D1223240

ESPN COLLEGE BASKETBALL ENCYCLOPEDIA

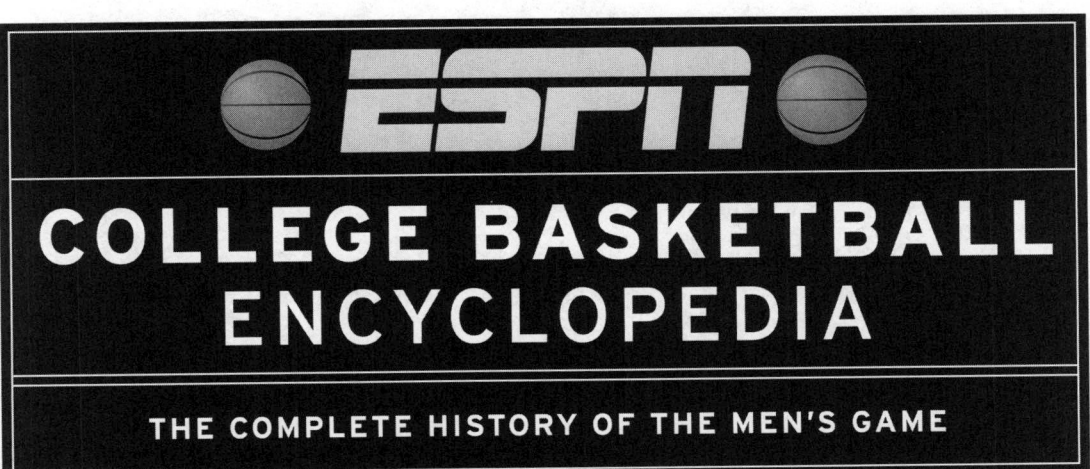

ESPN COLLEGE BASKETBALL ENCYCLOPEDIA

THE COMPLETE HISTORY OF THE MEN'S GAME

BY THE

EDITORS OF ESPN

INTRODUCTION BY

BILL BRADLEY

ESPN BOOKS

BALLANTINE BOOKS • NEW YORK

ESPN College Basketball Encyclopedia is an editorial work created independently by ESPN Books, an imprint of ESPN, Inc., New York. It was not published or produced with any conference or school. The team logos on the book cover are registered trademarks of the individual institutions and cannot be reproduced without permission from the respective institutions.

Copyright © 2009 by ESPN Books

All rights reserved.

Published in the United States by ESPN Books, an imprint of ESPN, Inc., New York, and Ballantine Books, an imprint of The Random House Publishing Group, a division of Random House, Inc., New York.

BALLANTINE and colophon are registered trademarks of Random House, Inc.
The ESPN Books name and logo are registered trademarks of ESPN, Inc.

ISBN: 978-0-345-51392-2

Printed in the United States of America on acid-free paper

www.ballantinebooks.com
www.espnbooks.com

9 8 7 6 5 4 3 2 1

First Edition

CONTENTS

ABOUT THE COVER

IF YOU ARE AN ASTUTE COLLEGE basketball fan, you probably recognize all 64 school logos on our cover jacket (reproduced on the opposite page). But can you guess the rationale behind their arrangement? Even if you can, there's a very good chance you won't entirely agree with it—and isn't that the greatest thing about being a fan?

Now, before you Kentucky cats go too wild or you Florida fans start baring your chompers (not to mention you Ramblin' Wrecks from Georgia Tech, which *almost* made the cover), we need to tell you that the school logos shown on the jacket were chosen *not* by any college basketball expert or by any committee's vote. They came out of a computer, so you really have no one to be mad at.

What you see on the cover of the *ESPN College Basketball Encyclopedia* are, in order—left to right, top to bottom—the 64 most successful college basketball programs in the history of college basketball. And, as you will discover in these pages, that history began with the first college game in 1895 (the Minnesota School of Agriculture d. Hamline, 9-3), picked up steam with the NIT and the first NCAA Tournament in the late 1930s, and exploded into a major American passion in the 1960s and '70s, long before an American president filled out his NCAA Tournament bracket on national TV.

To come up with the ESPN/Sagarin historical program ranking, mathematician and computer expert Jeff Sagarin, along with research support from Doug Kern of the ESPN Stats & Information Group, fed into a special program all the regular-season and postseason results for every one of the 330 teams that played NCAA Division I basketball as of April 2009, beginning with the 1937-38 season—the first in which a postseason tournament (the NIT) determined the national champion. For each season, the computer highly rewarded a school for winning a national championship and having an excellent record (such as the 30–0 UCLA Bruins of 1972-73), but also considered the results of all of its opponents during that season. Teams that have played the toughest opponents and have done so for many, many seasons tend to place highly in the ESPN/Sagarin ranking. On the basis of strength of scheduling and longevity, Kentucky (winner of seven NCAA titles) nips UCLA (11) for the No. 1 spot. And that's why you see eight Big Ten programs—led by Indiana (five titles)—among the top 15. Similarly, Southern California played many brilliant seasons totally eclipsed by UCLA, so although the Trojans have never won an NCAA title, they are No. 25 in the ESPN/Sagarin ranking.

Some teams are helped into the Top 64 by virtue of their strength in bygone seasons. No. 39 Bradley, a proud mid-major these days, was a national power in the 1950s and '60s, won the NIT four times and was twice runner-up in the NCAA Tournament. On the other hand, another once-great team, Bill Russell's San Francisco Dons, back-to-back NCAA champs in 1955 and '56, have had only enough success since to reach No. 75.

So be proud, Gators fans. Florida winning back-to-back NCAA titles in 2006 and '07 was an accomplishment matched by only six other schools in the entire course of college basketball history. But pay attention to that last phrase. Viewed in the context of *the entire course of college basketball history*, your team's feat was the equivalent of a buzzer-beater. Welcome to the Top 64.

You'll find the ESPN/Sagarin ranking for each team in its alphabetical entry in the section titled "The Schools." In "The Ratings Are In," beginning on page 1,194, you will find more about the process of compiling the rankings, followed by a complete numerical listing, Top 40 listings for each decade and a few more surprises.

ESPN

COLLEGE BASKETBALL ENCYCLOPEDIA

THE COMPLETE HISTORY OF THE MEN'S GAME

1. Kentucky
2. UCLA
3. Kansas
4. North Carolina
5. Indiana
6. Illinois
7. Duke
8. Purdue
9. Ohio State
10. Iowa
11. Louisville
12. Notre Dame
13. Michigan
14. Minnesota
15. Michigan State
16. St. John's
17. Cincinnati
18. Oklahoma State
19. Utah
20. Oklahoma
21. Villanova
22. NC State
23. Syracuse
24. Marquette
25. Southern California
26. DePaul
27. Kansas State
28. Wisconsin
29. Missouri
30. Stanford
31. Temple
32. Arkansas
33. Tennessee
34. California
35. Washington
36. West Virginia
37. Wake Forest
38. Maryland
39. Bradley
40. Oregon State
41. Brigham Young
42. Georgetown
43. Alabama
44. Western Kentucky
45. Alabama-Birmingham
46. Vanderbilt
47. Texas
48. Dayton
49. Arizona
50. Oregon
51. Colorado
52. Iowa State
53. Saint Louis
54. Connecticut
55. Houston
56. Saint Joseph's
57. Nebraska
58. Nevada-Las Vegas
59. Xavier
60. Pittsburgh
61. Memphis
62. Louisiana State
63. Wyoming
64. Florida

HOW TO USE THIS BOOK

THE SCHOOLS

Pages 62–520

The program's all-time ESPN/ Sagarin ranking

First-round pro draft choices and consensus All-Americas

Each coach's cumulative record

Each major program is profiled in a quick-read format, featuring entries for Best Team, Best Player, Best Coach, Fiercest Rival, etc.

Key data about the university and its basketball history

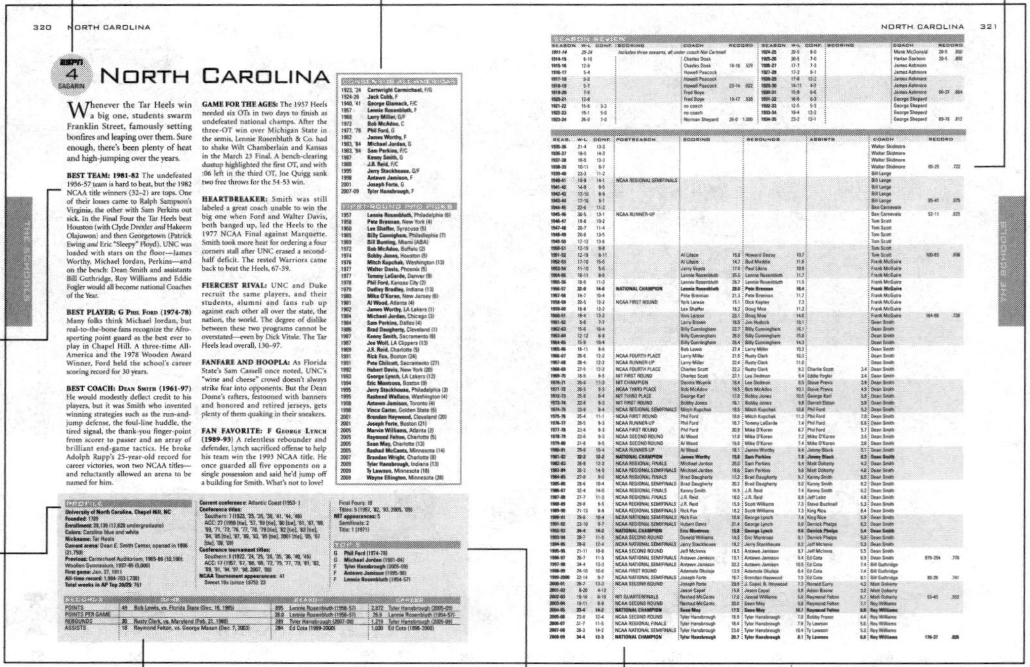

Game, single-season and career records for points, rebounds and assists

The program's all-time top five players

Season-by-season summary including coach, record, team leaders and postseason results

Early years are summarized with a composite win-loss record and a comment

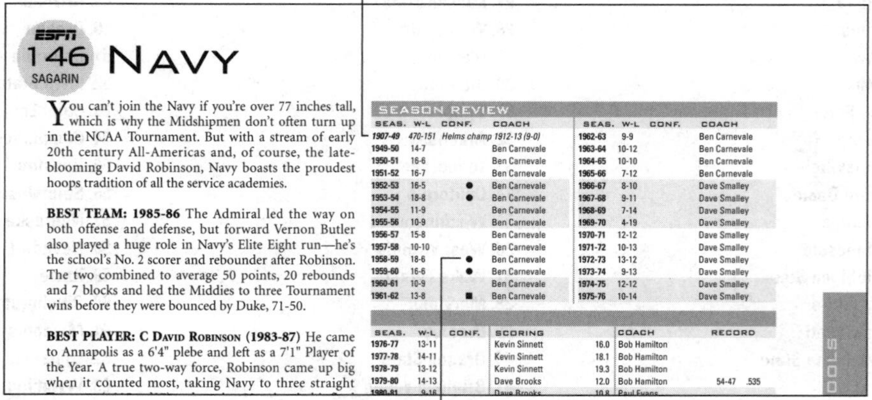

ESPN 146 SAGARIN

NAVY

You can't join the Navy if you're over 77 inches tall, which is why the Midshipmen don't often turn up in the NCAA Tournament. But with a stream of early 20th century All-Americas and, of course, the late-blooming David Robinson, Navy boasts the proudest hoops tradition of all the service academies.

BEST TEAM: 1985-86 The Admiral led the way on both offense and defense, but forward Vernon Butler also played a huge role in Navy's Elite Eight run—he's the school's No. 2 scorer and rebounder after Robinson. The two combined to average 50 points, 20 rebounds and 7 blocks and led the Middies to three Tournament wins before they were bounced by Duke, 71-50.

BEST PLAYER: C DAVID ROBINSON (1983-87) He came to Annapolis as a 6'4" plebe and left as a 7'1" Player of the Year. A true two-way force, Robinson came up big when it counted most, taking Navy to three straight

SEASON REVIEW

SEAS.	W-L	CONF.	COACH	SEAS.	W-L	CONF.	COACH
1907-49	470-151		Helms champ 1912-13 (9-0)	1962-63	9-9		Ben Carnevale
1949-50	14-7		Ben Carnevale	1963-64	10-12		Ben Carnevale
1950-51	16-6		Ben Carnevale	1964-65	10-10		Ben Carnevale
1951-52	16-7		Ben Carnevale	1965-66	7-12		Ben Carnevale
1952-53	16-5	●	Ben Carnevale	1966-67	8-10		Dave Smalley
1953-54	18-8	●	Ben Carnevale	1967-68	9-11		Dave Smalley
1954-55	11-9		Ben Carnevale	1968-69	7-14		Dave Smalley
1955-56	10-9		Ben Carnevale	1969-70	4-19		Dave Smalley
1956-57	15-8		Ben Carnevale	1970-71	12-12		Dave Smalley
1957-58	10-10		Ben Carnevale	1971-72	10-13		Dave Smalley
1958-59	18-6	●	Ben Carnevale	1972-73	13-12		Dave Smalley
1959-60	16-6	●	Ben Carnevale	1973-74	9-13		Dave Smalley
1960-61	10-9		Ben Carnevale	1974-75	12-12		Dave Smalley
1961-62	13-8	■	Ben Carnevale	1975-76	10-14		Dave Smalley

SEAS.	W-L	CONF.	SCORING		COACH	RECORD	
1976-77	13-11		Kevin Sinnett	16.0	Bob Hamilton		
1977-78	14-11		Kevin Sinnett	18.1	Bob Hamilton		
1978-79	13-12		Kevin Sinnett	19.3	Bob Hamilton		
1979-80	14-13		Dave Brooks	12.0	Bob Hamilton	54-47	.535
1980-81	9-16		Dave Brooks	10.8	Paul Evans		

Programs with ESPN/Sagarin rankings from 129 to 330 have symbols that show postseason tournament appearances

Annual Review

Pages 529–1191

Season summary

Conference standings show at a glance which schools received automatic and at-large NCAA Tournament bids and which went to the NIT

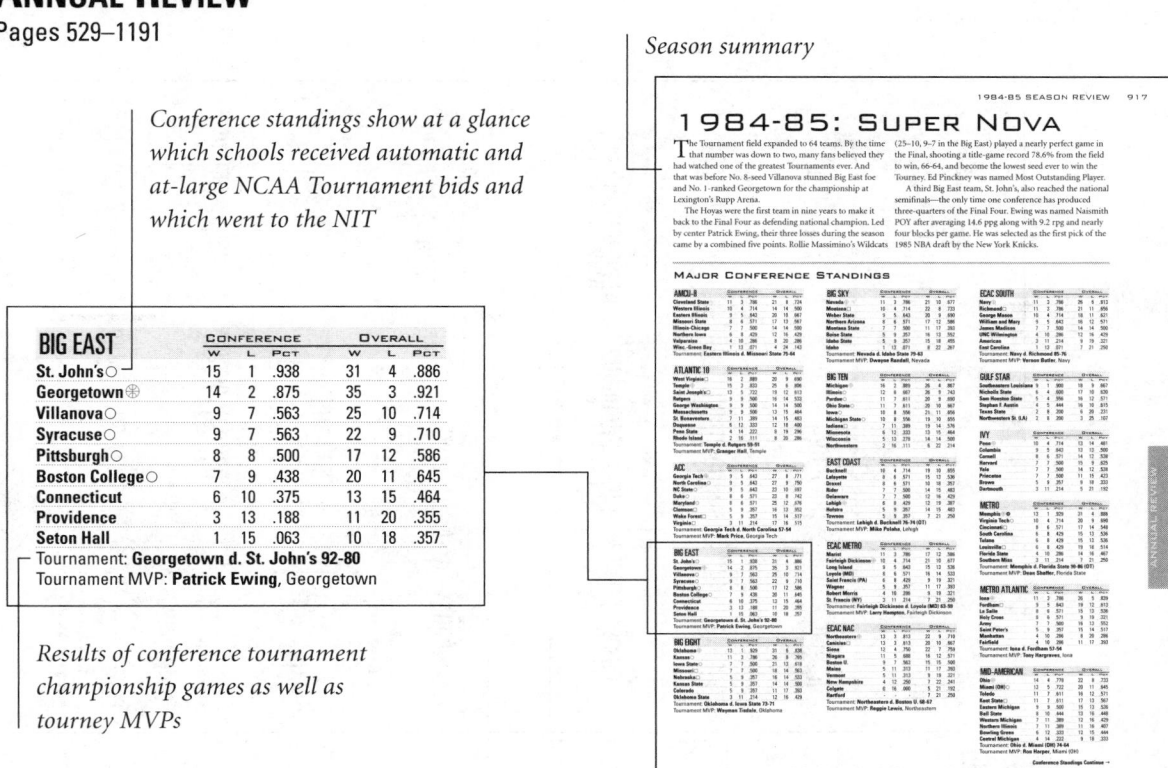

BIG EAST	Conference W	Conference L	Conference Pct	Overall W	Overall L	Overall Pct
St. John's○	15	1	.938	31	4	.886
Georgetown⊛	14	2	.875	35	3	.921
Villanova○	9	7	.563	25	10	.714
Syracuse○	9	7	.563	22	9	.710
Pittsburgh○	8	8	.500	17	12	.586
Boston College○	7	9	.438	20	11	.645
Connecticut	6	10	.375	13	15	.464
Providence	3	13	.188	11	20	.355
Seton Hall	1	15	.063	10	18	.357

Tournament: **Georgetown d. St. John's 92-80**
Tournament MVP: **Patrick Ewing**, Georgetown

Results of conference tournament championship games as well as tourney MVPs

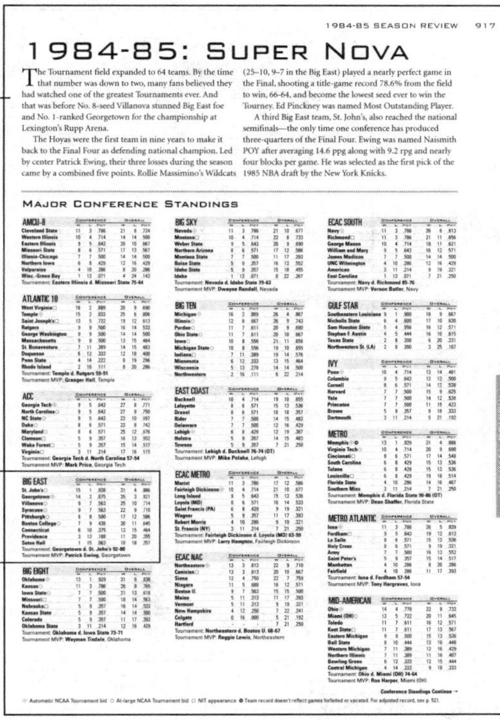

NCAA Division I individual and team leaders

Consensus All-Americas

Major award winners

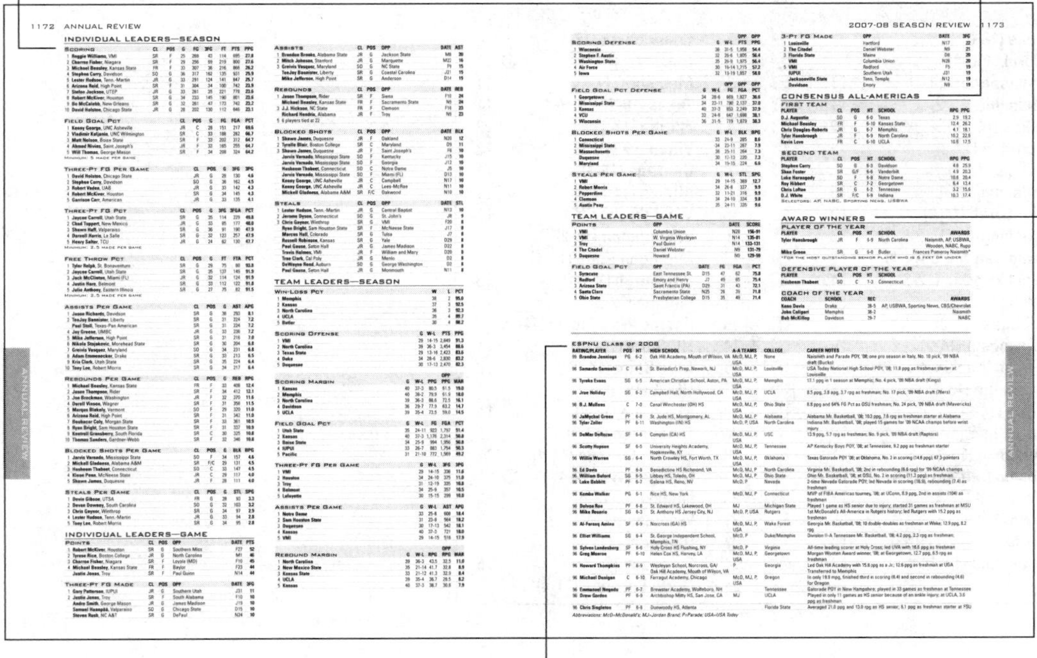

Top high school recruits for each season

Week-by-week AP and coaches polls let you relive the drive to March Madness

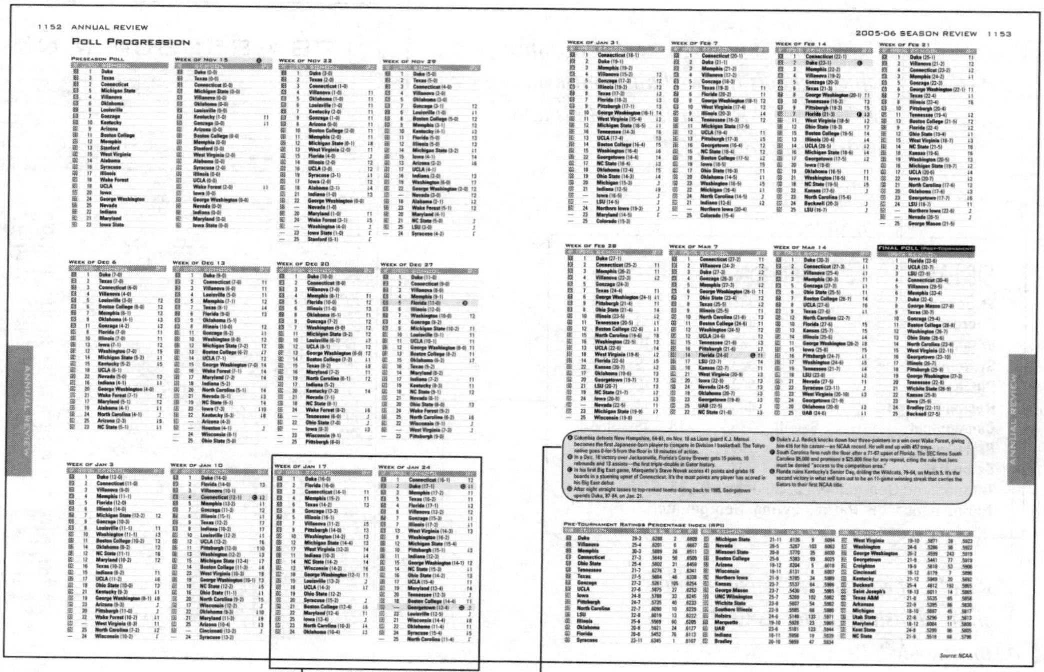

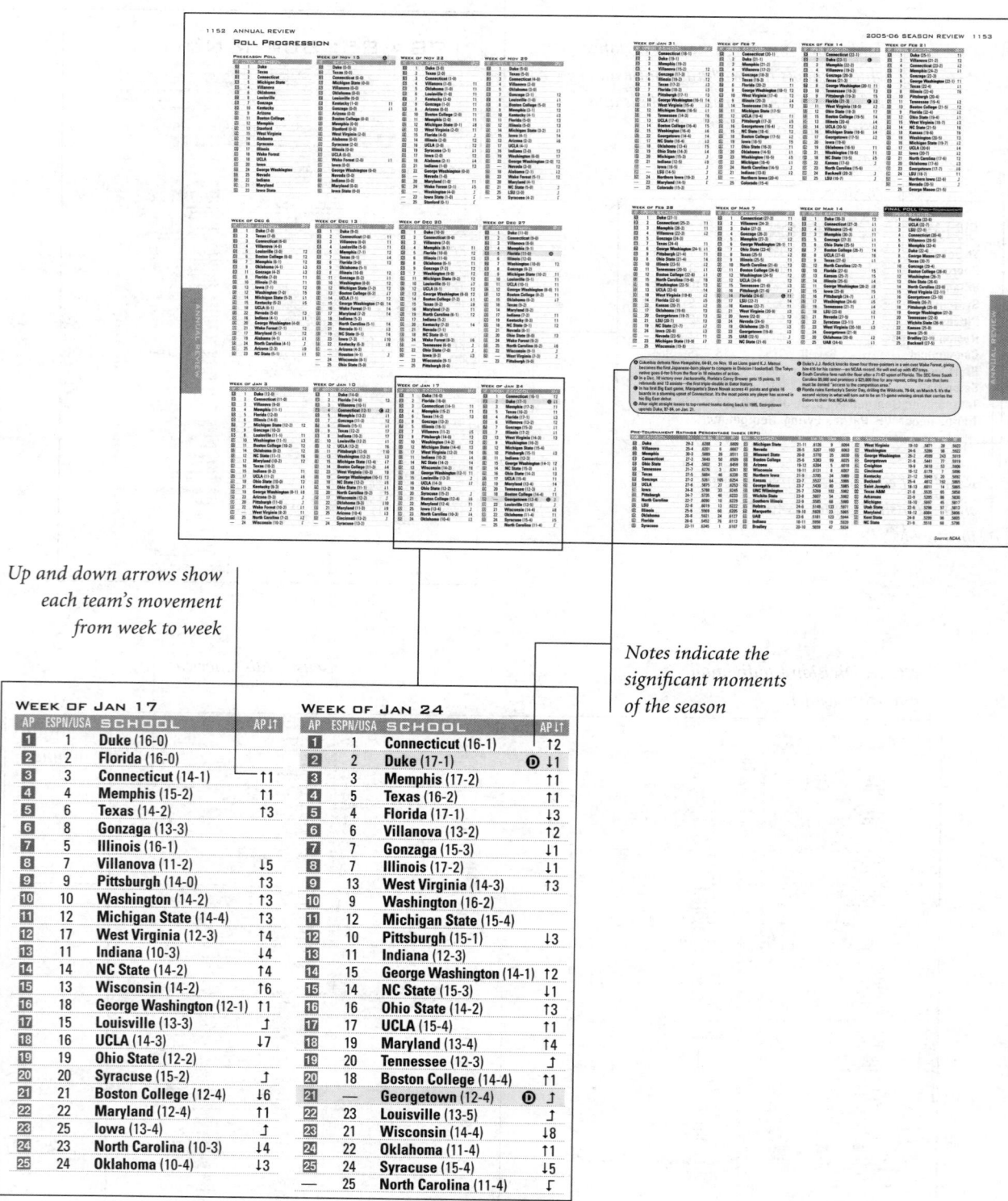

Up and down arrows show each team's movement from week to week

Notes indicate the significant moments of the season

WEEK OF JAN 17

AP	ESPN/USA	SCHOOL	AP↓↑
1	1	**Duke** (16-0)	
2	2	**Florida** (16-0)	
3	3	**Connecticut** (14-1)	↑1
4	4	**Memphis** (15-2)	↑1
5	6	**Texas** (14-2)	↑3
6	8	**Gonzaga** (13-3)	
7	5	**Illinois** (16-1)	
8	7	**Villanova** (11-2)	↓5
9	9	**Pittsburgh** (14-0)	↑3
10	10	**Washington** (14-2)	↑3
11	12	**Michigan State** (14-4)	↑3
12	17	**West Virginia** (12-3)	↑4
13	11	**Indiana** (10-3)	↓4
14	14	**NC State** (14-2)	↑4
15	13	**Wisconsin** (14-2)	↑6
16	18	**George Washington** (12-1)	↑1
17	15	**Louisville** (13-3)	⤴
18	16	**UCLA** (14-3)	↓7
19	19	**Ohio State** (12-2)	
20	20	**Syracuse** (15-2)	⤴
21	21	**Boston College** (12-4)	↓6
22	22	**Maryland** (12-4)	↑1
23	25	**Iowa** (13-4)	⤴
24	23	**North Carolina** (10-3)	↓4
25	24	**Oklahoma** (10-4)	↓3

WEEK OF JAN 24

AP	ESPN/USA	SCHOOL	AP↓↑
1	1	**Connecticut** (16-1)	↑2
2	2	**Duke** (17-1) Ⓓ	↓1
3	3	**Memphis** (17-2)	↑1
4	5	**Texas** (16-2)	↑1
5	4	**Florida** (17-1)	↓3
6	6	**Villanova** (13-2)	↑2
7	7	**Gonzaga** (15-3)	↓1
8	7	**Illinois** (17-2)	↓1
9	13	**West Virginia** (14-3)	↑3
10	9	**Washington** (16-2)	
11	12	**Michigan State** (15-4)	
12	10	**Pittsburgh** (15-1)	↓3
13	11	**Indiana** (12-3)	
14	15	**George Washington** (14-1)	↑2
15	14	**NC State** (15-3)	↓1
16	16	**Ohio State** (14-2)	↑3
17	17	**UCLA** (15-4)	↑1
18	19	**Maryland** (13-4)	↑4
19	20	**Tennessee** (12-3)	⤴
20	18	**Boston College** (14-4)	↑1
21	—	**Georgetown** (12-4) Ⓓ	⤴
22	23	**Louisville** (13-5)	⤴
23	21	**Wisconsin** (14-4)	↓8
24	22	**Oklahoma** (11-4)	↑1
25	24	**Syracuse** (15-4)	↓5
—	25	**North Carolina** (11-4)	⤵

Brackets for every NCAA Tournament, with seedings and results

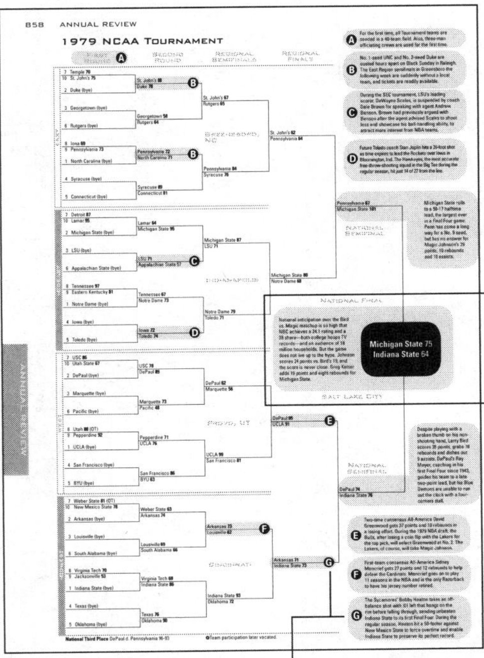

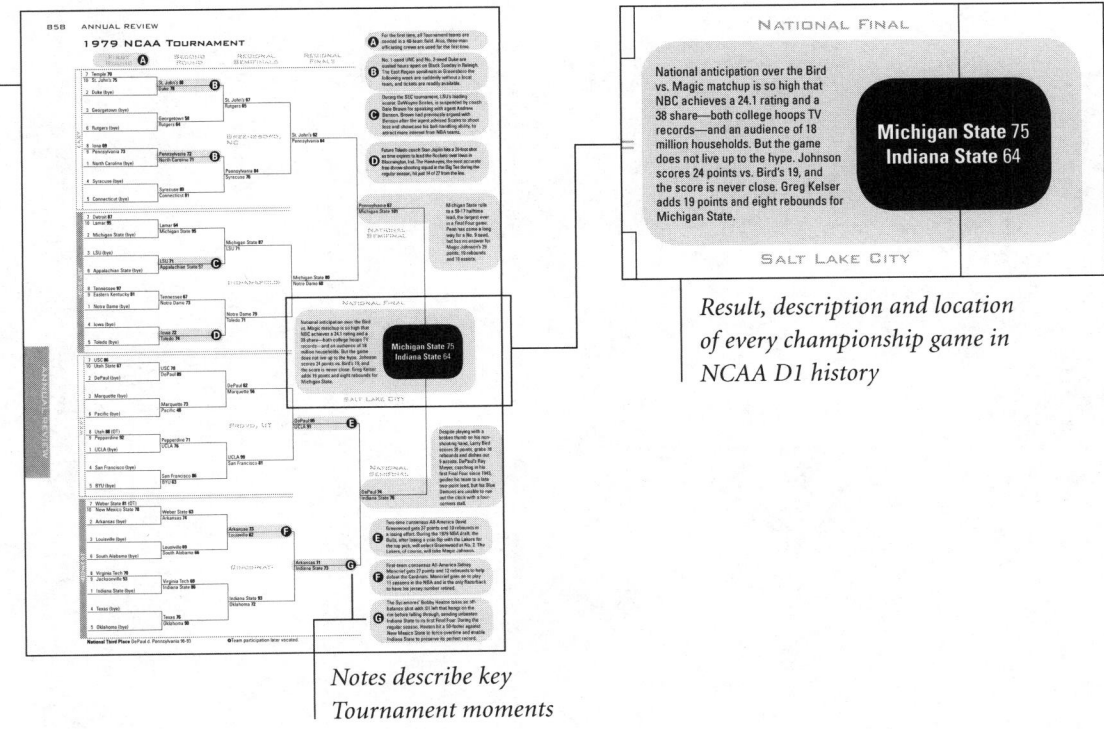

Result, description and location of every championship game in NCAA D1 history

Notes describe key Tournament moments

Top perfoming players and teams for each Tournament

Box scores for every Tournament game from the Sweet 16 to the Final

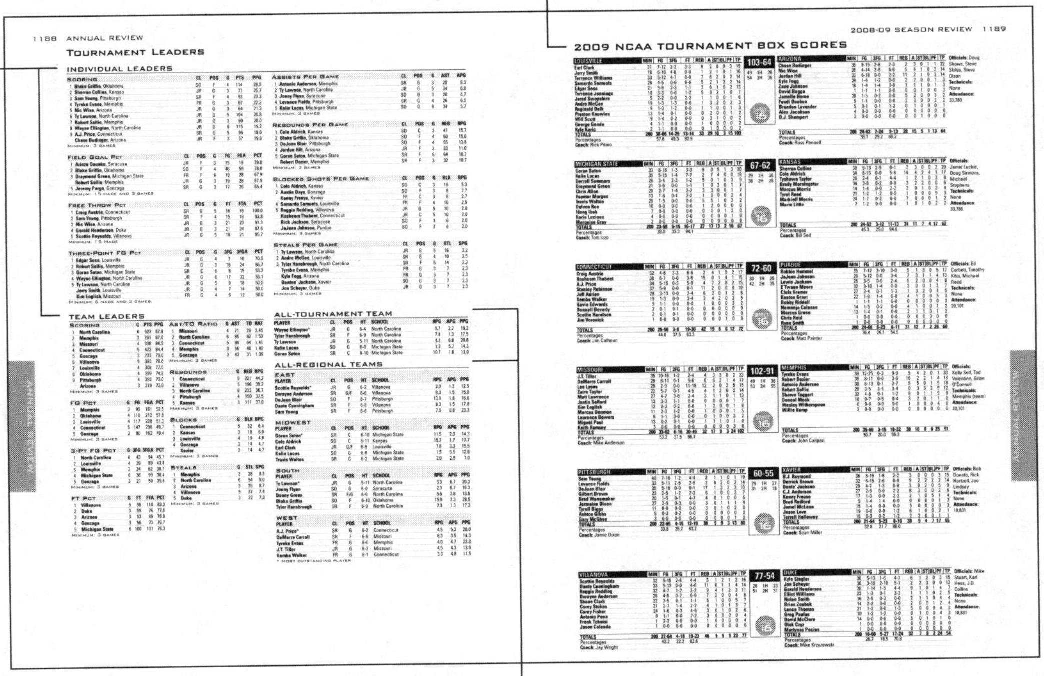

All-Tournament and All-Regional teams

Introduction

After 118 years, college basketball is the sport that best represents America, where anything is possible and everybody gets involved

BY BILL BRADLEY
U.S. SENATOR (1979-97), NAISMITH HALL OF FAME (1983)

By the time I reached the seventh grade, the game of basketball had seized my imagination. Although I knew that I would always be interested in life beyond basketball, the sport became my primary passion for the next 20 years. What was it about basketball that fascinated me so?

It began with the simplicity of the game itself. All you needed was a ball, a hoop and your imagination. If you spent enough time alone practicing, you could make the ball do whatever you wanted it to do. You could challenge yourself for hours on end—shooting baskets, dribbling around chairs, bouncing passes off a wall, going through your moves: a reverse pivot, a crossover dribble, a rocker step followed by a head fake and a drive to the basket. But the ball was also the focus of a complex web of 10 players, each of whom acted in relation to the ball—shooting it, passing or receiving a pass, screening away from the ball, moving without the ball, rebounding the ball, moving into the passing lane and double-teaming the ball on defense. All this took place on offense with set pieces (plays) in which each player had a role similar to a dancer in a choreographed routine. A play was not rigid because there were many options within it, depending on the response of the defense. Other times the game flowed freelance—without plays—meaning a player was smart enough and unselfish enough to see a pattern and an opening for himself or a teammate within the kaleidoscope of movement. Here the analogy was to jazz. Whether it was dance or jazz, each player had to be master of his or her technique. Winning a championship was what moved a good team. Each player knew that he or she was but one point on a five-pointed star. A team, not an individual—however great—won the NCAA title.

The game of basketball and its 118-year-old tradition has seeped into many corners of American life. Basketball can inspire silly chants, unite the passions of millions, divide the loyalties of an entire state's population, create cultural heroes, help heal racial discrimination, grow academic institutions, build a multi-billion-dollar business and maybe even help (a little) to elect an American president.

The best basketball in America today is played in the NBA, but the level at which the game means the most, to the most people in the most places, is college basketball.

Among the many reasons to love college basketball is that it's an equal opportunity sport. Did you know that, in all divisions, America's four-year colleges have more than 31,000 players competing for more than 2,600 men's and women's teams? In many places, women's games draw as much or more attention than the men's, as at the University of Connecticut, where, in 2009, the female Huskies won their sixth national championship while the men's team, in quest of its third title, reached the Final Four. While the crowds may get smaller as you move from Kentucky's Rupp Arena to, say, the College of Idaho, I guarantee you that the magic of the game for player and fan alike is the same as that which motivated me when I first discovered basketball in my small Missouri hometown as a seventh grader, or when I played for Princeton in the Final Four, or for the New York Knicks in the NBA Finals.

And speaking of equal opportunity, there is nothing in sports quite like the NCAA Tournament, otherwise known as March Madness. Any one of the 334 Division I teams has a shot at making the 65-team Tournament field and, once there, an underdog can heat up and win its way to the national championship. NC State did just that in 1983; Villanova in 1985. Every year a "Cinderella" or two reaches the Sweet 16 or Elite Eight (see Valparaiso 1998; Davidson 2008) or breaks through to the Final Four, as George Mason did in 2006. It's a beautiful thing, as Pat Forde describes in "The Sweetest 16" on page 28.

Of course, before college basketball arrived at this era of inclusiveness, the sport paralleled American society in a far more troubling way. In "One Sport, Two Games" (page 12), Hall of Famer and six-time NBA Most Valuable Player Kareem Abdul-Jabbar chronicles the racial segregation that until the 1960s denied African-American students the opportunity to play basketball at most of the country's colleges and universities. The perseverance of men such as Ed Henderson, John McLendon, Paul Robeson, Cumberland Posey, Bill Garrett, Oscar Robertson, Bill Russell, John Wooden and others eventually brought down the wall that separated white and black players. Their success in finally integrating the sport helped to change racial attitudes in American society as a whole. Several crucial moments in that struggle are recounted in Kareem's essay. In 1963, Loyola-Chicago coach George Ireland broke a "gentleman's agreement" not to play more than three African-Americans at any one time and started four black players on the team that won the NCAA championship. And in 1966, coach Don Haskins of Texas Western sent out an all-black starting five to win the title over the legendary Adolph Rupp and the Wildcats of Kentucky—a school that would not allow an African-American onto its team until 1969.

Even as these changes were slowly taking place, an entirely separate, and spectacular, college basketball culture took root and flourished among the so-called historically black college and universities (HBCUs) of the South and East. If they were of college age today, players like Earl "the Pearl" Monroe, Dick Barnett, Zelmo Beaty, Willis Reed and the many more featured in "Shadow Play" (page 20) would be national superstars. But in their day they were virtually unknown to most white fans, even those who lived near HBCU schools.

Basketball can inspire silly chants, unite the passions of millions, divide the loyalties of an entire state's population, maybe even help (a little) to elect an American president.

Why, of all the institutions in America, is the basketball court the place where the ideal of racial equality first came closest to being achieved? As I wrote in my 1998 book, *Values of the Game*, I believe it's always been because the community of a basketball team is so close that players have to talk with one another; they spend so much time together practicing and traveling that they have to interact with one another; the competition is so intense that they have to challenge one another; the game is so fluid that they have to depend on one another; the high and low moments are so frequent that they learn to share them.

Another watershed moment described in Kareem's essay is the "Secret Game of 1944," when a team of all-white medical students from Duke traveled to the campus of the North Carolina College for Negroes in absolute secrecy, not because such a thing "just wasn't done" in the American South of the 1940s, but because *it was against the law*. After the NCC team waxed the white boys 88-44 in an otherwise empty and locked gym, they chose up sides and played a second, integrated game—shirts vs. skins. Then they went for sodas together in the black players' dorm.

Beyond the racial integration of the sport, the emergence of women's college basketball as a big-time sport has given a whole new dimension to the game. In 1972, President Richard Nixon signed Title IX, federal legislation that prohibits gender discrimination in public institutions. The law had the effect of creating gym space, practice fields and weight rooms, and providing coaches for women athletes. It also led directly to the explosion of women's basketball (see "The Women's Game," page 40). At Tennessee, the Lady Vols home games attract 14,000 fans. At Missouri State in Springfield, a town of about 155,000 people, the average attendance at women's games a few years ago was around 7,400. Great stars emerged: Carol Blazejowski, Nancy Lieberman, Cheryl Miller, Teresa Edwards, Ann Meyers, Diana Taurasi and Candace Parker. Cynthia Cooper, Lisa Leslie, and Rebecca Lobo became media stars. Old Dominion, Texas and Louisiana Tech made early commitments to the women's game. Pat Summitt at Tennessee, Geno Auriemma at Connecticut, Theresa Grentz at Illinois, Tara VanDerveer at Stanford, Vivian Stringer at Rutgers were every bit as good as the great men's coaches. The women's game in some ways is much more interesting than the men's. I love the passing and movement away from the ball as well as the intensity, the unselfishness, the competitive fire and the unabashed joy.

Look at the list of the 50 greatest male college players on page 52. Lew Alcindor (as Kareem Abdul-Jabbar was then known), Oscar Robertson, Bill Russell, Pete Maravich, Wilt Chamberlain, Jerry West, Magic Johnson, Larry Bird and the rest performed at their schools for only a few years and then went on to the pros. Now look at the list of the outstanding coaches. Each lasted for decades. Most led the development of a unique basketball culture that simultaneously shaped their schools' overall public image: John Wooden (27 seasons at UCLA), Dean Smith (36 at North Carolina), Mike Krzyzewski (29 at Duke), Adolph Rupp (41 at Kentucky), Bob Knight (29 at Indiana), Phog Allen (39 at Kansas), Pete Carril (29 at Princeton), John Thompson (27 at Georgetown).

As William F. Reed writes in "The Teachers" (page 2), the basketball pedigrees of these men could all be traced back to Dr. James Naismith, and each, in turn, influenced his own line of coaching descendants. But not all of the greats were flawless, as Reed and Gene Wojciechowksi, in "Too Many Fouls" (page 34), point out. Over decades, dozens of coaches either wittingly or unwittingly presided over programs that were infected by gambling scandals or had victories forfeited and/or Tournament games expunged for violating NCAA rules. Rupp's legacy is stained by his longstanding unwillingness to integrate his team; Knight's by his dismissal for purported abusive behavior toward players and students. (Still, I admire Knight's devotion to the game.)

In 1971, the U.S. Supreme Court struck down an NBA rule that required young basketball players, no matter how good they were, to wait a full four years after high school—whether or not they attended college—before they could sign to play in the league. I had no interest in playing pro ball while I was in college from 1962 to '65, but one can understand the lure of the NBA for young players, especially those who live in poverty. Many of today's NBA stars, such as Kevin Garnett, Kobe Bryant, LeBron James and Dwight Howard, turned pro right out of high school. Their long-term futures, as well as those of every player, will be determined by what each does with his free time. Only he can decide to use his new wealth to continue learning the skills he'll need for a lifetime. A young draftee out of high school might reach the pros at 19 but it is certain that the same player will leave the league by time he's 39, and in most cases much earlier. At that point the player either faces life with terror, unable to ever regain the enthusiasm of his lost youth, or happily moves on to his post-playing days prepared by what he did outside of the game during his pro years. One of the most moving moments for me in the last several years was when Shaquille O'Neal went back as an NBA All-Star to complete his college degree at Louisiana State.

Yes, college basketball is different from what it was in 1969 and 1939 and 1909. But it has never been more popular. Is the game better today? Is *America* better today? To me the short answer to both questions is the same: Yes. We live in the greatest country in the world, and within the higher education system of that country resonates the most magical game ever invented.

THE GAME

The Teachers

From Naismith to Allen to McLendon to Rupp to Knight to Thompson to Donovan—a 120-year evolutionary chain

BY WILLIAM F. REED

"This roundball game is so simple. The boys come out. You hand them a ball and point to the hoop. 'Put it through the net,' you tell 'em. And that's about all there is to it. The boys who put it through there the most will be the winners."

—Coach E.A. Diddle,
Western Kentucky University, 1922-64

WE BRING YOU THE above quote as a public service, just to remind you right off the bat that no matter what Dick Vitale or Billy Packer might have you believe, coaching basketball is not on the same intellectual level as, say, rocket science. Granted, the job has become a lot more complicated since Diddle's day. Coaches of his generation never had to deal with agents, talk radio or the RPI. Still, many of today's coaches are getting paid upwards of $1 million a year to do the same things that coaches have always done—convince talented teenagers that their system or program is the best path to championships and college degrees, not to mention the NBA.

There's no surefire way to become a successful college basketball coach. Some coaches just bring in a lot of studs and roll out the balls. Others grind away over game tape, breaking down opponents' various tendencies, until their eyeballs turn inside out and they begin calling plays in their sleep. Some coaches are free spirits, in the fashion of Al McGuire, the streetwise coach at Marquette in the 1960s and '70s, but the majority, today more than ever, could easily be mistaken for accountants or bankers or slick salesmen.

Basketball genealogists love to amuse themselves by tracing the family trees of coaching icons to show how various sainted mentors have had an impact on and shaped the game by passing along their wisdom through generations of assistants and players. Yet this is a largely futile endeavor, sort of like trying to figure out what Irish poets or Greek philosophers are really trying to say. After a generation or so, the bloodlines get blurrier and more mixed than a warren of rabbits, making it really difficult to figure out who invented what and who merely copied and/or tweaked it.

Take the fast break, for example. In the East, Frank Keaney of Rhode Island is generally given credit for inventing the classic speed tactic and using it to win 401 games from 1920 to '48. But you might get an argument in the Midwest, where Purdue's Ward "Piggy" Lambert used a dazzling fast break that, in the early 1930s, was built around a ball-handling wizard named John Wooden. Out West, fans could be forgiven for believing the fast break was invented by Oregon's Howard Hobson, who won the first NCAA Tournament in 1939 with a big and fast team known as the Tall Firs.

So you see the problem with bloodlines and family trees. The lone exception is Kansas, where the coaching pedigree clearly goes back to the game's inventor. Dr. James Naismith plunked himself down in Lawrence, Kan., in 1898, only seven years after he wrote out his original 13 rules and oversaw the first game at the YMCA in Springfield, Mass. Naismith, however, never saw himself as a coach. There's a famous story in which he called in one of his pupils, Forrest Allen, in the spring of 1905. "I've got a good joke on you," Naismith told him. "They want you to coach basketball down at Baker."

"What's so funny about that?" Allen asked.

"Why, you can't *coach* basketball," Naismith said. "You just play it."

But Allen respectfully disagreed, and took the job at Baker University. It was the beginning of a 49-year coaching career that saw him return to his alma mater in 1919 and become, arguably, the father of big-time college basketball. His 1922 and '23 Kansas teams were named national champions by the Helms Foundation, and he won the NCAA title in 1952, the 14th year of the event that has evolved into what we know today as March Madness.

Known as Phog because of his foghorn voice or Doc because of his degree in osteopathy, Allen proved that basketball very definitely could be coached. He believed so strongly in the man-to-man defense that he couldn't bring himself to admit it when he used a zone; he insisted on describing the alignment as a "stratified, transitional man-for-man with a zone principle." Aside from his own success, Allen's greatest gifts to the basketball world were a couple of KU benchwarmers: Adolph Rupp (1923) and Dean Smith (1953). Both went on to surpass Allen's records and establish their own dynasties, at Kentucky and North Carolina, respectively.

Yet neither Rupp nor Smith had a more profound impact on the game than a student named John McLendon, who came to Lawrence in the 1930s not to play for Allen—as an African-American, he was not allowed to play for the all-white varsity team—but to study at the feet of Naismith, who then was an old man with only a few years remaining (he died on Nov. 28, 1939, only months after the first NCAA Tournament). McLendon was prepared to travel to Springfield from his home in Hiawatha, Kan., to seek out Naismith; he was thrilled to learn that the great teacher had moved to Lawrence, just 90 miles south of him.

"You're going to be my advisor," the brash youngster told Naismith.

"Who told you that?" the coach asked.

"My father," McLendon said.

"Well," said Naismith, chuckling, "fathers are always right, aren't they?"

After McLendon's three years at Kansas, Naismith helped him get a job as coach of the black team in a racially mixed Kansas high school. Two years later, McLendon took an assistant's job at the North Carolina College for Negroes (now North Carolina Central University) in Durham and in 1940 he became head coach.

And so began the remarkable, and largely underappreciated, career of the man who became known as the Father of Black College Basketball. More than Allen, Rupp or Smith, McLendon remained true to Naismith's belief that basketball should be played more than coached. So his teams ran, ran and ran some more. And they entertained. Long before Earl "The Pearl" Monroe or "Pistol" Pete Maravich, McLendon encouraged creativity instead of trying to stifle it.

More than Allen, Rupp or Smith, McLendon remained true to Naismith's belief that basketball should be played more than coached. So his teams ran, ran and ran some more.

Still, because America was racially segregated throughout his career, the historically black colleges existed in a parallel universe (see "Shadow Play," page 20) and McLendon never received the credit he was due for being an innovator. His variation of the fast break never received as much attention as Rupp's, which won the Baron four NCAA titles and made his book, *Rupp's Championship Basketball*, a bible for many young coaches. McLendon's teams were not allowed to compete in any of the whites-only tournaments and most white sports fans knew nothing about them.

It was Rupp's belief that "basketball styles of play, as a rule, are controlled by the geographic locations of the teams using them." He noted that Midwestern and Southern giants such as Kentucky, Iowa and Dayton played a "rugged" style of basketball that revolved around the fast break. In the West, he wrote, successful programs such as Oklahoma A&M (today's Oklahoma State) and San Francisco embraced a style that emphasized a ball-control offense and tenacious defense.

And in the East, Rupp wrote, "the game most widely played is the 'give-and-go' game. It is a variation of the so-called 'pro style' perfected by the Original Celtics of New York City. This style calls for fine ball handling and lends itself to freelancing or 'situation' basketball." It was, in other words, playground ball—the kind that was anathema to a disciplinarian like Rupp.

"Basketball is New York's game. It was the sport of the ghettos long before the ghettos were black. Even in the summer, when the pavement sizzles, New York kids are playing basketball. It requires no expensive equipment, no wide-open spaces—just a hoop, a ball and a boy. Once it was the game of the Irish and Italian-Catholics in Rockaway and the Jews on Fordham Road in the Bronx. It was recreation, status and a way out."

—David Wolf, author of *Foul! The Connie Hawkins Story*

Organized as a New York City settlement-house team in 1914, the Original Celtics did much to popularize basketball in the East, South and Midwest in the 1920s and '30s. The Celtics took on all comers, playing in all manner of arenas, gyms, field houses, dance halls, even cages outside coal mines. Their star players made as much as $10,000 a year (good money in those days) and they sometimes drew crowds of 10,000 or so in the big cities. After their playing days, two Celtics—Nat Holman and Joe Lapchick—went into coaching at City College of New York and St. John's University, respectively. They joined Clair Bee of Long Island University and John "Honey" Russell (another former barnstorming pro) of Seton Hall in developing the smart and sophisticated "give-and-go" style that spread to colleges in Boston and Philadelphia.

In the early 1930s, Ned Irish was among the first to recognize the money-making potential of college basketball. A former sportswriter, Irish began staging and promoting college doubleheaders in Madison Square Garden, giving large crowds the chance to watch the area's famous coaches and their teams. The success of these events encouraged Irish to bring in college teams from Chicago and elsewhere in the Midwest. Rupp loved to bring his Kentucky Wildcats to the Garden because he'd get to hold court with the New York City sports columnists, many of whom were syndicated in papers across America. He also liked to dine at the fine restaurants, drink whiskey and talk strategy with colleagues and writers well into the night.

The Garden doubleheaders led to the creation of the postseason National Invitation Tournament in 1938, which remained more prestigious than the NCAA Tournament until the point-shaving scandals of the early 1950s rocked basketball and all but ruined the game in New York (see "Too Many Fouls," page 34). Players from Holman's 1949-50 CCNY team, the first and still the only team to win both titles in the same season, and Bee's powerhouse Long Island University program, were implicated in the scandals, staining both coaches' records and Eastern basketball in general. In time, the NIT became a second-rate event and Madison Square Garden lost some of its luster as the mecca of college hoops.

> ***McGuire's Underground Railroad was the first wave in a new model for seeking out the best players.***

Although no St. John's players were touched by the scandal, coach Frank McGuire, who succeeded Lapchick in the 1947-48 season, left in 1952 to become coach at North Carolina. The fans on Tobacco Road weren't sure what to make of the smiling, charming, Irish-American carpetbagger and the Eastern style of play that he brought to the Southern and, the following season, the newborn Atlantic Coast Conferences. McGuire's Underground Railroad, as his recruiting pipeline between Chapel Hill and his old stomping ground in the talent-rich New York City area came to be known, was the first wave in a new model for seeking out the best players. What had always been essentially a local endeavor was now becoming regional and even national.

Many were stunned in 1955 when Allen convinced Wilt "The Stilt" Chamberlain the powerful 7'1" center, to leave his native Philadelphia to play college ball in Kansas. Some of Allen's rivals immediately screamed foul. Why, after all, would a black man from Philadelphia choose the culture shock of lily-white Lawrence when he could have his pick of five excellent college programs—La Salle, Villanova, Penn, Saint Joseph's and Temple—in the Philadelphia area? Besides, Allen still was still under a cloud of suspicion for the way he slipped into Terre Haute, Ind., in 1948 and stole 6'9" Clyde Lovellette right out from under Indiana coach Branch McCracken's nose. Having committed to IU, Lovellette went home to pick up some clothes and was next seen in Lawrence, signing a grant to play for the Jayhawks.

"There was nothing irregular in my recruitment of Wilt Chamberlain," Allen later told Ted O'Leary of the *Kansas City Star*. "But Clyde Lovellette—well, that's another story." It was a story he never got around to telling, but Lovellette helped Allen win his only NCAA title, in 1952. A year later, however, McCracken got sweet revenge, denying Allen a repeat title with a 69-68 championship game victory in, of all places, Kansas City.

Unfortunately for Allen, he never got to coach Chamberlain. Since freshmen were ineligible for varsity play in those days, Wilt had to watch what turned out to be Allen's last Kansas team from the sidelines. Allen reached the university's mandatory retirement age after the 1955-56 season, but he petitioned the Board of Regents to make an exception, just so he could coach Chamberlain. Despite Allen's 746 victories (590 at KU), the board refused. So when Chamberlain played his first varsity game—a 52-point, 31-rebound barrage against Northwestern—the Kansas coach was Dick Harp, Allen's former top assistant.

As agile as he was strong, Chamberlain was one of two stories that dominated the national sports media in 1956-57. The other was North Carolina's bid for a perfect season with a team built around five products of McGuire's New York area pipeline: Lennie Rosenbluth, Tommy Kearns, Pete Brennan, Joe Quigg and Bob Cunningham. Inevitably, the two forces collided for the NCAA championship in Kansas City. It was the southern fried version of Eastern basketball (North Carolina) against the classic inside power game that characterized the Midwest (Kansas). In what may be the greatest title game ever, the Tar Heels needed three overtimes to subdue Chamberlain and the Jayhawks, 54-53. Although four Tar Heels scored in double figures, led by Rosenbluth's 20, the game revolved around North Carolina's efforts to double-, triple-, even quadruple-team Chamberlain, who nevertheless managed 23 points and 14 rebounds.

The victory was celebrated just as avidly in New York as it was in Chapel Hill. Once again, the Eastern style of basketball ruled the college world.

"There'd be jazz mixed in with the games. After the first half, there'd be a warm-up band. After the second half, people would dance to Count Basie until three or four in the morning."

—Kareem Abdul-Jabbar, on Harlem's Renaissance Ballroom

Long before Frank McGuire came to Tobacco Road, John McLendon already was there coaching in the shadows at the North Carolina College for Negroes. At the time, young black coaches really had only two professional teams for role models. The most popular, at least in the eyes of white America, was the Harlem Globetrotters, basketball's touring minstrels. But the New York Rens—their nickname came from Harlem's Renaissance Ballroom—were the African-American version of the Original Celtics.

Between 1922 and '49, the Rens compiled a record of 2,588–529. They more than held their own in exhibitions against the Original Celtics and other white pro squads. But most important, from a cultural standpoint, they brought jazz to basketball. Rather than run rigid set plays, they improvised, riffed, let their imaginations soar. It was the kind of basketball Naismith envisioned when he invented the game, and the kind he passed along to the young McLendon.

It was Naismith's belief that "the game should be played from baseline to baseline" and that the team that was in the best shape would win most games because it could run its opponents into the floor. Right from the start, McLendon's teams averaged around 70 points a game, a stunning number considering that a typical game ended with scores in the 40s. The excitement surrounding the North Carolina College for Negroes grew so great that a secret game was arranged—games between blacks and whites were illegal in North Carolina at that time—between McLendon's team and a crack team of white players from the Duke University Medical School. McLendon's team humiliated the Duke team, 88-44 (see "One Sport, Two Games," page 12).

By the late 1940s, McLendon's abundant success was a magnet that drew many coaches, black and white, to Durham to pick his brain, take notes and copy his style. One man who paid him no attention was Clarence "Big House" Gaines, the young coach at historically black Winston-Salem (N.C.) Teachers College—until Gaines brought his team to Durham in 1949 and got shellacked, 119-65. Gaines was so embarrassed that he eventually quit his football coaching duties so that he could concentrate full time on basketball. He also decided that whatever it was that McLendon had, he wanted the same.

Generous as always, McLendon liked Gaines so much that he suggested they go on recruiting trips together. "John thought we were riding together to save gas money," Gaines wrote in his autobiography, "but the truth is I wanted to get him alone to talk about basketball plays, strategy on the court and how to motivate players to do exactly what I wanted them to do when I wanted them to do it."

They worked out a deal. When they were working the territory around Gaines' hometown of Paducah, Ky., or nearby southern Illinois, McLendon would stay in the car while Big House tried to sell recruits on Winston-Salem. Then, when they got into McLendon's territory around Kansas City and Chicago, Gaines would stay back while McLendon sold the North Carolina College for Negroes.

The two friends had to go their separate ways in 1952, when McLendon moved on to Hampton Institute in Virginia and then to Tennessee A&I (today's Tennessee State) in Nashville, where he won three consecutive NAIA championships from 1957 to '59—a first for a college basketball coach at any level. McLendon's title teams were crowd-pleasing, high-scoring machines built around Dick Barnett, a sleepy-eyed swingman whose signature move was a deadly accurate fallaway jumper from the deep corners, his heels kicking up behind him. Now McLendon was impossible to ignore, and he was hired to coach a pro team in Cleveland. After feuding with the meddlesome young owner, George Steinbrenner, he quit and moved on to Kentucky State and Cleveland State, where he distinguished himself as the first African-American head coach at a predominately white school.

Meanwhile, in 1966-67, McLendon's old rival, pupil and friend, Big House Gaines, became the first African-American coach to win an NCAA title in any sport, leading Winston-Salem to the NCAA College Division championship largely on the brilliance of Earl Monroe. A slouching 6'4" guard who ran as if his feet hurt, Monroe was such a magician with the ball that he was known as Black Jesus on the Philadelphia playgrounds from whence he sprang. He could shoot any shot from anywhere, with either hand. His dribbling and passing were sleight-of-hand at its most befuddling. Soon he was the Pearl, and anyone who saw him score at his 41.5 points-per-game clip during the 1966-67 season might have felt that LSU's Pete Maravich (the NCAA's scoring leader with a 40-plus average each of the next three seasons) was another case of a white artist covering a black artist's material—as singer Pat Boone had done to Little Richard and Fats Domino on the '50s rock-'n-roll charts. In truth, Pistol Pete was just as much of an original as the Pearl.

Trouble was, very few fans at the time ever saw—or even heard of—Monroe, while Maravich became a national icon.

Pistol Pete's version of showtime was rivaled by the likes of Purdue's Rick Mount, Niagara's Calvin Murphy and Notre Dame's Austin Carr, each of whom hit 30-point-or-better averages and generated unprecedented demand for college hoops on TV. Through the 1970s, more and more black players were being recruited by schools that had previously shunned them, and the historically black college teams began to lose their distinctiveness. McLendon's style also fell out of favor. The white coaches who still dominated the game identified more with John Philip Sousa's marches than with James Brown's stage moves. They clearly felt the need to regain control of a game that was in danger of being played more than it was coached.

"Walter was an extraordinary player, but one who liked to use fancy moves such as dribbling behind his back or between his legs. Some called him East Coast because the style of play back there was more given to showboating. This show-business type of play was unacceptable to me because it drew attention away from the team and onto the player."

—UCLA's John Wooden, on coaching Walt Hazzard

West Coast teams always have been hurt by the zone—not the 1-3-1 or the 2-1-2, but the Pacific time zone, where their games often end long after fans and newspapers have gone to bed in the East and the New York-based TV networks have ended their programming. Even in the era of 24-hour cable TV and the Internet, outstanding players and teams on the West Coast still don't get as much recognition as players in the East and the Midwest, with the result that some team from the West—a Gonzaga or a Loyola Marymount, for example—often emerges as a "sleeper" or "surprise" team when March Madness rolls around.

In the early years of the NCAA Tournament, travel was also a problem; it was costly both in money and time away from the classroom. So, with rare exceptions, teams didn't stray far to play each other until the postseason. It was thus a great surprise, at least to those Easterners who believed that the basketball world began and ended at Madison Square Garden, when four of the first six NCAA Tournament champions came from west of the Rockies: Oregon (1939), Stanford (1942), Wyoming (1943) and Utah (1944).

The sport was about to tilt even more toward the West. When Indiana State Teachers College coach John Wooden accepted an offer from UCLA in 1948, the Bruins program was a mess. Home games were played in the dank campus gym known as B.O. Barn for the overpowering odor that permeated the place. The returning talent was equally depressing, giving Wooden severe misgivings about taking such a misbegotten job so far from his roots in rural Indiana. Wooden was an anomaly in Los Angeles. He and his wife, Nell, might easily have been the models for Grant Wood's *American Gothic*—prim, straitlaced, God-fearing products of small-town USA. They recoiled from the fast-paced lifestyle, the traffic-jammed freeways, the glitz and gaudiness of Tinseltown. "Living in Los Angeles was not an easy adjustment," Wooden wrote in his 2004 book, *My Personal Best*. "Socially, I often didn't fit in, because I was a teetotaler who didn't smoke or swear and on many occasions was made to feel uncomfortable about it. On top of everything else, the traffic scared us. One day while I was driving very cautiously on the Pasadena Freeway, I looked at Nell and said, 'What in the world are we doing here, honey?' She was kind enough not to remind me that it was all my doing."

At the time, the dominant West Coast university in sports was San Francisco. Under Pete Newell, who favored a passing offense known as "reverse-action" and a tough man-to-man defense, the Dons won the 1949 NIT title. When Newell left for Michigan State in 1950, his successor, Phil Woolpert, had the good fortune to recruit a pair of talented players named Bill Russell and K.C. Jones. The game had never seen a big man as quick and agile as the 6'9" Russell, who was a force on defense as well as offense, and the Dons proceeded to win back-to-back NCAA titles in 1955 and '56, going 57–1 over those two seasons.

At UCLA, Wooden eschewed Newell's reverse-action offense in favor of the fast-break attack and high-post offense that he had learned from Piggy Lambert at Purdue in the 1930s. He turned the once-dismal UCLA program into a consistent winner, but did not reach the NCAA Final Four until 1962, when the Bruins lost in the semifinals to defending national champion Cincinnati, 72-70. "We just as easily could have won," said Wooden. Nonetheless, he felt that something was missing—something that he needed to find if the Bruins were ever to win a championship.

Before the 1962-63 season, at the suggestion of assistant coach Jerry Norman, Wooden added a 2-2-1 zone press to UCLA's repertoire. "The combination of conditioning and execution, with the Bruins' fast break and full-court press, could be very destructive," Wooden wrote in *My Personal Best*. "In tandem, they would allow us to set the speed of the game—fast—which would ultimately give the team in better condition an edge. Conditioning, of course, was a priority I learned from Piggy Lambert at Purdue."

The change paid off almost immediately. In the 12 seasons beginning in 1964 and ending in 1975, the Bruins won 10 national championships, including an almost unfathomable seven in a row from 1967 through '73. In four of those seasons,

UCLA never lost a single game. Wooden won his first two championships with small, quick teams built around guards—Walt Hazzard and Gail Goodrich in 1964 and Goodrich again in '65. When he had dominant big men, like 7'2" Lew Alcindor (the future Kareem Abdul-Jabbar) from 1966 to '69 and 6'11" Bill Walton from 1971 to '74, Wooden ditched his high-post offense in favor of a low-post set. UCLA won either way.

After NC State ended UCLA's consecutive-titles run in the 1974 NCAA national semis, the Bruins came back and won Wooden his 10th title in 1975. Wooden considers this one of his favorite championships because nobody expected it and because it was his final season. He had announced his retirement after the Bruins' semifinal win over Louisville, which was coached by his former assistant, Denny Crum.

Unlike Naismith, Allen, McLendon and others before him, and unlike Bob Knight and Dean Smith, who succeeded him as the college game's top coaches, Wooden did not spawn a large legacy of young coaches to carry on his methods. His only highly successful protégé was Crum, who applied the Wooden system to win titles at Louisville in 1980 and '86. Beyond his trademark zone press and high-post offense, Wooden had a knack for relating to his players in ways that made powerful and lasting impressions. He believed in discipline, organization, fundamentals and repetition. Every year, he would begin practice by showing his players the proper way to put on their socks, the underlying message being that no detail was too small in his famous Pyramid of Success.

> ***Every year, Wooden would begin practice by showing his players the proper way to put on their socks. No detail was too small in his famous Pyramid of Success.***

Greg Lee, who played alongside Walton on those championship teams, is fond of saying that coach Wooden motivated players from the *Ozzie and Harriet* generation to the Woodstock generation. "The principles are timeless," Walton wrote in his book, *Nothing But Net*, "and they help explain why John Wooden was able to relate to players in four different decades. As players changed, so did John Wooden."

> **"Bob reminds me of Alexander the Great, who conquered the world and then sat down and cried because there was nothing left to conquer."**
>
> —Al McGuire, on Bob Knight

Nobody has ever taken himself or the coaching profession more seriously than Bob Knight, who became a coaching icon during his stormy 42-year career as head man at Army, Indiana and Texas Tech. He always saw the game as an intellectual exercise, somewhat akin to chess or war maneuvers, and he respected only those coaches whom he regarded as thinkers and philosophers. For example, he never had much respect for those coaches he regarded mostly as recruiters—Allen, Rupp and even McCracken, his Indiana forebear. But he revered the men who had invented and reinvented aspects of the game—men like Clair Bee, Joe Lapchick, Nat Holman, Pete Newell and Red Auerbach. Indeed one of Knight's greatest contributions to the sport was his service as a loyal living conduit to its past.

Like Rupp and Smith during their playing days at Kansas, Knight was mostly a benchwarmer during his three-year varsity career at Ohio State (1959-62). He was fortunate to be in the same class as Jerry Lucas and John Havlicek, who led the Buckeyes to a 75-55 win over Newell's defending champion California Golden Bears in the 1960 NCAA championship game. Ohio State returned to the final in each of the next two years, only to be upset each time by Cincinnati.

"I first heard about Pete Newell because [longtime Ohio State coach] Fred Taylor had spent a lot of time with him, talking mostly about defense," Knight said. "We had a very simple offense with a lot of fast breaks, and Lucas was a very big part of it. We scored a lot of points, but we were really better defensively."

From the moment he became an assistant to Taylor "Tates" Locke at the U.S. Military Academy at West Point, Knight made it a point to attend as many games as possible in Madison Square Garden, 50 miles to the south, so he could visit with the forgotten old coaches who had invented the Eastern style of play. He was especially interested in Bee, the former Long Island University coach and author whose Chip Hilton sports novels Knight had read while growing up in rural Ohio. "I introduced myself to Clair Bee and really pestered him from then on," Knight said. "Bee had a great grasp of basketball and he was a very autocratic coach. He just *understood*, that's all. He had this farm in upstate New York, in a really beautiful area, and I'd go up and dig fence post holes with him and talk about basketball. I took him to his induction into the Basketball Hall of Fame in Springfield."

In 1965, when Locke left West Point (taking the Miami of Ohio job a year later), Knight became, at age 24, the youngest head coach in the nation. He didn't have the talent to win with the system he had learned under Taylor at Ohio State, so he used a form of the reverse-action offense that Newell had put to good use at Cal. He also tried to add some elements from the offense that Butch van Breda Kolff had coached at Princeton with Bill Bradley. Instead of running set plays, the Princeton players would make their cuts according to the movements of the defenders.

Through Havlicek, by then a star with the Boston Celtics, Knight got to know Auerbach, the cigar-chomping genius who coached the Celtics to nine NBA titles. "I learned a lot from Red," said Knight. "He knew how to handle players better than anyone. I guess Red and Vince Lombardi—and maybe Knute Rockne—had to be sports' all-time best motivators."

Knight still says his Army days were the happiest of his career. The old coaches would come to see him when they could, because everyone else seemed to have forgotten them. Any time Lapchick was in the stands, Knight would look up to see Lapchick giving him a keep-your-chin-up sign. Knight called Bee constantly for advice, and he also got to know Alvin "Doggie" Julian, who coached Holy Cross to the 1947 NCAA title, and John "Honey" Russell, coach of the great Walter Dukes at Seton Hall in the early '50s. "Mr. Lapchick told me two things that were guidelines my entire life," Knight said. "The first was to not have any training rules. He said that if you had rules, you were going to get hurt with good kids who might screw up once. He said, 'Just tell them that if you do something I don't like, I'll handle it however I want to.' The second thing he said was, 'Do you care if people like you?' I told him that I wanted to be like him and Clair Bee and have people respect me, but liking me wasn't a big issue with me. He said, 'That's good. If you care whether people like you, you can't coach, because you'll make a lot of bad decisions based on that.' When he died, I took Bee and Holman to the wake. That's when Mrs. Lapchick took me aside and said, 'You didn't play for Joe, but you were one of his favorite boys.' That meant a lot."

In the late 1960s, Knight met two more of his coaching idols, Newell and Hank Iba. He was introduced to Newell at the St. Francis Hotel in San Francisco when Army was there to play in the Cable Car Classic. As Knight tells it, he immediately buttonholed Newell for a five-hour discussion about post play and defense.

At about that same time, give or take a few months, Knight met Iba when the old coach was giving a speech to the Touchdown Club in Akron, Ohio.

"Son," said Iba, approaching Knight to shake his hand, "I'm Henry Iba."

"I know who you are, Mr. Iba," Knight replied, "but I'm surprised you know who I am."

"Well," said Iba, "the boys back East tell me you're doing a pretty good job of playing defense."

After Knight moved to Indiana in 1971, he added yet another old-timer, Everett Dean, to his "coaching cabinet." A native of Salem, Ind., Dean had played for the Hoosiers and preceded McCracken as IU's coach from 1924 to '38. Dean then left for Stanford, which he coached to the 1942 NCAA title. Upon retiring, he moved back to Indiana and bought a farm near his hometown. "I spent a lot of time with Everett," Knight said. "I'd take him on road trips and he'd come to practices a lot."

In 1972, Knight accepted Iba's offer to help him at the Olympic trials because he wanted to learn more about Iba's passing game, a system in which a player would pass and then screen away from the ball. "Henry would reverse the ball through the center," said Knight, "and I wanted to kind of take the center out of it. I wanted all five players to be able to pass, cut and screen. I wanted the cutters to read the defense and have options. I never wanted anybody to go to an area they couldn't shoot from, and I wanted dribbling kept to a minimum."

In only his second year in Bloomington, Knight took the Hoosiers to the 1973 NCAA semifinals in St. Louis, the program's first Final Four appearance since McCracken had won his second title in 1953. Unfortunately, IU's opponent was Bill Walton's unbeaten junior-year UCLA juggernaut. To this day, Knight contends that the Hoosiers might have won the game had a charge-block call gone against Walton rather than IU center Steve Downing. The foul was Downing's fourth instead of Walton's fifth, and only a few moments later Downing fouled out. Although he outscored the Bruins' big redhead 26-14, UCLA pulled out to a 70-59 victory. Said Knight, "I've always considered that fourth foul on Downing one of the worst big calls my teams have ever had." The Bruins then rode a virtuoso performance by Walton—he made 21 of 22 shots and scored 44 points—to rout Memphis State (today's Memphis), 87-66, in the title game.

Knight never got another crack at Wooden. His 1973-74 team didn't make the NCAA Tournament. The following season, Knight's unbeaten Hoosiers were upset by Kentucky in the Mideast Regional final, and Wooden's last team beat the same Wildcats to give the Wizard his 10th and final championship. In 1975-76, Knight's perfect team went 32–0, including the NCAA title game over Michigan, which took much of the sting out of the previous season's disaster.

With Wooden gone, Knight and North Carolina's Dean Smith became the dominant figures in college coaching.

Their approaches to the game certainly were different: Knight continued to refine the "motion" offense that combined principles he had learned from Iba, Newell and others, while Smith fine-tuned tactics such as mass substitutions and his famous "four-corner" delay offense. Even more than Wooden, though, both were perfectionists obsessed with details.

Still, they managed to more or less stay out of each other's way until the 1981 NCAA championship game in Philadelphia, when, on the day that President Ronald Reagan was shot in Washington, D.C., Knight's splendid sophomore guard, Isiah Thomas, led the late-blooming Hoosiers to a 63-50 victory over Smith's Tar Heels and Knight's second national title. By the time that game was played, Smith had strayed far from his Kansas roots. Unlike Naismith and Allen, he was, at times, accused of overcoaching his gifted players, denying them their imagination and creativity. When Michael Jordan played for North Carolina, the joke was that the only person who could stop him was Dean Smith.

With Wooden gone, Knight and Smith became the dominant figures in coaching. Their approaches were different, but both were perfectionists obsessed with details.

In 1982, Smith finally got his first national title when Jordan, then a freshman, hit a jumper from the side to beat Georgetown, 63-62, in the New Orleans Superdome. But never had Smith's obsession to control been more obvious than earlier that year in the ACC tournament championship game against Virginia. The Cavaliers were led by 7'4" Ralph Sampson, while the Tar Heels had Jordan, Sam Perkins and James Worthy. By rights, it should have been a high-scoring, up-and-down game just like McLendon and his rivals at the historically black colleges used to play. Instead, with Carolina leading 44-43 and 7:34 remaining, Smith went into his delay game and Virginia coach Terry Holland refused to come out of his zone. For 7:06, Carolina didn't shoot. The Tar Heels won the game 47-45, which suited Smith just fine. But that game, more than any other, pushed the NCAA toward adopting a 45-second shot clock by the 1985-86 season. (The time was reduced to 35 seconds in 1993-94.)

Because fans—and therefore TV broadcasters—craved more scoring, the NCAA also added the three-point-shot arc before the 1986-87 season. Predictably, Knight hated the new rules because they diminished a coach's control. He also felt the three-point shot cheapened the game by rewarding good shooting instead of good team play. It was ironic, then, that in the first season with the new rules, the Hoosiers won Knight his third NCAA title. There were few better three-point shooters than Steve Alford, and Knight adjusted his motion offense to guarantee that Alford would get plenty of open shots coming off screens.

When Georgetown's John Thompson became the first African-American coach to win the NCAA Division I title in 1984, his Hoyas beat Houston 84-75 by playing in a style that was closer to Knight's or Smith's than to McLendon's. The 6'10" Thompson had learned the Eastern game during his collegiate days at Providence, after which he joined the Celtics as Bill Russell's backup. His Georgetown teams—anchored by 7-foot center Patrick Ewing—were physical, both in their half-court offense and their man-to-man defense. Thompson was all about discipline, not jazz riffs.

After 1987, Knight took only one more team back to the Final Four, but he never won another national championship. He became a grumpy old man in his last few seasons in Bloomington. Finally, after enduring its fill of loutish tantrums, altercations, an infamous chair throw and other objectionable conduct, the university fired him on Sept. 10, 2000, ending his Indiana career after 29 seasons. The disgraceful exit left a sad stain on Knight's legacy.

After a year out of coaching, Knight resurfaced at Texas Tech, which was so far off basketball's beaten path that it became a kind of exile for him. Although he built a respectable program there, barely anyone noticed, including Tech's football-loving sports fans, who filled the basketball arena mostly to witness Knight's milestones. On Jan. 1, 2007, he notched his 880th career victory to supplant Smith atop the all-time victory list in Division I. A year later, Jan. 16, 2008, Knight became the first Division I coach to win 900 games with a 68-53 victory over Texas A&M. Soon after that Knight abruptly resigned, turning the team over in midseason to his son, Pat.

Fran Fraschilla, an ESPN analyst and former coach, estimated that at the time of Knight's retirement, *every* Division I team ran some form of his motion offense, which Fraschilla defined as "random movement with rules." Even Knight's biggest detractors had to give him credit for revolutionizing the game.

"John Calipari has signed an eight-year contract that will pay him $31.65 million over the life of the deal, a stunning total to lead the storied [Kentucky] program back to prominence ... In a sure sign of the magnitude of Calipari's presence at UK, his annual average salary of $3.96 million will exceed that of Florida coach Billy Donovan, who ... made $3.3 million with the Gators this season."

—*Cats Pause,* a publication devoted to Kentucky athletics

As college basketball headed into its second century, the money at stake and the pressure to win reached extravagant levels, with the result that contracts between coaches and universities seemed hardly to be worth the paper on which they were printed. Midway through the 2008-09 season, Alabama parted ways with coach (and alumnus) Mark Gottfried and Georgia dumped Dennis Felton. After the season, Kentucky fired Billy Clyde Gillispie after only two seasons and Sean Miller bolted Xavier for Arizona while the ink was still drying on his long-term contract. Loyalty, on both sides, was as dead as the two-handed set shot.

Instead of getting together with their peers to draw up X's and O's, today's coaches are more apt to spend time with their agents, accountants and stockbrokers. The business side has gotten so big that few coaches seem to devote much time to coming up with new ideas. "In the old days, coaches could be friends," Knight said. "They got along well and enjoyed each other. They exchanged ideas. We don't see that today in this multimillion-dollar business we're in."

The coach whose philosophy most closely mirrors Knight's, perhaps not surprisingly, is Duke's Mike Krzyzewski, who played for Knight at Army in the late 1960s and spent a year coaching under him at Indiana. A tough kid from Chicago, Krzyzewski thrived under Knight's demanding regimen at West Point. Knight recommended that Army hire Krzyzewski as its coach in 1975, and he recommended him again to Duke in 1980. For nearly three decades, Krzyzewski has been one of the college game's most respected spokesmen and tacticians. His Duke teams use much of the offense and defense he learned under Knight, but it took a long time before sportswriters stopped reflexively identifying him as a "Knight disciple"—a change that both Coach K's appreciated.

Although Krzyzewski won his third NCAA title in 2001, the period from 1999 to 2009 was dominated by three coaches who won two championships each: Jim Calhoun of Connecticut (1999 and 2004), Donovan of Florida (2006 and '07), and Roy Williams of North Carolina (2005 and '09).

When UConn hired Calhoun away from Northeastern in 1986, it had no idea it was getting a coach who would muscle and finesse his way into the college game's elite. Before Calhoun, the Huskies had a 4–14 record in 13 NCAA Tournaments and had never advanced beyond a regional final. Under Calhoun, however, UConn became a part of the national championship conversation almost every season. A spiritual descendant of the Eastern coaches of the 1930s and '40s, Calhoun developed teams known for their toughness. By 2009, he and UConn women's coach Geno Auriemma were the highest-paid public employees in Connecticut, each earning $1.6 million per year. But all the attention on UConn basketball also brought scrutiny; investigations into the possibility of recruiting violations rattled Calhoun and led him to begin musing about retirement.

Donovan was known as Billy the Kid when he played at Providence under Rick Pitino because of his boyish looks and willingness to pull the trigger from three-point range. He led the Friars to the 1987 Final Four and then became Pitino's assistant at Kentucky. After five seasons in Lexington, Donovan took the head job at Marshall, then moved to Florida in 1996. The Gators' back-to-back national championships made Donovan the first coach to accomplish the feat since Krzyzewski at Duke in 1991 and '92, and he did it by employing the freewheeling style he learned from Pitino.

Pitino himself is a product of Eastern basketball combined with a touch of Rupp. After learning the game in his native New York City and on Long Island, Pitino played college ball at Massachusetts, where, as a freshman, he watched the electrifying Julius Erving's senior team. From UMass, Pitino served apprenticeships at Hawaii and Syracuse and held the head job at Boston University before moving to Providence just as the Big East was becoming one of the nation's top conferences. When the 45-second shot clock and three-point field goal went into effect, Pitino reacted more adroitly than any other coach in the nation, combining a high-octane offense that relied on long-range shooting with a trapping defense that used a full-court press. Like McLendon, Pitino jazzed up the sport at a time when it was beginning to look more like a waltz.

After a two-year stint in the NBA with the Knicks, Pitino brought to Lexington the freewheeling style he had used at Providence, and Kentucky fans welcomed the return of the fast-paced game—so similar to the style Rupp had favored while making Kentucky the nation's premier program in the 1940s and '50s. Modifying the system as his talent pool grew, Pitino reached the Final Four in 1993 (his fourth year in Lexington), won the NCAA title in 1996 and nearly won a second consecutive title in 1997 before losing to Arizona in overtime. He then decided to take another crack at the NBA but, after three miserable years with the Celtics, came back to the college ranks—this time at Kentucky's hated instate rival, Louisville.

When the Cardinals reached the 2005 Final Four in St. Louis, Pitino became the first coach to take three different programs to the college game's biggest stage. He also could take pride in the fact that his former assistants and players were putting him in the class of Dean Smith and Bob Knight as a mentor. Besides Donovan with his back-to-back titles, Tubby Smith won the 1998 championship—the seventh for Kentucky, the team he inherited from Pitino.

As for Williams, he became the most recent headliner in the incestuous North Carolina-Kansas relationship. He joined Smith's staff in the early 1980s and was on the bench for the Tar Heels' 1982 title; he moved to Kansas in 1988 and took the Jayhawks to four Final Fours and two championship games; then he returned to Carolina in 2003 to revive a program that had slipped under Smith's successor, Bill Guthridge, and slid even more drastically under former Tar Heel Matt Doherty.

> ***As a new era at the game's most storied university was about to begin, observers were feeling that Kentucky and Calipari either deserved each other or were destined for each other.***

Even after North Carolina routed Michigan State, 89-72, to win the 2009 championship and tie him with Smith at two national titles, the modest Williams said, "I can't put Roy Williams and Dean Smith into the same sentence, and I'm not being humble." In at least one way, he was right. Smith never earned the sort of money North Carolina was paying Williams—an estimated $2.6 million-plus per year. And that still wasn't as much as Kansas was paying Williams' successor, Bill Self, who did in 2008 what Williams never could in Lawrence—win the national title.

Almost as soon as Self won that championship, he was approached by Oklahoma State, his alma mater and the school made famous by Iba, about its head coaching vacancy. It was reported that oil magnate and Oklahoma State booster T. Boone Pickens, who had already contributed $165 million to the Cowboys athletic program, was prepared to offer Self a blank check. In the new era of coach-as-businessman, Self, then 45, shocked a lot of people by opting to stay at Kansas, replacing the three years remaining on his contract with a new deal reportedly worth $30 million over 10 years.

The 2009 Final Four at Detroit's Ford Field was almost overshadowed by gossip about the huge contract Calipari received to leave Memphis for Kentucky. At 50, he was one of the hottest coaches in the nation, having led Memphis to four consecutive 30-win seasons and the 2008 title game (where the Tigers had Kansas on the ropes before missing a bunch of free throws down the stretch in regulation and losing in overtime). Those Kentucky fans who had never gotten over the way Pitino jilted them in 1997 were thrilled. Besides sounding and acting like Pitino, Calipari favors an up-tempo style of play—the old fast break evolved into the dribble-drive motion offense—that the most gifted athletes love nearly as much as they love Calipari's gift of gab.

Some critics are wary of Calipari's close relationships with so-called "street agents" and AAU coaches, who have increasingly replaced high school coaches as the primary advisors of many top prospects. These men establish close bonds with players who are still in their teens and help steer (some cynics believe "shop" is a more accurate verb) them to big-time colleges. More of today's college stars are "one-and-done" players who have little or no interest in academics and seek only to showcase their talent for a single season to increase their value as professionals. At Memphis, for example, Calipari recruited guard Derrick Rose through his friendship with a highly influential, if somewhat mysterious, man named William Wesley, known throughout basketball as Worldwide Wes. Rose starred as a freshman on the Tigers' 2008 national runner-up team, then opted for the NBA draft, in which Chicago made him the No. 1 overall pick.

As a new era at the game's most storied university was about to begin, many close observers were feeling that Kentucky and Calipari either deserve each other or were destined for each other—take your pick. Beyond the politics, jealousies and questionable ethics and that are now entwined with the sport, the Rupp style of basketball—*winning* basketball—is back in vogue in Lexington. Calipari knows he's expected to start hanging more championship banners in the rafters at Lexington. And he hasn't flinched. Why should he? Basketball is such a simple game.

As Coach Diddle might have told him, all he needs to do is make sure he can keep getting enough boys who can toss the ball in the basket more often than the boys on the other teams.

One Sport, Two Games

How college basketball has reflected—and helped heal—America's racial divide

BY KAREEM ABDUL-JABBAR

Basketball's pedigree has always had a spiritual component. After all, the game was invented by a teacher with advanced degrees in philosophy and religion who later divided his time between his spiritual calling as a chapel director and his physical calling as a basketball coach. So it's appropriate that basketball would come to symbolize both the physical and spiritual ambitions of America. The game first conceived by 30-year-old James Naismith in 1891 wasn't just a clever new activity designed to give athletes an interesting indoor outlet in the winter. It came to be a proving ground for bringing the disenfranchised African-American athlete out of the cold gulag of segregation.

Throughout the first half of the 20th century, black adults, hardened by lifetimes of enduring institutionalized discrimination, would take to the voting booths, the media and the streets in their long and grinding battle for recognition and integration. But the more vulnerable—and less patient—black youth of America tended to begin their struggles for acceptance in school playgrounds and gymnasiums.

Perhaps nowhere was this struggle for integration more intense or heartfelt than in colleges and universities, because these were the institutions organized to represent the collective intellect, learning and rational thinking of thousands of years of civilization. If the schools that were meant to produce the leaders of tomorrow practiced segregation, what did that say about the true soul of America—and what hope did they offer for the future? If not here, where else could young African-Americans expect fair play?

As a boy growing up in the 1950s in Harlem, the sport I loved most was baseball. I knew nothing about basketball until I was well into grade school, but baseball was part of my life in a big way. My mother's friend, Mary Mitchell, used to babysit me, and she was a big baseball fan. She lived only a short walk from the Polo Grounds, where the New York Giants played, and Yankee Stadium was just a 10-minute bus ride away. As a lucky result, I got to see Willie Mays play as a rookie and Joe DiMaggio in his final year.

I first saw basketball played at the park in my neighborhood, but the players weren't very good and the game didn't interest me. I knew nothing about the history of the game in my own community, including the fact that Harlem was home to the Rens, the team that won the very first World Professional Basketball Tournament, in Chicago in 1939. And I was certainly unaware of the important role basketball had already played in integrating American society. For me it was just a game. It would take a while before I learned about how long and difficult the path to integration had been, and would continue to be.

As the 1950s and '60s unfolded—and I unfolded along with it, into a 7'2" basketball prodigy—I became more aware of what was at stake as civil rights issues dominated American political activity. In 1965, the year I graduated from Power Memorial Academy, I had to consider the racial policies of the many universities that offered me scholarships. Some were willing to admit black students, but only to benefit from their athletic skills. Some colleges—the entire Southeastern Conference, for example—still had no black players at all. It had been 74 years since basketball was invented, but the top high school player in the country—me—was still not free to play for the college of his choice. Not that I would have chosen any school that had exhibited such racist policies.

It was 13 years after Professor Naismith nailed up the first peach baskets at a Springfield, Mass., YMCA that another instructor, Edwin Henderson, began teaching basketball to young black kids in Washington, D.C. Because basketball was strictly segregated in his time, Henderson formed the first athletic conference just for black players. The Interscholastic Athletic Association (ISAA) included all-black teams throughout the mid-Atlantic states from every available source—public schools, athletic clubs, churches and colleges. By 1915, black kids were passing pumpkin-size balls with finger-thick laces around high school and college courts in virtually every major city in America.

Among the first predominantly black universities to form basketball teams were Virginia's Hampton Institute and Virginia Union, Pennsylvania's Lincoln University and Ohio's Wilberforce University. In 1912, Howard University of Washington, D.C., and Shaw University of North Carolina joined Hampton, Virginia Union and Lincoln to form the all-black Colored Intercollegiate Athletic Association (known since 1952 as the *Central* Intercollegiate Athletic Association).

Copyright © 2009 by Kareem Abdul-Jabbar. All rights reserved.

Despite the standout athletic abilities and playing talents of the African-American students, college basketball teams more resembled the Sharks and Jets of *West Side Story* than today's Bruins and Trojans. In the 1950s musical, Anita warned Maria to "stick to your own kind," and that's exactly what colleges and universities did. Black players were confined to the "historically black" colleges and universities of the East and South, while the teams that were members of the NCAA or NAIA were virtually all-white. Because of Jim Crow laws and tradition, the "historically black" schools operated in their own world, mostly beyond the coverage of mainstream newspapers, radio and television. These schools produced dazzling superstars such as Sam Jones, Earl Monroe, Dick Barnett, Willis Reed and Zelmo Beaty, but their accomplishments don't appear in any NCAA record books or tournament histories—simply because their teams were not allowed to compete in NCAA events (see "Shadow Play," page 20).

It had been 74 years since basketball was invented, but the top high school player in the country—me—was still not free to play for the college of his choice.

Occasionally, a particularly outstanding black player got a chance to play for a white school. In the years before World War I, Paul Robeson played for Rutgers, Wilbur Wood for Nebraska, Fenwick Watkins for the University of Vermont and Cumberland Posey for Penn State. Robeson and Posey would become major figures in African-American sports history by helping to change the way black athletes were viewed by white America.

As an adult, Robeson (1898-1976) was an internationally recognized Renaissance Man who spoke more than 20 languages, acted in popular movies such as *Showboat* and *The Emperor Jones*, sang in concerts around the world and was intensely active in the civil rights movement. During his years at Rutgers, Robeson's achievements were equally impressive. Enrolled on an academic scholarship and the only black student on campus, he was one of just three members of his class accepted into Phi Beta Kappa and one of four chosen for the exclusive honor society Cap and Skull. He graduated as the Class of 1919 valedictorian. That would be more than enough for most students, but not Robeson. He was also a star athlete, earning 15 varsity letters in football, baseball, basketball and track and field.

But integration didn't come with a free pass, even for someone as talented as Robeson. In his first football scrimmage, some of his teammates savagely beat him, even ripping off his fingernails. Undaunted, he went on to become a two-time All-America and was called by his coach, Walter Camp, "the greatest end to ever trod the gridiron." In basketball, the 6'2" Robeson was a powerful forward who lettered at Rutgers for three seasons and led the Knights in scoring in 1918 with eight points per game.

After Rutgers, Robeson took seriously the class prophecy that he would one day be "the leader of the colored race in America." He went to Columbia University Law School, supporting himself by playing in the American Professional Football League and acting in New York and London. He quit a prominent law firm when a white secretary refused to take dictation from him. Then he abandoned law and focused on his acting and singing, the better to promote African-American history and culture. He became the target of persecution, not just by racist mobs, but also by the federal and state governments, in part because he was a highly vocal supporter of Soviet communism. After one of his concerts, in Peekskill, N.Y., was disrupted by white demonstrators while police stood by and did nothing, Robeson declared, "I'm going to sing wherever the people want me to sing … and I won't be frightened by crosses burning in Peekskill or anywhere else." A few years later, Albert Einstein sought Robeson's counsel on world peace.

Cumberland Willis "Cum" Posey Jr. (1890-1946) was also a gifted college athlete, considered by some to be the greatest basketball player of his time. Born and raised in Homestead, Pa., Posey led his high school team to the 1908 Pittsburgh city championship, then went on to play for two years at Penn State. In 1912 his all-black Monticello Athletic Association team was declared the first unofficial "Colored Basketball World's Champion" by a New York sportswriter. Posey later returned to play college ball again, this time under the alias Charles Cumbert, at the University of the Holy Ghost (today's Duquesne). After that, he led a Pittsburgh team called the Loendi Big Five to four straight championships in a tournament organized for the nation's best black teams.

Posey was also an excellent outfielder for the Murdock Grays, a semipro baseball team made up of black Pittsburgh-area steelworkers. By 1916 he was the manager, and a few years later he bought the team, by then known as the Homestead Grays. The Grays eventually won nine consecutive Negro National League pennants (1937-45) and three Negro World Series titles. Ironically, Posey was *against* integration because—according to Brad Snyder, author of *Beyond the Shadow of the Senators*—he believed it would cause him to lose all his best players to white teams and bring about the collapse of the Negro National League.

Posey was right. On April 18, 1946, less than a month after his death, the Brooklyn Dodgers signed Jackie Robinson, and in 1949 the Negro National League disbanded. Despite Posey's desire to keep his successful segregated world successfully segregated, by developing and showcasing such talented black athletes he helped make the integration of college and professional sports inevitable.

Although Posey and Robeson didn't directly force the full integration of college basketball, each played a pivotal role in its eventuality. They were part of a much larger movement that helped redefine the way white America thought about African-Americans. The Harlem Renaissance of the 1920s and '30s had popularized the idea of the "New Negro," black men and women who rose to prominence during this time. White America was forced to sit up and take notice of the many black Americans who were now publishing acclaimed books, playing jazz, exhibiting innovative works of art and passionately voicing the hopes and dreams of those who had never before been heard. But not all of white America was happy about it.

While the Harlem Renaissance may have made for good public relations among the more educated segments of white society, Ed Henderson, a black man who worked daily with black kids in the segregated public schools of Washington, D.C., was skeptical of the impact such advancements would have on the hearts and minds of the average white American. In Henderson's view, only if large numbers of blacks were able to demonstrate their excellence in sports would white working men and women finally wake up and begin to shed their prejudices. Henderson explained his belief in a 1927 interview: "I doubt much whether the mere acquisition of hundreds of degrees or academic honors have influenced the mass mind of America as much as the soul appeal made in a thrilling run for a touchdown by a colored athlete ... Fairness creeps out of the soul in the athletic world to a larger extent than anywhere else."

Given the great chuffing locomotive of civil rights that seemed to be barreling through American history before midcentury, integration might have looked like a forgone conclusion that was right around the next bend. Well, there is *Integration* and *integration*. The first form—Integration with an uppercase I—is an official and public policy that usually involves some form of tokenism. Laws are passed by well-meaning legislators, and businesses and institutions, suddenly compelled, begin hiring one or two members of an oppressed minority. The tokens can be paraded about any time a particular institution's commitment to integration is questioned. Never mind that the same institution may employ 500 whites and two African-Americans.

The second form is integration—with a lowercase i—which reflects integration as it is meant to be: without need to enforce it through law, but a natural state of existence within a society because it prizes and celebrates differences rather than fears and attacks them. Unfortunately, despite the enormous athletic achievements of black college students during the early part of the 20th century, true integration remained a dream. What came instead, with the 1954 U.S. Supreme Court decision in *Brown v. Board of Education of Topeka*, was Integration. Separate could no longer be considered equal, but at most colleges it merely meant that some occasional tokens would be allowed to play, not that they'd be truly accepted as part of the college's community.

The integration of college basketball didn't arrive with a sudden burst of enlightenment, as if 110 million lightbulbs flashed on above white America's heads; it wasn't a locked door suddenly being kicked open to let in fresh air and sunlight. It was a trickle of drop after drop after drop, until the rancid bucket toppled over, ending

In Henderson's view, only if large numbers of blacks were able to demonstrate their excellence in sports would white working men and women finally wake up and begin to shed their prejudices.

segregation forever. One such drop was George Gregory Jr. (1906-1994), who, in 1931, became the first African-American basketball player to be chosen as All-America. Just the second African-American to play for Columbia, Gregory scored 191 points in 23 games as the Lions went 21–2 in the pre-Ivy Eastern Collegiate League. He was again named All-America the following year (joining, among others, a guard out of Purdue named John Wooden, who would go on to become not only the greatest coach in the history of college basketball but also a major force for integration.)

Between the 1920s and the 1960s college basketball continued to integrate, not at the locomotive speed civil rights activists had hoped for, but at the glacial pace they had feared. Perhaps the popularity of all things Negro during the Harlem Renaissance produced what the Pulitzer-prize-winning journalist Susan Faludi refers to as a backlash effect. In her 1991 book *Backlash*, Faludi argues that each time in American history an oppressed group gains significant headway in society, a phalanx of frightened reactionary activists creates a backlash to strip away those gains. Certainly that seemed to be the case during those decades when segregation seemed to be as divisive and resilient as the Berlin Wall. But history tells us that walls, no matter how thick or long or sturdy, always ultimately fail in their purpose. Hadrian's Wall did not keep the Roman Empire in power in Britain. The Great Wall of China did not keep out the Manchus or the Mongols. And the Berlin Wall did not keep democracy out of Eastern Europe. Neither would the wall of segregation stand intact in America. But for the middle decades of the 20th century, all anyone could do was chip away at it.

Sometimes events that lead to social change are sudden, violent and very public. Sometimes they are private and secret, affecting only a few people at the time but generating a domino effect on many others. One such event was the Secret Game of 1944, the existence of which was publicly revealed only in 1996. Most of the best college players of 1944 were on the battlefields of World War II. But Duke University, because it offered an accelerated medical education program, attracted some highly intelligent students from across the country, some of whom happened to be top-notch basketball players. A group of these would-be doctors—all white, of course—put together a team that routinely trounced local church and city-league teams. They were so good, in fact, that they traveled extensively from their Durham, N.C., campus to compete against, and usually beat, semi-pro teams.

One Sunday in March, the team from Duke piled into a couple of borrowed cars and started driving, following a long and deliberately complex route, snaking through town until they finally arrived in the black district of Durham. The cloak-and-dagger journey was meant to discourage anyone who may have wanted to follow them. And anyone who had followed would have been shocked when the players pulled onto the campus of the North Carolina College for Negroes (now North Carolina Central University). Wary black faces peered down from dorm windows at the visitors, because whites were very rarely seen on campus. The Duke players were sneaked into the gym through the women's dressing room. NCC coach John McLendon, who had learned the game from Naismith in Kansas (see "The Teachers," page 2) and whose 1944 team was 19–1 in the Colored Intercollegiate Athletic Association, locked the gym doors. No spectators were permitted. This was not going to be just a secret game between two proud teams; under North Carolina law, a crime was about to be committed.

No spectators were permitted. This was not going to be just a secret game between two proud teams; under North Carolina law, a crime was about to be committed.

When the teams lined up for the opening tap, palpable tension filled the gym because most of the black players had never been permitted to touch a white person. "For the first five minutes, you felt like the biggest sinner in the world, in the biggest church in the world," said Edward "Pee Wee" Boyd, the NCC team manager. "But then we found out that the black wouldn't rub off and the white wouldn't rub off." NCC trounced the Duke med students, 88-44. After the humiliation, the two teams did something even more radical: They split up into integrated sides and played a shirts vs. skins pickup game. Afterward, the NCC players brought the Duke players to their dorm to shower, share some sodas and get acquainted. The med students never spoke of the secret game when they returned to Duke, for fear of being ostracized by their classmates and triggering possible reprisals against the

NCC players. The Ku Klux Klan was still quite active in North Carolina and exposure could have led to violence. The NCC players kept quiet for the same reason.

No one kept quiet about the phenomenal Bill Garrett (1929-74), who is sometimes called the Jackie Robinson of college basketball. While Garrett didn't topple the wall, he certainly punched a hole through it big enough for people to glimpse the future of the game—and of America. After he earned the coveted title of Indiana's Mr. Basketball while leading his Shelbyville High School team to the state title, Garrett became the first African-American to play at Indiana University—but only after black leaders in Bloomington persuaded coach Branch McCracken and IU president Herman B. Wells to offer Garrett a scholarship. Also the first African-American to play regularly in the Big Ten, Garrett led the Hoosiers in scoring and rebounding for three seasons, earned Most Valuable Player and All-America honors in 1951, and left Indiana as the school's career scoring leader with 792 points.

But as had happened so many times before, Garrett's achievements came with a personal cost: ugly racism and discrimination. A few days after his final college game, Garrett and two white teammates who were also close friends were driving back to campus from Indianapolis when they stopped for lunch at a diner outside Bloomington. A big sign reading "Hurryin' Hoosiers Fans Welcome" promised that Garrett and his mates would be fed and treated well, since he was the best-known Hoosier of them all. But when the men sat down to order, a waiter told Garrett's teammates, "I can feed the two of you, but not him." The three walked out and drove away, with Garrett in the back seat, weeping.

Garrett might have become the fourth African-American to play in the NBA after the Boston Celtics drafted him in 1951 (Earl Lloyd, Chuck Cooper and Nat "Sweetwater" Clifton had joined the league a year earlier). Unfortunately for the Celtics, a few months later Garrett was drafted by an even bigger team—the U.S. Army. When he was discharged in 1953, he found that the Celtics no longer wanted him—they had already filled their "unofficial quota" of two black players, Cooper and Don Barksdale. So Garrett joined the Harlem Globetrotters instead. Abandoning professional basketball three years later, he became a teacher and coach at the all-black Crispus Attucks High School in Indianapolis. Later he became dean of student activities at Indiana University-Purdue University Indianapolis. He died of a heart attack at the age of 45 in 1974, but his achievements served as a catalyst for the further integration of college basketball. By Garrett's senior year at Indiana, the freshman teams at Michigan and Michigan State each had their first black player.

"Just think if Bill Garrett hadn't worked out at IU," said the legendary Oscar Robertson. "Where would the black athlete have been?"

Perhaps Robertson understood the importance of Garrett's role in the integration of college basketball more than most. In 1955, Robertson's team at Crispus Attucks (Garrett's future employer) amassed a 31–1 record on the way to becoming the first all-black team in the nation to win an open state championship. The following year, Crispus Attucks improved its record to a perfect 31–0 and won a second Indiana state championship. But Robertson learned early about the mixed blessings that come with being a winner—when you're black. Even though Attucks' first state championship was also the first by any Indianapolis school, city officials decided to forgo the traditional downtown victory parade and forced the team to celebrate near the school in one of the city's black neighborhoods. The team and its supporters were outraged. Said Robertson, "I guess they felt black people would tear up downtown. I was part of Indiana basketball history. I wasn't an asterisk on the side, and neither were the other guys on the Crispus Attucks team. We were a part of the Indiana High School Athletic Association and we shouldn't have been treated that way."

"I guess they felt black people would tear up downtown," said Robertson. "I was part of Indiana basketball history. I wasn't an asterisk on the side."

After high school, Robertson starred at the University of Cincinnati, leading the nation in scoring in each of his three seasons. Over his career he averaged 33.8 points per game (still the third-highest average in NCAA history after Pete Maravich's 44.2 and Austin Carr's 34.6) and set 19 school and 14 NCAA records. He was a three-time consensus All-America and College Player of the Year in one poll or another in 1958, '59 and '60. But as with his forerunner, Garrett, Robertson's college successes were tainted by persistent racism. Though he declared in a

1999 interview that he would "never forgive" Indianapolis officials for disrespecting the 1955 champions from Crispus Attucks, he did receive a measure of satisfaction in 1998 when the U.S. Basketball Writers Association announced that the award given annually to the NCAA Division I Player of the Year would be named the Oscar Robertson Trophy.

The NBA's top draft pick in 1960, Robertson played 10 brilliant seasons with the Cincinnati Royals. In his second season he set an NBA standard that has yet to be matched: *averaging* a triple-double (double figures in scoring, assists and rebounding) for the entire season. But none of his Cincinnati teams—college or pro—was able to win a championship. Oscar was finally able to get his first title since high school in the 1970-71 season, his 11th in the NBA, when the Royals traded him to the Milwaukee Bucks. There, the distinguished veteran teamed up with a certain high-potential rookie center by the name of Kareem Abdul-Jabbar. Winning my first (of six) NBA championships while my great integration-pioneering teammate, Oscar Robertson, won his first and only was an especially poignant thrill for me.

Loyola made history in 1962 when it became the first team in NCAA Division I to field an all-black lineup. There was no turning back now.

The list of exceptional black college players from the mid-1950s through the start of the 1960s who endured endless racial taunts and cut a swath for other African-Americans to follow includes some of the greatest figures in the history of the sport. Bill Russell led the University of San Francisco to NCAA titles in 1955 and '56. The 6'9" Russell was so dominating that the NCAA instituted what became known as the Russell Rule—widening the foul lane from six to 12 feet to force centers to play farther from the basket. Wilt Chamberlain, the 7'1" Kansas All-America in 1957-58, was such a powerhouse that by the time he was 21, he'd been profiled in *Time*, *Look*, *Life* and *Newsweek* magazines.

These men, and many other African-American players, helped college basketball fashion an appearance of tolerance and integration at midcentury. But the reality was that they had to run head-first into that stone wall of racism every day, yet still persevere and play great basketball to justify their inclusion on mostly white teams. It was *Integration*—tokenism, quotas, restrictions—not *integration*, in which every player, regardless of race, would have an equal opportunity to play, based only on talent.

The 1960s finally began to bring some serious damage to that wall. In 1961, coach George Ireland of Loyola University in Chicago drove a bulldozer through it when he broke the time-honored "gentlemen's agreement" among coaches not to put more than three black players on the court at any one time. Ireland had the temerity to use as many as four black players at a time—in every game. Loyola made history in 1962 when it became first team in NCAA Division I to field an all-black lineup. Cincinnati won the 1962 Tournament (over Ohio State) using four black starters, and in the 1963 Final, Loyola beat Cincinnati, 60-58, in overtime. A great game, no doubt, but its historical significance stems from the fact that seven of the game's 10 starters (four for Loyola and three for Cincinnati) were African-American.

There was no turning back now. All around the country, people were kicking down that wall—African-American players from the one side, college coaches desperate to stay competitive from the other. By 1966, teams from the large Southern universities of the Southeastern and Atlantic Coast Conferences were among the last anti-integrationist holdouts. That folly was exposed when coach Don Haskins of Texas Western (now the University of Texas at El Paso) started five black players in the NCAA championship game against Adolph Rupp's highly favored—and all-white—Kentucky Wildcats. The result—Texas Western 72, Kentucky 65—shook the foundation of the sport.

On Jan. 20, 1968, my own UCLA Bruins met the University of Houston Cougars and their great forward, Elvin Hayes, in the so-called Game of the Century at the Houston Astrodome. The historical significance of this game wasn't a matter of how many blacks played for each team (for the record, each team started four) or that Houston beat us, 71-69, behind Elvin's 39 points to snap our 47-game winning streak. What mattered was that this was the first NCAA regular-season game to be shown nationally on prime-time television. The high ratings convinced network executives that there was big money to be made broadcasting college basketball.

This affected the integration of the sport in two significant ways: 1) Americans across the country could witness for themselves the extraordinary skills of black players, shattering the established prejudices of older fans and diminishing the chances of them taking hold in the younger generation; and 2) Southern schools had to watch as young black players left the region for points north and west to dazzle audiences and win championships for schools with less restrictive racial policies.

Quite suddenly, all-white teams from Southern schools began earnestly recruiting black players. No African-American had ever played in the ACC until Billy Jones entered his first varsity game for Maryland in December 1965. Vanderbilt integrated the Southeastern Conference in 1967 when it recruited Tennessee schoolboy Perry Wallace. Kentucky signed its first black player, Tom Payne, in 1969. Louisiana State's first black player was Collis Temple, in 1971.

In 1970, Illinois State made Will Robinson, a legendary Detroit high school coach, the first African-American to head an NCAA Division I program. In 1971, for the first time, every member of the consensus All-America first team was black—guards Austin Carr (Notre Dame) and Dean Meminger (Marquette), center Artis Gilmore (Jacksonville), and forwards Jim McDaniels (Western Kentucky) and Sidney Wicks (UCLA). In 1972, John Thompson, Bill Russell's former backup on the Boston Celtics, became coach at Georgetown. Twelve years later, he was the first African-American coach to win the NCAA Tournament.

When it came time for me to choose a college in 1965, I had a lot of choices. Why? One reason was that I was a good basketball player more than seven feet tall coming off a championship high school career. In my three years on the Power Memorial varsity, we went 96–6 (including a 71-game winning streak), won three straight New York City Catholic League titles, and I averaged 20.3 points per game. But there were other reasons, foremost among them people like Bill Garrett, Bill Russell, Wilt Chamberlain and Oscar Robertson suffering the slings and arrows of outraged segregationists before me. More than 100 universities expressed interest in me, but a number of schools with important basketball programs—Kentucky, North Carolina and most of the other SEC and ACC schools—expressed no interest at all.

That came as a shock. It hadn't occurred to me that certain schools still wanted nothing to do with black athletes. Oscar and others had felt intense racial hostility during their high school and college years, but I was fortunate to be part of the first group of black athletes who got to see significant barriers fall in the wake of successes in the civil rights movement. But, as I discovered, some barriers in the Deep South remained intact.

I chose UCLA mostly because of its basketball supremacy. I also received letters from two UCLA alumni who meant a great deal to me. Jackie Robinson had been a student there from 1939 to '41 and competed in baseball, football, basketball and track and field. And Dr. Ralph Bunche, who had played basketball for the Bruins in the 1920s, went on to win the Nobel Peace Prize in 1950 and the Medal of Freedom from President John F. Kennedy in 1963. Both men extolled UCLA's history of encouraging students of color to achieve in ways that were uncommon at other campuses. But a big part of my decision definitely had to do with coach John Wooden's attitude toward integration.

At UCLA we won not just games and NCAA championships—three in my three seasons; seven straight and 10 in 12 years for Coach Wooden—but also the minds of those white fans who were skeptical that blacks belonged on America's college teams.

Before he came to UCLA in 1948, Wooden had been the coach at Indiana State. At the end of the 1946-47 season, ISU was invited to compete in the NAIB (later to become the NAIA) tournament in Kansas City. But the invitation carried a condition: Wooden's team would have to come without its one black player, Clarence Walker. Coach Wooden thanked the tournament committee, but said that either his entire team would come, or it would stay home. The NAIB stood its ground and so did Coach Wooden. The following year, ISU was invited to the tournament once again—with the same condition, which elicited the same reply from Coach Wooden. This time, however, there was such a clamor to have the best teams in the tournament that the organizing committee backed down and allowed ISU to bring Walker.

But there were other problems. Though Walker could play, the NAIB still insisted that he not stay in the same hotel as his white teammates nor attend any publicity functions. Wooden nearly declined the conditional invitation again, but reconsidered after consulting with local NAACP leaders and with Walker and his family. He found a black minister who would house Walker in Kansas City, but while traveling to and from the tournament, the team had trouble finding restaurants that would serve blacks. Indiana State lost in the final to Louisville, 92-70, but the NAIB/NAIA tournament was never again segregated. Ten years later, when Tennessee State, an all-black team coached by John McLendon and led by Dick Barnett, won three straight NAIA titles (1957-59), Coach Wooden received hate mail blaming him for forcing the integration of the tournament. But his earlier resolve meant that the best athletes would get to compete in that tournament, and he never had a single misgiving about what he had done.

Oscar described Coach Wooden's importance in 2005: "What really pushed African-Americans to fully integrate was UCLA. [Most] other teams had one black player, maybe two. Coach Wooden had five or six. And they won."

I decided to become one of those five or six players. And we did, indeed, win, not just games and NCAA championships—three in my three seasons on the varsity; seven straight and 10 in 12 years for Coach Wooden—but also the minds of those white fans who were skeptical that blacks belonged on America's college teams.

Compared to those players who came before me, I had a fairly mild time as an African-American player at UCLA. Yes, there were the occasional racial slurs and demeaning comments, but for the most part I was untouched. Perhaps I was *too* untouched, forgetting that being a basketball star on an insular Southern California campus lined with palm trees wasn't the real world for a young African-American man in late-1960s America. It was only in the summer of 1966, when I was visiting Harlem, that I saw myself as racists saw me: as a target. That experience helped me realize that real integration didn't exist just because a lucky few of us had the opportunity to have our dreams come true. It would only exist when *everybody* had that opportunity. And I realized that college integration wasn't just about how many black students *matriculated* at a particular school; it was about how they were *treated* at that school.

So when African-American students and athletes at San Jose State threatened in 1967 to boycott the school's football games unless their grievances concerning racial discrimination on campus were addressed, I threw my support behind them. I had come to realize—as had so many black athletes before me and since—that sports provides a platform from which to address a wider audience than we would get by standing on street corners holding up signs railing about injustice. We used that platform in two ways: We exposed through our athletic abilities the ridiculousness of old racist notions that we weren't good enough to compete against white athletes, and we used our voices to reveal and accentuate the racial injustices that many might otherwise choose not to see.

We forced them to see the truth.

For us, college basketball integration was the first step toward universal integration, because we were fighting to create a world that wasn't just integrated, but that no longer even needed the word "integration."

Shadow Play

The game we know today was shaped by men the white world and the record books shunned

While college basketball boomed from the 1940s through the '60s, with its star players and teams glorified in print and on radio and TV, another version of the game was being played literally in the shadows. All but ignored by the NCAA, the NIT, most of the media and the record books—and therefore most fans—were the teams and players from what were then called Negro colleges. Today, they are known as Historically Black Colleges and Universities (HBCU). Many of them trace their origins to the second half of the 19th century, when the 13th and 14th amendments to the U.S. Constitution abolished slavery and promised equal rights for all citizens, regardless of race.

Equal? Not close. For most African-Americans, the HBCU schools were the only game in town. The 1896 U.S. Supreme Court decision in the case of *Plessy v. Ferguson* allowed states to operate "separate but equal" public facilities and schools, a ruling that left most African-Americans with the choice of attending either a Negro college or no college at all.

Basketball began taking root at the HBCUs in the early 1900s, just as it did in white colleges. But the game, as played and coached in all-black communities, developed differently than the all-white version. Not unlike the way black musicians expressed their creativity through jazz, combining the exuberant rhythms of African music with more structured European styles, black players at schools like North Carolina College for Negroes and Winston-Salem (N.C.) Teachers College, coached by John McLendon and Clarence "Big House" Gaines, respectively, played an up-tempo game that produced higher scores and much more movement than the more static "white" game. The fast breaks, quick shots and acrobatic moves of the players fed energy to the crowds, who, in turn, motivated the players to be even more creative. The game they played was anathema to that being taught by most coaches at white colleges.

Dozens of colleges today still proudly consider themselves "historically black." But when the Supreme Court struck down "separate but equal" and ordered integration with its 1954 decision in *Brown v. Board of Education*, the HBCUs began to lose their special basketball luster. In the mid 1960s, many top NCAA programs broke their de facto whites-only policies and began aggressively recruiting black players.

Many basketball legends came up through the HBCU system. Here are the top 10, as chosen an ESPN panel of experts, along with other notables.

1. EARL MONROE, 6'4" G
Winston-Salem (N.C.) State, 1963-67

As a 6'3" center at Philadelphia's John Bartram High School, Monroe was such a genius with his skills that he was given the nickname Thomas Edison. Later he would become knows as Black Jesus and, of course, the Pearl for his silky smoothness. He followed another Philly schoolboy star, Leon Whitley, to Winston-Salem, after Whitley became a recruiter for Hall of Fame coach Clarence "Big House" Gaines, who had never seen Monroe play. Whitley's word proved to be good enough—and then some. Monroe was a scoring machine, averaging 23.2 and 29.8 points per game in his sophomore and junior seasons. But as a senior he exploded into a sensation—at least for those fans who heard about him or saw him play—averaging 41.5 points per game on 60.7% shooting. In the 1967 NCAA College Division championship game, he hit 16 of 30 shots for 40 points in a 77-74 win over Southwest Missouri State. The Baltimore Bullets made him their No. 1 pick in the 1967 NBA draft and he went on to a Hall of Fame career with the Bullets and New York Knicks.

2. DICK BARNETT, 6'4" G/F, Tennessee A&I, 1955-59

Barnett was known for his stylish left-handed jump shot, distinguished by the way he'd kick up his heels as he drifted backwards, sometimes (famously) chanting "Fall back, baby!" as the ball swished. Barnett is still his school's (now Tennessee State) all-time leading scorer with 3,209 career points. The three-time Little All-America led the Tigers to three straight NAIA championships (1957-59) under the tutelage of Hall of Fame coach John McLendon. Barnett later starred on the New York Knicks' 1970 NBA championship team.

3. WILLIS REED, 6'10" C, Grambling (La.) College, 1960-64

A native of Bernice, La., Reed decided to play basketball at nearby Grambling College, best known for turning out football talent. At 6'10" and 240 pounds, Reed might have been a formidable tight end, but he was an awesome basketball center. Smaller than Wilt Chamberlain—to whom he was often compared—but almost as potent, Reed was rugged under the boards and nearly unstoppable inside, with a nice lefty turnaround jumper. With Reed in the middle, Grambling won three Southwestern Athletic Conference championships and the 1961 NAIA title. As a senior, he averaged 26.6 points and 21.3 rebounds a game and scored 265 points in 12 NAIA tournament games. He finished his career with 2,280 points and 1,851 rebounds, after which he played 10 seasons with the New York Knicks, forever highlighted by his inspired performance, hobbled by a severe knee injury, in the Knicks' 1970 upset NBA championship victory over the Los Angeles Lakers—led by the mighty Chamberlain.

4. SAM JONES, 6'4" G
North Carolina College, 1951-54, 1956-57

Known for his sweet bank shot and unusually strong rebounding for a guard, Jones was a major star in the Central Intercollegiate Athletic Association, where he played one season for legendary coach John McLendon. A three-time All-CIAA selection, Jones scored 1,770 points and grabbed 578 rebounds in his NCC career and was inducted into the NAIA Hall of Fame in 1962. Jones achieved great fame as a pro, starring on 10 Boston Celtics NBA championship teams between 1959 and '69, partnering in the backcourt with the great (and unrelated) K.C. Jones.

The fast breaks, quick shots and acrobatic moves fed energy to the crowds, who motivated the players to be even more creative. The game they played was anathema to that being taught by most coaches at white colleges.

5. TRAVIS GRANT, 6'8" F
Kentucky State, 1968-72

The nickname Machine Gun came naturally: Grant regularly shot the lights out for the small teaching college in Frankfort, Ky., that opened in 1887 as the State Normal School for Colored Persons. In his four-year career, Grant set NCAA all-divisions career scoring records with 4,045 points and 1,760 field goals. He still owns the NAIA tournament all-time highest career scoring average of 34.5 points a game, amassed while leading Kentucky State to three consecutive NAIA championships. In one 1970 game, Grant machine-gunned Northwood Institute with 75 points.

6. EARL LLOYD, 6'6" F/C, West Virginia State, 1946-50

Known as Big Cat, Lloyd was a three-time selection to what was then known as the All-Colored Intercollegiate Athletic Association team, and later became the first African-American to play in an NBA game. His 1947-48 WVS squad was the nation's only undefeated team (23–0), finishing atop the CIAA and winning its postseason tournament, as it did again the following year. After averaging 14 points and eight rebounds per game as a senior, Lloyd was drafted by the NBA Washington Capitols and played in his first game on Oct. 31, 1950, breaking the NBA's racial barrier just one day before the Celtics' Chuck Cooper and four days before the Knicks' Nat "Sweetwater" Clifton played their first games.

7. ZELMO BEATY, 6'9" C, Prairie View (Tex.) A&M, 1958-62

The Big Z was among the HBCU's most dominant big men in the early 1960s. A fierce rebounder and prolific scorer, Beaty collected 2,285 points and 1,916 rebounds (19.4 per game) in his career. He was chosen Most Valuable Player after leading the Panthers to the 1962 NAIA tournament title. But he was relatively unknown, even among NBA coaches and executives, when the St. Louis Hawks made him the No. 3 pick in the 1962 draft. "I shocked a lot of people when I selected him," said Marty Blake, then the team's general manager. "A lot of the scouts weren't making the effort to see the black colleges back then." Beaty ended up as a star—in every way—with the ABA Utah Stars.

8. BOB HOPKINS, 6'9" C
Grambling (La.), 1952-56

Only three players in the history of college basketball have scored more points than Hopkins' 3,759 (29.8 per game). The big center played his college basketball for Eddie Robinson, Grambling's legendary football coach, who also doubled and tripled as the men's and women's basketball coach. A bruising 205-pounder, Hopkins also pulled down 2,191 rebounds in his career. He played four seasons for the NBA Syracuse Nationals, averaging 8.2 points per game, and then turned to coaching, with stops at Prairie View A&M, Alcorn State and Xavier in New Orleans, among others. He joined the NBA Seattle SuperSonics as his cousin Bill Russell's assistant, then succeeded him as head coach—briefly. He was fired midway through his first (and only) season.

9. CLEO HILL, 6'1" G
Winston-Salem (N.C.) Teacher's College, 1957-61

Many who saw Hill play thought he was the best shooting guard of his era, black or white. He was one of the first superstars to play for Hall of Fame coach Clarence "Big House" Gaines—two years before the arrival of Earl Monroe. Hill scored 2,488 points during his college career, averaging 26.7 points a game as a senior. He was drafted by the St. Louis Hawks in 1961, but was never able to fit in. He believed the team's white scoring stars, Bob Pettit and Cliff Hagan, felt threatened by him, and that he was subsequently blackballed by the NBA.

10 (tie). MARQUES HAYNES, 6'0" G
Langston (Okla.) University, 1942-46

Haynes (see "They Were There," page 44) estimated that he played in some 12,500 basketball games over a 51-year span in 106 countries, thrilling crowds in most of them with his dazzling displays of ballhandling brilliance as "the world's greatest dribbler" and star of the Harlem Globetrotters. But before Haynes became a showman, he played the game for real at Langston, as the leading scorer on a team that achieved an amazing four-year record of 112–3, including a 59-game winning streak. After dribbling out the final minutes of the Negro National College title game against a frustrated Southern University team in 1946, Haynes scored 26 points for Langston in an exhibition against the Globetrotters, who immediately offered him a contract.

> ***"I shocked a lot of people when I selected Zelmo Beaty. A lot of NBA scouts weren't making the effort to see the black colleges back then."***

10 (tie). PURVIS SHORT, 6'7" G/F
Jackson (Miss.) State, 1974-78

Short scored 2,434 points in his career, averaging 25.5, 24.9 and 29.5 points per game in his final three seasons for the Tigers and earning All-America honors each year: Division II second team (1976); D2 first team ('77); Division I honorable mention ('78). He was a first-round draft choice of the Golden State Warriors, and averaged 17.3 points per game in a 12-year NBA career.

OTHER NOTABLES:

AL ATTLES, 6'0" G, North Carolina A&T, 1956-60

With his quick feet and long, powerful arms, Attles helped the Aggies win two CIAA championships, scoring 944 points in his career. His average of 6.5 assists per game still ranks as the highest in the history of the program.

JOHN CHANEY, 6'1" G, Bethune-Cookman (Fla.), 1951-55

Most fans know Chaney for his legendary coaching career at Temple, but few know he was one of the greatest college basketball players of the 1950s. Most of his college statistics were either never officially recorded or lost, but he is believed to have scored well over 3,000 points, including 57 in a game against Knoxville College.

NAT CLIFTON, 6'6" C, Xavier (La.), 1942-43

The man known as Sweetwater played only one college season but made quite an impact, leading Xavier to a 15–3 record before losing to South Carolina State in the Southern Intercollegiate Athletic Conference tournament. After serving in the army, Clifton played for the Harlem Globetrotters and other barnstorming teams before joining the New York Knicks in the NBA's first integrated season, 1950-51.

BOB DANDRIDGE, 6'6" F
Norfolk (Va.) State, 1965-69

With Dandridge averaging 32.3 points per game, Norfolk State was the highest-scoring team in the entire NCAA College Division in 1968-69. He set single-season school records for points (808) and rebounds (425)—since surpassed—and field goals made (333) and attempted (601)—which still stand. As a pro, he starred on NBA championship teams in Milwaukee (1970-71, with Kareem Abdul-Jabbar) and Washington (1977-78, with Elvin Hayes and Wes Unseld).

MIKE DAVIS, 6'4" G, Virginia Union, 1965-69

Virginia Union's all-time leading scorer with 2,872 points, Davis, nicknamed Crusher, was the CIAA Player of the Year in 1969. (The "C" in CIAA stood for "Central" rather than "Colored," beginning in 1950.) He is the CIAA's No. 2 all-time points leader, behind Winston-Salem's Earl Monroe.

EARL GLASS, 6'0" G
Mississippi Industrial College, 1959-63

Mississippi Industrial College, founded in Holly Springs in 1905 "for the literary and industrial training of the

Negro youth," closed in 1982. But older folks in northern Mississippi still remember Glass, the school's greatest player. During the 1962-63 season, he averaged an astounding 42.9 points per game, including a 60-point explosion against Texas College—all of it in the *second half.*

MAJOR JONES, 6'10" F, Albany (Ga.) State, 1972-76
Major was one of six Jones brothers to play for Albany State, four of whom (Major, Wilbert, Caldwell and Charles) also played in the NBA. By 1976, he was considered one of the top small-college players in the country. A rebounding superpower, he averaged more than 19 per game in each of his four seasons and is still second on the all-time NCAA list with 2,052.

RICK MAHORN, 6'11" C, Hampton (Va.), 1976-80
A three-time NAIA All-America, Mahorn averaged 20.3 points and 12.3 rebounds over his career. As a senior, he led NCAA Division II in rebounding, grabbing 15.8 boards a game. He spent 18 seasons in the NBA, including a stint with the championship Detroit Pistons "Bad Boys."

FRED "CURLY" NEAL, 6'1" G
Johnson C. Smith (N.C.) University, 1959-63
The man who followed in the footsteps of Marques Haynes as a star with the Harlem Globetrotters also followed Haynes as a serious player in the HBCU system. Neal averaged 23.1 points per game in his senior year and led the Golden Bulls to the 1963 CIAA semifinals, where they lost to Big House Gaines' Winston-Salem Teacher's College, 54-49. Neal played more than 6,000 games for the Globetrotters from 1963 to '85.

CHARLES OAKLEY, 6'9", Virginia Union, 1981-85
Virtually unstoppable as a collegian, Oakley stands as Virginia Union's all-time leading rebounder (1,664) and No. 3 scorer (2,379). In 1984-85, he was named NCAA Division II Player of the Year after leading the Panthers to the CIAA championship and an overall 31–1 record while averaging 24.3 points and 17.3 rebounds per game. Oakley was an NBA standout for 19 seasons (10 of them with the New York Knicks).

LEONARD ROBINSON, 6'7" F, Tennessee State, 1970-74
So wide and strong that his nickname, Truck, might as well have been inscribed on his birth certificate, Robinson played a power game but could score with an outside jump shot. He collected 2,249 points and 1,501 rebounds in his career, while his Tigers compiled an overall 94–19 record. Robinson went on to average 15.5 points per game in 11 NBA seasons.

WILLIE SHAW, 6'1" G, Lane College (Tenn.), 1960-64
One of the most explosive players of the early 1960s, Shaw was a phenomenal shooter, deadly from 20 feet. He amassed 2,379 points in his career, averaging 32.8 as a sophomore, 35.4 points as a junior and 40.7 as a senior, and stands seventh among the all-time NAIA career scoring leaders.

ELMORE SMITH, 7'0" C, Kentucky State, 1968-71
A center often compared—less than favorably—with Wilt Chamberlain and Lew Alcindor, Smith and teammate Travis "Machine Gun" Grant guided Kentucky State to NAIA championships in 1970 and 1971. Smith still holds NAIA records for rebounds in a season (799) and career rebounding average (22.6). He finished his college career with 1,917 rebounds. Smith played only one high school game before becoming a college player, and ended up an eight-year NBA veteran.

BEN WALLACE, 6'9" C, Virginia Union, 1994-96
Wallace transferred to Virginia Union after two seasons at Cuyahoga C.C. in Cleveland, and wound up leading the Panthers to the NCAA Division II final four with a 28–3 record. A powerful inside player, Wallace averaged 13.4 points and 10 rebounds for the Panthers. After going undrafted by the NBA, he played briefly in Italy before signing as a free agent with the Washington Bullets; he later played for Orlando, Detroit, Chicago and Cleveland.

DONALD "SLICK" WATTS, 6'1" G, Xavier (La.), 1970-73
Nicknamed for his quick hands and later famous for his gleaming bald pate, Watts averaged 18 points and 3.4 assists during his career, and eight steals per game as a senior. Because of his small stature, Watts was ignored in the 1973 NBA draft. But Xavier coach Bob Hopkins persuaded his cousin Bill Russell, then coach and GM of the Seattle SuperSonics, to sign Watts. "I didn't know a thing about him," said Russell. "Just that Hop sent him and said he could play. I did know that he was about the funniest looking guy I had ever seen."

MARVIN WEBSTER, 7'0", Morgan State (Md.), 1971-75
In 1974, the Human Eraser led Morgan State to the NCAA College Division national championship. He was the AP College Division Player of the Year in 1974 and again in '75, after averaging 15.6 points and 17.0 rebounds per game. Blocked shots—his specialty—were not then officially counted in box scores. As a senior, he is said by former teammate and ex-Morgan State sports information director Joe McIver to have "averaged something like 13 a game."

The Bracket Racket

How a simple geometric scrawl went forth and multiplied into an annual, national—even presidential—obsession

BY STEVE RUSHIN

The English word *bracket* comes from the French *braguette* and the Spanish *bragueta*, both of which mean the same thing: codpiece.

A codpiece, in medieval menswear, was a cloth pouch on the front of the pants that both concealed and called attention to the wearer's private parts. And so, this much can be said with absolute certainty: Men have been filling out brackets since at least the Middle Ages.

In the beginning, there were all manner of brackets. The architectural bracket got its name because it resembled a codpiece in profile. But brackets also supported bookshelves and enclosed arcane algebraic equations. They literally embraced [placed an editorial afterthought between braces, like these] and *were* embraced, by anyone who aspired to a higher tax bracket.

It wasn't until the late 20th century that the word bracket became synonymous with one thing: the NCAA Basketball Tournament schematic we fill out every March—32 typographical brackets that give way to the single, long-stemmed bracket of the championship game, which on paper resembles a toppled football goalpost:

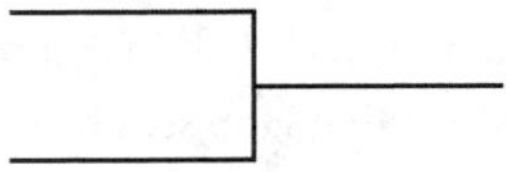

That metaphor is at once terribly wrong—college football is bereft of brackets, which is precisely its problem, say playoff advocates—and so very right: The toppled goalpost, like the basketball bracket it resembles, signifies epic celebration in college sports.

The Tournament bracket both embraces (think of NC State coach Jim Valvano looking for someone to hug after winning the big one in 1983) and is embraced (by a nation that sacrifices $3.8 billion a year in productivity to brood over its picks in one office pool or another).

Brackets once supported bookshelves. Now it's the other way around. Among the 21st-century volumes devoted to brackets is *The Enlightened Bracketologist: The Final Four of Everything*. In it, authors Mark Reiter and Richard Sandomir place the whole of human existence into brackets, then winnow each category—everything from Frank Sinatra songs to Shakespearean insults—down to a single Darwinian champion. And so, "Survey said ...!" beat "Come on down!" in the championship for Best Game Show Catchphrase.

Manifold magazines, newspapers and websites do the same, placing into the crucible of brackets everything from cars to beers to unusual names. And so, a professional basketball player in France named Steeve Ho You Fat battled a former University of Kansas softball shortstop named Destiny Frankenstein in an annual online, 64-entry Name of the Year bracket competition.

Both were upset by eventual champion Spaceman Africa. But then, brackets are a kind of sodium pentothal. Brackets force the truth—a concept that elevates college basketball over other sports.

There are no fluke champions. Brackets make sure of that. Selection Sunday might better be called *Natural* Selection Sunday, for brackets brutally illustrate survival of the fittest, a concept central to earthly existence since at least the Old Testament when Cain eliminated Abel in the East-of-Eden Regional.

And yet, the tournament bracket has no Darwin, no Edison, no founding genius who imposed order where once chaos reigned.

In 1933, an electrical draftsman named Harry Beck, inspired by circuit diagrams, drew a schematic map of the London Underground. Using little more than a few simple lines, Beck created an icon of international design—still used as a map, but also emblazoned on shopping bags and coffee mugs and T-shirts—for which he was paid five guineas.

Alas, the bracket has no Harry Beck, who was five guineas richer than the anonymous draftsman who ingeniously sketched the first brackets for a single-elimination tournament—or knockout competition, as it's known in England—where brackets or something like them have been in use at Wimbledon since the tournament began with 22 participants in 1877.

And yet, when we talk about Wimbledon, if we talk about it at all these days, we speak of its "draw," not its brackets. The same goes for the other Grand Slam tennis events. It was in the NCAA Basketball Tournament—with its alliteratively Darwinian descent from Sweet 16 to Elite Eight to Final Four—that the bracket found its highest purpose.

Even then, it wasn't until after 1984 that brackets became a cultural touchstone, when the NCAA expanded its field of teams to 64 (after diddling with various sizes growing from the seminal eight in 1939). More teams meant broader interest, of course, and a greater need for the organizational genius of brackets.

But more than that, there is something elemental about the number 64, something hardwired into the human race. Something to do with competition and status and desire. Sixty-four is the number of squares on a chess board, the number of positions in the *Kama Sutra*, the number of colors in the big box of Crayolas—the one you longed for in grade school but couldn't have; the one with the built-in sharpener.

The number 128—the number of men and women, respectively, in the Wimbledon singles draw—signifies nothing. And never mind that the NCAA technically invites 65 teams to the Tournament: That 65th—the loser of the play-in game—never makes it to the bracket, in the way that "the 51st state," Puerto Rico, never makes the weather map.

All of the following elements come into play when you complete a bracket, whether or not you realize it: chess, sex, envy and mortality. Brackets are life.

Whatever number the ever-avaricious NCAA might expand its field to in the future, 64 was an unmistakable milestone, as John Lennon and Paul McCartney well knew. *Will you still need me, will you still feed me, when I'm 64?*

All of the following elements come into play when you complete a bracket, whether or not you realize it: chess, sex, envy and mortality. Brackets are life. They give office bragging rights to pool winners every April. They've made a few people rich and others poor. Countless American men equate their brackets with their manhood.

It's worth remembering: When you endeavor to fill out a bracket, you are attempting to fill out a codpiece, and not *only* in an etymological sense. "My wife has a better bracket than I do," one of innumerable posters to one of innumerable online bracket contests lamented in 2008. "Thanks, Georgetown, for letting down the entire male gender."

The Hoyas that year were upset losers to Davidson, which instantly entered the pantheon of "bracketbusters." It is a perfect name for those teams that upend the traditional powers of college basketball—and not only because the bracket for each NCAA region resembles a toppled pyramid.

Bracketbuster is one more neologism in the alliterative lexicon of March Madness, that glorious period bracketed [if you will] by Selection Sunday and the Final Four, when Americans wager an estimated $7 billion on the outcomes of the games laid out in those brackets.

How ever did this happen? That is the (here's that number again) $64,000 question.

Nineteen fifty-nine was a revolutionary year, and not only in Cuba. It was an *annus mirabilis* for college basketball fans, who witnessed their own reinvention of the wheel with the introduction into the American workplace of the Xerox 914, the world's first commercially successful plain-paper copier.

Though we didn't know it then, the basketball bracket would become an enduring and iconic offspring of the office copy machine, ranking alongside the photocopied keister from the Christmas party as the most memorable fruits of xerography.

But we only know that in hindsight. In 1959, the NCAA Tournament consisted of 23 teams, nine of which had first-round byes, and brackets didn't have the neat symmetry they have today in which each half of the Tournament draw, turned on its side, resembles an inverted tower of champagne glasses.

Predicting the winner of the NCAA Tournament was not yet a national parlor game. On the contrary. For a good while, a chimpanzee with a four-letter alphabet—U, C, L and A-could accurately forecast the national champion every year.

In 1964, the Bruins began their run of 10 titles in 12 seasons, a Dark Age for the office pool. But three bracket-building phenomena occurred at the conclusion of that streak in 1975: 1) The UCLA dynasty ended with John Wooden's retirement; 2) The Tournament field expanded to a symmetrical, bracket-friendly field of 32; and 3) Cleveland *Plain Dealer* sportswriter Ed Chay coined the phrase "Final Four." The Tournament, and its attendant hype, was growing.

Four years later, the field grew again, to 40, and a Larry Bird vs. Magic Johnson final pulled the highest television rating ever for an NCAA Tournament game. College basketball's championship playoff, at last, was unpredictable. And people desperately wanted to predict it.

Exactly halfway between those watershed Tournaments of '75 and '79—when an Irish ex-bartender from New York named Al McGuire led Marquette to the '77 title—an Irish bar in Staten Island, N.Y., named Jody's Club Forest started a Tournament pool with 88 filled-out brackets. Patrons paid $10 per entry, winner take all.

Each regional bracket resembles a genealogy chart, a family tree in which every couple gives birth to an only child. And in the early 1980s, those brackets went forth and multiplied. The Tournament expanded to 48 teams in 1980, to 53 in '84, to 64 in '85, all the while stringing together a charm bracelet of memorable championship games.

Freshman "Mike" Jordan's jumper won the title for North Carolina in 1982—the year the phrase "March Madness" was uttered on national television for the first time, by CBS announcer Brent Musburger. (The phrase had been used by H.V. Porter of the Illinois High School Association as early as 1939, referring to that state's high school tourney.)

In the wine cellar of history, Jordan '82 was followed by other unforgettable vintages: that '83 Jimmy V, the '85 Villanova, the '90 UNLV. On Staten Island, the lines outside Jody Haggerty's tavern grew longer, a living bar graph of the Tournament's growth.

For a good while, a chimpanzee with a four-letter alphabet—U, C, L and A—could accurately forecast the national champion every year.

Published in newspapers, photocopied in offices, pored over in cubicles, brackets were becoming huge, and not only in a metaphorical sense. By 2004, pedestrians in downtown San Antonio would find themselves looking up—awestruck Earthlings in a sci-fi flick—at a six-story bracket hung on the side of the city's Convention Center.

This monster—*Attack of the 72-Foot Bracket*—was nurtured in the 1990s by the epoch-making arrival of the Internet, which would put brackets on every desk- and laptop. The annual office pool became so wedded to the PC that downloadable brackets for the men's and women's Tournaments were offered online by Microsoft, whose founder, Bill Gates, was more renowned for his tax bracket than his basketball bracket.

But the computer turned out to be much more than a mega-mimeograph machine. For the World Wide Web put expert advice at every desk jockey's fingertips, quite literally, and allowed all of humanity to join a single office pool. In 2003, ESPN.com started an online bracket competition that attracted 875,000 entries. And of course, the queues for Jody's Pool on Staten Island continued to grow, a joyous conga line of hoop junkies down Forest Avenue.

By 2009, according to a poll by CareerBuilders.com, 18% of American office workers participated in an NCAA Tournament pool, leaving many of us to wonder who the other 82% were. Even to those who cared nothing about basketball, brackets represented an irresistible intersection of money and soothsaying. Of that $7 billion wagered nationally on the Tournament, the state of Nevada—the only place where it's legal—accounts for only about 3%.

An online betting site in 2008 offered an $11 million prize to anyone who picked a perfect bracket, secure in the knowledge that the odds of doing so have been calculated at one in 9 million *trillion*.

Of course, participants don't have to pick them all right to win big: Rick Neuheisel reportedly won $20,000 in a high-stakes bracket competition in 2002. That revelation got him fired as football coach at the University of Washington, which ended up paying him $4.5 million in a legal settlement, almost certainly the biggest bracket prize in history.

The second-biggest prize may well have been the one at Jody's Club Forest. By 2005, Jody's Pool had 150,000 $10 entries, a prize of $1.5 million and prominent press coverage after the winner was identified as "Noe Body." That, in turn, drew the interest of the Internal Revenue Service. And though Jody's Pool was legal, the bar shut it down in 2006, ending the happy queues on Forest Avenue in Staten Island.

Bracket pools aren't legal in every state—a fact that offends many lawmakers. "It's a crime we consider [them] a crime," said Michigan state legislator Kim Meltzer in 2007. And indeed prosecutors—often participants in their own office pools—have been loath to indict millions of Americans on charges of bracketeering.

The biggest bracket pool by far is ESPN.com's, which in 2009 drew more than five million entries. (Four other sites combined to attract at least another four million entries.) And though ESPN's own expert, Joe Lunardi—Joey Brackets to the basketball mafia—coined the term "bracketology," filling in brackets is much more an art than a science. Consider: In 2006, only four of ESPN.com's 3.1 million brackets correctly predicted the Final Four, the year bracketbuster George

Mason made it all the way to the national semis. Two of the responsible geniuses were George Mason alumni. A third—Russell Pleasant of Omaha, Neb.—could not tell a lie: He meant to select George *Washington*. The Pleasant error won him $10,000.

Brackets don't just link the round of 64 to the round of 32 to the round of 16. They link people, lined up at a bar and connected at the elbow like paper dolls.

Dozens of websites now offer bracket tip sheets every March, and so-called bracketologists are so ubiquitous that the satirical newspaper *The Onion* ran the following headline: BRACKETIATRIST MISTAKEN FOR BRACKETOLOGIST.

And still, Johnny Gilbert of Salt Lake City was one of only two entrants to pick all Sweet 16 teams in ESPN.com's 2008 pool, even though Gilbert was 13 years old and didn't get ESPN or any other channel that wasn't carried over the airwaves; his family didn't have cable TV.

Bracketology, like theology, is a faith-based discipline. It requires belief—in what you hear on TV, in what you read on the Internet, in the guy two stools down at the bar using his bracket as a beer coaster on the first day of the Tournament, when 64 teams and a few trillion combinations are still alive. Hold down a barstool for 12 consecutive hours at Vaughan's Public House across from Hartford's XL Center, home of the two-time NCAA champion Connecticut Huskies, and you'll see them—hooky-playing office workers filing in all day, fingering their brackets like worry beads.

Tom Steed fled his office at Prudential with two co-workers. The systems analyst ducked into Vaughan's, where he found himself systematically analyzing a pint of Harp.

"Two years ago," said Steed, "we went into McKinnon's to get a quick beer and catch up on the scores. When we walked out, we ran into our boss on the street. She asked us where we'd been and one of my buddies said, 'We just gave blood at the Red Cross.'"

That's what brackets are all about. They don't just link the round of 64 to the round of 32 to the round of 16. They link people, lined up at a bar and connected at the elbow like paper dolls.

In 2009, the basketball-loving Barack Obama—that first name practically an anagram of *bracket*—made good on a campaign promise to fill out a tournament sheet for ESPN. In doing so, Obama became responsible for another milestone in presidential history: the first *Oval* Office pool.

Alas, finishing first on Election Day is no predictor of success on Selection Day: Obama *did* pick eventual champion North Carolina to win it all, but was right on only 65% of his other choices—good enough to place him 903,125th in the ESPN.com pool. The audacity of hoop.

More Americans might vote each November if political candidates were placed into brackets. There is a simple joy in filling in the empty lines, in making multiple office pool entries—like playing two bingo cards at once—and in the little epiphanies they elicit as the Tournament rolls on.

When Bradley played Pittsburgh in the 2006 Tournament, brackets—and the CBS scoreboard graphic—revealed the name of the biggest movie star in the world and gave a whole new meaning to the phrase *marquee matchup*:

BRAD

PITT

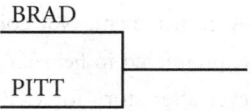

The names were inked in by millions of men, women and children from every region (and subregion) of the continent and points overseas—a diversity of interest that is the ultimate testament to the brilliance of brackets.

Each individual bracket resembles a tuning fork. And for people all over this pebble-grained globe, brackets do exactly what tuning forks do: They resonate.

The Sweetest 16

Nobody loves a Cinderella story more than a college hoops fan. Here are some of the best

BY PAT FORDE

Here in the Western world, the Brothers Grimm are widely credited with popularizing the Cinderella story. In 1812, they published the macabre German folklore version in which a toe is amputated, a heel is mutilated and eyeballs are plucked out by avenging birds. Soothing bedtime material for the kids.

In the nearly two centuries since, only Walt Disney has done more than college basketball to keep Cinderella in the American mainstream. For some reason, the slipper fits March Madness as it does no other event in sports. The NCAA Tournament has become an annual romp through the meadow of Cinderella metaphors. You can't swing a magic wand without hitting a triumphant underdog being likened to the beautiful heroine who overcame adversity and cruelty while living out the very definition of "fairy tale."

The usage dates back at least to 1939, when Lubbock (Tex.) *Avalanche Journal* reporter Jay Harris called the upstart Lubbock High football team the "Cinderella Kids." The phrase attained wide circulation in 1950 when the City College of New York improbably became the first and only school to win both postseason basketball championships: the NIT and NCAA Tournament. Not coincidentally, Disney's animated classic premiered in February of that year. (It was not a happily-ever-after story for CCNY, however. In later years, seven players from that 1949-50 team, including the entire starting five, pleaded guilty to point-shaving charges during their college careers. See "Too Many Fouls," page 34.)

Over the years, the virtuous young girl with petite feet has lent her name to surprising squads led by 7-foot he-men (Navy's David Robinson) and tattooed widebodies (George Mason's Jai Lewis). She's fronted for fives featuring budding basketball deities (Indiana State's Larry Bird) and shamed drug abusers (Villanova's Gary McLain, who admitted playing in the 1985 national semifinals under the influence). She's hitched a ride on the Tournament's greatest inbounds pass (1998: Valparaiso's Jamie Sykes to Bill Jenkins to Bryce Drew, on a play drawn up by Bryce's dad, Homer); on its most memorable backdoor pass (1996: Princeton's Steve Goodrich to Gabe Lewullis, to dethrone defending champ UCLA, on a play drawn up by the brilliant Pete Carril); and on its most famous unintentional pass (1983: Dereck Whittenburg's air ball caught and dunked by teammate Lorenzo Charles, on a play drawn up by God).

These Cinderella moments have punctuated so much of college hoops history, it's no wonder that the stage on which they annually play out has become a spin-off cliché. The NCAA Tournament is now routinely called the Big Dance, because that's where Cinderella met her fella, of course—at the royal ball.

How and why did college hoops and everyone's favorite fairy tale become so intertwined? Two main reasons.

First, college basketball lends itself to improbable upset stories more than, say, football, for the simple fact that small and obscure schools compete in the same championship event as the massive powerhouses. Bucknell is never going to play Kansas in the Fiesta Bowl, but the two disparate programs *might* meet in the NCAA Tournament. And Bucknell *might* win. And if it does, it *might* trigger that unique explosion of March Madness endorphins that will turn a sports bar full of TV-watching strangers into hugging comrades celebrating the epic feat of the underdog. *Might*? Jillian's of Indianapolis, 2005: Bucknell 64, Kansas 63. The place went nuts.

Second, in college hoops, a single special player can create a Cinderella circumstance. It's not like most other team sports, where a nowhere program needs a half-dozen studs and a few years of seasoning to somehow climb through the cracks and suddenly find itself in the same league with the biggest boys. In rare instances, one player can significantly alter the balance of power, however briefly. As former Indiana State coach Bill Hodges said, "You don't get many Larry Birds."

That's really part of the charm; most of the great Cinderella stories aren't built to last. They're a lightning-in-a-bottle experience, a comet streaking through March, a pinch-me moment that, for a Bucknell or an Indiana State, may never come again. The preciousness is in the impermanence.

You can only hope the out-of-nowhere schools properly appreciated their brief bursts of glory when they had them—schools like Lebanon Valley and Wayne State, each of which celebrated its one and only NCAA Tournament victory in 1953 and '56, respectively. Or Tufts, which made the 1945 Tournament with a 10–6 record, lost twice (back in the era of consolation games) and never got to the Dance again.

Or Springfield (Mass.), which made its only appearance in the second Tournament (1940), losing to eventual champ Indiana. (There's no record of Springfield having a Homer Simpson on its roster, but it did register a Tournament record-low eight field goals in that game. *D'oh!*)

Fame could hardly have been more fleeting for Hodges, who became Indiana State's head coach four days before practice started in 1978—Bird's senior season—and was fired by the school after the 1981-82 campaign. Before coming to Terre Haute, he was a small-college golf coach. After leaving, he sold insurance, taught at middle schools and coached basketball at Mercer University for six years. In 2008 he was teaching history at William Fleming High School in Roanoke, Va.

Nothing in Hodges' life matched the experience he had that very first season as a head coach. He was promoted to the job after his boss, Bob King, suffered an aneurysm and had to step down. Hodges' fellow assistant coach, Stan Evans, quit when he lost out on the promotion, so Hodges was left with very little help running the team (although he did have former Indiana Pacers star Mel Daniels as a grad assistant).

Cinderella stories aren't built to last. They're a lightning-in-a-bottle experience, a comet streaking through March, a pinch-me moment that, for a Bucknell or an Indiana State, may never come again. The preciousness is in the impermanence.

But how much coaching do you need when you have Larry Bird?

During Bird's year of ineligibility—he had transferred after an unhappy freshman experience at Indiana—Daniels got into a pickup game with him on the ISU campus. Afterward, Daniels walked into King's office and proclaimed, "Coach, that kid's as good as anyone in the ABA right now."

"Wait a minute," said Hodges, who was there with King. "Have you ever heard of Julius Erving?"

"I said *anybody*," Daniels replied.

"Okay, Mel," said Hodges. "We'll see."

More than 30 years later, Hodges chuckled while recalling the conversation. "Well, Mel was right," he said.

The Sycamores had never been to an NCAA Tournament before Bird's senior season. And having to replace four starters from the previous year's team, Indiana State wasn't even picked to win the Missouri Valley Conference. Hodges had to talk the ultra-shy Bird into coming to the league's media day in Wichita—and, after claiming he was misquoted in a subsequent newspaper story, Bird stopped talking to the press altogether. Hodges believed that Bird's reticence actually helped bring his team together because it forced secondary players like Carl Nicks, Alex Gilbert and Bob Heaton to step into public leadership roles.

As the season went along the victories started piling up, and by March the secret of Bird and the Sycamores was out. Heading into the Tournament, the team was a perfect 29–0. When the NCAA selection committee announced the Tournament seedings, Indiana State stood as a No. 1 alongside powerhouse programs North Carolina, UCLA and Notre Dame. Michigan State, with its exuberant sophomore star Magic Johnson, was a No. 2.

By the time Johnson and Bird met for the first time in the national championship game in Salt Lake City, college basketball's popularity was booming. The Spartans' zone defense frustrated Indiana State and Bird vs. Magic turned out to be a minor anticlimax, with Bird making just 7 of 21 shots and being outscored by Johnson 24-19 as the Spartans won, 75-64. But the real story was in the television Nielsen rating which, at 24.1, has stood for three decades as the highest in NCAA Tournament history. It was the beginning of a 12-year Magic-Bird Era that breathed new life into basketball, college and professional.

That was small consolation to the 36-year-old rookie—and losing—head coach. "I hadn't even watched the game until its 25th anniversary," Hodges said. "When I did, I got really upset." Hodges has maintained contact with Bird through the years, but one subject has never come up. "We've never talked about the championship game," Hodges said.

In case you were wondering, the Sycamores were referred to more than once that year as Cinderella.

"Oh, yeah," said Hodges, who recalled one headline that read *Cinderella Comes From Terre Haute*. "If the clock hadn't struck 12, we'd have been better off."

As improbable and unpredictable as Cinderella stories may seem, they follow the same general script our girl followed to the ball. If you subscribe to the Disney version of the fairy tale, it took a mixture of magic, fairy godmother ingenuity and old-fashioned pluck for Cindy to shine. It takes the same magical blend of ingredients to achieve *One Shining Moment*. Here are our sweetest 16 surprises in NCAA Tournament history. (To make the list, a team had to win at least three Tournament games.)

The Unsung Program That Lucks Into a Superstar

St. Bonaventure and Jacksonville 1970

(Half the Final Four)

Star Players Centers Bob Lanier and Artis Gilmore, respectively. Lanier grew up in Buffalo idolizing St. Bonaventure's Stith brothers, Tom and Sam, which isn't something you hear every day. Gilmore spent two years at Gardner-Webb (then a North Carolina junior college) before transferring to Jacksonville and becoming the NCAA's career rebounding leader at 22.7 boards per game.

The Run The Bonnies went 25–1 before losing to 26–1 Jacksonville in the national semis—without Lanier, who had been injured in the previous game. Gilmore's Dolphins then lost in the title game to UCLA. Neither school has won a Tournament game since.

Cinderella Moments For Bonaventure, it was avenging its only regular-season loss by walloping Villanova, 97-74, in the East Regional final—though it paid a heavy price. Lanier injured a knee in that game, ending his college career before the Final Four. Later he would be the No. 1 overall pick (by Detroit) in the NBA draft. For Jacksonville, the Cindy Moment came when it upset No. 1-ranked blueblood Kentucky, 106-100, in the Mideast Regional final, preventing the greatest player in Wildcats history, Dan Issel, from playing in a Final Four. Gilmore and Issel would go on to win an ABA title together as teammates on the Kentucky Colonels. St. Bonaventure and Jacksonville became the second- and third-smallest schools (after Holy Cross) to reach a Final Four.

Indiana State 1979

Star Player Larry Bird, the Hick from French Lick, wound up in little ol' Terre Haute after leaving Indiana as a homesick freshman and working on the back of a garbage truck back in his southern Indiana home town.

The Run ISU was 33–0, ranked No. 1 and undefeated until the very last game of the season, the NCAA championship against Magic Johnson and Michigan State. The Sycamores have won only one other Tournament game in their history.

Cinderella Moment In the Midwest Regional final against Arkansas, Sycamores sub Bob Heaton—a natural righty—put up a short lefthanded runner that bounced twice on the rim and dropped at the buzzer for a 73-71 victory over a Razorbacks team that had made the previous Final Four. Earlier in the season, Heaton had kept Indiana State's unbeaten streak alive with a half-court shot against New Mexico State that sent the game into overtime.

Navy 1984-87

Star Player David Robinson, who grew from 5'9" in junior high to 6'4" in high school to 7'1" as a Midshipman and ultimately an NBA superstar.

The Run Never a hoops power, Navy went 82–17 over Robinson's three seasons, including four Tournament victories. Three of those came in 1986, as the No. 7-seed Middies made the East Regional final before losing to Mike Krzyzewski's first Final Four Duke team. It remains the greatest NCAA run in service academy history. In fact, Navy is the *only* service academy ever to win a game in the Tournament.

Cinderella Moment Robinson turned a second-round game against No. 2-seed Syracuse into an upset romp on the Orangemen's home floor. His 35 points, 11 rebounds and 7 blocked shots led the 97-85 slaughter in the Carrier Dome, prompting Syracuse coach Jim Boeheim to proclaim, "He's a better shot-blocker than anybody we've ever played against. That includes [Patrick] Ewing, [Ed] Pinckney—all those guys. Based on what I've seen, Navy can beat anybody in the Tourney with him. Without him, they can't beat anybody." Robinson averaged 27.5 points per game throughout the Tournament.

Loyola Marymount 1987-90

Star Players Hank Gathers and Bo Kimble, a pair of Philly kids who went to USC and then transferred to nearby Loyola Marymount after Trojans coach Stan Morrison was fired.

The Run LMU went 74–21 over three seasons, including four Tournament victories, while plugged into coach Paul Westhead's frantic full-court running style. The Lions haven't been back to the Big Dance since then.

Cinderella Moments Three of those NCAA wins came as a No. 11 seed in 1990, after Gathers collapsed on the court and died of sudden heart failure during the West Coast Conference tournament. Everyone who watched Kimble shoot some of his free throws left-handed during the NCAAs to honor his friend Gathers (a converted lefty foul shooter) will never forget the sight. An inspired Kimble averaged 35.8 points per game in that Tournament. The highlight was a stunning 149-115 second-round detonation of defending national champion and No. 3-seed Michigan.

Davidson 2006-08

Star Player Guard Stephen Curry, the son of former NBA shooter deluxe Dell. Curry was not offered a scholarship by any ACC school despite playing high school ball in Charlotte.

The Run Davidson went 58–12 over the two seasons, including a delightful dash to the Elite Eight in 2008 as a No. 10 seed.

Cinderella Moment In the coolest administrative gesture ever, the school paid for hotel, transportation and game tickets for any Davidson student who wanted to make the trek from the small, idyllic campus near Charlotte to Detroit for the Sweet 16. More than 500 students took up the offer. The Wildcats made the trip worthwhile by routing Big Ten–champion Wisconsin in their Midwest Regional semifinal, with NBA star LeBron James on his feet cheering Curry's shooting brilliance. In the regional final, they came up an errant three-pointer short of beating eventual national champion Kansas. During that run, Curry shot No. 7-seed Gonzaga, No. 2 Georgetown and the No. 3 Badgers out of the Tournament. He averaged 32 points per game in the Tourney, and in Davidson's three upset victories he averaged 25.7 points—*in the second half.*

Everyone who watched Kimble shoot some of his free throws left-handed during the NCAA Tournament to honor his friend Gathers will never forget the sight.

The Unsung Program That Somehow Puts It Together Without a Superstar

Dayton 1967

The Run The Flyers were hardly an out-of-nowhere program, having been a regular in both the NIT and NCAA Tournament in the 1950s and early '60s. But this team, which lost to Niagara during the regular season, managed to break through and reach the championship game despite being unranked all year. Dayton beat sixth-ranked Western Kentucky by two points in overtime, No. 8 Tennessee by a point in regulation and unranked Virginia Tech by five in OT to reach its first Final Four.

Cinderella Moment Against No. 4 North Carolina in the national semifinals, Dayton star Don May made 13 consecutive field goals in one stretch and amassed 34 points and 15 rebounds to lead the Flyers to a shocking 76-62 upset of Dean Smith's first Final Four team. A first-year varsity sophomore named Lew Alcindor and unbeaten UCLA brought Dayton back to Earth the next night, 79-64.

New Mexico State 1970

The Run With a core group of players from back East, Lou Henson took the Aggies to a 27–3 season that ended with a Final Four loss to untouchable UCLA.

Cinderella Moment Despite being ranked fifth in the nation heading into the Tournament, the Aggies had to win a first-round game against Rice to advance, while their next opponent, Kansas State, received a first-round bye and favorable geography. Playing in Lawrence, Kan., before a partisan K-State crowd, the Aggies pulled out a 70-66 victory. New Mexico State then beat Drake to reach its only Final Four.

North Carolina-Charlotte 1977

The Run The commuter-school 49ers had just joined the fledgling Sun Belt Conference and were accustomed to being overshadowed by the titans of Tobacco Road. But behind Cedric "Cornbread" Maxwell and a capable supporting cast, Charlotte made the NIT final in 1976 and then the Final Four a year later in its first NCAA appearance.

Cinderella Moments After barely surviving an overtime first-round game against Central Michigan, Charlotte put itself on the map in a three-day span in Lexington. First it routed sixth-ranked Syracuse, then it beat No. 1 Michigan. A last-second noncall of a would-be offensive goaltending violation against Marquette center Jerome Whitehead eliminated the 49ers, keeping them from a title-game showdown with a North Carolina program that had refused to schedule the new kids on the block.

Pennsylvania 1979

The Run The Quakers entered the Tournament with a 21–5 record but only a No. 9 seed—at a time when seeds went no deeper than 10. They won four games by a total of 15 points, capped by a two-point East Regional victory in what might have been the ultimate Cinderella Bowl matchup: against No. 10-seed St. John's, which had won *its* previous three games by a total of nine points. Penn became the first Ivy League team since 1965 to reach a Final Four. There have been none since, and none has come close.

Cinderella Moment: Behind 25 points and 9 rebounds from senior Tony Price, the Quakers held off a rally and shocked No. 1-seed North Carolina, 72-71, in the second round in Raleigh. In 23 more opportunities, the Tar Heels never again suffered a Tourney loss in their home state.

George Mason 2006

The Run The Patriots didn't make the Colonial Athletic Association tournament final and barely made the NCAA field, sneaking in as a No. 11 seed. But all they needed was the opportunity. Once in, a Mason team lacking NBA-quality talent shocked Michigan State and defending national champion North Carolina, and ultimately beat No. 1-seed Connecticut, 86-84, in overtime, to reach the Final Four.

Cinderella Moment Coach Jim Larranaga played the same five for the final 15:37 of the Washington, D.C., regional final against UConn, erasing a 12-point deficit near halftime and gritting out a stunner, 86-84, in overtime. "I think it's been working for us, calling us Cinderella," guard Tony Skinn said. "We were not supposed to get into the Tournament, we got into it. We were not supposed to beat Michigan State and we beat them. Weren't supposed to beat North Carolina and we beat them. We definitely weren't supposed to beat UConn … We don't mind being the Cinderella."

The Program That Achieves Karmic Destiny Capped Off by a Stupefying Upset

North Carolina State 1983

The Run The idea of a national title could not have been more remote for the Wolfpack in the quarterfinals of the ACC tournament that year. They were 17–10 overall, 8–6 in league play—and tied with Wake Forest, 70-70, with less than a minute to play. In other words, they were one loss away from the NIT. Wake was holding for the last shot, but NC State forced a turnover and sophomore Lorenzo Charles made one free throw with :03 left. Enough to win, but *not* his last crucial points of the season.

Cinderella Moment After that, the Pack won seven straight—including several narrow escapes in the NCAA Tournament—to somehow reach the title game against huge favorite Houston. Jim Valvano outcoached Guy Lewis and his Phi Slama Jama cast (led by Hakeem Olajuwon) to win 54-52 on that immortal fluke air ball-turned-dunk by Charles at the buzzer.

> ***If you want to know what the perfect game looks like, consult the box score from Villanova 66, Georgetown 64.***

Villanova 1985

The Run The Wildcats lost seven Big East games and 10 games overall—but they won the six that counted most on their way to becoming the highest-seeded team (No. 8) ever to capture the national title.

Cinderella Moment If you want to know what the perfect game looks like, consult the box score from Villanova 66, Georgetown 64: classic Cinderella prevails over defending national champion and heavily favored Goliath (in the person of 7-foot superstar Patrick Ewing). The Wildcats shot an otherworldly 78.6% from the field against a tremendous defensive team, capped by the previously unheralded Harold Jensen's five-for-five shooting night.

Louisiana State 1986

The Run Every Cinderella needs some luck, and the Tigers got theirs from the NCAA Tournament selection committee. It placed LSU on its home court in Baton Rouge for the early rounds, and the No. 11-seed Tigers responded by upsetting No. 6 Purdue in double overtime and No. 3 Memphis by two points. Then they faced a geographic turnabout, having to play Georgia Tech in Atlanta. Didn't matter. They shocked the No. 2 seed to reach the Southeast Regional final.

Cinderella Moment Now the stage was set for *Mission Impossible*: No. 1-seed Kentucky, which had already beaten LSU three times that season. But coach Dale Brown's Tigers turned the tables in the fourth meeting, winning by a basket, 59-57, and advancing to the Final Four by a four-game margin of 17 points. They lost to Louisville, 88-77, but no lower-seeded team has reached the national semifinals since, though No. 11-seed George Mason matched LSU 20 years later.

The Program That Is Ahead of Its Time

Loyola-Chicago 1963

The Run Coach George Ireland's team was the first to win the national title with four African-American starters. In a move that might have been spurred more by self-preservation than by principle, Ireland recruited talented black players from inner-city New York and Nashville. Then he dared to play them all at the same time. The result was unlike anything the small Jesuit college had experienced before or since.

Cinderella Moment The night before the title game in Louisville, the Loyola players stayed up almost all night psyching themselves for the meeting with two-time defending national champion Cincinnati. "We were hitting each other with pillows, busting into each other's rooms and shouting, 'We gotta win!'" recalls star forward Jerry Harkness. The psyche-up turned into a psyche-out as Loyola promptly fell behind by 15 points. But then its pressure defense began forcing turnovers—the Bearcats committed 16, which was more than in their previous two championship games combined—and converting them into layups. Harkness finally hit a jumper with :06 left to force overtime and Vic Rouse won it for Loyola in OT, 60-58, with a putback basket.

Texas Western 1966

The Run Don Haskins had no idea they'd one day write books and make a movie about the first team to start *five* African-Americans while beating all-white superpower Kentucky for the national championship. Like Ireland before him, Haskins just wanted to win games. His Miners won 28 of them and lost only once on their way to achieving a victory that would become known as the *Brown v. Board of Education* of College Basketball.

Cinderella Moment The Miners led top-ranked, solidly favored Kentucky, 10-9, when quicksilver guard Bobby Joe Hill stole the ball from Tommy Kron and scored an uncontested layup. On the next possession he did it again, fleecing Louie Dampier. The tone was set and the mismatch in speed was obvious. Texas Western opened a big lead on the way to its historic 72-65 victory.

Providence 1987

The Run Master strategist Rick Pitino got his No. 6-seed Friars to the Final Four by relying on the three-point field goal in its first year of nationwide implementation. Going into the 1986-87 season, Pitino had planned to have his shooters hoist about 15 threes a game, expecting they'd hit maybe five. But after a preseason game in which the Soviet National team made 9 of 28 threes and Providence hit 7 of 18, Pitino upped his quota. Providence went on to lead the nation in threes made per game (8.2) and Pitino had a calling card for the rest of his career.

Cinderella Moment Before the Tournament pairings were announced, Pitino said that the only opponent his team couldn't handle was Big East rival Georgetown, which had throttled the Friars twice after Providence's upset win in their first meeting. Sure enough, the two teams wound up in the Southeast Region, and each won three times to set up a fourth meeting in the regional final. So Pitino went to Motivational Plan B and told his players how lucky they were to face an opponent that would overlook them completely. Two days after his shooters had strafed Alabama, 103-82, with 14 threes, he ordered an inside-out attack on Georgetown. The switcheroo shocked the No. 1-seed Hoyas, and Providence won an 88-73 rout to reach the Final Four, where they finally went down at the hands of another Big East team, Syracuse.

So Cinderella has come in a variety of shapes, sizes and costumes over the years. We rarely see her coming, which is part of her charm. We always lament her leaving. At least we have the certainty of knowing that she'll always come back, as long as balls bounce in March.

Too Many Fouls

Sadly, Dr. Naismith's simple game has too frequently found itself a magnet for malevolence

BY GENE WOJCIECHOWSKI

College basketball and scandal have been dance partners almost since the first pair of Chuck Taylors squeaked across a wooden gym floor. The unfortunate truth is that of all team sports, few are more susceptible to the dark forces of gambling, greed and cheating than college basketball. Or, as longtime Associated Press sportswriter Hal Bock wrote in 1985, "If Dr. Naismith hadn't invented basketball, professional gamblers almost certainly would have."

The specific virus that has so often found college basketball to be such an accommodating host is known as point-shaving. Almost from its start, college hoops was a huge attraction for gamblers. Why? It was wildly popular, with lots of scoring and dozens of games across America every week throughout the long winter months. Gamblers always loved to wager on which team would win or lose a game, but the truly irresistible lure, especially in a high-scoring sport like basketball, was the point spread. Before every game, professional oddsmakers would determine the number of points the favored team was "expected" to win by and gamblers would bet on their chosen team based on that spread. If the spread was set correctly, each team would attract exactly half of the wagered money—guaranteeing a big profit for the bookmakers, who made their money by keeping the losers' bets, augmented by a 10% commission known as "the vigorish."

Fans who liked to gamble on their favorite teams loved the point spread, because they could still win their bets even if their team lost, as long as it lost by fewer points than the point spread. What a concept! But it did not take long to expose the formula's fatal flaw—or, depending upon one's point of view, reveal its brilliant potential for manipulation. Someone who wanted to ensure a winning bet would only have to load up on the underdog, then make sure that the favored team won by a margin that was smaller than the spread. He would simply enlist (read: *bribe*) a few key players on the favored side to deliberately "shave" a few points, by missing a shot or losing the ball late in a game to ensure a final score that was closer than the oddsmakers had predicted.

Sadly for college basketball, such manipulation has been all too easy to accomplish all too often, and always for the same reason: unscrupulous men with money and greedy for more, preying on unsophisticated and, most important, unpaid young college basketball players.

Pick a decade, almost any decade, and you will find college hoops infected by a point-shaving scandal. To this day, fear of the Fix remains the game's most disturbing constant.

- 1940s: Kentucky
- 1950s: Kentucky, City College of New York, New York University, Bradley, Manhattan College, Long Island University
- 1960s: Saint Joseph's (Pa.)
- 1970s: Boston College
- 1980s: Tulane
- 1990s: Arizona State, Northwestern

And those are just the documented cases, cracked by luck or as byproducts of other criminal investigations. Who knows how many manipulated point spreads over the years remain someone's dirty little secret? "We're naïve to think it's not going on now in a much more sophisticated way," said a former prominent Division I athletic director in 2007. "Done? Oh, no. We've had point-shaving in the '40s, '50s, '60s, '70s, '80s and '90s. I think it's just a matter of time before it comes along again."

Former Arizona State coach Bill Frieder, whose program was crippled by a 1993-94 scandal involving two of his players, often spoke of a simple formula related to the Fix. For every program that was caught, Frieder believed there was another school at which players were shaving points undetected. Many college basketball insiders agree.

For the NCAA as well as university athletics administrators, presidents and head coaches, the possibility of a gambling-related scandal is on the short list of worst-case scenarios. "It's a bomb ready to explode," Duke coach Mike Krzyzewski said in 1998. Said former Notre Dame coach Digger Phelps, "It's never going to end." And from Frieder that same year: "No one is immune."

Krzyzewski's and Frieder's warnings are no less true today. If anything, they take on greater relevance given the sheer weight of college basketball's importance in the intersecting worlds of broadcasting and gambling. In TV rights fees alone, the Division I men's tournament is a $6 billion source of revenue for the NCAA. That's how much CBS agreed to pay the NCAA for the right to televise the 11 tournaments from 2003 through 2013 (with an option to renegotiate after 2010). At the time the deal was signed, it was the third-highest rights fee ever paid by a broadcaster to a sports organization (only the NFL and the NBA earned more).

There is no more vulnerable person in the world of sports than the college athlete. If organized crime senses an opportunity to make money on a college campus, it can be there overnight.

But as staggering as that sum is, the figure pales in comparison to the amount of money wagered annually in America on college basketball, most of it during the NCAA Tournament. Experts estimate that in each of the last several years, nearly $7 billion has been bet illegally on the NCAA Tournament *alone*, with nearly 40% of that wagered on just the three Final Four games. Only the Super Bowl does more illegal action (about $8.5 billion). So appealing is the Tournament to gamblers that the March 2008 basketball handle in Nevada, the only state in which sports wagering is legal, rose to $239 million from February's $117 million. Such is the power of March Madness.

So much money, so much temptation. And remember: Fortunes may be made by everyone in the college basketball business *except the players*.

"There is no more vulnerable person in the world of sports than the college athlete," wrote FBI agent Mike Welch in a 2004 NCAA publication. "If organized crime senses an opportunity to make money on a college campus, it can be there overnight ... There is one thing that organized crime is interested in above all: money."

College basketball players are not only vulnerable, they are convenient. The mathematics of the lineup make it so. "Basketball would be the easiest sport to fix, with only five players on the court," said Kenny White, chief operating officer of Las Vegas Sports Consultants, which sets the betting lines and point spreads for a majority of Vegas sports books. "It's a game where one guy can make such a huge difference in a game." White's company also works with the NCAA in monitoring betting patterns for telltale signs that a game might be subject to point-shaving. An unusual amount of money suddenly bet on an underdog very close to game time might be one such sign.

Gambling scandals don't discriminate. They've struck basketball royalty in the heartland (Kentucky) and tough urban centers (CCNY, Saint Joseph's), private academic strongholds (Northwestern, Boston College, Tulane) and large public universities (Arizona State). And beyond the proven, suspicion has at one time or another cropped up almost everywhere.

"The thing that happens," said the former D1 athletic director, "is these kids think they're smarter than anybody else."

For both the guilty and many of the accused against whom charges were never definitively proved, the results were often the same—ruined reputations for players, coaches and athletic directors, and of course, the colleges and universities themselves.

¶ THE 1948-49 KENTUCKY Wildcats, coached by the legendary Adolph Rupp, were one of the most feared teams of their day. They won the NCAA championship that season, but inexplicably lost two earlier games: a regular-season game with Saint Louis University and the NIT opener against Loyola of Chicago (at the time, teams could play in both postseason tournaments). Rupp reportedly had his suspicions about the Saint Louis loss, which were pretty much confirmed in 1951 when not one but three Kentucky players—All-Americas Ralph Beard and Alex Groza, as well as the key backup player, Dale Barnstable—confessed to throwing the Loyola game. By the time of their confessions, Beard and Groza had already left Kentucky and played two years in the NBA, but after their guilty pleas in April 1952, they were permanently banned from the pro league. "My God, I paid," said Beard in a 1993 interview with the Syracuse *Post-Standard*. "I have paid ... Now my name will always be mud."

¶ THE 1950 CITY COLLEGE OF NEW YORK (CCNY) Beavers didn't share Kentucky's basketball pedigree, but they became the first and only team to win both the NIT and NCAA championships in the same year. But the even bigger shock—the one that kneecapped the sport and, for decades, toppled New York City from its exalted place atop the basketball world—came almost a year later. That's when seven CCNY players were accused by Manhattan District Attorney Frank Hogan of point-shaving, along with players from several other New York-area schools and Bradley University (of Peoria, Ill.), the team CCNY beat in the NCAA Final. The breadth and depth of the scandal caused a seismic wave that reverberated for years. It isn't a stretch to say that the future of the college game teetered as the list of implicated players and schools continued to expand before an outraged public. Between 1947 and 1950, 86 games were found to be fixed and 32 players, including Bradley's Gene Melchiorre and LIU's Sherman White, were involved. "It just tore apart New York in every aspect," said former Temple coach and Basketball Hall of Famer John Chaney in a 2007 *Philadelphia Inquirer* interview. "What it did was really take some of our historically great schools out of the Division I level forever."

¶ GUESS WHO FELL AGAIN in 1951? Despite Rupp's defiant announcement after Kentucky's 1949 scandal that gamblers "couldn't touch my boys with a 10-foot pole," the 1951 Kentucky team was implicated in the New York area point-shaving scandal. This time it was Wildcat All-America center Bill Spivey, who was accused of accepting money

Hall of Shame

It's as if the Fab Five and their fab impact—two consecutive Final Four appearances, wins galore, basketball high fashion—never existed. Instead, University of Michigan officials exiled a pair of maize and blue banners, a gallery of player photos, a trophy-case basketball, even a sideline chair, to their very own on-campus Elba: the Bentley Historical Library.

This is where the hoops artifacts of cheaters go to die. Those 1992 and 1993 Final Four banners are rolled up and sealed in a vinyl case and kept in a climate-controlled facility. "We're kind of storing them for the athletic department," said Greg Kinney, the U of M associate archivist.

Chris Webber, Jalen Rose, Jimmy King, Juwan Howard and Ray Jackson made two kinds of basketball history at Michigan. In 1992, the five freshman reconfigured the world of college hoops by reaching (and losing) the NCAA championship game to Duke. They made the Final again as sophomores, but lost again—this time to North Carolina—as Webber called his infamous unsanctioned time-out in the waning seconds.

But it was off-the-court NCAA violations involving Webber and a deep-pocketed booster named Ed Martin that ultimately brought down the program. Webber and three other players were accused of accepting more than $600,000 from Martin. Michigan basketball went into the doldrums for more than a decade.

Cheating remains college basketball's poison ivy. Painful. Pernicious. Contagious. Uncontrollable.

The list of coaches whose teams have been forced to vacate or forfeit games is nearly as long as an NCAA Tournament bracket: Jerry Tarkanian (Long Beach State, Fresno State); Jim Harrick (Georgia); Steve Fisher (Michigan); Clem Haskins (Minnesota); Mike Jarvis (St. John's); Eddie Sutton (Kentucky); Norm Stewart (Missouri); Gene Keady (Purdue); Larry Brown (UCLA); Jim O'Brien (Ohio State); John Calipari (UMass); Jim Calhoun (Connecticut). On and on it goes.

Their programs were undone by greed, by boosters, by money, by ignorance, by arrogance, by agents, by their own players.

Todd Bozeman was banished for eight years after offering money to the family of a University of California recruit. An academic fraud scandal cost Haskins his job at Minnesota. Tarkanian, a longtime target of NCAA investigators during his many years at UNLV, retired after the 2001-02 Fresno State season under a cloud of suspicion that would later result in NCAA sanctions. Kelvin Sampson lost his job at Indiana in 2008 because he violated NCAA rules regarding phone contact with recruits, as he had earlier in his career at Oklahoma.

Players have done their part to blow up programs. Villanova's 1971 runner-up finish in the national championship was vacated because Tournament MVP Howard Porter was found to have signed a professional contract before season's end. Lester Earl accepted money from an LSU assistant, got caught, and then transferred to Kansas during the 1996-97 season. As a result, LSU was placed on probation in 1998 and lost six scholarships. Several members of the 1989-90 UNLV national championship team were photographed in a hot tub with Richie Perry, a convicted game-fixer, and UNLV was banned from postseason play in 1990-91. And in 2008, USC star guard O.J. Mayo was implicated in a controversy involving alleged payoffs to an agent.

Because so many latter-day college stars, like Mayo, bolt for NBA riches after only one year in college, the pressure to land players (read: *cheat*) is greater than ever. "Everyone is feeling they have to get a player for a year and try to win big," Michigan State coach Tom Izzo told the Fort Wayne *Journal Gazette* in 2008. "We're in this profession where you're hired to get fired, too, and because of that, I think nationwide, cheating is getting worse."

And it won't be getting better any time soon.

from a Brooklyn gambler to shave points. Spivey claimed innocence before a grand jury and was charged with lying under oath. He escaped legal penalty after a mistrial, but Kentucky, and then the NBA, prohibited Spivey from playing again. Beard, looking back in a 2003 interview, said that the 1949 scandal "was really a blip on the screen for Kentucky basketball. You just can't kill something that big." But two scandals, only a few years apart, seriously wounded it. Kentucky became the first college basketball program to receive the NCAA's so-called "death penalty" and was banned from playing the entire 1952-53 season. The Wildcats wouldn't reach a Final Four or win another national championship until they did both in 1958. By the way, New York sportswriters were said to have sent Rupp an 11-foot pole after the '51 scandal became public.

¶ Saint Joseph's of Philadelphia reached the Final Four in 1961. But the program was forced to vacate its third-place finish when three members of coach Jack Ramsay's team were found to have participated in a point-shaving scheme.

¶ In 1962, 37 players from 22 schools (Utah, Bowling Green, Pacific and Alabama, among others) were implicated in point-shaving schemes.

¶ The 1978-79 Boston College Eagles were infiltrated by Henry Hill, a colorful mobster who inspired the movie *Goodfellas*. Hill and a notorious New York gambler named Richard "The Fixer" Perry paid BC players to shave points in as many as nine games. The Eagles players weren't always successful, prompting Hill to pass along a chilling warning from mobster Jimmy "The Gent" Burke. According to a 2007 *USA Today* interview with Hill, Burke's message was scarily direct: "Tell those Boston kids they can't play basketball with broken arms." Three players (Jim Sweeney, Ernie Cobb and Rick Kuhn) were later identified in the scandal, but only Kuhn was charged, convicted and served prison time.

¶ The 1984-85 Tulane team was undone by the alleged point-shaving activities of five players, including four starters. According to two starters who were granted immunity for their testimony, cash and cocaine were the incentives. Tulane star John "Hot Rod" Williams was indicted on five counts of conspiracy and bribery, but charges were later dropped after a mistrial was declared. The damage done to Tulane's 72-year-old basketball program, however, was immediate and profound. Nine days after Williams was arrested, university president Eamon Kelly disbanded the team and head coach Ned Fowler resigned, along with two of his assistants, as well as athletic director Hindman Wall. Tulane basketball would not return from its self-imposed penalties until 1989.

¶ The 1993-94 Arizona State Sun Devils were betrayed by team captain Stevin "Hedake" Smith, whose point-shaving efforts eventually snowballed into a gambling catastrophe. What began as a two-man on-campus operation—Smith conspiring with student bookmaker Benny Silman as a way of settling Smith's $10,000 gambling debt—later included teammate Isaac Burton, then cartwheeled out of control as word spread of the mob-financed fixed games. Those red flags that people like sports consultant White watch out for were flapping everywhere when more than $1 million poured into the Las Vegas sports books for a March 5, 1994, game between Arizona State and underdog Washington. Under normal circumstances, such a game would attract little more than $50,000 worth of betting business. "It was eye opening," said White. "ASU students were coming in with bags full of money." And they were betting on Washington. The point spread moved a total of 42 times, from 15 points in ASU's favor down to only three, a sure sign that the Fix was in. Smith later admitted that it was. But things didn't work out well for the Huskies backers: Although ASU missed its first 14 shots, the Wildcats rallied to win—and cover the spread—73-55. There were reports that the ASU players were told at halftime that the game was under scrutiny. Smith ended up pleading guilty to sports bribery charges—he was paid $20,000 for each of four point-shaved games—and spent almost a year in jail. Burton, who helped fix two of the games, was sentenced to two months in jail and was also ordered to serve home detention and community service, and pay an $8,000 fine. Federal law enforcement officials determined that more money was wagered on those fixed ASU games than on any other point-shaving scheme in college sports history.

¶ The 1994-95 Northwestern Wildcats earned the dubious distinction of being the last program known to be involved in a college basketball point-shaving scheme in the 20th century. This time it was two senior starters: Dion Lee, who owed money to a student bookie, and Dewey Williams, who took bribes to fix three Big Ten games. But this scheme had a twist. Unlike most point-shaving cases, where the favored team is expected to win but not cover the spread, Lee and Williams worked to ensure that Northwestern, a perennial doormat that had never made it to the NCAA Tournament, would *lose* games by *more* than the betting line. The scandal sickened Northwestern's president and angered its athletic director, Rick Taylor, who told reporters that point-shaving "purely and simply is betrayal—betrayal of self, teammate, family, coaches, university and the very game itself." He would later describe gambling as "America's stealth addiction." Taylor had reason to feel betrayed. Not only did he have to deal with Northwestern's basketball point-shaving scandal, but the school's investigation also uncovered an instance of football point-shaving during the same school year.

Northwestern was the latest case study, but the odds pretty much guarantee it won't be the last. (In 2008, federal prosecutors in Detroit charged former Toledo University player Sammy Villegas with shaving points in 2004-05 and 2005-06.) Justin Wolfers, an assistant professor of business and public policy at the University of Pennsylvania, analyzed the outcomes of more than 44,000 Division I basketball games between 1989 and 2005. In a 2006 research paper, he estimated that about 500 of those games featured what he called "gambling-related corruption," which is a nice way of saying the Fix was probably in. Wolfers also contends that a whopping 5% of games with large point spreads—13 points or higher—were compromised by similar "corruption."

The NCAA has disputed those figures, but it does not disagree that a problem exists. Nor would it likely take issue with Wolfers' comments in a 2007 *New York Times* op-ed piece in which he wrote, "Point-shaving is a crime of opportunity" because the opportunities are plentiful. A 2003 NCAA report titled *National Study on Collegiate Sports Wagering and Associated Behaviors* revealed that 1.5% of the 388 Division I men's basketball players polled answered "yes" when asked, "Have you ever known of a teammate who accepted money or other reward for playing poorly?" One percent of the players said they had affected the outcome of a game because of gambling debts. More than 20,000 NCAA athletes were involved in the overall study.

Point-shaving in college basketball went a perfect six-for-six during the last six decades of the 20th century, and appears to have continued into the 21st.

Arizona State's Smith said in a 1998 *Sports Illustrated* interview, "Having been there, I can tell you how easily players can be drawn into fixing games. Poor, naïve teenagers plus rich, greedy gamblers equals disaster." To an expert like White, Smith fit the profile of a point-shaving mark. "I think it all starts with leverage," said White. "I don't think a player really intends to go do this … I think what happens is that someone gets in debt gambling." In the cases of both Smith and Northwestern's Lee, a campus bookie offered a supposed get-out-of-debt-free card. "And the bookmaker says, 'Hey, I've got a way for you to work it off,'" said White. "It all goes back to the leverage."

Desperation can overpower logic. That's why players like Smith were able to rationalize their actions by repeatedly accepting the fixer's creed: You're not trying to lose the game, *you're just trying to win by fewer points than the point spread.* Where's the harm? Or sometimes the leverage is a four- or five-figure bribe, which is understandably difficult to ignore for some players who can't handle the irony of being unpaid "amateurs" in the multi-billion-dollar business of college basketball. "It's probably happened a hundred times in the last couple of years," said White. "Kids have been approached: 'Hey, you want to make some money? You don't have to do anything more than miss a shot, make a bad pass, and we'll pay you $5,000.'"

"They go to the most vulnerable," said the former athletic director. "They go to the kids they can get. Who would you go to—the affluent kid from Shaker Heights, or the kid scraping together enough money for a pizza on Saturday night?"

It is this vulnerability to gambling scandal that has forced the NCAA to declare a DEFCON 1 state of readiness. Part of the concern centers on protecting the student-athlete, but there is little doubt the NCAA is also trying to protect the brand name and revenue-producing power of its annual men's basketball tournament. Former NCAA executive director Cedric Dempsey once told *The Washington Post* that he was aware of studies that showed college students spent more on gambling than on alcohol. "If we find that we have a lot of point-shaving going on," said Dempsey, "our public will lose confidence in what's happening, and then certainly what we see here in terms of interest [in the Tournament] will wane."

In 2001, NCAA officials appeared before a U.S. Senate committee chaired by Arizona Senator John McCain and called for the elimination of the loophole that allows legal wagering in Nevada on American college sports, reasoning that even legal gambling requires an intense degree of policing and regulation that neither the NCAA nor any agency is equipped to provide. And legal gambling still invites point-shaving.

"We are not an organization poised to infiltrate illegal gambling networks," testified William S. Saum, the NCAA's then-director of agent, gambling and amateurism activities. "We have, and continue to process, cases involving sports wagering when they come within the authority of the organization. We have brought attention for more than five years to a problem we would rather not have exist: There is illegal gambling on college campuses, some involving student-athletes … We ask you to do what is right for our student-athletes and what is right for college games."

The request might have had merit, but it did not have enough support from lawmakers. Legal wagering on college sports continues to be big business for Nevada's sports books. Faced with that reality, the NCAA established a partnership of sorts with the American Gaming Association: The two organizations work together to monitor betting activity on college games. They watch to see whether betting lines move unexpectedly, or if there is a sudden increase in betting volume on a particular game. When they spot a suspicious trend, the NCAA may alert an involved school, conference or law enforcement agency.

The NCAA has also increased its efforts to educate players, coaches and administrators about the dangers of gambling and point-shaving, using a good cop/bad cop model. Good cop: a 24-hour, confidential help line for problem gamblers; pre-NCAA Tournament lectures by experts and the FBI; a 26-page booklet that not only details the dangers associated with gambling, but also includes a chapter titled "How to Become a Millionaire" with a series of worksheets to teach responsible saving and investing. Bad cop: the potential loss of scholarship; expulsion; permanent ineligibility; and/or arrest.

Wolfers advocates a course more daring than education and threats. His *New York Times* piece noted, "When faced with a betting scandal, a sports league usually hardens its anti-gambling stance. But that doesn't work." Instead, Wolfers suggested legal betting on which team wins or loses, but a ban on point spreads. He argued that "banning all bets on immaterial outcomes like point spreads would destroy the market for illegal bookmakers and make sporting events less corruptible by gamblers." Fat chance. Even Wolfers admitted, "We're unlikely to see this necessary reform any time soon."

So the NCAA waits for what has become almost as predictable as the paths of the planets: a point-shaving scandal every 10 or so years. White's company has developed a system of algorithms designed to detect patterns of suspicious betting, but no warning system is 100% foolproof. The NCAA Tournament continues to draw huge amounts of betting money to the sports books, legal and illegal. The more money from the general public is in play, said White, "the easier it is to disguise point-shaving" for a single Tournament game.

Easier, but not completely invisible. Even though it's the Final Four games that draw the most betting action, the point spreads do not normally grow larger than five or six points, making them, according to White, much less likely to be targets for point-shaving. That's why authorities pay very special attention to those first-round games between very high and very low seeds, when the point spreads frequently reach double digits. *Those* are the potential point-shavers' targets. Vigilance is comforting, but it provides no guarantee. Point-shaving in college basketball went a perfect six-for-six during the last six decades of the 20th century, and appears to have continued into the 21st.

"So why are we surprised that it happens again?" asked the former athletic director. "If we don't learn something from history, we're pretty stupid."

The Women's Game

For more than a century, females have fought against stereotypes to prove they belong on the court

By Eric Adelson

She has the most famous first name in women's college basketball: Pat. But family members and friends who've known Patricia Head since her school days call her Trish. And the story of how Trish Head became Pat Summitt is symbolic of the entire story of women's basketball.

A knee injury closed the door on Trish Head's playing career at Tennessee-Martin in 1974, but it opened another door to a vacant coaching position at Tennessee-Knoxville when she was 22. Dr. Helen Watson, chair of UT's phys ed department, introduced Head to the Lady Volunteers as "Pat," assuming she went by the common diminutive for her given name, Patricia. Head said nothing. "Absolutely overwhelmed and scared to death," she later admitted, and too shy to rock the boat by correcting the boss. So she remains Pat, not Trish, to this day.

The tension facing Trish Head on that day symbolizes the tension that has defined Pat Summitt's (she married R.B. Summitt in 1980; they divorced in 2008) sport since its inception in the 19th century. Is it better to remain in an expected role as defined by someone else, or is it better to fight for a truer identity, even if the fighting might turn somebody off? Stay within the mold, or break it?

That dilemma has faced female players and their supporters from the very beginning of the sport in 1892, when Senda Berenson adapted basketball for women at Smith College in Northampton, Mass., a year after Dr. James Naismith invented the game for young men at Springfield College just down the road. The first director of physical education at Smith (and the sister of Bernard Berenson, the famed art historian), Berenson was a staunch advocate of physical education without excessive aggression for women. She modified Naismith's game by dividing the court into three zones and stationing three players from each team in each zone. As if endorsing the predominant social rules for women at the time, Berenson decreed that players must never leave their zone and that sharing was mandatory; a player could hold the ball for no more than three seconds. (Unlimited dribbling would not be sanctioned until 1966.) Stealing the ball was not allowed.

Young women played Berenson's game for more than 20 years before coaching was permitted in games, and it wasn't until after World War I that the women's game began to incorporate more of the men's rules. And yet, even early on, some women's teams dared to break from Berenson's rules and play the game the way men played it.

The women's game grew in fits and starts. Stanford and Cal played the first intercollegiate contest in 1896, but three years later Stanford forbade women from playing at all. Elsewhere, new rules were designed because the game, despite Berenson's original intent, had become too physical. Certain forms of shooting were discouraged because they made a woman look "less feminine." (The two-handed set shot, critics claimed, flattened the chest.) In 1912, a widely respected physical education expert named Dudley Sargent wrote an article for *Ladies' Home Journal* titled, "Are Athletics Making Girls Masculine?" Women faced a barrier men never would encounter: the belief that sports were not ladylike.

Women pushed back, and all sorts of barriers began falling after the end of World War I. The biggest toppled in 1920, when the 19th Amendment to the U.S. Constitution gave women the right to vote; the cultural shift was widespread and extended all the way down to the basketball court. Varsity high school tournaments started popping up in most states, and the AAU began to create women's leagues in cities across the country.

Businesses began sponsoring teams in local leagues to call attention to their products and services. One such business, the Employers Casualty Company in Dallas, sponsored a team in a local AAU league that featured a young player from Beaumont, Texas, named Mildred Ella Didrikson, who went by the nickname Babe. Beginning in 1930, Babe Didrikson earned AAU All-America honors three straight years, leading her Employers Casualty team to victory in the 1931 AAU women's national championship game.

The tone and pace of women's basketball took a jolting leap forward in the middle of the decade with the arrival on the hardwood of a professional team called the All American Red Heads. Not all were natural redheads. Those who weren't were willing to dye for the team. They played a brand of aggressive, high-octane hoops hitherto unseen (or even imagined) in women's basketball. And they played it all around the country against anybody, anywhere, who would accept their challenge. Provided they were men.

A former basketball player named Connie Mack "Ole" Olson organized the first Red Heads in 1936 to help publicize a small string of beauty parlors his wife ran in Arkansas and Missouri. By the end of the decade, the Red Heads were regularly attracting crowds of 1,000 or more around the nation, mostly in small and midsize cities

The Red Heads embraced both brawn and beauty, wearing shiny outfits with short shorts to go with their flaming tresses and glamorous makeup. The result was to expand the conventional definition of femininity to include smart and strong along with sassy and sexy. They wowed audiences with their trick shots, fancy ballhandling and breathtaking athletic ability, staging Globetrotter-inspired routines at halftime while male opponents rested. The Red Heads were out to win—always—and they came out on top in about 70% of the 160 or so games they played each year.

But from the outset their No. 1 job was to entertain, and they succeeded beyond any reasonable expectation. The barnstorming tour was, at the time, one of the boldest ventures in women's sports history. It was also one of the most effective: The Red Heads stayed in business for 50 years.

Yet just when it seemed that the mold that so tightly encased women in sports might have busted, it hardened again—more strongly than ever. The post-World War II era brought a major retrenchment of gender roles. Men worked; women stayed home. If a girl took part in a sporting event, she was most likely to be a cheerleader. And basketball? Mostly a man's game.

The NCAA crowned its first men's champion in 1939. The forerunner to the NBA launched in 1946. Rules changes—such as widening the foul lane and the NBA's shot clock—sped up the sport, which further separated the men's game from the women's. So the women's game sagged and did not get fully on its feet for much of the rest of the century. President Richard Nixon signed a new federal anti-discrimination statute into law in 1972, but Title IX was a response to sex discrimination in educational institutions, not to any cry for leveling the playing fields for men's and women's sports. The NCAA, after opposing the new law, didn't hold a basketball tournament for women until 10 years after its passage. It would take the dedication and drive of a few individuals to overcome cultural inertia and apply Title IX's power to women's sports in the schools.

Is it better to remain in an expected role as defined by someone else, or to fight for a truer identity, even if the fighting might turn somebody off? Stay within the mold, or break it?

Any discussion of the modern era of women's basketball begins with Cathy Rush, a Pennsylvanian who coached tiny Immaculata (Pa.) College to the first three Association for Intercollegiate Athletics for Women (AIAW) titles. Within one month in 1975, Immaculata played in the first televised women's game and then in the first women's game in Madison Square Garden, which drew more than 11,000 fans.

A rash of milestones followed: Women played in the Olympics for the first time in 1976 (the U.S. won silver to the Soviet Union's gold); Mel Greenberg of *The Philadelphia Inquirer* published the first women's Top-20 poll; Karen Logan—a Red Head—beat former Los Angeles Lakers superstar Jerry West at H-O-R-S-E on national TV; and NBC broadcast the first AIAW final four in 1978. By 1982, the NCAA finally decided to hold its own tournament, and the AIAW, unable to compete, disbanded. In 1983, ESPN began televising women's NCAA Tournament games.

All of this was happening at a time when, largely because of television, the attention of fans was being refocused from the team to the individual. It was the era of the superstar. The men's game took off on the electricity generated by the likes of Julius Erving, Magic Johnson and Larry Bird. Women's basketball would now move forward (or not) depending on the flair and personality of its star players and even coaches. Enter Cheryl Miller.

Every bit as dynamic as any of the Red Heads in their day, Miller, of Riverside, Calif., became the first high school player, male or female, to be named a *Parade* All-America four times. In one game she scored *105* points. She could play all five positions, but started as a 6'2" forward during her spectacular college career at USC. In her eight seasons of high school and college ball, her teams won 244 games and lost only 24. She led USC to two national titles. A pair of knee injuries forced her to quit playing the age of 24, but she went on to coach at USC (44–14 in two seasons) the way she played—with the tempo and aggression of the best male players. (Many believe that Miller's brother, five-time NBA All-Star Reggie, was the second-best player in the family.)

Miller led the way for other high achievers. Cynthia Cooper led Team USA to Olympic gold in 1988. Bernadette Mattox became an assistant men's coach under Rick Pitino at Kentucky. Nancy Lieberman played with the otherwise all-male Washington Generals, perennial foe of the Harlem Globetrotters. Sheryl Swoopes endorsed her own line of Nike shoes in 1995. C. Vivian Stringer became the first women's coach to earn a $150,000 salary when she was wooed from Iowa to Rutgers the same year. But all were overshadowed by two coaches who would raise the game to its highest level.

And one of them was a man.

The first was the former Trish Head, a Tennessee farmer's daughter who became a household name among basketball fans as Pat Summitt, whose sideline intensity was matched only by her love for the game and her players. The second was Geno Auriemma, just as quick with a barb as with an in-game adjustment, who preached head as ardently as Summitt preached heart.

Their storied rivalry—Summitt with Tennessee, Auriemma with Connecticut—took off during the 1994-95 season, which ended in a national championship game between the two teams that drew a 5.7 television rating—a record that still stands. Both teams already had long and distinguished hoops histories: The Lady Vols and the Huskies had been playing women's basketball since the turn of the 20th century.

Summitt preached defense and rebounding, while Auriemma focused more on running the perfect system. Their differences allowed the growth of two superpowers that rarely recruited the same players. That 1995 NCAA title game ended with Connecticut on top, 70-64, to complete a perfect 35–0 season. Tennessee came back with championships the next three years, led by the greatest player since Miller—Chamique Holdsclaw—and achieved its own perfect season in 1997-98. By that point, the entire women's basketball culture had changed completely. After earlier start-ups had failed, two new women's pro leagues formed (the WNBA and the ABL), women's games became a staple on national television and a female Dream Team won Olympic gold in Atlanta.

Summitt excelled with her unyielding demand for defense and rebounding; Auriemma used a complex offense and motivation techniques ranging from telling war stories to using mind games.

Other coaches of women's teams also fared well—Tara VanDerveer at Stanford, Jody Conradt at Texas, Stringer at Rutgers, Gail Goestenkors at Duke and, later, Texas—but Summitt and Auriemma outdid them all. Summitt excelled with her unyielding demand for defense and rebounding; Auriemma used a complex offense and motivation techniques ranging from telling war stories to using mind games. Both coaches recruited nationally and both pushed players far beyond their comfort zones. It was common practice among coaches of women's teams to coddle players, allowing them room to err and heal. But both Summitt and Auriemma saw sexism in such a policy and demanded as much of women as they would of men.

Summitt pitted her team against men in practice—another throwback to the Red Heads—while Auriemma incorporated the Chicago Bulls' famed triangle offense. Both perennially fielded teams that would elevate their performance under extreme pressure, while would-be rivals habitually melted down. Summitt sometimes lacked in-game creativity and Auriemma sometimes annoyed everyone in sight, but neither coach's team ever choked. That, along with the simmering feud between the two, made games between the Huskies and the Lady Vols appeal to more than just die-hard women's basketball fans. TV ratings and attendance figures ballooned in the 1990s and early 2000s, with both schools bringing consistently great teams to Final Fours held in packed arenas and even domed stadiums. The 1990 NCAA women's Final Four in Knoxville outdrew that year's men's Final Four in Denver.

A century after women took up the game, young girls and their parents saw opportunities for college scholarships, national exposure, professional careers, Olympic glory and even endorsements.

Naturally, the gold rush had its dark side. Recruiting turned more competitive, and even ugly, as more money seeped into the sport. Some coaches accused others of exploiting players' sexual orientation as a recruiting tool. But the big picture shown by TV cameras looked nothing but inspiring—a huge ramping up of talent, as the mostly plodding players of the old days gave way to sleek, smooth, sexy athletes who could do it all, from throwing no-look passes to shooting NBA three-pointers to slamming down dunks.

Tennessee and Connecticut reeled in two of the most versatile and agile players in the game's history, Candace Parker and Diana Taurasi, respectively. Each won a national title for her team and then immediately transformed the WNBA club that drafted her: Taurasi the Phoenix Mercury and Parker the LA Sparks. At last, the decades-old notion that women were meant to play only a strictly defined game was shattered by the reality that some women—like some men—were capable of creating and dominating the action all by themselves. By the early 2000s, some in the sports media argued that the women's game, now blessed with more athleticism *without* sacrificing the beautiful basics of teamwork, had eclipsed the clear-out-and-drive-the-lane men's version of the game.

At last the decades-old notion that women were meant to play only a strictly defined game was shattered by the reality that some women were capable of creating and dominating the action all by themselves.

By that time, Summitt had won nearly 800 games, more than all but a few men's coaches. (She passed them all in 2009, when she notched her 1,000th win.) But her rivalry with Auriemma had become so fascinating that it began to devour the sport it helped build. No other coaches had the star power of Pat and Geno, and any title game not involving either of their teams seemed anticlimactic. And even though the WNBA teemed with former Lady Vols and Huskies, the pro league paled in comparison because it failed to develop the drama or tradition of Tennessee and Connecticut. The WNBA lacked not only the verve and color of the barnstorming Red Heads, but also the freshness and intensity the new college game. If not for the financial backing it received from the NBA, the league would likely have fallen apart quickly—as the ABL did after just two-plus seasons in 1998.

While games in Knoxville and Hartford continued to pack houses, neutral NCAA Tournament sites often yawned with empty sections. Sports fans in the 21st century demand larger-than-life personalities, and in college sports—where players, even great ones, constantly come and go—that means coaches. And women's basketball still only had two. Although closer than ever to the men's game in terms of talent, style and appeal, the women still needed fresh faces to take chances and push the sport to a higher level. The tension that Berenson faced in the 1890s—either define and polish a distinct women's game or emulate the men's—still remains.

The Summitt vs. Auriemma rivalry boiled over in 2006-07, as the Big Two finally faced enough competition from schools such as Duke, Maryland, Oklahoma and others that they could no longer operate in their separate, and largely private, recruiting spheres. A spat over one prized prep reportedly snowballed into harsh words and then dead silence between the two dynamos, with Summitt ultimately deciding to discontinue the greatest rivalry in the history of her sport. The move brought immediate and strong criticism of the Tennessee coach from media and fans, who never imagined a regular season without a Pat vs. Geno showdown. And it raised a hard truth: each was getting closer to leaving the bench (Summitt turned 57 in 2009, Auriemma 55) and neither had an obvious heir.

Tennessee won its seventh and eighth titles in 2007 and 2008, and Connecticut won its sixth in 2009—with its third perfect season. But growth in the game's popularity has slowed. Another boundary must be broken. Perhaps it's a rule change. Or a woman able to take on LeBron James. Or perhaps it's an athlete who has demonstrated the courage to question the way things have become. Maybe someone like Becky Hammon, the South Dakota native who infuriated many but inspired others by playing for Russia's 2008 Olympic team after she was overlooked by Team USA. Or someone like Swoopes, who risked career damage by publicly endorsing a cruise line that catered to lesbians. Or someone like Parker, who is showing that women can play above as well as below the rim. Or someone who is not yet on the national radar, a young woman with the talent to awe and the charisma to entertain modern sports fans.

Women are slowly but surely closing the gap with men in athletic ability, so that someone is coming. But she will have to combine the best of those two competing influences over her sport—play a game for women or play the game like men.

That new face of women's basketball has to be ready to take a little bit of Trish Head and a little bit of Pat Summitt and be completely comfortable with both.

They Were There

Fifteen witnesses describe their favorite moments in the game

AS TOLD TO CAL FUSSMAN

TOMMY KEARNS

Kearns was the North Carolina guard who lined up for the opening tip against Wilt Chamberlain in UNC's 54-53 triple-overtime victory over Kansas in the 1957 NCAA Final.

I have a picture of the moment in my office at home. I'm looking at it right now. The referee has just tossed the ball up at center court. I'm squatting, ready to jump. The ball is on its way up. And Wilt's standing there with his hands on his hips looking at me with this expression that says, "What are *you* doing here?"

I'm only 5'11".

The reality was that nobody on our team was going to get the jump from Wilt. He was 7'1", the first of the really big men. All of us at North Carolina knew how talented he was. A lot of us were from the New York area, and we were busboys in the Catskills during the summer. Wilt was from Philadelphia and he went to play in the Catskills, too. So we knew him.

When Coach [Frank] McGuire came to me and said, "Do you mind jumping against Wilt?" he knew what he was doing. He was saying to Wilt and everyone else at Kansas, "We know you. But you don't know us."

Of course, Wilt won the tip. But it was a great ploy. It set the tone of the game. We got off to an early lead.

We had to win the game strategically. Wilt had been a celebrity from the time he was in grammar school. He was supposed to win three national championships wherever he went to school. We weren't playing Kansas. We were playing Wilt.

You have to remember something else. Back then, you played the semifinal game on Friday night. And you came back and played the Final on Saturday night. It took us three overtimes to beat Michigan State on Friday night, and it was a grueling game. That same night, Kansas easily blew out San Francisco.

Another thing people don't realize about the Final against Kansas is that our star, Lennie Rosenbluth, fouled out with a minute to go in regulation. We had to play through three overtimes against Wilt without Lennie.

In retrospect, the outcome came down to strategy. We were looking for a clear shot and weren't going to take one unless we had it. Kansas seemed content to let us do just that. They didn't force us out of our game. As a result, we controlled the tempo through the three overtimes.

We had a one-point lead with a few seconds left in the third overtime, and they had the ball. We all knew that it was going inside to Wilt. They were counting on him scoring or getting fouled and winning the game at the line. I was turned around, looking in, when the pass came in toward Wilt, and the next thing I knew it was deflected and coming out to me.

I sensed that they were going to foul me. So I took a couple of quick bounces, threw the ball toward the rafters, and the clock ran out before it came down.

Looking back on that moment now, it amazes me how an event can change lives. It was one of the early NCAA championship games to be televised and it captured the imagination of just about every person in the state of North Carolina. We all became celebrities of a sort. I got into the securities business, and that win was a big plus for me.

On the other hand, I've heard that the guy who threw that last pass to Wilt still thinks about it every time he watches a basketball game. And the loss was devastating for Wilt. That night, there were chants from the crowd of "We wilted the Stilt!" From then on, Wilt got a bad rap. They called him a loser.

I got a chance to know Wilt well. I did some business deals with him. He was a great guy and he had a great sense of humor. But I don't think he ever saw the humor in that picture on my wall.

BILL WALTON

The UCLA center (1971-74) discusses the Bruins' dynasty and his basketball idol.

Jan. 20, 1968, I was a sophomore in high school. I remember it being so exciting because it was the first regular-season college basketball game televised nationally in prime time. Not that we knew what prime time meant or anything.

UCLA against Houston. Kareem Abdul-Jabbar against Elvin Hayes. Kareem was still Lew Alcindor then, but to me, even in my memory, he's Kareem. The Houston Astrodome. Largest crowd [52,693] ever to see a college basketball game.

Elvin Hayes was a great player, but he was no Kareem Abdul-Jabbar. Kareem had never lost a collegiate game up to that point. He was so powerful in all aspects. We all wore the number 33 in honor of the king. But he'd been poked in the eye and spent about a week in the UCLA eye center. We weren't even sure if he was going to play.

When he did, he shot only four for 18. It was the only game in Kareem's entire college career that he shot less than 50% from the field.

Meanwhile, Elvin Hayes had a monster game. Scored 39 points and took down 15 rebounds. Houston won, 71-69.

What made the game so special was that it showed that the giant could be brought down. There was a lot of trash talking as the rematch approached in the NCAA semifinals. But Kareem never said a word. He would never use the eye injury as an excuse. But in a documentary film about the UCLA dynasty, Lucius Allen says that to this very day Kareem does not like Elvin Hayes.

There was so much excitement and anticipation surrounding the rematch. Then the Bruins came out and just suffocated them. Houston couldn't even move the ball around. The Bruins were flawless in every aspect of the game. Houston had no chance from the opening tip. It ended 101-69.

UCLA's perfect performance was represented by the photo on the cover of *Sports Illustrated.* There was Kareem soaring for a skyhook, scoreboard in the background and everybody else riveted to the ground, helpless and in awe.

When I think of the UCLA dynasty, that's the image that comes to mind.

LOUIS "LULU" BENDER

Columbia's Lulu Bender led all Ivy Leaguers in scoring in 1930 and 1931 with averages of 9.8 and 9.6 points per game. He played in the first college basketball event at New York City's Madison Square Garden—a tripleheader.

I don't think there was college basketball at Madison Square Garden until we played there on Dec. 31, 1931. I'll tell you why: That Garden was built with a marble floor. I don't think basketball had been considered when it was built. Hockey had been considered; they were able to water over the marble surface and turn it into ice.

There was an event where the basketball teams from six schools around New York came together to play, with the proceeds going to help the unemployed. Our Columbia team played NYU, CCNY played Fordham and Manhattan played St. John's. Jimmy Walker was the mayor at the time. Do you go back that far? No? Oh, you're a baby. I'm 98.

Anyway, someone got the idea to host the tripleheader at Madison Square Garden. This was not the original Garden. And it's not the Garden people go to now. It was the Garden on 50th Street and Eighth Avenue. It was built in 1925. Boxing was big then, and that Garden was built without any existing basketball court.

I'll tell you how we got to play there. Bill Tilden, the famous tennis player, had put down a tarp over the marble surface to play tennis there. He loaned the tarp to the Garden. It was reversed and the outlines of a basketball court were painted on the other side.

They must have brought in movable baskets. I don't know how they did it. But more than 14,000 people showed up for the games. We had never seen such a large crowd for a college basketball game in the East before. Of course, we won our game, 22-17.

They put a wooden floor over the marble surface after that.

> ***"Coach V ran out on the court and I think he was trying to find Dereck, but Dereck had gone somewhere else. So Coach V didn't know where his hug was. That's why you see him looking around like that."***

SIDNEY LOWE

The NC State guard (and future head coach) describes the greatest finish of an NCAA title game, when Dereck Whittenberg threw up a 35-foot prayer that was guided in at the buzzer by Lorenzo Charles, giving coach Jim Valvano's team a 54-52 upset win over Houston in 1983.

You see the replay over and over and over, and it starts to become your memory of what happened. Over time, it replaces what you actually saw.

Everybody's seen it. Dereck going high for the pass near the midcourt line with time running out. Nearly losing the ball. Getting it on the bounce and throwing up that desperation shot. The ball coming down short and Lorenzo jumping up to put it in. Then Coach V running onto the court to celebrate. It looks like he's looking for somebody to hug—and he is. I've seen the replay so many times that I really have to stop and think to recall my own memory of the moment.

As soon as the ball went through, my eyes were on the officials. I didn't know if the shot counted or if it went through after the buzzer. When I saw the officials moving off the court, that's when I knew we'd won. That was the moment that sunk in for me. I remember rushing through the pandemonium and running into the stands to hug my mom. That wasn't on tape. That's how I know it's *my* memory.

The guys who come to play for me at NC State now weren't even born when we beat Houston. They see the replay and I don't think they quite get it. When they look at it, they try to imagine themselves in that last-second situation that gives them a chance to be a hero. But that's not what I want them to get out of it. I want them to understand what most people overlook—what's underneath what they're seeing, the mental toughness that it took *to get to* that moment, and then to get through it. We needed to win the ACC tournament just to get *into* the NCAA Tournament. We needed to beat a team that had Michael Jordan just to have a chance.

Then, in the opening round of the NCAAs, we were down six to Pepperdine with 24 seconds left. And you know how we won? We won because a guy on the bench stepped up and asked Coach V to put him in the game in a tense moment because he knew he could do something special for the team. And that was the great thing about Coach V—he knew just when to put a guy in. He read us. He put in Cozell McQueen, and Cozell came up with one of the biggest plays of the year to send that game into overtime. Cozell wanted it. We all wanted it. We just were *not* going to lose.

Not many people gave us a chance against Houston with Hakeem Olajuwon and Clyde Drexler. We were going up against two guys who would be selected among the Top 50 players in NBA history.

This was before the shot clock. All week before the game, Coach V was saying to the press that if we got the ball we might not shoot it—just to keep it out of their hands. I'm the point guard hearing this all week. My mindset was into controlling the game based on what he was saying: We may not shoot the ball.

When we got in the locker room just before the game, he changed up on us. I'm not going to repeat it exactly the way he said it. But the essence was that we'd come this far in front of millions of people to do what? Hold the ball? That's crazy. *We don't care who they are!*

We're laughing, smiling, all fired up. If you recall, I shot a jump shot right off the bat, just jacked it up—it bounced off the rim and Thurl Bailey dunked it. We came to play. You can talk all you want about talent—and talent is important—but nobody *wanted* it more than we did.

After every game in that tournament, Coach V and Dereck would somehow find each other after the buzzer and hug. It became sort of a superstition. When we beat Houston, Coach V ran out on the court and I think he was trying to find Dereck where Dereck threw up the shot. But Dereck had gone somewhere else. So Coach V didn't know where his hug was. That's why you see him looking around like that.

When I think of Coach V, I think of a lot of things. But it always gets down to those two words: mental toughness. It's exactly what I'm trying to pass on to my guys. It prepares you for life no matter what obstacles are in front of you.

When Coach V got cancer, look how he handled it. He fought it as hard as he could. He never asked anyone to feel sorry for him. As he was dying, you know what he was thinking? "There are people coming behind me; what can I do to stop this disease before it gets to them?"

The Jimmy V Foundation has now raised $80 million. That's what I'm talking about. *What can I do for the team*? In that case, his team was the world.

PETE NEWELL

The game's premier coach of big men, Newell saw one of the best when his University of California squads ran into Bill Russell on the San Francisco teams that won 60 straight games, including consecutive NCAA titles in 1955 and '56. Newell died on Nov. 17, 2008, at the age of 93.

To this day, we haven't really had a shotblocker who dominated the game the way Bill Russell did. There have been a lot of big jumpers, but many of them got into foul trouble. What Russell had was innate. He rarely got into foul trouble and he was impossible to get by.

Russell brought to basketball the importance of defense. You couldn't prepare for those USF teams. Russell's ability to jam your offense was something we had never run into. He would knock your players' shots down, and he not only affected their shots for the rest of that game, but the experience altered their shots two and three games down the road.

Russell was different from most shotblockers. He played with flexed knees. That was really important in a time when most players were stiff-legged. When you're crouched like he was, you're bound to go up and get the ball much quicker.

USF proved that defense could be the best way to win. The entire team was coordinated around Russell. The other players would try to knock the ball loose, knowing that if they didn't and their man got by them, they didn't have to worry—because their man wouldn't get by Russell.

We didn't have fast-break games out on the West Coast before Russell arrived. You were in new territory against those USF teams. When a shot went up, K.C. Jones knew that he could race down court and if Russell got the rebound, the ball was coming his way. I don't know how many times he ran the fast break off Bill's initial outlet pass.

I don't think there was a team to compare with USF in my time. But there's something else about Russell that's very important: Wherever Bill Russell went, he won.

If Bill Russell were playing today, his team would win.

DICK ENBERG

The veteran television commentator called the first matchup between Earvin "Magic" Johnson and Larry Bird, in the 1979 NCAA Final, for NBC.

We can't rewrite history. The 1979 Final between Michigan State and Indiana State was not a great game. But it did have the all elements to *be* a great game.

Magic made you reach out and care about him. When that smile came out, we all seemed to love the game and care more about it because of the way Magic loved and cared. That's a rare quality. There are very few athletes in any sport over the years who've had the ability to reach the fans in the very last row of the arena and make them care about you.

In Bird, you had somebody who was inward. His personality was his game. Larry didn't have amazing natural talents—he wasn't that quick or fast or strong—but his gift was that he knew how to play. He knew how to be in the right place at the right time, he knew where everyone else was supposed to be, he knew how to pass, and he was one of the great shooters of all time.

You also had an unbeaten team—Indiana State at 33–0—making it all the way to the Final against Michigan State. The build-up was like watching a real-life version of the movie *Hoosiers*, and it attracted a lot of people who love to see the underdog win.

The team they were up against not only had Magic, but another All-America in Greg Kelser, and Jay Vincent, who later played in the NBA. When Indiana State stepped on the court—not to demean the rest of the Sycamores—it looked like Larry Bird and four chemistry majors going up against this powerful Big Ten team.

If Indiana State had beaten Michigan State, the game would have rated as one of the greatest college basketball games of all time. But early in the second half, it was apparent that Michigan State was going to win. The outcome [75-64] was never really in doubt. So you have to look at why that game became so important in the history of college basketball. Part of the reason is television.

The marriage between college basketball and television really started with the 1968 UCLA-Houston game in the Astrodome that was shown in prime time. The build-up to the Magic-Bird matchup made the '79 Final the most-watched college basketball game ever at the time. It's still the highest-rated title game ever. It took what started in 1968 and shot it into the stratosphere at supersonic speed. College basketball was never the same again.

There's another reason that game is seen as one of the biggest college games ever: All of the great Magic-Bird encounters later in the NBA made people remember the first.

BEVO FRANCIS

He scored 116 points in a game for Rio Grande College of Ohio against Ashland (Ky.) Junior College on Jan. 9, 1953.

By the third shot, I knew I was on to something special. I didn't know I was going to score 116 points, but I never paid much attention to my totals anyway. My teammates would check the scorebook more than I would.

> **"By the third shot, I knew I was on to something special. I didn't know I was going to score 116 points. My teammates would check the scorebook more than I would."**

We had a good team at Rio Grande. It was all set up around me scoring. I'm 6'9" and the other teams' big men weren't accustomed to coming outside to guard me. My shot was honed on every basket hung on every barn in the area around Hammondsville, Ohio. There was no three-point line back in the '50s, but a lot of the time, that's where I was shooting from.

The team from Ashland tried everything to stop me. They were pushing. They were shoving. They even put three men on me. All my shots were falling.

We won, 150-85, but I didn't know that I'd scored 116 until I came out of the shower. They told me I'd made 47 field goals and 22 free throws. I'll tell you what I remember most. That night, calls from the press started coming in from around the country. Where I lived, there was only one phone, and that belonged to the landlady downstairs. She was up the whole night answering the telephone and coming to get me. And she had to go to work the next morning!

Our 1952-53 team went 39–0. The NAIA and NCAA wouldn't recognize our records because we didn't play all our games against four-year colleges. Ashland was a junior college. There was nothing that could be done about it. The schedule was made up before I got there.

I was a little disappointed for a while. But the next year, we scheduled a lot of big colleges. We didn't play any home games because our gym had room for only 200 fans and everybody wanted to see us. That year, I made my point when I scored 113 against Hillsdale College in Michigan.

Many years later, they looked at my shooting chart from that night and they said that if the three-point shot and the one-and-one rule had been in place, I would've scored 164.

AL SKINNER

The Boston College coach (1997-) was a Massachusetts teammate of Julius "Dr. J" Erving—perhaps the greatest dunk artist of all time—in the era when dunking was illegal in college basketball (1967-76).

Dunking was something we just knew we couldn't do in a game. So we really didn't talk much about the no-dunk rule at the time.

We all knew the undercurrent of the rule. Kareem Abdul-Jabbar—Lew Alcindor then—clearly had a tremendous advantage around the basket because of his size and athleticism. The rule seemed to be aimed at reducing that advantage. But at the end of the day, it really helped him develop his game.

It led to the skyhook, his signature shot, which helped make Kareem the all-time leading scorer in the NBA. There are tremendous advantages to not dunking the ball. It forces you to develop an interior game. It forces you to learn how to create opportunities around the basket.

The rule only made Julius Erving that much better. Those finger rolls you saw, they were a part of his game all along. But the creativity in the way they were delivered was enhanced in college because he couldn't finish with a dunk.

We didn't dunk during practice back then. Once practice was over, everyone took a turn at trying to be creative. So you could see what he was capable of doing.

The trick that was unique to Julius was dunking two balls at a time. He could do it because of the size of his hands. The other dunks he did after practice weren't as flamboyant as you'd think, because a lot of his greatest dunks came out of necessity.

For Julius, necessity was definitely the mother of invention.

I remember when he played in a tournament after college in Port Jefferson, New York. It was the first time I saw him dunk in an organized game, and it took me aback because it came so easily to him—and it came against professionals. All of a sudden he was able to complete the plays, and a tremendous talent was unleashed.

It all came together in the pros. But think about some of his best moves. Think about the move that Magic Johnson talks about, the most highlighted one there is, where Julius goes up, then underneath the basket against the Lakers, then comes around the other side of the basket to scoop it in. Think about that move and think of the setting. He was doing it in the NBA Finals with Kareem, Magic and a great defense on the court.

That was Julius at his finest—and it wasn't a dunk! You could make the case that his greatness came *because* of the no-dunk rule.

RONNIE CARR

The former Western Carolina guard made the first three-point basket in NCAA history.

> **"Just the other day a reporter said to me, 'That shot was like the first man to walk on the moon.'"**

Just the other day a reporter said to me, "That shot was like the first man to walk on the moon." I never thought of it like that. But it's true when you consider the evolution of the game. One shot for Western Carolina. One giant leap for college basketball.

You can't imagine the college game without the three-point shot now. But we didn't have it when I was coming up. It was introduced as an experiment in the Southern Conference when I was a sophomore.

This was big publicity for the Southern Conference. There was a lot of hype. We were playing at home against Middle Tennessee State on Nov. 29, 1980. The gym was packed. All the press was there. We got briefed before the game. The arc was set at 22 feet.

A few three-point shots were attempted early on, but they didn't fall. Then we took the ball out under our own basket. I got the pass as I moved to the far left corner of the court. Bobby Knight always said that the far left corner is the hardest shot in basketball.

You know how some guys look down to see where their feet are to check if they're behind the line? I didn't look. But I remember the sound. It's the same sound that comes now with every three-pointer. That silence where the crowd is in suspended animation—and then, when the ball goes through, everyone erupts.

It swished.

As soon as it went through, people started running out on the court going crazy. The media relations people wanted the ball. They wanted my jersey.

I said, "Hold on. Hold on! We've got a game to play."

I had no idea the ball would end up in the Hall of Fame.

The three-pointer changed the dynamics of the game. It's sped up the game. It's spread out the game. It's made coaches change their defensive strategy. Teams have won championships because one guy could hit the three-pointer.

There's no denying how much people love the shot. When I'm doing question-and-answer sessions at camps, people are always asking me to shoot it. The coaches get out the balls and there's a long line of kids challenging me. One day they might beat me. But I'll always be the first.

PETE CARRIL

The legendary Princeton coach (1967-96) explains the backdoor play.

I don't know why the backdoor play became associated with Princeton. I didn't invent it. It was around for many years before I coached it. But it's sort of how you hear about the Princeton offense. *The Princeton offense*? The Princeton offense is nothing more than sharing the ball.

The backdoor play is the antidote for being overplayed. Maybe there's an association with Princeton because we were overplayed a lot. That's what happens when you have good shooters.

Here's how I would explain the backdoor play to a kid in sixth grade: You're going toward the ball to receive a pass or to receive a dribble exchange, but you're being overplayed. That means the defender won't let you get the ball. If there's too much resistance, then you quickly change direction and cut toward the basket. As soon as the defender has lost sight of you, the guy with the ball throws it to you as you move toward the basket.

It's a great tool for anyone who's fast. Trust me, it worked for us . . . and we were *slow*.

RICH CLARKSON

***The Lawrence, Kan., native photographed more than 50 NCAA Tournaments for* Sports Illustrated.**

In more than a half-century of NCAA Tournament games, I've never screamed once. I guarantee you, through all those great moments, not even a gasp has come from my mouth. You can't be emotional in my profession. If you let the big moment overwhelm you, you'll never be able to capture it.

The first year I photographed the Tournament was 1952. I can give you an idea how far back that is. I remember getting a shot of Dean Smith in one of the semifinal games while he was playing for Kansas. The Jayhawks won it all that year.

The Final was played at the University of Washington's Hec Edmundson Pavilion. It wasn't on network television. There were only five photographers around the court. At the end of the game I was the only one, because the other four had left to process their film to meet deadlines.

One of my most memorable cover shots came during the Final between Michigan State and Indiana State—Magic Johnson vs. Larry Bird—in 1979. That's because a new managing editor had just taken over and he was at the game. In the second half, Magic made a huge dunk that epitomized the win. The new managing editor said he wanted that dunk on the cover before he even knew if the picture actually existed.

The film was being processed right after the game in Salt Lake City, where the cover picture would be chosen and then flown to the printer in Chicago. The managing editor came into the lab and said, "The picture I want for the cover is Magic Johnson making that dunk." A few minutes later they put my film on the light table and there it was.

It was in focus.

WILL BLYTHE

***The author discusses the subject of his book:* To Hate Like This Is to Be Happy Forever: A Thoroughly Obsessive, Intermittently Uplifting and Occasionally Unbiased Account of the Duke-North Carolina Basketball Rivalry.**

The rivalry is almost primeval. My father defined his love of the state of North Carolina against Duke. The way he saw it, a Duke man walked down the street as if he owned the whole world. The University of North Carolina was about the achievement of the community.

But when I researched my book, Dean Smith pointed out to me that in the '50s, the big rivalry wasn't North Carolina and Duke. It was North Carolina against NC State.

Duke had fallen off in the early '70s. At that time, you had David Thompson at NC State. Then Maryland became North Carolina's big rival under Lefty Driesell. In the early '80s, when Ralph Sampson came along, Virginia became North Carolina's big rival. That was back in the day when Terry Holland named his dog Dean because, he said, the dog whines so much. So over the years, North Carolina's rival really depended on which teams were successful.

Since Mike Krzyzewski came to town, Duke has been consistently successful. So you now have two incredibly successful teams only eight miles apart.

Krzyzewski brought the rivalry to its current level of intensity. Here's this brash guy from Chicago stepping into a state that prided itself on Carolinian gentility.

Dean Smith used to discourage fans behind the basket from waving their hands to distract an opponent trying to make a foul shot. He thought it was poor sportsmanship. Suddenly, you had Krzyzewski accusing officials of having a double standard when it came to Dean Smith. Of course, 20 years later everyone would be saying the same thing about Krzyzewski. But there was a real clash in styles, and it was exacerbated by the ascent of the Cameron Crazies and ESPN.

When you saw Dick Vitale on the tube exalting the Cameron Crazies as these geniuses, more spirited and clever than all the other students in America, that struck a nerve—not only in North Carolina but across the country.

At the same time, Duke conveyed an image of choir boys—as America's team. But it's sort of like the Dallas Cowboys in football: As time passes, everybody in America begins to hate America's team.

The fact that you could be distant from these people and scream at them through the glass wall of a television set really stoked the hatred for a lot of people in North Carolina.

The experiment behind my book was to test the degree of my hatred for Duke against actual human beings. I hung out with the guy the Cameron Crazies call the Crazy Towel Guy and found him to be sort of my alter ego at Duke. Then I met J.J. Redick, who was one of the most universally reviled college players, and I *liked* him. I even had an hour with Krzyzewski and went away thinking he was a decent guy.

But the thing about television is that it gives you the distance to go back to your primal, tribal hatreds.

UNC fans would say they wouldn't care if Duke went winless for the rest of time. But I think within their heart of hearts they would begin to miss Duke as a strong rival. There are so many psychological aspects—public vs. private, outsider vs. local, elite rich kids vs. the public school kids—that would not be expressed if Duke was not successful.

After a few years, people would miss that. And if the Duke program came back, the UNC fans would be rhapsodic to hate that way again.

BOB WIGGINS

Wiggins is Kentucky's number one fan.

Since the 1960-61 season, I've been at every Kentucky home game. That's 695 straight. I don't know if it's a record. But you tell me, you know anybody else crazy enough to go to that many straight games?

I saw my first home game when I was about 16 years old. That was 1944. There are high school gyms in this state that are bigger now than the building where I saw that game. Alumni Gym didn't hold but about 2,300 people.

I got my first season tickets for the 1953-54 season, after they moved to Memorial Coliseum, and I've had them ever since. It got to a point where I was going to every game, home and away. I saved my vacation days and used them to go on the road. I worked as a construction engineer for the state and I had a good boss.

Kentucky has won seven national championships. I've seen four of them in person. Those would be the highlights: Coach Rupp's last title in 1958, Coach Hall's in 1978 with the team that had Goose Givens, Coach Pitino's in 1996 and coach Tubby Smith's in 1998.

You've got to take the bad with the good. That Christian Laettner shot that beat us in the last second in the 1992 East Regional final was one of those things. The sad part about that situation is that he never should have been in the game. He should have been on the bench. One of our boys was on the floor under the basket and on purpose Laettner stepped right on his chest. They called a technical foul, but he should've been kicked out.

A lot of people say that game with Duke was one of the greatest games ever played in history. It just didn't turn out right.

I had a streak of 615 games home and away until 1996. Then I had a heart attack the morning we were leaving for the Great Alaska Shootout. So that broke that streak.

I'm 80 now and don't go on the road much anymore. But at home games you can always find me in Section 17, Row K.

What's that you say? You've never been to Rupp Arena? You better get there quick. Until you've seen a Kentucky basketball game at Rupp Arena, you ain't lived.

RICHIE FARMER

The former Kentucky player—elected in 2003 as the state's commissioner of agriculture—talks about the moment Christian Laettner's shot went through the hoop in Duke's 1992 East Regional final win over the Wildcats.

For the first 22 years of my life, all I'd done was play basketball. I was a gym rat. I dreamed of playing at the University of Kentucky. And I'm one of those few people who had an opportunity to live a dream.

Nobody really thought we'd be in the position to win that game. Duke had been No. 1 pretty much all season. And there we were, up by one with two seconds left.

I was guarding Thomas Hill in the lane. When the pass came from the other end of the court to Laettner, near the top of the key, I made sure that I was going to block out and get the rebound. How many times would that shot go in? One in a hundred? It's a strange thing: When I watch it on replay I keep expecting the ball not to go in. But somehow he keeps making that shot every time.

I was standing pretty much underneath the basket when the ball went through the net. As it did, a flood of emotion went through me. I can't say I was thinking, but instinctively I felt something like, "That's it. That's the end. That's the end of my career."

I took a couple of steps, then the emotion of it all hit me and I dropped to my knees.

You've heard people talk about how they remember where they were when they heard that JFK had been shot? Well, the moment that shot went through had the same kind of effect on the people of Kentucky. Everybody remembers where they were and who they were with. It's a moment in time that's frozen in their being.

My memory is being lifted to my feet. It was Coach K. Only afterward did I understand the depth of the moment.

He could have been celebrating with his team. But he came over to lift me up. He hugged me and said, "You guys are *not* losers. You guys are class. Even though the scoreboard says Duke won, you guys are winners and don't ever forget that."

And I never will forget that.

MARQUES HAYNES

The man known as the World's Greatest Dribbler and star of the Harlem Globetrotters explains how it all started for him—at Langston University in 1942.

I didn't get a scholarship to play college ball. Small town guy like me, coming out of Sands Springs, Oklahoma? UCLA sounded like a foreign country to me.

I got a $25 scholarship from the church and used it to go to Langston University. Only God knows what would have happened to me if I hadn't gone to Langston.

Langston was the closest school to my home; 80 miles from my front door to its front gates. Had to hitch-hike to get there back then. Left home right after sunup, got there at sundown. It was the 16th ride that dropped me off at the gate.

I was invited to try out for the basketball team and made it my freshman year. The coach was a stern disciplinarian. No behind-the-back passes, no between-the-leg bounces, nothing fancy. If Zip Gayles saw you doing it, it was 25 or 30 laps around the court. Or make 50 consecutive free throws. You hit 49 straight and miss the 50th, you'd have to start all over.

Many times while we were practicing, Zip would leave the gym for one reason or another. Once he left, we knew there was only one door he could get back in through. So we'd put a spotter at the door. While he was away, we'd do all kinds of fancy deals with the ball. When Zip came back, the spotter would give us the signal and we'd stop and be for real.

My senior year, we played a tournament at Southern University. Southern had put on a show against Sam Houston. It was embarrassing to the team and to Jackie Robinson—yes, *that* Jackie Robinson was Sam Houston's assistant coach.

"If we get Southern in the final in their own gym," I told myself, "I'm gonna put a dribbling show on *them*."

We got up on Southern in that championship game with the clock running down—and that's just what I did. I was dribbling all over the place. The crowd went wild. Southern players were chasing after me. But what I didn't know was that my own coach had run on the court and *he* was chasing after me.

When I saw him, I stopped real quick. I knew he had leather shoes on. He slid right on by and the crowd nearly tore the roof off when they saw that.

The referees both had their whistles down and were enjoying the heck out of it. As the clock ran out, I drove in, scored and ran straight to the dressing room. Zip was right behind me. He was cursing me up and down, saying, "You'll never play another game for Langston University!"

I looked him straight in the eye and said, "Coach, I know it."

He said, "What do you mean?"

I said, "This is the last game of the season and I'm a senior."

He said, "Hell, you're right," and walked away.

A few days later, the Harlem Globetrotters owner wired Zip. He came looking for me and there was a little fear in me as Zip approached. He said, "Haynes, I'd like to talk to you for a second." He pulled out a telegram. The Globetrotters were scheduled to play in Oklahoma City, but their opponent had cancelled on them. The Globetrotters wanted to know if our team would substitute.

I said, "Well, coach, you guys can beat them."

He said, "What do you mean, *you guys*. You're back on the team!"

So I scored 26 points against the Globetrotters and we won.

After the game, the Globetrotters tried to hire me right then and there. They wanted to take me back to school to pick up my clothes. But I turned them down. I was only a month and half from graduation. My mother would have killed me if I'd left school at that time. She would have found me somewhere. And I didn't want to die right then.

I started with the Globetrotters right after I graduated. If you go on the Internet now and call up Langston University, you'll see it says "Your Passport to the World." They got that right. That's how a kid from Sand Springs, Oklahoma, got to play basketball in 106 countries.

"If you look up Langston University, you'll see it says, 'Your Passport to the World.' They got that right. That's how a kid from Sand Springs, Oklahoma, got to play basketball in 106 countries."

THE SELECTION COMMITTEE SAYS ...

Every March a committee of experts convenes to select the 65 teams and determine the seedings for the NCAA Men's Basketball Tournament. Something similar occurs in the Vatican whenever a new pope must be chosen. We decided to convene our own special Selection Committee, charged with boiling down the game's history into a series of lists. The committee consists of former coaches and players, as well as expert reporters and analysts who cover college basketball for ESPN.

The committee: Dick Vitale, Jay Bilas, Bill Raftery, Howie Schwab, Stephen Bardo, Dan Steir, Tom Brennan, Doris Burke, Andy Katz, Jimmy Dykes, Len Elmore, Fran Fraschilla, Doug Gottlieb, Steve Lavin, Bob Valvano, Jay Williams, Rece Davis, Digger Phelps and William F. Reed

THE 50 GREATEST PLAYERS

1. **Lew Alcindor (Kareem Abdul-Jabbar), UCLA 1966-69** Led UCLA to three NCAA titles; two-time national Player of the Year; career averages 26.4 points and 15.5 rebounds per game; dunking was banned because of his dominance.
2. **Oscar Robertson, Cincinnati 1957-60** National POY and top scorer in each of three varsity seasons (33.8 ppg career); also averaged 15.2 rpg; one of only three players to achieve a triple-double in the Final Four.
3. **Bill Russell, San Francisco 1953-56** Led Dons to NCAA titles in 1955 and '56; 1955 Tournament MOP; 1956 National POY; one of five players in history to average a 20-20 for his career (20.7 ppg, 20.3 rpg).
4. **Bill Walton, UCLA 1971-74** Three-time national POY; Tournament MOP in 1972 and '73, when he led UCLA to back-to-back undefeated seasons and national championships; career averages 20.3 ppg, 15.7 rpg and 65.1 FG%.
5. **Pete Maravich, LSU 1967-70** Pistol Pete was 1970 national POY; holds D1 records for career points (3,667) and scoring average (44.2).
6. **Jerry West, West Virginia 1957-60** Tournament MOP in 1959, when he averaged 32 ppg and led Mountaineers to the national championship game; career averages 24.8 ppg and 13.3 rpg.
7. **Bill Bradley, Princeton 1962-65** National POY and Tournament MOP in 1965; scored a (then) Final Four record 58 points against Wichita State; career averages 30.2 ppg and 12.1 rpg.
8. **David Thompson, NC State 1972-75** Tournament MOP in 1974, when he led NC State to the national championship ending UCLA's seven-year reign; national POY in '75; career average 26.8 ppg; popularized the alley-oop (he was the oop).
9. **Wilt Chamberlain, Kansas 1956-58** Massive 7'1" Stilt was 1957 Tournament MOP, averaging 30.3 ppg for runner-up Jayhawks; career averages 29.9 ppg and 18.3 rpg in his two seasons.
10. **Earvin "Magic" Johnson, Michigan State 1977-79** Tournament MOP in 1979; one of three players to achieve a triple-double in Final Four (see Oscar Robertson); scored 24 in MSU's title win over Larry Bird's Indiana State in highest-rated college basketball telecast ever.
11. **Jerry Lucas, Ohio State 1959-62** Twice national POY and twice Tournament MOP; his Buckeyes were 1960 national champions and runners-up in '61 and '62; career averages 24.3 ppg and 17.2 rpg.
12. **Larry Bird, Indiana State 1976-79** National POY in 1979, when he led Indiana State to the NCAA Final against Michigan State; career averages 30.3 ppg, 13.3 rpg and 53.3 FG%.
13. **Christian Laettner, Duke 1988-92** National POY in 1992; led Duke to two national titles and is the only player to start in four consecutive Final Fours; hit game-winning shot in Duke's 1992 East Regional final win over Kentucky, capping 10-for-10 FG and 10-for-10 FT night.
14. **Patrick Ewing, Georgetown 1981-85** Co-national POY in 1985; led Georgetown to three NCAA Finals; Tournament MOP in 1984 when he led Hoyas to the title.
15. **Elvin Hayes, Houston 1965-68** National POY in 1968; career averages 31.0 ppg, 17.2 rpg and 53.6 FG%; NCAA Tournament career leader in rebounds and field goals made.
16. **Ralph Sampson, Virginia 1979-83** Three-time national POY; averaged a double-double in each of four seasons, including 19.1 ppg and 11.7 rpg in 1983.
17. **Michael Jordan, North Carolina 1981-84** National POY in 1984; career average 17.7 ppg; All-Tournament as freshman in '82, when he hit the game-winning jumper in UNC's championship victory over Georgetown.
18. **Tim Duncan, Wake Forest 1993-97** National POY in 1997; NCAA career leader (post-1972-73) in rebounds; holds Tournament career record for blocked shots; career averages 16.5 ppg, 12.3 rpg and 57.7 FG%.
19. **Elgin Baylor, Seattle 1956-58** Tournament MOP in 1958; career averages 31.2 ppg and 19.8 rpg; first of the high-scoring, airborne, artistic big men.
20. **Earl Monroe, Winston-Salem 1963-67** The Pearl averaged 41.5 ppg his senior year, shooting 60.7%; finished career

with nearly 3,000 points; 1967 College Division POY, leading Rams to College Division championship.

21. Hakeem Olajuwon, Houston 1981-84 Tournament MOP in 1983, when he led Houston to the NCAA Final; as a junior averaged 16.8 ppg, 13.5 rpg and 67.5 FG%.

22. David Robinson, Navy 1983-87 Grew from 6'4" to 7'1" during career; national POY in 1987, averaging 28.2 ppg and leading nation in blocks; career averages 21.0 ppg, 10.3 rpg and 61.3 FG%; holds NCAA record for blocks in a season (207).

23. Tom Gola, La Salle 1951-55 Tournament MOP in 1954, when he led La Salle to its only national championship; NCAA career leader (all-time) in rebounds; one of two players in history to amass 2,000 points and 2,000 rebounds (the other is George Washington's Joe Holup).

24. Austin Carr, Notre Dame 1968-71 National POY in 1971; holds Tournament records for career scoring average (41.3), single-year average (52.7 in 1970) and most points in a game (61 vs. Ohio in '70).

25. Danny Manning, Kansas 1984-88 Tournament MOP and co-national POY in 1988 when he led Jayhawks to the national title, averaging 24.8 ppg for season; career averages 20.1 ppg and 59.3 FG%.

26. George Mikan, DePaul 1942-46 At 6'9", one of the first great big men; led Blue Demons to NIT championship in 1945; career average 19.1 ppg.

27. Phil Ford, North Carolina 1974-78 Point guard was national POY in 1978; career average 18.6 ppg; UNC's all-time leading scorer until surpassed in 2009 by Tyler Hansbrough.

28. Calvin Murphy, Niagara 1967-70 Phenomenally fast and high-flying scorer at 5'9"; averaged 38.2 ppg in 1968; career average 33.1.

29. Julius Erving, Massachusetts 1969-71 One of only five players to average a 20-20 for his career (26.3 ppg, 20.2 rpg); never played in the Tournament and never dunked in a game—it was illegal from 1967-76.

30. Cazzie Russell, Michigan 1963-66 National POY in 1966; All-Tournament in '65 after leading Wolverines to NCAA Final vs. UCLA; career averages 27.1 ppg and 8.5 rpg.

31. Bob Kurland, Oklahoma A&M 1942-46 First of the great seven-footers; twice Tournament MOP, leading Oklahoma A&M (now Oklahoma State) to back-to-back national championships in 1945 and '46; averaged 22.8 ppg in Tournament games.

32. Wayman Tisdale, Oklahoma 1982-85 Three-time Big Eight POY; career averages 25.6 ppg, 10.1 rpg and 57.8 FG%.

33. Grant Hill, Duke 1990-94 Twice named All-Tournament, leading Blue Devils to national championships in 1991 and '92; Tournament leader in career steals (39); career average 14.9 ppg.

34. Dick Barnett, Tennessee State 1955-59 Led Tigers to three straight NAIA tournament championships, 1957-59; MVP in '58 and '59; TSU's all-time leading scorer with 3,209 points.

35. Hank Luisetti, Stanford 1935-38 When everyone else used two hands, Luisetti dazzled crowds with his one-handed shot; first player to score 50 points in a game (vs. Duquesne in 1938); career average 16.1 ppg.

36. Dan Issel, Kentucky 1967-70 Great center averaged 33.9 ppg and 13.2 rpg his senior year; career average 25.8 ppg; held Wildcats' single-game scoring record (53 points) for almost 40 years.

37. Darrell Griffith, Louisville 1976-80 Dr. Dunkenstein was Wooden Award winner and Tournament MOP in 1980, leading Cardinals to national title; Louisville's all-time leading scorer; career average 18.5 ppg.

38. Sidney Wicks, UCLA 1968-71 Led UCLA to three national titles (1969-71), connecting Alcindor and Walton eras; Tournament MOP in 1970; averaged 20 ppg and 12.3 rpg in last two seasons.

39. Clyde Lovellette, Kansas 1949-52 Only player to lead the nation in scoring (28.6 ppg) and earn Tournament MOP honors in same season, which he did in leading Jayhawks to 1952 national championship.

40. Chris Mullin, St. John's 1981-85 A co-national POY and Tournament leader in points scored in 1985; career averages 19.5 ppg and 55.0 FG%; three-time Big East POY, alone or shared.

41. Shaquille O'Neal, LSU 1989-92 A national POY and rebounding leader in 1991; national leader in blocked shots in '92; averaged 25.8 ppg and 14.3 rpg his final two seasons.

42. Wes Unseld, Louisville 1965-68 Bruising center had career averages of 20.6 ppg, 18.9 rpg and 55.8 FG%; pounded Boston College with 35 points and 26 rebounds in 1966 NIT triple-overtime loss.

43. Willis Reed, Grambling State 1960-64 Led Tigers to 1961 NAIA championship; as a senior, averaged 26.6 ppg and 21.3 rpg with a 61.9 FG%; career totals 2,280 points and 1,851 rebounds.

44. John Havlicek, Ohio State 1959-62 Teamed with Jerry Lucas on 1960 national champion and '61 and '62 runner-up Buckeyes; career average 14.6 ppg.

45. Art Heyman, Duke 1960-63 National POY and Tournament MOP in 1963, when he led Duke to its first Final Four; career averages 25.1 ppg and 10.9 rpg.

46. Len Bias, Maryland 1982-86 ACC POY in 1985 and '86; averaged 23.2 ppg his senior year; shot 52.8% or better his final three seasons; Maryland's No. 2 career scorer; died of overdose days after being drafted by Boston Celtics.

47. John Lucas, Maryland 1972-76 First four-year starter in Terrapins history; Maryland's No. 5 career scorer; ACC Athlete of the Year in 1976 when he was named All-America in both basketball and tennis.

48. Isiah Thomas, Indiana 1979-81 Tournament MOP in 1981 when he led Indiana to national championship; averaged 18.2 ppg in '81 Tournament while shooting 58.9%.

49. Larry Johnson, UNLV 1989-91 A national POY in 1991 on Final Four team; led UNLV to national title in '90; career averages 21.6 ppg and 11.2 rpg.

50. Bob Pettit, LSU 1951-54 Career averages 27.4 ppg and 14.8 rpg; averaged 30.5 ppg in his six NCAA Tournament games; scored 57 points vs. Georgia in 1954.

THE 15 GREATEST COACHES

1. **John Wooden** 29 seasons, two schools, 664–162, .804. Led UCLA to 10 NCAA titles in 12 seasons, including seven straight (1967-73). His teams hold NCAA Final Four records for most titles (10), appearances (12), consecutive appearances (9) and victories (21). From 1964 to '73, his Bruins won a record 38 straight NCAA Tourney games.

2. **Dean Smith** 36 seasons, one school, 879–254, .776. No. 2 in career wins. Holds major college record for most consecutive 20-win seasons (27) and has the second-most overall (30). His 11 Final Fours are second only to Wooden's 12; 27 NCAA appearances, two NCAA titles (1982 and '93) and one NIT ('71).

3. **Mike Krzyzewski** 34 seasons, two schools, 833-274, .752. Has most 30-win seasons (10) and NCAA Tourney wins (70). Has led Duke to 25 NCAA berths, 10 Final Fours, three titles (1991, '92, 2001). One of two coaches since Wooden to win back-to-back NCAA titles.
4. **Adolph Rupp** 41 seasons, one school, 876–190, .822. The Baron of the Bluegrass led Kentucky to four NCAA titles (1948, '49, '51, '58) and an NIT title ('46). His '33 and '48 Wildcats were named Helms Foundation national champions.
5. **Bob Knight** 42 seasons, three schools, 902–371 .709. Winningest coach in D1 men's history. Led Indiana to three NCAA titles (1976, '81, '87), one NIT title ('79) and 11 Big Ten titles. In seven years at Texas Tech (2001-08), averaged nearly 20 wins per season.
6. **Forrest "Phog" Allen** 48 seasons, four schools, 746–264, .739. Led Kansas to 1952 NCAA title; 1922 and '23 teams were designated national champions by Helms Foundation.
7. **John McLendon** 25 seasons, five schools, 496-179, .735. A disciple of James Naismith at Kansas, relegated early to historically black schools, McLendon helped develop fast break, zone press and four-corners. At Tennessee A&I, became first coach to win three straight national (NAIA) titles (1957-59). First African-American coach hired by predominantly white school (Cleveland State, 1966).
8. **Henry "Hank" Iba** 41 seasons, three schools, 764–339, .693. While at Oklahoma A&M, became first coach to guide team to back-to-back NCAA titles (1945, '46). His Cowboys topped the country in scoring defense seven times between '47-48 '56-57.
9. **Frank McGuire** 30 seasons, three schools, 549-236, .699. Led North Carolina to 32–0 season and 1957 NCAA title. First coach to win 100 games at three different schools (UNC, St. John's, South Carolina). Led St. John's baseball team to '49 College World Series.
10. **Rick Pitino** 23 seasons, four schools, 552–236, .737. Only coach to take three schools (Providence, Kentucky, Louisville) to the Final Four, and one of just five to take four schools to the NCAAs. Coached Kentucky to the 1996 NCAA championship.
11. **Jim Calhoun** 37 seasons, two schools, 805–342, .702. Led Connecticut to two NCAA titles (1999, 2004), 10 Big East regular-season titles (won or shared), six Big East tournament titles and the '88 NIT title.
12. **John Thompson** 26-plus seasons, one school, 596–239, .714. Led Georgetown to three Final Fours (1982, '84, '85) and '84 NCAA title. Teams made 24 consecutive postseason appearances, 20 of them in NCAA Tournament. Of his 78 four-year players, 76 graduated.
13. **Clair Bee** 21 seasons, two schools, 412–88, .824. Helped develop 1-3-1 zone and introduce the three-second rule in 1936. Guided Long Island U. to NIT titles in '39 and '41. His .824 career winning percentage tops all coaches.
14. **Denny Crum** 30 seasons, one school, 675-295, .696. In seven-year span (1980-86), led Louisville to four Final Fours and two NCAA titles. His Cardinals appeared in 23 NCAA tournaments, including six Final Fours. Began career as a UCLA assistant under John Wooden, helping guide Bruins to three straight NCAA titles from '69 to '71.
15. **Roy Williams** 21 seasons, two schools, 594–138, .811. Fastest ever to win 500 games. Led North Carolina to NCAA titles in 2005 and '09. His teams have won at least one NCAA Tournament game in 20 straight years. One of only three coaches to lead two schools (UNC and Kansas) to the NCAA Final.

THE 15 GREATEST TEAMS

1. **1972-73 UCLA, 30–0** With Bill Walton's near-perfect 44-point Final vs. Memphis State, the Bruins won their seventh straight title; also featured future pros Keith Wilkes and Swen Nater.
2. **1975-76 Indiana, 32–0** The last team to go undefeated, Bob Knight's Hoosiers were led by National POY Scott May and Tourney MOP Kent Benson.
3. **1967-68 UCLA, 29–1** The Bruins avenged their Jan. 20 Astrodome loss by blowing out Houston in the NCAA semis, then trounced North Carolina. Lew Alcindor won his second of three Tourney MOPs.
4. **1955-56 San Francisco, 29–0** The Dons had a 20-point average victory margin and ran their win streak to 55 games as Bill Russell averaged 20.5 points and 21 rebounds playing 24 minutes a game.
5. **1966-67 UCLA, 30–0** The first of John Wooden's seven straight NCAA title teams, led by sophomore Lew Alcindor with 29 ppg and 15.5 rpg.
6. **1981-82 North Carolina, 32–2** Freshman Michael Jordan hit the game-winner against Georgetown in the Final; also featured Sam Perkins and James Worthy.
7. **1991-92 Duke, 34–2** Christian Laettner stunned Kentucky with his buzzer-beater in the East final, then, along with Grant Hill and Tourney MOP Bobby Hurley, the Blue Devils beat Michigan for the title.
8. **1989-90 UNLV, 35–5** The Rebels, led by Tournament MOP Anderson Hunt and Larry Johnson, beat Duke in the NCAA Final, 103-73—the largest title-game margin ever.
9. **1973-74 NC State, 30–1** The Wolfpack ended UCLA's NCAA title string at seven, then beat Marquette in the Final; David Thompson won his second of three ACC POY crowns.
10. **1995-96 Kentucky, 34–2** The Wildcats featured nine future NBA players: Derek Anderson, Tony Delk, Walter McCarty, Ron Mercer, Nazr Mohammed, Antoine Walker, Mark Pope, Jeff Sheppard and Wayne Turner.
11. **1968-69 UCLA, 29–1** The Bruins defeated John Wooden's alma mater, Purdue, in the Final, 92-72, thanks to 37 points and 20 rebounds from Lew Alcindor in his final college game.
12. **1956-57 North Carolina, 32–0** Frank McGuire's Miracle, with Lennie Rosenbluth, Pete Brennan and Tommy Kearns, went to triple overtime two nights in a row to beat Michigan State and then Wilt Chamberlain's Kansas, 54-53, for the title.
13. **1947-48 Kentucky, 36–3** Adolph Rupp's Wildcats won the NCAA Tournament and became the core of the undefeated 1948 U.S. Olympic gold-medal team.
14. **2000-01 Duke, 35–4** Five future pros—Shane Battier, Carlos Boozer, Chris Duhon, Mike Dunleavy and Jay Williams—beat Arizona, 82-72, for the NCAA title.
15. **1953-54 Kentucky, 25–0** The Wildcats beat everybody, including eventual champ La Salle, but the NCAA declared Frank Ramsey, Cliff Hagan and Lou Tsioropoulos ineligible for the Tournament because they graduated before play began. Rather than proceed without their three best players, the Wildcats decided to stay home.

THE 10 BEST NCAA TOURNAMENTS

1. **1957 North Carolina went to triple overtime** twice in successive nights, first beating Michigan State, 74-70, and then heavily favored Kansas, 54-53, with its 7'1" super sophomore Wilt Chamberlain. UNC coach Frank McGuire set the tone by sending 5'11" Tommy Kearns up against Chamberlain for the opening tip.
2. **1966 Texas Western made history** by becoming the first team to win the Tournament with five African-Americans in its starting lineup, 72-65, over all-white Kentucky. The Wildcats had beaten another all-white team, Duke, to reach the Final.
3. **1975 After UCLA's overtime win** over Louisville in the semis, John Wooden announced he'd retire after the Final. Louisville, Kentucky and Indiana all may have had better teams than UCLA, but the Bruins beat the Wildcats to send the Wizard out a winner—for the 10th time in 12 seasons.
4. **1963 Loyola-Chicago had four black starters** and SEC champion Mississippi State had to defy its state legislature and sneak out of the state to play Loyola in the Mideast Regional semis. Loyola went all the way, ending Cincinnati's bid for a three-peat on Vic Rouse's last-second putback in OT.
5. **1955 Bill Russell totally dominated the West** and then led his San Francisco Dons to a 77-63 title-game pounding of La Salle, which had won its first three Tournament games by an average of 32 points.
6. **1974 UCLA losing was unthinkable** after its seven straight titles, but David Thompson's NC State Wolfpack shocked the Bruins, 80-77, in their double-OT semifinal, then beat Marquette, 76-64, for the title. The Pack became the last team to win without ever leaving their home state
7. **1985 Villanova was close to perfect,** shooting 78.6% from the floor and 81% from the line to upset Big East rival Georgetown, 66-64, for the title. A third Big East team, St. John's, also made the Final Four.
8. **1983 NC State made the most improbable trip,** winning one upset after another from the ACC tournament through the NCAAs, until finally coming up against heavily favored Houston and Hakeem Olajuwon in the Final. There, Lorenzo Charles converted a desperation 35-foot heave by Dereck Whittenburg into the Tournament's most famous game-winning dunk.
9. **1991 Duke avenged its humiliating 30-point loss** in the 1990 title game by beating undefeated defending champion UNLV in the semifinals, 79-77. Then the Blue Devils beat Kansas, 72-65, for their first national title.
10. **1979 Bird vs. Magic didn't live up to the hype,** but Michigan State's 75-64 win over Indiana State drew the Tournament's highest TV rating ever. Forgotten by many: Bob Heaton's off-balance buzzer-beater against Arkansas that got ISU into the Final Four with its undefeated season intact.

THE 10 GREATEST INDIVIDUAL TOURNAMENT PERFORMANCES

1. **Bill Walton, UCLA 1973** In a near-perfect Final, he scored 44 points on 21-for-22 shooting with 13 rebounds to beat Memphis State, 87-66, for UCLA's seventh straight title and second straight 30-0 season.
2. **Lew Alcindor, UCLA 1968** After the January loss that snapped UCLA's 47-game win streak, Alcindor took fierce revenge in the Final Four with 19 points and 18 rebounds while the Bruins held his nemesis, Elvin Hayes, to a mere 10 points in a 101-69 trouncing.
3. **Christian Laettner, Duke 1992** To get to his and Duke's fourth Final Four, he went 10-for-10 from the field and 10-for-10 from the free-throw line, and popped the buzzer-beating, game-winning 17-footer.
4. **Bill Russell, San Francisco 1956** A year after he led USF to its first national championship, Russell scored 26 points with 27 rebounds to beat Iowa, 83-71, for USF's second.
5. **Jack Givens, Kentucky 1978** He scored a career-high 41 points to lead the Wildcats to a 94-88 win over Duke in the Final.
6. **David Thompson, NC State 1974** UCLA's string of seven straight titles ended in the Final Four as the 6'4" Thompson soared and scored 28 points and picked 10 rebounds to upset the Bill Walton-led Bruins.
7. **Pervis Ellison, Louisville 1986** Just a freshman, "Never Nervous" Pervis amassed 25 points and 11 rebounds in the Cardinals' 72-69 title win over Duke.
8. **Sidney Wicks, UCLA 1970** The 6'8" Wicks outplayed Jacksonville's Artis Gilmore in the Final, outrebounding the 7'2" giant, 18-16, and forcing him to miss 20 of his 29 shots, while scoring 17 points himself.
9. **Bill Bradley, Princeton 1965** In the national third-place game against Wichita State, Bradley scored 58 points, shooting 22-for-29 from the field and 14-for-15 from the line, and grabbed 17 rebounds.
10. **Lew Alcindor, UCLA 1969** In his final game, the greatest player in college basketball history single-handedly shredded Purdue with 37 points and 20 rebounds to win his and UCLA's third straight national title, 92-72.

VITALE

"AS SPECIAL AS A DON LARSON MAGICAL PERFECT GAME. THE BIG REDHEAD, MR. WALTON, COMPLETELY SUFFOCATED MEMPHIS WITH HIS SUPER, SCINTILLATING, SENSATIONAL PERFORMANCE. HIS DOMINANT SHOW WILL GO DOWN IN HISTORY AS AWESOME BABY—WITH A CAPITAL A!"

THE 10 BEST NCAA TOURNAMENT BUZZER BEATERS

1. April 4, 1983: NC State's Dereck Whittenburg launches a desperation 35-foot heave that lands in the hands of **Lorenzo Charles,** who stuffs it home to beat Houston, 54-52, for the title.
2. March 28, 1992: With Duke trailing Kentucky by one, **Christian Laettner** takes a 75-foot pass from Grant Hill and swishes a 17-foot jumper to beat Kentucky in OT and send Duke to the Final Four and its second consecutive title.
3. March 13, 1998: Valparaiso's run to the Sweet 16 is made possible by the first-round upset of Ole Miss, thanks to a baseball-throw relay from Jamie Sykes to Bill Jenkins to **Bryce Drew,** who pops a three for a 70-69 win.
4. March 19, 1995: Down by one with 4.8 seconds left, UCLA's **Tyus Edney** goes coast to coast with a little behind-the-back, ending in a running bank shot to beat Missouri, 75-74, and send the Bruins to the Sweet 16.
5. March 30, 1987: Indiana's **Keith Smart,** benched earlier in the second half by Bob Knight, drills a 15-footer with :04 left to beat Syracuse for the title, 74-73.
6. March 22, 1990: Connecticut's **Tate George** leaps to catch a length-of-the-floor pass, lands, rises again and hits a turnaround jumper to beat Clemson, 71-70, and reach the Elite Eight.
7. March 19, 1981: BYU's **Danny Ainge** makes like a whirling dervish as he drives the length of the court and hits a finger roll as time expires to upset Notre Dame, 51-50, in the East Regional semifinals.
8. March 19, 1998: Down one to Washington in the Sweet 16, UConn misses two shots, but the third is the charm: **Richard Hamilton** gets the rebound and hits a fadeaway in the lane for the 75-74 win.
9. April 7, 2008: His Jayhawks trailing Memphis by three with 2.1 seconds left, **Mario Chalmers** hits a three-pointer to force overtime and enable Kansas to win its third national title.
10. March 14, 1981: Arkansas' **U.S. Reed** gets the inbounds pass, takes a few dribbles along the sideline, then launches and hits a 50-foot two-pointer to give the Razorbacks a 74-73 win over defending national champion Louisville in the second round.

THE 15 BEST PROGRAMS NEVER TO WIN IT ALL

Considering the entire sweep of college basketball history, which schools should have won a national championship but never did? The Committee decided.

1. **Illinois (27 NCAA Tournaments, 5 Final Fours, 1 Final lost)** The Illini's last best shot was the 2005 Final loss to North Carolina. In 1988-89, they beat Michigan twice in the regular season but lost to the Fab Five in the Final Four.
2. **Houston (18, 5, 2)** Who didn't love watching Jim Valvano go nuts after Dereck Whittenburg's title-winning dunk in 1983? Houston fans. Also ask them how they feel about Georgetown's Patrick Ewing and UCLA's Lew Alcindor.
3. **Oklahoma (26, 4, 2)** The Sooners would have won it all in 1988 if not for Danny Manning and the Miracles. And then there was that Final loss in 1947 to Holy Cross.
4. **St. John's (27, 2, 1)** National runner-up in 1952 and a Big East stalwart in the '80s, but Chris Mullin couldn't shoot the Johnnies past Georgetown in the '85 Final Four.
5. **Purdue (23, 2, 1)** Not even Rick Mount's rocket fire could take down UCLA in 1969; and the Big Dog (Glenn Robinson) never quite got near the Big One.
6. **Iowa (22, 3, 1)** The 1956 version of the Fabulous Five was snuffed by Bill Russell's San Francisco Dons. Many Hawkeye heartbreaks have followed.
7. **Kansas State (23, 4, 1)** Who remembers the Cats' four national semifinal teams between 1948 and '64? We do—and also their 1951 Final loss to Kentucky.
8. **Notre Dame (29, 1, 0)** Not a great Tourney team but a great giant-killer, most notably UCLA. For that alone, the Irish get our love.
9. **Memphis (22, 3, 2)** Start with the blown title in 2008 after leading Kansas by nine with 2:12 in regulation, then remember Bill Walton's 21-for-22 shooting in the '73 Final.
10. **Temple (27, 2, 0)** Why the Owls? A terrific program in business since 1894, missed the 1958 Final by a point (to Kentucky). Led for a quarter-century by the great John Chaney.
11. **West Virginia (22, 1, 1)** Jerry West was great enough to be the model for the NBA logo, but his Mountaineers were not quite good enough to cop an NCAA title. Came within a point though, losing to Cal 71-70 in 1959.
12. **Texas (27, 3, 0)** The Longhorns had their best shot in 1947, when they had a one-point lead :10 from the Final, only to lose by a point to eventual runner-up Oklahoma. Lost to Syracuse in the 2003 Final Four, 95-84.
13. **Bradley (8, 2, 2)** In 1950, when winning either the NIT or the NCAA Tournament allowed a school to call itself a national champion, the Braves lost the final of both—to the same CCNY team.
14. **Missouri (22, 0, 0)** Only BYU has been to more Tournaments without reaching a Final Four. The 1981-82 Tigers topped the polls for a time, but lost by a point in the Midwest Regional to Hakeem Olajuwon's Houston.
15. **Wake Forest (21, 1, 0)** Wake could have taken care of business as one of the eight teams in the very first NCAA Tournament in 1939, but it lost to Ohio State. Billy Packer's team had a shot in the '62 Final Four (against Ohio State, no less), but no shining moment then, either.

THE 50 BEST NICKNAMES

1. **The Owl Without a Vowel** Bill Mlkvy, Temple
2. **The Round Mound of Rebound** Charles Barkley, Auburn
3. **Dr. Dunkenstein** Darrell Griffith, Louisville
4. **Pistol Pete** Pete Maravich, LSU
5. **The Big O** Oscar Robertson, Cincinnati
6. **The Big E** Elvin Hayes, Houston
7. **Big House** Clarence Gaines, Winston-Salem State coach
8. **Magic** Earvin Johnson, Michigan State

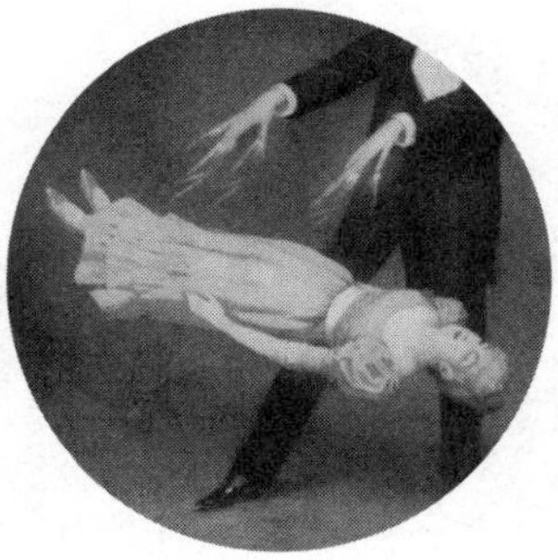

9. **Fly** James Williams, Austin Peay
10. **Hot Rod** Rod Hundley, West Virginia; John Williams, Tulane
11. **Hot Plate** John Williams, LSU

12. **The Pearl** Earl Monroe, Winston-Salem
13. **The Dream** Hakeem Olajuwon, Houston; Dean Meminger, Marquette
14. **The Admiral** David Robinson, Navy
15. **Sleepy** Eric Floyd, Georgetown
16. **Happy** Harold Hairston, NYU
17. **Doc** Glenn Rivers, Marquette

18. **Speedy** Craig Claxton, Hofstra
19. **Pooh** Jerome Richardson, UCLA
20. **Bimbo** Vernell Coles, Virginia Tech
21. **Spud** Anthony Webb, NC State
22. **Tiny** Nate Archibald, Loyola-Chicago
23. **Curly** Fred Neal, Johnson C. Smith
24. **Big Baby** Glen Davis, LSU

25. **Fall Back Baby** Dick Barnett, Tennessee A&I
26. **Big Dog** Glenn Robinson, Purdue
27. **Doggie** Alvin Julian, Holy Cross and Dartmouth coach
28. **Big Nasty** Corliss Williamson, Arkansas
29. **The Goat** Earl Manigault, Johnson C. Smith
30. **The Mailman** Karl Malone, Louisiana Tech
31. **The X-Man** Xavier McDaniel, Wichita State
32. **The Elevator Man** Ric Cobb, Marquette
33. **The Human Highlight Film** Dominique Wilkins, Georgia

34. **The Human Eraser** Marvin Webster, Morgan State
35. **The Glide** Clyde Drexler, Houston
36. **The Judge** Antoine Joubert, Michigan
37. **The Prince of Midair** Lloyd Free, Guilford
38. **Cornbread** Cedric Maxwell, Charlotte
39. **Cadillac** Greg Anderson, Houston
40. **Tractor** Robert Traylor, Michigan
41. **Zeke From Cabin Creek** Jerry West, West Virginia
42. **The Hick From French Lick** Larry Bird, Indiana State

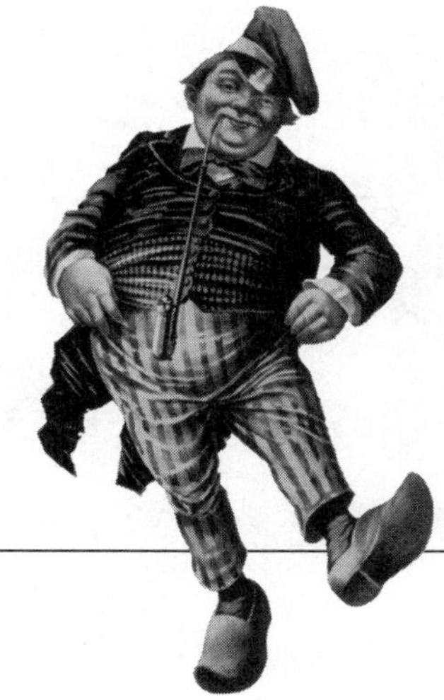

43. **The Alaskan Assassin** Trajan Langdon, Duke
44. **The Dunking Dutchman** Rik Smits, Marist
45. **Never Nervous** Pervis Ellison, Louisville
46. **Dinner Bell Mel** Mel Turpin, Kentucky
47. **Psycho T** Tyler Hansbrough, North Carolina

48. **White Lobster** Bryant Barr, Davidson
49. **The Vertical Hyphen** John Horan, Dayton
50. **Allah the Rim God** Alonza Allen, SW Louisiana

PHOTOGRAPHY AND ILLUSTRATION CREDITS Pages 52 and 55: all ESPN, Inc.
This page: Getty Images (lobster), iStockphoto (hot rod, dog, gavel), Library of Congress (magic, tractor, Dutchman).

THE SCHOOLS

The Schools

As of April 2009 there were 330 NCAA Division I men's teams playing a frenetic variation of James Naismith's original game. Four more will attain D1 status for the 2009-10 season. On paper, each team from No. 1 through No. 330 in our ESPN/Sagarin ranking is a champion of a sort—from the Sweet 16 regulars to the bracketbusters to those mired in the conference cellar with a past possibly brighter than their future—because each has fans who live and die with the fortunes of the program. Each has a Best Team that has set its school's historical standard, a Best Coach who will never be forgotten, a Best Player whose name still makes spines tingle and a Game for the Ages—that one victory that meant, and still means, the most to the fans.

We assigned two dozen college hoops diehards—who also happen to be writers—to become experts on each team's history and lore. They dove into the official records, pored through newspaper archives and spoke to former players, coaches and other experts. Our hope is that the histories and stories captured in these pages both settle debates (Mike Krzyzewski's record after three seasons at Duke? 38–47) and inflame them (Purdue's greatest player: Glenn "Big Dog" Robinson or Rick "the Rocket" Mount?). On these pages you'll also find the following information.

PROFILE: These give an overview of the school and of its historical basketball success through its all-time record, conference and conference tournament titles, and postseason tourney appearances. A few things to look out for:

- **All-time records** The historical records for some schools have been lost or are otherwise not available. In these instances, only verifiable win-loss records are included in the all-time total.
- **Total weeks in the AP Top 20/25** Ranked weeks were culled from the *NCAA Men's Basketball Records Book* and other sources. North Carolina has spent the most weeks in the polls—761. That's more than 14½ straight *years*.
- **Conference regular-season and tournament titles** Seasons listed include titles won in Division I conferences and conference tournaments only. If a title is vacated for rules violations, it is marked with a "v."
- **NCAA Tournament and NIT appearances** "Sweet 16s (since 1975)" refers to the beginning of the 32-team bracket era, before which the first game for all or for a majority of participating teams was in the Round of 16.

CONSENSUS ALL-AMERICAS: These include the NCAA's Division I and, before 1975, University Division first-team consensus players; consensus picks from Division II schools (marked "D2") and, pre-1975, from non-University Division ("College Division" or "Little A-A," for Little All-America) are also listed.

PRO PICKS: Our lists of first-round selections starts with the 1947 Basketball Association of America (BAA) draft and includes the NBA (1949-2009) and ABA (1967-76).

TOP 5: Each school's all-time team fills a standard lineup—with at least two guards and at least two frontcourt players.

RECORDS: When a number of players share a team record or a player has matched his own record, we include all such instances whenever possible. On some team pages we have had to abbreviate the list but have kept the most recent instance or instances. In the season records, as elsewhere in the book, seasons are given as fall-to-spring spans. Thus, 1992-93 is the season that began in the fall of '92 and ended in the spring of '93. A player's career is also rendered in fall-to-spring seasons. The career of an athlete who played the three seasons of 1990-91, '91-92 and '92-93 would be listed as 1990-93.

SEASON REVIEW: These charts include season-by-season team records, with postseason results and scoring leaders (and, for the top 128 ESPN/Sagarin-ranked teams, rebounds and assists), as well as coaches' records. The data was culled from the NCAA, conference records and school media guides and archives; win-loss discrepancies among the sources often had to be reconciled. After 1952, the NCAA considered games between its members and military bases, junior colleges, high schools and all-star teams to be exhibitions and does not count those results as part of the official record, even though many individual NCAA-affiliated universities do.

The first line of many Season Reviews is a composite win-loss record for the early years of the program. These are italicized, along with a note highlighting the team's early success (or lack of it).

If a team forfeited or vacated games because of NCAA or conference infractions during a season, or played an opponent that forfeited their match, a ⊗ appears between the overall and conference records. If a coach's record at a school has been affected by forfeits or vacated games, it's indicated with a ▼. (Season-by-season adjusted records for both schools and coaches can be found starting on page 521.) If per-game averages were not available, cumulative totals have been listed for scoring, rebounding and/or assist leaders.

ESPN 165 SAGARIN

AIR FORCE

In 1956, the Falcons started their inaugural season promisingly enough with a 72-64 win over Westminster. Five decades and 35 losing seasons later, the school that helped launch the careers of Dean Smith and Gregg Popovich is finally living up to that initial promise: The Falcons earned at-large bids to the Big Dance in 2004 and 2006, despite having lost in the first round of the Mountain West Conference tournament both years.

BEST TEAM: 2006-07 With an efficient motion offense and tricky matchup zone defense, coach Jeff Bzdelik's crew beat Stanford by 34 in mid-November. Blowout wins over Colorado, Texas Tech and Wake Forest followed, and though a late-season swoon cost them an NCAA bid, the Falcons rode the nation's second-best defense (56 ppg allowed) all the way to Madison Square Garden, where they lost to Clemson, 68-67, in the NIT semifinals.

BEST PLAYER: G Bob Beckel (1956-59) When he was inducted into the Falcons Hall of Fame in 2007, Beckel joked, "As my teammates will tell you, I just shot a lot." Maybe so, but he certainly made his fair share of them. He scored 50 against Arizona in 1959 and went for 45-plus on three other occasions.

BEST COACH: Bob Spear (1956-71) He didn't just launch the program and take it to two Tourneys. He helped give life to the careers of Smith, an Air Force assistant from 1956-58, and Popovich, a Falcons swingman from 1968 to '70.

GAME FOR THE AGES: On March 21, 2007, pandemonium broke out at Clune Arena when Jacob Burtschi took a nifty Tim Anderson pass and hit a layup with :07 left to help Air Force defeat DePaul, 52-51, and send the team to the NIT semifinals.

FIERCEST RIVAL: In-state MWC foe Colorado State used to own Air Force, winning 17 of 18 between 1995 and 2003. But the Falcons have won 12 of 15 from 2003-09—though one loss was a crushing first-round upset in the 2004 conference tourney. The Rams lead the series, 63–30.

SEASON REVIEW

SEAS.	W-L	CONF.	COACH	SEAS.	W-L	CONF.	COACH
1956-57	11-10		Bob Spear	1960-61	12-12		Bob Spear
1957-58	17-6		Bob Spear	1961-62	16-7	●	Bob Spear
1958-59	14-9		Bob Spear	1962-63	10-12		Bob Spear
1959-60	12-10	●	Bob Spear	1963-64	11-12		Bob Spear

SEAS.	W-L	CONF.	SCORING		COACH	RECORD
1964-65	9-14		Sam Peshut	14.2	Bob Spear	
1965-66	14-12		Sam Peshut	16.1	Bob Spear	
1966-67	6-18		Cliff Parsons	19.3	Bob Spear	
1967-68	9-15		Cliff Parsons	22.5	Bob Spear	
1968-69	11-13		Cliff Parsons	16.2	Bob Spear	
1969-70	12-12		G. Popovich, R. Weilert	14.3	Bob Spear	
1970-71	12-14		Ron Weilert	13.2	Bob Spear	177-175 .503
1971-72	12-13		Tom Blase	11.6	Hank Egan	
1972-73	14-10		Rich Nickelson	16.4	Hank Egan	
1973-74	11-13		Rich Nickelson	15.2	Hank Egan	
1974-75	13-12		Dan Kraft	16.3	Hank Egan	
1975-76	16-9		Randy Gricius	12.3	Hank Egan	
1976-77	11-16		Tom Schneeberger	18.3	Hank Egan	
1977-78	15-10		Tom Schneeberger	15.0	Hank Egan	
1978-79	12-13		Randy Gricius	18.3	Hank Egan	
1979-80	8-17		Tim Harris	17.5	Hank Egan	
1980-81	9-18	3-13	Tim Harris	18.1	Hank Egan	
1981-82	8-19	3-13	Rick Simmons	14.3	Hank Egan	
1982-83	11-16	2-14	Rick Simmons	16.0	Hank Egan	
1983-84	8-19	3-13	Maurice McDonald	13.1	Hank Egan	148-185 .444
1984-85	8-20	2-14	Maurice McDonald	12.6	Reggie Minton	
1985-86	10-19	3-13	Maurice McDonald	13.0	Reggie Minton	
1986-87	12-15	5-11	Raymond Dudley	13.6	Reggie Minton	
1987-88	11-17	4-12	Raymond Dudley	17.8	Reggie Minton	
1988-89	14-14	6-10	Raymond Dudley	26.6	Reggie Minton	
1989-90	12-20	3-13	Raymond Dudley	21.4	Reggie Minton	
1990-91	9-20	3-13	Chris Lowry	14.9	Reggie Minton	
1991-92	9-20	3-13	Dale French	13.6	Reggie Minton	
1992-93	9-19	3-15	Otis Jones	15.2	Reggie Minton	
1993-94	8-18	3-15	Otis Jones	25.5	Reggie Minton	
1994-95	8-20	4-14	Otis Jones	23.9	Reggie Minton	
1995-96	5-23	1-17	Jarmica Reese	14.8	Reggie Minton	
1996-97	7-19	2-14	Jarmica Reese	17.2	Reggie Minton	
1997-98	10-16	2-12	Jarmica Reese	18.8	Reggie Minton	
1998-99	10-16	2-12	Tyron Wright	18.2	Reggie Minton	
1999-2000	8-20	4-10	Jarvis Croff	17.3	Reggie Minton	150-296 .336
2000-01	8-21	3-11	Jarvis Croff	13.0	Joe Scott	
2001-02	9-19	3-11	Lamoni Yazzie	12.4	Joe Scott	
2002-03	12-16	3-11	Tim Keller	14.8	Joe Scott	
2003-04	22-7	12-2 ●	Nick Welch	11.4	Joe Scott	51-63 .447
2004-05	18-12	9-5	Antoine Hood	13.0	Chris Mooney	18-12 .600
2005-06	24-7	12-4 ●	Antoine Hood	14.9	Jeff Bzdelik	
2006-07	26-9	10-6 ■	Dan Nwaelele	14.3	Jeff Bzdelik	50-16 .758
2007-08	16-14	8-8	Tim Anderson	14.0	Jeff Reynolds	
2008-09	10-21	0-16	Andrew Henke	13.1	Jeff Reynolds	26-35 .426

● NCAA Tournament appearance ■ NIT appearance

PROFILE

United States Air Force Academy, Colorado Springs, CO
Founded: 1954
Enrollment: 4,226
Colors: Blue and silver
Nickname: Falcons
Current arena: Clune Arena, opened in 1968 (5,858)
Previous: Cadet Gymnasium, 1954-68 (N/A)
First game: Dec. 5, 1956
All-time record: 619-783 (.442)
Total weeks in AP Top 20/25: 13

Current conference: Mountain West (1999-)
Conference titles:
Mountain West: 1 (2004)
Conference tournament titles: 0
NCAA Tournament appearances: 4
NIT appearances: 1
Semifinals: 1

TOP 5

G **Bob Beckel** (1956-59)
G **Raymond Dudley** (1986-90)
G **Otis Jones** (1991-95)
F **Jacob Burtschi** (2003-07)
F **Cliff Parsons** (1966-69)

RECORDS	GAME		SEASON		CAREER	
POINTS	50	Bob Beckel, vs. Arizona (Feb. 28, 1959)	746	Raymond Dudley (1988-89)	2,178	Raymond Dudley (1986-90)
POINTS PER GAME			26.6	Raymond Dudley (1988-89)	22.8	Bob Beckel (1956-59)
REBOUNDS	21	Randy Gricius, vs. Washburn (Nov. 29, 1978); Ron Weilert, vs. Tulane (Feb. 28, 1970)	293	Cliff Parsons (1968-69)	776	Reggie Jones (1977-81)
ASSISTS	14	Jeff Bowling, vs. Pepperdine (Dec. 1, 1989); Bob Djokovich, vs. Oklahoma City (Feb. 5, 1977)	224	Jeff Bowling (1989-90)	447	Jeff Bowling (1986-87, '88-90)

ESPN 144 SAGARIN

AKRON

Has there been an era when the Zips weren't thrilling their fans? There were high-scoring Fritz Nagy and Jim Fenton in the 1940s and '50s, College Division final fours in the 1960s and '70s, Joe Jakubick, Bob Huggins and an NCAA Tournament bid in the '80s, a 96–41 record from 2005-06 to '08-09. Overlook a dry spell in the 1990s, and the answer is no.

BEST TEAM: 1971-72 Behind lefty big man Len Paul, a junior who broke 13 school records, the Zips advanced to the College Division title game, where they lost, 84-72, to Roanoke. Coach Wyatt Webb's team also featured sophomore playmaker Larry Jenkins and junior rebounding fiend Harvey Glover.

BEST PLAYER: G Joe Jakubick (1980-84) With range that extended to the cheap seats, the sweet-stroking guard led the nation with 30.1 ppg in 1983-84—a season that featured Jordan, Ewing, Olajuwon and Barkley. He wasn't a household name, but it wasn't for a lack of trying. To promote him for national awards—and win him more respect—the school put a photo of Jakubick alongside Rodney Dangerfield on its media guide cover.

BEST COACH: Bob Huggins (1984-89) In short order, Huggins established the Zips' cred just a few years after their D1 move in 1980, taking them to their first NCAA Tourney in 1986, and to the '87 and '89 NIT.

GAME FOR THE AGES: To reach the 1972 College Division title game, Len Paul and crew had to upend favored Tennessee State in the final four. They needed overtime, but they did it, 71-69. The Tigers' revenge? College Division final four wins over Akron in 1973 and '75.

FIERCEST RIVAL: Kent State and Akron have been going at it since the 1915-16 season, but it's gotten particularly contentious the past few seasons as the Zips have challenged the Golden Flashes' MAC dominance. The two Ohio foes, 14 miles apart, have drawn packed houses—and metaphorical blood, with Akron knocking Kent State out of the 2007 MAC tournament and the Flashes returning the favor in 2008. Kent State leads the series, 66–61.

SEASON REVIEW

SEAS.	W-L	CONF.	COACH	SEAS.	W-L	CONF.	COACH
1901-49	*454-230*		*Fred Sefton (1915-24), 92-27, .773*	1962-63	22-3		Tony Laterza
1949-50	14-11		Russell Beichly	1963-64	24-7		Tony Laterza
1950-51	3-20		Russell Beichly	1964-65	21-7		Tony Laterza
1951-52	4-20		Russell Beichly	1965-66	24-4		Tony Laterza
1952-53	17-7		Russell Beichly	1966-67	20-5		Tony Laterza
1953-54	10-11		Russell Beichly	1967-68	14-12		Tony Laterza
1954-55	17-5		Russell Beichly	1968-69	8-18		Wyatt Webb
1955-56	18-5		Russell Beichly	1969-70	12-11		Wyatt Webb
1956-57	18-7		Russell Beichly	1970-71	20-6		Wyatt Webb
1957-58	20-6		Russell Beichly	1971-72	26-5		Wyatt Webb
1958-59	21-2		Russell Beichly	1972-73	22-5		Wyatt Webb
1959-60	17-8		Tony Laterza	1973-74	18-6		Wyatt Webb
1960-61	18-7		Tony Laterza	1974-75	20-9		Wyatt Webb
1961-62	18-6		Tony Laterza	1975-76	10-14		Alex Adams

SEAS.	W-L	CONF.	SCORING		COACH	RECORD
1976-77	14-11		John Britton	18.7	Ken Cunningham	
1977-78	9-18		John Britton	19.3	Ken Cunningham	
1978-79	10-17		John Britton	25.0	Ken Cunningham	
1979-80	10-14		Wendell Bates	15.7	Ken Cunningham	43-60 .417
1980-81	8-18	5-9	Wendell Bates	14.7	Bob Rupert	
1981-82	7-19	3-13	Joe Jakubick	22.8	Bob Rupert	
1982-83	14-15	7-7	Joe Jakubick	28.5[a]	Bob Rupert	
1983-84	8-19	3-11	Joe Jakubick	30.1	Bob Rupert	37-71 .343
1984-85	12-14	6-8	Bryan Roth	15.1	Bob Huggins	
1985-86	22-8	10-4 ●	Marcel Boyce	17.5	Bob Huggins	
1986-87	21-9	9-5 ■	Marcel Boyce	20.0	Bob Huggins	
1987-88	21-7		Eric McLaughlin	18.1	Bob Huggins	
1988-89	21-8	■	Eric McLaughlin	22.5	Bob Huggins	97-46 .678
1989-90	16-12		Anthony Buford	19.8	Coleman Crawford	
1990-91	15-13	6-10	Pete Freeman	15.4	Coleman Crawford	
1991-92	16-12	10-6	Roy Coleman	18.4	Coleman Crawford	
1992-93	8-18	3-15	Mark Alberts	17.1	Coleman Crawford	
1993-94	8-18	2-16	Anthony Stanford	11.0	Coleman Crawford	
1994-95	8-18	4-14	Tron Jenkins	15.5	Coleman Crawford	71-91 .438
1995-96	3-23	0-18	George Phillips	9.8	Dan Hipsher	
1996-97	8-18	6-12	Jimmal Ball	17.1	Dan Hipsher	
1997-98	17-10	13-5	Jami Bosley	16.3	Dan Hipsher	
1998-99	18-9	12-6	Jami Bosley	18.6	Dan Hipsher	
1999-2000	17-11	11-7	Jami Bosley	16.2	Dan Hipsher	
2000-01	12-16	9-9	Nate Schindewolf	14.6	Dan Hipsher	
2001-02	10-21	5-13	Rashon Brown	16.7	Dan Hipsher	
2002-03	14-14	9-9	Derrick Tarver	20.6	Dan Hipsher	
2003-04	13-15	7-11	Derrick Tarver	22.7	Dan Hipsher	112-137 .450
2004-05	19-10	11-7	Darryl Peterson	12.9	Keith Dambrot	
2005-06	23-10	14-4 ■	Romeo Travis	13.8	Keith Dambrot	
2006-07	26-7	13-3	Romeo Travis	14.9	Keith Dambrot	
2007-08	24-11	11-5 ■	Jeremiah Wood	14.1	Keith Dambrot	
2008-09	23-13	10-6 ●	Brett McKnight	11.2	Keith Dambrot	115-51 .693

[a] In 1982-83, the OVC experimented with a 3-point line; Jakubick's listed ppg differs from his official NCAA average.

● NCAA Tournament appearance ■ NIT appearance

PROFILE

University of Akron, Akron, OH
Founded: 1870
Enrollment: 25,942 (21,635 undergraduate)
Colors: Blue and gold
Nickname: Zips
Current arena: James A. Rhodes Arena, opened in 1983 (5,500)
Previous: Memorial Hall, 1954-83 (4,000); Crouse Gymnasium, 1888-62 (N/A)
First game: 1901
All-time record: 1,385-913 (.603)
Total weeks in AP Top 20/25: 0

Current conference: Mid-American (1992-)
Conference titles:
Ohio Valley: 1 (1986 [tie])
Conference tournament titles:
Ohio Valley: 1 (1986)
MAC: 1 (2009)
NCAA Tournament appearances: 2
NIT appearances: 4

CONSENSUS ALL-AMERICAS

1967 **Bill Turner** (Little A-A), F
1972 **Len Paul** (Little A-A), F

TOP 5

G **Jim Fenton** (1951-54)
G **Fritz Nagy** (1943-47)
G **Joe Jakubick** (1980-84)
F **Len Paul** (1969-73)
F **Bill Turner** (1962-63, '64-67)

RECORDS

RECORDS	GAME		SEASON		CAREER	
POINTS	47	Joe Jakubick, vs. Murray State (Feb. 5, 1983)	827	Joe Jakubick (1982-83)	2,583	Joe Jakubick (1980-84)
POINTS PER GAME			30.1	Joe Jakubick (1983-84)	23.9	Joe Jakubick (1980-84)
REBOUNDS	28	Ray Pryear, vs. DePauw (Dec. 30, 1958); Mel Kiser, vs. Capital (Dec. 28, 1954)	400	Fred Golding (1956-57)	1,360	Fred Golding (1955-59)
ASSISTS	13	Reggie Hannah, vs. Western Illinois (Jan. 7, 1978)	165	Dru Joyce (2005-06)	503	Dru Joyce (2003-07)

THE SCHOOLS

ESPN 43 SAGARIN

ALABAMA

For years, Alabama had to cope with the knock that it just couldn't send teams to the NCAA Elite Eight—until Mark Gottfried's Crimson Tide finally got the program over that hump in 2004. But the proper retort all along should have been this: How many schools can match the eight Sweet 16 squads the Crimson Tide has put on the floor over the past 33 years?

BEST TEAM: 1929-30 Coach Hank Crisp (perhaps most famous for recruiting Bear Bryant to the football team) and star center James "Lindy" Hood (nicknamed for his resemblance to aviator Charles Lindbergh) took Alabama as far as it could go—to the 1930 Southern Conference championship. The only undefeated team in school history, the Tide beat Clemson, Georgia, Tennessee and Duke in succession to claim the crown.

BEST PLAYER: C LEON DOUGLAS (1972-76) The bruising 6'10", 230-pound center put Alabama back on the basketball map, leading the Crimson Tide to three SEC regular season titles—two shared (1974, '75), one solo (1976)—and its first Tourney appearances (1975 and the '76 Sweet 16). Douglas wound up his career with 1,909 points, 1,279 rebounds and 235 blocked shots. He became Alabama's first NBA first-round draft pick, going fourth in 1976 to the Detroit Pistons.

BEST COACH: WINFREY "WIMP" SANDERSON (1980-92) Arms flailing, feet stomping, face snarling—that was Wimp. As an assistant to Naismith Hall of Fame member C.M. Newton, Sanderson had to bite a towel to keep his emotions under control. But once Sanderson became Newton's successor, he was able to wean himself from the towel and transform himself into the animated-but-in-control coach who led Alabama to six Sweet 16s.

GAME FOR THE AGES: The Crimson Tide's Elite Eight run in the 2004 Tournament was made possible by a 70-67 second-round upset on March 20 over No. 1-seed Stanford. Kennedy Winston & Co. pounded the ball inside, fouled out Cardinal star Josh Childress, made 34 of 44 free throws and showed the world that an 18–12 team could take out a 30–1 squad using some old-fashioned grit.

HEARTBREAKER: In the 1990 Sweet 16, the Tide held a Loyola Marymount team that was averaging 125 points per game to only 22 in the first half, then took a 54-48 lead with fewer than six minutes to go. But a Lions rally and a missed 15-footer by Alabama go-to guy Robert Horry left the Tide with a dispiriting 62-60 loss.

FIERCEST RIVAL: As bitter as the Alabama-Auburn rivalry is on the football field, the two schools' basketball coaches usually have fun with it. Sanderson and Auburn's Sonny Smith even co-hosted a radio show for six years in the 1980s. "I know Sonny cheated to get Charles Barkley," Sanderson once joked, "because I was offering the opening bid to get him!" The Tide leads the series overall, 84–56.

FANFARE AND HOOPLA: The Coleman Coliseum is one of the SEC's toughest arenas for rivals to visit, and a portion of the credit goes to the 1,000-strong student booster club that called itself Mark's Madness—after Coach Gottfried, who resigned in 2009. The crazies clad in red T-shirts terrorize opponents from their floor-section seats near the opponent's second-half basket.

> ***"I know Sonny [Smith] cheated to get Charles Barkley," Wimp Sanderson once joked.***

FAN FAVORITE: F ROBERT HORRY (1988-92) The state of Alabama threw a Robert Horry Day at the Governor's Mansion in Montgomery in 2002. His hometown, Andalusia, named Robert Horry Park after him. That's what happens when you lead the Crimson Tide to two Sweet 16s, then go on to even greater heights as a pro (*seven* NBA titles).

FIRST-ROUND PRO PICKS

1976	**Leon Douglas,** Detroit (4)
1979	**Reggie King,** Kansas City (18)
1982	**Eddie Phillips,** New Jersey (21)
1983	**Ennis Whatley,** Kansas City (13)
1986	**Buck Johnson,** Houston (20)
1987	**Derrick McKey,** Seattle (9)
1987	**Jim Farmer,** Dallas (20)
1992	**Robert Horry,** Houston (11)
1992	**Latrell Sprewell,** Golden State (24)
1993	**James Robinson,** Portland (21)
1995	**Antonio McDyess,** LA Clippers (2)
1995	**Jason Caffey,** Chicago (20)
1996	**Roy Rogers,** Vancouver (22)
2001	**Gerald Wallace,** Sacramento (25)

PROFILE

University of Alabama, Tuscaloosa, AL
Founded: 1831
Enrollment: 25,580 (19,471 undergraduate)
Colors: Crimson and white
Nickname: Crimson Tide
Current arena: Coleman Coliseum, opened as Memorial Coliseum in 1968 (15,316)
Previous: Foster Auditorium, 1939-68 (2,000); Campus Gym, 1913-39 (N/A)
First game: 1913
All-time record: 1,484-903-1 (.622)

Total weeks in AP Top 20/25: 287
Current conference: Southeastern (1932-)
Conference titles:
Southern: 1 (1930)
SEC: 7 (1934, '56, '74 [tie], '75 [tie], '76, '87, 2002)
Conference tournament titles:
Southern: 1 (1930)
SEC: 6 (1934, '82, '87, '89, '90, '91)
NCAA Tournament appearances: 19
Sweet 16s (since 1975): 8
NIT appearances: 10
Semifinals: 5

TOP 5

G	**Ennis Whatley** (1981-83)
G/F	**T.R. Dunn** (1973-77)
F	**Reggie King** (1975-79)
F/C	**Derrick McKey** (1984-87)
C	**Leon Douglas** (1972-76)

RECORDS	GAME		SEASON		CAREER	
POINTS	50	Mike Nordholz, vs. Southern Mississippi (Dec. 12, 1966)	747	Reggie King (1978-79)	2,168	Reggie King (1975-79)
POINTS PER GAME			24.6	Jack Kubiszyn (1956-57)	20.1	Jerry Harper (1952-56)
REBOUNDS	33	Jerry Harper, vs. Louisiana College (Jan. 21, 1956)	517	Jerry Harper (1955-56)	1,688	Jerry Harper (1952-56)
ASSISTS	18	Ronald Steele, vs. East Tennessee State (Dec. 1, 2004)	241	Terry Coner (1985-86)	664	Terry Coner (1983-87)

THE SCHOOLS

SEASON REVIEW

SEASON	W-L	CONF.	SCORING	COACH	RECORD	
1912-18	*41-33*		*Alabama went 13-4 in 1915-16*			
1918-19	3-3-1			Yancey Goodall	3-3-1	.500
1919-20	5-7			Bill Moore	5-7	
1920-21	12-10			Charles Bernier		
1921-22	15-4	6-1		Charles Bernier		
1922-23	20-5	3-3		Charles Bernier	47-19	.712
1923-24	12-4	5-1		Hank Crisp		
1924-25	15-4	5-2		Hank Crisp		
1925-26	10-11	6-6		Hank Crisp		
1926-27	5-8	4-5		Hank Crisp		
1927-28	10-10	5-5		Hank Crisp		
1928-29	16-10	10-6		Hank Crisp		
1929-30	20-0	10-0		Hank Crisp		
1930-31	14-6	11-2		Hank Crisp		
1931-32	16-4	11-3		Hank Crisp		
1932-33	14-5	12-3		Hank Crisp		
1933-34	16-2	13-2		Hank Crisp		
1934-35	9-8	8-7		Hank Crisp		
1935-36	15-9	9-6		Hank Crisp		
1936-37	11-10	7-8		Hank Crisp		
1937-38	4-13	4-12		Hank Crisp		
1938-39	16-5	13-4		Hank Crisp		

SEAS.	W-L	CONF.	POSTSEASON	SCORING		REBOUNDS		ASSISTS		COACH	RECORD	
1939-40	18-5	14-4								Hank Crisp		
1940-41	14-8	11-7		Veo Storey	5.6					Hank Crisp		
1941-42	18-6	13-4		Louis Adair	6.3					Hank Crisp		
1942-43	10-10	9-9		Jim Homer	10.3					Paul Burnham	10-10	.500
1943-44	no team											
1944-45	10-5	5-3		Charley Teubert	13.1					Malcolm Laney	10-5	.667
1945-46	11-5	8-4		Carl Shaeffer	8.9					Hank Crisp	264-133	.665
1946-47	16-6	13-5		Jim Homer	14.9					Floyd Burdette		
1947-48	15-12	8-8		J.F. Sharp	8.8					Floyd Burdette		
1948-49	13-12	9-9		Dickie McKenzie	8.8					Floyd Burdette		
1949-50	9-12	8-9		Bryant Ivey	9.0					Floyd Burdette		
1950-51	15-8	10-4		Paul Sullivan	14.6					Floyd Burdette		
1951-52	13-9	9-5		Paul Sullivan	18.2	Paul Sullivan	12.9			Floyd Burdette	81-59	.579
1952-53	12-9	6-7		Jerry Harper	13.8	Jerry Harper	17.0			Johnny Dee		
1953-54	16-8	10-4		Jerry Harper	17.8	Jerry Harper	14.9			Johnny Dee		
1954-55	19-5	11-3		Jerry Harper	21.0	Jerry Harper	19.0			Johnny Dee		
1955-56	21-3	14-0		Jerry Harper	23.2	Jerry Harper	21.5			Johnny Dee	68-25	.731
1956-57	15-11	7-7		Jack Kubiszyn	24.6	Jim Fulmer	14.7			Eugene Lambert		
1957-58	17-9	9-5		Jack Kubiszyn	23.3	Jim Fulmer	8.6			Eugene Lambert		
1958-59	10-12	6-8		Lenny Kaplan	14.4	Clyde Frederick	9.7			Eugene Lambert		
1959-60	7-17	4-10		Porter Powers	15.8	Henry Hoskins	5.6			Eugene Lambert	49-49	.500
1960-61	7-18	5-9		Larry Pennington	17.2	Henry Hoskins	9.3			Hayden Riley		
1961-62	11-15	6-8		James Booth	11.2	James Booth	7.4			Hayden Riley		
1962-63	14-11	7-7		Bob Andrews	15.7	Bob Andrews	8.1			Hayden Riley		
1963-64	14-12	7-7		J.W. Berry	14.5	Bob Andrews	8.6			Hayden Riley		
1964-65	17-9	9-7		Bob Andrews	19.3	Harry Hammonds	9.4			Hayden Riley		
1965-66	16-10	9-7		Harry Hammonds	14.4	Harry Hammonds	11.6			Hayden Riley		
1966-67	13-13	6-12		Mike Nordholz	21.0	Rich Deppe	8.2			Hayden Riley		
1967-68	10-16	3-15		Mike Nordholz	20.1	Tom Jones	9.6			Hayden Riley	102-104	.495
1968-69	4-20	1-17		Gary Elliott	18.4	Rich Deppe	10.6	Gary Elliott	67	C.M. Newton		
1969-70	8-18	5-13		Jimmy Hollon	19.4	Alan House	10.1	Bobby Lynch	78	C.M. Newton		
1970-71	10-16	6-12		Alan House	19.4	Alan House	11.6	Bobby Lynch	123	C.M. Newton		
1971-72	18-8	13-5		Wendell Hudson	19.6	Wendell Hudson	13.1	Ray Odums	144	C.M. Newton		
1972-73	22-8	13-5	NIT FOURTH PLACE	Wendell Hudson	20.7	Wendell Hudson	12.1	Ray Odums	177	C.M. Newton		
1973-74	22-4	15-3		Charles Cleveland	17.1	Leon Douglas	9.9	Ray Odums	107	C.M. Newton		
1974-75	22-5	15-3	NCAA FIRST ROUND	Leon Douglas	20.7	Leon Douglas	13.1	Charles Cleveland	104	C.M. Newton		
1975-76	23-5	15-3	NCAA REGIONAL SEMIFINALS	Leon Douglas	20.6	Leon Douglas	12.4	Anthony Murray	142	C.M. Newton		
1976-77	25-6	14-4	NIT FOURTH PLACE	Reggie King	18.1	Reggie King	10.9	Anthony Murray	102	C.M. Newton		
1977-78	17-10	11-7		Reggie King	21.2	Reggie King	13.3	Anthony Murray	127	C.M. Newton		
1978-79	22-11	11-7	NIT THIRD PLACE	Reggie King	22.6	Reggie King	9.9	Robert Scott	191	C.M. Newton		
1979-80	18-12	12-6	NIT SECOND ROUND	Eddie Phillips	16.7	Eddie Phillips	11.4	Robert Scott	125	C.M. Newton	211-123	.632
1980-81	18-11	10-8	NIT SECOND ROUND	Eddie Phillips	17.0	Eddie Phillips	9.8	Eric Richardson	87	Wimp Sanderson		
1981-82	24-7	12-6	NCAA REGIONAL SEMIFINALS	Eddie Phillips	15.5	Eddie Phillips	8.6	Ennis Whatley	178	Wimp Sanderson		
1982-83	20-12	8-10	NCAA FIRST ROUND	Bobby Lee Hurt	15.3	Bobby Lee Hurt	8.9	Ennis Whatley	220	Wimp Sanderson		
1983-84	18-12	10-8	NCAA FIRST ROUND	Buck Johnson	17.0	Bobby Lee Hurt	9.1	Eric Richardson	186	Wimp Sanderson		
1984-85	23-10	11-7	NCAA REGIONAL SEMIFINALS	Buck Johnson	16.0	Buck Johnson	9.4	Terry Coner	184	Wimp Sanderson		
1985-86	24-9	13-5	NCAA REGIONAL SEMIFINALS	Buck Johnson	20.7	Buck Johnson	8.3	Terry Coner	241	Wimp Sanderson		
1986-87	28-5 ⊗	16-2	NCAA REGIONAL SEMIFINALS	Derrick McKey	18.6	Michael Ansley	7.8	Terry Coner	173	Wimp Sanderson		
1987-88	14-17	6-12		Michael Ansley	18.1	Michael Ansley	9.2	Craig Dudley	99	Wimp Sanderson		
1988-89	23-8	12-6	NCAA FIRST ROUND	Michael Ansley	20.3	Michael Ansley	9.2	Gary Waites	191	Wimp Sanderson		
1989-90	26-9	12-6	NCAA REGIONAL SEMIFINALS	Melvin Cheatum	15.7	Melvin Cheatum	6.7	Gary Waites	168	Wimp Sanderson		
1990-91	23-10	12-6	NCAA REGIONAL SEMIFINALS	James Robinson	16.8	Melvin Cheatum	7.7	Gary Waites	176	Wimp Sanderson		
1991-92	26-9	10-6	NCAA SECOND ROUND	James Robinson	19.4	Robert Horry	8.5	Robert Horry	80	Wimp Sanderson	267-119	.692▼
1992-93	16-13	7-9	NIT FIRST ROUND	James Robinson	20.6	Jason Caffey	8.7	James Robinson	68	David Hobbs		
1993-94	20-10	12-4	NCAA SECOND ROUND	Jamal Faulkner	13.5	Antonio McDyess	8.1	Artie Griffin	90	David Hobbs		
1994-95	23-10	10-6	NCAA SECOND ROUND	Antonio McDyess	13.9	Antonio McDyess	10.2	Marvin Orange	139	David Hobbs		
1995-96	19-13	9-7	NIT FOURTH PLACE	Eric Washington	18.6	Roy Rogers	9.3	Marco Whitfield	88	David Hobbs		
1996-97	17-14	6-10		Eric Washington	16.1	Washington, Alexander	6.3	Brian Williams	120	David Hobbs		
1997-98	15-16	6-10		Brian Williams	16.1	Demetrius Alexander	8.3	Chauncey Jones	109	David Hobbs	110-76	.591
1998-99	17-15	6-10	NIT FIRST ROUND	Brian Williams	17.3	Jeremy Hays	8.4	Chauncey Jones	98	Mark Gottfried		
1999-2000	13-16	6-10		Schea Cotton	15.5	Erwin Dudley	8.1	Tarik London	3.8	Mark Gottfried		
2000-01	25-11	8-8	NIT RUNNER-UP	Rod Grizzard	17.0	Erwin Dudley	10.0	Rod Grizzard	2.5	Mark Gottfried		
2001-02	27-8	12-4	NCAA SECOND ROUND	Erwin Dudley	15.2	Erwin Dudley	8.9	Mo Williams	4.5	Mark Gottfried		
2002-03	17-12	7-9	NCAA FIRST ROUND	Mo Williams	16.4	Erwin Dudley	9.5	Mo Williams	3.9	Mark Gottfried		
2003-04	20-13	8-8	NCAA REGIONAL FINALS	Kennedy Winston	17.1	Chuck Davis	5.9	Antoine Pettway	3.5	Mark Gottfried		
2004-05	24-8	12-4	NCAA FIRST ROUND	Kennedy Winston	17.9	Jermareo Davidson	7.0	Ronald Steele	5.0	Mark Gottfried		
2005-06	18-13	10-6	NCAA SECOND ROUND	Chuck Davis	16.5	Jermareo Davidson	8.9	Ronald Steele	4.3	Mark Gottfried		
2006-07	20-12	7-9	NIT FIRST ROUND	Richard Hendrix	14.6	Richard Hendrix	8.7	Ronald Steele	4.0	Mark Gottfried		
2007-08	17-16	5-11		Richard Hendrix	17.8	Richard Hendrix	10.1	Rico Pickett	3.3	Mark Gottfried		
2008-09	18-14	7-9		Alonzo Gee	15.0	JaMychal Green	7.6	Ronald Steele	3.7	Mark Gottfried[a]	210-131	.616

Cumulative totals listed when per game averages not available.

[a] Mark Gottfried (12-7) and Philip Pearson (6-7) both coached during the 2008-09 season.

⊗ Records don't reflect games forfeited or vacated. For adjusted records, see p. 521.

▼ Coach's record adjusted to reflect games forfeited or vacated: 265-118, .692. For yearly totals, see p.521.

ESPN 249 SAGARIN

ALABAMA A&M

After Ben Jobe passed the coaching reins to 29-year-old L. Vann Pettaway in 1986, the Bulldogs notched eight 20-win seasons and reached four D2 elite eights and one NCAA Tournament. Pettaway's challenge is to make AAMU a consistent winner in Division I the way it was in its D2 years.

BEST TEAM: 1987-88 Led by Willie Hayes, Ondray Wagner and Frank Sillmon, Alabama A&M streaked to the D2 national tournament after losing early-season contests to Jacksonville State and Alabama State, each by one point. After knocking off Ashland and Kentucky Wesleyan to reach the quarters, the No. 3-ranked Bulldogs shot a paltry 3 for 21 from long range in a 76-68 loss to the eventual champs, Massachusetts-Lowell.

BEST PLAYER: G Obie Trotter (2002-06) Though he was recruited by higher mid-majors, Trotter landed at AAMU because his mother wanted him to be coached by a "godly man." Advantage Pettaway. In leading the Bulldogs to their first NCAA D1 Tournament in 2005, Trotter led the nation with 125 steals and was SWAC Player of the Year. He ranks seventh on the NCAA's career steals list (346).

BEST COACH: L. Vann Pettaway (1986-) A disciple of transition basketball as a Jobe assistant, Pettaway is a defensive mastermind as coach, employing a variety of attacking schemes with full- and half-court traps. He is the winningest coach in AAMU history.

GAME FOR THE AGES: Playing on the daunting home court of Kentucky Wesleyan in the second round of the 1988 D2 tourney, Ondray Wagner hit a 22-footer from the corner with seconds left to give AAMU the 92-88 win.

FIERCEST RIVAL: Football's Magic City Classic between Alabama State and AAMU is one of the most passionate series on the gridiron, so it's no surprise that the rivalry extends to the hardwood. Bulldogs fans still growl over the "phantom foul" in a 1988 matchup that stopped an AAMU breakaway dunk and left them with a one-point loss. The Hornets lead the series 19–17 in D1 play.

SEASON REVIEW

SEAS.	W-L	CONF.	COACH	SEAS.	W-L	CONF.	COACH
1950-55	*37-70*	*No winning seasons*		1958-59	6-10		Frank E. Lewis
1955-56	5-15		Frank E. Lewis	1959-60	12-10		Frank E. Lewis
1956-57	8-13		Frank E. Lewis	1960-61	N/A		
1957-58	7-10		Frank E. Lewis	1961-62	7-15		Frank E. Lewis

SEAS.	W-L	CONF.	SCORING		COACH	RECORD
1962-63	6-14				Frank E. Lewis	88-157 .359
1963-64	N/A					
1964-65	N/A					
1965-66	N/A					
1966-67	N/A					
1967-68	N/A					
1968-69	11-16				Duane F. Gordon	
1969-70	13-12				Duane F. Gordon	
1970-71	16-8				Duane F. Gordon	
1971-72	4-20				Duane F. Gordon	44-56 .440
1972-73	7-15				Clarence Blackmon	
1973-74	7-16				Clarence Blackmon	
1974-75	18-11				Clarence Blackmon	
1975-76	18-10				Clarence Blackmon	
1976-77	17-8				Clarence Blackmon	
1977-78	9-13				Clarence Blackmon	
1978-79	10-17				Clarence Blackmon	
1979-80	9-18				Clarence Blackmon	
1980-81	16-11				Clarence Blackmon	111-119 .483
1981-82	N/A				Ben Jobe	
1982-83	18-9				Ben Jobe	
1983-84	21-8				Ben Jobe	
1984-85	21-10				Ben Jobe	
1985-86	23-9				Ben Jobe	83-36 .697
1986-87	23-7				L. Vann Pettaway	
1987-88	29-3		Frank Sillmon	20.6	L. Vann Pettaway	
1988-89	26-6		Frank Sillmon	23.0	L. Vann Pettaway	
1989-90	18-9				L. Vann Pettaway	
1990-91	16-14				L. Vann Pettaway	
1991-92	15-15				L. Vann Pettaway	
1992-93	28-3				L. Vann Pettaway	
1993-94	27-5				L. Vann Pettaway	
1994-95	29-3				L. Vann Pettaway	
1995-96	28-3				L. Vann Pettaway	
1996-97	24-6				L. Vann Pettaway	
1997-98	18-9		Miguel Smith	15.8	L. Vann Pettaway	
1998-99	10-17		Terrance Vanlier	19.3	L. Vann Pettaway	
1999-2000	18-10	14-4	Terrance Vanlier	17.8	L. Vann Pettaway	
2000-01	17-11	13-5	Desmond Cambridge	18.6	L. Vann Pettaway	
2001-02	19-10	12-6	Desmond Cambridge	20.6	L. Vann Pettaway	
2002-03	8-19	4-14	Anthony Hayes	14.4	L. Vann Pettaway	
2003-04	13-17	9-9	Obie Trotter	18.1	L. Vann Pettaway	
2004-05	18-14	12-6 ●	Obie Trotter	15.3	L. Vann Pettaway	
2005-06	13-13	11-7	Obie Trotter	19.2	L. Vann Pettaway	
2006-07	10-20	4-14	Trant Simpson	13.0	L. Vann Pettaway	
2007-08	14-15	11-7	Trant Simpson	15.5	L. Vann Pettaway	
2008-09	8-19	6-12	Trant Simpson	16.1	L. Vann Pettaway	429-248 .634

● **NCAA Tournament appearance**

PROFILE

Alabama A&M University, Normal, AL
Founded: 1875 as Huntsville Normal School; 1969, renamed Alabama Agricultural and Mechanical University
Enrollment: 5,124 (4,297 undergraduate)
Colors: Maroon and white
Nickname: Bulldogs
Current arena: T.M. Elmore Gymnasium, opened in 1974 (6,000)
Previous: Frank Lewis Gym, 1982 (N/A)

First game: 1950
All-time record: 755-616 (.551)
Total weeks in AP Top 20/25: 0
Current conference: Southwestern Athletic (1999-)
Conference titles:
SWAC: 1 (2005)
Conference tournament titles:
SWAC: 1 (2005)
NCAA Tournament appearances: 1
NIT appearances: 0

TOP 5

G **Deartrus Goodman** (1992-96)
G **Obie Trotter** (2002-06)
G **Ondray Wagner** (1984-88)
F **Frank Sillmon** (1987-89)
F/C **Mickell Gladness** (2005-08)

RECORDS

	GAME	SEASON		CAREER	
POINTS	N/A	736	Frank Sillmon (1988-89)	2,183	Deartrus Goodman (1992-96)
POINTS PER GAME		23.0	Frank Sillmon (1988-89)	21.9	Frank Sillmon (1987-89)
REBOUNDS	N/A	310	Fred Clemon (1990-91)	968	Fred Clemon (1989-93)
ASSISTS	N/A	287	Craig Lotte (1994-95)	673	Craig Lotte (1992-95)

ESPN 45 SAGARIN

ALABAMA-BIRMINGHAM

Pop quiz: Which Alabama school has made 22 postseason appearances, including 13 trips to the NCAA Tournament, since 1980? Hint: It's not an SEC school. Answer: It's the Blazers, who made the NIT field in 1979-80—just one season after starting their program from scratch.

BEST TEAM: 1981-82 Led by the supremely athletic wingman Oliver Robinson, UAB catapulted itself all the way into the NCAA Elite Eight, cutting down two giants along the way. In the second round, the Blazers put on a shooting clinic to beat Bob Knight's Indiana Hoosiers, 80-70. In the Sweet 16, they dropped Virginia and its 7'4" star, Ralph Sampson. Unfortunately, Alabama-Birmingham ran out of magic in the Mideast Regional final against Louisville, losing 75-68.

BEST PLAYER: G/F OLIVER ROBINSON (1978-82) A Birmingham native, Robinson was the first student to receive an athletic scholarship from UAB. After learning how to play the wing while facing the basket, Robinson served as the catalyst for the Blazers' Sweet 16 run in 1981 and Elite Eight run the following year. His signature game came against UVa in the 1982 Tournament, when he scored 23 points.

BEST COACH: GENE BARTOW (1978-96) Folks in Birmingham call Bartow the Father of UAB Athletics, and it isn't an exaggeration. Coming to B-ham after two seasons trying to succeed as John Wooden's successor at UCLA (NCAA runner-up and Sweet 16 finishes weren't good enough), Bartow built the UAB program—and, really, the entire athletic department—from the ground up. Virtually overnight, he made the Blazers relevant at the national level with wins in the program's first four seasons over Western Kentucky, Kentucky and Indiana, among others.

GAME FOR THE AGES: Few experts gave UAB a chance against Virginia in the round of 16 at the 1982 NCAA Tournament. After all, which Blazer could possibly match up against dominant All-America center Ralph Sampson? But with the advantage of playing the game on its home court, the Blazers were unfazed. Before the game, Robinson said, "Wilt Chamberlain's been defeated. Kareem Abdul-Jabbar's been defeated. And so will Ralph Sampson." The Blazers didn't exactly shut the big man down; Sampson had 19 points and 21 rebounds. But Robinson's hot touch proved to be a decisive factor in the 68-66 win.

Few experts gave UAB a chance against Virginia in the round of 16 at the 1982 NCAA Tournament.

HEARTBREAKER: After a second-round upset of No.1-seed Kentucky in the 2004 NCAA Tournament, No. 9-seed UAB conjured up memories of its 1981-82 team. Then came Kansas. The No. 4 seed, although dogged by injuries, still managed to run around, through and past the Blazers' usually withering press, while pounding the ball inside on offense and scoring seemingly at will. UAB coach Mike Anderson grew so frustrated with the officiating during the 100-74 rout that he drew his second technical with 5:24 left, ending his Tournament early.

FIERCEST RIVAL: UAB and Memphis have only been Conference USA mates since 1995, but the hatred runs deep. Witness Feb. 16, 2008, when the host Blazers lost to the No. 1-ranked Tigers, 79-78. In a game full of trash talk and intense physical play, the Blazers appeared to have pulled off the upset with a buzzer-beating trey. UAB fans even rushed onto the court. But officials ruled the shot came after the buzzer, leading to several altercations between the Memphis players and the home crowd. Memphis leads the rivalry, 28–10.

FANFARE AND HOOPLA: Think Birmingham was ready for some D1 hoops? In its home debut on Nov. 24, 1978, UAB drew more than 14,000 fans to the Birmingham-Jefferson arena, including governor George Wallace.

FAN FAVORITE: G CARLDELL JOHNSON (2003-06) How did they love him? Let us count the ways: 1) Nickname: Squeaky; 2) Diminutive stature: 5'10"; 3) Distinctive hairstyle: natty dreads. What's not to love?

THE SCHOOLS

PROFILE

University of Alabama at Birmingham, Birmingham, AL
Founded: 1969
Enrollment: 16,149 (10,369 undergraduate)
Colors: Green, white and gold
Nickname: Blazers
Current arena: Bartow Arena, opened in 1988 (8,508)
Previous: Birmingham-Jefferson Civic Center Coliseum, 1978-88 (19,000)
First game: Nov. 24, 1978
All-time record: 617-367 (.627)
Total weeks in AP Top 20/25: 32

Current conference: Conference USA (1995-)
Conference titles:
Sun Belt: 3 (1981, '82, '90)
C-USA: 1 (2004 [tie])
Conference tournament titles:
Sun Belt: 4 (1982, '83, '84, '87)
NCAA Tournament appearances: 13
Sweet 16s (since 1975): 3
NIT appearances: 9
Semifinals: 2

TOP 5

G **Morris Finley** (1999-2000, '01-04)
G **Steve Mitchell** (1982-86)
G/F **Oliver Robinson** (1978-82)
F **Jerome Mincy** (1982-86)
C **Andy Kennedy** (1988-91)

RECORDS	GAME		SEASON		CAREER	
POINTS	41	Robert Vaden, vs. UTEP (Feb. 27, 2008); Andy Kennedy, vs. Saint Louis (Jan. 3, 1991)	695	Robert Vaden (2007-08)	1,867	Steve Mitchell (1982-86)
POINTS PER GAME			21.8	Andy Kennedy (1990-91)	19.4	Carlos Williams (1994-97)
REBOUNDS	20	Will Campbell, vs. Houston (Jan. 31, 2001)	318	Carlos Williams (1996-97)	933	Jerome Mincy (1982-86)
ASSISTS	14	Jack Kramer, vs. Alabama State (Nov. 23, 1990)	209	Jack Kramer (1990-91)	597	Steve Mitchell (1982-86)

SEASON REVIEW

SEAS.	W-L	CONF.	POSTSEASON	SCORING		REBOUNDS		ASSISTS		COACH	RECORD	
1978-79	15-11			Larry Spicer	14.9	Larry Spicer	8.2	Greg Leet	3.3	Gene Bartow		
1979-80	18-12	10-4	NIT FIRST ROUND	Keith McCord	18.2	Keith McCord	7.2	Keith McCord	2.8	Gene Bartow		
1980-81	23-9	9-3	NCAA REGIONAL SEMIFINALS	Oliver Robinson	15.9	Chris Giles	7.8	Glenn Marcus	4.1	Gene Bartow		
1981-82	25-6	9-1	NCAA REGIONAL FINALS	Oliver Robinson	21.1	Chris Giles	7.6	Oliver Robinson	2.7	Gene Bartow		
1982-83	19-14	9-5	NCAA FIRST ROUND	Cliff Pruitt	16.4	Cliff Pruitt	5.8	Steve Mitchell	3.1	Gene Bartow		
1983-84	23-11	8-6	NCAA FIRST ROUND	McKinley Singleton	14.6	Jerome Mincy	6.0	Steve Mitchell	4.8	Gene Bartow		
1984-85	25-9	11-3	NCAA SECOND ROUND	Steve Mitchell	18.1	Jerome Mincy	8.5	Steve Mitchell	4.3	Gene Bartow		
1985-86	25-11	9-5	NCAA SECOND ROUND	Steve Mitchell	16.8	Jerome Mincy	8.4	Steve Mitchell	5.3	Gene Bartow		
1986-87	21-11	10-4	NCAA FIRST ROUND	Tracy Foster	17.3	Michael Charles	7.8	Tracy Foster	3.9	Gene Bartow		
1987-88	16-15	7-7		Michael Charles	18.7	Larry Rembert	5.7	Jeremy Bearden	5.5	Gene Bartow		
1988-89	22-12	8-6	NIT THIRD PLACE	Reginald Turner	19.5	Reginald Turner	7.4	Jack Kramer	5.8	Gene Bartow		
1989-90	22-9	12-2	NCAA FIRST ROUND	Andy Kennedy	16.9	Alan Ogg	6.2	Jack Kramer	5.7	Gene Bartow		
1990-91	18-13	9-5	NIT FIRST ROUND	Andy Kennedy	21.8	Elbert Rogers	6.5	Jack Kramer	6.7	Gene Bartow		
1991-92	20-9	4-6	NIT FIRST ROUND	Elbert Rogers	20.4	Elbert Rogers	7.1	Corey Jackson	5.0	Gene Bartow		
1992-93	21-14	5-5	NIT THIRD PLACE	Stanley Jackson	16.3	Clarence Thrash	5.2	Corey Jackson	5.0	Gene Bartow		
1993-94	22-8	8-4	NCAA FIRST ROUND	Robert Shannon	19.0	Clarence Thrash	6.6	Corey Jackson	3.6	Gene Bartow		
1994-95	14-16 ⊗	5-7		Carlos Williams	17.0	Anthony Thomas	7.2	Leonard Bush	3.0	Gene Bartow		
1995-96	16-14	6-8		Carlos Williams	20.2	Carlos Williams	8.4	Cedric Dixon	3.1	Gene Bartow	365-204	.641▼
1996-97	18-14	7-7	NIT FIRST ROUND	Carlos Williams	19.7	Carlos Williams	9.9	Will Bailey	2.4	Murry Bartow		
1997-98	21-12	10-6	NIT SECOND ROUND	Cedric Dixon	13.3	Fred Williams	7.0	Cedric Dixon	3.2	Murry Bartow		
1998-99	20-12	10-6	NCAA FIRST ROUND	Fred Williams	15.5	Torrey Ward	5.2	Eric Holmes	3.1	Murry Bartow		
1999-2000	14-14	7-9		Eric Holmes	16.6	Myron Ransom	5.9	LeAndrew Bass	3.2	Murry Bartow		
2000-01	17-14	8-8		LeAndrew Bass	14.6	Will Campbell	8.1	LeAndrew Bass	4.7	Murry Bartow		
2001-02	13-17	6-10		Will Campbell	12.7	Will Campbell	8.8	Eric Bush	5.4	Murry Bartow	103-83	.554
2002-03	21-13	8-8	NIT QUARTERFINALS	Morris Finley	18.3	Sidney Ball	5.4	Eric Bush	3.6	Mike Anderson		
2003-04	22-10	12-4	NCAA REGIONAL SEMIFINALS	Morris Finley	13.9	Sidney Ball	5.3	Carldell Johnson	4.3	Mike Anderson		
2004-05	22-11	10-6	NCAA SECOND ROUND	Donell Taylor	15.5	Demario Eddins	4.8	Carldell Johnson	4.6	Mike Anderson		
2005-06	24-7	12-2	NCAA FIRST ROUND	Marvett McDonald	14.8	Frank Holmes	4.8	Carldell Johnson	6.3	Mike Anderson	89-41	.685
2006-07	15-16	7-9		Paul Delaney III	15.5	Lawrence Kinnard	6.2	Paul Delaney III	5.2	Mike Davis		
2007-08	23-11	12-4		Robert Vaden	21.1	Lawrence Kinnard	6.8	Paul Delaney III	5.0	Mike Davis		
2008-09	22-12	11-5	NIT FIRST ROUND	Robert Vaden	17.6	Lawrence Kinnard	9.2	Aaron Johnson	3.6	Mike Davis	60-39	.606

⊗ Records don't reflect games forfeited or vacated. For adjusted records, see p. 521.

▼ Coach's record adjusted to reflect games forfeited or vacated: 366-203, .643. For yearly totals, see p. 521.

LATE GREAT

CAL STATE LA, 1969-75

During their brief tenure in the University Division, the team was known as the Diablos (they became the Golden Eagles in 1981) and were a member of the PCAA (now Big West) from 1969-70 to '73-74. They were independent during the 1974-75 season. In their six seasons at the major college level, the team made one NCAA Tournament appearance, an 88-80 first-round loss to Dayton in 1974. They received the PCAA's automatic bid because conference champ Long Beach State was on probation.

NOTABLE PLAYER: G Raymond Lewis (1972-73) The 6'1" Lewis is one of the best players never to play in the NBA. After leading Verbum Dei High to three straight California Interscholastic Federation titles, he stunned everyone in 1971 by choosing Cal State LA over UCLA and Long Beach State. He led all freshmen in scoring in 1971-72, then averaged 32.9 ppg in his only varsity season. He declared for the NBA, but bad judgment and contract problems derailed his career before it began. Cal State LA's major college aspirations also flatlined soon after.

ESPN 213 SAGARIN

ALABAMA STATE

They kept it close for a half. But while the Hornets were eventually routed by Michigan State in their NCAA Tournament debut in 2001, it was a landmark moment all the same. Since the program was launched in 1935, the historically black college has fielded some of the game's most entertaining teams, even if few people outside the football-crazy region knew it. Now that Alabama State is going national—and is a perennial SWAC contender—the secret is getting out.

BEST TEAM: 1979-80 Pity the team that had to play these guys in the old C.J. Dunn Arena, a.k.a. the Sweatbox. With the rafters shaking, the Hornets ran foes straight out of the gym. ASU averaged 82 points on the way to becoming NAIA national runner-up.

BEST PLAYER: G LEWIS JACKSON (1981-84) Ask contemporaries to describe Jackson and they'll all use the same word: quick. Four games into his freshman season, Jackson was a starter. By the time his career was done, the future Hornets coach had led ASU to consecutive SWAC titles.

BEST COACH: JAMES OLIVER (1978-95) Yes, his teams could score with the best. But it was Oliver's emphasis on defensive toughness that translated into the NAIA runner-up finish in 1980, back-to-back SWAC co-championships in 1983 and '84 and an NIT bid in 1983.

GAME FOR THE AGES: In the annual grudge match with Alabama A&M on Jan. 16, 2006, the Hornets built a 15-point, first-half lead in front of a sellout crowd at the ASU Acadome. Then a nearby traffic accident knocked out the arena's power. When the lights came back on 24 minutes later, A&M went on a huge run to tie the score at 44. After the power went out for another 10 or 15 minutes, the Hornets surged again and won, 81-68. Electric.

FIERCEST RIVAL: Epic. There's no other way to describe the longstanding A&M-ASU football feud. It's so big that it spills onto the basketball court. The home-and-home contests are guaranteed sellouts each season (ASU leads, 50–7), with fans from both schools stepping and dancing during games.

SEASON REVIEW

SEAS.	W-L	CONF.	COACH	SEAS.	W-L	CONF.	COACH
1934-45	*86-73*	*16-4 in 1936-37*		1958-59	9-10		C.J. Dunn
1945-46	8-12		C.J. Dunn	1959-60	N/A		C.J. Dunn
1946-47	8-2		C.J. Dunn	1960-61	12-10		C.J. Dunn
1947-48	14-9		C.J. Dunn	1961-62	10-12		C.J. Dunn
1948-49	18-11		C.J. Dunn	1962-63	10-8		C.J. Dunn
1949-50	7-5		C.J. Dunn	1963-64	15-14		Lucias Mitchell
1950-51	17-8		C.J. Dunn	1964-65	14-11		Lucias Mitchell
1951-52	13-12		C.J. Dunn	1965-66	19-9		Lucias Mitchell
1952-53	17-9		C.J. Dunn	1966-67	17-7		Lucias Mitchell
1953-54	15-4		C.J. Dunn	1967-68	18-7		Ben Jobe
1954-55	13-8		C.J. Dunn	1968-69	19-9		Willie Parker
1955-56	16-5		C.J. Dunn	1969-70	17-10		Bernard Boozer
1956-57	12-1		C.J. Dunn	1970-71	24-5		Bernard Boozer
1957-58	13-10		C.J. Dunn	1971-72	22-3		Bernard Boozer

SEAS.	W-L	CONF.	SCORING		COACH	RECORD	
1972-73	19-9				Bernard Boozer	82-27	.752
1973-74	19-9				Floyd Laisure		
1974-75	16-13				Floyd Laisure		
1975-76	19-8				Floyd Laisure		
1976-77	17-11				Floyd Laisure	71-41	.634
1977-78	no team						
1978-79	23-2				James Oliver		
1979-80	32-2				James Oliver		
1980-81	19-9				James Oliver		
1981-82	22-6				James Oliver		
1982-83	22-6	12-2 ■			James Oliver		
1983-84	22-6	11-3			James Oliver		
1984-85	14-17	4-10			James Oliver		
1985-86	11-17	7-7			James Oliver		
1986-87	14-14	5-9			James Oliver		
1987-88	8-20	7-7			James Oliver		
1988-89	13-16	7-7			James Oliver		
1989-90	15-13	7-7			James Oliver		
1990-91	18-11	7-5			James Oliver		
1991-92	14-14	8-6			James Oliver		
1992-93	14-13	9-5			James Oliver		
1993-94	19-10	10-4			James Oliver		
1994-95	11-15	8-6			James Oliver	291-191	.604
1995-96	9-18	5-9			Rob Spivery		
1996-97	8-21	5-9			Rob Spivery		
1997-98	11-17	6-10			Rob Spivery		
1998-99	11-16	8-8	Corey Williams	10.6	Rob Spivery		
1999-2000	13-15	14-4	Tyrone Levett	14.9	Rob Spivery		
2000-01	22-9	15-3 ●	Tyrone Levett	15.8	Rob Spivery		
2001-02	19-13	12-6	Tyrone Levett	13.6	Rob Spivery		
2002-03	13-14	10-7	Malcolm Campbell	13.5	Rob Spivery		
2003-04	16-15	11-7 ●	Malcolm Campbell	13.4	Rob Spivery		
2004-05	15-15	11-7	Ralfeal Golden	12.9	Rob Spivery	137-153	.472
2005-06	12-18	10-8	Akeim Claborn	14.7	Lewis Jackson		
2006-07	10-20	8-10	Andrew Hayles	14.5	Lewis Jackson		
2007-08	20-11	15-3 ■	Andrew Hayles	14.6	Lewis Jackson		
2008-09	22-10	16-2 ●	Brandon Brooks	13.7	Lewis Jackson	64-59	.520

■ NIT appearance ● NCAA Tournament appearance

PROFILE

Alabama State University, Montgomery, AL
Founded: 1867 as Lincoln Normal School; 1969, renamed Alabama State University
Enrollment: 5,269 (4,348 undergraduate)
Colors: Old gold and black
Nickname: Hornets
Current arena: Joe L. Reed Acadome (7,400)
First game: N/A
All-time record: 1,045-737 (.586)
Total weeks in AP Top 20/25: 0

Current conference: Southwestern Athletic (1982-)
Conference titles:
SWAC: 5 (1983 [tie], '84 [tie], 2001, '08, '09)
Conference tournament titles:
SWAC: 3 (2001, '04, '09)
NCAA Tournament appearances: 3
NIT appearances: 2

FIRST-ROUND PRO PICKS

1981 **Kevin Loder**, Kansas City (17)

TOP 5

G **Danny Crenshaw** (1967-70)
G **Lewis Jackson** (1980-84)
G **Willie Scott** (1966-69)
F **Kevin Loder** (1979-81)
F **Steve Rogers** (1989-92)

RECORDS

RECORDS	GAME		SEASON		CAREER	
POINTS	55	Greg Northington, vs. Savannah State (1972)	889	Willie Scott (1967-68)	3,155	Willie Scott (1966-69)
POINTS PER GAME			35.9	Willie Scott (1967-68)	30.6	Willie Scott (1966-69)
REBOUNDS		N/A	645	Eric Bain (1965-66)	944	Tyrone Levett (1998-2002)
ASSISTS	17	Michael Freeney, vs. S.C. State (Dec. 13, 1982)	203	Michael Freeney (1982-83)	770	Michael Freeney (1981-85)

ESPN 316 SAGARIN

ALBANY

For five decades, Richard "Doc" Sauers *was* Albany basketball. The coach's winning ways, dating back to the team's D3 days in the 1950s, helped shepherd the Great Danes' rise to D1 in 1999. Now the team has a new identity: Cinderella.

BEST TEAM: 2005-06 The Great Danes not only had their first winning season as a D1 team, they also won their first America East regular-season crown and conference tournament title. To top it off, in its NCAA Tourney debut, No. 16-seed Albany scared the daylights out of No. 1-seed UConn by opening a 12-point lead midway through the second half before bowing out, 72-59.

BEST PLAYER: G Jamar Wilson (2002-03, '04-07) This do-it-all guard put a charge into the fledgling D1 program, earning All-America honorable mentions in 2006 and 2007. He was equally capable of getting his points (a school-record 2,164) and making sure teammates got theirs (488 assists, second all-time).

BEST COACH: Richard "Doc" Sauers (1955-87, '88-97) Sauers liked to say that coaching was the most fun a person could have without working. Clearly, he meant it. After retiring, having endured only one losing season in 41 campaigns, he took over as coach of the Albany women's golf team, a position he still held as of 2009.

GAME FOR THE AGES: Never mind that Vermont entered the 2006 America East tournament final as the three-time defending conference tournament champs. Before a home crowd of 4,538 fans—many of whom had camped out for tickets the night before—the Great Danes upset the Catamounts, 80-67, to earn their first NCAA bid.

FIERCEST RIVAL: Since the turn of the millennium, Vermont has owned the America East. And when the Great Danes moved to the conference in 2001, the Catamounts owned them too. But by beating Vermont in the 2006 and '07 conference tournament title games, Albany served notice that despite being down 17–8 in the overall series, it's starting to measure up as a worthy adversary.

SEASON REVIEW

SEAS.	W-L	CONF.	COACH
1909-48	*178-212*	*Best early season, 1926-27 (10-1)*	
1948-49	7-14		Merlin Hathaway
1949-50	4-15		Merlin Hathaway
1950-51	6-13		Merlin Hathaway
1951-52	12-6		Merlin Hathaway
1952-53	11-9		Merlin Hathaway
1953-54	13-7		Merlin Hathaway
1954-55	2-16		Merlin Hathaway
1955-56	11-9		Richard Sauers
1956-57	17-5		Richard Sauers
1957-58	17-5		Richard Sauers
1958-59	17-8		Richard Sauers
1959-60	16-10		Richard Sauers
1960-61	22-6		Richard Sauers
1961-62	19-6		Richard Sauers
1962-63	14-12		Richard Sauers
1963-64	11-11		Richard Sauers
1964-65	16-6		Richard Sauers
1965-66	13-9		Richard Sauers
1966-67	15-7		Richard Sauers
1967-68	18-4		Richard Sauers
1968-69	18-6		Richard Sauers
1969-70	13-9		Richard Sauers
1970-71	17-5		Richard Sauers
1971-72	17-6		Richard Sauers
1972-73	17-8		Richard Sauers
1973-74	17-8		Richard Sauers
1974-75	15-10		Richard Sauers

SEAS.	W-L	CONF.	SCORING		COACH	RECORD	
1975-76	12-11		Barry Cavanaugh	13.5	Richard Sauers		
1976-77	19-7		Barry Cavanaugh	13.8	Richard Sauers		
1977-78	15-9		Barry Cavanaugh	15.8	Richard Sauers		
1978-79	20-7		Carmelo Verdejo	17.6	Richard Sauers		
1979-80	21-6		Winston Royal	13.3	Richard Sauers		
1980-81	23-5		John Dieckelman	13.4	Richard Sauers		
1981-82	18-10		John Dieckelman	16.2	Richard Sauers		
1982-83	17-10		John Dieckelman	17.1	Richard Sauers		
1983-84	14-11		Wilson Thomas	12.0	Richard Sauers		
1984-85	22-6		Adam Ursprung	13.6	Richard Sauers		
1985-86	18-9		Adam Ursprung	14.3	Richard Sauers		
1986-87	21-7		Adam Ursprung	17.7	Richard Sauers		
1987-88	16-10		Morrison Teague	18.5	Barry Cavanaugh	16-10	.615
1988-89	20-8		Morrison Teague	19.9	Richard Sauers		
1989-90	20-9		Micheal Shene	14.9	Richard Sauers		
1990-91	14-12		Micheal Shene	13.5	Richard Sauers		
1991-92	21-7		Jason Graber	17.5	Richard Sauers		
1992-93	15-10		Jason Graber	21.5	Richard Sauers		
1993-94	25-3		Jason Graber	20.3	Richard Sauers		
1994-95	18-8		Ted Hotaling	17.9	Richard Sauers		
1995-96	12-15		Andre Duncan	14.0	Richard Sauers		
1996-97	17-10		Andre Duncan	14.3	Richard Sauers	702-330	.680
1997-98	19-8		Andre Duncan	19.3	Scott Hicks		
1998-99	14-14		Todd Cetnar	16.2	Scott Hicks		
1999-2000	11-17		Todd Cetnar	16.1	Scott Hicks	44-39	.530
2000-01	6-22		E.J. Gallup	17.4	Scott Beeten		
2001-02	8-20	5-11	Antione Johnson	11.3	Scott Beeten[a]	7-29	.194
2002-03	7-21	3-13	Jamar Wilson	18.9	Will Brown		
2003-04	5-23	3-15	Levi Levine	14.3	Will Brown		
2004-05	13-15	9-9	Jamar Wilson	16.9	Will Brown		
2005-06	21-11	13-3 ●	Jamar Wilson	17.7	Will Brown		
2006-07	23-10	13-3 ●	Jamar Wilson	18.8	Will Brown		
2007-08	15-15	10-6	Brian Lillis	16.1	Will Brown		
2008-09	15-16	6-10	Tim Ambrose	14.3	Will Brown	106-124	.461

[a] Scott Beeten (1-7) and Will Brown (7-13) both coached during the 2001-02 season.
● NCAA Tournament appearance

PROFILE

University at Albany (State University of New York), Albany, NY
Founded: 1844
Enrollment: 17,684 (12,748 undergraduate)
Colors: Purple and gold
Nickname: Great Danes
Current arena: Recreation and Convocation Center, opened in 1992 (5,000)
First game: 1909
All-time record: 1,108-824 (.573)
Total weeks in AP Top 20/25: 0

Current conference: America East (2001-)
Conference titles:
America East: 1 (2006)
Conference tournament titles:
America East: 2 (2006, '07)
NCAA Tournament appearances: 2
NIT appearances: 0

TOP 5

G **Adam Ursprung** (1983-87)
G **Jamar Wilson** (2002-03, '04-07)
F **Jason Graber** (1990-94)
F **Gary Holway** (1955-59)
F **Morrison Teague** (1985-89)

RECORDS	GAME		SEASON		CAREER	
POINTS	40	Gary Holway, vs. Utica (Feb. 27, 1957)	620	Jamar Wilson (2006-07)	2,164	Jamar Wilson (2002-03, '04-07)
POINTS PER GAME			24.9	Gary Holway (1955-56)	21.0	Rich Margison (1966-69)
REBOUNDS	28	Gary Holway, vs. Utica (Feb. 27, 1957)	462	Don Cohen (1960-61)	1,317	Don Cohen (1957-61)
ASSISTS	15	Stephen Sauers, vs. Trinity (Feb. 27, 1988)	197	Mike Cinque (1985-86)	644	Dan Croutier (1981-85)

ESPN 204 SAGARIN

Alcorn State

Alcorn State can't seem to get much respect. The small, historically black college's location is often misidentified as Lorman, Miss. (The school's in Alcorn State, about eight miles away.) And though the basketball program has a rich tradition, including two NAIA final fours, 16 SWAC titles and six NCAA bids, the NIT once declared its gym too small to host a tourney game, turning the favored Braves into visitors against Mississippi State. No matter. The Braves won anyway.

BEST TEAM: 1978-79 The Braves went 27–0 during the regular season, but few noticed because Larry Bird and Indiana State were going 33–0. The Braves ended up in the NIT, defeating "host" Mississippi State, 80-78, on a buzzer-beating Larry Smith jumper, before falling to Indiana, 73-69. The lineup included 1,000-point scorers Smith, Alfredo Monroe, James Horton, Ronnie Smith and Joe Jenkins.

BEST PLAYER: F Larry Smith (1976-80) Nicknamed Mr. Mean because of his thunderous dunks and intimidating demeanor, Smith led the nation with 15.1 rpg in 1979-80 and was a two-time SWAC player of the year.

BEST COACH: Davey L. Whitney (1969-89, 1996-2003) He led Alcorn to the first NCAA Tourney win by a historically black college (see Game for the Ages). One of the first coaches to regularly use a trapping press, Whitney won 12 SWAC titles, four NAIA district titles and took the Braves to the 1974 NAIA championship game and six NCAA Tournaments.

GAME FOR THE AGES: In 1980, the 28–2 Braves made their first NCAA Tournament appearance and the first for any HBCU, at the expense of South Alabama, 70-62. The team featured 1,000-point scorers Larry Smith, Joe Jenkins, Eddie Baker and Albert Irving, along with Clinton Wyatt (1,002 rebounds).

FIERCEST RIVAL: SWAC East and in-state rival Jackson State has battled Alcorn State 147 times, with JSU holding an 86–61 lead. The Braves had their best run from 1975 to '81, winning eight straight and 12 of 14 overall.

SEASON REVIEW

SEAS.	W-L	CONF.	COACH	SEAS.	W-L	CONF.	COACH
1945-47	*14-6*	*12-2 in 1946-47 under L.T. Harris*		1960-61	19-8		E.E. Simmons
1947-48	16-7		L.T. Harris	1961-62	25-10		E.E. Simmons
1948-49	20-7		Dwight Fisher	1962-63	14-12		E.E. Simmons
1949-50	22-5		Dwight Fisher	1963-64	13-12		E.E. Simmons
1950-51	28-3		Dwight Fisher	1964-65	13-13		E.E. Simmons
1951-52	32-9		Dwight Fisher	1965-66	21-8		E.E. Simmons
1952-53	34-21		Dwight Fisher	1966-67	20-8		Robert Hopkins
1953-54	21-22		Dwight Fisher	1967-68	24-3		Robert Hopkins
1954-55	25-17		Dwight Fisher	1968-69	26-1		Robert Hopkins
1955-56	8-16		Dwight Fisher	1969-70	16-9		Davey L. Whitney
1956-57	12-12		W.A. Broadus	1970-71	16-9		Davey L. Whitney
1957-58	19-15		W.A. Broadus	1971-72	14-10		Davey L. Whitney
1958-59	18-13		W.A. Broadus	1972-73	24-5		Davey L. Whitney
1959-60	18-13		E.E. Simmons	1973-74	29-6		Davey L. Whitney

SEAS.	W-L	CONF.		SCORING		COACH	RECORD	
1974-75	25-10					Davey L. Whitney		
1975-76	27-4					Davey L. Whitney		
1976-77	26-9					Davey L. Whitney		
1977-78	22-7	8-4				Davey L. Whitney		
1978-79	28-1	12-0	■			Davey L. Whitney		
1979-80	28-2	12-0	●			Davey L. Whitney		
1980-81	17-12	8-4				Davey L. Whitney		
1981-82	22-8	10-2	●			Davey L. Whitney		
1982-83	22-10	10-4	●			Davey L. Whitney		
1983-84	21-10	11-3	●			Davey L. Whitney		
1984-85	23-7	13-1	■			Davey L. Whitney		
1985-86	16-13	11-3				Davey L. Whitney		
1986-87	5-23	3-11				Davey L. Whitney		
1987-88	8-21	5-9				Davey L. Whitney		
1988-89	5-23	4-10				Davey L. Whitney		
1989-90	7-22	6-8				Lonnie Walker		
1990-91	8-21	3-9				Lonnie Walker		
1991-92	15-14	8-6				Lonnie Walker		
1992-93	7-20	5-9				Lonnie Walker	37-77	.325
1993-94	3-24	3-11				Sam Weaver		
1994-95	7-19	4-10				Sam Weaver		
1995-96	10-15	7-7				Sam Weaver	20-58	.256
1996-97	11-17	8-6				Davey L. Whitney		
1997-98	12-15	8-8				Davey L. Whitney		
1998-99	23-7	14-2	●	Reuben Stiff	12.1	Davey L. Whitney		
1999-2000	19-10	15-3		Marcus Fleming	16.5	Davey L. Whitney		
2000-01	15-15	13-5		Marcus Fleming	16.7	Davey L. Whitney		
2001-02	21-10	16-2	●	Marcus Fleming	14.9	Davey L. Whitney		
2002-03	14-19	10-8		Lee Cook	16.7	Davey L. Whitney	509-292	.635
2003-04	11-18	9-9		Brian Jackson	13.9	Samuel West		
2004-05	7-22	6-12		Delvin Thompson	14.8	Samuel West		
2005-06	8-20	8-10		Delvin Thompson	17.1	Samuel West		
2006-07	11-19	10-8		Delvin Thompson	15.4	Samuel West		
2007-08	7-24	6-12		Troy Jackson	15.5	Samuel West	44-103	.299
2008-09	6-25	4-14		Troy Jackson	20.0	Larry Smith	6-25	.194

● NCAA Tournament appearance ■ NIT appearance

PROFILE

Alcorn State University, Alcorn State, MS
Founded: 1871
Enrollment: 3,583 (2,705 undergraduate)
Colors: Purple and gold
Nickname: Braves
Current arena: Davey L. Whitney Complex, opened in 1975 (7,000)
First game: 1945
All-time record: 1,078-796 (.575)
Total weeks in AP Top 20/25: 0

Current conference: Southwestern Athletic (1962-)
Conference titles:
SWAC: 16 (1966 [tie], '67 [tie], '68 [tie], '69, '73, '76, '79, '80, '81 [tie], '82 [tie], '84, '85, '86 [tie], '99, 2000, '02)
Conference tournament titles:
SWAC: 7 (1979, '80, '82, '83, '84, '99, 2002)
NCAA Tournament appearances: 6
NIT appearances: 2

TOP 5

G **Johnny McGill** (1974-76)
G **Richard Smith** (1951-55)
F **Nathaniel Archibald** (1970-74)
F **Willie Norwood** (1965-69)
F **Larry Smith** (1976-80)

RECORDS

	GAME		SEASON		CAREER	
POINTS	46	Richard Smith, vs. Texas College (Feb. 2, 1953)	933	Vernon Purnell (1952-53)	2,527	Richard Smith (1951-55)
POINTS PER GAME			24.8	Odell Agnew (1963-64)	N/A	
REBOUNDS	34	Alfred Milton, vs. Dillard (Dec. 22, 1971)	480	Walter Ned (1965-66)	1,432	Alfred Milton (1971-75)
ASSISTS	15	Eddie Archie, vs. Alabama State (1985); vs. Alabama State (1984); vs. North Texas (Jan. 28, 1982)	229	Eddie Archie (1982-83)	766	Eddie Archie (1981-85)

ESPN 211 SAGARIN

AMERICAN

Since joining D1 in 1966-67, American had never Danced until 2008, when the Eagles defeated Colgate for the school's first Patriot League title and NCAA berth. American has traditionally been a training ground for talented coaches: Jim Lynam, Fran Dunphy and Gary Williams all made stops on the Eagles' bench.

BEST TEAM: 1980-81 Gary Williams' third season was a smash: 24 wins, best in Eagles history, and an 11–0 record in the East Coast Conference, despite career scoring leader and senior forward Russell "Boo" Bowers missing 19 games with a knee injury. Bowers returned for American's first-round NIT matchup against Toledo, but shot only two of nine from the field as the Eagles' season came crashing down, 91-83.

BEST PLAYER: C Kermit Washington (1970-73) He may be most famous for the 1977 NBA incident known as the Punch (he crushed the face of Rudy Tomjanovich), but he was one of only five players in NCAA D1 history to average at least 20 ppg and 20 rpg for his career. No one has achieved the feat since.

BEST COACH: Gary Williams (1978-82) Before his NCAA championship in Maryland, Williams coached American to two NIT appearances and a 72–42 record in his first head coaching job. After he left, American didn't make another postseason tournament until the Jeff Jones-helmed 2007-08 squad.

GAME FOR THE AGES: On Dec. 15, 1982, a 19-point lead over No. 5 Georgetown had collapsed to just one with four minutes left after point guard Gordon Austin blew by Patrick Ewing for a layup. Austin, recovering from a thigh injury suffered during practice, scored seven points down the stretch and the Eagles held on to complete the 62-61 shocker.

FIERCEST RIVAL: In 2001-02 and '02-03, Holy Cross eliminated American from the Patriot League final. The annual matchup between the two schools has become a raucous event now known as the Phil Bender game—so-called because the game is the only one to routinely fill Bender Arena.

SEASON REVIEW

SEAS.	W-L	CONF.	COACH	SEAS.	W-L	CONF.	COACH
1926-48	*193-167*	*Arthur Boyd (1944-46), 32-5, .865*		1961-62	10-11		David Carrasco
1948-49	17-9		Stafford Cassell	1962-63	10-14		Jimmy Williams
1949-50	22-7		Stafford Cassell	1963-64	6-18		Jimmy Williams
1950-51	18-10		Stafford Cassell	1964-65	4-19		Jimmy Williams
1951-52	18-7		Stafford Cassell	1965-66	8-14		Alan Kyber
1952-53	15-8		Dutch Schulze	1966-67	16-8		Alan Kyber
1953-54	12-13		Dutch Schulze	1967-68	14-12		Alan Kyber
1954-55	8-18		Dutch Schulze	1968-69	4-19		Alan Kyber
1955-56	11-11		Dutch Schulze	1969-70	11-12	2-3	Tom Young
1956-57	10-13		David Carrasco	1970-71	13-12	2-4	Tom Young
1957-58	24-6		David Carrasco	1971-72	16-8	3-3	Tom Young
1958-59	22-7		David Carrasco	1972-73	21-5	4-2 ■	Tom Young
1959-60	22-7		David Carrasco	1973-74	16-10	4-2	Jim Lynam
1960-61	15-7		David Carrasco	1974-75	16-10	5-1	Jim Lynam

SEAS.	W-L	CONF.	SCORING		COACH	RECORD
1975-76	9-16	1-4	Calvin Brown	14.8	Jim Lynam	
1976-77	13-13	2-3	Calvin Brown	20.1	Jim Lynam	
1977-78	16-12	2-3	Russell Bowers	16.9	Jim Lynam	70-61 .534
1978-79	14-13	7-5	Russell Bowers	22.6	Gary Williams	
1979-80	13-14	5-6	Russell Bowers	26.9	Gary Williams	
1980-81	24-6	11-0 ■	Mark Nickens	15.4	Gary Williams	
1981-82	21-9	8-3 ■	Mark Nickens	19.2	Gary Williams	72-42 .632
1982-83	20-10	7-2	Mark Nickens	15.9	Ed Tapscott	
1983-84	6-22	5-11	Fernando Aunon	16.5	Ed Tapscott	
1984-85	9-19	3-11	Frank Ross	14.7	Ed Tapscott	
1985-86	10-18	3-11	Frank Ross	23.0	Ed Tapscott	
1986-87	13-14	5-9	Frank Ross	25.3	Ed Tapscott	
1987-88	14-14	9-5	Mike Sampson	14.5	Ed Tapscott	
1988-89	17-11	9-5	Ron Draper	16.4	Ed Tapscott	
1989-90	20-9	10-4	Ron Draper	16.1	Ed Tapscott	109-117 .482
1990-91	15-14	8-6	Brian Gilgeous	18.1	Chris Knoche	
1991-92	11-18	8-6	Brian Gilgeous	18.9	Chris Knoche	
1992-93	11-17	6-8	Brian Gilgeous	22.7	Chris Knoche	
1993-94	8-19	5-9	Tim Fudd	19.0	Chris Knoche	
1994-95	9-19	7-7	Christian Ast	18.7	Chris Knoche	
1995-96	12-15	8-8	Darryl Franklin	15.4	Chris Knoche	
1996-97	11-16	7-9	Nathan Smith	17.3	Chris Knoche	77-118 .395
1997-98	9-19	5-11	Nathan Smith	16.3	Art Perry	
1998-99	7-21	2-14	Patrick Doctor	11.0	Art Perry	
1999-2000	11-18	5-11	Patrick Doctor	15.4	Art Perry	27-58 .318
2000-01	7-20	3-13	Patrick Doctor	16.1	Jeff Jones	
2001-02	18-12	10-4	Patrick Doctor	15.0	Jeff Jones	
2002-03	16-14	9-5	Steven Miles	16.4	Jeff Jones	
2003-04	18-13	10-4	Andre Ingram	13.6	Jeff Jones	
2004-05	16-12 ⊗	8-6	Andre Ingram	15.3	Jeff Jones	
2005-06	12-17	7-7	Andre Ingram	12.0	Jeff Jones	
2006-07	16-14	7-7	Andre Ingram	15.2	Jeff Jones	
2007-08	21-12	10-4 ●	Garrison Carr	18.4	Jeff Jones	
2008-09	24-8	13-1 ●	Garrison Carr	17.9	Jeff Jones	148-122 .548

⊗ Records don't reflect games forfeited or vacated. For adjusted records, see p. 521.

● NCAA Tournament appearance ■ NIT appearance

PROFILE

American University, Washington, DC
Founded: 1893
Enrollment: 3,936 (1,444 undergraduate)
Colors: Red, white and blue
Nickname: Eagles
Current arena: Bender Arena, opened in 1988 (4,500)
Previous: Fort Myer Ceremonial Hall 1969-88 (N/A)
First game: 1926
All-time record: 1,043-960 (.521)
Total weeks in AP Top 20/25: 0

Current conference: Patriot League (2001-)
Conference titles:
East Coast: 1 (1981)
Patriot: 4 (2002, '04 [tie], '08, '09)
Conference tournament titles:
Patriot: 2 (2008, '09)
NCAA Tournament appearances: 2
NIT appearances: 3

CONSENSUS ALL-AMERICAS

1960 **Willie Jones** (Little A-A), G

FIRST-ROUND PRO PICKS

1969 **Art Beatty,** Houston (ABA)
1973 **Kermit Washington,** LA Lakers (4)

TOP 5

G **Gordon Austin** (1979-83)
G **Willie Jones** (1957-60)
F **Russell Bowers** (1977-81)
F **Brian Gilgeous** (1989-93)
C **Kermit Washington** (1970-73)

RECORDS

	GAME		SEASON		CAREER	
POINTS	54	Willie Jones, vs. Evansville (March 9, 1960)	726	Russell Bowers (1979-80)	2,056	Russell Bowers (1977-81)
POINTS PER GAME			26.9	Russell Bowers (1979-80)	22.1	Russell Bowers (1977-81)
REBOUNDS	34	Kermit Washington, vs. Georgetown (Feb. 6, 1971)	512	Kermit Washington (1970-71)	1,478	Kermit Washington (1970-73)
ASSISTS	19	Andres Rodriguez, vs. Navy (Jan. 14, 2004)	247	Gordon Austin (1982-83)	691	Gordon Austin (1979-83)

ESPN 262 SAGARIN

APPALACHIAN STATE

ASU, which started its hoops program in 1919 and joined D1 in 1973, has made just two NCAA Tournament appearances. But there's no denying the Mountaineers' lasting imprint. Belus Smawley, a 1943 NAIA All-America, is one of the game's original jump shooters. And while at ASU, coach Press Maravich nurtured the talent of his son, Pete, who became one of the greatest college players of all time.

BEST TEAM: 1999-2000 Coming off two straight 21-win seasons—and two straight losses in the Southern tournament final—ASU, with four senior starters, rattled off 22 wins and then soared past top-seed College of Charleston in the conference tourney final to earn the school's second NCAA Tournament bid.

BEST PLAYER: G Tyson Patterson (1996-2000) Listed generously at 5'8", Patterson was a quick, pass-first guard who often electrified the crowd with his signature half-court alley-oop lobs. His 638 assists are 130 more than anyone else on the school's all-time list. He also led his team in steals his final three seasons.

BEST COACH: Bobby Cremins (1975-81) Before moving on to fame at Georgia Tech, Cremins established his coaching chops by winning 100 games in six seasons at ASU and leading the school in 1979 to its first NCAA Tournament.

GAME FOR THE AGES: ASU fans remember the 2000 Southern Conference tournament semifinal against Furman as the win that almost wasn't. Playing at home, the heavily favored Mountaineers found themselves down by two with less than a minute to play. That's when Tyson Patterson took a rebound coast to coast for a game-tying layup. ASU went on to win, 60-56.

FIERCEST RIVAL: ASU and Western Carolina were the only public schools playing basketball in the western half of the state until 1964. They have played at least twice every season since 1935, and all that familiarity and proximity breeds contempt. ASU holds the overall edge, either 108–63 (according to ASU) or 104–57 (WCU).

SEASON REVIEW

SEAS.	W-L	CONF.	COACH	SEAS.	W-L	CONF.	COACH
1919-47	*232-122*	*22-3 in 1940-41 under Clyde Canipe*		1960-61	17-10		Bob Light
1947-48	20-8		Francis Hoover	1961-62	11-13		Bob Light
1948-49	14-6		Francis Hoover	1962-63	14-12		Bob Light
1949-50	21-9		Francis Hoover	1963-64	14-12		Bob Light
1950-51	16-8		Francis Hoover	1964-65	14-10		Bob Light
1951-52	18-6		Francis Hoover	1965-66	17-10		Bob Light
1952-53	5-18		Francis Hoover	1966-67	21-8		Bob Light
1953-54	4-20		Francis Hoover	1967-68	14-13		Bob Light
1954-55	12-12		Francis Hoover	1968-69	12-15		Bob Light
1955-56	8-13		Francis Hoover	1969-70	15-12		Bob Light
1956-57	4-20		Francis Hoover	1970-71	8-16		Bob Light
1957-58	12-12		Bob Light	1971-72	8-18		Bob Light
1958-59	16-9		Bob Light	1972-73	6-20	3-8	Press Maravich
1959-60	19-8		Bob Light	1973-74	5-20	1-11	Press Maravich

SEAS.	W-L	CONF.	SCORING		COACH	RECORD	
1974-75	3-23	1-11	Ed Kane	15.6	Press Maravich[a]	14-63	.182
1975-76	13-14	6-6	Darryl Robinson	15.1	Bobby Cremins		
1976-77	17-12	8-4	Walter Anderson	13.2	Bobby Cremins		
1977-78	15-13	9-3	Darryl Robinson	17.9	Bobby Cremins		
1978-79	23-6	11-3 ●	Darryl Robinson	15.1	Bobby Cremins		
1979-80	12-16	6-10	Walter Anderson	14.5	Bobby Cremins		
1980-81	20-9	11-5	Charles Payton	17.1	Bobby Cremins	100-70	.588
1981-82	11-15	6-10	John Fitch	15.0	Kevin Cantwell		
1982-83	6-21	3-13	David Lawrence	15.3	Kevin Cantwell		
1983-84	13-16	8-8	David Lawrence	14.5	Kevin Cantwell		
1984-85	14-14	7-9	Glenn Clyburn	16.1	Kevin Cantwell		
1985-86	17-12	9-7	Rob Davis	14.7	Kevin Cantwell	61-78	.439
1986-87	7-21	3-13	Darryl Person	10.6	Tom Apke		
1987-88	16-13	8-8	Kemp Phillips	14.2	Tom Apke		
1988-89	20-8	8-6	Sam Gibson	16.7	Tom Apke		
1989-90	19-11	8-6	Sam Gibson	15.2	Tom Apke		
1990-91	16-14	7-7	Steve Spurlock	18.6	Tom Apke		
1991-92	15-14	9-5	Billy Ross	15.9	Tom Apke		
1992-93	13-15	8-10	Billy Ross	24.4	Tom Apke		
1993-94	16-11	12-6	Chad McClendon	17.1	Tom Apke		
1994-95	9-20	4-10	Chad McClendon	18.4	Tom Apke		
1995-96	8-20	3-11	Kareem Livingston	15.6	Tom Apke	139-147	.486
1996-97	14-14	8-6	Junior Braswell	20.3	Buzz Peterson		
1997-98	21-8	13-2	Kareem Livingston	12.4	Buzz Peterson		
1998-99	21-8	13-3	Marshall Phillips	15.9	Buzz Peterson		
1999-2000	23-9	13-3 ●	Rufus Leach	16.4	Buzz Peterson	79-39	.670
2000-01	11-20	7-9	Josh Shehan	11.3	Houston Fancher		
2001-02	10-18	5-11	Donald Payne	9.0	Houston Fancher		
2002-03	19-10	11-5	Shawn Hall	20.5	Houston Fancher		
2003-04	9-21	4-12	Noah Brown	13.1	Houston Fancher		
2004-05	18-12	9-7	Noah Brown	12.6	Houston Fancher		
2005-06	14-16	6-8	D.J. Thompson	19.1	Houston Fancher		
2006-07	25-8	15-3 ■	D.J. Thompson	15.6	Houston Fancher		
2007-08	18-13	13-7	Donte Minter	13.9	Houston Fancher		
2008-09	13-18	9-11	Kellen Brand	14.8	Houston Fancher	137-136	.502

[a] **Russ Bergman also coached during the 1974-75 season, but the entire record is credited to Press Maravich.**

● NCAA Tournament appearance ■ NIT appearance

PROFILE

Appalachian State University, Boone, NC
Founded: 1899
Enrollment: 15,871 (13,997 undergraduate)
Colors: Black and gold
Nickname: Mountaineers
Current arena: Holmes Center, opened in 2000 (8,325)
Previous: Varsity Gym, 1968-2000 (8,000); Broome-Kirk Gym, 1950s-68 (N/A); University Gym, 1919-50s (N/A)
First game: 1919
All-time record: 1,096-953 (.535)
Total weeks in AP Top 20/25: 0

Current conference: Southern (1971-)
Conference titles:
Southern: 9 (1978, '79, '81 [tie], '98 [tie], '99 [tie], 2000 [tie], '03 [tie], '07 [tie], '08 [tie])
Conference tournament titles:
Southern: 2 (1979, 2000)
NCAA Tournament appearances: 2
NIT appearances: 1

TOP 5

G **Walter Anderson** (1976-80)
G **Tyson Patterson** (1996-2000)
G **D.J. Thompson** (2002-06)
F **Charles Payton** (1978-82)
F **Darryl Robinson** (1975-79)

RECORDS

RECORDS	GAME		SEASON		CAREER	
POINTS	56	Stan Davis, vs. Carson-Newman (Jan. 24, 1974)	683	Billy Ross (1992-93)	1,794	Don King (1957-61)
POINTS PER GAME			26.6	Dave Abernathy (1955-56)	21.0	John Pyecha (1951-55)
REBOUNDS	24	Larry Dudas, vs. UNC Wilmington (Feb. 26, 1972); Tony Searcy, vs. High Point (Feb. 20, 1978)	359	Tony Searcy (1977-78)	1,108	Wayne Duncan (1961-65)
ASSISTS	14	Tyson Patterson, vs. Lees-McRae (Nov. 27, 1999)	218	Tyson Patterson (1999-2000)	638	Tyson Patterson (1996-2000)

ESPN 49 SAGARIN

ARIZONA

Dr. Naismith surely could not have imagined a basketball powerhouse blooming in the Arizona desert, but that's what happened in Tucson after Lute Olson's arrival in 1983, as the Wildcats rose dramatically from Pac-10 doormat to NCAA champs. From Damon Stoudamire to Mike Bibby to Jerryd Bayless, the Silver Fox landed so many outstanding lead guards that Arizona is known as Point Guard U.

BEST TEAM: 1987-88 The first of Olson's quartet of Final Four Wildcat squads went 35–3, powered by Sean Elliott and Steve Kerr. Racing out of the blocks, the Cats defeated three Top-10 opponents to rise to the No. 1 national ranking for the first time in the program's history. The Pac-10 regular-season and tournament champions also featured Tom Tolbert, Jud Buechler and future MLB centerfielder Kenny Lofton. The Wildcats met their end in the NCAA semis at the hands of Oklahoma, 86-78, despite 31 points from Elliott.

BEST PLAYER: G/F SEAN ELLIOTT (1985-89) Tucson's own, Elliott is Arizona's all-time leading scorer (2,555), an all-the-more impressive stat considering that the three-point shot was not introduced to the college game until his sophomore season. A true inside-outside threat (140 career treys) who was twice named the Pac-10 Player of the Year, he's the only Cat to lead the team in scoring four straight seasons. Elliott led UA to 105 wins and the 1988 Final Four, and was the 1989 Wooden Award winner.

BEST COACH: LUTE OLSON (1983-2007) Just 11–17 his first season in the Old Pueblo, Olson's Cats won the Pac-10 regular-season title two years later. Arizona missed the NCAA Tournament just once in Olson's tenure, while making four trips to the Final Four and winning the 1997 title. For 20 straight seasons (1987-2007), his Cats achieved at least 20 wins.

GAME FOR THE AGES: On March 8, 2001, in the final week of the regular season, Arizona defeated No. 1 Stanford, 76-75, at Maples Pavilion. With :12 remaining, the Wildcats' Loren Woods found Michael Wright, who split Stanford's Collins twins and drove for the winning basket. Arizona rode the momentum all the way to NCAA championship game in Minneapolis, but lost to Duke, 82-72.

HEARTBREAKER: Vying for their fourth Final Four appearance in 12 seasons, the Wildcats led No.1-seed Illinois by 15 with four minutes left in their 2005 Elite Eight matchup. Then four Arizona turnovers and four Illinois three-pointers lifted the Illini to tie the game at 80 with :39 left. Illinois went on to win in overtime, 90-89.

FIERCEST RIVAL: Since Olson's arrival, UCLA has supplanted the Cats' natural rival, Arizona State. Some of Arizona's best players, such as Luke Walton (son of UCLA great Bill), have come from the Bruins' backyard. As a result, either the Bruins or the Wildcats have won at least a share of the Pac-10 regular-season title in 19 of the 24 seasons between 1985-86 and 2008-09.

FANFARE AND HOOPLA: John "Button" Salmon is Arizona's own version of the Gipper. Hospitalized in 1926 after a serious car accident, the quarterback and student body president delivered a message from his deathbed, instructing the Wildcats to "bear down." Thus, Bear Down became the official school slogan and the name of the Cats' fight song.

FAN FAVORITE: G STEVE KERR (1983-86, '87-88) An All-America as a senior and for years a member of Michael Jordan's NBA champion Chicago Bulls, Kerr is most loved for the courage he exhibited in the wake of the 1984 terrorist assassination of his father, Malcolm, president of the American University in Beirut, Lebanon.

CONSENSUS ALL-AMERICAS

1988, '89	**Sean Elliott,** G/F
1995	**Damon Stoudamire,** G
1998	**Mike Bibby,** G
1998	**Miles Simon,** G
1999	**Jason Terry,** G

FIRST-ROUND PRO PICKS

1979	**Larry Demic,** New York (9)
1989	**Sean Elliott,** San Antonio (3)
1989	**Anthony Cook,** Phoenix (24)
1991	**Brian Williams,** Orlando (10)
1993	**Chris Mills,** Cleveland (22)
1994	**Khalid Reeves,** Miami (12)
1995	**Damon Stoudamire,** Toronto (7)
1998	**Mike Bibby,** Vancouver (2)
1998	**Michael Dickerson,** Houston (14)
1999	**Jason Terry,** Atlanta (10)
2001	**Richard Jefferson,** Houston (13)
2004	**Andre Iguodala,** Philadelphia (9)
2005	**Channing Frye,** New York (8)
2008	**Jerryd Bayless,** Indiana (11)
2009	**Jordan Hill,** New York (8)

PROFILE

University of Arizona, Tucson, AZ
Founded: 1885
Enrollment: 38,057 (28,422 undergraduate)
Colors: Cardinal and navy
Nickname: Wildcats
Current arena: McKale Memorial Center, opened in 1973 (14,545)
Previous: Bear Down Gym, opened as University Gymnasium, 1927-73 (3,600)
First game: 1904
All-time record: 1,566-860-1 (.645)
Total weeks in AP Top 20/25: 412

Current conference: Pacific-10 (1978-)
Conference titles:
Border: 11 (1932, '36, '40 [tie], '43, '46, '47, '48, '49, '50, '51, '53 [tie])
WAC: 1 (1976)
Pac-10: 11 (1986, '88, '89, '90 [tie], '91, '93, '94, '98, 2000 [tie], '03, '05)
Conference tournament titles:
Pac-10: 4 (1988, '89, '90, 2002)
NCAA Tournaments: 28 (1 appearance vacated)
Sweet 16s (since 1975): 13
Final Fours: 4
Titles: 1 (1997)

NIT appearances: 3

TOP 5

G	**Jason Gardner** (1999-2003)
G	**Damon Stoudamire** (1991-95)
G/F	**Sean Elliott** (1985-89)
F	**Chris Mills** (1990-93)
C	**Bob Elliott** (1973-77)

RECORDS	GAME		SEASON		CAREER	
POINTS	46	Ernie McCray, vs. Cal State LA (Feb. 6, 1960)	848	Khalid Reeves (1993-94)	2,555	Sean Elliott (1985-89)
POINTS PER GAME			24.2	Khalid Reeves (1993-94)	23.9	Coniel Norman (1972-74)
REBOUNDS	26	Joe Skaisgir, vs. Cal State LA (Jan. 31, 1962); Bill Reeves, vs. UC Santa Barbara (Feb. 1, 1956)	373	Leo Johnson (1951-52)	1,190	Al Fleming (1972-76)
ASSISTS	19	Russell Brown, vs. Grand Canyon (Dec. 8, 1979)	247	Russell Brown (1978-79)	810	Russell Brown (1977-81)

SEASON REVIEW

SEASON	W-L	CONF.	COMMENTS		COACH	RECORD	
1904-17	*47-13-1*		*Undefeated in back-to-back seasons, 1914-15 and '15-16 (9-0, 5-0)*				
1917-18	3-2				J.F. McKale		
1918-19	6-3				J.F. McKale		
1919-20	9-5				J.F. McKale		
1920-21	7-0		A.L. Slonaker	23.7	J.F. McKale	49-12	.803
1921-22	10-2		A.L. Slonaker	7.5	James H. Pierce	10-2	.833
1922-23	17-3		Harold Tovrea	15.8	Basil Stanley		
1923-24	14-3		Harold Tovrea	17.3	Basil Stanley	31-6	.838
1924-25	7-4		Clarence Skousen	8.4	Walter Davis	7-4	.636
1925-26	6-7		Byron Drachman	9.0	Fred A. Enke		
1926-27	13-4		Charles Miller	8.9	Fred A. Enke		
1927-28	13-3		Larry Edwards	7.9	Fred A. Enke		
1928-29	19-4		Neal Goodman	9.6	Fred A. Enke		
1929-30	15-6		Neal Goodman	8.4	Fred A. Enke		
1930-31	9-6		Jack Raffety	10.9	Fred A. Enke		
1931-32	18-2	8-2	Howard Abbott	11.2	Fred A. Enke		
1932-33	19-5	7-3	Jack Raffety	8.0	Fred A. Enke		
1933-34	18-9	9-3	Vince Byrne	10.2	Fred A. Enke		
1934-35	11-8	5-7	Walt Scholtzhauer	11.6	Fred A. Enke		
1935-36	16-7	11-5	Lorry DiGrazia	8.3	Fred A. Enke		
1936-37	14-11	9-7	Lorry DiGrazia	8.4	Fred A. Enke		
1937-38	13-8	9-7	Lorry DiGrazia	10.0	Fred A. Enke		

SEAS.	W-L	CONF.	POSTSEASON	SCORING		REBOUNDS		ASSISTS		COACH	RECORD	
1938-39	12-11	8-10		George Jordan	8.7					Fred A. Enke		
1939-40	15-10	12-4		George Jordan	9.2					Fred A. Enke		
1940-41	11-7			Vince Cullen	11.0					Fred A. Enke		
1941-42	9-13	6-10		Vince Cullen	10.4					Fred A. Enke		
1942-43	22-2	16-2		Bob Ruman	11.4					Fred A. Enke		
1943-44	12-2			George Genung	13.6					Fred A. Enke		
1944-45	7-11	3-4		Jimmy Steele	12.1					Fred A. Enke		
1945-46	25-5	15-2	NIT QUARTERFINALS	Link Richmond	14.8					Fred A. Enke		
1946-47	21-3	14-2		Link Richmond	17.9					Fred A. Enke		
1947-48	19-10	12-4		Morris Udall	13.2					Fred A. Enke		
1948-49	17-11	13-3		Leon Blevins	13.5					Fred A. Enke		
1949-50	26-5	14-2	NIT FIRST ROUND	Leon Blevins	14.9					Fred A. Enke		
1950-51	24-6	15-1	NCAA 1ST RD, NIT QUARTERS	Bob Honea	12.8	Leo Johnson	12.4	Leo Johnson	4.9	Fred A. Enke		
1951-52	11-16	6-8		Bill Kermmeries	14.1	Jerry Dillon	7.9	Roger Johnson	3.2	Fred A. Enke		
1952-53	13-11	11-3		Bill Kermmeries	13.8	Teddy Lazovich	6.3			Fred A. Enke		
1953-54	14-10	8-4		Hadie Redd	13.2	Hadie Redd	7.0			Fred A. Enke		
1954-55	8-17	3-9		Hadie Redd	13.6	Hadie Redd	9.8			Fred A. Enke		
1955-56	11-15	6-6		Ed Nymeyer	15.6	Bill Reeves	13.2			Fred A. Enke		
1956-57	13-13	5-5		Ed Nymeyer	15.7	Bill Reeves	10.7			Fred A. Enke		
1957-58	10-15	4-6		Ed Nymeyer	15.7	Ernie McCray	10.7			Fred A. Enke		
1958-59	4-22	1-9		Ernie McCray	15.9	Ernie McCray	9.8			Fred A. Enke		
1959-60	10-14	4-6		Ernie McCray	23.9	Ernie McCray	12.2			Fred A. Enke		
1960-61	11-15	5-5		Joe Skaisgir	19.4	Joe Skaisgir	10.3			Fred A. Enke	509-324	.611
1961-62	12-14			Joe Skaisgir	20.3	Joe Skaisgir	12.1			Bruce Larson		
1962-63	13-13	3-7		Albert Johnson	12.9	Albert Johnson	9.7			Bruce Larson		
1963-64	15-11	4-6		Albert Johnson	15.2	Albert Johnson	11.0			Bruce Larson		
1964-65	17-9	5-5		Warren Rustand	14.2	Albert Johnson	9.0			Bruce Larson		
1965-66	15-11	5-5		Ted Pickett	16.5	Mike Aboud	8.4			Bruce Larson		
1966-67	8-17	3-7		Bill Davis	15.4	Bill Davis	7.7			Bruce Larson		
1967-68	11-13	4-6		Bill Davis	17.5	Bill Davis	10.6			Bruce Larson		
1968-69	17-10	5-5		Bill Warner	15.0	Eddie Myers	10.3			Bruce Larson		
1969-70	12-14	8-6		Bill Warner	20.3	Tom Lee	9.9			Bruce Larson		
1970-71	10-16	3-11		Bill Warner	20.9	Eddie Myers	9.2			Bruce Larson		
1971-72	6-20	4-10		Jim Huckestein	17.3	Lynard Harris	9.4			Bruce Larson	136-148	.479
1972-73	16-10	9-5		Coniel Norman	24.0	Al Fleming	9.9	Eric Money	3.7	Fred Snowden		
1973-74	19-7	9-5		Coniel Norman	23.8	Bob Elliott	10.7	Eric Money	5.5	Fred Snowden		
1974-75	22-7	9-5		Bob Elliott	23.3	Al Fleming	11.8	Gilbert Myles	5.5	Fred Snowden		
1975-76	24-9	11-3	NCAA REGIONAL FINALS	Bob Elliott	18.0	Bob Elliott	10.3	Jim Rappis	3.5	Fred Snowden		
1976-77	21-6	10-4	NCAA FIRST ROUND	Herman Harris	20.0	Philip Taylor	10.8	Gary Harrison	4.7	Fred Snowden		
1977-78	15-11	6-8		Philip Taylor	16.6	Philip Taylor	8.1	Russell Brown	7.6	Fred Snowden		
1978-79	16-11	10-8		Larry Demic	19.3	Larry Demic	10.3	Russell Brown	9.1	Fred Snowden		
1979-80	12-15	6-12		Joe Nehls	19.3	Frank Smith	6.0	Russell Brown	7.4	Fred Snowden		
1980-81	13-14	8-10		Ron Davis	19.6	Robbie Dosty	6.6	Russell Brown	6.1	Fred Snowden		
1981-82	9-18	4-14		Greg Cook	14.5	Frank Smith	7.8	Ricky Walker	3.3	Fred Snowden	167-108	.607
1982-83	4-24	1-17		Frank Smith	13.7	Frank Smith	7.6	Brock Brunkhorst	4.6	Ben Lindsey	4-24	.143
1983-84	11-17	8-10		Peter Williams	14.5	Peter Williams	9.9	Brock Brunkhorst	3.5	Lute Olson		
1984-85	21-10	12-6	NCAA FIRST ROUND	Eddie Smith	16.1	Peter Williams	8.5	Brock Brunkhorst	5.2	Lute Olson		
1985-86	23-9	14-4	NCAA FIRST ROUND	Sean Elliott	15.6	John Edgar	7.3	Steve Kerr	3.9	Lute Olson		
1986-87	18-12	13-5	NCAA FIRST ROUND	Sean Elliott	19.3	Anthony Cook	7.2	Sean Elliott	3.7	Lute Olson		
1987-88	35-3	17-1	NCAA NATIONAL SEMIFINALS	Sean Elliott	19.6	Anthony Cook	7.1	Steve Kerr	3.9	Lute Olson		
1988-89	29-4	17-1	NCAA REGIONAL SEMIFINALS	Sean Elliott	22.3	Anthony Cook	7.2	Kenny Lofton	4.1	Lute Olson		
1989-90	25-7	15-3	NCAA SECOND ROUND	Jud Buechler	14.9	Jud Buechler	8.3	Matt Muehlebach	5.3	Lute Olson		
1990-91	28-7	14-4	NCAA REGIONAL SEMIFINALS	Chris Mills	15.6	Brian Williams	7.8	Matt Othick	5.2	Lute Olson		
1991-92	24-7	13-5	NCAA FIRST ROUND	Sean Rooks	16.3	Chris Mills	7.9	Matt Othick	5.3	Lute Olson		
1992-93	24-4	17-1	NCAA FIRST ROUND	Chris Mills	20.4	Chris Mills	7.9	Damon Stoudamire	5.7	Lute Olson		
1993-94	29-6	14-4	NCAA NATIONAL SEMIFINALS	Khalid Reeves	24.2	Ray Owes	8.1	Damon Stoudamire	5.9	Lute Olson		
1994-95	23-8	⊗ 13-5	NCAA FIRST ROUND	Damon Stoudamire	22.8	Ray Owes	8.1	Damon Stoudamire	7.3	Lute Olson		
1995-96	26-7	⊗ 13-5	NCAA REGIONAL SEMIFINALS	Ben Davis	14.2	Ben Davis	9.5	Reggie Geary	7.0	Lute Olson		
1996-97	**25-9**	**11-7**	**NATIONAL CHAMPION**	**Michael Dickerson**	**18.9**	**A.J. Bramlett**	**6.9**	**Mike Bibby**	**5.2**	**Lute Olson**		
1997-98	30-5	17-1	NCAA REGIONAL FINALS	Michael Dickerson	18.0	A.J. Bramlett	7.7	Mike Bibby	5.7	Lute Olson		
1998-99	22-7	⊗ 13-5	NCAA FIRST ROUND	Jason Terry	21.9	A.J. Bramlett	9.4	Jason Terry	5.5	Lute Olson		
1999-2000	27-7	15-3	NCAA SECOND ROUND	Loren Woods	15.6	Michael Wright	8.7	Jason Gardner	4.8	Lute Olson		
2000-01	28-8	15-3	NCAA RUNNER-UP	Gilbert Arenas	16.2	Michael Wright	7.8	Jason Gardner	4.1	Lute Olson		
2001-02	24-10	12-6	NCAA REGIONAL SEMIFINALS	Jason Gardner	20.4	Luke Walton	7.3	Luke Walton	6.3	Lute Olson		
2002-03	28-4	17-1	NCAA REGIONAL FINALS	Jason Gardner	14.8	Channing Frye	8.0	Jason Gardner	4.9	Lute Olson		
2003-04	20-10	11-7	NCAA FIRST ROUND	Hassan Adams	17.2	Andre Iguodala	8.4	Andre Iguodala	4.9	Lute Olson		
2004-05	30-7	15-3	NCAA REGIONAL FINALS	Salim Stoudamire	18.4	Channing Frye	7.6	Mustafa Shakur	4.5	Lute Olson		
2005-06	20-13	11-7	NCAA SECOND ROUND	Hassan Adams	17.5	Ivan Radenovic	6.3	Mustafa Shakur	4.7	Lute Olson		
2006-07	20-11	11-7	NCAA FIRST ROUND	Marcus Williams	16.6	Ivan Radenovic	7.6	Mustafa Shakur	6.9	Lute Olson	587-190	.755▼
2007-08	19-15	9-9	NCAA FIRST ROUND	Jerryd Bayless	19.7	Jordan Hill	7.9	Nic Wise	4.4	Kevin O'Neill	19-15	.559
2008-09	21-14	9-9	NCAA REGIONAL SEMIFINALS	Jordan Hill	18.3	Jordan Hill	11.0	Nic Wise	4.6	Russ Pennell	21-14	.600

⊗ Records don't reflect games forfeited or vacated. For adjusted records, see p. 521.

▼ Coach's record adjusted to reflect games forfeited or vacated: 589-187, .759. For yearly totals, see p. 521.

ESPN 94 SAGARIN

ARIZONA STATE

The Sun Devils morphed from also-ran to desert power in the early 1960s, while UCLA's star was still ascendant. Contenders in three conferences (Border, WAC, Pac-10) under coach Ned Wulk, Arizona State came within a game of the Final Four three times (1961, '63, '75). The program has had its struggles since Wulk's departure in 1982, including damage from the discovery of a devastating point-shaving scandal in the mid-1990s.

BEST TEAM: 1980-81 In just its third season as a member of the Pac-10, ASU went 24–4 and finished second in the conference. Led by future pros Byron Scott (16.6 ppg), Lafayette "Fat" Lever, Sam Williams and Alton Lister, Wulk's team was ranked as high as No. 3 in the nation and beat three Top-10 teams, including No. 8 UCLA in triple-overtime and No. 1 Oregon State on its home court in Corvallis. But the No. 2-seed Sun Devils were upset by No. 7-seed Kansas, 88-71, in the second round of the NCAA Tournament.

BEST PLAYER: G Byron Scott (1979-81, '82-83) A sweet-shooting guard from Inglewood, Calif., Scott was the 1980 Pac-10 Rookie of the Year and left ASU as its all-time leading scorer (1,572 points, now No. 7). Averaging 17.5 ppg over his three-year career, Scott led the Sun Devils to their best season (24–4) as a sophomore, scoring 25 in the 87-67 upset of No. 1 Oregon State. The fourth pick in the 1983 NBA draft, he won three titles with the Lakers and later became an NBA head coach.

BEST COACH: Ned Wulk (1957-82) By far the winningest coach in ASU history (405–273), Wulk had 16 winning records in his 25 seasons, guiding the Sun Devils to nine NCAA Tournaments, including three Elite Eights. The Wells Fargo Arena floor is named in his honor.

GAME FOR THE AGES: ASU shellacked undefeated Oregon State, 87-67, in Corvallis on March 7, 1981, the final game of the regular season. It was the program's first and only victory over a No. 1 team. Led by Scott's 25 points, the Sun Devils shot a blistering 77% in the first half (64% for game).

HEARTBREAKER: On March 2, 2000, Oregon scored six points in four seconds to stun the Sun Devils, 76-74, in what Ducks fans still fondly remember as the Miracle at Mac Court. After Oregon's Alex Scales hit a three-pointer, ASU's inbounds pass skimmed off the hands of Eddie House. Darius Wright's subsequent 22-foot three-pointer won it for OU at the buzzer.

FIERCEST RIVAL: The basketball version of ASU's annual gridiron Duel in the Desert with Arizona has not been pretty for the Sun Devils, who trail in the series, 78–138. ASU held its own during Wulk's tenure in Tempe, but since his retirement the Sun Devils have won just 13 of 56 contests.

FANFARE AND HOOPLA: No, that's not a gang sign. Often mistaken for the University of Texas' digital Hook 'Em Horns sign or Wichita State's louche Shocker gesture, the Sun Devils' Pitchfork hand formation has certainly caught on. A three-finger lopsided W is formed by touching your ring finger to your thumb and then urging the Sun Devils to "fork 'em."

Byron Scott led the Sun Devils to their best season (24–4) as a sophomore, scoring 25 in the 87-67 upset of No. 1 Oregon State.

FAN FAVORITE: G Eddie House (1996-2000) ASU's all-time leading scorer, House was a trash-talking gunner with game to match. On Jan. 8, 2000, he put up a school-record 61 points in a double-OT win at Cal, and scored 40 or more three other times that season.

FIRST-ROUND PRO PICKS

1964	**Joe Caldwell,** Detroit (2)
1975	**Lionel Hollins,** Portland (6)
1981	**Alton Lister,** Milwaukee (21)
1982	**Lafayette Lever,** Portland (11)
1983	**Byron Scott,** San Diego (4)
1995	**Mario Bennett,** Phoenix (27)
2005	**Ike Diogu,** Golden State (9)
2009	**James Harden,** Oklahoma City (3)

PROFILE

Arizona State University, Tempe, AZ
Founded: 1885
Enrollment: 50,397 (41,626 undergraduate)
Colors: Maroon and gold
Nickname: Sun Devils
Current arena: Wells Fargo Arena, opened in 1974 (14,088)
First game: 1911
All-time record: 1,205-1,082 (.527)
Total weeks in AP Top 20/25: 94

Current conference: Pacific-10 (1978-)
Conference titles:
Border: 4 (1958, '59 [tie], '61 [tie], '62)
WAC: 4 (1963, '64 [tie], '73, '75)
Conference tournament titles: 0
NCAA Tournament appearances: 13
Sweet 16s (since 1975): 2
NIT appearances: 10

CONSENSUS ALL-AMERICAS

2009 **James Harden,** G

TOP 5

G **Eddie House** (1996-2000)
G **Lafayette Lever** (1978-82)
G **Byron Scott** (1979-81, '82-83)
F **Joe Caldwell** (1961-64)
F **Ike Diogu** (2002-05)

RECORDS

	GAME		SEASON		CAREER	
POINTS	61	Eddie House, vs. California (Jan. 8, 2000)	736	Eddie House (1999-2000)	2,044	Eddie House (1996-2000)
POINTS PER GAME			23.0	Eddie House (1999-2000)	21.4	Ike Diogu (2002-05)
REBOUNDS	27	Mark Landsberger, vs. San Diego State (Dec. 3, 1976)	415	Tony Cerkvenik (1960-61)	1,022	Tony Cerkvenik (1960-63)
ASSISTS	16	Ahlon Lewis, vs. Northern Arizona (Dec. 3, 1997)	294	Ahlon Lewis (1997-98)	454	Bobby Thompson (1983-87)

SEASON REVIEW

SEASON	W-L	CONF.	COMMENTS	COACH	RECORD	
1911-18	*33-17*		*One losing season, 0-1 in 1916-17 under coach George Schaeffer*			
1918-19	3-4			George Cooper		
1919-20	5-3			George Cooper		
1920-21	11-3			George Cooper		
1921-22	10-1			George Cooper	43-15	.741
1922-23	8-4			Ernest Willis	8-4	.667
1923-24	3-9			Aaron McCreary		
1924-25	11-6			Aaron McCreary		
1925-26	9-3			Aaron McCreary		
1926-27	4-8			Aaron McCreary		
1927-28	10-5			Aaron McCreary		

SEASON	W-L	CONF.	COMMENTS	COACH	RECORD	
1928-29	5-12			Aaron McCreary		
1929-30	6-11			Aaron McCreary	48-54	.471
1930-31	12-6	8-4		Ted Shipkey		
1931-32	7-12	4-8		Ted Shipkey		
1932-33	13-12	7-9		Ted Shipkey	32-30	.516
1933-34	9-11	8-10		Rudy Lavik		
1934-35	8-11	3-9		Rudy Lavik		
1935-36	12-14	11-7		Earl Pomeroy		
1936-37	8-12	7-11		Earl Pomeroy		
1937-38	11-12	9-9		Earl Pomeroy		
1938-39	13-13	11-11		Earl Pomeroy	44-51	.463

SEAS.	W-L	CONF.	POSTSEASON	SCORING		REBOUNDS		ASSISTS		COACH	RECORD	
1939-40	8-13	7-11								Rudy Lavik		
1940-41	8-11									Rudy Lavik		
1941-42	10-10	10-6								Rudy Lavik		
1942-43	10-9	6-6								Rudy Lavik		
1943-44	12-2	12-2								Rudy Lavik		
1944-45	5-9	3-5								Rudy Lavik		
1945-46	12-16	6-8								Rudy Lavik		
1946-47	7-13	6-11								Rudy Lavik		
1947-48	13-11	9-7								Rudy Lavik	102-116	.468
1948-49	12-17	4-12								Bill Kajikawa		
1949-50	12-14	10-6								Bill Kajikawa		
1950-51	8-16	6-10								Bill Kajikawa		
1951-52	8-16	6-8								Bill Kajikawa		
1952-53	12-7	10-4		Lester Dean	13.1	Lester Dean	4.3			Bill Kajikawa		
1953-54	5-18	3-9		Dick Daugherty	16.5					Bill Kajikawa		
1954-55	9-13	8-4		Don Weischedel	15.9					Bill Kajikawa		
1955-56	11-15	5-7		Royce Youree	13.9					Bill Kajikawa		
1956-57	10-15	4-6		Jim Newman	15.6	Garth Wilson	11.0			Bill Kajikawa	87-131	.399
1957-58	13-13	8-2	NCAA FIRST ROUND	Jim Newman	16.1	Al Nealey	9.1			Ned Wulk		
1958-59	17-9	7-3		Al Nealey	17.7	Al Nealey	10.3			Ned Wulk		
1959-60	16-7	7-3		Al Nealey	18.4	Al Nealey	11.9			Ned Wulk		
1960-61	23-6	9-1	NCAA REGIONAL FINALS	Larry Armstrong	19.9	Tony Cerkvenik	14.3			Ned Wulk		
1961-62	23-4	10-0	NCAA FIRST ROUND	Larry Armstrong	17.2	Tony Cerkvenik	12.2			Ned Wulk		
1962-63	26-3	9-1	NCAA REGIONAL FINALS	Joe Caldwell	19.7	Art Becker	11.2			Ned Wulk		
1963-64	16-11	7-3	NCAA FIRST ROUND	Joe Caldwell	21.8	Joe Caldwell	12.2			Ned Wulk		
1964-65	13-14	4-6		Dennis Dairman	20.5	Dennis Hamilton	8.0			Ned Wulk		
1965-66	12-14	3-7		Freddie Lewis	22.7	Dennis Hamilton	8.5			Ned Wulk		
1966-67	5-21	1-9		Randy Lindner	12.5	Bob Edwards	7.2			Ned Wulk		
1967-68	11-17	4-6		Seabern Hill	14.9	Bob Edwards	8.5			Ned Wulk		
1968-69	11-15	4-6		Seabern Hill	20.2	Gerhard Schreur	8.5	Roger Detter	2.6	Ned Wulk		
1969-70	4-22	2-12		Seabern Hill	22.8	Gerhard Schreur	11.2	Jim Owens	2.5	Ned Wulk		
1970-71	16-10	8-6		Paul Stovall	16.3	Paul Stovall	11.4	Jim Owens	2.3	Ned Wulk		
1971-72	18-8	9-5		Paul Stovall	21.3	Paul Stovall	13.5	Mike Contreras	3.0	Ned Wulk		
1972-73	19-9	10-4	NCAA REGIONAL SEMIFINALS	Mike Contreras	16.7	Ron Kennedy	8.7	Jim Owens	3.0	Ned Wulk		
1973-74	18-9	9-5		Lionel Hollins	17.3	Mark Wasley	6.9	Lionel Hollins	3.1	Ned Wulk		
1974-75	25-4	12-2	NCAA REGIONAL FINALS	Lionel Hollins	16.7	Jack Schrader	7.4	Lionel Hollins	5.1	Ned Wulk		
1975-76	16-11 ⊗	5-9		Scott Lloyd	18.1	Scott Lloyd	7.7	Gary Jackson	2.6	Ned Wulk		
1976-77	15-13	6-8		Mark Landsberger	17.2	Mark Landsberger	14.4	James Holliman	3.2	Ned Wulk		
1977-78	13-14	6-8		Blake Taylor	14.1	Tony Zeno	8.7	Rick Taylor	2.9	Ned Wulk		
1978-79	16-14	7-11		Tony Zeno	12.2	Tony Zeno	9.2	Greg Goorjian	3.0	Ned Wulk		
1979-80	22-7	15-3	NCAA SECOND ROUND	Kurt Nimphius	16.6	Kurt Nimphius	9.6	Lafayette Lever	4.9	Ned Wulk		
1980-81	24-4	16-2	NCAA SECOND ROUND	Byron Scott	16.6	Alton Lister	9.7	Lafayette Lever	5.3	Ned Wulk		
1981-82	13-14	8-10		Paul Williams	17.0	Paul Williams	5.8	Lafayette Lever	3.9	Ned Wulk	405-273	.597▼
1982-83	19-14	12-6	NIT SECOND ROUND	Byron Scott	21.6	Paul Williams	7.1	Byron Scott	4.2	Bob Weinhauer		
1983-84	13-15	8-10		Chris Beasley	18.3	Jim Deines	6.8	Bobby Thompson	4.1	Bob Weinhauer		
1984-85	12-16	7-11		Steve Beck	11.2	Jim Deines	6.3	Bobby Thompson	5.4	Bob Weinhauer	44-45	.494
1985-86	14-14	8-10		Steve Beck	14.9	Mark Carlino	4.9	Bobby Thompson	4.0	Steve Patterson		
1986-87	11-17	6-12		Steve Beck	19.0	Tarre Isiah	6.2	Arthur Thomas	2.9	Steve Patterson		
1987-88	13-16	6-12		Arthur Thomas	14.2	Mark Becker	5.5	Tarence Wheeler	4.4	Steve Patterson		
1988-89	12-16	5-13		Trent Edwards	19.5	Trent Edwards	8.2	Alex Austin	4.3	Steve Patterson[a]	48-56	.462
1989-90	15-16	6-12	NIT FIRST ROUND	Alex Austin	18.0	Alex Austin	7.7	Mike Redhair	6.0	Bill Frieder		
1990-91	20-10	10-8	NCAA SECOND ROUND	Isaac Austin	16.2	Isaac Austin	8.7	Lynn Collins	5.2	Bill Frieder		
1991-92	19-14	9-9	NIT SECOND ROUND	Jamal Faulkner	12.6	Lester Neal	7.5	Lynn Collins	6.1	Bill Frieder		
1992-93	18-10	11-7	NIT FIRST ROUND	Stevin Smith	20.0	Lester Neal	9.0	Marcell Capers	7.1	Bill Frieder		
1993-94	15-13	10-8	NIT FIRST ROUND	Stevin Smith	18.5	Dwayne Fontana	8.6	Stevin Smith	5.1	Bill Frieder		
1994-95	24-9 ⊗	12-6	NCAA REGIONAL SEMIFINALS	Mario Bennett	18.7	Mario Bennett	8.2	Marcell Capers	7.1	Bill Frieder		
1995-96	11-16 ⊗	6-12		Ron Riley	20.1	Ron Riley	6.1	Quincy Brewer	4.3	Bill Frieder		
1996-97	10-20	2-16		Jeremy Veal	18.7	Rodger Farrington	7.1	Jeremy Veal	4.7	Bill Frieder	132-108	.550▼
1997-98	18-14	8-10	NIT FIRST ROUND	Jeremy Veal	20.8	Bobby Lazor	7.8	Ahlon Lewis	9.2	Don Newman	18-14	.563
1998-99	14-16	6-12		Eddie House	18.9	Bobby Lazor	8.7	Alton Mason	4.1	Rob Evans		
1999-00	19-13	10-8	NIT SECOND ROUND	Eddie House	23.0	Awvee Storey	7.6	Eddie House	3.5	Rob Evans		
2000-01	13-16	5-13		Alton Mason	13.4	Awvee Storey	9.1	Alton Mason	3.8	Rob Evans		
2001-02	14-15	7-11	NIT FIRST ROUND	Chad Prewitt	17.0	Chad Prewitt	7.3	Curtis Millage	2.5	Rob Evans		
2002-03	20-12	11-7	NCAA SECOND ROUND	Ike Diogu	19.0	Ike Diogu	7.8	Kyle Dodd	3.3	Rob Evans		
2003-04	10-17	4-14		Ike Diogu	22.8	Ike Diogu	8.9	Jason Braxton	4.8	Rob Evans		
2004-05	18-14	7-11	NIT FIRST ROUND	Ike Diogu	22.6	Ike Diogu	9.8	Jason Braxton	3.6	Rob Evans		
2005-06	11-17	5-13		Kevin Kruger	15.0	Jeff Pendergraph	6.1	Antwi Atuahene	3.9	Rob Evans	119-120	.498
2006-07	8-22	2-16		Jeff Pendergraph	12.1	Jeff Pendergraph	9.1	Derek Glasser	3.2	Herb Sendek		
2007-08	21-13	9-9	NIT QUARTERFINALS	James Harden	17.8	Jeff Pendergraph	6.4	Derek Glasser	3.9	Herb Sendek		
2008-09	25-10	11-7	NCAA SECOND ROUND	James Harden	20.1	Jeff Pendergraph	8.2	Derek Glasser	4.8	Herb Sendek	54-45	.545

[a] Steve Patterson (10-9) and Bob Schermerhorn (2-7) both coached during the 1988-89 season.

⊗ Records don't reflect games forfeited or vacated. For adjusted records, see p. 521.

▼ Coaches' records adjusted to reflect games forfeited or vacated: Ned Wulk, 406-272, .599; Bill Frieder, 131-106, .553. For yearly totals, see p. 521.

ESPN 32 SAGARIN

ARKANSAS

Francis Schmidt's Southwest Conference powers in the 1920s; Eddie Sutton's Triplets; Nolan Richardson's 40 Minutes of Hell. Era in and era out, the Razorbacks have been the toast of the Ozarks for more than 80 years. The results: 29 NCAA Tournament appearances, six Final Fours and the 1994 national championship.

BEST TEAM: 1993-94 Who needs seniors when you've got a deep bench, a dogged backcourt defense and a furious offensive pace? Sophomores Scotty Thurman and Corliss Williamson (team-high 20.4 ppg) led a Razorbacks team ranked No. 1 for nearly half the season. After their 13-game winning streak was snapped in the SEC tournament, the Hogs stormed their way to their first NCAA championship, 76-72, while denying Duke a third title in four years.

BEST PLAYER: G Sidney Moncrief (1975-79) The best of the famed Triplets (along with Ron Brewer and Marvin Delph), Moncrief could do it all. But he was most famous for his shooting smarts and touch (62% for his career) and air-tight defense. Exhibit A: He held Larry Bird to four points over the last seven minutes of Arkansas' 73-71 Elite Eight loss to Indiana State in 1979.

BEST COACH: Nolan Richardson (1985-2002) To prepare his players for the 40 Minutes of Hell defense that tortured so many opponents, Richardson subjected the Razorbacks to a grueling practice routine. It paid off. From 1988 to '95, Arkansas won 200 games, made three Final Fours and claimed the 1994 national championship.

GAME FOR THE AGES: The Razorbacks trailed Duke by 10 early in the second half of the 1994 NCAA championship game. But they turned up the tempo to mount a furious comeback, setting up the Shot. With :51 to go and the game tied at 70, Scotty Thurman sank a three that barely cleared the outstretched arm of Blue Devil Antonio Lang. Arkansas held on for a 76-72 win.

HEARTBREAKER: The Razorbacks' attempt to make back-to-back Final Fours fell short in the 1979 Midwest Regional final against No. 1-ranked and undefeated Indiana State, 73-71. After Arkansas' U.S. Reed was called for traveling with a minute left, ISU's Bob Heaton hit an off-hand shot that bounced around the rim before dropping in for the Sycamores' victory.

FIERCEST RIVAL: Texas and Arkansas were sworn enemies when both played in the now-defunct Southwest Conference. Today, fellow SEC member LSU plays the Longhorns' former role. The bad blood first bubbled up on March 3, 1992, when the Shaquille O'Neal-led Tigers visited Fayetteville with the SEC title on the line and came away 106-92 overtime losers. It reached a boiling point in the Tigers' 85-56 win over the Razorbacks in the first round of the 2003 conference tournament, when LSU coach John Brady got into a shouting match with Arkansas guard Eric Ferguson, leading to the player's expulsion. The Hogs lead, 28–20, in their annual get-togethers.

FANFARE AND HOOPLA: "Woooooooo, Pig! Sooie!" The Hog Call became the school yell in the 1920s, some say after a group of farmers attended a Razorbacks football game. The coaxing of pork, complete with precise arm movements, is chanted three times and finished with a shout of "Razorbacks!"

> ***It wasn't just the Shot. Scotty Thurman built his Arkansas career on crowd-thrilling last-second heroics.***

FAN FAVORITE: G/F Scotty Thurman (1992-95) It wasn't just the Shot. Thurman built his Arkansas career on crowd-thrilling last-second heroics, like his game winner over Kentucky on Jan. 29, 1995, that thwarted the Cats' hopes for a perfect SEC season.

CONSENSUS ALL-AMERICAS

1928	**Glen Rose,** F
1936	**Ike Poole,** C
1941	**John Adams,** F
1979	**Sidney Moncrief,** G

FIRST-ROUND PRO PICKS

1948	**George Kok,** Indianapolis (2)
1978	**Ron Brewer,** Portland (7)
1979	**Sidney Moncrief,** Milwaukee (5)
1983	**Darrell Walker,** New York (12)
1984	**Alvin Robertson,** San Antonio (7)
1985	**Joe Kleine,** Sacramento (6)
1992	**Todd Day,** Milwaukee (8)
1992	**Oliver Miller,** Phoenix (22)
1992	**Lee Mayberry,** Milwaukee (23)
1995	**Corliss Williamson,** Sacramento (13)
2001	**Joe Johnson,** Boston (10)
2006	**Ronnie Brewer,** Utah (14)

PROFILE

University of Arkansas, Fayetteville, AR
Founded: 1871
Enrollment: 19,191 (11,498 undergraduate)
Colors: Cardinal and white
Nickname: Razorbacks
Current arena: Bud Walton Arena, opened in 1993 (19,200)
Previous: Barnhill Arena, 1957-93 (9,000); Schmitty's Barn, 1923-57 (N/A)
First game: 1923
All-time record: 1,487-822 (.644)
Total weeks in AP Top 20/25: 255

Current conference: Southeastern (1991-)
Conference titles:
Southwest: 22 (1926, '27, '28, '29, '30, '35 [tie], '36, '38, '41, '42 [tie], '44 [tie], '49 [tie], '50 [tie], '58 [tie], '77, '78 [tie], '79 [tie], '81, '82, '89, '90, '91)
SEC: 2 (1992, '94)
Conference tournament titles:
Southwest: 6 (1977, '79, '82, '89, '90, '91)
SEC: 1 (2000)
NCAA Tournament appearances: 29
Sweet 16s (since 1975): 10
Final Fours: 6
Titles: 1 (1994)

NIT appearances: 2
Semifinals: 1

TOP 5

G	**Lee Mayberry** (1988-92)
G	**Sidney Moncrief** (1975-79)
F	**Todd Day** (1988-92)
F	**Corliss Williamson** (1992-95)
C	**Joe Kleine** (1982-85)

RECORDS	GAME		SEASON		CAREER	
POINTS	47	Martin Terry, vs. SMU (1973)	786	Todd Day (1990-91)	2,395	Todd Day (1988-92)
POINTS PER GAME			28.3	Martin Terry (1972-73)	26.3	Martin Terry (1971-73)
REBOUNDS	23	Nick Davis, vs. Jackson State (Nov. 22, 1996)	349	Derek Hood (1998-99)	1,015	Sidney Moncrief (1975-79)
ASSISTS	15	Dontell Jefferson, vs. Portland State (Nov. 18, 2005); Kareem Reid, vs. Jackson State (Nov. 22, 1996)	219	Kareem Reid (1995-96)	748	Kareem Reid (1995-99)

SEASON REVIEW

SEASON	W-L	CONF.	SCORING	COACH	RECORD
1923-24	17-11	3-9		Francis Schmidt	
1924-25	21-5	10-4		Francis Schmidt	
1925-26	23-2	11-1		Francis Schmidt	
1926-27	14-2	8-2		Francis Schmidt	
1927-28	19-1	12-0		Francis Schmidt	
1928-29	19-1	11-1		Francis Schmidt	113-22 .837
1929-30	16-7	10-2		Charles Bassett	
1930-31	14-9	7-5		Charles Bassett	
1931-32	18-6	8-4		Charles Bassett	
1932-33	14-7	6-6		Charles Bassett	62-29 .681
1933-34	16-8	6-6		Glen Rose	
1934-35	14-5	9-3		Glen Rose	
1935-36	24-3	11-1		Glen Rose	
1936-37	12-6	8-4		Glen Rose	

SEAS.	W-L	CONF.	POSTSEASON	SCORING		REBOUNDS		ASSISTS		COACH	RECORD
1937-38	19-3	11-1								Glen Rose	
1938-39	18-5	9-3								Glen Rose	
1939-40	12-10	6-6								Glen Rose	
1940-41	20-3	12-0	NATIONAL SEMIFINALS							Glen Rose	
1941-42	19-4	10-2								Glen Rose	
1942-43	19-7	8-4								Eugene Lambert	
1943-44	16-8	11-1								Eugene Lambert	
1944-45	17-9	9-3	NATIONAL SEMIFINALS							Eugene Lambert	
1945-46	16-7	9-3								Eugene Lambert	
1946-47	14-10	8-4		Al Williams	15.8					Eugene Lambert	
1947-48	16-8	8-4		George Kok	19.5					Eugene Lambert	
1948-49	15-11	9-3	NCAA REGIONAL SEMIFINALS	Bob Ambler	10.0					Eugene Lambert	113-60 .653
1949-50	12-12	8-4		Jim Cathcart	10.1					Presley Askew	
1950-51	13-11	7-5		Billy Hester	9.1					Presley Askew	
1951-52	10-14	4-8		Walter Kearns	9.0					Presley Askew	35-37 .486
1952-53	10-11	4-8		Eugene Lambert Jr	12.9	Walter Kearns	6.8			Glen Rose	
1953-54	13-9	6-6		Jerald Barnett	9.8	Raymond Shaw	6.0			Glen Rose	
1954-55	14-9	8-4		Jerald Barnett	10.3	Pete Butler	7.2			Glen Rose	
1955-56	11-12	9-3		Manuel Whitley	17.0	Manuel Whitley	9.7			Glen Rose	
1956-57	11-12	5-7		Terry Day	12.5	Terry Day	9.0			Glen Rose	
1957-58	17-10	9-5	NCAA REGIONAL SEMIFINALS	Fred Grim	14.1	Harry Thompson	8.5			Glen Rose	
1958-59	9-14	6-8		Clyde Rhoden	14.6	Jay Carpenter	8.8			Glen Rose	
1959-60	12-11	7-7		Clyde Rhoden	16.2	Ronnie Garner	9.6			Glen Rose	
1960-61	16-7	9-5		Pat Foster	15.4	Ronnie Garner	7.8			Glen Rose	
1961-62	14-10	5-9		Jerry Carlton	18.2	Jim Wilson	6.6			Glen Rose	
1962-63	13-11	8-6		Tommy Boyer	18.3	Jim Wilson	7.5			Glen Rose	
1963-64	9-14	6-8		Jim Magness	14.8	Jim Magness	5.6			Glen Rose	
1964-65	9-14	5-9		Ricky Sugg	14.2	J.D. McConnell	7.0			Glen Rose	
1965-66	13-10	7-7		Ricky Sugg	13.6	McConnell, J. Talkington	8.5			Glen Rose	325-201 .618
1966-67	6-17	4-10		Tommy Rowland	18.5	Tommy Rowland	9.0			Duddy Waller	
1967-68	10-14	7-7		James Eldridge	16.6	Gary Stephens	7.6			Duddy Waller	
1968-69	10-14	4-10		James Eldridge	13.7	James Eldridge	7.0			Duddy Waller	
1969-70	5-19	3-11		Almer Lee	17.0	Robert McKenzie	7.5			Duddy Waller	31-64 .326
1970-71	5-21	1-13		Almer Lee	19.2	Vernon Murphy	8.8			Lanny Van Eman	
1971-72	8-18	5-9		Martin Terry	24.3	Dean Tolson	9.9			Lanny Van Eman	
1972-73	16-10	9-5		Martin Terry	28.3	Dean Tolson	12.4			Lanny Van Eman	
1973-74	10-16	6-8		Dean Tolson	22.5	Dean Tolson	13.2			Lanny Van Eman	39-65 .375
1974-75	17-9	11-3		Kent Allison	15.1	Kent Allison	8.2			Eddie Sutton	
1975-76	19-9	9-7		Marvin Delph	16.3	Sidney Moncrief	7.6			Eddie Sutton	
1976-77	26-2	16-0	NCAA FIRST ROUND	Marvin Delph	19.7	Sidney Moncrief	8.4			Eddie Sutton	
1977-78	32-4	14-2	NCAA THIRD PLACE	Ron Brewer	18.0	Sidney Moncrief	7.7	Jim Counce	3.3	Eddie Sutton	
1978-79	25-5	13-3	NCAA REGIONAL FINALS	Sidney Moncrief	22.0	Sidney Moncrief	9.6	Sidney Moncrief	2.7	Eddie Sutton	
1979-80	21-8	13-3	NCAA FIRST ROUND	Scott Hastings	16.2	Scott Hastings	6.7	Alan Zahn	2.6	Eddie Sutton	
1980-81	24-8	13-3	NCAA REGIONAL SEMIFINALS	Scott Hastings	16.3	Scott Hastings	5.4	Darrell Walker	3.3	Eddie Sutton	
1981-82	23-6	12-4	NCAA SECOND ROUND	Scott Hastings	18.6	Scott Hastings	6.0	Darrell Walker	3.5	Eddie Sutton	
1982-83	26-4	14-2	NCAA REGIONAL SEMIFINALS	Darrell Walker	18.2	Joe Kleine	7.3	Alvin Robertson	3.6	Eddie Sutton	
1983-84	25-7	14-2	NCAA SECOND ROUND	Joe Kleine	18.2	Joe Kleine	9.2	Alvin Robertson	6.0	Eddie Sutton	
1984-85	22-13	10-6	NCAA SECOND ROUND	Joe Kleine	22.1	Joe Kleine	8.4	William Mills	4.5	Eddie Sutton	260-75 .776
1985-86	12-16	4-12		Mike Ratliff	13.1	Andrew Lang	6.5	Scott Rose	2.5	Nolan Richardson	
1986-87	19-14	8-8	NIT SECOND ROUND	Tim Scott	11.9	Andrew Lang	7.5	Ron Huery	2.7	Nolan Richardson	
1987-88	21-9	11-5	NCAA FIRST ROUND	Ron Huery	13.4	Andrew Lang	7.3	Keith Wilson	2.9	Nolan Richardson	
1988-89	25-7	13-3	NCAA SECOND ROUND	Lenzie Howell	14.6	Lenzie Howell	7.0	Keith Wilson	4.3	Nolan Richardson	
1989-90	30-5	14-2	NCAA NATIONAL SEMIFINALS	Todd Day	19.5	Oliver Miller	6.3	Lee Mayberry	5.2	Nolan Richardson	
1990-91	34-4	15-1	NCAA REGIONAL FINALS	Todd Day	20.7	Oliver Miller	7.7	Lee Mayberry	5.5	Nolan Richardson	
1991-92	26-8	13-3	NCAA SECOND ROUND	Lee Mayberry	15.2	Oliver Miller	7.7	Lee Mayberry	5.9	Nolan Richardson	
1992-93	22-9	10-6	NCAA REGIONAL SEMIFINALS	Scotty Thurman	17.4	Darrell Hawkins	4.5	Corey Beck	3.6	Nolan Richardson	
1993-94	**31-3**	**14-2**	**NATIONAL CHAMPION**	**Corliss Williamson**	**20.4**	**Corliss Williamson**	**7.7**	**Corey Beck**	**5.0**	**Nolan Richardson**	
1994-95	32-7	12-4	NCAA RUNNER-UP	Corliss Williamson	19.7	Corliss Williamson	7.5	Corey Beck	5.3	Nolan Richardson	
1995-96	20-13	9-7	NCAA REGIONAL SEMIFINALS	Kareem Reid	12.9	Derek Hood	6.1	Kareem Reid	6.6	Nolan Richardson	
1996-97	18-14	8-8	NIT FOURTH PLACE	Pat Bradley	14.4	Derek Hood	8.0	Kareem Reid	5.7	Nolan Richardson	
1997-98	24-9	11-5	NCAA SECOND ROUND	Pat Bradley	14.8	Nick Davis	9.8	Kareem Reid	5.2	Nolan Richardson	
1998-99	23-11	9-7	NCAA SECOND ROUND	Pat Bradley	14.1	Derek Hood	10.3	Kareem Reid	5.3	Nolan Richardson	
1999-2000	19-15	7-9	NCAA FIRST ROUND	Joe Johnson	16.0	Joe Johnson	5.7	T.J. Cleveland	2.9	Nolan Richardson	
2000-01	20-11	10-6	NCAA FIRST ROUND	Joe Johnson	14.2	Joe Johnson	6.4	T.J. Cleveland	2.7	Nolan Richardson	
2001-02	14-15	6-10		Jannero Pargo	16.6	Dionisio Gomez	5.0	Jannero Pargo	3.3	Nolan Richardson[a]	389-169 .697
2002-03	9-19	4-12		Jonathon Modica	11.5	Dionisio Gomez	6.6	Eric Ferguson	3.3	Stan Heath	
2003-04	12-16	4-12		Jonathon Modica	16.5	Ronnie Brewer	5.5	Ronnie Brewer	3.4	Stan Heath	
2004-05	18-12	6-10		Ronnie Brewer	16.2	Ronnie Brewer	4.8	Eric Ferguson	4.3	Stan Heath	
2005-06	22-10	10-6	NCAA FIRST ROUND	Ronnie Brewer	18.4	Darian Townes	5.1	Dontell Jefferson	4.4	Stan Heath	
2006-07	21-14	7-9	NCAA FIRST ROUND	Patrick Beverley	13.9	Charles Thomas	5.7	Gary Ervin	4.8	Stan Heath	82-71 .536
2007-08	23-12	9-7	NCAA SECOND ROUND	Sonny Weems	15.0	Patrick Beverley	6.6	Gary Ervin	3.7	John Pelphrey	
2008-09	14-16	2-14		Michael Washington	15.5	Michael Washington	9.8	Courtney Fortson	6.0	John Pelphrey	37-28 .569

[a] Nolan Richardson (13-14) and Mike Anderson (1-1) both coached during the 2001-02 season.

ESPN 196 SAGARIN

ARKANSAS STATE

Arthur Agee, star of the 1994 documentary *Hoop Dreams*, ran point at ASU for two seasons. But otherwise, the team formerly known as the Indians—now the Red Wolves—haven't seen much glory since their inception in 1926. They've had just five 20-win seasons; four were produced by Nelson Catalina's NIT teams from 1986-87 to '90-91.

BEST TEAM: 1998-99 Coming off a 20-win season, the Indians started 1–3 but finished strong, dominating the Sun Belt tournament and reaching the NCAAs for the only time in school history. Chico Fletcher & Co. gave No. 2-seed Utah a good run, trailing 39-38 with 16:28 left before running out of gas and losing, 80-58.

BEST PLAYER: F Jerry Rook (1961-65) The Arkansas native turned down a chance to play for Adolph Rupp at Kentucky so he could stay close to home. Good move. He averaged 19.8 ppg as a freshman, playing primarily in the post. As a junior he moved to the perimeter, where he used his deadly jump shot to average 25.3 ppg. He was the Southland Conference POY in 1964 and '65, when he also made the Little All-America team.

BEST COACH: Nelson Catalina (1984-95) He never made it to the Big Dance, but Catalina did lead the Indians to four NITs, where his teams went 4–4, including victories over Stanford and Memphis and a near-upset of Arkansas in 1987.

GAME FOR THE AGES: After trouncing New Orleans by 17 and Florida International by 18 in the 1999 Sun Belt tournament, all that stood between the Indians and their first NCAA bid was Western Kentucky—only the most storied program in the conference. It wasn't close. Behind Fletcher's 21 points and eight assists, the Indians won, 65-48.

FIERCEST RIVAL: Arkansas-Little Rock battles the Red Wolves for recruits, Sun Belt bragging rights and the ALLTEL Classic Trophy, awarded to the winner of each Little Rock meeting. ASU won five of the last eight games and holds a 42–24 advantage in a series that started in 1928.

THE SCHOOLS

SEASON REVIEW

SEAS.	W-L	CONF.	COACH	SEAS.	W-L	CONF.	COACH
1926-53	*238-276*	*Consecutive winning seasons, '33-36*		1966-67	17-7	8-0	Marvin Speight
1953-54	14-11		John Rauth	1967-68	6-17	4-4	Marvin Speight
1954-55	13-11		John Rauth	1968-69	6-16	3-5	Marvin Speight
1955-56	14-11		John Rauth	1969-70	14-9	4-4	John Rose
1956-57	7-14		John Rauth	1970-71	15-9	6-2	John Rose
1957-58	18-9		John Rauth	1971-72	12-14	5-3	John Rose
1958-59	10-13		John Rauth	1972-73	7-17 ⊘	2-10	John Rose
1959-60	14-13		John Rauth	1973-74	17-8	4-0	John Rose
1960-61	11-11		John Rauth	1974-75	13-12	3-5	John Rose
1961-62	17-7		John Rauth	1975-76	10-15	3-7	John Rose
1962-63	15-11		John Rauth	1976-77	14-13	4-6	Marvin Adams
1963-64	16-9	5-3	Marvin Speight	1977-78	9-18	2-8	Marvin Adams
1964-65	13-9	6-2	Marvin Speight	1978-79	15-12	5-5	Marvin Adams
1965-66	17-9	4-4	Marvin Speight	1979-80	15-12	5-5	Marvin Adams

SEAS.	W-L	CONF.	SCORING		COACH	RECORD
1980-81	12-15	2-8	Anthony Myles	15.2	Marvin Adams	
1981-82	15-11	3-7	Mike Sailes	11.8	Marvin Adams	
1982-83	17-12	5-7	Jay Hansen	13.0	Marvin Adams	
1983-84	13-15	4-8	Scott Horrell	14.1	Marvin Adams	110-108 .505
1984-85	14-14	6-6	Tim Norman	15.0	Nelson Catalina	
1985-86	18-11	7-5	Reggie Gordon	12.5	Nelson Catalina	
1986-87	21-13	5-5 ■	John Tate	15.7	Nelson Catalina	
1987-88	21-14	4-6 ■	John Tate	16.1	Nelson Catalina	
1988-89	20-10	6-4 ■	John Tate	15.7	Nelson Catalina	
1989-90	15-13	2-8	Greg Williams	12.2	Nelson Catalina	
1990-91	23-9	9-3 ■	Bobby Gross	15.4	Nelson Catalina	
1991-92	17-11	11-5	Fred Shepherd	12.1	Nelson Catalina	
1992-93	16-12	11-7	Jeff Clifton	17.6	Nelson Catalina	
1993-94	15-12	10-8	Jeff Clifton	21.3	Nelson Catalina	
1994-95	8-20	3-15	Vernall Cole	10.8	Nelson Catalina	188-139 .575
1995-96	9-18	7-11	Ron Darrett	11.8	Dickey Nutt	
1996-97	15-12	8-10	Mark Kiehne	16.8	Dickey Nutt	
1997-98	20-9	14-4	Micah Marsh	15.1	Dickey Nutt	
1998-99	18-12	9-5 ●	Chico Fletcher	17.0	Dickey Nutt	
1999-2000	10-18	7-9	C.J. Pepper	14.6	Dickey Nutt	
2000-01	17-13	10-6	Jason Jennings	13.9	Dickey Nutt	
2001-02	15-16	5-9	Nick Rivers	17.1	Dickey Nutt	
2002-03	13-15	6-8	Tevoris Thompson	15.3	Dickey Nutt	
2003-04	17-11	7-7	Dewarick Spencer	19.0	Dickey Nutt	
2004-05	16-13	7-7	Dewarick Spencer	18.6	Dickey Nutt	
2005-06	12-18	7-7	Isaac Wells	14.4	Dickey Nutt	
2006-07	18-15	11-7	Adrian Banks	21.1	Dickey Nutt	
2007-08	10-20	5-13	Adrian Banks	18.4	Dickey Nutt[a]	189-187 .503
2008-09	13-17	5-13	Donald Boone	13.6	John Brady	13-17 .433

[a] Dickey Nutt coached the first part of the season (9-17); Shawn Forrest and Al Grushkin were co-interim coaches for the remainder of the 2007-08 season (1-3).

⊘ Records do not reflect games forfeited or vacated. For adjusted records, see p. 521.

● NCAA Tournament appearance ■ NIT appearance

PROFILE

Arkansas State University, Jonesboro, AR
Founded: 1909
Enrollment: 10,869 (9,385 undergraduate)
Colors: Scarlet and black
Nickname: Red Wolves
Current arena: Convocation Center, opened in 1987 (10,038)
Previous: Indian Field House, 1961-87 (4,000); The Armory, 1939-61 (N/A)
First game: Dec. 14, 1926
All-time record: 1,035-992 (.511)

Total weeks in AP Top 20/25: 0
Current conference: Sun Belt (1991-)
Conference titles:
Southland: 4 (1965 [tie], '67, '71, '74)
American South: 1 (1991 [tie])
Sun Belt: 2 (1998 [tie], 2007 [tie])
Conference tournament titles:
Sun Belt: 1 (1999)
NCAA Tournament appearances: 1
NIT appearances: 4

CONSENSUS ALL-AMERICAS

1965 **Jerry Rook** (Little A-A), F

TOP 5

G **Chico Fletcher** (1996-2000)
G **Don Scaife** (1972-75)
F **Dan Henderson** (1973-77)
F **Jerry Rook** (1961-65)
C **John Dickson** (1963-67)

RECORDS

RECORDS	GAME		SEASON		CAREER	
POINTS	47	John Dickson, vs. Chattanooga (Jan. 14, 1967); vs. Texas-Arlington (1967)	695	Adrian Banks (2006-07)	2,153	Jerry Rook (1961-65)
POINTS PER GAME			27.1	Don Scaife (1974-75)	22.9	Jerry Rook (1961-65)
REBOUNDS	28	Jim Ward, vs. Union (Tenn.), (1954-55)	354	John Dickson (1965-66)	1,166	John Belcher (1968-72)
ASSISTS	17	Chico Fletcher, vs. TCU (Nov. 23, 1998)	250	Chico Fletcher (1998-99)	893	Chico Fletcher (1996-2000)

ESPN 258 SAGARIN

ARKANSAS-LITTLE ROCK

In 1990, on the heels of five straight postseason bids, coach Mike Newell left for Lamar. UALR immediately crashed, and over the next 19 seasons churned through five coaches—while capturing zero NCAA bids. The low point was a memorable-for-all-the-wrong-reasons season under Little Rock favorite son Sidney Moncrief in 1999-2000, in which the Trojans won four games.

BEST TEAM: 1985-86 Their opponents knew what was coming: a spread offense featuring quick ball movement. Yet few teams could stop the Trojans, largely because the system was built around a trio—Ken Worthy, Pete Myers and Michael Clarke—who had been balling together since junior high. After the Trojans upset No. 3-seed Notre Dame in the Tourney's first round, it took NC State two OTs to oust them.

BEST PLAYER: G Derek Fisher (1992-96) He finished his UALR career with 184 steals and 472 assists, both second all time in school history. Although Fisher stood only 6'1", the LA Lakers fell in love with his game and took him as the 24th overall pick of the 1996 draft.

BEST COACH: Mike Newell (1984-90) This former Billy Tubbs assistant put UALR on the map by mining Detroit recruits and by pumping up the pace on both ends of the court. In six seasons, he won three TAAC championships and achieved five 20-win campaigns.

GAME FOR THE AGES: In the first round of the 1986 Tournament, the No. 14-seed Trojans overcame Notre Dame and Digger Phelps' match-up zone defense to pull off a 90-83 upset. Clarke and Myers combined for 56 points, while the team collectively drained 15 of 19 shots in the second half.

FIERCEST RIVAL: Arkansas is the undisputed king of the Razorback State, leaving UALR and Arkansas State to battle for second-fiddle status. Fans of the two schools take this struggle very seriously—the Trojans-Red Wolves matchup on Feb. 2, 2002, set an SBC single-game attendance record with 12,985 fans. (UALR's Mark Green hit a three with 3.1 seconds left to win the game, 65-63.) The Red Wolves lead the series, 42–24.

SEASON REVIEW

SEAS.	W-L	CONF.	COACH	SEAS.	W-L	CONF.	COACH
1930-49	*97-151*		*Herman Bogan (1942-46), 39-24, .619*	1962-63	12-14		Bill Ballard
1949-50	1-20		John Floyd	1963-64	15-14		Bill Ballard
1950-51	7-13		Jim Bearden	1964-65	9-14		Bill Ballard
1951-52	10-15		John Kincannon	1965-66	14-13		Cleve Branscum
1952-53	9-15		John Kincannon	1966-67	8-14		Cleve Branscum
1953-54	12-14		Woody Johnson	1967-68	2-23		Happy Mahfouz
1954-55	10-13		Woody Johnson	1968-69	6-20		Happy Mahfouz
1955-56	3-17		Woody Johnson	1969-70	8-17		Happy Mahfouz
1956-57	no team			1970-71	9-14		Happy Mahfouz
1957-58	no team			1971-72	16-9		Happy Mahfouz
1958-59	no team			1972-73	15-10		Happy Mahfouz
1959-60	no team			1973-74	18-6		Happy Mahfouz
1960-61	no team			1974-75	13-12		Happy Mahfouz
1961-62	6-12		Bill Ballard	1975-76	11-15		Happy Mahfouz

SEAS.	W-L	CONF.		SCORING		COACH	RECORD
1976-77	9-17					Happy Mahfouz	
1977-78	9-13					Happy Mahfouz	
1978-79	6-20					Happy Mahfouz	122-176 .409
1979-80	16-10			Marty Laguerre	16.1	Ron Kestenbaum	
1980-81	13-13	5-6		Jessey Massey	13.5	Ron Kestenbaum	
1981-82	19-8	12-4		Jimmy Lampley	15.4	Ron Kestenbaum	
1982-83	23-6	12-2		Vaughn Williams	15.5	Ron Kestenbaum	
1983-84	14-15	7-7		Mike Rivers	17.6	Ron Kestenbaum	85-52 .620
1984-85	17-13	9-5		Michael Clarke	18.8	Mike Newell	
1985-86	23-11	12-2	●	Myron Jackson	19.4	Mike Newell	
1986-87	26-11	16-2	■	Curtis Kidd	15.6	Mike Newell	
1987-88	24-7	15-3	■	James Scott	16.0	Mike Newell	
1988-89	23-8	14-4	●	Johnnie Bell	17.5	Mike Newell	
1989-90	20-10	12-4	●	Carl Brown	18.4	Mike Newell	133-60 .689
1990-91	10-20	6-8		James Scott	15.4	Jim Platt	
1991-92	17-13 ⊗	9-7		Tony Martin	18.8	Jim Platt	
1992-93	15-12	10-8		Tony Martin	19.2	Jim Platt	
1993-94	13-15	6-12		Derrick Hall	19.4	Jim Platt	55-60 .478
1994-95	17-12	9-9		Derek Fisher	17.7	Wimp Sanderson	
1995-96	23-7	14-4	■	Malik Dixon	17.8	Wimp Sanderson	
1996-97	18-11	11-7		Malik Dixon	20.8	Wimp Sanderson	
1997-98	15-13	10-8		Chris Green	15.2	Wimp Sanderson	
1998-99	12-15	5-9		Alan Barksdale	14.8	Wimp Sanderson	85-58 .594
1999-2000	4-24	1-15		Stan Blackmon	15.9	Sidney Moncrief	4-24 .143
2000-01	18-11	9-7		Stan Blackmon	18.4	Porter Moser	
2001-02	18-11	8-6		Nick Zachery	16.1	Porter Moser	
2002-03	18-12	8-6		Nick Zachery	14.1	Porter Moser	54-34 .614
2003-04	17-12	9-5		Brandon Freeman	13.5	Steve Shields	
2004-05	18-10	10-4		Brandon Freeman	16.3	Steve Shields	
2005-06	14-15	5-9		Zack Wright	12.3	Steve Shields	
2006-07	13-17	8-10		Rashad Jones-Jennings	12.5	Steve Shields	
2007-08	20-11	11-7		Steven Moore	9.9	Steve Shields	
2008-09	23-8	15-3		Shane Edwards	11.8	Steve Shields	105-73 .590

⊗ **Records do not reflect games forfeited or vacated. For adjusted records,** **see p. 521.**

● **NCAA Tournament appearance** ■ **NIT appearance**

THE SCHOOLS

PROFILE

University of Arkansas-Little Rock, Little Rock, AR
Founded: 1927
Enrollment: 12,135 (9,494 undergraduate)
Colors: Maroon, silver and black
Nickname: Trojans
Current arena: Jack Stephens Center, opened in 2005 (5,600)
Previous: Alltel Arena, 1999-05 (18,000); Barton Coliseum, 1979-84, '87-99 (8,600); Statehouse Convention Center, 1984-87 (4,500); Trojan Fieldhouse, 1930-79 (2,400)
First game: Dec. 9, 1930

All-time record: 856-876 (.494)
Total weeks in AP Top 20/25: 0
Current conference: Sun Belt (1991-)
Conference titles:
Trans America: 5 (1982, '83, '86, '87, '88 [tie])
Sun Belt: 5 (1996 [tie], 2004 [tie], '05 [tie], '08 [tie], '09 [tie])
Conference tournament titles:
Trans America: 3 (1986, '89, '90)
NCAA Tournament appearances: 3
NIT appearances: 3
Semifinals: 1

FIRST-ROUND PRO PICKS

1996 **Derek Fisher,** LA Lakers (24)

TOP 5

G **Derek Fisher** (1992-96)
G **James Scott** (1987-91)
G/F **Pete Myers** (1984-86)
F/C **Larry Johnson** (1974-78)
C **Muntrelle Dobbins** (1993-97)

RECORDS

	GAME		SEASON		CAREER	
POINTS	47	Tom Brown, vs. Southern (Jan. 26, 1976)	661	Myron Jackson (1985-86)	1,731	James Scott (1987-91)
POINTS PER GAME			25.2	Tom Brown (1975-76)	21.2	Tom Brown (1974-76)
REBOUNDS	31	Charlie Johnson, vs. Baptist Christian (Jan. 23, 1973)	402	Larry Johnson (1975-76)	1,315	Larry Johnson (1974-78)
ASSISTS	18	Carl Brown, vs. Centenary (Jan. 14, 1989)	217	Juric Brown (1986-87)	534	Vaughn Williams (1979-83)

ESPN 305 SAGARIN

ARKANSAS-PINE BLUFF

It was nearly madness. In 2006, UAPB came one win short of making its first NCAA Tournament, losing to Southern in the SWAC tournament title game. But while Division I success has proved elusive, the Golden Lions' College Division and NAIA achievements in the 1960s routinely had them playing in front of overflow crowds.

BEST TEAM: 1966-67 Led by high-flying big man Charles Hentz, the high-scoring Golden Lions won the SWAC title and advanced to the NCAA College Division national tournament. Hentz created easy scoring opportunities—both for himself with his athleticism and for his teammates with his passing touch out of double teams.

BEST PLAYER: G James "Mack" Allen (1960-64) With lockdown defensive ability, exceptional touch and the speed to create his own shot, Allen was a four-time All-SWAC selection and three-time NAIA All-America.

BEST COACH: Hubert O. Clemmons (1955-77) The architect of a free-flowing, high-scoring offense, Clemmons led the Lions to their only SWAC championship in 1967. That season was part of a run from 1964 to '68 that saw the Golden Lions notch a 99–36 record.

GAME FOR THE AGES: On Nov. 23, 1996, in their first game as a provisional D1 team, the Golden Lions sprung a 66-64 upset of Houston at Hofheinz Pavilion. With the game tied at 64, senior guard Shawn Forrest penetrated inside the free throw line and drilled the 12-foot game winner as time expired.

FIERCEST RIVAL: During the 1960s, Grambling State and UAPB tangled 22 times in SWAC competition. Most memorable was the Golden Lions' 129-124 double-OT win in 1964, in which James Allen scored 56 points. The series was renewed in 1997 when UAPB rejoined the SWAC after a 27-year hiatus. More classics followed, including the 2007 SWAC tournament game in which the Cinderella Golden Lions blew a 15-point lead before holding on for a 51-48 win. On Jan. 31, 2009, UAPB pulled off a 62-61 overtime victory thanks to a layup by Tavaris Washington with :21 left.

SEASON REVIEW

SEAS.	W-L	CONF.	COACH	SEAS.	W-L	CONF.	COACH
1956-57[a]	9-15			1960-61	9-15		Hubert O. Clemmons
1957-58	10-14		Hubert O. Clemmons	1961-62	14-10		Hubert O. Clemmons
1958-59	14-13		Hubert O. Clemmons	1962-63	14-12		Hubert O. Clemmons
1959-60	10-17		Hubert O. Clemmons	1963-64	18-7		Hubert O. Clemmons

SEAS.	W-L	CONF.	SCORING		COACH	RECORD
1964-65	22-4				Hubert O. Clemmons	
1965-66	17-11				Hubert O. Clemmons	
1966-67	24-7				Hubert O. Clemmons	
1967-68	18-7				Hubert O. Clemmons	
1968-69	13-14				Hubert O. Clemmons	
1969-70	17-9				Hubert O. Clemmons	
1970-71	14-10				Hubert O. Clemmons	
1971-72	19-8				Hubert O. Clemmons	
1972-73	15-7				Hubert O. Clemmons	
1973-74	15-11				Hubert O. Clemmons	
1974-75	12-13				Hubert O. Clemmons	
1975-76	12-13				Hubert O. Clemmons	
1976-77	14-12				Hubert O. Clemmons	310-229 .575
1977-78	13-14				Steve Smith	
1978-79	17-10				Steve Smith	
1979-80	21-4				Steve Smith	
1980-81	16-9				Steve Smith	
1981-82	15-12				Steve Smith	
1982-83	20-7				Steve Smith	102-56 .646
1983-84	N/A					
1984-85	N/A					
1985-86	N/A					
1986-87	N/A					
1987-88	N/A					
1988-89	N/A					
1989-90	N/A					
1990-91	N/A					
1991-92	N/A					
1992-93	N/A					
1993-94	N/A					
1994-95	N/A				Harold Blevins	
1995-96	9-12				Harold Blevins	
1996-97	10-16				Harold Blevins	
1997-98	4-23	3-13			Harold Blevins	
1998-99	3-24	1-15	Jeremy Jefferson	13.4	Harold Blevins	
1999-2000	6-21	5-13	Patrick Chambers	16.6	Harold Blevins	
2000-01	2-25	2-16	Jeremy Jefferson	12.4	Harold Blevins	
2001-02	2-26	2-16	Kory McKee	11.6	Harold Blevins	36-147 .197
2002-03	4-24	4-14	Kory McKee	10.1	Van Holt	
2003-04	1-26	1-17	Michael Kendrick	7.5	Van Holt	
2004-05	7-21 ⊗	5-13	Tamarius Brown	14.1	Van Holt	
2005-06	13-16	8-10	Tamarius Brown	13.7	Van Holt	
2006-07	12-19	9-9	William Byrd	13.0	Van Holt	
2007-08	13-18	8-10	Larry Williams	12.3	Van Holt	50-124 .287
2008-09	13-18	11-7	Terrance Calvin	12.0	George Ivory	13-18 .419

[a] Records from before 1956-57 have been lost.

⊗ Conference record doesn't reflect games forfeited or vacated. For adjusted record, see p. 521.

PROFILE

University of Arkansas at Pine Bluff, Pine Bluff, AR
Founded: 1873 as Branch Normal College; joined University of Arkansas system, 1972
Enrollment: 3,331 (3,232 undergraduate)
Colors: Black and gold
Nickname: Golden Lions
Current arena: H.O. Clemmons Arena, opened in 1984 (4,500)
First game: 1931
All-time record: 511-574 (.471)
Total weeks in AP Top 20/25: 0

Current conference: Southwestern Athletic (1936-70, '97-)
Conference titles:
SWAC: 1 (1967)
Conference tournament titles: 0
NCAA Tournament appearances: 0
NIT appearances: 0

TOP 5

G **James "Mack" Allen** (1960-64)
G **Harold Blevins** (1961-65)
F **Joe Bynes** (1968-72)
F **Jesse Mason** (1956-60)
F/C **Charles Hentz** (1963-67)

RECORDS

	GAME	SEASON	CAREER
POINTS	N/A	N/A	N/A
POINTS PER GAME		N/A	N/A
REBOUNDS	N/A	N/A	N/A
ASSISTS	N/A	N/A	N/A

ESPN 198 SAGARIN

ARMY

The U.S. Military Academy helped launch the coaching careers of Bob Knight and Mike Krzyzewski, and the Cadets have eight trips to the NIT to their credit. That's the bright side. The dark? Pretty much everything else. Army has never played in the NCAA Tournament, despite being a D1 member since 1935-36—a dubious distinction it shares with only four other schools.

BEST TEAM: 1969-70 Jim Oxley took over as captain for the departed guard Krzyzewski and averaged 15.6 ppg, playing with a tenacity that impressed even Knight. Army didn't lose consecutive games all season, scored road wins over Maryland and Syracuse, and beat Cincinnati and Manhattan in the NIT before losing to St. John's, then beating LSU for third place.

BEST PLAYER: C MIKE SILLIMAN (1963-66) Knight wrote in 2002 that Silliman "may still be the best player I've ever coached." Kentucky's 1962 Mr. Basketball, Silliman led Army in scoring and rebounding three consecutive seasons and is the only Cadet to play in the NBA.

BEST COACH: BOB KNIGHT (1965-71) At 25, he became the youngest head coach in major college history. While taking the Cadets to four NITs, he developed the patient offense and man-to-man D that would lead to much greater heights at Indiana.

GAME FOR THE AGES: The Cadets had never won a postseason game before the 1964 NIT. They ended that streak in dramatic style by rallying from a nine-point deficit to edge St. Bonaventure, 64-62, in the first round. But that was only a prelude to their greatest feat. In the quarterfinals on March 17, the undersized Cadets rallied from a 16-point deficit late in the first half to beat Duquesne in OT, 67-65.

FIERCEST RIVAL: Army-Navy is not just a football rivalry. The two service academies first clashed on the hardwood in 1920, and have met at least twice a year since becoming Patriot League mates in 1991-92. The second meeting each season is the Star Game or Trophy Game, with each member of the winning team earning a star for his letterman jacket. Navy leads overall, 68–42.

SEASON REVIEW

SEAS.	W-L	CONF.	COACH	SEAS.	W-L	CONF.	COACH
1902-49	*439-207*	*21 non-losing seasons, 1919-40*		**1962-63**	8-11		George Hunter
1949-50	9-8		John Mauer	**1963-64**	19-7	■	Taylor "Tates" Locke
1950-51	9-8		John Mauer	**1964-65**	21-8	■	Taylor "Tates" Locke
1951-52	8-9		Elmer Ripley	**1965-66**	18-8	■	Bob Knight
1952-53	11-8		Elmer Ripley	**1966-67**	13-8		Bob Knight
1953-54	15-7		Bob Vanatta	**1967-68**	20-5	■	Bob Knight
1954-55	9-9		Orvis Sigler	**1968-69**	18-10	■	Bob Knight
1955-56	10-13		Orvis Sigler	**1969-70**	22-6	■	Bob Knight
1956-57	7-13		Orvis Sigler	**1970-71**	11-13		Bob Knight
1957-58	13-12		Orvis Sigler	**1971-72**	11-13		Dan Dougherty
1958-59	14-10		George Hunter	**1972-73**	11-13		Dan Dougherty
1959-60	14-9		George Hunter	**1973-74**	6-18		Dan Dougherty
1960-61	17-7	■	George Hunter	**1974-75**	3-22		Dan Dougherty
1961-62	10-11		George Hunter	**1975-76**	11-14		Mike Krzyzewski

SEAS.	W-L	CONF.	SCORING		COACH	RECORD	
1976-77	20-8		Gary Winton	22.5	Mike Krzyzewski		
1977-78	19-9	■	Gary Winton	23.0	Mike Krzyzewski		
1978-79	14-11		Matt Brown	18.2	Mike Krzyzewski		
1979-80	9-17		Bob Brown	16.4	Mike Krzyzewski	73-59	.553
1980-81	7-19		Marty Coyne	16.5	Pete Gaudet		
1981-82	5-22	0-10	Dennis Schlitt	12.1	Pete Gaudet	12-41	.226
1982-83	11-18	2-8	Randy Cozzens	16.7	Les Wothke		
1983-84	11-17	4-10	Randy Cozzens	14.9	Les Wothke		
1984-85	16-13	7-7	Randy Cozzens	23.5	Les Wothke		
1985-86	9-18	5-9	Kevin Houston	22.2	Les Wothke		
1986-87	14-15	8-6	Kevin Houston	32.9	Les Wothke		
1987-88	9-19	4-10	Derrick Canada	13.9	Les Wothke		
1988-89	12-16	6-8	Derrick Canada	15.5	Les Wothke		
1989-90	10-19	5-11	Derrick Canada	15.4	Les Wothke	92-135	.405
1990-91	6-22	3-9	James Collins	16.0	Tom Miller		
1991-92	4-24	2-12	Spencer Staggs	10.5	Tom Miller		
1992-93	4-22	2-12	David Ardayfio	15.3	Tom Miller[a]	13-61	.176
1993-94	7-20	4-10	Mark Lueking	23.1	Dino Gaudio		
1994-95	12-16	4-10	Mark Lueking	24.4	Dino Gaudio		
1995-96	7-20	2-10	Mark Lueking	19.3	Dino Gaudio		
1996-97	10-16	4-8	George Tatum	17.5	Dino Gaudio	36-72	.333
1997-98	8-19	2-10	George Tatum	13.1	Pat Harris		
1998-99	8-19	4-8	George Tatum	14.8	Pat Harris		
1999-2000	5-23	2-10	Chris Spatola	12.1	Pat Harris		
2000-01	9-19	3-9	Chris Spatola	18.5	Pat Harris		
2001-02	12-16	6-8	Chris Spatola	16.5	Pat Harris	42-96	.304
2002-03	5-22	0-14	Andy Smith	9.6	Jim Crews		
2003-04	6-21	3-11	Josh Wilson	11.2	Jim Crews		
2004-05	3-24 ⊗	1-13	Matt Bell	14.3	Jim Crews		
2005-06	5-22	1-13	Jarell Brown	14.3	Jim Crews		
2006-07	15-16	4-10	Jarell Brown	16.9	Jim Crews		
2007-08	14-16	6-8	Jarell Brown	18.2	Jim Crews		
2008-09	11-19	6-8	Cleveland Richard	12.0	Jim Crews	59-140	.296

[a] **Tom Miller (3-15) and Mike Connors (1-7) both coached during the 1992-93 season.**

⊗ **Records do not reflect games forfeited or vacated. For adjusted records,** **see p. 521.**

■ **NIT appearance**

PROFILE

United States Military Academy, West Point, NY
Founded: 1802
Enrollment: 4,400 (4,400 undergraduate)
Colors: Black, gold and gray
Nicknames: Cadets, Black Knights
Current arena: Christl Arena, opened in 1985 (5,043)
Previous: USMA Fieldhouse, 1938-85 (3,500); Cadet Gymnasium, 1919-38 (N/A)
First game: 1903
All-time record: 1,094-1,084 (.502)
Total weeks in AP Top 20/25: 1
Current conference: Patriot League (1990-)

Conference titles: 0
Conference tournament titles: 0
NCAA Tournament appearances: 0
NIT appearances: 8
Semifinals: 5

CONSENSUS ALL-AMERICAS

1910	**William Copthorne**, G
1913	**William Roberts**, C
1915	**Elmer Oliphant**, G
1918	**Gene Vidal**, C
1927	**Harry Wilson**, G

TOP 5

G	**Kevin Houston** (1983-87)
G	**Mark Lueking** (1992-96)
G/F	**John Roosma** (1921-26)
F	**Gary Winton** (1974-78)
C	**Mike Silliman** (1963-66)

RECORDS

RECORDS	GAME		SEASON		CAREER	
POINTS	53	Kevin Houston, vs. Fordham (Feb. 28, 1987)	953	Kevin Houston (1986-87)	2,325	Kevin Houston (1983-87)
POINTS PER GAME			32.9	Kevin Houston (1986-87)	21.9	Gary Winton (1974-78)
REBOUNDS	27	Bill Hannon, vs. Pittsburgh (Feb. 22, 1954)	381	Bill Hannon (1953-54)	1,168	Gary Winton (1974-78)
ASSISTS	15	Ron Wilson, vs. Holy Cross (Feb. 12, 1988)	162	Ron Wilson (1988-89)	430	Randy Cozzens (1981-85)

ESPN 80 SAGARIN

AUBURN

The Tigers have won just one SEC tournament title and have a better conference winning percentage than only four current SEC members. But from Snow White and the Seven Dwarfs to the Round Mound of Rebound to the Cliff Dwellers, Auburn has rarely finished in the second division in terms of entertainment value.

BEST TEAM: 1998-99 The Tigers didn't have just one team MVP or even two co-MVPs. All five starters—center Mamadou N'diaye, forwards Chris Porter and Bryant Smith, guards Doc Robinson and Scott Pohlman—shared the honor, a testament to the team's balance and chemistry. Of course, the biggest factor wasn't a player at all, but the Cliff Dwellers—Auburn's rabid home fans, named in honor of coach Cliff Ellis. The Tigers went 15–0 at home to spur a run to the Sweet 16.

BEST PLAYER: F Charles Barkley (1981-84) The Round Mound of Rebound weighed as much as 300 pounds as a freshman and stood a good two inches shorter than his listed 6'6" height. But Barkley had fun with his pudgy image, eating pizza out of a box for a photo shoot one day and dunking on opponents the next. After trimming down to 265 pounds as a junior, he was named SEC Player of the Year and launched himself to a Hall of Fame NBA career.

BEST COACH: Joel Eaves (1949-63) The white-haired Eaves and his smallish Tigers—a.k.a. Snow White and the Seven Dwarfs—outworked opponents in the 1950s and '60s by running the shuffle offense, designed to produce layups resulting from a series of cuts to the basket. The result was the 1960 SEC title and three seasons ranked in the AP final Top 20.

GAME FOR THE AGES: On Feb. 20, 1960, the Tigers hosted Adolph Rupp's Wildcats, who had never lost at Auburn. Kentucky held a 60-59 lead with :04 left when Tigers forward Jimmy Fibbe stepped to the line for a one-and-one. Did we mention this was the first televised game in Tigers history? No big deal. Fibbe made both shots to pull off the upset.

HEARTBREAKER: In 1984, the Tigers made their first Big Dance and had the look of a contender. But No. 12-seed Richmond squashed that by pulling off a 72-71 first-round upset. Sophomore forward Chuck Person admitted that his teammates had looked past the Spiders, with their eyes on Indiana in the second round. Oops.

FIERCEST RIVAL: Of course it's Alabama. How could it not be? Consider Iron Bowl trophy presentation day. That's when the losing school in the annual November football clash presents the Iron Bowl to the winning school—on the victor's home court during halftime of the hoops matchup. When Bama beat Auburn on the gridiron in 2008, it snapped a five-year streak in which Tigers hoops coach Jeff Lebo hosted the event.

FANFARE AND HOOPLA: Aubie, who first took form as a cartoon on Auburn football game programs in 1959, came to life on Feb. 28, 1979, when the dancing Tony the Tiger look-alike entered the Birmingham Jefferson Civic Center basketball arena. Aubie is now a member of the Mascot Hall of Fame.

FAN FAVORITE: F Chuck Person (1982-86) Just like Barkley, the Rifleman was personable and energetic. But while Barkley went pro after his junior season, Person took the Tigers to the NCAA Elite Eight as a senior.

> ***Barkley had fun with his pudgy image, eating pizza for a photo shoot one day and dunking on opponents the next.***

FIRST-ROUND PRO PICKS

1978	**Mike Mitchell,** Cleveland (15)
1984	**Charles Barkley,** Philadelphia (5)
1986	**Chuck Person,** Indiana (4)
1988	**Chris Morris,** New Jersey (4)
1994	**Wesley Person,** Phoenix (23)
2000	**Mamadou N'diaye,** Denver (26)

PROFILE

Auburn University, Auburn, AL
Founded: 1856
Enrollment: 24,547 (19,812 undergraduate)
Colors: Burnt orange and navy blue
Nickname: Tigers
Current arena: Beard-Eaves-Memorial Coliseum, opened in 1969 (10,500)
Previous: The Sports Arena, 1948-69 (2,500); Alumni Gym, 1916-48 (N/A); The Gymnasium, 1906-16 (N/A)
First game: Jan. 19, 1906
All-time record: 1,203-1,042-1 (.536)
Total weeks in AP Top 20/25: 89
Current conference: Southeastern (1932-)
Conference titles:
SEC: 2 (1960, '99)
Conference tournament titles:
SEC: 1 (1985)
NCAA Tournament appearances: 8
Sweet 16s (since 1975): 4
NIT appearances: 6

TOP 5

G	**John Mengelt** (1968-71)
G/F	**Wesley Person** (1990-94)
F	**Charles Barkley** (1981-84)
F	**Chuck Person** (1982-86)
C	**Rex Frederick** (1956-59)

RECORDS	GAME		SEASON		CAREER	
POINTS	60	John Mengelt, vs. Alabama (Feb. 14, 1970)	747	Chuck Person (1984-85)	2,311	Chuck Person (1982-86)
POINTS PER GAME			28.4	John Mengelt (1970-71)	24.8	John Mengelt (1968-71)
REBOUNDS	27	Rex Frederick, vs. SMU (Dec. 19, 1957)	347	Korvotney Barber (2008-09)	996	Mike Mitchell (1974-78)
ASSISTS	15	Eddie Johnson, vs. LSU (1976)	221	Gerald White (1985-86)	624	Gerald White (1983-87)

SEASON REVIEW

SEASON	W-L	CONF.	SCORING	COACH	RECORD
1905-16	*50-57-1*		*Went 5-1-1 in their first season, including a 64-8 win over Mercer*		
1916-17	2-2			Mike Donahue	
1917-18	2-3			Mike Donahue	
1918-19	4-3			Mike Donahue	
1919-20	11-7			Mike Donahue	
1920-21	5-8			Mike Donahue	74-80-1 .481
1921-22	5-8	2-1		Wilbur Hutsell	
1922-23	7-7	2-3		Wilbur Hutsell	
1923-24	4-9	0-6		Wilbur Hutsell	16-24 .400
1924-25	3-11	1-5		Herb Bunker	3-11 .214
1925-26	5-10	1-7		Mike Papke	
1926-27	13-6	12-4		Mike Papke	
1927-28	20-2	12-1		Mike Papke	38-18 .679
1928-29	6-15	3-9		George Bohler	6-15 .286
1929-30	1-10	1-10		Hal Lee	1-10 .091
1930-31	9-6	7-4		Sam McAllister	
1931-32	12-3	9-2		Sam McAllister	
1932-33	4-9	4-7		Sam McAllister	25-18 .581
1933-34	2-11	2-9		Ralph Jordan	
1934-35	4-13	3-9		Ralph Jordan	
1935-36	10-7	7-4		Ralph Jordan	
1936-37	11-4	7-4		Ralph Jordan	

SEAS.	W-L	CONF.	POSTSEASON	SCORING		REBOUNDS		ASSISTS		COACH	RECORD
1937-38	14-5	6-3								Ralph Jordan	
1938-39	16-6	8-4								Ralph Jordan	
1939-40	7-10	6-7								Ralph Jordan	
1940-41	13-6	6-5								Ralph Jordan	
1941-42	11-6	9-5								Ralph Jordan	
1942-43	1-14	1-12								Bob Evans	
1943-44	no team										
1944-45	3-14	2-6								Bob Evans	4-28 .125
1945-46	7-9	7-6								Ralph Jordan	95-77 .552
1946-47	3-18	1-15								V.J. Edney	3-18 .143
1947-48	12-10	7-7								Danny Doyle	
1948-49	9-15	5-11								Danny Doyle	21-25 .457
1949-50	17-7	12-6		Bill Lynn	14.7					Joel Eaves	
1950-51	12-10	6-8		Dan Pridgen	12.6	Dan Pridgen	9.1			Joel Eaves	
1951-52	14-12	6-8		Inman Veal	10.9	Bob Fenn	7.8			Joel Eaves	
1952-53	13-8	6-7		Bob Miller	15.8	Bob Miller	12.3			Joel Eaves	
1953-54	16-8	8-6		Bob Miller	17.8	Bob Miller	11.5			Joel Eaves	
1954-55	11-9	6-8		Bill Kirkpatrick	18.7	Jim O'Donnell	8.6			Joel Eaves	
1955-56	11-10	8-6		Bill McGriff	15.9	Bill McGriff	10.2			Joel Eaves	
1956-57	13-8	8-6		Jimmy Lee	15.9	Rex Frederick	15.3			Joel Eaves	
1957-58	16-6	11-3		Rex Frederick	16.1	Rex Frederick	14.8			Joel Eaves	
1958-59	20-2	12-2		Jimmy Lee	13.1	Rex Frederick	12.9			Joel Eaves	
1959-60	19-3	12-2		Henry Hart	15.5	Jimmy Fibbe	6.9			Joel Eaves	
1960-61	15-7	8-6		Jimmy Fibbe	14.7	Jimmy Fibbe	6.5			Joel Eaves	
1961-62	18-6	11-3		Layton Johns	15.7	Layton Johns	11.3			Joel Eaves	
1962-63	18-4	10-4		Layton Johns	15.0	Layton Johns	12.4			Joel Eaves[a]	213-100 .681
1963-64	11-12	6-8		Lee DeFore	17.7	Freddie Guy	11.1			Bill Lynn	
1964-65	16-9	11-5		Lee DeFore	15.8	Freddie Guy	12.2			Bill Lynn	
1965-66	16-10	8-8		Lee DeFore	23.7	Lee DeFore	9.6	Bobby Buisson	4.2	Bill Lynn	
1966-67	17-8	12-6		Alex Howell	14.0	Wally Tinker	8.4	Bobby Buisson	2.9	Bill Lynn	
1967-68	13-13	8-10		Wally Tinker	14.5	Bill Alexander	7.4	Tom Perry	4.0	Bill Lynn	
1968-69	15-10	10-8		John Mengelt	19.4	Wally Tinker	7.8	Wally Tinker	5.2	Bill Lynn	
1969-70	15-11	11-7		John Mengelt	26.8	Bill Alexander	12.1	Carl Shetler	2.6	Bill Lynn	
1970-71	11-15	8-10		John Mengelt	28.4	Jim Retseck	11.3	John Mengelt	3.5	Bill Lynn	
1971-72	10-16	6-12		Jim Retseck	16.5	Jim Retseck	9.2	Henry Harris	2.7	Bill Lynn	
1972-73	6-20	4-14		Gary England	12.8	Gary Redding	8.2	Gary England	3.2	Bill Lynn	130-124 .512
1973-74	10-16	5-13		Eddie Johnson	21.8	Pepto Bolden	11.6	Mike Christian	3.6	Bob Davis	
1974-75	18-8	12-6		Eddie Johnson	20.9	Mike Mitchell	11.4	Eddie Johnson	5.8	Bob Davis	
1975-76	16-10	11-7		Eddie Johnson	19.7	Mike Mitchell	9.6	Eddie Johnson	5.7	Bob Davis	
1976-77	13-13	6-12		Mike Mitchell	19.4	Pepto Bolden	9.0	Eddie Johnson	5.2	Bob Davis	
1977-78	13-14	8-10		Mike Mitchell	24.9	Mike Mitchell	8.9	Stan Pietkiewicz	4.7	Bob Davis	70-61 .534
1978-79	13-16	5-13		Bobby Cattage	15.9	Bobby Cattage	9.3	Bubba Price	4.1	Sonny Smith	
1979-80	10-18	5-13		Bubba Price	10.9	Earl Banks	5.9	Eric Stringer	3.7	Sonny Smith	
1980-81	11-16	4-14		Earl Banks	11.9	Earl Banks	7.0	Byron Henson	2.4	Sonny Smith	
1981-82	14-14	7-11		Odell Mosteller	15.9	Charles Barkley	9.8	Paul Daniels	4.9	Sonny Smith	
1982-83	15-13	8-10		Charles Barkley	14.4	Charles Barkley	9.5	Paul Daniels	4.8	Sonny Smith	
1983-84	20-11	12-6	NCAA FIRST ROUND	Chuck Person	19.1	Charles Barkley	9.5	Paul Daniels	4.4	Sonny Smith	
1984-85	22-12	8-10	NCAA REGIONAL SEMIFINALS	Chuck Person	22.0	Chuck Person	8.9	Gerald White	5.4	Sonny Smith	
1985-86	22-11	13-5	NCAA REGIONAL FINALS	Chuck Person	21.5	Chuck Person	7.9	Gerald White	6.7	Sonny Smith	
1986-87	18-13	9-9	NCAA SECOND ROUND	Jeff Moore	17.4	Jeff Moore	9.5	Gerald White	5.2	Sonny Smith	
1987-88	19-11	11-7	NCAA SECOND ROUND	Chris Morris	20.7	Chris Morris	9.8	Terrance Howard	5.3	Sonny Smith	
1988-89	9-19	2-16		Keenan Carpenter	19.0	Matt Geiger	6.6	Derrick Dennison	4.3	Sonny Smith	173-154 .529
1989-90	13-18	8-10		Ronnie Battle	17.0	John Caylor	6.8	Reggie Gallon	3.8	Tommy Joe Eagles	
1990-91	13-16	5-13		Ronnie Battle	17.0	Robert McKie	5.9	Reggie Gallon	4.1	Tommy Joe Eagles	
1991-92	12-15	5-11		Wesley Person	19.9	Aaron Swinson	7.5	Champ Wrencher	4.5	Tommy Joe Eagles	
1992-93	15-12	8-8	NIT FIRST ROUND	Wesley Person	18.8	Aaron Swinson	7.7	Reggie Gallon	4.5	Tommy Joe Eagles	
1993-94	11-17	3-13		Wesley Person	22.2	Aubrey Wiley	9.3	Wes Flanigan	4.9	Tommy Joe Eagles	64-78 .451
1994-95	16-13	7-9	NIT FIRST ROUND	Lance Weems	13.2	Chris Davis	6.1	Moochie Norris	4.9	Cliff Ellis	
1995-96	19-13	6-10	NIT FIRST ROUND	Lance Weems	13.4	Pat Burke	8.7	Wes Flanigan	6.7	Cliff Ellis	
1996-97	16-15	6-10		Wes Flanigan	11.0	Pat Burke	7.0	Wes Flanigan	4.5	Cliff Ellis	
1997-98	16-14	7-9	NIT SECOND ROUND	Doc Robinson	12.4	Mamadou N'diaye	6.9	Doc Robinson	4.4	Cliff Ellis	
1998-99	29-4	14-2	NCAA REGIONAL SEMIFINALS	Chris Porter	16.0	Chris Porter	8.6	Doc Robinson	5.0	Cliff Ellis	
1999-2000	24-10	9-7	NCAA SECOND ROUND	Chris Porter	14.6	Mamadou N'diaye	7.9	Doc Robinson	5.1	Cliff Ellis	
2000-01	18-14	7-9	NIT SECOND ROUND	Marquis Daniels	15.7	Jamison Brewer	7.2	Jamison Brewer	5.8	Cliff Ellis	
2001-02	12-16	4-12		Marquis Daniels	11.6	Marquis Daniels	5.3	Marquis Daniels	4.1	Cliff Ellis	
2002-03	22-12	8-8	NCAA REGIONAL SEMIFINALS	Marquis Daniels	18.4	Marco Killingsworth	6.4	Marquis Daniels	3.3	Cliff Ellis	
2003-04	14-14	5-11		Marco Killingsworth	13.7	Marco Killingsworth	6.9	Ian Young	2.4	Cliff Ellis	186-125 .598
2004-05	14-17	4-12		Toney Douglas	16.9	Quinnel Brown	6.0	Ian Young	4.0	Jeff Lebo	
2005-06	12-16	4-12		Ronny LeMelle	12.8	Korvotney Barber	4.8	Quantez Robertson	4.6	Jeff Lebo	
2006-07	17-15	7-9		Josh Dollard	12.5	Josh Dollard	7.0	Quantez Robertson	5.1	Jeff Lebo	
2007-08	14-16	4-12		Quan Prowell	15.0	Korvotney Barber	6.9	Quantez Robertson	4.1	Jeff Lebo	
2008-09	24-12	10-6	NIT QUARTERFINALS	DeWayne Reed	13.2	Korvotney Barber	9.6	DeWayne Reed	3.7	Jeff Lebo	81-76 .516

[a] During the 1962-63 season Bill Lynn (5-2) took over as coach after Joel Eaves had a heart attack, but the entire record is credited to Eaves.

ESPN 212 SAGARIN

AUSTIN PEAY

"Let's go Peay! Let's go Peay!" Attend any Governors home game and you'll hear one of college hoops' most colorful chants. The call became popular in the early 1970s, when coach Lake Kelly turned a sleepy also-ran from Tennessee into a high-scoring dynamo, led by the prolific James "Fly" Williams. In those days, the chant had two parts. The first was, "The Fly is open!"

BEST TEAM: 1972-73 Freshman scoring sensation James "Fly" Williams teamed with Danny Odums and Howard Jackson to win the Governors' first OVC title and bring the Memorial Health Gymnasium—a.k.a. the Little Red Barn—to life. The thrills continued in the NCAA Tournament, where APSU beat Jacksonville before falling to Kentucky in OT, 106-100. (Austin Peay's participation in the 1973 Tournament was later vacated by the NCAA for rules violations.)

BEST PLAYER: G James "Fly" Williams (1972-74) He was skinny as a backboard, but the flamboyant 6'5" Brooklyn street-ball legend could score at will and with great creativity. His freshman average of 29.4 ppg stood as a D1 record until LSU'S Chris Jackson broke it in 1988-89. Although Williams left APSU after his sophomore season for academic reasons, he still ranks ninth on the school's all-time scoring list with 1,541 points.

BEST COACH: Dave Loos (1990-) The Govs named their home floor after Loos for good reason. Since 1993-94, APSU has finished no worse than .500 in its conference and has made three Tournament appearances.

GAME FOR THE AGES: Before the 1987 Big Dance, Dick Vitale vowed to stand on his head if Illinois lost its March 12 opener to No. 14-seed APSU. Sure enough, Tony Raye hit two free throws with :02 left to spring the 68-67 upset—and turn Dickie V upside down.

FIERCEST RIVAL: "Flush the Peay! Flush the Peay!" For every great chant there's a counter chant, this one made famous by the Murray State student section. Peay has seen a lot of games go down the drain against their rivals from Kentucky. Murray says it's won 69 of 109; Peay says Murray has won 72 of 112.

SEASON REVIEW

SEAS.	W-L	CONF.	COACH	SEAS.	W-L	CONF.	COACH
1929-49	*187-129*	*Seven non-losing seasons, 1929-36*		**1962-63**	18-11		George Fisher
1949-50	14-11		David B. Aaron	**1963-64**	14-9	7-7	George Fisher
1950-51	13-12		David B. Aaron	**1964-65**	4-17	2-12	George Fisher
1951-52	11-17		David B. Aaron	**1965-66**	7-14	3-11	George Fisher
1952-53	14-12		David B. Aaron	**1966-67**	14-9	7-7	George Fisher
1953-54	14-13		David B. Aaron	**1967-68**	8-16	4-10	George Fisher
1954-55	7-17		David B. Aaron	**1968-69**	10-14	3-11	George Fisher
1955-56	16-11		David B. Aaron	**1969-70**	5-21	2-12	George Fisher
1956-57	24-9		David B. Aaron	**1970-71**	10-14	5-9	George Fisher
1957-58	17-9		David B. Aaron	**1971-72**	10-14	5-9	Lake Kelly
1958-59	14-10		David B. Aaron	**1972-73**	22-7 ⊗	11-3 ●	Lake Kelly
1959-60	22-5		David B. Aaron	**1973-74**	17-10	10-4 ●	Lake Kelly
1960-61	22-9		David B. Aaron	**1974-75**	17-10	10-4	Lake Kelly
1961-62	14-12		David B. Aaron	**1975-76**	20-7	10-4	Lake Kelly

SEAS.	W-L	CONF.	SCORING		COACH	RECORD
1976-77	24-4	13-1	Calvin Garrett	17.4	Lake Kelly	
1977-78	15-12	8-6	Otis Howard	21.1	Ed Thompson	
1978-79	8-18	3-9	Alfred Barney	17.6	Ed Thompson	23-30 .434
1979-80	8-18	2-10	Roosevelt Sanders	15.4	Ron Bargatze	
1980-81	14-13	7-7	Andrew Burton	20.4	Ron Bargatze	
1981-82	6-20	4-12	Lenny Manning	18.7	Ron Bargatze	
1982-83	11-16	4-10	Lenny Manning	16.1	Ron Bargatze	39-67 .368
1983-84	11-16	5-9	Lenny Manning	18.7	Howard Jackson	
1984-85	8-19	4-10	Robert Biggers	13.3	Howard Jackson	19-35 .352
1985-86	14-14	8-6	Gerald Gray	15.1	Lake Kelly	
1986-87	20-12	8-6 ●	Lawrence Mitchell	21.9	Lake Kelly	
1987-88	17-13	10-4	Barry Sumpter	15.3	Lake Kelly	
1988-89	18-12	8-4	Keith Rawls	19.5	Lake Kelly	
1989-90	10-19	2-10	Donald Tivis	18.3	Lake Kelly	189-122 .608▼
1990-91	15-14	6-6	Tommy Brown	17.7	Dave Loos	
1991-92	11-17	6-8	Geoff Herman	17.9	Dave Loos	
1992-93	7-20	4-12	Rick Yudt	16.7	Dave Loos	
1993-94	11-16	10-6	Tyrone Beck	15.9	Dave Loos	
1994-95	13-16	8-8	Bubba Wells	19.3	Dave Loos	
1995-96	19-11	10-6 ●	Bubba Wells	26.3	Dave Loos	
1996-97	17-14	12-6	Bubba Wells	31.7	Dave Loos	
1997-98	17-11	11-7	Jerome Jackson	13.4	Dave Loos	
1998-99	11-16	9-9	Trenton Hassell	17.8	Dave Loos	
1999-2000	18-10	11-7	Trenton Hassell	18.1	Dave Loos	
2000-01	22-10	10-6	Trenton Hassell	21.7	Dave Loos	
2001-02	14-18	8-8	Nick Stapleton	23.2	Dave Loos	
2002-03	23-8	13-3 ●	Adrian Henning	15.5	Dave Loos	
2003-04	22-10	16-0 ■	Adrian Henning	13.7	Dave Loos	
2004-05	13-19	9-7	Maurice Hampton	14.7	Dave Loos	
2005-06	17-14	11-9	Maurice Hampton	16.4	Dave Loos	
2006-07	21-12	16-4 ■	Drake Reed	15.8	Dave Loos	
2007-08	24-11	16-4 ●	Drake Reed	14.4	Dave Loos	
2008-09	19-14	13-5	Drake Reed	21.9	Dave Loos	314-261 .546

⊗ Records do not reflect games forfeited or vacated. For adjusted records, see p. 521.
▼ Coach's record adjusted to reflect games forfeited or vacated: 188-120, .610. For yearly totals, see p. 521.
● NCAA Tournament appearance ■ NIT appearance

PROFILE

Austin Peay State University, Clarksville, TN
Founded: 1927
Enrollment: 9,207 (8,341 undergraduate)
Colors: Red and white
Nickname: Governors
Current arena: Winfield Dunn Center (Dave Aaron Arena), opened in 1975 (7,275)
Previous: Memorial Health Gymnasium, a.k.a. the Little Red Barn, 1952-75 (2,500)
First game: 1929
All-time record: 1,063-916 (.537)

Total weeks in AP Top 20/25: 3
Current conference: Ohio Valley (1963-)
Conference titles:
OVC: 8 (1973, '74 [tie], '77, '97 [tie], 2003 [tie], '04, '07, '08)
Conference tournament titles:
OVC: 4 (1987, '96, 2003, '08)
NCAA Tournament appearances: 6
NIT appearances: 2

FIRST-ROUND PRO PICKS

1974 **James "Fly" Williams,** Denver (ABA, 4)

TOP 5

G **James "Fly" Williams** (1972-74)
G/F **Trenton Hassell** (1998-2001)
F **Otis Howard** (1974-78)
F **Bubba Wells** (1993-97)
C **Tom Morgan** (1952-53, '55-58)

RECORDS

	GAME		SEASON		CAREER	
POINTS	51	James "Fly" Williams, vs. Tennessee Tech (Jan. 20, 1973); vs. Georgia Southern (Dec. 20, 1972)	854	James "Fly" Williams (1972-73)	2,267	Bubba Wells (1993-97)
POINTS PER GAME			31.7	Bubba Wells (1996-97)	28.5	James "Fly" Williams (1972-74)
REBOUNDS	28	Greg Kinman, vs. Chattanooga (Dec. 1, 1970)	561	Tom Morgan (1956-57)	1,431	Tom Morgan (1952-53, '55-58)
ASSISTS	16	Norman Jackson, vs. Southern Miss (Jan. 5, 1976)	211	Norman Jackson (1976-77)	637	Norman Jackson (1974-78)

ESPN 148 SAGARIN

BALL STATE

Some programs are defined by triumph. Ball State is defined by a near upset. In the 1990 NCAA Sweet 16, down 69-67 against eventual national champion UNLV, the Cardinals held the ball for the last shot. After taking a pass on the right wing, Paris McCurdy slipped to the floor and Ball State couldn't get a shot off before the buzzer. BSU hasn't won a Tournament game in three tries since.

BEST TEAM: 1989-90 First-year coach Dick Hunsaker led the senior-laden Cardinals to the Sweet 16 as a No. 12 seed, thanks to two thrilling upsets: a 54-53 victory over Oregon State in the first round and a 62-60 win over Louisville in the second.

BEST PLAYER: F Bonzi Wells (1994-98) When Cardinals great Ray McCallum became head coach in 1993, the first recruit he went after was this local product. Funny how it worked out: McCallum's and Wells' jerseys are the only two hanging from the Worthen Arena rafters. Wells is the all-time BSU leader in points and steals, and is the only Cardinal to be a first-round NBA draft pick.

BEST COACH: Rick Majerus (1987-89) He ran highly structured practices, pushed his players to commit to hard-nosed defense and was a tireless recruiter. In his second and final season, the formula paid dividends, as the Cardinals won the MAC, then upset Pittsburgh in the Tournament's first round. During his short tenure, Majerus established a winning tradition that would last into Hunsaker's and McCallum's tenures.

GAME FOR THE AGES: In the first round of the 1990 Tournament, the Cardinals trailed Oregon State, 53-51, when Paris McCurdy rose in traffic and unleashed a shot at the buzzer. Not only was it good, but McCurdy was fouled on the play. The senior forward sank the game-winner, setting off a celebration for the ages.

FIERCEST RIVAL: MAC rivals separated by 90 miles, Miami of Ohio and Ball State have been duking it out since 1935, with the RedHawks leading the series, 57–35. Nine of those games have gone to OT, most memorably Miami's triple-overtime, 86-84 win on Jan. 12, 2000.

SEASON REVIEW

SEAS.	W-L	CONF.	COACH	SEAS.	W-L	CONF.	COACH
1921-47	*239-190*		*Paul Parker (1925-30), 55-34, .618*	1960-61	12-11		Jim Hinga
1947-48	12-5		Pete Phillips	1961-62	12-10		Jim Hinga
1948-49	12-6		Dick Stealy	1962-63	15-9		Jim Hinga
1949-50	9-9		Dick Stealy	1963-64	17-8		Jim Hinga
1950-51	8-12		Dick Stealy	1964-65	9-13		Jim Hinga
1951-52	7-15		Dick Stealy	1965-66	10-15		Jim Hinga
1952-53	11-11		Robert Primmer	1966-67	7-14		Jim Hinga
1953-54	9-12		Robert Primmer	1967-68	10-12		Jim Hinga
1954-55	8-12		Jim Hinga	1968-69	7-16		Bud Getchell
1955-56	10-14		Jim Hinga	1969-70	8-16		Bud Getchell
1956-57	19-8		Jim Hinga	1970-71	6-20		Bud Getchell
1957-58	13-11		Jim Hinga	1971-72	9-15		Bud Getchell
1958-59	7-15		Jim Hinga	1972-73	9-15		Jim Holstein
1959-60	5-17		Jim Hinga	1973-74	14-12		Jim Holstein

SEAS.	W-L	CONF.		SCORING		COACH	RECORD	
1974-75	10-15			Kim Kaufman	18.0	Jim Holstein		
1975-76	11-14	5-11		Jim Fields	14.7	Jim Holstein		
1976-77	11-14	7-9		Randy Boarden	11.8	Jim Holstein	55-70	.440
1977-78	10-15	6-10		Mike Drews	12.5	Steve Yoder		
1978-79	16-11	9-7		Mike Drews	16.2	Steve Yoder		
1979-80	14-15	7-9		Ray McCallum	16.5	Steve Yoder		
1980-81	20-10	10-6	●	Ray McCallum	18.4	Steve Yoder		
1981-82	17-11	12-4		Ray McCallum	17.6	Steve Yoder	77-62	.554
1982-83	17-12	10-8		Ray McCallum	20.7	Al Brown		
1983-84	8-19	5-13		Jeff Furlin	10.6	Al Brown		
1984-85	13-16	8-10		Dan Palombizio	26.3	Al Brown		
1985-86	21-10	11-7	●	Dan Palombizio	20.2	Al Brown		
1986-87	9-18	4-12		Charles Smith	21.2	Al Brown	68-75	.476
1987-88	14-14	8-8		Derrick Wesley	20.6	Rick Majerus		
1988-89	29-3	14-2	●	Curtis Kidd	14.0	Rick Majerus	43-17	.717
1989-90	26-7	13-3	●	Paris McCurdy	11.8	Dick Hunsaker		
1990-91	21-10	10-6	■	Emanuel Cross	15.6	Dick Hunsaker		
1991-92	24-9	11-5	■	Keith Stalling	13.2	Dick Hunsaker		
1992-93	26-8	14-4	●	Jeermal Sylvester	14.1	Dick Hunsaker	97-34	.740
1993-94	16-12	11-7		Steve Payne	20.5	Ray McCallum		
1994-95	19-11	11-7	●	Steve Payne	17.3	Ray McCallum		
1995-96	16-12	11-7		Bonzi Wells	25.4	Ray McCallum		
1996-97	16-13	9-9		Bonzi Wells	22.0	Ray McCallum		
1997-98	21-8	14-4	■	Bonzi Wells	22.8	Ray McCallum		
1998-99	16-11	10-8		Duane Clemens	16.3	Ray McCallum		
1999-2000	22-9	11-7	●	Duane Clemens	18.7	Ray McCallum	126-76	.624
2000-01	18-12	11-7		Theron Smith	16.3	Tim Buckley		
2001-02	23-12	12-6	■	Theron Smith	19.6	Tim Buckley		
2002-03	13-17	8-10		Chris Williams	24.5	Tim Buckley		
2003-04	14-15	10-8		Dennis Trammell	13.2	Tim Buckley		
2004-05	15-13	10-8		Peyton Stovall	16.7	Tim Buckley		
2005-06	10-18	6-12		Skip Mills	18.6	Tim Buckley	93-87	.517
2006-07	9-22	5-11		Skip Mills	13.7	Ronny Thompson	9-22	.290
2007-08	6-24	5-11		Anthony Newell	16.9	Billy Taylor		
2008-09	14-17	7-9		Jarrod Jones	11.2	Billy Taylor	20-41	.328

● NCAA Tournament appearance ■ NIT appearance

PROFILE

Ball State University, Muncie, IN
Founded: 1918
Enrollment: 19,000 (15,083 undergraduate)
Colors: Cardinal and white
Nickname: Cardinals
Current arena: John E. Worthen Arena, opened as University Arena in 1992 (11,500)
Previous: Irving Gymnasium, 1962-92 (N/A)
First game: Jan. 7, 1921
All-time record: 1,079-980 (.524)
Total weeks in AP Top 20/25: 8

Current conference: Mid-American (1975-)
Conference titles:
MAC: 6 (1981 [tie], '82, '89, '90, '93 [tie], '98 [tie])
Conference tournament titles:
MAC: 7 (1981, '86, '89, '90, '93, '95, 2000)
NCAA Tournament appearances: 7
Sweet 16s (since 1975): 1
NIT appearances: 4

FIRST-ROUND NBA PICKS

1998 **Bonzi Wells,** Detroit (11)

TOP 5

G **Larry Bullington** (1971-74)
G **Ray McCallum** (1979-83)
G **Scott Nichols** (1986-90)
F **Paris McCurdy** (1988-90)
F **Bonzi Wells** (1994-98)

RECORDS

RECORDS	GAME		SEASON		CAREER	
POINTS	48	Chris Williams, vs. Akron (Jan. 4, 2003)	762	Dan Palombizio (1984-85)	2,485	Bonzi Wells (1994-98)
POINTS PER GAME			27.5	Jim Regenold (1970-71)	23.6	Larry Bullington (1971-74)
REBOUNDS	27	Ed Butler, vs. Valparaiso (Jan. 12, 1963); vs. Northern Illinois (Dec. 28, 1961)	442	Ed Butler (1963-64)	1,231	Ed Butler (1961-64)
ASSISTS	19	Bob Faulkner, vs. Racine (Feb. 2, 1974)	207	Jamie Matthews (1992-93)	573	Jim Hahn (1975-79)

ESPN 117 SAGARIN

BAYLOR

On Jan. 22, 1927, the lead headline of the *Waco Times-Herald* read, "Ten Baylor Stars Killed." The deaths resulted from a collision between a train and the bus carrying the Bears to a game against Texas. Seventy-six years later, the murder of reserve Patrick Dennehy by teammate Carlton Dotson, along with the revelation of numerous improprieties within the program, caused a national firestorm. But while Baylor basketball has been blighted by darkness, it's also been defined by resiliency. In 2008, Scott Drew led the Bears to their first NCAA Tournament in 20 years, and in '09 they finished as NIT runner-up.

BEST TEAM: 1947-48 Sometimes, the right coach makes all the difference. Bill Henderson took over a team that went 0–17 in 1944-45 and improved it to 25–5 in his first full season. Then in '47-48, Henderson won his second Southwest Conference title and his 24–8 Bears took out Washington and Kansas State in the NCAA Tournament, before losing to Kentucky in the Final, 58-42.

BEST PLAYER: G VINNIE JOHNSON (1977-79) As a 13-year pro, he was known as the Microwave for his ability to instantly heat up on offense. It's a trait he showed off at Baylor the minute he arrived from McLennan Community College. Although he played just two seasons, Johnson ranks 11th on Baylor's all-time scoring list with 1,231 career points (24.1 ppg).

BEST COACH: BILL HENDERSON (1941-43, '45-61) No drinking. No cursing. No smoking. Those were the three cardinal rules Henderson set down for his players. But that doesn't mean the Bears didn't have fun on the court. Playing tight defense and outpacing many opponents on offense, Baylor went to three NCAA tournaments under Henderson.

GAME FOR THE AGES: Baylor's 1950 West Regional semifinal game against BYU produced one of the most shocking endings in Tourney history. Down by four with two minutes left, the Bears took the lead after a field goal by Don Heathington and a three-point play by Gerald Cobb. Each team hit one more free throw, leaving Baylor the 56-55 victors.

HEARTBREAKER: After that 1950 miracle win over BYU, the Bears' luck ran out in the Final Four against Bradley. Baylor trailed by eight with 3:30 left, then rallied to within two, thanks to Heathington's clutch shooting. But the Bears' potential game-tying shot at the buzzer fell short and Bradley won, 68-66.

FIERCEST RIVAL: Texas has won 24 straight over the Bears—and Baylor's longstanding hatred for UT has grown with each loss. No game was more devastating than the 68-67 home defeat in 2007, when a shot by Mark Shepherd rimmed out at the buzzer. Texas leads overall, 155–75.

FANFARE AND HOOPLA: Baylor's resurgence is reflected in the antics of the Bear Pit, the student section started in 2005 with more than 500 members. Dressed in black-and-gold striped shirts, students mix in "Sic 'Em Bears" yells with the Bear Claw (hold your hand over your head and curl your fingers slightly, as if grabbing a grapefruit), creating a rowdy basketball atmosphere—once unthinkable at the world's largest Baptist university.

Skinner could ignite even the sleepiest of home crowds with one of his monster blocks, then keep them stoked with his rugged inside play.

FAN FAVORITE: C BRIAN SKINNER (1994-98) He could ignite even the sleepiest of home crowds with one of his signature monster blocks, then keep them stoked with his rugged inside play and all-out hustle—attributes that have made him a fan favorite in each of his seven NBA stops, as well.

PROFILE

Baylor University, Waco, TX
Founded: 1845
Enrollment: 14,541 (11,902 undergraduate)
Colors: Green and gold
Nickname: Bears
Current arena: Ferrell Center, opened in 1988 (10,284)
Previous: Heart O' Texas Coliseum, 1960-88 (N/A)
First game: Oct. 12, 1906
All-time record: 1,116-1,260 (.470)
Total weeks in AP Top 20/25: 12

Current conference: Big 12 (1996-)
Conference titles:
Southwest: 5 (1932, '46, '48, '49 [tie], '50 [tie])
Conference tournament titles: 0
NCAA Tournament appearances: 5
Final Fours: 2
NIT appearances: 4
Semifinals: 1

FIRST-ROUND PRO PICKS

1967	**Darrell Hardy**, Anaheim (ABA)
1979	**Vinnie Johnson**, Seattle (7)
1982	**Terry Teagle**, Houston (16)
1998	**Brian Skinner**, LA Clippers (22)

TOP 5

G	**Vinnie Johnson** (1977-79)
G	**Terry Teagle** (1978-82)
F	**Darrell Hardy** (1964-67)
F/C	**William Chatmon** (1969-71)
C	**Brian Skinner** (1994-98)

RECORDS

RECORDS	GAME		SEASON		CAREER	
POINTS	50	Vinnie Johnson, vs. TCU (Feb. 20, 1979)	666	Darryl Middleton (1987-88)	2,189	Terry Teagle (1978-82)
POINTS PER GAME			25.2	Vinnie Johnson (1978-79)	24.1	Vinnie Johnson (1977-79)
REBOUNDS	27	Jerry Mallett, vs. North Texas (Feb. 1, 1955)	375	Charlie McKinney (1973-74)	915	Brian Skinner (1994-98)
ASSISTS	19	Nelson Haggerty, vs. Oral Roberts (Feb. 27, 1993)	284	Nelson Haggerty (1994-95)	699	Nelson Haggerty (1991-95)

SEASON REVIEW

SEASON	W-L	CONF.	SCORING	COACH	RECORD	
1906-16	*65-53*		*Undefeated (13-0) under Ralph Glaze in 1911-12*			
1916-17	7-10	0-6		Charles Moseley		
1917-18	2-15	2-7		Charles Moseley		
1918-19	2-11	2-8		Charles Moseley		
1919-20	8-13	1-7		Charles Moseley	28-68	.292
1920-21	13-11	8-4		Frank Bridges		
1921-22	10-8	8-8		Frank Bridges		
1922-23	7-16	7-13		Frank Bridges		
1923-24	11-23	7-17		Frank Bridges		
1924-25	3-12	2-12		Frank Bridges		
1925-26	7-8	5-7		Frank Bridges	51-78	.395
1926-27	8-4	0-3		Ralph Wolf		
1927-28	9-9	2-8		Ralph Wolf		
1928-29	7-9	2-8		Ralph Wolf		
1929-30	10-6	4-6		Ralph Wolf		
1930-31	12-8	7-5		Ralph Wolf		
1931-32	14-4	10-2		Ralph Wolf		
1932-33	4-13	1-11		Ralph Wolf		
1933-34	8-10	2-10		Ralph Wolf		
1934-35	8-9	4-8		Ralph Wolf		
1935-36	12-13	6-6		Ralph Wolf		
1936-37	11-9	6-6		Ralph Wolf		

SEAS.	W-L	CONF.	POSTSEASON	SCORING		REBOUNDS		ASSISTS		COACH	RECORD	
1937-38	10-6	9-3								Ralph Wolf		
1938-39	15-6	7-5								Ralph Wolf		
1939-40	12-9	7-5								Ralph Wolf		
1940-41	11-11	6-6								Ralph Wolf	151-126	.545
1941-42	11-9	6-6								Bill Henderson		
1942-43	6-14	3-9								Bill Henderson		
1943-44	6-12	2-10								Van Sweet		
1944-45	0-17	0-12								Van Sweet[a]	6-23	.207
1945-46	25-5	11-1	NCAA REGIONAL SEMIFINALS							Bill Henderson		
1946-47	11-11	6-6								Bill Henderson		
1947-48	24-8	11-1	NCAA RUNNER-UP	James Owens	10.3					Bill Henderson		
1948-49	14-10	9-3		Don Heathington	12.0					Bill Henderson		
1949-50	14-13	8-4	NCAA FOURTH PLACE	Don Heathington	10.9					Bill Henderson		
1950-51	8-16	3-9		Ralph Johnson	12.8					Bill Henderson		
1951-52	6-18	5-7		Ralph Johnson	14.1					Bill Henderson		
1952-53	10-11	6-6		John Starkey	16.6	John Starkey	7.5			Bill Henderson		
1953-54	12-11	6-6		Murray Bailey	13.5	Don Dickson	6.6			Bill Henderson		
1954-55	13-11	7-5		Murray Bailey	18.6	Jerry Mallett	12.9			Bill Henderson		
1955-56	6-17	3-9		Louis Estes	16.7	Jerry Mallett	10.6			Bill Henderson		
1956-57	9-15	6-6		Jerry Mallett	16.5	Jerry Mallett	14.4			Bill Henderson		
1957-58	5-19	3-11		Tom Kelly	11.0	Tom Kelly	6.9			Bill Henderson		
1958-59	11-13	7-7		Carroll Dawson	13.3	Carroll Dawson	7.3			Bill Henderson		
1959-60	12-12	6-8		Carroll Dawson	16.4	Carroll Dawson	8.8			Bill Henderson		
1960-61	4-20	2-12		Richard Tinsley	12.8	Richard Tinsley	7.2			Bill Henderson	201-239	.457
1961-62	4-20	1-13		Herbert Barritt	12.0	Herbert Barritt	5.3			Bill Menefee		
1962-63	7-17	4-10		Winston Moore	16.7	Winston Moore	8.7			Bill Menefee		
1963-64	7-17	2-12		Spencer Carlson	16.2	Spencer Carlson	8.9			Bill Menefee		
1964-65	15-9	8-6		Darrell Hardy	14.9	Darrell Hardy	10.3			Bill Menefee		
1965-66	8-16	6-8		Darrell Hardy	20.7	Darrell Hardy	13.0			Bill Menefee		
1966-67	14-10	8-6		Darrell Hardy	21.1	Darrell Hardy	11.5			Bill Menefee		
1967-68	15-9	8-6		Tommy Bowman	13.5	Tommy Bowman	13.5			Bill Menefee		
1968-69	18-6	10-4		Larry Gatewood	19.5	Tommy Bowman	10.9			Bill Menefee		
1969-70	15-9	8-6		William Chatmon	20.7	William Chatmon	12.7			Bill Menefee		
1970-71	18-8	10-4		William Chatmon	23.3	William Chatmon	14.2			Bill Menefee		
1971-72	14-12	4-10		Roy Thomas	17.6	Adam West	8.2			Bill Menefee		
1972-73	14-11	8-6		Jerry Ahart	20.2	Charlie McKinney	11.3			Bill Menefee	149-144	.509
1973-74	12-13	5-9		Charlie McKinney	18.7	Charlie McKinney	15.0			Carroll Dawson		
1974-75	10-16	6-8		Tony Rufus	13.2	Tony Rufus	8.2			Carroll Dawson		
1975-76	12-15	8-8		Larry Spicer	15.4	Larry Spicer	8.4			Carroll Dawson		
1976-77	11-17	5-11		Larry Spicer	17.9	Arthur Edwards	7.8	Larry Rogowski	3.5	Carroll Dawson[b]	42-51	.452
1977-78	14-13	8-8		Vinnie Johnson	23.0	Edwards, Mays, Oliver	7.8	Vinnie Johnson	6.0	Jim Haller		
1978-79	16-12	9-7		Vinnie Johnson	25.2	Wendell Mays	7.8	Vinnie Johnson	6.1	Jim Haller		
1979-80	11-16	6-10		Terry Teagle	23.0	Terry Teagle	8.2	Mike Little	3.2	Jim Haller		
1980-81	15-12	10-6		Terry Teagle	20.0	Terry Teagle	7.0	Jay Shakir	3.7	Jim Haller		
1981-82	17-11	9-7		Terry Teagle	22.2	Terry Teagle	7.5	Jay Shakir	2.5	Jim Haller		
1982-83	12-16	4-12		Daryl Baucham	13.9	Daryl Baucham	8.1	Jay Shakir	3.5	Jim Haller		
1983-84	5-23	1-15		James Sterns	13.2	David Glover	5.8	James Sterns	3.2	Jim Haller		
1984-85	11-17	4-12		Carlos Briggs	20.4	Edwin Mitchell	5.7	Carlos Briggs	3.4	Jim Haller	104-130	.444
1985-86	11-16	3-13		Darryl Middleton	15.7	Darryl Middleton	6.9	Dave Reichert	2.6	Gene Iba		
1986-87	18-13	10-6	NIT FIRST ROUND	Darryl Middleton	18.3	Darryl Middleton	7.3	Micheal Williams	5.1	Gene Iba		
1987-88	23-11	11-5	NCAA FIRST ROUND	Darryl Middleton	19.6	Darryl Middleton	8.3	Micheal Williams	5.4	Gene Iba		
1988-89	5-22	1-15		Julius Denton	13.9	Joey Fatta	5.6	Julius Denton	2.7	Gene Iba		
1989-90	16-14	7-9	NIT FIRST ROUND	Julius Denton	16.4	Ivan Jones	7.0	Julius Denton	3.9	Gene Iba		
1990-91	12-15	4-12		David Wesley	16.5	Kelvin Chalmers	6.4	David Wesley	5.7	Gene Iba		
1991-92	13-15	5-9		David Wesley	20.9	Kelvin Chalmers	9.0	David Wesley	4.7	Gene Iba	98-106	.480
1992-93	16-11	7-7		Alex Holcombe	19.2	Alex Holcombe	9.4	Nelson Haggerty	7.3	Darrel Johnson		
1993-94	16-11	7-7		Aundre Branch	19.0	Jerome Lambert	14.8	Nelson Haggerty	7.3	Darrel Johnson	32-22	.593
1994-95	9-19	3-11		Aundre Branch	21.7	David Hamilton	8.5	Nelson Haggerty	10.1	Harry Miller		
1995-96	9-18	4-10		Brian Skinner	17.6	Brian Skinner	9.3	Damond Mannon	3.6	Harry Miller		
1996-97	18-12	6-10		Brian Skinner	16.1	Brian Skinner	8.4	Patrick Hunter	3.3	Harry Miller		
1997-98	14-14	8-8		Brian Skinner	18.1	Brian Skinner	9.5	Patrick Hunter	4.0	Harry Miller		
1998-99	6-24	0-16		Kish Lewis	14.3	Kish Lewis	8.9	Leon Morris	1.5	Harry Miller	56-87	.392
1999-2000	14-15	4-12		Tevis Stukes	17.6	Terry Black	7.7	DeMarcus Minor	5.8	Dave Bliss		
2000-01	19-12	6-10	NIT FIRST ROUND	Terry Black	15.4	Terry Black	8.4	DeMarcus Minor	4.6	Dave Bliss		
2001-02	14-16	4-12		Lawrence Roberts	16.6	Lawrence Roberts	8.2	John Lucas III	4.0	Dave Bliss		
2002-03	14-14	5-11		Lawrence Roberts	16.0	Lawrence Roberts	10.4	John Lucas III	4.3	Dave Bliss	61-57	.517
2003-04	8-21	3-13		Terrance Thomas	15.9	Terrance Thomas	6.9	Matt Sayman	4.0	Scott Drew		
2004-05	9-19	1-15		Aaron Bruce	18.2	Tommy Swanson	5.8	Aaron Bruce	3.8	Scott Drew		
2005-06	4-13	4-12		Curtis Jerrells	13.5	Mamadou Diene	5.8	Curtis Jerrells	3.3	Scott Drew		
2006-07	15-16	4-12		Curtis Jerrells	15.0	Kevin Rogers	7.6	Curtis Jerrells	3.8	Scott Drew		
2007-08	21-11	9-7	NCAA FIRST ROUND	Curtis Jerrells	15.3	Kevin Rogers	8.5	Curtis Jerrells	3.8	Scott Drew		
2008-09	24-15	5-11	NIT RUNNER-UP	Curtis Jerrells	16.3	Kevin Rogers	7.6	Curtis Jerrells	4.9	Scott Drew	81-95	.460

[a] Van Sweet (0-11) and Bill Henderson (0-6) both coached during the 1944-45 season.
[b] Carroll Dawson (8-7) and Jim Haller (3-10) both coached during the 1976-77 season.

ESPN 307 SAGARIN

BELMONT

A dozen or so years ago, the Bruins were playing the likes of Freed-Hardeman and Trevecca Nazarene in NAIA competition. Flash forward to 2008, when Belmont, a small Baptist school in Nashville, took on Duke in the first round of the NCAA Tournament—and nearly beat the Blue Devils. You can't grow up any faster than that.

BEST TEAM: 2007-08 Equally adept at scoring from beyond the arc and by the backdoor cut, the Bruins led the Atlantic Sun with a 79.8 ppg average to return to the Big Dance for the third straight season. There they scared the britches off Duke (see Game for the Ages).

BEST PLAYER: G JUSTIN HARE (2004-08) There's clutch, then there's this 6'2" guard from Cleveland, Tenn. The two-time A-Sun tourney MVP hit 14 game-winning or -tying last-second shots, including a three-point play against Lipscomb in the 2006 conference final that got Belmont to its first Big Dance.

BEST COACH: RICK BYRD (1986-) He's led Belmont to unlikely heights, but his greatest accomplishment might have been simply keeping the team from crashing and burning when it moved to D1 in 1999. By 2003-04, the Bruins had arrived: They upset No. 11-ranked Missouri to make the NIT.

GAME FOR THE AGES: Before No. 15-seed Belmont met No. 2-seed Duke on March 20 in the 2008 NCAA Tourney, Byrd hoped his team would be competitive. When the Blue Devils opened a 10-point lead, the coach hoped it wouldn't get ugly. But when the Bruins rallied to grab the lead with two minutes left, Byrd said he was lifted higher than he'd ever been as a coach. He landed when Gerald Henderson hit the deciding layup with 11.9 seconds left in Duke's 71-70 win.

FIERCEST RIVAL: The Battle of the Boulevard between Nashville foes Belmont and Lipscomb (the two campuses share a street) isn't some quaint small-school affair. They drew nearly 16,000 to a 1990 game. In 2006, they faced off in the A-Sun tournament final, with the Bruins claiming an NCAA bid with a 74-69 overtime victory. Lipscomb leads overall, 69–55.

SEASON REVIEW

SEAS.	W-L	CONF.	COACH	SEAS.	W-L	CONF.	COACH
1952-53	7-10		Larry Striplin	1959-60	10-11		George Kelley
1953-54	17-13		Larry Striplin	1960-61	12-10		George Kelley
1954-55	18-11		Larry Striplin	1961-62	11-9		George Kelley
1955-56	16-8		Larry Striplin	1962-63	4-15		Ken Sidwell
1956-57	10-15		George Kelley	1963-64	10-8		Ken Sidwell
1957-58	4-15		George Kelley	1964-65	21-7		Wayne Dobbs
1958-59	8-12		George Kelley	1965-66	14-12		Wayne Dobbs

SEAS.	W-L	CONF.	SCORING		COACH	RECORD
1966-67	9-16				Jack Young	9-16 .360
1967-68	12-17				Dewey Jones	
1968-69	9-18				Dewey Jones	
1969-70	15-17				Dewey Jones	
1970-71	15-16				Dewey Jones	
1971-72	18-8				Dewey Jones	69-76 .476
1972-73	8-18				Ken Sidwell	
1973-74	14-12				Ken Sidwell	36-53 .404
1974-75	15-13				Dick Campbell	
1975-76	15-13				Dick Campbell	
1976-77	10-19				Dick Campbell	
1977-78	8-23		Bernard Childress	22.9	Dick Campbell	48-68 .414
1978-79	13-23				Don Purdy	
1979-80	14-17				Don Purdy	
1980-81	9-22				Don Purdy	
1981-82	18-12				Don Purdy	
1982-83	22-9				Don Purdy	
1983-84	10-21				Don Purdy	
1984-85	12-19				Don Purdy	
1985-86	18-15				Don Purdy	116-138 .457
1986-87	15-15		Reggie Little	19.4	Rick Byrd	
1987-88	22-9		Joe Behling	23.6	Rick Byrd	
1988-89	25-10		Joe Behling	31.5	Rick Byrd	
1989-90	27-7		Joe Behling	29.1	Rick Byrd	
1990-91	23-9		Greg Thurman	18.9	Rick Byrd	
1991-92	22-10		Greg Thurman	27.1	Rick Byrd	
1992-93	30-6		Shad Smith	17.6	Rick Byrd	
1993-94	30-7		Al Allen	18.5	Rick Byrd	
1994-95	37-2		Al Allen	20.6	Rick Byrd	
1995-96	29-11		DaQuinn Goff	23.3	Rick Byrd	
1996-97	15-11		Ryan Steger	15.5	Rick Byrd	
1997-98	9-18		Ryan Steger	12.6	Rick Byrd	
1998-99	14-13		Wes Burtner	14.5	Rick Byrd	
1999-2000	7-21		Wes Burtner	14.3	Rick Byrd	
2000-01	13-15		Wes Burtner	20.1	Rick Byrd	
2001-02	11-17	8-12	Adam Sonn	18.8	Rick Byrd	
2002-03	17-12	12-4	Adam Mark	16.4	Rick Byrd	
2003-04	21-9	15-5 ■	Adam Mark	18.6	Rick Byrd	
2004-05	14-16	12-8	Jese Snyder	11.8	Rick Byrd	
2005-06	20-11	15-5 ●	Justin Hare	15.6	Rick Byrd	
2006-07	23-10	14-4 ●	Justin Hare	14.3	Rick Byrd	
2007-08	25-9	14-2 ●	Justin Hare	14.9	Rick Byrd	
2008-09	20-13	14-6	Alex Renfroe	16.2	Rick Byrd	469-261 .642

● NCAA Tournament appearance ■ NIT appearance

PROFILE

Belmont University, Nashville, TN
Founded: 1951
Enrollment: 5,017 (4,174 undergraduate)
Colors: Navy, red and white
Nickname: Bruins
Current arena: Curb Event Center, opened in 2003 (5,000)
Previous: Physical Education Plant Gymnasium, later renamed the Striplin Gymnasium, 1964-2003 (2,800); Blanton Hall Annex Gymnasium, 1952-64 (N/A)
First game: Nov. 20, 1952

All-time record: 895-745 (.546)
Total weeks in AP Top 20/25: 0
Current conference: Atlantic Sun (2001-)
Conference titles:
Atlantic Sun: 3 (2003 [tie], '06 [tie], '08)
Conference tournament titles:
Atlantic Sun: 3 (2006, '07, '08)
NCAA Tournament appearances: 3
NIT appearances: 1

TOP 5

G **Wes Burtner** (1998-2002)
G **Justin Hare** (2004-08)
G **Alex Renfroe** (2007-09)
F **Adam Mark** (2001-04)
F **Adam Sonn** (1999-2003)

RECORDS

	GAME		SEASON		CAREER	
POINTS	58	Joe Behling, vs. Lipscomb (March 4, 1989)	1,071	Joe Behling (1988-89)	1,833	Joe Behling (1986-90)
POINTS PER GAME			31.5	Joe Behling (1988-89)	28.1	Robert Barnes (1954-57)
REBOUNDS	30	Joe Gaines, vs. Lipscomb (Jan. 31, 1970); Jerry Sullivan, vs. Bethel (N/A)	578	Joe Gaines (1970-71)	1,895	Joe Gaines (1968-72)
ASSISTS	17	Tommy Dalley, vs. Christian Brothers (Feb. 27, 1992); Scott Speedy, vs. Lincoln Memorial (Dec. 9, 1988)	327	Scott Speedy (1988-89)	1,164	Scott Speedy (1987-91)

ESPN 306 SAGARIN

BETHUNE-COOKMAN

This Florida school served as the launching pad for one of college basketball's greatest careers. John Chaney was a lightning-fast guard who played on some marvelous Wildcats teams in the 1950s and went on to a legendary coaching career. After joining the MEAC and D1 in 1980, however, B-CU endured almost a generation of failure, posting just five winning conference seasons in 29 years.

BEST TEAM: 1952-53 Coach Rudolph Matthews' squad won the Southern Intercollegiate Athletic Conference (SIAC) title thanks to center Jack "Cy" McClairen, forwards Mike Ardis and Wycliffe Martin and guard Hubert Hemsley. But the team's star was a scoring machine and ball-handling whiz named John Chaney.

BEST PLAYER: G JOHN CHANEY (1951-55) Philadelphia's Public League player of the year in 1951 found no local collegiate takers, so Chaney went on to be a star at Bethune-Cookman. He was elected to the Basketball Hall of Fame in 2001 on the strength of his coaching résumé, but his rep as a player surely didn't hurt.

BEST COACH: JACK "CY" MCCLAIREN (1961-66, '67-93) A multi-sport star who earned 12 varsity letters and became Bethune-Cookman's first pro draft pick—by the Pittsburgh Steelers—McClairen returned to his alma mater to coach basketball, football and golf and to serve as athletic director. He is the school's winningest coach (397) and was MEAC coach of the year in 1989.

GAME FOR THE AGES: Chaney & Co.'s 1953 SIAC championship victory over Xavier (La.)—payback for a regular-season loss to Xavier in Daytona Beach—kicked off a couple of decades of strong Bethune-Cookman teams, including three league title winners and one stretch of 17 consecutive winning seasons.

FIERCEST RIVAL: On the gridiron, few rivalries match the Florida Classic—played between B-CU and Florida A&M—which regularly draws 70,000 to the Citrus Bowl. The intensity has spilled onto the hardwood; six basketball games since 2000 have been decided by four points or less. FAMU leads the series, 57–32.

SEASON REVIEW

SEAS.	W-L	CONF.	SCORING		COACH	RECORD	
1961-62[a]	14-12				Jack "Cy" McClairen		
1962-63	14-7				Jack "Cy" McClairen		
1963-64	18-5		Calvin Johnson	25.9	Jack "Cy" McClairen		
1964-65	18-9		Jerome Hamler	22.9	Jack "Cy" McClairen		
1965-66	20-8		Johnnie Allen	27.1	Jack "Cy" McClairen		
1966-67	19-10		Johnnie Allen	22.8	Raymond McDoogle	19-10	.655
1967-68	24-7		Johnnie Allen	32.1	Jack "Cy" McClairen		
1968-69	16-9		Johnnie Allen	28.0	Jack "Cy" McClairen		
1969-70	20-7		Warren Baker	22.5	Jack "Cy" McClairen		
1970-71	14-10		Vernon Taylor	23.1	Jack "Cy" McClairen		
1971-72	18-9		Vernon Taylor	23.6	Jack "Cy" McClairen		
1972-73	16-8		Aulcie Perry	27.0	Jack "Cy" McClairen		
1973-74	14-11		Jake Savis	15.2	Jack "Cy" McClairen		
1974-75	13-9				Jack "Cy" McClairen		
1975-76	16-7		Glenn Reeves	16.7	Jack "Cy" McClairen		
1976-77	21-5				Jack "Cy" McClairen		
1977-78	17-9				Jack "Cy" McClairen		
1978-79	12-15				Jack "Cy" McClairen		
1979-80	13-16		Anthony Chester	24.7	Jack "Cy" McClairen		
1980-81	13-15	4-6	Jarvis Smith	13.2	Jack "Cy" McClairen		
1981-82	10-18	4-8	Jarvis Smith	18.6	Jack "Cy" McClairen		
1982-83	5-21	3-9	Jarvis Smith	19.4	Jack "Cy" McClairen		
1983-84	6-22	2-8	Ronnie Weston	13.9	Jack "Cy" McClairen		
1984-85	8-19	4-7	Kevin Bradshaw	19.0	Jack "Cy" McClairen		
1985-86	7-22	4-10	Don Hill	19.9	Jack "Cy" McClairen		
1986-87	10-19	6-8	John Williams	10.4	Jack "Cy" McClairen		
1987-88	6-21	4-12	Anthony Anderson	16.4	Jack "Cy" McClairen		
1988-89	12-16	8-8	James Turner	14.6	Jack "Cy" McClairen		
1989-90	10-18	8-8	Clifford Reed Jr.	20.1	Jack "Cy" McClairen		
1990-91	5-24	3-13	Clifford Reed Jr.	22.2	Jack "Cy" McClairen		
1991-92	4-25	3-13	Reggie Cunningham	25.6	Jack "Cy" McClairen		
1992-93	3-24	2-14	Latroy Strong	16.1	Jack "Cy" McClairen	397-427	.482
1993-94	9-18	8-8	LaMont Parish	11.5	Tony Sheals		
1994-95	12-16	9-7	Latroy Strong	16.4	Tony Sheals		
1995-96	12-15	8-8	Jaime Grant	11.4	Tony Sheals		
1996-97	12-16	9-9	Freddie Cole	11.1	Tony Sheals	45-65	.409
1997-98	1-26	1-17	Johnny McClenton	13.1	Horace Broadnax		
1998-99	11-16	10-9	Freddie Cole	17.7	Horace Broadnax		
1999-2000	14-15	12-6	Freddie Cole	16.9	Horace Broadnax		
2000-01	10-19	5-13	Tyree Harris	14.6	Horace Broadnax		
2001-02	12-17	8-10	Richard Toussaint	21.6	Horace Broadnax[b]	42-89	.321
2002-03	8-22	5-13	Richard Toussaint	18.2	Clifford Reed Jr.		
2003-04	8-21	7-11	Diondre Larmond	10.7	Clifford Reed Jr.		
2004-05	13-17	8-10	Antonio Webb	14.9	Clifford Reed Jr.		
2005-06	15-15	11-7	Antonio Webb	16.6	Clifford Reed Jr.		
2006-07	9-21	6-12	Jimmy Hudson	11.4	Clifford Reed Jr.		
2007-08	11-21	5-11	John Holmes	13.8	Clifford Reed Jr.		
2008-09	17-16	9-7	C.J. Reed	15.0	Clifford Reed Jr.	87-137	.388

[a] Records from before 1961-62 have been lost.
[b] Horace Broadnax (6-13) and Clifford Reed Jr. (6-4) both coached during the 2001-02 season.

PROFILE

Bethune-Cookman University, Daytona Beach, FL
Founded: 1904 as Daytona Educational and Industrial School for Negro Girls; 1947, renamed Bethune-Cookman College; 2007, renamed Bethune-Cookman University
Enrollment: 2,895 (2,895 undergraduate)
Colors: Maroon and gold
Nickname: Wildcats
Current arena: Moore Gymnasium, opened in 1953 (3,000)
Previous: Campbell Street High School, then known as Dickinson Recreation Center, 1950-53 (600); PAL Recreation Center, then known as Cyphers Street Recreation Center, 1950-53 (400); White Hall Auditorium, 1948-49 (200)
First game: Feb. 14, 1942
All-time record: 590-728 (.448)
Total weeks in AP Top 20/25: 0
Current conference: Mid-Eastern Athletic (1980-)
Conference titles: 0
Conference tournament titles: 0
NCAA appearances: 0
NIT appearances: 0

TOP 5

G **John Chaney** (1951-55)
G **Reggie Cunningham** (1988-92)
G/F **Anthony Chester** (1975-80)
F **Johnnie Allen** (1965-69)
C **Carl Fuller** (1964-68)

RECORDS

	GAME		SEASON		CAREER	
POINTS	60	Carl Fuller, vs. Fisk (1968-69)	994	Johnnie Allen (1967-68)	3,000+	John Chaney (1951-55)
POINTS PER GAME			32.1	Johnnie Allen (1967-68)	27.6	Johnnie Allen (1965-69)
REBOUNDS	40	Carl Fuller, vs. Fisk (1967)	488	Carl Fuller (1964-65)	1,645	Carl Fuller (1964-68)
ASSISTS	17	Percy Williamson, vs. Rollins (Dec. 10, 1975)	174	Tyris Livas (1998-99)	373	Julious Grant (1986-90)

ESPN 330 SAGARIN

BINGHAMTON

The Bearcats' underwhelming history took a turn for the better in 2008-09, with their first 20-win D1 season and a Tournament bid. Before that, three straight D3 conference titles in the early-1990s had been the zenith of Binghamton hoops. Now the fans who pack the Events Center (the Bearcats led the America East in attendance every season since 2003-04, setting a league record in '08-09) can root for a winner.

BEST TEAM: 2008-09 Binghamton hadn't won a conference title or qualified for the NCAA Tournament. Then Kevin Broadus found some help for senior forward Reggie Fuller in junior college transfers D.J. Rivera and Emanuel Mayben. The season culminated in an 11-game win streak before the Bearcats fell to Duke, 86-62, in the first round of the Tourney.

BEST PLAYER: G Sherwin Telford (1991-94) It's no accident that the best multiseason stretch in Bearcats history coincided with the arrival of Telford, a trigger-happy transfer from Rochester. In three seasons, he became the school's No. 2 scorer (1,685 points).

BEST COACH: Dick Baldwin (1991-96) As coach at Broome Community College, Baldwin broke Adolph Rupp's unofficial record for most wins at any collegiate level. After taking four years off following his first retirement in 1987, the player-friendly coach padded his record in five seasons at Binghamton, finishing with 961 wins.

GAME FOR THE AGES: Junior guard Mike Gordon cemented his place in Bearcats lore in a 66-65 win over Stony Brook on Jan. 31, 2007. Trailing by one, Gordon inbounded the ball to himself off a defender, then hit the game-winning layup—all with 0.6 seconds left.

FIERCEST RIVAL: Since the first meeting between Albany and Binghamton in 1949, the Great Danes lead the Bearcats either 56–27 (according to Albany) or 55–29 (per Binghamton). Resentment boiled over after an Albany victory on Feb. 27, 2008. Head coaches Kevin Broadus and Will Brown exchanged words in the handshake line. Then Broadus and Albany assistant Chad O'Donnell pushed each other, resulting in one-game suspensions for both.

SEASON REVIEW

SEAS.	W-L	CONF.	COACH	SEAS.	W-L	CONF.	COACH
1946-47	7-4		Bert Broder	1960-61	11-6		Frank Pollard
1947-48	5-14		Gene Welborn	1961-62	14-3		Frank Pollard
1948-49	8-12		Gene Welborn	1962-63	6-10		Frank Pollard
1949-50	14-8		Gene Welborn	1963-64	2-13		Frank Pollard
1950-51	10-12		Gene Welborn	1964-65	4-12		Frank Pollard
1951-52	5-18		Richard Powell	1965-66	4-12		Frank Pollard
1952-53	1-17		John Natale	1966-67	10-6		Frank Pollard
1953-54	3-14		John Natale	1967-68	6-10		Frank Pollard
1954-55	7-11		John Natale	1968-69	7-10		Frank Pollard
1955-56	1-15		John Natale	1969-70	5-12		Frank Pollard
1956-57	1-14		Frank Pollard	1970-71	6-11		Frank Pollard
1957-58	1-13		Frank Pollard	1971-72	6-12		Frank Pollard
1958-59	3-12		Frank Pollard	1972-73	11-9		John Affleck
1959-60	6-8		Frank Pollard	1973-74	9-15		John Affleck

SEAS.	W-L	CONF.	SCORING		COACH	RECORD
1974-75	13-10		Glen McIver	15.0	John Affleck	
1975-76	14-10		Kurt Mohney	18.7	John Affleck	
1976-77	8-16		Ted Hull	16.0	John Affleck	
1977-78	10-14		Glen McIver	19.0	John Affleck	
1978-79	7-17		Kurt Atherton	15.5	John Affleck	
1979-80	5-19		Charlie Heins	14.7	John Affleck	
1980-81	10-15		Charlie Heins	16.9	John Affleck	
1981-82	3-18		Derek Pankey	12.0	John Affleck	
1982-83	9-15		Kevin Ziesig	13.8	John Affleck	99-159 .384
1983-84	16-10		Marty Young	11.4	Dave Archer	
1984-85	14-11		Greg Fleming	19.8	Dave Archer	
1985-86	14-14		Mark Jones	13.0	Dave Archer	
1986-87	10-15		Mark Jones	18.9	Dave Archer	
1987-88	9-17		Chris Jackey	24.2	Dave Archer	
1988-89	7-18		Chris Jackey	21.0	Dave Archer	
1989-90	8-17		Chris Jackey	21.4	Dace Archer	
1990-91	9-16		John Dormer	12.8	Dave Archer	87-118 .424
1991-92	19-7		Sherwin Telford	19.4	Dick Baldwin	
1992-93	19-9		Sherwin Telford	21.4	Dick Baldwin	
1993-94	23-7		Sherwin Telford	20.1	Dick Baldwin	
1994-95	11-13		Elbridge James	11.9	Dick Baldwin	
1995-96	10-15		Daye Kaba	12.0	Dick Baldwin	82-51 .617
1996-97	8-17		Daye Kaba	15.6	Jim Norris	
1997-98	17-10		Brad Nelson	16.8	Jim Norris	
1998-99	13-14		Nitai Spiro	12.0	Jim Norris	
1999-2000	14-12		Jeffrey St. Fort	14.4	Jim Norris	52-53 .495
2000-01	14-14		Jeffrey St. Fort	13.0	Al Walker	
2001-02	9-19	6-10	Jeffrey St. Fort	12.9	Al Walker	
2002-03	14-13	9-7	Anthony Green	16.7	Al Walker	
2003-04	14-16	10-8	Nick Billings	12.5	Al Walker	
2004-05	12-17	8-10	Andre Heard	14.3	Al Walker	
2005-06	16-13	12-4	Andre Heard	17.1	Al Walker	
2006-07	13-16	6-10	Steve Proctor	11.8	Al Walker	92-108 .460
2007-08	14-16	9-7	Lazar Trifunovic	14.0	Kevin Broadus	
2008-09	23-9	13-3 ●	D.J. Rivera	20.0	Kevin Broadus	37-25 .597

● NCAA Tournament appearance

PROFILE

Binghamton University (State University of New York), Binghamton, NY
Founded: 1946
Enrollment: 14,373 (11,523 undergraduate)
Colors: Dark green, black and white
Nickname: Bearcats
Current arena: Events Center, opened in 2004 (5,142)
Previous: West Gym, 1946-2004 (2,523)
First game: Jan. 10, 1947
All-time record: 602-802 (.429)
Total weeks in AP Top 20/25: 0

Current conference: America East (2001-)
Conference titles:
America East: 1 (2009 [tie])
Conference tournament titles:
America East: 1 (2009)
NCAA Tournament appearances: 1
NIT appearances: 0

TOP 5

G **Mike Gordon** (2004-08)
G **Sherwin Telford** (1991-94)
F **Andre Heard** (2004-06)
F **Jeff Merrill** (1990-94)
C **Nick Billings** (2001-05)

RECORDS

RECORDS	GAME		SEASON		CAREER	
POINTS	45	Tom Gomulka, vs. Geneseo (Dec. 13, 1969); Mickey Greenberg, vs. Utica (March 5, 1963)	639	D.J. Rivera (2008-29)	1,721	Chris Jackey (1986-90)
POINTS PER GAME			28.7	Tom Gomulka (1969-70)	24.1	Tom Gomulka (1967-71)
REBOUNDS	31	Derek Pankey, vs. Geneseo (Dec. 2, 1983)	323	Todd Jost (1988-89)	757	Jeff Merrill (1990-94)
ASSISTS	16	Mark Jones, vs. Cortland (Jan. 25, 1986)	217	Chris Ballerini (1997-98)	586	Jeremy Greenberg (1990-94)

ESPN 161 SAGARIN

BOISE STATE

When the Boise State Broncos get rolling, they're beautiful to watch—that is, unless you're wearing the opponents' colors. Cases in point: the 2007-08 team's WAC tourney run that culminated in a three-overtime title-game upset of New Mexico State; and the Chris Childs-led 1987-88 team's blazing 16–1 start on the way to Big Sky Conference domination.

BEST TEAM: 1987-88 The Broncos started 16–1, losing only to No. 5-ranked Wyoming by four points, finished 24–6 and won the Big Sky title. Conference POY Arnell Jones (16.4 ppg, 7.2 rpg) led the team, which lost to Michigan in the first round of the NCAA Tourney.

BEST PLAYER: G Chris Childs (1985-89) He led BSU to two NITs and the 1988 NCAA Tourney, was the '88 Big Sky tourney MVP and the '89 overall MVP. When he finished, Childs was tops all-time in steals (215)—since surpassed—second in scoring (1,602) and assists (392).

BEST COACH: Bobby Dye (1983-95) A defense-first coach who took Cal State Fullerton to the Sweet 16 in 1978, Dye worked his magic at BSU for 12 years, setting school marks in wins (213) and percentage (.616). He led the Broncos to three NCAAs and three NITs, and notched the school's first postseason victory.

GAME FOR THE AGES: By beating New Mexico State in the 2008 WAC championship, 107-102, in triple overtime, the underdog Broncos reached the NCAA Tournament for the first time since 1994. The Broncos squandered a 16-point lead during the final, but tourney MVP Reggie Larry (31 points, 16 boards) sank a free throw to send the game to OT. Finally, PG Anthony Thomas sealed the deal with a twisting reverse layup and two free throws with :05 left.

FIERCEST RIVAL: Boise State and Idaho aren't just in-state rivals, the two have faced off in three different conferences over the years—the Big Sky, Big West and WAC. BSU leads the series, 47–34. Its most memorable win? The 80-68 1993 Big Sky championship upset of No. 1-seed Idaho on national TV. The drubbing paid back a double-OT 107-99 loss to Idaho a month earlier.

SEASON REVIEW

SEAS.	W-L	CONF.	COACH	SEAS.	W-L	CONF.	COACH
1933-48	*133-145*	*24-9 in 1946-47*		1962-63	15-9		Dale Chatterton
1948-49	17-9		George Blankley	1963-64	13-13		Dale Chatterton
1949-50	16-10		George Blankley	1964-65	8-15		Dale Chatterton
1950-51	8-16		George Blankley	1965-66	14-11		Murray Satterfield
1951-52	10-8		George Blankley	1966-67	26-9		Murray Satterfield
1952-53	14-8		George Blankley	1967-68	26-5		Murray Satterfield
1953-54	14-12		George Blankley	1968-69	19-8		Murray Satterfield
1954-55	18-11		George Blankley	1969-70	20-8		Murray Satterfield
1955-56	18-11		George Blankley	1970-71	10-16	5-9	Murray Satterfield
1956-57	25-6		George Blankley	1971-72	14-12	7-7	Murray Satterfield
1957-58	17-5		George Blankley	1972-73	11-15	5-9	Murray Satterfield[a]
1958-59	6-13		George Blankley	1973-74	12-14	6-8	Bus Connor
1959-60	15-9		George Blankley	1974-75	13-13	7-7	Bus Connor
1960-61	9-13		George Blankley	1975-76	18-11	9-5 ●	Bus Connor
1961-62	19-8		George Blankley	1976-77	10-16	5-9	Bus Connor

SEAS.	W-L	CONF.	SCORING		COACH	RECORD
1977-78	13-14	8-6	Steve Connor	19.6	Bus Connor	
1978-79	11-15	6-8	Sean McKenna	15.7	Bus Connor	
1979-80	10-16	4-10	Dave Williams	15.1	Bus Connor	87-99 .468
1980-81	7-19	4-10	Eric Bailey	17.3	Dave Leach	
1981-82	12-14	6-8	Terry Lee	13.3	Dave Leach	
1982-83	10-17	5-9	Vince Hinchen	17.7	Dave Leach	29-50 .367
1983-84	15-13	6-8	Vince Hinchen	17.6	Bobby Dye	
1984-85	16-13	5-9	Frank Jackson	13.4	Bobby Dye	
1985-86	12-16	6-8	Chris Childs	10.7	Bobby Dye	
1986-87	22-8	10-4 ■	Arnell Jones	15.8	Bobby Dye	
1987-88	24-6	13-3 ●	Arnell Jones	16.4	Bobby Dye	
1988-89	23-7	13-3 ■	Wilson Foster	15.4	Bobby Dye	
1989-90	12-15	7-9	Tanoka Beard	13.6	Bobby Dye	
1990-91	18-11	10-6 ■	Tanoka Beard	17.7	Bobby Dye	
1991-92	16-13	7-9	Tanoka Beard	18.1	Bobby Dye	
1992-93	21-8	10-4 ●	Tanoka Beard	21.0	Bobby Dye	
1993-94	17-13 ⊗	7-7 ●	John Coker	17.4	Bobby Dye	
1994-95	17-10	7-7	John Coker	15.9	Bobby Dye	213-133 .616
1995-96	15-13	10-4	Joe Wyatt	11.6	Rod Jensen	
1996-97	14-13	9-7	Joe Wyatt	16.0	Rod Jensen	
1997-98	17-13	9-7	Roberto Bergersen	19.4	Rod Jensen	
1998-99	21-8	12-4	Roberto Bergersen	22.2	Rod Jensen	
1999-2000	12-15	6-10	Abe Jackson	16.2	Rod Jensen	
2000-01	17-14	8-8	Abe Jackson	17.4	Rod Jensen	
2001-02	13-17	6-12	Abe Jackson	18.6	Rod Jensen	109-93 .540
2002-03	13-16	7-11	Aaron Haynes	14.7	Greg Graham	
2003-04	23-10	12-6 ■	Aaron Haynes	14.8	Greg Graham	
2004-05	16-18	6-12	Jermaine Blackburn	15.4	Greg Graham	
2005-06	14-15	6-10	Coby Karl	17.2	Greg Graham	
2006-07	17-14	8-8	Coby Karl	14.8	Greg Graham	
2007-08	25-9	12-4 ●	Reggie Larry	19.4	Greg Graham	
2008-09	19-13	9-7	Mark Sanchez	13.0	Greg Graham	127-95 .572

[a] **Murray Satterfield (5-8) and Bus Connor (6-7) both coached during the 1972-73 season.**

⊗ **Conference record doesn't reflect games forfeited or vacated. For adjusted record,** **see p. 521.**

● **NCAA Tournament appearance** ■ **NIT appearance**

PROFILE

Boise State University, Boise, ID
Founded: 1932
Enrollment: 18,963 (15,593 undergraduate)
Colors: Blue and orange
Nickname: Broncos
Current arena: Taco Bell Arena, opened in 1982 (12,380)
Previous: Bronco Gym, 1968-82 (4,500)
First game: 1933
All-time record: 1,061-862 (.552)
Total weeks in AP Top 20/25: 0

Current conference: Western Athletic (2001-)
Conference titles:
Big Sky: 3 (1976 [tie], '88, '89)
WAC: 1 (2008 [tie])
Conference tournament titles:
Big Sky: 4 (1976, '88, '93, '94)
WAC: 1 (2008)
NCAA Tournament appearances: 5
NIT appearances: 4

TOP 5

G **Roberto Bergersen** (1996-99)
G **Chris Childs** (1985-89)
F **Ron Austin** (1968-71)
F **Reggie Larry** (2006-08)
C **Tanoka Beard** (1989-93)

RECORDS

RECORDS	GAME		SEASON		CAREER	
POINTS	42	Ron Austin, vs. Montana (Feb. 13, 1971)	661	Reggie Larry (2007-08)	1,944	Tanoka Beard (1989-93)
POINTS PER GAME			24.5	Ron Austin (1970-71)	18.0	Steve Connor (1974-78)
REBOUNDS	24	Bill Otey, vs. Eastern Washington (Jan. 31, 1969); vs. Northwest Nazarene (Feb. 10, 1969)	467	Bill Otey (1968-69)	948	Jason Ellis (2001-05)
ASSISTS	13	Bryan Defares, vs. UNLV (March 17, 2004)	145	Doug Usitalo (1987-88); Steve Connor (1976-77)	502	Steve Connor (1974-78)

ESPN 73 SAGARIN

BOSTON COLLEGE

When Boston College joined the Atlantic Coast Conference for the 2005-06 season, longtime Eagles fans couldn't help but think that BC was abandoning its Eastern basketball roots in favor of a foreign (read *Southern*) hoops culture. No worries. The Eagles, charter members of the Big East, have a proud basketball history that stands up well against much of Tobacco Road's storied tradition.

BEST TEAM: 1981-82 Dr. Tom Davis' 22–10 Eagles earned a No. 8 seed in the NCAA Tournament and advanced to a regional final for the first time since 1967. To get there, they knocked off No. 1-seed DePaul and No. 5-seed Kansas State. Davis had a talented core that consisted of Michael Adams, John Bagley, Jay Murphy and John Garris, the first three of whom are among the school's top-12 all-time scorers. Houston shot the Eagles down in the regional final, 99-92.

BEST PLAYER: G Michael Adams (1981-85) More than almost any college player of his generation, Hartford native Michael Adams was the victim of bad timing. Born too soon to have a three-point line to shoot from, Adams falls short of the Eagles' Top 10 scorers list with 1,650 points in 119 games. Many—maybe most—of his shots would have been threes if he'd made them in 1986-87. Still, the 5'11" guard left his mark as the Eagles made the postseason in each of his four seasons in the Heights (three NCAAs and one NIT).

BEST COACH: Bob Cousy (1963-69) The former Celtics (and Holy Cross) star brought the luck (and skill) of the Irish to BC during six seasons as head coach. Cousy's Eagles squads went 114–38; his .750 winning percentage is the best of any coach in school history by a wide margin. He coached BC to four 20-win seasons and five postseason appearances, including a title-game loss in the 1969 NIT.

GAME FOR THE AGES: Their March 20, 1994, upset of North Carolina earned a local Boston kid, Billy Curley, the cover of *Sports Illustrated* and knocked the defending national champions out of the NCAA Tournament. The Eagles' 75-72 second-round shocker over the Tar Heels was the second monumental upset of the athletic year at BC; the football team stunned top-ranked Notre Dame in November 1993.

HEARTBREAKER: With its highest Tournament seeding ever in 2001, the No. 3-seed Eagles lost a second-round game to No. 6-seed Southern California, 74-71. Sophomore Troy Bell, who went on to finish as the Eagles' all-time leading scorer, had 32 points, but BC failed to get off what could have been a game-tying three-pointer in the closing seconds.

FIERCEST RIVAL: Trailing Holy Cross in their series, 57–52, Boston College finds itself playing catch-up ball with the little school from Worcester, Mass. (For clarification, Holy Cross is the New England school that prides itself on never abandoning its New England basketball roots.) The two first played during the 1905-06 season, and the rivalry probably peaked in intensity during the 1950s and '60s. They last met in the 2005-06 season.

FANFARE AND HOOPLA: Greater Boston, a big-time sports town with many teams for fans to choose from, seems to embrace the Eagles only when they make a deep run into the NCAA Tournament. That, however, doesn't stop all-time Boston College football legend Doug Flutie from attending several games a year at Conte Forum. "Hail Mary" Flutie still lives in the Boston area and is a constant presence at school events.

FAN FAVORITE: G John Bagley (1979-82) A fireplug guard with a fearless attitude, the Bridgeport, Conn., native became a Son of Boston for coach Tom Davis' Eagles.

FIRST-ROUND PRO PICKS

1963	**Gerry Ward,** St. Louis (6)
1969	**Terry Driscoll,** Detroit (4)
1971	**Jim O'Brien,** Pittsburgh (ABA)
1982	**John Bagley,** Cleveland (12)
1989	**Dana Barros,** Seattle (16)
1994	**Bill Curley,** San Antonio (22)
2003	**Troy Bell,** Boston (16)
2007	**Sean Williams,** New Jersey (17)
2007	**Jared Dudley,** Charlotte (22)

PROFILE

Boston College, Chestnut Hill, MA
Founded: 1863
Enrollment: 14,500 (8,900 undergraduate)
Colors: Maroon and gold
Nickname: Eagles
Current arena: Silvio O. Conte Forum, opened in 1988 (8,606)
Previous: Roberts Center, 1958-88 (4,400)
First game: Dec. 26, 1904
All-time record: 1,071-816 (.568)
Total weeks in AP Top 20/25: 110

Current conference: Atlantic Coast (2005-)
Conference titles:
Big East: 6 (1981, '83 [tie], '97 [tie], 2001 [tie], '03 [tie] '05 [tie])
Conference tournament titles:
Big East: 2 (1997, 2001)
NCAA Tournament appearances: 18
Sweet 16s (since 1975): 7
NIT appearances: 10
Semifinals: 3

TOP 5

G	**Michael Adams** (1981-85)
G	**John Bagley** (1979-82)
F	**Terry Driscoll** (1966-69)
F	**Craig Smith** (2002-06)
C	**Jay Murphy** (1980-84)

RECORDS

RECORDS	GAME		SEASON		CAREER	
POINTS	49	John Austin, vs. Georgetown (Feb. 21, 1964)	781	Troy Bell (2002-03)	2,632	Troy Bell (1999-2003)
POINTS PER GAME			29.2	John Austin (1963-64)	27.1	John Austin (1963-66)
REBOUNDS	31	Terry Driscoll, vs. Fordham (Feb. 8, 1969)	498	Terry Driscoll (1968-69)	1,114	Craig Smith (2002-06)
ASSISTS	18	Jim O'Brien, vs. LeMoyne (Dec. 16, 1970)	276	Billy Evans (1966-67)	669	Billy Evans (1966-69)

SEASON REVIEW

SEASON	W-L	CONF.	COMMENTS	COACH	RECORD
1904-18	*19-36*		*Played only five seasons, all with losing records*		
1918-19	4-1			Luke Urban	
1919-20	6-4			Luke Urban	
1920-21	9-6			Luke Urban	19-11 .633
1921-22	3-9			William Coady	
1922-23	4-5			William Coady	
1923-24	8-3			William Coady	
1924-25	6-5			William Coady	21-22 .488
1925-45	no team				
1945-46	3-11			Al McClellan	
1946-47	12-10			Al McClellan	
1947-48	13-10			Al McClellan	
1948-49	9-9			Al McClellan	
1949-50	11-9			Al McClellan	

SEAS.	W-L	CONF.	POSTSEASON	SCORING		REBOUNDS		ASSISTS		COACH	RECORD	
1950-51	17-11									Al McClellan		
1951-52	22-5							Tom O'Toole	7.9	Al McClellan		
1952-53	7-15									Al McClellan	94-80	.540
1953-54	11-11									Don Martin		
1954-55	8-18					Phil Powell	19.0			Don Martin		
1955-56	6-17									Don Martin		
1956-57	12-11									Don Martin		
1957-58	15-6		NCAA FIRST ROUND							Don Martin		
1958-59	17-9									Don Martin		
1959-60	11-14									Don Martin		
1960-61	14-9									Don Martin		
1961-62	15-7									Don Martin	109-102	.517
1962-63	10-16									Frank Power	10-16	.385
1963-64	10-11			John Austin	29.2					Bob Cousy		
1964-65	21-7		NIT FIRST ROUND	John Austin	26.9	Willie Wolters	12.6			Bob Cousy		
1965-66	21-5		NIT QUARTERFINALS	John Austin	25.4	Willie Wolters	16.6			Bob Cousy		
1966-67	21-3		NCAA REGIONAL FINALS	Steve Adelman	18.9	Terry Driscoll	10.5			Bob Cousy		
1967-68	17-8		NCAA FIRST ROUND	Terry Driscoll	17.8	Terry Driscoll	12.9	Billy Evans	8.6	Bob Cousy		
1968-69	24-4		NIT RUNNER-UP	Terry Driscoll	23.3	Terry Driscoll	17.8	Billy Evans	8.2	Bob Cousy	114-38	.750
1969-70	11-13			Jim O'Brien	16.5	Tom Veronneau	9.0	Jim O'Brien	9.2	Chuck Daly		
1970-71	15-11			Jim O'Brien	18.9	Frank Fitzgerald	7.8	Jim O'Brien	8.9	Chuck Daly	26-24	.520
1971-72	13-13			D. Kilcullen, P. Schmid	14.0	Dave Walker	9.2	Bob Smith	5.2	Bob Zuffelato		
1972-73	11-14			Mark Raterink	13.1	Mark Raterink	7.2	Jere Nolan	6.9	Bob Zuffelato		
1973-74	21-9		NIT THIRD PLACE	Bob Carrington	19.4	Bill Collins	9.3	Jere Nolan	8.2	Bob Zuffelato		
1974-75	21-9		NCAA REGIONAL SEMIFINALS	Bob Carrington	20.9	Bill Collins	10.4	Mel Weldon	5.7	Bob Zuffelato		
1975-76	9-17			Bob Carrington	20.9	Bill Collins	10.1	Mike Shirey	2.2	Bob Zuffelato		
1976-77	8-18			Ernie Cobb	17.4	Michael Bowie	7.8	Jim Sweeney	3.2	Bob Zuffelato	83-80	.509
1977-78	15-11			Ernie Cobb	22.8	Bob Bennifield	8.9	Jim Sweeney	4.2	Tom Davis		
1978-79	21-9			Ernie Cobb	21.3	Joe Beaulieu	6.7	Jim Sweeney	4.1	Tom Davis		
1979-80	19-10	2-4	NIT SECOND ROUND	John Bagley	11.8	Joe Beaulieu	5.2	Jim Sweeney	4.6	Tom Davis		
1980-81	23-7	10-4	NCAA REGIONAL SEMIFINALS	John Bagley	20.4	Martin Clark	4.7	John Bagley	3.4	Tom Davis		
1981-82	22-10	8-6	NCAA REGIONAL FINALS	John Bagley	21.1	Martin Clark	5.2	John Bagley	3.8	Tom Davis	100-47	.680
1982-83	25-7	12-4	NCAA REGIONAL SEMIFINALS	John Garris	19.7	Jay Murphy	8.1	Michael Adams	5.3	Gary Williams		
1983-84	18-12	8-8	NIT SECOND ROUND	Jay Murphy	19.8	Jay Murphy	7.3	Michael Adams	3.5	Gary Williams		
1984-85	20-11	7-9	NCAA REGIONAL SEMIFINALS	Michael Adams	15.3	Trevor Gordon	5.2	Michael Adams	5.2	Gary Williams		
1985-86	13-15	4-12		Roger McCready	18.1	Roger McCready	5.5	Dana Barros	3.5	Gary Williams	76-45	.628
1986-87	11-18	3-13		Dana Barros	18.7	Skip Barry	5.2	Dana Barros	3.8	Jim O'Brien		
1987-88	18-15	6-10	NIT FOURTH PLACE	Dana Barros	21.9	Steve Benton	5.1	Dana Barros	4.1	Jim O'Brien		
1988-89	12-17	3-13		Dana Barros	23.9	Steve Benton	5.3	Dana Barros	3.3	Jim O'Brien		
1989-90	8-20	1-15		Doug Able	12.0	Doug Able	7.4	Bryan Edwards	3.3	Jim O'Brien		
1990-91	11-19	1-15		Bill Curley	12.6	Bill Curley	6.9	Howard Eisley	3.3	Jim O'Brien		
1991-92	17-14	7-11	NIT SECOND ROUND	Bill Curley	17.8	Bill Curley	8.1	Howard Eisley	4.4	Jim O'Brien		
1992-93	18-13	9-9	NIT QUARTERFINALS	Bill Curley	15.8	Bill Curley	7.6	Howard Eisley	4.9	Jim O'Brien		
1993-94	23-11	11-7	NCAA REGIONAL FINALS	Bill Curley	20.0	Bill Curley	9.0	Howard Eisley	4.6	Jim O'Brien		
1994-95	9-19	2-16		Danya Abrams	22.1	Danya Abrams	9.1	Duane Woodward	4.3	Jim O'Brien		
1995-96	19-11	10-8	NCAA SECOND ROUND	Danya Abrams	19.6	Danya Abrams	9.6	Scoonie Penn	3.5	Jim O'Brien		
1996-97	22-9	12-6	NCAA SECOND ROUND	Danya Abrams	16.4	Danya Abrams	8.2	Duane Woodward	3.9	Jim O'Brien	168-166	.503
1997-98	15-16	6-12		Antonio Granger	17.9	Kostas Maglos	6.7	Duane Woodward	5.1	Al Skinner		
1998-99	6-21	3-15		Kenny Harley	11.2	Brian Ross	4.9	Dwayne Pina	4.3	Al Skinner		
1999-2000	11-19	3-13		Troy Bell	18.8	Uka Agbai	5.0	Troy Bell	2.1	Al Skinner		
2000-01	27-5	13-3	NCAA SECOND ROUND	Troy Bell	20.4	Uka Agbai	5.6	Troy Bell	4.2	Al Skinner		
2001-02	20-12	8-8	NCAA FIRST ROUND	Troy Bell	21.6	Ryan Sidney	7.8	Ryan Sidney	4.3	Al Skinner		
2002-03	19-12	10-6	NIT FIRST ROUND	Troy Bell	25.2	Craig Smith	7.9	Ryan Sidney	4.6	Al Skinner		
2003-04	24-10	10-6	NCAA SECOND ROUND	Craig Smith	16.9	Craig Smith	8.3	Louis Hinnant	3.3	Al Skinner		
2004-05	25-5	13-3	NCAA SECOND ROUND	Craig Smith	18.0	Craig Smith	8.5	Louis Hinnant	4.8	Al Skinner		
2005-06	28-8	11-5	NCAA REGIONAL SEMIFINALS	Craig Smith	17.6	Craig Smith	9.4	Louis Hinnant	4.6	Al Skinner		
2006-07	21-12	10-6	NCAA SECOND ROUND	Jared Dudley	19.0	Jared Dudley	8.3	Tyrese Rice	5.4	Al Skinner		
2007-08	14-17	4-12		Tyrese Rice	21.0	Shamari Spears	6.1	Tyrese Rice	5.0	Al Skinner		
2008-09	22-12	9-7	NCAA FIRST ROUND	Tyrese Rice	16.9	Joe Trapani	6.6	Tyrese Rice	5.3	Al Skinner	232-149	.609

LATE GREAT

CITY COLLEGE OF NEW YORK
1934-63

CCNY's 1949-50 squad is the only team in history to win both the NCAA Tournament and the postseason NIT in the same year. Coached by Hall of Famer Nat Holman and led by NCAA Tournament MOP Irwin Dambrot and NIT MVP Ed Warner, the Beavers defeated No. 1-ranked Bradley in both title games. Unfortunately, the joy surrounding the program was short-lived. Seven CCNY players were found guilty the following year of shaving points during their championship season. Within a couple of years, CCNY was no longer a major power and today it plays in Division III—a sad twist of events for a proud program that began its intercollegiate basketball history at the beginning of the 20th century and was the 10th-winningest team of the 1930s.

NOTABLE PLAYER: F/C IRWIN DAMBROT (1946-50) The 6'4" frontcourt standout was captain of the historic 1950 team. In his 98 career games he averaged an impressive-for-the-era 10.0 ppg and came up huge in the team's championship run, scoring 23 in the NIT final. Though drafted by the Knicks as the seventh pick of the 1950 NBA draft, he chose to become a dentist instead. He pleaded guilty to misdemeanor charges of point shaving and received a suspended sentence.

220
SAGARIN

BOSTON UNIVERSITY

For nearly 20 years after their first NCAA Tournament appearance in 1959, the Terriers lost their bite, enduring losing season after losing season. Then a 25-year-old former UMass point guard took over as coach in 1978 and the team immediately shed its losing ways. Rick Pitino may not be the best coach in school history, but—with apologies to Matt Zunic, Mike Jarvis and Dennis Wolff—his legacy might be the most enduring.

BEST TEAM: 1958-59 It took no less of a player than West Virginia's Jerry West to stop the Terriers' roll in the NCAA Tournament. Before that 86-82 regional final loss, Matt Zunic's crew, sparked by captain and future UMass coach Jack Leaman, knocked off UConn at Madison Square Garden and UPI No. 18 Navy in Charlotte, to notch BU's first 20-win season.

BEST PLAYER: F/C TUNJI AWOJOBI (1993-97) Before starring for the Terriers, Awojobi was a boxer on the Nigerian Olympic team. That helps explain how someone just 6'7" could be the first New England player to score 2,000 points and grab 1,000 rebounds.

BEST COACH: DENNIS WOLFF (1994-2009) Even his worst teams are rarely much fun to play against. With his signature hard-nosed defense, Wolff has led BU to two NCAA Tourneys and three NITs, and has won more games than any other Terriers head man has even coached.

GAME FOR THE AGES: Using his sweet hook shot, Bob Cumings (22 points) carved up the Mountaineers in the third round of the 1959 NCAA Tournament. Too bad he couldn't slow down Jerry West; Mr. Clutch scored 14 straight at one point and finished with 33 points and 17 rebounds. To BU's credit, the Mountaineers didn't close out the game until they grabbed a rebound off their own missed free throw while up two with :10 left.

FIERCEST RIVAL: BU and Northeastern are connected by Boston's Green rail line—and by nearly 100 years of hoops history. In 135 meetings over 87 years, the Huskies have twice had 11-game winning streaks, yet the Terriers hold a 70–66 all-time lead.

SEASON REVIEW

SEAS.	W-L	CONF.	COACH	SEAS.	W-L	CONF.	COACH
1901-47	*175-205*	*Best season was 1945-46 (12-2)*		**1960-61**	9-14		John Burke
1947-48	10-9		Russ Peterson	**1961-62**	5-15		John Burke
1948-49	6-12		Charles Cummings	**1962-63**	10-9		John Burke
1949-50	7-9		Vin Cronin	**1963-64**	16-7		John Burke
1950-51	7-12		Vin Cronin	**1964-65**	10-10		John Burke
1951-52	9-8		Vin Cronin	**1965-66**	4-19		John Burke
1952-53	10-10		Matt Zunic	**1966-67**	4-18		Charles Luce
1953-54	9-11		Matt Zunic	**1967-68**	10-14		Charles Luce
1954-55	12-9		Matt Zunic	**1968-69**	14-10		Charles Luce
1955-56	17-6		Matt Zunic	**1969-70**	14-10		Charles Luce
1956-57	13-10		Matt Zunic	**1970-71**	7-18		Charles Luce
1957-58	15-5		Matt Zunic	**1971-72**	7-16		Ron Mitchell
1958-59	20-7	●	Matt Zunic	**1972-73**	15-10	7-4	Ron Mitchell
1959-60	14-10		John Burke	**1973-74**	9-16	2-9	Ron Mitchell

SEAS.	W-L	CONF.	SCORING		COACH	RECORD
1974-75	12-13	7-4	Kenny Walker	17.3	Roy Sigler	
1975-76	7-19	3-9	Neil Burns	18.6	Roy Sigler	
1976-77	7-19		Phil Andrews	13.5	Roy Sigler	
1977-78	10-15		Phil Andrews	14.0	Roy Sigler	36-66 .353
1978-79	17-9		Steve Wright	20.8	Rick Pitino	
1979-80	21-9	19-7 ■	Steve Wright	19.8	Rick Pitino	
1980-81	13-14	13-13	Tony Simms	14.7	Rick Pitino	
1981-82	19-9	6-2	Arturo Brown	14.7	Rick Pitino	
1982-83	21-10	8-2 ●	Tony Simms	18.6	Rick Pitino	91-51 .641
1983-84	16-13	9-5	Gary Plummer	17.0	John Kuester	
1984-85	15-15	9-7	Paul Hendricks	16.0	John Kuester	31-28 .525
1985-86	21-10	13-5 ■	Drederick Irving	18.0	Mike Jarvis	
1986-87	18-12	12-6	Drederick Irving	18.8	Mike Jarvis	
1987-88	23-8	14-4 ●	Drederick Irving	19.9	Mike Jarvis	
1988-89	21-9	14-4	Tony DaCosta	14.4	Mike Jarvis	
1989-90	18-12	9-3 ●	Steven Key	16.6	Mike Jarvis	101-51 .664
1990-91	11-18	5-5	Reggie Stewart	17.8	Bob Brown	
1991-92	10-18	5-9	Danny Delgado	14.8	Bob Brown	
1992-93	6-21	3-11	David Stiff	12.4	Bob Brown	
1993-94	11-16	4-10	Tunji Awojobi	18.9	Bob Brown	38-73 .342
1994-95	15-16	7-9	Tunji Awojobi	19.8	Dennis Wolff	
1995-96	18-11	13-5	Tunji Awojobi	22.7	Dennis Wolff	
1996-97	25-5	17-1 ●	Tunji Awojobi	19.4	Dennis Wolff	
1997-98	19-11	12-6	Walter Brown	14.7	Dennis Wolff	
1998-99	9-18	5-13	LeVar Folk	12.7	Dennis Wolff	
1999-2000	7-22	5-13	Paul Seymour	12.1	Dennis Wolff	
2000-01	14-14	9-9	Jason Grochowalski	12.7	Dennis Wolff	
2001-02	22-10	13-3 ●	Chaz Carr	13.5	Dennis Wolff	
2002-03	20-11	13-3 ■	Rashad Bell	12.0	Dennis Wolff	
2003-04	23-6	17-1 ■	Chaz Carr	13.0	Dennis Wolff	
2004-05	20-9	14-4 ■	Rashad Bell	15.6	Dennis Wolff	
2005-06	12-16	9-7	Kevin Gardner	13.7	Dennis Wolff	
2006-07	12-18	8-8	Corey Lowe	14.1	Dennis Wolff	
2007-08	14-17	9-7	Corey Lowe	18.1	Dennis Wolff	
2008-09	17-13	11-5	John Holland	18.1	Dennis Wolff	247-187 .569

● NCAA Tournament appearance ■ NIT appearance

PROFILE

Boston University, Boston, MA
Founded: 1869
Enrollment: 29,620 (16,572 undergraduate)
Colors: Scarlet and white
Nickname: Terriers
Current arena: Agganis Arena, opened in 2005 (7,200); Case Gymnasium, opened in 1972 (1,800)
Previous: Walter Brown Arena and the Boston Garden, 1983, 1985-93
First game: 1901
All-time record: 1,002-975 (.507)
Total weeks in AP Top 20/25: 0

Current conference: America East (1979-)
Conference titles:
America East: 7 (1980 [tie], '83 [tie], '97, '98 [tie], 2002 [tie], '03, '04)
Conference tournament titles:
America East: 5 (1983, '88, '90, '97, 2002)
NCAA Tournament appearances: 6
NIT appearances: 5

TOP 5

G **Jim Hayes** (1967-70)
G **Drederick Irving** (1984-88)
F **Rashad Bell** (2001-05)
F **Steve Wright** (1976-80)
F/C **Tunji Awojobi** (1993-97)

RECORDS

	GAME		SEASON		CAREER	
POINTS	47	Jim Hayes, vs. Springfield (Feb. 23, 1970)	658	Tunji Awojobi (1995-96)	2,308	Tunji Awojobi (1993-97)
POINTS PER GAME			25.7	Jim Hayes (1968-69)	24.3	Jim Hayes (1967-70)
REBOUNDS	34	Kevin Thomas, vs. Boston College (March 5, 1958)	382	Ed Washington (1958-59)	1,237	Tunji Awojobi (1993-97)
ASSISTS	16	Ken Leary, vs. Colby (Feb. 8, 1964)	238	Jeff Timberlake (1988-89)	772	Jeff Timberlake (1985-89)

ESPN 93 SAGARIN

BOWLING GREEN

The program began in 1916, but the Falcons didn't take off until Harold Anderson walked through the door in 1942 to coach the orange and brown. BGSU became a national powerhouse thanks to his single-pivot fast break; 10 of his players went on to play in the NBA. No wonder the team's arena is named after him.

BEST TEAM: 1962-63 Nate Thurmond's final season at BGSU wasn't going as planned when, after a Jan. 28 loss to DePaul, the Falcons were 8–6. But 10 straight wins later, the Falcons were MAC champs. Behind Howard "Butch" Komives' sharpshooting and Thurmond's inside dominance, Bowling Green beat Notre Dame, 77-72, in the first round of the NCAA Tournament. The winning streak came to an end with a 70-67 loss to Illinois in the next round.

BEST PLAYER: C NATE THURMOND (1960-63) Armed with a freakishly long wingspan and superior quickness, Thurmond thrived in Anderson's up-tempo system. He's one of only two players to lead the MAC in rebounding in three consecutive seasons, and he grabbed a school-record 31 in his final game. The San Francisco Warriors selected him third overall in the 1963 NBA draft, making him the earliest pick in MAC history. He averaged 15.0 points and 15.0 rebounds per game in 14 NBA seasons, and made seven All-Star teams.

BEST COACH: HAROLD ANDERSON (1942-63) Employing his trademark run-and-gun, Anderson guided the Falcons to their first NIT in 1944, then to four more over the next five seasons. By the time he retired almost two decades later, he'd led BGSU to three MAC titles and won a school-record 367 games. In 1985, he was enshrined in the Naismith Hall of Fame alongside Thurmond.

GAME FOR THE AGES: On Feb. 16, 1963, a then-record crowd of 5,734 at Anderson Arena broke into an ear-splitting pregame chant: "We Want Loyola!" The 21–0 Ramblers were the No. 2 team in the nation, but they proved no match for the Falcons' inside-out play. The end result: a 92-75 stomping of the eventual national champs.

HEARTBREAKER: Say the name Grunkemeyer on the BGSU campus and be prepared for a withering scowl. The No. 1-seed Falcons took a six-game winning streak into the 2000 MAC tournament, but played flat against No. 9-seed Miami, opening the door for Jason Grunkemeyer's 35-footer at the end of regulation that sent the game to overtime. Bowling Green's defense remained stingy, but the Falcons could muster only one bucket in the extra frame and lost, 58-56.

FIERCEST RIVAL: Toledo and Bowling Green, separated by a 25-mile strip of I-75, just don't get along in any sport. In 1935, the Rockets football team roughed up the Falcons, 63-0, triggering a fan riot. In 1942, BGSU hired Anderson away from Toledo, where he had gone 142–41. In 1948, to quell the animosity, the two schools started exchanging a peace pipe given to the winner of each hoops game, but that tradition ended in 1969 when the pipe was stolen. You get the picture. The Rockets lead the series, 83–76.

Armed with a freakishly long wingspan and superior quickness, Nate Thurmond thrived in Harold Anderson's up-tempo system.

FANFARE AND HOOPLA: A lot of history will be left behind at Anderson Arena when the Falcons move into the new Stroh Center in 2012. One of the oldest arenas currently in use in the MAC (opened in 1960), it is one of a small number of facilities in Division I to allow the students to actually stand on the playing floor during games.

FAN FAVORITE: G ANTONIO DANIELS (1993-97) The sweet-shooting guard led the Falcons to a share of their first MAC regular-season title in more than a decade and then became the first NBA top-5 draftee from Bowling Green since Thurmond. But before Daniels was on the NBA's radar, he was known as the younger brother of Dayton's Chris Daniels. Eight days before Chris was to see his brother's first college game, he died in his sleep of cardiac arrhythmia. Antonio went ahead and played against Eastern Michigan—and hit the game-winner on a coast-to-coast layup after his defender tripped and fell for no obvious reason (unless one believes in ghosts).

PROFILE

Bowling Green State University, Bowling Green, OH
Founded: 1910
Enrollment: 15,356 (13,968 undergraduate)
Colors: Orange and brown
Nickname: Falcons
Current arena: Anderson Arena, opened as Memorial Hall in 1960 (4,700)
First game: Jan. 8, 1916
All-time record: 1,230-1,019 (.547)
Total weeks in AP Top 20/25: 19

Current conference: Mid-American (1953-)
Conference titles:
MAC: 9 (1959, '62, '63, '68, '81 [tie], 83, '97 [tie], 2000, '09 [tie])
Conference tournament titles: 0
NCAA Tournament appearances: 4
NIT appearances: 14
Semifinals: 2

CONSENSUS ALL-AMERICAS

1945 **Wyndol Gray**, F

FIRST-ROUND PRO PICKS

1950	**Chuck Share**, Boston (1)
1963	**Nate Thurmond**, San Francisco (3)
1997	**Antonio Daniels**, Vancouver (4)

TOP 5

G	**Antonio Daniels** (1993-97)
G	**Howard "Butch" Komives** (1961-64)
F	**Wyndol Gray** (1942-43, '44-45)
F	**Walt Piatkowski** (1965-68)
C	**Nate Thurmond** (1960-63)

RECORDS	GAME		SEASON		CAREER	
POINTS	52	Jim Darrow, vs. Marshall (Feb. 27, 1960); vs. Toledo (Jan. 13, 1960)	844	Howard Komives (1963-64)	1,938	Anthony Stacey (1995-2000)
POINTS PER GAME			36.7	Howard Komives (1963-64)	25.8	Howard Komives (1961-64)
REBOUNDS	31	Al Dixon, vs. Northern Illinois (Jan 20, 1966); Nate Thurmond, vs. Mississippi State (March 16, 1963)	452	Nate Thurmond (1962-63)	1,295	Nate Thurmond (1960-63)
ASSISTS	15	David Greer, vs. Marshall (Dec. 30, 1980)	242	David Greer (1981-82)	768	David Greer (1979-83)

SEASON REVIEW

SEASON	W-L	CONF.	SCORING		COACH	RECORD
1915-16	3-8		Charles Branigan	10.4	F.G. Beyerman	
1916-17	2-6		Reeme Dillery	7.8	F.G. Beyerman	
1917-18	6-5		Claitus Stough	16.4	F.G. Beyerman	
1918-19	2-5		Claitus Stough	17.3	F.G. Beyerman	
1919-20	4-9		Claitus Stough	15.6	F.G. Beyerman	
1920-21	8-7		Franklin Skibbie	8.7	F.G. Beyerman	25-40 .385
1921-22	4-10		Franklin Skibbie	8.4	Earl Krieger	4-10 .286
1922-23	9-4		Carl Bachman	14.1	Allen Snyder	9-4 .692
1923-24	3-15		Carl Bachman	6.8	R.B. McCandless	3-15 .167
1924-25	9-5		Dale Huffman	7.0	Warren Steller	9-5 .643
1925-26	10-3		Carl Bachman	12.7	Paul Landis	
1926-27	12-7		Hayden Olds	8.9	Paul Landis	
1927-28	9-7		Marvin Steen	11.2	Paul Landis	
1928-29	6-11		Lloyd Jump	7.1	Paul Landis	
1929-30	5-11		Ross Cox	8.9	Paul Landis	
1930-31	10-5		John Swearingen	7.1	Paul Landis	
1931-32	6-12		Lewis Miller	6.5	Paul Landis	
1932-33	9-5		Thurl Shupe	8.5	Paul Landis	
1933-34	10-5		Paul Shafer	7.7	Paul Landis	
1934-35	6-9		Paul Shafer	9.9	Paul Landis	
1935-36	7-8		Kenneth Weber	7.9	Paul Landis	
1936-37	4-11		Cliff Conrad	7.4	Paul Landis	

SEAS.	W-L	CONF.	POSTSEASON	SCORING		REBOUNDS		ASSISTS		COACH	RECORD
1937-38	16-4			James Zechman	12.1					Paul Landis	
1938-39	12-7			James Zechman	8.6					Paul Landis	
1939-40	16-5			Michael Kormas	10.8					Paul Landis	
1940-41	10-11			Dewey Johnson	11.3					Paul Landis	
1941-42	8-12			Michael Kish	8.6					Paul Landis	156-133 .540
1942-43	18-5			Wyndol Gray	22.9					Harold Anderson	
1943-44	22-4		NIT QUARTERFINALS	Don Otten	11.8					Harold Anderson	
1944-45	24-4		NIT RUNNER-UP	Don Otten	16.1					Harold Anderson	
1945-46	27-5		NIT QUARTERFINALS	Don Otten	14.7					Harold Anderson	
1946-47	28-7			Charles Share	9.1					Harold Anderson	
1947-48	27-6		NIT QUARTERFINALS	Charles Share	11.1					Harold Anderson	
1948-49	24-7		NIT THIRD PLACE	Charles Share	16.8					Harold Anderson	
1949-50	19-11			Charles Share	19.9					Harold Anderson	
1950-51	15-12			James Gerber	17.3					Harold Anderson	
1951-52	17-10			James Gerber	20.6					Harold Anderson	
1952-53	12-15			Al Bianchi	22.1					Harold Anderson	
1953-54	17-7	10-3	NIT QUARTERFINALS	Al Bianchi	25.0	Clarence Yackey	267			Harold Anderson	
1954-55	6-16	5-9		Jim Tucker	15.4	Max Chapman	12.4			Harold Anderson	
1955-56	4-19	1-11		Eugene Ray	15.9	Crystal Ellis	8.6			Harold Anderson	
1956-57	14-9	7-5		Rex Leach	14.7	Rex Leach	13.0			Harold Anderson	
1957-58	15-8	6-6		Jim Darrow	22.1	Chuck McCampbell	10.4			Harold Anderson	
1958-59	18-8	9-3	NCAA FIRST ROUND	Jim Darrow	21.1	Rex Leach	8.3			Harold Anderson	
1959-60	10-14	6-6		Jim Darrow	29.4	Rex Leach	8.3			Harold Anderson	
1960-61	10-14	4-8		Nate Thurmond	17.8	Nate Thurmond	18.7			Harold Anderson	
1961-62	21-4	11-1	NCAA FIRST ROUND	Howard Komives	21.0	Nate Thurmond	15.9			Harold Anderson	
1962-63	19-8	9-3	NCAA REGIONAL SEMIFINALS	Howard Komives	20.2	Nate Thurmond	16.7			Harold Anderson	367-193 .655
1963-64	14-9	7-5		Howard Komives	36.7	Bob Dwors	205			Warren Scholler	
1964-65	9-15	6-6		Bob Dwors	23.1	Bob Dwors	251			Warren Scholler	
1965-66	9-15	6-6		Walt Piatkowski	18.4	Al Dixon	11.0			Warren Scholler	
1966-67	11-13	5-7		Walt Piatkowski	22.3	Al Dixon	11.3			Warren Scholler	43-52 .453
1967-68	18-7	10-2	NCAA FIRST ROUND	Walt Piatkowski	24.0	Al Dixon	10.9			Bill Fitch	18-7 .720
1968-69	9-15	3-9		Dick Rudgers	16.0	Dan McLemore	10.5			Bob Conibear	
1969-70	15-9	7-3		Jim Penix	19.5	Jim Connally	10.6			Bob Conibear	
1970-71	7-18	2-8		Rich Walker	20.1	Jim Connally	13.8			Bob Conibear	31-42 .425
1971-72	4-20	1-9		Brian Scanlan	13.9	Brian Scanlan	7.2			Pat Haley	
1972-73	13-13	7-5		Cornelius Cash	18.0	Cornelius Cash	15.2	Jeff Montgomery	3.4	Pat Haley	
1973-74	15-11	7-5		Cornelius Cash	13.9	Cornelius Cash	12.4	Jeff Montgomery	3.1	Pat Haley	
1974-75	18-10	9-5		Jeff Montgomery	19.8	Cornelius Cash	13.0	Tommy Harris	86	Pat Haley	
1975-76	12-15	8-8		Tommy Harris	19.0	Ron Hammye	9.1	Jim Feckley	3.3	Pat Haley	62-69 .473
1976-77	9-18	5-11		Tommy Harris	23.1	Ron Hammye	8.3	Dan Shumaker	5.4	John Weinert	
1977-78	12-15	10-6		Duane Gray	13.9	Ron Hammye	9.5	Duane Gray	3.6	John Weinert	
1978-79	14-13	6-10		Duane Gray	16.0	Mike Miday	6.3	Rosie Barnes	6.3	John Weinert	
1979-80	20-10	11-5	NIT FIRST ROUND	Joe Faine	16.5	Colin Irish	8.2	Rosie Barnes	4.7	John Weinert	
1980-81	15-12	10-6		Joe Faine	18.2	Colin Irish	7.4	David Greer	7.6	John Weinert	
1981-82	18-11	10-6		Marcus Newbern	20.1	Lamar Jackson	6.8	David Greer	8.6	John Weinert	
1982-83	21-9	15-3	NIT FIRST ROUND	David Jenkins	18.7	Bill Faine	7.2	David Greer	7.2	John Weinert	
1983-84	18-10	11-7		David Jenkins	17.9	Colin Irish	9.3	Brian Miller	6.4	John Weinert	
1984-85	12-15	6-12		Keith Taylor	22.2	Anthony Robinson	7.4	Brian Miller	3.3	John Weinert	
1985-86	7-20	5-13		Brian Miller	15.1	Anthony Robinson	5.8	Brian Miller	3.6	John Weinert	146-133 .523
1986-87	15-14	10-6		Frank Booker	14.0	Anthony Robinson	4.8	Joe Gregory	3.9	Jim Larranaga	
1987-88	12-16	7-9		Anthony Robinson	14.5	Anthony Robinson	5.0	Joe Gregory	3.9	Jim Larranaga	
1988-89	12-16 ⊗	7-9		Joe Gregory	13.2	Ed Colbert	6.1	Darrell McLane	3.5	Jim Larranaga	
1989-90	18-11	9-7	NIT FIRST ROUND	Clinton Venable	16.8	Joe Moore	7.3	Clinton Venable	4.6	Jim Larranaga	
1990-91	17-13	9-7	NIT FIRST ROUND	Clinton Venable	17.4	Joe Moore	7.4	Clinton Venable	4.6	Jim Larranaga	
1991-92	14-15	8-8		Michael Huger	12.1	Tom Hall	7.6	Michael Huger	3.2	Jim Larranaga	
1992-93	11-16	8-10		Michael Huger	16.0	Shane Kline-Ruminski	5.4	Michael Huger	4.1	Jim Larranaga	
1993-94	18-10	12-6		Shane Kline-Ruminski	17.7	Floyd Miller	152	Antonio Daniels	3.9	Jim Larranaga	
1994-95	16-11	10-8		Shane Kline-Ruminski	17.2	Shane Kline-Ruminski	7.3	Antonio Daniels	3.6	Jim Larranaga	
1995-96	14-13	9-9		Anthony Stacey	16.0	Anthony Stacey	7.6	Antonio Daniels	5.9	Jim Larranaga	
1996-97	22-10	13-5	NIT FIRST ROUND	Antonio Daniels	24.0	Anthony Stacey	6.5	Antonio Daniels	6.8	Jim Larranaga	169-145 .538▼
1997-98	10-16	7-11		Tony Reid	16.7	Kirk Cowan	8.7	DeMar Moore	3.5	Dan Dakich	
1998-99	18-10	12-6		Anthony Stacey	18.5	Anthony Stacey	5.6	DeMar Moore	3.9	Dan Dakich	
1999-2000	22-8	14-4	NIT FIRST ROUND	Anthony Stacey	16.8	Len Matela	7.7	Keith McLeod	2.6	Dan Dakich	
2000-01	15-14	10-8		Keith McLeod	18.1	Len Matela	8.8	Brandon Pardon	7.0	Dan Dakich	
2001-02	24-9	12-6	NIT FIRST ROUND	Keith McLeod	22.9	Len Matela	7.9	Brandon Pardon	6.3	Dan Dakich	
2002-03	13-16	8-10		Kevin Netter	15.3	Ron Lewis	5.0	Jabari Mattox	4.4	Dan Dakich	
2003-04	14-17	8-10		Ron Lewis	17.0	Josh Almanson	4.8	Steven Wright	4.0	Dan Dakich	
2004-05	18-11	10-8		John Reimold	18.5	John Reimold	5.1	John Floyd	5.2	Dan Dakich	
2005-06	9-21	5-13		Martin Samarco	18.9	Mawel Soler	4.9	Steven Wright	3.5	Dan Dakich	
2006-07	13-18	3-13		Martin Samarco	19.5	Nate Miller	7.7	Ryne Hamblet	4.2	Dan Dakich	156-140 .527
2007-08	13-17	7-9		Nate Miller	13.2	Chris Knight	7.3	Joe Jakubowski	3.0	Louis Orr	
2008-09	19-14	11-5	NIT FIRST ROUND	Nate Miller	13.8	Nate Miller	7.3	Joe Jakubowski	3.5	Louis Orr	32-31 .508

Cumulative totals listed when per game averages not available.

⊗ Records don't reflect games forfeited or vacated. For adjusted records, see p. 521.

▼ Coach's record adjusted to reflect games forfeited or vacated: 170-144, .541. For yearly totals, see p. 521.

ESPN 39 SAGARIN

BRADLEY

With no football team since 1970, the Bradley faithful save up all their energy for basketball season, regularly packing famed Carver Arena. They've had plenty to cheer about for a century in Peoria. The Missouri Valley's most storied program includes four NIT titles, two NCAA runner-up finishes and one of the game's greatest scorers.

BEST TEAM: 1949-50 Led by the inside-outside game of guard Gene "Squeaky" Melchiorre and center Paul Unruh, Bradley played for both the NIT and the NCAA championships at Madison Square Garden, but fell both times to the City College of New York. Adolph Rupp himself declared that Melchiorre was the "greatest small man in the history of basketball." His local hero status took a blow on July 24, 1951, when Melchiorre and four other Bradley players were caught up in a point-shaving scandal and admitted to having taken bribes from gamblers.

BEST PLAYER: G Hersey Hawkins (1984-88) After averaging 20.0 ppg over his first three seasons, Hawk took his silky-smooth jumper to a whole other level as a senior. The AP Player of the Year carried the Braves to the NCAA Tournament with a sensational 36.3 ppg. His season was highlighted by a 63-point explosion at Detroit, still a record for the Missouri Valley.

BEST COACH: Chuck Orsborn (1956-65) No one can match John Wooden, the Wizard of Westwood—but the Wizard of Oz wasn't too shabby in his time. The iron-fisted Orsborn took a .500 team and won the NIT title in his first season. He won two more NITs during his nine years. In 2003, Orsborn was honored as the Braves' Coach of the Century.

GAMES FOR THE AGES: In what was voted Bradley's Game of the Century, the No. 4-ranked Braves beat No. 1 Cincinnati and Oscar Robertson, 91-90, on Jan. 16, 1960. Bradley star Chet Walker had 28 points and 12 boards to offset a 46-point, 10-rebound performance by the Big O. Robertson appeared unstoppable until the final moments when, trailing 89-88, he accidentally stepped out of bounds and sent Bradley fans into hysterics.

HEARTBREAKER: Having lost to CCNY 69-61 in the NIT final 10 days earlier, the Braves sought revenge—and the NCAA title—on March 28, 1950. After a City College turnover with seconds left, Melchiorre drove to the hoop, but had the ball swatted away by a swarm of defenders. Bradley lost, 71-68, and you better believe the people of Peoria are still crying foul.

FIERCEST RIVAL: One of the oldest matchups in college basketball, the Bradley-Illinois State series dates to 1904-05. Dubbed the Interstate 74 Rivalry, the games are almost always sold out, and, although Bradley holds a 61–47 series lead, it's rare that the game isn't close. Witness the three consecutive contests that went to overtime in 1998-99 and 1999-2000.

FANFARE AND HOOPLA: Nearly 60 years after his playing days, Melchiorre's legacy still divides the program. Due to his involvement in the 1951 point-shaving scandal that rocked college basketball, his jersey has not been retired. In 2003, that drew the ire of former Bradley coach Orsborn who pointed out the severity of the punishment by saying, "Murderers don't serve 53 years!"

Adolph Rupp declared that Melchiorre was the "greatest small man in the history of basketball."

FAN FAVORITE: G Jim Les (1983-86) As a teen, he was Bradley's ball boy. Les grew up to become a scrappy point guard who became the 1986 MVC Player of the Year and won the Frances Pomeroy Naismith award the same year. He returned to coach Bradley in 2002, guiding the Braves to the Sweet 16 in 2006.

CONSENSUS ALL-AMERICAS

1950	**Paul Unruh**, C
1951	**Gene Melchiorre**, G
1961, '62	**Chet Walker**, F
1988	**Hersey Hawkins**, G

FIRST-ROUND PRO PICKS

1951	**Gene Melchiorre**, Baltimore (1)
1968	**Joe Allen**, New York (ABA)
1969	**L.C. Bowen**, Carolina (ABA)
1978	**Roger Phegley**, Washington (14)
1982	**David Thirdkill**, Phoenix (15)
1988	**Hersey Hawkins**, LA Clippers (6)
1997	**Anthony Parker**, New Jersey (21)
2006	**Patrick O'Bryant**, Golden State (9)

PROFILE

Bradley University, Peoria, IL
Founded: 1897
Enrollment: 5,873 (5,057 undergraduate)
Colors: Red and white
Nickname: Braves
Current arena: Carver Arena, opened in 1982 (11,060)
Previous: Robertson Memorial Fieldhouse, 1949-82 (8,300); Woodruff High School Gym, 1941-43 (N/A); Peoria Armory, 1924-1941, 1946-49 (N/A)
First game: Jan. 1, 1902
All-time record: 1,536-1,006 (.604)
Total weeks in AP Top 20/25: 128
Current conference: Missouri Valley (1948-51, 1955-)
Conference titles:
MVC: 5 (1950, '80, '82, '86, '96)
Conference tournament titles:
MVC: 2 (1980, '88)
NCAA Tournament appearances: 8
Sweet 16s (since 1975): 1
Final Fours: 2
NIT appearances: 21
Semifinals: 8
Titles: 4 (1957, '60, '64, '82)

TOP 5

G	**Hersey Hawkins** (1984-88)
G	**Gene Melchiorre** (1947-51)
G/F	**Roger Phegley** (1974-78)
F	**Chet Walker** (1959-62)
C	**Paul Unruh** (1946-50)

RECORDS

	GAME		SEASON		CAREER	
POINTS	63	Hersey Hawkins, vs. Detroit (Feb. 22, 1988)	1,125	Hersey Hawkins (1987-88)	3,008	Hersey Hawkins (1984-88)
POINTS PER GAME			36.3	Hersey Hawkins (1987-88)	24.5	Curtis Stuckey (1989-91)
REBOUNDS	28	Barney Cable, vs. Marquette (Jan. 28, 1956); vs. Canisius (Dec. 13, 1955)	540	Dick Estergard (1852-53)	1,414	Dick Estergard (1951-54)
ASSISTS	21	Anthony Manuel, vs. UC Irvine (Dec. 19, 1987)	373	Anthony Manuel (1987-88)	855	Anthony Manuel (1985-89)

SEASON REVIEW

SEASON	W-L	CONF.	SCORING		COACH	RECORD	
1902-16	*107-78*		*Bradley went 14-4 in 1912-13*				
1916-17	10-6				Fred Brown		
1917-18	6-8				Fred Brown		
1918-19	6-9				Harold Olsen	6-9	.400
1919-20	5-10				Fred Brown[a]	91-65	.583
1920-21	7-9				A.J. Robertson		
1921-22	12-6				A.J. Robertson		
1922-23	14-5				A.J. Robertson		
1923-24	11-10				A.J. Robertson		
1924-25	11-10				A.J. Robertson		
1925-26	15-4				A.J. Robertson		
1926-27	7-8				A.J. Robertson		
1927-28	14-5				A.J. Robertson		
1928-29	8-8				A.J. Robertson		
1929-30	13-4				A.J. Robertson		
1930-31	10-9				A.J. Robertson		
1931-32	7-10				A.J. Robertson		
1932-33	8-5				A.J. Robertson		
1933-34	3-14		William Getz	7.2	A.J. Robertson		
1934-35	1-13		Ed Davis	9.6	A.J. Robertson		
1935-36	6-10		Willard Norval	6.6	A.J. Robertson		
1936-37	15-4		Carl Schunk	9.7	A.J. Robertson		

SEAS.	W-L	CONF.	POSTSEASON	SCORING		REBOUNDS		ASSISTS		COACH	RECORD	
1937-38	18-2		NIT QUARTERFINALS	Carl Schunk	9.5					A.J. Robertson		
1938-39	19-3		NIT THIRD PLACE	Dar Hutchins	11.2					A.J. Robertson		
1939-40	14-6			Chris Hansen	10.1					A.J. Robertson		
1940-41	16-4			Chris Hansen	12.0					A.J. Robertson		
1941-42	15-5			Ray Ramsey	12.3					A.J. Robertson		
1942-43	8-11			Ray Ramsey	13.3					A.J. Robertson		
1943-44	no team											
1944-45	no team											
1945-46	11-12			Jack Eakle	8.3					A.J. Robertson		
1946-47	25-7		NIT QUARTERFINALS	Paul Unruh	11.9					A.J. Robertson		
1947-48	28-3			Paul Unruh	15.7					A.J. Robertson	316-187	.628
1948-49	27-8	6-4	NIT FOURTH PLACE	Paul Unruh	14.5					Forddy Anderson		
1949-50	32-5	11-1	NIT RUNNER-UP, NCAA R-UP	Paul Unruh	12.8					Forddy Anderson		
1950-51	32-6	11-3		Gene Melchiorre	11.3					Forddy Anderson		
1951-52	17-12			Bob Carney	13.3	Dick Estergard	16.5			Forddy Anderson		
1952-53	15-12			Bob Carney	17.2	Dick Estergard	20.0			Forddy Anderson		
1953-54	19-13		NCAA RUNNER-UP	Bob Carney	16.1	Dick Estergard	12.3			Forddy Anderson	142-56	.717
1954-55	9-20		NCAA REGIONAL FINALS	Harvey Babetch	16.9					Bob Vanatta		
1955-56	13-13	3-9		Lee Utt	11.5	Barney Cable	18.6			Bob Vanatta	22-33	.400
1956-57	22-7	9-5	NIT CHAMPION	Barney Cable	18.0	Barney Cable	13.2			Chuck Orsborn		
1957-58	20-7	12-2	NIT QUARTERFINALS	Shellie McMillon	16.4	Barney Cable	11.1			Chuck Orsborn		
1958-59	25-4	12-2	NIT THIRD PLACE	Bobby Joe Mason	15.2	Joe Billy McDade	8.8			Chuck Orsborn		
1959-60	27-2	12-2	NIT CHAMPION	Chet Walker	21.7	Chet Walker	13.4			Chuck Orsborn		
1960-61	21-5	9-3		Chet Walker	25.2	Chet Walker	12.5			Chuck Orsborn		
1961-62	21-7	10-2	NIT QUARTERFINALS	Chet Walker	26.4	Chet Walker	12.3			Chuck Orsborn		
1962-63	17-9	6-6		Mack Herndon	22.7	Mack Herndon	10.5			Chuck Orsborn		
1963-64	23-6	7-5	NIT CHAMPION	Levern Tart	17.5	Joe Strawder	10.8			Chuck Orsborn		
1964-65	18-9	9-5	NIT FIRST ROUND	Eddie Jackson	17.4	Eddie Jackson	8.7			Chuck Orsborn	194-56	.776
1965-66	20-6	9-5		Joe Allen	18.5	Joe Allen	11.0			Joe Stowell		
1966-67	17-9	6-8		Joe Allen	22.8	Joe Allen	11.3	Al Smith	3.2	Joe Stowell		
1967-68	19-9	12-4	NIT FIRST ROUND	Joe Allen	24.5	Joe Allen	10.4	Al Smith	3.4	Joe Stowell		
1968-69	14-12	7-9		L.C. Bowen, S. Kuberski	23.0	Steve Kuberski	10.1	Dave Lundstrom	4.1	Joe Stowell		
1969-70	14-12	7-9		Gene Gathers	17.9	Gene Gathers	7.4	Frank Sylvester	3.8	Joe Stowell		
1970-71	13-12	6-8		Al Smith	18.9	Gene Gathers	9.2	Frank Sylvester	3.9	Joe Stowell		
1971-72	17-9	8-6		Sam Simmons	21.3	Seymour Reed	7.5	Sam Simmons	3.3	Joe Stowell		
1972-73	12-14	4-10		Seymour Reed	15.1	Seymour Reed	9.2	Dave Klobucher	3.0	Joe Stowell		
1973-74	20-8	9-3		Greg Smith	17.9	Seymour Reed	8.6	Jim Caruthers	3.3	Joe Stowell		
1974-75	15-11	7-7		Mike Davis	18.0	Mike Davis	7.3	Tom Les	8.4	Joe Stowell		
1975-76	13-13	4-8		Mike Davis	20.0	Mike Davis	9.3	Jim Caruthers	5.7	Joe Stowell		
1976-77	9-18	4-8		Roger Phegley	27.4	Harold McMath	7.7	Bobby Humbles	4.4	Joe Stowell		
1977-78	14-14	8-8		Roger Phegley	27.6	Harold McMath	8.4	Bobby Humbles	5.7	Joe Stowell	197-147	.573
1978-79	9-17	3-13		Mitchell Anderson	21.0	Harold McMath	9.6	Carl Maniscalco	5.1	Dick Versace		
1979-80	23-10	13-3	NCAA FIRST ROUND	Mitchell Anderson	20.6	Mitchell Anderson	8.8	David Thirdkill	2.5	Dick Versace		
1980-81	18-9	10-6		Mitchell Anderson	19.4	Mitchell Anderson	8.8	Eric Duhart	3.1	Dick Versace		
1981-82	26-10	13-3	NIT CHAMPION	Mitchell Anderson	16.4	Mitchell Anderson	7.6	Willie Scott	6.2	Dick Versace		
1982-83	16-13	10-8		Voise Winters	15.4	Voise Winters	6.3	Willie Scott	6.6	Dick Versace		
1983-84	15-13	7-9		Voise Winters	15.4	Voise Winters	6.6	Jim Les	7.2	Dick Versace		
1984-85	17-13	9-7	NIT FIRST ROUND	Voise Winters	20.9	Voise Winters	6.5	Jim Les	8.8	Dick Versace		
1985-86	32-3	16-0	NCAA SECOND ROUND	Hersey Hawkins	18.7	Mike Williams	7.1	Jim Les	7.9	Dick Versace	156-88	.639
1986-87	17-12	10-4		Hersey Hawkins	27.2	Hersey Hawkins	6.7	Anthony Manuel	8.8	Stan Albeck		
1987-88	26-5	12-2	NCAA FIRST ROUND	Hersey Hawkins	36.3	Hersey Hawkins	7.8	Anthony Manuel	12.0	Stan Albeck		
1988-89	13-14	7-7		Anthony Manuel	21.1	Luke Jackson	9.4	Anthony Manuel	8.0	Stan Albeck		
1989-90	11-20	6-8		Curtis Stuckey	23.7	Luke Jackson	8.7	Charles White	3.9	Stan Albeck		
1990-91	8-20	6-10		Curtis Stuckey	25.1	Xanthus Houston	7.3	Charles White	4.6	Stan Albeck	75-71	.514
1991-92	7-23	3-15		James Hamilton	13.5	James Hamilton	7.3	Charles White	2.5	Jim Molinari		
1992-93	11-16	7-11		Deon Jackson	12.3	Marcus Pollard	5.3	Billy Wright	4.4	Jim Molinari		
1993-94	23-8	14-4	NIT QUARTERFINALS	Deon Jackson	14.3	Deon Jackson	5.1	Billy Wright	4.8	Jim Molinari		
1994-95	20-10	12-6	NIT SECOND ROUND	Anthony Parker	14.2	Anthony Parker	6.6	Billy Wright	5.3	Jim Molinari		
1995-96	22-8	15-3	NCAA FIRST ROUND	Anthony Parker	18.9	Anthony Parker	6.5	Billy Wright	5.5	Jim Molinari		
1996-97	17-13	12-6	NIT SECOND ROUND	Aaron Zobrist	13.4	Adebayo Akinkunle	6.0	Anthony Parker	3.4	Jim Molinari		
1997-98	15-14	9-9		Adebayo Akinkunle	15.4	Adebayo Akinkunle	8.2	Eric Roberson	3.6	Jim Molinari		
1998-99	17-12	11-7	NIT FIRST ROUND	Rob Dye	17.4	Eric Roberson	5.5	Eric Roberson	3.2	Jim Molinari		
1999-2000	14-16	10-8		Rob Dye	16.6	Eric Roberson	5.6	Eric Roberson	3.0	Jim Molinari		
2000-01	19-12	12-6	NIT FIRST ROUND	Jerome Robinson	16.9	Jeffrey Rabey	7.3	Jerome Robinson	2.6	Jim Molinari		
2001-02	9-20	5-13		Phillip Gilbert	14.1	Danny Granger	7.1	Marcello Robinson	3.6	Jim Molinari	174-152	.534
2002-03	12-18	8-10		Phillip Gilbert	18.9	Mike Suggs	4.7	Marcello Robinson	4.6	Jim Les		
2003-04	15-16	7-11		Phillip Gilbert	16.0	Marcellus Sommerville	7.3	Marcello Robinson	3.9	Jim Les		
2004-05	13-15	6-12		Marcellus Sommerville	17.5	Marcellus Sommerville	7.5	Daniel Ruffin	4.7	Jim Les		
2005-06	22-11	11-7	NCAA REGIONAL SEMIFINALS	Marcellus Sommerville	15.7	Patrick O'Bryant	8.3	Daniel Ruffin	5.2	Jim Les		
2006-07	22-13	10-8	NIT SECOND ROUND	Will Franklin	14.6	Zach Andrews	7.0	Daniel Ruffin	5.4	Jim Les		
2007-08	21-17	9-9		Jeremy Crouch	15.8	Matt Salley	6.9	Daniel Ruffin	5.8	Jim Les		
2008-09	21-15	10-8		Theron Wilson	14.0	Theron Wilson	7.3	Eddren McCain	3.1	Jim Les	126-105	.545

[a] Fred Brown (3-6) and Bill Allen (2-4) both coached during the 1919-20 season.

ESPN 41 SAGARIN

BRIGHAM YOUNG

As successful as the school's teams have been (24 NCAA Tournaments, two NIT titles, 44 All-Americas), BYU made its mark by being the first program to recruit foreign players, beginning with Finland's Timo Lampen in 1958. From 1970 to '73, the Cougars' best player was the Yugoslavian center Kresimir Cosic. After Cosic died from non-Hodgkins lymphoma in 1995, TV analyst Billy Packer referred to him as "the first great international player to play college basketball in the United States."

BEST TEAM: 1950-51 Renowned for its home-court advantage, BYU's greatest team won a national title without playing a single game on campus. With the Smith Fieldhouse under construction, coach Stan Watts' Cougars hosted visitors at either Springville High or the University of Utah. With All-Americas Mel Hutchins, a center, and Roland Minson, a forward, the 28–9 Cougars had all the advantages they needed. BYU charged through the then-dominant NIT, knocking off Saint Louis and Seton Hall before trouncing No. 4 Dayton, 62-43, in the championship game.

BEST PLAYER: G DANNY AINGE (1977-81) His coast-to-coast drive to beat Notre Dame in the 1981 East Regional semifinal is one of the most remembered NCAA moments—and the signature note to a season in which Ainge took home the Wooden and National Association of Basketball Coaches awards. But it's not even his most impressive accomplishment. He set an NCAA Division I record by scoring in double-digits for 112 straight games (later surpassed by La Salle's Lionel Simmons). Ainge also played three seasons of baseball in the Toronto Blue Jays system while a BYU student and went on to have a storied NBA career as a player and executive.

BEST COACH: STAN WATTS (1949-72) The man with the horn-rim glasses was one tough hombre. Watts led Brigham Young to the 1971 Western Athletic Conference championship just one year after beating cancer. Watts, a pioneer of the fast break, also led BYU to NIT titles in 1951 and 1966.

GAME FOR THE AGES: March 19, 1981. Brigham Young is down 50-49 to Notre Dame with :08 left in the East Regional semifinal. Senior guard Danny Ainge takes the inbounds, drives the length of the floor, dribbles between defenders and lofts the ball over the outstretched hands of Irish forward Orlando Woolridge. The ball drops through the net as time expires and BYU advances to the Elite Eight.

HEARTBREAKER: A week after winning the 1951 NIT, BYU's championship glow was snuffed out at the NCAA Tournament. In their regional semifinal, the Cougars were trounced by Kansas State, 64-54. In the next night's consolation game, BYU lost again, 80-67, to Washington.

FIERCEST RIVAL: The BYU-Utah rivalry started on the baseball diamond in 1895, during a tie game that was capped by a bench-clearing brawl. Fourteen years later, the Holy War extended to the basketball court. The two schools have played countless classics since, most notably a 2002 matchup in which BYU overcame a 21-point deficit to beat the Utes, 63-61. Overall Utah holds a narrow edge on the series, 125–123.

FANFARE AND HOOPLA: There's loud. There's deafening. Then there's a sellout crowd at the Marriott Center, the nation's fourth-largest on-campus arena (22,700). It's no coincidence that since the court opened in 1971, the Cougars have won more than 78% of their home games.

FAN FAVORITE: C KRESIMIR COSIC (1970-73) On March 4, 2006, BYU unveiled Cosic's No. 11 jersey from the rafters at the Marriott Center. The sold-out crowd broke into a Cosic chant to honor the charasmatic Cougars great, who died of non-Hodgkins lymphoma in 1995. The 6'11" center led his team to two WAC titles while flashing an inside-out game that was ahead of its time.

THE SCHOOLS

CONSENSUS ALL-AMERICAS

1931 **Elwood Romney,** F
1981 **Danny Ainge,** G

FIRST-ROUND PRO PICKS

1951 **Mel Hutchins,** Tri-Cities (2)
1967 **Craig Raymond,** Philadelphia (12)
1983 **Greg Kite,** Boston (21)
1989 **Michael Smith,** Boston (13)
1993 **Shawn Bradley,** Philadelphia (2)
2004 **Rafael Araujo,** Toronto (8)

PROFILE

Brigham Young University, Provo, UT
Founded: 1875
Enrollment: 34,126 (30,847 undergraduate)
Colors: Dark blue, white and tan
Nickname: Cougars
Current arena: Marriott Center, opened in 1971 (22,700)
Previous: Smith Fieldhouse, 1951-71 (10,200); Springville High, 1950-51 (1,500)
First game: Feb. 6, 1903
All-time record: 1,580-994 (.614)
Total weeks in AP Top 20/25: 99

Current conference: Mountain West (1999-)
Conference titles:
Rocky Mountain: 2 (1924, '33)
Skyline: 5 (1943, '48, '50, '51, '57)
WAC: 12 (1965, '67 [tie], '69, '71,'72, '79, '80, '83 [tie], '88, '90 [tie], '92, '93)
Mountain West: 5 (2001 [tie], '03 [tie], '07, '08, '09 [tie])
Conference tournament titles:
WAC: 2 (1991, '92)
Mountain West: 1 (2001)
NCAA Tournament appearances: 24
Sweet 16s (since 1975): 1

NIT appearances: 10
Semifinals: 2
Titles: 2 (1951, '66)

TOP 5

G **Danny Ainge** (1977-81)
G **Dick Nemelka** (1963-66)
F **Devin Durrant** (1978-80, '82-84)
F **Michael Smith** (1983-84, '86-89)
C **Kresimir Cosic** (1970-73)

RECORDS

	GAME		SEASON		CAREER	
POINTS	47	Bob Skousen, vs. UCLA (Dec. 1, 1961)	866	Devin Durrant (1983-84)	2,467	Danny Ainge (1977-81)
POINTS PER GAME			27.9	Devin Durrant (1983-84)	20.9	John Fairchild (1963-65)
REBOUNDS	27	Scott Warner, vs. Texas Tech (Dec. 18, 1969)	471	Mel Hutchins (1950-51)	922	Michael Smith (1983-84,'86-89)
ASSISTS	16	Mike May, vs. Niagara (Dec. 11, 1976)	217	Matt Montague (2001-02)	570	Matt Montague (1996-97, 1999-2002)

SEASON REVIEW

SEASON	W-L	CONF.	SCORING	COACH	RECORD		SEASON	W-L	CONF.	SCORING	COACH	RECORD	
1902-16	*95-33*		*4-5 in 1902-03; 11-1 in 1905-06*				1926-27	5-14	1-11		E.L. Roberts		
1916-17	14-2			E.L. Roberts			1927-28	13-10	3-9		E.L. Roberts	90-49	.647
1917-18	5-3			E.L. Roberts			1928-29	20-10	6-6		G. Ott Romney		
1918-19	5-3			E.L. Roberts			1929-30	23-7	6-6		G. Ott Romney		
1919-20	4-2			E.L. Roberts			1930-31	20-13	7-5		G. Ott Romney		
1920-21	10-2			Alvin Twitchell			1931-32	20-12	8-4		G. Ott Romney		
1921-22	9-3			Alvin Twitchell			1932-33	20-7	9-3		G. Ott Romney		
1922-23	7-5			Alvin Twitchell			1933-34	18-12	9-3		G. Ott Romney		
1923-24	14-4	7-1		Alvin Twitchell			1934-35	18-10	6-6		G. Ott Romney	139-71	.662
1924-25	10-6	5-3		Alvin Twitchell	50-20	.714	1935-36	16-9	6-6		Edwin R. Kimball		
1925-26	11-5	7-5		E.L. Roberts			1936-37	17-10	5-7		Fred Dixon		

SEAS.	W-L	CONF.	POSTSEASON	SCORING		REBOUNDS		ASSISTS		COACH	RECORD	
1937-38	8-13	4-8								Fred Dixon	25-23	.521
1938-39	12-12	4-8								Edwin R. Kimball		
1939-40	17-8	7-5								Edwin R. Kimball		
1940-41	14-9	6-6								Edwin R. Kimball	59-38	.608
1941-42	17-3	9-3								Floyd Millet		
1942-43	15-7	7-1								Floyd Millet		
1943-44	3-2									Floyd Millet		
1944-45	11-12	5-5								Floyd Millet		
1945-46	12-13	6-6								Floyd Millet		
1946-47	9-16	3-9								Floyd Millet		
1947-48	16-11	8-2								Floyd Millet		
1948-49	21-13	11-9								Floyd Millet	104-77	.575
1949-50	22-12	14-6	NCAA REGIONAL SEMIFINALS	Joe Nelson	14.5					Stan Watts		
1950-51	28-9	15-5	NIT CHAMP, NCAA REG. SEMIS	Roland Minson	16.7	Mel Hutchins	12.7	Roland Minson	2.7	Stan Watts		
1951-52	14-10	9-5		Joe Richey	14.6	Joe Richey	7.0	Jerry Romney	1.6	Stan Watts		
1952-53	22-8	11-3	NIT FIRST ROUND	Joe Richey	17.6	Nick Mateljan	9.7			Stan Watts		
1953-54	18-11	9-5	NIT FIRST ROUND	Dean Larsen	15.2	Nick Mateljan	10.6			Stan Watts		
1954-55	13-13	10-4		Herschel Pedersen	16.1	Herschel Pedersen	11.3			Stan Watts		
1955-56	18-8	10-4		Terry Tebbs	19.5	Herschel Pedersen	12.1			Stan Watts		
1956-57	19-9	11-3	NCAA REGIONAL SEMIFINALS	John Benson	18.4	John Benson	11.3			Stan Watts		
1957-58	13-13	9-5		John Nicholls	17.8	John Nicholls	11.8			Stan Watts		
1958-59	15-11	8-6		Bob Skousen	17.7	Bob Skousen	9.2			Stan Watts		
1959-60	8-17	5-9		Dave Eastis	20.1	Dave Eastis	10.2			Stan Watts		
1960-61	15-11	9-5		Gary Earnest	16.5	Dave Eastis	9.3			Stan Watts		
1961-62	10-16	5-9		Bob Skousen	15.9	Bruce Burton	10.4			Stan Watts		
1962-63	12-14	6-4		Bruce Burton	17.1	Bruce Burton	10.4			Stan Watts		
1963-64	13-12	5-5		John Fairchild	20.3	John Fairchild	13.2			Stan Watts		
1964-65	21-7	8-2	NCAA REGIONAL SEMIFINALS	John Fairchild	21.5	John Fairchild	12.4			Stan Watts		
1965-66	20-5	6-4	NIT CHAMPION	Dick Nemelka	24.0	Craig Raymond	9.9			Stan Watts		
1966-67	14-10	8-2		Craig Raymond	14.2	Craig Raymond	7.6			Stan Watts		
1967-68	13-12	4-6		Kari Liimo	17.0	Jim Eakins	10.1			Stan Watts		
1968-69	16-12	6-4	NCAA FIRST ROUND	Doug Howard	15.4	Paul Ruffner	9.6			Stan Watts		
1969-70	8-18	4-10		Doug Howard	18.2	Paul Ruffner	9.8			Stan Watts		
1970-71	18-11	10-4	NCAA REGIONAL SEMIFINALS	Bernie Fryer	19.2	Kresimir Cosic	12.6			Stan Watts		
1971-72	21-5	12-2	NCAA FIRST ROUND	Kresimir Cosic	22.3	Kresimir Cosic	12.8			Stan Watts	371-254	.594
1972-73	19-7	9-5		Kresimir Cosic	20.2	Kresimir Cosic	9.5			Glenn Potter		
1973-74	11-15	6-8		Doug Richards	20.3	Mark Handy	8.7			Glenn Potter		
1974-75	12-14	5-9		Brian Frishman	15.4	Mark Handy	9.1			Glenn Potter	42-36	.538
1975-76	12-14	6-8		Jay Cheesman	17.6	Jay Cheesman	9.3	Verne Thompson	3.0	Frank Arnold		
1976-77	12-15	4-10		Jay Cheesman	15.9	Jay Cheesman	8.3	Mike May	4.2	Frank Arnold		
1977-78	12-18	6-8		Danny Ainge	21.1	Alan Taylor	8.5	Danny Ainge	5.3	Frank Arnold		
1978-79	20-8	10-2	NCAA SECOND ROUND	Danny Ainge	18.4	Alan Taylor	9.5	Danny Ainge	4.5	Frank Arnold		
1979-80	24-5	13-1	NCAA SECOND ROUND	Danny Ainge	19.1	Alan Taylor	10.9	Danny Ainge	4.6	Frank Arnold		
1980-81	25-7	12-4	NCAA REGIONAL FINALS	Danny Ainge	24.4	Steve Trumbo	10.7	Danny Ainge	4.0	Frank Arnold		
1981-82	17-13	9-7	NIT FIRST ROUND	Fred Roberts	15.5	Steve Trumbo	11.5	Scott Sinek	3.3	Frank Arnold		
1982-83	15-14	11-5		Devin Durrant	22.8	Greg Kite	8.8	Marty Perry	3.4	Frank Arnold	137-94	.593
1983-84	20-11	12-4	NCAA SECOND ROUND	Devin Durrant	27.9	Brett Applegate	11.4	Chris Nikchevich	3.9	Ladell Andersen		
1984-85	15-14	9-7		Timo Saarelainen	22.0	Alan Pollard	6.5	Marty Perry	4.2	Ladell Andersen		
1985-86	18-14	11-5	NIT QUARTERFINALS	Jeff Chatman	17.5	Tom Gneiting	7.4	Bob Capener	3.3	Ladell Andersen		
1986-87	21-11	12-4	NCAA FIRST ROUND	Michael Smith	20.1	Michael Smith	8.5	Brian Taylor	3.7	Ladell Andersen		
1987-88	26-6	13-3	NCAA SECOND ROUND	Michael Smith	21.2	Michael Smith	7.8	Brian Taylor	4.7	Ladell Andersen		
1988-89	14-15	7-9		Michael Smith	26.4	Michael Smith	8.6	Marty Haws	5.1	Ladell Andersen	114-71	.616
1989-90	21-9	11-5	NCAA FIRST ROUND	Marty Haws	18.5	Andy Toolson	6.6	Marty Haws	4.1	Roger Reid		
1990-91	21-13	11-5	NCAA SECOND ROUND	Shawn Bradley	14.8	Shawn Bradley	7.7	Nathan Call	4.8	Roger Reid		
1991-92	25-7	12-4	NCAA FIRST ROUND	Gary Trost	14.2	Gary Trost	6.3	Nathan Call	6.4	Roger Reid		
1992-93	25-9	15-3	NCAA SECOND ROUND	Gary Trost	15.2	Gary Trost	6.9	Randy Reid	4.1	Roger Reid		
1993-94	22-10	12-6	NIT SECOND ROUND	Russell Larson	19.9	Russell Larson	9.1	Randy Reid	2.7	Roger Reid		
1994-95	22-10	13-5	NCAA FIRST ROUND	Russell Larson	17.9	Russell Larson	6.9	Robbie Reid	4.9	Roger Reid		
1995-96	15-13	9-9		Kenneth Roberts	19.3	Justin Weidauer	7.3	Randy Reid	5.1	Roger Reid		
1996-97	1-25	0-16		Jeff Campbell	15.3	Justin Weidauer	8.3	Matt Montague	5.0	Roger Reid[a]	152-77	.664
1997-98	9-21	4-10		Ron Selleaze	16.8	Ron Selleaze	7.0	Brian Dignan	4.0	Steve Cleveland		
1998-99	12-16	6-8		Mark Bigelow	15.0	Mark Bigelow	6.3	Michael Vranes	2.9	Steve Cleveland		
1999-2000	22-11	7-7	NIT QUARTERFINALS	Terrell Lyday	17.1	Mekeli Wesley	5.8	Matt Montague	3.8	Steve Cleveland		
2000-01	24-9	10-4	NCAA FIRST ROUND	Mekeli Wesley	17.2	Mekeli Wesley	5.5	Matt Montague	2.9	Steve Cleveland		
2001-02	18-12	7-7	NIT SECOND ROUND	Travis Hansen	15.6	Travis Hansen	6.2	Matt Montague	7.2	Steve Cleveland		
2002-03	23-9	11-3	NCAA FIRST ROUND	Travis Hansen	16.8	Rafael Araujo	8.9	Kevin Woodberry	2.5	Steve Cleveland		
2003-04	21-9	10-4	NCAA FIRST ROUND	Rafael Araujo	18.4	Rafael Araujo	10.1	Luiz Lemes	4.5	Steve Cleveland		
2004-05	9-21	3-11		Mike Hall	13.9	Keena Young	5.6	Austin Ainge	4.1	Steve Cleveland	138-108	.561
2005-06	20-9	12-4	NIT FIRST ROUND	Trent Plaisted	13.6	Trent Plaisted	6.9	Rashaun Broadus	3.6	Dave Rose		
2006-07	25-9	13-3	NCAA FIRST ROUND	Keena Young	17.4	Keena Young	6.6	Austin Ainge	4.4	Dave Rose		
2007-08	27-8	14-2	NCAA FIRST ROUND	Lee Cummard	15.8	Trent Plaisted	7.7	Ben Murdock	3.6	Dave Rose		
2008-09	25-8	12-4	NCAA FIRST ROUND	Lee Cummard	16.8	Jonathan Tavernari	7.2	Jimmer Fredette	4.1	Dave Rose	97-34	.740

[a] **Tony Ingle (0-19) and Roger Reid (1-6) both coached during the 1996-97 season.**

ESPN 246 SAGARIN

BROWN

What can Brown do in the new millennium? Deliver victories, apparently. The Bears' team-record 19-win season in 2007-08 was their fifth winning campaign in eight years, after just 19 in the entire 20th century. Not that those first 100 years were completely devoid of highlights: There was Mike Cingiser's Ivy League title in 1986, and Brown played the very first game in the inaugural 1939 NCAA Tournament (a 42-30 loss to Villanova).

BEST TEAM: 2002-03 Although the Bears finished second in the conference to unbeaten Penn, their 12–2 league mark earned them a rare NIT bid (rare for the Ivy, anyway). The team featured perhaps the most accomplished trio in school history: guards Earl Hunt (19.1 ppg) and Jason Forte (13.0 ppg, 5.3 apg), and forward Alai Nuualiitia (12.7 ppg, 1.4 bpg).

BEST PLAYER: F/C Arnie Berman (1969-72) If you watched the awkward freshman in his first college practice, you never would have envisioned the dominant post player he became. A consummate gym rat, Berman was a prolific inside scorer—and he made a robust second living at the line. His 22 free throws in a 1972 win over Columbia broke Bill Bradley's nine-year-old Ivy League record. Later that season, Berman made 25 in a game.

BEST COACH: Glen Miller (1999-2006) Using a four-guard motion offense fueled by high-scoring recruits, Miller guided the Bears to two straight 17-win seasons and an NIT bid, plus two other winning seasons.

GAME FOR THE AGES: On Valentine's Day 2003, Brown walked into Princeton's Jadwin Gymnasium as the holder of the nation's longest road losing streak against a single opponent—52 straight, to be exact. Thanks to 61% shooting, the Bears walked out 80-73 winners. Sure beats a card and chocolates.

FIERCEST RIVAL: Penn and Princeton pack the gym, and Providence is a geographic natural. But except for the past few years, the Bears have never been close to the same level as those three. Enter travel partner Yale, which Brown has managed to beat a relatively robust 34% of the time since their first meeting in 1905.

SEASON REVIEW

SEAS.	W-L	CONF.	COACH	SEAS.	W-L	CONF.	COACH
1901-47	*318-378-1*	*Made NCAA Tournament in 1938-39*		1960-61	11-14	8-6	L. Stanley Ward
1947-48	6-14		Robert B. Morris	1961-62	11-14	6-8	L. Stanley Ward
1948-49	13-8		Robert B. Morris	1962-63	11-13	6-8	L. Stanley Ward
1949-50	11-14		Robert B. Morris	1963-64	6-19	2-12	L. Stanley Ward
1950-51	8-11		Robert B. Morris	1964-65	7-17	3-11	L. Stanley Ward
1951-52	5-15		Robert B. Morris	1965-66	9-17	3-11	L. Stanley Ward
1952-53	5-14		Robert B. Morris	1966-67	10-16	3-11	L. Stanley Ward
1953-54	13-11	4-10	Robert B. Morris	1967-68	9-16	4-10	L. Stanley Ward
1954-55	7-16	3-11	L. Stanley Ward	1968-69	3-23	1-13	L. Stanley Ward
1955-56	7-18	3-11	L. Stanley Ward	1969-70	6-20	3-11	J. Gerald Alaimo
1956-57	8-16	4-10	L. Stanley Ward	1970-71	10-15	5-9	J. Gerald Alaimo
1957-58	10-15	5-9	L. Stanley Ward	1971-72	10-16	6-8	J. Gerald Alaimo
1958-59	11-13	6-8	L. Stanley Ward	1972-73	14-12	10-4	J. Gerald Alaimo
1959-60	13-12	8-6	L. Stanley Ward	1973-74	17-9	11-3	J. Gerald Alaimo

SEAS.	W-L	CONF.	SCORING		COACH	RECORD
1974-75	14-12	9-5			J. Gerald Alaimo	
1975-76	7-19	6-8	Brian Saunders	19.8	J. Gerald Alaimo	
1976-77	6-20	5-9	Brian Saunders	20.0	J. Gerald Alaimo	
1977-78	4-22	2-12			J. Gerald Alaimo	88-145 .378
1978-79	8-18	6-8			Joseph Mullaney	
1979-80	12-14	6-8	Peter Moss	20.8	Joseph Mullaney	
1980-81	9-17	5-9			Joseph Mullaney	29-49 .372
1981-82	5-21	5-9			Mike Cingiser	
1982-83	9-17	6-8			Mike Cingiser	
1983-84	11-15	6-8			Mike Cingiser	
1984-85	9-18	5-9			Mike Cingiser	
1985-86	16-11	10-4 ●			Mike Cingiser	
1986-87	9-18	4-10			Mike Cingiser	
1987-88	6-20	2-12			Mike Cingiser	
1988-89	7-19	2-12			Mike Cingiser	
1989-90	10-16	7-7			Mike Cingiser	
1990-91	11-15	6-8			Mike Cingiser	93-170 .354
1991-92	11-15	5-9			Frank Dobbs	
1992-93	7-19	2-12			Frank Dobbs	
1993-94	12-14	6-8			Frank Dobbs	
1994-95	13-13	8-6			Frank Dobbs	
1995-96	10-16	5-9			Frank Dobbs	
1996-97	4-22	3-11			Frank Dobbs	
1997-98	6-20	3-11			Frank Dobbs	
1998-99	4-22	2-12			Frank Dobbs	67-141 .322
1999-2000	8-19	4-10	Earl Hunt	17.0	Glen Miller	
2000-01	15-12	9-5	Earl Hunt	19.7	Glen Miller	
2001-02	17-10	8-6	Earl Hunt	19.7	Glen Miller	
2002-03	17-12	12-2 ■	Earl Hunt	19.1	Glen Miller	
2003-04	14-13	10-4	Jason Forte	16.8	Glen Miller	
2004-05	12-16	5-9	Jason Forte	18.4	Glen Miller	
2005-06	10-17	6-8	Keenan Jeppesen	11.1	Glen Miller	93-99 .484
2006-07	11-18	6-8	Mark McAndrew	15.8	Craig Robinson	
2007-08	19-10	11-3	Mark McAndrew	16.5	Craig Robinson	30-28 .517
2008-09	9-19	3-11	Matt Mullery	16.1	Jesse Agel	9-19 .321

● NCAA Tournament appearance ■ NIT appearance

PROFILE

Brown University, Providence, RI
Founded: 1764
Enrollment: 8,020 (5,874 undergraduate)
Colors: Seal brown, cardinal and white
Nickname: Bears
Current arena: Paul Bailey Pizzitola Memorial Sports Center, opened in 1989 (2,800)
Previous: Marvel Gymnasium, 1927-89 (N/A), Lyman Gymnasium, 1901-27
First game: Feb. 17, 1901
All-time record: 921-1,355-1 (.405)

Total weeks in AP Top 20/25: 0
Current conference: Ivy League (1953-)
Conference titles:
Ivy: 1 (1986)
NCAA Tournament appearances: 2
NIT appearances: 1

CONSENSUS ALL-AMERICAS

1908 **Don Pryor,** F/C

TOP 5

G **Earl Hunt** (1999-2003)
G **Mike Waitkus** (1982-86)
F **Mike Cingiser** (1959-62)
F/C **Arnie Berman** (1969-72)
C **Phil Brown** (1972-75)

RECORDS

	GAME		SEASON		CAREER	
POINTS	48	Harry Platt, vs. Northeastern (Feb. 2, 1938)	658	Arnie Berman (1971-72)	2,041	Earl Hunt (1999-2003)
POINTS PER GAME			25.3	Arnie Berman (1971-72)	21.6	Arnie Berman (1969-72)
REBOUNDS	32	Ed Tooley, vs. Northeastern (Feb. 9, 1955)	436	Ed Tooley (1954-55)	931	Phil Brown (1972-75)
ASSISTS	15	Jim Burke, vs. Dartmouth (Feb. 11, 1972)	155	Jason Forte (2002-03)	577	Mike Waitkus (1982-86)

ESPN 232 SAGARIN

BUCKNELL

Bucknell busted brackets everywhere by knocking off No. 3-seed Kansas in the 2005 NCAA Tournament. The upset was the signature moment of a remarkable two-year run that saw the Bison make consecutive Tourney appearances while winning 50 games. But this is no upstart program: Bucknell launched its team in 1896 and counts Hall-of-Fame pitcher Christy Mathewson (1898-1902) among its most famous hoopsters.

BEST TEAM: 2005-06 With :90 to play in the Patriot League tournament finals, the crowd started chanting "undefeated." But Bucknell's 74-59 victory over Holy Cross, which capped a 14–0 regular-season conference mark, was only the beginning. As a No. 9 seed in the NCAA Tournament, the experienced and disciplined Bison knocked off Arkansas in the first round, 59-55, before running out of steam in a 72-56 loss to Memphis in the second round.

BEST PLAYER: G Al Leslie (1977-81) The 6'3" Leslie played both guard positions and even some small forward, and scored in double digits in all but 11 of his 105 starts. A second-round pick of the Pacers, he is the first Bison to be drafted by an NBA team.

BEST COACH: Charlie Woollum (1975-94) A fun fact about Bucknell's longest-tenured coach: After Woollum succeeded Jim Valvano, his first recruit was Pat Flannery, who took over coaching duties from his mentor in 1994-95 and won 233 games, second only to—you guessed it—Woollum.

GAME FOR THE AGES: With 10.5 seconds left in the first round of the 2005 Tournament, Bison center Chris McNaughton hit a short jump-hook to upend Kansas, 64-63. The upset marked the first victory in the Big Dance for a Patriot League team.

FIERCEST RIVAL: Bucknell and Holy Cross, two of college hoops' oldest programs, didn't meet up until the formation of the Patriot League in 1990-91. They've been making up for lost time ever since, facing off 12 times in the postseason alone. Bucknell leads overall, 27–23.

SEASON REVIEW

SEAS.	W-L	CONF.	COACH	SEAS.	W-L	CONF.	COACH
1895-1948	*424-329-1*	*99-28*	*under student coaches till '08*	1961-62	7-15	2-9	Ben Kribbs
1948-49	2-18	0-8	Jack Guy	1962-63	7-16	2-8	Gene Evans
1949-50	5-16		Jack Guy	1963-64	8-13	3-7	Gene Evans
1950-51	9-13		Jack Guy	1964-65	11-13		Don Smith
1951-52	8-16		Jack Guy	1965-66	15-10		Don Smith
1952-53	3-16		Ben Kribbs	1966-67	11-11		Don Smith
1953-54	4-16		Ben Kribbs	1967-68	12-11		Don Smith
1954-55	3-18		Ben Kribbs	1968-69	13-11		Don Smith
1955-56	10-14		Ben Kribbs	1969-70	6-17	3-7	Don Smith
1956-57	16-8		Ben Kribbs	1970-71	9-14	4-6	Don Smith
1957-58	16-8		Ben Kribbs	1971-72	5-18	3-7	Don Smith
1958-59	16-7	6-5	Ben Kribbs	1972-73	11-14	6-4	Jim Valvano
1959-60	10-11	6-5	Ben Kribbs	1973-74	8-16	2-8	Jim Valvano
1960-61	12-11	5-6	Ben Kribbs	1974-75	14-12	4-4	Jim Valvano

SEAS.	W-L	CONF.	SCORING		COACH	RECORD
1975-76	13-13	5-5	Gerald Purnell	16.3	Charlie Woollum	
1976-77	10-15	5-5	Bob Barry	17.6	Charlie Woollum	
1977-78	13-15	5-5	Bob Barry	14.5	Charlie Woollum	
1978-79	18-9	12-6	Bob Barry, Al Leslie	18.7	Charlie Woollum	
1979-80	20-7	13-3	Al Leslie	20.9	Charlie Woollum	
1980-81	12-16	6-10	Al Leslie	19.2	Charlie Woollum	
1981-82	7-20	3-13	Jay Wright	11.9	Charlie Woollum	
1982-83	17-11	8-5	Jaye Andrews	13.7	Charlie Woollum	
1983-84	24-5	14-2	Jaye Andrews	15.3	Charlie Woollum	
1984-85	19-10	10-4	Jaye Andrews	16.8	Charlie Woollum	
1985-86	17-12	8-6	Mark Allsteadt	12.5	Charlie Woollum	
1986-87	22-9	11-3 ●	Mark Atkinson	14.9	Charlie Woollum	
1987-88	16-12	7-7	Mike Butts	17.5	Charlie Woollum	
1988-89	23-8	11-3 ●	Mike Butts	14.1	Charlie Woollum	
1989-90	15-14	6-8	Greg Leggett	20.2	Charlie Woollum	
1990-91	18-13	7-5	Bill Courtney	20.0	Charlie Woollum	
1991-92	21-9	11-3	Patrick King	20.3	Charlie Woollum	
1992-93	23-6	13-1	Chris Simpson	16.9	Charlie Woollum	
1993-94	10-17	6-8	Chris Simpson	20.5	Charlie Woollum	318-221 .590
1994-95	13-14	11-3	Brian Anderson	12.2	Pat Flannery	
1995-96	17-11	8-4	Brian Anderson	13.4	Pat Flannery	
1996-97	18-11	9-3	J.R. Holden	17.8	Pat Flannery	
1997-98	13-15	8-4	J.R. Holden	18.2	Pat Flannery	
1998-99	16-13	9-3	Valter Karavanic	11.2	Pat Flannery	
1999-2000	17-11	8-4	Dan Bowen	15.7	Pat Flannery	
2000-01	14-15	4-8	Bryan Bailey	17.7	Pat Flannery	
2001-02	13-16	8-6	Bryan Bailey	17.4	Pat Flannery	
2002-03	14-15	7-7	Boakai Lalugba	15.1	Pat Flannery	
2003-04	14-15	9-5	Kevin Bettencourt	14.9	Pat Flannery	
2004-05	23-10 ⊗	10-4 ●	Kevin Bettencourt	12.6	Pat Flannery	
2005-06	27-5	14-0 ●	Charles Lee	13.2	Pat Flannery	
2006-07	22-9	13-1	Chris McNaughton	12.0	Pat Flannery	
2007-08	12-19	6-8	John Griffin	13.1	Pat Flannery	233-179 .566
2008-09	7-23	4-10	Patrick Behan	13.8	Dave Paulsen	7-23 .233

⊗ Records do not reflect games forfeited or vacated. For adjusted records, see p. 521.

● NCAA Tournament appearance

PROFILE

Bucknell University, Lewisburg, PA
Founded: 1846
Enrollment: 3,609 (3,454 undergraduate)
Colors: Orange and blue
Nickname: Bison
Current arena: Sojka Pavilion, opened in 2003 (4,000)
Previous: Davis Gym, 1939-2003 (1,800); Tustin Gymnasium, 1896-1938 (N/A)
First game: Feb. 14, 1896
All-time record: 1,233-1,115-1 (.525)
Total weeks in AP Top 20/25: 1

Current conference: Patriot League (1990-)
Conference titles:
East Coast: 5 (1980 [tie],'84,'85,'87,'89)
Patriot: 5 (1992 [tie], '93, '95 [tie], 2006, '07 [tie])
Conference tournament titles:
East Coast: 2 (1987,'89)
Patriot: 2 (2005,'06)
NCAA Tournament appearances: 4
NIT appearances: 0

TOP 5

G **Charles Lee** (2002-06)
G **Al Leslie** (1977-81)
F **Mike Bright** (1989-93)
F/C **Hal Danzig** (1956-59)
C **Chris McNaughton** (2003-07)

RECORDS

RECORDS	GAME		SEASON		CAREER	
POINTS	45	Al Leslie, vs. American (Jan. 12, 1980)	619	Bill Courtney (1990-91)	1,973	Al Leslie (1977-81)
POINTS PER GAME			22.0	Joe Steiner (1960-61)	19.2	Jim Wherry (1967-70)
REBOUNDS	28	Craig Greenwood, vs. DePauw (Dec. 14, 1968)	387	Hal Danzig (1957-58)	1,134	Hal Danzig (1956-59)
ASSISTS	16	Russell Peyton, vs. UMBC (Jan. 27, 1992)	197	Chris Seneca (1986-87)	565	Mike Joseph (1986-90)

THE SCHOOLS

ESPN 263 SAGARIN

BUFFALO

Buffalo ran off 20 straight winning seasons from 1946-47 to '65-66, and made each of the first four College Division tournaments (1957-60) behind greats such as Jim Horne and Hal Kuhn. Since joining D1 in 1991-92, the road has been tough for Buff, with the notable exceptions of 2004-05 and '08-09.

BEST TEAM: 2004-05 Coach Reggie Witherspoon's 23–10 squad was Buffalo's first 20-win team, reaching the school's first (and only) postseason tournament behind MAC player of the year Turner Battle. The Bulls even won an NIT game before losing to eventual runner-up Saint Joseph's.

BEST PLAYER: G/F Jim Horne (1951-55) He exploded onto the scene alongside the legendary Kuhn on a powerful 1951-52 team that went 18–6 and set 11 scoring records at Buffalo. Horne owns three of the school's top four single-season scoring averages and finished as the all-time points leader with 1,833 (since surpassed by Rasaun Young).

BEST COACH: Leonard Serfustini (1956-70) The school's winningest coach (206), Serfustini led the Bulls to four straight College Division tournaments and six overall. He put together two awesome teams: the 18–7 1956-57 squad that made the College Division semifinals behind Joe Tontillo and Chuck Daniels; and the 19–3 1964-65 unit that included Dan Bazzani and Harvey Poe.

GAME FOR THE AGES: Buffalo's first D1 postseason game was memorable: a 2005 NIT overtime defeat of Drexel. Battle scored with 1.7 seconds left in regulation to send it to OT, during which the Bulls hit 8 of 10 free throws to pull away. Mark Bortz (20 points, 9 rebounds) and Battle (who scored 19 with 6 dishes) led the way.

FIERCEST RIVAL: Buffalo, Canisius, Niagara and St. Bonaventure make up the Buffalo-area Big Four, but of the group, Niagara stands out as the Bulls' principal foe. The Purple Eagles lead the series 55–26, including a 2007 80-63 victory that stopped a five-game Buffalo series winning streak. Included in that string was a thrilling 95-92 double-overtime Bulls win in 2004.

SEASON REVIEW

SEAS.	W-L	CONF.	COACH	SEAS.	W-L	CONF.	COACH
1915-48	228-212		*Arthur Powell, 198-189 from 1915-43*	1961-62	14-7		Leonard Serfustini
1948-49	11-9		Malcolm Eiken	1962-63	16-7		Leonard Serfustini
1949-50	15-10		Malcolm Eiken	1963-64	14-8		Leonard Serfustini
1950-51	13-8		Malcolm Eiken	1964-65	19-3		Leonard Serfustini
1951-52	18-6		Malcolm Eiken	1965-66	14-8		Leonard Serfustini
1952-53	10-9		Malcolm Eiken	1966-67	9-11		Leonard Serfustini
1953-54	15-8		Malcolm Eiken	1967-68	11-10		Leonard Serfustini
1954-55	16-6		Malcolm Eiken	1968-69	12-9		Leonard Serfustini
1955-56	17-3		Malcolm Eiken	1969-70	11-11		Leonard Serfustini
1956-57	18-7		Leonard Serfustini	1970-71	8-13		Edwin Muto
1957-58	17-5		Leonard Serfustini	1971-72	11-12		Edwin Muto
1958-59	16-7		Leonard Serfustini	1972-73	16-8		Edwin Muto
1959-60	15-6		Leonard Serfustini	1973-74	5-20		Leo Richardson
1960-61	18-5		Leonard Serfustini	1974-75	8-17		Leo Richardson

SEAS.	W-L	CONF.	SCORING		COACH	RECORD	
1975-76	10-16		Sam Pellom	14.9	Leo Richardson		
1976-77	5-21		Ed Johnson	16.0	Leo Richardson		
1977-78	6-18		Ed Johnson	18.0	Leo Richardson	34-92	.270
1978-79	7-18		Tony Smith	11.0	Virgil William Hughes		
1979-80	17-10		Nate Bouie	13.4	Virgil William Hughes		
1980-81	12-15		Tom Parsons	12.9	Virgil William Hughes		
1981-82	13-17		John Fitzpatrick	16.4	Virgil William Hughes	49-60	.450
1982-83	12-15		John Fitzpatrick	14.4	Kenneth Pope	12-15	.444
1983-84	14-13		Vince Brown	16.8	Dan Bazzani		
1984-85	5-19		Vince Brown	12.4	Dan Bazzani		
1985-86	14-11		Wayne James	18.2	Dan Bazzani		
1986-87	15-10		Anthony Miller	14.6	Dan Bazzani		
1987-88	14-13		Darryl Hall	16.1	Dan Bazzani		
1988-89	16-14		Brian Houston	15.7	Dan Bazzani		
1989-90	14-13		Rob Middlebrooks	16.0	Dan Bazzani		
1990-91	13-14		Rick Coleman	16.2	Dan Bazzani		
1991-92	2-26	0-12	John Blalock	21.1	Dan Bazzani		
1992-93	5-22		Kelvin Brown	12.8	Dan Bazzani	112-155	.419
1993-94	10-18	3-2	Modie Cox	12.6	Tim Cohane		
1994-95	18-10	12-6	Rasaun Young	18.0	Tim Cohane		
1995-96	13-14	10-8	Mike Martinho	17.7	Tim Cohane		
1996-97	17-11	11-5	Rasaun Young	19.6	Tim Cohane		
1997-98	15-13	9-7	Rasaun Young	19.8	Tim Cohane		
1998-99	5-24	1-17	Louis Campbell	12.4	Tim Cohane		
1999-2000	5-23	3-15	Louis Campbell	10.9	Tim Cohane[a]	80-93	.462
2000-01	4-24	2-16	Robert Brown	15.3	Reggie Witherspoon		
2001-02	12-18	7-11	Darcel Williams	15.1	Reggie Witherspoon		
2002-03	5-23	2-16	Turner Battle	12.7	Reggie Witherspoon		
2003-04	17-12	11-7	Turner Battle	14.5	Reggie Witherspoon		
2004-05	23-10	11-7 ■	Turner Battle	15.5	Reggie Witherspoon		
2005-06	19-13	8-10	Calvin Cage	18.5	Reggie Witherspoon		
2006-07	12-19	4-12	Yassin Idbihi	15.8	Reggie Witherspoon		
2007-08	10-20	3-13	Andy Robinson	13.1	Reggie Witherspoon		
2008-09	21-12	11-5	Rodney Pierce	14.3	Reggie Witherspoon	126-171	.424

[a] Tim Cohane (2-3) and Reggie Witherspoon (3-20) both coached during the 1999-2000 season.
■ NIT appearance

PROFILE

State University of New York at Buffalo (University at Buffalo), Buffalo, NY
Founded: 1846
Enrollment: 26,996 (18,263 undergraduate)
Colors: Royal blue and white
Nickname: Bulls
Current arena: Alumni Arena, opened in 1982 (6,100)
Previous: Clark Hall, 1938-82 (N/A)
First game: 1915
All-time record: 995-994 (.500)

Total weeks in AP Top 20/25: 0
Current conference: Mid-American (1998-)
Conference titles:
MAC: 1 (2009 [tie])
Conference tournament titles: 0
NCAA Tournament appearances: 0
NIT appearances: 1

TOP 5

G **Turner Battle** (2001-05)
G **Rasaun Young** (1993-98)
G/F **Jim Horne** (1951-55)
F/C **Curtis Blackmore** (1970-73)
C **Sam Pellom** (1974-78)

RECORDS

RECORDS	GAME		SEASON		CAREER	
POINTS	44	Mike Martinho, vs. Rochester (Feb. 3, 1998)	592	Calvin Cage (2005-06)	1,908	Rasaun Young (1993-98)
POINTS PER GAME			24.9	Jim Horne (1954-55)	20.8	Jim Horne (1951-55)
REBOUNDS	32	Curtis Blackmore, vs. Chattanooga (Feb. 19, 1973)	427	Curtis Blackmore (1972-73)	1,297	Sam Pellom (1974-78)
ASSISTS	22	Gary Domzalski, vs. Youngstown State (Feb. 8, 1975)	235	Gary Domzalski (1974-75)	565	Gary Domzalski (1972-76)

THE SCHOOLS

ESPN 98 SAGARIN

BUTLER

Walk into the Bulldogs locker room and you'll find a sign that reads, "The Butler Way demands commitment, denies selfishness, accepts reality, yet seeks constant improvement and placing the good of the team above self." Created by legendary coach Paul D. "Tony" Hinkle, the Butler Way has shaped one of the best mid-major programs of all time. The Bulldogs ruled the Indiana Collegiate Conference for parts of the 1950's through the '70s, and since 2000-01 they've won 20 or more games seven times.

BEST TEAM: 2006-07 The Bulldogs rarely outsized their opponents, but they almost always outhustled and outexecuted them on their way to the Sweet 16 and the school's first Top 10 ranking. Coach Todd Lickliter's team, led by juniors A.J. Graves (16.9 ppg) and Mike Green (13.9 ppg), set a Horizon League record with 29 wins (which the Bulldogs topped the following season), and gave defending national champion Florida all it could handle in a 65-57 loss in the NCAA Midwest Regional semifinals.

BEST PLAYER: F CHAD TUCKER (1983-88) Butler's all-time leading scorer, Tucker shot 50% or better from the field in each of his full seasons. He was an honorable mention All-America in 1984-85, when the Bulldogs advanced to the postseason for the first time in 23 years with an NIT bid. Tucker is first on the school's field goals made list (912) and second all-time in free throws made (468).

BEST COACH: PAUL D. "TONY" HINKLE (1926-42, '45-70) Deliberate. Methodical. Careful. When it came to offense, Hinkle didn't want his players freelancing or showboating; he wanted them to patiently work for open shots, then crash the boards in search of follow-up opportunities. The Hinkle System may not sound exciting, but the results were. He won three conference titles and 558 games, ranking him among the NCAA's top 50 winningest coaches. Hinkle also coached football and baseball at Butler.

GAME FOR THE AGES: No. 12-seed Butler had already upset Mississippi State in the 2003 NCAA Tournament, and in its second-round game against No. 4-seed Louisville on March 23, Darnell Archey couldn't be stopped. In the second half, the senior shooting guard made the Cardinals pay for overplaying his teammate, point guard Brandon Miller, by hitting all six of his three-pointers (Archey hit eight of nine for the entire game). As a team, the Bulldogs knocked down 14 of their 22 three-point attempts in their 79-71 victory—which sent Butler to the Sweet 16 for the first time in the school's history.

HEARTBREAKER: The 2000 NCAA Tournament runner-up, Florida, would not have gotten past the first round if not for Bulldogs guard LaVall Jordan's two missed free throws followed by the driving overtime buzzer-beater by Gator Mike Miller. Totally shocked, the Bulldogs suddenly found themselves 69-68 losers; the Gators barely crawled away with their lives.

FIERCEST RIVAL: In a series that dates all the way back to the 1903-04 season, Butler leads Indiana State, 67–56. The matchup has gone to extra frames 10 times, including a classic four-overtime thriller on Dec. 27, 1986. Butler won that one, 95-92, but not without controversy. With :02 left in the second overtime, Indiana State guard Richie Adderley hit a long shot that officials originally ruled a two-pointer—leaving the Sycamores trailing by a point. But after deliberating for 10 minutes, the officials reversed their original call and ruled the shot a game-tying three. It took the Bulldogs two more overtimes before they were able to get the lead back for good.

FANFARE AND HOOPLA: Originally known as the Butler Fieldhouse, the Bulldogs' home gym was renamed in 1966 to honor former coach Tony Hinkle. Constructed in 1928, the building has played host to six visiting U.S. presidents as well as all-star basketball games for both the NBA and ABA. For many years it was the home of the annual Indiana state high school tournament final, and played a feature role as such in the 1986 film *Hoosiers*.

FAN FAVORITE: G BOBBY PLUMP (1954-58) Plump was an Indiana sensation even before he became a star at Butler. That's because he scored the winning basket in the 1954 Indiana high school championship game for tiny Milan High, the team that inspired *Hoosiers*.

PROFILE

Butler University, Indianapolis, IN
Founded: 1855
Enrollment: 4,415 (3,907 undergraduate)
Colors: Blue and white
Nickname: Bulldogs
Current arena: Hinkle Fieldhouse, opened as Butler Fieldhouse in 1928 (10,000)
First game: 1897
All-time record: 1,371-1,027 (.572)
Total weeks in AP Top 20/25: 58

Current conference: Horizon League (1979-)
Conference titles:
Missouri Valley: 2 (1933, '34)
Mid-American: 1 (1947 [tie])
Midwestern Collegiate: 3 (1997, 2000, '01)
Horizon: 5 (2002, '03, '07 [tie], '08, '09)
Conference tournament titles:
Midwestern Collegiate: 4 (1997, '98, 2000, '01)
Horizon: 1 (2008)
NCAA Tournament appearances: 9
Sweet 16s (since 1975): 2
NIT appearances: 8

CONSENSUS ALL-AMERICAS

1924 **Hugh Middlesworth**, G

TOP 5

G **Darin Archbold** (1988-92)
G **A.J. Graves** (2004-08)
F **Lynn Mitchem** (1979-83)
F **Chad Tucker** (1983-88)
C **Jeff Blue** (1961-64)

RECORDS

RECORDS	GAME		SEASON		CAREER	
POINTS	54	Darrin Fitzgerald, vs. Detroit (Feb. 9, 1987)	770	Darin Archbold (1991-92)	2,321	Chad Tucker (1983-88)
POINTS PER GAME			27.8	Billy Shepherd (1969-70)	24.1	Billy Shepherd (1969-72)
REBOUNDS	26	Daryl Mason, vs. Evansville (Jan. 1, 1973)	354	Daryl Mason (1972-73)	961	Daryl Mason (1971-74)
ASSISTS	15	Thomas Jackson, vs. Detroit (March 7, 2000)	172	Mike Green (2007-08)	540	Thomas Jackson (1998-2002)

THE SCHOOLS

SEASON REVIEW

SEASON	W-L	CONF.	SCORING	COACH	RECORD	
1896-1916	*51-60*		*Best early season: 6-2 in 1904-05 under coach Edgar Wingard*			
1916-17	7-6			G. Cullen Thomas		
1917-18	0-6			G. Cullen Thomas	16-28	.364
1918-19	1-9			Joe Mullane	1-9	.100
1919-20	2-4			F.E. Ellis	2-4	.333
1920-21	16-4			Harlan O. "Pat" Page		
1921-22	24-6			Harlan O. "Pat" Page		
1922-23	17-3			Harlan O. "Pat" Page		
1923-24	12-7			Harlan O. "Pat" Page		
1924-25	20-4			Harlan O. "Pat" Page		
1925-26	16-5			Harlan O. "Pat" Page	105-29	.784
1926-27	17-4			Paul D. "Tony" Hinkle		
1927-28	19-3			Paul D. "Tony" Hinkle		
1928-29	17-2			Paul D. "Tony" Hinkle		
1929-30	12-8			Paul D. "Tony" Hinkle		
1930-31	17-2			Paul D. "Tony" Hinkle		
1931-32	14-5			Paul D. "Tony" Hinkle		
1932-33	16-5	9-1		Paul D. "Tony" Hinkle		
1933-34	14-7	9-1		Paul D. "Tony" Hinkle		
1934-35	13-7			Paul D. "Tony" Hinkle		
1935-36	6-15			Paul D. "Tony" Hinkle		
1936-37	6-14			Paul D. "Tony" Hinkle		

SEAS.	W-L	CONF.	POSTSEASON	SCORING		REBOUNDS		ASSISTS		COACH	RECORD	
1937-38	11-12									Paul D. "Tony" Hinkle		
1938-39	14-6									Paul D. "Tony" Hinkle		
1939-40	17-6									Paul D. "Tony" Hinkle		
1940-41	13-9									Paul D. "Tony" Hinkle		
1941-42	13-9									Paul D. "Tony" Hinkle		
1942-43	4-9									Frank Hedden		
1943-44	no team											
1944-45	14-6									Frank Hedden	18-15	.545
1945-46	12-8									Paul D. "Tony" Hinkle		
1946-47	16-7	6-2		Charles Maas	11.3					Paul D. "Tony" Hinkle		
1947-48	14-7	4-2		Ralph O'Brien	11.9					Paul D. "Tony" Hinkle		
1948-49	18-5	8-2		Ralph O'Brien	15.8					Paul D. "Tony" Hinkle		
1949-50	12-12	6-4		Ralph O'Brien	18.3					Paul D. "Tony" Hinkle		
1950-51	5-19			Orvis Burdsall	10.9					Paul D. "Tony" Hinkle		
1951-52	12-12			Orvis Burdsall	10.8					Paul D. "Tony" Hinkle		
1952-53	14-9			Keith Greve	17.1					Paul D. "Tony" Hinkle		
1953-54	13-12			Keith Greve	17.1					Paul D. "Tony" Hinkle		
1954-55	10-14			Wally Cox	10.6					Paul D. "Tony" Hinkle		
1955-56	14-9			Ted Guzek	15.9					Paul D. "Tony" Hinkle		
1956-57	11-14			Ted Guzek	21.2					Paul D. "Tony" Hinkle		
1957-58	15-10		NIT FIRST ROUND	Bobby Plump	19.6	Ken Pennington	8.2			Paul D. "Tony" Hinkle		
1958-59	19-9		NIT QUARTERFINALS	Bill Scott	18.3	John Jones	8.9			Paul D. "Tony" Hinkle		
1959-60	15-11			Ken Pennington	18.4	Ken Pennington	9.8			Paul D. "Tony" Hinkle		
1960-61	15-11			Gerry Williams	16.5	Tom Bowman	7.9			Paul D. "Tony" Hinkle		
1961-62	22-6		NCAA REGIONAL SEMIFINALS	Tom Bowman	18.4	Jeff Blue	12.0			Paul D. "Tony" Hinkle		
1962-63	16-10			Jeff Blue	17.7	Jeff Blue	11.7			Paul D. "Tony" Hinkle		
1963-64	13-13			Jeff Blue	18.6	Jeff Blue	12.0			Paul D. "Tony" Hinkle		
1964-65	11-15			Dave Sanders	20.6	Dave Sanders	8.9			Paul D. "Tony" Hinkle		
1965-66	16-10			Ed Schilling	20.7	Ed Schilling	12.3			Paul D. "Tony" Hinkle		
1966-67	9-17			Ed Schilling	14.7	Ed Schilling	9.5			Paul D. "Tony" Hinkle		
1967-68	11-14			Doug Wininger	14.9	Clarence Harper	7.8			Paul D. "Tony" Hinkle		
1968-69	11-15			Steve Norris	17.5	Garry Hoyt	10.3			Paul D. "Tony" Hinkle		
1969-70	15-11			Billy Shepherd	27.8	Dave Bennett	10.7			Paul D. "Tony" Hinkle	558-394	.586
1970-71	10-16			Billy Shepherd	24.0	Oscar Evans	9.2			George Theofanis		
1971-72	6-20			Oscar Evans	20.1	Daryl Mason	11.1	Billy Shepherd	5.8	George Theofanis		
1972-73	14-12			Kent Ehret	16.9	Daryl Mason	13.6	Clarence Crain	3.1	George Theofanis		
1973-74	14-12			Marty Monserez	13.2	Daryl Mason	12.2	Marty Monserez	2.1	George Theofanis		
1974-75	10-16			Wayne Burris	13.2	Barry Collier	5.9	John Dunn	2.3	George Theofanis		
1975-76	12-15			Wayne Burris	17.4	Barry Collier	7.5	Bill Lynch	4.5	George Theofanis		
1976-77	13-14			Wayne Burris	15.3	Ed Thompson	6.8	Wayne Burris	3.0	George Theofanis	79-105	.429
1977-78	15-11			Tom Orner	18.4	Joe Maloney	7.6	Doug Mitchell	3.0	Joe Sexson		
1978-79	11-16			Tom Orner	15.9	Mike Miller	9.8	Tom Orner	4.7	Joe Sexson		
1979-80	12-15	2-3		Tony Warren	17.4	Mike Miller	6.9	Dave Bastian	3.1	Joe Sexson		
1980-81	5-22	1-10		Lynn Mitchem	16.7	Lynn Mitchem	7.3	Claude Davis	3.4	Joe Sexson		
1981-82	7-20	3-9		Lynn Mitchem	19.8	Lynn Mitchem	7.2	Danny Jarrett	2.3	Joe Sexson		
1982-83	15-13	9-5		Lynn Mitchem	16.4	Lynn Mitchem	6.9	Skip Jones	4.1	Joe Sexson		
1983-84	13-15	7-7		Tim McRoberts	21.9	Tim Haseley	6.8	Darrin Fitzgerald	4.2	Joe Sexson		
1984-85	19-10	9-5	NIT FIRST ROUND	Chad Tucker	19.8	Tim Haseley	6.9	Darrin Fitzgerald	4.0	Joe Sexson		
1985-86	9-19	2-10		Chad Tucker	21.8	Tony Gallahar	6.1	Darrin Fitzgerald	2.8	Joe Sexson		
1986-87	12-16	5-7		Darrin Fitzgerald	26.2	Darren Fowlkes	8.3	Darrin Fitzgerald	3.6	Joe Sexson		
1987-88	14-14	5-5		Chad Tucker	24.1	Darren Fowlkes	7.0	Thad Matta	3.6	Joe Sexson		
1988-89	11-17	3-9		Darren Fowlkes	18.8	Darren Fowlkes	7.6	Darren Fowlkes	3.2	Joe Sexson	143-188	.432
1989-90	6-22	2-12		Darin Archbold	11.9	Rodney Haywood	6.3	Tim Bowen	2.9	Barry Collier		
1990-91	18-11	10-4	NIT FIRST ROUND	Darin Archbold	21.8	J.P. Brens	6.9	Tim Bowen	5.8	Barry Collier		
1991-92	21-10	7-3	NIT FIRST ROUND	Darin Archbold	24.8	J.P. Brens	6.2	Tim Bowen	4.1	Barry Collier		
1992-93	11-17	5-9		Jermaine Guice	17.3	Brian Beauford	6.7	Tim Bowen	3.6	Barry Collier		
1993-94	16-13	6-4		Jermaine Guice	18.2	John Taylor	7.5	Travis Trice	4.9	Barry Collier		
1994-95	15-12	8-7		Chris Miskel	13.9	Jon Neuhouser	6.4	Travis Trice	5.2	Barry Collier		
1995-96	19-8	12-4		Jon Neuhouser	12.6	Jon Neuhouser	6.9	Jeff Rogers	3.3	Barry Collier		
1996-97	23-10	12-4	NCAA FIRST ROUND	Jon Neuhouser	15.3	Jon Neuhouser	5.6	Jeff Rogers	5.2	Barry Collier		
1997-98	22-11	8-6	NCAA FIRST ROUND	Jon Neuhouser	12.6	Jon Neuhouser	5.3	Jeff Rogers	4.5	Barry Collier		
1998-99	22-10	11-3	NIT QUARTERFINALS	Mike Marshall	9.6	Mike Marshall	6.8	Thomas Jackson	3.0	Barry Collier		
1999-2000	23-8	12-2	NCAA FIRST ROUND	LaVall Jordan	11.7	Mike Marshall	6.9	Thomas Jackson	5.3	Barry Collier	196-132	.598
2000-01	24-8	11-3	NCAA SECOND ROUND	Thomas Jackson	13.0	Joel Cornette	5.9	Thomas Jackson	4.3	Thad Matta	24-8	.750
2001-02	26-6	12-4	NIT SECOND ROUND	Rylan Hainje	15.2	Joel Cornette	6.2	Thomas Jackson	4.6	Todd Lickliter		
2002-03	27-6	14-2	NCAA REGIONAL SEMIFINALS	Brandon Miller	11.9	Joel Cornette	6.5	Brandon Miller	3.4	Todd Lickliter		
2003-04	16-14	8-8		Duane Lightfoot	11.9	Mike Monserez	6.1	Mike Monserez	4.7	Todd Lickliter		
2004-05	13-15	7-9		Brandon Polk	13.6	Brandon Polk	4.6	Avery Sheets	4.0	Todd Lickliter		
2005-06	20-13	11-5	NIT FIRST ROUND	Brandon Polk	18.0	Brandon Crone	5.0	Avery Sheets	3.3	Todd Lickliter		
2006-07	29-7	13-3	NCAA REGIONAL SEMIFINALS	A.J. Graves	16.9	Mike Green	6.0	Mike Green	4.0	Todd Lickliter	131-61	.682
2007-08	30-4	16-2	NCAA SECOND ROUND	Mike Green	14.6	Mike Green	6.5	Mike Green	5.1	Brad Stevens		
2008-09	26-6	15-3	NCAA FIRST ROUND	Matt Howard	14.8	Matt Howard	6.8	Shelvin Mack	3.5	Brad Stevens	56-10	.848

ESPN 34 SAGARIN

CALIFORNIA

Former Stanford coach Mike Montgomery crossed San Francisco Bay in April 2008 to take over the head coaching job at Cal and immediately injected new life into one of the Pac-10's also-ran programs. The Golden Bears have certainly had their golden moments: back-to-back NCAA Tournament Final appearances in 1959 and '60 (winning one), an NIT championship in 1999, and great performances from several eventual first-round NBA picks. Monty's move to Berkeley has fans hopeful for more than just their memories and sporadic successes.

BEST TEAM: 1958-59 Heading into the Final Four, the Eastern basketball establishment laughed off Cal's chances of winning the national title. Considering that Cincinnati's Oscar Robertson and West Virginia's Jerry West stood in the Golden Bears' way, that skepticism was warranted. But Pete Newell's crew held the Big O to 5 of 16 shooting to win its semifinal, 64-58. The next day, the Bears overcame West's 28 points—Denny Fitzpatrick had 20, Bob Dalton 15 and Darrall Imhoff 10—to win their only NCAA title, 71-70.

BEST PLAYER: G JASON KIDD (1992-94) The husky 6'4" point guard from Oakland needed only two years to leave an indelible mark at Cal. Kidd was named national Freshman of the Year in 1993, when he led the nation in steals and carried the Bears past LSU and Duke in the NCAA Tournament. As a sophomore he was a first-team consensus All-America after leading D1 in assists (9.1 per game).

BEST COACH: PETE NEWELL (1954-60) The Newell Era lasted just six seasons at Cal, but the inventive coach later known for his Big Man Camp left Berkeley on top. His tough-minded D slowed down opposing offenses (the Bears allowed the fewest points per game in the nation in both 1958-59 and '59-60) and enabled his scrappy teams, like the 1959 champs, to beat more talented opponents.

GAME FOR THE AGES: The 1959 Tournament Final fits the bill for sure, with Imhoff making a tip-in with :17 left for an improbable 71-70 victory. But the 50 years that have gone by since Cal's sole championship have had their shining moments as well. Chief among them is March 20, 1993. Duke had won NCAA titles in both 1991 and '92, but in the second round of the Tournament, the Bears' Lamond Murray (28 points) and Kidd (11 points, 14 assists) helped put a stop to talk of a three-peat. No. 6-seed Cal pulled off a stunning 82-77 upset of the No. 3-seed Blue Devils.

HEARTBREAKER: On March 8, 2008, Cal held an 11-point lead with nine minutes to go against No. 3 UCLA at Pauley Pavilion. But after Bruins big man Kevin Love hit a three-pointer to cut the lead to one with :20 left, UCLA stripped Ryan Anderson of the inbounds pass (or brutally fouled him, depending on your point of view). Nineteen seconds later, Josh Shipp sank a baseline jumper that improbably arced over the backboard to give the Bruins an 81-80 win.

FIERCEST RIVAL: The Big Game (of football fame) gets all the publicity, but the Stanford-Cal hoops rivalry stirs up plenty of animosity too, especially with Montgomery's recent move. (Some Cardinal fans have taken to calling the coach Traitor Mike.) The Bears lead the series, 140–113.

FANFARE AND HOOPLA: The Bench, Cal's student section at Haas Pavilion, is most famous for texting and e-mailing USC guard Gabe Pruitt a week before a Trojans-Bears game in 2006, pretending to be a fictitious UCLA co-ed named Victoria. Pruitt and Victoria were to meet after the Cal game for a date. Instead, The Bench chanted "VIC-TO-RI-A!" throughout the game, rattling Pruitt into 3-of-13 shooting.

FAN FAVORITE: F ALFRED GRIGSBY (1991-97) The oft-injured Grigsby is the only Golden Bear to be named Most Inspirational Player four times—and also the only Cal player to be granted six years of eligibility.

CONSENSUS ALL-AMERICAS

1917	**George Hjelte**, G
1926, '27	**George Dixon**, G
1929	**Vern Corbin**, C
1960	**Darrall Imhoff**, C
1994	**Jason Kidd**, G

FIRST-ROUND PRO PICKS

1948	**Chuck Hanger**, Minneapolis (9)
1960	**Darrall Imhoff**, New York (3)
1969	**Bob Presley**, Denver (ABA)
1982	**Mark McNamara**, Philadelphia (22)
1987	**Kevin Johnson**, Cleveland (7)
1994	**Jason Kidd**, Dallas (2)
1994	**Lamond Murray**, LA Clippers (7)
1996	**Shareef Abdur-Rahim**, Vancouver (3)
1997	**Ed Gray**, Atlanta (22)
2008	**Ryan Anderson**, New Jersey (21)

PROFILE

University of California, Berkeley, Berkeley, CA
Founded: 1868
Enrollment: 35,409 (25,151 undergraduate)
Colors: Blue and gold
Nickname: Golden Bears
Current arena: Walter A. Haas Jr. Pavilion, opened 1999 (11,877)
Previous: New Arena, 1997-99 (19,200); Harmon Gymnasium, 1933-97 (6,578)
First game: 1908
All-time record: 1,428-1,033 (.580)
Total weeks in AP Top 20/25: 84
Current conference: Pacific-10 (1915-)
Conference titles:
Pacific Coast: 13 (1916 [tie], '21 [tie], '24, '25, '26, '27, '29, '32, '44 [tie], '46, '57, '58 [tie], '59)
AAWU: 1 (1960)
Conference tournament titles: 0
NCAA Tournaments: 15 (1 appearance vacated)
Sweet 16s (since 1975): 2
Final Fours: 3
Titles: 1 (1959)
NIT appearances: 6
Semifinals: 1
Titles: 1 (1999)

TOP 5

G	**Kevin Johnson** (1983-87)
G	**Jason Kidd** (1992-94)
F	**Sean Lampley** (1997-2001)
F	**Lamond Murray** (1991-94)
C	**Darrall Imhoff** (1957-60)

RECORDS	GAME		SEASON		CAREER	
POINTS	48	Ed Gray, vs. Washington State (Feb. 22, 1997)	729	Lamond Murray (1993-94)	1,776	Sean Lampley (1997-2001)
POINTS PER GAME			24.8	Ed Gray (1996-97)	20.0	Ed Gray (1995-97)
REBOUNDS	27	Bob Presley, vs. Saint Mary's (Calif.), (Dec. 6, 1967)	382	Ansley Truitt (1971-72)	1,019	Bob McKeen (1951-55)
ASSISTS	18	Jason Kidd, vs. Stanford (Jan. 20, 1994)	272	Jason Kidd (1993-94)	546	Keith Smith (1986-90)

SEASON REVIEW

SEASON	W-L	CONF.	SCORING		COACH	RECORD	
1907-18	*55-8*		*No losing seasons; program was undefeated through 1914-15 (21-0)*				
1918-19	6-3	2-2			William Hollender		
1919-20	8-5	5-5			William Hollender	14-8	.636
1920-21	19-4	8-3			E.H. Wright		
1921-22	19-6	10-4			E.H. Wright		
1922-23	12-6	5-3			E.H. Wright		
1923-24	14-4	5-3			E.H. Wright	64-20	.762
1924-25	11-4	3-1			Clarence "Nibs" Price		
1925-26	14-0	5-0			Clarence "Nibs" Price		
1926-27	17-0	5-0			Clarence "Nibs" Price		
1927-28	9-6	6-3			Clarence "Nibs" Price		
1928-29	17-3	9-0			Clarence "Nibs" Price		
1929-30	9-8	6-3	Kent Pursell	9.2	Clarence "Nibs" Price		
1930-31	12-10	6-3	Joe Kintana	6.1	Clarence "Nibs" Price		
1931-32	16-8	8-3	Joe Kintana	7.3	Clarence "Nibs" Price		
1932-33	18-7	8-3			Clarence "Nibs" Price		
1933-34	19-7	8-4	Harold Eifert	252	Clarence "Nibs" Price		
1934-35	11-14	5-7			Clarence "Nibs" Price		
1935-36	13-16	6-6			Clarence "Nibs" Price		
1936-37	17-10	4-8			Clarence "Nibs" Price		
1937-38	18-11	8-4			Clarence "Nibs" Price		
1938-39	24-8	9-3			Clarence "Nibs" Price		

SEAS.	W-L	CONF.	POSTSEASON	SCORING		REBOUNDS		ASSISTS		COACH	RECORD	
1939-40	15-17	5-7								Clarence "Nibs" Price		
1940-41	15-12	6-6								Clarence "Nibs" Price		
1941-42	11-19	4-8								Clarence "Nibs" Price		
1942-43	9-15	1-7								Clarence "Nibs" Price		
1943-44	7-3	4-0		Jim Smith	8.5					Clarence "Nibs" Price		
1944-45	7-8	1-3		Gus Mota	11.3					Clarence "Nibs" Price		
1945-46	30-6	11-1	NCAA FOURTH PLACE	Andy Wolfe	13.4					Clarence "Nibs" Price		
1946-47	20-11	8-4		Chuck Hanger	10.1					Clarence "Nibs" Price		
1947-48	25-9	11-1		Chuck Hanger	14.5					Clarence "Nibs" Price		
1948-49	14-19	1-11		Mike O'Neill	11.0					Clarence "Nibs" Price		
1949-50	10-17	4-8		Bill Hagler	10.7					Clarence "Nibs" Price		
1950-51	16-16	3-9		Bill Hagler	13.3					Clarence "Nibs" Price		
1951-52	17-13	6-6		Bob McKeen	9.8					Clarence "Nibs" Price		
1952-53	15-10	9-3		Bob McKeen	17.6					Clarence "Nibs" Price		
1953-54	17-7	6-6		Bob McKeen	16.0					Clarence "Nibs" Price	453-294	.606
1954-55	9-16	1-11		Bob McKeen	19.8					Pete Newell		
1955-56	17-8	10-6		Larry Friend	13.0					Pete Newell		
1956-57	21-5	14-2	NCAA REGIONAL FINALS	Larry Friend	18.9					Pete Newell		
1957-58	19-9	12-4	NCAA REGIONAL FINALS	Don McIntosh	11.7	Don McIntosh	8.0			Pete Newell		
1958-59	**25-4**	**14-2**	**NATIONAL CHAMPION**	**Denny Fitzpatrick**	**13.3**	**Darrall Imhoff**	**11.0**			**Pete Newell**		
1959-60	28-2	11-1	NCAA RUNNER-UP	Darrall Imhoff	13.7	Darrall Imhoff	12.4			Pete Newell	119-44	.730
1960-61	13-9	5-7		Bill McClintock	10.8	Bill McClintock	10.6			Rene Herrerias		
1961-62	8-17	2-10		Dick Smith	12.0	Don Lauer	6.3			Rene Herrerias		
1962-63	13-11	4-8		Dick Smith	14.6	Camden Wall	9.4			Rene Herrerias		
1963-64	11-13	8-7		Dan Wolthers	14.3	Camden Wall	8.9			Rene Herrerias		
1964-65	8-15	4-10		Dan Wolthers	17.7	Dan Wolthers	7.7			Rene Herrerias		
1965-66	9-16	4-10		Russ Critchfield	15.5	Bob Wolfe	7.0	Russ Critchfield	1.4	Rene Herrerias		
1966-67	15-10	6-8		Russ Critchfield	21.0	Stu Watterson	9.1	Russ Critchfield	2.3	Rene Herrerias		
1967-68	15-9	7-7		Russ Critchfield	22.0	Bob Presley	14.5	Russ Critchfield	1.5	Rene Herrerias	92-100	.479
1968-69	12-13	4-10		Jackie Ridgle	20.0	Bob Presley	11.3	Charlie Johnson	3.6	Jim Padgett		
1969-70	11-15	5-9		Jackie Ridgle	16.6	Ansley Truitt	9.7	Phil Chenier	3.4	Jim Padgett		
1970-71	16-9	8-6		Jackie Ridgle	17.3	Ansley Truitt	12.2	Charlie Johnson	4.3	Jim Padgett		
1971-72	13-16	6-8		Ansley Truitt	18.8	Ansley Truitt	13.2	Eric Ling	5.1	Jim Padgett	52-53	.495
1972-73	11-15	4-10		John Coughran	15.5	John Coughran	9.2	Brady Allen	3.5	Dick Edwards		
1973-74	9-17	3-11		Rickie Hawthorne	14.1	Carl Meier	7.0	Brady Allen	2.7	Dick Edwards		
1974-75	17-9	7-7		Rickie Hawthorne	16.2	Jay Young	7.5	Rickie Hawthorne	4.7	Dick Edwards		
1975-76	12-14 ⊗	4-10		Carl Bird	15.2	Jay Young	6.3	Gene Ransom	3.3	Dick Edwards		
1976-77	12-15	7-7		Ray Murry	17.4	Tom Schneiderjohn	8.2	Gene Ransom	5.1	Dick Edwards		
1977-78	11-16	4-10		Gene Ransom	17.0	Doug True	8.9	Gene Ransom	4.9	Dick Edwards	72-84	.462▼
1978-79	6-21	4-14		Kevin Singleton	16.1	Doug True	7.3	Kevin Sparks	3.0	Dick Kuchen		
1979-80	8-19	3-15		Doug True	15.1	Doug True	9.1	Michael Chavez	3.3	Dick Kuchen		
1980-81	13-14	5-13		Mark McNamara	17.2	Mark McNamara	10.5	Butch Hays	3.1	Dick Kuchen		
1981-82	14-13	8-10		Mark McNamara	22.0	Mark McNamara	12.6	Butch Hays	4.4	Dick Kuchen		
1982-83	14-14	7-11		Michael Pitts	14.4	Michael Pitts	6.1	Butch Hays	4.5	Dick Kuchen		
1983-84	12-16	5-13		Butch Hays	12.6	Dave Butler	6.6	Butch Hays	2.5	Dick Kuchen		
1984-85	13-15	5-13		Chris Washington	13.1	Leonard Taylor	6.1	Kevin Johnson	4.1	Dick Kuchen	80-112	.417
1985-86	19-10	11-7	NIT FIRST ROUND	Kevin Johnson	15.6	Dave Butler	7.9	Kevin Johnson	6.0	Lou Campanelli		
1986-87	20-15	10-8	NIT QUARTERFINALS	Kevin Johnson	17.2	Dave Butler	7.0	Kevin Johnson	5.0	Lou Campanelli		
1987-88	9-20	5-13		Matt Beeuwsaert	13.9	Matt Beeuwsaert	7.0	Keith Smith	3.9	Lou Campanelli		
1988-89	20-13	10-8	NIT SECOND ROUND	Leonard Taylor	19.7	Leonard Taylor	8.2	Keith Smith	5.8	Lou Campanelli		
1989-90	22-10	12-6	NCAA SECOND ROUND	Keith Smith	16.6	Brian Hendrick	7.6	Keith Smith	6.4	Lou Campanelli		
1990-91	13-15	8-10		Brian Hendrick	17.6	Brian Hendrick	9.0	Roy Fisher	4.2	Lou Campanelli		
1991-92	10-18	4-14		Brian Hendrick	16.1	Brian Hendrick	10.7	K.J. Roberts	4.5	Lou Campanelli		
1992-93	21-9	12-6	NCAA REGIONAL SEMIFINALS	Lamond Murray	19.1	Brian Hendrick	7.4	Jason Kidd	7.7	Lou Campanelli[a]	123-108	.532
1993-94	22-8	13-5	NCAA FIRST ROUND	Lamond Murray	24.3	Lamond Murray	7.9	Jason Kidd	9.1	Todd Bozeman		
1994-95	13-14 ⊗	5-13		Monty Buckley	16.1	Tremaine Fowlkes	6.7	Jelani Gardner	6.5	Todd Bozeman		
1995-96	17-11 ⊗	11-7	NCAA FIRST ROUND	Shareef Abdur-Rahim	21.1	Shareef Abdur-Rahim	8.4	Jelani Gardner	3.9	Todd Bozeman	63-35	.643▼
1996-97	23-9	12-6	NCAA REGIONAL SEMIFINALS	Ed Gray	24.8	Alfred Grigsby	6.1	Prentice McGruder	6.4	Ben Braun		
1997-98	12-15	8-10		Geno Carlisle	17.9	Sean Marks	7.6	Raymond King	3.3	Ben Braun		
1998-99	22-11	8-10	NIT CHAMPION	Geno Carlisle	15.9	Sean Lampley	8.8	Geno Carlisle	3.9	Ben Braun		
1999-2000	18-15	7-11	NIT QUARTERFINALS	Sean Lampley	16.6	Sean Lampley	7.4	Shantay Legans	3.7	Ben Braun		
2000-01	20-11	11-7	NCAA FIRST ROUND	Sean Lampley	19.5	Sean Lampley	7.2	Shantay Legans	4.8	Ben Braun		
2001-02	23-9	12-6	NCAA SECOND ROUND	Joe Shipp	14.8	Jamal Sampson	6.5	Shantay Legans	3.8	Ben Braun		
2002-03	22-9	13-5	NCAA SECOND ROUND	Joe Shipp	20.4	Amit Tamir	6.5	Brian Wethers	3.0	Ben Braun		
2003-04	13-15	9-9		Leon Powe	15.1	Leon Powe	9.5	Ayinde Ubaka	3.9	Ben Braun		
2004-05	13-16	6-12		Rod Benson	13.3	Rod Benson	6.3	Martin Smith	3.9	Ben Braun		
2005-06	20-11	12-6	NCAA FIRST ROUND	Leon Powe	20.5	Leon Powe	10.1	Ayinde Ubaka	3.8	Ben Braun		
2006-07	16-17	6-12		Ryan Anderson	16.4	Ryan Anderson	8.3	Ayinde Ubaka	4.3	Ben Braun		
2007-08	17-16	6-12	NIT SECOND ROUND	Ryan Anderson	21.1	Ryan Anderson	9.9	Jerome Randle	3.7	Ben Braun	219-154	.587
2008-09	22-11	11-7	NCAA FIRST ROUND	Jerome Randle	18.3	Jamal Boykin	6.4	Jerome Randle	5.0	Mike Montgomery	22-11	.667

Cumulative totals listed when per game averages not available.

[a] Lou Campanelli (10-7) and Todd Bozeman (11-2) both coached during the 1992-93 season.

⊗ Records don't reflect games forfeited or vacated. For adjusted records, **see p. 521.**

▼ Coaches' records adjusted to reflect games forfeited or vacated: Dick Edwards, 73-85, .462; Todd Bozeman, 35-62, .361. For yearly totals, **see p. 521.**

ESPN 245 SAGARIN

CAL POLY

What's so scary about a team that's never been to the NCAA Tournament? Plenty—if you're playing Cal Poly at Mott Gym. The Mustangs have won more than 68% of their home games, thanks to a raucous crowd (capacity: 3,032) that sits practically on top of the court.

BEST TEAM: 2006-07 After a 6–8 start, it looked like a lost season. Then Cal Poly's up-tempo style started working. Fueled by a school-record three-point shooting percentage of 39%, the Mustangs made it all the way to the Big West tournament finals, where their quest for their first D1 Tourney bid was denied by Long Beach State in a 94-83 shootout.

BEST PLAYER: F Derek Stockalper (2004-07) In back-to-back seasons, the San Diego transfer led the Mustangs in points and rebounds, despite being forced to play out of position as a 6'5" power forward.

BEST COACH: Ernie Wheeler (1972-86) He guided the Mustangs to five postseason appearances with a tough-love coaching style and a deliberate, ball-control offense. That stretch included a trip to the 1981 D2 semifinals, where they lost to Florida Southern.

GAME FOR THE AGES: On Feb. 12, 1972, Cal Poly hosted Cal State Northridge in what had the makings of a routine, low-stakes conference matchup. As it turned out, both teams played like their lives were on the line. The game went to one overtime. Then another. Then another. Then another. And yes, then one more—a fifth—at which point the Mustangs finally put the Matadors away, 124-116. The game still ranks as the longest in either school's history.

FIERCEST RIVAL: Two decades after US Highway 101 first connected Cal Poly to UC Santa Barbara some 100 miles away, the two schools met for the first time on the hardwood on Jan. 10, 1947. Although the UCSB Gauchos hold a commanding 53–30 series lead, the meetings are seldom short on intensity, as fans from each school routinely make the highway run to infiltrate their adversary's home court.

SEASON REVIEW

SEAS.	W-L	CONF.	COACH	SEAS.	W-L	CONF.	COACH
1907-47	*84-119*	*15-3 in 1932-33*		1960-61	13-10		Ed Jorgensen
1947-48	12-13		Ed Jorgensen	1961-62	16-6		Ed Jorgensen
1948-49	12-12		Ed Jorgensen	1962-63	11-13		Ed Jorgensen
1949-50	13-15		Ed Jorgensen	1963-64	4-14		Ed Jorgensen
1950-51	22-9		Ed Jorgensen	1964-65	8-17		Ed Jorgensen
1951-52	14-16		Ed Jorgensen	1965-66	8-16		Ed Jorgensen
1952-53	21-6		Ed Jorgensen	1966-67	12-11		Stuart Chestnut
1953-54	11-11		Ed Jorgensen	1967-68	10-12		Stuart Chestnut
1954-55	13-13		Ed Jorgensen	1968-69	7-19		Stuart Chestnut
1955-56	15-12		Ed Jorgensen	1969-70	13-13		Neale Stoner
1956-57	12-11		Ed Jorgensen	1970-71	17-11		Neale Stoner
1957-58	8-17		Ed Jorgensen	1971-72	17-9		Neale Stoner
1958-59	16-9		Ed Jorgensen	1972-73	13-13		Ernie Wheeler
1959-60	15-9		Ed Jorgensen	1973-74	18-10		Ernie Wheeler

SEAS.	W-L	CONF.	SCORING		COACH	RECORD	
1974-75	15-11				Ernie Wheeler		
1975-76	13-13				Ernie Wheeler		
1976-77	19-11		Andre Keys	16.1	Ernie Wheeler		
1977-78	17-10				Ernie Wheeler		
1978-79	13-14				Ernie Wheeler		
1979-80	22-7				Ernie Wheeler		
1980-81	24-8				Ernie Wheeler		
1981-82	23-6		Kevin Lucas	19.9	Ernie Wheeler		
1982-83	18-10				Ernie Wheeler		
1983-84	20-8				Ernie Wheeler		
1984-85	16-10				Ernie Wheeler		
1985-86	23-6				Ernie Wheeler	254-137	.650
1986-87	19-10		Sean Chambers	18.3	Steve Beason		
1987-88	17-10				Steve Beason		
1988-89	14-12				Steve Beason		
1989-90	19-9		Stuart Thomas	17.0	Steve Beason		
1990-91	14-14		Stuart Thomas	23.5	Steve Beason		
1991-92	19-8				Steve Beason		
1992-93	9-17				Steve Beason		
1993-94	9-16				Steve Beason		
1994-95	1-26	0-6	Damien Levesque	11.7	Steve Beason	121-122	.498
1995-96	16-13	5-1	Shanta Cotright	16.8	Jeff Schneider		
1996-97	14-16	6-10	Chris Bjorklund	17.9	Jeff Schneider		
1997-98	14-14	7-9	Mike Wozniak	20.3	Jeff Schneider		
1998-99	11-16	6-10	Chris Bjorklund	18.1	Jeff Schneider		
1999-2000	10-18	5-11	Chris Bjorklund	19.4	Jeff Schneider		
2000-01	9-19	3-13	Chris Bjorklund	18.1	Jeff Schneider[a]	70-84	.455
2001-02	15-12	9-9	Varnie Dennis	14.7	Kevin Bromley		
2002-03	16-14	10-8	Varnie Dennis	17.5	Kevin Bromley		
2003-04	11-16	6-12	Varnie Dennis	18.3	Kevin Bromley		
2004-05	5-22	3-15	Dawin Whiten	11.4	Kevin Bromley		
2005-06	10-19	7-7	Derek Stockalper	12.9	Kevin Bromley		
2006-07	19-11	9-5	Derek Stockalper	14.4	Kevin Bromley		
2007-08	12-18	7-9	Trae Clark, Lorenzo Keeler	10.3	Kevin Bromley		
2008-09	7-21	3-13	Lorenzo Keeler	12.7	Kevin Bromley	99-145	.406

[a] Jeff Schneider (5-7) and Kevin Bromley (4-12) both coached during the 2000-01 season.

PROFILE

California Polytechnic State University, San Luis Obispo, CA
Founded: 1901
Enrollment: 19,777 (18,842 undergraduate)
Colors: Forest green and gold
Nickname: Mustangs
Current arena: Mott Gymnasium, opened in 1960 (3,032)
Previous: Crandall Gymnasium, 1928-60 (1,200)
First game: Oct. 19, 1907
All-time record: 948-911 (.510)
Total weeks in AP Top 20/25: 0

Current conference: Big West (1996-)
Conference titles:
American West: 1 (1996)
Conference tournament titles: 0
NCAA Tournament appearances: 0
NIT appearances: 0

TOP 5

G **Jim Schultz** (1979-81)
G **Mike Wozniak** (1996-2000)
F **Mike LaRoche** (1965-68)
F **Derek Stockalper** (2004-07)
C **Varnie Dennis** (2000-04)

RECORDS

RECORDS	GAME		SEASON		CAREER	
POINTS	43	Shanta Cotright, vs. George Mason (Jan. 13, 1996); Larry Madsen, vs. Cal Poly Pomona (1953-54)	658	Stuart Thomas (1990-91)	2,006	Chris Bjorklund (1996-2001)
POINTS PER GAME			23.9	Mike LaRoche (1966-67)	21.4	Mike LaRoche (1965-68)
REBOUNDS	25	Les Rogers, vs. Fresno State (March 1, 1968)	293	Theo Dunn (1956-57)	737	Robert Jennings (1970-73)
ASSISTS	16	Keith Wheeler, vs. Sacramento State (Nov. 23, 1983); Lewis Cohen, vs. San Francisco State (1976-77)	295	Jim Schultz (1980-81)	552	Jim Schultz (1979-81)

ESPN 194 SAGARIN

CAL STATE FULLERTON

A homecoming event in February 2008 brought back to campus members of the Titans who went to the school's first NCAA Tournament in 1978. Apparently, the winning vibe rubbed off on the 2007-08 team, which earned the school's second Tourney bid.

BEST TEAM: 1977-78 These Cinderellas from Orange County nearly made the Final Four, earning the temporary nickname Cal State Disneyland. Using a six-man rotation powered by working-class hero Greg Bunch, the Titans knocked off Michael Cooper and New Mexico and then Bill Cartwright-led San Francisco, before losing to an Arkansas squad that featured Sidney Moncrief.

BEST PLAYER: G Leon Wood (1981-84) You won't see Charles Barkley challenging this All-America to a race any time soon. The NBA's most famous player-turned-ref was quite the star guard at Fullerton, using his 6'3", 185-pound frame to overpower smaller point guards to the tune of 20.6 ppg and 8.2 apg in three seasons.

BEST COACH: Bob Burton (2003-) In the three seasons before Burton took over the Titans, the school had won a total of 20 games. The coach's let-it-fly offense turned things around in a hurry—the Titans posted back-to-back 20-win seasons in 2006-07 and 2007-08.

GAME FOR THE AGES: The Titans pulled off so many comeback wins in 1977-78 that their fans began chanting "We believe!" at the end of each game. Their faith was rewarded when it mattered most. In the second round of the Tournament, CSF trailed San Francisco by as many as 15. But the Titans stormed back and, on a Keith Anderson jumper, took a 74-72 lead with :03 left. USF called a timeout it didn't have, resulting in a technical and a Titans free throw that iced the 75-72 upset.

FIERCEST RIVAL: It's been said that CSF wins so many games at Cal State Northridge that the Matadors should rename their gym the Titandome. But even with Fullerton's recent dominance of its Big West rival—winning 10 of 12 meetings between 2004-09, including one in the 2008 conference tournament semifinals—it still only leads the series 33–25.

SEASON REVIEW

SEAS.	W-L	CONF.		SCORING		COACH	RECORD	
1960-61	14-12					Alex Omalev		
1961-62	24-6					Alex Omalev		
1962-63	17-6					Alex Omalev		
1963-64	7-16			Leonard Guinn	27.4	Alex Omalev		
1964-65	1-24					Alex Omalev		
1965-66	13-11					Alex Omalev		
1966-67	7-18					Alex Omalev		
1967-68	6-18					Alex Omalev		
1968-69	11-13					Alex Omalev		
1969-70	6-18					Alex Omalev		
1970-71	13-13					Alex Omalev		
1971-72	9-17					Alex Omalev	128-172	.427
1972-73	9-17					Moe Radovich	9-17	.346
1973-74	16-10					Bobby Dye		
1974-75	13-11	4-6		Greg Bunch	10.3	Bobby Dye		
1975-76	15-10	6-4		Greg Bunch	16.0	Bobby Dye		
1976-77	16-10	7-5		Greg Bunch	15.9	Bobby Dye		
1977-78	23-9	9-5	●	Greg Bunch	15.8	Bobby Dye		
1978-79	16-11	7-7		Calvin Roberts	15.3	Bobby Dye		
1979-80	10-17	4-10		Calvin Roberts	16.2	Bobby Dye	109-78	.583
1980-81	4-23	2-12		Dave Wear	17.7	George McQuarn		
1981-82	18-14	9-5		Leon Wood	19.7	George McQuarn		
1982-83	21-8	12-4	■	Leon Wood	18.1	George McQuarn		
1983-84	17-13	8-10		Leon Wood	24.0	George McQuarn		
1984-85	17-13	11-7		Kevin Henderson	17.3	George McQuarn		
1985-86	16-16	8-10		Kevin Henderson	16.6	George McQuarn		
1986-87	17-13	9-9	■	Richard Morton	18.4	George McQuarn		
1987-88	12-17	7-11		Richard Morton	22.0	George McQuarn	122-117	.510
1988-89	16-13	10-8		Cedric Ceballos	21.2	John Sneed		
1989-90	13-16	6-12		Cedric Ceballos	23.1	John Sneed		
1990-91	14-14	7-11		Joe Small	21.8	John Sneed		
1991-92	12-16	8-10		Agee Ward	18.0	John Sneed	55-59	.482
1992-93	15-12	10-8		Bruce Bowen	16.3	Brad Holland		
1993-94	8-19	6-12		Winston Peterson	15.3	Brad Holland	23-31	.426
1994-95	7-20	5-13		Winston Peterson	17.6	Bob Hawking		
1995-96	6-20	5-13		Chuck Overton	15.8	Bob Hawking		
1996-97	13-14	6-10		John Williams	16.9	Bob Hawking		
1997-98	12-16	6-10		Chris Dade	17.0	Bob Hawking		
1998-99	13-14	7-9		Ike Harmon	15.7	Bob Hawking		
1999-2000	8-19	3-13		Ike Harmon	18.7	Bob Hawking	59-103	.364
2000-01	5-23	3-13		Ike Harmon	12.9	Donny Daniels		
2001-02	5-22	2-16		Pape Sow	15.5	Donny Daniels		
2002-03	10-19	8-10		Ralphy Holmes	17.4	Donny Daniels	20-64	.238
2003-04	11-17	7-11		Pape Sow	17.3	Bob Burton		
2004-05	21-11	12-6	■	Ralphy Holmes	16.9	Bob Burton		
2005-06	16-13	5-9		Bobby Brown	17.5	Bob Burton		
2006-07	20-10	9-5		Bobby Brown	20.2	Bob Burton		
2007-08	24-9	12-4	●	Josh Akognon	19.9	Bob Burton		
2008-09	15-17	7-9		Josh Akognon	23.9	Bob Burton	107-77	.582

● NCAA Tournament appearance ■ NIT appearance

PROFILE

California State University, Fullerton, Fullerton, CA
Founded: 1957
Enrollment: 36,018 (31,673 undergraduate)
Colors: Navy, orange and white
Nickname: Titans
Current arena: Titan Gym, opened in 1964 (4,000)
Previous: The Fullerton Junior College North Gymnasium, 1960-64 (1,500)
First game: Dec. 1, 1960
All-time record: 632-718 (.468)
Total weeks in AP Top 20/25: 0

Current conference: Big West (1974-)
Conference titles:
Pacific Coast: 1 (1976 [tie])
Conference tournament titles:
Pacific Coast: 1 (1978)
Big West: 1 (2008)
NCAA Tournament appearances: 2
Sweet 16s (since 1975): 1
NIT appearances: 3

FIRST-ROUND PRO PICKS

1984 **Leon Wood**, Philadelphia (10)

TOP 5

G **Bobby Brown** (2003-07)
G **Leon Wood** (1981-84)
F **Greg Bunch** (1974-78)
F **Cedric Ceballos** (1988-90)
F **Scott Cutley** (2006-08)

RECORDS

RECORDS	GAME		SEASON		CAREER	
POINTS	47	Bobby Brown, vs. Bethune-Cookman (Dec. 16, 2006)	764	Josh Akognon (2008-09)	1,961	Bobby Brown (2003-07)
POINTS PER GAME			27.4	Leonard Guinn (1963-64)	22.1	Cedric Ceballos (1988-90)
REBOUNDS	27	Kerry Davis, vs. Central Michigan (Dec. 15, 1975)	362	Cedric Ceballos (1989-90)	1,115	Tony Neal (1981-85)
ASSISTS	21	Leon Wood, vs. UC Santa Barbara (March 3, 1983); vs. Long Beach State (Jan. 8, 1983)	319	Leon Wood (1982-83)	744	Leon Wood (1981-84)

ESPN 248 SAGARIN

CAL STATE NORTHRIDGE

Shadows don't get any longer or darker than the one cast by UCLA in Los Angeles. But the Matadors—who have struggled to draw national notice as a small college since 1958 and then in D1 starting in 1990—are finally basking in a little sunshine of their own, thanks in large part to lighting up those Bruins in 2000.

BEST TEAM: 2000-01 In their final season in the Big Sky, the high-energy Matadors served notice that there was a new LA force to reckon with by knocking off No. 15 UCLA, 78-74, at Pauley Pavilion in November 2000. Three months later, Cal State Northridge won the conference's regular-season and tournament titles, before losing to Kansas, 99-75, in its first NCAA Tournament game.

BEST PLAYER: C Brian Heinle (1997-2001) The Matadors' first D1 honorable mention All-America was equally adept at beating big men off the dribble, banging 'em in down low and shooting jumpers from outside. Heinle averaged 20.2 points per game and 9.2 rebounds in the Matadors' history-making 2000-01 season, and left the school as its all-time leading scorer and second-leading rebounder and shot-blocker.

BEST COACH: Bobby Braswell (1996-) The Northridge alum stunned the experts when his nine-man recruiting class of 1997 was ranked by guru Bob Gibbons as the 36th best in the country. The newcomers instantly clicked in Braswell's highly active offense and defense, and laid the foundation for a program that has become one of the Big West's best.

GAME FOR THE AGES: On March 10, 2001, the Mata-maniacs went wild. Playing in front of many faces painted the school colors of red and black, the Matadors knocked off Eastern Washington, 73-58, in the 2001 Big Sky tournament final. After the win, fans stormed the court to celebrate the school's first NCAA Tourney bid.

FIERCEST RIVAL: The Matadors' emergence under Braswell has neatly coincided with Cal State Fullerton's resurgence under Bob Burton, providing LA with a second entertaining local grudge match to go along with UCLA-USC.

SEASON REVIEW

SEAS.	W-L	CONF.	SCORING		COACH	RECORD
1958-59	3-13				Paul Thomas	
1959-60	14-15		Jim Malkin	19.7	Paul Thomas	
1960-61	10-24		Jim Malkin	15.3	Paul Thomas	
1961-62	3-22		Jim Malkin	17.5	Paul Thomas	
1962-63	3-23		Jim Wagner	16.4	Paul Thomas	33-97 .254
1963-64	9-17		Paul Edmondson	14.2	Jerry Ball	
1964-65	18-8		Ollie Carter	21.1	Jerry Ball	
1965-66	9-16		Ollie Carter	22.7	Jerry Ball	
1966-67	17-9		Mark Cooley	19.7	Jerry Ball	
1967-68	14-12		Loren Bracci	16.7	Jerry Ball	
1968-69	12-13		Loren Bracci	23.1	Jerry Ball	
1969-70	11-14		Emerson Carr	22.5	Jerry Ball	
1970-71	14-12		Emerson Carr	18.0	Jerry Ball	104-101 .507
1971-72	16-9		Paul McCracken	18.0	Pete Cassidy	
1972-73	11-15		Louis Hamm	13.4	Pete Cassidy	
1973-74	11-14		George Robnett	24.9	Pete Cassidy	
1974-75	12-14		Jack Dyck	16.4	Pete Cassidy	
1975-76	13-13		Ron Kruidhof	15.2	Pete Cassidy	
1976-77	13-14		Larry Singleton	12.2	Pete Cassidy	
1977-78	22-7		Larry Singleton	15.9	Pete Cassidy	
1978-79	20-9		Charles Evans	11.2	Pete Cassidy	
1979-80	16-10		Eric Marquez	16.2	Pete Cassidy	
1980-81	13-14		Eric Marquez	13.3	Pete Cassidy	
1981-82	17-7		Ben Balke	11.1	Pete Cassidy	
1982-83	16-10		Cliff Higgins	17.3	Pete Cassidy	
1983-84	15-12		Cliff Higgins	19.2	Pete Cassidy	
1984-85	20-10		Mike Almeido	13.3	Pete Cassidy	
1985-86	11-15		Paul Drecksel	13.7	Pete Cassidy	
1986-87	12-15		Ray Horwath	12.8	Pete Cassidy	
1987-88	15-12		Pat Bolden	16.4	Pete Cassidy	
1988-89	16-11		Derrick Gathers	16.9	Pete Cassidy	
1989-90	12-15		Derrick Gathers	17.6	Pete Cassidy	
1990-91	8-20		Kyle Kerlegan	12.9	Pete Cassidy	
1991-92	11-17		Keith Gibbs	15.2	Pete Cassidy	
1992-93	10-17		Andre Chevalier	13.9	Pete Cassidy	
1993-94	8-18		Andre Chevalier	14.9	Pete Cassidy	
1994-95	8-20 ⊗	4-2	Michael Dorsey	12.7	Pete Cassidy	
1995-96	7-20	2-4	Eric Gray	10.9	Pete Cassidy	333-338 .496▼
1996-97	14-15	8-8	Derrick Higgins	11.6	Bobby Braswell	
1997-98	12-16	7-9	Mike O'Quinn	16.7	Bobby Braswell	
1998-99	17-12	9-7	Derrick Higgins	13.9	Bobby Braswell	
1999-2000	20-10	10-6	Brian Heinle	14.6	Bobby Braswell	
2000-01	22-10	13-3 ●	Brian Heinle	20.2	Bobby Braswell	
2001-02	12-16	11-7	Markus Carr	16.0	Bobby Braswell	
2002-03	14-15	8-10	Ian Boylan	15.8	Bobby Braswell	
2003-04	14-16	7-11	Ian Boylan	14.5	Bobby Braswell	
2004-05	18-13	12-6	Ian Boylan	15.5	Bobby Braswell	
2005-06	11-17	4-10	Mike Efevberha	17.1	Bobby Braswell	
2006-07	14-17	5-9	Jonathan Heard	13.5	Bobby Braswell	
2007-08	20-10	12-4	Deon Tresvant	13.9	Bobby Braswell	
2008-09	17-14	11-5 ●	Deon Tresvant	13.3	Bobby Braswell	205-181 .531

⊗ Records do not reflect games forfeited or vacated. For adjusted record, see p. 521.
▼ Coach's record adjusted to reflect games forfeited or vacated: 334-337, .498. For yearly totals, see p. 521.
● NCAA Tournament appearance

PROFILE

California State University, Northridge, Northridge, CA
Founded: 1958
Enrollment: 35,446 (29,484 undergraduate)
Colors: Red, white and black
Nickname: Matadors
Current arena: The Matadome, opened in 1962 (1,600)
First game: Dec. 1, 1958
All-time record: 675-717 (.485)
Total weeks ranked in AP Top 20/25: 0

Current conference: Big West (2001-)
Conference titles:
Big Sky: 1 (2001)
Big West: 2 (2008 [tie], '09)
Conference tournament titles:
Big Sky: 1 (2001)
Big West: 1 (2009)
NCAA Tournament appearances: 2
NIT appearances: 0

TOP 5

G **Ian Boylan** (2001-05)
G **Markus Carr** (1998-2002)
F **Cliff Higgins** (1981-84)
F **Paul McCracken** (1970-72)
C **Brian Heinle** (1997-2001)

RECORDS

RECORDS	GAME		SEASON		CAREER	
POINTS	47	Ollie Carter, vs. Westmont (Feb. 1, 1966)	646	Brian Heinle (2000-01)	1,641	Brian Heinle (1997-2001)
POINTS PER GAME			24.9	George Robnett (1973-74)	21.8	Ollie Carter (1964-66)
REBOUNDS	24	George Robnett, vs. UC Irvine (Jan. 16, 1971)	330	Paul McCracken (1970-71)	807	Jerry Joseph (1967-70)
ASSISTS	15	Markus Carr, vs. Montana State (Feb. 24, 2001); vs. Wyoming (Dec. 7, 2000); Keith Gibbs, vs. Colorado (Nov. 23, 1990)	286	Markus Carr (2000-01)	767	Markus Carr (1998-2002)

ESPN 291 SAGARIN

CAMPBELL

How loud can 947 fans get? When those fans were stuffed into the wooden rafters of the Carter Gym, the home of the Camels until 2008-09, the answer was deafening. The old gym also gave birth to the summer camp craze; at one point, Fred McCall's program, which was founded in 1954, hosted 1,500 players over two weeks, including a young Pete Maravich.

BEST TEAM: 1955-56 Coach McCall's team gleefully fired at will (eight 100-point games) and won the North Carolina Junior College tournament. The Camels featured junior-college All-America Bob Vernon and 1970 AL Cy Young winner Jim Perry.

BEST PLAYER: F Joe Spinks (1990-94) The Asheboro, N.C., native proved he could bang with the best of them as a freshman, averaging 9.4 boards per game. He rounded out his skills the next three years, leading the team in scoring, rebounding, assists, steals and blocks at one point midway through his junior season. He took the Camels to their only Tournament berth in 1992.

BEST COACH: Fred McCall (1953-68) McCall didn't sweat defense too much. As he once put it, "I have never seen a defense put the ball through the hoop." Not surprisingly, his teams put up a lot of shots—and missed a lot too. But the coach didn't sweat that either. He simply invented a machine (used worldwide today) to help hone his players' rebounding skills. Hey, it worked: McCall led the Camels to five junior college state championships.

GAME FOR THE AGES: Campbell's 72-69 overtime win at NC State on Dec. 4, 1993—led by Spinks' 25 points, including seven in OT—was a stunning upset of an ACC giant by a small private school.

FIERCEST RIVAL: Campbell has battled UNC Wilmington, one of just three D1 schools in eastern North Carolina, throughout their junior college, NAIA and D1 days. Separated by 100 miles and routinely targeting the same recruits, the teams have played 91 times since 1951 (the series is on hiatus), with the Seahawks winning 52 games.

SEASON REVIEW

SEAS.	W-L	CONF.	COACH	SEAS.	W-L	CONF.	COACH
1951-52	18-6		Earl Smith	1960-61	16-7		Fred McCall
1952-53	11-14		Earl Smith	1961-62	16-7		Fred McCall
1953-54	17-6		Fred McCall	1962-63	11-13		Fred McCall
1954-55	23-3		Fred McCall	1963-64	17-11		Fred McCall
1955-56	23-2		Fred McCall	1964-65	11-16		Fred McCall
1956-57	9-11		Fred McCall	1965-66	10-15		Fred McCall
1957-58	17-7		Fred McCall	1966-67	10-17		Fred McCall
1958-59	12-11		Fred McCall	1967-68	16-10		Fred McCall
1959-60	16-7		Fred McCall	1968-69	20-10		Fred McCall[a]

SEAS.	W-L	CONF.	SCORING		COACH	RECORD
1969-70	24-7				Danny Roberts	
1970-71	15-12				Danny Roberts	
1971-72	18-11				Danny Roberts	
1972-73	16-11				Danny Roberts	
1973-74	9-19				Danny Roberts	
1974-75	25-6				Danny Roberts	
1975-76	23-4				Danny Roberts	
1976-77	23-10				Danny Roberts	
1977-78	9-15		John Heckstall	12.9	Danny Roberts	
1978-79	10-16		John Heckstall	12.7	Danny Roberts	
1979-80	15-12		Fred Whitfield	16.2	Danny Roberts	
1980-81	11-16		Ron Curtis	12.9	Danny Roberts	
1981-82	11-16		Tony Britto	15.0	Danny Roberts	
1982-83	11-17		Larry Canady	12.7	Danny Roberts	233-178 .567
1983-84	10-18		L. Canady, Andrea McGee	13.4	Jerry Smith	
1984-85	5-22		Andrea McGee	15.3	Jerry Smith	15-40 .273
1985-86	8-19	3-5	Clarence Grier	14.5	Billy Lee	
1986-87	17-13	10-4	Clarence Grier	24.6	Billy Lee	
1987-88	11-16	3-9	Henry Wilson	18.3	Billy Lee	
1988-89	18-12	8-4	Henry Wilson	18.5	Billy Lee	
1989-90	15-13	7-5	Mark Mocnik	13.5	Billy Lee	
1990-91	9-19	3-11	Rod Gourdine	19.1	Billy Lee	
1991-92	19-12	7-7 ●	Mark Mocnik	16.0	Billy Lee	
1992-93	12-15	10-6	Joe Spinks	18.9	Billy Lee	
1993-94	20-9	12-4	Joe Spinks	20.9	Billy Lee	
1994-95	8-18	4-12	Dennis Hurst	10.8	Billy Lee	
1995-96	17-11	11-5	Scott Neely	15.1	Billy Lee	
1996-97	11-16	8-8	Corey Best	13.5	Billy Lee	
1997-98	10-17	4-12	George Miller	13.1	Billy Lee	
1998-99	9-18	6-10	Jamie Simmons	10.8	Billy Lee	
1999-2000	12-16	10-8	Adam Fellers	15.7	Billy Lee	
2000-01	7-21	5-13	Adam Fellers	15.5	Billy Lee	
2001-02	8-19	6-14	Jonte' Edwards	14.9	Billy Lee	
2002-03	5-22	1-15	Tarick Johnson	17.1	Billy Lee	216-286 .430
2003-04	3-24	3-17	Tarick Johnson	12.3	Robbie Laing	
2004-05	2-25	0-20	Ruell Pringle	12.6	Robbie Laing	
2005-06	10-18	9-11	Maurice Latham	18.0	Robbie Laing	
2006-07	14-17	7-11	Jonathan Rodriguez	17.3	Robbie Laing	
2007-08	10-20	5-11	Jonathan Rodriguez	17.3	Robbie Laing	
2008-09	14-16	11-9	Jonathan Rodriguez	15.6	Robbie Laing	53-120 .306

[a] Fred McCall (7-4) and Danny Roberts (13-6) both coached during the 1968-69 season.

● NCAA Tournament appearance

PROFILE

Campbell University, Buies Creek, NC
Founded: 1887
Enrollment: 4,663 (3,034 undergraduate)
Colors: Orange and black
Nickname: Fighting Camels
Current arena: John W. Pope Jr. Convocation Center, opened in 2008 (3,000)
Previous: Carter Gymnasium, 1953-2008 (947); Cumberland County Civic Center (5,000); The Old Gymnasium, 1951-52 (N/A)
First game: Nov. 10, 1951

All-time record: 777-791 (.496)
Total weeks in AP Top 20/25: 0
Current conference: Atlantic Sun (1994-)
Conference titles: 0
Conference tournament titles:
Big South: 1 (1992)
NCAA Tournament appearances: 1
NIT appearances: 0

TOP 5

G **George Lehmann** (1959-60)
G **Bob Vernon** (1954-56)
F **Jonathan Rodriguez** (2006-)
F **Joe Spinks** (1990-94)
F/C **Sam Staggers** (1973-77)

RECORDS

RECORDS	GAME		SEASON		CAREER	
POINTS	39	Clarence Grier, vs. Virginia Wesleyan (Jan. 7, 1987)	739	Clarence Grier (1986-87)	1,711	Joe Spinks (1990-94)
POINTS PER GAME			24.6	Clarence Grier (1986-87)	19.0	Jonathan Rodriguez (2006-)
REBOUNDS	19	Henry Wilson, vs. Methodist (Dec. 1, 1986)	304	Jonathan Rodriguez (2007-08)	954	Joe Spinks (1990-94)
ASSISTS	16	Dan Pogue, vs. UNC Asheville (Feb. 8, 1993)	207	Dan Pogue (1993-94)	701	Dan Pogue (1992-96)

ESPN 145 SAGARIN

CANISIUS

For much of its 106-year history, Canisius has been a small-school success story. But for three unforgettable seasons in the 1950s, the Golden Griffins weren't just a regional wonder—they were a legit national force.

BEST TEAM: 1955-56 With G John McCarthy setting them up and F Hank Nowak knocking them down, Canisius won 10 of its last 11 and climbed as high as No. 18 in the UP poll. Coach Joseph Curran's undersized-but-never-outhustled Griffs made waves in the NCAA Tournament, knocking off NC State and Dartmouth before finally succumbing to Temple in the East Regional final.

BEST PLAYER: G JOHN MCCARTHY (1953-56) The Buffalo native rode his precision passing and metronomic scoring consistency (he averaged 17.9, 18.7 and 19.8 ppg in his three seasons) all the way to the NBA, where, playing for the St. Louis Hawks in 1960, he became the first pro to achieve a triple-double in his playoff debut.

BEST COACH: JOHN BEILEIN (1992-97) He inherited a team coming off five straight losing seasons. By his second year, his signature motion offense and 1-3-1 zone got results: two NIT trips and an NCAA Tournament berth between 1993-94 and '95-96.

GAME FOR THE AGES: Forty minutes and three overtimes passed in the 1956 NCAA Tournament game between Canisius and No. 2-ranked NC State, and Griffs reserve Fran Corcoran had not made a field goal. Finally, with :04 left in the fourth OT and with three Griffs starters having fouled out, Corcoran hit a long one-handed jumper. It merely won the game, 79-78.

FIERCEST RIVAL: Canisius, St. Bonaventure and Niagara make up the Western NY Little Three, a group that's been battling each other for upstate New York bragging rights since the early 20th century. The series between the Griffs and Purple Eagles, who play for the Canal Cup in the Battle of the Bridge, hasn't always been sporting. Niagara boycotted Canisius at Buffalo's famed Aud from 1957 to '66 in a dispute over gate receipts. Niagara leads the ancient series—either 90–73 (by Canisius' count) or 94–71 (Niagara's).

SEASON REVIEW

SEAS.	W-L	CONF.	COACH	SEAS.	W-L	CONF.	COACH
1903-48	*376-249*	*15-6 team went to the 1944 NIT*		1961-62	12-9		Bob MacKinnon
1948-49	16-12	2-2	Joseph Niland	1962-63	19-7	■	Bob MacKinnon
1949-50	17-8	2-2	Joseph Niland	1963-64	10-14		Bob MacKinnon
1950-51	15-10	1-3	Joseph Niland	1964-65	10-12		Bob MacKinnon
1951-52	15-9	3-1	Joseph Niland	1965-66	7-15		Bob MacKinnon
1952-53	9-14	1-3	Joseph Niland	1966-67	14-10		Bob MacKinnon
1953-54	9-14	1-3	Joseph Curran	1967-68	7-17		Bob MacKinnon
1954-55	18-7	2-2 ●	Joseph Curran	1968-69	7-16		Bob MacKinnon
1955-56	19-7	4-0 ●	Joseph Curran	1969-70	9-13		Bob MacKinnon
1956-57	22-6	3-1 ●	Joseph Curran	1970-71	8-13		Bob MacKinnon
1957-58	2-19	0-2	Joseph Curran	1971-72	15-11		Bob MacKinnon
1958-59	7-16		Joseph Curran	1972-73	13-11		John Morrison
1959-60	10-13		Bob MacKinnon	1973-74	14-12		John Morrison
1960-61	13-10		Bob MacKinnon	1974-75	15-10		John McCarthy

SEAS.	W-L	CONF.	SCORING		COACH	RECORD	
1975-76	10-17		Tim Stokes	21.1	John McCarthy		
1976-77	3-22		Dave Spiller	10.5	John McCarthy	28-49	.364
1977-78	7-19		Ron Peaks	22.5	Nick Macarchuk		
1978-79	12-14		Ron Peaks	23.9	Nick Macarchuk		
1979-80	13-14	13-13	Barry Moore	13.1	Nick Macarchuk		
1980-81	11-15	11-15	Phil Seymore	15.9	Nick Macarchuk		
1981-82	19-8	7-2	Ray Hall	16.8	Nick Macarchuk		
1982-83	11-17	3-6	Ray Hall	19.9	Nick Macarchuk		
1983-84	19-11	9-5	Ray Hall	19.6	Nick Macarchuk		
1984-85	20-10	13-3 ■	Ray Hall	20.9	Nick Macarchuk		
1985-86	21-8	14-4	Tim Harvey	10.8	Nick Macarchuk		
1986-87	16-12	12-6	Brian Smith	14.4	Nick Macarchuk	149-128	.538
1987-88	7-20	7-11	Brian Smith	17.0	Marty Marbach		
1988-89	13-15	11-7	Ed Book	10.9	Marty Marbach		
1989-90	11-18	5-11	Jeff Priah	11.9	Marty Marbach		
1990-91	10-19	3-13	Harry Seymour	11.9	Marty Marbach		
1991-92	8-22	3-13	Ed Book	17.8	Marty Marbach	49-94	.343
1992-93	10-18	5-9	Craig Wise	15.8	John Beilein		
1993-94	22-7	12-2 ■	Craig Wise	16.1	John Beilein		
1994-95	21-14	10-4 ■	Craig Wise	16.4	John Beilein		
1995-96	19-11	7-7 ●	Micheal Meeks	16.2	John Beilein		
1996-97	17-12	10-4	Kevin Thompson	15.4	John Beilein	89-62	.589
1997-98	13-14	9-9	Jamie Cammaert	13.9	Mike MacDonald		
1998-99	15-12	11-7	Keith Lambkin	13.8	Mike MacDonald		
1999-2000	10-20	8-10	Darren Fenn	17.6	Mike MacDonald		
2000-01	20-11	9-9	Darren Fenn	13.8	Mike MacDonald		
2001-02	10-20	5-13	Hodari Mallory	10.8	Mike MacDonald		
2002-03	10-18	6-12	Hodari Mallory	16.7	Mike MacDonald		
2003-04	10-20	5-13	Kevin Downey	13.1	Mike MacDonald		
2004-05	11-18	8-10	Kevin Downey	16.5	Mike MacDonald		
2005-06	9-20	6-12	Kevin Downey	15.6	Mike MacDonald	108-153	.414
2006-07	12-19	6-12	Chuck Harris	14.3	Tom Parrotta		
2007-08	6-25	2-16	Frank Turner	12.9	Tom Parrotta		
2008-09	11-20	4-14	Frank Turner	15.6	Tom Parrotta	29-64	.312

● NCAA Tournament appearance ■ NIT appearance

PROFILE

Canisius College, Buffalo, NY
Founded: 1870
Enrollment: 4,916 (3,346 undergraduate)
Colors: Blue and gold
Nickname: Golden Griffins
Current arena: Koessler Athletic Center, opened in 1968 (2,176)
Previous: Memorial Auditorium, 1940-1996 (17,300)
First game: Dec. 7, 1903
All-time record: 1,145-1,104 (.509)
Total weeks in AP Top 20/25: 11

Current conference: Metro Atlantic Athletic (1989-)
Conference titles:
Western NY Little Three: 5 (1947, '50 [tie], '52 [tie], '56, '57)
Eastern Collegiate Athletic North Atlantic: 1 (1985 [tie])
MAAC: 1 (1994)
Conference tournament titles:
MAAC: 1 (1996)
NCAA Tournament appearances: 4
NIT appearances: 5
Semifinals: 2

TOP 5

G **Ray Hall** (1981-85)
G **John McCarthy** (1953-56)
F **Larry Fogle** (1973-75)
F **Hank Nowak** (1954-57)
F **Bill O'Connor** (1960-63)

RECORDS	GAME		SEASON		CAREER	
POINTS	55	Larry Fogle, vs. Saint Peter's (Feb. 9, 1974)	835	Larry Fogle (1973-74)	2,226	Ray Hall (1981-85)
POINTS PER GAME			33.4	Larry Fogle (1973-74)	29.8	Larry Fogle (1973-75)
REBOUNDS	26	Larry Fogle, vs. Catholic (Dec. 8, 1973)	369	Herm Hedderick (1951-52)	880	Hank Nowak (1954-57)
ASSISTS	15	Jim Schofield, vs. Saint Peter's (Feb. 9, 1974)	215	Duke Richardson (1978-79)	550	Javone Moore (1993-97)

ESPN 206 SAGARIN

CENTENARY

Not that it's an official stat, but Centenary almost certainly leads the country in ratio of pro draft picks (14) to student body (just over 900). Hall of Famer Robert Parish is the first Gentlemen that usually comes to fans' minds, but Connie Mack Rea and Tom Kerwin also enjoyed NBA careers (albeit brief ones).

BEST TEAM: 1975-76 Parish had one of the greatest senior seasons in NCAA history (24.8 ppg, 18.0 rpg), leading Centenary to a best-ever No. 19 final national ranking. But the Gentlemen, who were ineligible for the NCAA Tournament because of rules violations, were far from a one-man team. Taking advantage of Parish's skilled passes out of double-teams, Bobby White, Nate Bland and future Bulls draft pick Barry McLeod lit up the scoreboard.

BEST PLAYER: C ROBERT PARISH (1972-76) A local high school star, Parish arrived at Centenary in a cloud of controversy, with the NCAA maintaining he was academically ineligible. When Centenary refused to sideline him, the NCAA placed the school on probation for six years and refused to count Parish's stats. But the 7'1" center didn't let that slow him down, unofficially leading the nation in rebounding twice and his team in scoring in every season except his junior one.

BEST COACH: LARRY LITTLE (1971-76) The personable Little recruited five players who would be drafted by the NBA or ABA, resulting in five straight winning seasons and 16 weeks ranked in the AP Top 20.

GAME FOR THE AGES: Centenary's bid to beat Arkansas on Jan. 3, 1974, presumably came to a crashing halt when Parish fouled out five minutes into the second half. But the Gentlemen hung tough behind McLeod (13 points) and Bland (15), setting up Leon Johnson's buzzer-beating putback for the 98-96 win.

FIERCEST RIVAL: Centenary and Northwestern State carry on the oldest active series in Louisiana, playing 153 times since 1938. The Gents lead 83–70 overall, but four of the past 10 games have been decided by three points or fewer.

SEASON REVIEW

SEAS.	W-L	CONF.	COACH	SEAS.	W-L	CONF.	COACH
1921-48	*240-213*	*13-1 in 1937-38 under Curtis Parker*		**1961-62**	17-9		Orvis Sigler
1948-49	21-15		Ab Young	**1962-63**	12-14		Orvis Sigler
1949-50	15-11		F.H. Delaney	**1963-64**	16-8		Orvis Sigler
1950-51	16-13		F.H. Delaney	**1964-65**	13-11		Orvis Sigler
1951-52	17-17		F.H. Delaney	**1965-66**	12-14		Orvis Sigler
1952-53	21-10		F.H. Delaney	**1966-67**	9-17		Orvis Sigler
1953-54	13-12		F.H. Delaney	**1967-68**	3-23		Orvis Sigler
1954-55	14-12		F.H. Delaney	**1968-69**	9-18		Joe Swank
1955-56	20-7		Harold Mooty	**1969-70**	8-16		Joe Swank
1956-57	16-9		Harold Mooty	**1970-71**	13-13		Joe Swank
1957-58	13-12		Harold Mooty	**1971-72**	13-12		Larry Little
1958-59	14-14		Orvis Sigler	**1972-73**	19-8		Larry Little
1959-60	12-12		Orvis Sigler	**1973-74**	21-4		Larry Little
1960-61	14-12		Orvis Sigler	**1974-75**	25-4		Larry Little

SEAS.	W-L	CONF.	SCORING		COACH	RECORD	
1975-76	22-5		Robert Parish	24.8	Larry Little	100-33	.752
1976-77	11-19		Bobby White	20.2	Riley Wallace		
1977-78	10-17		George Lett	19.3	Riley Wallace[a]	15-27	.357
1978-79	9-20		George Lett	23.1	Tommy Canterbury		
1979-80	15-14	3-3	George Lett	21.2	Tommy Canterbury		
1980-81	16-12	7-5	Cherokee Rhone	18.4	Tommy Canterbury		
1981-82	17-12	9-7	Willie Jackson	23.9	Tommy Canterbury		
1982-83	16-13	8-6	Willie Jackson	24.0	Tommy Canterbury		
1983-84	12-16	7-7	Willie Jackson	23.7	Tommy Canterbury		
1984-85	7-21	2-12	Albert Thomas	16.9	Tommy Canterbury		
1985-86	13-17	6-8	Albert Thomas	15.9	Tommy Canterbury		
1986-87	10-17	5-13	Gene Vandenlangenberg	16.1	Tommy Canterbury		
1987-88	13-15	8-10	Fred McNealey	12.1	Tommy Canterbury		
1988-89	16-14	9-9	Larry Robinson	18.6	Tommy Canterbury	150-180	.455
1989-90	22-8	14-2	Larry Robinson	22.9	Tommy Vardeman		
1990-91	17-12	10-4	Patrick Greer	20.6	Tommy Vardeman		
1991-92	10-18	5-9	Nate Taylor	15.8	Tommy Vardeman		
1992-93	9-18	4-8	Nate Taylor	13.9	Tommy Vardeman		
1993-94	16-12	8-8	Nate Taylor	15.9	Tommy Vardeman		
1994-95	10-17	7-9	Jamar Comeaux	15.1	Tommy Vardeman		
1995-96	11-16	8-8	Lincoln Abrams	18.3	Tommy Vardeman		
1996-97	9-18	6-10	Herbert Lang	19.6	Tommy Vardeman	104-119	.466
1997-98	10-20	8-8	Ronnie McCollum	17.5	Billy Kennedy		
1998-99	14-14	9-7	Ronnie McCollum	19.4	Billy Kennedy	24-34	.414
1999-2000	10-18		Ronnie McCollum	23.8	Kevin Johnson		
2000-01	8-19		Ronnie McCollum	29.1	Kevin Johnson		
2001-02	14-13		Andrew Wisniewski	19.6	Kevin Johnson		
2002-03	14-14		Andrew Wisniewski	22.0	Kevin Johnson		
2003-04	16-12	10-6	Andrew Wisniewski	21.9	Kevin Johnson		
2004-05	3-24	1-15	Chad Maclies	18.0	Kevin Johnson	65-100	.394
2005-06	4-23	2-14	Chris Watson	14.0	Rob Flaska		
2006-07	10-21	3-11	Tyrone Hamilton	15.8	Rob Flaska		
2007-08	10-21	4-14	Nick Stallings	15.9	Rob Flaska	24-65	.270
2008-09	8-23	6-12	Nick Stallings	15.3	Greg Gary	8-23	.258

[a] Riley Wallace (4-8) and Tommy Canterbury (6-9) both coached during the 1977-78 season.

PROFILE

Centenary College of Louisiana, Shreveport, LA
Founded: 1825
Enrollment: 910 (854 undergraduate)
Colors: Maroon and white
Nickname: Gentlemen (Gents)
Current arena: Gold Dome, opened in 1970 (3,000)
Previous: Haynes Gymnasium, 1936-69 (1,700); The Gymnasium, 1926-35 (N/A)
First game: 1921
All-time record: 1,048-1,093 (.489)
Total weeks in AP Top 20/25: 16

Current conference: Summit League (2003-)
Conference titles:
Trans America: 1 (1990)
Conference tournament titles:
Trans America: 1 (1980)
NCAA Tournament appearances: 0
NIT appearances: 0

CONSENSUS ALL-AMERICAS

1957 **Milt Williams** (Little A-A), G

FIRST-ROUND PRO PICKS

1973 **Robert Parish,** Utah (ABA, 8)
1976 **Robert Parish,** Golden State (8)

TOP 5

G **Ronnie McCollum** (1997-2001)
G **Larry Robinson** (1988-90)
F **Willie Jackson** (1980-84)
F **Tom Kerwin** (1963-66)
C **Robert Parish** (1972-76)

RECORDS

RECORDS	GAME		SEASON		CAREER	
POINTS	50	Robert Parish, vs. Lamar (Dec. 12, 1972)	787	Ronnie McCollum (2000-01)	2,535	Willie Jackson (1980-84)
POINTS PER GAME			29.1	Ronnie McCollum (2000-01)	25.8	Tom Kerwin (1963-66)
REBOUNDS	33	Robert Parish, vs. Southern Miss (Jan. 27, 1973)	505	Robert Parish (1972-73)	1,820	Robert Parish (1972-76)
ASSISTS	17	Melvin Russell, vs. New Orleans (Feb. 24, 1973)	184	Melvin Russell (1972-73)	613	Napoleon Byrdsong (1979-83)

ESPN 298 SAGARIN

CENTRAL CONNECTICUT ST.

In a state dominated by UConn, Central Connecticut State has long been relegated to the agate type of the local sports pages. But there's always room for one more darling, and three times since 2000 the commuter-school Blue Devils have danced their way to the NCAA Tournament under former Jim Calhoun assistant Howie Dickenman.

BEST TEAM: 2001-02 CCSU set a school record with 27 wins to earn a No. 14 seed in the NCAA Tournament. Two of the Blue Devils' five losses came to teams that finished the season ranked in the Top 10; their first-round NCAA opponent, No. 3-seed Pittsburgh, beat Central, 71-54, en route to the Sweet 16.

BEST PLAYER: F CORSLEY EDWARDS (1998-2002) The second-leading scorer in Central Connecticut history was a beast inside, averaging 14.1 points and 7.9 rebounds a game in his four years in New Britain. After he was named the 2001-02 Northeast Conference Player of the Year, Edwards was chosen in the second round of the 2002 NBA draft by the Sacramento Kings.

BEST COACH: BILL DETRICK (1959-87) After a standout career as a three-sport star at CCSU in the late 1940s, Detrick returned to his alma mater to coach the Blue Devils for nearly three decades. His 468 wins are a school record, and his teams made the D2 tournament six times.

GAME FOR THE AGES: Two years after a 4–22 season and a year after losing to Mount St. Mary's in the NEC title game, the Blue Devils earned their first NCAA Tournament berth by thumping Robert Morris 63-46 in the 2000 NEC title game. A late 11-2 run sealed the game for CCSU.

FIERCEST RIVAL: Whenever Central Connecticut State and Monmouth face off, you can count on at least one of two things: a slugfest and/or high stakes. In the 1997-98 season, Monmouth and Central Connecticut State battled to a draw—for last place in the Northeast. Since then, the Blue Devils and Hawks have each won three conference tourney titles.

SEASON REVIEW

SEAS.	W-L	CONF.	COACH	SEAS.	W-L	CONF.	COACH
1934-46	*88-60*	*16-3 in 1936-37*		1959-60	16-5		Bill Detrick
1946-47	17-3		Ross Merrick	1960-61	17-5		Bill Detrick
1947-48	17-5		Ross Merrick	1961-62	14-9		Bill Detrick
1948-49	20-4		Ross Merrick	1962-63	22-1		Bill Detrick
1949-50	16-6		Ross Merrick	1963-64	25-1		Bill Detrick
1950-51	12-5		Ross Merrick	1964-65	19-5		Bill Detrick
1951-52	8-8		Ross Merrick	1965-66	23-3		Bill Detrick
1952-53	9-5		Ross Merrick	1966-67	17-8		Bill Detrick
1953-54	10-5		Bill Moore	1967-68	13-10		Bill Detrick
1954-55	5-11		Bill Moore	1968-69	20-8		Bill Detrick
1955-56	10-8		Bill Moore	1969-70	12-14		Bill Detrick
1956-57	12-7		Bill Moore	1970-71	20-7		Bill Detrick
1957-58	16-8		Bill Moore	1971-72	17-8		Bill Detrick
1958-59	19-4		Bill Moore	1972-73	15-11		Bill Detrick

SEAS.	W-L	CONF.	SCORING		COACH	RECORD
1973-74	13-12		Rich Ortiz	19.4	Bill Detrick	
1974-75	12-13		Dan Jones	19.8	Bill Detrick	
1975-76	15-11		Rob Charbonneau	16.9	Bill Detrick	
1976-77	14-12		Rob Charbonneau	20.5	Bill Detrick	
1977-78	12-15		Greg Roberts	19.6	Bill Detrick	
1978-79	14-13		Chris White	14.3	Bill Detrick	
1979-80	14-13		Chris White	17.7	Bill Detrick	
1980-81	18-9		Steve Ayers	20.0	Bill Detrick	
1981-82	18-9		Steve Ayers	20.1	Bill Detrick	
1982-83	21-9		Rich Leonard	14.8	Bill Detrick	
1983-84	26-6		Johnny Pruitt	19.9	Bill Detrick	
1984-85	16-12		Tony Little	15.2	Bill Detrick	
1985-86	15-13		Tyrone Canino	14.4	Bill Detrick	
1986-87	8-21		Bryan Heron	14.6	Bill Detrick	
1987-88	10-18		Tyrone Canino	14.3	Bill Detrick[a]	468-266 .638
1988-89	10-18		Bryan Heron	21.9	Mike Brown	
1989-90	6-22		Kevin Swann	14.5	Mike Brown	
1990-91	4-24	2-10	Kevin Swann	19.7	Mike Brown	20-64 .238
1991-92	7-21	3-9	Damian Johnson	20.5	Mark Adams	
1992-93	8-19		Damian Johnson	23.3	Mark Adams	
1993-94	4-22	0-5	Scott Hasenjaeger	11.8	Mark Adams	
1994-95	8-18	6-12	Robert Burrage	13.5	Mark Adams	
1995-96	13-15	9-9	Bill Langheim	13.7	Mark Adams	40-95 .296
1996-97	8-19	4-12	Sean Scott	13.8	Howie Dickenman	
1997-98	4-22	3-13	Rick Mickens	19.8	Howie Dickenman	
1998-99	19-13	11-9	Charron Watson	16.3	Howie Dickenman	
1999-2000	25-6	15-3 ●	Rick Mickens	17.8	Howie Dickenman	
2000-01	14-14	11-9	Corsley Edwards	16.2	Howie Dickenman	
2001-02	27-5	19-1 ●	Corsley Edwards	15.4	Howie Dickenman	
2002-03	15-13	12-6	Ricardo Scott	12.9	Howie Dickenman	
2003-04	14-14	9-9	Ron Robinson	18.0	Howie Dickenman	
2004-05	12-16	8-10	DeMario Anderson	14.1	Howie Dickenman	
2005-06	18-11	13-5	Tristan Blackwood	14.3	Howie Dickenman	
2006-07	22-12	16-2 ●	Tristan Blackwood	17.1	Howie Dickenman	
2007-08	14-16	10-8	Tristan Blackwood	16.4	Howie Dickenman	
2008-09	13-17	8-10	Ken Horton	16.5	Howie Dickenman	205-178 .535

[a] Bill Detrick (2-3) and Charles Jones (8-15) both coached during the 1987-88 season.

● NCAA Tournament appearance

PROFILE

Central Connecticut State University, New Britain, CT
Founded: 1849
Enrollment: 12,233 (9,906 undergraduate)
Colors: Blue and white
Nickname: Blue Devils
Current arena: Detrick Gymnasium, opened in 1965 (3,200)
First game: 1934
All-time record: 1,000-757 (.569)
Total weeks in AP Top 20/25: 0

Current conference: Northeast (1997-)
Conference titles:
Northeast: 3 (2000, '02, '07)
Conference tournament titles:
Northeast: 3 (2000, '02, '07)
NCAA Tournament appearances: 3
NIT appearances: 0

CONSENSUS ALL-AMERICAS

1969 **Howie Dickenman** (Little A-A), C

TOP 5

G **Damian Johnson** (1989-93)
G **Rick Mickens** (1996-2000)
F **Tyrone Canino** (1983-88)
F **Corsley Edwards** (1998-2002)
C **Howie Dickenman** (1966-69)

RECORDS

RECORDS	GAME		SEASON		CAREER	
POINTS	47	Paul Zajac, vs. St. Anselm's (Feb. 18, 1967)	645	Bill Reaves (1969-70)	1,734	Damian Johnson (1989-93)
POINTS PER GAME			24.8	Bill Reaves (1969-70)	21.1	Bill Reaves (1968-71)
REBOUNDS	32	Howie Dickenman, vs. Trenton State (Dec. 12, 1967)	420	Ken Hightower (1983-84)	1,243	Tyrone Canino (1983-88)
ASSISTS	18	Jere Quinn, vs. Sacred Heart (March 2, 1976)	227	Jere Quinn (1975-76)	567	Johnny Kidd (1980-85)

ESPN 230 SAGARIN

CENTRAL FLORIDA

UCF basketball turned 40 in 2008-09 and shows no signs of aging; coach Kirk Speraw's teams won 118 games and reached two NCAA Tourneys between 2003-04 and 2008-09. That's reminiscent of original Knights coach Torchy Clark's Division II dominance: his teams won more than 75% of their games.

BEST TEAM: 1977-78 They went 26–4 with 19 double-digit wins. Two of the Knights' losses were in road games to D1 teams. All-America Jerry Prather and Cleveland Jackson led the way. Their 24-game winning streak ended in the D2 final four with a 79-63 loss to Cheyney State.

BEST PLAYER: G Bo Clark (1975-77, '78-80) Coach Clark's second son was a two-time Division II All-America who regularly torched opponents, scoring 70 in one game and averaging a D2-best 31.6 ppg in 1978-79. He holds the UCF career scoring mark (2,886 points) and never averaged fewer than 24.1 ppg.

BEST COACH: Eugene "Torchy" Clark (1969-83) UCF could stand for University of the Clark Family; Torchy started the program, leading it through its college division and D2 glory days, while sons Bo and Mike stand one-two among the school's leading scorers. Torchy went 268–84 with six 20-win seasons, and led UCF to six Division II tourneys, including the '78 final four.

GAME FOR THE AGES: In coach Kirk Speraw's debut season of 1993-94, UCF went 21–9 and won the Trans America Athletic Conference (the precursor to today's Atlantic Sun) tourney with a dramatic 70-67 win over Stetson. Victor Saxton scored 17 points and Patrick Butts sank two free throws with :03 left to wrap it up. After nine losing seasons in D1, the Knights had made it to their first NCAA Tournament.

FIERCEST RIVAL: The Knights' fast D1 rise has meant multiple affiliations (independent, Sun Belt, Atlantic Sun, C-USA) and no true rivalry. Still, Stetson, located 45 minutes away, used to rough up the Knights in the mid to late 1980s. So it's sweet indeed that UCF turned the tables on the Hatters with 10 straight wins between 2001-02 and 2006-07. The teams haven't played since.

SEASON REVIEW

SEAS.	W-L	CONF.		SCORING		COACH	RECORD	
1969-70	11-3			Mike Clark	24.4	Torchy Clark		
1970-71	13-6			Mike Clark	27.6	Torchy Clark		
1971-72	18-6			Mike Clark	23.3	Torchy Clark		
1972-73	19-7			Arnett Hall	20.2	Torchy Clark		
1973-74	16-8			Arnett Hall	20.7	Torchy Clark		
1974-75	14-10			Bennie Shaw	25.4	Torchy Clark		
1975-76	20-3			Bennie Shaw	25.4	Torchy Clark		
1976-77	24-4			Bo Clark	28.8	Torchy Clark		
1977-78	26-4			Jerry Prather	21.0	Torchy Clark		
1978-79	19-7			Bo Clark	31.6	Torchy Clark		
1979-80	25-4			Bo Clark	26.8	Torchy Clark		
1980-81	23-5			Roland Ebron	15.2	Torchy Clark		
1981-82	21-8			Willie Edison	17.7	Torchy Clark		
1982-83	19-9			Dan Faison	16.7	Torchy Clark	268-84	.761
1983-84	15-13			Dan Faison	15.1	Chuck Machock		
1984-85	10-18			Stan Kimbrough	18.1	Chuck Machock	25-31	.446
1985-86	6-22			Pat Crocklin	11.7	Phil Carter		
1986-87	12-15			Pat Crocklin	13.3	Phil Carter		
1987-88	9-19			Ben Morton	15.6	Phil Carter		
1988-89	7-20			Ken Leeks	14.7	Phil Carter	34-76	.309
1989-90	7-21			Ken Leeks	15.0	Joe Dean		
1990-91	10-17	3-9		Ken Leeks	17.5	Joe Dean		
1991-92	10-18	3-13		Ken Leeks	18.5	Joe Dean		
1992-93	10-17			Darryl Davis	18.1	Joe Dean	37-73	.336
1993-94	21-9	11-5	●	Ochiel Swaby	18.3	Kirk Speraw		
1994-95	11-16	7-9		Ochiel Swaby	19.0	Kirk Speraw		
1995-96	11-19	6-10	●	Harry Kennedy	17.2	Kirk Speraw		
1996-97	7-19	4-12		Harry Kennedy	17.5	Kirk Speraw		
1997-98	17-11	11-5		Mark Jones	20.8	Kirk Speraw		
1998-99	19-10	13-3		Brad Traina	16.7	Kirk Speraw		
1999-2000	14-18	10-8		D'Quarius Stewart	16.1	Kirk Speraw		
2000-01	8-23	3-15		Paul Reed	14.0	Kirk Speraw		
2001-02	17-12	12-8		Paul Reed	13.8	Kirk Speraw		
2002-03	21-11	11-5		Ray Abellard	16.3	Kirk Speraw		
2003-04	25-6	17-3	●	Dexter Lyons	18.3	Kirk Speraw		
2004-05	24-9	13-7	●	Gary Johnson	13.6	Kirk Speraw		
2005-06	14-15	7-7		Josh Peppers	13.7	Kirk Speraw		
2006-07	22-9	11-5		Josh Peppers	14.3	Kirk Speraw		
2007-08	16-15	9-7		Jermaine Taylor	20.8	Kirk Speraw		
2008-09	17-14	7-9		Jermaine Taylor	26.2	Kirk Speraw	264-216	.550

● NCAA Tournament appearance

PROFILE

University of Central Florida, Orlando, FL
Founded: 1963
Enrollment: 50,275 (42,933 undergraduate)
Colors: Black and gold
Nickname: Golden Knights
Current arena: New UCF Arena, opened in 2007 (10,000)
Previous: UCF Arena, 1991-2007 (5,100); UCF Gymnasium, 1973-91 (2,456)
First game: Nov. 21, 1969
All-time record: 628-480 (.567)
Total weeks in AP Top 20/25: 0

Current conference: Conference USA (2005-)
Conference titles:
Atlantic Sun: 1 (2005)
Conference tournament titles:
Trans America: 2 (1994, '96)
Atlantic Sun: 2 (2004, '05)
NCAA Tournament appearances: 4
NIT appearances: 0

CONSENSUS ALL-AMERICAS

1979, '80 **Bo Clark** (D2), G

TOP 5

G **Bo Clark** (1975-77, '78-80)
G **Mike Clark** (1969-73)
G **Bennie Shaw** (1974-76)
F **Jerry Prather** (1974-78)
F/C **Ken Leeks** (1988-92)

RECORDS

RECORDS	GAME		SEASON		CAREER	
POINTS	70	Bo Clark, vs. Florida Memorial (Jan. 31, 1977)	812	Jermaine Taylor (2008-09)	2,886	Bo Clark (1975-77, '78-80)
POINTS PER GAME			31.6	Bo Clark (1978-79)	27.8	Bo Clark (1975-77, '78-80)
REBOUNDS	23	Ronnie Thornton, vs. Edward Waters (Nov. 24, 1981); Ed Fluitt, vs. Embry-Riddle (Dec. 1, 1971)	364	Ed Fluitt (1971-72)	942	Ken Leeks (1988-92)
ASSISTS	14	Kingsley Edwards, vs. Troy (Jan. 16, 2005)	183	Sinua Phillips (1991-92)	531	Sinua Phillips (1990-94)

ESPN 183 SAGARIN

CENTRAL MICHIGAN

Midway through the 1948-49 season, the Chippewas were ranked No. 1 in D2—until they lost to Northern Michigan. They have yet to return to such heights. But Central Michigan has been sneaky good from time to time, thanks to a steady stream of elite mid-major players, from Dan Roundfield to Chris Kaman.

BEST TEAM: 1974-75 When Central "upset" Georgetown in the first round of the NCAA Tournament, it was really a matter of superior talent prevailing. The Chippewas featured three future NBA players: high-flying forward Roundfield, do-everything guard James McElroy and shot-blocking terror Ben Poquette.

BEST PLAYER: G/F Dan Majerle (1984-88) Before he became Thunder Dan in the NBA, the sharpshooting swingman inspired an unusual Rose Arena tradition: After the first CMU basket of each game (often a long-range Majerle jumper), thousands of fans would launch rolls of toilet paper onto the court.

BEST COACH: Ted Kjolhede (1956-71) He didn't find success immediately upon becoming head coach. But CMU stuck with Kjolhede, and he went on to win four Interstate Intercollegiate Athletic Conference championships (1964, '66, '67, '70).

GAME FOR THE AGES: Nearly 30 years after its last postseason victory, CMU had a 26-point lead on No. 6 seed Creighton in the first round of the 2003 NCAA Tourney. Then center Chris Kaman got into foul trouble, Bluejays gunner Kyle Korver found his shot, and the lead was down to two with fewer than two minutes to play. But Creighton went cold and the Chippewas held on for a 79-73 win.

FIERCEST RIVAL: Three times, Central Michigan has drawn a standing-room-only crowd of 6,400-plus to the Rose Arena. All three were games against Western Michigan. Each season since 2005-06, the Broncos, the Chippewas and the Eagles of Eastern Michigan battle for the Michigan MAC Trophy. Western won the first two trophies, held onto it when the three teams battled to a draw in 2007-08, and then reclaimed the outright title in 2008-09.

SEASON REVIEW

SEAS.	W-L	CONF.	COACH	SEAS.	W-L	CONF.	COACH
1904-48	*317-240-1*	*17-3 in 1947-48*		1961-62	8-14		Ted Kjolhede
1948-49	15-1		Dan Rose	1962-63	11-11		Ted Kjolhede
1949-50	11-5		Dan Rose	1963-64	18-6		Ted Kjolhede
1950-51	8-12		Dan Rose	1964-65	19-7		Ted Kjolhede
1951-52	12-10		Dan Rose	1965-66	23-6		Ted Kjolhede
1952-53	10-12		Dan Rose	1966-67	23-3		Ted Kjolhede
1953-54	13-8		Dan Rose	1967-68	14-12		Ted Kjolhede
1954-55	11-9		Bill Kelly	1968-69	11-12		Ted Kjolhede
1955-56	11-11		Bill Kelly	1969-70	22-5		Ted Kjolhede
1956-57	14-11		Ted Kjolhede	1970-71	18-9		Ted Kjolhede
1957-58	11-13		Ted Kjolhede	1971-72	15-11		Dick Parfitt
1958-59	9-15		Ted Kjolhede	1972-73	13-13	4-6	Dick Parfitt
1959-60	12-14		Ted Kjolhede	1973-74	14-12	6-6	Dick Parfitt
1960-61	3-19		Ted Kjolhede	1974-75	22-6	10-4 ●	Dick Parfitt

SEAS.	W-L	CONF.	SCORING		COACH	RECORD
1975-76	12-14	8-8	Leonard Drake	18.2	Dick Parfitt	
1976-77	18-10	13-3 ●	Leonard Drake	16.9	Dick Parfitt	
1977-78	16-10	11-5	Jeff Tropf	17.3	Dick Parfitt	
1978-79	19-9	13-3 ■	Dave Grauzer	14.4	Dick Parfitt	
1979-80	12-13	6-10	Mike Robinson	14.4	Dick Parfitt	
1980-81	12-14	5-11	Melvin McLaughlin	20.8	Dick Parfitt	
1981-82	10-16	4-12	Melvin McLaughlin	23.2	Dick Parfitt	
1982-83	10-17	5-13	Melvin McLaughlin	24.1	Dick Parfitt	
1983-84	11-16	6-12	Derek Boldon	14.2	Dick Parfitt	
1984-85	9-18	4-14	Derek Boldon	15.7	Dick Parfitt	193-179 .519
1985-86	11-17	7-11	Dan Majerle	21.4	Charlie Coles	
1986-87	22-8	14-2 ●	Dan Majerle	21.1	Charlie Coles	
1987-88	19-13	10-6	Dan Majerle	23.7	Charlie Coles	
1988-89	12-16 ⊘	7-9	Carter Briggs	13.8	Charlie Coles	
1989-90	13-17	6-10	Jeff Majerle	12.9	Charlie Coles	
1990-91	14-14	8-8	Sean Waters	15.3	Charlie Coles	91-85 .517▼
1991-92	12-16	6-10	Darian McKinney	17.7	Keith Dambrot	
1992-93	8-18	4-14	Sander Scott	16.7	Keith Dambrot	20-34 .370
1993-94	5-21	4-14	Rob DeCook	12.7	Leonard Drake	
1994-95	3-23	0-18	Thomas Kilgore	18.9	Leonard Drake	
1995-96	6-20	3-15	Charles Macon	16.4	Leonard Drake	
1996-97	7-19	4-14	Charles Macon	18.2	Leonard Drake	21-83 .202
1997-98	5-21	3-15	Tim Kisner	12.1	Jay Smith	
1998-99	10-16	7-11	Mike Manciel	17.5	Jay Smith	
1999-2000	6-23	2-16	David Webber	19.2	Jay Smith	
2000-01	20-8	14-4	David Webber	18.4	Jay Smith	
2001-02	9-19	5-13	David Webber	17.7	Jay Smith	
2002-03	25-7	14-4 ●	Chris Kaman	22.4	Jay Smith	
2003-04	6-24	2-16	Gerrit Brigitha	17.1	Jay Smith	
2004-05	10-18	4-14	Kevin Nelson	17.0	Jay Smith	
2005-06	4-24	1-17	Giordan Watson	13.8	Jay Smith	95-160 .373
2006-07	13-18	7-9	Giordan Watson	18.8	Ernie Zeigler	
2007-08	14-17	8-8	Giordan Watson	16.4	Ernie Zeigler	
2008-09	12-19	7-9	Marcus Van	13.0	Ernie Zeigler	39-54 .419

⊘ **Records don't reflect games forfeited or vacated. For adjusted records, see p. 521.**
▼ **Coach's record adjusted to reflect games forfeited or vacated: 92-84, .523. For yearly totals, see p. 521.**
● **NCAA Tournament appearance** ■ **NIT appearance**

PROFILE

Central Michigan University, Mount Pleasant, MI
Founded: 1892
Enrollment: 27,354 (18,454 undergraduate)
Colors: Maroon and gold
Nickname: Chippewas
Current arena: Rose Arena, opened in 1973, (5,200)
First game: 1904
All-time record: 1,083-1,060-1 (.505)
Total weeks in AP Top 20/25: 0
Current conference: Mid-American (1972-)

Conference titles:
MAC: 5 (1975, '77, '87, 2001, '03)
Conference tournament titles:
MAC: 2 (1987, 2003)
NCAA Tournament appearances: 4
Sweet 16s (since 1975): 1
NIT appearances: 1

FIRST-ROUND PRO PICKS

1975 **Dan Roundfield**, Indiana (ABA, 6)
1988 **Dan Majerle**, Phoenix (14)
2003 **Chris Kaman**, LA Clippers (6)

TOP 5

G **Ben Kelso** (1970-73)
G **Melvin McLaughlin** (1979-83)
G/F **Dan Majerle** (1984-88)
F **Dan Roundfield** (1972-75)
C **Chris Kaman** (2000-03)

RECORDS

RECORDS	GAME		SEASON		CAREER	
POINTS	53	Tommie Johnson, vs. Wright State (Dec. 22, 1987)	759	Dan Majerle (1987-88)	2,071	Melvin McLaughlin (1979-83)
POINTS PER GAME			25.4	Ben Kelso (1971-72)	22.3	Ben Kelso (1970-73)
REBOUNDS	26	Dan Roundfield, vs. Northern Michigan (Feb. 5, 1974); Stan Breidinger, vs. Ohio Northern (Jan. 18, 1964); Don Kelly, vs. Northern Illinois (Feb. 27, 1953)	373	Chris Kaman (2002-03)	1,031	Dan Roundfield (1972-75)
ASSISTS	16	Derrick Richmond, vs. Youngstown State (Dec. 15, 1988)	196	Dave Grauzer (1977-78)	489	Giordan Watson (2004-08)

ESPN 329 SAGARIN

COLLEGE OF CHARLESTON

There's nothing gentle about the way this program from the genteel South tore through the NAIA for years, before storming into the NCAA in 1991. The College of Charleston wasted no time becoming a Tournament regular, winning at least 19 games in every one of its first 13 Division I seasons.

BEST TEAM: 1996-97 In its sixth Division I season, the red-hot senior-heavy squad rode the superb outside-inside punch of Anthony Johnson (40.5% three-point shooting) and Thaddeous Delaney (6'8", 250 pounds) to 23 consecutive wins. The team carried that momentum into the Tournament with a first-round victory over Maryland, before falling by four to eventual champ Arizona.

BEST PLAYER: G ANTHONY JOHNSON (1992-93, '94-97) The savvy point guard was the best of the talented class of '97 that led the Cougars to a 101–17 four-year record, including four straight Trans America titles. A dazzling ballhandler, Johnson was a TAAC Player of the Year before going on to a long NBA career.

BEST COACH: JOHN KRESSE (1979-2002) If you have an arena named after you, you probably had a stellar career. If, like Kresse, you were still working there when they named it after you, you're a *legend*. Indeed, Kresse (560–143) won 30 games four times, captured the 1983 NAIA title and led the transition to the NCAA.

GAME FOR THE AGES: The Cougars had West Virginia Wesleyan down by 15 points in the 1983 NAIA championship game before the Bobcats closed the gap to two with less than a minute to go. But G Stephen Yetman drew a crucial charge with seconds on the clock to save the day. What a fitting way for this team-oriented group to clinch a national title.

FIERCEST RIVAL: Sure, C of C shares a city with Charleston Southern, but the Cougars share a conference and a division with Citadel. Although the two teams played just once in a 40-year span when Charleston competed in the NAIA, they remained sworn enemies. Could it be because Citadel's cadets insisted on competing for C of C coeds?

SEASON REVIEW

SEAS.	W-L	CONF.	COACH	SEAS.	W-L	CONF.	COACH
1898-46	*100-242*	*Two year record of 0-20 in 1920-22*		1959-60	3-12		Jerry Callahan
1946-47	11-9		Henry Anderson	1960-61	3-11		Archie Jenkins
1947-48	9-10		Willard Silcox	1961-62	7-15		Archie Jenkins
1948-49	7-15		Willard Silcox	1962-63	6-12		Pat Harden
1949-50	7-12		Willard Silcox	1963-64	11-16		Pat Harden
1950-51	4-19		Willard Silcox	1964-65	7-13		Pat Harden
1951-52	6-8		Willard Silcox	1965-66	4-17		Pat Harden
1952-53	7-9		Willard Silcox	1966-67	0-19		Pat Harden
1953-54	4-14		Vincent Price	1967-68	6-17		Pat Harden
1954-55	3-14		Vincent Price	1968-69	9-15		Fred Daniels
1955-56	3-15		Willard Silcox	1969-70	9-18		Fred Daniels
1956-57	1-13		Bernard Puckhaber	1970-71	11-16		Alan LeForce
1957-58	1-12		Ernest Wehman	1971-72	11-11		Alan LeForce
1958-59	2-11		Jerry Callahan	1972-73	16-10		Alan LeForce

SEAS.	W-L	CONF.		SCORING		COACH	RECORD	
1973-74	18-9			Ken Gustafson	22.4	Alan LeForce		
1974-75	19-9			Ken Gustafson	21.5	Alan LeForce		
1975-76	18-11			Kevan Elliott	15.4	Alan LeForce		
1976-77	13-12			Muzon Cheeks	16.9	Alan LeForce		
1977-78	14-14					Alan LeForce		
1978-79	11-17					Alan LeForce	131-109	.546
1979-80	17-11					John Kresse		
1980-81	25-5			Sam Hare	14.8	John Kresse		
1981-82	25-5			Larry Butler	13.7	John Kresse		
1982-83	33-5		◆	Greg Mack	15.8	John Kresse		
1983-84	25-7			T.C. Sabbs	13.6	John Kresse		
1984-85	30-4			Greg Mack	21.8	John Kresse		
1985-86	26-9			Dwayne Grace	12.8	John Kresse		
1986-87	31-2			Steven Johnson	15.5	John Kresse		
1987-88	30-5			Steven Johnson	14.9	John Kresse		
1988-89	26-6			Derald Preston	14.7	John Kresse		
1989-90	19-8			Donnelly McCants	20.9	John Kresse		
1990-91	15-12			Mike Beckett	13.3	John Kresse		
1991-92	19-8			Ahdonus Cofer	15.6	John Kresse		
1992-93	19-8			Marion Busby	14.0	John Kresse		
1993-94	24-4	14-2	●	Marion Busby	16.6	John Kresse		
1994-95	23-6	15-1	■	Marion Busby	16.9	John Kresse		
1995-96	25-4	15-1	■	Thaddeous Delaney	14.6	John Kresse		
1996-97	29-3	16-0	●	Thaddeous Delaney	15.8	John Kresse		
1997-98	24-6	14-2	●	Sedric Webber	15.1	John Kresse		
1998-99	28-3	16-0	●	Sedric Webber	13.8	John Kresse		
1999-2000	24-6	13-3		Jody Lumpkin	15.1	John Kresse		
2000-01	22-7	12-4		Jody Lumpkin	17.1	John Kresse		
2001-02	21-9	9-7		Jeff Bolton	18.2	John Kresse	560-143	.797
2002-03	25-8	13-3	■	Troy Wheless	15.2	Tom Herrion		
2003-04	20-9	11-5		Thomas Mobley	15.7	Tom Herrion		
2004-05	18-10	10-6		Tony Mitchell	14.9	Tom Herrion		
2005-06	17-11	9-6		Dontaye Draper	18.5	Tom Herrion	80-38	.678
2006-07	22-11	13-5		Dontaye Draper	16.2	Bobby Cremins		
2007-08	16-17	9-11		T. White Jr./A.Goudelock	13.2	Bobby Cremins		
2008-09	27-9	15-5		Andrew Goudelock	16.7	Bobby Cremins	65-37	.637

● NCAA Tournament appearance ■ NIT appearance ◆ NAIA championship

THE SCHOOLS

PROFILE

College of Charleston, Charleston, S.C.
Founded: 1770
Enrollment: 11,088 (9,679 undergraduate)
Colors: Maroon and white
Nickname: Cougars
Current arena: John Kresse Arena at the F. Mitchell Johnson Center, opened in 1982 (3,500)
Previous: College Athletics Center, 1940-82 (1,000)
First game: Jan. 26, 1900
All-time record: 1,066-895 (.544)
Total weeks in AP Top 20/25: 12

Current conference: Southern (1998-)
Conference titles:
Trans America: 5 (1994, '95, '96, '97, '98)
Southern: 7 (1999 [tie], 2000 [tie], '01 [tie], '02 [tie] '03 [tie], '04 [tie], '05 [tie])
Conference tournament titles:
Trans America: 2 (1997, '98)
Southern: 1 (1999)
NCAA Tournament appearances: 4
NIT appearances: 3

TOP 5

G **Marion Busby** (1991-95)
G **Anthony Johnson** (1992-93, '94-97)
F **Thaddeous Delaney** (1993-97)
F **Greg Mack** (1981-85)
C **Ken Gustafson** (1971-75)

RECORDS

	GAME		SEASON		CAREER	
POINTS	45	Sam Meade, vs. Clinch Valley (Jan. 15, 1971)	740	Greg Mack (1984-85)	2,135	Ken Gustafson (1971-75)
POINTS PER GAME			23.1	Ken Gustafson (1972-73)	21.1	Ken Gustafson (1971-75)
REBOUNDS	31	Tom Gamble, vs. NC Wesleyan (Dec. 16, 1965)	440	Ken Gustafson (1974-75)	1,148	Ken Gustafson (1971-75)
ASSISTS	14	Mark McClam, vs. Pfeiffer (Jan. 9, 1980)	229	Anthony Johnson (1996-97)	520	Anthony Johnson (1992-93, '94-97)

ESPN 309 SAGARIN

CHARLESTON SOUTHERN

Charleston Southern, once Baptist College, is actually in North Charleston, but the important thing to remember is that hoops in South Carolina's low country isn't all about John Kresse, Bobby Cremins and that other college with Charleston in its name. The Buccaneers have made the Big Dance (in 1997) and have often beaten the College of Charleston through the years.

BEST TEAM: 1985-86 CSU won its final six games, including a run through the Big South tournament. Unfortunately, back then, winning the league tourney didn't mean an automatic NCAA berth. The Buccaneers were true road warriors: At one point, CSU had seven consecutive road games and won five.

BEST PLAYER: G Ben Hinson (1983-87) A couple of decades have passed since Hinson set the record for career points (2,295), but he's still got the field lapped. The next closest, Brett Larrick (1993-97), is 557 behind. Hinson also was Big South tourney MVP in '86 and '87.

BEST COACH: Tommy Gaither (1983-87) He was only at the school four seasons, but Gaither used a tenacious man-to-man D and a fast pace to win back-to-back Big South regular-season and tournament titles. It also helped that his stay at CSU coincided with Hinson's.

GAME FOR THE AGES: The 1996-97 team ended up just 17–13, but it got hot at the right time and took the Big South tourney by storm, reaching the title game against No. 2-seed Liberty. The Lynchburg, Va., crowd went wild as the home team led 40-29 in the second half. But F Rolando Hourruitiner and G Adam Larrick sparked the Bucs on a 20-4 run and won going away, 64-54. A few days later, more than 500 students and fans joined the team to watch the NCAA Tournament selection broadcast. Their reward: No. 2-seed UCLA and a 109-75 bruising. Hey, at least CSU was Dancing.

FIERCEST RIVAL: CSU and the College of Charleston compete early in the season in the Charleston City Championship. The Cougars lead the series but the Bucs have been competitive, winning 23 of 70 meetings. The two squads also play pick-up games during the summer.

SEASON REVIEW

SEAS.	W-L	CONF.	SCORING		COACH	RECORD	
1965-66	13-7		Jim Gardner	27.6	Howard Bagwell		
1966-67	14-9		Jim Gardner	22.2	Howard Bagwell	27-16	.628
1967-68	11-11		Marion Salerni	16.5	Mel Gibson		
1968-69	15-10		Marion Salerni	27.5	Mel Gibson		
1969-70	18-7		Jim Rooney	15.8	Mel Gibson		
1970-71	13-10		Dan Franz	16.8	Mel Gibson	57-38	.600
1971-72	10-14		Dave Kirk	17.3	Al Ferner		
1972-73	15-14		Robert Thomas	20.5	Al Ferner	25-28	.472
1973-74	5-22		John Johnson	18.8	Billy Henry		
1974-75	4-16		Mike Henry	20.2	Billy Henry	9-38	.191
1975-76	3-23		Mike Akers	14.6	Danny Monk		
1976-77	8-19		Joe Nix	14.7	Danny Monk		
1977-78	8-19		Vic Watkins	13.5	Danny Monk	19-61	.238
1978-79	2-25		James Clemens	15.3	David Reese		
1979-80	2-23		Eddie Talley	17.7	David Reese	4-48	.077
1980-81	8-19		Eddie Talley	14.6	Phil Carter		
1981-82	13-13		Eddie Talley	11.5	Phil Carter		
1982-83	13-14		Reggie Walker	12.7	Phil Carter	34-46	.425
1983-84	15-13		Jose Lara	15.1	Tommy Gaither		
1984-85	13-15		Ben Hinson	21.6	Tommy Gaither		
1985-86	21-9	5-1	Ben Hinson	19.7	Tommy Gaither		
1986-87	21-9	12-2	Ben Hinson	22.6	Tommy Gaither	70-46	.603
1987-88	17-12	8-4	Oliver Johnson	18.5	Gary Edwards		
1988-89	12-16	6-6	Heder Ambroise	15.3	Gary Edwards		
1989-90	11-17	4-8	Daryl Hall	18.2	Gary Edwards		
1990-91	9-19	4-10	Harvey Minor	13.7	Gary Edwards		
1991-92	16-14	7-7	Darnell Sneed	20.6	Gary Edwards		
1992-93	9-18	5-11	Darnell Sneed	23.0	Gary Edwards		
1993-94	9-18	8-10	Eric Burks	19.5	Gary Edwards		
1994-95	19-10	12-4	Eric Burks	21.1	Gary Edwards		
1995-96	15-13	9-5	T.L. Latson	18.2	Gary Edwards	117-137	.461
1996-97	17-13	7-7 ●	Brett Larrick	20.0	Tom Conrad		
1997-98	5-22	2-10	Adam Larrick	15.4	Tom Conrad		
1998-99	12-16	4-6	Adam Larrick	19.1	Tom Conrad		
1999-2000	8-21	3-11	Nick Mitchell	14.7	Tom Conrad	42-72	.368
2000-01	10-19	6-8	O.J. Linney	10.5	Jim Platt		
2001-02	12-17	8-6	Charles White	9.1	Jim Platt		
2002-03	14-14	8-6	Kevin Warzynski	13.8	Jim Platt		
2003-04	6-22	3-13	Kurtis Rice	13.1	Jim Platt		
2004-05	13-17	7-9	Kurtis Rice	12.8	Jim Platt	55-89	.382
2005-06	13-16	7-9	Chris Moore	13.0	Barclay Radebaugh		
2006-07	8-22	2-12	Dwayne Jackson	14.4	Barclay Radebaugh		
2007-08	10-20	4-10	Omar Carter	15.5	Barclay Radebaugh		
2008-09	9-20	4-14	Jamarco Warren	17.8	Barclay Radebaugh	40-78	.339

● NCAA Tournament appearance

PROFILE

Charleston Southern University, Charleston, SC
Founded: 1964
Enrollment: 3,201 (2,759 undergraduate)
Colors: Blue and gold
Nickname: Buccaneers
Current arena: CSU Field House, opened in 1965 (798)
First game: 1965
All-time record: 499-697 (.417)
Total weeks in AP Top 20/25: 0

Current conference: Big South (1985-)
Conference titles:
Big South: 2 (1986, '87)
Conference tournament titles:
Big South: 4 (1986, '87, '95, '97)
NCAA Tournament appearances: 1
NIT appearances: 0

TOP 5

G **Ben Hinson** (1983-87)
G **Brett Larrick** (1993-97)
G **Ed O'Neil** (2000-04)
F **Dan Franz** (1967-71)
F **Jim Gardner** (1965-68)

RECORDS

RECORDS	GAME		SEASON		CAREER	
POINTS	52	Marion Salerni, vs. Wofford (Jan. 7, 1969)	688	Marion Salerni (1968-69)	2,295	Ben Hinson (1983-87)
POINTS PER GAME			27.6	Jim Gardner (1965-66)	23.6	Jim Gardner (1965-68)
REBOUNDS	30	Dan Franz, vs. UNC Wilmington (Feb. 24, 1968)	390	Dan Franz (1969-70)	1,258	Dan Franz (1967-71)
ASSISTS	22	Tony Fairley, vs. Armstrong State (Feb. 9, 1987)	270	Tony Fairley (1986-87)	471	Ed O'Neil (2000-04)

ESPN 152 SAGARIN

CHARLOTTE

At the Final Four in 1977, Marquette's Al McGuire stopped UNC Charlotte coach, Lee Rose, before their national semifinal match and said, "There are a hundred [not very prominent state] schools in the country with names like yours and I can beat them all. But I'm not sure I can beat yours." Marquette did win by two points on the way to a national title, but a talented 49ers cast helped turn Charlotte into a pillar of the mid-major ranks. UNCC has gone to eight NCAA Tournaments and four NITs since 1994.

BEST TEAM: 1976-77 Coming off a trip to the NIT final in 1976, Rose decided to ditch the team's helter-skelter style for a more controlled pace that suited star Cedric "Cornbread" Maxwell, point guard Melvin Watkins & Co. It worked. The 49ers out-zoned No. 6-ranked Syracuse in the NCAA regional semis, then took out one of the tournament's favorites, Michigan, to reach the Final Four, before losing to Marquette.

BEST PLAYER: C Cedric "Cornbread" Maxwell (1973-77) Overlooked by the big schools because he played just one season of high school ball, four years later Maxwell was the nation's best pound-for-pound talent according to Coach Rose. He could play every position and graduated as the school's all-time leader with 1,824 points (since surpassed) and 1,117 rebounds.

BEST COACH: Lee Rose (1975-78) Adolph Rupp called on Rose's behalf to help him land the UNCC job—and the 49ers were lucky he did. Charlotte notched 20 wins in every one of his three seasons and reached the NCAA Final Four and the NIT championship match.

GAME FOR THE AGES: Early in the first half of Charlotte's 1977 Elite Eight contest with the top-ranked Wolverines, freshman Chad Kinch drove baseline and dunked over All-America Phil Hubbard. Michigan was slow to recover, and the Niners won, 75-68.

FIERCEST RIVAL: Charlotte and Davidson have played every year between 1979 and 2008 (though scheduling issues didn't allow a game in '09). The winner takes home the Hornet's Nest Trophy. Charlotte leads 26–10.

SEASON REVIEW

SEAS.	W-L	CONF.		SCORING		COACH	RECORD	
1965-66	6-17					Harvey Murphy		
1966-67	7-21					Harvey Murphy		
1967-68	5-17			Jerry Anthony	13.7	Harvey Murphy		
1968-69	12-10			Ben Basinger	16.5	Harvey Murphy		
1969-70	14-16			Norris Dae	15.8	Harvey Murphy	44-81	.352
1970-71	15-8			Norris Dae	13.9	Bill Foster		
1971-72	14-11			Robert Earl Blue	21.6	Bill Foster		
1972-73	14-12			Robert Earl Blue	20.8	Bill Foster		
1973-74	22-4			Robert Earl Blue	17.5	Bill Foster		
1974-75	23-3			George Jackson	24.5	Bill Foster	88-38	.698
1975-76	24-6		■	Lew Massey	22.5	Lee Rose		
1976-77	28-5	5-1	●	Cedric Maxwell	22.2	Lee Rose		
1977-78	20-7	9-1		Lew Massey	21.8	Lee Rose	72-18	.800
1978-79	16-11	6-4		Chad Kinch	20.6	Mike Pratt		
1979-80	15-12	9-5		Chad Kinch	18.9	Mike Pratt		
1980-81	10-17	3-9		Phil Ward	14.3	Mike Pratt		
1981-82	15-12	3-7		Bobby Potts	20.9	Mike Pratt	56-52	.519
1982-83	8-20	5-9		Melvin Johnson	16.3	Hal Wissel		
1983-84	9-19	2-12		Melvin Johnson	19.6	Hal Wissel		
1984-85	5-23	1-13		Clinton Hinton	16.8	Hal Wissel	22-62	.262
1985-86	8-20	1-13		Michael Milling	19.6	Jeff Mullins		
1986-87	18-14	6-8		Byron Dinkins	13.5	Jeff Mullins		
1987-88	22-9	11-3	●	Byron Dinkins	21.5	Jeff Mullins		
1988-89	17-12	10-4	■	Byron Dinkins	17.6	Jeff Mullins		
1989-90	16-14	6-8		Henry Williams	21.0	Jeff Mullins		
1990-91	14-14	6-8		Henry Williams	21.6	Jeff Mullins		
1991-92	23-9	7-5	●	Henry Williams	20.8	Jeff Mullins		
1992-93	15-13	6-6		Jarvis Lang	13.7	Jeff Mullins		
1993-94	16-13	7-5	■	Jarvis Lang	16.4	Jeff Mullins		
1994-95	19-9	8-4	●	Jarvis Lang	16.4	Jeff Mullins		
1995-96	14-15 ⊗	6-8		DeMarco Johnson	18.1	Jeff Mullins	182-142	.562▼
1996-97	22-9	10-4	●	DeMarco Johnson	18.8	Melvin Watkins		
1997-98	20-11	13-3	●	DeMarco Johnson	21.1	Melvin Watkins	42-20	.677
1998-99	23-11	10-6	●	Galen Young	14.7	Bobby Lutz		
1999-2000	17-16	7-9	■	Jobey Thomas	13.9	Bobby Lutz		
2000-01	22-11	10-6	●	Rodney White	18.7	Bobby Lutz		
2001-02	18-12	11-5	●	Jobey Thomas	18.5	Bobby Lutz		
2002-03	13-16	8-8		Demon Brown	16.8	Bobby Lutz		
2003-04	21-9	12-4	●	Curtis Withers	16.3	Bobby Lutz		
2004-05	21-8	12-4	●	Curtis Withers	18.0	Bobby Lutz		
2005-06	19-13	11-5	■	De'Angelo Alexander	17.0	Bobby Lutz		
2006-07	14-16	7-9		De'Angelo Alexander	17.6	Bobby Lutz		
2007-08	20-14	9-7	■	Leemire Goldwire	18.6	Bobby Lutz		
2008-09	11-20	5-12		Lamont Mack	15.2	Bobby Lutz	199-146	.577

⊗ Records do not reflect games forfeited or vacated. For adjusted records, see p. 521.

▼ Coach's record adjusted to reflect games forfeited or vacated: 183-141, .565. For yearly totals, see p. 521.

● NCAA Tournament appearance ■ NIT appearance

PROFILE

University of North Carolina at Charlotte, Charlotte, NC
Founded: 1946
Enrollment: 19,846 (15,875 undergraduate)
Colors: Green and white
Nickname: 49ers
Current arena: Halton Arena, opened in 1996 (9,105)
First game: Nov. 26, 1965
All-time record: 705-559 (.558)
Total weeks in AP Top 20/25: 23
Current conference: Atlantic 10 (2005-)

Conference titles:
Sun Belt: 3 (1977, '78 '88)
Metro: 1 (1995)
Conference USA: 1 (2004 [tie])
Conference tournament titles:
Sun Belt: 2 (1977, '88)
Metro: 1 (1992)
Conference USA: 2 (1999, 2001)
NCAA Tournament appearances: 11
Sweet 16s (since 1975): 1
Final Fours: 1
NIT appearances: 6
Semifinals: 1

FIRST-ROUND PRO PICKS

1977	**Cedric Maxwell,** Boston (12)
1980	**Chad Kinch,** Cleveland (22)
2001	**Rodney White,** Detroit (9)

TOP 5

G	**Melvin Watkins** (1973-77)
G	**Henry Williams** (1988-92)
F	**DeMarco Johnson** (1994-98)
F	**Jarvis Lang** (1990-91, '92-95)
C	**Cedric "Cornbread" Maxwell** (1973-77)

RECORDS

RECORDS	GAME		SEASON		CAREER	
POINTS	44	George Jackson, vs. Samford (Feb. 8, 1975)	690	Cedric Maxwell (1976-77)	2,383	Henry Williams (1988-92)
POINTS PER GAME			24.5	George Jackson (1974-75)	20.4	George Jackson (1973-75)
REBOUNDS	24	Cedric Maxwell, vs. Seton Hall (Feb. 19, 1977); Ben Basinger, vs. Florida Presbyterian (Dec. 3, 1970)	417	Norris Dae (1969-70)	1,117	Cedric Maxwell (1973-77)
ASSISTS	18	Sean Colson, vs. Houston (Feb. 28, 1998)	231	Sean Colson (1997-98)	515	Keith Williams (1983-87)

ESPN 244 SAGARIN

CHATTANOOGA

There's more to Chattanooga basketball than just the Mocs' 1997 fairy tale run to the Sweet 16; the school has made 10 NCAA Tournament appearances since 1981 and tradition runs deeper than its Division I days, punctuated by a 1977 D2 national title under coach Ron Shumate.

BEST TEAM: 1982-83 The 1996-97 Sweet 16 team was good, but this one was better. Led by shooting guard Willie White and future Knick Gerald Wilkins, the Mocs went 26–4, and 15–1 in the Southern Conference. They won 14 straight before a one-point loss to Lefty Driesell and Maryland in the NCAA Tournament sent them home with a No. 15 ranking in the final AP poll.

BEST PLAYER: G WILLIE WHITE (1980-84) Upon his arrival, White predicted he would lead the Mocs to four straight conference titles. Not quite: a double-OT loss to Marshall in the SoCon final his senior year held him to three. As a sophomore, White iced Chattanooga's first Tournament win, against NC State, from the free throw line. When he paired up with Wilkins—yikes, look out. The duo averaged nearly 36 ppg in 1983-84 and are one-two in almost every offensive category at UTC.

BEST COACH: MACK McCARTHY (1985-97) His first two seasons ended with NIT invites, and there were five NCAA runs during the next decade. By the time McCarthy left UTC, he had racked up the most wins in school and Southern Conference history (243).

GAME FOR THE AGES: After upending No. 3-seed Georgia in the 1997 Tourney first round, Chattanooga faced No. 6-seed Illinois. Before the game, the Mocs heard celebratory noises from the Illinois locker room—Providence had just knocked off Duke and the Illini thought their path to the Elite Eight was clear. Not so. An angry Chattanooga team exacted revenge, 75-63, with five players scoring in double figures.

FIERCEST RIVAL: In some ways, 1991-92 was typical. Of UTC's three conference losses, two came at the hands of in-state rival East Tennessee State, including the SoCon tournament final. ETSU took some heat out of the long-standing rivalry by moving to the Atlantic Sun in 2005. But the schools still meet up, and it's still contentious.

SEASON REVIEW

SEAS.	W-L	CONF.	COACH	SEAS.	W-L	CONF.	COACH
1915-45	*161-154*	*13-3 in 1926-27*		1958-59	14-7		Tommy Bartlett
1945-46	10-5		Perron Shoemaker	1959-60	14-9		Tommy Bartlett
1946-47	4-15		Bill O'Brien	1960-61	17-8		Tommy Bartlett
1947-48	5-12		Bill O'Brien	1961-62	15-10		Tommy Bartlett
1948-49	3-9		Bill O'Brien	1962-63	16-10		Leon Ford
1949-50	5-19		Bill O'Brien	1963-64	13-13		Leon Ford
1950-51	7-7		Bill O'Brien	1964-65	17-10		Leon Ford
1951-52	2-10		Bill O'Brien	1965-66	4-19		Leon Ford
1952-53	9-13		Bill O'Brien	1966-67	8-18		Leon Ford
1953-54	5-8		Bill O'Brien	1967-68	12-13		Leon Ford
1954-55	3-15		Bill O'Brien[a]	1968-69	16-10		Leon Ford
1955-56	3-15		Ben Boulware	1969-70	12-12		Leon Ford
1956-57	0-15		Ben Boulware	1970-71	18-5		Leon Ford
1957-58	4-12		Ben Boulware	1971-72	13-13		Leon Ford

SEAS.	W-L	CONF.		SCORING		COACH	RECORD	
1972-73	19-9					Ron Shumate		
1973-74	21-5					Ron Shumate		
1974-75	19-9					Ron Shumate		
1975-76	23-9					Ron Shumate		
1976-77	27-5		◆			Ron Shumate		
1977-78	16-11	7-5		Edsel Brooks	16.1	Ron Shumate		
1978-79	14-13	3-8		Keith Parker	17.3	Ron Shumate	139-61	.695
1979-80	13-14	7-9		Eric Smith	13.0	Murray Arnold		
1980-81	21-9	11-5	●	Eric Smith	16.4	Murray Arnold		
1981-82	27-4	15-1	●	Willie White	15.8	Murray Arnold		
1982-83	26-4	15-1	●	Willie White	18.4	Murray Arnold		
1983-84	24-7	12-4	■	Willie White	18.5	Murray Arnold		
1984-85	24-8	14-2	■	Gerald Wilkins	21.0	Murray Arnold	135-46	.746
1985-86	21-10	12-4	■	Carliss Jeter	12.3	Mack McCarthy		
1986-87	21-8	14-2	■	Lance Fulse	14.9	Mack McCarthy		
1987-88	20-13	8-8	●	Benny Green	17.2	Mack McCarthy		
1988-89	18-12	10-4		Daren Chandler	18.0	Mack McCarthy		
1989-90	14-14	7-7		Derrick Kirce	20.1	Mack McCarthy		
1990-91	19-10	11-3		Keith Nelson	20.0	Mack McCarthy		
1991-92	23-7	12-2		Keith Nelson	16.7	Mack McCarthy		
1992-93	26-7	16-2	●	Tim Brooks	16.5	Mack McCarthy		
1993-94	23-7	14-4	●	Chad Copeland	20.1	Mack McCarthy		
1994-95	19-11	11-3	●	Brandon Born	17.3	Mack McCarthy		
1995-96	15-12	9-5		Johnny Taylor	18.2	Mack McCarthy		
1996-97	24-11	11-3	●	Johnny Taylor	16.5	Mack McCarthy	243-122	.666
1997-98	13-15	7-7		David Phillips	12.5	Henry Dickerson		
1998-99	16-12	9-7		Mark Smith	9.4	Henry Dickerson		
1999-2000	10-19	6-10		Rashun Coleman	16.5	Henry Dickerson		
2000-01	17-13	9-7		Toot Young	12.5	Henry Dickerson		
2001-02	16-14	9-7		Toot Young	12.3	Henry Dickerson	72-73	.497
2002-03	21-9	11-5		Ashley Champion	15.4	Jeff Lebo		
2003-04	19-11	10-6		Ashley Champion	18.1	Jeff Lebo	40-20	.667
2004-05	20-11	10-6	●	Mindaugas Katelynas	11.8	John Shulman		
2005-06	19-13	8-6		Keddric Mays	11.0	John Shulman		
2006-07	15-18	6-12		Keddric Mays	14.3	John Shulman		
2007-08	18-13	13-7		Stephen McDowell	14.3	John Shulman		
2008-09	18-17	11-9	●	Stephen McDowell	18.1	John Shulman	90-72	.556

[a] Bill O'Brien (1-8) and Ben Boulware (2-7) both coached during the 1954-55 season.

● NCAA Tournament appearance ■ NIT appearance ◆ Division II championship

PROFILE

University of Tennessee at Chattanooga, Chattanooga, TN
Founded: 1886
Enrollment: 9,558 (8,194 undergraduate)
Colors: Navy, old gold and silver
Nickname: Mocs
Current arena: McKenzie Arena, originally UTC Arena, opened in 1982 (11,234)
Previous: Maclellan Gym, 1961-82 (4,177)
First game: 1915
All-time record: 1,129-860 (.568)

Total weeks in AP Top 20/25: 3
Current conference: Southern (1976-)
Conference titles:
Southern: 16 (1981 [tie], '82, '83, '85, '86, '89, '91 [tie], '92 [tie], '93, '94, '95 [tie], '97 [tie], '98 [tie], 2002 [tie], '08 [tie], '09 [tie])
Conference tournament titles:
Southern: 10 (1981, '82, '83, '88, '93, '94, '95, '97, 2005, '09)
NCAA Tournament appearances: 10
Sweet 16s (since 1975): 1
NIT appearances: 4

CONSENSUS ALL-AMERICAS

1977 **Wayne Golden** (D2), F

FIRST-ROUND PRO PICKS

1997 **Johnny Taylor**, Orlando (17)

TOP 5

G **Tim Brooks** (1991-93)
G **Willie White** (1980-84)
F **Brandon Born** (1991-95)
F **Lance Fulse** (1984-88)
F **Gerald Wilkins** (1982-85)

RECORDS

RECORDS	GAME		SEASON		CAREER	
POINTS	50	Oliver Morton, vs. Pikeville (Jan. 25, 2001)	672	Gerald Wilkins (1984-85)	1,972	Willie White (1980-84)
POINTS PER GAME			21.0	Gerald Wilkins (1984-85)	19.5	Derrick Kirce (1989-91)
REBOUNDS	21	Mindaugas Katelynas, vs. Appalachian State (March 4, 2005)	302	Nicchaeus Doaks (2008-09)	818	Nicchaeus Doaks (2005-09)
ASSISTS	17	Gary Robb, vs. Southern U. (Dec. 29, 1992)	209	Tim Brooks (1991-92)	414	Wes Moore (1995-99); Tim Brooks (1991-93)

ESPN 285 SAGARIN

CHICAGO STATE

Winning hasn't come easy for the Cougars lately. But it wasn't always that way. After cementing a reputation as an NAIA power from the 1960s to the early '80s, Chicago State jumped to D1 in 1984 and averaged 19 wins its first two seasons. Twenty-plus losing seasons followed. But the team recovered its winning ways in 2008-09, just in time for the Cougars' move to the Great West Conference.

BEST TEAM: 1983-84 They were known as the Heart Attack Kids for a reason. The Cougars rode the quick defensive hands of guards Darron Brittman and Charles Perry all the way to the NAIA national semifinals before bowing to Fort Hays State, 86-84, in OT—one of three overtime games they played in the tournament.

BEST PLAYER: G David Holston (2005-09) The Cougars ended 2005-06 with a losing record, as they had the 19 seasons before. Who could have known that the fix was already on the roster in the form of a 5'8" freshman with a walk-on scholarship? In 2008-09 Holston's lightning moves and deadly shooting range propelled the Cougars to a 19–13 record as an independent. The godson of Detroit Pistons guard Lindsey Hunter, he led the country in three-pointers as a junior and senior and broke most of Chicago State's scoring and assists records.

BEST COACH: Bob Hallberg (1977-87) He installed an up-tempo, guard-oriented offense and a disciplined zone D. Hallberg's game plan worked; the Cougars enjoyed a 75-game home winning streak from 1981 to '86.

GAME FOR THE AGES: In the second round of the 1984 NAIA tournament, the Cougars needed two OTs to beat Kearney State, 105-104, in a game that featured 69 fouls. Trailing early by 13, Hallberg grabbed the jerseys of his two star guards, Brittman and Perry, excoriating them on the sidelines. Brittman finished with 31 points and Perry had 22.

FIERCEST RIVALRY: At the top of Chicago State's list of bitter foes is former Mid-Continent rival Valparaiso. The Crusaders lead the series 30–3, most recently handing the Cougars a 90-61 thrashing on Dec. 15, 2007.

SEASON REVIEW

SEAS.	W-L	CONF.	SCORING		COACH	RECORD
1966-67	6-13				Isadoore Salario	
1967-68	14-11				Isadoore Salario	
1968-69	18-9				Isadoore Salario	
1969-70	10-12				Isadoore Salario	48-45 .516
1970-71	11-14				Robert Griggas	
1971-72	11-15				Robert Griggas	
1972-73	6-22				Robert Griggas	
1973-74	10-17				Robert Griggas	38-68 .358
1974-75	17-9		Jerome Holland	20.8	Joseph Buckhalter	
1975-76	8-16				Joseph Buckhalter	
1976-77	11-16		Ken Cyrus	24.9	Joseph Buckhalter	36-41 .468
1977-78	25-5		Ken Cyrus	22.3	Bob Hallberg	
1978-79	24-7		Ken Dancy	20.4	Bob Hallberg	
1979-80	26-6		Ken Dancy	18.4	Bob Hallberg	
1980-81	23-9				Bob Hallberg	
1981-82	17-13		Zeke Rand	17.7	Bob Hallberg	
1982-83	28-5		Sherrod Arnold	16.6	Bob Hallberg	
1983-84	31-5		Learandro Drake	16.2	Bob Hallberg	
1984-85	16-11		Charles Perry	18.6	Bob Hallberg	
1985-86	22-6		Darron Brittman	19.0	Bob Hallberg	
1986-87	11-17				Bob Hallberg	223-84 .726
1987-88	8-20		Stanley Jones	13.6	Tommy Suitts	
1988-89	12-16				Tommy Suitts	
1989-90	6-22		James Parker	16.9	Tommy Suitts	26-58 .310
1990-91	4-24		Rod Parker	22.1	Rick Pryor	
1991-92	7-21		Reggie Burcy	16.8	Rick Pryor	
1992-93	4-23		Jason Hodges	17.9	Rick Pryor	
1993-94	4-23	2-3	Ryan Malone	18.4	Rick Pryor	19-91 .173
1994-95	6-20	6-12	Kory Billups	16.0	Craig Hodges	
1995-96	2-25	2-16	Kory Billups	16.1	Craig Hodges	
1996-97	4-23	4-12	Kory Billups	17.3	Craig Hodges[a]	8-51 .136
1997-98	2-25	2-14	Jermaine Hicks	17.7	Phillip Gary	6-42 .125
1998-99	3-24	3-11	Jermaine Hicks	14.5	Bo Ellis	
1999-2000	10-18	7-9	Tim Bryant	14.2	Bo Ellis	
2000-01	5-23	2-14	Tony Jones	14.3	Bo Ellis	
2001-02	2-26	0-14	Clark Bone	12.3	Bo Ellis	
2002-03	3-27	0-14	Craig Franklin	13.6	Bo Ellis[b]	23-106 .178
2003-04	12-20	9-7	Craig Franklin	14.3	Kevin Jones	
2004-05	9-19	7-9	Tony Weeden	13.1	Kevin Jones	
2005-06	11-19	8-8	Royce Parran	18.1	Kevin Jones	
2006-07	9-20		David Holston	15.6	Kevin Jones	41-90 .313
2007-08	11-17		David Holston	23.1	Benjy Taylor	
2008-09	19-13		David Holston	25.9	Benjy Taylor	30-30 .500

[a] Craig Hodges (0-6) and Phillip Gary (4-17) both coached during the 1996-97 season.
[b] Bo Ellis (3-15) and Kevin Jones (0-12) both coached during the 2002-03 season.

PROFILE

Chicago State University, Chicago, IL
Founded: 1867 as Cook County Normal School
Enrollment: 7,200 (5,217 undergraduate)
Colors: Evergreen and white
Nickname: Cougars
Current arena: Emil and Patricia Jones Convocation Center, opened in 2007 (7,000)
Previous: Jacoby Dickens Center, 1971-2007 (2,500)
First game: 1966
All-time record: 498-706 (.414)
Total weeks in AP Top 20/25: 0

Current conference: Great West (2009-)
Conference titles: 0
Conference tournament titles: 0
NCAA Tournament appearances: 0
NIT appearances: 0

TOP 5

G **Darron Brittman** (1983-86)
G **Ken Cyrus** (1974-78)
G **David Holston** (2005-09)
F **Kory Billups** (1993-97)
F **Mike Eversley** (1976-79)

RECORDS	GAME		SEASON		CAREER	
POINTS	49	Ken Cyrus, vs. Northeastern Illinois (Jan. 18, 1977)	830	David Holston (2008-09)	2,331	David Holston (2005-09)
POINTS PER GAME			25.9	David Holston (2008-09)	19.6	David Holston (2005-09)
REBOUNDS	26	Ken Dancy, vs. Northeastern Illinois (Jan. 18, 1980)	304	Kory Billups (1996-97)	852	Kory Billups (1993-97)
ASSISTS	14	Anthony Figueroa, vs. UMKC (Feb. 12, 1997); David Holston, vs. Houston Baptist (March 2, 2009)	204	David Holston (2008-09)	529	David Holston (2005-09)

ESPN 17 SAGARIN

CINCINNATI

Home of the Big O, Ed and Huggs, Cincinnati has long had one of the Midwest's greatest programs. Jump-started by Oscar Robertson in the late 1950s, the Bearcats rolled to five straight Final Fours, winning back-to-back NCAA titles (1961, '62) under the guidance of Ed Jucker. The fiery Bob Huggins returned Cincy to the Final Four in 1992.

BEST TEAM: 1961-62 After two national third-place finishes in the Robertson years, followed by its first title in 1961, the 1961-62 team won a second straight NCAA crown, ending up 29–2, its two losses coming by a total of just three points. Led by All-America center Paul Hogue, the Bearcats avenged one of those defeats by crushing Bradley in the Missouri Valley Conference title playoff, 61-46. From there they cruised to the Final Four and easily beat Ohio State, 71-59. They would reach the NCAA Final yet again in 1963 (see Heartbreaker).

BEST PLAYER: G/F Oscar Robertson (1957-60) Considered by many to be the greatest player ever, the Big O is the Bearcats' all-time leading scorer (2,973), second in history only to LSU's Pete Maravich for players with three-year careers. Robertson's 33.8 ppg average is third-best in NCAA history. A three-time national POY who led the Cats to the Final Four in each of his last two seasons, Robertson holds Cincinnati season and career rebounding records and is third in career assists—despite the fact that Cincy didn't count assists until Oscar's junior season. Robertson played 14 seasons in the NBA, winning a title with the Milwaukee Bucks in 1971, and was inducted into the Naismith Hall of Fame in 1980.

BEST COACH: Bob Huggins (1989-2005) The school's all-time winningest coach with 398, Huggins revitalized the once-great UC program and guided the Bearcats to the 1992 Final Four in just his third season. Known for their rebounding and lockdown defense, Huggs' teams won 10 regular-season C-USA titles and eight conference tournament championships, and made 14 consecutive NCAA appearances.

GAME FOR THE AGES: On March 25, 1961, in their third straight trip to the Final Four (and first since the departure of Robertson), the Bearcats faced 27–0 Ohio State, a team some called unbeatable, for the NCAA championship. A layup by OSU's Bob Knight sent the game into overtime, but Cincinnati recovered, winning 70-65 to claim its first national title behind 17 points from Bob Wiesenhahn.

HEARTBREAKER: The 1963 NCAA title game was the first in which the majority of players on the floor for the opening tap were African-American. Cincinnati, bidding to become the first team to win three consecutive titles, lost a 15-point second-half lead to Loyola-Chicago, then lost the game in overtime, 60-58, when Vic Rouse scored on a last-second midair putback.

FIERCEST RIVAL: The annual Crosstown Shootout with Xavier dates back to 1928, though the teams didn't meet again until the 1942-43 season. Cincinnati has dominated the series, which alternates between the two teams' home courts, 47–29. However, XU did beat a No.1-ranked ranked Bearcats team in 1999-2000.

FANFARE AND HOOPLA: The Bearcats mascot is inspired not by the actual animal, but by former Cincy fullback Leonard K. "Teddy" Baehr. In a 1914 football game against Kentucky, a UC cheerleader created a chant that went: "They may be the Wildcats, but we have a Baehr-cat on our side." The press started referring to Cincinatti teams as Bearcats in 1919, and the name stuck.

FAN FAVORITE: F Jack Twyman (1951-55) The All-America forward averaged 24.6 points and 16.5 rebounds as a senior while leading the Bearcats to a third-place finish in the NIT. But he was loved all the more as a pro star and broadcaster—and because he became the legal guardian of his NBA teammate Maurice Stokes, who suffered a paralyzing brain injury.

CONSENSUS ALL-AMERICAS

1958-60	**Oscar Robertson**, G/F
1963	**Ron Bonham**, F
1963	**Tom Thacker**, G/F
1997	**Danny Fortson**, C
2000	**Kenyon Martin**, F
2002	**Steve Logan**, G

FIRST-ROUND PRO PICKS

1958	**Connie Dierking**, Syracuse (6)
1960	**Oscar Robertson**, Cincinnati (1)
1962	**Paul Hogue**, New York (2)
1963	**Tom Thacker**, Cincinnati (5)
1964	**George Wilson**, Cincinnati (8)
1969	**Rick Roberson**, LA Lakers (15)
1970	**Jim Ard**, Seattle (6)
1970	**Jim Ard**, New York (ABA)
1993	**Corie Blount**, Chicago (25)
1997	**Danny Fortson**, Milwaukee (10)
2000	**Kenyon Martin**, New Jersey (1)
2000	**DerMarr Johnson**, Atlanta (6)
2005	**Jason Maxiell**, Detroit (26)

PROFILE

University of Cincinnati, Cincinnati, OH
Founded: 1819
Enrollment: 36,518 (27,700 undergraduate)
Colors: Red and black
Nickname: Bearcats
Current arena: Fifth Third Arena, opened in 1989 (13,176)
First game: Dec. 12, 1901
All-time record: 1,561-921 (.629)
Total weeks in AP Top 20/25: 351
Current conference: Big East (2005-)

Conference titles:
Mid-American: 5 (1947 [tie], '48, '49, '50, '51)
Missouri Valley: 7 (1958, '59, '60, '61, '62, '63, '66)
Metro: 1 (1976)
Great Midwest: 2 (1992 [tie], '93)
Conference USA: 8 (1996 [tie], '97, '98, '99, 2000, '01 [tie], '02, '04 [tie])
Conference tournament titles:
Metro: 2 (1976, '77)
Great Midwest: 4 (1992, '93, '94, '95)
Conference USA: 4 (1996, '98, 2002, '04)
NCAA Tournament appearances: 24
Sweet 16s (since 1975): 5
Final Fours: 6
Titles: 2 (1961, '62)
NIT appearances: 9
Semifinals: 1

TOP 5

G	**Steve Logan** (1998-2002)
G/F	**Oscar Robertson** (1957-60)
F	**Kenyon Martin** (1996-2000)
F	**Jack Twyman** (1951-55)
C	**Danny Fortson** (1994-97)

RECORDS	GAME		SEASON		CAREER	
POINTS	62	Oscar Robertson, vs. North Texas (Feb. 8, 1960)	1,011	Oscar Robertson (1959-60)	2,973	Oscar Robertson (1957-60)
POINTS PER GAME			35.1	Oscar Robertson (1957-58)	33.8	Oscar Robertson (1957-60)
REBOUNDS	33	Connie Dierking, vs. Loyola (La.) (Feb. 16, 1957)	489	Oscar Robertson (1958-59)	1,338	Oscar Robertson (1957-60)
ASSISTS	16	Steve Logan, vs. Coppin State (Dec. 8, 2001)	219	Oscar Robertson (1959-60)	500	Eddie Lee (1976-80)

SEASON REVIEW

SEASON	W-L	CONF.	SCORING		COACH	RECORD	
1901-17	*68-81*		*Coach Amos Foster went 30-10 in five seasons (1904-09)*				
1917-18	2-6				Whitelaw Morrison	2-6	.250
1918-19	3-11				Boyd Chambers		
1919-20	5-9				Boyd Chambers		
1920-21	10-11				Boyd Chambers		
1921-22	15-8				Boyd Chambers		
1922-23	13-9				Boyd Chambers		
1923-24	11-8				Boyd Chambers		
1924-25	5-14				Boyd Chambers		
1925-26	17-2		Richard Bolton	10.7	Boyd Chambers		
1926-27	13-5		Richard Bolton	13.8	Boyd Chambers		
1927-28	14-4		Richard Bolton	9.4	Boyd Chambers	106-81	.567
1928-29	13-4		William Popp	9.5	Frank Rice		
1929-30	14-4		William Popp	10.2	Frank Rice		
1930-31	2-15		Howard Nelson	4.2	Frank Rice		
1931-32	4-11		Olen Grandle	6.9	Frank Rice	33-34	.493
1932-33	9-9		Olen Grandle	7.2	John Halliday	9-9	.500
1933-34	12-7		Carl Austing	13.5	Tay Brown		
1934-35	16-3		Carl Austing	11.7	Tay Brown		
1935-36	10-7		Lou Capelle	8.9	Tay Brown		
1936-37	9-10		Lou Capelle	8.9	Tay Brown	47-27	.635
1937-38	6-11		Gordon Iliff	7.4	Walter Van Winkle		

SEAS.	W-L	CONF.	POSTSEASON	SCORING		REBOUNDS		ASSISTS		COACH	RECORD	
1938-39	12-5			Lou Capelle	11.9					Walter Van Winkle	18-16	.529
1939-40	8-9			Ted Deskins	9.7					Clark Ballard		
1940-41	6-12			Don Davis	8.2					Clark Ballard		
1941-42	10-10			Nate Kabakoff	8.2					Clark Ballard	24-31	.436
1942-43	9-10			Harold Schneider	10.2					Bob Ruess		
1943-44	6-5			Harold Schneider	13.9					Bob Ruess	15-15	.500
1944-45	8-9			John Mueller	11.5					Ray Farnham		
1945-46	8-13			Bill Westerfeld	12.6					Ray Farnham	16-22	.421
1946-47	17-9	6-2		Bill Westerfeld	13.8					John Weithe		
1947-48	17-7	7-2		Ralph Richter	13.5					John Weithe		
1948-49	23-5	9-1		Ralph Richter	16.4					John Weithe		
1949-50	20-6	10-0		Jim Holstein	13.4					John Weithe		
1950-51	18-4	7-1	NIT FIRST ROUND	Jim Holstein	17.0					John Weithe		
1951-52	11-16	5-5		Jim Holstein	15.7	Jim Holstein	12.0			John Weithe	106-47	.693
1952-53	11-13	9-3		Jack Twyman	15.0	Jack Twyman	15.1			George Smith		
1953-54	11-10			Jack Twyman	21.8	Jack Twyman	16.5			George Smith		
1954-55	21-8		NIT THIRD PLACE	Jack Twyman	24.6	Jack Twyman	16.5			George Smith		
1955-56	17-7			Phil Wheeler	21.5	Wayne Stevens	13.9			George Smith		
1956-57	15-9		NIT FIRST ROUND	Connie Dierking	18.5	Connie Dierking	18.8			George Smith		
1957-58	25-3	13-1	NCAA REGIONAL SEMIFINALS	Oscar Robertson	35.1	Oscar Robertson	15.2			George Smith		
1958-59	26-4	13-1	NCAA THIRD PLACE	Oscar Robertson	32.6	Oscar Robertson	16.3	Oscar Robertson	6.9	George Smith		
1959-60	28-2	13-1	NCAA THIRD PLACE	Oscar Robertson	33.7	Oscar Robertson	14.1	Oscar Robertson	7.3	George Smith	154-56	.733
1960-61	**27-3**	**10-2**	**NATIONAL CHAMPION**	**Bob Wiesenhahn**	**17.1**	**Paul Hogue**	**12.5**	**Tom Thacker**	**3.8**	**Ed Jucker**		
1961-62	**29-2**	**10-2**	**NATIONAL CHAMPION**	**Paul Hogue**	**16.9**	**Paul Hogue**	**12.4**	**Tony Yates**	**4.3**	**Ed Jucker**		
1962-63	26-2	11-1	NCAA RUNNER-UP	Ron Bonham	21.0	George Wilson	11.2	Tom Thacker	4.0	Ed Jucker		
1963-64	17-9	6-6		Ron Bonham	24.4	George Wilson	12.5	Ken Cunningham	2.2	Ed Jucker		
1964-65	14-12	5-9		Don Rolfes	13.7	Ron Krick	8.9	Roland West	2.6	Ed Jucker	113-28	.801
1965-66	21-7	10-4	NCAA REGIONAL SEMIFINALS	Don Rolfes	16.4	Roland West	9.4	Dean Foster	4.9	Tay Baker		
1966-67	17-9	6-8		Rick Roberson	14.3	Rick Roberson	12.5	Dean Foster	3.4	Tay Baker		
1967-68	18-8	11-5		Rick Roberson	16.3	Rick Roberson	12.3	Dean Foster	2.7	Tay Baker		
1968-69	17-9	8-8		Rick Roberson	16.1	Rick Roberson	12.6	Don Ogletree	2.9	Tay Baker		
1969-70	21-6	12-4	NIT FIRST ROUND	Jim Ard	19.2	Jim Ard	15.2	Don Ogletree	3.3	Tay Baker		
1970-71	14-12			Derrek Dickey	17.9	Derrek Dickey	12.1	Charley Snow	2.3	Tay Baker		
1971-72	17-9			Lloyd Batts	18.7	Derrek Dickey	10.9	Lloyd Batts	2.3	Tay Baker	125-60	.676
1972-73	17-9			Lloyd Batts	20.1	Derrek Dickey	10.0	Dan Murphy	2.3	Gale Catlett		
1973-74	19-8		NIT FIRST ROUND	Lloyd Batts	21.3	Mike Franklin	8.6	Lloyd Batts	1.8	Gale Catlett		
1974-75	23-6		NCAA REGIONAL SEMIFINALS	Steve Collier	13.8	Mike Franklin	8.6	Steve Collier	3.3	Gale Catlett		
1975-76	25-6		NCAA FIRST ROUND	Robert Miller	15.2	Robert Miller	10.8	Gary Yoder	2.9	Gale Catlett		
1976-77	25-5	4-2	NCAA FIRST ROUND	Robert Miller	14.2	Robert Miller	10.6	Gary Yoder	3.9	Gale Catlett		
1977-78	17-10	6-6		Pat Cummings	18.0	Robert Miller	8.5	Steve Collier	3.2	Gale Catlett	126-44	.741
1978-79	13-14	4-6		Pat Cummings	24.5	Pat Cummings	11.3	Eddie Lee	6.9	Ed Badger		
1979-80	13-15	3-9		Eddie Lee	15.6	Dwight Jones	7.5	Eddie Lee	5.7	Ed Badger		
1980-81	16-13	6-6		David Kennedy	14.6	Doc Holden	8.1	David Kennedy	5.8	Ed Badger		
1981-82	15-12	4-8		Dwight Jones	15.0	Dwight Jones	10.0	Junior Johnson	3.1	Ed Badger		
1982-83	11-17	1-11		Dwight Jones	16.9	Dwight Jones	10.1	Junior Johnson	3.3	Ed Badger	68-71	.489
1983-84	3-25	0-14		Mark Dorris	16.3	Mark Dorris	6.8	Calvin Phiffer	1.9	Tony Yates		
1984-85	17-14	8-6	NIT SECOND ROUND	Roger McClendon	12.4	Myron Hughes	8.1	Derrick McMillan	3.8	Tony Yates		
1985-86	12-16	5-7		Roger McClendon	16.5	Myron Hughes	7.2	Tony Wilson	3.4	Tony Yates		
1986-87	12-16	3-9		Roger McClendon	19.9	Joe Stiffend	7.0	Romell Shorter	3.6	Tony Yates		
1987-88	11-17	3-9		Cedric Glover	18.9	Cedric Glover	8.3	Elnardo Givens	3.3	Tony Yates		
1988-89	15-12	5-7		Cedric Glover	14.5	Cedric Glover	8.5	Elnardo Givens	4.2	Tony Yates	70-100	.412
1989-90	20-14	9-5	NIT SECOND ROUND	Louis Banks	17.9	Levertis Robinson	7.8	Andre Tate	3.4	Bob Huggins		
1990-91	18-12	8-6	NIT SECOND ROUND	Herb Jones	16.1	Herb Jones	7.8	Louis Banks	3.3	Bob Huggins		
1991-92	29-5	8-2	NCAA NATIONAL SEMIFINALS	Herb Jones	18.1	Herb Jones	7.1	Nick Van Exel	2.9	Bob Huggins		
1992-93	27-5	8-2	NCAA REGIONAL FINALS	Nick Van Exel	18.3	Erik Martin	6.7	Nick Van Exel	4.5	Bob Huggins		
1993-94	22-10	7-5	NCAA FIRST ROUND	LaZelle Durden	17.8	Dontonio Wingfield	9.0	Damon Flint	2.8	Bob Huggins		
1994-95	22-12 ⊗	7-5	NCAA SECOND ROUND	LaZelle Durden	17.9	Art Long	8.3	Keith LeGree	4.5	Bob Huggins		
1995-96	28-5	11-3	NCAA REGIONAL FINALS	Danny Fortson	20.1	Danny Fortson	9.6	Keith LeGree	5.7	Bob Huggins		
1996-97	26-8	12-2	NCAA SECOND ROUND	Danny Fortson	21.3	Danny Fortson	9.1	Damon Flint	4.0	Bob Huggins		
1997-98	27-6	14-2	NCAA SECOND ROUND	Ruben Patterson	16.5	Bobby Brannen	8.1	Michael Horton	4.8	Bob Huggins		
1998-99	27-6	12-4	NCAA SECOND ROUND	Pete Mickeal	14.9	Pete Mickeal	7.2	Michael Horton	3.5	Bob Huggins		
1999-2000	29-4	16-0	NCAA SECOND ROUND	Kenyon Martin	18.9	Kenyon Martin	9.7	Kenny Satterfield	5.4	Bob Huggins		
2000-01	25-10	11-5	NCAA REGIONAL SEMIFINALS	Steve Logan	17.6	Donald Little	5.6	Kenny Satterfield	5.1	Bob Huggins		
2001-02	31-4	14-2	NCAA SECOND ROUND	Steve Logan	22.0	Donald Little	6.9	Steve Logan	5.3	Bob Huggins		
2002-03	17-12	9-7	NCAA FIRST ROUND	Leonard Stokes	15.7	Jason Maxiell	6.7	Taron Barker	5.0	Bob Huggins		
2003-04	25-7	12-4	NCAA SECOND ROUND	Jason Maxiell	13.6	Jason Maxiell	6.9	James White	3.6	Bob Huggins		
2004-05	25-8	12-4	NCAA SECOND ROUND	Jason Maxiell	15.3	Eric Hicks	9.0	James White	3.1	Bob Huggins	398-128	.757▼
2005-06	21-13	8-8	NIT QUARTERFINALS	James White	16.3	Eric Hicks	9.7	Devan Downey	4.3	Andy Kennedy	21-13	.618
2006-07	11-19	2-14		Deonta Vaughn	14.5	John Williamson	7.3	Deonta Vaughn	3.5	Mick Cronin		
2007-08	13-19	8-10		Deonta Vaughn	17.3	John Williamson	6.3	Deonta Vaughn	4.2	Mick Cronin		
2008-09	18-14	8-10		Deonta Vaughn	15.3	Yancy Gates	4.7	Deonta Vaughn	4.7	Mick Cronin	42-52	.447

⊗ Records do not reflect games forfeited or vacated. For adjusted records, see p. 521.

▼ Coach's record adjusted to reflect games forfeited or vacated: 399-127, .759. For yearly totals, see p. 521.

ESPN 293 SAGARIN

THE CITADEL

Author Pat Conroy brought notoriety to the Bulldogs with *My Losing Season*, the 2002 book based on his experiences as a Citadel guard in the 1966-67 season. It's a rocky, often painful memoir, reflecting the turmoil of a team that's still awaiting its first NCAA berth.

BEST TEAM: 1958-59 Exit the memory of one of the worst stretches in Citadel history, in which the Bulldogs won just 14 games from 1953-54 through '56-57. Enter the Blitz Kids, an exciting crew led by Ray Graves, Art Musselman and Dick Wherry. Playing intense defense and scoring plenty, the team marched all the way to the Southern Conference finals before Jerry West and West Virginia sent them packing, 85-66.

BEST PLAYER: F Art Musselman (1956-60) Musselman was the spark to the Blitz Kids squads of the late 1950s, leading the team in scoring three of his four seasons. The only Bulldog to have his jersey retired, Musselman graduated as The Citadel's career leading scorer (1,504).

BEST COACH: Les Robinson (1974-85) Never mind the .449 winning clip. An eternal optimist, Robinson turned the Bulldogs into a genuine fan attraction, with his 1978-79 team routinely packing the usually vacant McAlister Field House.

GAME FOR THE AGES: South Carolina had won 37 straight games (going back to World War II) against The Citadel when the Bulldogs finally bit back on Feb. 22, 1989. Undeterred by the hostile Carolina Coliseum crowd, The Citadel went 8-for-16 from the three-point line to pull off an 88-87 upset. Afterward, various Gamecocks called the loss "embarrassing," "a disgrace" and "crap."

FIERCEST RIVAL: The Furman-Citadel basketball rivalry isn't quite as famous as the football one, but don't tell that to the Furman mascot. In the 1960s, the Paladins' horse was stuffed into a car by Citadel hooligans and met its early demise. The Paladins have dominated the Southern Conference's longest-running series of late, winning 11 of 15 from 2002-03 to '08-09, and lead overall, 110–81.

SEASON REVIEW

SEAS.	W-L	CONF.	COACH	SEAS.	W-L	CONF.	COACH
1900-46	*259-201*	*20-0 over two seasons (1918-20)*		1959-60	15-8	8-4	Norm Sloan
1946-47	5-11	1-11	Whitey Piro	1960-61	17-8	10-3	Mel Thompson
1947-48	8-9	4-8	Bernard O'Neil	1961-62	8-15	4-8	Mel Thompson
1948-49	1-17	0-11	Bernard O'Neil	1962-63	3-20	2-10	Mel Thompson
1949-50	4-16	2-10	Bernard O'Neil	1963-64	11-10	4-8	Mel Thompson
1950-51	7-10	2-7	Bernard O'Neil	1964-65	13-11	8-5	Mel Thompson
1951-52	8-20	1-11	Bernard O'Neil	1965-66	7-16	4-9	Mel Thompson
1952-53	4-14	0-11	Leo Zack	1966-67	8-16	6-7	Mel Thompson
1953-54	1-18	1-7	Leo Zack	1967-68	11-14	6-5	Dick Campbell
1954-55	0-17	0-10	Jim Browning	1968-69	13-12	5-8	Dick Campbell
1955-56	2-19	0-10	Hank Witt	1969-70	8-16	4-8	Dick Campbell
1956-57	11-14	5-9	Norm Sloan	1970-71	13-12	6-5	Dick Campbell
1957-58	16-11	9-6	Norm Sloan	1971-72	12-13	5-6	George Hill
1958-59	15-5	7-4	Norm Sloan	1972-73	11-15	6-7	George Hill

SEAS.	W-L	CONF.	SCORING		COACH	RECORD	
1973-74	10-14	4-9	Rodney McKeever	15.0	George Hill	33-42	.440
1974-75	5-15	2-11	Rodney McKeever	23.0	Les Robinson		
1975-76	10-17	6-7	Rodney McKeever	20.5	Les Robinson		
1976-77	8-19	2-9	Rick Swing	16.6	Les Robinson		
1977-78	8-19	2-11	Rick Swing	13.3	Les Robinson		
1978-79	20-7	10-4	Tom Slawson	17.1	Les Robinson		
1979-80	14-13	6-10	Tom Slawson	15.4	Les Robinson		
1980-81	9-17	2-14	Wells Holland	10.8	Les Robinson		
1981-82	14-14	7-9	Felipe de las Pozas	13.5	Les Robinson		
1982-83	12-16	7-9	Felipe de las Pozas	16.5	Les Robinson		
1983-84	14-14	8-8	Regan Truesdale	22.0	Les Robinson		
1984-85	18-11	11-5	Regan Truesdale	21.5	Les Robinson	132-162	.449
1985-86	10-18	5-11	Craig Bardo	16.5	Randy Nesbit		
1986-87	13-15	6-10	Craig Burgess	17.6	Randy Nesbit		
1987-88	8-20	5-11	Kent Hill	14.4	Randy Nesbit		
1988-89	16-12	7-7	Patrick Elmore	18.0	Randy Nesbit		
1989-90	12-16	5-9	Patrick Elmore	20.8	Randy Nesbit		
1990-91	6-22	1-13	Ted Mosay	17.5	Randy Nesbit		
1991-92	10-18	3-11	Andre Harris	14.8	Randy Nesbit	75-121	.383
1992-93	10-17	8-10	Andre Harris	10.5	Pat Dennis		
1993-94	11-16	6-12	D. Stevens, R. Jones	13.3	Pat Dennis		
1994-95	11-16	6-8	Moncrief Michael	13.8	Pat Dennis		
1995-96	10-16	5-9	Noy Castillo	14.0	Pat Dennis		
1996-97	13-14	6-8	Virgil Stevens	14.4	Pat Dennis		
1997-98	15-13	6-8	Jamie Jenkins	14.7	Pat Dennis		
1998-99	9-18	3-13	Alan Puckett	9.0	Pat Dennis		
1999-2000	10-20	5-10	Alan Puckett	12.3	Pat Dennis		
2000-01	16-12	9-7	Travis Cantrell	12.7	Pat Dennis		
2001-02	17-12	8-8	Travis Cantrell	16.6	Pat Dennis		
2002-03	8-20	3-13	Max Mombollet	12.0	Pat Dennis		
2003-04	6-22	2-14	Dante Terry	11.3	Pat Dennis		
2004-05	12-16	4-12	Warren McLendon	12.8	Pat Dennis		
2005-06	10-21	1-14	Dante Terry	12.6	Pat Dennis	158-233	.404
2006-07	7-23	4-14	Kevin Hammack	13.0	Ed Conroy		
2007-08	6-24	1-19	Cameron Wells	14.4	Ed Conroy		
2008-09	20-13	15-5	Demetrius Nelson	16.4	Ed Conroy	33-60	.355

PROFILE

The Citadel, Charleston, SC
Founded: 1842
Enrollment: 3,313 (2,374 undergraduate)
Colors: Citadel blue and white
Nickname: Bulldogs, Cadets
Current arena: McAlister Field House (originally The Citadel Armory), opened in 1939 (6,000)
Previous: Alumni Hall, 1900-39 (N/A)
First game: 1900

All-time record: 899-1,158 (.437)
Total weeks in AP Top 20/25: 0
Current conference: Southern (1936-)
Conference titles: 0
Conference tournament titles: 0
NCAA Tournament appearances: 0
NIT appearances: 0

TOP 5

G **Regan Truesdale** (1981-85)
G/F **Rick Swing** (1975-79)
F **Gary Daniels** (1959-62)
F **Art Musselman** (1956-60)
C **Tom Slawson** (1976-80)

RECORDS

	GAME		SEASON		CAREER	
POINTS	51	Jerry Varn, vs. Piedmont (Feb. 1, 1953)	624	Regan Truesdale (1984-85)	1,661	Regan Truesdale (1981-85)
POINTS PER GAME			23.9	Gary Daniels (1961-62)	19.4	Rodney McKeever (1973-76); Gary Daniels (1959-62)
REBOUNDS	23	Keith Stowers, vs. Richmond (1961)	329	Gary Daniels (1960-61)	924	Ray Graves (1956-60)
ASSISTS	13	Jimmy Tharpe, vs. Western Carolina (1986); Greer Huguley, vs. USC-Aiken (1982); Randy Nesbit, vs. Marshall (1979); Rodney McKeever, vs. Davidson (1976)	179	Jimmy Tharpe (1985-86)	387	Jimmy Tharpe (1982-86)

ESPN 103 SAGARIN

CLEMSON

It's tough being a basketball team in football country, an ACC member in SEC land, the lone South Carolina representative in a North Carolina-dominated conference. All of which makes Clemson's hardcourt success that much more remarkable. The landmarks include the 1939 Southern Conference tournament title, the 1990 ACC regular-season championship, three Sweet 16 appearances, an Elite Eight trip in 1980 and a runner-up finish in the 1999 NIT.

BEST TEAM: 1989-90 Led by the imposing Duo of Doom—Dale Davis and Elden Campbell—the Tigers kept their fans on the edge all the way to the NCAA Sweet 16. The ACC regular-season champs rallied from halftime deficits to victories six times, including a climb back from a 16-point hole against La Salle in the second round of the NCAA Tournament (the largest halftime deficit overcome in school history). Too bad that in 1992, the NCAA stripped Clemson of its two '90 Tournament wins for using an academically ineligible player, Wayne Buckingham.

BEST PLAYER: F Elden Campbell (1986-90) Although Horace Grant and Tree Rollins were the only Tigers named to the ACC's 50th Anniversary Team, Campbell was Clemson's most complete player. In addition to ranking as the school's all-time leading scorer, he's the only Tiger with more than 100 career blocks, steals and assists.

BEST COACH: Cliff Ellis (1984-94) A former ostrich farmer and lead singer for a beach music group, Ellis's calling card was the 1-3-1 zone press, which the Tigers rode to the postseason eight times. He was named ACC Coach of the Year in 1986-87 and 1989-90—the only Clemson coach to win that award.

GAME FOR THE AGES: On Feb. 28, 1990, Clemson clinched a share of its first ACC regular-season title when Kirkland Howling hit four free throws in the final :17 for a 97-93 triumph over Duke at Littlejohn Coliseum. The real highlight came after the game, as the Tigers cut down the nets and celebrated on the court with their fans.

HEARTBREAKER: In their 1990 Sweet 16 matchup against No. 1-seed Connecticut, the Tigers erased a 19-point deficit, capped by David Young's three-pointer, which gave them a 70-69 lead with :11 left. Nine seconds later, the upset seemed in hand when Clemson's Sean Tyson was fouled after grabbing a rebound. But Tyson missed the front end of the one-and-one and Scott Burrell, a top pitching prospect who would be picked in the first round of both the NBA and MLB drafts, threw a full-court pass to Tate George, who turned around and drained the winning jumper as the buzzer went off. Oh, the agony!

FIERCEST RIVAL: The institutional bad blood between Clemson and South Carolina most famously plays out on the gridiron (for example, see their 2004 brawl). But the hoops teams have had some wars of their own. Exhibit A: Dec. 4, 2004, when freshman Cheyenne Moore's three-pointer with 3.4 seconds left in OT lifted the Tigers to a 63-62 victory. The Gamecocks lead overall, 86–73.

> *A former ostrich farmer and lead singer for a beach music group, Ellis's calling card was the 1-3-1 zone press, which the Tigers rode to the post-season eight times.*

FANFARE AND HOOPLA: Football will always be No. 1 at Clemson, but that doesn't mean Littlejohn is a fun place for visitors—not with those crazed orange-overall-wearing fans camped under the basket. Since it opened in 1968, Tigers faithful have been rewarded with 51 home wins over ranked teams.

FAN FAVORITE: F Sam Perry (2004-08) The Greenville, S.C., product never averaged more than 6.3 ppg in any season, but he captured the hearts of the home crowd with his hustle, fancy dunks and timely blocks.

FIRST-ROUND PRO PICKS

1977	**Tree Rollins,** Atlanta (14)
1981	**Larry Nance,** Phoenix (20)
1987	**Horace Grant,** Chicago (10)
1990	**Elden Campbell,** LA Lakers (27)
1991	**Dale Davis,** Indiana (13)
1994	**Sharone Wright,** Philadelphia (6)

PROFILE

Clemson University, Clemson, SC
Founded: 1889
Enrollment: 17,585 (14,270 undergraduate)
Colors: Burnt orange and northwest purple
Nickname: Tigers
Current arena: Littlejohn Coliseum, opened in 1968 (9,850)
First game: 1911
All-time record: 1,140-1,166-2 (.494)
Total weeks in AP Top 20/25: 117

Current conference: Atlantic Coast (1953-)
Conference titles:
ACC: 1 (1990)
Conference tournament titles:
Southern: 1 (1939)
NCAA Tournaments: 9 (1 appearance vacated)
Sweet 16s (since 1975): 3
NIT appearances: 14
Semifinals: 2

TOP 5

G **Greg Buckner** (1994-98)
G **Terrell McIntyre** (1995-99)
F **Elden Campbell** (1986-90)
F **Horace Grant** (1983-87)
C **Tree Rollins** (1973-77)

RECORDS

RECORDS	GAME		SEASON		CAREER	
POINTS	58	J.O. Erwin, vs. Butler Guards (Feb. 9, 1912)	651	Horace Grant (1986-87); Bill Yarborough (1954-55)	1,880	Elden Campbell (1986-90)
POINTS PER GAME			28.3	Bill Yarborough (1954-55)	23.5	Butch Zatezalo (1967-70)
REBOUNDS	30	Tommy Smith, vs. Georgia (Feb. 21, 1955)	395	Dale Davis (1989-90)	1,311	Tree Rollins (1973-77)
ASSISTS	20	Grayson Marshall, vs. UMES (Nov. 25, 1985)	262	Grayson Marshall (1985-86)	857	Grayson Marshall (1984-88)

SEASON REVIEW

SEASON	W-L	CONF.	COMMENTS	COACH	RECORD	
1911-18	*29-23-2*		*Undefeated (4-0) in inaugural season*			
1918-19	3-1			Jiggs Donahue	6-3	.667
1919-20	8-6			Country Morris	16-8	.667
1920-21	10-4			Larry Conover	10-4	.714
1921-22	8-13	0-3		E.R. Stewart		
1922-23	11-6	3-3		E.R. Stewart	19-19	.500
1923-24	2-14	0-6		Bud Saunders		
1924-25	4-14	3-2		Bud Saunders	6-28	.176
1925-26	4-17	1-7		A.A. Gilliam	4-17	.190
1926-27	2-13	1-7		Josh Cody		
1927-28	9-14	5-7		Josh Cody		
1928-29	15-12	6-4		Josh Cody		
1929-30	16-9	8-4		Josh Cody		
1930-31	6-7	3-5		Josh Cody	48-55	.466
1931-32	7-13	2-9		Joe Davis		
1932-33	10-9	0-2		Joe Davis		
1933-34	7-12	0-6		Joe Davis		
1934-35	15-3	3-1		Joe Davis		
1935-36	15-7	5-5		Joe Davis		
1936-37	6-15	2-7		Joe Davis		
1937-38	16-7	9-4	Banks McFadden 13.3	Joe Davis		
1938-39	16-8	6-6	Banks McFadden 11.8	Joe Davis		

SEAS.	W-L	CONF.	POSTSEASON	SCORING		REBOUNDS		ASSISTS		COACH	RECORD	
1939-40	9-12	9-7		Banks McFadden	13.7					Joe Davis	101-86	.540
1940-41	8-14	7-8		Marion Craig	12.7					Rock Norman		
1941-42	3-14	2-10		C.C. Graham	6.3					Rock Norman		
1942-43	3-13	0-10		Marion Craig	13.1					Rock Norman		
1943-44	1-10	1-2		Leonard Riddle	11.4					Rock Norman		
1944-45	8-8	3-5		Eddis Freeman	11.1					Rock Norman		
1945-46	9-11	5-7		June Pruitt	12.3					Rock Norman	32-70	.314
1946-47	7-13	2-12		June Pruitt	10.4					Banks McFadden		
1947-48	6-17	3-14		Leonard Riddle	11.5					Banks McFadden		
1948-49	10-11	6-9		Doug Haugk	10.9					Banks McFadden		
1949-50	10-10	8-8		Johnny Snee	13.9					Banks McFadden		
1950-51	11-7	9-4		Johnny Snee	17.5					Banks McFadden		
1951-52	17-7	11-4		Johnny Snee	14.7					Banks McFadden		
1952-53	8-10	6-8		John McGraw	13.8	John McGraw	11.1			Banks McFadden		
1953-54	5-18	0-9		Ames Wells	15.2	Charley Gage	11.3			Banks McFadden		
1954-55	2-21	0-14		Bill Yarborough	28.3	Tommy Smith	8.5			Banks McFadden		
1955-56	9-17	1-13		Vince Yockel	20.9	Gene Seay	10.5			Banks McFadden	85-131	.394
1956-57	7-17	3-11		Vince Yockel	19.8	Gene Seay	7.5			Press Maravich		
1957-58	8-16	4-10		Vince Yockel	13.8	George Krajack	6.9			Press Maravich		
1958-59	8-16	5-9		George Krajack	13.0	George Krajack	6.4			Press Maravich		
1959-60	10-16	4-10		Choppy Patterson	16.4	Tommy Mahaffey	7.5			Press Maravich		
1960-61	10-16	5-9		Choppy Patterson	19.0	Tommy Mahaffey	11.3			Press Maravich		
1961-62	12-15	4-10		Jim Brennan	17.1	Donnie Mahaffey	6.8			Press Maravich	55-96	.364
1962-63	12-13	5-9		Jim Brennan	16.6	Donnie Mahaffey	10.7			Bobby Roberts		
1963-64	13-12	8-6		Jim Brennan	18.3	Donnie Mahaffey	8.9			Bobby Roberts		
1964-65	8-15	4-10		Randy Mahaffey	17.3	Randy Mahaffey	9.7			Bobby Roberts		
1965-66	15-10	8-6		Garry Helms	19.2	Randy Mahaffey	10.2			Bobby Roberts		
1966-67	17-8	9-5		Jim Sutherland	18.8	Randy Mahaffey	9.0			Bobby Roberts		
1967-68	4-20	3-11		Butch Zatezalo	23.0	Richie Mahaffey	11.5			Bobby Roberts		
1968-69	6-19	2-12		Butch Zatezalo	25.8	Ronnie Yates	6.4			Bobby Roberts		
1969-70	7-19	2-12		Butch Zatezalo	21.7	Richie Mahaffey	9.1	Butch Zatezalo	80	Bobby Roberts	82-116	.414
1970-71	9-17	3-11		Dave Angel	13.7	Dave Angel	6.9	John Coakley	38	Taylor "Tates" Locke		
1971-72	10-16	2-10		Dave Angel	13.9	Dave Angel	9.7	Terrell Suit	40	Taylor "Tates" Locke		
1972-73	12-14	4-8		Van Gregg	13.6	Dave Angel	6.7	Ron DiPasquale	42	Taylor "Tates" Locke		
1973-74	14-12	3-9		Van Gregg	13.8	Tree Rollins	12.2	Jeff Reisinger	45	Taylor "Tates" Locke		
1974-75	17-11	8-4	NIT FIRST ROUND	Skip Wise	18.5	Tree Rollins	11.7	Jo Jo Bethea	81	Taylor "Tates" Locke	62-70	.470
1975-76	18-10	5-7		Tree Rollins	13.7	Tree Rollins	11.0	Derrick Johnson	98	Bill Foster		
1976-77	22-6	8-4		Stan Rome	15.3	Tree Rollins	12.8	Derrick Johnson	169	Bill Foster		
1977-78	15-12	3-9		Stan Rome	12.7	John Campbell	7.2	Derrick Johnson	132	Bill Foster		
1978-79	19-10	5-7	NIT SECOND ROUND	Billy Williams	13.2	Larry Nance	7.2	Bobby Conrad	101	Bill Foster		
1979-80	23-9	8-6	NCAA REGIONAL FINALS	Billy Williams	17.6	Larry Nance	8.1	Bobby Conrad	157	Bill Foster		
1980-81	20-11	6-8	NIT FIRST ROUND	Larry Nance	15.9	Larry Nance	7.6	Chris Dodds	187	Bill Foster		
1981-82	14-14	4-10	NIT FIRST ROUND	Vincent Hamilton	15.0	Horace Wyatt	6.7	Mike Eppley	89	Bill Foster		
1982-83	11-20	2-12		Raymond Jones	11.5	Raymond Jones	7.1	Marc Campbell	124	Bill Foster		
1983-84	14-14	3-11		Murray Jarman	15.0	Murray Jarman	5.5	Marc Campbell	104	Bill Foster	156-106	.595
1984-85	16-13	5-9	NIT FIRST ROUND	Vincent Hamilton	15.1	Vincent Hamilton	6.9	Grayson Marshall	192	Cliff Ellis		
1985-86	19-15	3-11	NIT QUARTERFINALS	Horace Grant	16.4	Horace Grant	10.5	Grayson Marshall	262	Cliff Ellis		
1986-87	25-6	10-4	NCAA FIRST ROUND	Horace Grant	21.0	Horace Grant	9.6	Grayson Marshall	221	Cliff Ellis		
1987-88	14-15	4-10	NIT FIRST ROUND	Elden Campbell	18.8	Dale Davis	7.7	Grayson Marshall	182	Cliff Ellis		
1988-89	19-11	7-7	NCAA SECOND ROUND	Elden Campbell	17.5	Dale Davis	8.9	Marion Cash	161	Cliff Ellis		
1989-90	26-9 ⊗	10-4	NCAA REGIONAL SEMIFINALS	Elden Campbell	16.4	Dale Davis	11.3	Marion Cash	174	Cliff Ellis		
1990-91	11-17	2-12		Dale Davis	17.9	Dale Davis	12.1	David Young	100	Cliff Ellis		
1991-92	14-14	4-12		Chris Whitney	13.4	Sharone Wright	8.1	Chris Whitney	161	Cliff Ellis		
1992-93	17-13	5-11	NIT SECOND ROUND	Devin Gray	16.7	Sharone Wright	10.5	Chris Whitney	193	Cliff Ellis		
1993-94	18-16	6-10	NIT QUARTERFINALS	Sharone Wright	15.4	Sharone Wright	10.6	Lou Richie	182	Cliff Ellis	179-129	.581▼
1994-95	15-13	5-11	NIT FIRST ROUND	Greg Buckner	12.0	Greg Buckner	5.9	Merl Code	111	Rick Barnes		
1995-96	18-11	7-9	NCAA FIRST ROUND	Greg Buckner	13.1	Harold Jamison	5.9	Terrell McIntyre	90	Rick Barnes		
1996-97	23-10	9-7	NCAA REGIONAL SEMIFINALS	Greg Buckner	15.6	Harold Jamison	5.7	Terrell McIntyre	145	Rick Barnes		
1997-98	18-14	7-9	NCAA FIRST ROUND	Greg Buckner	16.3	Harold Jamison	7.3	Terrell McIntyre	154	Rick Barnes	74-48	.607
1998-99	20-15	5-11	NIT RUNNER-UP	Terrell McIntyre	17.9	Harold Jamison	9.9	Terrell McIntyre	5.4	Larry Shyatt		
1999-2000	10-20	4-12		Will Solomon	20.9	Adam Allenspach	7.1	Will Solomon	3.2	Larry Shyatt		
2000-01	12-19	2-14		Will Solomon	19.7	Chris Hobbs	6.3	Edward Scott	4.2	Larry Shyatt		
2001-02	13-17	4-12		Jamar McKnight	12.5	Ray Henderson	8.8	Edward Scott	7.9	Larry Shyatt		
2002-03	15-13	5-11		Edward Scott	17.7	Sharrod Ford	6.8	Edward Scott	5.8	Larry Shyatt	70-84	.455
2003-04	10-18	3-13		Sharrod Ford	11.9	Sharrod Ford	7.1	Vernon Hamilton	3.2	Oliver Purnell		
2004-05	16-16	5-11	NIT FIRST ROUND	Sharrod Ford	14.9	Sharrod Ford	8.2	Shawan Robinson	2.9	Oliver Purnell		
2005-06	19-13	7-9	NIT SECOND ROUND	Shawan Robinson	12.3	Akin Akingbala	8.2	Cliff Hammonds	3.3	Oliver Purnell		
2006-07	25-11	7-9	NIT RUNNER-UP	K.C Rivers	14.0	T. Booker, J. Mays	6.4	Cliff Hammonds	4.1	Oliver Purnell		
2007-08	24-10	10-6	NCAA FIRST ROUND	K.C Rivers	14.7	Trevor Booker	7.4	Cliff Hammonds	4.0	Oliver Purnell		
2008-09	23-9	9-7	NCAA FIRST ROUND	Trevor Booker	15.3	Trevor Booker	9.7	Demontez Stitt	3.8	Oliver Purnell	117-77	.603

Cumulative totals listed when per game averages not available.

⊗ Record does not reflect games forfeited or vacated. For adjusted records, see p. 521.

▼ Coach's record adjusted to reflect games forfeited or vacated: 177-128, .580. For yearly totals, see p. 521.

ESPN 265 SAGARIN

CLEVELAND STATE

It's a program with a long history but only a couple of miracle moments. Most recently, there was the upset of Wake Forest in the first round of the 2009 NCAA Tournament. And few March Madness Cinderellas have captured America's heart the way the Vikings did in 1986, led by a point guard called Mouse and a pair of Clintons (Ransey and Smith).

BEST TEAM: 1985-86 The 27–3 regular-season and tournament champions of the AMCU-8 (now the Summit League, though CSU bolted for the Horizon League in 1994-95) knocked off Indiana in the first round of the NCAA Tournament, then dismissed Saint Joseph's with 23 points from freshman Ken "Mouse" McFadden. Only a last-second bucket by Navy's David Robinson kept the Vikings from the Elite Eight.

BEST PLAYER: G Franklin Edwards (1977-81) He could score from anywhere. Edwards is Cleveland State's all-time season and career ppg leader and set a school record when he drained 49 against Xavier in 1981. He went on to win an NBA title with the Philadelphia 76ers.

BEST COACH: Kevin Mackey (1983-90) He led the Vikings to four straight 20-win seasons and a thrilling Sweet 16 NCAA run, and achieved the highest winning percentage in school history. His tenure came to an abrupt end in 1990, when he was arrested outside a crack house accompanied by a prostitute. In 2003, after 13 years of sobriety and minor-league coaching around the world, he was hired by the Indiana Pacers as a scout.

GAME FOR THE AGES: CSU stunned Indiana in the first round of the 1986 Tourney, 83-79, behind 27 points from Clinton Ransey and spectacular passing by Clinton Smith. IU's Bob Knight was so upset at the loss that, despite being eliminated, he made his team practice every day while the Tournament lasted.

FIERCEST RIVAL: In the battle for northeast Ohio, CSU and Akron have battled more than 60 times. Akron fans still haven't forgiven CSU for shorting the Zips a point on the scoreboard during a 1983 game that Lee Reed won for Cleveland State at the buzzer, 83-82.

SEASON REVIEW

SEAS.	W-L	CONF.	COACH	SEAS.	W-L	CONF.	COACH
1929-47	*71-155*	*0-13 in 1942-43*		**1960-61**	4-15		Jim Rodriguez
1947-48	10-8		George McKinnon	**1961-62**	6-13		Jim Rodriguez
1948-49	4-14		George McKinnon	**1962-63**	9-9		Jim Rodriguez
1949-50	9-8		George Rung	**1963-64**	10-9		Jim Rodriguez
1950-51	6-11		George Rung	**1964-65**	10-9		Jim Rodriguez
1951-52	4-12		George Rung	**1965-66**	4-14		Jim Rodriguez
1952-53	2-15		Homer Woodling	**1966-67**	8-13		John McLendon
1953-54	1-18		George Rung	**1967-68**	7-15		John McLendon
1954-55	2-15		George Rung	**1968-69**	12-14		John McLendon
1955-56	3-15		George Rung	**1969-70**	5-21		Ray Dieringer
1956-57	3-15		George Rung	**1970-71**	5-20		Ray Dieringer
1957-58	6-13		George Rung	**1971-72**	8-18		Ray Dieringer
1958-59	7-12		Bill Gallagher	**1972-73**	9-14		Ray Dieringer
1959-60	0-19		Jim Rodriguez	**1973-74**	6-20		Ray Dieringer

SEAS.	W-L	CONF.	SCORING		COACH	RECORD	
1974-75	13-11		Wilbur Starks	17.8	Ray Dieringer		
1975-76	6-19		Dave Kyle	24.5	Ray Dieringer		
1976-77	10-17		Dave Kyle	15.8	Ray Dieringer		
1977-78	12-13		Franklin Edwards	18.7	Ray Dieringer		
1978-79	15-10		Franklin Edwards	18.7	Ray Dieringer		
1979-80	18-8		Franklin Edwards	25.5	Ray Dieringer		
1980-81	18-9		Franklin Edwards	24.6	Ray Dieringer		
1981-82	17-10		Darren Tillis	17.3	Ray Dieringer		
1982-83	8-20	1-4	Dave Youdath	16.6	Ray Dieringer	150-210	.417
1983-84	14-16	4-10	Dave Youdath	13.7	Kevin Mackey		
1984-85	21-8	11-3	Clinton Ransey	18.4	Kevin Mackey		
1985-86	29-4	13-1 ●	Clinton Smith	16.2	Kevin Mackey		
1986-87	25-8	10-4 ■	Ken McFadden	21.5	Kevin Mackey		
1987-88	22-8	11-3 ■	Ken McFadden	20.5	Kevin Mackey		
1988-89	16-12		Ken McFadden	22.9	Kevin Mackey		
1989-90	15-13		Brian Parker	16.5	Kevin Mackey	142-69	.673
1990-91	12-16	8-8	Mike Wawrzyniak	13.5	Mike Boyd		
1991-92	16-13	7-9	Anthony Reed	13.2	Mike Boyd		
1992-93	22-6	15-1	Sam Mitchell	16.8	Mike Boyd		
1993-94	14-15	9-9	Sam Mitchell	16.9	Mike Boyd		
1994-95	10-17	3-11	Jamal Jackson	16.4	Mike Boyd		
1995-96	5-21	3-13	Eric Nichelson	11.5	Mike Boyd	79-88	.473
1996-97	9-19	6-10	Malcolm Sims	14.1	Rollie Massimino		
1997-98	12-15	6-8	James Madison	15.3	Rollie Massimino		
1998-99	14-14	6-8	James Madison	15.0	Rollie Massimino		
1999-2000	16-14	9-5	Damon Stringer	19.1	Rollie Massimino		
2000-01	19-13	9-5	Theo Dixon	18.0	Rollie Massimino		
2001-02	12-16	6-10	Jamaal Harris	15.5	Rollie Massimino		
2002-03	8-22	3-13	Modibo Niakate	11.9	Rollie Massimino	90-113	.443
2003-04	4-25	0-16	Jermaine Robinson	19.6	Mike Garland		
2004-05	9-17	6-10	Omari Westley	17.1	Mike Garland		
2005-06	10-18	5-11	J'Nathan Bullock	11.3	Mike Garland	23-60	.277
2006-07	10-21	3-13	J'Nathan Bullock	13.5	Gary Waters		
2007-08	21-13	12-6 ■	J'Nathan Bullock	14.8	Gary Waters		
2008-09	26-10	12-6 ●	J'Nathan Bullock	15.4	Gary Waters	57-44	.564

● NCAA Tournament appearance ■ NIT appearance

PROFILE

Cleveland State University, Cleveland, OH
Founded: 1964
Enrollment: 15,664 (9,833 undergraduate)
Colors: Forest green and white
Nickname: Vikings
Current arena: Wolstein Center, opened in 1991, (13,610)
Previous: Woodling Gym, 1973-91 (3,000); Public Hall, 1970-84 (N/A)
First game: Dec. 6, 1929
All-time record: 739-1,025 (.419)
Total weeks in AP Top 20/25: 1

Current conference: Horizon League (1994-)
Conference titles:
Mid-Continent: 3 (1985, '86, '93)
Conference tournament titles:
Mid-Continent: 1 (1986)
Horizon: 1 (2009)
NCAA Tournament appearances: 2
Sweet 16s (since 1975): 1
NIT appearances: 3

FIRST-ROUND PRO PICKS

1981 **Franklin Edwards,** Philadelphia (22)
1982 **Darren Tillis,** Boston (23)

TOP 5

G **Franklin Edwards** (1977-81)
G **Ken"Mouse" McFadden** (1985-89)
F **J'Nathan Bullock** (2005-09)
F **Clinton Ransey** (1983-87)
C **Weldon Kytle** (1961-65)

RECORDS	GAME		SEASON		CAREER	
POINTS	49	Franklin Edwards, vs. Xavier (Feb. 25, 1981)	708	Ken McFadden (1986-87)	2,256	Ken McFadden (1985-89)
POINTS PER GAME			25.5	Franklin Edwards (1979-80)	21.9	Franklin Edwards (1977-81)
REBOUNDS	30	Weldon Kytle, vs. Malone (Feb. 13, 1964)	346	Darren Tillis (1981-82)	1,241	Weldon Kytle (1961-65)
ASSISTS	16	Ken McFadden, vs. Northern Iowa (Feb. 18, 1989)	198	Cedric Jackson (2008-09)	463	Ken McFadden (1985-89)

ESPN 294 SAGARIN

Coastal Carolina

Students flock to Coastal Carolina because, well, it's coastal. Nearby Myrtle Beach is a great playground, and CCU is home to a basketball program that's working to find its place in Palmetto State lore. The Chanticleers (a kind of rooster) haven't had a lot to crow about since their heyday in the early 1990s.

BEST TEAM: 1990-91 The plan was for a tough nonconference schedule to prepare the Chanticleers for a big run in the Big South, and that's exactly how it played out. At 6–5 entering league play, Coastal went 13–1 in-conference—the only loss coming in overtime—and then took the Big South tournament. The Chants fell to Indiana in the NCAAs, but they had set a precedent for the program.

BEST PLAYER: F Tony Dunkin (1989-93) All you need to know: T.D. was the first player in D1 history to be named MVP in his conference all four seasons. He finished as the CCU and Big South scoring leader, with 2,151 points.

BEST COACH: Russ Bergmann (1975-94) The five other coaches in Coastal history have 165 combined wins; Bergmann has 306. He recruited a talented crew that included Robert Dowdell and Dunkin, who carried the Chants to their only NCAA Tournament appearances in 1991 and 1993. His teams won four consecutive league titles from 1988 to 1991.

GAME FOR THE AGES: Winning the 1991 Big South title wasn't quite enough to get the Chants into the Big Dance. Coastal first had to face Jackson State in the NCAA's play-in game, on Jackson's home court. No problem: Dowdell and DuWayne Cheatam each scored 19 points to lead Coastal to a 78-59 victory.

FIERCEST RIVAL: U.S. Route 17 runs parallel to the Atlantic Ocean and leads from Coastal Carolina to Charleston Southern, which nowadays meet at least a twice each season. Most years they split, settling things only if they meet in the Big South tourney. Charleston Southern holds a 29–26 edge overall.

SEASON REVIEW

SEAS.	W-L	CONF.		SCORING		COACH	RECORD	
1974-75	6-17			Howard White	24.0	Dan Selwa	6-17	.261
1975-76	10-16			Howard White	29.6	Russ Bergman		
1976-77	21-10			Manuel Jessup	17.6	Russ Bergman		
1977-78	20-9			Manuel Jessup	20.4	Russ Bergman		
1978-79	18-13			Forrest Junck	18.6	Russ Bergman		
1979-80	10-19			James Brown	12.9	Russ Bergman		
1980-81	15-11			Tommy Rollins	15.3	Russ Bergman		
1981-82	21-9			Michael Hopkins	15.7	Russ Bergman		
1982-83	21-10			Tony Whittington	16.0	Russ Bergman		
1983-84	14-16			Robert Gray	13.0	Russ Bergman		
1984-85	7-21			William Calvin	12.7	Russ Bergman		
1985-86	10-17	1-7		Ricky Rutherford	12.6	Russ Bergman		
1986-87	12-16	4-4		Dave Mooney	13.9	Russ Bergman		
1987-88	17-11	9-3		William Calvin	16.4	Russ Bergman		
1988-89	14-14	9-3		Brian Penny	13.7	Russ Bergman		
1989-90	23-6	11-1		Tony Dunkin	18.1	Russ Bergman		
1990-91	24-8	13-1	●	Tony Dunkin	18.0	Russ Bergman		
1991-92	12-19	6-8		Tony Dunkin	22.5	Russ Bergman		
1992-93	22-10	12-4	●	Tony Dunkin	23.7	Russ Bergman		
1993-94	15-11	10-8		KeKe Hicks	22.4	Russ Bergman	306-246	.554
1994-95	6-20	3-13		KeKe Hicks	21.1	Michael Hopkins		
1995-96	5-21	1-13		Ben Avery	16.7	Michael Hopkins		
1996-97	11-16	6-8		Ben Avery	12.6	Michael Hopkins		
1997-98	8-19	4-8		Rodney Dupré	12.7	Michael Hopkins	30-76	.283
1998-99	7-20	4-6		Marcus Stewart	13.3	Pete Strickland		
1999-2000	10-18	7-7		Matt Gladieux	16.6	Pete Strickland		
2000-01	8-20	6-8		Torrey Butler	19.4	Pete Strickland		
2001-02	8-20	5-9		Brandon Newby	14.2	Pete Strickland		
2002-03	13-15	5-9		Torrey Butler	18.6	Pete Strickland		
2003-04	14-15	8-8		E.J. Gallup	17.2	Pete Strickland		
2004-05	10-19	7-9		Pele Paelay	16.8	Pete Strickland	70-127	.355
2005-06	20-10	12-4		Jack Leasure	17.8	Buzz Peterson		
2006-07	15-15	7-7		Jack Leasure	15.6	Buzz Peterson	35-25	.583
2007-08	13-15	6-8		Jack Leasure	16.8	Cliff Ellis		
2008-09	11-20	5-13		Joseph Harris	15.2	Cliff Ellis	24-35	.407

● NCAA Tournament appearance

PROFILE

Coastal Carolina University, Conway, SC
Founded: 1954
Enrollment: 8,300 (6,800 undergraduate)
Colors: Coastal green, bronze and black
Nickname: Chanticleers
Current arena: Kimbel Arena, opened in 1974 (1,039)
First game: Oct. 18, 1974
All-time record: 471-526 (.472)
Total weeks in AP Top 20/25: 0

Current conference: Big South (1985-)
Conference titles:
Big South: 4 (1988, '89, '90, '91)
Conference tournament titles:
Big South: 3 (1990, '91, '93)
NCAA Tournament appearances: 2
NIT appearances: 0

TOP 5

G **Robert Dowdell** (1987-91)
G **Howard White** (1974-76)
F **William Calvin** (1984-88)
F **Tony Dunkin** (1989-93)
F **Tony Whittington** (1979-83)

RECORDS

	GAME		SEASON		CAREER	
POINTS	52	Howard White, vs. College of Charleston (1974-75)	770	Howard White (1975-76)	2,151	Tony Dunkin (1989-93)
POINTS PER GAME			29.6	Howard White (1975-76)	26.9	Howard White (1974-76)
REBOUNDS	22	Moses Sonko, vs. VMI (Feb. 3, 2007)	356	Forrest Junck (1978-79)	888	William Calvin (1984-88)
ASSISTS	16	Dwight Lighty, vs. Wesleyan (1978-79)	241	Robert Smith (1977-78)	561	Robert Dowdell (1987-91)

ESPN 235 SAGARIN

COLGATE

The Raiders may have had less hoops success than any school in the Patriot League, but they have had good fortune. During the summer of 1991, two Colgate professors, Joan and Jay Mandle, went on a research trip to tiny Dominica, an island in the Caribbean, where they officiated at a hoops tournament featuring a tall native named Adonal Foyle. After moving in with the Mandles back in Hamilton, N.Y., Foyle became a prep star and spurned teams such as Syracuse and Duke to play for the Raiders. The rest is history.

BEST TEAM: 1994-95 The Raiders had the perfect combination of experience (senior Tucker Neale), talent (freshman Foyle) and brains (coach Jack Bruen). Neale and Foyle combined for 45 points as Colgate topped Navy, 68-63, to win the Patriot League tournament and earn its first NCAA bid. In the first round against No. 1-seed Kansas, Foyle scored 16 points, pulled down 13 rebounds and received a standing ovation when he fouled out with :54 left in a 82-68 loss.

BEST PLAYER: C ADONAL FOYLE (1994-97) The 6'10", 250-pound Foyle was a two-time Patriot League Player of the Year and finished his career as the NCAA's all-time leader in blocked shots (492, since surpassed). The Golden State Warriors selected him eighth overall in the 1997 NBA draft.

BEST COACH: JACK BRUEN (1989-97) He elevated Colgate to respectability in his nearly nine seasons as coach. He was on the bench for his last win, 80-69 over Marist, just a week before his death at age 48 from pancreatic cancer on Dec. 19, 1997.

GAME FOR THE AGES: In a Madison Square Garden showdown against NYU on Dec. 6, 1948, the Raiders were one point down when Colgate's Curt Norris made a miracle steal and glided home for a driving layup with :02 left for a 64-63 victory.

FIERCEST RIVAL: The Raiders have faced their central New York neighbor (and tormentor) Syracuse 161 times going back to 1902—and have lost 116 of those games, including the past 43 meetings.

SEASON REVIEW

SEAS.	W-L	CONF.	COACH	SEAS.	W-L	CONF.	COACH
1900-49	*513-323*	*14 straight winning seasons ('18-32)*		1962-63	5-13		Bob Dewey
1949-50	10-8		Howard Hartman	1963-64	7-16		Bob Dewey
1950-51	12-10		Howard Hartman	1964-65	7-16		Bob Duffy
1951-52	10-12		Howard Hartman	1965-66	8-14		Bob Duffy
1952-53	18-9		Howard Hartman	1966-67	10-13		Bob Duffy
1953-54	5-12		Howard Hartman	1967-68	10-16		Ed Ashnault
1954-55	11-9		Howard Hartman	1968-69	11-14		Ed Ashnault
1955-56	17-9		Howard Hartman	1969-70	14-11		Ed Ashnault
1956-57	14-10		Howard Hartman	1970-71	15-10		Ed Ashnault
1957-58	6-16		Howard Hartman	1971-72	15-8		Ed Ashnault
1958-59	7-12		Howard Hartman	1972-73	11-14		Bill Vesp
1959-60	11-12		Howard Hartman	1973-74	15-10		Bill Vesp
1960-61	14-12		Howard Hartman	1974-75	8-16		Bill Vesp
1961-62	8-15		Howard Hartman	1975-76	13-11		Bill Vesp

SEAS.	W-L	CONF.	SCORING		COACH	RECORD
1976-77	13-11		Chris Fagan	16.1	Mike Griffin	
1977-78	9-17		Dave Hargett	15.5	Mike Griffin	
1978-79	12-14		Dave Hargett	19.8	Mike Griffin	
1979-80	8-17	8-17	Mike Ferrara	22.8	Mike Griffin	
1980-81	11-18	11-17	Mike Ferrara	28.6	Mike Griffin	
1981-82	8-17	2-8	Kevin Ryan	11.3	Mike Griffin	61-94 .394
1982-83	3-24	0-8	Eric Jones	15.9	Tony Relvas	
1983-84	5-22	1-13	Tad Brown	11.9	Tony Relvas	
1984-85	5-21	0-16	Bob Bamford	14.2	Tony Relvas	
1985-86	1-24	0-18	Bob Bamford	13.8	Tony Relvas	14-91 .133
1986-87	4-23	3-15	Bob Bamford	13.6	Joe Baker	
1987-88	4-23	3-15	Carver Glezen	9.9	Joe Baker	
1988-89	6-22	5-13	Jay Armstrong	13.1	Joe Baker	14-68 .171
1989-90	8-21	3-9	Jonathan Stone	11.2	Jack Bruen	
1990-91	5-23	2-10	Jonathan Stone	16.1	Jack Bruen	
1991-92	14-14	7-7	Jonathan Stone	19.2	Jack Bruen	
1992-93	18-10	9-5	Tucker Neale	21.9	Jack Bruen	
1993-94	17-12	9-5	Tucker Neale	26.6	Jack Bruen	
1994-95	17-13	11-3 ●	Tucker Neale	23.1	Jack Bruen	
1995-96	15-15	9-3 ●	Adonal Foyle	20.2	Jack Bruen	
1996-97	12-16	8-4	Adonal Foyle	24.4	Jack Bruen	
1997-98	10-18	5-7	Seth Schaeffer	17.6	Jack Bruen[a]	113-139 .448
1998-99	14-14	7-5	Pat Campolieta	13.7	Emmett Davis	
1999-2000	13-16	4-8	Pat Campolieta	14.3	Emmett Davis	
2000-01	13-15	6-6	Pat Campolieta	14.4	Emmett Davis	
2001-02	17-11	8-6	Pat Campolieta	14.8	Emmett Davis	
2002-03	14-14	9-5	Mark Linebaugh	13.1	Emmett Davis	
2003-04	15-14	6-8	Mark Linebaugh	12.8	Emmett Davis	
2004-05	12-16 ⊗	7-7	Alvin Reed	12.8	Emmett Davis	
2005-06	10-19	4-10	Kyle Roemer	11.4	Emmett Davis	
2006-07	10-19	5-9	Jon Simon	13.4	Emmett Davis	
2007-08	18-14	7-7	Kyle Roemer	16.2	Emmett Davis	
2008-09	10-20	5-9	Mike Venezia	10.8	Emmett Davis	146-172 .459

[a] Jack Bruen (7-15) and Paul Aiello (3-3) both coached during the 1997-98 season.
⊗ Records don't reflect games forfeited or vacated. For adjusted records, see p. 521.
● NCAA Tournament appearance

PROFILE

Colgate University, Hamilton, NY
Founded: 1819
Enrollment: 2,809 (2,803 undergraduate)
Colors: Maroon, gray and white
Nickname: Raiders
Current arena: Cotterell Court, opened in 1966 (2,600)
Previous: Huntington Gymnasium, 1926-59 (N/A)
First game: 1900
All-time record: 1,156-1,218 (.487)
Total weeks in AP Top 20/25: 0

Current conference: Patriot League (1990-)
Conference titles:
Patriot: 3 (1994 [tie], '95 [tie], '96 [tie])
Conference tournament titles:
Patriot: 2 (1995, '96)
NCAA Tournament appearances: 2
NIT appearances: 0

CONSENSUS ALL-AMERICAS

1905 **Walter Runge,** F
1910 **Leon Campbell,** G
1912 **Emil Schradieck,** F

FIRST-ROUND PRO PICKS

1997 **Adonal Foyle,** Golden State (8)

TOP 5

G **Robert Duffy** (1959-62)
G **Mike Ferrara** (1978-81)
G **Tucker Neale** (1992-95)
F **Ernie Vandeweghe** (1945-49)
C **Adonal Foyle** (1994-97)

RECORDS

RECORDS	GAME		SEASON		CAREER	
POINTS	52	Jonathan Stone, vs. Brooklyn (March 2, 1992)	772	Mike Ferrara (1980-81)	2,075	Tucker Neale (1992-95)
POINTS PER GAME			28.6	Mike Ferrara (1980-81)	23.9	Tucker Neale (1992-95)
REBOUNDS	26	Jack Nichols, vs. Cornell (Dec. 8, 1956); Dick Osborn, vs. Yale (Dec. 15, 1951)	422	Jack Nichols (1955-56)	1,103	Adonal Foyle (1994-97)
ASSISTS	13	Hasan Brown, vs. Cornell (Feb. 24, 1992); Mike Ferrara, vs. Rensselaer (Feb. 4, 1980)	139	Hasan Brown (1993-94)	484	Hasan Brown (1990-94)

ESPN 51 SAGARIN

COLORADO

Whether it was Big Burd posting up or a young Mr. Big Shot putting it up, Colorado has had its share of big-time players creating buzz on the national scene. But what may be the team's most consistent weapon is Boulder—a scenic, thriving hometown that attracts many top recruits into giving the Buffaloes a long look.

BEST TEAM: 1954-55 After a 3–4 start, the Buffaloes rolled to their fifth Big Seven title and a third-place national finish by relentlessly feeding the ball inside to seniors Burdette Haldorson (21.0 ppg) and Bob Jeangerard (16.0 ppg). In fact, after that slow start, the only team to hold CU under 60 points was Bill Russell-led San Francisco in the Buffaloes' 62-50 Final Four loss.

BEST PLAYER: C BURDETTE HALDORSON (1951-55) At Colorado, Big Burd dropped in lefty hooks at will against even the toughest opponents. And he was *right*-handed. After bypassing the NBA to maintain his amateur status, Haldorson won two Olympic gold medals with Team USA, then led his AAU team to three outright National Industrial Basketball League titles before retiring.

BEST COACH: FORREST B. "FROSTY" COX (1935-42, '44-50) Cox coached one All-America after another, and they all had one thing in common: They played hard-nosed defense. Between 1936-37 and '41-42, his Buffaloes won four shared or outright titles in the Big Seven and Mountain States conferences. World War II forced the cancellation of the 1942-43 and '43-44 seasons, and Colorado wasn't nearly as strong in the years that followed, but Cox still owns the highest career winning percentage (.623) of any Buffaloes coach with more than one season at the helm.

GAME FOR THE AGES: In 2002-03, the Buffaloes beat four ranked opponents. But their most rousing win was nearly an upset loss in the opening round of the Big 12 tournament. With his team holding the ball and a 76-74 lead in the final seconds, Kansas State forward Pervis Pasco celebrated too early and was called for traveling. That gave Colorado one last shot with 1.8 seconds left. Just enough time for James "Mookie" Wright to nail a 19'9" trey.

HEARTBREAKER: Winning the 1940 NIT was priceless, but the Buffaloes' shining accomplishment lost some of its luster at the 1940 NCAA Tournament a week later. In the West Regional semifinals, Southern California took the air out of the ball and slowed down second-team All-America Jack Harvey and the fast-breaking Buffaloes (who shot a dismal 16% from the field), coming away with a 38-32 victory.

FIERCEST RIVAL: More than a century old, the series between Colorado and Colorado State has rarely lacked for drama—from 1914, when the Buffaloes edged the Rams, 26-23, during the infancy of the Rocky Mountain Conference, to Colorado State's 64-56 victory in the 1969 NCAA Tournament Mideast Regional semifinal and its 86-76 win in the second round of the 1999 NIT. Colorado leads overall, 87–33.

Big Burd dropped in lefty hooks at will—and he was right-handed.

FANFARE AND HOOPLA: Arapahoes, Big Horns, Bison, Buffs, Golden Avalanche, Golden Buffaloes, Frontiersman, Grizzlies, Hornets, Silver and Gold, Silver Helmets, Stampeding Herd, Thundering Herd, Yellow Jackets. At one time or another, Colorado has gone by all those nicknames—most of them informal. Since 1934, they've officially been the Buffaloes.

FAN FAVORITE: G CHAUNCEY BILLUPS (1995-97) The 6'3" Billups left CU after his sophomore season to join the NBA, where his clutch play for the Detroit Pistons and later the Denver Nuggets earned him the nickname Mr. Big Shot. But his impact is still being felt at Colorado through Chauncey's Kids Roundup, a program Billups funds that brings thousands of children to Buffaloes games each season.

FIRST-ROUND PRO PICKS

1971	**Cliff Meely,** San Diego (7)
1971	**Cliff Meely,** Denver (ABA)
1974	**Scott Wedman,** KC-Omaha (6)
1974	**Scott Wedman,** Memphis (ABA, 2)
1984	**Jay Humphries,** Phoenix (13)
1991	**Shaun Vandiver,** Golden State (25)
1997	**Chauncey Billups,** Boston (3)
2004	**David Harrison,** Indiana (29)

PROFILE

University of Colorado, Boulder, CO
Founded: 1876
Enrollment: 29,624 (24,473 undergraduate)
Colors: Silver, black and gold
Nickname: Buffaloes
Current arena: Coors Events/Conference Center, opened in 1979 (11,064)
Previous: Balch Fieldhouse, 1937-79 (4,000)
First game: Jan. 10, 1902
All-time record: 1,113-1,074 (.509)
Total weeks in AP Top 20/25: 31

Current conference: Big 12 (1996-)
Conference titles:
Rocky Mountain: 1 (1929 [tie])
Big Seven: 5 (1938 [tie], '39, '40, '54 [tie], '55)
Mountain States: 1 (1942)
Big Eight: 3 (1962, '63 [tie], '69)
Conference tournament titles: 0
NCAA Tournament appearances: 10
Final Fours: 2
NIT appearances: 8
Semifinals: 3
Titles: 1 (1940)

TOP 5

G	**Chauncey Billups** (1995-97)
G	**Jay Humphries** (1980-84)
F	**Cliff Meely** (1968-71)
F/C	**Jack Harvey** (1937-40)
C	**Burdette Haldorson** (1951-55)

RECORDS	GAME		SEASON		CAREER	
POINTS	47	Cliff Meely, vs. Oklahoma (Feb. 13, 1971)	729	Cliff Meely (1970-71)	2,001	Richard Roby (2004-08)
POINTS PER GAME			28.0	Cliff Meely (1970-71)	24.3	Cliff Meely (1968-71)
REBOUNDS	31	Burdette Haldorson, vs. Oklahoma (Dec. 29, 1952)	346	Burdette Haldorson (1954-55)	1,054	Stephane Pelle (1999-2003)
ASSISTS	15	Jose Winston, vs. Coppin State (Jan. 2, 2001)	194	Jose Winston (2000-01)	562	Jay Humphries (1980-84)

SEASON REVIEW

SEASON	W-L	CONF.	SCORING	COACH	RECORD	SEASON	W-L	CONF.	SCORING	COACH	RECORD
1902-17	*78-54*		*Only two losing seasons, 1902-03 (2-4) and 1914-15 (4-6)*			**1927-28**	5-7	5-7		Howard Beresford	
1917-18	9-2			Melbourne C. Evans	9-2 .818	**1928-29**	10-2	10-2		Howard Beresford	
1918-19	8-1			Joe Mills		**1929-30**	11-6	11-3		Howard Beresford	
1919-20	6-4			Joe Mills		**1930-31**	8-7	8-4		Howard Beresford	
1920-21	8-0			Joe Mills		**1931-32**	10-7	9-5		Howard Beresford	
1921-22	3-5			Joe Mills		**1932-33**	8-8	7-7		Howard Beresford	76-52 .594
1922-23	1-7	1-5		Joe Mills		**1933-34**	9-8	7-5		Hank Iba	9-8 .529
1923-24	4-7			Joe Mills	30-24 .556	**1934-35**	3-9	3-9		Earl Clark	3-9 .250
1924-25	9-5	7-4		Howard Beresford		**1935-36**	6-8	6-8		Forrest B. "Frosty" Cox	
1925-26	8-5	7-5		Howard Beresford		**1936-37**	10-5	10-2		Forrest B. "Frosty" Cox	
1926-27	7-5	7-5		Howard Beresford		**1937-38**	15-6	10-2	NIT RUNNER-UP	Forrest B. "Frosty" Cox	

SEAS.	W-L	CONF.	POSTSEASON	SCORING		REBOUNDS		ASSISTS		COACH	RECORD	
1938-39	14-4	10-2								Forrest B. "Frosty" Cox		
1939-40	17-4	11-1	NCAA REG. SEMIS, NIT CHAMP							Forrest B. "Frosty" Cox		
1940-41	10-6	7-5								Forrest B. "Frosty" Cox		
1941-42	16-2	11-1	NCAA REGIONAL FINALS							Forrest B. "Frosty" Cox		
1942-43	no team											
1943-44	no team											
1944-45	13-3	9-1								Forrest B. "Frosty" Cox		
1945-46	12-6	9-3	NCAA NATIONAL SEMIFINALS							Forrest B. "Frosty" Cox		
1946-47	7-11	5-7								Forrest B. "Frosty" Cox		
1947-48	7-14	4-8								Forrest B. "Frosty" Cox		
1948-49	6-12	4-8								Forrest B. "Frosty" Cox		
1949-50	14-8	6-6								Forrest B. "Frosty" Cox	147-89	.623
1950-51	4-20	2-10								H.B. Lee		
1951-52	8-16	4-8								H.B. Lee		
1952-53	10-11	3-9		Art Bunte	19.1	Art Bunte	8.5			H.B. Lee		
1953-54	11-11	10-2	NCAA REGIONAL SEMIFINALS	Burdette Haldorson	16.7	Burdette Haldorson	9.0			H.B. Lee		
1954-55	19-6	11-1	NCAA THIRD PLACE	Burdette Haldorson	21.0	Burdette Haldorson	13.8			H.B. Lee		
1955-56	11-10	7-5		Jim Ranglos	14.8	George Hannah	9.9			H.B. Lee	63-74	.460
1956-57	14-9	5-7		Dave Mowbray	11.9	Leo Hayward	6.3			Russell "Sox" Walseth		
1957-58	8-15	3-9		Gerry Schroeder	13.2	Don Walker	6.6			Russell "Sox" Walseth		
1958-59	14-10	8-6		Gerry Schroeder	13.4	Don Walker	8.5			Russell "Sox" Walseth		
1959-60	13-11	9-7		Wilky Gilmore	13.9	Wilky Gilmore	10.6			Russell "Sox" Walseth		
1960-61	15-10 ⊗	7-7		Roger Voss	17.6	Roger Voss	10.1			Russell "Sox" Walseth		
1961-62	19-7	13-1	NCAA REGIONAL FINALS	Ken Charlton	19.9	Ken Charlton	9.5			Russell "Sox" Walseth		
1962-63	19-7	11-3	NCAA REGIONAL FINALS	Ken Charlton	19.8	Jim Davis	12.7			Russell "Sox" Walseth		
1963-64	15-10	9-5		Jim Davis	18.5	Jim Davis	12.7			Russell "Sox" Walseth		
1964-65	13-12	8-6		Pat Frink	15.0	Chuck Gardner	8.1			Russell "Sox" Walseth		
1965-66	12-13	6-8		Chuck Gardner	20.2	Chuck Gardner	9.8			Russell "Sox" Walseth		
1966-67	17-8	10-4		Pat Frink	18.3	Bob Bauers	7.4			Russell "Sox" Walseth		
1967-68	9-16	3-11		Pat Frink	18.9	Mike Rebich	6.1			Russell "Sox" Walseth		
1968-69	21-7	10-4	NCAA REGIONAL SEMIFINALS	Cliff Meely	23.9	Cliff Meely	12.0			Russell "Sox" Walseth		
1969-70	14-12	7-7		Cliff Meely	20.9	Cliff Meely	12.8			Russell "Sox" Walseth		
1970-71	14-12	6-8		Cliff Meely	28.0	Cliff Meely	11.6			Russell "Sox" Walseth		
1971-72	7-19	4-10		Jim Creighton	17.5	Jim Creighton	10.2			Russell "Sox" Walseth		
1972-73	13-13	9-5		Scott Wedman	17.7	Scott Wedman	9.3			Russell "Sox" Walseth		
1973-74	9-17	4-10		Scott Wedman	20.0	Scott Wedman	9.3			Russell "Sox" Walseth		
1974-75	7-19	4-10		Tony Lawrence	15.7	Ron Wrigley	7.2			Russell "Sox" Walseth		
1975-76	7-19	4-10		Emmett Lewis	15.0	Larry Vaculik	7.2			Russell "Sox" Walseth	260-246	.514
1976-77	11-16	5-9		Emmett Lewis	19.6	Larry Vaculik	6.6	Toney Ellis	5.1	Bill Blair		
1977-78	9-18	3-11		Larry Vaculik	12.0	Larry Vaculik	6.9	Toney Ellis	3.2	Bill Blair		
1978-79	14-13	4-10		Emmett Lewis	16.9	Brian Johnson	7.1	Toney Ellis	2.6	Bill Blair		
1979-80	17-10	7-7		Jo Jo Hunter	14.9	Brian Johnson	7.0	Toney Ellis	4.2	Bill Blair		
1980-81	16-12	5-9		Jo Jo Hunter	19.1	Joe Cooper	7.1	Jay Humphries	3.5	Bill Blair	67-69	.493
1981-82	11-16	3-11		Jacques Tuz	13.9	Jacques Tuz	7.5	Jay Humphries	4.3	Tom Apke		
1982-83	13-15	3-11		Jay Humphries	14.3	Vince Kelley	9.1	Jay Humphries	6.2	Tom Apke		
1983-84	16-13	6-8		Jay Humphries	15.4	Alex Stivrins	9.2	Jay Humphries	6.0	Tom Apke		
1984-85	11-17	5-9		Randy Downs	16.4	Alex Stivrins	11.7	Mike Reid	5.6	Tom Apke		
1985-86	8-20	0-14		Matt Bullard	12.7	M. Bullard, R. Downs	6.4	Mike Reid	6.0	Tom Apke	59-81	.421
1986-87	9-19	3-11		Matt Bullard	16.6	Matt Bullard	9.3	Kenny Countryman	2.6	Tom Miller		
1987-88	7-21	3-11		Scott Wilke	21.5	Scott Wilke	8.4	Steve Wise	2.8	Tom Miller		
1988-89	7-21	2-12		Shaun Vandiver	18.2	Shaun Vandiver	10.5	Reggie Morton	3.6	Tom Miller		
1989-90	12-18	2-12		Shaun Vandiver	22.3	Shaun Vandiver	11.2	Reggie Morton	4.8	Tom Miller	35-79	.307
1990-91	19-14	5-9	NIT THIRD PLACE	Shaun Vandiver	21.2	Shaun Vandiver	10.0	Billy Law	5.2	Joe Harrington		
1991-92	13-15	4-10		Donnie Boyce	14.9	Poncho Hodges	6.1	Billy Law	5.4	Joe Harrington		
1992-93	10-17	2-12		Donnie Boyce	19.1	Poncho Hodges	7.5	Donnie Boyce	3.6	Joe Harrington		
1993-94	10-17	2-12		Donnie Boyce	22.4	Mark Dean	9.5	Donnie Boyce	4.5	Joe Harrington		
1994-95	15-13	5-9	NIT FIRST ROUND	Donnie Boyce	18.5	Donnie Boyce	6.5	Donnie Boyce	4.1	Joe Harrington		
1995-96	9-18	3-11		Chauncey Billups	17.9	Martice Moore	7.6	Chauncey Billups	5.5	Joe Harrington[a]	72-85	.459
1996-97	22-10	11-5	NCAA SECOND ROUND	Chauncey Billups	19.1	Fred Edmonds	6.4	Chauncey Billups	4.8	Ricardo Patton		
1997-98	13-14	7-9		Kenny Price	14.5	Charlie Melvin	7.6	Howard Frier	3.8	Ricardo Patton		
1998-99	18-15	7-9	NIT SECOND ROUND	Kenny Price	14.6	Carlton Carter	4.4	Jaquay Walls	3.9	Ricardo Patton		
1999-2000	18-14	7-9	NIT FIRST ROUND	Jaquay Walls	17.0	Jamahl Mosley	7.1	Jaquay Walls	4.5	Ricardo Patton		
2000-01	15-15	5-11		D.J. Harrison	15.2	Jamahl Mosley	7.5	Jose Winston	6.5	Ricardo Patton		
2001-02	15-14	5-11		David Harrison	13.9	Stephane Pelle	10.8	James Wright	4.9	Ricardo Patton		
2002-03	20-12	9-7	NCAA FIRST ROUND	Michel Morandais	16.9	Stephane Pelle	9.3	Michel Morandais	3.4	Ricardo Patton		
2003-04	18-11	10-6	NIT FIRST ROUND	David Harrison	17.1	David Harrison	8.8	Michel Morandais	3.1	Ricardo Patton		
2004-05	14-16	4-12		Richard Roby	16.0	Chris Copeland	5.6	Marcus Hall	4.4	Ricardo Patton		
2005-06	20-10	9-7	NIT FIRST ROUND	Richard Roby	17.0	Richard Roby	5.5	Marcus Hall	4.1	Ricardo Patton		
2006-07	7-20	3-13		Richard Roby	17.3	Dominique Coleman	6.9	Dominique Coleman	3.4	Ricardo Patton	184-160	.535
2007-08	12-20	3-13		Richard Roby	17.0	Richard Roby	6.7	Marcus Hall	4.0	Jeff Bzdelik		
2008-09	9-22	1-15		Cory Higgins	17.4	Cory Higgins	5.4	Nate Tomlinson	3.0	Jeff Bzdelik	21-42	.333

[a] Joe Harrington (5-9) and Ricardo Patton (4-9) both coached during the 1995-96 season.

⊗ Records don't reflect games forfeited or vacated. For adjusted records, see p. 521.

ESPN 102 SAGARIN

COLORADO STATE

If you're talking about CSU basketball, you're talking first about Jim Williams. The coach recruited and developed All-America Bill Green, engineered the triumphant win over rival Colorado in the 1969 NCAA Tournament, and took the Rams to three other Big Dances. But Williams isn't all you're talking about—not with four other Tourney bids and 2007 NBA first-rounder Jason Smith demanding your attention.

BEST TEAM: 1968-69 For the Rams, it doesn't get any sweeter than beating the Buffaloes in the NCAA Tournament. With their 64-56 Midwest Regional semifinal upset, the Rams advanced to their first and only Elite Eight, where they fell to Drake, 84-77. Many of the key players that season—including twins Lloyd and Floyd Kerr, Cliff Shegogg and Mike Davis—were honored during halftime of a 2004 home game.

BEST PLAYER: C Bill Green (1960-63) He quit the Celtics before his rookie season in 1963 because he was afraid of flying. Really. Too bad, because the first first-round draft pick in Colorado State hoops history clearly belonged on the big stage. He owns five of the top nine highest-scoring games in Rams history and was third nationally in scoring in 1963 (28.2 ppg)—ahead of Bill Bradley, among others.

BEST COACH: Jim Williams (1954-80) "Fiery" doesn't even begin to describe a coach who once received *seven* technical fouls in a game against Tulsa. (Although the school isn't sure which season this happened, it was before two technicals in a game resulted in a mandatory ejection). But JJ was beloved by his players for his dedication to making them better and for his strategical savvy. His Rams twice upset John Wooden-coached UCLA teams, one of them Walt Hazzard's Final Four-bound Bruins in 1961-62.

GAME FOR THE AGES: Colorado State and Colorado hadn't met on the hardwood for a decade before their NCAA Midwest Regional semifinal in 1969. For the Rams, it was well worth the wait. Williams orchestrated a balanced attack in the 64-56 upset of the No. 18-ranked Buffaloes, with four CSU players scoring in double digits: Shegogg (20), Davis (10), Floyd Kerr (14) and Lloyd Kerr (12).

HEARTBREAKER: In the first round of the 1965 NCAA Tournament, Colorado State trailed Abe Lemons' Oklahoma City Chiefs most of the game before Sonny Bustion (30 points, 20 rebounds) rallied the Rams to a 68-68 tie with :51 on the clock. When it got down to :01, the Chiefs scored to win, 70-68.

FIERCEST RIVAL: In a Border War that started in 1911, CSU and Mountain West rival Wyoming have squared off 210 times. Five of the Rams' largest home crowds have been for Cowboys games, and the teams have met three times in the MWC playoffs since 2000. The Rams have won twice, most recently a 68-63 victory in 2008.

"Fiery" doesn't even begin to describe a coach who once received seven technical fouls in a game.

FANFARE AND HOOPLA: The whale-shaped Moby Arena has been CSU's home since 1966, and the Rams have had four seasons in which they lost just once there (1968-69, '77-78, '89-90, '98-99). In 1976, Moby Arena and the CSU campus served as the setting for the basketball movie *One on One*, starring Robby Benson.

FAN FAVORITE: G Lonnie Wright (1963-66) A three-time season scoring leader, Wright in 1967 went on to be the first athlete to compete *simultaneously* in pro football and pro hoops. (He played safety for the Denver Broncos and guard for the ABA's Denver Rockets.)

PROFILE

Colorado State University, Fort Collins, CO
Founded: 1870
Enrollment: 24,484 (20,829 undergraduate)
Colors: Green and gold
Nickname: Rams
Current arena: Moby Arena, opened in 1966 (8,745)
First game: 1902
All-time record: 1,074-1,129 (.488)
Total weeks in AP Top 20/25: 4

Current conference: Mountain West (1999-)
Conference titles:
Skyline Eight: 2 (1954, '61 [tie])
WAC: 2 (1989, '90 [tie])
Conference tournament titles:
Mountain West: 1 (2003)
NCAA Tournament appearances: 8
NIT appearances: 6
Semifinals: 1

FIRST-ROUND PRO PICKS

1963	**Bill Green,** Boston (9)
1971	**Rick Fisher,** Utah (ABA)
2007	**Jason Smith,** Miami (20)

TOP 5

G	**Milt Palacio** (1996-99)
G	**Lonnie Wright** (1963-66)
F	**Pat Durham** (1985-89)
F	**Jason Smith** (2004-07)
C	**Bill Green** (1960-63)

RECORDS	GAME		SEASON		CAREER	
POINTS	48	Bill Green, vs. Denver (Feb. 9, 1963)	676	Pat Durham (1987-88)	1,980	Pat Durham (1985-89)
POINTS PER GAME			28.2	Bill Green (1962-63)	22.1	Bill Green (1960-63)
REBOUNDS	26	Mike Childress, vs. Rice (Dec. 10, 1970); vs. San Jose State (Dec. 22, 1969)	392	Mike Childress (1969-70)	851	Pat Durham (1985-89)
ASSISTS	12	Ryan Yoder, vs. Fort Lewis (Dec. 30, 1993); Rudy Carey, vs. Wisconsin-Milwaukee (Feb. 11, 1974)	204	Ryan Yoder (1992-93)	529	Ryan Yoder (1990-94)

THE SCHOOLS

SEASON REVIEW

SEASON	W-L	CONF.	SCORING	COACH	RECORD	
1901-16	*45-37*		*First coach of record was Claude Rothgeb (10-10 in four seasons)*			
1916-17	8-5			Harry Hughes		
1917-18	5-5			Harry Hughes		
1918-19	1-13			Harry Hughes		
1919-20	5-5			Harry Hughes		
1920-21	4-7			Harry Hughes		
1921-22	4-7			Harry Hughes		
1922-23	0-1			Harry Hughes		
1923-24	6-5	6-4		Harry Hughes		
1924-25	2-10	2-9		Harry Hughes	60-79	.432
1925-26	2-11	2-10		P.E. Lavik		

SEASON	W-L	CONF.	SCORING	COACH	RECORD	
1926-27	4-8	4-8		P.E. Lavik		
1927-28	5-7	5-7		P.E. Lavik	11-26	.297
1928-29	6-6	6-6		Joe Ryan		
1929-30	4-10	4-10		Joe Ryan		
1930-31	4-8	4-8		Joe Ryan		
1931-32	4-8	4-8		Joe Ryan		
1932-33	7-5	7-5		Joe Ryan		
1933-34	5-7	5-7		Joe Ryan	30-44	.405
1934-35	6-6	6-6		Saaly Salwachter	6-6	.500
1935-36	3-9	3-9		Sam Campbell		
1936-37	7-6	7-5		Sam Campbell	10-15	.400

SEAS.	W-L	CONF.	POSTSEASON	SCORING		REBOUNDS		ASSISTS		COACH	RECORD	
1937-38	7-9	3-9								John Davis		
1938-39	2-14	2-10								John Davis		
1939-40	6-12	3-9								John Davis		
1940-41	10-9	4-8								John Davis		
1941-42	3-16	1-11								John Davis		
1942-43	7-9	0-4								John Davis		
1943-44	no team											
1944-45	7-11	1-5								John Davis	42-80	.344
1945-46	15-9	6-6								E.D. Taylor		
1946-47	3-18	1-11								E.D. Taylor		
1947-48	6-15	1-9		Don Dobler	13.1					E.D. Taylor		
1948-49	14-21	3-17		Don Dobler	10.8					E.D. Taylor	38-63	.376
1949-50	7-23	2-18		Glen Anderson	12.2					H.B. Lee	7-23	.233
1950-51	13-20	6-14		Bill Gossett	14.2					Bill Strannigan		
1951-52	13-15	3-11		Bob Betz	10.4					Bill Strannigan		
1952-53	12-14	5-9		Dennis Stuehm	11.4					Bill Strannigan		
1953-54	22-7	12-2	NCAA REGIONAL SEMIFINALS	Dennis Stuehm	16.6					Bill Strannigan	60-56	.517
1954-55	11-12	5-9		Hal Kinard	13.3	Dennis Stuehm	9.6			Jim Williams		
1955-56	12-13	7-7		Gary Hibbard	17.0	Gary Hibbard	12.5			Jim Williams		
1956-57	9-16	6-8		Stan Albert	15.2	Richard Gregory	9.2			Jim Williams		
1957-58	14-11	9-5		Chuck Newcomb	13.8	Chuck Newcomb	7.6			Jim Williams		
1958-59	8-14	6-8		Chuck Newcomb	15.6	Larry Hoffner	234			Jim Williams		
1959-60	13-10	10-4		Chuck Newcomb	17.2	Larry Hoffner	236			Jim Williams		
1960-61	17-9	12-2	NIT QUARTERFINALS	Bill Green	17.7	Bill Green	9.9			Jim Williams		
1961-62	18-9	10-4	NIT FIRST ROUND	Bill Green	21.2	Bill Green	9.6			Jim Williams		
1962-63	18-5		NCAA FIRST ROUND	Bill Green	28.2	Bill Green	9.2			Jim Williams		
1963-64	16-9			Lonnie Wright	14.1	Sonny Bustion	7.7			Jim Williams		
1964-65	16-8		NCAA FIRST ROUND	Lonnie Wright	19.7	Sonny Bustion	10.1			Jim Williams		
1965-66	14-8		NCAA FIRST ROUND	Lonnie Wright	20.9	Bob Rule	9.8			Jim Williams		
1966-67	13-10			Bob Rule	14.8	Bob Rule	8.6			Jim Williams		
1967-68	11-13			Lloyd Kerr	14.6	Mike Davis	7.4			Jim Williams		
1968-69	17-7		NCAA REGIONAL FINALS	Cliff Shegogg	16.6	Cliff Shegogg	6.1			Jim Williams		
1969-70	14-9	7-7		Cliff Shegogg	18.9	Mike Childress	17.0			Jim Williams		
1970-71	15-10	7-7		Rick Fisher	18.7	Mike Childress	13.9			Jim Williams		
1971-72	15-9	7-7		George Price	19.4	Travis Lackey	11.1			Jim Williams		
1972-73	13-15	5-9		Gary Rhoades	21.3	Gary Rhoades	7.9			Jim Williams		
1973-74	12-14	5-9		Tim Hall	15.7	Tim Hall	7.1	Rudy Carey	140	Jim Williams		
1974-75	14-12	6-8		Barry Sabas	14.2	Tim Hall	7.3	Fred Anzures	47	Jim Williams		
1975-76	10-16	6-8		Lorenzo Cash	18.7	Lorenzo Cash	6.0	Fred Anzures	114	Jim Williams		
1976-77	13-12	6-8		Alan Cunningham	19.0	Larry Paige	8.7	Fred Anzures	100	Jim Williams		
1977-78	18-9	8-6		Barry Young	20.2	Alan Cunningham	9.1	Alton Brandon	84	Jim Williams		
1978-79	11-16	3-9		Barry Young	17.5	Rudy Watley	6.1	Alton Brandon	110	Jim Williams		
1979-80	10-17	5-9		Barry Young	14.7	Rudy Watley	7.0	Eddie Hughes	77	Jim Williams	352-293	.546
1980-81	3-24	1-15		Eddie Hughes	13.7	Rick Semin	4.8	Kevin Bromley	106	Tony McAndrews		
1981-82	8-19	2-14		Mark Steele	11.7	Mark Steele	6.0	Eddie Hughes	94	Tony McAndrews		
1982-83	11-17	6-10		Mark Steele	13.5	Mark Steele	7.1	Ray Lego	84	Tony McAndrews		
1983-84	16-14	9-7		Rich Strong	13.3	Rich Strong	6.6	Rich Strong	88	Tony McAndrews		
1984-85	18-12	9-7		Rich Strong	13.3	Rich Strong	7.0	Rich Strong	107	Tony McAndrews		
1985-86	11-18	6-10		Rich Strong	16.9	Rich Strong	7.6	David Turcotte	91	Tony McAndrews		
1986-87	13-16	7-9		Pat Durham	18.1	Pat Durham	9.4	Anthony Lee	104	Tony McAndrews	80-120	.400
1987-88	22-13	8-8	NIT THIRD PLACE	Pat Durham	19.3	Pat Durham	6.5	David Turcotte	115	Boyd Grant		
1988-89	23-10	12-4	NCAA SECOND ROUND	Pat Durham	18.5	Pat Durham	7.6	Trent Shippen	97	Boyd Grant		
1989-90	21-9	11-5	NCAA FIRST ROUND	Mike Mitchell	19.5	Mike Mitchell	6.7	Lynn Tryon	109	Boyd Grant		
1990-91	15-14	6-10		Chuckie White	14.5	Chuckie White	6.0	Lynn Tryon	77	Boyd Grant	81-46	.638
1991-92	14-17	8-8		Aaron Atkinson	13.5	Doug Larson	5.7	Ryan Yoder	126	Stew Morrill		
1992-93	17-12	9-9		Keith Bonds	13.4	Doug Larson	5.1	Ryan Yoder	204	Stew Morrill		
1993-94	15-13	8-10		Damon Crawford	16.8	Jeff Shelley	7.9	Ryan Yoder	187	Stew Morrill		
1994-95	17-14	7-11		David Evans	17.1	Kish Lewis	5.7	Bobby Sellers	109	Stew Morrill		
1995-96	18-12	11-7	NIT FIRST ROUND	David Evans	18.9	Matt Barnett	6.5	Bobby Sellers	155	Stew Morrill		
1996-97	20-9	10-6		Bryan Christiansen	15.6	Matt Barnett	7.8	Milt Palacio	147	Stew Morrill		
1997-98	20-9	8-6	NIT FIRST ROUND	Jameel Mahmud	13.7	Matt Barnett	7.6	Milt Palacio	148	Stew Morrill	121-86	.585
1998-99	19-11	7-7	NIT FIRST ROUND	Milt Palacio	18.4	Garrett Patik	5.2	Milt Palacio	4.3	Ritchie McKay		
1999-2000	18-12	8-6		Ceedric Goodwyn	17.8	Garrett Patik	5.6	Aki Palmer	2.6	Ritchie McKay	37-23	.617
2000-01	15-13	6-8		John Sivesind	12.6	Garrett Patik	6.0	Aki Palmer	3.2	Dale Layer		
2001-02	12-18	3-11		Brian Greene	16.2	Brian Greene	7.5	Andy Birley	3.9	Dale Layer		
2002-03	19-14	5-9	NCAA FIRST ROUND	Matt Nelson	17.0	Brian Greene	6.2	Micheal Morris	3.7	Dale Layer		
2003-04	13-16	4-10		Matt Nelson	15.6	Matt Nelson	5.7	Micheal Morris	4.0	Dale Layer		
2004-05	11-17	3-11		Matt Nelson	15.8	Matt Nelson	5.9	Micheal Morris	3.1	Dale Layer		
2005-06	16-15	4-10		Jason Smith	16.2	Jason Smith	7.3	Corey Lewis	4.5	Dale Layer		
2006-07	17-13	6-10		Jason Smith	16.8	Jason Smith	10.1	Corey Lewis	4.5	Dale Layer	103-106	.493
2007-08	7-25	0-16		Marcus Walker	17.1	Ronnie Aguilar	6.1	Willis Gardner	2.9	Tim Miles		
2008-09	9-22	4-12		Marcus Walker	17.1	Andy Ogide	5.8	Jesse Carr	2.5	Tim Miles	16-47	.254

Cumulative totals listed when per game averages not available.

ESPN 192 SAGARIN

COLUMBIA

The Lions haven't won an Ivy League title in more than 40 years. They've finished above .500 just twice since 1982-83. But there have been bright moments, some great players and plenty of fun for Lions fans.

BEST TEAM: 1967-68 With apologies to the 1950-51 team that went undefeated before a first-round NCAA Tournament loss to Illinois, this squad was more accomplished, performing in a much tougher era. Led by F Jim McMillian, the Lions won the annual ECAC Holiday Festival at Madison Square Garden, beat Princeton in a playoff to win the Ivy's NCAA Tournament bid and knocked off La Salle, 83-69, in the first round before falling to Davidson, 61-59, in overtime.

BEST PLAYER: G Chet Forte (1954-57) As a senior, Forte was the national POY—beating out Kansas soph Wilt Chamberlain. With his two-handed set shot, Forte averaged 28.9 ppg (24.8 for his career). After his playing days he became an award-winning director of ABC-TV's *Monday Night Football.*

BEST COACH: Lou Rossini (1950-58) Before the 1950-51 season, Lions coach Gordon Ridings had a heart attack, leaving the team in the hands of his 29-year-old assistant. After Rossini guided the Lions to a 23–1 finish, he stuck around for another seven seasons. He's the last Lions coach to finish with a winning career record.

GAME FOR THE AGES: The 1967-68 Ivy League title was in Columbia's hands until a 68-57 loss to Princeton in the final regular-season game. That set up a one-game playoff between the two schools at St. John's Alumni Hall, where the Lions walloped the Tigers, 92-74, on the strength of McMillian's 37 points.

FIERCEST RIVAL: The way Penn and Princeton have dominated the Ivy League makes them everyone's rivals, but Columbia has an extra ounce of hatred for the Quakers. Penn and Columbia are the two Ivy programs with true urban campuses, and the fact that the Lions haven't come close to replicating the Quakers' success (they've lost 63 of the last 78 meetings) just adds to fans' frustrations.

SEASON REVIEW

SEAS.	W-L	CONF.	COACH
1900-50	*546-325*	*21-3 in 1947-48; NCAA appearance*	
1950-51	23-1	12-0 ●	Lou Rossini
1951-52	12-10	7-5	Lou Rossini
1952-53	17-6	8-4	Lou Rossini
1953-54	11-13	6-8	Lou Rossini
1954-55	17-8	10-4	Lou Rossini
1955-56	15-9	9-5	Lou Rossini
1956-57	18-6	9-5	Lou Rossini
1957-58	6-18	2-12	Lou Rossini
1958-59	3-21	2-12	Archie Oldham
1959-60	9-14	2-12	Archie Oldham
1960-61	8-15	4-10	Archie Oldham
1961-62	3-21	1-13	Jack Rohan
1962-63	10-12	4-9	Jack Rohan
1963-64	11-12	6-8	Jack Rohan
1964-65	7-15	5-9	Jack Rohan
1965-66	18-6	10-4	Jack Rohan
1966-67	11-14	6-8	Jack Rohan
1967-68	23-5	12-2 ●	Jack Rohan
1968-69	20-4	11-3	Jack Rohan
1969-70	20-5	11-3	Jack Rohan
1970-71	15-9	9-5	Jack Rohan
1971-72	4-20	3-11	Jack Rohan
1972-73	7-18	5-9	Jack Rohan
1973-74	5-20	4-10	Jack Rohan
1974-75	4-22	2-12	Tom Penders
1975-76	8-17	6-8	Tom Penders
1976-77	16-10	8-6	Tom Penders

SEAS.	W-L	CONF.	SCORING		COACH	RECORD	
1977-78	15-11	11-3	Ricky Free	14.2	Tom Penders	43-60	.417
1978-79	17-9	10-4	Ricky Free	15.8	Arthur Mahar		
1979-80	10-16	5-9	Kurt Mahoney	12.5	Arthur Mahar		
1980-81	9-17	5-9	Kurt Mahoney	10.6	Arthur Mahar		
1981-82	16-10	9-5	Darren Burnett	13.7	Arthur Mahar		
1982-83	10-16	7-7	Darren Burnett	13.6	Arthur Mahar		
1983-84	8-18	5-9	George Meikle	12.6	Arthur Mahar	70-86	.449
1984-85	13-13	9-5	Tom Gwydir	10.9	Wayne Szoke		
1985-86	12-14	6-8	Tom Gwydir	13.7	Wayne Szoke		
1986-87	12-14	6-8	Sean Couch	21.1	Wayne Szoke	37-41	.474
1987-88	6-20	2-12	Matt Shannon	17.4	Wally Halas		
1988-89	8-18	4-10	Matt Shannon	12.8	Wally Halas		
1989-90	4-22	2-12	Eric Speaker	11.9	Wally Halas	18-60	.231
1990-91	7-19	5-9	Buck Jenkins	18.0	John P. Rohan		
1991-92	10-16	8-6	Buck Jenkins	16.8	John P. Rohan		
1992-93	16-10	10-4	Buck Jenkins	22.2	John P. Rohan		
1993-94	6-20	4-10	Jamal Adams	13.7	John P. Rohan		
1994-95	4-22 ⊘	1-13	Chad Brown	16.0	John P. Rohan	197-248	.443▼
1995-96	7-19	3-11	C.J. Thompkins	14.8	Armond Hill		
1996-97	6-20	1-13	C.J. Thompkins	20.2	Armond Hill		
1997-98	11-15	6-8	Gary Raimondo	14.7	Armond Hill		
1998-99	10-16	5-9	Gary Raimondo	17.2	Armond Hill		
1999-2000	13-14	7-7	Craig Austin	14.2	Armond Hill		
2000-01	12-15	7-7	Craig Austin	18.4	Armond Hill		
2001-02	11-17	4-10	Craig Austin	16.0	Armond Hill		
2002-03	2-25	0-14	Marco McCottry	9.0	Armond Hill	72-141	.338
2003-04	10-17	6-8	Matt Preston	15.3	Joe Jones		
2004-05	12-15	3-11	Matt Preston	13.7	Joe Jones		
2005-06	11-16	4-10	John Baumann	13.7	Joe Jones		
2006-07	16-12	7-7	John Baumann	13.3	Joe Jones		
2007-08	14-15	7-7	John Baumann	16.1	Joe Jones		
2008-09	12-16	7-7	Patrick Foley	10.9	Joe Jones	75-91	.452

⊘ **Records do not reflect games forfeited or vacated. For adjusted records, see p. 521.**
▼ **Coach's record adjusted to reflect games forfeited or vacated: 198-247, .445. For yearly totals, see p. 521.**
● **NCAA Tournament appearance**

PROFILE

Columbia University, New York, NY
Founded: 1754
Enrollment: 25,459 (7,584 undergraduate)
Colors: Columbia blue and white
Nickname: Lions
Current arena: Francis A. Levien Gymnasium, opened in 1974 (2,700)
Previous: University Gym (1,700)
First game: 1900
All-time record: 1,197-1,173 (.505)
Total weeks in AP Top 20/25: 31
Current conference: Ivy League (1901-)
Conference titles:
Ivy: 13 (1904, '05, '11, '12, '14 [tie], '26, '30, '31, '36, '47, '48, '51, '68); NJ-NY7: 1 (1977 [tie])

NCAA Tournament appearances: 3
NIT appearances: 0

CONSENSUS ALL-AMERICAS

1905	**Harry Fisher**, F
1905-07	**Marcus Hurley**, G/F
1907-09	**John Ryan**, C
1909	**Biaggio Gerussi**, G
1909-11	**Ted Kiendl**, F
1911	**A.D. Alexander**, C
1911	**W.M. Lee**, G
1912	**Claus D. Benson**, G
1914	**Dan Meenan**, F
1915	**Charlie Lee**, G/F
1927	**Jack Lorch**, G
1931	**George Gregory**, C
1957	**Chet Forte**, G

FIRST-ROUND PRO PICKS

1948	**Walter Budko**, Baltimore (6)
1953	**Jack Molinas**, Fort Wayne (4)
1970	**Jim McMillian**, LA Lakers (13)

TOP 5

G	**Alton Byrd** (1976-79)
G	**Chet Forte** (1954-57)
G/F	**Buck Jenkins** (1989-93)
F	**Jim McMillian** (1967-70)
C	**Dave Newmark** (1965-68)

RECORDS

RECORDS	GAME		SEASON		CAREER	
POINTS	47	Buck Jenkins, vs. Harvard (Feb. 15, 1991)	694	Chet Forte (1956-57)	1,767	Buck Jenkins (1989-93)
POINTS PER GAME			28.9	Chet Forte (1956-57)	24.8	Chet Forte (1954-57)
REBOUNDS	31	Jack Molinas, vs. Brown (Jan. 29, 1953)	408	Frank Thomas (1954-55)	1,022	Frank Thomas (1953-56)
ASSISTS	18	Tony Chiles, vs. Merchant Marine Academy (Jan. 9, 1988)	210	Alton Byrd (1976-77)	526	Alton Byrd (1976-79)

ESPN 54 SAGARIN

CONNECTICUT

Long a regional power in the old Yankee Conference and throughout New England, UConn stepped up to become one of the elite teams in all of college basketball soon after the arrival in 1986 of coach Jim Calhoun. The Huskies became the dominant force in the Big East in the early 1990s, won their first national title in '99 and maintained superiority through their second championship (2004) and beyond.

BEST TEAM: 1998-99 The Huskies went 34–2 (including 11–0 on the road) to win the school's first NCAA championship, after falling just shy of the Final Four on three occasions in the 1990s. Behind Richard Hamilton (21.5 ppg) and Khalid El-Amin (13.8), Connecticut also won the Big East regular-season and tournament titles for Coach Calhoun.

BEST PLAYER: G Ray Allen (1993-96) The school's first two-time first-team All-America and 1995-96 Big East Player of the Year ranks fourth all-time on the Connecticut scoring list with 1,922 points. As a junior, Allen scored 818, second-most in a season to Donyell Marshall's 855 in 1993-94. That same season, Allen set the UConn mark for field goal attempts (618) and three-pointers made (115). Not only is Allen a nine-time NBA All-Star and a member of the 2008 champion Boston Celtics, he also played Jesus Shuttlesworth in Spike Lee's 1998 film *He Got Game*.

BEST COACH: Jim Calhoun (1986-) Hall-of-Famer Calhoun has won 805 games in 37-plus seasons as a head coach at Northeastern and Connecticut—including more than a third of all the wins in Huskies history. A great recruiter and talent developer, in his more than two decades at UConn, Calhoun has delivered 15 first-round draft picks to the NBA.

GAME FOR THE AGES: In their first NCAA Tournament in more than a decade, Connecticut stunned Clemson in the 1990 Sweet 16 when Tate George took an inbounds pass from Scott Burrell in the final second and buried a near-impossible 15-footer for a 71-70 win.

HEARTBREAKER: In 2006, the 30–3 Huskies found themselves between super-Cinderella George Mason and a date for the Final Four. But even UConn could not derail Mason Madness. The Patriots pushed the game into overtime and prevailed, 86-84.

FIERCEST RIVAL: For the first few decades of a series that began in 1956, the Connecticut-Syracuse rivalry had a decidedly Orange tint. But shortly after Calhoun's arrival, the Huskies began regularly putting the bite on the Orangemen. Since 1990, many of their battles have had a direct impact on the Big East regular-season and/or tournament championship. Their March 12, 2009, Big East tournament quarterfinal was epic: It took nearly four hours, six overtimes and eight players fouling out before Syracuse prevailed, 127-117. Syracuse holds a 48–36 edge in the series.

FANFARE AND HOOPLA: Depending on which story you believe, a Siberian Husky named Jonathan was chosen as UConn's mascot in 1935 because either the winters in Connecticut were as cold as Siberia or a member of the school's board of trustees found a Siberian Husky puppy at a local breeder. Named in honor of the state's Revolutionary War-era governor, Jonathan Trumbull, there have been 12 more Jonathans since that first pup. None was more famous than Jonathan III, chosen in 1947 as one of 50 Huskies to escort Admiral Richard Byrd to Antarctica.

FAN FAVORITE: F Nadav Henefeld (1989-90) This Israeli-born deep threat played just one season in Storrs, but it turned out to be UConn's Dream Season which ended with a run to the Elite Eight. Henefeld is the Huskies' single-season record-holder for steals (138).

CONSENSUS ALL-AMERICA

1994	**Donyell Marshall,** F
1996	**Ray Allen,** G
1999	**Richard Hamilton,** G/F
2004	**Emeka Okafor,** C

FIRST-ROUND PRO PICKS

1947	**Walt Dropo,** Providence (4)
1967	**Wes Bialosuknia,** Oakland (ABA)
1990	**Tate George,** New Jersey (22)
1993	**Scott Burrell,** Charlotte (20)
1994	**Donyell Marshall,** Minnesota (4)
1996	**Ray Allen,** Minnesota (5)
1996	**Travis Knight,** Chicago (29)
1999	**Richard Hamilton,** Washington (7)
2002	**Caron Butler,** Miami (10)
2004	**Emeka Okafor,** Charlotte (2)
2004	**Ben Gordon,** Chicago (3)
2005	**Charlie Villanueva,** Toronto (7)
2006	**Rudy Gay,** Houston (8)
2006	**Hilton Armstrong,** New Orleans (12)
2006	**Marcus Williams,** New Jersey (22)
2006	**Josh Boone,** New Jersey (23)
2009	**Hasheem Thabeet,** Memphis (2)

PROFILE

University of Connecticut, Storrs, CT
Founded: 1881
Enrollment: 28,677 (20,784 undergraduate)
Colors: National flag blue and white
Nickname: Huskies
Current arena: Harry A. Gampel Pavilion, opened in 1990 (10,027)
First game: 1901
All-time record: 1,501-836 (.642)
Total weeks in AP Top 20/25: 278

Current conference: Big East (1979-)
Conference titles:
New England: 1 (1941 [tie])
Yankee: 18 (1948, '49, '51, '52, '53, '54, '55, '56, '57, '58, '59, '60, '63, '64 [tie], '65, '66 [tie], '67, '70 [tie])
Big East: 10 (1990 [tie], '94, '95, '96 [tie], '98 [tie], '99, 2002 [tie], '03 [tie], '05 [tie], '06 [tie])
Conference tournament titles:
Big East: 6 (1990, '96, '98, '99, 2002, '04)
NCAA Tournaments: 29 (1 appearance vacated)
Sweet 16s (since 1975): 13
Final Fours: 3
Titles: 2 (1999, 2004)

NIT appearances: 11
Semifinals: 2
Titles: 1 (1988)

TOP 5

G	**Ray Allen** (1993-96)
G	**Chris Smith** (1988-92)
G/F	**Richard Hamilton** (1996-99)
F	**Walt Dropo** (1942-43, '45-47)
C	**Emeka Okafor** (2001-04)

RECORDS

RECORDS	GAME		SEASON		CAREER	
POINTS	51	Bill Corley, vs. New Hampshire (Jan. 10, 1968)	855	Donyell Marshall (1993-94)	2,145	Chris Smith (1988-92)
POINTS PER GAME			28.0	Wes Bialosuknia (1966-67)	23.6	Wes Bialosuknia (1964-67)
REBOUNDS	40	Art Quimby, vs. Boston University (Jan. 11, 1955)	611	Art Quimby (1954-55)	1,716	Art Quimby (1951-55)
ASSISTS	16	Marcus Williams, vs. Notre Dame (Jan. 30, 2005); vs. Central Connecticut State (Dec. 22, 2004)	253	Taliek Brown (2003-04)	722	Taliek Brown (2000-04)

SEASON REVIEW

SEASON	W-L	CONF.	SCORING	COACH	RECORD
1901-18	*55-59*		*First coach was John F. Donahue in 1915-16; 45-44, .506 with no coach*		
1918-19	1-8			John F. Donahue	11-23 .324
1919-20	7-5			M.R. Schwartz	
1920-21	7-9			M.R. Schwartz	14-14 .500
1921-22	15-4			J.W. Tasker	
1922-23	8-7			J.W. Tasker[a]	15-5 .750
1923-24	4-8			Sumner A. Dole	
1924-25	10-4			Sumner A. Dole	
1925-26	11-3			Sumner A. Dole	
1926-27	9-7			Sumner A. Dole	39-25 .609
1927-28	11-3			Louis A. Alexander	
1928-29	11-6			Louis A. Alexander	
1929-30	8-7			Louis A. Alexander	
1930-31	10-6			Louis A. Alexander[b]	35-19 .648
1931-32	3-11			John J. Heldman Jr.	
1932-33	4-12			J. Wilder Tasker	
1933-34	5-10			J. Wilder Tasker	
1934-35	7-8			John J. Heldman Jr.	
1935-36	3-11			John J. Heldman Jr.[c]	19-42 .311
1936-37	11-7			Don White	
1937-38	13-5	4-4		Don White	
1938-39	12-6	6-2		Don White	

SEAS.	W-L	CONF.	POSTSEASON	SCORING		REBOUNDS		ASSISTS		COACH	RECORD
1939-40	9-7	6-2								Don White	
1940-41	14-2	7-1								Don White	
1941-42	12-5	6-2								Don White	
1942-43	8-7	5-3		Walt Dropo	21.7					Don White	
1943-44	10-9									Don White	
1944-45	5-11									Don White	94-59 .614
1945-46	11-6	4-2		Walt Dropo	21.0					Blair Gullion	
1946-47	16-2	6-1								Blair Gullion[d]	15-8 .652
1947-48	17-6	6-1								Hugh S. Greer	
1948-49	19-6	7-1		Pete Lind	9.7					Hugh S. Greer	
1949-50	17-8	5-2		Vince Yokabaskas	16.7					Hugh S. Greer	
1950-51	22-4	6-1	NCAA FIRST ROUND	Vince Yokabaskas	15.5	William Ebel	9.0			Hugh S. Greer	
1951-52	20-7	6-1		Vince Yokabaskas	16.8	Burr Carlson	14.5			Hugh S. Greer	
1952-53	17-4	5-1		Art Quimby	16.7	Art Quimby	20.5			Hugh S. Greer	
1953-54	23-3	7-0	NCAA FIRST ROUND	Art Quimby	16.3	Art Quimby	22.6			Hugh S. Greer	
1954-55	20-5	7-0	NIT FIRST ROUND	Art Quimby	23.2	Art Quimby	24.4			Hugh S. Greer	
1955-56	17-11	6-1	NCAA REGIONAL SEMIFINALS	Gordon Ruddy	16.6					Hugh S. Greer	
1956-57	17-8	8-0	NCAA FIRST ROUND	Bob Osborne	15.6	Al Cooper	11.8			Hugh S. Greer	
1957-58	17-10	9-1	NCAA FIRST ROUND	Jack Rose	13.0	Al Cooper	11.0			Hugh S. Greer	
1958-59	17-7	8-2	NCAA FIRST ROUND	Jack Rose	16.0	Ed Martin	12.1			Hugh S. Greer	
1959-60	17-9	8-2	NCAA FIRST ROUND	John Pipczynski	15.2	Walt Griffin	11.5			Hugh S. Greer	
1960-61	11-13	6-4		Lenny Carlson	13.5	Bob Haines	8.7			Hugh S. Greer	
1961-62	16-8	7-3		Lenny Carlson	15.1	Ed Slomcenski	9.5			Hugh S. Greer	
1962-63	18-7	9-1	NCAA FIRST ROUND	Toby Kimball	15.1	Toby Kimball	15.6			Hugh S. Greer[e]	286-112 .719
1963-64	16-11	8-2	NCAA REGIONAL FINALS	Toby Kimball	20.1	Toby Kimball	17.3			Fred A. Shabel	
1964-65	23-3	10-0	NCAA FIRST ROUND	Wes Bialosuknia	21.3	Toby Kimball	21.0			Fred A. Shabel	
1965-66	16-8	9-1		Wes Bialosuknia	21.3	Bill Corley	14.0			Fred A. Shabel	
1966-67	17-7	9-1	NCAA FIRST ROUND	Wes Bialosuknia	28.0	Bill Corley	11.9			Fred A. Shabel	72-29 .713
1967-68	11-13	7-3		Bill Corley	21.1	Bill Corley	15.2			Burr Carlson	
1968-69	5-19	3-7		Bob Staak	17.0	Ron Hrubala	10.3			Burr Carlson	16-32 .333
1969-70	14-9	8-2		Bob Boyd	23.4	Ron Hrubala	11.7	Bobby Boyd	5.5	Donald "Dee" Rowe	
1970-71	10-14	5-5		Bob Staak	20.9	Ron Hrubala	10.9	Bobby Boyd	4.5	Donald "Dee" Rowe	
1971-72	8-17	5-5		Gary Custick	18.3	Cal Chapman	8.8	Doug Melody	4.5	Donald "Dee" Rowe	
1972-73	15-10	9-3		Jimmy Foster	15.7	Cal Chapman	9.9	Al Weston	3.7	Donald "Dee" Rowe	
1973-74	19-8	9-3	NIT QUARTERFINALS	Jimmy Foster	16.3	John Thomas	10.4	Jimmy Foster	4.2	Donald "Dee" Rowe	
1974-75	18-10	9-3	NIT FIRST ROUND	Tony Hanson	16.7	John Thomas	10.8	Joe Whelton	3.1	Donald "Dee" Rowe	
1975-76	19-10	7-5	NCAA REGIONAL SEMIFINALS	Tony Hanson	19.1	John Thomas	13.9	Joe Whelton	4.8	Donald "Dee" Rowe	
1976-77	17-10			Tony Hanson	26.0	Tony Hanson	10.5	Randy LaVigne	3.6	Donald "Dee" Rowe	120-88 .577
1977-78	11-15			Joe Whelton	15.3	Jim Abromaitis	8.8	Joe Whelton	4.3	Dominic "Dom" Perno	
1978-79	21-8		NCAA SECOND ROUND	Corny Thompson	18.6	Corny Thompson	10.0	Randy LaVigne	3.9	Dominic "Dom" Perno	
1979-80	20-9	3-3	NIT FIRST ROUND	Mike McKay	16.7	Corny Thompson	9.3	Bobby Dulin	4.3	Dominic "Dom" Perno	
1980-81	20-9	8-6	NIT SECOND ROUND	Corny Thompson	15.0	Corny Thompson	8.1	Karl Hobbs	4.7	Dominic "Dom" Perno	
1981-82	17-11	7-7	NIT FIRST ROUND	Mike McKay	14.3	Corny Thompson	8.3	Karl Hobbs	3.8	Dominic "Dom" Perno	
1982-83	12-16	5-11		Earl Kelley	16.7	Bruce Kuczenski	6.8	Karl Hobbs	4.1	Dominic "Dom" Perno	
1983-84	13-15	5-11		Earl Kelley	14.4	Tim Coles	7.9	Karl Hobbs	6.4	Dominic "Dom" Perno	
1984-85	13-15	6-10		Earl Kelley	16.8	Tim Coles	7.0	Earl Kelley	4.8	Dominic "Dom" Perno	
1985-86	12-16	3-13		Earl Kelley	19.6	Tim Coles	9.3	Earl Kelley	6.4	Dominic "Dom" Perno	139-114 .549
1986-87	9-19	3-13		Cliff Robinson	18.1	Gerry Besselink	10.7	Tate George	6.0	Jim Calhoun	
1987-88	20-14	4-12	NIT CHAMPION	Cliff Robinson	17.6	Cliff Robinson	6.9	Tate George	5.6	Jim Calhoun	
1988-89	18-13	6-10	NIT QUARTERFINALS	Cliff Robinson	20.0	Cliff Robinson	7.4	Tate George	4.9	Jim Calhoun	
1989-90	31-6	12-4	NCAA REGIONAL FINALS	Chris Smith	17.2	Nadav Henefeld	5.6	Tate George	4.8	Jim Calhoun	
1990-91	20-11	9-7	NCAA REGIONAL SEMIFINALS	Chris Smith	21.2	Rod Sellers	8.0	Chris Smith	3.4	Jim Calhoun	
1991-92	20-10	10-8	NCAA SECOND ROUND	Chris Smith	21.2	Rod Sellers	8.7	Chris Smith	3.7	Jim Calhoun	
1992-93	15-13	9-9	NIT FIRST ROUND	Donyell Marshall	17.0	Donyell Marshall	7.8	Kevin Ollie	5.6	Jim Calhoun	
1993-94	29-5	16-2	NCAA REGIONAL SEMIFINALS	Donyell Marshall	25.1	Donyell Marshall	8.9	Kevin Ollie	6.2	Jim Calhoun	
1994-95	28-5	16-2	NCAA REGIONAL FINALS	Ray Allen	21.1	Travis Knight	8.2	Kevin Ollie	6.4	Jim Calhoun	
1995-96	32-3	⊗ 17-1	NCAA REGIONAL SEMIFINALS	Ray Allen	23.4	Travis Knight	9.3	Doron Sheffer	6.1	Jim Calhoun	
1996-97	18-15	7-11	NIT THIRD PLACE	Richard Hamilton	15.9	Kevin Freeman	6.4	Ricky Moore	5.4	Jim Calhoun	
1997-98	32-5	15-3	NCAA REGIONAL FINALS	Richard Hamilton	21.5	Jake Voskuhl	7.1	Khalid El-Amin	4.2	Jim Calhoun	
1998-99	**34-2**	**16-2**	**NATIONAL CHAMPION**	**Richard Hamilton**	**21.5**	**Kevin Freeman**	**7.3**	**Khalid El-Amin**	**3.9**	**Jim Calhoun**	
1999-2000	25-10	10-6	NCAA SECOND ROUND	Khalid El-Amin	16.0	Jake Voskuhl	6.4	Khalid El-Amin	5.2	Jim Calhoun	
2000-01	20-12	8-8	NIT SECOND ROUND	Caron Butler	15.3	Caron Butler	7.6	Taliek Brown	4.9	Jim Calhoun	
2001-02	27-7	13-3	NCAA REGIONAL FINALS	Caron Butler	20.3	Emeka Okafor	9.0	Taliek Brown	5.1	Jim Calhoun	
2002-03	23-10	10-6	NCAA REGIONAL SEMIFINALS	Ben Gordon	19.5	Emeka Okafor	11.2	Ben Gordon	4.7	Jim Calhoun	
2003-04	**33-6**	**12-4**	**NATIONAL CHAMPION**	**Ben Gordon**	**18.5**	**Emeka Okafor**	**11.5**	**Taliek Brown**	**6.5**	**Jim Calhoun**	
2004-05	23-8	13-3	NCAA SECOND ROUND	Charlie Villanueva	13.6	Josh Boone	8.4	Marcus Williams	7.8	Jim Calhoun	
2005-06	30-4	14-2	NCAA REGIONAL FINALS	Rudy Gay	15.2	Josh Boone	7.0	Marcus Williams	8.6	Jim Calhoun	
2006-07	17-14	6-10		Jerome Dyson	13.8	Jeff Adrien	9.7	A.J. Price	3.6	Jim Calhoun	
2007-08	24-9	13-5	NCAA FIRST ROUND	Jeff Adrien	14.8	Jeff Adrien	9.1	A.J. Price	5.8	Jim Calhoun	
2008-09	31-5	15-3	NCAA NATIONAL SEMIFINALS	A.J. Price	14.7	Hasheem Thabeet	10.8	A.J. Price	4.7	Jim Calhoun	559-206 .731▼

[a] J.W. Tasker (0-1) and Roy Guyer (8-6) both coached during the 1922-23 season. [b] Louis A. Alexander (5-3) and Sumner Dole (5-3) both coached during the 1930-31 season.
[c] John J. Heldman Jr. (0-1) and J.O. Christian (3-10) both coached during the 1935-36 season. [d] Blair Guillon (4-2) and Hugh S. Greer (12-0) both coached during the 1946-47 season.
[e] Hugh S. Greer (7-3) and George Wigton (11-4) both coached during the 1962-63 season.
⊗ Records don't reflect games forfeited or vacated. For adjusted records, see p. 521.
▼ Coach's record adjusted to reflect games forfeited or vacated: 557-205, .731. For yearly totals, see p. 521.

ESPN 302 SAGARIN

Coppin State

If you're a small-conference team, what can top knocking off the regular-season SEC champ in the NCAA Tournament, as the Eagles did in 1997? Well, you can make the Big Dance after starting the year 4–19, as Ron "Fang" Mitchell's crew did in 2008. No wonder so many big-time coaches name the Eagles as one of the underdogs they most fear to face.

BEST TEAM: 1975-76 Coach John Bates' team won 30 straight to end the season as NAIA national champs. Star big man Joe Pace scored 43 in the 96-91 title-game victory over Henderson State.

BEST PLAYER: C Joe Pace (1974-76) See if you can spot a pattern: Pace played on the 1973 NAIA runner-up at Maryland-Eastern Shore before transferring to CSU after the 1973-74 season. He averaged 22.3 ppg and 18.6 rpg in two seasons at Coppin State, where he led the Eagles to their 1976 title. Then, in 1978, Pace won a championship with the NBA's Washington Bullets. One word: winner.

BEST COACH: Ron "Fang" Mitchell (1986-) He didn't get his nickname by being cuddly. But Mitchell, a six-time MEAC Coach of the Year, usually brings out the best in his teams. Credit both his X's and O's acumen and the fact that his out-of-conference schedules routinely rank among the nation's toughest.

GAME FOR THE AGES: Vegas oddsmakers had Coppin State as a 30-point underdog in its first-round matchup with No. 2-seed South Carolina in the 1997 Tournament. But the Eagles crashed the boards and attacked the rim with abandon, taking a 55-54 lead with 6:12 left. The stunned Gamecocks crumbled and Coppin State coasted to a 78-65 win.

FIERCEST RIVAL: Coppin State is located on Baltimore's west side, while Morgan State is on the east. Which is why you can forget about the lopsidedness of the Eagles' 49–18 series lead; when these two teams meet, it's always a dogfight for city pride. Witness the Eagles' 62-60 MEAC tourney title victory over the Bears in 2008, after having been swept by them in the regular season.

SEASON REVIEW

SEAS.	W-L	CONF.		SCORING		COACH	RECORD	
1964-65	1-13					Cyril Byron	1-13	.071
1965-66	4-12					Joseph Jones		
1966-67	9-7					Joseph Jones		
1967-68	12-7					Joseph Jones		
1968-69	7-12					Joseph Jones		
1969-70	12-11					Joseph Jones	44-49	.473
1970-71	14-6					Charles Hardnett		
1971-72	15-8					Charles Hardnett		
1972-73	16-13					Charles Hardnett		
1973-74	14-12					Charles Hardnett	59-39	.602
1974-75	19-7					John Bates		
1975-76	39-2		◆	Tony Carter	894	John Bates		
1976-77	32-2					John Bates		
1977-78	14-6					John Bates		
1978-79	19-5					John Bates		
1979-80	10-17					John Bates		
1980-81	18-7			Milton Young	388	John Bates		
1981-82	10-15			Leroy Choice	526	John Bates		
1982-83	15-12			Kevin Bribson	424	John Bates		
1983-84	13-16			Jeff Churchwell	538	John Bates		
1984-85	10-15			Keith Mercer	320	John Bates		
1985-86	10-17	7-7		Earl Lee	388	John Bates	209-121	.633
1986-87	8-19	7-6		Steve Miller	433	Ron "Fang" Mitchell		
1987-88	13-14	8-7		Phil Booth	521	Ron "Fang" Mitchell		
1988-89	18-11	11-5		Reggie Isaac	527	Ron "Fang" Mitchell		
1989-90	26-7	15-1	●	Reggie Isaac	699	Ron "Fang" Mitchell		
1990-91	19-11	14-2	■	Larry Stewart	23.9	Ron "Fang" Mitchell		
1991-92	15-13	9-7		Tariq Saunders	466	Ron "Fang" Mitchell		
1992-93	22-8	16-0	●	Stephen Stewart	400	Ron "Fang" Mitchell		
1993-94	22-8	16-0		Stephen Stewart	546	Ron "Fang" Mitchell		
1994-95	21-10	15-1	■	Sidney Goodman	459	Ron "Fang" Mitchell		
1995-96	19-10	14-2		Terquin Mott	532	Ron "Fang" Mitchell		
1996-97	22-9	15-3	●	Antoine Brockington	510	Ron "Fang" Mitchell		
1997-98	21-8	17-1		Antoine Brockington	590	Ron "Fang" Mitchell		
1998-99	15-14	14-4		Fred Warrick	20.9	Ron "Fang" Mitchell		
1999-2000	15-15	13-5		Jorge Cajigas	14.7	Ron "Fang" Mitchell		
2000-01	13-15	11-8		Joe Brown	18.4	Ron "Fang" Mitchell		
2001-02	6-25	3-15		Larry Tucker	16.5	Ron "Fang" Mitchell		
2002-03	11-17	11-7		Larry Tucker	15.3	Ron "Fang" Mitchell		
2003-04	18-14	14-4		Jimmy Boykin	13.9	Ron "Fang" Mitchell		
2004-05	14-15	13-5		Nicholas King	14.1	Ron "Fang" Mitchell		
2005-06	12-18	12-6		Tywain McKee	15.4	Ron "Fang" Mitchell		
2006-07	12-20	9-9		Tywain McKee	17.4	Ron "Fang" Mitchell		
2007-08	16-21	7-9	●	Tywain McKee	16.6	Ron "Fang" Mitchell		
2008-09	13-19	9-7		Tywain McKee	18.4	Ron "Fang" Mitchell	371-321	.536

Cumulative totals listed when per game averages not available.
● NCAA Tournament appearance ■ NIT appearance ◆ NAIA championship

PROFILE

Coppin State University, Baltimore, MD
Founded: 1900 as part of Colored High School; previous names include Fanny Jackson Coppin Normal School and Coppin State College
Enrollment: 3,932 (3,242 undergraduate)
Colors: Royal blue and gold
Nickname: Eagles
Current arena: Coppin Center, opened in 1987 (1,720)
Previous: Baltimore City Community College gym, 1985-87 (2,013); Pullen Gymnasium, 1964-85 (N/A)
First game: Dec. 2, 1964
All-time record: 684-543 (.557)

Total weeks in AP Top 20/25: 0
Current conference: Mid-Eastern Athletic (1985-)
Conference titles:
MEAC: 10 (1990, '91, '93, '94, '95, '96 [tie], '97, '98, '99 [tie], 2004 [tie])
Conference tournament titles:
MEAC: 4 (1990, '93, '97, 2008)
NCAA Tournament appearances: 4
NIT appearances: 2

TOP 5

G **Antoine Brockington** (1995-98)
G **Tywain McKee** (2005-09)
G/F **Reggie Isaac** (1988-91)
F **Larry Stewart** (1988-91)
C **Joe Pace** (1974-76)

RECORDS

RECORDS	GAME		SEASON		CAREER	
POINTS	46	Tony Carter, vs. Bowie State (Feb. 7, 1976)	894	Tony Carter (1975-76)	2,158	Tywain McKee (2005-09)
POINTS PER GAME			23.9	Larry Stewart (1990-91)	22.3	Joe Pace (1974-76)
REBOUNDS	32	Joe Pace, vs. Federal City (Feb. 12, 1976)	670	Joe Pace (1975-76)	1,052	Larry Stewart (1988-91)
ASSISTS	17	Gary Barnes, vs. Rutgers-Camden (Nov. 29, 1975)	398	Gary Barnes (1975-76)	622	Larry Yarbray (1988-92)

ESPN 179 SAGARIN

CORNELL

The westernmost Ivy League school made its NCAA Tourney debut way back in 1954, but in truth, its program has taken a back seat to Penn and Princeton ever since. Cornell is enjoying a renaissance in this, the third century in which the Big Red has played basketball, winning back-to-back conference titles in 2007-08 and '08-09, serving notice that the league might just need to make room for a new power.

BEST TEAM: 2007-08 Ryan Wittman lit it up deep. Jeff Foote—all seven feet of him—took it to 'em down low. And point guard Louis Dale tied the balanced attack together with his expert dishes and leadership. The team set a school record with a 16-game winning streak, including a 14–0 mark in Ivy play, en route to their third NCAA berth. Unfortunately, Stanford handed Cornell a 77-53 reality check in the first round.

BEST PLAYER: G Chuck Rolles (1953-56) The 5'6" Rolles was consistently the most feared man on the court thanks to his quickness, ball handling and pinpoint one-handed set shot. A two-time All-Ivy selection, he led the Big Red to the Ivy title in 1954—the last one the school would win for more than three decades.

BEST COACH: Sam MacNeil (1959-68) A backcourt whiz for the Big Red in the early 1950s, MacNeil forged quick and sharp teams with his no-nonsense, fiery coaching style. He never endured a losing season in his nine years and scored road upsets over Illinois in 1961, Kentucky in '66 and Ohio State in '68.

GAME FOR THE AGES: On Dec. 28, 1966, Cornell trotted out before a sellout crowd of 11,500 at Kentucky's Memorial Coliseum as 25-point underdogs. Leading up to the game, *The Cincinnati Post* even openly wondered why the players would want to subject themselves to certain humiliation. It was a rout all right. Behind Gregg Morris' 37 points, Cornell won, 92-77.

FIERCEST RIVAL: Cornell first played Colgate during the 1901-02 season, winning 39-29. The two central New York schools have played 122 times since, with the Big Red holding a 70–53 overall series lead.

SEASON REVIEW

SEAS.	W-L	CONF.	COACH	SEAS.	W-L	CONF.	COACH
1898-1950	*465-438-2*	*Albert Sharpe, 78-32 in 1912-19*		1963-64	15-10	9-5	Sam MacNeil
1950-51	20-5	10-2	Royner Greene	1964-65	19-5	11-3	Sam MacNeil
1951-52	16-9	8-4	Royner Greene	1965-66	15-9	10-4	Sam MacNeil
1952-53	9-12	6-6	Royner Greene	1966-67	19-5	11-3	Sam MacNeil
1953-54	17-7	12-3 ●	Royner Greene	1967-68	14-11	6-8	Sam MacNeil
1954-55	10-13	8-6	Royner Greene	1968-69	12-13	7-7	Jerry Lace
1955-56	11-13	8-6	Royner Greene	1969-70	7-16	4-10	Jerry Lace
1956-57	4-19	2-12	Royner Greene	1970-71	5-21	1-13	Jerry Lace
1957-58	11-11	5-9	Royner Greene	1971-72	5-19	1-13	Jerry Lace
1958-59	8-15	4-10	Royner Greene	1972-73	4-22	1-13	Tony Coma
1959-60	13-10	8-6	Sam MacNeil	1973-74	3-23	1-13	Tony Coma[a]
1960-61	14-10	7-7	Sam MacNeil	1974-75	7-18	4-10	Ben Bluitt
1961-62	18-7	9-5	Sam MacNeil	1975-76	8-18	4-10	Ben Bluitt
1962-63	12-12	6-7	Sam MacNeil	1976-77	8-18 ✪	5-9	Ben Bluitt

SEAS.	W-L	CONF.	SCORING		COACH	RECORD	
1977-78	9-17	5-9	Mike Davis	21.4	Ben Bluitt		
1978-79	8-18	3-11	Mike Davis	19.0	Ben Bluitt		
1979-80	5-19	3-11	Mike Davis	15.2	Ben Bluitt	46-107	.301▼
1980-81	7-19	4-10	Alex Reynolds	11.9	Tom Miller		
1981-82	10-16	7-7	Mike Lucas	14.7	Tom Miller		
1982-83	10-16	6-8	Ken Bantum	14.5	Tom Miller		
1983-84	16-10	9-5	Ken Bantum	14.2	Tom Miller		
1984-85	14-12	8-6	Ken Bantum	20.0	Tom Miller		
1985-86	14-12	9-5	John Bajusz	18.4	Tom Miller	71-85	.455
1986-87	15-11	9-5	John Bajusz	19.4	Mike Dement		
1987-88	17-10	11-3 ●	Sam Jacobs	15.5	Mike Dement		
1988-89	10-16	7-7	Bernard Jackson	10.3	Mike Dement		
1989-90	12-17	5-9	Shawn Maharaj	12.6	Mike Dement		
1990-91	13-13	6-8	Shawn Maharaj	12.2	Mike Dement	67-67	.500
1991-92	7-19	5-9	Jeff Gaca	14.5	Jan van Breda Kolff		
1992-93	16-10	10-4	Jeff Gaca	15.7	Jan van Breda Kolff	23-29	.442
1993-94	8-18	3-11	Zeke Marshall	14.8	Al Walker		
1994-95	9-17	4-10	Brandt Schuckman	13.0	Al Walker		
1995-96	10-16	5-9	Eddie Samuel	13.4	Al Walker	27-51	.346
1996-97	15-11	7-7	John McCord	18.1	Scott Thompson		
1997-98	9-17	6-8	Ray Mercedes	12.6	Scott Thompson		
1998-99	11-15	6-8	Ray Mercedes	14.2	Scott Thompson		
1999-2000	10-17	3-11	Ray Mercedes	14.8	Scott Thompson	45-60	.429
2000-01	7-20	3-11	Ray Mercedes	13.9	Steve Donahue		
2001-02	5-22	2-12	Wallace Prather	11.4	Steve Donahue		
2002-03	9-18	4-10	Ka'Ron Barnes	14.0	Steve Donahue		
2003-04	11-16	6-8	Ka'Ron Barnes	20.1	Steve Donahue		
2004-05	13-14	8-6	Lenny Collins	13.3	Steve Donahue		
2005-06	13-15	8-6	Adam Gore	12.9	Steve Donahue		
2006-07	16-12	9-5	Ryan Wittman	15.6	Steve Donahue		
2007-08	22-6	14-0 ●	Ryan Wittman	15.4	Steve Donahue		
2008-09	21-10	11-3 ●	Ryan Wittman	18.5	Steve Donahue	117-133	.468

[a] Tony Coma (3-14) and Tom Allen (0-9) both coached during the 1973-74 season.

✪ Records don't reflect games forfeited or vacated. For adjusted records, see p. 521.

▼ Coach's record adjusted to reflect games forfeited or vacated; 47-106, .307. For yearly totals see p. 521.

● NCAA Tournament appearance

PROFILE

Cornell University, Ithaca, NY
Founded: 1865
Enrollment: 20,273 (13,486 undergraduate)
Colors: Carnelian and white
Nickname: Big Red
Current arena: Newman Arena, opened in 1990 (4,473)
Previous: Barton Hall, 1915-90 (5,500)
First game: Dec. 13, 1898
All-time record: 1,141-1,268-2 (.474)
Total weeks in AP Top 20/25: 3
Current conference: Ivy League (1901-)

Conference titles:
Ivy: 7 (1913, '14 [tie], '24, '54, '88, 2008, '09)
NCAA Tournament appearances: 4
NIT appearances: 0

CONSENSUS ALL-AMERICAS

1913, '14 **Gil Halstead,** G
1914 **Walter Lunden,** F
1915 **Leslie Brown,** F
1923 **John Luther,** C

FIRST-ROUND PRO PICKS

1948 **Bob Gale,** St. Louis (7)

TOP 5

G **John Bajusz** (1983-87)
G **Chuck Rolles** (1953-56)
G **Gregg Morris** (1965-68)
F **George Farley** (1957-60)
C **Ken Bantum** (1981-85)

RECORDS

RECORDS	GAME		SEASON		CAREER	
POINTS	47	George Farley, vs. Princeton (March 5, 1960)	572	Ryan Wittman (2008-09)	1,663	John Bajusz (1983-87)
POINTS PER GAME			23.0	Chuck Rolles (1955-56)	18.7	Mike Davis (1977-80)
REBOUNDS	26	George Farley, vs. Brown (Feb. 26, 1960)	466	George Farley (1959-60)	1,089	George Farley (1957-60)
ASSISTS	13	Ka'Ron Barnes, vs. Lafayette (Jan. 5, 2003)	171	Roger Chadwick (1951-52)	441	Roger Chadwick (1949-52)

ESPN 86 SAGARIN

CREIGHTON

Don't mess with the Bluejays. Save for a few stretches here and there, Creighton has long been one of the feistiest underdogs around. Actually, considering the Jays have been to 16 NCAA Tournaments and 10 NITs—more postseason appearances than many major conference teams—*top* dogs might be a better description.

BEST TEAM: 1961-62 How did the Bluejays go from 8–17 one season to 21–5 the next? Simple: They let a first-year big man named Paul Silas go to work. Behind his 22.0 ppg and 22.5 rpg, Creighton entered the NCAA Tournament on a nine-game winning streak. The team extended it to 10 with an 87-83 victory over Memphis State. Unfortunately, in the next round Silas picked up two early fouls in a 66-46 loss to eventual national champ Cincinnati.

BEST PLAYER: F/C PAUL SILAS (1961-64) At 6'7", he wasn't the most physically gifted player who ever stepped onto the hardwood. But he battled for every rebound and usually won, thanks to his timing and relentlessness. His 21.6 rpg career average ranks third in NCAA history, and he grabbed a career-high 38 in a 1962 game against Centenary. He carried Creighton on offense too, scoring 20.5 ppg over his career and leading the Bluejays to two NCAA regional semifinals. He went on to a 16-year NBA career.

BEST COACH: DANA ALTMAN (1994-) You can usually count on two things from an Altman-led team: lots of three-pointers and all kinds of defensive pressure. His system has resulted in 12 straight postseason berths, including two trips to the second round of the NCAA Tourney.

GAME FOR THE AGES: Terrell Taylor grew up idolizing Michael Jordan, and when he got a chance to play on the Chicago Bulls' United Center home court during the 2002 NCAA Tournament, he did a pretty good MJ impersonation. Facing No. 5-seed Florida in the first round, the Creighton junior guard scored 28 points, most of that on eight three-pointers. The last trey came with 0.2 seconds left in the second overtime, giving No. 12-seed Creighton an 83-82 win. Taylor, by the way, wore No. 23.

HEARTBREAKER: In the 1974 NCAA Midwest Regional semifinals, the Bluejays led No. 14-ranked Kansas 54-53 with 1:21 left. But then KU's Tommie Smith took a Tom Kivisto pass and hit a layup to put Kansas up 55-54, and the Jayhawks D held the rest of the way.

FIERCEST RIVAL: Whose fans have suffered more in the Creighton vs. Southern Illinois feud? Bluejays backers can point to eight straight losses to the Salukis from February 2004 to March 2007. SIU rooters can talk about coming up short against Creighton in the MVC tournament final in 2002, '03 and '07, and the 1989 regular-season matchup in which the Bluejays beat SIU, 102-100, in overtime after trailing by six with :45 left in regulation. The decider: Creighton leads overall, 45–36.

FANFARE AND HOOPLA: The first inductee into the Creighton Hall of Fame was none other than late-1950s star guard Bob Gibson, one of two former Bluejays hoops standouts to go on to MLB careers. Who else, besides the former St. Louis Cardinals ace? Dennis Rasmussen, a forward from 1977-80, and lefthanded pitcher for the Padres, Yankees, Reds, Cubs and Royals.

> ***Silas battled for every rebound and usually won, thanks to his timing and relentlessness. His 21.6 rpg career average ranks third in history.***

FAN FAVORITE: G RYAN SEARS (1997-2001) Starting all 124 games during his four seasons at Creighton, point guard Sears helped break the Bluejays out of their 1990s doldrums. In the process, he set school records for three-pointers (since surpassed by Kyle Korver), assists and steals.

THE SCHOOLS

CONSENSUS ALL-AMERICAS

1923, '24	**Jimmy Lovley,** F
1927	**Sidney Corenman,** G
1943	**Ed Beisser,** F/C

FIRST-ROUND PRO PICKS

1969	**Bob Portman,** San Francisco (7)
1985	**Benoit Benjamin,** LA Clippers (3)

PROFILE

Creighton University, Omaha, NE
Founded: 1878
Enrollment: 6,992 (4,104 undergraduate)
Colors: Blue and white
Nickname: Bluejays
Current arena: Qwest Center Omaha, opened in 2003 (17,272)
Previous: Omaha Civic Auditorium, 1961-2003 (9,377); University "Old" Gymnasium, 1916-60 (3,000)
First game: Jan. 12, 1917
All-time record: 1,352-919 (.595)
Total weeks in AP Top 20/25: 28
Current conference: Missouri Valley (1928-48, 1977-)
Conference titles:
MVC: 14 (1930 [tie], '31 [tie], '32, '35 [tie], '36 [tie], '41, '42 [tie], '43, '78, '89, '91, 2001, '02 [tie], '09 [tie])
Conference tournament titles:
MVC: 10 (1978, '81, '89, '91, '99, 2000, '02, '03, '05, '07)
NCAA Tournament appearances: 16
NIT appearances: 10
Semifinals: 1

TOP 5

G/F	**Rodney Buford** (1995-99)
G/F	**Kyle Korver** (1999-2003)
F	**Bob Portman** (1966-69)
F/C	**Paul Silas** (1961-64)
C	**Benoit Benjamin** (1982-85)

RECORDS

RECORDS	GAME		SEASON		CAREER	
POINTS	51	Bob Portman, vs. Wisconsin-Milwaukee (Dec. 16, 1967)	738	Bob Portman (1967-68)	2,116	Rodney Buford (1995-99)
POINTS PER GAME			29.5	Bob Portman (1967-68)	24.7	Bob Portman (1966-69)
REBOUNDS	38	Paul Silas, vs. Centenary (Feb. 19, 1962)	631	Paul Silas (1963-64)	1,751	Paul Silas (1961-64)
ASSISTS	17	Ralph Bobik, vs. Bradley, (Jan. 22, 1974); vs. Saint Francis (Pa.), (Feb. 23, 1973)	252	Ralph Bobik (1973-74)	570	Ryan Sears (1997-2001)

SEASON REVIEW

SEASON	W-L	CONF.	SCORING	COACH	RECORD
1916-17	17-3			Thomas E. Mills	
1917-18	11-0		Chuck Kearney 16.1	Thomas E. Mills	
1918-19	10-0			Thomas E. Mills	
1919-20	15-3			Thomas E. Mills	53-6 .898
1920-21	13-6			Charles Kearney[a]	
1921-22	23-5			Charles Kearney	31-10 .756
1922-23	12-5			Arthur A. Schabinger	
1923-24	13-2			Arthur A. Schabinger	
1924-25	14-2			Arthur A. Schabinger	
1925-26	11-9		Al Brown 6.4	Arthur A. Schabinger	
1926-27	14-5			Arthur A. Schabinger	
1927-28	13-2			Arthur A. Schabinger	
1928-29	13-4	4-1		Arthur A. Schabinger	
1929-30	12-7	6-2	M. Van Ackeren 8.2	Arthur A. Schabinger	
1930-31	8-10	5-3		Arthur A. Schabinger	
1931-32	17-4	8-0		Arthur A. Schabinger	
1932-33	12-5	8-2		Arthur A. Schabinger	
1933-34	14-3	7-3		Arthur A. Schabinger	
1934-35	12-8	8-4		Arthur A. Schabinger	165-66 .714
1935-36	13-6	8-4	Emil Engelbretson 9.5	Eddie Hickey	

SEAS.	W-L	CONF.	POSTSEASON	SCORING	REBOUNDS	ASSISTS	COACH	RECORD
1936-37	11-9	8-4		Richard Shaw 6.7			Eddie Hickey	
1937-38	11-14	7-7		Richard Shaw 5.9			Eddie Hickey	
1938-39	11-12	7-7		Carl Roh 7.0			Eddie Hickey	
1939-40	11-9	8-4					Eddie Hickey	
1940-41	18-7	9-3	NCAA REGIONAL SEMIFINALS	Brownie Jaquay 9.0			Eddie Hickey	
1941-42	18-5	9-1	NIT THIRD PLACE	Ralph Langer 10.5			Eddie Hickey	
1942-43	16-1	10-0	NIT QUARTERFINALS	Ralph Langer 11.2			Eddie Hickey	
1943-44	no team							
1944-45	no team							
1945-46	9-10	3-7		Jerry Caveny 12.4			Duce Belford	
1946-47	17-8	7-5		Ward Gibson 14.3			Eddie Hickey	126-71 .640
1947-48	10-13	4-6					Duce Belford	
1948-49	9-14						Duce Belford	
1949-50	13-13			Francis Miller 15.6			Duce Belford	
1950-51	9-18			Francis Miller 15.1			Duce Belford	
1951-52	6-15			Bill Heyden 12.9			Duce Belford	56-83 .403
1952-53	11-14			Elton Tuttle 18.8			Sebastian Salerno	
1953-54	14-17			Ray Yost 19.9			Sebastian Salerno	
1954-55	5-14			Eddie Cole 23.6			Sebastian Salerno	30-45 .400
1955-56	11-12			Bob Gibson 22.0	Bob Gibson 7.6		Theron Thomsen	
1956-57	15-6			Bob Gibson 17.7			Theron Thomsen	
1957-58	10-12			Jim Berry 11.3			Theron Thomsen	
1958-59	13-9			Dick Harvey 14.1	Dick Hartmann 15.1		Theron Thomsen	49-39 .557
1959-60	13-11			Dick Harvey 20.2			John J. McManus	
1960-61	8-17			Chuck Officer 16.1	Carl Silvestrini 9.4		John J. McManus	
1961-62	21-5		NCAA REGIONAL SEMIFINALS	Paul Silas 22.0	Paul Silas 22.5		John J. McManus	
1962-63	14-13			Paul Silas 21.2	Paul Silas 20.6		John J. McManus	
1963-64	22-7		NCAA REGIONAL SEMIFINALS	Paul Silas 18.5	Paul Silas 21.8		John J. McManus	
1964-65	13-10			Elton McGriff 15.0	Elton McGriff 13.8		John J. McManus	
1965-66	14-12			Tim Powers 21.5	Neil Johnson 12.1		John J. McManus	
1966-67	12-13			Bob Portman 18.3	Bob Portman 11.4		John J. McManus	
1967-68	8-17			Bob Portman 29.5	Bob Portman 15.4		John J. McManus	
1968-69	13-13			Bob Portman 26.2	Bob Portman 11.8		John J. McManus	138-118 .539
1969-70	15-10			Cyril Baptiste 18.9	Cyril Baptiste 11.7		Eddie Sutton	
1970-71	14-11			Cyril Baptiste 20.2	Cyril Baptiste 11.2	Michael Caruso 4.3	Eddie Sutton	
1971-72	15-11			Gene Harmon 15.8	Ted Wuebben 9.8	Ralph Bobik 5.2	Eddie Sutton	
1972-73	15-11			Gene Harmon 15.8	Ted Wuebben 8.4	Ralph Bobik 6.2	Eddie Sutton	
1973-74	23-7		NCAA REGIONAL SEMIFINALS	Gene Harmon 18.3	Ted Wuebben 6.8	Ralph Bobik 8.4	Eddie Sutton	82-50 .621
1974-75	20-7		NCAA FIRST ROUND	Doug Brookins 16.3	Doug Brookins 7.1	Charles Butler 3.4	Tom Apke	
1975-76	19-7			Rick Apke 16.8	Rick Apke 7.7	Randy Eccker 4.0	Tom Apke	
1976-77	21-7		NIT FIRST ROUND	Rick Apke 19.8	Cornell Smith 7.0	Randy Eccker 7.3	Tom Apke	
1977-78	19-9	12-4	NCAA FIRST ROUND	Rick Apke 18.3	Rick Apke 7.8	Randy Eccker 5.4	Tom Apke	
1978-79	14-13	8-8		John C. Johnson 17.9	David Wesely 9.7	David Wesely 4.0	Tom Apke	
1979-80	16-12	9-7		Kevin McKenna 16.5	George Morrow 10.0	Kevin McKenna 3.7	Tom Apke	
1980-81	21-9	11-5	NCAA FIRST ROUND	Kevin McKenna 15.8	George Morrow 11.0	George Morrow 3.1	Tom Apke	130-64 .670
1981-82	7-20	4-12		Daryl Stovall 15.6	Alex Stivrins 7.5	Alex Stivrins 3.0	Willis Reed	
1982-83	8-19	4-14		Benoit Benjamin 14.9	Benoit Benjamin 9.6	Vernon Moore 3.7	Willis Reed	
1983-84	17-14	8-8	NIT FIRST ROUND	Benoit Benjamin 16.2	Gregory Brandon 10.7	Vernon Moore 4.1	Willis Reed	
1984-85	20-12	9-7		Benoit Benjamin 21.5	Benoit Benjamin 14.1	Vernon Moore 5.0	Willis Reed	52-65 .444
1985-86	12-16	7-9		Reggie Morris 14.0	Kenny Evans 8.5	Bernard Edwards 2.7	Tony Barone	
1986-87	9-19	4-10		Gary Swain 17.3	Kenny Evans 7.3	Rod Mason 3.0	Tony Barone	
1987-88	16-16	6-8		Rod Mason 20.3	Bob Harstad 8.5	James Farr 4.0	Tony Barone	
1988-89	20-11	11-3	NCAA FIRST ROUND	Bob Harstad 16.7	Bob Harstad 9.4	James Farr 5.0	Tony Barone	
1989-90	21-12	9-5	NIT FIRST ROUND	Bob Harstad 22.2	Bob Harstad 8.8	Duan Cole 3.9	Tony Barone	
1990-91	24-8	12-4	NCAA SECOND ROUND	Chad Gallagher 19.4	Chad Gallagher 8.8	Duan Cole 4.0	Tony Barone	102-82 .554
1991-92	9-19	7-11		Duan Cole 19.2	Mike Amos 4.1	Latrell Wrightsell 5.4	Rick Johnson	
1992-93	8-18	6-12		Matt Petty 17.2	Mike Amos 7.5	Matt Petty 3.1	Rick Johnson	
1993-94	7-22	3-15		Nate King 15.7	Nate King 9.0	Denny Halligan 2.7	Rick Johnson	24-59 .289
1994-95	7-19	4-14		Tad Ackerman 13.0	Randall Crutcher 6.6	Marcus Lockett 3.3	Dana Altman	
1995-96	14-15	9-9		Rodney Buford 14.5	Chuckie Johnson 6.6	Edward St. Fleur 4.7	Dana Altman	
1996-97	15-15	10-8		Rodney Buford 19.6	Randall Crutcher 6.8	Edward St. Fleur 5.2	Dana Altman	
1997-98	18-10	12-6	NIT FIRST ROUND	Rodney Buford 18.9	Rodney Buford 7.3	Ryan Sears 4.8	Dana Altman	
1998-99	22-9	11-7	NCAA SECOND ROUND	Rodney Buford 18.6	Rodney Buford 7.2	Ryan Sears 4.0	Dana Altman	
1999-2000	23-10	11-7	NCAA FIRST ROUND	Ben Walker 12.0	Ben Walker 6.3	Ryan Sears 5.3	Dana Altman	
2000-01	24-8	14-4	NCAA FIRST ROUND	Kyle Korver 14.6	Ben Walker 6.3	Ryan Sears 4.3	Dana Altman	
2001-02	23-9	14-4	NCAA SECOND ROUND	Kyle Korver 15.1	Brody Deren 5.1	Kyle Korver 3.3	Dana Altman	
2002-03	29-5	15-3	NCAA FIRST ROUND	Kyle Korver 17.8	Kyle Korver 6.4	Tyler McKinney 4.1	Dana Altman	
2003-04	20-9	12-6	NIT OPENING ROUND	Nate Funk 11.1	Brody Deren 6.6	Nate Funk 2.7	Dana Altman	
2004-05	23-11	11-7	NCAA FIRST ROUND	Nate Funk 17.8	Nate Funk 5.1	Tyler McKinney 5.4	Dana Altman	
2005-06	20-10	12-6	NIT SECOND ROUND	Johnny Mathies 13.5	Anthony Tolliver 6.7	Josh Dotzler 4.2	Dana Altman	
2006-07	22-11	13-5	NCAA FIRST ROUND	Nate Funk 17.7	Anthony Tolliver 6.7	Nate Funk 3.0	Dana Altman	
2007-08	22-11	10-8	NIT SECOND ROUND	P'Allen Stinnett 12.6	Dane Watts 6.4	Josh Dotzler 3.6	Dana Altman	
2008-09	27-8	14-4	NIT SECOND ROUND	Booker Woodfox 15.8	Justin Carter 5.5	Josh Dotzler 3.5	Dana Altman	309-160 .659

[a] **Eddie Mulholland (5-1) and Charles Kearney (8-5) both coached during the 1920-21 season.**

ESPN 217 SAGARIN

DARTMOUTH

You have to feel for the Big Green faithful: Their team won more than 14 games only once from 1960-61 through '85-86, and the last winning season came in '98-99. But here's a cheery reminder: Dartmouth has made more Final Fours than Notre Dame, Tennessee, BYU and Missouri *combined* (two vs. one).

BEST TEAM: 1943-44 Dartmouth reached its peak during World War II, losing the 1944 national title game to Utah, 42-40 in overtime. All-America Aud Brindley scored 11 in the big game; St. John's star and Hall of Famer Dick McGuire, playing for Dartmouth while doing his military training, added six.

BEST PLAYER: C Rudy LaRusso (1956-59) As both a junior and a senior, LaRusso was first-team All-Ivy and led Dartmouth to a league title and an NCAA appearance. The Big Green reached the Elite Eight in 1958, and in '59 lost to Jerry West's national runner-up West Virginia in the first round, 82-68. LaRusso, a five-time NBA All-Star, averaged 14.6 points and 15.5 rebounds at Dartmouth.

BEST COACH: Osborne Cowles (1936-43, '44-46) In nine seasons, he had three 20-win campaigns, reached the NCAA title game twice and had Dartmouth, in the retroactive Premo-Poretta Power Poll, among the top 15 schools in the country three seasons.

GAME FOR THE AGES: When Dartmouth was a national power, it would easily beat lower-ranked opponents and rarely lost. Its March 7, 1959, matchup with Princeton proved to be an exception to the first rule—but, fortunately for Big Green fans, not to the second. Both teams finished with 13–1 league records, setting up a final showdown for the Ivy title and an NCAA berth. Dartmouth pulled it out, 69-68, thanks to LaRusso's 25 points, including the last-second game-winner.

FIERCEST RIVAL: Harvard is Dartmouth's travel partner, so the teams typically play twice within a week, often leading to all kinds of peculiar results. The most recent example: On Jan. 10, 2009, the Big Green lost at home to Harvard, 63-62. Two weeks later the Big Green won in Cambridge, 75-66. Dartmouth leads overall (94–74).

SEASON REVIEW

SEAS.	W-L	CONF.	COACH	SEAS.	W-L	CONF.	COACH
1900-49	*579-375*	*Reached Final Four in 1942 and '44*		**1962-63**	7-18	2-12	Alvin "Doggie" Julian
1949-50	8-17	1-11	Elmer Lampe	**1963-64**	2-23	0-14	Alvin "Doggie" Julian
1950-51	3-23	1-11	Alvin "Doggie" Julian	**1964-65**	4-21	1-13	Alvin "Doggie" Julian
1951-52	11-19	4-8	Alvin "Doggie" Julian	**1965-66**	3-21	0-14	Alvin "Doggie" Julian
1952-53	12-14	5-7	Alvin "Doggie" Julian	**1966-67**	7-17	1-13	Alvin "Doggie" Julian
1953-54	13-13	5-9	Alvin "Doggie" Julian	**1967-68**	8-18	6-8	Dave Gavitt
1954-55	18-7	9-5	Alvin "Doggie" Julian	**1968-69**	10-15	4-10	Dave Gavitt
1955-56	18-11	10-4 ●	Alvin "Doggie" Julian	**1969-70**	13-12	7-7	George Blaney
1956-57	18-7	10-4	Alvin "Doggie" Julian	**1970-71**	10-16	5-9	George Blaney
1957-58	22-5	11-3 ●	Alvin "Doggie" Julian	**1971-72**	14-12	8-6	George Blaney
1958-59	22-6	13-1 ●	Alvin "Doggie" Julian	**1972-73**	6-20	4-10	Tom O'Connor
1959-60	14-9	10-4	Alvin "Doggie" Julian	**1973-74**	4-22	2-12	Tom O'Connor
1960-61	5-19	4-10	Alvin "Doggie" Julian	**1974-75**	8-18	5-9	Marcus Jackson
1961-62	6-18	3-11	Alvin "Doggie" Julian	**1975-76**	16-10	7-7	Gary Walters

SEAS.	W-L	CONF.	SCORING		COACH	RECORD	
1976-77	4-22	3-11	Larry Cubas	16.5	Gary Walters		
1977-78	10-16	5-9	Sterling Edmonds	19.6	Gary Walters		
1978-79	14-12	6-8	Larry Lawrence	16.4	Gary Walters	44-60	.423
1979-80	6-20	3-11	Cleotha Robertson	13.3	Tim Cohane		
1980-81	10-16	3-11	Larry Lawrence	21.8	Tim Cohane		
1981-82	7-19	1-13	Paul Anderson	14.0	Tim Cohane		
1982-83	7-19	3-11	Paul Anderson	18.2	Tim Cohane	30-74	.288
1983-84	11-15	6-8	Brian Burke	17.6	Reggie Minton	11-15	.423
1984-85	5-21	3-11	Bryan Randall	10.3	Paul Cormier		
1985-86	11-15	6-8	Jim Barton	13.6	Paul Cormier		
1986-87	15-11	7-7	Jim Barton	21.4	Paul Cormier		
1987-88	18-8	10-4	Jim Barton	24.4	Paul Cormier		
1988-89	17-9	10-4	Jim Barton	23.5	Paul Cormier		
1989-90	12-14	7-7	Walter Palmer	16.5	Paul Cormier		
1990-91	9-17	4-10	James Blackwell	19.3	Paul Cormier	87-95	.478
1991-92	10-16	5-9	Gregg Frame	11.3	Dave Faucher		
1992-93	11-15	5-9	Crawford Palmer	17.3	Dave Faucher		
1993-94	10-16	6-8	Gregg Frame	16.9	Dave Faucher		
1994-95	13-13	10-4	Sea Lonergan	17.3	Dave Faucher		
1995-96	16-10	9-5	Sea Lonergan	16.9	Dave Faucher		
1996-97	18-8	10-4	Sea Lonergan	17.0	Dave Faucher		
1997-98	7-19	4-10	Shaun Gee	18.3	Dave Faucher		
1998-99	14-12	10-4	Shaun Gee	17.4	Dave Faucher		
1999-2000	9-18	5-9	Shaun Gee	18.1	Dave Faucher		
2000-01	8-19	3-11	Greg Buth	16.3	Dave Faucher		
2001-02	9-18	2-12	Flinder Boyd	14.4	Dave Faucher		
2002-03	8-19	4-10	Charles Harris	12.2	Dave Faucher		
2003-04	3-25	1-13	Leon Pattman	13.2	Dave Faucher	136-208	.395
2004-05	10-17	7-7	Mike Lang	11.8	Terry Dunn		
2005-06	6-21	4-10	Leon Pattman	10.9	Terry Dunn		
2006-07	9-18	4-10	Leon Pattman	15.3	Terry Dunn		
2007-08	10-18	3-11	Alex Barnett	15.6	Terry Dunn		
2008-09	9-19	7-7	Alex Barnett	19.4	Terry Dunn	44-93	.321

● NCAA Tournament appearance

PROFILE

Dartmouth College, Hanover, NH
Founded: 1769
Enrollment: 5,800 (4,100 undergraduate)
Colors: Dartmouth green and white
Nickname: Big Green
Current arena: Edward Leede Arena, opened in 1987 (2,100)
Previous: Alumni Gym, 1909-87 (2,250)
First game: 1900
All-time record: 1,197-1,321 (.475)
Total weeks in AP Top 20/25: 5

Current conference: Ivy League (1911-)
Conference titles:
Ivy: 12 (1927, '38, '39, '40, '41, '42, '43, '44, '46, '56, '58, '59)
NCAA Tournament appearances: 7
Final Fours: 2
NIT appearances: 0

CONSENSUS ALL-AMERICAS

1906 **George Grebenstein,** F
1912 **Ernst Mensel,** G
1912 **Rufus Sisson,** F
1940, '41 **Gus Broberg,** G/F
1944 **Aud Brindley,** F/C

TOP 5

G **Jim Barton** (1985-89)
G/F **Gus Broberg** (1938-41)
F **Paul Erland** (1969-72)
F/C **Aud Brindley** (1942-44, '46-47)
C **Rudy LaRusso** (1956-59)

RECORDS	GAME		SEASON		CAREER	
POINTS	48	Jim Barton, vs. Brown (Feb. 7, 1987)	636	Jim Barton (1987-88)	2,158	Jim Barton (1985-89)
POINTS PER GAME			24.4	Jim Barton (1987-88)	21.2	Paul Erland (1969-72)
REBOUNDS	32	Rudy LaRusso, vs. Columbia (Feb. 8, 1958)	503	Rudy LaRusso (1957-58)	1,239	Rudy LaRusso (1956-59)
ASSISTS	16	Flinder Boyd, vs. Albany (Jan. 20, 2001)	203	Kenny Mitchell (1996-97)	585	Flinder Boyd (1998-2002)

ESPN 174 SAGARIN

DAVIDSON

This sleepy, bookish school half an hour's drive north of Charlotte has distinguished itself in huge ways on the court under Lefty Driesell and, more recently, Bob McKillop. Only the Wildcats' proximity to the ACC mighties kept Davidson's accomplishments in the shadows for so long before Stephen Curry and the 2007-08 team exploded into the Elite Eight.

BEST TEAM: 1964-65 *Sports Illustrated* anointed Davidson the nation's top team in its season preview, and Fred Hetzel, Dick Snyder & Co. breezed through the schedule with one loss. But, ranked No. 6 at the end of the regular season, Davidson came up short in the Southern Conference tournament, falling to West Virginia in OT and losing its NCAA spot. Driesell always insisted that this team was good enough to win it all.

BEST PLAYER: F/C FRED HETZEL (1962-65) Fans of Snyder, Mike Maloy and Curry all can make cases, but Hetzel is the best. He averaged 25.7 points and 13.8 boards a game over his three seasons, and was a three-time SoCon Player of the Year. No wonder he was the No. 1 pick in the 1965 NBA draft.

BEST COACH: CHARLES "LEFTY" DRIESELL (1960-69) The former door-to-door encyclopedia salesman came to Davidson from the high school ranks. A creative recruiter, he quickly transformed the Wildcats into a national power before moving on to Maryland.

GAME FOR THE AGES: In the second round of the 2008 Tournament, Davidson trailed No. 2-seed Georgetown by 17 in the second half. Then, before an awe-struck Raleigh crowd, Curry dropped 25 points after halftime to propel the Wildcats to a 74-70 win.

FIERCEST RIVAL: The Wildcats' success since the early 1990s and back in Driesell's day often minimized the importance of regular conference foes, and Davidson fans don't mind saying so. If you force them to circle a name on the schedule, it might be Marshall, Furman, West Virginia or—most often these days—the College of Charleston, especially with silver fox Bobby Cremins on the sideline to balance Bob McKillop's white locks.

SEASON REVIEW

SEAS.	W-L	CONF.	COACH	SEAS.	W-L	CONF.		COACH
1907-48	*349-312*	*Monk Younger 83-61 (1923-31)*		1961-62	14-11	5-6		Lefty Driesell
1948-49	18-8	11-6	Norman Shepard	1962-63	20-7	8-3		Lefty Driesell
1949-50	10-16	6-12	Boyd Baird	1963-64	22-4	9-2		Lefty Driesell
1950-51	7-19	5-15	Boyd Baird	1964-65	24-2	12-0		Lefty Driesell
1951-52	7-18	4-15	Boyd Baird	1965-66	21-7	11-1	●	Lefty Driesell
1952-53	4-16	3-14	Danny Miller	1966-67	15-12	8-4		Lefty Driesell
1953-54	7-15	3-5	Danny Miller	1967-68	24-5	9-1	●	Lefty Driesell
1954-55	8-13	4-6	Danny Miller	1968-69	27-3	9-0	●	Lefty Driesell
1955-56	10-15	5-7	Tom Scott	1969-70	22-5	10-0	●	Terry Holland
1956-57	7-20	4-8	Tom Scott	1970-71	15-11	9-1		Terry Holland
1957-58	9-15	4-8	Tom Scott	1971-72	19-9	8-2	■	Terry Holland
1958-59	9-15	2-8	Tom Scott	1972-73	18-9	9-1		Terry Holland
1959-60	5-19	0-10	Tom Scott	1973-74	18-9	7-3		Terry Holland
1960-61	9-14	2-10	Lefty Driesell	1974-75	7-19	4-6		Bo Brickels

SEAS.	W-L	CONF.		SCORING		COACH	RECORD	
1975-76	5-21	1-9		John Gerdy	17.9	Bo Brickels	12-40	.231
1976-77	5-22	2-8		John Gerdy	23.2	Dave Pritchett		
1977-78	9-18	3-7		John Gerdy	25.8	Dave Pritchett	14-40	.259
1978-79	8-19	3-7		John Gerdy	26.7	Eddie Biedenbach		
1979-80	8-18	4-11		Rich DiBenedetto	20.0	Eddie Biedenbach		
1980-81	13-14	11-5		Todd Haynes	19.8	Eddie Biedenbach	29-51	.362
1981-82	14-15	9-7		Cliff Tribus	15.7	Bobby Hussey		
1982-83	13-15	8-8		Kenny Wilson	17.4	Bobby Hussey		
1983-84	9-19	5-11		Kenny Wilson	18.3	Bobby Hussey		
1984-85	10-20	6-10		Derek Rucker	12.8	Bobby Hussey		
1985-86	20-11	10-6	●	Derek Rucker	14.0	Bobby Hussey		
1986-87	20-10	12-4		Jeff Himes	18.1	Bobby Hussey		
1987-88	15-13	9-7		Derek Rucker	21.7	Bobby Hussey		
1988-89	7-24 ⊗			Bruce Elder	17.2	Bobby Hussey	108-127	.460▼
1989-90	4-24			Paul Denmond	13.4	Bob McKillop		
1990-91	10-19	6-8		Jason Zimmerman	12.5	Bob McKillop		
1991-92	11-17	6-8		Janko Narat	14.0	Bob McKillop		
1992-93	14-14	10-8		Detlef Musch	15.0	Bob McKillop		
1993-94	22-8	13-5	■	Janko Narat	17.7	Bob McKillop		
1994-95	14-13	7-7		Brandon Williams	14.2	Bob McKillop		
1995-96	25-5	14-0	■	Brandon Williams	18.2	Bob McKillop		
1996-97	18-10	10-4		Narcisse Ewodo	15.8	Bob McKillop		
1997-98	20-10	13-2	●	Mark Donnelly	14.6	Bob McKillop		
1998-99	16-11	11-5		Landry Kosmalski	13.9	Bob McKillop		
1999-2000	15-13	10-6		Stephen Marshall	15.9	Bob McKillop		
2000-01	15-17	7-9		Wayne Bernard	13.7	Bob McKillop		
2001-02	21-10	11-5	●	Emeka Erege	13.6	Bob McKillop		
2002-03	17-10	11-5		Wayne Bernard	15.1	Bob McKillop		
2003-04	17-12	11-5		Brendan Winters	17.8	Bob McKillop		
2004-05	23-9	16-0	■	Brendan Winters	16.7	Bob McKillop		
2005-06	20-11	10-5	●	Brendan Winters	16.9	Bob McKillop		
2006-07	29-5	17-1	●	Stephen Curry	21.5	Bob McKillop		
2007-08	29-7	20-0	●	Stephen Curry	25.9	Bob McKillop		
2008-09	27-8	18-2	■	Stephen Curry	28.6	Bob McKillop	367-233	.612

⊗ **Record does not reflect games forfeited or vacated. For adjusted records, see p. 521.**
▼ **Coach's record adjusted to reflect games forfeited or vacated: 109-125, .466. For yearly totals, see p. 521.**
● **NCAA Tournament appearance** ■ **NIT appearance**

PROFILE

Davidson College, Davidson, NC
Founded: 1837
Enrollment: 1,714 undergraduate
Colors: Red and black
Nickname: Wildcats
Current arena: John M. Belk Arena, opened in 1989 (5,700)
First game: 1907
All-time record: 1,248-1,101 (.531)
Total weeks in AP Top 20/25: 70
Current conference: Southern (1936-88, '92-)

Conference titles:
Southern: 20 (1964, '65, '66, '68, '69, '70, '71, '72, '73, '81 [tie], '96 [tie], '97 [tie], '98 [tie], 2002 [tie], '03 [tie], '04 [tie], '05 [tie], '07 [tie], '08 [tie], '09 [tie])
Conference tournament titles:
Southern: 10 (1966, '68, '69, '70, '86, '98, 2002, '06, '07, '08)
NCAA Tournament appearances: 10
Sweet 16s (since 1975): 1
NIT appearances: 5

CONSENSUS ALL-AMERICAS

1965 **Fred Hetzel,** F/C
2009 **Stephen Curry,** G

FIRST-ROUND PRO PICKS

1965 **Fred Hetzel,** San Francisco (1)
2009 **Stephen Curry,** Golden State (7)

TOP 5

G **Stephen Curry** (2006-09)
G **Dick Snyder** (1963-66)
F **John Gerdy** (1975-79)
F **Mike Maloy** (1967-70)
F/C **Fred Hetzel** (1962-65)

RECORDS

RECORDS	GAME		SEASON		CAREER	
POINTS	53	Fred Hetzel, vs. Furman (Dec. 8, 1964)	974	Stephen Curry (2008-09)	2,635	Stephen Curry (2006-09)
POINTS PER GAME			28.6	Stephen Curry (2008-09)	25.7	Fred Hetzel (1962-65)
REBOUNDS	27	Fred Hetzel, vs. Furman (Feb. 8, 1964)	385	Fred Hetzel (1964-65)	1,111	Mike Maloy (1967-70)
ASSISTS	19	Jason Richards, vs. Mount St. Mary's (Dec. 15, 2006)	293	Jason Richards (2007-08)	663	Jason Richards (2004-08)

ESPN 48 SAGARIN

DAYTON

An early Midwestern power, the Flyers have been regular participants in college basketball's postseason since the 1950s, winning the NIT in 1962 and '68 and reaching the NCAA Final in 1967, where they lost to UCLA. They made their last significant run in 1984 behind their all-time great, Roosevelt Chapman.

BEST TEAM: 1966-67 Coach Don Donoher's squad, coming off back-to-back Sweet 16 appearances, went 25–6 and advanced to the Final Four for the only time in the school's history. Led by junior Don May, who averaged 22.2 points and 16.7 rebounds per game, the Flyers eked out a two-point overtime win over Western Kentucky in the first round and a one-point win over Tennessee in the second before rolling over North Carolina, 76-62, in the national semifinal on their way to the UCLA loss (see Heartbreaker).

BEST PLAYER: F Roosevelt Chapman (1980-84) The Flyers' all-time leading scorer (2,233 points), Chapman stands among the program's top 10 in more than 30 categories. The Brooklyn, N.Y., native was known as Velvet for his ultra-smooth moves. As a senior, he led the Flyers on an improbable run through the 1984 Tourney, scoring 105 points in four games, including 41 in an upset win over Oklahoma.

BEST COACH: Don Donoher (1964-89) A former Dayton player under the man he succeeded, Tom Blackburn, Donoher is the school's all-time winningest coach (437–275). He took each of his first three teams, including the storied 1966-67 squad, to the NCAA Tournament. The following season, his Flyers beat Kansas to win the NIT.

GAME FOR THE AGES: The Flyers entered the 1984 NCAA Tournament West Regional in Salt Lake City as a No. 10 seed with an 18–10 record. They upset No. 7-seed LSU, 74-66, in the first round and then, on March 17, stunned No. 2-seed Oklahoma, 89-85, in the second round, as Chapman scored a career-high 41 points, hitting 13 of 22 shots from the field and 15 of 19 from the foul line.

HEARTBREAKER: When UCLA faced Dayton in the second round of the 1974 Tournament, the Bruins had won seven straight NCAA titles dating to their 1967 Final victory over the Flyers. Dayton fans went wild when Don Smith appeared to give the Flyers the lead with :14 left in regulation, but a Donoher time-out nullified the shot. The game went through three overtimes before UCLA pulled it out, 111-100. At least Dayton softened Bill Walton's last Bruins team for NC State, which beat UCLA in the national semis.

FIERCEST RIVAL: Dayton and Xavier have met 149 times—the most games Dayton has played against any opponent—dating back to 1920. The Flyers lead the series, 81–68, and the current Atlantic 10 foes continue to meet at least twice a year.

FANFARE AND HOOPLA: The UD Arena has given the Flyers a distinct home court advantage for three decades running. The building has also gained fame for serving annually since 2001 as the site of the NCAA Tournament Opening Round—more popularly known as the play-in game.

Chapman, the Brooklyn native known as Velvet, led the Flyers on an improbable run through the 1984 Tourney.

FAN FAVORITE: C Chris Daniels (1991-96) The immensely likeable Daniels was shooting 69% during the 1995-96 season, when, tragically, he died in his sleep on Feb. 8 of cardiac arrhythmia. His memory is vividly maintained at Dayton and in the Atlantic 10; both the school and the conference annually present their most improved player with an award named in Daniels' honor.

CONSENSUS ALL-AMERICAS

1912, '13 **Alphonse Schumacher,** C

FIRST-ROUND PRO PICKS

1955	**John Horan,** Fort Wayne (8)
1956	**Jim Paxson Sr.,** Minneapolis (3)
1973	**Don Smith,** Kentucky (ABA, 10)
1979	**Jim Paxson Jr.,** Portland (12)

PROFILE

University of Dayton, Dayton, OH
Founded: 1850 as Saint Mary's School for Boys; changed to Dayton in 1920
Enrollment: 10,920 (7,731 undergraduate)
Colors: Red and blue
Nickname: Flyers
Current arena: University of Dayton Arena, opened in 1969 (13,455)
First game: 1903
All-time record: 1,424-1,000 (.587)
Total weeks in AP Top 20/25: 90

Current conference: Atlantic 10 (1995-)
Conference titles:
Atlantic 10: 3 (1998 [tie], 2000 [tie], '04 [tie])
Conference tournament titles:
Midwestern: 1 (1990)
Atlantic 10: 1 (2003)
NCAA Tournament appearances: 14
Sweet 16s (since 1975): 1
Final Fours: 1
NIT appearances: 21
Semifinals: 8
Titles: 2 (1962, '68)

TOP 5

G	**Jim Paxson Jr.** (1975-79)
G	**Don Smith** (1971-74)
F	**Roosevelt Chapman** (1980-84)
F	**Don May** (1965-68)
C	**Henry Finkel** (1963-66)

RECORDS

RECORDS	GAME		SEASON		CAREER	
POINTS	52	Don Smith, vs. Loyola-Chicago (Feb. 3, 1973)	733	Henry Finkel (1964-65)	2,233	Roosevelt Chapman (1980-84)
POINTS PER GAME			25.3	Henry Finkel (1964-65)	23.7	Henry Finkel (1963-66)
REBOUNDS	32	Garry Roggenburk, vs. Miami (Ohio) (Dec. 9, 1959)	519	Don May (1966-67)	1,341	John Horan (1951-55)
ASSISTS	15	Negele Knight, vs. Xavier (March 10, 1990)	216	Negele Knight (1989-90)	663	Negele Knight (1985-86, '87-90)

THE SCHOOLS

SEASON REVIEW

SEASON	W-L	CONF.	SCORING	COACH	RECORD
1903-16	*113-25*		*Three consecutive undefeated seasons (1910-13): 10-0, 13-0, 11-0*		
1916-17	8-3			Alfred McCray	19-5 .792
1917-18	2-4			Al Mahrt	
1918-19	3-4			Al Mahrt	9-12 .429
1919-20	5-8			Harry Solimano	34-12 .739
1920-21	6-16			Dutch Thiele	6-16 .273
1921-22	6-8			William Sherry	6-8 .429
1922-23	8-8			Van Hill	8-8 .500
1923-24	9-5			Harry Baujan	
1924-25	9-11			Harry Baujan	
1925-26	7-8			Harry Baujan	
1926-27	10-9			Harry Baujan	
1927-28	11-5			Harry Baujan	46-38 .548
1928-29	9-10			George Fitzgerald	9-10 .474
1929-30	4-14			Bill Belanich	
1930-31	2-15			Bill Belanich	
1931-32	3-12			Bill Belanich	
1932-33	7-7			Bill Belanich	16-48 .250
1933-34	9-7			Louis Tschudi	
1934-35	4-11			Louis Tschudi	13-18 .419
1935-36	3-13			Joe Holsinger	
1936-37	7-12			Joe Holsinger	

SEAS.	W-L	CONF.	POSTSEASON	SCORING		REBOUNDS		ASSISTS		COACH	RECORD	
1937-38	6-11									Joe Holsinger		
1938-39	2-12									Joe Holsinger	18-48	.273
1939-40	4-17									James Carter		
1940-41	9-14									James Carter		
1941-42	12-6									James Carter		
1942-43	9-8									James Carter		
1943-44	no team											
1944-45	no team											
1945-46	3-13									James Carter		
1946-47	4-17									James Carter	41-75	.353
1947-48	12-14									Tom Blackburn		
1948-49	16-14									Tom Blackburn		
1949-50	24-8			Don Meineke	16.5					Tom Blackburn		
1950-51	27-5		NIT RUNNER-UP	Don Meineke	20.6	Don Meineke	11.3			Tom Blackburn		
1951-52	28-5		NIT R-UP, NCAA REG. SEMIS	Don Meineke	21.1	Don Meineke	11.8			Tom Blackburn		
1952-53	16-13			Jack Sallee	19.0	John Horan	10.9			Tom Blackburn		
1953-54	25-7		NIT QUARTERFINALS	Bill Uhl	18.4	Bill Uhl	15.3			Tom Blackburn		
1954-55	25-4		NIT RUNNER-UP	Bill Uhl	18.6	Bill Uhl	13.8			Tom Blackburn		
1955-56	25-4		NIT RUNNER-UP	Bill Uhl	18.4	Bill Uhl	14.7			Tom Blackburn		
1956-57	19-9		NIT QUARTERFINALS	Al Sicking	13.8	Jim Palmer	12.5			Tom Blackburn		
1957-58	25-4		NIT RUNNER-UP	Jack McCarthy	14.6	Bucky Bockhorn	12.4			Tom Blackburn		
1958-59	14-12			Frank Case	16.7	Joe Kennelly	11.7			Tom Blackburn		
1959-60	21-7		NIT QUARTERFINALS	Garry Roggenburk	16.1	Garry Roggenburk	13.8			Tom Blackburn		
1960-61	20-9		NIT FOURTH PLACE	Garry Roggenburk	16.1	Garry Roggenburk	12.5			Tom Blackburn		
1961-62	24-6		NIT CHAMPION	Garry Roggenburk	16.0	Bill Chmielewski	11.4			Tom Blackburn		
1962-63	16-10			Gordy Hatton	15.7	Bill Westerkamp	9.0			Tom Blackburn		
1963-64	15-10			Henry Finkel	23.0	Henry Finkel	13.0			Tom Blackburn[a]	352-141	.714
1964-65	22-7		NCAA REGIONAL SEMIFINALS	Henry Finkel	25.3	Henry Finkel	14.9			Don Donoher		
1965-66	23-6		NCAA REGIONAL SEMIFINALS	Henry Finkel	22.7	Henry Finkel	12.1			Don Donoher		
1966-67	25-6		NCAA RUNNER-UP	Don May	22.2	Don May	16.7			Don Donoher		
1967-68	21-9		NIT CHAMPION	Don May	23.4	Don May	15.0			Don Donoher		
1968-69	20-7		NCAA FIRST ROUND	Dan Sadlier	18.2	Dan Sadlier	9.3			Don Donoher		
1969-70	19-8		NCAA FIRST ROUND	Ken May	17.0	George Jackson	14.5			Don Donoher		
1970-71	18-9		NIT FIRST ROUND	Ken May	18.9	George Jackson	14.5			Don Donoher		
1971-72	13-13			Donald Smith	20.2	John Bitter	9.5			Don Donoher		
1972-73	13-13			Donald Smith	23.4	John Von Lehman	7.3			Don Donoher		
1973-74	20-9		NCAA REGIONAL SEMIFINALS	Donald Smith	18.0	Allen Elijah	10.0	Johnny Davis	4.1	Don Donoher		
1974-75	10-16			Johnny Davis	22.3	Allen Elijah	9.7	Johnny Davis	3.9	Don Donoher		
1975-76	14-13			Johnny Davis	21.8	Erv Giddings	10.9	Johnny Davis	4.0	Don Donoher		
1976-77	16-11			Jim Paxson	18.8	Erv Giddings	10.9	Jack Zimmerman	4.6	Don Donoher		
1977-78	19-10		NIT QUARTERFINALS	Jim Paxson	17.4	Erv Giddings	9.8	Jim Paxson	5.5	Don Donoher		
1978-79	19-10		NIT SECOND ROUND	Jim Paxson	23.2	Mike Kanieski	8.7	Jim Paxson	5.7	Don Donoher		
1979-80	13-14			Jack Zimmerman	17.2	Richard Montague	8.4	Jack Zimmerman	4.9	Don Donoher		
1980-81	18-11		NIT SECOND ROUND	Mike Kanieski	16.9	Mike Kanieski	8.0	Kevin Conrad	6.2	Don Donoher		
1981-82	21-9		NIT QUARTERFINALS	Mike Kanieski	18.4	Roosevelt Chapman	8.0	Kevin Conrad	6.3	Don Donoher		
1982-83	18-10			Roosevelt Chapman	23.0	Roosevelt Chapman	9.6	Kevin Conrad	5.1	Don Donoher		
1983-84	21-11		NCAA REGIONAL FINALS	Roosevelt Chapman	21.8	Roosevelt Chapman	9.1	Larry Schellenberg	4.4	Don Donoher		
1984-85	19-10		NCAA FIRST ROUND	Dave Colbert	16.7	Dave Colbert	7.7	Larry Schellenberg	5.2	Don Donoher		
1985-86	17-13		NIT FIRST ROUND	Dave Colbert	18.8	Dave Colbert	8.2	Negele Knight	4.3	Don Donoher		
1986-87	13-15			Anthony Grant	13.0	Anthony Grant	6.0	Dan Christie	5.3	Don Donoher		
1987-88	13-18			Anthony Corbitt	15.9	Anthony Corbitt	6.9	Ray Springer	5.2	Don Donoher		
1988-89	12-17	6-6		Anthony Corbitt	15.6	Anthony Corbitt	7..0	Negele Knight	5.8	Don Donoher	437-275	.614
1989-90	22-10	10-4	NCAA SECOND ROUND	Negele Knight	22.8	Anthony Corbitt	8.3	Negele Knight	6.8	Jim O'Brien		
1990-91	14-15	8-6		Chip Jones	20.2	Makor Shayok	6.3	Derrick Dukes	4.3	Jim O'Brien		
1991-92	15-15	5-5		Alex Robertson	11.6	Chip Hare	6.6	Derrick Dukes	4.0	Jim O'Brien		
1992-93	4-26	3-11		Chip Hare	17.8	Chip Hare	6.3	Derrick Dukes	4.1	Jim O'Brien		
1993-94	6-21	1-11		Alex Robertson	12.7	Alex Robertson	5.9	Derrick Dukes	4.8	Jim O'Brien	61-87	.412
1994-95	7-20	0-12		Andy Meyer	10.3	Ryan Perryman	7.7	Jeffrey Brookins	3.0	Oliver Purnell		
1995-96	15-14	6-10		Ryan Perryman	13.4	Ryan Perryman	9.3	Jeffrey Brookins	3.6	Oliver Purnell		
1996-97	13-14	6-10		Darnell Hoskins	14.1	Ryan Perryman	9.9	Darnell Hoskins	4.7	Oliver Purnell		
1997-98	21-12	11-5	NIT SECOND ROUND	Ryan Perryman	15.2	Ryan Perryman	12.5	Edwin Young	4.1	Oliver Purnell		
1998-99	11-17	5-11		Mark Ashman	15.2	Mark Ashman	5.8	Edwin Young	4.4	Oliver Purnell		
1999-2000	22-9	11-5	NCAA FIRST ROUND	Tony Stanley	14.7	Mark Ashman	5.8	Edwin Young	3.5	Oliver Purnell		
2000-01	21-13	9-7	NIT THIRD ROUND	Tony Stanley	15.9	Keith Waleskowski	7.7	David Morris	5.1	Oliver Purnell		
2001-02	21-11	10-6	NIT FIRST ROUND	Ramod Marshall	13.3	Keith Waleskowski	8.0	David Morris	6.0	Oliver Purnell		
2002-03	24-6	14-2	NCAA FIRST ROUND	Brooks Hall	12.8	Keith Waleskowski	8.2	Ramod Marshall	4.8	Oliver Purnell	155-116	.572
2003-04	24-9	12-4	NCAA FIRST ROUND	Ramod Marshall	14.6	Keith Waleskowski	9.9	Ramod Marshall	5.2	Brian Gregory		
2004-05	18-11	10-6		Monty Scott	11.1	Monty Scott	4.6	Warren Williams	3.4	Brian Gregory		
2005-06	14-17	6-10		Brian Roberts	16.0	Norman Plummer	6.5	Warren Williams	4.3	Brian Gregory		
2006-07	19-12	8-8		Brian Roberts	18.5	Charles Little	5.2	Brian Roberts	2.6	Brian Gregory		
2007-08	23-11	8-8	NIT QUARTERFINALS	Brian Roberts	18.4	Chris Wright	5.7	Brian Roberts	3.4	Brian Gregory		
2008-09	27-8	11-5	NCAA SECOND ROUND	Chris Wright	13.3	Chris Wright	6.6	London Warren	4.4	Brian Gregory	125-68	.648

[a] Don Donoher coached the last three games of the 1963-64 season, but all games were credited to Tom Blackburn's record.

ESPN 268 SAGARIN

DELAWARE

The Barber of Seville was no match for this. On Jan. 13, 1906, with their basketball gym still under construction, the Blue Hens made their debut at the Wilmington Opera House, losing to Pennsylvania Medical, 32-18. Delaware has hit just a few sporadic high notes since—notably Fred Emmerson's Middle Atlantic Southern Division title teams in the early 1950s and the Spencer Dunkley-led NCAA Tournament crashers of the 1990s.

BEST TEAM: 1991-92 The Blue Hens made their last season in the Delaware Field House one to remember. With five 1,000-point scorers—Mark Murray, Brian Pearl, Alex Coles, Anthony Wright and Dunkley—Delaware won 20 straight entering the Tournament. But Steve Steinwedel's crew ran out of ammo in the first round, losing to No. 4-seed Cincinnati, 85-47.

BEST PLAYER: F Mike Pegues (1996-2000) With his sweet touch, Pegues rewrote Delaware's record book: He's the school's all-time leading scorer (2,030 points), fifth-leading rebounder (785) and ranks in the top 15 in assists and steals. He was the America East Player of the Year as a junior and was first-team all-league three times, the first Blue Hen to achieve that honor.

BEST COACH: Mike Brey (1995-2000) The former Duke assistant and self-described nice guy had a simple message for his players: Compete every day, communicate, have no fear of failure. Brey's philosophy resonated with the Blue Hens, who made both the NCAA Tournament and the NIT in his five seasons.

GAME FOR THE AGES: The Blue Hens knew they were stronger and tougher than Drexel heading into the 1992 NAC title game. But they had no idea they'd be 20 rebounds stronger and 24 points tougher. With its 92-68 win, Delaware capped a perfect league season.

FIERCEST RIVAL: Delaware and Drexel have been dance partners through several conferences, and the Blue Hens keep stepping on Drexel's toes. With its 60-51 2008 CAA tourney win, Delaware claimed its sixth straight postseason win over the Dragons (dating to 1991-92) and holds a 72–68 series lead.

SEASON REVIEW

SEAS.	W-L	CONF.	COACH	SEAS.	W-L	CONF.	COACH
1905-46	*233-333-2*	*13-2 in 1919-20 under H.B. Shipley*		1959-60	7-16	1-9	Irvin C. Wisniewski
1946-47	9-7		Joseph Brunansky	1960-61	8-11	2-7	Irvin C. Wisniewski
1947-48	10-8		Joseph Brunansky	1961-62	18-5	9-3	Irvin C. Wisniewski
1948-49	5-15		Joseph Brunansky	1962-63	14-8	7-3	Irvin C. Wisniewski
1949-50	8-8		Fred Emmerson	1963-64	13-10	4-3	Irvin C. Wisniewski
1950-51	14-7		Fred Emmerson	1964-65	3-17		Irvin C. Wisniewski
1951-52	17-6		Fred Emmerson	1965-66	9-15		Irvin C. Wisniewski
1952-53	18-7		Fred Emmerson	1966-67	15-9		Daniel L. Peterson
1953-54	9-13		Fred Emmerson	1967-68	16-7		Daniel L. Peterson
1954-55	6-16		Irvin C. Wisniewski	1968-69	11-10		Daniel L. Peterson
1955-56	8-15		Irvin C. Wisniewski	1969-70	16-9	6-4	Daniel L. Peterson
1956-57	8-16		Irvin C. Wisniewski	1970-71	11-14	5-5	Daniel L. Peterson
1957-58	8-12		Irvin C. Wisniewski	1971-72	18-7	7-3	Donald J. Harnum
1958-59	9-13	4-6	Irvin C. Wisniewski	1972-73	14-11	6-4	Donald J. Harnum

SEAS.	W-L	CONF.		SCORING		COACH	RECORD	
1973-74	15-11	7-3		Wolfgang Fengler	12.7	Donald J. Harnum		
1974-75	12-13	4-4		Bill Sullivan	13.3	Donald J. Harnum		
1975-76	10-15	4-6		Bob Cook	13.4	Donald J. Harnum	69-57	.548
1976-77	12-13	7-3		Bob Cook	11.8	Ronald G. Rainey		
1977-78	16-11	5-5		Tom Carluccio	15.8	Ronald G. Rainey		
1978-79	5-22	3-15		Mark Mancini	14.1	Ronald G. Rainey		
1979-80	9-19	7-9		Ken Luck	13.2	Ronald G. Rainey		
1980-81	6-19	3-13		Ken Luck	13.2	Ronald G. Rainey		
1981-82	9-17	6-10		Ken Luck	20.0	Ronald G. Rainey		
1982-83	11-14	4-9		Tim Carr	13.8	Ronald G. Rainey		
1983-84	11-16	6-10		Oscar Jones	13.6	Ronald G. Rainey		
1984-85	12-16	7-7		Oscar Jones	16.9	Ronald G. Rainey	91-147	.382
1985-86	11-16	4-10		Oscar Jones	20.2	Steven C. Steinwedel		
1986-87	12-16	3-11		Tony Tucker	14.9	Steven C. Steinwedel		
1987-88	19-9	9-5		Tony Tucker	16.7	Steven C. Steinwedel		
1988-89	14-14	6-8		Elsworth Bowers	15.0	Steven C. Steinwedel		
1989-90	16-13	7-7		Mark Murray	13.0	Steven C. Steinwedel		
1990-91	16-13	8-4		Mark Murray	16.3	Steven C. Steinwedel		
1991-92	27-4	14-0	●	Alex Coles	14.3	Steven C. Steinwedel		
1992-93	22-8	10-4	●	Spencer Dunkley	19.2	Steven C. Steinwedel		
1993-94	14-13	7-7		Brian Pearl	16.7	Steven C. Steinwedel		
1994-95	12-15	7-9		Brian Pearl	14.8	Steven C. Steinwedel	163-121	.574
1995-96	15-12	11-7		Peca Arsic	17.4	Mike Brey		
1996-97	15-16	8-10		Greg Smith	21.3	Mike Brey		
1997-98	20-10	12-6	●	Mike Pegues	16.8	Mike Brey		
1998-99	25-6	15-3	●	Mike Pegues	21.8	Mike Brey		
1999-2000	24-8	14-4	■	Mike Pegues	20.8	Mike Brey	99-52	.656
2000-01	20-10	14-4		Ajmal Basit	15.2	David Henderson		
2001-02	14-16	9-9		Mike Ames	12.1	David Henderson		
2002-03	15-14	9-9		Mike Ames	14.0	David Henderson		
2003-04	16-12	10-8		Mike Ames	15.3	David Henderson		
2004-05	11-20	7-11		Harding Nana	18.5	David Henderson		
2005-06	9-21	4-14		Harding Nana	19.0	David Henderson	85-93	.478
2006-07	5-26	3-15		Herb Courtney	18.1	Monté Ross		
2007-08	14-17	9-9		Herb Courtney	14.1	Monté Ross		
2008-09	13-19	6-12		Marc Egerson	15.4	Monté Ross	32-62	.340

● **NCAA Tournament appearance** ■ **NIT appearance**

PROFILE

University of Delaware, Newark, DE
Founded: 1743
Enrollment: 20,500 (16,075 undergraduate)
Colors: Royal blue and gold
Nickname: Fightin' Blue Hens
Current arena: Bob Carpenter Center (Frank Acierno Arena), opened in 1992 (5,000)
Previous: Delaware Field House, 1967-92 (4,000); Carpenter Sports Building, 1943-66 (N/A); Taylor Gym, 1907-42 (N/A); Wilmington Opera House, 1906 (N/A)
First game: Jan. 13, 1906

All-time record: 1,042-1,139-2 (.478)
Total weeks in AP Top 20/25: 0
Current conference: Colonial Athletic Association (2001-)
Conference titles:
North Atlantic: 1 (1992)
America East: 2 (1998 [tie], '99 [tie])
Conference tournament titles:
North Atlantic Conference: 2 (1992, '93)
America East: 2 (1998, '99)
NCAA Tournament appearances: 4
NIT appearances: 1

TOP 5

G **Taurence Chisholm** (1984-88)
G/F **Ken Luck** (1978-82)
F **Mike Pegues** (1996-2000)
F **Greg Smith** (1993-97)
C **Spencer Dunkley** (1989-93)

RECORDS

RECORDS	GAME		SEASON		CAREER	
POINTS	52	Liston Houston, vs. Lebanon Valley (Feb. 19, 1910)	675	Mike Pegues (1998-99)	2,030	Mike Pegues (1996-2000)
POINTS PER GAME			23.9	Dave Sysko (1963-64)	19.6	Kenn Barnett (1966-68)
REBOUNDS	31	Jack Waddington, vs. Rutgers (Jan. 4, 1956)	367	Spencer Dunkley (1992-93)	916	Spencer Dunkley (1989-93)
ASSISTS	17	John Staudenmayer, vs. Lehigh (Feb. 6, 1982)	231	Taurence Chisholm (1985-86)	877	Taurence Chisholm (1984-88)

THE SCHOOLS

ESPN 315 SAGARIN

DELAWARE STATE

After three painful decades, Delaware State has taken a walk on the winning side since the turn of this century. The Hornets won three straight MEAC regular-season crowns from 2005 to '07, made their first Big Dance in 2005, and went to the NIT in '06 and '07.

BEST TEAM: 2004-05 Who are you calling an underdog? Even though they ran roughshod over the MEAC, the Hornets only earned a No. 16 seed in the NCAA Tourney. But while the undersized team didn't beat Duke—which was favored by 26—the Hornets gave the Blue Devils all they could handle, going on an 11-0 second-half run to pull within nine with just under two minutes left, before falling 57-46.

BEST PLAYER: F Tom Davis (1987-91) Thanks to his ability to both overpower defenders and blow past them, Davis achieved the two top scoring seasons in school history (706 in 1988-89 and 740 in '90-91). The '89 MEAC POY also owns the Hornets' top two single-game scoring marks: 50 against Brooklyn College in '88-89 and 47 against Florida A&M that same season.

BEST COACH: Greg Jackson (2000-) He never has the biggest teams, but Jackson's players make life miserable for almost any opponent with their trademark defensive pressure. In addition to a 2005 Tourney appearance, Jackson guided the program to its first 20-win season (in 2005-06) and postseason victory (over Northern Arizona in the '06 NIT).

GAME FOR THE AGES: In the 2005 MEAC tournament title game against Hampton, Delaware State rallied from a 13-point, first-half deficit to tie it late. On the Hornets' last possession, Jahsha Bluntt tipped a rebound to Aaron Williams, who hit a fall-away jumper with 1.6 seconds on the clock, clinching a 55-53 win.

FIERCEST RIVAL: In the late 1980s and early '90s, Delaware State and Howard got into fights almost every time they played football. The hoops feud isn't nearly as nasty, but it is competitive. During a 30-game stretch from 1990-91 through 2004-05, 14 games were decided by three points or less or in OT.

SEASON REVIEW

SEAS.	W-L	CONF.	COACH	SEAS.	W-L	CONF.	COACH
1956-60	*53-40*	*Records before 1956-57 lost*		1963-64	12-9		Bennie George
1960-61	12-8		Bennie George	1964-65	7-13		Bennie George
1961-62	12-9		Bennie George	1965-66	N/A		
1962-63	5-14		Bennie George	1966-67	5-15		Bennie George

SEAS.	W-L	CONF.		SCORING		COACH	RECORD	
1967-68	11-12					Bennie George		
1968-69	11-11					Bennie George		
1969-70	17-8			Dave Withers	25.5	Bennie George		
1970-71	10-13					Bennie George[a]	201-219	.479
1971-72	7-15	2-10				Ira Mitchell		
1972-73	10-13	3-9				Ira Mitchell		
1973-74	18-11	5-7				Ira Mitchell		
1974-75	15-9	7-5				Ira Mitchell		
1975-76	6-17	4-8				Ira Mitchell	56-65	.463
1976-77	2-25	0-12				Marshall Emery		
1977-78	10-15	5-7				Marshall Emery		
1978-79	18-10	7-5				Ajac Triplett		
1979-80	15-12					Ajac Triplett		
1980-81	8-18	3-7				Ajac Triplett		
1981-82	13-13	4-8				Ajac Triplett		
1982-83	8-19	5-7				Ajac Triplett	62-72	.463
1983-84	12-16	3-7				Joe Dean Davidson		
1984-85	12-17	8-4				Joe Dean Davidson	24-33	.421
1985-86	11-17	7-7				Marshall Emery		
1986-87	4-24	3-11				Marshall Emery		
1987-88	3-25	1-15				Marshall Emery	30-106	.221
1988-89	11-17	6-10				Jeff Jones		
1989-90	14-14	9-7				Jeff Jones		
1990-91	19-11	10-6				Jeff Jones		
1991-92	12-16	9-7				Jeff Jones		
1992-93	13-16	6-10				Jeff Jones		
1993-94	8-19	5-11				Jeff Jones	77-93	.453
1994-95	7-21	3-13				Fred Goodman		
1995-96	11-17	8-8				Fred Goodman	18-38	.321
1996-97	7-20	7-11				Art Perry	7-20	.259
1997-98	9-18	7-11				Jimmy DuBose		
1998-99	8-19	5-13		Terence Hood	20.3	Jimmy DuBose	17-37	.315
1999-2000	6-22	5-13		Stefan Malliet	11.5	Tony Sheals[b]	6-22	.200
2000-01	13-15	11-7		Andre Matthews	14.8	Greg Jackson		
2001-02	16-13	12-6		Andre Matthews	14.2	Greg Jackson		
2002-03	15-12	13-5		Andre Matthews	12.9	Greg Jackson		
2003-04	13-15	11-7		Terrance Hunter	12.1	Greg Jackson		
2004-05	19-14	14-4	●	Jahsha Bluntt	13.6	Greg Jackson		
2005-06	21-14	16-2	■	Jahsha Bluntt	14.6	Greg Jackson		
2006-07	21-13	16-2	■	Roy Bright, Jahsha Bluntt	15.5	Greg Jackson		
2007-08	14-16	10-6		Roy Bright	19.1	Greg Jackson		
2008-09	8-24	6-10		Donald Johnson	12.3	Greg Jackson	140-136	.507

[a] Bennie George's career at Delaware State began in 1949-50 but only his 1956-71 record is available.
[b] Stephen Wilson coached the last three games of the 1999-2000 season (1-2) but all games were credited to Tony Sheals' record.
● NCAA Tournament appearance ■ NIT appearance

PROFILE

Delaware State University, Dover, DE
Founded: 1891
Enrollment: 3,750 (3,374 undergraduate)
Colors: Columbia blue and red
Nickname: Hornets
Current arena: Memorial Hall, opened in 1967 (3,000)
First game: 1949
All-time record: 592-774 (.433)
Total weeks in AP Top 20/25: 0

Current conference: Mid-Eastern Athletic (1971-)
Conference titles:
MEAC: 3 (2005, '06, '07)
Conference tournament titles:
MEAC: 1 (2005)
NCAA Tournament appearances: 1
NIT appearances: 2

TOP 5

G **Jahsha Bluntt** (2003-07)
G **Emanual Davis** (1988-91)
F **Tom Davis** (1987-91)
F **Ronald Horton** (1964-68)
F **Dave Withers** (1967-71)

RECORDS

RECORDS	GAME		SEASON		CAREER	
POINTS	50	Tom Davis, vs. Brooklyn (Feb. 1, 1989)	740	Tom Davis (1990-91)	2,275	Tom Davis (1987-91)
POINTS PER GAME			25.5	Dave Withers (1969-70)	23.9	Tom Davis (1987-91)
REBOUNDS	26	Dave Withers, vs. St. Paul's (Dec. 15, 1969)	543	Ronald Horton (1967-68)	1,211	Dave Withers (1967-71)
ASSISTS	13	Antoine Morris (1995-96 twice, opponents N/A)	156	Darrin Shine (2006-07); Emanual Davis (1989-90)	420	Darrin Shine (2004-07)

163
SAGARIN

DENVER

Think you don't know any Denver players? Think again. David Adkins, better known as the comedian Sinbad, played for the Pioneers in the 1970s. But he's not Denver's only claim to basketball fame. DU had strong teams during the 1940s, and four decades later ran up a 79-game home winning streak.

BEST TEAM: 2004-05 This 20–11 Denver squad actually outperformed the 1983-84 team (28–4 against NAIA competition) by winning the Sun Belt West Division title and coming ever-so-close to the school's first NCAA bid, but for a loss in the conference tournament title game to Louisiana-Lafayette.

BEST PLAYER: F Vince Boryla (1948-49) A transfer from Notre Dame, Boryla must have seemed to Denver fans like a gift from heaven. Still the school's only consensus All-America, he played on the 1948 gold-medal-winning U.S. Olympic team, was decorated as the best visiting collegian to play in Madison Square Garden in 1948-49 and went on to an NBA career with the New York Knicks.

BEST COACH: Floyd Theard (1980-85) The future looked bright for the 40-year-old Theard after he led DU to 107 wins, including 72 of the Pioneers' 79 consecutive home victories from 1980 to '85. But tragedy struck when he died of a heart attack following the 1984-85 season.

GAME FOR THE AGES: Led by conference POY Yemi Nicholson, the Pioneers found themselves on the verge of the 2005 Sun Belt West title heading into the regular season finale. After falling behind New Orleans 30-24 at halftime, Rodney Billups (younger brother of Colorado and NBA star Chauncey) carried DU to the division crown, 63-61.

FIERCEST RIVAL: Denver and Wyoming have engaged 141 times in the Pack the House game, dating back to 1920. The raucous fans from Laramie enjoy their annual visits to Denver's Magness Arena, especially when the Cowboys add to their 98–43 advantage over the Pioneers.

SEASON REVIEW

SEAS.	W-L	CONF.	COACH	SEAS.	W-L	CONF.	COACH
1903-47	*271-337*	*Went 4-16 in 1941-42; 19-8 in '42-43*		**1960-61**	12-14	6-8	Hoyt Brawner
1947-48	18-11	6-4	Ellison Ketchum	**1961-62**	8-17	5-9	Hoyt Brawner
1948-49	18-15	13-7	Ellison Ketchum[a]	**1962-63**	6-19		Troy Bledsoe
1949-50	18-13	13-7	Hoyt Brawner	**1963-64**	6-20		Troy Bledsoe
1950-51	14-16	8-12	Hoyt Brawner	**1964-65**	11-14		Troy Bledsoe
1951-52	11-15	6-8	Hoyt Brawner	**1965-66**	14-11		Troy Bledsoe
1952-53	9-16	5-9	Hoyt Brawner	**1966-67**	13-12		Troy Bledsoe
1953-54	6-21	3-11	Hoyt Brawner	**1967-68**	11-14		Troy Bledsoe
1954-55	9-14	4-10	Hoyt Brawner	**1968-69**	2-24		Stan Albeck
1955-56	13-12	6-8	Hoyt Brawner	**1969-70**	13-11		Stan Albeck
1956-57	11-12	8-6	Hoyt Brawner	**1970-71**	17-9		Jim Karabetsos
1957-58	13-12	8-6	Hoyt Brawner	**1971-72**	11-15		Jim Karabetsos
1958-59	14-10	10-4 ■	Hoyt Brawner	**1972-73**	17-9		Al Harden
1959-60	13-11	8-6	Hoyt Brawner	**1973-74**	11-15		Al Harden

SEAS.	W-L	CONF.	SCORING		COACH	RECORD	
1974-75	9-16		George Zumbro	16.1	Al Harden		
1975-76	12-15		Steve Cribari	15.8	Al Harden		
1976-77	12-15		Bob Heaton	11.7	Al Harden	61-70	.466
1977-78	10-17		Steve Bajema	16.7	Bill Weimar	10-17	.370
1978-79	15-12		Matt Teahan	25.3	Ben Jobe		
1979-80	19-10		Alonzo Weatherly	23.2	Ben Jobe	34-22	.607
1980-81	22-7		Alonzo Weatherly	15.8	Floyd Theard		
1981-82	22-7		Dwayne Russell	11.9	Floyd Theard		
1982-83	21-7		Mark Langkamp	14.6	Floyd Theard		
1983-84	28-4		Mark Langkamp	19.6	Floyd Theard		
1984-85	14-13		Casey Carrabine	14.6	Floyd Theard	107-38	.738
1985-86	17-12		Stan Adams	12.2	Dick Peth		
1986-87	20-9		Peter Faller	15.8	Dick Peth		
1987-88	19-9		Peter Faller	16.6	Dick Peth		
1988-89	18-12		Dave Collignon	19.8	Dick Peth		
1989-90	16-12		Scott Williams	24.0	Dick Peth		
1990-91	19-10		Alex Sund	15.2	Dick Peth		
1991-92	26-6		Alex Sund	16.2	Dick Peth		
1992-93	15-11		Mark Ziegler	13.7	Dick Peth		
1993-94	17-13		Lars Van Etten	17.0	Dick Peth		
1994-95	18-10		Ashley Day	16.3	Dick Peth		
1995-96	22-7		Ashley Day	21.1	Dick Peth		
1996-97	14-12		Doug Price	20.7	Dick Peth	221-123	.642
1997-98	7-20		Russell Martin	16.3	Marty Fletcher		
1998-99	10-17		Arthur Ireland	17.1	Marty Fletcher		
1999-2000	6-22	3-13	Wahhab Carter	17.4	Marty Fletcher		
2000-01	10-18	5-11	B.J. Pratt	16.2	Marty Fletcher	33-77	.300
2001-02	8-20	3-12	B.J. Pratt	13.9	Terry Carroll		
2002-03	17-15	7-8	B.J. Pratt	16.0	Terry Carroll		
2003-04	14-13	6-9	Erik Benzel	14.4	Terry Carroll		
2004-05	20-11	12-3 ■	Yemi Nicholson	18.1	Terry Carroll		
2005-06	16-15	7-8	Yemi Nicholson	19.9	Terry Carroll		
2006-07	4-25	3-15	DaShawn Walker	14.9	Terry Carroll	79-99	.444
2007-08	11-19	7-11	Adam Tanner	10.8	Joe Scott		
2008-09	15-16	9-9	Nate Rohnert	15.3	Joe Scott	26-35	.426

[a] Ellison Ketchum (6-9) and Hoyt Brawner (12-6) coached during the 1948-49 season.
■ NIT appearance

PROFILE

University of Denver, Denver, CO
Founded: 1864
Enrollment: 11,053 (5,285 undergraduate)
Colors: Crimson and gold
Nickname: Pioneers
Current arena: Magness Arena, opened in 1999 (7,200)
Previous: DU Fieldhouse, 1948-99 (2,000); DU Gymnasium, 1911-48 (N/A)
First game: Jan. 16, 1904
All-time record: 1,133-1,176 (.491)

Total weeks in AP Top 20/25: 0
Current conference: Sun Belt (1999-)
Conference titles:
Sun Belt: 1 (2005)
Conference tournament titles: 0
NCAA Tournament appearances: 0
NIT appearances: 2

CONSENSUS ALL-AMERICAS

1949 **Vince Boryla, F**

TOP 5

G **Harry Hollines** (1965-68)
G **B.J. Pratt** (1999-2003)
F **Vince Boryla** (1948-49)
F **Dave Bustion** (1970-72)
C **Yemi Nicholson** (2003-06)

RECORDS

RECORDS	GAME		SEASON		CAREER	
POINTS	61	Matt Teahan, vs. Nebraska Wesleyan (Feb. 26, 1979)	659	Matt Teahan (1978-79)	1,879	Harry Hollines (1965-68)
POINTS PER GAME			25.3	Matt Teahan (1978-79)	25.1	Harry Hollines (1965-68)
REBOUNDS	38	Dick Brott, vs. Evansville (Dec. 29, 1956)	425	Dick Brott (1956-57)	1,067	Dick Brott (1954-57)
ASSISTS	18	Tom Jorgensen, vs. Houston Baptist (Feb. 16, 1979)	224	Tom Jorgensen (1979-80)	560	Doug Wilson (1981-84)

ESPN 26 SAGARIN

DEPAUL

Known by Chicagoans as "the little school under the El," DePaul's best days in college basketball came during the 1940s, when the city game held sway and George Mikan ruled under the basket. The Blue Demons rose again in the late 1970s, but playing in three different conferences since the 1990s has stalled their success. Now a member of the Big East, fans are hoping for a third Blue Demons reign.

BEST TEAM: 1944-45 With apologies to the Mark Aguirre-led Iron Five that carried DePaul to the 1979 Final Four, there's no denying the 21–3 team that won the 1945 NIT championship. Mikan scored 120 points in three tournament games, including 53 in a 97-53 semifinal win over Rhode Island and 34 in a 71-54 victory over Bowling Green in the final.

BEST PLAYER: C GEORGE MIKAN (1942-46) At 6'9", he was so unusually tall for his time that his own teammates used to tease him, singing, "Mikan's girl is 10 feet tall. She sleeps in the kitchen with her feet in the hall." The joke, of course, was usually on his overmatched opponents. The three-time All-America and two-time Player of the Year blocked so many shots and was such a defensive force, as was Oklahoma State big man Bob Kurland, that the NCAA instituted a defensive goaltending rule in 1944.

BEST COACH: RAY MEYER (1942-84) Meyer took over a team that practiced in a drafty former theater known as the Barn and, over the next 42 seasons, built it into a national contender showcased at the 18,500-seat Rosemont Horizon (as the Allstate Arena was then known). He was inducted into the Naismith Hall of Fame in 1979.

GAME FOR THE AGES: On Feb. 12, 1978, DePaul announced to the nation that the Blue Demons were once again a force to be reckoned with, going on the road and beating Notre Dame, 69-68, in overtime. DePaul-Notre Dame shared a national telecast window with another game, but the combined audiences watched as Gary Garland drained the winning basket with :03 left in OT.

HEARTBREAKER: A No.1-seed in the 1981 NCAA Tournament coming off a first-round bye, DePaul led Saint Joseph's 48-47 with :12 to go when the Blue Demons' Skip Dillard missed the front end of a one-and-one. Lonnie McFarlan of Saint Joe's found John Smith under the basket with :03 left for the game-winner.

FIERCEST RIVAL: DePaul basketball coach Jerry Wainwright grew up Catholic in Chicago. He was a Notre Dame fan when it came to football, but stuck to his hometown team for hoops. "DePaul was Chicago's team, so I didn't even think about Notre Dame basketball," Wainwright said. "They were Darth Vader in my mind." With both teams in the Big East, this series, which the Irish lead, 55–44, has never been more intense.

"DePaul was Chicago's team, so I didn't even think about Notre Dame basketball," Blue Demons coach Jerry Wainwright said. "They were Darth Vader in my mind."

FANFARE AND HOOPLA: During the Digger Phelps era at Notre Dame (1971-91), the Blue Demons student section would begin to chant, "Sit Down, Digger!" the moment the coach strode onto the sidelines. The tradition continues whenever Phelps works a DePaul game as a TV analyst.

FAN FAVORITE: G/F TOM KLEINSCHMIDT (1991-95) He arrived at DePaul already a Chicago hero, having led Gordon Tech High to the 1990 Class AA state finals. He left an icon, his gritty play underscoring his undeniable talent.

CONSENSUS ALL-AMERICAS

1944-46	**George Mikan**, C
1980, '81	**Mark Aguirre**, F
1982	**Terry Cummings**, F

FIRST-ROUND PRO PICKS

1948	**Ed Mikan**, Chicago (5)
1956	**Ron Sobie**, Fort Wayne (7)
1975	**Bill Robinzine**, KC-Omaha (10)
1978	**Dave Corzine**, Washington (18)
1981	**Mark Aguirre**, Dallas (1)
1982	**Terry Cummings**, San Diego (2)
1987	**Dallas Comegys**, Atlanta (21)
1988	**Rod Strickland**, New York (19)
1988	**Kevin Edwards**, Miami (20)
2000	**Quentin Richardson**, LA Clippers (18)
2001	**Steve Hunter**, Orlando (15)
2007	**Wilson Chandler**, New York (23)

PROFILE

DePaul University, Chicago, IL
Founded: 1898
Enrollment: 23,401 (15,024 undergraduate)
Colors: Royal blue and scarlet
Nickname: Blue Demons
Current arena: Ray and Marge Meyer Court at Allstate Arena, opened in 1980 (18,500); McGrath Arena (3,000)
Previous: United Center, 1994-2002 (21,000); Alumni Hall, 1956-99 (5,300); DePaul Auditorium (the Barn) 1942-56 (1,000)
First game: 1923

All-time record: 1,357-814 (.625)
Total weeks in AP Top 20/25: 156
Current conference: Big East (2005-)
Conference titles:
Great Midwest: 1 (1992)
Conference USA: 1 (2004 [tie])
Conference tournament titles: 0
NCAA Tournament appearances: 22
Sweet 16s (since 1975): 6
Final Fours: 2
NIT appearances: 16
Semifinals: 5
Titles: 1 (1945)

TOP 5

G	**David Booth** (1988-92)
G/F	**Tom Kleinschmidt** (1991-95)
F	**Mark Aguirre** (1978-81)
F	**Dave Corzine** (1974-78)
C	**George Mikan** (1942-46)

RECORDS	GAME		SEASON		CAREER	
POINTS	53	George Mikan, vs. Rhode Island (March 21, 1945)	767	Mark Aguirre (1978-79)	2,182	Mark Aguirre (1978-81)
POINTS PER GAME			26.8	Mark Aguirre (1979-80)	24.5	Mark Aguirre (1978-81)
REBOUNDS	28	Ken Warzynski, vs. Harvard (Jan. 3, 1970)	379	Ken Warzynski (1969-70)	1,151	Dave Corzine (1974-78)
ASSISTS	17	Imari Sawyer, vs. Youngstown State (Nov. 25, 2001)	215	Clyde Bradshaw (1979-80)	669	Kenny Patterson (1981-85)

SEASON REVIEW

SEASON	W-L	CONF.	SCORING	COACH	RECORD
1923-24	8-6			Robert L. Stevenson	8-6 .571
1924-25	6-13			Harry Adams	6-13 .316
1925-26	11-5			Eddie Anderson	
1926-27	7-7			Eddie Anderson	
1927-28	2-5			Eddie Anderson	
1928-29	5-4			Eddie Anderson	25-21 .543
1929-30	15-5			Jim Kelly	
1930-31	13-3			Jim Kelly	
1931-32	9-6			Jim Kelly	
1932-33	12-3			Jim Kelly	
1933-34	17-0			Jim Kelly	
1934-35	15-1			Jim Kelly	
1935-36	18-4			Jim Kelly	99-22 .818
1936-37	15-6			Tom Haggarty	
1937-38	12-10			Tom Haggarty	
1938-39	15-7			Tom Haggarty	

SEAS.	W-L	CONF.	POSTSEASON	SCORING	REBOUNDS	ASSISTS	COACH	RECORD
1939-40	22-6		NIT FOURTH PLACE				Tom Haggarty	64-29 .688
1940-41	13-8						Bill Wendt	
1941-42	10-12						Bill Wendt	23-20 .535
1942-43	19-5		NATIONAL SEMIFINALS				Ray Meyer	
1943-44	22-4		NIT RUNNER-UP				Ray Meyer	
1944-45	21-3		NIT CHAMPION	George Mikan 23.3			Ray Meyer	
1945-46	19-5			George Mikan 23.1			Ray Meyer	
1946-47	16-9			Ed Mikan 15.7			Ray Meyer	
1947-48	22-8		NIT FOURTH PLACE	Ed Mikan 15.4			Ray Meyer	
1948-49	16-9			Bato Govedarica 8.5			Ray Meyer	
1949-50	12-13			Bato Govedarica 12.9			Ray Meyer	
1950-51	13-12			Bato Govedarica 14.0			Ray Meyer	
1951-52	19-8			Gene Dyker 14.8			Ray Meyer	
1952-53	19-9		NCAA REGIONAL SEMIFINALS	Ron Feiereisel 18.0			Ray Meyer	
1953-54	11-10			Jim Lamkin 19.3			Ray Meyer	
1954-55	16-6			Ron Sobieszczyk 17.3			Ray Meyer	
1955-56	16-8		NCAA FIRST ROUND	Ron Sobieszczyk 22.5			Ray Meyer	
1956-57	8-14			Dick Heise 24.3	Dick Heise 10.5		Ray Meyer	
1957-58	8-12			Paul Ruddy 12.2	Bill Coglianese 9.5		Ray Meyer	
1958-59	13-11		NCAA REGIONAL SEMIFINALS	Howie Carl 19.2	Jim Flemming 10.7		Ray Meyer	
1959-60	17-7		NCAA REGIONAL SEMIFINALS	Howie Carl 19.7	McKinley Cowsen 10.2		Ray Meyer	
1960-61	17-8		NIT FIRST ROUND	Howie Carl 16.3	M.C. Thompson 13.3		Ray Meyer	
1961-62	13-10			M.C. Thompson 16.3	M.C. Thompson 15.4		Ray Meyer	
1962-63	15-8		NIT FIRST ROUND	M.C. Thompson 15.6	M.C. Thompson 12.4		Ray Meyer	
1963-64	21-4		NIT QUARTERFINALS	Jesse Nash 17.5	Jesse Nash 12.3		Ray Meyer	
1964-65	17-10		NCAA REGIONAL SEMIFINALS	Jim Murphy 17.5	Errol Palmer 11.2		Ray Meyer	
1965-66	18-8		NIT FIRST ROUND	Don Swanson 18.0	Errol Palmer 12.5		Ray Meyer	
1966-67	17-8			Mike Norris 17.2	Errol Palmer 11.3		Ray Meyer	
1967-68	13-12			Al Zetzsche 15.3	Ken Warzynski 9.4		Ray Meyer	
1968-69	14-11			Al Zetzsche 17.4	Ken Warzynski 11.0		Ray Meyer	
1969-70	12-13			Ken Warzynski 19.6	Ken Warzynski 15.2		Ray Meyer	
1970-71	8-17			Joey Meyer 19.2	Al Burks 9.7		Ray Meyer	
1971-72	12-11			Al Burks 20.3	Al Burks 8.3		Ray Meyer	
1972-73	14-11			Greg Boyd 17.5	Bill Robinzine 10.1		Ray Meyer	
1973-74	16-9			Bill Robinzine 16.8	Bill Robinzine 10.2	Mike Gillepsie 128	Ray Meyer	
1974-75	15-10			Bill Robinzine 19.4	Bill Robinzine 13.5	Ron Norwood 97	Ray Meyer	
1975-76	20-9		NCAA REGIONAL SEMIFINALS	Ron Norwood 19.3	Dave Corzine 8.8	Ron Norwood 133	Ray Meyer	
1976-77	15-12			Dave Corzine 19.0	Dave Corzine 12.6	Ron Norwood 126	Ray Meyer	
1977-78	27-3		NCAA REGIONAL FINALS	Dave Corzine 21.0	Dave Corzine 13.5	Joe Ponsetto 119	Ray Meyer	
1978-79	26-6		NCAA THIRD PLACE	Mark Aguirre 24.0	Curtis Watkins 8.1	Gary Garland 188	Ray Meyer	
1979-80	26-2		NCAA SECOND ROUND	Mark Aguirre 26.8	Terry Cummings 9.4	Clyde Bradshaw 215	Ray Meyer	
1980-81	27-2		NCAA SECOND ROUND	Mark Aguirre 23.0	Terry Cummings 9.0	Clyde Bradshaw 188	Ray Meyer	
1981-82	26-2		NCAA SECOND ROUND	Terry Cummings 22.3	Terry Cummings 11.9	Kenny Patterson 92	Ray Meyer	
1982-83	21-12		NIT RUNNER-UP	Bernard Randolph 13.7	Tyrone Corbin 7.9	Kenny Patterson 187	Ray Meyer	
1983-84	27-3		NCAA REGIONAL SEMIFINALS	Tyrone Corbin 14.1	Tyrone Corbin 7.4	Kenny Patterson 189	Ray Meyer	724-354 .672
1984-85	19-10		NCAA FIRST ROUND	Tyrone Corbin 15.8	Tyrone Corbin 8.1	Kenny Patterson 201	Joey Meyer	
1985-86	18-13 ⊗		NCAA REGIONAL SEMIFINALS	Rod Strickland 14.1	Marty Embry 7.3	Rod Strickland 159	Joey Meyer	
1986-87	28-3 ⊗		NCAA REGIONAL SEMIFINALS	Dallas Comegys 17.5	Dallas Comegys 7.5	Rod Strickland 196	Joey Meyer	
1987-88	22-8 ⊗		NCAA SECOND ROUND	Rod Strickland 20.0	Stanley Brundy 8.7	Rod Strickland 202	Joey Meyer	
1988-89	21-12 ⊗		NCAA SECOND ROUND	Stanley Brundy 19.5	Stanley Brundy 10.2	Terence Greene 168	Joey Meyer	
1989-90	20-15		NIT QUARTERFINALS	David Booth 16.9	Stephen Howard 8.1	Melvon Foster 127	Joey Meyer	
1990-91	20-9		NCAA FIRST ROUND	David Booth 18.7	David Booth 6.8	Joe Daughrity 134	Joey Meyer	
1991-92	20-9	8-2	NCAA FIRST ROUND	David Booth 17.4	Stephen Howard 8.7	Joe Daughrity 145	Joey Meyer	
1992-93	16-15	3-7		Tom Kleinschmidt 17.7	Kris Hill 8.3	Brandon Cole 135	Joey Meyer	
1993-94	16-12	4-8	NIT FIRST ROUND	Tom Kleinschmidt 20.5	Kris Hill 7.2	Tom Kleinschmidt 107	Joey Meyer	
1994-95	17-11	6-6	NIT FIRST ROUND	Tom Kleinschmidt 21.4	Will Macon 9.0	Tom Kleinschmidt 127	Joey Meyer	
1995-96	11-18 ⊗	2-12		Jermaine Watts 16.2	Bryant Bowden 7.8	Jermaine Watts 154	Joey Meyer	
1996-97	3-23	1-13		Charles Gelatt 12.9	Charles Gelatt 7.0	Thomas Cooper 61	Joey Meyer	231-158 .594▼
1997-98	7-23	3-13		Jermaine Watts 15.9	Demarcus Gaines 7.9	Willie Coleman 84	Pat Kennedy	
1998-99	18-13	10-6	NIT SECOND ROUND	Quentin Richardson 18.9	Quentin Richardson 10.5	Kerry Hartfield 3.1	Pat Kennedy	
1999-2000	21-12	9-7	NCAA FIRST ROUND	Quentin Richardson 17.0	Quentin Richardson 9.8	Rashon Burno 4.6	Pat Kennedy	
2000-01	12-18	4-12		Bobby Simmons 16.7	Bobby Simmons 8.6	Imari Sawyer 6.0	Pat Kennedy	
2001-02	9-19	2-14		Andre Brown 14.5	Andre Brown 9.4	Imari Sawyer 5.4	Pat Kennedy	67-85 .441
2002-03	16-13	8-8	NIT FIRST ROUND	Sam Hoskin 15.6	Andre Brown 9.0	Drake Diener 3.4	Dave Leitao	
2003-04	22-10	12-4	NCAA SECOND ROUND	Delonte Holland 16.5	Andre Brown 9.2	Sammy Mejia 4.4	Dave Leitao	
2004-05	20-11	10-6	NIT SECOND ROUND	Quemont Greer 18.3	Quemont Greer 7.6	Cliff Clinkscales 3.4	Dave Leitao	58-34 .630
2005-06	12-15	5-11		Sammy Mejia 15.1	Wilson Chandler 7.2	Jabari Currie 2.8	Jerry Wainwright	
2006-07	20-14	9-7	NIT QUARTERFINALS	Wilson Chandler 14.6	Wilson Chandler 6.9	Jabari Currie 3.0	Jerry Wainwright	
2007-08	11-19	6-12		Draelon Burns 17.6	Mac Koshwal 8.4	Cliff Clinkscales 4.1	Jerry Wainwright	
2008-09	9-24	0-18		Dar Tucker 18.5	Mac Koshwal 9.6	Jeremiah Kelly 2.4	Jerry Wainwright	52-72 .419

Cumulative totals listed when per game averages not available.

⊗ Records do not reflect games forfeited or vacated. For adjusted records, see p. 521.

▼ Coach's record adjusted to reflect games forfeited or vacated: 226-153, .596. For yearly totals, see p. 521.

ESPN 107 SAGARIN

DETROIT

The city has many nicknames, including Hockeytown, but don't be fooled. Few places are more talent-rich or passionate about hoops than the Motor City. The UDM Titans (the school changed its name to Detroit Mercy in 1990, but it's still referred to simply as Detroit) have done Motown proud with a history that dates back more than 100 years and includes two all-time greats, plus an exuberant coach now synonymous with NCAA basketball, Dick Vitale.

BEST TEAM: 1976-77 On Feb. 16, after the Titans beat Marquette—the team that would eventually win the Tournament—all but clinching an NCAA bid, Vitale and his players boogied on the Warriors' home floor. Following a first-round win over Middle Tennessee State, Detroit faced in-state rival and 1976 national runner-up Michigan. Falling behind early, the Titans tied the game at 68 but eventually ran out of gas in an 86-81 loss. It would be Vitale's final game as coach.

BEST PLAYER: F DAVE DEBUSSCHERE (1959-62) The Detroit native was known as Big D for his name and for his defensive prowess, but he could truly do it all (including pitch in the major leagues). He averaged 24.8 points and 19.4 rebounds over three seasons, before going on to a Hall-of-Fame career in the NBA. His tenacious play made him so beloved in Detroit that after his death, the city declared Feb. 14, 2004, Dave DeBusschere Day.

BEST COACH: BOB CALIHAN (1948-69) Often stocked with supreme talents such as DeBusschere, Dick Dzik and the great Spencer Haywood, Calihan's teams always had players who could score in bunches. This was best exemplified by the Titans' 1963-64 crew, which led the NCAA with 96.1 points per game—more than 20 above the national average. Calihan endured only five losing seasons in 21 years and leads all Titans coaches in career victories (304) by a significant margin.

GAME FOR THE AGES: Already 0–3 against his idol, Vitale got one last shot at Al McGuire on Feb. 16, 1977, before the legendary Marquette coach retired. Detroit's Dennis Boyd hit a 20-footer at the buzzer for the 64-63 road win. After the game, Vitale said, "I haven't been this choked up since I lost my eye when I was a kid." In a fitting twist, both coaches would go on to memorable TV careers.

HEARTBREAKER: After a rough regular season, UDM made a run to the 2005 Horizon League title game against Bruce Pearl's Wisconsin-Milwaukee squad. Sparked by 21 points from freshman guard Brandon Cotton, the Titans led for much of the game, which was played on the Panthers' home floor. But UWM forward Adrian Tigert hit two free throws with 4.2 seconds left for a 59-58 lead, and Cotton's shot at the buzzer missed to ruin Detroit's Cinderella dreams.

FIERCEST RIVAL: In a series that dates back to 1935-36, the Titans always amp up to play a Butler team that has dominated the Horizon League in recent years. Butler leads the series, 39–27. No UDM loss was more bitter than a 58-55 defeat at the hands of the Bulldogs in the semifinals of the 2003 conference tournament. Afterward, Detroit coach Perry Watson called the officiating "a joke."

> ***DeBusschere was known as Big D—for his name as well as for his defensive prowess.***

FANFARE AND HOOPLA: After serving as a Rutgers assistant for two years, Dickie V was virtually unknown when he arrived at Detroit in 1973. But he soon became a local—then national—celebrity with his loud mouth and crazy antics. In 1979, just over a year after heading across town to coach the NBA Pistons, he was a part of ESPN's first college basketball broadcast. He was elected to the Basketball Hall of Fame in 2008 as a contributor.

FAN FAVORITE: G BERNIE FUHS (1999-2003) A walk-on player, Fuhs (pronounced *Foose*) was the recipient of many a "Put in Fuhs!" chant during his career. As a senior, the Grand Rapids native averaged 2.3 ppg, his every score sending UDM fans into a frenzy.

PROFILE

University of Detroit Mercy, Detroit, MI
Founded: 1877
Enrollment: 5,723 (3,254 undergraduate)
Colors: Red, white and blue
Nickname: Titans
Current arena: Calihan Hall, opened as the Memorial Building in 1952 (8,295)
First game: 1906
All-time record: 1,267-1,061-3 (.544)
Total weeks in AP Top 20/25: 41

Current conference: Horizon League (1980-)
Conference titles:
Midwestern Collegiate: 2 (1998 [tie]. '99)
Conference tournament titles:
Midwestern Collegiate: 2 (1994, '99)
NCAA Tournament appearances: 5
Sweet 16s (since 1975): 1
NIT appearances: 6
Semifinals: 1

CONSENSUS ALL-AMERICAS

1969 **Spencer Haywood,** F

FIRST-ROUND PRO PICKS

1962 **Dave DeBusschere,** Detroit (4)
1970 **Spencer Haywood,** Denver (ABA)

TOP 5

G **Willie Green** (1999-2003)
G **Rashad Phillips** (1997-2001)
F **Dave DeBusschere** (1959-62)
F **Spencer Haywood** (1968-69)
F **John Long** (1974-78)

RECORDS

RECORDS	GAME		SEASON		CAREER	
POINTS	49	Archie Tullos, vs. Bradley (Feb. 22, 1988)	785	Rashad Phillips (2000-01)	2,319	Rashad Phillips (1997-2001)
POINTS PER GAME			32.1	Spencer Haywood (1968-69)	24.8	Dave DeBusschere (1959-62)
REBOUNDS	39	Dave DeBusschere, vs. Central Michigan (Jan. 30, 1960)	540	Dave DeBusschere (1959-60)	1,552	Dave DeBusschere (1959-62)
ASSISTS	19	Wilbert McCormick, vs. Canisius (Feb. 18, 1978)	220	Wilbert McCormick (1977-78)	615	Kevin McAdoo (1982-86)

SEASON REVIEW

SEASON	W-L	CONF.	COMMENTS	COACH	RECORD
1905-20	*81-44-1*		*Royal Campbell was 49-22 in two stints as coach (1909-13, '16-19)*		
1920-21	10-8		Walter Voss 8.7	James Brown	
1921-22	2-13-1		P. D'Arcy 3.5	James Brown	24-28-1 .462
1922-23	9-7		P. D'Arcy 8.5	Paul Harbrecht	9-7 .563
1923-24	9-8		Eddie Harrigan 4.6	John Barrett	
1924-25	6-6-1		Eddie Harrigan 7.7	John Barrett	15-14-1 .517
1925-26	13-6		Joe Fasce 8.5	Charles "Gus" Dorais	
1926-27	8-9			Charles "Gus" Dorais	
1927-28	11-4		Bill Butcher 7.0	Charles "Gus" Dorais	
1928-29	4-11		Lloyd Brazil 4.8	Charles "Gus" Dorais	36-30 .545
1929-30	10-9		Ed Gracey 5.9	Louis Conroy	10-9 .526

SEASON	W-L	CONF.	COMMENTS	COACH	RECORD
1930-31	10-9		Roger Lau 4.3	Lloyd Brazil	
1931-32	8-8		Ed Skrzycki 8.0	Lloyd Brazil	
1932-33	12-5		Bill Pegan 6.2	Lloyd Brazil	
1933-34	7-8		Larry Bleach 6.6	Lloyd Brazil	
1934-35	4-10		Walter Cavanaugh 6.4	Lloyd Brazil	
1935-36	12-5		Chet Laske 9.6	Lloyd Brazil	
1936-37	11-5		Chet Laske 8.7	Lloyd Brazil	
1937-38	16-4		Bob Calihan 9.8	Lloyd Brazil	
1938-39	15-5		Bob Calihan 13.3	Lloyd Brazil	
1939-40	14-9		Bob Calihan 13.8	Lloyd Brazil	
1940-41	11-10		Charles O'Brien 5.4	Lloyd Brazil	

SEAS.	W-L	CONF.	POSTSEASON	SCORING	REBOUNDS	ASSISTS	COACH	RECORD
1941-42	13-8			Arthur Stokley 6.3			Lloyd Brazil	
1942-43	15-5			Lee Knorek 12.1			Lloyd Brazil	
1943-44	13-7			Joey Smith 7.6			Lloyd Brazil	
1944-45	8-12			Tom Molitor 9.9			Lloyd Brazil	
1945-46	15-8			Gino Sovran 8.9			Lloyd Brazil	184-118 .609
1946-47	11-13			Sam Fortino 12.5			John Shada	
1947-48	7-15			Brendan McNamara 7.3			John Shada	18-28 .391
1948-49	12-10			John Kirwan 9.2			Bob Calihan	
1949-50	20-6	7-5		Norm Swanson 14.9			Bob Calihan	
1950-51	17-14	7-7		Norm Swanson 12.5			Bob Calihan	
1951-52	14-12	4-6		Norm Swanson 19.2			Bob Calihan	
1952-53	12-14	4-6		Walter Poff 16.7			Bob Calihan	
1953-54	11-17	1-9		Guy Sparrow 19.6			Bob Calihan	
1954-55	15-11	2-8		Guy Sparrow 23.1	Guy Sparrow 18.8		Bob Calihan	
1955-56	13-12	3-9		Bill Ebben 23.6			Bob Calihan	
1956-57	11-15	5-9		Bill Ebben 27.8			Bob Calihan	
1957-58	13-12			Mike Walsh 15.8	Don Haase 375		Bob Calihan	
1958-59	11-14			Ray Albee 13.7			Bob Calihan	
1959-60	20-7		NIT FIRST ROUND	Dave DeBusschere 25.6	Dave DeBusschere 540		Bob Calihan	
1960-61	18-9		NIT FIRST ROUND	Dave DeBusschere 22.1	Dave DeBusschere 514		Bob Calihan	
1961-62	15-12		NCAA FIRST ROUND	Dave DeBusschere 26.8	Dave DeBusschere 498		Bob Calihan	
1962-63	14-12			Dick Dzik 16.3	Dick Dzik 385		Bob Calihan	
1963-64	14-11			Dick Dzik 21.7	Dick Dzik 20.8		Bob Calihan	
1964-65	20-8		NIT QUARTERFINALS	Lou Hyatt 17.6	Dorie Murrey 366		Bob Calihan	
1965-66	17-8			Dorie Murrey 22.3	Dorie Murrey 16.6		Bob Calihan	
1966-67	10-15			Jerry Swartzfager 17.0			Bob Calihan	
1967-68	13-12			Ralph Brisker 15.4			Bob Calihan	
1968-69	14-10			Spencer Haywood 32.1	Spencer Haywood 22.1		Bob Calihan	304-241 .558
1969-70	7-18			Frank Russell 15.5			Jim Harding	
1970-71	14-12			Frank Russell 15.8			Jim Harding	
1971-72	18-6			Bill Pleas 16.6			Jim Harding	
1972-73	16-9			Gerald Smith 14.7			Jim Harding	55-45 .550
1973-74	17-9			Owen Wells 20.6			Dick Vitale	
1974-75	17-9			John Long 17.1			Dick Vitale	
1975-76	19-8			John Long 19.5			Dick Vitale	
1976-77	25-4 ⊘		NCAA REGIONAL SEMIFINALS	John Long 20.3		Dennis Boyd 219	Dick Vitale	78-30 .722▼
1977-78	25-4		NIT SECOND ROUND	John Long 21.4		Wilbert McCormick 220	Smokey Gaines	
1978-79	22-6		NCAA FIRST ROUND	Terry Duerod 23.3		Wilbert McCormick 184	Smokey Gaines	47-10 .825
1979-80	14-13			Earl Cureton 20.0			Willie McCarter	
1980-81	9-18	1-5		Joe Kopicki 19.9			Willie McCarter	
1981-82	10-17	6-6		Joe Kopicki 18.6			Willie McCarter	33-48 .407
1982-83	12-17	6-8		Doug Chappell 17.6			Don Sicko	
1983-84	8-20	4-10		Keith Gray 17.0		Kevin McAdoo 157	Don Sicko	
1984-85	16-12	8-6		Keith Gray 17.5		Kevin McAdoo 147	Don Sicko	
1985-86	14-15	7-5		Brian Humes 14.1		Kevin McAdoo 215	Don Sicko	
1986-87	7-21	2-10		Archie Tullos 19.7			Don Sicko	
1987-88	7-23	2-8		Archie Tullos 25.1			Don Sicko[a]	57-88 .393
1988-89	7-21	4-8		Darian McKinney 16.1		Bill Wood 158	Ricky Byrdsong	
1989-90	10-18	3-11		Shawn Williams 12.4			Ricky Byrdsong	
1990-91	9-19	2-12		Dwayne Kelley 15.9			Ricky Byrdsong	
1991-92	12-17	1-9		Dwayne Kelley 16.1			Ricky Byrdsong	
1992-93	15-12	7-7		Tony Tolbert 20.4			Ricky Byrdsong	53-87 .379
1993-94	16-13	5-5		Tony Tolbert 23.6			Perry Watson	
1994-95	13-15	9-5		Carl Pickett 12.4			Perry Watson	
1995-96	18-11	8-8		Carl Pickett 14.3			Perry Watson	
1996-97	16-13	11-5		Derrick Hayes 15.9			Perry Watson	
1997-98	25-6	12-2	NCAA SECOND ROUND	Derrick Hayes 13.7			Perry Watson	
1998-99	25-6	12-2	NCAA SECOND ROUND	Rashad Phillips 15.7	Jermaine Jackson 6.4	Jermaine Jackson 4.5	Perry Watson	
1999-2000	20-12	8-6		Rashad Phillips 23.0	Terrell Riggs 6.8	Rashad Phillips 5.3	Perry Watson	
2000-01	25-12	10-4	NIT FOURTH PLACE	Rashad Phillips 22.4	Terrell Riggs 6.5	Rashad Phillips 4.1	Perry Watson	
2001-02	18-13	11-5	NIT OPENING ROUND	Greg Grays 17.8	Terrell Riggs 7.5	Jimmy Twyman 2.2	Perry Watson	
2002-03	18-12	9-7		Willie Green 22.6	Terrell Riggs 5.9	Willie Green 2.5	Perry Watson	
2003-04	19-11	10-6		Elijah Warren 11.6	Willie Wallace 5.1	James Thues 3.6	Perry Watson	
2004-05	14-16	9-7		Brandon Cotton 18.8	Torvoris Baker 5.8	James Thues 2.6	Perry Watson	
2005-06	16-16	8-8		Brandon Cotton 17.5	Torvoris Baker 7.6	Jon Goode 3.3	Perry Watson	
2006-07	11-19	6-10		Brandon Cotton 18.1	Ryvon Covile 10.6	Brandon Bell 2.9	Perry Watson	
2007-08	7-23	3-15		Jon Goode 19.3	Chris Hayes 6.2	Jon Goode 2.7	Perry Watson[b]	261-198 .569
2008-09	7-23	2-16		Thomas Kennedy 11.6	Thomas Kennedy 4.5	Woody Payne 3.6	Ray McCallum	7-23 .233

Cumulative totals listed when per game averages not available.

[a] Don Sicko (0-3) and John Mulroy (7-20) both coached during 1987-88.

[b] Perry Watson (4-10) and Kevin Mondro (3-13) both coached during 2007-08, but all games are credited to Watson.

⊘ Record does not reflect games forfeited or vacated. For adjusted record, see p. 521.

▼ Coach's record adjusted to reflect games forfeited or vacated: 79-29, .731. For yearly totals, see p. 521.

ESPN 104 SAGARIN

DRAKE

If not for a harsh dry spell from 1987-88 to 2005-06 that saw the Bulldogs go 19 straight seasons without a winning record, Drake would have a good argument for ranking among the very best of the mid-majors. There's the 1969 Final Four, a school-record 28 wins in 2007-08, and one of the greatest—and wildest—coaches of his time, Maury John. But it takes a long time to live down that kind of drought.

BEST TEAM: 1968-69 The Bulldogs had finished tied for dead last in the Missouri Valley Conference just two seasons before, but that didn't stop Drake from matching Louisville's first-place conference record, topping the Cards in a playoff for the MVC regular-season crown, and charging to the NCAA Final Four with wins over Texas A&M and Colorado State. There, the Willie McCarter-led Bulldogs lost to UCLA, 85-82. Said Bruins coach John Wooden, "Drake gave us as much trouble—maybe more—than any team we've ever played in [any of] the Tournaments." In the third-place game, Drake crushed North Carolina, 104-84.

BEST PLAYER: G Willie McCarter (1966-69) While being recruited by Drake, future defensive star Dolph Pulliam lobbied Coach John to also take McCarter, his high school teammate in Gary, Ind. Pulliam said, "Coach, listen to me, Willie McCarter is going to make you famous." Those words proved prophetic. McCarter was the leading scorer (20.4 ppg) on the 1969 Final Four team and ranks third all-time at the school in points (1,626). He was chosen 12th in the 1969 NBA draft (LA Lakers).

BEST COACH: Maury John (1958-71) During his final three seasons before departing for Iowa State, John led the Bulldogs to the Final Four once (1969) and the regional finals twice (1970, '71). He used a ferocious brand of man-to-man known as "belly button defense" and was not above motivational ploys such as faking negative news clippings about his team.

GAME FOR THE AGES: To many Bulldogs backers, when Drake lost to Lew Alcindor and UCLA, 85-82, in the 1969 Final Four, the program won something nearly as important—national respect. McCarter finished with 24 points, but missed 17 of his 27 shots. Later, whenever the two players faced off in the NBA, McCarter reminded Alcindor (at that point, Kareem Abdul-Jabbar) that if only he had shot a bit better, "We would have kicked your a--."

HEARTBREAKER: In 2007-08, Drake sailed through the regular season 28–4 and earned a No. 5 seed in the NCAA Tournament. But in the first round, the Bulldogs had to claw their way back from 16 points down in the final minutes to tie No. 12-seed Western Kentucky in regulation. Drake led by a point in the waning seconds of the extra session, but WKU's Ty Rogers hit a miracle, buzzer-beating three with several hands in his face to end Drake's season, 101-99. The two teams combined for a record 70 three-point attempts in the manic contest, with Klayton Korver leading the Bulldogs by hitting 6-of-14 treys on his way to 21 points.

Dolph Pulliam said, "Coach, listen to me, Willie McCarter is going to make you famous."

FIERCEST RIVAL: The campus of MVC foe Creighton is just 135 miles away, so the rivalry has been known to divide families in half, as it did with the Korvers—Kyle and Kaleb picked Creighton, Klayton went to Drake. Creighton leads the series, 87–56.

FANFARE AND HOOPLA: In 1881, an editorial in the student literary magazine asked, "Are we to have a class of weak, puny, stoop-shouldered, sallow-skinned, sunken-eyed men or a grade which can be compared with any men in the west?" Two decades later, the first Drake basketball team began to answer that question.

FAN FAVORITE: F Dolph Pulliam (1966-69) He could have been a top scorer, but Coach John asked him to turn the offense over to McCarter and become Drake's defensive stopper. So Pulliam did all the dirty work for the 1969 Final Four team, taking charges and snatching up loose balls. Still bleeding school colors, he became a Bulldogs radio analyst.

PROFILE

Drake University, Des Moines, IA
Founded: 1881
Enrollment: 5,617 (3,441 undergraduate)
Colors: Blue and white
Nickname: Bulldogs
Current arena: Knapp Center, opened in 1992 (7,002)
Previous: Veterans Memorial Coliseum, 1957-92 (12,000); Drake Fieldhouse, 1926-62 (5,000); Des Moines Coliseum, 1923-26 (N/A); Alumni Gymnasium, 1909-25 (N/A)
First game: Jan. 26, 1907

All-time record: 1,104-1,304 (.458)
Total weeks in AP Top 20/25: 32
Current conference: Missouri Valley (1907-51, '56-)
Conference titles:
MVC: 7 (1935 [tie], '36 [tie], '39 [tie], '69, '70, '71, 2008)
Conference tournament titles:
MVC: 1 (2008)
NCAA Tournament appearances: 4
Final Fours: 1
NIT appearances: 3

FIRST-ROUND PRO PICKS

1969 **Willie McCarter,** LA Lakers (12)

TOP 5

G **Willie McCarter** (1966-69)
G/F **Jeff Halliburton** (1969-71)
F **Lewis Lloyd** (1979-81)
F **Melvin Mathis** (1982-86)
F **Red Murrell** (1955-58)

RECORDS	GAME		SEASON		CAREER	
POINTS	51	Red Murrell, vs. Houston (March 3, 1958)	815	Lewis Lloyd (1979-80)	1,657	Red Murrell (1955-58)
POINTS PER GAME			30.2	Lewis Lloyd (1979-80)	28.2	Lewis Lloyd (1979-81)
REBOUNDS	26	Ken Harris, vs. Tulsa (Feb. 12, 1977)	406	Lewis Lloyd (1979-80)	854	Melvin Mathis (1982-86)
ASSISTS	15	Jeff Hill, vs. Wisconsin-Superior (Jan. 5, 1980); vs. Memphis (Dec. 16, 1978)	213	Adam Emmenecker (2007-08)	384	Glenn Martin (1984-88)

SEASON REVIEW

SEASON	W-L	CONF.	SCORING	COACH	RECORD
1907-15	*15-61*		*0-18 over two seasons (1909-11)*		
1915-16	3-9	1-5		Ray Whisman	8-15 .348
1916-17	5-7	0-4		Ralph Glaze	5-7 .417
1917-18	2-17	0-10		S.W. Hobbs	2-17 .105
1918-19	10-18	2-9		M.B. Banks	
1919-20	12-11	3-7		M.B. Banks	
1920-21	10-8	5-8		M.B. Banks	32-37 .464
1921-22	14-4	12-4		Ossie Solem	
1922-23	10-6	10-6		Ossie Solem	
1923-24	9-9	8-8		Ossie Solem	
1924-25	4-13	4-12		Ossie Solem	37-32 .536
1925-26	9-9	7-9		Bill Boelter	
1926-27	8-10	7-7		Bill Boelter	
1927-28	7-13	7-11		Bill Boelter	
1928-29	6-13	3-4		Bill Boelter	
1929-30	10-9	4-4		Bill Boelter	
1930-31	4-15	2-6		Bill Boelter	
1931-32	2-17	2-6		Bill Boelter	46-86 .348
1932-33	4-12	2-8		Bill Williams	
1933-34	6-12	4-6		Bill Williams	
1934-35	14-11	8-4		Bill Williams	
1935-36	16-12	8-4		Bill Williams	

SEAS.	W-L	CONF.	POSTSEASON	SCORING		REBOUNDS		ASSISTS		COACH	RECORD
1936-37	13-10	7-5								Bill Williams	
1937-38	14-6	10-4								Bill Williams	
1938-39	14-7	11-3								Bill Williams	
1939-40	13-12	7-5								Bill Williams	
1940-41	9-11	6-6								Bill Williams	
1941-42	2-13	1-9								Bill Williams	
1942-43	8-9	3-7								Bill Williams	113-115 .496
1943-44	7-13									Bill Easton	7-13 .350
1944-45	11-13									Vee Green	
1945-46	10-16	5-7		Gordon Flick	10.0					Vee Green	21-29 .420
1946-47	18-11	8-4		John Pritchard	10.8					Forddy Anderson	
1947-48	14-12	5-5		John Pritchard	12.3					Forddy Anderson	32-23 .582
1948-49	13-13	4-6		John Pritchard	11.7					Jack McClelland	
1949-50	14-12	5-7		John Rennicke	18.0					Jack McClelland	
1950-51	11-14	4-10		John Rennicke	13.3	Dan DeRuyter	4.4			Jack McClelland	
1951-52	13-12			Gus Ollrich, Tom Hyland	12.1	Dan DeRuyter	7.3			Jack McClelland	
1952-53	13-12			Gus Ollrich	16.9	Jim Thomas	7.9			Jack McClelland	
1953-54	7-16			Ben Bumbry	17.4	Willie Cerf	7.3			Jack McClelland	
1954-55	9-12			Willie Cerf	20.9	Willie Cerf	12.1			Jack McClelland	
1955-56	10-14			Red Murrell	16.6	Willie Cerf	11.8			Jack McClelland	90-105 .462
1956-57	8-16	4-10		Red Murrell	24.5	Red Murrell	12.2			John Benington	
1957-58	13-12	7-7		Red Murrell	26.7	Bob Tealer	11.5			John Benington	21-28 .429
1958-59	9-15	4-10		Bob Tealer	17.1	Bob Tealer	10.9			Maury John	
1959-60	11-14	4-10		Gus Guydon	18.5	Dave Terre	10.6			Maury John	
1960-61	19-7	7-5		Gus Guydon	18.5	Marv Torrence	11.4			Maury John	
1961-62	16-8	6-6		Jerry Foster	17.2	Marv Torrence	10.7			Maury John	
1962-63	11-14	3-9		McCoy McLemore	13.4	McCoy McLemore	10.6			Maury John	
1963-64	21-7	10-2	NIT QUARTERFINALS	McCoy McLemore	15.0	McCoy McLemore	11.8			Maury John	
1964-65	15-10	6-8		Gene West	16.8	Bob Netolicky	9.4			Maury John	
1965-66	13-12	6-8		Bob Netolicky	16.8	Bob Netolicky	10.9			Maury John	
1966-67	9-16	4-10		Bob Netolicky	17.6	Bob Netolicky	12.0			Maury John	
1967-68	18-8	9-7		Willie McCarter	23.2	Willie Wise	11.1			Maury John	
1968-69	26-5	13-3	NCAA THIRD PLACE	Willie McCarter	20.4	Willie Wise	11.4			Maury John	
1969-70	22-7	14-2	NCAA REGIONAL FINALS	Jeff Halliburton	16.2	Al Williams	13.0			Maury John	
1970-71	21-8	9-5	NCAA REGIONAL FINALS	Jeff Halliburton	18.0	Tom Bush	12.7			Maury John	211-131 .617
1971-72	7-19	2-12		Leon Huff	11.6	Leon Huff	7.7			Howard Stacey	
1972-73	14-12	5-9		Dennis Bell	16.3	Dennis Bell	11.3			Howard Stacey	
1973-74	13-13	3-9		Larry Haralson	15.6	Andy Graham	8.8			Howard Stacey	34-44 .436
1974-75	19-10	9-5		Larry Haralson	20.1	Terry McKissick	8.4			Bob Ortegel	
1975-76	8-19	3-9		Ken Harris	18.1	Ken Harris	9.8			Bob Ortegel	
1976-77	10-17	5-7		Ken Harris	19.1	Ken Harris	9.1			Bob Ortegel	
1977-78	6-22	2-14		Wayne Kreklow	15.2	Gregory Johns	9.7			Bob Ortegel	
1978-79	15-12	8-8		Wayne Kreklow	19.5	Ernie Banks	7.0			Bob Ortegel	
1979-80	15-12	6-10		Lewis Lloyd	30.2	Lewis Lloyd	15.0			Bob Ortegel	
1980-81	18-11	10-6	NIT FIRST ROUND	Lewis Lloyd	26.3	Lewis Lloyd	10.0			Bob Ortegel	91-103 .469
1981-82	12-15	7-9		Donnie Earl	9.8	Donnie Earl	6.7			Gary Garner	
1982-83	13-15	9-9		Melvin Mathis	11.8	Melvin Mathis	5.7			Gary Garner	
1983-84	8-20	4-12		Melvin Mathis	19.1	Melvin Mathis	8.6			Gary Garner	
1984-85	12-15	4-12		Daryl Lloyd	17.9	Melvin Mathis	8.1			Gary Garner	
1985-86	19-11	10-6	NIT FIRST ROUND	David Miller	15.2	Melvin Mathis	8.6			Gary Garner	
1986-87	17-14	6-8		Michael Morgan	15.4	Michael Morgan	8.4			Gary Garner	
1987-88	14-14	5-9		Sam Roark	13.8	Sam Roark	9.1			Gary Garner	95-104 .477
1988-89	12-17	6-8		Eric Berger	15.0	Sam Roark	8.6			Tom Abatemarco	
1989-90	13-18	5-9		Sam Roark	16.1	Sam Roark	9.3			Tom Abatemarco[a]	23-29 .442
1990-91	8-21	4-12		Chris Jones	10.7	Calvin Tillis	5.8			Rudy Washington	
1991-92	6-21	3-15		Kevin Sams	15.5	William Celestine	5.2			Rudy Washington	
1992-93	14-14	9-9		Curt Smith	21.1	William Celestine	6.6			Rudy Washington	
1993-94	11-16	6-12		Jeff Allen	16.0	William Celestine	8.3			Rudy Washington	
1994-95	12-15	9-9		Lynnrick Rogers	18.1	Kevin Bennett	5.9			Rudy Washington	
1995-96	12-15	8-10		Lynnrick Rogers	16.3	Ken Maxey	6.9			Rudy Washington	63-102 .382
1996-97	2-26	0-18		Lynnrick Rogers	15.6	Rashaad Thomas	6.0			Kurt Kanaskie	
1997-98	3-24	0-18		Armand LeVasseur	10.9	Rashaad Thomas	5.3			Kurt Kanaskie	
1998-99	10-17	5-13		Matt Woodley	12.2	Dontay Harris	7.5	Matt Woodley	2.9	Kurt Kanaskie	
1999-2000	11-18	4-14		Dontay Harris	11.5	Dontay Harris	6.0	Lamont Evans	5.1	Kurt Kanaskie	
2000-01	12-16	8-10		Luke McDonald	14.7	Greg Danielson	6.2	Lamont Evans	7.3	Kurt Kanaskie	
2001-02	14-15	9-9		Luke McDonald	17.9	Greg Danielson	7.5	Lonnie Randolph	2.9	Kurt Kanaskie	
2002-03	10-20	5-13		J.J. Sola	14.4	Greg Danielson	8.9	Lonnie Randolph	3.5	Kurt Kanaskie	62-136 .313
2003-04	12-16	7-11		Lonnie Randolph	12.0	Josh Powell	4.4	Lonnie Randolph	3.8	Tom Davis	
2004-05	13-16	7-11		Pete Eggers	11.2	Aliou Keita	7.1	Chaun Brooks	3.4	Tom Davis	
2005-06	12-19	5-13		Chaun Brooks	10.4	Ajay Calvin	5.3	Al Stewart	4.6	Tom Davis	
2006-07	17-15	6-12		Ajay Calvin	16.2	Ajay Calvin	6.1	Al Stewart	5.4	Tom Davis	54-66 .450
2007-08	28-5	15-3	NCAA FIRST ROUND	Josh Young	15.9	Jonathan Cox	8.5	Adam Emmenecker	6.5	Keno Davis	28-5 .848
2008-09	17-16	7-11		Josh Young	15.4	Jonathan Cox	8.5	Craig Stanley	3.8	Mark Phelps	17-16 .515

[a] **Tom Abatemarco (11-12) and Eddie Fields (2-6) both coached during the 1989-90 season.**

ESPN 255 SAGARIN

DREXEL

Isn't it about time that Philadelphia's Big 5 becomes the Bigger 6? Granted, Drexel can't match the history of Penn, Saint Joseph's, Villanova, La Salle and Temple, having only joined D1 in 1973. The Dragons did make three straight NCAA Tournaments in the 1990s, but have had a tough time trying to repeat their North Atlantic success in the Colonial Athletic Association.

BEST TEAM: 1995-96 They were often outsized, but led by 6'7" Malik Rose (20.2 ppg, 13.2 rpg), the Dragons were rarely pushed around. Rose, a Philly native who couldn't even dunk in high school, embodied coach Bill Herrion's brand of hoops: relentless, smart, hard-working. As a No. 12 seed, Drexel beat Memphis, 75-63, in the NCAA Tournament's first round before losing to eventual national runner-up Syracuse.

BEST PLAYER: G MICHAEL ANDERSON (1984-88) He stood a shade under six feet, but he didn't play like he was undersized. Anderson was a smooth passer, scored in bunches and had quick hands—and he was a nifty rebounder to boot. He achieved six triple-doubles and ranks as the school's all-time leader in points, assists, steals and free throws made.

BEST COACH: BILL HERRION (1991-99) Pity the player who didn't give it his all under Herrion, whether in a blowout loss or a crack-of-dawn practice. With his intensity, the four-time conference coach of the year guided the Dragons to four postseason appearances.

GAME FOR THE AGES: In the end, all the Memphis players could do was bow their heads in shock. In the first round of the 1996 Tournament, Drexel outshot, outhustled and outdefended the No. 5 seed, while easily breaking the Tigers' pressure defense. The result was a 75-63 upset that felt more like a routine case of the better team winning.

FIERCEST RIVAL: According to Dragons coach Bruiser Flint, the Drexel-Delaware rivalry is their Duke-North Carolina. With 140 meetings dating back to 1911-12, it's the longest-running series between current CAA teams, with Delaware leading 72–68.

THE SCHOOLS

SEASON REVIEW

SEAS.	W-L	CONF.	COACH	SEAS.	W-L	CONF.	COACH
1895-1949	*267-350*		*W.S. Brokaw (1905-07), 21-7, .750*	1962-63	18-5		Sam Cozen
1949-50	11-5		Harold Kollar	1963-64	17-5		Sam Cozen
1950-51	5-12		Harold Kollar	1964-65	18-4		Sam Cozen
1951-52	9-10		Harold Kollar	1965-66	20-4		Sam Cozen
1952-53	9-8		Sam Cozen	1966-67	13-10		Sam Cozen
1953-54	15-3		Sam Cozen	1967-68	12-9		Sam Cozen[a]
1954-55	14-5		Sam Cozen	1968-69	8-11		Frank Syzmanski
1955-56	10-8		Sam Cozen	1969-70	11-11		Frank Syzmanski
1956-57	14-3		Sam Cozen	1970-71	7-17	0-6	Frank Szymanski
1957-58	11-8		Sam Cozen	1971-72	11-14	2-4	Ray Haesler
1958-59	10-8		Sam Cozen	1972-73	14-7	2-4	Ray Haesler
1959-60	12-8		Sam Cozen	1973-74	15-9	2-4	Ray Haesler
1960-61	11-6		Sam Cozen	1974-75	12-11	0-6	Ray Haesler
1961-62	11-7		Sam Cozen	1975-76	17-6	3-2	Ray Haesler

SEAS.	W-L	CONF.	SCORING		COACH	RECORD	
1976-77	11-13	0-5	Bob Stephens	16.5	Ray Haesler	80-60	.571
1977-78	13-13	2-3	Bob Stephens	14.5	Eddie Burke		
1978-79	18-9	7-6	Bob Stephens	18.9	Eddie Burke		
1979-80	12-15	4-7	David Broadus	17.8	Eddie Burke		
1980-81	14-13	6-5	Len Hatzenbeller	21.8	Eddie Burke		
1981-82	19-11	7-4	Randy Burkert	12.5	Eddie Burke		
1982-83	14-15	5-4	Richard Congo	13.8	Eddie Burke		
1983-84	17-12	10-6	Richard Congo	16.6	Eddie Burke		
1984-85	10-18	8-6	Michael Anderson	14.0	Eddie Burke		
1985-86	19-12	11-3 ●	Michael Anderson	18.8	Eddie Burke		
1986-87	14-14	7-7	Michael Anderson	20.1	Eddie Burke		
1987-88	18-10	9-5	Michael Anderson	23.9	Eddie Burke		
1988-89	12-16	7-7	John Rankin	23.6	Eddie Burke		
1989-90	13-15	7-7	Todd Lehmann	16.6	Eddie Burke		
1990-91	12-16	7-5	Michael Thompson	18.1	Eddie Burke	205-189	.520
1991-92	16-14	9-5	Michael Thompson	16.5	Bill Herrion		
1992-93	22-7	12-2	Brian Holden	16.9	Bill Herrion		
1993-94	25-5	12-2 ●	Brian Holden	16.2	Bill Herrion		
1994-95	22-8	12-4 ●	Malik Rose	19.5	Bill Herrion		
1995-96	27-4	17-1 ●	Malik Rose	20.2	Bill Herrion		
1996-97	22-9	16-2 ■	Jeff Myers	16.3	Bill Herrion		
1997-98	13-15	10-8	Joe Linderman	18.4	Bill Herrion		
1998-99	20-9	15-3	Joe Linderman	17.2	Bill Herrion	167-71	.702
1999-2000	13-17	9-9	Mike Kouser	15.9	Steve Seymour		
2000-01	15-12	12-6	Stephen Starks	19.4	Steve Seymour	28-29	.491
2001-02	14-14	11-7	Robert Battle	14.5	Bruiser Flint		
2002-03	19-12	12-6 ■	Robert Battle	15.1	Bruiser Flint		
2003-04	18-11	13-5 ■	Sean Brooks	14.4	Bruiser Flint		
2004-05	17-12	12-6 ■	Phil Goss	14.4	Bruiser Flint		
2005-06	15-16	8-10	Dominick Mejia	15.3	Bruiser Flint		
2006-07	23-9	13-5 ■	Frank Elegar	16.0	Bruiser Flint		
2007-08	12-20	5-13	Frank Elegar	14.0	Bruiser Flint		
2008-09	15-14	10-8	Scott Rodgers	13.6	Bruiser Flint	133-108	.552

[a] Sam Cozen (10-2) and Robert Morgan (2-7) both coached during the 1967-68 season.
● NCAA Tournament appearance ■ NIT appearance

PROFILE

Drexel University, Philadelphia, PA
Founded: 1891
Enrollment: 20,659 (12,906 undergraduate)
Colors: Navy blue and gold
Nickname: Dragons
Current arena: Daskalakis Athletic Center, opened in 1975 (2,532)
First game: 1895
All-time record: 1,146-974 (.541)
Total weeks in AP Top 20/25: 0

Current conference: Colonial Athletic Association (2001-)
Conference titles:
East Coast: 1 (1986)
North Atlantic: 4 (1993 [tie], '94, '95, '96)
America East: 1 (1999 [tie])
Conference tournament titles:
East Coast: 1 (1986)
North Atlantic: 3 (1994, '95, '96)
NCAA Tournament appearances: 4
NIT appearances: 5

TOP 5

G **Michael Anderson** (1984-88)
G **Jeff Myers** (1994-97)
F **Bob Buckley** (1954-57)
F **Malik Rose** (1992-96)
F **Bob Stephens** (1975-79)

RECORDS

RECORDS	GAME		SEASON		CAREER	
POINTS	44	John Rankin, vs. Rider (Jan. 6, 1988)	670	Michael Anderson (1987-88)	2,208	Michael Anderson (1984-88)
POINTS PER GAME			23.9	Michael Anderson (1987-88)	19.2	John Rankin (1985-89); Michael Anderson (1984-88)
REBOUNDS	30	Steve Lilly, vs. Muhlenberg (Jan. 5, 1972)	409	Malik Rose (1995-96)	1,514	Malik Rose (1992-96)
ASSISTS	19	Todd Lehmann, vs. Liberty (Feb. 5, 1990)	260	Todd Lehmann (1989-90)	724	Michael Anderson (1984-88)

ESPN 7 SAGARIN

DUKE

There's no middle ground: You either love the Blue Devils or you hate 'em. It's Coach K and Christian Laettner and the Shot. It's Bobby Hurley slapping the floor and Shane Battier drawing charges, Art Heyman fighting UNC's Larry Brown and the Cameron Crazies tormenting visitors. It's 18 regular-season ACC crowns, 17 ACC tourney titles, 14 Final Fours and three national titles.

BEST TEAM: 1991-92 After a surprising title run in 1991, Duke returned almost all its key players—including Christian Laettner, Grant Hill and Bobby Hurley—and was everyone's No. 1. The Dukies didn't disappoint, going 34–2 and winning the ACC regular-season and tourney titles. Then, after surviving an overtime scare against Kentucky in the East Regional final, they capped a remarkable season with a 20-point blowout of Michigan in the national title game, becoming the NCAA's first back-to-back champs since UCLA in 1972 and '73.

BEST PLAYER: C CHRISTIAN LAETTNER (1988-92) No Blue Devil made more of a name for himself in March. The accomplishments are staggering: two national championships, four Final Fours and the Tourney's career scoring record (407 points). Plus a buzzer-beater vs. UConn to send Duke to the 1990 Final Four and another vs. Kentucky to do the same in '92 that capped a perfect day: 10-for-10 from the field, 10-for-10 from the line.

BEST COACH: MIKE KRZYZEWSKI (1980-) After three seasons, the little-known Army grad and was 38–47 and Duke fans wanted his head. Three national championships and 10 Final Fours later, he's Coach K, a living legend whose name adorns the floor of Cameron Indoor Stadium.

GAME FOR THE AGES: Duke had all but been anointed repeat champion when it met Kentucky in the 1992 East Regional final. But the Wildcats pushed Duke into overtime, then took a 103-102 lead on Sean Woods' runner with 1.8 seconds left. After Duke took a timeout, history: Hill to Laettner—swish!— to immortality.

HEARTBREAKER: On March 2, 1974, Duke led its hated archrival, North Carolina, 86-78 with :17 left. Climaxing a miraculous Tar Heels rally, Walter Davis thrust a knife into Duke's heart with a game-tying 35-footer at the buzzer—and the Blue Devils bled to death in overtime, 96-92.

FIERCEST RIVAL: Duke and North Carolina are separated by eight miles, so fans of each shop at the same stores, just as the schools recruit the same players. Both rank in the top five in all-time wins; they have combined to claim eight national titles and 34 ACC tournament titles. North Carolina leads the series, 130–97.

FANFARE AND HOOPLA: You surely know about Duke's student section, the Cameron Crazies. From tenting overnight before big games in Krzyzewskiville to distracting opponents with brilliant chants and props—they continue to set the standard for all other college crowds.

FAN FAVORITE: F SHANE BATTIER (1997-2001) He once credited a scoring binge against Maryland to a film he'd seen about Shaolin monks. He performed in a campus improv show. And oh, he led Duke to the 2001 national title.

CONSENSUS ALL-AMERICAS

1952	**Dick Groat**, G
1963	**Art Heyman**, F/G
1967	**Bob Verga**, G
1979	**Mike Gminski**, C
1985, '86	**Johnny Dawkins**, G
1989	**Danny Ferry**, F
1992	**Christian Laettner**, C
1993	**Bobby Hurley**, G
1994	**Grant Hill**, F
1999	**Elton Brand**, F
2000	**Chris Carrawell**, F
2001	**Shane Battier**, F
2001, '02	**Jason Williams**, G
2005, '06	**J.J. Redick**, G
2006	**Shelden Williams**, F

FIRST-ROUND PRO PICKS

1952	**Dick Groat**, Fort Wayne (3)
1963	**Art Heyman**, New York (1)
1964	**Jeff Mullins**, St. Louis (6)
1966	**Jack Marin**, Baltimore (5)
1971	**Randy Denton**, Memphis (ABA)
1977	**Tate Armstrong**, Chicago (13)
1979	**Jim Spanarkel**, Philadelphia (16)
1980	**Mike Gminski**, New Jersey (7)
1986	**Johnny Dawkins**, San Antonio (10)
1986	**Mark Alarie**, Denver (18)
1989	**Danny Ferry**, LA Clippers (2)
1990	**Alaa Abdelnaby**, Portland (25)
1992	**Christian Laettner**, Minnesota (3)
1993	**Bobby Hurley**, Sacramento (7)
1994	**Grant Hill**, Detroit (3)
1995	**Cherokee Parks**, Dallas (12)
1998	**Roshown McLeod**, Atlanta (20)
1999	**Elton Brand**, Chicago (1)
1999	**Trajan Langdon**, Cleveland (11)
1999	**Corey Maggette**, Seattle (13)
1999	**William Avery**, Minnesota (14)
2001	**Shane Battier**, Vancouver (6)
2002	**Jason Williams**, Chicago (2)
2002	**Mike Dunleavy**, Golden State (3)
2003	**Dahntay Jones**, Boston (20)
2004	**Luol Deng**, Phoenix (7)
2006	**Shelden Williams**, Atlanta (5)
2006	**J.J. Redick**, Orlando (11)
2009	**Gerald Henderson**, Charlotte (12)

PROFILE

Duke University, Durham, NC
Founded: 1838 as Trinity College
Enrollment: 13,088 (6,244 undergraduate)
Colors: Royal blue and white
Nickname: Blue Devils
Current arena: Cameron Indoor Stadium, opened as Duke Indoor Stadium in 1940 (9,314)
Previous: Card Gym, 1930-39 (3,500); Alumni Memorial Gym, 1924-30 (2,000); Angier B. Duke Gym, a.k.a. the Ark, 1906-23 (N/A)
First game: March 2, 1906

All-time record: 1,877-817 (.697)
Total weeks in AP Top 20/25: 621
Current conference: Atlantic Coast (1953-)
Conference titles:
Southern: 3 (1940, '42, '43)
ACC: 18 (1954, '58, '63, '64, '65, '66, '79 [tie], '86, '91, '92, '94, '97, '98, '99, 2000, '01 [tie], '04, '06)
Conference tournament titles:
Southern: 5 (1938, '41, '42, '44, '46)
ACC: 17 (1960, '63, '64, '66, '78, '80, '86, '88, '92, '99, 2000, '01, '02, '03, '05, '06, '09)
NCAA Tournament appearances: 33
Sweet 16s (since 1975): 20
Final Fours: 14
Titles: 3 (1991, '92, 2001)
NIT appearances: 5
Semifinals: 1

TOP 5

G	**Johnny Dawkins** (1982-86)
G	**Bobby Hurley** (1989-93)
G/F	**Art Heyman** (1960-63)
G/F	**Grant Hill** (1990-94)
C	**Christian Laettner** (1988-92)

RECORDS

RECORDS	GAME		SEASON		CAREER	
POINTS	58	Danny Ferry, vs. Miami (Fla.) (Dec. 10, 1988)	964	J.J. Redick (2005-06)	2,769	J.J. Redick (2002-06)
POINTS PER GAME			26.8	J.J. Redick (2005-06)	25.1	Art Heyman (1960-63)
REBOUNDS	31	Bernie Janicki, vs. North Carolina (Feb. 29, 1952)	476	Bernie Janicki (1951-52)	1,262	Shelden Williams (2002-06)
ASSISTS	16	Bobby Hurley, vs. Florida State (Feb. 24, 1993)	289	Bobby Hurley (1990-91)	1,076	Bobby Hurley (1989-93)

SEASON REVIEW

SEASON	W-L	CONF.	SCORING		COACH	RECORD	
1905-16	*72-55*		*W.W. "Cap" Card started the program and coached 7 seasons (30-17)*				
1916-17	20-4				Chick Doak		
1917-18	10-5				Chick Doak	39-20	.661
1918-19	6-5				Henry P. Cole	6-5	.545
1919-20	10-4				Walter J. Rothensies	10-4	.714
1920-21	9-6				Floyd Egan	9-6	.600
1921-22	6-12				James Baldwin	6-12	.333
1922-23	15-7				Jesse S. Burbage		
1923-24	19-6				Jesse S. Burbage	34-13	.723
1924-25	4-9				George Buckheit		
1925-26	8-12				George Buckheit		
1926-27	4-10				George Buckheit		
1927-28	9-5				George Buckheit	25-36	.410
1928-29	12-8	5-4	Joe Croson	8.7	Eddie Cameron		
1929-30	18-2	9-1	Joe Croson	9.5	Eddie Cameron		
1930-31	14-7	5-4	Joe Croson	9.3	Eddie Cameron		
1931-32	14-11	6-5	James Thompson	7.2	Eddie Cameron		
1932-33	17-5	7-3	James Thompson	9.5	Eddie Cameron		
1933-34	18-6	9-4	James Thompson	9.6	Eddie Cameron		
1934-35	18-8	10-4	Charles Kunkle	4.8	Eddie Cameron		
1935-36	20-6	4-5	Kenneth Podger	6.5	Eddie Cameron		
1936-37	15-8	11-6	Kenneth Podger	8.5	Eddie Cameron		

SEAS.	W-L	CONF.	POSTSEASON	SCORING		REBOUNDS		ASSISTS		COACH	RECORD	
1937-38	15-9	9-5		Edwin Swindell	8.6					Eddie Cameron		
1938-39	10-12	8-8		Edwin Swindell	8.6					Eddie Cameron		
1939-40	19-7	13-2		Bill Mock	7.1					Eddie Cameron		
1940-41	14-8	8-4		Charles Holley	9.2					Eddie Cameron		
1941-42	22-2	15-1		Cedric Loftis	8.3					Eddie Cameron	226-99	.695
1942-43	20-6	12-1		Gordon Carver	11.9					Gerry Gerard		
1943-44	13-13	4-2		Gordon Carver	13.3					Gerry Gerard		
1944-45	13-9	6-1		Bill Sapp	11.6					Gerry Gerard		
1945-46	21-6	12-2		Ed Koffenberger	11.7					Gerry Gerard		
1946-47	19-8	10-4		Ed Koffenberger	15.4					Gerry Gerard		
1947-48	17-12	8-6		Corren Youmans	12.1					Gerry Gerard		
1948-49	13-9	5-7		Corren Youmans	11.5					Gerry Gerard		
1949-50	15-15	9-7		Corren Youmans	11.8					Gerry Gerard	131-78	.627
1950-51	20-13	13-6		Dick Groat	25.2					Harold Bradley		
1951-52	24-6	13-3		Dick Groat	26.0	Bernie Janicki	15.9	Dick Groat	7.6	Harold Bradley		
1952-53	17-8	12-4		Bernie Janicki	16.8	Bernie Janicki	10.5			Harold Bradley		
1953-54	21-6	9-1		Bernie Janicki	13.5	Ronnie Mayer	9.8			Harold Bradley		
1954-55	20-8	11-3	NCAA FIRST ROUND	Ronnie Mayer	21.7	Ronnie Mayer	12.4			Harold Bradley		
1955-56	19-7	10-4		Ronnie Mayer	22.1	Junior Morgan	9.8			Harold Bradley		
1956-57	13-11	8-6		Jim Newcome	14.5	Jim Newcome	11.4			Harold Bradley		
1957-58	18-7	11-3		Jim Newcome	13.2	Jim Newcome	9.5			Harold Bradley		
1958-59	13-12	7-7		Carroll Youngkin	15.9	Carroll Youngkin	11.1			Harold Bradley	165-78	.679
1959-60	17-11	7-7	NCAA REGIONAL FINALS	H. Hurt, C. Youngkin	13.4	Carroll Youngkin	9.9			Vic Bubas		
1960-61	22-6	10-4		Art Heyman	25.2	Carroll Youngkin	9.8			Vic Bubas		
1961-62	20-5	11-3		Art Heyman	25.3	Art Heyman	11.2			Vic Bubas		
1962-63	27-3	14-0	NCAA THIRD PLACE	Art Heyman	24.9	Art Heyman	10.8			Vic Bubas		
1963-64	26-5	13-1	NCAA RUNNER-UP	Jeff Mullins	24.2	Jay Buckley	9.0			Vic Bubas		
1964-65	20-5	11-3		Bob Verga	21.4	Jack Marin	10.3			Vic Bubas		
1965-66	26-4	12-2	NCAA THIRD PLACE	Jack Marin	18.9	Mike Lewis	11.0			Vic Bubas		
1966-67	18-9	9-3	NIT QUARTERFINALS	Bob Verga	26.1	Mike Lewis	12.3			Vic Bubas		
1967-68	22-6	11-3	NIT QUARTERFINALS	Mike Lewis	21.7	Mike Lewis	14.4			Vic Bubas		
1968-69	15-13	8-6		Randy Denton	17.4	Randy Denton	12.8	Dick DeVenzio	6.0	Vic Bubas	213-67	.761
1969-70	17-9	8-6	NIT FIRST ROUND	Randy Denton	21.5	Randy Denton	12.5	Dick DeVenzio	4.5	Bucky Waters		
1970-71	20-10	9-5	NIT FOURTH PLACE	Randy Denton	20.4	Randy Denton	12.8	Dick DeVenzio	3.8	Bucky Waters		
1971-72	14-12	6-6		Richie O'Conner	15.4	Alan Shaw	11.8	Gary Melchionni	2.6	Bucky Waters		
1972-73	12-14	4-8		Chris Redding	16.9	Bob Fleischer	8.5	Gary Melchionni	3.2	Bucky Waters	63-45	.583
1973-74	10-16	2-10		Bob Fleischer	15.7	Bob Fleischer	12.4	Kevin Billerman	4.3	Neill McGeachy	10-16	.385
1974-75	13-13	2-10		Bob Fleischer	17.2	Bob Fleischer	10.5	Kevin Billerman	3.8	Bill Foster		
1975-76	13-14	3-9		Tate Armstrong	24.2	George Moses	9.7	Tate Armstrong	4.4	Bill Foster		
1976-77	14-13	2-10		Tate Armstrong	22.7	Mike Gminski	10.7	Jim Spanarkel	3.6	Bill Foster		
1977-78	27-7	8-4	NCAA RUNNER-UP	Jim Spanarkel	20.8	Mike Gminski	10.0	Jim Spanarkel	3.7	Bill Foster		
1978-79	22-8	9-3	NCAA SECOND ROUND	Mike Gminski	18.8	Mike Gminski	9.2	Jim Spanarkel	3.7	Bill Foster		
1979-80	24-9	7-7	NCAA REGIONAL FINALS	Mike Gminski	21.3	Mike Gminski	10.9	Bob Bender	4.8	Bill Foster	113-64	.638
1980-81	17-13	6-8	NIT QUARTERFINALS	Gene Banks	18.5	Kenny Dennard	6.9	Tom Emma	2.4	Mike Krzyzewski		
1981-82	10-17	4-10		Vince Taylor	20.3	Vince Taylor	4.9	Tom Emma	3.3	Mike Krzyzewski		
1982-83	11-17	3-11		Johnny Dawkins	18.1	Mark Alarie	6.5	Johnny Dawkins	4.8	Mike Krzyzewski		
1983-84	24-10	7-7	NCAA SECOND ROUND	Johnny Dawkins	19.4	Mark Alarie	7.2	Tommy Amaker	4.8	Mike Krzyzewski		
1984-85	23-8	8-6	NCAA SECOND ROUND	Johnny Dawkins	18.8	Jay Bilas	6.0	Tommy Amaker	5.9	Mike Krzyzewski		
1985-86	37-3	12-2	NCAA RUNNER-UP	Johnny Dawkins	20.2	Mark Alarie	6.2	Tommy Amaker	6.0	Mike Krzyzewski		
1986-87	24-9	9-5	NCAA REGIONAL SEMIFINALS	Danny Ferry	14.0	Danny Ferry	7.8	Danny Ferry	4.3	Mike Krzyzewski		
1987-88	28-7	9-5	NCAA NATIONAL SEMIFINALS	Danny Ferry	19.1	Danny Ferry	7.6	Quin Snyder	5.7	Mike Krzyzewski		
1988-89	28-8	9-5	NCAA NATIONAL SEMIFINALS	Danny Ferry	22.6	Danny Ferry	7.4	Quin Snyder	6.2	Mike Krzyzewski		
1989-90	29-9	9-5	NCAA RUNNER-UP	Phil Henderson	18.5	Christian Laettner	9.6	Bobby Hurley	7.6	Mike Krzyzewski		
1990-91	**32-7**	**11-3**	**NATIONAL CHAMPION**	**Christian Laettner**	**19.8**	**Christian Laettner**	**8.7**	**Bobby Hurley**	**7.4**	**Mike Krzyzewski**		
1991-92	**34-2**	**14-2**	**NATIONAL CHAMPION**	**Christian Laettner**	**21.5**	**Christian Laettner**	**7.9**	**Bobby Hurley**	**7.6**	**Mike Krzyzewski**		
1992-93	24-8	10-6	NCAA SECOND ROUND	Grant Hill	18.0	Cherokee Parks	6.9	Bobby Hurley	8.2	Mike Krzyzewski		
1993-94	28-6	12-4	NCAA RUNNER-UP	Grant Hill	17.4	Cherokee Parks	8.4	Grant Hill	5.2	Mike Krzyzewski		
1994-95	13-18	2-14		Cherokee Parks	19.0	Cherokee Parks	9.3	Jeff Capel	4.1	Mike Krzyzewski[a]		
1995-96	18-13	8-8	NCAA FIRST ROUND	Jeff Capel	16.6	Greg Newton	8.2	Chris Collins	4.6	Mike Krzyzewski		
1996-97	24-9	12-4	NCAA SECOND ROUND	Trajan Langdon	14.3	Greg Newton	6.1	Steve Wojciechowski	5.3	Mike Krzyzewski		
1997-98	32-4	15-1	NCAA REGIONAL FINALS	Roshown McLeod	15.3	Shane Battier	6.4	Steve Wojciechowski	4.6	Mike Krzyzewski		
1998-99	37-2	16-0	NCAA RUNNER-UP	Elton Brand	17.7	Elton Brand	9.8	William Avery	5.0	Mike Krzyzewski		
1999-2000	29-5	15-1	NCAA REGIONAL SEMIFINALS	Shane Battier	17.4	Carlos Boozer	6.3	Jason Williams	6.5	Mike Krzyzewski		
2000-01	**35-4**	**13-3**	**NATIONAL CHAMPION**	**Jason Williams**	**21.6**	**Shane Battier**	**7.3**	**Jason Williams**	**6.1**	**Mike Krzyzewski**		
2001-02	31-4	13-3	NCAA REGIONAL SEMIFINALS	Jason Williams	21.3	Carlos Boozer	8.7	Chris Duhon	5.9	Mike Krzyzewski		
2002-03	26-7	11-5	NCAA REGIONAL SEMIFINALS	Dahntay Jones	17.7	Shelden Williams	5.9	Chris Duhon	6.4	Mike Krzyzewski		
2003-04	31-6	13-3	NCAA NATIONAL SEMIFINALS	J.J. Redick	15.9	Shelden Williams	8.5	Chris Duhon	6.1	Mike Krzyzewski		
2004-05	27-6	11-5	NCAA REGIONAL SEMIFINALS	J.J. Redick	21.8	Shelden Williams	11.2	Daniel Ewing	4.0	Mike Krzyzewski		
2005-06	32-4	14-2	NCAA REGIONAL SEMIFINALS	J.J. Redick	26.8	Shelden Williams	10.7	Greg Paulus	5.2	Mike Krzyzewski		
2006-07	22-11	8-8	NCAA FIRST ROUND	DeMarcus Nelson	14.1	Josh McRoberts	7.9	Greg Paulus	3.8	Mike Krzyzewski		
2007-08	28-6	13-3	NCAA SECOND ROUND	DeMarcus Nelson	15.2	DeMarcus Nelson	6.0	Greg Paulus	3.3	Mike Krzyzewski		
2008-09	30-7	11-5	NCAA REGIONAL SEMIFINALS	Gerald Henderson	16.5	Kyle Singler	7.7	John Scheyer	2.8	Mike Krzyzewski	760-215	.779

[a] Mike Krzyzewski (9-3) and Pete Gaudet (4-15) both coached during the 1994-95 season.

THE SCHOOLS

ESPN 67 SAGARIN

DUQUESNE

The Dukes have spent more time in the AP Top 10 than any other Atlantic 10 school (64 weeks), are the only team to have had back-to-back No. 1 overall pro draft picks (Dick Ricketts in 1955 and Sihugo Green in 1956), and have made 22 postseason appearances. But Duquesne's proudest achievements are about breaking racial boundaries: In 1915-16, future Negro National League managerial icon Cumberland Posey was a member of the DU starting five, and in 1950 center Chuck Cooper became the first African-American drafted by an NBA team (Boston Celtics).

BEST TEAM: 1954-55 Lead by first-team All-Americas Ricketts and Green, the Dukes were ranked in the Top 10 every week of the season. Playing suffocating defense, DU put the clamps on La Salle star Tom Gola to win the ECAC Holiday Festival title on Dec. 31, then a few months later beat Louisville, Cincinnati and Dayton to claim the NIT crown.

BEST PLAYER: F SIHUGO GREEN (1953-56) He was one of the supremely athletic, artistic and slashing drivers whose style would inspire players such as Julius "Dr. J" Erving and other midsize dunk specialists. A three-time All-America, the 6'2" Green averaged 19.8 ppg and 11.5 rpg, and was chosen by Rochester ahead of Bill Russell in the 1956 NBA draft.

BEST COACH: CHARLES "CHICK" DAVIES (1924-1943, '46-48) The Dean of Duquesne coaches endured just one losing season, had a 42–27 career mark in games against Hall of Fame coaches and mentored six All-Americas. In 1940, Davies guided the Dukes to the NIT final and the NCAA national semifinals despite a thin bench that limited him to using six players in most games.

GAME FOR THE AGES: Dick Ricketts and Bronx native Green put on a show at Madison Square Garden in the 1955 NIT title game against No. 9-ranked Dayton. The two combined for all of Duquesne's 35 first-half points (as well as the team's first 44). Green finished with 33 as DU won, 70-58, to claim the school's only national title.

HEARTBREAKER: Down 67-53 to No. 4-ranked North Carolina in the 1969 East Regional semifinals, the Dukes rallied to get to within one with :30 to go. Then Tar Heels big man Lee Dedmon caught an 85-foot pass and scored, and UNC held on to win, 79-78.

FIERCEST RIVAL: It's called the City Game—the annual grudge match between Pittsburgh and Duquesne, schools that are separated by two miles along Forbes Avenue. Pittsburghers believe the rivalry reached its peak in the 1970s, when the two teams battled it out in the Eastern 8. Still, with players from both teams often sparring during summer league runs and both coaching staffs covering most of the same recruiting turf, there's plenty of edge left to a series that dates back to 1932. Pitt leads overall, 46–31.

Sihugo Green was chosen by Rochester ahead of Bill Russell in the 1956 NBA draft.

FANFARE AND HOOPLA: First fan Mossie Murphy began his famous rallying cry—"Shoo Shoo, Rah Rah"—in the 1950s and later belted it out from a seat opposite the student section until his death in 1997. His seat at the Palumbo Center is now adorned with a plaque in his honor and kept vacant for all home games.

FAN FAVORITE: F MIKE RICE (1960-62) The 6'2", 170-pounder was revered for his scrappy, physical play. In a game against St. Bonaventure, Rice put his foot through a drum belonging to a Bonnies fan who was pounding the instrument every time his team scored.

CONSENSUS ALL-AMERICAS

1955, '56	**Sihugo Green,** F
1955	**Dick Ricketts,** F/C

FIRST-ROUND PRO PICKS

1955	**Dick Ricketts,** Milwaukee (1)
1956	**Sihugo Green,** Rochester (1)
1977	**Norm Nixon,** LA Lakers (22)

PROFILE

Duquesne University, Pittsburgh, PA
Founded: 1878
Enrollment: 10,160 (5,710 undergraduate)
Colors: Red and blue
Nickname: Dukes
Current arena: A.J. Palumbo Center, opened in 1988 (5,358)
First game: 1913
All-time record: 1,256-953 (.569)
Total weeks in AP Top 20/25: 91

Current conference: Atlantic 10 (1976-)
Conference titles:
Eastern Athletic: 2 (1980 [tie], '81[tie])
Conference tournament titles:
Eastern Collegiate: 1 (1977)
NCAA Tournament appearances: 5
Final Fours: 1
NIT appearances: 17
Semifinals: 7
Titles: 1 (1955)

TOP 5

G	**Norm Nixon** (1973-77)
G	**Willie Somerset** (1961-62, '63-65)
F	**Sihugo Green** (1953-56)
F/C	**Dick Ricketts** (1951-55)
C	**Chuck Cooper** (1946-50)

RECORDS	GAME		SEASON		CAREER	
POINTS	50	Ron Guziak, vs. Saint Francis (Pa.) (March 6, 1968)	788	Mark Stevenson (1989-90)	1,963	Dick Ricketts (1951-55)
POINTS PER GAME			27.2	Mark Stevenson (1989-90)	22.7	Willie Somerset (1961-62, '63-65)
REBOUNDS	29	Lionel Billingy, vs. Wheeling (Jan. 16, 1973)	450	Dick Ricketts (1954-55)	1,359	Dick Ricketts (1951-55)
ASSISTS	12	Bryant McAllister, vs. Fordham (Feb. 4, 2006); Martin Osimani, vs. Ohio (Jan. 7, 2004); Clayton Adams, vs. Indiana (Pa.) (Dec. 3, 1987); Brian Shanahan, vs. Iona (Dec. 14, 1986)	194	Aaron Jackson (2008-09)	577	Norm Nixon (1973-77)

SEASON REVIEW

SEASON	W-L	CONF.	SCORING	COACH	RECORD	
1913-17	*33-9*		*Best early season was 1914-15, when Duquesne went 12-2*			
1917-18	4-4			Rev. E. McGuigan		
1918-19	4-6			Rev. E. McGuigan		
1919-20	6-10			Rev. E. McGuigan		
1920-21	11-6			Ben Lubic	11-6	.647
1921-22	10-6			Rev. E. McGuigan		
1922-23	16-2			Rev. E. McGuigan	66-35	.653
1923-24	8-6			Bill Campbell	8-6	.571
1924-25	11-7			Charles "Chick" Davies		
1925-26	15-3			Charles "Chick" Davies		
1926-27	16-4			Charles "Chick" Davies		
1927-28	15-7			Charles "Chick" Davies		
1928-29	12-8			Charles "Chick" Davies		
1929-30	18-10			Charles "Chick" Davies		
1930-31	12-6			Charles "Chick" Davies		
1931-32	14-6			Charles "Chick" Davies		
1932-33	15-1			Charles "Chick" Davies		
1933-34	19-2			Charles "Chick" Davies		
1934-35	18-1			Charles "Chick" Davies		
1935-36	14-3			Charles "Chick" Davies		
1936-37	13-6			Charles "Chick" Davies		
1937-38	6-11			Charles "Chick" Davies		

SEAS.	W-L	CONF.	POSTSEASON	SCORING		REBOUNDS		ASSISTS		COACH	RECORD	
1938-39	14-4									Charles "Chick" Davies		
1939-40	20-3		NATIONAL SEMIS; NIT R-UP							Charles "Chick" Davies		
1940-41	17-3		NIT QUARTERFINALS							Charles "Chick" Davies		
1941-42	15-6									Charles "Chick" Davies		
1942-43	12-7									Charles "Chick" Davies		
1943-44	no team											
1944-45	no team											
1945-46	no team											
1946-47	20-2[a]		NIT QUARTERFINALS							Charles "Chick" Davies		
1947-48	17-6			Ed Dahler	9.3					Charles "Chick" Davies	314-106	.748
1948-49	17-5			Chuck Cooper	13.5					Dudey Moore		
1949-50	23-6		NIT FOURTH PLACE	Ed Dahler	16.9					Dudey Moore		
1950-51	16-11			Carl Pacacha	14.2					Dudey Moore		
1951-52	23-4		NCAA REG. FINALS, NIT 4TH PL	Jim Tucker	19.6					Dudey Moore		
1952-53	21-8		NIT THIRD PLACE	Dick Ricketts	20.9					Dudey Moore		
1953-54	26-3		NIT RUNNER-UP	Dick Ricketts	17.2	Jim Tucker	13.6			Dudey Moore		
1954-55	22-4		NIT CHAMPION	Sihugo Green	22.0	Dick Ricketts	17.3			Dudey Moore		
1955-56	17-10		NIT QUARTERFINALS	Sihugo Green	24.5	Sihugo Green	13.6			Dudey Moore		
1956-57	16-7			Dave Ricketts	17.9	Bob DePalma	13.0			Dudey Moore		
1957-58	10-12			Bernie Matthews	14.1	Bob DePalma	9.1			Dudey Moore	191-70	.732
1958-59	13-11			Bernie Matthews	15.3	Bob Slobodnik	12.8			Red Manning		
1959-60	8-15			George Brown	15.8	Bob Slobodnik	13.4			Red Manning		
1960-61	15-7			Ned Twyman	20.8	Bob Slobodnik	13.3			Red Manning		
1961-62	22-7		NIT FOURTH PLACE	Willie Somerset	19.5	Clyde Arnold	8.8			Red Manning		
1962-63	13-9			Ron Willard	16.0	Dennis Cuff	9.8			Red Manning		
1963-64	16-7		NIT QUARTERFINALS	Willie Somerset	24.7	Dennis Cuff	11.6			Red Manning		
1964-65	14-10			Willie Somerset	24.7	Willie Ross	10.6			Red Manning		
1965-66	14-9			Jim Smith	17.9	Phil Washington	10.6			Red Manning		
1966-67	7-15			Moe Barr	14.7	Ron Guziak	9.4			Red Manning		
1967-68	18-7		NIT FIRST ROUND	Ron Guziak	18.6	Phil Washington	13.4			Red Manning		
1968-69	21-5		NCAA REGIONAL SEMIFINALS	Jarrett Durham	17.1	Garry Nelson	8.3			Red Manning		
1969-70	17-7		NIT FIRST ROUND	Jarrett Durham	18.9	Garry Nelson	11.9			Red Manning		
1970-71	21-4		NCAA FIRST ROUND	Mickey Davis	19.1	Mickey Davis	9.5	Mickey Davis	5.6	Red Manning		
1971-72	20-5			Lionel Billingy	21.7	Lionel Billingy	14.2	Mike Barr	5.7	Red Manning		
1972-73	16-8			Ruben Montanez	17.8	Lionel Billingy	13.6	Jack Wojdowski	4.9	Red Manning		
1973-74	12-12			Lionel Billingy	15.9	Lionel Billingy	13.1	Norm Nixon	6.0	Red Manning	247-138	.642
1974-75	14-11			Kip McLane	14.7	Kip McLane	8.1	Norm Nixon	4.2	John Cinicola		
1975-76	12-13			Norm Nixon	21.0	Jesse Hubbard	9.2	Norm Nixon	6.0	John Cinicola		
1976-77	15-15	3-7	NCAA FIRST ROUND	Norm Nixon	22.0	Rich Cotton	7.3	Norm Nixon	5.9	John Cinicola		
1977-78	11-17	5-5		B.B. Flenory	14.4	Jesse Hubbard	8.4	B.B. Flenory	5.0	John Cinicola	52-56	.481
1978-79	13-13	2-8		B.B. Flenory	14.4	Bruce Atkins	9.8	B.B. Flenory	2.4	Mike Rice		
1979-80	18-10	7-3	NIT SECOND ROUND	B.B. Flenory	20.4	Bruce Atkins	9.3	B.B. Flenory	3.6	Mike Rice		
1980-81	20-10	10-3	NIT FIRST ROUND	Ronnie Dixon	16.8	Bruce Atkins	11.7	Tom Cvitkovic	3.1	Mike Rice		
1981-82	11-16	5-9		Bruce Atkins	16.1	Bruce Atkins	10.4	Tom Cvitkovic	3.2	Mike Rice	62-49	.559
1982-83	12-16	6-8		Billy Searles	14.8	Joey Myers	9.2	Andy Sisinni	3.5	Jim Satalin		
1983-84	10-18	8-10		Emmett Sellers	17.9	Greg Harrison	5.7	Andy Sisinni	5.1	Jim Satalin		
1984-85	12-18	6-12		Rick Suder	17.7	Dwayne Rawls	5.9	Pat Farrell	4.3	Jim Satalin		
1985-86	15-14	9-9		Rick Suder	20.4	Dwayne Rawls	8.0	Brian Shanahan	4.7	Jim Satalin		
1986-87	12-17	7-11		Emmett Sellers	17.7	Pete Freeman	5.7	Tony Petrarca	3.7	Jim Satalin		
1987-88	11-21	6-12		Collins Dobbs	17.3	Brian Shanahan	5.5	Clayton Adams	5.1	Jim Satalin		
1988-89	13-16	7-11		Brian Shanahan	12.9	Brian Anselmino	6.6	Clayton Adams	5.5	Jim Satalin	85-120	.415
1989-90	7-22	5-13		Mark Stevenson	27.2	Brian Anselmino	9.3	Clayton Adams	5.6	John Carroll		
1990-91	13-15	10-8		James Hargrove	13.6	Derrick Alston	6.3	Clayton Adams	5.0	John Carroll		
1991-92	13-15	6-10		James Hargrove	20.7	Derrick Alston	8.0	Effrem Whitehead	3.3	John Carroll		
1992-93	13-15	5-9		Derrick Alston	19.9	Derrick Alston	9.3	Kenya Hunter	5.3	John Carroll		
1993-94	17-13	8-8	NIT SECOND ROUND	Derrick Alston	21.3	Derrick Alston	7.3	Kenya Hunter	3.5	John Carroll		
1994-95	10-18	5-11		Tom Pipkins	17.4	Kevin Price	5.7	Kenya Hunter	4.0	John Carroll	73-98	.427
1995-96	9-18	3-13		Kevin Price	14.7	Kevin Price	6.7	Mike James	3.9	Scott Edgar		
1996-97	9-18	5-11		Tom Pipkins	19.3	Kevin Price	5.6	Mike James	4.1	Scott Edgar		
1997-98	11-19	5-11		Mike James	17.5	Nick Bosnic	5.7	Mike James	3.5	Scott Edgar	29-55	.345
1998-99	5-23	1-15		Wayne Smith	16.6	Wayne Smith	6.2	Courtney Wallace	3.9	Darelle Porter		
1999-2000	9-20	4-12		Wayne Smith	16.7	Wayne Smith	7.0	Devin Montgomery	3.8	Darelle Porter		
2000-01	9-21	3-13		Courtney Wallace	16.6	Wayne Smith	5.7	Courtney Wallace	3.4	Darelle Porter	23-64	.264
2001-02	9-19	4-12		Wayne Smith	16.4	Aaron Lovelace	6.3	Jamal Hunter	2.9	Danny Nee		
2002-03	9-21	4-12		Kevin Forney	13.4	Elijah Palmer	5.5	Bryant McAllister	2.6	Danny Nee		
2003-04	12-17	6-10		Elijah Palmer	13.9	Elijah Palmer	5.9	Martin Osimani	5.9	Danny Nee		
2004-05	8-22	5-11		Bryant McAllister	16.1	Kieron Achara	6.7	Martin Osimani	5.0	Danny Nee		
2005-06	3-24	1-15		Bryant McAllister	19.7	DeVario Hudson	5.4	Bryant McAllister	4.8	Danny Nee	41-103	.285
2006-07	10-19	6-10		Robert Mitchell	16.4	Kieron Achara	7.3	Aaron Jackson	3.8	Ron Everhart		
2007-08	17-13	7-9		Shawn James	12.6	Shawn James	6.9	Aaron Jackson	3.5	Ron Everhart		
2008-09	21-13	9-7	NIT FIRST ROUND	Aaron Jackson	19.3	Damian Saunders	7.6	Aaron Jackson	5.7	Ron Everhart	48-45	.516

[a] **Does not include a victory by forfeit against Tennessee (which refused to play unless Duquesne's African-American center, Chuck Cooper, sat out) not recognized by the NCAA.**

ESPN 225 SAGARIN

East Carolina

The Pirates have had 10 different coaches since 1974 and only one of them, Joe Dooley in the mid-'90s, finished his tenure on the good side of .500. Conference titles in 1972 (Southern) and 1993 (Colonial Athletic) led to the school's only NCAA appearances.

BEST TEAM: 1974-75 A few years after their '72 NCAA appearance, the Pirates had a team deserving of another bid. But ECU, 18–7 during the regular season, slipped against William and Mary in the Southern Conference tourney. An invite to the short-lived Collegiate Commissioners Tournament was appreciated, but not quite what the Pirates had hoped for.

BEST PLAYER: G Blue Edwards (1986-87, '88-89) In just two seasons he rewrote the Pirates record book—though there's also the small matter of a yearlong sophomore suspension for breaking and entering. Edwards really lit it up in his junior season: 26.7 ppg, 6.9 rpg, Colonial POY, ECU season records for most points (773) and most field goals made (297).

BEST COACH: Howard Porter (1947-59) He's the only ECU coach to last more than 10 years on the job. His Pirates never had a losing season and his 1952-53 and '53-54 squads reached the NAIA national tournament.

GAME FOR THE AGES: By all rights, the Pirates had no chance. They were the No. 7 seed in the 1993 Colonial Athletic Association tournament, but a couple of upsets left them facing Lefty Driesell's No. 1-seed James Madison in the final. The Pirates slowed the tempo to a crawl and Driesell's team missed nine free throws down the stretch to help seal a 54-49 win that sent East Carolina to the NCAAs with a not-very-pretty 13–16 mark.

FIERCEST RIVAL: UNC Wilmington has a nearby beach, five postseason appearances since 2000 and a 33–27 overall record in the series. That leaves East Carolina with a lot of envy. The teams' rivalry had more heat before ECU left the CAA for Conference USA in 2001. Now, they meet annually for The War at the Shore and local bragging rights in the early part of the season.

SEASON REVIEW

SEAS.	W-L	CONF.	COACH	SEAS.	W-L	CONF.	COACH
1931-46	*139-112*	*Best season 1940-41 (15-4)*		1959-60	14-9		Earl Smith
1946-47	17-10		Jim Johnson	1960-61	12-9		Earl Smith
1947-48	13-11		Howard Porter	1961-62	15-12		Earl Smith
1948-49	10-9		Howard Porter	1962-63	12-10		Earl Smith
1949-50	16-7		Howard Porter	1963-64	9-15		Wendell Carr
1950-51	13-11		Howard Porter	1964-65	12-10		Wendell Carr
1951-52	14-11		Howard Porter	1965-66	11-15	5-7	Wendell Carr
1952-53	18-5		Howard Porter	1966-67	7-17	4-8	Tom Quinn
1953-54	23-2		Howard Porter	1967-68	9-16	6-7	Tom Quinn
1954-55	16-8		Howard Porter	1968-69	17-11	9-2	Tom Quinn
1955-56	18-9		Howard Porter	1969-70	16-10	9-2	Tom Quinn
1956-57	13-13		Howard Porter	1970-71	13-12	7-4	Tom Quinn
1957-58	15-7		Howard Porter	1971-72	14-15	7-5 ●	Tom Quinn
1958-59	13-9		Howard Porter	1972-73	13-13	7-7	Tom Quinn

SEAS.	W-L	CONF.	SCORING		COACH	RECORD	
1973-74	13-12	8-6	Nicky White	13.2	Tom Quinn	102-106	.490
1974-75	19-9	11-3	Gregg Ashorn	15.2	Dave Patton		
1975-76	11-15	7-7	Earl Garner	15.4	Dave Patton		
1976-77	10-18	3-9	Larry Hunt	12.4	Dave Patton	40-42	.488
1977-78	9-17		Oliver Mack	28.0	Larry Gillman		
1978-79	12-15		Oliver Mack	18.3	Larry Gillman	21-32	.396
1979-80	15-12		George Maynor	17.0	Dave Odom		
1980-81	12-14		Charles Watkins	12.8	Dave Odom		
1981-82	10-17		Morris Hargrove	11.5	Dave Odom	37-43	.463
1982-83	16-13	3-7	Johnny Edwards	18.6	Charlie Harrison		
1983-84	4-24	1-9	Curt Vanderhorst	11.6	Charlie Harrison		
1984-85	7-21	1-13	Curt Vanderhorst	17.0	Charlie Harrison		
1985-86	12-16	6-8	Marchell Henry	15.6	Charlie Harrison		
1986-87	12-16	4-10	Marchell Henry	19.1	Charlie Harrison	51-90	.362
1987-88	8-20	3-11	Gus Hill	19.3	Mike Steele		
1988-89	15-14	6-8	Blue Edwards	26.7	Mike Steele		
1989-90	13-18	6-8	Reed Lose	12.7	Mike Steele		
1990-91	12-16	4-10	Lester Lyons	17.6	Mike Steele	48-68	.414
1991-92	10-18	4-10	Lester Lyons	15.6	Eddie Payne		
1992-93	13-17	4-10 ●	Lester Lyons	15.4	Eddie Payne		
1993-94	15-12	7-7	Lester Lyons	16.5	Eddie Payne		
1994-95	18-11	7-7	Anton Gill	16.8	Eddie Payne	56-58	.491
1995-96	17-11	8-8	Tim Basham	13.5	Joe Dooley		
1996-97	17-10	9-7	Raphael Edwards	13.2	Joe Dooley		
1997-98	10-17	5-11	Raphael Edwards	16.7	Joe Dooley		
1998-99	13-14	7-9	Evaldas Jocys	13.8	Joe Dooley	57-52	.523
1999-2000	10-18	5-11	Garrett Blackwelder	10.5	Bill Herrion		
2000-01	14-14	6-10	Gabriel Mikulas	15.0	Bill Herrion		
2001-02	12-18	5-11	Erroyl Bing	12.6	Bill Herrion		
2002-03	12-15	3-13	Derrick Wiley	14.0	Bill Herrion		
2003-04	13-14	5-11	Derrick Wiley	14.8	Bill Herrion		
2004-05	9-19	4-12	Mike Cook	15.0	Bill Herrion	70-98	.417
2005-06	8-20	2-12	Corey Rouse	14.3	Ricky Stokes		
2006-07	6-24	1-15	Darrell Jenkins	12.3	Ricky Stokes	14-44	.241
2007-08	11-19	5-11	Sam Hinnant	11.0	Mack McCarthy		
2008-09	13-17	5-11	Sam Hinnant	15.0	Mack McCarthy	24-36	.400

● **NCAA Tournament appearance**

PROFILE

East Carolina University, Greenville, NC
Founded: 1907
Enrollment: 25,990 (17,728 undergraduate)
Colors: Purple and gold
Nickname: Pirates
Current arena: Williams Arena at Minges Coliseum, opened in 1968 (8,000)
Previous: Christenbury Gym, 1952-1967 (N/A)
First game: Dec. 15, 1931
All-time record: 943-973 (.492)
Total weeks in AP Top 20/25: 0

Current conference: Conference USA (2001-)
Conference titles: 0
Conference tournament titles:
Southern: 1 (1972)
Colonial Athletic: 1 (1993)
NCAA Tournament appearances: 2
NIT appearances: 0

TOP 5

G **Blue Edwards** (1986-87, '88-89)
G **Lester Lyons** (1990-94)
F **Erroyl Bing** (2000-04)
F **Bobby Hodges** (1950-54)
F **Bill Otte** (1960-64)

FIRST-ROUND PRO PICKS

1989 **Blue Edwards**, Utah (21)

RECORDS

RECORDS	GAME		SEASON		CAREER	
POINTS	47	Oliver Mack, vs. USC-Aiken (Feb. 11, 1978)	773	Blue Edwards (1988-89)	2,018	Bobby Hodges (1950-54)
POINTS PER GAME			28.0	Oliver Mack (1977-78)	23.0	Oliver Mack (1977-79)
REBOUNDS	24	Erroyl Bing, vs. South Florida (Jan. 25, 2003); Jim Fairley, vs. Belmont Abbey (Jan. 21, 1970); Bill Otte, vs. Atlantic Christian (Feb. 3, 1962)	332	Bill Otte (1961-62)	969	Bill Otte (1960-64)
ASSISTS	14	Tom Miller vs. East Tenn. St. (Jan. 8, 1969); Brock Young, vs. Rice (Feb. 14, 2009)	227	Brock Young (2008-09)	413	Travis Holcomb-Faye (1999 -2003)

ESPN 173 SAGARIN

East Tennessee State

Making the NCAA Tournament used to be almost routine for East Tennessee State. After moving to a new conference, the Atlantic Sun, for 2005-06, the Buccaneers are working to regain their old swagger.

BEST TEAM: 1991-92 The season started off tragically, with PG recruit Chris White dying in his sleep. On the floor, the Bucs ran down opponents with a relentlessly up-tempo game. The sweetest of their 24 wins was the last—a first-round upset of No. 3-seed Arizona in the NCAA Tourney. The Bucs hit 11 first-half threes and won, 87-80, behind F Rodney English's 21 points.

BEST PLAYER: C Greg Dennis (1987-90, '91-92) It's no coincidence that his career coincides with the best four-year run in ETSU history, with four conference tourney titles and four NCAA bids. The 6'11" Dennis was tough to stop—he finished as the school's leading scorer (2,204).

BEST COACH: Madison Brooks (1948-73) He coached for 25 seasons in Johnson City, and through 2008-09 Brooks was credited with an astonishing 34% of the school's 1,109 all-time victories. He took three teams to the NAIA national tournament and one to the NCAA Tourney.

GAME FOR THE AGES: In the first round of the 1989 NCAA Tournament, ETSU came within a bucket of being the only No. 16-seed to topple a No. 1. The Bucs started three sophs and two freshmen but still sprinted to a 17-point lead over powerful Oklahoma. But OU's pressure D wore them down, and PG Keith "Mister" Jennings, a 5'7" dynamo, fouled out. With :08 left and ETSU down 72-71, Oklahoma's Mookie Blaylock missed the front end of a one-and-one. The Bucs called timeout with :04 left, but it wasn't enough time. A half-court air ball was the best they could manage.

FIERCEST RIVAL: Through the 1980s and '90s, ETSU and Chattanooga scrapped for the Southern Conference title nearly every year. (One or the other represented the SoCon in the NCAAs 12 out of 17 seasons between 1981-97). When the Bucs jetted to the Atlantic Sun, one school that stayed on the schedule was their eastern Tennessee rival.

SEASON REVIEW

SEAS.	W-L	CONF.	COACH
1918-46	*153-159*	*23-12 record in first four seasons*	
1946-47	13-3		Gene McMurray
1947-48	9-8		L.T. Roberts
1948-49	19-6		Madison Brooks
1949-50	17-5		Madison Brooks
1950-51	22-9		Madison Brooks
1951-52	24-7		Madison Brooks
1952-53	26-4		Madison Brooks
1953-54	23-4		Madison Brooks
1954-55	17-8		Madison Brooks
1955-56	20-7		Madison Brooks
1956-57	17-11		Madison Brooks
1957-58	6-19		Madison Brooks
1958-59	13-10	5-7	Madison Brooks
1959-60	9-14	2-10	Madison Brooks
1960-61	9-15	1-11	Madison Brooks
1961-62	11-14	3-9	Madison Brooks
1962-63	14-8	7-5	Madison Brooks
1963-64	12-10	8-6	Madison Brooks
1964-65	6-17	4-10	Madison Brooks
1965-66	7-14	3-11	Madison Brooks
1966-67	17-9	8-6	Madison Brooks
1967-68	19-8	10-4 ●	Madison Brooks
1968-69	15-11	6-8	Madison Brooks
1969-70	15-11	8-6	Madison Brooks
1970-71	12-12	8-6	Madison Brooks
1971-72	11-14	6-8	Madison Brooks
1972-73	9-17	2-12	Madison Brooks

SEAS.	W-L	CONF.	SCORING		COACH	RECORD
1973-74	8-18	3-11	Kenny Reynolds	16.7	Leroy Fisher	
1974-75	9-14	5-9	Kenny Reynolds	21.5	Leroy Fisher	
1975-76	6-20	4-10	Bob Brown	16.8	Leroy Fisher	23-52 .307
1976-77	12-14	6-8	Bob Brown	15.5	Sonny Smith	
1977-78	18-9	10-4	Jim Smith	15.5	Sonny Smith	30-23 .566
1978-79	16-11		Scott Place	12.7	Jim Halihan	
1979-80	15-13	8-7	Troy Mikell	16.5	Jim Halihan	
1980-81	13-14	9-7	Troy Mikell	14.1	Jim Halihan	
1981-82	13-15	8-8	Troy Mikell	14.2	Jim Halihan	57-53 .518
1982-83	22-9	12-4 ■	Troy Mikell	16.2	Barry Dowd	
1983-84	9-19	6-10	James Tandy	16.2	Barry Dowd	
1984-85	9-18	3-13	Mark Watkins	13.8	Barry Dowd	40-46 .465
1985-86	13-16	8-8	Wes Stallings	19.2	Les Robinson	
1986-87	7-21	3-13	Carniel Manuel	12.8	Les Robinson	
1987-88	14-15	9-7	Greg Dennis	16.4	Les Robinson	
1988-89	20-11	7-7 ●	Greg Dennis	16.3	Les Robinson	
1989-90	27-7	12-2 ●	Greg Dennis	19.7	Les Robinson	81-70 .536
1990-91	28-5	11-3 ●	Keith Jennings	20.1	Alan LeForce	
1991-92	24-7	12-2 ●	Rodney English	17.5	Alan LeForce	
1992-93	19-10	12-6	Jerry Pelphrey	15.0	Alan LeForce	
1993-94	16-14	13-5	Trazel Silvers	17.3	Alan LeForce	
1994-95	14-14	9-5	Tony Patterson	14.1	Alan LeForce	
1995-96	7-20	3-11	Shahid Perkins	10.4	Alan LeForce	108-70 .607
1996-97	7-20	2-12	Kyle Keeton	10.8	Ed DeChellis	
1997-98	11-16	6-9	Greg Stephens	17.2	Ed DeChellis	
1998-99	17-11	9-7	Greg Stephens	16.1	Ed DeChellis	
1999-2000	14-15	8-8	Leo Murray	11.0	Ed DeChellis	
2000-01	18-10	13-3	Dimeco Childress	13.2	Ed DeChellis	
2001-02	18-10	11-5	Dimeco Childress	17.5	Ed DeChellis	
2002-03	20-11	11-5 ●	Tiras Wade	16.3	Ed DeChellis	105-93 .530
2003-04	27-6	15-1 ●	Tim Smith	17.7	Murry Bartow	
2004-05	10-19	4-12	Tim Smith	22.2	Murry Bartow	
2005-06	15-13	12-8	Tim Smith	22.0	Murry Bartow	
2006-07	24-10	16-2 ■	Courtney Pigram	18.1	Murry Bartow	
2007-08	19-13	11-5	Courtney Pigram	15.8	Murry Bartow	
2008-09	23-11	14-6 ●	Courtney Pigram	17.6	Murry Bartow	118-72 .621

● NCAA Tournament appearance ■ NIT appearance

PROFILE

East Tennessee State University, Johnson City, TN
Founded: 1911 as East Tennessee State Normal School
Enrollment: 13,300
Colors: Navy blue and old gold
Nickname: Buccaneers
Current arena: Memorial Center, opened in 1977 (5,740)
Previous: Brooks Gym, 1918-77 (2,800)
First game: 1918
All-time record: 1,107-913 (.548)
Total weeks in AP Top 20/25: 14

Current conference: Atlantic Sun (2005-)
Conference titles:
Ohio Valley: 2 (1968 [tie], '78 [tie])
Southern: 7 (1990, '91 [tie], '92 [tie], 2001 [tie], '02 [tie], '03 [tie], '04 [tie])
Atlantic Sun: 1 (2007)
Conference tournament titles:
Southern: 6 (1989, '90, '91, '92, 2003, '04)
Atlantic Sun: 1 (2009)
NCAA Tournament appearances: 8
NIT appearances: 2

TOP 5

G **Keith Jennings** (1987-91)
G **Tim Smith** (2002-06)
F **Tom Chilton** (1958-61)
F **Tommy Woods** (1964-67)
C **Greg Dennis** (1987-90, '91-92)

RECORDS

RECORDS	GAME		SEASON		CAREER	
POINTS	52	Tom Chilton, vs. Austin Peay (Feb. 5, 1961)	771	Tom Chilton (1960-61)	2,300	Tim Smith (2002-06)
POINTS PER GAME			32.1	Tom Chilton (1960-61)	26.1	Tom Chilton (1958-61)
REBOUNDS	38	Tommy Woods, vs. Middle Tennessee State (1964-65)	607	Herb Weaver (1956-57)	1,034	Tommy Woods (1964-67)
ASSISTS	19	Keith Jennings, vs. Appalachian State (Feb. 2, 1991)	301	Keith Jennings (1990-91)	983	Keith Jennings (1987-91)

ESPN 189 SAGARIN

EASTERN ILLINOIS

Want to rile up a group of Panthers fans? Ask them to pinpoint the glory days. Some will insist they were during Bill Healey's reign from 1946 to '53. Others will make a case for the 1970s, when Jeff Furry and Charlie Thomas led the Panthers to two D2 final fours in three years. And the younger set will focus on the high-wattage teams featuring nationally ranked scorers Kyle Hill and Henry Domercant.

BEST TEAM: 1975-76 Behind Thomas' perfect-form jump shot and Furry's sound all-around game, the Panthers won 15 straight at one point, and beat Saint Joseph's College, Evansville, Bridgeport and Old Dominion to claim third place in the D2 tournament.

BEST PLAYER: G/F Henry Domercant (1999-2003) As solid as Kevin Duckworth was as an NBA center, his Panthers career never approached Domercant's dominance. An athletic catch-and-shoot artist, the shooting guard finished in the nation's Top 5 in scoring three straight years, is 32nd all-time in D1 points (2,602) and ranks as the Ohio Valley's all-time leading scorer.

BEST COACH: Don Eddy (1968-80) He didn't believe in defensive gimmicks or whiz-bang offensive schemes. But in large part by emphasizing fundamentals and all-out effort, he took eight of 12 teams to the postseason, including two D2 final fours (1976 and '78).

GAME FOR THE AGES: The game was over. With less than seven minutes left in the 2001 OVC tourney championship, Eastern Illinois was down 21 to Austin Peay. But shot by amazing shot, the Panthers furiously whittled down that lead, scoring on 13 of their final 16 possessions, including the most improbable of game-winners: center Jan Thompson's tip-in with under a second left, which counted only because the refs called goaltending on the Governors.

FIERCEST RIVAL: Even if they were from different states, the Eastern Illinois-Western Illinois series would still be a doozy because of how evenly matched the teams are. Each has defended its home court the past seven seasons, leaving the series tied at 76–76.

SEASON REVIEW

SEAS.	W-L	CONF.	COACH	SEAS.	W-L	CONF.	COACH
1908-46	*272-333*	*Charles Lantz coached 24 seasons*		1959-60	13-12		Robert Carey
1946-47	17-8		Bill Healey	1960-61	10-13		Robert Carey
1947-48	16-7		Bill Healey	1961-62	11-12		Rex Darling
1948-49	23-6		Bill Healey	1962-63	8-16		Robert Carey
1949-50	21-5		Bill Healey	1963-64	11-12		Robert Carey
1950-51	19-4		Bill Healey	1964-65	18-7		Rex Darling
1951-52	24-2		Bill Healey	1965-66	7-18		Rex Darling
1952-53	16-9		Bill Healey	1966-67	6-18		Rex Darling
1953-54	17-5		Robert Carey	1967-68	9-16		John Caine
1954-55	11-10		Robert Carey	1968-69	13-13		Don Eddy
1955-56	17-8		Robert Carey	1969-70	10-15		Don Eddy
1956-57	17-14		Robert Carey	1970-71	18-9		Don Eddy
1957-58	17-9		Robert Carey	1971-72	20-10		Don Eddy
1958-59	14-9		Robert Carey	1972-73	10-16		Don Eddy

SEAS.	W-L	CONF.	SCORING		COACH	RECORD
1973-74	14-12				Don Eddy	
1974-75	20-8				Don Eddy	
1975-76	23-8				Don Eddy	
1976-77	18-11				Don Eddy	
1977-78	21-10				Don Eddy	
1978-79	19-10				Don Eddy	
1979-80	22-7				Don Eddy	208-129 .617
1980-81	16-11		Ricky Robinson	17.3	Rick Samuels	
1981-82	14-13		Ricky Robinson	14.1	Rick Samuels	
1982-83	13-18	8-4	Kevin Jones	17.4	Rick Samuels	
1983-84	15-13	7-7	Kevin Duckworth	19.1	Rick Samuels	
1984-85	20-10	9-5	Jon Collins	18.6	Rick Samuels	
1985-86	19-13	8-6	Jon Collins	19.7	Rick Samuels	
1986-87	9-19	3-11	Jay Taylor	14.7	Rick Samuels	
1987-88	17-11	7-7	Jay Taylor	20.2	Rick Samuels	
1988-89	16-16	7-5	Jay Taylor	23.4	Rick Samuels	
1989-90	10-18	3-9	Barry Johnson	17.2	Rick Samuels	
1990-91	17-12	10-6	Steve Rowe	15.2	Rick Samuels	
1991-92	17-14	9-7 ●	Steve Rowe	15.1	Rick Samuels	
1992-93	10-17	7-9	Louis Jordan	14.7	Rick Samuels	
1993-94	12-15	7-11	L. Jordan, D. Landrus	12.0	Rick Samuels	
1994-95	16-13	10-8	Derrick Landrus	15.6	Rick Samuels	
1995-96	13-15	9-9	Andre Rodriguez	16.1	Rick Samuels	
1996-97	12-15	9-9	Rick Kaye	16.8	Rick Samuels	
1997-98	16-11	13-5	Rick Kaye	21.1	Rick Samuels	
1998-99	13-16	8-10	Kyle Hill	16.6	Rick Samuels	
1999-2000	17-12	11-7	Kyle Hill	19.1	Rick Samuels	
2000-01	21-10	11-5 ●	Kyle Hill	23.8	Rick Samuels	
2001-02	15-16	7-9	Henry Domercant	26.4	Rick Samuels	
2002-03	14-15	9-7	Henry Domercant	27.9	Rick Samuels	
2003-04	6-21	4-12	Josh Gomes	13.6	Rick Samuels	
2004-05	12-16	7-9	Josh Gomes	16.8	Rick Samuels	360-360 .500
2005-06	6-21	5-15	Josh Gomes	15.1	Mike Miller	
2006-07	10-20	6-14	Romain Martin	14.8	Mike Miller	
2007-08	7-22	6-14	Bobby Catchings	10.8	Mike Miller	
2008-09	12-18	8-10	Romain Martin	15.4	Mike Miller	35-81 .302

● NCAA Tournament appearance

PROFILE

Eastern Illinois University, Charleston, IL
Founded: 1895
Enrollment: 12,349 (10,410 undergraduate)
Colors: Blue, gray and white
Nickname: Panthers
Current arena: Lantz Arena, opened in 1966 (5,300)
Previous: Lantz Gym, 1938-66 (N/A); Pemberton Hall, 1909-38 (N/A)
First game: 1908
All-time record: 1,197-1,123 (.516)
Total weeks in AP Top 20/25: 0

Current conference: Ohio Valley (1996-)
Conference titles: 0
Conference tournament titles:
Assoc. of Mid-Continent Universities–8: 1 (1985)
Mid-Continent: 1 (1992)
OVC: 1 (2001)
NCAA Tournament appearances: 2
NIT appearances: 0

TOP 5

G **Jon Collins** (1983-86)
G **Jay Taylor** (1985-89)
G/F **Henry Domercant** (1999-2003)
F **Tom Katsimpalis** (1948-52)
C **Kevin Duckworth** (1982-86)

RECORDS

RECORDS	GAME		SEASON		CAREER	
POINTS	56	B.J. Smith, vs. Millikin (Feb. 28, 1959)	817	Henry Domercant (2001-02)	2,602	Henry Domercant (1999-2003)
POINTS PER GAME			27.9	Henry Domercant (2002-03)	21.7	Henry Domercant (1999-2003)
REBOUNDS	24	Scott Keeve, vs. Western Illinois (Jan. 16, 1971); Howard Long, vs. Northern Illinois (Jan. 10, 1958)	314	Jim Kitchen (1969-70)	867	Kevin Duckworth (1982-86)
ASSISTS	18	Chad Peckinpaugh, vs. Southeast Missouri State (Feb. 22, 1997)	197	Troy Richardson (1984-85)	415	Johnny Hernandez (1992-96)

ESPN 136 SAGARIN

EASTERN KENTUCKY

Seven times the Colonels (formerly the Maroons) have gone to the NCAA Tournament. Seven times they have lost—but not without putting up a fight nearly every time. Their most recent appearance in the Big Dance, against No. 1-seed North Carolina in 2007, captures the team's spunk. Down 28 points in the first half, Eastern went on a 32-9 run to close the deficit to 48-44 early in the second half, before fading late.

BEST TEAM: 1964-65 Eddie Bodkin's teammates called him the Machine because he performed his hook shot and other great moves without flash or emotion. He more than lived up to the nickname as a junior, leading the Maroons to 15 double-digit wins, plus victories over Dave Bing-led Syracuse and Clem Haskins' Western Kentucky before an NCAA Tourney loss to DePaul.

BEST PLAYER: F Jack Adams (1952-56) James "Turk" Tillman could light it up; he finished fourth nationally in scoring in 1979 (26.9 ppg) and fifth in 1980 (27.2). But Adams set 13 school records, is among the Top 10 in career scoring (1,460) and rebounding (870), averaged a career double-double (20.6, 12.3) and is the first Colonel to have his jersey retired.

BEST COACH: Paul McBrayer (1946-62) The former Kentucky All-America and assistant coach won his first 11 games at EKU and never looked back, going to two NCAA Tournaments and winning three OVC regular-season and two tournament crowns.

GAME FOR THE AGES: Every EKU fan knows about the controversial 78-77 OVC tourney title win over Western Kentucky in 1979. Colonels guard Dave Tierney was fouled on a follow-up—but did the hack come before the final buzzer? The refs huddled and awarded Tierney two shots with an empty lane. He nailed both to send host EKU to the NCAA Tournament. A later replay revealed the foul occurred after time ran out.

FIERCEST RIVAL: Historically, Western Kentucky has been the school's biggest rival. But with WKU's 1982 move to the Sun Belt, OVC foe Morehead State assumed that role. EKU leads the series, 101–70.

SEASON REVIEW

SEAS.	W-L	CONF.	COACH	SEAS.	W-L	CONF.	COACH
1909-46	*288-209*	*Third in the 1945 NAIB tourney*		1959-60	14-8	9-3	Paul McBrayer
1946-47	21-4		Paul McBrayer	1960-61	15-9	9-3	Paul McBrayer
1947-48	17-7		Paul McBrayer	1961-62	10-6	7-5	Paul McBrayer[a]
1948-49	16-4	7-3	Paul McBrayer	1962-63	9-12	6-6	Jim Baechtold
1949-50	16-6	7-3	Paul McBrayer	1963-64	15-9	9-5	Jim Baechtold
1950-51	18-8	8-3	Paul McBrayer	1964-65	19-6	13-1 ●	Jim Baechtold
1951-52	13-11	10-2	Paul McBrayer	1965-66	16-9	9-5	Jim Baechtold
1952-53	16-9	9-1 ●	Paul McBrayer	1966-67	5-18	2-12	Jim Baechtold
1953-54	7-16	4-6	Paul McBrayer	1967-68	10-14	6-8	Guy Strong
1954-55	15-8	6-4	Paul McBrayer	1968-69	13-9	7-7	Guy Strong
1955-56	9-16	3-7	Paul McBrayer	1969-70	12-10	8-6	Guy Strong
1956-57	6-15	4-6	Paul McBrayer	1970-71	16-8	10-4	Guy Strong
1957-58	8-11	3-7	Paul McBrayer	1971-72	15-11	9-5 ●	Guy Strong
1958-59	16-6	10-2 ●	Paul McBrayer	1972-73	12-13	7-7	Guy Strong

SEAS.	W-L	CONF.	SCORING		COACH	RECORD	
1973-74	8-15	6-8	Carl Brown	17.1	Bob Mulcahy		
1974-75	7-18	3-11	Carl Brown	18.8	Bob Mulcahy		
1975-76	10-15	6-8	Carl Brown	18.6	Bob Mulcahy	25-48	.342
1976-77	8-16	3-11	Dave Bootcheck	19.7	Ed Byhre		
1977-78	15-11	8-6	Lovell Joiner	17.4	Ed Byhre		
1978-79	21-8	9-3 ●	James Tillman	26.9	Ed Byhre		
1979-80	15-12	7-5	James Tillman	27.2	Ed Byhre		
1980-81	10-16	7-7	Tommy Baker	16.8	Ed Byhre	69-63	.523
1981-82	5-21	3-13	Jim Chambers, J. Stepp	12.2	Max Good		
1982-83	10-17	7-7	Jimmy Stepp	14.3	Max Good		
1983-84	11-16	5-9	Antonio Parris	18.8	Max Good		
1984-85	16-13	9-5	Antonio Parris	14.5	Max Good		
1985-86	10-18	5-9	Lewis Spence	14.5	Max Good		
1986-87	19-11	9-5	Antonio Parris	20.5	Max Good		
1987-88	18-11	10-4	Jeff McGill	18.6	Max Good		
1988-89	7-22	4-8	Darrin O'Bryant	15.1	Max Good	96-129	.427
1989-90	13-17	7-5	Randolph Taylor	14.2	Mike Pollio		
1990-91	19-10	9-3	Jamie Ross	12.8	Mike Pollio		
1991-92	19-14	9-5	John Allen	13.5	Mike Pollio	51-41	.554
1992-93	15-12	11-5	John Allen	17.2	Mike Calhoun		
1993-94	13-14	9-7	John Allen	15.6	Mike Calhoun		
1994-95	9-19	6-10	Arlando Johnson	18.2	Mike Calhoun		
1995-96	13-14	7-9	DeMarkus Doss	16.4	Mike Calhoun		
1996-97	8-18	6-12	Daniel Sutton	14.1	Mike Calhoun	58-77	.430
1997-98	10-17	8-10	Mark Williams	13.3	Scott Perry		
1998-99	3-23	2-16	Whitney Robinson	17.8	Scott Perry		
1999-2000	6-21	2-16	Sam Hoskin	15.7	Scott Perry	19-61	.238
2000-01	7-19	1-15	Lavoris Jerry	17.8	Travis Ford		
2001-02	7-20	3-13	Shawn Fields	16.4	Travis Ford		
2002-03	11-17	5-11	Shawn Fields	16.1	Travis Ford		
2003-04	14-15	8-8	Matt Witt	15.6	Travis Ford		
2004-05	22-9	11-5 ●	Matt Witt	14.4	Travis Ford	61-80	.433
2005-06	14-16	11-9	Matt Witt	18.5	Jeff Neubauer		
2006-07	21-12	13-7 ●	Mike Rose	15.1	Jeff Neubauer		
2007-08	14-16	10-10	Mike Rose	15.3	Jeff Neubauer		
2008-09	18-13	10-8	Mike Rose	20.0	Jeff Neubauer	67-57	.540

[a] **Paul McBrayer (4-3) and Jim Baechtold (6-3) both coached during the 1961-62 season.**

● **NCAA Tournament appearance**

PROFILE

Eastern Kentucky University, Richmond, KY
Founded: 1906
Enrollment: 16,000 (13,659 undergraduate)
Colors: Maroon and white
Nickname: Colonels
Current arena: Alumni Coliseum (Paul S. McBrayer Arena), opened in 1963 (6,500)
Previous: Weaver Gymnasium, 1931-63 (3,700); The Barn, 1923-30 (N/A); Memorial Hall, 1920-22 (N/A)
First game played: 1909

All-time record: 1,093-1,028 (.515)
Total weeks in AP Top 20/25: 6
Current conference: Ohio Valley (1948-)
Conference titles:
OVC: 6 (1953, '59, '61 [tie], '65, '72 [tie], '79)
Conference tournament titles:
OVC: 5 (1950, '55, '79, 2005, '07)
NCAA Tournament appearances: 7
NIT appearances: 0

FIRST-ROUND PRO PICKS

1952 **Jim Baechtold**, Baltimore (2)

TOP 5

G **Antonio Parris** (1983-87)
G/F **Charlie Mitchell** (1969-73)
F **Jack Adams** (1952-56)
F **Eddie Bodkin** (1963-66)
F **James Tillman** (1978-80)

RECORDS	GAME		SEASON		CAREER	
POINTS	49	Jack Adams, vs. Union (Dec. 1, 1955)	780	James Tillman (1978-79)	1,832	Matt Witt (2002-06)
POINTS PER GAME			27.2	James Tillman (1979-80)	27.0	James Tillman (1978-80)
REBOUNDS	33	Garfield Smith, vs. Marshall (Dec. 13, 1967)	472	Garfield Smith (1967-68)	977	Mike Smith (1988-92)
ASSISTS	12	Matt Witt, vs. Alabama A&M (Dec. 30, 2003)	243	Bruce Jones (1978-79)	699	Bruce Jones (1977-81)

ESPN 227 SAGARIN

EASTERN MICHIGAN

George Gervin. Grant Long. Earl Boykins. For a mid-major in the shadow of the University of Michigan, just 10 miles away, Eastern Michigan has fielded its fair share of transcendent players—and produced a good number of transcendent moments, too. EMU fans won't soon forget the 1991 Sweet 16 run or the 1996 Tournament victory over Duke.

BEST TEAM: 1990-91 Marcus Kennedy pounded it down low. Twins Carl and Charles Thomas took it to the air. Lorenzo Neely controlled the pace. Behind the versatile, senior-laden lineup, Eastern swept the Mid-American Conference regular-season and tournament titles, then bounced No. 5-seed Mississippi State and No. 13-seed Penn State to crash the Sweet 16. There, despite Carl Thomas' 27 points, No. 1-seed North Carolina sent them packing, 93-67.

BEST PLAYER: G GEORGE GERVIN (1971-72) He transferred from Long Beach State with eight games left in the 1970-71 season. The next year Gervin, who was nearly unstoppable one-on-one, set EMU single-season records for points (886) and rebounds (458). Although he was dismissed from the team after sucker-punching Roanoke's Jay Piccola during the 1972 College Division final four, the Ice Man went on to a Hall of Fame pro career.

BEST COACH: BEN BRAUN (1986-96) He didn't have the biggest lineups or the deepest benches, but his teams overflowed with energy. One story from Braun's high school playing days says it all about his intensity: During a pregame meal, he spotted a teammate indulging in ice cream, took it for a lack of discipline and spit in the dessert.

GAME FOR THE AGES: It took a 5'7" (later listed as 5'5") guard to slay a giant in the 1996 Tourney. Duke hadn't lost an opener since 1955, but No. 9-seed EMU, led by Earl Boykins' 23, won 75-60. EMU next gave No. 1-seed UConn a good run before falling 95-81.

FIERCEST RIVAL: Don't try to tell Eastern and Central Michigan that Michigan-Michigan State is the state's top rivalry. The two "directionals" have been going at it since 1906. CMU leads overall, 93–84.

SEASON REVIEW

SEAS.	W-L	CONF.	COACH	SEAS.	W-L	CONF.	COACH
1898-1949	*374-319*	*Went 29-2 from 1916-18 (.935)*		1962-63	10-10		J. Richard Adams
1949-50	6-12		William Crouch	1963-64	9-9		J. Richard Adams
1950-51	7-13		William Crouch	1964-65	11-7		J. Richard Adams
1951-52	9-11		William Crouch	1965-66	15-3		J. Richard Adams
1952-53	14-6		William Crouch	1966-67	16-7		Jim Dutcher
1953-54	8-12		Robert Hollway	1967-68	18-9		Jim Dutcher
1954-55	14-8		James Skala	1968-69	20-9		Jim Dutcher
1955-56	4-18		James Skala	1969-70	22-7		Jim Dutcher
1956-57	9-14		James Skala	1970-71	22-11		Jim Dutcher
1957-58	1-20		James Skala	1971-72	24-7		Jim Dutcher
1958-59	7-17		James Skala	1972-73	8-17		Allan Freund
1959-60	6-13		James Skala	1973-74	8-18		Allan Freund
1960-61	5-18		J. Richard Adams	1974-75	12-14	4-9	Allan Freund
1961-62	8-12		J. Richard Adams	1975-76	7-20	1-15	Allan Freund

SEAS.	W-L	CONF.		SCORING		COACH	RECORD	
1976-77	9-18	4-12		Bill Weaver	12.7	Ray Scott		
1977-78	11-16	7-9		Gary Green	15.7	Ray Scott		
1978-79	9-18	5-11		Gary Green	18.6	Ray Scott	29-52	.358
1979-80	11-16	5-11		Kelvin Blakely	17.3	Jim Boyce		
1980-81	13-14	8-8		Jeff Zatkoff	17.5	Jim Boyce		
1981-82	15-12	8-8		Jeff Zatkoff	16.6	Jim Boyce		
1982-83	12-16	8-10		Marlow McClain	16.2	Jim Boyce		
1983-84	12-17	8-10		Fred Cofield	15.6	Jim Boyce		
1984-85	15-13	9-9		Fred Cofield	20.6	Jim Boyce		
1985-86	9-18	5-13		Percy Cooper	13.9	Jim Boyce[a]	82-96	.461
1986-87	14-15	8-8		Grant Long	14.9	Ben Braun		
1987-88	22-8	14-2	●	Grant Long	23.0	Ben Braun		
1988-89	16-13 ⊗	5-11		Lorenzo Neely	13.1	Ben Braun		
1989-90	19-13	8-8		Lorenzo Neely	13.4	Ben Braun		
1990-91	26-7	13-3	●	Marcus Kennedy	20.0	Ben Braun		
1991-92	9-22	4-12		Kory Hallas	20.0	Ben Braun		
1992-93	13-17	8-10		Ellery Morgan	15.5	Ben Braun		
1993-94	15-12	10-8		Kareem Carpenter	18.4	Ben Braun		
1994-95	20-10	12-6	■	Brian Tolbert	17.0	Ben Braun		
1995-96	25-6	14-4	●	Brian Tolbert	20.5	Ben Braun	184-133	.580▼
1996-97	22-10	11-7		Earl Boykins	19.1	Milton Barnes		
1997-98	20-10	13-5	●	Earl Boykins	25.7	Milton Barnes		
1998-99	5-20	5-13		Craig Erquhart	11.0	Milton Barnes		
1999-2000	15-13	9-9		Calvin Warner	14.6	Milton Barnes	62-53	.539
2000-01	3-25	1-17		Melvin Hicks	13.1	Jim Boone		
2001-02	6-24	2-16		Ricky Cottrill	19.4	Jim Boone		
2002-03	14-14	8-10		Ryan Prillman	17.1	Jim Boone		
2003-04	13-15	7-11		Markus Austin	13.5	Jim Boone		
2004-05	12-18	5-13		Markus Austin	13.8	Jim Boone	48-96	.333
2005-06	7-21	3-15		John Bowler	20.1	Charles Ramsey		
2006-07	13-19	6-10		Carlos Medlock	13.2	Charles Ramsey		
2007-08	14-17	8-8		Carlos Medlock	14.8	Charles Ramsey		
2008-09	8-24	6-10		Brandon Bowdry	14.8	Charles Ramsey	42-81	.341

[a] Jim Boyce (4-8) and Ben Braun (5-10) both coached during the 1985-86 season.

⊗ Records don't reflect games forfeited or vacated. For adjusted records, see p. 521.

▼ Coach's record adjusted to reflect games forfeited or vacated: 185-132. .584. For yearly totals, see p. 521.

● NCAA Tournament appearance ■ NIT appearance

PROFILE

Eastern Michigan University, Ypsilanti, MI
Founded: 1849
Enrollment: 21,926 (17,213 undergraduate)
Colors: Dark green and white
Nickname: Eagles
Current arena: Convocation Center, opened in 1998 (8,824)
Previous: Bowen Field House, 1955-98 (N/A)
First game: 1898
All-time record: 1,121-1,152 (.493)
Total weeks in AP Top 20/25: 3

Current conference: Mid-American (1974-)
Conference titles:
MAC: 3 (1988, '91, '96)
Conference tournament titles:
MAC: 4 (1988, '91, '96, '98)
NCAA Tournament appearances: 4
Sweet 16s (since 1975): 1
NIT appearances: 1

FIRST-ROUND PRO PICKS

1971 **Kennedy McIntosh,** Chicago (15)

TOP 5

G **Earl Boykins** (1994-98)
G **George Gervin** (1971-72)
F **Earle Higgins** (1967-70)
F **Grant Long** (1984-88)
C **Kennedy McIntosh** (1967-71)

RECORDS	GAME		SEASON		CAREER	
POINTS	47	Gary Tyson, vs. Wheaton (March 2, 1974)	886	George Gervin (1971-72)	2,219	Kennedy McIntosh (1967-71)
POINTS PER GAME			29.5	George Gervin (1971-72)	26.8	George Gervin (1971-72)
REBOUNDS	27	Kareem Carpenter, vs. Western Michigan (Feb. 8, 1995)	458	George Gervin (1971-72)	1,426	Kennedy McIntosh (1967-71)
ASSISTS	18	Harvey Marlatt, vs. Ferris State (March 4, 1970)	182	Percy Cooper (1985-86)	624	Earl Boykins (1994-98)

THE SCHOOLS

ESPN 208 SAGARIN

EASTERN WASHINGTON

One shining moment in a storied history: EWU students carrying unlikely star Gregg Smith on their shoulders after his second-half heroics helped the Eagles secure the 2004 Big Sky title and the school's first NCAA Tournament bid. Other legends for the longtime NAIA and D2 power: Red Reese, Jerry Krause, Irv Leifer and Rodney Stuckey.

BEST TEAM: 1945-46 Coach Red Reese's Eagles went 31–4 and reached the NAIB elite eight behind NAIB Hall of Famer and 1947 tourney MVP Irv Leifer. With other leading players Jack Roffler and George Gablehouse, the team won 27 straight games and had an average victory margin of 22.4 points.

BEST PLAYER: G RODNEY STUCKEY (2005-07) A two-time honorable mention All-America, Stuckey scored 1,438 points in his two seasons at Eastern and broke 10 school records. His 24.4-ppg career scoring average is third-best in Big Sky Conference history.

BEST COACH: RED REESE (1930-42, '45-64) He served as basketball, football and track coach—as well as athletic director—during his EWU tenure. Reese is the school's all-time winningest hoops coach, with 12 conference titles, three NAIA tourney berths and six 20-win seasons. Eastern's Reese Court is named in his honor.

GAME FOR THE AGES: After losing three straight Big Sky title games on foreign courts, the 71-59 victory over Northern Arizona in 2004 earned the Eagles their lone NCAA bid—on their own Reese Court. The top scorers were Brendon Merritt (22) and Marc Axton (19). But Gregg Smith, a little-used reserve, helped guide EWU in the second half with six points, four rebounds, a blocked shot and a steal.

FIERCEST RIVAL: Central Washington lingers as a bad nightmare. EWU's former NAIA foe leads their all-time rivalry, 93–75. But, more memorably, Central knocked Eastern from four NAIA district playoffs (1976, '77, '78, '80) before the Eagles moved to D2 in 1981. Since the move to D1, Eastern leads 6–2 and Big Sky foe Montana has become a more important rival.

SEASON REVIEW

SEAS.	W-L	CONF.	COACH	SEAS.	W-L	CONF.	COACH
1903-48	*480-208*		*Bob Brumblay 73-18 (1942-45)*	1961-62	15-12		Red Reese
1948-49	16-9		Red Reese	1962-63	9-15		Red Reese
1949-50	23-7		Red Reese	1963-64	7-19		Red Reese
1950-51	22-6		Red Reese	1964-65	9-16		Ernie McKie
1951-52	8-18		Red Reese	1965-66	8-18		Ernie McKie
1952-53	23-5		Red Reese	1966-67	6-18		Ernie McKie
1953-54	9-16		Red Reese	1967-68	8-17		Jerry Krause
1954-55	9-15		Red Reese	1968-69	14-11		Jerry Krause
1955-56	12-14		Red Reese	1969-70	8-18		Jerry Krause
1956-57	9-17		Red Reese	1970-71	16-12		Jerry Krause
1957-58	12-14		Red Reese	1971-72	22-7		Jerry Krause
1958-59	17-9		Red Reese	1972-73	15-10		Jerry Krause
1959-60	11-15		Red Reese	1973-74	14-11		Jerry Krause
1960-61	16-11		Red Reese	1974-75	17-8		Jerry Krause

SEAS.	W-L	CONF.	SCORING		COACH	RECORD	
1975-76	21-7		Ron Cox	20.5	Jerry Krause		
1976-77	25-4		Ron Cox	16.7	Jerry Krause		
1977-78	20-8		Paul Hungenberg	20.0	Jerry Krause		
1978-79	10-18		Roger Boesel	13.6	Jerry Krause		
1979-80	18-12		George Abrams	11.8	Jerry Krause		
1980-81	18-9		George Abrams	13.9	Jerry Krause		
1981-82	19-8		Don Garves	14.1	Jerry Krause		
1982-83	17-11		Matt Piper	13.8	Joe Folda		
1983-84	4-22		Tony Chrisman	17.7	Jerry Krause		
1984-85	12-15		Tony Chrisman	14.7	Jerry Krause	259-193	.573
1985-86	20-8		Roosevelt Brown	16.3	Joe Folda		
1986-87	5-23		Dexter Griffen	13.0	Joe Folda	42-42	.500
1987-88	6-21	2-14	Kevin Sattler	15.0	Bob Hofman		
1988-89	8-22	5-11	David Peed	20.9	Bob Hofman		
1989-90	18-11	11-5	David Peed	17.2	Bob Hofman	32-54	.372
1990-91	11-16	5-11	Brian Sullivan	16.1	John Wade		
1991-92	6-21	3-13	Miguel Johnson	12.7	John Wade		
1992-93	6-20	3-11	Brad Sebree	14.0	John Wade		
1993-94	5-21 ⊘	0-14	Brad Sebree	16.2	John Wade		
1994-95	6-20	2-12	Melvin Lewis	11.9	John Wade	34-98	.258
1995-96	3-23	0-14	D'mitri Rideout	11.4	Steve Aggers		
1996-97	7-19	3-13	Travis King	12.4	Steve Aggers		
1997-98	16-11	10-6	Karim Scott	17.4	Steve Aggers		
1998-99	10-17	7-9	Shannon Taylor	16.8	Steve Aggers		
1999-2000	15-12	12-4	Ryan Hansen	12.3	Steve Aggers	51-82	.383
2000-01	17-11	11-5	Aaron Olson	13.8	Ray Giacoletti		
2001-02	17-13	10-4	Chris Hester	13.5	Ray Giacoletti		
2002-03	18-13	9-5 ■	Chris Hester	14.0	Ray Giacoletti		
2003-04	17-13	11-3 ●	Alvin Snow	14.7	Ray Giacoletti	69-50	.580
2004-05	8-20	5-9	Marc Axton	16.2	Mike Burns		
2005-06	15-15	9-5	Rodney Stuckey	24.2	Mike Burns		
2006-07	15-14	8-8	Rodney Stuckey	24.6	Mike Burns	38-49	.437
2007-08	11-19	6-10	Kellen Williams	13.5	Kirk Earlywine		
2008-09	12-18	6-10	Benny Valentine	15.1	Kirk Earlywine	23-37	.383

⊘ Records don't reflect games forfeited or vacated. For adjusted records, see p. 521.
● NCAA Tournament appearance ■ NIT appearance

PROFILE

Eastern Washington University, Cheney, WA
Founded: 1882
Enrollment: 10,809 (9,897 undergraduate)
Colors: Red and white
Nickname: Eagles
Current arena: Reese Court, opened in 1975 (6,000)
Previous: The Fieldhouse, 1949-75 (5,000)
First game: 1903
All-time record: 1,271-1,071 (.543)
Total weeks in AP Top 20/25: 0

Current conference: Big Sky (1987-)
Conference titles:
Big Sky: 2 (2000 [tie], '04)
Conference tournament titles:
Big Sky: 1 (2004)
NCAA Tournament appearances: 1
NIT appearances: 1

FIRST-ROUND PRO PICKS

2007 **Rodney Stuckey,** Detroit (15)

TOP 5

G **Irv Leifer** (1941-43, '45-47)
G **Alvin Snow** (2000-04)
G **Rodney Stuckey** (2005-07)
F **Dick Eicher** (1947-51)
F/C **Ron Cox** (1973-77)

RECORDS

	GAME		SEASON		CAREER	
POINTS	45	Rodney Stuckey, vs. Northern Arizona (Jan. 5, 2006)	726	Rodney Stuckey (2005-06)	1,741	Ron Cox (1973-77)
POINTS PER GAME			24.6	Rodney Stuckey (2006-07)	24.4	Rodney Stuckey (2005-07)
REBOUNDS	28	Dave Hayden, vs. Oregon Tech (Jan. 15, 1972)	436	Dick Eicher (1950-51)	1,273	Ron Cox (1973-77)
ASSISTS	18	Ronn McMahon, vs. UC Irvine (Dec. 13, 1989)	292	Ed Waters (1975-76)	763	Ed Waters (1973-77)

ESPN 284 SAGARIN

ELON

Few teams can match the cast of characters that have coached the Phoenix—including D.C. "Peahead" Walker, who in the 1930s doubled and tripled as the school's football and baseball coach; his successor, Horace "Horse" Hendrickson, the onetime Duke football star; and Ernie Nestor, who led the school to its first winning D1 season in 2005-06. And we haven't mentioned the best and most interesting Elon coach of them all.

BEST TEAM: 1996-97 Other Elon teams have had better records, but this squad peaked when it mattered most. Behind marksman Chris Kiger and free throw machine Chris King, the Phoenix pulled off three consecutive upsets to win the South Atlantic Conference tourney and advance to the D2 tournament.

BEST PLAYER: F JESSE BRANSON (1961-65) With a dead-on jump hook that he could shoot with either hand, this two-time NAIA All-America broke nearly every Elon scoring record.

BEST COACH: BILL MILLER (1959-79) A shrinking violet, he was not. But Miller's teams usually responded to his sideline intensity, as evidenced by their conference championships in 1971 and '74 and league tournament titles in 1965, '71 and '72. He remains the school's all-time winningest coach.

GAME FOR THE AGES: It should have been a mauling. Entering their Dec. 30, 2005, matchup against Clemson, the Phoenix were 2–9, with both wins coming over non-D1 opponents, while the Tigers were 11–1. Did we mention that Clemson was at home? But thanks to some hot three-point shooting (7-for-14), Elon pulled off its first win over an ACC team, 74-69.

FIERCEST RIVAL: Over the past two decades, Elon has played in three different levels (NAIA, D2, D1) and in four different conferences (Carolinas, South Atlantic, Big South, Southern). Amazingly, High Point has shadowed them nearly every step of the way, routinely drawing a raucous house whenever they make the 25-minute trek east to Alumni Gym. The Panthers lead the series, 89–83.

SEASON REVIEW

SEAS.	W-L	CONF.	COACH	SEAS.	W-L	CONF.	COACH
1907-46	*352-279*	*95-21 from 1937-38 to 1941-42*		**1959-60**	9-17		Bill Miller
1946-47	16-10		L.J. "Hap" Perry	**1960-61**	17-13		Bill Miller
1947-48	10-12		Garland Causey	**1961-62**	19-11		Bill Miller
1948-49	7-22		Harold Pope	**1962-63**	17-9		Bill Miller
1949-50	11-18		G. L. "Doc" Mathis	**1963-64**	21-7		Bill Miller
1950-51	12-11		G. L. "Doc" Mathis	**1964-65**	17-12		Bill Miller
1951-52	25-11		G. L. "Doc" Mathis	**1965-66**	13-11		Bill Miller
1952-53	25-11		G. L. "Doc" Mathis	**1966-67**	12-15		Bill Miller
1953-54	11-13		G. L. "Doc" Mathis	**1967-68**	13-15		Bill Miller
1954-55	17-11		G. L. "Doc" Mathis	**1968-69**	23-8		Bill Miller
1955-56	25-7		G. L. "Doc" Mathis	**1969-70**	22-8		Bill Miller
1956-57	21-6		G. L. "Doc" Mathis	**1970-71**	21-8		Bill Miller
1957-58	5-16		G. L. "Doc" Mathis	**1971-72**	21-8		Bill Miller
1958-59	7-16		G. L. "Doc" Mathis	**1972-73**	21-9		Bill Miller

SEAS.	W-L	CONF.	SCORING		COACH	RECORD
1973-74	23-7				Bill Miller	
1974-75	13-14				Bill Miller	
1975-76	13-11				Bill Miller	
1976-77	10-14				Bill Miller	
1977-78	15-11				Bill Miller	
1978-79	11-17				Bill Miller	331-225 .595
1979-80	15-13				William Morningstar	
1980-81	14-16				William Morningstar	
1981-82	7-21				William Morningstar	
1982-83	12-17				William Morningstar	
1983-84	17-11				William Morningstar	
1984-85	18-11				William Morningstar	
1985-86	16-14				William Morningstar	99-103 .490
1986-87	20-11				Robert Burton	
1987-88	20-10				Robert Burton	
1988-89	11-19				Robert Burton	
1989-90	19-10				Robert Burton	
1990-91	16-10				Robert Burton	
1991-92	17-11				Robert Burton	
1992-93	13-13				Robert Burton	116-84 .580
1993-94	5-21				Mark Simons	
1994-95	3-24				Mark Simons	
1995-96	14-14				Mark Simons	
1996-97	16-14				Mark Simons	
1997-98	13-14		Chris Kiger	18.5	Mark Simons	
1998-99	11-16		Brendon Rowell	14.7	Mark Simons	
1999-2000	13-15	7-7	Andrew Toole	14.6	Mark Simons	
2000-01	9-20	4-10	Brendon Rowell	18.8	Mark Simons	
2001-02	13-16	7-7	Brendon Rowell	13.9	Mark Simons	
2002-03	12-15	8-6	Scottie Rice	11.8	Mark Simons	109-169 .392
2003-04	12-18	7-9	Jackson Atoyebi	16.1	Ernie Nestor	
2004-05	8-23	5-11	Jackson Atoyebi	14.0	Ernie Nestor	
2005-06	15-14	10-4	Chris Chalko	12.6	Ernie Nestor	
2006-07	7-23	5-13	LeVonn Jordan	14.5	Ernie Nestor	
2007-08	14-19	9-11	Brett James	12.4	Ernie Nestor	
2008-09	11-20	7-13	Ola Atoyebi	13.9	Ernie Nestor	67-117 .364

PROFILE

Elon University, Elon, NC
Founded: 1889
Enrollment: 5,628 (4,992 undergraduate)
Colors: Maroon and gold
Nickname: Phoenix
Current arena: Alumni Gym, opened in 1940 (1,558)
Previous: West Building, prior to 1940 (N/A)
First game: 1907
All-time record: 1,266-1,141 (.526)
Total weeks in AP Top 20/25: 0

Current conference: Southern (2003-)
Conference titles:
Southern: 1 (2006 [tie])
Conference tournament titles: 0
NCAA Tournament appearances: 0
NIT appearances: 0

TOP 5

G **Lee Allison** (1977-81)
G **Dee Atkinson** (1952-54, '55-57)
F **Jesse Branson** (1961-65)
F **Tommy Cole** (1968-72)
C **Henry Goedeck** (1965-69)

RECORDS

RECORDS	GAME		SEASON		CAREER	
POINTS	44	Jesse Branson, vs. Wofford (Jan. 7, 1964)	780	Jesse Branson (1964-65)	2,241	Jesse Branson (1961-65)
POINTS PER GAME			26.9	Jesse Branson (1964-65)	20.0	Jesse Branson (1961-65)
REBOUNDS	27	Charlie Williamson vs. Atlantic Christian (1977); Larry Trautwein vs. North Carolina A&T (1971); Jesse Branson vs. Loyola (Md.) (Dec. 29, 1964)	550	Ed Juratic (1964-65)	1,969	Jesse Branson (1961-65)
ASSISTS		N/A	220	Duke Madsen (1975-76)	705	Tommy Cole (1968-72)

ESPN 106 SAGARIN

EVANSVILLE

Sadly, Evansville's first D1 season will always be remembered for the Dec. 13, 1977, plane crash that took the lives of the entire team, along with coach Bobby Watson. But that dark chapter is just a small part of the Purple Aces story. One of the best all-time small college programs, the Aces rebounded after the tragedy to carve out a winning niche in the Missouri Valley Conference.

BEST TEAM: 1964-65 The College Division power had 21 double-digit victories, averaged 95 points per game and defended its 1964 national title with an 85-82 overtime title win over Southern Illinois. But the undefeated Aces didn't just beat up on College Division foes. All-America swingman Jerry Sloan (the future NBA star and coach) and all-time leading scorer Larry Humes also led them to victories over Notre Dame, Iowa and LSU.

BEST PLAYER: G/F JERRY SLOAN (1962-65) It's easy to single out Sloan for his eye-popping stats (he's the only Purple Ace with more than 1,300 points and 1,000 rebounds), awards (a three-time first-team Little All-America) and accomplishments (two College Division championships). But there's no obvious measure for what was his best attribute: ferocious defense, his ticket to an 11-year NBA career as a player and 24 more as a coach.

BEST COACH: ARAD MCCUTCHAN (1946-77) He won five national titles, was a 12-time conference coach of the year, was the first College Division coach inducted into the Basketball Hall of Fame and was one of two coaches (along with Winston-Salem State's Clarence "Big House" Gaines) chosen for the Division II 50th Anniversary All-Elite Eight team in 2006. Any questions?

GAME FOR THE AGES: Three times during the 1964-65 season, Sloan and Evansville took on guard Walt Frazier and Southern Illinois. The Aces won the first two matchups by one point each. Then, when it counted the most, Sloan once again got the best of his future NBA rival by helping his team outlast the Salukis in overtime in a College Division title-game thriller, 85-82.

HEARTBREAKER: Evansville beat Drexel and Iona to reach the 1996 Preseason NIT semifinals at Madison Square Garden against in-state rival and national power Indiana. The Aces led 73-72 and were looking good for their first win ever against the Hoosiers when IU's Andrae Patterson hit a turnaround 15-footer with :01 left.

FIERCEST RIVAL: It's a short trip on Highway 41 to Indiana State, a route Evansville has taken nearly every year since 1920. Although the Sycamores barely lead the series, 75–74, each team has dominated in stretches, with the Aces going 18–3 from 1986 to '99 and the Sycamores going 13–3 from 1974 to '86. MVC foes since 1994, they've met only once in the playoffs (UE's 63-59, first-round win in 2004).

FANFARE AND HOOPLA: Because of strong fan support in Evansville, the University's 11,600-seat Roberts Stadium—the Purple Aces' home arena since 1956—hosted 21 straight NCAA College Division/D2 finals from 1957 to '77.

> ***There's no measure for what was Jerry Sloan's best attribute: ferocious defense.***

FAN FAVORITE: F MARTY SIMMONS (1986-88) Simmons transferred to Evansville from Indiana, averaged 22.4 and 25.9 ppg in his two seasons there, and helped spark a turnaround—an 8–19 team in 1985-86 went 37–20 over the next two seasons for coach Jim Crews. Simmons returned to Evansville in 2007 to coach the Aces.

CONSENSUS ALL-AMERICAS

1959	**Hugh Ahlering** (Little A-A), G
1960	**Ed Smallwood** (Little A-A), F
1965	**Jerry Sloan** (Little A-A), G/F
1965, '66	**Larry Humes** (Little A-A), F

FIRST-ROUND PRO PICKS

1965	**Jerry Sloan**, Baltimore (6)

PROFILE

University of Evansville, Evansville, IN
Founded: 1854 as Moores Hill Male and Female Collegiate Institute
Enrollment: 2,647 (2,434 undergraduate)
Colors: Purple and white
Nickname: Purple Aces
Current arena: Arad A. McCutchan Court at Roberts Stadium, opened in 1956 (11,600)
Previous: Evansville National Guard Armory, 1939-56 (N/A); Agoga Tabernacle, 1922-39 (N/A)
First game: Feb. 21, 1920

All-time record: 1,221-935 (.566)
Total weeks in AP Top 20/25 poll: 0
Current conference: Missouri Valley (1994-)
Conference titles:
Midwestern City: 1 (1982)
Midwestern Collegiate: 4 (1987 [tie], '89, '92, '93 [tie])
MVC: 1 (1999)
Conference tournament titles:
Midwestern City: 1 (1982)
Midwestern Collegiate: 2 (1992, '93)
NCAA Tournament appearances: 5
NIT appearances: 2

TOP 5

G	**Don Buse** (1969-72)
G	**Marcus Wilson** (1995-99)
G/F	**Jerry Sloan** (1962-65)
F	**Larry Humes** (1963-66)
F	**Ed Smallwood** (1957-60)

RECORDS	GAME		SEASON		CAREER	
POINTS	65	Scott Haffner, vs. Dayton (Feb. 18, 1989)	941	Larry Humes (1964-65)	2,236	Larry Humes (1963-66)
POINTS PER GAME			32.5	Larry Humes (1964-65)	26.4	Larry Humes (1963-66)
REBOUNDS	31	Dale Wise, vs. Ball State (Jan. 30, 1960); vs. Kentucky Wesleyan (Jan. 13, 1960); Jim Smallins, vs. Kentucky Wesleyan (Feb. 27, 1957)	496	Dale Wise (1959-60)	1,197	Dale Wise (1958-61)
ASSISTS	15	Jeremy Stanton, vs. Illinois State (March 3, 2001); Tyrone Scott, vs. Oklahoma City (Jan. 7, 1984)	211	Reed Crafton (1988-89)	601	Jeremy Stanton (1997-2001)

SEASON REVIEW

SEASON	W-L	CONF.	SCORING	COACH	RECORD	
1919-20	1-3			G.B. Schnurr	1-3	.250
1920-21	2-8			Clem McGinness	2-8	.200
1921-22	2-9			Harlan Miller	2-9	.182
1922-23	2-8			Charles Holton	2-8	.200
1923-24	5-9			John Harmon		
1924-25	11-2			John Harmon		
1925-26	8-3			John Harmon		
1926-27	16-4			John Harmon		
1927-28	14-3			John Harmon		
1928-29	2-14			John Harmon		
1929-30	3-15			John Harmon	59-50	.541
1930-31	4-10			Bill Slyker		
1931-32	8-7			Bill Slyker		
1932-33	11-6			Bill Slyker		
1933-34	15-4			Bill Slyker		
1934-35	11-7			Bill Slyker		
1935-36	11-8			Bill Slyker		
1936-37	2-9			Bill Slyker		

SEAS.	W-L	CONF.	POSTSEASON	SCORING		REBOUNDS		ASSISTS		COACH	RECORD	
1937-38	4-13									Bill Slyker		
1938-39	8-8									Bill Slyker		
1939-40	10-7									Bill Slyker		
1940-41	13-4									Bill Slyker		
1941-42	13-6			Gus Doerner	24.4					Bill Slyker		
1942-43	13-7									Bill Slyker	123-96	.562
1943-44	3-7									Emerson Henke		
1944-45	10-7									Emerson Henke		
1945-46	16-8									Emerson Henke	29-22	.569
1946-47	7-15									Arad McCutchan		
1947-48	8-18									Arad McCutchan		
1948-49	14-11	4-5								Arad McCutchan		
1949-50	14-14	2-7								Arad McCutchan		
1950-51	23-7	5-4								Arad McCutchan		
1951-52	7-20	2-10								Arad McCutchan		
1952-53	10-15									Arad McCutchan		
1953-54	12-12									Arad McCutchan		
1954-55	20-6									Arad McCutchan		
1955-56	16-7									Arad McCutchan		
1956-57	18-8			John Harrawood	23.0					Arad McCutchan		
1957-58	23-4			Ed Smallwood	23.5	Ed Smallwood	12.8			Arad McCutchan		
1958-59	21-6		COLLEGE DIV. CHAMPION			Dale Wise	11.7			Arad McCutchan		
1959-60	25-4		COLLEGE DIV. CHAMPION	Ed Smallwood	26.1	Dale Wise	17.1			Arad McCutchan		
1960-61	11-16					Dale Wise	14.7			Arad McCutchan		
1961-62	14-11					Marty Herthel	12.6			Arad McCutchan		
1962-63	21-6									Arad McCutchan		
1963-64	26-3		COLLEGE DIV. CHAMPION			Jerry Sloan	11.2			Arad McCutchan		
1964-65	29-0		COLLEGE DIV. CHAMPION	Larry Humes	32.5	Jerry Sloan	14.6			Arad McCutchan		
1965-66	18-9			Larry Humes	31.0					Arad McCutchan		
1966-67	8-17									Arad McCutchan		
1967-68	20-8									Arad McCutchan		
1968-69	12-14									Arad McCutchan		
1969-70	12-14									Arad McCutchan		
1970-71	22-8		COLLEGE DIV. CHAMPION							Arad McCutchan		
1971-72	22-6									Arad McCutchan		
1972-73	14-12									Arad McCutchan		
1973-74	19-9									Arad McCutchan		
1974-75	13-13									Arad McCutchan		
1975-76	20-9									Arad McCutchan		
1976-77	15-12									Arad McCutchan	514-314	.622
1977-78	1-3									Bobby Watson	1-3	.250
1978-79	13-16									Dick Walters		
1979-80	18-10	1-4								Dick Walters		
1980-81	19-9	6-5								Dick Walters		
1981-82	23-6	10-2	NCAA FIRST ROUND							Dick Walters		
1982-83	13-16	6-8								Dick Walters		
1983-84	15-14	7-7								Dick Walters		
1984-85	13-16	4-10								Dick Walters	114-87	.567
1985-86	8-19	3-9								Jim Crews		
1986-87	16-12	8-4		Marty Simmons	22.4	Marty Simmons	7.0			Jim Crews		
1987-88	21-8	6-4	NIT SECOND ROUND	Marty Simmons	25.9	Dan Godfread	8.5			Jim Crews		
1988-89	25-6	10-2	NCAA SECOND ROUND	Scott Haffner	24.5	Dan Godfread	8.0			Jim Crews		
1989-90	17-15	8-6		Dan Godfread	19.9	Dan Godfread	8.3			Jim Crews		
1990-91	14-14	7-7		Parrish Casebier	15.0	Parrish Casebier	7.2			Jim Crews		
1991-92	24-6	8-2	NCAA FIRST ROUND	Parrish Casebier	25.4	Parrish Casebier	9.5			Jim Crews		
1992-93	23-7	12-2	NCAA FIRST ROUND	Parrish Casebier	20.1	Sascha Hupman	10.6			Jim Crews		
1993-94	21-11	6-4	NIT FIRST ROUND	Andy Elkins	21.5	Andy Elkins	8.3			Jim Crews		
1994-95	18-9	11-7		Andy Elkins	20.3	Reed Jackson	9.0			Jim Crews		
1995-96	13-14	9-9		Marcus Wilson	13.4	Scott Sparks	4.6			Jim Crews		
1996-97	17-14	11-7		Marcus Wilson	15.7	Chris Hollender	5.7			Jim Crews		
1997-98	15-15	9-9		Marcus Wilson	18.3	Chris Hollender	7.4			Jim Crews		
1998-99	23-10	13-5	NCAA FIRST ROUND	Marcus Wilson	20.7	Craig Snow	5.7	Jeremy Stanton	4.5	Jim Crews		
1999-2000	18-12	9-9		Craig Snow	16.3	Craig Snow	6.0	Jeremy Stanton	5.1	Jim Crews		
2000-01	14-16	9-9		Craig Snow	14.6	Craig Snow	4.6	Jeremy Stanton	7.0	Jim Crews		
2001-02	7-21	4-14		Dan Lytle	11.6	Dan Lytle	4.3	Mark Allaria	5.4	Jim Crews	294-209	.584
2002-03	12-16	8-10		Clint Cuffle	16.5	Ian Hanavan	7.3	Lucious Wagner	3.2	Steve Merfeld		
2003-04	7-22	5-13		Clint Cuffle	13.8	Clint Cuffle	6.2	Lucious Wagner	4.6	Steve Merfeld		
2004-05	11-17	5-13		Lucious Wagner	14.1	Andre Burton	5.4	Lucious Wagner	5.1	Steve Merfeld		
2005-06	10-19	5-13		Matt Webster	14.2	Matt Webster	6.4	Jason Holsinger	4.1	Steve Merfeld		
2006-07	14-17	6-12		Matt Webster	16.9	Bradley Strickland	6.2	Jason Holsinger	5.1	Steve Merfeld	54-91	.372
2007-08	9-21	3-15		Shy Ely	14.4	Nate Garner	5.3	Jason Holsinger	4.6	Marty Simmons		
2008-09	17-14	8-10		Shy Ely	18.9	Nate Garner	6.2	Kaylon Williams	4.9	Marty Simmons	26-35	.426

ESPN
199
SAGARIN

FAIRFIELD

Sixty-one seasons of Fairfield hoops has proven one thing: Don't count out the Stags. They had a memorable upset of No. 14-ranked Holy Cross in 1978 and, of their three NCAA Tournament appearances, two resulted from miraculous MAAC tourney runs, the first in 1987 and the second 10 years later—and that '97 Tourney team led No. 1-seed North Carolina at halftime.

BEST TEAM: 1985-86 The Stags were coming off four straight losing seasons when Villanova assistant Mitch Buonaguro took over the reins. Importing a little Rollie Massimino-style attitude and a whole lot of discipline, the rookie coach transformed Tony George & Co. into school-record winners of 24 games and the MAAC tournament title before losing in the NCAAs to Illinois, 75-51.

BEST PLAYER: G JOE DESANTIS (1975-79) The 6'2" Bronx native combined with center Mark Young for one of the most potent inside-outside combos of the era. DeSantis helped keep the old Alumni Hall bleachers packed, with his scoring and passing theatrics. Joey D averaged 18.4 ppg for his career and is second in Fairfield history with 1,916 points.

BEST COACH: FRED BARAKAT (1970-81) He may have followed a more famous coach (Jim Lynam), but nobody at Fairfield has produced better results: five winning Division I seasons, the Stags' first D1 20-win campaign and three trips to the NIT.

GAME FOR THE AGES: The 1986-87 Stags lost heartbreaker after heartbreaker, and entered the MAAC tourney as the No. 7 seed. After upsetting La Salle and Army to reach the final, they trailed Iona by 18 with 14:25 left. Cue the furious comeback, capped by A.J. Wynder's game-tying buzzer-beater from just inside the three-point line. Then the Stags closed it out, 73-70, to make the NCAA Tournament for the second straight year.

FIERCEST RIVAL: After losing to Loyola (Md.) in the 2008 MAAC tournament, Stags coach Ed Cooley said, "When I see [Loyola] green, I get sick." No wonder: Though the Stags lead the series 32–14, four of Loyola's wins were in the MAAC tourney (1999, 2001, '07, '08).

THE SCHOOLS

SEASON REVIEW

SEAS.	W-L	CONF.	COACH	SEAS.	W-L	CONF.	COACH
1948-49	9-14		Joe Dunn	1959-60	17-9		George Bisacca
1949-50	5-16		Bob Noonan	1960-61	17-7		George Bisacca
1950-51	16-11		Jim Hanrahan	1961-62	20-5		George Bisacca
1951-52	10-9		Jim Hanrahan	1962-63	11-13		George Bisacca
1952-53	9-9		Jim Hanrahan	1963-64	14-11		George Bisacca
1953-54	12-8		Jim Hanrahan	1964-65	14-7		George Bisacca
1954-55	12-8		Jim Hanrahan	1965-66	19-5		George Bisacca
1955-56	6-10		Jim Hanrahan	1966-67	12-9		George Bisacca
1956-57	5-15		Jim Hanrahan	1967-68	16-10		George Bisacca
1957-58	12-9		Jim Hanrahan	1968-69	10-16		Jim Lynam
1958-59	11-11		George Bisacca	1969-70	13-13		Jim Lynam

SEAS.	W-L	CONF.		SCORING		COACH	RECORD	
1970-71	9-15					Fred Barakat		
1971-72	12-13					Fred Barakat		
1972-73	18-9		■			Fred Barakat		
1973-74	17-9		■			Fred Barakat		
1974-75	13-14					Fred Barakat		
1975-76	12-14					Fred Barakat		
1976-77	16-11					Fred Barakat		
1977-78	22-5		■	Joe DeSantis	20.1	Fred Barakat		
1978-79	17-9			Mark Young	20.9	Fred Barakat		
1979-80	11-16					Fred Barakat		
1980-81	13-13					Fred Barakat	160-128	.556
1981-82	11-18	3-7				Terry O'Connor		
1982-83	13-15	2-8				Terry O'Connor		
1983-84	10-18	5-9				Terry O'Connor		
1984-85	11-17	4-10				Terry O'Connor	45-68	.398
1985-86	24-7	13-1	●	Tony George	20.3	Mitch Buonaguro		
1986-87	15-16	5-9	●	Jeff Gromos	20.2	Mitch Buonaguro		
1987-88	8-20	4-10		Tony Bradford	22.7	Mitch Buonaguro		
1988-89	7-21	2-12		Tony Bradford	20.4	Mitch Buonaguro		
1989-90	10-19	6-10				Mitch Buonaguro		
1990-91	8-20	4-12				Mitch Buonaguro	72-103	.411
1991-92	8-20	4-12				Paul Cormier		
1992-93	14-13	7-7				Paul Cormier		
1993-94	8-19	4-10				Paul Cormier		
1994-95	13-15	6-8				Paul Cormier		
1995-96	20-10	10-4	■			Paul Cormier		
1996-97	11-19	2-12	●			Paul Cormier		
1997-98	12-15	7-11				Paul Cormier	86-111	.437
1998-99	12-15	7-11		Darren Phillip	16.7	Tim O'Toole		
1999-2000	14-15	11-7		Darren Phillip	15.9	Tim O'Toole		
2000-01	12-16	8-10		Sam Spann	15.0	Tim O'Toole		
2001-02	12-17	9-9		Ajou Deng	13.7	Tim O'Toole		
2002-03	19-12	13-5	■	Deng Gai	12.8	Tim O'Toole		
2003-04	19-11	12-6		Terrence Todd	14.9	Tim O'Toole		
2004-05	15-15	11-7		Terrence Todd	15.9	Tim O'Toole		
2005-06	9-19	7-11		Terrence Todd	18.8	Tim O'Toole	112-120	.483
2006-07	13-19	10-8		Michael Van Schaick	15.4	Ed Cooley		
2007-08	14-16	11-7		Jonathan Han	11.7	Ed Cooley		
2008-09	17-15	9-9		Jonathan Han	12.5	Ed Cooley	44-50	.468

● NCAA Tournament appearance ■ NIT appearance

PROFILE

Fairfield University, Fairfield, CT
Founded: 1942
Enrollment: 5,128 (4,084 undergraduate)
Colors: Cardinal red
Nickname: Stags
Current arena: The Arena at Harbor Yard, opened in 2001 (9,500)
Previous: Alumni Hall, 1959-2001 (N/A)
First game: December 1, 1948
All-time record: 789-805 (.495)

Total weeks in AP Top 20/25: 0
Current conference: Metro Atlantic Athletic (1981-)
Conference titles:
MAAC: 2 (1986, '96 [tie])
Conference tournament titles:
MAAC: 3 (1986, '87, '97)
NCAA Tournament appearances: 3
NIT appearances: 5

TOP 5

G **Joe DeSantis** (1975-79)
G **Tony George** (1982-86)
F **Deng Gai** (2001-05)
F **Darren Phillip** (1996-2000)
C **Mark Young** (1975-79)

RECORDS

RECORDS	GAME		SEASON		CAREER	
POINTS	41	George Groom, vs. Assumption (March 6, 1972)	630	Tony George (1985-86)	2,006	Tony George (1982-86)
POINTS PER GAME			22.7	Tony Bradford (1987-88)	19.8	George Groom (1970-73)
REBOUNDS	28	Art Crawford, vs. American International (Feb. 6, 1960)	405	Darren Phillip (1999-2000)	1,080	Drew Henderson (1989-93)
ASSISTS	23	John Ryan, vs. William and Mary (Dec. 22, 1973)	301	John Ryan (1973-74)	675	John Ryan (1971-74)

ESPN 242 SAGARIN

FAIRLEIGH DICKINSON

Four NCAA Tournament bids, zero wins. It doesn't sound much like a proud hoops history. But in fact, Fairleigh Dickinson has played the role of feisty underdog to near-perfection, losing to No. 1-seed Michigan by four in 1985, to No. 1-seed Purdue by 15 in '88, to No. 2-seed UConn by eight in '98 and to No. 1-seed Illinois by 12 in 2005.

BEST TEAM: 1951-52 Just two years after launching the FDU basketball program, coach Dick Holub took his team all the way to the NAIA national tournament, where it lost to 1950 champs Indiana State, 79-72. Leading up to the tournament, the Knights won 18 straight behind sure shot John Scholl.

BEST PLAYER: G Elijah Allen (1993-98) As great as his career was, the 6'1" point guard will forever be defined by one game. In the first round of the 1998 Tourney, against UConn, Allen was the best player on the floor—by a mile. In the eight-point loss, he scored 43 points and grabbed eight rebounds.

BEST COACH: Tom Green (1983-2009) When Green first took the FDU job, his son Brad was only a year old. Twenty-two years later, Brad was a grad student playing for his dad's fourth Tourney team. It's a testament to the coach's ability to win with many different styles.

GAME FOR THE AGES: Before the 1985 Tournament, broadcaster Dick Vitale said the Knights would be blown out by the top-seeded Wolverines in the first round. But despite having four starters foul out, FDU took Michigan to the limit before finally being undone by two late Roy Tarpley free throws. Take that, Dickie V.

FIERCEST RIVAL: How intense is the Garden State Rivalry Series between FDU and Monmouth, which dates back to 1972? On Jan. 17, 1998, the night Dave Calloway was making his coaching debut for the Hawks, Knights star Rahshon Turner got into a scrap with a Monmouth player, casting a pall over FDU's 85-57 win. Shortly afterward, Turner wrote an apology note to Calloway. Hey, who said rivalries can't be tempered by a little class? The Knights lead overall, 36-27.

SEASON REVIEW

SEAS.	W-L	CONF.	COACH	SEAS.	W-L	CONF.	COACH
1949-50	10-7		Dick Holub	1961-62	12-11		Dick Holub
1950-51	16-6		Dick Holub	1962-63	16-12		Dick Holub
1951-52	22-4		Dick Holub	1963-64	12-10		Dick Holub
1952-53	20-1		Dick Holub	1964-65	9-15		Dick Holub
1953-54	17-3		Dick Holub	1965-66	15-10	5-4	Dick Holub
1954-55	10-14		Dick Holub	1966-67	4-19	0-9	Jack Devine
1955-56	9-15		Dick Holub	1967-68	10-12	4-4	Jack Devine
1956-57	12-12		Dick Holub	1968-69	9-13	2-6	Jack Devine
1957-58	9-15		Dick Holub	1969-70	13-10		Al LoBalbo
1958-59	17-11		Dick Holub	1970-71	16-7		Al LoBalbo
1959-60	14-11		Dick Holub	1971-72	15-9		Al LoBalbo
1960-61	13-10		Dick Holub	1972-73	13-13		Al LoBalbo

SEAS.	W-L	CONF.		SCORING		COACH	RECORD	
1973-74	11-14			Glenn Bolduc	13.9	Al LoBalbo		
1974-75	11-13			Rich Conrad	19.2	Al LoBalbo		
1975-76	9-13			Steve Solop	10.9	Al LoBalbo		
1976-77	13-13					Al LoBalbo		
1977-78	6-18					Al LoBalbo		
1978-79	8-18			Dan McLaughlin	19.4	Al LoBalbo		
1979-80	13-14					Al LoBalbo	128-142	.474
1980-81	12-14			Ken Webb	20.9	Don Feeley		
1981-82	16-11	12-3		Marcus Gaither	20.4	Don Feeley		
1982-83	17-12	9-5		Marcus Gaither	22.9	Don Feeley	45-37	.549
1983-84	17-12	10-6		Marcus Gaither	14.9	Tom Green		
1984-85	21-10	10-4	●	Larry Hampton	14.9	Tom Green		
1985-86	22-8	13-3		Damari Riddick	13.9	Tom Green		
1986-87	19-10	11-5		Damari Riddick	17.7	Tom Green		
1987-88	23-7	13-3	●	Damari Riddick	17.2	Tom Green		
1988-89	17-12	11-5		Desi Wilson	17.9	Tom Green		
1989-90	16-13	8-8		Desi Wilson	22.3	Tom Green		
1990-91	22-9	13-3	■	Desi Wilson	23.8	Tom Green		
1991-92	14-14	11-5		Wendell Brereton	15.5	Tom Green		
1992-93	11-17	8-10		Antwan Dasher	15.0	Tom Green		
1993-94	14-13	10-8		Antwan Dasher	16.9	Tom Green		
1994-95	16-12	11-7		Antwan Dasher	17.6	Tom Green		
1995-96	7-20	6-12		Rahshon Turner	14.4	Tom Green		
1996-97	18-10	13-5		Rahshon Turner	15.5	Tom Green		
1997-98	23-7	13-3	●	R. Turner, Elijah Allen	17.8	Tom Green		
1998-99	12-16	9-11		Daryl Todd	10.8	Tom Green		
1999-2000	17-11	13-5		Chris Ekwe	13.6	Tom Green		
2000-01	13-15	10-10		Chris Ekwe	15.7	Tom Green		
2001-02	4-25	4-16		Matt Hammond	14.1	Tom Green		
2002-03	15-14	9-9		Lionel Bomayako	12.4	Tom Green		
2003-04	17-12	11-7		Gordon Klaiber	16.5	Tom Green		
2004-05	20-13	13-5	●	Gordon Klaiber	16.0	Tom Green		
2005-06	20-12	14-4	■	Chad Timberlake	15.2	Tom Green		
2006-07	14-16	9-9		Andre Harris	18.8	Tom Green		
2007-08	8-20	4-14		Manny Ubilla	20.8	Tom Green		
2008-09	7-23	6-12		Sean Baptiste	16.3	Tom Green	407-351	.537

● NCAA Tournament appearance ■ NIT appearance

PROFILE

Fairleigh Dickinson University, Teaneck, NJ
Founded: 1942
Enrollment: 12,112 (8,585 undergraduate)
Colors: Burgundy and blue
Nickname: Knights
Current arena: Stratis Arena at the George & Phyllis Rothman Center, opened in 1987 (5,000)
First game: Dec. 5, 1949
All-time record: 836-741 (.530)
Total weeks in AP Top 20/25: 0

Current conference: Northeast (1979-)
Conference titles:
Eastern Collegiate Athletic Metro: 3 (1982 [tie], '86, '88 [tie])
Northeast: 2 (1991 [tie], 2006)
Conference tournament titles:
Eastern Collegiate Athletic Metro: 2 (1985, '88)
Northeast: 2 (1998, 2005)
NCAA Tournament appearances: 4
NIT appearances: 2

TOP 5

G **Elijah Allen** (1993-98)
G **Marcus Gaither** (1980-84)
F **Desi Wilson** (1988-91)
F/C **Reggie Foster** (1965-68)
C **Greg Foster** (1980-84)

RECORDS

RECORDS	GAME		SEASON		CAREER	
POINTS	48	Tom Fox, vs. Upsala (March 1, 1962)	738	Desi Wilson (1990-91)	1,902	Desi Wilson (1988-91)
POINTS PER GAME			23.8	Desi Wilson (1990-91)	21.4	Desi Wilson (1988-91)
REBOUNDS	20	Rahshon Turner, vs. Monmouth (Feb. 19, 1998)	359	Reggie Foster (1966-67)	1,194	Greg Foster (1980-84)
ASSISTS	10	Cameron Tyler, vs. Sacred Heart (Jan. 30, 2007); Tamien Trent, vs. St. Francis (N.Y.), (Feb. 21, 2005); vs. Long Island (Jan. 31, 2005); Marcus Whitaker, vs. Wagner (March. 6, 2004)	223	Mel Hawkins (1990-91)	508	Mel Hawkins (1987-91)

ESPN 64 SAGARIN

FLORIDA

For a school that first got a taste of March Madness only in 1987, Florida certainly has made a big impact in a relatively short time. Long a football power, in 2006 and '07 the Gators became only the seventh school to win consecutive NCAA Tournaments.

BEST TEAM: 2006-07 Since UCLA won seven straight national titles (1967-73), only Duke had won back-to-back crowns (1991-92) until Billy Donovan's Gators did it in 2006 and '07. Florida (35–5) started and finished its season ranked No. 1 in the nation and also took home its third straight SEC tournament title. Led by Joakim Noah, Corey Brewer, Al Horford, Taurean Green and Lee Humphrey, the Gators rolled through the NCAA Tournament, winning each of their six games by seven or more points.

BEST PLAYER: G Ronnie Williams (1980-84) Florida's all-time leading scorer with 2,090 points, Williams is the only player in Gators history to lead the team in scoring four straight seasons. While only one of those teams finished above .500, Williams managed to reach the 1,000-point mark faster than any other Gator. He also holds the school record for free throws made (546) and attempted (785).

BEST COACH: Billy Donovan (1996-) A protégé of Rick Pitino, first as a tough Providence point guard and then as a young assistant at Kentucky, Donovan is the all-time winningest coach in Florida history (310–126). He has led the Gators to 22 NCAA Tournament wins—more than triple their total before his arrival—and three Final Fours, including two national championships, as well as three SEC tournament titles.

GAME FOR THE AGES: With their suffocating defense, the SEC-champion Gators made a convincing run through the 2006 NCAA Tournament, winning their six games by an average of 16 points, and snagged the school's first national championship, 73-57, over UCLA on April 3. Joakim Noah earned Final Four Most Outstanding Player honors after finishing with 16 points, nine rebounds and an NCAA title-game record six blocked shots. Donovan's squad won its first 17 games of the season and its last 11 to finish with a then-school-record 33 wins against six losses, proving it was, indeed, Great … to … be … a … Florida Gator.

Billy Donovan has led the Gators to 22 NCAA Tournament wins—more than triple their total before his arrival.

HEARTBREAKER: Florida was pushing on the door to greatness by 2002, when it entered the NCAA Tournament as a No. 5 seed, facing No. 12-seed Creighton. The Gators were about to chomp down an 82-80 double OT win when the Bluejays' Terrell Taylor launched a three with 0.2 seconds left that swished and badly upset the Gators' hoped-for meal.

FIERCEST RIVAL: Florida has been playing SEC archrival Kentucky since 1927 and it's no surprise that the NCAA's all-time winningest team has skinned the Gators by nearly a 3-to-1 margin (86–32). However, in recent seasons Florida has begun to bite back much more often, winning eight out of nine from 2004-05 through 2008-09.

FANFARE AND HOOPLA: A rowdy, raucous atmosphere awaits teams visiting the Stephen C. O'Connell Center, also known as the O'Dome. The Gators have won 13 or more home games in 10 of the last 11 seasons, including all 18 in 2006-07.

FAN FAVORITE: C Dwayne Schintzius (1986-90) A highly spirited 1989 All-America honorable mention, Schintzius—famed for his memorable mullet—is the only player in SEC history to score more than 1,000 points, grab 800 rebounds and amass 250 assists and 250 blocks.

FIRST-ROUND PRO PICKS

1969	**Neal Walk,** Phoenix (2)
1990	**Dwayne Schintzius,** San Antonio (24)
1998	**Jason Williams,** Sacramento (7)
2000	**Mike Miller,** Orlando (5)
2000	**Donnell Harvey,** New York (22)
2005	**David Lee,** New York (30)
2007	**Al Horford,** Atlanta (3)
2007	**Corey Brewer,** Minnesota (7)
2007	**Joakim Noah,** Chicago (9)
2008	**Marreese Speights,** Philadelphia (16)

PROFILE

University of Florida, Gainesville, FL
Founded: 1853
Enrollment: 51,520 (36,163 undergraduate)
Colors: Orange and blue
Nickname: Gators
Current arena: O'Connell Center, opened in 1980 (12,000)
Previous: Florida Gym, 1950-80 (7,000); The New Gym, 1928-49 (N/A); The Gym, 1920-27 (N/A)
First game: Dec. 15, 1915
All-time record: 1,192-1,002 (.543)
Total weeks in AP Top 20/25: 185

Current conference: Southeastern (1932-)
Conference titles:
SEC: 4 (1989, 2000 [tie], '01 [tie], '07)
Conference tournament titles:
SEC: 3 (2005, '06, '07)
NCAA Tournaments: 14 (2 appearances vacated)
Sweet 16s (since 1975): 6
Final Fours: 4
Titles: 2 (2006, '07)
NIT appearances: 9
Semifinals: 3

TOP 5

G	**Andrew Moten** (1983-87)
G	**Ronnie Williams** (1980-84)
F	**Udonis Haslem** (1998-2002)
F	**Al Horford** (2004-07)
C	**Neal Walk** (1966-69)

RECORDS	GAME		SEASON		CAREER	
POINTS	54	Tony Miller, vs. Chicago State (Feb. 29, 1972)	676	Andy Owens (1969-70)	2,090	Ronnie Williams (1980-84)
POINTS PER GAME			27.0	Andy Owens (1969-70)	20.8	Neal Walk (1966-69)
REBOUNDS	31	Neal Walk, vs. Alabama (Jan. 27, 1968); Jim Zinn, vs. Mississippi (Feb. 18, 1957)	494	Neal Walk (1967-68)	1,181	Neal Walk (1966-69)
ASSISTS	17	Jason Williams, vs. Duquesne (Dec. 3, 1997)	231	Nick Calathes (2008-09)	503	Ronnie Montgomery (1984-88)

SEASON REVIEW

SEASON	W-L	CONF.	SCORING	COACH	RECORD	SEASON	W-L	CONF.	SCORING	COACH	RECORD
1915-16	5-1			C.J. McCoy	5-1 .833	1926-27	6-20	1-8		Brady Cowell	
1916-17	no team					1927-28	5-16	2-10		Brady Cowell	
1917-18	no team					1928-29	7-13	4-11		Brady Cowell	
1918-19	no team					1929-30	10-4	2-3		Brady Cowell	
1919-20	2-5			no coach		1930-31	10-9	5-7		Brady Cowell	
1920-21	5-6			W.G.Klein		1931-32	8-12	4-10		Brady Cowell	
1921-22	5-5			W.G.Klein	10-11 .476	1932-33	9-5	4-4		Brady Cowell	62-86 .419
1922-23	2-5	0-3		C.Y. Byrd	2-5 .286	1933-34	11-7	4-2		Ben Clemmons	
1923-24	5-10	0-2		J.L. White		1934-35	8-7	4-3		Ben Clemmons	
1924-25	2-7	0-0		J.L. White	7-17 .292	1935-36	4-11	2-8		Ben Clemmons	23-25 .479
1925-26	7-7	0-3		Brady Cowell		1936-37	5-13	1-9		Josh Cody	5-13 .278

SEAS.	W-L	CONF.	POSTSEASON	SCORING		REBOUNDS		ASSISTS		COACH	RECORD	
1937-38	11-9	3-7								Sam McAllister		
1938-39	9-6	5-4								Sam McAllister		
1939-40	13-9	5-4								Sam McAllister		
1940-41	15-3	6-2								Sam McAllister		
1941-42	8-9	3-8								Sam McAllister		
1942-43	8-7	0-6								Spurgeon Cherry		
1943-44	no team											
1944-45	7-12	4-2								Spurgeon Cherry		
1945-46	7-14	2-6								Spurgeon Cherry	22-33	.400
1946-47	17-9	4-4								Sam McAllister		
1947-48	15-10	5-7		Hans Tanzler	13.2					Sam McAllister		
1948-49	11-15	4-8		Harry Hamilton	12.6					Sam McAllister		
1949-50	9-14	4-10		Julian Miller	14.4					Sam McAllister		
1950-51	11-12	6-8		Harry Hamilton	16.6					Sam McAllister	119-96	.553
1951-52	15-9	7-7		Rick Casares	14.9					John Mauer		
1952-53	13-6	8-5		Rick Casares	15.5					John Mauer		
1953-54	7-15	3-11		Bob Emrick	16.4					John Mauer		
1954-55	12-10	5-9		Bob Emrick	17.8					John Mauer		
1955-56	11-12	4-10		Bob Emrick	17.8					John Mauer		
1956-57	14-10	6-8		Joe Hobbs	18.8					John Mauer		
1957-58	12-9	5-9		Joe Hobbs	23.9	Jim Zinn	15.5			John Mauer		
1958-59	8-15	2-12		Bobby Sherwood	13.5	Bob Sherwood	9.4			John Mauer		
1959-60	6-16	3-11		Bob Shiver	17.5	Bob Sherwood	10.5			John Mauer	98-102	.490
1960-61	15-11	9-5		Lou Merchant	17.6	Cliff Luyk	14.2			Norm Sloan		
1961-62	12-11	8-6		Cliff Luyk	21.3	Cliff Luyk	15.3			Norm Sloan		
1962-63	12-14	5-9		Tom Baxley	16.2	Dick Tomlinson	7.0			Norm Sloan		
1963-64	12-10	6-8		Brooks Henderson	17.3	Mont Highley	10.7			Norm Sloan		
1964-65	18-7	11-5		Brooks Henderson	14.0	Gary Keller	9.9			Norm Sloan		
1965-66	16-10	9-7		Gary Keller	15.9	Gary Keller	12.5			Norm Sloan		
1966-67	21-4	14-4		Gary Keller	15.1	Gary Keller	11.3			Tommy Bartlett		
1967-68	15-10	11-7		Neal Walk	26.5	Neal Walk	19.8	Mike Leatherwood	3.2	Tommy Bartlett		
1968-69	18-9	12-6	NIT FIRST ROUND	Neal Walk	24.0	Neal Walk	17.8	Mike Leatherwood	5.0	Tommy Bartlett		
1969-70	9-17	6-12		Andy Owens	27.0	Andy Owens	9.1	Jerry Hoover	2.9	Tommy Bartlett		
1970-71	11-15	8-10		Tony Miller	16.4	Earl Findley	9.5	Jerry Hoover	4.8	Tommy Bartlett		
1971-72	10-15	4-14		Tony Miller	26.7	Dan Boe	9.9	Jerry Hoover	4.7	Tommy Bartlett		
1972-73	11-15	7-11		Tony Miller	17.2	Chip Williams	12.1	Steve Williams	4.5	Tommy Bartlett	95-85	.528
1973-74	15-11	9-9		Chip Williams	20.6	Chip Williams	11.1	Norm Caldwell	3.8	John Lotz		
1974-75	12-16	8-10		Gene Shy	15.8	Chip Williams	7.8	Norm Caldwell	3.9	John Lotz		
1975-76	12-14	7-11		Gene Shy	16.0	Bob Smyth	12.7	Mike Lederman	3.3	John Lotz		
1976-77	17-9	10-8		Bob Smyth	15.1	Bob Smyth	9.1	Richard Glasper	4.5	John Lotz		
1977-78	15-12	8-10		Reggie Hannah	13.6	Reggie Hannah	9.2	Richard Glasper	4.0	John Lotz		
1978-79	8-19	3-15		Malcolm Cesare	16.9	Reggie Hannah	8.6	Mike Milligan	3.1	John Lotz	79-81	.494
1979-80	7-21	2-16		Reggie Hannah	17.0	Reggie Hannah	8.9	Mike Milligan	3.9	Ed Visscher	7-21	.250
1980-81	12-16	5-13		Ronnie Williams	19.4	Ronnie Williams	9.0	Mike Moses	4.0	Norm Sloan		
1981-82	5-22	2-16		Ronnie Williams	21.3	Eugene McDowell	8.8	Mike Moses	3.9	Norm Sloan		
1982-83	13-18	5-13		Ronnie Williams	18.6	Ronnie Williams	8.8	Vernon Delancy	5.9	Norm Sloan		
1983-84	16-13	11-7	NIT FIRST ROUND	Ronnie Williams	16.6	Eugene McDowell	9.2	Vernon Delancy	4.6	Norm Sloan		
1984-85	18-12	9-9	NIT FIRST ROUND	Andrew Moten	16.6	Eugene McDowell	9.8	Andrew Moten	3.5	Norm Sloan		
1985-86	19-14	10-8	NIT FOURTH PLACE	Vernon Maxwell	19.6	Kenny McClary	5.6	Ronnie Montgomery	4.8	Norm Sloan		
1986-87	23-11 ✪	12-6	NCAA REGIONAL SEMIFINALS	Andrew Moten	16.0	Dwayne Schintzius	6.1	Andrew Moten	4.7	Norm Sloan		
1987-88	23-12 ✪	11-7	NCAA SECOND ROUND	Dwayne Schintzius	14.4	Dwayne Schintzius	6.5	Ronnie Montgomery	5.6	Norm Sloan		
1988-89	21-13	13-5	NCAA FIRST ROUND	Dwayne Schintzius	18.0	Dwayne Schintzius	9.7	Clifford Left	4.3	Norm Sloan	235-194	.548▼
1989-90	7-21	3-15		Dwayne Davis	12.3	Dwayne Davis	8.5	B.J. Carter	2.8	Don DeVoe	7-21	.250
1990-91	11-17	7-11		Dwayne Davis	15.1	Dwayne Davis	7.4	Renaldo Garcia	2.9	Lon Kruger		
1991-92	19-14	9-7	NIT FOURTH PLACE	Stacey Poole	17.8	Stacey Poole	7.3	Scott Stewart	2.5	Lon Kruger		
1992-93	16-12	9-7	NIT FIRST ROUND	Stacey Poole	16.4	Andrew DeClercq	7.1	Scott Stewart	3.0	Lon Kruger		
1993-94	29-8	12-4	NCAA NATIONAL SEMIFINALS	Dan Cross	15.7	Andrew DeClercq	7.9	Dan Cross	3.9	Lon Kruger		
1994-95	17-13	8-8	NCAA FIRST ROUND	Dan Cross	18.0	Andrew DeClercq	8.8	Greg Williams	4.0	Lon Kruger		
1995-96	12-16	6-10		Dametri Hill	17.6	Dametri Hill	7.8	Greg Williams	5.0	Lon Kruger	104-80	.565
1996-97	13-17	5-11		Greg Stolt	13.9	Greg Stolt	6.1	Eddie Shannon	4.2	Billy Donovan		
1997-98	14-15	6-10	NIT FIRST ROUND	Kenyan Weaks	12.7	Damen Maddox	5.4	Jason Williams	6.7	Billy Donovan		
1998-99	22-9	10-6	NCAA REGIONAL SEMIFINALS	Mike Miller	12.2	Brent Wright	5.9	Eddie Shannon	4.8	Billy Donovan		
1999-2000	29-8	12-4	NCAA RUNNER-UP	Mike Miller	14.1	Donnell Harvey	7.0	Brett Nelson	3.0	Billy Donovan		
2000-01	24-7	12-4	NCAA SECOND ROUND	Udonis Haslem	16.8	Matt Bonner	7.7	Brett Nelson	4.3	Billy Donovan		
2001-02	22-9	10-6	NCAA FIRST ROUND	Udonis Haslem	16.4	Udonis Haslem	8.3	Justin Hamilton	3.8	Billy Donovan		
2002-03	25-8	12-4	NCAA SECOND ROUND	Matt Bonner	15.2	David Lee	6.8	Justin Hamilton	3.6	Billy Donovan		
2003-04	20-11	9-7	NCAA FIRST ROUND	Anthony Roberson	17.9	David Lee	7.3	Anthony Roberson	3.6	Billy Donovan		
2004-05	24-8	12-4	NCAA SECOND ROUND	Anthony Roberson	17.5	David Lee	9.0	Matt Walsh	2.7	Billy Donovan		
2005-06	**33-6**	**10-6**	**NATIONAL CHAMPION**	**Joakim Noah**	**14.2**	**Al Horford**	**7.6**	**Taurean Green**	**4.7**	**Billy Donovan**		
2006-07	**35-5**	**13-3**	**NATIONAL CHAMPION**	**Taurean Green**	**13.3**	**Al Horford**	**9.5**	**Taurean Green**	**3.7**	**Billy Donovan**		
2007-08	24-12	8-8	NIT SEMIFINALS	Nick Calathes	15.7	Marreese Speights	7.9	Nick Calathes	6.0	Billy Donovan		
2008-09	25-11	9-7	NIT QUARTERFINALS	Nick Calathes	17.2	Alex Tyus	6.2	Nick Calathes	6.4	Billy Donovan	310-126	.711

✪ Records don't reflect games forfeited or vacated. For adjusted records, see p. 521.

▼ Coach's record adjusted to reflect games forfeited or vacated: 232-192 .547. For yearly totals, see p. 521.

ESPN 260 SAGARIN

FLORIDA A&M

During the 1950s and '60s, the dominant Rattlers were as disliked among historically black colleges as Duke is in Chapel Hill. Since moving to D1, however, the team has been mired in mediocrity, slogging through 22 losing seasons since 1979-80.

BEST TEAM: 1961-62 Featuring stud swingman Waite Bellamy and big man Jack Barnes, the fast-paced Rattlers averaged 91 ppg and breezed through the Southern Intercollegiate Athletic Conference with 24 straight wins. In the regional finals of the College Division tournament, FAMU stalled against slower paced Wittenberg, 33-31.

BEST PLAYER: G Willie Collier (1961-65) A West Palm Beach product, the brash but vertically-challenged (read: 5'9") Collier started as a frosh, immediately taking the reins of the team's racehorse style. During four prolific seasons he constantly attacked the rim.

BEST COACH: Ed "Rockjaw" Oglesby (1950-70, '71-72) Known as Rockjaw because he refused to smile, his fast-break offense inspired another great name: "Run It, Gun It and Never Shun It."

GAME FOR THE AGES: Facing Alabama State in the 1952 SIAC championship, all but four Rattlers fouled out. Thomas Hogan, Willie Irvin, Chuck White and John Cuyler played the final 3:30 of regulation and two OTs shorthanded. Even so, the Famed Final Four, as they became known, pulled out a 71-67 win. Afterward, White collapsed from exhaustion. AD Jake Gaither yelled at him, "If you're a true Rattler, get on your feet!" White jumped up and responded, "I'm a true Rattler!"

FIERCEST RIVAL: Since moving to D1, the Rattlers have been searching for a rival to match SIAC foe Alabama State. They do share a hometown and a dubious distinction with Florida State. On Dec. 7, 1991, a shoving match between FAMU's Reginald Finney and FSU's Doug Edwards led to a bench-clearing fight and an NCAA-record 18 ejections. With only three players left in uniform, the Rattlers forfeited. Despite the bad blood, or perhaps because of it, the teams have played only five times, with the Seminoles winning every game.

SEASON REVIEW

SEAS.	W-L	CONF.	COACH	SEAS.	W-L	CONF.	COACH
1950-52	*47-6*	*Records before 1950-51 lost*		1962-63	19-6		Ed "Rockjaw" Oglesby
1952-53	18-5		Ed "Rockjaw" Oglesby	1963-64	14-12		Ed "Rockjaw" Oglesby
1953-54	19-7		Ed "Rockjaw" Oglesby	1964-65	12-9		Ed "Rockjaw" Oglesby
1954-55	20-2		Ed "Rockjaw" Oglesby	1965-66	17-9		Ed "Rockjaw" Oglesby
1955-56	16-10		Ed "Rockjaw" Oglesby	1966-67	21-7		Ed "Rockjaw" Oglesby
1956-57	17-3		Ed "Rockjaw" Oglesby	1967-68	18-8		Ed "Rockjaw" Oglesby
1957-58	21-6		Ed "Rockjaw" Oglesby	1968-69	12-6		Ed "Rockjaw" Oglesby
1958-59	22-6		Ed "Rockjaw" Oglesby	1969-70	12-12		Ed "Rockjaw" Oglesby
1959-60	22-4		Ed "Rockjaw" Oglesby	1970-71	8-13		Dennis Jefferson
1960-61	15-9		Ed "Rockjaw" Oglesby	1971-72	18-10		Ed "Rockjaw" Oglesby
1961-62	26-1		Ed "Rockjaw" Oglesby	1972-73	17-9		Wendell Meeks

SEAS.	W-L	CONF.	SCORING		COACH	RECORD
1973-74	22-6		John Andrews	18.7	Ajac Triplett	
1974-75	17-9				Ajac Triplett	
1975-76	17-10				Ajac Triplett	
1976-77	18-12		Curtis Brooks	19.7	Ajac Triplett	
1977-78	23-6		Clemon Johnson	17.5	Ajac Triplett	
1978-79	18-9		Paul Grady	16.0	Ajac Triplett	115-52 .689
1979-80	7-22		Paul Grady	15.5	James Giles	
1980-81	17-11	6-4	Pete Taylor	16.6	James Giles	
1981-82	10-17	5-7	Darryl Spence	18.9	James Giles	
1982-83	7-21	4-8	Michael Toomer	11.6	James Giles	41-71 .366
1983-84	7-19		Michael Toomer	14.2	Anthony Fields	7-19 .269
1984-85	10-18		Mervin Jones	19.7	Willie Booker	
1985-86	12-16		Doug Cook	16.5	Willie Booker	
1986-87	12-16		Leonard King	17.9	Willie Booker	
1987-88	22-8	11-5	Aldwin Ware	19.5	Willie Booker	
1988-89	20-10	12-4	Leonard King	22.3	Willie Booker	
1989-90	18-11	13-3	Terry Giles	17.6	Willie Booker	
1990-91	17-14	9-7 ●	Kevin Daniels	16.8	Willie Booker	
1991-92	16-14	11-5	DeLon Turner	19.7	Willie Booker	
1992-93	10-18	8-8	DeLon Turner	21.5	Willie Booker	137-125 .523
1993-94	4-23	2-14	Joey McGear	11.9	Ron Brown	
1994-95	5-22	2-14	Ricky Davis	19.2	Ron Brown	
1995-96	8-19	3-13	Jerome James	11.9	Ron Brown[a]	15-58 .200
1996-97	8-19	8-10	Jerome James	16.1	Mickey Clayton	
1997-98	11-17	8-10	Jerome James	19.9	Mickey Clayton	
1998-99	12-19	8-11 ●	Monroe Pippins	20.5	Mickey Clayton	
1999-2000	9-22	7-11	Travis Grant	9.7	Mickey Clayton	
2000-01	6-22	4-14	Demarcus Wilkins	13.6	Mickey Clayton	48-105 .314
2001-02	9-19	8-10	Michael Griffith	15.3	Mike Gillespie	
2002-03	17-12	11-7	Terrence Woods	20.5	Mike Gillespie	
2003-04	15-17	10-8 ●	Terrence Woods	20.3	Mike Gillespie	
2004-05	14-15	9-8	Tony Tate	15.4	Mike Gillespie	
2005-06	14-17	10-8	Tony Tate	16.4	Mike Gillespie	
2006-07	21-14	12-6 ●	Rome Sanders	15.2	Mike Gillespie	90-94 .489
2007-08	15-17	9-7	Leslie Robinson	15.0	Eugene Harris	
2008-09	10-21	6-10	Lamar Twitty	11.0	Eugene Harris	25-38 .397

[a] Ron Brown (6-13) and Mickey Clayton (2-6) both coached during the 1995-96 season.
● NCAA Tournament appearance

PROFILE

Florida Agricultural and Mechanical University, Tallahassee, FL
Founded: 1887
Enrollment: 13,067 (11,450 undergraduate)
Colors: Orange and green
Nickname: Rattlers
Current arena: Jake Gaither Athletic Center, opened in 1963 (3,365)
Previous: The Hangar, 1948-63 (400); outside clay/dirt courts, 1933-48 (N/A)
First game: 1932

All-time record: 889-722 (.552)
Total weeks in AP Top 20/25: 0
Current conference: Mid-Eastern Athletic (1979-84, '86-)
Conference titles: 0
Conference tournament titles:
MEAC: 4 (1991, '99, 2004, '07)
NCAA Tournament appearances: 4
NIT appearances: 0

TOP 5

G **Willie Collier** (1961-65)
G **Aldwin Ware** (1983-88)
G/F **Waite Bellamy** (1960-63)
F **DeLon Turner** (1989-93)
C **Clemon Johnson** (1974-78)

RECORDS

RECORDS	GAME		SEASON		CAREER	
POINTS	53	Waite Bellamy, vs. Bethune-Cookman (Feb. 11, 1963)	709	Willie Collier (1964-65)	2,029	David Wright (1966-70)
POINTS PER GAME			22.3	Leonard King (1988-89)	31.2	Willie Collier (1961-65)
REBOUNDS	25	Clemon Johnson, vs. Morris Brown (Feb. 9, 1976)	412	Clemon Johnson (1977-78)	1,494	Clemon Johnson (1974-78)
ASSISTS	8	Tony Tate, vs. Hampton (March 1, 2006)	220	Kenny Robinson (1977-78)	603	Terry Giles (1986-90)

ESPN 311 SAGARIN

FLORIDA ATLANTIC

Step outside the FAU Arena and you can practically hear the Atlantic Ocean crashing on the shores of Boca Raton. Step inside and you'll see a team fighting to build some allure of its own.

BEST TEAM: 2001-02 In Sidney Green's first season as coach, the Owls won two games. The next season, seven. The third season, everything changed. With Raheim Brown patrolling the paint and Earnest Crumbley leading the attack, the Owls scored the third-most points (2,303) in school history. In the first round of the NCAA Tournament, FAU matched No. 2-seed Alabama shot for shot before succumbing late, 86-78.

BEST PLAYER: F CRAIG BUCHANAN (1993-97) A brute low-post scorer and versatile defender, Buchanan was the first Owl to break the 1,000-point barrier. He also led the team in scoring in three of his four seasons. In 2007, he was enshrined in the FAU Hall of Fame.

BEST COACH: SIDNEY GREEN (1999-2005) His Forida Atlantic coaching career started badly and ended even more painfully, with his firing in 2005. But he cemented his place in Owls lore by winning the Atlantic Sun title in 2002 to earn the school's lone Tourney bid. His common-man appeal (plus the fact that he was a former NBA teammate of Michael Jordan and Isiah Thomas) helped him land two of the best players in team history, forward Mike Bell and guard Earnest Crumbley.

GAME FOR THE AGES: How in the world did FAU snap Oklahoma State's 80-game home nonconference winning streak on Dec. 1, 1998? It was about grit, hot shooting and plain old clutch play. With the score tied at 81, Owls high-flyer Gary Durrant picked Joe Adkins' pocket and laid the ball in with 1.1 seconds left for the game-winner.

FIERCEST RIVAL: Only 56 miles and a single letter separate FAU and FIU (Florida International). Most of the games between the teams are even closer than that. Since the two started playing in 1990-91, seven contests have been decided by four points or less. FIU's Golden Panthers lead the series, 15–9.

SEASON REVIEW

SEAS.	W-L	CONF.	SCORING		COACH	RECORD	
1988-89	9-19		Ron McLin	19.4	Lonnie Williams	9-19	.321
1989-90	21-7		Daryl Kanning	15.0	Tim Loomis		
1990-91	7-10		Shane Taylor	20.0	Tim Loomis		
1991-92	14-14		Dexter Hill	12.8	Tim Loomis		
1992-93	3-25		Elvin Hazell	14.6	Tim Loomis		
1993-94	3-24		Marlon Jemerson	14.1	Tim Loomis		
1994-95	9-18		Craig Buchanan	14.2	Tim Loomis	67-98	.406
1995-96	9-18	5-11	Craig Buchanan	16.4	Kevin Billerman		
1996-97	16-11	11-5	Craig Buchanan	16.8	Kevin Billerman		
1997-98	5-22	5-11	Damon Arnette	16.1	Kevin Billerman		
1998-99	6-20	3-13	Damon Arnette	21.9	Kevin Billerman	36-71	.336
1999-2000	2-28	0-18	Ryan Hercek	14.6	Sidney Green		
2000-01	7-24	5-13	Jeff Cowans	13.7	Sidney Green		
2001-02	19-12	13-7 ●	Raheim Brown	16.4	Sidney Green		
2002-03	7-21	3-13	Earnest Crumbley	16.2	Sidney Green		
2003-04	9-19	6-14	Mike Bell	18.0	Sidney Green		
2004-05	10-17	10-10	Mike Bell	19.1	Sidney Green	54-121	.309
2005-06	15-13	14-6	DeAndre Rice	16.1	Matt Doherty	15-13	.536
2006-07	16-15	10-8	DeAndre Rice	20.5	Rex Walters		
2007-08	15-18	8-10	Carlos Monroe	15.4	Rex Walters	31-33	.484
2008-09	6-26	2-16	Paul Graham III	18.5	Mike Jarvis	6-26	.188

● NCAA Tournament appearance

PROFILE

Florida Atlantic University, Boca Raton, FL
Founded: 1961
Enrollment: 26,525 (20,623 undergraduate)
Colors: Blue and red
Nickname: Owls
Present Arena: FAU Arena, opened in 1988 (5,000)
First game: Nov. 18, 1984
All-time record: 208-381 (.353)
Total weeks in AP 20/25: 0

Current conference: Sun Belt (2006-)
Conference titles: 0
Conference tournament titles:
Atlantic Sun: 1 (2002)
NCAA Tournament appearances: 1
NIT appearances: 0

TOP 5

G **Damon Arnette** (1996-99)
G **Earnest Crumbley** (2000-04)
F **Mike Bell** (2003-05)
F **Craig Buchanan** (1993-97)
F **Carlos Monroe** (2005-09)

RECORDS	GAME		SEASON		CAREER	
POINTS	39	DeAndre Rice, vs. Troy (Feb. 3, 2007); Earnest Crumbley, vs. Campbell (Feb. 26, 2004)	575	Paul Graham III (2008-09)	1,559	Earnest Crumbley (2000-04)
POINTS PER GAME			21.9	Damon Arnette (1998-99)	18.5	Mike Bell (2003-05)
REBOUNDS	23	Mike Bell, vs. Stetson (Feb. 12, 2004)	312	Carlos Monroe (2007-08)	717	Carlos Monroe (2005-09)
ASSISTS	11	Alex Tucker, vs. New Orleans (Feb. 5, 2009); achieved four other times	145	Earnest Crumbley (2003-04)	505	Earnest Crumbley (2000-04)

ESPN 277 SAGARIN

FLORIDA INTERNATIONAL

The Panthers have four winning seasons since going D1 in 1987-88, which may not sound all that impressive. But FIU history boasts a surprising number of highlights—and future NBA players—for a commuter school that for many years relied largely on in-state talent. And with Isiah Thomas taking over as coach for the 2009-10 season, the Panthers are guaranteed to generate their fair share of headlines.

BEST TEAM: 1992-93 Behind the slow, disciplined brand of ball instilled by former Texas and Ole Miss coach Bob Weltlich, the Panthers achieved two firsts: a 20-win season and a Trans America Athletic Conference crown. But because the conference lacked an automatic NCAA bid, the emotional apex of the season was a last-second, game-winning shot by Clarence "Bobo" Flournory that beat conference foe Mercer, 67-65.

BEST PLAYER: F Dwight Stewart (1988-93) Sure, Raja Bell and Carlos Arroyo are household names, but Stewart holds nine school records. The big man lacked glitz but had a complete game and always gave max effort.

BEST COACH: Marcos "Shakey" Rodriguez (1995-2000) A legendary Miami prep coach, Rodriguez used his local fame to help recruit Arroyo and Bell. He upset big boys such as Alabama, Penn State and Michigan behind a fast-break offense and the mantra that "relentless pressure for 40 minutes equals success."

GAME FOR THE AGES: Entering the 1995 TAAC tournament, FIU was 8–18 and Coach Weltlich had already announced his resignation, effective at the end of the season. Little did anyone know the end would take so long. After knocking off No. 1-seed Stetson, then Southeastern Louisiana in overtime, the Panthers defeated heavily favored Mercer in the final, 68-57, to earn their first NCAA berth.

FIERCEST RIVAL: In football, Florida Atlantic and FIU battle for the Don Shula Award. In basketball, the stakes are much more basic: conference and regional pride. Although the Panthers lead the series 15–13, the Owls bounced them from the 2007 and '08 Sun Belt tourneys.

SEASON REVIEW

SEAS.	W-L	CONF.	SCORING		COACH	RECORD
1981-82	11-16		Eric Carithers	16.6	Rich Walker	
1982-83	15-12		Clyde Corley	16.3	Rich Walker	
1983-84	13-13		Patrick McDonald	16.0	Rich Walker	
1984-85	19-8		Mark Hollin	17.2	Rich Walker	
1985-86	17-9		Patrick McDonald	15.6	Rich Walker	
1986-87	7-18		Jerry Nash	14.7	Rich Walker	
1987-88	9-19		Sylvester Whigham	16.9	Rich Walker	
1988-89	10-18		Doug Johnson	17.5	Rich Walker	
1989-90	7-21		Ruben Colon	12.8	Rich Walker	108-134 .446
1990-91	6-22		Dwight Stewart	19.3	Bob Weltlich	
1991-92	11-17	7-7	Dwight Stewart	18.3	Bob Weltlich	
1992-93	20-10	9-3	Dwight Stewart	16.3	Bob Weltlich	
1993-94	11-16	7-9	Chuck Stuart	17.0	Bob Weltlich	
1994-95	11-19	4-12 ●	James Mazyck	16.4	Bob Weltlich	59-84 .413
1995-96	13-15	6-10	Scott Forbes	17.3	M. "Shakey" Rodriguez	
1996-97	16-13	12-4	Dedric Taylor	18.3	M. "Shakey" Rodriguez	
1997-98	21-8	13-3	Raja Bell	16.6	M. "Shakey" Rodriguez	
1998-99	13-16	7-7	Raja Bell	16.7	M. "Shakey" Rodriguez	
1999-2000	16-14	9-7	Carlos Arroyo	17.7	M. "Shakey" Rodriguez	79-66 .545
2000-01	8-21	5-11	Carlos Arroyo	21.2	Donnie Marsh	
2001-02	10-20	4-10	Taurance Johnson	14.7	Donnie Marsh	
2002-03	8-21 ⊗	1-13	Eulis Baez	12.7	Donnie Marsh	
2003-04	5-22 ⊗	1-13	Carlos Morban	12.0	Donnie Marsh	31-84 .270▼
2004-05	13-17 ⊗	4-10	Ivan Almonte	17.2	Sergio Rouco	
2005-06	8-20 ⊗	4-10	Ivan Almonte	14.7	Sergio Rouco	
2006-07	12-17	7-11	Alex Galindo	13.9	Sergio Rouco	
2007-08	9-20	6-12	Alex Galindo	13.3	Sergio Rouco	
2008-09	13-20	7-11	Michael Dominguez	10.1	Sergio Rouco	55-94 .369▼

⊗ Records do not reflect games forfeited or vacated. For adjusted records, see p. 521.

▼ Coaches' records adjusted to reflect games forfeited or vacated: Donnie Marsh, 19-84, .184; Sergio Ruoco, 35-94, .271. For yearly totals, see p. 521.

● NCAA Tournament appearance

PROFILE

Florida International University, Miami, FL
Founded: 1965
Enrollment: 39,146 (30,248 undergraduate)
Colors: Blue and gold
Nickname: Golden Panthers
Current arena: U.S. Century Bank Arena, opened as the Sunblazer Arena in 1986 (5,000)
First game: Nov. 20, 1981
All-time record: 332-462 (.418)
Total weeks in the AP Top 20/25: 0

Current conference: Sun Belt (1998-)
Conference titles:
Trans America: 1 (1993)
Conference tournament titles:
Trans America: 1 (1995)
NCAA Tournament appearances: 1
NIT appearances: 0

TOP 5

G **Carlos Arroyo** (1997-2001)
G **Raja Bell** (1997-99)
F **Ivan Almonte** (2004-06)
F **Dwight Stewart** (1988-93)
C **Russell Hicks** (2007-09)

RECORDS	GAME		SEASON		CAREER	
POINTS	39	Carlos Arroyo, vs. North Texas (Dec. 30, 2000)	615	Carlos Arroyo (2000-01)	2,101	Dwight Stewart (1988-93)
POINTS PER GAME			21.2	Carlos Arroyo (2000-01)	17.8	Dwight Stewart (1988-93)
REBOUNDS	22	Carlton Phoenix, vs. Northern Illinois (Feb. 23, 1987)	297	Ivan Almonte (2004-05)	875	Patrick McDonald (1982-86)
ASSISTS	13	Carlos Arroyo, vs. Northern Illinois (Nov. 29, 1998)	135	Carlos Arroyo (1997-98)	459	Carlos Arroyo (1997-2001)

THE SCHOOLS

ESPN 74 SAGARIN

FLORIDA STATE

They are one of the newest ACC teams and many seasons get treated like the little, picked-on brother. But every so often, the Seminoles prove capable of sparring with the big boys, making it to the NCAA Final in 1972, the Elite Eight in 1993 and returning to the NCAA Tournament in 2009 after a decade-long drought.

BEST TEAM: 1971-72 They were coming off probation, had never won an NCAA Tournament game, had no conference to call home, no cheerleaders, no band and the smallest of fan bases. But thanks to Ron King's shooting and Reggie Royals' rebounding, FSU was the story of the 1972 NCAA Tournament. After shocking Kentucky and North Carolina to reach the title game, the Seminoles took a 21-14 lead on unbeaten UCLA at Memorial Sports Arena in LA before falling, 81-76.

BEST PLAYER: C Dave Cowens (1967-70) With his red hair and infectious energy, the Kentucky native immediately stood out at Florida State. The 6'9" Cowens owned the paint from day one, averaging 19.0 points and 17.2 rebounds. He is still the school's all-time leading rebounder despite playing just three seasons. Cowens had a Hall-of-Fame career with the Celtics, averaging 17.6 points and 13.6 rebounds over his 11 seasons, and was named one of the 50 Greatest Players in NBA history.

BEST COACH: Hugh Durham (1966-78) Bud Kennedy built the foundation for FSU's program, but Durham took it to national prominence. In his 12 years, the Noles had just one losing season—his first—and went to three NCAA Tournaments, including the runner-up finish in 1972.

GAME FOR THE AGES: Infuriated by critics like Jerry Tarkanian, who said Florida State lacked "patience and discipline," the Seminoles took out Bob McAdoo and North Carolina, 79-75, in the 1972 Final Four. The team put on a clinic in mental toughness, overcoming the Tar Heels' pressure defense and gamely holding on for the win after taking a 45-32 halftime lead.

HEARTBREAKER: There were 26 ties and 17 lead changes, yet the result of the Feb. 4, 2006, matchup between Duke and Florida State was very familiar for the Seminoles: a loss at Cameron Indoor Stadium, where they'd never won. Florida State big man Al Thornton scored 37 and Todd Galloway hit a running three-pointer at the buzzer to force overtime. But the Seminoles had no answer for J.J. Redick's clutch shooting in the extra time, and fell 97-96.

FIERCEST RIVAL: Forget Florida. Like so many other ACC teams, the Seminoles reserve a special hatred in their hearts for the Blue Devils. When FSU finally won at Duke on Feb. 4, 2007, the players danced on the floor. It was just the sixth FSU victory in 31 tries against Duke since their first matchup on Jan. 3, 1954. Unfortunately, it doesn't seem to have started a trend; Florida State followed up with four straight losses to the Blue Devils.

FANFARE AND HOOPLA: Taking a cue from Krzyzewskiville, a dozen or so FSU students camped out overnight in Hamiltonville (named after coach Leonard Hamilton) before the Jan. 10, 2009, home loss to Duke.

The 6'9" Cowens owned the paint from day one, averaging 19.0 points and 17.2 rebounds over his three seasons.

FAN FAVORITE: G Charlie Ward (1990-94) There will never be another. In March 1993, Ward helped lead the Noles to the Elite Eight. That winter, the 190-pound QB won the Heisman Trophy and FSU won the national football title.

FIRST-ROUND PRO PICKS

1970	**Dave Cowens,** Boston (4)
1983	**Mitchell Wiggins,** Indiana (23)
1989	**George McCloud,** Indiana (7)
1993	**Doug Edwards,** Atlanta (15)
1993	**Sam Cassell,** Houston (24)
1994	**Charlie Ward,** New York (26)
1995	**Bob Sura,** Cleveland (17)
2007	**Al Thornton,** LA Clippers (14)
2009	**Toney Douglas,** LA Lakers (29)

PROFILE

Florida State University, Tallahassee, FL
Founded: 1851
Enrollment: 41,575 (32,525 undergraduate)
Colors: Garnet and gold
Nickname: Seminoles
Current arena: Donald L. Tucker Center, opened in 1981 (12,100)
First game: Dec. 10, 1947
All-time record: 993-735 (.575)
Total weeks in AP Top 20/25: 96

Current conference: Atlantic Coast (1991-)
Conference titles:
Metro 7: 1 (1978)
Metro: 1 (1989)
Conference tournament titles:
Metro: 1 (1991)
NCAA Tournament appearances: 11
Sweet 16s (since 1975): 2
Final Fours: 1
NIT appearances: 7
Semifinals: 1

TOP 5

G	**Sam Cassell** (1991-93)
G	**Jim Oler** (1952-56)
F	**Ron King** (1970-73)
F	**Reggie Royals** (1970-73)
C	**Dave Cowens** (1967-70)

RECORDS	GAME		SEASON		CAREER	
POINTS	46	Ron King, vs. Georgia Southern (Feb. 11, 1971)	751	Toney Douglas (2008-09)	2,130	Bob Sura (1991-95)
POINTS PER GAME			29.7	Jim Oler (1955-56)	23.2	Mitchell Wiggins (1981-83)
REBOUNDS	32	Rick Benson, vs. Florida Southern (Jan. 7, 1955)	456	Dave Cowens (1967-68)	1,340	Dave Cowens (1967-70)
ASSISTS	16	Tony William, vs. Jacksonville (Feb. 12, 1983); Otto Petty, vs. South Alabama (Jan. 19, 1972)	227	Otto Petty (1970-71)	688	Delvon Arrington (1998-2002)

SEASON REVIEW

SEAS.	W-L	CONF.	POSTSEASON	SCORING		REBOUNDS		ASSISTS		COACH	RECORD	
1947-48	5-13			Bill Kratzert	9.7					Don Loucks	5-13	.278
1948-49	12-12			Lee Benjamin	18.9					Bud Kennedy		
1949-50	15-10									Bud Kennedy		
1950-51	18-9			Bill Hartman	18.3					Bud Kennedy		
1951-52	5-20			McLaughlin, Whitmer	12.0					Bud Kennedy		
1952-53	11-11			Ham Wernke	21.3					Bud Kennedy		
1953-54	13-7			Ham Wernke	18.6					Bud Kennedy		
1954-55	22-4			Jim Oler	21.1	Rick Benson	16.6			Bud Kennedy		
1955-56	16-9			Jim Oler	29.7	Gary Wold	9.5			Bud Kennedy		
1956-57	9-17			Hugh Durham	19.6	Larry Strom	9.1			Bud Kennedy		
1957-58	9-16			Burt Deckel	17.0	Dan Boltz	12.1			Bud Kennedy		
1958-59	8-15			Hugh Durham	21.9	Dan Boltz	11.5			Bud Kennedy		
1959-60	10-15			Dave Fedor	21.1	Dave Fedor	16.0			Bud Kennedy		
1960-61	14-10			Dave Fedor	19.0	Dave Fedor	14.0			Bud Kennedy		
1961-62	15-8			Dave Fedor	20.4	Dave Fedor	10.1			Bud Kennedy		
1962-63	15-10			Charlie Long	16.5	Jerry Shirley	7.9			Bud Kennedy		
1963-64	11-14			Gary Schull	12.9	Gary Schull	7.2			Bud Kennedy		
1964-65	16-10			Jerry Shirley	15.2	Gary Schull	10.5			Bud Kennedy		
1965-66	14-11			Gary Schull	19.0	Gary Schull	12.7			Bud Kennedy	233-208	.528
1966-67	11-15			Bill Glenn	15.6	Dick Danford	3.2			Hugh Durham		
1967-68	19-8		NCAA FIRST ROUND	Dave Cowens	18.8	Dave Cowens	16.9			Hugh Durham		
1968-69	18-8			Dave Cowens	20.3	Dave Cowens	17.5	Skip Young	6.0	Hugh Durham		
1969-70	23-3			Dave Cowens	17.8	Dave Cowens	17.2	Skip Young	4.9	Hugh Durham		
1970-71	17-9			Ron King	22.7	Reggie Royals	15.0	Otto Petty	8.7	Hugh Durham		
1971-72	27-6		NCAA RUNNER-UP	Ron King	17.9	Reggie Royals	11.0	Otto Petty	5.6	Hugh Durham		
1972-73	18-8			Reggie Royals	16.5	Reggie Royals	10.2	Otto Petty	8.1	Hugh Durham		
1973-74	18-8			Larry Warren	16.9	Lawrence McCray	9.8	Otis Cole	3.7	Hugh Durham		
1974-75	18-8			Larry Warren	16.0	Greg Grady	10.3	Wayne Smalls	4.2	Hugh Durham		
1975-76	21-6 ⊗			David Thompson	14.4	G. Grady, D. Thompson	7.5	Carlton Byrd	3.5	Hugh Durham		
1976-77	16-11	2-4		David Thompson	18.5	Harry Davis	7.8	Carlton Byrd	5.9	Hugh Durham		
1977-78	23-6	11-1	NCAA FIRST ROUND	Harry Davis	19.5	David Thompson	7.2	Tony Jackson	5.7	Hugh Durham	229-96	.705▼
1978-79	19-10	7-3		Murray Brown	21.7	Murray Brown	8.3	Tony Jackson	5.4	Joe Williams		
1979-80	22-9	7-5	NCAA SECOND ROUND	Mickey Dillard	20.4	Elvis Rolle	7.9	Tony Jackson	6.9	Joe Williams		
1980-81	17-11	7-5		Mickey Dillard	18.3	Elvis Rolle	9.1	M. Dillard, Bobby Parks	3.3	Joe Williams		
1981-82	11-17	4-8		Mitchell Wiggins	23.8	Mitchell Wiggins	9.7	Tony William	4.0	Joe Williams		
1982-83	14-14	5-7		Mitchell Wiggins	22.7	Mitchell Wiggins	8.2	Tony William	5.6	Joe Williams		
1983-84	20-11	9-5	NIT SECOND ROUND	Alton Lee Gipson	20.2	Alton Lee Gipson	6.7	Tony William	7.7	Joe Williams		
1984-85	14-16	4-10		Alton Lee Gipson	18.9	Alton Lee Gipson	7.8	Dean Schaffer	6.1	Joe Williams		
1985-86	12-17	3-9		Pee Wee Barber	16.8	Randy Allen	6.2	Pee Wee Barber	5.0	Joe Williams	129-105	.551
1986-87	19-11	6-6	NIT SECOND ROUND	Pee Wee Barber	19.2	Randy Allen	7.8	Pee Wee Barber	4.8	Pat Kennedy		
1987-88	19-11	7-5	NCAA FIRST ROUND	George McCloud	18.2	Tat Hunter	9.0	George McCloud	3.5	Pat Kennedy		
1988-89	22-8	9-3	NCAA FIRST ROUND	George McCloud	22.8	Tat Hunter	8.3	George McCloud	4.2	Pat Kennedy		
1989-90	16-15	6-8		Tharon Mayes	23.3	Michael Polite	8.5	Tharon Mayes	3.9	Pat Kennedy		
1990-91	21-11	9-5	NCAA SECOND ROUND	Doug Edwards	16.4	Michael Polite	8.5	Charlie Ward	3.4	Pat Kennedy		
1991-92	22-10	11-5	NCAA REGIONAL SEMIFINALS	Sam Cassell	18.4	Doug Edwards	9.0	Charlie Ward	4.4	Pat Kennedy		
1992-93	25-10	12-4	NCAA REGIONAL FINALS	Bob Sura	19.9	Doug Edwards	9.4	Sam Cassell	4.9	Pat Kennedy		
1993-94	13-14	6-10		Bob Sura	21.2	Bob Sura	7.9	Bob Sura	4.5	Pat Kennedy		
1994-95	12-15	5-11		Bob Sura	18.6	Corey Louis	7.8	Bob Sura	5.4	Pat Kennedy		
1995-96	13-14	5-11		James Collins	18.3	Corey Louis	6.5	LaMarr Greer	4.9	Pat Kennedy		
1996-97	20-12	6-10	NIT RUNNER-UP	James Collins	16.6	Corey Louis	6.8	Kerry Thompson	5.8	Pat Kennedy	202-131	.607
1997-98	18-14	6-10	NCAA SECOND ROUND	Randell Jackson	12.7	Corey Louis	7.0	Kerry Thompson	5.4	Steve Robinson		
1998-99	13-17	5-11		Ron Hale	16.0	Ron Hale	5.6	Delvon Arrington	6.0	Steve Robinson		
1999-2000	12-17	6-10		Ron Hale	15.6	Oliver Simmons	4.9	Delvon Arrington	6.3	Steve Robinson		
2000-01	9-21	4-12		Delvon Arrington	11.5	Michael Joiner	6.0	Delvon Arrington	4.8	Steve Robinson		
2001-02	12-17	4-12		Monte Cummings	15.5	Nigel Dixon	6.4	Delvon Arrington	6.3	Steve Robinson	64-86	.427
2002-03	14-15	4-12		Tim Pickett	17.1	Tim Pickett	5.7	Todd Galloway	3.3	Leonard Hamilton		
2003-04	19-14	6-10	NIT SECOND ROUND	Tim Pickett	16.5	Adam Waleskowski	5.4	Nate Johnson	3.8	Leonard Hamilton		
2004-05	12-19	4-12		Von Wafer	12.5	Waleskowski, A. Thornton	4.4	Todd Galloway	3.0	Leonard Hamilton		
2005-06	20-10	9-7	NIT SECOND ROUND	Al Thornton	16.1	Alexander Johnson	7.4	Todd Galloway	3.1	Leonard Hamilton		
2006-07	22-13	7-9	NIT QUARTERFINALS	Al Thornton	19.7	Al Thornton	7.2	Isaiah Swann	3.1	Leonard Hamilton		
2007-08	19-15	7-9	NIT FIRST ROUND	Toney Douglas	15.6	Uche Echefu	7.2	T. Douglas, I. Swann	2.9	Leonard Hamilton		
2008-09	25-10	10-6	NCAA FIRST ROUND	Toney Douglas	21.5	Soloman Alabi	5.6	Soloman Alabi	2.9	Leonard Hamilton	131-96	.577

⊗ Record does not reflect games forfeited or vacated. For adjusted record, see p. 521.

▼ Coach's record adjusted to reflect games forfeited or vacated: 230-95, .708. For yearly totals, see p. 521.

LATE GREAT

LOYOLA UNIVERSITY OF NEW ORLEANS

1951-72

During its major college tenure, it was often relegated to second-fiddle status and largely ignored by the national press. Never mind that Loyola was the first institution in Louisiana to have won a national basketball championship (the 1945 NAIB title). Or that the Loyola Field House used to be the largest venue in New Orleans; built in 1954, the Field House seated 6,500, featured an elevated floor and defied state law by allowing integrated seating. Always at the forefront of racial issues, Loyola hosted Bradley and San Francisco—both integrated teams—during the 1955-56 season and signed All-America guard Charley Powell to an athletic scholarship in 1965, making him the first African-American athlete to sign with any Louisiana college. Powell held the school's single-season record for points (651 in 1967-68) for 35 years. The 1970-71 team went 16–10 and averaged 92.1 points a game, fifth in the nation. In 1972, Loyola discontinued intercollegiate athletics; they were reinstated in 1991, with the school joining the NAIA.

NOTABLE PLAYER: C TYRONE "TY" MARIONEAUX (1968-71) The 7'0" big man, also known around the campus as Ty the Guy, scored 1,628 points in three seasons—tops in Loyola's major college era and second all-time. His 53 points against VCU in 1970 is still a school record.

ESPN 133 SAGARIN

FORDHAM

Rose Hill Gym in the Bronx, opened in 1925, is the oldest D1 gym still in use. A subway ride away in Manhattan, Fordham played in the first college basketball game to be televised, in 1940 (a 57-37 loss to Pitt) at the old Madison Square Garden. But for many fans, the greatest Rams moment occurred at the Apple Invitational in Palo Alto, Calif., on Dec. 2, 1983, when point guard Jerry Hobbie stripped the ball from North Carolina's Michael Jordan and went the length of the court for a layup. (So what if Fordham lost, 73-56?)

BEST TEAM: 1970-71 Digger Phelps, at the ripe old age of 29, often used four guards and 6'4" center Tom Sullivan, but the undersized combo paid dividends. The 26–3 team ranked as high as No. 9 in the AP poll, drew the first two college basketball sellouts at the new Madison Square Garden, and advanced to the second round of the NCAA Tournament East Regional semifinals.

BEST PLAYER: F Ed Conlin (1951-55) He led the way to two of the Rams' four Tourney trips (1953 and '54) and remains Fordham's top scorer (1,886) and rebounder (1,930). The first Ram to score 40 in a game, he had a 36-rebound performance against Colgate.

BEST COACH: John Bach (1950-68) Just 25 when he took over, he led the Rams to seven postseason appearances over 18 years and is the school's all-time winningest coach.

GAME FOR THE AGES: "New York basketball was reborn" wrote the *Daily News* after Fordham beat Notre Dame, 94-88, before a sold-out Garden on Feb. 18, 1971. Charlie Yelverton scored 28 before fouling out, and Bill Mainor had 27 while guarding Irish star Austin Carr.

FIERCEST RIVAL: Fordham's departure to the Atlantic 10 dimmed the luster of several local rivalries, but the ties continue with Manhattan College. Although the series was never more intense than in the 1950s and '60s, in 2004 former Jaspers coach Fran Fraschilla called the Rams game a "two-shirter," meaning he would sweat through the first one by halftime. Manhattan leads overall, 52–49.

SEASON REVIEW

SEAS.	W-L	CONF.		COACH	SEAS.	W-L	CONF.		COACH
1902-47	*636-310*	*First losing season was '34-35 (7-9)*			1960-61	7-16	0-3		John Bach
1947-48	20-4	4-2		Frank Adams	1961-62	10-14	1-3		John Bach
1948-49	11-15	1-5		Frank Adams	1962-63	18-8	4-1	■	John Bach
1949-50	16-12	3-2		Frank Adams	1963-64	9-11			John Bach
1950-51	20-8	4-2		John Bach	1964-65	15-12		■	John Bach
1951-52	20-8	3-3		John Bach	1965-66	10-15			John Bach
1952-53	19-8	5-1	●	John Bach	1966-67	14-11			John Bach
1953-54	18-6	3-1	●	John Bach	1967-68	19-8		■	John Bach
1954-55	18-9	3-2		John Bach	1968-69	17-9		■	Ed Conlin
1955-56	11-14	2-2		John Bach	1969-70	10-15			Ed Conlin
1956-57	16-10	2-2		John Bach	1970-71	26-3		●	Digger Phelps
1957-58	16-9	1-3	■	John Bach	1971-72	18-9		■	Hal Wissel
1958-59	17-8	2-2	■	John Bach	1972-73	12-16			Hal Wissel
1959-60	8-18	1-3		John Bach	1973-74	8-17			Hal Wissel

SEAS.	W-L	CONF.		SCORING		COACH	RECORD	
1974-75	12-13			Darryl Brown	20.0	Hal Wissel		
1975-76	7-19			Stan Frankoski	13.4	Hal Wissel	57-74	.435
1976-77	5-21	0-5		John O'Neill	15.3	Dick Stewart		
1977-78	8-18	0-6		Paul Williams	14.8	Dick Stewart	13-39	.250
1978-79	7-22	1-5		Dud Tongal	12.0	Tom Penders		
1979-80	11-17			Bill Calhoun	12.0	Tom Penders		
1980-81	19-9		■	David Maxwell	12.0	Tom Penders		
1981-82	18-11	8-2	■	David Maxwell	10.4	Tom Penders		
1982-83	19-11	7-3	■	David Maxwell	14.7	Tom Penders		
1983-84	19-15	7-7	■	Steve Samuels	14.6	Tom Penders		
1984-85	19-12	9-5	■	Tony McIntosh	19.1	Tom Penders		
1985-86	13-17	7-7		Joe Paterno	12.4	Tom Penders	125-114	.523
1986-87	14-16	6-8		Joe Franco	13.5	Bob Quinn	14-16	.467
1987-88	18-15	9-5	■	Joe Paterno	14.7	Nick Macarchuk		
1988-89	14-15	8-6		Joe Paterno	20.0	Nick Macarchuk		
1989-90	20-13	10-6	■	Andre McClendon	17.3	Nick Macarchuk		
1990-91	25-8	11-1	■	Damon Lopez	17.7	Nick Macarchuk		
1991-92	18-13	11-3	●	Fred Herzog	17.9	Nick Macarchuk		
1992-93	15-16	9-5		Dave Buckner	14.9	Nick Macarchuk		
1993-94	12-15	9-5		Sherwin Content	15.7	Nick Macarchuk		
1994-95	11-17	6-8		Ryan Hunter	15.1	Nick Macarchuk		
1995-96	4-23	2-14		Darren Deschryver	8.9	Nick Macarchuk		
1996-97	6-21	1-15		Maurice Curtis	14.9	Nick Macarchuk		
1997-98	6-21	2-14		Bevon Robin	18.3	Nick Macarchuk		
1998-99	12-15	5-11		Bevon Robin	17.0	Nick Macarchuk	161-192	.456
1999-2000	14-15	7-9		Bevon Robin	15.7	Bob Hill		
2000-01	12-17	4-12		Bevon Robin	14.3	Bob Hill		
2001-02	8-20	4-12		Smush Parker	16.5	Bob Hill		
2002-03	2-26	1-15		Michael Haynes	15.1	Bob Hill	36-78	.316
2003-04	6-22	3-13		Michael Haynes	18.6	Dereck Whittenburg		
2004-05	13-16	8-8		Bryant Dunston	14.9	Dereck Whittenburg		
2005-06	16-16	9-7		Bryant Dunston	16.1	Dereck Whittenburg		
2006-07	18-12	10-6		Marcus Stout	15.3	Dereck Whittenburg		
2007-08	12-17	6-10		Bryant Dunston	15.5	Dereck Whittenburg		
2008-09	3-25	1-15		Jio Fontan	15.3	Dereck Whittenburg	68-108	.386

● NCAA Tournament appearance ■ NIT appearance

PROFILE

Fordham University, Bronx, NY
Founded: 1841
Enrollment: 14,861 (7,394 undergraduate)
Colors: Maroon and white
Nickname: Rams
Current arena: Rose Hill Gymnasium, opened in 1925 (3,200)
First game: Jan. 11, 1902
All-time record: 1,475-1,182 (.555)
Total weeks in AP Top 20/25: 19

Current conference: Atlantic 10 (1995-)
Conference titles:
Metro: 1 (1963)
Patriot: 3 (1991, '92 [tie], '94)
Conference tournament titles:
MAAC: 1 (1983)
Patriot: 2 (1991, '92)
NCAA Tournament appearances: 4
NIT appearances: 16
Semifinals: 1

FIRST-ROUND PRO PICKS

1955 **Ed Conlin,** Syracuse (7)

TOP 5

G **Ken Charles** (1970-73)
G **Charlie Yelverton** (1968-71)
F **Ed Conlin** (1951-55)
F **Jim Cunningham** (1955-58)
F **Bryant Dunston** (2004-08)

RECORDS

RECORDS	GAME		SEASON		CAREER	
POINTS	46	Ken Charles, vs. Saint Peter's (Jan. 20, 1973); Charlie Yelverton, vs. Rochester (Dec. 30, 1970)	679	Ken Charles (1972-73)	1,886	Ed Conlin (1951-55)
POINTS PER GAME			25.0	Ed Conlin (1954-55)	22.9	Jim Cunningham (1955-58)
REBOUNDS	36	Ed Conlin, vs. Colgate (Feb. 4, 1953)	612	Ed Conlin (1952-53)	1,930	Ed Conlin (1951-55)
ASSISTS	15	Jerry Hobbie, vs. La Salle (Dec. 28, 1984)	188	Jay Fazande (1992-93)	548	Jay Fazande (1989-93)

THE SCHOOLS

ESPN 126 SAGARIN

FRESNO STATE

The pride of the San Joaquin Valley burst onto the national scene under coach Boyd Grant in the early 1980s, appearing in three NCAA Tournaments and winning the 1983 NIT title. Starting in 1995, Jerry Tarkanian led a revival, posting six consecutive 20-win seasons before ultimately landing his alma mater on probation. That dubious tradition was carried on by Tark's successor, Ray Lopes, whose recruiting violations dating from 2002-04 will keep the Bulldogs on probation through 2009-10.

BEST TEAM: 1981-82 Boyd Grant called his team's deliberate style of play "tempo programming." The 1983 Bulldogs won the NIT championship, but the 1982 squad was even better at controlling the opposition. They gave up the fewest points per game (47.1) of any team since 1951-52, won a school-record 27 games (13–1 in the PCAA) and advanced to the NCAA Sweet 16.

BEST PLAYER: C MELVIN ELY (1998-2002) Fresno State's all-time leading scorer (1,951) and shot blocker (362), Ely led the Bulldogs to the postseason four straight seasons (although the Dogs' 2000 NCAA appearance was later vacated). Under Tarkanian, the 6'10" center from Illinois blossomed. His strong low-post offense, interior defense and surprising agility for a big man made him a perfect fit for the Bulldogs' system. Ely won WAC Player of the Year in 2001 and '02, and was the 12th overall pick in the 2002 NBA draft.

BEST COACH: BOYD GRANT (1977-86) Heading into the 1982-83 season, Grant had earned a reputation as a defensive mastermind—and an offensive curmudgeon. But he revved up the tempo midway through the 1982-83 season and the result was an NIT title run. Grant also guided the Bulldogs to two regular-season PCAA titles, three tournament titles, and the 1982 Sweet 16. The Bulldogs were especially tough at home under Grant, earning old Selland Arena the nickname Grant's Tomb.

GAME FOR THE AGES: In the last game at Selland, more than 10,000 fans watched Fresno State and Nevada duke it out on March 1, 2003. The stakes were high: Fresno State had a chance to clinch the regular-season WAC title. The action was furious: Damon Jackson made a tying three-pointer with :38 left, then Nevada's Kirk Snyder hit a jumper with :15 left to put Nevada up 73-71. Next, Terry Pettis made a layup with :06 on the clock to force overtime. With time running out in the extra frame, Jackson hit another three to send the game to a second OT. The Bulldogs went on a tear in the final five minutes to secure a 107-99 victory. The celebration was grand: Rookie coach Ray Lopes and some players cut down the nets, while others danced on the scorer's table.

HEARTBREAKER: In the 1996 WAC tournament semifinals, New Mexico's Charles Smith scored 29 points, including three game-tying free throws that forced a third and final overtime, helping the Lobos beat the Bulldogs, 104-99. The loss knocked Fresno State into the NIT in Tark's first season.

Boyd Grant called his team's deliberate style of play "tempo programming."

FIERCEST RIVAL: Fresno State first played San Jose State in 1922, and while the two schools are separated by only 150 miles, culturally they are poles apart. The Bulldogs represent the predominantly agrarian San Joaquin Valley, while the Spartans hail from the more urban Silicon Valley area. Fresno leads the series overall, 76-72.

FANFARE AND HOOPLA: The Bulldogs' ultra-loyal fans are known as the Red Wave, a tip to how well they travel. Starting with their 1983 NIT title run, Fresno State fans have been known to flock en masse to such neutral sites as Madison Square Garden.

FAN FAVORITE: F ROD HIGGINS (1978-82) The two-time All-America honorable mention with an inside-outside game ushered in the Boyd Grant era by leading the Bulldogs to back-to-back NCAA Tournament appearances in 1981 and '82.

FIRST-ROUND NBA PICKS

1984	**Bernard Thompson,** Portland (19)
2000	**Courtney Alexander,** Orlando (13)
2002	**Melvin Ely,** LA Clippers (12)
2002	**Chris Jefferies,** LA Lakers (27)

PROFILE

California State University, Fresno; Fresno, CA
Founded: 1911
Enrollment: 22,572 (19,245 undergraduate)
Colors: Cardinal red and blue
Nickname: Bulldogs
Current arena: Save Mart Center, opened in 2003 (15,596)
Previous: Selland Arena, 1966-2003 (11,300); North Gym, 1953-66 (1,551)
First game: 1921
All-time record: 1,214-978-1 (.554)

Total weeks in AP Top 20/25: 32
Current conference: Western Athletic (1992-)
Conference titles:
Pacific Coast Athletic Association: 2 (1981, '82)
WAC: 3 (1997 [tie] 2001, '03)
Conference tournament titles:
Pacific Coast Athletic Association: 3 (1981, '82, '84)
WAC: 1 (2000-v)
NCAA Tournaments: 5 (1 appearance vacated)
Sweet 16s (since 1975): 1

NIT appearances: 9
Semifinals: 2
Titles: 1 (1983)

TOP 5

G	**Courtney Alexander** (1998-2000)
G	**Ron Anderson** (1982-84)
F	**Rod Higgins** (1978-82)
F	**Bernard Thompson** (1980-84)
C	**Melvin Ely** (1998-2002)

RECORDS	GAME		SEASON		CAREER	
POINTS	45	Charles Bailey, vs. North Texas (Dec. 20, 1973)	694	Carl Ray Harris (1993-94)	1,951	Melvin Ely (1998-2002)
POINTS PER GAME			24.8	Courtney Alexander (1999-2000)	22.6	Courtney Alexander (1998-2000)
REBOUNDS	35	Larry Abney, vs. SMU (Feb. 17, 2000)	452	Lonnie Hughey (1965-66)	1,080	Gary Alcorn (1956-59)
ASSISTS	17	Tito Maddox, vs. TCU (Jan. 10, 2001)	240	Rafer Alston (1997-98)	598	Dominick Young (1994-97)

SEASON REVIEW

SEASON	W-L	CONF.	SCORING	COACH	RECORD
1921-22	6-5			Arthur W. Jones	
1922-23	14-7			Arthur W. Jones	
1923-24	7-6			Arthur W. Jones	
1924-25	12-7			Arthur W. Jones	
1925-26	11-3			Arthur W. Jones	
1926-27	12-8			Arthur W. Jones	
1927-28	6-11			Arthur W. Jones	
1928-29	12-6			Arthur W. Jones	80-53 .602
1929-30	11-5			J. Flint Hanner	
1930-31	8-6			J. Flint Hanner	
1931-32	6-9			J. Flint Hanner	
1932-33	7-7			Leo A. Harris	7-7 .500
1933-34	0-2			no coach	
1934-35	12-8			Stan Borleske	
1935-36	10-17			Stan Borleske	
1936-37	4-13			Stan Borleske	

SEAS.	W-L	CONF.	POSTSEASON	SCORING		REBOUNDS		ASSISTS		COACH	RECORD	
1937-38	11-10									Stan Borleske		
1938-39	6-13									Stan Borleske	43-61	.414
1939-40	8-11									Hal Beatty		
1940-41	9-14									Hal Beatty		
1941-42	11-9									Hal Beatty		
1942-43	6-6-1									Pix Pierson	6-6-1	.500
1943-44	no team											
1944-45	2-6									J. Flint Hanner	27-26	.509
1945-46	10-13									Hal Beatty		
1946-47	11-10									Hal Beatty	49-57	.462
1947-48	10-16									Dutch Warmerdam		
1948-49	14-16									Dutch Warmerdam		
1949-50	7-19									Dutch Warmerdam		
1950-51	5-19			Flip Darrow	11.4					Dutch Warmerdam		
1951-52	9-18			Fred Bartels	10.7					Dutch Warmerdam		
1952-53	10-19			Len Tucker	15.5					Dutch Warmerdam	55-107	.340
1953-54	12-16			Rolland Todd	14.0					Clark Van Galder	12-16	.429
1954-55	11-13			Don Boline	12.9					Bill Vandenburgh		
1955-56	9-17			Len Brown	14.4	Len Brown	9.6			Bill Vandenburgh		
1956-57	16-10			Gary Alcorn	21.4	Gary Alcorn	13.7			Bill Vandenburgh		
1957-58	19-8			Gary Alcorn	15.4	Gary Alcorn	13.6			Bill Vandenburgh		
1958-59	18-5			Gary Alcorn	17.1	Gary Alcorn	14.2			Bill Vandenburgh		
1959-60	18-10			Al Brown	13.2	Vern Chrissman	8.6			Bill Vandenburgh	91-63	.591
1960-61	14-12			Mike McFerson	20.4	Vern Chrissman	9.2			Harry Miller		
1961-62	19-7			Mike McFerson	20.6	Ron Neff	9.1			Harry Miller		
1962-63	20-8			Tony Burr	15.4	Maurice Talbot	9.8			Harry Miller		
1963-64	20-5			Maurice Talbot	22.2	Maurice Talbot	13.4			Harry Miller		
1964-65	20-7			Lonnie Hughey	23.2	Lonnie Hughey	14.4			Harry Miller	93-39	.705
1965-66	21-8			Lonnie Hughey	19.4	Lonnie Hughey	15.6			Ed Gregory		
1966-67	17-9			Jack Kennedy	17.2	Ron Riegel	10.5			Ed Gregory		
1967-68	18-8			Lucius Davis	17.6	Wes Russell	10.0			Ed Gregory		
1968-69	17-8			Lucius Davis	18.2	Ron Riegel	8.8			Ed Gregory		
1969-70	14-12	5-5		Lucius Davis	22.9	Larry Henricksen	11.6			Ed Gregory		
1970-71	15-11	4-6		Jerry Pender	22.6	Larry Henricksen	9.3			Ed Gregory		
1971-72	9-17	2-10		Jerry Pender	22.2	Neal McCoy	10.5			Ed Gregory		
1972-73	10-16	1-11		Clarence Metcalfe	15.6	Darryl Thompson	6.5			Ed Gregory		
1973-74	16-9	5-7		Charles Bailey	23.0	Roy Jones	7.0			Ed Gregory		
1974-75	16-10	5-5		Roy Jones	20.6	Roy Jones	8.5			Ed Gregory		
1975-76	12-14	4-6		Roy Jones	17.7	Roy Jones	7.7			Ed Gregory		
1976-77	7-20	1-11		Eddie Adams	14.8	Eddie Adams	6.1			Ed Gregory	172-142	.548
1977-78	21-6	11-3		Art Williams	12.9	Art Williams	6.7			Boyd Grant		
1978-79	16-12	9-5		Art Williams	13.9	Art Williams	8.1			Boyd Grant		
1979-80	17-7	8-4		Rod Higgins	12.9	Art Williams	7.6			Boyd Grant		
1980-81	25-4	12-2	NCAA FIRST ROUND	Rod Higgins	15.4	Rod Higgins	5.4			Boyd Grant		
1981-82	27-3	13-1	NCAA REGIONAL SEMIFINALS	Rod Higgins	15.1	Rod Higgins	6.3			Boyd Grant		
1982-83	25-10	9-7	NIT CHAMPION	Ron Anderson	16.3	Bernard Thompson	5.9			Boyd Grant		
1983-84	25-8	13-5	NCAA FIRST ROUND	Ron Anderson	17.6	Ron Anderson	6.1			Boyd Grant		
1984-85	23-9	15-3	NIT QUARTERFINALS	Mitch Arnold	14.7	Scott Barnes	7.4			Boyd Grant		
1985-86	15-15	8-10		Brian Salone	13.1	Jos Kuipers	6.0			Boyd Grant	194-74	.724
1986-87	9-20	4-14		Jervis Cole	12.4	Derrick Barden	7.1			Ron Adams		
1987-88	9-19	6-12		Jervis Cole	16.1	Derrick Barden	7.4			Ron Adams		
1988-89	15-14	9-9		Jervis Cole	18.5	Derrick Barden	6.1			Ron Adams		
1989-90	10-19	4-14		Wil Hooker	15.5	Chris Henderson	6.3			Ron Adams	43-72	.374
1990-91	14-16	7-11		Tod Bernard	19.2	Tod Bernard	7.5			Gary Colson		
1991-92	15-16	6-12		Wil Hooker	15.6	Lee Mayberry	5.8			Gary Colson		
1992-93	13-15	8-10		Travis Stel	12.0	Lee Mayberry	7.2			Gary Colson		
1993-94	21-11	13-5	NIT QUARTERFINALS	Carl Ray Harris	21.7	Lee Mayberry	10.6			Gary Colson		
1994-95	13-15	7-11		Dominick Young	15.6	Anthony Pelle	8.0			Gary Colson	76-73	.510
1995-96	22-11	13-5	NIT QUARTERFINALS	Kendric Brooks	19.4	Rahsaan Smith	7.2			Jerry Tarkanian		
1996-97	20-12	12-4	NIT FIRST ROUND	Chris Herren	17.5	Daymond Forney	6.6			Jerry Tarkanian		
1997-98	21-13	10-4	NIT FOURTH PLACE	Chris Herren	15.6	Tremaine Fowlkes	11.2	Rafer Alston	7.3	Jerry Tarkanian		
1998-99	21-12 ⊗	9-5	NIT FIRST ROUND	Courtney Alexander	21.4	Terrance Roberson	7.0	Chris Herren	7.2	Jerry Tarkanian		
1999-2000	24-10 ⊗	11-3	NCAA FIRST ROUND	Courtney Alexander	24.8	Larry Abney	11.8	Demetrius Porter	6.2	Jerry Tarkanian		
2000-01	26-7 ⊗	13-3	NCAA SECOND ROUND	Melvin Ely	16.5	Melvin Ely	7.5	Tito Maddox	8.0	Jerry Tarkanian		
2001-02	19-15	9-9	NIT FIRST ROUND	Melvin Ely	23.3	Melvin Ely	9.1	Chris Sandy	5.8	Jerry Tarkanian	153-80	.657▼
2002-03	20-8	13-5		Damon Jackson	13.3	Hiram Fuller	7.4	Ronaldo Todd	4.3	Ray Lopes		
2003-04	14-15	10-8		Shantay Legans	15.0	Mustafa Al-Sayyad	7.3	Shantay Legans	5.6	Ray Lopes		
2004-05	16-14	9-9		Ja'Vance Coleman	16.9	Mustafa Al-Sayyad	7.4	Dominique White	3.2	Ray Lopes	50-37	.575
2005-06	15-13	8-8		Quinton Hosley	18.6	Quinton Hosley	9.2	Kevin Bell	5.9	Steve Cleveland		
2006-07	22-10	10-6	NIT FIRST ROUND	Quinton Hosley	13.9	Dominic McGuire	9.8	Kevin Bell	5.6	Steve Cleveland		
2007-08	13-19	5-11		Kevin Bell	18.3	Hector Hernandez	7.3	Kevin Bell	5.8	Steve Cleveland		
2008-09	13-21	3-13		Sylvester Seay	15.3	Paul George	6.2	Dwight O'Neil	4.7	Steve Cleveland	63-63	.500

⊗ Records don't reflect games forfeited or vacated. For adjusted records, see p. 521.

▼ Coach's record adjusted to reflect games forfeited or vacated: 104-79, .568. For yearly totals, see p. 521.

ESPN 223 SAGARIN

FURMAN

A member of the Southern Conference since 1936, the Paladins enjoyed two golden eras. From 1952-53 to '55-56, Frank Selvy and Darrell Floyd held a lock on the NCAA scoring title, treating fans to 50-plus-point outings on 13 occasions. And from 1970-71 to '79-80, Furman dominated the SoCon, taking home six conference tournament crowns and making as many trips to the NCAA Tournament.

BEST TEAM: 1974-75 Led by All-America forward and two-time conference POY Clyde Mayes, and bolstered by the frontcourt play of 7'1" center Fessor "Moose" Leonard (15.5 ppg) and 6'7" Craig Lynch (16.1 ppg), the SoCon champs went undefeated both at home (11–0) and in league play (12–0) en route to an NCAA Tourney appearance.

BEST PLAYER: G FRANK SELVY (1951-54) Before there was Wilt the Stilt, there was the Corbin Comet. Selvy led the nation in scoring in 1952-53 (29.5 ppg) and '53-54 (41.7 ppg), won All-America honors three straight seasons and was the first overall NBA pick in 1954. It's been written that Adolph Rupp's greatest mistake was failing to bring this Kentuckian to Lexington.

BEST COACH: JOE WILLIAMS (1970-78) In eight seasons, Williams earned five NCAA Tournament trips. In the 1973-74 season, the Paladins scored the only Tourney win in school history, downing South Carolina 75-67. In Williams' final season, Furman knocked off North Carolina (89-83) and NC State (68-67) on back-to-back nights in Charlotte.

GAME FOR THE AGES: On Feb. 13, 1954, viewers of the first live local sports telecast in upstate South Carolina were treated to a show. Selvy drained 41 field goals and hit 18 of 22 from the stripe in a 149-95 drubbing of Newberry. Selvy's final field goal—a 40-foot heave as time expired—brought his total to 100 points, still the NCAA record.

FIERCEST RIVAL: Not only are Furman and Citadel cross-state rivals, they are the two longest standing continuous members of the SoCon. Dating back to 1919-20, the two have squared off 190 times, with Furman holding a 110–80 series edge.

SEASON REVIEW

SEAS.	W-L	CONF.	COACH
1908-47	*262-234*	*15-1 in 1931-32*	
1947-48	11-15	3-10	Lyles Alley
1948-49	8-14	4-11	Lyles Alley
1949-50	9-12	4-8	Melvin Bell
1950-51	3-20	1-13	Lyles Alley
1951-52	18-6	9-5	Lyles Alley
1952-53	21-6	10-3	Lyles Alley
1953-54	20-9	6-1	Lyles Alley
1954-55	17-10	6-4	Lyles Alley
1955-56	12-16	7-7	Lyles Alley
1956-57	10-17	7-5	Lyles Alley
1957-58	10-16	4-8	Lyles Alley
1958-59	14-12	5-7	Lyles Alley
1959-60	9-16	6-7	Lyles Alley
1960-61	15-11	6-7	Lyles Alley
1961-62	15-12	8-5	Lyles Alley
1962-63	14-14	9-6	Lyles Alley
1963-64	11-15	7-8	Lyles Alley
1964-65	6-19	1-13	Lyles Alley
1965-66	9-17	4-8	Lyles Alley
1966-67	9-15	4-6	Frank Selvy
1967-68	13-14	6-6	Frank Selvy
1968-69	9-17	5-6	Frank Selvy
1969-70	13-13	5-6	Frank Selvy
1970-71	15-12	5-5 ●	Joe Williams
1971-72	17-11	8-3	Joe Williams
1972-73	20-9	11-2 ●	Joe Williams
1973-74	22-9	11-1 ●	Joe Williams

SEAS.	W-L	CONF.	SCORING		COACH	RECORD	
1974-75	22-7	12-0 ●	Clyde Mayes	21.1	Joe Williams		
1975-76	9-18	5-7	Ray Miller	21.6	Joe Williams		
1976-77	18-10	8-2	Bruce Grimm	24.0	Joe Williams		
1977-78	19-11	7-5 ●	Jonathan Moore	18.3	Joe Williams	142-87	.620
1978-79	20-9	9-3	Jonathan Moore	21.9	Eddie Holbrook		
1979-80	23-7	14-1 ●	Jonathan Moore	18.4	Eddie Holbrook		
1980-81	11-16	8-8	Mel Daniel	22.0	Eddie Holbrook		
1981-82	11-16	7-9	Mel Daniel	17.6	Eddie Holbrook	65-48	.575
1982-83	9-20	4-12	George Singleton	16.1	Jene Davis		
1983-84	12-17	7-9	George Singleton	17.6	Jene Davis		
1984-85	7-21	4-12	Noel Gilliard	14.4	Jene Davis	28-58	.326
1985-86	10-17	5-11	Shawn Reid	13.4	Butch Estes		
1986-87	17-12	10-6	David Brown	15.2	Butch Estes		
1987-88	18-10	11-5	David Brown	14.8	Butch Estes		
1988-89	17-12	9-5	David Brown	17.8	Butch Estes		
1989-90	15-16	5-9	Bruce Evans	15.1	Butch Estes		
1990-91	20-9	11-3 ■	Bruce Evans	16.2	Butch Estes		
1991-92	17-11	9-5	Bruce Evans	16.4	Butch Estes		
1992-93	11-17	8-10	Derek Waugh	14.6	Butch Estes		
1993-94	10-18	6-12	Brian Edwards	13.4	Butch Estes	135-122	.525
1994-95	10-17	6-8	Steve Harris	15.8	Joe Cantafio		
1995-96	10-17	6-8	Chuck Vincent	15.0	Joe Cantafio		
1996-97	10-17	4-10	Chuck Vincent	16.2	Joe Cantafio	30-51	.370
1997-98	9-20	5-9	Chuck Vincent	17.2	Larry Davis		
1998-99	12-16	5-11	Stanislav Makshantsev	14.5	Larry Davis		
1999-2000	14-18	5-10	Karim Souchu	15.8	Larry Davis		
2000-01	10-16	5-11	Karim Souchu	18.9	Larry Davis		
2001-02	17-14	7-9	Karim Souchu	14.8	Larry Davis		
2002-03	14-17	8-8	Karim Souchu	19.5	Larry Davis		
2003-04	17-12	8-8	Maleye Ndoye	16.0	Larry Davis		
2004-05	16-13	9-7	Moussa Diagne	12.3	Larry Davis		
2005-06	15-13	8-7	Robby Bostain	14.1	Larry Davis	124-139	.471
2006-07	15-16	8-10	Moussa Diagne	13.3	Jeff Jackson		
2007-08	7-23	6-14	Alex Opacic	10.5	Jeff Jackson		
2008-09	6-24	4-16	Jordan Miller	13-8	Jeff Jackson	28-63	.308

● NCAA Tournament appearance ■ NIT appearance

PROFILE

Furman University, Greenville, SC
Founded: 1826
Enrollment: 3,042 (2,625 undergraduate)
Colors: Purple and white
Nickname: Paladins
Current arena: Timmons Arena, opened in 1997 (5,000)
Previous: Physical Activity Center, 1996-97 (2,000); Memorial Auditorium, 1958-96 (6,500)
First game: Oct. 30, 1908
All-time record: 1,090-1,118 (.494)
Total weeks in AP Top 20/25: 0

Current conference: Southern (1936-)
Conference titles:
Southern: 5 (1974, '75, '77 [tie], '80, '91 [tie])
Conference tournament titles:
Southern: 6 (1971, '73, '74, '75, '78, '80)
NCAA Tournament appearances: 6
NIT appearances: 1

CONSENSUS ALL-AMERICAS

1954 **Frank Selvy,** G

FIRST-ROUND PRO PICKS

1954 **Frank Selvy,** Baltimore (1)

TOP 5

G **Darrell Floyd** (1953-56)
G **Frank Selvy** (1951-54)
F **Clyde Mayes** (1972-75)
F **Jonathan Moore** (1976-80)
C **George Singleton** (1980-84)

RECORDS

RECORDS	GAME		SEASON		CAREER	
POINTS	100	Frank Selvy, vs. Newberry (Feb. 13, 1954)	1,209	Frank Selvy (1953-54)	2,538	Frank Selvy (1951-54)
POINTS PER GAME			41.7	Frank Selvy (1953-54)	32.5	Frank Selvy (1951-54)
REBOUNDS	35	Bob Thomas, vs. The Citadel (Jan. 14, 1954)	488	Gerald Glur (1961-62)	1,242	Jonathan Moore (1976-80)
ASSISTS	14	Guilherme Da Luz, vs. Coastal Carolina (Dec. 16, 1999)	206	Guilherme Da Luz (2001-02)	668	Guilherme Da Luz (1999-2003)

ESPN 214 SAGARIN

GARDNER-WEBB

To modern-day Gardner-Webb diehards, one moment clearly stands out: the night the Runnin' Bulldogs dominated Kentucky from start to finish in 2007. But for those who have been following the team since its junior college and NAIA days, it's the collection of highlights from George Adams and Artis Gilmore that leave the most lasting impression.

BEST TEAM: 1976-77 Coach Eddie Holbrook was a stickler for conditioning, and it showed. The Runnin' Bulldogs scored 100 or more points 18 times—fueling their scoring output with relentless board work—before losing to St. Augustine in the NAIA tournament. With his 40-inch vertical and daring shotmaking, G Dave Bormann engineered the frenetic pace.

BEST PLAYER: F George Adams (1968-72) With apologies to Artis Gilmore, who played two seasons at Gardner-Webb, there's no denying the 6'5" Adams. Impossibly strong, he broke nearly every scoring and rebounding record in the school's books.

BEST COACH: Eddie Holbrook (1964-78) If his teams couldn't outrace an opponent, they'd try to outmuscle them or smother them with full-court defense. The Bulldogs consistently ranked among the NJCAA and NAIA's scoring leaders under Holbrook's watch, and he developed greats such as Adams, Bormann, Gilmore and future NBA star John Drew.

GAME FOR THE AGES: Who cares that the 2007-08 Wildcats hardly ranked as one of Kentucky's all-time great teams? They were still ranked in the Top 25 and playing at home when the Bulldogs crushed them, 84-68, on Nov. 7, 2007. Gardner-Webb scored the first 14 points to silence the Rupp Arena crowd.

FIERCEST RIVAL: When Campbell wanted to open its new arena against Gardner-Webb in 2008, Bulldogs coach Rick Scruggs declined, thinking it would be an ambush. Fans come from all across North Carolina to see this matchup, which is almost always close—with the notable exception of the first in the series, a 1954 tilt won by the Camels, 100-69. Gardner-Webb leads, 9–8.

SEASON REVIEW

SEAS.	W-L	CONF.	SCORING		COACH	RECORD	
1969-70	18-7				Eddie Holbrook		
1970-71	20-4				Eddie Holbrook		
1971-72	28-5				Eddie Holbrook		
1972-73	18-8		George Adams	34.3	Eddie Holbrook		
1973-74	27-4				Eddie Holbrook		
1974-75	23-3				Eddie Holbrook		
1975-76	27-4		Dave Bormann	23.2	Eddie Holbrook		
1976-77	30-3		Dave Bormann	29.8	Eddie Holbrook		
1977-78	27-3				Eddie Holbrook	218-41	.842
1978-79	24-6				Jim Wiles		
1979-80	23-12				Jim Wiles		
1980-81	25-11				Jim Wiles		
1981-82	17-15				Jim Wiles		
1982-83	25-7				Jim Wiles		
1983-84	14-15				Jim Wiles		
1984-85	18-10				Jim Wiles		
1985-86	15-17				Jim Wiles		
1986-87	17-15				Jim Wiles		
1987-88	22-10				Jim Wiles		
1988-89	15-11				Jim Wiles		
1989-90	7-19				Jim Wiles	221-149	.597
1990-91	15-14				Jim Johnson		
1991-92	19-11				Jim Johnson		
1992-93	13-14				Jim Johnson		
1993-94	11-15				Jim Johnson		
1994-95	11-16				Jim Johnson	69-70	.496
1995-96	15-12				Rick Scruggs		
1996-97	17-10				Rick Scruggs		
1997-98	13-14		Dusty Mason	12.7	Rick Scruggs		
1998-99	11-16		Antoine Wilkerson	13.6	Rick Scruggs		
1999-2000	25-5		Carlos Webb	18.1	Rick Scruggs		
2000-01	22-10		Carlos Webb	16.3	Rick Scruggs		
2001-02	23-9		Bruce Fields	12.4	Rick Scruggs		
2002-03	5-24	2-14	Tim Behrendorff	10.5	Rick Scruggs		
2003-04	9-20	6-14	Brian Bender	12.7	Rick Scruggs		
2004-05	18-12	13-7	Brian Bender	15.4	Rick Scruggs		
2005-06	17-12	14-6	Simon Conn	15.1	Rick Scruggs		
2006-07	9-21	7-11	Chris Gash	12.3	Rick Scruggs		
2007-08	16-16	9-7	Thomas Sanders	18.1	Rick Scruggs		
2008-09	13-17	9-9	Grayson Flittner	14.5	Rick Scruggs	213-198	.518

PROFILE

Gardner-Webb University, Boiling Springs, NC
Founded: 1905
Enrollment: 3,797 (2,770 undergraduate)
Colors: Red and black
Nickname: Runnin' Bulldogs
Current arena: Paul Porter Arena, opened in 1984 (4,500)
Previous: Bost Gymnasium, 1970-84 (1,500)
First game: 1969
All-time record: 722-457 (.612)
Total weeks in AP Top 20/25: 0

Current conference: Big South (2008-)
Conference titles:
Atlantic Sun: 1 (2005 [tie])
Conference tournament titles: 0
NCAA Tournament appearances: 0
NIT appearances: 0

TOP 5

G **Dave Bormann** (1975-77)
G **John Drew** (1972-74)
F **George Adams** (1968-72)
F **Eddie Wilkins** (1980-84)
C **Artis Gilmore** (1967-69)

RECORDS

	GAME		SEASON		CAREER	
POINTS	57	George Adams, vs. Voorhees (Jan. 27, 1972)	986	George Adams (1971-72)	2,404	George Adams (1968-72)
POINTS PER GAME			34.3	George Adams (1971-72)	31.2	George Adams (1968-72)
REBOUNDS	26	George Adams, vs. Warren Wilson College (Feb. 9, 1970)	407	George Adams (1971-72)	1,113	George Adams (1968-72)
ASSISTS	13	T.J. McCullough, vs. Florida Atlantic (Feb. 26, 2005)	237	Chuck Nesbit (1979-80)	N/A	Brad Smith (1983-87)

ESPN 252 SAGARIN

GEORGE MASON

Having a miraculous NCAA Tournament run now has a name: It's called pulling a George Mason. The Patriots have actually made the Tournament four times since 1998-99, but Patriots fans will always remember the magical journey to the 2006 Final Four.

BEST TEAM: 2005-06 On Selection Sunday, Billy Packer ridiculed the committee for awarding Mason an at-large bid. Three weeks later, the joke was on the CBS analyst, when he found himself courtside for George Mason's Final Four game against Florida. The Patriots lost, but the No. 11 seed had already made history by knocking off Michigan State, North Carolina, Wichita State and Connecticut to win its region.

BEST PLAYER: F GEORGE EVANS (1997-2001) By the time Evans finished his career, he was a three-time Colonial Athletic Association POY, Mason's No. 3 all-time scorer and rebounder—and 30 years old. The burly 6'7" forward was a Gulf War vet who spent seven years in the Army, where he grew six inches.

BEST COACH: JIM LARRANAGA (1997-) His 9–18 rookie season is the last in which the Patriots had a losing record. Since then, Larranaga has nabbed three CAA tourney titles and four NCAA bids. And as accomplished as he is as a coach, he's equally skilled with a microphone; his playful quips were among the most memorable parts of Mason's Final Four run.

GAME FOR THE AGES: Leading up to the 2006 Elite Eight matchup vs. No. 1-seed UConn, Larranaga kept his players loose by playing up the way their conference had been mocked, declaring that CAA stood for "Connecticut Assassin Association." His team proved him right, hitting five shots in OT to win, 86-84.

FIERCEST RIVAL: The proximity between two Virginia schools, James Madison and George Mason, breeds contempt—not to mention a classic chant at the end of Mason's home victories. To get the Dukes out of Fairfax and home to Harrisonburg as quickly as possible, Patriot Center crowds yell out highway directions, "66 West, 81 South!" JMU leads the series, 49–37.

SEASON REVIEW

SEAS.	W-L	CONF.		SCORING		COACH	RECORD	
1966-67	6-12					Arnold Siegfried	6-12	.333
1967-68	5-17			Hal Woodside	24.8	Raymond Spuhler		
1968-69	2-20					Raymond Spuhler		
1969-70	4-23					Raymond Spuhler	11-60	.155
1970-71	9-17					John Linn		
1971-72	12-18			Rudolph Jones	26.6	John Linn		
1972-73	15-16			Rudolph Jones	25.1	John Linn		
1973-74	19-10			Herb Estes	23.2	John Linn		
1974-75	19-8					John Linn		
1975-76	16-13			Levester Berry	20.1	John Linn		
1976-77	9-19					John Linn		
1977-78	9-17					John Linn		
1978-79	17-8			Andre Gaddy	20.3	John Linn		
1979-80	5-21					John Linn	130-147	.469
1980-81	10-16			Dave Skaff	20.1	Joe Harrington		
1981-82	13-14	2-6				Joe Harrington		
1982-83	15-12	3-6		Carlos Yates	26.8	Joe Harrington		
1983-84	21-7	5-5		Carlos Yates	22.1	Joe Harrington		
1984-85	18-11	10-4		Carlos Yates	23.9	Joe Harrington		
1985-86	20-12	10-4	■			Joe Harrington		
1986-87	15-13	7-7				Joe Harrington	112-85	.569
1987-88	20-10	9-5		Kenny Sanders	22.0	Rick Barnes	20-10	.667
1988-89	20-11	10-4	●	Kenny Sanders	22.7	Ernie Nestor		
1989-90	20-12	10-4				Ernie Nestor		
1990-91	14-16	8-6				Ernie Nestor		
1991-92	7-21	3-11		Byron Tucker	20.7	Ernie Nestor		
1992-93	7-21	2-12				Ernie Nestor	68-81	.456
1993-94	10-17	5-9				Paul Westhead		
1994-95	7-20	2-12				Paul Westhead		
1995-96	11-16	6-10		Curtis McCants	22.0	Paul Westhead		
1996-97	10-17	4-12		Nate Langley	20.9	Paul Westhead	38-70	.352
1997-98	9-18	6-10		Jason Miskiri	15.9	Jim Larranaga		
1998-99	19-11	13-3	●	George Evans	17.2	Jim Larranaga		
1999-2000	19-11	12-4		George Evans	18.1	Jim Larranaga		
2000-01	18-12	11-5	●	George Evans	18.4	Jim Larranaga		
2001-02	19-10	13-5	■	Jesse Young	14.6	Jim Larranaga		
2002-03	16-12	11-7		Mark Davis	15.5	Jim Larranaga		
2003-04	23-10	12-6	■	Jai Lewis	14.5	Jim Larranaga		
2004-05	16-13	10-8		Lamar Butler	15.7	Jim Larranaga		
2005-06	27-8	15-3	●	Jai Lewis	13.7	Jim Larranaga		
2006-07	18-15	9-9		Folarin Campbell	13.9	Jim Larranaga		
2007-08	23-11	12-6	●	Will Thomas	16.1	Jim Larranaga		
2008-09	22-11	13-5	■	Cam Long	11.7	Jim Larranaga	229-142	.617

● NCAA Tournament appearance ■ NIT appearance

PROFILE

George Mason University, Fairfax, VA
Founded: 1957
Enrollment: 30,714 (18,809 undergraduate)
Colors: Green and gold
Nickname: Patriots
Current arena: Patriot Center, opened in 1985 (10,000)
First game: Dec. 6, 1966
All-time record: 614-607 (.503)
Total weeks in AP Top 20/25: 0

Current conference: Colonial Athletic Association (1979-)
Conference titles:
CAA: 3 (1999, 2000 [tie], '06 [tie])
Conference tournament titles:
CAA: 4 (1989, '99, 2001, '08)
NCAA Tournament appearances: 5
Sweet 16s (since 1975): 1
Final Fours: 1
NIT appearances: 4

TOP 5

G **Jason Miskiri** (1997-99)
G **Carlos Yates** (1981-85)
F **George Evans** (1997-2001)
F **Kenny Sanders** (1985-89)
F **Will Thomas** (2004-08)

RECORDS

RECORDS	GAME		SEASON		CAREER	
POINTS	42	Carlos Yates, vs. Navy (Feb. 27, 1985)	779	Rudolph Jones (1972-73)	2,420	Carlos Yates (1981-85)
POINTS PER GAME			26.8	Carlos Yates (1982-83)	25.8	Rudolph Jones (1971-73)
REBOUNDS	24	Jim Nowers, vs. D.C. Teachers (Feb. 23, 1974)	353	Will Thomas (2007-08)	1,048	Jim Nowers (1972-76)
ASSISTS	15	Curtis McCants, vs. Richmond (Feb. 22, 1995)	251	Curtis McCants (1994-95)	598	Curtis McCants (1993-96)

ESPN 97 SAGARIN

GEORGE WASHINGTON

Red Auerbach never let it go. As a GW sophomore in the 1937-38 season, he felt his team was overlooked for the first NIT because the organizers didn't want the Colonials beating any of the favored New York City teams. As writer Dan Shaughnessy recounted five decades later, the legendary coach viewed every Celtics victory at Madison Square Garden as payback for that slight. If he were alive today, Auerbach would be pleased to know that it's not often GW is overlooked in the postseason these days. The Colonials have made eight NCAA Tournaments and three NITs since 1993.

BEST TEAM: 1992-93 The formative moment in the Colonials' Sweet 16 run actually occurred in 1991, when a GW assistant fell for the game of a Nigerian teenager named Yinka Dare. Two years later, the "next Olajuwon" was patrolling the paint for Mike Jarvis' squad, with his rebounding and shot-blocking setting the tone. As a No. 12 seed, GW upset No. 5-seed New Mexico, 82-68, in the NCAA Tournament's first round, then got past Southern before falling to No. 1-seed Michigan, 72-64.

BEST PLAYER: C Joe Holup (1952-56) GW's No. 2 all-time scorer (2,226 points) and its all-time leading rebounder (2,030), Holup led the Colonials' first NCAA Tournament team in 1954. He's one of only two players in NCAA history to amass more than 2,000 points and 2,000 rebounds. (La Salle's Tom Gola is the other.)

BEST COACH: Bill Reinhart (1935-42, '49-66) Auerbach credited Reinhart with inventing the fast break and with influencing his overall coaching philosophy. Thanks to Reinhart's highly structured practices, his teams routinely ranked among the nation's best in scoring, rebounding and field-goal percentage. He led the Colonials to their first two NCAA Tournament appearances (1954, '61) and also to their first national ranking, during the 1953-54 season.

GAME FOR THE AGES: On Feb. 4, 1995, top-ranked Massachusetts came to town in a nationally televised game, and Hoops-Fan-in-Chief Bill Clinton was in attendance. Coach Jarvis, a man-to-man stalwart, surprised counterpart John Calipari with an effective zone defense in the Colonials' 78-75 upset. Afterward, GW students stormed the floor while the president gave a thumbs up.

HEARTBREAKER: During the 1970s, D.C. rivals Georgetown and George Washington engaged in a series of intense matchups, none more dramatic than host GU's 78-77 OT win on Feb. 23, 1978. GW thought it had the game won at the end of regulation, when Les Anderson's shot put the Colonials up two, and even started celebrating. But the refs ruled that :02 still remained—enough time for Hoyas guard Craig Esherick to hit a miracle 25-footer.

FIERCEST RIVAL: GW was a thorn in UMass' side during Calipari's mid-1990s heyday, and more recently has waged a war for Atlantic 10 supremacy with Xavier. But its most heated rivalry is a dormant one. GU and GW stopped playing in 1983, because—as Colonials fans see it—John Thompson didn't want to risk losing to the perpetual underdog Colonials. Maybe his heart simply couldn't handle it. Eight of their last 13 games were decided by five points or less, and three of the last eight contests went to overtime.

Holup is one of only two players to amass more than 2,000 points and 2,000 rebounds.

FANFARE AND HOOPLA: It's hard enough for opposing free throw shooters to concentrate as the 5,000-seat Charles E. Smith Center pulsates with fan noise. It's nearly impossible when facing a GW student section whose members are often decked out in tricornered Styrofoam hats.

FAN FAVORITE: G Shawnta Rogers (1995-99) Standing just a shade under 5'4", the 1999 A-10 Player of the Year endeared himself to the Colonials faithful as a mighty mite, finishing as GW's all-time assists leader with 634 (5.6 apg) and all-time steals leader with 310 (2.7 spg).

THE SCHOOLS

PROFILE

The George Washington University, Washington, D.C.
Founded: 1821
Enrollment: 24,092 (10,967)
Colors: Buff and blue
Nickname: Colonials
Current arena: Charles E. Smith Athletic Center, opened in 1975 (5,000)
First game: 1906
All-time record: 1,187-1,012 (.540)
Total weeks in AP Top 20/25: 72
Current conference: Atlantic 10 (1976-)

Conference titles:
Southern: 2 (1954, '56 [tie]); Atlantic 10: 5 (1996 [tie], '98 [tie], '99 [tie], 2005 [tie], '06)
Conference tournament titles:
Southern: 3 (1943, '54, '61); Atlantic 10: 2 (2005, '07)
NCAA Tournament appearances: 10
Sweet 16s (since 1975): 1
NIT appearances: 4

CONSENSUS ALL-AMERICAS

1976 **Pat Tallent**, G
1986 **Steve Frick**, F/C

FIRST-ROUND PRO PICKS

1956 **Joe Holup**, Syracuse (5)
1994 **Yinka Dare**, New Jersey (14)

TOP 5

G **Shawnta Rogers** (1995-99)
G **Pat Tallent** (1972-73, '74-76)
F **Mike Hall** (2002-06)
F **Yegor Mescheriakov** (1995-99)
C **Joe Holup** (1952-56)

RECORDS	GAME		SEASON		CAREER	
POINTS	49	Joe Holup, vs. Furman (Feb. 17, 1956)	738	SirValiant Brown (1999-2000)	2,249	Chris Monroe (1999-2003)
POINTS PER GAME			28.9	Bob Tallent (1968-69)	21.4	Joe Holup (1952-56)
REBOUNDS	33	Clyde Burwell, vs. Mount St. Mary's (Dec. 10, 1973)	604	Joe Holup (1955-56)	2,030	Joe Holup (1952-56)
ASSISTS	15	Ellis McKennie, vs. St. Bonaventure (March 4, 1990)	196	Shawnta Rogers (1998-99)	634	Shawnta Rogers (1995-99)

SEASON REVIEW

SEASON	W-L	CONF.	SCORING		COACH	RECORD	
1906-15	*16-37*		*No winning seasons*				
1915-16	2-10				George Colliflower		
1916-17	7-8				George Colliflower	9-18	.333
1917-18	5-6				B. Groesbeck, Murphy[a]	5-6	.455
1918-19	no team						
1919-20	no team						
1920-21	4-10				Bryan Morse		
1921-22	8-6				Bryan Morse		
1922-23	4-11				Bryan Morse	16-27	.372
1923-24	1-9				Jack Dailey		
1924-25	7-5				Jack Dailey	8-14	.364
1925-26	5-9				James Lemon		
1926-27	8-7				James Lemon	13-16	.448
1927-28	11-6				Maud Crum		
1928-29	2-8				Maud Crum	13-14	.482
1929-30	9-7				Joe Mitchell	9-7	.563
1930-31	11-5		Forrest Burgess	12.3	Jim Pixlee		
1931-32	11-4		Forrest Burgess	11.1	Jim Pixlee		
1932-33	15-5		Forrest Burgess	10.7	Ted O'Leary		
1933-34	11-4		Jimmy Howell	12.0	Ted O'Leary	26-9	.743
1934-35	14-6		Ben Goldfaden	8.9	Jim Pixlee[b]	36-15	.706
1935-36	16-3		Tommy O'Brien	10.2	Bill Reinhart		

SEAS.	W-L	CONF.	POSTSEASON	SCORING		REBOUNDS		ASSISTS		COACH	RECORD	
1936-37	16-4			Hal Kiesel	8.2					Bill Reinhart		
1937-38	13-4			Robert Faris	10.1					Bill Reinhart		
1938-39	13-8			Robert Faris	12.1					Bill Reinhart		
1939-40	13-6			Red Auerbach	8.5					Bill Reinhart		
1940-41	18-4			Matt Zunic	11.5					Bill Reinhart		
1941-42	11-9	8-3		Matt Zunic	13.3					Bill Reinhart		
1942-43	17-6	8-2		Jim Rausch	9.8					Arthur "Otts" Zahn		
1943-44	no team											
1944-45	no team											
1945-46	7-8	4-5								Arthur "Otts" Zahn		
1946-47	21-7	9-4		Bill Cantwell	10.6					Arthur "Otts" Zahn	45-21	.682
1947-48	19-7	13-3		Bill Cantwell	11.7					George Garber		
1948-49	18-8	9-4		Maynard Haithcock	9.8					George Garber	37-15	.712
1949-50	17-8	12-4		John Moffatt	12.4					Bill Reinhart		
1950-51	12-12	8-9		Art Cerra	13.3					Bill Reinhart		
1951-52	15-9	12-6		John Holup	13.6					Bill Reinhart		
1952-53	15-7	12-6		Joe Holup	19.4					Bill Reinhart		
1953-54	23-3	10-0	NCAA FIRST ROUND	Corky Devlin	21.2	Joe Holup	18.6			Bill Reinhart		
1954-55	24-6	8-2		Corky Devlin	22.6	Joe Holup	18.2			Bill Reinhart		
1955-56	19-7	10-2		Joe Holup	25.0	Joe Holup	23.0			Bill Reinhart		
1956-57	3-21	3-9		Gene Guarilia	17.1	Gene Guarilia	12.2			Bill Reinhart		
1957-58	12-11	8-4		Bucky McDonald	17.8	Gene Guarilia	11.1			Bill Reinhart		
1958-59	14-11	4-7		Bucky McDonald	17.8	Gene Guarilia	18.6			Bill Reinhart		
1959-60	15-11	7-5		Jon Feldman	21.0	Dick Markowitz	9.9			Bill Reinhart		
1960-61	9-17	3-9	NCAA FIRST ROUND	Jon Feldman	20.4	Dick Markowitz	10.3			Bill Reinhart		
1961-62	9-15	6-7		Jon Feldman	21.7	Joe Adamitis	11.8			Bill Reinhart		
1962-63	8-15	6-6		Kenny Legins	15.4	Joe Adamitis	11.5			Bill Reinhart		
1963-64	11-15	5-7		Joe Adamitis	17.8	Joe Adamitis	16.0			Bill Reinhart		
1964-65	10-13	6-7		Phil Aruscavage	15.9	Kenny Legins	10.3			Bill Reinhart		
1965-66	3-18	3-9		Joe Lalli	16.9	Dick Ballard	8.4			Bill Reinhart	319-237	.574
1966-67	6-18	5-7		Joe Lalli, Terry Grefe	17.5	Dick Ballard	7.6			Babe McCarthy	6-18	.250
1967-68	5-19	2-12		Roger Strong	14.2	Roger Strong	9.5			Wayne Dobbs		
1968-69	14-11	7-5		Bob Tallent	28.9	Bill Knorr	11.7			Wayne Dobbs		
1969-70	12-15	6-4		Mike Tallent	21.1	Walt Szczerbiak	11.7			Wayne Dobbs	31-45	.408
1970-71	11-14			Walt Szczerbiak	22.8	Walt Szczerbiak	13.0			Carl Slone		
1971-72	11-14			Ronnie Nunn	15.4	Mike Battle	9.5			Carl Slone		
1972-73	17-9			Pat Tallent	18.8	Clyde Burwell	10.7	Pat Tallent	4.0	Carl Slone		
1973-74	15-11			Keith Morris	16.2	Clyde Burwell	12.5	Keith Morris	4.1	Carl Slone	54-48	.529
1974-75	17-10			Pat Tallent	20.3	Clyde Burwell	11.3	Pat Tallent	3.1	Bob Tallent		
1975-76	20-7			Pat Tallent	23.0	Les Anderson	8.5	John Holloran	5.5	Bob Tallent		
1976-77	14-12	5-3		John Holloran	21.4	Les Anderson	9.2	John Holloran	4.9	Bob Tallent		
1977-78	15-11	4-6		Mike Zagardo	15.6	Mike Zagardo	8.7	Tom Tate	4.6	Bob Tallent		
1978-79	13-14	5-5		Mike Zagardo	16.0	Mike Zagardo	9.2	Tom Tate	4.7	Bob Tallent		
1979-80	15-11	5-5		Brian Magid	15.6	Mike Zagardo	8.6	Curtis Jeffries	3.6	Bob Tallent		
1980-81	8-19	4-9		Randy Davis	13.9	Paul Gracza	6.6	Randy Davis	3.8	Bob Tallent	102-84	.548
1981-82	13-14	7-7		Mike Brown	15.6	Mike Brown	8.5	Mike Brey	4.8	Gerry Gimelstob		
1982-83	14-15	4-10		T. Webster, M. Brown	17.1	Mike Brown	10.3	Mike O'Reilly	4.2	Gerry Gimelstob		
1983-84	17-12	11-7		Mike Brown	19.6	Mike Brown	12.1	Troy Webster	3.8	Gerry Gimelstob		
1984-85	14-14	9-9		Mike Brown	16.6	Mike Brown	11.0	Mike O'Reilly	4.0	Gerry Gimelstob	58-55	.513
1985-86	12-16	7-11		Troy Webster	14.6	Steve Frick	5.8	Mike O'Reilly	4.6	John Kuester		
1986-87	10-19	6-12		Gerald Jackson	13.7	Steve Frick	6.0	Gerald Jackson	4.9	John Kuester		
1987-88	13-15	7-11		Gerald Jackson	14.2	Mike Jones	6.9	Ellis McKennie	2.5	John Kuester		
1988-89	1-27	1-17		Glen Sitney	14.3	Mike Jones	7.3	Rodney Patterson	4.6	John Kuester		
1989-90	14-17	6-12		Ellis McKennie	16.3	Mike Jones	8.5	Ellis McKennie	5.8	John Kuester	50-94	.347
1990-91	19-12	10-8	NIT FIRST ROUND	Dirkk Surles	14.4	Ellis McKennie	5.1	Alvin Pearsall	5.3	Mike Jarvis		
1991-92	16-12	8-8		Dirkk Surles	19.9	Bill Brigham	8.2	Alvin Pearsall	6.3	Mike Jarvis		
1992-93	21-9	8-6	NCAA REGIONAL SEMIFINALS	Dirkk Surles	14.5	Yinka Dare	10.3	Alvin Pearsall	3.1	Mike Jarvis		
1993-94	18-12	8-8	NCAA SECOND ROUND	Yinka Dare	15.4	Yinka Dare	10.3	Alvin Pearsall	2.7	Mike Jarvis		
1994-95	18-14	10-6	NIT FIRST ROUND	Kwame Evans	19.4	Alexander Koul	6.6	Nimbo Hammons	3.6	Mike Jarvis		
1995-96	21-8	13-3	NCAA FIRST ROUND	Kwame Evans	18.7	Alexander Koul	7.8	Shawnta Rogers	6.5	Mike Jarvis		
1996-97	15-14	8-8	NIT FIRST ROUND	Yegor Mescheriakov	16.6	Alexander Koul	7.8	Shawnta Rogers	4.4	Mike Jarvis		
1997-98	24-9	11-5	NCAA FIRST ROUND	Shawnta Rogers	14.7	Alexander Koul	6.8	Shawnta Rogers	4.8	Mike Jarvis	152-90	.628
1998-99	20-9	13-3	NCAA FIRST ROUND	Shawnta Rogers	20.7	Yegor Mescheriakov	6.8	Shawnta Rogers	6.8	Tom Penders		
1999-2000	15-15	9-7		SirValiant Brown	24.6	Chris Monroe	6.8	Bernard Barrow	5.2	Tom Penders		
2000-01	14-18	6-10		Chris Monroe	18.7	Attila Cosby	7.2	Bernard Barrow	3.9	Tom Penders	49-42	.539
2001-02	12-16	5-11		Chris Monroe	21.1	Jaason Smith	7.8	T.J. Thompson	4.2	Karl Hobbs		
2002-03	12-17	5-11		Chris Monroe	20.3	Mike Hall	8.2	T.J. Thompson	6.1	Karl Hobbs		
2003-04	18-12	11-5	NIT FIRST ROUND	T.J. Thompson	13.2	Mike Hall	7.8	Carl Elliott	4.3	Karl Hobbs		
2004-05	22-8	11-5	NCAA FIRST ROUND	T.J. Thompson	13.6	Mike Hall	8.0	Carl Elliott	4.6	Karl Hobbs		
2005-06	27-3	16-0	NCAA SECOND ROUND	Danilo Pinnock	14.5	Mike Hall	7.6	Carl Elliott	3.9	Karl Hobbs		
2006-07	23-9	11-5	NCAA FIRST ROUND	Maureece Rice	15.1	Dokun Akingbade	5.6	Carl Elliott	4.8	Karl Hobbs		
2007-08	9-17	5-11		Rob Diggs	13.9	Rob Diggs	7.7	Maureece Rice	2.7	Karl Hobbs		
2008-09	10-18	4-12		Rob Diggs	13.4	Rob Diggs	7.3	Tony Taylor	2.8	Karl Hobbs	133-100	.571

[a] Bertram Groesbeck and Murphy served as co-coaches during the 1917-18 season. [b] Jim Pixlee and Logan Wilson both coached during the 1934-35 season.

ESPN 42 SAGARIN

GEORGETOWN

Georgetown basketball is a family business. Beginning in the 1970s, John Thompson Jr. turned a small Jesuit school into a national power. Then, just as the program seemed to fade in the early 2000s, his son, John Thompson III, restored Hoyas glory. That sense of family has been passed down to the players, with a who's-who of great centers returning to campus year after year to tutor the next generation.

BEST TEAM: 1983-84 Hoya Paranoia reached a pinnacle as junior center Patrick Ewing took the team on a national rampage, winning a school-record 34 games (to be broken the following season), capped by an 84-75 victory over Houston in an epic NCAA championship game that pitted Ewing against Hakeem Olajuwon. Although the Dream won the head-to-head battle, 15 points to 10, Ewing had more help, as four of his teammates scored in double figures.

BEST PLAYER: C PATRICK EWING (1981-85) Still the school's all-time leading rebounder and shot blocker, Ewing carried the Hoyas to the NCAA Final in three of his four seasons, including the 1984 championship. In doing so, he solidified Georgetown as a marquee team, setting the stage for the likes of big men Alonzo Mourning and Dikembe Mutombo. John Thompson always said Ewing could score more than the 15.3 points he averaged at Georgetown; sure enough, he averaged 21.0 a game in 17 NBA seasons.

BEST COACH: JOHN THOMPSON JR. (1972-99) In 27 seasons, the sideline giant (and former NBA center) reached the Final Four three times and won a national title. He did all of this at a school that had little winning tradition—the Hoyas were 3–23 the season before Thompson arrived. The Hall of Famer's legacy was built by dominating big men and rugged, relentless defense.

GAME FOR THE AGES: It's known as the Sweater Game. Mounted police surrounded Madison Square Garden on Feb. 27, 1985, as No. 2-ranked Georgetown looked to avenge a one-point loss to top-ranked St. John's earlier that season. But they didn't bar good humor from the building. St. John's coach Lou Carnesecca had taken to wearing a colorful lucky sweater, so Thompson answered with a replica under his blazer. The game turned into a laugher, too, as the Hoyas won, 85-69.

HEARTBREAKER: While the image of Fred Brown mistakenly throwing a pass to North Carolina's James Worthy in the 1982 national title game is shown every March, that moment pales in comparison to the 1985 NCAA Final. The Hoyas were heavy favorites over Big East rival Villanova. But what was supposed to be the crowning moment of Ewing's career turned into a nightmare, as Nova missed just one shot in the second half to pull off a stunning 66-64 upset.

FIERCEST RIVAL: It started when Thompson declared, "Manley Field House is officially closed," a dig at Syracuse after winning the final game on the Orange's then-home court on Feb. 13, 1980. Since that time, the Hoyas and the Orange have routinely battled for Big East titles—or at least bragging rights. Syracuse leads the series, 44–37.

FANFARE AND HOOPLA: In the early 1980s, the Big East's many large, multipurpose arenas (with ice rinks beneath the court) left Ewing feeling cold, so he started wearing a gray T-shirt under his jersey, unintentionally giving birth to a fashion trend.

FAN FAVORITE: C DIKEMBE MUTOMBO (1988-91) As a freshman at Midnight Madness, the 7'2" Congolese center extended his arms, waving to the crowd like a presidential candidate. Mutombo's goofy grin never disappeared in his three seasons in D.C., and his charitable work during an often-standout 18-year NBA career has endeared him even more to his alma mater.

CONSENSUS ALL-AMERICAS

1982	**Eric Floyd**, G
1983-85	**Patrick Ewing**, C
1987	**Reggie Williams**, F
1992	**Alonzo Mourning**, F/C
1996	**Allen Iverson**, G

FIRST-ROUND PRO PICKS

1980	**John Duren**, Utah (19)
1982	**Eric Floyd**, New Jersey (13)
1985	**Patrick Ewing**, New York (1)
1987	**Reggie Williams**, LA Clippers (4)
1991	**Dikembe Mutombo**, Denver (4)
1992	**Alonzo Mourning**, Charlotte (2)
1996	**Allen Iverson**, Philadelphia (1)
1996	**Jerome Williams**, Detroit (26)
2003	**Mike Sweetney**, New York (9)
2007	**Jeff Green**, Seattle (5)
2008	**Roy Hibbert**, Toronto (17)

PROFILE

Georgetown University, Washington, D.C.
Founded: 1789
Enrollment: 15,318 (7,092 undergraduate)
Colors: Blue and gray
Nickname: Hoyas
Current arena: Verizon Center, opened in 1997 (20,600); McDonough Arena, opened in 1951 (2,400)
First game: 1906
All-time record: 1,476-924 (.615)
Total weeks in AP Top 20/25: 326

Current conference: Big East (1979-)
Conference titles:
Big East: 9 (1980, '84, '87, '89, '92, '96, '97, 2007, '08)
Conference tournament titles:
Big East: 7 (1980, '82, '84, '85, '87, '89, 2007)
NCAA Tournament appearances: 25
Sweet 16s (since 1975): 11
Final Fours: 5
Titles: 1 (1984)
NIT appearances: 11
Semifinals: 3

TOP 5

G	**Eric Floyd** (1978-82)
G	**Allen Iverson** (1994-96)
F	**Reggie Williams** (1983-87)
F/C	**Alonzo Mourning** (1988-92)
C	**Patrick Ewing** (1981-85)

RECORDS	GAME		SEASON		CAREER	
POINTS	46	Jim Barry, vs. Fairleigh Dickinson (Feb. 27, 1965)	926	Allen Iverson (1995-96)	2,304	Eric Floyd (1978-82)
POINTS PER GAME			25.0	Allen Iverson (1995-96)	23.0	Allen Iverson (1994-96)
REBOUNDS	29	Charlie Adrion, vs. George Washington (Feb. 10, 1968)	389	Dikembe Mutombo (1990-91)	1,316	Patrick Ewing (1981-85)
ASSISTS	16	Kevin Braswell, vs. Rutgers (Mar. 2, 2002); Charles Smith, vs. St. Leo (Dec. 7, 1988)	242	Michael Jackson (1984-85)	695	Kevin Braswell (1998-2002)

THE SCHOOLS

SEASON REVIEW

SEASON	W-L	CONF.	SCORING	COACH	RECORD		SEASON	W-L	CONF.	SCORING	COACH	RECORD	
1906-15	*74-47*		*Includes only one losing season (5-7 in 1909-10)*				**1925-26**	5-8			John O'Reilly		
1915-16	9-6			John O'Reilly			**1926-27**	5-4			John O'Reilly	87-47	.649
1916-17	8-4			John O'Reilly			**1927-28**	12-1			Elmer Ripley		
1917-18	8-6			John O'Reilly			**1928-29**	12-5			Elmer Ripley		
1918-19	9-1			John O'Reilly			**1929-30**	13-12			Bill Dudak	13-12	.520
1919-20	13-1			John O'Reilly			**1930-31**	5-16			John Colrick	5-16	.238
1920-21	10-4			John O'Reilly			**1931-32**	6-11			Fred Mesmer		
1921-22	11-3			James Colliflower	43-20	.683	**1932-33**	6-11	3-5		Fred Mesmer		
1922-23	8-3			Jock Maloney	8-3	.727	**1933-34**	12-11	5-5		Fred Mesmer		
1923-24	6-3			John O'Reilly			**1934-35**	6-13	1-7		Fred Mesmer		
1924-25	6-2			John O'Reilly			**1935-36**	7-11	4-6		Fred Mesmer		

SEAS.	W-L	CONF.	POSTSEASON	SCORING		REBOUNDS		ASSISTS		COACH	RECORD	
1936-37	9-8	3-7								Fred Mesmer		
1937-38	7-11	5-5								Fred Mesmer	53-76	.411
1938-39	13-9	6-4								Elmer Ripley		
1939-40	8-10									Elmer Ripley		
1940-41	16-4									Elmer Ripley		
1941-42	9-11									Elmer Ripley		
1942-43	22-5		NCAA RUNNER-UP	John Mahnken	15.4					Elmer Ripley		
1943-44	no team											
1944-45	no team											
1945-46	11-9			Edward Drysgula	10.0					Ken Engles	11-9	.550
1946-47	19-7			Andy Kostecka	17.8					Elmer Ripley		
1947-48	13-15			Tom O'Keefe	9.6					Elmer Ripley		
1948-49	9-15			Tom O'Keefe	12.3					Elmer Ripley	133-82	.619
1949-50	12-12			Tom O'Keefe	14.5					Buddy O'Grady		
1950-51	8-14			Barry Sullivan	16.1					Buddy O'Grady		
1951-52	15-10			Bill Bolger	17.4					Buddy O'Grady	35-36	.493
1952-53	13-7		NIT FIRST ROUND	Bill Bolger	18.3					Harry Jeannette		
1953-54	11-18			Warren Buehler	18.2	Jack Vail	10.0			Harry Jeannette		
1954-55	12-13			Warren Buehler	15.4	Joe Missett	9.8			Harry Jeannette		
1955-56	13-11			Joe Missett	18.4	Joe Missett	13.5			Harry Jeannette	49-49	.500
1956-57	11-11			Joe Missett	15.9	Joe Missett	7.5			Tommy Nolan		
1957-58	10-11			Ken Pichette	16.6	Ken Pichette	7.0			Tommy Nolan		
1958-59	8-15			Brian Sheehan	18.6	Tom Coleman	7.1			Tommy Nolan		
1959-60	11-12			Brian Sheehan	15.7	Paul Tagliabue	8.9			Tommy Nolan	40-49	.449
1960-61	11-10			Brian Sheehan	14.1	Paul Tagliabue	8.2			Tom O'Keefe		
1961-62	14-9			Bob Sharpenter	18.0	Bob Sharpenter	12.5			Tom O'Keefe		
1962-63	13-13			Jim Barry	22.6	Jim Barry	8.2			Tom O'Keefe		
1963-64	15-10			Jim Christy	17.5	Owen Gillen	9.1			Tom O'Keefe		
1964-65	13-10			Jim Barry	19.1	Jim Barry	6.2			Tom O'Keefe		
1965-66	16-8			Steve Sullivan	15.1	Steve Sullivan	9.7			Tom O'Keefe	82-60	.577
1966-67	12-11			Steve Sullivan	18.6	Steve Sullivan	11.8			Jack Magee		
1967-68	11-12			Charlie Adrion	14.0	Charlie Adrion	10.2			Jack Magee		
1968-69	12-12			Jim Supple	16.5	Charlie Adrion	11.8			Jack Magee		
1969-70	18-7		NIT FIRST ROUND	Art White	15.1	Mike Laughna	10.4			Jack Magee		
1970-71	12-14			Mike Laughna	17.7	Mike Laughna	10.9			Jack Magee		
1971-72	3-23			Mike Laughna	16.8	Mike Laughna	11.0			Jack Magee	68-79	.463
1972-73	12-14			Jon Smith	14.0	Merlin Wilson	14.1			John Thompson Jr.		
1973-74	13-13			Jon Smith	17.9	Merlin Wilson	15.5			John Thompson Jr.		
1974-75	18-10		NCAA FIRST ROUND	Jon Smith	10.9	Merlin Wilson	8.6			John Thompson Jr.		
1975-76	21-7		NCAA FIRST ROUND	Derrick Jackson	17.0	Merlin Wilson	9.8			John Thompson Jr.		
1976-77	19-9		NIT FIRST ROUND	Derrick Jackson	16.8	Ed Hopkins	8.4			John Thompson Jr.		
1977-78	23-8		NIT FOURTH PLACE	Derrick Jackson	17.8	Craig Shelton	8.3			John Thompson Jr.		
1978-79	24-5		NCAA SECOND ROUND	Eric Floyd	16.6	Craig Shelton	8.2			John Thompson Jr.		
1979-80	26-6	5-1	NCAA REGIONAL FINALS	Eric Floyd	18.7	Craig Shelton	7.0			John Thompson Jr.		
1980-81	20-12	9-5	NCAA FIRST ROUND	Eric Floyd	19.0	Ed Spriggs	4.2			John Thompson Jr.		
1981-82	30-7	10-4	NCAA RUNNER-UP	Eric Floyd	16.7	Patrick Ewing	7.5			John Thompson Jr.		
1982-83	22-10	11-5	NCAA SECOND ROUND	Patrick Ewing	17.7	Patrick Ewing	10.2			John Thompson Jr.		
1983-84	**34-3**	**14-2**	**NATIONAL CHAMPION**	**Patrick Ewing**	**16.4**	**Patrick Ewing**	**10.0**			**John Thompson Jr.**		
1984-85	35-3	14-2	NCAA RUNNER-UP	Patrick Ewing	14.6	Patrick Ewing	9.2			John Thompson Jr.		
1985-86	24-8	11-5	NCAA SECOND ROUND	Reggie Williams	17.6	Reggie Williams	8.2			John Thompson Jr.		
1986-87	29-5	12-4	NCAA REGIONAL FINALS	Reggie Williams	23.0	Reggie Williams	8.7			John Thompson Jr.		
1987-88	20-10	9-7	NCAA SECOND ROUND	Charles Smith	15.7	Perry McDonald	6.3			John Thompson Jr.		
1988-89	29-5	13-3	NCAA REGIONAL FINALS	Charles Smith	18.7	Alonzo Mourning	7.3			John Thompson Jr.		
1989-90	24-7	11-5	NCAA SECOND ROUND	Mark Tillmon	19.8	Dikembe Mutombo	10.5			John Thompson Jr.		
1990-91	19-13	8-8	NCAA SECOND ROUND	Dikembe Mutombo	15.2	Dikembe Mutombo	12.2			John Thompson Jr.		
1991-92	22-10	12-6	NCAA SECOND ROUND	Alonzo Mourning	21.3	Alonzo Mourning	10.7			John Thompson Jr.		
1992-93	20-13	8-10	NIT RUNNER-UP	Othella Harrington	16.8	Othella Harrington	8.8			John Thompson Jr.		
1993-94	19-12	10-8	NCAA SECOND ROUND	Othella Harrington	14.7	Othella Harrington	8.0			John Thompson Jr.		
1994-95	21-10	11-7	NCAA REGIONAL SEMIFINALS	Allen Iverson	20.4	Jerome Williams	10.0			John Thompson Jr.		
1995-96	29-8	13-5	NCAA REGIONAL FINALS	Allen Iverson	25.0	Jerome Williams	8.9			John Thompson Jr.		
1996-97	20-10	11-7	NCAA FIRST ROUND	Victor Page	22.7	Ya Ya Dia	10.1			John Thompson Jr.		
1997-98	16-15	6-12	NIT SECOND ROUND	Shernard Long	13.1	Boubacar Aw	6.2			John Thompson Jr.		
1998-99	15-16	6-12	NIT FIRST ROUND	Anthony Perry	14.0	Jameel Watkins	8.2	Kevin Braswell	4.5	John Thompson Jr.		
1999-2000	19-15	6-10	NIT SECOND ROUND	Kevin Braswell	14.8	Ruben Boumtje-Boumtje	7.7	Kevin Braswell	5.3	John Thompson Jr.[a]	596-239	.714
2000-01	25-8	10-6	NCAA REGIONAL SEMIFINALS	Mike Sweetney	12.8	Mike Sweetney	7.4	Kevin Braswell	6.1	Craig Esherick		
2001-02	19-11	9-7		Mike Sweetney	19.0	Mike Sweetney	10.0	Kevin Braswell	4.8	Craig Esherick		
2002-03	19-15	6-10	NIT RUNNER-UP	Mike Sweetney	22.8	Mike Sweetney	10.4	Tony Bethel	3.6	Craig Esherick		
2003-04	13-15	4-12		Gerald Riley	17.0	Brandon Bowman	8.1	Ashanti Cook	3.8	Craig Esherick	103-74	.582
2004-05	19-13	8-8	NIT QUARTERFINALS	Brandon Bowman	15.1	Jeff Green	6.6	Jeff Green	2.9	John Thompson III		
2005-06	23-10	10-6	NCAA REGIONAL SEMIFINALS	Jeff Green	11.9	Roy Hibbert	6.9	Jeff Green	3.2	John Thompson III		
2006-07	30-7	13-3	NCAA NATIONAL SEMIFINALS	Jeff Green	14.3	Roy Hibbert	6.9	Jessie Sapp	3.5	John Thompson III		
2007-08	28-6	15-3	NCAA SECOND ROUND	Roy Hibbert	13.4	Roy Hibbert	6.4	Jessie Sapp	3.2	John Thompson III		
2008-09	16-15	7-11	NIT FIRST ROUND	DaJuan Summers	13.6	Greg Monroe	6.5	Chris Wright	3.8	John Thompson III	116-51	.695

[a] Craig Esherick (8-10) and John Thompson Jr. (7-6) both coached during the 1999-2000 season.

ESPN 101 SAGARIN

GEORGIA

It would be a huge mistake to think the Bulldogs' legacy begins and ends with Dominique Wilkins. Consider arena namesake Herman J. Stegeman's 12 teams in the early 20th century that went 170–78 (.685). And the 1953 All-America honorable mention, Zippy Morocco. Or the two-time All-America honorable mention, forward Bob Lienhard, who averaged at least 21 points and 13 rebounds for three straight seasons from 1967 to '70. And we're still just skimming the surface.

BEST TEAM: 1982-83 No height, no shooters, no tradition—so what? All-America guard Vern Fleming was the catalyst (16.9 ppg) on an unselfish team that got strength-in-numbers leadership from spirited forward James Banks (14.0 ppg), defensive stalwart Terry Fair (13.7), complementary guard Gerald Crosby (11.0) and assertive forward Lamar Heard (7.1). The Bulldogs rode this wave of chemistry to runaway wins in the tough Southeastern Conference tournament, qualified for their first NCAA Tournament and made the Final Four, knocking off top East Regional seeds St. John's and North Carolina along the way.

BEST PLAYER: F DOMINIQUE WILKINS (1979-82) The Human Highlight Film turned Georgia into an instant winner and himself into a legend with his acrobatic abilities. The All-America's best showings came in 1980-81 and '81-82, when he averaged 23.6 and 21.3 points, respectively, for squads that went 19–12 each season and made the NIT.

BEST COACH: HUGH DURHAM (1978-95) In 17 seasons, Durham used many different styles to get the Bulldogs to five NCAA Tournaments and seven NITs—the first postseason appearances in Georgia's history.

GAME FOR THE AGES: The Bulldogs found themselves down 10 to St. John's in the 1983 NCAA Sweet 16 before they finally got to work, relentlessly pressing Chris Mullin and the rest of the Redmen into submission. At the same time, Terry Fair proved that small centers can play big against a national power by scoring 27 in the 70-67 win.

HEARTBREAKER: Georgia coach Tubby Smith once lost a seven-overtime game in high school and said that the 1996 Sweet 16 OT loss to Syracuse was almost as tough to take. A last-second jumper from the Orangemen's Jason Cipolla sent the game into extra frames. There, John Wallace (30 points) made all the difference for Cuse. With 15 seconds left, the forward banked in a two-footer, giving Syracuse a 80-78 lead. After Bulldog Pertha Robinson (21 points) hit a three, Wallace took the inbounds coast to coast and splashed in a three to sink Georgia, 83-81.

FIERCEST RIVAL: "Clean, Old-Fashioned Hate." That's the name down South for a century-old rivalry between Georgia and Georgia Tech in which passions routinely overflow. Exhibit A: Jonas Hayes scored a career-high 25 points in a double-OT 83-80 win over the No. 3-ranked Yellow Jackets on Jan. 3, 2004, after which Georgia fans mobbed the Bulldogs at halfcourt. Both schools agree that Tech leads the series; it's either 100–84 (per UGA) or 101–84 (GT).

The Human Highlight Film turned Georgia into an instant winner and himself into a legend.

FANFARE AND HOOPLA: When Wilkins, a star at Washington (N.C.) High School, unexpectedly signed with Georgia in 1979, the furor in his home state was so fever-pitched that *Time* wrote a special dispatch about it called "The Strange Case of Dr. Dunk."

FAN FAVORITE: G VERN FLEMING (1980-84) He couldn't dunk like Nique—but then, who could? The point guard could still score in bunches, play tough defense, confidently run the show and bring out the best in his teammates. All these talents came together in 1983, when Fleming led the Bulldogs to their one and only Final Four appearance.

FIRST-ROUND PRO PICKS

1970	**Bob Lienhard,** Carolina (ABA)
1982	**Dominique Wilkins,** Utah (3)
1984	**Vern Fleming,** Indiana (18)
1988	**Willie Anderson,** San Antonio (10)
1990	**Alec Kessler,** Houston (12)
1999	**Jumaine Jones,** Atlanta (27)
2003	**Jarvis Hayes,** Washington (10)

PROFILE

University of Georgia, Athens, GA
Founded: 1785
Enrollment: 34,180 (25,002 undergraduate)
Colors: Red and black
Nickname: Bulldogs
Current arena: Stegeman Coliseum, opened as Georgia Coliseum in 1964 (10,523)
All-time record: 1,249-1,158 (.519)
First game: March 3, 1906
Total weeks in AP Top 20/25: 65

Current conference: Southeastern (1932-)
Conference titles:
Southern: 1 (1931)
SEC: 1 (1990)
Conference tournament titles:
Southern: 1 (1932)
SEC: 2 (1983, 2008)
NCAA Tournaments: 10 (2 appearances vacated)
Sweet 16s (since 1975): 2
Final Fours: 1
NIT appearances: 11
Semifinals: 2

TOP 5

G **Vern Fleming** (1980-84)
G **Litterial Green** (1988-92)
F **Bob Lienhard** (1967-70)
F **Dominique Wilkins** (1979-82)
C **Alec Kessler** (1986-90)

RECORDS	GAME		SEASON		CAREER	
POINTS	46	Ronnie Hogue, vs. LSU (Dec. 20, 1971)	732	Dominique Wilkins (1980-81)	2,111	Litterial Green (1988-92)
POINTS PER GAME			25.8	Jacky Dorsey (1974-75)	23.7	Jacky Dorsey (1974-76)
REBOUNDS	32	Bob Lienhard, vs. Sewanee (Dec. 3, 1968)	396	Bob Lienhard (1968-69)	1,116	Bob Lienhard (1967-70)
ASSISTS	15	Gino Gianfrancesco, vs. Georgia Tech (March 12, 1972)	169	Pertha Robinson (1994-95)	493	Rashad Wright (2000-04)

THE SCHOOLS

SEASON REVIEW

SEASON	W-L	CONF.	SCORING	COACH	RECORD	SEASON	W-L	CONF.	SCORING	COACH	RECORD
1905-18	*64-22*		*25-3 over three seasons from 1911-12 to 1913-14*			1928-29	18-6	13-4		Herman J. Stegeman	
1918-19	5-3			Kennon Mott	5-3 .625	1929-30	17-6	7-3		Herman J. Stegeman	
1919-20	9-7			Herman J. Stegeman		1930-31	23-2	15-1		Herman J. Stegeman	170-78 .685
1920-21	13-4			Herman J. Stegeman		1931-32	19-7	7-4		Vernon Smith	20-8 .714
1921-22	10-5	4-1		Herman J. Stegeman		1932-33	9-10	5-6		Rex Enright	
1922-23	11-8	3-3		Herman J. Stegeman		1933-34	10-9	3-6		Rex Enright	
1923-24	16-5	7-0		Herman J. Stegeman		1934-35	12-8	4-5		Rex Enright	
1924-25	9-11	4-4		Herman J. Stegeman		1935-36	9-11	6-7		Rex Enright	
1925-26	18-6	9-4		Herman J. Stegeman		1936-37	10-6	5-3		Rex Enright	
1926-27	14-8	3-6		Herman J. Stegeman		1937-38	12-10	4-6		Rex Enright[a]	52-49 .515
1927-28	12-10	8-5		Herman J. Stegeman		1938-39	11-6	8-3		Elmer Lampe	

SEAS.	W-L	CONF.	POSTSEASON	SCORING	REBOUNDS	ASSISTS	COACH	RECORD
1939-40	20-6	9-4					Elmer Lampe	
1940-41	13-11	6-7					Elmer Lampe	
1941-42	7-10	5-8					Elmer Lampe	
1942-43	4-13	1-8					Elmer Lampe	
1943-44	7-10	0-2					Elmer Lampe	
1944-45	5-16	2-9					Elmer Lampe	
1945-46	12-9	6-6					Elmer Lampe	
1946-47	5-14	4-9					Elmer Lampe[b]	81-86 .485
1947-48	18-10	6-8					Ralph Jordan	
1948-49	17-13	6-9					Ralph Jordan	
1949-50	15-9	6-7					Ralph Jordan[c]	44-39 .530
1950-51	13-11	6-8					Jim Whatley	24-18 .571
1951-52	3-22	2-12					Harbin Lawson	
1952-53	7-18	3-10		Zippy Morocco 23.6			Harbin Lawson	
1953-54	7-18	2-12					Harbin Lawson	
1954-55	9-16	7-7					Harbin Lawson	
1955-56	3-21	1-13					Harbin Lawson	
1956-57	8-16	4-10					Harbin Lawson	
1957-58	7-19	3-11					Harbin Lawson	
1958-59	11-15	5-9					Harbin Lawson	
1959-60	12-13	6-8		Phillip Simpson 14.1	Phillip Simpson 10.2		Harbin Lawson	
1960-61	8-18	4-10		Allan Johnson 14.9	John Johnson 10.0		Harbin Lawson	
1961-62	8-16	3-11		Allan Johnson 17.6	Carlton Gill 9.4		Harbin Lawson	
1962-63	9-17	4-10		Billy Rado 19.0	Chuck Adamek 7.5		Harbin Lawson	
1963-64	12-14	8-6		Jimmy Pitts 18.7	Jerry Waller 13.7		Harbin Lawson	
1964-65	8-18	4-12		Jimmy Pitts 18.5	Jerry Waller 10.8		Harbin Lawson	112-241 .317
1965-66	10-15	5-11		Jerry Waller 14.9	Jerry Waller 10.1		Ken Rosemond	
1966-67	9-17	5-13		Jim Youngblood 15.1	Don Wix 7.5		Ken Rosemond	
1967-68	17-8	11-7		Bob Lienhard 21.3	Bob Lienhard 14.9		Ken Rosemond	
1968-69	13-12	9-9		Bob Lienhard 23.8	Bob Lienhard 15.8		Ken Rosemond	
1969-70	13-12	11-7		Bob Lienhard 21.3	Bob Lienhard 13.9		Ken Rosemond	
1970-71	6-19	5-13		Ronnie Hogue 16.2	Cauthen Westbrook 7.8		Ken Rosemond	
1971-72	14-12	9-9		Ronnie Hogue 20.5	Tim Bassett 13.0		Ken Rosemond	
1972-73	10-16	5-13		Tim Bassett 17.0	Tim Bassett 14.2		Ken Rosemond	92-111 .453
1973-74	6-20	2-16		Billy Magarity 16.8	Billy Magarity 6.6		John Guthrie	
1974-75	8-17	3-15		Jacky Dorsey 25.8	Jacky Dorsey 11.8		John Guthrie	
1975-76	12-15	7-11		Jacky Dorsey 21.8	Jacky Dorsey 9.4		John Guthrie	
1976-77	9-18	3-15		David Reavis 14.3	Lavon Mercer 7.6		John Guthrie	
1977-78	11-16	5-13		Walter Daniels 16.4	Lavon Mercer 8.6	Walter Daniels 3.3	John Guthrie	46-86 .348
1978-79	14-14	7-11		Walter Daniels 21.9	Lavon Mercer 7.7	Jimmy Daughtry 3.5	Hugh Durham	
1979-80	14-13	7-11		Dominique Wilkins 18.6	Terry Fair 10.0	Jimmy Daughtry 2.9	Hugh Durham	
1980-81	19-12	9-9	NIT SECOND ROUND	Dominique Wilkins 23.6	Terry Fair 7.7	Vern Fleming 2.9	Hugh Durham	
1981-82	19-12	10-8	NIT SEMIFINALS	Dominique Wilkins 21.3	Dominique Wilkins 8.1	Vern Fleming 3.5	Hugh Durham	
1982-83	24-10	9-9	NCAA NATIONAL SEMIFINALS	Vern Fleming 16.9	Terry Fair 6.6	Vern Fleming 3.1	Hugh Durham	
1983-84	17-13	8-10	NIT FIRST ROUND	Vern Fleming 19.8	Richard Corhen 6.3	Gerald Crosby 4.0	Hugh Durham	
1984-85	22-9 ⊗	12-6	NCAA SECOND ROUND	Cedric Henderson 15.5	Cedric Henderson 7.1	Gerald Crosby 4.6	Hugh Durham	
1985-86	17-13	9-9	NIT SECOND ROUND	Joe Ward 15.6	Horace McMillan 5.9	Donald Hartry 5.1	Hugh Durham	
1986-87	18-12	10-8	NCAA FIRST ROUND	Willie Anderson 15.9	Chad Kessler 5.7	Willie Anderson 5.0	Hugh Durham	
1987-88	20-16	8-10	NIT SECOND ROUND	Willie Anderson 16.7	Alec Kessler 5.6	Willie Anderson 4.0	Hugh Durham	
1988-89	15-16	6-12		Alec Kessler 19.2	Alec Kessler 9.7	Litterial Green 4.3	Hugh Durham	
1989-90	20-9	13-5	NCAA FIRST ROUND	Alec Kessler 21.0	Alec Kessler 10.4	Rod Cole 4.3	Hugh Durham	
1990-91	17-13	9-9	NCAA FIRST ROUND	Litterial Green 20.6	Neville Austin 5.3	Rod Cole 3.9	Hugh Durham	
1991-92	15-14	7-9		Litterial Green 19.5	Kendall Rhine 6.6	Litterial Green 4.0	Hugh Durham	
1992-93	15-14	8-8	NIT FIRST ROUND	Charles Claxton 11.5	Charles Claxton 6.6	Bernard Davis 4.0	Hugh Durham	
1993-94	14-16	7-9		Shandon Anderson 13.8	Charles Claxton 7.9	Shandon Anderson 3.8	Hugh Durham	
1994-95	18-10	9-7	NIT FIRST ROUND	Carlos Strong 14.2	Charles Claxton 7.9	Pertha Robinson 6.3	Hugh Durham	298-216 .579▼
1995-96	21-10	9-7	NCAA REGIONAL SEMIFINALS	Katu Davis 15.8	Carlos Strong 6.3	Pertha Robinson 4.8	Tubby Smith	
1996-97	24-9	10-6	NCAA FIRST ROUND	Michael Chadwick 12.4	Michael Chadwick 5.5	G.G. Smith 4.5	Tubby Smith	45-19 .703
1997-98	20-15	7-9	NIT THIRD PLACE	Jumaine Jones 14.7	Jumaine Jones 8.5	G.G. Smith 4.2	Ron Jirsa	
1998-99	15-15	6-10	NIT FIRST ROUND	Jumaine Jones 18.8	Jumaine Jones 9.5	G.G. Smith 3.9	Ron Jirsa	35-30 .538
1999-2000	10-20	3-13		D.A. Layne 18.3	Anthony Evans 8.7	Moses White 3.6	Jim Harrick	
2000-01	16-15	9-7	NCAA FIRST ROUND	D.A. Layne 16.8	Anthony Evans 7.5	D.A. Layne 3.5	Jim Harrick	
2001-02	22-10 ⊗	10-6	NCAA SECOND ROUND	Jarvis Hayes 18.6	Chris Daniels 8.0	Rashad Wright 4.8	Jim Harrick	
2002-03	19-8	11-5		Jarvis Hayes 18.3	Steve Thomas 7.3	Rashad Wright 5.5	Jim Harrick	67-53 .558▼
2003-04	16-14	7-9	NIT FIRST ROUND	Rashad Wright 14.4	Chris Daniels 8.1	Rashad Wright 3.0	Dennis Felton	
2004-05	8-20	2-14		Levi Stukes 15.2	Dave Bliss 5.4	Sundiata Gaines 2.9	Dennis Felton	
2005-06	15-15	5-11		Levi Stukes 11.6	Sundiata Gaines 5.1	Sundiata Gaines 3.4	Dennis Felton	
2006-07	19-14	8-8	NIT SECOND ROUND	Takais Brown 14.2	Sundiata Gaines 5.7	Sundiata Gaines 4.8	Dennis Felton	
2007-08	17-17	4-12	NCAA FIRST ROUND	Sundiata Gaines 14.8	Sundiata Gaines 6.1	Sundiata Gaines 4.2	Dennis Felton	
2008-09	12-20	3-13		Terrance Woodbury 14.0	Howard Thompkins III 7.4	Dustin Ware 3.4	Dennis Felton[d]	84-91 .480

[a] Rex Enright (2-5), Vernon Smith (1-1), and Emil Breitkruetz (9-4) coached during the 1937-38 season.

[b] Ralph Jordan (2-3) and Elmer Lampe (3-11) both coached during the 1946-47 season.

[c] Ralph Jordan (4-2) and Jim Whatley (11-7) both coached during the 1949-50 season.

[d] Dennis Felton (9-11) and Pete Herrmann (3-9) both coached during the 2008-09 season.

⊗ Records don't reflect games forfeited or vacated. For adjusted records, see p. 521.

▼ Coaches' record adjusted to reflect games forfeited or vacated: Hugh Durham 297-215 .580; Jim Harrick 66-52 .559. For yearly totals, see p. 521.

THE SCHOOLS

ESPN 229 SAGARIN

GEORGIA SOUTHERN

Even though Georgia Southern began playing in 1926, entered Division I in 1971 and made six postseason appearances from 1983 to 2006, the Eagles have never won an NIT or NCAA Tournament game. They haven't made the NCAAs since joining the Southern Conference in 1992.

BEST TEAM: 1991-92 The Eagles left the Trans America Athletic Conference on top. Led by conference MVP Charlton Young, they went 25–6 in their last TAAC season, including a run through the league tourney in which they won their games by an average of 17.7 points. Their reward was an NCAA date with No. 2-seed Oklahoma State, which ended their season, 100-73.

BEST PLAYER: G ELTON NESBITT (2003-06) The 5'9" gunner owns every three-point record at the school: 11 in one game, 103 in a season and 262 for his career. He led the Soutnern Conference in scoring his senior year (21.7 ppg) and was conference Player of the Year.

BEST COACH: FRANK KERNS (1981-95) He took a five-win team and immediately turned it into a perennial contender. Under his watch, the Eagles had five 20-win campaigns, and the program's only visits to the NCAA Tournament (1983, '87 and '92).

GAME FOR THE AGES: The 1992 TAAC title game was the program's high-water mark, with Southern breezing past Georgia State, 95-82, at Hanner Fieldhouse. Charlton Young led with 20 points and 8 assists and was tourney MVP. Even the usually dour-faced Kerns was caught smiling after the Eagles' seventh victory in a row put them into the NCAA Tourney.

FIERCEST RIVAL: Mercer and GSU have been butting heads since 1933—sometimes literally. They've played 112 times, with the Eagles taking about two-thirds of those meetings, but that doesn't mean things don't get heated. After Mercer beat Southern 80-72 on Dec. 5, 2002 for the first time in 14 years, a brawl broke out that included fans and players and punches and tackles and both coaches in the middle of the scrum, trying to restore order.

SEASON REVIEW

SEAS.	W-L	CONF.	COACH	SEAS.	W-L	CONF.	COACH
1926-48	*158-97*	*27-5 over two seasons (1933-35)*		1961-62	14-13		J.B. Scearce
1948-49	21-3		J.B. Scearce	1962-63	14-13		J.B. Scearce
1949-50	27-3		J.B. Scearce	1963-64	19-12		J.B. Scearce
1950-51	24-5		J.B. Scearce	1964-65	22-5		J.B. Scearce
1951-52	22-6		J.B. Scearce	1965-66	26-6		J.B. Scearce
1952-53	15-14		J.B. Scearce	1966-67	17-11		J.B. Scearce
1953-54	13-11		J.B. Scearce	1967-68	13-11		Frank Radovich
1954-55	20-4		J.B. Scearce	1968-69	18-7		Frank Radovich
1955-56	21-7		J.B. Scearce	1969-70	17-6		Frank Radovich
1956-57	18-7		J.B. Scearce	1970-71	13-12		J.E. Rowe
1957-58	12-15		J.B. Scearce	1971-72	17-9		J.E. Rowe
1958-59	19-12		J.B. Scearce	1972-73	8-18		J.E. Rowe
1959-60	19-6		J.B. Scearce	1973-74	19-7		J.E. Rowe
1960-61	11-19		J.B. Scearce	1974-75	8-18		Larry Chapman

SEAS.	W-L	CONF.	SCORING		COACH	RECORD
1975-76	11-16		Kevin Anderson	13.6	Larry Chapman	
1976-77	16-11		Kevin Anderson	17.8	Larry Chapman	35-45 .438
1977-78	12-15		Kevin Anderson	19.6	J.B. Scearce	
1978-79	9-18		Matt Simpkins	22.0	J.B. Scearce	
1979-80	5-22		John Fowler	15.7	J.B. Scearce[a]	396-225 .638
1980-81	5-22	2-10	Reggie Cofer	16.3	John Nelson	7-29 .194
1981-82	14-13	8-8	Dennis Murphy	9.7	Frank Kerns	
1982-83	18-12	8-6 ●	Eric Hightower	15.4	Frank Kerns	
1983-84	16-12	8-6	Eric Hightower	14.8	Frank Kerns	
1984-85	24-5	11-3	Morris Hargrove	15.2	Frank Kerns	
1985-86	15-13	6-8	Brian Newton	14.7	Frank Kerns	
1986-87	20-11	12-6 ●	Brian Newton	14.7	Frank Kerns	
1987-88	24-7	15-3 ■	Jeff Sanders	18.1	Frank Kerns	
1988-89	23-6	16-2 ■	Jeff Sanders	23.2	Frank Kerns	
1989-90	17-11	11-5	Michael Curry	16.6	Frank Kerns	
1990-91	14-13	9-5	Tony Windless	15.4	Frank Kerns	
1991-92	25-6	13-1 ●	Tony Windless	17.6	Frank Kerns	
1992-93	19-9	12-6	Charlton Young	17.1	Frank Kerns	
1993-94	14-14	9-9	Dante Gay	13.8	Frank Kerns	
1994-95	8-20	3-11	Dante Gay	14.7	Frank Kerns[b]	244-132 .649
1995-96	3-23	2-12	Fernando Daniel	11.8	Gregg Polinsky	
1996-97	10-18	5-9	Elvardo Rolle	11.1	Gregg Polinsky	
1997-98	10-18	4-10	Cedric McGinnis	12.8	Gregg Polinsky	
1998-99	11-17	6-10	Fernando Daniel	13.6	Gregg Polinsky	34-76 .309
1999-2000	16-12	10-6	Julius Jenkins	15.5	Jeff Price	
2000-01	15-15	9-7	Julius Jenkins	16.7	Jeff Price	
2001-02	16-12	9-7	Sean Peterson	16.9	Jeff Price	
2002-03	16-13	8-8	Julius Jenkins	21.6	Jeff Price	
2003-04	21-8	11-5	Elton Nesbitt	15.7	Jeff Price	
2004-05	18-13	10-6	Elton Nesbitt	20.2	Jeff Price	
2005-06	20-10	11-4 ■	Elton Nesbitt	21.7	Jeff Price	
2006-07	15-16	7-11	Donte Gennie	16.2	Jeff Price	
2007-08	20-12	13-7	Louis Graham	16.8	Jeff Price	
2008-09	8-22	5-15	Antonio Hanson	12.0	Jeff Price	165-133 .554

[a] J.B. Scearce (3-15) and John Nelson (2-7) both coached during the 1979-80 season.
[b] Frank Kerns (1-0) and Doug Durham (7-20) both coached during the 1994-95 season.
● NCAA Tournament appearance ■ NIT appearance

PROFILE

Georgia Southern University, Statesboro, GA
Founded: 1906
Enrollment: 16,841 (14,820 undergraduate)
Colors: Blue and white
Nickname: Eagles
Current arena: Hanner Fieldhouse, opened in 1969 (4,358)
Previous: Hanner Gym, 1955-69 (N/A); Alumni Building, 1932-55 (N/A)
First game: 1926
All-time record: 1,133-822 (.580)
Total weeks in AP Top 20/25: 0

Current conference: Southern (1992-)
Conference titles:
Trans America: 4 (1985, '88 [tie], '89, '92)
Southern: 4 (2002 [tie], '04 [tie], '05 [tie] '06 [tie])
Conference tournament titles:
Trans America: 3 (1983, '87, '92)
NCAA Tournament appearances: 3
NIT appearances: 3

FIRST-ROUND PRO PICKS

1989 **Jeff Sanders,** Chicago (20)

TOP 5

G **Michael Curry** (1986-90)
G **Julius Jenkins** (1999-2003)
G **Elton Nesbitt** (2003-06)
F **Kevin Anderson** (1975-79)
F **Jeff Sanders** (1985-89)

RECORDS

	GAME		SEASON		CAREER	
POINTS	60	Fran Florian, vs. Jacksonville (Jan. 22, 1964)	883	Chester Webb (1955-56)	2,542	Chester Webb (1952-56)
POINTS PER GAME			30.5	Chester Webb (1955-56)	24.0	Chester Webb (1952-56)
REBOUNDS	33	Carlton Gill, vs. Toronto (Jan. 10, 1959)	524	Chester Webb (1955-56)	1,685	Chester Webb (1952-56)
ASSISTS	23	Don Adler, vs. Jacksonville (Jan. 22, 1964)	223	Don Wallen (1954-55)	588	Dwayne Foreman (2004-08)

THE SCHOOLS

ESPN 326 SAGARIN

GEORGIA STATE

The first 34 years of Georgia State basketball were downright ugly. The Panthers went 1–21 in their inaugural season of 1963-64, and didn't win more than 10 games until '75-76. Then the man they call Lefty showed up in 1997 and changed everything.

BEST TEAM: 2000-01 Panthers fans knew Lefty Driesell's team could be special after a road victory over Georgia in the season opener. GSU rolled to the Trans America regular-season and tournament titles with impressive scoring balance—four players averaged double digits. In the school's second NCAA Tourney, Georgia State stunned No. 6-seed Wisconsin, 50-49, before falling to Lefty's former school, Maryland.

BEST PLAYER: F Thomas Terrell (2000-02) This transfer from Mississippi's Copiah-Lincoln Community College came out of nowhere to lead Georgia State to the Tourney in 2001 and the NIT a year later. Although just 6'7", Terrell routinely outmuscled and outrebounded his competition down low, while keeping them guessing with a surprisingly decent three-point touch.

BEST COACH: Charles "Lefty" Driesell (1997-2003) Best known for building Maryland into a hoops powerhouse, Lefty took over a dismal GSU program and immediately delivered a winning season. Building success on transfers from major programs, he became just the second coach (Eddie Sutton was the first) to lead four schools to the NCAA Tournament.

GAME FOR THE AGES: Down 16 in the first half to a rock-solid defensive team a year removed from a Final Four appearance, Georgia State seemed doomed in its 2001 first-round NCAA Tournament game against Wisconsin. But the Panthers stormed back, and the Badgers' Mark Vershaw missed two free throws with 3.2 seconds left to gift-wrap a 50-49 win.

FIERCEST RIVAL: Georgia State's crosstown rival, longtime hoops powerhouse Georgia Tech, has routinely run the Panthers out of the building when the two have met. The Ramblin' Wreck holds a 17–2 series lead, with GSU's last win coming in the 1975-76 season.

SEASON REVIEW

SEAS.	W-L	CONF.	SCORING		COACH	RECORD	
1963-64	1-21		Virlyn Gaynes	15.6	Herbert "Stoney" Burgess	1-21	.045
1964-65	2-19		Virlyn Gaynes	13.3	Richard Wehr		
1965-66	2-18		Tom Mullins	10.8	Richard Wehr		
1966-67	4-20		Jim Jacobs	11.2	Richard Wehr	8-57	.123
1967-68	2-20		Jim Jacobs	18.1	Clyde H. "Jack" Waters		
1968-69	6-14		Ken Brewer	18.1	Clyde H. "Jack" Waters		
1969-70	8-14		Ken Brewer	19.8	Clyde H. "Jack" Waters		
1970-71	5-16		Ron Ricketts	21.1	Frank Davis	5-16	.238
1971-72	5-19		Jackie Poag	19.5	Roger McDowell	5-19	.208
1972-73	5-20		Walker Atrice	13.0	Clyde H. "Jack" Waters		
1973-74	1-25		Jackie Poag	14.4	Clyde H. "Jack" Waters		
1974-75	8-18		Jim Atkinson	16.6	Clyde H. "Jack" Waters		
1975-76	12-11		Bob Pierson	19.2	Clyde H. "Jack" Waters		
1976-77	10-18	2-4	George Pendleton	20.1	Clyde H. "Jack" Waters	52-140	.271
1977-78	5-21	2-8	Jerome Scott	14.8	Roger Couch		
1978-79	7-20	0-10	Mark Gulmire	11.9	Roger Couch		
1979-80	6-21	4-10	Rondy Tucker	15.8	Roger Couch		
1980-81	4-23	1-11	Don Ross	13.0	Roger Couch	22-85	.206
1981-82	4-23		Rondy Tucker	12.1	Jim Jarrett		
1982-83	9-19		Chavelo Holmes	18.3	Jim Jarrett	13-42	.236
1983-84	6-22		Chavelo Holmes	13.1	Tom Pugliese		
1984-85	2-26	0-14	Chris Jackson	15.5	Tom Pugliese[a]	7-24	.226
1985-86	10-18	4-10	Dewey Haley	13.9	Bob Reinhart		
1986-87	11-17	7-11	Harlen Graham	19.7	Bob Reinhart		
1987-88	9-19	5-13	James Andrews	15.1	Bob Reinhart		
1988-89	14-14	9-9	James Andrews	18.8	Bob Reinhart		
1989-90	5-23	3-13	Matt O'Brien	18.4	Bob Reinhart		
1990-91	16-15	7-7 ●	Phillip Luckydo	20.2	Bob Reinhart		
1991-92	16-14	8-6	Phillip Luckydo	21.0	Bob Reinhart		
1992-93	13-14	5-7	Mike Nalls	17.4	Bob Reinhart		
1993-94	13-14	9-7	Zavian Smith	15.6	Bob Reinhart	107-148	.420
1994-95	11-17	6-10	Terrence Brandon	18.7	Carter Wilson		
1995-96	10-16	6-10	Terrence Brandon	20.8	Carter Wilson		
1996-97	10-17	6-10	Rodney Hamilton	18.0	Carter Wilson	31-50	.383
1997-98	16-12	11-5	Rodney Hamilton	16.0	Lefty Driesell		
1998-99	17-13	11-5	Kevin Morris	16.6	Lefty Driesell		
1999-2000	17-12	13-5	Shernard Long	16.9	Lefty Driesell		
2000-01	29-5	16-2 ●	Shernard Long	18.0	Lefty Driesell		
2001-02	20-11	14-6 ■	Thomas Terrell	20.5	Lefty Driesell		
2002-03	14-15	8-8	Nate Williams	18.0	Lefty Driesell[b]	103-59	.636
2003-04	20-9	14-6	Nate Williams	14.7	Michael Perry		
2004-05	14-15	11-9	Marcus Brown	14.9	Michael Perry		
2005-06	7-22	3-15	Herman Favors	12.5	Michael Perry		
2006-07	11-20	5-13	Lance Perique	15.6	Michael Perry	62-75	.453
2007-08	9-21	5-13	Leonard Mendez	16.0	Rod Barnes		
2008-09	12-20	8-10	Joe Dukes	12.8	Rod Barnes	21-41	.339

[a] Tom Pugliese (1-2) and Mark Slonaker (1-24) both coached during the 1984-85 season.
[b] Lefty Driesell (4-6) and Michael Perry (10-9) both coached during the 2002-03 season.
● NCAA Tournament appearance ■ NIT appearance

PROFILE

Georgia State University, Atlanta, GA
Founded: 1913
Enrollment: 27,137 (19,904 undergraduate)
Colors: Blue and white
Nickname: Panthers
Current arena: GSU Sports Arena, opened in 1972 (3,400)
First game: 1963
All-time record: 438-801 (.354)
Total weeks in AP Top 20/25: 0

Current conference: Colonial Athletic Association (2005-)
Conference titles:
Trans America: 2 (2000 [tie], '01)
Atlantic Sun: 1 (2002 [tie])
Conference tournament titles:
Trans America: 2 (1991, 2001)
NCAA Tournament appearances: 2
NIT appearances: 1

TOP 5

G **Rodney Hamilton** (1994-98)
G **Kevin Morris** (1998-2001)
G/F **Shernard Long** (1999-2001)
F **Thomas Terrell** (2000-02)
C **Chris Collier** (1989-91)

RECORDS

RECORDS	GAME		SEASON		CAREER	
POINTS	49	Chris Collier, vs. Butler (Jan. 2, 1991)	635	Thomas Terrell (2001-02)	1,515	Rodney Hamilton (1994-98)
POINTS PER GAME			21.1	Ron Ricketts (1970-71)	20.6	Phillip Luckydo (1990-92)
REBOUNDS	28	Ron Ricketts, vs. Baptist (Jan. 8, 1972)	328	Chris Collier (1990-91)	750	Terrence Brandon (1991-92, '93-96)
ASSISTS	15	Howie Jarvis, vs. South Florida (Feb. 19, 1979)	222	Eric Ervin (1982-83)	535	Rodney Hamilton (1994-98)

ESPN 65 SAGARIN

GEORGIA TECH

Mark Price, Kenny Anderson, Dennis Scott, Travis Best, Stephon Marbury, Jarrett Jack. Few schools can match the run of NBA-caliber guards the Yellow Jackets have put on the court since the mid-1980s. Fewer still can equal Tech's flair for the dramatic—from the 59-58 win that snapped Kentucky's 129-game home winning streak in 1955 to unlikely Final Four runs in 1990 and 2004.

BEST TEAM: 1989-90 Nicknamed Lethal Weapon 3, the triumvirate of Anderson, Scott and Brian Oliver led the Yellow Jackets to the ACC tournament title and then to the Final Four. Anderson was named most outstanding player in the Southeast Regional, averaging 27.0 points in four games. As an overweight freshman, the 6'8" Scott had been kept out of the starting lineup by coach Bobby Cremins. The motivational technique worked. Scott became a brilliant all-around player, with his 970 points in 1989-90 breaking the ACC single-season record.

BEST PLAYER: G MARK PRICE (1982-86) Assistant coach George Felton spotted the Oklahoma schoolboy at an AAU tournament in Jacksonville, and pleaded with Cremins to sign Price. "How can I sign a player from Oklahoma—I don't even know one person from that state," Cremins joked. But he took the gamble and it paid off. Price was the first freshman to lead the ACC in scoring (20.3 ppg), and his 2,193 career points rank third all-time in Tech history. Price has been named one of the Top 50 athletes in ACC history.

BEST COACH: BOBBY CREMINS (1981-2000) He was best known for two things: brilliant recruiting and coaching great point guards (Price, Anderson, Best, Drew Barry, Marbury). The payoff was nine straight NCAA Tournament appearances from 1985 to '93, including one Final Four, an Elite Eight and two Sweet 16s.

GAME FOR THE AGES: With :05 left and Tech trailing by two to No. 1-seed Michigan State in the 1990 Southeast Regional semifinals, Kenny Anderson drove full-court and launched a 20-footer that went in at the buzzer. Initially judged a game-winning three, officials then ruled that one of Anderson's feet was on the line, sending the game into overtime. This time Dennis Scott hit a shot with :04 left to secure the 81-80 Tech win.

HEARTBREAKER: In the ACC tournament final against Duke on March 9, 1986, the Yellow Jackets rallied from a nine-point deficit and trailed 66-65 with :44 left. But the Blue Devils prevented Price from penetrating, and Craig Neal missed an open shot. Duke's Johnny Dawkins grabbed the rebound, was fouled and hit both free throws to send Tech home a 68-67 loser.

FIERCEST RIVAL: Home-court advantage means everything in the Georgia-Georgia Tech rivalry. Although the Final Four-bound Jackets started 12–0 in 2003-04, they lost on the road to the NIT-bound Bulldogs in double overtime. Tech has lost 12 straight in Athens and hasn't won there since 1976. Even so, the Jackets lead overall, either 101–84 (according to them), or 100–84 (if you ask the Bulldogs).

FANFARE AND HOOPLA: The Alexander Memorial Coliseum is called the Thriller Dome for a good reason: With sound reverberating off the domed ceiling, the 9,000-plus fans who fill the arena make for one of the game's loudest and most intimidating home venues.

FAN FAVORITE: F TOM HAMMONDS (1985-89) He was a ballyhooed prep school star who was recruited by more than 100 schools. But the 6'9" Hammonds really won the fans over with his intensity on the court (his nickname was the Terminator) and his friendliness off it. The school retired his jersey at his final home game in 1989. Hammonds became a driver on the NHRA circuit.

CONSENSUS ALL-AMERICAS

1961	**Roger Kaiser,** G
1991	**Kenny Anderson,** G

FIRST-ROUND PRO PICKS

1982	**Brook Steppe,** Kansas City (17)
1986	**John Salley,** Detroit (11)
1989	**Tom Hammonds,** Washington (9)
1990	**Dennis Scott,** Orlando (4)
1991	**Kenny Anderson,** New Jersey (2)
1992	**Jon Barry,** Boston (21)
1993	**Malcolm Mackey,** Phoenix (27)
1995	**Travis Best,** Indiana (23)
1996	**Stephon Marbury,** Milwaukee (4)
1998	**Matt Harpring,** Orlando (15)
1999	**Dion Glover,** Atlanta (20)
2000	**Jason Collier,** Milwaukee (15)
2003	**Chris Bosh,** Toronto (4)
2005	**Jarrett Jack,** Denver (22)
2007	**Thaddeus Young,** Philadelphia (12)
2007	**Javaris Crittenton,** LA Lakers (19)

PROFILE

Georgia Institute of Technology, Atlanta, GA
Founded: 1885
Enrollment: 19,393 (12,966 undergraduate)
Colors: Old gold and white
Nicknames: Yellow Jackets, Ramblin' Wreck
Current arena: Alexander Memorial Coliseum, opened in 1956 (9,191)
Previous: Heisman Gym, 1938-56 (1,800)
First game: Feb.17, 1906
All-time record: 1,207-1,060 (.532)
Total weeks in AP Top 20/25: 201

Current conference: Atlantic Coast (1979-)
Conference titles:
SEC: 1 (1938)
ACC: 2 (1985 [tie], '96)
Conference tournament titles:
SEC: 1 (1938)
ACC: 3 (1985, '90, '93)
NCAA Tournament appearances: 15
Sweet 16s (since 1975): 6
Final Fours: 2
NIT appearances: 7
Semifinals: 1

TOP 5

G	**Mark Price** (1982-86)
G	**Dennis Scott** (1987-90)
F	**Tom Hammonds** (1985-89)
F	**Matt Harpring** (1994-98)
C	**Rich Yunkus** (1968-71)

RECORDS

RECORDS	GAME		SEASON		CAREER	
POINTS	50	Kenny Anderson, vs. Loyola Marymount (Dec. 22, 1990)	970	Dennis Scott (1989-90)	2,232	Rich Yunkus (1968-71)
POINTS PER GAME			30.1	Rich Yunkus (1969-70)	26.6	Rich Yunkus (1968-71)
REBOUNDS	27	Eric Crake, vs. Georgia (Feb. 4, 1953)	364	Jim Caldwell (1963-64)	1,205	Malcolm Mackey (1989-93)
ASSISTS	19	Craig Neal, vs. Duke (Feb. 28, 1988)	303	Craig Neal (1987-88)	724	Drew Barry (1992-96)

SEASON REVIEW

SEASON	W-L	CONF.	SCORING	COACH	RECORD
1905-08	*2-1*		*No team in 1906-07 or 1907-08*		
1908-09	1-6			John Heisman	
1909-12	no team				
1912-13	2-6			John Heisman	
1913-14	6-2			John Heisman	9-14 .391
1914-19	no team				
1919-20	7-10			William Alexander	
1920-21	4-10			Joe Bean	4-10 .286
1921-22	11-6	2-3		William Alexander	
1922-23	9-9	5-3		William Alexander	
1923-24	9-13	4-5		William Alexander	36-38 .486
1924-25	4-12	2-7		Harold Hansen	
1925-26	6-11	4-10		Harold Hansen	10-23 .303
1926-27	17-10	8-2		Roy Mundorff	
1927-28	10-7	8-4		Roy Mundorff	
1928-29	15-6	10-2		Roy Mundorff	
1929-30	10-13	5-8		Roy Mundorff	
1930-31	11-13	8-7		Roy Mundorff	
1931-32	7-6	5-3		Roy Mundorff	
1932-33	9-6	7-5		Roy Mundorff	
1933-34	6-12	5-8		Roy Mundorff	
1934-35	6-8	5-6		Roy Mundorff	

SEAS.	W-L	CONF.	POSTSEASON	SCORING		REBOUNDS		ASSISTS		COACH	RECORD
1935-36	10-8	7-5								Roy Mundorff	
1936-37	13-2	10-0								Roy Mundorff	
1937-38	18-2	9-2								Roy Mundorff	
1938-39	6-9	4-7								Roy Mundorff	
1939-40	7-8	6-6								Roy Mundorff	
1940-41	8-11	4-8								Roy Mundorff	
1941-42	8-8	4-7								Roy Mundorff	
1942-43	11-5	7-4								Roy Mundorff	172-134 .562
1943-44	14-4	2-0								Dwight Keith	
1944-45	11-6	7-4								Dwight Keith	
1945-46	10-11	7-7								Dwight Keith	35-21 .625
1946-47	12-11	6-6								Roy McArthur	
1947-48	12-16	6-10								Roy McArthur	
1948-49	11-13	7-9								Roy McArthur	
1949-50	14-13	7-9								Roy McArthur	
1950-51	8-19	6-8								Roy McArthur	57-72 .442
1951-52	7-15	2-12								Whack Hyder	
1952-53	5-17	4-9		Pete Silas	17.0	Pete Silas	13.7			Whack Hyder	
1953-54	2-22	0-14		Dick Lenholt	12.5					Whack Hyder	
1954-55	12-13	7-7		Joe Helms	14.5	Dick Lenholt	10.6			Whack Hyder	
1955-56	12-11	6-8		Bobby Kimmel	18.8	Lenny Cohen	9.3			Whack Hyder	
1956-57	18-8	9-5		Bud Blemker	16.4	Lenny Cohen	11.1			Whack Hyder	
1957-58	15-11	8-6		Bud Blemker	17.4	Dave Denton	10.9			Whack Hyder	
1958-59	17-9	9-5		Bud Blemker	14.9	Frank Inman	7.2			Whack Hyder	
1959-60	22-6	11-3	NCAA REGIONAL FINALS	Roger Kaiser	22.8	Dave Denton	8.5			Whack Hyder	
1960-61	13-13	6-8		Roger Kaiser	23.4	Alan Nass	10.4			Whack Hyder	
1961-62	10-16	4-10		Mike Tomasovich	13.2	Alan Nass	9.4			Whack Hyder	
1962-63	21-5	10-4		Jim Caldwell	13.7	Jim Caldwell	10.9			Whack Hyder	
1963-64	17-9	9-5		Jim Caldwell	14.0	Jim Caldwell	14.0			Whack Hyder	
1964-65	14-11			Jim Caldwell	17.4	Jim Caldwell	13.8			Whack Hyder	
1965-66	13-13			Phil Wagner	14.9	Pete Thorne	7.1	Phil Wagner	3.8	Whack Hyder	
1966-67	17-9			Phil Wagner	19.5	Pete Thorne	6.5	Phil Wagner	4.2	Whack Hyder	
1967-68	12-13			Phil Wagner	19.6	Phil Wagner	6.6	Phil Wagner	3.9	Whack Hyder	
1968-69	12-13			Rich Yunkus	24.1	Rich Yunkus	11.0	Jim Thorne	3.7	Whack Hyder	
1969-70	17-10		NIT QUARTERFINALS	Rich Yunkus	30.1	Rich Yunkus	12.0	Jim Thorne	6.0	Whack Hyder	
1970-71	23-9		NIT RUNNER-UP	Rich Yunkus	25.5	Rich Yunkus	11.1	Jim Thorne	5.3	Whack Hyder	
1971-72	6-20			Steve Post	15.2	Karl Binns	6.5	Frank Samoylo	3.5	Whack Hyder	
1972-73	7-18			Steve Sherbak	14.8	Andy McCain	8.0	Steve Sherbak	5.6	Whack Hyder	292-271 .519
1973-74	5-21			Jim Wood	11.1	Harry Allen	5.9	Steve Sherbak	3.4	Dwane Morrison	
1974-75	11-15			Jim Wood	15.0	Jim Wood	9.6	Mike Bottorf	2.8	Dwane Morrison	
1975-76	13-14			Jim Wood	14.7	Mike Green	6.3	Mike Bottorf	2.6	Dwane Morrison	
1976-77	18-10	3-3		Tico Brown	16.4	Jim Wood	6.7	Ray Schnitzer	2.1	Dwane Morrison	
1977-78	15-12	6-6		Sammy Drummer	21.0	Lenny Horton	7.5	Billy Smith	2.3	Dwane Morrison	
1978-79	17-9			Sammy Drummer	23.7	Lenny Horton	7.6	Billy Smith	2.0	Dwane Morrison	
1979-80	8-18	1-13		Brook Steppe	18.9	Lenny Horton	6.5	Brook Steppe	2.5	Dwane Morrison	
1980-81	4-23	0-14		Fred Hall	12.2	Lee Goza	6.6	George Thomas	3.0	Dwane Morrison	91-122 .427
1981-82	10-16	3-11		Brook Steppe	17.8	Brook Steppe	5.4	Brian Howard	2.5	Bobby Cremins	
1982-83	13-15	4-10		Mark Price	20.3	John Salley	5.7	Mark Price	3.3	Bobby Cremins	
1983-84	18-11	6-8	NIT FIRST ROUND	Mark Price	15.6	Yvon Joseph	7.2	Mark Price	4.2	Bobby Cremins	
1984-85	27-8	9-5	NCAA REGIONAL FINALS	Mark Price	16.7	John Salley	7.1	Mark Price	4.3	Bobby Cremins	
1985-86	27-7	11-3	NCAA REGIONAL SEMIFINALS	Mark Price	17.4	John Salley	6.7	Mark Price	4.4	Bobby Cremins	
1986-87	16-13	7-7	NCAA FIRST ROUND	Duane Ferrell	17.9	Tom Hammonds	7.2	Craig Neal	5.9	Bobby Cremins	
1987-88	22-10	8-6	NCAA SECOND ROUND	Tom Hammonds	18.9	Tom Hammonds	7.2	Craig Neal	9.5	Bobby Cremins	
1988-89	20-12	8-6	NCAA FIRST ROUND	Tom Hammonds	20.9	Tom Hammonds	8.1	Brian Oliver	7.0	Bobby Cremins	
1989-90	28-7	8-6	NCAA NATIONAL SEMIFINALS	Dennis Scott	27.7	Malcolm Mackey	7.5	Kenny Anderson	8.1	Bobby Cremins	
1990-91	17-13	6-8	NCAA SECOND ROUND	Kenny Anderson	25.9	Malcolm Mackey	10.7	Kenny Anderson	5.6	Bobby Cremins	
1991-92	23-12	8-8	NCAA REGIONAL SEMIFINALS	Jon Barry	17.2	Malcolm Mackey	9.0	Jon Barry	5.9	Bobby Cremins	
1992-93	19-11	8-8	NCAA FIRST ROUND	James Forrest	19.5	Malcolm Mackey	10.2	Travis Best	5.9	Bobby Cremins	
1993-94	16-13	7-9	NIT FIRST ROUND	James Forrest	19.0	James Forrest	7.9	Drew Barry	5.9	Bobby Cremins	
1994-95	18-12	8-8		Travis Best	20.2	James Forrest	8.3	Drew Barry	6.7	Bobby Cremins	
1995-96	24-12	13-3	NCAA REGIONAL SEMIFINALS	Stephon Marbury	18.9	Matt Harpring	8.1	Drew Barry	6.6	Bobby Cremins	
1996-97	9-18	3-13		Matt Harpring	19.0	M. Harpring, E. Elisma	8.2	Kevin Morris	3.1	Bobby Cremins	
1997-98	19-14	6-10	NIT QUARTERFINALS	Matt Harpring	21.6	Matt Harpring	9.4	Travis Spivey	4.3	Bobby Cremins	
1998-99	15-16	6-10	NIT FIRST ROUND	Jason Collier	17.2	Alvin Jones	9.7	Tony Akins	4.8	Bobby Cremins	
1999-2000	13-17	5-11		Jason Collier	17.0	Jason Collier	9.2	Tony Akins	3.6	Bobby Cremins	354-237 .599
2000-01	17-13	8-8	NCAA FIRST ROUND	Tony Akins	14.5	Alvin Jones	10.4	Tony Akins	4.3	Paul Hewitt	
2001-02	15-16	7-9		Tony Akins	17.0	Ed Nelson	6.9	Tony Akins	5.7	Paul Hewitt	
2002-03	16-15	7-9	NIT QUARTERFINALS	Chris Bosh	15.6	Chris Bosh	9.0	Jarrett Jack	6.0	Paul Hewitt	
2003-04	28-10	9-7	NCAA RUNNER-UP	B.J. Elder	14.9	Luke Schenscher	6.6	Jarrett Jack	5.6	Paul Hewitt	
2004-05	20-12	8-8	NCAA SECOND ROUND	Jarrett Jack	15.5	Luke Schenscher	7.3	Jarrett Jack	4.5	Paul Hewitt	
2005-06	11-17	4-12		Anthony Morrow	16.0	Jeremis Smith	8.2	Zam Fredrick	3.9	Paul Hewitt	
2006-07	20-12	8-8	NCAA FIRST ROUND	Javaris Crittenton	14.4	Jeremis Smith	5.9	Javaris Crittenton	5.8	Paul Hewitt	
2007-08	15-17	7-9		Anthony Morrow	14.3	Jeremis Smith	7.3	Matt Causey	3.7	Paul Hewitt	
2008-09	12-19	2-14		Lewis Clinch	15.5	Gani Lawal	9.5	Iman Shumpert	5.0	Paul Hewitt	154-131 .540

ESPN 127 SAGARIN

GONZAGA

Once the quintessential Cinderella team, Gonzaga in recent years has recast itself as not just a party crasher at the Big Dance, but a regularly invited, elite-level program. Between 1999 and 2009, the Bulldogs made 11 straight Tournament appearances.

BEST TEAM: 1998-99 These Zags became the darlings of college basketball. Led by three of the school's all-time leading scorers—Matt Santangelo, Richie Frahm and Casey Calvary—Gonzaga finished 28–7 for head coach Dan Monson. As a No. 10 seed in the Tournament, Gonzaga beat Minnesota, Stanford and Florida before falling to eventual national champion Connecticut in the Elite Eight—the Zags' deepest run ever.

BEST PLAYER: G JOHN STOCKTON (1980-84) The player most identified with the Gonzaga program, Stockton was the first Bulldog to eclipse 1,000 points and 500 assists during his career. Stockton's 1,340 points place him among the school's Top 20 scorers, and he is fourth on the Zags' assist list with 554. As a senior, he was the West Coast Athletic Conference Player of the Year. Along with Frank Burgess, Stockton is one of just two Bulldogs to have their numbers retired. The 16th pick in the first round of the 1984 NBA draft, he was a 10-time All-Star in his 19 seasons with the Jazz.

BEST COACH: MARK FEW (1999-) After 10 years as an assistant coach, Few has compiled a 10-year head coaching record of 264–66 and has made the NCAA Tournament in every season, with four Sweet 16 runs to his credit. His .800 winning percentage is the highest among all who have coached Gonzaga for more than one season.

GAME FOR THE AGES: With a trip to the Elite Eight on the line on March 18, 1999, No. 10-seed Gonzaga locked horns with No. 6-seed Florida. With his team leading by a point, Florida's Brent Wright was called for traveling while trying to call a timeout with :15 left. The Zags put the ball in the hands of diminutive guard Quentin Hall, who hoisted a shot from the lane that bounced off the rim, only to be tipped in by a charging Casey Calvary with 4.4 seconds left, clinching the game for the Zags, 73-72. Frahm led the Zags with 17 points and four assists and Santangelo added seven assists of his own.

HEARTBREAKER: While they've suffered their share of gut-wrenching Tournament exits, the most enduring image of Gonzaga heartbreak is that of All-America Adam Morrison sitting on the floor, head buried between his knees, crying after the 73-71 Sweet 16 loss to UCLA in 2006. The Zags led by 13 at halftime and by nine with just over three minutes to go. But UCLA closed with an 11-0 run, seizing the lead for the only time in the game with :10 left.

FIERCEST RIVAL: Each renewal is known simply as the Game. Gonzaga and Washington State have met 144 times and WSU holds a 97–47 edge. But Gonzaga has been the power in recent seasons, having won eight of ten between 1998-99 and 2008-09.

FANFARE AND HOOPLA: Technically, the McCarthey Athletic Center replaced Kennedy Pavilion as the Zags' home court in 2004, but in local parlance, that's when the team moved from the Kennel to the New Kennel. Both arenas have been headquarters for the rowdy student bunch called the Kennel Club, whose fervor has helped Gonzaga to eight undefeated home campaigns since 1992-93, including a 50-game home win streak from 2002 to '07.

John Stockton was the first Bulldog to eclipse 1,000 points and 500 assists during his career.

FAN FAVORITE: F/C RONNY TURIAF (2001-05) Known for his friendly smile and his talk-to-anyone attitude, the Martinique native helped Gonzaga to 107 wins in his four seasons in Spokane. Turiaf was WCC Player of the Year as a senior in 2004-05.

CONSENSUS ALL-AMERICAS

2002	**Dan Dickau,** G
2006	**Adam Morrison,** G/F

FIRST-ROUND PRO PICKS

1984	**John Stockton,** Utah (16)
2002	**Dan Dickau,** Sacramento (28)
2006	**Adam Morrison,** Charlotte (3)
2009	**Austin Daye,** Detroit (15)

PROFILE

Gonzaga University, Spokane, WA
Founded: 1887
Enrollment: 6,375 (4,386 undergraduate)
Colors: Navy blue, white and red
Nicknames: Bulldogs, Zags
Current arena: McCarthey Athletic Center, opened in 2004 (6,000)
Previous: Kennedy Pavilion, 1965-2004 (renamed the Martin Centre in 1987) (4,000)
First game: 1908
All-time record: 1,369-1,059 (.564)
Total weeks in AP Top 20/25: 111
Current conference: West Coast (1979-)
Conference titles:
Big Sky: 2 (1966 [tie], '67 [tie])
West Coast: 13 (1994, '96 [tie], '98, '99, 2001, '02 [tie], '03, '04, '05, '06, '07, '08, '09)
Conference tournament titles:
West Coast: 10 (1995, '99, 2000, '01, '02, '04, '05, '06, '07, '09)
NCAA Tournament appearances: 12
Sweet 16s (since 1975): 5
NIT appearances: 3

TOP 5

G	**Frank Burgess** (1958-61)
G	**John Stockton** (1980-84)
G/F	**Adam Morrison** (2003-06)
F/C	**Ronny Turiaf** (2001-05)
C	**Jerry Vermillion** (1951-55)

RECORDS	GAME		SEASON		CAREER	
POINTS	52	Frank Burgess, vs. UC Davis (Jan. 26, 1961)	926	Adam Morrison (2005-06)	2,196	Frank Burgess (1958-61)
POINTS PER GAME			32.4	Frank Burgess (1960-61)	N/A	
REBOUNDS	33	Jim Dixon, vs. Eastern Washington (Jan. 23, 1961)	456	Jerry Vermillion (1952-53)	1,670	Jerry Vermillion (1951-55)
ASSISTS	16	Blake Stepp, vs. Long Beach State (Dec. 20, 2002)	225	Matt Santangelo (1999-2000)	668	Matt Santangelo (1996-2000)

SEASON REVIEW

SEASON	W-L	CONF.	SCORING	COACH	RECORD	SEASON	W-L	CONF.	SCORING	COACH	RECORD
1907-16	*58-23*		*38-8 over 4 seasons (1907-11)*			1926-27	8-16			Maurice Smith	
1916-17	4-5			John McGough	4-5 .444	1927-28	9-16			Maurice Smith	
1917-18	3-2			Condon	3-2 .600	1928-29	14-12			Maurice Smith	
1918-19	8-4			Edward Geheves		1929-30	8-7			Maurice Smith	
1919-20	1-13			Edward Geheves	9-17 .346	1930-31	7-8			Maurice Smith	46-59 .438
1920-21	4-8			Charles "Gus" Dorais		1931-32	4-7			S. Dagly	4-7 .364
1921-22	2-15			Charles "Gus" Dorais		1932-33	4-15			Perry Teneyck	4-15 .211
1922-23	10-8			Charles "Gus" Dorais		1933-34	7-16			Claude McGrath	
1923-24	9-10			Charles "Gus" Dorais		1934-35	6-14			Claude McGrath	
1924-25	9-12			Charles "Gus" Dorais		1935-36	9-10			Claude McGrath	
1925-26	16-7			Charles "Gus" Dorais	50-60 .455	1936-37	1-5			Claude McGrath	

SEAS.	W-L	CONF.	POSTSEASON	SCORING	REBOUNDS	ASSISTS	COACH	RECORD
1937-38	0-4						Claude McGrath	
1938-39	7-10						Claude McGrath	
1939-40	9-15						Claude McGrath	
1940-41	13-14						Claude McGrath	
1941-42	16-13						Claude McGrath	
1942-43	2-9						B. Frasier	2-9 .182
1943-44	22-4						Charles Henry	22-4 .846
1944-45	12-19						Eugene Wozny	12-19 .387
1945-46	6-14						Gordon White	6-14 .300
1946-47	20-9						Claude McGrath	
1947-48	24-11						Claude McGrath	
1948-49	17-12						Claude McGrath	129-133 .492
1949-50	18-11						L.T. Underwood	
1950-51	8-22						L.T. Underwood	26-33 .441
1951-52	19-16				Jerry Vermillion 372		Hank Anderson	
1952-53	15-14				Jerry Vermillion 456		Hank Anderson	
1953-54	12-16			Jerry Vermillion 21.2	Jerry Vermillion 402		Hank Anderson	
1954-55	15-11				Jerry Vermillion 440		Hank Anderson	
1955-56	13-15						Hank Anderson	
1956-57	11-16						Hank Anderson	
1957-58	16-10						Hank Anderson	
1958-59	11-15			Frank Burgess 23.2			Hank Anderson	
1959-60	14-12			Frank Burgess 28.9	Charlie Jordan 367		Hank Anderson	
1960-61	11-15			Frank Burgess 32.4			Hank Anderson	
1961-62	14-12			Bob Hunt 20.3	Jim Dixon 313		Hank Anderson	
1962-63	14-12				Jim Dixon 353		Hank Anderson	
1963-64	10-15	5-5		Bill Wilson 21.0			Hank Anderson	
1964-65	18-8	6-4					Hank Anderson	
1965-66	19-7	8-2		Gary Lechman 21.3			Hank Anderson	
1966-67	19-6	7-3		Gary Lechman 23.1	Gary Lechman 354		Hank Anderson	
1967-68	9-17	6-9					Hank Anderson	
1968-69	11-15	6-9					Hank Anderson	
1969-70	10-16	7-8					Hank Anderson	
1970-71	13-13	6-8					Hank Anderson	
1971-72	14-12	8-6			Joe Clayton 339		Hank Anderson	288-273 .513
1972-73	14-12	6-8					Adrian Buoncristiani	
1973-74	13-13	7-7					Adrian Buoncristiani	
1974-75	13-13	7-7				Ken Tyler 149	Adrian Buoncristiani	
1975-76	13-13	5-9					Adrian Buoncristiani	
1976-77	11-16	7-7					Adrian Buoncristiani	
1977-78	14-15	7-7			Paul Cathey 333		Adrian Buoncristiani	78-82 .488
1978-79	16-10	7-7					Dan Fitzgerald	
1979-80	14-13 ⊗	8-8					Dan Fitzgerald	
1980-81	19-8	9-5					Dan Fitzgerald	
1981-82	15-12	7-7					Jay Hillock	
1982-83	13-14	5-7				John Stockton 184	Jay Hillock	
1983-84	17-11	6-6		John Stockton 20.9		John Stockton 7.2	Jay Hillock	
1984-85	15-13	4-8					Jay Hillock	60-50 .545
1985-86	15-13	8-6					Dan Fitzgerald	
1986-87	18-10	9-5		Doug Spradley 21.6			Dan Fitzgerald	
1987-88	16-12	7-7					Dan Fitzgerald	
1988-89	14-14	5-9		Doug Spradley 605			Dan Fitzgerald	
1989-90	8-20	3-11		Jim McPhee 23.6			Dan Fitzgerald	
1990-91	14-14	5-9					Dan Fitzgerald	
1991-92	20-10	8-6					Dan Fitzgerald	
1992-93	19-9	10-4					Dan Fitzgerald	
1993-94	22-8	12-2	NIT SECOND ROUND	Jeff Brown 21.0			Dan Fitzgerald	
1994-95	21-9	7-7	NCAA FIRST ROUND				Dan Fitzgerald	
1995-96	21-9	10-4	NIT FIRST ROUND			Kyle Dixon 172	Dan Fitzgerald	
1996-97	15-12	8-6					Dan Fitzgerald	252-171 .596
1997-98	24-10	10-4	NIT SECOND ROUND	Bakari Hendrix 19.8			Dan Monson	
1998-99	28-7	12-2	NCAA REGIONAL FINALS	Richie Frahm 14.4	Casey Calvary 6.9	Matt Santangelo 5.3	Dan Monson	52-17 .754
1999-2000	26-9	11-3	NCAA REGIONAL SEMIFINALS	Richie Frahm 16.9	Casey Calvary 6.4	Matt Santangelo 6.4	Mark Few	
2000-01	26-7	13-1	NCAA REGIONAL SEMIFINALS	Casey Calvary 19.0	Casey Calvary 6.7	Dan Dickau 6.3	Mark Few	
2001-02	29-4	13-1	NCAA FIRST ROUND	Dan Dickau 20.3	Cory Violette 8.3	Dan Dickau 4.7	Mark Few	
2002-03	24-9	12-2	NCAA SECOND ROUND	Blake Stepp 18.0	Cory Violette 8.0	Blake Stepp 6.0	Mark Few	
2003-04	28-3	14-0	NCAA SECOND ROUND	Glen McGowan 17.8	Cory Violette 8.2	Blake Stepp 6.7	Mark Few	
2004-05	26-5	12-2	NCAA SECOND ROUND	Adam Morrison 19.0	Ronny Turiaf 9.5	Derek Raivio 4.8	Mark Few	
2005-06	29-4	14-0	NCAA REGIONAL SEMIFINALS	Adam Morrison 28.1	J.P. Batista 9.4	Derek Raivio 2.8	Mark Few	
2006-07	23-11	11-3	NCAA FIRST ROUND	Derek Raivio 18.0	Abdullahi Kuso 4.6	Jeremy Pargo 4.6	Mark Few	
2007-08	25-8	13-1	NCAA FIRST ROUND	Matt Bouldin 12.7	Josh Heytvelt 4.8	Jeremy Pargo 6.0	Mark Few	
2008-09	28-6	14-0	NCAA REGIONAL SEMIFINALS	Josh Heytvelt 14.9	Austin Daye 6.8	Jeremy Pargo 4.9	Mark Few	264-66 .800

Cumulative totals listed when per game averages not available.

⊗ Records don't reflect games forfeited or vacated. For adjusted records, see p. 521.

ESPN 247 SAGARIN

GRAMBLING STATE

Tiger fans are still holding out for their team's first NCAA Tournament. Until it happens, they can at least daydream on a host of sweet memories from Grambling's NAIA heyday in the 1960s. The Tigers won the national title in 1961, finished third in '63 and '66, and produced three NAIA Hall of Famers, including big man Willis Reed.

BEST TEAM: 1960-61 Fabled for their supreme conditioning, the Tigers raced their way to the 1961 NAIA title behind a Who's Who of the greatest players in school history: Reed, tourney MVP and NAIA Hall of Fame forward-center Charles Hardnett, and scintillating guard Hershell West.

BEST PLAYER: C Willis Reed (1960-64) With apologies to forward Bob Hopkins (1952-56), the second-leading scorer in NCAA history (3,759), Mr. Reed from rural Louisiana takes the honors. Stats don't always tell the whole story, but in Reed's case, his senior numbers—26.6 ppg, 21.3 rpg—speak loud and clear.

BEST COACH: Fred Hobby (1956-86) He coached 26 All-Americas, won eight conference championships and is the winningest coach in the state of Louisiana with 571 victories. Talk to any of his players now and what they'll remember most are Lefty's sweat-drenched practices—and his patient mentoring when those practices were finally, mercifully, over.

GAME FOR THE AGES: The Tigers entered the 1961 NAIA tournament as the No. 13 seed out of 32 teams. But with a well-rounded lineup, they were able to outlast No. 1 Westminster and advance to the finals. There, Grambling revved up its trademark fast break to crush No. 3-seed Georgetown (Ky.), 95-75.

FIERCEST RIVAL: Grambling's famed football rivalry with Southern carries over to the hardwood. Fans pack the gyms when the two teams play. (The 1959 game drew a school-record 5,601 to GSU's 4,500-seat arena.) Since 1995-96, the teams have played 18 games that were decided by fewer than six points.

SEASON REVIEW

SEAS.	W-L	CONF.		SCORING		COACH	RECORD	
1956-57[a]	28-8					Fred Hobdy		
1957-58	28-4					Fred Hobdy		
1958-59	28-1					Fred Hobdy		
1959-60	26-5					Fred Hobdy		
1960-61	32-4		◆			Fred Hobdy		
1961-62	20-6					Fred Hobdy		
1962-63	30-3					Fred Hobdy		
1963-64	26-4			Willis Reed	26.6	Fred Hobdy		
1964-65	21-5					Fred Hobdy		
1965-66	27-6					Fred Hobdy		
1966-67	20-7					Fred Hobdy		
1967-68	11-14					Fred Hobdy		
1968-69	20-8					Fred Hobdy		
1969-70	16-8					Fred Hobdy		
1970-71	20-9					Fred Hobdy		
1971-72	19-8					Fred Hobdy		
1972-73	6-18					Fred Hobdy		
1973-74	16-11					Fred Hobdy		
1974-75	16-12					Fred Hobdy		
1975-76	22-9					Fred Hobdy		
1976-77	16-11					Fred Hobdy		
1977-78	10-14	3-9				Fred Hobdy		
1978-79	16-11	6-6				Fred Hobdy		
1979-80	22-8	8-4	■			Fred Hobdy		
1980-81	18-11	7-5				Fred Hobdy		
1981-82	12-17	8-4				Fred Hobdy		
1982-83	6-22	3-11				Fred Hobdy		
1983-84	17-12	7-7				Fred Hobdy		
1984-85	8-19	4-10				Fred Hobdy		
1985-86	14-12	4-10				Fred Hobdy	571-287	.666
1986-87	16-14	11-3				Robert Hopkins		
1987-88	13-17	9-5				Robert Hopkins		
1988-89	15-14	10-4				Robert Hopkins	44-45	.494
1989-90	9-19	5-9				Aaron James		
1990-91	6-22	3-9				Aaron James		
1991-92	4-24	2-12				Aaron James		
1992-93	13-14	5-9				Aaron James		
1993-94	9-18	4-10				Aaron James		
1994-95	11-17	5-9				Aaron James	52-114	.313
1995-96	12-16	6-7				Lacey Reynolds		
1996-97	10-17	5-9		Mark Meredith	14.9	Lacey Reynolds		
1997-98	16-12	10-6		Chris Thomas	13.4	Lacey Reynolds		
1998-99	6-21	5-11		Chris Thomas	17.9	Lacey Reynolds	44-66	.400
1999-2000	1-30	0-18		Chris Thomas	15.2	Larry Wright		
2000-01	8-18	8-10		Paul Haynes	13.9	Larry Wright		
2001-02	9-19	7-11		Paul Haynes	20.2	Larry Wright		
2002-03	12-18	9-9		Paul Haynes	17.3	Larry Wright		
2003-04	11-18	9-9		Brion Rush	19.3	Larry Wright		
2004-05	14-12	11-7		Brion Rush	17.6	Larry Wright		
2005-06	14-13	11-7		Brion Rush	25.7	Larry Wright		
2006-07	12-14	10-8		Andre' Ratliffe	16.4	Larry Wright		
2007-08	7-19	7-11		Anthony Williams	14.5	Larry Wright	88-161	.353
2008-09	6-23	4-14		Ariece Perkins	11.3	Ricky Duckett	6-23	.207

[a] **Records from before 1956-57 have been lost.**

■ NIT appearance ◆ NAIA championship

PROFILE

Grambling State University, Grambling, LA
Founded: 1901 as the Colored Industrial and Agricultural School; named Grambling College in 1946
Enrollment: 5,253 (4,440 undergraduate)
Colors: Black and gold
Nickname: Tigers
Current arena: Health and Physical Education Building, opened in 2007 (7,500)
First game: Dec. 2, 1937
All-time record: 805-696 (.536)
Total weeks in AP Top 20/25: 0

Current conference: Southwestern Athletic (1958-)
Conference titles:
SWAC: 10 (1959, '60, '63, '64 [tie], '66 [tie] , '67 [tie], '71, '72, '87, '89 [tie])
Conference tournament titles: 0
NCAA Tournament appearances: 0
NIT appearances: 1

CONSENSUS ALL-AMERICAS

1961, '62	**Charles Hardnett** (Little A-A), F/C
1963, '64	**Willis Reed** (Little A-A), C
1966	**Johnny Comeaux** (Little A-A), F
1976	**Larry Wright** (D2), G

FIRST-ROUND PRO PICKS

1976	**Larry Wright**, Washington (14)

TOP 5

G	**James Hooper** (1955-59)
G	**Larry Wright** (1973-76)
F	**Bob Hopkins** (1952-56)
F/C	**Charles Hardnett** (1958-62)
C	**Willis Reed** (1960-64)

RECORDS

RECORDS	GAME		SEASON		CAREER	
POINTS	62	Bob Hopkins, vs. Texas College (1955)	1,036	Bob Hopkins (1954-55)	3,759	Bob Hopkins (1952-56)
POINTS PER GAME			32.4	Bob Hopkins (1954-55)	29.1	Bob Hopkins (1952-56)
REBOUNDS	34	Bob McCoy, vs. Tougaloo (1954)	589	Charles Hardnett (1960-61)	2,191	Bob Hopkins (1952-56)
ASSISTS		N/A		N/A		N/A

ESPN 280 SAGARIN

HAMPTON

Hampton's up-tempo style has produced 80 games of 100 or more points over the years, but only one between 1984 and 2008. No matter: The Pirates have found new ways to win, earning three trips to the Big Dance since the turn of the century while producing some of the Tourney's most inspired moments.

BEST TEAM: 2001-02 The season began with an upset of North Carolina. It continued with a 17–1 rampage of the MEAC. The Pirates' magical year ended in the first round of the NCAA Tourney against UConn, 78-67, but not before they nearly pulled off an upset of a No. 2 seed for the second straight season.

BEST PLAYER: C Rick Mahorn (1976-80) Before becoming the Detroit Pistons' baddest Bad Boy, Ricky, as he was known in college, swung that sizeable rump of his for the Pirates, scoring and rebounding at a madman's pace. He's the only Hampton player with 2,000 points (2,418); he pulled down 21 boards or more nine times in his career.

BEST COACH: Hank Ford (1975-87) He took over a 2–21 team and guided it to a stretch of five seasons with 21-plus wins in six years. Having exceeded all others at Hampton in longevity and productivity, Ford's place in Pirates history can't be denied, even if he did go on to become athletic director ... at Howard. (Gasp!)

GAME FOR THE AGES: In the 2001 Tournament, Hampton became just the fourth No. 15 seed to upset a No. 2 seed when Tarvis Williams sank a four-footer with 6.9 seconds left against Iowa State. Coach Steve Merfeld ran around the court aimlessly, à la Jim Valvano, until reserve David Johnson hoisted him into the air.

FIERCEST RIVAL: They share initials and a tradition as historically black colleges, and the Battle of the Real HU between Hampton and Howard is so big now that it's played at New York's Madison Square Garden. There's a blue-collar, white-collar aspect to the competition, as Howard alums needle Hampton folk about their Johnny-come-lately university status. Hampton leads the series, 24–4, since moving to Division I in 1995.

SEASON REVIEW

SEAS.	W-L	CONF.	COACH	SEAS.	W-L	CONF.	COACH
1952-53	16-6		John McLendon	1961-62	7-15		Willie Smith
1953-54	16-13		John McLendon	1962-63	6-15		Frank Enty
1954-55	10-15		Ben Whaley	1963-64	11-8		Lee Royster
1955-56	5-17		Ben Whaley	1964-65	10-10		Ike Moorehead
1956-57	5-17		Ben Whaley	1965-66	10-11		Ike Moorehead
1957-58	8-14		Frank Enty	1966-67	13-10		Ike Moorehead
1958-59	17-10		Frank Enty	1967-68	11-15		Ike Moorehead
1959-60	17-8		Frank Enty	1968-69	13-11		Ike Moorehead
1960-61	15-7		Frank Enty	1969-70	9-17		Ike Moorehead

SEAS.	W-L	CONF.	SCORING		COACH	RECORD
1970-71	10-15				Isaac Tom Moorehead	76-89 .461
1971-72	8-15		Walter Martin	14.8	Louis Shackleford	
1972-73	11-13		W. Martin, W. Youngblood	11.0	Louis Shackleford	19-28 .404
1973-74	12-14		Wayne Britt	17.7	Solomon Frazier	
1974-75	2-21		Tyrone Best	16.5	Solomon Frazier[a]	14-30 .318
1975-76	8-16		Randy White	18.3	Hank Ford	
1976-77	13-15		Marvin Payne	21.2	Hank Ford	
1977-78	24-7		Rick Mahorn	24.0	Hank Ford	
1978-79	24-6		Rick Mahorn	22.8	Hank Ford	
1979-80	21-10		Rick Mahorn	27.6	Hank Ford	
1980-81	17-11		Darryl Warwick	21.9	Hank Ford	
1981-82	28-8		Tony Washington	18.8	Hank Ford	
1982-83	23-7		Tony Washington	20.4	Hank Ford	
1983-84	18-11		Larry Garrick	11.8	Hank Ford	
1984-85	19-8				Hank Ford	
1985-86	16-9		John Stevens	14.9	Hank Ford	
1986-87	17-12				Hank Ford	228-120 .655
1987-88	14-12		Peltre Williams	16.7	Malcolm Avery	
1988-89	17-9		Stacy Clark	14.7	Malcolm Avery	
1989-90	18-11		Kenneth Brown	14.3	Malcolm Avery	
1990-91	22-10		Kenneth Brown	17.2	Malcolm Avery	
1991-92	14-12		Kenneth Brown	18.1	Malcolm Avery	
1992-93	15-12		Kevin Gregory	15.6	Malcolm Avery	
1993-94	21-8		Derett Boyd	16.0	Malcolm Avery	
1994-95	19-7		JaFonde Williams	22.5	Malcolm Avery	140-81 .633
1995-96	9-17		JaFonde Williams	25.7	Byron Samuels	
1996-97	8-19	7-11	Al Bell	12.4	Byron Samuels	17-36 .321
1997-98	14-12	11-7	Torrey Farrington	12.9	Steve Merfeld	
1998-99	8-19	8-10	Torrey Farrington	16.1	Steve Merfeld	
1999-00	17-12	13-5	Marseilles Brown	16.0	Steve Merfeld	
2000-01	25-7	14-4 ●	Tarvis Williams	21.9	Steve Merfeld	
2001-02	26-7	17-1 ●	Tommy Adams	19.8	Steve Merfeld	90-57 .612
2002-03	19-11	13-5	Devin Green	14.9	Bobby Collins	
2003-04	13-17	11-7	Devin Green	15.2	Bobby Collins	
2004-05	17-13	13-5	Bruce Brown	14.3	Bobby Collins	
2005-06	16-16	10-8 ●	Jaz Cowan	13.1	Bobby Collins	65-57 .533
2006-07	15-16	10-8	Rashad West	17.8	Kevin Nickelberry	
2007-08	18-12	11-5	Rashad West	17.2	Kevin Nickelberry	
2008-09	16-16	8-8	Vincent Simpson	11.7	Kevin Nickelberry	49-44 .527

[a] Solomon Frazier (2-16) and Joe Buggs (0-5) both coached during the 1974-75 season.

● NCAA Tournament appearance

PROFILE

Hampton University, Hampton, VA
Founded: 1868
Enrollment: 5,427 (4,700 undergraduate)
Colors: Royal blue and white
Nickname: Pirates
Current arena: Hampton University Convocation Center, opened in 1993 (7,200)
Previous: Holland Hall Gymnasium, 1969-72, 1973-93 (2,600); Hampton High School, 1972-73 (N/A); Williams Gymnasium, 1952-69 (1,000)
First game: 1952

All-time record: 831-692 (.546)
Total weeks in AP Top 20/25: 0
Current conference: Mid-Eastern Athletic (1995-)
Conference titles:
MEAC: 2 (2001 [tie], 2002)
Conference tournament titles:
MEAC: 3 (2001, '02, '06)
NCAA Tournament appearances: 3
NIT appearances: 0

TOP 5

G **Tommy Adams** (1998-2002)
G **JaFonde Williams** (1992-96)
F **Greg Hines** (1979-83)
F **Tarvis Williams** (1997-2001)
C **Rick Mahorn** (1976-80)

RECORDS

RECORDS	GAME		SEASON		CAREER	
POINTS	48	Rick Mahorn, vs. St. Augustine's (Feb. 22, 1980)	855	Rick Mahorn (1979-80)	2,418	Rick Mahorn (1976-80)
POINTS PER GAME			27.6	Rick Mahorn (1979-80)	20.3	Rick Mahorn (1976-80)
REBOUNDS	28	Rick Mahorn, vs. Winston-Salem State (Feb. 24, 1979)	490	Rick Mahorn (1979-80)	1,465	Rick Mahorn (1976-80)
ASSISTS	18	Tony Threatt, vs. Winston-Salem State (Feb. 7, 1977)	214	Darryl Warwick (1979-80)	722	Darryl Warwick (1977-81)

ESPN 322 SAGARIN

HARTFORD

Memories of Vin Baker, coach Gordon McCullough's D2 tourney teams and a stunning 1986 upset of UConn keep Hawks fans warm during the long, cold winters. Going on its third decade in D1, Hartford is still looking for its first NCAA or NIT appearance.

BEST TEAM: 1973-74 The best of Hartford's four straight D2 tournament teams was led by Peter Egan (20.8 ppg, 10.6 rpg); the school's all-time assist co-leader, Chuck Harding; and 1,000-point scorer Bill Brown. Egan and Harding were high school teammates in West Hartford and their chemistry carried the Hawks to their second 20-win season.

BEST PLAYER: F Vin Baker (1989-93) Baker was the ultimate scout's secret: a kid who didn't start in high school until his senior season, yet somehow could do it all for Hartford. He scored in the blocks and from the three-point line, ran the floor, cleaned up on the glass and sent shots packing. He ranked second nationally with 27.6 ppg as a junior and fourth with 28.3 ppg as a senior, and after Milwaukee made him the eighth overall pick of the 1993 draft, was a four-time NBA All-Star.

BEST COACH: Gordon McCullough (1962-76) He led the Hawks to nine straight winning seasons and four straight D2 tournaments. McCullough's players included three of the school's all-time leading scorers (Egan, Mark Noon and Gary Palladino).

GAME FOR THE AGES: In-state big brother UConn owns Hartford, having won 13 of 14 games through 2008-09. Ahh, but that one Hartford victory! On Dec. 29, 1986, coach Jack Phelan's team took a five-game winning streak into a packed Hartford Civic Center and upset Jim Calhoun's Huskies, 49-48.

FIERCEST RIVAL: Hartford used to play the nail to Boston University's hammer, losing 13 of 14 from 2000 to '06. But after a mojo-turning 80-75 double-overtime victory on Jan. 6, 2007, the Hawks have won three of the last seven. That includes a gritty 59-52 win in the 2008 America East tournament semis. BU still holds a commanding series lead, 38–18.

SEASON REVIEW

SEAS.	W-L	CONF.	COACH	SEAS.	W-L	CONF.	COACH
1949-50	7-13		A. Peter LoMaglio	1959-60	7-13		Roy Spear
1950-51	13-7		A. Peter LoMaglio	1960-61	7-14		Roy Spear
1951-52	14-6		A. Peter LoMaglio	1961-62	7-13		Roy Spear
1952-53	20-7		A. Peter LoMaglio	1962-63	11-11		Gordon McCullough
1953-54	11-8		A. Peter LoMaglio	1963-64	10-11		Gordon McCullough
1954-55	10-11		A. Peter LoMaglio	1964-65	12-10		Gordon McCullough
1955-56	10-11		Abe Silverman	1965-66	9-14		Gordon McCullough
1956-57	5-14		Abe Silverman	1966-67	9-11		Gordon McCullough
1957-58	9-13		Roy Spear	1967-68	12-11		Gordon McCullough
1958-59	10-15		Roy Spear	1968-69	17-7		Gordon McCullough

SEAS.	W-L	CONF.	SCORING		COACH	RECORD
1969-70	19-3		Wayne Augustine	20.0	Gordon McCullough	
1970-71	15-8		Tom Meade	22.7	Gordon McCullough	
1971-72	18-6		Edward Hill	21.9	Gordon McCullough	
1972-73	17-7		Peter Egan	18.4	Gordon McCullough	
1973-74	20-4		Peter Egan	20.8	Gordon McCullough	
1974-75	18-7		Peter Egan	19.1	Gordon McCullough	
1975-76	14-7		Mark Noon	20.6	Gordon McCullough	201-117 .632
1976-77	19-8		Mark Noon	21.3	Gary Palladino	
1977-78	15-11		Mark Noon	22.1	Gary Palladino	
1978-79	12-14		Mark Noon	23.7	Gary Palladino	
1979-80	6-21		Bob Tanguay	13.1	Gary Palladino	
1980-81	9-16		Bob Tanguay	18.2	Gary Palladino	61-70 .466
1981-82	8-20		Bob Tanguay	17.7	Jack Phelan	
1982-83	9-18		Ulysses Garcia	18.0	Jack Phelan	
1983-84	12-15		Ulysses Garcia	17.0	Jack Phelan	
1984-85	7-21		Ulysses Garcia	13.0	Jack Phelan	
1985-86	12-16	10-8	Ulysses Garcia	14.2	Jack Phelan	
1986-87	14-14	8-10	Anthony Moye	15.4	Jack Phelan	
1987-88	15-16	12-6	Anthony Moye	19.4	Jack Phelan	
1988-89	15-13	10-7	Lamont Middleton	16.4	Jack Phelan	
1989-90	17-11	8-4	Lamont Middleton	18.9	Jack Phelan	
1990-91	13-16	5-5	Vin Baker	19.6	Jack Phelan	
1991-92	6-21	3-11	Vin Baker	27.6	Jack Phelan	128-181 .414
1992-93	14-14	7-7	Vin Baker	28.3	Paul Brazeau	
1993-94	16-12	9-5	Mike Bond	19.4	Paul Brazeau	
1994-95	11-16	7-9	Mike Bond	20.2	Paul Brazeau	
1995-96	6-22	5-13	Ryan Howse	16.0	Paul Brazeau	
1996-97	17-11	11-7	Anthony Bethune	15.0	Paul Brazeau	
1997-98	15-12	11-7	Justin Bailey	20.1	Paul Brazeau	
1998-99	11-16	9-9	Justin Bailey	20.1	Paul Brazeau	
1999-2000	10-19	6-12	Darrick Jackson	15.8	Paul Brazeau	100-122 .450
2000-01	4-24	1-17	Keyon Smith	12.6	Larry Harrison	
2001-02	14-18	10-6	Deon Saunders	10.9	Larry Harrison	
2002-03	16-13	10-6	Jerell Parker	13.6	Larry Harrison	
2003-04	12-17	6-12	Aaron Cook	15.0	Larry Harrison	
2004-05	8-20	4-14	Aaron Cook	14.9	Larry Harrison	
2005-06	13-15	9-7	Kenny Adeleke	20.7	Larry Harrison	67-107 .385
2006-07	13-18	6-10	Bo Taylor	14.9	Dan Leibovitz	
2007-08	18-16	10-6	Joe Zeglinski	16.2	Dan Leibovitz	
2008-09	7-26	2-14	Joe Zeglinski	15.3	Dan Leibovitz	38-60 .388

PROFILE

University of Hartford, West Hartford, CT
Founded: 1877
Enrollment: 7,366 (5,695 undergraduate)
Colors: Scarlet and white
Nickname: Hawks
Current arena: Chase Arena at Reich Family Pavilion, opened in 1990 (3,508)
First game: 1949
All-time record: 725-802 (.475)
Total weeks in AP Top 20/25: 0

Current conference: America East (1985-)
Conference titles: 0
Conference tournament titles: 0
NCAA Tournament appearances: 0
NIT appearances: 0

CONSENSUS ALL-AMERICAS

1979 **Mark Noon** (D2), G

FIRST-ROUND PRO PICKS

1993 **Vin Baker,** Milwaukee (8)

TOP 5

G **Justin Bailey** (1995-99)
G **Mark Noon** (1975-79)
F **Vin Baker** (1989-93)
F **Ken Gwozdz** (1966-69)
C **Peter Egan** (1971-75)

RECORDS

RECORDS	GAME		SEASON		CAREER	
POINTS	45	Mark Noon, vs. Lowell (Feb. 20, 1978); Gary Palladino, vs. CCNY (Feb. 26, 1966)	792	Vin Baker (1992-93)	2,238	Vin Baker (1989-93)
POINTS PER GAME			28.5	Gary Palladino (1965-66)	25.3	Gary Palladino (1964-67)
REBOUNDS	34	Ken Gwozdz, vs. Yeshiva (Feb. 21, 1968)	418	Ken Gwozdz (1968-69)	1,054	Peter Egan (1971-75)
ASSISTS	15	Ron Berger, vs. Bridgeport (Feb. 14, 1970)	181	Ron Berger (1969-70)	586	Mark Noon (1975-79); Chuck Harding (1971-75)

ESPN 236 SAGARIN

HARVARD

Harvard is associated with greatness everywhere in the world. Except, perhaps, in Lavietes Pavilion, home of the Crimson basketball team, which made its one and only NCAA Tournament appearance in 1946. On the bright side, a few Harvard hoopsters have made names for themselves—albeit in other walks of life—among them former vice president Al Gore, TV analyst James Brown and the late author Michael Crichton.

BEST TEAM: 1945-46 Harvard's greatest season climaxed with a 39-37 defeat of Yale in a packed Boston Arena. The win helped get Harvard to the NCAA Tournament, where it fell to Ohio State in the East Regional semis. But the Crimson's 19–3 finish set a school record for wins that still stands.

BEST PLAYER: F Joe Carrabino (1980-82, '83-85) After sitting out the 1982-83 season with an injury, the 6'7" junior (22.0 ppg) was named Ivy League Player of the Year—Harvard's only winner—and nearly led the Crimson to an upset of Coach K and Duke.

BEST COACH: Edward A. Wachter (1920-33) A true iron man, Wachter played 25 seasons of pre-NBA professional basketball and then coached another 25. He is one of only two Harvard coaches with a winning record in more than one season at the helm (the other is John Clark, who achieved a 20–13 mark from 1900-02). Wachter was inducted into the Naismith Hall of Fame in 1961.

GAME FOR THE AGES: Harvard had one chance of defeating Bill Bradley and NCAA Tournament-bound Princeton on Feb. 7, 1964: shoot the lights out. And that they did. Keith Sedlacek and Merle McClung combined for 61 points to upset the Tigers in Cambridge, 88-82.

FIERCEST RIVAL: Harvard-Yale is an eternal battle over bragging rights as the nation's best (if not athletic, at least academic) college. Alas for the Crimson, the Bulldogs have a lopsided series lead. Not that the two schools agree on the precise numbers; that would be too amicable. Harvard's records have Yale winning 112 of 178 contests; Yale claims 113 victories. Let the schools' debate teams settle the matter.

SEASON REVIEW

SEAS.	W-L	CONF.	COACH	SEAS.	W-L	CONF.	COACH
1900-46	*285-300*	*NCAA Tournament in 1945-46*		1959-60	12-11	6-8	Floyd S. Wilson
1946-47	16-9	5-7	William C. Barclay	1960-61	11-13	4-10	Floyd S. Wilson
1947-48	5-20	1-11	William C. Barclay	1961-62	10-14	3-11	Floyd S. Wilson
1948-49	3-20	0-12	William C. Barclay	1962-63	6-15	5-9	Floyd S. Wilson
1949-50	9-15	3-9	Norman Shepard	1963-64	12-10	6-8	Floyd S. Wilson
1950-51	8-18	3-9	Norman Shepard	1964-65	11-12	6-8	Floyd S. Wilson
1951-52	5-17	0-12	Norman Shepard	1965-66	10-14	6-8	Floyd S. Wilson
1952-53	7-16	2-10	Norman Shepard	1966-67	10-14	4-10	Floyd S. Wilson
1953-54	9-16	2-12	Norman Shepard	1967-68	7-14	4-10	Floyd S. Wilson
1954-55	7-16	3-11	Floyd S. Wilson	1968-69	7-18	3-11	Robert W. Harrison
1955-56	8-16	3-11	Floyd S. Wilson	1969-70	7-19	1-13	Robert W. Harrison
1956-57	12-9	7-7	Floyd S. Wilson	1970-71	16-10	11-3	Robert W. Harrison
1957-58	16-9	7-7	Floyd S. Wilson	1971-72	15-11	8-6	Robert W. Harrison
1958-59	10-15	4-10	Floyd S. Wilson	1972-73	14-12	7-7	Robert W. Harrison

SEAS.	W-L	CONF.	SCORING		COACH	RECORD
1973-74	11-13	9-5	Lou Silver	16.2	Thomas Sanders	
1974-75	12-13	9-5	Lou Silver	16.1	Thomas Sanders	
1975-76	8-18	3-11	Brian Banks	14.9	Thomas Sanders	
1976-77	9-16	6-8	Steve Irion	14.3	Thomas Sanders	40-60 .400
1977-78	11-15	7-7	Brian Banks	15.6	Frank McLaughlin	
1978-79	8-21	6-8	Bob Hooft	15.1	Frank McLaughlin	
1979-80	11-15	6-8	Don Fleming	19.9	Frank McLaughlin	
1980-81	16-10	9-5	Don Fleming	19.1	Frank McLaughlin	
1981-82	11-15	6-8	Don Fleming	16.8	Frank McLaughlin	
1982-83	12-14	4-10	Bob Ferry	14.7	Frank McLaughlin	
1983-84	15-11	9-5	Joe Carrabino	22.0	Frank McLaughlin	
1984-85	15-9	7-7	Joe Carrabino	21.4	Frank McLaughlin	99-110 .474
1985-86	6-20	2-12	Keith Webster	11.6	Peter Roby	
1986-87	9-17	4-10	Arne Duncan	16.9	Peter Roby	
1987-88	11-15	6-8	Ralph James	14.5	Peter Roby	
1988-89	11-15	7-7	Ralph James	14.2	Peter Roby	
1989-90	12-14	7-7	Ralph James	20.1	Peter Roby	
1990-91	9-17	6-8	Ralph James	18.0	Peter Roby	58-98 .372
1991-92	6-20	5-9	Tyler Rullman	15.4	Frank Sullivan	
1992-93	6-20	3-11	Tyler Rullman	22.4	Frank Sullivan	
1993-94	9-17	5-9	Darren Rankin	12.3	Frank Sullivan	
1994-95	6-20	4-10	Kyle Snowden	13.9	Frank Sullivan	
1995-96	15-11	7-7	Kyle Snowden	15.1	Frank Sullivan	
1996-97	17-9	10-4	Kyle Snowden	16.4	Frank Sullivan	
1997-98	13-13	6-8	Mike Scott	15.1	Frank Sullivan	
1998-99	13-13	7-7	Tim Hill	16.0	Frank Sullivan	
1999-2000	12-15	7-7	Dan Clemente	18.6	Frank Sullivan	
2000-01	14-12	7-7	Dan Clemente	18.7	Frank Sullivan	
2001-02	14-12	7-7	Patrick Harvey	18.1	Frank Sullivan	
2002-03	12-15	4-10	Patrick Harvey	16.7	Frank Sullivan	
2003-04	4-23	3-11	Kevin Rogus	14.7	Frank Sullivan	
2004-05	12-15	7-7	Matt Stehle	13.7	Frank Sullivan	
2005-06	13-14	5-9	Jim Goffredo	14.9	Frank Sullivan	
2006-07	12-16	5-9	Brian Cusworth	17.4	Frank Sullivan	178-245 .421
2007-08	8-22	3-11	Jeremy Lin	12.6	Tommy Amaker	
2008-09	14-14	6-8	Jeremy Lin	17.8	Tommy Amaker	22-36 .379

PROFILE

Harvard University, Cambridge, MA
Founded: 1636
Enrollment: 20,042 (6,715 undergraduate)
Colors: Crimson
Nickname: Crimson
Current arena: Ray Lavietes Pavilion, opened as the Briggs Athletic Center in 1926 (2,050)
Previous: Indoor Athletic Building, 1930-82 (N/A)
First game: Dec. 11, 1900
All-time record: 945-1,232 (.434)
Total weeks in AP Top 20/25: 0

Current conference: Ivy League (1901-07, '33-)
Conference titles: 0
NCAA Tournament appearances: 1
NIT appearances: 0

CONSENSUS ALL-AMERICAS

1906 **Harold Amberg**, C
1906 **Ralph Griffiths**, G

FIRST-ROUND PRO PICKS

1948 **George Hauptfuhrer**, Boston (3)
1951 **Ed Smith**, New York (6)

TOP 5

G **Tim Hill** (1995-99)
G **Ralph James** (1987-91)
F **Joe Carrabino** (1980-82, '83-85)
F **Don Fleming** (1978-82)
F **Wyndol Gray** (1945-46)

RECORDS	GAME		SEASON		CAREER	
POINTS	45	Brady Merchant, vs. Brown (March 8, 2003)	629	Jim Fitzsimmons (1971-72)	1,880	Joe Carrabino (1980-82, '83-85)
POINTS PER GAME			24.2	Jim Fitzsimmons (1971-72)	18.4	Joe Carrabino (1980-82, '83-85)
REBOUNDS	31	Bob Canty, vs. Boston College (Feb. 8, 1955)	343	Floyd Lewis (1970-71)	913	Kyle Snowden (1993-97)
ASSISTS	16	Elliott Prasse-Freeman, vs. Mercer (Dec. 19, 2002)	207	Elliott Prasse-Freeman (2002-03) Glenn Fine (1978-79)	705	Elliott Prasse-Freeman (1999-2003)

ESPN 150 SAGARIN

HAWAII

Every now and then, the sun shines on the Rainbow Warriors. It seems that the key to each of UH's periods of success was luring big-time junior-college recruits to the islands—most notably in the 1970s when Red Rocha brought the Fabulous Five, and in the 1990s when Riley Wallace signed Anthony Carter.

BEST TEAM: 1971-72 Behind the Fabulous Five—center and future coach Bob Nash, guards Jerome Freeman and Dwight Holiday and forwards Al Davis and John Penebacker—the Rainbows raced past opponents to the tune of 91.7 ppg. They were truly inspired at home, routinely selling out the 7,500-seat Honolulu International Center (as Blaisdell Arena was known then) and winning all 19 of their home games to help seal the team's first NCAA Tournament bid.

BEST PLAYER: G TOM HENDERSON (1972-74) Henderson was chosen as a member of the 1972 U.S. Olympic team before he even suited up for Hawaii. Once he became a Warrior, he showed his two-way skills, leaving Hawaii as the school's all-time leader in scoring average (20.0 ppg) and steals (160).

BEST COACH: RILEY WALLACE (1987-2007) He was notorious for barking at players from the sideline. But Wallace got results; witness his 334 wins at Hawaii and the three NCAA Tournament and six NIT invitations his teams earned.

GAME FOR THE AGES: In the title game of its own Outrigger Hotels Rainbow Classic on Dec. 30, 1997, Hawaii used a 1-2-2 zone to stifle No. 2-ranked Kansas, 76-65. As the *Honolulu Star-Bulletin* suggested, "If you want to see a bigger win—and one as odds-defying—go rent *Hoosiers*."

FIERCEST RIVAL: After Hawaii lost to Fresno State, 85-83, in the quarterfinals of the 1998 NIT, Bulldogs guard Chris Herren danced on the scorers' table. A Hawaii fan responded by throwing a beer at his head. It was the culmination of a bitter feud between Herren and Rainbows rooters, who often taunted him for having a troubled past. The bad blood between the WAC foes lingers. Fresno leads overall, 23–16.

SEASON REVIEW

SEAS.	W-L	CONF.	COACH	SEAS.	W-L	CONF.	COACH
1912-47[a]	*119-89*	*17-0 over two seasons (1930-32)*		1960-61	6-9		Al Saake
1947-48	2-3		Art Gallon	1961-62	2-10		Al Saake
1948-49	1-3		Art Gallon	1962-63	5-13		Al Saake
1949-50	1-14		Art Gallon	1963-64	2-9		Red Rocha
1950-51	0-3		Art Gallon	1964-65	1-12		Red Rocha
1951-52	3-5		Al Saake	1965-66	0-18		Red Rocha
1952-53	5-10		Al Saake	1966-67	2-20		Red Rocha
1953-54	7-13		Al Saake	1967-68	13-8		Red Rocha
1954-55	2-15		Ah Chew Goo	1968-69	7-16		Red Rocha
1955-56	0-2		Ah Chew Goo	1969-70	6-20		Red Rocha
1956-57	3-10		Ah Chew Goo	1970-71	23-5	■	Red Rocha
1957-58	0-4		Al Saake	1971-72	24-3	●	Red Rocha
1958-59	6-9		Al Saake	1972-73	15-11		Red Rocha
1959-60	6-18		Al Saake	1973-74	19-9	■	Bruce O'Neil

SEAS.	W-L	CONF.	SCORING		COACH	RECORD
1974-75	14-11		Jimmie Baker	15.1	Bruce O'Neil	
1975-76	11-16		Reggie Carter	16.6	Bruce O'Neil	44-36 .550
1976-77	9-18		Gavin Smith	23.4	Larry Little	
1977-78	1-26		Tony Wells	14.8	Larry Little	
1978-79	10-17		Eric Bowman	12.5	Larry Little	
1979-80	13-14	4-10	Aaron Strayhorn	15.9	Larry Little	
1980-81	14-13	7-9	Aaron Strayhorn	13.4	Larry Little	
1981-82	17-10	9-7	Clarence Dickerson	17.0	Larry Little	
1982-83	17-11	9-7	Tony Webster	13.5	Larry Little	
1983-84	12-16	6-10	Jack Miller	15.4	Larry Little	
1984-85	10-18	5-11	Andre Morgan	16.4	Larry Little	103-143 .419
1985-86	4-24	1-15	Andre Morgan	14.6	Frank Arnold	
1986-87	7-21	2-14	Chris Gaines	17.1	Frank Arnold	11-45 .196
1987-88	4-25	2-14	Chris Gaines	16.3	Riley Wallace	
1988-89	17-13	9-7 ■	Reggie Cross	18.6	Riley Wallace	
1989-90	25-10	10-6 ■	Chris Gaines	17.6	Riley Wallace	
1990-91	16-13	7-9	Ray Reed	19.9	Riley Wallace	
1991-92	16-12	9-7	Phil Lott	18.5	Riley Wallace	
1992-93	12-16	7-11	Fabio Ribeiro	14.1	Riley Wallace	
1993-94	18-15	11-7 ●	Trevor Ruffin	20.8	Riley Wallace	
1994-95	16-13	8-10	Tes Whitlock	16.3	Riley Wallace	
1995-96	10-18	7-11	Anthony Harris	22.4	Riley Wallace	
1996-97	21-8	12-4 ■	Anthony Carter	18.7	Riley Wallace	
1997-98	21-9	8-6 ■	Alika Smith	18.2	Riley Wallace	
1998-99	6-20	3-11	Marquette Alexander	13.4	Riley Wallace	
1999-2000	17-12	5-9	Marquette Alexander	15.0	Riley Wallace	
2000-01	17-14	8-8 ●	Predrag Savovic	17.6	Riley Wallace	
2001-02	27-6	15-3 ●	Predrag Savovic	20.3	Riley Wallace	
2002-03	19-12	9-9 ■	Carl English	19.6	Riley Wallace	
2003-04	21-12	11-7 ■	Michael Kuebler	18.1	Riley Wallace	
2004-05	16-13	7-11	Matt Gibson	13.0	Riley Wallace	
2005-06	17-11	10-6	Julian Sensley	17.6	Riley Wallace	
2006-07	18-13	8-8	Matt Lojeski	16.9	Riley Wallace	334-265 .558
2007-08	11-19	7-9	Matt Gibson	17.0	Bob Nash	
2008-09	13-17	5-11	Roderick Flemings	16.6	Bob Nash	24-36 .400

[a] Records until 1968-69 include only games played against collegiate teams.

● NCAA Tournament appearance ■ NIT appearance

PROFILE

University of Hawaii at Manoa, Manoa, HI
Founded: 1907
Enrollment: 18,972 (12,787 undergraduate)
Colors: Green, black, silver and white
Nickname: Rainbow Warriors
Current arena: Stan Sheriff Center, opened in 1994 (10,300)
Previous: Neal S. Blaisdell Center Arena, 1967-94 (7,500); Otto Klum Gym, 1958-67 (3,800)
First game: 1912
All-time record: 777-877 (.470)
Total weeks in AP Top 20/25: 16

Current conference: Western Athletic (1979-)
Conference titles:
WAC: 2 (1997 [tie], 2002 [tie])
Conference tournament titles:
WAC: 3 (1994, 2001, '02)
NCAA Tournament appearances: 4
NIT appearances: 8

FIRST-ROUND PRO PICKS

1972 **Bob Nash,** Detroit (9)
1974 **Tom Henderson,** Atlanta (7)
1975 **Jimmie Baker,** Kentucky (ABA, 10)

TOP 5

G **Anthony Carter** (1996-98)
G **Chris Gaines** (1986-90)
G **Tom Henderson** (1972-74)
F **Julian Sensley** (2003-06)
F/C **Bob Nash** (1970-72)

RECORDS

	GAME		SEASON		CAREER	
POINTS	45	Tony Davis, vs. Cal State L.A., (Feb. 6, 1959)	626	Anthony Harris (1995-96)	1,734	Chris Gaines (1986-90)
POINTS PER GAME			23.4	Gavin Smith (1976-77)	20.0	Tom Henderson (1972-74)
REBOUNDS	30	Bob Nash, vs. Arizona State (Dec. 30, 1971)	361	Bob Nash (1971-72)	1,098	Melton Werts (1972-76)
ASSISTS	19	Reggie Carter, vs. San Francisco (Dec. 12, 1975)	212	Anthony Carter (1997-98)	412	Troy Bowe (1988-91)

THE SCHOOLS

ESPN 270 SAGARIN

HIGH POINT

NCAA Tournament bids? National TV games? First-round draft picks? These achievements are not part of High Point lore just yet. But how many programs can boast a story this sweet: On April 14, 2004, F Danny Gathings attended a convocation service at conference rival Liberty and handed over his 2004 Big South tournament MVP trophy to Flames guard Larry Blair—simply because Gathings felt Blair was more deserving.

BEST TEAM: 1964-65 In his third year at High Point, coach Thomas Quinn revved up the Panthers' attack, to great success. The team scored 100-plus points three times. Unfortunately, High Point ran out of gas in the second round of the NAIA tournament, losing to Winston-Salem State and the great Earl Monroe, 78-62.

BEST PLAYER: F Arizona Reid (2004-08) This hard-working forward could fill it up from three and post up, beat guys off the dribble and outmuscle them for boards. He's the only conference player to finish his career with both 2,000 points and 1,000 rebounds.

BEST COACH: Bart Lundy (2003-) His glasses and bald head make this 30-something look like a grizzled hoops veteran. So do his results. Upon his arrival, he cranked up the pace on both offense (his teams have led the Big South in scoring twice) and defense (the Panthers perennially rank among the league leaders in field goal percentage defense).

GAME FOR THE AGES: In a 130-71 victory over Belmont Abbey on Jan. 2, 1965, Kirk Stewart was sick—both literally ill and sick as in "unstoppable." Before the game, the lefty was so far under the weather he wasn't even sure he'd be able to play. He scored 51 points.

FIERCEST RIVAL: Whenever the big, bad bullies from Winthrop show up in High Point, it's a standing-room-only affair at the Millis Athletic Center. In the event of an upset victory (the Eagles lead the series, 22–4), the place goes bonkers. Witness the YouTube video of the High Point faithful shaking the gym when Eagles guard Antwon Harris missed a last-second bank shot to give the Panthers a 63-62 win on Jan. 12, 2008.

SEASON REVIEW

SEAS.	W-L	CONF.	COACH	SEAS.	W-L	CONF.	COACH
1927-46	*260-141*	*24-1 under Virgil Yow in 1941-42*		1959-60	16-7		Virgil Yow
1946-47	14-8		Ralph James	1960-61	14-10		Virgil Yow
1947-48	15-6		Ralph James	1961-62	14-12		Virgil Yow
1948-49	16-8		Ralph James	1962-63	22-7		Thomas Quinn
1949-50	25-2		Ralph James	1963-64	25-7		Thomas Quinn
1950-51	19-11		Bob Davis	1964-65	29-4		Thomas Quinn
1951-52	20-10		Bob Davis	1965-66	19-7		Thomas Quinn
1952-53	17-13		Bob Davis	1966-67	5-18		Bob Vaughn
1953-54	7-23		Virgil Yow	1967-68	15-11		Bob Vaughn
1954-55	14-17		Virgil Yow	1968-69	28-3		Bob Vaughn
1955-56	16-17		Virgil Yow	1969-70	13-17		Bob Vaughn
1956-57	20-10		Virgil Yow	1970-71	12-18		Bob Vaughn
1957-58	17-9		Virgil Yow	1971-72	13-16		J.D. Barnett
1958-59	15-12		Virgil Yow	1972-73	11-15		Jerry Steele

SEAS.	W-L	CONF.	SCORING		COACH	RECORD	
1973-74	8-19		Pete Collins	23.6	Jerry Steele		
1974-75	16-15		Pearlee Shaw	13.9	Jerry Steele		
1975-76	12-14		Pearlee Shaw	13.0	Jerry Steele		
1976-77	13-14		Ray Coble	15.3	Jerry Steele		
1977-78	16-14		Danny Anderson	15.1	Jerry Steele		
1978-79	27-6		Charlie Floyd	20.7	Jerry Steele		
1979-80	22-8		Bruce Floyd	11.3	Jerry Steele		
1980-81	16-12		Jeff Anderson	12.0	Jerry Steele		
1981-82	15-10		Bruce Floyd	11.3	Jerry Steele		
1982-83	6-19		Danny Murphy	14.5	Jerry Steele		
1983-84	15-9		Mike Everett	12.5	Jerry Steele		
1984-85	18-12		Odell Walker	14.0	Jerry Steele		
1985-86	11-17		Tony Bolde	12.0	Jerry Steele		
1986-87	18-11		Roy Smith	15.7	Jerry Steele		
1987-88	22-6		Roy Smith	15.8	Jerry Steele		
1988-89	22-6		Kenny Drummond	21.5	Jerry Steele		
1989-90	8-17		George Byers	20.5	Jerry Steele		
1990-91	12-18		Jay Witmer	15.9	Jerry Steele		
1991-92	16-14				Jerry Steele		
1992-93	12-15				Jerry Steele		
1993-94	21-8				Jerry Steele		
1994-95	20-9		Robert Martin	22.4	Jerry Steele		
1995-96	24-7		Brett Speight	16.6	Jerry Steele		
1996-97	18-12		Brett Speight	21.6	Jerry Steele		
1997-98	12-13		Brian Wise	17.6	Jerry Steele		
1998-99	10-16		Geordie Cullen	18.3	Jerry Steele		
1999-2000	11-17	5-9	Geordie Cullen	15.4	Jerry Steele		
2000-01	8-20	3-11	Dus Van Weerdhuizen	11.8	Jerry Steele		
2001-02	11-19	5-9	Dus Van Weerdhuizen	16.4	Jerry Steele		
2002-03	7-20	3-11	Danny Gathings	18.7	Jerry Steele	458-412	.526
2003-04	19-11	10-6	Danny Gathings	15.8	Bart Lundy		
2004-05	13-18	7-9	Zione White	12.0	Bart Lundy		
2005-06	16-13	8-8	Arizona Reid	18.3	Bart Lundy		
2006-07	22-10	11-3	Arizona Reid	21.0	Bart Lundy		
2007-08	17-14	8-6	Arizona Reid	23.9	Bart Lundy		
2008-09	9-21	4-14	Nick Barbour	14.2	Bart Lundy	96-87	.525

PROFILE

High Point University, High Point, NC
Founded: 1924
Enrollment: 3,250 (2,330 undergraduate)
Colors: Purple and white
Nickname: Panthers
Current arena: Millis Athletic Center, opened in 1992 (2,565)
Previous: Alumni Gym, 1957-92 (N/A); Harrison Hall, 1927-57 (N/A)
First game: 1927
All-time record: 1,254-923 (.576)
Total weeks in AP Top 20/25: 0

Current conference: Big South (1999-)
Conference titles: 0
Conference tournament titles: 0
NCAA Tournament appearances: 0
NIT appearances: 0

TOP 5

G **Gene Littles** (1965-69)
G **Tubby Smith** (1969-1973)
F **Danny Gathings** (2002-05)
F **Arizona Reid** (2004-08)
F **Kirk Stewart** (1962-65)

RECORDS	GAME		SEASON		CAREER	
POINTS	51	Kirk Stewart, vs. Belmont Abbey (Jan. 2, 1965)	779	Danny Witt (1969-70)	2,398	Gene Littles (1965-69)
POINTS PER GAME			25.9	Danny Witt (1969-70)	23.3	Gene Littles (1965-69)
REBOUNDS	31	Steve Afendis, vs. Newberry (1957)	424	Jim Picks (1968-69)	1,268	Pete Collins (1970-74)
ASSISTS		N/A	185	Tracy Gross (1996-97)	376	Landon Quick (2003-07)

ESPN 184 SAGARIN

HOFSTRA

It's hard to be a mid-major college hoops team in Hempstead, N.Y., where the Jets used to train and the Islanders play. But every once in a while, the Pride—known as the Flying Dutchmen until 2000—steal a few headlines. Such as: *Hofstra Doing Wright Thing … Greedy for Speedy … Van Breda Kolff Exits a Champion.*

BEST TEAM: 1999-2000 With two future NBA players in guard Craig "Speedy" Claxton and swingman Norman Richardson, coach Jay Wright scheduled a brutal nonconference schedule that included opponents from the Big East, Pac-10 and SEC. Hofstra didn't spring any upsets, but it emerged battle-tested and tore through the America East to reach its first NCAA Tournament in 23 years. There it fell in the first round to Elite Eight-bound Oklahoma State, 86-66.

BEST PLAYER: F/C BILL THIEBEN (1953-56) At 6'6", he could score nearly at will, averaging 26.9 ppg in his three seasons. But rebounding was his true calling; no other Flying Dutchman or Pride has come within 150 boards of Thieben's *worst* season (590).

BEST COACH: BUTCH VAN BREDA KOLFF (1955-62, '88-94) Before and after the fiery vagabond clashed with Wilt Chamberlain as the Lakers head coach and became one of the innovators of the Princeton offense, van Breda Kolff was squeezing every last win possible out of mixed-bag lineups at Hofstra.

GAME FOR THE AGES: The final seconds ticked off, the fans rushed the court and Claxton stood atop the scorer's table to soak it all in. In the 2000 America East title game against Delaware, the 5'10" guard scored 24 points and handed out eight assists to send Hofstra to the NCAA Tournament, 76-69.

FIERCEST RIVAL: Manhattan and Hofstra haven't played every year since their first meeting in 1937. But from the Flying Dutchmen's 1958 upset of the Jaspers on Ray Cunneen's last-second free throws to their intense and usually evenly matched battles now, the two teams prove that New York metro bragging rights bring out their best. Manhattan leads overall, 37-20.

SEASON REVIEW

SEAS.	W-L	CONF.	COACH	SEAS.	W-L	CONF.	COACH
1936-47	*127-88*		*Jack McDonald, 100-56 in 8 seasons*	1960-61	21-4		B. van Breda Kolff
1947-48	13-6		Frank Reilly	1961-62	24-4		B. van Breda Kolff
1948-49	18-8		Frank Reilly	1962-63	23-7		Paul Lynner
1949-50	17-9		Frank Reilly	1963-64	23-6		Paul Lynner
1950-51	18-11		Frank Reilly	1964-65	11-14		Paul Lynner
1951-52	26-3		Frank Reilly	1965-66	16-10	6-3	Paul Lynner
1952-53	20-7		Frank Reilly	1966-67	12-13	2-7	Paul Lynner
1953-54	15-9		Frank Reilly	1967-68	13-12	1-7	Paul Lynner
1954-55	19-7		Frank Reilly	1968-69	12-13	4-4	Paul Lynner
1955-56	22-4		B. van Breda Kolff	1969-70	13-13	2-3	Paul Lynner
1956-57	11-15		B. van Breda Kolff	1970-71	16-8	4-2	Paul Lynner
1957-58	15-8		B. van Breda Kolff	1971-72	11-14	2-4	Paul Lynner
1958-59	20-7		B. van Breda Kolff	1972-73	8-16	1-5	Roger Gaeckler
1959-60	23-1		B. van Breda Kolff	1973-74	8-16	1-5	Roger Gaeckler

SEAS.	W-L	CONF.		SCORING		COACH	RECORD	
1974-75	11-13	3-3		Bernard Tomlin	19.8	Roger Gaeckler		
1975-76	18-12	3-2	●	Rich Laurel	20.3	Roger Gaeckler		
1976-77	23-7	4-1	●	Rich Laurel	30.3	Roger Gaeckler		
1977-78	8-19	0-5		Doug Swanson	12.5	Roger Gaeckler		
1978-79	8-19	3-9		Henry Hollingsworth	21.5	Roger Gaeckler	84-102	.452
1979-80	14-14	6-5		David Taylor	17.6	Joe Harrington	14-14	.500
1980-81	12-15	5-6		David Taylor	16.2	Dick Berg		
1981-82	12-16	4-7		David Taylor	17.9	Dick Berg		
1982-83	18-9	7-2		David Taylor	16.3	Dick Berg		
1983-84	14-14	9-7		Doug Mills	16.6	Dick Berg		
1984-85	14-15	5-9		Tom Schreyer	15.4	Dick Berg		
1985-86	17-13	9-5		Luke Murphy	14.6	Dick Berg		
1986-87	10-18	4-10		Leroy Allen	15.7	Dick Berg		
1987-88	6-21	2-12		Frank Walker	15.6	Dick Berg	103-121	.460
1988-89	14-15	7-7		Derrick Flowers	13.3	Butch van Breda Kolff		
1989-90	13-15	8-6		Frank Walker	15.0	Butch van Breda Kolff		
1990-91	14-14	7-5		Erroll Flanigan	12.7	Butch van Breda Kolff		
1991-92	20-9	10-2		Demetrius Dudley	21.7	Butch van Breda Kolff		
1992-93	9-18			Demetrius Dudley	22.7	Butch van Breda Kolff		
1993-94	9-20	1-4		James Shaffer	15.4	Butch van Breda Kolff	215-134	.616
1994-95	10-18	5-11		John Mavroukas	15.1	Jay Wright		
1995-96	9-18	5-13		Lawrence Thomas	14.4	Jay Wright		
1996-97	12-15	9-9		Craig "Speedy" Claxton	15.0	Jay Wright		
1997-98	19-12	11-7		Craig "Speedy" Claxton	16.3	Jay Wright		
1998-99	22-10	14-4	■	Norman Richardson	13.9	Jay Wright		
1999-2000	24-7	16-2	●	Craig "Speedy" Claxton	22.8	Jay Wright		
2000-01	26-5	16-2	●	Norman Richardson	16.7	Jay Wright	122-85	.589
2001-02	12-20	5-13		Rick Apodaca	17.7	Tom Pecora		
2002-03	8-21	6-12		Kenny Adeleke	16.1	Tom Pecora		
2003-04	14-15	10-8		Wendell Gibson	14.3	Tom Pecora		
2004-05	21-9	12-6	■	Loren Stokes	18.3	Tom Pecora		
2005-06	26-7	14-4	■	Loren Stokes	17.4	Tom Pecora		
2006-07	22-10	14-4	■	Loren Stokes	20.3	Tom Pecora		
2007-08	12-18	8-10		Antoine Agudio	22.7	Tom Pecora		
2008-09	21-11	11-7		Charles Jenkins	19.7	Tom Pecora	136-111	.551

● NCAA Tournament appearance ■ NIT appearance

PROFILE

Hofstra University, Hempstead, NY
Founded: 1935
Enrollment: 12,999 (9,053 undergraduate)
Colors: Gold, white and blue
Nickname: Pride
Current arena: David S. Mack Sports and Exhibition Complex, opened in 2000 as Hofstra Arena (5,047)
Previous: Physical Fitness Center, 1970-99 (N/A); Calkins Gymnasium, 1938-70 (N/A)
First game: Dec. 17, 1936
All-time record: 1,097-825 (.571)
Total weeks in AP Top 20/25: 0

Current conference: Colonial Athletic Association (2001-)
Conference titles:
East Coast: 1 (1992)
America East: 2 (2000, '01)
Conference tournament titles:
East Coast: 3 (1976, '77, '94)
America East: 2 (2000, '01)
NCAA Tournament appearances: 4
NIT appearances: 4

FIRST-ROUND PRO PICKS

1977 **Rich Laurel,** Portland (19)
2000 **Craig "Speedy" Claxton,** Philadelphia (20)

TOP 5

G **Craig "Speedy" Claxton** (1996-2000)
G **Rich Laurel** (1973-77)
G **Steve Nisenson** (1962-65)
F **John Irving** (1974-77)
F/C **Bill Thieben** (1953-56)

RECORDS

	GAME		SEASON		CAREER	
POINTS	48	Bill Thieben, vs. Union (Dec. 11, 1954)	908	Rich Laurel (1976-77)	2,276	Antoine Agudio (2004-08)
POINTS PER GAME			30.3	Rich Laurel (1976-77)	26.9	Bill Thieben (1953-56)
REBOUNDS	43	Bill Thieben, vs. Springfield (1954-55)	627	Bill Thieben (1954-55)	1,837	Bill Thieben (1953-56)
ASSISTS	16	Robbie Weingard, vs. Bloomfield (Jan. 19, 1984)	228	Robbie Weingard (1984-85)	660	Craig "Speedy" Claxton (1996-2000)

ESPN 100 SAGARIN

HOLY CROSS

Holy Cross is inextricably linked by alums Bob Cousy and Tom Heinsohn to the Boston Celtics' reign of the late 1950s and early '60s. But the Crusaders, NCAA champion in 1947 and NIT champ in 1954, have been relegated to small-school anonymity in recent decades, competing for the Patriot League's automatic Tournament bid. That the Big East considered adding Holy Cross in 1979 seems almost unfathomable today.

BEST TEAM: 1946-47 Even though the Crusaders didn't have an on-campus gym, they set new standards for speed and creativity, fueled by veteran guard Joe Mullaney, athletic big man George Kaftan and freshman sparkplug Cousy. After dispatching Navy and CCNY in the NCAA Tournament, the Cross beat Oklahoma to win it all.

BEST PLAYER: G BOB COUSY (1946-50) He arrived in Worcester as a showboating New Yorker known for his behind-the-back dribbling and fancy passing. Even though he came off the bench as a freshman after butting heads with coach Alvin "Doggie" Julian, Cousy helped the Crusaders win the NCAA title. He continued to struggle with his coach's rotation the following season, even contemplating a transfer to St. John's, but eventually his talent won out. The three-time All-America broke the school's scoring record before going on to a legendary pro career as the Cooz with the Celtics.

BEST COACH: GEORGE BLANEY (1972-94) He was the face of Holy Cross basketball for 22 years, returning the Crusaders to prominence (and the postseason) following their mid-century peak. Blaney was New England Coach of the Year after taking the Cross to the 1975 NIT. Holy Cross made the NCAA Tournament three times during his tenure.

GAME FOR THE AGES: In the NCAA Final on March 25, 1947, a smaller, faster Holy Cross team held off Oklahoma to win the championship, 58-47. Kaftan—the tallest of the Crusaders at 6'3"—finished with a team-high 18 points. He also made another valuable contribution when, to break the tension during Coach Julian's halftime talk, he picked up a trash can and rolled it through the locker room.

HEARTBREAKER: In the 1948 Final Four, Holy Cross' short lineup was no match for Kentucky's Fabulous Five and its imposing 6'7" center, Alex Groza, in a 60-52 loss. Defended by Dale Barnstable and Kenneth Rollins, Cousy struggled mightily, making just one field goal and ending up with only five points.

FIERCEST RIVAL: For years, the Crusaders' biggest rival was Boston College. The two schools engaged in one of the nation's first football series, and when Holy Cross stopped playing basketball in 1909, it took BC's urging to revive the program 11 years later. In 1979, when BC got the Big East nod instead of Holy Cross, the rivalry deepened. Even though the two teams stopped playing in 2006, school officials have promised the series will start anew. Holy Cross leads overall, 57–52.

Cousy continued to struggle with his coach's rotation, even contemplating a transfer, but eventually his talent won out.

FANFARE AND HOOPLA: Holy Cross alumni like to reminisce about the effect Crusaders fans had on making the old Boston Garden such an advantageous home court when Cousy and Heinsohn were winning NBA rings. These days, the on-campus Hart Center could use a little bit of that creative ardor; when students got rowdy in a 2006 game against Bucknell, the Catholic school's administration was quick to reprimand their "crude language" and "catcalls."

FAN FAVORITE: G RONALD PERRY (1951-54) All he did was pitch the Crusaders to the 1952 College World Series baseball title, then lead the hoops team to the 1954 NIT championship. He also served as AD for 26 years.

CONSENSUS ALL-AMERICAS

1950 **Bob Cousy,** G
1956 **Tom Heinsohn,** F

FIRST-ROUND PRO PICKS

1950 **Bob Cousy,** Tri-Cities (4)
1954 **Togo Palazzi,** Boston (5)
1956 **Tom Heinsohn,** Boston (6)

PROFILE

College of the Holy Cross, Worcester, MA
Founded: 1843
Enrollment: 2,800 (2,800 undergraduate)
Colors: Royal purple
Nickname: Crusaders
Current arena: Hart Recreation Center, opened in 1975 (3,600)
Previous: Worcester Auditorium, 1949-75 (3,200)
First game: Jan. 11, 1901
All-time record: 1,279-828 (.607)
Total weeks in AP Top 20/25: 79

Current conference: Patriot League (1990-)
Conference titles:
Patriot: 5 (1994 [tie], 2001, '03, '05, '07 [tie])
Conference tournament titles:
Eastern Collegiate Athletic North: 1 (1980)
Patriot: 5 (1993, 2001, '02, '03, '07)
NCAA Tournament appearances: 12
Final Fours: 2
Titles: 1 (1947)
NIT appearances: 12
Semifinals: 2
Titles: 1 (1954)

TOP 5

G **Bob Cousy** (1946-50)
G **Ronnie Perry** (1976-80)
F **Tom Heinsohn** (1953-56)
F **Togo Palazzi** (1951-54)
C **George Kaftan** (1945-49)

RECORDS	GAME		SEASON		CAREER	
POINTS	56	Jack Foley, vs. Connecticut (Feb. 17, 1962)	866	Jack Foley (1961-62)	2,524	Ronnie Perry (1976-80)
POINTS PER GAME			33.3	Jack Foley (1961-62)	28.4	Jack Foley (1959-62)
REBOUNDS	42	Tom Heinsohn, vs. Boston College (March 1, 1956)	569	Tom Heinsohn (1955-56)	1,254	Tom Heinsohn (1953-56)
ASSISTS	17	Glenn Williams, vs. Army (Feb. 12, 1988)	278	Glenn Williams (1988-89)	714	Glenn Williams (1985-89)

SEASON REVIEW

SEASON	W-L	CONF.	SCORING	COACH	RECORD
1901-16	*60-39*		*Did not field a team from 1909-1916*		
1916-17	no team				
1917-18	no team				
1918-19	no team				
1919-20	no team				
1920-21	2-0			William Casey	
1921-22	14-3			William Casey	
1922-23	7-13			William Casey	
1923-24	5-9			William Casey	28-25 .528
1924-25	10-5			Ken Simendinger	10-5 .667
1925-26	8-9			John Reed	
1926-27	7-6			John Reed	
1927-28	13-6			John Reed	
1928-29	10-7			John Reed	
1929-30	12-7			John Reed	
1930-31	10-6			John Reed	60-41 .594
1931-32	no team				
1932-33	no team				
1933-34	no team				
1934-35	3-12			Albert Riopel	
1935-36	no team				
1936-37	no team				

SEAS.	W-L	CONF.	POSTSEASON	SCORING		REBOUNDS		ASSISTS		COACH	RECORD	
1937-38	no team											
1938-39	no team											
1939-40	2-3									Edward Krause		
1940-41	4-7									Edward Krause		
1941-42	5-4									Edward Krause	11-14	.440
1942-43	1-5									Albert Riopel		
1943-44	6-8									Albert Riopel		
1944-45	4-9									Albert Riopel	14-34	.292
1945-46	12-3			George Kaftan	15.8					Alvin "Doggie" Julian		
1946-47	**27-3**		**NATIONAL CHAMPION**	**George Kaftan**	**11.1**					**Alvin "Doggie" Julian**		
1947-48	26-4		NCAA THIRD PLACE	Bob Cousy	16.2					Alvin "Doggie" Julian	65-10	.867
1948-49	19-8			Bob Cousy	17.8					Lester Sheary		
1949-50	27-4		NCAA REGIONAL SEMIFINALS	Bob Cousy	19.4					Lester Sheary		
1950-51	20-5			Earle Markey	12.7					Lester Sheary		
1951-52	24-4		NIT QUARTERFINALS	Togo Palazzi	13.7	Jim Dilling	11.8			Lester Sheary		
1952-53	20-6		NCAA REGIONAL FINALS	Togo Palazzi	22.8	Togo Palazzi	16.2			Lester Sheary		
1953-54	26-2		NIT CHAMPION	Togo Palazzi	24.8	Togo Palazzi	13.5			Lester Sheary		
1954-55	19-7		NIT QUARTERFINALS	Tom Heinsohn	23.3	Tom Heinsohn	14.8			Lester Sheary	155-36	.812
1955-56	22-5		NCAA FIRST ROUND	Tom Heinsohn	27.4	Tom Heinsohn	21.1			Roy Leenig		
1956-57	11-12			George Waddleton	18.5	Joe Hughes	14.4			Roy Leenig		
1957-58	16-9			Joe Hughes	14.9	Joe Hughes	13.9			Roy Leenig		
1958-59	14-11			Tim Shea	15.0	Ralph Brandt	14.9			Roy Leenig		
1959-60	20-6		NIT FIRST ROUND	Jack Foley	24.6	Ralph Brandt	12.3			Roy Leenig		
1960-61	21-5		NIT THIRD PLACE	Jack Foley	26.5	Jack Foley	10.5			Roy Leenig	104-48	.684
1961-62	20-6		NIT QUARTERFINALS	Jack Foley	33.3	Jack Foley	8.3			Frank Oftring		
1962-63	16-9			Pat Gallagher	16.2	Pat Gallagher	6.9			Frank Oftring		
1963-64	15-8			John Wendelken	21.6	John Sullivan	7.6			Frank Oftring		
1964-65	13-10			John Wendelken	21.2	Greg Hochstein	8.6			Frank Oftring	64-33	.660
1965-66	10-13			Richard Murphy	17.3	Keith Hochstein	14.6			Jack Donohue		
1966-67	16-9			Ed Siudut	20.4	Ed Siudut	11.2			Jack Donohue		
1967-68	15-8			Ed Siudut	23.2	Ed Siudut	14.2			Jack Donohue		
1968-69	16-8			Ed Siudut	23.6	Ed Siudut	11.7			Jack Donohue		
1969-70	16-9			Bob Kissane	22.0	Bob Kissane	12.0	Jack Adams	3.8	Jack Donohue		
1970-71	18-8			Bob Kissane	17.1	Bob Kissane	10.1	Jack Adams	2.9	Jack Donohue		
1971-72	15-11			Gene Doyle	21.8	Gene Doyle	12.4	Bruce Grentz	5.1	Jack Donohue	106-66	.616
1972-73	9-17			Gene Doyle	20.8	Gene Doyle	13.1	King Gaskins	4.8	George Blaney		
1973-74	8-18			Malcolm Moulton	18.0	Marty Halsey	7.1	Ed Reilly	6.1	George Blaney		
1974-75	20-8		NIT FIRST ROUND	Chris Potter, M. Vicens	14.6	Chris Potter	7.6	Kevin McAuley	5.2	George Blaney		
1975-76	22-10		NIT QUARTERFINALS	Michael Vicens	15.0	Chris Potter	8.0	Kevin McAuley	4.6	George Blaney		
1976-77	23-6		NCAA FIRST ROUND	Ronnie Perry	23.0	Chris Potter	9.7	Chris Potter	5.4	George Blaney		
1977-78	20-7			Ronnie Perry	21.7	Chris Potter	10.2	Chris Potter	5.2	George Blaney		
1978-79	17-11		NIT FIRST ROUND	Ronnie Perry	25.0	David Mulquin	6.8	Bob Kelly	7.1	George Blaney		
1979-80	19-11	16-10	NCAA FIRST ROUND	Ronnie Perry	22.9	Ernie Floyd	6.7	Bob Kelly	5.8	George Blaney		
1980-81	20-10	18-8	NIT SECOND ROUND	Garry Witts	15.1	Tom Seaman	5.4	Eddie Thurman	5.1	George Blaney		
1981-82	16-11	4-4		Kevin Greaney	14.4	Chris Logan	5.9	Eddie Thurman	4.8	George Blaney		
1982-83	17-13	5-3		Chris Logan	15.6	Pat Elzie	8.1	Larry Westbrook	4.1	George Blaney		
1983-84	12-18	5-9		Ernie Floyd	15.6	Pat Elzie	8.9	Larry Westbrook	4.2	George Blaney		
1984-85	9-19	8-6		Jim McCaffrey	21.6	Walter Coates	6.8	Jim McCaffrey	4.2	George Blaney		
1985-86	12-18	6-8		Jim McCaffrey	22.8	Paul Durkee	5.3	Jim McCaffrey	3.7	George Blaney		
1986-87	9-19	6-8		Glenn Tropf	11.9	Glenn Tropf	7.1	Glenn Williams	4.4	George Blaney		
1987-88	14-15	8-6		Dwight Pernell	15.7	Glenn Tropf	7.0	Glenn Williams	8.1	George Blaney		
1988-89	13-15	5-9		Dwight Pernell	19.5	Grant Evans	6.6	Glenn Williams	9.9	George Blaney		
1989-90	24-6	14-2	NIT FIRST ROUND	Dwight Pernell	21.6	Jim Nairus	5.9	Dwight Pernell	5.3	George Blaney		
1990-91	18-12	8-4		Jim Nairus	18.3	Jim Nairus	7.8	Aaron Jordan	5.8	George Blaney		
1991-92	18-11	10-4		Rick Mashburn	16.1	Rick Mashburn	5.9	Roger Breslin	6.4	George Blaney		
1992-93	23-7	12-2	NCAA FIRST ROUND	Rob Feaster	17.7	Rick Mashburn	7.4	Roger Breslin	7.1	George Blaney		
1993-94	14-14	9-5		Rob Feaster	28.0	John Young	8.1	Gordon Hamilton	4.1	George Blaney	357-276	.564
1994-95	15-12	9-5		Rob Feaster	25.0	Rob Feaster	6.9	Gordon Hamilton	3.0	Bill Raynor		
1995-96	16-13 ⊗	8-4		Walter Brown	17.3	Walter Brown	7.6	Brian Lockhart	4.4	Bill Raynor		
1996-97	8-19	5-7		Chris Rojik	13.6	Chris Rojik	5.9	John Hightower	3.8	Bill Raynor		
1997-98	7-20	3-9		Jon Kerr	15.4	Jon Kerr	6.2	John Hightower	3.7	Bill Raynor		
1998-99	7-20	3-9		Ryan Serravalle	11.6	Juan Pegues	6.8	John Hightower	3.2	Bill Raynor	53-84	.387▼
1999-2000	10-18	3-9		Josh Sankes	14.1	Josh Sankes	11.9	Ryan Serravalle	2.7	Ralph Willard		
2000-01	22-8	10-2	NCAA FIRST ROUND	Josh Sankes	12.8	Josh Sankes	9.6	Jave Meade	3.1	Ralph Willard		
2001-02	18-15	9-5	NCAA FIRST ROUND	Tim Szatko	13.6	Tim Szatko	6.7	Jave Meade	4.9	Ralph Willard		
2002-03	26-5	13-1	NCAA FIRST ROUND	Patrick Whearty	12.4	Patrick Whearty	6.6	Jave Meade	6.2	Ralph Willard		
2003-04	13-15	7-7		Kevin Hamilton	11.0	John Hurley	5.0	Jave Meade	5.5	Ralph Willard		
2004-05	25-7	13-1	NIT SECOND ROUND	Kevin Hamilton	15.7	John Hurley	6.0	Torey Thomas	3.7	Ralph Willard		
2005-06	20-12	11-3		Kevin Hamilton	17.6	Kevin Hamilton	6.3	Torey Thomas	4.8	Ralph Willard		
2006-07	25-9	13-1	NCAA FIRST ROUND	Keith Simmons	16.9	Keith Simmons	5.8	Torey Thomas	4.7	Ralph Willard		
2007-08	15-14	5-9		Tim Clifford	18.0	Tim Clifford	5.4	Pat Doherty	4.3	Ralph Willard		
2008-09	18-14	11-3		R.J. Evans	13.4	Andrew Keister	6.3	Pat Doherty	3.7	Ralph Willard	192-117	.621

⊗ Records don't reflect games forfeited or vacated. For adjusted records, see p. 521.

▼ Coach's record adjusted to reflect games forfeited or vacated: 54-83, .394. For yearly totals, see p. 521.

ESPN 55 SAGARIN

HOUSTON

Calling Houston a storied program is like saying the Gulf of Mexico is a wet spot. The Cougars secured a permanent place in hoops lore by playing in the Game of the Century in 1968, and have been embellishing their legacy ever since, from Guy V. Lewis to Phi Slama Jama to Hakeem "the Dream" Olajuwon's last Dance in 1984. And don't forget the other all-time greats, from the Big E to Otis Birdsong to Clyde the Glide and Don Chaney.

BEST TEAM: 1982-83 *Houston Post* columnist Thomas Bonk came up with the funky faux frat name, Phi Slama Jama, for the high-scoring, high-flying squad led by All-Americas Clyde "the Glide" Drexler and Olajuwon. After back-to-back losses in mid-December, Guy V. Lewis' team won 26 straight, including a 94-81 win over fellow No. 1-seed Louisville in the Final Four, before an unforgettable last-second loss to NC State in the NCAA Final (see Heartbreaker).

BEST PLAYER: F Elvin Hayes (1965-68) The Big E made his legend in a fabled 1968 win at the Astrodome that snapped UCLA's 47-game winning streak. Hayes went for 39 points and 15 rebounds—albeit against an injured Lew Alcindor. The dominant power forward was a three-time All-America and a spectacular scorer who hit 40 or more 18 times, including four games of 50 or more points. Following a 16-year pro career in which he averaged 21.0 points and 12.5 rebounds per game, he was named one of the NBA's 50 Greatest Players.

BEST COACH: Guy V. Lewis (1956-86) He started out playing at Rice, but after a stint in the Army, Lewis wound up on Houston's first team during the 1945-46 season, and he put the Cougars on the hoops map more than a decade later as coach. All five of the school's Final Four trips came under Lewis. A colorful dresser, the two-time Coach of the Year had equally flashy teams, including a Player of the Year (Hayes in 1968), a Tournament MOP (Olajuwon in '83) and 11 NBA first-round draftees.

GAME FOR THE AGES: College basketball went from being a game to a spectacle on Jan. 20, 1968, when 52,693 fans filled the Astrodome—and half of all the TV sets in use in America tuned in to the prime-time telecast—to watch the No. 2-ranked Cougars stun the undefeated four-time defending NCAA champion Bruins, 71-69. Thanks to Lewis' scheming, Houston broke UCLA's full-court pressure, and the Cougars outlasted the Bruins—in no small measure because UCLA's great Alcindor was impaired by an eye injury. Hayes had 39 points and 15 rebounds in a game that lived up to its intense pregame hype. UCLA exacted its revenge when it destroyed Houston, 101-69, in that season's Final Four.

HEARTBREAKER: After blowing a six-point lead with a little more than three minutes to go in the 1983 NCAA Final, the Cougars thought they were headed for overtime when NC State guard Dereck Whittenburg's last-second desperation 35-footer missed by several feet. But Lorenzo Charles leaped for the ball and dunked it home, giving the Wolfpack a most memorable 54-52 win.

FIERCEST RIVAL: Lewis famously hated losing to his original team, Rice. Former Cougar Reid Gettys once said, "It wasn't a pretty sight when you lost to them, and you just never did." Relations haven't gotten any warmer since, with both teams now duking it out in Conference USA. Houston leads overall, 55–14.

FANFARE AND HOOPLA: During the Phi Slama Jama era, fans began grading Cougars dunks during warmups—and all would receive a perfect 10. Pregame dunking is now banned, but a few scorecards still break out in Hofheinz Pavilion after a Cougars player dunks.

FAN FAVORITE: G/F Michael Young (1980-84) The Houston native and the only Cougar to start on four teams that earned NCAA Tournament berths has been a member of the school's basketball staff since 1998 and is always warmly cheered when introduced.

CONSENSUS ALL-AMERICAS

1967, '68	**Elvin Hayes**, F
1977	**Otis Birdsong**, G
1984	**Hakeem Olajuwon**, C

FIRST-ROUND PRO PICKS

1961	**Gary Phillips**, Boston (9)
1968	**Elvin Hayes**, San Diego (1)
1968	**Don Chaney**, Boston (12)
1972	**Dwight Davis**, Cleveland (3)
1972	**Dwight Davis**, Florida (ABA)
1973	**Dwight Jones**, Atlanta (9)
1977	**Otis Birdsong**, Kansas City (2)
1982	**Rob Williams**, Denver (19)
1983	**Clyde Drexler**, Portland (14)
1984	**Hakeem Olajuwon**, Houston (1)
1984	**Michael Young**, Boston (24)
1987	**Greg Anderson**, San Antonio (23)

PROFILE

University of Houston, Houston, TX
Founded: 1927 as Houston Junior College
Enrollment: 36,104 (27,602 undergraduate)
Colors: Scarlet and white with navy trim
Nickname: Cougars
Current arena: Hofheinz Pavilion, opened in 1969 (8,479)
Previous: Jeppesen Field House, 1946-66 (2,500); Delmar Gym, 1966-69 (5,300); Sam Houston Coliseum (Houston Coliseum), 1960-69 (7,700)
First game: Jan. 10, 1946

All-time record: 1,088-725 (.600)
Total weeks in AP Top 20/25: 126
Current conference: Conference USA (1996-)
Conference titles:
Missouri Valley: 1 (1956)
Southwest: 3 (1983, '84, '92 [tie])
Conference tournament titles:
Southwest: 5 (1978, '81, '83, '84, '92)
NCAA Tournament appearances: 18
Sweet 16s (since 1975): 3
Final Fours: 5
NIT appearances: 9
Semifinals: 1

TOP 5

G	**Otis Birdsong** (1973-77)
G	**Don Chaney** (1965-68)
F	**Clyde Drexler** (1980-83)
F	**Elvin Hayes** (1965-68)
C	**Hakeem Olajuwon** (1981-84)

RECORDS

RECORDS	GAME		SEASON		CAREER	
POINTS	62	Elvin Hayes, vs. Valparaiso (Feb. 24, 1968)	1,214	Elvin Hayes (1967-68)	2,884	Elvin Hayes (1965-68)
POINTS PER GAME			36.8	Elvin Hayes (1967-68)	31.0	Elvin Hayes (1965-68)
REBOUNDS	37	Elvin Hayes, vs. Centenary (Feb. 10, 1968)	624	Elvin Hayes (1967-68)	1,602	Elvin Hayes (1965-68)
ASSISTS	17	Reid Gettys, vs. Rice (Feb. 17, 1985)	309	Reid Gettys (1983-84)	740	Reid Gettys (1981-85)

SEASON REVIEW

SEAS.	W-L	CONF.	POSTSEASON	SCORING		REBOUNDS		ASSISTS		COACH	RECORD	
1945-46	10-4			Guy V. Lewis	21.1					Alden Pasche		
1946-47	15-7			Guy V. Lewis	19.7					Alden Pasche		
1947-48	11-11			Dick Berg	8.4					Alden Pasche		
1948-49	11-11			Lloyd Hendrix	12.0					Alden Pasche		
1949-50	16-7			Lloyd Hendrix	13.0					Alden Pasche		
1950-51	11-17	2-12		Lloyd Hendrix	13.3					Alden Pasche		
1951-52	7-14	3-7		Royce Ray	11.9					Alden Pasche		
1952-53	9-13	5-5		Jack Mosher	12.0					Alden Pasche		
1953-54	11-15	3-7		Gary Shivers	15.6	Gary Shivers	12.7			Alden Pasche		
1954-55	15-10	3-7		Don Boldebuck	24.2	Don Boldebuck	18.1			Alden Pasche		
1955-56	19-7	9-3	NCAA REGIONAL SEMIFINALS	Don Boldebuck	21.4	Don Boldebuck	15.8			Alden Pasche	135-116	.538
1956-57	10-16	5-9		Dan Dotson	15.3	Russell Boone	8.4			Guy V. Lewis		
1957-58	9-16	4-10		Russell Boone	16.6	Russell Boone	9.4			Guy V. Lewis		
1958-59	12-14	6-8		Gary Phillips	16.8	Ted Luckenbill	9.8			Guy V. Lewis		
1959-60	13-12	6-8		Gary Phillips	20.5	Ted Luckenbill	9.3			Guy V. Lewis		
1960-61	17-11		NCAA REGIONAL SEMIFINALS	Ted Luckenbill	18.0	Ted Luckenbill	10.1			Guy V. Lewis		
1961-62	21-6		NIT QUARTERFINALS	Lyle Harger	15.9	Lyle Harger	10.6			Guy V. Lewis		
1962-63	15-11			Lyle Harger	21.5	Lyle Harger	13.8	Don Schverak	3.0	Guy V. Lewis		
1963-64	16-10			Chet Oliver	10.9	Don Schverak	7.8	Chet Oliver	3.5	Guy V. Lewis		
1964-65	19-10		NCAA REGIONAL SEMIFINALS	Joe Hamood	17.3	Leary Lentz	8.6	Joe Hamood	4.1	Guy V. Lewis		
1965-66	23-6		NCAA REGIONAL SEMIFINALS	Elvin Hayes	27.2	Elvin Hayes	16.9	Joe Hamood	6.6	Guy V. Lewis		
1966-67	27-4		NCAA THIRD PLACE	Elvin Hayes	28.4	Elvin Hayes	15.7	Gary Grider	5.1	Guy V. Lewis		
1967-68	31-2		NCAA FOURTH PLACE	Elvin Hayes	36.8	Elvin Hayes	18.9	George Reynolds	5.6	Guy V. Lewis		
1968-69	16-10			Ollie Taylor	19.2	Ken Spain	11.6	George Reynolds	4.5	Guy V. Lewis		
1969-70	25-5		NCAA REGIONAL SEMIFINALS	Ollie Taylor	24.4	Ollie Taylor	11.5	Poo Welch	6.0	Guy V. Lewis		
1970-71	22-7		NCAA REGIONAL SEMIFINALS	Dwight Davis	20.3	Dwight Davis	12.3	Poo Welch	4.6	Guy V. Lewis		
1971-72	20-7		NCAA FIRST ROUND	Dwight Davis	24.4	Dwight Jones	13.3	Steve Newsome	4.2	Guy V. Lewis		
1972-73	23-4		NCAA FIRST ROUND	Louis Dunbar	21.1	Dwight Jones	14.1	Steve Newsome	4.5	Guy V. Lewis		
1973-74	17-9			Louis Dunbar	21.7	Maurice Presley	10.4	Donnell Hayes	6.2	Guy V. Lewis		
1974-75	16-10			Otis Birdsong	24.6	Maurice Presley	10.7	Louis Dunbar	3.6	Guy V. Lewis		
1975-76	17-11	7-9		Otis Birdsong	26.1	David Marrs	10.3	Otis Birdsong	3.5	Guy V. Lewis		
1976-77	29-8	13-3	NIT RUNNER-UP	Otis Birdsong	30.3	Mike Schultz	9.8	Ken Ciolli	5.4	Guy V. Lewis		
1977-78	25-8	11-5	NCAA FIRST ROUND	Cecile Rose	17.6	Mike Schultz	10.0	Ken Ciolli	4.8	Guy V. Lewis		
1978-79	16-15	6-10		Kenneth Williams	30.3	George Walker	9.3	Ken Ciolli	5.6	Guy V. Lewis		
1979-80	14-14	8-8		Rob Williams	16.3	Larry Rogers	6.0	Rob Williams	4.5	Guy V. Lewis		
1980-81	21-9	10-6	NCAA FIRST ROUND	Rob Williams	25.0	Clyde Drexler	10.5	Rob Williams	4.9	Guy V. Lewis		
1981-82	25-8	11-5	NCAA NATIONAL SEMIFINALS	Rob Williams	21.1	Clyde Drexler	10.5	Rob Williams	4.5	Guy V. Lewis		
1982-83	31-3	16-0	NCAA RUNNER-UP	Michael Young	17.3	Hakeem Olajuwon	11.4	Reid Gettys	6.1	Guy V. Lewis		
1983-84	32-5	15-1	NCAA RUNNER-UP	Michael Young	19.8	Hakeem Olajuwon	13.5	Reid Gettys	8.3	Guy V. Lewis		
1984-85	16-14	8-8	NIT FIRST ROUND	Alvin Franklin	16.9	Rickie Winslow	8.8	Reid Gettys	6.9	Guy V. Lewis		
1985-86	14-14	8-8		Alvin Franklin	20.5	Greg Anderson	12.9	Alvin Franklin	4.5	Guy V. Lewis	592-279	.680
1986-87	18-12	9-7	NCAA FIRST ROUND	Greg Anderson	18.2	Greg Anderson	10.6	Darrell McArthur	3.1	Pat Foster		
1987-88	18-13	10-6	NIT SECOND ROUND	Richard Hollis	17.0	Rolando Ferreira	6.8	Randy Brown	5.6	Pat Foster		
1988-89	17-14	8-8		Craig Upchurch	18.8	Richard Hollis	8.4	Derrick Daniels	5.8	Pat Foster		
1989-90	25-8	13-3	NCAA FIRST ROUND	Carl Herrera	16.7	Carl Herrera	9.2	Derrick Daniels	5.9	Pat Foster		
1990-91	18-11	10-6	NIT SECOND ROUND	Byron Smith	17.7	Darrell Mickens	8.5	Derrick Daniels	6.2	Pat Foster		
1991-92	25-6	11-3	NCAA FIRST ROUND	Sam Mack	17.5	Bo Outlaw	8.2	Derrick Daniels	5.0	Pat Foster		
1992-93	21-9	9-5	NIT FIRST ROUND	David Diaz	17.7	Bo Outlaw	10.0	Anthony Goldwire	5.7	Pat Foster	142-73	.660
1993-94	8-19	5-9		Tim Moore	17.7	Tim Moore	8.5	Anthony Goldwire	6.1	Alvin Brooks		
1994-95	9-19	5-9		Tim Moore	20.1	Tim Moore	10.6	Tommie Davis	4.3	Alvin Brooks		
1995-96	17-10	11-3		Tim Moore	17.3	Tim Moore	10.9	Damon Jones	3.9	Alvin Brooks		
1996-97	11-16	3-11		Galen Robinson	17.0	Galen Robinson	9.0	Damon Jones	4.9	Alvin Brooks		
1997-98	9-20	2-14		Galen Robinson	13.8	Galen Robinson	8.0	Shamahn McBride	2.5	Alvin Brooks	54-84	.391
1998-99	10-17	5-11		Gee Gervin	20.6	William Stringfellow	9.6	Gee Gervin	3.9	Clyde Drexler		
1999-2000	9-22	2-14		Gee Gervin	18.0	George Williams	8.5	Gee Gervin	3.1	Clyde Drexler	19-39	.328
2000-01	9-20	6-10		George Willams	13.5	Patrick Okafor	8.6	Dominic Smith	3.8	Ray McCallum		
2001-02	18-15	9-7	NIT FIRST ROUND	Dominic Smith	15.1	Louis Truscott	9.3	Kevin Gaines	5.5	Ray McCallum		
2002-03	8-20	6-10		Louis Truscott	15.3	Louis Truscott	11.3	Andre Owens	3.2	Ray McCallum		
2003-04	9-18	3-13		Andre Owens	16.0	Anwar Ferguson	7.4	Lanny Smith	3.2	Ray McCallum	44-73	.376
2004-05	18-14	9-7	NIT OPENING ROUND	Andre Owens	18.3	Ramon Dyer	5.6	Lanny Smith	4.2	Tom Penders		
2005-06	21-10	9-5	NIT SECOND ROUND	Oliver Lafayette	15.7	Ramon Dyer	6.1	Lanny Smith	5.4	Tom Penders		
2006-07	18-15	10-6		Robert McKiver	19.2	Jahmar Thorpe	6.1	Robert McKiver	3.4	Tom Penders		
2007-08	24-10	11-5		Robert McKiver	23.6	Dion Dowell	6.8	Lanny Smith	3.7	Tom Penders		
2008-09	21-12	10-6		Aubrey Coleman	19.4	Marcus Cousin	8.4	Desmond Wade	3.4	Tom Penders	102-61	.626

LATE GREAT

MUHLENBERG (PA.) 1935-63

This small school in eastern Pennsylvania definitely had some bright basketball moments. Before he took Holy Cross to the 1947 NCAA title, Alvin "Doggie" Julian spent nine seasons on the Mules' bench and guided the 1944 squad to a quarterfinal NIT matchup with DePaul, led by George Mikan. Unfortunately, Mikan blocked at least 20 shots in Muhlenberg's loss. Before dropping to the College Division, Muhlenberg owed much of its success to the U.S. Marine Corps. The campus featured a Corps officers training program and a number of players on the 1946 squad had been Marines during the war. The 1946 Mules raced to a 23–5 record, defeating such high-profile programs as Syracuse, La Salle, Princeton and Saint Joseph's, before settling for a fourth-place finish in the NIT.

NOTABLE PLAYER: G Harry Donovan (1945-49) The 6'0" Donovan scored 1,521 points during his career at Muhlenberg and was named to the All-Pennsylvania team all four years. He played one season in the NBA with the New York Knicks (1949-50).

ESPN 317 SAGARIN

HOWARD

Better known for its academic excellence, this historically black university in Washington, D.C., is no slouch on the court. Bison highlights include a miracle comeback in the 1992 Mid-Eastern Athletic Conference tournament final and the memorable frontcourt of Larry Spriggs, James Ratliff and James Terry.

BEST TEAM: 1979-80 They didn't quite become the first Howard squad to make the NCAA Tournament, but A.B. Williamson's team won its last six regular season games and rolled through the MEAC tourney to finish 21–7. Too bad for Spriggs, Ratliff and crew that the MEAC champs didn't then receive an automatic bid to the Dance.

BEST PLAYER: F LARRY SPRIGGS (1978-81) Part of a front line that called itself the Dunk Patrol, the 6'7" Spriggs steered Howard to its first NCAA bid in 1981 and won the MEAC tournament MVP title every year he played.

BEST COACH: A.B. WILLIAMSON (1975-90) He holds the school's all-time record for wins and was named MEAC Coach of the Year three times. But Williamson never completely shook the criticism that he couldn't win big games—his teams lost the conference tournament final eight times.

GAME FOR THE AGES: After starting the 1991-92 season 1–9, Howard fought its way back to a respectable 16–13 and made it to the MEAC tournament championship game against Florida A&M. Things looked bleak once more for the Bison as they fell behind by 19 in the second half, only to mount a brilliant comeback to win, 67-65. An NCAA first-round matchup with Kansas was their reward (alas, a 100-67 loss).

FIERCEST RIVAL: Howard and North Carolina A&T are 300 miles apart, but the rivalry is much closer than that. Their mutual history includes fights on the court, name-calling in the stands and back-and-forth battles on the scoreboard. From 1978 to '88, no other school won the MEAC tournament; the Aggies won nine and Howard won two. Howard trails in the series, 36–57, according to the school's count.

SEASON REVIEW

SEAS.	W-L	CONF.	COACH	SEAS.	W-L	CONF.	COACH
1952-53[a]	15-11		Thomas A. Hart	**1964-65**	11-11		James M. Thompson
1953-54	1-8		Thomas A. Hart	**1965-66**	16-10		James M. Thompson
1954-55	11-11		Thomas A. Hart	**1966-67**	21-6		Marshall Emery
1955-56	13-10		Thomas A. Hart	**1967-68**	14-10		Marshall Emery
1956-57	12-9		Thomas A. Hart	**1968-69**	5-15		Marshall Emery
1957-58	13-8		Thomas A. Hart	**1969-70**	14-11		Marshall Emery
1958-59	11-1		Thomas A. Hart	**1970-71**	20-6		Marshall Emery
1959-60	13-21		William L. Jones	**1971-72**	18-9	8-4	Marshall Emery
1960-61	N/A			**1972-73**	22-6	9-3	Marshall Emery
1961-62	N/A			**1973-74**	11-15	4-8	Marshall Emery
1962-63	10-14		James M. Thompson	**1974-75**	13-13	6-6	Marshall Emery
1963-64	10-14		James M. Thompson	**1975-76**	9-19	5-7	A.B. Williamson

SEAS.	W-L	CONF.	SCORING		COACH	RECORD
1976-77	18-10	8-4	Gerald Glover	18.8	A.B. Williamson	
1977-78	15-9	8-4	Gerald Glover	18.4	A.B. Williamson	
1978-79	16-12	6-6			A.B. Williamson	
1979-80	21-7				A.B. Williamson	
1980-81	17-12	6-4 ●			A.B. Williamson	
1981-82	17-11	9-3			A.B. Williamson	
1982-83	19-9	11-1			A.B. Williamson	
1983-84	15-14	7-3			A.B. Williamson	
1984-85	16-12	9-3			A.B. Williamson	
1985-86	19-10	11-3			A.B. Williamson	
1986-87	25-5	13-1			A.B. Williamson	
1987-88	16-13	9-7			A.B. Williamson	
1988-89	9-19	5-11			A.B. Williamson	
1989-90	8-20	5-11			A.B. Williamson	240-182 .569
1990-91	8-20	7-9			Butch Beard	
1991-92	17-14	12-4 ●			Butch Beard	
1992-93	10-18	6-10			Butch Beard	
1993-94	10-17	7-9			Butch Beard	45-69 .395
1994-95	9-18	8-8			Mike McLeese	
1995-96	7-20	6-10			Mike McLeese	
1996-97	7-20	7-11			Mike McLeese	
1997-98	8-20	5-13	Xavier Singletary	22.3	Mike McLeese	31-78 .284
1998-99	2-25	2-16	Melvin Watson	14.1	Kirk Saulny	
1999-2000	1-27	1-17	Bryan Alvin	9.3	Kirk Saulny[b]	2-34 .056
2000-01	10-18	8-10	Ron Williamson	19.2	Frankie Allen	
2001-02	18-13	11-7	Kyle Williams	18.7	Frankie Allen	
2002-03	13-17	9-9	Ron Williamson	21.7	Frankie Allen	
2003-04	6-22	4-14	James Wilkerson	13.0	Frankie Allen	
2004-05	5-23	2-16	Will Gant	14.0	Frankie Allen	52-93 .359
2005-06	7-22	5-13	Darryl Hudson	12.1	Gil Jackson	
2006-07	9-22	5-13	Darryl Hudson	14.4	Gil Jackson	
2007-08	6-26	3-13	Eugene Myatt	14.1	Gil Jackson	
2008-09	8-23	6-10	Eugene Myatt	15.8	Gil Jackson	30-93 .244

[a] **Reliable data before 1952-53 is not available.**
[b] **Kirk Saulny (0-9) and Willie E. Coward (1-18) both coached during the 1999-2000 season.**
● **NCAA Tournament appearance**

PROFILE

Howard University, Washington, DC
Founded: 1867
Enrollment: 11,227 (7,480 undergraduate)
Colors: Blue, red and white
Nickname: Bison
Current arena: Burr Gymnasium, opened in 1963 (2,700)
First game: March 8, 1912
All-time record: 675-786 (.462)
Total weeks in AP Top 20/25: 0

Current conference: Mid-Eastern Athletic (1971-)
Conference titles:
MEAC: 4 (1980, '83, '87, '92 [tie])
Conference tournament titles:
MEAC: 3 (1980, '81, '92)
NCAA Tournament appearances: 2
NIT appearances: 0

TOP 5

G **Bernard Perry** (1979-83)
G **Ron Williamson** (1999-2003)
F **James Ratliff** (1979-82)
F **Larry Spriggs** (1978-81)
F/C **Gerald Glover** (1974-78)

RECORDS

	GAME		SEASON		CAREER	
POINTS	41	Eugene Myatt, vs. VMI (Nov. 25, 2006); vs. Coppin State (Feb. 23, 2009)	650	Ron Williamson (2002-03)	1,712	Gerald Glover (1974-78)
POINTS PER GAME			22.3	Xavier Singletary (1997-98)		N/A
REBOUNDS	30	Aaron Shingler, vs. Virginia State (1965)	425	Karl Hodges (1966-67)	1,003	William Holland (1962-65)
ASSISTS	13	Chuck Smalley, vs. South Carolina State (1989); Gerald Glover, vs. North Carolina A&T (1977)	195	Rodney Wright (1981-82)	445	Milan Brown (1989-93)

ESPN 147 SAGARIN

IDAHO

When the Vandals are bad, they are really, really bad. Try 22 seasons of fewer than four conference wins. But when the Vandals are good, they are often electrifying. Try four NCAA Tournament appearances between 1981 and '90 and a coaching pipeline that's produced such notables as Tim Floyd, Kermit Davis and Larry Eustachy.

BEST TEAM: 1981-82 The Vandals climbed as high as No. 6 nationally, won the Big Sky and advanced to the NCAA Sweet 16—all because coach Don Monson insulted his best player. In 1980, Monson told juco star Ken Owens he might not be good enough to play for Idaho. Owens signed with the Vandals anyway and, with a chip on his shoulder, was conference MVP as a senior.

BEST PLAYER: F Gus Johnson (1962-63) In his one season, Johnson averaged 19.0 ppg and 20.3 rpg, and carried Idaho to its only 20-win season over a 34-year stretch. The five-time NBA All-Star's leaping ability was immortalized for decades at Main Street's Corner Club—Gus Johnson's Nail marked the spot 11'6" off the floor where he once touched a roof beam.

BEST COACH: Don Monson (1978-83) Monson pushed his players hard. He took over a team that finished last in the Big Sky four straight seasons and won two league titles, went to two NCAA Tournaments and was cited as a national Coach of the Year in 1982.

GAME FOR THE AGES: In Idaho's only NCAA Tournament win, the No. 3 seed beat No. 6-seed Iowa 69-67 in overtime to reach the 1982 Sweet 16. Phil Hopson had 21 points, reserve Pete Prigge hit two clutch free throws in the last minute of OT and Brian Kellerman scored 14, including the buzzer-beating, rim-toying game-winner.

FIERCEST RIVAL: When the Vandals travel south to the Treasure Valley to play Boise State, there's usually plenty of resentment in tow. Boise dominates its Panhandle rivals in both football and hoops. In the latter, Boise State leads, 47–34 overall, winning 14 in a row before the Vandals swept the season series in 2008-09, Don Verlin's first year as head coach.

SEASON REVIEW

SEAS.	W-L	CONF.	COACH	SEAS.	W-L	CONF.	COACH
1905-46	*372-399*	*Best season: 19-2 in 1921-22*		1959-60	11-15		Dave Strack
1946-47	4-24	1-15	Guy Wicks	1960-61	10-16		Joe Cipriano
1947-48	12-18	3-13	Charles Finley	1961-62	13-13		Joe Cipriano
1948-49	17-15	7-9	Charles Finley	1962-63	20-6		Joe Cipriano
1949-50	15-17	7-9	Charles Finley	1963-64	7-19	4-6	Jim Goddard
1950-51	15-14	6-10	Charles Finley	1964-65	6-19	4-6	Jim Goddard
1951-52	19-13	9-7	Charles Finley	1965-66	12-14	2-8	Jim Goddard
1952-53	14-11	8-8	Charles Finley	1966-67	14-11	5-5	Wayne Anderson
1953-54	15-8	9-7	Charles Finley	1967-68	15-11	9-6	Wayne Anderson
1954-55	8-18	5-11	Harlan Hodges	1968-69	11-15	6-9	Wayne Anderson
1955-56	6-19	4-12	Harlan Hodges	1969-70	10-15	6-9	Wayne Anderson
1956-57	10-16	4-12	Harlan Hodges	1970-71	14-12	8-6	Wayne Anderson
1957-58	17-9	9-7	Harlan Hodges	1971-72	5-20	2-12	Wayne Anderson
1958-59	11-15	6-10	Harlan Hodges	1972-73	7-19	3-11	Wayne Anderson

SEAS.	W-L	CONF.	SCORING		COACH	RECORD	
1973-74	12-14	5-9	Steve Weist	15.3	Wayne Anderson	88-117	.429
1974-75	10-16	4-10	Henry Harris	19.8	Jim Jarvis		
1975-76	7-19	3-11	Steve Weist	13.0	Jim Jarvis		
1976-77	5-21	3-11	James Smith	17.0	Jim Jarvis		
1977-78	4-22	1-13	Reed Jaussi	17.0	Jim Jarvis	26-78	.250
1978-79	11-15	4-10	Don Newman	17.6	Don Monson		
1979-80	17-10	9-5	Don Newman	18.3	Don Monson		
1980-81	25-4	12-2 ●	Brian Kellerman	16.0	Don Monson		
1981-82	27-3	13-1 ●	Ken Owens	15.6	Don Monson		
1982-83	20-9	9-5 ■	Brian Kellerman	17.9	Don Monson	100-41	.709
1983-84	9-19	4-10	Stan Arnold	12.6	Bill Trumbo		
1984-85	8-22	1-13	Frank Garza	14.3	Bill Trumbo		
1985-86	11-18	4-10	Ken Luckett	17.7	Bill Trumbo	28-59	.322
1986-87	16-14	5-9	Andrew Jackson	14.1	Tim Floyd		
1987-88	19-11	11-5	Raymond Brown	16.1	Tim Floyd	35-25	.583
1988-89	25-6	13-3 ●	Riley Smith	15.9	Kermit Davis		
1989-90	25-6	13-3 ●	Riley Smith	22.6	Kermit Davis		
1990-91	19-11	11-5	Sammie Freeman	12.3	Larry Eustachy		
1991-92	18-14	10-6	Orlando Lightfoot	21.8	Larry Eustachy		
1992-93	24-8	11-3	Orlando Lightfoot	22.3	Larry Eustachy	61-33	.649
1993-94	18-10	9-5	Orlando Lightfoot	25.4	Joe Cravens		
1994-95	12-15	6-8	Mark Leslie	15.2	Joe Cravens		
1995-96	12-16	5-9	Reggie Rose	13.9	Joe Cravens	42-41	.506
1996-97	13-17	5-11	Jason Jackman	17.0	Kermit Davis	63-29	.685
1997-98	15-12	9-7	Avery Curry	19.7	David Farrar		
1998-99	16-11	11-5	Avery Curry	16.5	David Farrar		
1999-2000	12-17	6-10	Gordon Scott	17.6	David Farrar		
2000-01	6-21	3-13	Matt Gerschefske	11.0	David Farrar	49-61	.445
2001-02	9-19	6-12	Justin Logan	8.7	Leonard Perry		
2002-03	13-15	9-9	Tyrone Hayes	13.1	Leonard Perry		
2003-04	14-16	9-9	Tyrone Hayes	13.5	Leonard Perry		
2004-05	8-22	6-12	Dandrick Jones	16.8	Leonard Perry		
2005-06	4-25	1-15	Tanoris Shepard	15.4	Leonard Perry	48-97	.331
2006-07	4-27	1-15	Keoni Watson	18.1	George Pfeifer		
2007-08	8-21	5-11	Jordan Brooks	12.4	George Pfeifer	12-48	.200
2008-09	17-16	9-7	Mac Hopson	16.4	Don Verlin	17-16	.515

● NCAA Tournament appearance ■ NIT appearance

PROFILE

University of Idaho, Moscow, ID
Founded: 1889
Enrollment: 11,192 (7,961 undergraduate)
Colors: Silver and vandal gold
Nickname: Vandals
Current arena: Cowan Spectrum, opened in 1975 (7,000)
Previous: Memorial Gym, 1928-75 (1,500)
First game: 1905
All-time record: 1,183-1,343 (.468)
Total weeks in AP Top 20/25: 15

Current conference: Western Athletic (2005-)
Conference titles:
Big Sky: 5 (1981, '82, '89 [tie], '90, '93)
Conference tournament titles:
Big Sky: 4 (1981, '82, '89, '90)
NCAA Tournament appearances: 4
Sweet 16s (since 1975): 1
NIT appearances: 1

CONSENSUS ALL-AMERICAS

1923 **Al Fox**, F

TOP 5

G **Orlando Lightfoot** (1991-94)
G **Ken Owens** (1980-82)
G **Gary Simmons** (1954-58)
F **Gus Johnson** (1962-63)
F **Riley Smith** (1989-90)

RECORDS	GAME		SEASON		CAREER	
POINTS	50	Orlando Lightfoot, vs. Gonzaga (Dec. 21, 1993)	715	Orlando Lightfoot (1992-93)	2,102	Orlando Lightfoot (1991-94)
POINTS PER GAME			25.4	Orlando Lightfoot (1993-94)	23.1	Orlando Lightfoot (1991-94)
REBOUNDS	31	Tom Moreland, vs. Whitworth (Feb. 11, 1964); Gus Johnson, vs. Oregon (Feb. 9, 1963)	466	Gus Johnson (1962-63)	877	Deon Watson (1990-94)
ASSISTS	16	Otis Livingston, vs. Montana State (Feb. 8, 1990)	262	Otis Livingston (1989-90)	390	Brian Kellerman (1979-83)

ESPN
181
SAGARIN

IDAHO STATE

Few small schools have played bigger than Idaho State. Consider the eight straight NCAA Tourney appearances from 1953 to '60; the UCLA upset and the whatever-it-takes style of the 1976-77 team; the fiery Jim Killingsworth and the rivalry with Weber State; Steve Hayes playing like Shaq before there was a Shaq. Big.

BEST TEAM: 1976-77 No one gave ISU any chance of beating UCLA in the Sweet 16. But Killingsworth's crew pulled it off, 76-75. If you want to know how, go back to their regular-season game with Montana State. Facing a stall, the Bengals gritted out a 31-11 win. Yes, 31-11. This was one feisty team that, until its NCAA West Regional final loss to UNLV, always seemed to find a way to win.

BEST PLAYER: C Steve Hayes (1973-77) The Aberdeen, Idaho, native introduced himself to the nation during the 1977 Tournament, dominating the defensive paint with his shotblocking. The seven-footer also scored 27 points in the Bengals' Sweet 16 upset of the Bruins, and ranks second in school history with 1,933 points.

BEST COACH: Steve Belko (1950-56) He inherited a team that went 5–24 and guided the school to four NCAA Tournaments in six seasons. Belko's success coincided with the opening of Reed Gym—one of the nation's first multimillion-dollar athletic facilities—and helped fill its seats for seasons to come.

GAME FOR THE AGES: With Idaho State clinging to a 72-69 lead over UCLA in the 1977 Sweet 16, freshman guard Ernie Wheeler twice went to the line for a one-and-one. He hit all four free throws to ice the upset.

FIERCEST RIVAL: Idaho State and Big Sky rival Weber State haven't always played nice, and the animosity can get creative. During a Jan. 9, 1997, game at WSU, Idaho State coaches turned to the fans—whose team was under NCAA probation for recruiting violations—waving money and saying, "Why don't you buy some better players?" The crowd pulled out its own greenery and, referring to five ISU players who had been arrested for shoplifting, shot back, "Why don't you bail your players out of jail?" Weber leads overall, 70-46.

SEASON REVIEW

SEAS.	W-L	CONF.	COACH	SEAS.	W-L	CONF.	COACH
1926-48	*250-176*	*Guy Wicks, 168-71 from 1931-41*		1961-62	17-9		John Evans
1948-49	10-17		Ed Willet	1962-63	9-15		John Evans
1949-50	5-24		Ed Willet	1963-64	11-13	5-5	James Nau
1950-51	17-12		Steve Belko	1964-65	7-19	4-6	James Nau
1951-52	16-11		Steve Belko	1965-66	7-19	1-9	Claude Retherford
1952-53	18-7	●	Steve Belko	1966-67	10-15	5-5	Claude Retherford
1953-54	22-5	●	Steve Belko	1967-68	13-13	7-8	Danny Miller
1954-55	18-8	●	Steve Belko	1968-69	8-18	3-12	Danny Miller
1955-56	18-8	●	Steve Belko	1969-70	13-11	11-4	Danny Miller
1956-57	25-4	●	John Grayson	1970-71	9-15	7-7	Danny Miller
1957-58	22-6	●	John Grayson	1971-72	14-12	8-6	Jim Killingsworth
1958-59	21-7	●	John Grayson	1972-73	18-8	10-4	Jim Killingsworth
1959-60	21-5	●	John Evans	1973-74	20-8	11-3 ●	Jim Killingsworth
1960-61	13-12		John Evans	1974-75	16-10	9-5	Jim Killingsworth

SEAS.	W-L	CONF.	SCORING		COACH	RECORD	
1975-76	16-11	9-5	Steve Hayes	19.7	Jim Killingsworth		
1976-77	25-5	13-1 ●	Steve Hayes	20.2	Jim Killingsworth	109-54	.669
1977-78	16-10	11-3	Lawrence Butler	23.7	Lynn Archibald		
1978-79	14-13	8-6	Lawrence Butler	30.1	Lynn Archibald		
1979-80	9-17	5-9	Joe Fazekas	13.0	Lynn Archibald		
1980-81	12-14	6-8	Robert Tate	16.3	Lynn Archibald		
1981-82	14-12	5-9	Robert Tate	16.6	Lynn Archibald	65-66	.496
1982-83	10-17	7-7	Jackie Fleury	15.0	Wayne Ballard		
1983-84	12-20	6-8	Mike Williams	13.2	Wayne Ballard		
1984-85	15-18	5-9	Nelson Peterson	18.3	Wayne Ballard	37-55	.402
1985-86	15-12	8-6	Donn Holston	18.7	Dr. Jim Boutin		
1986-87	15-16	5-9 ●	Donn Holston	18.8	Dr. Jim Boutin		
1987-88	15-13	8-8	Chase Brown	12.2	Dr. Jim Boutin		
1988-89	9-18	4-12	Steven Garrity	16.9	Dr. Jim Boutin		
1989-90	6-21	3-13	Steven Garrity	12.0	Dr. Jim Boutin	60-80	.429
1990-91	11-18	7-9	Alex Kreps	17.8	Herb Williams		
1991-92	9-21	6-10	Herman Smith	17.8	Herb Williams		
1992-93	10-18	5-9	Jim Potter	18.8	Herb Williams		
1993-94	18-9 ⊗	9-5	Jim Potter	18.2	Herb Williams		
1994-95	18-10	7-7	Jim Potter	18.9	Herb Williams		
1995-96	11-15	7-7	Nate Green	14.6	Herb Williams		
1996-97	14-13	9-7	Nate Green	16.4	Herb Williams		
1997-98	6-20	2-14	Tywan Meadows	20.9	Herb Williams	97-124	.439
1998-99	6-20	4-12	Kevin Sweetwyne	17.3	Doug Oliver		
1999-00	8-19	3-13	Kevin Sweetwyne	16.3	Doug Oliver		
2000-01	14-14	10-6	Jordie McTavish	15.6	Doug Oliver		
2001-02	10-17	3-11	Jeremy Brown	15.8	Doug Oliver		
2002-03	15-14	7-7	Scott Henry	11.7	Doug Oliver		
2003-04	13-18	7-7	Marquis Poole	19.0	Doug Oliver		
2004-05	9-18	3-11	Jeff Gardner	12.0	Doug Oliver		
2005-06	13-14	4-10	Slim Millien	15.5	Doug Oliver	88-134	.382
2006-07	13-17	8-8	David Schroeder	16.8	Joe O'Brien		
2007-08	12-19	8-8	Matt Stucki	11.9	Joe O'Brien		
2008-09	13-19	9-7	Amorrow Morgan	13.6	Joe O'Brien	38-55	.409

⊗ Records don't reflect games forfeited or vacated. For adjusted record, see p. 521.
● NCAA Tournament appearance

PROFILE

Idaho State University, Pocatello, ID
Founded: 1901
Enrollment: 14,209 (9,755 undergraduate)
Colors: Orange and black
Nickname: Bengals
Current arenas: Holt Arena, opened in 1971 (8,000); Reed Gym, opened in 1951 (3,040)
First game: 1926
All-time record: 1,074-1,017 (.514)
Total weeks in AP Top 20/25: 6

Current conference: Big Sky (1963-)
Conference titles:
Big Sky: 4 (1974 [tie], '76 [tie], '77, '94 [tie])
Conference tournament titles:
Big Sky: 2 (1977, '87)
NCAA Tournament appearances: 11
Sweet 16s (since 1975): 1
NIT appearances: 0

TOP 5

G **Tyrone Buckmon** (1990-92)
G **Lawrence Butler** (1977-79)
G **Willie Humes** (1969-71)
F **Jim Potter** (1991-95)
C **Steve Hayes** (1973-77)

RECORDS

	GAME		SEASON		CAREER	
POINTS	53	Willie Humes, vs. Montana State (Feb. 20, 1971)	845	Dave Wagnon (1965-66)	1,964	Les Roh (1952-56)
POINTS PER GAME			32.5	Dave Wagnon (1965-66)	31.5	Willie Humes (1969-71)
REBOUNDS	30	Ed Wilson, vs. Texas-Pan American (Dec. 16, 1967)	420	Ed Wilson (1967-68)	1,147	Steve Hayes (1973-77)
ASSISTS	17	Tyrone Buckmon, vs. Weber State (Feb. 16, 1991)	195	Tyrone Buckmon (1990-91)	349	Tyrone Buckmon (1990-92)

ESPN 6 SAGARIN

ILLINOIS

The Orange Krush mystique was born in 1894, more than a decade before the first basketball season, when the football Illini switched uniform colors from Dartmouth green to their signature bright orange. It reached an early crescendo on the hardcourt in 1914-15, when the Illini won the first of 17 Big Ten titles and were named national champs by the Helms Foundation, and was revitalized during Illinois' Final Four run in 1989 and national runner-up finish in 2005. There's only one way left to elevate the Krush mystique even higher: win an NCAA title.

BEST TEAM: 2004-05 Backcourt stars Deron Williams and Dee Brown ran the offense to perfection while playing ferocious defense. James Augustine and Roger Powell formed a tough, hard-working frontcourt, while Luther Head's threes kept opponents on their toes. The result was a 29–0 run to start the season, a No. 1 ranking for most of the campaign, a Big Ten title and a trip to the NCAA Final, where the Illini lost, 75-70, to North Carolina.

BEST PLAYER: G DERON WILLIAMS (2002-05) Williams learned to play point guard from his mom, Denise, a former college player who discouraged her son from shooting too much and demanded that he play tough defense. It was easy to see the fruits of her labor when, as a junior, Williams shut down two big scorers—Arizona's Salim Stoudamire (nine points) and Louisville's Francisco Garcia (four)—on the way to the NCAA Final. Williams is Illinois' career Tournament assists leader.

BEST COACH: LOU HENSON (1975-96) Known for his enthusiasm, teaching skills and the way he badgered officials, Henson led the Illini to 12 NCAA Tournament appearances. In fact, Bob Knight once said that he probably never met anyone who loved basketball more than Henson.

GAME FOR THE AGES: In the 2005 Elite Eight against Arizona, Illinois trailed 75-60 with just over four minutes remaining before going on a 20-5 run to force overtime. Williams then hit two three-pointers in the extra frame to seal the Illini's 90-89 win. A blowup image of Williams' game-tying three with :38 left in regulation hangs in coach Bruce Weber's office.

HEARTBREAKER: In the 1989 Final Four, Illinois lost to Michigan—a team the Illini had beaten twice during the regular season—in an 83-81 classic that featured 33 lead changes. With time winding down, Wolverines forward Terry Mills missed a shot, but teammate Sean Higgins grabbed the rebound and scored the game-winner with :02 left.

FIERCEST RIVAL: On March 10, 1991, Henson called Knight a "classic bully" after the Hoosiers coach refused to shake his hand as he was exiting the court. Knight thought Henson's assistants were using overly aggressive tactics in recruiting players. Both coaches moved on, but the recruiting wars between the schools still rage. In 2006, they fought over prep star Eric Gordon, who chose Indiana after making a verbal commitment to Illinois. The Hoosiers lead the series overall, 82–80.

FANFARE AND HOOPLA: In 2005, the Orange Krush student fan group was able to buy a block of seats for a game at Michigan by posing as a youth group from Chicago. The Krush arrived in Ann Arbor in disguise, declined an offer of a campus tour but did have their photo taken with Michigan coach Tommy Amaker. They didn't reveal their true colors until tip-off.

FAN FAVORITE: G DEE BROWN (2002-06) Assembly Hall was at its loudest during Brown's introduction. One 80-year-old fan even wore Brown's signature orange headband as a tribute to the player's hustle.

CONSENSUS ALL-AMERICAS

1915-17	**Ray Woods**, G
1917	**Clyde Alwood**, C
1918	**Earl Anderson**, F
1920, '22	**Charles Carney**, F
1940	**Bill Hapac**, F
1942, '43	**Andy Phillip**, G
1945	**Walton Kirk**, G
1952	**Rod Fletcher**, G
2005	**Dee Brown**, G

FIRST-ROUND PRO PICKS

1951	**Don Sunderlage**, Philadelphia (9)
1954	**John Kerr**, Syracuse (6)
1957	**George Bon Salle**, Syracuse (7)
1970	**Mike Price**, New York (17)
1973	**Nick Weatherspoon**, Washington (13)
1983	**Derek Harper**, Dallas (11)
1987	**Ken Norman**, LA Clippers (19)
1989	**Nick Anderson**, Orlando (11)
1989	**Kenny Battle**, Detroit (27)
1990	**Kendall Gill**, Charlotte (5)
2002	**Frank Williams**, Denver (25)
2003	**Brian Cook**, LA Lakers (24)
2005	**Deron Williams**, Utah (3)
2005	**Luther Head**, Houston (24)

PROFILE

University of Illinois at Urbana-Champaign, Urbana-Champaign, IL
Founded: 1867
Enrollment: 41,379 (31,173 undergraduate)
Colors: Orange and blue
Nickname: Fighting Illini
Current arena: Assembly Hall, opened in 1963 (16,450)
Previous: Huff Gym, opened as New Gymnasium, 1925-63 (7,000); Men's Old Gym Annex, 1915-25 (3,500); Men's Old Gym, 1906-14 (1,500)
First game: Jan. 12, 1906

All-time record: 1,607-855 (.653)
Total weeks in AP Top 20/25: 415
Current conference: Big Ten (1905-)
Conference titles:
Big Ten: 17 (1915, '17 [tie], '24 [tie], '35 [tie], '37 [tie], '42, '43, '49, '51, '52, '63 [tie], '84 [tie], '98 [tie], 2001 [tie], '02 [tie], '04, '05)
Conference tournament titles:
Big Ten: 2 (2003, '05)
NCAA Tournament appearances: 28
Sweet 16s (since 1975): 8
Final Fours: 5

NIT appearances: 3
Semifinals: 1

TOP 5

G **Derek Harper** (1980-83)
G **Deron Williams** (2002-05)
F **Nick Anderson** (1987-89)
F **Ken Norman** (1984-87)
C **John Kerr** (1951-54)

RECORDS

RECORDS	GAME		SEASON		CAREER	
POINTS	53	Dave Downey, vs. Indiana (Feb. 16, 1963)	668	Don Freeman (1965-66)	2,129	Deon Thomas (1990-94)
POINTS PER GAME			27.8	Don Freeman (1965-66)	20.9	Nick Weatherspoon (1970-73)
REBOUNDS	24	Skip Thoren, vs. UCLA (Dec. 28, 1963)	349	Skip Thoren (1964-65)	1,023	James Augustine (2002-06)
ASSISTS	16	Tony Wysinger, vs. Pittsburgh (Dec. 6, 1986)	264	Deron Williams (2004-05)	765	Bruce Douglas (1982-86)

SEASON REVIEW

SEASON	W-L	CONF.	SCORING		COACH	RECORD	
1906-16	*101-61*		*Helms Foundation champion 1914-15 under Ralph R. Jones (16-0)*				
1916-17	13-3	10-2	Ralf Woods	10.3	Ralph R. Jones		
1917-18	9-6	6-6	Earl Anderson	13.4	Ralph R. Jones		
1918-19	6-8	5-7	Ken Wilson	8.5	Ralph R. Jones		
1919-20	9-4	8-4	Charles Carney	16.5	Ralph R. Jones	85-34	.714
1920-21	11-7	7-5	Charles Vail Jr.	6.0	Frank J. Winters		
1921-22	14-5	7-5	Charles Carney	13.1	Frank J. Winters	25-12	.676
1922-23	9-6	7-5	Walter Roettger	8.9	J. Craig Ruby		
1923-24	11-6	8-4	Leland Stilwell	7.6	J. Craig Ruby		
1924-25	11-6	8-4	Russell Daugherity	6.5	J. Craig Ruby		
1925-26	9-8	6-6	Russell Daugherity	5.8	J. Craig Ruby		
1926-27	10-7	7-5	Russell Daugherity	7.9	J. Craig Ruby		
1927-28	5-12	2-10	John How	7.4	J. Craig Ruby		
1928-29	10-7	6-6	John How	6.0	J. Craig Ruby		
1929-30	8-8	7-5	Charles Harper	4.8	J. Craig Ruby		
1930-31	12-5	7-5	Charles Harper	7.3	J. Craig Ruby		
1931-32	11-6	7-5	Caslon Bennett	6.2	J. Craig Ruby		
1932-33	11-7	6-6	Frank Froschauer	7.8	J. Craig Ruby		
1933-34	13-6	7-5	Frank Froschauer	8.9	J. Craig Ruby		
1934-35	15-5	9-3	F. Froschauer, B. Riegel	7.4	J. Craig Ruby		
1935-36	13-6	7-5	Harry Combes	8.1	J. Craig Ruby	148-95	.609
1936-37	14-4	10-2	Lou Boudreau	8.7	Douglas R. Mills		

SEAS.	W-L	CONF.	POSTSEASON	SCORING		REBOUNDS		ASSISTS		COACH	RECORD	
1937-38	9-9	4-8		Louis Dehner	12.4					Douglas R. Mills		
1938-39	14-5	8-4		Louis Dehner	12.6					Douglas R. Mills		
1939-40	14-6	7-5		Bill Hapac	12.2					Douglas R. Mills		
1940-41	13-7	7-5		Art Mathisen	8.9					Douglas R. Mills		
1941-42	18-5	13-2	NCAA REGIONAL SEMIFINALS	Andy Phillip	10.1					Douglas R. Mills		
1942-43	17-1	12-0		Andy Phillip	16.9					Douglas R. Mills		
1943-44	11-9	5-7		Stan Patrick	12.0					Douglas R. Mills		
1944-45	13-7	7-5		Walton Kirk	10.6					Douglas R. Mills		
1945-46	14-7	7-5		Bob Doster	13.0					Douglas R. Mills		
1946-47	14-6	8-4		Andy Phillip	9.6					Douglas R. Mills	151-66	.696
1947-48	15-5	7-5		Dwight Eddleman	13.9					Harry Combes		
1948-49	21-4	10-2	NCAA THIRD PLACE	Dwight Eddleman	13.1					Harry Combes		
1949-50	14-8	7-5		Wally Osterkorn	15.1					Harry Combes		
1950-51	22-5	13-1	NCAA THIRD PLACE	Don Sunderlage	17.4					Harry Combes		
1951-52	22-4	12-2	NCAA THIRD PLACE	John Kerr	13.7					Harry Combes		
1952-53	18-4	14-4		John Kerr	17.5					Harry Combes		
1953-54	17-5	10-4		John Kerr	25.3					Harry Combes		
1954-55	17-5	10-4		Paul Judson	16.5					Harry Combes		
1955-56	18-4	11-3		George BonSalle	22.9					Harry Combes		
1956-57	14-8	7-7		Harv Schmidt	18.8					Harry Combes		
1957-58	11-11	5-9		Don Ohl	19.6					Harry Combes		
1958-59	12-10	7-7		Roger Taylor	17.9	John Wessels	9.3			Harry Combes		
1959-60	16-7	8-6		Govoner Vaughn	17.9	Govoner Vaughn	8.1			Harry Combes		
1960-61	9-15	5-9		Dave Downey	16.8	Dave Downey	11.1			Harry Combes		
1961-62	15-8	7-7		Dave Downey	20.2	Dave Downey	12.2			Harry Combes		
1962-63	20-6	11-3	NCAA REGIONAL FINALS	Dave Downey	19.7	Dave Downey	9.8			Harry Combes		
1963-64	13-11	6-8		Skip Thoren	20.3	Skip Thoren	13.8			Harry Combes		
1964-65	18-6	10-4		Skip Thoren	22.2	Skip Thoren	14.5			Harry Combes		
1965-66	12-12	8-6		Don Freeman	27.8	Don Freeman	11.9			Harry Combes		
1966-67	12-12	6-8		Jim Dawson	21.7	Dave Scholz	10.9			Harry Combes	316-150	.678
1967-68	11-13	6-8		Dave Scholz	22.0	Dave Scholz	9.6			Harv Schmidt		
1968-69	19-5	9-5		Dave Scholz	19.1	Dave Scholz	8.7			Harv Schmidt		
1969-70	15-9	8-6		Greg Jackson	17.0	Greg Jackson	9.8			Harv Schmidt		
1970-71	11-12	5-9		Rick Howat	20.6	Nick Weatherspoon	10.7			Harv Schmidt		
1971-72	14-10	5-9		Nick Weatherspoon	20.8	Nick Weatherspoon	11.0			Harv Schmidt		
1972-73	14-10	8-6		Nick Weatherspoon	25.0	Nick Weatherspoon	12.3			Harv Schmidt		
1973-74	5-18	2-12		Rick Schmidt	21.4	Rick Schmidt	7.2	Jeff Dawson	3.2	Harv Schmidt	89-77	.536
1974-75	8-18	4-14		Rick Schmidt	20.2	Rick Schmidt	5.3	Rick Schmidt	2.8	Gene Bartow	8-18	.308
1975-76	14-13	7-11		Rich Adams	15.9	Rich Adams	5.9	Otho Tucker	3.2	Lou Henson		
1976-77	14-16 ⊗	8-10		Audie Matthews	16.0	Levi Cobb	6.4	Steve Lanter	3.4	Lou Henson		
1977-78	13-14	7-11		Audie Matthews	12.1	Neil Bresnahan	7.2	Neil Bresnahan	2.5	Lou Henson		
1978-79	19-11	7-11		Mark Smith	13.5	Neil Bresnahan	7.9	Mark Smith	4.0	Lou Henson		
1979-80	22-13	8-10	NIT THIRD PLACE	Eddie Johnson	17.4	Eddie Johnson	8.9	Reno Gray	3.1	Lou Henson		
1980-81	21-8	12-6	NCAA REGIONAL SEMIFINALS	Eddie Johnson	17.2	Eddie Johnson	9.2	Derek Harper	5.4	Lou Henson		
1981-82	18-11	10-8	NIT SECOND ROUND	Craig Tucker	15.5	James Griffin	7.0	Derek Harper	5.0	Lou Henson		
1982-83	21-11	11-7	NCAA FIRST ROUND	Derek Harper	15.4	Efrem Winters	6.9	Bruce Douglas	5.9	Lou Henson		
1983-84	26-5	15-3	NCAA REGIONAL FINALS	Efrem Winters	14.7	George Montgomery	7.2	Bruce Douglas	5.7	Lou Henson		
1984-85	26-9	12-6	NCAA REGIONAL SEMIFINALS	Anthony Welch	11.9	Efrem Winters	7.2	Bruce Douglas	5.7	Lou Henson		
1985-86	22-10	11-7	NCAA SECOND ROUND	Ken Norman	16.4	Ken Norman	7.1	Bruce Douglas	6.2	Lou Henson		
1986-87	23-8	13-5	NCAA FIRST ROUND	Ken Norman	20.7	Ken Norman	9.8	Tony Wysinger	6.4	Lou Henson		
1987-88	23-10	12-6	NCAA SECOND ROUND	Nick Anderson	15.9	Nick Anderson	6.6	Kendall Gill	4.2	Lou Henson		
1988-89	31-5	14-4	NCAA NATIONAL SEMIFINALS	Nick Anderson	18.0	Nick Anderson	7.9	Larry Smith	4.4	Lou Henson		
1989-90	21-8	11-7	NCAA FIRST ROUND	Kendall Gill	20.0	Marcus Liberty	7.7	Stephen Bardo	4.7	Lou Henson		
1990-91	21-10	11-7		Andy Kaufmann	21.3	Deon Thomas	6.8	Larry Smith	5.0	Lou Henson		
1991-92	13-15	7-11		Deon Thomas	19.4	Deon Thomas	6.9	Rennie Clemons	4.9	Lou Henson		
1992-93	19-13	11-7	NCAA SECOND ROUND	Deon Thomas	18.3	Deon Thomas	8.0	Rennie Clemons	4.2	Lou Henson		
1993-94	17-11	10-8	NCAA FIRST ROUND	Deon Thomas	19.6	Deon Thomas	6.9	Richard Keene	4.0	Lou Henson		
1994-95	19-12	10-8	NCAA FIRST ROUND	Kiwane Garris	15.9	Shelly Clark	8.3	Kiwane Garris	3.8	Lou Henson		
1995-96	18-13	7-11	NIT FIRST ROUND	Kiwane Garris	15.4	Bryant Notree, J. Gee	6.1	Richard Keene	5.2	Lou Henson	421-226	.651▼
1996-97	22-10	11-7	NCAA SECOND ROUND	Kiwane Garris	19.4	Chris Gandy	5.7	Kiwane Garris	5.6	Lon Kruger		
1997-98	23-10	13-3	NCAA SECOND ROUND	Kevin Turner	17.7	Jerry Hester, Jarrod Gee	5.3	Matt Heldman	4.0	Lon Kruger		
1998-99	14-18	3-13		Cory Bradford	15.4	Fess Hawkins	5.1	Sergio McClain	2.6	Lon Kruger		
1999-2000	22-10	11-5	NCAA SECOND ROUND	Cory Bradford	15.3	Brian Cook	4.5	Frank Williams	4.1	Lon Kruger	81-48	.628
2000-01	27-8	13-3	NCAA REGIONAL FINALS	Frank Williams	14.9	Brian Cook	6.1	Frank Williams	4.4	Bill Self		
2001-02	26-9	11-5	NCAA REGIONAL SEMIFINALS	Frank Williams	16.2	Brian Cook	6.7	Frank Williams	4.4	Bill Self		
2002-03	25-7	11-5	NCAA SECOND ROUND	Brian Cook	20.0	Brian Cook	7.6	Dee Brown	5.0	Bill Self	78-24	.765
2003-04	26-7	13-3	NCAA REGIONAL SEMIFINALS	Deron Williams	14.0	James Augustine	7.3	Deron Williams	6.2	Bruce Weber		
2004-05	37-2	15-1	NCAA RUNNER-UP	Luther Head	15.9	James Augustine	7.6	Deron Williams	6.8	Bruce Weber		
2005-06	26-7	11-5	NCAA SECOND ROUND	Dee Brown	14.2	James Augustine	9.1	Dee Brown	5.8	Bruce Weber		
2006-07	23-12	9-7	NCAA FIRST ROUND	Warren Carter	13.7	Shaun Pruitt	7.5	Chester Frazier	4.5	Bruce Weber		
2007-08	16-19	5-13		Shaun Pruitt	12.6	Shaun Pruitt	7.3	Chester Frazier	3.6	Bruce Weber		
2008-09	24-10	11-7	NCAA FIRST ROUND	Demetri McCamey	11.5	Mike Davis	8.1	Chester Frazier	5.3	Bruce Weber	152-57	.727

⊗ Records don't reflect games forfeited or vacated. For adjusted records, see p. 521.

▼ Coach's record adjusted to reflect games forfeited or vacated: 423-224, .654. For yearly totals, see p. 521.

ESPN 113 SAGARIN

ILLINOIS STATE

Four years after finishing fourth in the 1967 College Division tournament, the Redbirds played their first season in D1. Behind the scoring theatrics of Doug Collins, the first Illinois State player to receive a full basketball scholarship, the Redbirds were instant winners, finishing above .500 in each of his three seasons. That laid the groundwork for a program that would become one of the toughest mid-majors, earning six NCAA Tournament and 10 NIT bids.

BEST TEAM: 1997-98 All 14 players returned from the team that suffered a first-round loss to Iowa State in the 1997 NCAA Tournament. The continuity paid off. Coach Kevin Stallings' squad tied a school record with 25 wins and a No. 9 seed in the Big Dance, where the Redbirds advanced to the second round. The 6'6" Rico Hill was listed as the team's starting power forward, but could play both inside and out, knocking down 45 threes for the season while averaging 18.4 ppg and 7.5 rpg. He got plenty of support from fellow big man Dan Muller, a defensive terror who averaged 13 points.

BEST PLAYER: G Doug Collins (1970-73) In 1968, Collins was a high school junior who didn't start. By the summer of '72, he was a star who nailed the free throws that appeared to seal the gold for Team USA over the Soviets at the Munich Olympics, before controversy and a loss ensued (that's a whole other story). A year later, after averaging 29.1 ppg over his three seasons at Illinois State—still the 20th-best scoring average in NCAA history—he was the first pick in the NBA draft (Philadelphia 76ers).

BEST COACH: Bob Donewald (1978-89) Few opponents liked playing Donewald's teams. Instead of operating an up-tempo system like many of his Missouri Valley rivals, the former Bob Knight assistant emphasized relentless, hard-nosed, man-to-man defense. In fact, at many of his notoriously rugged practices, his players sometimes didn't take any shots for the first hour. ISU went to three straight Tournaments from 1983 to '85, beating Alabama in the first round in '84.

GAME FOR THE AGES: In the first round of the 1998 NCAA Tournament, the Redbirds faced Tennessee, which had passed over Stallings for its coaching vacancy before the season. The coach's revenge was dramatic and sweet: With 15.3 seconds left in overtime, UT's C.J. Black scored for an 81-80 advantage. But seconds later, ISU guard Kyle Cartmill drove the baseline and found Muller under the basket for an easy lay-in, giving the Redbirds the 82-81 win.

HEARTBREAKER: The Redbirds opened a six-point second-half lead over Ohio in the first round of the 1983 Tourney. But missed free throws and turnovers let the Bobcats back into it. Tied at 47 with 1:38 to go, the Redbirds spread their offense to play for the last shot. But OU's Robert Tatum somehow stole the ball and scored. ISU's Raynard Malaine responded by scoring with :03 left, but Tatum wasn't done. He collected a loose ball after a floor-length inbounds pass and lobbed in the game-winner.

FIERCEST RIVAL: Separated by just 40 miles on I-74, Bradley and Illinois State aren't always evenly matched (Bradley won five straight from 2005 to '08), except in one category: intensity. As Bradley coach Jim Les put it after his team pulled out a 76-75 thriller on Jan. 23, 2008, "It's a game that brings out a lot of emotion in everybody: coaches, players, fans." Bradley leads the series overall, 61–47.

FANFARE AND HOOPLA: Much the way Clemson football players rub Howard's Rock before each game, all ISU athletes touch the Battle Bird before each home contest. The coconut-size bronze cardinal head was unveiled in October 2000. Fans bid each year to be the Keeper of the Bird.

FAN FAVORITE: G Tarise Bryson (1998-2002) After a spectacular junior season, Bryson suffered a season-ending wrist injury just 22 minutes into his senior year. He was denied a hardship waiver, and ISU fans are still bitter over the way his career ended.

CONSENSUS ALL-AMERICAS

1968 **Jerry McGreal** (Little A-A), G
1973 **Doug Collins**, G

FIRST-ROUND PRO PICKS

1973 **Doug Collins**, Philadelphia (1)
1973 **Doug Collins**, New York (ABA, 4)

PROFILE

Illinois State University, Normal, IL
Founded: 1857
Enrollment: 20,799 (18,065 undergraduate)
Colors: Red and white
Nickname: Redbirds
Current arena: Redbird Arena, opened in 1989 (10,200)
Previous: Horton Field House, 1963-89 (7,700); McCormick Gymnasium, 1956-63 (N/A)
First game: 1898

All-time record: 1,445-1,036 (.582)
Total weeks in the AP Top 20/25: 11
Current conference: Missouri Valley (1981-)
Conference titles:
MVC: 5 (1984 [tie], '92 [tie], '93, '97, '98)
Conference tournament titles:
MVC: 4 (1983, '90, '97, '98)
NCAA Tournament appearances: 6
NIT appearances: 10

TOP 5

G **Tarise Bryson** (1998-2002)
G **Doug Collins** (1970-73)
F **Billy Lewis** (1974-78)
F **Fred Marberry** (1953-57)
C **Jeff Wilkins** (1974-77)

RECORDS	GAME		SEASON		CAREER	
POINTS	58	Robert Hawkins, vs. Northern Illinois (Feb. 20, 1974)	847	Doug Collins (1971-72)	2,240	Doug Collins (1970-73)
POINTS PER GAME			32.6	Doug Collins (1971-72)	29.1	Doug Collins (1970-73)
REBOUNDS	24	Ron deVries, vs. Pacific (Jan. 19, 1974); Mike Akin, vs. Sioux Falls (Dec. 30, 1964); Wardell Vaughn, vs. Eastern Illinois (Jan. 5, 1963); John Swart, vs. Eastern Illinois (Feb. 6, 1960)	373	Ron deVries (1973-74)	1,033	Ron deVries (1971-74)
ASSISTS	23	Mike Bonczyk, vs. Northern Illinois (Jan. 25, 1975)	243	Todd Starks (1986-87)	740	Jamar Smiley (1994-98)

SEASON REVIEW

SEASON	W-L	CONF.	SCORING	COACH	RECORD	
1898-1916	*105-67*		*Includes three undefeated seasons, 1898-99, 1899-1900, and 1908-09*			
1916-17	8-7			Harrison Russell		
1917-18	7-7			Harrison Russell		
1918-19	4-8			Harrison Russell		
1919-20	11-5			Harrison Russell		
1920-21	5-11			Harrison Russell		
1921-22	2-11			Harrison Russell		
1922-23	8-6			Harrison Russell	89-101	.468
1923-24	8-6			Clifford E. Horton		
1924-25	0-14			Clifford E. Horton	8-20	.286
1925-26	3-10			Don Karnes		
1926-27	6-10			Don Karnes	9-20	.310
1927-28	2-13			Joseph Cogdal		
1928-29	13-8			Joseph Cogdal		
1929-30	11-7			Joseph Cogdal		
1930-31	17-3			Joseph Cogdal		
1931-32	20-5			Joseph Cogdal		
1932-33	9-16			Joseph Cogdal		
1933-34	13-8			Joseph Cogdal		
1934-35	12-5			Joseph Cogdal		
1935-36	12-6			Joseph Cogdal		
1936-37	20-3			Joseph Cogdal		

SEAS.	W-L	CONF.	POSTSEASON	SCORING		REBOUNDS		ASSISTS		COACH	RECORD	
1937-38	15-4									Joseph Cogdal		
1938-39	17-6									Joseph Cogdal		
1939-40	20-5									Joseph Cogdal		
1940-41	15-4									Joseph Cogdal		
1941-42	17-5									Joseph Cogdal		
1942-43	14-4									Joseph Cogdal		
1943-44	16-7									Joseph Cogdal		
1944-45	7-15									Joseph Cogdal		
1945-46	7-14									Joseph Cogdal		
1946-47	7-13									Joseph Cogdal		
1947-48	7-15									Joseph Cogdal		
1948-49	9-11									Joseph Cogdal	280-177	.613
1949-50	9-15									James "Pim" Goff		
1950-51	14-12									James "Pim" Goff		
1951-52	17-7									James "Pim" Goff		
1952-53	12-12									James "Pim" Goff		
1953-54	9-12									James "Pim" Goff		
1954-55	13-12									James "Pim" Goff		
1955-56	10-14			Fred Marberry	26.9	Fred Marberry	13.8			James "Pim" Goff		
1956-57	14-13			Fred Marberry	29.5	Tony Cadle	11.7			James "Pim" Goff	98-97	.503
1957-58	13-14					Dave Schertz	11.3			James Collie		
1958-59	24-5					Ed Koch	10.6			James Collie		
1959-60	18-8					Ron English	14.9			James Collie		
1960-61	19-7					John Swart	9.5			James Collie		
1961-62	16-11					Wardell Vaughn	8.2			James Collie		
1962-63	15-10					Wardell Vaughn	8.3			James Collie		
1963-64	15-10					Preston Jordan	12.2			James Collie		
1964-65	6-18					Duane Bruninga	8.9			James Collie		
1965-66	12-14					Steve Arends	8.8			James Collie		
1966-67	18-13			Jerry McGreal	18.0	Steve Arends	11.1			James Collie		
1967-68	25-3			George Terry	22.6	Steve Arends	11.2			James Collie		
1968-69	19-10			Blaine Royer	20.1	Tom Taulbee	9.8			James Collie		
1969-70	9-16			Greg Guy	18.5	Myron Litwiller	9.4			James Collie	209-139	.601
1970-71	16-10			Doug Collins	28.6	Jim Smith	9.4			Will Robinson		
1971-72	16-10			Doug Collins	32.6	Ron deVries	14.3			Will Robinson		
1972-73	13-12			Doug Collins	26.0	Ron deVries	14.8			Will Robinson		
1973-74	17-9			Rick Whitlow	21.8	Ron deVries	14.3	Mike Bonczyk	4.4	Will Robinson		
1974-75	16-10			Rick Whitlow	22.2	Billy Lewis	8.3	Mike Bonczyk	7.2	Will Robinson	78-51	.605
1975-76	20-7			Roger Powell	19.2	Jeff Wilkins	10.6	Mike Bonczyk	7.0	Gene Smithson		
1976-77	22-7		NIT QUARTERFINALS	Jeff Wilkins	21.8	Jeff Wilkins	11.1	Ron Jones	7.3	Gene Smithson		
1977-78	24-4		NIT FIRST ROUND	Billy Lewis	21.4	Billy Lewis	8.6	Derrick Mayes	5.4	Gene Smithson	66-18	.786
1978-79	20-10			Derrick Mayes	19.8	Joe Galvin	8.5	Rick Ferina	5.5	Bob Donewald		
1979-80	20-9		NIT SECOND ROUND	Ron Jones	17.5	Del Yarbrough	7.9	Dave Nussbaumer	5.4	Bob Donewald		
1980-81	17-10			Rick Lamb	13.3	Rick Lamb	7.3	McKay Smith	2.4	Bob Donewald		
1981-82	17-12	9-7		Rick Lamb	14.3	Rick Lamb	8.7	Dwayne Tyus	3.2	Bob Donewald		
1982-83	24-7	13-5	NCAA FIRST ROUND	Rick Lamb	14.1	Rick Lamb	8.5	Michael McKenny	3.4	Bob Donewald		
1983-84	23-8	13-3	NCAA SECOND ROUND	Hank Cornley	14.8	Hank Cornley	7.6	Michael McKenny	4.4	Bob Donewald		
1984-85	22-8	11-5	NCAA SECOND ROUND	Lou Stefanovic	17.5	Lou Stefanovic	7.0	Michael McKenny	4.6	Bob Donewald		
1985-86	15-14	9-7		Derrick Sanders	12.6	Derrick Sanders	7.4	Mark Kraatz	3.0	Bob Donewald		
1986-87	19-13	7-7	NIT QUARTERFINALS	Derrick Sanders	15.8	Derrick Sanders	8.1	Todd Starks	7.8	Bob Donewald		
1987-88	18-13	9-5	NIT FIRST ROUND	Tony Holifield	14.8	Cliff Peterson	7.0	Rickey Jackson	3.7	Bob Donewald		
1988-89	13-17	6-8		Jarrod Coleman	16.0	Jarrod Coleman	6.7	Randy Blair	5.2	Bob Donewald	208-121	.632
1989-90	18-13	9-5	NCAA FIRST ROUND	Rickey Jackson	15.2	Jarrod Coleman	6.4	Randy Blair	3.9	Bob Bender		
1990-91	5-23	4-12		Reggie Wilson	15.2	Reggie Wilson	7.0	Richard Thomas	3.0	Bob Bender		
1991-92	18-11	14-4		Scott Fowler	11.7	Scott Fowler	5.0	Todd Wemhoener	3.7	Bob Bender		
1992-93	19-10	13-5		Mike VandeGarde	15.3	Mike VandeGarde	5.0	Richard Thomas	3.2	Bob Bender	60-57	.513
1993-94	16-11	12-6		Mike VandeGarde	13.5	Thomas Hunter	6.1	David Cason	4.9	Kevin Stallings		
1994-95	20-13	13-5	NIT SECOND ROUND	Maurice Trotter	11.4	Dan Muller	4.8	David Cason	6.8	Kevin Stallings		
1995-96	22-12	13-5	NIT QUARTERFINALS	Maurice Trotter	14.9	Dan Muller	5.7	Jamar Smiley	6.7	Kevin Stallings		
1996-97	24-6	14-4	NCAA FIRST ROUND	Rico Hill	18.8	Rico Hill	8.2	Jamar Smiley	7.3	Kevin Stallings		
1997-98	25-6	16-2	NCAA SECOND ROUND	Rico Hill	18.4	Rico Hill	7.5	Jamar Smiley	6.4	Kevin Stallings		
1998-99	16-15	7-11		Tarise Bryson	15.5	LeRoy Watkins	5.5	Victor Williams	3.3	Kevin Stallings	123-63	.661
1999-2000	10-20	5-13		Tarise Bryson	19.3	Tarise Bryson	4.1	Tarise Bryson	3.5	Tom Richardson		
2000-01	21-9	12-6	NIT FIRST ROUND	Tarise Bryson	22.8	Shedrick Ford	5.8	Randy Rice	4.4	Tom Richardson		
2001-02	17-14	12-6		Baboucarr Bojang	13.2	Baboucarr Bojang	7.6	Randy Rice	4.1	Tom Richardson		
2002-03	8-21	5-13		Vince Greene	12.3	Baboucarr Bojang	5.0	Vince Greene	4.4	Tom Richardson	56-64	.467
2003-04	10-19	4-14		Trey Guidry	15.2	Marcus Arnold	4.6	Vince Greene	3.8	Porter Moser		
2004-05	17-13	8-10		Lorenzo Gordon	16.3	Lorenzo Gordon	6.5	Vince Greene	4.4	Porter Moser		
2005-06	9-19	4-14		Greg Dilligard	9.9	Greg Dilligard	5.9	Neil Plank	2.8	Porter Moser		
2006-07	15-16	6-12		Levi Dyer	12.1	Greg Dilligard	5.8	Boo Richardson	4.9	Porter Moser	51-67	.432
2007-08	25-10	13-5	NIT SECOND ROUND	Osiris Eldridge	15.8	Anthony Slack	7.1	Boo Richardson	3.7	Tim Jankovich		
2008-09	24-10	11-7	NIT FIRST ROUND	Champ Oguchi	15.2	Dinma Odiakosa	7.5	Lloyd Phillips	3.6	Tim Jankovich	49-20	.710

ESPN 233 SAGARIN

ILLINOIS-CHICAGO

Sure, there were Flames highlights before coach Jimmy Collins got to the West Side in 1996—Sherell Ford, Kenny Williams and Craig Lathen produced many of them. But the program never burned as brightly as it has since Collins arrived and UIC began to pile up NCAA Tourney appearances and 20-win seasons.

BEST TEAM: 2003-04 The Flames won the Horizon League tourney and a school-record 24 games behind the trio of Cedrick Banks (2,097 career points), Martell Bailey (second nationally with 7.8 apg) and 1,000-point scorer Armond Williams. Their NCAA trip was UIC's third straight postseason tourney—a school first.

BEST PLAYER: F SHERELL FORD (1992-95) He sat out his freshman year before leading Illinois-Chicago in scoring two seasons and in rebounding three seasons. The Illinois native was Midwestern Collegiate (now the Horizon League) POY for 1994-95. He finished his career with 2,012 points and 807 rebounds.

BEST COACH: JIMMY COLLINS (1996-) In its first 49 years, UIC had no postseason appearances and just two 20-win seasons. Since Collins took over, the Flames have made three NCAAs and one NIT, had four 20-win seasons and racked up memorable upsets like a 70-58 drubbing of co-Big Ten champ Michigan State in 1997.

GAME FOR THE AGES: The Flames' 76-75 OT win over Loyola-Chicago in the 2002 Horizon League title game pitted brother against brother. David Bailey scored 35 points for Loyola-Chicago, while UIC's Martell Bailey scored nine with six assists. The killing blow was a last-second jumper by Cedrick Banks (17 points).

FIERCEST RIVAL: When coach Bruce Pearl arrived at Wisconsin-Milwaukee in 2001, a white-hot rivalry was born. Collins held a long grudge against Pearl over a 1989 allegation of recruiting violations. He refused to shake the UWM coach's hand after games. But it wasn't so easy to ignore the Panthers on the floor. In the early 2000s, UIC and UWM knocked each other out of the Horizon League tourney three times, with each winning two titles.

SEASON REVIEW

SEAS.	W-L	CONF.	COACH	SEAS.	W-L	CONF.	COACH
1947-48	1-15		Leo Gedvilas	1961-62	11-15		Mike Maksud
1948-49	6-12		Leo Gedvilas	1962-63	9-9		Tom Russo
1949-50	12-6		Leo Gedvilas	1963-64	9-9		Tom Russo
1950-51	11-6		Leo Gedvilas	1964-65	9-9		Tom Russo
1951-52	8-8		Leo Gedvilas	1965-66	6-15		Tom Russo
1952-53	9-8		Leo Gedvilas	1966-67	8-7		Tom Russo
1953-54	13-3		Leo Gedvilas	1967-68	12-5		Tom Russo
1954-55	15-2		Leo Gedvilas	1968-69	11-11		Tom Russo
1955-56	8-7		Leo Gedvilas	1969-70	10-9		Tom Russo
1956-57	9-7		Leo Gedvilas	1970-71	4-21		Tom Russo
1957-58	10-6		Leo Gedvilas	1971-72	4-17		Tom Russo
1958-59	8-6		Dick Rader	1972-73	6-16		Ed McQuillan
1959-60	11-10		Dick Rader	1973-74	8-18		Ed McQuillan
1960-61	10-11		Mike Maksud	1974-75	8-18		Ed McQuillan

SEAS.	W-L	CONF.		SCORING		COACH	RECORD
1975-76	8-18					Ed McQuillan	
1976-77	8-18			Ed Stacks	12.8	Ed McQuillan	38-88 .302
1977-78	13-14			Tom Goodalis	17.9	Tom Meyer	
1978-79	13-14			Joe Hedger	13.4	Tom Meyer	
1979-80	11-16			Andrew Cooper	14.5	Tom Meyer	
1980-81	10-17			Tim Anderson	13.1	Tom Meyer	
1981-82	14-13			John Ellis	16.9	Tom Meyer	
1982-83	16-12	7-4		John Ellis	15.6	Tom Meyer	77-86 .472
1983-84	22-7	12-2		John Ellis	14.7	Willie Little	
1984-85	14-14	7-7		Ivan Daniels	17.7	Willie Little	
1985-86	13-16	7-7		Eric Longino	18.0	Willie Little	
1986-87	17-15	9-5		Bobby Locke	21.1	Willie Little	66-52 .559
1987-88	8-20	4-10		Nate Chambers	16.5	Bob Hallberg	
1988-89	13-17	3-9		Tony Freeman	14.5	Bob Hallberg	
1989-90	16-12	6-6		Corwin Hunt	16.8	Bob Hallberg	
1990-91	15-15	5-11		Brian Hill	15.1	Bob Hallberg	
1991-92	16-14	10-6		Brian Hill	15.9	Bob Hallberg	
1992-93	17-15	9-7		Kenny Williams	21.7	Bob Hallberg	
1993-94	20-9	14-4		Sherell Ford	24.3	Bob Hallberg	
1994-95	18-9	11-4		Sherell Ford	26.2	Bob Hallberg	
1995-96	10-18 ⊗	5-11		Mark Miller	17.9	Bob Hallberg	133-129 .508▼
1996-97	15-14	11-5		Mark Miller	14.7	Jimmy Collins	
1997-98	22-6	12-2	●	Mark Miller	19.7	Jimmy Collins	
1998-99	7-21	2-12		Bryant Notree	15.0	Jimmy Collins	
1999-2000	11-20	5-9		Theandre Kimbrough	13.6	Jimmy Collins	
2000-01	11-17	5-9		Maurice Brown, Joe Scott	10.4	Jimmy Collins	
2001-02	20-14	8-8	●	Cedrick Banks	13.9	Jimmy Collins	
2002-03	21-9	12-4	■	Cedrick Banks	19.0	Jimmy Collins	
2003-04	24-8	12-4	●	Cedrick Banks	18.4	Jimmy Collins	
2004-05	15-14	8-8		Cedrick Banks	18.7	Jimmy Collins	
2005-06	16-15	8-8		Justin Bowen	14.7	Jimmy Collins	
2006-07	14-18	7-9		Othyus Jeffers	15.4	Jimmy Collins	
2007-08	18-15	9-9		Josh Mayo	17.1	Jimmy Collins	
2008-09	16-15	7-11		Josh Mayo	17.0	Jimmy Collins	210-186 .530

⊗ Records don't reflect games forfeited or vacated. For adjusted records, see p. 521.
▼ Coach's record adjusted to reflect games forfeited or vacated: 134-128, .511. For yearly totals, see p. 521.
● NCAA Tournament appearance ■ NIT appearance

PROFILE

University of Illinois at Chicago, Chicago, IL
Founded: 1896
Enrollment: 25,125 (15,672 undergraduate)
Colors: Nave blue and fire engine red
Nickname: Flames
Current arena: UIC Pavilion, opened in 1982 (8,000)
Previous: UIC Physical Education Building, 1965-82 (3,200); Men's Gym, 1947-65 (N/A)
First game: 1947
All-time record: 748-775 (.491)
Total weeks in AP Top 20/25: 0

Current conference: Horizon League (1994-)
Conference titles:
Assoc. of Mid-Continent Universities-8: 1 (1984)
Midwestern Collegiate: 1 (1998 [tie])
Conference tournament titles:
Horizon: 2 (2002, '04)
NCAA Tournament appearances: 3
NIT appearances: 1

TOP 5

G **Craig Lathen** (1981-85)
G **Kenny Williams** (1990-94)
G/F **Cedrick Banks** (2001-05)
F **Sherell Ford** (1992-95)
F/C **Chuck Lambert** (1971-75)

FIRST-ROUND PRO PICKS

1995 **Sherell Ford,** Seattle (26)

RECORDS

RECORDS	GAME		SEASON		CAREER	
POINTS	43	Chuck Lambert, vs. Trinity Christian (Jan. 27, 1974)	707	Sherell Ford (1994-95)	2,097	Cedrick Banks (2001-05)
POINTS PER GAME			26.2	Sherell Ford (1994-95)	22.9	Sherell Ford (1992-95)
REBOUNDS	25	Greg Olsen, vs. Chicago State (Feb. 20, 1969)	348	Chuck Lambert (1972-73)	1,181	Chuck Lambert (1971-75)
ASSISTS	17	Craig Lathen, vs. Cleveland State (Jan. 21, 1984)	274	Craig Lathen (1983-84)	755	Craig Lathen (1981-85)

ESPN 5 SAGARIN

INDIANA

Long before Bob Knight began ranting at refs, a 1906 *Indiana Daily Student* said this following an 18-17 loss to the New Albany (Ind.) YMCA: "Everybody unites in agreeing that the work of the official who reigned with a tyrannic hand was the vilest and most unfair ever perpetrated." Five national titles later, a famous Knight quote still rings true: "Basketball may have been invented in Massachusetts, but it was made for Indiana."

BEST TEAM: 1975-76 After their perfect 1974-75 season was ruined by Kentucky in the NCAA Mideast Regional final, the '75-76 Hoosiers had a mission: follow 31–1 with 32–0. IU opened with a 20-point pounding of defending champ UCLA, then cruised to their fourth straight Big Ten title and a third meeting with conference rival Michigan in the NCAA Final. There, national POY Scott May had 26 points and eight rebounds in an 86-68 romp. Mission accomplished.

BEST PLAYER: F Scott May (1973-76) With his great strength, quickness, shooting and passing, the 6'7" May was the perfect Knight player. A two-time Big Ten POY, he scored a then-record 752 points as a senior and was the No. 2 pick (Chicago) in the 1976 NBA draft.

BEST COACH: Bob Knight (1971-2000) His infamous temper made him a lightning rod for attention, and his IU career came to an inglorious end in 2000 when he violated a "zero tolerance" warning and was dismissed for grabbing a student by the arm. But there's no arguing the weight of his accomplishments—24 Tournament bids, three national titles (1976, '81, '87) and that perfect 1975-76 season—all fueled by his genius motion offense and relentless man-to-man defense.

GAME FOR THE AGES: The 1986-87 Hoosiers were far from Knight's best team, but they might have been the most resilient. After eking out victories over LSU and UNLV to advance to the NCAA Final on March 30, the Hoosiers won their fifth national title by beating Syracuse, 74-73, on Keith Smart's 17-foot jumper with :05 on the clock.

HEARTBREAKER: Playing for the first time since breaking his left arm four weeks earlier, May saw just seven minutes of action in the 1975 NCAA Mideast Regional final, ending up with more turnovers (three) than points (two) in a 92-90 loss to Kentucky.

FIERCEST RIVAL: Indiana vs. Purdue spans more than a century. The Boliermakers won the first nine games, including a 22-21 victory for the 1904 state title. The rivalry became downright nasty when coach Gene Keady arrived in West Lafayette in 1980. In his first game at IU's Assembly Hall, a message on the visiting locker room chalkboard—supposedly written by one of the Hoosiers—read, "Keady, we're gonna kick your a--." Purdue leads overall, 108–84.

FANFARE AND HOOPLA: In 1987, upset over Merriam-Webster's definition of a Hoosier as an "unskilled person," Indiana senator (and future U.S. vice president) Dan Quayle urged the dictionary's editors to give the word a more positive connotation. The slight didn't prevent IU from winning the NCAA championship that year. The definition was changed in 1993; it now reads, "a native or resident of Indiana."

FAN FAVORITE: G Steve Alford (1983-87) In a reader poll conducted in 1999 by the *Bloomington Herald-Times*, Alford was named IU's Athlete of the Century over nine-time Olympic gold-medal-winning swimmer Mark Spitz.

CONSENSUS ALL-AMERICAS

1921	**Everett Dean,** C
1930	**Branch McCracken,** F
1936	**Vern Huffman,** G
1939	**Ernie Andres,** G
1947	**Ralph Hamilton,** F
1954	**Don Schlundt,** C
1975, '76	**Scott May,** F
1976, '77	**Kent Benson,** C
1981	**Isiah Thomas,** G
1986, '87	**Steve Alford,** G
1993	**Calbert Cheaney,** G/F
2000	**A.J. Guyton,** G

FIRST-ROUND PRO PICKS

1948	**Ward Williams,** Fort Wayne (8)
1958	**Archie Dees,** Cincinnati (2)
1961	**Walt Bellamy,** Chicago (1)
1973	**Steve Downing,** Boston (17)
1973	**Steve Downing,** Indiana (ABA, 7)
1975	**Steve Green,** Utah (ABA, 5)
1976	**Scott May,** Chicago (2)
1976	**Quinn Buckner,** Milwaukee (7)
1976	**Bob Wilkerson,** Seattle (11)
1977	**Kent Benson,** Milwaukee (1)
1980	**Mike Woodson,** New York (12)
1981	**Isiah Thomas,** Detroit (2)
1981	**Ray Tolbert,** New Jersey (18)
1983	**Randy Wittman,** Washington (22)
1985	**Uwe Blab,** Dallas (17)
1993	**Calbert Cheaney,** Washington (6)
1993	**Greg Graham,** Charlotte (17)
1995	**Alan Henderson,** Atlanta (16)
1996	**Brian Evans,** Orlando (27)
2001	**Kirk Haston,** Charlotte (16)
2002	**Jared Jeffries,** Washington (11)
2008	**Eric Gordon,** LA Clippers (7)
2008	**D.J. White,** Detroit (29)

PROFILE

Indiana University, Bloomington, IN
Founded: 1820
Enrollment: 40,354 (31,626 undergraduate)
Colors: Cream and crimson
Nickname: Hoosiers
Current arena: Assembly Hall, opened in 1971 (17,456)
Previous: New Fieldhouse, 1960-71 (9,236); Old Fieldhouse, 1928-60 (10,000); Men's Gymnasium, 1917-28 (2,400); Assembly Hall, 1901-17 (600)
First game: Feb. 8, 1901

All-time record: 1638-912 (.642)
Total weeks in AP Top 20/25: 498
Current conference: Big Ten (1905-)
Conferences titles:
Big Ten: 20 (1926 [tie], '28 [tie], '36 [tie], '53, '54, '57 [tie], '58, '67 [tie], '73, '74 [tie], '75, '76, '80, '81, '83, '87 [tie], '89, '91 [tie], '93, 2002 [tie])
Conference tournament titles: 0
NCAA Tournament appearances: 35
Sweet 16s (since 1975): 14
Final Fours: 8
Titles: 5 (1940, '53, '76, '81, '87)

NIT appearances: 4
Semifinals: 2
Titles: 1 (1979)

TOP 5

G	**Steve Alford** (1983-87)
G	**Isiah Thomas** (1979-81)
F	**Scott May** (1973-76)
F/C	**George McGinnis** (1970-71)
C	**Walt Bellamy** (1958-61)

RECORDS	GAME		SEASON		CAREER	
POINTS	56	Jimmy Rayl, vs. Michigan State (Feb. 23, 1963); vs. Minnesota (Jan. 27, 1962)	785	Calbert Cheaney (1992-93)	2,613	Calbert Cheaney (1989-93)
POINTS PER GAME			30.0	George McGinnis (1970-71)	30.0	George McGinnis (1970-71)
REBOUNDS	33	Walt Bellamy, vs. Michigan (Mar. 11, 1961)	428	Walt Bellamy (1960-61)	1,091	Alan Henderson (1991-95)
ASSISTS	15	Michael Lewis, vs. Iowa (Feb. 28, 1998); Keith Smart, vs. Auburn (Mar. 14, 1987)	197	Isiah Thomas (1980-81)	545	Michael Lewis (1996-2000)

SEASON REVIEW

SEASON	W-L	CONF.	SCORING	COACH	RECORD
1901-17	*105-126*		*Had 2-20 conference record from 1911-12 to '14-15*		
1917-18	10-4	3-3		Dana M. Evans	
1918-19	10-7	4-6		Dana M. Evans	20-11 .645
1919-20	13-8	6-4		Ewald O. Stiehm	13-8 .619
1920-21	15-6	6-5		George W. Lewis	
1921-22	10-10	3-7		George W. Lewis	25-16 .610
1922-23	8-7	5-7		Leslie Mann	
1923-24	11-6	7-5		Leslie Mann	19-13 .594
1924-25	12-5	8-4		Everett S. Dean	
1925-26	12-5	8-4		Everett S. Dean	
1926-27	13-4	9-3		Everett S. Dean	
1927-28	15-2	10-2		Everett S. Dean	
1928-29	7-10	4-8		Everett S. Dean	
1929-30	8-9	7-5		Everett S. Dean	
1930-31	9-8	5-7		Everett S. Dean	
1931-32	8-10	4-8		Everett S. Dean	
1932-33	10-8	6-6		Everett S. Dean	
1933-34	13-7	6-6		Everett S. Dean	
1934-35	14-6	8-4		Everett S. Dean	
1935-36	18-2	11-1		Everett S. Dean	
1936-37	13-7	6-6		Everett S. Dean	
1937-38	10-10	4-8		Everett S. Dean	162-93 .635

SEAS.	W-L	CONF.	POSTSEASON	SCORING	REBOUNDS	ASSISTS	COACH	RECORD
1938-39	17-3	9-3					Branch McCracken	
1939-40	**20-3**	**9-3**	**NATIONAL CHAMPION**	**Paul Armstrong 8.8**			**Branch McCracken**	
1940-41	17-3	10-2		William Menke 8.8			Branch McCracken	
1941-42	15-6	10-5		Ed Denton 8.2			Branch McCracken	
1942-43	18-2	11-2		Ralph Hamilton 12.5			Branch McCracken	
1943-44	7-15	2-10		Paul Shields 8.5			Harry C. Good	
1944-45	10-11	3-9		Al Kralovansky 9.2			Harry C. Good	
1945-46	18-3	9-3		John Wallace 14.4			Harry C. Good	35-29 .547
1946-47	12-8	8-4		Ralph Hamilton 13.4			Branch McCracken	
1947-48	8-12	3-9		Don Ritter 13.8			Branch McCracken	
1948-49	14-8	6-6		Bill Garrett 10.0			Branch McCracken	
1949-50	17-5	7-5		Bill Garrett 12.9			Branch McCracken	
1950-51	19-3	12-2		Bill Garrett 13.1	Bill Garrett 8.5		Branch McCracken	
1951-52	16-6	9-5		Don Schlundt 17.1	Don Schlundt 7.2		Branch McCracken	
1952-53	**23-3**	**17-1**	**NATIONAL CHAMPION**	**Don Schlundt 25.4**	**Charles Kraak 10.7**		**Branch McCracken**	
1953-54	20-4	12-2	NCAA REGIONAL SEMIFINALS	Don Schlundt 24.3	Don Schlundt 11.1		Branch McCracken	
1954-55	8-14	5-9		Don Schlundt 26.0	Don Schlundt 9.8		Branch McCracken	
1955-56	13-9	6-8		Wally Choice 21.0	Archie Dees 12.6		Branch McCracken	
1956-57	14-8	10-4		Archie Dees 25.0	Archie Dees 14.4		Branch McCracken	
1957-58	13-11	10-4	NCAA REGIONAL SEMIFINALS	Archie Dees 25.5	Archie Dees 14.4		Branch McCracken	
1958-59	11-11	7-7		Walt Bellamy 17.4	Walt Bellamy 15.2		Branch McCracken	
1959-60	20-4	11-3		Walt Bellamy 22.4	Walt Bellamy 13.5		Branch McCracken	
1960-61	15-9	8-6		Walt Bellamy 21.8	Walt Bellamy 17.8		Branch McCracken	
1961-62	13-11	7-7		Jimmy Rayl 29.8	Charley Hall 10.3		Branch McCracken	
1962-63	13-11	9-5		Jimmy Rayl 25.3	Tom Van Arsdale 9.3		Branch McCracken	
1963-64	9-15	5-9		Dick Van Arsdale 22.3	Dick Van Arsdale 12.4		Branch McCracken	
1964-65	19-5	9-5		Tom Van Arsdale 18.4	Dick Van Arsdale 8.7		Branch McCracken	364-174 .677
1965-66	8-16	4-10		Max Walker 16.5	Butch Joyner 7.9		Lou Watson	
1966-67	18-8	10-4	NCAA REGIONAL SEMIFINALS	Butch Joyner 18.5	Butch Joyner 10.5		Lou Watson	
1967-68	10-14	4-10		Vern Payne 14.8	Bill DeHeer 10.4		Lou Watson	
1968-69	9-15	4-10		Joe Cooke 21.8	Ken Johnson 12.1		Lou Watson	
1969-70	7-17	3-11		Jim Harris 18.1	Ken Johnson 10.5		Jerry Oliver	7-17 .292
1970-71	17-7	9-5		George McGinnis 30.0	George McGinnis 14.7	Jim Harris 3.0	Lou Watson	62-60 .508
1971-72	17-8	9-5	NIT FIRST ROUND	Joby Wright 19.9	Steve Downing 15.1	Bootsie White 4.3	Bob Knight	
1972-73	22-6	11-3	NCAA THIRD PLACE	Steve Downing 20.1	Steve Downing 10.6	Quinn Buckner 2.9	Bob Knight	
1973-74	23-5	12-2		Steve Green 16.7	Kent Benson 8.2	Quinn Buckner 5.4	Bob Knight	
1974-75	31-1	18-0	NCAA REGIONAL FINALS	Steve Green 16.6	Kent Benson 8.9	Quinn Buckner 5.5	Bob Knight	
1975-76	**32-0**	**18-0**	**NATIONAL CHAMPION**	**Scott May 23.5**	**Kent Benson 8.8**	**Bobby Wilkerson 5.3**	**Bob Knight**	
1976-77	14-13 ⊗	11-7		Mike Woodson 18.5	Kent Benson 10.8	Jim Wisman 5.0	Bob Knight	
1977-78	21-8	12-6	NCAA REGIONAL SEMIFINALS	Mike Woodson 19.9	Ray Tolbert 6.9	Jim Wisman 4.0	Bob Knight	
1978-79	22-12	10-8	NIT CHAMPION	Mike Woodson 21.0	Ray Tolbert 7.1	Butch Carter 4.6	Bob Knight	
1979-80	21-8	13-5	NCAA REGIONAL SEMIFINALS	Isiah Thomas 14.6	Ray Tolbert 7.2	Isiah Thomas 5.5	Bob Knight	
1980-81	**26-9**	**14-4**	**NATIONAL CHAMPION**	**Isiah Thomas 16.0**	**Ray Tolbert 6.4**	**Isiah Thomas 5.8**	**Bob Knight**	
1981-82	19-10	12-6	NCAA SECOND ROUND	Ted Kitchel 19.6	Jim Thomas 6.2	Jim Thomas 3.5	Bob Knight	
1982-83	24-6	13-5	NCAA REGIONAL SEMIFINALS	Randy Wittman 19.0	Jim Thomas 5.3	Tony Brown 4.0	Bob Knight	
1983-84	22-9	13-5	NCAA REGIONAL FINALS	Steve Alford 15.5	Uwe Blab 6.1	Stew Robinson 3.5	Bob Knight	
1984-85	19-14	7-11	NIT RUNNER-UP	Steve Alford 18.1	Uwe Blab 6.3	Stew Robinson 4.6	Bob Knight	
1985-86	21-8	13-5	NCAA FIRST ROUND	Steve Alford 22.5	Andre Harris 5.6	Winston Morgan 4.6	Bob Knight	
1986-87	**30-4**	**15-3**	**NATIONAL CHAMPION**	**Steve Alford 22.0**	**Dean Garrett 8.5**	**Steve Alford 3.6**	**Bob Knight**	
1987-88	19-10	11-7	NCAA FIRST ROUND	Dean Garrett 16.1	Dean Garrett 8.5	Joe Hillman 3.9	Bob Knight	
1988-89	27-8	15-3	NCAA REGIONAL SEMIFINALS	Jay Edwards 20.0	Eric Anderson 6.1	Joe Hillman 3.9	Bob Knight	
1989-90	18-11	8-10	NCAA FIRST ROUND	Calbert Cheaney 17.1	Eric Anderson 7.0	Jamal Meeks 3.8	Bob Knight	
1990-91	29-5	15-3	NCAA REGIONAL SEMIFINALS	Calbert Cheaney 21.6	Eric Anderson 7.1	Jamal Meeks 4.9	Bob Knight	
1991-92	27-7	14-4	NCAA NATIONAL SEMIFINALS	Calbert Cheaney 17.6	Alan Henderson 7.2	Jamal Meeks 4.2	Bob Knight	
1992-93	31-4	17-1	NCAA REGIONAL FINALS	Calbert Cheaney 22.4	Alan Henderson 8.1	Damon Bailey 4.1	Bob Knight	
1993-94	21-9	12-6	NCAA REGIONAL SEMIFINALS	Damon Bailey 19.6	Alan Henderson 10.3	Damon Bailey 4.3	Bob Knight	
1994-95	19-12	11-7	NCAA FIRST ROUND	Alan Henderson 23.5	Alan Henderson 9.7	Brian Evans 3.9	Bob Knight	
1995-96	19-12 ⊗	12-6	NCAA FIRST ROUND	Brian Evans 21.2	Brian Evans 7.1	Neil Reed 4.4	Bob Knight	
1996-97	22-11	9-9	NCAA FIRST ROUND	Andrae Patterson 13.7	Andrae Patterson 6.7	A.J. Guyton 3.9	Bob Knight	
1997-98	20-12	9-7	NCAA SECOND ROUND	A.J. Guyton 16.8	Andrae Patterson 5.8	Michael Lewis 4.7	Bob Knight	
1998-99	23-11	9-7	NCAA SECOND ROUND	Luke Recker 16.1	Kirk Haston 6.5	Michael Lewis 4.6	Bob Knight	
1999-2000	20-9	10-6	NCAA FIRST ROUND	A.J. Guyton 19.7	Kirk Haston 8.3	Michael Lewis 5.3	Bob Knight	659-242 .731▼
2000-01	21-13	10-6	NCAA FIRST ROUND	Kirk Haston 19.0	Kirk Haston 8.7	Tom Coverdale 4.8	Mike Davis	
2001-02	25-12	11-5	NCAA RUNNER-UP	Jared Jeffries 15.0	Jared Jeffries 7.6	Tom Coverdale 4.8	Mike Davis	
2002-03	21-13	8-8	NCAA SECOND ROUND	Bracey Wright 16.2	Jeff Newton 8.2	Tom Coverdale 4.5	Mike Davis	
2003-04	14-15	7-9		Bracey Wright 18.5	A.J. Moye 6.4	Marshall Strickland 2.7	Mike Davis	
2004-05	15-14	10-6	NIT FIRST ROUND	Bracey Wright 18.3	D.J. White 4.9	Marshall Strickland 3.4	Mike Davis	
2005-06	19-12	9-7	NCAA SECOND ROUND	Marco Killingsworth 17.1	Marco Killingsworth 7.8	Robert Vaden 3.5	Mike Davis	115-79 .593
2006-07	21-11	10-6	NCAA SECOND ROUND	D.J. White 13.8	D.J. White 7.3	Earl Calloway 4.3	Kelvin Sampson	
2007-08	25-8	14-4	NCAA FIRST ROUND	Eric Gordon 20.9	D.J. White 10.3	Jamarcus Ellis 3.4	Kelvin Sampson[a]	43-15 .741
2008-09	6-25	1-17		Devan Dumes 12.7	Tom Pritchard 6.4	Verdell Jones III 3.6	Tom Crean	6-25 .194

[a] Kelvin Sampson (22-4) and Dan Dakich (3-4) both coached during the 2007-08 season.

⊗ Records don't reflect games forfeited or vacated. For adjusted records, see p. 521.

▼ Coach's record adjusted to reflect games forfeited or vacated: 662-239, .735. For yearly records, see p. 521.

ESPN 125 SAGARIN

INDIANA STATE

John Wooden launched his head-coaching career at Indiana State, but that's only the second-most important chapter in Sycamores history. There is simply no adequate way to measure the awe with which the city of Terre Haute beheld Larry Bird as he led his home-state team to the 1979 NCAA Championship game.

BEST TEAM: 1978-79 It's still known as the Dream Season—when the entire basketball world focused on a small Missouri Valley school led by a country boy straight out of folklore. Entering the NCAA Tournament unbeaten at 29–0, Indiana State appeared to be a team of destiny when Bob Heaton hit a miraculous shot in the Elite Eight to beat Arkansas. Even though the Sycamores lost to Michigan State, 75-64, in the Final, the team's and the star player's legends were secure.

BEST PLAYER: F Larry Bird (1976-79) After dropping out of Indiana in his freshman year before ever playing a game for the Hoosiers, Bird drove a garbage truck in his hometown until Indiana State assistant Bill Hodges lured him to play for the Sycamores. Three years later, the Hick from French Lick was the 14th-leading scorer in NCAA history (30.3 ppg) and was well on his way to becoming Larry Legend—with a legendary NBA All-Star and championship career with the Boston Celtics still to come.

BEST COACH: Bob King (1975-78) The former New Mexico coach took over the downtrodden Sycamores in 1975 and struck gold by landing Bird. King had to step aside for health reasons right before the 1978-79 season, but the players, the fans and especially Hodges, who took over for him, were always quick to credit King with making the Dream possible.

GAME FOR THE AGES: Even at 31–0, it wasn't until the Elite Eight game against Arkansas on March 17, 1979, that the Sycamores convinced skeptics they were for real. Although Bird was spectacular as usual (31 points, 10 rebounds), the game was tied at 71 in the final seconds. That's when "Miracle Man" Heaton drove the lane, took to the air, switched the ball between his hands in midair and hit the 10-foot runner at the buzzer that sent Indiana State to its first Final Four—and its championship date with America's other favorite team and player, Michigan State and Ervin "Magic" Johnson.

HEARTBREAKER: On March 26, 1979, 35 million television viewers tuned in to watch Indiana State vs. Michigan State in what remains the highest-rated NCAA Final. The hype from Salt Lake City was enormous, but the game never reached the intensity level that everyone expected. In fact, ISU never really challenged the Spartans in the 75-64 loss. Bird left the court in tears after scoring just 19 points to Magic Johnson's 24. The loss eats at him to this day, along with the thought that he let Terre Haute down that night.

FIERCEST RIVAL: Indiana State and Indiana have played only 22 times since their first meeting on Jan. 24, 1902 (the Hoosiers lead, 17–5). But lately the series has become the state's version of David vs. Goliath, with the Sycamores winning three of five games since 1999. That includes a miraculous 59-58 win in 2000,

> ***There is simply no way to measure the awe with which Terre Haute beheld Larry Bird.***

when Michael Menser scored six points in the final 8.5 seconds and blew the roof off the Hulman Center.

FANFARE AND HOOPLA: In 1948, Clarence Walker became the first African-American to play in a postseason college basketball tournament—a milestone Wooden helped ensure. A year earlier, NAIB organizers had told the coach to leave Walker at home, but Wooden withdrew his team instead. In 1948, the tournament reluctantly allowed Walker to play.

FAN FAVORITE: G Kelyn Block (1998-2002) They don't get any tougher. During a 2001 NCAA first-round game against Oklahoma, Block took an elbow that shattered three lower front teeth, yet returned in overtime to score five points in a 70-68 victory.

CONSENSUS ALL-AMERICAS

1968	**Jerry Newsome** (Little A-A), F
1978, '79	**Larry Bird,** F

FIRST-ROUND PRO PICKS

1978	**Larry Bird,** Boston (6)
1980	**Carl Nicks,** Denver (23)

PROFILE

Indiana State University, Terre Haute, IN
Founded: 1865 as Indiana State Normal School
Enrollment: 10,487 (8,386 undergraduate)
Colors: Royal blue and white
Nickname: Sycamores
Current arena: Hulman Center, opened in 1973 (10,200)
Previous: The Arena, 1962-73 (4,800); The Gymnasium, 1928-62 (3,000); Wiley High School Gymnasium, 1923-28 (1,600)
First game: Nov. 10, 1899
All-time record: 1,331-1,132 (.540)
Total weeks in AP Top 20/25: 22
Current conference: Missouri Valley (1977-)
Conference titles:
MVC: 2 (1979, 2000)
Conference tournament titles:
MVC: 2 (1979, 2001)
NCAA Tournament appearances: 3
Sweet 16s (since 1975): 1
Final Fours: 1
NIT appearances: 2

TOP 5

G	**David Moss** (2002-06)
G	**Butch Wade** (1964-67)
F	**Larry Bird** (1976-79)
F	**Jerry Newsom** (1965-68)
F	**John Sherman Williams** (1982-86)

RECORDS

RECORDS	GAME		SEASON		CAREER	
POINTS	49	Larry Bird, vs. Wichita State (Feb. 25, 1979)	973	Larry Bird (1978-79)	2,850	Larry Bird (1976-79)
POINTS PER GAME			32.8	Larry Bird (1976-77)	30.3	Larry Bird (1976-79)
REBOUNDS	25	Jim Cruse, vs. Drake (Jan. 18, 1997)	505	Larry Bird (1978-79)	1,247	Larry Bird (1976-79)
ASSISTS	16	Jim Smith, vs. Drake (Jan. 14, 1978)	239	Steve Reed (1978-79)	616	Steve Reed (1977-81)

SEASON REVIEW

SEASON	W-L	CONF.	COMMENTS	COACH	RECORD	SEASON	W-L	CONF.	COMMENTS	COACH	RECORD
1899-1916	*71-104*		*First winning season was Bertram Wiggins' only, 1911-12 (7-6)*			1926-27	3-13			David A. Glascock	
1916-17	13-4			Alfred Westphal	47-23 .671	1927-28	12-5			Walter E. Marks	
1917-18	8-8			O.E. Sink	8-8 .500	1928-29	15-4			Walter E. Marks	
1918-19	6-3			Birch E. Bayh		1929-30	16-2			Walter E. Marks	
1919-20	4-6			Birch E. Bayh		1930-31	7-8			Walter E. Marks	
1920-21	15-7			Birch E. Bayh		1931-32	10-5			J. Roy Goodland	10-5 .667
1921-22	12-3			Birch E. Bayh		1932-33	10-6			David A. Glascock	33-32 .508
1922-23	20-5			Birch E. Bayh	57-24 .704	1933-34	8-9			Walter E. Marks	
1923-24	16-7			Arthur L. Strum	16-7 .696	1934-35	13-4			Walter E. Marks	
1924-25	11-4			David A. Glascock		1935-36	11-3			Walter E. Marks	
1925-26	9-9			David A. Glascock		1936-37	7-6			Walter E. Marks	

SEAS.	W-L	CONF.	POSTSEASON	SCORING	REBOUNDS	ASSISTS	COACH	RECORD
1937-38	1-17						Walter E. Marks	90-58 .608
1938-39	10-9						Glenn M. Curtis	
1939-40	15-3						Glenn M. Curtis	
1940-41	11-8						Glenn M. Curtis	
1941-42	17-4						Glenn M. Curtis	
1942-43	13-4						Glenn M. Curtis	
1943-44	17-4						Glenn M. Curtis	
1944-45	18-6						Glenn M. Curtis	
1945-46	21-7						Glenn M. Curtis	122-45 .731
1946-47	17-8						John Wooden	
1947-48	27-7			Duane Klueh 17.6			John Wooden	44-15 .746
1948-49	24-8						John Longfellow	
1949-50	27-8		NAIB CHAMPION				John Longfellow	
1950-51	15-10			Cliff Murray 13.1			John Longfellow	
1951-52	19-10			Dick Atha 12.3			John Longfellow	
1952-53	23-8			Dick Atha 14.9			John Longfellow	
1953-54	12-15			Joe Lee 16.3			John Longfellow	120-59 .670
1954-55	9-15			Joe Lee 11.8			Paul Wolf[a]	9-15 .375
1955-56	8-16			Sam Richardson 16.7			Duane Klueh	
1956-57	12-13			Jim Bates 15.2			Duane Klueh	
1957-58	11-14			Jim Bates 16.4			Duane Klueh	
1958-59	17-10			Jim Gangloff 15.7	Jim Gangloff 7.6		Duane Klueh	
1959-60	7-13			Arley Andrews 17.9	Arley Andrews 7.2		Duane Klueh	
1960-61	17-9			John Dow 10.6	Howard Dardeen 9.3		Duane Klueh	
1961-62	19-11			Howard Dardeen 21.1	Howard Dardeen 10.8		Duane Klueh	
1962-63	18-7			John Robbins 17.0	Wayne Allison 10.6		Duane Klueh	
1963-64	17-8			Wayne Allison 17.7	Lennie Long 10.0		Duane Klueh	
1964-65	13-10			Butch Wade 27.3	Butch Wade 9.7		Duane Klueh	
1965-66	22-6			Jerry Newsom 26.6	Jerry Newsom 11.1		Duane Klueh	
1966-67	21-5			Jerry Newsom 22.8	Jerry Newsom 12.2		Duane Klueh	182-122 .599
1967-68	23-8			Jerry Newsom 26.1	Jerry Newsom 10.5		Gordon Stauffer	
1968-69	13-13			Mike Cooper 17.8	George Pillow 9.0		Gordon Stauffer	
1969-70	16-10			Bob Barker 17.1	George Pillow 9.8		Gordon Stauffer	
1970-71	17-9			George Pillow 18.8	George Pillow 10.0		Gordon Stauffer	
1971-72	12-14			Dan Bush 18.4	Rick Peckinpaugh 6.5		Gordon Stauffer	
1972-73	16-10			Carl Macon 15.4	Carl Moon 11.1		Gordon Stauffer	
1973-74	12-14			Rick Williams 16.8	Rick Williams 9.3		Gordon Stauffer	
1974-75	12-14			Rick Williams 20.0	Rick Williams 8.3		Gordon Stauffer	121-92 .568
1975-76	13-12			Rick Williams 15.7	DeCarsta Webster 13.6		Bob King	
1976-77	25-3		NIT FIRST ROUND	Larry Bird 32.8	Larry Bird 13.3		Bob King	
1977-78	23-9	11-5	NIT QUARTERFINALS	Larry Bird 30.0	Larry Bird 11.5		Bob King	61-24 .718
1978-79	33-1	16-0	NCAA RUNNER-UP	Larry Bird 28.6	Larry Bird 14.9	Steve Reed 239	Bill Hodges	
1979-80	16-11	8-8		Carl Nicks 26.7	Alex Gilbert 8.9		Bill Hodges	
1980-81	9-18	4-12		Robert McField 14.7	Dale Brakins 5.7		Bill Hodges	
1981-82	9-18	2-14		Ken Bannister 13.9	James Smith 9.1		Bill Hodges	67-48 .583
1982-83	9-19	5-13		John Williams 18.6	James Smith 9.4		Dave Schellhase	
1983-84	14-14	6-10		John Williams 21.8	Matt Brundige 6.4		Dave Schellhase	
1984-85	14-15	6-10		John Williams 22.8	Johnny Edwards 10.4		Dave Schellhase	37-48 .435
1985-86	11-17	5-11		John Williams 20.8	John Williams 5.9		Ron Greene	
1986-87	9-20	4-10		Benji Frazier 9.7	Larry Bush 7.5		Ron Greene	
1987-88	7-21	2-12		Eddie Bird 15.3	Rotimi Alakija 5.4		Ron Greene	
1988-89	4-24	0-14		Eddie Bird 13.1	Luke Gross 4.1		Ron Greene	31-82 .274
1989-90	8-20	2-12		Eddie Bird 14.6	Luke Gross 5.0		Tates Locke	
1990-91	14-14	9-7		Eddie Bird 12.9	Mike Land 4.3		Tates Locke	
1991-92	13-15	12-6		Travis Inman 12.2	Jason Edwards 5.6		Tates Locke	
1992-93	11-17	7-11		Greg Thomas 17.1	Jason Edwards 5.1		Tates Locke	
1993-94	4-22	3-15		Mario Clark 12.0	Jim Cruse 4.7		Tates Locke	50-88 .362
1994-95	7-19	3-15		Mike Jovanovich 11.8	Denny Hinson 5.8		Sherman Dillard	
1995-96	10-16	6-12		Cory DeGroote 12.5	Jim Cruse 9.0		Sherman Dillard	
1996-97	12-16	6-12		Jim Cruse 14.0	Jim Cruse 10.6		Sherman Dillard	29-51 .363
1997-98	16-11	10-8		Jayson Wells 16.7	Jayson Wells 8.4		Royce Waltman	
1998-99	15-12	10-8		Matt Renn 11.6	Matt Renn 7.1	Nate Green 4.6	Royce Waltman	
1999-2000	22-10	14-4	NCAA FIRST ROUND	Nate Green 13.8	Matt Renn 7.3	Matt Renn 7.3	Royce Waltman	
2000-01	22-12	10-8	NCAA SECOND ROUND	Matt Renn 15.8	Matt Renn 7.5	Matt Renn 7.5	Royce Waltman	
2001-02	6-22	4-14		Kelyn Block 11.0	Djibril Kante 8.5	Lamar Grimes 2.6	Royce Waltman	
2002-03	7-24	2-16		David Moss 13.2	Brian Giesen 5.1	Wilfred Antoine 3.2	Royce Waltman	
2003-04	9-19	5-13		David Moss 13.6	Amani Daanish 5.0	David Moss 3.5	Royce Waltman	
2004-05	11-20	5-13		David Moss 14.9	Amani Daanish 6.6	David Moss 3.5	Royce Waltman	
2005-06	13-16	4-14		David Moss 16.6	Trent Wurtz 5.9	David Moss 4.0	Royce Waltman	
2006-07	13-18	5-13		Gabe Moore 11.5	Adam Arnold 6.2	Gabe Moore 3.9	Royce Waltman	134-164 .450
2007-08	15-16	8-10		Gabe Moore 12.1	Jay Tunnell 4.7	Gabe Moore 4.5	Kevin McKenna	
2008-09	11-21	7-11		Harry Marshall 13.6	Jay Tunnell 6.2	Harry Marshall 4.2	Kevin McKenna	26-37 .413

Cumulative totals listed when per game averages not available.

[a] Paul Wolf and John Longfellow served as co-coaches during the 1954-55 season.

THE SCHOOLS

ESPN 324 SAGARIN

IPFW

Since it started playing hoops in 1973, Indiana University-Purdue University Fort Wayne has been better known for its odd nickname—the Mastodons—and the school's strange, dual-university affiliation than for its performance. That changed somewhat in 2005, when IPFW hired 25-year-old Dane Fife, a former Indiana guard who became the youngest head coach in Division I. On the sideline Fife proved precocious—in '05-06, the Mastodons reached double-digit victories for the first time in D1.

BEST TEAM: 1992-93 Led by the Gibson brothers, Sean and Shane, IPFW tallied a school-record 23 wins and reached the D2 tournament. Along the way, the Mastodons climbed to a school-best No. 4 in the national rankings and took the Great Lakes Valley title.

BEST PLAYER: C David Simon (2002-05) Before his junior season, some experts rated the 6'10" Simon as the nation's No. 2 center, after UConn's Emeka Okafor. Simon averaged 18.0 ppg and 9.8 rpg that year. An ACL injury kept him from jumping to the NBA; he returned to lead the team in points, rebounds and blocks.

BEST COACH: Andy Piazza (1987-96) After a brief look from the San Antonio Spurs at their rookie camp, this Saginaw, Mich., native played two seasons of pro hoops in, of all places, Iceland. But he found his real niche as a coach in Fort Wayne. IPFW reached 20 wins four times in its brief history, each time under Piazza.

GAME FOR THE AGES: The Mastodons began 2001-02, their first year in Division I, with 13 straight losses against D1 opponents. Considering that they'd ended the previous season with seven straight losses, things weren't looking so hot. But then, on Jan. 8, the Mastodons ran into Chicago State—and came away with a 79-62 victory and reason to celebrate.

FIERCEST RIVAL: IPFW is always looking up at its bigger sister school, IUPUI. Not only have the Jaguars made the NCAA Tourney and produced an NBA first-round pick (George Hill in 2008), they also whipped IPFW consistently in the new millennium, winning eight times in a row from 2002-03 to '08-09.

SEASON REVIEW

SEAS.	W-L	CONF.	SCORING		COACH	RECORD	
1973-74	5-21				George Wehrmeister	5-21	.192
1974-75	12-12		Mitch Easterly	23.4	Gene Hany	12-12	.500
1975-76	15-12				Gordon Stauffer		
1976-77	8-19				Gordon Stauffer		
1977-78	8-16				Gordon Stauffer		
1978-79	6-21				Gordon Stauffer	37-68	.352
1979-80	3-21				Ken Workman		
1980-81	9-17		Rickie Smith	23.2	Ken Workman		
1981-82	2-24				Ken Workman	14-62	.184
1982-83	15-13				Tim Russell		
1983-84	18-10		Jeff Fullove	18.5	Tim Russell		
1984-85	16-11				Tim Russell		
1985-86	10-18				Tim Russell		
1986-87	9-19				Tim Russell	68-71	.489
1987-88	15-13		Bruce Roland	24.0	Andy Piazza		
1988-89	21-7				Andy Piazza		
1989-90	20-8		Sean Gibson	10.3	Andy Piazza		
1990-91	16-12		Sean Gibson	15.6	Andy Piazza		
1991-92	21-7		Sean Gibson	15.9	Andy Piazza		
1992-93	23-6		Sean Gibson	20.9	Andy Piazza		
1993-94	8-19				Andy Piazza		
1994-95	10-17				Andy Piazza		
1995-96	9-20				Andy Piazza	143-109	.567
1996-97	12-15				John Williams		
1997-98	8-18		Adam Moore	17.3	John Williams		
1998-99	10-17		Adam Moore	16.0	John Williams	30-50	.375
1999-2000	11-16		Steve Griffin	19.1	Doug Noll		
2000-01	7-23		Nick Wise	17.8	Doug Noll		
2001-02	7-21		Nick Wise	18.0	Doug Noll		
2002-03	9-21		Ric Wyand	12.6	Doug Noll		
2003-04	3-25		David Simon	18.0	Doug Noll		
2004-05	7-22		David Simon	16.6	Doug Noll[a]	40-119	.252
2005-06	10-18		DeWitt Scott	14.2	Dane Fife		
2006-07	12-17		DeWitt Scott	11.1	Dane Fife		
2007-08	13-18	9-9	Jaraun Burrows	13.7	Dane Fife		
2008-09	13-17	8-10	David Carson	14.8	Dane Fife	48-70	.407

[a] Doug Noll (3-13) and Joe Pechota (4-9) both coached during the 2004-05 season.

PROFILE

Indiana University-Purdue University Fort Wayne, Fort Wayne, IN
Founded: 1964
Enrollment: 11,943 (11,110 undergraduate)
Colors: Royal Blue and white
Nickname: Mastodons
Current arena: Allen County War Memorial Coliseum, opened in 1964 (11,500)
Previous: Hilliard Gates Sports Center, 1981-2003 (2,800)
First game: 1973
All-time record: 401-591 (.404)

Total weeks in AP Top 20/25: 0
Current conference: Summit League (2007-)
Conference titles: 0
Conference tournament titles: 0
NCAA Tournament appearances: 0
NIT appearances: 0

TOP 5

G **Lawrence Jordan** (1985-86, '87-90)
G **Nick Wise** (1999-2002)
F **Sean Gibson** (1989-93)
F **Bruce Roland** (1986-89)
C **David Simon** (2002-05)

RECORDS

RECORDS	GAME		SEASON		CAREER	
POINTS	41	Bruce Roland, vs. Southern Indiana (Jan. 30, 1988)	672	Bruce Roland (1987-88)	1,765	Sean Gibson (1989-93)
POINTS PER GAME			24.0	Bruce Roland (1987-88)	15.8	Sean Gibson (1989-93)
REBOUNDS	22	Rickie Smith, vs. Indiana Tech (Jan. 31, 1981)	303	Rickie Smith (1980-81)	965	Sean Gibson (1989-93)
ASSISTS	19	Russ Marcinek, vs. IUPUI (Dec. 20, 1993)	266	Lawrence Jordan (1989-90)	913	Lawrence Jordan (1985-86, '87-90)

ESPN 278 SAGARIN

IUPUI

As casual fans struggle to figure out what IUPUI actually stands for (it's Indiana University-Purdue University Indianapolis), the Jaguars struggle for relevance in the heart of hoops country. But the 11-year D1 program already has one NCAA Tourney appearance and a first-round NBA draftee to boast about.

BEST TEAM: 2002 -03 The Jaguars not only finished with a winning record for the first time in D1 play, they also made their Tournament debut. Led by the rugged 6'4" F Odell Bradley, the Jags won the Mid-Continent conference tourney, earning a No. 16 seed and the right to be blown out by No. 1 Kentucky, 95-64.

BEST PLAYER: G George Hill (2004-06, '07-08) It took this quick, explosive combo guard just three years to become the school's No. 4 all-time leading scorer (1,619 points). In 2008, he became the first player in IUPUI history to be chosen in the NBA draft when the Spurs selected him with the 26th pick.

BEST COACH: Ron Hunter (1994-) Not only did the Jags make their first NCAA Tourney under Hunter's watch, they also moved from D2 to D1, thanks in large part to his encouragement. Nevertheless, he is perhaps best known for having coached games barefoot to raise awareness for Samaritan's Feet, a nonprofit organization that donates shoes to needy people.

GAME FOR THE AGES: With a trip to the 2003 Big Dance on the line, Matt Crenshaw banged home a last-second jumper to lift the Jaguars over Valparaiso and win the 2003 Mid-Con conference tourney, 66-64. Hunter was so excited that he belly-flopped onto the court—burning a hole in his pants in the process.

FIERCEST RIVAL: IUPUI's sister school, IPFW, is only 130 miles away in Fort Wayne. The two schools first played each other in basketball in 1972, and since then the Jaguars have won 21 of 30. But you can forget about overzealous booster alumni: All 42,000 students at the two schools actually receive degrees from either Indiana or Purdue, leaving IUPUI and IPFW with no true alums to call their own.

SEASON REVIEW

SEAS.	W-L	CONF.	SCORING		COACH	RECORD
1971-72	1-6				George Dickison	
1972-73	11-14		Charlie Battle	13.8	George Dickison	
1973-74	11-14		Bob Woodford	16.3	George Dickison	
1974-75	12-13		Bob Woodford	14.5	George Dickison	35-47 .427
1975-76	13-14		Dale Taylor	17.7	Kirby Overman	
1976-77	9-17		Julius Norman	21.2	Kirby Overman	
1977-78	11-16		Julius Norman	16.1	Kirby Overman	
1978-79	5-21		Kim King	19.3	Kirby Overman	38-68 .358
1979-80	10-21		Mike Herr	13.2	Mel Garland	
1980-81	14-12		Ron Angevine	16.0	Mel Garland	
1981-82	10-14		Ron Angevine	13.7	Mel Garland	34-47 .420
1982-83	14-13		Ron Angevine	17.4	Bob Lovell	
1983-84	16-15		Aldray Gibson	14.6	Bob Lovell	
1984-85	21-15		Aldray Gibson	18.3	Bob Lovell	
1985-86	11-19		Aldray Gibson	18.7	Bob Lovell	
1986-87	20-13		Aldray Gibson	27.0	Bob Lovell	
1987-88	24-12		Jesse Bingham	20.2	Bob Lovell	
1988-89	19-18		Jesse Bingham	21.3	Bob Lovell	
1989-90	23-14		Greg Wright	15.0	Bob Lovell	
1990-91	9-23		James Vaughn	17.3	Bob Lovell	
1991-92	15-16		Chad Pate	14.0	Bob Lovell	
1992-93	14-15		Chad Pate	21.7	Bob Lovell	
1993-94	9-18		Lamar Morton	16.3	Bob Lovell	195-191 .505
1994-95	16-13		Carlos Knox	28.4	Ron Hunter	
1995-96	22-7		Carlos Knox	32.0	Ron Hunter	
1996-97	16-11		Anthony Winburn	17.3	Ron Hunter	
1997-98	17-9		Carlos Knox	30.0	Ron Hunter	
1998-99	11-16	6-8	Don Carlisle	13.9	Ron Hunter	
1999-2000	7-21	4-12	Don Carlisle	12.8	Ron Hunter	
2000-01	11-18	6-10	Don Carlisle	15.5	Ron Hunter	
2001-02	15-15	6-8	Charles Price	12.4	Ron Hunter	
2002-03	20-14	10-4 ●	Odell Bradley	14.7	Ron Hunter	
2003-04	21-11	10-6	Odell Bradley	23.1	Ron Hunter	
2004-05	16-13	9-7	Brandon Cole	14.3	Ron Hunter	
2005-06	19-10	13-3	George Hill	18.9	Ron Hunter	
2006-07	15-15	7-7	Austin Montgomery	13.7	Ron Hunter	
2007-08	26-7	15-3	George Hill	21.5	Ron Hunter	
2008-09	16-14	9-9	Robert Glenn	13.9	Ron Hunter	248-194 .561

● **NCAA Tournament appearance**

PROFILE

Indiana University-Purdue University Indianapolis, Indianapolis, IN
Founded: 1969
Enrollment: 29,933 (21,202 undergraduate)
Colors: Red, gold and black
Nickname: Jaguars
Current arena: IUPUI Gymnasium, a.k.a. The Jungle, opened in 1982 (1,215)
Previous: Harry E. Wood Continuing Education Center Market Square Arena, 1978-82 (16,530); Indiana Fairgrounds Coliseum, 1977-78 (N/A); Bishop Chatard High School, 1976-77 (N/A); The Armory, 1972-76 (N/A)

First game: Jan. 22, 1972
All-time record: 550-547 (.501)
Total weeks in AP Top 20/25: 0
Current conference: Summit League (1998-)
Conference titles:
Mid-Continent: 1 (2006 [tie])
Conference tournament titles:
Mid-Continent: 1 (2003)
NCAA Tournament appearances: 1
NIT appearances: 0

FIRST-ROUND PRO PICKS

2008 **George Hill,** San Antonio (26)

TOP 5

G **George Hill** (2004-06, '07-08)
G **Carlos Knox** (1994-98)
F **Jesse Bingham** (1986-89)
F **Eric McKay** (1982-85)
C **Don Carlisle** (1997-2001)

RECORDS

RECORDS	GAME		SEASON		CAREER	
POINTS	51	Carlos Knox, vs. Oklahoma-Panhandle State (Jan. 5, 1998)	927	Carlos Knox (1995-96)	2,556	Carlos Knox (1994-98)
POINTS PER GAME			32.0	Carlos Knox (1995-96)	30.1	Carlos Knox (1994-98)
REBOUNDS	20	Austris Purvlicis, vs. IPFW (Jan. 18, 1975); Michael Boles, vs. IU-South Bend (March 7, 1993)	337	Dale Taylor (1975-76)	769	Don Carlisle (1997-2001)
ASSISTS	14	Johnny Miller, vs. Southern Utah (Feb. 5, 2005)	194	Greg Simmons (1989-90)	510	Matt Crenshaw (2000-04)

THE SCHOOLS

ESPN 164 SAGARIN

IONA

Like many of the metropolitan New York programs, Iona's best years were in the 1970s and '80s. The Gaels hit their peak when a young coach named Jim Valvano arrived in New Rochelle.

BEST TEAM: 1979-80 Coached by Valvano and led by Jeff Ruland, the 29–5 Gaels ended up No. 19 in the AP poll. They won their first-round NCAA Tournament matchup with Holy Cross, 84-78, but the season ended with a heartbreaking 74-71 loss to No. 11 Georgetown. (The NCAA later vacated Iona's Tourney participation because of Ruland's dealings with an agent.)

BEST PLAYER: C JEFF RULAND (1977-80) One of the best—and biggest—players ever to wear the Iona uniform, the 6'10" Ruland was a truly dominant force. He burst onto the scene in 1977-78 to lead the Gaels and the nation's freshmen in scoring (22.3 ppg) and rebounding (12.8). After an eight-year NBA career, Ruland turned to coaching, including a nine-year stint (1998-2007) at Iona.

BEST COACH: JIM VALVANO (1975-80) Jimmy V taught a lesson at Iona he would later share with the nation: Dare to dream. He recruited great talent, including Ruland, and achieved a 94–45 (.676) record. After the 1980 Tournament he left for NC State, for which he won the thrilling national title of 1983.

GAME FOR THE AGES: The Gaels' first victory over a nationally ranked opponent came at Madison Square Garden on Feb. 21, 1980, when Iona spanked Louisville, 77-60, behind Ruland's 30 points and 21 rebounds. The win took on further luster when the Cardinals went on to win the NCAA championship.

FIERCEST RIVAL: Fordham and Iona are nearly dead even after 61 meetings in the annual holy war between schools separated by less than 10 miles. At one point during the 1980s, the rivalry was so fierce that games had to be moved to New Jersey's Brendan Byrne Arena or Madison Square Garden to accommodate the large crowds—as well as alleviate the tensions that led to fights at the on-campus venues.

SEASON REVIEW

SEAS.	W-L	CONF.	COACH	SEAS.	W-L	CONF.	COACH
1945-49	*61-33*		*Arthur Loftus, 44-25 in 3 seasons*	1962-63	12-7		Jim McDermott
1949-50	21-4		Jim McDermott	1963-64	15-5		Jim McDermott
1950-51	18-8		Jim McDermott	1964-65	12-11		Jim McDermott
1951-52	16-10		Jim McDermott	1965-66	5-16	3-6	Jim McDermott
1952-53	17-3		Jim McDermott	1966-67	11-10	4-5	Jim McDermott
1953-54	11-10		Jim McDermott	1967-68	13-9	4-4	Jim McDermott
1954-55	10-11		Jim McDermott	1968-69	11-11	4-4	Jim McDermott
1955-56	8-14		Jim McDermott	1969-70	12-12		Jim McDermott
1956-57	12-7		Jim McDermott	1970-71	10-12		Jim McDermott
1957-58	18-6		Jim McDermott	1971-72	6-17		Jim McDermott
1958-59	14-7		Jim McDermott	1972-73	6-16		Jim McDermott
1959-60	13-5		Jim McDermott	1973-74	11-13		Gene Roberti
1960-61	10-11		Jim McDermott	1974-75	4-19		Gene Roberti
1961-62	8-11		Jim McDermott	1975-76	11-15		Jim Valvano

SEAS.	W-L	CONF.	SCORING		COACH	RECORD
1976-77	15-10		Glenn Vickers	17.9	Jim Valvano	
1977-78	17-10		Jeff Ruland	22.3	Jim Valvano	
1978-79	23-6	●	Jeff Ruland	20.3	Jim Valvano	
1979-80	29-5 ✪	●	Jeff Ruland	20.1	Jim Valvano	95-46 .674▼
1980-81	15-14		Gary Springer	19.9	Pat Kennedy	
1981-82	24-9	7-3 ■	Steve Burtt Sr.	22.1	Pat Kennedy	
1982-83	22-9	8-2 ■	Steve Burtt Sr.	23.2	Pat Kennedy	
1983-84	23-8	11-3 ●	Steve Burtt Sr.	24.2	Pat Kennedy	
1984-85	26-5	11-3 ●	Rory Grimes	16.5	Pat Kennedy	
1985-86	14-15	9-5	Bob Coleman	17.5	Pat Kennedy	124-60 .674
1986-87	16-14	8-6	Richie Simmonds	17.4	Gary Brokaw	
1987-88	11-16	5-9	Richie Simmonds	16.2	Gary Brokaw	
1988-89	15-16	8-6	Chip Langdon	13.7	Gary Brokaw	
1989-90	13-15	8-8	Sean Green	19.8	Gary Brokaw	
1990-91	17-13	11-5	Sean Green	23.2	Gary Brokaw	72-74 .493
1991-92	14-15	8-8	Derrick Canada	18.4	Jerry Welsh	
1992-93	16-11	9-5	Harry Hart	16.2	Jerry Welsh	
1993-94	7-20	3-11	Mikkel Larsen	17.6	Jerry Welsh	
1994-95	10-17	6-8	Mikkel Larsen	17.5	Jerry Welsh	47-63 .427
1995-96	21-8	10-4 ■	Bryan Matthew	14.5	Tim Welsh	
1996-97	22-8	11-3 ■	Bryan Matthew	18.7	Tim Welsh	
1997-98	27-6	15-3 ●	Kashif Hameed	15.3	Tim Welsh	70-22 .761
1998-99	16-14	12-6	Tariq Kirksay	13.8	Jeff Ruland	
1999-2000	20-11	13-5 ●	Tariq Kirksay	19.2	Jeff Ruland	
2000-01	22-11	12-6 ●	Nakiea Miller	15.1	Jeff Ruland	
2001-02	13-17	10-8	Courtney Fields	12.8	Jeff Ruland	
2002-03	17-12	11-7	Courtney Fields	13.2	Jeff Ruland	
2003-04	11-18	8-10	Steve Burtt Jr.	13.5	Jeff Ruland	
2004-05	15-16	9-9	Steve Burtt Jr.	19.3	Jeff Ruland	
2005-06	23-8	13-5 ●	Steve Burtt Jr.	25.2	Jeff Ruland	
2006-07	2-28	1-17	Anthony Bruin	12.0	Jeff Ruland	139-135 .507
2007-08	12-20	8-10	Dexter Gray	11.3	Kevin Willard	
2008-09	12-19	7-11	Gary Springer	11.8	Kevin Willard	24-39 .381

✪ Record does not reflect games forfeited or vacated. For adjusted record, see p. 521.

▼ Coach's record adjusted to reflect games forfeited or vacated, 94-45, .676. For yearly totals, see p. 521.

● NCAA Tournament appearance ■ NIT appearance

PROFILE

Iona College, New Rochelle, NY
Founded: 1940
Enrollment: 4,250 (3,246 undergraduate)
Colors: Maroon and gold
Nickname: Gaels
Current arena: Hynes Athletics Center, opened in 1974 (2,611)
Previous: O'Connell Gym, 1945-74 (N/A)
First game: 1945
All-time record: 936-737 (.559)
Total weeks in AP Top 20/25: 1

Current conference: Metro Atlantic Athletic (1981-)
Conference titles:
Eastern Collegiate Athletic Metro: 1 (1930)
MAAC: 7 (1983, '84 [tie], '85, '96 [tie], '97, '98, 2001 [tie])
Conference tournament titles:
MAAC: 7 (1982, '84, '85, '98, 2000, '01, '06)
NCAA Tournaments: 8 (1 appearance vacated)
NIT appearances: 4

TOP 5

G **Steve Burtt Sr.** (1980-84)
G **Richie Guerin** (1951-54)
F **Warren Isaac** (1962-65)
F **Gary Springer** (1980-84)
C **Jeff Ruland** (1977-80)

RECORDS

RECORDS	GAME		SEASON		CAREER	
POINTS	50	Warren Isaac, vs. Bates (Dec. 18, 1964)	780	Steve Burtt Jr. (2005-06)	2,534	Steve Burtt Sr. (1980-84)
POINTS PER GAME			25.2	Steve Burtt Jr. (2005-06)	21.5	Warren Isaac (1962-65)
REBOUNDS	33	Larry Blaney, vs. Siena (Feb. 20, 1957);	480	Warren Isaac (1964-65)	1,124	Warren Isaac (1962-65)
ASSISTS	17	Danny Doyle, vs. Fairfield (Feb. 19, 1994)	194	Glenn Grant (1988-89)	558	Rory Grimes (1981-85)

ESPN 10 SAGARIN

IOWA

The Hawkeyes have yet to reach the heights of some of their Big Ten rivals; they've made three Final Fours without ever winning a national title. On the other hand, the program made famous by the likes of Don Nelson, Sam H. Williams and Ronnie Lester hasn't endured a lot of hardship either; only three of its 20 former coaches finished with losing records.

BEST TEAM: 1955-56 Known in their time as the Fabulous Five, Bill Seaberg, Bill Logan, Carl Cain, Sharm Scheuerman and Bill Schoof dropped their Big Ten opener before winning the next 14 for Iowa's second straight conference title. The Hawkeyes then knocked off Morehead State, Kentucky and Temple to earn a berth in the NCAA Final against San Francisco. Iowa hung tough with Bill Russell & Co. in the first half but faded late and lost, 83-71.

BEST PLAYER: G RONNIE LESTER (1976-80) He was a scoring and passing whiz, but Iowa's floor leader also had a knack for bringing out the best in his teammates. That became clear when he missed 15 games in 1979-80 with a knee injury and returned to help the Hawks make the Tournament, only to reinjure the knee during an 80-72 Final Four loss to Louisville. Years later, teammate Bobby Hansen told the *Des Moines Register*, "There's absolutely no doubt in my mind that if Ronnie didn't go down, we would've been national champions." Hawkeyes fans don't doubt it either. A first-round pick in the 1980 draft, Lester played six years in the NBA.

BEST COACH: TOM DAVIS (1986-99) If the opponent had a weakness, his Hawkeyes were sure to expose it with their pressure defense and strong fundamentals. In Davis' 13 seasons before Iowa controversially declined to renew his contract, he never won a Big Ten title, but he did make nine NCAA Tournaments and won at least one game each time.

GAME FOR THE AGES: In what Lute Olson considers one of the greatest games in Tournament history, his No. 5-seed Hawkeyes stunned Georgetown with an 81-80 victory in the 1980 Elite Eight. Trailing by 14 early in the second half, Iowa shot 71% and turned the ball over just once in the final 20 minutes, winning on a three-point play by Steve Waite with :05 left.

HEARTBREAKER: No. 3-seed Iowa appeared poised for a deep run in the 2006 Big Dance; it was fresh off the Big Ten tournament title and flush with veteran leadership in Jeff Horner and Greg Brunner. And everything was going to plan in the first round, as the Hawkeyes took a 17-point lead with 8:30 remaining against No. 14-seed Northwestern State. But Steve Alford's team collapsed, opening the door for Jermaine Wallace's fadeaway three with less than a second left. The result was a 64-63 loss.

FIERCEST RIVAL: If you want to raise the ire of Illini backers, mention the name Bruce Pearl, the Iowa assistant coach who claimed Illinois cheated in recruiting Deon Thomas in 1988 and '89. An investigation turned up no offenses relating to Thomas, but the NCAA did penalize Illinois for other violations the investigation uncovered. If you want to send a shiver down the backs of Hawkeyes fans, mention Andy Kaufmann. He's the Illini who sunk a buzzer-beating three to stun Iowa, 78-77, on Feb. 4, 1993. The Illini lead the 101-year series, 76–66.

FANFARE AND HOOPLA: Herky the Hawk has been called one of the 10 worst-dressed college mascots. SI.com judged his black-and-gold outfit a "mom-made Halloween job." Don't tell that to Iowa fans, who have been cheering on Herky (short for Hercules) since his first appearance in 1959.

FAN FAVORITE: F CHRIS STREET (1990-93) Every year the Chris Street Award goes to the Hawkeye who best exemplifies the "spirit, enthusiasm and intensity" of Street, who died in a car accident on Jan. 19, 1993, midway through his junior season.

CONSENSUS ALL-AMERICAS

1948	**Murray Wier,** G
1952	**Chuck Darling,** C

FIRST-ROUND PRO PICKS

1952	**Chuck Darling,** Rochester (9)
1970	**John Johnson,** Cleveland (7)
1971	**Fred Brown,** Seattle (6)
1973	**Kevin Kunnert,** Chicago (12)
1980	**Ronnie Lester,** Portland (10)
1989	**B.J. Armstrong,** Chicago (18)
1989	**Roy Marble,** Atlanta (23)
1993	**Acie Earl,** Boston (19)
1998	**Ricky Davis,** Charlotte (21)

PROFILE

University of Iowa, Iowa City, IA
Founded: 1847
Enrollment: 30,561 (20,823 undergraduate)
Colors: Gold and black
Nickname: Hawkeyes
Current arena: Carver-Hawkeye Arena, opened in 1983 (15,500)
Previous: Iowa Fieldhouse, 1927-83 (13,365); Armory, 1922-25 (N/A); Men's Gym, 1904-22 (N/A); Close Hall, 1893-1904 (500)
First game: Jan. 18, 1901

All-time record: 1,463-1,009 (.592)
Total weeks in AP Top 20/25: 314
Current conference: Big Ten (1905-)
Conference titles:
Big Ten: 8 (1923 [tie], '26 [tie], '45, '55, '56, '68 [tie], '70, '79 [tie])
Conference tournament titles:
Big Ten: 2 (2001, '06)
NCAA Tournament appearances: 22
Sweet 16s (since 1975): 5
Final Fours: 3
NIT appearances: 5

TOP 5

G	**B.J. Armstrong** (1985-89)
G	**Ronnie Lester** (1976-80)
G	**Bill Seaberg** (1953-56)
G/F	**Sam H. Williams** (1966-68)
F	**Don Nelson** (1959-62)

RECORDS

RECORDS	GAME		SEASON		CAREER	
POINTS	49	John Johnson, vs. Northwestern (Feb. 24, 1970)	699	John Johnson (1969-1970)	2,116	Roy Marble (1985-89)
POINTS PER GAME			27.9	John Johnson (1969-1970)	24.0	Sam H. Williams (1966-68)
REBOUNDS	30	Chuck Darling, vs. Wisconsin (March 3, 1952)	416	Reggie Evans (2000-01)	990	Greg Brunner (2002-06)
ASSISTS	16	Cal Wulfsberg, vs. Ohio State (Jan. 24, 1976)	193	Andre Woolridge (1995-96)	612	Jeff Horner (2002-06)

THE SCHOOLS

SEASON REVIEW

SEASON	W-L	CONF.	SCORING	COACH	RECORD	
1901-17	*131-94*		*Ed Rule coached Iowa in four non-consecutive seasons*			
1917-18	6-8	4-6		Maury Kent	42-36	.538
1918-19	8-7	4-7		Edwin Bannick	8-7	.533
1919-20	9-10	6-6		James Ashmore		
1920-21	9-9	6-5		James Ashmore		
1921-22	11-7	5-6		James Ashmore	29-26	.527
1922-23	13-2	11-1		Sam Barry		
1923-24	7-10	4-8		Sam Barry		
1924-25	6-10	5-7		Sam Barry		
1925-26	12-5	8-4		Sam Barry		
1926-27	9-8	7-5		Sam Barry		
1927-28	6-11	3-9		Sam Barry		
1928-29	9-8	5-7		Sam Barry	62-54	.534
1929-30	4-13			Rollie Williams		
1930-31	5-12	2-10		Rollie Williams		
1931-32	5-12	3-9		Rollie Williams		
1932-33	15-5	8-4		Rollie Williams		
1933-34	13-6	6-6		Rollie Williams		
1934-35	10-9	6-6		Rollie Williams		
1935-36	9-10	5-7		Rollie Williams		
1936-37	11-9	3-9		Rollie Williams		
1937-38	11-9	6-6		Rollie Williams		

SEAS.	W-L	CONF.	POSTSEASON	SCORING		REBOUNDS		ASSISTS		COACH	RECORD	
1938-39	8-11	3-9		Ben Stephens	13.4					Rollie Williams		
1939-40	9-12	4-8		Vic Siegel	9.0					Rollie Williams		
1940-41	12-8	4-8		Vic Siegel	9.7					Rollie Williams		
1941-42	12-8	10-5		Tom Chapman	12.3					Rollie Williams		
1942-43	7-10	3-9		Ben Trickey	13.5					Pops Harrison		
1943-44	14-4	9-3		Dick Ives	18.2					Pops Harrison		
1944-45	17-1	11-1		Dick Ives	12.1					Pops Harrison		
1945-46	14-4	8-4		Dick Ives	10.3					Pops Harrison		
1946-47	12-7	5-7		Murray Wier	15.1					Pops Harrison		
1947-48	15-4	8-4		Murray Wier	21.0					Pops Harrison		
1948-49	10-10	3-9		Charlie Mason	7.8					Pops Harrison		
1949-50	15-7	6-6		Frank Calsbeek	15.1					Pops Harrison[a]	98-42	.700
1950-51	15-7	9-5		Chuck Darling	16.3	Chuck Darling	17.6			Rollie Williams	139-131	.515
1951-52	19-3	11-3		Chuck Darling	25.5					Bucky O'Connor		
1952-53	12-10	9-9		Deacon Davis	14.9					Bucky O'Connor		
1953-54	17-5	11-3		Bill Logan	14.3					Bucky O'Connor		
1954-55	19-7	11-3	NCAA FOURTH PLACE	Bill Logan	15.9	Bill Logan	11.0			Bucky O'Connor		
1955-56	20-6	13-1	NCAA RUNNER-UP	Bill Logan	17.7	Bill Logan	10.3			Bucky O'Connor		
1956-57	8-14	4-10		Dave Gunther	12.3	Dave Gunther	8.9			Bucky O'Connor		
1957-58	13-9	7-7		Dave Gunther	19.8	Nolden Gentry	10.9			Bucky O'Connor	114-59	.659
1958-59	10-12	7-7		Dave Gunther	21.9	Dave Gunther	12.1			Sharm Scheuerman		
1959-60	14-10	6-8		Don Nelson	15.8	Don Nelson	10.0			Sharm Scheuerman		
1960-61	18-6	10-4		Don Nelson	23.7	Don Nelson	10.8			Sharm Scheuerman		
1961-62	13-11	7-7		Don Nelson	23.8	Don Nelson	11.9			Sharm Scheuerman		
1962-63	9-15	5-9		Dave Roach	12.0	Dave Roach	6.8			Sharm Scheuerman		
1963-64	8-15	3-11		Dave Roach	15.9	Dave Roach	7.0			Sharm Scheuerman	72-69	.511
1964-65	14-10	8-6		Chris Pervall	21.1	George Peeples	10.4			Ralph Miller		
1965-66	17-7	8-6		Chris Pervall	19.1	George Peeples	10.8			Ralph Miller		
1966-67	16-8	9-5		Sam H. Williams	22.6	Gerry Jones	10.7			Ralph Miller		
1967-68	16-9	10-4		Sam H. Williams	25.3	Sam H. Williams	10.9			Ralph Miller		
1968-69	12-12	5-9		John Johnson	19.7	John Johnson	10.7			Ralph Miller		
1969-70	20-5	14-0	NCAA REGIONAL SEMIFINALS	John Johnson	27.9	John Johnson	10.1			Ralph Miller	95-51	.651
1970-71	9-15	4-10		Fred Brown	27.6	Kevin Kunnert	9.4			Dick Schultz		
1971-72	11-13	5-9		Rick Williams	19.5	Kevin Kunnert	14.7			Dick Schultz		
1972-73	13-11	6-8		Kevin Kunnert	19.2	Kevin Kunnert	13.9			Dick Schultz		
1973-74	8-16	5-9		Candy LaPrince	19.0	Neil Fegebank	6.8			Dick Schultz	41-55	.427
1974-75	10-16	7-11		Bruce King	11.5	Bruce King	8.8	Larry Moore	2.7	Lute Olson		
1975-76	19-10	9-9		Scott Thompson	19.5	Bruce King	10.1	Cal Wulfsberg	9.0	Lute Olson		
1976-77	18-9 ⊗	12-6		Bruce King	21.0	Bruce King	13.3	Cal Wulfsberg	4.1	Lute Olson		
1977-78	12-15	5-13		Ronnie Lester	19.9	Clay Hargrave	9.9	Ronnie Lester	6.1	Lute Olson		
1978-79	20-8	13-5	NCAA SECOND ROUND	Ronnie Lester	18.7	William Mayfield	8.4	Ronnie Lester	5.3	Lute Olson		
1979-80	23-10	10-8	NCAA FOURTH PLACE	Kenny Arnold	13.5	Steve Krafcisin	6.4	Kenny Arnold	4.3	Lute Olson		
1980-81	21-7	13-5	NCAA SECOND ROUND	Vince Brookins	14.7	Steve Krafcisin	6.4	Kenny Arnold	3.9	Lute Olson		
1981-82	21-8	12-6	NCAA SECOND ROUND	Michael Payne	11.4	Michael Payne	6.9	Kevin Boyle	3.5	Lute Olson		
1982-83	21-10	11-7	NCAA REGIONAL SEMIFINALS	Greg Stokes	17.7	Michael Payne	7.5	Steve Carfino	4.3	Lute Olson	165-93	.640▼
1983-84	13-15	6-12		Greg Stokes	14.9	Greg Stokes	6.9	Andre Banks	3.3	George Raveling		
1984-85	21-11	10-8	NCAA FIRST ROUND	Greg Stokes	19.9	Greg Stokes	8.4	Andre Banks	3.5	George Raveling		
1985-86	20-12	10-8	NCAA FIRST ROUND	Roy Marble	12.5	Gerry Wright	6.6	Andre Banks	3.7	George Raveling	54-38	.587
1986-87	30-5	14-4	NCAA REGIONAL FINALS	Roy Marble	14.9	Brad Lohaus	7.7	B.J. Armstrong	4.2	Tom Davis		
1987-88	24-10	12-6	NCAA REGIONAL SEMIFINALS	B.J. Armstrong	17.4	Kent Hill	6.5	B.J. Armstrong	4.6	Tom Davis		
1988-89	23-10	10-8	NCAA SECOND ROUND	Roy Marble	20.5	Ed Horton	10.6	B.J. Armstrong	5.4	Tom Davis		
1989-90	12-16	4-14		Les Jepsen	14.9	Les Jepsen	10.0	Troy Skinner	3.8	Tom Davis		
1990-91	21-11	9-9	NCAA SECOND ROUND	Acie Earl	16.3	Acie Earl	6.7	Troy Skinner	3.4	Tom Davis		
1991-92	19-11	10-8	NCAA SECOND ROUND	Acie Earl	19.5	Chris Street	8.2	Kevin Smith	4.8	Tom Davis		
1992-93	23-9	11-7	NCAA SECOND ROUND	Acie Earl	16.9	Acie Earl	8.9	Kevin Smith	3.9	Tom Davis		
1993-94	11-16	5-13		James Winters	18.0	Jess Settles	7.5	Mon'ter Glasper	5.2	Tom Davis		
1994-95	21-12	9-9	NIT QUARTERFINALS	Chris Kinsbury	16.8	Jim Bartels	6.2	Andre Woolridge	5.8	Tom Davis		
1995-96	23-9 ⊗	11-7	NCAA SECOND ROUND	Jess Settles	15.1	Jess Settles	7.5	Andre Woolridge	6.0	Tom Davis		
1996-97	22-10	12-6	NCAA SECOND ROUND	Andre Woolridge	20.2	Ryan Bowen	9.1	Andre Woolridge	6.0	Tom Davis		
1997-98	20-11	9-7	NIT FIRST ROUND	Ricky Davis	15.0	Ryan Bowen	8.7	Dean Oliver	4.2	Tom Davis		
1998-99	20-10	9-7	NCAA REGIONAL SEMIFINALS	Dean Oliver	11.9	Jess Settles	4.8	Dean Oliver	4.5	Tom Davis	269-140	.658▼
1999-2000	14-16	6-10		Dean Oliver	13.6	Jacob Jaacks	7.3	Dean Oliver	4.2	Steve Alford		
2000-01	23-12	7-9	NCAA SECOND ROUND	Reggie Evans	15.1	Reggie Evans	11.9	Dean Oliver	4.8	Steve Alford		
2001-02	19-16	5-11	NIT FIRST ROUND	Luke Recker	17.1	Reggie Evans	11.1	Pierre Pierce	3.2	Steve Alford		
2002-03	17-14	7-9	NIT SECOND ROUND	Chauncey Leslie	15.8	Jared Reiner	8.3	Jeff Horner	4.5	Steve Alford		
2003-04	16-13	9-7	NIT FIRST ROUND	Pierre Pierce	16.1	Greg Brunner	8.2	Jeff Horner	4.2	Steve Alford		
2004-05	21-12	7-9	NCAA FIRST ROUND	Greg Brunner	14.7	Greg Brunner	8.3	Jeff Horner	5.5	Steve Alford		
2005-06	25-9	11-5	NCAA FIRST ROUND	Greg Brunner	14.1	Greg Brunner	9.2	Jeff Horner	5.6	Steve Alford		
2006-07	17-14	9-7		Adam Haluska	20.5	Tyler Smith	4.9	Tony Freeman	3.7	Steve Alford	152-106	.589
2007-08	13-19	6-12		Tony Freeman	13.8	Cyrus Tate	5.4	Tony Freeman	3.2	Todd Lickliter		
2008-09	15-17	5-13		Jake Kelly	11.6	Cyrus Tate	5.7	Jeff Peterson	4.2	Todd Lickliter	28-36	.438

[a] Pops Harrison (9-2) and Bucky O'Connor (6-5) both coached during the 1949-50 season.

⊗ Records don't reflect games forfeited or vacated. For adjusted records, see p. 521.

▼ Coaches records adjusted to reflect games forfeited or vacated: Lute Olson, 167-91, .647; Tom Davis, 270-139, .660. For yearly totals, see p. 521.

ESPN 52 SAGARIN

IOWA STATE

Cyclones fans have come to expect the unexpected. And why not? So many overachieving teams, so many miracle wins. Plus there's been a long string of surprise stars, from Gary Thompson, who was passed over by archrival Iowa before he became an ISU star, to Jeff Hornacek, who rose above expectations to become an NBA All-Star, to Jamaal Tinsley, a junior college transfer who had the best season in Cyclones history.

BEST TEAM: 1999-2000 Most everyone picked the Cyclones to finish in the bottom half of the Big 12. Little did they anticipate the instant impact Tinsley would make, power forward Marcus Fizer's ability to carry his team, and the potency of coach Larry Eustachy's in-your-face defense. All three factors came together in the team's NCAA Elite Eight run, which saw the Cyclones blow out Central Connecticut State, Auburn and UCLA before falling to eventual national champion Michigan State.

BEST PLAYER: G Gary Thompson (1954-57) The 5'10" Hawkeye State high school star known as the Roland Rocket did not get an offer from Iowa because the coaches thought he was too small. Hawkeyes' loss, Cyclones' gain. Thompson's senior season was one to remember: He averaged 20.7 points, led Iowa State to a No. 3 national ranking and was a second-team All-America.

BEST COACH: Tim Floyd (1994-98) A disciple of UTEP legend Don Haskins, Floyd leaned heavily on junior college players such as Dedric Willoughby on his 1996-97 Sweet 16 team. Floyd won at least one NCAA Tournament game in three of his four seasons at ISU.

GAME FOR THE AGES: The Jan. 14, 1957, game was so hard-fought that Kansas star Wilt Chamberlain went into the Cyclones locker room afterward and congratulated each player for upsetting his No. 1 Jayhawks, 39-37. With time winding down and the score tied at 37, KU swarmed Gary Thompson to prevent the star guard from getting off a last shot. But that left center Don Medsker alone at the top of the key. He drained a buzzer-beater and 8,000 Cyclone fans rushed onto the court to celebrate.

HEARTBREAKER: During World War II, many of the 13–3 Cyclones were enlisted in the school's Navy training program and were not allowed to be away from the base more than 48 hours. So ISU turned down a bid to the 1944 NCAA Tournament—until the Navy granted them the time to go to Kansas City for the West Regional. There, they beat Pepperdine (playing only because Iowa backed out of the Tourney to avoid the Cyclones) and were preparing for the national semifinals when the Navy ruled that even if they won, they wouldn't be allowed to go to New York for the national championship game. Playing only for the championship of the West was no motivation; star center Price Brookfield missed all 14 of his shots in the second half and the Cyclones lost to eventual champ Utah, 40-31.

FIERCEST RIVAL: How deep is the Iowa vs. Iowa State enmity? Iowa reneged on its acceptance of a 1944 Tournament bid rather than play Iowa State (see Heartbreaker). In fact, the two Hawkeye State schools didn't play each other between 1935 and '70. Iowa leads the series, 42–20.

Wilt Chamberlain personally congratulated each Cyclones player for upsetting his No. 1 Jayhawks in '57.

FANFARE AND HOOPLA: Iowa State has pulled out an unnatural number of unlikely victories at Hilton Coliseum; so many that in 1989 a local sportswriter gave the phenomenon a name: Hilton Magic.

FAN FAVORITE: G Jeff Hornacek (1982-86) He was working at a paper cup company in Chicago when his father asked a fellow prep school basketball coach to persuade Iowa State coach Johnny Orr to let his boy walk on for the second semester of the 1981-82 season. Four years later, Horny left as the school's all-time assists leader on the way to a solid NBA career.

CONSENSUS ALL-AMERICAS

2000 **Marcus Fizer**, F

FIRST-ROUND PRO PICKS

1968	**Don Smith**, Cincinnati (5)
1988	**Jeff Grayer**, Milwaukee (13)
1991	**Victor Alexander**, Golden State (17)
1995	**Loren Meyer**, Dallas (24)
1997	**Kelvin Cato**, Dallas (15)
2000	**Marcus Fizer**, Chicago (4)
2001	**Jamaal Tinsley**, Vancouver (27)

PROFILE

Iowa State University, Ames, IA
Founded: 1858
Enrollment: 24,445 (21,004 undergraduate)
Colors: Cardinal and gold
Nickname: Cyclones
Current arena: James H. Hilton Coliseum, opened in 1971 (14,356)
Previous: The Armory, 1947-71 (7,500); State Gymnasium, 1913-46 (N/A)
First game: Feb. 20, 1908
All-time record: 1,161-1,197 (.492)

Total weeks in AP Top 20/25: 88
Current conference: Big 12 (1996-)
Conference titles:
Big Six: 4 (1935, '41 [tie], '44 [tie], '45)
Big 12: 2 (2000, '01)
Conference tournament titles:
Big Eight: 1 (1996)
Big 12: 1 (2000)
NCAA Tournament appearances: 13
Sweet 16s (since 1975): 3
Final Fours: 1
NIT appearances: 3
Semifinals: 1

TOP 5

G	**Gary Thompson** (1954-57)
G	**Jamaal Tinsley** (1999-2001)
F	**Marcus Fizer** (1997-2000)
F	**Jeff Grayer** (1984-88)
C	**Don Smith** (1965-68)

RECORDS	GAME		SEASON		CAREER	
POINTS	54	Lafester Rhodes, vs. Iowa (Dec. 19, 1987)	844	Marcus Fizer (1999-2000)	2,502	Jeff Grayer (1984-88)
POINTS PER GAME			28.3	Hercle Ivy (1974-75)	22.3	Don Smith (1965-68)
REBOUNDS	26	Bill Cain, vs. Minnesota (Dec. 9, 1969)	396	Bill Cain (1969-70)	1,233	Dean Uthoff (1976-80)
ASSISTS	16	Eric Heft, vs. Nebraska (Feb. 5, 1974)	244	Jamaal Tinsley (1999-2000)	665	Jeff Hornacek (1982-86)

SEASON REVIEW

SEASON	W-L	CONF.	SCORING		COACH	RECORD	
1908-18	*63-96*		*Both coaches before H.H. Walters also finished with losing records*				
1918-19	5-11	3-8			H.H. Walters	27-38	.415
1919-20	6-12	2-10			R.N. Berryman	6-12	.333
1920-21	10-8	6-8			Maury Kent	10-8	.556
1921-22	10-8	8-8			Bill Chandler		
1922-23	10-8	9-7			Bill Chandler		
1923-24	2-16	2-14			Bill Chandler		
1924-25	2-15	1-15			Bill Chandler		
1925-26	4-14	3-11	Nick Elliott	8.3	Bill Chandler		
1926-27	9-9	7-8	Nick Elliott	6.4	Bill Chandler		
1927-28	3-15	3-15			Bill Chandler	40-85	.320

SEASON	W-L	CONF.	SCORING		COACH	RECORD
1928-29	8-7	4-6	Lester Lande	11.6	Louis Menze	
1929-30	9-8	5-5	Jack Roadcap	9.2	Louis Menze	
1930-31	8-8	4-6	Jack Roadcap	9.3	Louis Menze	
1931-32	9-6	4-6	Al Heitman	9.0	Louis Menze	
1932-33	6-10	2-8	Waldo Wegner	8.4	Louis Menze	
1933-34	6-11	2-8	Waldo Wegner	8.1	Louis Menze	
1934-35	13-3	8-2	Waldo Wegner	10.6	Louis Menze	
1935-36	8-8	3-7	Jack Flemming	9.8	Louis Menze	
1936-37	3-15	0-10	Jack Flemming	11.9	Louis Menze	
1937-38	6-9	2-8	Robert Blahnik	12.6	Louis Menze	
1938-39	8-9	5-5	Robert Harris	9.5	Louis Menze	

SEAS.	W-L	CONF.	POSTSEASON	SCORING		REBOUNDS		ASSISTS		COACH	RECORD	
1939-40	9-9	2-8		Gordon Nicholas	8.9					Louis Menze		
1940-41	15-4	7-3		Gordon Nicholas	10.9					Louis Menze		
1941-42	11-6	5-5		Al Budolfson	12.3					Louis Menze		
1942-43	7-9	2-8		Ray Wehde	7.8					Louis Menze		
1943-44	14-4	9-1	NCAA NATIONAL SEMIFINALS	Price Brookfield	11.6					Louis Menze		
1944-45	11-5	8-2		James Myers	13.2					Louis Menze		
1945-46	8-8	5-5		James Stark	12.3					Louis Menze		
1946-47	7-14	5-5		Ray Wehde	8.3					Louis Menze	166-153	.520
1947-48	14-9	6-6		Ray Wehde	9.1					Clay Sutherland		
1948-49	8-14	3-9		Bob Peterson	10.1					Clay Sutherland		
1949-50	6-17	2-10		Dudley Ruisch	9.4					Clay Sutherland		
1950-51	9-12	3-9		Sy Wilhelmi	11.1					Clay Sutherland		
1951-52	10-11	4-8		Jim Strange	14.2					Clay Sutherland		
1952-53	10-11	5-7		Delmer Diercks	17.7					Clay Sutherland		
1953-54	6-15	2-10		Chuck Duncan	14.3	Chuck Duncan	7.3			Clay Sutherland	63-89	.414
1954-55	11-10	4-8		Chuck Duncan	21.9	Chuck Duncan	12.0			Bill Strannigan		
1955-56	18-5	8-4		Gary Thompson	19.1	John Crawford	9.7			Bill Strannigan		
1956-57	16-7	6-6		Gary Thompson	20.7	John Crawford	10.2			Bill Strannigan		
1957-58	15-8	8-4		John Crawford	14.1	John Crawford	9.1			Bill Strannigan		
1958-59	9-16	4-10		John Krocheski	14.4	John Krocheski	8.3			Bill Strannigan	69-46	.600
1959-60	15-9	7-7		Vince Brewer	15.3	Vince Brewer	9.3			Glen Anderson		
1960-61	13-12 ✪	6-8		Henry Whitney	17.4	Henry Whitney	12.1			Glen Anderson		
1961-62	13-12	8-6		Vince Brewer	13.7	Vince Brewer	9.9			Glen Anderson		
1962-63	14-11	8-6		Marv Straw	14.3	Gary Kleven	8.3			Glen Anderson		
1963-64	9-16	5-9		Rick Froistad	10.2	Steve Harmon	7.0			Glen Anderson		
1964-65	9-16	6-8		Al Koch	17.8	Al Koch	5.9			Glen Anderson		
1965-66	11-14	6-8		Don Smith	18.0	Don Smith	13.0			Glen Anderson		
1966-67	13-12	6-8		Don Smith	24.8	Don Smith	13.4			Glen Anderson		
1967-68	12-13	8-6		Don Smith	24.2	Don Smith	14.6			Glen Anderson		
1968-69	14-12	8-6		Bill Cain	21.8	Bill Cain	13.5			Glen Anderson		
1969-70	12-14	5-9		Bill Cain	19.8	Bill Cain	15.2			Glen Anderson		
1970-71	5-21	2-12		Gene Mack	19.8	Bob Moser	5.7			Glen Anderson	140-162	.464
1971-72	12-14	5-9		Martinez Denmon	16.8	Clint Harris	10.4			Maury John		
1972-73	16-10	7-7		Clint Harris	17.5	Clint Harris	11.0			Maury John		
1973-74	15-11	6-8		Hercle Ivy	18.1	Wes Harris	8.8	Eric Heft	4.1	Maury John[a]	32-25	.561
1974-75	10-16	4-10		Hercle Ivy	28.3	Art Johnson	9.7	Jeff Branstetter	4.8	Ken Trickey		
1975-76	3-24	3-11		Hercle Ivy	22.8	Art Johnson	9.9	Hercle Ivy	3.3	Ken Trickey	13-40	.245
1976-77	8-19	3-11		Dean Uthoff	11.5	Dean Uthoff	11.3	Carlton Evans	1.9	Lynn Nance		
1977-78	14-13	9-5		Andrew Parker	22.4	Dean Uthoff	14.0	Dean Uthoff	2.4	Lynn Nance		
1978-79	11-16	6-8		Andrew Parker	20.3	Dean Uthoff	11.4	Jon Ness	3.1	Lynn Nance		
1979-80	11-16	5-9		Chuck Harmison	12.5	Dean Uthoff	9.0	Charles Harris	2.6	Lynn Nance[b]	41-58	.414
1980-81	9-18	2-12		Robert Estes	14.9	Robert Estes	6.7	Lefty Moore	4.6	Johnny Orr		
1981-82	10-17	5-9		Ron Harris	13.3	Robert Estes	5.8	Terrence Allen	3.1	Johnny Orr		
1982-83	13-15	5-9		Barry Stevens	16.5	Barry Stevens	5.2	Terrence Allen	3.2	Johnny Orr		
1983-84	16-13	6-8	NIT FIRST ROUND	Barry Stevens	22.2	Barry Stevens	5.0	Jeff Hornacek	6.8	Johnny Orr		
1984-85	21-13	7-7	NCAA FIRST ROUND	Barry Stevens	21.7	Sam Hill	7.3	Jeff Hornacek	4.9	Johnny Orr		
1985-86	22-11	9-5	NCAA REGIONAL SEMIFINALS	Jeff Grayer	20.7	Sam Hill	6.7	Jeff Hornacek	6.6	Johnny Orr		
1986-87	13-15	5-9		Jeff Grayer	22.4	Tom Schafer	8.0	Gary Thompkins	5.9	Johnny Orr		
1987-88	20-12	6-8	NCAA FIRST ROUND	Jeff Grayer	25.3	Jeff Grayer	9.4	Gary Thompkins	5.7	Johnny Orr		
1988-89	17-12	7-7	NCAA FIRST ROUND	Victor Alexander	19.9	Victor Alexander	8.8	Terry Woods	5.4	Johnny Orr		
1989-90	10-18	4-10		Victor Alexander	19.7	Victor Alexander	8.7	Terry Woods	6.2	Johnny Orr		
1990-91	12-19	6-8		Victor Alexander	23.4	Victor Alexander	9.0	Doug Collins	5.8	Johnny Orr		
1991-92	21-13	5-9	NCAA SECOND ROUND	Justus Thigpen	16.3	Julius Michalik	5.7	Ron Bayless	4.0	Johnny Orr		
1992-93	20-11	8-6	NCAA FIRST ROUND	Justus Thigpen	17.6	Fred Hoiberg	6.3	Ron Bayless	5.1	Johnny Orr		
1993-94	14-13	4-10		Fred Hoiberg	20.2	Fred Hoiberg	6.7	Fred Hoiberg	3.6	Johnny Orr	218-200	.522
1994-95	23-11	6-8	NCAA SECOND ROUND	Fred Hoiberg	19.9	Loren Meyer	8.9	Jacy Holloway	4.9	Tim Floyd		
1995-96	24-9 ✪	9-5	NCAA SECOND ROUND	Dedric Willoughby	20.5	Kelvin Cato	7.7	Jacy Holloway	4.5	Tim Floyd		
1996-97	22-9	10-6	NCAA REGIONAL SEMIFINALS	Dedric Willoughby	18.9	Kelvin Cato	8.4	Jacy Holloway	5.9	Tim Floyd		
1997-98	12-18	5-11		Marcus Fizer	14.9	Klay Edwards	7.7	Lee Love	3.7	Tim Floyd	81-47	.633▼
1998-99	15-15	6-10		Marcus Fizer	18.0	Marcus Fizer	7.6	Stevie Johnson	3.1	Larry Eustachy		
1999-2000	32-5	14-2	NCAA REGIONAL FINALS	Marcus Fizer	22.8	Marcus Fizer	7.7	Jamaal Tinsley	6.6	Larry Eustachy		
2000-01	25-6	13-3	NCAA FIRST ROUND	Jamaal Tinsley	14.3	Paul Shirley	6.9	Jamaal Tinsley	6.0	Larry Eustachy		
2001-02	12-19	4-12		Tyray Pearson	18.7	Tyray Pearson	7.8	Ricky Morgan	3.1	Larry Eustachy		
2002-03	17-14	5-11	NIT FIRST ROUND	Jake Sullivan	17.0	Jackson Vroman	9.4	Tim Barnes	5.0	Larry Eustachy	101-59	.631
2003-04	20-13	7-9	NIT SEMIFINALS	Curtis Stinson	16.2	Jackson Vroman	9.6	Curtis Stinson	4.3	Wayne Morgan		
2004-05	19-12	9-7	NCAA SECOND ROUND	Curtis Stinson	17.2	Jared Homan	8.7	Will Blalock	4.8	Wayne Morgan		
2005-06	16-14	6-10		Curtis Stinson	19.4	Rahshon Clark	5.5	Will Blalock	6.1	Wayne Morgan	55-39	.585
2006-07	15-16	6-10		Mike Taylor	16.0	Wesley Johnson	7.9	Mike Taylor	4.5	Greg McDermott		
2007-08	14-18	4-12		Jiri Hubalek	12.4	Jiri Hubalek	7.3	Bryan Petersen	2.9	Greg McDermott		
2008-09	15-17	4-12		Craig Brackins	20.2	Craig Brackins	9.5	Diante Garrett	5.0	Greg McDermott	44-51	.463

[a] Maury John (4-1) and Gus Guydon (11-10) both coached during the 1973-74 season.

[b] Lynn Nance (8-10) and Rick Samuels (3-6) both coached during the 1979-80 season.

✪ Records don't reflect games forfeited or vacated. For adjusted records, see p. 521.

▼ Coach's record adjusted to reflect games forfeited or vacated: 82-46, .640. For yearly totals, see p. 521.

ESPN 205 SAGARIN

JACKSON STATE

Walter Payton's alma mater can brag about its hoops heritage, too: 14 Southwestern Athletic Conference regular-season or tourney championships, three top-10 NBA draft picks (Lindsey Hunter, Purvis and Eugene Short), and 23 20-win seasons. And they're still talking about that 1993 NIT upset of UConn.

BEST TEAM: 1974-75 The 25–4 SWAC champion Tigers featured the Short brothers, both of whom were NAIA first-team All-Americas, two other 1,000-point scorers (Alphonso Smith and Ricky Berry) and another future NBAer (Henry Ward).

BEST PLAYER: G Lindsey Hunter (1990-93) Despite playing only three seasons at JSU (he transferred from Alcorn State after his freshman year), Hunter scored 2,226 points for the Tigers, second to Purvis Short. He was the nation's fifth-best scorer as a senior (26.0 ppg) as his team went 25–9 and won the SWAC regular-season championship. He was the 10th overall pick (Detroit Pistons) in the '93 NBA draft.

BEST COACH: Harrison B. Wilson (1950-67) JSU started its program with nine straight 20-win seasons—eight of those under Wilson, who became head coach when he was only 23. His 1956-57 team went 24–1 and reached the NAIA tournament, and his 1963-64 team (29–5) was SWAC regular-season co-champion.

GAME FOR THE AGES: Jackson State had never played a D1 postseason game before the 1993 NIT. But opposing coach Jim Calhoun warned his powerful UConn Huskies that no lead would be safe against the Tigers' Hunter. He was so right. After a five-point first half, Hunter caught fire and finished with 39 in the 90-88 upset, including 9 of JSU's 10 points in OT.

FIERCEST RIVAL: Jackson State has played no team more often than in-state and SWAC East rival Alcorn State: 154 times in all, with the Tigers leading, 90–64. The schools can sometimes get too close for comfort. Case in point: Hunter transferred from ASU to JSU after his freshman year, helping the Tigers program reach new heights.

SEASON REVIEW

SEAS.	W-L	CONF.	COACH	SEAS.	W-L	CONF.	COACH
1949-50	22-5		T. B. Ellis	**1962-63**	17-7		Harrison B. Wilson
1950-51	20-5		Harrison B. Wilson	**1963-64**	29-5		Harrison B. Wilson
1951-52	22-9		Harrison B. Wilson	**1964-65**	19-7		Harrison B. Wilson
1952-53	23-4		Harrison B. Wilson	**1965-66**	24-5		Harrison B. Wilson
1953-54	20-6		Harrison B. Wilson	**1966-67**	20-9		Harrison B. Wilson
1954-55	23-5		Harrison B. Wilson	**1967-68**	24-3		Paul Covington
1955-56	29-4		Harrison B. Wilson	**1968-69**	15-6		Paul Covington
1956-57	24-1		Harrison B. Wilson	**1969-70**	23-3		Paul Covington
1957-58	22-4		Harrison B. Wilson	**1970-71**	20-4		Paul Covington
1958-59	19-7		Harrison B. Wilson	**1971-72**	15-11		Paul Covington
1959-60	21-4		Harrison B. Wilson	**1972-73**	21-7		Paul Covington
1960-61	20-4		Harrison B. Wilson	**1973-74**	22-4		Paul Covington
1961-62	19-7		Harrison B. Wilson	**1974-75**	25-4		Paul Covington

SEAS.	W-L	CONF.	SCORING		COACH	RECORD
1975-76	17-7				Paul Covington	
1976-77	19-8				Paul Covington	
1977-78	21-5	9-3			Paul Covington	
1978-79	13-14	4-8			Paul Covington	
1979-80	15-14	7-5			Paul Covington	
1980-81	16-13	7-5			Paul Covington	
1981-82	19-9	10-2			Paul Covington	
1982-83	6-24	4-10			Paul Covington	
1983-84	10-18	5-9			Paul Covington	
1984-85	10-16	6-8			Paul Covington	
1985-86	14-15	9-5			Paul Covington	325-185 .637
1986-87	15-14	8-6			John Prince	
1987-88	13-15	7-7			John Prince	
1988-89	15-13	7-7			John Prince	43-42 .505
1989-90	9-19	4-10			Andy Stoglin	
1990-91	17-13	10-2			Andy Stoglin	
1991-92	12-16	7-7			Andy Stoglin	
1992-93	25-9	13-1 ■			Andy Stoglin	
1993-94	19-10	11-3			Andy Stoglin	
1994-95	12-19	7-7			Andy Stoglin	
1995-96	16-13	11-3			Andy Stoglin	
1996-97	14-16	9-5 ●			Andy Stoglin	
1997-98	14-13	11-5			Andy Stoglin	
1998-99	16-12	11-5	Vincent Jones	12.7	Andy Stoglin	
1999-2000	17-16	10-8 ●	Vincent Jones	13.2	Andy Stoglin	
2000-01	7-23	7-11	Richard Bradley	15.3	Andy Stoglin	
2001-02	9-19	8-10	Tim Henderson	17.5	Andy Stoglin	
2002-03	10-18	9-9	Tim Henderson	17.5	Andy Stoglin	197-216 .477
2003-04	12-17	9-9	Ishmael Joyce	15.5	Tevester Anderson	
2004-05	15-17 ✪	10-8	Kelly Ross	10.2	Tevester Anderson	
2005-06	15-17	10-8	Trey Johnson	23.4	Tevester Anderson	
2006-07	21-14	12-6 ●	Trey Johnson	27.0	Tevester Anderson	
2007-08	14-20	10-8	Grant Maxey	14.7	Tevester Anderson	
2008-09	18-15	15-3	Grant Maxey	16.4	Tevester Anderson	95-100 .487

✪ Records don't reflect games forfeited or vacated. For adjusted records, see p. 521.
● NCAA Tournament appearance ■ NIT appearance

PROFILE

Jackson State University, Jackson, MS
Founded: 1877 as Natchez Seminary; renamed Jackson College in 1899
Enrollment: 8,699 (6,992 undergraduate)
Colors: Royal blue and white
Nickname: Tigers
Current arena: Lee E. Williams Athletics and Assembly Center, opened in 1981 (8,000)
First game: 1949
All-time record: 1,053-641 (.622)
Total weeks in AP Top 20/25: 0

Current conference: Southwestern Athletic (1958-)
Conference titles:
SWAC: 9 (1964, '68, '70, '74, '75, '82, '91, '93, '96)
Conference tournament titles:
SWAC: 5 (1978, '91, '97, 2000, '07)
NCAA Tournament appearances: 3
NIT appearances: 1

CONSENSUS ALL-AMERICAS

1974, '75	**Eugene Short** (Little A-A), F
1977	**Purvis Short** (D2), G/F

FIRST-ROUND PRO PICKS

1975	**Eugene Short,** New York (9)
1978	**Purvis Short,** Golden State (5)
1993	**Lindsey Hunter,** Detroit (10)

TOP 5

G	**Lindsey Hunter** (1990-93)
G	**Trey Johnson** (2005-07)
G/F	**Purvis Short** (1974-78)
F	**Eugene Short** (1972-75)
C	**Audie Norris** (1978-81)

RECORDS	GAME		SEASON		CAREER	
POINTS	48	Lindsey Hunter, vs. Kansas (Dec. 12, 1992)	947	Trey Johnson (2006-07)	2,434	Purvis Short (1974-78)
POINTS PER GAME			29.6	Purvis Short (1977-78)	25.3	Trey Johnson (2005-07)
REBOUNDS	30	Cornell Warner, vs. Boston College (Dec. 21, 1969)	341	Audie Norris (1981-82)	1,610	Cornell Warner (1966-70)
ASSISTS		N/A	179	Kirk Mitchell (1987-88)	514	John Taylor (1990-94)

ESPN 193 SAGARIN

JACKSONVILLE

Cinderellas don't get more colorful than the Dolphins. Fifteen years removed from being a junior college, the team advanced to the 1970 NCAA title game sporting mutton chops, Afros and green-and-yellow bell-bottom warmups. The Dolphins have appeared in four other NCAAs and five NITs.

BEST TEAM: 1969-70 All five starters from '68-69 were back, with the addition of two seven-foot juco transfers, Artis Gilmore and Pembrook Burrows. The result was carnage, as the Dolphins became the first NCAA team to average more than 100 points (100.4 ppg, to be exact) over a season. In the Tourney, they dropped 109 on Western Kentucky, 104 on Iowa, 106 on top-ranked Kentucky, and 91 on St. Bonaventure to set up a Final showdown with UCLA. There, Sidney Wicks put the clamps on Gilmore in the Bruins' 80-69 win.

BEST PLAYER: C ARTIS GILMORE (1969-71) The 7'2" lefty boasted an imposing 'fro and an even more imposing game. He led the NCAA in rebounding in both of his seasons, averaged 10.6 blocks per game as a senior and was a consensus All-America.

BEST COACH: JOE WILLIAMS (1964-70) He was no slouch as a tactician but also appreciated keeping things loose. Before the 1970 Tourney, the Dolphins presented him with a white sport coat, blue pants and a deep pink shirt. He wore the ensemble for every game.

GAME FOR THE AGES: Were the 1970 Dolphins for real? Gilmore & Co. answered that question the most emphatic way possible by beating Kentucky, 106-100, in the Tournament's Mideast Regional final. Wildcats star Dan Issel fouled out with minutes remaining on a controversial charging call. UK's Adolph Rupp declared the loss the worst of his coaching career.

FIERCEST RIVAL: When the Atlantic Sun added the Dolphins to its mix in 1998, the longstanding in-state rivalry between Jacksonville and Stetson became an in-conference one, too. The result: great basketball. Consider the Dolphins' triple-OT 98-94 win over the Hatters on Jan. 3, 2008. Jacksonville holds a 39–30 series lead.

SEASON REVIEW

SEAS.	W-L	CONF.	COACH	SEAS.	W-L	CONF.	COACH
1948-49	17-1		John Geilen	**1961-62**	12-13		Dick Kendall
1949-50	20-3		John Geilen	**1962-63**	14-12		Dick Kendall
1950-51	9-12		John Geilen	**1963-64**	13-13		Dick Kendall
1951-52	6-11		John Geilen	**1964-65**	15-11		Joe Williams
1952-53	15-5		John Geilen	**1965-66**	12-11		Joe Williams
1953-54	17-7		Rollie Rourke	**1966-67**	8-17		Joe Williams
1954-55	15-8		Rollie Rourke	**1967-68**	13-13		Joe Williams
1955-56	23-3		Rollie Rourke	**1968-69**	17-7		Joe Williams
1956-57	19-6		Rollie Rourke	**1969-70**	27-2	●	Joe Williams
1957-58	11-5		Rollie Rourke	**1970-71**	22-4	●	Tom Wasdin
1958-59	11-8		Rollie Rourke	**1971-72**	20-8	■	Tom Wasdin
1959-60	11-10		Rollie Rourke	**1972-73**	21-6	●	Tom Wasdin
1960-61	12-11		Dick Kendall	**1973-74**	20-10	■	Bob Gottlieb

SEAS.	W-L	CONF.		SCORING		COACH	RECORD	
1974-75	15-11			Ricky Coleman	21.2	Bob Gottlieb	35-21	.625
1975-76	13-13			Kent Glover	17.8	Don Beasley		
1976-77	10-19	2-4		Kent Glover	15.1	Don Beasley		
1977-78	14-14	6-4		Ron Anthony	19.4	Don Beasley	37-46	.446
1978-79	19-11	5-5	●	James Ray	16.1	Taylor "Tates" Locke		
1979-80	20-9	10-4	■	James Ray	17.2	Taylor "Tates" Locke		
1980-81	8-19	4-8		Mike Hackett	12.1	Taylor "Tates" Locke	47-39	.547
1981-82	14-13	5-5		Mike Hackett	20.8	Bob Wenzel		
1982-83	7-22	0-14		Otis Smith	14.3	Bob Wenzel		
1983-84	12-16	3-11		Ronnie Murphy	17.9	Bob Wenzel		
1984-85	15-14	6-8		Otis Smith	12.9	Bob Wenzel		
1985-86	21-10	9-5	●	Otis Smith	15.3	Bob Wenzel		
1986-87	19-11	11-3	■	Ronnie Murphy	22.0	Bob Wenzel	88-86	.506
1987-88	8-21	2-12		Troy Mundine	14.9	Rich Haddad		
1988-89	14-16	5-9		Dee Brown	19.6	Rich Haddad		
1989-90	13-16	5-9		Dee Brown	19.3	Rich Haddad		
1990-91	6-22	2-12		Reggie Law	17.6	Rich Haddad	41-75	.353
1991-92	12-17	6-10		Tim Burroughs	15.6	Matt Kilcullen		
1992-93	5-22	3-15		Barry Brown	17.3	Matt Kilcullen		
1993-94	17-11	11-7		Barry Brown	20.8	Matt Kilcullen	34-50	.405
1994-95	18-9	12-6		Artemus McClary	20.5	George Scholz		
1995-96	15-13	10-8		Artemus McClary	18.5	George Scholz		
1996-97	5-23	4-14		John Knox	18.7	George Scholz[a]	33-28	.541
1997-98	8-19	6-12		Micah Ross	12.6	Hugh Durham		
1998-99	12-15	7-9		Calvin Slaughter	15.8	Hugh Durham		
1999-2000	8-19	5-13		Calvin Slaughter	16.2	Hugh Durham		
2000-01	18-10	11-7		B. Williams, Shawn Platts	14.5	Hugh Durham		
2001-02	18-12	12-8		Travis Robinson	14.0	Hugh Durham		
2002-03	13-16	8-8		Calvin Warner	16.9	Hugh Durham		
2003-04	13-15	8-12		Haminn Quaintance	14.3	Hugh Durham		
2004-05	16-13	11-9		Haminn Quaintance	13.6	Hugh Durham	106-119	.471
2005-06	1-26	1-19		Antonio Cool	15.4	Cliff Warren		
2006-07	15-14	11-7		Jesse Kimbrough	14.0	Cliff Warren		
2007-08	18-13	12-4		Ben Smith	15.8	Cliff Warren		
2008-09	18-14	15-5	■	Ben Smith	16.9	Cliff Warren	52-67	.437

[a] **George Scholz (0-6) and Buster Harvey (5-17) both coached during the 1996-97 season.**

● NCAA Tournament appearance ■ NIT appearance

PROFILE

Jacksonville University, Jacksonville, FL
Founded: 1934
Enrollment: 3,436 (2,982 undergraduate)
Colors: Green and gold
Nickname: Dolphins
Current arena: Jacksonville Veterans Memorial Arena, opened in 2004 (5,191); Swisher Gymnasium, opened in 1953 (1,500)
Previous: Jacksonville Coliseum, 1959-2000 (10,000); Robert E. Lee High School, 1948-53 (1,500); Julia Landon Middle School (250)
First game: Dec. 2, 1948
All-time record: 858-755 (.532)
Total weeks in AP Top 20/25: 49

Current conference: Atlantic Sun (1998-)
Conference titles:
Atlantic Sun: 1 (2009)
Conference tournament titles:
Sun Belt: 2 (1979, '86)
NCAA Tournament appearances: 5
Final Four: 1
NIT appearances: 5
Semifinals: 2

CONSENSUS ALL-AMERICAS

1962, '63	**Roger Strickland** (Little A-A), F
1971	**Artis Gilmore**, C

FIRST-ROUND PRO PICKS

1963	**Roger Strickland,** LA Lakers (8)
1971	**Artis Gilmore,** Kentucky (ABA)
1972	**David Brent,** Memphis (ABA)
1973	**Henry Williams,** New York (ABA, 4)
1980	**James Ray,** Denver (5)
1987	**Ronnie Murphy,** Portland (17)
1990	**Dee Brown,** Boston (19)

TOP 5

G	**Dee Brown** (1986-90)
G	**Rex Morgan** (1968-70)
F	**James Ray** (1976-80)
F	**Roger Strickland** (1960-63)
C	**Artis Gilmore** (1969-71)

RECORDS

RECORDS	GAME		SEASON		CAREER	
POINTS	59	Ernie Fleming, vs. St. Peter's (Jan. 29, 1972)	783	Roger Strickland (1961-62)	2,184	Ralph Tiner (1961-65)
POINTS PER GAME			32.6	Roger Strickland (1961-62)	27.3	Roger Strickland (1960-63)
REBOUNDS	34	Artis Gilmore, vs. St. Peter's (Dec. 3, 1970)	621	Artis Gilmore (1969-70)	1,224	Artis Gilmore (1969-71)
ASSISTS	20	Roger Strickland, vs. Rollins (Dec. 5, 1962)	259	Danny Tirado (1990-91)	507	Jeremy Livingston (1991-95)

ESPN 295 SAGARIN

JACKSONVILLE STATE

JSU's pre-Division I years include the 31–1 squad that won the 1985 D2 tournament and another final four appearance. But since joining D1 for the 1995-96 season, Gamecocks highlights have been on a more modest scale—three seasons with above-.500 records and the all-around play of Walker Russell Jr.

BEST TEAM: 1984-85 Led by their backcourt stars, Earl Warren and Melvin Allen, the Gamecocks won 30 straight games and reached the D2 national final, thanks to the Shot Heard 'Round Calhoun County—a 40-foot bomb by Allen that sealed a 80-79 win over Southeast Missouri State. The 74-73 title win over South Dakota State was another nail-biter, with last-minute heroics by Allen (go-ahead layup) and Warren (two steals).

BEST PLAYER: G Walker Russell Jr. (2003-06) The son of a former NBA player, Russell is all over the Gamecocks' D1 career record book. He's first in free throw percentage, assists and games started, and second in steals. He's also just the second player in JSU history to score more than 1,000 points in three seasons.

BEST COACH: Mike LaPlante (2000-08) He ran an up-tempo, guard-driven offense. Despite some lean years, LaPlante holds D1-era school records for most career wins (95) and most wins in a season (20). He has also been a consultant to Senegal's national team.

GAME FOR THE AGES: The 2006 Gamecocks finished the regular season 15–12 and hosted their first Ohio Valley Conference tournament game at Mathews Coliseum. Russell led JSU to an 86-59 blowout over Eastern Kentucky with a 21-11-11 triple double—the first in Gamecocks history. In their next game, they nearly stole a win from top-seed and eventual champ Murray State.

FIERCEST RIVAL: Wanted: a new adversary. Jacksonville State faced off with Troy 109 times in their D2 years, 12 times in D1, but not once since 2003. And there used to be a sparkling animosity against Samford, but then the Bulldogs left the OVC. One likely contender for the near future is Tennessee Tech, and a football rivalry with Alabama A&M could spread to hoops.

SEASON REVIEW

SEAS.	W-L	CONF.	COACH	SEAS.	W-L	CONF.	COACH
1925-48	*67-28*	*26-5 in '46-47; 25-5 the next year*		1961-62	12-8		Tom Roberson
1948-49	17-10		J.W. Stephenson	1962-63	15-5		Tom Roberson
1949-50	23-6		J.W. Stephenson	1963-64	12-8		Tom Roberson
1950-51	20-8		J.W. Stephenson	1964-65	16-6		Tom Roberson
1951-52	17-7		Ray Wedgeworth	1965-66	16-13		Tom Roberson
1952-53	15-7		Ray Wedgeworth	1966-67	18-7		Tom Roberson
1953-54	8-14		Tom Roberson	1967-68	15-11		Tom Roberson
1954-55	19-6		Tom Roberson	1968-69	19-5		Tom Roberson
1955-56	12-8		Tom Roberson	1969-70	22-5		Tom Roberson
1956-57	8-13		Tom Roberson	1970-71	11-12		Tom Roberson
1957-58	12-9		Tom Roberson	1971-72	11-14		Mitchell Caldwell
1958-59	11-13		Tom Roberson	1972-73	17-9		Mitchell Caldwell
1959-60	9-9		Tom Roberson	1973-74	10-15		Mitchell Caldwell
1960-61	16-6		Tom Roberson	1974-75	20-7		Bill Jones

SEAS.	W-L	CONF.	SCORING		COACH	RECORD
1975-76	16-8		Eddie Butler	15.4	Bill Jones	
1976-77	13-14		Greg Davis	16.4	Bill Jones	
1977-78	11-13		David Thomas	19.5	Bill Jones	
1978-79	17-8		Robert Clements	16.4	Bill Jones	
1979-80	20-7		Tommy Bonds	18.8	Bill Jones	
1980-81	22-8		Randy Albright	15.9	Bill Jones	
1981-82	16-10		Doug Creel	13.4	Bill Jones	
1982-83	24-8		Andre King	12.1	Bill Jones	
1983-84	23-8		Melvin Allen	18.5	Bill Jones	
1984-85	31-1	◆	Melvin Allen	17.0	Bill Jones	
1985-86	19-8		Pat Williams	18.2	Bill Jones	
1986-87	12-12		Terry Rutledge	14.9	Bill Jones	
1987-88	17-11		Robert Lee Sanders	16.5	Bill Jones	
1988-89	27-6		Robert Lee Sanders	19.3	Bill Jones	
1989-90	24-5		Robert Lee Sanders	22.7	Bill Jones	
1990-91	20-6		Charles Burkette	19.0	Bill Jones	
1991-92	28-2		David Edmond	18.5	Bill Jones	
1992-93	16-10		Anthony Kingston	17.7	Bill Jones	
1993-94	17-8		Pat Armour	21.1	Bill Jones	
1994-95	24-1		Pat Armour	18.9	Bill Jones	
1995-96	10-17	4-12	Aaron Kelley	15.1	Bill Jones	
1996-97	10-17	9-7	Kenny Sorenson	15.2	Bill Jones	
1997-98	12-14	6-10	Derrell Johnson	16.9	Bill Jones	449-209 .682
1998-99	8-18	3-13	Marlon Gurley	14.0	Mark Turgeon	
1999-2000	17-11	12-6	Mike McDaniel	12.9	Mark Turgeon	25-29 .463
2000-01	9-19	6-12	Mike McDaniel	17.5	Mike LaPlante	
2001-02	13-16	8-12	Poonie Richardson	14.4	Mike LaPlante	
2002-03	20-10	10-6	Omar Barlett	15.0	Mike LaPlante	
2003-04	14-14	7-9	Trent Eager	13.4	Mike LaPlante	
2004-05	7-22	2-14	Walker Russell Jr.	14.5	Mike LaPlante	
2005-06	16-13	12-8	Courtney Bradley	15.3	Mike LaPlante	
2006-07	9-21	7-13	Courtney Bradley	17.0	Mike LaPlante	
2007-08	7-22	5-15	Nick Murphy	13.0	Mike LaPlante	95-137 .409
2008-09	11-17	5-13	Jeremy Bynum	12.9	James Green	11-17 .393

◆ **Division II championship**

PROFILE

Jacksonville State University, Jacksonville, AL
Founded: 1883 as Jacksonville State Normal School; renamed Jacksonville State University in 1966
Enrollment: 9,481 (7,485 undergraduate)
Nickname: Gamecocks
Current arena: Pete Mathews Coliseum, opened in 1974 (5,500)
First game: 1925-26
All-time record: 1,028-654 (.611)
Total weeks in AP Top 20/25: 0

Current conference: Ohio Valley (2003-)
Conference titles: 0
Conference tournament titles: 0
NCAA Tournament appearances: 0
NIT appearances: 0

TOP 5

G **Aaron Kelly** (1993-97)
G **Walker Russell Jr.** (2003-06)
F **Courtney Bradley** (2005-07)
F **Jay Knowlton** (1994-98)
C **Rusty Brand** (1993-97)

RECORDS

RECORDS	GAME		SEASON		CAREER	
POINTS	33	Jay Knowlton, vs. Alabama State (1997-98)	510	Courtney Bradley (2006-07)	1,233	Jay Knowlton (1994-98)
POINTS PER GAME			17.5	Mike McDaniel (2000-01)	16.2	Courtney Bradley (2005-07)
REBOUNDS	18	Rusty Brand, vs. Alabama State (1995-96); Brant Harriman, vs. Clayton State (Dec. 30, 1999); Nick Murphy, vs. Murray State (Feb. 2, 2008)	239	Rusty Brand (1995-96)	543	Rusty Brand (1993-97)
ASSISTS	13	DeAndre Bray, vs. Southeast Missouri St. (Dec. 20, 2007); vs. Tennessee-Martin (Dec. 8, 2007)	211	Walker Russell Jr. (2004-05)	590	Walker Russell Jr. (2003-06)

ESPN 221 SAGARIN

JAMES MADISON

Just a few years after joining D1, the Dukes were already giving the big boys trouble in three straight NCAA Tournament trips from 1981 to '83, most memorably upsetting Georgetown in the first round in 1981. Chalk it up to coach Lou Campanelli, who left for Cal in 1985. Another charismatic coach, Lefty Driesell, arrived in Harrisonburg to revive the program in the late 1980s and early '90s, but the highlights have been scarce since.

BEST TEAM: 1981-82 Even though the Dukes lost in the ECAC South tournament final, they received an at-large Tournament bid and a No. 9 seed. Then they proved they deserved that honor by playing smothering defense in a 55-48 first-round victory over Ohio State, before falling 52-50 to Michael Jordan & Co.

BEST PLAYER: F Steve Stielper (1976-80) He was a scruffy, self-admitted hard partier, but he could play a little ball too. As a junior, the 6'8" forward set the JMU single-season scoring average record (25.7 ppg) on the way to finishing with the most points in team history, and he led the Dukes in rebounds all four seasons.

BEST COACH: Lou Campanelli (1972-85) Whether playing zone or man-to-man, Campanelli's teams regularly overachieved by virtue of their intense defense. Outspoken and driven, the New Jersey native wore his emotions on his sleeve, his eyes welling with tears in the postgame press conference after JMU came just short of upsetting North Carolina in the 1982 Tournament.

GAME FOR THE AGES: They were no match for Georgetown's size or quickness in the first round of the 1981 Tournament. But playing a 2-3 zone and making 17 of 20 free throws, the Dukes proved to be physically and mentally tougher than the Hoyas in their 61-55 upset.

FIERCEST RIVAL: JMU and William and Mary have been locking up since they were rivals in the ECAC, and they brought their grudge match to the Colonial in 1985. It's been a streaky series, with the Dukes winning 18 straight from 1988 to '95, and the Tribe winning eight in a row from 2005 to '07. JMU leads overall, 42–32.

SEASON REVIEW

SEAS.	W-L	CONF.	SCORING		COACH	RECORD
1969-70	11-9				Charles Branscom	
1970-71	9-8				Charles Branscom	20-17 .541
1971-72	16-7		Tim Meyers	17.0	Dean Ehlers	16-7 .696
1972-73	16-10		David Correll	13.2	Lou Campanelli	
1973-74	20-6		Sherman Dillard	21.0	Lou Campanelli	
1974-75	19-6		Sherman Dillard	20.2	Lou Campanelli	
1975-76	18-9		Sherman Dillard	22.4	Lou Campanelli	
1976-77	17-9		Steve Stielper	20.9	Lou Campanelli	
1977-78	18-8	6-2	Sherman Dillard	19.2	Lou Campanelli	
1978-79	18-8	9-5	Steve Stielper	25.7	Lou Campanelli	
1979-80	18-8	7-3	Steve Stielper	18.4	Lou Campanelli	
1980-81	21-9	11-2 ●	Linton Townes	15.3	Lou Campanelli	
1981-82	24-6	10-1 ●	Linton Townes	16.3	Lou Campanelli	
1982-83	20-11	6-3 ●	Dan Ruland	15.1	Lou Campanelli	
1983-84	15-14	5-5	Derek Steele	11.9	Lou Campanelli	
1984-85	14-14	7-7	John Newman	12.6	Lou Campanelli	238-118 .669
1985-86	5-23	3-11	Eric Brent	14.3	John Thurston	
1986-87	20-10	8-6 ■	Eric Brent	15.3	John Thurston	
1987-88	10-18	5-9	Kennard Winchester	16.1	John Thurston[a]	31-44 .413
1988-89	16-14	6-8	William Davis	15.7	Lefty Driesell	
1989-90	20-11	11-3 ■	Steve Hood	22.0	Lefty Driesell	
1990-91	19-10	12-2 ■	Steve Hood	20.7	Lefty Driesell	
1991-92	21-11	12-2 ■	Bryan Edwards	15.7	Lefty Driesell	
1992-93	21-9	11-3 ■	William Davis	16.0	Lefty Driesell	
1993-94	20-10	10-4 ●	Clayton Ritter	18.3	Lefty Driesell	
1994-95	16-13	9-5	Louis Rowe	21.7	Lefty Driesell	
1995-96	10-20	6-10	Darren McLinton	22.7	Lefty Driesell	
1996-97	16-13	8-8	Chatney Howard	16.3	Lefty Driesell	159-111 .589
1997-98	11-16	6-10	Eugene Atkinson	14.2	Sherman Dillard	
1998-99	16-11	9-7	Jabari Outtz	15.0	Sherman Dillard	
1999-2000	20-9	12-4	Jabari Outtz	17.2	Sherman Dillard	
2000-01	12-17	6-10	Tim Lyle	11.6	Sherman Dillard	
2001-02	14-15	6-12	David Fanning	18.0	Sherman Dillard	
2002-03	13-17	8-10	David Fanning	15.1	Sherman Dillard	
2003-04	7-21	3-15	Dwayne Broyles	15.4	Sherman Dillard	93-106 .467
2004-05	6-22	3-15	Ray Barbosa	14.9	Dean Keener	
2005-06	5-23	2-16	Juwann James	12.7	Dean Keener	
2006-07	7-23	4-14	Juwann James	13.0	Dean Keener	
2007-08	13-17	5-13	Abdulai Jalloh	15.6	Dean Keener	31-85 .267
2008-09	21-15	9-9	Juwann James	14.1	Matt Brady	21-15 .583

[a] **John Thurston (6-11) and Tom McCorry (4-7) both coached during the 1987-88 season.**
● NCAA Tournament appearance ■ NIT appearance

PROFILE

James Madison University, Harrisonburg, VA
Founded: 1908
Enrollment: 17,078 (16,619 undergraduate)
Colors: Purple and gold
Nickname: Dukes
Current arena: JMU Convocation Center, opened in 1982 (7,156)
Previous: Godwin Hall, 1972-82 (5,100); Harrisonburg High School, 1969-72 (N/A)
First game: Dec. 3, 1969
All-time record: 613-510 (.546)
Total weeks in AP Top 20/25: 0

Current conference: Colonial Athletic Association (1979-)
Conference titles:
East Coast Athletic South: 1 (1982)
CAA: 6 (1990, '91, '92 [tie], '93 [tie], '94 [tie], 2000 [tie])
Conference tournament titles:
East Coast Athletic South: 2 (1981, '83)
CAA: 1 (1994)
NCAA Tournament appearances: 4
NIT appearances: 5

TOP 5

G **Kent Culuko** (1991-95)
G **Sherman Dillard** (1973-76, '77-78)
G **Steve Hood** (1989-91)
F **Pat Dosh** (1974-78)
F **Steve Stielper** (1976-80)

RECORDS

RECORDS	GAME		SEASON		CAREER	
POINTS	51	Steve Stielper, vs. Robert Morris (Jan. 27, 1979)	682	Steve Hood (1989-90)	2,126	Steve Stielper (1976-80)
POINTS PER GAME			25.7	Steve Stielper (1978-79)	21.4	Steve Hood (1989-91)
REBOUNDS	22	Steve Stielper, vs. Baptist (Jan. 17, 1977); Joe Frye, vs. Eastern Mennonite (Dec. 4, 1972)	279	Steve Stielper (1976-77)	917	Steve Stielper (1976-80)
ASSISTS	16	Jeff Cross, vs. Wilmington College (Jan. 29, 1977)	221	Ben Gordon (1986-87)	420	Joe Pfahler (1972-76)

ESPN 3 SAGARIN

KANSAS

There can be no doubt—Kansas *is* college basketball. The game's inventor, Dr. James Naismith, was the Jayhawks' first coach. His pupil, Phog Allen, coached both Adolph Rupp and Dean Smith. And the players? From Wilt the Stilt to Danny and the Miracles to Paul Pierce, KU has been the heartland's best program for more than 100 years.

BEST TEAM: 2007-08 Kansas won its third NCAA championship in thrilling fashion over Memphis, 75-68. The Jayhawks erased a nine-point deficit in the final two minutes of regulation, capped by a three from "Super Mario" Chalmers with 2.1 seconds left to send the game into overtime. Four players averaged double figures on Bill Self's 37–3 team, which started the season 20–0 and finished by winning its final 13 games.

BEST PLAYER: C Wilt Chamberlain (1956-58) A two-time consensus All-America, the 7'1" colossus scored 52 points and grabbed 31 rebounds in his varsity *debut*. But forget about the stats. Chamberlain changed the game with his finger roll, fadeaway jumper, passing and shot blocking. He was named Most Outstanding Player of the 1957 Tourney despite a title-game loss to North Carolina (54-53 in triple overtime) in which the Tar Heels triple-teamed him.

BEST COACH: Dr. F.C. "Phog" Allen (1907-09, '19-56) Allen far exceeded his mentor, Dr. James Naismith, winning 24 conference championships, two Helms Foundation national championships (1922 and '23) and the NCAA title in 1952. Allen also helped organize the first NCAA Tournament. KU's historic Allen Fieldhouse is named in his honor.

GAME FOR THE AGES: On April 4, 1988, Larry Brown's Jayhawks completed a miraculous turnaround from unranked team to NCAA champs. In the title game, Danny Manning poured in 31 points, including four clutch free throws in the final :14 seconds, to lead KU to an 83-79 win over conference rival Oklahoma.

HEARTBREAKER: No. 1-ranked Kansas stormed through the 1996-97 season losing just one game. But the Jayhawks were shocked by Arizona in the Sweet 16, 85-82. Trailing by 10 with less than two minutes left, the Jayhawks battled back, only to miss three game-tying three-point attempts in the final 18 seconds.

FIERCEST RIVAL: The Border Showdown (changed from Border War in the wake of 9/11) is the name of Kansas' longstanding feud with Missouri in all sports. The animosity dates back to the days of Bloody Kansas, when the two states fought over slavery in the 1850s. Kansas leads the hoops series, 167–94.

FANFARE AND HOOPLA: *Rock, Chalk, Jayhawk, KU.* Composed by a KU chemistry professor in 1886, the Rock Chalk chant's cadence, heard at games when a win is deemed certain, mimics the sound of a train picking up speed. Rock Chalk is a reference to the chalky limestone of Kansas' Mount Oread.

FAN FAVORITE: F Danny Manning (1984-88) While he remains the Jayhawks' all-time leading scorer and rebounder, it was Manning's orchestration of KU's 1988 NCAA title run that made him a legend in Lawrence.

CONSENSUS ALL-AMERICAS

1909	**Tommy Johnson,** F
1915	**Ralph Sproull,** F
1919	**Dutch Lonborg,** G
1922, '23	**Paul Endacott,** G
1924, '25	**Arthur Ackerman,** F/C
1924	**Charlie T. Black,** G/F
1926	**Gale Gordon,** F
1926	**Al Petersen,** C
1938	**Fred Pralle,** G
1941	**Howard Engleman,** F
1943	**Charlie Black,** F
1951, '52	**Clyde Lovellette,** C
1957, '58	**Wilt Chamberlain,** C
1987, '88	**Danny Manning,** F
1997, '98	**Raef LaFrentz,** F
1998	**Paul Pierce,** G/F
2002	**Drew Gooden,** F
2003	**Nick Collison,** F
2005	**Wayne Simien,** F

FIRST-ROUND PRO PICKS

1952	**Clyde Lovellette,** Minneapolis (10)
1959	**Wilt Chamberlain,** Philadelphia (3)
1962	**Wayne Hightower,** Philadelphia (7)
1966	**Walt Wesley,** Cincinnati (6)
1969	**Jo Jo White,** Boston (9)
1971	**Roger Brown,** Dallas (ABA)
1972	**Bud Stallworth,** Seattle (7)
1972	**Bud Stallworth,** Denver (ABA)
1976	**Norman Cook,** Boston (16)
1981	**Darnell Valentine,** Portland (16)
1988	**Danny Manning,** LA Clippers (1)
1991	**Mark Randall,** Chicago (26)
1993	**Rex Walters,** New Jersey (16)
1995	**Greg Ostertag,** Utah (28)
1997	**Scot Pollard,** Detroit (19)
1997	**Jacque Vaughn,** Utah (27)
1998	**Raef LaFrentz,** Denver (3)
1998	**Paul Pierce,** Boston (10)
2002	**Drew Gooden,** Memphis (4)
2003	**Kirk Hinrich,** Chicago (7)
2003	**Nick Collison,** Seattle (12)
2005	**Wayne Simien,** Miami (29)
2007	**Julian Wright,** New Orleans (13)
2008	**Brandon Rush,** Portland (13)
2008	**Darrell Arthur,** New Orleans (27)

PROFILE

University of Kansas, Lawrence, KS
Founded: 1866
Enrollment: 30,644 (27,875 undergraduate)
Colors: Crimson and blue
Nickname: Jayhawks
Current arena: Allen Fieldhouse, opened in 1955 (16,300)
Previous arenas: Hoch Auditorium, 1928-55 (3,800); Robinson Gym, 1907-28 (900); Snow Hall, 1899-1907 (250)
First game: Feb. 3, 1899
All-time record: 1,970-793 (.713)
Total weeks in AP Top 20/25: 572
Current conference: Big 12 (1996-)
Conference titles:
Missouri Valley: 13 (1908, '09, '10, '11, '12 [tie], '14 [tie], '15, '22 [tie], '23, '24, '25, '26, '27); Big Six: 12 (1931, '32, '33, '34, '36, '37 [tie], '38, '40 [tie], '41 [tie], '42 [tie], '43, '46); Big Seven: 5 (1950 [tie], '52, '53, '54 [tie], '57); Big Eight: 13 (1960 [tie], '66, '67, '71, '74, '75, '78, '86, '91 [tie], '92, '93, 95, '96); Big 12: 9 (1997, '98, 2002, '03, '05 [tie], '06 [tie], '07, '08 [tie], '09)
Conference tournament titles:
Big Eight: 4 (1981, '84, '86, '92); Big 12: 6 (1997, '98, '99, 2006, '07, '08)
NCAA Tournament appearances: 38
Sweet 16s (since 1975): 17
Final Fours: 13
Titles: 3 (1952, '88, 2008)
NIT appearances: 2
Semifinals: 1

TOP 5

G	**Jo Jo White** (1965-69)
G/F	**Paul Pierce** (1995-98)
F	**Danny Manning** (1984-88)
C	**Wilt Chamberlain** (1956-58)
C	**Clyde Lovelette** (1949-52)

RECORDS	GAME		SEASON		CAREER	
POINTS	52	Wilt Chamberlain, vs. Northwestern (Dec. 3, 1956)	942	Danny Manning (1987-88)	2,951	Danny Manning (1984-88)
POINTS PER GAME			30.1	Wilt Chamberlain (1957-58)	29.9	Wilt Chamberlain (1956-58)
REBOUNDS	36	Wilt Chamberlain, vs. Iowa State (Feb. 15, 1958)	510	Wilt Chamberlain (1956-57)	1,187	Danny Manning (1984-88)
ASSISTS	18	Tom Kivisto, vs. Nebraska (Dec. 29, 1973)	278	Cedric Hunter (1985-86)	954	Aaron Miles (2001-05)

SEASON REVIEW

SEASON	W-L	CONF.	COMMENTS		COACH	RECORD	
1899-1915	*188-91*		*First coach was Dr. James Naismith who went 55-60 from 1898-1907*				
1915-16	6-12	5-11			W.O. Hamilton		
1916-17	12-8	9-7			W.O. Hamilton		
1917-18	10-8	9-8			W.O. Hamilton		
1918-19	7-9	5-9			W.O. Hamilton	125-59	.679
1919-20	11-7	9-7			Forrest "Phog" Allen		
1920-21	10-8	10-8			Forrest "Phog" Allen		
1921-22	16-2	15-1	George Rody	14.7	Forrest "Phog" Allen		
1922-23	17-1	16-0	Arthur Ackerman	9.0	Forrest "Phog" Allen		
1923-24	16-3	15-1	Arthur Ackerman	8.4	Forrest "Phog" Allen		
1924-25	17-1	15-1	Arthur Ackerman	10.2	Forrest "Phog" Allen		
1925-26	16-2	16-2	Al Petersen	9.1	Forrest "Phog" Allen		
1926-27	15-2	11-2	Al Petersen	10.3	Forrest "Phog" Allen		
1927-28	9-9	9-9	Russell Thomson	11.3	Forrest "Phog" Allen		
1928-29	3-15	2-8	Russell Thomson	8.5	Forrest "Phog" Allen		
1929-30	14-4	7-3	Tom Bishop	9.7	Forrest "Phog" Allen		
1930-31	15-3	7-3	Tom Bishop	9.1	Forrest "Phog" Allen		
1931-32	13-5	7-3	Ted O'Leary	11.0	Forrest "Phog" Allen		
1932-33	13-4	8-2	Bill Johnson	10.7	Forrest "Phog" Allen		
1933-34	16-1	9-1	Ray Ebling	10.7	Forrest "Phog" Allen		
1934-35	15-5	12-4	Ray Ebling	10.9	Forrest "Phog" Allen		
1935-36	21-2	10-0	Ray Ebling	12.2	Forrest "Phog" Allen		

SEAS.	W-L	CONF.	POSTSEASON	SCORING		REBOUNDS		ASSISTS		COACH	RECORD	
1936-37	15-4	8-2		Fred Pralle	8.8					Forrest "Phog" Allen		
1937-38	18-2	9-1		Fred Pralle	10.7					Forrest "Phog" Allen		
1938-39	13-7	6-4		Howard Engleman	6.4					Forrest "Phog" Allen		
1939-40	19-6	8-2	NCAA RUNNER-UP	Ralph Miller	9.1					Forrest "Phog" Allen		
1940-41	12-6	7-3		Howard Engleman	16.1					Forrest "Phog" Allen		
1941-42	17-5	8-2	NCAA REGIONAL SEMIFINALS	Ralph Miller	13.4					Forrest "Phog" Allen		
1942-43	22-6	10-0		Otto Schnellbacher	16.3					Forrest "Phog" Allen		
1943-44	17-9	5-5		Don Barrington	9.7					Forrest "Phog" Allen		
1944-45	12-5	8-4		Charlie Moffett	9.7					Forrest "Phog" Allen		
1945-46	19-2	10-0		Charlie Black	16.3					Forrest "Phog" Allen		
1946-47	16-11	5-5		Charlie Black	11.3					Forrest "Phog" Allen		
1947-48	9-15	4-8		Otto Schnellbacher	13.5					Forrest "Phog" Allen		
1948-49	12-12	3-9		Gene Peterson	11.6					Forrest "Phog" Allen		
1949-50	14-11	8-4		Clyde Lovellette	21.8					Forrest "Phog" Allen		
1950-51	16-8	8-4		Clyde Lovellette	22.8					Forrest "Phog" Allen		
1951-52	**28-3**	**11-1**	**NATIONAL CHAMPION**	**Clyde Lovellette**	**28.6**	**Clyde Lovellette**	**13.2**			**Forrest "Phog" Allen**		
1952-53	19-6	10-2	NCAA RUNNER-UP	B.H. Born	18.9	B.H. Born	11.2			Forrest "Phog" Allen		
1953-54	16-5	10-2		B.H. Born	19.0					Forrest "Phog" Allen		
1954-55	11-10	5-7		Dallas Dobbs	15.9					Forrest "Phog" Allen		
1955-56	14-9	6-6		Maurice King	14.0	Lew Johnson	10.0			Forrest "Phog" Allen	590-219	.729
1956-57	24-3	11-1	NCAA RUNNER-UP	Wilt Chamberlain	29.6	Wilt Chamberlain	18.9			Dick Harp		
1957-58	18-5	8-4		Wilt Chamberlain	30.1	Wilt Chamberlain	17.5			Dick Harp		
1958-59	11-14	8-6		Ron Loneski	19.0	Bill Bridges	13.7			Dick Harp		
1959-60	19-9	10-4	NCAA REGIONAL FINALS	Wayne Hightower	21.8	Bill Bridges	13.8			Dick Harp		
1960-61	17-8	10-4		Wayne Hightower	20.7	Bill Bridges	14.1			Dick Harp		
1961-62	7-18	3-11		Jerry Gardner	20.7	Joe Dumas	9.1			Dick Harp		
1962-63	12-13	5-9		George Unseld	17.2	George Unseld	8.0			Dick Harp		
1963-64	13-12	8-6		George Unseld	18.4	George Unseld	7.4			Dick Harp	121-82	.596
1964-65	17-8	9-5		Walt Wesley	23.5	Walt Wesley	8.8			Ted Owens		
1965-66	23-4	13-1	NCAA REGIONAL FINALS	Walt Wesley	20.7	Walt Wesley	9.3			Ted Owens		
1966-67	23-4	13-1	NCAA REGIONAL SEMIFINALS	Rodger Bohnenstiehl	16.4	Ron Franz	6.9			Ted Owens		
1967-68	22-8	10-4	NIT RUNNER-UP	Jo Jo White	15.3	Dave Nash	6.5			Ted Owens		
1968-69	20-7	9-5	NIT FIRST ROUND	Dave Robisch	18.1	Dave Robisch	7.4			Ted Owens		
1969-70	17-9	8-6		Dave Robisch	26.5	Dave Robisch	12.1			Ted Owens		
1970-71	27-3	14-0	NCAA FOURTH PLACE	Dave Robisch	19.2	Roger Brown	11.1			Ted Owens		
1971-72	11-15	7-7		Bud Stallworth	25.3	Bud Stallworth	7.7			Ted Owens		
1972-73	8-18	4-10		Richard Suttle	16.3	Richard Suttle	8.2			Ted Owens		
1973-74	23-7	13-1	NCAA FOURTH PLACE	Danny Knight	12.4	Danny Knight	7.1			Ted Owens		
1974-75	19-8	11-3	NCAA FIRST ROUND	Richard Suttle	14.6	Norman Cook	8.2	Dale Greenlee	3.7	Ted Owens		
1975-76	13-13	6-8		Norman Cook	14.8	Norman Cook	7.9	Clint Johnson	2.5	Ted Owens		
1976-77	18-10	8-6		John Douglas	19.2	Herb Nobles	8.2	Herb Nobles	2.8	Ted Owens		
1977-78	24-5	13-1	NCAA FIRST ROUND	Darnell Valentine	13.5	Paul Mokeski	8.5	Darnell Valentine	4.5	Ted Owens		
1978-79	18-11	8-6		Darnell Valentine	16.1	Paul Mokeski	8.3	Darnell Valentine	5.8	Ted Owens		
1979-80	15-14	7-7		Darnell Valentine	16.5	John Crawford	4.8	Darnell Valentine	4.8	Ted Owens		
1980-81	24-8	9-5	NCAA REGIONAL SEMIFINALS	Tony Guy	15.8	Art Housey	6.5	Darnell Valentine	5.3	Ted Owens		
1981-82	13-14	4-10		David Magley	17.3	David Magley	8.4	Tony Guy	3.8	Ted Owens		
1982-83	13-16	4-10		Carl Henry	17.4	Kelly Knight	7.2	Jeff Guiot	3.0	Ted Owens	348-182	.657
1983-84	22-10	9-5	NCAA SECOND ROUND	Carl Henry	16.8	Kelly Knight	7.0	Mark Turgeon	4.3	Larry Brown		
1984-85	26-8	11-3	NCAA SECOND ROUND	Ronald Kellogg	17.6	Danny Manning	7.6	Cedric Hunter	4.3	Larry Brown		
1985-86	35-4	13-1	NCAA NATIONAL SEMIFINALS	Danny Manning	16.7	Danny Manning	6.3	Cedric Hunter	7.1	Larry Brown		
1986-87	25-11	9-5	NCAA REGIONAL SEMIFINALS	Danny Manning	23.9	Danny Manning	9.5	Cedric Hunter	5.8	Larry Brown		
1987-88	**27-11**	**9-5**	**NATIONAL CHAMPION**	**Danny Manning**	**24.8**	**Danny Manning**	**9.0**	**Kevin Pritchard**	**2.9**	**Larry Brown**	**135-44**	**.754**
1988-89	19-12	6-8		Milt Newton	17.7	Mark Randall	6.7	Scooter Barry	5.7	Roy Williams		
1989-90	30-5	11-3	NCAA SECOND ROUND	Kevin Pritchard	14.5	Mark Randall	6.2	Kevin Pritchard	5.1	Roy Williams		
1990-91	27-8	10-4	NCAA RUNNER-UP	Terry Brown	16.0	Alonzo Jamison	6.4	Adonis Jordan	4.5	Roy Williams		
1991-92	27-5	11-3	NCAA SECOND ROUND	Rex Walters	16.0	Richard Scott	4.7	Adonis Jordan	4.4	Roy Williams		
1992-93	29-7	11-3	NCAA NATIONAL SEMIFINALS	Rex Walters	15.3	Richard Scott	5.3	Adonis Jordan	4.5	Roy Williams		
1993-94	27-8	9-5	NCAA REGIONAL SEMIFINALS	Steve Woodberry	15.5	Greg Ostertag	8.8	Jacque Vaughn	5.2	Roy Williams		
1994-95	25-6	11-3	NCAA REGIONAL SEMIFINALS	Jerod Haase	15.0	Greg Ostertag	7.5	Jacque Vaughn	7.7	Roy Williams		
1995-96	29-5	12-2	NCAA REGIONAL FINALS	Raef LaFrentz	13.4	Raef LaFrentz	8.2	Jacque Vaughn	6.6	Roy Williams		
1996-97	34-2	15-1	NCAA REGIONAL SEMIFINALS	Raef LaFrentz	18.5	Raef LaFrentz	9.3	Jacque Vaughn	6.2	Roy Williams		
1997-98	35-4	15-1	NCAA SECOND ROUND	Paul Pierce	20.4	Raef LaFrentz	11.4	Ryan Robertson	6.4	Roy Williams		
1998-99	23-10	11-5	NCAA SECOND ROUND	Eric Chenowith	13.5	Eric Chenowith	9.1	Jeff Boschee	3.7	Roy Williams		
1999-2000	24-10	11-5	NCAA SECOND ROUND	Kenny Gregory	12.8	Drew Gooden	7.5	Kirk Hinrich	3.6	Roy Williams		
2000-01	26-7	12-4	NCAA REGIONAL SEMIFINALS	Kenny Gregory	15.6	Eric Chenowith	7.6	Kirk Hinrich	6.9	Roy Williams		
2001-02	33-4	16-0	NCAA NATIONAL SEMIFINALS	Drew Gooden	19.8	Drew Gooden	11.4	Aaron Miles	6.8	Roy Williams		
2002-03	30-8	14-2	NCAA RUNNER-UP	Nick Collison	18.5	Nick Collison	10.0	Aaron Miles	6.4	Roy Williams	418-101	.805
2003-04	24-9	12-4	NCAA REGIONAL FINALS	Wayne Simien	17.8	Wayne Simien	9.3	Aaron Miles	7.3	Bill Self		
2004-05	23-7	12-4	NCAA FIRST ROUND	Wayne Simien	20.3	Wayne Simien	11.0	Aaron Miles	7.2	Bill Self		
2005-06	25-8	13-3	NCAA FIRST ROUND	Brandon Rush	13.5	Brandon Rush	5.9	Russell Robinson	4.6	Bill Self		
2006-07	33-5	14-2	NCAA REGIONAL FINALS	Brandon Rush	13.8	Julian Wright	7.8	Russell Robinson	4.4	Bill Self		
2007-08	**37-3**	**13-3**	**NATIONAL CHAMPION**	**Brandon Rush**	**13.3**	**Darnell Jackson**	**6.7**	**Mario Chalmers**	**4.3**	**Bill Self**		
2008-09	27-8	14-2	NCAA REGIONAL SEMIFINALS	Sherron Collins	18.9	Cole Aldrich	11.1	Sherron Collins	5.0	Bill Self	169-40	.809

ESPN 27 SAGARIN

Kansas State

The K-State coaching lineage reads like a biblical role call: Jack Gardner begat Tex Winter who begat Cotton Fitzsimmons who begat Jack Hartman who begat Lon Kruger who begat Dana Altman. That coaching legacy, as much as the school's long list of playing greats, is why the Wildcats boast more than 1,300 wins, plus 23 Tournament appearances and four Final Four showings.

BEST TEAM: 1950-51 It was nearly the perfect storybook season. K-State opened fabled Ahearn Field House, an arena that rang with deafening noise from the very first game. Senior captain Ernie Barrett used his long-range touch to earn second-team All-America honors. And the balanced Wildcats (25–4) won the Big Seven, then beat Arizona, BYU and Oklahoma A&M (now Oklahoma State) in the NCAA Tournament, before losing to Kentucky in the Final.

BEST PLAYER: F Bob Boozer (1956-59) The 6'8", 215-pound power forward came off double picks time and time again to nail 20-foot jumpers. And even though he was oh-so-predictable, nobody could stop him. The two-time All-America averaged 21.9 ppg and 10.7 rpg in his career.

BEST COACH: Jack Gardner (1939-42, '46-53) Known as the Father of Kansas State Basketball, Gardner was a tactical innovator who tutored another hoops genius, his Wildcats assistant Tex Winter, the triangle offense specialist. But Gardner also knew how to inspire brilliant team play, with his leading scorer sometimes averaging only 10 points per game.

GAME FOR THE AGES: In the Midwest Regional semifinals of the 1958 NCAA Tournament, Kansas State found a brilliant way to thwart Cincinnati star Oscar Robertson: Leave it to the refs. In the closing seconds of regulation, the Big O was fouled. He tied the game with his first free throw, but before his second shot Robertson put the ball down and walked the length of the court to calm himself. An official started counting—a player only has 10 seconds in which to take a foul shot—and Robertson rushed back to the line. He missed, sending the game into overtime. The Wildcats pulled it out in the extra frame, 83-80.

HEARTBREAKER: Kansas' Jay Roberts scored only 29 points in his college career, but two of them ruined K-State's holiday. In a Big Eight Holiday Tournament game on Dec. 29, 1962, the Wildcats took the Jayhawks to four overtimes. When Kansas State triple-teamed star Nolen Ellison on the final possession, Roberts made an open 12-footer that clinched a 90-88 KU win.

FIERCEST RIVAL: The Sunflower Showdown between Kansas State and Kansas dates back to 1857, when the communities of Manhattan and Lawrence started arguing about which was the better site for the official state university. Since the feud took to the basketball court in 1907, it has featured such memorable clashes as Mitch Richmond vs. Danny Manning, Rolando Blackman vs. Darnell Valentine and Bob Boozer vs. Wilt Chamberlain. Although KU leads 177–90, K-State fans have had their share of fun: To mock the Jayhawks and their nickname, students would throw live chickens on the floor during pregame introductions, until the university cracked down on the practice.

FANFARE AND HOOPLA: Dubbed the Octagon of Doom because of its eight-sided design, the Bramlage Coliseum turns into a wall of noise when fans break into the "Wildcat Victory" or the "Wabash Cannonball" fight songs.

FAN FAVORITE: G Ernie Barrett (1948-51) The long-range bomber with the feathery touch later became the Kansas State athletic director with a strong-as-oak handshake and always-welcoming smile. A statue of Barrett, who was known as Mr. K-State, was erected in 1999, fittingly, in front of Bramlage Coliseum.

THE SCHOOLS

CONSENSUS ALL-AMERICAS

1917	**F.I. Reynolds**, F
1958, '59	**Bob Boozer**, F
2008	**Michael Beasley**, F

FIRST-ROUND PRO PICKS

1949	**Howie Shannon**, Providence (1)
1951	**Ernie Barrett**, Boston (7)
1959	**Bob Boozer**, Cincinnati (1)
1976	**Chuckie Williams**, Cleveland (15)
1978	**Mike Evans**, Denver (21)
1981	**Rolando Blackman**, Dallas (9)
1988	**Mitch Richmond**, Golden State (5)
2008	**Michael Beasley**, Miami (2)

PROFILE

Kansas State University, Manhattan, KS
Founded: 1863
Enrollment: 23,520 (18,761 undergraduate)
Colors: Purple and white
Nickname: Wildcats
Current arena: Bramlage Coliseum, opened in 1988 (13,344)
Previous arenas: Ahearn Field House, 1950-88 (11,220); Nichols Gym, 1911-50 (2,800)
First game: Jan. 16, 1903
All-time record: 1,433-1,040 (.579)
Total weeks in AP Top 20/25: 162
Current conference: Big 12 (1996-)
Conference titles:
Missouri Valley: 2 (1917, '19)
Big Seven: 4 (1948, '50 [tie], '51, '56)
Big Eight: 11 (1958, '59, '60 [tie], '61, '63 [tie], '64, '68, '70, '72, '73, '77)
Conference tournament titles:
Big Eight: 2 (1977, '80)
NCAA Tournament appearances: 23
Sweet 16s (since 1975): 5
Final Fours: 4
NIT appearances: 7
Semifinals: 1

TOP 5

G	**Rolando Blackman** (1977-81)
G	**Mitch Richmond** (1986-88)
G	**Chuckie Williams** (1972-76)
F	**Michael Beasley** (2007-08)
F	**Bob Boozer** (1956-59)

RECORDS

RECORDS	GAME		SEASON		CAREER	
POINTS	62	Askia Jones, vs. Fresno State (March 24, 1994)	866	Michael Beasley (2007-08)	2,115	Mike Evans (1974-78)
POINTS PER GAME			26.2	Michael Beasley (2007-08)	21.9	Bob Boozer (1956-59)
REBOUNDS	27	David Hall, vs. Oklahoma (Jan. 25, 1971)	408	Michael Beasley (2007-08)	1,069	Ed Nealy (1978-82)
ASSISTS	16	Keith Frazier, vs. Central Missouri State (Dec. 18, 1976)	186	Steve Henson (1987-88)	582	Steve Henson (1986-90)

SEASON REVIEW

SEASON	W-L	CONF.	SCORING	COACH	RECORD
1903-16	*87-72*		*Only early coach with losing record, C.W. Melick (6-9 in 1905-06)*		
1916-17	15-2	10-2		Zora G. Clevenger	
1917-18	12-5	10-5		Zora G. Clevenger	
1918-19	17-2	10-2		Zora G. Clevenger	
1919-20	10-8	8-8		Zora G. Clevenger	54-17 .761
1920-21	14-5	11-5		E.A. Knoth	14-5 .737
1921-22	3-14	3-13		E.C. Curtis	
1922-23	2-14	2-14		E.C. Curtis	5-28 .152
1923-24	8-8	8-8		Charles Corsaut	
1924-25	10-8	10-6		Charles Corsaut	
1925-26	11-7	9-3		Charles Corsaut	
1926-27	10-8	6-6		Charles Corsaut	
1927-28	8-10	8-10		Charles Corsaut	
1928-29	6-10	2-8		Charles Corsaut	
1929-30	9-7	4-6		Charles Corsaut	
1930-31	11-6	5-5		Charles Corsaut	
1931-32	7-8	5-5		Charles Corsaut	
1932-33	9-9	4-6		Charles Corsaut	89-81 .524
1933-34	3-15	2-8		Frank Root	
1934-35	5-15	4-12		Frank Root	
1935-36	9-9	3-7		Frank Root	
1936-37	9-9	5-5		Frank Root	

SEAS.	W-L	CONF.	POSTSEASON	SCORING	REBOUNDS	ASSISTS	COACH	RECORD
1937-38	7-11	3-7					Frank Root	
1938-39	5-13	2-8					Frank Root	38-72 .345
1939-40	6-12	2-8					Jack Gardner	
1940-41	6-12	3-7					Jack Gardner	
1941-42	8-10	3-7					Jack Gardner	
1942-43	6-14	1-9					Chili Cochrane	6-14 .300
1943-44	7-15	1-9					Cliff Rock	7-15 .318
1944-45	10-13	5-7					Fritz Knorr	
1945-46	4-20	2-8					Fritz Knorr	14-33 .298
1946-47	14-10	3-7		Harold Howey 10.1			Jack Gardner	
1947-48	22-6	9-3	NCAA FOURTH PLACE	Howie Shannon 9.8			Jack Gardner	
1948-49	13-11	8-4		Rick Harman 11.1			Jack Gardner	
1949-50	17-7	8-4		Rick Harman 11.2			Jack Gardner	
1950-51	25-4	11-1	NCAA RUNNER-UP	Ernie Barrett 10.3	Lew Hitch 8.7		Jack Gardner	
1951-52	19-5	10-2		Dick Knostman 16.3	Dick Knostman 13.3		Jack Gardner	
1952-53	17-4	9-3		Dick Knostman 22.7	Dick Knostman 11.9		Jack Gardner	147-81 .645
1953-54	11-10	5-7		Jesse Prisock 14.8	Jesse Prisock 6.0		Tex Winter	
1954-55	11-10	6-6		Roger Craft 12.1	Roger Craft 8.0		Tex Winter	
1955-56	17-8	9-3	NCAA REGIONAL SEMIFINALS	Jack Parr 17.4	Jack Parr 13.6		Tex Winter	
1956-57	15-8	8-4		Bob Boozer, Jack Parr 20.6	Bob Boozer 10.3		Tex Winter	
1957-58	22-5	10-2	NCAA FOURTH PLACE	Bob Boozer 20.1	Bob Boozer 10.4		Tex Winter	
1958-59	25-2	14-0	NCAA REGIONAL FINALS	Bob Boozer 25.6	Bob Boozer 11.3		Tex Winter	
1959-60	16-10	10-4		Wally Frank 14.7	Wally Frank 7.4		Tex Winter	
1960-61	22-5 ⊗	12-2	NCAA REGIONAL FINALS	Larry Comley 18.3	Larry Comley 11.7		Tex Winter	
1961-62	22-3	12-2		Mike Wroblewski 19.0	Pat McKenzie 9.4		Tex Winter	
1962-63	16-9	11-3		Willie Murrell 18.6	Willie Murrell 10.2		Tex Winter	
1963-64	22-7	12-2	NCAA FOURTH PLACE	Willie Murrell 22.3	Willie Murrell 11.1		Tex Winter	
1964-65	12-13	5-9		Ron Paradis 12.3	Roy Smith 8.9		Tex Winter	
1965-66	14-11	9-5		Nick Pino 10.9	Nick Pino 7.0		Tex Winter	
1966-67	17-8	9-5		D. Berkholtz, E. Seyfert 13.8	Earl Seyfert 8.2		Tex Winter	
1967-68	19-9	11-3	NCAA REGIONAL SEMIFINALS	Steven Honeycutt 14.4	Gene Williams 10.1		Tex Winter	261-118 .689
1968-69	14-12	9-5		Jerry Venable 14.8	Gene Williams 11.4		Cotton Fitzsimmons	
1969-70	20-8	10-4	NCAA REGIONAL SEMIFINALS	Jerry Venable 16.1	David Hall 9.8		Cotton Fitzsimmons	34-20 .630
1970-71	11-15	6-8		Steve Mitchell 14.3	David Hall 10.9		Jack Hartman	
1971-72	19-9	12-2	NCAA REGIONAL FINALS	David Hall 13.2	David Hall 9.5		Jack Hartman	
1972-73	23-5	12-2	NCAA REGIONAL FINALS	Steve Mitchell 15.2	Steve Mitchell 8.9		Jack Hartman	
1973-74	19-8	11-3		Lon Kruger 17.6	Larry Williams 7.4		Jack Hartman	
1974-75	20-9	10-4	NCAA REGIONAL FINALS	Chuckie Williams 22.1	Carl Gerlach 8.6		Jack Hartman	
1975-76	20-8	11-3	NIT QUARTERFINALS	Chuckie Williams 20.9	Carl Gerlach 8.8		Jack Hartman	
1976-77	23-8 ⊗	11-3	NCAA REGIONAL SEMIFINALS	Mike Evans 18.3	Larry Dassie 8.7	Mike Evans 2.9	Jack Hartman	
1977-78	18-11	7-7		Mike Evans 19.1	Steve Soldner 7.4	Mike Evans 3.1	Jack Hartman	
1978-79	16-12	8-6		Rolando Blackman 17.3	Ed Nealy 8.2	Glenn Marshall 3.1	Jack Hartman	
1979-80	22-9	8-6	NCAA SECOND ROUND	Rolando Blackman 17.9	Ed Nealy 8.7	Rolando Blackman 3.0	Jack Hartman	
1980-81	24-9	9-5	NCAA REGIONAL FINALS	Rolando Blackman 15.0	Ed Nealy 9.1	Tim Jankovich 3.6	Jack Hartman	
1981-82	23-8	10-4	NCAA REGIONAL SEMIFINALS	Tyrone Adams 14.9	Ed Nealy 8.7	Tyrone Adams 4.2	Jack Hartman	
1982-83	12-16	4-10		Les Craft 11.7	Les Craft 5.3	Ed Galvao 3.5	Jack Hartman	
1983-84	14-15	5-9		Eddie Elder 13.1	Eddie Elder 7.1	Jim Roder 5.6	Jack Hartman	
1984-85	14-14	5-9		Tom Alfaro 13.7	Eddie Elder 7.1	Tom Alfaro, Mark Bohm 2.6	Jack Hartman	
1985-86	16-14	4-10		Norris Coleman 21.8	Norris Coleman 8.0	Ron Meyer 3.0	Jack Hartman	294-170 .634▼
1986-87	20-11	8-6	NCAA SECOND ROUND	N. Coleman, M. Richmond 20.7	Norris Coleman 8.4	Steve Henson 3.7	Lon Kruger	
1987-88	25-9	11-3	NCAA REGIONAL FINALS	Mitch Richmond 22.6	Charles Bledsoe 7.4	Steve Henson 5.5	Lon Kruger	
1988-89	19-11	8-6	NCAA FIRST ROUND	Steve Henson 18.5	Fred McCoy 6.6	Steve Henson 4.7	Lon Kruger	
1989-90	17-15	7-7	NCAA FIRST ROUND	Steve Henson 17.4	Tony Massop 6.6	Steve Henson 4.4	Lon Kruger	81-46 .638
1990-91	13-15	3-11		Jean Derouillere 17.2	Keith Amerson 6.1	Jeff Wires 3.8	Dana Altman	
1991-92	16-14	5-9	NIT SECOND ROUND	Askia Jones 15.5	Wylie Howard 6.6	Marcus Zeigler 5.4	Dana Altman	
1992-93	19-11	7-7	NCAA FIRST ROUND	Vincent Jackson 13.7	Deryl Cunningham 8.3	Anthony Beane 4.6	Dana Altman	
1993-94	20-14	4-10	NIT FOURTH PLACE	Askia Jones 22.1	Deryl Cunningham 8.7	Anthony Beane 4.5	Dana Altman	68-54 .557
1994-95	12-15	3-11		Elliot Hatcher 13.4	T. Davis, Demond Davis 6.2	Elliot Hatcher 3.1	Tom Asbury	
1995-96	17-12	7-7	NCAA FIRST ROUND	Elliot Hatcher 16.4	Tyrone Davis 8.2	Elliot Hatcher 3.3	Tom Asbury	
1996-97	10-17	3-13		Mark Young 12.9	Shawn Rhodes 6.4	Aaron Swartzendruber 2.9	Tom Asbury	
1997-98	17-12	7-9	NIT FIRST ROUND	Manny Dies 15.7	Manny Dies 7.6	Aaron Swartzendruber 3.4	Tom Asbury	
1998-99	20-13	7-9	NIT FIRST ROUND	Manny Dies 10.0	Tony Kitt 7.6	Chris Griffin 4.1	Tom Asbury	
1999-2000	9-19	2-14		Cortez Groves 16.1	Tony Kitt 9.1	Galen Morrison 2.7	Tom Asbury	85-88 .491
2000-01	11-18	4-12		Phineas Atchison 11.7	Travis Reynolds 7.7	Larry Reid 3.8	Jim Wooldridge	
2001-02	13-16	6-10		Larry Reid 14.4	Pervis Pasco 8.4	Larry Reid 5.3	Jim Wooldridge	
2002-03	13-17	4-12		Gilson DeJesus 11.2	Pervis Pasco 7.5	Frank Richards 4.9	Jim Wooldridge	
2003-04	14-14	6-10		Jeremiah Massey 14.7	Jeremiah Massey 7.8	Frank Richards 3.6	Jim Wooldridge	
2004-05	17-12	6-10		Jeremiah Massey 17.9	Jeremiah Massey 6.9	Clent Stewart 4.0	Jim Wooldridge	
2005-06	15-13	6-10		Cartier Martin 18.0	Cartier Martin 6.6	Clent Stewart 3.1	Jim Wooldridge	83-90 .480
2006-07	23-12	10-6	NIT SECOND ROUND	Cartier Martin 17.1	Akeem Wright 6.3	Clent Stewart 2.9	Bob Huggins	23-12 .657
2007-08	21-12	10-6	NCAA SECOND ROUND	Michael Beasley 26.2	Michael Beasley 12.4	Jacob Pullen 3.2	Frank Martin	
2008-09	22-12	9-7	NIT SECOND ROUND	Denis Clemente 15.0	Darren Kent 5.8	Denis Clemente 3.5	Frank Martin	43-24 .642

⊗ Record does not reflect games forfeited or vacated. For adjusted records, see p. 521.

▼ Coach's record adjusted to reflect games forfeited or vacated: 295-169, .636. For yearly totals, see p. 521.

ESPN 141 SAGARIN

KENT STATE

In 2008-09, the Golden Flashes fell one win shy of an 11th straight 20-win season. It's been a defining stretch for a mid-major which, for much of its nearly 100-year existence, has struggled to achieve and sustain success. In fact, it wasn't until 1986-87 that KSU finished as high as second in the Mid-American Conference and 2001-02 that it won its first regular-season league title.

BEST TEAM: 2001-02 The proof is in the NCAA bracket: The No. 10-seed Golden Flashes upset Oklahoma State (No. 7), Alabama (No. 2) and Pittsburgh (No. 3) before finally falling to Indiana in the Elite Eight. Led by Antonio Gates, a do-it-all point forward who went on to a Pro Bowl career as a tight end for the San Diego Chargers, KSU won 30 games for the first time.

BEST PLAYER: G Trevor Huffman (1998-2002) The 6'1" Huffman played a low-key, inconspicuous game, at least until it came time to blow by a defender or whiz a no-look pass past his face. The Michigan native finished as the Kent State career leader in points (1,820), three-pointers (210) and free throws (524).

BEST COACH: Gary Waters (1996-2001) He waited 22 years for his first head-coaching gig, then made it count. He led the Flashes to MAC tournament titles in 1999 and 2001 and engineered an upset of Indiana in the first round of the 2001 NCAA Tournament in what proved to be his last season on the KSU sideline.

GAME FOR THE AGES: "A validation of our place in history." That's how Huffman described KSU's 78-73 OT victory over Pitt in the Sweet 16 on March 21, 2002. He scored 17, Gates tallied 22 and the Golden Flashes forced 11 first-half turnovers and 17 for the game.

FIERCEST RIVAL: KSU's long-simmering rivalry with Akron, dating back to 1915, boiled over on Jan. 23, 2008, when the Golden Flashes erased a 10-point deficit to win, 75-69. After a late skirmish and unruly behavior by some M.A.C. Center fans, KSU senior Haminn Quaintance laughed and danced in the postgame handshake line until he was led from the court by his angry coach, Jim Christian. Kent State leads overall, 66–61.

SEASON REVIEW

SEAS.	W-L	CONF.	COACH	SEAS.	W-L	CONF.	COACH
1913-50	*268-288*	*18-4 in 1949-50*		1963-64	11-13	5-7	Bob Doll
1950-51	18-8		Dave McDowell	1964-65	9-11	4-8	Bob Doll
1951-52	14-10	3-7	Clarence Haerr	1965-66	8-16	3-9	Bob Doll
1952-53	7-15	3-9	Clarence Haerr	1966-67	5-18	1-11	Frank Truitt
1953-54	8-13	3-9	Clarence Haerr	1967-68	9-15	3-9	Frank Truitt
1954-55	8-14	5-9	Clarence Haerr	1968-69	14-10	6-6	Frank Truitt
1955-56	10-11	5-7	Dave McDowell	1969-70	7-17	2-8	Frank Truitt
1956-57	5-18	2-10	Dave McDowell	1970-71	13-11	4-6	Frank Truitt
1957-58	9-14	3-9	Bill Bertka	1971-72	7-17	6-4	Frank Truitt
1958-59	11-13	6-6	Bill Bertka	1972-73	10-16	5-7	Frank Truitt
1959-60	7-16	2-10	Bill Bertka	1973-74	9-17	1-11	Frank Truitt
1960-61	9-14	4-8	Bill Bertka	1974-75	6-20	3-11	Rex Hughes
1961-62	2-19	1-11	Bob Doll	1975-76	12-14	7-9	Rex Hughes
1962-63	3-18	1-11	Bob Doll	1976-77	8-19	4-12	Rex Hughes

SEAS.	W-L	CONF.		SCORING		COACH	RECORD	
1977-78	6-21	4-12		Burrell McGhee	22.8	Rex Hughes[a]	27-63	.300
1978-79	13-14	7-9		Burrell McGhee	22.4	Ed Douma		
1979-80	16-11	7-9		Trent Grooms	16.2	Ed Douma		
1980-81	7-19	5-11		Geoff Warren	9.8	Ed Douma		
1981-82	10-16	6-10		Dave Zeigler	13.3	Ed Douma	46-60	.434
1982-83	15-13	9-9		Dave Zeigler	18.4	Jim McDonald		
1983-84	15-14	8-10		Larry Robbins	17.3	Jim McDonald		
1984-85	17-13	11-7	■	Anthony Grier	20.9	Jim McDonald		
1985-86	11-16	7-11		Terry Wearsch	13.6	Jim McDonald		
1986-87	19-10	11-5		Jay Peters	17.3	Jim McDonald		
1987-88	10-18	6-10		Reggie Adams	14.8	Jim McDonald		
1988-89	20-11 ⊗	12-4	■	Eric Glenn	14.5	Jim McDonald		
1989-90	21-8	12-4	■	Ric Blevins	18.2	Jim McDonald		
1990-91	10-18	4-12		Tony Banks	15.3	Jim McDonald		
1991-92	9-19	6-10		Tony Banks	14.3	Jim McDonald	147-140	.512▼
1992-93	10-17	7-11		Greg Holman	14.7	Dave Grube		
1993-94	13-14	8-10		Nate Reinking	13.1	Dave Grube		
1994-95	8-19	5-13		Nate Reinking	14.8	Dave Grube		
1995-96	14-13	8-10		Nate Reinking	18.7	Dave Grube	45-63	.417
1996-97	9-18	7-11		D.J. Bosse	13.7	Gary Waters		
1997-98	13-17	9-9		Kyrem Massey	12.0	Gary Waters		
1998-99	23-7	13-5	●	John Whorton	12.8	Gary Waters		
1999-2000	23-8	13-5	■	Trevor Huffman	13.1	Gary Waters		
2000-01	24-10	13-5	●	Trevor Huffman	16.8	Gary Waters	92-60	.605
2001-02	30-6	17-1	●	Trevor Huffman	16.0	Stan Heath	30-6	.833
2002-03	21-10	12-6	■	Antonio Gates	20.6	Jim Christian		
2003-04	22-9	13-5	■	John Edwards	13.2	Jim Christian		
2004-05	20-13	11-7	■	Jason Edwin	12.2	Jim Christian		
2005-06	25-9	15-3	●	Jay Youngblood	14.6	Jim Christian		
2006-07	21-11	12-4		Omni Smith	13.9	Jim Christian		
2007-08	28-7	13-3	●	Al Fisher	13.9	Jim Christian	137-59	.699
2008-09	19-15	10-6		Al Fisher	15.1	Geno Ford	19-15	.599

[a] Rex Hughes (1-10) Mike Boyd (5-11) both coached during the 1977-78 season.

⊗ Records don't reflect games forfeited or vacated. For adjusted records, see p. 521.

▼ Coach's records adjusted to reflect games forfeited or vacated: 148-139, .516. For yearly totals, see p. 521.

● NCAA Tournament appearance ■ NIT appearance

PROFILE

Kent State University, Kent, OH
Founded: 1910
Enrollment: 22,819 (18,090 undergraduate)
Colors: Navy blue and gold
Nickname: Golden Flashes
Current arena: M.A.C. Center, opened in 1950 (6,327)
Previous: Wills Gymnasium, 1923-50 (N/A)
First game: 1913
All-time record: 1,029-1,109 (.481)
Total weeks in AP Top 20/25: 1

Current conference: Mid-American (1951-)
Conference titles:
MAC: 3 (2002, '06, '08)
Conference tournament titles:
MAC: 5 (1999, 2001, '02, '06, '08)
NCAA Tournament appearances: 5
Sweet 16s (since 1975): 1
NIT appearances: 7

TOP 5

G **DeAndre Haynes** (2002-06)
G **Trevor Huffman** (1998-2002)
F **Eric Glenn** (1986-90)
F **Trent Grooms** (1976-80)
F **Burrell McGhee** (1976-79)

RECORDS

RECORDS	GAME		SEASON		CAREER	
POINTS	49	Dan Potopsky, vs. Western Michigan (Feb. 5, 1955)	640	Antonio Gates (2002-03)	1,820	Trevor Huffman (1998-2002)
POINTS PER GAME			23.4	Dan Potopsky (1954-55)	21.6	Burrell McGhee (1976-79)
REBOUNDS	31	Leroy Thompson, vs. Case Western (Dec. 12, 1948); Fred Klaisner, vs. Western Reserve (1948)	423	Brad Robinson (1973-74)	1,012	Trent Grooms (1976-80)
ASSISTS	15	Joe McKeown, vs. Bowling Green (March 1, 1978)	180	DeAndre Haynes (2004-05)	625	DeAndre Haynes (2002-06)

THE SCHOOLS

ESPN 1 SAGARIN

KENTUCKY

Rick Pitino once called Kentucky the Roman Empire of college basketball—remarkable considering the Wildcats' humble beginnings. Legend has it that the First Five of J. White Guyn, R.H. Arnett, Joe Coons, H.J. Wurtele and Lee Andrus pooled their money to buy a $3 basketball. They lost their first game to Georgetown (Ky.), 15-6, on Feb. 6, 1903, and didn't have a winning season until 1909. In 1912 they were "Southern Champions" and the rest is pure hoops history: most NCAA victories, 45 conference titles and seven national championships.

BEST TEAM: 1995-96 Tony Delk and Antoine Walker, a.k.a. the Untouchables, kept UK at No. 1 for most of the season on the strength of a 27-game winning streak, then tore through the NCAA field. After UK avenged a regular-season loss to UMass in the Final Four, Delk tied a Final record with seven treys in the 76-67 title win over Syracuse.

BEST PLAYER: C DAN ISSEL (1967-70) Slick, smooth, athletic—that wasn't Issel. Yet, armed with an accurate outside shot and legendary engine—he was called Horse—the 6'8" center was a consensus All-America as a senior and remains UK's all-time leader in points and rebounds.

BEST COACH: ADOLPH RUPP (1930-72) While a player at Kansas, he learned from the game's seminal legends, Phog Allen and Dr. James Naismith. Rupp then became a legend himself, even though his Wildcats were the first recipient of the NCAA's death penalty—barred from play in 1952-53 in the wake of revelations resulting from point-shaving charges. Rupp's final numbers: 876 wins, 27 SEC regular-season titles, four NCAA titles, one NIT championship and an Olympic gold medal.

GAME FOR THE AGES: With a Final Four spot on the line against Duke on March 22, 1998, Cat fans had to suffer through endless replays of Christian Laettner's miracle game-winner six years earlier. But UK overcame a 17-point second-half deficit to win, 86-84.

HEARTBREAKER: Speaking of the Shot, in the 1992 Elite Eight, Kentucky's Sean Woods hit a bucket with :02 remaining in OT to put UK up 103-102. After a timeout, Laettner caught Grant Hill's inbounds pass at the Duke free throw line, turned, let fly—and ripped the heart out of the Bluegrass State.

FIERCEST RIVAL: Rupp refused to play Louisville again after losing to the Cardinals in the 1959 NCAA Tournament. When the teams were finally forced together in the 1983 Elite Eight, UL triumphed once more in an overtime classic. Since Pitino took the Cardinals helm in 2001, things have gotten downright ugly. Once considered UK's savior, Pitino is now Benedict Rick and is booed mercilessly in Rupp Arena. Kentucky leads overall, 26–14.

FANFARE AND HOOPLA: A 15-year-old Louisville native named Scott Padgett was one of those UK fans who felt the thrust of Laettner's dagger in 1992. Six years later, Padgett got his revenge on Duke, hitting the game-winning three with :39 left in the Sequel.

FAN FAVORITE: F COTTON NASH (1961-64) He could score from pretty much anywhere and played every position—later including first base and outfield (White Sox, Twins) while moonlighting from the NBA and ABA (Lakers, Warriors, Colonels).

CONSENSUS ALL-AMERICAS

1921	**Basil Hayden,** G/F
1925	**Burgess Carey,** G
1932, '33	**Forest Sale,** C/F
1935	**LeRoy Edwards,** C
1944	**Bob Brannum,** C
1947, '49	**Alex Groza,** C
1947-49	**Ralph Beard,** G
1951	**Bill Spivey,** C
1952, '54	**Cliff Hagan,** C/F
1959	**Johnny Cox,** F
1964	**Cotton Nash,** F
1970	**Dan Issel,** C
1980	**Kyle Macy,** G
1986	**Kenny Walker,** F
1993	**Jamal Mashburn,** F
1996	**Tony Delk,** G
1997	**Ron Mercer,** G/F

FIRST-ROUND PRO PICKS

1949	**Alex Groza,** Indianapolis (2)
1949	**Wallace Jones,** Washington (9)
1953	**Frank Ramsey,** Boston (6)
1967	**Louie Dampier,** Kentucky (ABA)
1967	**Pat Riley,** San Diego (7)
1975	**Kevin Grevey,** Washington (18)
1975	**Kevin Grevey,** San Diego (ABA, 8)
1978	**Rick Robey,** Indiana (3)
1978	**Jack Givens,** Atlanta (16)
1979	**Kyle Macy,** Phoenix (22)
1984	**Sam Bowie,** Portland (2)
1984	**Mel Turpin,** Washington (6)
1986	**Kenny Walker,** New York (5)
1988	**Rex Chapman,** Charlotte (8)
1993	**Jamal Mashburn,** Dallas (4)
1996	**Antoine Walker,** Boston (6)
1996	**Tony Delk,** Charlotte (16)
1996	**Walter McCarty,** New York (19)
1997	**Ron Mercer,** Boston (6)
1997	**Derek Anderson,** Cleveland (13)
1998	**Nazr Mohammed,** Utah (29)
1999	**Scott Padgett,** Utah (28)
2000	**Jamaal Magloire,** Charlotte (19)
2002	**Tayshaun Prince,** Detroit (23)
2006	**Rajon Rondo,** Phoenix (21)

PROFILE

University of Kentucky, Lexington, KY
Founded: 1865
Enrollment: 27,000 (18,434 undergraduate)
Colors: Blue and white
Nickname: Wildcats
Current arena: Rupp Arena, opened in 1976 (23,000)
Previous: Memorial Coliseum, 1950-76 (8,700); Alumni Gym, 1924-50 (3,500); Pre-Alumni Gym, 1903-24 (N/A)
First game: Feb. 6, 1903
All-time record: 1,990-636-1 (.758)
Total weeks in AP Top 20/25: 726
Current conference: Southeastern (1932-)

Conference titles:
Southern: 2 (1926, '32 [tie]); SEC: 44 (1933, '35 [tie], '37, '39, '40, '42, '44, '45, '46, '47, '48, '49, '50, '51, '52, '54 [tie], '55, '57, '58, '62 [tie], '64, '66, '68, '69, '70, '71, '72 [tie], '73, '75 [tie], '77 [tie], '78, '80, '82 [tie], '83, '84, '86, '88-v, '95, '96, '98, 2000 [tie], '01 [tie], '03, '05)
Conference tournament titles:
Southern: 1 (1921); SEC: 26 (1933, '37, '39, '40, '42, '44, '45, '46, '47, '48, '49, '50, '52, '84, '86, '88-v, '92, '93, '94, '95, '97, '98, '99, 2001, '03, '04)
NCAA Tournaments: 50 (1 appearance vacated)
Sweet 16s (since 1975): 20
Final Fours: 13
Titles: 7 (1948, '49, '51, '58, '78, '96, '98)

NIT appearances: 7
Semifinals: 4
Titles: 2 (1946, '76)
v – title vacated

TOP 5

G	**Ralph Beard** (1945-49)
G	**Frank Ramsey** (1950-52, '53-54)
F	**Jack Givens** (1974-78)
F/C	**Cliff Hagan** (1950-52, '53-54)
C	**Dan Issel** (1967-70)

RECORDS

RECORDS	GAME		SEASON		CAREER	
POINTS	54	Jodie Meeks, vs. Tennessee (Jan. 13, 2009)	948	Dan Issel (1969-70)	2,138	Dan Issel (1967-70)
POINTS PER GAME			33.9	Dan Issel (1969-70)	25.8	Dan Issel (1967-70)
REBOUNDS	34	Bob Burrow, vs. Temple (Dec. 10, 1955); Bill Spivey, vs. Xavier (Feb. 13, 1951)	567	Bill Spivey (1950-51)	1,078	Dan Issel (1967-70)
ASSISTS	15	Travis Ford, vs. Eastern Kentucky (Dec. 8, 1993)	232	Roger Harden (1985-86)	646	Dirk Minniefield (1979-83)

SEASON REVIEW

SEASON	W-L	CONF.	SCORING		COACH	RECORD	
1903-17	*75-71*		*Went 9-0 in 1911-12 and were proclaimed "Southern Champions"*				
1917-18	9-2-1				S.A. Boles	9-2-1	.818
1918-19	6-8				Andrew Gill	6-8	.429
1919-20	5-7				George C. Buchheit		
1920-21	13-1				George C. Buchheit		
1921-22	10-6	3-1			George C. Buchheit		
1922-23	3-10	0-5	Carl Riefkin	10.2	George C. Buchheit		
1923-24	13-3	6-2	Jim McFarland	9.8	George C. Buchheit	44-27	.620
1924-25	13-8	6-2	Jim McFarland	7.2	C.O. Applegran	13-8	.619
1925-26	15-3	8-0	Gayle Mohney	11.1	Ray Eklund	15-3	.833
1926-27	3-13	1-6	Paul Jenkins	6.1	Basil Hayden	3-13	.188
1927-28	12-6	8-1	Cecil Combs	10.3	John Mauer		
1928-29	12-5	7-4	Stan Milward	6.8	John Mauer		
1929-30	16-3	9-1	Cecil Combs	6.6	John Mauer	40-14	.741
1930-31	15-3	8-2	Carey Spicer	10.6	Adolph Rupp		
1931-32	15-2	9-1	Forest Sale	13.8	Adolph Rupp		
1932-33	21-3	8-0	Forest Sale	13.5	Adolph Rupp		
1933-34	16-1	11-0	John DeMoisey	12.5	Adolph Rupp		
1934-35	19-2	11-0	LeRoy Edwards	16.3	Adolph Rupp		
1935-36	15-6	6-2	Ralph Carlisle	11.5	Adolph Rupp		
1936-37	17-5	5-3	Ralph Carlisle	9.9	Adolph Rupp		
1937-38	13-5	6-0	Joe Hagan	10.2	Adolph Rupp		

SEAS.	W-L	CONF.	POSTSEASON	SCORING		REBOUNDS		ASSISTS		COACH	RECORD	
1938-39	16-4	5-2		Fred Curtis	9.2					Adolph Rupp		
1939-40	15-6	4-4		Mickey Rouse	8.3					Adolph Rupp		
1940-41	17-8	8-1		Jim King	6.0					Adolph Rupp		
1941-42	19-6	6-2	NCAA NATIONAL SEMIFINALS	Marvin Akers	7.6					Adolph Rupp		
1942-43	17-6	8-1		Milt Ticco	10.1					Adolph Rupp		
1943-44	19-2		NIT THIRD PLACE	Bob Brannum	12.1					Adolph Rupp		
1944-45	22-4	4-1	NCAA REGIONAL SEMIFINALS	Jack Tingle	11.3					Adolph Rupp		
1945-46	28-2	6-0	NIT CHAMPION	Jack Parkinson	11.3					Adolph Rupp		
1946-47	34-3	11-0	NIT RUNNER-UP	Alex Groza	10.6					Adolph Rupp		
1947-48	**36-3**	**9-0**	**NATIONAL CHAMPION**	**Ralph Beard**	**12.5**					**Adolph Rupp**		
1948-49	**32-2**	**13-0**	**NAT'L CHAMP, NIT QUARTERS**	**Alex Groza**	**20.5**					**Adolph Rupp**		
1949-50	25-5	11-2	NIT QUARTERFINALS	Bill Spivey	19.3					Adolph Rupp		
1950-51	**32-2**	**14-0**	**NATIONAL CHAMPION**	**Bill Spivey**	**19.2**	**Bill Spivey**	**17.2**			**Adolph Rupp**		
1951-52	29-3	14-0	NCAA REGIONAL FINALS	Cliff Hagan	21.6	Cliff Hagan	16.5			Adolph Rupp		
1952-53	no team											
1953-54	25-0	14-0		Cliff Hagan	24.0	Cliff Hagan	13.5			Adolph Rupp		
1954-55	23-3	12-2	NCAA REGIONAL SEMIFINALS	Bob Burrow	19.0	Bob Burrow	17.7			Adolph Rupp		
1955-56	20-6	12-2	NCAA REGIONAL FINALS	Bob Burrow	21.1	Bob Burrow	14.6			Adolph Rupp		
1956-57	23-5	12-2	NCAA REGIONAL FINALS	Johnny Cox	19.4	Ed Beck	14.1			Adolph Rupp		
1957-58	**23-6**	**12-2**	**NATIONAL CHAMPION**	**Vernon Hatton**	**17.1**	**Johnny Cox**	**12.6**			**Adolph Rupp**		
1958-59	24-3	12-2	NCAA REGIONAL SEMIFINALS	Johnny Cox	17.9	Johnny Cox	12.2			Adolph Rupp		
1959-60	18-7	10-4		Bill Lickert	14.4	Don Mills	12.9			Adolph Rupp		
1960-61	19-9	10-4	NCAA REGIONAL FINALS	Bill Lickert	16.0	Roger Newman	9.5			Adolph Rupp		
1961-62	23-3	13-1	NCAA REGIONAL FINALS	Cotton Nash	23.4	Cotton Nash	13.3	Scotty Baesler	4.3	Adolph Rupp		
1962-63	16-9	8-6		Cotton Nash	20.6	Cotton Nash	12.0	Cotton Nash	2.6	Adolph Rupp		
1963-64	21-6	11-3	NCAA REGIONAL SEMIFINALS	Cotton Nash	24.0	Cotton Nash	11.7	Larry Conley	4.2	Adolph Rupp		
1964-65	15-10	10-6		Louie Dampier	17.0	John Adams	8.6	Larry Conley	3.2	Adolph Rupp		
1965-66	27-2	15-1	NCAA RUNNER-UP	Pat Riley	22.0	Pat Riley	8.9	Larry Conley	3.4	Adolph Rupp		
1966-67	13-13	8-10		Louie Dampier	20.6	Thad Jaracz	8.3	Pat Riley	2.6	Adolph Rupp		
1967-68	22-5	15-3	NCAA REGIONAL FINALS	Mike Casey	20.1	Dan Issel	12.1	Mike Pratt	3.0	Adolph Rupp		
1968-69	23-5	16-2	NCAA REGIONAL SEMIFINALS	Dan Issel	26.6	Dan Issel	13.6	Mike Casey	4.6	Adolph Rupp		
1969-70	26-2	17-1	NCAA REGIONAL FINALS	Dan Issel	33.9	Dan Issel	13.2	Mike Pratt	3.5	Adolph Rupp		
1970-71	22-6	16-2	NCAA REGIONAL SEMIFINALS	Tom Parker	17.6	Tom Payne	10.1	Larry Steele	3.9	Adolph Rupp		
1971-72	21-7	14-4	NCAA REGIONAL FINALS	Jim Andrews	21.5	Jim Andrews	11.3	Stan Key	3.2	Adolph Rupp	876-190	.822
1972-73	20-8	14-4	NCAA REGIONAL FINALS	Jim Andrews	20.1	Jim Andrews	12.4	Jimmy Dan Conner	3.0	Joe B. Hall		
1973-74	13-13	9-9		Kevin Grevey	21.9	Bob Guyette	7.9	Mike Flynn	3.2	Joe B. Hall		
1974-75	26-5	15-3	NCAA RUNNER-UP	Kevin Grevey	23.6	Rick Robey	6.9	J. D. Conner, M. Flynn	3.4	Joe B. Hall		
1975-76	20-10	11-7	NIT CHAMPION	Jack Givens	20.1	Mike Phillips	9.8	Larry Johnson	3.3	Joe B. Hall		
1976-77	26-4	16-2	NCAA REGIONAL FINALS	Jack Givens	18.9	Rick Robey	9.1	Larry Johnson	4.8	Joe B. Hall		
1977-78	**30-2**	**16-2**	**NATIONAL CHAMPION**	**Jack Givens**	**18.1**	**Rick Robey**	**8.2**	**Kyle Macy**	**5.6**	**Joe B. Hall**		
1978-79	19-12	10-8	NIT FIRST ROUND	Kyle Macy	15.2	LaVon Williams	6.9	Kyle Macy	4.2	Joe B. Hall		
1979-80	29-6	15-3	NCAA REGIONAL SEMIFINALS	Kyle Macy	15.4	Sam Bowie	8.1	Kyle Macy	4.7	Joe B. Hall		
1980-81	22-6	15-3	NCAA SECOND ROUND	Sam Bowie	17.4	Sam Bowie	9.1	Dirk Minniefield	5.4	Joe B. Hall		
1981-82	22-8	13-5	NCAA FIRST ROUND	Derrick Hord	16.3	Mel Turpin	7.1	Dirk Minniefield	6.3	Joe B. Hall		
1982-83	23-8	13-5	NCAA REGIONAL FINALS	Mel Turpin	15.1	Mel Turpin	6.3	Dirk Minniefield	5.8	Joe B. Hall		
1983-84	29-5	14-4	NCAA NATIONAL SEMIFINALS	Mel Turpin	15.2	Sam Bowie	9.2	Dickey Beal	4.4	Joe B. Hall		
1984-85	18-13	11-7	NCAA REGIONAL SEMIFINALS	Kenny Walker	22.9	Kenny Walker	10.2	Roger Harden	4.7	Joe B. Hall	297-100	.748
1985-86	32-4	17-1	NCAA REGIONAL FINALS	Kenny Walker	20.0	Kenny Walker	7.7	Roger Harden	6.4	Eddie Sutton		
1986-87	18-11	10-8	NCAA FIRST ROUND	Rex Chapman	16.0	Richard Madison	7.4	Rex Chapman	3.6	Eddie Sutton		
1987-88	27-6 ⊗	13-5	NCAA REGIONAL SEMIFINALS	Rex Chapman	19.0	Winston Bennett	7.8	Ed Davender	4.0	Eddie Sutton		
1988-89	13-19	8-10		LeRon Ellis	16.0	Chris Mills	8.7	Sean Sutton	4.7	Eddie Sutton	90-40	.692▼
1989-90	14-14	10-8		Derrick Miller	19.2	Reggie Hanson	7.1	Sean Woods	5.9	Rick Pitino		
1990-91	22-6	14-4		John Pelphrey	14.4	Reggie Hanson	7.2	Sean Woods	5.6	Rick Pitino		
1991-92	29-7	12-4	NCAA REGIONAL FINALS	Jamal Mashburn	21.3	Jamal Mashburn	7.8	Sean Woods	4.6	Rick Pitino		
1992-93	30-4	13-3	NCAA NATIONAL SEMIFINALS	Jamal Mashburn	21.0	Jamal Mashburn	8.3	Travis Ford	4.9	Rick Pitino		
1993-94	27-7	12-4	NCAA SECOND ROUND	Tony Delk	16.6	Jared Prickett	7.0	Travis Ford	5.8	Rick Pitino		
1994-95	28-5	14-2	NCAA REGIONAL FINALS	Tony Delk	16.7	Mark Pope	6.3	Anthony Epps	4.2	Rick Pitino		
1995-96	**34-2**	**16-0**	**NATIONAL CHAMPION**	**Tony Delk**	**17.8**	**Antoine Walker**	**8.4**	**Anthony Epps**	**4.9**	**Rick Pitino**		
1996-97	35-5	13-3	NCAA RUNNER-UP	Ron Mercer	18.1	Jared Prickett	5.9	Anthony Epps	4.8	Rick Pitino	219-50	.814
1997-98	**35-4**	**14-2**	**NATIONAL CHAMPION**	**Jeff Sheppard**	**13.7**	**Nazr Mohammed**	**7.2**	**Wayne Turner**	**4.4**	**Tubby Smith**		
1998-99	28-9	11-5	NCAA REGIONAL FINALS	Scott Padgett	12.6	Scott Padgett	5.9	Wayne Turner	3.9	Tubby Smith		
1999-2000	23-10	12-4	NCAA SECOND ROUND	Tayshaun Prince	13.3	Jamaal Magloire	9.1	Saul Smith	3.5	Tubby Smith		
2000-01	24-10	12-4	NCAA REGIONAL SEMIFINALS	Keith Bogans	17.0	Tayshaun Prince	6.5	Saul Smith	3.9	Tubby Smith		
2001-02	22-10	10-6	NCAA REGIONAL SEMIFINALS	Tayshaun Prince	17.5	Tayshaun Prince	6.3	Cliff Hawkins	4.3	Tubby Smith		
2002-03	32-4	16-0	NCAA REGIONAL FINALS	Keith Bogans	15.7	Chuck Hayes	6.8	Cliff Hawkins	3.8	Tubby Smith		
2003-04	27-5	13-3	NCAA SECOND ROUND	Gerald Fitch	16.2	Chuck Hayes	8.1	Cliff Hawkins	5.2	Tubby Smith		
2004-05	28-6	14-2	NCAA REGIONAL FINALS	Kelenna Azubuike	14.7	Chuck Hayes	7.7	Patrick Sparks	3.6	Tubby Smith		
2005-06	22-13	9-7	NCAA SECOND ROUND	Randolph Morris	13.3	Rajon Rondo	6.1	Rajon Rondo	4.9	Tubby Smith		
2006-07	22-12	9-7	NCAA SECOND ROUND	Randolph Morris	16.1	Randolph Morris	7.8	Ramel Bradley	3.8	Tubby Smith	263-83	.760
2007-08	18-13	12-4	NCAA FIRST ROUND	Joe Crawford	17.3	Patrick Patterson	7.7	Ramel Bradley	3.3	Billy Gillispie		
2008-09	22-14	8-8	NIT QUARTERFINALS	Jodie Meeks	23.7	Patrick Patterson	9.3	DeAndre Liggins	2.8	Billy Gillispie	40-27	.597

⊗ Records don't reflect games forfeited or vacated. For adjusted records, see p. 521.

▼ Coach's record adjusted to reflect games forfeited or vacated: 88-39, .693. For yearly totals, see p. 521.

ESPN 71 SAGARIN

LA SALLE

Start with Naismith Hall of Fame superstar Tom Gola and 1980 U.S. Olympic team captain Michael Brooks. Add 11 NCAA and 11 NIT appearances, one 30-win season, 20 NBA players and two national titles. Toss in 1990 national Player of the Year Lionel Simmons. It all adds up to a team that's helped make Philadelphia an epicenter of college basketball lore.

BEST TEAM: 1968-69 Gola returned to the school that made his name one of the most famous in the game to coach a team with all five starters returning, including All-Americas Larry Cannon and Ken Durrett. Playing an up-tempo style with a weaving half-court offense, the Explorers dominated all season long, beating Florida State, Indiana, Loyola, Penn State and Villanova, among others. Unfortunately, La Salle was banned from postseason play because of rules infractions under previous coach Jim Harding, leaving Explorers fans to forever wonder, "What if?"

BEST PLAYER: C Tom Gola (1951-55) His coach, Ken Loeffler, dubbed him Mr. All Around for a reason: The Philly native, who played every position, possessed the ball skills of a guard, the post-up game of a center and supreme defensive ability. A three-time consensus All-America, Gola led La Salle to the 1952 NIT title, the 1954 NCAA title and the 1955 national championship game while being named Player of the Year as a senior. His 2,201 career rebounds remain a Division I record.

BEST COACH: Ken Loeffler (1949-55) He was best known for his figure-8 motion offense and emphasis on teamwork, but Loeffler was also a shrewd in-game tactician. In the 1954 NCAA Final against Bradley, Gola picked up four first-half fouls, forcing Loeffler to install a zone defense to protect his star from fouling out. The Explorers rolled to the title, 92-76. Loeffler won 20-plus games and made the postseason in each of his six seasons, and was enshrined in the Naismith Hall of Fame in 1964.

GAME FOR THE AGES: In the 1952 NIT final, the Explorers executed Loeffler's offense to perfection: Gola, Buddy Donnelly, Norm Grekin and Fred Iehle all scored in double digits, and Jackie Moore (the first African-American basketball player at La Salle) added eight points in a 75-64 win over Dayton.

HEARTBREAKER: The defending NCAA champion Explorers looked primed to repeat after blowing past Princeton, Canisius and Iowa in the 1955 Tournament to face San Francisco and Bill Russell for the title. Billed as Gola the Great vs. Russell the Remarkable, it was 6'1" K.C. Jones who shackled Gola (16 points) on the perimeter, while Russell (23 points) dominated the La Salle star in the post and on the boards in the Dons' 77-63 win.

FIERCEST RIVAL: Saint Joseph's and La Salle have provided some of the most dramatic moments in the Philadelphia Big 5 series, including the Explorers' 98-95 double-overtime win on Jan. 23, 1999—one of five straight games between the two Atlantic 10 rivals that were decided by four or fewer points. The Hawks lead overall, 63–50.

Tom Gola played every position, possessed the ball skills of a guard, the post-up game of a center and supreme defensive ability.

FANFARE AND HOOPLA: After every home game, win or lose, La Salle players wade into the gold-shirt-wearing student section—the Explorer Entourage—and join in singing the school fight song.

FAN FAVORITE: F Lionel Simmons (1986-90) Even opposing fans couldn't take their eyes off of the L-Train, because they never knew when or how he was going to score next. Simmons led the Explorers to either the NIT or NCAA Tournament in all four of his seasons—and was the seventh player chosen (by Sacramento) in the 1990 NBA draft.

CONSENSUS ALL-AMERICAS

1953-55	**Tom Gola,** C
1980	**Michael Brooks,** F
1990	**Lionel Simmons,** F

FIRST-ROUND PRO PICKS

1950	**Larry Foust,** Chicago (6)
1955	**Tom Gola,** Philadelphia (3)
1969	**Larry Cannon,** Chicago (5)
1971	**Ken Durrett,** Cincinnati (4)
1975	**Joe Bryant,** Golden State (14)
1980	**Michael Brooks,** San Diego (9)
1990	**Lionel Simmons,** Sacramento (7)
1992	**Randy Woods,** LA Clippers (16)

PROFILE

La Salle University, Philadelphia, PA
Founded: 1863
Enrollment: 7,554 (4,773 undergraduate)
Colors: Blue and gold
Nickname: Explorers
Current arena: Tom Gola Arena, opened in 1998 (4,000)
First game: 1930
All-time record: 1,237-828 (.599)
Total weeks in AP Top 20/25: 107
Current conference: Atlantic 10 (1995-)

Conference titles:
Middle Atlantic: 3 (1968, '69, '74 [tie])
East Coast: 3 (1975 [tie], '78 [tie], '83 [tie])
MAAC: 5 (1984 [tie], 1988, '89, '90 [tie], '91 [tie])
Conference tournament titles:
East Coast: 4 (1975, '78, '80, '83)
MAAC: 4 (1988, '89, '90, '92)
NCAA Tournament appearances: 11
Final Fours: 2
Titles: 1 (1954)
NIT appearances: 11
Semifinals: 2
Titles: 1 (1952)

TOP 5

G	**Larry Cannon** (1966-69)
G	**Ken Durrett** (1968-71)
F	**Michael Brooks** (1976-80)
F	**Lionel Simmons** (1986-90)
C	**Tom Gola** (1951-55)

RECORDS

RECORDS	GAME		SEASON		CAREER	
POINTS	52	Kareem Townes, vs. Loyola-Chicago, (Feb. 4, 1995)	908	Lionel Simmons (1988-89)	3,217	Lionel Simmons (1986-90)
POINTS PER GAME			28.4	Lionel Simmons (1988-89)	24.6	Lionel Simmons (1986-90)
REBOUNDS	37	Tom Gola, vs. Lebanon Valley (Jan. 15, 1955)	652	Tom Gola (1953-54)	2,201	Tom Gola (1951-55)
ASSISTS	18	Doug Overton, vs. Holy Cross (Feb. 13, 1989)	244	Doug Overton (1988-89)	671	Doug Overton (1987-91)

SEASON REVIEW

SEAS.	W-L	CONF.	POSTSEASON	SCORING		REBOUNDS		ASSISTS		COACH	RECORD	
1930-31	15-4									James Henry	15-4	.790
1931-32	15-8									Thomas Conley		
1932-33	13-3									Thomas Conley	28-11	.718
1933-34	14-3									Leonard Tanseer		
1934-35	15-6									Leonard Tanseer		
1935-36	4-13									Leonard Tanseer		
1936-37	12-7									Leonard Tanseer		
1937-38	9-8									Leonard Tanseer		
1938-39	13-6									Leonard Tanseer		
1939-40	12-8									Leonard Tanseer		
1940-41	11-8									Leonard Tanseer	90-59	.604
1941-42	12-11									Charles "Obie" O'Brien		
1942-43	13-10									Charles "Obie" O'Brien	25-21	.544
1943-44	8-8									Joseph Meehan		
1944-45	11-8			Bob Walters	13.4					Joseph Meehan		
1945-46	9-14			Bob Walters	13.8					Joseph Meehan	28-30	.483
1946-47	20-6			Bob Walters	16.0					Charles McGlone		
1947-48	20-4		NIT FIRST ROUND	Bob Walters	13.4					Charles McGlone		
1948-49	21-7			Larry Foust	16.2					Charles McGlone	61-17	.782
1949-50	21-4		NIT QUARTERFINALS	Larry Foust	14.2					Ken Loeffler		
1950-51	22-7		NIT FIRST ROUND	Jack George	16.2					Ken Loeffler		
1951-52	24-5		NIT CHAMPION	Tom Gola	15.8	Tom Gola	15.5			Ken Loeffler		
1952-53	25-3		NIT QUARTERFINALS	Tom Gola	18.5	Tom Gola	15.5			Ken Loeffler		
1953-54	**26-4**		**NATIONAL CHAMPION**	**Tom Gola**	**23.0**	**Tom Gola**	**21.7**			**Ken Loeffler**		
1954-55	26-5		NCAA RUNNER-UP	Tom Gola	24.2	Tom Gola	19.9			Ken Loeffler	144-28	.837
1955-56	15-10			Alonzo Lewis	13.0	Fran O'Malley	14.1			Jim Pollard		
1956-57	17-9			Alonzo Lewis	17.2	Wally Fredericks	8.7			Jim Pollard		
1957-58	16-9			Bill Katheder	13.0	Bob Alden	9.3			Jim Pollard	48-28	.632
1958-59	16-7	5-2		Joey Heyer	17.4	Bob Herdelin	14.1			Donald "Dudey" Moore		
1959-60	16-6	6-1		Robert Alden	16.4	Bob Alden	14.5			Donald "Dudey" Moore		
1960-61	15-7	7-2		Bill Raftery	17.8	Joe Carey	9.6			Donald "Dudey" Moore		
1961-62	16-9	5-3		Bob McAteer	21.7	Walt Sampson	11.2			Donald "Dudey" Moore		
1962-63	16-8	7-1	NIT FIRST ROUND	Frank Corace	18.4	George Sutor	11.5			Donald "Dudey" Moore	79-37	.681
1963-64	16-9	5-1		Frank Corace	24.0	George Sutor	11.3			Bob Walters		
1964-65	15-8		NIT FIRST ROUND	Curt Fromal	19.2	George Sutor	11.6			Bob Walters	31-17	.646
1965-66	10-15			Hubie Marshall	27.0	George Paull	8.8	Hubie Marshall	3.9	Joe Heyer		
1966-67	14-12			Hubie Marshall	21.1	Stan Wlodarczyk	9.9	Hubie Marshall	4.1	Joe Heyer	24-27	.471
1967-68	20-8		NCAA FIRST ROUND	Larry Cannon	19.5	Ed Szczesny	10.0	Larry Cannon	4.8	Jim Harding	20-8	.714
1968-69	23-1			Ken Durrett	20.0	Ken Durrett	11.8	Larry Cannon	5.8	Tom Gola		
1969-70	14-12	3-2		Ken Durrett	24.3	Ken Durrett	12.1	Fran Dunphy	4.4	Tom Gola	37-13	.740
1970-71	20-7	5-1	NIT FIRST ROUND	Ken Durrett	27.0	Ken Durrett	9.3	Greg Cannon	5.2	Paul Westhead		
1971-72	6-19	2-4		Jim Crawford	15.7	Jim Crawford	10.9	Jim Crawford	2.7	Paul Westhead		
1972-73	15-10	3-3		Jim Crawford	19.6	Joe DiCocco	9.5	Jim Crawford	3.2	Paul Westhead		
1973-74	18-10	5-1		Bill Taylor	19.7	Joe Bryant	10.8	Charlie Wise	3.9	Paul Westhead		
1974-75	22-7	5-1	NCAA FIRST ROUND	Joe Bryant	21.8	Joe Bryant	11.4	Charlie Wise	4.4	Paul Westhead		
1975-76	11-15	1-4		Donn Wilber	17.2	Donn Wilber	10.0	Charlie Wise	5.2	Paul Westhead		
1976-77	17-12	3-2		Michael Brooks	19.9	Michael Brooks	10.7	Tony DiLeo	3.6	Paul Westhead		
1977-78	18-12	5-0	NCAA FIRST ROUND	Michael Brooks	24.9	Michael Brooks	12.8	Darryl Gladden	6.4	Paul Westhead		
1978-79	15-13	10-3		Michael Brooks	23.3	Michael Brooks	13.3	Darryl Gladden	5.6	Paul Westhead	142-105	.575
1979-80	22-9	7-4	NCAA FIRST ROUND	Michael Brooks	24.1	Michael Brooks	11.5	Kevin Lynam	4.2	Dave "Lefty" Ervin		
1980-81	14-13	8-3		Stan Williams	16.6	Stan Williams	9.2	Greg Webster	6.4	Dave "Lefty" Ervin		
1981-82	16-13	7-4		Steve Black	20.0	Albert Butts	8.8	Steve Black	2.9	Dave "Lefty" Ervin		
1982-83	18-14	7-2	NCAA SECOND ROUND	Steve Black	20.1	Albert Butts	9.6	Chip Greenberg	3.6	Dave "Lefty" Ervin		
1983-84	20-11	11-3	NIT FIRST ROUND	Ralph Lewis	20.6	Ralph Lewis	9.1	Chip Greenberg	4.9	Dave "Lefty" Ervin		
1984-85	15-13	8-6		Steve Black	19.7	Ralph Lewis	9.6	Chip Greenberg	4.4	Dave "Lefty" Ervin		
1985-86	14-14	8-6		Chip Greenberg	16.8	Chip Greenberg	5.2	Chip Greenberg	3.8	Dave "Lefty" Ervin	119-87	.578
1986-87	20-13	10-4	NIT RUNNER-UP	Lionel Simmons	20.3	Lionel Simmons	9.8	Rich Tarr	5.7	William "Speedy" Morris		
1987-88	24-10	14-0	NCAA FIRST ROUND	Lionel Simmons	23.3	Lionel Simmons	11.4	Rich Tarr	4.9	William "Speedy" Morris		
1988-89	26-6	13-1	NCAA FIRST ROUND	Lionel Simmons	28.4	Lionel Simmons	11.4	Doug Overton	7.6	William "Speedy" Morris		
1989-90	30-2	16-0	NCAA SECOND ROUND	Lionel Simmons	26.5	Lionel Simmons	11.1	Doug Overton	6.6	William "Speedy" Morris		
1990-91	19-10	12-4	NIT FIRST ROUND	Doug Overton	22.3	Milko Lieverst	8.0	Doug Overton	5.0	William "Speedy" Morris		
1991-92	20-11	12-4	NCAA FIRST ROUND	Randy Woods	27.3	Milko Lieverst	7.9	Randy Woods	5.2	William "Speedy" Morris		
1992-93	14-13	9-5		Kareem Townes	22.5	Blitz Wooten	6.4	Paul Burke	4.9	William "Speedy" Morris		
1993-94	11-16	4-6		Kareem Townes	22.9	Romaine Haywood	6.4	Paul Burke	6.7	William "Speedy" Morris		
1994-95	13-14	7-7		Kareem Townes	25.9	Romaine Haywood	6.7	Paul Burke	6.2	William "Speedy" Morris		
1995-96	6-24	3-13		Romaine Haywood	18.1	Romaine Haywood	7.2	Shawn Smith	5.9	William "Speedy" Morris		
1996-97	10-17	5-11		Donnie Carr	23.9	Travar Johnson	5.8	Shawn Smith	4.9	William "Speedy" Morris		
1997-98	9-18	5-11		Donnie Carr	18.0	K'Zell Wesson	10.7	Donnie Carr	4.2	William "Speedy" Morris		
1998-99	13-15	8-8		Donnie Carr	18.7	K'Zell Wesson	10.8	Donnie Carr	4.9	William "Speedy" Morris		
1999-2000	11-17	5-11		Rasual Butler	18.4	Victor Thomas	8.7	Julian Blanks	4.8	William "Speedy" Morris		
2000-01	12-17	5-11		Rasual Butler	22.1	Victor Thomas	6.8	Julian Blanks	6.0	William "Speedy" Morris	238-203	.540
2001-02	15-17	6-10		Rasual Butler	20.9	Rasual Butler	8.8	Julian Blanks	5.1	Billy Hahn		
2002-03	12-17	6-10		Gary Neal	18.6	Steven Smith	8.1	Jermaine Thomas	4.3	Billy Hahn		
2003-04	10-20	5-11		Steven Smith	17.1	Steven Smith	8.0	Mike Cleaves	2.5	Billy Hahn	37-54	.407
2004-05	10-19	5-11		Steven Smith	20.3	Steven Smith	7.3	Tabby Cunningham	4.6	John Giannini		
2005-06	18-10	10-6		Steven Smith	19.7	Steven Smith	7.9	Jermaine Thomas	3.9	John Giannini		
2006-07	10-20	3-13		Darnell Harris	14.0	Mike St. John	5.7	Mike St. John	2.8	John Giannini		
2007-08	15-17	8-8		Darnell Harris	16.6	Joe Jerrell	6.4	Rodney Green	3.2	John Giannini		
2008-09	18-13	9-7		Rodney Green	17.8	Yves Mekongo Mbala	6.0	Rodney Green	3.4	John Giannini	71-79	.473

ESPN 200 SAGARIN

LAFAYETTE

Behold, the virtue of patience. Watching Lafayette's first game, on Feb. 1, 1901, cost fans a quarter. After seven scoreless minutes, Ed Haldeman finally made a basket to spark the Leopards' 12-4 win. Lafayette appeared in its first NCAA Tournament 56 years later, went another 15 years before making the NIT, then finally returned to the NCAAs in 1999 and 2000.

BEST TEAM: 1999-2000 Fran O'Hanlon's team was led by two former Patriot League POYs: G Brian Ehlers (1998-99 and 1999-2000) and C Stefan Ciosici (1997-98). The Leopards won a school-record 24 games, the last an 87-61 dismantling of Navy that avenged their lone conference loss. In their second straight NCAA Tourney, the Leopards lost to No. 2-seed Temple, 73-47.

BEST PLAYER: F Tracy Tripucka (1969-72) The product of an athletic dynasty (father Frank was a Notre Dame quarterback, brother Kelly was a hoops star at Notre Dame), Tracy set Lafayette career records for points, scoring average (25.0 ppg), field goals, free throws and field goal percentage (the last two have since been broken). The sweet shooter scored 40 or more three times, including 41 against Syracuse on Jan. 14, 1971.

BEST COACH: Tom Davis (1971-77) In his first head coaching gig, Dr. Tom guided the Leopards to the 1972 and '75 NIT. His 1971-72 team beat Virginia, 72-71, in the first round—the Leopards' only postseason win.

GAME FOR THE AGES: Tyson Whitfield's three-quarter-court heave swished at the end of the first half of the 1999 Patriot League tournament final against Bucknell. Free throws by Tim Bieg and Brian Ehlers sealed a 67-63 victory, sending the Leopards to the Dance for the first time in 42 years. At the time, it was the nation's second-longest span between NCAA appearances.

FIERCEST RIVAL: The hoops series between Lafayette and Lehigh isn't quite as old as the football matchup, which dates to 1884. But the two teams have played 210 times since 1902, with the Leopards winning 137 of those, thanks, in part, to a 34-game win streak that stretched from 1944 to '61.

SEASON REVIEW

SEAS.	W-L	CONF.		COACH	SEAS.	W-L	CONF.		COACH
1901-50	*361-339*			*Bill Anderson 139-82 in 11 seasons*	1963-64	15-8	4-4		George Davidson
1950-51	14-11	2-2		Ray Stanley	1964-65	12-8			George Davidson
1951-52	15-9	3-0		B. van Breda Kolff	1965-66	9-11			George Davidson
1952-53	13-12			B. van Breda Kolff	1966-67	4-21			George Davidson
1953-54	17-10			B. van Breda Kolff	1967-68	5-19			Hal Wissel
1954-55	23-3		■	B. van Breda Kolff	1968-69	9-17			Hal Wissel
1955-56	20-7		■	George Davidson	1969-70	12-14	7-3		Hal Wissel
1956-57	22-5		●	George Davidson	1970-71	17-9	9-1		Hal Wissel
1957-58	16-10			George Davidson	1971-72	21-6	7-3	■	Tom Davis
1958-59	13-8	7-6		George Davidson	1972-73	16-10	7-3		Tom Davis
1959-60	12-13	6-7		George Davidson	1973-74	17-9	7-3		Tom Davis
1960-61	16-8	6-6		George Davidson	1974-75	22-6	7-1	■	Tom Davis
1961-62	18-6	9-3		George Davidson	1975-76	19-7	9-1		Tom Davis
1962-63	13-11	6-4		George Davidson	1976-77	21-6	9-1		Tom Davis

SEAS.	W-L	CONF.		SCORING		COACH	RECORD	
1977-78	23-8	10-0		Phil Ness	18.4	Roy Chipman		
1978-79	16-12	9-9		Bob Falconiero	13.4	Roy Chipman		
1979-80	21-8	13-3	■	Bob Falconiero	14.2	Roy Chipman	60-28	.682
1980-81	15-13	8-8		Thomas Best	15.2	Will Rackley		
1981-82	12-15	7-9		Mike Whitman	15.4	Will Rackley		
1982-83	7-21	3-10		Stan Morse	13.0	Will Rackley		
1983-84	12-17	9-7		Stan Morse	12.6	Will Rackley	46-66	.411
1984-85	15-13	8-6		Tony Duckett	15.0	Butch van Breda Kolff		
1985-86	14-15	8-6		Gary Bennett	17.9	Butch van Breda Kolff		
1986-87	16-13	10-4		Otis Ellis	21.0	Butch van Breda Kolff		
1987-88	19-10	11-3		Otis Ellis	17.0	Butch van Breda Kolff	132-85	.608
1988-89	20-10	8-6		Otis Ellis	14.1	John Leone		
1989-90	15-13	7-7		Andy Wescoe	14.9	John Leone		
1990-91	7-21	1-11		Bruce Stankavage	18.2	John Leone		
1991-92	8-20	6-8		Craig White	16.5	John Leone		
1992-93	7-20	4-10		Keith Brazzo	17.5	John Leone		
1993-94	9-19	4-10		Keith Brazzo	18.6	John Leone		
1994-95	2-25	0-14		Craig Kowadla	18.3	John Leone	68-128	.347
1995-96	7-20	4-8		Craig Kowadla	18.4	Fran O'Hanlon		
1996-97	11-17	5-7		Stefan Ciosici	13.7	Fran O'Hanlon		
1997-98	19-9	10-2		Stefan Ciosici	17.0	Fran O'Hanlon		
1998-99	22-8	10-2	●	Brian Ehlers	18.1	Fran O'Hanlon		
1999-2000	24-7	11-1	●	Brian Ehlers	17.3	Fran O'Hanlon		
2000-01	12-16	4-8		Tyson Whitfield	15.1	Fran O'Hanlon		
2001-02	15-14	8-6		Brian Burke	15.5	Fran O'Hanlon		
2002-03	13-16	6-8		Justin DeBerry	16.3	Fran O'Hanlon		
2003-04	18-10	9-5		Justin DeBerry	14.8	Fran O'Hanlon		
2004-05	9-19 ⊗	5-9		Sean Knitter	10.9	Fran O'Hanlon		
2005-06	11-17	5-9		Andrei Capusan	12.0	Fran O'Hanlon		
2006-07	9-21	3-11		Matt Betley	10.9	Fran O'Hanlon		
2007-08	15-15	6-8		Andrew Brown	15.9	Fran O'Hanlon		
2008-09	8-22	4-10		Andrew Brown	13.6	Fran O'Hanlon	193-211	.478

⊗ Records don't not reflect games forfeited or vacated. For adjusted records, see p. 521.

● NCAA Tournament appearance ■ NIT appearance

PROFILE

Lafayette College, Easton, PA
Founded: 1826
Enrollment: 2,279 (2,279 undergraduate)
Colors: Maroon and white
Nickname: Leopards
Current arena: Allan P. Kirby Sports Center, opened in 1973 (3,500)
Previous: Alumni Gym, 1924-73 (N/A)
First game: Feb. 1, 1901
All-time record: 1,203-1,087 (.525)
Total weeks in AP Top 20/25: 0

Current conference: Patriot League (1990-)
Conference titles:
Middle Atlantic States-Northern: 1 (1949 [tie])
Middle Three: 3 (1949 [tie], '50 [tie], '52)
East Coast: 5 (1975, '76, '77, '78, '88)
Patriot: 3 (1998 [tie], '99, 2000 [tie])
Conference tournament titles:
Patriot: 2 (1999, 2000)
NCAA Tournament appearances: 3
NIT appearances: 5

TOP 5

G **Pete Carril** (1949-52)
G **Brian Ehlers** (1996-2000)
F **Otis Ellis** (1985-89)
F **Tracy Tripucka** (1969-72)
C **Stefan Ciosici** (1995-2000)

RECORDS

RECORDS	GAME		SEASON		CAREER	
POINTS	47	Bob Mantz, vs. Wilkes (March 5, 1958)	679	Todd Tripucka (1975-76)	1,973	Tracy Tripucka (1969-72)
POINTS PER GAME			26.1	Todd Tripucka (1975-76)	25.0	Tracy Tripucka (1969-72)
REBOUNDS	33	Ron Moyer, vs. Gettysburg (Dec. 9, 1970)	450	Jim Radcliffe (1954-55)	1,262	Bob Mantz (1955-58)
ASSISTS	17	Gerry Kavanaugh, vs. Columbia (Jan. 20, 1976)	192	Tony Duckett (1983-84)	622	Tony Duckett (1981-85)

ESPN 168 SAGARIN

LAMAR

What coach Jack Martin started in D2 in the 1950s and '60s, D1 NCAA Tournament favorites came to fear in the '80s: Lamar in the postseason. From 1978 to '84 the Cardinals upset five Tourney teams, including Alabama, Oregon State and Missouri, while winning 80 straight on their home court over the same span.

BEST TEAM: 1979-80 Coach Billy Tubbs' 22–11 team featured three of Lamar's top four all-time leading scorers: Mike Olliver (2,518 points), B.B. Davis (2,084) and Clarence Kea (1,814). The Cardinals beat three Top-20 opponents during the season and barely lost to No. 1 DePaul, 63-61. They reached the NCAA Sweet 16 before falling to Clemson (led by Larry Nance and John Campbell), 74-66.

BEST PLAYER: G Mike Olliver (1977-81) Lamar's top scorer averaged 20.6 ppg for his career, during which the Cardinals went to three straight NCAA Tourneys. Olliver's arrival also coincided with the start of Lamar's 80-game homecourt winning streak—the seventh-longest in NCAA history.

BEST COACH: Jack Martin (1951-76) A pilot during WW II, Martin led the Cardinals for 25 years, winning a school-record 334 games. The height of his success (1958-66) was a run of eight straight winning seasons that featured five conference titles (three Lone Star and two Southland), two 20-win seasons and five College Division national tourney appearances.

GAME FOR THE AGES: The 1979-80 team, a No. 10 seed, reached the Sweet 16 with a shocking 81-77 victory over No. 2-seed Oregon State and All-America Steve Johnson. Never had an SLC team gone so far in the NCAA Tournament. Five Cardinals hit double figures, led by Olliver and Davis with 18.

FIERCEST RIVAL: Lamar has played McNeese State more than any other Southland foe, with the Cardinals ahead overall, 47–39. The Cowboys, however, lead 14–6 since Lamar returned to the SLC in 1998 after an 11-year absence.

SEASON REVIEW

SEAS.	W-L	CONF.	COACH	SEAS.	W-L	CONF.	COACH
1951-53	*18-28*			1960-61	19-8		Jack Martin
1953-54	13-11		Jack Martin	1961-62	20-8		Jack Martin
1954-55	11-14		Jack Martin	1962-63	22-5		Jack Martin
1955-56	12-12		Jack Martin	1963-64	19-6	7-1	Jack Martin
1956-57	14-11		Jack Martin	1964-65	18-6	5-3	Jack Martin
1957-58	10-12		Jack Martin	1965-66	17-9	4-4	Jack Martin
1958-59	17-7		Jack Martin	1966-67	5-19	0-8	Jack Martin
1959-60	18-9		Jack Martin	1967-68	8-17	3-5	Jack Martin

SEAS.	W-L	CONF.		SCORING		COACH	RECORD	
1968-69	20-4	6-2		Earl Dow	23.3	Jack Martin		
1969-70	15-9	7-1		Luke Adams	15.5	Jack Martin		
1970-71	11-13	5-3		Luke Adams	23.0	Jack Martin		
1971-72	13-13	7-1		Trennis Jones	15.9	Jack Martin		
1972-73	11-13	6-6		Danny Bromley	19.2	Jack Martin		
1973-74	6-19	0-4		Danny Bromley	16.9	Jack Martin		
1974-75	7-16	4-4		Alfred Nickson	13.2	Jack Martin		
1975-76	10-14	6-4		Henry Jones	13.4	Jack Martin	334-283	.541
1976-77	12-17	6-4		Clarence Kea	15.7	Billy Tubbs		
1977-78	18-9	8-2		B.B. Davis	17.6	Billy Tubbs		
1978-79	23-9	9-1	●	Mike Olliver	22.0	Billy Tubbs		
1979-80	22-11	8-2	●	Mike Olliver	21.7	Billy Tubbs		
1980-81	25-5	8-2	●	Mike Olliver	22.3	Pat Foster		
1981-82	22-7	7-3	■	Terry Long	14.8	Pat Foster		
1982-83	23-8	9-3	●	Tom Sewell	18.6	Pat Foster		
1983-84	26-5	11-1	■	Tom Sewell	22.9	Pat Foster		
1984-85	20-12	8-4	■	Jerry Everett	16.9	Pat Foster		
1985-86	18-12	6-6	■	Anthony Todd	15.4	Pat Foster	134-49	.732
1986-87	14-15	4-6		James Gulley	19.8	Tom Abatemarco		
1987-88	20-11	5-5		James Gulley	17.6	Tom Abatemarco	34-26	.567
1988-89	12-16	3-7		Adrian Caldwell	14.7	Tony Branch		
1989-90	7-21	1-9		Daryl Reed	15.8	Tony Branch	19-37	.339
1990-91	15-13	4-8		Anthony Bledsoe	16.1	Mike Newell		
1991-92	12-19	7-9		Shawn Copes	14.5	Mike Newell		
1992-93	15-12	9-9		Keith Veney	16.6	Mike Newell	42-44	.488
1993-94	10-17	6-12		Atiim Browne	16.3	Grey Giovanine		
1994-95	11-16	6-12		Ron Coleman	16.9	Grey Giovanine		
1995-96	12-15	7-11		Ron Coleman	15.7	Grey Giovanine		
1996-97	15-12	10-8		Ron Coleman	16.1	Grey Giovanine		
1997-98	15-14	7-11		Ronad Nunnery	14.4	Grey Giovanine		
1998-99	17-11	11-7		Matt Sundblad	13.7	Grey Giovanine	80-85	.485
1999-2000	15-16	8-10	●	Landon Rowe	15.2	Mike Deane		
2000-01	9-18	7-13		Joey Ray	11.3	Mike Deane		
2001-02	15-14	11-9		Damany Hendrix	17.7	Mike Deane		
2002-03	13-14	10-10		Ron Austin	15.7	Mike Deane	52-62	.456
2003-04	11-18	5-11		Raymond Anthony	15.5	Billy Tubbs		
2004-05	18-11	9-7		Alan Daniels	19.9	Billy Tubbs		
2005-06	17-14	9-7		Alan Daniels	23.5	Billy Tubbs	121-89	.576
2006-07	15-17	8-8		James Davis	15.4	Steve Roccaforte		
2007-08	19-11	13-3		Kenny Dawkins	14.6	Steve Roccaforte		
2008-09	15-15	6-10		Kenny Dawkins	15.2	Steve Roccaforte	49-43	.533

● NCAA Tournament appearance ■ NIT appearance

PROFILE

Lamar University, Beaumont, TX
Founded: 1923
Enrollment: 13,280 (8,550 undergraduate)
Colors: Red and white
Nickname: Cardinals
Current arena: Montagne Center, opened in 1984 (10,800)
Previous: Beaumont Civic Center, 1980-84 (5,600); McDonald Gym, 1958-81 (3,500); MacArthur and Union Gyms, 1951-58 (N/A)
First game: Nov. 28, 1951
All-time record: 865-718 (.546)

Total weeks in AP Top 20/25: 1
Current conference: Southland (1963-87, '98-)
Conference titles:
Southland: 9 (1964, '70, '78 [tie], '79, '80, '81, '83, '84, '08 [tie])
Conference tournament titles:
Southland: 3 (1981, '83, 2000)
NCAA Tournament appearances: 5
Sweet 16s (since 1975): 1
NIT appearances: 4

TOP 5

G **Atiim Browne** (1990-94)
G **Mike Olliver** (1977-81)
F **Alan Daniels** (2004-06)
F **B.B. Davis** (1977-81)
C **Don Bryson** (1962-65)

RECORDS

RECORDS	GAME		SEASON		CAREER	
POINTS	50	Mike Olliver, vs. Portland State (Jan. 12, 1980)	730	Alan Daniels (2005-06)	2,518	Mike Olliver (1977-81)
POINTS PER GAME			23.5	Alan Daniels (2005-06)	20.6	Mike Olliver (1977-81)
REBOUNDS	28	Odis Booker, vs. Texas Wesleyan (Dec. 10, 1965)	421	Johnny Johnston (1960-61)	1,143	Clarence Kea (1976-80)
ASSISTS	21	Alvin Brooks, vs. Texas-Pan American (Jan. 15, 1981)	249	Alvin Brooks (1980-81)	641	Atiim Browne (1990-94)

ESPN 312 SAGARIN

LEHIGH

Lehigh added a special project to one of its marketing classes in 2008: promoting Mountain Hawks hoops, with the syllabus calling for students to attend games at Stabler Arena and figure out ways to improve the fan experience. Not that fans really needed the help. Fact is, the Lehigh program could be a major unto itself, with a team dating back to 1901 that has produced such coaching luminaries as Tony Packer (father of Billy), Brian Hill and Pete Carril.

BEST TEAM: 1987-88 Led by the top two scorers in Lehigh history, G/F Daren Queenan and G Mike Polaha, Lehigh won a school-best 21 games on its way to the East Coast Conference tournament title and second NCAA Tournament. As a No. 16 seed, Lehigh put a scare into in-state power Temple, with Queenan and Polaha dissecting John Chaney's famed match-up zone, only to have the Owls take command late to win, 87-73.

BEST PLAYER: G/F DAREN QUEENAN (1984-88) A slashing swingman known simply as Q, the 6'5" Queenan was a scoring machine who was unafraid to mix it up with the big boys. He finished second in the nation with 28.5 ppg as a senior, and his 1,013 career rebounds are best in school history.

BEST COACH: FRAN MCCAFFERY (1985-88) He was the nation's youngest D1 coach at 26. But the Philly native, known as White Magic as a player, had a veteran's touch on the bench, taking a longtime laughingstock to the Big Dance in his third and final season at the school.

GAME FOR THE AGES: With :05 left in the 2004 Patriot League title game, frosh guard Jose Olivero hit a jumper to beat American, 59-57, and send the Mountain Hawks to their first NCAA Tournament in 16 seasons.

FIERCEST RIVAL: It's often said around Bethlehem that Mountain Hawks fans consider their two favorite teams to be Lehigh and whoever is playing against Lafayette. While the football series, the oldest in the nation, is the stuff of PBS documentaries, the two basketball teams have been court rivals for more than a century. The Leopards lead the series, 137–73.

SEASON REVIEW

SEAS.	W-L	CONF.	COACH	SEAS.	W-L	CONF.	COACH
1901-49	*344-345*			1962-63	6-19	3-10	Tony Packer
1949-50	4-14	0-4	Dan Yarbo	1963-64	5-17	1-10	Tony Packer
1950-51	6-13	1-3	Tony Packer	1964-65	7-13		Tony Packer
1951-52	7-12	1-3	Tony Packer	1965-66	4-17		Tony Packer
1952-53	12-8		Tony Packer	1966-67	11-12		Pete Carril
1953-54	8-12		Tony Packer	1967-68	12-11		Roy Heckman
1954-55	10-11		Tony Packer	1968-69	7-17		Roy Heckman
1955-56	7-11		Tony Packer	1969-70	13-14	7-3	Roy Heckman
1956-57	8-10		Tony Packer	1970-71	10-16	4-6	Roy Heckman
1957-58	8-10		Tony Packer	1971-72	10-14	3-7	Roy Heckman
1958-59	6-16	4-10	Tony Packer	1972-73	8-17	3-7	Tom Pugliese
1959-60	6-16	4-10	Tony Packer	1973-74	3-21	2-8	Tom Pugliese
1960-61	5-16	4-10	Tony Packer	1974-75	1-23	0-8	Tom Pugliese
1961-62	7-12	4-10	Tony Packer	1975-76	9-15	2-8	Brian Hill

SEAS.	W-L	CONF.	SCORING		COACH	RECORD
1976-77	12-15	6-4			Brian Hill	
1977-78	8-18	5-5			Brian Hill	
1978-79	8-18	4-13			Brian Hill	
1979-80	5-20	2-14			Brian Hill	
1980-81	14-12	6-10			Brian Hill	
1981-82	9-17	3-13			Brian Hill	
1982-83	10-16	2-11			Brian Hill	75-131 .364
1983-84	4-23	3-13			Tom Schneider	
1984-85	12-19	6-8 ●	Daren Queenan	18.2	Tom Schneider	16-42 .276
1985-86	13-15	6-8	Daren Queenan	19.8	Fran McCaffery	
1986-87	15-14	8-6	Daren Queenan	24.8	Fran McCaffery	
1987-88	21-10	8-6 ●	Daren Queenan	28.5	Fran McCaffery	49-39 .557
1988-89	10-18	5-9			Dave Duke	
1989-90	18-12	8-6			Dave Duke	
1990-91	19-10	10-2			Dave Duke	
1991-92	14-15	8-6			Dave Duke	
1992-93	4-23	2-12	Chuck Penn	21.5	Dave Duke	
1993-94	10-17	6-8	Rashawne Glenn	19.5	Dave Duke	
1994-95	11-16	5-9			Dave Duke	
1995-96	4-23	2-10			Dave Duke	90-134 .402
1996-97	1-26	1-11	Brett Eppehimer	20.3	Sal Mentesana	
1997-98	10-17	4-8	Brett Eppehimer	24.7	Sal Mentesana	
1998-99	6-22	0-12	Jared Hess	12.8	Sal Mentesana	
1999-2000	8-21	3-9	Jared Hess	12.6	Sal Mentesana	
2000-01	13-16	6-6	Matt Logie	14.1	Sal Mentesana	
2001-02	5-23	2-12	Matt Logie	15.8	Sal Mentesana	43-125 .256
2002-03	16-12	8-6	Matt Logie	15.5	Billy Taylor	
2003-04	20-11	10-4 ●	Austen Rowland	15.5	Billy Taylor	
2004-05	14-15 ⊗	7-7	Joe Knight	13.6	Billy Taylor	
2005-06	19-12	11-3	Jose Olivero	17.1	Billy Taylor	
2006-07	12-19	7-7	Jose Olivero	16.4	Billy Taylor	81-69 .540
2007-08	14-15	7-7	Marquis Hall	14.1	Brett Reed	
2008-09	15-14	5-9	Zahir Carrington	14.0	Brett Reed	29-29 .500

⊗ Records don't reflect games forfeited or vacated. For adjusted records, see p. 521.
● NCAA Tournament appearance

PROFILE

Lehigh University, Bethlehem, PA
Founded: 1865
Enrollment: 6,605 (4,633 undergraduate)
Colors: Brown and white
Nickname: Mountain Hawks
Current arena: Stabler Arena, opened in 1979 (5,600)
First game: 1902
All-time record: 918-1,286 (.417)
Total weeks in AP Top 20/25: 0

Current conference: Patriot League (1990-)
Conference titles:
East Coast: 1 (1990 [tie])
Patriot: 1 (2004 [tie])
Conference tournament titles:
East Coast: 2 (1985, '88)
Patriot: 1 (2004)
NCAA Tournament appearances: 3
NIT appearances: 0

TOP 5

G **Mike Polaha** (1983-88)
G/F **Daren Queenan** (1984-88)
F **Bob Krizansky** (1988-92)
F **Dozie Mbonu** (1988-92)
C **Greg Falkenbach** (1969-72)

RECORDS

RECORDS	GAME		SEASON		CAREER	
POINTS	49	Daren Queenan, vs. Bucknell (March 7, 1987)	882	Daren Queenan (1987-88)	2,703	Daren Queenan (1984-88)
POINTS PER GAME			28.5	Daren Queenan (1987-88)	22.9	Daren Queenan (1984-88)
REBOUNDS	25	Greg Falkenbach, vs. Drexel (Dec. 19, 1970); vs. Franklin and Marshall (Jan. 31, 1969)	360	Greg Falkenbach (1969-70)	1,013	Daren Queenan (1984-88)
ASSISTS	13	Mike McKee, vs. Holy Cross (Feb. 9, 1994)	160	Mike McKee (1993-94)	452	Scott Layer (1986-90)

ESPN 304 SAGARIN

LIBERTY

The Flames have the transition game down pat. Just not the one that helps you get easy buckets. Liberty started as a National Christian College Athletic Association team in 1972, then moved to NAIA and D2 before going Division I in 1988. Unfortunately, success has proven a bit more elusive. Although Liberty won the Big South twice, in 1994 and 2004, it had only six winning D1 seasons before going 23–12 and making the College Insider Tournament in 2008-09.

BEST TEAM: 1996-97 The Flames enjoyed their second 20-win season (the first came in 1991-92) and tied for first in the Big South. They had a scrappy style on both ends of the court, but fell short of an NCAA Tournament bid when Charleston Southern upset them in the conference tournament. The team featured Nigerian center and future Globetrotter Peter Aluma, who is the Big South's all-time leading shotblocker (366).

BEST PLAYER: G Larry Blair (2003-07) He was a shooter's shooter, often following one three with another from four steps farther back. He finished his career as the Big South all-time leading scorer (currently No. 2) with 2,211 career points. He also ranks first in Liberty history in three-pointers (227) and games played (122) and third in field goals made (801).

BEST COACH: Jeff Meyer (1981-97) The school's all-time leader in coaching victories, Meyer guided the Flames into D1, then to the Big South tournament crown in 1994. His teams were known for defensive toughness and balanced offensive schemes.

GAME FOR THE AGES: In the 1980 NCCAA title game, the Flames controlled the tempo in the first half and opened a 35-26 lead over Point Loma College. With 2:40 left to play, the Crusaders pulled to within one, 58-57. But Roger Webb hit eight free throws in a row over the last 1:35 to seal a 68-65 victory.

FIERCEST RIVAL: Just 95 miles separate Liberty from Radford, and that proximity has bred contempt, dating back to both Virginia schools' NCCAA days. Radford leads the series, 31–23.

SEASON REVIEW

SEAS.	W-L	CONF.	SCORING		COACH	RECORD
1972-73	13-14		George Sweet	20.8	Dan Manley	
1973-74	11-12		Mike Goad	22.2	Dan Manley	
1974-75	17-11		Mike Goad	17.9	Dan Manley	
1975-76	12-15		Mark Chafin	16.0	Dan Manley	
1976-77	5-22		Mark Chafin	21.6	Dan Manley	58-74 .439
1977-78	7-22		Mark Chafin	22.0	Harley Swift	7-22 .241
1978-79	15-16		Karl Hess	27.0	Dale Gibson	
1979-80	28-11		Karl Hess	24.9	Dale Gibson	
1980-81	5-19		Steve Isaacs	19.6	Dale Gibson	48-46 .511
1981-82	15-11		Greg McCauley	15.2	Jeff Meyer	
1982-83	23-9		Steve Isaacs	18.2	Jeff Meyer	
1983-84	19-10	6-6	Eric Gordon	18.1	Jeff Meyer	
1984-85	19-10	7-5	Cliff Webber	18.6	Jeff Meyer	
1985-86	18-13	6-5	Mike Minett	17.0	Jeff Meyer	
1986-87	18-11	4-6	Brad Hamersley	11.9	Jeff Meyer	
1987-88	13-15	4-6	Bailey Alston	27.0	Jeff Meyer	
1988-89	10-17		Bailey Alston	23.9	Jeff Meyer	
1989-90	11-17		Bailey Alston	25.5	Jeff Meyer	
1990-91	5-23		Mike Coleman	15.8	Jeff Meyer	
1991-92	22-7	10-4	Julius Nwosu	13.7	Jeff Meyer	
1992-93	16-14	9-7	Julius Nwosu	18.1	Jeff Meyer	
1993-94	18-12	13-5 ●	Matt Hildebrand	18.1	Jeff Meyer	
1994-95	12-16	7-9	Peter Aluma	15.7	Jeff Meyer	
1995-96	17-12	9-5	Peter Aluma	18.9	Jeff Meyer	
1996-97	23-9	11-3	Peter Aluma	15.7	Jeff Meyer	259-206 .557
1997-98	11-17	5-7	Larry Jackson	16.7	Randy Dunton	
1998-99	4-23	0-10	Delawn Grandison	16.0	Mel Hankinson	
1999-2000	14-14	4-10	Carl Williams	15.3	Mel Hankinson	
2000-01	13-15	5-9	Chris Caldwell	16.7	Mel Hankinson	
2001-02	5-25	2-12	Chris Caldwell	15.4	Mel Hankinson	36-77 .319
2002-03	14-15	8-6	Gabe Martin	15.1	Randy Dunton	
2003-04	18-15	12-4 ●	Gabe Martin	13.7	Randy Dunton	
2004-05	13-15	11-5	Larry Blair	16.6	Randy Dunton	
2005-06	7-23	3-13	Larry Blair	22.6	Randy Dunton	
2006-07	14-17	8-6	Larry Blair	20.4	Randy Dunton	77-102 .430
2007-08	16-16	7-7	Anthony Smith	16.0	Ritchie McKay	
2008-09	23-12	12-6	Seth Curry	20.2	Ritchie McKay	39-28 .582

● NCAA Tournament appearance

PROFILE

Liberty University, Lynchburg, VA
Founded: 1971
Enrollment: 28,000 (11,300 undergraduate)
Colors: Red, white and blue
Nickname: Flames
Current arena: The Vines Center, opened in 1990 (8,500)
Previous: Liberty Gym, 1979-90 (N/A); Jefferson Forest High School, 1972-79 (N/A)
First game: 1972
All-time record: 524-555 (.486)
Total weeks in AP Top 20/25: 0

Current conference: Big South (1991-)
Conference titles:
Big South: 2 (1997 [tie], 2004 [tie])
Conference tournament titles:
Big South: 2 (1994, 2004)
NCAA Tournament appearances: 2
NIT appearances: 0

TOP 5

G **Larry Blair** (2003-07)
G **Karl Hess** (1976-80)
G **Larry Jackson** (1994-98)
F **Mike Coleman** (1988-92)
F **Julius Nwosu** (1990-93)

RECORDS

RECORDS	GAME		SEASON		CAREER	
POINTS	46	Bailey Alston, vs. Ferrum (Va.) (Feb. 26, 1988)	972	Karl Hess (1979-80)	2,373	Karl Hess (1976-80)
POINTS PER GAME			27.0	Bailey Alston (1987-88); Karl Hess (1978-79)	25.4	Bailey Alston (1987-90)
REBOUNDS	23	Ed Vickers, vs. Presbyterian (Jan. 4, 1979); Ed Vickers, vs. Bowie State (Dec. 7, 1978); Willard DeShazor, vs. Shenandoah (Jan. 26, 1974)	416	Ed Vickers (1979-80)	1,130	Steve Isaacs (1979-83)
ASSISTS	20	Kenny Gunn, vs. Roberts Wesleyan (Dec. 30, 1983)	256	Ed Gomes (1978-79)	648	Karl Hess (1976-80)

ESPN 313 SAGARIN

LIPSCOMB

The small Nashville school has played basketball since 1926, and the Bisons take pride in their 1986 NAIA tournament championship and a 1989-90 team that won 41 games. Lipscomb began the process of joining the NCAA in 1999 and became a full member of the Atlantic Sun Conference in 2003.

BEST TEAM: 1985-86 The Bisons won their first 18 games to attain the school's first No. 1 (NAIA) ranking, and closed with a 13-game run to finish 35–4. In the NAIA tourney, Lipscomb was the only team to surpass 100 points (102-91 over St. Thomas Aquinas). In the title game, 6'10" C John Kimbrell had 22 points and 11 rebounds to defeat Arkansas Monticello, 67-54.

BEST PLAYER: F JOHN PIERCE (1990-94) A redshirt freshman when Lipscomb's Philip Hutcheson became the NAIA's and college basketball's all-time leading scorer, Pierce passed his former roomie four years later and became the top scorer on any collegiate level with 4,230 points. (The school's D1 scoring leader is Brian Fisk.) Pierce's No. 50 and Hutcheson's No. 44 are Lipscomb's only retired jerseys.

BEST COACH: DON MEYER (1975-99) On Jan. 10, 2009, while coaching Northern State (S.D.), Meyer won career game No. 903, surpassing Bob Knight's 902 victories at the top of the NCAA all-time men's list. But Meyer's remarkable legacy was forged mainly at Lipscomb. During 24 seasons, the Bisons won at least 25 games 18 times and averaged 36 wins a year between 1988-89 and '92-93.

GAME FOR THE AGES: Lipscomb's McQuiddy gym served as home court for Vanderbilt for three seasons, and it was there that the Bisons stunned the heavily favored Commodores, 59-57, on Jan. 2, 1951.

FIERCEST RIVAL: Lipscomb and Belmont tangle each year in the Battle of the Boulevard—Belmont Boulevard, along which the two Christian schools are separated by less than three miles. The rivalry, dating back to 1953, took a hiatus from 1997-2003, but the Battle's back and better than ever, with regular sellout crowds. After 122 meetings, Lipscomb has a 69–55 edge.

SEASON REVIEW

SEAS.	W-L	CONF.	COACH	SEAS.	W-L	CONF.	COACH
1926-46	*181-131*	*60-19 from 1929-30 to 1931-32*		1959-60	11-14		Charles Morris
1946-47	9-10		Fessor Boyce	1960-61	16-10		Charles Morris
1947-48	16-10		Fessor Boyce	1961-62	8-13		Charles Morris
1948-49	11-9		Fessor Boyce	1962-63	15-11		Charles Morris
1949-50	16-11		Herman Waddell	1963-64	5-19		Charles Morris
1950-51	21-6		Herman Waddell	1964-65	14-11		Charles Morris
1951-52	23-11		Herman Waddell	1965-66	20-4		Charles Morris
1952-53	14-15		Elvis Sherrill	1966-67	8-14		Guy Phipps
1953-54	8-19		Elvis Sherrill	1967-68	9-14		Ken Dugan
1954-55	8-15		Elvis Sherrill	1968-69	9-15		Ken Dugan
1955-56	15-16		Charles Morris	1969-70	6-19		Ken Dugan
1956-57	6-18		Charles Morris	1970-71	8-14		Mike Clark
1957-58	6-16		Charles Morris	1971-72	16-11		Mike Clark
1958-59	12-12		Charles Morris	1972-73	4-20		Mike Clark

SEAS.	W-L	CONF.	SCORING		COACH	RECORD
1973-74	15-15				Charles Strasburger	
1974-75	11-19		Steve Flatt	17.7	Charles Strasburger	26-34 .433
1975-76	11-19		Billy Bennett	13.5	Don Meyer	
1976-77	17-10		Steve Flatt	18.8	Don Meyer	
1977-78	21-6				Don Meyer	
1978-79	21-12		Kenny Neal	13.7	Don Meyer	
1979-80	15-15		Alan Banks	15.1	Don Meyer	
1980-81	25-11				Don Meyer	
1981-82	32-5				Don Meyer	
1982-83	19-14				Don Meyer	
1983-84	30-5				Don Meyer	
1984-85	25-9				Don Meyer	
1985-86	35-4	◆			Don Meyer	
1986-87	27-6		Philip Hutcheson	24.4	Don Meyer	
1987-88	33-3		Philip Hutcheson	25.1	Don Meyer	
1988-89	38-2		Philip Hutcheson	28.0	Don Meyer	
1989-90	41-5		Philip Hutcheson	27.7	Don Meyer	
1990-91	35-4		John Pierce	26.7	Don Meyer	
1991-92	31-5		John Pierce	28.5	Don Meyer	
1992-93	34-4		John Pierce	31.9	Don Meyer	
1993-94	29-6		John Pierce	27.9	Don Meyer	
1994-95	30-7		R. Page	18.3	Don Meyer	
1995-96	33-6		Kenyata Perry	22.6	Don Meyer	
1996-97	30-6		Kenyata Perry	17.9	Don Meyer	
1997-98	26-8		Bryan Farmer	13.4	Don Meyer	
1998-99	25-9		Adam Sonn	10.9	Don Meyer	663-181 .786
1999-2000	34-4		Lorenzo Withrite	17.3	Scott Sanderson	
2000-01	21-7		Lorenzo Withrite	16.7	Scott Sanderson	
2001-02	6-21		Jeff Dancy	10.3	Scott Sanderson	
2002-03	8-20		Ryan Roller	13.1	Scott Sanderson	
2003-04	7-21	4-16	Brian Fisk	11.5	Scott Sanderson	
2004-05	16-12	11-9	Brian Fisk	14.1	Scott Sanderson	
2005-06	21-11	15-5 ■	Eddie Ard	16.2	Scott Sanderson	
2006-07	18-13	11-7	Eddie Ard	15.0	Scott Sanderson	
2007-08	15-16	9-7	Eddie Ard	15.1	Scott Sanderson	
2008-09	17-14	12-8	Adnan Hodzic	17.1	Scott Sanderson	163-139 .540

■ NIT appearance ◆ NAIA championship

PROFILE

Lipscomb University, Nashville, TN
Founded: 1891
Enrollment: 3,054 (2,420 undergraduate)
Colors: Purple and gold
Nickname: Bisons
Current arena: Allen Arena, opened in 2001 (5,028)
Previous: McQuiddy Physical Education Building, 1949-2001 (3,247); Burton Gymnasium, 1924-49 (200)
First game: 1926
All-time record: 1,347-842 (.615)
Total weeks in AP Top 20/25: 0

Current conference: Atlantic Sun (2003-)
Conference titles:
Atlantic Sun: 1 (2006 [tie])
Conference tournament titles: 0
NCAA Tournament appearances: 0
NIT appearances: 1

CONSENSUS ALL-AMERICAS

1988-90 **Philip Hutcheson** (D2), F/C
1992 **John Pierce** (D2), F

TOP 5

G **Brian Fisk** (2003-07)
G **Andy McQueen** (1991-94)
F **John Pierce** (1990-94)
F/C **Philip Hutcheson** (1986-90)
C **John Kimbrell** (1982-86)

RECORDS

RECORDS	GAME		SEASON		CAREER	
POINTS	38	Jeff Dancy, vs. Tennessee State (Jan. 14, 2002)	658	Lorenzo Withrite (1999-2000)	1,633	Brian Fisk (2003-07)
POINTS PER GAME			17.3	Lorenzo Withrite (1999-2000)	17.1	Lorenzo Withrite (1999-2001)
REBOUNDS	17	Cameron Robinson, vs. Jackson State (Dec. 8, 2005)	229	Shaun Durant (2005-06)	577	Eddie Ard (2004-08)
ASSISTS	10	Josh Slater, vs. East Tennessee State (Feb. 16, 2009) Trey Williams, vs. Campbell (Feb. 16, 2006) Craig Schoen, vs. Tennessee-Martin (Dec. 7, 2002)	125	Trey Williams (2005-06)	362	Brian Fisk (2003-07)

ESPN 156 SAGARIN

LONG BEACH STATE

Seven NCAA Tournament victories, five trips to the NIT, a coaching legacy that includes Jerry Tarkanian, Lute Olson and Tex Winter—if only the Long Beach story ended there. Unfortunately, you can't talk about the 49ers without delving into the dark side. The NCAA placed the program on probation twice, once for recruiting violations in the early 1970s and again for myriad violations from 2002 to '07.

BEST TEAM: 1973-74 Led by freshman forward Cliff Pondexter and guard Glenn McDonald, the 49ers went 24–2 (12–0 in the PCAA) and finished third nationally in scoring margin (19.1). But a three-year NCAA probation imposed at midseason dashed hopes for a national title and ultimately cost them their coach, Olson, who bolted for Iowa after just one season.

BEST PLAYER: G/F ED RATLEFF (1970-73) He could defend and score with the best of them (21.4 ppg in three seasons). And when Tarkanian needed a point guard during the 1972-73 season, Ratleff moved over from shooting guard to lead the 49ers to their fourth straight Tourney appearance.

BEST COACH: JERRY TARKANIAN (1968-73) In his five seasons, he guided the 49ers to four consecutive Tournaments (1970-73), two regional finals and a 116–17 record—and *never* lost a home game. How? His army of junior college transfers—unique at the time (and also a source of his recruiting troubles)—enabled him to push the pace; the 1972-73 49ers averaged 90.1 ppg.

GAME FOR THE AGES: In the West Regional final of the 1971 Tournament, Long Beach had a shot to break UCLA's run of four straight titles, holding a 52-50 lead with 5:46 left. Then Ratleff (18 points) fouled out and the Bruins scored seven of the final 10 to win, 57-55—on their way to another championship.

FIERCEST RIVAL: Located only 25 minutes away, Cal State Fullerton has proven to be the 49ers' most competitive rival in recent years. Since 2003-04, Long Beach has a 7–6 overall record against the Titans, and 10 of those games have been decided by 10 points or less.

SEASON REVIEW

SEAS.	W-L	CONF.	COACH	SEAS.	W-L	CONF.	COACH
1950-51	3-14		Herm Schwarzkopf	**1962-63**	10-15		Dick Perry
1951-52	10-13		Herm Schwarzkopf	**1963-64**	8-16		Dick Perry
1952-53	12-10		Earl Kidd	**1964-65**	17-9		Dick Perry
1953-54	5-15		Earl Kidd	**1965-66**	8-17		Dick Perry
1954-55	10-7		Earl Kidd	**1966-67**	11-16		Dick Perry
1955-56	6-15		Earl Kidd	**1967-68**	12-13		Randy Sandefur
1956-57	7-19		Earl Kidd	**1968-69**	23-3		Jerry Tarkanian
1957-58	10-13		Bill Patterson	**1969-70**	24-5	10-0 ●	Jerry Tarkanian
1958-59	8-13		Bill Patterson	**1970-71**	24-5 ⊗	10-0 ●	Jerry Tarkanian
1959-60	15-7		Bill Patterson	**1971-72**	25-4 ⊗	10-2 ●	Jerry Tarkanian
1960-61	15-11		Dick Perry	**1972-73**	26-3 ⊗	10-2 ●	Jerry Tarkanian
1961-62	14-12		Dick Perry	**1973-74**	24-2	12-0	Lute Olson

SEAS.	W-L	CONF.	SCORING		COACH	RECORD	
1974-75	19-7	8-2	Richard Johnson	17.8	Dwight Jones		
1975-76	14-12	6-4	Anthony McGee	14.8	Dwight Jones		
1976-77	21-8	9-3 ●	Lloyd McMillian	15.8	Dwight Jones		
1977-78	16-13	7-7	Michael Wiley	20.5	Dwight Jones	70-40	.636
1978-79	16-12	7-7	Rickey Williams	18.1	Tex Winter		
1979-80	22-12	11-3 ■	Michael Wiley	20.5	Tex Winter		
1980-81	15-13	9-5	Dino Gregory	16.0	Tex Winter		
1981-82	12-16	7-7	D. Gregory, C. Hodges	17.5	Tex Winter		
1982-83	13-16	6-10	Joedy Gardner	15.7	Tex Winter	78-69	.531
1983-84	9-19	6-12	Joedy Gardner	15.8	Dave Buss	9-19	.321
1984-85	4-23	2-16	Darryl Adams	11.9	Ron Palmer		
1985-86	7-22	3-15	M. Wiley, D. Langston	11.1	Ron Palmer		
1986-87	12-19	7-11	Morlon Wiley	12.8	Ron Palmer	23-64	.264
1987-88	17-12	11-7 ■	Morlon Wiley	19.9	Joe Harrington		
1988-89	13-15	10-8	John Hatten	13.8	Joe Harrington		
1989-90	23-9	12-6 ■	Lucious Harris	14.3	Joe Harrington	53-36	.596
1990-91	11-17	7-11	Lucious Harris	19.7	Seth Greenberg		
1991-92	18-12	11-7 ■	Lucious Harris	18.8	Seth Greenberg		
1992-93	22-10	11-7 ●	Lucious Harris	23.1	Seth Greenberg		
1993-94	17-10	11-7	Rod Hannibal	15.7	Seth Greenberg		
1994-95	20-10	13-5 ●	Joe McNaull	12.7	Seth Greenberg		
1995-96	17-11	12-6	James Cotton	19.5	Seth Greenberg	105-70	.600
1996-97	13-14	9-7	James Cotton	23.5	Wayne Morgan		
1997-98	10-19	5-11	Andrew Betts	18.7	Wayne Morgan		
1998-99	13-15	9-7	Ramel Lloyd	18.0	Wayne Morgan		
1999-2000	24-6	15-1 ■	Mate Milisa	18.5	Wayne Morgan		
2000-01	18-13	10-6	Ramel Lloyd	19.4	Wayne Morgan		
2001-02	13-17	9-9	Travis Reed	14.7	Wayne Morgan	91-84	.520
2002-03	5-22	4-14	Tony Darden	15.9	Larry Reynolds		
2003-04	6-21	4-14	Kevin Roberts	15.7	Larry Reynolds		
2004-05	10-20	7-11	Jibril Hodges	12.7	Larry Reynolds		
2005-06	18-12 ⊗	9-5	Aaron Nixon	14.7	Larry Reynolds		
2006-07	24-8	12-2 ●	Aaron Nixon	18.8	Larry Reynolds	63-83	.432▼
2007-08	6-25	3-13	Donovan Morris	21.2	Dan Monson		
2008-09	15-15	10-6	Donovan Morris	14.8	Dan Monson	21-40	.344

⊗ Records don't reflect games forfeited or vacated. For adjusted records, see p. 521.
▼ Coach's record adjusted to reflect games forfeited or vacated: 45-83, .352. For yearly totals, see p. 521.
● NCAA Tournament appearance ■ NIT appearance

PROFILE

Cal State University, Long Beach; Long Beach, CA
Founded: 1949
Enrollment: 37,890 (31,564 undergraduate)
Colors: Black and gold
Nickname: 49ers
Current arena: The Walter Pyramid, opened 1994 (5,000)
Previous: Long Beach Arena, 1972-1985 (12,000); The Gold Mine, 1950-1972, '85-94 (2,000)
First game: Nov. 18, 1950
All-time record: 840-762 (.524)
Total weeks in AP Top 20/25: 60

Current conference: Big West (1969-)
Conference titles:
Pacific Coast Athletic: 8 (1970, '71, '72, '73, '74, '75, '76 [tie], '77 [tie])
Big West: 2 (1996, 2007)
Conference tournament titles:
Pacific Coast Athletic: 1 (1977)
Big West: 3 (1993, '95, 2007)
NCAA Tournaments: 8 (3 appearances vacated)
NIT appearances: 5

CONSENSUS ALL-AMERICAS

1972, '73 **Ed Ratleff**, G/F

FIRST-ROUND PRO PICKS

1971 **George Trapp**, Atlanta (5)
1972 **Ed Ratleff**, Indiana (ABA)
1973 **Ed Ratleff**, Houston (6)
1974 **Cliff Pondexter**, Chicago (16)
1974 **Cliff Pondexter**, San Diego (ABA, 8)
1974 **Glenn McDonald**, Boston (17)

TOP 5

G **Lucious Harris** (1989-93)
G/F **Ed Ratleff** (1970-73)
F **George Trapp** (1969-71)
F **Michael Wiley** (1976-80)
F **Francois Wise** (1976-80)

RECORDS

	GAME		SEASON		CAREER	
POINTS	45	Ed Ratleff, vs. Saint Mary's (Calif.), (Dec. 10, 1970)	739	Lucious Harris (1992-93)	2,312	Lucious Harris (1989-93)
POINTS PER GAME			23.5	James Cotton (1996-97)	21.4	Ed Ratleff (1970-73)
REBOUNDS	38	Dave Jones, vs. Cal State LA (Jan. 28, 1961)	358	Dave Jones (1960-61)	896	Francois Wise (1976-80)
ASSISTS	15	Rick Aberegg, vs. Northern Illinois (Jan. 26, 1974)	189	Ed Ratleff (1971-72)	507	Billy Walker (1984-88)

ESPN 175 SAGARIN

LONG ISLAND

It was called Operation Rebound—a mission to resurrect the LIU program after it was shut down between 1951-52 and 1956-57 following a point-shaving scandal involving Blackbirds players. Consider the mission a modest success: the Brooklyn school, which won the 1939 and '41 NIT titles, was a force in the 1960s and has played in three NCAA Tournaments since returning to Division I in 1969.

BEST TEAM: 1938-39 The Blackbirds' leading scorer was All-America Irving Torgoff, a 6'3" sharpshooter who averaged 9.5 ppg. But as well-known as Clair Bee's teams were for their inside play and set shooting, LIU could play some rugged defense, too. The team held fellow unbeaten Loyola-Chicago well below its season average to win the NIT final, 44-32.

BEST PLAYER: G CHARLES JONES (1996-98) If not for the point-shaving scandal that marred his career, forward Sherman White (1948-51) might deserve this honor. Instead, we turn to the modern era and anoint Jones, who scored 30.1 ppg as a junior and 29.0 ppg as a senior—both tops in the nation.

BEST COACH: CLAIR BEE (1931-43, '45-51) He holds the NCAA record for highest all-time D1 college winning percentage (.824), but Bee's impact runs far deeper than his two NIT titles. The Hall of Famer invented the 1-3-1 zone and the three-second rule, and was an advocate of the NBA's 24-second clock. He also wrote the best-selling series of Chip Hilton sports novels.

GAME FOR THE AGES: Sometimes it's the game you don't play that matters most. In 1936, the U.S. Olympic Committee held a tournament to determine which team would represent the nation at the Berlin games. The powerhouse Blackbirds refused to participate because of Nazi Germany's anti-Semitism.

FIERCEST RIVAL: Long Island and St. Francis (N.Y.) have competed since 1928, spanning the Blackbirds' days as a national power, a D1 independent and now as a fellow member of the Northeast Conference. LIU leads in the Battle of Brooklyn, 55–35.

SEASON REVIEW

SEAS.	W-L	CONF.	COACH	SEAS.	W-L	CONF.	COACH
1928-44	*305-69-2*	*Won NIT in 1939, '41 under Clair Bee*		1962-63	10-14		Roy Rubin
1944-45	14-5		George Wolfe	1963-64	14-9		Roy Rubin
1945-46	14-9		Clair F. Bee	1964-65	16-7		Roy Rubin
1946-47	17-5	■	Clair F. Bee	1965-66	22-4	7-1[a]	Roy Rubin
1947-48	17-4		Clair F. Bee	1966-67	22-7	6-0[a]	Roy Rubin
1948-49	18-12		Clair F. Bee	1967-68	22-2	7-1 ■	Roy Rubin
1949-50	20-5	■	Clair F. Bee	1968-69	17-6	6-2	Roy Rubin
1950-51	20-4		Clair F. Bee	1969-70	16-9		Roy Rubin
1951-57	no team			1970-71	10-15		Roy Rubin
1957-58	12-6		William T. Lai	1971-72	13-12		Roy Rubin
1958-59	7-14		William T. Lai	1972-73	13-12		Ron Smalls
1959-60	12-9		William T. Lai	1973-74	13-12		Ron Smalls
1960-61	13-10		William T. Lai	1974-75	13-12		Ron Smalls
1961-62	12-9		Roy Rubin	1975-76	15-12		Paul Lizzo

SEAS.	W-L	CONF.		SCORING		COACH	RECORD
1976-77	9-16			Kim Malcolm	19.1	Paul Lizzo	
1977-78	8-18			John Bailey	13.9	Paul Lizzo	
1978-79	12-13			John Bailey	17.0	Paul Lizzo	
1979-80	14-12			Riley Clarida	14.1	Paul Lizzo	
1980-81	18-11		●	Robert Cole	15.0	Paul Lizzo	
1981-82	20-10	11-4	■	Robert Cole	18.0	Paul Lizzo	
1982-83	20-9	11-3		Robert Cole	18.4	Paul Lizzo	
1983-84	20-11	11-5	●	Robert Brown	19.5	Paul Lizzo	
1984-85	15-13	9-5		Carey Scurry	21.1	Paul Lizzo	
1985-86	9-19	4-12		Andre Ervin	21.6	Paul Lizzo	
1986-87	13-14	5-11		Calvin Lamb	19.2	Paul Lizzo	
1987-88	14-14	8-8		Calvin Lamb	20.2	Paul Lizzo	
1988-89	9-19	7-9		Freddie Burton	21.9	Paul Lizzo	
1989-90	3-23	1-15		Brent McCollin	19.0	Paul Lizzo	
1990-91	10-18	4-12		Brent McCollin	21.5	Paul Lizzo	
1991-92	11-18	7-9		Joe Griffin	15.5	Paul Lizzo	
1992-93	11-17	7-11		Joe Griffin	20.0	Paul Lizzo	
1993-94	3-24	2-16		Dave Masciale	12.3	Paul Lizzo	
1994-95	11-17	8-10		Joe Griffin	25.8	Paul Lizzo	245-308 .443
1995-96	9-19	5-13		Dave Masciale	17.1	Ray Haskins	
1996-97	21-9	15-3	●	Charles Jones	30.1	Ray Haskins	
1997-98	21-11	14-2	■	Charles Jones	29.0	Ray Haskins	51-39 .567
1998-99	10-17	10-10		Richie Parker	15.4	Ray Martin	
1999-2000	8-19	5-13		Antawn Dobie	13.4	Ray Martin	
2000-01	12-16	12-8		Ray Rivera	14.5	Ray Martin	
2001-02	5-22	5-15		Antawn Dobie	21.2	Ray Martin[b]	30-61 .330
2002-03	9-19	7-11		Antawn Dobie	19.1	Jim Ferry	
2003-04	8-19	4-14		Brandon Thomas	12.3	Jim Ferry	
2004-05	14-15	10-8		James Williams	16.3	Jim Ferry	
2005-06	12-16	9-9		James Williams	16.6	Jim Ferry	
2006-07	10-19	6-12		James Williams	16.2	Jim Ferry	
2007-08	15-15	7-11		Jaytornah Wisseh	15.8	Jim Ferry	
2008-09	16-14	12-6		Jaytornah Wisseh	15.2	Jim Ferry	84-117 .418

[a] **Record for Tri-State League; Metropolitan League records: 1965-66, 7-2; 1966-67, 5-4.**
[b] **Ray Martin (0-9) and Roy Brown (5-13) both coached during the 2001-02 season.**
● NCAA Tournament appearance ■ NIT appearance

PROFILE

Long Island University, Brooklyn, NY
Founded: 1926
Enrollment: 24,170 (10,634 undergraduate)
Colors: Black and silver
Nickname: Blackbirds
Current arena: Wellness, Recreation and Athletic Center, opened in 2006 (2,500)
Previous: Arnold and Marie Schwartz Athletic Center, 1963-2006 (1,000)
First game: 1928
All-time record: 1,097-820-2 (.572)
Total weeks in AP Top 20/25: 20
Current conference: Northeast (1981-)

Conference titles:
Metro: 4 (1936, '37, '38, '39); ECAC Metro: 2 (1983 [tie], '84 [tie]); Northeast: 2 (1997, '98)
Conference tournament titles:
ECAC Metro: 1 (1984)
Northeast: 1 (1997)
NCAA Tournament appearances: 3
NIT appearances: 10
Semifinals: 2
Titles: 2 (1939, '41)

CONSENSUS ALL-AMERICAS

1937 **Jules Bender**, G
1939 **Irving Torgoff**, F
1968 **Luther Green** (Little A-A), C
1968 **Larry Newbold** (Little A-A), G

FIRST-ROUND PRO PICKS

1947 **Dick Holub**, New York (5)
1953 **Ray Felix**, Baltimore (2)

TOP 5

G **Charles Jones** (1996-98)
G **Ossie Schectman** (1938-41)
F **Albie Grant** (1963-66)
F **Irving Torgoff** (1936-39)
F **Sherman White** (1948-51)

RECORDS

	GAME		SEASON		CAREER	
POINTS	63	Sherman White, vs. John Marshall (NJ) (Feb. 28, 1950)	903	Charles Jones (1996-97)	1,830	Joe Griffin (1991-95)
POINTS PER GAME			30.1	Charles Jones (1996-97)	29.5	Charles Jones (1996-98)
REBOUNDS	26	Charles Scurry, vs. Marist (Feb. 2, 1983)	418	Carey Scurry (1983-84)	1,013	Carey Scurry (1982-85)
ASSISTS	17	Antawn Dobie, vs. St. Francis (NY), (Dec. 15, 2002)	221	Charles Jones (1997-98)	610	Robert Cole (1979-83)

ESPN 300 SAGARIN

LONGWOOD

Longwood is the little team that could. Only four seasons after the program's founding, the Lancers reached the 1980 D3 final four. By 2001 they were a D2 power, with three NCAA trips, and in 2004-05 they began provisional Division I play. Little Longwood University in Farmville, Va., was now playing with the big boys. Such dizzying team success has almost overshadowed stars like NBAer Jerome Kersey and 2001 D2 Player of the Year Colin Ducharme. Almost.

BEST TEAM: 1979-80 Barely out of diapers, the four-year old Lancers went 28–3 with an astonishing 21 double-digit victories. Coach Ron Bash's D3 final four team was led by Shack Leonard and three 1,000-point scorers (Ken Ford, Joe Remar, Ron Orr). The Lancers' two postseason tourney semifinal losses were by a combined three points.

BEST PLAYER: F Jerome Kersey (1980-84) He did it all for Longwood and still ranks as the school's second all-time leading scorer (1,756) and the leader in rebounds (1,162), steals (255) and blocks (142). An All-America as a senior, Kersey averaged a D2-best 14.2 rebounds per game. He went on to play 17 NBA seasons, winning a championship ring with San Antonio in 1999.

BEST COACH: Cal Luther (1981-90) The school's winningest coach (136–105) took over in the second year of Longwood's transition from D3 to D2 and coached five of the top six all-time scoring leaders, including Kersey and career leader Kevin Jefferson (1,806).

GAME FOR THE AGES: The Lancers hadn't officially finished their move to D1 when, on Feb. 18, 2006, they beat longtime force James Madison, which had NCAA Tourney wins over Georgetown, Ohio State and West Virginia in the 1980s. Longwood's Maurice Sumter scored 27 points and Brandon Giles 21 in the 77-73 win.

FIERCEST RIVAL: Longwood and in-state rival Liberty are 50 miles apart, but it's an extra-long trip for the Flames, who dropped 10 straight at Longwood over one stretch. The Lancers lead the series, 17–8.

SEASON REVIEW

SEAS.	W-L	CONF.	SCORING		COACH	RECORD	
1976-77	2-9		Jimmy Yarbrough	22.5	Allen McNamee	2-9	.182
1977-78	8-16		Jimmy Yarbrough	16.8	Bill McAdams	8-16	.333
1978-79	19-8		Shack Leonard	16.1	Dr. Ron Bash		
1979-80	28-3		Ken Ford	15.9	Dr. Ron Bash		
1980-81	19-9		Jerome Kersey	16.9	Dr. Ron Bash	66-20	.767
1981-82	15-8		Jerome Kersey	17.0	Cal Luther		
1982-83	15-10		Joe Remar	18.7	Cal Luther		
1983-84	15-12		Jerome Kersey	19.6	Cal Luther		
1984-85	11-17		David Strothers	12.9	Cal Luther		
1985-86	14-13		Kenneth Fields	18.3	Cal Luther		
1986-87	13-14		Art Monroe	16.8	Cal Luther		
1987-88	19-10		Kevin Jefferson	23.7	Cal Luther		
1988-89	20-7		Kevin Jefferson	18.6	Cal Luther		
1989-90	14-14		Kevin Jefferson	25.6	Cal Luther	136-105	.564
1990-91	11-17		Billy Dunn	17.0	Ron Carr		
1991-92	14-14		Charles Brown	13.4	Ron Carr		
1992-93	17-10		Charles Brown	13.3	Ron Carr		
1993-94	23-6		Charles Brown	12.6	Ron Carr		
1994-95	19-9		Joe Jones	14.9	Ron Carr		
1995-96	11-17		Joe Jones	19.7	Ron Carr		
1996-97	11-17		Jason Outlaw	12.1	Ron Carr		
1997-98	13-15		Lee Farrior	20.2	Ron Carr		
1998-99	8-19		Jon Hughes	15.6	Ron Carr	127-124	.506
1999-2000	4-22		Lee Farrior	13.7	Mike Leeder		
2000-01	23-8		Jason Pryor	24.8	Mike Leeder		
2001-02	13-13		Marques Cunningham	19.3	Mike Leeder		
2002-03	15-14		Charles Stephens	22.7	Mike Leeder	55-57	.491
2003-04	5-22		Michael Jefferson	15.1	Mike Gillian		
2004-05	1-30		Michael Jefferson	15.4	Mike Gillian		
2005-06	10-20		Maurice Sumter	15.5	Mike Gillian		
2006-07	9-22		Maurice Sumter	16.7	Mike Gillian		
2007-08	9-22		Kirk Williams	16.9	Mike Gillian		
2008-09	17-14		Dana Smith	14.8	Mike Gillian	51-130	.282

THE SCHOOLS

PROFILE

Longwood University, Farmville, VA
Founded: 1839
Enrollment: 4,700 (4,044 undergraduate)
Colors: Blue and white
Nickname: Lancers
Current arena: Willett Hall, opened in 1980 (1,729)
Previous: French Gym, 1976-80 (500)
First game: Nov. 30, 1976
All-time record: 445-461 (.491)
Total weeks in AP Top 20/25: 0

Current conference: Independent (2004-)
Conference titles: 0
Conference tournament titles: 0
NCAA Tournament appearances: 0
NIT appearances: 0

CONSENSUS ALL-AMERICAS

1984 **Jerome Kersey** (D2), F
2001 **Colin Ducharme** (D2), C

TOP 5

G **Joe Remar** (1979-83)
G **Maurice Sumter** (2003-07)
F **Kevin Jefferson** (1986-90)
F **Jerome Kersey** (1980-84)
C **Colin Ducharme** (2000-01)

RECORDS

RECORDS	GAME		SEASON		CAREER	
POINTS	46	Jimmy Yarbrough, vs. Bluefield (Feb. 24, 1977)	745	Jason Pryor (2000-01)	1,806	Kevin Jefferson (1986-90)
POINTS PER GAME			25.6	Kevin Jefferson (1989-90)	25.5	Jason Pryor (2000-02)
REBOUNDS	26	Jerome Kersey, vs. Mount St. Mary's (Feb. 25, 1984); vs. UMBC (Feb. 13, 1984)	490	Colin Ducharme (2000-01)	1,162	Jerome Kersey (1980-84)
ASSISTS	15	Joe Remar, vs. Liberty (Feb. 16, 1981)	147	Ryan Earl (2002-03)	531	Joe Remar (1979-83)

ESPN 153 SAGARIN

LOUISIANA-LAFAYETTE

Few teams have made a bigger impact in their first Division I season than the Ragin' Cajuns did in 1971-72, with the longtime NAIA power making the NCAA Tournament. Few teams have crashed as hard and as fast, with the NCAA shutting down the program for two seasons in the '70s for recruiting violations. Since their return, the Cajuns have become one of the Sun Belt's more successful teams, but the NCAA also vacated many of their wins in the 2003-04 and '04-05 seasons for using an ineligible player.

BEST TEAM: 1972-73 Thanks to a nearly unstoppable transition game led by All-America guard Dwight "Bo" Lamar, the Cajuns won the Southland, rose to as high as No. 7 nationally and made the NCAA Tournament's Midwest Regional semifinals. In addition to Lamar, the Cajuns featured four other future NBA draft picks: guards Jerry Bisbano, Fred Saunders and Larry Fogle, and center Roy Ebron.

BEST PLAYER: G Dwight "Bo" Lamar (1969-73) Lighting it up from all over the court, the quick and creative Lamar is the only player in NCAA history to lead the nation in scoring at both the D1 and D2 levels.

BEST COACH: Beryl Shipley (1957-73) Shipley guided UL-Lafayette to its most successful stretch in school history, winning 293 games in 16 seasons and appearing in two NCAA Tournaments. His Cajuns coaching career came to an ignominious end, though, when the team got hit with the death penalty following the 1972-73 season, for myriad violations.

GAME FOR THE AGES: In the first round of the 1992 Tournament, the Cajuns knocked off No. 4-seed Oklahoma, 87-83. Five players hit both ends of one-and-one attempts in the final 1:48, including four in a row by Eric Mouton in the final 11 seconds.

FIERCEST RIVAL: Good luck finding a seat in the Cajundome when in-state and Sun Belt rival New Orleans is in town. UNO almost always gives the Cajuns a run for their money. Louisiana-Lafayette leads the series, 36–32, and six of those games have gone to OT.

SEASON REVIEW

SEAS.	W-L	CONF.	COACH	SEAS.	W-L	CONF.	COACH
1911-48	*312-275*	*Two 20-win seasons ('22-23, '39-40)*		**1961-62**	17-8		Beryl Shipley
1948-49	12-8		J.C. Reinhardt	**1962-63**	12-13		Beryl Shipley
1949-50	13-13		J.C. Reinhardt	**1963-64**	13-10		Beryl Shipley
1950-51	8-10		J.C. Reinhardt	**1964-65**	20-10		Beryl Shipley
1951-52	11-16		J.C. Reinhardt	**1965-66**	17-8		Beryl Shipley
1952-53	8-15		J.C. Reinhardt	**1966-67**	20-11		Beryl Shipley
1953-54	6-13		J.C. Reinhardt	**1967-68**	19-5		Beryl Shipley
1954-55	10-14		J.C. Reinhardt	**1968-69**	20-7		Beryl Shipley
1955-56	5-17		J.C. Reinhardt	**1969-70**	16-10		Beryl Shipley
1956-57	7-19		J.C. Reinhardt	**1970-71**	25-4		Beryl Shipley
1957-58	16-11		Beryl Shipley	**1971-72**	25-4 ⊗	8-0 ●	Beryl Shipley
1958-59	14-10		Beryl Shipley	**1972-73**	24-5 ⊗	12-0 ●	Beryl Shipley
1959-60	20-8		Beryl Shipley	**1973-75**	no team		
1960-61	18-5		Beryl Shipley	**1975-76**	7-19	4-6	Jim Hatfield

SEAS.	W-L	CONF.	SCORING		COACH	RECORD
1976-77	21-8	8-2	Andrew Toney	21.0	Jim Hatfield	
1977-78	19-8	7-3	Andrew Toney	24.5	Jim Hatfield	47-35 .573
1978-79	16-11	6-4	Andrew Toney	23.3	Bobby Paschal	
1979-80	21-9	5-5 ■	Andrew Toney	26.1	Bobby Paschal	
1980-81	15-13	6-4	Kevin Figaro	22.8	Bobby Paschal	
1981-82	24-8	8-2 ●	Alford Turner	17.6	Bobby Paschal	
1982-83	22-7	●	Graylin Warner	16.6	Bobby Paschal	
1983-84	23-10	■	George Almones	16.9	Bobby Paschal	
1984-85	17-14	■	George Almones	17.7	Bobby Paschal	
1985-86	15-13		Cedric Hill	21.0	Bobby Paschal	153-85 .643
1986-87	11-17		Randal Smith	18.4	Marty Fletcher	
1987-88	12-16	3-7	Earl Watkins	17.5	Marty Fletcher	
1988-89	17-12	4-6	Sydney Grider	23.4	Marty Fletcher	
1989-90	20-9	4-6	Sydney Grider	25.5	Marty Fletcher	
1990-91	21-10	6-6	Kevin Brooks	21.2	Marty Fletcher	
1991-92	21-11	12-4 ●	Todd Hill	14.1	Marty Fletcher	
1992-93	17-13	11-7	Michael Allen	20.9	Marty Fletcher	
1993-94	22-8	13-5 ●	Michael Allen	22.7	Marty Fletcher	
1994-95	7-22	4-14	Bryan Collins	13.3	Marty Fletcher	
1995-96	16-12	9-9	Conley Verdun	16.8	Marty Fletcher	
1996-97	12-16	9-9	Reginald Poole	16.0	Marty Fletcher	176-146 .547
1997-98	18-13	12-6	Casey Green	16.9	Jessie Evans	
1998-99	13-16	7-7	Reginald Poole	14.7	Jessie Evans	
1999-2000	25-9	13-3 ●	Orlando Butler	13.1	Jessie Evans	
2000-01	16-13	10-6	Anthony Johnson	15.5	Jessie Evans	
2001-02	20-11	11-4 ■	Anthony Johnson	14.9	Jessie Evans	
2002-03	20-10	12-3 ■	Brad Boyd	16.8	Jessie Evans	
2003-04	20-9 ⊗	12-3 ●	Antoine Landry	13.3	Jessie Evans	132-81 .620▼
2004-05	20-11 ⊗	11-4 ●	Tiras Wade	20.3	Robert Lee	
2005-06	13-16	7-8	Dwayne Mitchell	16.6	Robert Lee	
2006-07	9-21	7-11	Ross Mouton	17.1	Robert Lee	
2007-08	15-15	11-7	Chris Gradnigo	9.6	Robert Lee	
2008-09	10-20	7-11	Chris Gradnigo	13.3	Robert Lee	67-82 .450▼

⊗ Records don't reflect games forfeited or vacated. **For adjusted records, see p. 521.**

▼ Coaches' records adjusted to reflect games forfeited or vacated: Jessie Evans, 118-80, .605; Robert Lee, 50-82, .379. **For yearly totals, see p. 521.**

● NCAA Tournament appearance ■ NIT appearance

PROFILE

University of Louisiana at Lafayette, Lafayette, LA
Founded: 1900
Enrollment: 16,345 (14,931 undergraduate)
Colors: Vermilion and white
Nickname: Ragin' Cajuns
Current arena: Cajundome, opened in 1985 (11,550)
Previous: Blackham Coliseum, 1948-85 (5,000); Earl K. Long Gymnasium, 1936-48 (2,000); SLI Gymnasium, 1926-36 (1,000)
First game: 1911
All-time record: 1,263-959 (.568)
Total weeks in AP Top 20/25: 32
Current conference: Sun Belt (1991-)

Conference titles:
Southland: 4 (1972-v, '73-v, '77, '82)
Sun Belt: 6 (1992 [tie], 2000 [tie], '02 [tie], '03 [tie], '04 [tie]-v, '08 [tie])
Conference tournament titles:
Southland: 1 (1982)
Sun Belt: 5 (1992, '94, 2000, '04-v, '05-v)
NCAA Tournaments: 9 (4 appearances vacated)
NIT appearances: 5
Semifinals: 1
v – title vacated

CONSENSUS ALL-AMERICAS

1965	**Dean Church** (Little A-A), G
1970	**Marvin Winkler** (Little A-A), G
1971	**Dwight "Bo" Lamar** (Little A-A), G
1972, '73	**Dwight "Bo" Lamar**, G

FIRST-ROUND PRO PICKS

1973	**Dwight "Bo" Lamar**, San Diego (ABA, 1)
1980	**Andrew Toney**, Philadelphia (8)
1991	**Kevin Brooks**, Milwaukee (18)

TOP 5

G	**Dwight "Bo" Lamar** (1969-73)
G	**Andrew Toney** (1976-80)
F	**Kevin Brooks** (1987-91)
F	**Jerry Flake** (1965-69)
C	**Roy Ebron** (1970-73)

RECORDS

	GAME		SEASON		CAREER	
POINTS	62	Dwight "Bo" Lamar, vs. Louisiana-Monroe (Feb. 25, 1971)	1,054	Dwight "Bo" Lamar (1971-72)	3,493	Dwight "Bo" Lamar (1969-73)
POINTS PER GAME			36.3	Dwight "Bo" Lamar (1971-72)	31.2	Dwight "Bo" Lamar (1969-73)
REBOUNDS	28	Roy Ebron, vs. Northwestern State (Jan. 10, 1972)	500	Elvin Ivory (1966-67)	1,064	Roy Ebron (1970-73)
ASSISTS	18	Ted Lyles, vs. Houston Baptist (Dec. 10, 1975)	264	Aaron Mitchell (1989-90)	674	Aaron Mitchell (1987-91)

ESPN 257 SAGARIN

LOUISIANA-MONROE

The 2006-07 season brought a lot of changes to ULM. For one thing, the school became full members of the Sun Belt (it had been football-only since 2001). For another, the school retired the old Indians mascot and became the Warhawks. Still, Louisiana-Monroe's basketball tradition runs deep: They've won nine regular-season titles in two different D1 conferences (TAAC, Southland). For all the success, though, one thing has eluded the program: an NCAA Tournament win. ULM has never come within eight points of victory in seven tries.

BEST TEAM: 1978-79 After eight games, the Indians were .500, having lost their last two in OT. Calvin Natt and crew won the next 17, riding that momentum to the TAAC tournament title. That earned them a berth in the NIT, where they fell to Virginia, 79-78, on a baseline jumper with :07 left.

BEST PLAYER: F Calvin Natt (1975-79) A son of a Baptist minister, the 6'6" Natt became a fan favorite for his ability to score both in the paint and off of the dribble and for his rebounding mastery. Natt is the only player in ULM history with 2,000 points and 1,000 boards. He was picked eighth overall in the 1979 NBA draft.

BEST COACH: Mike Vining (1981-2005) He allowed players freedom in his motion-oriented system, with fine results: six 20-win seasons, seven regular-season conference championships and seven NCAA Tourneys. Vining was also a four-time Southland Coach of the Year.

GAME FOR THE AGES: On Jan. 15, 1976, Centenary entered Ewing Coliseum ranked No. 18 in the nation behind center Robert Parish. ULM sprung a 59-57 upset for the school's first victory over a ranked opponent. Natt hit a layup with :05 left to win the game.

FIERCEST RIVAL: The 2008-09 season marked the return of Louisiana-Monroe's feud with Louisiana Tech, just 37 miles down I-20. The series, which the Bulldogs lead 47–36, began in 1954 but had been suspended after the 1990-91 season, when Tech joined the Sun Belt.

SEASON REVIEW

SEAS.	W-L	CONF.	COACH	SEAS.	W-L	CONF.	COACH
1951-52	2-15		Carl Phillips	1959-60	3-21		Lenny Fant
1952-53	6-18		Carl Phillips	1960-61	12-13		Lenny Fant
1953-54	7-16		Arnold Kilpatrick	1961-62	17-8		Lenny Fant
1954-55	21-13		Arnold Kilpatrick	1962-63	15-11		Lenny Fant
1955-56	16-13		Arnold Kilpatrick	1963-64	14-11		Lenny Fant
1956-57	14-10		Arnold Kilpatrick	1964-65	18-4		Lenny Fant
1957-58	8-15		Lenny Fant	1965-66	16-8		Lenny Fant
1958-59	12-13		Lenny Fant	1966-67	13-11		Lenny Fant

SEAS.	W-L	CONF.		SCORING		COACH	RECORD
1967-68	12-11			Glynn Saulters	31.3	Lenny Fant	
1968-69	12-11			Roger Stockton	19.0	Lenny Fant	
1969-70	20-9			Henry Steele	20.9	Lenny Fant	
1970-71	16-6			Henry Steele	22.5	Lenny Fant	
1971-72	16-7			Henry Steele	18.4	Lenny Fant	
1972-73	15-10			Mike Rose	18.4	Lenny Fant	
1973-74	16-10			Mike Rose	18.3	Lenny Fant	
1974-75	15-10			David Pickett	21.3	Lenny Fant	
1975-76	18-7			Jerry Jingles	20.8	Lenny Fant	
1976-77	15-12			Calvin Natt	29.0	Lenny Fant	
1977-78	20-7			Calvin Natt	21.3	Lenny Fant	
1978-79	23-6		■	Calvin Natt	24.4	Lenny Fant	326-221 .596
1979-80	18-10	6-0		Kenny Natt	20.1	Benny Hollis	
1980-81	15-13	8-4		Donald Wilson	17.3	Benny Hollis	33-23 .589
1981-82	19-11	9-7	●	Donald Wilson	16.3	Mike Vining	
1982-83	14-14	6-6		Terry Martin	15.1	Mike Vining	
1983-84	17-12	9-3		Bruce Williams	13.6	Mike Vining	
1984-85	17-12	4-8		Arthur Hayes	15.5	Mike Vining	
1985-86	20-10	9-3	●	Bobby Jenkins	19.4	Mike Vining	
1986-87	13-15	3-7		Michael Saulsberry	14.2	Mike Vining	
1987-88	21-9	10-4	■	Michael Saulsberry	16.5	Mike Vining	
1988-89	17-12	9-5		Anthony Jones	15.0	Mike Vining	
1989-90	22-8	13-1	●	Fred Thompson	16.4	Mike Vining	
1990-91	25-8	13-1	●	Anthony Jones	15.0	Mike Vining	
1991-92	19-10	12-6	●	Ryan Stuart	21.6	Mike Vining	
1992-93	26-5	17-1	●	Ryan Stuart	21.1	Mike Vining	
1993-94	19-9	15-3		Larry Carr	18.6	Mike Vining	
1994-95	14-18	11-7		Larry Carr	17.0	Mike Vining	
1995-96	16-14	13-5	●	Paul Marshall	21.3	Mike Vining	
1996-97	14-14	10-6		Anthony Cook	14.8	Mike Vining	
1997-98	13-16	8-8		Maurice Bell	15.3	Mike Vining	
1998-99	13-14	12-6		Mike Smith	18.5	Mike Vining	
1999-2000	19-9	13-5		Maurice Bell	21.9	Mike Vining	
2000-01	11-17	8-12		Brian Lubeck	13.7	Mike Vining	
2001-02	20-12	15-5		Brian Lubeck	14.6	Mike Vining	
2002-03	12-16	10-10		Kirby Lemons	16.7	Mike Vining	
2003-04	12-19	8-8		John Andrews	9.9	Mike Vining	
2004-05	8-19	2-14		Cecil Hood	9.9	Mike Vining	401-303 .570
2005-06	10-18	6-10		Tony Hooper	10.6	Orlando Early	
2006-07	18-14	11-7		Tony Hooper	15.4	Orlando Early	
2007-08	10-21	4-14		Tony Hooper	15.1	Orlando Early	
2008-09	10-20	6-12		Malcolm Thomas	12.3	Orlando Early	48-73 .397

● NCAA Tournament appearance ■ NIT appearance

PROFILE

University of Louisiana at Monroe, Monroe, LA
Founded: 1931
Enrollment: 8,541 (7,296 undergraduate)
Colors: Maroon and gold
Nickname: Warhawks
Current arena: Fant-Ewing Coliseum, opened in 1971 (8,000)
Previous: Monroe Civic Center Arena, 1969-71 (7,000); Brown Gymnasium, 1951-69 (1,200)
First game: Dec. 6, 1951
All-time record: 874-705 (.554)

Total weeks in AP Top 20/25: 0
Current conference: Sun Belt (2006-)
Conference titles:
Trans America: 2 (1979, '80)
Southland: 7 (1986, '90, '91, '93, '94, '96, '97 [tie])
Sun Belt: 1 (2007 [tie])
Conference tournament titles:
Trans America: 2 (1979, '82)
Southland: 6 (1986, '90, '91, '92, '93, '96)
NCAA Tournament appearances: 7
NIT appearances: 2

FIRST-ROUND PRO PICKS

1979 **Calvin Natt,** New Jersey (8)

TOP 5

G **Lanny Johnson** (1958-62)
G **Glynn Saulters** (1964-68)
F **Calvin Natt** (1975-79)
F **Ryan Stuart** (1991-93)
C **Wojciech Myrda** (1998-2002)

RECORDS

RECORDS	GAME		SEASON		CAREER	
POINTS	51	Glynn Saulters, vs. Nicholls State (Feb. 1, 1968)	782	Calvin Natt (1976-77)	2,581	Calvin Natt (1975-79)
POINTS PER GAME			31.3	Glynn Saulters (1967-68)	23.9	Calvin Natt (1975-79)
REBOUNDS	31	Calvin Natt, vs. Georgia Southern (Dec. 29, 1976); Billy May, vs. Southeastern La. (Jan. 10, 1959)	473	Bill Bradley (1954-55)	1,285	Calvin Natt (1975-79)
ASSISTS	19	Larry Saulters, vs. Mississippi College (Feb. 28, 1970)	251	Larry Saulters (1969-70)	437	Bob Patterson (1954-58)

ESPN 62 SAGARIN

LOUISIANA STATE

Never won a national championship in hoops? Playing basketball in a football-crazy town? Doesn't matter. The Tigers consistently generate plenty of buzz. Credit is largely owed to three players who dominated with distinctly different styles in different eras: Bob Pettit, the 6'9" pivot man who reigned supreme in the early 1950s; "Pistol" Pete Maravich, the dazzling showman and deadly sharpshooter of the late 1960s; and Shaquille O'Neal, the unstoppable inside force who ruled in the early 1990s.

BEST TEAM: 1980-81 The Tigers won 31 games, including 26 straight. For the first three games of the NCAA Tournament, they lived up to their No. 1 seed, too. But standout forward Rudy Macklin broke a finger in LSU's Elite Eight win over Wichita State, leaving him at less than 100% for the Final Four matchup against Indiana. The Tigers were overwhelmed 67-49—the third straight year they were eliminated by the eventual champs.

BEST PLAYER: G "Pistol" Pete Maravich (1967-70) Coach Press Maravich's son was such a finished product when he reached college that many Tigers fans filled the stands for Pete's freshman-team games, then left before the varsity took the floor. With an unrivaled combination of athleticism, shooting skill, artistry and hoops IQ, Maravich holds NCAA Division I career records for points (3,667), scoring average (44.2 ppg) and most games with 50 or more points (28). After a long NBA career, Maravich was inducted into the Naismith Hall of Fame in 1987. He died of a sudden heart attack in 1988 at age 40.

BEST COACH: Dale Brown (1972-97) Without question, he improved the program: Before Brown arrived, Louisiana State hadn't made the NCAA Tournament since 1954. In 25 seasons, he guided the Tigers to 13 appearances. And he could inspire. In 1987, Brown vowed not to sleep until the 18–13 Tigers won the SEC tournament. (Four sleepless days later, LSU lost in the final.)

GAME FOR THE AGES: When No. 14-ranked LSU played host to No. 20 Loyola Marymount on Feb. 3, 1990, the action was so crazy that the electric typewriter the school used to log the play-by-play summary couldn't keep up with the frenzied typist and eventually burned out. The Tigers, on the other hand, kept attacking. Led by O'Neal and Chris Jackson, they outran and outgunned Hank Gathers, Bo Kimble and the rest of the Lions to win, 148-141, in overtime.

HEARTBREAKER: Kentucky fans call it the Mardi Gras Miracle, but to LSU fans it's more like the Mardi Gras Meltdown. On Fat Tuesday, Feb. 15, 1994, the host Tigers ran up a 68-37 lead over Kentucky. Insurmountable? It should have been, but the Wildcats pulled out a 99-95 shocker, the biggest second-half comeback in NCAA history.

FIERCEST RIVAL: From the moment Brown took the reins at Louisiana State in the early 1970s, he obsessed over how the Tigers fared against SEC power Kentucky. During his tenure, the Tigers managed to go 19–34 against the Wildcats, a record that's more respectable than it looks considering that, through 2008-09, LSU has beaten UK only five other times against 44 losses *without* Brown at the helm.

FANFARE AND HOOPLA: Louisiana State tickets are free to students and are handed out on a first-come, first-served basis, so Maravich Maniacs—even after all these years—often spend their nights camped outside the Palace That Pete Built.

FAN FAVORITE: C Shaquille O'Neal (1989-92) It was comical how easily he dominated the competition, and the 7'1", 300-pound man-mountain was even funnier off the court. As he once put it, LSU stands for "Love Shaq University."

CONSENSUS ALL-AMERICAS

1954	**Bob Pettit**, F/C
1968-70	**Pete Maravich**, G
1989, '90	**Chris Jackson**, G
1991, '92	**Shaquille O'Neal**, C

FIRST-ROUND PRO PICKS

1952	**Joe Dean**, Indianapolis (5)
1954	**Bob Pettit**, Milwaukee (2)
1970	**Pete Maravich**, Atlanta (3)
1983	**Howard Carter**, Denver (15)
1985	**Jerry Reynolds**, Milwaukee (22)
1986	**John Williams**, Washington (12)
1990	**Chris Jackson**, Denver (3)
1991	**Stanley Roberts**, Orlando (23)
1992	**Shaquille O'Neal**, Orlando (1)
1993	**Geert Hammink**, Orlando (26)
2000	**Stromile Swift**, Vancouver (2)
2006	**Tyrus Thomas**, Portland (4)
2008	**Anthony Randolph**, Golden State (14)

PROFILE

Louisiana State University, Baton Rouge, LA
Founded: 1860
Enrollment: 29,317 (21,811 undergraduate)
Colors: Purple and gold
Nicknames: Tigers, Fighting Tigers
Current arena: Pete Maravich Assembly Center, opened in 1971 (13,215)
Previous: Field House, later named Huey Long Field House, 1932-71 (3,000)
First game: Jan. 30, 1909
All-time record: 1,386-1,036 (.572)
Total weeks in AP Top 20/25: 195
Current conference: Southeastern (1932-)
Conference titles:
SEC: 10 (1935 [tie], '53, '54, [tie] '79, '81, '85, '91 [tie], 2000 [tie], '06, '09)
Conference tournament titles:
SEC: 1 (1980)
NCAA Tournament appearances: 20
Sweet 16s (since 1975): 7
Final Fours: 4
NIT appearances: 5
Semifinals: 1

TOP 5

G	**Chris Jackson** (1988-90)
G	**Pete Maravich** (1967-70)
F	**Rudy Macklin** (1976-78, '79-81)
F/C	**Bob Pettit** (1951-54)
C	**Shaquille O'Neal** (1989-92)

RECORDS	GAME		SEASON		CAREER	
POINTS	69	Pete Maravich, vs. Alabama (Feb. 7, 1970)	1,381	Pete Maravich (1969-70)	3,667	Pete Maravich (1967-70)
POINTS PER GAME			44.5	Pete Maravich (1969-70)	44.2	Pete Maravich (1967-70)
REBOUNDS	32	Rudy Macklin, vs. Tulane (Nov. 26, 1976)	474	Al Sanders (1969-70)	1,276	Rudy Macklin (1976-78, '79-81)
ASSISTS	19	Kenny Higgs, vs. Georgia (Jan. 17, 1977)	239	Kenny Higgs (1976-77)	645	Kenny Higgs (1974-78)

SEASON REVIEW

SEASON	W-L	CONF.	SCORING	COACH	RECORD		SEASON	W-L	CONF.	SCORING	COACH	RECORD
1909-16	*53-31*		*Only losing coach of early era, F.M. Long, was 6-9 in 1911-12, '12-13*				1926-27	7-9	3-5		Harry Rabenhorst	
1916-17	20-2			Dr. C. C. Stroud			1927-28	14-4	7-3		Harry Rabenhorst	
1917-18	12-1			Dr. C. C. Stroud			1928-29	8-13	5-9		Harry Rabenhorst	
1918-19	1-0			R.E. Edmonds	1-0	1.000	1929-30	10-11	6-7		Harry Rabenhorst	
1919-20	19-2			Dr. C. C. Stroud	82-21	.796	1930-31	7-8	4-4		Harry Rabenhorst	
1920-21	19-4			Branch Bocock	19-4	.826	1931-32	11-9	8-8		Harry Rabenhorst	
1921-22	15-1			Tad Gormley			1932-33	15-8	13-7		Harry Rabenhorst	
1922-23	10-10	0-6		Tad Gormley	25-11	.694	1933-34	13-4	13-3		Harry Rabenhorst	
1923-24	8-12	0-7		Moon Ducote	8-12	.400	1934-35	14-1	12-0		Harry Rabenhorst	
1924-25	10-7	1-4		Gob Wilson	10-7	.588	1935-36	10-10	9-6		Harry Rabenhorst	
1925-26	9-9	4-5		Harry Rabenhorst			1936-37	13-7	7-6		Harry Rabenhorst	

SEAS.	W-L	CONF.	POSTSEASON	SCORING		REBOUNDS		ASSISTS		COACH	RECORD	
1937-38	10-10	7-6								Harry Rabenhorst		
1938-39	13-7	10-5								Harry Rabenhorst		
1939-40	10-8	8-4								Harry Rabenhorst		
1940-41	9-9	7-5								Harry Rabenhorst		
1941-42	8-7	8-3								Harry Rabenhorst		
1942-43	18-4	11-2								Dale Morey		
1943-44	10-15	0-4								Dale Morey	28-19	.596
1944-45	15-9	3-3		Clyde Lindsey	15.7					Jesse Fatherree[a]	11-7	.611
1945-46	18-3	8-0		Joe Bill Adcock	18.6					Harry Rabenhorst		
1946-47	17-4	8-2		Frank Brian	16.2					Harry Rabenhorst		
1947-48	8-18	4-10		Bob Meador	9.8					Harry Rabenhorst		
1948-49	15-10	7-6		Bob Meador	12.2					Harry Rabenhorst		
1949-50	13-12	5-8		Joe Dean	10.8					Harry Rabenhorst		
1950-51	10-14	6-8		Joe Dean	15.1					Harry Rabenhorst		
1951-52	17-7	9-5		Bob Pettit	25.5	Bob Pettit	13.7			Harry Rabenhorst		
1952-53	22-3	13-0	NCAA FOURTH PLACE	Bob Pettit	24.7	Bob Pettit	11.9			Harry Rabenhorst		
1953-54	20-5	14-0	NCAA REGIONAL SEMIFINALS	Bob Pettit	31.4	Bob Pettit	17.3			Harry Rabenhorst		
1954-55	6-18	3-11		Roger Sigler	15.0	Ned Clark	15.8			Harry Rabenhorst		
1955-56	7-17	5-9		Roger Sigler	25.1	Roger Sigler	13.8			Harry Rabenhorst		
1956-57	6-19	1-13		Roger Sigler	18.4	Troy Rushing	10.3			Harry Rabenhorst	340-264	.563
1957-58	7-18	3-11		Dom Merle	12.3	Jim Crisco	9.0			Jay McCreary		
1958-59	10-15	2-12		Jim Crisco	12.2	Jim Crisco	7.6			Jay McCreary		
1959-60	5-18	3-11		Dick Davies	12.4	Tom Conklin	6.2			Jay McCreary		
1960-61	11-14	6-8		George Nattin	16.5	Tom Conklin	9.0			Jay McCreary		
1961-62	13-11	7-7		George Nattin	12.8	Maury Drummond	12.5			Jay McCreary		
1962-63	12-12	5-9		Dick Maile	14.0	Dick Maile	10.9			Jay McCreary		
1963-64	12-13	8-6		Dick Maile	20.7	Dick Maile	10.5			Jay McCreary		
1964-65	12-14	7-9		Dick Maile	17.1	Dick Maile	9.8			Jay McCreary	82-115	.416
1965-66	6-20	2-14		Harry Heroman	17.6	Harry Heroman	7.7			Frank Truitt	6-20	.231
1966-67	3-23	1-17		Kenny Drost	16.5	Ralph Jukkola	7.2			Press Maravich		
1967-68	14-12	8-10		Pete Maravich	43.8	Ralph Jukkola	8.6	Pete Maravich	4.0	Press Maravich		
1968-69	13-13	7-11		Pete Maravich	44.2	Dave Ramsden	10.8	Pete Maravich	4.9	Press Maravich		
1969-70	22-10	13-5	NIT FOURTH PLACE	Pete Maravich	44.5	Al Sanders	14.8	Pete Maravich	6.1	Press Maravich		
1970-71	14-12	10-8		Al Sanders	20.9	Al Sanders	14.7	Tommy Hess	5.0	Press Maravich		
1971-72	10-16	6-12		Bill Newton	18.9	Al Sanders	12.5	Tommy Hess	5.0	Press Maravich	76-86	.469
1972-73	14-10	9-9		Eddie Palubinskas	18.6	Collis Temple	6.9	Eddie Palubinskas	4.1	Dale Brown		
1973-74	12-14	6-12		Glenn Hansen	19.4	Collis Temple	10.5	Eddie Palubinskas	3.7	Dale Brown		
1974-75	10-16	6-12		Glenn Hansen	21.7	Glenn Hansen	10.0	Mike Darnall	6.6	Dale Brown		
1975-76	12-14	5-13		Kenny Higgs	22.2	Ed LeBlanc	10.4	Kenny Higgs	6.6	Dale Brown		
1976-77	15-12	8-10		Kenny Higgs	17.7	Rudy Macklin	11.8	Kenny Higgs	8.8	Dale Brown		
1977-78	18-9	12-6		Rudy Macklin	19.0	Rudy Macklin	10.6	Ethan Martin	4.5	Dale Brown		
1978-79	23-6	14-4	NCAA REGIONAL SEMIFINALS	Al Green	17.7	Lionel Green	11.1	Ethan Martin	5.3	Dale Brown		
1979-80	26-6	14-4	NCAA REGIONAL FINALS	Rudy Macklin	17.6	Rudy Macklin	9.7	Ethan Martin	5.4	Dale Brown		
1980-81	31-5	17-1	NCAA FOURTH PLACE	Howard Carter	16.0	Rudy Macklin	9.8	Ethan Martin	5.5	Dale Brown		
1981-82	14-14	11-7	NIT FIRST ROUND	Howard Carter	16.7	Leonard Mitchell	7.6	Derrick Taylor	3.2	Dale Brown		
1982-83	19-13	10-8	NIT FIRST ROUND	Howard Carter	17.6	Leonard Mitchell	9.1	Johnny Jones	4.0	Dale Brown		
1983-84	18-11	11-7	NCAA FIRST ROUND	Jerry Reynolds	14.2	Jerry Reynolds	8.2	John Tudor	3.5	Dale Brown		
1984-85	19-10	13-5	NCAA FIRST ROUND	Nikita Wilson	15.0	Nikita Wilson	6.9	Jerry Reynolds	3.6	Dale Brown		
1985-86	26-12	9-9	NCAA NATIONAL SEMIFINALS	John Williams	17.8	John Williams	8.5	Derrick Taylor	3.8	Dale Brown		
1986-87	24-15	8-10	NCAA REGIONAL FINALS	Anthony Wilson	16.6	Oliver Brown	7.3	Bernard Woodside	2.9	Dale Brown		
1987-88	16-14	10-8	NCAA FIRST ROUND	Ricky Blanton	17.0	Ricky Blanton	8.8	Bernard Woodside	4.5	Dale Brown		
1988-89	20-12	11-7	NCAA FIRST ROUND	Chris Jackson	30.2	Ricky Blanton	8.2	Ricky Blanton	4.6	Dale Brown		
1989-90	23-9	12-6	NCAA SECOND ROUND	Chris Jackson	27.8	Shaquille O'Neal	12.0	Maurice Williamson	3.8	Dale Brown		
1990-91	20-10	13-5	NCAA FIRST ROUND	Shaquille O'Neal	27.6	Shaquille O'Neal	14.7	T.J. Pugh	6.5	Dale Brown		
1991-92	21-10	12-4	NCAA SECOND ROUND	Shaquille O'Neal	24.1	Shaquille O'Neal	14.0	Jamie Brandon	3.6	Dale Brown		
1992-93	22-11	9-7	NCAA FIRST ROUND	Geert Hammink	15.2	Geert Hammink	10.2	Andre Owens	2.7	Dale Brown		
1993-94	11-16	5-11		Jamie Brandon	16.5	Clarence Ceasar	6.3	Andre Owens	4.0	Dale Brown		
1994-95	12-15	6-10		Ronnie Henderson	23.3	Clarence Ceasar	7.0	Randy Livingston	9.4	Dale Brown		
1995-96	12-17	4-12		Ronnie Henderson	21.8	Roman Rubchenko	6.9	Gene Nabors	3.3	Dale Brown		
1996-97	10-20	3-13		Duane Spencer	15.1	Duane Spencer	7.7	Gene Nabors	2.4	Dale Brown	448-301	.598
1997-98	9-18	2-14		Maurice Carter	14.4	Cedric Carter	6.1	DeJuan Collins	3.4	John Brady		
1998-99	12-15	4-12		Maurice Carter	17.3	Jabari Smith	9.7	Jamaal Wolfe	2.5	John Brady		
1999-2000	28-6	12-4	NCAA REGIONAL SEMIFINALS	Stromile Swift	16.2	Stromile Swift	8.2	Torris Bright	4.3	John Brady		
2000-01	13-16	2-14		Ronald Dupree	17.3	Ronald Dupree	8.8	Torris Bright	4.1	John Brady		
2001-02	19-15	6-10	NIT SECOND ROUND	Ronald Dupree	16.2	Ronald Dupree	8.5	Torris Bright	3.8	John Brady		
2002-03	21-11	8-8	NCAA FIRST ROUND	Ronald Dupree	15.8	Jaime Lloreda	9.0	Torris Bright	4.7	John Brady		
2003-04	18-11	8-8	NIT FIRST ROUND	Jaime Lloreda	16.9	Jaime Lloreda	11.6	Xavier Whipple	3.0	John Brady		
2004-05	20-10	12-4	NCAA FIRST ROUND	Brandon Bass	17.3	Brandon Bass	9.1	Tack Minor	4.6	John Brady		
2005-06	27-9	14-2	NCAA NATIONAL SEMIFINALS	Glen Davis	18.6	Glen Davis	9.7	Darrel Mitchell	4.4	John Brady		
2006-07	17-15	5-11		Glen Davis	17.7	Glen Davis	10.4	Garrett Temple	4.3	John Brady		
2007-08	13-18	6-10		Marcus Thornton	19.6	Anthony Randolph	8.5	Garrett Temple	3.6	John Brady[b]	192-139	.580
2008-09	27-8	13-3	NCAA SECOND ROUND	Marcus Thornton	21.1	T. Mitchell, C. Johnson	7.2	Garrett Temple	3.8	Trent Johnson	27-8	.771

[a] Jesse Fatherree (11-7) and A.L. Swanson (4-2) both coached during the 1944-45 season.

[b] John Brady (8-13) and Butch Pierre (5-5) both coached during the 2007-08 season.

ESPN 162 SAGARIN

LOUISIANA TECH

Randy White, P.J. Brown, Paul Millsap. Few mid-majors come even close to Louisiana Tech's legacy of NBA-worthy big men. Who knows? The next great one could be working out right now in the weight room named after the man who started it all, Karl Malone.

BEST TEAM: 1984-85 With the Mailman punishing opponents in the paint, Tech averaged more than 5,000 fans per game for the first and only time in school history. But Malone didn't carry the Bulldogs to the Sweet 16 all by himself. They had a savvy point guard in Wayne Smith, a good shot-blocker in Willie Simmons and a revved-up fast break that backed up the nickname the Dunkin' Dawgs.

BEST PLAYER: F KARL MALONE (1982-85) The muscle-bound country kid averaged 20.9 points during his first season (he was academically ineligible as a freshman in 1981-82). Malone's power game elevated his teammates, as evidenced by the school's first Tourney win in 1984 and its first Sweet 16 trip in 1985.

BEST COACH: ANDY RUSSO (1979-85) This Don Haskins disciple wasn't nearly satisfied by Tech's one Tourney win in 1984. So in the off-season he made a pilgrimage to Fresno State to learn a few things from defensive guru Boyd Grant. *Voilà!* The next March, Tech used its new assortment of match-up zone schemes and half-court man defenses to make the Sweet 16.

GAME FOR THE AGES: When the Sooners and the Bulldogs met in the 1985 Sweet 16, it was a much-hyped battle of the titans, Wayman Tisdale and Malone. The Mailman muscled his way to 20 points, but Tisdale sank the last shot in Oklahoma's 86-84 OT win.

FIERCEST RIVAL: There's something about Tech that gets under Fresno State's skin. Maybe it's the shared nickname, or the annual 1,816-mile trek since the two packs of Bulldogs joined the WAC in 2001. Whatever the reason, one game started it all: On Feb. 21, 2002, Tech guard Gerrod Henderson hit a buzzer-beater three to top Fresno. It's been a dogfight ever since, with Fresno leading the series 11–10.

THE SCHOOLS

SEASON REVIEW

SEAS.	W-L	CONF.	COACH	SEAS.	W-L	CONF.	COACH
1925-47	*198-183*	*Best team, 1945-46 (16-8)*		**1960-61**	7-16		Cecil Crowley
1947-48	14-10		Cecil Crowley	**1961-62**	6-17		Cecil Crowley
1948-49	11-11		Cecil Crowley	**1962-63**	10-13		Cecil Crowley
1949-50	11-9		Cecil Crowley	**1963-64**	12-10		Cecil Crowley
1950-51	11-10		Cecil Crowley	**1964-65**	10-11		Scotty Robertson
1951-52	13-11		Cecil Crowley	**1965-66**	14-11		Scotty Robertson
1952-53	17-10		Cecil Crowley	**1966-67**	20-8		Scotty Robertson
1953-54	11-14		Cecil Crowley	**1967-68**	16-9		Scotty Robertson
1954-55	20-10		Cecil Crowley	**1968-69**	12-13		Scotty Robertson
1955-56	11-14		Cecil Crowley	**1969-70**	17-5		Scotty Robertson
1956-57	14-11		Cecil Crowley	**1970-71**	23-5		Scotty Robertson
1957-58	15-10		Cecil Crowley	**1971-72**	23-3	6-2	Scotty Robertson
1958-59	21-4		Cecil Crowley	**1972-73**	18-8	8-4	Scotty Robertson
1959-60	17-9		Cecil Crowley	**1973-74**	8-13	0-0[a]	Scotty Robertson

SEAS.	W-L	CONF.		SCORING		COACH	RECORD	
1974-75	12-13	5-3		Lanky Wells	460	Emmett Hendricks		
1975-76	15-11	9-1		Mike McConathy	642	Emmett Hendricks		
1976-77	13-13	4-6		Mike McConathy	716	Emmett Hendricks	40-37	.519
1977-78	6-21	2-8		Victor King	356	J.D. Barnett		
1978-79	17-8	6-4		Victor King	509	J.D. Barnett	23-29	.442
1979-80	17-10	10-5		Joe Ivory	468	Andy Russo		
1980-81	20-10	7-3		Dave Simmons	498	Andy Russo		
1981-82	11-16	2-8		Ken Roberson	303	Andy Russo		
1982-83	19-9	8-4		Karl Malone	20.9	Andy Russo		
1983-84	26-7	8-4	●	Karl Malone	18.8	Andy Russo		
1984-85	29-3	11-1	●	Karl Malone	16.5	Andy Russo	122-55	.689
1985-86	20-14	6-6	■	Robert Godbolt	448	Tommy Eagles		
1986-87	22-8	9-1	●	Robert Godbolt	483	Tommy Eagles		
1987-88	22-9	7-3	■	Randy White	578	Tommy Eagles		
1988-89	23-9	6-4	●	Randy White	678	Tommy Eagles	87-40	.685
1989-90	20-8	8-2	■	Anthony Dade	488	Jerry Loyd		
1990-91	21-10	8-4	■	Anthony Dade	447	Jerry Loyd		
1991-92	22-9	13-3	■	Ron Ellis	486	Jerry Loyd		
1992-93	7-21	4-16		Andre Jackson	264	Jerry Loyd		
1993-94	2-25	0-18		Ryan Bond	278	Jerry Loyd	72-73	.497
1994-95	14-13	9-9		Doug Annison	427	Jim Woolridge		
1995-96	11-17	6-12		Johnny Miller	376	Jim Woolridge		
1996-97	15-14	10-8		Lonnie Cooper	398	Jim Woolridge		
1997-98	12-15	9-9		Lonnie Cooper	459	Jim Woolridge	52-59	.468
1998-99	19-9	10-4		Craig Jackson	15.6	Keith Richard		
1999-2000	21-8	13-5		Gerrod Henderson	18.4	Keith Richard		
2000-01	17-12	10-6		Gerrod Henderson	18.4	Keith Richard		
2001-02	22-10	14-4	■	Gerrod Henderson	17.3	Keith Richard		
2002-03	12-15	9-9		Antonio Meeking	17.9	Keith Richard		
2003-04	15-15	8-10		Paul Millsap	15.6	Keith Richard		
2004-05	14-15	9-9		Paul Millsap	20.4	Keith Richard		
2005-06	20-13	11-5	■	Paul Millsap	19.6	Keith Richard		
2006-07	10-20	7-9		Trey McDowell	13.7	Keith Richard	150-117	.562
2007-08	6-24	3-13		Kyle Gibson	16.5	Kerry Rupp		
2008-09	15-18	6-10		Kyle Gibson	16.1	Kerry Rupp	21-42	.333

Cumulative totals listed when per game averages not available.
[a] Ineligible for conference competition due to recruiting violations.
● NCAA Tournament appearance ■ NIT appearance

PROFILE

Louisiana Tech University, Ruston, LA
Founded: 1894
Enrollment: 11,710 (9.331 undergraduate)
Colors: Blue and red
Nickname: Bulldogs
Current arena: Thomas Assembly Center, opened in 1982 (8,000)
Previous: Memorial Gym, 1952-82 (3,000)
First game: 1925
All-time record: 1,147-910 (.558)
Total weeks in AP Top 20/25: 13
Current conference: Western Athletic (2001-)

Conference titles:
Southland: 3 (1976, '85, '87); American South: 2 (1988, '90); Sun Belt: 2 (1992, '99)
Conference tournament titles:
Southland: 3 (1984, '85, '87); American South: 3 (1988, '89, '91)
NCAA Tournament appearances: 5
Sweet 16s (since 1975): 1
NIT appearances: 6
Semifinals: 1

CONSENSUS ALL-AMERICAS

1973 **Mike Green** (Little A-A), C

FIRST-ROUND PRO PICKS

1960	**Jackie Moreland,** Detroit (4)
1973	**Mike Green,** Seattle (4)
1973	**Mike Green,** Indiana (ABA, 2)
1985	**Karl Malone,** Utah (13)
1989	**Randy White,** Dallas (8)

TOP 5

G	**Gerrod Henderson** (1998-2002)
G	**Mike McConathy** (1973-77)
F	**Karl Malone** (1982-85)
F	**Jackie Moreland** (1957-60)
C	**Mike Green** (1969-73)

RECORDS	GAME		SEASON		CAREER	
POINTS	47	Mike McConathy, vs. Lamar (Feb. 23, 1976); Mike Green, vs. Lamar (Jan. 22, 1973)	803	Mike Green (1972-73)	2,340	Mike Green (1969-73)
POINTS PER GAME			30.9	Mike Green (1972-73)	22.9	Mike Green (1969-73)
REBOUNDS	33	Charlie Bishop, vs. Centenary (Feb. 28, 1967)	468	Jackie Moreland (1958-59)	1,575	Mike Green (1969-73)
ASSISTS	14	Bud Dean, vs. Nicholls State (Jan. 17, 1969)	218	Wayne Smith (1984-85)	712	Wayne Smith (1982-86)

ESPN 11 SAGARIN

LOUISVILLE

With apologies to Georgetown, Duke and Indiana, the Cardinals were the team of the 1980s, with four Final Four appearances, two national titles and the best Tournament winning percentage (23–6, .793). But of course, Louisville's success is not limited merely to one decade. In fact, UL is the only team to have won three different major national postseason tournaments: the 1948 NAIB, the 1956 NIT and the 1980 and '86 NCAAs.

BEST TEAM: 1979-80 The 33–3 Cardinals, a.k.a. the Doctors of Dunk used full-court pressure to run foes ragged and generated fast breaks that were capped by high-flying jams. Senior Darrell Griffith led a young lineup, featuring one freshman and three sophomores, to the NCAA championship game against UCLA, setting up a story for the ages: Hours before the Final, star forward Wiley Brown, who, as a child, had accidentally cut off a thumb, left his artificial digit on the breakfast table at the team's hotel. A trainer retrieved the thumb from the garbage just in time for the tip and the Cardinals won, 59-54.

BEST PLAYER: G DARRELL GRIFFITH (1976-80) Several times a game, Dr. Dunkenstein would launch into a 48-inch vertical leap and electrify the crowd with a sizzling slam. But Griffith could score in myriad ways, as he proved in averaging a team-best 22.9 ppg in 1979-80 while winning the Wooden Award.

BEST COACH: DENNY CRUM (1971-2001) Dubbed Cool Hand Luke by TV analyst Al McGuire, the even-keeled Crum led Louisville to six Final Fours and two NCAA titles during his Hall-of-Fame career. He's one of only 13 coaches in NCAA history to win two or more titles.

GAME FOR THE AGES: They avoided playing each other for 24 years. Finally, Louisville and Kentucky met in the NCAA Elite Eight on March 26, 1983, and put on an electrifying show that revitalized their ancient rivalry. The Wildcats' Jim Master hit a jumper with :01 left in regulation to tie it, but the Cardinals ran off the first 14 points in overtime to win, 80-68.

HEARTBREAKER: In the 1975 Final Four, Crum came up short against his mentor, John Wooden, and UCLA in the most agonizing fashion possible. Junior Bridgeman, Ricky Gallon and Philip Bond, who entered the game with a combined shooting percentage above 50%, hit on just six of 24 shots. Meanwhile, after converting all 28 of his free throws during the season, reserve guard Terry Howard missed the front end of a one-and-one in the waning seconds of overtime and the Cardinals lost to the eventual champs, 75-74.

FIERCEST RIVAL: Separated by 75 miles, Louisville and Kentucky divide the loyalties of many towns straight down the middle. As sportswriter Dave Kindred once described the Battle for the Bluegrass, "Louisville fans dismiss Kentucky zealots as insufferably arrogant dolts, and Kentucky fans consider Louisville zealots hopelessly deluded elitists." The Wildcats lead overall, 26–14.

FANFARE AND HOOPLA: Louisville claims the high five was invented—or at least became popular—at Freedom Hall. Wiley Brown, Derek Smith and Daryl Cleveland are credited with initiating the habit of high-fiving each other during practice. That led to the entire team joining in on the ritual during the run to the 1980 title.

FAN FAVORITES: F SCOOTER MCCRAY (1978-83), F RODNEY MCCRAY (1979-83) Scooter and younger brother Rodney won over Cardinals faithful with their emotional leadership, solid inside play and unselfishness in one of the greatest eras of UL hoops.

CONSENSUS ALL-AMERICAS

1957	**Charlie Tyra**, C
1967, '68	**Wes Unseld**, C
1980	**Darrell Griffith**, G
1989	**Pervis Ellison**, F/C
1994	**Clifford Rozier**, F/C

FIRST-ROUND PRO PICKS

1952	**Bob Lochmueller**, Syracuse (8)
1957	**Charlie Tyra**, Detroit (2)
1968	**Wes Unseld**, Baltimore (2)
1969	**Butch Beard**, Atlanta (10)
1975	**Junior Bridgeman**, LA Lakers (8)
1977	**Wesley Cox**, Golden State (18)
1980	**Darrell Griffith**, Utah (2)
1983	**Rodney McCray**, Houston (3)
1984	**Lancaster Gordon**, LA Clippers (8)
1986	**Billy Thompson**, Atlanta, (19)
1989	**Pervis Ellison**, Sacramento (1)
1989	**Kenny Payne**, Philadelphia (19)
1990	**Felton Spencer**, Minnesota (6)
1991	**LaBradford Smith**, Washington (19)
1994	**Clifford Rozier**, Golden State (16)
1994	**Greg Minor**, LA Clippers (25)
1996	**Samaki Walker**, Dallas (9)
2003	**Reece Gaines**, Orlando (15)
2005	**Francisco Garcia**, Sacramento (23)
2009	**Terrence Williams**, New Jersey (11)
2009	**Earl Clark**, Phoenix (14)

PROFILE

University of Louisville, Louisville, KY
Founded: 1798
Enrollment: 20,521 (14,467 undergraduate)
Colors: Red and black
Nickname: Cardinals
Current arena: Freedom Hall, opened in 1956 (18,865)
Previous: Jefferson County Armory, 1949-72 (N/A)
First game: Jan. 28, 1912
All-time record: 1,587-831 (.656)
Total weeks in AP Top 20/25: 495

Current conference: Big East (2005-)
Conference titles:
Missouri Valley: 5 (1967, '68, '72, '74, '75)
Metro 7: 1 (1977)
Metro: 11 (1979, '80, '81, '83, '84 [tie], '86, '87, '88, '90, '93, '94)
Conference USA: 1 (2005)
Big East: 1 (2009)
Conference tournament titles:
Metro 7: 1 (1978)
Metro: 10 (1980, '81, '83, '86, '88, '89, '90, '93, '94, '95)
Conference USA: 2 (2003, '05)
Big East: 1 (2009)

NCAA Tournament appearances: 35
Sweet 16s (since 1975): 17
Final Fours: 8
Titles: 2 (1980, '86)
NIT appearances: 14
Semifinals: 3; Titles: 1 (1956)

TOP 5

G	**Darrell Griffith** (1976-80)
G	**LaBradford Smith** (1987-91)
F/C	**Pervis Ellison** (1985-89)
C	**Charlie Tyra** (1953-57)
C	**Wes Unseld** (1965-68)

RECORDS	GAME		SEASON		CAREER	
POINTS	45	Wes Unseld, vs. Georgetown College (Dec. 1, 1967)	825	Darrell Griffith (1979-80)	2,333	Darrell Griffith (1976-80)
POINTS PER GAME			23.8	Charlie Tyra (1955-56)	20.6	Wes Unseld (1965-68)
REBOUNDS	38	Charlie Tyra, vs. Canisius (Dec. 10, 1955)	645	Charlie Tyra (1955-56)	1,617	Charlie Tyra (1953-57)
ASSISTS	15	Francisco Garcia, vs. Murray State (Jan. 3, 2004)	226	LaBradford Smith (1989-90)	713	LaBradford Smith (1987-91)

THE SCHOOLS

SEASON REVIEW

SEASON	W-L	CONF.	SCORING		COACH	RECORD	
1911-15	*8-17*		*No winning seasons*				
1915-16	8-3		Edwin Kornfeld	11.1	Ed Bowman		
1916-17	no team						
1917-18	3-4		Sam Morgan	17.3	Ed Bowman	11-7	.611
1918-19	7-4		Sam Morgan	12.7	Earl Ford	7-4	.636
1919-20	6-5		Don Butler	7.6	Tuley Brucker	6-5	.545
1920-21	3-8		Don Butler	10.1	Jimmie Powers	3-8	.273
1921-22	1-13		Phillip Silverstein	4.8	Dr. John T. O'Rourke	1-13	.071
1922-23	no team						
1923-24	4-13		Lynn Miller	7.7	Fred A. Enke		
1924-25	10-7		Fred Koster	10.0	Fred A. Enke	14-20	.412
1925-26	4-8		Lynn Miller	13.0	Tom King		
1926-27	7-5		Fred Koster	8.0	Tom King		
1927-28	12-4		Edward Weber	7.7	Tom King		
1928-29	12-8		Burt Libbey	5.6	Tom King		
1929-30	9-6		Kenny Bott	5.9	Tom King	44-31	.587
1930-31	5-11		Kenny Bott	7.8	Edward Weber		
1931-32	15-7		Ray Judy	5.4	Edward Weber	20-18	.526
1932-33	11-11		Les Wright	8.5	C.V. Money		
1933-34	16-9		Les Wright	7.4	C.V. Money		
1934-35	5-9		Harry Long	7.0	C.V. Money		
1935-36	14-11		Ches Masterson	7.8	C.V. Money	46-40	.535

SEAS.	W-L	CONF.	POSTSEASON	SCORING		REBOUNDS		ASSISTS		COACH	RECORD	
1936-37	4-8			Si Monen	12.1					Lawrence Apitz		
1937-38	4-11			Bob Meyer	10.1					Lawrence Apitz		
1938-39	1-15			Bob Meyer	5.5					Lawrence Apitz		
1939-40	1-18			Bob King	9.1					Lawrence Apitz	10-52	.161
1940-41	2-14			Aaron Andrews	11.2					John C. Heldman, Jr.		
1941-42	7-10			Frank Epley	17.6					John C. Heldman, Jr	9-24	.273
1942-43	no team											
1943-44	10-10			Cal Johnson	8.6					H. Church, Walter Casey	10-10	.500
1944-45	16-3			George Hauptfuhrer	16.2					Bernard "Peck" Hickman		
1945-46	22-6			George Hauptfuhrer	13.2					Bernard "Peck" Hickman		
1946-47	17-6			Jack Coleman	11.0					Bernard "Peck" Hickman		
1947-48	29-6		NAIB CHAMPION	Jack Coleman	12.1					Bernard "Peck" Hickman		
1948-49	23-10	6-3		Jack Coleman	14.6					Bernard "Peck" Hickman		
1949-50	21-11			Kenny Reeves	13.6					Bernard "Peck" Hickman		
1950-51	19-7		NCAA FIRST ROUND	Bob Lochmueller	19.0					Bernard "Peck" Hickman		
1951-52	20-6		NIT FIRST ROUND	Bob Brown	17.0					Bernard "Peck" Hickman		
1952-53	22-6		NIT QUARTERFINALS	Chuck Noble	17.0	Vlad Gastevich	8.1			Bernard "Peck" Hickman		
1953-54	22-7		NIT FIRST ROUND	Chuck Noble	17.2	John Prudhoe	10.7			Bernard "Peck" Hickman		
1954-55	19-8		NIT QUARTERFINALS	Charlie Tyra	14.7	Charlie Tyra	13.6			Bernard "Peck" Hickman		
1955-56	26-3		NIT CHAMPION	Charlie Tyra	23.8	Charlie Tyra	22.2			Bernard "Peck" Hickman		
1956-57	21-5			Charlie Tyra	21.4	Charlie Tyra	20.0			Bernard "Peck" Hickman		
1957-58	13-12			Jerry DuPont	15.2	Jerry DuPont	16.0			Bernard "Peck" Hickman		
1958-59	19-12		NCAA FOURTH PLACE	John Turner	14.0	Fred Sawyer	11.5			Bernard "Peck" Hickman		
1959-60	15-11			John Turner	13.4	Fred Sawyer	14.1			Bernard "Peck" Hickman		
1960-61	21-8		NCAA REGIONAL SEMIFINALS	John Turner	23.1	John Turner	11.4			Bernard "Peck" Hickman		
1961-62	15-10			Bud Olsen	20.8	Bud Olsen	13.2			Bernard "Peck" Hickman		
1962-63	14-11			John Reuther	16.2	John Reuther	10.3			Bernard "Peck" Hickman		
1963-64	15-10		NCAA FIRST ROUND	John Reuther	19.6	John Reuther	10.2			Bernard "Peck" Hickman		
1964-65	15-10	8-6		John Reuther	18.8	John Reuther	11.1			Bernard "Peck" Hickman		
1965-66	16-10	8-6	NIT FIRST ROUND	Wes Unseld	19.9	Wes Unseld	19.4			Bernard "Peck" Hickman		
1966-67	23-5	12-2	NCAA REGIONAL SEMIFINALS	Butch Beard	20.5	Wes Unseld	19.0			Bernard "Peck" Hickman	443-183	.708
1967-68	21-7	14-2	NCAA REGIONAL SEMIFINALS	Wes Unseld	23.0	Wes Unseld	18.3			John Dromo		
1968-69	21-6	13-3	NIT QUARTERFINALS	Butch Beard	20.6	Mike Grosso	16.0			John Dromo		
1969-70	18-9	11-5	NIT FIRST ROUND	Mike Grosso	18.6	Mike Grosso	13.9	Jim Price	4.7	John Dromo		
1970-71	20-9	9-5	NIT FIRST ROUND	Jim Price	16.5	Ron Thomas	12.6	Jim Price	4.0	John Dromo[a]	68-23	.747
1971-72	26-5	12-2	NCAA FOURTH PLACE	Jim Price	21.0	Ron Thomas	13.5	Jim Price	4.4	Denny Crum		
1972-73	23-7	11-3	NIT QUARTERFINALS	Allen Murphy	16.1	Bill Bunton	9.6	Terry Howard	3.8	Denny Crum		
1973-74	21-7	11-1	NCAA REGIONAL SEMIFINALS	Allen Murphy	16.6	Junior Bridgeman	8.4	Terry Howard	3.9	Denny Crum		
1974-75	28-3	12-2	NCAA THIRD PLACE	Allen Murphy	16.3	Bill Bunton	7.6	Phillip Bond	4.7	Denny Crum		
1975-76	20-8	2-2	NIT QUARTERFINALS	Ricky Gallon	15.3	Ricky Gallon	7.0	Phillip Bond	5.4	Denny Crum		
1976-77	21-7	6-1	NCAA FIRST ROUND	Wesley Cox	16.5	Larry Williams	9.0	Phillip Bond	5.6	Denny Crum		
1977-78	23-7	9-3	NCAA REGIONAL SEMIFINALS	Darrell Griffith	18.6	Ricky Gallon	8.2	Rick Wilson	4.5	Denny Crum		
1978-79	24-8	9-1	NCAA REGIONAL SEMIFINALS	Darrell Griffith	18.5	Larry Williams	7.8	Scooter McCray	3.1	Denny Crum		
1979-80	**33-3**	**12-0**	**NATIONAL CHAMPION**	**Darrell Griffith**	**22.9**	**Derek Smith**	**8.3**	**Darrell Griffith**	**3.8**	**Denny Crum**		
1980-81	21-9	11-1	NCAA SECOND ROUND	Derek Smith	15.5	Derek Smith	7.8	Jerry Eaves	3.3	Denny Crum		
1981-82	23-10	8-4	NCAA NATIONAL SEMIFINALS	Derek Smith	15.7	Rodney McCray	7.1	Jerry Eaves	3.3	Denny Crum		
1982-83	32-4	12-0	NCAA NATIONAL SEMIFINALS	Milt Wagner	14.4	Rodney McCray	8.4	Scooter McCray	3.5	Denny Crum		
1983-84	24-11	11-3	NCAA REGIONAL SEMIFINALS	Milt Wagner	16.6	Charles Jones	9.7	Milt Wagner	3.9	Denny Crum		
1984-85	19-18	6-8	NIT FOURTH PLACE	Billy Thompson	15.1	Billy Thompson	8.4	Billy Thompson	4.2	Denny Crum		
1985-86	**32-7**	**10-2**	**NATIONAL CHAMPION**	**Billy Thompson**	**14.9**	**Pervis Ellison**	**8.2**	**Milt Wagner**	**4.2**	**Denny Crum**		
1986-87	18-14	9-3		Herbert Crook	15.5	Pervis Ellison	8.7	Herbert Crook	3.0	Denny Crum		
1987-88	24-11	9-3	NCAA REGIONAL SEMIFINALS	Pervis Ellison	17.6	Pervis Ellison	8.3	LaBradford Smith	4.5	Denny Crum		
1988-89	24-9	8-4	NCAA REGIONAL SEMIFINALS	Pervis Ellison	17.6	Pervis Ellison	8.7	LaBradford Smith	5.6	Denny Crum		
1989-90	27-8	12-2	NCAA SECOND ROUND	Felton Spencer	14.9	Felton Spencer	8.5	LaBradford Smith	6.5	Denny Crum		
1990-91	14-16	4-10		LaBradford Smith	16.6	Cornelius Holden	8.2	LaBradford Smith	4.9	Denny Crum		
1991-92	19-11	7-5	NCAA SECOND ROUND	Everick Sullivan	13.7	Cornelius Holden	6.7	Everick Sullivan	3.6	Denny Crum		
1992-93	22-9	11-1	NCAA REGIONAL SEMIFINALS	Dwayne Morton	16.1	Clifford Rozier	10.9	Keith LeGree	3.8	Denny Crum		
1993-94	28-6	10-2	NCAA REGIONAL SEMIFINALS	Clifford Rozier	18.1	Clifford Rozier	11.1	Jason Osborne	4.1	Denny Crum		
1994-95	19-14	7-5	NCAA FIRST ROUND	DeJuan Wheat	16.5	Samaki Walker	7.2	DeJuan Wheat	3.2	Denny Crum		
1995-96	22-12	10-4	NCAA REGIONAL SEMIFINALS	DeJuan Wheat	17.7	Samaki Walker	7.5	DeJuan Wheat	3.9	Denny Crum		
1996-97	26-9	9-5	NCAA REGIONAL FINALS	DeJuan Wheat	17.3	Alvin Sims	5.8	DeJuan Wheat	4.3	Denny Crum		
1997-98	12-20	5-11		Nate Johnson	12.3	Damion Dantzler	6.2	Cameron Murray	4.2	Denny Crum		
1998-99	19-11	11-5	NCAA FIRST ROUND	Nate Johnson	12.3	Alex Sanders	6.3	Cameron Murray	3.9	Denny Crum		
1999-2000	19-12	10-6	NCAA FIRST ROUND	Marques Maybin	14.7	Dion Edward	7.4	Reece Gaines	3.4	Denny Crum		
2000-01	12-19	8-8		Marques Maybin	17.7	Joseph N'Sima	5.6	Reece Gaines	3.3	Denny Crum	675-295	.696
2001-02	19-13	8-8	NIT SECOND ROUND	Reece Gaines	21.0	Ellis Myles	9.3	Reece Gaines	3.6	Rick Pitino		
2002-03	25-7	11-5	NCAA SECOND ROUND	Reece Gaines	17.9	Elllis Myles	7.9	Reece Gaines	5.0	Rick Pitino		
2003-04	20-10	9-7	NCAA FIRST ROUND	Francisco Garcia	16.4	Luke Whitehead	7.7	Francisco Garcia	4.7	Rick Pitino		
2004-05	33-5	14-2	NCAA NATIONAL SEMIFINALS	Francisco Garcia	15.7	Ellis Myles	9.2	Francisco Garcia	3.9	Rick Pitino		
2005-06	21-13	6-10	NIT SEMIFINALS	Taquan Dean	17.1	Juan Palacios	6.3	Taquan Dean	3.5	Rick Pitino		
2006-07	24-10	12-4	NCAA SECOND ROUND	Terrence Williams	12.4	Terrence Williams	7.0	Terrence Williams	3.8	Rick Pitino		
2007-08	27-9	14-4	NCAA REGIONAL FINALS	David Padgett	11.2	Earl Clark	8.1	Terrence Williams	4.5	Rick Pitino		
2008-09	31-6	16-2	NCAA REGIONAL FINALS	Earl Clark	14.2	Earl Clark	8.7	Terrence Williams	5.0	Rick Pitino	200-73	.733

[a] **John Dromo (8-1) and Howard Stacey (12-8) both coached during the 1970-71 season.**

ESPN 267 SAGARIN

LOYOLA (MD.)

Jim Lacy, Emil "Lefty" Reitz, Skip Prosser and the 1994 MAAC tourney miracle, plus the longest rivalry in state hoops history are all reminders that Loyola has made its mark after 99 seasons. The program might have peaked in the 1940s, but there also might be great moments yet to come.

BEST TEAM: 1948-49 The two-time defending Mason-Dixon Conference champs went 25–9 to set the school record for wins and capture another league tournament title. Coach Lefty Reitz, Bob Anderson and school Hall of Famers Jim Lacy, Andy O'Donnell and Mike Zedalis led Loyola to the NAIA tournament and three National Catholic tournament victories.

BEST PLAYER: F Jim Lacy (1943-44, '46-49) The first player in college basketball history to reach 2,000 points (finishing with 2,199), Lacy led Loyola to 84 wins over four seasons, three league championships, three NAIA tourneys and its first NAIA tourney win. He's the school's all-time leading scorer and shares the single-game high scoring mark (44).

BEST COACH: Emil "Lefty" Reitz (1937-44, '45-61) Reitz, for whom the school's arena is named, is Loyola's winningest coach (349) with the highest percentage (.605). He led the Greyhounds to three 20-win seasons (their only ones), five league titles and four NAIA tournaments.

GAME FOR THE AGES: Loyola's three upsets in the 1994 Metro Atlantic Athletic Conference tournament secured its only NCAA Tourney berth. Skip Prosser's No. 5-seed Greyhounds beat St. Peter's and upset top-seeded Canisius before their stunning March 7 win over defending champ Manhattan, 80-75, behind tourney MVP Tracy Bergan and all-tourney pick Michael Reese.

FIERCEST RIVAL: The most-played in-state rivalry in Maryland history pits Loyola against Mount St. Mary's, which leads the series, 95–69. The teams first played in 1910 and were in the Mason-Dixon Conference from 1940 to '77. Their nonconference games have continued, with Loyola coming up short in seven of the last 11.

SEASON REVIEW

SEAS.	W-L	CONF.	COACH	SEAS.	W-L	CONF.	COACH
1907-48	*379-296*	*20-12 in 1946-47*		1961-62	10-9		Nap Doherty
1948-49	25-8		Emil "Lefty" Reitz	1962-63	12-10		Nap Doherty
1949-50	19-9		Emil "Lefty" Reitz	1963-64	10-13		Nap Doherty
1950-51	12-17		Emil "Lefty" Reitz	1964-65	13-11		Nap Doherty
1951-52	16-12		Emil "Lefty" Reitz	1965-66	15-10		Nap Doherty
1952-53	17-9		Emil "Lefty" Reitz	1966-67	9-11		Nap Doherty
1953-54	12-11		Emil "Lefty" Reitz	1967-68	8-17		Nap Doherty
1954-55	18-8		Emil "Lefty" Reitz	1968-69	11-14		Nap Doherty
1955-56	19-9		Emil "Lefty" Reitz	1969-70	12-14		Nap Doherty
1956-57	17-9		Emil "Lefty" Reitz	1970-71	19-7		Nap Doherty
1957-58	12-12		Emil "Lefty" Reitz	1971-72	17-10		Nap Doherty
1958-59	13-11		Emil "Lefty" Reitz	1972-73	16-13		Nap Doherty
1959-60	10-10		Emil "Lefty" Reitz	1973-74	12-14		Nap Doherty
1960-61	5-13		Emil "Lefty" Reitz	1974-75	16-11		Tom O'Connor

SEAS.	W-L	CONF.	SCORING		COACH	RECORD	
1975-76	14-12				Tom O'Connor	30-23	.566
1976-77	11-15				Gary Dicovitsky		
1977-78	17-10				Gary Dicovitsky		
1978-79	17-11				Gary Dicovitsky		
1979-80	13-12				Gary Dicovitsky		
1980-81	14-11				Gary Dicovitsky	72-59	.550
1981-82	11-16	7-7			William Burke	11-16	.407
1982-83	4-24	3-11			Mark Amatucci		
1983-84	16-12	10-6			Mark Amatucci		
1984-85	16-14	8-6			Mark Amatucci		
1985-86	16-12	10-6			Mark Amatucci		
1986-87	15-14	10-6			Mark Amatucci		
1987-88	8-22	6-10	Mike Morrison	667	Mark Amatucci		
1988-89	10-18	7-9			Mark Amatucci	85-116	.423
1989-90	4-24	2-14	Kevin Green	543	Tom Schneider		
1990-91	12-16	5-11	Kevin Green	620	Tom Schneider		
1991-92	14-14	10-6	Kevin Green	561	Tom Schneider		
1992-93	2-25	1-13			Tom Schneider[a]	32-79	.288
1993-94	17-13	6-8 ●			Skip Prosser	17-13	.567
1994-95	9-18	5-9			Brian Ellerbe		
1995-96	12-15	8-6	Mike Powell	538	Brian Ellerbe		
1996-97	13-14	10-4			Brian Ellerbe	34-47	.420
1997-98	12-16	9-9	Mike Powell	23.1	Dino Gaudio		
1998-99	13-15	6-12	Jason Rowe	21.9	Dino Gaudio		
1999-2000	7-21	4-14	Jason Rowe	17.9	Dino Gaudio	32-52	.381
2000-01	6-23	2-16	John Reimold	15.5	Scott Hicks		
2001-02	5-23	4-14	Lucious Jordan	13.0	Scott Hicks		
2002-03	4-24	1-17	Lucious Jordan	13.2	Scott Hicks		
2003-04	1-27	1-17	Charlie Bell	15.3	Scott Hicks	16-97	.142
2004-05	6-22	5-13	Charlie Bell	10.3	Jimmy Patsos		
2005-06	15-13	8-10	Andre Collins	26.1	Jimmy Patsos		
2006-07	18-13	12-6	Gerald Brown	22.2	Jimmy Patsos		
2007-08	19-14	12-6	Gerald Brown	18.8	Jimmy Patsos		
2008-09	12-20	7-11	Jamal Barney	18.1	Jimmy Patsos	70-82	.461

Cumulative totals listed when per game averages not available.

[a] Joe Boylan also coached during the 1992-93 season, but all games are credited to Tom Schneider.

● NCAA Tournament appearance

PROFILE

Loyola College in Maryland, Baltimore, MD
Founded: 1852
Enrollment: 6,080 (3,716 undergraduate)
Colors: Green and grey
Nickname: Greyhounds
Current arena: Reitz Arena, opened in 1984 (3,253)
Previous: Evergreen Gym, prior to 1984 (N/A)
First game: 1907
All-time record: 1,137-1,171 (.493)
Total weeks in AP Top 20/25: 0

Current conference: Metro Atlantic Athletic (1989-)
Conference titles: 0
Conference tournament titles:
MAAC: 1 (1994)
NCAA Tournament appearances: 1
NIT appearances: 0

TOP 5

G **David Gately** (1983-87)
G **Kevin Green** (1988-92)
G **Mike Morrison** (1985-89)
F **Jim Lacy** (1943-44, '46-49)
F/C **Mike Krawczyk** (1968-72)

RECORDS	GAME		SEASON		CAREER	
POINTS	44	Joel Hittleman, vs. Catholic (Dec. 17, 1954); Jim Lacy, vs. Western Maryland (Feb. 14, 1948)	731	Andre Collins (2005-06)	2,199	Jim Lacy (1943-44, '46-49)
POINTS PER GAME			26.1	Andre Collins (2005-06)	26.1	Andre Collins (2005-06)
REBOUNDS	44	Charles McCullough, vs. Western Maryland (Feb. 17, 1955)	616	Charles McCullough (1954-55)	1,244	Mike Krawczyk (1968-72)
ASSISTS	15	Ed Butler, vs. American (Feb. 14, 1973)	178	Tracy Bergan (1991-92); Ed Butler (1971-72)	538	Tracy Bergan (1989-94)

ESPN 95 SAGARIN

LOYOLA-CHICAGO

We won! We won! We won! Those were the only words Ramblers radio broadcaster Red Rush could muster after Loyola-Chicago upset Cincinnati to win the 1963 national championship. Sure, the hoops team has lost a bit of its luster in recent years, but with a legacy that includes an unbeaten season (16–0 in 1928-29), a first overall pick in the NBA draft (LaRue Martin in 1972), a Hall of Fame coach (Lenny Sachs) and the NCAA's No. 10 all-time leading scorer (Alfredrick Hughes), the Ramblers are certainly not one-hit wonders.

BEST TEAM: 1962-63 After the first semester, the Ramblers lost two of their top bench players to bad grades. But that didn't slow down their furious up-tempo offense. Thanks to the emergence of the Iron Men—rarely rested starters Jerry Harkness, Les Hunter, Ron Miller, Vic Rouse and Johnny Egan—Loyola led the nation in scoring and set a still-standing NCAA Tournament record for margin of victory by beating Tennessee Tech 111-42 in the first round. The Ramblers' 60-58 overtime title victory over Cincinnati didn't come quite as easily, but it only proved the Iron Men were as resilient as they were energetic.

BEST PLAYER: F JERRY HARKNESS (1960-63) The Ramblers' legendary offenses from the early 1960s never would have made it out of first gear if not for Harkness' savvy ballhandling and deadly jumper. The 1963 All-America led Loyola-Chicago in scoring all three seasons, and he averaged 21.4 points and 7.6 rebounds in the championship season.

BEST COACH: GEORGE IRELAND (1951-75) Ireland was decades ahead of today's high-flying style. His fast-break offense created what he labeled "organized confusion," and his full-court press was no picnic either. He also made history, foreshadowing Texas Western's historic 1966 championship team by starting a quartet of African-Americans during the 1962-63 title season.

GAME FOR THE AGES: What happens when an unstoppable offense meets an immovable defense? For much of 1963 NCAA Final, the grind-it-down Bearcats got the best of the Ramblers' attack, opening a 15-point second-half lead. Then Harkness got hot, scoring 12 points in the final 4:30, including a 12-foot jumper with :06 on the clock, to send the game into overtime. There, with time running out, Hunter missed a shot from the foul line, but Rouse tipped it in as the final buzzer sounded to win the title.

HEARTBREAKER: The 1965-66 team looked every bit as dangerous as the outfit that won the title three seasons earlier. But the No. 6 Ramblers weren't merely upset by Western Kentucky in the first round of the Tournament—they were *routed*, 105-86.

FIERCEST RIVAL: In a city overflowing with hoops talent and D1 teams, Illinois-Chicago and Loyola-Chicago have sparked one of the most entertaining turf wars, fanned by their Horizon League membership. The Flames lead the series, 29–13, but have taken a few blows on the chin of late, including losses in the 2005 and 2007 conference tournaments.

Ireland made history by starting a quartet of African-Americans during the 1963-63 championship season.

FANFARE AND HOOPLA: Closed to hoops since 1996, the old Alumni Gym still merits a reverential full page in the program's media guide, so legendary was the home-court advantage it once conferred upon the Ramblers. Loyola-Chicago won 78.1% of its games at the Big Brown Box That Rocks, thanks in large part to a wall of fans who were so close to the floor they could practically breathe on the players as they ran by.

FAN FAVORITE: G ANDRE WAKEFIELD (1976-78) Fans still approach the outgoing Wakefield to talk about the 1978 Indiana State game: With time winding down, the 6'1" guard drew a foul from Larry Bird, then hit one of two free throws to spring the home upset.

CONSENSUS ALL-AMERICAS

1963	**Jerry Harkness,** F

FIRST-ROUND PRO PICKS

1949	**Jack Kerris,** Chicago (10)
1972	**LaRue Martin,** Portland (1)
1972	**LaRue Martin,** Dallas (ABA)
1979	**Larry Knight,** Utah (20)
1985	**Alfredrick Hughes,** San Antonio (14)

PROFILE

Loyola University Chicago, Chicago, IL
Founded: 1870
Enrollment: 15,545 (9,732 undergraduate)
Colors: Maroon and gold
Nickname: Ramblers
Current arena: Joseph J. Gentile Center, opened in 1996 (5,200)
Previous: Alumni Gym, 1924-96 (2,000)
First game: 1914
All-time record: 1,168-1,010 (.536)
Total weeks in AP Top 20/25: 49

Current conference: Horizon League (1979-)
Conference titles:
Midwestern City: 3 (1980, '83, '85)
Midwestern Collegiate: 1 (1987 [tie])
Conference tournament titles:
Midwestern City: 1 (1985)
NCAA Tournament appearances: 5
Sweet 16s (since 1975): 1
Final Fours: 1
Titles: 1 (1963)
NIT appearances: 4
Semifinals: 3

TOP 5

G	**Johnny Egan** (1961-64)
G/F	**Alfredrick Hughes** (1981-85)
F	**Jerry Harkness** (1960-63)
F/C	**Jack Kerris** (1945-49)
C	**LaRue Martin** (1969-72)

RECORDS	GAME		SEASON		CAREER	
POINTS	47	Alfredrick Hughes, vs. Detroit (Feb. 9, 1985)	868	Alfredrick Hughes (1984-85)	2,914	Alfredrick Hughes (1981-85)
POINTS PER GAME			27.6	Alfredrick Hughes (1983-84)	24.7	Keith Gailes (1988-91)
REBOUNDS	32	LaRue Martin, vs. Ohio (Feb. 8, 1971)	427	Les Hunter (1963-64)	1,062	LaRue Martin (1969-72)
ASSISTS	19	Darius Clemons, vs. Northwestern (Dec. 19, 1981)	305	Carl Golston (1984-85)	703	Darius Clemons (1978-82)

SEASON REVIEW

SEASON	W-L	CONF.	SCORING	COACH	RECORD	
1913-14	0-2			unknown		
1915-16	8-3			unknown		
1915-16	10-3			Percy Moore	10-3	.769
1916-17	1-3			unknown		
1917-20	no team					
1920-21	7-4			Bill Feeney	7-4	.636
1921-22	0-6			Harry Rhodes	0-6	.000
1922-23	5-7			Jack Tierney	5-7	.417
1923-24	8-11			Lenny Sachs		
1924-25	4-11			Lenny Sachs		
1925-26	13-8			Lenny Sachs		
1926-27	13-4			Lenny Sachs		
1927-28	16-4			Lenny Sachs		
1928-29	16-0			Lenny Sachs		
1929-30	13-5			Lenny Sachs		
1930-31	8-7			Lenny Sachs		
1931-32	15-2			Lenny Sachs		
1932-33	14-7			Lenny Sachs		
1933-34	7-8			Lenny Sachs		
1934-35	5-14			Lenny Sachs		
1935-36	8-8			Lenny Sachs		
1936-37	16-3			Lenny Sachs		

SEAS.	W-L	CONF.	POSTSEASON	SCORING		REBOUNDS		ASSISTS		COACH	RECORD	
1937-38	12-8									Lenny Sachs		
1938-39	21-1		NIT RUNNER-UP							Lenny Sachs		
1939-40	5-14									Lenny Sachs		
1940-41	13-8									Lenny Sachs		
1941-42	17-6									Lenny Sachs	224-129	.635
1942-43	12-10									John Connelly	12-10	.545
1943-44	no team											
1944-45	no team											
1945-46	23-4									Tom Haggerty		
1946-47	20-9			Jack Kerris	14.5					Tom Haggerty		
1947-48	26-9			Jack Kerris	15.3					Tom Haggerty		
1948-49	25-6		NIT RUNNER-UP	Jack Kerris	15.1					Tom Haggerty		
1949-50	17-13			Ed Dawson	12.4					Tom Haggerty	111-41	.730
1950-51	15-14			Nick Kladis	15.7					John Jordan	15-14	.517
1951-52	17-8			Nick Kladis	17.6					George Ireland		
1952-53	8-15			Elwood Sigwards	13.0					George Ireland		
1953-54	8-15			Bill Palka	12.8	Bill Palka	8.7			George Ireland		
1954-55	13-11			Art Schalk	15.8	Art Schalk	11.2			George Ireland		
1955-56	10-14			Jack Carpenter	12.8	Jack Carpenter	12.2			George Ireland		
1956-57	14-10			Paul Krucker	15.7	Art McZier	13.5			George Ireland		
1957-58	16-8			Al Norville	18.0	Art McZier	15.7			George Ireland		
1958-59	11-13			Clarence Red	20.3	Clarence Red	16.8			George Ireland		
1959-60	10-12			Clarence Red	16.9	Clarence Red	11.0			George Ireland		
1960-61	15-8			Jerry Harkness	22.6	Clarence Red	10.6			George Ireland		
1961-62	23-4		NIT THIRD PLACE	Jerry Harkness	21.0	Vic Rouse	11.3			George Ireland		
1962-63	**29-2**		**NATIONAL CHAMPION**	**Jerry Harkness**	**21.4**	**Vic Rouse**	**12.1**			**George Ireland**		
1963-64	22-6		NCAA REGIONAL SEMIFINALS	Ron Miller	21.9	Les Hunter	15.3			George Ireland		
1964-65	11-14			Jim Coleman	17.6	Frank Perez	9.3			George Ireland		
1965-66	22-3		NCAA FIRST ROUND	Billy Smith	18.8	Billy Smith	13.3			George Ireland		
1966-67	13-9			Jim Tillman	24.7	Corky Bell	11.7			George Ireland		
1967-68	15-9		NCAA FIRST ROUND	Jim Tillman	17.7	Corky Bell	9.2			George Ireland		
1968-69	9-14			Walter Robertson	22.6	Billy Moody	9.0			George Ireland		
1969-70	13-11			Walter Robertson	18.1	LaRue Martin	14.4			George Ireland		
1970-71	4-20			LaRue Martin	18.7	LaRue Martin	17.6			George Ireland		
1971-72	8-14			LaRue Martin	19.5	LaRue Martin	15.7			George Ireland		
1972-73	8-15			Nate Hayes	22.0	Paul Cohen	13.8			George Ireland		
1973-74	12-14			Tony Parker	17.1	Paul Cohen	12.7			George Ireland		
1974-75	10-15			Ralph Vallot	18.8	Ralph Vallot	8.5			George Ireland[a]	319-255	.556
1975-76	10-16			Ralph Vallot	21.2	Ralph Vallot	9.4			Jerry Lyne		
1976-77	13-13			Tony Parker	17.7	John Hunter	9.2			Jerry Lyne		
1977-78	16-11			Andre Wakefield	17.0	Larry Knight	12.7	Andre Wakefield	5.2	Jerry Lyne		
1978-79	12-15			Larry Knight	21.5	Larry Knight	14.3	Dan Bush	4.2	Jerry Lyne		
1979-80	19-10	5-0	NIT FIRST ROUND	LeRoy Stampley	20.3	Kevin Sprewer	9.8	Dan Bush	4.3	Jerry Lyne	72-74	.493
1980-81	13-15	7-4		Darius Clemons	21.9	Wayne Sappleton	13.4	Darius Clemons	7.8	Gene Sullivan		
1981-82	17-12	8-4		Wayne Sappleton	22.0	Wayne Sappleton	13.0	Darius Clemons	9.9	Gene Sullivan		
1982-83	19-10	12-2		Alfredrick Hughes	25.7	Chris Rogers	9.3			Gene Sullivan		
1983-84	20-9	10-4		Alfredrick Hughes	27.6	Alfredrick Hughes	8.2	Carl Golston	5.8	Gene Sullivan		
1984-85	27-6	13-1	NCAA REGIONAL SEMIFINALS	Alfredrick Hughes	26.3	Andre Moore	10.3	Carl Golston	9.2	Gene Sullivan		
1985-86	13-16	7-5		Carl Golston	19.6	Andre Moore	9.9	Carl Golston	6.1	Gene Sullivan		
1986-87	16-13	8-4		Bernard Jackson	22.8	Andre Moore	12.4	Keith Carter	5.0	Gene Sullivan		
1987-88	13-16	3-7		Gerald Hayward	26.1	Kenny Miller	13.6	Keith Carter	5.7	Gene Sullivan		
1988-89	11-17	4-8		Keith Gailes	22.5	Keith Gailes	7.6	Keith Carter	5.6	Gene Sullivan	149-114	.567
1989-90	7-22	3-11		Keith Gailes	26.3	Keir Rogers	8.6	Don Sobczak	3.9	Will Rey		
1990-91	10-19	3-11		Keith Gailes	25.3	Eric Dolezal	6.2	Don Sobczak	4.1	Will Rey		
1991-92	13-16	2-8		Keir Rogers	19.0	Keir Rogers	7.2	Don Sobczak	4.0	Will Rey		
1992-93	7-20	3-11		Kerman Ali	14.1	Kerman Ali	6.4	Chris Wilburn	4.7	Will Rey		
1993-94	8-19	1-9		Vernell Brent	10.9	Marlon Burton	5.7	Vernell Brent	5.8	Will Rey	45-96	.319
1994-95	5-22	2-13		Bernie Salthe	15.7	Bernie Salthe	6.3	Chris Wilburn	4.4	Ken Burmeister		
1995-96	8-19	5-11		Derek Molis	14.9	Javan Goodman	7.9	Theodis Owens	5.3	Ken Burmeister		
1996-97	12-15	7-9		Derek Molis	12.6	Javan Goodman	7.6	Charles Smith	3.0	Ken Burmeister		
1997-98	15-15	6-8		Javan Goodman	16.8	Javan Goodman	8.4	Earl Brown	5.6	Ken Burmeister	40-71	.360
1998-99	9-18	7-7		Javan Goodman	18.5	Javan Goodman	8.8	Earl Brown	5.0	Larry Farmer		
1999-2000	14-14	4-10		Earl Brown	14.3	Schin Kerr	5.0	David Bailey	4.1	Larry Farmer		
2000-01	7-21	2-12		David Bailey	17.3	Schin Kerr	6.3	David Bailey	6.1	Larry Farmer		
2001-02	17-13	9-7		David Bailey	21.7	Ryan Blankson	10.1	David Bailey	4.6	Larry Farmer		
2002-03	15-16	9-7		David Bailey	18.4	Paul McMillan	9.0	David Bailey	5.3	Larry Farmer		
2003-04	9-20	4-12		Paul McMillan	17.0	Paul McMillan	7.4	Blake Schilb	2.5	Larry Farmer	71-102	.410
2004-05	13-17	8-8		Blake Schilb	17.9	Blake Schilb	5.5	Blake Schilb	4.0	Jim Whitesell		
2005-06	19-11	8-8		Blake Schilb	19.1	Leon Young	7.2	Blake Schilb	3.9	Jim Whitesell		
2006-07	21-11	10-6		Blake Schilb	17.0	Andy Polka	7.2	Blake Schilb	4.0	Jim Whitesell		
2007-08	12-19	6-12		J.R. Blount	15.1	Andy Polka	6.7	J.R. Blount	2.6	Jim Whitesell		
2008-09	14-18	6-12		J.R. Blount	14.1	Darrin Williams	4.9	J.R. Blount	4.3	Jim Whitesell	79-76	.510

[a] **George Ireland (8-6) and Jerry Lyne (2-9) both coached during the 1974-75 season.**

ESPN 154 SAGARIN

LOYOLA MARYMOUNT

It's been two decades since the Lions were the story of the 1989-90 season, and some of their fans still haven't caught their breath. But the Bo and Hank Show is far from the team's lone contribution to hoops lore. Coaching standouts Pete Newell, Phil Woolpert and Rick Adelman all played here, as did two-sport star Jerry Grote.

BEST TEAM: 1989-90 One of the most entertaining teams—26–6, an NCAA D1 record 122.4 points per game—in basketball history was brought to a standstill when star Hank Gathers suddenly collapsed on the court on March 4, 1990, during the West Coast conference tournament, and died from a heart-muscle disorder. But Bo Kimble, Gathers' teammate since their high school days, refused to let the Lions' season come to a halt. Shooting his first free throw in each Tournament game left-handed as a tribute to Gathers, Kimble led the Lions on a rousing run to the Elite Eight.

BEST PLAYER: F Hank Gathers (1987-90) Supremely talented, the 6'7", 210-pound power forward was also a relentless competitor. Going toe-to-toe with LSU giants Shaquille O'Neal and Stanley Roberts on Feb. 3, 1990, Gathers had his first seven shots blocked—yet finished with 48 points in a 148-141 overtime loss.

BEST COACH: Paul Westhead (1985-90) He took run-and-gun to new levels, capitalizing on the relentless strengths of Gathers, Kimble and long-range bomber Jeff Fryer. Westhead came to LMU from the NBA and went back after the Lions' 1990 Tournament run, having won two regular-season West Coast titles.

GAME FOR THE AGES: "Inspired" doesn't begin to describe the Lions' play in their 149-115 drubbing of Michigan in the second round of the 1990 Tournament, after the loss of Gathers. Kimble scored 37.

FIERCEST RIVAL: Whether they are good or bad (and of late, the two have been mostly bad), LMU and Pepperdine always bring their A-game against each other. The crosstown-LA series started with a 30-18 LMU victory in 1940-41 and reached its peak during the Gathers-Doug Christie days. Pepperdine leads, 89–60.

SEASON REVIEW

SEAS.	W-L	CONF.	COACH	SEAS.	W-L	CONF.	COACH
1906-50	*203-202*	*Went 3-13 with no coach in '42-43*		1963-64	12-13	6-6	John Arndt
1950-51	14-11		Scotty McDonald	1964-65	6-20	2-12	John Arndt
1951-52	12-14		Scotty McDonald	1965-66	11-15	7-7	John Arndt
1952-53	14-14		Edwin Powell	1966-67	16-10	10-4	John Arndt
1953-54	14-16		William Donovan	1967-68	19-6	11-3	John Arndt
1954-55	16-9		William Donovan	1968-69	6-19	3-11	Richard Baker
1955-56	13-12	9-5	William Donovan	1969-70	13-13	7-7	Richard Baker
1956-57	11-16	5-9	William Donovan	1970-71	15-10	10-4	Richard Baker
1957-58	6-18	1-11	William Donovan	1971-72	11-15	6-8	Richard Baker
1958-59	8-15	4-8	William Donovan	1972-73	10-16	7-7	Richard Baker
1959-60	19-8	9-3	William Donovan	1973-74	13-14	6-8	Dave Benaderet
1960-61	20-7	10-2 ●	William Donovan	1974-75	14-12	7-7	Dave Benaderet
1961-62	18-9	6-6	John Arndt	1975-76	7-19	4-8	Dave Benaderet
1962-63	9-17	3-9	John Arndt	1976-77	11-15	4-10	Dave Benaderet

SEAS.	W-L	CONF.	SCORING		COACH	RECORD	
1977-78	11-15	4-10	Greg Hunter	18.2	Dave Benaderet		
1978-79	5-21	1-13	Greg Hunter	16.7	Dave Benaderet	61-96	.389
1979-80	14-14 ⊗	10-6	Jim McCloskey	22.2	Ron Jacobs	14-14	.500▼
1980-81	9-19	5-9	Jim McCloskey	22.4	Ed Goorjian		
1981-82	3-24	1-13	Forrest McKenzie	13.9	Ed Goorjian		
1982-83	9-18	2-10	Greg Goorjian	26.1	Ed Goorjian		
1983-84	12-15	5-7	Forrest McKenzie	20.9	Ed Goorjian		
1984-85	11-16	3-9	Keith Smith	25.1	Ed Goorjian	44-92	.324
1985-86	19-11	10-4 ■	Keith Smith	21.0	Paul Westhead		
1986-87	12-16	4-10	Mike Yoest	19.3	Paul Westhead		
1987-88	28-4	14-0 ●	Hank Gathers	22.5	Paul Westhead		
1988-89	20-11	10-4 ●	Hank Gathers	32.7	Paul Westhead		
1989-90	26-6	13-1 ●	Bo Kimble	35.3	Paul Westhead	105-48	.686
1990-91	16-15	9-5	Terrell Lowery	28.5	Jay Hillock		
1991-92	15-13	8-6	Terrell Lowery	26.0	Jay Hillock	31-28	.525
1992-93	7-20	2-12	Zan Mason	14.3	John Olive		
1993-94	6-21	4-10	Wyking Jones	19.7	John Olive		
1994-95	13-15	4-10	Wyking Jones	13.1	John Olive		
1995-96	18-11	8-6	Ime Oduok	13.5	John Olive		
1996-97	7-21	3-11	Jim Williamson	16.4	John Olive	51-88	.367
1997-98	7-20	3-11	Haywood Eaddy	15.2	Charles Bradley		
1998-99	11-16	6-8	Haywood Eaddy	14.8	Charles Bradley		
1999-2000	2-26	0-14	Rupert McClendon	12.7	Charles Bradley	20-62	.244
2000-01	9-19	5-9	Robert Davis	11.9	Steve Aggers		
2001-02	9-20	2-12	Greg Lakey	11.1	Steve Aggers		
2002-03	11-20	4-10	Charles Brown	11.1	Steve Aggers		
2003-04	15-14	5-9	Sherman Gay	16.1	Steve Aggers		
2004-05	11-17	3-11	Matthew Knight	15.4	Steve Aggers	55-90	.379
2005-06	12-18	8-6	Matthew Knight	16.2	Rodney Tention		
2006-07	13-18	5-9	Brandon Worthy	18.5	Rodney Tention		
2007-08	5-26	2-12	Orlando Johnson	12.4	Rodney Tention	30-62	.326
2008-09	3-28	2-12	Vernon Teel	14.6	Bill Bayno[a]	0-3	.000

[a] Bill Bayno (0-3) and Max Good (3-25) both coached during the 2008-09 season.
⊗ Records don't reflect games forfeited or vacated. For adjusted records, see p. 521.
▼ Coach's record adjusted to reflect games forfeited or vacated: 14-13, .519. For yearly totals, see p. 521.
● NCAA Tournament appearance ■ NIT appearance

PROFILE

Loyola Marymount University, Los Angeles, CA
Founded: 1865 as St. Vincent's College For Boys in Los Angeles
Enrollment: 8,845 (5,509 undergraduate)
Colors: Crimson, navy and gray
Nickname: Lions
Current arena: Albert Gersten Pavilion, opened in 1981 (4,156)
Previous: Loyola Memorial Gymnasium, 1947-81 (1,500)
First game: 1906
All-time record: 910-1,113 (.450)
Total weeks in AP Top 20/25: 16

Current conference: West Coast (1955-)
Conference titles:
West Coast Athletic: 2 (1961, '88)
West Coast: 1 (1990)
Conference tournament titles:
West Coast Athletic: 1 (1988)
West Coast: 1 (1989)
NCAA Tournament appearances: 4
Sweet 16s (since 1975): 1
NIT appearances: 1

FIRST-ROUND PRO PICKS

1990 **Bo Kimble,** LA Clippers (8)

TOP 5

G **Rick Adelman** (1965-68)
G **Terrell Lowery** (1988-92)
F **Hank Gathers** (1987-90)
F **Jim Haderlein** (1968-71)
F **Bo Kimble** (1987-90)

RECORDS

RECORDS	GAME		SEASON		CAREER	
POINTS	54	Bo Kimble, vs. Saint Joseph's (Jan. 4, 1990)	1,131	Bo Kimble (1989-90)	2,490	Hank Gathers (1987-90)
POINTS PER GAME			35.3	Bo Kimble (1989-90)	28.0	Hank Gathers (1987-90)
REBOUNDS	29	Hank Gathers, vs. U.S. International (Jan. 31, 1989)	442	Jim Haderlein (1969-70)	1,161	Jim Haderlein (1968-71)
ASSISTS	18	Terrell Lowery, vs. Saint Joseph's (Dec. 29, 1990)	283	Terrell Lowery (1990-91)	689	Terrell Lowery (1988-92)

ESPN
286
SAGARIN

MAINE

There's plenty to celebrate in Orono, even if there has yet to be an NCAA or NIT Black Bear sighting. There's the brilliance of the 1959-60 (Skip Chappelle and Don Sturgeon) and 1999-2000 (Nate Fox and Andy Bedard) teams; the out-of-nowhere 1997 upset of Marquette; the transcendent star Rufus Harris; and, best of all, Maine's continued domination of New Hampshire.

BEST TEAM: 1959-60 Coach Brian McCall's squad went 19–4 and finished second in the Yankee Conference. Led by Chappelle (20.7 ppg) and Sturgeon (12.0 ppg, 9.7 rpg), plus top rebounder Larry Schiner (10.0 rpg), Black Bear highlights included wins over Rhode Island and NCAA Tourney-bound Connecticut.

BEST PLAYER: G RUFUS HARRIS (1976-80) The school's all-time leading scorer (2,206 points) led the Black Bears for three straight seasons, including a school-record 25.6 ppg in 1979-80. He's also fourth all-time in rebounds and ninth in assists. Harris was a three-time All-District selection and a fifth-round pick of the Boston Celtics.

BEST COACH: BRIAN MCCALL (1958-68) Former star player Skip Chappelle coached the most wins (217) and seasons (17), but McCall's teams had a better winning percentage (.529), and he righted a program that had enjoyed only one winning season in the previous decade. Under McCall (120 victories), the Black Bears won six Maine State Series championships and finished second in the Yankee Conference three times.

GAME FOR THE AGES: Maine's unusual road trip on Feb. 5, 1997—an out-of-conference game during the conference season—resulted in a memorable payoff. Maine beat eventual C-USA tourney champ and NCAA-bound Marquette, 68-59, on the defensive strength of seven steals by Ramone Jones. Maine finished 11–20 that year, while Marquette went 22–9.

FIERCEST RIVAL: Maine and cross-border foe New Hampshire have battled for more than 104 years—so long that the schools cannot agree on how many times they've played. Either way, Maine rules, 110–64 (by its count) or 109–62 (by New Hampshire's).

SEASON REVIEW

SEAS.	W-L	CONF.	COACH	SEAS.	W-L	CONF.	COACH
1904-46	*156-165*	*No team 1910-17, '19-20, '29-35*		**1959-60**	19-4	6-4	Brian McCall
1946-47	9-8	2-4	George Allen	**1960-61**	18-5	7-3	Brian McCall
1947-48	11-7	2-5	George Allen	**1961-62**	11-13	4-6	Brian McCall
1948-49	4-14	0-7	George Allen	**1962-63**	8-15	3-7	Brian McCall
1949-50	13-6	3-5	Dr. Rome Rankin	**1963-64**	12-11	2-8	Brian McCall
1950-51	5-13	2-5	Dr. Rome Rankin	**1964-65**	13-10	4-6	Brian McCall
1951-52	7-12	2-6	Dr. Rome Rankin	**1965-66**	9-13	4-6	Brian McCall
1952-53	7-10	3-4	Dr. Rome Rankin	**1966-67**	8-12	1-9	Brian McCall
1953-54	6-12	1-7	Dr. Rome Rankin	**1967-68**	7-17	2-8	Brian McCall
1954-55	4-13	1-7	Russell DeVette	**1968-69**	10-13	5-5	Gil Philbrick
1955-56	6-12	3-5	Harold Woodbury	**1969-70**	7-17	1-9	Gil Philbrick
1956-57	6-14	2-6	Harold Woodbury	**1970-71**	8-16	3-7	Gil Philbrick
1957-58	8-12	4-6	Harold Woodbury	**1971-72**	15-10	6-4	Skip Chappelle
1958-59	15-7	7-3	Brian McCall	**1972-73**	13-10	6-6	Skip Chappelle

SEAS.	W-L	CONF.	SCORING		COACH	RECORD
1973-74	14-10	2-10	Robert Warner	18.0	Skip Chappelle	
1974-75	11-14	1-10	Robert Warner	19.7	Skip Chappelle	
1975-76	14-11	5-7	Paul Wholey	22.1	Skip Chappelle	
1976-77	13-13		Roger Lapham	16.7	Skip Chappelle	
1977-78	17-8		Rufus Harris	22.8	Skip Chappelle	
1978-79	14-10		Rufus Harris	21.5	Skip Chappelle	
1979-80	15-13	14-12	Rufus Harris	25.6	Skip Chappelle	
1980-81	14-14	13-13	Wilford Godbolt, Jr.	18.8	Skip Chappelle	
1981-82	7-19	3-7	Clayton Pickering	15.6	Skip Chappelle	
1982-83	12-14	6-4	Jeff Cross	19.2	Skip Chappelle	
1983-84	17-10	7-7	Jeff Cross	16.8	Skip Chappelle	
1984-85	11-17	5-11	Rich Henry	14.1	Skip Chappelle	
1985-86	7-20	5-13	Rich Henry	13.9	Skip Chappelle	
1986-87	10-18	6-12	James Boylan	21.1	Skip Chappelle	
1987-88	13-15	10-8	Reggie Banks	18.1	Skip Chappelle	217-226 .490
1988-89	9-19	7-11	Matt Rossignol	13.8	Rudy Keeling	
1989-90	11-17	6-6	Dean Smith	19.1	Rudy Keeling	
1990-91	13-16	7-3	Derrick Hodge	13.9	Rudy Keeling	
1991-92	17-15	8-6	Francois Bouchard	13.5	Rudy Keeling	
1992-93	10-17	4-10	Francois Bouchard	13.0	Rudy Keeling	
1993-94	20-9	11-3	Francois Bouchard	15.7	Rudy Keeling	
1994-95	11-16	6-10	Casey Arena	17.9	Rudy Keeling	
1995-96	15-13	11-7	John Gordon	13.2	Rudy Keeling	106-122 .465
1996-97	11-20	6-12	Terry Hunt	15.4	Dr. John Giannini	
1997-98	7-20	4-14	Fred Meeks	19.5	Dr. John Giannini	
1998-99	19-9	13-5	Nate Fox	18.2	Dr. John Giannini	
1999-2000	24-7	15-3	Nate Fox	17.6	Dr. John Giannini	
2000-01	18-11	10-8	Julian Dunkley	16.6	Dr. John Giannini	
2001-02	12-18	7-9	Errick Greene	16.4	Dr. John Giannini	
2002-03	14-16	8-8	Rickey White	13.2	Dr. John Giannini	
2003-04	20-10	12-6	Kevin Reed	14.5	Dr. John Giannini	125-111 .530
2004-05	14-15	8-10	Ernest Turner	13.7	Ted Woodward	
2005-06	12-16	7-9	Ernest Turner	15.2	Ted Woodward	
2006-07	12-18	7-9	Kevin Reed	14.1	Ted Woodward	
2007-08	7-23	3-13	Mark Socoby	14.6	Ted Woodward	
2008-09	9-21	4-12	Mark Socoby	12.3	Ted Woodward	54-93 .367

PROFILE

University of Maine, Orono, ME
Founded: 1865
Enrollment: 12,000 (9,000 undergraduate)
Colors: Blue and white
Nickname: Black Bears
Current arena: Harold Alfond Sports Arena, opened in 1977 (5,712)
First game: 1904
All-time record: 889-1,003 (.470)
Total weeks in AP Top 20/25: 0

Current conference: America East (1996-)
Conference titles: 0
Conference tournament titles: 0
NCAA Tournament appearances: 0
NIT appearances: 0

CONSENSUS ALL-AMERICAS

1961 **Skip Chappelle** (Little A-A), G

TOP 5

G **Rufus Harris** (1976-80)
G **Keith Mahaney** (1952-54, '56-57)
G **Jim Stephenson** (1966-69)
F **Skip Chappelle** (1959-62)
F **Bob Warner** (1972-76)

RECORDS

RECORDS	GAME		SEASON		CAREER	
POINTS	54	Jim Stephenson, vs. Colby (March 3, 1969)	718	Rufus Harris (1979-80)	2,206	Rufus Harris (1976-80)
POINTS PER GAME			25.6	Rufus Harris (1979-80)	22.7	Jim Stephenson (1966-69)
REBOUNDS	28	Bob Warner, vs. Trinity (Jan. 15, 1974)	352	Bob Warner (1974-75)	1,304	Bob Warner (1972-76)
ASSISTS	16	Jeff Sturgeon, vs. Niagara (1982-83)	193	Andy Bedard (1999-2000)	619	Marty Higgins (1988-92)

THE SCHOOLS

ESPN 131 SAGARIN

MANHATTAN

An early power in New York basketball circles, the Jaspers routinely made the NIT in the 1950s—and routinely lost before advancing very far. But they made a far greater contribution to the game than titles. In January 1951, forward Junius Kellogg not only refused an offer to fix a game, he reported it to his coach then the district attorney's office, helping to unravel a gambling scandal that rocked college basketball.

BEST TEAM: 1994-95 Manhattan ran off winning streaks of eight and 14 games on its way to the Metro Atlantic Athletic Conference regular-season crown. The Jaspers' résumé was so strong that they made the Big Dance despite losing in the MAAC tournament finals; their at-large bid was a conference first. As a No. 13 seed, the Jaspers upset No. 4-seed Oklahoma, 77-67, before falling in the second round to Arizona State.

BEST PLAYER: G Luis Flores (2001-04) The Rutgers transfer played only three seasons at Manhattan, yet is its all-time leading scorer. In the 2003 MAAC tournament semis, he played all 50 minutes of the Jaspers' double-OT victory over Niagara, scoring 30. One year later, the two-time MAAC Player of the Year went for 26 in Manhattan's first-round Tournament upset of Florida.

BEST COACH: Kenneth Norton (1946-68) Despite being limited to recruiting mostly New York City players, Norton turned the Jaspers into a consistent winner, largely by stressing fundamentals and smarts. His teams made 10 postseason appearances, most memorably beating No. 1-ranked West Virginia in the 1958 Tourney.

GAME FOR THE AGES: The No. 12-seed Jaspers didn't just upset Florida, 75-60, in the first round of the 2004 Tourney. They outplayed, outhustled and outmuscled them. Afterward, Gators coach Billy Donovan said his team had a deer-in-the-headlights look.

FIERCEST RIVAL: It's called the Battle of the Bronx, a series between Manhattan and Fordham that dates to 1911-12. Although the Jaspers lead 52–49 overall, they've lost their share of heartbreakers, such as a 44-42 OT loss in the 1985 MAAC tournament.

SEASON REVIEW

SEAS.	W-L	CONF.		COACH	SEAS.	W-L	CONF.		COACH
1904-47	*380-287*	*Went to NIT in '43, finished 18-3*			1960-61	8-11	1-2		Kenneth Norton
1947-48	22-6	3-3		Kenneth Norton	1961-62	12-10	1-3		Kenneth Norton
1948-49	18-8	5-1	■	Kenneth Norton	1962-63	9-14	0-4		Kenneth Norton
1949-50	14-11	3-3		Kenneth Norton	1963-64	11-11			Kenneth Norton
1950-51	16-6	3-2		Kenneth Norton	1964-65	13-9		■	Kenneth Norton
1951-52	12-9	4-2		Kenneth Norton	1965-66	13-9	8-1	■	Kenneth Norton
1952-53	20-6	6-0	■	Kenneth Norton	1966-67	13-8	7-2		Kenneth Norton
1953-54	15-11	3-3	■	Kenneth Norton	1967-68	8-14	3-5		Kenneth Norton
1954-55	18-5	6-0	■	Kenneth Norton	1968-69	13-9	7-1		Jack Powers
1955-56	16-8	4-1	●	Kenneth Norton	1969-70	18-8		■	Jack Powers
1956-57	15-9	2-2	■	Kenneth Norton	1970-71	13-11			Jack Powers
1957-58	16-10	3-1	●	Kenneth Norton	1971-72	11-13			Jack Powers
1958-59	15-6	4-0	■	Kenneth Norton	1972-73	16-10		■	Jack Powers
1959-60	13-11	2-2		Kenneth Norton	1973-74	18-9		■	Jack Powers

SEAS.	W-L	CONF.		SCORING		COACH	RECORD	
1974-75	14-12		■			Jack Powers		
1975-76	14-14					Jack Powers		
1976-77	13-14	3-2				Jack Powers		
1977-78	12-14	3-2		Steve Grant	23.6	Jack Powers	142-114	.555
1978-79	6-20	1-6		JoJo Walters	22.7	Brian Mahoney		
1979-80	4-22					Brian Mahoney		
1980-81	6-20					Brian Mahoney	16-62	.205
1981-82	11-16	3-7				Gordon Chiesa		
1982-83	15-13	4-6				Gordon Chiesa		
1983-84	9-19	2-12		Tim Cain	20.9	Gordon Chiesa		
1984-85	8-20	4-10				Gordon Chiesa	43-68	.387
1985-86	2-26	1-13				Tom Sullivan	2-26	.071
1986-87	6-21	2-12				Bob Delle Bovi		
1987-88	7-23	1-13		Bill Wheeler	22.6	Bob Delle Bovi	13-44	.228
1988-89	7-21	3-11				Steve Lappas		
1989-90	11-17	7-9				Steve Lappas		
1990-91	13-15	8-8				Steve Lappas		
1991-92	25-9	13-3	■			Steve Lappas	56-62	.475
1992-93	23-7	12-2	●			Fran Fraschilla		
1993-94	20-10	10-4	■			Fran Fraschilla		
1994-95	26-5	12-2	●			Fran Fraschilla		
1995-96	17-12	9-5	■			Fran Fraschilla	86-34	.716
1996-97	9-18	5-9				John Leonard		
1997-98	12-17	7-11				John Leonard		
1998-99	5-22	3-15		Ken Kavanagh	14.5	John Leonard	26-57	.313
1999-2000	12-15	9-9		Durelle Brown	21.3	Bobby Gonzalez		
2000-01	14-15	11-7		Durelle Brown	17.8	Bobby Gonzalez		
2001-02	20-9	12-6	■	Luis Flores	19.4	Bobby Gonzalez		
2002-03	23-7	14-4	●	Luis Flores	24.6	Bobby Gonzalez		
2003-04	25-6	16-2	●	Luis Flores	24.0	Bobby Gonzalez		
2004-05	15-14	9-9		Peter Mulligan	19.3	Bobby Gonzalez		
2005-06	20-11	14-4	■	C.J. Anderson	18.8	Bobby Gonzalez	129-77	.626
2006-07	13-17	10-8		Devon Austin	12.4	Barry Rohrssen		
2007-08	12-19	5-13		Antoine Pearson	12.2	Barry Rohrssen		
2008-09	16-14	9-9		Darryl Crawford	14.4	Barry Rohrssen	41-50	.451

● NCAA Tournament appearance ■ NIT appearance

PROFILE

Manhattan College, Riverdale, NY
Founded: 1853
Enrollment: 3,299 (2,909 undergraduate)
Colors: Kelly green and white
Nickname: Jaspers
Current arena: Draddy Gymnasium, opened in 1978 (2,500)
First game: 1904
All-time record: 1,231-1,073 (.534)
Total weeks in AP Top 20/25: 8

Current conference: Metro Atlantic Athletic (1981-)
Conference titles:
Metro NY: 4 (1949 [tie], '53, '55, '59)
Metro: 3 (1966, '67 [tie], '69 [tie])
MAAC: 6 (1992, '93, '95, 2003, '04, '06)
Conference tournament titles:
MAAC: 3 (1993, 2003, '04)
NCAA Tournament appearances: 6
NIT appearances: 18
Semifinals: 1

TOP 5

G **Luis Flores** (2001-04)
G/F **Keith Bullock** (1989-93)
F **Jamal Marshall** (1991-95)
F **Jack Powers** (1955-58)
C **Ed O'Connor** (1951-55)

RECORDS

RECORDS	GAME		SEASON		CAREER	
POINTS	51	Bob Mealy, vs. CCNY (Feb. 22, 1960)	744	Luis Flores (2003-04)	2,046	Luis Flores (2001-04)
POINTS PER GAME			25.7	Larry Lembo (1963-64)	22.7	Luis Flores (2001-04)
REBOUNDS	30	Bill Campion, vs. Hofstra (Feb. 10, 1973)	419	Bill Campion (1973-74)	1,070	Bill Campion (1972-75)
ASSISTS	15	Tom Courtney, vs. Columbia (Dec. 5, 1978)	176	Phil Lane (1999-2000)	447	Ed Lawson (1983-88)

ESPN 308 SAGARIN

MARIST

The long and the short of it: Two great teams dominate Marist's 48-year history. The first centered around 7'4" Rik Smits and reached the NCAA Tournament in 1986 and 1987. The second, led by guards Jared Jordan and Will Whittington, upset Oklahoma State in the 2007 NIT for the school's only postseason win.

BEST TEAM: 1986-87 First-year coach Dave Magarity landed a dream job: Smits and quicksilver guard Drafton Davis were juniors, bangers Mark Shamley and Miroslav Pecarski supported Smits, and the Red Foxes had reached the NCAA Tourney the previous year. The nightmare reality: a 6–9 start. But Marist righted itself, took 14 straight and the ECAC Metro tourney, and claimed another NCAA Tourney bid—though it lost its first-rounder to Pittsburgh.

BEST PLAYER: C Rik Smits (1984-88) The Dunking Dutchman was born and raised in Eindhoven, the Netherlands, and arrived at Marist as a (very) raw talent. But Smits learned fast and carried the Red Foxes to two league tourney titles with his smooth jumper and inside prowess—he was second nationally in blocks (3.9 bpg) in 1987-88. He was the NBA's second overall pick in 1988 and a 12-year star with the Indiana Pacers.

BEST COACH: Dave Magarity (1986-2004) Matt Brady (2004-08) certainly revitalized Marist, but Magarity was the face of the program, having led Marist for all but 10 of the its 28 D1 seasons and amassing 253 wins. Smits, Davis, Alan Tomidy and Izett Buchanan are just a few of the Red Foxes who thrived under Magarity.

GAME FOR THE AGES: With Marist down 54-52 to top-seed Fairleigh Dickinson in the 1986 ECAC Metro tournament final, Smits hit a jumper with :24 left to force overtime. Then, after missing three free throws in overtime, Smits finally hit one with :14 seconds left to win it for the Red Foxes, 57-56.

FIERCEST RIVAL: Marist is tired of meeting Siena in the league tournament. The in-state rivals played five MAAC tournament games from 1999 to 2009 and the Red Foxes were bounced by the Saints each time.

SEASON REVIEW

SEAS.	W-L	CONF.		SCORING		COACH	RECORD	
1961-62	6-7					George Sturba	6-7	.462
1962-63	14-9					Tom Wade		
1963-64	4-15					Tom Wade	18-24	.429
1964-65	6-17					Paul Arnold		
1965-66	6-17					Paul Arnold	12-34	.261
1966-67	9-16					Ron Petro		
1967-68	11-13					Ron Petro		
1968-69	19-8					Ron Petro		
1969-70	15-9					Ron Petro		
1970-71	20-7					Ron Petro		
1971-72	16-9					Ron Petro		
1972-73	15-12					Ron Petro		
1973-74	9-16					Ron Petro		
1974-75	16-10					Ron Petro		
1975-76	15-10					Ron Petro		
1976-77	8-16					Ron Petro		
1977-78	7-19					Ron Petro		
1978-79	8-16					Ron Petro		
1979-80	9-17					Ron Petro		
1980-81	12-15					Ron Petro		
1981-82	12-14	6-9		Steve Smith	21.0	Ron Petro		
1982-83	14-15	7-7		Steve Smith	20.4	Ron Petro		
1983-84	14-15	8-8		Tom Meekins	12.2	Ron Petro	229-237	.491
1984-85	17-12	11-3		Steve Eggink	15.3	Matt Furjanic		
1985-86	19-12	11-5	●	Rik Smits	17.7	Matt Furjanic	36-24	.600
1986-87	20-10	15-1	●	Rik Smits	20.1	Dave Magarity		
1987-88	18-9	13-3		Rik Smits	24.7	Dave Magarity		
1988-89	13-15	9-7		Miroslav Pecarski	19.6	Dave Magarity		
1989-90	17-11	10-6		Steve Paterno	14.2	Dave Magarity		
1990-91	6-22	4-12		Fred Ingles	18.1	Dave Magarity		
1991-92	10-20	6-10		Izett Buchanan	17.5	Dave Magarity		
1992-93	14-16	10-8		Izett Buchanan	14.8	Dave Magarity		
1993-94	14-13	10-8		Izett Buchanan	25.4	Dave Magarity		
1994-95	17-11	12-6		Danny Basile	17.3	Dave Magarity		
1995-96	22-7	14-4	■	Alan Tomidy	16.8	Dave Magarity		
1996-97	6-22	4-14		Bobby Joe Hatton	12.4	Dave Magarity		
1997-98	11-17	7-11		Bobby Joe Hatton	14.9	Dave Magarity		
1998-99	16-12	8-10		Bobby Joe Hatton	14.7	Dave Magarity		
1999-2000	14-14	10-8		Tom Kenney	14.2	Dave Magarity		
2000-01	17-13	11-7		Drew Samuels	15.4	Dave Magarity		
2001-02	19-9	13-5		Sean Kennedy	14.7	Dave Magarity		
2002-03	13-16	8-10		Nick Eppehimer	17.0	Dave Magarity		
2003-04	6-22	4-14		Will McClurkin	10.8	Dave Magarity	253-259	.494
2004-05	11-17	8-10		Will Whittington	16.1	Matt Brady		
2005-06	19-10	12-6		Jared Jordan	16.1	Matt Brady		
2006-07	25-9	14-4	■	Will Whittington	17.6	Matt Brady		
2007-08	18-14	11-7		Jay Gavin	12.3	Matt Brady	73-50	.593
2008-09	10-23	4-14		Ryan Schneider	15.9	Chuck Martin	10-23	.303

● NCAA Tournament appearance ■ NIT appearance

PROFILE

Marist College, Poughkeepsie, NY
Founded: 1929
Enrollment: 5,829 (5,032 undergraduate)
Colors: Red and white
Nickname: Red Foxes
Current arena: McCann Recreation Center, opened in 1977 (3,200)
First game: 1961
All-time record: 637-658 (.492)
Total weeks in AP Top 20/25: 0

Current conference: Metro Atlantic Athletic (1997-)
Conference titles:
East Coast Athletic Metro: 3 (1985, '87, '88 [tie])
MAAC: 2 (2002 [tie], '07)
Conference tournament titles:
East Coast Athletic Metro: 2 (1986, '87)
NCAA Tournament appearances: 2
NIT appearances: 2

FIRST-ROUND PRO PICKS

1988 **Rik Smits,** Indiana (2)

TOP 5

G **Jared Jordan** (2003-07)
G **Will Whittington** (2003-07)
G/F **Steve Smith** (1979-83)
F **Alan Tomidy** (1992-96)
C **Rik Smits** (1984-88)

RECORDS

RECORDS	GAME		SEASON		CAREER	
POINTS	51	Izett Buchanan, vs. Long Island (Feb. 12, 1994)	685	Izett Buchanan (1993-94)	2,077	Steve Smith (1979-83)
POINTS PER GAME			25.4	Izett Buchanan (1993-94)	19.4	Steve Smith (1979-83)
REBOUNDS	22	Alan Tomidy, vs. Long Island (Feb. 8, 1996)	329	Alan Tomidy (1995-96)	923	Ted Taylor (1981-85)
ASSISTS	17	Sean Kennedy, vs. Saint Peter's (Feb. 21, 2002)	286	Jared Jordan (2006-07)	813	Jared Jordan (2003-07)

ESPN 24 SAGARIN

MARQUETTE

Greatest program? Even though the Golden Eagles are one of only 18 schools to have won both an NIT and an NCAA title, not even their biggest boosters would claim that. But most colorful? That's an argument Marquette might win. There's Al McGuire, as entertaining as a coach as he was as a broadcaster. There's the long line of trendsetting uniforms, most famously the early 1970s bumblebee look, which the NCAA eventually banned out of concern that it was too distracting for opponents. And of course, there's the legacy of transcendent talents, from Jim Chones and Maurice Lucas to Bo Ellis, Butch Lee and Dwyane Wade.

BEST TEAM: 1975-76 McGuire famously said his 1977 national title team wasn't even one of his half-dozen best. That leaves this well-balanced squad to claim to honors. Led by Earl Tatum and Bo Ellis, the Warriors (now known as the Golden Eagles) lost just twice—in overtime to Minnesota in the regular season and to unbeaten Indiana in the Elite Eight. They played with trademark quickness and defensive intensity, but Tatum's scoring (18.3 ppg) gave them surprising sizzle for a McGuire team.

BEST PLAYER: G Butch Lee (1974-78) Visiting Lee in his Harlem home on a recruiting trip, McGuire called the prep star the best guard in America. When Lee noted that the coach hadn't even seen him play, Maguire quipped that since Lee was the best guard in New York, that also meant he was the best guard in America. A four-year starter, Lee lived up to his billing. After nearly leading Puerto Rico to an upset of the gold-medal-winning U.S. basketball team in the 1976 Olympics, Lee capped off his Marquette career as the then-second all-time leading scorer while splitting national POY honors with North Carolina's Phil Ford.

BEST COACH: Al McGuire (1964-77) He's legendary for his metaphors (according to some accounts, he was the first to call refs "zebras" and top recruits "blue-chippers"), love of colorful uniforms, battles with refs, noisy practices and unique motivational tactics. During halftime of Marquette's first-round matchup with Cincinnati in the 1977 Tourney, McGuire slapped star shooter Bernard Toone after the coach became infuriated by his play and his talking back. The team rolled over the Bearcats in the second half—then to the NCAA title.

GAME FOR THE AGES: Using a 2-3 zone and fueled by considerable swagger, the Warriors overcame North Carolina's vaunted four-corners offense to win the 1977 NCAA title, 67-59. As the last seconds ticked off, McGuire, coaching his last game, cried on the sideline while the crowd started to chant "Al's Last Hurrah."

HEARTBREAKER: Facing undefeated Indiana in the 1976 Elite Eight, the Warriors made a spirited comeback from 10 down to close within three points late. But McGuire drew a technical foul with :25 left—his second T of the game—sinking the Warriors' cause. The Hoosiers won, 65-56.

FIERCEST RIVAL: How big a deal is it for Marquette to beat Wisconsin? Shortly after the Golden Eagles upset Duke in November 2006, guard Dominic James was walking around campus when a student approached him—not to congratulate him on the momentous win but to implore him to beat the Badgers in December. Wisconsin leads overall, 62–53.

FANFARE AND HOOPLA: Whenever the Golden Eagles win a big game, students pour out of dorms and apartments and run down Wisconsin Avenue toward Lake Michigan. The most memorable such run came after the school's 1977 national title win.

FAN FAVORITE: G Dwyane Wade (2001-03) As a high school senior, he finished *seventh* in the voting for Illinois' Mr. Basketball. But coach Tom Crean saw the potential in Wade's then-quiet game, and soon the guard became an alley-ooping, jump-shooting, ball-hawking star beloved by fans. After leading Marquette to an upset of Cincinnati on Feb. 2, 2002, fans stormed the floor and carried Wade on their shoulders.

CONSENSUS ALL-AMERICAS

1971 **Dean Meminger,** G
1972 **Jim Chones,** C
1978 **Butch Lee,** G
2003 **Dwyane Wade,** G

FIRST ROUND PRO PICKS

1971 **Dean Meminger,** New York (16)
1972 **Jim Chones,** New York (ABA)
1974 **Maurice Lucas,** Chicago (14)
1977 **Bo Ellis,** Washington (17)
1978 **Butch Lee,** Atlanta (10)
2003 **Dwyane Wade,** Miami (5)

PROFILE

Marquette University, Milwaukee, WI
Founded: 1881
Enrollment: 11,548 (8,048 undergraduate)
Colors: Blue and gold
Nickname: Golden Eagles
Current arena: Bradley Center, opened in 1988 (18,850)
Previous arena: MECCA, opened as Milwaukee Arena, 1950-88 (11,000); Marquette Gym, N/A (2,100); Milwaukee Auditorium, N/A (6,200)
First game: Jan. 13, 1917

All-time record: 1,422-878 (.618)
Total weeks in AP Top 20/25: 327
Current conference: Big East (2005-)
Conference titles:
Great Midwest: 1 (1994)
Conference USA: 1 (2003)
Conference tournament titles:
Conference USA: 1 (1997)
NCAA Tournament appearances: 27
Sweet 16s (since 1975): 5
Final Fours: 3
Titles: 1 (1977)

NIT appearances: 15
Semifinals: 4
Titles: 1 (1970)

TOP 5

G **Butch Lee** (1974-78)
G **George Thompson** (1966-69)
G **Dwyane Wade** (2001-03)
F **Bo Ellis** (1973-77)
C **Jim Chones** (1970-72)

RECORDS

RECORDS	GAME		SEASON		CAREER	
POINTS	44	Tony Smith, vs. Wisconsin (Feb. 19, 1990); Mike Moran, vs. Creighton (Feb. 5, 1958)	710	Dwyane Wade (2002-03)	1,985	Jerel McNeal (2005-09)
POINTS PER GAME			23.8	Tony Smith (1989-90)	20.4	George Thompson (1966-69)
REBOUNDS	28	Pat Smith, vs. Loyola-Chicago (Feb. 8, 1967)	462	Don Kojis (1960-61)	1,222	Don Kojis (1958-61)
ASSISTS	17	Tony Miller, vs. Memphis (Mar. 4, 1995)	274	Tony Miller (1993-94)	956	Tony Miller (1991-95)

SEASON REVIEW

SEASON	W-L	CONF.	SCORING		COACH	RECORD	
1916-17	8-2		Al Delmore	7.3	Ralph Risch	8-2	.800
1917-18	4-6		Al Delmore	5.1	Jack Ryan		
1918-19	no team						
1919-20	9-3				Jack Ryan	13-9	.591
1920-21	14-3				Frank Murray		
1921-22	15-5		Dick Quinn	7.0	Frank Murray		
1922-23	19-2				Frank Murray		
1923-24	10-10				Frank Murray		
1924-25	8-11		Robert Demoling	3.6	Frank Murray		
1925-26	8-13				Frank Murray		
1926-27	5-10		Floyd Razner	4.5	Frank Murray		
1927-28	7-11		Jim O'Donnell	6.3	Frank Murray		
1928-29	8-8		Roy Andrews	5.3	Frank Murray	94-73	.563
1929-30	11-12		Roy Andrews	6.7	Cord Lipe	11-12	.478
1930-31	11-7		Whitey Budrunas	8.9	Bill Chandler		
1931-32	11-8		Whitey Budrunas	8.9	Bill Chandler		
1932-33	14-3		Ray Morstadt	9.6	Bill Chandler		
1933-34	15-4		Ray Morstadt	8.5	Bill Chandler		
1934-35	11-7		Ray Morstadt	10.9	Bill Chandler		
1935-36	7-12		Charles Eirich	5.7	Bill Chandler		
1936-37	8-8		Glenn Adams	5.0	Bill Chandler		
1937-38	14-5		Paul Sokody	6.7	Bill Chandler		

SEAS.	W-L	CONF.	POSTSEASON	SCORING		REBOUNDS		ASSISTS		COACH	RECORD	
1938-39	12-5			Bob Deneen	11.4					Bill Chandler		
1939-40	7-9			Bob Deneen	9.7					Bill Chandler		
1940-41	2-13			Bill Komenich	7.2					Bill Chandler		
1941-42	6-11			Ray Kuffel	8.4					Bill Chandler		
1942-43	9-10			Ray Kuffel	8.9					Bill Chandler		
1943-44	8-6			Howie Kallenberger	12.1					Bill Chandler		
1944-45	7-10			Gene Berce	13.4					Bill Chandler		
1945-46	11-7			Howie Kallenberger	9.3					Bill Chandler		
1946-47	9-14			Gene Berce	14.7					Bill Chandler		
1947-48	9-15			Gene Berce	17.7					Bill Chandler		
1948-49	8-13			Frank McCabe	12.7					Bill Chandler		
1949-50	6-17			Mel Peterson	10.1					Bill Chandler		
1950-51	8-14			Grant Wittberger	12.8	Grant Wittberger	10.5			Bill Chandler	193-198	.494
1951-52	12-14			Russ Wittberger	12.0	Grant Wittberger	9.1			Tex Winter		
1952-53	13-11			Russ Wittberger	19.4	Russ Wittberger	8.5			Tex Winter	25-25	.500
1953-54	11-15			Terry Rand	15.2	Terry Rand	10.3			Jack Nagle		
1954-55	24-3		NCAA REGIONAL FINALS	Terry Rand	15.9	Terry Rand	14.7			Jack Nagle		
1955-56	13-11		NIT FIRST ROUND	Terry Rand	20.3	Terry Rand	13.1			Jack Nagle		
1956-57	10-15			Mike Moran	20.4	John Glaser	14.0			Jack Nagle		
1957-58	11-11			Mike Moran	17.1	Walt Mangham	10.2			Jack Nagle	69-55	.556
1958-59	23-6		NCAA REGIONAL SEMIFINALS	Mike Moran	18.1	Don Kojis	13.0			Eddie Hickey		
1959-60	13-12			Don Kojis	20.9	Don Kojis	15.4			Eddie Hickey		
1960-61	16-11		NCAA FIRST ROUND	Don Kojis	21.4	Don Kojis	17.1			Eddie Hickey		
1961-62	15-11			Ron Glaser	16.4	Dave Erickson	8.4			Eddie Hickey		
1962-63	20-9		NIT THIRD PLACE	Ron Glaser	17.6	Dave Erickson	8.8			Eddie Hickey		
1963-64	5-21			Tom Flynn	17.3	Tom Flynn	10.2			Eddie Hickey	92-70	.568
1964-65	8-18			Tom Flynn	16.5	Paul Carbins	11.7			Al McGuire		
1965-66	14-12			Bob Wolf	22.0	Paul Carbins	11.4			Al McGuire		
1966-67	21-9		NIT RUNNER-UP	Bob Wolf	18.4	Brian Brunkhorst	7.8			Al McGuire		
1967-68	23-6		NCAA REGIONAL SEMIFINALS	George Thompson	22.9	George Thompson	8.6			Al McGuire		
1968-69	24-5		NCAA REGIONAL FINALS	George Thompson	20.2	Ric Cobb	9.7			Al McGuire		
1969-70	26-3		NIT CHAMPION	Dean Meminger	18.8	Ric Cobb	9.1			Al McGuire		
1970-71	28-1		NCAA REGIONAL SEMIFINALS	Dean Meminger	21.2	Jim Chones	11.5			Al McGuire		
1971-72	25-4		NCAA REGIONAL SEMIFINALS	Jim Chones	20.6	Jim Chones	11.9			Al McGuire		
1972-73	25-4		NCAA REGIONAL SEMIFINALS	Larry McNeill	17.6	Maurice Lucas	10.9			Al McGuire		
1973-74	26-5		NCAA RUNNER-UP	Maurice Lucas	15.8	Maurice Lucas	10.6			Al McGuire		
1974-75	23-4		NCAA FIRST ROUND	Bo Ellis	16.3	Bo Ellis	10.5			Al McGuire		
1975-76	27-2		NCAA REGIONAL FINALS	Earl Tatum	18.3	Bo Ellis	9.3			Al McGuire		
1976-77	**25-7** ⊘		**NATIONAL CHAMPION**	**Butch Lee**	**19.6**	**Bo Ellis**	**8.3**			**Al McGuire**	**295-80**	**.787▼**
1977-78	24-4		NCAA FIRST ROUND	Butch Lee	17.7	Jerome Whitehead	8.3			Hank Raymonds		
1978-79	22-7		NCAA REGIONAL SEMIFINALS	Bernard Toone	18.7	Bernard Toone	6.7			Hank Raymonds		
1979-80	18-9		NCAA FIRST ROUND	Sam Worthen	16.9	Robert Byrd	10.0			Hank Raymonds		
1980-81	20-11		NIT FIRST ROUND	Oliver Lee	17.7	Oliver Lee	6.5			Hank Raymonds		
1981-82	23-9		NCAA SECOND ROUND	Michael Wilson	16.1	Dean Marquardt	6.6			Hank Raymonds		
1982-83	19-10		NCAA FIRST ROUND	Glenn Rivers	13.2	Marc Marotta	6.0			Hank Raymonds	126-50	.716
1983-84	17-13		NIT SECOND ROUND	Dwayne Johnson	14.0	Marc Marotta	7.1			Rick Majerus		
1984-85	20-11		NIT QUARTERFINALS	Kerry Trotter	12.4	Kerry Trotter	6.2			Rick Majerus		
1985-86	19-11		NIT SECOND ROUND	David Boone	15.3	David Boone	10.6			Rick Majerus	56-35	.615
1986-87	16-13		NIT FIRST ROUND	David Boone	15.9	David Boone	8.8			Bob Dukiet		
1987-88	10-18			Tony Smith	13.1	Trevor Powell	6.0			Bob Dukiet		
1988-89	13-15			Trevor Powell	15.1	Trevor Powell	6.3			Bob Dukiet	39-46	.459
1989-90	15-14	9-5	NIT FIRST ROUND	Tony Smith	23.8	Trevor Powell	7.8			Kevin O'Neill		
1990-91	11-18	7-7		Damon Key	13.2	Trevor Powell	7.3			Kevin O'Neill		
1991-92	16-13	5-5		Damon Key	13.6	Ron Curry	7.2	Tony Miller	7.6	Kevin O'Neill		
1992-93	20-8	6-4	NCAA FIRST ROUND	Ron Curry	14.4	Ron Curry	8.1	Tony Miller	7.6	Kevin O'Neill		
1993-94	24-9	10-2	NCAA REGIONAL SEMIFINALS	Damon Key	15.6	Jim McIlvaine	8.3	Tony Miller	8.3	Kevin O'Neill	86-62	.581
1994-95	21-12	7-5	NIT RUNNER-UP	Roney Eford	13.2	Amal McCaskill	8.5	Tony Miller	7.5	Mike Deane		
1995-96	23-8	10-4	NCAA SECOND ROUND	Aaron Hutchins	14.0	Amal McCaskill	8.9	Aaron Hutchins	6.9	Mike Deane		
1996-97	22-9	9-5	NCAA FIRST ROUND	Chris Crawford	14.9	Faisal Abraham	6.5			Mike Deane		
1997-98	20-11	8-8	NIT QUARTERFINALS	Aaron Hutchins	15.2	Jarrod Lovette	6.9			Mike Deane		
1998-99	14-15	6-10		Brian Wardle	12.3	Mike Bargen	5.4	Cordell Henry	3.2	Mike Deane	100-55	.645
1999-2000	15-14	8-8	NIT FIRST ROUND	Brian Wardle	16.6	Oluoma Nnamaka	6.7	Cordell Henry	3.5	Tom Crean		
2000-01	15-14	9-7		Brian Wardle	18.8	Odartey Blankson	5.5	Cordell Henry	4.4	Tom Crean		
2001-02	26-7	13-3	NCAA FIRST ROUND	Dwyane Wade	17.8	Dwyane Wade	6.6	Dwyane Wade	3.4	Tom Crean		
2002-03	27-6	14-2	NCAA NATIONAL SEMIFINALS	Dwyane Wade	21.5	Robert Jackson	7.5	Travis Diener	5.6	Tom Crean		
2003-04	19-12	8-8	NIT QUARTERFINALS	Travis Diener	18.8	Scott Merritt	7.1	Travis Diener	6.0	Tom Crean		
2004-05	19-12	7-9	NIT FIRST ROUND	Travis Diener	19.7	Marcus Jackson	8.5	Travis Diener	7.0	Tom Crean		
2005-06	20-11	10-6	NCAA FIRST ROUND	Steve Novak	17.5	Steve Novak	5.9	Dominic James	5.4	Tom Crean		
2006-07	24-10	10-6	NCAA FIRST ROUND	Dominic James	14.9	Ousmane Barro	6.9	Dominic James	4.9	Tom Crean		
2007-08	25-10	11-7	NCAA SECOND ROUND	Jerel McNeal	14.9	Lazar Hayward	6.5	Dominic James	4.4	Tom Crean	190-96	.664
2008-09	25-10	12-6	NCAA SECOND ROUND	Jerel McNeal	19.8	Lazar Hayward	8.6	Dominic James	5.0	Buzz Williams	25-10	.714

⊘ Record does not reflect games forfeited or vacated. For adjusted record, see p. 521.

▼ Coach's record adjusted to reflect games forfeited or vacated: 296-79, .789. For yearly totals, see p. 521.

ESPN 108 SAGARIN

MARSHALL

Hall-of-Famer Hal Greer, NBA coach Mike D'Antoni and Billy Donovan share a common bond: *They are Marshall.* Greer and D'Antoni played for the Thundering Herd, while the school was the first stop in Donovan's impressive head coaching career. Known more for football—and a tragic 1970 team plane crash—the Thundering Herd has managed to make some noise on the hardwood as well.

BEST TEAM: 1946-47 Led by the high-scoring tandem of Andy Tonkovich and Bill Toothman, the Thundering Herd went 32–5 and won the national championship of the NAIB (the precursor to the NAIA). But that achievement did not come easily. Marshall could only afford to take eight players to the tournament in Kansas City, and had to mount two comeback victories before beating Mankato State in the final, 73-59.

BEST PLAYER: G/F Harold Everett "Hal" Greer (1955-58) A Huntington native, Greer was the first African-American to receive a scholarship from Marshall and the first to play intercollegiate sports in the state of West Virginia. He averaged 19.4 points per game at Marshall. In 1996, after a 15-year career with the Syracuse Nationals and Philadelphia 76ers, Greer was named one of the 50 greatest players in NBA history. Today, the only street in downtown Huntington that isn't numbered is Hal Greer Boulevard.

BEST COACH: Eli Camden "Cam" Henderson (1935-55) Marshall named its basketball arena after Henderson as much for his 361 wins and the 1947 championship as for his influence on the game. Henderson pioneered the fast break and zone defense, while also somehow managing to coach the school's football team.

GAME FOR THE AGES: In the semifinals of the 1947 NAIB tournament, a crowd of 8,000 watched Emporia try to run out the final 2:30 of overtime while leading 55-54. But the Hornets missed a chippy with :20 left, Bill Toothman got the rebound and sank a shot from just beyond halfcourt. One steal of an inbounds pass later, and the Herd was on its improbable way to the final.

HEARTBREAKER: Marshall's first NCAA Tournament appearance in 10 years was hanging in the balance on March 2, 1997, in the Southern Conference tournament final against Chattanooga. The Herd had overcome a 10-point deficit in the game's final 12 minutes and the teams were tied at 64 with :14 left when Marshall senior point guard Sidney Coles took a shot that rolled tantalizingly around the rim and bounced out. The overtime was a back-and-forth struggle that wasn't settled until a Chris Mims putback with :03 on the clock gave Chattanooga a 71-70 victory.

FIERCEST RIVAL: Constantly in the shadow of in-state rival West Virginia, Marshall has pulled off a few memorable wins in the series, including a stunning Jan. 11, 2005, upset of the No. 24-ranked Mountaineers, who eventually made the NCAA Elite Eight. Still, West Virginia holds an overall 27–10 edge.

Greer was the first African-American to receive a scholarship from Marshall and the first to play intercollegiate sports in the state of West Virginia.

FANFARE AND HOOPLA: It's one of the most memorable chants in college sports, vocalized by one of the most intense student sections in the land. The Marshall Maniacs are a relatively new phenomenon, but they are impossible to ignore, dressed in green and white and going gaga for every Herd score. And no arena rocks harder than Cam Henderson when the Maniacs lead the crowd in a chorus of "We are . . . Marshall!"

FAN FAVORITE: F/C Charlie Slack (1952-56) Pomeroy, Ohio, native Slack was the 1954-55 NCAA rebounding champ with an astonishing NCAA-record 25.6 rpg. He tops Marshall in career boards with 1,916—about 800 more than the No. 2, J.R. VanHoose (1,086).

PROFILE

Marshall University, Huntington, WV
Founded: 1837
Enrollment: 13,584 (9,314 undergraduate)
Colors: Green and white
Nickname: Thundering Herd
Current arena: Cam Henderson Center, opened in 1981 (9,600)
Previous: Memorial Field House, 1950-81 (6,532); Huntington East Gymnasium, Late 1940s (1,000); Radio Center/Vanity Fair, 1930s (2,500)
First game: Dec. 14, 1906

All-time record: 1317-968-2 (.576)
Total weeks in AP Top 20/25: 14
Current conference: Conference USA (2005-)
Conference titles:
Mid-American Conference: 1 (1956)
Southern: 5 (1984, '87, '88, '95 [tie], '97 [tie])
Conference tournament titles:
Southern: 3 (1984, '85, '87)
NCAA Tournament appearances: 5
NIT appearances: 4
Semifinals: 1

FIRST-ROUND PRO PICKS

1948	**Andy Tonkovich,** Providence (1)
1972	**Russell Lee,** Milwaukee (6)
1973	**Mike D'Antoni,** San Antonio (ABA, 3)

TOP 5

G	**Mike D'Antoni** (1970-73)
G	**Skip Henderson** (1984-88)
G/F	**Hal Greer** (1955-58)
G/F	**Tamar Slay** (1998-2002)
F/C	**Charlie Slack** (1952-56)

RECORDS	GAME		SEASON		CAREER	
POINTS	55	Skip Henderson, vs. The Citadel (March 3, 1988)	804	Skip Henderson (1987-88)	2,574	Skip Henderson (1984-88)
POINTS PER GAME			29.3	Leo Byrd (1958-59)	23.9	Russell Lee (1969-72)
REBOUNDS	43	Charlie Slack, vs. Morris Harvey (Jan. 12, 1954)	538	Charlie Slack (1954-55)	1,916	Charlie Slack (1952-56)
ASSISTS	18	Greg White, vs. CCNY (Dec. 8, 1979)	241	Mike D'Antoni (1971-72)	701	Greg White (1977-81)

SEASON REVIEW

SEASON	W-L	CONF.	SCORING	COACH	RECORD	
1906-13	17-11-1		*First coach, L.B. Crotty, had 5-1-1 record over two seasons (1906-08)*			
1913-14	2-6			Boyd Chambers	14-16	.467
1914-18	no team					
1918-19	2-5			Archer Reilly	2-5	.286
1919-20	no team					
1920-21	6-9			Kemper Shelton	6-9	.400
1921-22	5-4-1			Herbert Cramer	5-4-1	.550
1922-23	1-3			J.E.R. Barnes	1-3	.250
1923-24	8-7			Bill Strickling		
1924-25	12-6			Russ Meredith	12-6	.667
1925-26	10-7			Charles Tallman	10-7	.588

SEASON	W-L	CONF.	SCORING	COACH	RECORD	
1926-27	7-10			Bill Strickling	15-17	.469
1927-28	11-10			Johnny Stuart		
1928-29	14-8			Johnny Stuart		
1929-30	12-3			Johnny Stuart		
1930-31	9-8			Johnny Stuart	46-29	.613
1931-32	8-10			Tom Dandelet		
1932-33	10-9			Tom Dandelet		
1933-34	13-8			Tom Dandelet		
1934-35	12-9			Tom Dandelet	43-36	.544
1935-36	6-10			Cam Henderson		
1936-37	21-8			Cam Henderson		

SEAS.	W-L	CONF.	POSTSEASON	SCORING		REBOUNDS		ASSISTS		COACH	RECORD	
1937-38	28-4									Cam Henderson		
1938-39	22-5									Cam Henderson		
1939-40	26-3									Cam Henderson		
1940-41	14-9									Cam Henderson		
1941-42	15-9									Cam Henderson		
1942-43	10-7									Cam Henderson		
1943-44	15-7									Cam Henderson		
1944-45	17-9									Cam Henderson		
1945-46	25-10									Cam Henderson		
1946-47	32-5		NAIB CHAMPION							Cam Henderson		
1947-48	22-11									Cam Henderson		
1948-49	16-12	2-2								Cam Henderson		
1949-50	15-9	5-4								Cam Henderson		
1950-51	13-13	2-6		Bob Koontz	16.5					Cam Henderson		
1951-52	15-11	5-7		Walt Walowac	22.3	Lewis Burns	6.4			Cam Henderson		
1952-53	20-4			Walt Walowac	29.1	Charlie Slack	16.3			Cam Henderson		
1953-54	12-9	6-7		Walt Walowac	26.1	Charlie Slack	22.1			Cam Henderson		
1954-55	17-4	10-4		Cebe Price	23.6	Charlie Slack	25.6			Cam Henderson	361-159	.694
1955-56	18-5	10-2	NCAA FIRST ROUND	Charlie Slack	22.5	Charlie Slack	23.6			Jule Rivlin		
1956-57	15-9	8-4		Cebe Price	19.3	Hal Greer	13.8			Jule Rivlin		
1957-58	17-7	9-3		Leo Byrd	23.6	Hal Greer	11.7			Jule Rivlin		
1958-59	12-12	6-6		Leo Byrd	29.3	Ivan Mielke	10.0			Jule Rivlin		
1959-60	10-13	4-8		John Milhoan	23.3	Bob Burgess	15.5			Jule Rivlin		
1960-61	11-13	5-7		Bob Burgess	14.5	Bob Burgess	14.1			Jule Rivlin		
1961-62	10-13	6-6		Mickey Sydenstricker	18.1	Bob Burgess	13.9			Jule Rivlin		
1962-63	7-16	1-11		Phil Carter	13.4	Phil Carter	10.9			Jule Rivlin	100-88	.532
1963-64	6-17	1-11		Tom Langfitt	15.5	Bruce Belcher	7.3			Ellis Johnson		
1964-65	4-20	1-11		Tom Langfitt	21.2	George Hicks	9.8			Ellis Johnson		
1965-66	12-12	4-8		George Stone	18.6	George Stone	11.5			Ellis Johnson		
1966-67	20-8	10-2	NIT FOURTH PLACE	George Stone	24.4	Bob Allen	13.8			Ellis Johnson		
1967-68	17-8	9-3	NIT FIRST ROUND	George Stone	23.7	Bob Allen	14.2			Ellis Johnson		
1968-69	9-15	3-9		Danny D'Antoni	17.5	Dave Smith	11.7			Ellis Johnson	68-80	.459
1969-70	9-14			Russell Lee	24.1	Dave Smith	10.3			Stewart Way		
1970-71	16-10			Russell Lee	25.3	Russell Lee	12.4	Mike D'Antoni	7.3	Stewart Way	25-24	.510
1971-72	23-4		NCAA FIRST ROUND	Russell Lee	22.3	Randy Noll	12.6	Mike D'Antoni	8.9	Carl Tacy	23-4	.852
1972-73	20-7		NIT FIRST ROUND	Randy Noll	19.6	Randy Noll	12.1	Mike D'Antoni	8.4	Bob Daniels		
1973-74	17-9			Tom Ferrell	15.5	Jack Battle	10.4	Joe Hickman	5.9	Bob Daniels		
1974-75	13-13			Bob Williams	13.9	Bob Williams	10.5	Joe Hickman	7.4	Bob Daniels		
1975-76	13-14			Frank Steele	14.8	Dave Miller	7.5	Joe Hickman	6.5	Bob Daniels		
1976-77	8-19			Greg Young	16.1	Harley Major	9.1	Bunny Gibson	3.7	Bob Daniels	71-62	.534
1977-78	14-15	8-5		Bunny Gibson	20.4	Harley Major	8.5	Greg White	6.8	Stu Aberdeen		
1978-79	11-16	5-8		Bunny Gibson	16.4	Ken Labanowski	8.9	Greg White	6.2	Stu Aberdeen	25-31	.446
1979-80	17-12	10-6		James Campbell	14.5	Ken Labanowski	6.2	Greg White	5.7	Bob Zuffelato		
1980-81	18-10	8-8		George Washington	14.5	Ken Labanowski	6.8	Greg White	6.1	Bob Zuffelato		
1981-82	16-11	8-8		George Washington	14.3	David Wade	6.9	Sam Henry	7.0	Bob Zuffelato		
1982-83	20-8	13-3		B. Kincaid, L. Evans	13.8	Charles Jones	8.9	Sam Henry	5.8	Bob Zuffelato	71-41	.634
1983-84	25-6	13-3	NCAA FIRST ROUND	LaVerne Evans	20.5	David Wade	4.6	Jeff Battle	4.5	Rick Huckabay		
1984-85	21-13	12-4	NCAA FIRST ROUND	Skip Henderson	17.7	Jeff Guthrie	7.3	Jeff Battle	5.2	Rick Huckabay		
1985-86	19-11	10-6		Skip Henderson	18.4	Rodney Holden	8.7	Skip Henderson	4.2	Rick Huckabay		
1986-87	25-6 ⊗	15-1	NCAA FIRST ROUND	Skip Henderson	21.0	Rodney Holden	8.8	Dwayne Lewis	4.7	Rick Huckabay		
1987-88	24-8	14-2	NIT FIRST ROUND	Skip Henderson	25.1	Rodney Holden	9.0	Andy Paul Williamson	5.3	Rick Huckabay		
1988-89	15-15	6-8		John Taft	26.0	Omar Roland	7.9	Andy Paul Williamson	4.2	Rick Huckabay	129-59	.686▼
1989-90	15-13	9-5		John Taft	23.4	Omar Roland	7.8	John Taft	2.6	Dana Altman	15-13	.536
1990-91	14-14	7-7		John Taft	27.3	John Taft	6.9	Brett Vincent	3.4	Dwight Freeman		
1991-92	7-22	3-11		Tyrone Phillips	16.9	Tyrone Phillips	6.4	Frank Martin	2.9	Dwight Freeman		
1992-93	16-11	11-7		Tyrone Phillips	22.4	Tyrone Phillips	5.9	Tink Brown	3.0	Dwight Freeman		
1993-94	9-18	7-11		Shawn Moore	17.3	Shawn Moore	6.8	Tink Brown	3.5	Dwight Freeman	46-65	.414
1994-95	18-9	10-4		Shawn Moore	19.9	Shawn Moore	6.9	Tink Brown	3.4	Billy Donovan		
1995-96	17-11	8-6		Keith Veney	19.6	John Brown	6.9	Jason Williams	6.4	Billy Donovan	35-20	.636
1996-97	20-9	10-4		John Brannen	20.9	Derrick Wright	6.3	Sidney Coles	6.3	Greg White		
1997-98	11-16	7-11		Carlton King	13.7	D. Wright, T. McKelvy	6.9	Travis Young	4.3	Greg White		
1998-99	16-11	11-7		J.R. VanHoose	14.7	J.R. VanHoose	8.1	Cornelius Jackson	5.4	Greg White		
1999-2000	21-9	11-7		Tamar Slay	19.9	J.R. VanHoose	8.6	Cornelius Jackson	7.3	Greg White		
2000-01	18-9	12-6		Tamar Slay	17.3	J.R. VanHoose	11.1	Cornelius Jackson	5.7	Greg White		
2001-02	15-15	8-10		Tamar Slay	18.9	J.R. VanHoose	10.6	Monty Wright	3.7	Greg White		
2002-03	14-15	9-9		Ronald Blackshear	20.3	Marvin Black	7.8	A.W. Hamilton	5.5	Greg White	115-84	.578
2003-04	12-17	8-10		Marvin Black	14.4	Marvin Black	7.8	A.W. Hamilton	5.5	Ron Jirsa		
2004-05	6-22	3-15		M. Patton, A.W. Hamilton	11.0	Mark Patton	8.1	A.W. Hamilton	4.1	Ron Jirsa		
2005-06	12-16	5-9		Mark Patton	14.9	Mark Patton	6.8	Chris Ross	4.6	Ron Jirsa		
2006-07	13-19	7-9		Markel Humphrey	14.0	Markel Humphrey	6.5	Chris Ross	4.1	Ron Jirsa	43-74	.368
2007-08	16-14	8-8		Mark Dorris	13.6	Tyler Wilkerson	5.9	P.-M. Altidor Cespedes	2.8	Donnie Jones		
2008-09	15-17	7-9		Markel Humphrey	12.5	Tyler Wilkerson	6.2	Damier Pitts	3.2	Donnie Jones	31-31	.500

⊗ Records do not reflect games forfeited or vacated. For adjusted records, see p. 521.

▼ Coach's record adjusted to reflect games forfeited or vacated: 129-58, .690. For yearly totals, see p. 521.

ESPN 38 SAGARIN

MARYLAND

After winning the ACC tournament in 1984, Terrapins coach Lefty Driesell boasted that he would put the trophy on the hood of his Cadillac and drive across Tobacco Road with it. That's Maryland basketball: successful—and never happier than when bucking the Carolina-centricity of its conference.

BEST TEAM: 2001-02 The 2002 national champs had four future NBAers in its starting lineup. ACC Player of the Year Juan Dixon averaged 20.4 ppg; Lonny Baxter compensated for his height (6'8") in the low post with strength and savvy; Steve Blake drove the high-powered offense; and Chris Wilcox played best in the biggest moments, blocking five shots in two Final Four games. They ground out a 64-52 victory over Indiana to win it all.

BEST PLAYER: G JOHN LUCAS (1972-76) The stylish guard made everyone around him better with his energy and defense. But despite his no-jump, one-handed shot (he was said to be so fast that he didn't need to learn to shoot a jumper), he could light up the scoreboard. The first freshman to play on the Terps varsity, Lucas averaged more than 19 ppg in each of his final three seasons and was a three-time All-America.

BEST COACH: GARY WILLIAMS (1989-) He returned to his alma mater in 1989 and brought new vitality to a team that had lost much of its Driesell-era swagger. Williams, a master of the flex offense, has led the Terps to 13 NCAA Tournaments, seven Sweet 16s and two Final Fours (including the 2002 title).

GAME FOR THE AGES: In the semifinals of the 2004 ACC tournament, No. 6-seed Maryland trailed No. 2-seed NC State by as many as 21 points. But John Gilchrist scored 23 of his 30 points in the second half to lead the greatest ACC tourney comeback ever. The 85-82 win led to the Terps' first conference tournament title in 20 years.

HEARTBREAKER: Every heart in the Maryland family was broken on June 19, 1986, when star Len Bias died of a drug overdose less than 48 hours after the Boston Celtics made him the second player chosen in the NBA draft. For on-court disappointment, nothing tops the 1974 ACC tournament final, one of the sport's greatest games. Led by Tom McMillen (22 points), Mo Howard (22), Len Elmore (18) and Lucas (18 and 10 assists), the Terps blew a 25-12 lead over NC State but hung tough before losing 103-100 in overtime. David Thompson's Wolfpack went on to win the NCAA championship, while Maryland, crushed, got no NCAA bid and turned down the NIT.

FIERCEST RIVAL: The Maryland-Duke series is one of game's most intense, not because of geographic proximity or longevity but because the two fan bases so despise one another. Fevers rose in the teams' 2001 Final Four matchup when Williams yelled at a courtside official, "How badly do you want Duke to win this game?" (Duke won, 95-84.) Cameron Crazies routinely serenade the hyperactive Williams with "Sweat, Gary, sweat!" Sweat, perhaps, but from 2004 to '07 the Terps won five of seven encounters with the Blue Devils, including two at Cameron. Duke commands the series all-time, though, 106–60.

FANFARE AND HOOPLA: Midnight Madness was invented at Maryland in 1970 by Lefty Driesell. "The NCAA told us we could start practice on October 15," the coach once recounted. "Well, I said, that means we can start practicing one minute past midnight." Word leaked out on campus and a few hundred spectators showed up to watch the Terps take laps around the track that used to encircle the field at Byrd Stadium.

FAN FAVORITE: G JUAN DIXON (1998-2002) It was impossible not to be inspired by his story. Dixon rebounded from a traumatic childhood (his parents were heroin addicts who died of AIDS-related illnesses before Dixon was 18) to lead the Terps to the 2002 NCAA title.

CONSENSUS ALL-AMERICAS

1932	**Louis Berger,** G
1975, '76	**John Lucas,** G
1986	**Len Bias,** F
1995	**Joe Smith,** F/C
2002	**Juan Dixon,** G

FIRST-ROUND PRO PICKS

1954	**Gene Shue,** Philadelphia (3)
1960	**Al Bunge,** Philadelphia (7)
1974	**Tom McMillen,** Buffalo (9)
1974	**Tom McMillen,** Virginia (ABA, 1)
1974	**Len Elmore,** Washington (13)
1974	**John Lucas,** Carolina (ABA, 7)
1975	**John Lucas,** New York (ABA, 8)
1976	**John Lucas,** Houston (1)
1977	**Brad Davis,** LA Lakers (15)
1981	**Buck Williams,** New Jersey (3)
1981	**Albert King,** New Jersey (10)
1986	**Len Bias,** Boston (2)
1990	**Jerrod Mustaf,** New York (17)
1992	**Walt Williams,** Sacramento (7)
1995	**Joe Smith,** Golden State (1)
1997	**Keith Booth,** Chicago (28)
1999	**Steve Francis,** Vancouver (2)
2002	**Chris Wilcox,** LA Clippers (8)
2002	**Juan Dixon,** Washington (17)

PROFILE

University of Maryland, College Park, MD
Founded: 1807
Enrollment: 36,014 (25,857 undergraduate)
Colors: Red, white, black and gold
Nickname: Terrapins
Current arena: Comcast Center, opened in 2002 (17,950)
Previous: Cole Field House, 1955-2002 (14,596); Ritchie Coliseum, 1931-55 (1,500); The Gymnasium, 1923-31 (N/A)
First game: 1904
All-time record: 1,344-952 (.585)

Total weeks in AP Top 20/25: 352
Current conference: Atlantic Coast (1953-)
Conference titles:
Southern: 1 (1932 [tie])
ACC: 4 (1975, '80, '95 [tie], 2002)
Conference tournament titles:
Southern: 1 (1931)
ACC: 3 (1958, '84, 2004)
NCAA Tournament: 23 (1 appearance vacated)
Sweet 16s (since 1975): 11
Final Fours: 2
Titles: 1 (2002)

NIT appearances: 7
Semifinals: 2
Titles: 1 (1972)

TOP 5

G	**Juan Dixon** (1998-2002)
G	**John Lucas** (1972-76)
F	**Len Bias** (1982-86)
F	**Buck Williams** (1978-81)
C	**Len Elmore** (1971-74)

RECORDS

RECORDS	GAME		SEASON		CAREER	
POINTS	44	Ernest Graham, vs. NC State (Dec. 20, 1978)	776	Walt Williams (1991-92)	2,269	Juan Dixon (1998-2002)
POINTS PER GAME			26.8	Walt Williams (1991-92)	20.5	Tom McMillen (1971-74)
REBOUNDS	26	Len Elmore, vs. Wake Forest (Feb. 27, 1974)	412	Len Elmore (1973-74)	1,053	Len Elmore (1971-74)
ASSISTS	15	Greivis Vazquez, vs. NC State (Feb. 9, 2008); Terrell Stokes, vs. Western Carolina (Nov. 14, 1998)	286	Steve Blake (2001-02)	972	Steve Blake (1999-2003)

SEASON REVIEW

SEASON	W-L	CONF.	SCORING	COACH	RECORD
1904-05	0-2			Unknown	
1905-10	no team				
1910-11	3-9			Unknown	
1911-13	no team				
1913-14	0-16			Unknown	
1914-18	no team				
1918-19	1-5			Unknown	
1919-23	no team				
1923-24	5-7	1-2		H. Burton Shipley	
1924-25	12-5	3-1		H. Burton Shipley	
1925-26	14-3	7-1		H. Burton Shipley	
1926-27	10-10	6-4		H. Burton Shipley	
1927-28	14-4	8-1		H. Burton Shipley	
1928-29	7-9	2-6		H. Burton Shipley	
1929-30	16-6	8-5		H. Burton Shipley	
1930-31	18-4	8-1		H. Burton Shipley	
1931-32	16-4	9-1		H. Burton Shipley	
1932-33	11-9	7-3		H. Burton Shipley	
1933-34	11-8	6-1		H. Burton Shipley	
1934-35	8-10	4-3		H. Burton Shipley	
1935-36	14-6	4-3		H. Burton Shipley	
1936-37	8-12	5-8		H. Burton Shipley	

SEAS.	W-L	CONF.	POSTSEASON	SCORING		REBOUNDS		ASSISTS		COACH	RECORD	
1937-38	15-9	6-4								H. Burton Shipley		
1938-39	15-9	8-3								H. Burton Shipley		
1939-40	14-9	7-5								H. Burton Shipley		
1940-41	1-21	0-13								H. Burton Shipley		
1941-42	7-15	3-8								H. Burton Shipley		
1942-43	8-8	5-5								H. Burton Shipley		
1943-44	4-14	2-1								H. Burton Shipley		
1944-45	2-14	2-5								H. Burton Shipley		
1945-46	9-12	5-4								H. Burton Shipley		
1946-47	14-10	9-5								H. Burton Shipley	253-218	.537
1947-48	11-14	9-6								Flucie Stewart		
1948-49	9-17	7-7								Flucie Stewart		
1949-50	7-18	5-13								Flucie Stewart	27-44	.380
1950-51	15-10	11-8		Lee Brawley	15.0					Bud Millikan		
1951-52	13-9	9-5								Bud Millikan		
1952-53	15-8	12-3		Gene Shue	22.1					Bud Millikan		
1953-54	23-7	7-2		Gene Shue	21.8					Bud Millikan		
1954-55	17-7	10-4		Bob Kessler	20.3					Bud Millikan		
1955-56	14-10	7-7		Bob Kessler	20.4	Bob Kessler	14.0			Bud Millikan		
1956-57	16-10	9-5		Bob O'Brien	13.2	Jim Halleck	7.5			Bud Millikan		
1957-58	22-7	9-5	NCAA REGIONAL SEMIFINALS	Charles McNeil	14.8	Al Bunge	9.1			Bud Millikan		
1958-59	10-13	7-7		Charles McNeil	14.8	Al Bunge	10.5			Bud Millikan		
1959-60	15-8	9-5		Al Bunge	16.6	Al Bunge	12.6			Bud Millikan		
1960-61	14-12	6-8		Bob McDonald	13.4	Bob McDonald	10.7			Bud Millikan		
1961-62	8-17	3-11		Jerry Greenspan	15.2	Jerry Greenspan	9.4			Bud Millikan		
1962-63	8-13	4-10		Jerry Greenspan	17.4	Jerry Greenspan	8.8			Bud Millikan		
1963-64	9-17	5-9		George Suder	13.0	Gary Ward	7.4			Bud Millikan		
1964-65	18-8	10-4		Jay McMillen	19.7	Gary Ward	10.4			Bud Millikan		
1965-66	14-11	7-7		Gary Ward	17.2	Gary Ward	9.6			Bud Millikan		
1966-67	11-14	5-9		Jay McMillen	16.3	Jay McMillen	8.1			Bud Millikan	243-182	.572
1967-68	8-16	4-10		Pete Johnson	15.0	Jay McMillen	8.1			Frank Fellows		
1968-69	8-18	2-12		Will Hetzel	23.3	Will Hetzel	12.2			Frank Fellows	16-34	.320
1969-70	13-13	5-9		Rod Horst	16.5	Rod Horst	9.9	Mickey Wiles	5.2	Lefty Driesell		
1970-71	14-12	5-9		Jim O'Brien	16.3	Barry Yates	8.6	Jim O'Brien	3.3	Lefty Driesell		
1971-72	27-5	8-4	NIT CHAMPION	Tom McMillen	20.8	Len Elmore	11.0	Howard White	2.9	Lefty Driesell		
1972-73	23-7	7-5	NCAA REGIONAL FINALS	Tom McMillen	21.2	Len Elmore	11.2	John Lucas	5.9	Lefty Driesell		
1973-74	23-5	9-3		John Lucas	20.1	Len Elmore	14.7	John Lucas	5.7	Lefty Driesell		
1974-75	24-5	10-2	NCAA REGIONAL FINALS	John Lucas	19.5	Tom Roy	11.1	Brad Davis	4.6	Lefty Driesell		
1975-76	22-6	7-5		John Lucas	19.9	Larry Gibson	9.8	Brad Davis	5.9	Lefty Driesell		
1976-77	19-8	7-5		Steve Sheppard	16.2	Larry Gibson	8.4	Brad Davis	4.9	Lefty Driesell		
1977-78	15-13	3-9		Lawrence Boston	15.5	Larry Gibson	9.0	Greg Manning	2.6	Lefty Driesell		
1978-79	19-11	6-6	NIT SECOND ROUND	Ernest Graham	16.6	Buck Williams	10.8	Dutch Morley	4.3	Lefty Driesell		
1979-80	24-7	11-3	NCAA REGIONAL SEMIFINALS	Albert King	21.7	Buck Williams	10.1	Ernest Graham	4.4	Lefty Driesell		
1980-81	21-10	8-6	NCAA SECOND ROUND	Albert King	18.0	Buck Williams	11.7	Ernest Graham	3.9	Lefty Driesell		
1981-82	16-13	5-9	NIT SECOND ROUND	Adrian Branch	15.2	Herman Veal	7.3	Dutch Morley	4.3	Lefty Driesell		
1982-83	20-10	8-6	NCAA SECOND ROUND	Adrian Branch	18.7	Ben Coleman	8.1	Jeff Adkins	4.0	Lefty Driesell		
1983-84	24-8	9-5	NCAA REGIONAL SEMIFINALS	Ben Coleman	15.3	Ben Coleman	8.4	Keith Gatlin	4.6	Lefty Driesell		
1984-85	25-12	8-6	NCAA REGIONAL SEMIFINALS	Len Bias	18.9	Len Bias	6.8	Keith Gatlin	6.0	Lefty Driesell		
1985-86	19-14	6-8	NCAA SECOND ROUND	Len Bias	23.2	Len Bias	7.0	Keith Gatlin	6.4	Lefty Driesell	348-159	.686
1986-87	9-17	0-14		Derrick Lewis	19.6	Derrick Lewis	9.5	Teyon McCoy	4.3	Bob Wade		
1987-88	18-13 ⊗	6-8	NCAA SECOND ROUND	Derrick Lewis	15.0	Derrick Lewis	7.6	Rudy Archer	5.5	Bob Wade		
1988-89	9-20	1-13		Tony Massenburg	16.6	Tony Massenburg	7.8	Greg Nared	4.8	Bob Wade	36-50	.419▼
1989-90	19-14	6-8	NIT SECOND ROUND	Jerrod Mustaf	18.5	Tony Massenburg	10.1	Walt Williams	4.5	Gary Williams		
1990-91	16-12	5-9		Walt Williams	18.7	Cedric Lewis	8.3	Walt Williams	5.4	Gary Williams		
1991-92	14-15	5-11		Walt Williams	26.8	Evers Burns	7.1	Kevin McLinton	5.3	Gary Williams		
1992-93	12-16	2-14		Evers Burns	18.5	Evers Burns	8.9	Kevin McLinton	5.3	Gary Williams		
1993-94	18-12	8-8	NCAA REGIONAL SEMIFINALS	Joe Smith	19.4	Joe Smith	10.7	Duane Simpkins	4.5	Gary Williams		
1994-95	26-8	12-4	NCAA REGIONAL SEMIFINALS	Joe Smith	20.4	Joe Smith	10.7	Duane Simpkins	4.8	Gary Williams		
1995-96	17-13	8-8	NCAA FIRST ROUND	Johnny Rhodes	16.7	Keith Booth	7.8	Duane Simpkins	4.4	Gary Williams		
1996-97	21-11	9-7	NCAA FIRST ROUND	Keith Booth	19.5	Keith Booth	7.9	Terrell Stokes	4.5	Gary Williams		
1997-98	21-11	10-6	NCAA REGIONAL SEMIFINALS	Laron Profit	15.8	Rodney Elliott	7.4	Terrell Stokes	4.7	Gary Williams		
1998-99	28-6	13-3	NCAA REGIONAL SEMIFINALS	Steve Francis	17.0	Terence Morris	7.1	Terrell Stokes	6.3	Gary Williams		
1999-2000	25-10	11-5	NCAA SECOND ROUND	Juan Dixon	18.0	Lonny Baxter	8.8	Steve Blake	6.2	Gary Williams		
2000-01	25-11	10-6	NCAA NATIONAL SEMIFINALS	Juan Dixon	18.2	Lonny Baxter	7.9	Steve Blake	6.9	Gary Williams		
2001-02	**32-4**	**15-1**	**NATIONAL CHAMPION**	**Juan Dixon**	**20.4**	**Lonny Baxter**	**8.2**	**Steve Blake**	**7.9**	**Gary Williams**		
2002-03	21-10	11-5	NCAA REGIONAL SEMIFINALS	Drew Nicholas	17.8	Ryan Randle	7.2	Steve Blake	7.1	Gary Williams		
2003-04	20-12	7-9	NCAA SECOND ROUND	John Gilchrist	15.4	Jamar Smith	8.8	John Gilchrist	5.0	Gary Williams		
2004-05	19-13	7-9	NIT SEMIFINALS	Nik Caner-Medley	16.0	Travis Garrison	6.5	John Gilchrist	5.5	Gary Williams		
2005-06	19-13	8-8	NIT FIRST ROUND	Nik Caner-Medley	15.3	Ekene Ibekwe	6.6	D.J. Strawberry	4.0	Gary Williams		
2006-07	25-9	10-6	NCAA SECOND ROUND	D.J. Strawberry	14.9	Ekene Ibekwe	7.8	Greivis Vasquez	4.6	Gary Williams		
2007-08	19-15	8-8	NIT SECOND ROUND	Greivis Vasquez	17.0	James Gist	7.8	Greivis Vasquez	6.8	Gary Williams		
2008-09	21-14	7-9	NCAA SECOND ROUND	Greivis Vasquez	17.5	Greivis Vasquez	5.4	Greivis Vasquez	5.0	Gary Williams	418-229	.646

⊗ Records don't reflect games forfeited or vacated. For adjusted record, see p. 521.

▼ Coach's record adjusted to reflect games forfeited or vacated: 35-49, .417. For yearly totals, see p. 521.

ESPN 327 SAGARIN

MARYLAND-BALTIMORE COUNTY

UMBC makes news every decade or so. The program started in 1967. The Retrievers reached the D2 elite eight in '79. They jumped to D1 in '86. They won the Northeast Conference regular-season title in '99. And they got their NCAA Tournament bid in 2008.

BEST TEAM: 2007-08 Coach Randy Monroe parlayed a bold move—bringing in a couple of transfers from James Madison who each had only one season of eligibility—into a 24-9 season. Ray Barbosa and Cavell Johnson joined Brian Hodges (1,472 points) in leading the Retrievers to America East regular-season and tourney titles. And UMBC finally went to the Dance.

BEST PLAYER: G Larry Simmons (1986-90) As a freshman, the Indiana native led the Retrievers with 20 points in their first D1 victory, a 69-66 win over Northern Arizona, and Simmons only got better. He became the school's all-time leader in scoring (1,805) and steals (240), averaged 20.4 ppg as a senior, and was named to the All-Independent team.

BEST COACH: Billy Jones (1974-86) The first African-American varsity player in the ACC (Maryland), Jones went on to coach the Retrievers to their first winning season (1977-78) and, shortly after that, to two NCAA D2 tournaments. He guided UMBC to five of its 10 winning seasons and two of its four 20-win seasons.

GAME FOR THE AGES: Students who packed UMBC's sold-out RAC Arena two hours before tip-off on March 15, 2008, were rewarded with the school's first America East league title, thanks to an 82-65 thrashing of Hartford, set up by a ferocious 20-0 first-half run. Tournament MOP Jay Greene had 12 points, 8 assists and 6 rebounds, while Darryl Proctor led the Retrievers with 23 points.

FIERCEST RIVAL: UMBC played in two defunct metro tournaments—the Baltimore Beltway Classic (1988-92) and the Battle of Baltimore (1998-2005)—against area teams such as Towson, Loyola, Morgan State, Coppin State and Mount St. Mary's. The Retrievers won the Battle of Baltimore four times.

SEASON REVIEW

SEAS.	W-L	CONF.	SCORING		COACH	RECORD	
1967-68	4-7				Joe Phillip	4-7	.364
1968-69	5-10				John Frank		
1969-70	5-16				John Frank		
1970-71	3-17		Bill Wade	14.2	John Frank		
1971-72	9-15		Rick Bellamy	15.5	John Frank		
1972-73	14-15		James Drew	12.8	John Frank		
1973-74	10-16		Emmerson Small	16.5	John Frank	46-89	.341
1974-75	7-14		Henry McCaskill	17.1	Billy Jones		
1975-76	5-19		John Goedeke	16.5	Billy Jones		
1976-77	12-13		John Goedeke	18.0	Billy Jones		
1977-78	15-13		John Goedeke	17.3	Billy Jones		
1978-79	21-8		Howie Kane	17.2	Billy Jones		
1979-80	23-5		Reggie Nance	17.8	Billy Jones		
1980-81	14-12		Reggie Nance	16.5	Billy Jones		
1981-82	17-8		Rick Moreland	18.5	Billy Jones		
1982-83	9-18		Rick Moreland	22.6	Billy Jones		
1983-84	9-19		Henry McMullen	14.7	Billy Jones		
1984-85	6-21		Jim Pearce	17.3	Billy Jones		
1985-86	5-23		Breck Robinson	15.8	Billy Jones	143-173	.453
1986-87	12-16		Gamel Spencer	13.8	Jeff Bzdelik		
1987-88	13-15		Kenny Reynolds	18.4	Jeff Bzdelik	25-31	.446
1988-89	17-11		Larry Simmons	15.9	Earl Hawkins		
1989-90	12-16		Larry Simmons	20.4	Earl Hawkins		
1990-91	7-22	4-8	Jim Frantz	11.8	Earl Hawkins		
1991-92	10-19	8-4	Derell Thompson	15.5	Earl Hawkins		
1992-93	12-16	7-9	Skip Saunders	15.6	Earl Hawkins		
1993-94	6-21	5-13	Skip Saunders	12.4	Earl Hawkins		
1994-95	13-14	10-6	Tony Thompson	12.6	Earl Hawkins	77-119	.393
1995-96	5-22	3-11	Tony Thompson	16.7	Tom Sullivan		
1996-97	5-22	2-12	Issac Green	8.6	Tom Sullivan		
1997-98	14-14	6-6	Rich Giddens	15.5	Tom Sullivan		
1998-99	19-9	17-3	Terence Ward	14.8	Tom Sullivan		
1999-2000	11-18	7-11	Terence Ward	15.9	Tom Sullivan		
2000-01	18-11	13-7	Terence Ward	15.7	Tom Sullivan		
2001-02	20-9	15-5	Peter Mulligan	16.0	Tom Sullivan		
2002-03	7-20	5-13	Kareem Washington	15.8	Tom Sullivan		
2003-04	7-21	4-14	Kareem Washington	11.6	Tom Sullivan[a]	106-145	.422
2004-05	11-18	5-13	Andrew Feeley	9.6	Randy Monroe		
2005-06	10-19	5-11	John Zito	13.5	Randy Monroe		
2006-07	12-19	7-9	Brian Hodges	14.7	Randy Monroe		
2007-08	24-9	13-3 ●	Ray Barbosa	16.5	Randy Monroe		
2008-09	15-17	7-9	Darryl Proctor	20.0	Randy Monroe	72-82	.468

[a] Tom Sullivan (7-20) and Randy Monroe (0-1) both coached during the 2003-04 season.

● NCAA Tournament appearance

PROFILE

University of Maryland, Baltimore County, MD
Founded: 1966
Enrollment: 12,041 (9,464 undergraduate)
Colors: Black and gold
Nickname: Retrievers
Current arena: RAC (Retriever Activities Center) Arena, opened in 1973 (4,000)
First game: 1967
All-time record: 473-647 (.422)
Total weeks in AP Top 20/25: 0

Current conference: America East (2003-)
Conference titles:
Northeast: 1 (1999)
America East: 1 (2008)
Conference tournament titles:
America East: 1 (2008)
NCAA Tournament appearances: 1
NIT appearances: 0

TOP 5

G **Larry Simmons** (1986-90)
G **Terence Ward** (1997-2001)
G/F **Reggie Nance** (1977-81)
F **John Goedeke** (1975-79)
F **Rick Moreland** (1979-83)

RECORDS

	GAME		SEASON		CAREER	
POINTS	43	Derell Thompson, vs. Towson (Feb. 15, 1992)	639	Darryl Proctor (2008-09)	1,805	Larry Simmons (1986-90)
POINTS PER GAME			22.6	Rick Moreland (1982-83)	17.5	Darryl Proctor (2004-'06, '07-09)
REBOUNDS	24	Henry McCaskill, vs. George Mason (Feb. 22, 1975); vs. Washington (Md.) (Jan. 18, 1975); vs. George Mason (Dec. 1973)	312	Breck Robinson (1985-86)	985	Kennedy Okafor (1997-2001)
ASSISTS	20	Dana Harris, vs. St. Mary's (Md.) (Dec. 12, 1992)	236	Jay Greene (2007-08)	683	Jay Greene (2005-09)

ESPN 301 SAGARIN

MARYLAND EASTERN SHORE

The school once known as Maryland State has accomplished much: two NAIA tourney title games (1969, '73); small-school dominance in the 1950s, '60s and early '70s; and the proud achievement of being the first historically black school to play in the postseason NIT.

BEST TEAM: 1973-74 Fresh from their runner-up finish in the 1973 NAIA tourney, the Hawks went 27–2, won the MEAC and a first-round NIT game. UMES led all D1 schools in scoring offense (97.6 ppg) and won more games than all but two teams, one of which was NCAA champ NC State (30–1). Three Hawks—Rubin Collins, Talvin Skinner and William Gordon—became NBA draft picks.

BEST PLAYER: G Jake Ford (1966-70) The school's all-time leading scorer (2,218) was twice an NAIA All-America and was named MVP of the 1969 NAIA tournament even though the Hawks lost the title game to Eastern New Mexico, 99-76.

BEST COACH: Nathaniel "Nate" Taylor (1954-66) As a player he followed his Oklahoma City high school coach, Vernon "Skip" McCain, to Maryland State, then succeeded McCain as coach. Taylor's 1954-55 team went 19–5, and the next season's squad went 23–2. Taylor was on his way to becoming the school's winningest coach.

GAME FOR THE AGES: In 1974, UMES became the first historically black college team invited to the NIT. The Hawks, led by Collins, Skinner, Gordon and sophomore Joe Pace, spurned the NAIA playoffs for the chance to play in Madison Square Garden and upset home-team Manhattan, 84-81. They were knocked out in the next round by Jacksonville, 85-83.

FIERCEST RIVAL: UMES has played MEAC and in-state foe Morgan State 93 times since 1954. The Hawks won 18 of the first 19 games but now hold a slim 48–46 series lead. Both were powerhouses among historically black colleges. UMES defeated MSU in the '74 MEAC tournament final before heading off to the NIT (while MSU went on to win the College Division national championship).

SEASON REVIEW

SEAS.	W-L	CONF.	COACH	SEAS.	W-L	CONF.	COACH
1947-50[a]	*43-11*	*19-3 in 1949-50*		1963-64	11-9		N. "Nate" Taylor
1950-51	19-2		V. "Skip" McCain	1964-65	16-6		N. "Nate" Taylor
1951-52	18-4		V. "Skip" McCain	1965-66	8-10		N. "Nate" Taylor
1952-53	13-4		V. "Skip" McCain	1966-67	12-10		Joe Robinson
1953-54	19-2		V. "Skip" McCain	1967-68	16-6		Joe Robinson
1954-55	19-5		N. "Nate" Taylor	1968-69	27-5		Joe Robinson
1955-56	23-2		N. "Nate" Taylor	1969-70	29-2		Joe Robinson
1956-57	7-15		N. "Nate" Taylor	1970-71	17-10		Joe Robinson
1957-58	7-11		N. "Nate" Taylor	1971-72	20-7	7-5	John Bates
1958-59	9-9		N. "Nate" Taylor	1972-73	26-5	10-2	John Bates
1959-60	22-6		N. "Nate" Taylor	1973-74	27-2	11-1 ■	John Bates
1960-61	17-7		N. "Nate" Taylor	1974-75	2-24	0-12	Dan Jones
1961-62	21-5		N. "Nate" Taylor	1975-76	2-21	1-11	Dan Jones
1962-63	14-5		N. "Nate" Taylor	1976-77	7-19	6-6	Dan Jones[b]

SEAS.	W-L	CONF.	SCORING		COACH	RECORD	
1977-78	7-19	2-10			Kirkland Hall		
1978-79	7-16	5-7			Kirkland Hall		
1979-80	16-9				Kirkland Hall		
1980-81	17-15				Kirkland Hall		
1981-82	6-20	3-9			Kirkland Hall		
1982-83	10-19	5-7			Kirkland Hall		
1983-84	7-21	3-7			Kirkland Hall	76-131	.367
1984-85	3-25	2-10			Howie Evans		
1985-86	5-23	3-11			Howie Evans		
1986-87	2-24	0-13			Howie Evans	10-72	.122
1987-88	7-20	5-11			Steve Williams		
1988-89	1-26	1-15			Steve Williams		
1989-90	10-17	4-12			Steve Williams	18-63	.222
1990-91	5-23	3-13			Bob Hopkins		
1991-92	3-25	2-14			Bob Hopkins[c]	5-30	.143
1992-93	13-14	7-9			Rob Chavez		
1993-94	16-12	10-6			Rob Chavez	29-26	.527
1994-95	13-14	9-7			Jeff Menday		
1995-96	11-16	6-10			Jeff Menday	24-30	.444
1996-97	11-17	6-12			Lonnie Williams		
1997-98	9-18	7-11			Lonnie Williams		
1998-99	10-17	7-11	Demetric Reese	14.1	Lonnie Williams		
1999-2000	12-17	8-10	Demetric Reese	19.7	Lonnie Williams	42-69	.378
2000-01	12-16	10-8	Thomas Trotter	14.2	Thomas Trotter		
2001-02	11-18	7-11	Thomas Trotter	16.7	Thomas Trotter		
2002-03	5-23	5-13	Thomas Trotter	20.5	Thomas Trotter		
2003-04	8-21	6-12	Thomas Trotter	19.3	Thomas Trotter	36-78	.316
2004-05	2-26	1-17	Corey Brown	12.7	Larry Lessett		
2005-06	7-22	4-14	Tim Parham	14.0	Larry Lessett		
2006-07	4-27	1-17	Ed Tyson	16.4	Larry Lessett	13-75	.148
2007-08	4-28	2-14	Ed Tyson	20.2	Meredith Smith	4-28	.125
2008-09	7-23	3-13	Neal Pitt	16.0	Frankie Allen	7-23	.233

[a] Records from before 1947-48 have been lost.
[b] Dan Jones (1-7) and Kirkland Hall (6-12) both coached during the 1976-77 season.
[c] Bob Hopkins (0-7) and Bobby Wilkerson (3-18) both coached during the 1991-92 season.
■ NIT appearance

THE SCHOOLS

PROFILE

University of Maryland Eastern Shore, Princess Anne, MD
Founded: 1886 as Delaware Conference Academy
Enrollment: 4,290 (3,815 undergraduate)
Colors: Maroon and gray
Nickname: Hawks
Current arena: William Hytche Athletic Center, opened in 1999 (5,500)
Previous: Tawes Gymnasium, 1960s-99 (1,500); Kiah "the Matchbox" Gymnasium, before 1960 (500)
First game: Jan. 7, 1933
All-time record: 732-855 (.461)
Total weeks in AP Top 20/25: 1
Current conference: Mid-Eastern Athletic (1971-79, 1981-)
Conference titles:
MEAC: 2 (1973, '74 [tie])
Conference tournament titles:
MEAC: 1 (1974)
NCAA Tournament appearances: 0
NIT appearances: 1

TOP 5

G **Jake Ford** (1966-70)
G **Ken McBride** (1948-52)
G **Ken Simmons** (1975-78)
F/C **James Morgan** (1966-70)
F/C **Talvin Skinner** (1970-74)

RECORDS	GAME		SEASON		CAREER	
POINTS	52	Ken Simmons, vs. St. Mary's College (Jan. 20, 1978)	669	Ken Simmons (1977-78)	2,218	Jake Ford (1966-70)
POINTS PER GAME			36.6	Eddie Williams (1963-64)	21.7	Jake Ford (1966-70)
REBOUNDS	37	James Morgan, vs. Virginia State (Dec. 18, 1967)	518	James Morgan (1969-70)	1,741	James Morgan (1966-70)
ASSISTS		N/A	142	Jesse Brooks (2005-06)		N/A

ESPN 157 SAGARIN

MASSACHUSETTS

UMass basketball didn't begin with the arrival of John Calipari in 1988, but for many fans beyond New England it might have seemed that way. Legendary coach Jack Leaman won 217 games from 1966 to '79, and there was that future doctor, Julius Erving, whom many had heard of but few had seen play as a collegian.

BEST TEAM: 1995-96 UMass reached the Elite Eight in 1995, but the 1995-96 Minutemen (32–2), led by Marcus Camby, broke through to the school's first Final Four—where they lost to No. 1 seed Kentucky, 81-74 (although the NCAA later vacated UMass' appearance because of rules violations).

BEST PLAYER: F Julius Erving (1969-71) The game's best-kept secret until he scored 25.7 ppg as a sophomore and then 26.9 as a junior (a season in which he also averaged more than 20 rpg), the 6'6" forward remains a mythic figure in Amherst even though he played just two seasons there. Ironically, the man who became world famous for his stupefying dunks never scored with one for UMass—during his entire college career, dunking was illegal.

BEST COACH: John Calipari (1988-96) Jack Leaman has more wins than Calipari (217 to 193), but Cal has the big edge in winning percentage (.731 to .633) and is the coach most closely associated with UMass. He led the school to five consecutive Atlantic 10 tournament titles (1992-96) and seven straight postseasons.

GAME FOR THE AGES: CBS' *60 Minutes* was delayed while the Minutemen finished the most important 45 minutes of the program's history on March 22, 1992. With a 77-71 OT win over Syracuse, Calipari's crew reached the school's first Sweet 16 and, by pre-empting Andy Rooney and friends, received an unprecedented level of national recognition.

FIERCEST RIVAL: UMass vs. Temple began in 1983, and in their first 20 meetings the Minutemen couldn't notch a win against John Chaney's crew. With a breakthrough victory in 1992, UMass and Calipari then went on to win 12 of 14 from the Owls, and a simmering feud became a full-fledged rivalry. Temple leads, 40–20.

SEASON REVIEW

SEAS.	W-L	CONF.	COACH	SEAS.	W-L	CONF.	COACH
1899-49	*243-257*	*Harold Gore, 85-53 between 1916-29*		**1962-63**	12-12	6-4	Matthew Zunic
1949-50	8-11	2-3	Lorin Ball	**1963-64**	15-9	5-5	Johnny Orr
1950-51	6-14	1-3	Lorin Ball	**1964-65**	13-11	8-2	Johnny Orr
1951-52	4-17	0-6	Lorin Ball	**1965-66**	11-13	5-5	Johnny Orr
1952-53	4-15	1-4	Robert Curran	**1966-67**	11-14	7-3	Jack Leaman
1953-54	13-9	5-1	Robert Curran	**1967-68**	14-11	8-2	Jack Leaman
1954-55	10-14	4-2	Robert Curran	**1968-69**	17-7	9-1	Jack Leaman
1955-56	17-6	5-1	Robert Curran	**1969-70**	18-7	8-2 ■	Jack Leaman
1956-57	13-11	4-4	Robert Curran	**1970-71**	23-4	10-0 ■	Jack Leaman
1957-58	13-12	5-5	Robert Curran	**1971-72**	14-12	6-4	Jack Leaman
1958-59	11-13	5-5	Robert Curran	**1972-73**	20-7	10-2 ■	Jack Leaman
1959-60	14-10	6-4	Matthew Zunic	**1973-74**	21-5	11-1 ■	Jack Leaman
1960-61	16-10	4-6	Matthew Zunic	**1974-75**	18-8	10-2 ■	Jack Leaman
1961-62	15-9	8-2 ●	Matthew Zunic	**1975-76**	21-6	11-1	Jack Leaman

SEAS.	W-L	CONF.	SCORING		COACH	RECORD	
1976-77	20-11	3-4 ■	Jim Town	16.2	Jack Leaman		
1977-78	15-12	5-5	Mike Pyatt	16.8	Jack Leaman		
1978-79	5-22	0-10	Mark Haymore	17.1	Jack Leaman	217-126	.633
1979-80	2-24	0-10	Curtis Phauls	15.5	Ray Wilson		
1980-81	3-24	0-13	Edwin Green	14.3	Ray Wilson	5-48	.094
1981-82	7-20	3-11	Donald Russell	16.4	Tom McLaughlin		
1982-83	9-20	4-10	John Hempel	16.2	Tom McLaughlin	16-40	.286
1983-84	12-17	6-12	John Hempel	15.8	Ron Gerlufsen		
1984-85	13-15	9-9	Donald Russell	15.2	Ron Gerlufsen		
1985-86	9-19	6-12	Lorenzo Sutton	17.8	Ron Gerlufsen		
1986-87	11-16	7-11	Lorenzo Sutton	19.4	Ron Gerlufsen		
1987-88	10-17	5-13	Lorenzo Sutton	19.4	Ron Gerlufsen	55-84	.396
1988-89	10-18	5-13	Jim McCoy	19.8	John Calipari		
1989-90	17-14	10-8 ■	Jim McCoy	20.6	John Calipari		
1990-91	20-13	10-8 ■	Jim McCoy	18.9	John Calipari		
1991-92	30-5	13-3 ●	Jim McCoy	16.4	John Calipari		
1992-93	24-7	11-3 ●	Lou Roe	13.8	John Calipari		
1993-94	28-7	14-2 ●	Lou Roe	18.6	John Calipari		
1994-95	29-5	13-3 ●	Lou Roe	16.5	John Calipari		
1995-96	35-2 ⊗	15-1 ●	Marcus Camby	20.5	John Calipari	193-71	.731▼
1996-97	19-14	11-5 ●	Carmelo Travieso	14.8	Bruiser Flint		
1997-98	21-11	12-4 ●	Lari Ketner	15.2	Bruiser Flint		
1998-99	14-16	9-7	Monty Mack	18.1	Bruiser Flint		
1999-2000	17-16	9-7 ■	Monty Mack	19.8	Bruiser Flint		
2000-01	15-15	11-5	Monty Mack	19.5	Bruiser Flint	86-72	.544
2001-02	13-16	6-10	Shannon Crooks	14.6	Steve Lappas		
2002-03	11-18	6-10	Jackie Rogers	12.9	Steve Lappas		
2003-04	10-19	4-12	Rashaun Freeman	15.4	Steve Lappas		
2004-05	16-12	9-7	Rashaun Freeman	15.4	Steve Lappas	50-65	.435
2005-06	13-15	8-8	Rashaun Freeman	13.6	Travis Ford		
2006-07	24-9	13-3 ■	Rashaun Freeman	14.7	Travis Ford		
2007-08	25-11	10-6 ■	Gary Forbes	19.4	Travis Ford	62-35	.639
2008-09	12-18	7-9	Ricky Harris	18.2	Derek Kellogg	12-18	.400

⊗ Records don't reflect games forfeited or vacated. For adjusted records, see p. 521.
▼ Coach's record adjusted to reflect games forfeited or vacated: 189-70, .730. For yearly totals, see p. 521.
● NCAA Tournament appearance ■ NIT appearance

PROFILE

University of Massachusetts, Amherst, MA
Founded: 1863
Enrollment: 25,633 (19,934 undergraduate)
Colors: Maroon and white
Nickname: Minutemen
Current arena: Mullins Center, opened in 1993 (9,493)
First game: 1899
All-time record: 1,134-1,012 (.528)
Total weeks in AP Top 20/25: 78
Current conference: Atlantic 10 (1976-)

Conference titles:
Yankee: 9 (1962, '68 [tie], '69, '70 [tie], '71, '73, '74, '75, '76); Atlantic 10: 6 (1992, '93, '94, '95, '96 [tie], 2007 [tie])
Conference tournament titles:
Atlantic 10: 5 (1992, '93, '94, '95, '96)
NCAA Tournaments: 8 (1 appearance vacated)
Sweet 16s (since 1975): 3
Final Fours: 1
NIT appearances: 11
Semifinals: 2

CONSENSUS ALL-AMERICAS

1996 **Marcus Camby,** F/C

FIRST-ROUND PRO PICKS

1972 **Julius Erving,** Milwaukee (12)
1996 **Marcus Camby,** Toronto (2)

TOP 5

G **Monty Mack** (1997-2001)
G **Jim McCoy** (1988-92)
F **Julius Erving** (1969-71)
F **Lou Roe** (1991-95)
F/C **Marcus Camby** (1993-96)

RECORDS

	GAME		SEASON		CAREER	
POINTS	41	Billy Tindall, vs. Vermont (Feb. 10, 1968)	727	Julius Erving (1970-71)	2,374	Jim McCoy (1988-92)
POINTS PER GAME			26.9	Julius Erving (1970-71)	26.3	Julius Erving (1969-71)
REBOUNDS	32	Julius Erving, vs. Syracuse (Feb. 22, 1971)	527	Julius Erving (1970-71)	1,070	Lou Roe (1991-95)
ASSISTS	15	Carl Smith, vs. Duquesne (Jan. 23, 1986); Alex Eldridge, vs. Connecticut (Dec. 14, 1977); Joe DiSarcina, vs. Maine (Dec. 19, 1968)	247	Edgar Padilla (1995-96)	647	Chris Lowe (2005-09)

ESPN 188 SAGARIN

McNEESE STATE

Two great eras, each led by an extraordinary player, stand out in McNeese State history. The first leader was the unstoppable Bill Reigel who, with a handful of other U.S. Army vets, took coach Ralph Ward's 1956 Cowboys to the NAIA national title. The second was the scoring genius Joe Dumars, who went on to achieve prominence as a star player and executive in the NBA.

BEST TEAM: 1955-56 The NAIA title-winning squad went 33–3, winning its last 18 games. All-America Bill Reigel was the NAIA's leading scorer with an amazing 33.9 points per game, supported by '57 All-America Frank Glenn, plus Charles Decker and Dudley Carver.

BEST PLAYER: G Joe Dumars (1981-85) Hall of Famer Dumars was No. 4 in the nation in scoring in 1984-85 (25.8 ppg), No. 6 in 1983-84 (26.4) and finished No. 11 among the NCAA's all-time scoring leaders. The school's top scorer by far (2,607), he became a six-time NBA All-Star, two-time title winner and team president—all with the Detroit Pistons.

BEST COACH: Ralph Ward (1952-71) He won six Gulf State Conference titles, the 1956 NAIA title and a school-record 281 games while coaching Reigel, Glenn and their mates.

GAME FOR THE AGES: No McNeese victory can top the 1956 NAIA championship game over Texas Southern in Kansas City, which the Cowboys won, 60-55, behind Reigel's 21 and Glenn's 14 points. But *the* game for locals took place on Feb. 16, 1985, when fans as well as NBA GMs and scouts crammed into the Thomas Assembly Center at Louisiana Tech to see Dumars take on Karl Malone's Bulldogs. In a defensive battle, Tech won, 59-58, on Malone's last-second tip-in.

FIERCEST RIVAL: Packed houses and multisport battles fire up the hoops encounters of McNeese State and historical nemesis Louisiana-Lafayette, which leads 50–33. But since UL-Lafayette's move to the Sun Belt in 1991, Southland foe Northwestern State has become the main antagonist, even bumping the Cowboys from the 2001 Southland Conference tourney title game, 72-71.

SEASON REVIEW

SEAS.	W-L	CONF.	COACH	SEAS.	W-L	CONF.	COACH
1943-50	*101-44*	*7 winning seasons, '43-'50, W. Cusic*		1963-64	10-16		Ralph Ward
1950-51	8-10		Wayne Cusic	1964-65	10-15		Ralph Ward
1951-52	15-4		Wayne Cusic	1965-66	7-16		Ralph Ward
1952-53	17-13		Ralph Ward	1966-67	12-10		Ralph Ward
1953-54	11-11		Ralph Ward	1967-68	20-5		Ralph Ward
1954-55	17-12		Ralph Ward	1968-69	9-12		Ralph Ward
1955-56	33-3	◆	Ralph Ward	1969-70	8-13		Ralph Ward
1956-57	21-5		Ralph Ward	1970-71	12-12		Ralph Ward
1957-58	19-4		Ralph Ward	1971-72	13-12		Bill Reigel
1958-59	14-7		Ralph Ward	1972-73	19-7 ⊗	8-4	Bill Reigel
1959-60	12-15		Ralph Ward	1973-74	20-5	0-0[a]	Bill Reigel
1960-61	16-7		Ralph Ward	1974-75	16-8	6-2	E.W. Foy
1961-62	17-8		Ralph Ward	1975-76	16-11	7-3	E.W. Foy
1962-63	16-9		Ralph Ward	1976-77	20-7	7-3	E.W. Foy

SEAS.	W-L	CONF.	SCORING		COACH	RECORD
1977-78	20-8	8-2	David Lawrence	15.5	Glenn Duhon	
1978-79	10-17	3-7	David Lawrence	22.4	Glenn Duhon	
1979-80	15-12	5-5	David Lawrence	20.6	Glenn Duhon	
1980-81	11-21	0-10			Glenn Duhon	
1981-82	14-15	4-6	Joe Dumars	21.5	Glenn Duhon	
1982-83	16-13	6-6	Joe Dumars	19.6	Glenn Duhon	
1983-84	16-15	6-6	Joe Dumars	26.4	Glenn Duhon	
1984-85	18-10	9-3	Joe Dumars	25.8	Glenn Duhon	
1985-86	21-11	8-4 ■	Jerome Batiste	18.4	Glenn Duhon	
1986-87	14-14	5-5	Jerome Batiste	21.9	Glenn Duhon	155-136 .533
1987-88	7-22	4-10	Anthony Pullard	16.0	Steve Welch	
1988-89	16-14	9-5 ●	Michael Cutright	20.4	Steve Welch	
1989-90	14-13	11-3	Anthony Pullard	22.5	Steve Welch	
1990-91	8-19	4-10	Derrick Turner	16.8	Steve Welch	
1991-92	7-22	4-14	Derek Haywood	18.8	Steve Welch	
1992-93	12-15	9-9	Melvin Johnson	16.2	Steve Welch	
1993-94	11-16	9-9	Alvydas Pazdrazdis	13.2	Steve Welch	75-121 .383
1994-95	11-16	7-11	Alvydas Pazdrazdis	16.0	Ron Everhart	
1995-96	15-12	11-7	Robert Palmer	16.1	Ron Everhart	
1996-97	18-12	10-6	Rosell Ellis	18.5	Ron Everhart	
1997-98	7-19	4-12	Demond Mallet	18.9	Ron Everhart	
1998-99	13-15	11-7	Demond Mallet	17.6	Ron Everhart	
1999-2000	6-21	5-13	Tierre Brown	22.0	Ron Everhart	
2000-01	22-9	17-3 ■	Demond Mallet	21.3	Ron Everhart	92-104 .469
2001-02	21-9	17-3 ●	Jason Coleman	14.4	Tic Price	
2002-03	15-14	10-10	Jason Coleman	14.9	Tic Price	
2003-04	11-16	7-9	Edward Garriet	14.0	Tic Price	
2004-05	13-15	8-8	Edward Garriet	11.0	Tic Price	
2005-06	14-14	9-7	J.T. Williams	15.8	Tic Price	74-68 .521
2006-07	15-17	9-7	Jarvis Bradley	15.1	Dave Simmons	
2007-08	13-16	7-9	Jarvis Bradley	12.8	Dave Simmons	
2008-09	11-18	5-11	Diego Kapelan	11.7	Dave Simmons	39-51 .433

[a] Ineligible for conference competition due to recruiting violations.
⊗ Record does not reflect games forfeited or vacated. For adjusted records, see p. 521.
● NCAA Tournament appearance ■ NIT appearance ◆ NAIA championship

PROFILE

McNeese State University, Lake Charles, LA
Founded: 1939
Enrollment: 8,800 (7,053 undergraduate)
Colors: Blue and gold
Nickname: Cowboys
Current arena: Burton Coliseum, opened in 1986 (8,000)
Previous: Lake Charles Civic Center, 1973-87 (6,500); McNeese Arena, 1956-73 (5,000); McNeese Memorial Gym, 1946-56 (1,000)
First game: 1943
All-time record: 944-781 (.547)

Total weeks in AP Top 20/25: 0
Current conference: Southland (1972-)
Conference titles:
Southland: 5 (1975, '78 [tie], '97 [tie], 2001, '02)
Conference tournament titles:
Southland: 2 (1989, 2002)
NCAA Tournament appearances: 2
NIT appearances: 2

FIRST-ROUND PRO PICKS

1985 **Joe Dumars**, Detroit (18)

TOP 5

G **Joe Dumars** (1981-85)
G **Stan Kernan** (1956-58, '60-61)
F **Frank Glenn** (1955-58)
F **Bill Reigel** (1954-56)
F **John Rudd** (1974-78)

RECORDS

	GAME		SEASON		CAREER	
POINTS	57	Bill Reigel, vs. Southeastern Louisiana (Feb. 22, 1956)	1,220	Bill Reigel (1955-56)	2,607	Joe Dumars (1981-85)
POINTS PER GAME			33.9	Bill Reigel (1955-56)	31.9	Bill Reigel (1954-56)
REBOUNDS	27	Henry Ray, vs. Texas-Arlington (Feb. 18, 1974)	451	Frank Glenn (1955-56)	1,212	Edmond Lawrence (1972-76)
ASSISTS	15	Pointer Williams, vs. Nicholls State (Feb. 29, 1996)	243	Girard Harmon (1985-86)	605	David Green (1980-84)

THE SCHOOLS

ESPN 61 SAGARIN

MEMPHIS

Home of the Blues? Absolutely. But in every decade since the 1970s, the Tigers have risen up to remind the nation that Memphis is also home to a pretty special college basketball tradition. Relying on local talent like Larry Finch, Anfernee "Penny" Hardaway and Andre Turner, the Tigers made Final Four trips in 1973, '85 and 2008 and reached the NCAA Final in '73 and '08 (losing both times).

BEST TEAM: 2007-08 With a nine-point lead over Kansas at San Antonio's Alamodome, these Tigers were 2:12 away from the school's first national title. Then the wheels fell off. Turnovers, missed free throws and defensive lapses resulted in a crushing 75-68 overtime loss. Led by junior Chris Douglas-Roberts and freshman sensation Derrick Rose, John Calipari's squad had to "settle" for a two-loss season, against the most wins of any team in NCAA history (38).

BEST PLAYER: C KEITH LEE (1981-85) A 6'10" wizard from West Memphis, Ark., Lee led his high school team to two undefeated seasons before leading Memphis (then known as Memphis State) to 104 wins and four NCAA trips in his four seasons. Lee finished his career with the all-time school record of 2,408 points and 1,336 rebounds.

BEST COACH: LARRY FINCH (1986-97) An All-America guard on the Tigers' first Final Four team in 1973, Finch took over the Memphis program in 1986 and proceeded to win 220 games in his 11 seasons. All told, Finch competed in more than 500 games as a Tiger player and coach, and participated in more than 300 wins.

GAME FOR THE AGES: In Finch's first season as head coach—a year dubbed the Season of Miracles—his Cardiac Kids had several come-from-behind wins. But perhaps none was as improbable as the Jan. 14, 1987, 59-58 win over Oral Roberts. Memphis trailed by seven points with :15 left, but wound up winning on John Wilfong's last-second three-pointer.

HEARTBREAKER: The difference between the verge of ecstasy and the edge of despair? For Memphis, that would be the last few ticks in the April 7, 2008, NCAA title game. The Tigers led Kansas by three when, with 2.1 seconds left, the Jayhawks' Mario Chalmers hit a miracle jumper. A desperation heave from Robert Dozier sailed wide and Kansas dominated overtime to win by seven.

FIERCEST RIVAL: Memphis and its in-state foe, Tennessee, met only 18 times from 1969 until their epic battle of Feb. 23, 2008, won by Tennessee, 66-62. Because of the proximity of the schools (382 miles), the Big Conference-Smaller Conference discrepancy and the alumni rivalries, these two schools—surprise!—simply don't like each other. More than half their meetings have been decided by four points or fewer. UT leads, 12–8.

FANFARE AND HOOPLA: Playing in the NBA home of the Memphis Grizzlies—the FedExForum—gives Memphis games a big-time feel. Nearby is one of the nation's biggest party destinations—Beale Street. Pre- and postgame revelry floods the downtown area on game days, making for one of the college basketball's best parties.

The difference between the verge of ecstasy and the edge of despair? That would be the last few ticks on April 7, 2008.

FAN FAVORITE: F JOEY DORSEY (2004-08) Often prompting chants of "Joey! Joey! Joey!" during his career, the big teddy bear of a bruiser endeared himself to the Tigers faithful like few others. Though he was allegedly involved in several off-the-court altercations, Dorsey's supporters never gave up on him and serenaded him with one final round of "Joeys" during his last college game at the FedEx Forum in 2008.

CONSENSUS ALL-AMERICAS

1983, '85	**Keith Lee,** C
1993	**Anfernee Hardaway,** G/F
2008	**Chris Douglas-Roberts,** G

FIRST-ROUND PRO PICKS

1957	**Win Wilfong,** St. Louis (5)
1961	**Wayne Yates,** LA Lakers (4)
1969	**Mike Butler,** New Orleans (ABA)
1985	**Keith Lee,** Chicago (11)
1986	**William Bedford,** Phoenix (6)
1993	**Anfernee Hardaway,** Golden State (3)
1995	**David Vaughn,** Orlando (25)
1996	**Lorenzen Wright,** LA Clippers (7)
2002	**Dajuan Wagner,** Cleveland (6)
2006	**Rodney Carney,** Chicago (16)
2006	**Shawne Williams,** Indiana (17)
2008	**Derrick Rose,** Chicago (1)
2009	**Tyreke Evans,** Sacramento (4)

PROFILE

University of Memphis, Memphis, TN
Founded: 1912
Enrollment: 20,214 (15,813 undergraduate)
Colors: Royal blue and gray
Nickname: Tigers
Current arena: FedExForum, opened in 2004 (18,400)
Previous: Pyramid Arena, 1991-2004 (21,000); Mid-South Coliseum, 1964-91 (11,200); Memorial Fieldhouse, 1964-91 (4,000); Memorial Gym, 1929-51 (4,000); Normal Cage/YMCA/Messick HS Gym, 1920-29 (N/A)
First game: Dec. 14, 1920
All-time record: 1,382-810-1 (.630)

Total weeks in AP Top 20/25: 253
Current conference: Conference USA (1995-)
Conference titles:
Missouri Valley: 1 (1973)
Metro Conference: 3 (1982, '84 [tie], '85)
Great Midwest: 1 (1995)
C-USA: 6 (1996 [tie], 2004 [tie], '06, '07, '08, '09)
Conference tournament titles:
Metro Conference: 4 (1982, '84, '85, '87)
C-USA: 4 (2006, '07, '08, '09)
NCAA Tournaments: 22 (5 appearances vacated)
Sweet 16s (since 1975): 10
Final Fours: 3

NIT appearances: 16
Semifinals: 4
Titles: 1 (2002)

TOP 5

G	**Larry Finch** (1970-73)
G/F	**Anfernee Hardaway** (1991-93)
F	**Forest Arnold** (1952-56)
F	**Ronnie Robinson** (1970-73)
C	**Keith Lee** (1981-85)

RECORDS

RECORDS	GAME		SEASON		CAREER	
POINTS	48	Larry Finch, vs. Saint Joseph's (Jan. 20, 1973)	762	Dajuan Wagner (2001-02)	2,408	Keith Lee (1981-85)
POINTS PER GAME			24.0	Larry Finch (1972-73)	22.3	Larry Finch (1970-73)
REBOUNDS	28	Ronnie Robinson, vs. Tulsa (Feb. 25 1971)	501	Larry Kenon (1972-73)	1,336	Keith Lee (1981-85)
ASSISTS	15	Andre Turner, vs. South Carolina (March 7, 1986)	262	Andre Turner (1985-86)	763	Andre Turner (1982-86)

SEASON REVIEW

SEASON	W-L	CONF.	SCORING	COACH	RECORD	
1920-21	22-7-1			Fred Grantham	22-7-1	.750
1921-22	1-7			W.H. DePriest	1-7	.125
1922-23	6-4			Lester Barnhard		
1923-24	4-9			Lester Barnhard	10-13	.435
1924-25	3-5			Zach Curlin		
1925-26	4-5			Zach Curlin		
1926-27	5-7			Zach Curlin		
1927-28	10-11			Zach Curlin		
1928-29	15-3			Zach Curlin		
1929-30	16-8			Zach Curlin		
1930-31	14-2			Zach Curlin		
1931-32	11-10			Zach Curlin		
1932-33	7-6			Zach Curlin		
1933-34	5-14			Zach Curlin		
1934-35	5-15			Zach Curlin		
1935-36	7-7			Zach Curlin		

SEAS.	W-L	CONF.	POSTSEASON	SCORING		REBOUNDS		ASSISTS		COACH	RECORD	
1936-37	5-7									Zach Curlin		
1937-38	0-14									Zach Curlin		
1938-39	2-13									Zach Curlin		
1939-40	7-9									Zach Curlin		
1940-41	9-8									Zach Curlin		
1941-42	7-9									Zach Curlin		
1942-43	7-4									Zach Curlin		
1943-44	no team											
1944-45	3-6									Zach Curlin		
1945-46	7-4									Zach Curlin		
1946-47	11-7									Zach Curlin		
1947-48	13-10									Zach Curlin	173-184	.485
1948-49	11-10									McCoy Tarry		
1949-50	12-9									McCoy Tarry		
1950-51	17-8									McCoy Tarry	40-27	.597
1951-52	25-10									Eugene Lambert		
1952-53	10-14									Eugene Lambert		
1953-54	15-9									Eugene Lambert		
1954-55	17-5		NCAA FIRST ROUND							Eugene Lambert		
1955-56	20-7		NCAA FIRST ROUND							Eugene Lambert	87-45	.659
1956-57	24-6		NIT RUNNER-UP	Win Wilfong	21.0	Win Wilfong	12.4			Bob Vanatta		
1957-58	15-7									Bob Vanatta		
1958-59	17-6									Bob Vanatta		
1959-60	18-5		NIT FIRST ROUND							Bob Vanatta		
1960-61	20-3		NIT QUARTERFINALS	Wayne Yates	17.5	Wayne Yates	14.4			Bob Vanatta		
1961-62	15-7		NCAA FIRST ROUND	Hunter Beckman	21.3	Bob Neumann	10.5			Bob Vanatta	109-34	.762
1962-63	19-7		NIT QUARTERFINALS	Hunter Beckman	18.5	Hunter Beckman	7.4			Dean Ehlers		
1963-64	14-11			Bob Neumann	20.7	John Hillman	9.4			Dean Ehlers		
1964-65	10-14			John Hillman	20.1	John Hillman	9.6			Dean Ehlers		
1965-66	10-15			Mike Butler	19.2	Jimmy Hawkins	7.5			Dean Ehlers	53-47	.530
1966-67	17-9		NIT FIRST ROUND	Mike Butler	17.1	Chuck Neal	6.6			Moe Iba		
1967-68	8-17	2-14		Mike Butler	19.4	Mackie Don Smith	7.7			Moe Iba		
1968-69	6-19	0-16		Richard Jones	21.7	Richard Jones	11.1	Richard Jones	2.5	Moe Iba		
1969-70	6-20	1-15		James Douglas	17.1	Don Holcomb	11.4	Jesse Buckman	3.4	Moe Iba	37-65	.363
1970-71	18-8	8-6		Larry Finch	18.4	Ronnie Robinson	14.2	Larry Finch	2.5	Gene Bartow		
1971-72	21-7	12-2	NIT FIRST ROUND	Larry Finch	23.9	Ronnie Robinson	13.3	Larry Finch	4.2	Gene Bartow		
1972-73	24-6	12-2	NCAA RUNNER-UP	Larry Finch	24.0	Larry Kenon	16.7	Larry Finch	3.9	Gene Bartow		
1973-74	19-11		NIT QUARTERFINALS	Dexter Reed	18.4	John Washington	7.8	Bill Cook	3.3	Gene Bartow	82-32	.719
1974-75	20-7		NIT FIRST ROUND	Bill Cook	19.0	Marion Hillard	12.5	Alvin Wright	4.7	Wayne Yates		
1975-76	21-9		NCAA FIRST ROUND	Bill Cook	18.8	Marion Hillard	11.2	Alvin Wright	5.3	Wayne Yates		
1976-77	20-9	2-4	NIT FIRST ROUND	Dexter Reed	17.0	John Washington	9.3	Alvin Wright	6.1	Wayne Yates		
1977-78	19-9	7-5		James Bradley	18.3	James Bradley	9.8	Alvin Wright	5.4	Wayne Yates		
1978-79	13-15	5-5		Rodney Lee	12.0	James Bradley	9.2	Otis Jackson	3.4	Wayne Yates	93-49	.655
1979-80	13-14	5-7		Otis Jackson	12.1	Hank McDowell	7.5	Otis Jackson	4.2	Dana Kirk		
1980-81	13-14	5-7		Hank McDowell	11.9	Hank McDowell	7.6	Otis Jackson	4.3	Dana Kirk		
1981-82	24-5 ⊗	10-2	NCAA REGIONAL SEMIFINALS	Keith Lee	18.3	Keith Lee	11.0	Otis Jackson	6.0	Dana Kirk		
1982-83	23-8 ⊗	6-6	NCAA REGIONAL SEMIFINALS	Keith Lee	18.7	Keith Lee	10.8	Andre Turner	4.1	Dana Kirk		
1983-84	26-7 ⊗	11-3	NCAA REGIONAL SEMIFINALS	Keith Lee	18.4	Keith Lee	10.8	Andre Turner	4.5	Dana Kirk		
1984-85	31-4 ⊗	13-1	NCAA NATIONAL SEMIFINALS	Keith Lee	19.7	Keith Lee	9.2	Andre Turner	6.6	Dana Kirk		
1985-86	28-6 ⊗	9-3	NCAA SECOND ROUND	William Bedford	17.3	William Bedford	8.5	Andre Turner	7.7	Dana Kirk	158-58	.731▼
1986-87	26-8	8-4		Vincent Askew	15.1	Sylvester Gray	7.6	John Wilfong	5.8	Larry Finch		
1987-88	20-12	6-6	NCAA SECOND ROUND	Dwight Boyd	15.2	Dewayne Bailey	5.8	Elliot Perry	4.1	Larry Finch		
1988-89	21-11	8-4	NCAA FIRST ROUND	Elliot Perry	19.4	Steve Ballard	6.8	Elliot Perry	3.7	Larry Finch		
1989-90	18-12	8-6	NIT FIRST ROUND	Elliot Perry	16.8	Ernest Smith	5.7	Elliot Perry	5.0	Larry Finch		
1990-91	17-15	7-7	NIT SECOND ROUND	Elliot Perry	20.8	Anthony Douglas	4.9	Elliot Perry	4.6	Larry Finch		
1991-92	23-11	5-5	NCAA REGIONAL FINALS	Anfernee Hardaway	17.4	David Vaughn	8.3	Anfernee Hardaway	5.5	Larry Finch		
1992-93	20-12	7-3	NCAA FIRST ROUND	Anfernee Hardaway	22.8	Anfernee Hardaway	8.5	Anfernee Hardaway	6.4	Larry Finch		
1993-94	13-16	4-8		David Vaughn	16.6	David Vaughn	12.0	Chris Garner	4.4	Larry Finch		
1994-95	24-10	9-3	NCAA REGIONAL SEMIFINALS	Lorenzen Wright	14.8	Lorenzen Wright	10.2	Chris Garner	6.4	Larry Finch		
1995-96	22-8	11-3	NCAA FIRST ROUND	Lorenzen Wright	17.4	Lorenzen Wright	10.4	Chris Garner	5.7	Larry Finch		
1996-97	16-15	10-4	NIT FIRST ROUND	Cedric Henderson	16.0	Sunday Adebayo	7.0	Chris Garner	4.1	Larry Finch	220-130	.629
1997-98	17-12	12-4	NIT SECOND ROUND	Omar Sneed	20.9	Omar Sneed	9.2	Detric Golden	3.0	Tic Price		
1998-99	13-15	6-10		Omar Sneed	16.7	Omar Sneed	7.5	Dinno Daniels	3.3	Tic Price	30-27	.526
1999-2000	15-16	7-9		Kelly Wise	14.5	Kelly Wise	8.6	Courtney Trask	4.5	Johnny Jones	15-16	.484
2000-01	21-15	10-6	NIT THIRD PLACE	Kelly Wise	15.3	Kelly Wise	10.1	Shyrone Chatman	4.6	John Calipari		
2001-02	27-9	12-4	NIT CHAMPION	Dajuan Wagner	21.2	Kelly Wise	10.3	Antonio Burks	5.1	John Calipari		
2002-03	23-7	13-3	NCAA FIRST ROUND	Chris Massie	16.7	Chris Massie	10.8	Antonio Burks	5.6	John Calipari		
2003-04	22-8	12-4	NCAA SECOND ROUND	Sean Banks	17.4	Sean Banks	6.5	Antonio Burks	5.5	John Calipari		
2004-05	22-16	9-7	NIT SEMIFINALS	Rodney Carney	16.0	Duane Erwin	6.3	Darius Washington Jr	3.8	John Calipari		
2005-06	33-4	13-1	NCAA REGIONAL FINALS	Rodney Carney	17.2	Joey Dorsey	7.5	Andre Allen	3.0	John Calipari		
2006-07	33-4	16-0	NCAA REGIONAL FINALS	Chris Douglas-Roberts	15.4	Joey Dorsey	9.4	Antonio Anderson	3.6	John Calipari		
2007-08	38-2	16-0	NCAA RUNNER-UP	Chris Douglas-Roberts	18.1	Joey Dorsey	9.5	Derrick Rose	4.7	John Calipari		
2008-09	33-4	16-0	NCAA REGIONAL SEMIFINALS	Tyreke Evans	17.1	Shawn Taggart	7.6	Antonio Anderson	4.5	John Calipari	252-69	.785

⊗ Records don't reflect games forfeited or vacated. For adjusted records, see p. 521.

▼ Coach's record adjusted to reflect games forfeited or vacated: 149-53, .738. For yearly totals, see p. 521.

THE SCHOOLS

ESPN 283 SAGARIN

MERCER

The high points have come often enough to leave a string of lasting memories: the wondrous talents of Sam Mitchell; mid-century stars Tommy Mixon and Glenn Wilkes; coach Bill Bibb's NCAA Tourney teams; the big-time playmaking of James Florence; the eye-opening upset of USC in 2007. Plus any victory over Stetson makes for a good season.

BEST TEAM: 1984-85 Bibb's 1984-85 Atlantic Sun tournament champs featured the high-scoring Mitchell (774 points) and Earl Walker (597), plus guard Elston Harris (6.4 apg). They beat Stanford, suffered one-point losses at Auburn and Texas, and defeated Arkansas-Little Rock, 105-96, for the A-Sun title and an NCAA bid.

BEST PLAYER: F Sam Mitchell (1981-85) Mercer's all-time leading scorer (1,986) was the 1984-85 A-Sun POY and carried the Bears to their tourney title and NCAA berth. Mitchell went on to a 13-year NBA career—Mercer's only NBA player to date. In 2004 he became coach of the Toronto Raptors.

BEST COACH: Bill Bibb (1974-89) He took over to start the school's second D1 season and guided the Bears to nine winning campaigns (the most by any Mercer coach), two 20-win seasons, two A-Sun tourney titles and both of Mercer's NCAA Tournament bids. He's the school's winningest coach (222) and the only one with more than 150 victories.

GAME FOR THE AGES: The Nov. 10, 2007, season-opening upset of 18th-ranked host USC—led by NBA first-rounder O.J. Mayo—is Mercer's most remarkable. The Bears (11–19) jumped out to a 47-30 halftime lead and never looked back, winning 96-81. James Florence (30 points), Calvin Henry (14) and Shaddean Aaron (13) led the way over Mayo (32) and the Trojans.

FIERCEST RIVAL: Stetson (113 games) and Georgia Southern (107) have both played Mercer more than 100 times, but Stetson, still a league rival, plays the Bears twice each year. The Hatters had a pair of two-point wins in 2007-08 to raise their overall series lead to 67–46; Mercer had won eight of the previous 10 encounters.

SEASON REVIEW

SEAS.	W-L	CONF.	COACH	SEAS.	W-L	CONF.	COACH
1908-48	*284-214*			1961-62	12-12		Robert Wilder
1948-49	15-8		James Cowan	1962-63	12-12		Robert Wilder
1949-50	19-7		James Cowan	1963-64	10-14		Robert Wilder
1950-51	16-9		James Cowan	1964-65	12-12		Robert Wilder
1951-52	19-10		Dan Nymicz	1965-66	13-10		Robert Wilder
1952-53	21-6		Dan Nymicz	1966-67	15-6		Robert Wilder
1953-54	19-9		James Cowan	1967-68	9-14		Robert Wilder
1954-55	8-14		James Cowan	1968-69	14-12		Robert Wilder
1955-56	10-12		James Cowan	1969-70	6-18		Robert Wilder
1956-57	8-16		James Cowan[a]	1970-71	14-9		Dwayne Morrison
1957-58	13-7		Robert Wilder	1971-72	19-7		Dwayne Morrison
1958-59	9-13		Robert Wilder	1972-73	15-6		Dwayne Morrison
1959-60	9-14		Robert Wilder	1973-74	16-8		Joe Dan Gold
1960-61	7-16		Robert Wilder	1974-75	9-17		Bill Bibb

SEAS.	W-L	CONF.	SCORING		COACH	RECORD
1975-76	15-10		Steve Hendrickson	16.1	Bill Bibb	
1976-77	6-19		Jerry Thruston	16.2	Bill Bibb	
1977-78	16-11		Stewart Reese	15.8	Bill Bibb	
1978-79	21-6		Stewart Reese	17.4	Bill Bibb	
1979-80	16-12	3-3	Benton Wade	15.1	Bill Bibb	
1980-81	18-12	7-4 ●	Tony Gattis	16.2	Bill Bibb	
1981-82	16-11	8-8	Tony Gattis	14.4	Bill Bibb	
1982-83	13-15	6-8	Tony Gattis	20.4	Bill Bibb	
1983-84	14-14	6-8	Sam Mitchell	21.5	Bill Bibb	
1984-85	22-9	10-4 ●	Sam Mitchell	25.0	Bill Bibb	
1985-86	15-14	6-8	Chris Moore	16.2	Bill Bibb	
1986-87	12-16	7-11	Chris Moore	17.7	Bill Bibb	
1987-88	15-14	8-10	Ben Wilson	18.6	Bill Bibb	
1988-89	14-14	9-9	Scott Bailey	16.4	Bill Bibb	222-194 .534
1989-90	7-20	2-14	Scott Bailey	20.0	Brad Siegfried	
1990-91	2-25	1-13	Mike Smith	14.0	Brad Siegfried	9-45 .167
1991-92	11-18	6-8	Shaun Thompson	19.2	Bill Hodges	
1992-93	13-14	7-5	Kenny Brown	22.1	Bill Hodges	
1993-94	5-24	3-13	Will Tuttle	13.0	Bill Hodges	
1994-95	15-14	8-8	Chance Solomon	19.3	Bill Hodges	
1995-96	15-14	7-9	Reggie Elliott	21.9	Bill Hodges	
1996-97	3-23	1-15	Bruce Simms	15.2	Bill Hodges	62-107 .367
1997-98	5-21	2-14	Mark Johnson	13.2	Mark Slonaker	
1998-99	8-18	5-11	Earnest Brown	12.6	Mark Slonaker	
1999-2000	12-21	7-11	Scott Emerson	15.2	Mark Slonaker	
2000-01	13-15	10-8	Rodney Kirtz	17.4	Mark Slonaker	
2001-02	6-23	4-16	Aleem Muhammad	17.2	Mark Slonaker	
2002-03	23-6	14-2	Aleem Muhammad	15.5	Mark Slonaker	
2003-04	12-18	9-11	Delmar Wilson	13.4	Mark Slonaker	
2004-05	16-12	11-9	Will Emerson	15.6	Mark Slonaker	
2005-06	9-19	7-13	Andrew Brown	15.5	Mark Slonaker	
2006-07	13-17	8-10	James Florence	19.3	Mark Slonaker	
2007-08	11-19	6-10	James Florence	19.0	Mark Slonaker	128-189 .404
2008-09	17-15	11-9	James Florence	20.8	Bob Hoffman	17-15 .531

[a] James Cowan (2-7) and Robert Wilder (6-9) both coached during the 1956-57 season.
● NCAA Tournament appearance

PROFILE

Mercer University, Macon, GA
Founded: 1833
Enrollment: 7,180 (4,628 undergraduate)
Colors: Orange and black
Nickname: Bears
Current arena: University Center, opened in 2004 (3,200)
Previous: Porter Gymnasium, 1937-2004 (500)
First game: 1908
All-time record: 1,062-1,045 (.504)
Total weeks in AP Top 20/25: 0

Current conference: Atlantic Sun (1979-)
Conference titles:
Atlantic Sun: 1 (2003 [tie])
Conference tournament titles:
Trans America: 2 (1981, '85)
NCAA Tournament appearances: 2
NIT appearances: 0

TOP 5

- G **James Florence** (2006-)
- G **Tommy Mixon** (1951-55)
- F **Scott Emerson** (1999-2004)
- F **Sam Mitchell** (1981-85)
- F **Glenn Wilkes** (1946-50)

RECORDS

RECORDS	GAME		SEASON		CAREER	
POINTS	39	James Florence, vs. Jacksonville (Feb. 16, 2007)	774	Sam Mitchell (1984-85)	1,986	Sam Mitchell (1981-85)
POINTS PER GAME			25.7	Tommy Mixon (1954-55)	22.5	Tommy Mixon (1951-55)
REBOUNDS	22	Calvin Henry, vs. VMI (Dec. 9, 2006); Scott Farley, vs. Alabama (Dec. 16, 1995)	349	Scott Farley (1994-95)	1,058	Steve Moody (1963-67)
ASSISTS	16	Elston Harris, vs. Georgia State (Jan. 12, 1985)	224	Damitrius Coleman (2004-05)	470	Elston Harris (1982-86)

ESPN 132 SAGARIN

MIAMI

The ibis may seem a peculiar mascot for a team nicknamed the Hurricanes, but according to folklore, it's the last animal to take shelter before violent weather and the first to return afterward. Sebastian the Ibis has been cheering on the Canes for more than four decades, and has survived many stormy periods, including a 14-year hiatus following the 1970-71 season. But as an ACC member, Miami has become a legitimate force.

BEST TEAM: 1964-65 Future ABA and NBA legend Rick Barry averaged 37.4 ppg, and the Canes set a new NCAA DI scoring mark by averaging 98.4 points per contest. But Miami was not allowed to compete in the NCAA Tournament because of recruiting violations.

BEST PLAYER: F Rick Barry (1962-65) He scored more than 25,000 points as a pro, so imagine the futility of trying to guard Barry in college. The school's leading scorer, he averaged 29.8 points over his three seasons. He still holds UM's eight highest single-game scoring totals, topped by his 59 points against Rollins in 1965.

BEST COACH: Bruce Hale (1954-67) Known as Slick for the way he combed his hair straight back, the retired Air Force captain had just one losing campaign in Coral Gables—his first. Hale led Miami to its first Tournament appearance in 1960 and finished as the school's winningest coach.

GAME FOR THE AGES: Facing a team that had been to the Final Four the year before, Miami held Ohio State to 36% shooting in the second round of the 2000 Tourney. Meanwhile, reserve UM guard Johnny Hemsley hit one clutch basket after another on his way to 24 points. The Canes won, 75-62, and advanced to their first Sweet 16.

FIERCEST RIVAL: As if the Miami-Florida State rivalry wasn't already fierce enough, the two teams became conference foes in 2004. The Canes broke a five-game losing streak against the Seminoles on Jan. 21, 2009, with a 75-69 win, but UM fans like to point out that their team leads in Tournament appearances since the turn of the century (three to one).

SEASON REVIEW

SEAS.	W-L	CONF.	COACH	SEAS.	W-L	CONF.	COACH
1926-47	*107-62*		*T. McCann 30-7 between '28 and '32*	1960-61	20-7	■	Bruce Hale
1947-48	11-7		Hart Morris	1961-62	14-12		Bruce Hale
1948-49	19-8		Hart Morris	1962-63	23-5	■	Bruce Hale
1949-50	14-9		Hart Morris	1963-64	20-7	■	Bruce Hale
1950-51	10-12		Hart Morris	1964-65	22-4		Bruce Hale
1951-52	14-8		Hart Morris	1965-66	15-11		Bruce Hale
1952-53	8-12		Dave Wike	1966-67	15-11		Bruce Hale
1953-54	5-10		Dave Wike	1967-68	17-11		Ron Godfrey
1954-55	9-11		Bruce Hale	1968-69	14-10		Ron Godfrey
1955-56	14-12		Bruce Hale	1969-70	9-17		Ron Godfrey
1956-57	13-13		Bruce Hale	1970-71	7-19		Ron Godfrey
1957-58	14-8		Bruce Hale	1971-72	no team		
1958-59	18-7		Bruce Hale	1972-73	no team		
1959-60	23-4	●	Bruce Hale	1973-74	no team		

SEAS.	W-L	CONF.	SCORING		COACH	RECORD	
1974-75	no team						
1975-76	no team						
1976-77	no team						
1977-78	no team						
1978-79	no team						
1979-80	no team						
1980-81	no team						
1981-82	no team						
1982-83	no team						
1983-84	no team						
1984-85	no team						
1985-86	14-14		Eric Brown	460	Bill Foster		
1986-87	15-16		Eric Brown	460	Bill Foster		
1987-88	17-14		Eric Brown	551	Bill Foster		
1988-89	19-12		Eric Brown	765	Bill Foster		
1989-90	13-15		Joe Wylie	514	Bill Foster	78-71	.523
1990-91	9-19		Joe Wylie	514	Leonard Hamilton		
1991-92	8-24	1-17	Jerome Scott	515	Leonard Hamilton		
1992-93	10-17	7-11	Steven Edwards	430	Leonard Hamilton		
1993-94	7-20	0-18	Jamal Johnson	257	Leonard Hamilton		
1994-95	15-13	9-9 ■	Steven Edwards	359	Leonard Hamilton		
1995-96	15-13	8-10	Steven Edwards	361	Leonard Hamilton		
1996-97	16-13	9-9 ■	Tim James	405	Leonard Hamilton		
1997-98	18-10	11-7 ●	Tim James	469	Leonard Hamilton		
1998-99	23-7	15-3 ●	Tim James	18.6	Leonard Hamilton		
1999-2000	23-11	13-3 ●	Johnny Hemsley	18.1	Leonard Hamilton	144-147	.495
2000-01	16-13	8-8 ■	Darius Rice	14.1	Perry Clark		
2001-02	24-8	10-6 ●	Darius Rice	14.9	Perry Clark		
2002-03	11-17	4-12	Darius Rice	18.7	Perry Clark		
2003-04	14-16	4-12	Darius Rice	16.9	Perry Clark	65-54	.546
2004-05	16-13	7-9 ■	Guillermo Diaz	18.6	Frank Haith		
2005-06	18-16	7-9 ■	Guillermo Diaz	17.2	Frank Haith		
2006-07	12-20	4-12	Jack McClinton	16.7	Frank Haith		
2007-08	23-11	8-8 ●	Jack McClinton	17.7	Frank Haith		
2008-09	19-13	7-9 ■	Jack McClinton	19.3	Frank Haith	88-73	.547

Cumulative totals listed when per game averages not available.
● NCAA Tournament appearance ■ NIT appearance

PROFILE

University of Miami, Coral Gables, FL
Founded: 1925
Enrollment: 14,685 (9,751 undergraduate)
Colors: Orange, green and white
Nickname: Hurricanes
Current arena: BankUnited Center, opened in 2003 (7,200)
Previous: Miami Arena, 1988-2003 (16,640); Knight Center, 1985-88 (4,686)
First game: 1926
All-time record: 830-642 (.564)
Total weeks in AP Top 20/25: 42

Current conference: Atlantic Coast (2004-)
Conference titles:
Big East: 1 (2000 [tie])
Conference tournament titles: 0
NCAA Tournament appearances: 6
Sweet 16s (since 1975): 1
NIT appearances: 9

CONSENSUS ALL-AMERICAS

1965 **Rick Barry,** F

FIRST-ROUND PRO PICKS

1965 **Rick Barry,** San Francisco (4)
1999 **Tim James,** Miami (25)
2002 **John Salmons,** San Antonio (26)

TOP 5

G **Don Curnutt** (1967-70)
G **Dick Hickox** (1958-61)
F **Rick Barry** (1962-65)
F **Eric Brown** (1985-89)
F **Tim James** (1995-99)

RECORDS

RECORDS	GAME		SEASON		CAREER	
POINTS	59	Rick Barry, vs. Rollins (Feb. 23, 1965)	973	Rick Barry (1964-65)	2,298	Rick Barry (1962-65)
POINTS PER GAME			37.4	Rick Barry (1964-65)	29.8	Rick Barry (1962-65)
REBOUNDS	29	Rick Barry, vs. Oklahoma City (Jan. 30, 1965)	475	Rick Barry (1964-65)	1,274	Rick Barry (1962-65)
ASSISTS	14	Michael Gardner, vs. Pittsburgh (Jan. 23, 1993)	218	Vernon Jennings (1999-2000)	520	Vernon Jennings (1996-2000)

ESPN 69 SAGARIN

MIAMI (OHIO)

Miami was once described by *The New York Times* as a "hidden gem" among public universities. The same might be said about many of the athletes recruited over the years to play there. Before they were national names, Ron Harper, Wally Szczerbiak and Wayne Embry flew under the radar in Oxford. And the teams haven't done badly, either: Miami has been to 17 NCAA Tournaments—although only one in the 21st century.

BEST TEAM: 1998-99 To Miami fans it will be remembered as the year the MAC regular-season champions turned the NCAA Tournament—at least for a while—into Wally's World. In a first-round 59-58 upset of No. 7-seed Washington, Szczerbiak scored 43 points and made a game-saving block in the waning seconds. In the next round against No. 2-seed Utah's relentless man-to-man defense, the sharpshooter dished out five assists and went 10 for 10 from the line in a 66-58 win. Kentucky ended Miami's run in the Sweet 16, 58-43, but Szczerbiak's legend was assured.

BEST PLAYER: G/F RON HARPER (1982-86) The 6'6" Harper scored inside and out, showed remarkable speed in transition after collecting a rebound and was a terrific passer. Not bad for the kid many D1 programs rejected because of a stuttering problem they thought would interfere with his college workload. He went on to a solid 15-year NBA career.

BEST COACH: DARRELL HEDRIC (1970-84) In a school known as the Cradle of Coaches (although mainly in football), this former Miami assistant stands out for his in-your-face aggressiveness and winning ways (four NCAA Tourney bids). He was also well-known for pithy one-liners, which his staff called Darrell-isms. Describing the pugnacity of his most prized recruit, Harper, he said, "If you give him a rash of crap, you'd better buckle your chin strap."

GAME FOR THE AGES: In the 1978 NCAA Tournament, Miami delivered a first-round knockout to defending champ Marquette, 84-81, in overtime. In fact, a literal knockout led to the victory. With 3:38 to go and his team down 10, Miami's John Shoemaker was floored by an elbow to the face from Jerome Whitehead. The Marquette center was ejected for a flagrant foul, Miami rallied, tied it in regulation and won in OT.

HEARTBREAKER: Many fans still can't comprehend the 69-68 first-round overtime loss to Maryland in the 1985 NCAA Tournament. Miami had possession with the score tied and :46 left in regulation when Harper threw the ball away to Len Bias. Then the team blew a three-point lead in the final minute of OT. Worse, the game was played in Dayton, Miami's backyard.

FIERCEST RIVAL: When the RedHawks travel to Athens to face Ohio University, they don't expect to sleep: Bobcats fans have a knack for tracking down Miami players' cell numbers and dialing them until the wee hours. It's all part of the Battle of the Bricks; both schools add up their wins in all athletic events, with the higher number taking home a trophy with a brick (matching the signature architectural material of both campuses) on top of it. Ohio leads the basketball series, 95–88.

1998-99 will be remembered as the year the MAC champions turned the NCAA Tournament—at least for a while—into Wally's World.

FANFARE AND HOOPLA: The RedHawks' assistants so respected coach Charlie Coles (1996-) for fighting through numerous health problems that they organized the Miami faithful into Charlie's Army. Students now attend games dressed in red-and-black camouflage tees and black helmets.

FAN FAVORITE: F MIKE ENSMINGER (1997-2001) If basketball had a position called enforcer, Ensminger would have fit the bill perfectly. He set screens for Szczerbiak, threw subtle elbows and psyched up teammates by shaving his head for the Tournament.

PROFILE

Miami University, Oxford, OH
Founded: 1809
Enrollment: 17,161 (15,069 undergraduate)
Colors: Red and white
Nickname: RedHawks
Current arena: Millett Hall, opened in 1968 (6,400)
First game: 1905
All-time record: 1,257-1,007 (.555)
Total weeks in AP Top 20/25: 7

Current conference: Mid-American (1947-)
Conference titles:
MAC: 18 (1952 [tie], '53, '55, '57, '58, '66, '69, '71, '73, '78, '84, '86, '92, '93 [tie], '95, '97 [tie], '99, 2005)
Conference tournament titles:
MAC: 4 (1984, '92, '97, 2007)
NCAA Tournament appearances: 17
Sweet 16s (since 1975): 2
NIT appearances: 6

FIRST-ROUND PRO PICKS

1986 **Ron Harper,** Cleveland (8)
1999 **Wally Szczerbiak,** Minnesota (6)

TOP 5

G **Damon Frierson** (1995-99)
G **Eric Newsome** (1983-88)
G/F **Ron Harper** (1982-86)
F **Wally Szczerbiak** (1995-99)
C **Wayne Embry** (1955-58)

RECORDS	GAME		SEASON		CAREER	
POINTS	45	Ron Harper, vs. Ball State (Mar. 8, 1985)	775	Wally Szczerbiak (1998-99)	2,377	Ron Harper (1982-86)
POINTS PER GAME			26.8	Fred Foster (1967-68)	19.8	Ron Harper (1982-86)
REBOUNDS	34	Wayne Embry, vs. Kent State (Feb. 16, 1957); vs. Eastern Kentucky (Feb. 14, 1957)	488	Wayne Embry (1957-58)	1,119	Ron Harper (1982-86)
ASSISTS	17	Eddie Schilling, vs. Kent State (Feb. 4, 1987)	241	Eddie Schilling (1984-85)	629	Eddie Schilling (1984-88)

SEASON REVIEW

SEASON	W-L	CONF.	SCORING	COACH	RECORD
1905-17	*53-70*		*12-3 in 1916-17 under George Little, first winning season since 1910-11*		
1917-18	10-0			George Rider	
1918-19	7-5			George Rider	17-5 .773
1919-20	9-5			George Little	
1920-21	9-6			George Little	
1921-22	13-7			George Little	43-21 .672
1922-23	9-6			Harry Ewing	
1923-24	2-9			Harry Ewing	11-15 .423
1924-25	3-10			Roy Tillotson	
1925-26	7-9			Roy Tillotson	
1926-27	9-6			Roy Tillotson	
1927-28	13-3			Roy Tillotson	
1928-29	7-11			Roy Tillotson	
1929-30	5-10			Roy Tillotson	44-49 .473
1930-31	5-10			John Mauer	
1931-32	6-10			John Mauer	
1932-33	3-13			John Mauer	
1933-34	4-11			John Mauer	
1934-35	3-12			John Mauer	
1935-36	9-8			John Mauer	
1936-37	5-11			John Mauer	
1937-38	11-5			John Mauer	46-80 .365

SEAS.	W-L	CONF.	POSTSEASON	SCORING		REBOUNDS		ASSISTS		COACH	RECORD
1938-39	5-13									Wilbur "Weeb" Ewbank	5-13 .278
1939-40	12-6									Walter Van Winkle	
1940-41	10-7									Walter Van Winkle	
1941-42	6-9									Walter Van Winkle	28-22 .560
1942-43	10-6									W.J. "Blue" Foster	
1943-44	10-2									W.J. "Blue" Foster	
1944-45	8-7									W.J. "Blue" Foster	
1945-46	10-9									W.J. "Blue" Foster	
1946-47	15-7			Bob Brown	19.9					W.J. "Blue" Foster	
1947-48	13-15	3-5		Bob Brown	16.5					W.J. "Blue" Foster	
1948-49	8-13	3-7		Bob Brown	10.9					W.J. "Blue" Foster	74-59 .556
1949-50	5-15	3-7		Frank Peticca	7.0					John Brickels	
1950-51	10-13	4-4		Dick Walls	12.1	Dick Walls	14.3			John Brickels	15-28 .349
1951-52	19-6	9-3		Dick Walls	14.9	Dick Walls	13.3			William Rohr	
1952-53	17-6	10-2	NCAA FIRST ROUND	Dick Walls	21.1	Dick Walls	14.5			William Rohr	
1953-54	12-10	7-5		Dick Klitch	16.0	Ed Gunderson	10.2			William Rohr	
1954-55	14-9	11-3	NCAA FIRST ROUND	Tom Bryant	15.3	Tom Bryant	9.7			William Rohr	
1955-56	12-8	8-4		Bill Kennon	17.0	Bill Kennon	10.3			William Rohr	
1956-57	17-8	11-1	NCAA FIRST ROUND	Wayne Embry	23.1	Wayne Embry	17.2			William Rohr	91-47 .659
1957-58	18-9	12-0	NCAA REGIONAL SEMIFINALS	Wayne Embry	24.9	Wayne Embry	18.0			Richard Shrider	
1958-59	14-11	9-3		Jim Thomas	13.3	Ed Wingard	12.2			Richard Shrider	
1959-60	8-16	6-6		Vernon Lawson	15.8	Vernon Lawson	10.8			Richard Shrider	
1960-61	12-12	7-5		Dave Zeller	22.3	Dave Mack	10.4			Richard Shrider	
1961-62	7-17	3-9		LeVern Benson	24.6	Ralph Wright	10.2			Richard Shrider	
1962-63	12-12	8-4		Jeff Gehring	17.1	Charley Dinkins	9.1			Richard Shrider	
1963-64	17-7	9-3		Jeff Gehring	19.9	Charley Dinkins	10.9			Richard Shrider	
1964-65	20-5	11-1		Jeff Gehring	17.1	Charley Dinkins	8.2			Richard Shrider	
1965-66	18-7	11-1	NCAA FIRST ROUND	Jim Patterson	15.6	Jim Patterson	12.0			Richard Shrider	126-96 .568
1966-67	14-10	7-5		Fred Foster	21.3	Fred Foster	10.1			Taylor "Tates" Locke	
1967-68	11-12	4-8		Fred Foster	26.8	Fred Foster	12.5			Taylor "Tates" Locke	
1968-69	15-12	10-2	NCAA REGIONAL SEMIFINALS	Frank Lukacs	12.5	Walt Williams	7.4			Taylor "Tates" Locke	
1969-70	16-8	7-3	NIT FIRST ROUND	Terry Martin	12.5	Terry Martin	8.5			Taylor "Tates" Locke	56-42 .571
1970-71	20-5	9-1	NCAA FIRST ROUND	Gerry Spears	12.3	Tom Roberts	7.2			Darrell Hedric	
1971-72	12-12	4-6		Phil Lumpkin	16.7	Tom Roberts	5.9	Phil Lumpkin	3.5	Darrell Hedric	
1972-73	18-9	9-2	NCAA FIRST ROUND	Rich Hampton	14.9	Rich Hampton	9.2	Phil Lumpkin	5.7	Darrell Hedric	
1973-74	13-13	6-6		Phil Lumpkin	18.1	Dave Elmer	10.0	Phil Lumpkin	5.7	Darrell Hedric	
1974-75	19-7	8-5		Steve Fields	15.1	Steve Fields	7.4	Rod Dieringer	4.2	Darrell Hedric	
1975-76	18-8	14-2		Chuck Goodyear	18.1	Archie Aldridge	6.6	John Shoemaker	3.9	Darrell Hedric	
1976-77	20-6	13-3		Archie Aldridge	19.1	Archie Aldridge	8.6	John Shoemaker	4.2	Darrell Hedric	
1977-78	19-9	12-4	NCAA REGIONAL SEMIFINALS	Archie Aldridge	20.8	Archie Aldridge	7.8	Randy Ayers	4.5	Darrell Hedric	
1978-79	9-18	6-10		Rick Goins	16.4	Todd Jones	5.3	Tom Dunn	4.5	Darrell Hedric	
1979-80	9-18	7-9		Rick Goins	15.4	George Sweigert	5.7	Tom Dunn	3.7	Darrell Hedric	
1980-81	11-15	6-10		Al Watkins	15.6	George Sweigert	7.6	Al Watkins	2.0	Darrell Hedric	
1981-82	11-16	8-8		George Sweigert	16.9	George Sweigert	8.5	Chuck Stahl	2.3	Darrell Hedric	
1982-83	13-15	10-8		Craig Tubbs	14.9	Ron Harper	7.0	Ron Harper	2.2	Darrell Hedric	
1983-84	24-6	16-2	NCAA FIRST ROUND	Ron Harper	16.3	Ron Harper	7.6	John Willoughby	4.5	Darrell Hedric	216-157 .579
1984-85	20-11	13-5	NCAA FIRST ROUND	Ron Harper	24.9	Ron Harper	10.7	Eddie Schilling	6.9	Jerry Peirson	
1985-86	24-7	16-2	NCAA FIRST ROUND	Ron Harper	24.4	Ron Harper	11.7	Ron Harper	4.3	Jerry Peirson	
1986-87	13-15	7-9		Trimill Haywood	17.1	Trimill Haywood	7.1	Eddie Schilling	7.3	Jerry Peirson	
1987-88	9-18	6-10		Eric Newsome	20.2	Jim Paul	7.6	Eddie Schilling	4.2	Jerry Peirson	
1988-89	13-15 ⊗	8-8		Karlton Clayborne	13.6	Lamont Hanna	6.6	Jamie Mercurio	4.9	Jerry Peirson	
1989-90	14-15	9-7		David Scott	14.3	Jim Paul	7.6	Derek Walton	4.3	Jerry Peirson	93-81 .534▼
1990-91	16-12	10-6		David Scott	17.4	Craig Michaelis	4.8	Jamie Mercurio	3.6	Joby Wright	
1991-92	23-8	13-3	NCAA FIRST ROUND	David Scott	15.0	John McKenna	4.5	Jamie Mercurio	4.0	Joby Wright	
1992-93	22-9	14-4	NIT QUARTERFINALS	Matt Kramer	11.2	Jamie Mahaffey	7.5	Derrick Cross	3.8	Joby Wright	61-29 .678
1993-94	19-11	12-6	NIT FIRST ROUND	Landon Hackim	16.6	Devin Davis	7.7	Derrick Cross	4.0	Herb Sendek	
1994-95	23-7	16-2	NCAA SECOND ROUND	Devin Davis	16.9	Jamie Mahaffey	8.7	Derrick Cross	3.7	Herb Sendek	
1995-96	21-8	12-6	NIT FIRST ROUND	Devin Davis	17.8	Devin Davis	9.9	Chris McGuire	3.0	Herb Sendek	63-26 .708
1996-97	21-9	13-5	NCAA FIRST ROUND	Devin Davis	16.9	Devin Davis	9.4	Rob Mestas	4.6	Charlie Coles	
1997-98	17-12	9-9		Damon Frierson	18.8	John Estick	7.9	Damon Frierson	4.1	Charlie Coles	
1998-99	24-8	15-3	NCAA REGIONAL SEMIFINALS	Wally Szczerbiak	24.2	Wally Szczerbiak	8.5	Damon Frierson	3.3	Charlie Coles	
1999-00	15-15	8-10		Anthony Taylor	16.4	Refiloe Lethunya	6.2	Rob Mestas	5.5	Charlie Coles	
2000-01	17-16	10-8		Alex Shorts	15.7	Mike Ensminger	5.9	Jason Grunkemeyer	2.4	Charlie Coles	
2001-02	13-18	9-9		Alex Shorts	13.6	Danny Horace	5.8	Doug Davis	2.9	Charlie Coles	
2002-03	13-15	11-7		Juby Johnson	14.8	Chet Mason	6.2	Chet Mason	2.4	Charlie Coles	
2003-04	18-11	12-6		Juby Johnson	17.4	Chet Mason	7.9	Chet Mason	2.9	Charlie Coles	
2004-05	19-11	12-6	NIT FIRST ROUND	Danny Horace	15.4	Danny Horace	9.5	William Hatcher	3.3	Charlie Coles	
2005-06	18-11	14-4	NIT FIRST ROUND	William Hatcher	14.3	Nathan Peavy	6.9	William Hatcher	4.3	Charlie Coles	
2006-07	18-15	10-6	NCAA FIRST ROUND	Tim Pollitz	16.1	Nathan Peavy	6.3	Alex Moosmann	3.8	Charlie Coles	
2007-08	17-16	9-7		Michael Bramos	16.3	Tim Pollitz	7.1	Tim Pollitz	3.1	Charlie Coles[a]	
2008-09	17-13	10-6		Michael Bramos	17.9	Tyler Dierkers	7.3	Kenny Hayes	3.8	Charlie Coles	224-168 .571

[a] Charlie Coles (14-14) and Jermaine Henderson (3-2) both coached during the 2007-08 season.

⊗ Records don't reflect games forfeited or vacated. For adjusted records, see p. 521.

▼ Coach's record adjusted to reflect games forfeited or vacated: 85-89, .489. For yearly totals, see p. 521.

ESPN 13 SAGARIN

MICHIGAN

Black socks, baggy shorts, shaved heads—history won't soon forget the trendsetting Fab Five of Chris Webber, Jalen Rose, Juwan Howard, Jimmy King and Ray Jackson. Never mind that they never won a national title, a Big Ten crown or anything else for that matter, since the NCAA voided most of their actual accomplishments because of rules violations. But with stars over the past 50 years such as Cazzie Russell, Rudy Tomjanovich and Glen Rice, and an NCAA title in 1989, there's plenty of other substance to back up Michigan's style.

BEST TEAM: 1988-89 Before the NCAA Tournament, coach Bill Frieder accepted an offer to coach Arizona State in 1989-90 but said he would finish the current season at UM. Not so fast, said AD and football legend Bo Schembechler, who replaced Frieder with assistant Steve Fisher. Behind one of the greatest individual Tournaments of all time by star forward Rice (NCAA-record 184 points), and clutch moments from his supporting cast, the No. 3-seed Wolverines won it all.

BEST PLAYER: G/F Cazzie Russell (1963-66) Crisler Arena is called the House That Cazzie Built even though Russell never played a game there. As the story goes, so many fans flocked to see the flashy 6'5" Russell at old Yost Fieldhouse that UM decided to build a new hoops venue. In his three seasons, Russell averaged 27.1 ppg and led the Wolverines to three Big Ten titles and two Final Fours. The first pick in the 1966 NBA draft (Knicks), Russell never quite reached superstardom as a pro.

BEST COACH: Dave Strack (1960-68) With the help of Russell, Bill Buntin, Oliver Darden and an aggressive, crowd-pleasing style, Strack turned a football school's afterthought into a hot ticket. From 1964 to '66, the Wolverines won three straight Big Ten titles, highlighted by a 1965 team that battled UCLA for the NCAA title (and lost, 91-80).

GAME FOR THE AGES: Their motto was "Shock the World" so it was fitting that Michigan's 1989 NCAA Final against Seton Hall went to overtime. Trailing by one with :03 left, point guard Rumeal Robinson slashed through the lane and was fouled. Just a 67% career free throw shooter, he calmly drained both and the Wolverines won, 80-79.

HEARTBREAKER: The coda to the 1993 NCAA Final was bad enough (Michigan's appearance at the Tourney was wiped out), but the end of the actual game was murder. Trailing North Carolina by two, Webber grabbed a rebound, got away with a travel and, with :11 on the clock, called a timeout that the team didn't have. UNC's Donald Williams hit four free throws to close it out, 77-71. The miscue haunted Webber throughout his standout NBA career.

FIERCEST RIVAL: UM didn't make the Tournament from 1999 to 2008. During that same stretch, Michigan State went to four Final Fours, won the 2000 national title and handed the Wolverines numerous drubbings. In fact, UM hasn't won in Izzoville since 1998. Michigan does lead overall, 91–72.

FANFARE AND HOOPLA: Before the season opener on Dec. 1, 1992, the Fab Five rounded out what would soon become the sport's standard look by deciding to wear black socks—without informing their coach or inviting any other teammates to join in. After the 75-71 win over Rice, no one was in much of a mood to complain.

FAN FAVORITE: C Rudy Tomjanovich (1967-70) When Rudy T returned to Ann Arbor in 2003 to have his jersey retired, Crisler Arena echoed with chants of "Rudy! Rudy! Rudy!"—a fitting tribute to one of the greatest scorers in Michigan history. After his Wolverines career, Tomjanovich played 11 seasons in the NBA, followed by a 13-year coaching career in which he won two titles.

CONSENSUS ALL-AMERICAS

1924	**Harry Kipke**, G
1926	**Richard Doyle**, C
1927, '28	**Bennie Oosterbaan**, F
1965, '66	**Cazzie Russell**, G/F
1977	**Rickey Green**, G
1988	**Gary Grant**, G
1993	**Chris Webber**, F/C*

* Honor vacated due to NCAA and school sanctions.

FIRST-ROUND PRO PICKS

1965	**Bill Buntin**, Detroit (3)
1966	**Cazzie Russell**, New York (1)
1970	**Rudy Tomjanovich**, San Diego (2)
1974	**Campy Russell**, Cleveland (8)
1977	**Rickey Green**, Golden State (16)
1979	**Phil Hubbard**, Detroit (15)
1981	**Mike McGee**, LA Lakers (19)
1984	**Tim McCormick**, Cleveland (12)
1986	**Roy Tarpley**, Dallas (7)
1988	**Gary Grant**, Seattle (15)
1989	**Glen Rice**, Miami (4)
1990	**Rumeal Robinson**, Atlanta (10)
1990	**Loy Vaught**, LA Clippers (13)
1990	**Terry Mills**, Milwaukee (16)
1993	**Chris Webber**, Orlando (1)
1994	**Juwan Howard**, Washington (5)
1994	**Jalen Rose**, Denver (13)
1997	**Maurice Taylor**, LA Clippers (14)
1998	**Robert Traylor**, Dallas (6)
2000	**Jamal Crawford**, Chicago (8)

PROFILE

University of Michigan, Ann Arbor, MI
Founded: 1817
Enrollment: 41,042 (26,083 undergraduate)
Colors: Maize and blue
Nickname: Wolverines
Current arena: Crisler Arena, opened in 1967 (13,751)
Previous: Yost Field House, 1924-67 (6,637)
First game: Jan. 9, 1908
All-time record: 1,366-931 (.595)
Total weeks in AP Top 20/25: 315

Current conference: Big Ten (1917-)
Conference titles:
Big Ten: 12 (1921 [tie], '26 [tie], '27, '29 [tie], '48, '64 [tie], '65, '66, '74 [tie], '77, '85, '86)
Conference tournament titles:
Big Ten: 1 (1998-v)
NCAA Tournaments: 21 (4 appearances vacated)
Sweet 16s (since 1975): 7
Final Fours: 6
Titles: 1 (1989)

NIT appearances: 10 (1 appearance vacated)
Semifinals: 4
Titles: 3 (1984, '97-v, 2004)
v – title vacated

TOP 5

G **Gary Grant** (1984-88)
G/F **Cazzie Russell** (1963-66)
F **Glen Rice** (1985-89)
F/C **Chris Webber** (1991-93)
C **Rudy Tomjanovich** (1967-70)

RECORDS	GAME		SEASON		CAREER	
POINTS	48	Rudy Tomjanovich, vs. Indiana (Jan. 7, 1969); Cazzie Russell, vs. Northwestern (March 5, 1966)	949	Glen Rice (1988-89)	2,442	Glen Rice (1985-89)
POINTS PER GAME			30.8	Cazzie Russell (1965-66)	27.1	Cazzie Russell (1963-66)
REBOUNDS	30	Rudy Tomjanovich, vs. Loyola-Chicago (Feb. 1, 1969)	389	Phil Hubbard (1976-77)	1,044	Rudy Tomjanovich (1967-70)
ASSISTS	14	Gary Grant, vs. Northern Michigan (Dec. 19, 1987); vs. Western Michigan (Dec. 7, 1987)	234	Gary Grant (1987-88)	731	Gary Grant (1984-88)

SEASON REVIEW

SEASON	W-L	CONF.	SCORING		COACH	RECORD		SEASON	W-L	CONF.	SCORING		COACH	RECORD	
1908-09	1-4		Henry Farquhar	9.6	G.D. Corneal	1-4	.200	**1926-27**	14-3	10-2	Frank Harrigan	9.0	E.J. Mather		
1909-17	no team							**1927-28**	10-7	7-5	Bennie Oosterbaan	10.8	E.J. Mather	106-53	.667
1917-18	6-12	0-10	James McClintock	6.8	Elmer Mitchell			**1928-29**	13-3	10-2	Robert Chapman	7.1	George Veenker		
1918-19	18-6	5-5	Arthur Karpus	8.2	Elmer Mitchell	24-18	.571	**1929-30**	9-5	6-4	Joseph Truskowski	8.1	George Veenker		
1919-20	10-13	3-9	Walter Rea	5.8	E.J. Mather			**1930-31**	13-4	8-4	Norman Daniels	8.9	George Veenker	35-12	.745
1920-21	16-4	8-4	Arthur Karpus	9.2	E.J. Mather			**1931-32**	11-6	8-4	Norman Daniels	8.7	Franklin "Cappy" Cappon		
1921-22	15-4	8-4	William Miller	12.1	E.J. Mather			**1932-33**	10-8	8-4	DeForest Eveland	7.4	Franklin "Cappy" Cappon		
1922-23	11-4	8-4	Gilbert Ely	11.6	E.J. Mather			**1933-34**	6-14	4-8	Alfred Plummer	4.2	Franklin "Cappy" Cappon		
1923-24	10-7	6-6	George Haggarty	9.5	E.J. Mather			**1934-35**	8-12	2-10	Richard Joslin	3.9	Franklin "Cappy" Cappon		
1924-25	8-6	6-5	George Haggarty	10.4	E.J. Mather			**1935-36**	15-5	7-5	John Townsend	7.7	Franklin "Cappy" Cappon		
1925-26	12-5	8-4	Frank Harrigan	6.6	E.J. Mather			**1936-37**	16-4	9-3	John Townsend	9.6	Franklin "Cappy" Cappon		

SEAS.	W-L	CONF.	POSTSEASON	SCORING		REBOUNDS		ASSISTS		COACH	RECORD	
1937-38	12-8	6-6		John Townsend	11.3					Franklin "Cappy" Cappon	78-57	.578
1938-39	11-9	4-8		Edmund Thomas	7.0					Bennie Oosterbaan		
1939-40	13-7	6-6		James Rae	10.0					Bennie Oosterbaan		
1940-41	9-10	5-7		Michael Sofiak	10.1					Bennie Oosterbaan		
1941-42	6-14	5-10		James Mandler	11.5					Bennie Oosterbaan		
1942-43	10-8	4-8		James Mandler	8.9					Bennie Oosterbaan		
1943-44	8-10	5-7		Dave Strack	12.1					Bennie Oosterbaan		
1944-45	12-7	5-7		Robert Geahan	7.2					Bennie Oosterbaan		
1945-46	12-7	6-6		Glen Selbo	11.2					Bennie Oosterbaan	81-72	.529
1946-47	12-8	6-6		Mack Suprunowicz	11.4					Osborne Cowles		
1947-48	16-6	10-2	NCAA REGIONAL SEMIFINALS	Bob Harrison	11.1					Osborne Cowles	28-14	.667
1948-49	15-6	7-5		Mack Suprunowicz	11.8					Ernest McCoy		
1949-50	11-11	4-8		Mack Suprunowicz	12.6					Ernest McCoy		
1950-51	7-15	3-11		Leo VanderKuy	15.0					Ernest McCoy		
1951-52	7-15	4-10		Jim Skala	11.7					Ernest McCoy	40-47	.460
1952-53	6-16	3-15		Paul Groffsky	13.6					William Perigo		
1953-54	9-13	3-11		Jim Barron	17.1					William Perigo		
1954-55	11-11	5-9		Ron Kramer	16.0					William Perigo		
1955-56	9-13	4-10		Ron Kramer	20.3					William Perigo		
1956-57	13-9	8-6		George Lee	15.2					William Perigo		
1957-58	11-11	6-8		Pete Tillotson	18.8					William Perigo		
1958-59	15-7	8-6		M.C. Burton	20.9	M.C. Burton	17.2			William Perigo		
1959-60	4-20	1-13		John Tidwell	21.6	Lovell Farris	9.7			William Perigo	78-100	.438
1960-61	6-18	2-12		John Tidwell	19.1	Tom Cole	9.3			Dave Strack		
1961-62	7-17	5-9		Tom Cole	15.0	Tom Cole	9.3			Dave Strack		
1962-63	16-8	8-6		Bill Buntin	22.3	Bill Buntin	15.7			Dave Strack		
1963-64	23-5	11-3	NCAA THIRD PLACE	Cazzie Russell	24.8	Bill Buntin	12.5			Dave Strack		
1964-65	24-4	13-1	NCAA RUNNER-UP	Cazzie Russell	25.7	Bill Buntin	11.5			Dave Strack		
1965-66	18-8	11-3	NCAA REGIONAL FINALS	Cazzie Russell	30.8	Oliver Darden	9.6			Dave Strack		
1966-67	8-16	2-12		Craig Dill	19.6	Craig Dill	8.7			Dave Strack		
1967-68	11-13	6-8		Rudy Tomjanovich	19.5	Rudy Tomjanovich	13.5			Dave Strack	113-89	.559
1968-69	13-11	7-7		Rudy Tomjanovich	25.7	Rudy Tomjanovich	14.2			Johnny Orr		
1969-70	10-14	5-9		Rudy Tomjanovich	30.1	Rudy Tomjanovich	15.5			Johnny Orr		
1970-71	19-7	12-2	NIT QUARTERFINALS	Henry Wilmore	25.0	Ken Brady	10.3			Johnny Orr		
1971-72	14-10	9-5		Henry Wilmore	23.9	John Lockard	9.8			Johnny Orr		
1972-73	13-11	6-8		Henry Wilmore	21.8	Campy Russell	9.6			Johnny Orr		
1973-74	22-5	12-2	NCAA REGIONAL FINALS	Campy Russell	23.7	C.J. Kupec	11.6			Johnny Orr		
1974-75	19-8	12-6	NCAA FIRST ROUND	C.J. Kupec	18.1	C.J. Kupec	8.4			Johnny Orr		
1975-76	25-7	14-4	NCAA RUNNER-UP	Rickey Green	19.9	Phil Hubbard	11.0			Johnny Orr		
1976-77	26-4	16-2	NCAA REGIONAL FINALS	Phil Hubbard	19.6	Phil Hubbard	12.9			Johnny Orr		
1977-78	16-11	11-7		Mike McGee	19.7	Joel Thompson	8.7	Dave Baxter	6.6	Johnny Orr		
1978-79	15-12	8-10		Mike McGee	18.9	Phil Hubbard	9.2	Marty Bodnar	2.3	Johnny Orr		
1979-80	17-13	8-10	NIT QUARTERFINALS	Mike McGee	22.2	Thad Garner	6.7	Thad Garner	2.5	Johnny Orr	209-113	.649
1980-81	19-11	8-10	NIT QUARTERFINALS	Mike McGee	24.4	Thad Garner	5.6	Johnny Johnson	3.5	Bill Frieder		
1981-82	7-20	7-11		Eric Turner	14.7	Thad Garner	6.7	Eric Turner	4.4	Bill Frieder		
1982-83	15-13	7-11		Eric Turner	19.2	Tim McCormick	6.4	Eric Turner	5.9	Bill Frieder		
1983-84	23-10	11-7	NIT CHAMPION	Roy Tarpley	12.5	Roy Tarpley	8.1	Eric Turner	4.5	Bill Frieder		
1984-85	26-4	16-2	NCAA SECOND ROUND	Roy Tarpley	19.0	Roy Tarpley	10.4	Antoine Joubert	5.7	Bill Frieder		
1985-86	28-5	14-4	NCAA SECOND ROUND	Roy Tarpley	15.9	Roy Tarpley	8.8	Gary Grant	5.6	Bill Frieder		
1986-87	20-12	10-8	NCAA SECOND ROUND	Gary Grant	22.4	Glen Rice	9.2	Gary Grant	5.4	Bill Frieder		
1987-88	26-8	13-5	NCAA REGIONAL SEMIFINALS	Glen Rice	22.1	Glen Rice	7.2	Gary Grant	6.9	Bill Frieder	188-90	.676
1988-89	**30-7**	**12-6**	**NATIONAL CHAMPION**	**Glen Rice**	**25.6**	**Loy Vaught**	**8.0**	**Rumeal Robinson**	**6.3**	**Steve Fisher**[a]		
1989-90	23-8	12-6	NCAA SECOND ROUND	Rumeal Robinson	19.2	Loy Vaught	11.2	Rumeal Robinson	6.1	Steve Fisher		
1990-91	14-15	7-11	NIT FIRST ROUND	Demetrius Calip	20.5	Eric Riley	8.6	Demetrius Calip	3.5	Steve Fisher		
1991-92	25-9 ⊗	11-7	NCAA RUNNER-UP	Jalen Rose	17.6	Chris Webber	10.0	Jalen Rose	4.0	Steve Fisher		
1992-93	31-5 ⊗	15-3	NCAA RUNNER-UP	Chris Webber	19.2	Chris Webber	10.1	Jalen Rose	3.9	Steve Fisher		
1993-94	24-8	13-5	NCAA REGIONAL FINALS	Jalen Rose	19.9	Juwan Howard	8.9	Jalen Rose	3.9	Steve Fisher		
1994-95	17-14	11-7	NCAA FIRST ROUND	Ray Jackson	15.8	Maceo Baston	5.5	Ray Jackson	3.0	Steve Fisher		
1995-96	20-12 ⊗	10-8	NCAA FIRST ROUND	Maurice Taylor	14.0	Maurice Taylor	7.0	Travis Conlan	4.8	Steve Fisher		
1996-97	24-11 ⊗	9-9	NIT CHAMPION	Louis Bullock	16.3	Robert Traylor	7.7	Travis Conlan	4.5	Steve Fisher	184-80	.694▼
1997-98	25-9 ⊗	11-5	NCAA SECOND ROUND	Louis Bullock	17.1	Robert Traylor	10.1	Travis Conlan	4.2	Brian Ellerbe		
1998-99	12-19 ⊗	5-11		Louis Bullock	20.7	Peter Vignier	7.4	Robbie Reid	3.1	Brian Ellerbe		
1999-2000	15-14	6-10	NIT FIRST ROUND	LaVell Blanchard	14.4	LaVell Blanchard	7.9	Kevin Gaines	4.6	Brian Ellerbe		
2000-01	10-18	4-12		LaVell Blanchard	17.8	LaVell Blanchard	8.4	Avery Queen	4.3	Brian Ellerbe	62-60	.508▼
2001-02	11-18	5-11		LaVell Blanchard	14.8	LaVell Blanchard	6.3	Avery Queen	3.3	Tommy Amaker		
2002-03	17-13	10-6		LaVell Blanchard	16.2	LaVell Blanchard	6.8	Daniel Horton	4.5	Tommy Amaker		
2003-04	23-11	8-8	NIT CHAMPION	Lester Abram	13.1	Bernard Robinson Jr.	5.7	Bernard Robinson Jr.	3.8	Tommy Amaker		
2004-05	13-18	4-12		Dion Harris	14.3	Brent Petway	5.4	Dion Harris	3.5	Tommy Amaker		
2005-06	22-11	8-8	NIT RUNNER-UP	Daniel Horton	17.6	Graham Brown	7.4	Daniel Horton	5.3	Tommy Amaker		
2006-07	22-13	8-8	NIT SECOND ROUND	Dion Harris	13.4	Courtney Sims	6.2	Dion Harris	3.6	Tommy Amaker	108-84	.562
2007-08	10-22	5-13		Manny Harris	16.1	DeShawn Sims	5.4	Kelvin Grady	2.8	John Beilein		
2008-09	21-14	9-9	NCAA SECOND ROUND	Manny Harris	16.9	DeShawn Sims	6.8	Manny Harris	4.4	John Beilein	31-36	.463

[a] Bill Frieder (24-7) and Steve Fisher (6-0) both coached during the 1988-89 season.

⊗ Records don't reflect games forfeited or vacated. For adjusted records, see p. 521.

▼ Coaches' records adjusted to reflect games forfeited or vacated: Steve Fisher, 109-79, .580; Brian Ellerbe, 25-59, .298. For yearly totals, see p. 521.

ESPN 15 SAGARIN

MICHIGAN STATE

No matter how many times the Spartans return to the Final Four—and under Tom Izzo, it seems to happen almost every year—there may never be any topping the splash made by Magic Johnson & Co. in the 1979 NCAA Tournament. Their Final win over Larry Bird and Indiana State was the highest-rated televised game in college basketball history and was one of the seminal events that gave rise to March Madness.

BEST TEAM: 1978-79 The Spartans went 26–6 and romped through the NCAA Tournament field, culminating in a dominating 75-64 throttling of Indiana State in which they limited Bird to 7-of-21 shooting. The undisputed star of the squad was Johnson—who, despite five NBA titles with the Lakers, still considers the victory over the Sycamores the favorite of all his championships, the fulfillment of a childhood dream. The leading scorer for coach Jud Heathcote was forward Greg Kelser, a.k.a. Special K, who averaged 18.8 ppg and is the only player in Spartans history to amass more than 2,000 points and 1,000 rebounds.

BEST PLAYER: G EARVIN "MAGIC" JOHNSON (1977-79) Folks weren't drawn to Magic just because of his physical gifts, but also his unique style. Like Bird, Johnson was a great thinker and a terrific passer. Unlike Bird, the all-smiles 6'9" point guard delighted in the spotlight. Johnson, the only freshman in Spartans history to be named All-America, set an MSU single-season assist record (since surpassed) with 269 (8.4 per game) as a sophomore; he also averaged 17.1 points and 7.3 rebounds.

BEST COACH: TOM IZZO (1995-) He doesn't pride himself on fancy offenses, but rather on good old-fashioned defense and rebounding. It's hard to argue with the formula. Izzo's teams qualified for 12 straight NCAA Tournaments, beginning in 1998, including five Final Fours and the 2000 championship.

GAME FOR THE AGES: When the UCLA dynasty ended after 1975, many wondered if college basketball would ever again attract broad national attention. The 1979 NCAA Final provided the answer. Nearly a quarter all of U.S. households tuned in to see if upstart undefeated Indiana State, with a guy who looked like his name—Bird—could defeat famous Michigan State with a guy who *played* like his—Magic. That the Spartans totally dominated in their 75-64 win barely detracted from the spectacle.

HEARTBREAKER: The way the Spartans saw it, their 1986 Sweet 16 loss to Kansas was really a matter of bad timing—and bad officiating. With 2:21 remaining, KU inbounded but the clock didn't start running for about 15 seconds. Despite Jud Heathcote's protests, the refs refused to run off the time. Flash forward to :09 left in regulation. With his Jayhawks down two, Archie Marshall tipped the ball in to send the game to OT. There, Kansas ran away to win, 96-86.

FIERCEST RIVAL: In 2009, the *Detroit Free Press* declared there was no Michigan-Michigan State rivalry anymore because of the Spartans' dominance over the past decade and the Wolverines' mediocre play. Don't believe it. MSU faithful delighted in every minute of the Spartans' 12-point win over the revitalized Wolverines on Feb. 10, 2009, just as much as they did during State's 51-point blowout of UM on March 4, 2000. Michigan still leads overall, 91–72.

FANFARE AND HOOPLA: The Izzone student section, for all their famed chants and taunts, deserves the most props for their creative signs, such as "My Grandma Has the Hots for Shannon Brown," and "Chuck Norris + Vin Diesel = Tom Izzo."

FAN FAVORITE: G MATEEN CLEAVES (1996-2000) He didn't have the prettiest jump shot, but fans loved his toughness, epitomized by his gritting out the 2000 Final on one good leg.

CONSENSUS ALL-AMERICAS

1979	**Earvin "Magic" Johnson**, G
1995	**Shawn Respert**, G
1999	**Mateen Cleaves**, G

FIRST ROUND PRO PICKS

1959	**Johnny Green**, New York (6)
1967	**Matt Aitch**, Dallas (ABA)
1971	**Ralph Simpson**, Denver (ABA)
1972	**Ralph Simpson**, Chicago (11)
1976	**Terry Furlow**, Philadelphia (12)
1979	**Earvin "Magic" Johnson**, LA Lakers (1)
1979	**Greg Kelser**, Detroit (4)
1984	**Kevin Willis**, Atlanta (11)
1985	**Sam Vincent**, Boston (20)
1986	**Scott Skiles**, Milwaukee (22)
1991	**Steve Smith**, Miami (5)
1995	**Shawn Respert**, Portland (8)
2000	**Mateen Cleaves**, Detroit (14)
2000	**Morris Peterson**, Toronto (21)
2001	**Jason Richardson**, Golden State (5)
2001	**Zach Randolph**, Portland (19)
2006	**Shannon Brown**, Cleveland (25)
2006	**Maurice Ager**, Dallas (28)

PROFILE

Michigan State University, East Lansing, MI
Founded: 1855
Enrollment: 46,648 (36,337 undergraduate)
Colors: Green and white
Nickname: Spartans
Current arena: Breslin Center, opened in 1989 (14,759)
Previous: Jenison Fieldhouse, 1940-89 (10,004); Demonstration Hall, 1930-39 (3,000)
First game: Feb. 27, 1899
All-time record: 1,456-1,002 (.592)
Total weeks in AP Top 20/25: 299

Current conference: Big Ten (1950-)
Conference titles:
Big Ten: 11 (1957 [tie], '59, '67 [tie], '78, '79 [tie], '90, '98 [tie], '99, 2000 [tie], '01 [tie], '09)
Conference tournament titles:
Big Ten: 2 (1999, 2000)
NCAA Tournament appearances: 23
Sweet 16s (since 1975): 12
Final Fours: 7
Titles: 2 (1979, 2000)
NIT appearances: 5
Semifinals: 1

TOP 5

G	**Earvin "Magic" Johnson** (1977-79)
G	**Scott Skiles** (1982-86)
G	**Steve Smith** (1987-91)
F	**Greg Kelser** (1975-79)
F	**Johnny Green** (1956-59)

RECORDS

RECORDS	GAME		SEASON		CAREER	
POINTS	50	Terry Furlow, vs. Iowa (Jan. 5, 1976)	850	Scott Skiles (1985-86)	2,531	Shawn Respert (1990-95)
POINTS PER GAME			29.4	Terry Furlow (1975-76)	24.2	Mike Robinson (1971-74)
REBOUNDS	29	Horace Walker, vs. Butler (Dec. 28, 1959); Johnny Green, vs. Washington (Dec. 30, 1957)	392	Johnny Green (1957-58)	1,092	Greg Kelser (1975-79)
ASSISTS	20	Mateen Cleaves, vs. Michigan (March 4, 2000)	274	Mateen Cleaves (1998-99)	816	Mateen Cleaves (1996-2000)

SEASON REVIEW

SEASON	W-L	CONF.	SCORING	COACH	RECORD
1899-1918	*151-82*		*Coach Chester Brewer, 70-25, .737 from 1903-10*		
1918-19	9-9			George Gauthier	
1919-20	21-15			George Gauthier[a]	41-38 .519
1920-21	13-8			Lyman Frimodig	
1921-22	11-13			Lyman Frimodig	30-22 .577
1922-23	10-9			Fred Walker	
1923-24	10-10			Fred Walker	20-19 .513
1924-25	6-13			John H. Kobs	
1925-26	5-13			John H. Kobs	11-26 .297
1926-27	7-11		Verne Dickeson 162	Benjamin F. VanAlstyne	
1927-28	11-4		Verne Dickeson 100	Benjamin F. VanAlstyne	
1928-29	11-5		Arthur Haga 99	Benjamin F. VanAlstyne	
1929-30	12-4		Roger Grove 91	Benjamin F. VanAlstyne	
1930-31	16-1		Roger Grove 135	Benjamin F. VanAlstyne	
1931-32	12-5		Randy Boeskool 80	Benjamin F. VanAlstyne	
1932-33	10-7		Gerald McCaslin 92	Benjamin F. VanAlstyne	
1933-34	12-5		Maurice Buysse 126	Benjamin F. VanAlstyne	
1934-35	14-4		Arnold Van Faasen 133	Benjamin F. VanAlstyne	
1935-36	8-9		Ron Garlock 109	Benjamin F. VanAlstyne	
1936-37	5-12		Leonard Oesterink 112	Benjamin F. VanAlstyne	
1937-38	9-8		George Falkowski 173	Benjamin F. VanAlstyne	
1938-39	9-8		George Falkowski 119	Benjamin F. VanAlstyne	

SEAS.	W-L	CONF.	POSTSEASON	SCORING	REBOUNDS	ASSISTS	COACH	RECORD
1939-40	14-6			Chet Aubuchon 169			Benjamin F. VanAlstyne	
1940-41	11-6			Max Hindman 144			Benjamin F. VanAlstyne	
1941-42	15-6			Joe Gerard 239			Benjamin F. VanAlstyne	
1942-43	2-14			John Cawood 118			Benjamin F. VanAlstyne	
1943-44	no team							
1944-45	9-7			Sam Fortino 11.9			Benjamin F. VanAlstyne	
1945-46	12-9			Sam Fortino 12.0			Benjamin F. VanAlstyne	
1946-47	11-10			Bob Geahan 11.2			Benjamin F. VanAlstyne	
1947-48	12-10			Bob Brannum 15.6			Benjamin F. VanAlstyne	
1948-49	9-12			Bill Rapchak 10.6			Benjamin F. VanAlstyne	231-163 .586
1949-50	4-18			Dan Smith 9.4			Alton S. Kircher	4-18 .182
1950-51	10-11	5-9		Ray Steffen 8.9			Pete Newell	
1951-52	13-9	6-8		Keith Stackhouse 11.8			Pete Newell	
1952-53	13-9	11-7		Al Ferrari 16.0			Pete Newell	
1953-54	9-13	4-10		Julius McCoy 18.6			Pete Newell	45-42 .517
1954-55	13-9	8-6		Al Ferrari 20.1			Forddy Anderson	
1955-56	13-9	7-7		Julius McCoy 27.3	Julius McCoy 10.0		Forddy Anderson	
1956-57	16-10	10-4	NCAA FOURTH PLACE	Jack Quiggle 15.3	Johnny Green 14.6		Forddy Anderson	
1957-58	16-6	9-5		Johnny Green 18.0	Johnny Green 17.8		Forddy Anderson	
1958-59	19-4	12-2	NCAA REGIONAL FINALS	Bob Anderegg 19.5	Johnny Green 16.6		Forddy Anderson	
1959-60	10-11	5-9		Horace Walker 22.6	Horace Walker 17.7		Forddy Anderson	
1960-61	7-17	3-11		Dick Hall 16.2	Ted Williams 12.0		Forddy Anderson	
1961-62	8-14	3-11		Pete Gent 14.1	Pete Gent 9.3		Forddy Anderson	
1962-63	4-16	3-11		Pete Gent 16.4	Bill Berry 9.2		Forddy Anderson	
1963-64	14-10	8-6		Pete Gent 21.0	Stan Washington 10.2		Forddy Anderson	
1964-65	5-18	1-13		Stan Washington 21.3	Stan Washington 10.7		Forddy Anderson	125-124 .502
1965-66	15-7	10-4		Stan Washington 18.0	Stan Washington 10.6		John E. Benington	
1966-67	16-7	10-4		Matthew Aitch 16.3	Lee Lafayette 9.7		John E. Benington	
1967-68	12-12	6-8		Lee Lafayette 16.8	Lee Lafayette 10.5		John E. Benington	
1968-69	11-12	6-8		Lee Lafayette 18.7	Lee Lafayette 10.3		John E. Benington	54-38 .587
1969-70	9-15	5-9		Ralph Simpson 29.0	Ralph Simpson 10.3		Gus Ganakas	
1970-71	10-14	4-10		Rudy Benjamin 21.2	Bill Kilgore 12.8		Gus Ganakas	
1971-72	13-11	6-8		Mike Robinson 24.7	Bill Kilgore 11.1		Gus Ganakas	
1972-73	13-11	6-8		Mike Robinson 25.3	Bill Kilgore 9.9		Gus Ganakas	
1973-74	13-11	8-6		Mike Robinson 22.4	Lindsay Hairston 13.6		Gus Ganakas	
1974-75	17-9	10-8		Terry Furlow 20.4	Lindsay Hairston 11.5		Gus Ganakas	
1975-76	14-13	10-8		Terry Furlow 29.4	Greg Kelser 9.5	Benny White 3.9	Gus Ganakas	89-84 .514
1976-77	10-17 ❂	9-9		Greg Kelser 21.7	Greg Kelser 10.8	Edgar Wilson 3.4	Jud Heathcote	
1977-78	25-5	15-3	NCAA REGIONAL FINALS	Greg Kelser 17.7	Greg Kelser 9.1	Earvin "Magic" Johnson 7.4	Jud Heathcote	
1978-79	**26-6**	**13-5**	**NATIONAL CHAMPION**	**Greg Kelser 18.8**	**Greg Kelser 8.7**	**Earvin "Magic" Johnson 8.4**	**Jud Heathcote**	
1979-80	12-15	6-12		Jay Vincent 21.6	Ron Charles 8.9	Mike Brkovich 3.6	Jud Heathcote	
1980-81	13-14	7-11		Jay Vincent 22.6	Jay Vincent 8.5	Kevin Smith 4.8	Jud Heathcote	
1981-82	11-17	7-11		Kevin Smith 15.6	Derek Perry 5.4	Kevin Smith 4.5	Jud Heathcote	
1982-83	17-13	9-9	NIT SECOND ROUND	Sam Vincent 16.6	Kevin Willis 9.6	Scott Skiles 4.2	Jud Heathcote	
1983-84	15-13	9-9		Scott Skiles 14.5	Kevin Willis 7.7	Scott Skiles 4.6	Jud Heathcote	
1984-85	19-10	10-8	NCAA FIRST ROUND	Sam Vincent 23.0	Ken Johnson 10.2	Scott Skiles 5.8	Jud Heathcote	
1985-86	23-8	12-6	NCAA REGIONAL SEMIFINALS	Scott Skiles 27.4	Larry Polec 5.7	Scott Skiles 6.5	Jud Heathcote	
1986-87	11-17	6-12		Darryl Johnson 22.1	Carlton Valentine 5.6	Darryl Johnson 4.0	Jud Heathcote	
1987-88	10-18	5-13		Carlton Valentine 13.3	Carlton Valentine 5.6	Ed Wright 3.3	Jud Heathcote	
1988-89	18-15	6-12	NIT FOURTH PLACE	Steve Smith 17.7	Steve Smith 6.9	Ken Redfield 4.0	Jud Heathcote	
1989-90	28-6	15-3	NCAA REGIONAL SEMIFINALS	Steve Smith 20.2	Ken Redfield 6.8	Steve Smith 4.8	Jud Heathcote	
1990-91	19-11	11-7	NCAA SECOND ROUND	Steve Smith 25.1	Mike Peplowski 6.9	Mark Montgomery 5.8	Jud Heathcote	
1991-92	22-8	11-7	NCAA SECOND ROUND	Shawn Respert 15.8	Mike Peplowski 8.6	Mark Montgomery 6.3	Jud Heathcote	
1992-93	15-13	7-11	NIT FIRST ROUND	Shawn Respert 20.1	Mike Peplowski 10.0	Eric Snow 5.2	Jud Heathcote	
1993-94	20-12	10-8	NCAA SECOND ROUND	Shawn Respert 24.3	Anthony Miller 9.0	Eric Snow 6.7	Jud Heathcote	
1994-95	22-6	14-4	NCAA FIRST ROUND	Shawn Respert 25.6	Jamie Feick 10.1	Eric Snow 7.8	Jud Heathcote	336-224 .600▼
1995-96	16-16	9-9	NIT SECOND ROUND	Quinton Brooks 16.3	Jamie Feick 9.5	Thomas Kelley 3.6	Tom Izzo	
1996-97	17-12	9-9	NIT SECOND ROUND	Ray Weathers 13.6	Antonio Smith 10.6	Mateen Cleaves 5.0	Tom Izzo	
1997-98	22-8	13-3	NCAA REGIONAL SEMIFINALS	Mateen Cleaves 16.1	Antonio Smith 8.7	Mateen Cleaves 7.2	Tom Izzo	
1998-99	33-5	15-1	NCAA NATIONAL SEMIFINALS	Morris Peterson 13.6	Antonio Smith 8.4	Mateen Cleaves 7.2	Tom Izzo	
1999-2000	**32-7**	**13-3**	**NATIONAL CHAMPION**	**Morris Peterson 16.8**	**Andre Hutson 6.2**	**Mateen Cleaves 6.9**	**Tom Izzo**	
2000-01	28-5	13-3	NCAA NATIONAL SEMIFINALS	Jason Richardson 14.7	Andre Hutson 7.6	Charlie Bell 5.1	Tom Izzo	
2001-02	19-12	10-6	NCAA FIRST ROUND	Marcus Taylor 16.8	Aloysius Anagonye 6.3	Marcus Taylor 5.3	Tom Izzo	
2002-03	22-13	10-6	NCAA REGIONAL FINALS	Chris Hill 13.7	Aloysius Anagonye 5.3	Chris Hill 3.7	Tom Izzo	
2003-04	18-12	12-4	NCAA FIRST ROUND	Paul Davis 15.8	Paul Davis 6.2	Chris Hill 3.7	Tom Izzo	
2004-05	26-7	13-3	NCAA NATIONAL SEMIFINALS	Maurice Ager 14.1	Paul Davis 8.0	Chris Hill 4.3	Tom Izzo	
2005-06	22-12	8-8	NCAA FIRST ROUND	Maurice Ager 19.3	Paul Davis 9.1	Drew Neitzel 5.6	Tom Izzo	
2006-07	23-12	8-8	NCAA SECOND ROUND	Drew Neitzel 18.1	Goran Suton 6.7	Travis Walton 5.5	Tom Izzo	
2007-08	27-9	12-6	NCAA REGIONAL SEMIFINALS	Raymar Morgan 14.0	Goran Suton 8.2	Travis Walton 4.3	Tom Izzo	
2008-09	31-7	15-3	NCAA RUNNER-UP	Kalin Lucas 14.7	Goran Suton 8.4	Kalin Lucas 4.6	Tom Izzo	336-137 .710

Cumulative totals listed when per game averages not available.

[a] George Gauthier (15-14) and Lyman Frimodig (6-1) both coached during the 1919-20 season.

❂ Records don't reflect games forfeited or vacated. For adjusted totals, see p. 521.

▼ Coach's record adjusted to reflect games forfeited or vacated: 338-222, .604. For yearly totals, see p. 521.

ESPN 215 SAGARIN

MIDDLE TENNESSEE STATE

It is only appropriate that a team known as the Blue Raiders has historically made its mark in the paint—frontcourt stars have carried MTSU to stretches of Ohio Valley Conference dominance as well as unforgettable NCAA upsets of Kentucky and Florida State. Big men Warren Kidd, George Sorrell, Kerry Hammonds, Bob Burden and Desmond Yates all merit consideration for Middle Tennessee's all-time Top 5 list.

BEST TEAM: 1974-75 All five starters were eventual all-OVC picks and three Raiders would top 1,000 career points—Tim Sisneros (1,426), Sleepy Taylor (1,421) and Fred Allen (1,108). They went a school-best 23–5 and are MTSU's only outright winners of regular-season and OVC tourney titles.

BEST PLAYER: F JERRY BECK (1979-82) The two-time OVC Player of the Year led MTSU to a 1982 Tourney upset of Kentucky. He scored 1,401 points in just three full seasons, leading the Raiders in scoring and rebounding each year.

BEST COACH: BRUCE STEWART (1984-91) He transformed a program that had only three 20-win seasons into an OVC power. In Stewart's seven seasons, the Raiders topped 20 wins five times and reached three NCAA Tourneys and two NITs. His team's 1989 Tourney comeback from 17 down to beat No. 4-seed Florida State, 97-83, is legendary in Murfreesboro and environs.

GAME FOR THE AGES: After labeling his 21–7 team "sacrificial lambs," coach Stan Simpson's Raiders stunned Kentucky, 50-44, in the 1982 NCAA first round. After trailing 8-0, MTSU shut down the Melvin Turpin-led Wildcats. Rick Campbell (19 points) and Beck (14) directed MTSU's first Tourney win ever.

FIERCEST RIVAL: Old OVC foe Austin Peay remains No. 1 on the Raiders' Gotta Beat list; the two schools have played 137 times since 1939 (MTSU leads, 73–64). The Governors have won eight of the last 11—three in overtime—including the 78-75 nail-biter in 2008. MTSU won OVC tourney title games against the Governors three times (1975, '77, '89) to reach the NCAAs.

SEASON REVIEW

SEAS.	W-L	CONF.	COACH	SEAS.	W-L	CONF.	COACH
1914-48	*168-158*	*Alfred Miles (1922-24), 27-6, .818*		1961-62	6-12	2-10	Ed Diddle Jr
1948-49	11-12		Charles Murphy	1962-63	9-15	4-8	Bill Stokes
1949-50	14-13		Charles Greer	1963-64	11-10	5-9	Bill Stokes
1950-51	8-14		Charles Greer	1964-65	6-18	4-10	Bill Stokes
1951-52	19-12		Charles Greer	1965-66	7-17	3-11	Ken Trickey
1952-53	7-16	0-10	Charles Greer	1966-67	10-15	4-10	Ken Trickey
1953-54	12-17	1-9	Charles Greer	1967-68	15-9	7-7	Ken Trickey
1954-55	11-16	2-8	Charles Greer	1968-69	13-13	4-10	Ken Trickey
1955-56	6-15	0-10	Charles Greer	1969-70	15-11	6-8	Jimmy Earle
1956-57	12-13	2-8	Ed Diddle Jr.	1970-71	11-15	3-11	Jimmy Earle
1957-58	11-10	4-6	Ed Diddle Jr.	1971-72	15-11	5-9	Jimmy Earle
1958-59	9-17	4-8	Ed Diddle Jr.	1972-73	12-13	5-9	Jimmy Earle
1959-60	9-14	2-10	Ed Diddle Jr.	1973-74	18-8	9-5	Jimmy Earle
1960-61	9-14	4-8	Ed Diddle Jr.	1974-75	23-5	12-2 ●	Jimmy Earle

SEAS.	W-L	CONF.	SCORING		COACH	RECORD	
1975-76	16-12	6-8	Tim Sisneros	22.1	Jimmy Earle		
1976-77	20-9	9-5 ●	Bob Martin	17.9	Jimmy Earle		
1977-78	18-8	10-4	Sleepy Taylor	18.0	Jimmy Earle		
1978-79	16-11	7-5	Greg Joyner	20.9	Jimmy Earle	164-103	.614
1979-80	13-13	5-7	Jerry Beck	15.6	Stan Simpson		
1980-81	18-9	9-5	Jerry Beck	17.3	Stan Simpson		
1981-82	22-8	12-4 ●	Jerry Beck	17.5	Stan Simpson		
1982-83	7-20	3-11	Doug Lipscomb	12.8	Stan Simpson		
1983-84	11-16	4-10	Russell Smith	12.0	Stan Simpson	71-66	.518
1984-85	17-14	7-7 ●	Kim Cooksey	17.3	Bruce Stewart		
1985-86	23-11	10-4 ■	Kim Cooksey	18.9	Bruce Stewart		
1986-87	22-7	11-3 ●	D. Rainey, A. Tunstill	14.7	Bruce Stewart		
1987-88	23-11	11-3 ■	Chris Rainey	16.6	Bruce Stewart		
1988-89	23-8	10-2 ●	Randy Henry	19.5	Bruce Stewart		
1989-90	12-15	6-6[a]	Kevin Wallace	13.9	Bruce Stewart		
1990-91	21-9	6-6	Robert Taylor	15.3	Bruce Stewart	141-75	.653
1991-92	16-11	9-5	Robert Taylor	16.5	David Farrar		
1992-93	10-16	5-11	Robert Taylor	22.2	David Farrar		
1993-94	8-19	5-11	Milton Dean	22.1	David Farrar		
1994-95	12-15	5-11	Tim Gaither	14.2	David Farrar		
1995-96	15-12	9-7	Nod Carter	15.1	David Farrar	61-73	.455
1996-97	19-12	11-7	Nod Carter	16.8	Randy Wiel		
1997-98	19-9	12-6	Aylton Tesch	13.6	Randy Wiel		
1998-99	12-19	9-9	Cedrick Wallace	12.8	Randy Wiel		
1999-2000	15-13	10-8	Fernando Ortiz	15.3	Randy Wiel		
2000-01	5-22	1-15	Iiro Tenngren	9.6	Randy Wiel		
2001-02	14-15	6-8	Lee Nosse	12.6	Randy Wiel	84-90	.483
2002-03	16-14	9-5	Tommy Gunn	15.9	Kermit Davis		
2003-04	17-12	8-6	Tommy Gunn	16.0	Kermit Davis		
2004-05	19-12	7-7	Mike Dean	14.4	Kermit Davis		
2005-06	16-12	8-6	Adam Vogelsberg	12.4	Kermit Davis		
2006-07	15-17	8-10	Kevin Kanaskie	12.2	Kermit Davis		
2007-08	17-15	11-7	Desmond Yates	16.0	Kermit Davis		
2008-09	18-14	10-8	Desmond Yates	17.2	Kermit Davis	118-96	.551

[a] **Record includes a conference victory against Tennessee State that was later forfeited.**

● NCAA Tournament appearance ■ NIT appearance

PROFILE

Middle Tennessee State University, Murfreesboro, TN
Founded: 1911
Enrollment: 23,863 (20,883 undergraduate)
Colors: Royal blue and white
Nickname: Blue Raiders
Current arena: Murphy Center, opened in 1972 (11,520)
Previous: Alumni Memorial Gym, 1951-1972 (3,800); The Gym, 1914-51 (500)
First game: Jan. 10, 1914
All-time record: 1,022-953 (.517)
Total weeks in AP Top 20/25: 0

Current conference: Sun Belt (2000-)
Conference titles:
Ohio Valley: 5 (1975, '78 [tie], '86 [tie], '87, '89 [tie])
Conference tournament titles:
Ohio Valley: 5 (1975, '77, '82, '85, '89)
NCAA Tournament appearances: 6
NIT appearances: 2

FIRST-ROUND PRO PICKS

1969 **Willie Brown,** Dallas (ABA)

TOP 5

G **Tommy Gunn** (2000-04)
G **Robert Taylor** (1989-93)
F **Jerry Beck** (1979-82)
F **Greg Joyner** (1976-79)
C **Tim Sisneros** (1972-76)

RECORDS

RECORDS	GAME		SEASON		CAREER	
POINTS	44	Mike Milholland, vs. Austin Peay (Jan. 23, 1965)	623	Kim Cooksey (1985-86)	1,622	Robert Taylor (1989-93)
POINTS PER GAME			23.3	Willie Brown (1968-69)	20.3	Willie Brown (1966-69)
REBOUNDS	32	Mike Milholland, vs. Austin Peay (Jan. 4, 1965)	429	Booker Brown (1968-69)	1,048	Warren Kidd (1990-93)
ASSISTS	20	James Johnson, vs. Freed-Hardeman (Jan. 2, 1986)	255	Duane Washington (1986-87)	485	Kevin Kanaskie (2005-09)

ESPN 14 SAGARIN

MINNESOTA

Being a Gophers fan can have its moments—this is the school, after all, of Kevin McHale, Mychal Thompson, Jim Brewer and Voshon Lenard. But it also means having to experience regret and even embarrassment. In a 1972 game against Ohio State, Minnesota's Corky Taylor offered Ohio State's Luke Witte a hand up off the floor, only to knee him in the groin. Gopher Ron Behagen then stomped on Witte's head, sparking a brutal brawl that led to the rest of the game being canceled and OSU declared the winner. Nearly three decades later, Minnesota forfeited all its wins from 1993-94 to '97-98 over an academic fraud scandal.

BEST TEAM: 1996-97 You might not realize it from a quick perusal of the record book, but these Gophers made it to the Final Four. Led by Bobby Jackson and Sam Jacobson, the Big Ten champs always seemed to find a way to win the close ones, including a double-OT Midwest Regional semifinal victory over Clemson, 90-84. The Gophers ran out of gas in the national semifinals, falling to Kentucky by nine. But after an academic counselor claimed she had written 400 papers for Minnesota players, five seasons of team play were erased from the official record.

BEST PLAYER: F KEVIN MCHALE (1976-80) The Minnesota native grew up playing hockey as well as basketball until a growth spurt spurred him to hang up his skates for good in high school. He was only lightly recruited, but he grew to 6'11" at Minnesota and his game took off from there. He is still the school's fifth-leading scorer and second-leading rebounder.

BEST COACH: L.J. "DOC" COOKE (1896-1924) Cooke is perhaps most famous for his role in creating the Little Brown Jug football tradition between Minnesota and Michigan in 1903. But he is also the father of Minnesota hoops, coaching the Gophers to five Big Ten titles and two Helms Foundation national titles.

GAME FOR THE AGES: Shortly after his Gophers beat Iowa, 107-96, in triple overtime on March 5, 1994, coach Clem Haskins said, "I'm drained." For good reason: The Hawkeyes mounted furious comebacks in the first two OTs before Lenard's career-high 38 points won the day for Minnesota.

HEARTBREAKER: In the 1990 Elite Eight, star forward Willie Burton did everything in his power to help Minnesota advance to its first Final Four, scoring 35 points against Georgia Tech. But the Gophers had no answer for Lethal Weapon 3—Kenny Anderson, Dennis Scott, Brian Oliver—who combined for 89. Minnesota lost, 93-91.

FIERCEST RIVAL: Entering their Jan. 15, 2009, matchup, Minnesota hadn't won at Wisconsin in 15 seasons. But the Gophers' 78-74 Miracle in Madison overtime win—they trailed by nine with 3:24 left—reignited a classic rivalry. The Gophers lead the series overall, 99–88.

FANFARE AND HOOPLA: Set foot in the Gophers student section and you'll see fans who look like they just escaped from a farm or a petting zoo. Why? In in keeping with the theme of famed Williams Arena, of course, which is affectionately known as the Barn.

FAN FAVORITE: G HOSEA CRITTENDEN (1992-96) In high school, the 5'9" guard averaged seven points a game as a senior, yet made the Gophers as a freshman walk-on and played 21 games as a senior. Minnesota fans sported Crittenden masks and exercised their lungs whenever he took the floor.

CONSENSUS ALL-AMERICAS

1905	**George Tuck**, C
1906	**Garfield Brown**, G
1911	**Frank Lawler**, F
1917	**Francis Stadsvold**, F
1918	**Harold Gillen**, F
1919, '21	**Arnold Oss**, F
1919	**Erling Platou**, G
1948	**Jim McIntyre**, C
1955	**Dick Garmaker**, F
1978	**Mychal Thompson**, C

FIRST ROUND PRO PICKS

1951	**Whitey Skoog**, Minneapolis (10)
1954	**Ed Kalafat**, Minneapolis (9)
1955	**Dick Garmaker**, Minneapolis (6)
1966	**Lou Hudson**, St. Louis (4)
1968	**Tom Kondla**, Miami (ABA)
1973	**Jim Brewer**, Cleveland (2)
1973	**Jim Brewer**, New York (ABA)
1973	**Ron Behagen**, KC-Omaha (7)
1975	**Mark Olberding**, San Antonio (ABA)
1977	**Ray Williams**, New York (10)
1978	**Mychal Thompson**, Portland (1)
1980	**Kevin McHale**, Boston (3)
1982	**Trent Tucker**, New York (6)
1983	**Randy Breuer**, Milwaukee (18)
1990	**Willie Burton**, Miami (9)
1997	**Bobby Jackson**, Seattle (23)
1997	**John Thomas**, New York (25)
1998	**Sam Jacobson**, LA Lakers (26)
1999	**Quincy Lewis**, Utah (19)
2000	**Joel Przybilla**, Houston (9)
2004	**Kris Humphries**, Utah (14)

THE SCHOOLS

PROFILE

University of Minnesota, Twin Cities, Minneapolis, MN
Founded: 1851
Enrollment: 51,140 (28,505 undergraduate)
Colors: Maroon and gold
Nickname: Golden Gophers
Current arena: Williams Arena, opened in 1928 (14,625)
First game: Jan. 13, 1896
All-time record: 1,457-1,068-2 (.577)
Total weeks in AP Top 20/25: 202

Current conference: Big Ten (1905-)
Conference titles:
Big Ten: 9 (1906, '07 [tie], '11 [tie], '17 [tie], '19, '37 [tie] '72, '82, '97-v)
Conference tournament titles: 0
NCAA Tournaments: 10 (4 appearances vacated)
Sweet 16s (since 1975): 4
Final Fours: 1
NIT appearances: 13 (2 appearances vacated)
Semifinals: 4
Titles: 2 (1993, '98-v)
v – title vacated

TOP 5

G	**Voshon Lenard** (1991-95)
G	**Whitey Skoog** (1948-51)
F	**Jim Brewer** (1970-73)
F	**Kevin McHale** (1976-80)
C	**Mychal Thompson** (1974-78)

RECORDS	GAME		SEASON		CAREER	
POINTS	42	Oliver Shannon, vs. Wisconsin (March 6, 1971); Eric Magdanz, vs. Michigan (March 5, 1962)	647	Mychal Thompson (1975-76)	1,992	Mychal Thompson (1974-78)
POINTS PER GAME			25.9	Mychal Thompson (1975-76)	22.9	Dick Garmaker (1953-55)
REBOUNDS	28	Larry Mikan, vs. Michigan (March 3, 1970)	349	Larry Mikan (1969-70)	956	Mychal Thompson (1974-78)
ASSISTS	16	Arriel McDonald, vs. Wisconsin (Jan. 12, 1994)	179	Arriel McDonald (1993-94)	547	Arriel McDonald (1990-94)

SEASON REVIEW

SEASON	W-L	CONF.	SCORING	COACH	RECORD	SEASON	W-L	CONF.	SCORING	COACH	RECORD
1896-1918	*207-97-2*		*Helms Foundation champions in 1901-02 (15-0) and '18-19 (13-0)*			1928-29	4-13	1-11		Dave McMillan	
1918-19	13-0	10-0		L.J. "Doc" Cooke		1929-30	8-9	3-9		Dave McMillan	
1919-20	7-9	3-9		L.J. "Doc" Cooke		1930-31	13-4	8-4		Dave McMillan	
1920-21	10-5	7-5		L.J. "Doc" Cooke		1931-32	15-3	9-3		Dave McMillan	
1921-22	5-8	4-7		L.J. "Doc" Cooke		1932-33	5-15	1-11		Dave McMillan	
1922-23	2-13	1-11		L.J. "Doc" Cooke		1933-34	9-11	5-7		Dave McMillan	
1923-24	9-8	5-7		L.J. "Doc" Cooke	250-135-2 .649	1934-35	11-9	5-7		Dave McMillan	
1924-25	9-7	6-6		Harold Taylor		1935-36	7-17	3-9		Dave McMillan	
1925-26	7-10	5-7		Harold Taylor		1936-37	14-6	10-2		Dave McMillan	
1926-27	3-13	1-11		Harold Taylor	19-30 .388	1937-38	16-4	9-3		Dave McMillan	
1927-28	4-12	2-10		Dave McMillan		1938-39	14-6	7-5		Dave McMillan	

SEAS.	W-L	CONF.	POSTSEASON	SCORING		REBOUNDS		ASSISTS		COACH	RECORD
1939-40	12-8	5-7								Dave McMillan	
1940-41	11-9	7-5								Dave McMillan	
1941-42	15-6	9-6								Dave McMillan	
1942-43	10-9	5-7								Carl Nordly	
1943-44	7-14	2-10								Carl Nordly	17-23 .425
1944-45	8-13	4-8								Weston Mitchell	8-13 .381
1945-46	14-7	7-5								Dave McMillan	
1946-47	14-7	7-5								Dave McMillan	
1947-48	10-10	5-7		Jim McIntyre	18.9					Dave McMillan	196-156 .557
1948-49	18-3	9-3		Jim McIntyre	16.9					Osborne Cowles	
1949-50	13-9	4-8		Whitey Skoog	17.0					Osborne Cowles	
1950-51	13-9	7-7		Whitey Skoog	14.4					Osborne Cowles	
1951-52	15-7	10-4		Edward Kalafat	15.9	Edward Kalafat	9.2			Osborne Cowles	
1952-53	14-8	11-7		Charles Mencel	18.0	Edward Kalafat	10.3			Osborne Cowles	
1953-54	17-5	10-4		Dick Garmaker	21.6	Edward Kalafat	9.7			Osborne Cowles	
1954-55	15-7	10-4		Dick Garmaker	24.2	Bill Simonovich	10.9			Osborne Cowles	
1955-56	11-11	6-8		Jed Dommeyer	19.0	Dave Tucker	11.5			Osborne Cowles	
1956-57	14-8	9-5		George Kline	18.1	Dave Tucker	10.1			Osborne Cowles	
1957-58	9-12	5-9		George Kline	19.8	Ron Johnson	11.7			Osborne Cowles	
1958-59	8-14	5-9		Ron Johnson	20.2	Ron Johnson	12.8			Osborne Cowles	147-93 .613
1959-60	12-12	8-6		Ron Johnson	21.1	Ron Johnson	11.7			John Kundla	
1960-61	10-13	8-6		Thomas McGrann	14.2	Thomas McGrann	8.5			John Kundla	
1961-62	10-14	6-8		Eric Magdanz	23.0	Ray Cronk	11.9			John Kundla	
1962-63	12-12	8-6		Eric Magdanz	19.1	Mel Northway	10.1			John Kundla	
1963-64	17-7	10-4		Lou Hudson	18.1	Mel Northway	11.5			John Kundla	
1964-65	19-5	11-3		Lou Hudson	23.3	Lou Hudson	10.3			John Kundla	
1965-66	14-10	7-7		Archie Clark	24.5	Dennis Dvoracek	10.3			John Kundla	
1966-67	9-15	5-9		Tom Kondla	24.9	Tom Kondla	11.3			John Kundla	
1967-68	7-17	4-10		Tom Kondla	21.0	Tom Kondla	9.0			John Kundla	110-105 .512
1968-69	12-12	6-8		Larry Mikan	18.4	Larry Mikan	10.5			Bill Fitch	
1969-70	13-11	7-7		Eric Hill	18.9	Larry Mikan	14.5			Bill Fitch	25-23 .521
1970-71	11-13	5-9		Oliver Shannon	20.5	Jim Brewer	13.8			George Hanson	11-13 .458
1971-72	18-7 ⊗	11-3	NCAA REGIONAL SEMIFINALS	Clyde Turner	18.6	Jim Brewer	11.0			Bill Musselman	
1972-73	21-5	10-4	NIT QUARTERFINALS	Clyde Turner	18.1	Jim Brewer	11.6			Bill Musselman	
1973-74	12-12	6-8		Dennis Shaffer	17.2	Peter Gilcud	7.1			Bill Musselman	
1974-75	18-8	11-7		Mark Olberding	15.9	Mark Olberding	8.2			Bill Musselman	69-32 .683▼
1975-76	16-10	8-10		Mychal Thompson	25.9	Mychal Thompson	12.5			Jim Dutcher	
1976-77	24-3 ⊗	15-3		Mychal Thompson	22.0	Mychal Thompson	8.9	Ray Williams	6.1	Jim Dutcher	
1977-78	17-10	12-6		Mychal Thompson	22.0	Mychal Thompson	10.9	Osborne Lockhart	3.1	Jim Dutcher	
1978-79	11-16	6-12		Kevin McHale	17.9	Kevin McHale	9.6	Leo Rautins	3.9	Jim Dutcher	
1979-80	21-11	10-8	NIT RUNNER-UP	Kevin McHale	17.4	Kevin McHale	8.8	Mark Hall	1.9	Jim Dutcher	
1980-81	19-11	9-9	NIT QUARTERFINALS	Randy Breuer	15.2	Randy Breuer	5.5	Mark Hall	2.0	Jim Dutcher	
1981-82	23-6	14-4	NCAA REGIONAL SEMIFINALS	Randy Breuer	16.6	Randy Breuer	7.2	Darryl Mitchell	3.1	Jim Dutcher	
1982-83	18-11	9-9	NIT FIRST ROUND	Randy Breuer	20.4	Randy Breuer	8.9	Marc Wilson	3.9	Jim Dutcher	
1983-84	15-13	6-12		Tommy Davis	16.0	James Petersen	6.9	Marc Wilson	3.8	Jim Dutcher	
1984-85	13-15	6-12		Tommy Davis	19.1	John Shasky	6.8	Marc Wilson	2.5	Jim Dutcher	
1985-86	15-16	5-13		Marc Wilson	16.2	John Shasky	7.0	Marc Wilson	3.2	Jim Dutcher[a]	190-113 .627▼
1986-87	9-19	2-16		Terence Woods	12.0	Richard Coffey	6.5	Kim Zurcher	2.7	Clem Haskins	
1987-88	10-18	4-14		Willie Burton	13.7	Richard Coffey	8.7	M. Newbern, K. Zurcher	2.4	Clem Haskins	
1988-89	19-12	9-9	NCAA REGIONAL SEMIFINALS	Willie Burton	18.6	Richard Coffey	8.7	Melvin Newbern	4.4	Clem Haskins	
1989-90	23-9	11-7	NCAA REGIONAL FINAL	Willie Burton	19.3	Richard Coffey	9.3	Melvin Newbern	5.2	Clem Haskins	
1990-91	12-16	5-13		Kevin Lynch	18.1	Randy Carter	5.9	Arriel McDonald	4.5	Clem Haskins	
1991-92	16-16	8-10	NIT FIRST ROUND	Voshon Lenard	12.8	Randy Carter	5.6	Arriel McDonald	3.8	Clem Haskins	
1992-93	22-10	9-9	NIT CHAMPION	Voshon Lenard	17.1	Randy Carter	6.9	Arriel McDonald	3.8	Clem Haskins	
1993-94	22-13 ⊗	10-8	NCAA SECOND ROUND	Randy Carter	12.1	Randy Carter	7.6	Arriel McDonald	5.4	Clem Haskins	
1994-95	19-13 ⊗	10-8	NCAA FIRST ROUND	Sam Jacobson	7.7	Sam Jacobson	4.8	Sam Jacobson	1.2	Clem Haskins	
1995-96	19-13 ⊗	10-8	NIT SECOND ROUND	Sam Jacobson	12.8	Sam Jacobson	4.8	Sam Jacobson	2.0	Clem Haskins	
1996-97	35-5 ⊗	16-2	NCAA NATIONAL SEMIFINALS	Sam Jacobson	13.7	Sam Jacobson	4.5	Sam Jacobson	1.7	Clem Haskins	
1997-98	20-15 ⊗	6-10	NIT CHAMPION	Sam Jacobson	18.2	Quincy Lewis	5.6	Quincy Lewis	1.9	Clem Haskins	
1998-99	17-11	8-8	NCAA FIRST ROUND	Quincy Lewis	23.1	Quincy Lewis	5.9	Mitch Ohnstad	2.7	Clem Haskins	243-170 .588▼
1999-2000	12-16	4-12		Dusty Rychart	11.8	Dusty Rychart	7.9	Terrance Simmons	4.1	Dan Monson	
2000-01	18-14	5-11	NIT SECOND ROUND	Dusty Rychart	14.6	Dusty Rychart	8.0	Terrance Simmons	3.9	Dan Monson	
2001-02	18-13	9-7	NIT SECOND ROUND	Rick Rickert	14.2	Dusty Rychart	6.6	Kevin Burleson	4.7	Dan Monson	
2002-03	19-14	8-8	NIT FOURTH PLACE	Rick Rickert	15.6	Rick Rickert	6.2	Kevin Burleson	4.8	Dan Monson	
2003-04	12-18	3-13		Kris Humphries	21.7	Kris Humphries	10.1	Adam Boone	4.1	Dan Monson	
2004-05	21-11	10-6	NCAA FIRST ROUND	Vincent Grier	17.9	Jeff Hagen	6.1	Aaron Robinson	2.9	Dan Monson	
2005-06	16-15	5-11	NIT SECOND ROUND	Vincent Grier	15.7	Vincent Grier	6.3	Adam Boone	4.7	Dan Monson	
2006-07	9-22	3-13		Lawrence McKenzie	14.9	Dan Coleman	6.0	Lawrence McKenzie	2.8	Dan Monson[b]	118-106 .527
2007-08	20-14	8-10	NIT FIRST ROUND	Lawrence McKenzie	11.8	Dan Coleman	5.8	Al Nolen	3.5	Tubby Smith	
2008-09	22-11	9-9	NCAA FIRST ROUND	Lawrence Westbrook	12.6	Paul Carter	4.5	Al Nolen	4.3	Tubby Smith	42-25 .627

[a] Jim Dutcher (13-7) and Jimmy Williams (2-9) both coached during the 1985-86 season.

[b] Dan Monson (2-5) and Jim Molinari (7-17) both coached during the 2006-07 season.

⊗ Records don't reflect games forfeited or vacated. For adjusted records, see p. 521.

▼ Coaches' records adjusted to reflect games forfeited or vacated: Bill Musselman, 68-31, .687; Jim Dutcher, 166-137, .548; Clem Haskins, 232-167, .581. For yearly totals, see p. 521.

ESPN 115 SAGARIN

MISSISSIPPI

The Rebels don't come close to matching the likes of Kentucky or Arkansas in championship banners or all-time greats. But from winning the Southern Conference title in 1928 to its first nationally recognized star, B.L. "Country" Graham in 1938, to its consistent NCAA Tournament appearances in the late 1990s and early 2000s, Mississippi has at least afforded its fans several glimpses of college basketball greatness.

BEST TEAM: 2000-01 Coaching a team stocked with in-state talent such as forwards Justin Reed and Rahim Lockhart and guards Aaron Harper and David Sanders, Rod Barnes led Ole Miss to the most wins in school history (27–8) and its first Sweet 16 appearance. There, the No. 3-seed Rebels frustrated No. 2-seed Arizona with their trademark rugged defense. But with Lockhart bottled up by constant double-teaming, Ole Miss fell to the Wildcats, 66-56.

BEST PLAYER: F JOHN STROUD (1976-80) After watching their team lose 39 games over the previous two seasons, Rebels fans were praying for a player with a winning touch. They found one in Stroud, who as a senior led Ole Miss to its first postseason berth—in the still-important NIT. That capped a prolific career in which Stroud led the SEC in scoring in back-to-back seasons (1978-79 and '79-80).

BEST COACH: ROD BARNES (1998-2006) He simply knew how to get more out of less. As a Rebels point guard from 1984 to '88, he overcame an awkward shot and middling athleticism to become an All-SEC (second team) selection his senior season. As coach, he won the first three Tournament games in Rebels history, and finished behind only Graham in career wins.

GAME FOR THE AGES: In the second round of the 2001 NCAA Tournament Midwest Regional against No. 6-seed Notre Dame, the Rebels trailed by one with under a minute left. As the shot clock approached single digits, 5'5" junior Jason Harrison pulled up from the top of the arc and drilled a three-pointer. That proved to be the game-winner in the Rebels' 59-56 victory.

HEARTBREAKER: One team's Shining Moment is another's Stinking Memory. Ole Miss seemed to have tiny Valparaiso beaten in the first round of the 1998 NCAA Tournament, but with 4.1 seconds left and a 69-67 lead, the Rebs' Ansu Sesay missed two free throws, opening the door for Bryce Drew's immortal buzzer-beating three-pointer.

FIERCEST RIVAL: Naturally, the team that Ole Miss has played most in overtime is bitter in-state nemesis Mississippi State. Although the Bulldogs hold a 6–4 edge in extra-period games (and a 134–105 overall lead), the Rebels can at least claim supremacy in perhaps the most memorable of the overtime thrillers, a 59-52 victory on Jan. 24, 1981. Coach Bob Weltlich's crew won by hitting 11 free throws in the extra session, which left his counterpart, Jim Hatfield, fuming about the officiating.

Johnny Neumann, the Rebs' answer to Pete Maravich, pasted 63 points on the Pistol's alma mater, LSU, and 60 on Baylor.

FANFARE AND HOOPLA: Opposing teams hate it and don't understand it, but down in Oxford, it's all about the *Hotty Toddy* fight song. As any Reb fan knows, the song goes, "Hotty Toddy, gosh almighty, who the hell are we? Hey! Flim flam, bim bam, Ole Miss, by damn."

FAN FAVORITE: G/F JOHNNY NEUMANN (1970-71) He played just a single season in Oxford, but Neumann's legend is everlasting. The Rebels' answer to supreme showman Pete Maravich, Neumann pasted 63 points on the Pistol's alma mater, LSU, and 60 on Baylor, on his way to the Ole Miss single-season scoring records of 923 points and a whopping 40.1 ppg. Neumann, a pioneer of "one and done," had a merely mediocre pro career.

PROFILE

University of Mississippi, Oxford, MS
Founded: 1848
Enrollment: 17,601 (11,731 undergraduate)
Colors: Cardinal red and navy blue
Nickname: Rebels
Current arena: C.M. "Tad" Smith Coliseum, opened in 1966 (8,700)
Previous: Gymnasium, a.k.a. Old Gym, 1929-66 (2,400)
First game: Jan. 28, 1909
All-time record: 1,107-1,183 (.483)
Total weeks in AP Top 20/25: 38

Current conference: Southeastern (1932-)
Conference titles: 0
Conference tournament titles:
Southern: 1 (1928)
SEC: 1 (1981)
NCAA Tournament appearances: 6
Sweet 16s (since 1975): 1
NIT appearances: 8
Semifinals: 1

FIRST-ROUND PRO PICKS

1990 **Gerald Glass,** Minnesota (20)

TOP 5

G **Don Kessinger** (1961-64)
G/F **Johnny Neumann** (1970-71)
F **Gerald Glass** (1988-90)
F **Justin Reed** (2000-04)
F **John Stroud** (1976-80)

RECORDS

	GAME		SEASON		CAREER	
POINTS	63	Johnny Neumann, vs. LSU (Jan. 30, 1971)	923	Johnny Neumann (1970-71)	2,328	John Stroud (1976-80)
POINTS PER GAME			40.1	Johnny Neumann (1970-71)	40.1	Johnny Neumann (1970-71)
REBOUNDS	25	Ivan Richmann, vs. Tulane (Feb. 22, 1958)	337	Dwayne Curtis (2007-08)	945	Walter Actwood (1973-77)
ASSISTS	15	Sean Tuohy, vs. Auburn (Jan. 26, 1980)	260	Sean Tuohy (1979-80)	830	Sean Tuohy (1978-82)

SEASON REVIEW

SEASON	W-L	CONF.	SCORING	COACH	RECORD	
1909-14	*28-30*		*19-5 under E.R. Hubbard and B.Y. Walton; 9-25 with no coach*			
1914-15	0-3			no coach		
1915-16	4-7			no coach		
1916-17	11-7			no coach		
1917-18	no team					
1918-19	0-3			C.R. Noble	0-3	.000
1919-20	9-4			R.L. Sullivan		
1920-21	9-7			R.L. Sullivan		
1921-22	7-4			R.L. Sullivan		
1922-23	8-7	2-4		R.L. Sullivan		
1923-24	16-6	2-4		R.L. Sullivan		
1924-25	17-8	1-6		R.L. Sullivan	66-36	.647
1925-26	16-2	8-1		Homer Hazel		
1926-27	13-5	10-4		Homer Hazel		
1927-28	10-9	5-9		Homer Hazel		
1928-29	9-9	7-8		Homer Hazel		
1929-30	6-7	6-6		Homer Hazel	54-32	.628
1930-31	6-9	2-4		Ed Walker		
1931-32	9-6	8-5		Ed Walker		
1932-33	6-12	5-7		Ed Walker		
1933-34	7-9	2-8		Ed Walker		
1934-35	8-10	5-7		Ed Walker	36-46	.439

SEAS.	W-L	CONF.	POSTSEASON	SCORING		REBOUNDS		ASSISTS		COACH	RECORD	
1935-36	11-9	7-5								George Bohler		
1936-37	20-6	7-3		B.L. "Country" Graham	15.5					George Bohler		
1937-38	22-12	11-2		B.L. "Country" Graham	17.5					George Bohler	53-27	.663
1938-39	10-16	4-10		Burnell Egger	10.5					Frank Johnson	10-16	.385
1939-40	9-10	3-8		Burnell Egger	14.3					Charles Jaskwhich		
1940-41	2-18	2-15		Burnell Egger	11.1					Charles Jaskwhich		
1941-42	4-15	3-12		Harry Simpson	9.2					Charles Jaskwhich	15-43	.259
1942-43	8-10	6-8		Ray Poole	12.3					Edwin Hale		
1943-44	no team											
1944-45	15-8	3-1		Maxie McMullen	19.0					Edwin Hale	23-18	.561
1945-46	8-11	2-8		Jack Marshall	9.3					Buster Poole	8-11	.421
1946-47	7-14	2-11		Harold Kelly	9.4					Jim Whatley		
1947-48	11-12	5-9		Jack Marshall	12.2					Jim Whatley		
1948-49	8-13	4-12		Jack Marshall	13.5					Jim Whatley	26-39	.400
1949-50	8-17	4-13		R.B. Reeves	15.5					B.L. "Country" Graham		
1950-51	12-12	5-9		Ken Robbins	11.2					B.L. "Country" Graham		
1951-52	15-11	8-6		Cob Jarvis	15.5					B.L. "Country" Graham		
1952-53	14-11	5-8		Cob Jarvis	23.2	Ralph Ross	9.2			B.L. "Country" Graham		
1953-54	12-12	7-7		Denver Brackeen	22.1	Denver Brackeen	10.1			B.L. "Country" Graham		
1954-55	8-15	5-9		Denver Brackeen	27.2	Denver Brackeen	13.9			B.L. "Country" Graham		
1955-56	10-13	4-10		Joe Gibbon	22.2	Joe Gibbon	10.0			B.L. "Country" Graham		
1956-57	9-13	4-10		Joe Gibbon	30.0	Joe Gibbon	14.1			B.L. "Country" Graham		
1957-58	12-12	6-8		Carlton Garner	18.0	Louis Griffin	9.6			B.L. "Country" Graham		
1958-59	7-17	1-13		Jack Waters	18.6	Louis Griffin	9.6			B.L. "Country" Graham		
1959-60	15-9	8-6		Jack Waters	20.0	Ivan Richmann	10.4			B.L. "Country" Graham		
1960-61	10-14	5-9		Jack Waters	20.3	Sterling Ainsworth	10.1			B.L. "Country" Graham		
1961-62	12-13	5-9		Don Kessinger	21.4	Bill White	8.9			B.L. "Country" Graham	144-169	.460
1962-63	7-17	4-10		Don Kessinger	21.8	Bill Bolton	10.1			Eddie Crawford		
1963-64	10-12	7-7		Don Kessinger	23.5	Ron Davidson	8.7			Eddie Crawford		
1964-65	4-21	1-15		Eddie Dunn	10.9	Jim Robbins	4.9			Eddie Crawford		
1965-66	5-18	2-14		Mickey Williams	12.1	Mickey Williams	9.1			Eddie Crawford		
1966-67	13-12	7-11		Jerry Brawner	14.5	Jerry Brawner	9.2			Eddie Crawford		
1967-68	7-17	4-14		Ken Turner	13.8	Jerry Brawner	8.8			Eddie Crawford	46-97	.322
1968-69	10-14	7-11		Ken Turner	19.5	Jerry Brawner	8.8			Cob Jarvis		
1969-70	10-15	6-12		Ron Coleman	20.8	Tom Butler	9.0	Charlie Ward	2.0	Cob Jarvis		
1970-71	11-15	6-12		Johnny Neumann	40.1	Jim Farr	6.8	Johnny Neumann	3.2	Cob Jarvis		
1971-72	13-12	8-10		Coolidge Ball	16.8	Fred Cox	10.8	Coolidge Ball	1.7	Cob Jarvis		
1972-73	14-12	8-10		Fred Cox	14.2	Fred Cox	9.8	Bob Mahoney	4.9	Cob Jarvis		
1973-74	15-10	9-9		Dave Shepherd	14.3	Coolidge Ball	9.8	Dave Shepherd	4.2	Cob Jarvis		
1974-75	8-18	4-14		Dave Shepherd	20.7	Walter Actwood	11.3	Bob Mahoney	5.7	Cob Jarvis		
1975-76	6-21	2-16		Eugene Harris	14.8	Eugene Harris	9.8	Henry Jackson	3.3	Cob Jarvis	87-117	.426
1976-77	11-16	5-13		John Billips	17.3	John Billips	9.8	Henry Jackson	4.3	Bob Weltlich		
1977-78	10-17	5-13		John Stroud	18.1	John Stroud	8.5	Henry Jackson	4.3	Bob Weltlich		
1978-79	11-16	6-12		John Stroud	26.3	John Stroud	9.2	Sean Tuohy	6.2	Bob Weltlich		
1979-80	17-13	9-9	NIT SECOND ROUND	John Stroud	25.2	John Stroud	7.2	Sean Tuohy	8.7	Bob Weltlich		
1980-81	16-14	8-10	NCAA FIRST ROUND	Elston Turner	20.6	Elston Turner	8.1	Sean Tuohy	6.2	Bob Weltlich		
1981-82	18-12	11-7	NIT SECOND ROUND	Carlos Clark	21.1	Roger Stieg	5.0	Sean Tuohy	7.2	Bob Weltlich	83-88	.485
1982-83	18-13	10-8	NIT QUARTERFINALS	Carlos Clark	20.4	Michael Partridge	5.8	Cecil Dowell	4.1	Lee Hunt		
1983-84	8-20	3-15		Eric Laird	17.3	Sylvester Kincheon	3.4	Cecil Dowell	2.4	Lee Hunt		
1984-85	11-17	5-13		Curtis Ritchwood	14.3	Curtis Ritchwood	7.4	Andre Laird	3.7	Lee Hunt		
1985-86	12-17	4-14		Eric Smith	17.5	Eric Smith	6.8	Rod Barnes	5.3	Lee Hunt	49-67	.405
1986-87	15-14	8-10	NIT FIRST ROUND	Joe Ayers	13.7	Eric Smith	8.0	Rod Barnes	6.0	Ed Murphy		
1987-88	13-16	6-12		Rod Barnes	19.0	Charles Prater	6.9	Rod Barnes	3.9	Ed Murphy		
1988-89	15-15	8-10	NIT FIRST ROUND	Gerald Glass	28.0	Gerald Glass	8.5	John Matthews	3.7	Ed Murphy		
1989-90	13-17	8-10		Gerald Glass	24.1	Gerald Glass	7.6	Gerald Glass	4.0	Ed Murphy		
1990-91	9-19	3-15		Joe Harvell	17.4	Sean Murphy	6.1	Dondi Flemister	2.8	Ed Murphy		
1991-92	11-17	4-12		Joe Harvell	25.0	Joe Harvell	5.9	Dondi Flemister	3.6	Ed Murphy	76-98	.437
1992-93	10-18	4-12		Joe Harvell	17.7	Jarrell Evans	6.1	Kevin Watkins	2.6	Rob Evans		
1993-94	14-13	7-9		David Johnson	15.1	Jarrell Evans	6.6	Ervin Garnes	2.1	Rob Evans		
1994-95	8-19	3-13		David Johnson	13.5	John Jackson	5.1	Cedric Brim	4.9	Rob Evans		
1995-96	12-15	6-10		Keith Carter	13.8	Anthony Boone	6.2	Michael White	3.3	Rob Evans		
1996-97	20-9	11-5	NCAA FIRST ROUND	Ansu Sesay	14.8	Ansu Sesay	7.9	Michael White	3.4	Rob Evans		
1997-98	22-7	12-4	NCAA FIRST ROUND	Ansu Sesay	18.6	Ansu Sesay	7.6	Michael White	3.0	Rob Evans	86-81	.515
1998-99	20-13	8-8	NCAA SECOND ROUND	Keith Carter	16.4	Jason Smith	5.6	Michael White	3.0	Rod Barnes		
1999-2000	19-14	5-11	NIT QUARTERFINALS	Marcus Hicks	14.3	Rahim Lockhart	8.4	Jason Harrison	3.5	Rod Barnes		
2000-01	27-8	11-5	NCAA REGIONAL SEMIFINALS	Rahim Lockhart	13.0	Rahim Lockhart	8.1	Jason Harrison	3.0	Rod Barnes		
2001-02	20-11	9-7	NCAA FIRST ROUND	Justin Reed	14.6	Justin Reed	6.6	Jason Harrison	3.9	Rod Barnes		
2002-03	14-15	4-12		Justin Reed	15.4	Justin Reed	5.3	David Sanders	3.1	Rod Barnes		
2003-04	13-15	5-11		Justin Reed	18.5	Justin Reed	6.3	Aaron Harper	3.3	Rod Barnes		
2004-05	14-17	4-12		Tommie Eddie	11.3	T. Eddie, L. Nolen	4.4	Todd Abernethy	2.6	Rod Barnes		
2005-06	14-16	4-12		Dwayne Curtis	13.6	Dwayne Curtis	7.6	Todd Abernethy	2.9	Rod Barnes	141-109	.564
2006-07	21-13	8-8	NIT SECOND ROUND	Clarence Sanders	16.1	Dwayne Curtis	8.3	Todd Abernethy	5.5	Andy Kennedy		
2007-08	24-11	7-9	NIT SEMINFINALS	Chris Warren	15.8	Dwayne Curtis	9.6	Chris Warren	4.5	Andy Kennedy		
2008-09	16-15	7-9		Chris Warren	19.6	Murphy Holloway	6.6	Chris Warren	4.0	Andy Kennedy	61-39	.610

ESPN 90 SAGARIN

MISSISSIPPI STATE

It was the dictionary definition of bittersweet. Attending the Bulldogs' Final Four matchup against Syracuse during the 1996 NCAA Tournament, Hall of Famer Bailey Howell reveled in his former team's success. But Mississippi State's postseason run also served as a reminder of the lost 1958-59 season, in which Bailey and the Bulldogs (then known as the Maroons) were kept out of the NCAA Tournament because of the school's unwritten but rigidly enforced prohibition against playing integrated teams.

BEST TEAM: 1958-59 Many who saw the Maroons play thought they could have won it all. Just ask Adolph Rupp. Led by Howell's inside dominance, MSU knocked off top-ranked and defending national champs Kentucky on the way to winning the team's first SEC title and finishing No. 3 in the AP poll. But the school forbade the team from accepting an NCAA Tournament bid and Howell's amazing college career ended just like that.

BEST PLAYER: C BAILEY HOWELL (1956-59) Recruited out of Middleton, Tenn., the soft-spoken Howell was a dominating inside force from his very first game, averaging 25.9 points in his first season on the way to setting the school's all-time scoring record (since surpassed by Jeff Malone). In 1957-58, Howell averaged 27.8 points, fourth behind Oscar Robertson, Elgin Baylor and Wilt Chamberlain. He scored 27.5 ppg as a senior, again finishing fourth, and was a consensus All-America.

BEST COACH: BABE McCARTHY (1955-65) Known as the Magnolia Mouth of the South for his quick wit, McCarthy proved the depth of his character before the 1963 NCAA Tournament by helping his team skip town before an injunction could be served preventing them from playing integrated Loyola-Chicago. That the Maroons lost didn't tarnish the historical significance of McCarthy's bold defiance.

GAMES FOR THE AGES: The Bulldogs were given little chance in the 1996 SEC tournament title game on March 10. Their opponent? Top-ranked Kentucky, a.k.a. the Untouchables, led by Tony Delk and Antoine Walker. But sparked by Dontae' Jones' 28 points, MSU pulled off an 84-73 shocker for the program's first SEC tourney title. Howell called it the "greatest day in Mississippi State basketball history." Kentucky went on to win the national title.

HEARTBREAKER: It was bad enough that Mississippi State failed to make the 2007 Big Dance despite sharing the SEC West title. But as a No. 1 seed in the NIT semifinals, the Bulldogs lost in the most agonizing fashion possible, blowing a 14-point second-half lead to West Virginia. The final slap to the face in the 63-62 loss: Darris Nichols' stepback three-pointer at the buzzer.

FIERCEST RIVAL: It doesn't matter if it's football or tiddlywinks, MSU can't stand losing to Mississippi, a school it views as snobby and elitist. Like football's Egg Bowl, the basketball rivalry is one of the oldest in the country; the schools have played more than 235 times. Unlike football, MSU leads, 134–105.

McCarthy helped his team skip town before an injunction could stop them from playing integrated Loyola-Chicago.

FANFARE AND HOOPLA: SEC fans wondering why they can't bring any type of noisemaker into conference football or basketball games can blame the fans in Starkville. Cowbells became a trademark of MSU sports in the 1950s and '60s, until the SEC voted to ban artificial noisemakers in 1974. Of course, that just started a new Bulldogs tradition: sneaking cowbells into games.

FAN FAVORITE: F DONTAE' JONES (1995-96) A junior college transfer, Jones catapulted MSU to the 1996 Final Four with his freakish athleticism and highlight-reel plays. A first-round pick of the Knicks in the 1996 draft, his pro career was limited to 15 games with the Celtics in 1997-98.

CONSENSUS ALL-AMERICAS

1959	**Bailey Howell**, C
2004	**Lawrence Roberts**, F

FIRST-ROUND PRO PICKS

1959	**Bailey Howell**, Detroit (2)
1979	**Wiley Peck**, San Antonio (19)
1980	**Rickey Brown**, Golden State (13)
1983	**Jeff Malone**, Washington (10)
1996	**Erick Dampier**, Indiana (10)
1996	**Dontae' Jones**, New York (21)

PROFILE

Mississippi State University, Starkville, MS
Founded: 1878
Enrollment: 17,039 (13,208 undergraduate)
Colors: Maroon and white
Nickname: Bulldogs
Current arena: Humphrey Coliseum, opened in 1975 (10,500)
Previous: New Gym, later renamed McCarthy Gym, 1950-75 (5,000); Tin Gym, 1932-50 (1,800)
First game: Jan. 1, 1909
All-time record: 1,248-1,044 (.545)
Total weeks in AP Top 20/25: 125
Current conference: Southeastern (1932-)
Conference titles:
SEC: 6 (1959, '61, '62 [tie], '63, '91 [tie], 2004)
Conference tournament titles:
Southern: 1 (1923)
SEC: 3 (1996, 2002, '09)
NCAA Tournament appearances: 10
Sweet 16s (since 1975): 2
Final Fours: 1
NIT appearances: 6
Semifinals: 1

TOP 5

G	**Jim Ashmore** (1953-57)
G	**Jeff Malone** (1979-83)
G	**Darryl Wilson** (1993-96)
F	**Rickey Brown** (1976-80)
C	**Bailey Howell** (1956-59)

RECORDS	GAME		SEASON		CAREER	
POINTS	47	Bailey Howell, vs. Union (Dec. 4, 1958)	777	Jeff Malone (1982-83)	2,142	Jeff Malone (1979-83)
POINTS PER GAME			28.3	Jim Ashmore (1956-57)	27.1	Bailey Howell (1956-59)
REBOUNDS	34	Bailey Howell, vs. LSU (Feb. 1, 1957)	492	Bailey Howell (1956-57)	1,277	Bailey Howell (1956-59)
ASSISTS	16	Chuck Evans, vs. Missouri-Kansas City (Feb. 23, 1993)	235	Chuck Evans (1992-93)	514	Derrick Zimmerman (1999-2003)

SEASON REVIEW

SEASON	W-L	CONF.	SCORING	COACH	RECORD
1909-14	*40-12*		*33-3 in first three seasons (1911-14) under E.C. Hayes*		
1914-15	8-6			E.C. Hayes	
1915-16	11-5			E.C. Hayes	
1916-17	6-4			E.C. Hayes	
1917-18	no team				
1918-19	4-3			E.C. Hayes	
1919-20	12-5			E.C. Hayes	
1920-21	10-6			E.C. Hayes	
1921-22	12-10	0-4		E.C. Hayes	
1922-23	15-4	8-3		E.C. Hayes	
1923-24	13-8	8-4		E.C. Hayes	124-54 .697
1924-25	14-9	4-4		K.P. Gatchell	14-9 .609
1925-26	14-8	5-3		Bernie Bierman	
1926-27	17-7	7-5		Bernie Bierman	31-15 .674
1927-28	13-7	10-1		Ray G. Dauber	
1928-29	8-15	5-8		Ray G. Dauber	
1929-30	5-8	2-7		Ray G. Dauber	
1930-31	no team				
1931-32	5-10	4-7		Ray G. Dauber	
1932-33	6-13	3-9		Ray G. Dauber	37-53 .411
1933-34	8-11	4-8		Edwin Hale	
1934-35	12-6	5-5		Edwin Hale	20-17 .541

SEAS.	W-L	CONF.	POSTSEASON	SCORING		REBOUNDS		ASSISTS		COACH	RECORD
1935-36	11-6	9-5								Frank Carideo	
1936-37	15-9	6-7								Frank Carideo	
1937-38	9-12	7-9								Frank Carideo	
1938-39	8-12	5-10								Frank Carideo	43-39 .524
1939-40	9-6	4-5								Stanfield Hitt	
1940-41	12-10	6-6								Stanfield Hitt	
1941-42	13-7	9-6								Stanfield Hitt	
1942-43	14-8	13-7								Stanfield Hitt	
1943-44	no team										
1944-45	5-13	2-9								Stanfield Hitt	
1945-46	5-14	3-13								Stanfield Hitt	
1946-47	10-11	4-9								Stanfield Hitt	68-69 .496
1947-48	6-12	6-10		Willard Daley	14.2					Paul Gregory	
1948-49	4-13	3-12		Willard Daley	12.4					Paul Gregory	
1949-50	7-11	6-10		Willard Daley	10.9					Paul Gregory	
1950-51	3-16	2-12		Herb Hargett	18.8					Paul Gregory	
1951-52	12-11	4-10		Coyte Vance	20.5					Paul Gregory	
1952-53	9-10	5-8		Gerald Caveness	14.6					Paul Gregory	
1953-54	11-10	5-9		Gerald Caveness	17.8	Jack Houston	11.8			Paul Gregory	
1954-55	6-17	2-12		Jim Ashmore	22.3	Jack Houston	11.7			Paul Gregory	58-100 .367
1955-56	12-12	6-8		Jim Ashmore	22.3	Wayne Lemon	11.0			Babe McCarthy	
1956-57	17-8	9-5		Jim Ashmore	28.3	Bailey Howell	19.7			Babe McCarthy	
1957-58	20-5	9-5		Bailey Howell	27.8	Bailey Howell	16.2			Babe McCarthy	
1958-59	24-1	13-1		Bailey Howell	27.5	Bailey Howell	15.2			Babe McCarthy	
1959-60	12-13	5-9		Jerry Graves	18.6	Jerry Graves	10.4			Babe McCarthy	
1960-61	19-6	11-3		Jerry Graves	21.3	Jerry Graves	10.3			Babe McCarthy	
1961-62	24-1	13-1		Leland Mitchell	16.7	Leland Mitchell	8.9			Babe McCarthy	
1962-63	22-6	12-2	NCAA REGIONAL SEMIFINALS	Leland Mitchell	17.1	Leland Mitchell	9.8			Babe McCarthy	
1963-64	9-17	4-10		Doug Hutton	14.9	Stan Brinker	9.0			Babe McCarthy	
1964-65	10-16	6-10		Bill Chumbler	13.5	Richie Williams	5.8			Babe McCarthy	169-85 .665
1965-66	14-11	10-6		Dave Williams	19.7	Dave Williams	10.2			Joe Dan Gold	
1966-67	14-11	8-10		Dave Williams	15.7	Dave Williams	9.9			Joe Dan Gold	
1967-68	9-17	5-13		Tom Payne	15.8	Dave Williams	10.3			Joe Dan Gold	
1968-69	8-17	6-12		Manny Washington	15.4	John Guyton	7.2			Joe Dan Gold	
1969-70	6-18	3-15		John Guyton	16.3	Jim Martin	9.2			Joe Dan Gold	51-74 .408
1970-71	15-10	9-9		Jack Bouldin	19.1	Malcolm Wesson	7.4			Kermit Davis	
1971-72	13-13	6-12		Jack Bouldin	15.8	Terry Kusnierz	12.0			Kermit Davis	
1972-73	11-15	4-14		Rich Knarr	18.0	Larry Fry	7.7			Kermit Davis	
1973-74	16-10	8-10		Jerry Jenkins	18.1	Bill Singletary	8.7			Kermit Davis	
1974-75	9-17	5-13		Jerry Jenkins	22.1	Taylor Williams	9.4	Jeff Stroman	3.4	Kermit Davis	
1975-76	13-13	6-12		Ray White	18.3	Taylor Williams	7.9	Al Perry	8.0	Kermit Davis	
1976-77	14-13	6-12		Rickey Brown	19.3	Rickey Brown	10.8	Al Perry	7.4	Kermit Davis	91-91 .500
1977-78	18-9	13-5		Ray White	14.5	Wiley Peck	8.4	Ray White	3.5	Ron Greene	18-9 .667
1978-79	19-9	11-7	NIT FIRST ROUND	Ray White	17.1	Wiley Peck	11.3	Tom Schuberth	4.3	Jim Hatfield	
1979-80	13-14	7-11		Rickey Brown	20.5	Rickey Brown	14.4	Greg Grim	2.9	Jim Hatfield	
1980-81	8-19	3-15		Jeff Malone	20.1	Kalpatrick Wells	9.1	Terry Lewis	3.4	Jim Hatfield	40-42 .488
1981-82	8-19	4-14		Jeff Malone	18.6	Kalpatrick Wells	6.6	Butch Pierre	3.9	Bob Boyd	
1982-83	17-12	9-9		Jeff Malone	26.8	Kalpatrick Wells	6.8	Butch Pierre	4.5	Bob Boyd	
1983-84	9-19	4-14		Ken Harvey	12.7	Kelvin Hildreth	6.1	Ken Harvey	3.1	Bob Boyd	
1984-85	13-15	9-9		Ken Harvey	13.9	Raymond Brown	5.0	Jeff Norwood	4.5	Bob Boyd	
1985-86	8-22	3-15		Chauncey Robinson	14.0	Chauncey Robinson	7.0	Tracy Taylor	4.6	Bob Boyd	55-87 .387
1986-87	7-21	3-15		Hubert Henderson	14.9	Hubert Henderson	9.1	Tracy Taylor	3.4	Richard Williams	
1987-88	14-15	6-12		Greg Lockhart	9.9	Carl Nichols	6.6	Greg Lockhart	2.9	Richard Williams	
1988-89	13-15	7-11		Cameron Burns	15.1	Cameron Burns	6.3	Greg Lockhart	3.9	Richard Williams	
1989-90	16-14	7-11	NIT SECOND ROUND	Cameron Burns	18.2	Cameron Burns	7.3	Doug Hartsfield	5.3	Richard Williams	
1990-91	20-9	13-5	NCAA FIRST ROUND	Cameron Burns	16.9	Greg Carter	7.8	Doug Hartsfield	4.4	Richard Williams	
1991-92	15-13	7-9		Tony Watts	19.2	Johnny Walker	9.1	Chuck Evans	7.8	Richard Williams	
1992-93	13-16	5-11		Orien Watson	15.4	Johnny Walker	7.5	Chuck Evans	8.1	Richard Williams	
1993-94	18-11	9-7	NIT FIRST ROUND	Darryl Wilson	16.2	Erick Dampier	8.7	T.J. Honore	4.4	Richard Williams	
1994-95	22-8	12-4	NCAA REGIONAL SEMIFINALS	Darryl Wilson	17.8	Erick Dampier	9.7	T.J. Honore	3.8	Richard Williams	
1995-96	26-8	10-6	NCAA NATIONAL SEMIFINALS	Darryl Wilson	18.0	Erick Dampier	9.3	Marcus Bullard	5.2	Richard Williams	
1996-97	12-18	6-10		Horatio Webster	16.1	Tyrone Washington	7.9	Trey Moore	4.5	Richard Williams	
1997-98	15-15	4-12		Horatio Webster	17.0	Tyrone Washington	9.3	Detrick White	5.5	Richard Williams	191-163 .540
1998-99	20-13	8-8	NIT FIRST ROUND	Tyrone Washington	12.7	Tyrone Washington	8.4	Detrick White	5.6	Rick Stansbury	
1999-2000	14-16	5-11		Tang Hamilton	14.4	Robert Jackson	7.0	Todd Myles	4.4	Rick Stansbury	
2000-01	18-13	7-9	NIT QUARTERFINALS	Antonio Jackson	12.8	Robert Jackson	7.3	Antonio Jackson	3.2	Rick Stansbury	
2001-02	27-8	10-6	NCAA SECOND ROUND	Mario Austin	16.1	Mario Austin	7.6	Derrick Zimmerman	6.0	Rick Stansbury	
2002-03	21-10	9-7	NCAA FIRST ROUND	Mario Austin	15.5	Mario Austin	7.7	Derrick Zimmerman	5.5	Rick Stansbury	
2003-04	26-4	14-2	NCAA SECOND ROUND	Lawrence Roberts	16.9	Lawrence Roberts	10.1	Timmy Bowers	4.8	Rick Stansbury	
2004-05	23-11	9-7	NCAA SECOND ROUND	Lawrence Roberts	16.9	Lawrence Roberts	11.0	Gary Ervin	4.7	Rick Stansbury	
2005-06	15-15	5-11		Charles Rhodes	13.8	Charles Rhodes	7.1	Jamont Gordon	4.3	Rick Stansbury	
2006-07	21-14	8-8	NIT SEMIFINALS	Jamont Gordon	16.0	Jamont Gordon	7.1	Jamont Gordon	5.3	Rick Stansbury	
2007-08	23-11	12-4	NCAA SECOND ROUND	Charles Rhodes	17.4	Charles Rhodes	7.8	Jamont Gordon	4.8	Rick Stansbury	
2008-09	23-13	9-7	NCAA FIRST ROUND	Jarvis Varnado	12.9	Jarvis Varnado	8.8	Dee Bost	4.3	Rick Stansbury	241-128 .653

ESPN 259 SAGARIN

MISSISSIPPI VALLEY STATE

The names and memories are easily recalled: Alphonso Ford bombing away, Marcus Mann streaking down the lane, Herman Harris controlling the paint and, for more than two decades, coach Lafayette Stribling making the Delta Devils Dance. Was the first NCAA bid in 1986 the high point, or was it the 2008 miracle after an 0–8 start? It's all good.

BEST TEAM: 1995-96 The team featured SWAC Player of the Year Marcus Mann and set a school record for wins (22–7). The Delta Devils shared the regular-season title with Jackson State, then defeated JSU in the league tournament final. Playing in its third NCAA Tourney, MVSU lost to Elite Eight-bound Georgetown, 93-56.

BEST PLAYER: G ALPHONSO FORD (1989-93) He finished fourth in the nation in scoring as a freshman with 29.9 ppg, then second (32.7), third (27.5) and sixth (26.0). After brief stints in the NBA and CBA, Ford was a pro star in Greece until he died of leukemia at age 32. Today the Euroleague awards the Alphonso Ford Trophy to its leading scorer.

BEST COACH: LAFAYETTE STRIBLING (1983-2005) He took over a program that had yet to have a winning D1 season and led the Delta Devils to four SWAC regular-season titles (two outright, two shared), three conference tourney championships and three NCAA Tournaments. Stribling is the winningest coach in school history, with a 305–318 record.

GAME FOR THE AGES: The six-overtime game against Southern in 1983 is certainly memorable, but the 59-58 SWAC title win over Jackson State on March 15, 2008, was unforgettable. Chris Watson's three-pointer with :37 to go tied the game and Carl Lucas hit two free throws with :01 left for the win.

FIERCEST RIVAL: Alcorn State and Jackson State, the other two Mississippi-based SWAC schools, always draw big crowds. And for good reason. From 1996 to 2008 one of the three won the league's regular-season title seven times. MVSU has played five tourney finals against both teams and won four, including that '08 SWAC title game.

SEASON REVIEW

SEAS.	W-L	CONF.		SCORING		COACH	RECORD	
1961-62	18-12					Arthur J McAfee	18-12	.600
1962-63	N/A							
1963-64	N/A							
1964-65	15-11					Duane F. Gordon	15-11	.577
1965-66	N/A							
1966-67	N/A							
1967-68	N/A							
1968-69	N/A							
1969-70	N/A							
1970-71	7-13					Andrew Jackson		
1971-72	14-11					Andrew Jackson		
1972-73	10-14					Andrew Jackson		
1973-74	8-17					Andrew Jackson	39-55	.415
1974-75	15-14					William "Pop" Gaines		
1975-76	12-12					William "Pop" Gaines		
1976-77	15-11					William "Pop" Gaines		
1977-78	15-20	3-9				William "Pop" Gaines		
1978-79	15-16	5-7				William "Pop" Gaines		
1979-80	3-24	2-10				William "Pop" Gaines		
1980-81	11-16	4-8				William "Pop" Gaines		
1981-82	6-20	4-8				William "Pop" Gaines	92-133	.409
1982-83	11-17	6-8				Jerry Lewis	11-17	.393
1983-84	15-13	6-8				Lafayette Stribling		
1984-85	18-11	7-7				Lafayette Stribling		
1985-86	20-11	10-4	●			Lafayette Stribling		
1986-87	13-15	9-5				Lafayette Stribling		
1987-88	8-20	5-9				Lafayette Stribling		
1988-89	8-20	3-11		Alphonso Ford	29.9	Lafayette Stribling		
1989-90	11-18	7-7		Alphonso Ford	32.7	Lafayette Stribling		
1990-91	9-19	4-8		Alphonso Ford	27.5	Lafayette Stribling		
1991-92	16-14	11-3	●	Alphonso Ford	26.0	Lafayette Stribling		
1992-93	13-15	7-7				Lafayette Stribling		
1993-94	10-17	6-8				Lafayette Stribling		
1994-95	17-11	10-4				Lafayette Stribling		
1995-96	22-7	11-3	●			Lafayette Stribling		
1996-97	19-10	11-3				Lafayette Stribling		
1997-98	6-21	6-10				Lafayette Stribling		
1998-99	14-13	10-6		Faragi Phillips	20.9	Lafayette Stribling		
1999-2000	6-21	6-12		Dewayne Jefferson	17.8	Lafayette Stribling		
2000-01	18-9	14-4		Dewayne Jefferson	23.6	Lafayette Stribling		
2001-02	12-17	9-9		D'Jamel Jackson	16.3	Lafayette Stribling		
2002-03	15-14	13-5		Attarrius Norwood	16.8	Lafayette Stribling		
2003-04	22-7	16-2		Attarrius Norwood	14.3	Lafayette Stribling		
2004-05	13-15	11-7		Hosea Butler	13.0	Lafayette Stribling	305-318	.490
2005-06	9-19	9-9		Standford Speech	10.4	James Green		
2006-07	18-16	13-5		Standford Speech	12.3	James Green		
2007-08	17-16	12-6	●	Carl Lucas	12.5	James Green	44-51	.463
2008-09	7-25	7-11		Eric Perry	12.6	Sean Woods	7-25	.219

● NCAA Tournament appearance

THE SCHOOLS

PROFILE

Mississippi Valley State University, Itta Bena, MS
Founded: 1950 as Mississippi Vocational College; named changed to MVSU in 1974
Enrollment: 2,929 (2,513 undergraduate)
Colors: Forest green and white
Nickname: Delta Devils
Current arena: Robert W. Harrison HPER Complex, opened circa 1970 (6,000)
First game: 1961
All-time record: 531-622 (.461)
Total weeks in AP Top 20/25: 0

Current conference: Southwestern Athletic (1968-)
Conference titles:
SWAC: 5 (1992 [tie], '96 [tie], '97, 2004, '07)
Conference tournament titles:
SWAC: 4 (1986, '92, '96, 2008)
NCAA Tournament appearances: 4
NIT appearances: 0

TOP 5

G **Alphonso Ford** (1989-93)
G **Ashley Robinson** (1999-2003)
F **Marcus Mann** (1992-96)
F/C **Calvin Robinson** (1973-76)
C **Herman Harris** (1973-76)

RECORDS

RECORDS	GAME		SEASON		CAREER	
POINTS	51	Alphonso Ford, vs. Texas Southern (Feb. 19, 1990)	915	Alphonso Ford (1988-90)	3,165	Alphonso Ford (1989-93)
POINTS PER GAME			32.7	Alphonso Ford (1988-90)		N/A
REBOUNDS		N/A	518	Calvin Robinson (1975-76)	1,211	Calvin Robinson (1973-76)
ASSISTS		N/A	186	Ashley Robinson (2002-03)	593	Ashley Robinson (1999-2003)

ESPN 29 SAGARIN

MISSOURI

More than losing to Kansas, more than numerous embarrassing off-court scandals, this fact gnaws at Tigers fans: 22 NCAA Tournament appearances, zero Final Fours. In fact, only BYU has received more bids to the Big Dance without advancing to the national semifinals. Yet Missouri boosters have plenty to take pride in, too, most recently a trip to the 2009 Elite Eight in which the Tigers displayed the energy and grit of their classic teams.

BEST TEAM: 1981-82 The Tigers won the Big Eight thanks to fleet center Steve Stipanovich, guards Prince Bridges and Jon Sundvold, and swingman Ricky Frazier (16.1 points per game), who busted 2-3 zones with his foul line jumpers. But although the Tigers achieved a No. 1 ranking for the first time in team history, they lost to Houston in the NCAA's Midwest Regional semifinals, 79-78.

BEST PLAYER: G ANTHONY PEELER (1988-92) During Peeler's 43-point rampage against Kansas on March 8, 1992, Jayhawks coach Roy Williams considered fouling the free-spirited guard in the backcourt to slow him down. With a near-perfect shot and above-the-rim theatrics, Peeler averaged a Big Eight-best 23.4 points per game as a senior and finished as the Tigers' all-time leader in steals and assists.

BEST COACH: NORM STEWART (1967-99) Stormin' Norman once wore a woman's wig to speak at a banquet, performed a lewd pantomime after a Tigers player missed a free throw and regularly mocked the media. Supporters considered him colorful; one Chicago columnist called him a "poor excuse for a human being." Either way, nobody could deny that Stewart could coach. Emphasizing man-to-man defense and working for the good shot, he had 17 seasons of 20 or more wins. He was elected to the National Collegiate Basketball Hall of Fame in 2007.

GAME FOR THE AGES: On Feb. 4, 1997, top-ranked Kansas arrived at Missouri with a 22–0 record. The Tigers sent the Jayhawks home with their first loss, but not before two overtimes, numerous lead changes and one of the most unlikely big shots in the rivalry's long history. With 5.6 seconds left in the second extra frame and the score tied at 94, Corey Tate grabbed a loose ball near the free throw line and tossed in the game winner, sending Tigers fans onto the floor.

HEARTBREAKER: In the second round of the 1995 NCAA Tournament, Missouri led UCLA 74-73 with 4.8 seconds left when Bruins guard Tyus Edney drove the length of the floor, dissecting the Tigers defense along the way, and flipped in the game winner at the buzzer.

FIERCEST RIVAL: In the Border Showdown between Kansas and Missouri, neither team can claim the high road. Tigers supporters have been accused of spitting on Jayhawks players. KU fans once held up a sign referring to then-Tigers coach Quin Snyder that read, "For a Good Time Call Quin's Mom"—and thoughtfully provided a phone number. The coaches have gotten into the act, too: Stewart famously claimed that he never spent money in Kansas, staying and eating across the border in Kansas City, *Missouri*, whenever his team traveled to play the Jayhawks. KU leads the series overall, 167–94.

FANFARE AND HOOPLA: The often-rowdy Antlers student fan section was formed in 1976 and perhaps reached their height of notoriety—and creativity—in 1992 when they stuck a hog's head on a pole and waved it in front of Arkansas players as they entered the Hearnes Center for a game.

FAN FAVORITE: F DERRICK CHIEVOUS (1984-88) The frenetic forward was nicknamed Band-Aid for the strip he wore on his face, but it could have just as easily been for his bruising style of play, which put him on the foul line often and fired up the crowd.

CONSENSUS ALL-AMERICAS

1916	**Fred Williams,** G
1918, '19	**J. Craig Ruby,** F
1920, '21	**George Williams,** C
1921-23	**Herbert Bunker,** G
1922, '23	**Arthur Browning,** F

FIRST-ROUND PRO PICKS

1952	**Bill Stauffer,** Boston (7)
1973	**John Brown,** Atlanta (10)
1974	**Al Eberhard,** Detroit (15)
1980	**Larry Drew,** Detroit (17)
1983	**Steve Stipanovich,** Indiana (2)
1983	**Jon Sundvold,** Seattle (16)
1988	**Derrick Chievous,** Houston (16)
1989	**Byron Irvin,** Portland (22)
1991	**Doug Smith,** Dallas (6)
1992	**Anthony Peeler,** LA Lakers (15)
2000	**Keyon Dooling,** Orlando (10)
2002	**Kareem Rush,** Toronto (20)
2005	**Linas Kleiza,** Portland (27)
2009	**DeMarre Carroll,** Memphis (27)

PROFILE

University of Missouri, Columbia, MO
Founded: 1839
Enrollment: 28,477 (21,653 undergraduate)
Colors: Old gold and black
Nickname: Tigers
Current arena: Mizzou Arena, opened in 2004 (15,061)
Previous: Hearnes Center, 1972-2004 (13,300); Brewer Field House, 1929-72 (6,000)
First game: Jan. 12, 1907
All-time record: 1,452-1,021 (.587)
Total weeks in AP Top 20/25: 232

Current conference: Big 12 (1996-)
Conference titles:
Missouri Valley: 4 (1918, '20, '21, '22 [tie])
Big Six: 3 (1930, '39 [tie], '40 [tie])
Big Eight: 8 (1976, '80, '81, '82, '83, '87, '90, '94)
Conference tournament titles:
Big Eight: 6 (1978, '82, '87, '89, '91, '93)
Big 12: 1 (2009)
NCAA Tournaments: 22 (1 appearance vacated)
Sweet 16s (since 1975): 7
NIT appearances: 7

TOP 5

G **Anthony Peeler** (1988-92)
G **Jon Sundvold** (1979-83)
F **Derrick Chievous** (1984-88)
F **Doug Smith** (1987-91)
C **Steve Stipanovich** (1979-83)

RECORDS	GAME		SEASON		CAREER	
POINTS	46	Joe Scott, vs. Nebraska (March 6, 1961)	821	Derrick Chievous (1986-87)	2,580	Derrick Chievous (1984-88)
POINTS PER GAME			25.3	Willie Smith (1975-76)	23.9	Willie Smith (1974-76)
REBOUNDS	27	Bob Reiter, vs. Kansas State (Jan. 15, 1955)	379	Bill Stauffer (1951-52)	1,083	Arthur Johnson (2000-04)
ASSISTS	13	Stefhon Hannah, vs. Coppin State (Nov. 27, 2006); Melvin Booker, vs. Illinois (Dec. 22, 1993)	179	Anthony Peeler (1989-90)	497	Anthony Peeler (1988-92)

SEASON REVIEW

SEASON	W-L	CONF.	SCORING		COACH	RECORD	
1907-16	*83-75*		*Went 12-3 in 1915-16*				
1916-17	12-4	10-4			John Miller		
1917-18	17-1	15-1			W. "Doc" Meanwell		
1918-19	14-3	11-3			John Miller	26-7	.788
1919-20	17-1	17-1			W. "Doc" Meanwell	34-2	.944
1920-21	17-1	17-1			J. Craig Ruby		
1921-22	16-1	15-1			J. Craig Ruby	33-2	.943
1922-23	15-3	14-2			George Bond		
1923-24	4-14	4-12			George Bond		
1924-25	7-11	6-10			George Bond		
1925-26	8-10	8-8			George Bond	34-38	.472
1926-27	9-8	6-6			George Edwards		
1927-28	13-5	13-5			George Edwards		
1928-29	11-7	7-3			George Edwards		
1929-30	15-3	8-2			George Edwards		
1930-31	8-9	5-5			George Edwards		
1931-32	9-9	6-4	John Cooper	10.7	George Edwards		
1932-33	10-8	6-4	Norman Wagner	9.3	George Edwards		
1933-34	10-8	6-4			George Edwards		
1934-35	7-11	7-9	Ken Jorgensen	6.3	George Edwards		
1935-36	5-12	2-8	Evans Powell	5.1	George Edwards		
1936-37	7-9	2-8	Ralph Beer	5.7	George Edwards		

SEAS.	W-L	CONF.	POSTSEASON	SCORING		REBOUNDS		ASSISTS		COACH	RECORD	
1937-38	9-9	4-6		William Harvey	8.8					George Edwards		
1938-39	12-6	7-3		Harlan Keirsey	7.0					George Edwards		
1939-40	13-6	8-2		John Lobsiger	6.2					George Edwards		
1940-41	6-10	2-8		Loren Mills	6.1					George Edwards		
1941-42	6-12	2-8		Donald Harvey	8.1					George Edwards		
1942-43	7-10	5-5		Thornton Jenkins	11.5					George Edwards		
1943-44	10-9	5-5	NCAA REGIONAL SEMIFINALS	Dan Pippin	8.9					George Edwards		
1944-45	8-10	6-5		Eugene Kurash	8.3					George Edwards		
1945-46	6-11	3-7		Wendall Moulder	7.1					George Edwards	181-172	.513
1946-47	15-10	6-4		Thornton Jenkins	9.9					Wilbur Stalcup		
1947-48	14-10	7-5		Thornton Jenkins	10.3					Wilbur Stalcup		
1948-49	11-13	6-6		Dan Pippin	10.7					Wilbur Stalcup		
1949-50	14-10	4-8		Bud Heineman	9.6	Bill Stauffer	9.5			Wilbur Stalcup		
1950-51	16-8	8-4		Bud Heineman	11.8	Bill Stauffer	14.9			Wilbur Stalcup		
1951-52	14-10	6-6		Bill Stauffer	16.0	Bill Stauffer	15.8			Wilbur Stalcup		
1952-53	11-9	6-6		Bob Reiter	13.2	Bob Reiter	14.3			Wilbur Stalcup		
1953-54	11-10	6-6		Bob Reiter	19.6					Wilbur Stalcup		
1954-55	16-5	9-3		Bob Reiter	18.0	Bob Reiter	14.3			Wilbur Stalcup		
1955-56	15-7	8-4		Norm Stewart	24.1	Norm Stewart	10.7			Wilbur Stalcup		
1956-57	10-13	4-8		Lionel Smith	20.4					Wilbur Stalcup		
1957-58	9-13	3-9		Sonny Siebert	16.7	Roger Egelhoff	5.4			Wilbur Stalcup		
1958-59	6-19	3-11		Charles Henke	10.6	Al Abram	11.5			Wilbur Stalcup		
1959-60	12-13	5-9		Charles Henke	19.3	Charles Henke	11.5			Wilbur Stalcup		
1960-61	9-15 ⊗	7-7		Charles Henke	24.6	Charles Henke	10.8			Wilbur Stalcup		
1961-62	9-16	3-11		Ray Bob Carey	8.2	Ray Bob Carey	7.1			Wilbur Stalcup	192-181	.515
1962-63	10-15	5-9		Ray Bob Carey	14.2	Ray Bob Carey	8.5			Bob Vanatta		
1963-64	13-11	7-7		Ray Bob Carey	18.9	Ray Bob Carey	9.9			Bob Vanatta		
1964-65	13-11	8-6		Ron Coleman	11.3	Ron Coleman	2.5			Bob Vanatta		
1965-66	3-21	1-13		Ron Coleman	21.3	Ron Coleman	3.7			Bob Vanatta		
1966-67	3-22	1-13		Ron Coleman	20.4	Ron Coleman	4.0			Bob Vanatta	42-80	.344
1967-68	10-16	5-9		Don Tomlinson	15.2	Don Tomlinson	5.3			Norm Stewart		
1968-69	14-11	7-7		Don Tomlinson	17.4	Don Tomlinson	6.9			Norm Stewart		
1969-70	15-11	7-7		Don Tomlinson	14.2	Henry Smith	7.3			Norm Stewart		
1970-71	17-9	9-5		Henry Smith	22.3	Henry Smith	9.4			Norm Stewart		
1971-72	21-6	10-4	NIT FIRST ROUND	John Brown	21.7	John Brown	10.5			Norm Stewart		
1972-73	21-6	9-5	NIT FIRST ROUND	John Brown	21.0	John Brown	11.0			Norm Stewart		
1973-74	12-14	3-11		Al Eberhard	19.7	Al Eberhard	12.0			Norm Stewart		
1974-75	18-9	9-5		Willie Smith	22.4	Bill Flamank	8.1	Willie Smith	3.6	Norm Stewart		
1975-76	26-5	12-2	NCAA REGIONAL FINALS	Willie Smith	25.3	Stan Ray	8.3	Willie Smith	4.5	Norm Stewart		
1976-77	21-8	9-5		Kim Anderson	18.3	Clay Johnson	7.9	Scott Sims	4.9	Norm Stewart		
1977-78	14-16	4-10	NCAA FIRST ROUND	Clay Johnson	17.2	Clay Johnson	7.7	Larry Drew	2.6	Norm Stewart		
1978-79	13-15	8-6		Larry Drew	15.2	Curtis Berry	9.0	Larry Drew	4.3	Norm Stewart		
1979-80	25-6	11-3	NCAA REGIONAL SEMIFINALS	Steve Stipanovich	14.4	Steve Stipanovich	6.4	Larry Drew	5.0	Norm Stewart		
1980-81	22-10	10-4	NCAA FIRST ROUND	Ricky Frazier	16.3	Curtis Berry	8.1	Jon Sundvold	3.4	Norm Stewart		
1981-82	27-4	12-2	NCAA REGIONAL SEMIFINALS	Ricky Frazier	16.1	Steve Stipanovich	8.0	Prince Bridges	3.3	Norm Stewart		
1982-83	26-8	12-2	NCAA SECOND ROUND	Steve Stipanovich	18.4	Steve Stipanovich	8.8	Jon Sundvold	3.6	Norm Stewart		
1983-84	16-14	5-9		Malcolm Thomas	16.4	Greg Cavener	8.7	Greg Cavener	3.3	Norm Stewart		
1984-85	18-14	7-7	NIT FIRST ROUND	Malcolm Thomas	17.4	Malcolm Thomas	7.5	Greg Cavener	3.4	Norm Stewart		
1985-86	21-14	8-6	NCAA FIRST ROUND	Derrick Chievous	18.8	Derrick Chievous	7.7	Lynn Hardy	4.0	Norm Stewart		
1986-87	24-10	11-3	NCAA FIRST ROUND	Derrick Chievous	24.1	Derrick Chievous	8.6	L. Hardy, M. Sandbothe	3.4	Norm Stewart		
1987-88	19-11	7-7	NCAA FIRST ROUND	Derrick Chievous	23.4	Derrick Chievous	8.5	Lee Coward	4.2	Norm Stewart		
1988-89	29-8	10-4	NCAA REGIONAL SEMIFINALS	Byron Irvin	19.7	Doug Smith	6.9	Lee Coward	4.4	Norm Stewart		
1989-90	26-6	12-2	NCAA FIRST ROUND	Doug Smith	19.8	Nathan Buntin	9.5	Anthony Peeler	5.8	Norm Stewart		
1990-91	20-10	8-6		Doug Smith	23.6	Doug Smith	10.4	Melvin Booker	3.5	Norm Stewart		
1991-92	21-9	8-6	NCAA SECOND ROUND	Anthony Peeler	23.4	Jevon Crudup	8.2	Melvin Booker	3.9	Norm Stewart		
1992-93	19-14	5-9	NCAA FIRST ROUND	Melvin Booker	15.8	Jevon Crudup	8.3	Melvin Booker	3.7	Norm Stewart		
1993-94	28-4 ⊗	14-0	NCAA REGIONAL FINALS	Melvin Booker	18.1	Jevon Crudup	8.0	Melvin Booker	4.5	Norm Stewart		
1994-95	20-9	8-6	NCAA SECOND ROUND	Paul O'Liney	19.7	Julian Winfield	7.6	Kendrick Moore	2.5	Norm Stewart		
1995-96	18-15	6-8	NIT SECOND ROUND	Jason Sutherland	14.0	Simeon Haley	5.4	Julian Winfield	2.9	Norm Stewart		
1996-97	16-17	5-11		Kelly Thames	13.0	Kelly Thames	6.1	Dibi Ray	2.8	Norm Stewart		
1997-98	17-15	8-8	NIT FIRST ROUND	Kelly Thames	14.8	Kelly Thames	6.0	Dibi Ray	2.6	Norm Stewart		
1998-99	20-9	11-5	NCAA FIRST ROUND	Albert White	16.3	Albert White	8.7	Albert White	3.0	Norm Stewart	634-333	.565▼
1999-2000	18-13	10-6	NCAA FIRST ROUND	Keyon Dooling	15.3	Tajudeen Soyoye	6.3	Keyon Dooling	3.7	Quin Snyder		
2000-01	20-13	9-7	NCAA SECOND ROUND	Kareem Rush	21.1	Arthur Johnson	7.8	Clarence Gilbert	3.5	Quin Snyder		
2001-02	24-12	9-7	NCAA REGIONAL FINALS	Kareem Rush	19.8	Arthur Johnson	7.9	Wesley Stokes	4.1	Quin Snyder		
2002-03	22-11	9-7	NCAA SECOND ROUND	Rickey Paulding	17.4	Arthur Johnson	9.6	Ricky Clemons	3.8	Quin Snyder		
2003-04	16-14	9-7	NIT FIRST ROUND	Arthur Johnson	16.4	Arthur Johnson	7.5	Jimmy McKinney	3.2	Quin Snyder		
2004-05	16-17	7-9	NIT FIRST ROUND	Linas Kleiza	16.1	Linas Kleiza	7.6	Jason Horton	3.2	Quin Snyder		
2005-06	12-16	5-11		Thomas Gardner	19.7	Kevin Young	7.3	Jason Horton	4.5	Quin Snyder	128-96	.571
2006-07	18-12	7-9		Stefhon Hannah	15.4	Kalen Grimes	5.6	Stefhon Hannah	4.6	Mike Anderson		
2007-08	16-16	6-10		DeMarre Carroll	13.0	DeMarre Carroll	6.7	Stefhon Hannah	5.3	Mike Anderson		
2008-09	31-7	12-4	NCAA REGIONAL FINALS	DeMarre Carroll	16.6	DeMarre Carroll	7.2	J.T. Tiller	3.6	Mike Anderson	65-35	.650

⊗ Records don't reflect games forfeited or vacated. For adjusted records, see p. 521.
▼Coach's record adjusted to reflect games forfeited or vacated: 631-332, .655. For yearly totals, see p. 521.

ESPN 234 SAGARIN

MISSOURI-KANSAS CITY

The University of Missouri-Kansas City has been a member of Division I only since 1987-88; the program started in the NAIA in 1969, reached the '77 national tourney under coach Darrell Corwin and chalked up 27 wins in '84-85 with coach Bruce Carrier. The Kangaroos have had just six winning D1 seasons and one 20-win campaign ('91-92).

BEST TEAM: 1991-92 Two of UMKC's best, Tony Dumas and Ronnie Schmitz, played together for three seasons, leading the school's best run. In its fifth D1 season, the Independent 1991-92 team went 20–8 with wins over Texas A&M (twice), Baylor and Creighton.

BEST PLAYER: G Tony Dumas (1990-94) When Dumas finished at UMKC, he was the school's all-time leading scorer (2,459) and rebounder (576) and was second in assists and steals. He carried the Kangaroos to their best D1 seasons and was eighth nationally in scoring his senior year (26.0 ppg). The Dallas Mavericks' second first-round pick in 1994 (Jason Kidd was their first), Dumas played four NBA seasons.

BEST COACH: Lee Hunt (1986-96) When the NBA Kings left Kansas City for Sacramento in 1985, UMKC filled the big-time basketball void by moving to D1—a transition that fell to Hunt. In five seasons, his Kangaroos made the leap from being a 9–18 also-ran to a 20–8 legitmate D1 contender.

GAME FOR THE AGES: The school's 200th win couldn't have been more memorable. UMKC had lost all 14 of its games with Kansas State before their Dec. 30, 2003, meeting in Municipal Auditorium. That night the Kangaroos not only stunned the Wildcats, but blew them out, 93-52. The teams have not played since.

FIERCEST RIVAL: UMKC and Summit League foe Oral Roberts have taken turns riding series winning streaks. ORU, 18–10 in the rivalry, has won eight straight. UMKC's two biggest victories came in 2003: 91-86 in double-OT behind all-time scoring leader Michael Watson's school-record 54 points, then 76-73 to knock ORU from the league tourney.

SEASON REVIEW

SEAS.	W-L	CONF.	SCORING		COACH	RECORD	
1969-70[a]	11-13				Bill Ross		
1970-71	14-16				Bill Ross		
1971-72	19-8				Bill Ross		
1972-73	15-11				Bill Ross		
1973-74	15-12				Darrell Corwin		
1974-75	21-7				Darrell Corwin		
1975-76	16-10				Darrell Corwin		
1976-77	21-9				Darrell Corwin		
1977-78	15-15				Darrell Corwin		
1978-79	17-11				Darrell Corwin		
1979-80	13-14				Darrell Corwin	118-78	.602
1980-81	7-16				Byron Lehman		
1981-82	11-13				Byron Lehman		
1982-83	10-16				Byron Lehman	28-45	.384
1983-84	23-13				Bruce Carrier		
1984-85	27-9				Bruce Carrier	50-22	.694
1985-86	19-15				Bill Ross	78-63	.553
1986-87	no team						
1987-88	9-18		Mark Oliver	13.6	Lee Hunt		
1988-89	9-18		Napoleon Petteway	12.7	Lee Hunt		
1989-90	13-15		Ronnie Schmitz	16.8	Lee Hunt		
1990-91	15-14		Ronnie Schmitz	19.3	Lee Hunt		
1991-92	20-8		Tony Dumas	21.5	Lee Hunt		
1992-93	15-12		Tony Dumas	23.8	Lee Hunt		
1993-94	12-17		Tony Dumas	26.0	Lee Hunt		
1994-95	7-19	7-11	Darecko Rawlins	18.1	Lee Hunt		
1995-96	12-15	10-8	Darecko Rawlins	15.5	Lee Hunt	112-136	.452
1996-97	10-17	7-9	Vinson Smith	15.6	Bob Sundvold		
1997-98	9-18	7-9	Jimmy Keller	11.2	Bob Sundvold		
1998-99	8-22	3-11	Eddie Smith	16.1	Bob Sundvold		
1999-2000	16-13	10-6	Michael Jackson	19.8	Bob Sundvold	43-70	.381
2000-01	14-16	9-7	Michael Jackson	15.4	Dean Demopoulos	14-16	.467
2001-02	18-11	7-7	Michael Watson	21.9	Rich Zvosec		
2002-03	9-20	7-7	Michael Watson	25.5	Rich Zvosec		
2003-04	15-14	9-7	Michael Watson	23.4	Rich Zvosec		
2004-05	16-12	12-4	Mike English	15.8	Rich Zvosec		
2005-06	14-14	11-5	Quinton Day	20.3	Rich Zvosec		
2006-07	12-20	6-8	Quinton Day	16.9	Rich Zvosec	84-91	.480
2007-08	11-21	6-12	Dane Brumagin	17.1	Matt Brown		
2008-09	7-24	3-15	Dane Brumagin	15.3	Matt Brown	18-45	.286

[a] **Records from before 1969-70 not available.**

PROFILE

University of Missouri-Kansas City, Kansas City, MO
Founded: 1933
Enrollment: 14,221 (8,533 undergraduate)
Colors: Blue and gold
Nickname: Kangaroos
Current arena: Municipal Auditorium, opened in 1936 (9,827)
First game: Jan. 28, 1954
All-time record: 545-566 (.491)
Total weeks in AP Top 20/25: 0

Current conference: Summit League (1994-)
Conference titles: 0
Conference tournament titles: 0
NCAA Tournament appearances: 0
NIT appearances: 0

FIRST-ROUND PRO PICKS

1994 **Tony Dumas,** Dallas (19)

TOP 5

G **Tony Dumas** (1990-94)
G **Ronnie Schmitz** (1989-93)
G **Michael Watson** (2000-04)
F **Darecko Rawlins** (1992-96)
F/C **Michael Jackson** (1999-2002)

RECORDS

RECORDS	GAME		SEASON		CAREER	
POINTS	54	Michael Watson, vs. Oral Roberts (Feb. 22, 2003)	753	Tony Dumas (1993-94)	2,488	Michael Watson (2000-04)
POINTS PER GAME			26.0	Tony Dumas (1993-94)	22.0	Tony Dumas (1990-94)
REBOUNDS	23	Tony Berg, vs. Baylor (Dec. 3, 1996)	271	Carlton Aaron (2004-05)	639	Darecko Rawlins (1992-96)
ASSISTS	13	Marc Stricker, vs. Bellevue (Dec. 16, 1999)	131	Quinton Day (2006-07)	377	Quinton Day (2004-07)

ESPN 112 SAGARIN

MISSOURI STATE

MSU is one of only a handful of schools that can claim tournament wins in the NAIA, D2, NIT and NCAAs. Just as golden for Bears fans: In its 101-year hoops history (for much of that time, the school was known as Southwest Missouri State), the program has endured a mere 16 losing seasons, with only four of those coming since the move to D1 in 1982.

BEST TEAM: 1986-87 Coach Charlie Spoonhour started the same five players in all 34 games. Led by guard and Mid-Continent Player of the Year Winston Garland (21.2 points, 1.9 steals per game), the team's on-court chemistry showed when it counted the most. The Bears won 11 straight games to close the regular season at 24–5, reeled off another three straight to take the Mid-Continent tournament title, then knocked off No. 4-seed Clemson in the first round of the NCAA Tourney before finally falling to Kansas by four.

BEST PLAYER: F CURTIS PERRY (1966-70) A relentless physical force down low, Perry is Missouri State's all-time rebounding leader. No other Bear comes within 300 of his 1,424 boards. Perry also scored 1,835 points, ranking him second all-time at the school. He enjoyed an eight-year NBA career, averaging 9.5 points and 8.8 rebounds per game.

BEST COACH: ANDY MCDONALD (1925-50) With his precision motion offense, McDonald claimed six MIAA titles and won a school-record 301 games. His pedigree is hard to beat: He played for Phog Allen at Kansas, alongside another young man with a bright coaching future, Adolph Rupp.

GAME FOR THE AGES: Thirty years after opening the Hammons Student Center, Missouri State closed it down in style on Feb. 26, 2008, by knocking off No. 20 Drake. MSU employed a relentless D and led by as many as 17, but Drake's sharpshooters erupted for six late three-pointers, and it wasn't until forward Deven Mitchell (20 points) stole a long inbounds pass with :02 left that the Bears' 86-83 win was secure. The Bulldogs are the highest-ranked opponent the Bears ever beat at their venerable old court.

HEARTBREAKER: On March 4, 1978, the Bears hosted Lincoln (Mo.) in the regional finals of the Division II tournament. With one second to go and his team trailing 84-83, MSU's Harry Policape was fouled in the act of shooting. But Policape missed both shots, propelling Lincoln to the elite eight. Adding to the torment, the Hammons Student Center played host to the final four two weeks later.

FIERCEST RIVAL: Southern Illinois and Missouri State battled regularly at the D2 level back in the 1960s, and the rivalry only intensified when the Bears joined the Salukis in the Missouri Valley Conference in 1990. The two schools always have the largest fan bases in attendance at the conference tournament in St. Louis each March. The Bears are 20–25 in MVC play against SIU.

FANFARE AND HOOPLA: Marty "Sign Man" Prather has been a regular at MSU games since 1987 and has made close to 1,000 signs supporting the Bears and their players over the years. His large, colorful productions have been seen at sporting venues across the nation, including several World Series and MLB playoff games, and he always gives player-specific signs to graduating seniors. He was inducted into the Missouri Sports Hall of Fame in 2003.

No other Bear comes within 300 of Curtis Perry's 1,424 boards. Perry also scored 1,835 points, ranking him second all-time at the school.

FAN FAVORITE: G ARNOLD BERNARD (1989-91) The 5'6" dynamo earned a place in the hearts of Missouri State fans with his circus-like dribbling and passing. The A-Train helped guide the Bears to the 1990 NCAA Tournament and the 1991 NIT as the starting point guard. As a senior, he broke the school's single-season assist and steals record, and earned second-team All-MVC honors. He went on to play with the Harlem Globetrotters.

PROFILE

Missouri State University, Springfield, MO
Founded: 1905 as the Fourth District Normal School
Enrollment: 21,688 (17,671 undergraduate)
Colors: Maroon and white
Nickname: Bears
Current arena: JQH Arena 2008-present (11,000)
Previous: Hammons Student Center, 1976-2008 (8,846); McDonald Arena, 1940-76 (3,288); Administration Building's Basement Gymnasium, 1908-40 (N/A)
First game: 1908
All-time record: 1,499-833 (.643)
Total weeks in AP Top 20/25: 1
Current conference: Missouri Valley (1990-)
Conference titles:
Mid-Continent: 4 (1987, '88, '89, '90)
Conference tournament titles:
Mid-Continent: 2 (1987, '89)
MVC: 1 (1992)
NCAA Tournament appearances: 6
Sweet 16s (since 1975): 1
NIT appearances: 8

TOP 5

G **Jerry Anderson** (1951-55)
G **Winston Garland** (1985-87)
G **Daryel Garrison** (1971-75)
F **Danny Bolden** (1963-67)
F **Curtis Perry** (1966-70)

RECORDS

RECORDS	GAME		SEASON		CAREER	
POINTS	53	Jimmie Dull, vs. Kentucky Wesleyan (Feb. 7, 1977)	720	Winston Garland (1986-87)	1,975	Daryel Garrison (1971-75)
POINTS PER GAME			24.5	Zack Townsend (1971-72)	22.2	Mike Robinson (1978-80)
REBOUNDS	31	Curtis Perry, vs. UT Arlington (Feb. 10, 1970)	478	Curtis Perry (1969-70)	1,424	Curtis Perry (1966-70)
ASSISTS	21	Andy Newton, vs. Kentucky Wesleyan (March 1, 1975)	257	Arnold Bernard (1990-91)	507	Randy Towe (1974-79)

SEASON REVIEW

SEASON	W-L	CONF.	SCORING	COACH	RECORD	
1908-09	7-4			W.A. Daggett		
1909-10	4-5			W.A. Daggett	11-9	.550
1910-11	13-8			Corliss Buchanan	13-8	.619
1911-12	no team					
1912-13	no team					
1913-14	10-1			Arthur Briggs		
1914-15	11-8			Arthur Briggs		
1915-16	13-3			Arthur Briggs		
1916-17	12-3			Arthur Briggs		
1917-18	13-2			Arthur Briggs		
1918-19	2-4			Paul Andrews	2-4	.333
1919-20	16-3			Arthur Briggs		
1920-21	12-5			Arthur Briggs		
1921-22	10-3			Arthur Briggs		
1922-23	9-3			Arthur Briggs	106-31	.774
1923-24	13-1			Chester Barnard	13-1	.929
1924-25	9-6	3-5		Donald Holwerda	9-6	.600
1925-26	11-3	5-3		Andrew McDonald		
1926-27	11-10	5-7		Andrew McDonald		
1927-28	18-4	9-3		Andrew McDonald		
1928-29	16-6	10-6		Andrew McDonald		
1929-30	8-13	5-11		Andrew McDonald		
1930-31	8-5	7-1		Andrew McDonald		
1931-32	8-8	5-3		Andrew McDonald		
1932-33	9-6	4-4		Andrew McDonald		
1933-34	15-4	7-1		Andrew McDonald		
1934-35	16-3	6-2		Andrew McDonald		
1935-36	9-11	3-7		Andrew McDonald		
1936-37	11-8	4-6		Andrew McDonald		
1937-38	11-7	7-3		Andrew McDonald		
1938-39	15-6	7-3		Andrew McDonald		
1939-40	12-11	3-7		Andrew McDonald		

SEAS.	W-L	CONF.	POSTSEASON	SCORING		REBOUNDS		ASSISTS		COACH	RECORD	
1940-41	7-15	3-7								Andrew McDonald		
1941-42	13-12	7-3								Andrew McDonald		
1942-43	12-13									Andrew McDonald		
1943-44	no team											
1944-45	no team											
1945-46	9-4									Andrew McDonald		
1946-47	18-4	8-2								Andrew McDonald		
1947-48	21-6	6-4								Andrew McDonald		
1948-49	25-2	9-1								Andrew McDonald		
1949-50	19-5	8-2								Andrew McDonald	301-166	.645
1950-51	22-3	7-3								Bob Vanatta		
1951-52	27-4	10-0	NAIA CHAMPION							Bob Vanatta		
1952-53	24-4	8-2	NAIA CHAMPION							Bob Vanatta	73-11	.869
1953-54	22-7	8-2	NAIA THIRD PLACE							Edwin Matthews		
1954-55	11-9	5-5								Edwin Matthews		
1955-56	14-6	6-4								Edwin Matthews		
1956-57	12-7	7-3		Joe Reiter	14.6	Russ Robinson	8.5			Edwin Matthews		
1957-58	22-2	9-1		Jack Israel	14.1	Charles Taylor	12.1			Edwin Matthews		
1958-59	23-3	8-2	D2 RUNNER-UP	Jack Israel	15.7	Charles Taylor	9.9			Edwin Matthews		
1959-60	14-9	7-3		Jay Kinser	17.3	Carl Wilks	9.9			Edwin Matthews		
1960-61	10-13	5-5		Jerry Kirksey	17.7	Carl Wilks	10.9			Edwin Matthews		
1961-62	15-8	8-2		Charles Marshall	14.9	Carl Wilks	9.5			Edwin Matthews		
1962-63	8-15	2-8		Charles Marshall	14.6	Charles Marshall	6.9			Edwin Matthews		
1963-64	12-11	6-4		Charles Marshall	13.9	Danny Bolden	11.9			Edwin Matthews	162-90	.643
1964-65	15-8	6-4		Jim Gant	18.1	Don Carlson	12.7			Bill Thomas		
1965-66	19-6	10-0		Jim Gant	22.7	Don Carlson	11.3			Bill Thomas		
1966-67	23-5	10-0	D2 RUNNER-UP	Danny Bolden	19.6	Danny Bolden	11.0			Bill Thomas		
1967-68	19-6	9-1		Lou Shepherd	18.1	Curtis Perry	12.9			Bill Thomas		
1968-69	24-5	8-2	D2 RUNNER-UP	Curtis Perry	19.7	Curtis Perry	14.7			Bill Thomas		
1969-70	17-11	8-2		Curtis Perry	24.4	Curtis Perry	17.1			Bill Thomas		
1970-71	9-16	4-8		Chuck Williams	17.5	Tom Harshbarger	8.1			Bill Thomas		
1971-72	12-12	8-4		Zack Townsend	24.6	Zack Townsend	7.8	Daryel Garrison	3.6	Bill Thomas		
1972-73	20-8	9-3		Daryel Garrison	16.5	William Doolittle	13.4	Randy Magers	4.4	Bill Thomas		
1973-74	21-9	9-3	D2 RUNNER-UP	Daryel Garrison	20.6	William Doolittle	12.7	Randy Magers	4.8	Bill Thomas		
1974-75	13-13	6-6		Daryel Garrison	22.2	Dennis Hill	9.6	Andy Newton	6.5	Bill Thomas		
1975-76	15-11	7-5		Andy Newton	17.9	Scott Hawk	9.8	Andy Newton	5.4	Bill Thomas		
1976-77	11-14	4-8		Jimmie Dull	22.7	Jimmie Dull	8.0	Randy Towe	3.3	Bill Thomas		
1977-78	21-7	11-1		Jimmie Dull	22.0	Harry Policape	7.4	Randy Towe	7.1	Bill Thomas		
1978-79	16-10	5-7		Mike Robinson	21.0	Mike Robinson	11.3	Randy Towe	9.3	Bill Thomas		
1979-80	10-17	3-9		Mike Robinson	23.3	Mike Robinson	13.6	Wes Dunn	7.1	Bill Thomas	265-158	.626
1980-81	9-21	5-9		Joe Ward	12.0	Mark Bailey	5.5	Mark Lance	4.7	Bob Cleeland		
1981-82	17-10			Keith Hilliard	18.1	Ricky Johnson	7.6	Keith Hilliard	6.1	Bob Cleeland		
1982-83	13-15	6-3		Bobby Howard	15.1	Ricky Johnson	8.1	Brian Smith	4.9	Bob Cleeland	39-46	.459
1983-84	18-10	9-5		Chris Scott	13.6	Chris Scott	6.4	Brian Smith	3.7	Charlie Spoonhour		
1984-85	17-13	8-6		Handy Johnson	14.6	Chris Ward	6.3	Brian Smith	6.2	Charlie Spoonhour		
1985-86	24-8	10-4	NIT QUARTERFINALS	Winston Garland	16.5	Greg Bell	5.8	Basil Robinson	5.3	Charlie Spoonhour		
1986-87	28-6	13-1	NCAA SECOND ROUND	Winston Garland	21.2	Greg Bell	7.0	Basil Robinson	5.2	Charlie Spoonhour		
1987-88	22-7	12-2	NCAA FIRST ROUND	Kelby Stuckey	15.8	Kelby Stuckey	7.6	Doug Lewis	4.2	Charlie Spoonhour		
1988-89	21-10	10-2	NCAA FIRST ROUND	Hubert Henderson	17.2	Kelby Stuckey	7.5	Doug Lewis	6.1	Charlie Spoonhour		
1989-90	22-7	11-1	NCAA FIRST ROUND	Darryl Reid	19.0	Lee Campbell	12.5	Arnold Bernard	6.9	Charlie Spoonhour		
1990-91	22-12	11-5	NIT SECOND ROUND	Darryl Reid	16.3	Ryan Thornton	6.8	Arnold Bernard	7.6	Charlie Spoonhour		
1991-92	23-8	13-5	NCAA FIRST ROUND	Jackie Crawford	12.0	Clint Thomas	4.8	Jackie Crawford	4.5	Charlie Spoonhour	197-81	.709
1992-93	20-11	11-7	NIT QUARTERFINALS	Johnny Murdock	17.3	Clint Thomas	5.6	Jackie Crawford	3.2	Mark Bernsen		
1993-94	12-15	7-12		Johnny Murdock	18.7	Clint Thomas	6.9	Johnny Murdock	3.1	Mark Bernsen		
1994-95	16-11	9-9		Johnny Murdock	17.4	Johnny Epps	6.6	Johnny Murdock	4.5	Mark Bernsen	48-37	.565
1995-96	16-12	11-7		Ben Kandlbinder	14.8	Johnny Epps	7.2	Robert Wilkerson	4.2	Steve Alford		
1996-97	24-9	12-6	NIT FIRST ROUND	Danny Moore	19.5	Danny Moore	7.3	Ryan Bettenhausen	3.4	Steve Alford		
1997-98	16-16	11-7		Danny Moore	15.7	Danny Moore	6.0	William Fontleroy	4.2	Steve Alford		
1998-99	22-11	11-7	NCAA REGIONAL SEMIFINALS	Danny Moore	16.5	Danny Moore	6.1	William Fontleroy	4.0	Steve Alford	78-48	.619
1999-2000	23-11	13-5	NIT SECOND ROUND	Allen Phillips	13.0	Ron Bruton	6.7	William Fontleroy	3.1	Barry Hinson		
2000-01	13-16	8-10		Scott Brakebill	12.6	Mike Wallace	7.2	Robert Yanders	3.6	Barry Hinson		
2001-02	17-15	11-7		Scott Brakebill	14.4	Mike Wallace	9.8	Terrance McGee	3.2	Barry Hinson		
2002-03	17-12	12-6		Terrance McGee	14.9	Monwell Randle	7.1	Terrance McGee	3.7	Barry Hinson		
2003-04	19-14	9-9		Merrill Andrews	10.9	Monwell Randle	5.8	Merrill Andrews	3.2	Barry Hinson		
2004-05	19-13	10-8	NIT SECOND ROUND	Tamarr Maclin	10.9	Tamarr Maclin	7.9	Anthony Shavies	3.6	Barry Hinson		
2005-06	22-9	12-6	NIT QUARTERFINALS	Blake Ahearn	16.2	Nathan Bilyeu	6.5	Tyler Chaney	2.6	Barry Hinson		
2006-07	22-11	12-6	NIT FIRST ROUND	Blake Ahearn	15.4	Nathan Bilyeu	5.4	Spencer Laurie	4.3	Barry Hinson		
2007-08	17-16	8-10		Dale Lamberth	14.5	Deven Mitchell	6.1	Justin Fuehrmeyer	4.1	Barry Hinson	169-117	.591
2008-09	11-20	3-15		Chris Cooks	12.4	Chris Cooks	6.5	Justin Fuehrmeyer	2.8	Cuonzo Martin	11-20	.359

ESPN 228 SAGARIN

MONMOUTH

Two names stand out in Monmouth basketball history: program founder and longtime coach Bill Boylan and star player (and later coach) Ron Kornegay. Nine of the school's 13 20-win seasons involved one or both. An NAIA power in the 1960s, Monmouth later reached two NCAA Division II tournaments, and four more in D1 since 1996.

BEST TEAM: 1968-69 Boylan's 24–6 squad featured five players who would top 1,300 career points (including one who would win 55 major league baseball games): Kornegay, John Barone, Jim McIntyre, John Haas and Ed Halicki (who pitched for the Giants and the Angels). The Hawks chalked up 18 double-digit victories that season and won two NAIA tourney games.

BEST PLAYER: G Ron Kornegay (1965-69) A two-time NAIA All-America, Kornegay guided the Hawks' best four-year run (101–16), including three NAIA tournaments, averaging 25.2 ppg as a junior and finishing with 2,526 points (not a school record because Monmouth only counts D1 performances). He came back to coach the Hawks from 1977-78 into the '86-87 season.

BEST COACH: Bill Boylan (1956-77) The man who started Monmouth's program had winning records in 19 of his 21 seasons (368–155 overall), winning five NAIA district titles and reaching six national tourneys. His seven 20-win seasons are one more than the Hawks have had in the 32 years since.

GAME FOR THE AGES: A thrilling 60-59 victory over Rider for the Northeast Conference tournament title on March 8, 1996, sent Monmouth to its first NCAA Tournament. Four 1,000-point scorers (John Giraldo, Corey Albano, Mustafa Barksdale and Jack Gordon) helped the Hawks beat Rider three times that season.

FIERCEST RIVAL: Monmouth has evened things out against in-state foe Fairleigh Dickinson, after winning just two of their first 11 showdowns starting in 1972-73. The teams have split their last 16 games, as Monmouth has made three NCAA Tournaments in coach Dave Calloway's 11 full seasons. FDU still leads 36–26 overall.

SEASON REVIEW

SEAS.	W-L	CONF.		SCORING		COACH	RECORD
1956-58	*22-10*					Bill Boylan	
1958-59	12-2					Bill Boylan	
1959-60	13-8					Bill Boylan	
1960-61	15-6					Bill Boylan	
1961-62	22-3					Bill Boylan	
1962-63	11-11					Bill Boylan	
1963-64	15-10					Bill Boylan	
1964-65	14-11					Bill Boylan	
1965-66	27-3					Bill Boylan	
1966-67	23-5					Bill Boylan	
1967-68	27-2					Bill Boylan	
1968-69	24-6					Bill Boylan	
1969-70	17-11					Bill Boylan	
1970-71	17-10					Bill Boylan	
1971-72	18-9					Bill Boylan	
1972-73	13-14					Bill Boylan	
1973-74	19-9					Bill Boylan	
1974-75	22-7					Bill Boylan	
1975-76	22-5					Bill Boylan	
1976-77	15-13					Bill Boylan	368-155 .704
1977-78	8-17					Ron Kornegay	
1978-79	16-12					Ron Kornegay	
1979-80	19-10					Ron Kornegay	
1980-81	25-4					Ron Kornegay	
1981-82	21-9					Ron Kornegay	
1982-83	12-17					Ron Kornegay	
1983-84	6-21			Jesse Stout	14.6	Ron Kornegay	
1984-85	12-15			Rich Pass	21.3	Ron Kornegay	
1985-86	9-19	6-10		Mason McBride	16.6	Ron Kornegay	
1986-87	8-19	4-12		Ken Henry	12.6	Ron Kornegay[a]	129-130 .498
1987-88	16-13	11-5		Harrie Garris	16.4	Wayne Szoke	
1988-89	15-13	9-7		Fernando Sanders	17.2	Wayne Szoke	
1989-90	17-12	11-5		Alex Blackwell	19.7	Wayne Szoke	
1990-91	19-10	10-6		Alex Blackwell	22.9	Wayne Szoke	
1991-92	20-9	11-5		Alex Blackwell	18.4	Wayne Szoke	
1992-93	11-17	7-11		John Giraldo	14.2	Wayne Szoke	
1993-94	18-11	13-5		Glenn Stokes	15.3	Wayne Szoke	
1994-95	13-14	11-7		John Giraldo	18.7	Wayne Szoke	
1995-96	20-10	14-4	●	Corey Albano	17.2	Wayne Szoke	
1996-97	18-11	12-6		Corey Albano	19.3	Wayne Szoke	
1997-98	4-23	3-13		Joe Fermino	11.5	Wayne Szoke[b]	168-133 .558
1998-99	5-21	5-15		Alpha Bangura	18.0	Dave Calloway	
1999-2000	12-16	9-9		Rahsaan Johnson	17.7	Dave Calloway	
2000-01	21-10	15-5	●	Rahsaan Johnson	19.1	Dave Calloway	
2001-02	18-12	14-6		Rahsaan Johnson	19.2	Dave Calloway	
2002-03	15-13	13-5		Dwayne Byfield	14.9	Dave Calloway	
2003-04	21-12	12-6	●	Blake Hamilton	18.1	Dave Calloway	
2004-05	16-13	14-4		Blake Hamilton	16.2	Dave Calloway	
2005-06	19-15	12-6	●	Dejan Delic	12.3	Dave Calloway	
2006-07	12-18	7-11		Dejan Delic	14.6	Dave Calloway	
2007-08	7-24	4-14		Jhamar Youngblood	12.1	Dave Calloway	
2008-09	8-23	6-12		Travis Taylor	12.4	Dave Calloway	154-177 .465

[a] Ron Kornegay (1-6) and Ron Krayl (7-13) both coached during the 1986-87 season.
[b] Wayne Szoke (1-13) amd Dave Calloway (3-10) both coached during the 1997-98 season.
● NCAA Tournament appearance

PROFILE

Monmouth University, West Long Branch, NJ
Founded: 1933
Enrollment: 5,636 (4,194 undergraduate)
Colors: Royal blue and white
Nickname: Hawks
Current arena: Boylan Gymnasium, opened in 1962 (2,200)
First game: 1956
All-time record: 829-618 (.573)
Total weeks in AP Top 20/25: 0

Current conference: Northeast (1985-)
Conference titles:
Northeast: 2 (2004 [tie], '05)
Conference tournament titles:
Northeast: 4 (1996, 2001, '04, '06)
NCAA Tournament appearances: 4
NIT appearances: 0

TOP 5

G **Rahsaan Johnson** (1999-2002)
G **Ron Kornegay** (1965-69)
F **Alex Blackwell** (1989-92)
F **Ed Halicki** (1969-72)
F **Walt Mischler** (1959-62)

RECORDS

RECORDS	GAME		SEASON		CAREER	
POINTS	43	Rahsaan Johnson, vs. St. Francis (N.Y.) (Feb. 4, 2001)	663	Alex Blackwell (1990-91)	1,749	John Giraldo (1992-96); Alex Blackwell (1989-92)
POINTS PER GAME			22.9	Alex Blackwell (1990-91)		N/A
REBOUNDS	23	Karl Towns, vs. Morgan State (Jan. 12, 1985)	319	Karl Towns (1984-85)	779	Corey Albano (1994-97)
ASSISTS	17	Derric Thomas, vs. Long Island (Jan. 17, 1986)	205	Derric Thomas (1985-86)	524	Derric Thomas (1985-88)

ESPN 151 SAGARIN

MONTANA

A lot of big names have passed through the old logging town of Missoula. Pre-Michigan State coach Jud Heathcote, pre-Stanford coach Mike Montgomery, and pre-NBA players Micheal Ray Richardson and Larry Krystkowiak (the Grizzlies' all-time leading scorer and rebounder) are the biggest in a history that includes 25 straight winning seasons from 1973-74 through '97-98.

BEST TEAM: 1991-92 The Grizzlies got off to an 18–1 start and finished 27–4, beating Washington, Oregon and Doug Christie-led Pepperdine. Behind All-Big Sky picks Delvon Anderson, Roger Fasting and Daren Engellant, plus Nate Atchison, Montana won the league tourney before a 78-68 NCAA Tourney loss to No. 3-seed Florida State (Sam Cassell, Bob Sura, Charlie Ward).

BEST PLAYER: G MICHEAL RAY RICHARDSON (1974-78) Montana got lucky with the super-quick Richardson, who slipped under the recruiting radar as one of six 1974 D1 recruits from Denver's Manual High. Richardson ranks in Montana's top 10 in points (1,827), rebounds (670) and assists (372). He went on to become a four-time NBA All-Star with the Knicks and Nets.

BEST COACH: MIKE MONTGOMERY (1978-86) Heathcote started Montana's revitalization, but Montgomery took it up a notch, leading the team to four straight 20-win seasons, four Big Sky tourney finals and two NITs.

GAME FOR THE AGES: Montana didn't act much like a No. 12 seed in its March 16, 2006, NCAA Tourney 87-79 upset of 27-win Nevada. The Grizzlies never trailed, shooting 52% from the field and 85% from the line behind career 1,000-point scorers Andrew Strait (22 points), Kevin Criswell (18), and Jordan Hasquet (16)—as well as Virgil Matthews (20).

FIERCEST RIVAL: Montana and Montana State have played 279 times (with MSU ahead 145–134), and some meetings have strained families. In 1985, State beat Montana, 74-71, on a half-court buzzer beater by Scott Hurley. The two previous seasons, Scott's brother, Rob, had started for Montana. Scott's son, Tyler (Rob's nephew), joined the Montana roster in 2008-09.

SEASON REVIEW

SEAS.	W-L	CONF.	COACH	SEAS.	W-L	CONF.	COACH
1901-49	*365-405-1*	*Albion Findley, 7-3, .700, 1907-09*		1962-63	6-18		Ron Nord
1949-50	27-4		George Dahlberg	1963-64	6-17	1-9	Ron Nord
1950-51	13-18		George Dahlberg	1964-65	11-15	2-8	Ron Nord
1951-52	12-14	7-7	George Dahlberg	1965-66	14-10	6-4	Ron Nord
1952-53	14-11	6-8	George Dahlberg	1966-67	6-18	1-9	Ron Nord
1953-54	8-19	3-11	George Dahlberg	1967-68	8-17	5-10	Ron Nord
1954-55	12-14	4-10	George Dahlberg	1968-69	9-17	4-11	Bob Cope
1955-56	14-12	4-10	F.B. "Frosty" Cox	1969-70	8-18	5-10	Bob Cope
1956-57	13-9	9-5	F.B. "Frosty" Cox	1970-71	9-15	6-8	Lou Rocheleau
1957-58	12-10	8-6	F.B. "Frosty" Cox	1971-72	14-12	7-7	Jud Heathcote
1958-59	10-14	7-7	F.B. "Frosty" Cox	1972-73	13-13	7-7	Jud Heathcote
1959-60	7-17	3-11	F.B. "Frosty" Cox	1973-74	19-8	11-3	Jud Heathcote
1960-61	14-9	7-7	F.B. "Frosty" Cox	1974-75	19-8	13-1 ●	Jud Heathcote
1961-62	10-14	5-9	F.B. "Frosty" Cox	1975-76	13-12	7-7	Jud Heathcote

SEAS.	W-L	CONF.	SCORING		COACH	RECORD	
1976-77	18-8 ⊗	8-6	M.R. Richardson	19.2	Jim Brandenburg		
1977-78	20-9	12-2	M.R. Richardson	24.2	Jim Brandenburg	38-17	.691▼
1978-79	14-13	7-7	Allan Nielsen	13.9	Mike Montgomery		
1979-80	17-11	8-6	Craig Zanon	15.1	Mike Montgomery		
1980-81	19-9	11-3	Craig Zanon	17.0	Mike Montgomery		
1981-82	17-10	10-4	Derrick Pope	17.4	Mike Montgomery		
1982-83	22-7	9-5	Derrick Pope	17.9	Mike Montgomery		
1983-84	23-7	9-5	Larry Krystkowiak	18.0	Mike Montgomery		
1984-85	22-8	10-4 ■	Larry Krystkowiak	21.1	Mike Montgomery		
1985-86	21-11	9-5 ■	Larry Krystkowiak	22.2	Mike Montgomery	155-76	.671
1986-87	18-11	8-6	Scott Zanon	17.1	Stew Morrill		
1987-88	18-11	7-9	Wayne Tinkle	16.2	Stew Morrill		
1988-89	20-11	11-5	Wayne Tinkle	17.1	Stew Morrill		
1989-90	19-10	10-6	John Reckard	12.7	Stew Morrill		
1990-91	22-9	13-3 ●	Kevin Kearney	18.3	Stew Morrill	97-52	.651
1991-92	27-4	14-2 ●	Delvon Anderson	14.5	Blaine Taylor		
1992-93	17-11	8-6	Jeremy Lake	10.5	Blaine Taylor		
1993-94	19-9	6-8	Matt Kempfert	13.4	Blaine Taylor		
1994-95	21-9	11-3 ■	Matt Kempfert	14.0	Blaine Taylor		
1995-96	20-8	10-4	Shawn Samuelson	16.0	Blaine Taylor		
1996-97	21-11	11-5 ●	J.R. Camel	11.3	Blaine Taylor		
1997-98	16-14	9-7	J.R. Camel	11.8	Blaine Taylor	141-66	.681
1998-99	13-14	6-10	Matt Williams	15.2	Don Holst		
1999-2000	17-11	12-4	Matt Williams	19.2	Don Holst		
2000-01	11-16	6-10	Dan Trammel	12.4	Don Holst		
2001-02	16-15	7-7 ●	David Bell	13.7	Don Holst	57-56	.504
2002-03	13-17	7-7	David Bell	17.6	Pat Kennedy		
2003-04	10-18	6-8	Kamarr Davis	14.1	Pat Kennedy	23-35	.397
2004-05	18-13	9-5 ●	Kamarr Davis	15.2	Larry Krystkowiak		
2005-06	24-7	10-4 ●	Andrew Strait	16.6	Larry Krystkowiak	42-20	.677
2006-07	17-15	10-6	Andrew Strait	15.0	Wayne Tinkle		
2007-08	14-16	8-8	Jordan Hasquet	13.7	Wayne Tinkle		
2008-09	17-12	11-5	Anthony Johnson	17.6	Wayne Tinkle	48-43	.527

⊗ **Records don't reflect games forfeited or vacated. For adjusted records,** **see p. 521.**

▼ **Coach's record adjusted to reflect games forfeited or vacated: 39-16, .709. For yearly totals,** **see p. 521.**

● **NCAA Tournament appearance** ■ **NIT appearance**

PROFILE

University of Montana, Missoula, MT
Founded: 1893
Enrollment: 14,207 (10,780 undergraduate)
Colors: Copper, silver and gold
Nickname: Grizzlies
Current arena: Dahlberg Arena, opened in 1953 (7,500)
First game: 1901
All-time record: 1,287-1,281-1 (.533)
Total weeks in AP Top 20/25: 0

Current conference: Big Sky (1963-)
Conference titles:
Big Sky: 8 (1974 [tie], '75, '78, '86 [tie], '91, '92, '95 [tie], 2000 [tie])
Conference tournament titles:
Big Sky: 6 (1991, '92, '97, 2002, '05, '06)
NCAA Tournament appearances: 7
Sweet 16s (since 1975): 1
NIT appearances: 3

TOP 5

G **Kevin Criswell** (2002-06)
G **Micheal Ray Richardson** (1974-78)
F **Larry Krystkowiak** (1982-86)
F **Derrick Pope** (1979-83)
C **Bob Cope** (1946-50)

FIRST-ROUND PRO PICKS

1978 **Micheal Ray Richardson,** New York (4)

RECORDS

	GAME		SEASON		CAREER	
POINTS	40	Bob Cope, vs. Gonzaga (Feb. 21, 1948); Micheal Ray Richardson, vs. Montana St. (March 2, 1976)	709	Larry Krystkowiak (1985-86)	2,017	Larry Krystkowiak (1982-86)
POINTS PER GAME			24.2	Micheal Ray Richardson (1977-78)		N/A
REBOUNDS	26	Russ Sheriff, vs. Gonzaga (1958)	393	Ray Howard (1954-55)	1,105	Larry Krystkowiak (1982-86)
ASSISTS	14	Nate DuChesne, vs. Simon Fraser (1989)	199	Travis DeCuire (1993-94)	435	Travis DeCuire (1991-94)

ESPN 169 SAGARIN

MONTANA STATE

Montana State was one of the first schools to use the fast break, enabling the Bobcats of the 1920s to become a national power. The stream of highlights slowed when Montana State joined D1 in 1958. The school's All-Americas are of an era past, and its most recent NCAA Tournament berth was in 1996.

BEST TEAM: 1928-29 John "Cat" Thompson, Frank Ward and Brick Breeden led the 36–2 Wonder Team that was named national champions by the Helms Foundation. The run-and-gun Bobcats won five games by 60 or more points and one by a 100-point margin. Two wins in three tries against AAU champion Cook Painters established the team's national reputation.

BEST PLAYER: G John "Cat" Thompson (1926-30) The Helms Foundation named this four-time All-America one of the five greatest college hoops players of the first half of the 20th century. He was the leader of a team that won three straight Rocky Mountain Conference titles, and he averaged 15.4 points per game in an era when scoring was at a premium.

BEST COACH: G. Ott Romney (1922-28) He helped pioneer "racehorse basketball," the up-tempo, fast-breaking style that was the polar opposite of the short-passing, deliberate game of the day. Romney built a 144–31 record in six seasons while making basketball big in Bozeman. During World War I, he gave up a Rhodes Scholarship to join the U.S. Army Air Corps.

GAME FOR THE AGES: MSU fans stormed the Brick Breeden Fieldhouse court after the Bobcats beat Weber State in the 1996 Big Sky title game, 81-70. Freshman Danny Sprinkle scored 30 to lead the Bobcats to their first Tourney since 1986.

FIERCEST RIVAL: The football feud with Montana often includes fans throwing both profanities and punches, and the intensity has spread to the hardcourt as well. In 1988, officials called a technical foul against the home-team Bobcats when a full soda can was thrown on the court. The penalty resulted in a successful free throw and Montana ended up winning by one point.

SEASON REVIEW

SEAS.	W-L	CONF.	COACH	SEAS.	W-L	CONF.	COACH
1901-48	*586-304*	*1928-29 Helms champion (36-2)*		1961-62	10-13		Dobbie Lambert
1948-49	14-15		Brick Breeden	1962-63	13-13		Roger Craft
1949-50	20-12		Brick Breeden	1963-64	16-9	8-2	Roger Craft
1950-51	24-12	●	Brick Breeden	1964-65	15-10	6-4	Roger Craft
1951-52	22-14		Brick Breeden	1965-66	7-17	5-5	Roger Craft
1952-53	11-24		Brick Breeden	1966-67	14-11	7-3	Roger Craft
1953-54	18-11		Brick Breeden	1967-68	10-15	6-9	Roger Craft
1954-55	11-16		Wally Lemm	1968-69	17-8	11-4	Roger Craft
1955-56	15-14		Dobbie Lambert	1969-70	4-22	4-11	Gary Hulst
1956-57	12-13		Dobbie Lambert	1970-71	12-13	8-6	Gary Hulst
1957-58	18-8		Dobbie Lambert	1971-72	10-16	6-8	Gary Hulst
1958-59	12-13		Dobbie Lambert	1972-73	17-9	9-5	Hank Anderson
1959-60	11-14		Dobbie Lambert	1973-74	11-15	5-9	Hank Anderson
1960-61	10-15		Dobbie Lambert	1974-75	11-15	5-9	Rich Juarez

SEAS.	W-L	CONF.		SCORING		COACH	RECORD
1975-76	9-16	6-8		Daryl Ross	16.0	Rich Juarez	
1976-77	9-17	6-8		Craig Finberg	15.8	Rich Juarez	
1977-78	10-16	4-10		Craig Finberg	22.2	Rich Juarez	39-64 .379
1978-79	15-11	6-8		Craig Finberg	17.7	Bruce Haroldson	
1979-80	14-12	7-7		Doug Hashley	17.4	Bruce Haroldson	
1980-81	16-11	11-3		Doug Hashley	15.9	Bruce Haroldson	
1981-82	11-18	5-9		John Maclin	17.6	Bruce Haroldson	
1982-83	10-17	3-11		Jeff Epperly	12.7	Bruce Haroldson	66-69 .489
1983-84	14-15	7-7		Chris Brazier	12.5	Stu Starner	
1984-85	11-17	7-7		Tryg Johnson	11.9	Stu Starner	
1985-86	14-17	6-8	●	Kral Ferch	16.1	Stu Starner	
1986-87	21-8	12-2	■	Tom Domako	20.3	Stu Starner	
1987-88	19-11	10-6		Tom Domako	22.2	Stu Starner	
1988-89	14-15	6-10		Alonzo Stephens	18.4	Stu Starner	
1989-90	17-12	8-8		Alonzo Stephens	13.8	Stu Starner	110-95 .537
1990-91	12-16	6-10		Johnny Mack	16.8	Mick Durham	
1991-92	14-14	6-10		Johnny Mack	15.2	Mick Durham	
1992-93	9-18	5-9		Art Menefee	16.0	Mick Durham	
1993-94	16-11 ⊗	8-6		Eric Talley	14.0	Mick Durham	
1994-95	21-8	8-6		Kwesi Coleman	13.5	Mick Durham	
1995-96	21-9	11-3	●	Quadre Lollis	17.9	Mick Durham	
1996-97	16-14	10-6		Nate Holmstadt	17.6	Mick Durham	
1997-98	19-11	9-7		Nate Holmstadt	16.9	Mick Durham	
1998-99	16-13	9-7		Nate Holmstadt	20.8	Mick Durham	
1999-2000	12-17	4-12		Justin Brown	14.8	Mick Durham	
2000-01	16-14	8-8		John Lazosky	13.5	Mick Durham	
2001-02	20-10	12-2	■	Damir Latovic	11.2	Mick Durham	
2002-03	11-16	5-9		Pete Conway	14.3	Mick Durham	
2003-04	14-13	6-8		Jason Erickson	17.3	Mick Durham	
2004-05	14-14	9-5		Ja'Ron Jefferson	12.9	Mick Durham	
2005-06	15-15	7-7		Ja'Ron Jefferson	14.3	Mick Durham	246-213 .536
2006-07	11-19	8-8		Nick Dissly	14.3	Brad Huse	
2007-08	15-15	7-9		Carlos Taylor	18.3	Brad Huse	
2008-09	14-17	6-10		Will Bynum	10.7	Brad Huse	40-51 .440

⊗ Records don't reflect games forfeited or vacated. For adjusted records, see p. 521.

● NCAA Tournament appearance ■ NIT appearance

PROFILE

Montana State University, Bozeman, MT
Founded: 1893
Enrollment: 12,369 (10,519 undergraduate)
Colors: Blue and gold
Nickname: Bobcats
Current arena: Brick Breeden Fieldhouse at Worthington Arena, opened as the MSU Fieldhouse in 1956 (7,250)
Previous: Romney Gymnasium, 1926-56 (N/A)
First game: 1901
All-time record: 1,441-1,148 (.557)
Total weeks in AP Top 20/25: 0

Current conference: Big Sky (1963-)
Conference titles:
Rocky Mountain: 4 (1927 [tie], '28, '29 [tie], '37)
Big Sky: 5 (1964, '67 [tie], '87, '96, 2002)
Conference tournament titles:
Big Sky: 2 (1986, '96)
NCAA Tournament appearances: 3
NIT appearances: 2

CONSENSUS ALL-AMERICAS

1927-30 **John "Cat" Thompson,** G
1930 **Frank Ward,** C

FIRST-ROUND PRO PICKS

1969 **Jack Gillespie,** Oakland (ABA)

TOP 5

G **Brick Breeden** (1926-30)
G **John "Cat" Thompson** (1926-30)
F **Larry Chanay** (1956-60)
F **Quadre Lollis** (1994-96)
C **Jack Gillespie** (1965-69)

RECORDS

RECORDS	GAME		SEASON		CAREER	
POINTS	44	Tom Storm, vs. Portland State (Jan. 26, 1967)	667	Tom Domako (1987-88)	2,034	Larry Chanay (1956-60)
POINTS PER GAME			23.7	Larry Chanay (1959-60)	20.6	Jack Gillespie (1965-69)
REBOUNDS	24	Doug Hashley, vs. Nevada (Jan. 30, 1982)	383	Jack Gillespie (1968-69)	1,011	Jack Gillespie (1965-69)
ASSISTS	16	Craig Finberg, vs. St. Joseph's (Dec. 21, 1977); Paul Kinne, vs. Portland State (1976-77)	194	Chris Conway (1987-88)	608	Scott Hatler (1992-96)

ESPN 159 SAGARIN

MOREHEAD STATE

It started humbly in 1929. Morehead State, a fledgling school in the foothills of eastern Kentucky, lost its first game to in-state rival Sue Bennett, 37-25. Some 80 years later, Sue Bennett doesn't exist but the Eagles are still going strong, with six Tournament bids to their credit.

BEST TEAM: 1955-56 Bobby Laughlin's crew shared the OVC title, then beat Marshall in the NCAA Tournament and finished third in the Midwest Regional with a win over Wayne State. The team featured future Celtic Dan Swartz and Steve Hamilton—one of only two men to play in both an NBA championship (Lakers) and a World Series (Yankees). (Gene Conley is the other.)

BEST PLAYER: G Ricky Minard (2000-04) With his quickness, smarts and shooting precision, Minard led all four of his MSU teams in scoring, three in rebounding and one in assists. After being named first-team All-OVC as a sophomore, junior and senior, he was drafted in the second round in 2004 by the Sacramento Kings.

BEST COACH: Bobby Laughlin (1953-65) His teams were best known for their huge scoring numbers, but they were multidimensional. Some days the Eagles would spend entire practices pounding the boards; in 1956-57 they led the nation in rebounding.

GAME FOR THE AGES: Like drama? In the opening round of the 1984 NCAA Tournament, MSU's Guy Minnifield sank a shot with :04 left to beat North Carolina A&T, 70-69. And that wasn't even the most intense moment. With :26 left and the game tied at 68, Aggies guard Eric Boyd, an 85% free throw shooter, stepped to the line. But after reviewing the video, officials determined that it was James Horace who was fouled. Horace missed one of two shots, opening the door for Minnifield's game-winner.

FIERCEST RIVALRY: MSU has played Eastern Kentucky more times (168) than any other school, and all that familiarity has bred a heap of contempt. Friendly taunting? Hardly. MSU fans wear their sentiments on their T-shirts. Example: "Friends don't let friends go to EKU." Eastern Kentucky leads, 94–74.

SEASON REVIEW

SEAS.	W-L	CONF.	COACH	SEAS.	W-L	CONF.	COACH
1929-47	*181-138*			**1960-61**	19-12	9-3 ●	Bobby Laughlin
1947-48	10-17		Ellis T. Johnson	**1961-62**	14-8	7-5	Bobby Laughlin
1948-49	14-9	2-7	Ellis T. Johnson	**1962-63**	13-7	8-4	Bobby Laughlin
1949-50	12-10	5-6	Ellis T. Johnson	**1963-64**	10-11	6-8	Bobby Laughlin
1950-51	14-12	4-7	Ellis T. Johnson	**1964-65**	13-10	6-8	Bobby Laughlin
1951-52	11-14	3-9	Ellis T. Johnson	**1965-66**	12-12	8-6	Bob Wright
1952-53	13-12	3-7	Ellis T. Johnson	**1966-67**	16-8	8-6	Bob Wright
1953-54	16-8	6-4	Bobby Laughlin	**1967-68**	12-9	8-6	Bob Wright
1954-55	14-10	5-5	Bobby Laughlin	**1968-69**	18-9	11-3	Bob Wright
1955-56	19-10	7-3 ●	Bobby Laughlin	**1969-70**	13-11	5-9	Bill Harrell
1956-57	19-8	9-1 ●	Bobby Laughlin	**1970-71**	8-17	4-10	Bill Harrell
1957-58	13-10	6-4	Bobby Laughlin	**1971-72**	16-11	9-5	Bill Harrell
1958-59	11-12	5-7	Bobby Laughlin	**1972-73**	14-11	9-5	Bill Harrell
1959-60	5-14	3-7	Bobby Laughlin	**1973-74**	17-9	10-4	Bill Harrell

SEAS.	W-L	CONF.	SCORING		COACH	RECORD
1974-75	13-13	5-9	Arch Johnson	15.6	Jack Schalow	
1975-76	13-14	7-7	Ted Hundley	18.8	Jack Schalow	
1976-77	15-10	9-5	Herbie Stamper	21.9	Jack Schalow	
1977-78	4-19	0-14	Herbie Stamper	24.6	Jack Schalow	45-56 .446
1978-79	14-13	7-5	Herbie Stamper	19.6	Wayne Martin	
1979-80	15-12	7-5	Charlie Clay	14.9	Wayne Martin	
1980-81	11-15	4-10	Glen Napier	14.7	Wayne Martin	
1981-82	17-10	11-5	Guy Minnifield	15.0	Wayne Martin	
1982-83	19-11	10-4 ●	Guy Minnifield	15.8	Wayne Martin	
1983-84	25-6	12-2 ●	Earl Harrison	12.9	Wayne Martin	
1984-85	7-20	2-12	Bob McCann	17.1	Wayne Martin	
1985-86	8-19	1-13	Bob McCann	16.9	Wayne Martin	
1986-87	14-14	8-6	Bob McCann	18.6	Wayne Martin	130-120 .520
1987-88	5-22	1-13	Michael Mason	13.6	Tommy Gaither	
1988-89	15-16	5-7	Darrin Hale	14.2	Tommy Gaither	
1989-90	16-13	7-5	Elbert Boyd	19.2	Tommy Gaither	
1990-91	16-13	4-8	Rod Mitchell	17.3	Tommy Gaither	52-64 .448
1991-92	14-15	6-8	Brett Roberts	28.1	Dick Fick	
1992-93	6-21	6-10	Doug Bentz	20.7	Dick Fick	
1993-94	14-14	8-8	Johnnie Williams	14.0	Dick Fick	
1994-95	15-12	10-6	Tyrone Boardley	16.3	Dick Fick	
1995-96	7-20	2-14	Mark Kinnaird	13.8	Dick Fick	
1996-97	8-19	6-12	Doug Wyciscalla	15.8	Dick Fick	64-101 .388
1997-98	3-23	2-16	Aaron Knight	11.4	Kyle Macy	
1998-99	13-15	9-9	Erik Brown	19.2	Kyle Macy	
1999-2000	9-18	4-14	Brad Cleaver	16.7	Kyle Macy	
2000-01	12-16	6-10	Ricky Minard	16.7	Kyle Macy	
2001-02	18-11	11-5	Ricky Minard	22.3	Kyle Macy	
2002-03	20-9	13-3	Ricky Minard	22.5	Kyle Macy	
2003-04	16-13	10-6	Ricky Minard	21.8	Kyle Macy	
2004-05	11-16	5-11	Chad McKnight	16.9	Kyle Macy	
2005-06	4-23	3-17	Shaun Williams	16.4	Kyle Macy	106-144 .424
2006-07	12-18	8-12	Quentin Pryor	11.4	Donnie Tyndall	
2007-08	15-15	12-8	Leon Buchanan	13.2	Donnie Tyndall	
2008-09	20-16	12-6 ●	Leon Buchanan	15.1	Donnie Tyndall	47-49 .490

● NCAA Tournament appearance

PROFILE

Morehead State University, Morehead, KY
Founded: 1887 as Morehead Normal School
Enrollment: 9,278 (7,747 undergraduate)
Colors: Blue and gold
Nickname: Eagles
Current arena: Johnson Arena (6,500)
Previous: Wetherby Gymnasium, 1956-80 (N/A); Button Hall, 1929-56 (N/A)
First game: 1929
All-time record: 991-963 (.507)
Total weeks in AP Top 20/25: 0

Current conference: Ohio Valley (1948-)
Conference titles:
OVC: 9 (1956 [tie], '57 [tie], '61 [tie], '63 [tie], '69 [tie], '72 [tie], '74 [tie], '84, 2003 [tie])
Conference tournament titles:
OVC: 3 (1983, '84, 2009)
NCAA Tournament appearances: 6
NIT appearances: 0

TOP 5

G **Sonny Allen** (1946-50)
G **Ricky Minard** (2000-04)
F **Steve Hamilton** (1954-58)
F **Brett Roberts** (1988-92)
F **Dan Swartz** (1953-56)

RECORDS

RECORDS	GAME		SEASON		CAREER	
POINTS	53	Brett Roberts, vs. Middle Tennessee State (Feb. 10, 1992)	828	Dan Swartz (1955-56)	2,381	Ricky Minard (2000-04)
POINTS PER GAME			28.6	Dan Swartz (1955-56)	27.5	Dan Swartz (1953-56)
REBOUNDS	38	Steve Hamilton, vs. Florida State (Jan. 2, 1957)	543	Steve Hamilton (1956-57)	1,675	Steve Hamilton (1954-58)
ASSISTS	16	Marquis Sykes, vs. Tennessee State (Feb. 10, 2000); Jeff Fultz, vs. Middle Tennessee State (Dec. 16, 1984)	204	Nikola Stojakovic (2007-08)	606	Marquis Sykes (1999-2003)

ESPN 320 SAGARIN

MORGAN STATE

Marvin Webster. The mere mention of his name still makes men he played against flinch in fear of the Human Eraser. Webster's 1973-74 team won the College Division national title—a legacy that the Bears hope to approach someday on the Division I level.

BEST TEAM: 1973-74 Coach Nathaniel Frazier's Bears went 28–5 and took that national title with Webster and a supporting cast that included Billy Newton, Alvin O'Neal, Pat Edwards and Mike Streety. Webster, the school's all-time leading scorer, had his best season, averaging 21.4 points and 22.4 rebounds.

BEST PLAYER: C MARVIN WEBSTER (1971-75) The seven-foot center earned his nickname for the ferocity and frequency with which he wiped away opponents' shots. Webster played before blocked shots were officially counted, but it was not unusual for him to swat away a dozen or more in a game. Webster had a 10-year career in the ABA and NBA.

BEST COACH: NATHANIEL FRAZIER (1971-77, '85-89) He took the Bears to the '74 College Division title and, three years later, the school's first MEAC tournament title. He had two stints: His first featured six winning seasons—the school has had just eight others between 1960-61 and 2008-09—for a 123–50 record. The reprise was less sweet, a mere 43–70, and it ended after a much-publicized incident in which he refused to leave the gym after being ejected from a game against Florida A&M.

GAME FOR THE AGES: Morgan State capped off its brilliant 1973-74 season in the College division tournament final on March 15 against small-school power Southwest Missouri State (now Missouri State), which was appearing in its third title game in eight years. Webster and Co. barely broke a sweat in the 67-52 rout.

FIERCEST RIVAL: Morgan and in-state foe Maryland-Eastern Shore have met 94 times since 1954-55, with UMES leading the series, 48–46, thanks largely to its early dominance. But the Bears have been catching up fast, taking nine of 10 during a recent stretch, including a 87-52 victory on Jan. 31, 2009.

SEASON REVIEW

SEAS.	W-L	CONF.	COACH	SEAS.	W-L	CONF.	COACH
1930-48[a]	*158-66*	*15-0 in 1944-45*		1961-62	10-13		H. "Brutus" Wilson
1948-49	6-9		Talmadge Hill	1962-63	10-12		H. "Brutus" Wilson
1949-50	6-13		Talmadge Hill	1963-64	15-9		H. "Brutus" Wilson
1950-51	10-13		Talmadge Hill	1964-65	11-12		H. "Brutus" Wilson
1951-52	17-9		Talmadge Hill	1965-66	10-14		H. "Brutus" Wilson
1952-53	17-10		Talmadge Hill	1966-67	7-17		H. "Brutus" Wilson
1953-54	15-5		Talmadge Hill	1967-68	6-17		H. "Brutus" Wilson
1954-55	13-14		Talmadge Hill	1968-69	12-12		H. "Brutus" Wilson
1955-56	17-11		Talmadge Hill	1969-70	5-15		H. "Brutus" Wilson
1956-57	9-10		Talmadge Hill	1970-71	12-10		H. "Brutus" Wilson
1957-58	11-8		Talmadge Hill	1971-72	16-10	7-5	Nathaniel Frazier
1958-59	11-4		Talmadge Hill	1972-73	20-8	8-4	Nathaniel Frazier
1959-60	5-11		Talmadge Hill	1973-74	28-5	11-1 ◆	Nathaniel Frazier
1960-61	11-10		H."Brutus" Wilson	1974-75	19-10	8-4	Nathaniel Frazier

SEAS.	W-L	CONF.	SCORING		COACH	RECORD	
1975-76	22-6	11-1	Eric Evans	20.0	Nathaniel Frazier		
1976-77	18-11	7-5	Eric Evans	24.7	Nathaniel Frazier		
1977-78	15-12	9-3	Eric Evans	18.1	Aaron Johnson	15-12	.556
1978-79	18-12	6-6	Garcia Hopkins	19.2	Gus Guydon		
1979-80	7-16		Mike Warren	13.0	Gus Guydon		
1980-81	6-14		Yarharbrough Roberts	22.8	Gus Guydon	31-42	.425
1981-82	4-23		Yarharbrough Roberts	19.5	Billy Newton		
1982-83	8-20		Yarharbrough Roberts	20.1	Billy Newton		
1983-84	8-20		Jessie Jackson	19.2	Billy Newton	20-63	.241
1984-85	3-25	1-11	Thomas Foster	11.7	Nathaniel McMillian[b]	3-20	.130
1985-86	7-20	7-7	Troy Brown	15.4	Nathaniel Frazier		
1986-87	8-20	5-9	Troy Brown	14.3	Nathaniel Frazier		
1987-88	13-17	7-8	Troy Brown	17.5	Nathaniel Frazier		
1988-89	15-13	9-7	Anthony Reid	20.0	Nathaniel Frazier	166-120	.580
1989-90	8-20	4-12	Jermaine Williams	15.7	Nathaniel "Nate" Taylor	8-20	.286
1990-91	7-22	6-10	Glenn Smith	16.7	Michael Holmes		
1991-92	6-23	5-11	Obadiah Johnson	13.1	Michael Holmes		
1992-93	9-17	9-7	Chico Langston	15.5	Michael Holmes		
1993-94	8-21	4-12	Gerald Jordan	13.5	Michael Holmes	30-83	.265
1994-95	5-22	5-11	Terrance Wright	12.8	Lynn Ramage	5-22	.185
1995-96	7-20	6-10	Paul Grant	13.0	Chris Fuller		
1996-97	9-18	8-10	Tremaine Byrd	12.3	Chris Fuller		
1997-98	12-16	11-7	Tremaine Byrd	14.1	Chris Fuller		
1998-99	14-14	12-6	Rasheed Sparks	14.5	Chris Fuller		
1999-2000	5-24	5-13	Jimmy Fields	15.6	Chris Fuller		
2000-01	6-23	4-15	Curtis King	15.6	Chris Fuller	53-115	.315
2001-02	3-25	2-16	Curtis King	13.2	Butch Beard		
2002-03	7-22	6-12	Randy Dukes	14.9	Butch Beard		
2003-04	11-16	9-9	Aaron Andrews	11.0	Butch Beard		
2004-05	14-16	10-7	Sam Brand	13.1	Butch Beard		
2005-06	4-26	4-14	Joseph McLean	14.7	Butch Beard	39-105	.271
2006-07	13-18	10-8	Ronald Timus	14.5	Todd Bozeman		
2007-08	22-11	14-2 ■	Jamar Smith	16.6	Todd Bozeman		
2008-09	23-12	13-13 ●	Reggie Holmes	16.8	Todd Bozeman	58-41	.586

[a] Records from before 1930-31 have been lost.
[b] Nathaniel McMillian (3-20) and Tom Dean (0-5) both coached during the 1984-85 season.
● NCAA Tournament appearance ■ NIT appearance ◆ College Division championship

PROFILE

Morgan State University, Baltimore, MD
Founded: 1867
Enrollment: 7,005 (6,114 undergraduate)
Colors: Orange and blue
Nickname: Bears
Current arena: Talmadge Hill Field House, opened in 1974 (4,250)
Previous: Hurt Gymnasium, 1950-74 (1,000); 5th Regiment Armory/New Albert Hall, 1925-50 (N/A)
First game: Jan. 17, 1925
All-time record: 832-972 (.461)
Total weeks in AP Top 20/25: 0

Current conference: Mid-Eastern Athletic (1971-80, '84-)
Conference titles:
MEAC: 4 (1974 [tie], '76 [tie], 2008, '09)
Conference tournament titles:
MEAC: 2 (1977, 2009)
NCAA Tournament appearances: 1
NIT appearances: 1

CONSENSUS ALL-AMERICAS

1974, '75 **Marvin Webster** (College Div.), C

FIRST-ROUND PRO PICKS

1975 **Marvin Webster,** Atlanta (3)

TOP 5

G/F **Lee Cornish** (1963-66)
G/F **Yarharbrough Roberts** (1979-83)
F **Ernest Garrett** (1952-55)
F/C **Eric Evans** (1974-78)
C **Marvin Webster** (1971-75)

RECORDS

	GAME		SEASON		CAREER	
POINTS	48	Ernest Garrett, vs. Loyola (MD) (Feb. 12, 1954)	707	Marvin Webster (1973-74)	1,990	Marvin Webster (1971-75)
POINTS PER GAME			24.7	Eric Evans (1977-78)	20.7	Lee Cornish (1963-66)
REBOUNDS	32	Marvin Webster, vs. SC State (1973-74)	740	Marvin Webster (1973-74)	2,267	Marvin Webster (1971-75)
ASSISTS	14	Jerrell Green, vs. Coppin State (Dec. 6, 2006)	170	Jermaine Bolden (2008-09)	442	Jason McCoy (1987-91)

ESPN 243 SAGARIN

Mount St. Mary's

One of the best things to happen to this small Maryland Catholic school was the 1954 arrival of Jim Phelan and his trademark bowties. In nearly 50 years, Phelan's achievements rank him with coaching royalty.

BEST TEAM: 1980-81 It wasn't a team with a lot of stars, but Jim Rowe, Steve Rossignoli, Durelle Lewis and a deep rotation nearly took home a national title anyway. The Mountaineers lost just two regular-season games, but their third loss hurt most. It came to Florida Southern in the Division II championship game, 73-68.

BEST PLAYER: F Jack Sullivan (1953-57) The only Mountaineer to score 50 points or more in a game (twice), the 6'4" Sullivan averaged 25.4 ppg and 11.6 rpg for his career. He was from Washington, D.C., where he got to play against local star Elgin Baylor and Wilt Chamberlain, who spent a summer there.

BEST COACH: Jim Phelan (1954-2003) No, peach baskets were not still in use when Phelan took over at the Mount. He led the team to a 22–3 record his first season and would become the fourth coach to earn 800 wins, including the 1962 College Division national title. In 2006, the team's home floor—with painted bowties at each end—was renamed Coach Jim Phelan Court. Two years later, Phelan was inducted into the National Collegiate Basketball Hall of Fame.

GAME FOR THE AGES: The Mountaineers' 69-62 upset over Rider—after an anemic 16-point first half—in the 1995 Northeast Conference tournament final propelled the Mount into the NCAA Tournament for the first time. Silas Cheung scored all of his 19 points in the second half. If only that 113-67 loss to Kentucky hadn't followed.

FIERCEST RIVAL: Long-time foe Catholic University moved down to Divison III and the old rivalry has somewhat lapsed. The Mount has a long-standing yearly battle with Loyola (Md.). They've played in every season since 1931, a total of 163 games. The Mount leads overall, 95–68, but has just a 10–9 edge since 1988-89.

SEASON REVIEW

SEAS.	W-L	CONF.	COACH
1908-48	*395-246*	*9 straight winning seasons, '31-40*	
1948-49	10-10		Michael Kennedy
1949-50	7-15		John McMahon
1950-51	19-13		Pete Caruso
1951-52	5-16		Bill Clark
1952-53	20-7		Bill Clark
1953-54	15-11		Bill Clark
1954-55	22-3		Jim Phelan
1955-56	20-8		Jim Phelan
1956-57	27-5		Jim Phelan
1957-58	16-9		Jim Phelan
1958-59	15-12		Jim Phelan
1959-60	19-6		Jim Phelan
1960-61	26-5		Jim Phelan
1961-62	24-6	◆	Jim Phelan
1962-63	13-12		Jim Phelan
1963-64	18-7		Jim Phelan
1964-65	20-5		Jim Phelan
1965-66	21-6		Jim Phelan
1966-67	18-9		Jim Phelan
1967-68	22-4		Jim Phelan
1968-69	20-8		Jim Phelan
1969-70	20-6		Jim Phelan
1970-71	10-14		Jim Phelan
1971-72	6-17		Jim Phelan
1972-73	15-10		Jim Phelan
1973-74	17-10		Jim Phelan
1974-75	14-11		Jim Phelan

SEAS.	W-L	CONF.	SCORING		COACH	RECORD
1975-76	16-12		Mike Cataline	21.1	Jim Phelan	
1976-77	9-18		Mark Dwight	15.0	Jim Phelan	
1977-78	16-11		Steve Rossignoli	15.1	Jim Phelan	
1978-79	18-10		Jim Rowe	17.3	Jim Phelan	
1979-80	22-7		Jim Rowe	17.4	Jim Phelan	
1980-81	28-3		Jim Rowe	15.8	Jim Phelan	
1981-82	20-8		Durelle Lewis	16.4	Jim Phelan	
1982-83	18-9		Joe Reedy	19.0	Jim Phelan	
1983-84	21-9		Joe Reedy	18.7	Jim Phelan	
1984-85	28-5		Paul Edwards	12.9	Jim Phelan	
1985-86	26-4		Paul Edwards	17.0	Jim Phelan	
1986-87	26-5		Paul Edwards	17.8	Jim Phelan	
1987-88	20-8		Mike Tate	18.0	Jim Phelan	
1988-89	12-15		Mike Tate	16.9	Jim Phelan	
1989-90	16-12	10-6	Kevin Booth	18.5	Jim Phelan	
1990-91	8-19	6-10	John Miller	13.8	Jim Phelan	
1991-92	6-22	3-13	Kevin Booth	19.3	Jim Phelan	
1992-93	13-15	10-8	Chris McGuthrie	19.8	Jim Phelan	
1993-94	14-14	9-9	Chris McGuthrie	18.0	Jim Phelan	
1994-95	17-13	12-6 ●	Chris McGuthrie	19.7	Jim Phelan	
1995-96	21-8	16-2 ■	Chris McGuthrie	22.3	Jim Phelan	
1996-97	14-13	10-8	Gregory Harris	12.0	Jim Phelan	
1997-98	13-15	8-8	Gregory Harris	15.5	Jim Phelan	
1998-99	15-15	10-10 ●	Gregory Harris	17.0	Jim Phelan	
1999-2000	9-20	7-11	Gregory Harris	17.0	Jim Phelan	
2000-01	7-21	7-13	Aaron Herbert	12.4	Jim Phelan	
2001-02	3-24	2-18	Jamion Christian	11.3	Jim Phelan	
2002-03	11-16	6-12	Landy Thompson	15.6	Jim Phelan	830-524 .613
2003-04	10-19	8-10	Landy Thompson	17.7	Milan Brown	
2004-05	7-20	5-13	Landy Thompson	14.4	Milan Brown	
2005-06	13-17	11-7	Landy Thompson	13.7	Milan Brown	
2006-07	11-20	9-9	Chris Vann	13.6	Milan Brown	
2007-08	19-15	11-7 ●	Jeremy Goode	14.5	Milan Brown	
2008-09	19-14	12-6	Jeremy Goode	14.9	Milan Brown	79-105 .429

● NCAA Tournament appearance ■ NIT appearance ◆ College Division championship

PROFILE

Mount St. Mary's University, Emmitsburg, MD
Founded: 1808
Enrollment: 1,528 (1,100 undergraduate)
Colors: Blue and white
Nickname: Mountaineers
Current arena: Jim Phelan Court at Knott Arena, opened in 1987 (3,121)
First game: 1908
All-time record: 1,380-947 (.593)
Total weeks in AP Top 20/25: 0

Current conference: Northeast (1989-)
Conference titles:
Northeast: 1 (1996)
Conference tournament titles:
Northeast: 3 (1995, '99, 2008)
NCAA Tournament appearances: 3
NIT appearances: 1

CONSENSUS ALL-AMERICAS

1957 **Jack Sullivan** (Little A-A), F

TOP 5

G **Paul Edwards** (1982-87)
G **Gregory Harris** (1996-2000)
G **Chris McGuthrie** (1992-96)
F **Fred Carter** (1966-69)
F **Jack Sullivan** (1953-57)

RECORDS

RECORDS	GAME		SEASON		CAREER	
POINTS	55	Jack Sullivan, vs. Baltimore (Mar. 6, 1957)	1,070	Jack Sullivan (1956-57)	2,672	Jack Sullivan (1953-57)
POINTS PER GAME			33.4	Jack Sullivan (1956-57)	25.4	Jack Sullivan (1953-57)
REBOUNDS	34	Sal Angelo, vs. Gettysburg (Jan. 24, 1953)	609	Sal Angelo (1952-53)	1,368	Bob Sutor (1965-70)
ASSISTS	15	Riley Inge, vs. Robert Morris (Jan. 8, 1994); Jay Gallagher, vs. UMBC (Jan. 26, 1977)	225	Marlon Cook (1983-84)	529	Gregory Harris (1996-2000)

ESPN 99 SAGARIN

MURRAY STATE

Don't tell Kentucky fans, but the Bluegrass State school that stands fifth nationally with 22 straight winning seasons is Murray State. Only Syracuse, Oklahoma, Kansas and Arizona have more. The Racers' legacy includes a regular-season or tourney title in 14 of 20 years between 1988 and 2008, and standouts such as Joe Fulks, Popeye Jones and Jeff Martin.

BEST TEAM: 1997-98 Ohio Valley Conference Player of the Year De'Teri Mayes (21.5 ppg) led the Racers to 23 victories by double-digit margins, the conference regular-season and tournament titles and an AP Top 25 national ranking. Mayes' backcourt mate, Chad Townsend, along with forward Isaac Spencer, also made all-conference. But while Murray State was unbeaten at home, it couldn't translate its regular-season magic to the NCAA Tournament, where it lost to No. 8-seed (and Elite Eight-bound) Rhode Island, 97-74.

BEST PLAYER: F JEFF MARTIN (1985-89) No Division I basketball player in Kentucky has scored more points than Martin (2,484). The two-time OVC Player of the Year was the nation's fifth-leading scorer in 1988 (26.0 ppg), when he took the Racers to their first Tournament in 19 years. With his nifty outside touch, versatility (he could play shooting guard or small forward) and solid all-around game, he played two NBA seasons before enjoying a long career in Europe.

BEST COACH: CARLISLE CUTCHIN (1925-41) Before Murray State opened the Regional Special Events Center in 1998, it played its home games at Racer Arena in the Cutchin Fieldhouse, named after the coach who launched the program. In 1940-41, Cutchin led the Racers to the NAIB title game, where they lost to San Diego State and its four NAIB All-Americas, 36-34.

GAME FOR THE AGES: Coach Steve Newton's No. 14-seed Racers pulled off *the* upset of the 1988 Tournament, beating No. 3-seed NC State in the first round, 78-75, for the school's only Tourney win. The M&M Boys—Jeff Martin and Don Mann—led the way with 39 combined points, besting a Wolfpack team with six future NBAers, including the dream backcourt of Rodney Monroe and Chris Corchiani.

HEARTBREAKER: Murray State almost shocked the world in the 1990 Tournament, coming ever so close to becoming the first No. 16 seed to upset a No. 1. The Racers trailed Michigan State for most of regulation, but Popeye Jones' scoring barrage (37 points) kept things close, setting the stage for Greg Coble's buzzer-beater three that sent the game into OT. There, it took a crazy reverse layup from Spartans guard Kirk Manns to end the upset bid, 75-71.

FIERCEST RIVAL: It's not quite Kentucky-Louisville, but you can bet whenever Tennessee's Austin Peay travels 82 miles west to play Murray State, they'll be a raucous and relentless crowd awaiting. ("Flush the Peay" goes one of the more polite student chants.) Although the Racers lead the series 69–40, the Governors have played them tight since 1999-2000, winning 11 of 21.

> ***No Division I player in Kentucky has scored more points than Jeff Martin (2,484).***

FANFARE AND HOOPLA: Is it any wonder that Dunker, the Racers mascot, is so popular? Back in 1995, while returning home from an NCAA Tourney loss, the van carrying the team's cheerleaders blew a tire and flipped over. Jeff Piskos, the student playing Dunker at the time, was following in a pickup truck. He pulled over, climbed into the back of the van to retrieve one of the trapped cheerleaders, Brandon Vaughn, then wrapped up Vaughn's nearly severed arm with towels and sweatshirts. Physicians credited Piskos with saving Vaughn's life.

FAN FAVORITE: C POPEYE JONES (1988-92) Befitting his nickname, Ronald "Popeye" Jones never came up short in the effort department. The Racers had been to one NCAA Tournament in the 20 seasons before he arrived; with his grit and talent, he took them to three straight. Although he was only a second-round NBA draft pick, his determination paved the way for an 11-year pro career in which he averaged 7.0 ppg and 7.4 rpg.

THE SCHOOLS

PROFILE

Murray State University, Murray, KY
Founded: 1922
Enrollment: 10,350 (8,607 undergraduate)
Colors: Navy and gold
Nickname: Racers
Current arena: Regional Special Events Center, opened in 1998 (8,600)
Previous: Racer Arena, 1954-98 (5,500); Carr Health Building, 1950-54 (3,000); Lovett Auditorium, 1925-50 (1,500)
First game: Jan. 17, 1926

All-time record: 1394-810 (.632)
Total weeks in AP Top 20/25: 10
Current conference: Ohio Valley (1948-)
Conference titles:
OVC: 20 (1951, '64, '68 [tie], '69 [tie], '80 [tie], '82 [tie], '83, '88, '89 [tie], '90, '91, '92, '94, '95 [tie], '96, '97 [tie], '98, '99, 2000 [tie], '06)
Conference tournament titles:
OVC: 13 (1951, '64, '88, '90, '91, '92, '95, '97, '98, '99, 2002, '04, '06)
NCAA Tournament appearances: 13
NIT appearances: 6

TOP 5

G	**Marcus Brown** (1992-96)
G	**Howie Crittenden** (1952-56)
F	**Joe Fulks** (1941-43)
F	**Jeff Martin** (1985-89)
C	**Popeye Jones** (1988-92)

RECORDS

RECORDS	GAME		SEASON		CAREER	
POINTS	45	Marcus Brown, vs. Washington (Dec. 16, 1995)	806	Jeff Martin (1987-88)	2,484	Jeff Martin (1985-89)
POINTS PER GAME			26.4	Marcus Brown (1995-96)	21.3	De'Teri Mayes (1996-98)
REBOUNDS	36	Dick Cunningham, vs. MacMurray (Jan. 2, 1967)	479	Dick Cunningham (1966-67)	1,374	Popeye Jones (1988-92)
ASSISTS	16	Chad Townsend, vs. Eastern Illinois (Feb. 20, 1997)	212	Chad Townsend (1996-97)	531	Don Mann (1985-89)

SEASON REVIEW

SEASON	W-L	CONF.	SCORING		COACH	RECORD
1925-26	9-5		Ty Holland	11.1	Carlisle Cutchin	
1926-27	11-9		Ty Holland	11.0	Carlisle Cutchin	
1927-28	8-9		Ty Holland	9.3	Carlisle Cutchin	
1928-29	12-8		John Miller	10.2	Carlisle Cutchin	
1929-30	19-2		Jim Miller	10.6	Carlisle Cutchin	
1930-31	12-6		Jim Miller	11.2	Carlisle Cutchin	
1931-32	17-3		Willard Bagwell	14.5	Carlisle Cutchin	
1932-33	14-6		Willard Bagwell	17.3	Carlisle Cutchin	
1933-34	11-6		Basil Crider	7.5	Carlisle Cutchin	
1934-35	18-6		Ross Magruder	8.0	Carlisle Cutchin	
1935-36	23-2		Floyd Burdette	8.0	Carlisle Cutchin	
1936-37	22-3		Floyd Burdette	11.4	Carlisle Cutchin	

SEAS.	W-L	CONF.	POSTSEASON	SCORING		REBOUNDS		ASSISTS		COACH	RECORD	
1937-38	27-4			Floyd Burdette	10.7					Carlisle Cutchin		
1938-39	13-8			Ned Washer	13.1					Carlisle Cutchin		
1939-40	14-9			Bill Carneal	7.5					Carlisle Cutchin		
1940-41	26-5			Durwood Culp	11.1					Carlisle Cutchin	267-101	.726
1941-42	18-4			Joe Fulks	12.9					Rick Mountjoy	18-4	.818
1942-43	21-5			Joe Fulks	13.5					John Miller		
1943-44	5-9			Herb Hurley	12.0					John Miller		
1944-45	12-10			Johnny Reagan	11.6					John Miller		
1945-46	10-13			Zadia Herrold	10.9					John Miller		
1946-47	14-11			Johnny Reagan	12.0					John Miller		
1947-48	12-12			Johnny Reagan	9.0					John Miller[a]	74-60	.552
1948-49	13-12	3-9		Zadia Herrold	10.7					Harlan Hodges		
1949-50	18-13	5-7		Madison Stanford	10.3					Harlan Hodges		
1950-51	21-6	9-3		Garrett Beshear	13.6					Harlan Hodges		
1951-52	24-10	9-3		Bennie Purcell	18.3	Melvin Deweese	11.0			Harlan Hodges		
1952-53	18-9	7-3		Garrett Beshear	23.8	Garrett Beshear	9.4			Harlan Hodges		
1953-54	15-16	6-4		Howie Crittenden	21.0	Fran Watrous	7.8			Harlan Hodges	109-66	.622
1954-55	11-15	6-4		Howie Crittenden	21.3	Jim Gainey	9.7			Rex Alexander		
1955-56	15-10	6-4		Howie Crittenden	21.2	Joe Mikez	8.8			Rex Alexander		
1956-57	11-13	5-5		Quitman Sullins	16.7	Quitman Sullins	13.5			Rex Alexander		
1957-58	8-16	4-6		Quitman Sullins	12.8	Quitman Sullins	12.5			Rex Alexander	45-54	.455
1958-59	10-15	3-9		Terry Darnall	14.1	Ken Peterson	9.2			Cal Luther		
1959-60	12-11	7-4		Gene Herndon	15.5	Gene Herndon	11.6			Cal Luther		
1960-61	13-10	7-5		Gene Herndon	14.8	Gene Herndon	14.3			Cal Luther		
1961-62	13-12	5-7		Jim Jennings	20.5	Jim Jennings	17.2			Cal Luther		
1962-63	13-9	6-6		Jim Jennings	17.6	Jim Jennings	16.1			Cal Luther		
1963-64	16-9	11-3	NCAA FIRST ROUND	Jim Jennings	19.6	Jim Jennings	15.1			Cal Luther		
1964-65	19-7	9-5		S. Johnson, J. Namciu	20.0	Stewart Johnson	14.1			Cal Luther		
1965-66	13-12	8-6		Herb McPherson	21.2	Dick Cunningham	15.6			Cal Luther		
1966-67	14-9	8-6		Herb McPherson	21.8	Dick Cunningham	21.8			Cal Luther		
1967-68	16-8	10-4		Billy Chumbler	15.5	Dick Cunningham	18.4			Cal Luther		
1968-69	22-6	11-3	NCAA FIRST ROUND	Claude Virden	23.5	Claude Virden	11.4			Cal Luther		
1969-70	17-9	9-5		Claude Virden	20.4	Ron Johnson	12.5			Cal Luther		
1970-71	19-5	10-4		Jimmy Young	16.1	Ron Johnson	9.8			Cal Luther		
1971-72	15-11	6-8		Les Taylor	25.6	Marcelous Starks	10.9			Cal Luther		
1972-73	17-8	9-5		Les Taylor	22.4	Mike Coleman	11.9	Les Taylor	3.3	Cal Luther		
1973-74	12-13	6-8		Mike Coleman	24.1	Marcelous Starks	12.8	Darnell Adell	2.1	Cal Luther	241-154	.610
1974-75	10-15	3-11		Jesse Williams	20.8	Larry Moffett	10.3	Grover Woolard	4.7	Fred Overton		
1975-76	9-17	5-9		Jesse Williams	21.1	Jesse Williams	8.7	Grover Woolard	4.3	Fred Overton		
1976-77	17-10	9-5		Mike Muff	18.8	Mike Muff	8.4	Grover Woolard	4.3	Fred Overton		
1977-78	8-17	4-10		Mike Muff	23.6	Mike Muff	9.4	Mike Muff	2.7	Fred Overton	44-59	.427
1978-79	4-22	2-10		John Randall	13.1	John Randall	8.4	David Lowry	3.8	Ron Greene		
1979-80	23-8	10-2	NIT QUARTERFINALS	Gary Hooker	18.6	Gary Hooker	12.3	Lamont Sleets	5.1	Ron Greene		
1980-81	17-10	10-4		Lamont Sleets	16.7	Kenney Hammonds	6.4	Lamont Sleets	3.7	Ron Greene		
1981-82	20-8	13-3	NIT FIRST ROUND	Glen Green	14.9	Ricky Hood	8.9	Glen Green	4.9	Ron Greene		
1982-83	21-8	11-3	NIT FIRST ROUND	Glen Green	20.1	Ricky Hood	10.2	Lamont Sleets	4.0	Ron Greene		
1983-84	15-13	7-7		Lamont Sleets	18.3	Vada Martin	6.2	Brian Stewart	3.6	Ron Greene		
1984-85	19-9	8-6		Vada Martin	13.0	Vada Martin	6.3	Chuck Glass	4.0	Ron Greene	119-78	.604
1985-86	17-12	8-6		Chuck Glass	18.2	Chuck Glass	6.8	Don Mann	3.0	Steve Newton		
1986-87	13-15	6-8		Jeff Martin	21.2	Jeff Martin	5.6	Don Mann	4.6	Steve Newton		
1987-88	22-9	13-1	NCAA SECOND ROUND	Jeff Martin	26.0	Chris Ogden	6.8	Don Mann	6.0	Steve Newton		
1988-89	19-11	10-2	NIT FIRST ROUND	Jeff Martin	25.7	Linzie Foster	6.8	Don Mann	5.7	Steve Newton		
1989-90	21-9	10-2	NCAA FIRST ROUND	Popeye Jones	19.5	Popeye Jones	11.2	Frank Allen	3.6	Steve Newton		
1990-91	24-9	10-2	NCAA FIRST ROUND	Popeye Jones	20.2	Popeye Jones	14.2	Greg Coble	3.6	Steve Newton	116-65	.641
1991-92	17-13	11-3	NCAA FIRST ROUND	Popeye Jones	21.1	Popeye Jones	14.4	Maurice Cannon	3.7	Scott Edgar		
1992-93	18-12	11-5		Frank Allen	16.7	Jerry Wilson	4.8	Frank Allen	2.3	Scott Edgar		
1993-94	23-6	15-1	NIT FIRST ROUND	Marcus Brown	18.1	Antwan Hoard	5.0	Cedric Gumm	3.0	Scott Edgar		
1994-95	21-9	11-5	NCAA FIRST ROUND	Marcus Brown	22.4	Vincent Rainey	6.1	William Moore	3.3	Scott Edgar	79-40	.664
1995-96	19-10 ⊗	12-4	NIT FIRST ROUND	Marcus Brown	26.4	Fred Walker	7.5	Marcus Brown	4.1	Mark Gottfried		
1996-97	20-10	12-6	NCAA FIRST ROUND	Vincent Rainey	21.9	Vincent Rainey	8.2	Chad Townsend	7.1	Mark Gottfried		
1997-98	29-4	16-2	NCAA FIRST ROUND	De'Teri Mayes	21.5	Isaac Spencer	8.3	Chad Townsend	5.2	Mark Gottfried	68-24	.739▼
1998-99	27-6	16-2	NCAA FIRST ROUND	Isaac Spencer	16.0	Isaac Spencer	7.1	Aubrey Reese	4.9	Tevester Anderson		
1999-2000	23-9	14-4		Aubrey Reese	20.4	Isaac Spencer	8.2	Aubrey Reese	4.8	Tevester Anderson		
2000-01	17-12	11-5		Isaac Spencer	21.6	Antione Whelchel	7.8	Isaac Spencer	3.9	Tevester Anderson		
2001-02	19-13	10-6	NCAA FIRST ROUND	Justin Burdine	20.4	James Singleton	10.1	Kevin Paschel	3.9	Tevester Anderson		
2002-03	17-12	9-7		Cuthbert Victor	15.3	James Singleton	11.0	Mark Borders	3.1	Tevester Anderson	103-52	.665
2003-04	28-6	14-2	NCAA FIRST ROUND	Cuthbert Victor	14.6	Cuthbert Victor	10.2	Adam Chiles	4.6	Mick Cronin		
2004-05	17-11	11-5		Trey Pearson	14.5	Shawn Witherspoon	5.0	Keith Jenifer	4.0	Mick Cronin		
2005-06	24-7	17-3	NCAA FIRST ROUND	Shawn Witherspoon	10.6	Shawn Witherspoon	7.7	Keith Jenifer	3.4	Mick Cronin	69-24	.742
2006-07	16-14	13-7		Bruce Carter	12.1	Shawn Witherspoon	5.5	Ed Horton	3.2	Billy Kennedy		
2007-08	18-13	13-7		Bruce Carter	14.5	Bruce Carter	5.6	Kevin Thomas	4.5	Billy Kennedy		
2008-09	19-12	13-5		Danero Thomas	12.5	Ivan Aska	5.8	K. Thomas, I. Miles	3.1	Billy Kennedy	53-39	.576

[a] John Miller (1-2) and Carlisle Cutchin (11-10) both coached during the 1947-48 season.

⊗ Records don't reflect games forfeited or vacated. For adjusted records, see p. 521.

▼ Coach's record adjusted to reflect games forfeited or vacated: 69-23, .750. For yearly totals, see p. 521.

ESPN 146 SAGARIN

NAVY

You can't join the Navy if you're over 77 inches tall, which is why the Midshipmen don't often turn up in the NCAA Tournament. But with a stream of early 20th century All-Americas and, of course, the late-blooming David Robinson, Navy boasts the proudest hoops tradition of all the service academies.

BEST TEAM: 1985-86 The Admiral led the way on both offense and defense, but forward Vernon Butler also played a huge role in Navy's Elite Eight run—he's the school's No. 2 scorer and rebounder after Robinson. The two combined to average 50 points, 20 rebounds and 7 blocks and led the Middies to three Tournament wins before they were bounced by Duke, 71-50.

BEST PLAYER: C David Robinson (1983-87) He came to Annapolis as a 6'4" plebe and left as a 7'1" Player of the Year. A true two-way force, Robinson came up big when it counted most, taking Navy to three straight Tourneys (1985 to '87) and scoring 50 points in his final game, a first-round loss to Michigan on March 12, 1987. He was the NBA's top draft pick (Spurs) in 1987.

BEST COACH: Ben Carnevale (1946-66) A supreme tactician, Carnevale memorably outcoached North Carolina's Frank McGuire in a 76-63 upset of the No. 9-ranked Tar Heels in the 1959 NCAA Tournament. Carnevale led Navy to five other postseason appearances in his 20 years in Annapolis.

GAME FOR THE AGES: No. 2-seed Syracuse should have made easy work of the Middies in the second round of the 1986 NCAA Tournament, playing on its home court with an early-season romp over Navy already under its belt. But Robinson was spectacular, destroying the Orangemen with 35 points, 11 rebounds, 7 blocks and 3 steals in the 97-85 upset.

FIERCEST RIVAL: When the Midshipmen beat Army, each player gets an N-Star for his letter sweater. If that's not motivation enough, the "Go Navy! Beat Army!" chant is driven into their heads from Day 1. Naturally, Alumni Hall's top 10 crowds have all been for Navy-Army games. The Midshipmen lead overall, 68–42.

SEASON REVIEW

SEAS.	W-L	CONF.	COACH
1907-49	*470-151*	*Helms champ 1912-13 (9-0)*	
1949-50	14-7		Ben Carnevale
1950-51	16-6		Ben Carnevale
1951-52	16-7		Ben Carnevale
1952-53	16-5	●	Ben Carnevale
1953-54	18-8	●	Ben Carnevale
1954-55	11-9		Ben Carnevale
1955-56	10-9		Ben Carnevale
1956-57	15-8		Ben Carnevale
1957-58	10-10		Ben Carnevale
1958-59	18-6	●	Ben Carnevale
1959-60	16-6	●	Ben Carnevale
1960-61	10-9		Ben Carnevale
1961-62	13-8	■	Ben Carnevale
1962-63	9-9		Ben Carnevale
1963-64	10-12		Ben Carnevale
1964-65	10-10		Ben Carnevale
1965-66	7-12		Ben Carnevale
1966-67	8-10		Dave Smalley
1967-68	9-11		Dave Smalley
1968-69	7-14		Dave Smalley
1969-70	4-19		Dave Smalley
1970-71	12-12		Dave Smalley
1971-72	10-13		Dave Smalley
1972-73	13-12		Dave Smalley
1973-74	9-13		Dave Smalley
1974-75	12-12		Dave Smalley
1975-76	10-14		Dave Smalley

SEAS.	W-L	CONF.	SCORING		COACH	RECORD
1976-77	13-11		Kevin Sinnett	16.0	Bob Hamilton	
1977-78	14-11		Kevin Sinnett	18.1	Bob Hamilton	
1978-79	13-12		Kevin Sinnett	19.3	Bob Hamilton	
1979-80	14-13		Dave Brooks	12.0	Bob Hamilton	54-47 .535
1980-81	9-16		Dave Brooks	10.8	Paul Evans	
1981-82	12-14	2-4	Rob Romaine	14.9	Paul Evans	
1982-83	18-11	3-3	Dave Brooks	17.0	Paul Evans	
1983-84	24-8	6-4	Vernon Butler	14.7	Paul Evans	
1984-85	26-6	11-3 ●	David Robinson	23.6	Paul Evans	
1985-86	30-5	13-1 ●	David Robinson	22.7	Paul Evans	119-60 .665
1986-87	26-6	13-1 ●	David Robinson	28.2	Pete Herrmann	
1987-88	12-16	6-8	Cliff Rees	13.9	Pete Herrmann	
1988-89	6-22	1-13	Eddie Reddick	15.1	Pete Herrmann	
1989-90	5-23	4-10	Eddie Reddick	12.8	Pete Herrmann	
1990-91	8-21	2-12	Erik Harris	20.0	Pete Herrmann	
1991-92	6-22	1-13	John Haase	13.0	Pete Herrmann	63-110 .364
1992-93	8-19	5-9	Chuck Robinson	10.3	Don DeVoe	
1993-94	17-13	9-5 ●	T.J. Hall	13.7	Don DeVoe	
1994-95	20-9	10-4	Michael Heary	13.6	Don DeVoe	
1995-96	15-12	9-3	Michael Heary	11.0	Don DeVoe	
1996-97	20-9	10-2 ●	Michael Heary	17.9	Don DeVoe	
1997-98	19-11	10-2 ●	Michael Heary	13.6	Don DeVoe	
1998-99	20-7	9-3	Chris Williams	13.7	Don DeVoe	
1999-2000	23-6	11-1	Sitapha Savane	16.9	Don DeVoe	
2000-01	19-12	9-3	Chris Williams	17.9	Don DeVoe	
2001-02	10-20	5-9	Jason Jeanpierre	10.9	Don DeVoe	
2002-03	8-20	4-10	Jason Jeanpierre	11.3	Don DeVoe	
2003-04	5-23	2-12	David Hooper	7.8	Don DeVoe	184-161 .533
2004-05	9-19 ✪	5-9	Matt Fannin	10.9	Billy Lange	
2005-06	10-18	3-11	Greg Sprink	14.9	Billy Lange	
2006-07	14-16	4-10	Greg Sprink	16.9	Billy Lange	
2007-08	16-14	9-5	Greg Sprink	21.8	Billy Lange	
2008-09	19-11	8-6	Kaleo Kina	18.0	Billy Lange	68-78 .466

✪ **Records don't reflect games forfeited or vacated. For adjusted records,** **see p. 521.**
● **NCAA Tournament appearance** ■ **NIT appearance**

PROFILE

United States Naval Academy, Annapolis, MD
Founded: 1845
Enrollment: 4,200 (4,200 undergraduate)
Colors: Navy blue and gold
Nickname: Midshipmen
Current arena: Alumni Hall, opened in 1991 (5,710)
Previous: Halsey Field House, 1958-91 (6,400); Dahlgren Hall, 1907-58 (N/A)
First game: Dec.14, 1907
All-time record: 1,271-878 (.591)
Total weeks in AP Top 20/25: 23
Current conference: Patriot League (1991-)

Conference titles:
ECAC South: 1 (1985 [tie]); Colonial: 2 (1986, '87); Patriot: 5 (1994 [tie], '96 [tie], '97, '98 [tie], 2000 [tie])
Conference tournament titles:
ECAC South: 1 (1985); Colonial: 2 (1986, '87); Patriot: 3 (1994, '97, '98)
NCAA Tournament appearances: 11
Sweet 16s (since 1975): 1
NIT appearances: 1

CONSENSUS ALL-AMERICAS

1911 **Harry Hill,** F
1913 **Laurence Wild,** F
1919 **Knight Farwell,** G
1922, '23 **Ira McKee,** G
1933 **Elliott Loughlin,** G
1987 **David Robinson,** C

FIRST-ROUND PRO PICKS

1987 **David Robinson,** San Antonio (1)

TOP 5

G **Ira McKee** (1920-24)
G/F **John Clune** (1951-54)
F **Vernon Butler** (1982-86)
F **Don Lange** (1951-54)
C **David Robinson** (1983-87)

RECORDS

RECORDS	GAME		SEASON		CAREER	
POINTS	50	David Robinson, vs. Michigan (March 12, 1987)	903	David Robinson (1986-87)	2,669	David Robinson (1983-87)
POINTS PER GAME			28.2	David Robinson (1986-87)	22.3	John Clune (1951-54)
REBOUNDS	35	Don Lange, vs. Loyola (Md.) (Feb. 18, 1953)	455	David Robinson (1985-86)	1,314	David Robinson (1983-87)
ASSISTS	14	Erik Harris, vs. UNC Wilmington (Jan. 7, 1991); Doug Wojcik, vs. East Carolina (March 7, 1985); Doug Wojcik, vs. Loyola (Md.) (Jan. 5, 1985); achieved two other times	251	Doug Wojcik (1985-86)	714	Doug Wojcik (1984-87)

THE SCHOOLS

ESPN 57 SAGARIN

NEBRASKA

THE SCHOOLS

Trivia question: Of the 73 teams in BCS conferences, what three have never won an NCAA Tournament game? The answer: Northwestern has never even made the Big Dance, South Florida is 0–2 and Nebraska is 0–6. But don't dismiss the Cornhuskers as just another big-time football school. The Huskers did win the 1996 NIT, and they've made 15 other appearances in that tournament. And they've won 20-plus games 10 times since 1977-78, with only six losing seasons during that span.

BEST TEAM: 1990-91 Before the season began, Big Eight coaches predicted NU would finish last. In fact, the season ended in a more disappointing fashion than that, with a first-round NCAA Tournament loss to No. 14-seed Xavier. But nearly every moment leading up to that game was pure magic, highlighted by three wins over Oklahoma. The balanced Huskers featured eight future pros, including 7'2" Rich King (15.5 ppg) and freshman sixth man Eric Piatkowski (a.k.a. the Polish Rifle).

BEST PLAYER: C Dave Hoppen (1982-86) The Nebraska native started his college career with a bang, leading the Huskers to the NIT final four as a freshman while averaging a team-best 13.9 points. Three years later, he had broken or tied 19 school records, despite suffering a season-ending knee injury in February of his senior year that caused him to miss the school's first Tournament appearance. The three-time All-Big Eight player was the first basketball player to have his jersey retired at NU.

BEST COACH: Danny Nee (1986-2000) Nearly as famous for his loud ties as his up-tempo system, Nee stood in stark contrast to stoic Huskers football coach Tom Osborne. He sometimes took heat for his team's lack of execution and discipline, and was fired in 2000 after a 11–19 season. But it's hard to beat his record: Nee is tied with Joe Cipriano as the all-time school leader in wins, and his squads set a Nebraska record by making nine straight post-season appearances from 1990-91 through '98-99.

GAME FOR THE AGES: On Feb. 8, 1958, Kansas and Wilt Chamberlain handed NU its worst loss ever, a 102-46 laugher. Two weeks later, the Huskers laughed last. Coach Jerry Bush kept Chamberlain in check by slowing the game down. Meanwhile, with six minutes left, injured Huskers guard Jim Kubacki, who started the game in street clothes, persuaded Bush to let him play. You guessed it—with two seconds left and the score tied at 41, Kubacki fired a 15-footer over Chamberlain that swished through.

HEARTBREAKER: Anticipating the school's first Tournament win, Nebraska fans flocked to Minneapolis for the Huskers' 1991 first-round matchup with Xavier. But the team played shakily, hitting just 14 of 27 free throws, while the Musketeers made five free throws down the stretch to pull off the 89-84 upset. Fifteen years later, Piatkowski admitted to the *Lincoln Journal Star* that he and his mates had underestimated Xavier.

FIERCEST RIVAL: Oklahoma, Colorado, Texas, Iowa State—Nebraska always wants to beat its traditional football rivals. But the Huskers' most entertaining series of late has been with its only in-state D1 rival, Creighton. In the 2004 NIT, NU beat the Bluejays, 71-70, on Nate Johnson's last-second shot. Nine months later, Creighton won 50-48 on Kellen Miliner's shot with under a tick to go. Fast forward to Nov. 29, 2008, when the Huskers came back from 13 down to win 54-52. NU leads overall, 24–18.

FANFARE AND HOOPLA: Nebraska played so poorly in that 102-46 loss to Kansas in 1958 that Jayhawks fans at the Allen Fieldhouse threw popcorn boxes at Huskers players as they walked off the floor. That's just cold.

FAN FAVORITE: G Jack Moore (1978-82) Two years after winning the 1982 Frances Pomeroy Naismith Award, given annually to the top senior player 6'0" or under, the 5'9" Moore was killed in a plane crash. The team's Most Outstanding Player award is named after him.

CONSENSUS ALL-AMERICAS

1913	**Sam Carrier,** G

FIRST-ROUND PRO PICKS

1991	**Rich King,** Seattle (14)
1994	**Eric Piatkowski,** Indiana (15)
1998	**Tyronn Lue,** Denver (23)

PROFILE

University of Nebraska-Lincoln, Lincoln, NE
Founded: 1869
Enrollment: 22,973 (18,555 undergraduate)
Colors: Scarlet and cream
Nickname: Cornhuskers
Current arena: Bob Devaney Sports Center, opened in 1976 (13,595)
Previous: NU Coliseum, 1926-76 (8,000); Grant Memorial Hall, 1897-1926 (2,000)
First game: Feb. 2, 1897
All-time record: 1,353-1,203 (.529)
Total weeks in AP Top 20/25: 29
Current conference: Big 12 (1996-)
Conference titles:
Missouri Valley: 4 (1912 [tie], '13, '14 [tie], '16)
Big Six: 1 (1937 [tie])
Big Seven: 2 (1949 [tie], '50 [tie])
Conference tournament titles:
Big Eight: 1 (1994)
NCAA Tournament appearances: 6
NIT appearances: 16
Semifinals: 3
Titles: 1 (1996)

TOP 5

G **Jerry Fort** (1972-76)
G **Tyronn Lue** (1995-98)
G/F **Eric Piatkowski** (1990-94)
F/C **Andre Smith** (1977-81)
C **Dave Hoppen** (1982-86)

RECORDS	GAME		SEASON		CAREER	
POINTS	42	Eric Piatkowski, vs. Oklahoma (March 11, 1994)	704	Dave Hoppen (1984-85)	2,167	Dave Hoppen (1982-86)
POINTS PER GAME			23.5	Dave Hoppen (1984-85)	19.5	Dave Hoppen (1982-86)
REBOUNDS	26	Bill Johnson, vs. Iowa State (Jan. 4, 1954)	335	Aleks Maric (2007-08); Venson Hamilton (1998-99)	1,080	Venson Hamilton (1995-99)
ASSISTS	18	Brian Carr, vs. Evansville (Jan. 3, 1985)	237	Brian Carr (1984-85)	682	Brian Carr (1983-87)

SEASON REVIEW

SEASON	W-L	CONF.	SCORING	COACH	RECORD	
897-1916	170-93		56-14 (.800) under E.O. "Jumbo" Stiehm from 1911-15			
916-17	12-10	4-8		E.J. Stewart		
917-18	7-7	4-5		E.J. Stewart		
918-19	10-6	10-6		E.J. Stewart	29-23	.558
919-20	22-2			Paul Schlisser		
920-21	15-3	9-1		Paul Schlisser	37-5	.881
921-22	8-9	8-8		Owen A. Frank		
922-23	6-12	5-11		Owen A. Frank	14-21	.400
923-24	11-7	10-6		W.E. Kline		
924-25	14-4	13-3		W.E. Kline	25-11	.694
925-26	8-10	7-7		Ernest Bearg	8-10	.444
1926-27	12-6	7-5		Charlie T. Black		
1927-28	7-11	7-11		Charlie T. Black		
1928-29	11-5	5-5		Charlie T. Black		
1929-30	9-9	6-4		Charlie T. Black		
1930-31	9-9	6-4		Charlie T. Black		
1931-32	3-17	2-8		Charlie T. Black	51-57	.472
1932-33	3-13	2-8		William H. Browne		
1933-34	7-11	5-5		William H. Browne		
1934-35	6-12	3-7		William H. Browne		
1935-36	13-8	7-3		William H. Browne		
1936-37	13-7	8-2		William H. Browne		

SEAS.	W-L	CONF.	POSTSEASON	SCORING		REBOUNDS		ASSISTS		COACH	RECORD	
937-38	9-11	4-6								William H. Browne		
938-39	7-13	3-7								William H. Browne		
939-40	6-12	2-8								William H. Browne	64-87	.424
940-41	8-10	6-4								A.J. Lewandowski		
941-42	6-13	4-6								A.J. Lewandowski		
942-43	6-10	5-5								A.J. Lewandowski		
943-44	2-13	1-9								A.J. Lewandowski		
944-45	2-17	1-9								A.J. Lewandowski	24-63	.276
945-46	7-13	3-7								L.F. Klein	7-13	.350
946-47	10-14	3-7								Harry C. Good		
947-48	11-13	5-7		Claude Retherford	10.8					Harry C. Good		
948-49	16-10	9-3		Claude Retherford	12.0					Harry C. Good		
949-50	16-7	8-4		Bus Whitehead	15.7					Harry C. Good		
950-51	9-14	4-8		Bob Pierce	16.7					Harry C. Good		
951-52	7-17	3-9		Jim Buchanan	16.7	Bill Johnson	7.6			Harry C. Good		
952-53	9-11	4-8		Bill Johnson	13.9	Bill Johnson	9.4			Harry C. Good		
953-54	8-13	5-7		Bill Johnson	18.2	Bill Johnson	11.2			Harry C. Good	86-99	.465
954-55	9-12	6-6		Willard Fagler	13.6	Rex Ekwall	11.5			Jerry Bush		
955-56	7-16	3-9		Rex Ekwall	14.9	Rex Ekwall	10.7			Jerry Bush		
956-57	11-12	5-7		Rex Ekwall	13.3	Rex Ekwall	9.3			Jerry Bush		
957-58	10-13	5-7		G. Reimers, W. Fitzpatrick	11.5	Herschell Turner	8.2			Jerry Bush		
958-59	12-13	5-9		Herschell Turner	17.1	Herschell Turner	9.8			Jerry Bush		
959-60	7-17	4-10		Herschell Turner	15.9	Herschell Turner	8.0			Jerry Bush		
960-61	10-14 ⊗	4-10		Tom Russell	12.5	Tom Russell	9.7			Jerry Bush		
961-62	9-16	5-9		Tom Russell	16.5	Tom Russell	8.0			Jerry Bush		
962-63	6-19	1-13		Daryl Petsch	14.8	Charlie Jones	8.2			Jerry Bush	81-132	.380
963-64	7-18	5-9		Charlie Jones	12.9	Charlie Jones	6.8			Joe Cipriano		
964-65	10-15	5-9		Fred Hare	15.2	Fred Hare	7.4			Joe Cipriano		
965-66	20-5	12-2		Tom Baack	15.4	Stuart Lantz	8.0			Joe Cipriano		
966-67	16-9	10-4	NIT QUARTERFINALS	Stuart Lantz	19.2	Stuart Lantz	7.7			Joe Cipriano		
967-68	15-10	8-6		Stuart Lantz	19.3	Stuart Lantz	7.2			Joe Cipriano		
968-69	12-14	5-9		Marvin Stewart	14.6	Leroy Chalk	9.9			Joe Cipriano		
969-70	16-9	7-7		Tom Scantlebury	14.4	Leroy Chalk	9.4			Joe Cipriano		
970-71	18-8	8-6		Marvin Stewart	21.4	Leroy Chalk	11.2			Joe Cipriano		
971-72	14-12	7-7		Chuck Jura	21.2	Chuck Jura	11.7			Joe Cipriano		
972-73	9-17	4-10		Jerry Fort	14.5	Brendy Lee	7.1			Joe Cipriano		
973-74	14-12	7-7		Jerry Fort	18.0	Brendy Lee	7.6	Ricky Marsh	3.0	Joe Cipriano		
974-75	14-12	7-7		Jerry Fort	20.2	Bob Siegel	8.7	Steve Erwin	3.3	Joe Cipriano		
975-76	19-8	10-4		Jerry Fort	19.0	Larry Cox	6.1	Jerry Fort	3.1	Joe Cipriano		
976-77	15-14 ⊗	7-7		Carl McPipe	15.2	Carl McPipe	8.3	Allen Holder	4.1	Joe Cipriano		
977-78	22-8	9-5	NIT QUARTERFINALS	Carl McPipe	15.3	Carl McPipe	7.9	Brian Banks	3.2	Joe Cipriano		
978-79	14-13	7-7		Andre Smith	13.5	Carl McPipe	7.5	Bob Moore	3.0	Joe Cipriano		
979-80	18-13	8-6	NIT FIRST ROUND	Andre Smith	19.4	Andre Smith	8.1	Jack Moore	4.7	Joe Cipriano	253-197	.562▼
980-81	15-12	9-5		Andre Smith	18.3	Andre Smith	6.6	Jack Moore	4.0	Moe Iba		
981-82	16-12	7-7		Jack Moore	12.7	Jerry Shoecraft	4.4	Jack Moore	4.0	Moe Iba		
982-83	22-10	9-5	NIT SEMIFINALS	Dave Hoppen	13.9	Claude Renfro	5.5	Stan Cloudy	3.3	Moe Iba		
983-84	18-12	7-7	NIT SECOND ROUND	Dave Hoppen	19.9	Dave Hoppen	6.9	David Ponce	4.1	Moe Iba		
984-85	16-14	5-9	NIT SECOND ROUND	Dave Hoppen	23.5	Dave Hoppen	8.6	Brian Carr	7.9	Moe Iba		
985-86	19-11	8-6	NCAA FIRST ROUND	Dave Hoppen	22.1	Bernard Day	6.6	Brian Carr	6.7	Moe Iba	106-71	.599
986-87	21-12	7-7	NIT THIRD PLACE	Bernard Day	12.4	Bill Jackman	6.5	Brian Carr	5.0	Danny Nee		
987-88	13-18	4-10		Derrick Vick	11.2	Derrick Vick	5.2	Eric Johnson	3.6	Danny Nee		
988-89	17-16	4-10	NIT SECOND ROUND	Beau Reid	11.9	Pete Manning	6.1	Eric Johnson, Beau Reid	4.2	Danny Nee		
989-90	10-18	3-11		Rich King	16.1	Rich King	7.4	Clifford Scales	4.2	Danny Nee		
990-91	26-8	9-5	NCAA FIRST ROUND	Rich King	15.5	Rich King	8.1	Beau Reid	3.8	Danny Nee		
991-92	19-10	7-7	NCAA FIRST ROUND	Eric Piatkowski	14.3	Derrick Chandler	8.2	Jamar Johnson	4.6	Danny Nee		
992-93	20-11	8-6	NCAA FIRST ROUND	Eric Piatkowski	16.7	Derrick Chandler	8.1	Jamar Johnson	3.3	Danny Nee		
993-94	20-10	7-7	NCAA FIRST ROUND	Eric Piatkowski	21.5	Bruce Chubick	7.3	Jamar Johnson	4.4	Danny Nee		
994-95	18-14	4-10	NIT SECOND ROUND	Jaron Boone	17.5	Mikki Moore	6.2	Erick Strickland	4.3	Danny Nee		
995-96	21-14	4-10	NIT CHAMPION	Erick Strickland	14.7	Bernard Garner	6.3	Tyronn Lue	4.1	Danny Nee		
996-97	18-15	7-9	NIT QUARTERFINALS	Tyronn Lue	18.8	Venson Hamilton	8.4	Tyronn Lue	4.3	Danny Nee		
997-98	20-12	10-6	NCAA FIRST ROUND	Tyronn Lue	21.2	Venson Hamilton	9.8	Tyronn Lue	4.8	Danny Nee		
998-99	20-13	10-6	NIT SECOND ROUND	Venson Hamilton	15.7	Venson Hamilton	10.2	Cookie Belcher	4.3	Danny Nee		
999-2000	11-19	4-12		Larry Florence	13.0	Kimani Ffriend	8.8	Danny Walker	3.3	Danny Nee	254-190	.572
000-01	14-16	7-9		Cookie Belcher	16.4	Kimani Ffriend	8.2	Cookie Belcher	4.4	Barry Collier		
001-02	13-15	6-10		Cary Cochran	14.0	John Turek	6.2	Jake Muhleisen	3.8	Barry Collier		
002-03	11-19	3-13		Andrew Drevo	13.9	Andrew Drevo	7.3	Brennon Clemmons	2.6	Barry Collier		
003-04	18-13	6-10	NIT QUARTERFINALS	Nate Johnson	13.0	John Turek	5.9	Charles Richardson Jr.	2.1	Barry Collier		
004-05	14-14	7-9		Joe McCray	15.5	Aleks Maric	6.3	Marcus Neal	3.3	Barry Collier		
005-06	19-14	7-9	NIT FIRST ROUND	Wes Wilkinson	11.9	Aleks Maric	8.1	Charles Richardson Jr.	3.3	Barry Collier	89-91	.494
006-07	17-14	6-10		Aleks Maric	18.5	Aleks Maric	8.7	Charles Richardson Jr.	5.8	Doc Sadler		
007-08	20-13	7-9	NIT SECOND ROUND	Aleks Maric	15.7	Aleks Maric	10.2	Cookie Miller	3.6	Doc Sadler		
008-09	18-13	8-8	NIT FIRST ROUND	Ade Dagunduro	12.8	Ade Dagunduro	4.4	Cookie Miller	3.6	Doc Sadler	55-40	.579

Records don't reflect games forfeited or vacated. For adjusted records, see p. 521.

Coach's record adjusted to reflect games forfeited or vacated: 254-196, .564. For yearly totals, see p. 521.

ESPN 166 SAGARIN

NEVADA

Before the opening tip at each home game, Wolf Pack fans recite, in unison, an excerpt from Rudyard Kipling's *The Law for the Wolves*: "Now this is the law of the jungle, as old and as true as the sky/And the wolf that shall keep it may prosper, but the wolf that shall break it must die/For the strength of the pack is the wolf, and strength of the wolf is the pack." After years of futility, Nevada has lived up to those words.

BEST TEAM: 2006-07 After rolling to its fourth straight WAC title (the Wolf Pack ranked among the nation's Top 10 teams at one point in midseason), Nevada proved its mettle in its first-round Tournament win over Creighton. With leading scorer Nick Fazekas slowed by foul trouble, the rest of the Pack picked up the scoring load in the 77-71 overtime win.

BEST PLAYER: F Nick Fazekas (2003-07) "I set out to be an American European," Fazekas once said in describing his style—a reliable three-point shot, the ability to score off the dribble and a solid inside game. The Coloradan was WAC Player of the Year in 2005, '06 and '07 and is the team's all-time leader in scoring, blocked shots and free throws attempted and made.

BEST COACH: Mark Fox (2004-09) Fox went 123–43 in five seasons at Nevada, winning at least 20 games every year and taking the Wolf Pack to the NCAA Tournament three times. His teams won four regular-season WAC titles and the WAC tournament crown in '06.

GAME FOR THE AGES: Appearing in its first NCAA Tournament since 1985, No. 10-seed Nevada routed No. 2-seed Gonzaga, 91-72, on March 20, 2004, in the second round of the NCAA Tournament. Every Wolf Pack starter scored in double digits, led by Kevinn Pinkney's 20 and Fazekas' 16.

FIERCEST RIVAL: UNLV holds a 51–19 all-time lead against Nevada, a fact that grates on Wolf Pack fans to no end, especially since UNLV is an offshoot of the Reno school. But the rivalry has been more even since the turn of the century, with Nevada taking four of the nine games since 2000-01.

SEASON REVIEW

SEAS.	W-L	CONF.	COACH	SEAS.	W-L	CONF.	COACH
1913-47	*277-245*	*28-5 in 1945-46*		1960-61	12-8		Jack Spencer
1947-48	9-16		Jake Lawlor	1961-62	11-15		Jack Spencer
1948-49	12-14		Jake Lawlor	1962-63	11-13		Jack Spencer
1949-50	14-10		Jake Lawlor	1963-64	14-13		Jack Spencer
1950-51	9-14		Jake Lawlor	1964-65	12-12		Jack Spencer
1951-52	19-3		Jake Lawlor	1965-66	21-6		Jack Spencer
1952-53	12-10		Jake Lawlor	1966-67	5-20		Jack Spencer
1953-54	10-11		Jake Lawlor	1967-68	8-18		Jack Spencer
1954-55	8-15		Jake Lawlor	1968-69	10-16		Jack Spencer
1955-56	10-9		Jake Lawlor	1969-70	5-17	2-12	Jack Spencer
1956-57	16-8		Jake Lawlor	1970-71	3-23	1-13	Jack Spencer
1957-58	12-14		Jake Lawlor	1971-72	2-24	0-14	Jack Spencer
1958-59	12-10		Jake Lawlor	1972-73	10-16	5-9	Jim Padgett
1959-60	9-14		Jack Spencer	1973-74	11-15	4-10	Jim Padgett

SEAS.	W-L	CONF.		SCORING		COACH	RECORD	
1974-75	10-16	2-12		Perry Campbell	20.6	Jim Padgett		
1975-76	12-14	7-5		Edgar Jones	17.6	Jim Padgett	43-61	.413
1976-77	15-12	7-7		Edgar Jones	23.7	Jim Carey		
1977-78	19-8	10-4		Mike "Fly" Gray	17.7	Jim Carey		
1978-79	21-7	9-5	■	Mike "Fly" Gray	23.1	Jim Carey		
1979-80	10-19	5-9		Gene Ransom	17.3	Jim Carey	65-46	.586
1980-81	11-15	5-9		Greg Palm	18.0	Sonny Allen		
1981-82	19-9	9-5		Ken Green	18.4	Sonny Allen		
1982-83	18-11	10-4		Ken Green	24.0	Sonny Allen		
1983-84	17-14	7-7	●	Curtis High	13.3	Sonny Allen		
1984-85	21-10	11-3	●	Curtis High	17.8	Sonny Allen		
1985-86	13-15	7-7		Dwyane Randall	23.0	Sonny Allen		
1986-87	15-15	7-7		Boris King	18.5	Sonny Allen	114-89	.562
1987-88	15-13	8-8		Darryl Owens	18.5	Len Stevens		
1988-89	16-12	10-6		Darryl Owens	22.7	Len Stevens		
1989-90	15-13	9-7		Kevin Franklin	19.2	Len Stevens		
1990-91	17-14	12-4		Ric Herrin	18.2	Len Stevens		
1991-92	19-10	13-3		Bryan Thomasson	14.8	Len Stevens		
1992-93	9-17	4-14		Eric Morris	15.8	Len Stevens	91-79	.535
1993-94	11-17	6-12		Jimmy Moore	19.2	Pat Foster		
1994-95	18-11	12-6		Brian Green	15.1	Pat Foster		
1995-96	16-13	9-9		Brian Green	17.9	Pat Foster		
1996-97	21-10	12-4	■	Faron Hand	19.4	Pat Foster		
1997-98	16-12	11-5		Paul Culbertson	18.1	Pat Foster		
1998-99	8-18	4-12		John Burrell	16.4	Pat Foster	90-81	.526
1999-2000	9-20	6-10		Terrance Green	13.9	Trent Johnson		
2000-01	10-18	3-13		Terrance Green	11.8	Trent Johnson		
2001-02	17-13	9-9		Terrance Green	16.3	Trent Johnson		
2002-03	18-14	11-7	■	Kirk Snyder	16.3	Trent Johnson		
2003-04	25-9	13-5	●	Kirk Snyder	18.8	Trent Johnson	79-74	.516
2004-05	25-7	16-2	●	Nick Fazekas	20.7	Mark Fox		
2005-06	27-6	13-3	●	Nick Fazekas	21.8	Mark Fox		
2006-07	29-5	14-2	●	Nick Fazekas	20.4	Mark Fox		
2007-08	21-12	12-4		Marcelus Kemp	20.0	Mark Fox		
2008-09	21-13	11-5		Luke Babbitt	16.9	Mark Fox	123-43	.741

● NCAA Tournament appearance ■ NIT appearance

PROFILE

University of Nevada, Reno, NV
Founded: 1874
Enrollment: 16, 867 (13,367 undergraduate)
Colors: Navy blue and silver
Nickname: Wolf Pack
Current arena: Lawlor Events Center, opened in 1983 (11,536)
Previous: Centennial Coliseum, a.k.a. Reno-Sparks Convention Center, 1973-83 (5,600); Virginia Street Gym, a.k.a. the Old Gym, 1945-73, (3,500); Old Gymnasium, 1913-44 (N/A)
First game: 1913

All-time record: 1,148-1,051 (.522)
Total weeks in AP Top 20/25: 34
Current conference: Western Athletic (2000-)
Conference titles:
Big Sky: 2 (1983 [tie], '85)
Big West: 1 (1997 [tie])
WAC: 5 (2004 [tie], '05, '06, '07, '08 [tie])
Conference tournament titles:
Big Sky: 2 (1984, '85)
WAC: 2 (2004, '06)
NCAA Tournament appearances: 6
Sweet 16s (since 1975): 1
NIT appearances: 3

FIRST-ROUND PRO PICKS

2004 **Kirk Snyder,** Utah (16)
2008 **JaVale McGee,** Washington (18)

TOP 5

G **Billy Allen** (1981-83)
G **Mike "Fly" Gray** (1976-79)
F **Nick Fazekas** (2003-07)
F **Pete Padgett** (1971-76)
C **Edgar Jones** (1974-79)

RECORDS	GAME		SEASON		CAREER	
POINTS	49	Alex Boyd, vs. Willamette (Dec. 2, 1967)	721	Nick Fazekas (2005-06)	2,464	Nick Fazekas (2003-07)
POINTS PER GAME			26.5	Alex Boyd (1967-68)	23.7	Alex Boyd (1966-70)
REBOUNDS	30	Pete Padgett, vs. Loyola Marymount (Jan. 4, 1973)	462	Pete Padgett (1972-73)	1,464	Pete Padgett (1971-76)
ASSISTS	16	Eathan O'Bryant, vs. UC Irvine (Jan. 15, 1994); Billy Allen, vs. Detroit (Jan. 4, 1982); Billy Allen, vs. South Dakota State (Dec. 3, 1981)	240	Billy Allen (1981-82)	716	Kevin Soares (1988-92)

ESPN 58 SAGARIN

NEVADA-LAS VEGAS

UNLV, once known as Tumbleweed Tech, rose to power in the mid-1970s and grew along with the nearby Vegas Strip into a national story. With four Final Fours between 1977 and '91, the Runnin' Rebels revolutionized the college game with their flashy, up-tempo style, while under near-constant scrutiny by the NCAA, looking for rules violations.

BEST TEAM: 1990-91 Best team never to win it all? The debate starts here. Led by Larry Johnson, Greg Anthony and Stacey Augmon, the Rebels won their first game by 41, setting the tone for a perfect regular season. In fact, UNLV failed to win by at least a double-digit margin only once in the regular season (112-105 over Arkansas on Feb. 10). Jerry Tarkanian's crew continued that dominance in the Tournament (with a second-round blip—a mere eight-point win against Georgetown) until they were ambushed by Duke, 79-77, in the Final Four. Some fans still can't believe it.

BEST PLAYER: F LARRY JOHNSON (1989-91) Johnson accomplished in two seasons what few players have accomplished in four, taking the Runnin' Rebels to back-to-back Final Fours while winning the 1990 national title and the 1991 co-Player of the Year. The junior college transfer overwhelmed defenders inside with his physical prowess, yet also had a feathery touch—a combination that led to his selection by the Charlotte Hornets as the No. 1 overall draft pick in 1991. He played 10 years in the NBA and made two All-Star teams (1993, '95).

BEST COACH: JERRY TARKANIAN (1973-92) His ethics will forever be debated; where Tark the Shark went, controversy and the NCAA's watchful eye followed. But there's no denying his tactical genius. At previous stops he built his teams around zone defense and inside-out play, but at UNLV he designed some of the greatest college offenses of all time, often fueled by relentless full-court pressure.

GAME FOR THE AGES: Capping off a championship season in 1989-90, the Rebels recorded the most lopsided victory in title-game history in beating Duke 103-73. Using a swarming defense that Tarkanian dubbed the Amoeba, UNLV forced the Blue Devils into 23 turnovers and held them to 42.6% shooting. Rebels wing Anderson Hunt scored a game-high 29 points on 12-of-16 shooting and was named Most Outstanding Player at the Final Four. Larry Johnson added 22.

HEARTBREAKER: A year after running the Blue Devils out of the building, the Rebels lost in a Final Four rematch in the 1991 Tournament. The Blue Devils largely contained Johnson, while counterpart Christian Laettner riddled the Rebels with his inside-out play. The Duke center hit two free throws with 12.7 seconds left to give Duke the 79-77 lead, and Hunt's three-point attempt with :02 on the clock was way off. It was the Rebels' only loss of the season.

FIERCEST RIVAL: In 1957, UNLV opened as a satellite campus to the University of Nevada, Reno, creating a natural rivalry. During the Rebels' heyday, Tarkanian admits that he had to convince his team to take the Wolf Pack as seriously as they did all the national powers they would routinely dismantle. But Nevada fans have never needed any prodding to get up for UNLV; four of the school's biggest crowds have been for Rebels games. UNLV holds a commanding lead in the series, 51–19.

FANFARE AND HOOPLA: The UNLV mascot is a spirited, long-mustached cartoon Rebel known as Hey Reb. He replaced the original Rebel mascot, a Confederate-capped, fanged, winking, black-and-white cartoon wolf named Beauregard that struck more than a few fans as offensive.

FAN FAVORITE: G/F REGGIE THEUS (1975-78) With an oversized Afro and a smooth all-around game, Theus helped define Tarkanian's flashy, crowd-pleasing style of play. He was just as popular and prolific in the NBA, averaging 18.5 points over 13 seasons.

CONSENSUS ALL-AMERICAS

1990, '91	**Larry Johnson,** F

FIRST-ROUND PRO PICKS

1975	**Ricky Sobers,** Phoenix (16)
1978	**Reggie Theus,** Chicago (9)
1983	**Sidney Green,** Chicago (5)
1986	**Anthony Jones,** Washington (21)
1987	**Armon Gilliam,** Phoenix (2)
1991	**Larry Johnson,** Charlotte (1)
1991	**Stacey Augmon,** Atlanta (9)
1991	**Greg Anthony,** New York (12)
1992	**Elmore Spencer,** LA Clippers (25)
1993	**J.R. Rider,** Minnesota (5)
1998	**Keon Clark,** Orlando (13)
1999	**Shawn Marion,** Phoenix (9)
2003	**Marcus Banks,** Memphis (13)

PROFILE

University of Nevada, Las Vegas; Las Vegas, NV
Founded: 1957
Enrollment: 28,371 (22,108 undergraduate)
Colors: Scarlet and gray
Nickname: Runnin' Rebels
Current arena: Thomas & Mack Center, opened in 1983 (18,776)
Previous: Las Vegas Convention Center, 1966-83 (6,380); NSU Gymnasium, 1960-66 (2,000)
First game: Dec. 5, 1958
All-time record: 1,058-429 (.711)
Total weeks in AP Top 20/25: 227
Current conference: Mountain West (1999-)
Conference titles:
West Coast Athletic: 1 (1975)
Pacific Coast Athletic: 6 (1983, '84, '85, '86, '87, '88)
Big West: 4 (1989, '90 [tie], '91, '92)
WAC: 1 (1999 [tie])
Mountain West: 1 (2000 [tie])
Conference tournament titles:
Pacific Coast Athletic: 4 (1983, '85, '86, '87)
Big West: 3 (1989, '90, '91)
WAC: 1 (1998)
Mountain West: 3 (2000, '07, '08)
NCAA Tournament appearances: 16
Sweet 16s (since 1975): 10
Final Fours: 4
Titles: 1 (1990)
NIT appearances: 10
Semifinals: 1

TOP 5

G	**Greg Anthony** (1988-91)
G/F	**Stacey Augmon** (1987-91)
F	**Larry Johnson** (1989-91)
F	**Eddie Owens** (1973-77)
F/C	**Sidney Green** (1979-83)

RECORDS

RECORDS	GAME		SEASON		CAREER	
POINTS	55	Elburt Miller, vs. Portland (Feb. 12, 1967)	903	Armon Gilliam (1986-87)	2,221	Eddie Owens (1973-77)
POINTS PER GAME			31.9	Elburt Miller (1966-67)	29.1	Elburt Miller (1966-68)
REBOUNDS	26	Jimmie Baker, vs. San Francisco (Feb. 23, 1973)	457	Larry Johnson (1989-90)	1,276	Sidney Green (1979-83)
ASSISTS	21	Mark Wade, vs. Navy (Dec. 29, 1986)	406	Mark Wade (1986-87)	838	Greg Anthony (1988-91)

SEASON REVIEW

SEAS.	W-L	CONF.	POSTSEASON	SCORING		REBOUNDS		ASSISTS		COACH	RECORD	
1958-59	0-6			Bernie Fumagalli	17.6	Jim Jansen				Michael Drakulich		
1959-60	5-6			Bernie Fumagalli	20.1	George Namovich				Michael Drakulich		
1960-61	11-10			Bernie Fumagalli	17.3	Tim Leonard	12.3			Michael Drakulich		
1961-62	14-8			Tim Leonard	18.2	Tim Leonard				Michael Drakulich		
1962-63	16-4			Silas Stepp	17.9	Gary Tapper	14.1			Michael Drakulich	46-34	.575
1963-64	18-7			Silas Stepp	17.3	Silas Stepp	10.6			Ed Gregory		
1964-65	19-8			Silas Stepp	17.6	Silas Stepp	10.9			Ed Gregory	37-15	.712
1965-66	15-11			Silas Stepp	20.4	Silas Stepp	11.7			Rolland Todd		
1966-67	21-6			Elburt Miller	31.9	Vic Morton	9.8			Rolland Todd		
1967-68	22-7			Elburt Miller	26.7	John Q. Trapp	11.4			Rolland Todd		
1968-69	21-7			Curtis Watson	21.0	Cliff Findlay	11.3			Rolland Todd		
1969-70	17-9	9-5		Odis Allison	19.0	Cliff Findlay	10.8			Rolland Todd	96-40	.706
1970-71	16-10	9-5		Booker Washington	20.4	Toby Houston	10.5			John Bayer		
1971-72	14-12	8-6		Bob Florence	22.1	Jerry Baskerville	11.3			John Bayer		
1972-73	13-15	6-8		Bob Florence	24.6	Jimmie Baker	15.1			John Bayer	43-37	.538
1973-74	20-6	10-4		Bob Florence	18.1	Jimmie Baker	10.0	Ricky Sobers	103	Jerry Tarkanian		
1974-75	24-5	13-1	NCAA REGIONAL SEMIFINALS	Eddie Owens	18.4	Lewis Brown	11.7	Ricky Sobers	166	Jerry Tarkanian		
1975-76	29-2		NCAA REGIONAL SEMIFINALS	Eddie Owens	23.4	Jackie Robinson	8.9	Robert Smith	157	Jerry Tarkanian		
1976-77	29-3		NCAA THIRD PLACE	Eddie Owens	21.8	Glen Gondrezick	10.8	Robert Smith	195	Jerry Tarkanian		
1977-78	20-8			Reggie Theus	19.0	Earl Evans	10.2	Reggie Theus	126	Jerry Tarkanian		
1978-79	21-8			Earl Evans	17.9	Earl Evans	10.1	Flintie Ray Williams	193	Jerry Tarkanian		
1979-80	23-9		NIT FOURTH PLACE	Sidney Green	15.6	Sidney Green	11.1	Flintie Ray Williams	184	Jerry Tarkanian		
1980-81	16-12			Larry Anderson	15.5	Sidney Green	10.9	Michael Burns	168	Jerry Tarkanian		
1981-82	20-10		NIT SECOND ROUND	Larry Anderson	17.2	Sidney Green	9.0	Danny Tarkanian	262	Jerry Tarkanian		
1982-83	28-3	15-1	NCAA SECOND ROUND	Sidney Green	22.1	Sidney Green	11.9	Danny Tarkanian	286	Jerry Tarkanian		
1983-84	29-6	16-2	NCAA REGIONAL SEMIFINALS	Richie Adams	12.7	Richie Adams	6.7	Danny Tarkanian	289	Jerry Tarkanian		
1984-85	28-4	17-1	NCAA SECOND ROUND	Richie Adams	15.8	Richie Adams	7.9	Freddie Banks	186	Jerry Tarkanian		
1985-86	33-5	16-2	NCAA REGIONAL SEMIFINALS	Anthony Jones	18.0	Armon Gilliam	8.5	Mark Wade	283	Jerry Tarkanian		
1986-87	37-2	18-0	NCAA NATIONAL SEMIFINALS	Armon Gilliam	23.2	Armon Gilliam	9.3	Mark Wade	406	Jerry Tarkanian		
1987-88	28-6	15-3	NCAA SECOND ROUND	Gerald Paddio	19.4	Jarvis Basnight	6.9	Karl James	122	Jerry Tarkanian		
1988-89	29-8	16-2	NCAA REGIONAL FINALS	David Butler	15.4	Stacey Augmon	7.4	Greg Anthony	239	Jerry Tarkanian		
1989-90	**35-5**	**16-2**	**NATIONAL CHAMPION**	**Larry Johnson**	**20.6**	**Larry Johnson**	**11.4**	**Greg Anthony**	**7.4**	**Jerry Tarkanian**		
1990-91	34-1	18-0	NCAA NATIONAL SEMIFINALS	Larry Johnson	22.7	Larry Johnson	10.9	Greg Anthony	8.9	Jerry Tarkanian		
1991-92	26-2	18-0		J.R. Rider	20.7	Elmore Spencer	8.1	Dedan Thomas	3.4	Jerry Tarkanian	509-105	.829
1992-93	21-8	13-5	NIT FIRST ROUND	J.R. Rider	29.1	J.R. Rider	8.9	Dedan Thomas	8.6	Rollie Massimino		
1993-94	15-13	10-8		Reggie Manuel	17.2	Kebu Stewart	11.6	Dedan Thomas	7.3	Rollie Massimino	36-21	.632
1994-95	12-16	7-11		Patrick Savoy	14.7	Kebu Stewart	10.0	Jermaine Smith	3.7	Tim Grgurich[a]	2-5	.286
1995-96	10-16	7-11		Clayton Johnson	16.7	Warren Rosegreen	9.5	Chancellor Davis	3.3	Bill Bayno		
1996-97	22-10	11-5	NIT QUARTERFINALS	Tyrone Nesby	16.5	Keon Clark	10.0	M. Dickel, Kevin James	3.8	Bill Bayno		
1997-98	20-13	7-7	NCAA FIRST ROUND	Tyrone Nesby	15.8	Kaspars Kambala	7.4	Mark Dickel	5.5	Bill Bayno		
1998-99	16-13	9-5	NIT FIRST ROUND	Shawn Marion	18.7	Shawn Marion	9.3	Mark Dickel	6.6	Bill Bayno		
1999-2000	23-8	10-4	NCAA FIRST ROUND	Kaspars Kambala	18.5	Kaspars Kambala	9.3	Mark Dickel	9.0	Bill Bayno		
2000-01	16-13	7-7		Kaspars Kambala	16.9	Kaspars Kambala	9.1	Trevor Diggs	3.2	Bill Bayno[b]	94-64	.595
2001-02	21-11	9-5	NIT SECOND ROUND	Dalron Johnson	17.4	Dalron Johnson	7.0	Marcus Banks	3.0	Charlie Spoonhour		
2002-03	21-11	8-6	NIT FIRST ROUND	Marcus Banks	20.3	J.K. Edwards, D. Johnson	6.3	Marcus Banks	5.5	Charlie Spoonhour		
2003-04	18-13	7-7	NIT OPENING ROUND	Odartey Blankson	17.6	Odartey Blankson	10.2	Jerel Blassingame	6.6	Charlie Spoonhour[c]	54-31	.635
2004-05	17-14	7-7	NIT SECOND ROUND	Odartey Blankson	17.5	Odartey Blankson	8.1	Jerel Blassingame	5.5	Lon Kruger		
2005-06	17-13	10-6		Louis Amundson	14.3	Louis Amundson	8.6	Jason Petrimoulx	4.0	Lon Kruger		
2006-07	30-7	12-4	NCAA REGIONAL SEMIFINALS	Wendell White	14.4	Wendell White	6.1	Kevin Kruger	5.1	Lon Kruger		
2007-08	27-8	12-4	NCAA SECOND ROUND	Wink Adams	16.9	Rene Rougeau	6.2	Curtis Terry	4.8	Lon Kruger		
2008-09	21-11	9-7	NIT FIRST ROUND	Wink Adams	14.3	Rene Rougeau	6.7	Oscar Bellfield	3.4	Lon Kruger	112-53	.679

Cumulative totals listed when per game averages not available.

[a] Tim Grgurich (2-5), Howie Landa (5-2) and Cleveland Edwards (5-9) coached during the 1994-95 season.

[b] Bill Bayno (3-4) and Max Good (13-9) both coached during the 2000-01 season.

[c] Charlie Spoonhour (12-9) and Jay Spoonhour (6-4) both coached during the 2003-04 season.

LATE GREAT

NEW YORK UNIVERSITY 1933-72

One of the most important programs of college basketball's early years, NYU had undefeated runs in 1908-09 and '33-34 and one-loss seasons in '19-20, '20-21 and '39-40. Its best season, however, was 1934-35, when it went 18–1 and was named national champion by the Helms Foundation. On Jan. 5, 1935, the Violets beat a powerhouse Kentucky team by one point at Madison Square Garden. NYU made six NCAA Tournament appearances—including a 49-45 loss in the 1945 championship game to Hank Iba's Oklahoma A&M—and eight NIT appearances.

NOTABLE PLAYERS: C ADOLPH "DOLPH" SCHAYES (1944-48), F HAROLD "HAPPY" HAIRSTON (1961-64) As a freshman, the 6'8" Schayes had to face Oklahoma A&M's seven-foot Bob Kurland in the NCAA Final, and scored just six points to Kurland's 22 in NYU's loss. Schayes developed a keen outside shot, unusual for a man his size, and as a senior he received the Haggerty Memorial Award from New York City sportswriters as the most outstanding player in the metropolitan area. He was inducted into the Naismith Hall of Fame in 1973. The 6'7" Hairston led NYU in rebounds twice and graduated as the school's No. 2 scorer with 1,346 points. He won an NBA championship in 1972 with the Lakers.

ESPN 325 SAGARIN

NEW HAMPSHIRE

Since joining D1 in 1961, the Wildcats haven't made a single postseason tournament and have a total of seven winning seasons. But UNH fans can do a bit of boasting: Jim Boylan, the Chicago Bulls interim coach in 2007-08, got his first head coaching job at New Hampshire, and all-time leading scorer Al McClain was drafted by the Houston Rockets in 1984.

BEST TEAM: 1994-95 The Wildcats had never won more than 16 games in their 100-plus-year history, but Gib Chapman's squad won 11 North Atlantic Conference games and went 19–9 overall. That squad included members of the all-NAC first team (Scott Drapeau), second team (Matt Alosa) and rookie team (Matt Acres).

BEST PLAYER: G Matt Alosa (1994-96) The Providence transfer played just two seasons in New Hampshire but made a splash with his open-court wizardry, deft ballhandling and solid three-point shooting. The combo guard averaged 23.1 ppg, tops in UNH history.

BEST COACH: Gerry Friel (1969-89) When Friel was hired, UNH hadn't had a winning season since 1951-52. Friel changed that immediately, posting a 12–11 mark his inaugural season and leading the Wildcats to 188 victories in his era, tops in the program's history. He was NAC Coach of the Year in 1983.

GAME FOR THE AGES: UNH had been blown out by Siena twice during the 1987-88 season. But in the NAC tournament's opening round, the Wildcats shocked the top-seeded Indians with a 70-63 victory. Derek Counts' 26 points led the way.

FIERCEST RIVAL: There's no love lost between America East rivals Maine and New Hampshire. The schools can't even agree on the series record. (The Black Bears lead 110–64 according to Maine, while in the Wildcats' book it's 109–62.) In 1991, mired in a 31-game home losing streak and facing conference-leading Maine, UNH held a "Guaranteed Win" promotion. The biggest home crowd ever (2,551) had its hopes raised only to watch the Black Bears come from behind late to edge the Wildcats, 71-68. Guaranteed pain.

SEASON REVIEW

SEAS.	W-L	CONF.	COACH	SEAS.	W-L	CONF.	COACH
1902-47	*307-260*	*14-1 in '26-27 for coach Wm. Cowell*		1960-61	6-18	1-9	Bill Olsen
1947-48	5-12	2-5	Ed Stanczyk	1961-62	3-20	1-9	Bill Olsen
1948-49	7-10	2-6	Ed Stanczyk	1962-63	7-17	2-8	Bill Olsen
1949-50	4-11	1-5	Ed Stanczyk	1963-64	8-15	2-8	Bill Olsen
1950-51	4-12	2-6	Andy Mooradian	1964-65	2-19	1-9	Bill Olsen
1951-52	11-9	4-5	Dale Hall	1965-66	3-21	0-10	Bill Olsen
1952-53	8-10	2-5	Bob Kerr	1966-67	10-12	4-6	Bill Haubrich
1953-54	8-10	2-6	Bob Kerr	1967-68	1-22	0-10	Bill Haubrich
1954-55	4-14	1-9	Bob Kerr	1968-69	9-15	3-7	Bill Haubrich
1955-56	2-15	0-10	Bob Kerr	1969-70	12-11	3-7	Gerry Friel
1956-57	3-16	1-9	Bill Olsen	1970-71	11-12	3-7	Gerry Friel
1957-58	10-12	3-7	Bill Olsen	1971-72	14-9	5-5	Gerry Friel
1958-59	9-14	1-9	Bill Olsen	1972-73	11-15	2-10	Gerry Friel
1959-60	9-14	2-8	Bill Olsen	1973-74	16-9	8-4	Gerry Friel

SEAS.	W-L	CONF.	SCORING		COACH	RECORD	
1974-75	6-18	2-10			Gerry Friel		
1975-76	8-18	3-9			Gerry Friel		
1976-77	12-14				Gerry Friel		
1977-78	7-19				Gerry Friel		
1978-79	10-16				Gerry Friel		
1979-80	4-22	4-22			Gerry Friel		
1980-81	7-19	7-19			Gerry Friel		
1981-82	9-18	2-9			Gerry Friel		
1982-83	16-12	8-2	Robin Dixon	20.8	Gerry Friel		
1983-84	15-13	8-6	Al McClain	22.8	Gerry Friel		
1984-85	7-22	4-12	Dirk Koopman	10.8	Gerry Friel		
1985-86	11-17	5-13	Dirk Koopman	14.2	Gerry Friel		
1986-87	4-24	3-15	Greg Steele	15.6	Gerry Friel		
1987-88	4-25	3-15	Derek Counts	14.6	Gerry Friel		
1988-89	4-22	3-14	Derek Counts	15.3	Gerry Friel	188-335	.359
1989-90	5-23	3-9	Pat Manor	13.3	Jim Boylan		
1990-91	3-25	0-10	Tommy MacDonald	10.3	Jim Boylan		
1991-92	7-21	5-9	Jose Powell	12.1	Jim Boylan	15-69	.179
1992-93	6-21	4-10	Pat Manor	12.6	Gib Chapman		
1993-94	15-13	8-6	Scott Drapeau	22.9	Gib Chapman		
1994-95	19-9	11-5	Scott Drapeau	23.1	Gib Chapman		
1995-96	6-21	5-13	Matt Alosa	24.0	Gib Chapman	46-64	.418
1996-97	7-20	5-13	Matt Acres	13.2	Jeff Jackson		
1997-98	10-17	6-12	Matt Acres	13.4	Jeff Jackson		
1998-99	4-23	2-16	Ethan Cole	12.0	Jeff Jackson	21-60	.259
1999-2000	3-25	2-16	Marcelle Williams	13.6	Phil Rowe		
2000-01	7-21	6-12	Austin Ganly	13.3	Phil Rowe		
2001-02	11-17	8-8	Austin Ganly	15.5	Phil Rowe		
2002-03	5-23	3-13	Shejdie Childs	9.4	Phil Rowe		
2003-04	10-20	5-13	Ben Sturgill	13.1	Phil Rowe		
2004-05	9-19	5-13	Ben Sturgill	13.6	Phil Rowe	45-125	.265
2005-06	12-17	8-8	Blagoj Janev	14.4	Bill Herrion		
2006-07	10-20	6-10	Jermaine Anderson	14.5	Bill Herrion		
2007-08	9-20	6-10	Tyrece Gibbs	14.4	Bill Herrion		
2008-09	14-16	8-8	Tyrece Gibbs	14.6	Bill Herrion	45-73	.381

PROFILE

University of New Hampshire, Durham, NH
Founded: 1866
Enrollment: 14,370 (11,382 udergraduate)
Colors: Blue and white
Nickname: Wildcats
Current arena: Lundholm Gymnasium, opened in 1966 (3,000)
Previous: Field House, 1930-65 (N/A); New Hampshire Hall, 1905-29 (N/A)
First game: 1902
All-time record: 800-1,304 (.380)
Total weeks in AP Top 20/25: 0

Current conference: America East (1979-)
Conference titles: 0
Conference tournament titles: 0
NCAA Tournament appearances: 0
NIT appearances: 0

TOP 5

G **Matt Alosa** (1994-96)
G **Al McClain** (1980-84)
F **Blagoj Janev** (2003-07)
F **Dave Pemberton** (1969-72)
C **Rob Marquardt** (1997-2001)

RECORDS

RECORDS	GAME		SEASON		CAREER	
POINTS	44	Frank McLaughlin, vs. Massachusetts (Jan. 15, 1955)	648	Scott Drapeau (1994-95)	1,861	Al McClain (1980-84)
POINTS PER GAME			24.0	Matt Alosa (1995-96)	23.1	Matt Alosa (1994-96)
REBOUNDS	27	Pete Smilikis, vs. Middlebury (Jan. 2, 1960)	428	Pete Smilikis (1959-60)	897	Dave Pemberton (1969-72)
ASSISTS	19	Randy Kinzly, vs. Colgate (Feb. 2, 1981)	163	Wayne Morrison (1972-73)	505	Wayne Morrison (1972-76)

ESPN 110 SAGARIN

NEW MEXICO

Think of Lobos basketball and a lot of NBA names come to mind: Michael Cooper, Luc Longley, Charles Smith, Kenny Thomas, Danny Granger. But first and foremost, New Mexico is identified with the Pit, its raucous home court. In Albuquerque, they take their basketball super seriously—one reason why the NCAA regularly schedules March Madness regionals there.

BEST TEAM: 1977-78 Norm Ellenberger recruited Michael Cooper out of Pasadena City College, a move that really started paying off during Coop's second season at New Mexico. The All-America swingman contributed 16.1 points to a well-balanced offense that scored 97.5 per game. The Lobos climbed as high as No. 5 in the national rankings and, despite a first-round NCAA Tournament upset by Cal State Fullerton that ended the season, no one can take away the Lobos' then-school-record 24 wins and WAC championship.

BEST PLAYER: F KENNY THOMAS (1995-99) The All-America big man was a presence on both ends of the floor, earning All-WAC regular and All-WAC defensive team honors his last two seasons. New Mexico went 102–30 during his four seasons, including 71–3 at the Pit, and advanced to the second round of the NCAA Tournament four straight times. Thomas has played 10 years in the NBA, and averaged a double-double (13.6 ppg, 10.1 rpg) for the Philadelphia 76ers in 2003-04.

BEST COACH: BOB KING (1962-72) Before King, New Mexico had never made the NCAA Tourney and had a cumulative losing record. King's winning ways (two WAC titles, one Tournament appearance, three NITs) created excitement in the Johnson Center, which led to Lobomania, which led to the construction of the Pit—the court there was named in King's honor.

GAME FOR THE AGES: On Jan. 2, 1988, top-ranked Arizona entered the Pit undefeated and left just another victim of New Mexico's home-court advantage. The Lobos jumped out to a 25-9 lead, withstood a Wildcats rally led by Sean Elliott and Steve Kerr (38 points combined) and secured a 61-59 win, thanks to Hunter Greene's rejection of an Elliott three in the final seconds.

HEARTBREAKER: Say the words "Cup Game" in Albuquerque and you're bound to get sighs and gasps, even today. On Jan. 25, 1986, New Mexico led UTEP by one point with two seconds left in OT when Miner Wayne Campbell stepped to the line for a one-and-one. He missed the front end and the Lobos exploded in celebration. But the referee whistled the party to an abrupt end. A Lobos fan had thrown a paper cup at Campbell before the shot and he was awarded another one-and-one. Campbell made both and the Lobos lost, 71-70.

FIERCEST RIVAL: In a Lobos' list of the top 10 games in Pit history, three were against New Mexico State—not surprising, since state bragging rights are at stake when the two schools square off. First comes the double-overtime 112-104 Aggies win on Dec. 11, 1993, in which the Lobos blew a nine-point lead with 1:20 left in regulation. Next is the Feb. 1, 1969, game that Petie Gibson won for the Lobos, 68-66, with a 30-foot desperation buzzer-beater. Then there was the Feb. 7, 1968, thriller in which the lead changed hands 14 times in the Lobos' 72-71 win. New Mexico leads the series, 108–94.

Say the words "Cup Game" in Albuquerque and you're bound to get sighs and gasps.

FANFARE AND HOOPLA: An independent study conducted by the *St. Petersburg Times* declared the Pit the "loudest arena in the country," beating out Duke's Cameron Indoor Stadium and Indiana's Assembly Hall.

FAN FAVORITE: G TOBY ROYBAL (1952-56) The high-flying Albuquerque hometown hero could drop 45 on opponents one night, then, when facing triple teams the next game, set up his teammates just as successfully.

FIRST-ROUND PRO PICKS

1967	**Mel Daniels,** Cincinnati (9)
1967	**Mel Daniels,** Minnesota (ABA)
1970	**Greg Howard,** Phoenix (10)
1971	**Willie Long,** Floridians (ABA)
1991	**Luc Longley,** Minnesota (7)
1997	**Charles Smith,** Miami (26)
1999	**Kenny Thomas,** Houston (22)
2005	**Danny Granger,** Indiana (17)
2008	**J.R. Giddens,** Boston (30)

PROFILE

University of New Mexico, Albuquerque, NM
Founded: 1889
Enrollment: 25,820 (18,395 undergraduate)
Colors: Cherry and silver
Nickname: Lobos
Current arena: Bob King Court at University Arena, a.k.a. the Pit, opened in 1966 (18,018)
Previous: Johnson Center, 1957-66 (7,000)
First game: Feb. 2, 1900
All-time record: 1,310-1,016 (.563)
Total weeks in AP Top 20/25: 112

Current conference: Mountain West (1999-)
Conference titles:
Border: 2 (1944, '45)
WAC: 5 (1964 [tie], '68, '74, '78, '94)
Mountain West: 1 (2009 [tie])
Conference tournament titles:
WAC: 2 (1993, '96)
NCAA Tournament appearances: 11
NIT appearances: 18
Semifinals: 2

TOP 5

G **Michael Cooper** (1976-78)
G **Petie Gibson** (1968-71)
F **Kenny Thomas** (1995-99)
F/C **Luc Longley** (1987-91)
C **Mel Daniels** (1964-67)

RECORDS	GAME		SEASON		CAREER	
POINTS	50	Marvin Johnson, vs. Colorado State (March 2, 1978)	784	Kenny Page (1979-80)	1,993	Charles Smith (1993-97)
POINTS PER GAME			28.0	Kenny Page (1979-80)	26.2	Kenny Page (1979-81)
REBOUNDS	26	Tom King, vs. Wyoming (Feb. 13, 1960)	375	Tom King (1960-61)	1,032	Kenny Thomas (1995-99)
ASSISTS	21	Kelvin Scarborough, vs. Hawaii (Feb. 13, 1987)	243	Darrell McGee (1988-89)	684	Darrell McGee (1986-90)

SEASON REVIEW

SEASON	W-L	CONF.	COMMENTS	COACH	RECORD	
900-15	35-14		*Ralph Hutchinson started in 1910-11, the program's first coach*			
915-16	9-2			Ralph Hutchinson		
916-17	4-1			Ralph Hutchinson	32-8	.800
917-18	no team					
918-19	2-4			John McGough	2-4	.333
919-20	0-3			Roy Johnson		
920-21	no team					
921-22	0-2			Roy Johnson		
922-23	2-7			Roy Johnson		
923-24	5-3			Roy Johnson		
1924-25	12-1			Roy Johnson		
1925-26	12-2			Roy Johnson		
1926-27	13-4			Roy Johnson		
1927-28	12-7			Roy Johnson		
1928-29	14-9			Roy Johnson		
1929-30	16-4			Roy Johnson		
1930-31	9-7			Thomas Churchill		
1931-32	10-6	5-5		Thomas Churchill		
1932-33	13-6	8-6		Thomas Churchill	32-19	.627
1933-34	16-4	6-4		Roy Johnson		
1934-35	10-10	7-9		Roy Johnson		
1935-36	16-10	11-9		Roy Johnson		

SEAS.	W-L	CONF.	POSTSEASON	SCORING		REBOUNDS		ASSISTS		COACH	RECORD	
1936-37	12-14	10-10								Roy Johnson		
1937-38	9-16	6-10								Roy Johnson		
1938-39	4-21	4-16								Roy Johnson		
1939-40	3-22	1-15								Roy Johnson	156-139	.529
1940-41	5-18	4-14								Dr. Benjamin Sacks	5-18	.217
1941-42	9-13	5-11								Willis Barnes		
1942-43	3-17	1-11								Willis Barnes	12-30	.286
1943-44	11-2	3-0								George White	11-2	.846
1944-45	14-2	12-0								Woody Clements		
1945-46	16-9	13-8								Woody Clements		
1946-47	11-8	10-6		L.C. Cozzens	13.7					Woody Clements		
1947-48	14-15	8-8		L.C. Cozzens	11.2					Woody Clements		
1948-49	11-12	7-9		Ned Wallace	12.7					Woody Clements		
1949-50	5-19	4-12		Larry Tuttle	10.3					Woody Clements		
1950-51	13-11	9-7		Frank Kremer	10.1	Frank Kremer	8.4			Woody Clements		
1951-52	6-19	1-13		Larry Tuttle	14.4					Berl Huffman	6-19	.240
1952-53	10-14	5-9		Toby Roybal	12.6	Russ Nystedt	6.3			Woody Clements		
1953-54	11-11	5-9		Toby Roybal	15.6	Russ Nystedt	8.9			Woody Clements		
1954-55	7-17	2-12		Ray Esquibel	12.4	Bruce Wilson	8.0			Woody Clements	112-118	.487
1955-56	6-16	5-9		Toby Roybal	20.4	John Teel	9.9			Bill Stockton		
1956-57	5-21	1-13		John Teel	15.8	John Teel	10.5			Bill Stockton		
1957-58	3-21	0-14		John Teel	14.2	John Teel	8.5			Bill Stockton	14-58	.194
1958-59	3-19	1-13		Gig Brummell	10.5	Fred Sims	9.5			Bob Sweeney		
1959-60	6-19	3-11		Francis Grant	19.2	Tom King	14.9			Bob Sweeney		
1960-61	6-17	3-11		Francis Grant	15.7	Tom King	16.3			Bob Sweeney		
1961-62	6-20	3-11		Francis Grant	15.8	Mike Lucero	9.2			Bob Sweeney	21-75	.219
1962-63	16-9	4-6		Ira Harge	21.1	Ira Harge	13.2			Bob King		
1963-64	23-6	7-3	NIT RUNNER-UP	Ira Harge	16.8	Ira Harge	10.5			Bob King		
1964-65	19-8	5-5	NIT QUARTERFINALS	Mel Daniels	17.0	Mel Daniels	11.2			Bob King		
1965-66	16-8	4-6		Mel Daniels	21.2	Mel Daniels	10.3			Bob King		
1966-67	19-8	5-5	NIT QUARTERFINALS	Mel Daniels	21.5	Mel Daniels	11.6			Bob King		
1967-68	23-5	8-2	NCAA REGIONAL SEMIFINALS	Ron Nelson	19.5	Greg Howard	9.7			Bob King		
1968-69	17-9	4-6		Greg Howard	19.7	Ron Sanford	8.8	Petie Gibson	7.0	Bob King		
1969-70	13-13	7-7		Willie Long	23.9	Willie Long	12.9	Petie Gibson	6.9	Bob King		
1970-71	14-12	4-10		Willie Long	23.9	Willie Long	10.6	Petie Gibson	7.6	Bob King		
1971-72	15-11	7-7		Mike Faulkner	16.4	Darryl Minniefield	9.8	Tommy Roberts	4.2	Bob King	175-89	.663
1972-73	21-6	9-5	NIT FIRST ROUND	Darryl Minniefield	13.1	Darryl Minniefield	9.8	Tommy Roberts	3.3	Norm Ellenberger		
1973-74	22-7	10-4	NCAA REGIONAL SEMIFINALS	Bernard Hardin	17.1	Bill Hagins	9.0	Wendell Taylor	3.8	Norm Ellenberger		
1974-75	13-13	4-10		Bill Hagins	14.9	Bill Hagins	11.6	Pat King	3.9	Norm Ellenberger		
1975-76	16-11	8-6		Larry Gray	14.3	Larry Gray	10.4	Ricky Williams	3.9	Norm Ellenberger		
1976-77	19-11	8-6		Marvin Johnson	19.8	Jimmy Allen	8.7	Michael Cooper	3.4	Norm Ellenberger		
1977-78	24-4	13-1	NCAA FIRST ROUND	Marvin Johnson	24.0	Jimmy Allen	6.9	Russell Saunders	4.7	Norm Ellenberger		
1978-79	19-10	8-4	NIT FIRST ROUND	Phil Abney	16.2	Larry Belin	6.7	Russell Saunders	5.1	Norm Ellenberger	134-62	.684
1979-80	7-21	3-11		Kenny Page	28.0	Jim Williams	7.4	Everette Jefferson	5.7	Charlie Harrison	7-21	.250
1980-81	11-15	6-10		Kenny Page	24.1	Jerome Henderson	7.8	Phil Smith	6.8	Gary Colson		
1981-82	14-14	7-9		Phil Smith	15.9	Larry Tarrance	5.8	Phil Smith	6.1	Gary Colson		
1982-83	14-15	6-10		Phil Smith	12.9	George Scott	5.8	Phil Smith	5.1	Gary Colson		
1983-84	24-11	10-6	NIT FIRST ROUND	Tim Garrett	15.4	Alan Dolensky	6.3	Phil Smith	5.8	Gary Colson		
1984-85	19-13	9-7	NIT SECOND ROUND	Johnny Brown	18.8	George Scott	6.6	Kelvin Scarborough	5.5	Gary Colson		
1985-86	17-14	8-8	NIT FIRST ROUND	Johnny Brown	20.9	Johnny Brown	7.5	Kelvin Scarborough	4.9	Gary Colson		
1986-87	25-10	11-5	NIT FIRST ROUND	Hunter Greene	21.1	Hunter Greene	6.2	Kelvin Scarborough	6.1	Gary Colson		
1987-88	22-14	8-8	NIT QUARTERFINALS	Charlie Thomas	17.0	Charlie Thomas	7.5	Darrell McGee	5.1	Gary Colson	146-106	.579
1988-89	22-11	11-5	NIT QUARTERFINALS	Charlie Thomas	16.5	Charlie Thomas	7.8	Darrell McGee	7.4	Dave Bliss		
1989-90	20-14	9-7	NIT FOURTH PLACE	Luc Longley	18.4	Luc Longley	9.7	Darrell McGee	6.0	Dave Bliss		
1990-91	20-10	10-6	NCAA FIRST ROUND	Luc Longley	19.1	Luc Longley	9.2	Jimmy Taylor	3.8	Dave Bliss		
991-92	20-13	11-5	NIT QUARTERFINALS	Willie Banks	13.2	Khari Jaxon	7.4	Willie Banks	4.9	Dave Bliss		
992-93	24-7	13-5	NCAA FIRST ROUND	Ike Williams	15.9	Khari Jaxon	7.4	Steve Logan	4.5	Dave Bliss		
993-94	23-8	14-4	NCAA FIRST ROUND	Greg Brown	19.3	Lewis LaMar	10.3	Greg Brown	4.4	Dave Bliss		
994-95	15-15	9-9		Charles Smith	15.9	Brian Hayden	4.8	David Gibson	3.8	Dave Bliss		
995-96	28-5	14-4	NCAA SECOND ROUND	Charles Smith	19.5	Kenny Thomas	7.8	David Gibson	3.6	Dave Bliss		
996-97	25-8	11-5	NCAA SECOND ROUND	Charles Smith	17.5	Kenny Thomas	6.9	David Gibson	3.4	Dave Bliss		
997-98	24-8	11-3	NCAA SECOND ROUND	Kenny Thomas	16.8	Kenny Thomas	9.3	David Gibson	3.6	Dave Bliss		
998-99	25-9	9-5	NCAA SECOND ROUND	Kenny Thomas	17.8	Kenny Thomas	10.0	John Robinson II	4.8	Dave Bliss	246-108	.695
999-2000	18-14	9-5	NIT SECOND ROUND	Lamont Long	18.7	Damion Walker	6.1	Marlon Parmer	3.6	Fran Fraschilla		
000-01	21-13	6-8	NIT QUARTERFINALS	Ruben Douglas	16.3	Wayland White	6.0	Marlon Parmer	5.4	Fran Fraschilla		
001-02	16-14	6-8	NIT FIRST ROUND	Ruben Douglas	18.1	Patrick Dennehy	7.5	Senque Carey	3.2	Fran Fraschilla	55-41	.573
002-03	10-18	4-10		Ruben Douglas	28.0	Ruben Douglas	6.6	Javin Tindall	2.7	Ritchie McKay		
003-04	14-14	5-9		Danny Granger	19.5	Danny Granger	9.0	Javin Tindall	3.5	Ritchie McKay		
004-05	26-7	10-4	NCAA FIRST ROUND	Danny Granger	18.8	Danny Granger	8.9	Mark Walters	2.8	Ritchie McKay		
005-06	17-13	8-8		Mark Walters	15.5	David Chiotti	6.3	Mark Walters	3.1	Ritchie McKay		
006-07	15-17	4-12		J.R. Giddens	15.8	Aaron Johnson	7.3	Darren Prentice	3.3	Ritchie McKay	82-69	.543
007-08	24-9	11-5	NIT FIRST ROUND	J.R. Giddens	16.3	J.R. Giddens	8.8	Dairese Gary	3.2	Steve Alford		
008-09	22-12	12-4	NIT SECOND ROUND	Tony Danridge	15.0	Daniel Faris	6.4	Dairese Gary	4.1	Steve Alford	46-21	.687

ESPN 119 SAGARIN

NEW MEXICO STATE

On Feb. 9, 2002, New Mexico State dedicated its court to Lou Henson, an honor that was nearly 60 years in the making. Henson got his start in Las Cruces as a defensive specialist for Presley Askew's teams in the 1950s, then returned for his first stint as NMSU's coach starting in 1966. In 1997, Henson returned to his alma mater for a second run, rising to seventh on the list of all-time D1 coaching wins (779) before retiring in 2005. (He's now No. 11.) Long story short: Lou Henson *is* Aggies basketball.

BEST TEAM: 1969-70 The big guy was 6'10", 235-pound Sam Lacey, a rebounding and shot-blocking force. The little guy was 5'8" Charlie Criss, a dazzling playmaker. The skinny guy was 6'2" shooting guard Jimmy Collins, who averaged 24.3 points. Together, along with junior power forward Jeff Smith, the Aggies knocked off Rice, Kansas State and Drake in the first three rounds of the NCAA Tournament. Henson's crew finally met its match in the Final Four against a longtime thorn in their side, losing 93-77 to UCLA.

BEST PLAYER: C Sam Lacey (1967-70) He didn't start playing basketball until he was 14 years old, but by the time he arrived in Las Cruces, he was dominant. Lacey came up biggest in New Mexico State's greatest season, scoring 17.7 points and grabbing 15.9 rebounds to earn first-team All-America honors. Even after spraining his ankle a few minutes into the Final Four loss to UCLA, he went for eight points and 16 rebounds.

BEST COACH: Lou Henson (1966-75, 1997-2005) Nobody would have guessed five decades ago that the guard who averaged all of 5.5 ppg in his college career would one day have a hairstyle (the Lou-'do) and a basketball court named after him, and be one of the first inductees into New Mexico's Ring of Honor (along with Lacey and Billy Joe Price). "I am deeply humbled," he said at the court dedication.

GAME FOR THE AGES: On Jan. 8, 1990, the Larry Johnson-led Runnin' Rebels came to town riding a six-game win streak. But their road to the national championship hit a speed bump at the Pan American Center. With the Rebels protecting an 82-81 lead, Aggie Keith Hill let loose a fadeaway 18-footer that kissed the glass and dropped in for the upset win.

HEARTBREAKER: In the 1992 Sweet 16, NMSU lost to No. 4-ranked UCLA, 85-78, in a game that wasn't quite as close as the final score. What's so heartbreaking about that? It was a bitter reminder of the Bruins' legacy of bouncing talented Aggies teams from the Tournament: a 58-49 regional semifinal loss in 1968, a year later another regional semi loss (that one 53-38) and a 1970 Final Four loss. The Aggies are 0–7 all-time against the Bruins.

FIERCEST RIVAL: New Mexico State vs. New Mexico is the hoops equivalent of the wild, wild West. The Aggies lost on Feb 1, 1969, when Petie Gibson hit a late 30-footer—a heartbreaker surpassed on Dec. 16, 1995, when Clayton Shields sank a 55-foot Lobos' game-winner. New Mexico leads the series, 108–94.

Nobody would have guessed that the guard who averaged 5.5 ppg in his college career would one day have a hairstyle (the Lou-'do) and a basketball court named after him.

FANFARE AND HOOPLA: During the 2006-07 season, Cuyler Frank made history by becoming the first radio announcer to call college basketball games in Navajo. Cruising through the Las Cruces dials, you'll know Frank's call when you hear it; because there aren't Navajo words for many basketball terms (such as "zone defense" and "alley-oop"), his broadcasts are peppered with English.

FAN FAVORITE: G John Williamson (1971-73) "Supe! Supe! Supe!" That was the chant that broke out at the Pan American Center whenever Super John Williamson did the spectacular—which was often. Stocky and cocky, the 6'2", 180-pound guard averaged 27.1 ppg as a sophomore to earn first-team All-America honors.

PROFILE

New Mexico State, Las Cruces, NM
Founded: 1888
Enrollment: 16,428 (13,677 undergraduate)
Colors: Crimson and white
Nickname: Aggies
Current arena: Pan American Center, opened in 1968 (12,482)
Previous: Williams Gym, 1932-68 (2,500)
First game: Dec. 22, 1904
All-time record: 1,332-1,012-2 (.568)
Total weeks in AP Top 20/25: 64
Current conference: Western Athletic (2005-)

Conference titles:
Border: 8 (1937, '38, '39, '40 [tie], '52 [tie], '59 [tie], '60, '61 [tie])
Missouri Valley: 1 (1977 [tie])
Big West: 5 (1990 [tie], '93, '94, '97 [tie], '99 [tie])
WAC: 1 (2008 [tie])
Conference tournament titles:
Big West: 3 (1992, '94, '99)
WAC: 1 (2007)
NCAA Tournaments: 17 (3 appearances vacated)
Sweet 16s (since 1975): 1
Final Fours: 1
NIT appearances: 4

FIRST-ROUND PRO PICKS

1970 **Sam Lacey,** Cincinnati (5)
1970 **Jimmy Collins,** Chicago (11)

TOP 5

G **Jimmy Collins** (1967-70)
G **John Williamson** (1971-73)
F **George Knighton** (1959-62)
F **James Moore** (2000-04)
C **Sam Lacey** (1967-70)

RECORDS	GAME		SEASON		CAREER	
POINTS	48	John Williamson, vs. California (Jan. 17, 1972)	754	Jimmy Collins (1969-70)	1,862	Eric Channing (1998-2002)
POINTS PER GAME			27.1	John Williamson (1971-72)	27.2	John Williamson (1971-73)
REBOUNDS	27	Sam Lacey, vs. Hardin-Simmons (Dec. 19, 1969)	493	Sam Lacey (1969-70)	1,265	Sam Lacey (1967-70)
ASSISTS	20	Sam Crawford, vs. Sam Houston State (Dec. 21, 1992)	310	Sam Crawford (1992-93)	592	Sam Crawford (1991-93)

SEASON REVIEW

EASON	W-L	CONF.	SCORING	COACH	RECORD		SEASON	W-L	CONF.	SCORING	COACH	RECORD	
04-17	*32-45-1*		*Won 1 game each season (3-22) under Arthur Badenoch (1910-13)*				**1927-28**	3-11-1			Ted R. Coffman		
17-18	7-3			John G. Griffith			**1928-29**	6-9			Ted R. Coffman	9-20-1	.452
18-19	8-2			John G. Griffith			**1929-30**	12-14			Jerry Hines		
19-20	5-4			John G. Griffith	20-9	.690	**1930-31**	9-14			Jerry Hines		
20-21	9-1			Arthur Bergman			**1931-32**	9-10	1-7		Jerry Hines		
21-22	3-4			Arthur Bergman	12-5	.706	**1932-33**	7-11	2-10		Jerry Hines		
22-23	14-6			Robert R. Brown			**1933-34**	10-9	2-6		Jerry Hines		
23-24	10-9			Robert R. Brown			**1934-35**	12-6	4-6		Jerry Hines		
24-25	11-9			Robert R. Brown			**1935-36**	10-9	8-8		Jerry Hines		
25-26	13-7			Robert R. Brown	48-31	.608	**1936-37**	22-5	15-3		Jerry Hines		
26-27	6-13			A.L. Burkeholder	6-13	.316	**1937-38**	22-3	18-0		Jerry Hines		

EAS.	W-L	CONF.	POSTSEASON	SCORING		REBOUNDS		ASSISTS		COACH	RECORD	
38-39	20-4	14-2	NIT QUARTERFINALS							Jerry Hines		
39-40	16-7	12-4								Jerry Hines		
40-41	14-12	8-8								Julius Johnston		
41-42	8-18	2-14								Julius Johnston	22-30	.423
42-43	no team											
43-44	no team											
44-45	9-5	4-3								Kermit Laabs		
45-46	5-16	2-12								Kermit Laabs	14-21	.400
46-47	8-17	2-14								Jerry Hines	157-109	.590
47-48	13-11	6-10								John Gunn		
48-49	9-15	4-12								John Gunn	21-26	.447
49-50	17-13	7-9								George McCarty		
50-51	19-14	10-6								George McCarty		
51-52	22-10	12-2	NCAA REGIONAL SEMIFINALS							George McCarty		
52-53	7-17	5-9								George McCarty	65-54	.546
53-54	6-12	3-9								Presley Askew		
54-55	6-13	1-11								Presley Askew		
55-56	16-7	7-5								Presley Askew		
56-57	6-18	3-7		Bob Jarrett	12.7	Wayne Yates	9.4			Presley Askew		
57-58	14-9	7-3		Wayne Yates	13.4	Wayne Yates	9.9			Presley Askew		
58-59	17-11	7-3	NCAA FIRST ROUND	Billy Joe Price	19.0	Billy Joe Price	12.6			Presley Askew		
59-60	20-7	8-2	NCAA FIRST ROUND	George Knighton	21.4	George Knighton	10.7			Presley Askew		
60-61	19-5	9-1		George Knighton	22.0	George Knighton	13.2			Presley Askew		
61-62	10-14	3-5		George Knighton	23.1	George Knighton	10.8			Presley Askew		
62-63	4-17			Charles Lindsey	12.1	Willie Booker	6.3			Presley Askew		
63-64	8-15			Charles Lindsey	15.9	Don Henry	5.6			Presley Askew		
64-65	8-18			Mike Dabich	14.2	Mike Dabich	8.7			Presley Askew	134-146	.479
65-66	4-22			Mike Dabich	18.3	Mike Dabich	10.6			Jim McGregor	4-22	.154
66-67	15-11		NCAA FIRST ROUND	Ernest Turner	14.3	Wes Morehead	7.2			Lou Henson		
67-68	23-6		NCAA REGIONAL SEMIFINALS	Sam Lacey	15.1	Sam Lacey	11.6	Jimmy Collins	77	Lou Henson		
68-69	24-5		NCAA REGIONAL SEMIFINALS	Jimmy Collins	19.3	Sam Lacey	15.0	Charlie Criss	58	Lou Henson		
69-70	27-3		NCAA THIRD PLACE	Jimmy Collins	24.3	Sam Lacey	15.9	Milton Horne	110	Lou Henson		
970-71	19-8		NCAA FIRST ROUND	Truman Ward	14.5	Truman Ward	10.3	Alex Scott	92	Lou Henson		
971-72	19-6			John Williamson	27.1	Truman Ward	10.2	Alex Scott	149	Lou Henson		
972-73	12-14	6-8		John Williamson[a]	27.2	Jim Bostic	8.6	John DiBiase	67	Lou Henson		
973-74	14-11	7-6		Roland Grant	18.0	Roland Grant	10.3	Steve White	44	Lou Henson		
974-75	20-7	11-3	NCAA FIRST ROUND	Richard Robinson	14.7	Jim Bostic	10.7	Jim Bostic	64	Lou Henson		
975-76	15-12	4-8		Bill Allen	17.9	Bill Allen	8.1	John DiBiase	79	Ken Hayes		
976-77	17-10	8-4		Richard Robinson	19.0	Richard Robinson	7.4	Richard Robinson	90	Ken Hayes		
977-78	15-14	9-7		Slab Jones	14.3	Robert Gunn	7.6	Danny Lopez	103	Ken Hayes		
978-79	22-10	11-5	NCAA FIRST ROUND	Slab Jones	16.4	Robert Gunn	9.0	Bill Myers	137	Ken Hayes	69-46	.600
979-80	17-10	8-8		Slab Jones	18.0	Slab Jones	11.0	Greg Webb	93	Weldon Drew		
980-81	10-17	7-9		Jaime Peña	18.1	Renault Moultrie	7.1	Ernest Patterson	113	Weldon Drew		
981-82	17-11	10-6		Jaime Peña	17.5	Renault Moultrie	7.9	Ernest Patterson	100	Weldon Drew		
982-83	18-11	11-7		Ernest Patterson	19.5	Derek Sailors	7.3	Steve Colter	130	Weldon Drew		
983-84	13-15	9-9		Steve Colter	19.5	Andre Patterson	8.1	Steve Colter	127	Weldon Drew		
984-85	7-20	4-14		Gilbert Wilburn	23.6	Andre Patterson	9.6	Gerald Wright	89	Weldon Drew	82-84	.494
985-86	18-12	10-8		Gilbert Wilburn	19.1	Gilbert Wilburn	7.1	Jeff Williams	80	Neil McCarthy		
986-87	15-15	9-9		Kenny Travis	20.2	Kenny Travis	7.3	Kenny Travis	80	Neil McCarthy		
987-88	16-16	8-10		Willie Joseph	14.6	Steve McGlothin	6.7	Keith Hill	109	Neil McCarthy		
988-89	21-11	12-6	NIT FIRST ROUND	Johnny Roberson	14.1	Johnny Roberson	7.2	Willie Joseph	122	Neil McCarthy		
989-90	26-5	16-2	NCAA FIRST ROUND	James Anderson	13.6	James Anderson	6.9	Keith Hill	120	Neil McCarthy		
990-91	23-6	15-3	NCAA FIRST ROUND	Reggie Jordan	14.6	Reggie Jordan	7.8	Randy Brown	187	Neil McCarthy		
991-92	25-8	⊗ 12-6	NCAA REGIONAL SEMIFINALS	Sam Crawford	12.9	Malcolm Leak	7.5	Sam Crawford	282	Neil McCarthy		
992-93	26-8	⊗ 15-3	NCAA SECOND ROUND	Sam Crawford	12.9	Tracey Ware	7.1	Sam Crawford	310	Neil McCarthy		
993-94	23-8	⊗ 12-6	NCAA FIRST ROUND	James Dockery	13.1	James Dockery	8.5	Keith Johnson	151	Neil McCarthy		
994-95	25-10	13-5	NIT QUARTERFINALS	Rodney Walker	15.7	Clyde Jordan	7.6	Troy Brewer	144	Neil McCarthy		
995-96	11-15	8-10		Enoch Davis	15.8	Charles Gosa	5.9	Chewy Johnson	52	Neil McCarthy		
996-97	19-9	⊗ 12-4		Enoch Davis	12.5	Enoch Davis	5.2	Bostajan Leban	57	Neil McCarthy	248-123	.668▼
997-98	18-12	⊗ 8-8		Demark Reid	16.9	Charles Gosa	8.1	Dominic Ellison	165	Lou Henson		
998-99	23-10	12-4	NCAA FIRST ROUND	Charles Gosa	14.9	Charles Gosa	8.0	Billy Keys	4.8	Lou Henson		
999-2000	22-10	11-5	NIT FIRST ROUND	Billy Keys	17.3	Daveeno Hines	7.7	Billy Keys	4.7	Lou Henson		
000-01	14-14	10-6		Eric Channing	18.6	Daveeno Hines	9.1	Brandon Mason	2.9	Lou Henson		
001-02	20-12	11-4		Eric Channing	16.2	Chris Jackson	8.7	Brandon Mason	3.5	Lou Henson		
002-03	20-9	9-6		James Moore	18.8	Chris Jackson	10.0	Jason Fontenet	4.0	Lou Henson		
003-04	13-14	6-9		James Moore	15.4	James Moore	6.6	Detruis Roberson	2.9	Lou Henson		
004-05	6-24	1-14		Duane John	14.1	Jeff Jones	6.3	Josh Jenkins	3.5	Lou Henson[b]	307-164	.652▼
005-06	16-14	10-6		Tyrone Nelson	17.8	Tyrone Nelson	8.7	Elijah Ingram	3.1	Reggie Theus		
006-07	25-9	11-5	NCAA FIRST ROUND	Justin Hawkins	15.6	Justin Hawkins	6.6	Fred Peete	2.6	Reggie Theus	41-23	.641
007-08	21-14	12-4		Justin Hawkins	18.1	Hatila Passos	7.3	Fred Peete	4.1	Marvin Menzies		
008-09	17-15	9-7		Jahmar Young	17.9	Weldell McKines	10.0	Hernst Laroche	4.3	Marvin Menzies	38-29	.567

umulative totals listed when per game averages not available.
Williamson played only 18 games; NMSU considers his 1971-72 average its single-season record.
Lou Henson (4-12) and Tony Stubblefield (2-12) both coached during the 2004-05 season.
⊗ Records don't reflect games forfeited or vacated. For adjusted records, see p. 521.
▼ Coaches' records adjusted to reflect games forfeited or vacated: Neil McCarthy, 226-111, .671; Lou Henson, 289-152, .655. For yearly totals, see p. 521.

ESPN 121 SAGARIN

NEW ORLEANS

It's amazing what a one-time fledgling LSU offshoot can accomplish in just 40 years. The Privateers have enjoyed 14 20-win seasons, two D2 final fours, an unbeaten league season (1992-93), enough pro talent to start their own NBA alumni chapter, and impressive coaching talent (Ron Greene, Butch van Breda Kolff, Tim Floyd and Tic Price).

BEST TEAM: 1986-87 Statement games don't get any more emphatic than New Orleans' Dec. 20, 1986, road upset of LSU, 82-71. Behind future pros Ledell Eackles (22.6 ppg) and Ron Grandison (9.7 rpg), the independent Privateers won 21 of their next 22 to claim a No. 7 seed in the NCAA Tournament. There they edged BYU, 83-79, in the first round before getting swarmed by Alabama, 101-76. No matter: Their No. 16 ranking in the final AP poll was an all-time end-of-season high.

BEST PLAYER: C ERVIN JOHNSON (1989-93) It's fitting that the school's strength and conditioning center is named after this 6'11" intimidator. In November 1988, Johnson walked into coach Tim Floyd's office uninvited and said he wanted a spot on the team—never mind that the unenrolled 20-year-old hadn't played since 10th grade and was working at a Baton Rouge A&P. Floyd took a flier on the raw prospect and was glad he did. A workout warrior, Johnson transformed himself into a rebounding, shotblocking and scoring machine—and a future 13-year pro.

BEST COACH: TIM FLOYD (1988-94) On Sept. 25, 2007, the school held Tim Floyd Roast Day to benefit the basketball program. Maybe his NBA coaching career was a bit of a joke, but Floyd's six seasons at New Orleans were anything but: two NCAA Tournaments, three NITs and a No. 17 ranking in the final 1993 AP poll. He's apparently a pretty good sport, too, telling some of the funniest jokes at his own expense at that roast. Think Bob Knight would do that?

GAME FOR THE AGES: The 1995-96 Privateers won eight straight to reach the Sun Belt tournament championship at Arkansas-Little Rock, the site of their last loss. Behind tourney MVP Lewis Sims, all-league Tyrone Garris and all-tourney James Douglas, coach Tic Price's team beat Derek Fisher and the Trojans, 57-56, to reach the NCAAs.

HEARTBREAKER: Seven seconds remained in the 1975 D2 championship game, with Oliver Purnell-led Old Dominion guarding a 76-74 lead over UNO. The Privateers rebounded a missed one-and-one and guard Wilbur Holland got off a 15-footer ... that kissed the rim twice and bounced off.

FIERCEST RIVAL: Since rejoining the Sun Belt in 1991, the Privateers have generally gotten the best of their conference rivals—with one big exception: West Division nemesis Louisiana-Lafayette has won three of the conference tourney titles since the turn of the century (2000, '04, '05), including a 2004 title-game victory over New Orleans. The Cajuns have gone 13–4 against the Privateers since 2002 and lead the overall series, 36–32.

In November 1988, Ervin Johnson walked into coach Tim Floyd's office uninvited and said he wanted a spot on the team—never mind that the unenrolled 20-year-old hadn't played since 10th grade.

FANFARE AND HOOPLA: For their first 14 seasons, the Privateers played in the cramped, sweaty Human Performance Center, a.k.a. the Chamber of Horrors. The team had to return to that court from 2005 through the 2007-08 season, after Hurricane Katrina damaged the Kiefer Lakefront Arena—and opponents were the worse for it; UNO went 23–14 during that time.

FAN FAVORITE: G BO MCCALEBB (2003-08) The resilient do-everything six-footer stuck by the Privateers through a natural disaster and two coaching changes to become the Sun Belt's all-time leading scorer.

PROFILE

University of New Orleans, New Orleans, LA
Founded: 1958
Enrollment: 11,363 (8,653 undergraduate)
Colors: Royal blue and silver
Nickname: Privateers
Current arena: Kiefer Lakefront Arena (8,933)
Previous: Human Performance Center, a.k.a. the Chamber of Horrors, 1969-83, 2005-08 (1,200); Kiefer Lakefront Arena, 1983-2005 (8,818)
First game played: Dec. 1, 1969
All-time record: 686-467 (.595)
Total weeks in AP Top 20/25: 12

Current conference: Sun Belt (1976-80, '91-)
Conference titles:
American South: 4 (1988 [tie], '89, '90 [tie], '91 [tie])
Sun Belt: 3 (1993, '96 [tie], '97 [tie])
Conference tournament titles:
American South: 1 (1990)
Sun Belt: 2 (1978, '96)
NCAA Tournament appearances: 4
NIT appearances: 6

CONSENSUS ALL-AMERICAS

1971 **Xavier Webster** (Little A-A), F

FIRST-ROUND PRO PICKS

1993 **Ervin Johnson**, Seattle (23)

TOP 5

G **Ledell Eackles** (1986-88)
G **Wilbur Holland** (1973-75)
G **Bo McCalebb** (2003-08)
F/C **Wayne Cooper** (1974-78)
C **Ervin Johnson** (1989-93)

RECORDS

RECORDS	GAME	SEASON	CAREER
POINTS	48 Xavier Webster, vs. Ball State (Dec. 5, 1970)	776 Bo McCalebb (2006-07)	2,679 Bo McCalebb (2003-08)
POINTS PER GAME		26.7 Xavier Webster (1970-71)	25.2 Xavier Webster (1969-71)
REBOUNDS	27 Ervin Johnson, vs. Lamar (Feb. 18, 1993)	367 Ervin Johnson (1990-91)	1,287 Ervin Johnson (1989-93)
ASSISTS	18 Jordan Crump, vs. Savannah State (Nov. 30, 1974)	178 Jimmie Smith (1994-95)	456 Gabe Corchiani (1984-88)

SEASON REVIEW

SEAS.	W-L	CONF.	POSTSEASON	SCORING		REBOUNDS		ASSISTS		COACH	RECORD	
69-70	18-5			Xavier Webster	23.5	Xavier Webster	12.2	Duane Reboul	8.0	Ron Greene		
70-71	23-3			Xavier Webster	26.7	Xavier Webster	12.8	Duane Reboul	6.8	Ron Greene		
71-72	16-10			John Hamilton	26.5	C.B. Gordon	13.7	Terry Gill	6.2	Ron Greene		
72-73	9-13			Mel Henderson	21.2	Milton Cooper	8.4	Terry Gill	5.8	Ron Greene		
73-74	21-9			Wilbur Holland	20.3	Ernest Stackhouse	7.0	Terry Gill	4.9	Ron Greene		
74-75	23-7			Wilbur Holland	25.2	Ardith Wearren	6.9	Jordan Crump	5.5	Ron Greene		
75-76	18-8			Nate Mills	13.7	Wayne Cooper	9.4	Jordan Crump	4.2	Ron Greene		
76-77	18-10	4-2		Nate Mills	15.5	Wayne Cooper	10.1	Rico Weaver	3.7	Ron Greene	146-65	.692
77-78	21-6	8-2		Wayne Cooper	18.1	Wayne Cooper	12.7	Rico Weaver	3.7	Butch van Breda Kolff		
78-79	11-16	3-7		Mike Edwards	18.3	Mike Edwards	9.9	Mike Edwards	3.8	Butch van Breda Kolff	32-22	.593
79-80	5-21	2-12		Lloyd Terry	13.8	Lloyd Terry	9.5	Tim Owens	3.2	Don Smith		
80-81	13-14			Oscar Taylor	16.9	Oscar Taylor	8.7	Mitch Shuler	4.2	Don Smith		
81-82	18-8			Mark Petteway	15.2	Mark Petteway	9.5	Claude Butler	5.2	Don Smith		
82-83	23-7		NIT SECOND ROUND	Mark Petteway	17.1	Oscar Taylor	7.9	Claude Butler	3.5	Don Smith		
83-84	14-14			John Harris	18.6	John Harris	8.7	Eugene Washington	4.7	Don Smith		
84-85	11-19			John Harris	19.9	John Harris	9.7	Rocky Adrianson	4.5	Don Smith	84-83	.503
85-86	16-12			Ron Grandison	16.6	Ron Grandison	9.7	Gabe Corchiani	3.6	Benny Dees		
86-87	26-4		NCAA SECOND ROUND	Ledell Eackles	22.6	Ron Grandison	9.7	Gabe Corchiani	4.3	Benny Dees	42-16	.724
87-88	21-11	7-3	NIT FIRST ROUND	Ledell Eackles	23.4	Sam Jones	7.4	Gabe Corchiani	4.3	Art Tolis	21-11	.656
88-89	19-11	7-3	NIT FIRST ROUND	Tony Harris	17.2	Tony Harris	5.5	Lamont Thornton	5.1	Tim Floyd		
89-90	21-11	8-2	NIT QUARTERFINALS	Tony Harris	19.9	Ervin Johnson	6.8	Louweegi Dyer	3.4	Tim Floyd		
90-91	23-8	9-3	NCAA FIRST ROUND	Tank Collins	17.3	Ervin Johnson	12.2	Cass Clarke	2.9	Tim Floyd		
91-92	18-14 ⊗	9-7		Ervin Johnson	15.4	Ervin Johnson	11.1	Dwight Myvett	2.9	Tim Floyd		
92-93	26-4	18-0	NCAA FIRST ROUND	Ervin Johnson	18.4	Ervin Johnson	11.9	Reni Mason	4.0	Tim Floyd		
93-94	20-10	12-6	NIT SECOND ROUND	Melvin Simon	16.3	Melvin Simon	11.8	Gerald Williams	3.4	Tim Floyd	127-58	.686
94-95	20-11	13-5		Tyrone Garris	17.1	Michael McDonald	9.7	Jimmie Smith	5.7	Tic Price		
95-96	21-9	14-4	NCAA FIRST ROUND	Tyrone Garris	15.2	Lewis Sims	7.6	Tyrone Garris	3.7	Tic Price		
96-97	22-7	14-4	NIT FIRST ROUND	Kwan Johnson	14.0	DeWaune Wesley	7.8	Corey Brown	3.7	Tic Price	63-27	.700
97-98	15-12	9-9		DeWaune Wesley	17.8	DeWaune Wesley	8.4	Edderick Womack	3.8	Joey Stiebing		
98-99	14-16	5-9		Curtis Wilson	11.2	Curtis Wilson	5.7	Markell Sneed	2.6	Joey Stiebing		
99-2000	11-18	6-10		Tory Walker	12.7	Tory Walker	5.9	Desmond Baxter	3.3	Joey Stiebing		
00-01	17-12	10-6		Tory Walker	17.0	Clyde Ellis	6.3	Ben Adams	3.7	Joey Stiebing	57-58	.496
01-02	15-14	9-6		Hector Romero	20.2	Hector Romero	10.8	A.J. Meredith	4.6	Monte Towe		
02-03	15-14	7-8		Hector Romero	18.3	Hector Romero	9.1	A.J. Meredith	4.1	Monte Towe		
03-04	17-14	9-6		Bo McCalebb	13.1	Victor Brown	6.1	Johnell Smith	3.0	Monte Towe		
04-05	13-17	7-8		Bo McCalebb	22.6	Shawn Malloy	6.3	Bo McCalebb	3.7	Monte Towe		
05-06	10-19	6-9		James Parlow	10.6	Nathaniel Parker	6.3	Jamie McNeilly	5.6	Monte Towe	70-78	.473
06-07	14-17	9-9		Bo McCalebb	25.0	Bo McCalebb	6.8	Shaun Reynolds	3.5	Buzz Williams	14-17	.452
07-08	19-13	8-10		Bo McCalebb	23.2	Kyndall Dykes	5.3	Bo McCalebb	3.1	Joe Pasternack		
08-09	11-19	6-12		T.J. Worley	16.0	Jaroslav Tyrna	4.9	Darrian McKinstry	2.7	Joe Pasternack	30-32	.484

⊗ **Records don't reflect games forfeited or vacated. For adjusted records, see p. 521.**

LATE GREAT

OKLAHOMA CITY 1950-85

During his tenure as coach from 1947 to '55, Doyle Parrack built up the Chiefs (as OCU's teams were nicknamed back then) from a nonscholarship club team without its own gym to an NCAA contender. He led the team to the first four of six consecutive NCAA Tournament appearances between 1952 and '57. His successor, Abe Lemons, went 432–265 in two stints at OCU (1955-73 and 1983-90). Lemons led the Chiefs to seven NCAAs, including four in a row from 1963 to '66. OCU led the country in 1966-67 with 96.0 ppg. Between 1954 and '81, seven Chiefs finished in the top 10 in scoring eight different times. The school's best season was 1956-57, when Oklahoma City ended up No. 9 in the AP poll and No. 16 in the UP.

NOTABLE PLAYERS: C Hub Reed (1954-58) and G Allen Leavell (1975-79) The 6'10" Reed was a dominant big man when there were few of those around. No. 99 (a jersey number rarely used in the era) held his own against Wilt Chamberlain, scoring 26 in their 1957 NCAA Midwest Regional final head-to-head. The 6'1" Leavell was a product of legendary Muncie (Ind.) Central High School. Both Reed and Leavell went on to have long NBA careers.

ESPN 122 SAGARIN

NIAGARA

No, there's no such thing as a Purple Eagle. The nickname for the one-time Catholic seminary is derived from the eagles that used to perch on the university's buildings and a color associated with royalty throughout history. That's just the beginning of this program's quirky story. As a member of the Western New York Little Three, along with St. Bonaventure and Canisius, Niagara has been part of a rich hoops tradition for more than a century.

BEST TEAM: 1953-54 The starting five of Larry Costello, Baltico "Bo" Erias, Charlie Hoxie, Ed Fleming and Jim McConnell were all NBA draft picks after their careers at Niagara. They made it to the final four of the NIT, and, after disposing of Western Kentucky in the third-place game, 71-65, they also clinched their best finish (24–6) under coach John J. "Taps" Gallagher.

BEST PLAYER: G CALVIN MURPHY (1967-70) The three-time All-America was a 5'9" dynamo: devastating from the perimeter, fierce on D and an improbable dunk artist (although only in practice, because dunking was outlawed during games from 1967 to '76). Murphy scored 68 against Syracuse as a junior in 1968. The next season, he blazed Niagara's first trail to the Tourney.

BEST COACH: JOHN J. "TAPS" GALLAGHER (1931-43, '46-65) In 31 seasons, the Gentleman Coach led Niagara to 26 winning seasons and seven NITs. But the best testament to his ability is the list of his pupils: future NBA coaches Hubie Brown, Larry Costello and Frank Layden.

GAME FOR THE AGES: Sure, defeating Siena in six overtimes on Feb. 21, 1953, was impressive. But busting No. 2 St. Bonaventure's 99-game winning streak at the Olean Armory on Feb. 25, 1961, was epic.

HEARTBREAKER: In the 1993 MAAC tournament finals, Niagara was poised to make its first NCAA Tournament in 23 years, riding its trapping defense to a 10-point halftime lead over Manhattan. But the Purple Eagles paid the ultimate price for failing to put the game away in the second half. With nine seconds left and the game tied at 67, Jaspers star Keith Bullock (30 points) missed a five-footer off the front iron, setting off a loose-ball scramble that ended with a controversial Dwayne Daniel foul on Manhattan's Chris Williams in the left corner. Williams made one of two from the line for the 68-67 win, and Niagara stayed in bracketology exile for another 12 years.

FIERCEST RIVAL: Ever since 1907, Niagara and Canisius have been crossing over the Erie Canal to duke it out. While Niagara holds a 94–72 series lead, Canisius has come up big against the Purple Eagles at some very inopportune times. Canisius snapped Niagara's 37-game home winning streak in 1935 and spoiled the ribbon-cutting of the Niagara Falls Convention Center in 1974 by handing Niagara its first loss in its new home.

FANFARE AND HOOPLA: Don't call Niagara "chicken." That's the mistake St. Bonaventure made before a 1961 game in which it was going for its 100th straight home win. With the Purple Eagles about to come out for warmups, a purple-painted bird guided by a leash clucked all around the court, to the delight of the Olean Armory crowd. The Purple Eagles got the last laugh, however, winning 87-77. In fact, they are still laughing about it: In their trophy case, you'll find a stuffed replica of the faux-chicken.

FAN FAVORITE: G PHIL SCAFFIDI (1975-80) As captain of the 1978-79 squad, Scaffidi was on his way to setting the school's all-time assist record when he was diagnosed with adrenal cancer. After undergoing eight hours of surgery and grueling rehab, the six-foot guard returned to the court six times during the next season and set the career assist record (since surpassed) in a game against Cleveland State on Jan. 21, 1980. Sadly, two months later he died. After the season, the U.S. Basketball Writers Association posthumously honored Scaffidi with its Most Courageous Award. Today, his No. 3 hangs in the Gallagher Center and a campus gym has been named in his honor.

CONSENSUS ALL-AMERICAS

1969, '70 **Calvin Murphy,** G

FIRST-ROUND PRO PICKS

1951 **Zeke Sinicola,** Fort Wayne (4)

PROFILE

Niagara University, Niagara, NY
Founded: 1856
Enrollment: 3,825 (2,927 undergraduate)
Colors: Purple and white
Nickname: Purple Eagles
Current arena: John J. "Taps" Gallagher Center, opened in 1949 (2,400)
Previous: Niagara Falls Convention Center, 1974-82, 1988-96 (N/A); Buffalo Memorial Auditorium, 1941-96 (18,000); St. Vincent's Gym, 1906-49 (N/A)
First game: 1905

All-time record: 1,348-1,044-1 (.564)
Total weeks in AP Top 20/25: 20
Current conference: Metro Atlantic Athletic (1989-)
Conference titles:
Western NY Little Three: 6 (1948, '49, '50 [tie], '53, '54, '55)
MAAC: 3 (1999 [tie], 2001 [tie], '05 [tie])
Conference tournament titles:
MAAC: 2 (2005, '07)
NCAA Tournament appearances: 3
NIT appearances: 13
Semifinals: 2

TOP 5

G **Alvin Cruz** (2001-05)
G **Calvin Murphy** (1967-70)
F **Charlie Hoxie** (1951-55)
F **Juan Mendez** (2001-05)
C **Alex "Boo" Ellis** (1955-58)

RECORDS	GAME		SEASON		CAREER	
POINTS	68	Calvin Murphy, vs. Syracuse (Dec. 7, 1968)	916	Calvin Murphy (1967-68)	2,548	Calvin Murphy (1967-70)
POINTS PER GAME			38.2	Calvin Murphy (1967-68)	33.1	Calvin Murphy (1967-70)
REBOUNDS	31	Alex "Boo" Ellis, vs. Kent State (Jan. 7, 1957); vs. Villanova (Dec. 28, 1956)	526	Alex "Boo" Ellis (1957-58)	1,533	Alex "Boo" Ellis (1955-58)
ASSISTS	22	Jackie Knowles, vs. Iona (Jan. 19, 1974)	195	Gary Bossert (1986-87)	630	Alvin Cruz (2001-05)

SEASON REVIEW

SEASON	W-L	CONF.	SCORING	COACH	RECORD	
905-1914	*67-54-1*					
914-15	8-9			A.V. Barrett	37-33	.529
915-16	4-6			Tom Tracey		
916-17	2-5			Tom Tracey	6-11	.353
917-18	8-3			John O'Shea		
918-19	1-0			John O'Shea	9-3	.750
919-20	6-2			John Blake		
920-21	15-4			John Blake		
921-22	27-4			John Blake	48-10	.828
922-23	13-4			Peter Dwyer		
923-24	9-10			Peter Dwyer		
1924-25	12-7			Peter Dwyer		
1925-26	12-6			Peter Dwyer	46-27	.630
1926-27	8-7			William McCarthy		
1927-28	11-5			William McCarthy		
1928-29	12-9			William McCarthy		
1929-30	9-11			William McCarthy		
1930-31	12-10			William McCarthy	52-42	.553
1931-32	19-5			John J. "Taps" Gallagher		
1932-33	13-6			John J. "Taps" Gallagher		
1933-34	11-9			John J. "Taps" Gallagher		
1934-35	13-6			John J. "Taps" Gallagher		

SEAS.	W-L	CONF.	POSTSEASON	SCORING		REBOUNDS		ASSISTS		COACH	RECORD	
935-36	17-6									John J. "Taps" Gallagher		
936-37	12-10									John J. "Taps" Gallagher		
937-38	8-13									John J. "Taps" Gallagher		
938-39	11-8									John J. "Taps" Gallagher		
939-40	12-7									John J. "Taps" Gallagher		
940-41	13-7									John J. "Taps" Gallagher		
941-42	16-6									John J. "Taps" Gallagher		
942-43	20-6									John J. "Taps" Gallagher		
943-44	no team											
944-45	7-6									Edward Flynn		
945-46	11-8									Edward Flynn	18-14	.563
946-47	13-8	2-2								John J. "Taps" Gallagher		
947-48	15-9	3-1								John J. "Taps" Gallagher		
948-49	24-7	3-1								John J. "Taps" Gallagher		
949-50	20-7	2-2	NIT FIRST ROUND							John J. "Taps" Gallagher		
950-51	18-10	2-2								John J. "Taps" Gallagher		
951-52	8-21	0-4								John J. "Taps" Gallagher		
952-53	22-6	4-0	NIT QUARTERFINALS							John J. "Taps" Gallagher		
953-54	24-6	3-1	NIT THIRD PLACE							John J. "Taps" Gallagher		
954-55	20-6	3-1	NIT QUARTERFINALS			Ed Fleming	15.5			John J. "Taps" Gallagher		
955-56	20-7	2-2	NIT FIRST ROUND	Alex "Boo" Ellis	22.9	Alex "Boo" Ellis	18.0			John J. "Taps" Gallagher		
956-57	12-13	0-4		Alex "Boo" Ellis	24.3	Alex "Boo" Ellis	20.1			John J. "Taps" Gallagher		
957-58	18-7	0-2	NIT FIRST ROUND			Alex "Boo" Ellis	19.5			John J. "Taps" Gallagher		
958-59	15-7									John J. "Taps" Gallagher		
959-60	13-12			Al Butler	28.8					John J. "Taps" Gallagher		
960-61	16-5		NIT QUARTERFINALS							John J. "Taps" Gallagher		
961-62	16-8									John J. "Taps" Gallagher		
962-63	14-4									John J. "Taps" Gallagher		
963-64	8-12									John J. "Taps" Gallagher		
964-65	4-17									John J. "Taps" Gallagher	465-261	.640
965-66	11-13					Manny Leaks	15.3			James Maloney		
966-67	12-13					Manny Leaks	14.0			James Maloney		
967-68	12-12			Calvin Murphy	38.2	Manny Leaks	14.2			James Maloney	35-38	.479
968-69	11-13			Calvin Murphy	32.4					Frank Layden		
969-70	22-7		NCAA REGIONAL SEMIFINALS	Calvin Murphy	29.4					Frank Layden		
970-71	14-12									Frank Layden		
971-72	21-9		NIT RUNNER-UP							Frank Layden		
972-73	9-16							Al Williams	6.6	Frank Layden		
973-74	12-14									Frank Layden		
974-75	13-14									Frank Layden		
975-76	17-12		NIT FIRST ROUND							Frank Layden	119-97	.551
976-77	13-13									Dan Raskin		
977-78	14-12									Dan Raskin		
978-79	6-20									Dan Raskin		
979-80	11-16	11-15								Dan Raskin	44-61	.419
980-81	11-15	11-15								Pete Lonergan		
981-82	19-10	7-2								Pete Lonergan		
982-83	11-18	5-4						Mike Curran	5.2	Pete Lonergan		
983-84	10-18	5-9								Pete Lonergan		
984-85	16-12	11-5								Pete Lonergan	67-73	.479
985-86	14-14	10-8						Gary Bossert	5.4	Andy Walker		
986-87	21-10	14-4	NIT SECOND ROUND					Gary Bossert	6.3	Andy Walker		
987-88	15-15	12-6								Andy Walker		
988-89	9-19	6-12								Andy Walker	59-58	.504
989-90	6-22	5-11								Jack Armstrong		
990-91	8-20	6-10								Jack Armstrong		
991-92	14-14	8-8								Jack Armstrong		
992-93	23-7	11-3	NIT FIRST ROUND							Jack Armstrong		
993-94	6-21	3-11								Jack Armstrong		
994-95	5-25	2-12								Jack Armstrong		
995-96	13-15	6-8								Jack Armstrong		
996-97	11-17	5-9								Jack Armstrong		
997-98	14-13	10-8								Jack Armstrong	100-154	.394
998-99	17-12	13-5		Alvin Young	25.1	Kevin Jobity	7.7	Jeremiah Johnson	5.0	Joe Mihalich		
999-2000	17-12	10-8		Demond Stewart	22.9	Nate Bernosky	6.8	Daryl Greene	5.0	Joe Mihalich		
000-01	15-13	12-6		Demond Stewart	19.6	James Reaves	7.7	Daryl Greene	5.0	Joe Mihalich		
001-02	18-14	12-6		Daryl Greene	14.8	James Reaves	8.8	Alvin Cruz	2.5	Joe Mihalich		
002-03	17-12	12-6		Juan Mendez	18.4	Juan Mendez	9.0	Alvin Cruz	5.8	Joe Mihalich		
003-04	22-10	13-5	NIT FIRST ROUND	Juan Mendez	20.5	James Reaves	9.6	Alvin Cruz	6.0	Joe Mihalich		
004-05	20-10	13-5	NCAA FIRST ROUND	Juan Mendez	23.5	Juan Mendez	10.6	Alvin Cruz	6.4	Joe Mihalich		
005-06	11-18	7-11		Charron Fisher	18.3	Clif Brown	8.2	Stanley Hodge	3.8	Joe Mihalich		
006-07	23-12	13-5	NCAA FIRST ROUND	Charron Fisher	20.6	Clif Brown	9.7	Stanley Hodge	4.0	Joe Mihalich		
007-08	19-10	12-6		Charron Fisher	27.6	Charron Fisher	9.5	Anthony Nelson	5.1	Joe Mihalich		
008-09	26-9	14-4	NIT FIRST ROUND	Tyrone Lewis	16.2	Bilal Benn	9.3	Anthony Nelson	5.5	Joe Mihalich	205-132	.608

ESPN 292 SAGARIN

NICHOLLS STATE

Endless arguments could rage over Nicholls State's best team and best player, which tells you something about the program's strength. Best team: 1978-79 or '94-95? Does Larry Wilson deserve to be the most decorated Colonel, or does Reggie Jackson or Gerard King? But there's no questioning Nicholls' pile of wins and fine finishes—two D1 Tourneys and a D2 elite eight.

BEST TEAM: 1994-95 With apologies to the 1978-79 team, the '94-95 Colonels (school-record 24–6) get the nod. Led by Southland Conference POY Reggie Jackson (21.6 ppg), Gerard King (21.6) and Ray Washington (7.3 apg), coach Rickey Broussard's squad won 12 straight en route to a league title and an NCAA berth.

BEST PLAYER: F Larry Wilson (1975-79) A three-time D2 All-America, Wilson starred on two of the school's four 20-win teams. He scored 30 in NSU's 1979 D2 elite eight loss to eventual champ North Alabama, and is the Colonels' all-time leading scorer (2,569) and fourth-leading rebounder (982). Wilson was the Atlanta Hawks' second-round pick in 1979.

BEST COACH: Rickey Broussard (1990-2002) He led Nicholls to two SLC championships and the school's two NCAA Tourneys. The SLC Coach of the Year three times, his teams finished third or better seven times, and twice had just one conference loss. His 150 victories is second only to Don Landry's 170.

GAME FOR THE AGES: The first is always the sweetest—and the Colonels' 1995 win over rival Louisiana-Monroe (then called Northeast Louisiana) clinched both their first SLC title and first NCAA Tourney bid. Nicholls took a 20-3 lead, shot 64% and stifled a late rally to win, 98-87. Northeast had won four of the previous five league tourneys.

FIERCEST RIVAL: Louisiana-Monroe's move to the Sun Belt didn't end the rivalry, but it made Nicholls State's schedule a little easier. ULM leads the overall series, 54–17, although the Colonels won in 2007 after dropping the previous 10. Nicholls' 87-83 win on Dec. 11 that year was the first at ULM since 1999.

SEASON REVIEW

SEAS.	W-L	CONF.	SCORING		COACH	RECORD	
1958-59	11-10				Morris Osburn		
1959-60	13-12		Frank Etheridge	17.3	Morris Osburn	24-22	.522
1960-61	10-13		Frank Etheridge	20.0	Jack Holley		
1961-62	14-12		Jack Barton	19.2	Jack Holley	24-25	.490
1962-63	12-12		Gene Simmons	20.0	Billy Key	12-12	.500
1963-64	12-14		Gene Simmons	26.5	Jim Mahoney		
1964-65	8-15		John Summers	15.7	Jim Mahoney		
1965-66	7-18		Henry Gaudet	14.2	Jim Mahoney	27-47	.365
1966-67	8-15		Herb Gros	18.2	Don Landry		
1967-68	10-16		Phil Driskill	16.0	Don Landry		
1968-69	10-14		Phil Driskill	18.0	Don Landry		
1969-70	11-15		Cleveland Hill	20.8	Don Landry		
1970-71	10-16		Danny Smith	20.5	Don Landry		
1971-72	15-9		Cleveland Hill	20.8	Don Landry		
1972-73	14-13		Richard Polk	14.2	Don Landry		
1973-74	10-12		Shelby Hypolite	16.2	Don Landry		
1974-75	11-14		Richard Polk	17.1	Don Landry		
1975-76	22-4		Larry Wilson	21.8	Don Landry		
1976-77	11-15		Larry Wilson	25.8	Don Landry		
1977-78	17-8		Larry Wilson	28.1	Don Landry		
1978-79	21-7		Larry Wilson	27.0	Don Landry	170-158	.518
1979-80	18-8		Johnny Hall	23.6	Jerry Sanders		
1980-81	6-22		Chris Jennings	17.4	Jerry Sanders	24-30	.444
1981-82	6-20		Kevin Celestine	17.7	Gordon Stauffer		
1982-83	16-12		Cedric Robinson	15.4	Gordon Stauffer		
1983-84	19-7		Cedric Robinson	14.7	Gordon Stauffer		
1984-85	17-10	6-4	Cedric Robinson	16.9	Gordon Stauffer		
1985-86	8-16	2-8	Cedric Robinson	19.6	Gordon Stauffer		
1986-87	9-18	1-9	Ron Smith	15.9	Gordon Stauffer		
1987-88	10-18		Ron Smith	15.6	Gordon Stauffer		
1988-89	12-16		Durwin Jackson	15.6	Gordon Stauffer		
1989-90	4-23		Robert Lee	12.8	Gordon Stauffer	101-140	.419
1990-91	3-25		Jason Tucker	15.0	Rickey Broussard		
1991-92	15-13	12-6	Reggie Jackson	16.4	Rickey Broussard		
1992-93	14-12	11-7	Reggie Jackson	20.5	Rickey Broussard		
1993-94	19-9	12-6	Gerard King	18.5	Rickey Broussard		
1994-95	24-6	17-1 ●	R. Jackson, G. King	21.6	Rickey Broussard		
1995-96	5-21	5-13	Kenderick Franklin	18.1	Rickey Broussard		
1996-97	10-16	7-9	Kenderick Franklin	22.1	Rickey Broussard		
1997-98	19-10	15-1 ●	Russell McCutcheon	16.8	Rickey Broussard		
1998-99	14-15	12-6	Jason McCutcheon	14.6	Rickey Broussard		
1999-2000	11-17	8-10	James Banks	12.4	Rickey Broussard		
2000-01	14-14	12-8	Art Haralson	18.1	Rickey Broussard		
2001-02	2-25	1-19	Ronnie Price	11.3	Rickey Broussard	150-183	.450
2002-03	3-25	1-19	Earnest Porter	11.3	Ricky Blanton		
2003-04	6-21	1-15	Willie Depron	15.4	Ricky Blanton	9-46	.164
2004-05	6-21	1-15	Willie Depron	14.7	J.P. Piper		
2005-06	9-18	5-11	Stefan Blaszczynski	13.3	J.P. Piper		
2006-07	8-22	7-9	Stefan Blaszczynski	19.2	J.P. Piper		
2007-08	10-21	5-11	Ryan Bathie	13.6	J.P. Piper		
2008-09	20-11	12-4	Ryan Bathie	15.8	J.P. Piper	53-93	.363

● NCAA Tournament appearance

PROFILE

Nicholls State University, Thibodaux, LA
Founded: 1948
Enrollment: 6,926 (6,305 undergraduate)
Colors: Red and gray
Nickname: Colonels
Current arena: Stopher Gym, opened in 1967 (3,800)
Previous: Shaver Gym, 1958-67 (750)
First game: 1958
All-time record: 594-756 (.440)
Total weeks in AP Top 20/25: 0

Current conference: Southland (1991-)
Conference titles:
Southland: 2 (1995, '98)
Conference tournament titles:
Southland: 2 (1995, '98)
NCAA Tournament appearances: 2
NIT appearances: 0

CONSENSUS ALL-AMERICAS

1978 **Larry Wilson** (D2), F

TOP 5

G **Gene Simmons** (1960-64)
G/F **Gerard King** (1990-91, '92-95)
F **Kenderick Franklin** (1994-98)
F **Larry Wilson** (1975-79)
C **Reggie Jackson** (1991-95)

RECORDS

RECORDS	GAME		SEASON		CAREER	
POINTS	48	Larry Wilson, vs. Jacksonville State (Feb. 12, 1979)	730	Larry Wilson (1978-79)	2,569	Larry Wilson (1975-79)
POINTS PER GAME			28.1	Larry Wilson (1977-78)	25.7	Larry Wilson (1975-79)
REBOUNDS	26	Rogers Washington, vs. Mississippi College (Feb. 8. 1979); Cleveland Hill, vs. McNeese State (Jan. 11, 1971); Cleveland Hill, vs. Spring Hill (Jan. 27, 1970)	366	Rogers Washington (1978-79)	1,271	Reggie Jackson (1991-95)
ASSISTS	20	Ray Washington, vs. McNeese State (Jan. 28, 1995)	275	Sonny Charpentier (1978-79)	737	Sonny Charpentier (1975-79)

ESPN 219 SAGARIN

NORFOLK STATE

Don't know much about Norfolk State? Try this: The Spartans had a remarkable 35 straight winning seasons (1962-63 to '96-97); *five* players scored more than 2,000 points; no coach before the D1 era (which started in 1997-98) had a career losing record; and star Bob Dandridge was part of a seven-year, 154–30 stretch of dominance and explosive scoring unlikely to be seen anywhere again.

BEST TEAM: 1967-68 With a a nod to the 27–6 1994-95 D2 final four team (led by All-America Corey Williams), the 24–2 1967-68 College Division squad wins out. Dandridge, playground legend Richard "Pee Wee" Kirkland and Johnny McKinney formed a talented trio the likes of which most D1 teams can only dream about.

BEST PLAYER: F BOB DANDRIDGE (1965-69) In 1968-69, the Richmond native led the College Divion's highest-scoring offense (106.1), averaging 32.3 points and 17.0 rebounds. His teams went 87–16 and he finished as the school's all-time leading scorer (1,740, since surpassed). The four-time NBA All-Star won two league titles and averaged 18.5 points over a 13-year career.

BEST COACH: CHARLES CHRISTIAN (1973-78, '81-90) He made winning look so easy that the school turned to him for a second stretch, which was just as successful as the first. The four-time CIAA coach of the year had 11 20-win seasons, won seven CIAA tourneys and made eight D2 postseasons, including three elite eights.

GAME FOR THE AGES: The 1967-68 team took the CIAA tournament with a heart-stopping 134-132 triple-OT win over North Carolina A&T to reach the NCAA College Division tournament. Kirkland, with three FGs in the third OT, was tourney MVP, Dandridge pumped in 38, McKinney 26 and Charles Bonaparte 24.

FIERCEST RIVAL: Norfolk and Hampton battled for years in the CIAA before HU moved up to D1 in 1995, two years ahead of the Spartans. NSU won 14 of 16 from 1983-84 through 1989-90, but Hampton has won 15 of 27 D1 matchups, including three MEAC tourney games that closed out NSU seasons.

SEASON REVIEW

SEAS.	W-L	CONF.	COACH	SEAS.	W-L	CONF.	COACH
1953-54	11-12		John Turpin	1961-62	9-11		John Turpin
1954-55	13-9		John Turpin	1962-63	18-7		Ernie Fears
1955-56	17-7		John Turpin	1963-64	18-5		Ernie Fears
1956-57	21-7		John Turpin	1964-65	22-3		Ernie Fears
1957-58	16-9		John Turpin	1965-66	26-6		Ernie Fears
1958-59	17-9		John Turpin	1966-67	16-4		Ernie Fears
1959-60	13-10		John Turpin	1967-68	24-2		Ernie Fears
1960-61	19-7		John Turpin	1968-69	21-4		Ernie Fears

SEAS.	W-L	CONF.	SCORING		COACH	RECORD
1969-70	19-7				Bob Smith	
1970-71	26-4				Bob Smith	
1971-72	20-4				Bob Smith	
1972-73	21-10				Bob Smith	86-25 .775
1973-74	21-9				Charles Christian	
1974-75	23-5				Charles Christian	
1975-76	23-7				Charles Christian	
1976-77	18-8				Charles Christian	
1977-78	19-9				Charles Christian	
1978-79	23-8				Lucias Mitchell	
1979-80	19-10				Lucias Mitchell	
1980-81	19-10				Lucias Mitchell	61-28 .685
1981-82	14-13				Charles Christian	
1982-83	20-9				Charles Christian	
1983-84	29-2				Charles Christian	
1984-85	23-7				Charles Christian	
1985-86	26-5				Charles Christian	
1986-87	28-3				Charles Christian	
1987-88	23-8				Charles Christian	
1988-89	24-6				Charles Christian	
1989-90	27-4				Charles Christian	318-95 .770
1990-91	15-13				Isaac Moorhead	15-13 .536
1991-92	22-10				Mike Bernard	
1992-93	19-10				Mike Bernard	
1993-94	27-6				Mike Bernard	
1994-95	27-6				Mike Bernard	
1995-96	23-4				Mike Bernard	
1996-97	17-10				Mike Bernard	
1997-98	6-21				Mike Bernard	141-67 .678
1998-99	15-12	11-7	Damian Woolfolk	23.5	Mel Coleman	15-12 .556
1999-2000	12-16	11-7	Damian Woolfolk	20.9	Wil Jones	
2000-01	12-17	11-7	Darrell Neal	10.6	Wil Jones	
2001-02	10-19	9-8	Terrence Winston	16.6	Wil Jones	34-52 .395
2002-03	14-15	10-8	Chakowby Hicks	11.3	Dwight Freeman	
2003-04	12-17	10-8	Chakowby Hicks	15.9	Dwight Freeman	
2004-05	13-14	11-7	Chakowby Hicks	15.4	Dwight Freeman	
2005-06	13-18	10-8	Tony Murphy	15.6	Dwight Freeman	
2006-07	11-19	10-8	Tony Murphy	16.5	Dwight Freeman	63-83 .432
2007-08	16-15	11-5	Tony Murphy	19.9	Anthony Evans	
2008-09	13-18	9-7	Michael DeLoache	21.5	Anthony Evans	29-33 .468

PROFILE

Norfolk State University, Norfolk, VA
Founded: 1935
Enrollment: 6,325 (5,653 undergraduate)
Colors: Green and gold
Nickname: Spartans
Current arena: Joseph Echols Hall , opened in 1982 (7,000)
Previous: Gill Gymnasium, 1960-82 (3,200); Tidewater Gym, 1955-60 (N/A); Booker T. Washington High School Gym, 1946-55 (500)
First game: Dec. 19, 1953
All-time record: 1,043-520 (.667)

Total weeks in AP Top 20/25: 0
Current conference: Mid-Eastern Athletic (1997-)
Conference titles: 0
Conference tournament titles: 0
NCAA Tournament appearances: 0
NIT appearances: 0

FIRST-ROUND PRO PICKS

1969 **Bob Dandridge,** Kentucky (ABA)

CONSENSUS ALL-AMERICAS

1979 **Ken Evans** (D2), G
1984 **David Pope** (D2), F
1987 **Ralph Tally** (D2), G
1995 **Corey Williams** (D2), F

TOP 5

G **Richard "Pee Wee" Kirkland** (1967-68)
G **Ralph Tally** (1983-87)
F **Bob Dandridge** (1965-69)
F **David Pope** (1980-84)
F **Corey Williams** (1993-95)

RECORDS

RECORDS	GAME		SEASON		CAREER	
POINTS	54	Johnny McKinney, vs. Old Dominion (Feb. 23, 1970)	842	Ralph Tally (1986-87)	2,575	Ralph Tally (1983-87)
POINTS PER GAME			32.3	Bob Dandridge (1968-69)	25.9	Richard Pitts (1962-66)
REBOUNDS	27	Louis Thomas, vs. Morris Brown (Feb. 13, 1980)	485	Rudy Peele (1970-71)	1,335	Rudy Peele (1968-72)
ASSISTS	21	Billy Walker, vs. Hampton (Feb. 3, 1981)	273	Billy Walker (1980-81)	634	Billy Walker (1980-83, '84-85)

ESPN 4 SAGARIN

NORTH CAROLINA

Whenever the Tar Heels win a big one, students swarm Franklin Street, famously setting bonfires and leaping over them. Sure enough, there's been plenty of heat and high-jumping over the years.

BEST TEAM: 1981-82 The undefeated 1956-57 team is hard to beat, but the 1982 NCAA title winners (32–2) are tops. One of their losses came to Ralph Sampson's Virginia, the other with Sam Perkins out sick. In the Final Four the Tar Heels beat Houston (with Clyde Drexler *and* Hakeem Olajuwon) and then Georgetown (Patrick Ewing *and* Eric "Sleepy" Floyd). UNC was loaded with stars on the floor—James Worthy, Michael Jordan, Perkins—and on the bench: Dean Smith and assistants Bill Guthridge, Roy Williams and Eddie Fogler would all become national Coaches of the Year.

BEST PLAYER: G PHIL FORD (1974-78) Many folks think Michael Jordan, but real-to-the-bone fans recognize the Afro-sporting point guard as the best ever to play in Chapel Hill. A three-time All-America and the 1978 Wooden Award Winner, Ford held the school's career scoring record for 30 years.

BEST COACH: DEAN SMITH (1961-97) He would modestly deflect credit to his players, but it was Smith who invented winning strategies such as the run-and-jump defense, the foul-line huddle, the tired signal, the thank-you finger-point from scorer to passer and an array of brilliant end-game tactics. He broke Adolph Rupp's 25-year-old record for career victories, won two NCAA titles—and reluctantly allowed an arena to be named for him.

GAME FOR THE AGES: The 1957 Heels needed six OTs in two days to finish as undefeated national champs. After the three-OT win over Michigan State in the semis, Lennie Rosenbluth & Co. had to shake Wilt Chamberlain and Kansas in the March 23 Final. A bench-clearing dustup highlighted the first OT, and with :06 left in the third OT, Joe Quigg sank two free throws for the 54-53 win.

HEARTBREAKER: Smith was still labeled a great coach unable to win the big one when Ford and Walter Davis, both banged up, led the Heels to the 1977 NCAA Final against Marquette. Smith took more heat for ordering a four corners stall after UNC erased a second-half deficit. The rested Warriors came back to beat the Heels, 67-59.

FIERCEST RIVAL: UNC and Duke recruit the same players, and their students, alumni and fans rub up against each other all over the state, the nation, the world. The degree of dislike between these two programs cannot be overstated—even by Dick Vitale. The Tar Heels lead overall, 130–97.

FANFARE AND HOOPLA: As Florida State's Sam Cassell once noted, UNC's "wine and cheese" crowd doesn't always strike fear into opponents. But the Dean Dome's rafters, festooned with banners and honored and retired jerseys, gets plenty of them quaking in their sneakers.

FAN FAVORITE: F GEORGE LYNCH (1989-93) A relentless rebounder and defender, Lynch sacrificed offense to help his team win the 1993 NCAA title. He once guarded all five opponents on a single possession and said he'd jump off a building for Smith. What's not to love?

CONSENSUS ALL-AMERICAS

1923, '24	**Cartwright Carmichael,** F/G
1924-26	**Jack Cobb,** F
1940, '41	**George Glamack,** F/C
1957	**Lennie Rosenbluth,** F
1968	**Larry Miller,** G/F
1972	**Bob McAdoo,** C
1977, '78	**Phil Ford,** G
1982	**James Worthy,** F
1983, '84	**Michael Jordan,** G
1983, '84	**Sam Perkins,** F/C
1987	**Kenny Smith,** G
1988	**J.R. Reid,** F/C
1995	**Jerry Stackhouse,** G/F
1998	**Antawn Jamison,** F
2001	**Joseph Forte,** G
2007-09	**Tyler Hansbrough,** F

FIRST-ROUND PRO PICKS

1957	**Lennie Rosenbluth,** Philadelphia (6)
1958	**Pete Brennan,** New York (4)
1960	**Lee Shaffer,** Syracuse (5)
1965	**Billy Cunningham,** Philadelphia (7)
1969	**Bill Bunting,** Miami (ABA)
1972	**Bob McAdoo,** Buffalo (2)
1974	**Bobby Jones,** Houston (5)
1976	**Mitch Kupchak,** Washington (13)
1977	**Walter Davis,** Phoenix (5)
1977	**Tommy LaGarde,** Denver (9)
1978	**Phil Ford,** Kansas City (2)
1979	**Dudley Bradley,** Indiana (13)
1980	**Mike O'Koren,** New Jersey (6)
1981	**Al Wood,** Atlanta (4)
1982	**James Worthy,** LA Lakers (1)
1984	**Michael Jordan,** Chicago (3)
1984	**Sam Perkins,** Dallas (4)
1986	**Brad Daugherty,** Cleveland (1)
1987	**Kenny Smith,** Sacramento (6)
1987	**Joe Wolf,** LA Clippers (13)
1989	**J.R. Reid,** Charlotte (5)
1991	**Rick Fox,** Boston (24)
1991	**Pete Chilcutt,** Sacramento (27)
1992	**Hubert Davis,** New York (20)
1993	**George Lynch,** LA Lakers (12)
1994	**Eric Montross,** Boston (9)
1995	**Jerry Stackhouse,** Philadelphia (3)
1995	**Rasheed Wallace,** Washington (4)
1998	**Antawn Jamison,** Toronto (4)
1998	**Vince Carter,** Golden State (5)
2001	**Brendan Haywood,** Cleveland (20)
2001	**Joseph Forte,** Boston (21)
2005	**Marvin Williams,** Atlanta (2)
2005	**Raymond Felton,** Charlotte (5)
2005	**Sean May,** Charlotte (13)
2005	**Rashad McCants,** Minnesota (14)
2007	**Brandan Wright,** Charlotte (8)
2009	**Tyler Hansbrough,** Indiana (13)
2009	**Ty Lawson,** Minnesota (18)
2009	**Wayne Ellington,** Minnesota (28)

PROFILE

University of North Carolina, Chapel Hill, NC
Founded: 1789
Enrollment: 28,136 (17,628 undergraduate)
Colors: Carolina blue and white
Nickname: Tar Heels
Current arena: Dean E. Smith Center, opened in 1986 (21,750)
Previous: Carmichael Auditorium, 1965-86 (10,180); Woollen Gymnasium, 1937-65 (5,000)
First game: Jan. 27, 1911
All-time record: 1,984-703 (.738)
Total weeks in AP Top 20/25: 761

Current conference: Atlantic Coast (1953-)
Conference titles:
Southern: 7 (1923, '25, '35, '38, '41, '44, '46)
ACC: 27 (1956 [tie], '57, '59 [tie], '60 [tie], '61, '67, '68, '69, '71, '72, '76, '77, '78, '79 [tie], '82 [tie], '83 [tie], '84, '85 [tie], '87, '88, '93, '95 [tie], 2001 [tie], '05, '07 [tie], '08, '09)
Conference tournament titles:
Southern: 8 (1922, '24, '25, '26, '35, '36, '40, '45)
ACC: 17 (1957, '67, '68, '69, '72, '75, '77, '79, '81, '82, '89, '91, '94, '97, '98, 2007, '08)
NCAA Tournament appearances: 41
Sweet 16s (since 1975): 23
Final Fours: 18
Titles: 5 (1957, '82, '93, 2005, '09)
NIT appearances: 5
Semifinals: 2
Title: 1 (1971)

TOP 5

G	**Phil Ford** (1974-78)
G	**Michael Jordan** (1981-84)
F	**Tyler Hansbrough** (2005-09)
F	**Antawn Jamison** (1995-98)
F	**Lennie Rosenbluth** (1954-57)

RECORDS

RECORDS	GAME		SEASON		CAREER	
POINTS	49	Bob Lewis, vs. Florida State (Dec. 16, 1965)	895	Lennie Rosenbluth (1956-57)	2,872	Tyler Hansbrough (2005-09)
POINTS PER GAME			28.0	Lennie Rosenbluth (1956-57)	26.9	Lennie Rosenbluth (1954-57)
REBOUNDS	30	Rusty Clark, vs. Maryland (Feb. 21, 1968)	399	Tyler Hansbrough (2007-08)	1,219	Tyler Hansbrough (2005-09)
ASSISTS	18	Raymond Felton, vs. George Mason (Dec. 7, 2003)	284	Ed Cota (1999-2000)	1,030	Ed Cota (1996-2000)

SEASON REVIEW

EASON	W-L	CONF.	SCORING	COACH	RECORD	
911-14	*25-24*		*Includes three seasons, all under coach Nat Cartmell*			
914-15	6-10			Charles Doak		
915-16	12-6			Charles Doak	18-16	.529
916-17	5-4			Howell Peacock		
917-18	9-3			Howell Peacock		
918-19	9-7			Howell Peacock	23-14	.622
919-20	7-9			Fred Boye		
920-21	12-8			Fred Boye	19-17	.528
921-22	15-6	3-3		no coach		
922-23	15-1	5-0		no coach		
923-24	26-0	7-0		Norman Shepard	26-0	1.000
SEASON	**W-L**	**CONF.**	**SCORING**	**COACH**	**RECORD**	
1924-25	20-5	8-0		Monk McDonald	20-5	.800
1925-26	20-5	7-0		Harlan Sanborn	20-5	.800
1926-27	17-7	7-3		James Ashmore		
1927-28	17-2	8-1		James Ashmore		
1928-29	17-8	12-2		James Ashmore		
1929-30	14-11	4-7		James Ashmore		
1930-31	15-9	6-6		James Ashmore	80-37	.684
1931-32	16-5	6-3		George Shepard		
1932-33	12-5	5-3		George Shepard		
1933-34	18-4	12-2		George Shepard		
1934-35	23-2	12-1		George Shepard	69-16	.812

SEAS.	W-L	CONF.	POSTSEASON	SCORING		REBOUNDS		ASSISTS		COACH	RECORD	
935-36	21-4	13-3								Walter Skidmore		
936-37	18-5	14-3								Walter Skidmore		
937-38	16-5	13-3								Walter Skidmore		
938-39	10-11	8-7								Walter Skidmore	65-25	.722
939-40	23-3	11-2								Bill Lange		
940-41	19-9	14-1	NCAA REGIONAL SEMIFINALS							Bill Lange		
941-42	14-9	9-5								Bill Lange		
942-43	12-10	8-9								Bill Lange		
943-44	17-10	9-1								Bill Lange	85-41	.675
944-45	22-6	11-3								Ben Carnevale		
945-46	30-5	13-1	NCAA RUNNER-UP							Ben Carnevale	52-11	.825
946-47	19-8	10-2								Tom Scott		
947-48	20-7	11-4								Tom Scott		
948-49	20-8	13-5								Tom Scott		
949-50	17-12	13-6								Tom Scott		
950-51	12-15	9-8								Tom Scott		
951-52	12-15	8-11		Al Lifson	15.8	Howard Deasy	10.7			Tom Scott	100-65	.606
952-53	17-10	15-6		Al Lifson	14.7	Bud Maddie	11.6			Frank McGuire		
953-54	11-10	5-6		Jerry Vayda	17.0	Paul Likins	10.9			Frank McGuire		
954-55	10-11	8-6		Lennie Rosenbluth	25.5	Lennie Rosenbluth	11.7			Frank McGuire		
955-56	18-5	11-3		Lennie Rosenbluth	26.7	Lennie Rosenbluth	11.5			Frank McGuire		
956-57	**32-0**	**14-0**	**NATIONAL CHAMPION**	**Lennie Rosenbluth**	**28.0**	**Pete Brennan**	**10.4**			**Frank McGuire**		
957-58	19-7	10-4		Pete Brennan	21.3	Pete Brennan	11.7			Frank McGuire		
958-59	20-5	12-2	NCAA FIRST ROUND	York Larese	15.1	Dick Kepley	7.3			Frank McGuire		
959-60	18-6	12-2		Lee Shaffer	18.2	Doug Moe	11.3			Frank McGuire		
960-61	19-4	12-2		York Larese	23.1	Doug Moe	14.0			Frank McGuire	164-58	.739
961-62	8-9	7-7		Larry Brown	16.5	Jim Hudock	10.1			Dean Smith		
962-63	15-6	10-4		Billy Cunningham	22.7	Billy Cunningham	16.1			Dean Smith		
963-64	12-12	6-8		Billy Cunningham	26.0	Billy Cunningham	15.8			Dean Smith		
964-65	15-9	10-4		Billy Cunningham	25.4	Billy Cunningham	14.3			Dean Smith		
965-66	16-11	8-6		Bob Lewis	27.4	Larry Miller	10.3			Dean Smith		
966-67	26-6	12-2	NCAA FOURTH PLACE	Larry Miller	21.9	Rusty Clark	10.3			Dean Smith		
967-68	28-4	12-2	NCAA RUNNER-UP	Larry Miller	22.4	Rusty Clark	11.0			Dean Smith		
968-69	27-5	12-2	NCAA FOURTH PLACE	Charles Scott	22.3	Rusty Clark	9.2	Charlie Scott	3.4	Dean Smith		
969-70	18-9	9-5	NIT FIRST ROUND	Charles Scott	27.1	Lee Dedmon	9.4	Eddie Fogler	3.4	Dean Smith		
970-71	26-6	11-3	NIT CHAMPION	Dennis Wuycik	18.4	Lee Dedmon	8.5	Steve Previs	2.9	Dean Smith		
971-72	26-5	9-3	NCAA THIRD PLACE	Bob McAdoo	19.5	Bob McAdoo	10.1	Steve Previs	4.9	Dean Smith		
972-73	25-8	8-4	NIT THIRD PLACE	George Karl	17.0	Bobby Jones	10.5	George Karl	5.8	Dean Smith		
973-74	22-6	9-3	NIT FIRST ROUND	Bobby Jones	16.1	Bobby Jones	9.8	Darrell Elston	5.6	Dean Smith		
974-75	23-8	8-4	NCAA REGIONAL SEMIFINALS	Mitch Kupchak	18.5	Mitch Kupchak	10.8	Phil Ford	5.2	Dean Smith		
975-76	25-4	11-1	NCAA FIRST ROUND	Phil Ford	18.6	Mitch Kupchak	11.3	Phil Ford	7.0	Dean Smith		
976-77	28-5	9-3	NCAA RUNNER-UP	Phil Ford	18.7	Tommy LaGarde	7.4	Phil Ford	6.6	Dean Smith		
977-78	23-8	9-3	NCAA FIRST ROUND	Phil Ford	20.8	Mike O'Koren	6.7	Phil Ford	5.7	Dean Smith		
978-79	23-6	9-3	NCAA SECOND ROUND	Al Wood	17.8	Mike O'Koren	7.2	Mike O'Koren	3.5	Dean Smith		
979-80	21-8	9-5	NCAA SECOND ROUND	Al Wood	19.0	Mike O'Koren	7.4	Mike O'Koren	3.6	Dean Smith		
1980-81	29-8	10-4	NCAA RUNNER-UP	Al Wood	18.1	James Worthy	8.4	Jimmy Black	5.1	Dean Smith		
1981-82	**32-2**	**12-2**	**NATIONAL CHAMPION**	**James Worthy**	**15.6**	**Sam Perkins**	**7.8**	**Jimmy Black**	**6.3**	**Dean Smith**		
1982-83	28-8	12-2	NCAA REGIONAL FINALS	Michael Jordan	20.0	Sam Perkins	9.4	Matt Doherty	4.3	Dean Smith		
1983-84	28-3	14-0	NCAA REGIONAL SEMIFINALS	Michael Jordan	19.6	Sam Perkins	9.6	Matt Doherty	4.0	Dean Smith		
1984-85	27-9	9-5	NCAA REGIONAL FINALS	Brad Daugherty	17.3	Brad Daugherty	9.7	Kenny Smith	6.5	Dean Smith		
1985-86	28-6	10-4	NCAA REGIONAL SEMIFINALS	Brad Daugherty	20.2	Brad Daugherty	9.0	Kenny Smith	6.2	Dean Smith		
1986-87	32-4	14-0	NCAA REGIONAL FINALS	Kenny Smith	16.9	J.R. Reid	7.4	Kenny Smith	6.2	Dean Smith		
1987-88	27-7	11-3	NCAA REGIONAL FINALS	J.R. Reid	18.0	J.R. Reid	8.9	Jeff Lebo	4.8	Dean Smith		
1988-89	29-8	9-5	NCAA REGIONAL SEMIFINALS	J.R. Reid	15.9	Scott Williams	7.3	Steve Bucknall	5.3	Dean Smith		
1989-90	21-13	8-6	NCAA REGIONAL SEMIFINALS	Rick Fox	16.2	Scott Williams	7.3	King Rice	6.4	Dean Smith		
1990-91	29-6	10-4	NCAA NATIONAL SEMIFINALS	Rick Fox	16.9	George Lynch	7.4	King Rice	5.9	Dean Smith		
1991-92	23-10	9-7	NCAA REGIONAL SEMIFINALS	Hubert Davis	21.4	George Lynch	8.8	Derrick Phelps	6.3	Dean Smith		
1992-93	**34-4**	**14-2**	**NATIONAL CHAMPION**	**Eric Montross**	**15.8**	**George Lynch**	**9.6**	**Derrick Phelps**	**5.4**	**Dean Smith**		
1993-94	28-7	11-5	NCAA SECOND ROUND	Donald Williams	14.3	Eric Montross	8.1	Derrick Phelps	5.3	Dean Smith		
1994-95	28-6	12-4	NCAA NATIONAL SEMIFINALS	Jerry Stackhouse	19.2	Jerry Stackhouse	8.2	Jeff McInnis	5.3	Dean Smith		
1995-96	21-11	10-6	NCAA SECOND ROUND	Jeff McInnis	16.5	Antawn Jamison	9.7	Jeff McInnis	5.5	Dean Smith		
1996-97	28-7	11-5	NCAA NATIONAL SEMIFINALS	Antawn Jamison	19.1	Antawn Jamison	9.4	Ed Cota	6.9	Dean Smith	879-254	.776
1997-98	34-4	13-3	NCAA NATIONAL SEMIFINALS	Antawn Jamison	22.2	Antawn Jamison	10.5	Ed Cota	7.4	Bill Guthridge		
1998-99	24-10	10-6	NCAA FIRST ROUND	Ademola Okulaja	13.9	Ademola Okulaja	8.4	Ed Cota	7.4	Bill Guthridge		
1999-2000	22-14	9-7	NCAA NATIONAL SEMIFINALS	Joseph Forte	16.7	Brendan Haywood	7.5	Ed Cota	8.1	Bill Guthridge	80-28	.741
2000-01	26-7	13-3	NCAA SECOND ROUND	Joseph Forte	20.9	J. Capel, B. Haywood	7.3	Ronald Curry	4.3	Matt Doherty		
2001-02	8-20	4-12		Jason Capel	15.6	Jason Capel	8.6	Adam Boone	3.2	Matt Doherty		
2002-03	19-16	6-10	NIT QUARTERFINALS	Rashad McCants	17.0	Jawad Williams	5.6	Raymond Felton	6.7	Matt Doherty	53-43	.552
2003-04	19-11	8-8	NCAA SECOND ROUND	Rashad McCants	20.0	Sean May	9.8	Raymond Felton	7.1	Roy Williams		
2004-05	**33-4**	**14-2**	**NATIONAL CHAMPION**	**Sean May**	**17.5**	**Sean May**	**10.7**	**Raymond Felton**	**6.9**	**Roy Williams**		
2005-06	23-8	12-4	NCAA SECOND ROUND	Tyler Hansbrough	18.9	Tyler Hansbrough	7.8	Bobby Frasor	4.4	Roy Williams		
2006-07	31-7	11-5	NCAA REGIONAL FINALS	Tyler Hansbrough	18.4	Tyler Hansbrough	7.9	Ty Lawson	5.6	Roy Williams		
2007-08	36-3	14-2	NCAA NATIONAL SEMIFINALS	Tyler Hansbrough	23.0	Tyler Hansbrough	10.4	Ty Lawson	5.3	Roy Williams		
2008-09	**34-4**	**13-3**	**NATIONAL CHAMPION**	**Tyler Hansbrough**	**20.7**	**Tyler Hansbrough**	**8.1**	**Ty Lawson**	**6.6**	**Roy Williams**	**176-37**	**.826**

THE SCHOOLS

ESPN 231 SAGARIN

NORTH CAROLINA A&T

The Aggies from this historically black school have won 15 of 37 Mid-Eastern Athletic Conference tournament championships and played in 15 postseason events. The reason? Legendary coaches Cal Irvin and Don Corbett and stars such as the great Al Attles, and all-time leading scorer and rebounder Joe Binion.

BEST TEAM: 1987-88 Corbett's squad went a school-best 26–3 with 18 double-digit victories and claimed a seventh straight MEAC tourney title. Conference POY Claude Williams (1,648 points, 973 rebounds) and all-time assists and steals leader, Thomas Griffis, joined three other players who would top 900 career points: Carlton Becton, Corvin Davis and Glenn Taggart.

BEST PLAYER: G Al Attles (1956-60) The famously tough guard led the Aggies to two College Division national tourneys. Attles went on to play 11 seasons with the Philadelphia/San Francisco Warriors and coached them for another 14.

BEST COACH: Cal Irvin (1954-72) Rarely does a school have two career 400-win coaches in its history, but the Aggies' Irvin and Corbett left such a legacy that their court is named after both. Irvin (brother of Baseball Hall of Famer Monte Irvin) won six league titles, reached five national tourneys, two College Division final fours, and his 1958-59 team went 26–4.

GAME FOR THE AGES: Attles and Joe Cotton led the way to the 1959 NCAA College Division tourney. After running through Tuskegee and Florida A&M, the Aggies took down American, 87-70, to become the first historically black college to reach a final four. The run ended with a 110-92 loss to eventual champ Evansville.

FIERCEST RIVAL: Winston-Salem State's entry into the MEAC in 2007 renewed a classic rivalry between the North Carolina neighbors. For their game on Jan. 26, 2008, the gates to the Corbett Center in Greensboro had to be closed more than 20 minutes before tip-off. The Aggies won in a rout, 75-56, and then lost a month later, 71-63, after two last-minute technicals were called against them. WSSU leads overall, 36–31.

SEASON REVIEW

SEAS.	W-L	CONF.	COACH	SEAS.	W-L	CONF.	COACH
1952-55	*29-44*	*Records before 1952-53 lost*		1961-62	20-7		Cal Irvin
1955-56	15-8		Cal Irvin	1962-63	20-7		Cal Irvin
1956-57	17-8		Cal Irvin	1963-64	23-7		Cal Irvin
1957-58	21-4		Cal Irvin	1964-65	20-6		Cal Irvin
1958-59	26-4		Cal Irvin	1965-66	17-7		Cal Irvin
1959-60	19-6		Cal Irvin	1966-67	18-5		Cal Irvin
1960-61	18-7		Cal Irvin	1967-68	18-5		James Staggs

SEAS.	W-L	CONF.		SCORING		COACH	RECORD	
1968-69	17-4			Darryl Cherry	19.0	Cal Irvin		
1969-70	18-7			Melvin Evans	12.1	Cal Irvin		
1970-71	24-8			Elmer Austin	19.1	Cal Irvin		
1971-72	20-6	9-3		Elmer Austin	21.3	Cal Irvin	344-117	.746
1972-73	16-11	7-5		James Outlaw	16.6	Warren Reynolds		
1973-74	16-10	7-5		James Outlaw	24.9	Warren Reynolds		
1974-75	18-7	10-2		Allen Spruill	16.6	Warren Reynolds		
1975-76	20-6	11-1		James Sparrow	20.9	Warren Reynolds		
1976-77	3-24	3-9		L.J. Pipken	15.7	Warren Reynolds	73-58	.557
1977-78	20-8	11-1		James Sparrow	19.1	Gene Littles		
1978-79	20-7	11-1		James Sparrow	18.4	Gene Littles	40-15	.727
1979-80	8-19			Joe Brawner	20.6	Don Corbett		
1980-81	21-8	7-3	■	Joe Binion	19.1	Don Corbett		
1981-82	19-9	10-2	●	Joe Binion	14.4	Don Corbett		
1982-83	23-8	9-3	●	Joe Binion	19.9	Don Corbett		
1983-84	22-7	9-1	●	Joe Binion	20.4	Don Corbett		
1984-85	19-10	10-2	●	Jimmy Brown	18.2	Don Corbett		
1985-86	22-8	12-2	●	George Cale	14.8	Don Corbett		
1986-87	24-6	12-2	●	George Cale	15.9	Don Corbett		
1987-88	26-3	16-0	●	Claude Williams	16.2	Don Corbett		
1988-89	9-18	6-10		Carlton Becton	18.7	Don Corbett		
1989-90	12-17	6-10		Glenn Taggart	14.6	Don Corbett		
1990-91	17-10	10-6		Glenn Taggart	20.7	Don Corbett		
1991-92	18-9	12-4		Dana Elliott	16.8	Don Corbett		
1992-93	14-13	9-7		Jamaine Williams	21.4	Don Corbett	254-145	.637
1993-94	16-14	10-6	●	Phillip Allen	16.3	Jeff Capel	16-14	.533
1994-95	15-15	10-6	●	John Floyd	17.3	Roy Thomas		
1995-96	10-17	7-9		Kimani Stewart	11.2	Roy Thomas		
1996-97	15-13	11-7		Kimani Stewart	13.2	Roy Thomas		
1997-98	8-19	7-11		Jonathan Richmond	11.9	Roy Thomas		
1998-99	13-15	9-9		Jonathan Richmond	15.4	Roy Thomas	61-79	.436
1999-2000	14-15	11-8		Bruce Jenkins	14.5	Curtis Hunter		
2000-01	13-17	8-10		James Miller	16.0	Curtis Hunter		
2001-02	11-17	10-7		Bruce Jenkins	18.5	Curtis Hunter		
2002-03	1-26	1-17		Tyrone Green	13.2	Curtis Hunter	39-75	.342
2003-04	3-25	3-15		Sean Booker	14.6	Jerry Eaves		
2004-05	6-24	5-13		Sean Booker	16.1	Jerry Eaves		
2005-06	6-23	6-12		Jason Wills	14.7	Jerry Eaves		
2006-07	15-17	10-8		Steven Rush	17.2	Jerry Eaves		
2007-08	15-16	9-7		Steven Rush	14.3	Jerry Eaves		
2008-09	16-16	9-7		Ed Jones	12.8	Jerry Eaves	61-121	.335

● NCAA Tournament appearance ■ NIT appearance

PROFILE

North Carolina A&T State University, Greensboro, NC
Founded: 1891 as the Agricultural and Mechanical College for the Colored Race; renamed the Agricultural and Technical College of North Carolina in 1915
Enrollment: 10,388 (8,829 undergraduate)
Colors: Blue and gold
Nickname: Aggies
Current arena: Ellis Corbett Sports Center, opened in 1978 (5,700)
Previous: Moore Gymnasium, 1955-78 (800)
First game: Feb. 8, 1926

All-time record: 904-657 (.579)
Total weeks in AP Top 20/25: 0
Current conference: Mid-Eastern Athletic (1971-)
Conference titles:
MEAC: 11 (1972, '75, '76, '78, '79, '81, '82, '84, '85, '86, '88)
Conference tournament titles:
MEAC: 15 (1972, '73, '75, '76, '78, '79, '82, '83, '84, '85, '86, '87, '88, '94, '95)
NCAA Tournament appearances: 9
NIT appearances: 1

TOP 5

G **Al Attles** (1956-60)
G **James Sparrow** (1975-79)
F **Elmer Alston** (1969-72)
F **Joe Binion** (1980-84)
F **Claude Williams** (1983-88)

RECORDS

RECORDS	GAME		SEASON		CAREER	
POINTS	41	James Jackson, vs. St. Augustine (1963-64)	647	James Outlaw (1973-74)	2,143	Joe Binion (1980-84)
POINTS PER GAME			24.9	James Outlaw (1973-74)	18.8	James Sparrow (1975-79)
REBOUNDS	21	Bruce Jenkins, vs. James Madison (Nov. 18, 1998)	408	Elmer Alston (1970-71)	1,257	Joe Binion (1980-84)
ASSISTS	16	Glenn Taggart, vs. Morgan State (1988-89)	201	Glenn Taggart (1989-90)	582	Thomas Griffis (1984-88)

ESPN 287 SAGARIN

NORTH CAROLINA-ASHEVILLE

A member of Division I since only the mid-1980s, the Bulldogs took a big step toward making a name for themselves among the state's great college basketball programs in 2002-03, when they improbably won the Big South tournament and earned an NCAA berth—the 17th team ever to do so with a losing record.

BEST TEAM: 2002-03 It may be odd to declare a sub-.500 (15–17) squad the program's best, but it's the only time Asheville has been to the Big Dance. And the Bulldogs *did* win a Tournament game, even if it was the play-in game, over Texas Southern to earn the No. 16 seed in the South region.

BEST PLAYER: G JIM MCELHANEY (1966-69, '70-71) One of the program's pioneers, his freshman season was just the school's third. The 5'9" McElhaney could really light it up (1,904 career points), but he bugged opponents even more with his harassing defense. After he died in 2002, he was posthumously inducted into UNCA's Hall of Fame.

BEST COACH: JERRY GREEN (1979-88) He led UNCA to six consecutive winning seasons, including three 20-win campaigns in four years. Green used those good years coaching his alma mater (he played for the Bulldogs in the mid-1960s) to vault himself to bigger jobs at Oregon and later, Tennessee.

GAME FOR THE AGES: Getting to the NCAA Tournament should have been enough for a team that had never been there before. But the Bulldogs became the first Big South team to ever win an NCAA Tourney game by taking out Texas Southern, 92-84 in overtime, in the 2003 play-in game. Andre Smith scored a season-high 28 points, 10 of which came in OT. UNCA earned the opportunity to lose to No. 1-seed Texas, 82-61.

FIERCEST RIVAL: Asheville and High Point have been playing since before the completion of the I-40 corridor that connects the two cities. The rivalry jumped up a notch in 1999 when the schools became Big South rivals. High Point has knocked Asheville out of the conference tourney three times since 2002.

SEASON REVIEW

SEAS.	W-L	CONF.	SCORING		COACH	RECORD
1964-65	14-13				Bob Hartman	
1965-66	15-8		Jim Baker	19.7	Bob Hartman	
1966-67	17-8		Guy Batsel	21.3	Bob Hartman	
1967-68	16-9		Guy Batsel	22.6	Bob Hartman	
1968-69	19-9		Jim McElhaney	21.9	Bob Hartman	
1969-70	14-13		Mickey Gibson	23.3	Bob Hartman	
1970-71	20-10		Rod Healy	17.5	Bob Hartman	
1971-72	18-12		Dean Nanney	13.8	Bob Hartman	
1972-73	15-17		Doug Murray	14.0	Bob Hartman	
1973-74	17-18		Frank Rhyne	15.7	Bob Hartman	
1974-75	12-17		Prince Frazier	12.5	Bob Hartman	
1975-76	8-22		Bamford Jones	17.2	Bob Hartman	
1976-77	14-18		Bamford Jones	19.2	Bob Hartman	
1977-78	17-15		Bamford Jones	17.9	Bob Hartman	
1978-79	7-20		George Gilbert	13.0	Bob Hartman	223-209 .516
1979-80	11-16		George Gilbert	13.4	Jerry Green	
1980-81	14-15		Paul Allen	15.1	Jerry Green	
1981-82	19-10		Paul Allen	19.2	Jerry Green	
1982-83	22-9		Paul Allen	14.9	Jerry Green	
1983-84	21-10		Paul Allen	14.4	Jerry Green	
1984-85	15-13		Tom Haus	13.5	Jerry Green	
1985-86	20-9	4-2	Van Wilkins	16.8	Jerry Green	
1986-87	15-11	5-3	Van Wilkins	19.0	Jerry Green	
1987-88	13-15	5-7	Ricky Chatman	16.4	Jerry Green	150-108 .581
1988-89	16-14	6-6	Milton Moore	17.6	Don Doucette	
1989-90	18-12	7-5	Milton Moore	17.5	Don Doucette	
1990-91	8-20	4-10	Darryl Sanders	14.5	Don Doucette	
1991-92	9-19	6-8	Robert Watson	13.2	Don Doucette	
1992-93	4-23	2-14	Josh Kohn	11.5	Don Doucette	55-88 .385
1993-94	3-24	3-15	Josh Kohn	16.1	Randy Wiel	
1994-95	11-16	7-9	William Coley	13.8	Randy Wiel	
1995-96	18-10	9-5	Josh Kohn	14.1	Randy Wiel	32-50 .390
1996-97	18-10	11-3	Josh Pittman	18.1	Eddie Biedenbach	
1997-98	19-9	11-1	Josh Pittman	18.4	Eddie Biedenbach	
1998-99	11-18	5-5	Kevin Martin	21.9	Eddie Biedenbach	
1999-2000	11-19	7-7	Andre Smith	11.3	Eddie Biedenbach	
2000-01	15-13	9-5	Brett Carey	13.3	Eddie Biedenbach	
2001-02	13-15	10-4	Andre Smith	16.2	Eddie Biedenbach	
2002-03	15-17	7-7 ●	Andre Smith	15.9	Eddie Biedenbach	
2003-04	9-20	6-10	Bryan McCullough	10.0	Eddie Biedenbach	
2004-05	11-17	8-8	Bryan McCullough	13.5	Eddie Biedenbach	
2005-06	9-19	6-10	Joseph Barber	13.0	Eddie Biedenbach	
2006-07	12-19	6-8	Bryan Smithson	14.6	Eddie Biedenbach	
2007-08	23-10	10-4 ■	Bryan Smithson	16.4	Eddie Biedenbach	
2008-09	15-16	10-8	Reid Augst	15.4	Eddie Biedenbach	181-202 .473

● NCAA Tournament appearance ■ NIT appearance

PROFILE

University of North Carolina at Asheville, Asheville, NC
Founded: 1927
Enrollment: 3,500 (3,470 undergraduate)
Colors: Royal blue and white
Nickname: Bulldogs
Current arena: Justice Center, opened in 1964 (1,100)
First game: 1964
All-time record: 641-657 (.494)
Total weeks in AP Top 20/25: 0

Current conference: Big South (1985-)
Conference titles:
Big South: 4 (1997 [tie], '98, 2002 [tie], '08 [tie])
Conference tournament titles:
Big South: 2 (1989, 2003)
NCAA Tournament appearances: 1
NIT appearances: 1

TOP 5

G **Bamford Jones** (1974-78)
G **Jim McElhaney** (1966-69, '70-71)
G **Andre Smith** (1999-2003)
F **Tony Bumphus** (1974-78)
F **Rod Healy** (1967-71)

RECORDS

RECORDS	GAME		SEASON		CAREER	
POINTS	44	Mickey Gibson, vs. Washington and Lee (1969-70)	634	Kevin Martin (1998-99)	1,919	Bamford Jones (1974-78)
POINTS PER GAME			23.3	Mickey Gibson (1969-70)	21.9	Guy Batsel (1966-68)
REBOUNDS	30	Rod Healy, vs. Belmont-Abbey (1969-70)	393	Frank Rhyne (1973-74)	1,121	Rod Healy (1967-71)
ASSISTS	14	Jeff Lippard, vs. Charleston Southern (1990-91)	205	Mike Grace (1973-74)	520	K.J. Garland (2003-05, '06-08)

ESPN 319 SAGARIN

NORTH CAROLINA-GREENSBORO

It may not have an address on Tobacco Road, but UNC-Greensboro has certainly joined the neighborhood association. Soon after upgrading from D2, UNCG nearly made the 1995 Big Dance and then crashed the party the following year. More recently, Kyle Hines further increased the program's visibility by dominating the paint and joining an elite big men's club.

BEST TEAM: 1994-95 This band of Spartans just missed the NCAA Tourney, but went 23–6 thanks to G Scott Hartzell's grace and C Eric Cuthrell's tenacity around the basket. A one-point loss to Charleston Southern is all that kept them from something much bigger.

BEST PLAYER: F KYLE HINES (2004-08) Move over Pervis Ellison, David Robinson, Alonzo Mourning, Tim Duncan and Derrick Coleman. Add Kyle Hines to the ultra-impressive 2,000-point, 1,000-rebound, 300-block club. Though a mere 6'6", Hines was quite the enforcer, holding down the middle like a football defensive tackle. Just note his 349 blocks to grasp that concept.

BEST COACH: MIKE DEMENT (1991-95, 2005-) Consider Dement the bridge that connects Greensboro's past to its present. He left after that near-miss 1994-95 season to coach at SMU, turning over the team to his top assistant, Randy Peele, who took the Spartans to the Dance the next year. When Dement's welcome wore out in Dallas, UNCG held out open arms for his return.

GAME FOR THE AGES: The Spartans really had no business being in the 2001 NCAA Tourney. How'd they do it? In the Southern Conference final, David Schuck hauled in a 75-foot pass from Jay Joseph, spun around and nailed a jumper off the glass to beat Chattanooga 67-66. (They bowed to Stanford, 89-60, in the NCAAs.)

FIERCEST RIVAL: Hate thy neighbor. With campuses just 20 miles apart, Elon keeps getting in UNCG's face. In 2004, during the Phoenix's second season in the SoCon, they beat the Spartans in a painful triple-OT thriller. The only time they've met in the conference tourney, in 2006, Elon kicked UNCG out. Eight of the past 13 games have been decided by single digits. Elon leads the series, 14–12.

SEASON REVIEW

SEAS.	W-L	CONF.		SCORING		COACH	RECORD	
1967-68	2-11					Jim Swiggett		
1968-69	4-15					Jim Swiggett		
1969-70	4-16					Jim Swiggett		
1970-71	8-10					Jim Swiggett		
1971-72	10-15					Jim Swiggett		
1972-73	9-11					Jim Swiggett		
1973-74	2-19					Jim Swiggett		
1974-75	6-16					Jim Swiggett	45-113	.285
1975-76	8-11					Jack Mehl		
1976-77	11-15					Jack Mehl		
1977-78	8-15					Jack Mehl	27-41	.397
1978-79	8-16			Larry Moore	11.7	Larry G. Hargett		
1979-80	16-12			David Whiteside	17.8	Larry G. Hargett		
1980-81	17-8			Scott Harper	14.5	Larry G. Hargett		
1981-82	14-10			Esker Tatum	14.2	Larry G. Hargett	55-46	.545
1982-83	16-9			Esker Tatum	16.2	Ed Douma		
1983-84	11-15			Joe Monroe	18.6	Ed Douma	27-24	.529
1984-85	9-16			John Baker	18.0	Bob McEvoy		
1985-86	13-14			Robert Bryant	24.3	Bob McEvoy		
1986-87	22-6			Frazier Bryant	18.3	Bob McEvoy		
1987-88	19-8			Ron Sheppard	16.5	Bob McEvoy		
1988-89	14-13			Marvin Dawson	20.3	Bob McEvoy		
1989-90	6-22			Greg Stauffer	12.9	Bob McEvoy		
1990-91	9-17			Yusuf Stewart	20.7	Bob McEvoy	92-96	.489
1991-92	7-21			Yusuf Stewart	14.8	Mike Dement		
1992-93	10-17			Scott Hartzell	13.4	Mike Dement		
1993-94	15-12	11-7		Scott Hartzell	13.2	Mike Dement		
1994-95	23-6	14-2		Scott Hartzell	15.7	Mike Dement		
1995-96	20-10	11-3	●	Brian Brunson	12.4	Randy Peele		
1996-97	10-20	6-8		Tony Daughtry	12.5	Randy Peele		
1997-98	9-19	6-9		Derrick Nix	11.9	Randy Peele		
1998-99	7-20	5-11		Nathan Jameson	10.6	Randy Peele	46-69	.400
1999-2000	15-13	9-7		Demetrius Cherry	13.7	Fran McCaffery		
2000-01	19-12	10-6	●	Courtney Eldridge	14.6	Fran McCaffery		
2001-02	20-11	11-5	■	James Maye	13.8	Fran McCaffery		
2002-03	7-22	3-13		James Maye	16.3	Fran McCaffery		
2003-04	11-17	7-9		Jay Joseph	17.0	Fran McCaffery		
2004-05	18-12	9-7		Ronnie Burrell	15.0	Fran McCaffery	90-87	.508
2005-06	12-19	4-10		Kyle Hines	19.3	Mike Dement		
2006-07	16-14	12-6		Kyle Hines	20.9	Mike Dement		
2007-08	19-12	12-8		Kyle Hines	19.2	Mike Dement		
2008-09	5-25	4-16		Mikko Koivisto	12.4	Mike Dement	107-126	.459

● NCAA Tournament appearance ■ NIT appearance

PROFILE

University of North Carolina at Greensboro, Greensboro, NC
Founded: 1891
Enrollment: 17,157 (13,156 undergraduate)
Colors: Gold, white and navy
Nickname: Spartans
Current arena: Fleming Gymnasium, opened in 1989 (2,320)
Previous: Park Gym, prior to 1989 (N/A); Rosenthal Gym (N/A)
First game: 1967

All-time record: 489-602 (.448)
Total weeks in AP Top 20/25: 0
Current conference: Southern (1997-)
Conference titles:
Big South: 2 (1995, '96)
Southern: 1 (2002 [tie])
Conference tournament titles:
Big South: 1 (1996)
Southern: 1 (2001)
NCAA Tournament appearances: 2
NIT appearances: 1

TOP 5

- G **Courtney Eldridge** (1998-2002)
- G **Scott Hartzell** (1992-96)
- G **Jay Joseph** (2000-04)
- F **Kyle Hines** (2004-08)
- F **Bruce Shaw** (1968-73)

RECORDS

RECORDS	GAME		SEASON		CAREER	
POINTS	38	Kyle Hines, vs. Marshall (Nov. 11, 2006)	605	Kyle Hines (2006-07)	2,187	Kyle Hines (2004-08)
POINTS PER GAME			20.9	Kyle Hines (2006-07)	18.2	Kyle Hines (2004-08)
REBOUNDS	21	Kyle Hines, vs. College of Charleston (Dec. 3, 2005)	284	Eric Cuthrell (1994-95)	1,047	Kyle Hines (2004-08)
ASSISTS	12	Dwayne Johnson, vs. Bridgewater (Nov. 30, 2004)	182	Courtney Eldridge (2001-02)	584	Courtney Eldridge (1998-2002)

THE SCHOOLS

ESPN 22 SAGARIN

NORTH CAROLINA STATE

When Herb Sendek left NC State for Arizona State in 2006, there was much chatter about the unreasonable expectations in Raleigh driving him West. There's probably something to that. The Wolfpack's storied history—the David Thompson Era, Jimmy V's frantic search for a hug and the big upsets of their Research Triangle rivals, Duke and North Carolina—is difficult to live up to.

BEST TEAM: 1973-74 Coming off a 27–0 record in 1972-73, a season in which they were ineligible for postseason play, the Wolfpack looked like serious contenders to snap UCLA's string of seven straight NCAA titles. Norm Sloan's team avenged an early-season loss to the Bruins in the Final Four, bouncing Bill Walton & Co. in a double-overtime thriller, 80-77. By comparison, State's 76-64 title win over Marquette was anticlimactic.

BEST PLAYER: F David Thompson (1972-75) Legend has it he could pick quarters off the top of the backboard. But the man who would come to be known as Skywalker was more than just an athletic freak. One rival coach said that the 6'4", 190-pound forward was the best player in the ACC before he played a single varsity game. Thompson finished his career as a three-time ACC Player of the Year and the 1975 national POY, having twice turned down seven-figure offers to turn pro early. He went on to star for the Denver Nuggets in the ABA and NBA.

BEST COACH: Everett Case (1946-64) Thanks to his exciting, up-tempo style, Case helped popularize basketball in a region where football had been king. The Old Gray Fox won ACC Coach of the Year three times and started several indelible traditions, such as cutting down the nets after a championship.

GAME FOR THE AGES: Wolfpack fans are divided as to their favorite highlight from NC State's improbable 1983 NCAA title win over Houston, 54-52. Was it Lorenzo Charles' game-winning putback of a Dereck Whittenburg 35-foot air ball as the final seconds ticked off? Or Jim Valvano's manic sprint around the court afterward? The victory was so dramatic that it overshadows the Wolfpack's famed back-and-forth 103-100 ACC tournament title win over Maryland on March 9, 1974.

HEARTBREAKER: Between Case's arrival in Raleigh in 1946 and Jan. 24, 1953, NC State dominated North Carolina, winning every single matchup. But the Tar Heels shocked the Wolfpack in new coach Frank McGuire's UNC debut at Reynolds Coliseum, 70-69. Afterward, McGuire boldly had his team cut down the Reynolds nets, adding fuel to the rivalry's fire.

FIERCEST RIVAL: NC State's rivalry with North Carolina may not be as famous as UNC-Duke, but it may evoke even more passion in students. With the campuses 20 miles apart, there's no end to the pranking opportunities: The Free Expression Tunnel in Raleigh has been painted Carolina blue; Chapel Hill water fountains have run Wolfpack red; *The Technician*, NC State's student paper, once ran a foldout of a nude Dean Smith. The Wolfpack are only 75–140 against the Tar Heels, but they've come out on top 31 times when the Heels have been ranked in the AP poll.

FANFARE AND HOOPLA: Early in a second-half win over UNC-Charlotte on March 1, 1975, Thompson found himself alone on a breakaway. For the first and only time in his college career, he dunked—and drew a technical, since the shot was banned at the time. When Sloan pulled him from the game, the home fans gave Thompson a rousing ovation. That's entertainment.

FAN FAVORITE: G Chris Corchiani (1987-91) He graduated as the NCAA's all-time leader in assists and the ACC's in steals (both records since broken), but the emotional point guard is best remembered as the Fire to backcourt mate Rodney Monroe's Ice.

CONSENSUS ALL-AMERICAS

1951	**Sam Ranzino**, G
1956	**Ronnie Shavlik**, F/C
1973-75	**David Thompson**, F

FIRST-ROUND PRO PICKS

1951	**Sam Ranzino**, Rochester (8)
1956	**Ronnie Shavlik**, New York (4)
1959	**John Richter**, Boston (8)
1974	**Tom Burleson**, Seattle (3)
1975	**David Thompson**, Atlanta (1)
1975	**David Thompson**, Virginia (ABA)
1977	**Kenny Carr**, LA Lakers (6)
1980	**Hawkeye Whitney**, Kansas City (16)
1983	**Thurl Bailey**, Utah (7)
1986	**Chris Washburn**, Golden State (3)
1992	**Tom Gugliotta**, Washington (6)
1996	**Todd Fuller**, Golden State (11)
2005	**Julius Hodge**, Denver (20)
2006	**Cedric Simmons**, New Orleans (15)
2008	**J.J. Hickson**, Cleveland (19)

PROFILE

North Carolina State University, Raleigh, NC
Founded: 1887
Enrollment: 31,100 (23,730 undergraduate)
Colors: Red and white
Nickname: Wolfpack
Current arena: RBC Center, opened in 1999 (19,722)
Previous: Reynolds Coliseum, 1949-99 (12,000)
First game: Feb. 16, 1911
All-time record: 1,539-936 (.622)
Total weeks in AP Top 20/25: 326

Current conference: Atlantic Coast (1953-)
Conference titles:
Southern: 6 (1947, '48, '49, '50, '51, '53)
ACC: 7 (1955, '56 [tie], '59 [tie], '73, '74, '85 [tie], '89)
Conference tournament titles:
Southern: 7 (1929, '47, '48, '49, '50, '51, '52)
ACC: 10 (1954, '55, '56, '59, '65, '70, '73, '74, '83, '87)
NCAA Tournaments: 22 (2 appearances vacated)
Sweet 16s (since 1975): 5
Final Fours: 3
Titles: 2 (1974, '83)
NIT appearances: 11
Semifinals: 4

TOP 5

G **Rodney Monroe** (1987-91)
G/F **Julius Hodge** (2001-05)
F **David Thompson** (1972-75)
F/C **Ronnie Shavlik** (1953-56)
C **Tom Burleson** (1971-74)

RECORDS	GAME		SEASON		CAREER	
POINTS	57	David Thompson, vs. Buffalo St. (Dec. 5, 1974)	838	David Thompson (1974-75)	2,551	Rodney Monroe (1987-91)
POINTS PER GAME			29.9	David Thompson (1974-75)	26.8	David Thompson (1972-75)
REBOUNDS	35	Ronnie Shavlik, vs. Villanova (Jan. 1, 1955)	581	Ronnie Shavlik (1954-55)	1,598	Ronnie Shavlik (1953-56)
ASSISTS	20	Chris Corchiani, vs. Maryland (Feb. 27, 1991)	299	Chris Corchiani (1990-91)	1,038	Chris Corchiani (1987-91)

THE SCHOOLS

SEASON REVIEW

SEASON	W-L	CONF.	SCORING	COACH	RECORD		SEASON	W-L	CONF.	SCORING	COACH	RECORD	
1910-16	*22-33*		*Only one winning season: 7-6 under Chuck Sandborn in 1915-16*				1926-27	12-5	5-2		Gus Tebell		
1916-17	10-8			Harry Hartsell			1927-28	10-8	3-6		Gus Tebell		
1917-18	12-2			Harry Hartsell			1928-29	15-6	6-5		Gus Tebell		
1918-19	11-3			Tal Safford	11-3	.786	1929-30	11-6	7-5		Gus Tebell	79-36	.687
1919-20	11-5			Richard Crozier			1930-31	8-8	5-5		R.R. Sermon		
1920-21	6-14			Richard Crozier			1931-32	10-6	6-4		R.R. Sermon		
1921-22	6-13	1-5		Harry Hartsell			1932-33	11-8	6-3		R.R. Sermon		
1922-23	5-8	1-2		Harry Hartsell	33-31	.516	1933-34	11-6	6-5		R.R. Sermon		
1923-24	7-16	2-4		Richard Crozier	24-35	.407	1934-35	10-9	6-5		R.R. Sermon		
1924-25	11-7	1-4		Gus Tebell			1935-36	15-4	10-3		R.R. Sermon		
1925-26	20-4	5-3		Gus Tebell			1936-37	15-9	14-7		R.R. Sermon		

SEAS.	W-L	CONF.	POSTSEASON	SCORING		REBOUNDS		ASSISTS		COACH	RECORD	
1937-38	13-6	10-3								R.R. Sermon		
1938-39	10-7	7-6								R.R. Sermon		
1939-40	8-11	5-10								R.R. Sermon	111-74	.600
1940-41	6-9	6-9								Bob Warren		
1941-42	15-7	9-4								Bob Warren	21-16	.568
1942-43	7-9	7-5								Leroy Jay		
1943-44	5-13	2-5								Leroy Jay		
1944-45	10-11	7-5								Leroy Jay		
1945-46	6-12	5-7								Leroy Jay	28-45	.384
1946-47	26-5	11-2	NIT THIRD PLACE							Everett Case		
1947-48	29-3	12-0	NIT QUARTERFINALS							Everett Case		
1948-49	25-8	14-1								Everett Case		
1949-50	27-6	12-2	NCAA THIRD PLACE							Everett Case		
1950-51	30-7	13-1	NIT 1ST R, NCAA REG. SEMIS	Sam Ranzino	20.8					Everett Case		
1951-52	24-10	12-2	NCAA REGIONAL SEMIFINALS							Everett Case		
1952-53	26-6	13-3		Bobby Speight	16.9	Bobby Speight	11.1			Everett Case		
1953-54	26-7	5-3	NCAA REGIONAL SEMIFINALS	Mel Thompson	18.3	Ronnie Shavlik	13.5			Everett Case		
1954-55	28-4	12-2		Ronnie Shavlik	22.1	Ronnie Shavlik	18.2			Everett Case		
1955-56	24-4	11-3	NCAA FIRST ROUND	Ronnie Shavlik	18.2	Ronnie Shavlik	19.5			Everett Case		
1956-57	15-11	7-7		John Richter	15.5	John Richter	12.7			Everett Case		
1957-58	18-6	10-4		Lou Pucillo	15.8	John Richter	10.9			Everett Case		
1958-59	22-4	12-2		John Richter	17.0	John Richter	14.2			Everett Case		
1959-60	11-15	5-9		Bob DiStefano	12.7	Bob DiStefano	9.1			Everett Case		
1960-61	16-9	8-6		Bob DiStefano	13.2	Bob DiStefano	8.6			Everett Case		
1961-62	11-6	10-4		Jon Speaks	17.4	John Punger	9.5			Everett Case		
1962-63	10-11	5-9		Jon Speaks	12.5	Pete Auksel	7.6			Everett Case		
1963-64	8-11	4-10		Larry Lakins	20.8	Pete Auksel	8.4			Everett Case	377-134	.738
1964-65	21-5	10-4	NCAA REGIONAL SEMIFINALS	Larry Lakins	19.0	Pete Coker	10.0			Press Maravich		
1965-66	18-9	9-5		Eddie Biedenbach	16.2	Pete Coker	9.9			Press Maravich	38-13	.745
1966-67	7-19	2-12		Bill Kretzer	11.7	Bill Kretzer	7.2			Norm Sloan		
1967-68	16-10	9-5		Eddie Biedenbach	14.1	Vann Williford	8.1			Norm Sloan		
1968-69	15-10	8-6		Vann Williford	21.6	Vann Williford	10.0			Norm Sloan		
1969-70	23-7	9-5	NCAA REGIONAL SEMIFINALS	Vann Williford	23.7	Vann Williford	10.0			Norm Sloan		
1970-71	13-14	5-9		Ed Leftwich	16.4	Paul Coder	8.4			Norm Sloan		
1971-72	16-10	6-6		Tom Burleson	21.3	Tom Burleson	14.0			Norm Sloan		
1972-73	27-0	12-0		David Thompson	24.7	Tom Burleson	12.0	Monte Towe	4.2	Norm Sloan		
1973-74	**30-1**	**12-0**	**NATIONAL CHAMPION**	**David Thompson**	**26.0**	**Tom Burleson**	**12.2**	**Monte Towe**	**3.8**	**Norm Sloan**		
1974-75	22-6	8-4		David Thompson	29.9	Phil Spence	10.0	Monte Towe	4.1	Norm Sloan		
1975-76	21-9	7-5	NIT THIRD PLACE	Kenny Carr	26.6	Kenny Carr	10.3	Craig Davis	3.1	Norm Sloan		
1976-77	17-11	6-6		Kenny Carr	21.0	Kenny Carr	9.9	Clyde Austin	4.9	Norm Sloan		
1977-78	21-10	7-5	NIT RUNNER-UP	Hawkeye Whitney	15.3	Tiny Pinder	6.2	Clyde Austin	4.2	Norm Sloan		
1978-79	18-12	3-9		Hawkeye Whitney	18.7	Hawkeye Whitney	6.1	Clyde Austin	4.0	Norm Sloan		
1979-80	20-8	9-5	NCAA SECOND ROUND	Hawkeye Whitney	18.6	Hawkeye Whitney	4.9	Sidney Lowe	4.5	Norm Sloan	266-127	.677
1980-81	14-13	4-10		Thurl Bailey	12.3	Thurl Bailey	6.1	Sidney Lowe	7.7	Jim Valvano		
1981-82	22-10	7-7	NCAA FIRST ROUND	Thurl Bailey	13.7	Thurl Bailey	6.8	Sidney Lowe	5.7	Jim Valvano		
1982-83	**26-10**	**8-6**	**NATIONAL CHAMPION**	**Thurl Bailey**	**16.7**	**Thurl Bailey**	**7.7**	**Sidney Lowe**	**7.5**	**Jim Valvano**		
1983-84	19-14	4-10	NIT FIRST ROUND	Lorenzo Charles	18.0	Cozell McQueen	9.0	Spud Webb	6.0	Jim Valvano		
1984-85	23-10	9-5	NCAA REGIONAL FINALS	Lorenzo Charles	18.1	Cozell McQueen	6.9	Spud Webb	5.3	Jim Valvano		
1985-86	21-13	7-7	NCAA REGIONAL FINALS	Chris Washburn	17.6	Chris Washburn	6.7	Nate McMillan	6.8	Jim Valvano		
1986-87	20-15 ⊗	6-8	NCAA FIRST ROUND	Bennie Bolton	15.0	Charles Shackleford	7.6	Vinny Del Negro	2.9	Jim Valvano		
1987-88	24-7 ⊗	10-4	NCAA FIRST ROUND	Chucky Brown	16.6	Charles Shackleford	9.6	Chris Corchiani	7.3	Jim Valvano		
1988-89	22-9	10-4	NCAA REGIONAL SEMIFINALS	Rodney Monroe	21.4	Chucky Brown	8.8	Chris Corchiani	8.6	Jim Valvano		
1989-90	18-12	6-8		Rodney Monroe	23.2	Tom Gugliotta	7.0	Chris Corchiani	7.9	Jim Valvano	209-112	.651▼
1990-91	20-11	8-6	NCAA SECOND ROUND	Rodney Monroe	27.0	Tom Gugliotta	9.1	Chris Corchiani	9.6	Les Robinson		
1991-92	12-18	6-10		Tom Gugliotta	22.5	Tom Gugliotta	9.0	Donnie Seale	4.5	Les Robinson		
1992-93	8-19	2-14		Kevin Thompson	15.5	Kevin Thompson	9.1	Curtis Marshall	4.3	Les Robinson		
1993-94	11-19	5-11		Todd Fuller	11.8	Todd Fuller	8.4	Curtis Marshall	4.5	Les Robinson		
1994-95	12-15	4-12		Todd Fuller	16.4	Todd Fuller	8.6	Ishua Benjamin	4.6	Les Robinson		
1995-96	15-16	3-13		Todd Fuller	20.9	Todd Fuller	9.9	Curtis Marshall	3.5	Les Robinson	78-98	.443
1996-97	17-15	4-12	NIT SECOND ROUND	C.C. Harrison	15.7	Damon Thornton	7.0	Jeremy Hyatt	3.0	Herb Sendek		
1997-98	17-15	5-11	NIT SECOND ROUND	C.C. Harrison	16.6	Kenny Inge	7.4	Ishua Benjamin	3.8	Herb Sendek		
1998-99	19-14	6-10	NIT SECOND ROUND	Adam Harrington	11.6	Damon Thornton	6.3	Justin Gainey	3.8	Herb Sendek		
1999-2000	20-14	6-10	NIT FOURTH PLACE	Anthony Grundy	12.5	Damon Thornton	7.6	J. Gainey, A. Grundy	2.8	Herb Sendek		
2000-01	13-16	5-11		Anthony Grundy	14.6	D. Thornton, Kenny Inge	7.2	Clifford Crawford	3.5	Herb Sendek		
2001-02	23-11	9-7	NCAA SECOND ROUND	Anthony Grundy	17.8	Anthony Grundy	5.5	Anthony Grundy	3.5	Herb Sendek		
2002-03	18-13	9-7	NCAA FIRST ROUND	Julius Hodge	17.7	Julius Hodge	5.5	Clifford Crawford	4.2	Herb Sendek		
2003-04	21-10	11-5	NCAA SECOND ROUND	Julius Hodge	18.2	Marcus Melvin	8.1	Julius Hodge	3.6	Herb Sendek		
2004-05	21-14	7-9	NCAA REGIONAL SEMIFINALS	Julius Hodge	17.0	Julius Hodge	6.6	Julius Hodge	4.8	Herb Sendek		
2005-06	22-10	10-6	NCAA SECOND ROUND	Cameron Bennerman	14.1	Cedric Simmons	6.3	Engin Atsür	3.4	Herb Sendek	191-132	.591
2006-07	20-16	5-11	NIT QUARTERFINALS	Brandon Costner	16.8	Brandon Costner	7.3	Engin Atsür	4.2	Sidney Lowe		
2007-08	15-16	4-12		J.J. Hickson	14.8	J.J. Hickson	8.5	Gavin Grant	2.9	Sidney Lowe		
2008-09	16-14	6-10		Brandon Costner	13.3	Ben McCauley	7.8	Javier Gonzalez	3.3	Sidney Lowe	51-46	.526

⊗ Records don't reflect games forfeited or vacated. For adjusted records, see p. 521.

▼ Coach's record adjusted to reflect games forfeited or vacated: 209-110, .655. For yearly totals, see p. 521.

ESPN 218 SAGARIN

NORTH CAROLINA-WILMINGTON

A program slowly and steadily on the rise went meteoric at the beginning of the millennium, with four NCAA appearances from 2000 to '06.

BEST TEAM: 2001-02 The upperclassmen-laden Seahawks rolled through Colonial play, winning 17 conference games (regular-season and tournament) and 23 overall while following the motto, "Dream big, focus small." Both the dreaming and the focus paid off when UNCW knocked off Southern California in the NCAA's first round. There was no shame in losing by single digits to Indiana in the following round, especially after coming back from 17 down to cut the Hoosiers' lead to three in the second half.

BEST PLAYER: G Brett Blizzard (1999-2003) True to his name, Blizzard stormed through the CAA. His 2,144 points and 249 steals are Wilmington records, by far. He was named CAA tournament MVP three times and league POY twice. In 2008, ESPN analyst Jay Bilas named Blizzard one of the 25 greatest college three-point shooters of all time.

BEST COACH: Jerry Wainwright (1994-2002) The former Wake Forest assistant made Wilmington relevant not only inside the state but nationally with a 2002 upset of Southern California Wainwright took the Seahawks to the postseason in four of his eight seasons.

GAME FOR THE AGES: UNCW's first-round opponent in the 2002 NCAA Tournament was a senior-laden USC Trojans team that had been to the 2001 Elite Eight. Blizzard and Craig Callahan each notched 18 points in the Seahawks' 93-89 overtime victory, their first Tournament win in only their second game. Fans remember Stewart Hare hammering home a thunderous dunk to put the game out of reach.

FIERCEST RIVAL: Some of the most popular activity in North Carolina east of Raleigh occurs on the beaches. And then there's the War at the Shore, UNCW's rivalry with East Carolina. The series took a bit of a hit when ECU bolted the Colonial in 2001, but since the rivalry resumed five years later, plenty of heat remains.

SEASON REVIEW

SEAS.	W-L	CONF.	COACH	SEAS.	W-L	CONF.	COACH
1951-52	12-4		Bill Brooks	1960-61	24-6		Bill Brooks
1952-53	9-5		Bill Brooks	1961-62	21-6		Bill Brooks
1953-54	14-9		Bill Brooks	1962-63	17-10		Bill Brooks
1954-55	11-8		Bill Brooks	1963-64	9-8		Bill Brooks
1955-56	5-12		Bill Brooks	1964-65	11-10		Bill Brooks
1956-57	7-12		Bill Brooks	1965-66	13-11		Bill Brooks
1957-58	12-9		Bill Brooks	1966-67	9-18		Bill Brooks
1958-59	24-5		Bill Brooks	1967-68	9-16		Bill Brooks
1959-60	20-6		Bill Brooks	1968-69	6-23		Bill Brooks

SEAS.	W-L	CONF.	SCORING		COACH	RECORD
1969-70	8-16				Bill Brooks	
1970-71	8-18				Bill Brooks	
1971-72	7-16				Bill Brooks	256-228 .529
1972-73	10-14		Mike Cherry	18.4	Mel Gibson	
1973-74	14-10		Mike Cherry	21.4	Mel Gibson	
1974-75	8-17		Willy Jackson	20.2	Mel Gibson	
1975-76	13-15				Mel Gibson	
1976-77	16-10		Denny Fields	21.4	Mel Gibson	
1977-78	19-7		Denny Fields	22.5	Mel Gibson	
1978-79	19-8				Mel Gibson	
1979-80	19-10				Mel Gibson	
1980-81	13-13				Mel Gibson	
1981-82	13-14				Mel Gibson	
1982-83	11-16				Mel Gibson	
1983-84	11-17				Mel Gibson	
1984-85	12-16	4-10	Brian Rowsom	18.4	Mel Gibson	
1985-86	16-13	6-8	Brian Rowsom	20.3	Mel Gibson	194-180 .519
1986-87	18-12	9-5	Brian Rowsom	21.8	Robert McPherson	
1987-88	15-14	8-6			Robert McPherson	
1988-89	16-14	9-5	Antonio Howard	17.3	Robert McPherson	
1989-90	8-20	3-11			Robert McPherson	57-60 .487
1990-91	11-17	6-8			Kevin Eastman	
1991-92	13-15	6-8			Kevin Eastman	
1992-93	17-11	6-8			Kevin Eastman	
1993-94	18-10	9-5			Kevin Eastman	59-53 .527
1994-95	16-11	10-4			Jerry Wainwright	
1995-96	13-16	9-7			Jerry Wainwright	
1996-97	16-14	10-6			Jerry Wainwright	
1997-98	20-11	13-3 ■			Jerry Wainwright	
1998-99	11-17	9-7	Stan Simmons	16.3	Jerry Wainwright	
1999-2000	18-13	8-8 ●	Brett Blizzard	15.6	Jerry Wainwright	
2000-01	19-11	11-5 ■	Brett Blizzard	13.8	Jerry Wainwright	
2001-02	23-10	14-4 ●	Brett Blizzard	17.9	Jerry Wainwright	136-103 .569
2002-03	24-7	15-3 ●	Brett Blizzard	21.1	Brad Brownell	
2003-04	15-15	9-9	Ed Spencer	8.7	Brad Brownell	
2004-05	19-10	13-5	John Goldsberry	12.1	Brad Brownell	
2005-06	25-8	15-3 ●	T.J. Carter	13.6	Brad Brownell	83-40 .675
2006-07	7-22	4-14	Vladimir Kuljanin	13.6	Benny Moss	
2007-08	20-13	12-6	T.J. Carter	15.8	Benny Moss	
2008-09	7-25	3-16	Chad Tomko	15.6	Benny Moss	34-60 .362

● NCAA Tournament appearance ■ NIT appearance

PROFILE

University of North Carolina Wilmington, Wilmington, NC
Founded: 1947
Enrollment: 11,840 (10,753 undergraduate)
Colors: Teal, navy and gold
Nickname: Seahawks
Current arena: Trask Coliseum, opened in 1977 (6,100)
First game: Dec. 3, 1951
All-time record: 819-724 (.531)
Total weeks in AP Top 20/25: 0

Current conference: Colonial Athletic Association (1984-)
Conference titles:
CAA: 5 (1997 [tie], '98 [tie], '02, '03, '06 [tie])
Conference tournament titles:
CAA: 4 (2000, '02, '03, '06)
NCAA Tournament appearances: 4
NIT appearances: 2

TOP 5

G **Brett Blizzard** (1999-2003)
G **John Goldsberry** (2002-06)
F **Shawn Williams** (1979-83)
F **Dave Wohl** (1975-79)
C **Brian Rowsom** (1983-87)

RECORDS

RECORDS	GAME		SEASON		CAREER	
POINTS	39	Brian Rowsom, vs. East Carolina (Jan. 17, 1987)	655	Brett Blizzard (2002-03)	2,144	Brett Blizzard (1999-2003)
POINTS PER GAME			22.5	Denny Fields (1977-1978)	24.3	Jay Neary (1963-66)
REBOUNDS	20	Matt Fish, vs. American (Jan. 20, 1992)	345	Brian Rowsom (1986-87)	1,015	Brian Rowsom (1983-87)
ASSISTS	15	Chad Tomko, vs. Towson (Jan. 24, 2009)	244	Rick Alessi (1974-75)	530	John Goldsberry (2002-06)

ESPN 266 SAGARIN

NORTH DAKOTA STATE

In 113 years of Bison hoops, there's been something for everyone: College Division All-America Marv Bachmeier lighting it up in the late 1950s; D2 tourney teams galore under Erv Inniger and Tom Billeter; upsets of Wisconsin and Marquette; and, best of all, the dawning of a new era in 2008-09, when North Dakota State became D1 Tourney eligible.

BEST TEAM: 2008-09 Coach Tim Miles redshirted the 2004 recruiting class—Ben Woodside, Brett Winkelman, Lucas Moormann and Mike Nelson. The plan: Once NDSU lost its provisional status in 2008-09, the seniors would give the Bison a better shot at making the NCAA Tournament. Worked like a charm—except that Miles left in 2007 to take over Colorado State. The Bison won the Summit League's regular-season and tournament titles and then lost to No. 3-seed Kansas, 84-74, in the Tourney.

BEST PLAYER: G Marv Bachmeier (1958-61) A prolific scorer with 1,553 points, Bachmeier was a three-time Little All-America, including in 1960 when he averaged 27.0 ppg. He holds two of the school's top four single-season scoring averages.

BEST COACH: Tom Billeter (1992-97) His five seasons included four straight 20-win campaigns—outstanding, since there had been only five in the school's previous 95 seasons. His teams went 97–50 and made four straight D2 tournaments, winning six tourney games.

GAME FOR THE AGES: The 11:15 a.m. tip-off on Jan. 21, 2006, wasn't enough of a wake-up call for No. 15-ranked Wisconsin. The Bison had never beaten a ranked D1 team, but they shocked the host Badgers, 62-55. Woodside (24 points) and Andre Smith (16 points, 13 rebounds) led the way.

FIERCEST RIVAL: North Dakota was the enemy in Divison II; South Dakota State has filled that role as a Summit League opponent. The two schools first met in 1909-10, and NDSU leads the century-long series, 105–93. But the Bison have closed the gap with wins in eight of the last nine games, including season sweeps from 2006-07 to '08-09.

SEASON REVIEW

SEAS.	W-L	CONF.	COACH	SEAS.	W-L	CONF.	COACH
1897-47	*517-275*	*Best season, 22-3 in 1925-26*		1960-61	11-14		B.C. Bentson
1947-48	10-14		C.P. Reed	1961-62	8-17		B.C. Bentson
1948-49	10-14		C.P. Reed	1962-63	9-17		B.C. Bentson
1949-50	12-10		B.C. Bentson	1963-64	7-16		B.C. Bentson
1950-51	8-15		B.C. Bentson	1964-65	9-16		B.C. Bentson
1951-52	17-11		B.C. Bentson	1965-66	14-10		Doug Cowman
1952-53	10-12		B.C. Bentson	1966-67	13-11		Doug Cowman
1953-54	14-9		B.C. Bentson	1967-68	6-20		Doug Cowman
1954-55	16-8		B.C. Bentson	1968-69	9-17		Lyle "Bud" Belk
1955-56	12-11		B.C. Bentson	1969-70	15-11		Lyle "Bud" Belk
1956-57	9-14		B.C. Bentson	1970-71	18-9		Lyle "Bud" Belk
1957-58	9-14		B.C. Bentson	1971-72	8-18		Lyle "Bud" Belk
1958-59	8-13		B.C. Bentson	1972-73	14-12		Marv Skaar
1959-60	10-10		B.C. Bentson	1973-74	17-10		Marv Skaar

SEAS.	W-L	CONF.	SCORING		COACH	RECORD	
1974-75	15-11		Mark Gibbons	19.6	Marv Skaar		
1975-76	18-9		Steve Saladino	20.1	Marv Skaar		
1976-77	13-14		Bob Nagle	17.3	Marv Skaar		
1977-78	16-13		Paul Shogren	20.2	Marv Skaar	93-69	.574
1978-79	16-11		Paul Shogren	14.3	Erv Inniger		
1979-80	16-13		Brady Lipp	14.3	Erv Inniger		
1980-81	20-9		Jeff Giersch	16.1	Erv Inniger		
1981-82	18-11		Jeff Askew	15.5	Erv Inniger		
1982-83	21-9		Jeff Askew	18.3	Erv Inniger		
1983-84	19-9		Lance Berwald	21.4	Erv Inniger		
1984-85	19-9		Steve Stacy	15.9	Erv Inniger		
1985-86	16-12		Joe Regnier	10.8	Erv Inniger		
1986-87	19-9		Joe Regnier	16.1	Erv Inniger		
1987-88	19-9		Dan Wilberscheid	16.0	Erv Inniger		
1988-89	18-10		Joe Regnier	19.3	Erv Inniger		
1989-90	17-11		Ray McKenzie	14.7	Erv Inniger		
1990-91	14-13		Ray McKenzie	16.2	Erv Inniger		
1991-92	12-15		Bart Inniger	13.2	Erv Inniger	244-150	.619
1992-93	12-17		Jeff Griffin	11.0	Tom Billeter		
1993-94	21-9		Brian Sand	14.9	Tom Billeter		
1994-95	22-8		Brian Sand	15.0	Tom Billeter		
1995-96	20-9		Brian Sand	19.4	Tom Billeter		
1996-97	22-7		Mark McGehee	16.3	Tom Billeter	97-50	.660
1997-98	18-9		Mark McGehee	17.0	Ray Giacoletti		
1998-99	14-13		Derek Hodges	14.3	Ray Giacoletti		
1999-2000	16-11		Gary Hall	14.8	Ray Giacoletti	48-33	.593
2000-01	15-11		Denver TenBroek	18.8	Greg McDermott	15-11	.577
2001-02	11-15		Denver TenBroek	19.1	Tim Miles		
2002-03	20-11		Denver TenBroek	21.5	Tim Miles		
2003-04	16-13		CoCo Cofield	15.3	Tim Miles		
2004-05	16-12		Myron Green	16.2	Tim Miles		
2005-06	16-12		Ben Woodside	17.5	Tim Miles		
2006-07	20-8		Andre Smith	17.0	Tim Miles	99-71	.582
2007-08	16-13	10-8	Ben Woodside	20.7	Saul Phillips		
2008-09	26-7	16-2 ●	Ben Woodside	23.2	Saul Phillips	42-20	.677

● NCAA Tournament appearance

PROFILE

North Dakota State University, Fargo, ND
Founded: 1890
Enrollment: 12,527 (10,751 undergraduate)
Colors: Yellow and green
Nickname: Bison
Current arena: Bison Sports Arena, opened in 1970 (6,000)
Previous: Bentson-Bunker Fieldhouse, 1931-70 (3,600)
First game: 1897
All-time record: 1,427-1,010 (.586)
Total weeks in AP Top 20/25: 0

Current conference: Summit League (2007-)
Conference titles:
Summit: 1 (2009)
Conference tournament titles:
Summit: 1 (2009)
NCAA Tournament appearances: 1
NIT appearances: 0

CONSENSUS ALL-AMERICAS

1960 **Marv Bachmeier** (Little A-A), G

TOP 5

G **Marv Bachmeier** (1958-61)
G **Ben Woodside** (2005-09)
F **Mike Kuppich** (1969-72)
F **Denver TenBroek** (1999-2003)
C **Lance Berwald** (1982-84)

RECORDS

	GAME		SEASON		CAREER	
POINTS	60	Ben Woodside, vs. Stephen F. Austin (Dec. 12, 2008)	766	Ben Woodside (2008-09)	2,315	Ben Woodside (2005-09)
POINTS PER GAME			27.0	Marv Bachmeier (1959-60)	23.9	Marv Bachmeier (1958-61)
REBOUNDS	24	Robert Lauf, vs. Northern Iowa (Jan. 11, 1954); Gene Gamache, vs. North Dakota (Feb. 25, 1955); Roger Erickson, vs. North Dakota (Feb. 27, 1960)	298	John Wojtak (1970-71)	874	Brett Winkelman (2005-09)
ASSISTS	16	David Ryles, vs. Northern Colorado (Feb. 20, 1987)	230	David Ryles (1986-87)	684	Jeff Askew (1979-83)

THE SCHOOLS

ESPN 254 SAGARIN

NORTHEASTERN

Few small schools can match the Huskies' seven NCAA Tournament appearances. Fewer still can match Northeastern's lore. Not only does the team play its home games in Matthews Arena, the original home of Boston's Celtics and Bruins, but it has produced a string of great hoops minds and players.

BEST TEAM: 1983-84 This was the season a sweet-shooting freshman named Reggie Lewis introduced himself to the nation, leading the Huskies to an NCAA Tournament win over Long Island. Only a 20-foot buzzer-beater from the hands of Virginia Commonwealth's Rolando Lamb kept this team from advancing.

BEST PLAYER: F Reggie Lewis (1983-87) Quiet, unassuming, kind. Those are the words most typically used to describe Lewis as a person. But as a player, the appropriate adjectives are inventive, daring and passionate. The Huskies' all-time leading scorer stayed local after leaving NU, playing for the Celtics from 1987 to '93. But, tragically, in 1993 he died of a heart attack at age 27 during an off-season workout.

BEST COACH: Jim Calhoun (1972-86) Before winning two national titles at Connecticut, the charismatic Massachusetts native took his first steps toward the Naismith Hall of Fame while at Northeastern. During his tenure, the Huskies went to their first NCAA Tournament—then went to four more.

GAME FOR THE AGES: In an epic second-round 1982 Tourney matchup, Northeastern took Villanova to triple overtime before falling, 76-72. At the end of the first OT, Huskies forward Dave Leitao (the future Virginia coach) missed a six-foot jumper that bounced in and out.

FIERCEST RIVAL: Northeastern was founded in 1898 and counted among its students graduates of Boston University. Not that this history means the two schools, walking distance apart in the heart of Boston, get along on the hardcourt. The Huskies and the Terriers have met nearly every year since 1921, with BU holding a 70–65 series lead.

SEASON REVIEW

SEAS.	W-L	CONF.	COACH
1920-47	*168-264*	*5 straight winning seasons, '30-35*	
1947-48	10-8		William Grinnell
1948-49	12-6		Joe Zabilski
1949-50	6-10		Joe Zabilski
1950-51	8-9		Joe Zabilski
1951-52	12-7		Joe Zabilski
1952-53	7-11		Joe Zabilski
1953-54	11-8		Joe Zabilski
1954-55	5-16		Joe Zabilski
1955-56	10-11		Joe Zabilski
1956-57	6-17		Joe Zabilski
1957-58	5-15		Joe Zabilski
1958-59	10-8		Dick Dukeshire
1959-60	10-11		Dick Dukeshire
1960-61	10-10		Dick Dukeshire
1961-62	17-8		Dick Dukeshire
1962-63	21-6		Dick Dukeshire
1963-64	17-8		Dick Dukeshire
1964-65	13-11		Dick Dukeshire
1965-66	18-8		Dick Dukeshire
1966-67	22-4		Dick Dukeshire
1967-68	19-9		Dick Dukeshire
1968-69	16-5		Dick Dukeshire
1969-70	14-8		Dick Dukeshire
1970-71	17-4		Dick Dukeshire
1971-72	12-9		Jim Bowman
1972-73	19-7		Jim Calhoun
1973-74	12-11		Jim Calhoun

SEAS.	W-L	CONF.		SCORING		COACH	RECORD	
1974-75	12-12			John Clark	18.2	Jim Calhoun		
1975-76	12-13			John Clark	20.4	Jim Calhoun		
1976-77	12-14			Dave Caligaris	20.9	Jim Calhoun		
1977-78	14-12			Dave Caligaris	24.6	Jim Calhoun		
1978-79	13-13			Pete Harris	22.0	Jim Calhoun		
1979-80	19-8	19-7		Pete Harris	20.8	Jim Calhoun		
1980-81	24-6	21-5	●	Pete Harris	20.0	Jim Calhoun		
1981-82	23-7	8-1	●	Perry Moss	23.7	Jim Calhoun		
1982-83	13-15	4-6		Mark Halsel	19.5	Jim Calhoun		
1983-84	27-5	14-0	●	Mark Halsel	21.0	Jim Calhoun		
1984-85	22-9	13-3	●	Reggie Lewis	24.1	Jim Calhoun		
1985-86	26-5	16-2	●	Reggie Lewis	23.8	Jim Calhoun	250-137	.646
1986-87	27-7	17-1	●	Reggie Lewis	23.3	Karl Fogel		
1987-88	15-13	11-7		Derrick Lewis	14.6	Karl Fogel		
1988-89	17-11	12-5		Derrick Lewis	19.1	Karl Fogel		
1989-90	16-12	9-3		George Yuille	13.9	Karl Fogel		
1990-91	22-11	8-2	●	Dexter Jenkins	13.0	Karl Fogel		
1991-92	9-19	5-9		Ben Harlee	12.9	Karl Fogel		
1992-93	20-8	12-2		Ben Harlee	12.4	Karl Fogel		
1993-94	5-22	2-12		Anthony Brown	19.4	Karl Fogel	131-103	.560
1994-95	18-11	10-6		Lonnie Harrell	16.7	Dave Leitao		
1995-96	4-24	2-16		Lonnie Harrell	16.6	Dave Leitao	22-35	.386
1996-97	7-20	6-12		Ty Mack	16.7	Rudy Keeling		
1997-98	14-14	9-9		Ty Mack	17.3	Rudy Keeling		
1998-99	10-18	6-12		Marcus Blossom	16.3	Rudy Keeling		
1999-2000	7-21	5-13		Marcus Blossom	14.9	Rudy Keeling		
2000-01	10-19	8-10		Ricky Cranford	16.6	Rudy Keeling	48-92	.343
2001-02	7-21	5-11		Aaron Davis	11.4	Ron Everhart		
2002-03	16-15	8-8		Jose Juan Barea	17.0	Ron Everhart		
2003-04	19-11	13-5		Jose Juan Barea	20.7	Ron Everhart		
2004-05	21-10	15-3	■	Jose Juan Barea	22.2	Ron Everhart		
2005-06	19-11	12-6		Jose Juan Barea	21.0	Ron Everhart	82-68	.547
2006-07	13-19	9-9		Bennet Davis	15.0	Bill Coen		
2007-08	14-17	9-9		Matt Janning	16.1	Bill Coen		
2008-09	19-13	12-6		Matt Janning	14.3	Bill Coen	46-49	.484

● NCAA Tournament appearance ■ NIT appearance

PROFILE

Northeastern University, Boston, MA
Founded: 1898
Enrollment: 21,324 (15,521 undergraduate)
Colors: Red and black
Nickname: Huskies
Current arena: Matthews Arena, opened in 1910 (6,000)
Previous: Solomon Court at the Cabot Center, 1997-2005 (2,500); Cabot Center Gym, 1954-80 (3,000); Boston YMCA, 1920-54 (N/A)
First game: 1920
All-time record: 1,053-975 (.519)
Total weeks in AP Top 20/25: 1

Current conference: Colonial Athletic Association (2005-)
Conference titles:
Eastern Collegiate Athletic North: 3 (1980 [tie], '81, '82)
ECAC North Atlantic: 4 (1984, '85 [tie], '86, '87)
North Atlantic: 3 (1990, '91, '93 [tie])
Conference tournament titles:
Eastern Collegiate Athletic North: 2 (1981, '82)
ECAC North Atlantic: 4 (1984, '85, '86, '87)
North Atlantic: 1 (1991)
NCAA Tournament appearances: 7
NIT appearances: 1

FIRST-ROUND PRO PICKS

1987 **Reggie Lewis**, Boston (22)

TOP 5

G **Jose Juan Barea** (2002-06)
G **Perry Moss** (1978-82)
G/F **Dave Caligaris** (1974-78)
F **Reggie Lewis** (1983-87)
F **Francis "Inga" Walsh** (1944-45, 1946-49)

RECORDS	GAME		SEASON		CAREER	
POINTS	41	Jose Juan Barea, vs. Stony Brook (March 5, 2005); Reggie Lewis, vs. Siena (Feb. 19, 1986)	748	Reggie Lewis (1984-85)	2,709	Reggie Lewis (1983-87)
POINTS PER GAME			24.6	Dave Caligaris (1977-78)	22.2	Reggie Lewis (1983-87)
REBOUNDS	24	Fran Ryan, vs. Boston College (Feb. 11, 1964)	364	Dan Callahan (1994-95)	1,115	Mark Halsel (1980-84)
ASSISTS	15	Bill Loughnane, vs. Delaware (Dec. 29, 1977)	252	Andre LaFleur (1983-84)	894	Andre LaFleur (1983-87)

ESPN 250 SAGARIN

NORTHERN ARIZONA

If it's the Big Sky championship, Northern Arizona is probably playing. The Lumberjacks reached seven of 12 title games between 1998 and 2009. The run is reminiscent of NAU in the 1940s, when Wayne See's squad made it to an NAIA final four.

BEST TEAM: 1946-47 NAU became the first team from the state to reach the NAIA final four after wins of four points or fewer over Youngstown State, Houston and Northeast Missouri State. Coach Frank Brickey's 20–7 team, led by See and Vince Cisterna, lost in the semis to runner-up Mankato State, 52-46.

BEST PLAYER: G Wayne See (1941-42, '46-49) Ross Land could shoot, Walt Mannon could score and Ruben Boykin Jr. and Tom DeBerry could do it all, but the Man on NAU's best team was the 23-year-old former Marine who led Northern Arizona to the 1947 NAIB final four. Two years later, See signed with the Waterloo Hawks of the brand new NBA for a whopping $5,200.

BEST COACH: Mike Adras (1999-) Only four coaches have lasted more than five seasons at Northern Arizona, with Herb Gregg staying for 24. Adras made "recruit to shoot" the mantra of his run-and-gun style of play, and it helped him claim two Big Sky regular-season titles (in 2006 and '07), a league tourney title, an NIT berth and an NCAA bid in 2000.

GAME FOR THE AGES: NAU's second NCAA bid came courtesy of a rollicking March 11, 2000, 85-81 OT Big Sky championship victory over Cal State Northridge. Adam Lopez (22 points) and tourney MVP Ross Land (20) led the way for Adras' 20–11 team. Land hit five of nine three-pointers, including an 85-foot prayer just before the first-half buzzer, and the team shot 59% from behind the three-point arc. Land and Dan McClintock (17) each hit late free throws in OT to seal it.

FIERCEST RIVAL: Big Sky foes Idaho State and Northern Arizona are almost even after playing 84 games against each other. The Lumberjacks trail, barely, but they have reason to believe: They won 16 of 27 meetings since 1997.

SEASON REVIEW

SEAS.	W-L	CONF.	COACH
1909-50	*304-251*	*3rd place in 1947 NAIB tourney*	
1950-51	8-19	3-13	Herb Gregg
1951-52	4-23	1-13	Herb Gregg
1952-53	5-18	3-11	Herb Gregg
1953-54	20-7		Herb Gregg
1954-55	19-4		Herb Gregg
1955-56	11-10		Herb Gregg
1956-57	14-10		Herb Gregg
1957-58	16-7		Herb Gregg
1958-59	12-10		Herb Gregg
1959-60	14-9		Herb Gregg
1960-61	9-13		Herb Gregg
1961-62	18-9		Herb Gregg
1962-63	11-10		Herb Gregg
1963-64	12-10		Herb Gregg
1964-65	12-10		Herb Gregg
1965-66	13-12		Herb Gregg
1966-67	15-11		Herb Gregg
1967-68	13-12		Herb Gregg
1968-69	16-9		Herb Gregg
1969-70	17-6		Herb Gregg
1970-71	6-19	4-10	Herb Gregg
1971-72	13-10	8-6	Herb Gregg
1972-73	6-20	3-11	Herb Gregg
1973-74	6-20	3-11	Herb Gregg
1974-75	9-17	5-9	John Birkett
1975-76	14-13	8-6	John Birkett
1976-77	11-15	5-9	John Birkett

SEAS.	W-L	CONF.	SCORING		COACH	RECORD	
1977-78	10-15	4-10	David Henson	19.6	John Birkett	44-60	.423
1978-79	13-14	8-6	Mark Stevens	15.4	Joedy Gardner		
1979-80	14-12	5-9	Mark Stevens	17.2	Joedy Gardner		
1980-81	8-17	2-12	Elliott Jones	18.2	Joedy Gardner	35-43	.449
1981-82	6-20	2-12	Ted Plotts	12.3	Gene Visscher		
1982-83	10-16	3-11	Eric Wade	14.2	Gene Visscher	16-36	.308
1983-84	13-15	5-9	Andy Hurd	13.7	Jay Arnote		
1984-85	17-12	8-6	Andy Hurd	15.4	Jay Arnote		
1985-86	19-10	9-5 ■	Andre Spencer	18.9	Jay Arnote		
1986-87	11-17	5-9	David Duane	16.0	Jay Arnote		
1987-88	10-18	7-9	Mark Anderson	17.2	Jay Arnote	70-72	.493
1988-89	2-25	1-15	Steve Williams	12.7	Pat Rafferty		
1989-90	8-20	3-13	Steve Williams	13.0	Pat Rafferty[a]	10-41	.196
1990-91	4-23	1-15	Corey Rogers	15.0	Harold Merritt		
1991-92	7-20	3-13	Demetreus Robbins	12.2	Harold Merritt		
1992-93	10-16	4-10	Demetreus Robbins	13.0	Harold Merritt		
1993-94	13-13 ⊗	6-8	Jason Word	15.8	Harold Merritt	34-76	.309
1994-95	8-18 ⊗	4-10	John Rondeno	13.5	Ben Howland		
1995-96	6-20 ⊗	3-11	Charles Thomas	11.3	Ben Howland		
1996-97	21-7	14-2 ■	Andrew Mavis	15.0	Ben Howland		
1997-98	21-8	13-3 ●	Andrew Mavis	14.0	Ben Howland		
1998-99	21-8	12-4	Ross Land	13.7	Ben Howland	77-61	.558▼
1999-00	20-11	11-5 ●	Ross Land	16.6	Mike Adras		
2000-01	15-14	8-8	Cory Schwab	15.5	Mike Adras		
2001-02	14-14	7-7	Matt Gebhardt	11.8	Mike Adras		
2002-03	15-13	6-8	Ryan McDade	18.0	Mike Adras		
2003-04	15-14	7-7	Aaron Bond	17.4	Mike Adras		
2004-05	11-17	4-10	Stephen Sir	14.0	Mike Adras		
2005-06	21-11	12-2 ■	Kelly Golob	14.3	Mike Adras		
2006-07	18-12	11-5	Ruben Boykin Jr.	16.4	Mike Adras		
2007-08	21-11	11-5	Kyle Landry	17.5	Mike Adras		
2008-09	8-19	5-11	Cameron Jones	12.7	Mike Adras	158-136	.537

[a] **Pat Rafferty (8-16) and Harold Merritt (0-4) both coached during the 1989-90 season.**

⊗ Records don't reflect games forfeited or vacated. For adjusted records, see p. 521.

▼ Coach's record adjusted to reflect games forfeited or vacated: 79-59, .572. For yearly totals, see p. 521.

● NCAA Tournament appearance ■ NIT appearance

PROFILE

Northern Arizona University, Flagstaff, AZ
Founded: 1899
Enrollment: 21,352 (15,569 undergraduate)
Colors: Blue, gold and sage
Nickname: Lumberjacks
Current arena: J. Lawrence Walkup Skydome, opened in 1977 (7,000)
First game: 1909
All-time record: 1,038-1,064 (.494)
Total weeks in AP Top 20/25: 0

Current conference: Big Sky (1970-)
Conference titles:
Big Sky: 5 (1986, '97, '98, 2006, '07 [tie])
Conference tournament titles:
Big Sky: 2 (1998, 2000)
NCAA Tournament appearances: 2
NIT appearances: 3

TOP 5

G **Tom DeBerry** (1974-76)
G **Walt Mannon** (1968-72)
G **Wayne See** (1941-42, '46-49)
F **Ruben Boykin, Jr.** (2003-07)
F **Andre Spencer** (1984-86)

RECORDS

RECORDS	GAME		SEASON		CAREER	
POINTS	46	Frank Turley, vs. West New Mexico (1955-56)	561	Kyle Landry (2007-08)	1,550	Kelly Golob (2002-06)
POINTS PER GAME			20.4	Bill Lewis (1955-56)	19.8	Walter Mannon (1968-72)
REBOUNDS	25	Milt Jacobs, vs. Weber State (1965-66); Don Buttrum, vs. Santa Fe (1961-62); Carlos Moore, vs. Grand Canyon (1959-60)	376	Don Buttrum (1961-62)	1,044	Don Buttrum (1959-63)
ASSISTS	16	Tom DeBerry, vs. Portland State (1975-76)	195	Josh Wilson (2005-06)	636	Josh Wilson (2005-09)

ESPN 274 SAGARIN

NORTHERN COLORADO

Anyone wondering whether Northern Colorado was ready for its move to D1 in 2007-08 got a definitive answer when longtime rival Colorado State visited Greeley on Dec. 1, 2007—and the Bears sent them home losers. Fans of coach George Sage's great mid-1960s teams and Mike Higgins' late-1980s teams may have new reasons, and seasons, to celebrate.

BEST TEAM: 1988-89 Coach Ron Brillhart's Bears set a school record for wins (24-6), won the North Central Conference and reached the D2 regional title game—the school's first postseason trip since 1966. Higgins (25.0 ppg, 11.2 rpg), 1,000-point scorer Toby Moser and guard Scott Watson led the Bears.

BEST PLAYER: C MIKE HIGGINS (1985-89) He owns more than a dozen school records, including career points (2,112), rebounds (959) and blocks (302). A 1989 D2 All-America, Higgins was chosen all-conference three times and is the only Bears alum to play in the NBA (Lakers, Nuggets, Kings).

BEST COACH: GEORGE SAGE (1963-68) He guided Northern Colorado to its best era, during which the Bears went 95–36, won four straight league titles and reached three straight College Division tourneys (1964-66)—UNC's first postseason games. Among the top players he coached: Henry Clausen, Dennis Colson, Daryl Brumley and Don Meyer.

GAME FOR THE AGES: The 1988-89 team earned the right to host the NCAA D2 North Central Regional, and on March 17, Bears fans packed the house for the school's only tourney win. The second-largest Butler-Hancock Pavilion crowd to date (4,013) saw Northern Colorado break a halftime tie and pull away to a 92-70 win over Alaska-Fairbanks, behind Higgins' 26 points.

FIERCEST RIVAL: For years Northern was a doormat to its former Rocky Mountain Conference foe Colorado State, winner in 66 of their 103 meetings. When CSU came to town on Dec. 1, 2007, Northern had won only once since 1953 (in 1986). That made the Bears' 72-59 victory all the more stunning.

SEASON REVIEW

SEAS.	W-L	CONF.	COACH	SEAS.	W-L	CONF.	COACH
1901-46	*276-242*		*Coach George Cooper, 87-47 (9 yrs)*	1959-60	14-11		John W. Bunn
1946-47	11-8		L.C. "Pete" Butler	1960-61	8-16		John W. Bunn
1947-48	10-13		L.C. "Pete" Butler	1961-62	10-16		John W. Bunn
1948-49	13-4		L.C. "Pete" Butler	1962-63	10-16		John W. Bunn
1949-50	13-8		L.C. "Pete" Butler	1963-64	18-8		George Sage
1950-51	11-11		L.C. "Pete" Butler	1964-65	19-8		George Sage
1951-52	10-12		L.C. "Pete" Butler	1965-66	21-6		George Sage
1952-53	11-9		L.C. "Pete" Butler	1966-67	19-7		George Sage
1953-54	9-8		L.C. "Pete" Butler	1967-68	18-7		George Sage
1954-55	8-13		L.C. "Pete" Butler	1968-69	11-13		Thurm Wright
1955-56	10-8		L.C. "Pete" Butler	1969-70	9-15		Thurm Wright
1956-57	11-10		John W. Bunn	1970-71	12-12		Thurm Wright
1957-58	6-15		John W. Bunn	1971-72	4-19		Thurm Wright
1958-59	14-10		John W. Bunn	1972-73	12-12		Thurm Wright

SEAS.	W-L	CONF.	SCORING		COACH	RECORD	
1973-74	15-9				Thurm Wright		
1974-75	14-12				Thurm Wright		
1975-76	11-13				Thurm Wright		
1976-77	10-15				Thurm Wright		
1977-78	11-15				Thurm Wright		
1978-79	7-17				Thurm Wright		
1979-80	11-15				Thurm Wright		
1980-81	6-18				Thurm Wright		
1981-82	13-15				Thurm Wright		
1982-83	10-16				Thurm Wright	156-216	.419
1983-84	6-20				Ron Brillhart		
1984-85	16-12				Ron Brillhart		
1985-86	12-16				Ron Brillhart		
1986-87	18-10				Ron Brillhart		
1987-88	17-11		Mike Higgins	20.3	Ron Brillhart		
1988-89	24-6		Mike Higgins	25.0	Ron Brillhart		
1989-90	10-18				Ron Brillhart		
1990-91	3-24				Ron Brillhart		
1991-92	15-15				Ron Brillhart	121-132	.478
1992-93	12-15				Ken Smith		
1993-94	11-18				Ken Smith		
1994-95	10-16				Ken Smith		
1995-96	11-16				Ken Smith		
1996-97	8-18				Ken Smith		
1997-98	16-11		Antwine Williams	21.9	Ken Smith		
1998-99	10-17		Mickael Allen	14.9	Ken Smith	78-111	.413
1999-00	9-18		Pierre Elize	13.4	Craig Rasmuson		
2000-01	10-16		Michael Morse	12.5	Craig Rasmuson		
2001-02	14-13		Aaron Austin	15.7	Craig Rasmuson		
2002-03	11-15		Sean Nolen	18.1	Craig Rasmuson		
2003-04	6-22		Vincent Jackson	13.6	Craig Rasmuson		
2004-05	8-21		Kirk Archibeque	12.2	Craig Rasmuson		
2005-06	5-24		Sean Taibi	15.3	Craig Rasmuson	63-129	.328
2006-07	4-24	2-14	Sean Taibi	14.6	Tad Boyle		
2007-08	13-16	6-10	Jabril Banks	13.2	Tad Boyle		
2008-09	14-18	8-8	J. Banks, W. Figures	12.1	Tad Boyle	31-58	.348

PROFILE

University of Northern Colorado, Greeley, CO
Founded: 1889
Enrollment: 13,035 (11,509 undergraduate)
Colors: Navy blue and Vegas gold
Nickname: Bears
Current arena: Butler-Hancock Sports Pavilion, opened in 1975 (2,734)
Previous: Gunter Hall, 1926-75 (N/A)
First game: 1901
All-time record: 999-1,112 (.473)
Total weeks in AP Top 20/25: 0

Current conference: Big Sky (2007-)
Conference titles: 0
Conference tournament titles: 0
NCAA Tournament appearances: 0
NIT appearances: 0

TOP 5

G **Chuck Knostman** (1981-85)
G/F **Theo Holland** (1957-61)
F **Henry Clausen** (1966-69)
F **John McFarland** (1994-97)
C **Mike Higgins** (1985-89)

RECORDS	GAME		SEASON		CAREER	
POINTS	46	Mike Higgins, vs. Southern Colorado (Dec. 3, 1988)	751	Mike Higgins (1988-89)	2,112	Mike Higgins (1985-89)
POINTS PER GAME			25.0	Mike Higgins (1988-89)	20.2	Antwine Williams (1996-98)
REBOUNDS	24	Daryl Brumley, vs. Adams State (1966-67); Robert Skinner, vs. Southern Colorado (1978-79)	335	Mike Higgins (1988-89)	959	Mike Higgins (1985-89)
ASSISTS	14	Sean Nolen, vs. Kendall College (Nov. 28, 2003)	198	Troy Graefe (1984-85)	427	Sean Nolen (2000-05)

ESPN 171 SAGARIN

NORTHERN ILLINOIS

What do Bob Knight, Eddie Sutton and Ray Meyer have in common? Their teams were all eaten alive at the Chick Evans Field House, a.k.a. the Doghouse. The iconic stone structure was replaced by the Convocation Center in 2002, but fans still associate the best of Huskies hoops with the old court.

BEST TEAM: 1971-72 The Huskies started 12–1, including an upset of Knight's No. 5-ranked Hoosiers, to rise to No. 20 in a mid-January AP poll—their first national ranking. Tom Jorgensen's high-scoring lineup, led by frontcourt star Jim Bradley (22.9 ppg, 15.9 rpg) set a school record for wins (now second-best).

BEST PLAYER: F/C Jim Bradley (1971-73) With apologies to Kenny Battle, whose above-the-rim theatrics spawned Huskies fans' famed Dunk-O-Meter in the mid-1980s, Bradley takes this crown. In addition to patrolling the paint, the 6'10" big man had a guard's ball-handling and open-court ability. His two triple-doubles and 46 double-doubles say it all. If his college career wasn't cut one season short by academic issues, Bradley would probably own every Huskies record in the book.

BEST COACH: Tom Jorgensen (1966-73) The former Michigan assistant moved Northern Illinois into D1—and right into the Top 20 in 1972. Fans wore red-and-black "We Love Jorgy" buttons while watching his aggressive, fast-breaking teams.

GAME FOR THE AGES: On Jan. 4, 1972, in its fifth D1 year, NIU rocked Knight's visiting Hoosiers, 85-71—a game that was never in doubt. The Huskies led by 43-33 at halftime and 63-42 with 11 minutes left. Bradley (24 points, 20 rebounds) was unstoppable.

FIERCEST RIVAL: Since its D1 move, NIU has switched conference affiliations three times. Illinois State (two games since 1983) and Southern Illinois (twice since 1997) used to be big showdowns. Unfortunately, the MAC offers no in-state rival, so regional heavyweight DePaul (which owns a 22–6 series lead) has to do.

SEASON REVIEW

SEAS.	W-L	CONF.	COACH	SEAS.	W-L	CONF.	COACH
1901-48	*429-277*	*Best season, 17-1 in 1926-27*		1961-62	11-10		William Healey
1948-49	10-11		George Fekete	1962-63	15-8		William Healey
1949-50	4-17		Gilbert Wiilson	1963-64	11-11		Ev Cochrane
1950-51	12-7		Gilman Hertz	1964-65	12-10		Ev Cochrane
1951-52	5-16		Gilman Hertz	1965-66	10-13		Ev Cochrane
1952-53	13-7		Gilman Hertz	1966-67	8-12		Tom Jorgensen
1953-54	5-14		Gilman Hertz	1967-68	10-14		Tom Jorgensen
1954-55	9-11		William Healey	1968-69	13-11		Tom Jorgensen
1955-56	5-14		William Healey	1969-70	13-12		Tom Jorgensen
1956-57	7-13		William Healey	1970-71	13-10		Tom Jorgensen
1957-58	10-12		William Healey	1971-72	21-4		Tom Jorgensen
1958-59	11-11		William Healey	1972-73	17-8		Tom Jorgensen
1959-60	14-7		William Healey	1973-74	8-17		Emory Luck
1960-61	14-8		William Healey	1974-75	8-15		Emory Luck

SEAS.	W-L	CONF.	SCORING		COACH	RECORD	
1975-76	5-21	2-14	Matt Hicks	25.0	Emory Luck	21-53	.284
1976-77	13-14	10-6	Matt Hicks	25.3	John McDougal		
1977-78	11-16	9-7	Paul Dawkins	20.6	John McDougal		
1978-79	14-13	8-8	Paul Dawkins	26.7	John McDougal		
1979-80	16-13	9-7	Allen Rayhorn	19.9	John McDougal		
1980-81	17-12	10-6	Allen Rayhorn	18.8	John McDougal		
1981-82	16-14	9-7 ●	Allen Rayhorn	15.3	John McDougal		
1982-83	11-16	8-10	Tim Dillon	18.9	John McDougal		
1983-84	12-15	9-9	Tim Dillon	21.2	John McDougal		
1984-85	11-16	7-11	Kenny Battle	20.1	John McDougal		
1985-86	15-12	10-8	Kenny Battle	19.6	John McDougal	136-141	.491
1986-87	9-19		Rodney Davis	14.5	Jim Rosborough		
1987-88	8-20		Rodney Davis	18.3	Jim Rosborough		
1988-89	11-17		Stacy Arrington	18.1	Jim Rosborough	28-56	.333
1989-90	17-11		Donnell Thomas	17.8	Jim Molinari		
1990-91	25-6	14-2 ●	Donnell Thomas	17.0	Jim Molinari	42-17	.712
1991-92	11-17	7-9	Brian Molis	16.3	Brian Hammel		
1992-93	15-12	10-6	Mike Lipniski	13.9	Brian Hammel		
1993-94	10-17	7-11	Randy Tucker	16.0	Brian Hammel		
1994-95	19-10	7-8	Jamal Robinson	16.0	Brian Hammel		
1995-96	20-10	10-6 ●	T.J. Lux	15.2	Brian Hammel		
1996-97	12-15	6-10	Chris Coleman	17.3	Brian Hammel		
1997-98	10-16	6-12	T.J. Lux	18.6	Brian Hammel		
1998-99	6-20	2-16	Mike Brown	10.9	Brian Hammel		
1999-2000	13-15	7-11	T.J. Lux	19.9	Brian Hammel		
2000-01	5-23	4-14	Leon Rodgers	16.6	Brian Hammel[a]	117-138	.459
2001-02	12-16	8-10	Leon Rodgers	21.3	Rob Judson		
2002-03	17-14	11-7	P.J. Smith	14.7	Rob Judson		
2003-04	10-20	5-13	P.J. Smith	14.5	Rob Judson		
2004-05	11-17	7-11	Mike McKinney	12.6	Rob Judson		
2005-06	17-11	12-6	Todd Peterson	12.1	Rob Judson		
2006-07	7-23	4-12	Mike McKinney	12.6	Rob Judson	74-101	.423
2007-08	6-22	3-12	Darion Anderson	12.2	Ricardo Patton		
2008-09	10-20	5-11	Darion Anderson	16.9	Ricardo Patton	16-42	.276

[a] Brian Hammel (1-6) and Andrew Greer (4-17) both coached during the 2000-2001 season.

● NCAA Tournament appearance

PROFILE

Northern Illinois University, DeKalb, IL
Founded: 1895
Enrollment: 24,397 (18,431 undergraduate)
Colors: Cardinal and black
Nickname: Huskies
Current arena: Convocation Center, opened in 2002 (10,000)
Previous: Chick Evans Field House, a.k.a. the Doghouse, 1956-2002 (6,044); Still Gymnasium, 1928-56 (1,500)
First game: Feb. 9, 1901
All-time record: 1,140-1,113 (.506)
Total weeks in AP Top 20/25: 2

Current conference: Mid-American (1975-86, '97-)
Conference titles:
MAC: 1 (1981 [tie])
Mid-Continent: 1 (1991)
Conference tournament titles:
MAC: 1 (1982)
Midwestern Collegiate: 1 (1996)
NCAA Tournament appearances: 3
NIT appearances: 0

TOP 5

G **Billy Harris** (1970-73)
G **Donald Whiteside** (1987-91)
F **Kenny Battle** (1984-86)
F **Matt Hicks** (1974-77)
F/C **Jim Bradley** (1971-73)

RECORDS

	GAME		SEASON		CAREER	
POINTS	52	Larry Wyllie, vs. Eastern Michigan (Feb. 15, 1958)	695	Paul Dawkins (1978-79)	1,996	T.J. Lux (1995-2000)
POINTS PER GAME			26.7	Paul Dawkins (1978-79)	23.1	Jim Bradley (1971-73)
REBOUNDS	32	Abe Booker, vs. Eastern Michigan (Dec. 17, 1959)	426	Jim Bradley (1972-73)	1,110	T.J. Lux (1995-2000)
ASSISTS	13	Ray Clark, vs. Bowling Green (Dec. 9, 1978)	163	Jay Bryant (1979-80)	367	Jay Bryant (1976-80)

ESPN 195 SAGARIN

NORTHERN IOWA

Seven of the Panthers' top 10 all-time scorers come from the state of Iowa, a reflection of the school's regional recruiting focus. But that's not a bad thing in such a hoops-crazy place. UNI dominated College Division ball in the 1960s, surprised much bigger opponents in the 1990s and in the 2000s began vying for the unofficial crown as best team in Iowa.

BEST TEAM: 2005-06 What the Panthers lacked in size, they more than made up for in offensive precision, running coach Greg McDermott's half-court sets to near-perfection. Although Georgetown's brawn proved too much to overcome in the first round of the NCAA Tournament, Northern Iowa's 23 wins (including upsets of Iowa and LSU) tied a school record.

BEST PLAYER: F/C Pete Spoden (1959-62, '63-64) Just 6'6", he was a strong finisher nevertheless, averaging 17.7 points and 15.6 rebounds for his career. A fourth-round pick of the Baltimore Bullets in 1964, Spoden was the first of two Panthers drafted by NBA teams (the second was Bill McCoy in 1973).

BEST COACH: Norm Stewart (1961-67) Before he came to be known as Sit Down Norm! at Missouri, he was Norman Stewart, whiz-kid coach at Northern Iowa. Here he honed a wide-open offensive system that delivered two conference titles and a pair of wins over Iowa State.

GREATEST GAME: In 1990, the Panthers reached their first NCAA Tournament. And their first-round opponent? Missouri, with Norm Stewart at the helm. No. 14-seed UNI stunned the No. 3-seed Tigers, 74-71, on Maurice Newby's three-pointer with one tick left.

FIERCEST RIVAL: Panthers fans always get jacked when Iowa State or Iowa visits: Nine of the top 10 attendance figures at the old UNI-Dome have come against these two. Of course, UNI victories have been rare in both series, making the school's other in-state rivalry, against Drake, more of a crowd pleaser. They first played in 1907, and after a three-decade-plus lull, now cross paths twice a season as Missouri Valley members. The Panthers lead the series, 30–23.

SEASON REVIEW

SEAS.	W-L	CONF.	COACH	SEAS.	W-L	CONF.	COACH
1900-46	*274-215*	*13-2 in 1929-30 under A. Dickinson*		1959-60	15-8	8-4	James H. Witham
1946-47	6-14	3-4	O.M. "Hon" Nordly	1960-61	16-5	9-3	James H. Witham
1947-48	14-6	9-1	O.M. "Hon" Nordly	1961-62	19-5	8-4	Norman Stewart
1948-49	16-6	8-2	O.M. "Hon" Nordly	1962-63	15-8	8-4	Norman Stewart
1949-50	16-5	9-3	O.M. "Hon" Nordly	1963-64	23-4	11-1	Norman Stewart
1950-51	14-9	9-3	O.M. "Hon" Nordly	1964-65	16-7	8-4	Norman Stewart
1951-52	14-10	6-6	O.M. "Hon" Nordly	1965-66	13-7	9-3	Norman Stewart
1952-53	14-11	10-2	O.M. "Hon" Nordly	1966-67	11-11	6-6	Norman Stewart
1953-54	6-15	6-6	O.M. "Hon" Nordly	1967-68	15-7	8-4	Zeke Hogeland
1954-55	11-11	7-5	Stanley Hall	1968-69	15-9	9-3	Zeke Hogeland
1955-56	8-11	5-7	Stanley Hall	1969-70	13-12	8-6	Zeke Hogeland
1956-57	12-10	5-7	James H. Witham	1970-71	6-20	4-10	Zeke Hogeland
1957-58	9-14	3-9	James H. Witham	1971-72	10-13	8-6	Zeke Hogeland
1958-59	11-12	6-6	James H. Witham	1972-73	11-13	6-8	Zeke Hogeland

SEAS.	W-L	CONF.		SCORING		COACH	RECORD	
1973-74	4-22	1-13		Joe Ferguson	12.4	James Berry		
1974-75	6-20	4-10		Bill Runchey	12.4	James Berry		
1975-76	9-17	6-8		Mark Enright	16.4	James Berry		
1976-77	9-18	3-11		Ron Lemons	15.8	James Berry		
1977-78	15-12	9-5		Ron Lemons	16.1	James Berry		
1978-79	18-11			Ron Lemons	16.3	James Berry		
1979-80	12-13			Rod Underwood	15.0	James Berry		
1980-81	8-19			Rod Underwood	13.4	James Berry		
1981-82	12-15			Ray Storck	13.4	James Berry		
1982-83	13-18	6-5		Randy Kraayenbrink	12.4	James Berry		
1983-84	18-10	10-4		Randy Kraayenbrink	18.5	James Berry		
1984-85	12-16	6-8		Randy Kraayenbrink	21.0	James Berry		
1985-86	8-19	3-11		Scott Plondke	16.5	James Berry	144-210	.407
1986-87	13-15	7-7		Greg McDermott	13.8	Eldon Miller		
1987-88	10-18	4-10		James Parker	14.5	Eldon Miller		
1988-89	19-9	8-4		Jason Reese	22.3	Eldon Miller		
1989-90	23-9	6-6	●	Jason Reese	19.9	Eldon Miller		
1990-91	13-19	8-8		Troy Muilenburg	13.4	Eldon Miller		
1991-92	10-18	6-12		Dale Turner	13.8	Eldon Miller		
1992-93	12-15	8-10		Randy Blocker	18.9	Eldon Miller		
1993-94	16-13	10-8		Randy Blocker	23.0	Eldon Miller		
1994-95	8-20	4-14		Jason Daisy	14.7	Eldon Miller		
1995-96	14-13	8-10		Jason Daisy	22.3	Eldon Miller		
1996-97	16-12	11-7		Jason Daisy	21.2	Eldon Miller		
1997-98	10-17	4-14		Tony Brus	15.4	Eldon Miller	164-178	.480
1998-99	9-18	6-12		Sean Stackhouse	16.4	Sam Weaver		
1999-2000	14-15	7-11		Robbie Sieverding	16.3	Sam Weaver		
2000-01	7-24	3-15		Joe Breakenridge	13.3	Sam Weaver	30-57	.345
2001-02	14-15	8-10		Robbie Sieverding	17.1	Greg McDermott		
2002-03	11-17	7-11		David Gruber	13.3	Greg McDermott		
2003-04	21-10	12-6	●	Ben Jacobson	14.0	Greg McDermott		
2004-05	21-11	11-7	●	Ben Jacobson	17.9	Greg McDermott		
2005-06	23-10	11-7	●	Ben Jacobson	14.2	Greg McDermott	90-63	.588
2006-07	18-13	9-9		Eric Coleman	13.1	Ben Jacobson		
2007-08	18-14	9-9		Eric Coleman	12.3	Ben Jacobson		
2008-09	23-11	14-4	●	Adam Koch	12.1	Ben Jacobson	59-38	.608

● **NCAA Tournament appearance**

PROFILE

University of Northern Iowa, Cedar Falls, IA
Founded: 1876, as the Iowa State Normal School
Enrollment: 12,908 (11,047 undergraduate)
Colors: Purple and old gold
Nickname: Panthers
Current arena: McLeod Center, opened in 2006 (7,018)
Previous: UNI-Dome 1975-2006 (10,200); West Gymnasium 1925-75 (2,200); The Gymnasium (N/A) 1905-25
First game: 1900
All-time record: 1,110-1,024 (.520)

Total weeks in AP Top 20/25: 3
Current conference: Missouri Valley (1991-)
Conference titles:
Mid-Continent: 1 (1990)
MVC: 1 (2009 [tie])
Conference tournament titles:
MVC: 2 (2004, '09)
NCAA Tournament appearances: 5
NIT appearances: 0

TOP 5

G **Ben Jacobson** (2002-06)
G **Randy Kraayenbrink** (1982-86)
F **Randy Blocker** (1992-94)
F/C **Pete Spoden** (1959-62, '63-64)
C **Jason Reese** (1986-90)

RECORDS

	GAME		SEASON		CAREER	
POINTS	40	Cam Johnson, vs. Drake (Feb. 12, 1994); Jerry Waugh, vs. North Dakota (Feb. 27, 1968)	645	Randy Blocker (1993-94)	2,033	Jason Reese (1986-90)
POINTS PER GAME			23.0	Randy Blocker (1993-94)	21.0	Randy Blocker (1992-94)
REBOUNDS	34	Pete Spoden, vs. Winona State (Feb. 22, 1961)	418	Jim Jackson (1958-59)	1,097	Jim Jackson (1958-61)
ASSISTS	16	Jay Imhoff, vs. Centenary (Jan. 5, 1980)	179	Brooks McKowen (2006-07)	520	Dale Turner (1988-92)

ESPN 180 SAGARIN

NORTH TEXAS

After every game at the North Texas Coliseum (a.k.a. the Super Pit), Mean Green fans curl their thumb, index and middle finger forward to make the Eagle Talon sign while the alma mater plays. It may be the most famous fan ritual from a school that has memorable traditions both winning (two NCAA Tournament bids) and losing (12 seasons of five or fewer wins since 1940).

BEST TEAM: 2006-07 They lost to No. 2-seed Memphis in the first round of the NCAA Tournament, 73-58, but not before proving their moxie. The game was the culmination of a record-breaking season in which North Texas won the Sun Belt tournament as the No. 5 seed and set a school record for wins with a 23–11 finish.

BEST PLAYER: G CHRIS DAVIS (1999-2003) He could do it all—and sometimes had to, because his 1999-2000 team won just seven games. As a junior, he became the first Mean Green to lead his team in points, assists and rebounds in the same season, and finished ninth in the NCAA in scoring (22.5 ppg). If he hadn't fallen ill late in his senior season, Davis almost certainly would have finished as the school's all-time leading scorer.

BEST COACH: BILL BLAKELEY (1975-83) He inherited a team that won just six games the year before and led it to three straight 20-win seasons. During his first season, the Mean Green even cracked the AP Top 20, but didn't make the NCAA or NIT field primarily because they played as an independent.

GAME FOR THE AGES: With 2:42 left in the Sun Belt title game on March 6, 2007, 26-year-old Iraq war vet Rich Young threw down a one-handed jam, giving the Mean Green a 74-70 lead over Arkansas State and igniting the Cajun Dome crowd. Seven free throws later, North Texas players were dancing as 83-75 victors.

FIERCEST RIVAL: It was fitting that North Texas' road to the 2007 Sun Belt tourney title ran through Louisiana-Monroe, which the Mean Green beat in the quarterfinals, 77-71, in OT. In their first meeting, on Dec. 6, 1955, the Mean Green also won in OT, 88-85. Yet in the five decades since, the Warhawks lead the series 24–17.

SEASON REVIEW

SEAS.	W-L	CONF.	COACH	SEAS.	W-L	CONF.	COACH
1914-47	*293-221*	*13 straight winning seasons 1917-30*		**1960-61**	2-22	1-11	Charles Johnson
1947-48	15-10		Pete Shands	**1961-62**	3-23	0-12	Charles Johnson
1948-49	10-11		Pete Shands	**1962-63**	10-14	4-8	Charles Johnson
1949-50	10-16		Pete Shands	**1963-64**	7-17	1-11	Charles Johnson
1950-51	12-12		Pete Shands	**1964-65**	7-19	1-13	Charles Johnson
1951-52	15-8		Pete Shands	**1965-66**	5-20	0-14	Dan Spika
1952-53	18-4		Pete Shands	**1966-67**	12-13	4-10	Dan Spika
1953-54	19-9		Pete Shands	**1967-68**	8-18	3-13	Dan Spika
1954-55	8-16		Pete Shands	**1968-69**	15-10	8-8	Dan Spika
1955-56	9-13		Pete Shands	**1969-70**	18-8	11-5	Dan Spika
1956-57	3-20		Pete Shands	**1970-71**	10-15	4-10	Harry Miller
1957-58	3-18	1-13	Pete Shands	**1971-72**	8-18	2-12	Gene Robbins
1958-59	6-18	2-12	Pete Shands	**1972-73**	9-16	4-10	Gene Robbins
1959-60	7-19	1-13	Charles Johnson	**1973-74**	13-13	4-8	Gene Robbins

SEAS.	W-L	CONF.		SCORING		COACH	RECORD	
1974-75	6-20	3-11		Terry Bailey	15.6	Gene Robbins	36-67	.350
1975-76	22-4			Terry Bailey	19.3	Bill Blakeley		
1976-77	21-6			Fred Mitchell	18.4	Bill Blakeley		
1977-78	22-6			Fred Mitchell	16.8	Bill Blakeley		
1978-79	11-16			Jon Manning	25.9	Bill Blakeley		
1979-80	13-14			Kenneth Lyons	17.7	Bill Blakeley		
1980-81	15-12			Kenneth Lyons	21.7	Bill Blakeley		
1981-82	15-12			Kenneth Lyons	21.7	Bill Blakeley		
1982-83	15-15	5-7		Kenneth Lyons	24.3	Bill Blakeley	134-85	.607
1983-84	9-19	3-9		Javan Dupree	12.3	Tommy Newman		
1984-85	5-23	1-11		Vincent Greene	14.4	Tommy Newman		
1985-86	10-18	4-8		Keenan DeBose	14.0	Tommy Newman	24-60	.286
1986-87	11-17	4-6		Tony Worrell	20.0	Jimmy Gales		
1987-88	17-13	12-2	●	Tony Worrell	20.2	Jimmy Gales		
1988-89	14-15	10-4		Deon Hunter	17.9	Jimmy Gales		
1989-90	5-25	3-11		Ronnie Morgan	15.7	Jimmy Gales		
1990-91	17-13	11-3		Donnell Hayden	22.4	Jimmy Gales		
1991-92	15-14	12-6		Jesse Ratliff	19.3	Jimmy Gales		
1992-93	5-21	5-13		Jesse Ratliff	23.1	Jimmy Gales	84-118	.416
1993-94	14-15	9-9		Jesse Ratliff	19.7	Tim Jankovich		
1994-95	14-13	9-9		Adam Smith	19.6	Tim Jankovich		
1995-96	15-13	12-6		Chris Smith	13.3	Tim Jankovich		
1996-97	10-16	5-11		Chad Elstun	12.9	Tim Jankovich	53-57	.482
1997-98	5-21	4-12		David Miller	12.3	Vic Trilli		
1998-99	4-22	4-12		Deginald Erskin	12.3	Vic Trilli		
1999-2000	7-20	5-11		Chris Davis	21.7	Vic Trilli		
2000-01	4-24	1-15		Chris Davis	18.0	Vic Trilli	20-87	.187
2001-02	15-14	8-7		Chris Davis	22.5	Johnny Jones		
2002-03	7-21	2-13		Chris Davis	19.0	Johnny Jones		
2003-04	13-15	8-7		Leonard Hopkins	14.0	Johnny Jones		
2004-05	14-14	6-9		Leonard Hopkins	18.1	Johnny Jones		
2005-06	14-14	6-9		Kendrick Davis	16.8	Johnny Jones		
2006-07	23-11	10-8	●	Calvin Watson	15.7	Johnny Jones		
2007-08	20-11	10-8		Josh White	13.9	Johnny Jones		
2008-09	20-12	11-7		Eric Tramiel	12.0	Johnny Jones	126-112	.529

● NCAA Tournament appearance

PROFILE

University of North Texas, Denton, TX
Founded: 1890
Enrollment: 34,153 (27,242 undergraduate)
Colors: Green and white
Nickname: Mean Green
Current arena: North Texas Coliseum, a.k.a. the Super Pit, opened in 1973 (10,032)
Previous: North Texas Men's Gym, a.k.a. the Snake Pit, 1950-73 (5,000); Harriss Gym, 1923-50 (N/A)
First game: 1914
All-time record: 1,002-1,160 (.463)
Total weeks in AP Top 20/25: 2

Current conference: Sun Belt (2000-)
Conference titles:
Southland: 2 (1988, '89)
Conference tournament titles:
Southland: 1 (1988)
Sun Belt: 1 (2007)
NCAA Tournament appearances: 2
NIT appearances: 0

TOP 5

G **Chris Davis** (1999-2003)
G **Pat Hicks** (1979-83)
F **Kenneth Lyons** (1979-83)
F **Jim Mudd** (1958-60)
C **Ken Williams** (1974-78)

RECORDS

RECORDS	GAME		SEASON		CAREER	
POINTS	47	Kenneth Lyons, vs. Louisiana Tech (March 10, 1983)	728	Kenneth Lyons (1982-83)	2,291	Kenneth Lyons (1979-83)
POINTS PER GAME			25.9	Jon Manning (1978-79)	23.3	Jim Mudd (1958-60)
REBOUNDS	29	Ken Williams, vs. Lamar (Jan. 18, 1978)	411	Ken Williams (1977-78)	1,095	Ken Williams (1974-78)
ASSISTS	19	Pat Hicks, vs. Loyola Marymount (Dec. 22, 1981)	208	Walter Johnson (1976-77)	526	Pat Hicks (1979-83)

ESPN 77 SAGARIN

NORTHWESTERN

If Wildcats fans have heard it once, they've heard it a thousand times: Northwestern is the only BCS conference school never to make the NCAA Tournament. Winning seasons? Nearly as rare as postseason bids. But as any longtime diehard will tell you, there was actually a time when the Wildcats were the kings of the Big Ten.

BEST TEAM: 1930-31 With the offense flowing through 6'2" All-America forward Joseph Reiff, Northwestern dominated the Big Ten, beating Michigan four times while losing just once, to Illinois at home. The Helms Foundation retroactively named the Wildcats champions for the season. Reiff led the conference in scoring with 10.3 ppg in Big Ten play.

BEST PLAYER: C Evan Eschmeyer (1995-99) Reiff clearly stands as the greatest Wildcat of the pre-Tournament era, ranking first in the Big Ten in scoring in 1930-31 and '32-33 while guiding his team to at least a share of the conference title both seasons. But Eschmeyer gets the nod for the modern era. With an arsenal of classic post moves, the big man shot 59.5% for his career and averaged 16.1 points. Just as remarkable, he led the Wildcats to the brink of an NCAA Tournament bid as a senior. He played four years in the NBA with the Nets and Mavericks.

BEST COACH: Arthur "Dutch" Lonborg (1927-50) As a standout guard at Kansas, Dutch learned the game from one of the best: Phog Allen. After graduating, Lonborg considered a career in law but decided to give coaching a try first. He never looked back. Using a set offense that typically flowed through the pivot, his Wildcats won or shared two Big Ten titles. Just as notable, Lonborg was one of the five founders of the NCAA Tournament, the first of which was hosted by Northwestern in 1939.

GAME FOR THE AGES: It looked like business as usual on Jan. 11, 1988, when Bob Knight and defending national champion Indiana led host Northwestern by 10 points in the second half. But Wildcats guard Jeff Grose, a former Indiana Mr. Basketball whom the Hoosiers passed over, helped his team claw back, scoring 18 points. Northwestern finished off the 66-64 upset by hitting all 21 of its second-half free throws, including four from Grose in the final 28 seconds. Afterward, delirious Wildcats fans cut down the nets at Welsh-Ryan Arena.

HEARTBREAKER: On March 5, 1999, the 15–12 Wildcats still held out hope for the team's first NCAA bid, entering their quarterfinal Big Ten tournament game against top-seed Michigan State. Despite losing the battle of the boards (34-23) against the rugged Spartans, the Wildcats took a 59-56 lead with 3:06 left, thanks to Eschmeyer's inside scoring (30 points). But Mateen Cleaves hit a short jumper over Eschmeyer with :37 on the clock to give the Spartans a 61-59 lead, and Steve Lepore's last-second three bounced off the rim. Northwestern went to the NIT and the Spartans went to the Final Four.

FIERCEST RIVAL: It's infuriating enough that Northwestern has lost nearly 80% of its games to in-state Big Ten rival Illinois (the Illini lead overall, 126–34). The salt in the wound is that many of those losses have come at Welsh-Ryan Arena, where there's often as much orange in the crowd as there is purple.

As any longtime diehard will tell you, there was actually a time when the Wildcats were the kings of the Big Ten.

FANFARE AND HOOPLA: The best talent on the Welsh-Ryan Arena floor is often the Northwestern varsity dance team, known as the Ladycats. Performing for all home football and basketball games, they qualified for the Universal Dance Association College National Dance Team Championship for the first time in 2007 and finished 15th in the country.

FAN FAVORITE: G Michael Jenkins (2001-02, '03-06) The 5'9" walk-on guard earned his way to a scholarship, thanks to clutch plays like his game-winning three-pointer at the buzzer for a dramatic 75-74 OT victory against Iowa on Jan. 26, 2005.

PROFILE

Northwestern University, Evanston, IL
Founded: 1851
Enrollment: 15,631 (8,100 undergraduate)
Colors: Purple and white
Nickname: Wildcats
Current arena: Welsh-Ryan Arena, opened as McGaw Memorial Hall in 1952 (8,117)
Previous: Evanston High School, 1940-52 (N/A); Chicago Stadium, 1941-50 (N/A); Patten Gymnasium, 1910-40 (5,000)
First game: Feb. 24, 1905

All-time record: 913-1,365-1 (.401)
Total weeks in AP Top 20/25: 11
Current conference: Big Ten (1906-)
Conference titles:
Big Ten: 2 (1931, '33 [tie])
Conference tournament titles: 0
NCAA Tournament appearances: 0
NIT appearances: 4

CONSENSUS ALL-AMERICAS

1931, '33	**Joseph Reiff**, F/C
1944	**Otto Graham**, F
1946	**Max Morris**, F

TOP 5

G	**Jim Burns** (1964-67)
G	**Billy McKinney** (1973-77)
F	**Max Morris** (1944-46)
F/C	**Joseph Reiff** (1930-33)
C	**Evan Eschmeyer** (1995-99)

RECORDS	GAME		SEASON		CAREER	
POINTS	49	Rich Falk, vs. Iowa (Feb. 24, 1964)	585	Evan Eschmeyer (1997-98)	1,900	Billy McKinney (1973-77)
POINTS PER GAME			24.3	Dale Kelley (1969-70)	19.9	Joe Ruklick (1956-59)
REBOUNDS	29	Jim Pitts, vs. Indiana (Feb. 13, 1965)	321	Jim Pitts (1965-66)	995	Evan Eschmeyer (1995-99)
ASSISTS	14	Patrick Baldwin, vs. Youngstown State (Dec. 5, 1992)	157	Tim Doyle (2006-07)	452	Patrick Baldwin (1990-94)

SEASON REVIEW

SEASON	W-L	CONF.	SCORING	COACH	RECORD	SEASON	W-L	CONF.	SCORING	COACH	RECORD
1905-17	*66-88*		*No winning seasons until 1912-13 (0-9 in '09-10)*			1927-28	12-5	9-3		Arthur "Dutch" Lonborg	
1917-18	7-4	5-3		Norman Elliott		1928-29	12-5	7-5		Arthur "Dutch" Lonborg	
1918-19	7-6	6-4		Tom Robinson	7-6 .538	1929-30	8-8	6-6		Arthur "Dutch" Lonborg	
1919-20	3-7	2-6		Norman Elliott	10-11 .476	1930-31	16-1	11-1	*Helms Foundation champion*	Arthur "Dutch" Lonborg	
1920-21	2-12	1-11		Ray Elder	2-12 .143	1931-32	13-5	9-3		Arthur "Dutch" Lonborg	
1921-22	7-11	3-9		Dana Evans	7-11 .389	1932-33	15-4	10-2		Arthur "Dutch" Lonborg	
1922-23	5-11	3-9		Maury Kent		1933-34	11-8	8-4		Arthur "Dutch" Lonborg	
1923-24	0-16	0-12		Maury Kent		1934-35	10-10	3-9		Arthur "Dutch" Lonborg	
1924-25	6-10	4-8		Maury Kent		1935-36	13-6-1	7-5		Arthur "Dutch" Lonborg	
1925-26	5-12	3-9		Maury Kent		1936-37	11-9	4-8		Arthur "Dutch" Lonborg	
1926-27	3-14	1-11		Maury Kent	19-63 .232	1937-38	10-10	7-5		Arthur "Dutch" Lonborg	

SEAS.	W-L	CONF.	POSTSEASON	SCORING		REBOUNDS		ASSISTS		COACH	RECORD
1938-39	7-13	5-7								Arthur "Dutch" Lonborg	
1939-40	13-7	7-5								Arthur "Dutch" Lonborg	
1940-41	7-11	3-9								Arthur "Dutch" Lonborg	
1941-42	8-13	5-10								Arthur "Dutch" Lonborg	
1942-43	8-9	7-5								Arthur "Dutch" Lonborg	
1943-44	12-7	8-4								Arthur "Dutch" Lonborg	
1944-45	7-12	4-8								Arthur "Dutch" Lonborg	
1945-46	15-5	8-4								Arthur "Dutch" Lonborg	
1946-47	7-13	2-10								Arthur "Dutch" Lonborg	
1947-48	6-14	3-9								Arthur "Dutch" Lonborg	
1948-49	5-16	2-10								Arthur "Dutch" Lonborg	
1949-50	10-12	3-9		Ray Ragelis	15.4					Arthur "Dutch" Lonborg	236-203-1 .538
1950-51	12-10	7-7		Ray Ragelis	19.1	Ray Ragelis	11.1			Harold Olsen	
1951-52	7-15	4-10		Frank Petrancek	14.2	Frank Petrancek	9.5			Harold Olsen	19-25 .432
1952-53	6-16	5-13		Larry Kurka	12.4	John Biever	6.4			Waldo Fisher	
1953-54	9-13	6-8		Frank Ehmann	18.2	Hal Grant	6.7			Waldo Fisher	
1954-55	12-10	7-7		Frank Ehmann	23.9	Hal Grant	10.7			Waldo Fisher	
1955-56	2-20	1-13		Dick Mast	21.0	Bill Schulz	9.5			Waldo Fisher	
1956-57	6-16	2-12		Joe Ruklick	18.0	Joe Ruklick	12.5			Waldo Fisher	35-75 .318
1957-58	13-9	8-6		Joe Ruklick	18.2	Joe Ruklick	13.9			Bill Rohr	
1958-59	15-7	8-6		Joe Ruklick	23.0	Joe Ruklick	13.0			Bill Rohr	
1959-60	11-12	8-6		Willie Jones	17.5	Chuck Brandt	8.8			Bill Rohr	
1960-61	10-12	6-8		Ralph Wells	14.0	Brad Snyder	10.0			Bill Rohr	
1961-62	8-15	3-11		Ralph Wells	13.6	Phil Keeley	7.1			Bill Rohr	
1962-63	9-15	6-8		Rich Falk	15.5	Phil Keeley	7.4			Bill Rohr	66-70 .485
1963-64	8-13	6-8		Rich Falk	23.3	Jim Pitts	13.2			Larry Glass	
1964-65	7-17	3-11		Jim Burns	17.1	Jim Pitts	13.4			Larry Glass	
1965-66	12-12	7-7		Jim Burns	20.2	Jim Pitts	13.4			Larry Glass	
1966-67	11-11	7-7		Jim Burns	21.5	Mike Weaver	10.4			Larry Glass	
1967-68	13-10	8-6		Dale Kelley	16.4	Don Adams	11.1			Larry Glass	
1968-69	14-10	6-8		Dale Kelley	18.1	Don Adams	11.2			Larry Glass[a]	61-71 .462
1969-70	9-15	4-10		Dale Kelley	24.3	Don Adams	10.4			Brad Snyder	
1970-71	7-17	3-11		Barry Moran	17.5	Barry Moran	10.3	Mark Sibley	2.7	Brad Snyder	
1971-72	5-18	3-11		Mark Sibley	14.0	Barry Hentz	7.9	Mark Sibley	2.6	Brad Snyder	
1972-73	5-19	2-12		Mark Sibley	19.2	Greg Wells	9.2	Kevin Kachan	2.8	Brad Snyder	30-71 .297
1973-74	9-15	3-11		Billy McKinney	15.8	Bryan Ashbaugh	9.8	Bryan Ashbaugh	2.3	Tex Winter	
1974-75	6-20	4-14		Billy McKinney	18.2	Jim Wallace	7.0	Tim Teasley	1.8	Tex Winter	
1975-76	12-15	7-11		Billy McKinney	19.8	Jim Wallace	6.7	Billy McKinney	3.5	Tex Winter	
1976-77	7-20 ⊗	7-11		Billy McKinney	20.6	Bob Svete	5.4	Billy McKinney	2.6	Tex Winter	
1977-78	8-19	4-14		Tony Allen	15.1	Mike Campbell	6.8	Jerry Marifke	2.5	Tex Winter	42-89 .321▼
1978-79	6-21	2-16		Rod Roberson	10.4	Bob Klaas	5.0	Jerry Marifke	3.7	Rich Falk	
1979-80	10-17	5-13		Jim Stack	12.9	Mike Campbell	6.0	Brian Gibson	3.1	Rich Falk	
1980-81	9-18	3-15		Rod Roberson	17.2	Jim Stack	6.6	Michael Jenkins	3.5	Rich Falk	
1981-82	8-19	5-13		Jim Stack	14.9	Bob Grady	6.3	Michael Jenkins	2.7	Rich Falk	
1982-83	17-13	8-10	NIT SECOND ROUND	Jim Stack	14.9	Andre Goode	6.7	Michael Jenkins	4.4	Rich Falk	
1983-84	12-16	7-11		Art Aaron	16.9	Andre Goode	5.7	Shawn Watts	3.5	Rich Falk	
1984-85	6-22	2-16		Andre Goode	12.6	John Peterson	5.9	Shawn Watts	3.8	Rich Falk	
1985-86	7-20	2-16		Shon Morris	16.0	Shon Morris	7.5	Shawn Watts	2.7	Rich Falk	75-146 .339
1986-87	7-21	2-16		Shon Morris	13.5	Shon Morris	8.2	Shawn Watts	3.8	Bill Foster	
1987-88	7-21	2-16		Shon Morris	15.1	Shon Morris	7.0	Phil Styles	3.2	Bill Foster	
1988-89	9-19	2-16		Walker Lambiotte	18.0	Brian Schwabe	6.1	Rob Ross	3.2	Bill Foster	
1989-90	9-19	2-16		Rex Walters	17.6	Brian Schwabe	6.5	Rex Walters	4.5	Bill Foster	
1990-91	5-23	0-18		Todd Leslie	14.0	Kevin Rankin	7.4	Patrick Baldwin	3.8	Bill Foster	
1991-92	9-19	2-16		Cedric Neloms	14.4	Kevin Rankin	7.6	Kip Kirkpatrick	2.4	Bill Foster	
1992-93	8-19	3-15		Cedric Neloms	16.8	Kevin Rankin	8.4	Patrick Baldwin	5.4	Bill Foster	54-141 .277
1993-94	15-14	5-13	NIT SECOND ROUND	Kevin Rankin	15.3	Kevin Rankin	8.2	Patrick Baldwin	2.0	Ricky Byrdsong	
1994-95	5-22	1-17		Cedric Neloms	13.7	Brian Chamberlain	5.7	Geno Carlisle	3.9	Ricky Byrdsong	
1995-96	7-20 ⊗	2-16		Geno Carlisle	19.7	Evan Eschmeyer	6.6	Jevon Johnson	3.1	Ricky Byrdsong	
1996-97	7-22	2-16		Evan Eschmeyer	14.1	Evan Eschmeyer	8.1	Jevon Johnson	2.9	Ricky Byrdsong	34-78 .304▼
1997-98	10-17	3-13		Evan Eschmeyer	21.7	Evan Eschmeyer	10.7	Julian Bonner	4.1	Kevin O'Neill	
1998-99	15-14	6-10	NIT FIRST ROUND	Evan Eschmeyer	19.6	Evan Eschmeyer	10.1	Julian Bonner	2.7	Kevin O'Neill	
1999-2000	5-25	0-16		Ben Johnson	11.6	Tavaras Hardy	5.7	Ben Johnson	2.4	Kevin O'Neill	30-56 .349
2000-01	11-19	3-13		Winston Blake	11.9	Tavaras Hardy	5.7	Collier Drayton	3.4	Bill Carmody	
2001-02	16-13	7-9		Winston Blake	13.6	Tavaras Hardy	6.4	Collier Drayton	3.6	Bill Carmody	
2002-03	12-17	3-13		Jitim Young	13.4	Jitim Young	5.1	Jason Burke	2.7	Bill Carmody	
2003-04	14-15	8-8		Jitim Young	17.9	Jitim Young	6.0	T.J. Parker	4.0	Bill Carmody	
2004-05	15-16	6-10		Vedran Vukusic	16.8	Mohamed Hachad	4.4	Davor Duvancic	2.7	Bill Carmody	
2005-06	14-15	6-10		Vedran Vukusic	19.0	Mohamed Hachad	5.0	Tim Doyle	3.8	Bill Carmody	
2006-07	13-18	2-14		Kevin Coble	13.4	Kevin Coble	5.2	Tim Doyle	5.1	Bill Carmody	
2007-08	8-22	1-17		Kevin Coble	15.9	Kevin Coble	5.4	Michael Thompson	4.3	Bill Carmody	
2008-09	17-14	8-10	NIT FIRST ROUND	Kevin Coble	15.5	Kevin Coble	4.8	Michael Thompson	3.7	Bill Carmody	120-149 .446

[a] Larry Glass (10-8) and Brad Snyder (4-2) both coached during the 1968-69 season.

⊗ Records don't reflect games forfeited or vacated. For adjusted records, see p. 521.

▼ Coaches records adjusted to reflect games forfeited or vacated: Tex Winter, 44-87, .336; Ricky Byrdsong, 36-76, .321. For yearly totals, see p. 521.

THE SCHOOLS

ESPN 224 SAGARIN

NORTHWESTERN STATE

If political correctness ever compels the Demons to change their nickname, they might consider becoming the McConathys. Johnny McConathy was the school's all-time best player (1947-51); his brothers, Leslie and George, and distant relative Herschel, were also Demons. Then the program endured a four-decade decline, until Mike McConathy, Johnny's son and a former Louisiana Tech star (the horror!), came home to Natchitoches to coach the program back to health. The future looked brighter after coach McConathy made Demons of sons Logan and Michael.

BEST TEAM: 2005-06 Coach McConathy's 26–8 Southland Conference champs reached the second round of the NCAA Tournament by knocking off Iowa, after trailing by 17 (see Game for the Ages). The Demons danced deliriously after the 64-63 triumph, but they weren't entirely shocked: In the regular season, they'd won six games after being down by double digits.

BEST PLAYER: F JOHNNY MCCONATHY (1947-51) He missed his senior season at Bryceland (La.) High School with a broken ankle, and not one college cared about him. So McConathy hitchhiked 60 miles to Northwestern State and the rest is history—1,092 points' worth.

BEST COACH: MIKE MCCONATHY (1999-) The Demons were woeful before Mike McConathy came along. Johnny's oldest son took a listless program with five winning seasons in its 24 years in D1 to NCAA Tournament wins in each of its first two appearances (2001 and '06).

GAME FOR THE AGES: No. 14-seed NSU stunned No. 3-seed Iowa in the Tourney first round on March 17, 2006. After closing a 17-point gap, Jermaine Wallace heaved a three from the corner with a half-second left. As the Demons prayed, the ball swished. Wallace was a fitting hero: The New Orleans family home of his girlfriend, Katrina, had been destroyed seven months earlier by the catastrophic hurricane of the same name.

FIERCEST RIVAL: Northwestern State goes at it with Stephen F. Austin, two hours away, like, well, demons. The series dates back to 1926, with NSU leading 59–46.

SEASON REVIEW

SEAS.	W-L	CONF.	COACH	SEAS.	W-L	CONF.	COACH
1912-47	*332-133*		*H. Lee Prather coached all 35 years*	1960-61	16-11		Huey W. Cranford
1947-48	19-6		H. Lee Prather	1961-62	10-17		Huey W. Cranford
1948-49	23-5		H. Lee Prather	1962-63	8-17		Huey W. Cranford
1949-50	18-8		H. Lee Prather	1963-64	12-14		Huey W. Cranford
1950-51	15-11		Charles "Red" Thomas	1964-65	9-17		Huey W. Cranford
1951-52	17-14		Charles "Red" Thomas	1965-66	18-7		Tynes Hildebrand
1952-53	22-10		Charles "Red" Thomas	1966-67	8-17		Tynes Hildebrand
1953-54	23-9		Charles "Red" Thomas	1967-68	12-13		Tynes Hildebrand
1954-55	20-9		Charles "Red" Thomas	1968-69	16-13		Tynes Hildebrand
1955-56	18-10		Charles "Red" Thomas	1969-70	13-13		Tynes Hildebrand
1956-57	14-13		Charles "Red" Thomas	1970-71	14-11		Tynes Hildebrand
1957-58	20-7		Huey W. Cranford	1971-72	11-14		Tynes Hildebrand
1958-59	18-10		Huey W. Cranford	1972-73	6-19		Tynes Hildebrand
1959-60	23-5		Huey W. Cranford	1973-74	21-9		Tynes Hildebrand

SEAS.	W-L	CONF.	SCORING		COACH	RECORD
1974-75	13-14		Billy Reynolds	415	Tynes Hildebrand	
1975-76	14-10		Billy Reynolds	499	Tynes Hildebrand	
1976-77	17-9		Billy Reynolds	686	Tynes Hildebrand	
1977-78	12-15		Lester Elie	488	Tynes Hildebrand	
1978-79	7-19		Jerry Lewis	402	Tynes Hildebrand	
1979-80	5-20		Frederick Piper	325	Tynes Hildebrand	187-203 .479
1980-81	11-17	5-7	Wayne Waggoner	446	Wayne Yates	
1981-82	19-9	10-6	Wayne Waggoner	493	Wayne Yates	
1982-83	9-19	5-9	Kenny Hale	471	Wayne Yates	
1983-84	6-22	2-12	Fred Walker	293	Wayne Yates	
1984-85	3-25	2-8	George Jones	429	Wayne Yates	48-92 .343
1985-86	11-16	7-3	Victor Willis	391	Don Beasley	
1986-87	15-13	4-6	Victor Willis	423	Don Beasley	
1987-88	16-12	7-7	Byron Smith	354	Don Beasley	42-41 .506
1988-89	13-16	7-7	Terrance Rayford	591	Dan Bell	
1989-90	10-19	5-9	Roman Banks	425	Dan Bell	
1990-91	6-22	2-12	Jay Scherer	477	Dan Bell	
1991-92	15-13	9-9	Roman Banks	454	Dan Bell	
1992-93	13-13	7-11	Eric Kubel	539	Dan Bell	
1993-94	11-15	6-12	Eric Kubel	632	Dan Bell	68-98 .410
1994-95	13-14	8-10	Tarius Brown	488	J.D. Barnett	
1995-96	5-21	3-15	Charlie Johnson	314	J.D. Barnett	
1996-97	13-15	8-8	Charles Duncan	414	J.D. Barnett	
1997-98	13-14	10-6	Seth LeGrand	372	J.D. Barnett	
1998-99	11-15	8-10	Alann Polk	12.3	J.D. Barnett	55-79 .410
1999-2000	17-13	11-7	Richard Taylor	12.2	Mike McConathy	
2000-01	19-13	11-9 ●	Michael Byars-Dawson	13.2	Mike McConathy	
2001-02	13-18	9-11	Michael Byars-Dawson	15.8	Mike McConathy	
2002-03	6-21	6-14	Jermaine Wallace	11.0	Mike McConathy	
2003-04	11-17	8-8	Jermaine Wallace	15.5	Mike McConathy	
2004-05	21-12	13-3	Jermaine Wallace	11.9	Mike McConathy	
2005-06	26-8	15-1 ●	Clifton Lee	14.1	Mike McConathy	
2006-07	17-15	10-6	Luke Rogers	13.5	Mike McConathy	
2007-08	15-18	9-7	Trey Gilder	16.4	Mike McConathy	
2008-09	11-20	3-13	Damon Jones	12.2	Mike McConathy	156-155 .502

Cumulative totals listed when per game averages not available.
● NCAA Tournament appearance

PROFILE

Northwestern State University, Natchitoches, LA
Founded: 1884
Enrollment: 9,111 (8,018 undergraduate)
Colors: Purple and white
Nickname: Demons
Current arena: Prather Coliseum, opened in 1964 (3,600)
Previous: Demon Gym, 1913-64 (2,800)
First game: 1912
All-time record: 1,193-994 (.545)
Total weeks in AP Top 20/25: 0

Current conference: Southland (1987-)
Conference titles:
Southland: 2 (2005 [tie], '06)
Conference tournament titles:
Southland: 2 (2001, '06)
NCAA Tournament appearances: 2
NIT appearances: 0

FIRST-ROUND PRO PICKS

1951 **Johnny McConathy,** Syracuse (5)

TOP 5

G **Roman Banks** (1987-90, '91-92)
G **Jimmie Leach** (1955-59)
F **Johnny McConathy** (1947-51)
F **Billy Reynolds** (1973-77)
C **James Wyatt** (1965-69)

RECORDS

	GAME		SEASON		CAREER	
POINTS	54	Jimmy Leach, vs. Southwestern Louisiana (Feb. 27, 1959)	686	Billy Reynolds (1976-77)	2,009	Billy Reynolds (1973-77)
POINTS PER GAME			26.4	Billy Reynolds (1976-77)	20.6	Vernon Wilson (1970-73)
REBOUNDS	30	James Wyatt, vs. Northeast Louisiana (Feb. 19, 1969); vs. Nicholls State (Feb. 15, 1969); vs. Southwestern Louisiana (Feb. 5, 1968)	497	James Wyatt (1968-69)	1,549	James Wyatt (1965-69)
ASSISTS	16	Dwight Moody, vs. Sam Houston State (Jan. 25, 1986)	236	Howard Hughes (1973-74)	552	Ryan Bundy (1994-98)

ESPN 12 SAGARIN

NOTRE DAME

Notre Dame will always be known as a football school, of course, but basketball arrived in South Bend in 1898, just 11 years after the Irish first took to the gridiron. In fact, UND is among 14 schools in college hoops history with 1,600 wins all-time.

BEST TEAM: 1977-78 A series of standout recruiting classes for Digger Phelps came to fruition in the Irish's only Final Four season. All five starters, led by forward-center Dave Batton (14 ppg), scored 1,000 career points, and eight players went on to play in the NBA. Bill Laimbeer, Orlando Woolridge and Bill Hanzlik couldn't even crack the starting lineup. Sweetest of all, Notre Dame routed rival DePaul to make the NCAA semifinals (where it lost to Duke).

BEST PLAYER: G AUSTIN CARR (1968-71) A chunk of the NCAA Tournament record book belongs to Carr. His 61 points against Ohio in 1970 (*without* the three-point basket) remains the standard today, and he's the Tourney's all-time leading scorer with a 41.3 ppg average in seven games. Thanks to his sweet touch, the 6'3" guard was virtually double-team-proof, as his 23 games of 40-plus points attests. After averaging 38 points as a senior, Carr ran away with the voting for national Player of the Year.

BEST COACH: DIGGER PHELPS (1971-91) Phelps' Fordham team upset the Irish on Feb. 18, 1971. A few months later, he was introduced as the new Notre Dame coach, beginning a 20-year tenure that left him as the winningest coach in school history. The demanding Phelps had a flair for the dramatic, engineering a monumental upset of UCLA in 1974 (see Game for the Ages) and taking the Irish to the 1978 Final Four.

GAME FOR THE AGES: No matter that UCLA had won 88 straight games since its last loss, on Jan. 23, 1971—to Notre Dame. In practices leading up to the teams' Jan. 19, 1974 meeting at South Bend, Phelps had his players practice cutting down the nets. And sure enough, the Irish erased an 11-point deficit with 3:22 left by turning up the defensive pressure. They took the lead on a baseline jumper by Dwight Clay with :29 on the clock, Bill Walton missed a short turnaround in the final seconds, and No. 1 UCLA's winning streak ended with a 71-70 loss.

HEARTBREAKER: The Irish boasted a powerful lineup in 1980-81 featuring Kelly Tripucka, Woolridge and John Paxson. But it all went up in smoke in a 51-50 Sweet 16 loss to BYU. Notre Dame squandered a double-digit lead, setting the stage for Danny Ainge's coast-to-coast game-winning layup over Woolridge. "We should have blown out BYU by 20 to begin with," Tripucka said years later. Woulda, coulda, shoulda.

FIERCEST RIVAL: Big East members Notre Dame and Marquette have battled since 1920 and, in the early days of the Tournament, the two Catholic schools routinely jockeyed for at-large berths. Phelps' first notable win for the Irish came on Jan. 13, 1973, when 3–6 Notre Dame ended Marquette's 81-game home winning streak in a 71-69 thriller. UND's road to the 1978 Final Four included a regular-season win over Marquette. Notre Dame leads overall, 77–35.

FANFARE AND HOOPLA: Why did one veteran columnist name Notre Dame's Leprechaun Legion the nation's second best student section, behind Duke's Cameron Crazies? Opposing bench players can expect to be taunted with a "Rudy!" chant, for one.

FAN FAVORITE: F ORLANDO WOOLRIDGE (1977-81) One year after the dunking ban was lifted, Woolridge thrilled Irish faithful with his tremendous leaping ability and the delight he took in slamming the ball down.

CONSENSUS ALL-AMERICAS

1909	**Raymond Scanlon**, G
1925	**Noble Kizer**, G
1927	**John Nyikos**, C
1932-34	**Edward Krause**, C
1936-38	**John Moir**, F
1936-38	**Paul Nowak**, C
1944, '46	**Leo Klier**, F
1945	**Bill Hassett**, G
1948	**Kevin O'Shea**, G
1971	**Austin Carr**, G
1974	**John Shumate**, F/C
1975, '76	**Adrian Dantley**, F
2000, '01	**Troy Murphy**, F

FIRST ROUND PRO PICKS

1950	**Kevin O'Shea**, Minneapolis (11)
1954	**Dick Rosenthal**, Fort Wayne (4)
1959	**Tom Hawkins**, Minneapolis (4)
1969	**Bob Arnzen**, Indiana (ABA)
1971	**Austin Carr**, Cleveland (1)
1971	**Austin Carr**, Virginia (ABA)
1971	**Collis Jones**, Milwaukee (17)
1974	**John Shumate**, Phoenix (4)
1974	**Gary Brokaw**, Milwaukee (18)
1976	**Adrian Dantley**, Buffalo (6)
1980	**Bill Hanzlik**, Seattle (20)
1981	**Orlando Woolridge**, Chicago (6)
1981	**Kelly Tripucka**, Detroit (12)
1983	**John Paxson**, San Antonio (19)
1986	**Ken Barlow**, LA Lakers (23)
1988	**David Rivers**, LA Lakers (25)
1992	**LaPhonso Ellis**, Denver (5)
1994	**Monty Williams**, New York (24)
1998	**Pat Garrity**, Milwaukee (19)
2001	**Troy Murphy**, Golden State (14)
2002	**Ryan Humphrey**, Utah (19)

PROFILE

University of Notre Dame, South Bend, IN
Founded: 1842
Enrollment: 11,479 (8,332 undergraduate)
Colors: Gold and blue
Nickname: Fighting Irish
Current arena: Joyce Center, opened in 1968 as the Athletic and Convocation Center (11,418)
Previous: Notre Dame Fieldhouse, 1898-99, 1907-68 (6,000)
First game: Jan. 29, 1898
All-time record: 1,651-908-1 (.645)
Total weeks in AP Top 20/25: 296
Current conference: Big East (1995-)
Conference titles:
Big East: 1 (2001 [tie])
Conference tournament titles: 0
NCAA Tournament appearances: 29
Sweet 16s (since 1975): 8
Final Fours: 1
NIT appearances: 11
Semifinals: 6

TOP 5

G	**Austin Carr** (1968-71)
G	**Kevin O'Shea** (1946-50)
F	**Adrian Dantley** (1973-76)
F	**Troy Murphy** (1998-2001)
F/C	**John Shumate** (1972-74)

RECORDS

RECORDS	GAME		SEASON		CAREER	
POINTS	61	Austin Carr, vs. Ohio (March 7, 1970)	1,106	Austin Carr (1969-70)	2,560	Austin Carr (1968-71)
POINTS PER GAME			38.1	Austin Carr (1969-70)	34.6	Austin Carr (1968-71)
REBOUNDS	30	Bob Whitmore, vs. St. Norbert (Dec. 14, 1967); Walter Sahm, vs. Ball State (Dec. 4, 1964)	499	Tom Hawkins (1957-58)	1,318	Tom Hawkins (1956-59)
ASSISTS	17	Jackie Meehan, vs. Creighton (Feb. 16, 1971); vs. Ohio (March 7, 1970)	252	Chris Thomas (2001-02)	833	Chris Thomas (2001-05)

THE SCHOOLS

SEASON REVIEW

SEASON	W-L	CONF.	SCORING		COACH	RECORD	
[illegible]1915	119-32		*Eight consecutive winning seasons from 1907-15*				
1915-16	9-3		Freeman Fitzgerald		Jesse Harper		
1916-17	8-5		Frank McDermott	14.9	Jesse Harper		
1917-18	2-4		Peter Rochetti	6.5	Jesse Harper	44-20	.688
1918-19	2-10		Leonard Bahan		Charles "Gus" Dorais		
1919-20	5-13		Harry Mehre	12.2	Charles "Gus" Dorais	7-23	.233
1920-21	9-14		Harry Mehre		Walter Halas		
1921-22	6-13		Frank McDermott		Walter Halas		
1922-23	10-12		Noble Kizer	12.2	Walter Halas	25-39	.391
1923-24	15-8		Clem Crowe		George Keogan		
1924-25	11-11		John Nyikos	7.9	George Keogan		
1925-26	19-1		John Nyikos	8.2	George Keogan		
1926-27	19-1		John Nyikos	8.6	George Keogan		
1927-28	18-4		Francis Crowe	5.6	George Keogan		
1928-29	15-5		Francis Crowe	5.6	George Keogan		
1929-30	14-6		John McCarthy	5.5	George Keogan		
1930-31	12-8		Raymond DeCook	6.6	George Keogan		
1931-32	18-2		Edward Krause	7.7	George Keogan		
1932-33	16-6		Edward Krause	10.1	George Keogan		
1933-34	20-4		Edward Krause	8.5	George Keogan		
1934-35	13-9		Martin Peters	6.9	George Keogan		
1935-36	22-2-1		John Moir	11.3	George Keogan		

SEAS.	W-L	CONF.	POSTSEASON	SCORING		REBOUNDS		ASSISTS		COACH	RECORD	
1936-37	20-3			John Moir	13.2					George Keogan		
1937-38	20-3			John Moir	10.5					George Keogan		
1938-39	15-6			Eddie Riska	9.6					George Keogan		
1939-40	15-6			Eddie Riska	11.0					George Keogan		
1940-41	17-5			Eddie Riska	10.2					George Keogan		
1941-42	16-6			Bob Faught	9.5					George Keogan		
1942-43	18-2			Bob Faught	9.8					George Keogan[a]	327-97	.771
1943-44	10-9			Leo Klier	15.4					Edward Krause		
1944-45	15-5			Vince Boryla	16.1					Clem Crowe	15-5	.750
1945-46	17-4			Leo Klier	16.9					Elmer Ripley	17-4	.810
1946-47	20-4			John Brennan	12.0					Edward Krause		
1947-48	17-7			Leo Barnhorst	12.1					Edward Krause		
1948-49	17-7			Leo Barnhorst	11.8					Edward Krause		
1949-50	15-9			Kevin O'Shea	14.9					Edward Krause		
1950-51	13-11			Dan Bagley	13.3					Edward Krause	98-48	.671
1951-52	16-10			Leroy Leslie	14.1					John Jordan		
1952-53	19-5		NCAA REGIONAL FINALS	Dick Rosenthal	16.3					John Jordan		
1953-54	22-3		NCAA REGIONAL FINALS	Dick Rosenthal	20.2					John Jordan		
1954-55	14-10			Jack Stephens	20.9					John Jordan		
1955-56	9-15			Lloyd Aubrey	22.4					John Jordan		
1956-57	20-8		NCAA REGIONAL SEMIFINALS	Tom Hawkins	20.6	Tom Hawkins	17.3			John Jordan		
1957-58	24-5		NCAA REGIONAL FINALS	Tom Hawkins	25.2	Tom Hawkins	17.2			John Jordan		
1958-59	12-13			Tom Hawkins	23.4	Tom Hawkins	15.2			John Jordan		
1959-60	17-9		NCAA FIRST ROUND	Mike Graney	17.3	Mike Graney	13.5			John Jordan		
1960-61	12-14			Armand Reo	14.6	Armand Reo	10.7			John Jordan		
1961-62	7-16			Armand Reo	18.0	Armand Reo	11.5			John Jordan		
1962-63	17-9		NCAA FIRST ROUND	John Andreoli	15.0	Walter Sahm	16.8			John Jordan		
1963-64	10-14			Larry Sheffield	22.3	Ron Reed	17.7			John Jordan	199-131	.603
1964-65	15-12		NCAA FIRST ROUND	Ron Reed	21.0	Walter Sahm	16.4			Johnny Dee		
1965-66	5-21			Jim Monahan	15.1	Jim Monahan	9.7			Johnny Dee		
1966-67	14-14			Bob Arnzen	21.4	Bob Whitmore	13.7			Johnny Dee		
1967-68	21-9		NIT THIRD PLACE	Bob Whitmore	22.0	Bob Whitmore	13.8			Johnny Dee		
1968-69	20-7		NCAA FIRST ROUND	Bob Whitmore	17.1	Bob Arnzen	11.6			Johnny Dee		
1969-70	21-8		NCAA REGIONAL SEMIFINALS	Austin Carr	38.1	Collis Jones	12.4			Johnny Dee		
1970-71	20-9		NCAA REGIONAL SEMIFINALS	Austin Carr	38.0	Collis Jones	13.1			Johnny Dee	116-80	.592
1971-72	6-20			Gary Novak	19.5	Gary Novak	10.3			Digger Phelps		
1972-73	18-12		NIT RUNNER-UP	John Shumate	21.0	John Shumate	12.2			Digger Phelps		
1973-74	26-3		NCAA REGIONAL SEMIFINALS	John Shumate	24.2	John Shumate	11.0	Dwight Clay	3.8	Digger Phelps		
1974-75	19-10		NCAA REGIONAL SEMIFINALS	Adrian Dantley	30.4	Adrian Dantley	10.2	Dwight Clay	3.2	Digger Phelps		
1975-76	23-6		NCAA REGIONAL SEMIFINALS	Adrian Dantley	28.6	Adrian Dantley	10.1	Ray Martin	3.8	Digger Phelps		
1976-77	22-7		NCAA REGIONAL SEMIFINALS	Don Williams	18.1	Toby Knight	10.6	Rich Branning	4.7	Digger Phelps		
1977-78	23-8		NCAA FOURTH PLACE	Dave Batton	14.0	Dave Batton	6.8	Rich Branning	4.3	Digger Phelps		
1978-79	24-6		NCAA REGIONAL FINALS	Kelly Tripucka	14.3	Bill Laimbeer	5.5	Rich Branning	3.6	Digger Phelps		
1979-80	22-6		NCAA SECOND ROUND	Tracy Jackson	15.1	Tracy Jackson	7.1	Rich Branning	3.5	Digger Phelps		
1980-81	23-6		NCAA REGIONAL SEMIFINALS	Kelly Tripucka	18.2	Kelly Tripucka	5.8	John Paxson	4.7	Digger Phelps		
1981-82	10-17			John Paxson	16.4	Bill Varner	6.2	John Paxson	3.6	Digger Phelps		
1982-83	19-10		NIT FIRST ROUND	John Paxson	17.7	Tim Kempton	5.9	John Paxson	3.8	Digger Phelps		
1983-84	21-12		NIT RUNNER-UP	Tom Sluby	18.7	Jim Dolan	7.4	Jim Dolan	3.1	Digger Phelps		
1984-85	21-9		NCAA SECOND ROUND	David Rivers	15.8	Ken Barlow	6.5	David Rivers	4.2	Digger Phelps		
1985-86	23-6		NCAA FIRST ROUND	David Rivers	16.7	Ken Barlow	5.4	David Rivers	4.9	Digger Phelps		
1986-87	24-8		NCAA REGIONAL SEMIFINALS	David Rivers	15.7	Donald Royal	7.0	David Rivers	5.1	Digger Phelps		
1987-88	20-9		NCAA FIRST ROUND	David Rivers	22.0	Gary Voce	7.8	David Rivers	5.6	Digger Phelps		
1988-89	21-9		NCAA SECOND ROUND	Joe Fredrick	16.7	LaPhonso Ellis	9.4	Tim Singleton	6.9	Digger Phelps		
1989-90	16-13		NCAA FIRST ROUND	Keith Robinson	14.7	LaPhonso Ellis	12.6	Tim Singleton	4.7	Digger Phelps		
1990-91	12-20			Daimon Sweet	16.3	Keith Tower	7.0	Tim Singleton	6.5	Digger Phelps	393-197	.666
1991-92	18-15		NIT RUNNER-UP	LaPhonso Ellis	17.7	LaPhonso Ellis	11.7	Elmer Bennett	6.1	John MacLeod		
1992-93	9-18			Monty Williams	18.5	Monty Williams	9.3	Malik Russell	2.0	John MacLeod		
1993-94	12-17			Monty Williams	22.4	Monty Williams	8.2	Admore White	3.3	John MacLeod		
1994-95	15-12			Pat Garrity	13.4	Marcus Young	5.3	Lamarr Justice	3.8	John MacLeod		
1995-96	9-18	4-14		Pat Garrity	17.2	Pat Garrity	7.1	Doug Gottlieb	5.7	John MacLeod		
1996-97	16-14	8-10	NIT QUARTERFINALS	Pat Garrity	21.1	Pat Garrity	7.4	Admore White	6.7	John MacLeod		
1997-98	13-14	7-11		Pat Garrity	23.2	Pat Garrity	8.3	Martin Ingelsby	5.5	John MacLeod		
1998-99	14-16	8-10		Troy Murphy	19.2	Troy Murphy	9.9	Martin Ingelsby	4.2	John MacLeod	106-124	.461
1999-2000	22-15	8-8	NIT RUNNER-UP	Troy Murphy	22.7	Troy Murphy	10.3	Jimmy Dillon	5.7	Matt Doherty	22-15	.595
2000-01	20-10	11-5	NCAA SECOND ROUND	Troy Murphy	21.8	Troy Murphy	9.2	Martin Ingelsby	6.4	Mike Brey		
2001-02	22-11	10-6	NCAA SECOND ROUND	Ryan Humphrey	18.9	Ryan Humphrey	10.9	Chris Thomas	7.6	Mike Brey		
2002-03	24-10	10-6	NCAA REGIONAL SEMIFINALS	Matt Carroll	19.5	Torin Francis	8.4	Chris Thomas	6.9	Mike Brey		
2003-04	19-13	9-7	NIT QUARTERFINALS	Chris Thomas	19.7	Torin Francis	8.8	Chris Thomas	4.6	Mike Brey		
2004-05	17-12	9-7	NIT FIRST ROUND	Chris Thomas	14.2	Torin Francis	7.8	Chris Thomas	6.7	Mike Brey		
2005-06	16-14	6-10	NIT SECOND ROUND	Chris Quinn	17.7	Torin Francis	9.4	Chris Quinn	6.4	Mike Brey		
2006-07	24-8	11-5	NCAA FIRST ROUND	Russell Carter	17.1	Rob Kurz	8.0	Kyle McAlarney	5.4	Mike Brey		
2007-08	25-8	14-4	NCAA SECOND ROUND	Luke Harangody	20.4	Luke Harangody	10.6	Tory Jackson	5.8	Mike Brey		
2008-09	21-15	8-10	NIT SEMIFINALS	Luke Harangody	23.3	Luke Harangody	11.8	Tory Jackson	4.9	Mike Brey	188-101	.651

[a] George Keogan (12-1) and Edward Krause (6-1) both coached during the 1942-43 season.

ESPN 272 SAGARIN

OAKLAND

In the mid-1990s, the D2 Michigan school had a string of four 20-plus win seasons. Then it moved into D1 and, in its first year eligible, won the 1999-2000 Mid-Continent Conference regular season title. Add an NCAA Tourney bid in '05, and nobody's pining for Oakland's old D2 unofficial mascot, the buckskin-clad Pioneer Pete.

BEST TEAM: 1996-97 They lived and died by the three-point bomb. Mostly lived. Led by sharpshooting G Kevin Kovach, the Golden Grizzlies averaged 10.7 treys a game, finished 23–8 and reached the D2 round of 16.

BEST PLAYER: F Rawle Marshall (2002-05) The career scoring numbers are 18.6 ppg and 31.2% three-point shooting. But the most impressive thing about the 6'7" Marshall was his 7'1" wingspan—and he had the defensive stats to show for it. In only three campaigns, he finished second all-time in blocks (101) and first in steals (199).

BEST COACH: Greg Kampe (1984-) He has led the team to one Mid-Continent tournament and a regular-season title and proved himself a capable improviser. In a 1997 D2 tournament regional game against a Grand Valley State squad that had already beaten Oakland twice, Kampe dug 10 years into the film vault for a flat 3-2 zone that helped the Grizzlies pull off a 79-74 upset.

GAME FOR THE AGES: Top-seeded Oral Roberts seemed to have the 2005 Mid-Continent championship game wrapped up. Oakland, which had started the season 0–7, had been on a streak, though, and never let the game get entirely out of hand. After ORU missed some key free throws, Oakland guard Pierre Dukes hit a trey with 1.3 seconds remaining for a 61-60 victory and a ticket to the Dance. Not bad for a 12–18 team.

FIERCEST RIVAL: Though in-state rival Michigan State gets Golden Grizzlies fans' blood boiling, Oakland has its toughest games against Oral Roberts, especially after Oakland dashed the Golden Eagles' dreams in 2005. Two seasons later, ORU exacted revenge in the conference tournament final over Kampe's squad with a 71-67 victory in Tulsa. Oral Roberts leads the series, 16–8.

SEASON REVIEW

SEAS.	W-L	CONF.	SCORING		COACH	RECORD	
1967-68	6-15		Tom Allan	16.0	Dick Robinson	6-15	.286
1968-69	11-10		John Eley	18.9	Gene Boldon		
1969-70	9-14		Carvin Melson	19.8	Gene Boldon		
1970-71	14-12		Carvin Melson	23.0	Gene Boldon		
1971-72	14-12		Carvin Melson	27.2	Gene Boldon		
1972-73	15-11		Carvin Melson	26.7	Gene Boldon		
1973-74	17-11		Walter Johnson	19.1	Gene Boldon		
1974-75	4-22		Eulis Stephens	13.5	Gene Boldon		
1975-76	5-22		Eulis Stephens	17.5	Gene Boldon	89-114	.438
1976-77	8-18		Tim Kramer	16.7	Jim Mitchell		
1977-78	4-22		Tim Kramer	14.2	Jim Mitchell		
1978-79	11-15		Tim Kramer	19.3	Jim Mitchell[a]	17-48	.262
1979-80	12-14		Rich Brauer	16.6	Lee Frederick		
1980-81	8-19		Bill Peterson	15.5	Lee Frederick		
1981-82	18-9		Antoine Williams	15.2	Lee Frederick		
1982-83	11-16		Mike Mohn	16.7	Lee Frederick		
1983-84	13-14		Mike Mohn	20.1	Lee Frederick	68-79	.463
1984-85	13-15		Chris Howze	18.3	Greg Kampe		
1985-86	13-15		Chris Howze	17.3	Greg Kampe		
1986-87	19-9		Scott Bittinger	18.4	Greg Kampe		
1987-88	19-9		Scott Bittinger	26.4	Greg Kampe		
1988-89	20-8		John Henderson	22.1	Greg Kampe		
1989-90	19-9		Eric Taylor	23.3	Greg Kampe		
1990-91	16-13		Eric Taylor	23.6	Greg Kampe		
1991-92	16-13		Eric Taylor	20.3	Greg Kampe		
1992-93	15-11		Tom Eller	19.8	Greg Kampe		
1993-94	21-10		Tom Eller	21.6	Greg Kampe		
1994-95	20-9		Frank Zielinski	17.1	Greg Kampe		
1995-96	21-8		Kevin Kovach	18.5	Greg Kampe		
1996-97	23-8		Matt MacClellan	20.0	Greg Kampe		
1997-98	15-12		Dan Champagne	17.3	Greg Kampe		
1998-99	12-15		Dan Champagne	15.9	Greg Kampe		
1999-2000	13-17	11-5	Brad Buddenborg	17.4	Greg Kampe		
2000-01	12-16	8-8	Jason Rozycki	18.3	Greg Kampe		
2001-02	17-13	10-4	Mike Helms	18.4	Greg Kampe		
2002-03	17-11	10-4	Mike Helms	26.9	Greg Kampe		
2003-04	13-17	6-10	Mike Helms	23.2	Greg Kampe		
2004-05	13-19	7-9 ●	Rawle Marshall	19.9	Greg Kampe		
2005-06	11-18	6-10	Calvin Wooten	19.2	Greg Kampe		
2006-07	19-14	10-4	Vova Severovas	14.3	Greg Kampe		
2007-08	17-14	11-7	Derick Nelson	17.3	Greg Kampe		
2008-09	23-13	13-5	Erik Kangas	18.9	Greg Kampe	417-316	.569

[a] Jim Mitchell (5-8) and Lee Frederick (6-7) both coached during the 1978-79 season.

● NCAA Tournament appearance

PROFILE

Oakland University, Rochester, MI
Founded: 1957
Enrollment: 18,082 (14,090 undergraduate)
Colors: Gold and black
Nickname: Golden Grizzlies
Current arena: Athletics Center O'rena, opened in 1998 (4,000)
Previous: The Bubble, 1996-98 (500); Hollie Lepley Sports Center, 1967-96 (1,000)
First game: Dec. 2, 1967
All-time record: 597-572 (.511)

Total weeks in AP Top 20/25: 0
Current conference: Summit League (1999-)
Conference titles:
Mid-Continent: 1 (2000)
Conference tournament titles:
Mid-Continent: 1 (2005)
NCAA Tournament appearances: 1
NIT appearances: 0

TOP 5

- G **Brad Buddenborg** (1998-2002)
- G **Jason Rozycki** (1998-2002)
- F **Rawle Marshall** (2002-05)
- F **Vova Severovas** (2005-07)
- C **Dan Champagne** (1998-2002)

RECORDS

RECORDS	GAME		SEASON		CAREER	
POINTS	45	Mike Helms, vs. Western Michigan (Dec. 29, 2001)	752	Mike Helms (2002-03)	2,314	Mike Helms (2000-04)
POINTS PER GAME			26.9	Mike Helms (2002-03)	19.9	Mike Helms (2000-04)
REBOUNDS	21	Cortney Scott, vs. Saginaw Valley St. (Dec. 16, 2003)	280	Keith Benson (2008-09)	668	Cortney Scott (2002-05)
ASSISTS	15	Johnathon Jones, vs. IPFW (Feb. 14, 2009); vs. IUPUI (Feb. 21, 2009)	290	Johnathon Jones (2008-09)	595	Johnathon Jones (2006-)

ESPN 88 SAGARIN

OHIO

Oh, the players and teams that have wowed Athens: Gary "Shaq of the MAC" Trent, All-America Frank Baumholtz, Walter Luckett, coach Jim Snyder's 1964 Elite Eight squad, and the nation's No. 7-ranked 1940-41 team.

BEST TEAM: 1963-64 To commemorate the program's 100-year anniversary in 2007, Ohio raised a banner honoring Snyder's squad. How many teams can claim victories over Louisville and Kentucky in the same season, let alone in back-to-back NCAA Tournament games? After outlasting the Cardinals in the first round, 71-69, the Bobcats shocked the No. 4-ranked Wildcats, 85-69, before losing to Cazzie Russell and Michigan in the Mideast Regional finals, 69-57. It remains Ohio's best NCAA Tourney showing.

BEST PLAYER: G FRANK BAUMHOLTZ (1938-41) Nicknamed the Midvale Marvel in honor of his Ohio hometown, Baumholtz's marvels truly never ceased. The MVP of the 1941 NIT, he scored 53 points in three games to lead the Bobcats to the final, where they lost to top-ranked Long Island, 56-42. After a stint in the Navy, Baumholtz played one season of pro basketball for the Cleveland Rebels and 10 solid MLB seasons (lifetime BA: .290) with three clubs (Reds, Cubs, Phillies).

BEST COACH: JIM SNYDER (1949-74) Upon Snyder's death in 1994, one of his friends joked to a reporter that Gentleman Jim was far too nice to have been a coach. But while Snyder rarely yelled, his teams never lacked for drive, winning seven MAC titles, reeling off a string of 13 straight winning seasons and a school-record 29-game home winning streak, and appearing in seven NCAA Tourneys.

GAME FOR THE AGES: Ohio pulled off the upset of the 1964 NCAA Tournament, knocking out SEC champion Kentucky, 85-69, in their Mideast Regional semifinal. The Bobcats raced to a 16-point halftime lead over All-America Cotton Nash's Wildcats and never looked back.

HEARTBREAKER: Behind future NBA lottery pick Gary Trent, the Bobcats won 24 games and the preseason NIT in 1994-95, and were even nationally ranked for four weeks. But their bid for a second consecutive trip to the Big Dance was thwarted by Eastern Michigan in the MAC tournament semifinals, 78-72.

FIERCEST RIVAL: In the 1907-08 season, the Bobcats traveled 180 miles to Oxford to play Miami (Ohio) for the first time. Although they fell short of double figures in the 27-8 loss, they've continued playing the RedHawks nearly every season since. Ohio leads the series 95–88, racking up many emphatic victories, including an 89-66 rout to win the 1994 MAC tournament.

FANFARE AND HOOPLA: Ohio has played in four home arenas—not including the basement of Ewing Hall, which hosted the fledgling Bobcats in 1907-08. The current Convocation Center, a 13,080-capacity dome that opened in 1968, might just be the most inhospitable for visiting teams, especially of late. With Ohio's O-Zone student section creating a wall of noise, the team has won more than 80% of its home games since 2000.

FAN FAVORITE: G WALTER LUCKETT (1972-75) "Put it in the Bucket" Luckett was such a recruiting score for the Bobcats that he graced the cover of *Sports Illustrated* in his first week with the team. He proved worthy of the hype, averaging 20.6 points per game in his three seasons before declaring early for the NBA. Unfortunately, a knee injury derailed his pro career before it even began.

Upon Jim Snyder's death in 1994, one of his friends joked to a reporter that Gentleman Jim was far too nice to have been a coach.

PROFILE

Ohio University, Athens, OH
Founded: 1804
Enrollment: 20,537 (16,738 undergraduate)
Colors: Hunter green and white
Nickname: Bobcats
Current arena: Convocation Center, opened in 1968 (13,080)
Previous: Grover Center, 1960-68 (N/A); Men's Gymnasium, 1924-60 (N/A); Ohio Gymnasium, 1908-24 (N/A); Ewing Hall, 1907 (N/A)
First game: 1907

All-time record: 1,331-1,015 (.567)
Total weeks in AP Top 20/25: 15
Current conference: Mid-American (1946-)
Conference titles:
MAC: 9 (1960, '61, '64, '65, '70, '72, '74, '85, '94)
Conference tournament titles:
MAC: 4 (1983, '85, '94, 2005)
NCAA Tournament appearances: 11
NIT appearances: 4
Semifinals: 1

FIRST-ROUND PRO PICKS

1990 **Dave Jamerson,** Miami (15)
1995 **Gary Trent,** Milwaukee (11)

TOP 5

G **Frank Baumholtz** (1938-41)
G **Dave Jamerson** (1985-90)
G **Walter Luckett** (1972-75)
F **Paul Graham** (1985-89)
F **Gary Trent** (1992-95)

RECORDS	GAME		SEASON		CAREER	
POINTS	60	Dave Jamerson, vs. Charleston (W. Va.) (Dec. 21, 1989)	874	Dave Jamerson (1989-90)	2,336	Dave Jamerson (1985-90)
POINTS PER GAME			31.2	Dave Jamerson (1989-90)	22.7	Gary Trent (1992-95)
REBOUNDS	34	Dave Scott, vs. Marietta (March 2, 1959)	468	Howard Jolliff (1959-60)	1,103	Brandon Hunter (1999-2003)
ASSISTS	16	Dennis Whitaker, vs. Western Michigan (Feb. 20, 1988)	199	Dennis Whitaker (1987-88)	651	Dennis Whitaker (1986-90)

SEASON REVIEW

SEASON	W-L	CONF.	SCORING	COACH	RECORD		SEASON	W-L	CONF.	SCORING	COACH	RECORD
1907-16	*42-52*		*Five coaches in five seasons from 1909-10 to '13-14*				1926-27	8-13			Butch Grover	
1916-17	2-14			Mark B. Banks			1927-28	10-10			Butch Grover	
1917-18	4-8			Mark B. Banks	28-43	.394	1928-29	10-10			Butch Grover	
1918-19	5-4			Frank B. Gullum			1929-30	12-9			Butch Grover	
1919-20	5-6			Frank B. Gullum	10-10	.500	1930-31	12-4			Butch Grover	
1920-21	15-2			R.W. Finsterwald			1931-32	11-10			Butch Grover	
1921-22	19-4			R.W. Finsterwald	34-6	.850	1932-33	16-4			Butch Grover	
1922-23	11-8			Butch Grover			1933-34	5-14			Butch Grover	
1923-24	16-5			Butch Grover			1934-35	11-9			Butch Grover	
1924-25	12-6			Butch Grover			1935-36	13-7			Butch Grover	
1925-26	15-9			Butch Grover			1936-37	18-3			Butch Grover	

SEAS.	W-L	CONF.	POSTSEASON	SCORING		REBOUNDS		ASSISTS		COACH	RECORD	
1937-38	12-8									Butch Grover	192-129	.598
1938-39	12-8									Dutch Trautwein		
1939-40	19-6									Dutch Trautwein		
1940-41	18-4		NIT RUNNER-UP							Dutch Trautwein		
1941-42	12-9									Dutch Trautwein		
1942-43	11-7									Dutch Trautwein		
1943-44	9-7									Dutch Trautwein		
1944-45	11-8									Dutch Trautwein		
1945-46	15-5									Dutch Trautwein		
1946-47	13-10	5-3		Dick Shrider	11.4					Dutch Trautwein		
1947-48	10-10	4-4		Dick Shrider	16.4					Dutch Trautwein		
1948-49	6-16	2-8		Bob Johnson	11.0					Dutch Trautwein	136-90	.602
1949-50	6-14	3-7		Dick Garrison	13.1					Jim Snyder		
1950-51	13-11	4-4		Glen Hursey	12.8					Jim Snyder		
1951-52	12-12	6-6		Glen Hursey	15.5					Jim Snyder		
1952-53	9-13	4-8		Jim Betts	18.2	Jim Betts	14.1			Jim Snyder		
1953-54	12-10	5-7		Lou Sawchik	17.3	Lou Sawchik	13.9			Jim Snyder		
1954-55	16-5	9-5		Fred Moore	19.7	Dick Garrison	9.5			Jim Snyder		
1955-56	13-11	5-7		Scott Griesheimer	14.2	Scott Griesheimer	8.4			Jim Snyder		
1956-57	15-8	7-5		Fred Moore	19.7	Dave Scott	13.0			Jim Snyder		
1957-58	16-8	7-5		Bob Peters	12.4	Dave Scott	11.9			Jim Snyder		
1958-59	14-10	6-6		Bunk Adams	14.4	Dave Scott	13.3			Jim Snyder		
1959-60	16-8	10-2	NCAA REGIONAL SEMIFINALS	Bunk Adams	16.4	Howard Jolliff	18.7			Jim Snyder		
1960-61	17-7	10-2	NCAA FIRST ROUND	Larry Kruger	18.6	Bunk Adams	12.8			Jim Snyder		
1961-62	13-10	8-4		Jerry Jackson	15.8	Jerry Jackson	9.6			Jim Snyder		
1962-63	13-11	8-4		Jerry Jackson	15.3	Don Hilt	8.2			Jim Snyder		
1963-64	21-6	10-2	NCAA REGIONAL FINALS	Jerry Jackson	17.6	Don Hilt	10.4			Jim Snyder		
1964-65	19-7	11-1	NCAA FIRST ROUND	Don Hilt	19.0	Don Hilt	11.8			Jim Snyder		
1965-66	13-10	6-6		Ken Fowlkes	16.1	John Schroeder	11.9			Jim Snyder		
1966-67	8-15	4-8		Gerald McKee	17.7	John Schroeder	13.3			Jim Snyder		
1967-68	7-16	3-9		Gerald McKee	20.0	Gerald McKee	9.7			Jim Snyder		
1968-69	17-9	9-3	NIT QUARTERFINALS	Gerald McKee	18.7	Gerald McKee	9.6			Jim Snyder		
1969-70	20-5	9-1	NCAA FIRST ROUND	John Canine	18.8	Craig Love	12.9			Jim Snyder		
1970-71	17-7	6-4		Ken Kowall	20.9	Craig Love	12.1			Jim Snyder		
1971-72	15-11	7-3	NCAA FIRST ROUND	Tom Corde	17.3	Denny Rusch	6.8			Jim Snyder		
1972-73	16-10	6-5		George Green	14.1	Dave Ball	7.3			Jim Snyder		
1973-74	16-11	9-3	NCAA FIRST ROUND	Walter Luckett	22.8	George Green	10.3			Jim Snyder	354-245	.591
1974-75	12-14	4-10		Walter Luckett	25.2	George Green	9.3			Dale Bandy		
1975-76	11-15	7-9		Scott Love	15.7	Scott Love	8.5			Dale Bandy		
1976-77	9-17	4-12		Steve Skaggs	19.3	Steve Skaggs	7.1			Dale Bandy		
1977-78	13-14	6-10		Tim Joyce	21.9	Brewer Gray	8.5			Dale Bandy		
1978-79	16-11	10-6		Tim Joyce	22.0	Brewer Gray	8.3			Dale Bandy		
1979-80	8-18	5-11		Kirk Lehman	17.6	Spindle Graves	5.3			Dale Bandy	69-89	.437
1980-81	7-20	6-10		Tim Woodson	13.4	John Devereaux	6.7			Danny Nee		
1981-82	13-14	8-8		Kirk Lehman	12.3	John Devereaux	6.9			Danny Nee		
1982-83	23-9	12-6	NCAA SECOND ROUND	John Devereaux	14.2	John Devereaux	9.8			Danny Nee		
1983-84	20-8	14-4		Vic Alexander	12.8	John Devereaux	10.3			Danny Nee		
1984-85	22-8	14-4	NCAA FIRST ROUND	Vic Alexander	14.4	Vic Alexander	7.2			Danny Nee		
1985-86	22-8	14-4	NIT FIRST ROUND	Robert Tatum	17.2	John Rhodes	6.8			Danny Nee	107-67	.615
1986-87	14-14	7-9		Paul Graham	21.1	John Rhodes	8.1			Billy Hahn		
1987-88	16-14	9-7		Paul Graham	20.0	John Rhodes	9.4			Billy Hahn		
1988-89	12-17 ⊗	6-10		Paul Graham	22.2	Paul Graham	7.0			Billy Hahn	42-45	.482▼
1989-90	12-16	5-11		Dave Jamerson	31.2	Dave Jamerson	6.4			Larry Hunter		
1990-91	16-12	9-7		Lewis Geter	18.1	Lewis Geter	6.8			Larry Hunter		
1991-92	18-10	10-6		Lewis Geter	20.9	Lewis Geter	8.4			Larry Hunter		
1992-93	14-13	11-7		Gary Trent	19.0	Gary Trent	9.3			Larry Hunter		
1993-94	25-8	14-4	NCAA FIRST ROUND	Gary Trent	25.4	Gary Trent	11.4			Larry Hunter		
1994-95	24-10	13-5	NIT SECOND ROUND	Gary Trent	22.9	Gary Trent	12.8			Larry Hunter		
1995-96	16-14	11-7		Geno Ford	18.9	Curtis Simmons	7.9			Larry Hunter		
1996-97	17-10	12-6		Geno Ford	18.7	Ed Sears	6.5			Larry Hunter		
1997-98	5-21	3-15		Sanjay Adell	16.1	B. Fakhir, D. Flenorl	7.9			Larry Hunter		
1998-99	18-10	12-6		LaDrell Whitehead	18.9	Shaun Stonerook	9.1	Shaun Stonerook	3.6	Larry Hunter		
1999-2000	20-13	11-7		Sanjay Adell	16.1	Shaun Stonerook	11.7	Shaun Stonerook	4.2	Larry Hunter		
2000-01	19-11	12-6		Brandon Hunter	18.1	Brandon Hunter	9.4	Anthony Jones	3.4	Larry Hunter	204-148	.580
2001-02	17-11	11-7		Brandon Hunter	17.3	Brandon Hunter	9.1	Jaivon Harris	2.9	Tim O'Shea		
2002-03	14-16	8-10		Brandon Hunter	21.5	Brandon Hunter	12.6	Jaivon Harris	3.1	Tim O'Shea		
2003-04	10-20	7-11		Jaivon Harris	15.1	Jaivon Harris	4.6	Thomas Stephens	3.2	Tim O'Shea		
2004-05	21-11	11-7	NCAA FIRST ROUND	Mychal Green	15.0	Leon Williams	8.6	Jeremy Fears	3.7	Tim O'Shea		
2005-06	19-11	10-8		Mychal Green	12.7	Leon Williams	6.9	Jeremy Fears	4.2	Tim O'Shea		
2006-07	19-13	9-7		Jerome Tillman	14.6	Leon Williams	8.8	Sonny Troutman	4.4	Tim O'Shea		
2007-08	20-13	9-7		Leon Williams	16.4	Leon Williams	9.8	Michael Allen	4.4	Tim O'Shea	120-95	.558
2008-09	15-17	7-9		Jerome Tillman	17.7	Jerome Tillman	8.1	Michael Allen	4.3	John Groce	15-17	.469

⊗ Records don't reflect games forfeited or vacated. For adjusted records, see p. 521.

▼ Coach's record adjusted to reflect games forfeited or vacated: 43-44, .494. For yearly totals, see p. 521.

THE SCHOOLS

ESPN 9 SAGARIN

OHIO STATE

You might be surprised to know that Ohio State has been to the Final Four more often than any other Big Ten team—10 in total (nine if you don't count the NCAA-vacated 1999 appearance). Add on the 1960 national championship, a long list of NBA talents (and a benchwarmer named Bob Knight), and it's clear nobody should mistake Ohio State for a mere football school.

BEST TEAM: 1959-60 Sophomores Jerry Lucas and John Havlicek formed a devastating frontcourt, junior guard Larry Siegfried got them the ball and Knight chipped in off the bench. After losing to Utah and Kentucky in a span of three games in late December, the Buckeyes reeled off 13 straight wins. Ohio State then won each Tournament game by at least 17 points, including the 75-55 Final victory in San Francisco over defending national champion California.

BEST PLAYER: C JERRY LUCAS (1959-62) During practice for the 1960 Olympics, the legendary Pete Newell pointed to Lucas and said, "There's the most unselfish player that ever played the game." The only three-time Big Ten Most Valuable Player, Lucas went on to a Hall of Fame NBA career.

BEST COACH: FRED TAYLOR (1958-76) After going .500 his first year, Taylor guided OSU to the 1960 national title. His encore: back-to-back runner-up finishes in 1961 and '62—the third coach to lead his team to three straight Final Fours. Taylor was best known for his recruiting (he counted Lucas and Havlicek among his haul) and staunch defense. Knight credits Taylor with teaching him about great D and discipline.

GAME FOR THE AGES: In the 1999 Tournament, the Buckeyes pulled off the impossible: reaching the Final Four just one year after finishing dead last in the Big Ten. With OSU up two in the Elite Eight, St. John's Erick Barkley dribbled up the floor looking to tie. But Scoonie Penn knocked the ball loose, it squirted out of Barkley's hands and into the arms of Redd, and OSU won, 77-74. The joy didn't last, though. Not only did the Buckeyes lose in the national semis to Connecticut, but the NCAA vacated 29 regular-season games and their entire 1999 Tournament appearance for recruiting violations.

HEARTBREAKER: Looking for their first Final Four appearance in 24 years, No. 1-seed OSU ran into No. 6-seed Michigan in the 1992 Elite Eight, having already beaten the Wolverines twice during the season. OSU stormed from behind in the second half to force OT. But the Buckeyes ran out of gas, losing 75-71, and were forced to watch their nemesis go to the Final Four.

FIERCEST RIVAL: Words can't describe the hatred Ohio State fans hold in their hearts for Michigan. But as with football, OSU has dominated Michigan on the hardwood of late. After beating the Wolverines twice in 2008-09, the Buckeyes have won nine of the last 10 games and lead overall, 85–70.

FANFARE AND HOOPLA: Brutus Buckeye, the school's most visible fan, first appeared as Ohio State's mascot in 1965. Although OSU never had a mascot before Brutus, there were discussions many years earlier about the possibility of using a buck, but the idea was scrapped because deer have such a skittish nature. Brutus' head was designed by an art student of the era to resemble the nut from the state's official tree—the Buckeye—and the name was settled on in a campus-wide contest.

FAN FAVORITE: G JAY BURSON (1985-89) The two-time OSU MVP broke a bone in his neck during a game in February of his senior season and never played for the Buckeyes again. Burson received more than 8,000 cards and letters of support. Amazingly, he recovered to play in the CBA for a year.

CONSENSUS ALL-AMERICAS

1925	**Johnny Miner,** F
1931	**Wes Fesler,** G/C
1939	**Jimmy Hull,** F
1950	**Dick Schnittker,** F
1956	**Robin Freeman,** G
1960-62	**Jerry Lucas,** C
1964	**Gary Bradds,** C
1991, '92	**Jim Jackson,** G/F

FIRST-ROUND PRO PICKS

1947	**Jack Underman,** St. Louis (7)
1947	**Paul Huston,** Chicago (8)
1950	**Dick Schnittker,** Washington (5)
1961	**Larry Siegfried,** Cincinnati (3)
1962	**Jerry Lucas,** Cincinnati (6)
1962	**John Havlicek,** Boston (9)
1964	**Gary Bradds,** Baltimore (3)
1968	**Bill Hosket,** New York (10)
1968	**Bill Hosket,** Minnesota (ABA)
1971	**Jim Cleamons,** LA Lakers (13)
1980	**Kelvin Ransey,** Chicago (4)
1981	**Herb Williams,** Indiana (14)
1982	**Clark Kellogg,** Indiana (8)
1984	**Tony Campbell,** Detroit (20)
1986	**Brad Sellers,** Chicago (9)
1987	**Dennis Hopson,** New Jersey (3)
1992	**Jim Jackson,** Dallas (4)
2007	**Greg Oden,** Portland (1)
2007	**Mike Conley Jr.,** Memphis (4)
2007	**Daequan Cook,** Philadelphia (21)
2008	**Kosta Koufos,** Utah (23)
2009	**B.J. Mullens,** Dallas (24)

PROFILE

The Ohio State University, Columbus, OH
Founded: 1870
Enrollment: 53,715 (40,212 undergraduate)
Colors: Scarlet and gray
Nickname: Buckeyes
Current arena: Value City Arena at the Jerome Schottenstein Center, opened in 1998 (19,049)
Previous: St. John Arena, 1956-98 (13,276)
First game: Dec. 2, 1898
All-time record: 1,512-1,017 (.598)
Total weeks in AP Top 20/25: 273

Current conference: Big Ten (1912-)
Conference titles:
Big Ten: 19 (1925, '33 [tie], '39, '44, '46, '50, '60, '61, '62, '63 [tie], '64 [tie], '68 [tie], '71, '91 [tie], '92, 2000 [tie]-v, '02 [tie]-v, 2006, '07)
Conference tournament titles:
Big Ten: 2 (2002-v, '07)
NCAA Tournaments: 25 (4 appearances vacated)
Sweet 16s (since 1975): 6
Final Fours: 10
Titles: 1 (1960)

NIT appearances: 8
Semifinals: 4
Titles: 2 (1986, 2008)
v – title vacated

TOP 5

G	**Robin Freeman** (1953-56)
G/F	**Jim Jackson** (1989-92)
F	**John Havlicek** (1959-62)
F	**Dennis Hopson** (1983-87)
C	**Jerry Lucas** (1959-62)

RECORDS	GAME		SEASON		CAREER	
POINTS	49	Gary Bradds, vs. Illinois (Feb. 10, 1964)	958	Dennis Hopson (1986-87)	2,096	Dennis Hopson (1983-87)
POINTS PER GAME			32.9	Robin Freeman (1955-56)	28.0	Robin Freeman (1953-56)
REBOUNDS	32	Frank Howard, vs. BYU (Dec. 29, 1956)	499	Jerry Lucas (1961-62)	1,411	Jerry Lucas (1959-62)
ASSISTS	14	Curtis Wilson, vs. Purdue (Jan. 7, 1988)	238	Mike Conley Jr. (2006-07)	579	Jamar Butler (2004-08)

SEASON REVIEW

SEASON	W-L	CONF.	SCORING	COACH	RECORD	
1898-1916	*142-75*		*Includes back-to-back 11-1 seasons, 1908-09 and 1909-10*			
1916-17	15-11	3-9		Lynn W. St. John		
1917-18	13-7	5-5		Lynn W. St. John		
1918-19	7-12	2-6		Lynn W. St. John	80-69	.537
1919-20	17-10	3-9		George M. Trautman		
1920-21	4-13	2-10		George M. Trautman		
1921-22	8-10	5-7		George M. Trautman	29-33	.468
1922-23	4-11	1-11		Harold G. Olsen		
1923-24	12-5	7-5		Harold G. Olsen		
1924-25	14-2	11-1		Harold G. Olsen		
1925-26	10-7	6-6		Harold G. Olsen		
1926-27	11-6	6-6		Harold G. Olsen		
1927-28	5-12	3-9		Harold G. Olsen		
1928-29	9-8	6-6		Harold G. Olsen		
1929-30	4-11	1-9		Harold G. Olsen		
1930-31	4-13	3-9		Harold G. Olsen		
1931-32	9-9	5-7		Harold G. Olsen		
1932-33	17-3	10-2		Harold G. Olsen		
1933-34	8-12	4-8		Harold G. Olsen		
1934-35	12-7	8-4		Harold G. Olsen		
1935-36	12-8	5-7		Harold G. Olsen		
1936-37	13-7	7-5		Harold G. Olsen		

SEAS.	W-L	CONF.	POSTSEASON	SCORING		REBOUNDS		ASSISTS		COACH	RECORD	
1937-38	12-8	7-5								Harold G. Olsen		
1938-39	16-7	10-2	NCAA RUNNER-UP							Harold G. Olsen		
1939-40	13-7	8-4								Harold G. Olsen		
1940-41	10-10	7-5								Harold G. Olsen		
1941-42	6-14	4-11								Harold G. Olsen		
1942-43	8-9	5-7								Harold G. Olsen		
1943-44	15-6	10-2	NCAA NATIONAL SEMIFINALS							Harold G. Olsen		
1944-45	15-5	10-2	NCAA NATIONAL SEMIFINALS							Harold G. Olsen		
1945-46	16-5	10-2	NCAA THIRD PLACE							Harold G. Olsen	255-192	.570
1946-47	7-13	5-7								William H. "Tippy" Dye		
1947-48	10-10	5-7								William H. "Tippy" Dye		
1948-49	14-7	6-6								William H. "Tippy" Dye		
1949-50	22-4	11-1	NCAA REGIONAL SEMIFINALS	Dick Schnittker	21.3					William H. "Tippy" Dye	53-34	.609
1950-51	6-16	3-11		James Remington	8.5					Floyd S. Stahl		
1951-52	8-14	6-8		Paul Ebert	20.1					Floyd S. Stahl		
1952-53	10-12	7-11		Paul Ebert	21.7					Floyd S. Stahl		
1953-54	11-11	5-9		Paul Ebert	23.5					Floyd S. Stahl		
1954-55	10-12	4-10		John Miller	20.1					Floyd S. Stahl		
1955-56	16-6	9-5		Robin Freeman	32.9					Floyd S. Stahl		
1956-57	14-8	9-5		Frank Howard	20.1	Frank Howard	15.3			Floyd S. Stahl		
1957-58	9-13	8-6		Frank Howard	16.9	Frank Howard	13.6			Floyd S. Stahl	84-92	.477
1958-59	11-11	7-7		Larry Siegfried	19.6	Dick Furry	10.7			Fred Taylor		
1959-60	**25-3**	**13-1**	**NATIONAL CHAMPION**	**Jerry Lucas**	**26.3**	**Jerry Lucas**	**16.4**			**Fred Taylor**		
1960-61	27-1	14-0	NCAA RUNNER-UP	Jerry Lucas	24.9	Jerry Lucas	17.4			Fred Taylor		
1961-62	26-2	13-1	NCAA RUNNER-UP	Jerry Lucas	21.7	Jerry Lucas	17.8			Fred Taylor		
1962-63	20-4	11-3		Gary Bradds	28.0	Gary Bradds	13.0			Fred Taylor		
1963-64	16-8	11-3		Gary Bradds	30.6	Gary Bradds	13.4			Fred Taylor		
1964-65	12-12	6-8		Dick Ricketts	18.2	Ron Sepic	8.6			Fred Taylor		
1965-66	11-13	5-9		Bill Hosket	18.5	Bill Hosket	13.1			Fred Taylor		
1966-67	13-11	6-8		Bill Hosket	19.6	Bill Hosket	12.6			Fred Taylor		
1967-68	21-8	10-4	NCAA THIRD PLACE	Bill Hosket	20.1	Bill Hosket	11.4			Fred Taylor		
1968-69	17-7	9-5		Dave Sorenson	23.6	Dave Sorenson	10.6			Fred Taylor		
1969-70	17-7	8-6		Dave Sorenson	24.2	Dave Sorenson	9.0			Fred Taylor		
1970-71	20-6	13-1	NCAA REGIONAL FINALS	Allan Hornyak	22.5	Luke Witte	12.7			Fred Taylor		
1971-72	18-6	10-4		Allan Hornyak	21.6	Luke Witte	12.6			Fred Taylor		
1972-73	14-10	8-6		Allan Hornyak	24.0	Luke Witte	8.3			Fred Taylor		
1973-74	9-15	4-10		Bill Andreas	15.7	Steve Wenner	8.7	Larry Bolden	3.3	Fred Taylor		
1974-75	14-14	8-10		Bill Andreas	19.1	Craig Taylor	9.0	Larry Bolden	5.6	Fred Taylor		
1975-76	6-20	2-16		Craig Taylor	14.9	Craig Taylor	9.9	Jud Wood	3.4	Fred Taylor	297-158	.653
1976-77	9-18 ⊗	4-14		Kelvin Ransey	13.1	Jim Ellinghausen	6.4	Larry Bolden	3.8	Eldon Miller		
1977-78	16-11	9-9		Kelvin Ransey	17.6	Herb Williams	11.4	Kelvin Ransey	5.1	Eldon Miller		
1978-79	19-12	12-6	NIT FOURTH PLACE	Kelvin Ransey	21.4	Herb Williams	10.5	Kelvin Ransey	4.3	Eldon Miller		
1979-80	21-8	12-6	NCAA REGIONAL SEMIFINALS	Herb Williams	17.6	Herb Williams	9.0	Kelvin Ransey	6.3	Eldon Miller		
1980-81	14-13	9-9		Clark Kellogg	17.3	Clark Kellogg	12.0	Larry Huggins	3.6	Eldon Miller		
1981-82	21-10	12-6	NCAA FIRST ROUND	Clark Kellogg	16.1	Clark Kellogg	10.5	Troy Taylor	3.4	Eldon Miller		
1982-83	20-10	11-7	NCAA REGIONAL SEMIFINALS	Tony Campbell	18.9	Tony Campbell	8.3	Ron Stokes	3.4	Eldon Miller		
1983-84	15-14	8-10	NIT FIRST ROUND	Tony Campbell	18.6	Tony Campbell	7.4	Ron Stokes	3.4	Eldon Miller		
1984-85	20-10	11-7	NCAA SECOND ROUND	Troy Taylor	15.8	Brad Sellers	8.8	Troy Taylor	4.7	Eldon Miller		
1985-86	19-14	8-10	NIT CHAMPION	Dennis Hopson	20.9	Brad Sellers	12.6	Curtis Wilson	3.2	Eldon Miller	174-120	.592▼
1986-87	20-13	9-9	NCAA SECOND ROUND	Dennis Hopson	29.0	Dennis Hopson	8.2	Curtis Wilson	4.9	Gary Williams		
1987-88	20-13	9-9	NIT RUNNER-UP	Jay Burson	18.9	Perry Carter	7.2	Curtis Wilson	5.7	Gary Williams		
1988-89	19-15	6-12	NIT QUARTERFINALS	Jay Burson	22.1	Perry Carter	8.1	Jay Burson	4.0	Gary Williams	59-41	.590
1989-90	17-13	10-8	NCAA SECOND ROUND	Jim Jackson	16.1	Perry Carter	7.8	Jim Jackson	3.7	Randy Ayers		
1990-91	27-4	15-3	NCAA REGIONAL SEMIFINALS	Jim Jackson	18.9	Perry Carter	8.4	Mark Baker	5.0	Randy Ayers		
1991-92	26-6	15-3	NCAA REGIONAL FINALS	Jim Jackson	22.4	Jim Jackson	6.8	Mark Baker	5.2	Randy Ayers		
1992-93	15-13	8-10	NIT FIRST ROUND	Lawrence Funderburke	16.3	Lawrence Funderburke	6.8	Jamie Skelton	2.8	Randy Ayers		
1993-94	13-16	6-12		Lawrence Funderburke	15.2	Lawrence Funderburke	6.0	Jamie Skelton	3.8	Randy Ayers		
1994-95	6-22	2-16		Doug Etzler	16.3	Rickey Dudley	7.5	Doug Etzler	3.9	Randy Ayers		
1995-96	10-17 ⊗	3-15		Damon Stringer	11.3	J. Tate, S. Stonerook	6.9	Damon Stringer	4.6	Randy Ayers		
1996-97	10-17	5-13		Damon Stringer	15.1	Shaun Stonerook	7.7	Damon Stringer	4.4	Randy Ayers	124-108	.534▼
1997-98	8-22	1-15		Michael Redd	21.9	Michael Redd	6.4	Carlos Davis	4.2	Jim O'Brien		
1998-99	27-9 ⊗	12-4	NCAA NATIONAL SEMIFINALS	Michael Redd	19.5	Ken Johnson	5.7	Scoonie Penn	4.3	Jim O'Brien		
1999-2000	23-7 ⊗	13-3	NCAA SECOND ROUND	Michael Redd	17.1	Michael Redd	6.5	Scoonie Penn	4.3	Jim O'Brien		
2000-01	20-11 ⊗	11-5	NCAA FIRST ROUND	Brian Brown	14.6	Ken Johnson	7.3	Brian Brown	4.1	Jim O'Brien		
2001-02	24-8 ⊗	11-5	NCAA SECOND ROUND	Brian Brown	16.3	Zach Williams	5.8	Brian Brown	3.3	Jim O'Brien		
2002-03	17-15	7-9	NIT FIRST ROUND	Brent Darby	18.3	Velimir Radinovic	6.1	Brent Darby	4.4	Jim O'Brien		
2003-04	14-16	6-10		Tony Stockman	13.6	Terence Dials	6.6	Tony Stockman	2.6	Jim O'Brien	133-88	.602▼
2004-05	20-12	8-8		Terence Dials	15.9	Terence Dials	7.9	Brandon Fuss-Cheatham	3.1	Thad Matta		
2005-06	26-6	12-4	NCAA SECOND ROUND	Terence Dials	15.3	Terence Dials	8.0	Jamar Butler	4.6	Thad Matta		
2006-07	35-4	15-1	NCAA RUNNER-UP	Greg Oden	15.7	Greg Oden	9.6	Mike Conley Jr	6.1	Thad Matta		
2007-08	24-13	10-8	NIT CHAMPION	Jamar Butler	15.0	Kosta Koufos	6.7	Jamar Butler	5.9	Thad Matta		
2008-09	22-11	10-8	NCAA FIRST ROUND	Evan Turner	17.3	Evan Turner	7.1	Evan Turner	4.0	Thad Matta	127-46	.734

⊗ Records don't reflect games forfeited or vacated. For adjusted records, see p. 521.

▼ Coaches' records adjusted to reflect games forfeited or vacated: Eldon Miller, 176-118, .599; Randy Ayers, 126-106, .543; Jim O'Brien, 51-57, .472. For yearly totals, see p. 521.

ESPN 20 SAGARIN

OKLAHOMA

In their first 73 years, the Sooners enjoyed exactly two 20-win seasons. But ever since Billy Tubbs arrived in 1980, Oklahoma has been making up for lost winning time. From 1981-82 to 2005-06, the Sooners qualified for postseason play all 25 seasons. That includes two Elite Eights and two Final Fours, highlighted by a run to the 1988 national title game. Under coach Jeff Capel, the Sooners have a new streak going, having made the 2008 and '09 NCAA Tournaments and riding Blake Griffin all the way to the 2009 Elite Eight.

BEST TEAM: 1987-88 Starring three future first-round draft picks—Mookie Blaylock, Stacey King and Harvey Grant—the Sooners were a near-unstoppable offensive force, averaging a school-record 102.9 points. The Big Eight regular-season and tournament champions steamrolled their way through the NCAA Tournament, outscoring their opponents by an average of 17 points on their way to the Final. There, they lost a shocker to Danny Manning's Kansas squad, 83-79, immediately transforming them into one of the best teams never to win it all.

BEST PLAYER: F/C Wayman Tisdale (1982-85) The 6'9" lefty from Tulsa always had a smile on his face; so did every OU fan watching him play. Tisdale was the Big Eight Player of the Year in each of his three seasons in Norman, and he was the first freshman ever named to the AP All-America First Team. Tisdale averaged 25.6 points during his career and still holds Sooners records for total points and rebounds. After a long career in both the NBA and in music, he died of cancer in May 2009.

BEST COACH: Billy Tubbs (1980-94) His high-flying offense and full-court pressure defense—a.k.a. Billy Ball—transformed the also-ran Sooners into a legit national power. Tubbs led Oklahoma to four Sweet 16 appearances and a trip to the 1988 Final, but didn't make many friends along with the way with his brazen style. He was routinely accused of running up the score. He was also accused of flicking off Colorado fans after a game. He denies both charges to this day.

GAME FOR THE AGES: In the 2002 Big 12 tournament final, top-ranked Kansas looked to the entire hoops world like national title favorites. But Sooners coach Kelvin Sampson put the clamps down on Roy Williams' bunch in a 64-55 upset. Oklahoma held KU to 33.3% shooting and displayed the grit and defensive determination that would carry them to the Final Four.

HEARTBREAKER: Oklahoma entered the 1988 NCAA Final supremely confident, having beaten Kansas twice already that season. But KU legend Manning was unstoppable, racking up 31 points and 18 rebounds. His teammates, known to Jayhawks fans as simply the Miracles, shot 63.6% from the field as Kansas pulled off an 83-79 stunner.

FIERCEST RIVAL: No one has caused the Sooners more heartbreak than KU, but the Oklahoma State Cowboys in Stillwater will always be OU's archrival. Known as the Bedlam Rivalry, the series reached new heights when charismatic coaches Tubbs and Eddie Sutton strolled the sideline starting in the 1990s. Sooners coach Jeff Capel made himself persona non grata forever in Stillwater after he was caught on tape screaming out to his team after a 2008 road win, "Let's hurry up and get a shower and get the hell out of this hell hole!" OU leads, 125–90.

FANFARE AND HOOPLA: The OU Chant is sung after every hoops game by Sooners fans as a sign of unity. The Oklahoma faithful stand and raise their index fingers in unison while reciting the words written by a girl's glee club director in 1936. They go, "OU's chant will never die." Boomer Sooner.

FAN FAVORITE: F Eduardo Najera (1996-2000) Najera was the quintessential Sampson player, known for his bruising style on the glass and the defensive end. He went on to become only the second Mexican-born player drafted by the NBA.

CONSENSUS ALL-AMERICAS

1910	**Ernest Lambert,** F
1928	**Victor Holt,** C
1929	**Thomas Churchill,** F
1935	**Bud Browning,** G
1944	**Alva Paine,** G
1947	**Gerald Tucker,** C
1983-85	**Wayman Tisdale,** F/C
1989	**Stacey King,** C
2009	**Blake Griffin,** F

FIRST-ROUND PRO PICKS

1951	**Marcus Freiberger,** Indianapolis (3)
1970	**Garfield Heard,** Memphis (ABA)
1975	**Alvan Adams,** Phoenix (4)
1985	**Wayman Tisdale,** Indiana (2)
1988	**Harvey Grant,** Washington (12)
1989	**Stacey King,** Chicago (6)
1989	**Mookie Blaylock,** New Jersey (12)
2009	**Blake Griffin,** LA Clippers (1)

PROFILE

University of Oklahoma, Norman, OK
Founded: 1890
Enrollment: 29,721 (19,015 undergraduate)
Colors: Crimson and cream
Nickname: Sooners
Current arena: Lloyd Noble Center, opened in 1975 (12,000)
Previous: Field House, 1928-75 (2,000); Armory, 1919-28 (4,000); Gymnasium, 1907-19 (200)
First game: Nov. 26, 1907
All-time record: 1,498-942 (.614)
Total weeks in AP Top 20/25: 307
Current conference: Big 12 (1996-)
Conference titles:
Missouri Valley: 1 (1928)
Big Six: 6 (1929, '39 [tie], '40 [tie], '42 [tie], '44 [tie], '47)
Big Seven: 1 (1949 [tie])
Big Eight: 5 (1979, '84, '85, '88, '89)
Big 12: 1 (2005 [tie])
Conference tournament titles:
Big Eight: 4 (1979, '85, '88, '90)
Big 12: 3 (2001, '02, '03)
NCAA Tournament appearances: 26
Sweet 16s (since 1975): 9
Final Fours: 4
NIT appearances: 7
Semifinals: 2

TOP 5

G	**Mookie Blaylock** (1987-89)
G	**Tim McCalister** (1983-87)
F	**Blake Griffin** (2007-09)
F/C	**Wayman Tisdale** (1982-85)
C	**Stacey King** (1985-89)

RECORDS

RECORDS	GAME		SEASON		CAREER	
POINTS	61	Wayman Tisdale, vs. Texas-San Antonio (Dec. 28, 1983)	932	Wayman Tisdale (1984-85)	2,661	Wayman Tisdale (1982-85)
POINTS PER GAME			27.0	Wayman Tisdale (1983-84)	25.6	Wayman Tisdale (1982-85)
REBOUNDS	28	Alvan Adams, vs. Indiana State (Nov. 27, 1972)	504	Blake Griffin (2008-09)	1,048	Wayman Tisdale (1982-85)
ASSISTS	18	Michael Johnson, vs. North Texas (Dec. 22, 1997); Jan Pannell, vs. Oklahoma City (Jan. 12, 1983)	280	Ricky Grace (1987-88)	651	Terry Evans (1989-93)

SEASON REVIEW

SEASON	W-L	CONF.	SCORING	COACH	RECORD
1907-16	*64-26*		*Undefeated (8-0) in 1909-10 and 1912-13*		
1916-17	13-8			Bennie Owen	
1917-18	11-1			Bennie Owen	
1918-19	12-0			Bennie Owen	
1919-20	9-7	3-7		Bennie Owen	
1920-21	8-10	5-9		Bennie Owen	113-49 .698
1921-22	9-9	8-8		Hugh McDermott	
1922-23	6-12	5-11		Hugh McDermott	
1923-24	15-3	13-3		Hugh McDermott	
1924-25	10-8	9-7		Hugh McDermott	
1925-26	11-4	9-3		Hugh McDermott	
1926-27	12-5	8-4		Hugh McDermott	
1927-28	18-0	18-0		Hugh McDermott	
1928-29	13-2	10-0		Hugh McDermott	
1929-30	6-12	0-10		Hugh McDermott	
1930-31	10-8	3-7		Hugh McDermott	
1931-32	9-5	6-4		Hugh McDermott	
1932-33	12-5	7-3		Hugh McDermott	
1933-34	10-8	6-4		Hugh McDermott	
1934-35	9-9	8-8		Hugh McDermott	
1935-36	9-8	5-5		Hugh McDermott	
1936-37	12-4	7-3		Hugh McDermott	

SEAS.	W-L	CONF.	POSTSEASON	SCORING		REBOUNDS		ASSISTS		COACH	RECORD	
1937-38	14-4	8-2								Hugh McDermott	185-106	.636
1938-39	12-9	7-3	NCAA NATIONAL SEMIFINALS							Bruce Drake		
1939-40	12-7	8-2								Bruce Drake		
1940-41	6-12	5-5								Bruce Drake		
1941-42	11-7	8-2								Bruce Drake		
1942-43	18-9	7-3	NCAA REGIONAL SEMIFINALS	Gerald Tucker	14.3					Bruce Drake		
1943-44	15-8	9-1								Bruce Drake		
1944-45	12-13	5-5								Bruce Drake		
1945-46	11-10	7-3								Bruce Drake		
1946-47	24-7	8-2	NCAA RUNNER-UP	Gerald Tucker	10.5					Bruce Drake		
1947-48	13-9	7-5								Bruce Drake		
1948-49	14-10	9-3								Bruce Drake		
1949-50	12-10	6-6								Bruce Drake		
1950-51	14-10	6-6		Marcus Freiberger	15.8					Bruce Drake		
1951-52	7-17	4-8		Sherman Norton	15.1					Bruce Drake		
1952-53	8-13	5-7		Bob Waller	13.5					Bruce Drake		
1953-54	8-13	4-8		Lester Lane	18.8					Bruce Drake		
1954-55	3-18	1-11		Lester Lane	19.6	LeRoy Bacher	13.0			Bruce Drake	200-182	.524
1955-56	4-19	1-11		LeRoy Bacher	18.6	Joe King	9.5			Doyle Parrack		
1956-57	8-15	3-9		Joe King	16.0	Don Schwall	8.7			Doyle Parrack		
1957-58	13-10	5-7		Joe King	15.7	Joe King	7.7			Doyle Parrack		
1958-59	15-10	9-5		Dennis Price	13.1	Dennis Price	5.0			Doyle Parrack		
1959-60	14-11	9-5		Brian Etheridge	10.4	Brian Etheridge	5.1			Doyle Parrack		
1960-61	10-15 ⊗	2-12		Warren Fouts	11.1	Brian Etheridge	6.4			Doyle Parrack		
1961-62	7-17	5-9		Warren Fouts	12.4	Warren Fouts	7.3			Doyle Parrack	71-97	.423
1962-63	12-13	8-6		Eddie Evans	16.4	James Gatewood	6.9			Bob Stevens		
1963-64	7-18	3-11		James Gatewood	13.6	James Gatewood	7.8			Bob Stevens		
1964-65	8-17	3-11		James Gatewood	14.5	James Gatewood	8.0			Bob Stevens		
1965-66	11-14	7-7		Don Sidle	17.6	Don Sidle	9.1			Bob Stevens		
1966-67	8-17	5-9		Don Sidle	23.7	Don Sidle	11.0			Bob Stevens	46-79	.368
1967-68	13-13	8-6		Don Sidle	19.8	Don Sidle	10.0			John MacLeod		
1968-69	7-19	3-11		Garfield Heard	13.2	Garfield Heard	9.7			John MacLeod		
1969-70	19-9	7-7	NIT QUARTERFINALS	Garfield Heard	21.7	Garfield Heard	12.5			John MacLeod		
1970-71	19-8	9-5	NIT FIRST ROUND	Bobby Jack	17.3	Clifford Ray	12.0			John MacLeod		
1971-72	14-12	9-5		Bobby Jack	16.5	Bobby Jack	7.5			John MacLeod		
1972-73	18-8	8-6		Alvan Adams	22.1	Alvan Adams	13.2			John MacLeod	90-69	.566
1973-74	18-8	9-5		Alvan Adams	21.2	Alvan Adams	12.1			Joe Ramsey		
1974-75	13-13	6-8		Alvan Adams	26.6	Alvan Adams	13.3			Joe Ramsey	31-21	.596
1975-76	9-17	6-8		Rick McNeil	12.2	Kevin Jones	5.9			Dave Bliss		
1976-77	18-10	9-5		John McCullough	15.2	Al Beal	7.0	Eddie Fields	5.1	Dave Bliss		
1977-78	14-13	7-7		John McCullough	13.8	Al Beal	8.0	John McCullough	3.5	Dave Bliss		
1978-79	21-10	10-4	NCAA REGIONAL SEMIFINALS	John McCullough	16.1	Al Beal	9.1	Raymond Whitley	4.3	Dave Bliss		
1979-80	15-12	6-8		Terry Stotts	16.9	Al Beal	8.3	Raymond Whitley	4.4	Dave Bliss	77-62	.554
1980-81	9-18	4-10		Chucky Barnett	18.4	Steve Bajema	8.4	Bo Overton	4.1	Billy Tubbs		
1981-82	22-11	8-6	NIT SEMIFINALS	Chucky Barnett	18.9	Charles Jones	6.0	Bo Overton	4.5	Billy Tubbs		
1982-83	24-9	10-4	NCAA SECOND ROUND	Wayman Tisdale	24.5	Wayman Tisdale	10.3	Bo Overton	7.1	Billy Tubbs		
1983-84	29-5	13-1	NCAA SECOND ROUND	Wayman Tisdale	27.0	Wayman Tisdale	9.7	Jan Pannell	7.1	Billy Tubbs		
1984-85	31-6	13-1	NCAA REGIONAL FINALS	Wayman Tisdale	25.2	Wayman Tisdale	10.2	Anthony Bowie	5.3	Billy Tubbs		
1985-86	26-9	8-6	NCAA SECOND ROUND	Darryl Kennedy	21.0	Darryl Kennedy	8.2	Linwood Davis	5.0	Billy Tubbs		
1986-87	24-10	9-5	NCAA REGIONAL SEMIFINALS	Tim McCalister	19.8	Harvey Grant	9.9	Ricky Grace	5.6	Billy Tubbs		
1987-88	35-4	12-2	NCAA RUNNER-UP	Stacey King	22.3	Harvey Grant	9.4	Ricky Grace	7.2	Billy Tubbs		
1988-89	30-6	12-2	NCAA REGIONAL SEMIFINALS	Stacey King	26.0	Stacey King	10.1	Mookie Blaylock	6.7	Billy Tubbs		
1989-90	27-5	11-3	NCAA SECOND ROUND	Skeeter Henry	17.3	William Davis	8.5	T. Evans, Skeeter Henry	4.4	Billy Tubbs		
1990-91	20-15	5-9	NIT RUNNER-UP	Jeff Webster	18.3	Kermit Holmes	9.3	Brent Price	5.5	Billy Tubbs		
1991-92	21-9	8-6	NCAA FIRST ROUND	Damon Patterson	20.6	Bryan Sallier	9.1	Brent Price	6.2	Billy Tubbs		
1992-93	20-12	7-7	NIT SECOND ROUND	Bryatt Vann	16.9	Bryan Sallier	8.6	Terry Evans	5.8	Billy Tubbs		
1993-94	15-13	6-8	NIT FIRST ROUND	Jeff Webster	23.7	Jeff Webster	7.8	John Ontjes	6.5	Billy Tubbs	333-132	.716
1994-95	23-9	9-5	NCAA FIRST ROUND	Ryan Minor	23.6	Ryan Minor	8.4	John Ontjes	6.8	Kelvin Sampson		
1995-96	17-13 ⊗	8-6	NCAA FIRST ROUND	Ryan Minor	21.3	Ernie Abercrombie	10.1	Tyrone Foster	5.6	Kelvin Sampson		
1996-97	19-11	9-7	NCAA FIRST ROUND	Nate Erdmann	20.5	Eduardo Najera	5.6	Corey Brewer	3.5	Kelvin Sampson		
1997-98	22-11	11-5	NCAA FIRST ROUND	Corey Brewer	20.8	Ryan Humphery	6.5	Michael Johnson	4.3	Kelvin Sampson		
1998-99	22-11	11-5	NCAA REGIONAL SEMIFINALS	Eduardo Najera	15.5	Eduardo Najera	8.3	Michael Johnson	3.9	Kelvin Sampson		
1999-2000	27-7	12-4	NCAA SECOND ROUND	Eduardo Najera	18.4	Eduardo Najera	9.2	Hollis Price	3.5	Kelvin Sampson		
2000-01	26-7	12-4	NCAA FIRST ROUND	Nolan Johnson	13.2	Daryan Selvy	5.2	Hollis Price	4.6	Kelvin Sampson		
2001-02	31-5	13-3	NCAA NATIONAL SEMIFINALS	Hollis Price	16.5	Aaron McGhee	7.7	Quannas White	4.7	Kelvin Sampson		
2002-03	27-7	12-4	NCAA REGIONAL FINALS	Hollis Price	18.0	Kevin Bookout	5.9	Quannas White	4.1	Kelvin Sampson		
2003-04	20-11	8-8	NIT SECOND ROUND	Jason Detrick	11.4	Jabahri Brown	5.1	Drew Lavender	3.9	Kelvin Sampson		
2004-05	25-8	12-4	NCAA SECOND ROUND	Taj Gray	14.6	Taj Gray	8.2	Terrell Everett	5.0	Kelvin Sampson		
2005-06	20-9	11-5	NCAA FIRST ROUND	Taj Gray	14.2	Taj Gray	7.7	Terrell Everett	6.9	Kelvin Sampson	279-109	.719▼
2006-07	16-15	6-10		Nate Carter	11.6	Longar Longar	7.1	Austin Johnson	2.8	Jeff Capel		
2007-08	23-12	9-7	NCAA SECOND ROUND	Blake Griffin	14.7	Blake Griffin	9.1	Austin Johnson	2.7	Jeff Capel		
2008-09	30-6	13-3	NCAA REGIONAL FINALS	Blake Griffin	22.7	Blake Griffin	14.4	Austin Johnson	3.9	Jeff Capel	69-33	.676

⊗ Records don't reflect games forfeited or vacated. For adjusted records, see p. 521.

▼ Coach's record adjusted to reflect games forfeited or vacated: 280-108, .722. For yearly totals, see p. 521.

ESPN 18 SAGARIN

OKLAHOMA STATE

Under legendary coach Hank Iba, the agricultural school formerly known as Oklahoma A&M cultivated one of the heartland's most storied programs. As Aggies, they made it to four Final Fours and were the first team to win back-to-back NCAA titles. As Cowboys, they returned to the Final Four twice, both times coached by Iba protégé Eddie Sutton.

BEST TEAM: 1945-46 Hank Iba's Oklahoma A&M squad achieved a 31–2 record on its way to becoming the first team to win NCAA titles in consecutive years. After losing their second game of the season to DePaul, the Aggies reeled off 15 straight victories, lost to Bowling Green, then closed out the season with another string of 15 wins. While each member of the starting five was named first team all-conference, the Aggies were led by All-America center Bob Kurland, who scored 23 points in the 43-40 NCAA championship win over North Carolina.

BEST PLAYER: C Bob Kurland (1942-46) The school's only three-time All-America, the 7-foot Kurland led the Aggies to those back-to-back NCAA championships in 1945 and '46. Nicknamed Foothills, he was the leading scorer on both title teams and was named the Tournament's Most Outstanding Player each time. A dominating defensive force, his prowess for blocking shots that were on their way down to the basket led to the rule banning defensive goaltending. In his four seasons, Kurland scored 1,669 points (fifth all-time at OSU), including a school-record 58 against Saint Louis in 1946.

BEST COACH: Hank Iba (1934-70) The legendary Mr. Iba was the first coach to run the motion offense and promote "help" principles on a man-to-man defense known as the "swinging gate." One of the true giants of the game, he coached OSU to 653 wins (against 317 losses), 13 league championships, four Final Fours and back-to-back titles in 1945 and '46.

GAME FOR THE AGES: OSU's 105-103 triple-overtime win over Texas on Jan. 16, 2007, had it all. UT's D.J. Augustin pushed the game into a first OT, Longhorn Kevin Durant carried it into the third. But OSU's Mario Boggan had the final say. His three-pointer from near the OSU bench turned out to be the game-winner. Both Durant and Boggan finished the classic with 37 points.

HEARTBREAKER: The Cowboys' attempt to get Eddie Sutton to an NCAA championship game fell just short in a 67-65 national semifinal loss to Georgia Tech on April 3, 2004. John Lucas III's three-pointer pulled the Cowboys into a 65-65 tie, but Tech's Will Bynum scored on a layup with 1.5 seconds left to send the Yellow Jackets to the Final—and Sutton and the Cowboys home.

FIERCEST RIVAL: The Bedlam Series with Oklahoma is an expression of pure athletic hatred. For example, Iba so despised OU that he refused to set foot in Norman, except when he had to coach games against the Sooners. The rivalry actually has its roots in wrestling competition, but extends to all sports, pitting city (Oklahoma) against country (Oklahoma State). On the court, Oklahoma leads the series, 125–90.

Iba so despised OU that he refused to set foot in Norman, except when he had to coach games against the Sooners.

FANFARE AND HOOPLA: Called the Madison Square Garden of the Plains when it opened in 1938, Gallagher-Iba Arena is still one of the toughest places to play in college basketball. Originally named for OSU wrestling coach Ed Gallagher, Iba's name was added in 1987. Despite two renovations to the building, the Cowboys continue to play on the original white maple floor.

FAN FAVORITE: C Bryant Reeves (1991-95) A 7-foot hillbilly from tiny Gans, Okla., the aptly nicknamed Big Country morphed from a project to a two-time Big Eight Player of the Year.

CONSENSUS ALL-AMERICAS

1944-46 **Bob Kurland,** C

FIRST-ROUND PRO PICKS

1949	**Bob Harris,** Fort Wayne (3)
1992	**Byron Houston,** Chicago (27)
1994	**Brooks Thompson,** Orlando (27)
1995	**Bryant Reeves,** Vancouver (6)
2000	**Desmond Mason,** Seattle (17)
2004	**Tony Allen,** Boston (25)
2005	**Joey Graham,** Toronto (16)

PROFILE

Oklahoma State University, Stillwater, OK
Founded: 1890
Enrollment: 20,756 (16,395 undergraduate)
Colors: Orange and black
Nickname: Cowboys
Current arena: Gallagher-Iba Arena, opened in 1938 as the 4H Club and Student Activity Building, renamed Gallagher Hall (13,611)
Previous: New Armory, 1920-38 (1,500); Old Armory, 1907-19 (N/A)
First game: 1908
All-time record: 1,475-1,030 (.589)
Total weeks in AP Top 20/25: 237
Current conference: Big 12 (1996-)
Conference titles:
Southwest: 1 (1925)
Missouri Valley: 13 (1931 [tie], '36 [tie], '37, '38, '39 [tie], '40, '42 [tie], '46, '48, '49, '51, '53, '54)
Big Eight: 2 (1965, '91 [tie])
Big 12: 1 (2004)
Conference tournament titles:
Big Eight: 2 (1983, '95)
Big 12: 2 (2004, '05)
NCAA Tournament appearances: 23
Sweet 16s (since 1975): 6
Final Fours: 6
Titles: 2 (1945, '46)
NIT appearances: 10
Semifinals: 3

TOP 5

G	**Tony Allen** (2002-04)
G/F	**Desmond Mason** (1996-2000)
F	**Byron Houston** (1988-92)
C	**Bob Kurland** (1942-46)
C	**Bryant Reeves** (1991-95)

RECORDS

RECORDS	GAME		SEASON		CAREER	
POINTS	58	Bob Kurland, vs. Saint Louis (Feb. 22, 1946)	797	Bryant Reeves (1994-95)	2,379	Byron Houston (1988-92)
POINTS PER GAME			24.2	Ed Odom (1979-80)	18.7	Byron Houston (1988-92)
REBOUNDS	27	Andy Hopson, vs. Missouri (Jan. 30, 1973)	375	Andy Hopson (1973-74)	1,189	Byron Houston (1988-92)
ASSISTS	18	Doug Gottlieb, vs. Florida Atlantic (Dec. 1, 1998)	299	Doug Gottlieb (1998-99)	793	Doug Gottlieb (1997-2000)

SEASON REVIEW

SEASON	W-L	CONF.	SCORING		COACH	RECORD	
1907-16	*28-32*		*Includes one winning season (1914-15, 10-4)*				
1916-17	11-4				John G. Griffith	18-12	.600
1917-18	6-10	1-4			Earl A. Pritchard		
1918-19	5-5				Earl A. Pritchard	11-15	.423
1919-20	1-12				Jim Pixlee		
1920-21	2-9				Jim Pixlee	3-21	.125
1921-22	6-15	1-4			John F. Maulbetsch		
1922-23	12-11	7-8			John F. Maulbetsch		
1923-24	14-6	10-4			John F. Maulbetsch		
1924-25	15-3	12-2			John F. Maulbetsch		
1925-26	9-9	5-7			John F. Maulbetsch		
1926-27	8-9	6-6			John F. Maulbetsch		
1927-28	11-7	11-7			John F. Maulbetsch		
1928-29	1-14	0-4			John F. Maulbetsch	76-74	.507
1929-30	1-15	0-8			George Rody		
1930-31	7-9	5-3			George Rody	8-24	.250
1931-32	4-16	2-6			Harold James		
1932-33	5-12	3-7			Harold James		
1933-34	4-14	1-9			Harold James	13-42	.236
1934-35	9-9	5-7			Hank Iba		
1935-36	16-8	8-4	Merle Rousey	5.9	Hank Iba		
1936-37	19-3	11-1	Merle Rousey	6.1	Hank Iba		

SEAS.	W-L	CONF.	POSTSEASON	SCORING		REBOUNDS		ASSISTS		COACH	RECORD	
1937-38	25-3	13-1	NIT THIRD PLACE	Dick Krueger	9.5					Hank Iba		
1938-39	19-8	11-3		Jesse Renick	6.6					Hank Iba		
1939-40	26-3	12-0	NIT THIRD PLACE	Jesse Renick	7.7					Hank Iba		
1940-41	18-7	8-4		Leroy Floyd	7.4					Hank Iba		
1941-42	20-6	9-1		Lon Eggleston	10.5					Hank Iba		
1942-43	14-10	7-3		Vernon Yates	7.5					Hank Iba		
1943-44	27-6		NIT FOURTH PLACE	Bob Kurland	13.5					Hank Iba		
1944-45	**27-4**		**NATIONAL CHAMPION**	**Bob Kurland**	**17.1**					**Hank Iba**		
1945-46	**31-2**	**12-0**	**NATIONAL CHAMPION**	**Bob Kurland**	**19.5**					**Hank Iba**		
1946-47	24-8	8-4		A.L.Bennett	10.3					Hank Iba		
1947-48	27-4	10-0		Bob Harris	8.4					Hank Iba		
1948-49	23-5	9-1	NCAA RUNNER-UP	Bob Harris	11.7					Hank Iba		
1949-50	18-9	7-5		Jack Shelton	10.4					Hank Iba		
1950-51	29-6	12-2	NCAA FOURTH PLACE	Don Johnson	12.1	Don Johnson	6.7			Hank Iba		
1951-52	19-8	7-3		Don Johnson	14.0	Don Johnson	8.3			Hank Iba		
1952-53	23-7	8-2	NCAA REGIONAL FINALS	Bob Mattick	17.4	Bob Mattick	9.4			Hank Iba		
1953-54	24-5	9-1	NCAA REGIONAL FINALS	Bob Mattick	20.7	Bob Mattick	11.2			Hank Iba		
1954-55	12-13	5-5		Clayton Carter	12.2	Clayton Carter	7.1			Hank Iba		
1955-56	18-9	8-4	NIT FIRST ROUND	Clayton Carter	15.0	V.R. Barnhouse	6.4			Hank Iba		
1956-57	17-9	8-6		Henry Kemple	12.9	Henry Kemple	7.8			Hank Iba		
1957-58	21-8		NCAA REGIONAL FINALS	Arlen Clark	17.3	Arlen Clark	6.6			Hank Iba		
1958-59	11-14	5-9		Arlen Clark	20.4	Arlen Clark	5.7			Hank Iba		
1959-60	10-15	4-10		Don Heffington	8.0	Eddie Bunch	4.7			Hank Iba		
1960-61	14-11 ⊗	9-5		Fritz Greer	13.9	Cecil Epperley	8.2			Hank Iba		
1961-62	14-11	7-7		Eddie Bunch	14.3	Cecil Epperley	10.4			Hank Iba		
1962-63	16-9	7-7		Larry Hawk	13.2	James King	8.7			Hank Iba		
1963-64	15-10	7-7		Larry Hawk	13.9	James King	10.3			Hank Iba		
1964-65	20-7	12-2	NCAA REGIONAL FINALS	Gary Hassmann	12.6	James King	10.6			Hank Iba		
1965-66	4-21	2-12		Jim Feamster	11.8	Jim Feamster	5.8			Hank Iba		
1966-67	7-18	2-12		Jim Feamster	10.7	Joe Smith	5.5			Hank Iba		
1967-68	10-16	3-11		Joe Smith	13.0	Charlie Savall	6.6			Hank Iba		
1968-69	12-13	5-9		Amos Thomas	17.9	Charlie Savall	5.5			Hank Iba		
1969-70	14-12	5-9		Rick Cooper	13.0	Bob Buck	8.2			Hank Iba	653-317	.673
1970-71	7-19	2-12		Tony Kraus	12.2	Tony Kraus	6.4			Sam Aubrey		
1971-72	4-22	2-12		Ralph Rasmuson	14.1	Ralph Rasmuson	7.8			Sam Aubrey		
1972-73	7-19	3-11		Kevin Fitzgerald	18.6	Andy Hopson	13.5			Sam Aubrey	18-60	.231
1973-74	9-17	3-11		Kevin Fitzgerald	17.9	Andy Hopson	14.4			Guy Strong		
1974-75	10-16	5-9		Ronnie Daniel	17.5	Andy Hopson	11.3			Guy Strong		
1975-76	10-16	4-10		Ronnie Daniel	15.8	Olus Holder	7.2			Guy Strong		
1976-77	10-17	4-10		Olus Holder	16.8	Olus Holder	10.0	Ronnie Daniel	3.7	Guy Strong	39-66	.371
1977-78	10-16	4-10		Olus Holder	17.0	Olus Holder	10.3	Randy Wright	2.6	Jim Killingsworth		
1978-79	12-15	5-9		Mark Tucker	17.1	Don Youman	10.1	Randy Wright	5.0	Jim Killingsworth	22-31	.415
1979-80	10-17	4-10		Ed Odom	24.2	Don Youman	9.1	Randy Wright	5.1	Paul Hansen		
1980-81	18-9	8-6		Matt Clark	17.3	Leroy Combs	8.2	Eddie Hannon	4.7	Paul Hansen		
1981-82	15-12	7-7		Leroy Combs	12.1	Leroy Combs	7.2	Eddie Hannon	5.2	Paul Hansen		
1982-83	24-7	9-5	NCAA FIRST ROUND	Leroy Combs	17.3	Leroy Combs	8.7	Matt Clark	6.5	Paul Hansen		
1983-84	13-15	5-9		Joe Atkinson	18.0	Joe Atkinson	7.6	Bill Self	4.8	Paul Hansen		
1984-85	12-16	3-11		Joe Atkinson	13.5	Joe Atkinson	6.7	Bill Self	3.9	Paul Hansen		
1985-86	15-13	6-8		Terry Faggins	14.5	Andre Ivy	5.4	Roshon Patton	2.9	Paul Hansen	107-89	.546
1986-87	8-20	4-10		Todd Christian	13.7	Sylvester Kincheon	6.2	Jay Davis	5.5	Leonard Hamilton		
1987-88	14-16	4-10		Richard Dumas	17.4	Richard Dumas	6.4	John Starks	4.6	Leonard Hamilton		
1988-89	17-13	7-7	NIT SECOND ROUND	Richard Dumas	15.7	Byron Houston	8.4	Darwyn Alexander	3.5	Leonard Hamilton		
1989-90	17-14	6-8	NIT SECOND ROUND	Byron Houston	18.5	Byron Houston	10.0	Darwyn Alexander	3.7	Leonard Hamilton	56-63	.471
1990-91	24-8	10-4	NCAA REGIONAL SEMIFINALS	Byron Houston	22.7	Byron Houston	10.5	Sean Sutton	4.0	Eddie Sutton		
1991-92	28-8	8-6	NCAA REGIONAL SEMIFINALS	Byron Houston	20.2	Byron Houston	8.7	Sean Sutton	4.8	Eddie Sutton		
1992-93	20-9	8-6	NCAA SECOND ROUND	Bryant Reeves	19.5	Bryant Reeves	10.0	Brooks Thompson	5.0	Eddie Sutton		
1993-94	24-10	10-4	NCAA SECOND ROUND	Bryant Reeves	21.0	Bryant Reeves	9.7	Brooks Thompson	5.7	Eddie Sutton		
1994-95	27-10	10-4	NCAA NATIONAL SEMIFINALS	Bryant Reeves	21.5	Bryant Reeves	9.5	Andre Owens	6.9	Eddie Sutton		
1995-96	17-10	7-7		Jerome Lambert	13.0	Jerome Lambert	6.6	Andre Owens	5.4	Eddie Sutton		
1996-97	17-15	7-9	NIT SECOND ROUND	Adrian Peterson	14.0	Brett Robisch	6.4	Chianti Roberts	3.5	Eddie Sutton		
1997-98	22-7	11-5	NCAA SECOND ROUND	Adrian Peterson	17.7	Brett Robisch	8.2	Doug Gottlieb	6.9	Eddie Sutton		
1998-99	23-11	10-6	NCAA SECOND ROUND	Adrian Peterson	17.7	Desmond Mason	7.9	Doug Gottlieb	8.8	Eddie Sutton		
1999-2000	27-7	12-4	NCAA REGIONAL FINALS	Desmond Mason	18.0	Brian Montonati	7.2	Doug Gottlieb	8.6	Eddie Sutton		
2000-01	20-10	10-6	NCAA FIRST ROUND	Maurice Baker	19.8	Andre Williams	7.7	Maurice Baker	4.2	Eddie Sutton		
2001-02	23-9	10-6	NCAA FIRST ROUND	Victor Williams	13.1	Ivan McFarlin	7.7	Victor Williams	3.9	Eddie Sutton		
2002-03	22-10	10-6	NCAA SECOND ROUND	Victor Williams	15.5	Ivan McFarlin	7.8	Victor Williams	3.2	Eddie Sutton		
2003-04	31-4	14-2	NCAA NATIONAL SEMIFINALS	Tony Allen	16.0	Ivan McFarlin	6.7	John Lucas III	4.5	Eddie Sutton		
2004-05	26-7	11-5	NCAA REGIONAL SEMIFINALS	Joey Graham	17.7	Ivan McFarlin	7.4	John Lucas III	4.1	Eddie Sutton		
2005-06	17-16	6-10	NIT FIRST ROUND	Mario Boggan	14.8	Mario Boggan	5.7	JamesOn Curry	4.0	Eddie Sutton	368-151	.709
2006-07	22-13	6-10	NIT FIRST ROUND	Mario Boggan	19.0	Mario Boggan	7.6	JamesOn Curry	3.7	Sean Sutton		
2007-08	17-16	7-9	NIT FIRST ROUND	James Anderson	13.3	Marcus Dove	5.7	Byron Eaton	3.5	Sean Sutton	39-29	.574
2008-09	23-12	9-7	NCAA SECOND ROUND	James Anderson	18.2	Obi Muonelo	7.2	Byron Eaton	5.9	Travis Ford	23-12	.657

⊗ Records don't reflect games forfeited or vacated. For adjusted records, see p. 521.

ESPN 160 SAGARIN

OLD DOMINION

If it's mid-March, it's pretty much guaranteed that the Monarchs are still playing basketball somewhere. ODU has earned 19 postseason bids since joining D1 in 1976, including nine to the NCAA Tournament.

BEST TEAM: 1994-95 Jeff Capel sure wasn't shy as a first-year coach, scheduling Virginia, Southern Illinois, Washington and North Carolina, among others. Add in a knee injury that ended star forward Odell Hodge's season after just four games, and the result was an 11-loss regular season. The other result was a postseason-ready ODU team. The Monarchs survived an OT game in the semis before winning the CAA tournament. Then, as a No. 14 NCAA Tourney seed, ODU outlasted Villanova in triple OT, 89-81, to advance to the second round.

BEST PLAYER: G Leo Anthony (1957-61) No matter what opponents tried—box-and-ones, double-teams—it was no use against the six-foot guard. Anthony's quick feet helped him shake defenders, and he also used hook shots or scoops to get around and over hands and arms. He averaged 26.6 points per game for his career, capped by a 60-point showing against Lynchburg in his final game.

BEST COACH: Sonny Allen (1965-75) Allen's breakneck style of ball took the Monarchs to the College Division title game in 1971. Old Dominion then won the title in 1975, before Allen moved on to SMU. The 1967-68 team averaged 98.2 points per game, a school record that's all but untouchable.

GAME FOR THE AGES: On Jan. 10, 1981, Monarchs swingman Billy Mann stole a DePaul inbounds pass and laid in the ball at the horn to finish a 63-62 upset of the top-ranked and unbeaten Blue Demons in Chicago. It was DePaul's first home court loss in 49 games.

FIERCEST RIVAL: Two days before the Monarchs' home matchup with Virginia Commonwealth on Feb. 14, 2009, ODU students took turns smashing a minivan painted in the VCU colors and spray-painted with the slogan, "Slam the Rams." Backed by a sold-out home crowd, ODU won, 69-65, narrowing its deficit in the all-time series to 41–38.

SEASON REVIEW

SEAS.	W-L	CONF.	COACH	SEAS.	W-L	CONF.	COACH
1930-47	*138-151*	*0-14 in 1941-42*		1960-61	16-4		Bud Metheny
1947-48	21-8		Jack Callahan	1961-62	17-3		Bud Metheny
1948-49	11-5		Bud Metheny	1962-63	13-12		Bud Metheny
1949-50	9-10		Bud Metheny	1963-64	12-10		Bud Metheny
1950-51	11-10		Bud Metheny	1964-65	8-13		Bud Metheny
1951-52	12-13		Bud Metheny	1965-66	7-17		Sonny Allen
1952-53	3-3		Bud Metheny	1966-67	14-12		Sonny Allen
1953-54	5-1		Bud Metheny	1967-68	19-7		Sonny Allen
1954-55	4-4		Bud Metheny	1968-69	21-10		Sonny Allen
1955-56	6-9		Bud Metheny	1969-70	21-7		Sonny Allen
1956-57	11-9		Bud Metheny	1970-71	21-9		Sonny Allen
1957-58	13-7		Bud Metheny	1971-72	14-10		Sonny Allen
1958-59	15-7		Bud Metheny	1972-73	19-9		Sonny Allen
1959-60	12-6		Bud Metheny	1973-74	20-7		Sonny Allen

SEAS.	W-L	CONF.		SCORING		COACH	RECORD	
1974-75	25-6		◆	Jeff Fuhrmann	16.3	Sonny Allen	181-94	.658
1975-76	19-12			Jeff Fuhrmann	18.6	Paul Webb		
1976-77	25-4		■	Ronnie Valentine	22.4	Paul Webb		
1977-78	11-15			Ronnie Valentine	24.1	Paul Webb		
1978-79	23-7		■	Ronnie Valentine	23.4	Paul Webb		
1979-80	25-5		●	Ronnie Valentine	18.5	Paul Webb		
1980-81	18-10		■	Ronnie McAdoo	15.9	Paul Webb		
1981-82	18-12	5-4	●	Mark West	15.7	Paul Webb		
1982-83	19-10	12-2	■	Mark West	14.4	Paul Webb		
1983-84	19-12	9-5	■	Mark Davis	14.2	Paul Webb		
1984-85	19-12	9-5	●	Kenny Gattison	16.1	Paul Webb	196-99	.664
1985-86	23-8	11-3	●	Kenny Gattison	17.4	Tom Young		
1986-87	6-22	1-13		Anthony Carver	15.5	Tom Young		
1987-88	18-12	9-5	■	Anthony Carver	15.0	Tom Young		
1988-89	15-13	7-7		Chris Gatling	22.4	Tom Young		
1989-90	14-14	7-7		Anthony Carver	21.1	Tom Young		
1990-91	14-18	5-9		Chris Gatling	21.0	Tom Young	90-87	.508
1991-92	15-15	8-6	●	Ricardo Leonard	20.4	Oliver Purnell		
1992-93	21-8	11-3	■	K. Jackson, P. Sessoms	16.9	Oliver Purnell		
1993-94	21-10	10-4	■	Odell Hodge	19.4	Oliver Purnell	57-33	.633
1994-95	21-12	12-2	●	Petey Sessoms	22.1	Jeff Capel		
1995-96	18-13	12-4		Joe Bunn	16.1	Jeff Capel		
1996-97	22-11	10-6	●	Odell Hodge	18.1	Jeff Capel		
1997-98	12-16	8-8		Mark Poag	15.3	Jeff Capel		
1998-99	25-9	11-5	■	Cal Bowdler	14.7	Jeff Capel		
1999-2000	11-19	6-10		Andre McCullum	12.9	Jeff Capel		
2000-01	13-18	7-9		Andre McCullum	12.5	Jeff Capel	122-98	.555
2001-02	13-16	7-11		Ricardo Marsh	15.3	Blaine Taylor		
2002-03	12-15	9-9		Ricardo Marsh	16.7	Blaine Taylor		
2003-04	17-12	11-7		Alex Loughton	16.6	Blaine Taylor		
2004-05	28-6	15-3	●	Alex Loughton	14.1	Blaine Taylor		
2005-06	24-10	13-5	■	Isaiah Hunter	14.3	Blaine Taylor		
2006-07	24-9	15-3	●	Valdas Vasylius	15.6	Blaine Taylor		
2007-08	18-16	11-7		Gerald Lee	12.9	Blaine Taylor		
2008-09	25-10	12-6		Gerald Lee	15.5	Blaine Taylor	161-94	.631

● NCAA Tournament appearance ■ NIT appearance ◆ College Division championship

PROFILE

Old Dominion University, Norfolk, VA
Founded: 1930 (as the Norfolk Division of the College of William and Mary)
Enrollment: 23,500 (16,066 undergraduate)
Colors: Slate blue, silver and light blue
Nickname: Monarchs
Current arena: Ted Constant Convocation Center, opened in 2002 (8, 424)
Previous: ODU Fieldhouse, 1970-2002 (5,200)
First game: 1930
All-time record: 1,144-790 (.592)
Total weeks in AP Top 20/25: 0
Current conference: Colonial Athletic Association (1991-)
Conference titles:
Eastern Collegiate Athletic South: 1 (1980)
Sun Belt: 2 (1983 [tie], '86)
CAA: 5 (1993 [tie], '94 [tie], '95, '97 [tie], 2005)
Conference tournament titles:
Eastern Collegiate Athletic South: 2 (1980, '82)
CAA: 4 (1992, '95, '97, 2005)
NCAA Tournament appearances: 9
NIT appearances: 10
Semifinals: 1

CONSENSUS ALL-AMERICAS

1972 **Dave Twardzik** (Little A-A), G
1974 **Joel Copeland** (College Div.), F
1976 **Wilson Washington** (D2), C

FIRST-ROUND PRO PICKS

1991 **Chris Gatling,** Golden State (16)
1999 **Cal Bowdler,** Atlanta (17)

TOP 5

G **Leo Anthony** (1957-61)
G **Dave Twardzik** (1969-72)
F **Odell Hodge** (1992-97)
F **Ronnie Valentine** (1976-80)
C **Wilson Washington** (1974-77)

RECORDS

RECORDS	GAME		SEASON		CAREER	
POINTS	67	Bob Pritchett, vs. Richmond Professional Inst. (Feb. 14, 1968)	730	Petey Sessoms (1994-95)	2,204	Ronnie Valentine (1976-80)
POINTS PER GAME			31.0	Leo Anthony (1960-61)	26.6	Leo Anthony (1957-61)
REBOUNDS	33	Ron Drews, vs. Richmond Professional Inst. (Dec. 3, 1966)	443	Randy Leddy (1965-66)	1,153	Randy Leddy (1962-66)
ASSISTS	20	Dave Twardzik, vs. Mount St. Mary's (Feb. 24, 1972)	332	Dave Twardzik (1970-71)	883	Frank Smith (1984-88)

THE SCHOOLS

ESPN 118 SAGARIN

ORAL ROBERTS

Since joining the University Division in 1971-72, ORU has made 12 postseason appearances, including five NCAA Tournaments. And even though they only survived the first round once, the program follows the motto coined by the university's eponymous evangelical founder: "Expect a Miracle."

BEST TEAM: 1973-74 Ken Trickey's 23–6 squad, led by Sam McCants and Eddie Woods, upset Syracuse and Louisville in the NCAA Tournament to reach the Midwest Regional final, where they lost in overtime to Kansas, 93-90. ORU was No. 18 in the final AP poll.

BEST PLAYER: F Anthony Roberts (1973-77) He led ORU into three postseasons, including the 1974 run to the NCAA Elite Eight. In 1977, Roberts (no relation to the school's founder) scored 66 points against North Carolina A&T and 65 in ORU's NIT matchup against Oregon; he remains the only player to score 65 or more against D1 opponents twice in the same season.

BEST COACH: Scott Sutton (1999-) Son of coaching legend Eddie Sutton, Scott led the Golden Eagles to three NCAA Tourneys and four consecutive 20-win seasons. Other highlights include defeating Oklahoma State (coached by older brother Sean) in 2007-08 and No. 3 Kansas in '06-07. That win was especially sweet—Sutton defeated Bill Self, who hired him as an ORU assistant in 1995.

GAME FOR THE AGES: Oral Roberts lost a pair of two-point games to Xavier during the 1983-84 regular season, but the Titans (as the team was called at the time) got their revenge on the Musketeers in the Midwestern City Conference championship. With :11 left and the game tied at 66, Xavier's Victor Fleming was called for a backcourt violation. Butch Berry, who hadn't taken a single shot all game, then hit the game-winner—despite being fouled on the shot—with two ticks left on the clock. He missed the free throw but a desperation shot by Jeff Jenkins missed, and Oral Roberts had earned its first NCAA Tournament berth since 1974.

HEARTBREAKER: Two nights before ORU's March 16, 1974, Elite Eight game with Kansas, Coach Trickey was arrested for driving drunk and suspended himself, only to be reinstated by school president Oral Roberts himself. In the game, ORU was up by nine with four minutes left, but Kansas came back and won in OT, 93-90. A miracle finish, perhaps—but for Kansas.

FIERCEST RIVAL: Oral Roberts vies with crosstown Tulsa for the right to hoist the Mayor's Cup. Tulsa threw fuel on the fire by hiring Bill Self before the 1997-98 season. One of Sutton's first wins as Golden Eagles head coach came in December 1999 against Tulsa and his former boss. Tulsa leads the series, 29–16.

FANFARE AND HOOPLA: The Mabee Maniacs make every game a costume party by choosing a sartorial theme that ranges from camouflage to hip-hop to whiteout. Students are expected to dress as if every night is Halloween. Opponents, unsurprisingly, can get a bit spooked.

> ***Butch Berry, who hadn't taken a single shot all game, hit the game-winner with two ticks left on the clock.***

FAN FAVORITE: G Luke Spencer-Gardner (2000-03, '04-05) The first ORU athlete to be immortalized as a bobblehead doll was a diminutive Aussie (6'1", 190 lbs.) who spent his Oral Roberts career throwing his body around in an attempt to shut down the best player of every opposing team, regardless of size. Spencer-Gardner's best work may have come against Maryland's 6'8" forward, Nik Caner-Medley, in the first round of the 2005 NIT. The Terrapins won, but it wasn't Spencer-Gardner's fault—he held his fellow hyphenate scoreless on 0-for-7 shooting.

PROFILE

Oral Roberts University, Tulsa, OK
Founded: 1963
Enrollment: 5,109 (3,198 undergraduate)
Colors: Vegas gold, navy blue and white
Nickname: Golden Eagles
Current arena: Mabee Center, opened in 1972 (10,575)
First game: 1965-66
All-time record: 763-511 (.599)
Total weeks in AP Top 20/25: 15

Current conference: Summit League (1997-)
Conference titles:
Midwestern City: 1 (1984)
Mid-Continent: 4 (1999 [tie], 2005, '06 [tie], '07)
Summit: 1 (2008)
Conference tournament titles:
Midwestern City: 2 (1980, '84)
Mid-Continent Conference: 2 (2006, '07)
Summit: (2008)
NCAA Tournament appearances: 5
NIT appearances: 7

FIRST-ROUND PRO PICKS

1977 **Anthony Roberts**, Denver (21)

TOP 5

G **Greg Sutton** (1988-91)
G **Haywoode Workman** (1986-89)
F **Caleb Green** (2003-07)
F **Anthony Roberts** (1973-77)
C **Mark Acres** (1981-85)

RECORDS

RECORDS	GAME		SEASON		CAREER	
POINTS	68	Greg Sutton, vs. Oklahoma City (Dec. 15, 1990)	1,006	Richard Fuqua (1971-72)	3,070	Greg Sutton (1988-91)
POINTS PER GAME			35.9	Richard Fuqua (1971-72)	29.5	Greg Sutton (1988-91)
REBOUNDS	34	David Vaughn, vs. Brandeis (Jan. 8, 1973)	427	Howard Suggs (1989-90)	1,365	Eddie Woods (1970-74)
ASSISTS	16	Jonathan Bluitt, vs. Oakland (Jan. 20, 2005)	249	Greg Sutton (1989-90)	534	Luke Spencer-Gardner (2000-03, '04-05)

SEASON REVIEW

SEAS.	W-L	CONF.	POSTSEASON	SCORING		REBOUNDS		ASSISTS		COACH	RECORD	
1965-66	16-10									Bill White		
1966-67	17-9			Bobby Hodge, Mel Reed	16.1	Arnold Coles	10.8			Bill White		
1967-68	18-6			Dana Lewis	16.0	Dana Lewis	10.2			Bill White		
1968-69	14-10			Bill Hull	21.2	Carl Hardaway	9.6			Bill White	65-35	.650
1969-70	27-4			Richard Fuqua	18.1	Ingram Montgomery	10.8			Ken Trickey		
1970-71	21-5			Richard Fuqua	31.8	Eddie Woods	13.0			Ken Trickey		
1971-72	26-2		NIT QUARTERFINALS	Richard Fuqua	35.9	Eddie Woods	14.5			Ken Trickey		
1972-73	21-6		NIT FIRST ROUND	Richard Fuqua	23.5	David Vaughn	14.3			Ken Trickey		
1973-74	23-6		NCAA REGIONAL FINALS	Sam McCants	24.0	Eddie Woods	12.1			Ken Trickey		
1974-75	20-8		NIT QUARTERFINALS	Anthony Roberts	22.4	Harold Johnson	10.8	Arnold Dugger	5.9	Jerry Hale		
1975-76	20-6			Anthony Roberts	24.2	Alvin Scott	9.5	Arnold Dugger	5.4	Jerry Hale		
1976-77	21-7		NIT FIRST ROUND	Anthony Roberts	34.0	Anthony Roberts	9.2	Arnold Dugger	6.9	Jerry Hale	61-21	.744
1977-78	13-14			Lamont Reid	16.4	Antonio Martin	10.2	Rodney Wright	3.0	Lake Kelly		
1978-79	17-10			Calvin Garrett	21.0	Antonio Martin	9.5	Robert Griffin	4.8	Lake Kelly	30-24	.556
1979-80	18-10	4-1		Calvin Garrett	22.2	Antonio Martin	11.9	Gary "Cat" Johnson	5.2	Ken Hayes		
1980-81	11-16	6-5		Steve Bontrager	16.3	Jeff Acres	8.0	Gary "Cat" Johnson	6.1	Ken Hayes		
1981-82	18-12	8-4	NIT FIRST ROUND	Mark Acres	14.6	Mark Acres	8.1	Gary "Cat" Johnson	5.5	Ken Hayes		
1982-83	14-14	10-4		Mark Acres	18.8	Mark Acres	9.6	Mark Gottfried	3.4	Ken Hayes[a]	50-43	.538
1983-84	21-10	11-3	NCAA FIRST ROUND	Mark Acres	20.8	Mark Acres	10.5	Charles Dorsey	4.1	Dick Acres		
1984-85	15-15	8-6		Mark Acres	18.8	Mark Acres	9.7	Willie Irons	3.2	Dick Acres	47-34	.580
1985-86	10-18	5-7		Akin Akin-Otiko	14.1	Maurice Smith	7.8	Willie Irons	4.2	Ted Owens		
1986-87	11-17	5-7		Akin Akin-Otiko	15.0	Akin Akin-Otiko	7.2	Haywoode Workman	6.7	Ted Owens	21-35	.375
1987-88	8-21			Haywoode Workman	19.4	Marvin Washington	7.5	Willie Irons	3.8	Ken Trickey		
1988-89	8-20			Greg Sutton	21.9	Howard Suggs	9.1	Haywoode Workman	3.9	Ken Trickey		
1989-90	36-6			Greg Sutton	30.6	Howard Suggs	10.2	Greg Sutton	6.1	Ken Trickey		
1990-91	29-6			Greg Sutton	34.3	Sebastian Neal	12.5	Greg Sutton	4.3	Ken Trickey		
1991-92	10-18			Ray Thompson	25.5	Ray Thompson	9.8	Brian Garner	4.4	Ken Trickey		
1992-93	5-22			Ray Thompson	23.6	Ray Thompson	9.3	Ray Thompson	3.1	Ken Trickey	214-116	.648
1993-94	6-21			Fred Smith	14.6	Fred Smith	9.1	Kenny Bohanon	2.5	Bill Self		
1994-95	10-17			Tim Gill	16.3	Rocky Walls	7.4	Earl McClellan	3.5	Bill Self		
1995-96	18-9			Tim Gill	17.5	Rocky Walls	7.6	Earl McClellan	5.4	Bill Self		
1996-97	21-7		NIT FIRST ROUND	Tim Gill	17.9	Rocky Walls	7.8	Earl McClellan	4.9	Bill Self	55-54	.505
1997-98	19-12	12-4		Tim Gill	18.1	Rocky Walls	10.5	Tim Gill	4.5	Barry Hinson		
1998-99	17-11	10-4		Chad Wilkerson	16.4	Derrick Taylor	6.4	Chad Wilkerson	3.5	Barry Hinson	36-23	.610
1999-2000	13-17	8-8		Eric Perry, Derrick Taylor	14.0	Derrick Taylor	7.3	Eric Perry	5.2	Scott Sutton		
2000-01	10-19	5-11		Markius Barnes	16.0	Kyan Brown	6.3	Luke Spencer-Gardner	4.0	Scott Sutton		
2001-02	17-14	10-4		Reggie Borges	14.4	Reggie Borges	6.6	Luke Spencer-Gardner	5.0	Scott Sutton		
2002-03	18-10	9-5		Reggie Borges	18.0	Kendrick Moore	7.3	Luke Spencer-Gardner	5.9	Scott Sutton		
2003-04	17-11	10-6		Ken Tutt	20.7	Caleb Green	9.9	Jonathan Bluitt	6.1	Scott Sutton		
2004-05	25-8	13-3	NIT FIRST ROUND	Caleb Green	19.4	Caleb Green	9.3	Jonathan Bluitt	5.4	Scott Sutton		
2005-06	21-12	13-3	NCAA FIRST ROUND	Caleb Green	20.8	Caleb Green	8.8	Jonathan Bluitt	4.1	Scott Sutton		
2006-07	23-11	12-2	NCAA FIRST ROUND	Caleb Green	20.5	Caleb Green	9.3	Adam Liberty	2.9	Scott Sutton		
2007-08	24-9	16-2	NCAA FIRST ROUND	Robert Jarvis	16.1	Shawn King	6.5	Adam Liberty	3.3	Scott Sutton		
2008-09	16-15	14-4		Robert Jarvis	17.2	Marcus Lewis	7.2	Kelvin Sango	2.7	Scott Sutton	184-126	.594

[a] **Ken Hayes (3-5) and Dick Acres (11-9) both coached during the 1982-83 season.**

LATE GREAT

SEATTLE
1952-80

The 1952-53 Chieftains (the school changed its nickname to the Redhawks in 2000) went 29–4, still the NCAA record for wins by a first-year Major College or Division I program. Led by the great Elgin Baylor, Seattle made it to the 1958 NCAA championship game, losing to Kentucky, 84-72. A member of the West Coast Athletic Conference (now WCC) from 1971-72 to '79-80, Seattle had several Top 20 finishes in the polls; the best season was 1956-57, when it ended up No. 5 in both the AP and UPI rankings. Seattle is currently scheduled to regain full D1 status for the 2012-13 season.

NOTABLE PLAYERS: C Johnny O'Brien (1950-53), F/C Elgin Baylor (1956-58) The 5'9" O'Brien was third in the country in scoring in 1952-53 with 28.5 ppg and was a consensus All-America. His twin brother, Eddie, was also on the team. Excellent all-around athletes, the O'Briens became the first set of twins to play in a Major League Baseball game for the same team (Pittsburgh). The 6'5" Baylor averaged 31.2 ppg and 19.8 rpg in his Seattle career. In 1957-58 he was a consensus All-America and the Most Outstanding Player of the NCAA Tournament. He was enshrined in the Naismith Hall of Fame in 1977.

ESPN 50 SAGARIN

OREGON

Oregon has had its share of peaks and valleys. But from the Tall Firs' 1939 NCAA title to the Kamikaze Kids' 1970s run to the recent reign of the two Lukes (Ridnour and Jackson) to the low times in between, the one constant is the insane atmosphere at 82-year-old McArthur Court—a place known as the Pit.

BEST TEAM: 1938-39 Dubbed the Tall Firs for their towering (for their day) frontline, the 1938-39 Ducks own the distinction of being the very first NCAA Tournament champions. Led by All-Americas Lauren "Laddie" Gale (6'4"), Bobby Anet (5'8") and center Urgel "Slim" Wintermute (6'8"), the Firs went 29–5, including an impressive Christmas tour through the East and Midwest during which they beat Saint Joseph's, Canisius, Wayne State and Drake. In the eight-team NCAA Tournament, Howard Hobson's squad easily defeated Texas, Oklahoma and finally Ohio State, 46-33, to take the title, in Evanston, Ill.

BEST PLAYER: F Greg Ballard (1973-77) The brawny 6'7" power forward is the Ducks' all-time leading rebounder (1,114) and fourth all-time leading scorer (1,829). A major player in coach Dick Harter's Kamikaze Kids revival of the once-great program, Ballard led the Ducks to the NIT final four as a sophomore and was an All-America as a senior. He scored 40 or more points three times, including a then school-record 43 against Oral Roberts and 41 in Oregon's famous five-overtime loss to Cal in 1977—a game in which he played 63 minutes.

BEST COACH: Howard "Hobby" Hobson (1935-44, '45-47) A three-year team captain from 1923 to '26, Hobson won 212 games in 11 years coaching at his alma mater. One of the first coaches to promote intersectional play, Hobson and his Ducks topped the Pacific Coast Conference North Division in 1937 and '38, won the PCC title outright in '39 and topped off that season by winning the very first NCAA championship.

GAME FOR THE AGES: Dynastic UCLA had not lost consecutive games in eight years when the Bruins came to a frenzied Mac Court on Feb. 16, 1974. Having been shocked by Oregon State the previous night, the No. 1-ranked Bruins were slain again, this time by Harter's Kamikaze Kids, 56-51. The two games went down in Bruins lore as UCLA's Lost Weekend.

HEARTBREAKER: The Ducks were 15–3 when they hosted 16–2 UCLA at Mac Court on Feb. 8, 1975. In what would turn out to be coach John Wooden's last visit to the Pit, the Bruins shot the lights out in the second half and skewered the Ducks, 107-103. Oregon lost its next four games and had to settle for a berth in the NIT.

FIERCEST RIVAL: Oregon-Oregon State is college basketball's most contested rivalry. The teams have played an NCAA-record 331 times, with Oregon State holding a 181–150 lead. There have been many memorable moments, perhaps none more heated than in 1974, at the end of a game in Corvallis, when Harter tripped a male cheerleader who was running with the Chancellor's Trophy, given to the seasonal series winner. Whether it was an accident or not (opinion is divided on the matter), Harter required a police escort from Gill Coliseum. The dented cup was retired to an OSU trophy case.

FANFARE AND HOOPLA: McArthur Court, 82 years old and going strong, is one of greatest gyms the sport has ever known. It was named for Clifton N. "Pat" McArthur, the university's first student body president. Also lovingly known as the Pit, the building's triple-decked pavilion literally vibrates with the sound of 9,087 strong, sometimes causing the scoreboard suspended by wires above the court to "dance" on its supports.

FAN FAVORITE: G Ron Lee (1972-76) An All-America and the leading scorer in Ducks history, Lee is most remembered for a full-tilt style of play that helped his Oregon teams earn the nickname Kamikaze Kids.

CONSENSUS ALL-AMERICAS

1921	**Eddie Durno,** F
1924	**Hugh Latham,** C
1926	**Algot Westergren,** G
1939	**Urgel "Slim" Wintermute,** C
1940	**John Dick,** F

FIRST-ROUND PRO PICKS

1955	**Jim Loscutoff,** Boston (4)
1966	**Jim Barnett,** Boston (8)
1971	**Stan Love,** Baltimore (9)
1976	**Ron Lee,** Phoenix (10)
1977	**Greg Ballard,** Washington (4)
1985	**Blair Rasmussen,** Denver (15)
1991	**Terrell Brandon,** Cleveland (11)
2002	**Fred Jones,** Indianapolis (14)
2003	**Luke Ridnour,** Seattle (14)
2004	**Luke Jackson,** Cleveland (10)
2007	**Aaron Brooks,** Houston (26)

PROFILE

University of Oregon, Eugene, OR
Founded: 1876
Enrollment: 21,507 (17,358 undergraduate)
Colors: Green and yellow
Nickname: Ducks
Current arena: McArthur Court, a.k.a. the Pit, opened in 1927 (9,087)
Previous: Hayward Hall, 1910-26 (N/A); Oregon Men's Gymnasium, 1903-08 (N/A)
First game: Jan. 24, 1903
All-time record: 1,416-1,252 (.531)
Total weeks in AP Top 20/25: 73

Current conference: Pacific-10 (1916-59, 1964-)
Conference titles:
Pacific Coast: 3 (1919, '39, '45)
Pac-10: 1 (2002)
Conference tournament titles:
Pac-10: 2 (2003, '07)
NCAA Tournament appearances: 10
Sweet 16s (since 1975): 2
Final Fours: 1
Titles: 1 (1939)
NIT appearances: 9
Semifinals: 3

TOP 5

G	**Terrell Brandon** (1989-91)
G	**Ron Lee** (1972-76)
G/F	**Luke Jackson** (2000-04)
F	**Greg Ballard** (1973-77)
C	**Stan Love** (1968-71)

RECORDS

RECORDS	GAME		SEASON		CAREER	
POINTS	43	Greg Ballard, vs. Oral Roberts (March 9, 1977)	745	Terrell Brandon (1990-91)	2,085	Ron Lee (1972-76)
POINTS PER GAME			26.6	Terrell Brandon (1990-91)	22.2	Terrell Brandon (1989-91)
REBOUNDS	32	Jim Loscutoff, vs. BYU (Jan. 28, 1955)	465	Bob Peterson (1951-52)	1,114	Greg Ballard (1973-77)
ASSISTS	13	Darius Wright, vs. Arizona (Jan. 21, 1999); achieved 2 other times	218	Luke Ridnour (2002-03)	614	Kenya Wilkins (1993-97)

SEASON REVIEW

SEASON	W-L	CONF.	SCORING	COACH	RECORD	
1903-16	*56-65*		*No winning seasons until 1910-11*			
1916-17	0-11	0-8		Hugo Bezdek	17-35	.327
1917-18	3-8			Bill Hayward	34-29	.540
1918-19	13-4	11-3		Dean Walker	13-4	.765
1919-20	8-9	5-8		Hollis Huntington	8-9	.471
1920-21	15-5	8-4		George Bohler		
1921-22	7-24	0-16		George Bohler		
1922-23	15-10	2-6		George Bohler	37-39	.487
1923-24	15-5	4-4		Bill Reinhart		
1924-25	15-5	7-2		Bill Reinhart		
1925-26	18-4	10-0		Bill Reinhart		
1926-27	24-4	8-2		Bill Reinhart		
1927-28	18-3	8-2		Bill Reinhart		
1928-29	10-8	3-7		Bill Reinhart		
1929-30	14-12	8-8		Bill Reinhart		
1930-31	12-10	6-10		Bill Reinhart		
1931-32	13-11	7-9		Bill Reinhart		
1932-33	8-19	2-14		Bill Reinhart		
1933-34	17-8	9-7		Bill Reinhart		
1934-35	16-12	7-9		Bill Reinhart	180-101	.641
1935-36	20-11	7-9		Howard "Hobby" Hobson		
1936-37	20-9	11-5		Howard "Hobby" Hobson		

SEAS.	W-L	CONF.	POSTSEASON	SCORING		REBOUNDS		ASSISTS		COACH	RECORD	
1937-38	25-8	14-6								Howard "Hobby" Hobson		
1938-39	**29-5**	**14-2**	**NATIONAL CHAMPION**							**Howard "Hobby" Hobson**		
1939-40	19-12	10-6								Howard "Hobby" Hobson		
1940-41	18-18	7-9								Howard "Hobby" Hobson		
1941-42	12-15	7-9								Howard "Hobby" Hobson		
1942-43	19-10	10-6								Howard "Hobby" Hobson		
1943-44	16-10	11-5								Howard "Hobby" Hobson		
1944-45	30-15	11-5	NCAA REGIONAL SEMIFINALS							John A. Warren		
1945-46	16-17	8-8								Howard "Hobby" Hobson		
1946-47	18-9	7-9								Howard "Hobby" Hobson	212-124	.631
1947-48	18-11	8-8								John A. Warren		
1948-49	12-18	7-9								John A. Warren		
1949-50	9-19	6-10		Will Urban	11.1					John A. Warren		
1950-51	18-13	10-6		Bob Peterson	12.1	Jim Loscutoff	12.8			John A. Warren	87-76	.534
1951-52	14-16	8-8		Bob Peterson	12.6	Bob Peterson	16.6			Bill Borcher		
1952-53	14-14	8-8		Chet Noe	16.4	Chet Noe	14.6			Bill Borcher		
1953-54	17-10	9-7		Ed Halberg	12.3					Bill Borcher		
1954-55	13-13	8-8		Jim Loscutoff	19.4	Jim Loscutoff	17.2			Bill Borcher		
1955-56	11-15	5-11		Max Anderson	15.4	Max Anderson	12.1			Bill Borcher	69-68	.504
1956-57	4-21	2-14		Charlie Franklin	16.6	Hal Duffy	11.6			Steve Belko		
1957-58	13-11	6-10		Charlie Franklin	17.6					Steve Belko		
1958-59	9-16	3-13		Dale Herron	12.3					Steve Belko		
1959-60	19-10		NCAA REGIONAL FINALS	Glenn Moore	14.4					Steve Belko		
1960-61	15-12		NCAA FIRST ROUND	Charlie Warren	17.0					Steve Belko		
1961-62	9-17			Charlie Warren	22.2					Steve Belko		
1962-63	11-15			S. Jones, Jim Johnson	14.5					Steve Belko		
1963-64	14-12			Steve Jones	16.2					Steve Belko		
1964-65	9-17	3-11		Jim Barnett	19.0					Steve Belko		
1965-66	13-13	6-8		Jim Barnett	19.3					Steve Belko		
1966-67	9-17	1-13		Nick Jones	19.5					Steve Belko		
1967-68	7-19	2-12		Ken Smith	15.6					Steve Belko		
1968-69	13-13	5-9		Stan Love	17.8					Steve Belko		
1969-70	17-9	8-6		Stan Love	20.8					Steve Belko		
1970-71	17-9	8-6		Stan Love	24.6	Stan Love	11.3			Steve Belko	179-211	.459
1971-72	6-20	0-14		Doug Little	15.2					Dick Harter		
1972-73	16-10	8-6		Ron Lee	18.8					Dick Harter		
1973-74	15-11	9-5		Ron Lee	18.7					Dick Harter		
1974-75	21-9	6-8	NIT THIRD PLACE	Ron Lee	18.4					Dick Harter		
1975-76	19-11 ⊗	10-4	NIT QUARTERFINALS	Ron Lee	18.6	Greg Ballard	10.4			Dick Harter		
1976-77	19-10	9-5	NIT QUARTERFINALS	Greg Ballard	21.7					Dick Harter		
1977-78	16-11	6-8		Dan Hartshorne	9.3					Dick Harter	112-82	.577▼
1978-79	12-15	7-11		Rob Closs	10.3					Jim Haney		
1979-80	10-17	5-13		Mike Clark	11.3					Jim Haney		
1980-81	13-14	6-12		Mike Clark	15.5					Jim Haney		
1981-82	9-18	4-14		John Greig	15.8					Jim Haney		
1982-83	9-18	5-13		Blair Rasmussen	14.8					Jim Haney	53-82	.393
1983-84	16-13	11-7	NIT FIRST ROUND	Blair Rasmussen	16.6					Don Monson		
1984-85	15-16	8-10		Blair Rasmussen	16.1					Don Monson		
1985-86	11-17	6-12		Anthony Taylor	17.0					Don Monson		
1986-87	16-14	8-10		Anthony Taylor	19.6					Don Monson		
1987-88	16-14	10-8	NIT SECOND ROUND	Anthony Taylor	21.3					Don Monson		
1988-89	8-21	3-15		Frank Johnson	16.3					Don Monson		
1989-90	15-14	10-8	NIT FIRST ROUND	Terrell Brandon	17.9					Don Monson		
1990-91	13-15	8-10		Terrell Brandon	26.6					Don Monson		
1991-92	6-21	2-16		Antoine Stoudamire	20.5					Don Monson	116-145	.444
1992-93	10-20	3-15		Antoine Stoudamire	18.6					Jerry Green		
1993-94	10-17	6-12		Orlando Williams	18.6					Jerry Green		
1994-95	19-9	11-7	NCAA FIRST ROUND	Orlando Williams	18.7					Jerry Green		
1995-96	16-13 ⊗	9-9		K. Wilkins, J. Lawrence	13.7					Jerry Green		
1996-97	17-11	8-10	NIT FIRST ROUND	Kenya Wilkins	15.7					Jerry Green	72-70	.507▼
1997-98	13-14	8-10		Terik Brown	12.8					Ernie Kent		
1998-99	19-13	8-10	NIT FOURTH PLACE	Alex Scales	14.3	A.D. Smith	7.8	Darius Wright	4.7	Ernie Kent		
1999-2000	22-8	13-5	NCAA FIRST ROUND	Alex Scales	16.3	A.D. Smith	5.8	Darius Wright	4.7	Ernie Kent		
2000-01	14-14	5-13		Bryan Bracey	18.6	Bryan Bracey	7.1	Luke Ridnour	3.8	Ernie Kent		
2001-02	26-9	14-4	NCAA REGIONAL FINALS	Fred Jones	18.6	Robert Johnson	7.5	Luke Ridnour	5.0	Ernie Kent		
2002-03	23-10	10-8	NCAA FIRST ROUND	Luke Ridnour	19.7	Luke Jackson	6.9	Luke Ridnour	6.6	Ernie Kent		
2003-04	18-13	9-9	NIT SEMIFINALS	Luke Jackson	21.2	Luke Jackson	7.2	Luke Jackson	4.5	Ernie Kent		
2004-05	14-13	6-12		Aaron Brooks	14.7	Ian Crosswhite	5.7	Aaron Brooks	4.6	Ernie Kent		
2005-06	15-18	7-11		Malik Hairston	15.0	Maarty Leunen	6.1	Aaron Brooks	4.4	Ernie Kent		
2006-07	29-8	11-7	NCAA REGIONAL FINALS	Aaron Brooks	17.7	Maarty Leunen	8.2	Aaron Brooks	4.3	Ernie Kent		
2007-08	18-14	9-9	NCAA FIRST ROUND	Malik Hairston	16.3	Maarty Leunen	9.2	Kamyron Brown	3.1	Ernie Kent		
2008-09	8-23	2-16		Tajuan Porter	15.4	Joevan Catron	6.6	Joevan Catron	2.3	Ernie Kent	219-157	.582

⊗ Records don't reflect games forfeited or vacated. For adjusted records, see p. 521.
▼ Coaches' records adjusted to reflect games forfeited or vacated: Dick Harter, 113-81, .582; Jerry Green, 73-69, .514. For yearly totals, see p. 521.

ESPN 40 SAGARIN

OREGON STATE

The Beavers have been a Pacific Northwest power for more than half a century, first under Amory "Slats" Gill (599 wins, two Final Fours) and later Ralph Miller (359 victories, although NCAA sanctions cost him 17). A long list of All-Americas, including Mel Counts, Steve Johnson, A.C. Green and Gary Payton, wore the orange and black. In 2008-09, OSU's power pipeline intensified when the brother-in-law of first-year coach Craig Robinson became President Barack Obama.

BEST TEAM: 1980-81 Ralph Miller's Orange Express went 26–2, holding a No. 1 or No. 2 national ranking for nearly two months. Famed for their full-court pressure defense, the Beavers were led by All-America Steve Johnson, guard Mark Radford and newcomers Lester Conner and Charlie Sitton. OSU swept its two games with UCLA and cruised to the Pac-10 title, losing in the regular season only to Arizona State. After a first-round bye in the NCAA Tournament, the Beavers were stunned by underdog Kansas State, 50-48.

BEST PLAYER: G GARY PAYTON (1986-90) Payton was a defensive stopper for the Beavers from his freshman season—long before he was christened the Glove—when he was named the Pac-10 Defensive Player of the Year. But the Oakland native was known just as much for his offense, scoring a school-record 2,172 points, including an OSU-best 58 in one game. The 1990 Pac-10 POY, Payton still holds conference records for assists (938) and steals (321), and he led OSU to three NCAA Tournaments.

BEST COACH: RALPH MILLER (1970-89) He revolutionized Beavers basketball, preaching defense and ball movement. In his 19 seasons at OSU, Miller achieved 359 victories (of his 674 total) and four Pac-10 titles (one shared), and he was the AP Coach of the Year in 1980-81 and '81-82. The floor in OSU's Gill Coliseum is named in his honor.

GAME FOR THE AGES: OSU brought UCLA's 50-game conference winning streak to an end at Gill Coliseum on Feb. 15, 1974, as Beavers reserve forward Paul Miller scored 16 points to help Oregon State overcome a seven-point halftime deficit. UCLA rallied late to draw within a point, but freshman guard George Tucker hit four free throws in the final :25 to preserve the 61-57 upset.

HEARTBREAKER: The Beavers entered the 1981 NCAA Tournament at 26–1 and were cruising along against second-round foe Kansas State. But the Wildcats ignited a 16-6 run, OSU All-America Johnson fouled out and K-State's Rolando Blackman stepped up to hit a 16-foot jumper with :02 left to shock the Beavers, 50-48.

FIERCEST RIVAL: OSU has dominated Oregon (181–150) in the hoops version of what in football is known as the Civil War, and animosity for the Lemon Yellow runs deep. In 1947, Oregon offered the use of 8,000-seat McArthur Court for one game of OSU's playoff with UCLA that would decide the Pacific Coast Conference title. Beavers coach Slats Gill, wary of UO's intentions, turned down the offer.

FANFARE AND HOOPLA: According to university archives, the school's first mascot, for the 1892-93 football season, was Jimmie the Coyote. The lovable, buck-toothed, beanie-wearing Benny Beaver didn't come along until the 1950s, but he was an instant hit with fans. Perhaps it's no coincidence that, after some miserable seasons, OSU's fortunes took something of a turn for the better around the time that happy Benny was replaced by what's known as the "angry Beaver" in 2001.

FAN FAVORITE: F A.C. GREEN (1981-85) In addition to sporting a Hall-of-Fame set of Jheri curls, Green was a classy, hard-working star for four years in Corvallis and later as an iron man in the NBA.

CONSENSUS ALL-AMERICAS

1916	**Adolph "Ade" Sieberts,** F
1922	**Marshall Hjelte,** C
1924	**Slats Gill,** F
1925	**Carlos Steele,** G
1981	**Steve Johnson,** F/C
1990	**Gary Payton,** G

FIRST-ROUND PRO PICKS

1958	**Dave Gambee,** St. Louis (7)
1964	**Mel Counts,** Boston (9)
1970	**Gary Freeman,** Milwaukee (16)
1970	**Gary Freeman,** Virginia, (ABA)
1970	**Vic Bartolome,** Pittsburgh (ABA)
1972	**Freddie Boyd,** Phoenix (5)
1975	**Lonnie Shelton,** Memphis (ABA, 2)
1981	**Steve Johnson,** Kansas City (7)
1982	**Lester Conner,** Golden State (14)
1985	**A.C. Green,** LA Lakers (23)
1987	**Jose Ortiz,** Utah (15)
1990	**Gary Payton,** Seattle (2)
1993	**Scott Haskin,** Indiana (14)
1995	**Brent Barry,** Denver (15)
1998	**Corey Benjamin,** Chicago (28)

PROFILE

Oregon State University, Corvallis, OR
Founded: 1868
Enrollment: 19,753 (16,228 undergraduate)
Colors: Orange and black
Nickname: Beavers
Current arena: Ralph Miller Court at Gill Coliseum, opened in 1949 (10,400)
First game: 1901
All-time record: 1,609-1,170 (.579)
Total weeks in AP Top 20/25: 128

Current conference: Pacific-10 (1915-59, 1964-)
Conference titles:
Pacific Coast: 6 (1916 [tie], '33, '47, '49, '55, '58 [tie])
AAWU: 1 (1966)
Pac-10: 5 (1980, '81, '82, '84 [tie], '90 [tie])
Conference tournament titles: 0
NCAA Tournament appearances: 16
Sweet 16s (since 1975): 2
Final Fours: 2
NIT appearances: 4

TOP 5

G	**Gary Payton** (1986-90)
G/F	**Lester Conner** (1980-82)
F	**A.C. Green** (1981-85)
F/C	**Steve Johnson** (1976-81)
C	**Mel Counts** (1961-64)

RECORDS

	GAME		SEASON		CAREER	
POINTS	58	Gary Payton, vs. USC (Feb. 22, 1990)	775	Mel Counts (1963-64)	2,172	Gary Payton (1986-90)
POINTS PER GAME			26.7	Mel Counts (1963-64)	22.2	Mel Counts (1961-64)
REBOUNDS	36	Swede Halbrook, vs. Idaho (Feb. 15, 1955)	489	Mel Counts (1963-64)	1,375	Mel Counts (1961-64)
ASSISTS	15	Gary Payton, vs. Arizona State (Nov. 30, 1989)	244	Gary Payton (1988-89)	938	Gary Payton (1986-90)

SEASON REVIEW

SEASON	W-L	CONF.	SCORING	COACH	RECORD	
1901-19	*170-80*		*27-1 from 1905-07, includes undefeated season in '05-06 (10-0)*			
1919-20	7-12	5-7		H.W. Hargiss	10-25	.286
1920-21	6-17	2-14		R.B. Rutherford		
1921-22	21-2	10-2		R.B. Rutherford	27-19	.587
1922-23	19-7	4-4		Bob Hager		
1923-24	20-5	6-2		Bob Hager		
1924-25	29-8	7-2		Bob Hager		
1925-26	18-6	6-4		Bob Hager		
1926-27	14-11	4-6		Bob Hager		
1927-28	15-16	4-6		Bob Hager	115-53	.685
1928-29	12-8	4-6		Slats Gill		

SEASON	W-L	CONF.	SCORING	COACH	RECORD	
1929-30	14-13	7-9		Slats Gill		
1930-31	19-9	9-7		Slats Gill		
1931-32	12-12	8-8		Slats Gill		
1932-33	21-6	12-4		Slats Gill		
1933-34	14-10	7-9		Slats Gill		
1934-35	19-9	12-4		Slats Gill		
1935-36	16-9	10-6		Slats Gill		
1936-37	11-15	5-11		Slats Gill		
1937-38	17-16	6-14		Slats Gill		
1938-39	13-11	6-10		Slats Gill		
1939-40	27-11	12-4		Slats Gill		

SEAS.	W-L	CONF.	POSTSEASON	SCORING		REBOUNDS		ASSISTS		COACH	RECORD	
1940-41	19-9	9-7								Slats Gill		
1941-42	18-9	11-5								Slats Gill		
1942-43	19-9	8-8								Slats Gill		
1943-44	8-16	5-11								Slats Gill		
1944-45	20-8	10-6								Slats Gill		
1945-46	13-11	10-6								Slats Gill		
1946-47	28-5	13-3	NCAA REGIONAL SEMIFINALS							Slats Gill		
1947-48	21-13	10-6								Slats Gill		
1948-49	24-12	12-4	NCAA FOURTH PLACE							Slats Gill		
1949-50	13-14	8-8								Slats Gill		
1950-51	14-18	6-10								Slats Gill		
1951-52	9-19	3-13								Slats Gill		
1952-53	11-18	6-10								Slats Gill		
1953-54	19-10	11-5		Swede Halbrook	21.2	Swede Halbrook	11.9			Slats Gill		
1954-55	22-8	15-1	NCAA REGIONAL FINALS	Swede Halbrook	20.9	Swede Halbrook	14.1			Slats Gill		
1955-56	8-18	5-11		Dave Gambee	18.0	Dave Gambee	10.4			Slats Gill		
1956-57	11-15	6-10		Dave Gambee	20.2	Dave Gambee	10.5			Slats Gill		
1957-58	20-6	12-4		Dave Gambee	18.3	Dave Gambee	11.0			Slats Gill		
1958-59	13-13	7-9		Lee Harman	15.6	Karl Anderson	8.3			Slats Gill		
1959-60	15-11			Jim Woodland	10.5	Karl Anderson	9.9			Slats Gill[a]		
1960-61	14-12			Karl Anderson	10.2	Jay Carty	7.6			Slats Gill		
1961-62	24-5		NCAA REGIONAL FINALS	Mel Counts	18.5	Mel Counts	13.8			Slats Gill		
1962-63	22-9		NCAA FOURTH PLACE	Mel Counts	21.3	Mel Counts	15.6			Slats Gill		
1963-64	25-4		NCAA FIRST ROUND	Mel Counts	26.7	Mel Counts	16.9			Slats Gill	599-393	.604
1964-65	16-10	7-7		Jim Jarvis	21.1	Charlie White	7.0			Paul Valenti		
1965-66	21-7	12-2	NCAA REGIONAL FINALS	Loy Petersen	12.9	Ed Fredenburg	7.4			Paul Valenti		
1966-67	14-14	8-6		Vince Fritz	16.4	Loy Petersen	7.2			Paul Valenti		
1967-68	12-13	5-9		Vince Fritz	18.2	Gary Freeman	6.6			Paul Valenti		
1968-69	12-14	5-9		Gary Freeman	15.9	Gary Freeman	9.4			Paul Valenti		
1969-70	10-16	4-10		Vic Bartolome	16.1	Vic Bartolome	8.7			Paul Valenti	91-82	.526
1970-71	12-14	4-10		Freddie Boyd	17.8	Sam Whitehead	9.6	Freddie Boyd	6.8	Ralph Miller		
1971-72	18-10	9-5		Freddie Boyd	19.8	Sam Whitehead	8.0	Freddie Boyd	6.6	Ralph Miller		
1972-73	15-11	6-8		Sam Whitehead	13.8	Sam Whitehead	7.8	Charlie Neal	5.6	Ralph Miller		
1973-74	13-13	6-8		Lonnie Shelton	12.2	Lonnie Shelton	7.8	Charlie Neal	5.3	Ralph Miller		
1974-75	19-12	10-4	NCAA REGIONAL SEMIFINALS	Lonnie Shelton	18.3	Lonnie Shelton	9.4	George Tucker	5.1	Ralph Miller		
1975-76	18-9 ⊗	10-4		Rocky Smith	17.0	Paul Miller	5.9	George Tucker	5.3	Ralph Miller		
1976-77	16-13	8-6		Rocky Smith	19.8	Steve Johnson	5.6	George Tucker	6.0	Ralph Miller		
1977-78	16-11	9-5		Rickey Lee	13.7	Rickey Lee	6.8	Dwayne Allen	4.1	Ralph Miller		
1978-79	18-10	11-7	NIT FIRST ROUND	Steve Johnson	18.4	Steve Johnson	6.6	Dwayne Allen	5.5	Ralph Miller		
1979-80	26-4 ⊗	16-2	NCAA SECOND ROUND	Steve Johnson	17.0	Steve Johnson	6.9	Dwayne Allen	4.7	Ralph Miller		
1980-81	26-2 ⊗	17-1	NCAA SECOND ROUND	Steve Johnson	21.0	Steve Johnson	7.7	Lester Conner	4.0	Ralph Miller		
1981-82	25-5 ⊗	16-2	NCAA REGIONAL FINALS	Lester Conner	14.9	Lester Conner	5.4	Lester Conner	5.1	Ralph Miller		
1982-83	20-11	12-6	NIT QUARTERFINALS	Charlie Sitton	18.8	A.C. Green	7.6	W. Brew, Darryl Flowers	3.2	Ralph Miller		
1983-84	22-7	15-3	NCAA FIRST ROUND	Charlie Sitton	14.9	A.C. Green	8.7	Steve Woodside	3.4	Ralph Miller		
1984-85	22-9	12-6	NCAA FIRST ROUND	A.C. Green	19.1	A.C. Green	9.2	Darryl Flowers	4.2	Ralph Miller		
1985-86	12-15	8-10		Jose Ortiz	16.4	Jose Ortiz	8.5	Darryl Flowers	5.3	Ralph Miller		
1986-87	19-11	10-8	NIT SECOND ROUND	Jose Ortiz	22.3	Jose Ortiz	8.7	Gary Payton	7.6	Ralph Miller		
1987-88	20-11	12-6	NCAA FIRST ROUND	Gary Payton	14.5	Earl Martin	5.4	Gary Payton	7.4	Ralph Miller		
1988-89	22-8	13-5	NCAA FIRST ROUND	Gary Payton	20.1	Earl Martin	4.5	Gary Payton	8.1	Ralph Miller	359-186	.659▼
1989-90	22-7	15-3	NCAA FIRST ROUND	Gary Payton	25.7	Earl Martin	5.2	Gary Payton	8.1	Jim Anderson		
1990-91	14-14	8-10		Teo Alibegovic	18.1	Chad Scott	8.3	Charles McKinney	3.4	Jim Anderson		
1991-92	15-16	7-11		Scott Haskin	18.0	Scott Haskin	6.5	Charles McKinney	3.3	Jim Anderson		
1992-93	13-14	9-9		Scott Haskin	16.7	Scott Haskin	8.1	Charles McKinney	3.3	Jim Anderson		
1993-94	6-21	2-16		Brent Barry	15.2	Jerohn Brown	5.9	Stephane Brown	4.6	Jim Anderson		
1994-95	9-18	6-12		Brent Barry	21.0	Mustapha Hoff	7.5	Brent Barry	3.9	Jim Anderson	79-90	.467
1995-96	4-23 ⊗	2-16		J.D. Vetter	10.1	C. Benjamin, M. Brown	4.4	Markee Brown	2.9	Eddie Payne		
1996-97	7-20	3-15		Carson Cunningham	14.9	Terrill Woods	5.7	Carson Cunningham	4.7	Eddie Payne		
1997-98	13-17	3-15		Corey Benjamin	19.8	John-Blair Bickerstaff	4.7	John-Blair Bickerstaff	3.5	Eddie Payne		
1998-99	13-14	7-11		Deaundra Tanner	15.8	Clifton Jones	6.4	Deaundra Tanner	4.7	Eddie Payne		
1999-2000	13-16	5-13		Deaundra Tanner	14.2	Clifton Jones	5.7	Deaundra Tanner	5.1	Eddie Payne	50-90	.357▼
2000-01	10-20	4-14		Jason Heide	13.8	Jason Heide	5.5	Deaundra Tanner	3.5	Ritchie McKay		
2001-02	12-17	4-14		Philip Ricci	16.2	Philip Ricci	7.1	Adam Masten	2.9	Ritchie McKay	22-37	.373
2002-03	13-15	6-12		Philip Ricci	16.5	Philip Ricci	8.2	Lamar Hurd	3.8	Jay John		
2003-04	12-16	6-12		David Lucas	17.2	David Lucas	6.9	Lamar Hurd	4.9	Jay John		
2004-05	17-15	8-10	NIT OPENING ROUND	David Lucas	18.5	David Lucas	7.0	Jason Fontenet	3.0	Jay John		
2005-06	13-18	5-13		Sasa Cuic	13.5	Marcel Jones	6.7	Jason Fontenet	2.7	Jay John		
2006-07	11-21	3-15		Marcel Jones	15.3	Kyle Jeffers	5.8	Josh Tarver	3.8	Jay John		
2007-08	6-25	0-18		Marcel Jones	10.4	Marcel Jones	5.7	Josh Tarver	2.4	Jay John[b]	72-97	.426
2008-09	18-18	7-11		Calvin Haynes	13.0	Daniel Deane	4.1	Roeland Schaftenaar	3.3	Craig Robinson	18-18	.500

[a] Slats Gill (9-3) and Paul Valenti (6-8) both coached during the 1959-60 season.

[b] Jay John (6-12) and Kevin Mouton (0-12) both coached during the 2007-08 season.

⊗ Records don't reflect games forfeited or vacated. For adjusted records, see p. 521.

▼ Coaches' records adjusted to reflect games forfeited or vacated: Ralph Miller, 342-198, .633; Eddie Payne, 52-88, .371. For yearly totals, see p. 521.

ESPN 138 SAGARIN

PACIFIC

Is it any wonder that Pacific routinely attracts some of the best mid-major-bound talent from across the nation—and even from overseas? Reviewers routinely cite the Stockton, Calif., campus as among America's most beautiful. And it's hard to imagine a more lovely gameday walk than the one to the Spanos Center, tucked smack in the middle of that campus.

BEST TEAM: 1966-67 Coach Dick Edwards had a good rebounder in Keith Swagerty and two solid shooters in Bob Krulish and David Fox. That, combined with the Tigers' hustle and heart, brought Pacific the West Coast Athletic Conference title. After an early loss to Kansas, Pacific rolled all the way to the NCAA West Regional final, where it met UCLA. A hobbled Swagerty was held to 11 points in the 80-64 loss.

BEST PLAYER: C MICHAEL OLOWOKANDI (1995-98) As the 7'1" Englishman explained it, he chose UOP because the college directory he was looking at just happened to open to that page. Olowokandi, who didn't start playing hoops until he was 17, blossomed so fully at Pacific that the LA Clippers selected him as the first pick of the 1998 NBA draft.

BEST COACH: BOB THOMASON (1988-) The secret to his five Big West Coach of the Year awards? Ever since Olowokandi came to Stockton, Thomason has gone out of his way to recruit top-notch players from abroad. His 2004-05 team started four foreign-born players.

GAME FOR THE AGES: One year after Texas Western and its all-African-American starting lineup made history in the 1966 NCAA Tournament, UOP made a little history of its own by bouncing the defending champs in the West Regional semis, 72-63.

FIERCEST RIVAL: Pacific and San Jose State play every year for the Bell, a humongous—you guessed it—bell painted in the two schools' colors. At one time, the team that lost the game had to walk the Bell 78 miles from one campus to the other. Thank goodness for SJSU's sake they don't actually walk the walk anymore, beacause it has lost 18 of the last 22 games. The Tigers lead overall, 83–72.

SEASON REVIEW

SEAS.	W-L	CONF.	COACH	SEAS.	W-L	CONF.	COACH
1910-50	*298-297*		*Erwin Righter, 88-75 (1921-33)*	1963-64	15-11	7-5	Dick Edwards
1950-51	19-11		Chris Kjeldsen	1964-65	13-12	8-6	Dick Edwards
1951-52	9-14		Chris Kjeldsen	1965-66	22-6	13-1 ●	Dick Edwards
1952-53	2-18	0-8	Van Sweet	1966-67	24-4	14-0 ●	Dick Edwards
1953-54	9-17	3-9	Van Sweet	1967-68	17-9	6-8	Dick Edwards
1954-55	11-15	4-8	Van Sweet	1968-69	17-9	9-5	Dick Edwards
1955-56	15-11	9-5	Van Sweet	1969-70	21-6	11-3	Dick Edwards
1956-57	9-17	3-11	Van Sweet	1970-71	22-6	12-2 ●	Dick Edwards
1957-58	9-15	5-7	Van Sweet	1971-72	17-9	8-4	Dick Edwards
1958-59	11-15	6-6	Van Sweet	1972-73	14-12	6-6	Stan Morrison
1959-60	9-17	2-10	Van Sweet	1973-74	14-12	4-8	Stan Morrison
1960-61	5-21	0-12	Van Sweet	1974-75	12-14	3-7	Stan Morrison
1961-62	10-16	5-7	Van Sweet	1975-76	14-14	4-6	Stan Morrison
1962-63	4-22	0-12	Van Sweet	1976-77	11-14	5-7	Stan Morrison

SEAS.	W-L	CONF.	SCORING		COACH	RECORD
1977-78	17-10	9-5	Russ Coleman	17.6	Stan Morrison	
1978-79	18-12	11-3 ●	Terence Carney	15.6	Stan Morrison	100-88 .532
1979-80	15-16	7-7	Ron Cornelius	21.6	Dick Fichtner	
1980-81	14-13	4-10	Ron Cornelius	22.3	Dick Fichtner	
1981-82	7-20	3-11	Matt Waldron	20.1	Dick Fichtner	36-49 .424
1982-83	7-21	4-12	Rich Anema	12.9	Tom O'Neill	
1983-84	3-27	1-17	Rich Anema	12.7	Tom O'Neill	
1984-85	9-19	5-13	Domingo Rosario	14.1	Tom O'Neill	
1985-86	17-14	9-9	Rich Anema	15.6	Tom O'Neill	
1986-87	10-17	6-12	Brent Counts	17.2	Tom O'Neill	
1987-88	5-24	0-18	Christian Gray	15.6	Tom O'Neill[a]	51-110 .317
1988-89	7-21	3-15	Don Lyttle	12.5	Bob Thomason	
1989-90	15-14	7-11	Dell Demps	15.9	Bob Thomason	
1990-91	14-15	9-9	Dell Demps	18.8	Bob Thomason	
1991-92	14-16	8-10	Dell Demps	19.0	Bob Thomason	
1992-93	16-11	12-6	Tony Amundsen	15.3	Bob Thomason	
1993-94	17-14	10-8	Michael Jackson	17.9	Bob Thomason	
1994-95	14-13 ⊘	9-9	Charles Jones	18.0	Bob Thomason	
1995-96	15-12	11-7	Adam Jacobsen	14.1	Bob Thomason	
1996-97	24-6	12-4 ●	Mark Boelter	13.3	Bob Thomason	
1997-98	23-10	14-2 ■	Michael Olowokandi	22.2	Bob Thomason	
1998-99	14-13	9-7	Jason Williams	16.7	Bob Thomason	
1999-2000	11-18	6-10	Clay McKnight	11.8	Bob Thomason	
2000-01	18-12	8-8	Peter Heizer	12.5	Bob Thomason	
2001-02	20-10	11-7	Demetrius Jackson	13.2	Bob Thomason	
2002-03	12-16	7-11	Demetrius Jackson	13.6	Bob Thomason	
2003-04	25-8	17-1 ●	Miah Davis	14.7	Bob Thomason	
2004-05	27-4	18-0 ●	Guillaume Yango	13.2	Bob Thomason	
2005-06	24-8	12-2 ●	Christian Maraker	17.6	Bob Thomason	
2006-07	12-19	5-9	Anthony Brown	14.3	Bob Thomason	
2007-08	21-10	11-5	Steffan Johnson	14.5	Bob Thomason	
2008-09	21-13	10-6	Bryan LeDuc	11.4	Bob Thomason	364-263 .581▼

[a] Tom O'Neill (5-12) and Denis Willens (0-12) both coached during the 1987-88 season.
⊘ Records don't reflect games forfeited or vacated. For adjusted records, see p. 521.
▼ Coach's record adjusted to reflect games forfeited or vacated: 365-262, .582. For yearly totals, see p. 521.
● NCAA Tournament appearance ■ NIT appearance

PROFILE

University of the Pacific, Stockton, CA
Founded: 1851
Enrollment: 6,251 (3,457 undergraduate)
Colors: Orange and black
Nickname: Tigers
Current arena: Alex G. Spanos Center, opened in 1981 (6,150)
First game: 1910
All-time record: 1,139-1,100 (.509)
Total weeks in AP Top 20/25: 6

Current conference: Big West (1971-)
Conference titles:
West Coast Athletic: 4 (1966, '67, '70 [tie], '71)
Pacific Coast Athletic: 1 (1979)
Big West: 5 (1997 [tie], '98 [tie], 2004 [tie], '05, '06)
Conference tournament titles:
Pacific Coast Athletic: 1 (1979)
Big West: 3 (1997, 2004, '06)
NCAA Tournament appearances: 8
NIT appearances: 1

FIRST-ROUND PRO PICKS

1972 **John Gianelli,** Pittsburgh (ABA)
1998 **Michael Olowokandi,** LA Clippers (1)

TOP 5

G **Miah Davis** (2002-04)
G **Ken Stanley** (1959-62)
F **Ron Cornelius** (1977-81)
F **Keith Swagerty** (1964-67)
C **Michael Olowokandi** (1995-98)

RECORDS

	GAME		SEASON		CAREER	
POINTS	44	Bill Stricker, vs. Portland (Dec. 21, 1968)	732	Michael Olowokandi (1997-98)	2,065	Ron Cornelius (1977-81)
POINTS PER GAME			24.0	Ken Stanley (1960-61)	20.5	John Gianelli (1969-72)
REBOUNDS	39	Keith Swagerty, vs. UC Santa Barbara (March 5, 1965)	652	Leroy Wright (1958-59)	1,505	Keith Swagerty (1964-67)
ASSISTS	14	Dell Demps, vs. UC Irvine (Jan. 7, 1991)	178	Leonard Armato (1973-74)	436	Adam Jacobsen (1993-96, '97-98)

ESPN 87 SAGARIN

PENNSYLVANIA

Yes, Penn is an elite university, but it's one where a focus on academics hasn't hindered a certain athletic tradition. Start with the Quakers' hallowed home court, the aptly named Palestra (Greek for an ancient gym), multiply by 23 NCAA Tournaments, add in the ritual Big 5 rivalries and what you get is an Ivy League community that is proud to have its urban campus known as a basketball school.

BEST TEAM: 1970-71 The Quakers went 26–0 through the end of the regular season and had not totally crazy notions about challenging four-time defending champ UCLA for the NCAA title. Led by forwards Bob Morse and Corky Calhoun and guards Dave Wohl and Steve Bilsky, coach Dick Harter's crew won its first two Tournament games by an average of 10 points to set up a meeting with Big 5 rival Villanova in the East Regional final. There, Villanova avenged its regular-season loss to Penn with a 90-47 pasting (see Heartbreaker).

BEST PLAYER: C ERNIE BECK (1950-53) Penn's top career scorer accomplished the feat in only three seasons. The 6'4" Beck still holds nine school records. After leading Penn to the 1953 Tournament, he was drafted by the Philadelphia Warriors and played seven NBA seasons.

BEST COACH: FRAN DUNPHY (1989-2006) Penn has been a cradle of coaches: Chuck Daly, Dick Harter and Jack McCloskey all stalked the Palestra sideline. Best of them all was Dunphy, who in 17 seasons amassed a 310–163 record. But he never thought he'd make it past his second season when the Quakers finished 9–17. Instead of firing him, AD Paul Rubincam gave Dunphy a vote of confidence. The coach then won nine Ivy League titles and took the team to nine NCAA Tournaments.

GAME FOR THE AGES: In North Carolina they call it Black Sunday. In the second round of the NCAA Tournament in Raleigh on March 11, 1979, No. 9-seed Penn pulled off a miracle, beating No. 1-seed North Carolina, 72-71, behind Tony Price's 25 points and nine rebounds. Never before or since had UNC lost a Tournament game in its home state. Penn rolled on to the Final Four, where Magic Johnson and Michigan State ended the dream.

HEARTBREAKER: Losing any game to a Big 5 rival is painful, but this time a national title was within sight. On March 20, 1971, the undefeated Quakers, No. 3 in the nation, were mortally embarrassed in the NCAA East Regional final by Villanova, 90-47. Everything went wrong for the Quakers: They didn't make a field goal in the first six minutes and shot 20 for 67 overall, while the Wildcats shot out the lights—and Penn's hopes of a national title.

FIERCEST RIVAL: Philly's Big 5—Penn, Villanova, Temple, Saint Joseph's and La Salle—has been a round-robin league of its own since 1954. But no team riles Quaker blood the way Princeton does. The teams' two annual meetings almost always determine the Ivy League title (there's no postseason tournament). Either Penn or Princeton (or both) have worn the Ivy crown in all but four seasons from 1963 through 2009. Penn leads all-time, 122–98.

FANFARE AND HOOPLA: Since its opening in 1927, more college hoops games have been played at the Palestra than at any other arena in the country. Until 1977, all Big 5 games took place there and each set of fans would throw streamers on the court after its team scored its first bucket—until the NCAA banned the practice. Quakers fans still unfurl "roll-outs"—long banners with funny (or just off-color) messages meant to distract the opposition.

FAN FAVORITE: G STAN GREENE (1975-78) A 1977-78 captain, Greene was beloved for his tenacious D. Not only did students develop a cowbell-driven chant punctuated with "Go, Stan Greene!" while he was there, but they continued to do it after he graduated.

CONSENSUS ALL-AMERICAS

1906, '07	**George M. Flint,** F
1906-09	**Charles Keinath,** F
1911	**Lewis Walton,** G
1912	**William Turner,** F
1916	**Edward McNichol,** G
1918, '20	**Hubert Peck,** G
1918, '20	**George Sweeney,** F
1919-21	**Dan McNichol,** G
1919	**Andrew Stannard,** F
1922	**William Graves,** C
1925, '26	**Emanuel Goldblatt,** G
1928, '29	**Joe Schaaf,** G/F
1945	**Howie Dallmar,** F
1953	**Ernie Beck,** C

FIRST-ROUND PRO PICKS

1947	**Frank Crossin,** Philadelphia (6)
1953	**Ernie Beck,** Philadelphia (1)
1972	**Corky Calhoun,** Phoenix (4)
1972	**Corky Calhoun,** Kentucky (ABA)
1973	**Craig Littlepage,** San Antonio (ABA, 5)
1975	**Bob Bigelow,** KC-Omaha (13)

PROFILE

University of Pennsylvania, Philadelphia, PA
Founded: 1740
Enrollment: 20,128 (10,275 undergraduate)
Colors: Red and blue
Nickname: Quakers
Current arena: The Palestra, opened in 1927 (8,722)
Previous: Weightman Hall, 1897-1927 (2,000)
First game: March 20, 1897
All-time record: 1,658-949-2 (.636)
Total weeks in AP Top 20/25: 70

Current conference: Ivy League (1901-)
Conference titles:
Ivy: 36 (1906, '08, '16, '18, '20, '21, '28, '29, '34, '35, '37, '45, '53, '66, '70, '71, '72, '73, '74, '75, '78, '79, '80, '82, '85, '87, '93, '94, '95, '99, 2000, '02, '03, '05, '06, '07)
NCAA Tournament appearances: 23
Sweet 16s (since 1975): 2
Final Fours: 1
NIT appearances: 1

TOP 5

G **Jerome Allen** (1991-95)
G **Keven McDonald** (1975-78)
F **Bob Morse** (1969-72)
F **Ugonna Onyekwe** (1999-2003)
C **Ernie Beck** (1950-53)

RECORDS	GAME		SEASON		CAREER	
POINTS	47	Ernie Beck, vs. Duke (Dec. 30, 1952)	673	Ernie Beck (1952-53)	1,827	Ernie Beck (1950-53)
POINTS PER GAME			25.9	Ernie Beck (1952-53)	22.3	Ernie Beck (1950-53)
REBOUNDS	32	Barton Leach, vs. Harvard (Feb. 18, 1955)	556	Ernie Beck (1950-51)	1,557	Ernie Beck (1950-53)
ASSISTS	13	Tim Begley, vs. Lafayette (Jan. 18, 2005); Dave Wohl, vs. Brown (Feb. 14, 1970)	162	Ibrahim Jaaber (2006-07); David Klatsky (2000-01)	505	Jerome Allen (1991-95)

THE SCHOOLS

SEASON REVIEW

SEASON	W-L	CONF.	SCORING		COACH	RECORD	
1897-1914	*153-99-2*		*74-22 in four seasons under R.B. Smith (1905-06 to '08-09)*				
1914-15	9-10	3-7			Lon Jourdet		
1915-16	11-7	8-2			Lon Jourdet		
1916-17	11-7	5-5			Lon Jourdet		
1917-18	18-2	9-1			Lon Jourdet		
1918-19	15-1	7-1			Lon Jourdet		
1919-20	22-1	10-0	*Helms Foundation champion*		Lon Jourdet		
1920-21	21-2	9-1	*Helms Foundation champion*		Edward McNichol		
1921-22	24-3	8-3			Edward McNichol		
1922-23	14-11	3-7			Edward McNichol		
1923-24	18-8	3-7			Edward McNichol		
1924-25	17-5	6-4	James Carmack	6.7	Edward McNichol		
1925-26	14-7	5-5	Roger Lindsay	5.0	Edward McNichol		
1926-27	16-10	5-5	Paul Davenport	7.1	Edward McNichol		
1927-28	22-5	7-3	Joe Schaaf	12.1	Edward McNichol		
1928-29	20-6	8-2	Joe Schaaf	10.5	Edward McNichol		
1929-30	20-6	7-3	Leonard Tanseer	6.3	Edward McNichol	186-63	.747
1930-31	9-17	3-7	Harold Sander	5.2	Lon Jourdet		
1931-32	10-11	2-8	Leonard Tanseer	5.3	Lon Jourdet		
1932-33	12-6	6-4	Robert Freeman	7.7	Lon Jourdet		
1933-34	16-3	10-2	Kenneth Hashagen	7.0	Lon Jourdet		
1934-35	16-4	10-2	Robert Freeman	7.3	Lon Jourdet		

SEAS.	W-L	CONF.	POSTSEASON	SCORING		REBOUNDS		ASSISTS		COACH	RECORD	
1935-36	12-9	7-5		Roger Hanger	5.8					Lon Jourdet		
1936-37	17-3	12-0		Roy Menzel	7.3					Lon Jourdet		
1937-38	8-10	7-5		Robert Dougherty	9.2					Lon Jourdet		
1938-39	7-11	6-6		Tony Mischo	10.0					Lon Jourdet		
1939-40	5-13	2-10		Henry Soleliac	7.2					Lon Jourdet		
1940-41	5-12	3-9		Sidney Levinson	7.4					Lon Jourdet		
1941-42	9-9	5-7		Charles Viguers	10.1					Lon Jourdet		
1942-43	14-7	6-6		Frank Crossin	11.3					Lon Jourdet	226-143	.612
1943-44	10-4	6-2		Frank Crossin	13.6					Donald Kellett		
1944-45	12-5	5-1		Howie Dallmar	10.5					Donald Kellett		
1945-46	7-10	4-4		Herbert Lyon	11.5					Robert Dougherty	7-10	.412
1946-47	14-8	7-5		John Colbert	11.9					Donald Kellett		
1947-48	10-14	5-7		Herbert Lyon	15.0					Donald Kellett	46-31	.597
1948-49	15-8	8-4		Herbert Lyon	15.8					Howie Dallmar		
1949-50	11-14	4-8		Herbert Lyon	16.8					Howie Dallmar		
1950-51	19-8	7-5		Ernie Beck	20.7	Ernie Beck	20.6			Howie Dallmar		
1951-52	21-8	9-3		Ernie Beck	20.6	Ernie Beck	19.0			Howie Dallmar		
1952-53	22-5	10-2	NCAA REGIONAL SEMIFINALS	Ernie Beck	25.9					Howie Dallmar		
1953-54	17-8	10-4		Joe Sturgis	16.1					Howie Dallmar	105-51	.673
1954-55	19-6	10-4		Barton Leach	18.1					Ray Stanley		
1955-56	12-13	9-5		Joe Sturgis	18.6					Ray Stanley	31-19	.620
1956-57	7-19	3-11		Richard Csencsitz	17.7					Jack McCloskey		
1957-58	13-12	8-6		Richard Csencsitz	15.7					Jack McCloskey		
1958-59	12-14	5-9		George Schmidt	13.2					Jack McCloskey		
1959-60	14-11	8-6		Bob Mlkvy	18.9	Bob Mlkvy	10.0			Jack McCloskey		
1960-61	16-9	10-4		Bob Mlkvy	14.3	Bob Mlkvy	10.0			Jack McCloskey		
1961-62	17-8	11-3		John Wideman	13.2	John Wideman	7.6			Jack McCloskey		
1962-63	19-6	10-4		John Wideman	13.8	David Robinson	10.4			Jack McCloskey		
1963-64	14-10	10-4		Stan Pawlak	16.0	John Hellings	8.7			Jack McCloskey		
1964-65	15-10	10-4		Stan Pawlak	21.5	John Hellings	9.4			Jack McCloskey		
1965-66	19-6	12-2		Stan Pawlak	23.2	Frank Burgess	9.0			Jack McCloskey	146-105	.582
1966-67	11-14	7-7		Tom Northrup	12.1	Frank Burgess	10.9			Dick Harter		
1967-68	9-17	4-10		Tom Northrup	11.4	Carl Robbins	7.8			Dick Harter		
1968-69	15-10	10-4		Dave Wohl	16.1	Jim Wolf	9.9			Dick Harter		
1969-70	25-2	14-0	NCAA FIRST ROUND	Bob Morse	15.9	Corky Calhoun, Jim Wolf	8.9			Dick Harter		
1970-71	28-1	14-0	NCAA REGIONAL FINALS	Bob Morse	15.4	Corky Calhoun	8.6			Dick Harter	88-44	.667
1971-72	25-3	13-1	NCAA REGIONAL FINALS	Bob Morse	18.1	Phil Hankinson	8.3			Chuck Daly		
1972-73	21-7	12-2	NCAA REGIONAL SEMIFINALS	Phil Hankinson	18.3	Ronald Haigler	10.5			Chuck Daly		
1973-74	21-6	13-1	NCAA FIRST ROUND	Ronald Haigler	17.4	Ronald Haigler	10.6			Chuck Daly		
1974-75	23-5	13-1	NCAA FIRST ROUND	Ronald Haigler	21.6	Ronald Haigler	9.9			Chuck Daly		
1975-76	17-9	11-3		Keven McDonald	18.9	Bill Jones	8.0			Chuck Daly		
1976-77	18-8	12-2		Keven McDonald	21.2	Keven McDonald	9.2			Chuck Daly	125-38	.767
1977-78	20-8	12-2	NCAA REGIONAL SEMIFINALS	Keven McDonald	22.3	Tony Price	9.0			Bob Weinhauer		
1978-79	25-7	13-1	NCAA FOURTH PLACE	Tony Price	19.8	Tony Price	8.7	Bobby Willis	4.2	Bob Weinhauer		
1979-80	17-12	11-3	NCAA SECOND ROUND	James Salters	14.6	Vincent Ross	6.0	James Salters	3.5	Bob Weinhauer		
1980-81	20-8	13-1	NIT FIRST ROUND	Kenneth Hall	11.3	George Noon	5.4	Kenneth Hall	4.2	Bob Weinhauer		
1981-82	17-10	12-2	NCAA FIRST ROUND	Paul Little	11.6	Michael Brown	5.7	Fran McCaffery	3.9	Bob Weinhauer	99-45	.688
1982-83	17-9	11-3		Michael Brown	13.7	Michael Brown	8.0	Karl Racine	3.7	Craig Littlepage		
1983-84	10-16	7-7		Karl Racine	14.2	Bruce Lefkowitz	5.7	Anthony Arnolie	2.6	Craig Littlepage		
1984-85	13-14	10-4	NCAA FIRST ROUND	Perry Bromwell	15.3	Bruce Lefkowitz	7.0	Karl Racine	4.4	Craig Littlepage	40-39	.506
1985-86	15-11	9-5		Bruce Lefkowitz	14.2	Bruce Lefkowitz	7.8	John Wilson	5.7	Tom Schneider		
1986-87	13-14	10-4	NCAA FIRST ROUND	Bruce Lefkowitz	18.7	Bruce Lefkowitz	8.9	John Wilson	4.4	Tom Schneider		
1987-88	10-16	8-6		Tyrone Pitts	17.4	Tyrone Pitts	7.0	Walt Frazier	4.4	Tom Schneider		
1988-89	13-13	9-5		Walt Frazier	17.8	Hassan Duncombe	6.2	Walt Frazier	3.6	Tom Schneider	51-54	.486
1989-90	12-14	7-7		Hassan Duncombe	19.1	Hassan Duncombe	7.7	Paul Chambers	4.3	Fran Dunphy		
1990-91	9-17	6-8		Paul McMahon	13.8	Vince Curran	6.6	Paul Chambers	4.4	Fran Dunphy		
1991-92	16-10	9-5		Barry Pierce	12.9	Vince Curran	6.5	Paul Chambers	5.8	Fran Dunphy		
1992-93	22-5	14-0	NCAA FIRST ROUND	Matt Maloney	16.3	Eric Moore	6.6	Jerome Allen	4.9	Fran Dunphy		
1993-94	25-3	14-0	NCAA SECOND ROUND	Jerome Allen	14.5	LaShawn Trice	7.1	Jerome Allen	4.6	Fran Dunphy		
1994-95	22-6	14-0	NCAA FIRST ROUND	Matt Maloney	14.5	LaShawn Trice	7.0	Jerome Allen	5.7	Fran Dunphy		
1995-96	17-10	12-2		Ira Bowman	16.4	Tim Krug	8.9	Ira Bowman	5.3	Fran Dunphy		
1996-97	12-14	8-6		Garett Kreitz	12.7	Paul Romanczuk	5.1	Michael Jordan	2.8	Fran Dunphy		
1997-98	17-12	10-4		Michael Jordan	15.3	Paul Romanczuk	6.3	Michael Jordan	4.9	Fran Dunphy		
1998-99	21-6	13-1	NCAA FIRST ROUND	Michael Jordan	15.3	Geoff Owens	7.3	Michael Jordan	4.6	Fran Dunphy		
1999-2000	21-8	14-0	NCAA FIRST ROUND	Michael Jordan	16.0	Geoff Owens	7.3	Michael Jordan	4.9	Fran Dunphy		
2000-01	12-17	9-5		Lamar Plummer	14.9	Ugonna Onyekwe	7.4	David Klatsky	5.6	Fran Dunphy		
2001-02	25-7	11-3	NCAA FIRST ROUND	Ugonna Onyekwe	17.5	Ugonna Onyekwe	6.0	Andrew Toole	3.6	Fran Dunphy		
2002-03	22-6	14-0	NCAA FIRST ROUND	Ugonna Onyekwe	16.5	Ugonna Onyekwe	6.4	Andrew Toole	2.9	Fran Dunphy		
2003-04	17-10	10-4		Jeff Schiffner	14.4	Adam Chubb	7.5	Tim Begley	4.2	Fran Dunphy		
2004-05	20-9	13-1	NCAA FIRST ROUND	Tim Begley	13.9	Mark Zoller	6.4	Tim Begley	4.8	Fran Dunphy		
2005-06	20-9	12-2	NCAA FIRST ROUND	Ibrahim Jaaber	18.2	Mark Zoller	7.3	Steve Danley	3.0	Fran Dunphy	310-163	.655
2006-07	22-9	13-1	NCAA FIRST ROUND	Mark Zoller	18.2	Mark Zoller	7.5	Ibrahim Jaaber	5.2	Glen Miller		
2007-08	13-18	8-6		Brian Grandieri	13.2	Brian Grandieri	5.9	Harrison Gaines	3.6	Glen Miller		
2008-09	10-18	6-8		Tyler Bernardini	13.7	Jack Eggleston	5.9	Zack Rosen	5.0	Glen Miller	45-45	.500

ESPN 82 SAGARIN

PENN STATE

Shortly after the clock ran out in the Nittany Lions' 82-74 second-round NCAA Tournament victory over North Carolina in 2001, the players danced at midcourt. Their overflow of emotion was understandable, considering that Penn State hadn't advanced to the Sweet 16 since 1955 and had only made it to eight NCAA Tournaments overall. And while four losing seasons followed that game, an NIT title in 2009 proved that PSU can no longer be overlooked in the Big Ten.

BEST TEAM: 1953-54 Penn State bounced back from a three-game losing streak late in the season to qualify for the NCAA Tournament. Then the real magic happened. First, the Nittany Lions upset No. 8-ranked LSU, led by future Hall of Famer Bob Pettit. Then PSU stunned No. 6 Notre Dame, ending an 18-game Irish winning streak. In their only Final Four appearance, the Nittany Lions came up short against eventual national champion La Salle, 69-54, but salvaged third place by beating Southern California in the consolation game.

BEST PLAYER: F/C Jesse Arnelle (1951-55) He was originally recruited to play football in Happy Valley by gridiron coach Rip Engle and an assistant by the name of Joe Paterno. But after impressing a Nittany Lions basketball assistant in an impromptu game of one-on-one during a campus visit, Arnelle was invited to play hoops as well. An honorable mention All-America tight end, Arnelle proved to be even more dominant on the hardwood as a 6'5" frontcourt star, finishing as the school's all-time leading scorer and rebounder.

BEST COACH: Elmer Gross (1949-54) As captain of the Nittany Lions in 1941-42, he led his team to an 18–3 record and into the 1942 Tournament. He earned a Purple Heart in World War II at the battle of Saint-Lô before returning to coach Penn State. Playing an exciting brand of fast-break ball, his teams made three NCAA Tournaments in his five years on the sideline, including a third-place finish in 1954.

GAME FOR THE AGES: In the second round of the 2001 Tournament, No. 2-seed North Carolina owned the boards, holding the No. 7-seed Nittany Lions without an offensive rebound for the first 14:30. So how did PSU pull off an 82-74 upset that left Tar Heels coach Matt Doherty in tears? The Nittany Lions literally stole the game, picking the Tar Heels' pockets a school-record 18 times and forcing them into 22 turnovers.

How did PSU pull off an 82-74 upset that left Tar Heels coach Matt Doherty in tears? The Nittany Lions literally stole the game.

HEARTBREAKER: In 1990-91, PSU's last season in the Atlantic 10, the Nittany Lions won the conference tournament to advance to the Big Dance. But after upsetting UCLA in the first round, the No. 13 seed met its Cinderella match in No. 12-seed Eastern Michigan, losing 71-68 in overtime. The game featured 20 lead changes and eight ties, and ended with Penn State guard Freddie Barnes missing a pair of three-pointers.

FIERCEST RIVAL: Fans of both Penn State and Pittsburgh anxiously await the day when the two teams renew their hoops rivalry, which has lain dormant since the Panthers' 91-54 win on Dec. 10, 2005. Pitt fans used to shout "Penn State sucks!" during a lull in the PSU fight song, until the school reworked the tune to eliminate the break. It never made much difference: Of the 144 meetings between the two schools, the Nittany Lions have won 76.

FANFARE AND HOOPLA: Before each game, the Nittany Nation student fan club produces its own gameday publication called *Forty Minutes*. The newsletter drew the ire of Buckeyes coach Thad Matta in 2005 for mocking Ohio State's troubles with articles as "The Price Is Right Ohio State" and "Dirty Laundry."

FAN FAVORITES: G Joe Crispin (1997-2001), G Jon Crispin (1999-2001) The Crispin brothers made up the starting backcourt in the magical 2000-01 season, in which they combined to average 26.7 points per game.

PROFILE

Pennsylvania State University, University Park, PA
Founded: 1855
Enrollment: 44,112 (37,988 undergraduate)
Colors: Blue and white
Nickname: Nittany Lions
Current arena: Bryce Jordan Center, opened in 1996 (15,261)
Previous: Rec Hall, 1929-96 (6,846); The Armory, 1897-1928 (N/A)
First game: 1897
All-time record: 1,319-1,012-1 (.566)

Total weeks in AP Top 20/25: 15
Current conference: Big Ten (1992-)
Conference titles:
Eastern Collegiate: 1 (1977 [tie])
Conference tournament titles:
Atlantic 10: 1 (1991)
NCAA Tournament appearances: 8
Sweet 16s (since 1975): 1
Final Fours: 1
NIT appearances: 10
Semifinals: 5
Titles: 1 (2009)

TOP 5

G **Joe Crispin** (1997-2001)
G **Pete Lisicky** (1994-98)
G/F **Geary Claxton** (2004-08)
F/C **Jesse Arnelle** (1951-55)
C **John Amaechi** (1992-95)

RECORDS	GAME		SEASON		CAREER	
POINTS	46	Gene Harris, vs. Holy Cross (Dec. 27, 1961)	731	Jesse Arnelle (1954-55)	2,138	Jesse Arnelle (1951-55)
POINTS PER GAME			26.1	Jesse Arnelle (1954-55)	21.0	Jesse Arnelle (1951-55)
REBOUNDS	27	Jesse Arnelle, vs. Temple (Jan. 29, 1955)	428	Jesse Arnelle (1954-55)	1,238	Jesse Arnelle (1951-55)
ASSISTS	15	Tom Doaty, vs. Syracuse (Jan. 29, 1975)	189	Talor Battle (2008-09)	600	Freddie Barnes (1988-92)

SEASON REVIEW

SEASON	W-L	CONF.	SCORING		COACH	RECORD	
1897-1915	*119-65-1*		*Played without a coach through the 1914-15 season*				
1915-16	8-3				Burke Hermann		
1916-17	12-2				Burke Hermann		
1917-18	12-1				no coach		
1918-19	11-2				Hugo Bezdek	11-2	.846
1919-20	12-1				Burke Hermann		
1920-21	14-2				Burke Hermann		
1921-22	9-5		J.N. Reed	190	Burke Hermann		
1922-23	13-1		J.N. Reed	242	Burke Hermann		
1923-24	13-2		J.N. Reed	151	Burke Hermann		
1924-25	12-2		E.O. Gerhardt	144	Burke Hermann		
1925-26	7-7		Harold Von Neida	83	Burke Hermann		
1926-27	14-4		Michael Hamas	223	Burke Hermann		
1927-28	10-5		L.D. Reilly	111	Burke Hermann		
1928-29	10-9		J. Neil Stahley		Burke Hermann		
1929-30	5-9		Fred Brand	108	Burke Hermann		
1930-31	3-12		Fred Brand	120	Burke Hermann		
1931-32	6-9		Ed McMinn	141	Burke Hermann	148-73	.670
1932-33	7-4		Norrie McFarlane	114	Earl Leslie		
1933-34	8-4		Norrie McFarlane	169	Earl Leslie		
1934-35	8-9		John Stocker	121	Earl Leslie		
1935-36	6-11	0-10	Sol Miehoff	121	Earl Leslie	29-28	.509

SEAS.	W-L	CONF.	POSTSEASON	SCORING		REBOUNDS		ASSISTS		COACH	RECORD	
1936-37	10-7	6-4		Sol Miehoff	125					John Lawther		
1937-38	13-5	6-4		Sol Miehoff	175					John Lawther		
1938-39	13-10	5-5		Charlie Prosser	195					John Lawther		
1939-40	15-8			John Barr	231					John Lawther		
1940-41	15-5			John Barr	200					John Lawther		
1941-42	18-3		NCAA REGIONAL SEMIFINALS	H. Baltimore, E. Gross	179					John Lawther		
1942-43	15-4			David Hornstein	139					John Lawther		
1943-44	8-7			Don McNary	146					John Lawther		
1944-45	10-7			Irwin Batnick	113					John Lawther		
1945-46	7-9			Walt Hatkevich	216					John Lawther		
1946-47	10-8			Jack Biery	218					John Lawther		
1947-48	9-10			Jack Biery	260					John Lawther		
1948-49	7-10			Milt Simon	177					John Lawther	150-93	.617
1949-50	13-10			Marty Costa	299					Elmer Gross		
1950-51	14-9			Lou Lamie	14.5					Elmer Gross		
1951-52	20-6		NCAA REGIONAL SEMIFINALS	Jesse Arnelle	18.9	Jesse Arnelle	9.8			Elmer Gross		
1952-53	15-9			Jesse Arnelle	17.0	Jesse Arnelle	11.3			Elmer Gross		
1953-54	18-6		NCAA THIRD PLACE	Jesse Arnelle	21.1	Jesse Arnelle	11.9			Elmer Gross	80-40	.667
1954-55	18-10		NCAA REGIONAL SEMIFINALS	Jesse Arnelle	26.1	Jesse Arnelle	15.3			John Egli		
1955-56	12-14			Earl Fields	14.1					John Egli		
1956-57	15-10			Ron Rainey	15.1					John Egli		
1957-58	8-11			Ron Rainey	15.1					John Egli		
1958-59	11-9			Mark DuMars	16.8	Tom Hancock	10.2	Mark DuMars	1.1	John Egli		
1959-60	11-11			Mark DuMars	21.3	Gene Harris	10.0	Mark DuMars	1.4	John Egli		
1960-61	11-13			Gene Harris	15.4	Gene Harris	10.2	Mark DuMars	1.3	John Egli		
1961-62	12-11			Gene Harris	18.7	Gene Harris	13.0	Gene Harris	1.4	John Egli		
1962-63	15-5			Earl Hoffman	21.7	Earl Hoffman	7.8	Bob Weiss	1.9	John Egli		
1963-64	16-7			Bob Weiss	17.0	Carver Clinton	9.6	Bob Weiss	2.3	John Egli		
1964-65	20-4		NCAA FIRST ROUND	Carver Clinton	17.1	Carver Clinton	11.4	Bob Weiss	3.8	John Egli		
1965-66	18-6		NIT FIRST ROUND	Carver Clinton	18.9	Carver Clinton	9.9	Carver Clinton	1.1	John Egli		
1966-67	10-14			Jeff Persson	17.6	Paul Mickey	11.2	Jeff Persson	3.5	John Egli		
1967-68	10-10			Jeff Persson	17.0	Jeff Persson	8.2	Tom Daley	1.1	John Egli	187-135	.581
1968-69	13-9			Tom Daley	14.2	Bill Stansfield	13.1	Tom Daley	1.4	John Bach		
1969-70	13-11			Tom Daley	15.3	Bob Fittin	7.9	Tom Daley	4.2	John Bach		
1970-71	10-12			Bill Kunze	16.7	Paul Neumayer	11.1	Bruce Mello	2.7	John Bach		
1971-72	17-8			Ron Brown	18.1	Ron Brown	9.3	Ron Brown	4.6	John Bach		
1972-73	15-8			Randy Meister	14.7	Jon Marshall	11.4	Ron Brown	5.2	John Bach		
1973-74	14-12			Ron Brown	17.4	Jon Marshall	11.1	Ron Brown	4.6	John Bach		
1974-75	11-12			Randy Meister	15.0	Randy Meister	10.6	Tom Doaty	4.0	John Bach		
1975-76	10-15			Chris Erichsen	17.4	Chris Erichsen	8.2	Jim Ouderkirk	2.8	John Bach		
1976-77	11-15	5-5		Jeff Miller	13.3	Carvin Jefferson	8.4	Jeff Miller	3.1	John Bach		
1977-78	8-19	4-6		Jeff Miller	18.7	Carvin Jefferson	8.6	Tom Wilkinson	6.1	John Bach	122-121	.502
1978-79	12-18	4-6		Mike Edelman	11.4	Steve Kuhn	4.1	Tom Wilkinson	5.7	Dick Harter		
1979-80	18-10		NIT FIRST ROUND	Frank Brickowski	11.4	Frank Brickowski	7.8	Tom Wilkinson	3.9	Dick Harter		
1980-81	17-10			Frank Brickowski	13.0	Mike Lang	7.9	Rich Fetter	3.4	Dick Harter		
1981-82	15-12			Mike Lang	10.1	Mike Lang	8.8	Dwight Gibson	4.2	Dick Harter		
1982-83	17-11	9-5		Mike Lang	13.1	Mike Lang	10.0	Dwight Gibson	3.6	Dick Harter	79-61	.564
1983-84	5-22	3-15		Wally Choice	13.1	David Griffin	4.9	Jim Forjan	3.9	Bruce Parkhill		
1984-85	8-19	4-14		Craig Collins	14.9	Carl Chrabascz	5.2	Tony Ward	3.9	Bruce Parkhill		
1985-86	12-17	5-13		Paul Murphy	10.2	Mike Peapos	5.6	Paul Murphy	3.1	Bruce Parkhill		
1986-87	15-12	9-9		Tom Hovasse	13.0	Tom Hovasse	5.2	Tony Ward	3.3	Bruce Parkhill		
1987-88	13-14	9-9		Tom Hovasse	14.4	Tom Hovasse	6.7	Tony Ward	3.4	Bruce Parkhill		
1988-89	20-12	12-6	NIT SECOND ROUND	Tom Hovasse	17.8	Tom Hovasse	7.5	Freddie Barnes	3.5	Bruce Parkhill		
1989-90	25-9	13-5	NIT THIRD PLACE	Ed Fogell	15.3	James Barnes	6.7	Freddie Barnes	4.7	Bruce Parkhill		
1990-91	21-11	10-8	NCAA SECOND ROUND	DeRon Hayes	15.0	James Barnes	7.5	Freddie Barnes	4.8	Bruce Parkhill		
1991-92	21-8		NIT FIRST ROUND	Monroe Brown	14.6	David Degitz	5.1	Freddie Barnes	6.1	Bruce Parkhill		
1992-93	7-20	2-16		DeRon Hayes	13.9	John Amaechi	7.6	Michael Jennings	3.3	Bruce Parkhill		
1993-94	13-14	6-12		John Amaechi	16.9	John Amaechi	8.9	Dan Earl	4.2	Bruce Parkhill		
1994-95	21-11	9-9	NIT THIRD PLACE	John Amaechi	16.1	John Amaechi	9.9	Dan Earl	5.7	Bruce Parkhill	181-169	.517
1995-96	21-7	12-6	NCAA FIRST ROUND	Pete Lisicky	13.3	Matt Gaudio	6.4	Dan Earl	5.4	Jerry Dunn		
1996-97	10-17	3-15		Pete Lisicky	16.3	Phil Williams	6.8	Ryan Bailey	4.2	Jerry Dunn		
1997-98	19-13	8-8	NIT RUNNER-UP	Pete Lisicky	15.6	Calvin Booth	6.8	Pete Lisicky	3.5	Jerry Dunn		
1998-99	13-14	5-11		Calvin Booth	15.3	Calvin Booth	8.7	Dan Earl	4.1	Jerry Dunn		
1999-2000	19-16	5-11	NIT THIRD PLACE	Jarrett Stephens	18.8	Jarrett Stephens	10.5	Joe Crispin	5.1	Jerry Dunn		
2000-01	21-12	7-9	NCAA REGIONAL SEMIFINALS	Joe Crispin	19.5	Gyasi Cline-Heard	8.2	Titus Ivory	4.5	Jerry Dunn		
2001-02	7-21	3-13		Sharif Chambliss	14.6	Jan Jagla	5.8	Brandon Watkins	4.1	Jerry Dunn		
2002-03	7-21	2-14		Sharif Chambliss	14.7	Aaron Johnson	7.5	Brandon Watkins	3.7	Jerry Dunn	117-121	.492
2003-04	9-19	3-13		Jan Jagla	13.4	Jan Jagla	7.9	Ben Luber	4.1	Ed DeChellis		
2004-05	7-23	1-15		Geary Claxton	12.7	Aaron Johnson	9.9	Ben Luber	3.6	Ed DeChellis		
2005-06	15-15	6-10	NIT OPENING ROUND	Geary Claxton	15.2	Geary Claxton	7.5	Ben Luber	4.4	Ed DeChellis		
2006-07	11-19	2-14		Geary Claxton	16.3	Geary Claxton	8.0	Ben Luber	3.4	Ed DeChellis		
2007-08	15-16	7-11		Geary Claxton	17.5	Geary Claxton	8.4	Talor Battle	3.2	Ed DeChellis		
2008-09	27-11	10-8	NIT CHAMPION	Talor Battle	16.7	Jamelle Cornley	6.3	Talor Battle	5.0	Ed DeChellis	84-103	.449

Cumulative totals listed when per-game averages not available.

ESPN 124 SAGARIN

PEPPERDINE

Since making the 2002 NCAA Tournament, the Waves have fallen upon hard times, averaging just under nine wins per season since 2005-06. But there's plenty of consolation for Pepperdine, starting with its strong legacy (13 NCAA Tournaments, six NITs), cherished memories of former players (Doug Christie, Dennis Johnson)—and, of course, the fact that the school sits perched on the cliffs of Malibu, with views to die for.

BEST TEAM: 1975-76 Nobody knew what to expect from Dennis Johnson when he transferred to Pepperdine in 1975. After being discovered on a playground by his junior college coach, he proceeded to get kicked off his team three times in two seasons. But as it turned out, DJ proved to be a humble, hardworking, NBA-caliber backcourt ace. Coach Gary Colson paired him with big man Marcos Leite and the Waves made waves, winning Pepperdine's second regular-season West Coast Athletic Conference title. Then they beat Memphis State, 87-77, in the NCAA Tournament before losing to UCLA, 70-61.

BEST PLAYER: G Doug Christie (1989-92) He didn't have a textbook shot, he was slow to make an impact after sitting out his freshman season because of academics, and he underwent arthroscopic surgery on his right knee twice between his junior and senior seasons. Yet the long, lean, 6'6" guard ended up a first-round NBA pick. How? With unreal athleticism, scoring flair and defensive tenacity. Christie averaged 19.1 and 19.5 ppg his final two seasons and had potential that scouts couldn't ignore. They were right: Christie enjoyed an often-prolific 15-year NBA career.

BEST COACH: Al Duer (1939-48) He took over the Waves in their second season and guided them to postseason play in five of his nine campaigns, making the NCAA Tournament once and the NAIA tourney four times, finishing as runner-up (to Loyola, La.) in 1945. Duer, who championed racial integration when he became executive director of the NAIA (formerly known as the NAIB), was inducted into the Naismith Hall of Fame in 1982.

GAME FOR THE AGES: A Firestone Fieldhouse record crowd of 4,500 came to life on Feb. 6, 1976, when Pepperdine beat UNLV, 93-91, in a game that was expertly played from tip to buzzer. No surprise there: The Waves had Leite, Johnson and Ollie Matson, while Jerry Tarkanian's third-ranked Rebels were led by Glen Gondrezick and Reggie Theus.

HEARTBREAKER: Jim Valvano and NC State were the story of the 1983 Tourney. But Waves fans will never forget how Jim Harrick's crew had the Wolfpack beaten in the first round on March 18, 1983, before falling in double-overtime, 69-67. Pepperdine held a six-point lead with :24 left in the first OT, but star Dane Suttle, an 83.5% free throw shooter, twice missed front ends of one-and-ones. NC State's Cozell McQueen followed up a free throw miss by teammate Dereck Whittenburg with a putback to send the game into a second OT. NC State finally prevailed.

Discovered on a playground by his junior college coach, Dennis Johnson proceeded to get kicked off his team three times in two seasons.

FIERCEST RIVAL: Since the West Coast Conference began holding tournaments, Pepperdine and Gonzaga have won a combined 13 of 22 titles and one or the other has appeared in all but four finals. Lately, though, the battle has been more of a rout. Through 2008-09, the Zags have won 16 straight against the Waves and hold an overall 38–31 edge.

FANFARE AND HOOPLA: How often does a sitting U.S. president christen your gym? That's what happened on Sept. 20, 1975, when Gerald R. Ford was in Malibu for the dedication of Firestone Fieldhouse, which was named for his good friend and the U.S. ambassador to Belgium at the time, Leonard K. Firestone.

FAN FAVORITE: G Dennis Johnson (1975-76) Although he played only one season at Pepperdine, Johnson made an impact that still endures. Colson, for one, said the defensive ace was his hero.

THE SCHOOLS

PROFILE

Pepperdine University, Malibu, CA
Founded: 1937
Enrollment: 7,614 (3,404 undergraduate)
Colors: Blue, orange and white
Nickname: Waves
Current arena: Firestone Fieldhouse, opened in 1973 (3,104)
Previous: Campus Gym, 1947-71 (N/A)
First game: 1938
All-time record: 1,111-910 (.550)
Total weeks in AP Top 20/25: 1

Current conference: West Coast (1955-)
Conference titles:
West Coast Athletic: 7 (1962, '76, '81 [tie], '82, '83, '85, '86)
West Coast: 5 (1991, '92, '93, 2000, '02 [tie])
Conference tournament titles:
West Coast: 3 (1991, '92, '94)
NCAA Tournament appearances: 13
Sweet 16s (since 1975): 1
NIT appearances: 6

FIRST-ROUND PRO PICKS

1992	**Doug Christie,** Seattle (17)
2001	**Brandon Armstrong,** Houston (23)

TOP 5

G	**William "Bird" Averitt** (1971-73)
G	**Doug Christie** (1989-92)
G	**Dennis Johnson** (1975-76)
F	**Dana Jones** (1990-94)
C	**Marcos Leite** (1973-76)

RECORDS

RECORDS	GAME		SEASON		CAREER	
POINTS	57	William "Bird" Averitt, vs. Nevada (Jan. 6, 1973)	848	William "Bird" Averitt (1972-73)	1,702	Dane Suttle (1979-83)
POINTS PER GAME			33.9	William "Bird" Averitt (1972-73)	31.5	William "Bird" Averitt (1971-73)
REBOUNDS	36	Larry Dugan, vs. UC Santa Barbara (Jan. 11, 1955)	434	Hugh Faulkner (1950-51)	1,031	Dana Jones (1990-94)
ASSISTS	17	Bryan Parker, vs. Oral Roberts (Jan. 9, 1993)	208	Tezale Archie (1999-2000)	450	Mark Wilson (1980-84)

SEASON REVIEW

SEASON	W-L	CONF.	SCORING		COACH	RECORD	
1938-39	16-13		Elmore Price	13.7	Wade Ruby	16-13	.552
1939-40	15-11				Al Duer		
1940-41	10-15				Al Duer		
1941-42	19-7		Pete Fogo	18.1	Al Duer		
1942-43	26-9		Pete Fogo	18.5	Al Duer		
1943-44	20-14		Nick Buzolich	12.8	Al Duer		
1944-45	24-13		Nick Buzolich	16.7	Al Duer		
1945-46	26-9		Nick Buzolich	12.7	Al Duer		
1946-47	14-13		Joy Pace	9.7	Al Duer		
1947-48	22-11		Joy Pace	12.9	Al Duer	176-102	.633
1948-49	19-11		Hugh Faulkner	8.8	Robert Dowell		
1949-50	21-12		John Furlong	11.0	Robert Dowell		
1950-51	25-8		John Furlong	13.5	Robert Dowell		
1951-52	20-5		Dick Alvord	14.9	Robert Dowell		

SEAS.	W-L	CONF.	POSTSEASON	SCORING		REBOUNDS		ASSISTS		COACH	RECORD	
1952-53	18-8			Bob Morris	18.8	Bob Morris	8.0			Robert Dowell		
1953-54	15-10			Larry Dugan	15.4	Larry Dugan	9.6			Robert Dowell		
1954-55	16-9			Larry Dugan	17.4	Larry Dugan	13.6			Robert Dowell		
1955-56	2-23	0-14		Ermine Zappa	14.6	Ermine Zappa	9.8			Robert Dowell		
1956-57	7-18	2-12		Mack Taylor	21.9	John Kasser	11.0			Robert Dowell		
1957-58	15-11	5-7		Sterling Forbes	18.6	George Taylor	10.5			Robert Dowell		
1958-59	16-8	8-4		Sterling Forbes	18.3	Sterling Forbes	11.8			Robert Dowell		
1959-60	14-11	8-4		Sterling Forbes	17.7	Sterling Forbes	13.0			Robert Dowell		
1960-61	9-16	3-9		Noel Smith	13.6	Harry Dinnel	12.1			Robert Dowell		
1961-62	20-7	11-1	NCAA REGIONAL SEMIFINALS	Bob Warlick	16.4	Harry Dinnel	10.9			Robert Dowell		
1962-63	14-11	6-6		Bob Warlick	17.2	Bob Warlick	13.0			Robert Dowell		
1963-64	6-19	3-9		Roland Betts	17.8	Roland Betts	16.0			Robert Dowell		
1964-65	6-19	3-11		Roland Betts	16.3	Roland Betts	14.9			Robert Dowell		
1965-66	2-24	1-13		Tandy Holmes	20.3	Tandy Holmes	8.1			Robert Dowell		
1966-67	9-17	5-9		Hal Grant	17.7	Hal Grant	10.8			Robert Dowell		
1967-68	9-17	2-12		Steve Ebey	22.9	Hal Grant	11.0			Robert Dowell	263-264	.499
1968-69	14-12	6-8		Bob Sands	16.0	Jake Davis	9.5			Gary Colson		
1969-70	14-12	7-7		Bob Sands	19.8	Bob McKenney	10.6			Gary Colson		
1970-71	12-13	4-10		Steve Sims	16.8	Hiram Peterson	9.4			Gary Colson		
1971-72	10-15	5-9		Bird Averitt	28.9	Jeff Hendrix	9.4	Stanford Williams	3.9	Gary Colson		
1972-73	14-11	7-7		Bird Averitt	33.9	Dick Skophammer	10.5	Bird Averitt	4.6	Gary Colson		
1973-74	8-18	4-10		Dick Skophammer	14.1	Dick Skophammer	7.7	Billy Williams	4.5	Gary Colson		
1974-75	17-8	8-6		Marcos Leite	19.7	Marcos Leite	11.1	Art Allen	4.5	Gary Colson		
1975-76	22-6	10-2	NCAA REGIONAL SEMIFINALS	Marcos Leite	18.7	Marcos Leite	10.0	Flintie Ray Williams	3.8	Gary Colson		
1976-77	13-13	5-9		Flintie Ray Williams	16.3	Ollie Matson	9.2	Art Allen	3.9	Gary Colson		
1977-78	7-19	2-12		Michael Knight	16.2	Ray Ellis	11.0	Michael Knight	4.7	Gary Colson		
1978-79	22-10	10-4	NCAA SECOND ROUND	Ricardo Brown	17.4	Ollie Matson	9.0	Ricardo Brown	5.7	Gary Colson	153-137	.528
1979-80	17-11	9-7	NIT FIRST ROUND	Ricardo Brown	19.5	Tony Fuller	6.8	Ricardo Brown	6.0	Jim Harrick		
1980-81	16-12	11-3		Boot Bond	18.5	Victor Anger	7.4	Dane Suttle	3.5	Jim Harrick		
1981-82	22-7	14-0	NCAA SECOND ROUND	Boot Bond	18.3	Orlando Phillips	8.7	Dane Suttle	4.3	Jim Harrick		
1982-83	20-9	10-2	NCAA FIRST ROUND	Dane Suttle	23.5	Orlando Phillips	9.6	Mark Wilson	5.5	Jim Harrick		
1983-84	15-13	6-6		Grant Gondrezick	13.7	Scott McCollum	7.4	Mark Wilson	5.3	Jim Harrick		
1984-85	23-9	11-1	NCAA FIRST ROUND	Eric White	15.9	Eric White	9.2	Jon Korfas	5.5	Jim Harrick		
1985-86	25-5	13-1	NCAA FIRST ROUND	Dwayne Polee	15.7	Anthony Frederick	6.9	Jon Korfas	6.2	Jim Harrick		
1986-87	12-18	5-9		Eric White	19.3	Levy Middlebrooks	9.0	Donny Moore	4.0	Jim Harrick		
1987-88	17-13	8-6	NIT FIRST ROUND	Tom Lewis	22.9	Levy Middlebrooks	10.7	Lamar Wilson	6.5	Jim Harrick	167-97	.633
1988-89	20-13	10-4	NIT SECOND ROUND	Tom Lewis	16.2	Casey Crawford	7.5	Lamar Wilson	5.0	Tom Asbury		
1989-90	17-11	10-4		Dexter Howard	17.9	Geoff Lear	8.9	Doug Christie	4.0	Tom Asbury		
1990-91	22-9	13-1	NCAA FIRST ROUND	Doug Christie	19.1	Geoff Lear	9.8	Doug Christie	4.2	Tom Asbury		
1991-92	24-7	14-0	NCAA FIRST ROUND	Doug Christie	19.5	Dana Jones, Geoff Lear	7.1	Doug Christie	4.8	Tom Asbury		
1992-93	23-8	11-3	NIT SECOND ROUND	Dana Jones	15.6	Dana Jones	9.1	Bryan Parker	6.5	Tom Asbury		
1993-94	19-11	8-6	NCAA FIRST ROUND	Dana Jones	18.4	Dana Jones	9.7	Bryan Parker	5.1	Tom Asbury		
1994-95	8-19	4-10		Gerald Brown	16.5	Gavin Van Der Putten	5.3	Gerald Brown	2.7	Tony Fuller		
1995-96	10-18	2-12		Gerald Brown	17.8	Bryan Hill	7.3	Khary Hervey	4.0	Tony Fuller[a]	15-27	.357
1996-97	6-21	4-10		Bryan Hill	14.5	Bryan Hill	8.1	Khary Hervey	2.4	Lorenzo Romar		
1997-98	17-10	9-5		Gerald Brown	16.9	Bryan Hill	7.1	Jelani Gardner	5.4	Lorenzo Romar		
1998-99	19-13	9-5	NIT FIRST ROUND	Jelani Gardner	13.8	Kelvin Gibbs	7.3	Jelani Gardner	4.6	Lorenzo Romar	42-44	.488
1999-2000	25-9	12-2	NCAA SECOND ROUND	Brandon Armstrong	14.4	Kelvin Gibbs	7.0	Tezale Archie	6.1	Jan van Breda Kolff		
2000-01	22-9	12-2	NIT SECOND ROUND	Brandon Armstrong	22.1	Kelvin Gibbs	8.2	Micah McKinney	2.8	Jan van Breda Kolff	47-18	.723
2001-02	22-9	13-1	NCAA FIRST ROUND	Jimmy Miggins	14.9	Jimmy Miggins	7.5	Devin Montgomery	3.8	Paul Westphal		
2002-03	15-13	7-7		Jimmy Miggins	15.4	Boomer Brazzle	6.3	Jimmy Miggins	3.7	Paul Westphal		
2003-04	15-16	9-5		Glen McGowan	17.8	Glen McGowan	5.4	Shaun Davis	4.1	Paul Westphal		
2004-05	17-14	6-8		Glen McGowan	19.2	Glen McGowan	7.6	Marvin Lea	3.7	Paul Westphal		
2005-06	7-20	3-11		Tashaan Forehan-Kelly	15.5	Tashaan Forehan-Kelly	5.8	Michael Gerrity	3.4	Paul Westphal	76-72	.514
2006-07	8-23	4-10		Chase Griffin	15.7	Marvin Lea	4.8	Gregg Barlow	3.3	Vance Walberg		
2007-08	11-21	4-10		Tyrone Shelley	15.1	Malcolm Thomas	8.8	Rico Tucker	3.2	Vance Walberg[b]	14-35	.286
2008-09	9-23	5-9		Keion Bell	12.9	Taylor Darby	6.1	Keion Bell	2.2	Tom Asbury	134-82	.620

[a] Tony Fuller (7-8) and Marty Wilson (3-10) both coached during the 1995-96 season.

[b] Vance Walberg (6-12) and Eric Bridgeland (5-9) both coached during the 2007-08 season.

LATE GREAT — U.S. INTERNATIONAL 1981-91

USIU (known today as Alliant International) had a curious, though memorable, life as a D1 program. Playing most of their games on the road because the school had no permanent home gym, they didn't win much but sure scored a lot of points. On Jan. 31, 1989, the Gulls lost to Loyola Marymount, 181-150, an NCAA record for total points in a game. In a Jan. 5, 1991, meeting of the same teams, about two weeks after U.S. International declared bankruptcy and announced it would eliminate its basketball program, guard Kevin Bradshaw scored 72 points, breaking Pete Maravich's NCAA record for the most points against a Division I opponent. And those 72 came in a *loss;* this time Loyola beat the Gulls, 186-140, falling short of their record total by five points. **NOTABLE PLAYER: G Zach Lieberman (1982-85)** Although Bradshaw averaged 37.6 points per game in 1990-91, U.S. International's most famous player was a 5'2½" bearded point guard known as the Hully Gully Man. Always the shortest player on the court, Lieberman was known for his impressive ballhandling skills and was a big fan (and media) favorite.

ESPN 60 SAGARIN

PITTSBURGH

When you talk about the best teams never to win the NCAA Tournament, Pittsburgh deserves to be part of the conversation. Of course, that doesn't mean the Panthers have never won a national championship. But if the 1928 and '30 titles are little consolation to modern Pitt fans frustrated by their team's inability to reach the NCAA Final, they can always take solace in rooting for the Big East team with the most wins since 2002-03—and hope it portends a March Madness breakthrough.

BEST TEAM: 1927-28 Doc Carlson's squad was the only Pitt team to finish a season with an undefeated record, which earned them the Helms Foundation National Championship (awarded retroactively for the 1900-01 through '40-41 seasons). All-America sophomore Charley "Chuck" Hyatt preserved the perfect campaign on Feb. 18, 1928, when he took a pass from Paul Zehfuss and nailed a last-second basket to defeat Notre Dame, 24-22. It was Pittsburgh's only lead of the game.

BEST PLAYER: F/C Charles Smith (1984-88) While Hyatt is the best Panther before 1950, Smith stands tallest as Pitt's best player in the tougher Big East era. The smooth, versatile big man helped return the Panthers to the national spotlight in 1987-88, earning conference Player of the Year honors and leading his team to its first outright Big East regular-season championship. Smith started all 122 games in his four years, becoming Pitt's all-time leading scorer with 2,045 points.

BEST COACH: Henry "Doc" Carlson (1922-53) Colorful and innovative, Carlson earned a medical degree from Pitt before playing a season of pro football for the Cleveland Indians. Doc administered oxygen to players on the bench, presumably fueling them to run his figure-8 offense on the court. Whatever works. In 31 years at Pitt, Carlson coached two Helms national title teams (in 1927-28 and '29-30) and guided the Panthers to the NCAA national semifinals in 1941.

GAME FOR THE AGES: On Feb. 28, 1940, Pittsburgh defeated Fordham, 57-37, at Madison Square Garden in the first college basketball game to be televised (with a single camera). Same venue, 67 years later: Pitt pulled off a 65-64 overtime thriller over Duke as native New Yorker Levance Fields drained a three-pointer with 4.7 seconds left.

HEARTBREAKER: Many Pitt fans were convinced 2008-09 was their year. The Panthers tied a school record with 31 wins and were seeded No. 1 in the Tournament for the first time. But Villanova dashed those title hopes in the Elite Eight. After Fields' free throws with 5.5 seconds left tied the game at 76, Nova guard Scottie Reynolds hit a floater to send the Panthers packing, 78-76.

FIERCEST RIVAL: Pitt's rivalry with West Virginia started on the gridiron in 1895. But the hardwood version of the Backyard Brawl is nearly as colorful. At WVU in 1948, a Mountaineers fan dumped a bucket of water on Carlson from the balcony. The next year, the coach wore rain gear and Pitt pulled out a last-second OT win that snapped West Virginia's 57-game home winning streak. WVU leads overall, 94–84.

FANFARE AND HOOPLA: The Pitt student section is now known as the Oakland Zoo, named after the neighborhood where the school is located. But at the Fitzgerald Field House, the Panthers' former home, the Field House Fanatics cheerfully recorded opponent's losses on fake tombstones.

FAN FAVORITE: F Jerome Lane (1985-88) His glass-shattering dunk on Jan. 25 1988, in a home game against Providence sent Pitt fans into a frenzy, delayed the game for 32 minutes, and led to TV analyst Bill Raftery introducing "Send it in, Jerome," to the basketball lexicon.

CONSENSUS ALL-AMERICAS

1928-30	**Charley "Chuck" Hyatt**, F
1928	**Wallace Reed**, G
1933	**Don Smith**, G
1934, '35	**Claire Cribbs**, G
1958	**Don Hennon**, G
2009	**DeJuan Blair**, C/F

FIRST-ROUND PRO PICKS

1974	**Billy Knight**, Indiana (ABA, 6)
1975	**Mel Bennett**, Virginia (ABA, 9)
1988	**Charles Smith**, Philadelphia (3)
1988	**Jerome Lane**, Denver (23)
1994	**Eric Mobley**, Milwaukee (18)
1999	**Vonteego Cummings**, Indiana (26)

PROFILE

University of Pittsburgh, Pittsburgh, PA
Founded: 1787
Enrollment: 26,731 (17,181 undergraduate)
Colors: Blue and gold
Nickname: Panthers
Current arena: Petersen Events Center, opened in 2002 (12,508)
Previous: Fitzgerald Field House, 1951-2002 (6,798); Pitt Pavilion 1925-51 (N/A)
First game: 1905
All-time record: 1,413-1,032 (.578)
Total weeks in AP Top 20/25: 203

Current conference: Big East (1982-)
Conference titles:
Eastern Intercollegiate: 5 (1933, '34, '35 [tie], '36 [tie], '37 [tie]
Big East: 5 (1987 [tie], '88, 2002 [tie], '03 [tie], '04)
Conference tournament titles:
Eastern Athletic: 2 (1981, '82)
Big East: 2 (2003, '08)
NCAA Tournament appearances: 21
Sweet 16s (since 1975): 5
Final Fours: 1
NIT appearances: 8

TOP 5

G **Don Hennon** (1956-59)
G **Brandin Knight** (1999-2003)
F **Billy Knight** (1971-74)
F **Charley "Chuck" Hyatt** (1927-30)
F/C **Charles Smith** (1984-88)

RECORDS	GAME		SEASON		CAREER	
POINTS	45	Don Hennon, vs. Duke (Dec. 21, 1957)	690	Sam Young (2008-09)	2,045	Charles Smith (1984-88)
SCORING AVERAGE			26.0	Don Hennon (1957-58)	24.2	Don Hennon (1956-59)
REBOUNDS	26	Don Virostek, vs. Westminster (1952-53)	444	Jerome Lane (1986-87)	1,342	Sam Clancy (1977-81)
ASSISTS	16	Levance Fields, vs. DePaul (Feb. 7, 2009); Bob Shrewsbury, vs. South Carolina (Feb. 14, 1976)	270	Levance Fields (2008-09)	785	Brandin Knight (1999-2003)

SEASON REVIEW

SEASON	W-L	CONF.	SCORING	COACH	RECORD
1905-14	*56-50*				
1914-15	14-4			Dr. George M. Flint	
1915-16	15-2			Dr. George M. Flint	
1916-17	12-6			Dr. George M. Flint	
1917-18	5-9			Dr. George M. Flint	
1918-19	7-7			Dr. George M. Flint	
1919-20	9-6			Dr. George M. Flint	
1920-21	12-9			Dr. George M. Flint	106-67 .613
1921-22	12-8			Andy Kerr	12-8 .600
1922-23	10-5			Henry "Doc" Carlson	
1923-24	10-7			Henry "Doc" Carlson	
1924-25	4-10			Henry "Doc" Carlson	
1925-26	12-5			Henry "Doc" Carlson	
1926-27	10-7			Henry "Doc" Carlson	
1927-28	21-0		*Helms Foundation champion*	Henry "Doc" Carlson	
1928-29	16-5		Charley "Chuck" Hyatt 14.9	Henry "Doc" Carlson	
1929-30	23-2		*Helms Foundation champion*	Henry "Doc" Carlson	
1930-31	20-4			Henry "Doc" Carlson	
1931-32	14-16			Henry "Doc" Carlson	
1932-33	17-5	7-1		Henry "Doc" Carlson	
1933-34	18-4	8-0		Henry "Doc" Carlson	
1934-35	18-6	6-2		Henry "Doc" Carlson	

SEAS.	W-L	CONF.	POSTSEASON	SCORING		REBOUNDS		ASSISTS		COACH	RECORD
1935-36	18-9	7-3								Henry "Doc" Carlson	
1936-37	14-7	7-3								Henry "Doc" Carlson	
1937-38	9-12	5-5								Henry "Doc" Carlson	
1938-39	10-8	5-5								Henry "Doc" Carlson	
1939-40	8-9									Henry "Doc" Carlson	
1940-41	13-6		NCAA NATIONAL SEMIFINALS							Henry "Doc" Carlson	
1941-42	5-10									Henry "Doc" Carlson	
1942-43	10-5									Henry "Doc" Carlson	
1943-44	7-7			Tay Malarkey	11.9					Henry "Doc" Carlson	
1944-45	8-4			DoDo Canterna	13.1					Henry "Doc" Carlson	
1945-46	7-7			Hank Zeller	12.2					Henry "Doc" Carlson	
1946-47	8-10			Sam David	9.8					Henry "Doc" Carlson	
1947-48	10-11			DoDo Canterna	11.6					Henry "Doc" Carlson	
1948-49	12-13			Sam David	15.6					Henry "Doc" Carlson	
1949-50	4-14			George McCrossin	13.9					Henry "Doc" Carlson	
1950-51	9-17			Michael Belich	15.9					Henry "Doc" Carlson	
1951-52	10-12			Mickey Zernich	15.2	Don Virostek	8.6	Clarence Burch	6.0	Henry "Doc" Carlson	
1952-53	12-11			Mickey Zernich	13.4	Don Virostek	20.2			Henry "Doc" Carlson	367-248 .597
1953-54	9-14			Clarence Burch	15.8	Ed Pavlick	13.7			Robert Timmons	
1954-55	10-16			Ed Pavlick	23.9	Bob Lazor	12.6			Robert Timmons	
1955-56	15-10			Bob Lazor	19.8	Chuck Hursh	10.3			Robert Timmons	
1956-57	16-11		NCAA REGIONAL SEMIFINALS	Don Hennon	21.2	John Riser	10.5			Robert Timmons	
1957-58	18-7		NCAA FIRST ROUND	Don Hennon	26.0	Chuck Hursh	9.2			Robert Timmons	
1958-59	10-14			Don Hennon	25.7	John Fridley	10.2			Robert Timmons	
1959-60	11-14			John Mills	13.9	John Fridley	10.7			Robert Timmons	
1960-61	12-11			Ben Jinks	13.0	John Fridley	12.5			Robert Timmons	
1961-62	12-11			Calvin Sheffield	18.5	Brian Generalovich	9.2			Robert Timmons	
1962-63	19-6		NCAA FIRST ROUND	Dave Roman	15.0	Paul Krieger	10.4			Robert Timmons	
1963-64	17-8		NIT FIRST ROUND	Calvin Sheffield	16.3	Paul Krieger	8.7			Robert Timmons	
1964-65	7-16			Larry Szykowny	15.8	Bob Lovett	8.0			Robert Timmons	
1965-66	5-17			Larry Szykowny	15.4	Jim LaValley	9.1			Robert Timmons	
1966-67	6-19			Jim LaValley	11.9	Jim LaValley	12.2			Robert Timmons	
1967-68	7-15			Tony DeLisio	12.1	Mike Patcher	5.6			Robert Timmons	174-189 .479
1968-69	4-20			Mike Caldwell	11.6	Mike Patcher	8.7			Charles "Buzz" Ridl	
1969-70	12-12			Kent Scott	16.9	Paul O'Gorek	11.1			Charles "Buzz" Ridl	
1970-71	14-10			Kent Scott	13.6	Paul O'Gorek	10.2	Bill Downes	3.5	Charles "Buzz" Ridl	
1971-72	12-12			Billy Knight	21.0	Billy Knight	11.5	Cleveland Edwards	5.4	Charles "Buzz" Ridl	
1972-73	12-14			Billy Knight	23.7	Billy Knight	11.0	Billy Knight	3.0	Charles "Buzz" Ridl	
1973-74	25-4		NCAA REGIONAL FINALS	Billy Knight	21.8	Billy Knight	13.4	Tom Richards	3.5	Charles "Buzz" Ridl	
1974-75	18-11		NIT QUARTERFINALS	Kirk Bruce	17.1	Mel Bennett	10.2	Keith Starr	6.2	Charles "Buzz" Ridl	97-83 .539
1975-76	12-15			Larry Harris	22.1	Larry Harris	6.4	Bob Shrewsbury	5.7	Tim Grgurich	
1976-77	6-21	1-9		Larry Harris	22.9	Michael Rice	8.0	Pete Strickland	4.3	Tim Grgurich	
1977-78	16-11	5-5		Larry Harris	20.6	Sam Clancy	12.1	Pete Strickland	4.2	Tim Grgurich	
1978-79	18-11	6-4		Sam Clancy	15.4	Sam Clancy	12.5	Pete Strickland	3.8	Tim Grgurich	
1979-80	17-12	5-5	NIT FIRST ROUND	Sammie Ellis	17.4	Sam Clancy	11.1	Dwayne Wallace	4.3	Tim Grgurich	69-70 .496
1980-81	19-12	8-5	NCAA SECOND ROUND	Sam Clancy	16.3	Sam Clancy	10.7	Dwayne Wallace	4.4	Roy Chipman	
1981-82	20-10	8-6	NCAA FIRST ROUND	Clyde Vaughan	18.0	Clyde Vaughan	9.5	Dwayne Wallace	6.2	Roy Chipman	
1982-83	13-15	6-10		Clyde Vaughan	21.9	Clyde Vaughan	9.2	Billy Culbertson	5.1	Roy Chipman	
1983-84	18-13	6-10	NIT QUARTERFINALS	Clyde Vaughan	21.0	Clyde Vaughan	8.3	Billy Culbertson	5.5	Roy Chipman	
1984-85	17-12	8-8	NCAA FIRST ROUND	Charles Smith	15.0	Charles Smith	8.0	Curtis Aiken	4.2	Roy Chipman	
1985-86	15-14	6-10	NIT FIRST ROUND	Demetreus Gore	16.1	Charles Smith	8.1	Joey David	3.6	Roy Chipman	102-76 .573
1986-87	25-8	12-4	NCAA SECOND ROUND	Charles Smith	17.0	Jerome Lane	13.5	Mike Goodson	4.8	Paul Evans	
1987-88	24-7	12-4	NCAA SECOND ROUND	Charles Smith	18.9	Jerome Lane	12.2	Sean Miller	5.8	Paul Evans	
1988-89	17-13	9-7	NCAA FIRST ROUND	Brian Shorter	19.6	Brian Shorter	9.6	Sean Miller	6.0	Paul Evans	
1989-90	12-17	5-11		Brian Shorter	20.6	Brian Shorter	9.6	Darelle Porter	7.9	Paul Evans	
1990-91	21-12	9-7	NCAA SECOND ROUND	Jason Matthews	16.5	Brian Shorter	6.4	Darelle Porter	5.1	Paul Evans	
1991-92	18-16	9-9	NIT SECOND ROUND	Chris McNeal	14.5	Chris McNeal	9.1	Sean Miller	6.6	Paul Evans	
1992-93	17-11	9-9	NCAA FIRST ROUND	Jerry McCullough	15.3	Chris McNeal	8.5	Jerry McCullough	5.6	Paul Evans	
1993-94	13-14	7-11		Eric Mobley	13.7	Eric Mobley	8.8	Jerry McCullough	7.0	Paul Evans	147-98 .600
1994-95	10-18	5-13		Jaime Peterson	13.9	Jaime Peterson	9.4	Andre Alridge	5.8	Ralph Willard	
1995-96	10-17	5-13		Jerry McCullough	13.4	Chad Varga	6.3	Jerry McCullough	5.3	Ralph Willard	
1996-97	18-15	10-8	NIT SECOND ROUND	Vonteego Cummings	16.3	Mark Blount	6.8	Vonteego Cummings	4.2	Ralph Willard	
1997-98	11-16	6-12		Vonteego Cummings	19.5	Isaac Hawkins	9.2	Vonteego Cummings	5.9	Ralph Willard	
1998-99	14-16	5-13		Vonteego Cummings	16.1	Isaac Hawkins	8.9	Vonteego Cummings	4.3	Ralph Willard	63-82 .434
1999-2000	13-15	5-11		Ricardo Greer	18.1	Ricardo Greer	9.8	Brandin Knight	5.5	Ben Howland	
2000-01	19-14	7-9	NIT SECOND ROUND	Ricardo Greer	18.6	Isaac Hawkins	7.9	Brandin Knight	5.5	Ben Howland	
2001-02	29-6	13-3	NCAA REGIONAL SEMIFINALS	Brandin Knight	15.6	Jaron Brown	6.1	Brandin Knight	7.2	Ben Howland	
2002-03	28-5	13-3	NCAA REGIONAL SEMIFINALS	Julius Page	12.2	Chevon Troutman	5.1	Brandin Knight	6.3	Ben Howland	89-40 .690
2003-04	31-5	13-3	NCAA REGIONAL SEMIFINALS	Carl Krauser	15.4	Chris Taft	7.5	Carl Krauser	4.5	Jamie Dixon	
2004-05	20-9	10-6	NCAA FIRST ROUND	Carl Krauser	16.0	Chevon Troutman	8.0	Carl Krauser	5.9	Jamie Dixon	
2005-06	25-8	10-6	NCAA SECOND ROUND	Carl Krauser	15.0	Aaron Gray	10.5	Carl Krauser	4.8	Jamie Dixon	
2006-07	29-8	12-4	NCAA REGIONAL SEMIFINALS	Aaron Gray	13.9	Aaron Gray	9.5	Levance Fields	4.5	Jamie Dixon	
2007-08	27-10	10-8	NCAA SECOND ROUND	Sam Young	18.1	DeJuan Blair	9.1	Levance Fields	5.3	Jamie Dixon	
2008-09	31-5	15-3	NCAA REGIONAL FINALS	Sam Young	19.2	DeJuan Blair	12.3	Levance Fields	7.5	Jamie Dixon	163-45 .784

ESPN 178 SAGARIN

PORTLAND

The late 1940s and '50s were happy days for Portland. Mush Torson's 1952 NAIA national semifinal team was the best of a string of successful squads that made NAIA tourneys eight times in 11 years. Then came darker times, including two miserable seasons in the late '80s when the Pilots suffered through a school-record 21-game losing streak. Their 19–13 record in 2008-09 made it feel like happy days might be back again.

BEST TEAM: 1951-52 James "Mush" Torson's squad won a school-record 24 games en route to the NAIA final four. The team featured many of the program's NAIA-era best players, including 1,000-point scorers Jim Winters, Andy Johnson and Ray Foleen. After a string of impressive tourney wins, including a 72-48 dismantling of Memphis State, they fell to Murray State by a point in the national semis.

BEST PLAYER: G Darwin Cook (1976-80) He could do it all—and right away. As a freshman, Cook was named the Pilots' MVP. He finished as the school's all-time leader in scoring (1,678; now third), assists (573) and steals (206). Cook went on to play eight NBA seasons.

BEST COACH: Jack Avina (1970-87) Avina's first set of seniors were playing for their fourth coach in four years and had won just 12 games in the previous three seasons. Before long, Avina put together five straight winning campaigns (1977-78 to '81-82), including an unbeaten home schedule in '77-78.

GAME FOR THE AGES: Portland stunned Ralph Miller's No. 19-ranked, Elite Eight-bound Oregon State, 68-63, on Dec. 11, 1981. The Pilots featured honorable mention All-America Jose Slaughter (18.7 ppg, 5.9 rpg) and went 17–10 in Avina's last winning campaign.

FIERCEST RIVAL: Portland and Gonzaga first played one another in 1946. Gonzaga leads 83–65, and it's been especially one-sided lately, with Portland losing 26 of 27 between 1997 and 2009. The brightest moment in recent years was a 76-68 win over the Zags in the 1996 WCC tournament title game that earned the Pilots an NCAA Tourney bid.

SEASON REVIEW

SEAS.	W-L	CONF.	COACH	SEAS.	W-L	CONF.	COACH
1922-50	*328-235*	*Includes school-best 16-2 in '24-25*		1963-64	17-9		Al Negratti
1950-51	23-6		James "Mush" Torson	1964-65	12-13		Al Negratti
1951-52	24-11		James "Mush" Torson	1965-66	6-19		Al Negratti
1952-53	15-14		James "Mush" Torson	1966-67	10-16		Al Negratti
1953-54	9-19		James "Mush" Torson	1967-68	5-21		Bill Turner
1954-55	9-13		Art McLarney[a]	1968-69	3-23		Bill Turner
1955-56	20-8		Al Negratti	1969-70	4-22		Joe Etzel[b]
1956-57	18-12		Al Negratti	1970-71	5-21		Jack Avina
1957-58	18-11		Al Negratti	1971-72	10-16		Jack Avina
1958-59	19-8	●	Al Negratti	1972-73	9-19		Jack Avina
1959-60	11-15		Al Negratti	1973-74	15-11		Jack Avina
1960-61	16-9		Al Negratti	1974-75	13-16		Jack Avina
1961-62	8-18		Al Negratti	1975-76	9-18 ⊗		Jack Avina
1962-63	8-18		Al Negratti	1976-77	11-15	6-8	Jack Avina

SEAS.	W-L	CONF.	SCORING		COACH	RECORD	
1977-78	19-8	9-5	Reggie Logan	15.2	Jack Avina		
1978-79	18-10	5-9	Rick Raivio	21.0	Jack Avina		
1979-80	17-11	9-7	Rick Raivio	19.1	Jack Avina		
1980-81	17-10	7-7	Jose Slaughter	21.2	Jack Avina		
1981-82	17-10	9-5	Jose Slaughter	18.7	Jack Avina		
1982-83	10-18	4-8	Dennis Black	11.1	Jack Avina		
1983-84	11-17	2-10	Darran Jenkins	11.1	Jack Avina		
1984-85	14-14	3-9	Darran Jenkins	10.9	Jack Avina		
1985-86	13-15	4-10	Fred Harris	13.5	Jack Avina		
1986-87	14-14	6-8	Greg Anthony	15.3	Jack Avina	222-243	.477▼
1987-88	6-22	1-13	Adam Simmons	14.2	Larry Steele		
1988-89	2-26	2-12	Josh Lowery	16.0	Larry Steele		
1989-90	11-17	7-7	Josh Lowery	16.7	Larry Steele		
1990-91	5-23	3-11	David Roth	14.5	Larry Steele		
1991-92	10-18	3-11	Peter McKelvey	19.6	Larry Steele		
1992-93	9-18	3-11	Matt Houle	14.7	Larry Steele		
1993-94	13-17	6-8	Matt Houle	16.6	Larry Steele	56-141	.284
1994-95	21-8	10-4	Canaan Chatman	18.3	Rob Chavez		
1995-96	19-11	7-7 ●	Kweemada King	13.6	Rob Chavez		
1996-97	9-18	4-10	Greg Klosterman	15.6	Rob Chavez		
1997-98	14-13	7-7	Chivo Anderson	13.3	Rob Chavez		
1998-99	9-18	3-11	Jimmie Rainwater	12.1	Rob Chavez		
1999-2000	10-18	4-10	Ryan Jones	14.4	Rob Chavez		
2000-01	11-17	4-10	Tim Frost	14.9	Rob Chavez	93-103	.474
2001-02	6-24	2-12	Casey Frandsen	19.2	Michael Holton		
2002-03	11-17	4-10	Casey Frandsen	12.7	Michael Holton		
2003-04	11-17	5-9	Pooh Jeter	16.6	Michael Holton		
2004-05	15-15	4-10	Pooh Jeter	15.2	Michael Holton		
2005-06	11-18	5-9	Pooh Jeter	18.5	Michael Holton	54-91	.372
2006-07	9-23	4-10	Darren Cooper	12.1	Eric Reveno		
2007-08	9-22	3-11	Nik Raivio	12.6	Eric Reveno		
2008-09	19-13	9-5	Nik Raivio	16.0	Eric Reveno	37-58	.389

[a] Art McLarney (5-8) and Mike Tichy (4-5) both coached during the 1954-55 season.
[b] Ernie Smith, head coach for 1969-70, died of a heart attack before the start of the season.
⊗ Record does not reflect games forfeited or vacated. For adjusted records, see p. 521.
▼ Coach's record adjusted to reflect games forfeited or vacated: 223-242, .480. For yearly totals, see p. 521.
● NCAA Tournament appearance

PROFILE

University of Portland, Portland, OR
Founded: 1901
Enrollment: 3,300 (2,850 undergraduate)
Colors: Purple and white
Nickname: Pilots
Current arena: Chiles Center, opened in 1984 (4,852)
Previous: Memorial Coliseum, 1961-84 (12,666); Howard Hall, 1928-84 (1,200)
First game: 1922
All-time record: 1,045-1,156 (.478)
Total weeks in AP Top 20/25: 3

Current conference: West Coast (1976-)
Conference titles: 0
Conference tournament titles:
West Coast: 1 (1996)
NCAA Tournament appearances: 2
NIT appearances: 0

FIRST-ROUND PRO PICKS

1961 **Ray Scott,** Detroit (4)

TOP 5

G **Darwin Cook** (1976-80)
G **Jose Slaughter** (1978-82)
G **Jim Winters** (1950-53, '55-56)
G/F **Bill O'Donnell** (1935-39)
F **Rick Raivio** (1976-80)

RECORDS

RECORDS	GAME		SEASON		CAREER	
POINTS	43	Matt Houle, vs. San Francisco (Feb. 13, 1993)	587	Rick Raivio (1978-79)	1,940	Jose Slaughter (1978-82)
POINTS PER GAME			21.2	Jose Slaughter (1980-81)	19.4	Peter McKelvey (1991-93)
REBOUNDS	26	Don Lawson, vs. Nevada Southern (Feb. 12, 1967)	337	Rick Raivio (1978-79)	910	Rick Raivio (1976-80)
ASSISTS	14	Dionn Holton, vs. Southern Oregon (Dec. 9, 1995)	174	Darwin Cook (1979-80)	573	Darwin Cook (1976-80)

ESPN 191 SAGARIN

PORTLAND STATE

Three things stand out in Portland State hoops history: the legendary scorer Freeman Williams; the dropping of the basketball program for budgetary reasons between 1981 and '96; and the magical run to the 2008 NCAA Tournament.

BEST TEAM: 2007-08 They reached heights no other Vikings team had reached—the 20-win mark for the first time in NCAA competition, the Big Sky championship game and the Big Dance, behind league MVP Jeremiah Dominguez (who transferred to PSU after two frustrating seasons at archrival Portland) and all-conference picks Deonte Huff and Scott Morrison.

BEST PLAYER: G Freeman Williams (1974-78) Only LSU's Pete Maravich scored more points in Division I. The 6'4" guard didn't play much D, but Williams put PSU hoops on the map, leading the nation in scoring in each of his last two seasons (38.8 and 35.9 ppg). In 1978, he scored 81 points against Rocky Mountain College, the third-highest total for a Division I player against a non-D1 opponent. He went on to play six seasons in the NBA.

BEST COACH: Sharkey Nelson (1953-65) He notched the most wins in school history (162), despite the fact that Nelson's teams mostly played in a former high school gym known not so affectionately as the Black Hole of Calcutta.

GAME FOR THE AGES: On March 12, 2008, at the Rose Garden, the Vikings earned their first NCAA berth with a 67-51 Big Sky tourney victory over Northern Arizona. PSU never trailed, thanks to tourney MVP Deonte Huff, who scored 11 of PSU's first 20 points. He finished with 17 to go along with 7 rebounds and 3 steals.

FIERCEST RIVAL: They share a city and a name. Portland leads the series with Portland State, 31–16. On Nov. 28, 2007, the Vikings beat the Pilots, 78-73, winning at Portland's Chiles Center for the first time since PSU's program was restored. But the Vikes are ahead in a different sort of contest: Two of PSU's recent star players—Dominguez and F Jamie Jones—transferred from Portland.

SEASON REVIEW

SEAS.	W-L	CONF.	SCORING		COACH	RECORD	
1946-47	6-12		Phillips	9.0	John Jenkins	6-12	.333
1947-48	14-5				Joe Holland	14-5	.737
1948-49	6-7		Leroy Coleman, E. Baldini	10.6	Arba Ager		
1949-50	21-9		Don Koepke	14.8	Arba Ager		
1950-51	18-9		Lloyd Bergman	18.4	Arba Ager		
1951-52	18-9				Arba Ager		
1952-53	14-13		Don Koepke	17.7	Arba Ager	77-47	.621
1953-54	8-17		Don Porter	25.0	Sharkey Nelson		
1954-55	17-4		Jack Viskov	15.5	Sharkey Nelson		
1955-56	21-8		Jack Viskov	17.2	Sharkey Nelson		
1956-57	11-17		Jack Parker	15.0	Sharkey Nelson		
1957-58	14-14		John Winters	18.0	Sharkey Nelson		
1958-59	20-8		John Winters	12.4	Sharkey Nelson		
1959-60	14-14		Don Powell	11.9	Sharkey Nelson		
1960-61	17-10		Bill Turner	12.1	Sharkey Nelson		
1961-62	15-13		Bill Turner	12.3	Sharkey Nelson		
1962-63	7-18		John Nelson	16.0	Sharkey Nelson		
1963-64	10-15		John Nelson	17.2	Sharkey Nelson		
1964-65	8-18		John Nelson	25.0	Sharkey Nelson	162-156	.509
1965-66	6-19		John Nelson	25.8	Marion Pericin		
1966-67	16-9		Bill Wilkerson	24.8	Marion Pericin		
1967-68	13-9		Hal Dohling	19.0	Marion Pericin		
1968-69	8-16		Leon Edmonds	22.9	Marion Pericin		
1969-70	9-14		Willie Stoudamire	18.2	Marion Pericin		
1970-71	16-6		Willie Stoudamire	25.5	Marion Pericin		
1971-72	17-8		Willie Stoudamire	30.1	Marion Pericin	85-81	.512
1972-73	12-12		Leo Franz	20.4	Ken Edwards		
1973-74	16-11		Ed Buchanan	15.2	Ken Edwards		
1974-75	18-8		Freeman Williams	16.8	Ken Edwards		
1975-76	17-10 ⊗		Freeman Williams	30.9	Ken Edwards		
1976-77	16-10		Freeman Williams	38.8	Ken Edwards		
1977-78	14-13		Freeman Williams	35.9	Ken Edwards	93-64	.595▼
1978-79	6-21		Bob Sisul	14.4	Glen Kinney		
1979-80	5-21		Mike Babin	13.3	Glen Kinney		
1980-81	7-20		Doug Eilertson	16.3	Glen Kinney	18-62	.225
1981-96	no team						
1996-97	9-17	6-10	Brian Towne	12.4	Ritchie McKay		
1997-98	15-12	10-6	Jason Hartman	19.1	Ritchie McKay	24-29	.453
1998-99	17-11	9-7	Jason Hartman	22.8	Joel Sobotka		
1999-2000	15-14	7-9	Ime Udoka	14.5	Joel Sobotka		
2000-01	9-18	6-10	Anthony Lackey	14.5	Joel Sobotka		
2001-02	12-16	6-8	Anthony Lackey	16.4	Joel Sobotka	53-59	.473
2002-03	5-22	3-11	Jeb Ivey	15.0	Heath Schroyer		
2003-04	11-16	5-9	Blake Walker	16.1	Heath Schroyer		
2004-05	19-9	11-3	Seamus Boxley	20.6	Heath Schroyer	35-47	.427
2005-06	12-16	5-9	Jake Schroeder	12.5	Ken Bone		
2006-07	19-13	9-7	Dupree Lucas	13.2	Ken Bone		
2007-08	23-10	14-2 ●	Jeremiah Dominguez	14.2	Ken Bone		
2008-09	23-10	11-5 ●	Jeremiah Dominguez	12.9	Ken Bone	77-49	.611

⊗ Record does not reflect games forfeited or vacated. For adjusted records, see p. 521.
▼ Coach's record adjusted to reflect games forfeited or vacated: 94-63, .599. For yearly totals, see p. 521.
● NCAA Tournament appearance

PROFILE

Portland State University, Portland, OR
Founded: 1946
Enrollment: 26,587 (20,515 undergraduate)
Colors: Green, white and silver
Nickname: Vikings
Current arena: Peter W. Stott Center, opened in 1967 (1,500)
First game: 1946
All-time record: 646-609 (.515)
Total weeks in AP Top 20/25: 0

Current conference: Big Sky (1996-)
Conference titles:
Big Sky: 2 (2005, '08)
Conference tournament titles:
Big Sky: 2 (2008, '09)
NCAA Tournament appearances: 2
NIT appearances: 0

FIRST-ROUND PRO PICKS

1978 **Freeman Williams,** Boston (8)

TOP 5

G **John Nelson** (1962-66)
G **Willie Stoudamire** (1969-72)
G **Freeman Williams** (1974-78)
F **Bill Wilkerson** (1965-67)
F **John Winters** (1955-59)

RECORDS

	GAME		SEASON		CAREER	
POINTS	81	Freeman Williams, vs. Rocky Mountain (Feb. 3, 1978)	1,010	Freeman Williams (1976-77)	3,249	Freeman Williams (1974-78)
POINTS PER GAME			38.8	Freeman Williams, (1976-77)	30.4	Freeman Williams (1974-78)
REBOUNDS	26	Bernie Jones, vs. Oregon Coll. of Education (Jan. 20, 1959)	332	Bill Wilkerson (1966-67)	767	Bob Sisul (1976-79)
ASSISTS	19	Terry Adolph, vs. Saint Mary's (Calif.) (Dec. 27, 1977)	224	Will Funn (2004-05)	421	Terry Adolph (1976-78)

ESPN 290 SAGARIN

PRAIRIE VIEW A&M

How about a little Hoop Phi Hoop for Panthers history? The post-victory step dance commemorating Prairie View's stunning 1998 SWAC tourney title win over Texas Southern could also honor the 1962 NAIA national champs, all-time great Zelmo Beaty and any fan who endured the 1991-92 and '92-93 seasons, when the Panthers were a combined 1–54.

BEST TEAM: 1961-62 The 6'9" Beaty led the Panthers to the NAIA national title, setting a still-standing tournament record of 96 total rebounds while earning MVP honors. Coach Leroy Moore's loaded team also included Cornell Lackey (1,112 career points), Thomas Redman (1,366 rebounds) and Douglas Hines (1,231 rebounds).

BEST PLAYER: C Zelmo Beaty (1958-62) Panthers fans used to pack the school's old gym starting at 4:30 before a 7:00 tip-off just to watch Big Z warm up. Beaty rarely failed to send them home happy. After winning the 1962 NAIA title, the big man was picked No. 3 overall in the 1962 NBA draft (St. Louis), was an NBA or ABA All-Star five times, and reached the playoffs in 11 of his 12 pro seasons.

BEST COACH: Leroy Moore Jr. (1956-63, '65-66) Moore guided teams that featured Prairie View's three all-time top scorers—Beaty, Harold Grimes and Guy Manning. After leaving the bench with a 138–59 record, Moore served Prairie View as athletic director and acting dean of the College of Education.

GAME FOR THE AGES: The Panthers had a losing record entering the 1998 SWAC tournament, yet made it to the title game to face top-seeded Texas Southern. Prairie View rallied from a 41-21 halftime deficit and, after two free throws by Tamarron Sharpe, took its first lead of the game with 1:47 remaining. They held on, 59-57, to earn the Panthers' only Tourney bid.

FIERCEST RIVAL: Texas Southern, the other SWAC school located in Texas, has brought out some of Prairie View's best individual performances: Manning scoring 41 twice, Beaty netting 40 twice and Gregory Burks hitting 37. Oh, and there was that big 1998 SWAC tourney win.

SEASON REVIEW

SEAS.	W-L	CONF.	SCORING		COACH	RECORD	
1956-58	*24-20*	*Records from before 1956-57 have been lost*					
1958-59	17-8				Leroy Moore Jr.		
1959-60	21-5				Leroy Moore Jr.		
1960-61	25-2				Leroy Moore Jr.		
1961-62	20-3	◆			Leroy Moore Jr.		
1962-63	18-8				Leroy Moore Jr.		
1963-64	N/A						
1964-65	10-14				Robert Hopkins	10-14	.417
1965-66	13-13				Leroy Moore Jr.	138-59	.701
1966-67	N/A						
1967-68	N/A						
1968-69	N/A						
1969-70	10-17				Bill Cofield		
1970-71	14-12				Bill Cofield		
1971-72	14-11				Bill Cofield		
1972-73	19-8				Bill Cofield	57-48	.543
1973-74	7-17				Elwood Plummer		
1974-75	16-10				Elwood Plummer		
1975-76	13-11				Elwood Plummer		
1976-77	11-18				Elwood Plummer		
1977-78	14-13	3-9			Elwood Plummer		
1978-79	17-14	3-9			Elwood Plummer		
1979-80	10-18	2-10			Calvin White		
1980-81	2-23	1-11			Calvin White		
1981-82	2-23	1-11			Calvin White	14-64	.179
1982-83	4-22	2-12			Jim Duplantier		
1983-84	2-26	0-14			Jim Duplantier		
1984-85	5-22	4-10			Jim Duplantier		
1985-86	5-25	1-13			Jim Duplantier		
1986-87	6-22	2-12			Jim Duplantier		
1987-88	5-22	2-12			Jim Duplantier		
1988-89	11-16	5-9			Jim Duplantier		
1989-90	9-18	5-9			Jim Duplantier	47-173	.214
1990-91	4-21	0-0			Elwood Plummer		
1991-92	0-28	0-14			Elwood Plummer		
1992-93	1-26	0-14			Elwood Plummer		
1993-94	5-22	2-12			Elwood Plummer		
1994-95	6-21	3-11			Elwood Plummer		
1995-96	4-23	0-14			Elwood Plummer		
1996-97	10-17	7-7			Elwood Plummer		
1997-98	13-17	6-10 ●			Elwood Plummer		
1998-99	6-21	4-12	Jocquinn Arch	16.0	Elwood Plummer		
1999-2000	7-20	5-13	Gregory Burks	18.4	Elwood Plummer		
2000-01	6-22	5-13	Xavier Lee	17.7	Elwood Plummer		
2001-02	10-20	8-10	Gregory Burks	17.5	Elwood Plummer	150-341	.305
2002-03	17-12	14-4	Gregory Burks	18.0	Jerry Francis		
2003-04	7-20	7-11	Kevin Cooper	15.1	Jerry Francis		
2004-05	5-23 ⊘	6-12	Philip Scott	12.0	Jerry Francis	29-55	.345
2005-06	5-24	2-16	Anthony Oha	12.1	Darrell Hawkins	5-24	.172
2006-07	8-22	6-12	Brian Ezeh	10.6	Byron Rimm II		
2007-08	8-22	6-12	Brian Ezeh	13.1	Byron Rimm II		
2008-09	17-16	12-6	Darnell Hugee	12.0	Byron Rimm II	33-60	.355

⊘ Records don't reflect games forfeited or vacated. For adjusted records, see p. 521.
● NCAA Tournament appearance ◆ NAIA championship

PROFILE

Prairie View A&M University, Prairie View, TX
Founded: 1876
Enrollment: 8,382 (6,324 undergraduate)
Colors: Purple and gold
Nickname: Panthers
Current arena: William J. Nicks Building (5,520)
First game: 1920
All-time record: 483-838 (.366)
Total weeks in AP Top 20/25: 0

Current conference: Southwestern Athletic (1920-)
Conference titles:
SWAC: 3 (1961, '62, 2003)
Conference tournament titles:
SWAC: 1 (1998)
NCAA Tournament appearances: 1
NIT appearances: 0

CONSENSUS ALL-AMERICAS

1962 **Zelmo Beaty** (Little A-A), C

FIRST-ROUND PRO PICKS

1962 **Zelmo Beaty**, St. Louis (3)

TOP 5

G **Gregory Burks** (1998-2003)
G **Harold Grimes** (1956-60)
F **Guy Manning** (1962-66)
F/C **Clarence Ludd** (1950-54)
C **Zelmo Beaty** (1958-62)

RECORDS

RECORDS	GAME		SEASON		CAREER	
POINTS	N/A		N/A		2,285	Zelmo Beaty (1958-62)
POINTS PER GAME			N/A		23.1	Zelmo Beaty (1958-62)
REBOUNDS	N/A		519	Larry Johnson (1973-74)	1,916	Zelmo Beaty (1958-62)
ASSISTS	N/A		N/A		N/A	

ESPN 85 SAGARIN

PRINCETON

The Tigers have decimated Ivy League foes since the conference was founded, and they've provided some of March's most memorable moments. But Princeton being Princeton, the Tigers haven't limited their influence to the court. Princeton's best ever, Bill Bradley, was a U.S. senator, and another all-time great, Craig Robinson, is the brother-in-law of President Barack Obama.

BEST TEAM: 1964-65 With apologies to the 1997-98 team, which went 27–2 and earned a No. 5 Tournament seed, it's impossible to pick against the squad that made the 1965 Final Four. It was only fitting that Bradley's stellar college career ended on such a grand stage. In their East Regional seminfinal, the Tigers knocked off NC State, only to watch Providence presumptuously cut down the nets after beating St. Joseph's in the second game of the doubleheader. Big mistake. Princeton routed the Friars by 40 to advance to the national semis. There they lost to Michigan, before besting Wichita State in the third-place game, behind Bradley's 58 points.

BEST PLAYER: F Bill Bradley (1962-65) His career, immortalized in John McPhee's book *A Sense of Where You Are*, is the stuff of legend. The 6'5" forward out of Crystal City (Mo.) High received about 70 scholarship offers and backed out of a commitment to go to Duke to attend Princeton—which, like the other Ivies, didn't hand out athletic scholarships. Not only is Bradley the Tigers' all-time leading scorer and rebounder, not only did he captain the U.S. team that won gold at the 1964 Tokyo Olympics, not only did he star for the New York Knicks and win two championships, but he was a Rhodes Scholar who became a three-term senator from New Jersey.

BEST COACH: Pete Carril (1967-96) *Backdoor. Yoda. Legend.* The image of the squat curmudgeon stalking the sideline conjures one-word captions, but none do the man justice. In 29 seasons at Princeton, he won 11 Ivy championships, guided Princeton to the NCAA Tourney 11 times and won the 1975 NIT. He also perfected a system that came to be known simply as the Princeton Offense—a motion-based attack that involves quick passes, constant movement and yes, those signature backdoor cuts.

GAME FOR THE AGES: Carril earned his rep as a giant-killer when the No. 13-seeded Tigers faced defending champ UCLA in the first round of the 1996 Tournament. With the score tied at 41 and less than :10 remaining, Gabe Lewullis made a backdoor cut, caught a pinpoint pass from Steve Goodrich and put up the game-winning layup.

HEARTBREAKER: A No. 16-seed has never defeated a No. 1-seed in the Big Dance. If not for the long arm of Alonzo Mourning in 1989, that might not be the case. The Hoyas held a one-point lead with :06 left, when Zo swatted away attempts by Bob Scrabis and Kit Mueller (the latter a foul, according to Tigers faithful) to preserve a 50-49 victory.

FIERCEST RIVAL: With Penn and Princeton dominating the Ivy so thoroughly, is it any surprise that their rivalry is so intense? Tiger fans love chanting "Safety School" at their Quakers counterparts—almost as much as they enjoying reliving Feb. 9, 1999, when Princeton trailed 33-9 at the half and 40-13 early in the second, only to come back and win, 50-49. But Penn has had the last laugh 122 times in their 220 meetings.

FANFARE AND HOOPLA: When Jadwin Gym was being built in the late 1960s, Carril would sit outside smoking a stogie or drinking a beer and just gaze at the construction. Now the floor bears his name.

FAN FAVORITE: C Kit Mueller (1987-91) He was a 6'5" center who was graciously listed as two inches taller in the Tigers media guide. Yet Carril's words succinctly sum up the thoughts of all Princeton fans: "God smiled on me the day that kid walked into my life." Mueller was the quintessential high-post center critical to Carril's offensive approach; he ranks second in team history with 381 career assists. And he's well remembered for battling Mourning in Princeton's epic one-point loss to Georgetown in the first round of the 1989 NCAA Tournament.

CONSENSUS ALL-AMERICAS

1905	**Oliver DeGray Vanderbilt,** G
1913	**Hamilton Salmon,** F
1916, '17	**Cyril Haas,** G/F
1922, '23	**Arthur Loeb,** G
1926	**Carl Loeb,** G
1964, '65	**Bill Bradley,** F

FIRST-ROUND PRO PICKS

1965	**Bill Bradley,** New York (2)
1970	**Geoff Petrie,** Portland (8)
1970	**John Hummer,** Buffalo (15)
1970	**John Hummer,** Florida (ABA)
1976	**Armond Hill,** Atlanta (9)

PROFILE

Princeton University, Princeton, NJ
Founded: 1746
Enrollment: 7,497 (4,981 undergraduate)
Colors: Orange and black
Nickname: Tigers
Current arena: L. Stockwell Jadwin Gymnasium, opened in 1969 (6,854)
First game: Jan. 20, 1901
All-time record: 1,552-986 (.612)
Total weeks in AP Top 20/25: 41

Current conference: Ivy League (1901-)
Conference titles:
Ivy: 27 (1922, '25, '32, '50, '52, '55, '60, '61, '63, '64, '65, '67, '69, '76, '77, '81, '83, '84, '89, '90, '91, '92, '96, '97, '98, 2001, '04)
NCAA Tournament appearances: 23
Final Fours: 1
NIT appearances: 5
Semifinals: 1
Titles: 1 (1975)

TOP 5

G **Brian Taylor** (1970-72)
G/F **Geoff Petrie** (1967-70)
F **Bill Bradley** (1962-65)
F **Craig Robinson** (1979-83)
C **Kit Mueller** (1987-91)

RECORDS

	GAME		SEASON		CAREER	
POINTS	58	Bill Bradley, vs. Wichita State (March 20, 1965)	936	Bill Bradley (1963-64)	2,503	Bill Bradley (1962-65)
POINTS PER GAME			32.3	Bill Bradley (1963-64)	30.2	Bill Bradley (1962-65)
REBOUNDS	29	Carl Belz, vs. Rutgers (Jan. 31, 1959)	406	David Fulcomer (1955-56)	1,008	Bill Bradley (1962-65)
ASSISTS	12	William Ryan, vs. Columbia (Feb. 25, 1984); vs. Yale (Feb. 4, 1984); vs. Brown (Jan. 9, 1982)	161	William Ryan (1983-84)	413	William Ryan (1980-84)

SEASON REVIEW

SEASON	W-L	CONF.	SCORING	COACH	RECORD
1901-16	*138-122*		*10 different coaches in first 13 seasons*		
1916-17	15-5	8-2		Frederick Luehring	
1917-18	12-3	8-2		Frederick Luehring	
1918-19	5-5			Frederick Luehring	
1919-20	16-6	6-4		Frederick Luehring	100-43 .699
1920-21	14-9	4-6		Louis Sugarman[a]	11-4 .733
1921-22	20-5	8-2		J. Hill Zahn	
1922-23	16-4	6-4		J. Hill Zahn	36-9 .800
1923-24	11-6	6-4		Albert Wittmer	
1924-25	21-2	9-1		Albert Wittmer	
1925-26	9-13	5-5		Albert Wittmer	
1926-27	11-11	7-3		Albert Wittmer	
1927-28	14-10	7-3		Albert Wittmer	
1928-29	9-15	1-9		Albert Wittmer	
1929-30	13-12	3-7		Albert Wittmer	
1930-31	9-13	1-9		Albert Wittmer	
1931-32	18-4	8-2		Albert Wittmer	115-86 .572
1932-33	19-3	7-3		Herbert "Fritz" Crisler	
1933-34	13-8	7-5		Herbert "Fritz" Crisler	32-11 .744
1934-35	6-14	4-8		John Jeffries	6-14 .300
1935-36	9-14	5-7		Ken Fairman	
1936-37	6-14	2-10		Ken Fairman	

SEAS.	W-L	CONF.	POSTSEASON	SCORING	REBOUNDS	ASSISTS	COACH	RECORD
1937-38	10-10	5-7					Ken Fairman	25-38 .397
1938-39	10-9	6-6					Franklin "Cappy" Cappon	
1939-40	14-8	8-4					Franklin "Cappy" Cappon	
1940-41	10-13	4-8					Franklin "Cappy" Cappon	
1941-42	16-5	10-2					Franklin "Cappy" Cappon	
1942-43	14-6	9-3					Franklin "Cappy" Cappon[b]	
1943-44	6-12	2-6					William Logan	
1944-45	7-12						William Logan[c]	20-20 .500
1945-46	7-12	0-8					Wesley Fesler	7-12 .368
1946-47	7-16	2-10					Franklin "Cappy" Cappon	
1947-48	12-11	6-6					Franklin "Cappy" Cappon	
1948-49	13-9	8-4					Franklin "Cappy" Cappon	
1949-50	14-9	11-1					Franklin "Cappy" Cappon	
1950-51	15-7	5-7					Franklin "Cappy" Cappon	
1951-52	16-11	10-2	NCAA REGIONAL SEMIFINALS				Franklin "Cappy" Cappon	
1952-53	9-14	5-7					Franklin "Cappy" Cappon	
1953-54	16-9	11-4					Franklin "Cappy" Cappon	
1954-55	13-12	10-4	NCAA REGIONAL SEMIFINALS	Harold Haabestad 20.0			Franklin "Cappy" Cappon	
1955-56	11-13	7-7			David Fulcomer 16.9		Franklin "Cappy" Cappon	
1956-57	14-9	9-5			Carl Belz 328		Franklin "Cappy" Cappon	
1957-58	15-8	9-5			David Fulcomer 285		Franklin "Cappy" Cappon	
1958-59	19-5	13-1			Carl Belz 333		Franklin "Cappy" Cappon	
1959-60	15-9	11-3	NCAA FIRST ROUND	Peter Campbell 20.9			Franklin "Cappy" Cappon	
1960-61	18-8	11-3	NCAA REGIONAL SEMIFINALS		Alfred Kaemmerlen 335		Franklin "Cappy" Cappon[d]	250-181 .580
1961-62	13-10	10-4		Peter Campbell 19.7	Alfred Kaemmerlen 347		Jake McCandless	22-16 .579
1962-63	19-6	11-3	NCAA FIRST ROUND	Bill Bradley 27.3	Bill Bradley 12.2		Butch van Breda Kolff	
1963-64	20-9	12-2	NCAA REGIONAL SEMIFINALS	Bill Bradley 32.3	Bill Bradley 12.4		Butch van Breda Kolff	
1964-65	23-6	13-1	NCAA THIRD PLACE	Bill Bradley 30.5	Bill Bradley 11.8		Butch van Breda Kolff	
1965-66	16-7	9-5					Butch van Breda Kolff	
1966-67	25-3	13-1	NCAA REGIONAL SEMIFINALS				Butch van Breda Kolff	103-31 .769
1967-68	20-6	12-2					Pete Carril	
1968-69	19-7	14-0	NCAA FIRST ROUND	Geoff Petrie 20.8			Pete Carril	
1969-70	16-9	9-5		Geoff Petrie 22.3			Pete Carril	
1970-71	14-11	9-5		Brian Taylor 23.5			Pete Carril	
1971-72	20-7	12-2	NIT QUARTERFINALS	Brian Taylor 25.0			Pete Carril	
1972-73	16-9	11-3					Pete Carril	
1973-74	16-10	11-3					Pete Carril	
1974-75	22-8	12-2	NIT CHAMPION				Pete Carril	
1975-76	22-5	14-0	NCAA FIRST ROUND				Pete Carril	
1976-77	21-5	13-1	NCAA FIRST ROUND				Pete Carril	
1977-78	17-9	11-3					Pete Carril	
1978-79	14-12	7-7					Pete Carril	
1979-80	15-15	11-3					Pete Carril	
1980-81	18-10	13-1	NCAA FIRST ROUND				Pete Carril	
1981-82	13-13	9-5					Pete Carril	
1982-83	20-9	12-2	NCAA SECOND ROUND				Pete Carril	
1983-84	18-10	10-4	NCAA FIRST ROUND				Pete Carril	
1984-85	11-15	7-7					Pete Carril	
1985-86	13-13	7-7					Pete Carril	
1986-87	16-9	9-5					Pete Carril	
1987-88	17-9	9-5					Pete Carril	
1988-89	19-8	11-3	NCAA FIRST ROUND				Pete Carril	
1989-90	20-7	11-3	NCAA FIRST ROUND				Pete Carril	
1990-91	24-3	14-0	NCAA FIRST ROUND				Pete Carril	
1991-92	22-6	12-2	NCAA FIRST ROUND				Pete Carril	
1992-93	15-11	7-7					Pete Carril	
1993-94	18-8	11-3					Pete Carril	
1994-95	16-10	10-4					Pete Carril	
1995-96	22-7	12-2	NCAA SECOND ROUND				Pete Carril	514-261 .663
1996-97	24-4	14-0	NCAA FIRST ROUND				Bill Carmody	
1997-98	27-2	14-0	NCAA SECOND ROUND				Bill Carmody	
1998-99	22-8	11-3	NIT QUARTERFINALS	Gabe Lewullis 14.8	Mason Rocca 5.9	Brian Earl 3.5	Bill Carmody	
1999-2000	19-11	11-3	NIT FIRST ROUND	Chris Young 13.8	Chris Young 6.3	Nate Walton 4.0	Bill Carmody	92-25 .786
2000-01	16-11	11-3	NCAA FIRST ROUND		Nate Walton 5.6	Mike Bechtold 6.9	John Thompson III	
2001-02	16-12	11-3	NIT FIRST ROUND	Mike Bechtold 10.3	Mike Bechtold 4.4	Ahmed El-Nokali 2.4	John Thompson III	
2002-03	16-11	10-4		Spencer Gloger 15.7	Spencer Gloger 5.7	Kyle Wente 3.5	John Thompson III	
2003-04	20-8	13-1	NCAA FIRST ROUND	Judson Wallace 15.3	Judson Wallace 6.4	Ed Persia 3.1	John Thompson III	68-42 .618
2004-05	15-13	6-8		Judson Wallace 12.2	Judson Wallace 4.9	Will Venable 3.1	Joe Scott	
2005-06	12-15	10-4		Scott Greenman 10.8	Justin Conway 4.2	Justin Conway 3.1	Joe Scott	
2006-07	11-17	2-12		Kyle Koncz 8.0	Justin Conway 3.9	Marcus Schroeder 3.1	Joe Scott	38-45 .458
2007-08	6-23	3-11		Zach Finley 10.2	Kyle Koncz 4.9	Lincoln Gunn 3.1	Sydney Johnson	
2008-09	13-14	8-6		Doug Davis 12.3	Zach Finley 4.1	Marcus Schroeder 3.0	Sydney Johnson	19-37 .339

Cumulative totals listed when per game averages are not available.

[a] Louis Sugarman (11-4) and James Hynson (3-5) both coached during the 1920-21 season. [b] Franklin "Cappy" Cappon (2-2) and William Logan (12-4) both coached during the 1942-43 season.

[c] William Logan (2-4) and Leonard Hettinger (5-8) both coached during the 1944-45 season. [d] Franklin "Cappy" Cappon (9-2) and Jake McCandless (9-6) both coached during the 1960-61 season.

78 SAGARIN

PROVIDENCE

An early power in New England basketball, Providence burst out onto the national scene in 1972-73 with two of the most colorful players in the game's history, and again in 1987 under a young, spunky head coach named Rick Pitino. The Friars have earned more than 30 postseason appearances, 15 of them in the NCAA Tournament.

BEST TEAM: 1972-73 In their inaugural season playing in the Providence Civic Center, coach Dave Gavitt's Friars rolled through a 24–2 regular season behind PC legends Ernie DiGregorio and Marvin Barnes. DiGregorio (24.6 ppg, 8.6 apg) was a cocky ball-handling wizard in the mold of Bob Cousy, and Barnes (18.3 ppg, 19.0 rpg) was a 6'8" terror near the basket. (Barnes also made a name for himself with his off-court antics—Bad News. He infamously hit a teammate in the head with a tire iron in 1972 and had several other run-ins with the law.) Meanwhile, deadeye shooter Kevin Stacom (17.8 ppg) was always at the ready. The Friars reached the Final Four for the first time in school history, losing to Memphis State (see Heartbreaker). The impact of that team resonates in Rhode Island to this day.

BEST PLAYER: G JIMMY WALKER (1964-67) Providence's second-leading scorer with 2,045 points and a three-time All-America, in 1967 Walker became the only Friar to average more than 30 ppg, leading the nation with 30.4. He was the top pick in the 1967 NBA draft and became a two-time All-Star with the Detroit Pistons.

BEST COACH: JOE MULLANEY (1955-69, '81-85) Immortalized as the architect of PC basketball, Mullaney is the all-time winningest coach in Providence history (319–164 over 18 seasons). He led the Friars to nine postseason appearances, including three straight NCAA bids from 1964 to '66, and is credited with creating the match-up zone defense.

GAME FOR THE AGES: In the 1987 NCAA Tournament, No. 6-seed Providence ran up against a Cinderella on fire. No. 14-seed Austin Peay, fresh off a first-round upset of No. 3-seed Illinois, built a 10-point lead over Pitino's Friars. Providence went on a 15-4 run in the final minutes to help send the game into overtime, and came away with a 90-87 win on their way to the Final Four.

HEARTBREAKER: Playing in its first Final Four against Memphis State on March 24, 1973, Providence was dealt a crippling blow just eight minutes into the game when Barnes injured his right knee and was forced to sit out the rest of the game. The Friars forged on valiantly without their all-everything center, but even DiGregorio's 32 points could not offset the loss of Barnes. The Tigers won, 98-85, for the right to try (and fail) to unseat defending champ UCLA.

FIERCEST RIVAL: Intense in-state foes (with a private vs. public school twist), Providence and Rhode Island first met on the hardwood back in 1920, with PC leading series 66–53. The schools play annually, usually in November or December, when the state divides itself into black (PC) and blue (URI) camps.

FANFARE AND HOOPLA: Opened in 1972 as the Providence Civic Center, PC's home court is now called the Dunkin' Donuts Center, or more simply the Dunk. Frequent sellouts, especially for Big East games, give the Dunk a raucous atmosphere, presided over by the familiar PC mascot clad in his Friar's robe.

FAN FAVORITE: F RYAN GOMES (2001-05) The school's all-time leading scorer with 2,138 points, Gomes' legacy grew greater after he left PC and became the second-round draft pick of Rhode Island's favorite NBA team, the Boston Celtics.

CONSENSUS ALL-AMERICAS

1966, '67	**Jimmy Walker,** G
1973	**Ernie DiGregorio,** G
1974	**Marvin Barnes,** C
2004	**Ryan Gomes,** F

FIRST-ROUND PRO PICKS

1960	**Lenny Wilkens,** St. Louis (6)
1967	**Jimmy Walker,** Detroit (1)
1973	**Ernie DiGregorio,** Buffalo (3)
1973	**Marvin Barnes,** Denver (ABA, 6)
1974	**Marvin Barnes,** Philadelphia (2)
1984	**Otis Thorpe,** Kansas City (9)
1991	**Eric Murdock,** Utah (21)
1994	**Dickey Simpkins,** Chicago (21)
1995	**Eric Williams,** Boston (14)
1997	**Austin Croshere,** Indiana (12)

PROFILE

Providence College, Providence, RI
Founded: 1917
Enrollment: 5,098 (4,364 undergraduate)
Colors: Black, white and silver
Nickname: Friars
Current arena: Dunkin' Donuts Center (formerly Providence Civic Center) opened in 1972 (12,993)
Previous: Mullaney Gymnasium, 1955-72 (2,600)
First game: Dec. 4, 1920
All-time record: 1,274-847 (.601)
Total weeks in AP Top 20/25: 129

Current conference: Big East (1979-)
Conferences titles: 0
Conference tournament titles:
Big East: 1 (1994)
NCAA Tournament appearances: 15
Sweet 16s (since 1975): 2
Final Fours: 2
NIT appearances: 18
Semifinals: 7
Titles: 2 (1961, '63)

TOP 5

G	**Ernie DiGregorio** (1970-73)
G	**Jimmy Walker** (1964-67)
F	**Austin Croshere** (1993-97)
F	**Ryan Gomes** (2001-05)
C	**Marvin Barnes** (1971-74)

RECORDS

RECORDS	GAME		SEASON		CAREER	
POINTS	52	Marvin Barnes, vs. Austin Peay (Dec. 15, 1973)	851	Jimmy Walker (1966-67)	2,138	Ryan Gomes (2001-05)
POINTS PER GAME			30.4	Jimmy Walker (1966-67)	25.2	Jimmy Walker (1964-67)
REBOUNDS	34	Marvin Barnes, vs. Buffalo State (Dec. 8, 1971)	597	Marvin Barnes (1973-74)	1,592	Marvin Barnes (1971-74)
ASSISTS	16	Carlton Screen, vs. Syracuse (Jan. 20, 1990); Vinnie Ernst, vs. Catholic (Feb. 9, 1963); Ernst, vs. DePaul (Feb. 7, 1963)	267	Ernie DiGregorio (1972-73)	662	Ernie DiGregorio (1970-73)

SEASON REVIEW

SEASON	W-L	CONF.	SCORING		COACH	RECORD	
20-21	0-3		Fred Bentley	13.3	no coach		
21-22	0-6		Joseph McGee	8.3	William Donovan	0-6	.000
22-23	no team						
23-24	no team						
24-25	no team						
1925-26	no team						
1926-27	8-8		Hector Allen	7.3	Archie Golembeski	8-8	.500
1927-28	7-9		John Krieger	9.9	Al McClellan		
1928-29	17-3		Eddie Wineapple	13.9	Al McClellan		
1929-30	15-4		John Krieger	10.7	Al McClellan		
1930-31	14-5		Allen Brachen	9.5	Al McClellan		
1931-32	19-5		Allen Brachen	9.4	Al McClellan		
1932-33	13-3		Allen Brachen	13.0	Al McClellan		
1933-34	12-5		Allen Brachen	9.9	Al McClellan		
1934-35	17-5		Bill Kutniewski	8.0	Al McClellan		
1935-36	14-7		Ed Bobinski	10.1	Al McClellan		

SEAS.	W-L	CONF.	POSTSEASON	SCORING		REBOUNDS		ASSISTS		COACH	RECORD	
1936-37	12-10			Ed Bobinski	9.5					Al McClellan		
1937-38	7-9			John Crowley	9.8					Al McClellan	147-65	.693
1938-39	4-7			Steve Fallon	10.1					Edward Crotty		
1939-40	5-9			Joe Kwasniewski	9.7					Edward Crotty		
1940-41	11-6			John Lee	10.3					Edward Crotty		
1941-42	13-7			Ted McConnon	15.5					Edward Crotty		
1942-43	15-5			Ted McConnon	15.0					Edward Crotty		
1943-44	no team											
1944-45	5-7			John Arzoomanian	19.7					Edward Crotty		
1945-46	5-12			Henri Ethier	13.9					Edward Crotty	58-53	.523
1946-47	8-11			John Sullivan	8.2					Lawrence J. Drew		
1947-48	10-10			Ferdinand Sowa	10.7					Lawrence J. Drew		
1948-49	7-19									Lawrence J. Drew	25-40	.385
1949-50	14-9			James Schlimm	15.5					James V. Cuddy		
1950-51	14-10			James Schlimm	15.7					James V. Cuddy		
1951-52	14-9			Robert Moran	18.0	James Schlimm	8.3			James V. Cuddy		
1952-53	11-11			Robert Moran	20.8	Robert Prendergast	7.8			James V. Cuddy		
1953-54	13-13			Robert Moran	16.0					James V. Cuddy		
1954-55	9-12			Mike Pascale	17.8	John Ritch	14.2			James V. Cuddy	75-64	.540
1955-56	14-8			Mike Pascale	15.0	John Ritch	10.3			Joe Mullaney		
1956-57	15-9			John Ritch	14.4					Joe Mullaney		
1957-58	18-6			Lenny Wilkens	14.9	John Woods	8.4			Joe Mullaney		
1958-59	20-7		NIT FOURTH PLACE	John Egan	20.9	John Woods	9.6			Joe Mullaney		
1959-60	24-5		NIT RUNNER-UP	James Hadnot	14.8	James Hadnot	16.3			Joe Mullaney		
1960-61	24-5		NIT CHAMPION	James Hadnot	19.3	James Hadnot	16.4			Joe Mullaney		
1961-62	20-6		NIT FIRST ROUND	James Hadnot	18.3	James Hadnot	13.5			Joe Mullaney		
1962-63	24-4		NIT CHAMPION	R. Flynn, J. Thompson Jr.	18.9	John Thompson Jr.	14.0	Vinnie Ernst	8.7	Joe Mullaney		
1963-64	20-6		NCAA FIRST ROUND	John Thompson Jr.	26.2	John Thompson Jr.	14.5			Joe Mullaney		
1964-65	24-2		NCAA REGIONAL FINALS	Jimmy Walker	20.5	Dexter Westbrook	12.1	Jimmy Walker	5.2	Joe Mullaney		
1965-66	22-5		NCAA FIRST ROUND	Jimmy Walker	24.5	Michael Riordan	9.1	Jimmy Walker	5.5	Joe Mullaney		
1966-67	21-7		NIT QUARTERFINALS	Jimmy Walker	30.4	Anthony Koski	11.2	Jimmy Walker	5.1	Joe Mullaney		
1967-68	11-14			Alphonse Hayes	15.6	Anthony Koski	11.2			Joe Mullaney		
1968-69	14-10			Jim Larranaga	19.4	Raymond Johnson	10.4			Joe Mullaney		
1969-70	14-11			Jim Larranaga	16.3	Raymond Johnson	10.4	Jim Larranaga	3.2	Dave Gavitt		
1970-71	20-8		NIT QUARTERFINALS	Ernie DiGregorio	18.6	Nehru King	6.1	Ernie DiGregorio	6.5	Dave Gavitt		
1971-72	21-6		NCAA FIRST ROUND	Marvin Barnes	21.6	Marvin Barnes	15.7	Ernie DiGregorio	7.9	Dave Gavitt		
1972-73	27-4		NCAA NATIONAL SEMIFINALS	Ernie DiGregorio	24.6	Marvin Barnes	19.0	Ernie DiGregorio	8.6	Dave Gavitt		
1973-74	28-4		NCAA REGIONAL SEMIFINALS	Marvin Barnes	22.1	Marvin Barnes	18.7	Kevin Stacom	5.3	Dave Gavitt		
1974-75	20-11		NIT RUNNER-UP	Joe Hassett	16.5	Bill Eason	7.9	Rick Santos	4.5	Dave Gavitt		
1975-76	21-11		NIT FOURTH PLACE	Joe Hassett	17.0	Bruce Campbell	8.5	Bob Misevicius	4.8	Dave Gavitt		
1976-77	24-5		NCAA FIRST ROUND	Joe Hassett	18.8	Bruce Campbell	8.1	Dwight Williams	5.1	Dave Gavitt		
1977-78	24-8		NCAA FIRST ROUND	Bruce Campbell	17.4	Bill Eason	8.3	Bob Misevicius	5.5	Dave Gavitt		
1978-79	10-16			Rudy Williams	17.8	Rudy Williams	9.0	David Frye	5.0	Dave Gavitt	209-84	.713
1979-80	11-16	0-6		Jerry Scott	14.9	Rudy Williams	7.6	Ricky Tucker	5.3	Gary Walters		
1980-81	10-18	3-11		Rich Hunger	12.0	Rich Hunger	6.7	Jim Panaggio	3.9	Gary Walters	21-34	.382
1981-82	10-17	2-12		Ron Jackson	16.2	Otis Thorpe	8.0	Jim Panaggio	4.0	Joe Mullaney		
1982-83	12-19	4-12		Ron Jackson	18.3	Otis Thorpe	8.0	Ricky Tucker	6.1	Joe Mullaney		
1983-84	15-14	5-11		Otis Thorpe	17.1	Otis Thorpe	10.3	Harold Starks	3.3	Joe Mullaney		
1984-85	11-20	3-13		Donald Brown	9.5	Ray Knight	6.0	Harold Starks	3.8	Joe Mullaney	319-164	.660
1985-86	17-14	7-9	NIT QUARTERFINALS	Billy Donovan	15.1	Steve Wright	7.3	Billy Donovan	4.7	Rick Pitino		
1986-87	25-9	10-6	NCAA NATIONAL SEMIFINALS	Billy Donovan	20.6	David Kipfer	5.3	Billy Donovan	7.2	Rick Pitino	42-23	.646
1987-88	11-17	5-11		Delray Brooks	13.5	Steve Wright	6.5	Eric Murdock	3.8	Gordon Chiesa	11-17	.393
1988-89	18-11	7-9	NCAA FIRST ROUND	Eric Murdock	16.2	Marty Conlon	7.0	Carlton Screen	6.8	Rick Barnes		
1989-90	17-12	8-8	NCAA FIRST ROUND	Eric Murdock	15.4	Marty Conlon	7.5	Carlton Screen	7.0	Rick Barnes		
1990-91	19-13	7-9	NIT QUARTERFINALS	Eric Murdock	25.6	Marques Bragg	8.8	Eric Murdock	4.6	Rick Barnes		
1991-92	14-17	6-12		Marques Bragg	11.3	Michael Smith	10.3	Trent Forbes	3.4	Rick Barnes		
1992-93	20-13	9-9	NIT FOURTH PLACE	Michael Smith	11.8	Michael Smith	11.4	Abdul Abdullah	5.7	Rick Barnes		
1993-94	20-10	10-8	NCAA FIRST ROUND	Eric Williams	15.7	Michael Smith	11.5	Abdul Abdullah	8.0	Rick Barnes	108-76	.587
1994-95	17-13	7-11	NIT SECOND ROUND	Eric Williams	17.7	Troy Brown	7.9	Michael Brown	3.9	Pete Gillen		
1995-96	18-12	9-9	NIT SECOND ROUND	Austin Croshere	15.3	Ruben Garces	7.5	God Shammgod	6.5	Pete Gillen		
1996-97	24-12	10-8	NCAA REGIONAL FINALS	Austin Croshere	17.9	Ruben Garces	7.8	God Shammgod	6.6	Pete Gillen		
1997-98	13-16	7-11		Jamel Thomas	18.5	Jamel Thomas	6.9	Kendrick Moore	3.2	Pete Gillen	72-53	.576
1998-99	16-14	9-9	NIT FIRST ROUND	Jamel Thomas	22.0	Jamel Thomas	7.2	John Linehan	3.8	Tim Welsh		
1999-2000	11-19	4-12		Erron Maxey	14.8	Karim Shabazz	8.2	Abdul Mills	2.2	Tim Welsh		
2000-01	21-10	11-5	NCAA FIRST ROUND	Erron Maxey	11.4	Karim Shabazz	7.4	John Linehan	3.9	Tim Welsh		
2001-02	15-16	6-10		Abdul Mills	14.5	Ryan Gomes	7.8	John Linehan	4.4	Tim Welsh		
2002-03	18-14	8-8	NIT SECOND ROUND	Ryan Gomes	18.4	Ryan Gomes	9.7	Donnie McGrath	4.3	Tim Welsh		
2003-04	20-9	11-5	NCAA FIRST ROUND	Ryan Gomes	18.9	Ryan Gomes	9.4	Donnie McGrath	3.4	Tim Welsh		
2004-05	14-17	4-12		Ryan Gomes	21.6	Ryan Gomes	8.2	Donnie McGrath	3.7	Tim Welsh		
2005-06	12-15	5-11		Donnie McGrath	15.1	Geoff McDermott	9.0	Sharaud Curry	3.5	Tim Welsh		
2006-07	18-13	8-8	NIT FIRST ROUND	Herbert Hill	18.1	Geoff McDermott	9.1	Geoff McDermott	5.1	Tim Welsh		
2007-08	15-16	6-12		Jeff Xavier	12.4	Geoff McDermott	8.1	Geoff McDermott	4.9	Tim Welsh	160-143	.528
2008-09	19-14	10-8	NIT FIRST ROUND	Weyinmi Efejuku	15.7	Geoff McDermott	8.5	Sharaud Curry	4.2	Keno Davis	19-14	.576

ESPN 8 SAGARIN

PURDUE

A gang of Hoosiers two hours south of West Lafayette bask in the glory befitting one of college hoops' most storied programs. But the Boilermakers deserve their kudos, too. After all, while Purdue has never won a national title, it has won more Big Ten championships than any other school (21), *including* Indiana. And any team that produced John Wooden is worthy of admiration.

BEST TEAM: 1968-69 Purdue lost its first game to UCLA, 94-82, but provided a hint of the offensive fireworks to come. The team won 20 of its next 23 to claim the Big Ten title, while leading the nation in scoring (93.0 ppg). Then the Boilermakers cleaned house in the NCAA Tournament to set up a rematch with the Bruins in the NCAA Final. While junior sensation Rick Mount scored 28 points, it took him 36 shots to do so, and John Wooden's crew ran away with it, 92-72.

BEST PLAYER: G RICK MOUNT (1967-70) The Rocket, a prep legend from Lebanon, Ind., strongly considered committing to Miami (Fla.). But Mount changed his mind and stayed in-state, a decision that rewrote the Boilermakers history book. His debut against UCLA on Dec. 2, 1967 was covered by more than 30 newspapers, and he nearly led an upset, scoring 28 points in a 73-71 loss. With a picture-perfect outside shot, Mount went on to average more than 32 points a game in his career. He remains the Boilermakers' all-time leading scorer.

BEST COACH: GENE KEADY (1980-2005) He is legendary for his wicked comb-over, explosive temper, coaching smarts and unbelievable consistency. In 25 seasons, Keady made the postseason 22 times, won six Big Ten titles and was named conference Coach of the Year seven times—tied for the most with a Hoosier honcho named Bob Knight.

GAME FOR THE AGES: The Rocket knew it was good as soon as it left his hands. In the 1969 NCAA Mideast Regional final, Purdue and Marquette were deadlocked at 73 in the final seconds of OT when Mount came off a pick, took two dribbles and unleashed a deep shot from the baseline. It went in, sending Purdue to its first Final Four.

HEARTBREAKER: Playing No. 8-seed Wisconsin in the 2000 Elite Eight, the No. 6-seed Boilermakers desperately wanted to send Keady to his first Final Four. But after leading 50-49 with just under seven minutes to go, Purdue didn't hit another shot from the field until 57 ticks left, and lost 64-60. Afterward, in the locker room, many of the players had red eyes, while senior Brian Cardinal broke down in the postgame press conference. "My heart was broken," Keady later told the *Capital Times*.

FIERCEST RIVAL: Some coaches bring out the best in each other. Keady and Knight brought out the nasty. In Keady's first game against Knight, the two coaches both drew technicals for bickering with the refs. In Purdue's win over host IU on Feb. 23, 1985, Knight famously threw a chair on the floor to protest a technical called against him. In a pregame tirade before a Jan. 15, 1991, matchup, Knight told his players he was sick of losing to Purdue. Although Keady retired owning a 21–20 all-time edge over his adversary, IU fans are quick to point out he had to forfeit one of those wins for using an ineligible player. Purdue leads overall, 108–84.

FANFARE AND HOOPLA: Purdue's student section, known as the Paint Crew, is the largest student organization on campus. Formerly known as the Gene Pool, the crew is best known for its renditions of Bon Jovi's "Livin' on a Prayer" with the band during timeouts.

FAN FAVORITE: F BRIAN CARDINAL (1996-2000) With his trademark kneepads and reckless abandon, Cardinal endured so much punishment during his college career that he earned the nickname Citizen Pain. He's scored 5.7 ppg in his nine-year NBA career.

CONSENSUS ALL-AMERICAS

1910, '11	**Dave Charters,** C
1913	**Larry Teeple,** C
1914	**Elmer Oliphant,** G
1921	**Donald White,** G
1922	**Ray Miller,** G
1926	**George Spradling,** F
1928-30	**Charles "Stretch" Murphy,** C
1930-32	**John Wooden,** G
1934	**Norman Cottom,** F
1936	**Bob Kessler,** F
1937, '38	**Jewell Young,** F
1961, '62	**Terry Dischinger,** C
1966	**Dave Schellhase,** G/F
1969, '70	**Rick Mount,** G
1980	**Joe Barry Carroll,** C
1994	**Glenn Robinson,** F

FIRST-ROUND PRO PICKS

1947	**Ed Ehlers,** Boston (3)
1966	**Dave Schellhase,** Chicago (10)
1969	**Herm Gilliam,** Cincinnati (8)
1972	**Bill Franklin,** Virginia (ABA)
1980	**Joe Barry Carroll,** Golden State (1)
1982	**Keith Edmonson,** Atlanta (10)
1983	**Russell Cross,** Golden State (6)
1994	**Glenn Robinson,** Milwaukee (1)

PROFILE

Purdue University, West Lafayette, IN
Founded: 1869
Enrollment: 40,090 (31,761 undergraduate)
Colors: Old gold and black
Nickname: Boilermakers
Current arena: Mackey Arena, opened in 1967 (14,123)
Previous: Lambert Fieldhouse, 1937-67 (10,000); Lafayette Jefferson High School Gymnasium, 1934-37 (N/A); Memorial Gymnasium, 1910-34 (2,000); Lafayette Coliseum, 1907-09 (N/A); Military Hall and Gymnasium, 1897, 1900-09 (N/A)

First game: Jan. 23, 1897
All-time record: 1,583-911 (.635)
Total weeks in AP Top 20/25: 263
Current conference: Big Ten (1905-)
Conference titles:
Big Ten: 21 (1911 [tie], '12 [tie], '21 [tie], '22, '26 [tie], '28 [tie], '30, '32, '34, '35 [tie], '36 [tie], '38, '40, '69, '79 [tie], '84 [tie], '87 [tie], '88, '94, '95, '96)
Conference tournament titles:
Big Ten: 1 (2009)
NCAA Tournaments: 23 (1 appearance vacated)
Sweet 16s (since 1975): 7
Final Fours: 2

NIT appearances: 8
Semifinals: 4
Titles: 1 (1974)

TOP 5

G	**Rick Mount** (1967-70)
G/F	**Dave Schellhase** (1963-66)
F	**Glenn Robinson** (1992-94)
C	**Terry Dischinger** (1959-62)
C	**Joe Barry Carroll** (1976-80)

RECORDS	GAME		SEASON		CAREER	
POINTS	61	Rick Mount, vs. Iowa (Feb. 28, 1970)	1,030	Glenn Robinson (1993-94)	2,323	Rick Mount (1967-70)
POINTS PER GAME			35.4	Rick Mount (1969-70)	32.3	Rick Mount (1967-70)
REBOUNDS	27	Carl McNulty, vs. Minnesota (Feb. 19, 1951)	352	Joe Barry Carroll (1978-79)	1,148	Joe Barry Carroll (1976-80)
ASSISTS	18	Bruce Parkinson, vs. Minnesota (March 8, 1975)	207	Bruce Parkinson (1974-75)	690	Bruce Parkinson (1972-77)

SEASON REVIEW

SEASON	W-L	CONF.	SCORING		COACH	RECORD	
1897-1917	*133-85*		*12-0 in 1900-01 under coach Alpha P. Jamison*				
1917-18	11-5	5-5			J.J. Maloney	11-5	.688
1918-19	6-8	4-7			Ward "Piggy" Lambert		
1919-20	16-4	8-2			Ward "Piggy" Lambert		
1920-21	13-7	8-4			Ward "Piggy" Lambert		
1921-22	15-3	8-1			Ward "Piggy" Lambert		
[illegible]	9-6	7-5			Ward "Piggy" Lambert		
1923-24	12-5	7-5			Ward "Piggy" Lambert		
1924-25	9-5	7-4			Ward "Piggy" Lambert		
1925-26	13-4	8-4			Ward "Piggy" Lambert		
1926-27	12-5	9-3			Ward "Piggy" Lambert		
1927-28	15-2	10-2	C. "Stretch" Murphy	10.4	Ward "Piggy" Lambert		
1928-29	13-4	9-3	C. "Stretch" Murphy	11.8	Ward "Piggy" Lambert		
1929-30	13-2	10-0	C. "Stretch" Murphy	12.6	Ward "Piggy" Lambert		
1930-31	12-5	8-4	John Wooden	8.2	Ward "Piggy" Lambert		
1931-32	17-1	11-1	John Wooden	12.2	Ward "Piggy" Lambert		
1932-33	11-7	6-6	Norman Cottom	7.1	Ward "Piggy" Lambert		
1933-34	17-3	10-2	Norman Cottom	9.0	Ward "Piggy" Lambert		
1934-35	17-3	9-3	Bob Kessler	11.3	Ward "Piggy" Lambert		
1935-36	16-4	11-1	Bob Kessler	13.0	Ward "Piggy" Lambert		
1936-37	15-5	8-4	Jewell Young	12.1	Ward "Piggy" Lambert		
1937-38	18-2	10-2	Jewell Young	14.5	Ward "Piggy" Lambert		

SEAS.	W-L	CONF.	POSTSEASON	SCORING		REBOUNDS		ASSISTS		COACH	RECORD	
1938-39	12-7	6-6		Robert Igney	7.6					Ward "Piggy" Lambert		
1939-40	16-4	10-2		Donald Blanken	9.2					Ward "Piggy" Lambert		
1940-41	13-7	6-6		Forrest Sprowl	10.9					Ward "Piggy" Lambert		
1941-42	14-7	9-6		Forrest Sprowl	12.3					Ward "Piggy" Lambert		
1942-43	9-11	6-6		Edwin Ehlers	10.1					Ward "Piggy" Lambert		
1943-44	11-10	8-4		Paul Hoffman	10.9					Ward "Piggy" Lambert		
1944-45	9-11	6-6		Billy Gosewehr	12.2					Ward "Piggy" Lambert		
1945-46	10-11	4-8		Paul Hoffman	12.1					Ward "Piggy" Lambert[a]	371-152	.709
1946-47	9-11	4-8		Paul Hoffman	12.4					Mel Taube		
1947-48	11-9	6-6		Richard Axness	12.2					Mel Taube		
1948-49	13-9	6-6		Howard Williams	12.1					Mel Taube		
1949-50	9-13	3-9		Richard Axness	11.3					Mel Taube	45-46	.495
1950-51	8-14	4-10		Carl McNulty	17.1					Ray Eddy		
1951-52	8-14	3-11		Carl McNulty	18.1					Ray Eddy		
1952-53	4-18	3-15		Jack Runyan	13.6					Ray Eddy		
1953-54	9-13	3-11		Dennis Blind	14.4	Don Beck	9.5			Ray Eddy		
1954-55	12-10	5-9		Joe Sexson	16.9	Don Beck	11.0			Ray Eddy		
1955-56	16-6	9-5		Joe Sexson	19.1	Lamar Lundy	10.1			Ray Eddy		
1956-57	15-7	8-6		Bill Greve	13.8	Lamar Lundy	9.3			Ray Eddy		
1957-58	14-8	9-5		Willie Merriweather	14.5	Wilson Eison	10.4			Ray Eddy		
1958-59	15-7	8-6		Willie Merriweather	20.8	Wilson Eison	13.0			Ray Eddy		
1959-60	11-12	6-8		Terry Dischinger	26.3	Terry Dischinger	14.3			Ray Eddy		
1960-61	16-7	10-4		Terry Dischinger	28.2	Terry Dischinger	13.4			Ray Eddy		
1961-62	17-7	9-5		Terry Dischinger	30.3	Terry Dischinger	13.4			Ray Eddy		
1962-63	7-17	2-12		Mel Garland	21.8	Bill Jones	14.4			Ray Eddy		
1963-64	12-12	8-6		Dave Schellhase	24.5	Dave Schellhase	11.3			Ray Eddy		
1964-65	12-12	5-9		Dave Schellhase	29.3	Dave Schellhase	8.0			Ray Eddy	176-164	.518
1965-66	8-16	4-10		Dave Schellhase	32.5	Dave Schellhase	10.6			George King		
1966-67	15-9	7-7		Herman Gilliam	16.4	Herman Gilliam	9.6			George King		
1967-68	15-9	9-5		Rick Mount	28.5	Herman Gilliam	9.1			George King		
1968-69	23-5	13-1	NCAA RUNNER-UP	Rick Mount	33.3	Herman Gilliam	8.5			George King		
1969-70	18-6	11-3		Rick Mount	35.4	George Faerber	10.0			George King		
1970-71	18-7	11-3	NIT FIRST ROUND	Larry Weatherford	21.1	William Franklin	10.2	Larry Weatherford	4.2	George King		
1971-72	12-12	6-8		Bob Ford	19.6	Bob Ford	9.6	Dennis Gamauf	2.6	George King	109-64	.630
1972-73	15-9	8-6		Frank Kendrick	18.5	John Garrett	9.1	Bruce Parkinson	6.1	Fred Schaus		
1973-74	21-9	10-4	NIT CHAMPION	John Garrett	21.6	Frank Kendrick	10.1	Bruce Parkinson	6.1	Fred Schaus		
1974-75	17-11	11-7		John Garrett	19.8	John Garrett	10.0	Bruce Parkinson	7.4	Fred Schaus		
1975-76	16-11	11-7		Walter Jordan	16.9	Walter Jordan	9.2	Eugene Parker	3.9	Fred Schaus		
1976-77	19-9	⊗ 14-4	NCAA FIRST ROUND	Walter Jordan	18.6	Joe Barry Carroll	7.4	Bruce Parkinson	5.1	Fred Schaus		
1977-78	16-11	11-7		Walter Jordan	17.0	Joe Barry Carroll	10.7	Jerry Sichting	5.3	Fred Schaus	104-60	.634▼
1978-79	27-8	13-5	NIT RUNNER-UP	Joe Barry Carroll	22.8	Joe Barry Carroll	10.1	Brian Walker	5.7	Lee Rose		
1979-80	23-10	11-7	NCAA THIRD PLACE	Joe Barry Carroll	22.3	Joe Barry Carroll	9.2	Brian Walker	5.1	Lee Rose	50-18	.735
1980-81	21-11	10-8	NIT THIRD PLACE	Keith Edmonson	17.3	Russell Cross	6.3	Brian Walker	6.4	Gene Keady		
1981-82	18-14	11-7	NIT RUNNER-UP	Keith Edmonson	21.2	Michael Scearce	6.8	Kevin Stallings	3.5	Gene Keady		
1982-83	21-9	11-7	NCAA SECOND ROUND	Russell Cross	17.7	Russell Cross	7.4	Ricky Hall	4.5	Gene Keady		
1983-84	22-7	15-3	NCAA SECOND ROUND	Jim Rowinski	15.0	Jim Rowinski	6.7	Steve Reid	4.7	Gene Keady		
1984-85	20-9	11-7	NCAA FIRST ROUND	James Bullock	14.2	James Bullock	6.6	Steve Reid	5.9	Gene Keady		
1985-86	22-10	11-7	NCAA FIRST ROUND	Troy Lewis	18.4	Todd Mitchell	7.2	Mack Gadis	5.6	Gene Keady		
1986-87	25-5	15-3	NCAA SECOND ROUND	Troy Lewis	18.5	Todd Mitchell	6.5	Everette Stephens	6.3	Gene Keady		
1987-88	29-4	16-2	NCAA REGIONAL SEMIFINALS	Troy Lewis	17.9	Todd Mitchell	5.8	Everette Stephens	5.5	Gene Keady		
1988-89	15-16	8-10		Melvin McCants	13.4	Stephen Scheffler	6.0	Tony Jones	5.0	Gene Keady		
1989-90	22-8	13-5	NCAA SECOND ROUND	Stephen Scheffler	16.8	Stephen Scheffler	6.1	Tony Jones	5.7	Gene Keady		
1990-91	17-12	9-9	NCAA FIRST ROUND	Jimmy Oliver	19.2	Chuckie White	8.5	Jimmy Oliver	3.1	Gene Keady		
1991-92	18-15	8-10	NIT QUARTERFINALS	Woody Austin	18.5	Ian Stanback	5.8	Matt Waddell	3.4	Gene Keady		
1992-93	18-10	9-9	NCAA FIRST ROUND	Glenn Robinson	24.1	Glenn Robinson	9.2	Matt Painter	4.5	Gene Keady		
1993-94	29-5	14-4	NCAA REGIONAL FINALS	Glenn Robinson	30.3	Glenn Robinson	10.1	Matt Waddell	4.8	Gene Keady		
1994-95	25-7	15-3	NCAA SECOND ROUND	Cuonzo Martin	18.4	Brandon Brantley	6.1	Porter Roberts	3.8	Gene Keady		
1995-96	26-6	⊗ 15-3	NCAA SECOND ROUND	Chad Austin	12.8	Brandon Brantley	5.6	Porter Roberts	4.9	Gene Keady		
1996-97	18-12	12-6	NCAA SECOND ROUND	Chad Austin	17.0	Brad Miller	8.3	Brad Miller	2.9	Gene Keady		
1997-98	28-8	12-4	NCAA REGIONAL SEMIFINALS	Brad Miller	17.2	Brad Miller	8.9	Chad Austin	3.7	Gene Keady		
1998-99	21-13	7-9	NCAA REGIONAL SEMIFINALS	Jaraan Cornell	15.2	Brian Cardinal	5.5	Brian Cardinal	2.4	Gene Keady		
1999-2000	24-10	12-4	NCAA REGIONAL FINALS	Brian Cardinal	13.9	Mike Robinson	6.2	Carson Cunningham	4.1	Gene Keady		
2000-01	17-15	6-10	NIT QUARTERFINALS	Rodney Smith	13.9	John Allison	5.3	Carson Cunningham	4.4	Gene Keady		
2001-02	13-18	5-11		Willie Deane	17.3	John Allison	5.7	Austin Parkinson	4.8	Gene Keady		
2002-03	19-11	10-6	NCAA SECOND ROUND	Willie Deane	17.8	Chris Booker	5.7	Brandon McKnight	2.5	Gene Keady		
2003-04	17-14	7-9	NIT FIRST ROUND	Kenneth Lowe	13.3	Ivan Kartelo	6.0	Austin Parkinson	3.8	Gene Keady		
2004-05	7-21	3-13		Carl Landry	18.2	Carl Landry	7.1	Brandon McKnight	3.8	Gene Keady	512-270	.655▼
2005-06	9-19	3-13		Matt Kiefer	12.0	Matt Kiefer	7.5	Bryant Dillon	3.0	Matt Painter		
2006-07	22-12	9-7	NCAA SECOND ROUND	Carl Landry	18.9	Carl Landry	7.3	Chris Kramer	2.5	Matt Painter		
2007-08	25-9	15-3	NCAA SECOND ROUND	E'Twaun Moore	12.9	Robbie Hummel	6.1	Chris Kramer	2.9	Matt Painter		
2008-09	27-10	11-7	NCAA REGIONAL SEMIFINALS	E'Twaun Moore	13.8	Robbie Hummel	7.0	Lewis Jackson	3.3	Matt Painter	83-50	.624

[a] Ward "Piggy" Lambert (7-7) and Mel Taube (3-4) both coached during the 1945-46 season.

⊗ Records don't reflect games forfeited or vacated. For adjusted records, see p. 521.

▼ Coaches' records adjusted to reflect games forfeited or vacated: Fred Schaus, 105-59, .640; Gene Keady, 493-287, .632. For yearly totals, see p. 521.

THE SCHOOLS

ESPN 318 SAGARIN

QUINNIPIAC

Located at the foot of Sleeping Giant State Park in southwestern Connecticut, Quinnipiac is a regional recruiter that jumped to D1 in 1998. But that doesn't mean QU lacks big aspirations: In 2007, the school opened the $52 million TD Banknorth Sports Center and hired Tom Moore, UConn's top assistant, as coach.

BEST TEAM: 1999-2000 A year after moving up to D1 hoops, the Bobcats finished 18–10 overall and 12–6 in the NEC behind do-it-all guard Nate Pondexter. The 18 wins equalled QU's cumulative total in coach Joe DeSantis' first three seasons. Too bad the Bobcats weren't yet eligible for the NEC's postseason tourney.

BEST PLAYER: G Rob Monroe (2001-05) The 5'10", 160-pound Monroe was the first Quinnipiac player named a finalist for a national award (the 2005 Bob Cousy Award, for best male point guard). Monroe averaged 17.3 points and 5.4 assists a game over three seasons, and torched Longwood for 41 points in a double-OT win his senior year.

BEST COACH: Burt Kahn (1961-91) In 1961, Kahn became the third coach in the program's first 10 years. During his three decades of coaching Quinnipiac, he led the Bobcats to new NAIA heights (including several postseason appearances) and their move to NCAA D2 play. Before the Bobcats moved to TD Banknorth Sports Center, they played on Burt Kahn Court.

GAME FOR THE AGES: On Nov. 18, 1998, in its second D1 game, Quinnipiac stormed to a 20-point lead against Navy. But the Midshipmen battled back and eventually led by six with under five minutes to play. The Bobcats whittled the lead to one, and with :10 left, Pondexter hit the game-winner to give Quinnipiac its first big-time win.

FIERCEST RIVAL: On Dec. 20, 1960, Quinnipiac scored a school-record-low 40 points in a blowout loss to Central Connecticut. Fast forward to March 6, 2002, when the Blue Devils beat the Bobcats in the Northeast finals, putting an end to their underdog run for an NCAA Tournament bid. Yep, CCSU sure does enjoy tormenting its in-state rival, leading the series, 50–15.

SEASON REVIEW

SEAS.	W-L	CONF.	COACH	SEAS.	W-L	CONF.	COACH
1951-52	14-7		Red Verderame	1960-61	16-10		Tuffle Maroon
1952-53	12-7		Red Verderame	1961-62	16-6		Burt Kahn
1953-54	16-7		Tuffle Maroon	1962-63	17-11		Burt Kahn
1954-55	17-9		Tuffle Maroon	1963-64	20-8		Burt Kahn
1955-56	18-6		Tuffle Maroon	1964-65	18-7		Burt Kahn
1956-57	15-9		Tuffle Maroon	1965-66	21-5		Burt Kahn
1957-58	9-8		Tuffle Maroon	1966-67	15-10		Burt Kahn
1958-59	16-6		Tuffle Maroon	1967-68	15-9		Burt Kahn
1959-60	6-13		Tuffle Maroon	1968-69	18-8		Burt Kahn

SEAS.	W-L	CONF.	SCORING		COACH	RECORD
1969-70	18-6		George McDowell	13.6	Burt Kahn	
1970-71	14-12		Cliff Mosley	20.6	Burt Kahn	
1971-72	21-9		Robert Vacca	21.5	Burt Kahn	
1972-73	22-7		Ed Roulhac	15.8	Burt Kahn	
1973-74	9-16		Ed Roulhac	13.4	Burt Kahn	
1974-75	17-10		Harold Driver	16.4	Burt Kahn	
1975-76	19-9		Harold Driver	16.8	Burt Kahn	
1976-77	18-11		Harold Driver	13.4	Burt Kahn	
1977-78	17-11		Harold Driver	18.4	Burt Kahn	
1978-79	20-7		Al Carfora	19.7	Burt Kahn	
1979-80	22-7		Al Carfora	17.0	Burt Kahn	
1980-81	17-10		Frank Berretta	19.5	Burt Kahn	
1981-82	8-18	1-5	Kevin Woodward	17.4	Burt Kahn	
1982-83	11-17	3-9	Frank Berretta	18.0	Burt Kahn	
1983-84	7-20	2-12	Peter Gray	16.3	Burt Kahn	
1984-85	9-19	4-10	Peter Gray	21.2	Burt Kahn	
1985-86	11-17	3-9	Peter Gray	22.3	Burt Kahn	
1986-87	6-22	2-12	Troy Adams	16.5	Burt Kahn	
1987-88	18-13	10-8	Troy Adams	18.8	Burt Kahn	
1988-89	8-20	5-13	Lester Ayala	17.1	Burt Kahn	
1989-90	11-16	9-9	Kyle Leeman	15.8	Burt Kahn	
1990-91	16-14	11-7	Lester Ayala	16.7	Burt Kahn	459-355 .564
1991-92	7-18	6-12	Glenn Phillip	20.4	Bill Mecca	
1992-93	16-13	10-8	LeRon Gittens	15.3	Bill Mecca	
1993-94	13-13	10-8	Rick Barry	18.1	Bill Mecca	
1994-95	12-15	7-11	Rick Barry	23.5	Bill Mecca	
1995-96	5-22	1-15	Joe Trimarchi	13.1	Bill Mecca	53-81 .396
1996-97	5-20	4-14	Joe Trimarchi	13.8	Joe DeSantis	
1997-98	4-23	3-17	Myles Anderson	15.0	Joe DeSantis	
1998-99	9-18	6-14	Nate Pondexter	14.4	Joe DeSantis	
1999-2000	18-10	12-6	Nate Pondexter	16.6	Joe DeSantis	
2000-01	6-21	3-17	Collin Charles	17.5	Joe DeSantis	
2001-02	14-16	10-10	Bill Romano	17.3	Joe DeSantis	
2002-03	17-12	10-8	Kason Mims	13.4	Joe DeSantis	
2003-04	9-20	5-13	Rashaun Banjo	17.5	Joe DeSantis	
2004-05	10-17	6-12	Rob Monroe	22.7	Joe DeSantis	
2005-06	12-16	7-11	John Winchester	12.4	Joe DeSantis	
2006-07	14-15	11-7	DeMario Anderson	15.7	Joe DeSantis	118-188 .386
2007-08	15-15	11-7	DeMario Anderson	21.7	Tom Moore	
2008-09	15-16	10-8	James Feldeine	17.0	Tom Moore	30-31 .492

PROFILE

Quinnipiac University, Hamden, CT
Founded: 1929
Enrollment: 7,400 (5,400 undergraduate)
Colors: Blue and gold
Nickname: Bobcats
Current arena: TD Banknorth Sports Center, opened in 2007 (3,570)
Previous: Burt Kahn Court, 1970-2007 (2,000)
First game: 1951
All-time record: 799-737 (.520)
Total weeks in AP Top 20/25: 0

Current conference: Northeast (1998-)
Conference titles: 0
Conference tournament titles: 0
NCAA Tournament appearances: 0
NIT appearances: 0

TOP 5

G **Rob Monroe** (2001-05)
G **Frank Vieira** (1953-57)
F **Harold Driver** (1974-78)
F **Ed Skwara** (1966-69)
C **George McDowell** (1969-72)

RECORDS

RECORDS	GAME		SEASON		CAREER	
POINTS	68	Frank Vieira, vs. Brooklyn Poly (Feb. 3, 1957)	848	Frank Vieira (1956-57)	2,649	Frank Vieira (1953-57)
POINTS PER GAME			35.8	Frank Vieira (1953-54)		N/A
REBOUNDS	31	David Tuthill, vs. New Bedford Inst. of Tech. (Jan. 3, 1964)	500	David Tuthill (1963-64)	1,147	Harold Driver (1974-78)
ASSISTS	15	Nate Pondexter, vs. Brown (Jan. 11, 2000)	211	Mike Buscetto (1992-93)	624	Mike Buscetto (1991-93)

ESPN 256 SAGARIN

RADFORD

The highlight reel is long and colorful, befitting this school in the foothills of the Blue Ridge Mountains: Kevin Robinson's 10-foot jump hook to claim a 1998 NCAA bid; the 1993 upset of LSU; Doug Day setting an NCAA record for three-point rainbows.

BEST TEAM: 1993-94 Dr. Ron Bradley's Highlanders did the unimaginable: They beat LSU, participants in 10 straight NCAA Tourneys, 73-72, on a jumper by Don Burgess with 2.8 seconds left. The 20–8 team included 1,000-point scorers Burgess (1,452), Tyrone Travis (1,313), Anthony Walker (1,601) and Jason Landsdown (1,099). Only a 72-61 upset loss to Campbell in the Big South tournament kept Radford out of the NCAAs.

BEST PLAYER: G Doug Day (1989-93) Radford's all-time leading scorer (2,027 points) and No. 5 in Big South history, Day ended his career as the NCAA's D1 leader in career three-pointers with 401 (he's currently eighth). Today Radford rewards its hardest-working player with an award named for Day.

BEST COACH: Dr. Ron Bradley (1991-2002) The son of a hoops coach, Bradley has the most wins (192) and the highest percentage (.606) in school history. His teams finished first in the Big South three times, second twice, had eight straight winning seasons, won the school's first Big South championship and received its first NCAA Tournament bid.

GAME FOR THE AGES: After starting the 1997-98 season 3–6, the Highlanders won 16 of their next 19 to reach the Big South championship game against North Carolina-Asheville. Tournament MVP Kevin Robinson's last-second bucket off a miss by Chibi Johnson capped a rally from a 17-point deficit and sent Radford to the NCAAs.

FIERCEST RIVAL: Among the young program's in-conference rivals, Winthrop stands out. The Highlanders lead the overall series, 29–26, but Winthrop recently took 12 straight, including a 76-45 dismantling in the 2008 BSC tourney.

SEASON REVIEW

SEAS.	W-L	CONF.	SCORING		COACH	RECORD	
1974-75	11-10		Wallace Foster	22.4	Chuck Taylor		
1975-76	16-12		Wallace Foster	19.7	Chuck Taylor		
1976-77	15-10		Ed Cottrell	14.0	Chuck Taylor		
1977-78	14-11		Dan Wilbourne	17.7	Chuck Taylor	56-43	.566
1978-79	23-4		Dan Grubbs	16.4	Joe Davis		
1979-80	15-13		Dan Wilbourne	12.4	Joe Davis		
1980-81	16-12		Craig Rhew	13.1	Joe Davis		
1981-82	18-8		Ivey Cook	15.5	Joe Davis		
1982-83	15-11		Ivey Cook	13.2	Joe Davis		
1983-84	17-10		James Cooke	14.4	Joe Davis		
1984-85	16-12		James Cooke	14.6	Joe Davis		
1985-86	11-17	3-4	Pat DiServio	14.1	Joe Davis		
1986-87	15-14	7-7	Tim Penn	18.9	Joe Davis		
1987-88	16-14	8-4	Aswan Wainwright	13.6	Joe Davis	162-115	.585
1988-89	15-13	5-7	Phil Young	17.4	Oliver Purnell		
1989-90	7-22	3-9	Ron Shelburne	11.9	Oliver Purnell		
1990-91	22-7	12-2	Doug Day	20.2	Oliver Purnell	44-42	.512
1991-92	20-9	12-2	Doug Day	19.7	Dr. Ron Bradley		
1992-93	15-16	8-8	Doug Day	17.6	Dr. Ron Bradley		
1993-94	20-8	13-5	Tyrone Travis	16.4	Dr. Ron Bradley		
1994-95	16-12	9-7	Anthony Walker	15.3	Dr. Ron Bradley		
1995-96	14-13	8-6	Jason Lansdown	16.2	Dr. Ron Bradley		
1996-97	15-13	8-6	Anthony Walker	15.4	Dr. Ron Bradley		
1997-98	20-10	10-2 ●	Corey Reed	14.8	Dr. Ron Bradley		
1998-99	20-8	8-2	Ryan Charles	15.5	Dr. Ron Bradley		
1999-2000	18-10	12-2	Jason Williams	18.1	Dr. Ron Bradley		
2000-01	19-10	12-2	Jason Williams	17.0	Dr. Ron Bradley		
2001-02	15-16	9-5	Andrey Savtchenko	16.2	Dr. Ron Bradley	192-125	.606
2002-03	10-20	6-8	Raymond Arrington	14.8	Byron Samuels		
2003-04	12-16	7-9	Whit Holcomb-Faye	17.5	Byron Samuels		
2004-05	12-16	7-9	Whit Holcomb-Faye	15.1	Byron Samuels		
2005-06	16-13	9-7	Whit Holcomb-Faye	23.1	Byron Samuels		
2006-07	8-22	3-11	Chris Oliver	18.8	Byron Samuels	58-87	.400
2007-08	10-20	5-9	Martell McDuffy	14.4	Brad Greenberg		
2008-09	21-12	15-3 ●	Artsiom Parakhouski	16.2	Brad Greenberg	31-32	.492

● **NCAA Tournament appearance**

PROFILE

Radford University, Radford, VA
Founded: 1910
Enrollment: 9,157 (8,155 undergraduate)
Colors: Red, blue and white
Nickname: Highlanders
Current arena: Dedmon Center, opened in 1981 (5,000)
Previous: Peters Hall, 1974-81 (800)
First game: 1974
All-time record: 542-444 (.550)
Total weeks in AP Top 20/25: 0

Current conference: Big South (1985-)
Conference titles:
Big South: 4 (1992, 2000, '01, '09)
Conference tournament titles:
Big South: 2 (1998, 2009)
NCAA Tournament appearances: 2
NIT appearances: 0

TOP 5

G **Doug Day** (1989-93)
G **Whit Holcomb-Faye** (2002-06)
G **Anthony Walker** (1993-97)
F **Chris Oliver** (2003-07)
F **Jason Williams** (1997-2001)

RECORDS

RECORDS	GAME		SEASON		CAREER	
POINTS	43	Doug Day, vs. Central Connecticut State (Dec. 12, 1990)	669	Whit Holcomb-Faye (2005-06)	2,027	Doug Day (1989-93)
POINTS PER GAME			23.1	Whit Holcomb-Faye (2005-06)	21.0	Wallace Foster (1974-76)
REBOUNDS	20	Andrey Savtchenko, vs. Purdue (Nov. 21, 2001)	369	Artsiom Parakhouski (2008-09)	845	Chris Oliver (2003-07)
ASSISTS	15	Brian Schmall, vs. Campbell (Feb. 4, 1992)	216	Brian Schmall (1992-93)	510	Anthony Walker (1993-97)

ESPN 114 SAGARIN

RHODE ISLAND

We can thank Rhode Island—more specifically, legendary coach Frank Keaney—for revolutionizing basketball by being one of the early programs to employ the fast break. Before Keaney's time, teams would struggle to score 40 points in a game. His teams would dazzle crowds by sometimes scoring in the 80s. Soon enough, Keaney's style would become the standard for teams everywhere.

BEST TEAM: 1997-98 In Jim Harrick's first of two seasons in Kingston, the Rams came within 60 seconds of earning the school's first trip to the Final Four. The 25–9 crew did win Rhode Island's first Atlantic 10 title behind guards Tyson Wheeler and Cuttino Mobley and forward Antonio Reynolds-Dean. Then the No. 8-seed Rams shocked No. 1-seed Kansas, 80-75, in the second round of the NCAA Tournament, before taking out Valparaiso, 74-68, in the Sweet 16. Next came Stanford in the Elite Eight (see Heartbreaker).

BEST PLAYER: F Sylvester "Sly" Williams (1976-79) Before he played even one game for the Rams, Williams was a Rhode Island legend for having spurned archrival Providence (with whom he had signed a letter of intent) in order to enroll at URI. The Rams' No. 3 career scorer with 1,777 points, Williams led Rhode Island in 1978 to its first NCAA Tournament appearance in more than a decade. He was the first-round pick of the New York Knicks in the 1979 NBA draft.

BEST COACH: Frank Keaney (1920-48) Still the all-time winningest coach in Rhode Island history (401–124), Keaney was inducted into the Naismith Hall of Fame in 1960. His antidote to the slow games of the day was to "give the crowds action" with his up-tempo offense. His game plan: "If some coach puts up a screwy defense, use a screwier offense. You've got to stop us." Few could, as Keaney's teams made the prestigious NIT four times from 1941 through 1946, losing by just one point to Kentucky in the '46 final.

Frank Keaney's game plan: "If some coach puts up a screwy defense, use a screwier offense."

GAME FOR THE AGES: In the quarterfinals of the NIT at Madison Square Garden on March 14, 1946, Rhode Island trailed favored Bowling Green and its 6'11" All-America Don Otten, by two points with :08 left. The Rams' Ernie Calverley launched a rainbow the full length of the court. The shot—officially measured at 62 feet—swished, sending the game into overtime, and the Rams won, 82-79. Calverly's heave will live forever in Rhody lore as the Shot Heard 'Round the World.

HEARTBREAKER: On March 22, 1998, closing in on its first trip to the NCAA Final Four, Rhode Island blew an 11-point second-half lead over Stanford in the last minutes of the Midwest Regional final with untimely turnovers and three missed free throws. Final score: 79-77, Stanford.

FIERCEST RIVAL: Rhode Island trails its in-state nemesis, Providence, 66–55, in a series that dates back to 1920. The Rams haven't always lived in the shadow of their big-time Big East rival. They dominated in the Keaney era, and Rhode Island had already been playing basketball for 17 years when the Providence program began in 1920.

FANFARE AND HOOPLA: During the 2006-07 season, URI began a charitable promotion day called the Pink Out to benefit a local breast cancer foundation and spread awareness about the disease. Rhode Island was the first men's basketball team from a major conference to hold a breast cancer awareness night.

FAN FAVORITE: G Eddie "The Flea" Molloy (1968-71) Listed generously as 5'7", Molloy was a scrappy and quick point guard who endeared himself to the Rams faithful with his all-out, high-octane style.

PROFILE

Rhode Island University, Kingston, RI
Founded: 1892
Enrollment: 15,383 (12,205 undergraduate)
Colors: Keaney blue, dark blue and white
Nickname: Rams
Current arena: Thomas M. Ryan Center, opened in 2002 (7,657)
First game: 1903
All-time record: 1,335-990 (.574)
Total weeks in AP Top 20/25: 16
Current conference: Atlantic 10 (1980-)

Conference titles:
New England: 7 (1938, '39, '40, '41 [tie], '42, '43, '46)
Yankee: 6 (1950, '61, '64 [tie], '66 [tie], '68 [tie], '72)
Eastern Athletic: 1 (1981)
Conference tournament titles:
Atlantic 10: 1 (1999)
NCAA Tournament appearances: 8
Sweet 16s (since 1975): 2
NIT appearances: 13
Semifinals: 2

CONSENSUS ALL-AMERICAS

1939 **Chet Jaworski, G**

FIRST-ROUND PRO PICKS

1979 **Sylvester "Sly" Williams,** New York (21)
1999 **Lamar Odom,** LA Clippers (4)

TOP 5

G **Ernie Calverley** (1942-46)
G **Carlton "Silk" Owens** (1984-88)
F **Art Stephenson** (1965-68)
F **Sylvester "Sly" Williams** (1976-79)
C **Kenny Green** (1985-90)

RECORDS	GAME		SEASON		CAREER	
POINTS	50	Tom Garrick, vs. Rutgers (March 7, 1988); Tom Harrington, vs. Brandeis (Feb. 4, 1959)	762	Carlton Owens (1987-88)	2,114	Carlton "Silk" Owens (1984-88)
POINTS PER GAME			26.7	Ernie Calverley (1943-44)	22.6	Bill Von Weyhe (1954-57)
REBOUNDS	28	Art Stephenson, vs. Brown (Feb. 20, 1968)	420	Art Stephenson (1967-68)	1,048	Art Stephenson (1965-68)
ASSISTS	13	Tyson Wheeler, vs. Penn (Dec. 30, 1997)	205	Tyson Wheeler (1997-98)	712	Tyson Wheeler (1994-98)

SEASON REVIEW

SEASON	W-L	CONF.	SCORING	COACH	RECORD	SEASON	W-L	CONF.	SCORING	COACH	RECORD
1903-17	*50-33*		*Eight consecutive winning seasons from 1905-06 to '12-13*			**1927-28**	15-5			Frank Keaney	
1917-18	7-3			Jim Baldwin	12-14 .462	**1928-29**	15-1			Frank Keaney	
1918-19	7-1			Fred Walker	7-1 .875	**1929-30**	10-5			Frank Keaney	
1919-20	3-8			Fred Murray	3-8 .273	**1930-31**	13-4			Frank Keaney	
1920-21	9-8			Frank Keaney		**1931-32**	13-3			Frank Keaney	
1921-22	7-8			Frank Keaney		**1932-33**	14-4			Frank Keaney	
1922-23	9-4			Frank Keaney		**1933-34**	13-3			Frank Keaney	
1923-24	9-6			Frank Keaney		**1934-35**	12-6			Frank Keaney	
1924-25	11-5			Frank Keaney		**1935-36**	13-5			Frank Keaney	
1925-26	8-8			Frank Keaney		**1936-37**	18-3			Frank Keaney	
1926-27	13-3			Frank Keaney		**1937-38**	19-2	8-0		Frank Keaney	

SEAS.	W-L	CONF.	POSTSEASON	SCORING		REBOUNDS		ASSISTS		COACH	RECORD	
1938-39	17-4	7-1		Chet Jaworski	22.6					Frank Keaney		
1939-40	19-3	8-0		Stan Stutz	23.1					Frank Keaney		
1940-41	21-4	7-1	NIT QUARTERFINALS							Frank Keaney		
1941-42	18-4	8-0	NIT QUARTERFINALS							Frank Keaney		
1942-43	16-3	7-1								Frank Keaney		
1943-44	14-6			Ernie Calverley	26.7					Frank Keaney		
1944-45	20-5		NIT SEMIFINALS							Frank Keaney		
1945-46	21-3	4-0	NIT RUNNER-UP							Frank Keaney		
1946-47	17-3	4-1								Frank Keaney		
1947-48	17-6	5-1								Frank Keaney	401-124	.764
1948-49	16-6	5-1								Bob "Red" Haire		
1949-50	18-8	6-1								Bob "Red" Haire		
1950-51	13-15	5-2								Bob "Red" Haire		
1951-52	10-13	6-2								Bob "Red" Haire	57-42	.576
1952-53	13-10	6-2								Jack Guy		
1953-54	8-13	5-4								Jack Guy		
1954-55	17-10	5-3								Jack Guy		
1955-56	11-14	6-2								Jack Guy		
1956-57	11-11	6-3		Bill Von Weyhe	23.7					Jack Guy	60-58	.508
1957-58	4-17	3-7								Ernie Calverley		
1958-59	8-12	5-5				Don Brown	10.9			Ernie Calverley		
1959-60	12-14	6-4				Gary Koenig	10.4			Ernie Calverley		
1960-61	18-9	9-1	NCAA FIRST ROUND			Gary Koenig	14.6			Ernie Calverley		
1961-62	14-12	7-3				Gary Koenig	14.9			Ernie Calverley		
1962-63	15-11	8-2								Ernie Calverley		
1963-64	19-8	8-2								Ernie Calverley		
1964-65	15-11	6-4								Ernie Calverley		
1965-66	20-8	9-1	NCAA FIRST ROUND							Ernie Calverley		
1966-67	14-12	8-2		Steve Chubin	23.5	Art Stephenson	12.7			Ernie Calverley		
1967-68	15-11	8-2				Art Stephenson	16.2			Ernie Calverley	154-125	.552
1968-69	10-15	7-3				John Fultz	10.3			Tom Carmody		
1969-70	16-10	7-3		John Fultz	23.0	John Fultz	11.6			Tom Carmody		
1970-71	10-17	8-2								Tom Carmody		
1971-72	15-11	8-2								Tom Carmody		
1972-73	7-18	5-6								Tom Carmody	58-71	.450
1973-74	11-14	6-5		Steve Rowell	22.9					Jack Kraft		
1974-75	5-20	3-7								Jack Kraft		
1975-76	14-12	7-5								Jack Kraft		
1976-77	13-13									Jack Kraft		
1977-78	24-7		NCAA FIRST ROUND							Jack Kraft		
1978-79	20-9		NIT FIRST ROUND	Sylvester "Sly" Williams	23.9					Jack Kraft		
1979-80	15-13	14-12								Jack Kraft		
1980-81	21-8	10-3	NIT FIRST ROUND							Jack Kraft[a]	103-88	.539
1981-82	10-17	4-10				Roland Houston	10.0			Claude English		
1982-83	9-19	3-11								Claude English		
1983-84	6-22	5-13		Pappy Owens	22.3					Claude English	45-66	.405
1984-85	8-20	2-16								Brendan Malone		
1985-86	9-19	5-13								Brendan Malone	17-39	.304
1986-87	20-10	12-6	NIT FIRST ROUND					Tom Garrick	4.4	Tom Penders		
1987-88	28-7	14-4	NCAA REGIONAL SEMIFINALS					Carlton "Silk" Owens	5.1	Tom Penders	48-17	.738
1988-89	13-15	9-9						Herb Dixon	5.5	Al Skinner		
1989-90	15-13	11-7				Kenny Green	10.9	Carlos Easterling	5.1	Al Skinner		
1990-91	11-17	6-12		Eric Leslie	23.0					Al Skinner		
1991-92	22-10	9-7	NIT THIRD ROUND							Al Skinner		
1992-93	19-11	8-6	NCAA SECOND ROUND							Al Skinner		
1993-94	11-16	7-9								Al Skinner		
1994-95	7-20	2-14						Tyson Wheeler	5.0	Al Skinner		
1995-96	20-14	8-8	NIT THIRD ROUND					Tyson Wheeler	6.0	Al Skinner		
1996-97	20-10	12-4	NCAA FIRST ROUND					Tyson Wheeler	5.6	Al Skinner	138-126	.523
1997-98	25-9	12-4	NCAA REGIONAL FINALS	Cuttino Mobley	17.3			Tyson Wheeler	6.0	Jim Harrick		
1998-99	20-13	10-6	NCAA FIRST ROUND					Preston Murphy	4.0	Jim Harrick	45-22	.672
1999-2000	5-25	2-14		Zach Marbury	15.3	Luther Clay	8.0	Zach Marbury	3.4	Jerry DeGregorio		
2000-01	7-23	3-13		Tavorris Bell	19.1	Tavorris Bell	5.7	Howard Smith	3.5	Jerry DeGregorio	12-48	.200
2001-02	8-20	4-12		Troy Wiley	14.1	D. Hellenga, L. Adingono	3.9	Dinno Daniels	4.6	Jim Baron		
2002-03	19-12	10-6	NIT SECOND ROUND	Brian Woodward	14.1	Brian Woodward	6.0	Howard Smith	4.1	Jim Baron		
2003-04	20-14	7-9	NIT FIRST ROUND	Dawan Robinson	15.1	Brian Woodward	6.2	Dawan Robinson	3.5	Jim Baron		
2004-05	6-22	4-12		Scott Hazelton	15.5	Scott Hazelton	7.0	Jon Lucky	2.3	Jim Baron		
2005-06	14-14	8-8		Dawan Robinson	15.7	Jamaal Wise	5.9	Dawan Robinson	4.3	Jim Baron		
2006-07	19-14	10-6		Will Daniels	17.4	Kahiem Seawright	7.5	Parfait Bitee	3.2	Jim Baron		
2007-08	21-12	7-9	NIT FIRST ROUND	Will Daniels	18.6	Kahiem Seawright	8.4	Parfait Bitee	4.7	Jim Baron		
2008-09	23-11	11-5	NIT SECOND ROUND	Jimmy Baron	17.4	Kahiem Seawright	7.5	Marquis Jones	4.0	Jim Baron	130-119	.522

[a] Jack Kraft (1-0) and Claude English (20-8) both coached during the 1980-81 season.

ESPN 129 SAGARIN

RICE

Bob Kinney, Bill Tom Closs and Bill Henry in the 1940s. Gene Schwinger and Don Lance in the 1950s. Ricky Pierce in the 1980s, Brent Scott in the '90s, Michael Harris and Morris Almond in the 2000s. The Owls have boasted so much star power over the years, it's easy to forget that they've only been to four NCAA Tournaments and five NITs.

BEST TEAM: 1944-45 With big man Bill Henry manhandling the competition inside and savvy guard Murray Mendenhall directing the show from the perimeter, the Owls won 17 games by double digits en route to an undefeated Southwest Conference campaign. Their only loss came to eventual two-time NCAA champion Oklahoma A&M in late December.

BEST PLAYER: C BILL HENRY (1942-45) The 6'8" Henry used a killer hook shot to dominate in an era of smaller frontcourt players. The school's only two-time first-team All-America, he averaged 17.6 points as a sophomore and 20.7 points as a junior and played on three SWC first-place teams.

BEST COACH: BUSTER BRANNON (1938-42, '45-46) Before going on to even bigger things as the coach at TCU, Brannon actually managed to turn basketball at Rice into something more than just a way to kill time between football seasons. Known for his good humor, his teams were all business on the court, accounting for two of the school's four NCAA Tournaments.

GAME FOR THE AGES: Going into the 1969-70 season, pretty much every hoops insider picked the Owls to finish last in the SWC. Flash forward to Feb. 28, 1970. Having won six of seven, Rice had a chance to clinch the conference title with a victory over TCU. With guard Gary Reist leading the offensive charge, coach Don Knodel's crew did just that, winning 82-73.

FIERCEST RIVAL: Old SWC foe and current Conference USA mate Houston is just across town, but much to Rice's eternal frustration, the two have rarely been that close on the court. The Owls won just three of 42 games vs. the Cougars from 1972 to '91 and trail overall, 55–14.

SEASON REVIEW

SEAS.	W-L	CONF.	COACH	SEAS.	W-L	CONF.	COACH
1915-47	*300-284*	*NCAA Tourn. in 1940, '42; NIT in '43*		**1960-61**	11-12	7-7	John Frankie
1947-48	10-14	6-6	Joe Davis	**1961-62**	12-11	7-7	John Frankie
1948-49	13-11	9-3	Joe Davis	**1962-63**	12-11	9-5	John Frankie
1949-50	8-15	2-10	Don Suman	**1963-64**	15-9	8-6	George Carlisle
1950-51	8-15	2-10	Don Suman	**1964-65**	2-22	1-13	George Carlisle
1951-52	9-15	4-8	Don Suman	**1965-66**	1-22	1-13	George Carlisle
1952-53	15-6	8-4	Don Suman	**1966-67**	7-17	4-10	Don Knodel
1953-54	23-5	9-3 ●	Don Suman	**1967-68**	8-16	6-8	Don Knodel
1954-55	10-12	6-6	Don Suman	**1968-69**	10-14	6-8	Don Knodel
1955-56	19-5	8-4	Don Suman	**1969-70**	14-11	10-4 ●	Don Knodel
1956-57	16-8	8-4	Don Suman	**1970-71**	14-12	6-8	Don Knodel
1957-58	13-11	7-7	Don Suman	**1971-72**	6-20	1-13	Don Knodel
1958-59	11-13	5-9	Don Suman	**1972-73**	7-19	2-12	Don Knodel
1959-60	4-20	1-13	John Frankie	**1973-74**	11-17	5-9	Don Knodel

SEAS.	W-L	CONF.	SCORING		COACH	RECORD	
1974-75	5-21	2-12	Charles Daniels	16.8	Bob Polk		
1975-76	3-24	1-15	Elbert Darden	15.3	Bob Polk		
1976-77	9-18	3-13	Elbert Darden	17.8	Bob Polk	17-63	.213
1977-78	4-22	2-14	Elbert Darden	13.5	Mike Schuler		
1978-79	7-20	4-12	Elbert Darden	19.9	Mike Schuler		
1979-80	7-19	4-12	Ricky Pierce	19.2	Mike Schuler		
1980-81	12-15	7-9	Ricky Pierce	20.9	Mike Schuler	30-76	.283
1981-82	15-15	6-10	Ricky Pierce	26.8	Tommy Suitts		
1982-83	8-20	2-14	Renaldo O'Neal	10.3	Tommy Suitts		
1983-84	13-17	6-10	Tony Barnett	10.6	Tommy Suitts		
1984-85	11-16	3-13	Tony Barnett	16.0	Tommy Suitts		
1985-86	9-19	2-14	Greg Hines	16.7	Tommy Suitts		
1986-87	8-19	2-14	Greg Hines	18.2	Tommy Suitts[a]	63-99	.389
1987-88	6-21	3-13	David Willie	15.4	Scott Thompson		
1988-89	12-16	6-10	Andy Gilchrist	12.9	Scott Thompson		
1989-90	11-17	5-11	Brent Scott	15.3	Scott Thompson		
1990-91	16-14	9-7 ■	Brent Scott	16.9	Scott Thompson		
1991-92	20-11	8-6	Brent Scott	15.8	Scott Thompson	65-79	.451
1992-93	18-10	11-3 ■	Marvin Moore	17.4	Willis Wilson		
1993-94	15-14	6-8	Torrey Andrews	21.8	Willis Wilson		
1994-95	15-13	8-6	Adam Peakes	15.1	Willis Wilson		
1995-96	14-14	5-9	Tommy McGhee	20.5	Willis Wilson		
1996-97	12-15	6-10	Shaun Igo	16.9	Willis Wilson		
1997-98	6-22	3-11	Jarvis Kelley Sanni	14.8	Willis Wilson		
1998-99	18-10	8-6	Robert Johnson	22.0	Willis Wilson		
1999-2000	5-22	1-13	Mike Wilks	15.8	Willis Wilson		
2000-01	14-16	5-11	Mike Wilks	20.1	Willis Wilson		
2001-02	10-19	5-13	Michael Harris	12.8	Willis Wilson		
2002-03	19-10	11-7	Michael Harris	15.3	Willis Wilson		
2003-04	22-11	12-6 ■	Michael Harris	17.5	Willis Wilson		
2004-05	19-12	12-6 ■	Michael Harris	20.6	Willis Wilson		
2005-06	12-16	6-8	Morris Almond	21.9	Willis Wilson		
2006-07	16-16	8-8	Morris Almond	26.4	Willis Wilson		
2007-08	3-27	0-16	Patrick Britton	11.3	Willis Wilson	218-247	.469
2008-09	10-22	4-12	Rodney Foster	12.0	Ben Braun	10-22	.313

[a] **Tommy Suitts (7-12) and Greg Walcavich (1-7) both coached during the 1986-87 season.**

● NCAA Tournament appearance ■ NIT appearance

PROFILE

Rice University, Houston, TX
Founded: 1891
Enrollment: 5,339 (3,102 undergraduate)
Colors: Blue and gray
Nickname: Owls
Current arena: Autry Court at Tudor Fieldhouse, opened in 1950 (5,000)
First game: Jan. 16, 1915
All-time record: 993-1,240 (.445)
Total weeks in AP Top 20/25: 8

Current conference: Conference USA (2005-)
Conference titles:
Southwest: 10 (1918, '35 [tie], '40, '42 [tie], '43 [tie], '44 [tie], '45, '49 [tie], '54 [tie], '70)
Conference tournament titles: 0
NCAA Tournament appearances: 4
NIT appearances: 5

CONSENSUS ALL-AMERICAS

1942 **Bob Kinney**, F/C
1943 **Bill Tom Closs**, F
1945 **Bill Henry**, C

FIRST-ROUND PRO PICKS

1982 **Ricky Pierce**, Detroit (18)
2007 **Morris Almond**, Utah (25)

TOP 5

G/F **Morris Almond** (2003-07)
G/F **Ricky Pierce** (1979-82)
F **Michael Harris** (2001-05)
F/C **Bob Kinney** (1939-42)
C **Bill Henry** (1942-45)

RECORDS

RECORDS	GAME		SEASON		CAREER	
POINTS	47	Doug McKendrick, vs. Georgia Tech (Dec. 6, 1965)	844	Morris Almond (2006-07)	2,014	Michael Harris (2001-05)
POINTS PER GAME			26.8	Ricky Pierce (1981-82)	22.5	Ricky Pierce (1979-82)
REBOUNDS	30	Joe Durrenberger, vs. Baylor (Feb. 15, 1955)	363	Michael Harris (2004-05)	1,111	Michael Harris (2001-05)
ASSISTS	12	Rashid Smith, vs. UL-Lafayette (Feb. 21, 2004); vs. Connecticut (Jan. 2, 2004)	170	Lorenzo Williams (2005-06)	502	Dana Hardy (1988-92)

THE SCHOOLS

ESPN 158 SAGARIN

RICHMOND

It took the Spiders until 1982 to crawl into their first postseason tournament, but over the following 23 seasons they played in 13 postseasons (seven NCAAs, six NITs) and became the first school to win NCAA Tournament games as a No. 12, 13, 14 and 15 seed.

BEST TEAM: 1987-88 The 26–7 Spiders set program records for wins, assists and three-point percentage (43.8%) and, as a No. 13 seed, dumped defending champion Indiana, 72-69, in the first round of the Tournament. Peter Woolfolk's 27 points pushed Richmond past Georgia Tech, but the dream died with a 69-47 loss to Temple in the Sweet 16.

BEST PLAYER: F Johnny Newman (1982-86) He ruled the Robins Center just as UR stepped into the national spotlight. The CAA 1983 ROY and 1984 POY, Newman is still the school's all-time leading scorer. He notched 96 points in four NCAA games, including 26 in an upset of Charles Barkley's Auburn Tigers.

BEST COACH: Dick Tarrant (1981-93) His tenure began with an NIT berth in 1982 and encompassed almost every significant win in Richmond history. In his 12 seasons UR made five NCAAs and four NITs and won or shared five CAA titles. He has the most wins (239) and highest percentage (.655) of any Spiders coach, and eight of his teams won 20 or more games.

GAME FOR THE AGES: Of all Richmond's Tourney upsets, the March 14, 1991, 73-69 shocker over Billy Owens and Syracuse stands supreme. UR never trailed as Curtis Blair dropped 18 points and had six assists to kill the Orange zone, while the Spiders baffled Syracuse with their own match-up zone. Result: The first upset of a No. 2 seed by a No. 15 in NCAA history.

FIERCEST RIVAL: Although Richmond left the CAA for the Atlantic 10 in 2002, it still fiercely battles Virginia Commonwealth, just six miles away. Richmond is small, private and suburban with many out-of-state students, while VCU is large, public and urban. VCU holds a 39–24 advantage in the series—now called (fittingly) the Farm Bureau Insurance Black & Blue Classic.

SEASON REVIEW

SEAS.	W-L	CONF.	COACH	SEAS.	W-L	CONF.	COACH
1913-49	*347-237*	*8-15 in 1948-49*		1962-63	7-18	3-13	H. Lester Hooker Jr
1949-50	8-16	4-13	Malcolm Pitt	1963-64	6-16	4-12	Lewis Mills
1950-51	7-14	5-10	Malcolm Pitt	1964-65	10-16	6-10	Lewis Mills
1951-52	7-15	3-11	Malcolm Pitt	1965-66	12-13	9-7	Lewis Mills
1952-53	20-7	13-5	H. Lester Hooker Jr.	1966-67	11-12	9-7	Lewis Mills
1953-54	23-8	10-3	H. Lester Hooker Jr.	1967-68	12-13	8-8	Lewis Mills
1954-55	19-9	9-4	H. Lester Hooker Jr.	1968-69	13-14	6-7	Lewis Mills
1955-56	16-13	8-6	H. Lester Hooker Jr.	1969-70	9-18	4-9	Lewis Mills
1956-57	15-11	9-7	H. Lester Hooker Jr.	1970-71	7-21	3-9	Lewis Mills
1957-58	14-12	7-8	H. Lester Hooker Jr.	1971-72	6-19	3-9	Lewis Mills
1958-59	11-11	6-8	H. Lester Hooker Jr.	1972-73	8-16	5-9	Lewis Mills
1959-60	7-18	2-12	H. Lester Hooker Jr.	1973-74	16-12	10-4	Lewis Mills
1960-61	9-14	5-11	H. Lester Hooker Jr.	1974-75	10-16	7-7	Carl J. Slone
1961-62	6-21	5-11	H. Lester Hooker Jr.	1975-76	14-14	7-7	Jeff Butler

SEAS.	W-L	CONF.		SCORING		COACH	RECORD	
1976-77	15-11			Jeff Butler	16.1	Carl J. Slone		
1977-78	4-22			Mike Perry	19.0	Carl J. Slone	43-63	.406
1978-79	10-16			Mike Perry	18.3	Lou Goetz		
1979-80	13-14			Mike Perry	19.1	Lou Goetz		
1980-81	15-14			Mike Perry	22.8	Lou Goetz	38-44	.463
1981-82	18-11	6-4	■	John Schweitz	17.5	Dick Tarrant		
1982-83	12-16	2-7		Johnny Newman	12.2	Dick Tarrant		
1983-84	22-10	7-3	●	Johnny Newman	21.9	Dick Tarrant		
1984-85	21-11	11-3	■	Johnny Newman	21.3	Dick Tarrant		
1985-86	23-7	12-2	●	Johnny Newman	21.9	Dick Tarrant		
1986-87	15-14	8-6		Peter Woolfolk	13.9	Dick Tarrant		
1987-88	26-7	11-3	●	Peter Woolfolk	18.3	Dick Tarrant		
1988-89	21-10	13-1	■	Mike Winiecki	17.6	Dick Tarrant		
1989-90	22-10	10-4	●	Ken Atkinson	18.9	Dick Tarrant		
1990-91	22-10	10-4	●	Curtis Blair	16.1	Dick Tarrant		
1991-92	22-8	12-2	■	Curtis Blair	20.3	Dick Tarrant		
1992-93	15-12	10-4		Kenny Wood	15.9	Dick Tarrant	239-126	.655
1993-94	14-14	8-6		Michael Hodges	16.2	Bill Dooley		
1994-95	8-20	3-11		Kass Weaver	17.8	Bill Dooley		
1995-96	8-20	3-13		Jarod Stevenson	13.7	Bill Dooley		
1996-97	13-15	7-9		Rick Edwards	13.6	Bill Dooley	43-69	.384
1997-98	23-8	12-4	●	Jarod Stevenson	19.1	John Beilein		
1998-99	15-12	10-6		Charles Stephens	17.0	John Beilein		
1999-2000	18-12	11-5		Greg Stevenson	18.5	John Beilein		
2000-01	22-7	12-4	■	Greg Stevenson	19.7	John Beilein		
2001-02	22-14	11-5	■	Reggie Brown	14.4	John Beilein	100-53	.654
2002-03	15-14 ⊗	10-6	■	Mike Skrocki	11.2	Jerry Wainwright		
2003-04	20-13	10-6	●	Mike Skrocki	16.0	Jerry Wainwright		
2004-05	14-15	8-8		Kevin Steenberge	12.6	Jerry Wainwright	49-42	.538▼
2005-06	13-17	6-10		Jermaine Bucknor	13.5	Chris Mooney		
2006-07	8-22	4-12		Dan Geriot	11.9	Chris Mooney		
2007-08	16-15	9-7		Dan Geriot	14.3	Chris Mooney		
2008-09	20-16	9-7		Kevin Anderson	16.6	Chris Mooney	57-70	.448

⊗ Records don't reflect games forfeited or vacated. For adjusted records, see p. 521.
▼ Coach's record adjusted to reflect games forfeited or vacated: 50-41, .549. For yearly totals, see p. 521.
● NCAA Tournament appearance ■ NIT appearance

PROFILE

University of Richmond, Richmond, VA
Founded: 1830
Enrollment: 4,475 (3,651 undergraduate)
Colors: Red and blue
Nickname: Spiders
Current arena: Robins Center, opened in 1972 (9,071)
First game: 1913
All-time record: 1,195-1,071 (.527)
Total weeks in AP Top 20/25: 6

Current conference: Atlantic 10 (2001-)
Conference titles:
East Coast South: 2 (1984, '85 [tie])
Colonial Athletic: 4 (1988, '89, '92 [tie], 2001)
Conference tournament titles:
East Coast South: 1 (1984)
Colonial Athletic: 3 (1990, '91, '98)
NCAA Tournament appearances: 7
Sweet 16s (since 1975): 1
NIT appearances: 7

TOP 5

G **Curtis Blair** (1988-92)
G **Johnny Moates** (1964-67)
F **Bob McCurdy** (1973-75)
F **Johnny Newman** (1982-86)
F **Aron Stewart** (1972-74)

RECORDS

RECORDS	GAME		SEASON		CAREER	
POINTS	53	Bob McCurdy, vs. Appalachian State (Feb. 26, 1975)	855	Bob McCurdy (1974-75)	2,383	Johnny Newman (1982-86)
POINTS PER GAME			32.9	Bob McCurdy (1974-75)	28.1	Aron Stewart (1972-74)
REBOUNDS	35	Walt Lysaght, vs. North Carolina (Feb. 3, 1953)	421	Ken Daniel (1954-55)	1,255	Ken Daniel (1952-56)
ASSISTS	16	Greg Beckwith, vs. Navy (Feb. 25, 1986)	200	Greg Beckwith (1985-86)	573	Greg Beckwith (1982-86)

THE SCHOOLS

ESPN 237 SAGARIN

RIDER

The Broncs lay claim to a coach-turned-TV-icon (Digger Phelps, a forward from 1960-63), a legendary NBA ref (Jack Madden, a forward from 1956-59) and a true hoops pioneer (Clair Bee, a coach from 1928-31). Now they can lay claim to an NBA first-round pick, too, in Jason Thompson, a forward from 2004-08.

BEST TEAM: 2007-08 The winningest team in Rider history couldn't withstand a pressing Siena defense in its 74-53 MAAC tournament final loss. But that was one of the few blights in a stellar season. Do-everything Jason Thompson (20.4 ppg) led the Broncs to a share of the regular-season title and a berth in the first College Basketball Invitational tournament, where they lost to Old Dominion, 68-65, in the first round.

BEST PLAYER: F JASON THOMPSON (2004-08) With a reliable jumper, impressive athleticism and the ability to take his man off the dribble or down low, he became one of just 99 D1 players to amass 2,000 points and 1,000 boards. His reward? Going No. 12 overall in the 2008 draft to the Sacramento Kings.

BEST COACH: KEVIN BANNON (1989-97) He inherited a 5–23 team and was Northeast Conference champion four years later. The fastest Rider coach to get 100 victories, Bannon reached five league championship games, won two NEC tourney titles and went to two straight NCAA Tournaments (1993, '94).

GAME FOR THE AGES: In the 1993 NEC tourney title game, Broncs guard Darrick Suber's 33rd point sent the Rider home crowd into pandemonium. Following a full-court sprint, Suber hit "the Shot": a runner in the lane with no time on the clock to beat Wagner, 65-64, and send his team to their second NCAA Tournament.

FIERCEST RIVAL: Although the Broncs first started playing in 1928, they've only taken on two teams (Lafayette and Delaware) at least 60 times. But the Marist feud is shaping up to be a doozy. Conference rivals since 1992 (first in the NEC, then in the MAAC), the teams have split their two playoff showdowns, including Rider's 76-71 semifinal victory in 2008.

SEASON REVIEW

SEAS.	W-L	CONF.	COACH	SEAS.	W-L	CONF.	COACH
1928-47	*203-140*	*13-12 in 1946-47*		1960-61	13-12		Glenn Leach
1947-48	14-6		Thomas Leyden	1961-62	12-13		Glenn Leach
1948-49	14-9		Thomas Leyden	1962-63	20-8		Robert Greenwood
1949-50	11-9		Thomas Leyden	1963-64	15-10		Robert Greenwood
1950-51	6-13		Thomas Leyden	1964-65	13-11		Robert Greenwood
1951-52	9-5		Thomas Leyden	1965-66	16-9		Dick Harter
1952-53	9-10		Thomas Leyden	1966-67	11-12		John Carpenter
1953-54	12-12		Thomas Leyden	1967-68	9-15		John Carpenter
1954-55	9-14		Thomas Leyden	1968-69	11-14		John Carpenter
1955-56	15-7		Thomas Leyden	1969-70	16-10	7-3	John Carpenter
1956-57	20-7		Thomas Leyden	1970-71	20-6	8-2	John Carpenter
1957-58	17-8		Thomas Leyden	1971-72	15-11	8-2	John Carpenter
1958-59	12-14		Thomas Leyden	1972-73	12-14	2-8	John Carpenter
1959-60	12-14		Thomas Leyden	1973-74	13-13	8-2	John Carpenter

SEAS.	W-L	CONF.		SCORING		COACH	RECORD
1974-75	16-11	5-3				John Carpenter	
1975-76	14-13	6-4				John Carpenter	
1976-77	8-18	1-9				John Carpenter	
1977-78	11-16	4-6				John Carpenter	
1978-79	11-15	7-9				John Carpenter	
1979-80	10-18	5-11				John Carpenter	
1980-81	14-14	8-8				John Carpenter	
1981-82	11-16	7-9				John Carpenter	
1982-83	20-9	10-3				John Carpenter	
1983-84	20-11	11-5	●			John Carpenter	
1984-85	14-15	7-7				John Carpenter	
1985-86	9-19	5-9				John Carpenter	
1986-87	12-16	8-6				John Carpenter	
1987-88	10-19	6-8				John Carpenter	
1988-89	5-23	2-12				John Carpenter	292-328 .471
1989-90	10-18	5-9				Kevin Bannon	
1990-91	14-16	4-8				Kevin Bannon	
1991-92	16-13	9-3				Kevin Bannon	
1992-93	19-11	14-4	●			Kevin Bannon	
1993-94	21-9	14-4	●			Kevin Bannon	
1994-95	18-11	13-5				Kevin Bannon	
1995-96	19-11	12-6				Kevin Bannon	
1996-97	14-14	10-8				Kevin Bannon	131-103 .560
1997-98	18-10	12-6	■			Don Harnum	
1998-99	12-16	7-11		Greg Burston	15.1	Don Harnum	
1999-2000	16-14	8-10		Mario Porter	17.6	Don Harnum	
2000-01	16-12	11-7		Mario Porter	19.2	Don Harnum	
2001-02	17-11	13-5		Mario Porter	20.1	Don Harnum	
2002-03	12-16	7-11		Jerry Johnson	18.3	Don Harnum	
2003-04	17-14	10-8		Jerry Johnson	18.7	Don Harnum	
2004-05	19-11	13-5		Jerry Johnson	18.4	Don Harnum	127-104 .550
2005-06	8-20	4-14		Jason Thompson	16.6	Tommy Dempsey	
2006-07	16-15	9-9		Jason Thompson	20.1	Tommy Dempsey	
2007-08	23-11	13-5		Jason Thompson	20.4	Tommy Dempsey	
2008-09	19-13	12-6		Ryan Thompson	18.0	Tommy Dempsey	66-59 .528

● NCAA Tournament appearance ■ NIT appearance

PROFILE

Rider University, Lawrenceville, NJ
Founded: 1865
Enrollment: 5,974 (4,760 undergraduate)
Colors: Cranberry, white and gray
Nickname: Broncs
Current arena: Alumni Gymnasium, opened in 1958 (1,650)
First game: 1928
All-time record: 1,068-925 (.536)
Total weeks in AP Top 20/25: 0

Current conference: Metro Atlantic Athletic (1997-)
Conference titles:
Northeast: 3 (1993, '94, '95)
MAAC: 3 (2002 [tie], '05, '08 [tie])
Conference tournament titles: 3
East Coast: 1 (1984)
Northeast: 2 (1993, '94)
NCAA Tournament appearances: 3
NIT appearances: 1

FIRST-ROUND PRO PICKS

2008 **Jason Thompson**, Sacramento (12)

TOP 5

G **Jack Cryan** (1963-66)
G **Deon Hames** (1992-96)
G **Darrick Suber** (1989-93)
F **Herb Krautblatt** (1945-48)
F **Jason Thompson** (2004-08)

RECORDS

RECORDS	GAME		SEASON		CAREER	
POINTS	51	George Abel, vs. Cathedral (March 2, 1940)	694	Jason Thompson (2007-08)	2,219	Darrick Suber (1989-93)
POINTS PER GAME			25.8	Ray Walowski (1953-54)	20.9	Ron Simpson (1985-88)
REBOUNDS	24	Jason Thompson, vs. Siena (Feb. 10, 2008)	412	Jason Thompson (2007-08)	1,171	Jason Thompson (2004-08)
ASSISTS	18	Norm Hobbie, vs. Georgia State (Dec. 4, 1976); vs. Susquehanna (Dec. 30, 1975)	192	Deon Hames (1995-96)	598	Deon Hames (1992-96)

ESPN 264 SAGARIN

ROBERT MORRIS

If it wasn't for a man in blue, the Colonials would never have won five Northeast titles. Back in 1963, Robert Morris (then a junior college) tapped Gus Krop, a former prep coach and police chief, to launch their program. Krop went 19–5 in his first season, won another 268 games over the next 12 years, and retired in 1976 with the team poised to make the jump to D1.

BEST TEAM: 1982-83 Definition of a bad idea: getting into a shootout with coach Matt Furjanic's squad, which featured four 1,000-point scorers (G Chipper Harris, G Forest Grant, F Tom Parks and F Tom Underman). The Colonials won their conference games by an average of 14 points, then beat Georgia Southern, 64-54, in the opening round of the NCAA Tournament.

BEST PLAYER: G CHIPPER HARRIS (1980-84) As freshmen, Harris and Grant formed a promising backcourt—on a team that won nine games. Over the next three years, though, the two turned the Colonials into an Eastern Collegiate Metro power. With Grant setting him up from the point, Harris became the first Colonial to score at least 500 points in a season three times.

BEST COACH: JARRETT DURHAM (1984-96) Go ahead and forget those first two seasons, and also—*especially*—the last two. Remember instead Durham's three Northeast crowns and NCAA Tourney appearances.

GAME FOR THE AGES: The Colonials had been thoroughly trashed by top-seed Arizona the previous year, but No. 2-seed Kansas didn't find Robert Morris such easy prey in the first round of the 1990 NCAA Tournament. The Colonials nearly matched the balanced Jayhawks shot for shot well into the second half, before running out of firepower late in a 79-71 loss.

FIERCEST RIVAL: Robert Morris appeared destined for a 2008 Tourney bid, winning the Northeast regular-season crown and rolling over Monmouth in the conference tournament opener. But then Mount St. Mary's handed the Colonials an 83-65 ticket to the NIT—the third year in a row in which one of the two schools brought an end to the other's conference season.

SEASON REVIEW

SEAS.	W-L	CONF.		SCORING		COACH	RECORD	
1976-77	7-19			Earl Cureton	17.2	Tom Weirich		
1977-78	4-19			Charlie Gaines	19.0	Tom Weirich		
1978-79	13-14			Hosea Champine	17.6	Tom Weirich	24-52	.316
1979-80	7-19			Mike Morton	14.7	Matt Furjanic		
1980-81	9-18			Larry Downing	13.8	Matt Furjanic		
1981-82	17-13	9-5	●	Chipper Harris	17.6	Matt Furjanic		
1982-83	23-8	12-2	●	Chipper Harris	17.4	Matt Furjanic		
1983-84	17-13	11-5		Chipper Harris	18.4	Matt Furjanic	73-71	.507
1984-85	9-19	4-10		Tom Underman	17.3	Jarrett Durham		
1985-86	10-18	6-10		Ron Winbush	12.8	Jarrett Durham		
1986-87	13-14	7-9		Ron Winbush	12.4	Jarrett Durham		
1987-88	14-14	9-7		Vaughn Luton	13.3	Jarrett Durham		
1988-89	21-9	12-4	●	Vaughn Luton	17.9	Jarrett Durham		
1989-90	22-8	12-4	●	Anthony Dickens	12.5	Jarrett Durham		
1990-91	17-11	12-4		Myron Walker	16.3	Jarrett Durham		
1991-92	19-12	12-4	●	Myron Walker	19.8	Jarrett Durham		
1992-93	9-18	7-11		Myron Walker	17.8	Jarrett Durham		
1993-94	14-14	11-7		Myron Walker	20.1	Jarrett Durham		
1994-95	4-23	2-16		Gabe Jackson	18.3	Jarrett Durham		
1995-96	5-23	2-16		Javier Smith	9.0	Jarrett Durham	157-183	.462
1996-97	4-23	3-15		Javier Smith	12.0	Jim Boone		
1997-98	8-19	4-12		Keith Jones	12.0	Jim Boone		
1998-99	15-12	12-8		Gene Nabors	16.9	Jim Boone		
1999-2000	18-12	13-5		Gene Nabors	19.1	Jim Boone	45-66	.405
2000-01	7-22	7-13		Wesley Fluellen	16.7	Danny Nee	7-22	.241
2001-02	12-18	11-9		Tyler Bacon	12.9	Mark Schmidt		
2002-03	10-17	7-11		Maurice Carter	19.1	Mark Schmidt		
2003-04	14-15	10-8		Chaz McCrommon	17.0	Mark Schmidt		
2004-05	14-15	11-7		Chaz McCrommon	16.7	Mark Schmidt		
2005-06	15-14	10-8		A.J. Jackson	17.0	Mark Schmidt		
2006-07	17-11	9-9		A.J. Jackson	16.9	Mark Schmidt	82-90	.477
2007-08	26-8	16-2	■	Jeremy Chappell	14.9	Mike Rice		
2008-09	24-11	15-3	●	Jeremy Chappell	16.7	Mike Rice	50-19	.725

● NCAA Tournament appearance ■ NIT appearance

PROFILE

Robert Morris University, Moon Township, PA
Founded: 1921
Enrollment: 5,100 (4,000 undergraduate)
Colors: Blue and white with red
Nickname: Colonials
Current arena: Charles L. Sewall Center, opened in 1985 (3,056)
Previous: John Jay Center, 1976-85 (1,000)
First game: 1976
All-time record: 438-503 (.465)
Total weeks in AP Top 20/25: 0

Current conference: Northeast (1981-)
Conference titles:
Eastern Collegiate Metro: 3 (1982 [tie], '83 [tie], '84 [tie])
Northeast: 5 (1989, '90, '92, 2008, '09)
Conference tournament titles:
Eastern Collegiate Metro: 2 (1982, '83)
Northeast: 4 (1989, '90, '92, 2009)
NCAA Tournament appearances: 6
NIT appearances: 1

TOP 5

G **Chipper Harris** (1980-84)
G **Myron Walker** (1990-94)
G/F **Tony Lee** (2004-08)
F **Vaughn Luton** (1986-89)
C **Earl Cureton** (1975-77)

RECORDS

RECORDS	GAME		SEASON		CAREER	
POINTS	42	Maurice Carter, vs. Eastern Michigan (Nov. 26, 2002)	614	Myron Walker (1991-92)	1,965	Myron Walker (1990-94)
POINTS PER GAME			20.1	Myron Walker (1993-94)	18.7	Myron Walker (1990-94)
REBOUNDS	20	Mike Morton, vs. Baltimore (Jan. 12, 1980)	274	Earl Cureton (1976-77)	751	Anthony Dickens (1985-90); Tony Lee (2004-08)
ASSISTS	12	Ricky Richburg, vs. Sacred Heart (Dec. 20, 2000); Wade Timmerson, vs. Saint Francis (Pa.) (Feb. 15, 1992); achieved three other times	217	Tony Lee (2007-08)	555	Forest Grant (1980-84)

ESPN 149 SAGARIN

RUTGERS

Zero NCAA Tournaments since 1991. Zero above-.500 conference records since joining the Big East in 1995-96. Only four overall winning seasons since 1992-93. No matter how you slice it, the Scarlet Knights have struggled mightily since their heyday in the 1970s and early '80s. But rest assured that when they do put together a consistent winner, the RAC (as most fans still refer to the former Rutgers Athletic Center) will come alive. Even during Rutgers' darkest days, its fans make sure the team enjoys a sizable home-court advantage.

BEST TEAM: 1975-76 RU simply outran its opponents during an undefeated regular season, reaching the century mark 11 times. The team memorably came from behind against St. Bonaventure to finish the regular season 26–0, then beat Princeton, Connecticut and VMI to make its first and only Final Four.

BEST PLAYER: F PHIL SELLERS (1972-76) Phil the Thrill could do more than just light up the scoreboard—he handled the ball, passed like a guard and ignited his team with his unwavering energy. The All-America averaged 19.2 points and 10.1 rebounds as senior.

BEST COACH: TOM YOUNG (1973-85) Young got a big assist from his predecessor, Dick Lloyd, who recruited Sellers. Young took advantage of his good fortune by leading Rutgers to postseason appearances in his first six seasons. By the time he left for Old Dominion in 1985, he was the school's winningest coach.

GAME FOR THE AGES: With its perfect regular season on the line March 1, 1976, host Rutgers fell behind St. Bonaventure, 75-69, with 6:15 to go. But boosted by four layups, RU pulled off an 85-80 win. Fans stormed the court, then carried the party onto College Avenue.

FIERCEST RIVAL: Rutgers and Seton Hall first played in 1916 (a 40-20 RU win), but only met sporadically until the Scarlet Knights joined the Pirates in the Big East. The only two conference members from New Jersey have played a number of classics recently, with 14 of the last 21 meetings decided by fewer than 10 points. Seton Hall leads overall, 31–24.

SEASON REVIEW

SEAS.	W-L	CONF.	COACH	SEAS.	W-L	CONF.	COACH
1906-47	*262-208*			1960-61	11-10	3-6	Tony Kuolt
1947-48	14-9		Don White	1961-62	10-13	2-8	Tony Kuolt
1948-49	14-12	3-1	Don White	1962-63	7-16		Don White
1949-50	13-15	3-1	Don White	1963-64	5-17		Bill Foster
1950-51	7-14	3-1	Don White	1964-65	12-12		Bill Foster
1951-52	6-13	1-2	Don White	1965-66	17-7		Bill Foster
1952-53	8-13		Don White	1966-67	22-7	■	Bill Foster
1953-54	11-13		Don White	1967-68	14-10		Bill Foster
1954-55	2-22		Don White	1968-69	21-4	■	Bill Foster
1955-56	3-15		Don White	1969-70	13-11		Bill Foster
1956-57	8-15		Warren Harris	1970-71	16-7		Bill Foster
1957-58	7-15		Warren Harris	1971-72	14-11		Dick Lloyd
1958-59	9-15		Warren Harris	1972-73	15-11	■	Dick Lloyd
1959-60	11-14	4-4	Tony Kuolt	1973-74	18-8	■	Tom Young

SEAS.	W-L	CONF.	SCORING		COACH	RECORD
1974-75	22-7	●	Phil Sellers	22.7	Tom Young	
1975-76	31-2	●	Phil Sellers	19.2	Tom Young	
1976-77	18-10	7-1 ■	Eddie Jordan	17.7	Tom Young	
1977-78	24-7	7-3 ■	James Bailey	23.6	Tom Young	
1978-79	22-9	7-3 ●	James Bailey	18.5	Tom Young	
1979-80	14-14	7-3	Kelvin Troy	18.9	Tom Young	
1980-81	16-14	7-6	Kelvin Troy	15.2	Tom Young	
1981-82	20-10	9-5 ■	Roy Hinson	12.5	Tom Young	
1982-83	23-8	11-3 ●	Roy Hinson	16.6	Tom Young	
1983-84	15-13	9-9	John Battle	21.0	Tom Young	
1984-85	16-14	9-9	John Battle	21.0	Tom Young	239-116 .673
1985-86	8-21	2-16	Eric Riggins	15.7	Craig Littlepage	
1986-87	8-20	5-13	Eric Riggins	24.7	Craig Littlepage	
1987-88	7-22	3-15	Tom Savage	13.5	Craig Littlepage	23-63 .267
1988-89	18-13	13-5 ●	Tom Savage	20.0	Bob Wenzel	
1989-90	18-17	11-7 ■	Keith Hughes	18.5	Bob Wenzel	
1990-91	19-10	14-4 ●	Keith Hughes	21.0	Bob Wenzel	
1991-92	16-15	6-10 ■	Steve Worthy	18.8	Bob Wenzel	
1992-93	13-15	6-8	Steve Worthy	18.3	Bob Wenzel	
1993-94	11-16	6-10	Charles Jones	13.9	Bob Wenzel	
1994-95	13-15	7-9	Charles Jones	13.3	Bob Wenzel	
1995-96	9-18	6-12	Geoff Billet	11.6	Bob Wenzel	
1996-97	11-16	5-13	Geoff Billet	13.7	Bob Wenzel	128-135 .487
1997-98	14-15	6-12	Geoff Billet	13.9	Kevin Bannon	
1998-99	19-13	9-9 ■	Rob Hodgson	12.8	Kevin Bannon	
1999-2000	15-16	6-10 ■	Dahntay Jones	16.0	Kevin Bannon	
2000-01	11-16	3-13	Todd Billet	16.6	Kevin Bannon	59-60 .496
2001-02	18-13	8-8 ■	Jerome Coleman	16.8	Gary Waters	
2002-03	12-16	4-12	Jerome Coleman	16.0	Gary Waters	
2003-04	20-13	7-9 ■	Ricky Shields	15.5	Gary Waters	
2004-05	10-19	2-14	Quincy Douby	15.1	Gary Waters	
2005-06	19-14	7-9 ■	Quincy Douby	25.4	Gary Waters	79-75 .513
2006-07	10-19	3-13	J.R. Inman	12.0	Fred Hill	
2007-08	11-20	3-15	J.R. Inman	12.2	Fred Hill	
2008-09	11-21	2-16	Mike Rosario	16.2	Fred Hill	32-60 .348

● **NCAA Tournament appearance** ■ **NIT appearance**

PROFILE

Rutgers University, New Brunswick, NJ
Founded: 1766
Enrollment: 37,204 (26,691 undergraduate)
Color: Scarlet
Nickname: Scarlet Knights
Current arena: Louis Brown Athletic Center, a.k.a. the RAC, opened as Rutgers Athletic Center in 1977 (8,000)
Previous: College Avenue Gymnasium, 1931-77 (1,200)
First game: 1906
All-time record: 1,112-1,038 (.517)
Total weeks in AP Top 20/25: 26
Current conference: Big East (1995-)

Conference titles:
Middle Three: 4 (1943, '49 [tie], '50 [tie], '51)
Eastern Collegiate: 1 (1977 [tie])
Eastern 8: 1 (1978 [tie])
NJ-NY7: 2 (1978 [tie], '79)
Eastern Athletic: 1 (1980 [tie])
Atlantic 10: 2 (1983, '91)
Conference tournament titles:
Eastern 8: 1 (1979)
Atlantic 10: 1 (1989)
NCAA Tournament appearances: 6
Sweet 16s (since 1975): 1
Final Fours: 1
NIT appearances: 14
Semifinals: 3

CONSENSUS ALL-AMERICAS

1967 **Bob Lloyd,** G

FIRST-ROUND PRO PICKS

1979 **James Bailey,** Seattle (6)
1983 **Roy Hinson,** Cleveland (20)
2006 **Quincy Douby,** Sacramento (19)

TOP 5

G **Mike Dabney** (1972-76)
G **Bob Lloyd** (1964-67)
F **Phil Sellers** (1972-76)
F/C **Roy Hinson** (1979-83)
F/C **James Bailey** (1975-79)

RECORDS

RECORDS	GAME		SEASON		CAREER	
POINTS	51	Eric Riggins, vs. Penn State (Feb. 21, 1987); Bob Lloyd, vs. Delaware (Dec. 8, 1965)	839	Quincy Douby (2005-06)	2,399	Phil Sellers (1972-76)
POINTS PER GAME			27.9	Bob Lloyd (1966-67)	26.6	Bob Lloyd (1964-67)
REBOUNDS	30	George Sundstrom, vs. Army (Feb. 24, 1954); vs. Johns Hopkins (Feb. 3, 1953)	494	George Sundstrom (1953-54)	1,111	Phil Sellers (1972-76)
ASSISTS	16	Brian Ellerbe, vs. NC State (Dec. 27, 1984)	202	Eddie Jordan (1976-77)	585	Eddie Jordan (1973-77)

ESPN 310 SAGARIN

SACRAMENTO STATE

Sacramento State went D1 in 1991 and has exactly zero winning seasons to show for it. But hit the rewind button, go back a few decades, and you'll find a team that made the College Division tournament with semi-regularity—and rarely failed to entertain.

BEST TEAM: 1961-62 In the second half of the College Division title game, Hornets coach Everett Shelton suffered a minor heart attack. No big deal. After taking a breather, Shelton did push-ups to show the crowd he was fine. When the game resumed, the unranked Hornets took No. 5-ranked Mount St. Mary's to overtime, before losing 58-57. The Hornets still got a hero's welcome when 2,000 fans greeted them at the Sacramento Airport.

BEST PLAYER: G Robert "Money" Martin (1985-89) Winning was never more fun than in the 1980s, when Money was the lead gun of coach Joseph Anders' high-scoring crew. Martin's junior season was his most memorable; thanks to his outside touch, the Hornets scored a school-record 93.1 points per game.

BEST COACH: Everett Shelton (1959-68) Amazingly, coaching through a heart attack might have been his second-most noteworthy feat. When Hornets fans were trying to distract an opposing free throw shooter in a 1965 game, Shelton took the microphone and told his home crowd that he would forfeit the game if they didn't stop. They stopped.

GAME FOR THE AGES: Four years before it went D1, Sacramento State proved on Dec. 19, 1987, that it was worthy of a bigger stage by upsetting Texas A&M at ARCO Arena, 87-84. Alex Williams made seven of the Hornets' 12 three-pointers against the defending Southwest Conference tournament champs.

FIERCEST RIVAL: Even when Sacramento State and UC Davis are playing poorly, they never let up against one another. The 11 D1 games between them stand at 6–5 in favor of Sacramento State. The two northern California adversaries compete annually for the Causeway Cup, which is awarded to the school with the better head-to-head performance in 20 sports.

SEASON REVIEW

SEAS.	W-L	CONF.	COACH	SEAS.	W-L	CONF.	COACH
1948-49	6-11		Warren Conrad	1960-61	18-8		Everett Shelton
1949-50	15-9		Warren Conrad	1961-62	20-11		Everett Shelton
1950-51	8-13		Warren Conrad	1962-63	10-16		Everett Shelton
1951-52	18-10		Warren Conrad	1963-64	8-18		Everett Shelton
1952-53	18-8		Dr. Hal Wolf	1964-65	10-16		Everett Shelton
1953-54	9-9		Dr. Hal Wolf	1965-66	10-16		Everett Shelton
1954-55	8-17		Dr. Hal Wolf	1966-67	15-11		Everett Shelton
1955-56	10-10		Dr. Hal Wolf	1967-68	16-10		Everett Shelton
1956-57	10-12		Harvey Roloff	1968-69	13-12		Jack Heron
1957-58	10-14		Dr. Hal Wolf	1969-70	17-11		Jack Heron
1958-59	13-12		Dr. Hal Wolf	1970-71	17-8		Jack Heron
1959-60	11-14		Everett Shelton	1971-72	17-9		Jack Heron

SEAS.	W-L	CONF.	SCORING		COACH	RECORD	
1972-73	15-9				Jack Heron		
1973-74	10-16				Jack Heron		
1974-75	11-13				Jack Heron		
1975-76	16-13		Russ Carlson	13.9	Jack Heron		
1976-77	13-14		Nate Robinson	14.3	Jack Heron		
1977-78	14-13		Nate Robinson	18.9	Jack Heron[a]		
1978-79	13-13		Ted Borum	14.9	Elmo Slider	17-17	.500
1979-80	13-14		Darnell Anderson	20.5	Jack Heron		
1980-81	9-18		Tony Vaughn	10.2	Jack Heron		
1981-82	12-16		Jim Jansen	15.1	Jack Heron		
1982-83	10-17		Rovan Turner	13.9	Jack Heron		
1983-84	16-16		Vernon Durham	13.8	Jack Heron	199-195	.505
1984-85	7-23		Marvin Epps	11.7	Fred Lewis	7-23	.233
1985-86	13-15		Cassius Kelleybrew	11.6	Bill Brown		
1986-87	12-16		Alex Williams	16.9	Bill Brown[b]	17-21	.447
1987-88	22-8		Alex Williams	25.6	Joseph Anders		
1988-89	15-13		Robert "Money" Martin	21.5	Joseph Anders		
1989-90	15-16		Mike Kane	18.1	Joseph Anders		
1990-91	11-15		Greg Ballard	14.4	Joseph Anders		
1991-92	4-24		Charlo Davis	18.0	Joseph Anders	75-86	.466
1992-93	3-24		Charlo Davis	14.0	Don Newman		
1993-94	1-26		Michael Boyd	10.9	Don Newman		
1994-95	6-21	2-4	Damond Edwards	14.7	Don Newman		
1995-96	7-20	2-4	Abie Ramirez	13.7	Don Newman		
1996-97	3-23	2-14	Damond Edwards	14.8	Don Newman	20-114	.149
1997-98	1-25	0-16	Sedessa Fisher	13.9	Tom Abatemarco		
1998-99	3-23	3-13	Nate Murase	10.3	Tom Abatemarco		
1999-00	9-18	3-13	Anthony Flood	13.4	Tom Abatemarco	13-66	.165
2000-01	5-22	2-14	Rickie Glenn	15.4	Jerome Jenkins		
2001-02	9-19	3-11	Joseth Dawson	14.0	Jerome Jenkins		
2002-03	12-17	5-9	Derek Lambeth	13.0	Jerome Jenkins		
2003-04	13-15	7-7	Joseth Dawson	14.4	Jerome Jenkins		
2004-05	12-16	8-6	Jason Harris	17.5	Jerome Jenkins		
2005-06	15-15	5-9	Alex Bausley	13.6	Jerome Jenkins		
2006-07	10-19	5-11	Haron Hargrave	13.8	Jerome Jenkins		
2007-08	4-24	2-14	Loren Leath	13.1	Jerome Jenkins	80-147	.352
2008-09	2-27	1-15	Loren Leath	15.6	Brian Katz	2-27	.069

[a] **Jack Heron (10-9) and Elmo Slider (4-4) both coached during the 1977-78 season.**
[b] **Bill Brown (4-6) and Joseph Anders (8-10) both coached during the 1986-87 season.**

PROFILE

School: California State University, Sacramento, CA
Founded: 1947
Enrollment: 28,829 (23,724 undergraduate)
Colors: Green and gold
Nickname: Hornets
Current arena: Hornets Nest, opened in 1955 (1,200)
First game: 1948
All-time record: 673-941 (.417)
Total weeks in AP Top 20/25: 0

Current conference: Big Sky (1996-)
Conference titles: 0
Conference tournament titles: 0
NCAA Tournament appearances: 0
NIT appearances: 0

TOP 5

G **Lynn Livie** (1964-66)
G **Robert "Money" Martin** (1985-89)
G **Alex Williams** (1986-88)
F **Greg Reed** (1966-69)
F/C **Bill Whitaker** (1959-62)

RECORDS	GAME		SEASON		CAREER	
POINTS	51	Lynn Livie, vs. San Francisco State (Feb. 4, 1966)	779	Lynn Livie (1965-66)	1,774	Robert Martin (1985-89)
POINTS PER GAME			30.0	Lynn Livie (1965-66)	27.9	Lynn Livie (1964-66)
REBOUNDS	24	Bill Whitaker (1960-61)	482	Bill Whitaker (1960-61)	1,026	Bill Whitaker (1959-62)
ASSISTS	13	Nate Murase, vs. Fresno State (Dec. 1, 1998); Ryan Coleman, vs. Montana State (Jan. 29, 1998)	207	Chris Farr (1987-88)	501	DaShawn Freeman (2002-06)

ESPN 281 SAGARIN

SACRED HEART

Not many teams have 13 20-win seasons before their first losing year. But Sacred Heart isn't like most teams. The Pioneers began playing hoops in 1965, won the 1986 D2 national title, and reached six D2 tournament quarterfinals before moving to D1 in 1999. Seven losing seasons followed before Sacred Heart broke through to the winning side.

BEST TEAM: 1985-86 Dave Bike's crew wasn't just good—it was darned entertaining. Led by two-time All-America Roger Younger (18.9 ppg), the Pioneers scored at least 90 points 11 times, including their 93-87 D2 title game win over Southeast Missouri State.

BEST PLAYER: C Ed Czernota (1969-72) As a senior, this Waterbury, Conn., native set a school record with 45 points against American International College on Dec. 11, 1971. He tied that record a week later against Lehman, then broke it scoring 49 against Tufts on Feb. 7, 1972. For the season, the consensus Little All-America averaged 32.2 points and 16.2 rebounds.

BEST COACH: Dave Bike (1978-) To many Pioneers fans, just making it to the 2007 NEC title game against Central Connecticut State was a worthy accomplishment. But to Bike, being just four points short of the NCAA Tournament was cause for tears. It's that passion that's made the coach a 31-year institution at Sacred Heart.

GAME FOR THE AGES: The Pioneers' path through the 1986 D2 national tournament included a few thrillers: a 76-74 double-OT victory in the first round, and a fourth game against New Hampshire College—which had beaten the Pioneers twice during the year—in round two. But you can't top the 93-87 title game win over Southeast Missouri State. And you can't beat the sight of Pioneer Joe Jackson messing with Dick Vitale's hair afterward.

FIERCEST RIVAL: Before Sacred Heart's move to D1, Bridgeport used to be a thorn in the Pioneers' side. Now Central Connecticut State plays that role, having bumped Sacred Heart from the NEC tournament three times, including the 2007 title game. CCSU leads the series, 27–16, and has won 17 of the schools' 24 D1 matchups.

SEASON REVIEW

SEAS.	W-L	CONF.	SCORING		COACH	RECORD
1965-66	13-8		Mike Koritko	19.2	Don Feeley	
1966-67	12-12		Rich Pucciarello	22.4	Don Feeley	
1967-68	16-11		Rich Pucciarello	18.8	Don Feeley	
1968-69	16-8		Rich Pucciarello	22.3	Don Feeley	
1969-70	23-5		Rich Pucciarello	22.5	Don Feeley	
1970-71	22-6		Ed Czernota	23.1	Don Feeley	
1971-72	24-4		Ed Czernota	32.2	Don Feeley	
1972-73	17-11		Ray Vyzas	27.4	Don Feeley	
1973-74	14-13		Carl Winfree	21.1	Don Feeley	
1974-75	20-8		Carl Winfree	21.1	Don Feeley	
1975-76	14-12		T. Trimboli, H. Olivencia	22.0	Don Feeley	
1976-77	28-4		Hector Olivencia	20.8	Don Feeley	
1977-78	21-9		Hector Olivencia	25.2	Don Feeley	240-111 .684
1978-79	19-9		Cedric Cannon	21.7	Dave Bike	
1979-80	15-12		Greg Pritchett	17.6	Dave Bike	
1980-81	20-9		Keith Bennett	24.4	Dave Bike	
1981-82	26-6		Keith Bennett	22.2	Dave Bike	
1982-83	27-5		Keith Bennett	18.8	Dave Bike	
1983-84	26-7		Roger Younger	20.0	Dave Bike	
1984-85	25-7		Roger Younger	18.4	Dave Bike	
1985-86	30-4	◆	Roger Younger	18.9	Dave Bike	
1986-87	19-13		Keith Johnson	18.5	Dave Bike	
1987-88	16-13		Tony Judkins	22.3	Dave Bike	
1988-89	22-10		Tony Judkins	18.5	Dave Bike	
1989-90	15-14		T. Williams, D. Robinson	22.7	Dave Bike	
1990-91	12-18		T. Williams, D. Robinson	19.2	Dave Bike	
1991-92	10-18		Darrin Robinson	30.4	Dave Bike	
1992-93	14-13		Darrin Robinson	32.0	Dave Bike	
1993-94	10-17		Theodore Gadsden	19.0	Dave Bike	
1994-95	17-12		Brian Johnson	17.1	Dave Bike	
1995-96	13-14		Kevin Vulin	21.2	Dave Bike	
1996-97	12-16		Joe Doyle	16.3	Dave Bike	
1997-98	15-12		Louis Frye	17.8	Dave Bike	
1998-99	11-16		John Randazzo	17.6	Dave Bike	
1999-2000	3-25	2-16	D. Johnson, C. Watson	13.9	Dave Bike	
2000-01	7-21	6-14	Andrew Hunter	12.1	Dave Bike	
2001-02	8-20	7-13	Maurice Bailey	18.9	Dave Bike	
2002-03	8-21	6-12	Maurice Bailey	16.0	Dave Bike	
2003-04	12-15	8-10	Maurice Bailey	20.1	Dave Bike	
2004-05	4-23	3-15	Joey Henley	12.3	Dave Bike	
2005-06	11-17	8-10	Kibwe Trim	19.2	Dave Bike	
2006-07	18-14	12-6	Jarrid Frye	13.3	Dave Bike	
2007-08	18-14	13-5	Brice Brooks	12.6	Dave Bike	
2008-09	17-14	12-6	Joey Henley	15.7	Dave Bike	480-429 .528

◆ Division II championship

PROFILE

Sacred Heart University, Fairfield, CT
Founded: 1963
Enrollment: 5,801 (4,226 undergraduate)
Colors: Scarlet and white
Nickname: Pioneers
Current arena: Pitt Center, opened in 1997 (2,100)
First game: Nov. 22, 1965
All-time record: 720-540 (.571)
Total weeks in AP Top 20/25: 0

Current conference: Northeast (1999-)
Conference titles: 0
Conference tournament titles: 0
NCAA Tournament appearances: 0
NIT appearances: 0

CONSENSUS ALL-AMERICAS

1972	**Ed Czernota** (Little A-A), C
1978	**Hector Olivencia** (D2), F
1978	**Andre Means** (D2), C
1982, '83	**Keith Bennett** (D2), G
1986	**Roger Younger** (D2), G
1993	**Darrin Robinson** (D2), G

TOP 5

G	**Keith Bennett** (1979-83)
G	**Roger Younger** (1982-86)
F	**Tony Judkins** (1985-89)
F	**Hector Olivencia** (1974-78)
C	**Ed Czernota** (1969-72)

RECORDS

RECORDS	GAME		SEASON		CAREER	
POINTS	55	Darrin Robinson, vs. Husson (Dec. 6, 1991)	902	Ed Czernota (1971-72)	2,431	Keith Bennett (1979-83)
POINTS PER GAME			32.2	Ed Czernota (1971-72)	27.0	Darrin Robinson (1989-93)
REBOUNDS	29	Ed Czernota, vs. Tufts (Feb. 7, 1972)	516	Andre Means (1976-77)	1,317	Ed Czernota (1969-72)
ASSISTS	19	Bill Burke, vs. St. Michael's (Jan. 10, 1972)	271	Steve Zazuri (1983-84)	956	Steve Zazuri (1980-84)

ESPN 96 SAGARIN

St. Bonaventure

The tiny western New York town of Olean has enjoyed more than its fair share of hardwood excitement, thanks to a 99-game home winning streak, the "nervous defense" and the most famous size 22s in college basketball history.

BEST TEAM: 1969-70 A year after being banned from postseason play for minor NCAA rules violations, the Bonnies came back a determined powerhouse. They rolled to the East Regional final, where they avenged the single blemish on their 22–1 regular-season record by crushing Villanova, 97-74. With only Jacksonville standing between the Bonnies and UCLA—unusually vulnerable in its two-year gap between the Lew Alcindor and Bill Walton eras—Bonnies fans still believe the national title would have been theirs had their Final Four run not been cut short by Bob Lanier's untimely knee injury (see Heartbreaker).

BEST PLAYER: C Bob Lanier (1967-70) At 6'11", 265 pounds (and those boat-size sneakers), Big Cat marked his inside territory and then some, setting school career records for scoring (27.6 ppg) and rebounding (15.7) averages. A swooping left-handed hook shot and a smooth outside touch made the three-time All-America almost unstoppable. After his knee injury stopped the Bonnies during their 1970 Final Four run, Lanier was the first player selected in the NBA draft (Detroit). He became an eight-time All-Star with the Pistons and the Milwaukee Bucks, while averaging 20.1 points and 10.1 rebounds for his career.

BEST COACH: Larry Weise (1961-73) As a guard and floor general under legendary mentor Eddie Donovan, Weise concocted St. Bonaventure's "nervous defense," which pressed and terrorized opponents, ultimately earning him the full-time coaching gig at the tender age of 24. During his 12 seasons, the Sheriff accumulated a 202–90 record and four postseason appearances.

GAME FOR THE AGES: On New Year's Eve, 1960, inside the Mecca of basketball (Madison Square Garden) and up against the loaded defending national champs—Ohio State with John Havlicek, Jerry Lucas and Larry Siegfried—the team from tiny St. Bonaventure proved it could hang with the big boys. Despite the 84-82 loss, Tom Stith's 35 points gave the Buckeyes the scare of their undefeated regular season—and left Bonnies fans with a lasting memory and a portent of greatness to come.

HEARTBREAKER: While the Bonnies were finishing off Villanova on their way to their 1970 Final Four matchup with Jacksonville, Nova's Chris Ford got tripped up and put his shoulder into Lanier's right knee. Five days later, Jacksonville's 7'2" star center, Artis Gilmore, had his way with Lanier's replacement, 6'5" Matt Gantt, amassing 29 points and 21 rebounds in the Dolphins' 91-83 victory. ("Vulnerable" UCLA then decimated Jacksonville, 80-69, for the title.)

FIERCEST RIVAL: Over the years, the in-season battles among the Little Three (St. Bonaventure, Niagara and Canisius) have ignited more passions than the postseason. Though the Niagara leg of the rivalry has faded recently, the Bob Lanier vs. Calvin Murphy battles remain epic—and the Purple Eagles' 87-77 dramatic defeat of the Bonnies on Feb. 25, 1961, that ended their epic 99-home game winning streak still stings.

At 6'11", 265 pounds (and those boat-size sneakers), Big Cat Lanier marked his inside territory and then some.

FANFARE AND HOOPLA: In Lanier's day, the Bonnies would take the court to the tune of Ramsey Lewis' fusion-funk "Wade in the Water" and Lou Russo sang the national anthem. At a time when such an act would not generally be considered offensive, a group of black beret-wearing "pallbearers" carried a coffin holding a dummy representing the opponent to midcourt.

FAN FAVORITE: F Essie Hollis (1973-77) A dominant scorer off the glass, fierce on defense and an exemplary student and teammate, Hollis did it all—with a smile.

CONSENSUS ALL-AMERICAS

1960, '61 **Tom Stith**, F
1970 **Bob Lanier**, C

FIRST-ROUND PRO PICKS

1957 **Brendan McCann**, New York (5)
1961 **Tom Stith**, New York (2)
1970 **Bob Lanier**, Detroit (1)

PROFILE

St. Bonaventure University, St. Bonaventure, NY
Founded: 1858
Enrollment: 2,800 (2,202 undergraduate)
Colors: Brown and white
Nickname: Bonnies
Current arena: Reilly Center, opened in 1966 as University Center (5,780)
First game: 1919
All-time record: 1,174-908 (.564)
Total weeks in AP Top 20/25: 82

Current conference: Atlantic 10 (1979-)
Conference titles:
WNY Little Three: 5 (1950 [tie], '51, '52 [tie], '57 [tie], '58)
Atlantic 10: 1 (1983 [tie])
Conference tournament titles: 0
NCAA Tournament appearances: 5
Final Fours: 1
NIT appearances: 15
Semifinals: 6
Titles: 1 (1977)

TOP 5

G **Fred Crawford** (1960-61, '62-64)
G **Ronald "Whitey" Martin** (1958-61)
F **Essie Hollis** (1973-77)
F **Tom Stith** (1958-61)
C **Bob Lanier** (1967-70)

RECORDS	GAME		SEASON		CAREER	
POINTS	51	Bob Lanier, vs. Seton Hall (Feb. 24, 1969)	830	Tom Stith (1960-61)	2,238	Greg Sanders (1974-78)
POINTS PER GAME			31.5	Tom Stith (1959-60)	27.6	Bob Lanier (1967-70)
REBOUNDS	27	Bob Lanier, vs. Loyola (Md.) (Feb. 22, 1967)	416	Bob Lanier (1969-70)	1,180	Bob Lanier (1967-70)
ASSISTS	14	Marques Green, vs. La Salle (Jan. 18, 2003)	216	Marques Green (2002-03)	657	Marques Green (2000-04)

SEASON REVIEW

SEASON	W-L	CONF.	SCORING	COACH	RECORD		SEASON	W-L	CONF.	SCORING	COACH	RECORD	
1919-20	6-10			Richard Phelan	6-10	.375	1928-29	17-7			Mike Reilly		
1920-21	2-13			Al Carmont			1929-30	17-5			Mike Reilly		
1921-22	12-10			Al Carmont			1930-31	10-3			Mike Reilly		
1922-23	13-10			Al Carmont	27-33	.450	1931-32	4-6			Mike Reilly		
1923-24	7-4			Glenn Carberry			1932-33	7-3			Mike Reilly		
1924-25	13-11			Glenn Carberry			1933-34	3-3			Mike Reilly		
1925-26	15-6			Glenn Carberry	35-21	.625	1934-35	1-5			Mike Reilly		
1926-27	13-5			Jack Flavin	13-5	.722	1935-36	7-2			Mike Reilly		
1927-28	14-7			Fred Ostergren	14-7	.667	1936-37	4-7			Mike Reilly		

SEAS.	W-L	CONF.	POSTSEASON	SCORING		REBOUNDS		ASSISTS		COACH	RECORD	
1937-38	9-0									Mike Reilly		
1938-39	10-7									Mike Reilly		
1939-40	11-6									Mike Reilly		
1940-41	12-5									Mike Reilly		
1941-42	12-8									Mike Reilly		
1942-43	8-9									Mike Reilly	133-75	.639
1943-44	no team											
1944-45	3-7									Fr. Anselm Krieger		
1945-46	12-3									Fr. Anselm Krieger	15-10	.600
1946-47	10-11	0-3								Harry Singleton	10-11	.476
1947-48	12-10	1-3								Ed Melvin		
1948-49	18-8	1-3								Ed Melvin		
1949-50	17-5	2-2		Ken Murray	14.8					Ed Melvin		
1950-51	19-6	3-1	NIT QUARTERFINALS	Bob Sassone	12.5					Ed Melvin		
1951-52	21-6	3-1	NIT THIRD PLACE	Bob Sassone	13.1	Bill Kenville	11.4			Ed Melvin		
1952-53	10-11	1-3		Bill Kenville	19.0					Ed Melvin	97-46	.678
1953-54	12-11	2-2		Mal Duffy	21.1	Gerry Schlee	8.8			Eddie Donovan		
1954-55	13-10	1-3		Mal Duffy	22.0	Carl Saglimben	9.5			Eddie Donovan		
1955-56	11-12	0-4		Brendan McCann	16.3	Gerry Schlee	12.1			Eddie Donovan		
1956-57	17-7	3-1	NIT FOURTH PLACE	Larry Weise	13.5	John Connors	7.9			Eddie Donovan		
1957-58	21-5	4-0	NIT THIRD PLACE	Ken Fairfield	14.8	John Connors	10.4			Eddie Donovan		
1958-59	20-3		NIT QUARTERFINALS	Tom Stith	18.3	Tom Stith	10.2			Eddie Donovan		
1959-60	21-5		NIT FOURTH PLACE	Tom Stith	31.5	Tom Stith	10.6			Eddie Donovan		
1960-61	24-4		NCAA SECOND ROUND	Tom Stith	29.6	Fred Crawford	10.0			Eddie Donovan	139-57	.709
1961-62	14-7			Miles Aiken	23.6	Miles Aiken	11.0			Larry Weise		
1962-63	13-12			Fred Crawford	19.7	Fred Crawford	8.8			Larry Weise		
1963-64	16-8		NIT FIRST ROUND	Fred Crawford	17.5	Fred Crawford	12.0			Larry Weise		
1964-65	15-8			George Carter	17.5	George Carter	11.3			Larry Weise		
1965-66	16-7			George Carter	20.3	George Carter	12.4			Larry Weise		
1966-67	13-9			Bill Butler	22.0	George Carter	13.8			Larry Weise		
1967-68	23-2		NCAA REGIONAL SEMIFINALS	Bob Lanier	26.2	Bob Lanier	15.6			Larry Weise		
1968-69	17-7			Bob Lanier	27.2	Bob Lanier	15.5			Larry Weise		
1969-70	25-3		NCAA NATIONAL SEMIFINALS	Bob Lanier	29.1	Bob Lanier	16.0			Larry Weise		
1970-71	21-6		NIT THIRD PLACE	Greg Gary	18.0	Greg Gary	9.4			Larry Weise		
1971-72	16-8			Glenn Price	20.7	Glenn Price	10.5			Larry Weise		
1972-73	13-13			Glenn Price	21.5	Glenn Price	11.3			Larry Weise	202-90	.692
1973-74	17-9			Glenn Price	20.0	Glenn Price	14.4			Jim Satalin		
1974-75	14-13			Bob Rozyczko	18.5	Bob Rozyczko	9.4	Jim Baron	3.0	Jim Satalin		
1975-76	17-10			Greg Sanders	18.8	Essie Hollis	9.4	Glenn Hagan	4.7	Jim Satalin		
1976-77	23-6		NIT CHAMPION	Essie Hollis	21.7	Essie Hollis	10.1	Jim Baron	3.9	Jim Satalin		
1977-78	21-8		NCAA FIRST ROUND	Greg Sanders	22.1	Tim Waterman	10.0	Glenn Hagan	6.4	Jim Satalin		
1978-79	19-9		NIT FIRST ROUND	Earl Belcher	21.5	Tim Waterman	11.2	Jim Elenz	6.2	Jim Satalin		
1979-80	16-11	5-5		Earl Belcher	26.9	Delmar Harrod	9.1	Jim Elenz	3.8	Jim Satalin		
1980-81	14-13	6-7		Earl Belcher	24.5	Eric Stover	8.1	Mark Jones	3.7	Jim Satalin		
1981-82	14-14	7-7		Mark Jones	18.1	Rob Garbade	6.6	Norman Clarke	4.2	Jim Satalin	155-93	.625
1982-83	20-10	10-4	NIT FIRST ROUND	Mark Jones	16.4	Eric Stover	5.8	Mark Jones	4.2	Jim O'Brien		
1983-84	18-13	8-10		Barry Mungar	14.3	Barry Mungar	6.5	Alvin Lott	4.4	Jim O'Brien		
1984-85	14-15	7-11		Rob Samuels	13.8	Barry Mungar	5.8	Alvin Lott	4.7	Jim O'Brien		
1985-86	15-13	10-8		Barry Mungar	17.1	Barry Mungar	7.9	Elmer Anderson	5.5	Jim O'Brien	67-51	.568
1986-87	5-23	3-15		Rocky Llewellyn	14.3	Rocky Llewellyn	7.2	Richard McCormick	3.9	Ron DeCarli		
1987-88	13-15	7-11		Richard McCormick	13.8	Patrick Allen	6.3	Richard McCormick	5.6	Ron DeCarli		
1988-89	13-15	7-11		Rocky Llewellyn	20.2	Rocky Llewellyn	6.9	Rob Lanier	5.3	Ron DeCarli	31-53	.369
1989-90	8-20	3-15		Michael Burnett	14.6	Michael Burnett	4.9	Rob Lanier	3.6	Tom Chapman		
1990-91	5-23	0-18		Jason Brower	16.7	Jason Brower	6.7	Quinn Smith	4.2	Tom Chapman		
1991-92	9-19	3-13		Harry Moore	15.7	Harry Moore	6.0	David Vanterpool	3.6	Tom Chapman	22-62	.262
1992-93	10-17	0-14		Harry Moore	19.0	Harry Moore	8.2	David Vanterpool	4.3	Jim Baron		
1993-94	10-17	4-12		Harry Moore	20.5	Harry Moore	8.8	Shandue McNeill	5.3	Jim Baron		
1994-95	18-13	9-7	NIT SECOND ROUND	David Vanterpool	17.5	Jeff Quakenbush	6.0	Shandue McNeill	5.6	Jim Baron		
1995-96	10-18	4-12		Rashaan Palmer	16.2	Robert Blackwell Jr.	6.2	Shandue McNeill	5.1	Jim Baron		
1996-97	14-14	5-11		Rashaan Palmer	16.9	Terrence Durham	5.9	Shandue McNeill	5.7	Jim Baron		
1997-98	17-15	6-10	NIT FIRST ROUND	Rashaan Palmer	17.5	Terrence Durham	6.6	Tim Winn	4.1	Jim Baron		
1998-99	14-15	8-8		Tim Winn	13.0	Caswell Cyrus	6.9	Tim Winn	5.7	Jim Baron		
1999-2000	21-10	11-5	NCAA FIRST ROUND	Tim Winn	13.6	Peter Van Paassen	7.1	Tim Winn	4.2	Jim Baron		
2000-01	18-12	9-7	NIT FIRST ROUND	Kevin Houston	19.5	Kevin Houston	6.9	J.R. Bremer	4.2	Jim Baron	132-131	.502
2001-02	17-13	8-8	NIT FIRST ROUND	J.R. Bremer	24.6	Patricio Prato	5.0	Marques Green	5.9	Jan van Breda Kolff		
2002-03	13-14 ✪	7-9		Marques Green	21.3	Mike Gansey	5.0	Marques Green	8.0	Jan van Breda Kolff	30-27	.526▼
2003-04	7-21	3-13		Marques Green	19.4	Ahmad Smith	5.9	Marques Green	5.2	Anthony Solomon		
2004-05	2-26	1-15		Ahmad Smith	14.2	Ahmad Smith	6.2	Ahmad Smith	3.4	Anthony Solomon		
2005-06	8-19	2-14		Ahmad Smith	15.9	Paul Williams	7.1	Ahmad Smith	2.9	Anthony Solomon		
2006-07	7-22	4-12		Michael Lee	12.8	Michael Lee	6.2	Terron Diggs	2.6	Anthony Solomon	24-88	.214
2007-08	8-22	2-14		Michael Lee	17.5	Michael Lee	8.0	Tyler Relph	3.9	Mark Schmidt		
2008-09	15-15	6-10		Jonathan Hall	12.9	Jonathan Hall	6.3	Jonathan Hall	3.2	Mark Schmidt	23-37	.383

✪ Records don't reflect games forfeited or vacated. For adjusted records, see p. 521.

▼ Coach's record adjusted to reflect games forfeited or vacated: 18-27, .400. For yearly totals, see p. 521.

ESPN 241 SAGARIN

St. Francis (N.Y.)

This Brooklyn school's glory teams from the 1950s had it all: stars such as Al Inniss and Jim Luisi, national rankings, postseason success and a winning streak longer than today's average league schedule. Despite some lean years since, St. Francis has fought its way back, with two Northeast Conference title game appearances in seven years.

BEST TEAM: 1955-56 Led by Inniss, Dan Mannix, Walt Adamushko and Tony D'Elia, coach Daniel Lynch's 21–4 Terriers were the school's fifth straight 20-win team. They won 18 straight, at one point were ranked No. 13 nationally and upset Niagara to reach the NIT semifinals before falling to Dayton.

BEST PLAYER: C Al Inniss (1954-58) He was the biggest star during the school's most successful era (105 wins in five seasons). He set a still-intact school record with 37 rebounds in the 1956 NIT first round against Lafayette—the Terriers reached the semifinals that year—and finished with a then-school-record 1,503 points.

BEST COACH: Daniel Lynch (1948-69) He guided St. Francis to five straight 20-win seasons (going 105–32 from 1951-52 to '55-56), the '54 NIT quarterfinal (losing to eventual champ Holy Cross) and the '56 NIT final four. Today, the MVP of the annual Battle of Brooklyn (see Fiercest Rival) receives the Lai-Lynch Trophy, named for Lynch and another man with an impeccable reputation, longtime Long Island University coach Buck Lai.

GAME FOR THE AGES: St. Francis won the first double-overtime game in Madison Square Garden history, against Manhattan College on Feb. 11, 1939. Carl Malfitano, who was considered to have one of the best set shots in the country, scored 10 points and hit the game-winner, while Jim Naughton scored 11, including the insurance bucket, in the 53-49 win.

FIERCEST RIVAL: Each year since 1975-76, NEC foes St. Francis and LIU wage the Battle of Brooklyn (named after the first major battle of the American Revolution). Long Island leads the series, 20–15.

SEASON REVIEW

SEAS.	W-L	CONF.	COACH	SEAS.	W-L	CONF.	COACH
1901-47	*333-225*		*Rody Cooney 116-77 (1932-41)*	1960-61	10-10	2-1	Daniel Lynch
1947-48	16-9	2-3	Joseph Brennan	1961-62	8-15	2-3	Daniel Lynch
1948-49	20-13	2-2	Daniel Lynch	1962-63	16-7	4-2 ■	Daniel Lynch
1949-50	6-18	0-4	Daniel Lynch	1963-64	10-16		Daniel Lynch
1950-51	19-11	1-5	Daniel Lynch	1964-65	11-9		Daniel Lynch
1951-52	20-8	4-2	Daniel Lynch	1965-66	5-17	0-9	Daniel Lynch
1952-53	20-7	2-3	Daniel Lynch	1966-67	15-8	7-2	Daniel Lynch
1953-54	23-5	5-0 ■	Daniel Lynch	1967-68	7-16	0-8	Daniel Lynch
1954-55	21-8	2-3	Daniel Lynch	1968-69	7-16		Daniel Lynch
1955-56	21-4	4-0 ■	Daniel Lynch	1969-70	9-12		Lester Yellin
1956-57	12-14	1-2	Daniel Lynch	1970-71	8-17		Lester Yellin
1957-58	14-9	2-1	Daniel Lynch	1971-72	12-14		Lester Yellin
1958-59	5-18	0-3	Daniel Lynch	1972-73	8-16		Lester Yellin
1959-60	13-8	2-1	Daniel Lynch	1973-74	11-13		Jack Prenderville

SEAS.	W-L	CONF.	SCORING		COACH	RECORD	
1974-75	7-19				Jack Prenderville	18-32	.360
1975-76	13-13				Lucio Rossini		
1976-77	12-14				Lucio Rossini		
1977-78	16-9				Lucio Rossini		
1978-79	14-12				Lucio Rossini	55-48	.533
1979-80	11-15				Gene Roberti		
1980-81	10-16				Gene Roberti		
1981-82	10-17	8-7			Gene Roberti		
1982-83	10-18	7-7			Gene Roberti		
1983-84	2-26	1-15			Gene Roberti	43-92	.318
1984-85	7-21	3-11			Bob Valvano		
1985-86	9-19	4-12			Bob Valvano		
1986-87	11-16	5-11			Bob Valvano		
1987-88	11-18	5-11			Bob Valvano	38-74	.339
1988-89	14-16	5-11			Rich Zvosec		
1989-90	9-18	4-12			Rich Zvosec		
1990-91	15-14	8-8			Rich Zvosec	38-48	.441
1991-92	15-14	8-8			Ron Ganulin		
1992-93	9-18	8-10			Ron Ganulin		
1993-94	1-26	1-17			Ron Ganulin		
1994-95	9-18	5-13			Ron Ganulin		
1995-96	9-18	3-15			Ron Ganulin		
1996-97	13-15	7-11			Ron Ganulin		
1997-98	15-12	10-6			Ron Ganulin		
1998-99	20-8	16-4	Ray Minlend	24.3	Ron Ganulin		
1999-2000	18-12	12-6	Steven Howard	17.6	Ron Ganulin		
2000-01	18-11	16-4	Steven Howard	20.2	Ron Ganulin		
2001-02	18-11	13-7	Jason Morgan	17.4	Ron Ganulin		
2002-03	14-16	9-9	Bronski Dockery	15.4	Ron Ganulin		
2003-04	15-13	12-6	John Quintana	15.2	Ron Ganulin		
2004-05	13-15	9-9	Tory Cavalieri	15.6	Ron Ganulin	187-207	.474
2005-06	10-17	7-11	Allan Sheppard	11.6	Brian Nash		
2006-07	9-22	7-11	Robert Hines	16.5	Brian Nash		
2007-08	7-22	4-14	Robert Hines	15.0	Brian Nash		
2008-09	10-20	7-11	Ricky Cadell	15.3	Brian Nash	36-81	.308

■ NIT appearance

PROFILE

St. Francis College, Brooklyn, NY
Founded: 1859
Enrollment: 2,326 (2,326 undergraduate)
Colors: Red and blue
Nickname: Terriers
Current arena: Pope Center, opened in 1960 (1,200)
First game: 1901
All-time record: 1,084-1,112 (.494)
Total weeks in AP Top 20/25: 5

Current conference: Northeast (1981-)
Conference titles:
Metro NY: 2 (1954, '56)
Metro: 1 (1967)
Northeast: 2 (2001, '04 [tie])
Conference tournament titles: 0
NCAA Tournament appearances: 0
NIT appearances: 3
Semifinals: 1

TOP 5

G **John Conforti** (1967-70)
G/F **Jim Luisi** (1949-53)
F **Dennis McDermott** (1971-74)
F **Vernon Stokes** (1950-53)
C **Al Inniss** (1954-58)

RECORDS

RECORDS	GAME		SEASON		CAREER	
POINTS	45	John Conforti, vs. Wagner (Jan. 10, 1970)	680	Ray Minlend (1998-99)	1,613	Darrwin Purdie (1985-89)
POINTS PER GAME			24.3	Ray Minlend (1998-99)	21.3	Dennis McDermott (1971-74)
REBOUNDS	37	Al Inniss, vs. Lafayette (March 17, 1956)	311	Jerome Williams (1974-75)	1,018	Jerome Williams (1972-76)
ASSISTS	16	Jim Paguaga, vs. York College (Feb. 7, 1986)	223	Jim Paguaga (1985-86)	534	Greg Nunn (1997-2001)

ESPN 187 SAGARIN

SAINT FRANCIS (PA.)

What's in the water in Loretto, Pa.? This small Franciscan school has produced way more than its share of NBA talent—including Maurice Stokes, Norm Van Lier and Kevin Porter—along with an NIT final four team in 1955 and a 1991 NCAA Tourney squad. Fans are hungry for more.

BEST TEAM: 1990-91 Coach Jim Baron's 24–8 team employed a scorched-earth offense led by Penn State transfer Mike Iuzzolino (24.1 ppg) and all-time leading scorer Joe Anderson (2,301 career points). The Red Flash won their only Northeast Conference regular-season and tournament titles and made it to the NCAA Tournament.

BEST PLAYER: C MAURICE STOKES (1951-55) He finished as the school's top scorer (still second with 2,282 points) and top rebounder (1,819), led Saint Francis to a 78–24 mark and was named MVP of the 1955 NIT. Stokes was an NBA All Star in each of his three seasons, before a head injury suffered during a game left him paralyzed. Two years after his death in 1970, the school's athletic center was renamed in his honor.

BEST COACH: DR. WILLIAM "SKIP" HUGHES (1945-66) He led Saint Francis to nine consecutive winning seasons (1946-47 to '54-55), five of the school's nine 20-win campaigns and all three of its NIT appearances.

GAME FOR THE AGES: In 1991, the NCAA instituted a play-in game for six conference winners, so Saint Francis, 23–7 and representing the NEC, had to beat the Patriot League's Fordham (24–6) just to make it into the first round. The Red Flash responded, winning 70-64 behind 32 points from Joe Anderson.

FIERCEST RIVALS: Saint Francis has long-simmering hatreds for Northeast Conference rivals Duquesne and Robert Morris. And the records tell you why: Duquesne leads its series with the Red Flash 60–12 (*ouch!*), while Robert Morris, despite a more mundane 37–28 series advantage, has won every postseason game against Saint Francis, including NEC tournament oustings in 2000 and 2004.

SEASON REVIEW

SEAS.	W-L	CONF.	COACH	SEAS.	W-L	CONF.	COACH
1917-48	*204-154*	*Records from '05-17 lost in a fire*		1961-62	14-8		William Hughes
1948-49	16-11		William Hughes	1962-63	10-12		William Hughes
1949-50	18-9		William Hughes	1963-64	10-14		William Hughes
1950-51	19-4		William Hughes	1964-65	11-14		William Hughes
1951-52	23-7		William Hughes	1965-66	8-18		William Hughes
1952-53	13-5		William Hughes	1966-67	20-6		John Clark
1953-54	21-5	■	William Hughes	1967-68	19-6		John Clark
1954-55	21-7	■	William Hughes	1968-69	16-8		John Clark
1955-56	10-14		William Hughes	1969-70	12-12		John Hiller
1956-57	12-12		William Hughes	1970-71	15-10		John Hiller
1957-58	20-5	■	William Hughes	1971-72	12-13		Dick Conover
1958-59	20-5		William Hughes	1972-73	5-21		Dick Conover
1959-60	14-9		William Hughes	1973-74	15-11		Pete Lonergan
1960-61	6-19		William Hughes	1974-75	11-14		Pete Lonergan

SEAS.	W-L	CONF.	SCORING		COACH	RECORD	
1975-76	14-14		Jack Phelan	13.1	Pete Lonergan		
1976-77	15-11		Nick Leasure	16.8	Pete Lonergan		
1977-78	15-11		Nick Leasure	12.9	Pete Lonergan	70-61	.534
1978-79	13-13		Nick Leasure	15.9	Dave Magarity		
1979-80	12-16		Charlie Kates	14.4	Dave Magarity		
1980-81	17-10		Bob Convey	14.9	Dave Magarity		
1981-82	6-20	2-5	Jeff Hamilton	14.4	Dave Magarity		
1982-83	12-17	7-7	Jeff Hamilton	14.8	Dave Magarity	60-76	.441
1983-84	12-15	8-8	Jeff Hamilton	17.7	Kevin Porter		
1984-85	9-19	6-8	Jeff Hamilton	19.0	Kevin Porter		
1985-86	10-18	8-8	Lamont Harris	23.0	Kevin Porter		
1986-87	11-16	7-9	Bill Hughes	17.5	Kevin Porter	42-68	.382
1987-88	7-20	4-12	Joe Anderson	15.0	Jim Baron		
1988-89	13-16	6-10	Joe Anderson	22.0	Jim Baron		
1989-90	17-11	10-6	Mike Iuzzolino	21.3	Jim Baron		
1990-91	24-8	13-3 ●	Mike Iuzzolino	24.1	Jim Baron		
1991-92	13-16	5-11	Harkeem Dixon	16.8	Jim Baron	74-71	.510
1992-93	9-18	7-11	Deon George	18.3	Tom McConnell		
1993-94	13-15	9-9	Deon George	16.2	Tom McConnell		
1994-95	12-16	7-11	Rob Wooster	15.0	Tom McConnell		
1995-96	13-14	11-7	Rob Wooster	13.6	Tom McConnell		
1996-97	12-15	9-9	Eric Taylor	14.6	Tom McConnell		
1997-98	17-10	10-6	Eric Taylor	17.5	Tom McConnell		
1998-99	9-17	7-13	Sam Sutton	13.5	Tom McConnell	85-105	.447
1999-2000	10-18	7-11	Tom Fox	10.9	Bobby Jones		
2000-01	9-18	9-11	Melvin Scott	13.0	Bobby Jones		
2001-02	6-21	5-15	Reiner Mougnol	13.1	Bobby Jones		
2002-03	14-14	10-8	Darshan Luckey	21.6	Bobby Jones		
2003-04	13-15	10-8	Darshan Luckey	17.6	Bobby Jones		
2004-05	15-13	10-8	Darshan Luckey	21.5	Bobby Jones		
2005-06	4-24	2-16	Rahsaan Benton	12.5	Bobby Jones		
2006-07	8-21	5-13	Devin Sweetney	13.0	Bobby Jones		
2007-08	6-23	4-14	Chris Berry	11.2	Bobby Jones	85-167	.337
2008-09	6-23	3-15	Devin Sweetney	16.3	Don Friday	6-23	.207

● NCAA Tournament appearance ■ NIT appearance

PROFILE

Saint Francis University, Loretto, PA
Founded: 1847
Enrollment: 2,210 (1,612 undergraduate)
Colors: Red and white
Nickname: Red Flash
Current arena: DeGol Arena in the Maurice Stokes Athletics Center, opened in 1972 (3,500)
First game: 1905
All-time record: 991-979 (.503)
Total weeks in AP Top 20/25: 0

Current conference: Northeast (1981-)
Conference titles:
Northeast: 1 (1991 [tie])
Conference tournament titles:
Northeast: 1 (1991)
NCAA Tournament appearances: 1
NIT appearances: 3
Semifinals: 1

FIRST-ROUND PRO PICKS

1955 **Maurice Stokes,** Rochester (2)

TOP 5

G **Kevin Porter** (1968-72)
G **Norm Van Lier** (1966-69)
F **Joe Anderson** (1987-91)
F **Sandy Williams** (1961-64)
C **Maurice Stokes** (1951-55)

RECORDS

RECORDS	GAME		SEASON		CAREER	
POINTS	46	Larry Lewis, vs. St. Vincent (Feb. 10, 1969)	772	Mike Iuzzolino (1990-91)	2,301	Joe Anderson (1987-91)
POINTS PER GAME			27.1	Maurice Stokes (1954-55)	22.4	Maurice Stokes (1951-55)
REBOUNDS	39	Maurice Stokes, vs. John Carroll (Jan. 28, 1955)	733	Maurice Stokes (1954-55)	1,819	Maurice Stokes (1951-55)
ASSISTS	19	Pat McGeary, vs. Siena (Feb. 4, 1975)	290	Norm Van Lier (1967-68)	589	Napoleon Lightning (1981-85)

ESPN 16 SAGARIN

St. John's

It may surprise some to know that this Queens, N.Y., school's program is in the top 10 in all-time D1 victories and winning percentage. After all, the 2000s were a lean decade for the Red Storm (formerly the Redmen). But St. John's, especially under coaches Joe Lapchick and Lou Carnesecca, exemplified everything that's good about the City Game, playing in 27 NCAA Tournaments, reaching two Final Fours and winning six NITs.

BEST TEAM: 1984-85 Coach Carnesecca's star-studded team featured Chris Mullin, Walter Berry, Mark Jackson and Bill Wennington. The Redmen reached No. 1 in the rankings during the season and advanced to the Final Four. They finished 31–4, with three of their losses coming to Patrick Ewing and Georgetown—the last of those in the Final Four.

BEST PLAYER: G/F Chris Mullin (1981-85) The Brooklyn-born gym rat averaged 16.6 ppg as a freshman and only got better, blossoming into a three-time Big East Player (or co-Player) of the Year and Wooden Award winner in his senior season. The 6'6" Mullin was deadly accurate, shooting 55% from the floor and 84.7% from the line over his career. He led the Redmen to the 1985 Final Four; the previous summer, he also found time to win an Olympic gold medal.

BEST COACH: Lou Carnesecca (1965-70, '73-92) His personality was as luminous as the colorful sweaters he wore courtside. In 24 seasons, Carnesecca never failed to reach a postseason tournament (18 NCAAs, six NITs). His teams won 20 or more games 18 times. In 1992, he was inducted into the Naismith Hall of Fame.

GAME FOR THE AGES: The 1985 Elite Eight matchup between St. John's and NC State was dubbed the Spaghetti Western because of the ethnicity of the men in civvies prowling the sidelines (Carnesecca and Jim Valvano). It proved to be a back-and-forth affair that wasn't decided until a pair of buckets in the final minutes by Mullin, who finished with 25 points. Said Carnesecca after the 69-60 win punched St. John's ticket for the Final Four, "When I'm going to my grave, this I'll remember."

HEARTBREAKER: In 1999, his first season as head coach, Mike Jarvis had the Red Storm within one victory of the Final Four. St. John's was down by nine to Ohio State with 2:47 on the clock and rallied to within two with seconds left and the ball in the hands of point guard Erick Barkley. Bad time for Barkley to commit his first turnover of the game. The Buckeyes won, 77-74.

FIERCEST RIVAL: The Big East experienced a Golden Era in the mid-1980s and Georgetown vs. St. John's was one big reason why. Coaches Carnesecca and John Thompson Jr. would invariably play little head games with each other—in 1985, after Carnesecca took to wearing the same "lucky sweater" during a 19-game winning streak, Thompson showed up at a Madison Square Garden game wearing a replica. The Red Storm leads the series, 52–40.

FANFARE AND HOOPLA: Built in 1961 and holding just 6,008 fans, Carnesecca Arena (originally named Alumni Hall) is a cozy home venue, but it's too small for games against elite opponents. Then the scene shifts to Manhattan's Madison Square Garden, where opposing fans sometimes show up en masse and limit the Red Storm's home-court edge.

FAN FAVORITE: C Marco Baldi (1985-88) The 6'11" Italian center never fulfilled the high expectations set for him, but he always had a place in the hearts of the St. John's faithful. His best moment came in 1987, when he hit the game-winning shot in a first-round NCAA Tournament victory over Wichita State.

CONSENSUS ALL-AMERICAS

1911	**John Keenan,** F
1943	**Harry Boykoff,** C
1985	**Chris Mullin,** G/F
1986	**Walter Berry,** F

FIRST-ROUND PRO PICKS

1949	**Dick McGuire,** New York (8)
1962	**LeRoy Ellis,** LA Lakers (8)
1967	**Sonny Dove,** Detroit (4)
1967	**Sonny Dove,** New Jersey (ABA)
1969	**John Warren,** New York (11)
1973	**Mel Davis,** New York (14)
1973	**Mel Davis,** Carolina (ABA 10)
1978	**George Johnson,** Milwaukee (12)
1985	**Chris Mullin,** Golden State (7)
1985	**Bill Wennington,** Dallas (16)
1986	**Walter Berry,** Portland (14)
1987	**Mark Jackson,** New York (18)
1990	**Jayson Williams,** Phoenix (21)
1992	**Malik Sealy,** Indiana (14)
1998	**Felipe Lopez,** San Antonio (24)
1999	**Ron Artest,** Chicago (16)
2000	**Erick Barkley,** Portland (28)

PROFILE

St. John's University, Queens, NY
Founded: 1870
Enrollment: 20,069 (14,983 undergraduate)
Colors: Red and white
Nickname: Red Storm
Current arena: Carnesecca Arena, opened as Alumni Hall in 1961 (6,008)
Previous: DeGray Gymnasium, 1932-56 (900)
First game: Dec. 6, 1907
All-time record: 1,732-869 (.666)
Total weeks in AP Top 20/25: 281

Current conference: Big East (1979-)
Conference titles:
Metro New York: 9 (1943, '46 [tie], '47, '49 [tie], '51, '52, '58, '61, '62)
NJ-NY 7: 1 (1978 [tie])
Big East: 5 (1980 [tie], '83 [tie], '85, '86 [tie], '92 [tie])
Conference titles:
Big East: 3 (1983, '86, 2000)
NCAA Tournaments: 27 (1 appearance vacated)
Sweet 16s (since 1975): 5
Final Fours: 2

NIT appearances: 27 (1 vacated)
Semifinals: 16
Titles: 6 (1943, '44, '59, '65, '89, 2003-v)
v-title vacated

TOP 5

G	**Mark Jackson** (1983-87)
G	**Dick McGuire** (1943-44, '46-49)
G/F	**Chris Mullin** (1981-85)
F	**Walter Berry** (1984-86)
F	**Tony Jackson** (1958-61)

RECORDS

RECORDS	GAME		SEASON		CAREER	
POINTS	65	Bob Zawoluk, vs. Saint Peter's (March 3, 1950)	828	Walter Berry (1985-86)	2,440	Chris Mullin (1981-85)
POINTS PER GAME			24.7	Bill Schaeffer (1972-73)	21.2	Marcus Hatten (2001-03)
REBOUNDS	30	LeRoy Ellis, vs. NYU (Dec. 30, 1961)	479	Mel Davis (1970-71)	1,240	George Johnson (1974-78)
ASSISTS	17	Omar Cook, vs. Stony Brook (Nov. 18, 2000)	328	Mark Jackson (1985-86)	738	Mark Jackson (1983-87)

SEASON REVIEW

SEASON	W-L	CONF.	SCORING		COACH	RECORD
1907-18	*112-73*		*14-0 in 1910-11*			
1918-19	0-7		John Butler	5.8	John Crenny	
1919-20	9-14		Louis Damico	12.7	John Crenny	
1920-21	10-9		Louis Damico	12.7	John Crenny	
1921-22	10-11		Vincent O'Brien	15.8	Edward Kelleher	10-11 .476
1922-23	11-10		Charles Germain	9.4	John Crenny	
1923-24	16-15		J. Freeman, L. McCready	8.2	John Crenny	
1924-25	18-6		Carl Reiher	13.0	John Crenny	
1925-26	18-7		Dick Paige	8.0	John Crenny	
1926-27	15-10		James Freeman	6.8	John Crenny	105-86 .550
1927-28	18-4		James Collins	11.3	James Freeman	
1928-29	23-2		James Collins	10.2	James Freeman	
1929-30	23-1		Al Schuckman	7.9	James Freeman	
1930-31	21-1		M. Begovich, Schuckman	7.0	James Freeman	
1931-32	22-4		Nat Lazar	7.3	James Freeman	
1932-33	23-4		Nat Lazar	7.2	James Freeman	
1933-34	16-3	3-4	John McGuinness	6.9	James Freeman	
1934-35	13-8		Joseph Marchese	7.3	James Freeman	
1935-36	18-4	4-3	Reuben Kaplinsky	7.3	James Freeman	177-31 .851
1936-37	12-7	1-4	Gerard Bush	7.1	Joe Lapchick	
1937-38	15-4	4-2			Joe Lapchick	
1938-39	18-4	17-2	*NIT FOURTH PLACE*		Joe Lapchick	

SEAS.	W-L	CONF.	POSTSEASON	SCORING		REBOUNDS		ASSISTS		COACH	RECORD
1939-40	15-5		NIT QUARTERFINALS	James White	8.7					Joe Lapchick	
1940-41	11-6			James White	10.2					Joe Lapchick	
1941-42	16-5			James White	9.5					Joe Lapchick	
1942-43	21-3	6-1	NIT CHAMPION	Harry Boykoff	16.6					Joe Lapchick	
1943-44	18-5		NIT CHAMPION	Hy Gotkin	8.9					Joe Lapchick	
1944-45	21-3		NIT THIRD PLACE	Ray Wertis	14.7					Joe Lapchick	
1945-46	17-6	5-1	NIT QUARTERFINALS	Harry Boykoff	16.5					Joe Lapchick	
1946-47	16-7	6-0	NIT QUARTERFINALS	Harry Boykoff	16.7					Joe Lapchick	
1947-48	12-11	3-3		Dick McGuire	10.4					Frank McGuire	
1948-49	15-9	5-1	NIT FIRST ROUND	Dick McGuire	12.8					Frank McGuire	
1949-50	24-5	3-3	NIT THIRD PLACE	Bob Zawoluk	20.3					Frank McGuire	
1950-51	26-5	6-0	NIT 3RD PL, NCAA REG. SEMIS	Bob Zawoluk	21.1					Frank McGuire	
1951-52	25-6	6-0	NIT QUARTERS, NCAA R-UP	Bob Zawoluk	18.9	Bob Zawoluk	397			Frank McGuire	102-36 .739
1952-53	17-6	5-1	NIT RUNNER-UP	Dick Duckett	13.8	Jim Davis	231			Al DeStefano	
1953-54	9-11	2-3		Solly Walker	14.0	Solly Walker	243			Al DeStefano	
1954-55	11-9	5-1		Mike Parenti	16.0	Bill Chrystal	226			Al DeStefano	
1955-56	12-12	3-3		Mike Parenti	22.1	Mike Parenti	330			Al DeStefano	49-38 .563
1956-57	14-9	4-2		Bernie Pascal	12.4	Bill Chrystal	224			Joe Lapchick	
1957-58	18-8	6-0	NIT FOURTH PLACE	Alan Seiden	20.4	Louis Roethal	236			Joe Lapchick	
1958-59	20-6	4-2	NIT CHAMPION	Alan Seiden	21.9	Tony Jackson	401			Joe Lapchick	
1959-60	17-8	5-1	NIT QUARTERFINALS	Tony Jackson	21.2	Tony Jackson	322			Joe Lapchick	
1960-61	20-5	4-0	NCAA FIRST ROUND	Tony Jackson	22.0	Tony Jackson	10.7			Joe Lapchick	
1961-62	21-5	5-0	NIT RUNNER-UP	LeRoy Ellis	23.5	LeRoy Ellis	430			Joe Lapchick	
1962-63	9-15	2-2		Ken McIntyre	13.0	Fred Edelman	242			Joe Lapchick	
1963-64	14-11			Ken McIntyre	15.9	Robert McIntyre	225			Joe Lapchick	
1964-65	21-8		NIT CHAMPION	Ken McIntyre	17.9	Sonny Dove	338			Joe Lapchick	334-130 .720
1965-66	18-8		NIT FIRST ROUND	Sonny Dove	21.2	Sonny Dove	369			Lou Carnesecca	
1966-67	23-5		NCAA REGIONAL FINALS	Sonny Dove	22.4	Sonny Dove	14.8			Lou Carnesecca	
1967-68	19-8		NCAA FIRST ROUND	John Warren	15.8	Rudy Bogad	239			Lou Carnesecca	
1968-69	23-6		NCAA REGIONAL SEMIFINALS	John Warren	19.6	Ralph Abraham	251			Lou Carnesecca	
1969-70	21-8		NIT RUNNER-UP	Joe DePre	16.5	Billy Paultz	389			Lou Carnesecca	
1970-71	18-9		NIT FIRST ROUND	Mel Davis	21.0	Mel Davis	479	Rich Lyons	48	Frank Mulzoff	
1971-72	19-11		NIT THIRD PLACE	Mel Davis	21.1	Mel Davis	460	Rich Lyons	128	Frank Mulzoff	
1972-73	19-7		NCAA FIRST ROUND	Bill Schaeffer	24.7	Bill Schaeffer	290	Mel Utley	126	Frank Mulzoff	56-27 .675
1973-74	20-7		NIT FIRST ROUND	Mel Utley	17.6	Ed Searcy	308	Kevin Cluess	125	Lou Carnesecca	
1974-75	21-10		NIT FOURTH PLACE	Mel Utley	15.5	George Johnson	285	Mel Utley	133	Lou Carnesecca	
1975-76	23-6		NCAA FIRST ROUND	Glen Williams	14.8	George Johnson	296	Frank Alagia	182	Lou Carnesecca	
1976-77	22-9	3-2	NCAA FIRST ROUND	Glen Williams	21.5	George Johnson	335	Tom Calabrese	125	Lou Carnesecca	
1977-78	21-7	5-1	NCAA FIRST ROUND	George Johnson	19.4	George Johnson	324	Bernard Rencher	83	Lou Carnesecca	
1978-79	21-11	3-3	NCAA REGIONAL FINALS	Reggie Carter	15.0	Wayne McKoy	248	Bernard Rencher	126	Lou Carnesecca	
1979-80	24-5	5-1	NCAA SECOND ROUND	Reggie Carter	15.0	Wayne McKoy	205	Bernard Rencher	143	Lou Carnesecca	
1980-81	17-11	8-6	NIT FIRST ROUND	David Russell	14.8	David Russell	218	Bill Goodwin	59	Lou Carnesecca	
1981-82	21-9	9-5	NCAA SECOND ROUND	David Russell	17.4	David Russell	209	Bob Kelly	139	Lou Carnesecca	
1982-83	28-5	12-4	NCAA REGIONAL SEMIFINALS	Chris Mullin	19.1	David Russell	245	Bob Kelly	141	Lou Carnesecca	
1983-84	18-12	8-8	NCAA FIRST ROUND	Chris Mullin	22.9	Jeff Allen	198	Mike Moses	124	Lou Carnesecca	
1984-85	31-4	15-1	NCAA NATIONAL SEMIFINALS	Chris Mullin	19.8	Walter Berry	304	Chris Mullin	151	Lou Carnesecca	
1985-86	31-5	14-2	NCAA SECOND ROUND	Walter Berry	23.0	Walter Berry	11.1	Mark Jackson	9.1	Lou Carnesecca	
1986-87	21-9	10-6	NCAA SECOND ROUND	Mark Jackson	18.9	Shelton Jones	234	Mark Jackson	193	Lou Carnesecca	
1987-88	17-12	8-8	NCAA FIRST ROUND	Shelton Jones	18.6	Shelton Jones	256	Greg Harvey	131	Lou Carnesecca	
1988-89	20-13	6-10	NIT CHAMPION	Jayson Williams	19.5	Jayson Williams	246	Jason Buchanan	167	Lou Carnesecca	
1989-90	24-10	10-6	NCAA SECOND ROUND	Malik Sealy	18.1	Robert Werdann	260	Greg Harvey	180	Lou Carnesecca	
1990-91	23-9	10-6	NCAA REGIONAL FINALS	Malik Sealy	22.1	Malik Sealy	247	Jason Buchanan	188	Lou Carnesecca	
1991-92	19-11	12-6	NCAA FIRST ROUND	Malik Sealy	22.6	Malik Sealy	203	Jason Buchanan	187	Lou Carnesecca	526-200 .725
1992-93	19-11	12-6	NCAA SECOND ROUND	Shawnelle Scott	13.7	Shawnelle Scott	225	David Cain	213	Brian Mahoney	
1993-94	12-17	5-13		Shawnelle Scott	16.0	Charles Minlend	225	Maurice Brown	92	Brian Mahoney	
1994-95	14-14	7-11	NIT FIRST ROUND	Felipe Lopez	17.8	Charles Minlend	230	Maurice Brown	86	Brian Mahoney	
1995-96	11-16	5-13		Zendon Hamilton	20.8	Zendon Hamilton	277	Maurice Brown	90	Brian Mahoney	56-58 .491
1996-97	13-14	8-10		Zendon Hamilton	16.2	Zendon Hamilton	254	Tarik Turner	84	Fran Fraschilla	
1997-98	22-10	13-5	NCAA FIRST ROUND	Felipe Lopez	17.6	Zendon Hamilton	277	Collin Charles	95	Fran Fraschilla	35-24 .593
1998-99	28-9	14-4	NCAA REGIONAL FINALS	Bootsy Thornton	14.9	Tyrone Grant	8.6	Erick Barkley	4.7	Mike Jarvis	
1999-2000	25-8	12-4	NCAA SECOND ROUND	Erick Barkley	16.0	Lavor Postell	6.9	Erick Barkley	4.5	Mike Jarvis	
2000-01	14-15 ⊗	8-8		Omar Cook	15.3	Anthony Glover	5.9	Omar Cook	8.7	Mike Jarvis	
2001-02	20-12 ⊗	9-7	NCAA FIRST ROUND	Marcus Hatten	20.1	Anthony Glover	6.7	Marcus Hatten	4.5	Mike Jarvis	
2002-03	21-13 ⊗	7-9	NIT CHAMPION	Marcus Hatten	22.2	Anthony Glover	5.6	Marcus Hatten	4.1	Mike Jarvis	
2003-04	6-21 ⊗	1-15		Daryll Hill	14.8	Kyle Cuffe	7.2	Daryll Hill	3.7	Mike Jarvis[a]	110-61 .634▼
2004-05	9-18	3-13		Daryll Hill	20.7	Lamont Hamilton	7.5	Eugene Lawrence	3.9	Norm Roberts	
2005-06	12-15	5-11		Lamont Hamilton	12.6	Lamont Hamilton	7.6	Eugene Lawrence	4.9	Norm Roberts	
2006-07	16-15	7-9		Lamont Hamilton	13.4	Lamont Hamilton	6.5	Eugene Lawrence	5.6	Norm Roberts	
2007-08	11-19	5-13		Justin Burrell	10.8	Justin Burrell	5.9	Eugene Lawrence	3.7	Norm Roberts	
2008-09	16-18	6-12		Paris Horne	14.6	Sean Evans	7.1	Malik Boothe	4.4	Norm Roberts	64-85 .430

Cumulative totals listed when per game averages not available.

[a] Mike Jarvis (2-4) and Kevin Clark (4-17) both coached during the 2003-04 season.

⊗ Records don't reflect games forfeited or vacated. For adjusted records, **see p. 521.**

▼ Coach's record adjusted to reflect games forfeited or vacated: 68-60, .531. For adjusted records, **see p. 521.**

ESPN 56 SAGARIN

SAINT JOSEPH'S

With a proud history of college basketball excellence (and one very dark moment) dating back to the mid-1950s, Saint Joseph's has long been a powerhouse of Northeast basketball. With a rebirth in the late 1990s under head coach Phil Martelli, it's apparent that generations of St. Joe's fans have always had it right: The Hawk will *never* die.

BEST TEAM: 2003-04 Martelli's team went 27–0 in the regular season, earning the school's first No. 1 national ranking. The win streak—halted in the Atlantic 10 tournament by Xavier—also earned the Hawks their first No. 1 seed in the NCAA Tournament. They flew all the way into the Elite Eight before being shot down by Oklahoma State, 64-62. Both of the Hawks' guards, Jameer Nelson and Delonte West, were chosen in the first round of the 2004 NBA draft (by Denver and Boston, respectively).

BEST PLAYER: G JAMEER NELSON (2000-04) The consensus 2003-04 National Player of the Year, Nelson is the school's career leader in points (2,094), assists (713) and steals (256). He started all 125 games he appeared in, and he upped his scoring average each year—from 12.5 ppg as a freshman to 20.6 as a senior. He was the Atlantic 10 Rookie of the Year in 2001 and the league's Player of the Year in 2004.

BEST COACH: JACK RAMSAY (1955-66) Dr. Jack coached the Hawks to their lone Final Four in 1961. But he also shared their shame when the third-place finish was vacated after three of his players were found to have participated in a point-shaving scheme. Still, Ramsay has the highest winning percentage in school history with an 11-year mark of 234–72 (.765). The Naismith Hall of Famer (who also coached four NBA teams) led the Hawks to five consecutive NCAA berths (1959-63) and nine straight postseason bids—the most of any SJU coach.

GAME FOR THE AGES: On March 14, 1981, senior John Smith hit a layup at the buzzer as No. 9-seed Saint Joseph's stunned the nation's No. 1 team, DePaul, 49-48, in the second round of the NCAA Tournament. Though the Hawks went on to lose in the Elite Eight to eventual champion Indiana, the DePaul upset remains a shining moment for the program.

HEARTBREAKER: After an amazing undefeated 2003-04 regular season, the Hawks—playing in the nearby New Jersey Meadowlands—were 6.9 seconds away from the Final Four. But Oklahoma State's John Lucas III hit a three-pointer, and when Jameer Nelson's ensuing three-point attempt at the buzzer bounced off the rim, Saint Joseph's went home a 64-62 loser instead.

FIERCEST RIVAL: St. Joe's and Villanova are Catholic institutions located just 6.5 miles apart in the Philadelphia suburbs. Many families, neighborhoods and local offices are split in their loyalties to the schools. Villanova leads the rivalry, which dates back to 1921, 42–24.

FANFARE AND HOOPLA: One of the most famous mascots in college athletics, the Hawk is known for flapping its wings during the entire game as the embodiment of the team's motto and rally cry: "The Hawk Will Never Die!" The Hawk—with a lucky student inside the feathery costume—has been flapping since the 1954-55 season.

The Hawk—with a lucky student inside—has been flapping since the 1954-55 season.

FAN FAVORITE: G MATT GUOKAS JR. (1964-66) The two Matt Guokases—junior and senior—were not just father-son St. Joe's stars (senior was on a 1930s team dubbed the Mighty Mites). They were also the first two-generation professional champions, senior with Philadelphia of the BAA (precursor of the NBA) and junior with the NBA's Philadelphia 76ers.

CONSENSUS ALL-AMERICAS

1943 **George Senesky**, G/F
2004 **Jameer Nelson**, G

FIRST-ROUND PRO PICKS

1966 **Matt Guokas Jr.**, Philadelphia (9)
1967 **Cliff Anderson**, Pittsburgh (ABA)
1973 **Mike Bantom**, Phoenix (8)
1986 **Maurice Martin**, Denver (16)
2004 **Jameer Nelson**, Denver (20)
2004 **Delonte West**, Boston (24)

PROFILE

Saint Joseph's University, Philadelphia, PA
Founded: 1851
Enrollment: 7,542 (4,515 undergraduate)
Colors: Crimson and gray
Nickname: Hawks
Current arena: Michael J. Hagan '85 Arena, opened as Alumni Memorial Fieldhouse in 1949 (4,200)
Previous: The Palestra, 1926-48, 2008-09 (8,722)
First game: Dec. 10, 1909
All-time record: 1,482-967 (.605)
Total weeks in AP Top 20/25: 65

Current conference: Atlantic 10 (1982-)
Conference titles:
Middle Atlantic: 11 (1959, '60, '61, '62, '63, '65, '66, '70 [tie], '71 [tie], '73 [tie], '74 [tie])
East Coast Conference: 2 (1976 [tie], '80 [tie])
Atlantic 10: 7 (1986, '97 [tie], 2001, '02 [tie], '03 [tie], '04 [tie], '05 [tie])
Conference tournament titles:
East Coast Conference: 2 (1981, '82)
Atlantic 10: 2 (1986, '97)
NCAA Tournaments: 19 (1 appearance vacated)
Sweet 16s (since 1975): 3
Final Fours: 1

NIT appearances: 14
Semifinals: 3

TOP 5

G **Jameer Nelson** (2000-04)
G/F **George Senesky** (1939-43)
F **Mike Bantom** (1970-73)
F/C **Cliff Anderson** (1964-67)
C **Rodney Blake** (1984-88)

RECORDS	GAME		SEASON		CAREER	
POINTS	47	Tony Costner, vs. Alaska-Anchorage (Dec. 30, 1983); Jack Egan, vs. Gettysburg (Jan. 21, 1961)	706	Marvin O'Connor (2000-01)	2,094	Jameer Nelson (2000-04)
POINTS PER GAME			26.5	Cliff Anderson (1966-67)	20.7	Paul Senesky (1947-50)
REBOUNDS	34	John Doogan, vs. West Chester State (Feb. 18, 1953)	450	Cliff Anderson (1964-65)	1,228	Cliff Anderson (1964-67)
ASSISTS	14	Rap Curry, vs. Drexel (Nov. 28, 1990); Tom Haggerty, vs. Fairfield (Feb. 21, 1976)	213	Jameer Nelson (2000-01)	713	Jameer Nelson (2000-04)

SEASON REVIEW

SEASON	W-L	CONF.	SCORING	COACH	RECORD	SEASON	W-L	CONF.	SCORING	COACH	RECORD
1909-16	*68-54*		*14-1 in 1914-15*			1926-27	6-11			Tom Temple	
1916-17	18-5			John Donahue		1927-28	6-11			Tom Temple	12-22 .353
1917-18	5-2			John Donahue		1928-29	8-10			Bill Ferguson	
1918-19	3-3			John Donahue	78-52 .600	1929-30	12-9			Bill Ferguson	
1919-20	9-6			John Lavin		1930-31	16-5		Phil Zuber 6.6	Bill Ferguson	
1920-21	4-10		Dick Crean 7.8	John Lavin		1931-32	8-10		Phil Zuber 6.8	Bill Ferguson	
1921-22	8-9			John Lavin		1932-33	7-9			Bill Ferguson	
1922-23	7-8			John Lavin		1933-34	6-11			Bill Ferguson	
1923-24	9-9			John Lavin		1934-35	12-3			Bill Ferguson	
1924-25	9-9			John Lavin		1935-36	14-5			Bill Ferguson	
1925-26	4-11			John Lavin	50-62 .446	1936-37	15-4		Matt Guokas Sr. 7.7	Bill Ferguson	

SEAS.	W-L	CONF.	POSTSEASON	SCORING	REBOUNDS	ASSISTS	COACH	RECORD
1937-38	13-5			Matt Guokas Sr. 11.3		Matt Guokas Sr. 2.8	Bill Ferguson	
1938-39	9-12			Larry Kenney 11.2			Bill Ferguson	
1939-40	10-5			Larry Kenney 10.2			Bill Ferguson	
1940-41	12-6			Larry Kenney 15.4			Bill Ferguson	
1941-42	12-6			George Senesky 12.8			Bill Ferguson	
1942-43	18-4			George Senesky 23.4			Bill Ferguson	
1943-44	18-7			Jack Flannery 12.2			Bill Ferguson	
1944-45	12-11			Bob O'Neill 15.1			Bill Ferguson	
1945-46	9-11			Bill Poletti 8.1			Bill Ferguson	
1946-47	16-6			Norm Butz 9.3			Bill Ferguson	
1947-48	13-11			Paul Senesky 18.2			Bill Ferguson	
1948-49	12-11			Paul Senesky 21.0			Bill Ferguson	
1949-50	10-15			Paul Senesky 22.8			Bill Ferguson	
1950-51	13-14			Mike Fallon 12.4			Bill Ferguson	
1951-52	20-7			John Hughes 15.8			Bill Ferguson	
1952-53	14-11			Ed Garrity 15.8	John Doogan 14.1		Bill Ferguson	309-208 .598
1953-54	14-9			Bill Lynch 15.6	Bill Lynch 14.6		John McMenamin	
1954-55	12-14			Mike Fallon 14.3	Bill Lynch 11.0		John McMenamin	26-23 .531
1955-56	23-6		NIT THIRD PLACE	Kurt Engelbert 17.0	Bill Lynch 13.1		Jack Ramsay	
1956-57	17-7			Kurt Engelbert 20.3	Ray Radziszewski 15.5	Dan Dougherty 3.5	Jack Ramsay	
1957-58	18-9		NIT QUARTERFINALS	Bob McNeill 18.7	Bob Clarke 10.3	Bob McNeill 4.9	Jack Ramsay	
1958-59	22-5	7-0	NCAA REGIONAL SEMIFINALS	Bob McNeill 16.4	Bob Clarke 10.6	Bob McNeill 6.5	Jack Ramsay	
1959-60	20-7	7-1	NCAA REGIONAL SEMIFINALS	Bob McNeill 16.7	Jack Egan 11.0	Bob McNeill 4.3	Jack Ramsay	
1960-61	25-5 ⊗	8-0	NCAA THIRD PLACE	Jack Egan 21.9	Jack Egan 12.0		Jack Ramsay	
1961-62	18-10	9-1	NCAA REGIONAL SEMIFINALS	Tom Wynne 19.5	Tom Wynne 10.0		Jack Ramsay	
1962-63	23-5	8-0	NCAA REGIONAL FINALS	Tom Wynne 18.4	Jim Boyle 9.5		Jack Ramsay	
1963-64	18-10	5-1	NIT QUARTERFINALS	Steve Courtin 20.7	Larry Hofmann 10.9		Jack Ramsay	
1964-65	26-3		NCAA REGIONAL SEMIFINALS	Cliff Anderson 17.9	Cliff Anderson 15.5	Matt Guokas Jr. 5.3	Jack Ramsay	
1965-66	24-5		NCAA REGIONAL SEMIFINALS	Cliff Anderson 17.9	Cliff Anderson 14.0	Matt Guokas Jr. 6.1	Jack Ramsay	234-72 .765▼
1966-67	16-10			Cliff Anderson 26.5	Cliff Anderson 14.3	Steve Donches 2.7	Jack McKinney	
1967-68	17-9			Mike Hauer 17.8	Mike Hauer 13.8	Dan Kelly 3.1	Jack McKinney	
1968-69	17-11		NCAA FIRST ROUND	Mike Hauer 20.6	Mike Hauer 12.0	Dan Kelly 3.8	Jack McKinney	
1969-70	15-12	5-0		Dan Kelly 20.7	Mike Hauer 11.7	Tom Lynch 2.5	Jack McKinney	
1970-71	19-9	6-0	NCAA FIRST ROUND	Mike Bantom 18.1	Mike Bantom 13.2	Mike Moody 2.7	Jack McKinney	
1971-72	19-9	5-1	NIT FIRST ROUND	Mike Bantom 21.8	Mike Bantom 14.8	Jim O'Brien 4.1	Jack McKinney	
1972-73	22-6	6-0	NCAA FIRST ROUND	Pat McFarland 20.3	Mike Bantom 13.1	Jim O'Brien 3.8	Jack McKinney	
1973-74	19-11	5-1	NCAA FIRST ROUND	Ron Righter 12.1	Kevin Furey 6.9	Jim O'Brien 5.1	Jack McKinney	144-77 .652
1974-75	8-17	3-3		Ron Righter 16.1	Ron Righter 7.4	Frank Rafferty 3.0	Harry Booth	
1975-76	10-16	4-1		Norman Black 16.9	Norman Black 9.5	Tom Haggerty 2.6	Harry Booth	
1976-77	13-13	2-3		Norman Black 16.7	Mike Thomas 7.7	Luke Griffin 4.4	Harry Booth	
1977-78	13-15	2-3		Norman Black 17.6	Norman Black 9.6	Luke Griffin 4.6	Harry Booth	44-61 .419
1978-79	19-11	11-3	NIT FIRST ROUND	Norman Black 15.5	Norman Black 8.3	Luke Griffin 5.4	Jim Lynam	
1979-80	21-9	10-1	NIT FIRST ROUND	Boo Williams 13.9	Boo Williams 7.9	Luke Griffin 4.0	Jim Lynam	
1980-81	25-8	9-2	NCAA REGIONAL FINALS	Bryan Warrick 13.5	Boo Williams 6.6	Jeffery Clark 3.4	Jim Lynam	65-28 .699
1981-82	25-5	10-1	NCAA FIRST ROUND	Bryan Warrick 14.9	Tony Costner 7.5	Bryan Warrick 5.0	Jim Boyle	
1982-83	15-13	8-6		Bob Lojewski 18.2	Tony Costner 9.3	Maurice Martin 4.3	Jim Boyle	
1983-84	20-9	13-5	NIT FIRST ROUND	Tony Costner 18.6	Tony Costner 8.3	Maurice Martin 3.5	Jim Boyle	
1984-85	19-12	13-5	NIT SECOND ROUND	Maurice Martin 16.5	Bob Lojewski 6.4	Maurice Martin 3.2	Jim Boyle	
1985-86	26-6	16-2	NCAA SECOND ROUND	Maurice Martin 17.8	Greg Mullee 7.4	Geoff Arnold 4.2	Jim Boyle	
1986-87	16-13	9-9		Rodney Blake 17.6	Rodney Blake 7.1	Bruiser Flint 5.9	Jim Boyle	
1987-88	15-14	9-9		Rodney Blake 18.2	Henry Smith 8.8	Ivan Brown 4.7	Jim Boyle	
1988-89	8-21	4-14		Brian Leahy 16.5	Henry Smith 8.6	Ray Washington 2.2	Jim Boyle	
1989-90	7-21	5-13		Craig Amos 18.0	Craig Amos 6.4	Chris Gardler 3.6	Jim Boyle	151-114 .570
1990-91	13-17	7-11		Bernard Blunt 18.8	Bernard Blunt 6.5	Rap Curry 5.7	John Griffin	
1991-92	13-15	6-10		Bernard Blunt 19.7	Jason Warley 9.0	Bernard Blunt 3.1	John Griffin	
1992-93	18-11	8-6	NIT FIRST ROUND	Bernard Blunt 18.0	Carlin Warley 9.0	Rap Curry 5.1	John Griffin	
1993-94	14-14	5-11		Carlin Warley 16.4	Carlin Warley 11.4	Rap Curry 6.3	John Griffin	
1994-95	17-12	9-7	NIT FIRST ROUND	Reggie Townshend 14.7	Carlin Warley 10.7	Rashid Bey 2.3	John Griffin	75-69 .521
1995-96	19-13	9-7	NIT RUNNER-UP	Reggie Townshend 14.8	Will Johnson 10.2	Rashid Bey 5.0	Phil Martelli	
1996-97	26-7	13-3	NCAA REGIONAL SEMIFINALS	Rashid Bey 15.0	Nemanja Petrovic 5.2	Rashid Bey 4.6	Phil Martelli	
1997-98	11-17	3-13		Rashid Bey 16.9	Harold Rasul 8.8	Rashid Bey 4.6	Phil Martelli	
1998-99	12-18	5-11		Andre Howard 11.9	Andre Howard 8.4	Na'im Crenshaw 2.9	Phil Martelli	
1999-2000	13-16	7-9		Marvin O'Connor 16.6	Andre Howard 6.6	Tim Brown 3.3	Phil Martelli	
2000-01	26-7	14-2	NCAA SECOND ROUND	Marvin O'Connor 22.1	Bill Phillips 8.9	Jameer Nelson 6.5	Phil Martelli	
2001-02	19-12	12-4	NIT FIRST ROUND	Marvin O'Connor 17.5	Bill Phillips 7.6	Jameer Nelson 6.1	Phil Martelli	
2002-03	23-7	12-4	NCAA FIRST ROUND	Jameer Nelson 19.7	Dwayne Jones 6.3	Jameer Nelson 4.7	Phil Martelli	
2003-04	30-2	16-0	NCAA REGIONAL FINALS	Jameer Nelson 20.6	Dwayne Jones 7.0	Jameer Nelson 5.3	Phil Martelli	
2004-05	24-12	14-2	NIT RUNNER-UP	Pat Carroll 18.3	Dwayne Jones 11.6	Dwayne Lee 5.2	Phil Martelli	
2005-06	19-14	9-7	NIT SECOND ROUND	Abdulai Jalloh 15.0	Abdulai Jalloh 5.5	Dwayne Lee 4.3	Phil Martelli	
2006-07	18-14	9-7		Ahmad Nivins 16.2	Ahmad Nivins 7.4	Pat Calathes 3.9	Phil Martelli	
2007-08	21-13	9-7	NCAA FIRST ROUND	Pat Calathes 18.0	Pat Calathes 7.7	Tasheed Carr 5.0	Phil Martelli	
2008-09	17-15	9-7		Ahmad Nivins 19.2	Ahmad Nivins 11.8	Garrett Williamson 4.5	Phil Martelli	278-167 .625

⊗ Records don't reflect forfeited or vacated games. For adjusted records, see p. 521.

▼ Coach's record adjusted to reflect games forfeited or vacated: 231-71, .765. For yearly totals, see p. 521.

ESPN 53 SAGARIN

SAINT LOUIS

Saint Louis has one of the odder mascots in college sports—the chubby, elfin Billiken—and a basketball history that's almost as intriguing. An early power just as college hoops started to expand in the late 1940s, Saint Louis disappeared from the headlines for the next three decades before once again beginning to command national attention in the mid-1990s.

BEST TEAM: 1947-48 Led by first-year head coach Eddie Hickey, Saint Louis went 24–3 and made its first postseason appearance in the still-prominent NIT. Behind junior Ed Macauley, the Billikens beat Bowling Green, Western Kentucky and then NYU in the final to end up as SLU's only national championship team. Macauley was named tournament MVP and the Billikens finished with the highest single-season winning percentage (.889) in school history.

BEST PLAYER: F/C ED MACAULEY (1945-49) A former local high school star, "Easy" Ed Macauley was a first-team All-America in his final two seasons and the 1948-49 Associated Press Collegiate Player of the Year. In 1960, after retiring from a 10-year, seven-time NBA All-Star career, he became, at the age of 32, the youngest person inducted into the Naismith Hall of Fame.

BEST COACH: EDDIE HICKEY (1947-58) SLU's all-time winningest and longest-tenured coach (211–89, 11 seasons) guided the Billikens to two NCAA Tournaments and to the 1948 NIT championship, when the NIT was still the more important postseason event. A member of the Naismith Hall of Fame, Hickey never had a losing season and five times coached the Billikens to 20 or more victories.

GAME FOR THE AGES: On March 17, 1948, Saint Louis upset NYU, 66-52, to win the NIT at Madison Square Garden. In a battle between future Hall of Fame forwards, Macauley poured in a game-high 24 points while holding NYU All-America Dolph Schayes to eight. As NIT champ, Saint Louis was one of eight teams invited to compete in the U.S. Olympic basketball trials. No Billikens made the Olympic team, however.

HEARTBREAKER: In its final season in the Great Midwest before joining Conference USA, Saint Louis fell to Cincinnati in the 1995 GMW championship game, 67-65, on LaZelle Durden's three-pointer with 1.2 seconds left. The Billikens' Carl Turner heaved up a 60-foot shot of his own at the buzzer that hit the front of the rim and bounced away as time expired.

FIERCEST RIVAL: Saint Louis and Dayton didn't begin playing each other until 1952, and the Billikens have faced other opponents more often over more years. But the Dayton rivalry has escalated to a fever pitch in recent seasons, as four of the eight games since March 1, 2006, had to be decided in overtime—all in Dayton's favor. Dayton leads the series overall, 23–19.

FANFARE AND HOOPLA: The three-foot-tall bronze Billiken statue sits serenely smiling on a stone pedestal outside the Bauman-Eberhardt Center, the team's old home court (1926-45) and now a recreation center for students and staff. The students and fans are known to rub the belly of the chubby Buddha-like character—located there since 1996—for good luck before important Saint Louis games. The Billiken was designed and patented in 1908 by a Missouri art teacher named Florence Pretz and became extremely popular across the nation. No one is certain exactly how the character came to be connected with Saint Louis University.

"Easy" Ed Macauley became, at the age of 32, the youngest person inducted into the Naismith Hall of Fame.

FAN FAVORITE: F ANTHONY BONNER (1986-90) The St. Louis native is not only the school's all-time leading scorer (1,972) and rebounder (1,424), but also the most beloved Billiken, because of his continued involvement with the SLU program after a solid five-year NBA career.

PROFILE

Saint Louis University, St. Louis, MO
Founded: 1818
Enrollment: 10,211 (7,082 undergraduate)
Colors: Royal blue and white
Nickname: Billikens
Current arena: Chaifetz Arena, opened in 2008 (10,600)
Previous: Scottrade Center, 1994-2008 (20,000)
First game: 1915
All-time record: 1,241-1,075 (.536)
Total weeks in AP Top 20/25: 96

Current conference: Atlantic 10 (2005-)
Conference titles:
Missouri Valley: 4 (1947, '52, '55 [tie], '57)
Conference tournament titles:
Conference USA: 1 (2000)
NCAA Tournament appearances: 6
NIT appearances: 18
Semifinals: 4
Titles: 1 (1948)

CONSENSUS ALL-AMERICAS

1948, '49 **Ed Macauley,** F/C

FIRST-ROUND PRO PICKS

1949	**Ed Macauley,** St. Louis (5)
1959	**Bob Ferry,** St. Louis (7)
1990	**Anthony Bonner,** Sacramento (23)
1998	**Larry Hughes,** Philadelphia (8)

TOP 5

G	**Larry Hughes** (1997-98)
G	**H Waldman** (1993-95)
F	**Anthony Bonner** (1986-90)
F	**Bob Ferry** (1956-59)
F/C	**Ed Macauley** (1945-49)

RECORDS

RECORDS	GAME		SEASON		CAREER	
POINTS	45	Anthony Bonner, vs. Loyola-Chicago (March 1, 1990)	670	Larry Hughes (1997-98)	1,972	Anthony Bonner (1986-90)
POINTS PER GAME			24.5	Harry Rogers (1972-73)	19.4	David Burns (1979-81)
REBOUNDS	38	Jerry Koch, vs. Bradley (March 3, 1954)	502	Jerry Koch (1953-54)	1,424	Anthony Bonner (1986-90)
ASSISTS	18	Jim Roder, vs. Southern Mississippi (March 17, 1987)	235	Jim Roder (1986-87)	436	Josh Fisher (2000-04)

SEASON REVIEW

SEASON	W-L	CONF.	SCORING	COACH	RECORD	
1915-16	13-6			George Koegan	13-6	.684
1916-17	5-6			Armin Fischer		
1917-18	3-12			Armin Fischer		
1918-19	4-8			Armin Fischer		
1919-20	2-9			Armin Fischer		
1920-21	11-6			Armin Fischer	25-41	.379
1921-22	4-9			Steve O'Rourke	4-9	.308
1922-23	5-5			Dan Savage		
1923-24	8-2			Dan Savage		
1924-25	14-2			Dan Savage		
1925-26	9-4			Dan Savage	36-13	.735
1926-27	0-14			Squint Hunter	0-14	.000
1927-28	11-11			Harry Reget	11-11	.500
1928-29	14-4			Mike Nyikos		
1929-30	14-6			Mike Nyikos		
1930-31	13-6			Mike Nyikos		
1931-32	13-6			Mike Nyikos		
1932-33	9-9			Mike Nyikos		
1933-34	10-8			Mike Nyikos		
1934-35	11-5			Mike Nyikos		
1935-36	9-11			Mike Nyikos	93-55	.628
1936-37	6-15			Ed Davidson		

SEAS.	W-L	CONF.	POSTSEASON	SCORING		REBOUNDS		ASSISTS		COACH	RECORD	
1937-38	8-21	2-12								Ed Davidson	14-36	.280
1938-39	5-16	3-11								Jack Sterret		
1939-40	4-14	2-10								Jack Sterret	9-30	.231
1940-41	3-14	2-10								Bob Klenck		
1941-42	8-12	4-6								Bob Klenck		
1942-43	11-10	3-7								Bob Klenck	22-36	.379
1943-44	no team											
1944-45	10-4									Dukes Duford	10-4	.714
1945-46	13-11	6-5		Ed Macauley	10.0					John Flanigan		
1946-47	18-11	11-1		Ed Macauley	13.7					John Flanigan	31-22	.585
1947-48	24-3	8-2	NIT CHAMPION	Ed Macauley	13.4					Eddie Hickey		
1948-49	22-4	8-2	NIT QUARTERFINALS	Ed Macauley	15.5					Eddie Hickey		
1949-50	17-9	8-4		Joe Ossola	12.2					Eddie Hickey		
1950-51	22-8	11-3	NIT QUARTERFINALS	Ed Scott	10.7					Eddie Hickey		
1951-52	23-8	9-1	NCAA R. FINAL, NIT QUARTERS	Ray Steiner	12.2					Eddie Hickey		
1952-53	16-11	5-5	NIT FIRST ROUND	Dick Boushka	18.7	Jerry Koch	15.0			Eddie Hickey		
1953-54	14-12	4-6		Dick Boushka	21.4	Jerry Koch	20.1			Eddie Hickey		
1954-55	20-8	8-2	NIT QUARTERFINALS	Dick Boushka	19.6	Jim McLaughlin	16.5			Eddie Hickey		
1955-56	18-7	8-4	NIT FIRST ROUND	Grady Smith	17.0	Jim McLaughlin	18.2			Eddie Hickey		
1956-57	19-9	12-2	NCAA REGIONAL SEMIFINALS	Harold Alcorn	20.1	Calvin Burnett	14.9			Eddie Hickey		
1957-58	16-10	9-5		Jack Mimlitz	17.8					Eddie Hickey	211-89	.703
1958-59	20-6	10-4	NIT QUARTERFINALS	Bob Ferry	21.8	Bob Ferry	14.0			John Benington		
1959-60	19-8	9-5	NIT QUARTERFINALS	Bob Nordmann	16.3	Bob Nordmann	14.6			John Benington		
1960-61	21-9	7-5	NIT RUNNER-UP	Bob Nordmann	13.0	Tom Kieffer	5.1			John Benington		
1961-62	11-15	5-7		Tom Keiffer	11.2	Gary Garrison	9.8			John Benington		
1962-63	16-12	6-6	NIT QUARTERFINALS	Dave Harris	12.4	Donnell Reid	7.8			John Benington		
1963-64	13-12	6-6		Gil Beckemeier	13.3	Rich Parks	8.3			John Benington		
1964-65	18-9	9-5	NIT FIRST ROUND	Rick Naes	11.6	Rick Naes	9.1			John Benington	118-71	.624
1965-66	16-10	8-6		Rich Parks	18.6	Rich Parks	12.7			Joe "Buddy" Brehmer		
1966-67	13-13	5-9		Rich Niemann	18.1	Rich Niemann	12.3			Joe "Buddy" Brehmer		
1967-68	15-11	9-7		Rich Neimann	16.0	Rich Niemann	12.7			Joe "Buddy" Brehmer		
1968-69	6-20	5-11		Joe Wiley	16.5	Joe Wiley	10.9			Joe "Buddy" Brehmer	50-54	.481
1969-70	9-17	5-11		Joe Wiley	22.0	Joe Wiley	8.0	Jim Irving	3.4	Bob Polk		
1970-71	17-12	9-5		Jim Irving	20.8	Harry Rogers	8.8	Jim Irving	3.0	Bob Polk		
1971-72	18-8	9-5		Harry Rogers	18.8	Rich Stallworth	8.3	Rich Stallworth	3.2	Bob Polk		
1972-73	19-7	10-4		Harry Rogers	24.5	Harry Rogers	9.1	Bill Paradoski	3.7	Bob Polk		
1973-74	9-16	4-8		Bill Morris	17.3	Bill Morris	11.1	Leartha Scott	3.3	Bob Polk	72-60	.545
1974-75	12-14			Lewis McKinney	21.5	Robin Jones	7.2	Jim Hackmann	2.5	Randy Albrecht		
1975-76	13-14	0-2		Lewis McKinney	19.1	Carl Johnson	7.5	Bill Moulder	2.7	Randy Albrecht		
1976-77	7-19	1-5		Carl Johnson	13.8	Carl Johnson	7.9	Bill Moulder	5.0	Randy Albrecht	32-47	.405
1977-78	7-20	2-10		Ricky Frazier	13.7	Carl Johnson	9.0	Everne Carr	2.1	Ron Coleman	7-20	.259
1978-79	10-17	3-7		Jim Glass	14.1	Kelvin Henderson	8.3	Everne Carr	3.6	Ron Ekker		
1979-80	12-15	4-8		David Burns	17.4	Kelvin Henderson	9.4	David Burns	4.7	Ron Ekker		
1980-81	9-18	3-9		David Burns	21.4	Willie Becton	7.3	LaTodd Johnson	5.3	Ron Ekker		
1981-82	6-21	1-11		Willie Becton	12.2	Willie Becton	6.9	LaTodd Johnson	5.9	Ron Ekker	37-71	.343
1982-83	5-23	2-12		Luther Burden	15.5	Andre Craig	7.0	Kevin Williams	3.9	Rich Grawer		
1983-84	12-16	5-9		Luther Burden	13.2	Carvin Norman	6.8	Darryl Lenard	4.5	Rich Grawer		
1984-85	13-15	6-8		Luther Burden	19.6	Carvin Norman	7.3	Darryl Lenard	4.5	Rich Grawer		
1985-86	18-12	8-4		Monroe Douglass	14.5	Roland Gray	7.6	Darryl Lenard	4.0	Rich Grawer		
1986-87	25-10	7-5	NIT SECOND ROUND	Roland Gray	16.9	Anthony Bonner	9.6	Jim Roder	6.7	Rich Grawer		
1987-88	14-14	5-5		Monroe Douglass	15.9	Anthony Bonner	8.8	Charles Newberry	3.7	Rich Grawer		
1988-89	27-10	8-4	NIT RUNNER-UP	Anthony Bonner	15.5	Anthony Bonner	10.4	Charles Newberry	3.6	Rich Grawer		
1989-90	21-12	9-5	NIT RUNNER-UP	Anthony Bonner	19.8	Anthony Bonner	13.8	Charles Newberry	6.7	Rich Grawer		
1990-91	19-14	8-6		Quitman Dillard	14.0	Quitman Dillard	5.7	Jeff Luechtefeld	4.5	Rich Grawer		
1991-92	5-23	0-10		Quitman Dillard	14.4	Quitman Dillard	6.2	Julian Winfield	3.0	Rich Grawer	159-149	.516
1992-93	12-17	1-9		Erwin Claggett	19.7	Donnie Dobbs	6.5	Erwin Claggett	3.8	Charlie Spoonhour		
1993-94	23-6	8-4	NCAA FIRST ROUND	Erwin Claggett	17.4	Donnie Dobbs	6.1	H Waldman	5.2	Charlie Spoonhour		
1994-95	23-8	8-4	NCAA SECOND ROUND	Erwin Claggett	18.2	David Robinson	6.8	H Waldman	4.8	Charlie Spoonhour		
1995-96	16-14	4-10	NIT FIRST ROUND	Jeff Harris	12.9	Jeff Harris	7.9	Jeff Carlos McCauley	3.2	Charlie Spoonhour		
1996-97	11-18	4-10		Jeff Harris	12.9	Jeff Harris	7.1	Jamall Walker	2.6	Charlie Spoonhour		
1997-98	22-11	11-5	NCAA SECOND ROUND	Larry Hughes	20.9	Ryan Luechtefeld	5.7	Jamall Walker	3.9	Charlie Spoonhour		
1998-99	15-16	8-8		Justin Love	13.7	Ryan Luechtefeld	5.2	Jamall Walker	2.7	Charlie Spoonhour	122-90	.575
1999-2000	19-14	7-9	NCAA FIRST ROUND	Justin Love	18.2	Justin Tatum	6.0	Justin Love	2.5	Lorenzo Romar		
2000-01	17-14	8-8		Maurice Jeffers	16.0	Maurice Jeffers	6.1	Marque Perry	3.5	Lorenzo Romar		
2001-02	15-16	9-7		Marque Perry	14.1	Kenny Brown	6.2	Josh Fisher	3.3	Lorenzo Romar	51-44	.537
2002-03	16-14	9-7	NIT FIRST ROUND	Marque Perry	17.1	Kenny Brown	6.4	Josh Fisher	3.7	Brad Soderberg		
2003-04	19-13	9-7	NIT SECOND ROUND	Reggie Bryant	16.4	Chris Sloan	4.8	Josh Fisher	4.3	Brad Soderberg		
2004-05	9-21	6-10		Reggie Bryant	12.2	Izik Ohanon	5.4	Dwayne Polk	2.6	Brad Soderberg		
2005-06	16-13	10-6		Ian Vouyoukas	13.9	Ian Vouyoukas	7.4	Tommie Liddell	2.7	Brad Soderberg		
2006-07	20-13	8-8		Tommie Liddell III	15.4	Ian Vouyoukas	7.4	Kevin Lisch	3.5	Brad Soderberg	80-74	.519
2007-08	16-15	7-9		Kevin Lisch	14.6	Luke Meyer	5.4	Kevin Lisch	3.1	Rick Majerus		
2008-09	18-14	8-8		Kevin Lisch	14.1	Tommie Liddell III	5.7	Kwamain Mitchell	3.7	Rick Majerus	34-29	.540

ESPN 139 SAGARIN

SAINT MARY'S (CALIF.)

A 30-year hiatus between NCAA Tournament appearances finally ended in 1989 and three of the Gaels' five NCAA appearances have come since 1997. But the program's lone Tournament win came way back before the dry spell, in 1959.

BEST TEAM: 1988-89 Forget the lean years; the 25–5 Gaels won 16 of their first 17 games and set school marks for field goal shooting (.535) and victories (surpassed in 2008-09). Led by top scorer Al Lewis (392), they earned a No. 8 Tournament seed but lost in the first round to No. 9-seed Clemson, 83-70.

BEST PLAYER: F Tom Meschery (1958-61) The only Gael to be selected as an All-America, Meschery averaged 16.7 points and a school-record 13.5 rebounds per game, and is also the No. 2 all-time rebounder with 916. Meschery led Saint Mary's to its first NCAA Tournament in 1959 and that lone Tourney victory—80-71 over Idaho State. He then played 10 seasons as a bruising forward with the NBA Warriors and SuperSonics.

BEST COACH: Randy Bennett (2001-) He's the school's all-time winningest coach and the only one to lead Saint Mary's to multiple NCAA Tournament appearances. In each of his first eight seasons, Bennett led the Gaels as far as the semifinals of the West Coast Conference tournament, thrice reaching the final (2004, '05, '09).

GAME FOR THE AGES: Playing their conference rival, Gonzaga, in a nationally televised home game on Feb. 4, 2008, Saint Mary's rode the scoring of freshman Patty Mills to a wild 89-85 overtime win. It was the first time the Zags had faced a ranked conference opponent in nearly 20 years. Mills scored the Gaels' final 10 points in regulation and five more in overtime to finish with 23.

FIERCEST RIVAL: The Gaels' battles with Gonzaga for WCC supremacy have intensified this rivalry in recent seasons. Their March 1, 2008, encounter was the first in which both teams entered the game with a Top-25 national ranking. Gonzaga avenged its Feb. 4 loss with an 88-76 win—and leads the series (by its count) 48–23, including 26 wins in the last 29 meetings.

SEASON REVIEW

SEAS.	W-L	CONF.		COACH	SEAS.	W-L	CONF.	COACH
1907-50	*318-308*	*0-12 over 3 seasons (1920-22)*			1963-64	7-19	5-7	Mike Cimino
1950-51	9-11			Thomas Foley	1964-65	8-18	5-9	Mike Cimino
1951-52	16-10			Thomas Foley	1965-66	8-17	4-10	Mike Cimino
1952-53	9-11	4-4		Thomas Foley	1966-67	4-21	2-12	Mike Cimino
1953-54	10-14	4-8		Thomas Foley	1967-68	4-20	3-11	Mike Cimino
1954-55	6-19	1-11		Thomas Foley	1968-69	6-19	3-11	Mike Cimino
1955-56	16-10	8-6		James Weaver	1969-70	3-22	0-14	Mike Cimino
1956-57	17-9	10-4		James Weaver	1970-71	10-16	4-10	Bruce Hale
1957-58	11-15	8-4		James Weaver	1971-72	9-17	3-11	Bruce Hale
1958-59	19-6	11-1	●	James Weaver	1972-73	7-19	2-12	Bruce Hale
1959-60	15-11	7-5		James Weaver	1973-74	15-13	5-9	Frank LaPorte
1960-61	19-7	8-4		James Weaver	1974-75	14-12	7-7	Frank LaPorte
1961-62	13-11	8-4		James Weaver	1975-76	3-23	2-10	Frank LaPorte
1962-63	14-11	8-4		Mike Cimino	1976-77	11-16	4-10	Frank LaPorte

SEAS.	W-L	CONF.		SCORING		COACH	RECORD	
1977-78	13-14	5-9		Nick Pappageorge	492	Frank LaPorte		
1978-79	13-15	5-9		Kenny Jones	491	Frank LaPorte	69-93	.426
1979-80	13-14 ⊗	9-7		David Vann	452	Bill Oates		
1980-81	9-18	3-11		David Vann	472	Bill Oates		
1981-82	11-16	3-11		Peter Thibeaux	523	Bill Oates		
1982-83	14-12	7-5		Peter Thibeaux	19.8	Bill Oates		
1983-84	12-16	7-5		David Boone	428	Bill Oates		
1984-85	15-12	7-5		David Cooke	408	Bill Oates		
1985-86	10-17	3-11		Paul Robertson	396	Bill Oates	84-105	.444
1986-87	17-13	7-7		Paul Robertson	381	Lynn Nance		
1987-88	19-9	9-5		Robert Haugen	403	Lynn Nance		
1988-89	25-5	12-2	●	Al Lewis	392	Lynn Nance	61-27	.693
1989-90	7-20	4-10		Mike Vontoure	348	Paul Landreaux		
1990-91	13-17	7-7		Eric Bamberger	456	Paul Landreaux[a]	11-29	.275
1991-92	13-17	4-10		Eric Bamberger	411	Ernie Kent		
1992-93	11-16	6-8		Brian Brazier	316	Ernie Kent		
1993-94	13-14	5-9		Chris Johnson	351	Ernie Kent		
1994-95	18-10	10-4		Brent Farris	403	Ernie Kent		
1995-96	12-15	5-9		David Sivulich	423	Ernie Kent		
1996-97	23-8	10-4	●	Brad Millard	384	Ernie Kent	90-80	.529
1997-98	12-15	7-7		David Sivulich	19.4	Dave Bollwinkel		
1998-99	13-18	5-9		Eric Schraeder	19.8	Dave Bollwinkel		
1999-2000	8-20	3-11		Frank Allocco	12.1	Dave Bollwinkel		
2000-01	2-27	0-14		Jovan Harris	15.1	Dave Bollwinkel	35-80	.304
2001-02	9-20	3-11		Chase Poole	10.2	Randy Bennett		
2002-03	15-15	6-8		Daniel Kickert	12.7	Randy Bennett		
2003-04	19-12	9-5		Paul Marigney	16.0	Randy Bennett		
2004-05	25-9	11-3	●	Daniel Kickert	16.6	Randy Bennett		
2005-06	17-12	8-6		Daniel Kickert	16.7	Randy Bennett		
2006-07	17-15	8-6		Diamon Simpson	14.1	Randy Bennett		
2007-08	25-7	12-2	●	Patty Mills	14.8	Randy Bennett		
2008-09	28-7	10-4	■	Patty Mills	18.4	Randy Bennett	155-97	.615

Cumulative totals listed when per game averages not available.

[a] Paul Landreaux (4-9) and Dave Fehte (9-8) both coached during the 1990-91 season.

⊗ Records don't reflect games forfeited or vacated. For adjusted records, see p. 521.

● NCAA Tournament appearance ■ NIT appearance

PROFILE

Saint Mary's College of California, Moraga, CA
Founded: 1863
Enrollment: 3,916 (2,486 undergraduate)
Colors: Navy and red
Nickname: Gaels
Current arena: McKeon Pavilion, opened in 1978 (3,500)
First game: 1907
All-time record: 1,072-1,160 (.480)
Total weeks in AP Top 20/25: 13

Current conference: West Coast (1952-)
Conference titles:
West Coast Athletic: 2 (1959, '80 [tie])
West Coast: 2 (1989, '97 [tie])
Conference tournament titles:
West Coast: 1 (1997)
NCAA Tournament appearances: 5
NIT appearances: 1

FIRST-ROUND PRO PICKS

1961 **Tom Meschery,** Philadelphia (7)

TOP 5

G **Patty Mills** (2007-09)
G **David Vann** (1978-82)
F **Tom Meschery** (1958-61)
F **Diamon Simpson** (2005-09)
C **Daniel Kickert** (2002-06)

RECORDS

RECORDS	GAME		SEASON		CAREER	
POINTS	43	Jim Moore, vs. Sacramento State (Dec. 12, 1964)	614	Eric Schraeder (1998-99)	1,863	Daniel Kickert (2002-06)
POINTS PER GAME			23.8	Steve Gray (1962-63)	20.0	Sam Hill (1969-71)
REBOUNDS	24	Mike Wadsworth, vs. UC Davis (Dec. 11, 1953)	377	Diamon Simpson (2008-09)	1,130	Diamon Simpson (2005-09)
ASSISTS	16	Ray Orgill, vs. Southern Utah (Dec. 3, 1980)	213	Nick Pappageorge (1976-77)	507	Kamran Sufi (1993-97)

ESPN 177 SAGARIN

SAINT PETER'S

When you emerge from Saint Peter's basketball facility, you can see Manhattan glittering through the Jersey City haze. New York City has hosted some of the Peacocks' sweetest moments, but the team's success has rested largely on staying local and finding quality players passed over by the nationally ranked big boys.

BEST TEAM: 1967-68 Led by forward Elnardo Webster (25.0 ppg), the high-scoring, fast-breaking Peacocks earned the nickname Run, Baby, Run—and a devoted following. In the NIT quarterfinals, Saint Peter's routed No. 10-ranked Duke, 100-71, in front of largest NIT crowd to date. But Kansas silenced the de facto home team in the semifinals, 58-46, and Notre Dame did too, winning the third-place game, 81-78.

BEST PLAYER: G Keydren "KeeKee" Clark (2002-06) The Peacocks' all-time leader in 11 statistical categories, as a soph the 5'8" Clark was the shortest player ever to win the D1 scoring title with 26.7 ppg, An inch taller as a junior, Clark repeated as scoring champ with 25.8 ppg.

BEST COACH: Don Kennedy (1950-1972) He had a remarkable ability to find unheralded local talent, and used it to run a high-scoring fast break that powered his squads to five NITs.

GAME FOR THE AGES: In the 1995 MAAC tournament final, not only did the Peacocks avenge regular-season losses of 21 and 23 points to Manhattan with a wild 80-78 OT victory, they knocked off the No. 1 seed and booked their second trip to the NCAAs. Saint Peter's blew a nine-point lead in the final two minutes of regulation, but Mike Frensley's 14-footer with :04 remaining in the extra session closed the deal.

FIERCEST RIVAL: Saint Peter's is located in working-class Jersey City, and its fans always get their collective backs up when crossing paths (or PATH trains) with fans of Manhattan College, whose campus is in the affluent Riverdale section of the Bronx. The series dates back to the 1946-47 season, and the Jaspers lead overall, 64–45–1. But the Peacocks have the edge in MAAC tournament matchups, 5–4.

SEASON REVIEW

SEAS.	W-L	CONF.	COACH	SEAS.	W-L	CONF.	COACH
1930-46	*70-134*			1959-60	15-5		Don Kennedy
1946-47	5-16		George Babich	1960-61	14-9		Don Kennedy
1947-48	16-5		George Babich	1961-62	12-10		Don Kennedy
1948-49	18-5		George Babich	1962-63	12-11		Don Kennedy
1949-50	13-11-1		Pete Caruso	1963-64	13-9		Don Kennedy
1950-51	9-16		Don Kennedy	1964-65	10-10		Don Kennedy
1951-52	13-11		Don Kennedy	1965-66	11-12	5-4	Don Kennedy
1952-53	14-8		Don Kennedy	1966-67	18-6	7-2 ■	Don Kennedy
1953-54	17-7		Don Kennedy	1967-68	24-4	8-0 ■	Don Kennedy
1954-55	11-11		Don Kennedy	1968-69	21-7	7-1 ■	Don Kennedy
1955-56	14-7		Don Kennedy	1969-70	13-11		Don Kennedy
1956-57	18-4	■	Don Kennedy	1970-71	11-13		Don Kennedy
1957-58	20-4	■	Don Kennedy	1971-72	12-13		Don Kennedy
1958-59	15-6		Don Kennedy	1972-73	8-18		Bernie Ockene

SEAS.	W-L	CONF.	SCORING		COACH	RECORD	
1973-74	8-18		Ken Markowski	15.5	Bernie Ockene	16-36	.308
1974-75	15-12	■	Bob Fazio	17.5	Dick McDonald		
1975-76	19-11	■	Bob Fazio	21.9	Dick McDonald		
1976-77	13-13		Bob Fazio	17.7	Dick McDonald	47-36	.566
1977-78	8-18		Kevin Bannon	14.9	Bob Kelly		
1978-79	10-15		Kevin Bannon	14.3	Bob Kelly	18-33	.353
1979-80	22-9	■	Jim Brandon	15.7	Bob Dukiet		
1980-81	17-9		Kevin Rogers	14.8	Bob Dukiet		
1981-82	20-9	9-1 ■	William Brown	16.9	Bob Dukiet		
1982-83	22-5	7-3	Shelton Gibbs	19.0	Bob Dukiet		
1983-84	23-6	11-3 ■	Shelton Gibbs	17.0	Bob Dukiet		
1984-85	15-14	5-9	Leonard Hayes	20.4	Bob Dukiet		
1985-86	16-12	7-7	Willie Haynes	12.8	Bob Dukiet	135-64	.678
1986-87	21-8	11-3 ■	Willie Haynes	15.1	Ted Fiore		
1987-88	20-9	11-3	Alex Roberts	17.0	Ted Fiore		
1988-89	22-9	11-3 ■	Willie Haynes	16.9	Ted Fiore		
1989-90	14-14	7-9	Tony Walker	16.1	Ted Fiore		
1990-91	24-7	11-5 ●	Tony Walker	19.2	Ted Fiore		
1991-92	8-21	3-13	Chuck Veterano	15.0	Ted Fiore		
1992-93	9-18	3-11	Scott Weeden	17.4	Ted Fiore		
1993-94	14-13	8-6	Mike Frensley, A. Allen	10.5	Ted Fiore		
1994-95	19-11	10-4 ●	Luis Arrosa	15.3	Ted Fiore	151-110	.579
1995-96	15-12	5-9	Luis Arrosa	14.2	Rodger Blind		
1996-97	13-15	9-5	Ricky Bellinger	16.3	Rodger Blind		
1997-98	8-19	4-14	Ricky Bellinger	16.5	Rodger Blind		
1998-99	14-15	10-8	Ricky Bellinger	16.2	Rodger Blind		
1999-2000	5-23	2-16	Ricky Bellinger	15.1	Rodger Blind	55-84	.396
2000-01	4-24	2-16	Keith Sellers	18.7	Bob Leckie		
2001-02	4-24	3-15	Corien John	12.8	Bob Leckie		
2002-03	10-19	6-12	Keydren "KeeKee" Clark	24.9	Bob Leckie		
2003-04	17-12	12-6	Keydren "KeeKee" Clark	26.7	Bob Leckie		
2004-05	15-13	10-8	Keydren "KeeKee" Clark	25.8	Bob Leckie		
2005-06	17-15	9-9	Keydren "KeeKee" Clark	26.3	Bob Leckie	67-107	.421
2006-07	5-25	3-15	Raul Orta	13.3	John Dunne		
2007-08	6-24	3-15	Wesley Jenkins	13.0	John Dunne		
2008-09	11-19	8-10	Wesley Jenkins	15.7	John Dunne	22-68	.244

● NCAA Tournament appearance ■ NIT appearance

PROFILE

Saint Peter's College, Jersey City, NJ
Founded: 1872
Enrollment: 3,111 (2,436 undergraduate)
Colors: Blue and white
Nickname: Peacocks
Current arena: Yanitelli Center, opened in 1975 (3,200)
First game: Dec. 12, 1930
All-time record: 950-903-1 (.513)
Total weeks in AP Top 20/25: 0

Current conference: Metro Atlantic Athletic (1981-)
Conference titles:
Metropolitan Collegiate: 3 (1967 [tie], '68, '69 [tie])
MAAC: 3 (1982, '84 [tie], '87)
Conference tournament titles:
MAAC: 2 (1991, '95)
NCAA Tournament appearances: 2
NIT appearances: 12
Semifinals: 1

TOP 5

G **Keydren "KeeKee" Clark** (2002-06)
G **Rich Rinaldi** (1968-71)
F **Bob Fazio** (1974-77)
F **Elnardo Webster** (1967-69)
C **Pete O'Dea** (1965-68)

RECORDS

	GAME		SEASON		CAREER	
POINTS	54	Rich Rinaldi, vs. St. Francis (N.Y.) (Feb. 13, 1971)	840	Keydren Clark (2005-06)	3,058	Keydren Clark (2002-06)
POINTS PER GAME			28.6	Rich Rinaldi (1970-71)	25.9	Keydren Clark (2002-06)
REBOUNDS	28	Juan Jiminez, vs. Upsala (1969-70)	409	Pete O'Dea (1967-68)	1,022	Pete O'Dea (1965-68)
ASSISTS	20	Jasper Walker, vs. Holy Cross (Feb. 11, 1990)	204	Jasper Walker (1988-89)	674	Jasper Walker (1987-91)

ESPN 239 SAGARIN

SAM HOUSTON STATE

After a long and storied history in lower-division hoops dating back to 1917, Sam Houston State joined D1 in 1987. It took a few years (and coaches) to get the Bearkats rolling, but since 2000 the only D1 squad in Texas with more wins on the hardwood is the UT Longhorns.

BEST TEAM: 1972-73 At a time when integrated teams were still uncommon in East Texas, Sam Houston State recruited African-American players such as James Lister, Robert White and Ron Battle. As seniors, the trio helped the Bearkats win their first 28 games and finish atop both the final AP and UPI NAIA polls before losing in the second round of the NAIA tournament.

BEST PLAYER: C James Lister (1969-73) Scrawny and shy, Lister was lightly recruited out of high school. But he proved to be an efficient scorer and instinctual rebounder in his college career—which coincides with the best four-year stretch in SHSU history. No wonder people still call it the Lister Era.

BEST COACH: Bob Marlin (1998-) When Marlin took over, SHSU had finished in the bottom half of the Southland Conference every season since 1991. That quickly changed. The Bearkats won the regular-season crown in Marlin's second year and again in 2003, and in 2004-05 began a streak of four straight top-three finishes.

GAME FOR THE AGES: The largest home crowd in SHSU history (5,068) came out for the 2003 Southland title game to see the regular-season champs take on runner-up Stephen F. Austin. SHSU let a 14-point second half lead slip away before winning on a dramatic Donald Cole three-pointer in OT, 69-66, to earn the school's first NCAA Tournament bid.

FIERCEST RIVAL: Sam Houston State and Stephen F. Austin first met in the hardwood edition of the Battle of the Piney Woods during the 1924-25 season, and have clashed at least once every season since, even as both teams rose from the NAIA ranks to D1. Amazingly, Sam Houston trails the series by just one game, 91–90 (according to the school's own records).

SEASON REVIEW

SEAS.	W-L	CONF.	COACH	SEAS.	W-L	CONF.	COACH
1917-47	*278-188*	*Undefeated 1917-18 to '19-20 (24-0)*		1960-61	8-17	6-8	Bruce Craig
1947-48	10-8		Jack Williams	1961-62	9-16	6-8	Bruce Craig
1948-49	13-9		Jack Williams	1962-63	13-9	8-6	Bruce Craig
1949-50	11-13		Jack Williams	1963-64	8-15	1-11	Bruce Craig
1950-51	8-14		Jack Williams	1964-65	7-18	1-11	Archie Porter
1951-52	6-17		Jack Williams	1965-66	17-11	8-4	Archie Porter
1952-53	8-15	3-7	Jack Williams	1966-67	20-10	11-3	Archie Porter
1953-54	12-12	5-5	Jack Williams	1967-68	9-22	3-11	Archie Porter
1954-55	14-12	6-6	Jack Williams	1968-69	17-16	7-9	Archie Porter
1955-56	7-19	2-10	Jack Williams	1969-70	20-8	13-5	Archie Porter
1956-57	13-13	7-7	Bruce Craig	1970-71	18-9	14-4	Archie Porter
1957-58	14-12	6-8	Bruce Craig	1971-72	22-4	16-2	Archie Porter
1958-59	8-16	5-9	Bruce Craig	1972-73	28-1	18-0	Archie Porter
1959-60	11-15		Bruce Craig	1973-74	17-11	10-8	Archie Porter

SEAS.	W-L	CONF.	SCORING		COACH	RECORD	
1974-75	14-18	6-8	Melvin Moore	16.1	Archie Porter	189-128	.596
1975-76	12-15	7-8	Melvin Moore	17.1	Dennis Price		
1976-77	10-16	6-9	Larry Cockrel	14.1	Dennis Price		
1977-78	8-18	3-12	Alvin Brooks	13.4	Dennis Price		
1978-79	5-22	3-12	Donnie Haywood	13.8	Dennis Price	35-71	.330
1979-80	15-12	8-7	Anthony Carroll	13.0	Bob Derryberry		
1980-81	23-8	12-5	Willie Whittenberg	18.4	Bob Derryberry	38-20	.655
1981-82	22-9	13-4	Anthony Carroll	15.7	Robert McPherson		
1982-83	20-10	11-6	Reggie Harris	17.4	Robert McPherson		
1983-84	17-10	9-6	Yommy Sangodeyi	16.8	Robert McPherson		
1984-85	16-12	5-4	Bruce Allen	20.1	Robert McPherson		
1985-86	27-6	9-1	Bruce Allen	16.8	Robert McPherson	102-47	.685
1986-87	16-12	6-4	Tracy Pearson	16.3	Steve Tucker	16-12	.571
1987-88	14-14	9-5	Tracy Pearson	14.1	Gary Moss		
1988-89	12-16	8-6	Derrick Williams	16.0	Gary Moss[a]	16-22	.421
1989-90	10-18	8-6	Derrick Gilliam	18.6	Larry Brown		
1990-91	7-20	5-9	Gibbiarra Outten	16.6	Larry Brown	17-38	.309
1991-92	2-25	1-17	Roosevelt Moore	12.3	Jerry Hopkins		
1992-93	6-19	4-14	Roosevelt Moore	14.9	Jerry Hopkins		
1993-94	7-20	7-11	Derick Preston	18.0	Jerry Hopkins		
1994-95	7-19	4-14	Mike Dillard	13.5	Jerry Hopkins		
1995-96	11-16	9-9	Frank Mata	15.6	Jerry Hopkins		
1996-97	8-18	7-9	David Amaya	10.7	Jerry Hopkins		
1997-98	9-17	7-9	Mike Dillard	16.3	Jerry Hopkins	50-134	.272
1998-99	10-16	7-11	David Amaya	16.2	Bob Marlin		
1999-2000	22-7	15-3	Jeremy Burkhalter	15.9	Bob Marlin		
2000-01	16-13	11-9	Seneca Wall	19.1	Bob Marlin		
2001-02	14-14	9-11	Donald Cole	16.4	Bob Marlin		
2002-03	23-7	17-3 ●	Donald Cole	17.5	Bob Marlin		
2003-04	13-15	8-8	Joe Thompson	15.3	Bob Marlin		
2004-05	18-12	11-5	Joe Thompson	16.0	Bob Marlin		
2005-06	22-9	11-5	Chris Jordan	14.3	Bob Marlin		
2006-07	21-10	13-3	Ryan Bright	14.8	Bob Marlin		
2007-08	23-8	10-6	Ryan Bright	11.7	Bob Marlin		
2008-09	18-12	12-4	Corey Allmond	15.3	Bob Marlin	200-123	.619

[a] **Gary Moss (2-8) and Jeff Dittman (10-8) both coached during the 1988-89 season.**
● **NCAA Tournament appearance**

PROFILE

Sam Houston State, Huntsville, TX
Founded: 1879
Enrollment: 16,633 (14,302 undergraduate)
Colors: Orange and white
Nickname: Bearkats
Current arena: Bernard G. Johnson Coliseum, opened in 1976 (6,100)
Previous: Bearkat Gymnasium, 1956-75 (1,100); Sam Houston State Gymnasium, a.k.a. the Old Wooden Gym, 1917-55 (N/A)
First game: 1917
All-time record: 1,124-1,023 (.524)
Total weeks in AP Top 20/25: 0
Current conference: Southland (1987-)
Conference titles:
Gulf Star: 1 (1986)
Southland: 2 (2000, '03)
Conference tournament titles:
Southland: 1 (2003)
NCAA Tournament appearances: 1
NIT appearances: 0

CONSENSUS ALL-AMERICAS

1973 **James Lister** (Little A-A), C

TOP 5

G **Scott Horstman** (1980-84)
G **Boney Watson** (1996-2000)
F **Donald Cole** (2001-03)
F **Robert White** (1970-73)
C **James Lister** (1969-73)

RECORDS

RECORDS	GAME		SEASON		CAREER	
POINTS	47	James Lister, vs. East Texas (1970-71)	674	James Lister (1970-71)	2,304	James Lister (1969-73)
POINTS PER GAME			25.0	James Lister (1970-71)	21.9	James Lister (1969-73)
REBOUNDS	30	James Lister, vs. Stephen F. Austin (1971-72)	473	James Lister (1971-72)	1,682	James Lister (1969-73)
ASSISTS	18	Bill Froechtenicht, vs. Abilene Christian (1975-76); Scott Horstman, vs. Dallas Baptist (1983-84)	241	Scott Horstman (1983-84)	813	Scott Horstman (1980-84)

ESPN 288 SAGARIN

SAMFORD

If change is good, then things at this small Southern Baptist Church-affiliated school outside Birmingham are great: new arena in 2007-08, new league (Southern Conference) in 2008-09 and renewed hope for more teams like the Marc Salyers-Reed Rawlings-led crew that made back-to-back NCAA Tourney appearances.

BEST TEAM: 1999-2000 Coach Jimmy Tillette's 21–11 Bulldogs returned five starters from a 20-win team and came through with huge victories over No. 15 St. John's—avenging a 1999 NCAA Tourney loss—and Alabama. Marc Salyers (1,604 career points), Reed Rawlings (1,493), Will Daniel (1,421) and Mario Lopez (1,026) guided Samford to its second TAAC title and NCAA Tourney.

BEST PLAYER: F Craig Beard (1982-85) He had three monster seasons after transferring from Tulane, finishing as the school's all-time leading scorer (1,925 points, 21.9 ppg) and in the top 10 in rebounds (519), hitting double figures in scoring in 84 straight games. In 2003, he was named one of the 30 best players in Alabama history.

BEST COACH: Jimmy Tillette (1997-) Samford's winningest coach is also the only one to lead the Bulldogs to consecutive 20-win seasons and the only one to take them to the NCAA Tournament. As the Bulldogs got ready to move into Corts Arena for the 2007-08 season, Tillette quipped, "It eliminates one of only two negatives against us—the lack of a new facility and my dysfunctional personality. Now it's down to just one."

GAME FOR THE AGES: The Bulldogs hadn't won the TAAC championship in 16 years when they faced Central Florida on Feb. 27, 1999, with an NCAA bid on the line. UCF had knocked the Bulldogs from the 1998 tourney, but Samford exacted revenge, 89-61, behind Salyers (22 points) and reserve Chris Weaver (20).

FIERCEST RIVAL: Samford and Jacksonville State started playing each other in 1921, and Samford leads its in-state foe, 51–37. Between 2000-01 and '08-09, the Bulldogs won seven of eight, their best stretch against the Gamecocks.

SEASON REVIEW

SEAS.	W-L	CONF.	COACH	SEAS.	W-L	CONF.	COACH
1901-46	*213-257*	*Best season: 25-5 in 1938-39*		**1959-60**	13-21		Walt Barnes
1946-47	11-10		Donald Lance	**1960-61**	23-1		Walt Barnes
1947-48	13-14		Herman Roberson	**1961-62**	12-9		Walt Barnes
1948-49	15-12		Herman Roberson	**1962-63**	13-9		Walt Barnes
1949-50	14-11		Herman Roberson	**1963-64**	7-16		Virgil Ledbetter
1950-51	13-12		Earl Gartman	**1964-65**	11-11		Virgil Ledbetter
1951-52	11-13		Earl Gartman	**1965-66**	12-14		John Edwards
1952-53	15-16		Earl Gartman	**1966-67**	11-13		John Edwards
1953-54	16-18		Earl Gartman	**1967-68**	9-13		John Edwards
1954-55	16-14		Earl Gartman	**1968-69**	5-21		Van Washer
1955-56	15-14		Virgil Ledbetter	**1969-70**	16-9		Van Washer
1956-57	12-15		Virgil Ledbetter	**1970-71**	16-10		Van Washer
1957-58	7-17		Virgil Ledbetter	**1971-72**	8-15		Van Washer
1958-59	4-10		Virgil Ledbetter	**1972-73**	5-20		Ron Harris

SEAS.	W-L	CONF.		SCORING		COACH	RECORD	
1973-74	6-20			Randy Morgan	19.2	Ron Harris		
1974-75	9-17			Julius Norman	19.2	Ron Harris	20-57	.260
1975-76	3-23			Earl Hill	21.6	Fred Crowell		
1976-77	7-19			Ervin Terry	15.4	Fred Crowell		
1977-78	8-19			Robbin Bumbry	15.0	Fred Crowell		
1978-79	10-15			Steve Barker	15.6	Fred Crowell	28-76	.269
1979-80	8-19	3-3		Steve Barker	15.9	Cliff Wettig		
1980-81	10-17	5-6		Steve Barker	17.9	Cliff Wettig	18-36	.333
1981-82	11-15	6-10		Steve Barker	22.5	Mike Hanks		
1982-83	13-15	6-8		Craig Beard	20.2	Mike Hanks		
1983-84	22-8	10-4		Craig Beard	21.9	Mike Hanks	46-38	.548
1984-85	18-12	7-7		Craig Beard	23.4	Mel Hankinson		
1985-86	16-13	8-6		Rembert Martin	14.9	Mel Hankinson		
1986-87	4-22	1-17		Rembert Martin	19.1	Mel Hankinson	38-47	.447
1987-88	7-20	4-14		Arnold Hamilton	19.1	Ed McLean		
1988-89	8-19	5-13		Arnold Hamilton	15.5	Ed McLean		
1989-90	6-22	4-12		Arnold Hamilton	13.5	Ed McLean		
1990-91	6-22	2-12		Tim Donlon	15.1	Ed McLean	27-83	.245
1991-92	11-18	7-7		Bubba Sheafe	15.7	John Brady		
1992-93	17-10	7-5		Bubba Sheafe	14.9	John Brady		
1993-94	10-18	4-12		Joey Davenport	19.4	John Brady		
1994-95	16-11	11-5		Jonathan Pixley	17.9	John Brady		
1995-96	16-11	11-5		Jonathan Pixley	20.0	John Brady		
1996-97	19-9	11-5		Jonathan Pixley	17.7	John Brady	89-77	.536
1997-98	14-13	9-7		Will Daniel	13.0	Jimmy Tillette		
1998-99	24-6	15-1	●	Reed Rawlings	16.5	Jimmy Tillette		
1999-2000	21-11	12-6	●	Marc Salyers	16.8	Jimmy Tillette		
2000-01	15-14	11-7		Marc Salyers	17.2	Jimmy Tillette		
2001-02	15-14	12-8		Chris Weaver	13.7	Jimmy Tillette		
2002-03	13-15	9-7		Phillip Ramelli	11.5	Jimmy Tillette		
2003-04	12-16	7-9		Phillip Ramelli	13.1	Jimmy Tillette		
2004-05	15-13	10-6		J. Robert Merritt	16.5	Jimmy Tillette		
2005-06	20-11	14-6		J. Robert Merritt	17.6	Jimmy Tillette		
2006-07	16-16	12-8		Randall Gulina	18.1	Jimmy Tillette		
2007-08	14-16	10-10		Travis Peterson	13.2	Jimmy Tillette		
2008-09	16-16	9-11		Bryan Friday	12.5	Jimmy Tillette	195-161	.548

● NCAA Tournament appearance

PROFILE

Samford University, Birmingham, AL
Founded: 1841 as Howard College
Enrollment: 4,500 (2,860 undergraduate)
Colors: Red and blue
Nickname: Bulldogs
Current arena: Corts Arena in Pete Hanna Center, opened in 2007 (5,000)
Previous: Seibert Hall, 1959-2007 (4,000)
First game: 1901
All-time record: 992-1,170 (.459)
Total weeks in AP Top 20/25: 0

Current conference: Southern (2008-)
Conference titles:
Trans America: 1 (1999)
Conference tournament titles:
Trans America: 2 (1999, 2000)
NCAA Tournament appearances: 2
NIT appearances: 0

TOP 5

G **Steve Barker** (1978-82)
G/F **Bill Lankford** (1954-57)
F **Craig Beard** (1982-85)
F/C **Clyde Frederick** (1960-62)
C **Dwayne Barnette** (1972-76)

RECORDS

RECORDS	GAME		SEASON		CAREER	
POINTS	48	Jim Harrison, vs. Chattanooga (Jan. 6, 1956)	703	Craig Beard (1984-85)	1,925	Craig Beard (1982-85)
POINTS PER GAME			23.4	Craig Beard (1984-85); Bill Lankford (1957-58)	21.9	Craig Beard (1982-85)
REBOUNDS	30	Clyde Frederick, vs. Huntingdon (Jan. 12, 1961)	388	Clyde Frederick (1961-62)	1,008	Dwayne Barnette (1972-76)
ASSISTS	12	Ervin Terry, vs. South Carolina State (Feb. 7, 1978)	140	Ervin Terry (1978-79)	433	Jerry Smith (2003-07)

ESPN 197 SAGARIN

San Diego

If you happened to be watching the broadcast of the Toreros' win over Gonzaga in the 2008 West Coast tournament finals, you couldn't miss it—a student holding up a T-shirt that read "We Live Where You Spring Break." Forgive the taunt, but after many lean years, how can one not brag with such a successful team in such a beautiful location?

BEST TEAM: 2007-08 Coach Bill Grier expected the world of his senior-less squad, pushing relentlessly in practice and teaching a hard-nosed defensive system in preparation for a tough schedule. The payoff: USD shook off an 8–11 start by winning 14 of its last 17 games, including upsets of the Zags in the conference final and Connecticut in the NCAA first round.

BEST PLAYER: F Mike Whitmarsh (1982-84) He achieved fame as a 1996 Olympic silver medalist in beach volleyball, but Whitmarsh also put USD hoops on the map by leading the 1983-84 Toreros to their first WCAC championship and NCAA Tournament. The two-time all-conference forward is the only Torero to lead his team in points (18.8), rebounds (7.3) and assists (6.0) in a single season, a trifecta he accomplished as a senior. Tragically, he took his own life in 2009 at age 46.

BEST COACH: Hank Egan (1984-94) Shutting down offenses was Egan's trademark at USD, where he won WCAC coach of the year honors in 1986 and '87. It's no coincidence that the NBA Spurs and Cleveland Cavaliers were known for their defense in the 1990s and 2000s, after Egan joined their teams as an assistant coach.

GAME FOR THE AGES: There were 1.2 seconds left in OT of the 2008 NCAA first-round matchup between No. 4-seed UConn and No. 13-seed USD when sophomore guard De'Jon Jackson drained a jumper from just inside the arc. That clinched San Diego's 70-69 OT win.

FIERCEST RIVAL: Since 1999, Gonzaga has lost twice in the WCAC tournament—both times to USD. The Toreros' 2008 final win was especially sweet, coming on their home court and snapping a 13-game losing streak to the Zags. Afterward, USD fans, many wearing "Go Toreros Beat Gonzaga" T-shirts, stormed the court. Still, Gonzaga holds a huge series lead, 52–21.

SEASON REVIEW

SEAS.	W-L	CONF.	SCORING		COACH	RECORD	
1955-56	11-15				Fon Johnson		
1956-57	13-16		Ken Leslie	13.5	Fon Johnson	24-31	.436
1957-58	14-11		Ken Leslie	16.9	Bob McCutcheon	14-11	.560
1958-59	5-18		Ken Leslie	15.7	Les Harvey		
1959-60	10-18		Jim Fleming	15.6	Les Harvey	15-36	.294
1960-61	11-16		Jim Fleming	18.7	Ken Leslie	11-16	.407
1961-62	6-20		Russ Cravens	13.3	Ed Baron	6-20	.231
1962-63	6-19		Lymond Williams	13.1	Phil Woolpert		
1963-64	13-13		Cliff Ashford	17.7	Phil Woolpert		
1964-65	15-11		Cliff Ashford	19.0	Phil Woolpert		
1965-66	17-11		Rick Cabrera	17.2	Phil Woolpert		
1966-67	14-11		Ted Fields	17.2	Phil Woolpert		
1967-68	15-10		Rick Cabrera	17.1	Phil Woolpert		
1968-69	10-15		Jeff Filzenger	13.6	Phil Woolpert	90-90	.500
1969-70	14-12		Gus Magee	14.4	Bernie Bickerstaff		
1970-71	10-14		Oscar Foster	16.7	Bernie Bickerstaff		
1971-72	12-14		Stan Washington	18.1	Bernie Bickerstaff		
1972-73	19-9		Robert "Pinky" Smith	17.9	Bernie Bickerstaff	55-49	.529
1973-74	16-11		Stan Washington	19.2	Jim Brovelli		
1974-75	11-15		Neil Traub	13.8	Jim Brovelli		
1975-76	15-10		Ken Smith	14.8	Jim Brovelli		
1976-77	20-7		Ron Cole	13.9	Jim Brovelli		
1977-78	22-7		Ron Cole	16.8	Jim Brovelli		
1978-79	19-7		Bob Bartholomew	14.7	Jim Brovelli		
1979-80	5-20 ✪	1-15	Bob Bartholomew	15.4	Jim Brovelli		
1980-81	10-16	3-11	Bob Bartholomew	13.7	Jim Brovelli		
1981-82	11-15	4-10	Rusty Whitmarsh	10.2	Jim Brovelli		
1982-83	11-15	5-7	Mike Whitmarsh	15.3	Jim Brovelli		
1983-84	18-10	9-3 ●	Mike Whitmarsh	18.8	Jim Brovelli	158-133	.543
1984-85	16-11	5-7	Anthony Reuss	12.6	Hank Egan		
1985-86	19-9	9-5	Scott Thompson	14.4	Hank Egan		
1986-87	24-6	13-1 ●	Scott Thompson	15.9	Hank Egan		
1987-88	11-17	3-11	Marty Munn	14.5	Hank Egan		
1988-89	8-20	2-12	Craig Cottrell	12.2	Hank Egan		
1989-90	16-12	9-5	John Jerome	19.3	Hank Egan		
1990-91	17-12	8-6	Anthony Thomas	14.7	Hank Egan		
1991-92	14-14	6-8	Kelvin Woods	13.8	Hank Egan		
1992-93	13-14	7-7	Gylan Dottin	13.1	Hank Egan		
1993-94	18-11	7-7	Doug Harris	14.4	Hank Egan	156-126	.553
1994-95	11-16	5-9	Doug Harris	17.2	Brad Holland		
1995-96	14-14	6-8	Brian Miles	11.4	Brad Holland		
1996-97	17-11	8-6	Brian Miles	14.6	Brad Holland		
1997-98	14-14	5-9	Brian Miles	16.8	Brad Holland		
1998-99	18-9	9-5	Ryan Williams	15.7	Brad Holland		
1999-2000	20-9	10-4	Andre Laws	12.9	Brad Holland		
2000-01	16-13	7-7	Andre Laws	10.3	Brad Holland		
2001-02	16-13	7-7	Andre Laws	18.2	Brad Holland		
2002-03	18-12	10-4 ●	Jason Keep	18.0	Brad Holland		
2003-04	4-26	1-13	Brice Vounang	16.9	Brad Holland		
2004-05	16-13	7-7	Brandon Gay	17.4	Brad Holland		
2005-06	18-12	6-8	Nick Lewis	17.6	Brad Holland		
2006-07	18-14	6-8	Ross DeRogatis	15.7	Brad Holland	200-176	.532
2007-08	22-14	11-3 ●	Brandon Johnson	16.9	Bill Grier		
2008-09	16-16	6-8	Gyno Pomare	13.8	Bill Grier	38-30	.559

✪ Records don't reflect games forfeited or vacated. For adjusted records, see p. 521.

● NCAA Tournament appearance

PROFILE

University of San Diego, San Diego, CA
Founded: 1949
Enrollment: 7,600 (4,962 undergraduate)
Colors: Torero blue, navy and white
Nickname: Toreros
Current arena: The Jenny Craig Pavilion, opened in 2000 (5,100)
Previous: USD Sports Center, 1963-2000 (2,500)
First game: 1955
All-time record: 767-718 (.516)

Total weeks in AP Top 20/25: 0
Current conference: West Coast (1979-)
Conference titles:
West Coast Athletic: 2 (1984, '87)
Conference tournament titles:
West Coast Athletic: 2 (2003, '08)
NCAA Tournament appearances: 4
NIT appearances: 0

TOP 5

G **Andre Laws** (1998-2002)
G **Stan Washington** (1971-74)
F **Mike Whitmarsh** (1982-84)
F/C **Scott Thompson** (1983-87)
C **Gus Magee** (1966-70)

RECORDS

RECORDS	GAME		SEASON		CAREER	
POINTS	37	Marty Munn, vs. Loyola Marymount (Feb. 27, 1988); Mike Whitmarsh vs. Loyola Marymount (Feb. 26, 1983)	540	Jason Keep (2002-03); John Jerome (1989-90)	1,725	Gyno Pomare (2005-09)
POINTS PER GAME			19.3	John Jerome (1989-90)	17.2	Mike Whitmarsh (1982-84)
REBOUNDS	21	Robby Roberts, vs. Northern Arizona (Nov. 29, 1982)	274	Jason Keep (2002-03)	864	Gyno Pomare (2005-09)
ASSISTS	14	Mike McGrain, vs. Winthrop (Dec. 30, 2003)	195	David Fizdale (1995-96)	465	David Fizdale (1992-96)

THE SCHOOLS

ESPN 140 SAGARIN

SAN DIEGO STATE

San Diego State is fab again, thanks to Steve Fisher's revival of a program that had fallen on hard times. In their glory days, the Aztecs were an NAIA force—so good that they reached three straight championship games. Over the decades, SDSU has produced enough NBA-worthy players that a dozen or so draft picks don't crack the school's all-time starting lineup.

BEST TEAM: 1940-41 The 24–7 Aztecs were stacked with two first-team NAIA All-Americas (Milton Phelps, Kenny Hale) and two second-teamers (Dick Mitchell, Harry Hodgetts). For SDSU, the third time proved the charm: It won the NAIA title in its third straight championship game appearance, beating Murray State 36-34.

BEST PLAYER: G Milton "Milky" Phelps (1937-41) Because of all-time assist leader Tony Gwynn (yes, *that* Tony Gwynn) and two-time leading scorer Art Linkletter (yes, *that* Art Linkletter), the program's best player isn't its most famous alum. But Phelps, a two-time first-team All-America, led the Aztecs in scoring three times and took them to three NAIA finals.

BEST COACH: Morris Gross (1929-42) Okay, the competition may have been sketchy (the barnstorming Broadway Clowns and the New Mexico Mines), but Gross coached the Aztecs during a glorious three-year run that included one NAIA championship, two runner-up finishes, victories against Cal, BYU and Fresno State, and a 5–1 record against UCLA.

GAME FOR THE AGES: In their third season under Steve Fisher, the Aztecs went 20–11 and reached the 2002 Mountain West tourney final. Behind Randy Holcomb (20 points, 12 rebounds), SDSU led UNLV by 15 with five minutes left. The Rebels mounted a comeback, but Deandre Moore hit two free throws to secure a 78-75 win and an NCAA bid.

FIERCEST RIVAL: It's the way of the Mountain West—every program measures itself against UNLV and usually comes out on the short end. The Rebels twice ousted the Aztecs from the NCAA Tournament—and lead the series with SDSU, 31–15.

SEASON REVIEW

SEAS.	W-L	CONF.	COACH	SEAS.	W-L	CONF.	COACH
1921-49	*372-216-1 NAIA title, 1941; runner-up '39, '40*			**1962-63**	17-9		George Ziegenfuss
1949-50	14-10		George Ziegenfuss	**1963-64**	15-11		George Ziegenfuss
1950-51	9-19		George Ziegenfuss	**1964-65**	14-11		George Ziegenfuss
1951-52	11-12		George Ziegenfuss	**1965-66**	14-12		George Ziegenfuss
1952-53	16-12		George Ziegenfuss	**1966-67**	24-5		George Ziegenfuss
1953-54	17-7		George Ziegenfuss	**1967-68**	21-6		George Ziegenfuss
1954-55	17-9		George Ziegenfuss	**1968-69**	10-15		George Ziegenfuss
1955-56	23-6		George Ziegenfuss	**1969-70**	13-13	3-7	Dick Davis
1956-57	17-10		George Ziegenfuss	**1970-71**	12-14	3-7	Dick Davis
1957-58	17-8		George Ziegenfuss	**1971-72**	18-10	7-5	Dick Davis
1958-59	17-8		George Ziegenfuss	**1972-73**	15-11	7-5	Dick Davis
1959-60	9-17		George Ziegenfuss	**1973-74**	7-19	4-8	Dick Davis
1960-61	10-14		George Ziegenfuss	**1974-75**	14-13	6-4 ●	Tim Vezie
1961-62	10-16		George Ziegenfuss	**1975-76**	16-13	5-5 ●	Tim Vezie

SEAS.	W-L	CONF.	SCORING		COACH	RECORD
1976-77	13-15	9-3	Presnell Gilbert	15.4	Tim Vezie	
1977-78	19-9	11-3	Kim Goetz	16.9	Tim Vezie	
1978-79	15-12	4-8	Kim Goetz	20.5	Tim Vezie	77-62 .554
1979-80	6-21	3-11	Eddie Morris	13.3	Smokey Gaines	
1980-81	15-12	8-8	Zack Jones	17.1	Smokey Gaines	
1981-82	20-9	11-5 ■	Keith Smith	12.8	Smokey Gaines	
1982-83	18-10	8-8	Michael Cage	19.5	Smokey Gaines	
1983-84	15-13	6-10	Michael Cage	24.5	Smokey Gaines	
1984-85	23-8	11-5 ●	Anthony Watson	17.5	Smokey Gaines	
1985-86	10-19	7-9	Anthony Watson	22.5	Smokey Gaines	
1986-87	5-25	2-14	Tony Ross	16.3	Smokey Gaines	112-117 .489
1987-88	12-17	5-11	Tony Ross	15.9	Jim Brandenburg	
1988-89	12-17	4-12	Mitch McMullen	14.6	Jim Brandenburg	
1989-90	13-18	4-12	Shawn Jamison	16.8	Jim Brandenburg	
1990-91	13-16	6-10	Marty Dow	17.0	Jim Brandenburg	
1991-92	2-26	0-16	Joe McNaull	13.1	Jim Brandenburg[a]	52-87 .374
1992-93	8-21	3-15	Joe McNaull	11.7	Tony Fuller	
1993-94	12-16	6-12	Carlus Groves	18.3	Tony Fuller	20-37 .351
1994-95	11-17	5-13	Marc Carter	13.3	Fred Trenkle	
1995-96	15-14	8-10	Kareem Anderson	13.7	Fred Trenkle	
1996-97	12-15	4-12	Jason Richey	17.6	Fred Trenkle	
1997-98	13-15	5-9	Jason Richey	17.4	Fred Trenkle	
1998-99	4-22	2-12	Matt Watts	14.5	Fred Trenkle	55-83 .399
1999-2000	5-23	0-14	Myron Epps	14.4	Steve Fisher	
2000-01	14-14	4-10	Randy Holcomb	15.9	Steve Fisher	
2001-02	21-12	7-7 ●	Al Faux	17.0	Steve Fisher	
2002-03	16-14	6-8 ■	Tony Bland	16.4	Steve Fisher	
2003-04	14-16	5-9	Aerick Sanders	16.1	Steve Fisher	
2004-05	11-18	4-10	Brandon Heath	18.3	Steve Fisher	
2005-06	24-9	13-3 ●	Brandon Heath	18.4	Steve Fisher	
2006-07	22-11	10-6 ■	Brandon Heath	19.3	Steve Fisher	
2007-08	20-13	9-7 ■	Lorrenzo Wade	14.8	Steve Fisher	
2008-09	26-10	11-5 ■	Kyle Spain[b]	14.0	Steve Fisher	173-140 .553

[a] Jim Bradenburg (2-19) and Jim Harrick Jr. (0-7) both coached during the 1991-92 season.

[b] Lorrenzo Wade averaged 14.1 ppg in 26 games; SDSU considers Spain (36 games) the scoring leader.

● NCAA Tournament appearance ■ NIT appearance

PROFILE

San Diego State University, San Diego, CA
Founded: 1897 as San Diego Normal School
Enrollment: 35,832 (29,481 undergraduate)
Colors: Scarlet and black
Nickname: Aztecs
Current arena: Viejas Arena, opened as Cox Arena at Aztec Bowl in 1997 (12,845)
Previous: San Diego Sports Arena (13,741) and Peterson Gym (5,000), 1968-97
First game: Dec. 20, 1921
All-time record: 1,228-1,033-1 (.543)
Total weeks in AP Top 20/25: 0

Current conference: Mountain West (1999-)
Conference titles:
Pacific Coast Athletic: 2 (1977 [tie], '78 [tie])
Mountain West: 1 (2006)
Conference tournament titles:
Pacific Coast Athletic: 1 (1976)
WAC: 1 (1985)
Mountain West: 2 (2002, '06)
NCAA Tournament appearances: 5
NIT appearances: 5
Semifinals: 1

FIRST-ROUND PRO PICKS

1984 **Michael Cage**, LA Clippers (14)

TOP 5

G **Brandon Heath** (2003-07)
G **Milton "Milky" Phelps** (1937-41)
F **Michael Cage** (1980-84)
F **Tony Pinkins** (1954-57)
C **Al Skalecky** (1965-68)

RECORDS

RECORDS	GAME		SEASON		CAREER	
POINTS	54	Anthony Watson, vs. U.S. International (Feb. 20, 1986)	686	Michael Cage (1983-84)	2,189	Brandon Heath (2003-07)
POINTS PER GAME			24.5	Michael Cage (1983-84)	18.8	Bob Brady (1951-54)
REBOUNDS	26	Michael Cage, vs. La Salle (Dec. 29, 1980)	394	Al Skalecky (1966-67)	1,317	Michael Cage (1980-84)
ASSISTS	18	Tony Gwynn, vs. UNLV (Feb. 5, 1980); Eric Martensen, vs. Chapman (Feb. 8, 1969)	221	Tony Gwynn (1979-80)	590	Tony Gwynn (1977-81)

ESPN 75 SAGARIN

SAN FRANCISCO

Innovative coaches (Pete Newell, Phil Woolpert) and trailblazing talent (Bill Russell, K.C. Jones) turned USF into a midcentury national power. The Dons rose again to No. 1 in the nation behind Bill Cartwright in the late 1970s, but a scandal begat by an assault conviction against star guard Quintin Dailey shut down the once-great program from 1982 to '85.

BEST TEAM: 1955-56 Just the third team at the time to win back-to-back NCAA titles, the Dons were a perfect 29–0, extending their winning streak to 55 games. Led by senior center Bill Russell, guard K.C. Jones and newcomer forward Mike Farmer, Phil Woolpert's team outscored its opponents by a 20-point average margin during the season. Blowing through the NCAA Tournament without the ineligible fifth-year senior, Jones, USF finished off Iowa, 83-71, in the championship game on the strength of Russell's stunning 26 points and 27 rebounds.

BEST PLAYER: C BILL RUSSELL (1953-56) Perhaps the greatest defensive player of all time, Russell averaged 20.7 points and 20.3 rebounds in his USF career, collecting a school-record 1,606 career caroms in total. The 6'9" center led the Dons to back-to-back titles (1955, '56) and 55 of their then-record 60 straight wins. His effect on the game was so thorough that the NCAA adopted what came to be known as the Russell Rule—widening the lane from six to 12 feet to keep players like Russell from dominating the paint.

BEST COACH: PHIL WOOLPERT (1950-59) Assembling one of the nation's first racially integrated starting fives, which included Russell and Jones, Woolpert amassed a 153–78 record in nine seasons while winning those back-to-back titles in 1955 and '56. In 1956-57, after Russell and Jones graduated, USF's win streak reached 60 games and the Dons returned to the Final Four.

GAME FOR THE AGES: In an epic battle of big men on March 12, 1955, Russell squared off against Oregon State's 7'3" center Swede Halbrook, in the NCAA West Regional final in Corvallis, on the Beavers' home court. Russell scored 29 points to Halbrook's 18, but in the end the hero was the 6'1" Jones, who tied up Halbrook to force a jump ball, then somehow tapped the ball to teammate Hal Perry, who protected the ball for the final seven seconds to preserve a 57-56 win.

HEARTBREAKER: On March 5, 1977, the No. 1 Dons, led by Cartwright at center, brought a 29–0 record to the regular-season finale at Notre Dame. Just as the Fighting Irish had famously ended UCLA's 88-game winning streak in 1974, they rode the emotions of their home crowd to upset USF, 93-82.

FIERCEST RIVAL: Saint Mary's in nearby Moraga is one rival, but it's USF's fellow Jesuit school, Santa Clara, that truly raises the Dons' dander. The rivalry dates back to 1908 and came to a boil in '55 when the Broncos' Ken Sears was chosen by the Northern California sportswriters as the West Coast Athletic Conference Player of the Year over USF's All-America Russell. Santa Clara leads the series, 107–96.

Perhaps the greatest defensive player of all time, Russell averaged 20.7 points and 20.3 rebounds in his USF career.

FANFARE AND HOOPLA: The Dons' Victory Song, sung on the Hilltop for more than half a century, is a direct link to the championship teams of the 1950s. Penned by an alum, the song crows, "We're out to win this game, here's why. For the Green and Gold, the Dons are going in to do or die."

FAN FAVORITE: G PHIL SMITH (1971-74) He walked on at USF after coach Bob Gaillard supposedly spotted him in a pickup game. An All-America as a senior, Smith scored 1,523 points in his career, then continued to be a Bay Area favorite as a two-time NBA All-Star with the Golden State Warriors.

CONSENSUS ALL-AMERICAS

1955, '56	**Bill Russell,** C
1982	**Quintin Dailey,** G

FIRST-ROUND PRO PICKS

1950	**Joe McNamee,** Rochester (10)
1950	**Don Lofgran,** Syracuse (12)
1956	**Bill Russell,** St. Louis (2)
1958	**Mike Farmer,** New York (3)
1965	**Ollie Johnson,** Boston (11)
1970	**Pete Cross,** Kentucky (ABA)
1973	**Phil Smith,** Virginia (ABA)
1978	**James Hardy,** New Orleans (11)
1978	**Winford Boynes,** New Jersey (13)
1979	**Bill Cartwright,** New York (3)
1982	**Quintin Dailey,** Chicago (7)

PROFILE

University of San Francisco, San Francisco, CA
Founded: 1855
Enrollment: 8,772 (5,477 undergraduate)
Colors: Green and gold
Nickname: Dons
Current arena: War Memorial Gymnasium, opened in 1958 (4,500)
First game: 1923
All-time record: 1,207-863 (.583)
Total weeks in AP Top 20/25: 133

Current conference: West Coast (1952-82, '85-)
Conference titles:
California Basketball Association: 4 (1953 [tie], '55, '56, '57)
West Coast Athletic: 12 (1958, '63, '64, '65, '72, '73, '74, '77, '78, '79, '80 [tie], '81 [tie])
Conference tournament titles:
West Coast: 1 (1998)
NCAA Tournament appearances: 16
Sweet 16s (since 1975): 2
Final Fours: 3
Titles: 2 (1955, '56)

NIT appearances: 5
Semifinals: 1
Titles: 1 (1949)

TOP 5

G	**Quintin Dailey** (1979-82)
G	**K.C. Jones** (1951-56)
F	**Mike Farmer** (1955-58)
C	**Bill Cartwright** (1975-79)
C	**Bill Russell** (1953-56)

RECORDS	GAME		SEASON		CAREER	
POINTS	47	Keith Jackson, vs. Loyola Marymount (Feb. 13, 1988)	755	Quintin Dailey (1981-82)	2,116	Bill Cartwright (1975-79)
POINTS PER GAME			25.2	Quintin Dailey (1981-82)	20.7	Bill Russell (1953-56)
REBOUNDS	35	Bill Russell, vs. Loyola Marymount, (March 3, 1956)	609	Bill Russell (1955-56)	1,606	Bill Russell (1953-56)
ASSISTS	15	Orlando Smart, vs. Portland (Feb. 23, 1991); vs. Fairleigh Dickinson (Dec. 8, 1990)	241	Orlando Smart (1991-92)	902	Orlando Smart (1990-94)

SEASON REVIEW

SEASON	W-L	CONF.	SCORING	COACH	RECORD	SEASON	W-L	CONF.	SCORING	COACH	RECORD
1923-24	14-4			James Needles		1930-31	12-6			James Needles	
1924-25	4-8			James Needles		1931-32	11-5			Phil Morrissey	11-5 .688
1925-26	8-6			James Needles		1932-33	10-7			Wally Cameron	
1926-27	8-7			James Needles		1933-34	8-5			Wally Cameron	
1927-28	16-5			James Needles		1934-35	7-14			Wally Cameron	
1928-29	21-2			James Needles		1935-36	11-9			Wally Cameron	
1929-30	9-4			James Needles		1936-37	10-7			Wally Cameron	

SEAS.	W-L	CONF.	POSTSEASON	SCORING		REBOUNDS		ASSISTS		COACH	RECORD	
1937-38	10-12	3-5								Wally Cameron		
1938-39	7-10	4-4								Wally Cameron		
1939-40	9-8									Wally Cameron		
1940-41	2-13									Wally Cameron	74-85	.465
1941-42	14-10									Forrest Twogood	14-10	.583
1942-43	13-9									James Needles		
1943-44	8-11									James Needles	113-62	.646
1944-45	no team											
1945-46	9-12									William Bussenius	9-12	.429
1946-47	13-14									Pete Newell		
1947-48	13-11									Pete Newell		
1948-49	25-5		NIT CHAMPION	Don Lofgran	14.7					Pete Newell		
1949-50	19-7		NIT FIRST ROUND	Don Lofgran	14.7					Pete Newell	70-37	.654
1950-51	9-17			Jerry Hickey	7.9					Phil Woolpert		
1951-52	11-13			Frank Evangelho	11.5					Phil Woolpert		
1952-53	10-11	6-2		Phil Vukicevich	12.9					Phil Woolpert		
1953-54	14-7	8-4		Bill Russell	19.2	Bill Russell	19.2			Phil Woolpert		
1954-55	**28-1**	**12-0**	**NATIONAL CHAMPION**	**Bill Russell**	**21.4**	**Bill Russell**	**20.5**			**Phil Woolpert**		
1955-56	**29-0**	**14-0**	**NATIONAL CHAMPION**	**Bill Russell**	**20.5**	**Bill Russell**	**21.0**			**Phil Woolpert**		
1956-57	21-7	12-2	NCAA THIRD PLACE	Gene Brown	15.1	Art Day	10.0			Phil Woolpert		
1957-58	25-2	12-0	NCAA REGIONAL SEMIFINALS	Gene Brown	14.2	Art Day	10.3			Phil Woolpert		
1958-59	6-20	3-9		Fred LaCour	17.1					Phil Woolpert	153-78	.662
1959-60	9-16	5-7		Charlie Range	10.5					Ross Giudice	9-16	.360
1960-61	17-11	8-4		Bob Gaillard	12.1	Ed Thomas	8.6			Peter P. Peletta		
1961-62	10-15	4-8		Bob Gaillard	17.6	David Lee	7.9			Peter P. Peletta		
1962-63	18-9	10-2	NCAA REGIONAL SEMIFINALS	Ollie Johnson	17.3	Ollie Johnson	14.3			Peter P. Peletta		
1963-64	23-5	12-0	NCAA REGIONAL FINALS	Ollie Johnson	20.5	Ollie Johnson	16.7			Peter P. Peletta		
1964-65	24-5	13-1	NCAA REGIONAL FINALS	Ollie Johnson	21.6	Ollie Johnson	16.2			Peter P. Peletta		
1965-66	22-6	11-3	NIT QUARTERFINALS	Erwin Mueller	18.4	Joe Ellis	11.9			Peter P. Peletta	114-51	.691
1966-67	13-12	7-7		Dennis Black	19.3	Dennis Black	12.5			Phil Vukicevich		
1967-68	16-10	10-4		Dennis Black	19.9	Dennis Black	9.9			Phil Vukicevich		
1968-69	7-18	3-11		Pete Cross	24.6	Pete Cross	16.0	Charlie Dullea	2.6	Phil Vukicevich		
1969-70	15-11	9-5		Pete Cross	21.3	Pete Cross	18.0			Phil Vukicevich		
1970-71	10-16	8-6		John Burks	15.4					Phil Vukicevich[a]	51-57	.472
1971-72	20-8	13-1	NCAA REGIONAL SEMIFINALS	Phil Smith	15.0	Snake Jones	14.0			Bob Gaillard		
1972-73	23-5	12-2	NCAA REGIONAL FINALS	Phil Smith	18.7	Kevin Restani	12.7	Mike Quick	3.6	Bob Gaillard		
1973-74	19-9	12-2	NCAA REGIONAL FINALS	Phil Smith	10.7	Eric Fernsten	10.0	John Boro	3.5	Bob Gaillard		
1974-75	19-7	9-5		Tony Styles	19.0	Marlon Redmond	11.2	Russ Coleman	4.8	Bob Gaillard		
1975-76	22-8	9-3	NIT FIRST ROUND	Winford Boynes	18.1	James Hardy	9.0	Russ Coleman	5.1	Bob Gaillard		
1976-77	29-2	14-0	NCAA FIRST ROUND	Bill Cartwright	19.4	James Hardy	10.9	Chubby Cox	5.4	Bob Gaillard		
1977-78	23-6	12-2	NCAA REGIONAL SEMIFINALS	Winford Boynes	21.7	Doug Jemison	9.7	Chubby Cox	5.4	Bob Gaillard	165-55	.750
1978-79	22-7	12-2	NCAA REGIONAL SEMIFINALS	Bill Cartwright	19.4	Bill Cartwright	15.7	Billy Reid	5.4	Dan Belluomini		
1979-80	22-7	11-5		Quintin Dailey	13.6	Wallace Bryant	10.4	Quintin Dailey	3.6	Dan Belluomini	44-14	.759
1980-81	24-7	11-3	NCAA FIRST ROUND	Quintin Dailey	22.4	Wallace Bryant	9.2	Ken McAlister	3.4	Pete Barry		
1981-82	25-6	11-3	NCAA FIRST ROUND	Quintin Dailey	25.2	Wallace Bryant	10.9	Ken McAlister	3.0	Pete Barry	49-13	.790
1982-83	no team											
1983-84	no team											
1984-85	no team											
1985-86	7-21	2-12		Anthony Mann	10.4	Peter Reitz	5.3	Robbie Grigsby	2.8	Jim Brovelli		
1986-87	16-12	6-8		Pat Clardy	13.3	Mark McCathrion	6.4	Rodney Tention	5.0	Jim Brovelli		
1987-88	13-15	5-9		Mark McCathrion	14.8	Pat Clardy	6.1	Rodney Tention	3.8	Jim Brovelli		
1988-89	16-12	8-6		Mark McCathrion	16.5	Mark McCathrion	7.3	Kevin Mouton	5.3	Jim Brovelli		
1989-90	8-20	4-10		Joel DeBortoli	18.3	Joel DeBortoli	7.1	Kevin Bell	3.6	Jim Brovelli		
1990-91	12-17	4-10		Tim Owens	20.1	Darryl Johnson	9.5	Orlando Smart	8.2	Jim Brovelli		
1991-92	13-16	4-10		Tim Owens	16.0	Darryl Johnson	11.4	Orlando Smart	8.3	Jim Brovelli		
1992-93	19-12	8-6		Orlando Smart	14.6	Kent Bennett	5.7	Orlando Smart	7.1	Jim Brovelli		
1993-94	17-11	8-6		Gerald Walker	17.9	Kent Bennett	6.5	Orlando Smart	7.6	Jim Brovelli		
1994-95	10-19 ⊗	4-10		Gerald Walker	17.9	John Duggan	6.9	Gerald Walker	4.3	Jim Brovelli	131-155	.458▼
1995-96	15-12 ⊗	8-6		John Duggan	13.7	Zerrick Campbell	7.3	Gerald Walker	4.7	Philip Mathews		
1996-97	16-13	9-5		Hakeem Ward	15.3	Damian Cantrell	7.7	Jamal Cobbs	3.8	Philip Mathews		
1997-98	19-11	7-7	NCAA FIRST ROUND	Hakeem Ward	17.0	Damian Cantrell	9.7	Jamal Cobbs	4.0	Philip Mathews		
1998-99	12-18	4-10		Gerald Zimmerman	18.3	James Lee	6.0	LyRyan Russell	4.5	Philip Mathews		
1999-2000	19-9	7-7		Kenyon Jones	16.5	Kenyon Jones	9.0	LyRyan Russell	4.1	Philip Mathews		
2000-01	12-18	5-9		Darrell Tucker	16.5	Darrell Tucker	6.8	Ali Thomas	4.2	Philip Mathews		
2001-02	13-15	8-6		Darrell Tucker	18.9	Darrell Tucker	10.1	LyRyan Russell	4.5	Philip Mathews		
2002-03	15-14	9-5		Darrell Tucker	18.5	Darrell Tucker	8.1	Jason Gaines	5.1	Philip Mathews		
2003-04	17-14	7-7		James Bayless	12.4	Tyrone Riley	7.0	Andre Hazel	5.2	Philip Mathews	138-124	.527▼
2004-05	17-14	6-8	NIT FIRST ROUND	John Cox	20.0	Tyrone Riley	8.7	Andre Hazel	3.1	Jessie Evans		
2005-06	11-17	7-7		Armondo Surratt	14.2	Alan Wiggins Jr.	8.3	Armondo Surratt	5.1	Jessie Evans		
2006-07	13-18	8-6		Antonio Kellogg	15.2	Alan Wiggins Jr.	7.2	Antonio Kellogg	3.6	Jessie Evans		
2007-08	10-21	5-9		Dior Lowhorn	20.5	Dior Lowhorn	7.4	Manny Quezada	4.6	Jessie Evans[b]	45-57	.441
2008-09	11-19	3-11		Dior Lowhorn	20.1	Dior Lowhorn	6.9	Dontae Bryant	3.1	Rex Walters	11-19	.367

[a] Phil Vukicevich (0-6) and Bob Gaillard (10-10) both coached during the 1970-71 season.

[b] Jessie Evans (4-8) and Eddie Sutton (6-13) both coached during the 2007-08 season.

⊗ Records don't reflect games forfeited or vacated. For adjusted records, see p. 521.

▼ Coaches' records adjusted to reflect games forfeited or vacated: Philip Mathews, 139-123, .531; Jim Brovelli, 132-154, .462. For yearly totals, see p. 521.

ESPN 143 SAGARIN

San Jose State

San Jose State is winless in three NCAA Tournament appearances. That's the bright side of this program's long history. In January 1989, 10 Spartans quit, citing coach Bill Berry's harsh style. A few months later, after the team finished 5–23, Berry was fired. Then in August, Berry's son Ricky, a former Spartans star coming off his rookie NBA season, killed himself following a dispute with his wife.

BEST TEAM: 1979-80 Early in the season, the Spartans took out Ralph Sampson and Virginia. The team lived up to that early promise in the Pacific Coast Athletic Association tournament finals, when big men Wally Rank and Sid Williams outdueled Long Beach State's Francois Wise and Michael Wiley to earn the school's first Tourney spot since 1951.

BEST PLAYER: G/F Ricky Berry (1985-88) He transferred from Oregon State to play for his father, Bill Berry. Three seasons later, Berry left the Spartans a three-time honorable mention All-America, thanks to his jaw-dropping range (45.9% from three) and solid all-around game (7.2 rpg, 3.2 apg).

BEST COACH: Hovey McDonald (1923-35) Following the program's launch in 1909, no Spartans coach had lasted more than two seasons before McDonald's arrival. In just his second year, McDonald won the small-college California Coast Conference title, the first of his four conference crowns.

GAME FOR THE AGES: On Feb. 16, 1980, Long Beach State outgunned the Spartans, 82-74, thanks to the triangle offense of 49ers coach Tex Winter. On March 1, with an NCAA bid on the line in the PCAA tournament finals, Bill Berry & Co. got another crack at that system—and they cracked it indeed, holding Long Beach State to 55 points in a two-point win.

FIERCEST RIVAL: In 1925, San Jose State and Fresno State played a four-game tournament to decide the CCAA title, with the Spartans winning three of those games. The two schools have been going at it ever since. Fresno State holds the series edge, 78–70.

SEASON REVIEW

SEAS.	W-L	CONF.	COACH	SEAS.	W-L	CONF.	COACH
1909-48	*360-261*		*Hovey McDonald 142-81 (1923-35)*	1961-62	13-11	5-7	Stu Inman
1948-49	22-13		Walt McPherson	1962-63	14-10	6-6	Stu Inman
1949-50	21-7		Walt McPherson	1963-64	14-10	6-6	Stu Inman
1950-51	18-12	●	Walt McPherson	1964-65	14-10	9-5	Stu Inman
1951-52	15-10		Walt McPherson	1965-66	11-13	7-7	Stu Inman
1952-53	15-8	4-4	Walt McPherson	1966-67	9-15	4-10	Dan Glines
1953-54	12-15	6-6	Walt McPherson	1967-68	13-12	8-6	Dan Glines
1954-55	16-9	7-5	Walt McPherson	1968-69	16-8	11-3	Dan Glines
1955-56	15-10	8-6	Walt McPherson	1969-70	3-21	0-10	Dan Glines
1956-57	13-12	7-7	Walt McPherson	1970-71	2-24	0-10	Dan Glines
1957-58	13-13	5-7	Walt McPherson	1971-72	11-15	5-7	Ivan Guevara
1958-59	5-19	1-11	Walt McPherson	1972-73	11-14	6-6	Ivan Guevara
1959-60	6-19	2-10	Walt McPherson	1973-74	11-15	2-10	Ivan Guevara
1960-61	11-14	5-7	Stu Inman	1974-75	16-13	4-6	Ivan Guevara

SEAS.	W-L	CONF.		SCORING		COACH	RECORD
1975-76	17-10	5-5		Ron Fair	15.3	Ivan Guevara	
1976-77	17-12	8-4		Ken Mickey	14.8	Ivan Guevara	
1977-78	8-19	4-10		Wally Rank	14.7	Ivan Guevara	
1978-79	7-20	4-10		Wally Rank	15.1	Ivan Guevara	99-117 .458
1979-80	17-12	7-6	●	Wally Rank	16.3	Bill Berry	
1980-81	21-9	10-4	■	Sid Williams	15.1	Bill Berry	
1981-82	13-13	7-7		Chris McNealy	15.1	Bill Berry	
1982-83	14-15	7-9		Chris McNealy	19.3	Bill Berry	
1983-84	10-18	6-12		Stony Evans	9.9	Bill Berry	
1984-85	16-13	10-8		Matt Fleming	13.4	Bill Berry	
1985-86	16-12	9-9		Ricky Berry	18.6	Bill Berry	
1986-87	16-14	10-8		Ricky Berry	20.2	Bill Berry	
1987-88	14-15	8-10		Ricky Berry	24.2	Bill Berry	
1988-89	5-23	1-17		Steve Haney	16.8	Bill Berry	142-144 .497
1989-90	8-20	5-13		Kenne Young	14.2	Stan Morrison	
1990-91	7-20	5-13		Terry Cannon	12.6	Stan Morrison	
1991-92	2-24	1-17		Terry Cannon	13.0	Stan Morrison	
1992-93	7-19	4-14		Daryl Scott	14.6	Stan Morrison	
1993-94	15-12	11-7		Terry Cannon	14.9	Stan Morrison	
1994-95	4-23	3-15		Brad Quinet	13.0	Stan Morrison	
1995-96	13-17	9-9	●	Olivier Saint-Jean	17.2	Stan Morrison	
1996-97	13-14	5-11		Olivier Saint-Jean	23.8	Stan Morrison	
1997-98	3-23	1-13		Michael Quinney	15.8	Stan Morrison	72-172 .295
1998-99	12-16	5-9		Terrance Richmond	12.2	Phil Johnson	
1999-00	15-15	6-8		Cory Powell	12.8	Steve Barnes	
2000-01	14-14	6-10		Cory Powell	13.6	Steve Barnes	
2001-02	10-22	4-14		Brandon Hawkins	16.0	Steve Barnes	39-51 .433
2002-03	7-21	4-14		Brandon Hawkins	13.0	Phil Johnson	
2003-04	6-23	1-17		Eric Walton	11.8	Phil Johnson	
2004-05	6-23	3-15		Marquin Chandler	19.6	Phil Johnson	31-83 .272
2005-06	6-25	2-14		Demetrius Brown	13.9	George Nessman	
2006-07	5-25	4-12		Carlton Spencer	14.3	George Nessman	
2007-08	13-19	4-12		C.J. Webster	11.3	George Nessman	
2008-09	13-17	6-10		Adrian Oliver	17.1	George Nessman	37-86 .301

● NCAA Tournament appearance ■ NIT appearance

PROFILE

San Jose State University, San Jose, CA
Founded: 1857
Enrollment: 32,746 (25,187 undergraduate)
Colors: Gold, white and blue
Nickname: Spartans
Current arena: Walt McPherson Court, opened in 1989 (5,000)
Previous: San Jose Civic Auditorium, 1979-88 (2,412); Independence High School, 1976-82 (5,000); San Jose Civic Auditorium, 1961-76 (3,200); Spartan Gym, 1930s-1976 (N/A)
First game: Dec. 2, 1909

All-time record: 1,070-1,210 (.469)
Total weeks in AP Top 20/25: 3
Current conference: Western Athletic (1996-)
Conference titles: 0
Conference tournament titles:
Pacific Coast Athletic: 1 (1980)
Big West: 1 (1996)
NCAA Tournament appearances: 3
NIT appearances: 1

FIRST-ROUND PRO PICKS

1971 **Darnell Hillman,** Golden State (8)
1988 **Ricky Berry,** Sacramento (18)
1997 **Olivier Saint-Jean,** Sacramento (11)

TOP 5

G **Carroll Williams** (1952-55)
G/F **Ricky Berry** (1985-88)
F **Stu Inman** (1946-50)
F **Chris McNealy** (1980-83)
F **Olivier Saint-Jean** (1995-97)

RECORDS

RECORDS	GAME		SEASON		CAREER	
POINTS	40	Wally Rank, vs. Sacramento State (Jan. 3, 1980)	702	Ricky Berry (1987-88)	1,767	Ricky Berry (1985-88)
POINTS PER GAME			24.2	Ricky Berry (1987-88)	21.0	Ricky Berry (1985-88)
REBOUNDS	28	Marv Branstrom, vs. Arizona State (Dec. 4, 1956)	376	George Clark (1951-52)	864	Marv Branstrom (1955-58)
ASSISTS	17	Ken Mickey, vs. Illinois State (Jan. 12, 1977)	203	Ken Mickey (1976-77)	477	Michael Dixon (1981-85)

ESPN 79 SAGARIN

SANTA CLARA

Say Santa Clara to a college basketball diehard and two things immediately spring to mind: Steve Nash and the school's shocking upset of Arizona in the 1993 NCAA Tournament. But Santa Clara is nearly as proud of its Cable Car Classic. Founded in 1967 to make the Bay Area a destination for high-profile teams across the country, the event has become the nation's longest-running holiday tournament.

BEST TEAM: 1951-52 Coach Bob Feerick's zone defense, quick-cut offense and young lineup (only one senior) came to life in the NCAA Tournament. The Broncos, featuring freshman forward Bob Sears, who two years later became the first hoops player featured on *Sports Illustrated*'s cover, beat UCLA and Wyoming before falling, 74-55, to eventual champion Kansas.

BEST PLAYER: G Steve Nash (1992-96) As a freshman, the South Africa-born, Canada-raised Nash guided the Broncos to the West Coast conference title and a Tournament upset of Arizona. A sweet shooter with a gift for making his teammates better, the two-time WCC Player of the Year (1995, '96) rates at or near the top of SCUs all-time leaders in three-pointers (263), three-point percentage (.401), free throw percentage (.867) and assists (510).

BEST COACH: Carroll Williams (1970-92) Much of Williams' success can be traced back to the mid-1970s when he implemented and coined the name of the now-ubiquitous flex offense. Predicated on continuous cuts and nonstop movement by all five players, the flex got the Broncos into the NCAA Tournament in 1987.

GAME FOR THE AGES: It was fun while it lasted, but after hanging tough with No. 2-seed Arizona in the first round of the 1993 NCAA Tournament, SCU came apart early in the second half, allowing the Wildcats 25 unanswered points to fall behind 46-33 with 15:26 left. Game over, right? Not so fast. The Broncos went on a 19-7 run to pull within 53-52, took the lead on Pete Eisenrich's jumper with 2:40 left, and held on for a 64-61 win even though both Nash and Kevin Dunne each missed two free throws late.

HEARTBREAKER: Featuring three future pros—the Ogden brothers (Bud and Ralph) and Dennis Awtrey—the Broncos stormed through the 1967-68 regular season, winning 25 of 26 games, including a win over No. 12-ranked Houston, by an average scoring margin of 15.7 points per game. They beat New Mexico in the NCAA Tournament, but the last impediment to the school's first Final Four was a big one. Lew Alcindor and UCLA spoiled Santa Clara's Big Dance, 87-66.

FIERCEST RIVAL: Santa Clara's rivalry with Saint Mary's comes down to simple numbers: 50—the approximate distance, in miles, along the San Francisco Bay that separates the two schools; 1910—the year the two teams first faced off (Saint Mary's won, 42-13); 205—the number of times the Broncos and Gaels have matched up, the most in either program's history. SCU leads overall, 131–74.

> ***The last impediment to the 1968 Final Four was a big one—Lew Alcindor and UCLA.***

FANFARE AND HOOPLA: SCU's student section, the Ruff Riders, deservedly gets credit for making the Leavey Center such a tough place to play, but they don't *always* come up clutch. During the Broncos' 81-73 loss to Gonzaga on Feb. 26, 2009, the home crowd drew two technicals for throwing items onto the court.

FAN FAVORITE: G Brody Angley (2004-08) Opposing fans often referred to Angley as Harry Potter because on the floor the 5'11" guard looked like a precocious child among adults. (Not to mention that Angley bears a passing resemblance to actor Daniel Radcliffe.) But the boy wizard was a lovable underdog and the taunt only endeared him more to the Ruff Riders faithful.

FIRST-ROUND PRO PICKS

1947	**Dick O'Keefe,** Washington (9)
1955	**Ken Sears,** New York (5)
1969	**Bud Ogden,** Philadelphia (13)
1970	**Dennis Awtrey,** Indiana (ABA)
1996	**Steve Nash,** Phoenix (15)

PROFILE

Santa Clara University, Santa Clara, CA
Founded: 1851
Enrollment: 8,685 (5,261 undergrad)
Colors: Red and white
Nickname: Broncos
Current arena: Leavey Center, opened as Harold Toso Pavilion in 1975 (4,700)
First game: 1905
All-time record: 1,338-940 (.587)
Total weeks in AP Top 20/25: 23

Current conference: West Coast (1952-)
Conference titles:
Northern California: 2 (1938 [tie], '39)
California Basketball Association: 2 (1953 [tie], '54)
West Coast Athletic: 4 (1960, '68, '69, '70)
West Coast: 3 (1995, '96 [tie], '97 [tie])
Conference tournament titles:
West Coast Athletic: 1 (1987)
West Coast: 1 (1993)
NCAA Tournament appearances: 11
Final Fours: 1
NIT appearances: 4

TOP 5

G **Harold Keeling** (1982-85)
G **Steve Nash** (1992-96)
F **Dennis Awtrey** (1967-70)
F **Kurt Rambis** (1976-80)
C **Nick Vanos** (1981-85)

RECORDS	GAME		SEASON		CAREER	
POINTS	55	Bud Ogden, vs. Pepperdine (March 3, 1967)	619	Dennis Awtrey (1968-69)	1,735	Kurt Rambis (1976-80)
POINTS PER GAME			22.4	Russ Vrankovich (1963-64)	19.9	Dennis Awtrey (1967-70)
REBOUNDS	30	Ken Sears, vs. Pacific (March 4, 1955)	467	John Bryant (2008-09)	1,152	John Bryant (2005-09)
ASSISTS	15	Steve Nash, vs. Southern U. (Dec. 9, 1995)	190	John Woolery (1993-94)	517	Brian Jones (1997-2001)

SEASON REVIEW

EASON	W-L	CONF.	SCORING	COACH	RECORD		SEASON	W-L	CONF.	SCORING	COACH	RECORD	
04-15	49-32		*Best early season, 18-6 in 1911-12*				1925-26	5-10			Russell Wilson	5-10	.333
15-16	11-5						1926-27	7-6			Harlan Dykes		
16-17	8-2						1927-28	9-4			Harlan Dykes		
17-18	4-0			Jerry Desmond	4-0	1.000	1928-29	10-4			Harlan Dykes		
18-19	10-3			Norbert Keefe	10-3	.769	1929-30	14-6			Harlan Dykes		
19-20	2-4			Robert Harmon			1930-31	15-3			Harlan Dykes		
20-21	1-5			Robert Harmon	3-9	.250	1931-32	14-4			Harlan Dykes		
21-22	12-5			Joe Aurreocoecha			1932-33	9-10			Harlan Dykes		
22-23	10-6			Joe Aurreocoecha	22-11	.667	1933-34	10-7			Harlan Dykes		
23-24	1-10			Eddie Keinholz			1934-35	13-4			Harlan Dykes	101-48	.678
24-25	6-9			Eddie Keinholz	7-19	.269	1935-36	12-6			George Barsi		

SEAS.	W-L	CONF.	POSTSEASON	SCORING		REBOUNDS		ASSISTS		COACH	RECORD	
36-37	13-7									George Barsi		
37-38	12-6	6-2								George Barsi		
38-39	15-5	7-1								George Barsi		
39-40	17-3									George Barsi		
40-41	15-7									George Barsi		
41-42	10-9									George Barsi		
42-43	10-9									George Barsi		
43-44	no team											
44-45	0-11									George Barsi	104-63	.623
45-46	8-6									Ray Pesco		
46-47	21-4									Ray Pesco		
47-48	11-11									Ray Pesco		
48-49	8-15									Ray Pesco		
49-50	14-8			George Stein	10.6					Ray Pesco	62-44	.585
50-51	9-15			Andy Collins	8.8					Bob Feerick		
51-52	17-12		NCAA FOURTH PLACE	Jim Young	11.8					Bob Feerick		
52-53	20-7	6-2	NCAA REGIONAL FINALS	Ken Sears	14.2					Bob Feerick		
53-54	20-7	9-3	NCAA REGIONAL FINALS	Ken Sears	18.3					Bob Feerick		
54-55	13-11	6-6		Ken Sears	22.3					Bob Feerick		
55-56	8-16	6-8		Rich Montgomery	14.8	Rich Montgomery	11.1			Bob Feerick		
56-57	15-7	10-4		Rich Montgomery	15.7	Dick Garibaldi	11.3			Bob Feerick		
57-58	13-11	6-6		Frank Sobrero	15.7	Jerry Bachich	7.0			Bob Feerick		
58-59	16-9	9-3		Frank Sobrero	17.0	Mel Prescott	6.9			Bob Feerick		
59-60	21-10	9-3	NCAA REGIONAL SEMIFINALS	Jim Russi	15.3	Joe Sheaff	11.7			Bob Feerick		
60-61	18-9	8-4		Gene Shields	10.6	Leroy Jackson	6.9			Bob Feerick		
61-62	19-6	8-4		Gene Shields	10.8	Leroy Jackson	7.2			Bob Feerick	189-120	.612
62-63	16-9	9-3		Joe Weiss	13.9	Leroy Jackson	10.9			Dick Garibaldi		
63-64	6-20	3-9		Russ Vrankovich	22.4	John Turner	8.5			Dick Garibaldi		
64-65	14-12	9-5		Mike Gervasoni	16.9	John Turner	7.5			Dick Garibaldi		
65-66	16-11	8-6		Mike Gervasoni	16.0	Larry Dunlap	7.7			Dick Garibaldi		
66-67	13-13	8-6		Mike Gervasoni	20.1	Bud Ogden	9.5			Dick Garibaldi		
67-68	22-4	13-1	NCAA REGIONAL FINALS	Bud Ogden	20.5	Dennis Awtrey	13.1			Dick Garibaldi		
68-69	27-2	13-1	NCAA REGIONAL FINALS	Dennis Awtrey	21.3	Dennis Awtrey	13.3			Dick Garibaldi		
69-70	23-6	11-3	NCAA REGIONAL SEMIFINALS	Ralph Ogden	21.9	Dennis Awtrey	14.1			Dick Garibaldi	137-77	.640
70-71	11-15	8-6		Mike Stewart	15.7	Mike Stewart	9.8			Carroll Williams		
71-72	17-9	11-3		Mike Stewart	21.2	Mike Stewart	9.7			Carroll Williams		
72-73	19-7	11-3		Mike Stewart	18.7	Fred Lavaroni	10.6	Alan Hale	3.2	Carroll Williams		
73-74	9-18	4-10		Remel Diggs	12.7	Remel Diggs	7.8	Jerry Bellotti	2.8	Carroll Williams		
74-75	10-16	4-10		Vester Robinson	13.6	Jerry Bellotti	8.9	Jerry Bellotti	4.3	Carroll Williams		
75-76	10-16	4-8		Glen Hubbard	11.9	Glen Hubbard	5.6	Eddie Joe Chavez	5.1	Carroll Williams		
76-77	17-10	9-5		Kurt Rambis	15.3	Kurt Rambis	11.6	Eddie Joe Chavez	5.8	Carroll Williams		
77-78	21-8	8-6		Kurt Rambis	13.7	Kurt Rambis	8.6	Eddie Joe Chavez	5.3	Carroll Williams		
78-79	13-14	6-8		Londale Theus	20.1	Kurt Rambis	8.4	John Kovaleski	3.4	Carroll Williams		
79-80	15-12 ⊗	8-8		Kurt Rambis	19.6	Kurt Rambis	9.9	Gary Gower	3.2	Carroll Williams		
80-81	14-13	7-7		Gary Mendenhall	15.9	Michael Norman	8.5	Bill Duffy	2.7	Carroll Williams		
81-82	16-11	7-7		Bill Duffy	15.2	Michael Norman	4.8	Lance Jackson	2.4	Carroll Williams		
82-83	21-7	9-3		Harold Keeling	14.9	Nick Vanos	6.6	Harold Keeling	3.6	Carroll Williams		
83-84	22-10	7-5	NIT QUARTERFINALS	Harold Keeling	18.3	Nick Vanos	9.9	Harold Keeling	3.8	Carroll Williams		
84-85	20-9	9-3	NIT FIRST ROUND	Harold Keeling	19.8	Nick Vanos	10.8	Steve Kenilvort	4.7	Carroll Williams		
85-86	12-16	7-7		Steve Kenilvort	16.5	Steve Kenilvort	6.1	Steve Kenilvort	4.0	Carroll Williams		
86-87	18-14	6-8	NCAA FIRST ROUND	Jens Gordon	11.4	Jens Gordon	7.3	Chris Lane	4.7	Carroll Williams		
87-88	20-11	9-5	NIT FIRST ROUND	Dan Weiss	12.7	Jens Gordon	7.4	Chris Lane	4.5	Carroll Williams		
88-89	20-11	7-7	NIT FIRST ROUND	Jens Gordon	16.8	Jens Gordon	8.3	Mitch Burley	3.5	Carroll Williams		
89-90	9-19	6-8		Jeffty Connelly	16.2	Ron Reis	6.9	Jeffty Connelly	3.6	Carroll Williams		
90-91	16-13	7-7		Rhea Taylor	19.0	Ron Reis	7.4	Melvin Chinn	3.0	Carroll Williams		
91-92	14-15	9-5		Ron Reis	13.0	Ron Reis	8.8	LaCoby Phillips	3.0	Carroll Williams	344-274	.557
92-93	19-12	9-5	NCAA SECOND ROUND	Pete Eisenrich	14.4	Pete Eisenrich	6.4	John Woolery	5.2	Dick Davey		
93-94	13-14	6-8		Steve Nash	14.6	Pete Eisenrich	6.0	John Woolery	7.0	Dick Davey		
94-95	21-7	12-2	NCAA FIRST ROUND	Steve Nash	20.9	Kevin Dunne	6.2	Steve Nash	6.4	Dick Davey		
95-96	20-9	10-4	NCAA SECOND ROUND	Steve Nash	17.0	Brendan Graves	7.2	Steve Nash	6.0	Dick Davey		
96-97	16-11	10-4		Marlon Garnett	17.4	Todd Wuschnig	5.8	Brian Jones	4.1	Dick Davey		
97-98	18-10	8-6		Brian Jones	15.6	Todd Wuschnig	5.8	Brian Jones	4.1	Dick Davey		
98-99	14-15	8-6		Nathan Fast	15.7	Alex Lopez	5.7	Delano D'Oyen	3.3	Dick Davey		
99-2000	19-12	9-5		Nathan Fast	14.1	Todd Wuschnig	5.7	Brian Jones	5.0	Dick Davey		
00-01	20-12	10-4		Brian Jones	16.0	Jaime Holmes	7.4	Brian Jones	4.1	Dick Davey		
01-02	13-15	8-6		Steve Ross	15.7	Jordan Legge	5.0	Kyle Bailey	3.9	Dick Davey		
02-03	13-15	4-10		Brandon Rohe	10.6	Jim Howell	6.2	Brandon Rohe	2.4	Dick Davey		
03-04	16-16	6-8		Doron Perkins	13.3	Jim Howell	5.6	Kyle Bailey	3.7	Dick Davey		
04-05	15-16	7-7		Doron Perkins	15.4	Doron Perkins	6.0	Kyle Bailey	4.2	Dick Davey		
05-06	13-16	5-9		Travis Niesen	18.9	Travis Niesen	6.6	Brody Angley	4.9	Dick Davey		
06-07	21-10	10-4		Sean Denison	10.8	John Bryant	6.7	Danny Pariseau	4.7	Dick Davey	251-190	.569
07-08	15-16	6-8		John Bryant	18.0	John Bryant	9.6	Brody Angley	5.3	Kerry Keating		
08-09	16-17	7-7		John Bryant	18.1	John Bryant	14.2	Perry Petty	2.9	Kerry Keating	31-33	.484

Records don't reflect games forfeited or vacated. For adjusted records, see p. 521.

ESPN 299 SAGARIN

SAVANNAH STATE

There's no escaping it—the Tigers have endured some of the lowest of lows of any D1 team, including an 0–28 season in 2004-05. But in 2008-09, coach Horace Broadnax had SSU pointed in the right direction, harkening to an era when winning wasn't such a rarity at the historically black college.

BEST TEAM: 1961-62 Their official record has been lost to time, but the Tigers' high-flying ways are legend to longtime fans. The team was built around the Chicago Five—James Dixon, Redell Walton, Willie Tate, Ira Jackson and Stephen Kelley—the first four of whom had played together since elementary school.

BEST PLAYER: F Harold "Bobo" Hubbard (1976-80) The 6'8" inside intimidator unquestionably had the best single season in Tigers history in 1978-79, averaging 24.6 points and 13.1 rebounds a game in leading SSU to the Southern Intercollegiate Athletic Conference (SIAC) championship. Bobo went on to a long career with the Harlem Globetrotters.

BEST COACH: Russell Ellington (1976-85) He rode his reputation as one of Georgia's top prep coaches into the Savannah State job, then proved himself by leading the Tigers to three SIAC regular-season and tournament titles. The coach of the Harlem Globetrotters from 1984 to '93, he was inducted into the Georgia Sports Hall of Fame in 2007—to the tune of "Sweet Georgia Brown."

GAME FOR THE AGES: With three games to go in the 2008-09 season, the idea of the 12–14 Tigers finishing above .500 for the first time as a D1 team seemed far-fetched. But after knocking off Florida Atlantic and Carver Bible College, SSU pulled off the feat on March 2 by beating North Carolina Central, 69-64.

FIERCEST RIVAL: During John Chaney's heyday at Bethune-Cookman during the 1950s, the Tigers and the Wildcats routinely participated in knock-down, drag-out classics. Upon SSU's move to D1, the two schools picked up where they left off, with the Tigers beating the Wildcats for two of their seven victories from 2002-03 to '03-04. B-CU leads the series 22–13 overall.

SEASON REVIEW

SEAS.	W-L	CONF.	SCORING		COACH	RECORD	
1964-65[a]	9-20				Leo Richardson		
1965-66	17-6				Leo Richardson		
1966-67	15-13				Leo Richardson		
1967-68	20-9				Leo Richardson		
1968-69	15-16				Leo Richardson		
1969-70	18-9				Leo Richardson		
1970-71	18-11				Leo Richardson	112-84	571
1971-72	9-13				Mike Backus		
1972-73	14-10		Kelsey Stevens	17.5	Mike Backus		
1973-74	9-14				Mike Backus		
1974-75	12-16				Mike Backus		
1975-76	8-14				Mike Backus	52-67	.437
1976-77	8-17		Sherman Grant	13.5	Russell Ellington		
1977-78	11-10				Russell Ellington		
1978-79	20-10		Harold "Bobo" Hubbard	24.6	Russell Ellington		
1979-80	24-5				Russell Ellington		
1980-81	25-4		Teddy Riley	18.6	Russell Ellington		
1981-82	12-11		Michael Stocks	17.8	Russell Ellington		
1982-83	16-9		Michael Stocks	16.5	Russell Ellington		
1983-84	15-13		Charlie Askew	13.6	Russell Ellington		
1984-85	17-12		Charlie Askew	21.9	Russell Ellington	148-91	.619
1985-86	17-8		Willie Jones	22.6	Jimmie Westley		
1986-87	12-15		Calvin Laing	14.4	Jimmie Westley		
1987-88	8-19				Bob Eskew		
1988-89	11-16		Steve Kelly	15.7	Bob Eskew		
1989-90	5-21		Anthony Roper	13.5	Bob Eskew	24-56	.300
1990-91	6-20		Chad Faulkner	16.7	John L. Williams		
1991-92	5-21		Young Rucker	14.8	John L. Williams		
1992-93	12-15		Chad Faulkner	16.0	John L. Williams		
1993-94	13-14		Samuel Mumford	13.2	John L. Williams		
1994-95	7-20		Kendrick Layne	15.7	John L. Williams	43-90	.323
1995-96	13-14		Kendrick Layne	16.4	Jimmie Westley		
1996-97	10-18		Marquez Sterling	13.1	Jimmie Westley	52-55	.486
1997-98	11-16		Reggie Smith	13.8	Jacques Curtis		
1998-99	9-18		Marquez Sterling	21.3	Jacques Curtis	20-34	.370
1999-2000	8-18		Toyian Williams	12.3	Samuel Jackson	8-18	.308
2000-01	4-21		M. Belle, T. Williams	11.6	Jack Grant		
2001-02	2-26		Alvin Payton	10.1	Jack Grant	6-47	.113
2002-03	3-24		Jamal Daniels	10.4	Ed Daniels Jr.		
2003-04	4-24		Jamal Daniels	12.1	Ed Daniels Jr.		
2004-05	0-28		Mark Williams	16.6	Ed Daniels Jr	7-76	.084
2005-06	2-28		Javon Randolph	17.0	Horace Broadnax		
2006-07	12-18		Javon Randolph	14.6	Horace Broadnax		
2007-08	13-18		Joseph Flegler	8.8	Horace Broadnax		
2008-09	15-14		Chris Linton	9.9	Horace Broadnax	42-78	.350

[a] Records from before 1963-64 have been lost.

PROFILE

Savannah State University, Savannah, GA
Founded: 1890
Enrollment: 3,456 (3,340 undergraduate)
Colors: Burnt orange and reflex blue
Nickname: Tigers
Current arena: Tiger Arena, opened in 2000 (6,000)
Previous: Wiley-Wilcox Gymnasium, 1967-2000 (N/A)
First game: 1927
All-time record: 514-696 (.425)

Total weeks in AP Top 20/25: 0
Current conference: Independent (2002-)
NCAA Tournaments appearances: 0
NIT appearances: 0

TOP 5

G **Stephen Kelly** (1958-62)
G **Javon Randolph** (2005-07)
F **Harold "Bobo" Hubbard** (1976-80)
F **Redell Walton** (1958-62)
C **Vincent White** (1966-70)

RECORDS

	GAME		SEASON		CAREER	
POINTS	34	Javon Randolph, vs. Longwood (Jan. 21, 2006)	510	Javon Randolph (2005-06)	876	Javon Randolph (2005-07)
POINTS PER GAME			24.6	Harold "Bobo" Hubbard (1978-79)	15.9	Javon Randolph (2005-07)
REBOUNDS	17	Joshua Obiajunwa, vs. Southeastern (Nov. 19, 2006); Sherard Reddick, vs. Florida A&M (Feb. 14, 2005)	300	Lance Fulse (1987-88)	747	Lance Fulse (1984-88)
ASSISTS	9	Josh Barker, vs. Mercer (Dec. 20, 2004); vs. IPFW (Nov. 13, 2004)	142	RaSha Williams (1996-97)	212	Joseph Flegler (2005-08)

ESPN 76 SAGARIN

SETON HALL

It's amazing to think that when Seton Hall was invited to be a founding member of the Big East in 1979, the athletic department wasn't even sure the school would be willing to pay the $25,000 entry fee. That's just one slice of the Pirates' often-surprising, always-colorful history, which also includes two Big East tournament titles, a memorable run to the NCAA Final in 1989 and such transcendent personalities as Aussie star Andrew Gaze and coach Bill Raftery.

BEST TEAM: 1952-53 Playmaker extraordinaire Richie Regan ran the show, smooth low-post operator Walter Dukes dominated both ends of the floor and the Pirates made history—avenging their loss in the 1951 NIT third-place game by beating St. John's, 58-46, in front of the then-largest crowd in Madison Square Garden history (18,496).

BEST PLAYER: C Walter Dukes (1950-53) Dukes ran track for Seton Hall, and it showed when he took to the hardwood. With uncommon dexterity and mobility for a big man, he initiated many Pirates fast breaks with his rebounds and routinely finished around the basket with both hands. As a senior, the All-America grabbed an NCAA-record 734 rebounds (22.2 per game) and was named MVP of the NIT. He remains the Pirates' all-time leading rebounder and ranks eighth in points. His coach, John "Honey" Russell, called him the best player he ever saw.

BEST COACH: John "Honey" Russell (1936-43, '49-60) Seton Hall's all-time leader in games and wins, Russell guided the Pirates to their lone national title in 1953. His 18-year reign featured a 41-game winning streak from 1939 to '41. Russell became the first coach of the Boston Celtics (1946-48) when Seton Hall discontinued basketball during World War II. In 1964, the former ABL defensive standout was elected to the Naismith Hall of Fame as a player.

GAME FOR THE AGES: In the 1988-89 Big East preseason coaches poll, Seton Hall was picked seventh among nine teams. But the Pirates defied the experts by riding a wave of unselfish, defense-oriented play—coaxed by the excitable P.J. Carlesimo—to the 1989 Final Four. There, facing Duke and Danny Ferry, the Pirates were down 18 points after 11 minutes before storming back for a 95-78 upset. Senior forward Daryll Walker clamped down on Ferry, limiting the Naismith Player of the Year to 13 points in the second half, while Andrew Gaze scored 20 points.

HEARTBREAKER: The "phantom foul" game brought Seton Hall's wild ride in the 1989 NCAA Tournament to an end in the Final. The Pirates held a 79-78 lead over Michigan with :03 left in OT when referee John Clougherty whistled Hall guard Gerald Greene for a bump on Rumeal Robinson. The Wolverines guard made both ends of the one-and-one and Walker's 21-foot shot at the buzzer missed the mark—a fittingly dramatic end to a back-and-forth instant classic.

FIERCEST RIVAL: From 1915 to '18, then 1919 to '30, Seton Hall coach Frank Hill doubled as the coach at Rutgers. When the two New Jersey schools played each other, Hill said he wanted only a fair game and for the best team to win. These days, the Pirates usually have the better team—but that doesn't mean they always win. Witness the Knights' 64-61 stunner of the Hall on March 9, 2008, won on a buzzer-beater three that broke RU's nine-game losing streak. The Pirates lead overall, 31–24.

FANFARE AND HOOPLA: With the Pirates playing off-campus "home" games at the Meadowlands and now Newark's Prudential Center, the once-cherished student tradition of throwing streamers onto the floor after the first Seton Hall bucket in each game has been lost. The threat of drawing a technical certainly also played a part.

FAN FAVORITE: F Andrew Gaze (1988-89) He became the face of Australian basketball during the Hall's run to the NCAA Final in 1989, charming fans with his affable personality and igniting the Pirates' offense with his scoring prowess.

THE SCHOOLS

CONSENSUS ALL-AMERICAS

1942	**Bob Davies,** G
1953	**Walter Dukes,** C

FIRST-ROUND PRO PICKS

1948	**Bobby Wanzer,** Rochester (10)
1949	**Frank Saul,** Rochester (12)
1953	**Richie Regan,** Rochester (5)
1953	**Walter Dukes,** New York (8)
1977	**Glenn Mosley,** Philadelphia (20)
1988	**Mark Bryant,** Portland (21)
1989	**John Morton,** Cleveland (25)
1991	**Anthony Avent,** Atlanta (15)
1993	**Terry Dehere,** LA Clippers (13)
1993	**Luther Wright,** Utah (18)
2001	**Eddie Griffin,** New Jersey (7)
2001	**Samuel Dalembert,** Philadelphia (26)

PROFILE

Seton Hall University, South Orange, NJ
Founded: 1856
Enrollment: 9,522 (5,245 undergraduate)
Colors: Blue and white
Nickname: Pirates
Current arena: Prudential Center, a.k.a. the Rock, opened in 2007 (9,800)
Previous arena: Continental Airlines Arena, 1981-2007 (20,029); Walsh Gymnasium, 1941-81 (2,600)
First game: December 9, 1903
All-time record: 1327-946-2 (.584)

Total weeks in AP Top 20/25: 95
Current conference: Big East (1979-)
Conference titles:
NJ-NY 7: 1 (1977 [tie])
Big East: 2 (1992 [tie], '93)
Conference tournament titles:
Big East: 2 (1991, '93)
NCAA Tournament appearances: 9
Sweet 16s (since 1975): 4
Final Fours: 1
NIT appearances: 15
Semifinals: 3
Titles: 1 (1953)

TOP 5

G	**Terry Dehere** (1989-93)
G	**Richie Regan** (1950-53)
F	**Mark Bryant** (1984-88)
F	**Nick Werkman** (1961-64)
C	**Walter Dukes** (1950-53)

RECORDS	GAME		SEASON		CAREER	
POINTS	52	Nick Werkman, vs. Scranton (Jan. 29, 1964)	861	Walter Dukes (1952-53)	2,494	Terry Dehere (1989-93)
POINTS PER GAME			33.2	Nick Werkman (1963-64)	32.0	Nick Werkman (1961-64)
REBOUNDS	34	Walter Dukes, vs. King's (Pa.) (Dec. 13, 1952)	734	Walter Dukes (1952-53)	1,697	Walter Dukes (1950-53)
ASSISTS	17	Paul Lape, vs. Saint Peter's (March 1, 1973)	197	Golden Sunkett (1962-63)	681	Shaheen Holloway (1996-2000)

SEASON REVIEW

SEASON	W-L	CONF.	SCORING	COACH	RECORD	
1903-16	*84-25-2*		*No losing seasons after inaugural year in 1903-04 (2-3-1)*			
1916-17	13-3			Frank Hill		
1917-18	8-5			Frank Hill		
1918-19	no team					
1919-20	10-3			Frank Hill		
1920-21	13-4			Frank Hill		
1921-22	14-2			Frank Hill		
1922-23	8-4			Frank Hill		
1923-24	6-7			Frank Hill		
1924-25	8-6			Frank Hill		
1925-26	7-5			Frank Hill		
1926-27	10-3			Frank Hill		
1927-28	9-4			Frank Hill		
1928-29	11-4			Frank Hill		
1929-30	13-9			Frank Hill	192-75-1	.718
1930-31	12-11			Dan Steinberg	12-11	.522
1931-32	10-9			Les Fries		
1932-33	8-4			Les Fries	18-13	.581
1933-34	no team					
1934-35	4-11			John Colrick		
1935-36	4-11			John Colrick	8-22	.267
1936-37	5-10			John "Honey" Russell		

SEAS.	W-L	CONF.	POSTSEASON	SCORING		REBOUNDS		ASSISTS		COACH	RECORD	
1937-38	10-8									John "Honey" Russell		
1938-39	15-7									John "Honey" Russell		
1939-40	19-0									John "Honey" Russell		
1940-41	20-2		NIT FOURTH PLACE							John "Honey" Russell		
1941-42	16-3									John "Honey" Russell		
1942-43	16-2									John "Honey" Russell		
1943-44	no team											
1944-45	no team											
1945-46	no team											
1946-47	24-3			Frank "Pep" Saul	11.6					Bob Davies	24-3	.889
1947-48	18-4			Frank "Pep" Saul	13.8					Jack Reitemeier		
1948-49	16-8			Frank "Pep" Saul	13.3					Jack Reitemeier	34-12	.739
1949-50	11-15			Sam Lackaye	12.6					John "Honey" Russell		
1950-51	24-7		NIT FOURTH PLACE	Walter Dukes	13.0					John "Honey" Russell		
1951-52	25-3		NIT FIRST ROUND	Walter Dukes	20.2	Walter Dukes	19.7			John "Honey" Russell		
1952-53	31-2		NIT CHAMPION	Walter Dukes	26.1	Walter Dukes	22.2			John "Honey" Russell		
1953-54	13-10			Harry Brooks	15.0	Richie Long	10.3			John "Honey" Russell		
1954-55	17-9		NIT FIRST ROUND	Dick Gaines	17.2	Richie Long	9.8			John "Honey" Russell		
1955-56	20-5		NIT QUARTERFINALS	Dick Gaines	20.3	Richie Long	10.3			John "Honey" Russell		
1956-57	17-10		NIT FIRST ROUND	Dick Gaines	21.1	Marty Farrell	10.7			John "Honey" Russell		
1957-58	7-19			Tom Cross	12.4	Tom Cross	13.1			John "Honey" Russell		
1958-59	13-10			John Rowley	11.9	Tom Cross	9.3			John "Honey" Russell		
1959-60	16-7			Art Hicks	17.1	Art Hicks	12.1			John "Honey" Russell	295-129	.696
1960-61	15-9			Hank Gunter	20.9					Richie Regan		
1961-62	15-9			Nick Werkman	33.0	Nick Werkman	17.2	Golden Sunkett	8.6	Richie Regan		
1962-63	16-7			Nick Werkman	29.5	N. Werkman, H. Slaton	12.6			Richie Regan		
1963-64	13-12			Nick Werkman	33.2	Nick Werkman	13.8			Richie Regan		
1964-65	12-13			Richie Dec	16.9	Richie Dec	11.6			Richie Regan		
1965-66	6-18	3-6		Terry Morawski	16.6	Terry Morawski	8.3			Richie Regan		
1966-67	7-17	3-6		John Suminski	17.7	Bill Somerset	11.0			Richie Regan		
1967-68	9-15	4-4		Gerry Mackey	13.7	Bill Somerset	12.6			Richie Regan		
1968-69	9-16	4-4		Mel Knight	17.7	Gary Cavallo	6.9			Richie Regan		
1969-70	10-15			Ken House	18.8	Ken House	15.8	Frank Cortes	2.6	Richie Regan	112-131	.461
1970-71	11-15			Ken House	21.0	Ken House	14.2	Frank Cortes	4.2	Bill Raftery		
1971-72	10-16			Ken House	25.1	Ken House	14.8	Roger Kindel	7.2	Bill Raftery		
1972-73	8-17			John Ramsay	15.1	Ray Clark	7.7	Paul Lape	7.7	Bill Raftery		
1973-74	16-11		NIT FIRST ROUND	Bill Terry	13.8	Glenn Mosley	14.2	Paul Lape	7.2	Bill Raftery		
1974-75	16-11			John Ramsay	19.1	Glenn Mosley	16.3	Tom Flaherty	4.1	Bill Raftery		
1975-76	18-9			Greg Tynes	18.6	Glenn Mosley	13.9	Tom Flaherty	4.4	Bill Raftery		
1976-77	18-11	3-1	NIT FIRST ROUND	Greg Tynes	21.9	Glenn Mosley	16.3	Nick Galis	4.8	Bill Raftery		
1977-78	16-11	1-5		Greg Tynes	20.5	Dawan Scott	10.2	Nick Galis	4.5	Bill Raftery		
1978-79	16-11	5-1		Nick Galis	27.5	Howard McNeil	8.1	Dan Callandrillo	4.3	Bill Raftery		
1979-80	14-13	1-5		Dan Callandrillo	19.4	Darryl Devero	7.0	Dan Callandrillo	3.7	Bill Raftery		
1980-81	11-16	4-10		Dan Callandrillo	16.1	Sir John Collins	5.3	Dan Callandrillo	2.6	Bill Raftery	154-141	.522
1981-82	11-16	2-12		Dan Callandrillo	25.9	Mike Ingram	6.3	Dan Callandrillo	3.6	Hoddy Mahon	11-16	.407
1982-83	6-23	1-15		Andre McCloud	16.6	Andre McCloud	6.6	Ken Powell	4.2	P.J. Carlesimo		
1983-84	9-19	2-14		Andre McCloud	14.8	Andre McCloud	6.0	Mike Jones	6.5	P.J. Carlesimo		
1984-85	10-18	1-15		Andre McCloud	20.8	Andre McCloud	7.2	James Major	3.9	P.J. Carlesimo		
1985-86	14-18	3-13		Andre McCloud	15.6	Mark Bryant	7.5	Gerald Greene	5.2	P.J. Carlesimo		
1986-87	15-14	4-12	NIT FIRST ROUND	James Major	17.6	Mark Bryant	7.1	John Morton	4.2	P.J. Carlesimo		
1987-88	22-13	8-8	NCAA SECOND ROUND	Mark Bryant	20.5	Mark Bryant	9.1	John Morton	4.7	P.J. Carlesimo		
1988-89	31-7	11-5	NCAA RUNNER-UP	John Morton	17.3	Ramon Ramos	7.6	Gerald Greene	5.1	P.J. Carlesimo		
1989-90	12-16	5-11		Terry Dehere	16.1	Anthony Avent	9.4	Oliver Taylor	3.3	P.J. Carlesimo		
1990-91	25-9	9-7	NCAA REGIONAL FINALS	Terry Dehere	19.8	Anthony Avent	9.9	Oliver Taylor	3.4	P.J. Carlesimo		
1991-92	23-9	12-6	NCAA REGIONAL SEMIFINALS	Terry Dehere	19.4	Jerry Walker	7.4	Bryan Caver	4.3	P.J. Carlesimo		
1992-93	28-7	14-4	NCAA SECOND ROUND	Terry Dehere	22.0	Luther Wright	7.5	Danny Hurley	3.4	P.J. Carlesimo		
1993-94	17-13	8-10	NCAA FIRST ROUND	Arturas Karnishovas	18.3	Adrian Griffin	7.8	Bryan Caver	3.3	P.J. Carlesimo	212-166	.561
1994-95	16-14	7-11	NIT FIRST ROUND	Adrian Griffin	15.3	Adrian Griffin	7.2	Danny Hurley	5.3	George Blaney		
1995-96	12-16 ⊗	7-11		Adrian Griffin	19.5	Adrian Griffin	8.3	Danny Hurley	5.2	George Blaney		
1996-97	10-18	5-13		Shaheen Holloway	17.3	Bayonne Taty	6.4	Shaheen Holloway	6.3	George Blaney	38-48	.442▼
1997-98	15-15	9-9	NIT FIRST ROUND	Levell Sanders	15.6	Duane Jordan	6.7	Shaheen Holloway	6.5	Tommy Amaker		
1998-99	15-15	8-10	NIT FIRST ROUND	R. Kaukenas, G. Saunders	13.5	Duane Jordan	7.0	Shaheen Holloway	5.0	Tommy Amaker		
1999-2000	22-10	10-6	NCAA REGIONAL SEMIFINALS	Darius Lane	15.3	Samuel Dalembert	6.0	Shaheen Holloway	5.6	Tommy Amaker		
2000-01	16-15	5-11	NIT FIRST ROUND	Eddie Griffin	17.8	Eddie Griffin	10.8	Andre Barrett	5.5	Tommy Amaker	68-55	.553
2001-02	12-18	5-11		Andre Barrett	16.9	Charles Manga	6.8	Andre Barrett	5.0	Louis Orr		
2002-03	17-13	10-6	NIT FIRST ROUND	Andre Barrett	16.7	Kelly Whitney	6.1	Andre Barrett	5.3	Louis Orr		
2003-04	21-10	10-6	NCAA SECOND ROUND	Andre Barrett	17.3	Andre Sweet	6.0	Andre Barrett	5.9	Louis Orr		
2004-05	12-16	4-12		Kelly Whitney	11.9	Kelly Whitney	6.3	John Allen	2.6	Louis Orr		
2005-06	18-12	9-8	NCAA FIRST ROUND	Donald Copeland	16.1	Kelly Whitney	7.9	Donald Copeland	4.5	Louis Orr	80-69	.537
2006-07	13-16	4-12		Eugene Harvey, B. Laing	16.5	Brian Laing	6.7	Eugene Harvey	4.2	Bobby Gonzalez		
2007-08	17-15	7-11		Brian Laing	18.6	John Garcia	7.0	Eugene Harvey	4.9	Bobby Gonzalez		
2008-09	17-15	7-11		Jeremy Hazell	22.7	Robert Mitchell	8.0	Eugene Harvey	4.9	Bobby Gonzalez	47-46	.505

⊗ Records don't reflect games forfeited or vacated. For adjusted records, see p. 521.

▼ Coach's record adjusted to reflect games forfeited or vacated: 39-47, .453. For yearly totals, see p. 521.

ESPN 203 SAGARIN

SIENA

The absence of a major sports team in New York's capital makes Saints hoops one of the top tickets in the Albany area. The Saints enjoy a healthy home-court advantage at the Times Union Center, a rowdy following and consistently solid coaching—a formula that's spurred Siena to NCAA Tournament wins in 1989 (over Stanford), 2008 (Vanderbilt) and 2009 (Ohio State).

BEST TEAM: 1988-89 The Saints' 25–5 record and run to the NCAA Tournament's second round is all the more remarkable considering that an on-campus measles outbreak forced them to play nine games in empty arenas and cancel two others they almost certainly would have won (Brooklyn, Northeastern).

BEST PLAYER: G Marc Brown (1987-91) Quick, competitive and a terrific ballhandler, "Showbiz" was a natural for Mike Deane's guard-oriented system. As a senior, he earned MAAC Player of the Year honors, and he finished his career as one of only three D1 players to record 2,000 points and 750 assists.

BEST COACH: Mike Deane (1986-94) As hands-on as they come, Deane dictated that the Saints offense be controlled through the point guard and Brown obliged, resulting in NIT and NCAA Tournament victories.

GAME FOR THE AGES: Many Saints fans assumed Siena's 80-78 upset of Stanford in the 1989 NCAA Tournament would never be topped. But the 2008-09 team did just that with its first-round, 74-72 victory over No. 8-seed Ohio State on March 20. Ronald Moore hit a three to tie it late in the first OT, then nailed the game-winner with 3.9 seconds left in the second overtime—from nearly the same spot.

FIERCEST RIVAL: Siena has ended Marist's season in the MAAC tournament five times between 1999 and 2007—a fittingly bitter twist to this rivalry. A brawl between the teams during the 1983-84 season forced a three-year hiatus in the series. When it was renewed in 1987, Siena went on the road to face 7'4" Rik Smits and possibly the best Marist team ever. The outcome? An 87-66 Siena victory. The Saints lead overall, 41–22.

SEASON REVIEW

SEAS.	W-L	CONF.	COACH	SEAS.	W-L	CONF.	COACH
1938-48	*85-48*	*No losing seasons*		1961-62	14-8		Dan Cunha
1948-49	22-7		Dan Cunha	1962-63	13-10		Dan Cunha
1949-50	27-5		Dan Cunha	1963-64	8-13		Dan Cunha
1950-51	19-8		Dan Cunha	1964-65	9-10		Dan Cunha
1951-52	24-6		Dan Cunha	1965-66	6-16		Tom Hannon
1952-53	10-11		Dan Cunha	1966-67	12-11		Tom Hannon
1953-54	7-14		Dan Cunha	1967-68	9-16		Tom Hannon
1954-55	3-13		Dan Cunha	1968-69	10-13		Tom Hannon
1955-56	7-13		Dan Cunha	1969-70	7-16		Gene Culnan
1956-57	5-15		Dan Cunha	1970-71	8-17		Gene Culnan
1957-58	5-15		Dan Cunha	1971-72	12-14		Gene Culnan[a]
1958-59	3-16		Dan Cunha	1972-73	15-8		William Kirsch
1959-60	3-18		Dan Cunha	1973-74	18-9		William Kirsch
1960-61	11-13		Dan Cunha	1974-75	16-9		William Kirsch

SEAS.	W-L	CONF.		SCORING		COACH	RECORD	
1975-76	11-11			Gary Holle	20.6	William Kirsch		
1976-77	9-15			Nelson Richardson	13.9	William Kirsch		
1977-78	13-10			Michael Catino	16.2	William Kirsch		
1978-79	14-12			Michael Catino	15.2	William Kirsch		
1979-80	14-14			Rod Owens	16.8	William Kirsch		
1980-81	17-10			Kevin McGraw	16.2	William Kirsch		
1981-82	15-13	8-7		Kevin McGraw	16.7	William Kirsch	142-111	.561
1982-83	12-16	6-8		Rod Mullin	14.0	John Griffin		
1983-84	15-13	8-8		Eric Banks	16.5	John Griffin		
1984-85	22-7	12-4		Doug Poetzsch	18.9	John Griffin		
1985-86	21-8	12-6		Eric Banks	15.7	John Griffin	70-44	.614
1986-87	17-12	12-6		Matt Brady	14.1	Mike Deane		
1987-88	23-6	16-2	■	Rick Williams	20.8	Mike Deane		
1988-89	25-5	16-1	●	Jeffery Robinson	19.8	Mike Deane		
1989-90	16-13	11-5		Marc Brown	16.9	Mike Deane		
1990-91	25-10	12-4	■	Marc Brown	23.3	Mike Deane		
1991-92	19-10	11-5		Doremus Bennerman	16.9	Mike Deane		
1992-93	16-13	8-6		Doremus Bennerman	18.4	Mike Deane		
1993-94	25-8	10-4	■	Doremus Bennerman	26.0	Mike Deane	166-77	.683
1994-95	8-19	5-9		Matt Gras	13.8	Bob Beyer		
1995-96	5-22	1-13		Jim Secretarski	11.2	Bob Beyer		
1996-97	9-18	4-10		Geoff Walker	12.8	Bob Beyer	22-59	.272
1997-98	17-12	10-8		Marcus Faison	16.1	Paul Hewitt		
1998-99	25-6	13-5	●	Marcus Faison	14.7	Paul Hewitt		
1999-2000	24-9	15-3	■	Marcus Faison	17.3	Paul Hewitt	66-27	.710
2000-01	20-11	12-6		Dwayne Archbold	14.9	Louis Orr	20-11	.645
2001-02	17-19	9-9	●	Dwayne Archbold	19.9	Rob Lanier		
2002-03	21-11	12-6	■	Prosper Karangwa	16.6	Rob Lanier		
2003-04	14-16	9-9		Michael Haddix	15.6	Rob Lanier		
2004-05	6-24	4-14		Jack McClinton	13.6	Rob Lanier	58-70	.453
2005-06	15-13	10-8		Antoine Jordan	17.1	Fran McCaffery		
2006-07	20-12	12-6		Michael Haddix	16.3	Fran McCaffery		
2007-08	23-11	13-5	●	Edwin Ubiles	17.0	Fran McCaffery		
2008-09	27-8	16-2	●	Edwin Ubiles	15.0	Fran McCaffery	85-44	.659

[a] **Gene Culnan (10-9) and Rit Keith (2-5) both coached during the 1971-72 season.**

● NCAA Tournament appearance ■ NIT appearance

PROFILE

Siena College, Loudonville, NY
Founded: 1937
Enrollment: 3,338 (3,338 undergraduate)
Colors: Green and gold
Nickname: Saints
Current arena: Times Union Center, opened in 1990 (8,065)
Previous: Alumni Recreation Center, 1974-97 (4,000); Washington Avenue Armory,1945-76 (3,500); Gibbons Hall, 1938-74 (N/A)
First game: 1938
All-time record: 968-789 (.551)

Total weeks in AP Top 20/25: 13
Current conference: Metro Atlantic Athletic (1989-)
Conference titles:
ECAC North Atlantic: 2 (1988, '89)
MAAC: 5 (1991 [tie], '99 [tie], 2000, '08 [tie], '09)
Conference tournament titles:
ECAC North Atlantic: 1 (1989)
MAAC: 4 (1999, 2002, '08, '09)
NCAA Tournament appearances: 5
NIT appearances: 5
Semifinals: 1

TOP 5

G **Doremus Bennerman** (1990-94)
G **Marc Brown** (1987-91)
G **Kenny Hasbrouck** (2005-09)
F **Lee Matthews** (1989-93)
F **Steve McCoy** (1985-89)

RECORDS

	GAME		SEASON		CAREER	
POINTS	51	Doremus Bennerman, vs. Kansas State (March 30, 1994)	858	Doremus Bennerman (1993-94)	2,284	Marc Brown (1987-91)
POINTS PER GAME			26.0	Doremus Bennerman (1993-94)	20.6	Gary Holle (1974-76)
REBOUNDS	30	Jack Mulvey (1964-65)	387	Billy Harrell (1949-50)	1,037	Lee Matthews (1989-93)
ASSISTS	15	Marc Brown, vs. Army (Feb. 3, 1990)	224	Ronald Moore (2008-09)	796	Marc Brown (1987-91)

ESPN 130 SAGARIN

SOUTH ALABAMA

Ignore South Alabama at your own peril. Just ask that *other* Alabama up in Tuscaloosa about Jeff Hodge's Shot Heard 'Round the World in the 1989 NCAA Tourney. All the Jaguars need now is a better draw; in eight NCAA Tourneys, they've faced three eventual champs.

BEST TEAM: 2007-08 Four all-conference picks—Brandon Davis, Domonic Tilford and senior guards Demetric Bennett and Daon Merritt—led the Jags to a 26–7 record, a share of the Sun Belt regular-season title and the conference's first at-large NCAA bid since 1994.

BEST PLAYER: F TERRY CATLEDGE (1982-85) In just three seasons, "Cadillac" finished as the school's No. 2 all-time scorer (1,866) and No. 1 all-time rebounder (932). Catledge led the Jaguars to the 1984 NIT and went on to an eight-year NBA career.

BEST COACH: CLIFF ELLIS (1975-84) In 1975, the Jags were considering dropping to Division II. Instead, they hired the 29-year-old former lead singer of a beach music band who had never coached in D1. Ellis turned things around with six straight winning campaigns, including three regular-season conference titles (one shared), two NCAA Tournaments and two NIT appearances.

GAME FOR THE AGES: The University of Alabama never played the upstarts from Mobile until the NCAA selection committee paired them up in the first round of the 1989 Dance. The Jags roared back from a 19-point deficit, and guards Junie Lewis and Jeff Hodge, known collectively as Peanut Butter and Jelly, blended perfectly when it mattered most: Lewis (19 points) found Sun Belt POY Hodge (29) for a three-pointer that gave USA a stunning 86-84 upset over the SEC champs.

FIERCEST RIVAL: Until Jacksonville left the Sun Belt after the 1997-98 season, it was South Alabama's fiercest in-conference rival. USA leads the series 32–26. Three years later, Middle Tennessee State joined the league and quickly became a pain in South Alabama's side. The Blue Raiders knocked the Jags out of the Sun Belt tournament four times between and 2001-02 and '08-09.

SEASON REVIEW

SEAS.	W-L	CONF.		SCORING		COACH	RECORD	
1968-69	11-12			Roger Webb	21.0	Rex Frederick		
1969-70	8-17			Kent Carson	19.4	Rex Frederick	19-29	.396
1970-71	14-12			Roger Webb	18.0	Jimmy Taylor		
1971-72	7-17			Andy Denny	20.5	Jimmy Taylor		
1972-73	14-11			Eugene Oliver	18.5	Jimmy Taylor		
1973-74	22-6			Eugene Oliver	17.3	Jimmy Taylor		
1974-75	19-7			Glenn Selph	14.6	Jimmy Taylor	76-53	.589
1975-76	18-9			Rick Sinclair	16.0	Cliff Ellis		
1976-77	17-10	3-3		John Mallard	16.2	Cliff Ellis		
1977-78	18-10	3-7		Gary Reese	13.9	Cliff Ellis		
1978-79	20-7	10-0	●	Rory White	19.0	Cliff Ellis		
1979-80	23-6	12-2	●	Ed Rains	18.8	Cliff Ellis		
1980-81	25-6	9-3	■	Ed Rains	18.5	Cliff Ellis		
1981-82	12-16	2-8		Rory White	16.9	Cliff Ellis		
1982-83	16-12	6-8		Michael Gerren	20.1	Cliff Ellis		
1983-84	22-8	9-5	■	Terry Catledge	19.9	Cliff Ellis	171-84	.671
1984-85	15-13	6-8		Terry Catledge	25.6	Mike Hanks		
1985-86	16-16	5-9		Jeff Hodge	12.2	Mike Hanks		
1986-87	14-14	6-8		Jeff Hodge	19.0	Mike Hanks	45-43	.511
1987-88	15-14	8-6		Junie Lewis	21.7	Ronnie Arrow		
1988-89	23-9	11-3	●	Jeff Hodge	21.7	Ronnie Arrow		
1989-90	11-17	5-9		Derek Turner	14.3	Ronnie Arrow		
1990-91	22-9	11-3	●	Kevin McDaniels	13.4	Ronnie Arrow		
1991-92	14-14	9-7		Derek Turner	16.6	Ronnie Arrow		
1992-93	15-13	9-9		Charlie Burke	16.0	Ronnie Arrow		
1993-94	13-14	9-9		John Blake	13.8	Ronnie Arrow		
1994-95	9-18	7-11		Anthony Foster	15.1	Ronnie Arrow[a]		
1995-96	12-15	7-11		Mark Neal	12.8	Bill Musselman		
1996-97	23-7	14-4	●	Mark Neal	11.9	Bill Musselman	35-22	.614
1997-98	21-7	14-4	●	Toby Madison	15.0	Bob Weltlich		
1998-99	11-16	6-8		Darrian Evans	20.3	Bob Weltlich		
1999-2000	20-10	13-3		Virgil Stanescu	13.4	Bob Weltlich		
2000-01	22-11	11-5	■	Virgil Stanescu	14.0	Bob Weltlich		
2001-02	7-21	2-13		Demetrice Williams	13.4	Bob Weltlich	81-65	.555
2002-03	14-14	7-8		Chris Young	15.9	John Pelphrey		
2003-04	12-16	6-9		Chris Young	12.8	John Pelphrey		
2004-05	10-18	6-9		Mario Jointer	16.6	John Pelphrey		
2005-06	24-7	12-3	●	Mario Jointer	13.4	John Pelphrey		
2006-07	20-12	13-5	■	Demetric Bennett	15.5	John Pelphrey	80-67	.544
2007-08	26-7	16-2	●	Demetric Bennett	19.7	Ronnie Arrow		
2008-09	20-13	10-8		Dominic Tilford	16.3	Ronnie Arrow	160-113	.586

[a] Ronnie Arrow (1-3) and Judas Prada (8-15) both coached during the 1994-95 season.

● NCAA Tournament appearance ■ NIT appearance

PROFILE

University of South Alabama, Mobile, AL
Founded: 1963
Enrollment: 14,003 (10,690 undergraduate)
Colors: Blue, red and white
Nickname: Jaguars
Current arena: Mitchell Center, opened in 1999 (10,041)
Previous: Jaguar Gymnasium & Mobile Civic Center, 1968-99 (3,138; 10,000)
First game: Dec. 2, 1968
All-time record: 675-491 (.579)
Total weeks in AP Top 20/25: 8

Current conference: Sun Belt (1976-)
Conference titles:
Sun Belt: 12 (1979, '80, '81 [tie], 89, '91, '97 [tie], '98 [tie], 2000 [tie], '01 [tie], '06 [tie], '07 [tie], '08 [tie])
Conference tournament titles:
Sun Belt: 5 (1989, '91, '97, '98, 2006)
NCAA Tournament appearances: 8
NIT appearances: 4

FIRST-ROUND PRO PICKS

1985 **Terry Catledge**, Philadelphia (21)

TOP 5

G **Jeff Hodge** (1985-89)
G **Junie Lewis** (1986-89)
F **Terry Catledge** (1982-85)
F **Ed Rains** (1977-81)
F **Rory White** (1977-82)

RECORDS

RECORDS	GAME		SEASON		CAREER	
POINTS	46	Eugene Oliver, vs. Southern Miss (Feb. 14, 1974)	718	Terry Catledge (1984-85)	2,221	Jeff Hodge (1985-89)
POINTS PER GAME			25.6	Terry Catledge (1984-85)	21.7	Terry Catledge (1982-85)
REBOUNDS	28	Leon Williams, vs. Texas-Arlington (Dec. 30, 1972)	332	Terry Catledge (1983-84)	932	Terry Catledge (1982-85)
ASSISTS	19	Herb Andrew, vs. Mississippi Valley State (Feb. 2, 1981)	203	Anthony Foster (1994-95)	566	Cedric Yelding (1989-93)

THE SCHOOLS

ESPN 91 SAGARIN

SOUTH CAROLINA

Fans of a certain age remember when South Carolina could claim Atlantic Coast supremacy over North Carolina—mainly because the gruff New Yorker who made the Tar Heels a power in the 1950s did the same for the Gamecocks in the '60s and '70s. Frank McGuire simply made Columbia, rather than Chapel Hill, the terminus of his famous New York City area recruiting pipeline, turning tough city boys such as Bobby Cremins, John Roche, Brian Winters and Mike Dunleavy Sr. into proud—and productive—South Carolina Gamecocks.

BEST TEAM: 1970-71 You've got to hand it to the Gamecocks: They left the ACC on a high note. With two-time conference player of the year John Roche at the point, Kevin Joyce as the off guard and Tom Owens in the paint, McGuire's team got past rival North Carolina for the ACC tournament crown to inflate their record to 23–4. The run ended with a 79-64 loss to Penn in the NCAA East Regional semifinals.

BEST PLAYER: F ALEX ENGLISH (1972-76) South Carolina knew it had a star in English; the school retired his jersey in the season following his final game. English started every one of 111 games in his four seasons, scoring more points (1,972) than any Gamecock before him (B.J. McKie passed him 23 years later). English is still one of only five South Carolina players to total more than 1,000 points and rebounds. Only a second-round draft pick (Milwaukee), he ended up an eight-time NBA All-Star with the Denver Nuggets.

BEST COACH: FRANK MCGUIRE (1964-80) He had already attained legend status for his coaching at St. John's and North Carolina—where he ranks third in victories behind Roy Williams and Dean Smith. How many more wins did McGuire have left for South Carolina? Only 283 in 16 seasons, making him the winningest coach in school history. He took SC to four consecutive NCAA Tournaments from 1971 to '74, good enough to have the venue at Carolina Coliseum renamed the Frank McGuire Arena.

GAME FOR THE AGES: Nearly four decades later, folks in both Carolinas are still in awe of the way the ACC title game ended on March, 13, 1971. The Tar Heels held a 51-50 lead with :06 left when the Gamecocks' 6'3" Kevin Joyce forced a jump ball with 6'10" Lee Dedmon. Before the tip, McGuire told Joyce to "jump to the moon." Mission accomplished: Joyce tapped the ball to Tom Owens under the basket, who laid in the game winner.

HEARTBREAKER: The Gamecocks skated through a 14–0 ACC regular season in 1969-70 before NC State pulled the plug in the ACC tournament final. The 42-39 double OT loss kept South Carolina out of the NCAA Tournament.

FIERCEST RIVAL: Something about tiger paws and Clemson orange turns Gamecocks fans a deep shade of red. Just a few hours' drive apart, the teams meet every December with Palmetto State pride on the line. South Carolina leads the rivalry, 86–73.

FANFARE AND HOOPLA: The flag-waving, bearded superfan has patrolled an area behind one of the baskets since the very first game in the old Coliseum, in 1968. His name is Carlton Thompson, but fans know him as Baseline Jesus—although his frequent foot-to-floor activity inspires some to call him the Stomper.

FAN FAVORITE: G B.J. MCKIE (1995-99) His perpetual smile and easygoing playing style made fans love McKie, a native Columbian. Oh, and he's also the school's all-time leading scorer (2,119 points).

CONSENSUS ALL-AMERICAS

1972	**Tom Riker**, F

FIRST-ROUND PRO PICKS

1968	**Gary Gregor**, Phoenix (8)
1968	**Skip Harlicka**, Atlanta (13)
1971	**John Roche**, Phoenix (14)
1972	**Tom Riker**, New York (8)
1972	**Tom Riker**, Carolina (ABA)
1973	**Kevin Joyce**, Golden State (11)
1974	**Brian Winters**, L.A. Lakers (12)
1974	**Brian Winters**, New York (ABA)
1975	**Tom Boswell**, Boston (17)
2006	**Renaldo Balkman**, New York (20)

PROFILE

University of South Carolina, Columbia, SC
Founded: 1801
Enrollment: 25,077 (18,826 undergraduate)
Colors: Garnet and black
Nickname: Gamecocks
Current arena: The Colonial Center, opened in 2002 (18,000)
Previous: Carolina Coliseum, 1969-2002 (12,401); Carolina Fieldhouse, 1927-69 (3,200); Carolina Gymnasium, now Longstreet Theater, 1912-27 (N/A)
First game: Oct. 30, 1908

All-time record: 1,258-1,096-1 (.534)
Total weeks in AP Top 20/25: 118
Current conference: Southeastern (1991-)
Conference titles:
Southern: 4 (1927, '33, '34, '45)
ACC: 1 (1970)
SEC: 1 (1997)
Conference tournament titles:
Southern: 3 (1933, '35, '36)
ACC: 1 (1971)
NCAA Tournament appearances: 8

NIT appearances: 11
Semifinals: 3
Titles: 2 (2005, '06)

TOP 5

G	**B.J. McKie** (1995-99)
G	**John Roche** (1968-71)
F	**Alex English** (1972-76)
F	**Tom Owens** (1968-71)
F	**Grady Wallace** (1955-57)

RECORDS	GAME		SEASON		CAREER	
POINTS	56	John Roche, vs. Furman (Feb. 4, 1971)	906	Grady Wallace (1956-57)	2,119	B.J. McKie (1995-99)
POINTS PER GAME			31.2	Grady Wallace (1956-57)	28.0	Grady Wallace (1955-57)
REBOUNDS	35	Gary Gregor, vs. Elon (Dec. 19, 1966)	434	Lee Collins (1954-55)	1,159	Lee Collins (1952-56)
ASSISTS	17	Jack Gilloon, vs. Georgia Southern (Feb. 28, 1976)	182	Gerald Peacock (1982-83)	543	Melvin Watson (1994-98)

THE SCHOOLS

SEASON REVIEW

SEASON	W-L	CONF.	SCORING		COACH	RECORD	
1908-16	*17-29-1*		*Only one winning season (5-4-1 in 1913-14)*				
1916-17	7-8		R.L. Bowen	11.0	Dixon Foster		
1917-18	8-5		Clark Waring	12.2	Dixon Foster		
1918-19	4-7		Clark Waring	14.9	Dixon Foster		
1919-20	7-11		Rube Skinner	10.0	Dixon Foster	26-31	.456
1920-21	7-11		Thornton Sparkman	6.2	Sol Metzger	7-11	.389
1921-22	7-12		Thornton Sparkman	13.3	Lana A. Sims	7-12	.368
1922-23	6-13	0-3	Thornton Sparkman	13.0	Jack Crawford		
1923-24	11-9	2-2	Jack Wright	10.3	Jack Crawford	17-22	.436
1924-25	10-7	4-2	Jack Wright	14.0	Branch Bocock		
1925-26	9-5	4-2	Buster Holcombe	8.4	Branch Bocock		
1926-27	14-4	9-1	Buster Holcombe	10.0	Branch Bocock	33-16	.673
1927-28	8-12	4-7	Buster Holcombe	10.9	A. Burnet Stoney	8-12	.400
1928-29	8-13	4-9	Lou White	12.2	A.W. Norman		
1929-30	6-10	0-6	Dave Rembert	7.2	A.W. Norman		
1930-31	1-17	1-12	John DuPre	4.8	A.W. Norman		
1931-32	9-7	2-2	Grayson Wolf	7.7	A.W. Norman		
1932-33	17-2	4-0	Freddie Tompkins	14.2	Billy Laval	17-2	.895
1933-34	18-1	6-0	Freddie Tompkins	14.1	A.W. Norman		
1934-35	15-9	5-7	Dana Henderson	14.1	A.W. Norman	57-57	.500
1935-36	11-8	1-6	Bernard James	8.1	Ted Petoskey		
1936-37	13-7	7-4	Tom Hutto	8.5	Ted Petoskey		

SEAS.	W-L	CONF.	POSTSEASON	SCORING		REBOUNDS		ASSISTS		COACH	RECORD	
1937-38	3-21	1-13		Tom Hutto	9.3					Ted Petoskey		
1938-39	5-18	2-8		Tom Hutto	8.2					Ted Petoskey		
1939-40	5-13	3-10		Preston Westmoreland	10.8					Ted Petoskey	37-67	.356
1940-41	15-9	8-3		Preston Westmoreland	15.5					Frank Johnson		
1941-42	12-9	8-4		Preston Westmoreland	13.4					Frank Johnson		
1942-43	13-6	6-3		Henry Martin	10.1					Frank Johnson[a]		
1943-44	13-2	1-2		T.S. Ary	14.4					Lt. Henry Findley	13-2	.867
1944-45	19-3	9-0		Charley Sokol	13.0					Johnnie McMillan	19-3	.864
1945-46	9-11	4-7		Steve Trewhella	7.5					Dick Anderson[b]	4-8	.667
1946-47	16-9	7-5		Al Adams	11.8					Frank Johnson		
1947-48	12-11	8-7		Henry Martin	10.8					Frank Johnson		
1948-49	10-12	7-6		Jim Slaughter	17.3					Frank Johnson		
1949-50	13-9	12-5		Jim Slaughter	20.0					Frank Johnson		
1950-51	13-12	12-7		Jim Slaughter	22.8	Jim Slaughter	16.3	Don Cox	5.4	Frank Johnson		
1951-52	14-10	8-7		Dwane Morrison	19.8	Dwane Morrison	10.4	Don Cox	4.7	Frank Johnson		
1952-53	11-13	7-12		Joe Smith	15.7	Joe Smith	12.9			Frank Johnson		
1953-54	10-16	2-8		Joe Smith	16.6	Joe Smith	11.5			Frank Johnson		
1954-55	10-17	2-12		Lee Collins	16.1	Lee Collins	16.1			Frank Johnson		
1955-56	9-14	3-11		Grady Wallace	23.9	Lee Collins	17.6			Frank Johnson		
1956-57	17-12	5-9		Grady Wallace	31.2	Grady Wallace	14.4			Frank Johnson		
1957-58	5-19	3-11		Ray Pericola	15.1	Mike Callahan	7.6			Frank Johnson	174-175	.499[a]
1958-59	4-20	2-12		Ray Pericola	12.8	Mike Callahan	10.5			Walt Hambrick	4-20	.167
1959-60	10-16	6-8		Art Whisnant	17.0	Mike Callahan	11.8			Bob Stevens		
1960-61	9-17	2-12		Art Whisnant	19.1	Art Whisnant	9.2			Bob Stevens		
1961-62	15-12	7-7		Art Whisnant	21.0	Art Whisnant	7.2			Bob Stevens	34-45	.430
1962-63	9-15	4-10		Scotti Ward	17.6	Ronnie Collins	8.4			Chuck Noe		
1963-64	10-14	7-7		Ronnie Collins	23.7	Bill Yarbrough	9.9			Chuck Noe[c]	15-21	.417
1964-65	6-17	2-12		Jim Fox	17.8	Jim Fox	13.6			Frank McGuire		
1965-66	11-13	4-10		Skip Harlicka	14.3	Frank Standard	10.6			Frank McGuire		
1966-67	16-7	8-4		Skip Harlicka	16.7	Gary Gregor	13.3			Frank McGuire		
1967-68	15-7	9-5		Skip Harlicka	21.8	Gary Gregor	12.2			Frank McGuire		
1968-69	21-7	11-3	NIT QUARTERFINALS	John Roche	23.6	Tom Owens	13.0	John Roche	2.3	Frank McGuire		
1969-70	25-3	14-0		John Roche	22.3	Tom Owens	14.0			Frank McGuire		
1970-71	23-6	10-4	NCAA REGIONAL SEMIFINALS	John Roche	21.6	Tom Owens	12.9	John Roche	4.2	Frank McGuire		
1971-72	24-5		NCAA REGIONAL SEMIFINALS	Tom Riker	19.6	Danny Traylor	10.7	Kevin Joyce	4.2	Frank McGuire		
1972-73	22-7		NCAA REGIONAL SEMIFINALS	Kevin Joyce	20.4	A. English, D. Traylor	10.6	Kevin Joyce	5.2	Frank McGuire		
1973-74	22-5		NCAA FIRST ROUND	Brian Winters	20.0	Bob Mathias	9.7	Mike Dunleavy	3.5	Frank McGuire		
1974-75	19-9		NIT QUARTERFINALS	Tom Boswell	16.5	Alex English	8.7	Jack Gilloon	4.4	Frank McGuire		
1975-76	18-9			Alex English	22.6	Alex English	10.3	Jack Gilloon	6.5	Frank McGuire		
1976-77	14-12			Nate Davis	15.7	Jim Graziano	7.7	Jack Gilloon	4.5	Frank McGuire		
1977-78	16-12		NIT FIRST ROUND	Mike Doyle	13.7	Jim Graziano	7.6	Jack Gilloon	5.1	Frank McGuire		
1978-79	15-12			Cedrick Hordges	19.6	Cedrick Hordges	10.1	Kenny Reynolds	3.6	Frank McGuire		
1979-80	16-11			Cedrick Hordges	19.9	Jim Strickland	8.4	Kenny Reynolds	4.1	Frank McGuire	283-142	.666
1980-81	17-10			Zam Fredrick	28.9	Jimmy Foster	11.0	Kevin Dunleavy	3.7	Bill Foster		
1981-82	14-15			Jimmy Foster	15.4	Jimmy Foster	8.3	Gerald Peacock	4.8	Bill Foster		
1982-83	22-9		NIT QUARTERFINALS	Jimmy Foster	17.3	Jimmy Foster	8.9	Gerald Peacock	7.0	Bill Foster		
1983-84	12-16	5-9		Jimmy Foster	18.5	Jimmy Foster	9.4	Michael Foster	3.7	Bill Foster		
1984-85	15-13	6-8		Linwood Moye	15.3	Linwood Moye	8.5	Michael Foster	5.2	Bill Foster		
1985-86	12-16	2-10		Linwood Moye	15.0	Darryl Martin	9.0	Michael Foster	3.5	Bill Foster	92-79	.538
1986-87	15-14	5-7		Terry Dozier	17.0	Darryl Martin	9.3	Terry Gould	3.9	George Felton		
1987-88	19-10	6-6		John Hudson	13.5	Darryl Martin	8.2	Terry Gould	3.9	George Felton		
1988-89	19-11	8-4	NCAA FIRST ROUND	John Hudson	14.8	John Hudson	7.7	Brent Price	4.3	George Felton		
1989-90	14-14	6-8		Jo Jo English	15.3	Joe Rhett	7.9	Jo Jo English, B. Popovic	2.9	George Felton		
1990-91	20-13	5-9	NIT SECOND ROUND	Jo Jo English	15.0	Joe Rhett	6.9	Barry Manning	3.7	George Felton	87-62	.584
1991-92	11-17	3-13		Jo Jo English	15.8	Jeff Roulston	5.7	Barry Manning	4.1	Steve Newton		
1992-93	9-18	5-11		Jamie Watson	14.7	Emmett Hall	7.7	Carey Rich	4.7	Steve Newton	20-35	.364
1993-94	9-19	4-12		Jamie Watson	18.1	Emmett Hall	8.8	Carey Rich	5.2	Eddie Fogler		
1994-95	10-17	5-11		Carey Rich	13.4	Malik Russell	6.9	Melvin Watson	4.0	Eddie Fogler		
1995-96	19-12	8-8	NIT QUARTERFINALS	Larry Davis	18.0	Malik Russell	5.9	Melvin Watson	4.5	Eddie Fogler		
1996-97	24-8	15-1	NCAA FIRST ROUND	B.J. McKie	17.4	William Gallman	6.2	Mevlin Watson	5.1	Eddie Fogler		
1997-98	23-8	11-5	NCAA FIRST ROUND	B.J. McKie	18.8	Ryan Stack	6.0	Melvin Watson	4.7	Eddie Fogler		
1998-99	8-21	3-13		B.J. McKie	17.3	Bud Johnson	6.4	B.J. McKie	4.0	Eddie Fogler		
1999-2000	15-17	5-11		Herbert Lee Davis	9.4	Tony Kitchings	5.0	Chuck Eidson	4.0	Eddie Fogler		
2000-01	15-15	6-10	NIT FIRST ROUND	Jamel Bradley	11.5	Tony Kitchings	6.6	Aaron Lucas	3.9	Eddie Fogler	123-117	.513
2001-02	22-15	6-10	NIT RUNNER-UP	Jamel Bradley	13.1	Tony Kitchings	6.2	Aaron Lucas	3.9	Dave Odom		
2002-03	12-16	5-11		Carlos Powell	12.6	Rolando Howell	6.3	Chuck Eidson	4.5	Dave Odom		
2003-04	23-11	8-8	NCAA FIRST ROUND	Carlos Powell	12.2	Carlos Powell	6.2	Mike Boynton Jr	3.4	Dave Odom		
2004-05	20-13	7-9	NIT CHAMPION	Carlos Powell	16.4	Carlos Powell	6.5	Tre' Kelley	3.6	Dave Odom		
2005-06	23-15	6-10	NIT CHAMPION	Tarence Kinsey	15.8	Renaldo Balkman	6.3	Tre' Kelley	4.6	Dave Odom		
2006-07	14-16	4-12		Tre' Kelley	18.9	Brandon Wallace	9.4	Tre' Kelley	5.1	Dave Odom		
2007-08	14-18	5-11		Devan Downey	18.4	D. Archie, Mike Holmes	5.7	Devan Downey	5.4	Dave Odom	128-104	.552
2008-09	21-10	10-6	NIT FIRST ROUND	Devan Downey	19.8	Mike Holmes	7.7	Devan Downey	4.5	Darrin Horn	21-10	.677

[a] Frank Johnson (2-0) and Rex Enright (11-6) both coached during the 1942-43 season. [b] Johnson (5-3) and Dick Anderson (4-8) both coached during the 1945-46 season.
[c] Chuck Noe (6-6) and Dwayne Morrison (4-8) both coached during the 1963-64 season.

ESPN 253 SAGARIN

SOUTH CAROLINA STATE

It took awhile, but the Bulldogs seem to have gotten the hang of things at the Division I level. They jumped from the small-college ranks to the newly formed MEAC in 1971. Okay, so it wasn't until 1989 that they won the league and earned an NCAA Tournament trip, but they've been back four times since.

BEST TEAM: 1988-89 This wasn't just a team that got hot late. The Bulldogs spent their holidays in Puerto Rico and came home with the San Juan Shootout title, taking out a field that included No. 11-ranked Villanova. Behind five starters who all averaged double figures, SC State rolled to the MEAC title, earning the team a Big Dance date with—and 90-69 trouncing by—Duke and Danny Ferry.

BEST PLAYER: F Lindberg Moody (1958-62) He was nicknamed the Bird because of his grace on the floor. Defend him as a shooter, he'd go by you. Stop his driving, he'd pop a shot in your face. "Fly, Bird, fly," fans would chant as Moody did his thing. Following his college career, he became a well-known high school coach in South Carolina before a car accident took his life in 1980.

BEST COACH: Cy Alexander (1987-2003) In 1987, Alexander inherited a team coming off nine straight losing seasons. The Bulldogs went 16–13 in his first season, a mere hint of the five Tournament trips to come. Alexander's intensity and cunning defined him; Bulldogs faithful still smile about the way the coach harassed officials, yet somehow rarely drew a technical.

GAME FOR THE AGES: Conference title? Check. Tournament bid? Check. But it wasn't until Dec. 11, 1999, that South Carolina State checked off the biggest regular-season achievement of them all: knocking off an ACC foe. The Bulldogs hit 18 of 22 free throws in the game to finish off Clemson, 71-68.

FIERCEST RIVAL: For more than three decades on the gridiron, South Carolina State has concluded every regular season in a border war with North Carolina A&T, usually in front of overflow crowds. The meetings on the hardwood are just as intense, on the court and in the stands. Only a handful of times have the games not gone down to the wire and, fittingly, the series is tied at 40 wins apiece.

SEASON REVIEW

SEAS.	W-L	CONF.		SCORING		COACH	RECORD	
1955-56[a]	16-7					Edward Martin		
1956-57	15-10					Edward Martin		
1957-58	18-9					Edward Martin		
1958-59	9-10					Edward Martin		
1959-60	9-14					Edward Martin		
1960-61	23-7					Edward Martin		
1961-62	22-7					Edward Martin		
1962-63	19-8					Edward Martin		
1963-64	19-8					Edward Martin		
1964-65	16-9					Edward Martin		
1965-66	23-3					Edward Martin		
1966-67	18-5					Edward Martin		
1967-68	12-3					Edward Martin	219-100	.687
1968-69	20-5					Ben Jobe		
1969-70	21-7					Ben Jobe		
1970-71	20-7			Johnny Thornton	23.4	Ben Jobe		
1971-72	15-11	6-6		Johnny Thornton	19.5	Ben Jobe		
1972-73	17-14	3-9		Tommy Boswell	18.8	Ben Jobe	93-44	.679
1973-74	13-15	2-10		Alex Barron	19.7	Tim Autrey		
1974-75	14-11	7-5		Harry Nickens	21.1	Tim Autrey		
1975-76	17-8	8-4		Harry Nickens	15.0	Tim Autrey		
1976-77	15-11	10-2		Harry Nickens	16.5	Tim Autrey		
1977-78	16-12	5-7		Harry Nickens	20.1	Tim Autrey		
1978-79	8-19	3-9		Jonathan Robinson	15.0	Tim Autrey		
1979-80	12-17			Gregory Wilson	15.8	Tim Autrey	95-93	.505
1980-81	11-15	4-6		Gregory Wilson	15.0	Johnny Jones		
1981-82	10-15	7-5		Gregory Wilson	17.4	Johnny Jones		
1982-83	13-15	5-7		Marvin Haynes	19.6	Johnny Jones	34-45	.430
1983-84	13-16	6-4		Ralph Miller	14.9	Chico Caldwell		
1984-85	11-16	7-4		Ralph Miller	14.9	Chico Caldwell		
1985-86	10-18	5-9		Mack Joyner	17.7	Chico Caldwell		
1986-87	14-15	9-5		Mack Joyner	13.2	Chico Caldwell	48-65	.425
1987-88	16-13	10-6		Rodney Mack	16.2	Cy Alexander		
1988-89	25-8	14-2	●	Rodney Mack	15.2	Cy Alexander		
1989-90	13-16	8-8		Travis Williams	20.6	Cy Alexander		
1990-91	13-15	10-6		Travis Williams	21.7	Cy Alexander		
1991-92	14-15	9-7		Jackie Robinson	18.2	Cy Alexander		
1992-93	16-13	9-7		Jackie Robinson	20.2	Cy Alexander		
1993-94	16-13	10-6		Deon Murray	15.4	Cy Alexander		
1994-95	15-13	11-5		Derrick Patterson	17.8	Cy Alexander[b]		
1995-96	22-8	14-2	●	Derrick Patterson	16.9	Cy Alexander		
1996-97	14-14	12-6		Roderick Blakney	23.4	Cy Alexander		
1997-98	22-8	16-2	●	Roderick Blakney	20.7	Cy Alexander		
1998-99	17-12	14-4		Mike Wiatre	15.2	Cy Alexander		
1999-2000	20-14	14-5	●	Mike Wiatre	15.8	Cy Alexander		
2000-01	19-13	14-4		Vincent Whitt	16.0	Cy Alexander		
2001-02	15-16	10-7		Moses Malone Jr	14.9	Cy Alexander		
2002-03	20-11	15-3	●	Moses Malone Jr., Thurman Zimmerman	16.0	Cy Alexander	276-200	.580
2003-04	18-11	14-4		Thurman Zimmerman	18.8	Ben Betts Jr.		
2004-05	19-12	11-7		Thurman Zimmerman	14.7	Ben Betts Jr.		
2005-06	14-16	11-7		Brian Mason	14.3	Ben Betts Jr	52-41	.559
2006-07	13-17	10-8		Brian Mason	13.2	Jamal Brown	13-17	.433
2007-08	13-20	7-9		Jason Johnson	11.4	Tim Carter		
2008-09	17-14	10-6		Jason Johnson	13.8	Tim Carter	30-34	.469

[a] Records from before 1955-56 have been lost.
[b] Ben Betts Jr. coached three games (1-2) during the 1994-95 season due to Alexander's NCAA suspension.
● NCAA Tournament appearance

PROFILE

South Carolina State University, Orangeburg, SC
Founded: 1896
Enrollment: 4,294 (3,704 undergraduate)
Colors: Garnet and blue
Nickname: Bulldogs
Current arena: Smith-Hammond-Middleton Memorial Center, opened in 1968 (3,200)
Previous: Duke's Gym, prior to 1968 (N/A)
First game (with available data): 1955
All-time record: 860-639 (.574)

Total weeks in AP Top 20/25: 0
Current conference: Mid-Eastern Athletic (1971-)
Conference titles:
MEAC: 8 (1977, '89, '96 [tie], '99 [tie], 2000, '01 [tie], '03, '04 [tie])
Conference tournament titles:
MEAC: 5 (1989, '96, '98, 2000, '03)
NCAA Tournament appearances: 5
NIT appearances: 0

TOP 5

G **Roderick Blakney** (1994-98)
G **Bobby Lewis** (1964-68)
G **Harry Nickens** (1974-78)
F **Lindberg Moody** (1958-62)
F **Teddy Wright** (1955-59)

RECORDS

RECORDS	GAME		SEASON		CAREER	
POINTS	52	Lindberg Moody, vs. Allen University (1961-62)	884	Lindberg Moody (1959-60)	1,851	Harry Nickens (1974-78)
POINTS PER GAME			23.4	Roderick Blakney (1996-97), Johnny Thornton (1970-71)		N/A
REBOUNDS		N/A	534	Julius Keyes (1964-65)	1,055	Dexter Hall (1998-2002)

ESPN 226 SAGARIN

SOUTH DAKOTA STATE

What's not to love about the Jackrabbits? A College Division national championship—on a desperation heave, no less—multiple final fours (1961, '63, '85), several All-Americas and more than 1,000 total victories. The transition to D1, begun in 2004, was tough, but if 106 years of hoops success proves anything, it's that Jackrabbits know how to adapt.

BEST TEAM: 1962-63 A 4–4 start hardly augured what lay ahead for coach Jim Iverson's squad. After getting past the feeling-out period, newcomer and future All-America center Tom Black (17.3 ppg, 15.0 rpg), 1,000-point scorer Sid Bostic and Wayne Rasmussen won 18 of their last 19 and claimed the College Division championship.

BEST PLAYER: C MARK TETZLAFF (1981-85) While others perhaps have had better, shorter careers (Tom Black, Chris White), Tetzlaff transformed a 13–14 1982 team into the 26–7 1985 D2 championship runner-up (a 74-73 loss to Jacksonville State). He was the final four MVP and finished as the school's all-time leading scorer (1,931) and rebounder (1,132).

BEST COACH: SCOTT NAGY (1995-) Nagy's difficult transition from D2 to D1 (46–103) doesn't negate all his D2 success. Nagy has eight 20-win seasons, eight NCAA D2 regional appearances, one elite eight showing and he's the school's all-time winningest coach (256–162).

GAME FOR THE AGES: Two years after reaching the 1961 College Division final four, Iverson's Jackrabbits went a step farther, reaching the national title game behind Black, who would be named all-tournament, and Rasmussen, named final MVP. But Bostic was the hero, hitting a game-winning 40-foot shot at the buzzer for a 44-42 victory over Wittenberg (Ohio).

FIERCEST RIVAL: Long before South Dakota State and North Dakota State joined D1, the teams were battling for Dakotas bragging rights in the North Central Conference—and long, long before that (we're talking the first few decades of the 20th century) as two of the region's independent powers. The Bison lead the series, 105–92.

SEASON REVIEW

SEAS.	W-L	CONF.	COACH	SEAS.	W-L	CONF.	COACH
1903-47	*289-272*	*25-3 in 1921-22*		**1960-61**	21-6		Jim Iverson
1947-48	19-6		R.B. "Jack" Frost	**1961-62**	13-9		Jim Iverson
1948-49	11-14		R.B. "Jack" Frost	**1962-63**	22-5	◆	Jim Iverson
1949-50	9-12		R.B. "Jack" Frost	**1963-64**	14-7		Jim Iverson
1950-51	16-12		R.B. "Jack" Frost	**1964-65**	9-14		Jim Iverson[a]
1951-52	10-12		R.B. "Jack" Frost	**1965-66**	13-11		Jim Marking
1952-53	10-12		R.B. "Jack" Frost	**1966-67**	11-14		Jim Marking
1953-54	11-11		R.B. "Jack" Frost	**1967-68**	20-7		Jim Marking
1954-55	14-11		Russell "Sox" Walseth	**1968-69**	18-6		Jim Marking
1955-56	17-7		Russell "Sox" Walseth	**1969-70**	22-4		Jim Marking
1956-57	19-3		Jim Iverson	**1970-71**	15-7		Jim Marking
1957-58	12-11		Jim Iverson	**1971-72**	17-8		Jim Marking
1958-59	17-7		Jim Iverson	**1972-73**	18-8		Jim Marking
1959-60	17-7		Jim Iverson	**1973-74**	11-12		Jim Marking

SEAS.	W-L	CONF.	SCORING		COACH	RECORD	
1974-75	12-12		Ron Wiblemo	20.3	Gene Zulk		
1975-76	12-12		George Schroeder	15.2	Gene Zulk		
1976-77	10-16		Steve Brown	20.4	Gene Zulk		
1977-78	17-12		Steve Brown	19.8	Gene Zulk		
1978-79	13-14		Jim Walker	17.3	Gene Zulk		
1979-80	23-7		Jim Walker	18.2	Gene Zulk		
1980-81	13-14		Steve Lingenfelter	26.7	Gene Zulk		
1981-82	13-14		Bob Winzenburg	11.6	Gene Zulk		
1982-83	16-12		Mark Tetzlaff	19.9	Gene Zulk		
1983-84	21-9		Mark Tetzlaff	16.3	Gene Zulk		
1984-85	26-7		Mark Tetzlaff	18.6	Gene Zulk	176-129	.577
1985-86	8-20		Mark Schultz	17.4	Jim Thorson		
1986-87	16-12		Craig Jenkins, R. Suarez	14.2	Jim Thorson		
1987-88	21-9		Randy Suarez	13.8	Jim Thorson		
1988-89	16-12		Cullen Ober	13.6	Jim Thorson		
1989-90	8-19		Rich McClendon	12.2	Jim Thorson		
1990-91	24-8		Chris White	19.8	Jim Thorson		
1991-92	25-8		Chris White	22.6	Jim Thorson		
1992-93	19-12		Ryan Naatjes	13.2	Jim Thorson	137-100	.578
1993-94	19-8		Juriad Hughes	24.6	Brad Soderberg		
1994-95	17-10		Tom Rops	14.5	Brad Soderberg	36-18	.667
1995-96	24-5		Jermaine Showers	17.3	Scott Nagy		
1996-97	25-5		Jason Sempsrott	23.9	Scott Nagy		
1997-98	26-3		Kurt Meister	16.2	Scott Nagy		
1998-99	17-10		Bill Fischer	14.6	Scott Nagy		
1999-2000	21-9		Austin Hansen	13.5	Scott Nagy		
2000-01	22-7		Austin Hansen	14.1	Scott Nagy		
2001-02	24-6		Austin Hansen	15.2	Scott Nagy		
2002-03	24-7		Austin Hansen	18.0	Scott Nagy		
2003-04	27-7		Andy Moeller	17.6	Scott Nagy		
2004-05	10-18		Ben Beran	13.6	Scott Nagy		
2005-06	9-20		Matt Cadwell	15.6	Scott Nagy		
2006-07	6-24		Kai Williams	12.1	Scott Nagy		
2007-08	8-21	3-15	Kai Williams	14.0	Scott Nagy		
2008-09	13-20	7-11	Garrett Callahan	15.8	Scott Nagy	256-162	.612

[a] Jim Iverson (6-11) and Jim Marking (3-3) both coached during the 1964-65 season.

◆ College Division championship

PROFILE

South Dakota State University, Brookings, SD
Founded: 1881 as Dakota Agriculture College
Enrollment: 11,706 (9,897 undergraduate)
Colors: Yellow and blue
Nickname: Jackrabbits
Current arena: Frost Arena, opened in 1973 (6,500)
First game: 1903
All-time record: 1,300-924 (.585)
Total weeks in AP Top 20/25: 0

Current conference: Summit League (2007-)
Conference titles: 0
Conference tournament titles: 0
NCAA Tournament appearances: 0
NIT appearances: 0

CONSENSUS ALL-AMERICAS

1961 **Don Jacobsen** (Little A-A), G
1964 **Tom Black** (Little A-A), C

TOP 5

G **Don Jacobsen** (1958-61)
G **Chris White** (1990-92)
F **Sid Bostic** (1961-64)
F **Lee Colburn** (1969-73)
C **Mark Tetzlaff** (1981-85)

RECORDS

RECORDS	GAME		SEASON		CAREER	
POINTS	44	Dave Thomas, vs. Coe College (March 10, 1973)	747	Chris White (1991-92)	1,931	Mark Tetzlaff (1981-85)
POINTS PER GAME			26.7	Steve Lingenfelter (1980-81)	21.2	Chris White (1990-92)
REBOUNDS	29	Terry Slattery, vs. Lincoln University (Dec. 22, 1961)	404	Tom Black (1962-63)	1,132	Mark Tetzlaff (1981-85)
ASSISTS	17	Tom McDonald, vs. Morningside (Feb. 21, 1986)	225	Brian Norberg (1997-98)	605	Brian Norberg (1995-99)

ESPN 186 SAGARIN

SOUTHEAST MISSOURI STATE

For decades, Southeast fans considered the regular season just a prelude to postseason fun. There was an NAIB title team in 1943 and a 28–14 overall tournament record between the 1950s and the '90s.

BEST TEAM: 1942-43 Of all Southeast's terrific teams, only Charles P. Harris' 19–6 squad won a national title, with a 34-32 victory over Maryville Teacher's College (today's Northwest Missouri State) in the NAIB title game. All five Southeast starters were league all-stars: Jack Behrens, Jack Russell, Carl "Ben" Bidewell, Rolla Anderson and Jack Klosterman.

BEST PLAYER: G Carl Ritter (1958-61, '62-63) The local high school star led Southeast to a 25–3 record and college division national runner-up finish in 1960-61. The school's all-time leading scorer (1,916 points), Ritter is a member of the Missouri Basketball Hall of Fame.

BEST COACH: Ron Shumate (1981-97) He took Southeast to eight D2 tourneys in 10 seasons, including two title games (1986, '89). The school's all-time winningest coach (306–171), Shumate had seven straight 20-win seasons and oversaw the tough D1 transition in 1991-92. He was fired after NCAA infractions led to a three-year probation for Southeast from 1998-99 to 2000-01.

GAME FOR THE AGES: Some consider the 1989 D2 national semifinal between Southeast and California-Riverside the best D2 tourney game ever. UC Riverside, 30–4 and regular-season winners over D1 Iowa, led late, before Southeast's Mike Lewis tied it with a three. In overtime, Earnest Taylor banked a jumper with :09 left for an 84-83 Southeast win.

FIERCEST RIVAL: In the NAIB (precursor to the NAIA), College Division and D2 days, it was bitter MIAA rival Southwest Missouri State (now Missouri State), but the two teams have met only rarely since the D1 jump. Murray State wears the bull's-eye now, though it's slightly one-sided; the Racers won 15 straight at one point, including a buzzer-beater in the 1999 OVC title game. Southeast got some payback with a 61-58 first-round upset in the 2005 tourney.

SEASON REVIEW

SEAS.	W-L	CONF.	COACH	SEAS.	W-L	CONF.	COACH
1906-47	*183-168*	*1-30 over two seasons (1928-30)*		1960-61	25-3		Charles Parsley
1947-48	10-9		Joe J. McDonald	1961-62	18-7		Charles Parsley
1948-49	7-12		Joe J. McDonald	1962-63	21-4		Charles Parsley
1949-50	6-13		John J. Adams	1963-64	19-6		Charles Parsley
1950-51	3-16		John J. Adams	1964-65	15-8		Charles Parsley
1951-52	5-12		John J. Adams	1965-66	13-9		Charles Parsley
1952-53	13-8		Ralph Pink	1966-67	15-6		Charles Parsley
1953-54	13-7		Ralph Pink	1967-68	8-14		Charles Parsley
1954-55	12-6		Ralph Pink	1968-69	7-15		Charles Parsley
1955-56	12-8		Ralph Pink	1969-70	9-12		Charles Parsley
1956-57	7-13		Ralph Pink	1970-71	13-10		Bob Cradic
1957-58	11-9		Ralph Pink	1971-72	15-9		Bob Cradic
1958-59	11-9		Charles Parsley	1972-73	11-13		Bob Cradic
1959-60	12-8		Charles Parsley	1973-74	10-14		Bob Cradic

SEAS.	W-L	CONF.	SCORING		COACH	RECORD
1974-75	14-12		Steve Valli	15.4	Bob Cradic	
1975-76	5-21		Dave Shipley	8.2	Bob Cradic	68-79 .463
1976-77	8-18		Joe Cagle	16.5	Carroll Williams	
1977-78	11-15		Steve Tappmeyer	16.5	Carroll Williams	
1978-79	19-9		Desi Barmore, M. Harvey	15.4	Carroll Williams	
1979-80	14-12		Otto Porter	27.0	Carroll Williams	
1980-81	11-16		Otto Porter	25.1	Carroll Williams	63-70 .474
1981-82	21-10		Terry Mead	16.8	Ron Shumate	
1982-83	25-6		Terry Mead	15.1	Ron Shumate	
1983-84	16-12		Jewell Crawford	22.4	Ron Shumate	
1984-85	24-8		Ronny Rankin	20.6	Ron Shumate	
1985-86	27-7		Ronny Rankin	20.5	Ron Shumate	
1986-87	20-11		Derick Turner	17.6	Ron Shumate	
1987-88	28-4		Ray Pugh	17.9	Ron Shumate	
1988-89	27-6		Ray Pugh	17.9	Ron Shumate	
1989-90	26-5		Earnest Taylor	18.1	Ron Shumate	
1990-91	21-7		Danny Dohogne	17.4	Ron Shumate	
1991-92	12-16	5-9	Curtis Shelton	15.2	Ron Shumate	
1992-93	16-11	9-7	Devon Lake	11.9	Ron Shumate	
1993-94	10-17	5-11	Curtis Shelton	15.2	Ron Shumate	
1994-95	13-14	7-9	Jermall Morgan	17.2	Ron Shumate	
1995-96	8-19	5-11	William "Bud" Eley	17.2	Ron Shumate	
1996-97	12-18	9-9	William "Bud" Eley	17.9	Ron Shumate	306-171 .642
1997-98	14-13	10-8	Cory Johnson	14.5	Gary Garner	
1998-99	20-9	15-3	William "Bud" Eley	15.3	Gary Garner	
1999-2000	24-7	14-4 ●	Roderick Johnson	14.1	Gary Garner	
2000-01	18-12	8-8	Michael Stokes	15.0	Gary Garner	
2001-02	6-22	4-12	Derek Winans	14.9	Gary Garner	
2002-03	11-19	5-11	Derek Winans	15.3	Gary Garner	
2003-04	11-16	4-12	Derek Winans	14.5	Gary Garner	
2004-05	15-14	9-7	Dainmon Gonner	16.5	Gary Garner	
2005-06	7-20	4-16	Roy Booker	22.0	Gary Garner	126-132 .488
2006-07	11-20	9-11	Brandon Foust	12.0	Scott Edgar	
2007-08	12-19	7-13	Jaycen Herring	13.1	Scott Edgar	23-39 .371
2008-09	3-27	0-18	Kenard Moore	19.0	Zac Roman	3-27 .100

● NCAA Tournament appearance

PROFILE

Southeast Missouri State University, Cape Girardeau, MO
Founded: 1873
Enrollment: 10,126 (9,487 undergraduate)
Colors: Red and black
Nickname: Redhawks
Current arena: Show Me Center, opened in 1987 (7,000)
First game: 1906-07
All-time record: 1,044-900 (.537)
Total weeks in AP Top 20/25: 0

Current conference: Ohio Valley (1991-)
Conference titles:
OVC: 1 (2000 [tie])
Conference tournament titles:
OVC: 1 (2000)
NCAA Tournament appearances: 1
NIT appearances: 0

TOP 5

G **Michael Morris** (1984-88)
G **Carl Ritter** (1958-61, '62-63)
G/F **Bill Giessing** (1959-63)
F **Ray Pugh** (1985-89)
C **William "Bud" Eley** (1995-99)

RECORDS

RECORDS	GAME		SEASON		CAREER	
POINTS	52	Kermit Meystedt, vs. McKendree (Jan. 14, 1967)	667	Otto Porter (1980-81)	1,916	Carl Ritter (1958-61, '62-63)
POINTS PER GAME			27.0	Otto Porter (1979-80)	25.9	Otto Porter (1979-81)
REBOUNDS	29	Paul Ranson, vs. MacMurray (Dec. 8, 1961)	362	Kermit Meystedt (1966-67)	955	William "Bud" Eley (1995-99)
ASSISTS	13	Kevin Roberts, vs. Morehead State (Feb. 6, 2003); Jerry Freshwater, vs. Wisconsin-Milwaukee (Feb. 3, 1995)	200	Dwayne Rutherford (1988-89)	541	Dwayne Rutherford (1986-90)

ESPN 276 SAGARIN

SOUTHEASTERN LOUISIANA

None of the other 12 D1 teams in Louisiana—not even 2006 NCAA semifinalist LSU—could match the Lions' achievement of five straight winning seasons from 2003-04 to '07-08. There's a history, too: state Hall of Fame coach Luther Marlar, NAIA All-America C.A. Core, a 2005 Southland Conference title and an NCAA bid.

BEST TEAM: 2004-05 Coach Billy Kennedy's Lions set a school record for wins (24) and SLC victories (13), and earned the program's first NCAA Tourney appearance (a 63-50 loss to No.-2 seed Oklahoma State), led by Ricky Woods (17.2 ppg) and Nate Lofton (team leader in rebounding, assists, blocks and steals).

BEST PLAYER: C C.A. CORE (1964-68) Standing alone as the school's leader in scoring and rebounding both for career totals (2,046 and 1,475) and single-season averages (22.3 and 18.5), Core was a two-time second-team NAIA All-America and is a member of the Louisiana Basketball Hall of Fame.

BEST COACH: LUTHER MARLAR (1947-67) The school's first coach of the modern era, Marlar is Southeastern Louisiana's winningest coach (220) and a member of the Louisiana Basketball Hall of Fame. He took the Lions to their three NAIA national tournaments (1950, '51, '54) and was the first coach to achieve a 20-win season (22–10 in 1953-54).

GAME FOR THE AGES: No victory was greater than the March 13, 2005, 49-42 SLC tourney championship upset of No. 1-seed Northwestern State, which advanced Southeastern Louisiana to the NCAA Tournament. Kennedy's team held NSU to its lowest point total of the season. Woods (16 points, 8 rebounds), Lofton (9 and 10) and Jonathan Patton (13 points) led the Lions.

FIERCEST RIVAL: The Lions have played no team more often than in-state and SLC East Division rival Northwestern State, with the Demons holding a 77–42 advantage. Southeastern's 2005 SLC tourney win was its first over NSU in Natchitoches in 20 years. Since then, the Lions have dropped six of nine to the Demons, including an opening-round 71-51 tourney loss in 2008.

SEASON REVIEW

SEAS.	W-L	CONF.	COACH	SEAS.	W-L	CONF.	COACH
1947-48	5-15		Luther Marlar	**1961-62**	10-14		Luther Marlar
1948-49	12-12		Luther Marlar	**1962-63**	8-13		Luther Marlar
1949-50	13-11		Luther Marlar	**1963-64**	3-18		Luther Marlar
1950-51	13-10		Luther Marlar	**1964-65**	12-12		Luther Marlar
1951-52	10-14		Luther Marlar	**1965-66**	17-8		Luther Marlar
1952-53	12-10		Luther Marlar	**1966-67**	11-12		Luther Marlar
1953-54	22-10		Luther Marlar	**1967-68**	11-13		Bert Barnett
1954-55	8-10		Luther Marlar	**1968-69**	4-22		Bert Barnett
1955-56	14-10		Luther Marlar	**1969-70**	9-17		E.W. Foy
1956-57	15-11		Luther Marlar	**1970-71**	11-15		E.W. Foy
1957-58	8-17		Luther Marlar	**1971-72**	8-15		E.W. Foy
1958-59	7-16		Luther Marlar	**1972-73**	21-7		E.W. Foy
1959-60	12-12		Luther Marlar	**1973-74**	15-10		E.W. Foy
1960-61	8-16		Luther Marlar	**1974-75**	14-11		Ken Fortenberry

SEAS.	W-L	CONF.	SCORING		COACH	RECORD	
1975-76	12-11		Bruce Gilmore	16.1	Ken Fortenberry		
1976-77	16-11		Jeff Tyson	16.1	Ken Fortenberry		
1977-78	11-14		Jeff Tyson	18.4	Ken Fortenberry		
1978-79	7-19		David Williams	15.6	Ken Fortenberry		
1979-80	9-17		Deboy Johnson	12.9	Ken Fortenberry		
1980-81	14-13		Wayne Booker	16.3	Ken Fortenberry		
1981-82	16-11		Jerry Kelly	16.0	Ken Fortenberry		
1982-83	18-9		Jerry Kelly	17.3	Ken Fortenberry		
1983-84	11-17		Thelander Tillman	12.1	Ken Fortenberry	128-133	.490
1984-85	18-9	9-1	David Jones	12.9	Newton Chelette		
1985-86	10-18	3-5	Robert Cousin	14.5	Newton Chelette		
1986-87	10-21	4-6	Teddy Butler	16.5	Newton Chelette		
1987-88	7-21		Troy Thaggart	17.0	N.Chelette, L. McClure[a]	41-57	.418
1988-89	3-24		Stafford Riley	17.6	Leo McClure	7-36	.163
1989-90	no team						
1990-91	9-19		Hank Washington	16.9	Don Wilson		
1991-92	6-22	4-10	Hank Washington	19.0	Don Wilson	15-41	.268
1992-93	12-15	4-8	Hank Washington	21.5	Norm Picou		
1993-94	10-17	7-9	Harvey Baker	16.6	Norm Picou	22-32	.407
1994-95	12-16	7-9	Sam Bowie	19.6	John Lyles		
1995-96	15-12	11-5	Sam Bowie	21.9	John Lyles		
1996-97	10-18	7-9	Troy Green	14.0	John Lyles		
1997-98	6-20	2-14	Maurice Clark	11.9	John Lyles		
1998-99	6-20	3-15	Maurice Clark	10.8	John Lyles	49-86	.363
1999-2000	10-17	5-13	Marcus Kemp	13.3	Billy Kennedy		
2000-01	8-21	5-15	Jaron Singletary	10.0	Billy Kennedy		
2001-02	7-20	6-14	Amir Abdur-Rahim	15.9	Billy Kennedy		
2002-03	11-16	9-11	Amir Abdur-Rahim	15.4	Billy Kennedy		
2003-04	20-9	11-5	Amir Abdur-Rahim	15.1	Billy Kennedy		
2004-05	24-9	13-3 ●	Ricky Woods	17.2	Billy Kennedy	80-92	.465
2005-06	16-12	10-6	Ricky Woods	17.8	Jim Yarbrough		
2006-07	16-14	8-8	Daryl Cohen	15.1	Jim Yarbrough		
2007-08	17-13	9-7	Kevyn Green	15.4	Jim Yarbrough		
2008-09	13-17	7-9	Patrick Sullivan	12.1	Jim Yarbrough	62-56	.525

[a] **Newton Chelette (3-9) and Leo McClure (4-12) both coached during the 1987-88 season.**

● NCAA Tournament appearance

PROFILE

Southeastern Louisiana University, Hammond, LA
Founded: 1925
Enrollment: 15,622 (10,983 undergraduate)
Colors: Green and gold
Nickname: Lions
Current arena: University Center, opened in 1982 (7,500)
Previous: Cefalu Coliseum, 1956-82 (3,000); Old Men's Gym, 1947-56 (500)
First game: 1947
All-time record: 703-883 (.443)
Total weeks in AP Top 20/25: 0

Current conference: Southland (1997-)
Conference titles:
Gulf Star: 1 (1985)
Southland: 2 (2004 [tie], '05 [tie])
Conference tournament titles:
Southland: 1 (2005)
NCAA Tournament appearances: 1
NIT appearances: 0

TOP 5

G **Dick Sharp** (1951-55)
G **Hank Washington** (1990-93)
F **Ricky Woods** (2004-06)
F/C **Curlee Connors** (1969-71)
C **C.A. Core** (1964-68)

RECORDS

RECORDS	GAME		SEASON		CAREER	
POINTS	43	Jim McClain, vs. Mississippi College (Dec. 10, 1968)	590	Sam Bowie (1995-96)	2,046	C.A. Core (1964-68)
POINTS PER GAME			22.3	C.A. Core (1964-65)	21.3	C.A. Core (1964-68)
REBOUNDS	31	C.A. Core, vs. Mississippi College (Dec. 18, 1967)	439	C.A. Core (1967-68)	1,475	C.A. Core (1964-68)
ASSISTS	16	Kevin Fogg, vs. Pikeville College (Dec. 7, 1974)	188	Leo McClure (1976-77)	433	Leo McClure (1973-77)

ESPN 240 SAGARIN

SOUTHERN

There have been two periods of peak basketball prowess at this Baton Rouge, La., university. The first was in the early 1960s, behind the brilliant play of Bob Love. The second spanned the '80s and '90s, when Southern made six NCAA Tournaments—pulling off a major Tourney upset of Georgia Tech in 1993.

BEST TEAM: 1987-88 Future NBA stars Avery Johnson and Bobby Phills led a 24–7 team that was third in the nation in scoring (95.6 ppg) and had seven players averaging double figures. Johnson set the NCAA assist record with 13.3 per game, leading the nation for the second straight season.

BEST PLAYER: F Bob Love (1961-65) The 6'8" Love was one of the first players to combine size, speed and artistry to regularly explode for 30 or 40 points in a game. In his four seasons, he averaged 23.1 points a game and totaled 2,458. Very intelligent but deeply shy because of a severe stutter, Love endured years of discrimination to become an NBA star (Chicago Bulls), but could get only menial work after his career ended. Ultimately, he conquered his disability and became a motivational speaker.

BEST COACH: Ben Jobe (1986-96, 2001-'03) A dedicated coach who worked (and won) at nine colleges and in two foreign countries, his philosophy boiled down to, "Take more shots than the other team." His Jaguars, routinely among the nation's top five in scoring, notched four SWAC tournament championships, four NCAA bids and one NIT berth.

GAME FOR THE AGES: No. 13-seed Southern stunned ACC champ Georgia Tech in the first round of the 1993 Tournament, 93-78. Afterward, Jobe apologized to Bobby Cremins, his one-time boss, saying that the Tech coach "needed this game more than I did."

FIERCEST RIVAL: Southern and Grambling have a heated two-sport rivalry. From 1977-78 to '89-90, one of the two claimed a share of the SWAC hoops title in seven of 13 seasons. From 1995 to 2009, they played 18 games that were decided by five points or less.

SEASON REVIEW

SEAS.	W-L	CONF.		SCORING		COACH	RECORD	
1949-50	25-7					Robert Henry Lee		
1950-51	22-7					Robert Henry Lee		
1951-52	23-5					Robert Henry Lee		
1952-53	22-9					Robert Henry Lee		
1953-54	27-7					Robert Henry Lee		
1954-55	17-9					Robert Henry Lee		
1955-56	19-6					Robert Henry Lee	155-50	.756
1956-69	N/A							
1969-70	11-11					Richard Mack		
1970-71	9-17					Richard Mack		
1971-72	9-15					Richard Mack	29-43	.403
1972-73	8-12					Carl E. Stewart		
1973-74	17-13					Carl E. Stewart		
1974-75	19-8					Carl E. Stewart		
1975-76	13-14					Carl E. Stewart		
1976-77	19-11					Carl E. Stewart		
1977-78	23-5	9-3				Carl E. Stewart		
1978-79	16-12	6-6				Carl E. Stewart		
1979-80	14-15	6-6				Carl E. Stewart		
1980-81	17-11	8-4	●			Carl E. Stewart		
1981-82	7-18	3-9				Carl E. Stewart	153-119	.562
1982-83	16-14	7-7				Andy Stoglin		
1983-84	16-12	10-4				Andy Stoglin	32-26	.552
1984-85	19-11	9-5	●			Robert Hopkins		
1985-86	19-8	11-3				Robert Hopkins	38-19	.667
1986-87	19-12	9-5	●			Ben Jobe		
1987-88	24-7	12-2	●			Ben Jobe		
1988-89	20-11	10-4	●			Ben Jobe		
1989-90	25-6	12-2	■			Ben Jobe		
1990-91	19-9	8-4				Ben Jobe		
1991-92	18-12	9-5				Ben Jobe		
1992-93	21-10	9-5	●			Ben Jobe		
1993-94	16-11	8-6				Ben Jobe		
1994-95	13-13	7-7				Ben Jobe		
1995-96	17-11	8-5				Ben Jobe		
1996-97	10-17	5-9				Tommy Green		
1997-98	14-13	10-6				Tommy Green		
1998-99	21-7	13-3		Adarrial Smylie	19.0	Tommy Green		
1999-2000	18-11	14-4		Adarrial Smylie	18.2	Tommy Green		
2000-01	11-16	8-10		Courtney Henderson	16.4	Tommy Green	74-64	.536
2001-02	7-20	6-12		Victor Tarver	15.7	Ben Jobe		
2002-03	9-20	5-13		Victor Tarver	13.4	Ben Jobe	208-142	.594
2003-04	12-16	9-9		Deon Saunders	18.4	Michael Grant		
2004-05	14-15	10-8		Chris Alexander	14.5	Michael Grant	26-31	.456
2005-06	19-13	15-3	●	Chris Alexander	15.7	Rob Spivery		
2006-07	10-21	9-9		Deforrest Riley-Smith	13.9	Rob Spivery		
2007-08	11-19	9-9		Chris Davis	15.3	Rob Spivery		
2008-09	8-23	8-10		Chris Davis	14.9	Rob Spivery	48-76	.387

● NCAA Tournament appearance ■ NIT appearance

PROFILE

Southern University and A&M College, Baton Rouge, LA
Founded: 1881
Enrollment: 10,364 (8,964 undergraduate)
Colors: Columbia blue and gold
Nickname: Jaguars
Current arena: F.G. Clark Activity Center, opened in 1975 (7,500)
First game: 1949
All-time record: 763-570 (.572)
Total weeks in AP Top 20/25: 0

Current conference: Southwestern Athletic (1934-)
Conference titles:
SWAC: 8 (1965, '78, '81, '86, '88, '89, '90, 2006)
Conference tournament titles:
SWAC: 7 (1981, '85, '87, '88, '89, '93, 2006)
NCAA Tournament appearances: 7
NIT appearances: 1

FIRST-ROUND PRO PICKS

1978 **Frank Sanders**, San Antonio (20)

TOP 5

G **Tommy Green** (1974-78)
G **Avery Johnson** (1986-88)
G **Bobby Phills** (1987-91)
F **Bob Love** (1961-65)
F **Jervaughn Scales** (1991-94)

RECORDS

RECORDS	GAME		SEASON		CAREER
POINTS	56	Tim Roberts, vs. Faith Baptist (Dec. 12, 1994)	932	Tony Murphy (1979-80)	N/A
POINTS PER GAME			32.1	Tony Murphy (1979-80)	N/A
REBOUNDS	32	Jervaughn Scales, vs. Grambling (Feb. 7, 1994)	433	Lionell Garrett (1978-79)	N/A
ASSISTS	22	Avery Johnson, vs. Texas Southern (Jan. 25, 1988)	399	Avery Johnson (1987-88)	N/A

ESPN 25 SAGARIN

SOUTHERN CALIFORNIA

For years terribly overshadowed (and shut out of the NCAA Tournament) by the UCLA dynasty across town, USC has nevertheless made its mark on college basketball. Coach Sam Barry laid the groundwork for the triangle offense. Bob Boyd consistently fielded top squads before the Tournament issued any at-large bids. And several Trojans have ranked among the game's greatest talents, among them Bill Sharman, Paul Westphal and Gus Williams.

BEST TEAM: 1970-71 The Trojans, led by Paul Westphal, Dennis "Mo" Layton and Ron Riley, were 16–0 and ranked No. 1 by the UPI before No. 2 (UPI) UCLA rallied for a 64-60 win at the Los Angeles Sports Arena in early February. Boyd's team had a chance to tie UCLA for the Pac-8 championship but lost the rematch at Pauley Pavilion, 73-62, and ended up 24–2—still a school record for best winning percentage. In those years, second place meant no postseason, so while USC watched, the hated Bruins won their seventh NCAA title.

BEST PLAYER: F Bill Sharman (1946-50) Known as Bull's-Eye Bill for his accuracy from the foul line (80.3% for his career), Sharman was a four-year letterman, an All-America as a senior and an all-Pacific Coast Conference first-teamer in both 1949 and '50. He went on to star on four NBA champion Boston Celtics teams and coached both the ABA Utah Stars and the NBA LA Lakers. And as if that wasn't enough, Sharman also played the outfield in the Dodgers organization.

BEST COACH: Sam Barry (1929-41, '45-50) USC's all-time winningest coach with 260 victories, Barry is one of only three coaches to lead a school to the Final Four and the College World Series in baseball. An advocate of eliminating jump balls following each basket, he created the forerunner to the triangle offense, later refined by one of his players, Tex Winter, who, as an assistant to Phil Jackson, made it the signature style of the NBA Bulls and Lakers.

GAME FOR THE AGES: "Stalls Are for Horses" read one sign in Pauley Pavilion on March 8, 1969. But the visiting Trojans ignored such sentiment, bringing the game to a virtual halt for large stretches of a 46-44 win. (The shot clock was not used in the college game until 1985-86.) It was the last regular-season game—and only the second loss—for UCLA's Lew Alcindor.

HEARTBREAKER: Led by Harold Miner, George Raveling's No. 2-seed Trojans steamed into their 1992 NCAA second-round matchup with No. 7-seed Georgia Tech. After Rodney Chatman scored to put USC ahead, 78-76, the Yellow Jackets' James Forrest hit a turn-around three-pointer at the buzzer to upset the Men of Troy, 79-78.

FIERCEST RIVAL: It's no surprise that UCLA holds a substantial edge in its series with the Trojans (128–101), but early on USC had the upper hand. From 1932 to '43, the Trojans won 42 straight over the men from Westwood, by far the longest streak in the history of the rivalry.

FANFARE AND HOOPLA: "Fight On" is great and "Conquest" quite majestic, but a Trojan fight song without a troupe of sweater-wearing, victory-sign-flashing song girls is just noise. For 43 years, the USC song girls have brightened the sidelines in their trademark white sweaters and skirts trimmed in cardinal and gold. The Bruins have nothing on that.

FAN FAVORITE: G Harold Miner (1989-92) Nicknamed Baby Jordan, the skywalking 6'8" Miner is USC's all-time leading scorer and the only Trojan to top the 2,000-point mark (2,048). The lefthander pumped in 176 career threes and scored 30 or more points 19 times in three seasons. Pac-10 Freshman of the Year in 1990, Miner was an All-America and Pac-10 POY as a junior, when he totaled 789 points and led Southern California to a No. 2 seed in the NCAA Tournament.

CONSENSUS ALL-AMERICAS

1933	**Jerry Nemer,** F
1935	**Lee Guttero,** C
1940	**Ralph Vaughn,** F
1950	**Bill Sharman,** F
1992	**Harold Miner,** G

FIRST-ROUND PRO PICKS

1968	**Bill Hewitt,** LA Lakers (11)
1972	**Paul Westphal,** Boston (10)
1975	**John Lambert,** Cleveland (15)
1975	**Gus Williams,** St. Louis (ABA, 4)
1979	**Cliff Robinson,** New Jersey (11)
1992	**Harold Miner,** Miami (12)
1997	**Rodrick Rhodes,** Houston (24)
2007	**Nick Young,** Washington (16)
2008	**O.J. Mayo,** Minnesota (3)
2009	**DeMar DeRozan,** Toronto (9)
2009	**Taj Gibson,** Chicago (26)

PROFILE

University of Southern California, Los Angeles, CA
Founded: 1880
Enrollment: 33,500 (16,500 undergraduate)
Colors: Cardinal and gold
Nickname: Trojans
Current arena: Galen Center, opened in 2006 (10,258)
Previous: The Los Angeles Sports Arena, 1959-2006 (16,161)
First game: 1906
All-time record: 1,454-1,047 (.581)
Total weeks in AP Top 20/25: 167

Current conference: Pacific-10 (1921-)
Conference titles:
Pacific Coast: 5 (1928, '30, '35, '40, '54)
AAWU: 1 (1961)
Pac-10: 1 (1985 [tie])
Conference tournament titles:
Pac-10: 1 (2009)
NCAA Tournament appearances: 14
Sweet 16s (since 1975): 2
Final Fours: 2
NIT appearances: 4

TOP 5

G	**Paul Westphal** (1969-72)
G	**Gus Williams** (1972-75)
F	**Bill Sharman** (1946-50)
F	**Sam Clancy** (1998-2002)
C	**John Rudometkin** (1959-62)

RECORDS	GAME		SEASON		CAREER	
POINTS	45	John Block, vs. Washington (Feb. 11, 1966)	789	Harold Miner (1991-92)	2,048	Harold Miner (1989-92)
POINTS PER GAME			26.3	Harold Miner (1991-92)	23.5	Harold Miner (1989-92)
REBOUNDS	28	David Bluthenthal, vs. Arizona State (Jan. 20, 2000); Cliff Robinson, vs. Portland State (Jan. 20, 1978)	398	Ron Riley (1970-71)	1,067	Ron Riley (1969-72)
ASSISTS	15	Brandon Granville, vs. Memphis (Nov. 23, 1999)	248	Brandon Granville (1999-2000)	779	Brandon Granville (1998-2002)

SEASON REVIEW

SEASON	W-L	CONF.	SCORING		COACH	RECORD	
1906-18	93-71		*21-3 in 1908-09 without a coach*				
1918-19	3-8				Motts Blair	11-20	.355
1919-20	8-2				Elmer Henderson		
1920-21	10-4				Elmer Henderson	18-6	.750
1921-22	7-5	1-3			Bill Hunter	7-5	.583
1922-23	5-12	2-6			Les Turner		
1923-24	15-4	4-4			Les Turner		
1924-25	14-4				Les Turner		
1925-26	4-8	0-6			Les Turner		
1926-27	10-8	0-6			Les Turner	48-36	.571
1927-28	22-4	6-3			Leo Calland		
1928-29	16-6	3-6			Leo Calland	38-10	.792
1929-30	15-5	7-2	Jack Gardner	8.9	Sam Barry		
1930-31	8-8	5-4	William Pierce	5.6	Sam Barry		
1931-32	10-12	8-3	Jerry Nemer	10.1	Sam Barry		
1932-33	18-5	10-1	Lee Guttero	11.5	Sam Barry		
1933-34	16-8	9-3	Lee Guttero	11.9	Sam Barry		
1934-35	20-6	11-1	Lee Guttero	13.7	Sam Barry		
1935-36	14-12	8-4	Jack Hupp	10.3	Sam Barry		
1936-37	19-6	8-4	Jerry Gracin	8.0	Sam Barry		
1937-38	17-9	6-6	Ralph Vaughn	12.9	Sam Barry		
1938-39	20-5	9-3	Ralph Vaughn	12.8	Sam Barry		

SEAS.	W-L	CONF.	POSTSEASON	SCORING		REBOUNDS		ASSISTS		COACH	RECORD	
1939-40	20-3	10-2	NCAA REGIONAL FINAL	Ralph Vaughn	11.5					Sam Barry		
1940-41	15-10	6-6		Robert Ormsby	9.4					Sam Barry		
1941-42	12-8	7-5		Robert Ormsby	9.4					Julie Bescos	12-8	.600
1942-43	23-5	7-1		Eugene Rock	12.6					Ernie Holbrook		
1943-44	8-12	1-5		Bob Howard	8.6					Ernie Holbrook[a]	29-9	.763
1944-45	15-9	3-3		Jack Nichols	9.5					Bobby Muth	17-17	.500
1945-46	14-7	8-4		Bob Kloppenburg	10.9					Sam Barry		
1946-47	10-14	2-10		Eugene Rock	11.1					Sam Barry		
1947-48	14-10	7-5		Alex Hannum	11.4					Sam Barry		
1948-49	14-10	8-4		Bill Sharman	15.9					Sam Barry		
1949-50	16-8	7-5		Bill Sharman	18.6					Sam Barry	260-138	.653
1950-51	21-6	8-4		Bob Boyd	9.2					Forrest Twogood		
1951-52	16-14	4-8		Bob Boyd	12.1					Forrest Twogood		
1952-53	17-5	7-5		Ken Flower	13.8					Forrest Twogood		
1953-54	19-14	8-4	NCAA FOURTH PLACE	Roy Irvin	13.0					Forrest Twogood		
1954-55	14-11	5-7		Dick Welsh	14.5	Roy Irvin	12.4			Forrest Twogood		
1955-56	14-12	9-7		Jack Dunne	14.6					Forrest Twogood		
1956-57	16-12	9-7		Dan Rogers	16.5					Forrest Twogood		
1957-58	12-13	8-8		Jim Hanna	12.2					Forrest Twogood		
1958-59	15-11	8-8		John Werhas	14.3					Forrest Twogood		
1959-60	16-11	5-7	NCAA FIRST ROUND	John Rudometkin	11.7					Forrest Twogood		
1960-61	21-8	9-3	NCAA REGIONAL SEMIFINALS	John Rudometkin	23.9	John Rudometkin	12.0			Forrest Twogood		
1961-62	14-11	5-7		John Rudometkin	21.0	John Rudometkin	11.6			Forrest Twogood		
1962-63	20-9	6-6		Gordon Martin	19.3					Forrest Twogood		
1963-64	10-16	6-9		Allen Young	17.4	Allen Young	12.1			Forrest Twogood		
1964-65	14-12	8-6		Allen Young	16.1					Forrest Twogood		
1965-66	13-13	6-8		John Block	25.2					Forrest Twogood	252-178	.586
1966-67	13-12	6-8		Bill Hewitt	19.5					Bob Boyd		
1967-68	18-8	11-3		Bill Hewitt	18.8	Bill Hewitt	11.8			Bob Boyd		
1968-69	15-11	8-6		Ernest Powell	14.8					Bob Boyd		
1969-70	18-8	9-5		Dennis "Mo" Layton	16.6	Ron Riley	11.5			Bob Boyd		
1970-71	24-2	12-2		Dennis "Mo" Layton	17.6	Ron Riley	15.3			Bob Boyd		
1971-72	16-10	9-5		Paul Westphal	20.3	Ron Riley	14.2			Bob Boyd		
1972-73	18-10	9-5	NIT FIRST ROUND	Clint Chapman	15.2					Bob Boyd		
1973-74	24-5	11-3		Gus Williams	15.5					Bob Boyd		
1974-75	18-8	8-6		Gus Williams	21.2					Bob Boyd		
1975-76	11-16 ⊗	0-14		Marv Safford	18.0					Bob Boyd		
1976-77	6-20	2-12		Greg White	15.8					Bob Boyd		
1977-78	14-13	7-7		Cliff Robinson	18.4					Bob Boyd		
1978-79	20-9	14-4	NCAA SECOND ROUND	Cliff Robinson	18.8					Bob Boyd	215-132	.620▼
1979-80	12-15	5-13		Purvis Miller	16.4					Stan Morrison		
1980-81	14-13	9-9		Dwight Anderson	19.3					Stan Morrison		
1981-82	19-9	13-5	NCAA FIRST ROUND	Dwight Anderson	20.3					Stan Morrison		
1982-83	17-11	11-7		Wayne Carlander	13.1					Stan Morrison		
1983-84	11-20	6-12		Wayne Carlander	14.6					Stan Morrison		
1984-85	19-10	13-5	NCAA FIRST ROUND	Wayne Carlander	16.0					Stan Morrison		
1985-86	11-17	5-13		Tom Lewis	17.6					Stan Morrison	103-95	.520
1986-87	9-19	4-14		Derrick Dowell	20.9					George Raveling		
1987-88	7-21	5-13		Chris Moore	12.3					George Raveling		
1988-89	10-22	2-16		Ronnie Coleman	15.3					George Raveling		
1989-90	12-16	6-12		Harold Miner	20.6					George Raveling		
1990-91	19-10	10-8	NCAA FIRST ROUND	Harold Miner	23.5					George Raveling		
1991-92	24-6	15-3	NCAA SECOND ROUND	Harold Miner	26.3					George Raveling		
1992-93	18-12	9-9	NIT QUARTERFINALS	Phil Glenn	12.9					George Raveling		
1993-94	16-12	9-9	NIT FIRST ROUND	Lorenzo Orr	13.4					George Raveling	115-118	.494
1994-95	7-21 ⊗	2-16		Lorenzo Orr	16.9					Charlie Parker		
1995-96	11-19 ⊗	4-14		Stais Boseman	15.2					Charlie Parker[b]	16-31	.340▼
1996-97	17-11	12-6	NCAA FIRST ROUND	Stais Boseman	16.0					Henry Bibby		
1997-98	9-19	5-13		Gary Johnson	13.3					Henry Bibby		
1998-99	15-13	7-11	NIT FIRST ROUND	Brian Scalabrine	14.6	Brian Scalabrine	6.4	Brandon Granville	5.0	Henry Bibby		
1999-2000	16-14	9-9		Brian Scalabrine	17.8	David Bluthenthal	8.3	Brandon Granville	8.3	Henry Bibby		
2000-01	24-10	11-7	NCAA REGIONAL FINALS	Sam Clancy	17.3	Sam Clancy	7.5	Brandon Granville	6.1	Henry Bibby		
2001-02	22-10	12-6	NCAA FIRST ROUND	Sam Clancy	19.1	Sam Clancy	9.4	Brandon Granville	5.8	Henry Bibby		
2002-03	13-17	6-12		Desmon Farmer	18.7	Errick Craven	5.3	Brandon Brooks	3.5	Henry Bibby		
2003-04	13-15	8-10		Desmon Farmer	19.4	Jeff McMillan	8.6	Errick Craven	3.0	Henry Bibby		
2004-05	12-17	5-13		Gabe Pruitt	12.3	Jeff McMillan	6.9	Gabe Pruitt	3.2	Henry Bibby[c]	131-120	.522▼
2005-06	17-13	8-10		Nick Young	17.3	Nick Young	6.6	Ryan Francis	3.7	Tim Floyd		
2006-07	25-12	11-7	NCAA REGIONAL SEMIFINALS	Nick Young	17.5	Taj Gibson	8.7	Gabe Pruitt	4.3	Tim Floyd		
2007-08	21-12	11-7	NCAA FIRST ROUND	O.J. Mayo	20.7	Taj Gibson	7.8	O.J. Mayo	3.3	Tim Floyd		
2008-09	22-13	9-9	NCAA SECOND ROUND	Dwight Lewis	14.4	Taj Gibson	9.0	Daniel Hackett	4.7	Tim Floyd	85-50	.630

[a] Ernie Holbrook (6-4) and Bobby Muth (2-8) both coached during the 1943-44 season. [b] Charlie Parker (10-9) and Henry Bibby (1-8) both coached during the 1995-96 season.

[c] Henry Bibby (2-2) and Jim Saia (10-15) both coached during the 2004-05 season.

⊗ Records don't reflect games forfeited or vacated. For adjusted records, see p. 521.

▼ Coaches' records adjusted to reflect games forfeited or vacated: Bob Boyd, 216-131, .622; Charlie Parker, 19-28, .404; Henry Bibby, 132-119, .526. For yearly totals, see p. 521.

THE SCHOOLS

ESPN 84 SAGARIN

SOUTHERN ILLINOIS

With a history that includes an NAIB championship, two Division II runner-up finishes and an NIT championship team led by Walt Frazier, Southern Illinois was already a successful small program steeped in tradition at the turn of the 21st century. But that was only a stepping stone. Since then, the Salukis have become a mid-major dynasty, winning four straight (and five of six) MVC titles and making three NCAA Sweet 16 appearances.

BEST TEAM: 2006-07 As a No. 4-seed, the highest in school history, the 27–6 Salukis could no longer be considered a sleeper when they entered the 2007 NCAA Tournament. Led by Jamaal Tatum, SIU's suffocating defense held its first two victims, Holy Cross and Virginia Tech, to 51 and 48 points, respectively. In the Sweet 16, No. 1-seed Kansas—which had opened the Tourney scoring 107 points against Niagara—could reach only 61 against the rabid Salukis, but that was enough to eke out a three-point win and deny SIU a trip to the Elite Eight.

BEST PLAYER: C JOE C. MERIWEATHER (1973-75) Charlie Vaughn is the school's all-time leading scorer, but that was against D2 competition. And great as he was in the NBA, Walt Frazier played only two seasons at SIU. The 6'10" Meriweather was a monster in the middle during his three seasons, averaging 19.7 points, 12.9 rebounds and 2.1 blocks per game (the last two are school records). After single-handedly carrying SIU to the 1975 NIT, he was the 11th player chosen in the NBA draft (Houston Rockets).

BEST COACH: JACK HARTMAN (1962-70) He led Southern Illinois to two Division II national runner-up finishes and the 1967 NIT title in just eight seasons (142–64) at the helm. For his successes, *The Sporting News* named Hartman its 1967 Coach of the Year. Hartman left Southern Illinois in 1970 to become head coach at Kansas State, where he went 294–170 in 16 seasons.

GAME FOR THE AGES: In a dream 1966-67 season that saw unheralded SIU take down No. 2 Louisville and defending national champion Texas Western, Frazier and Dick Garrett officially lifted Salukis basketball to national prominence by defeating coach Al McGuire's vaunted Marquette Warriors, 71-56, for the NIT crown. Frazier dazzled the Madison Square Garden crowd (as he would for the next decade with the Knicks) with 21 points and 11 rebounds and was named tournament MVP.

HEARTBREAKER: Led by Darren Brooks' 25 points, No. 9-seed SIU had a 64-63 lead over No. 8-seed Alabama in the first round of the 2004 Tournament when the Tide's Antoine Pettway hit the game-winner with :05 left. Bama went all the way to the Elite Eight, leaving Salukis fans to ponder, "What if?"

FIERCEST RIVAL: When ESPN's *College GameDay* crew visited Carbondale in January 2008 for Creighton vs. Southern Illinois, MVC commissioner Doug Elgin said, "It's our Duke-North Carolina." The conference's two best programs since 2000 had another epic battle that day, as SIU rallied from 10 down for the 48-44 win. Creighton leads the series overall, 45–36.

Frazier dazzled the Madison Square Garden crowd (as he would for the next decade with the Knicks).

FANFARE AND HOOPLA: Salukis are Middle Eastern hunting dogs and said to be the oldest pure domesticated breed in the world. SIU's first Saluki mascot, appropriately named King Tut (1943-54), is entombed in the school's football stadium. When Khalila, SIU's 22nd mascot, died in 2005, many Southern Illinois fans volunteered their own dogs for service. The athletic department selected as the primary mascot a cousin of Khalila named Fabian.

FAN FAVORITE: G TONY YOUNG (2003-07) Named to the MVC All-Defensive Team three times and known in Carbondale as the Secretary of Defense, Young won Salukis fans over—and over—with his gritty play.

CONSENSUS ALL-AMERICAS

1966 **George McNeil** (Little A-A), G
1967 **Walt Frazier** (Little A-A), G

FIRST-ROUND PRO PICKS

1967 **Walt Frazier**, New York (5)
1967 **Walt Frazier**, Denver (ABA)
1975 **Joe C. Meriweather**, Houston (11)

PROFILE

Southern Illinois University Carbondale, Carbondale, IL
Founded: 1869
Enrollment: 20,673 (15,980 undergraduate)
Colors: Maroon and white
Nickname: Salukis
Current arena: SIU Arena, opened in 1964 (9,628)
Previous: Davies Gym, 1925-64 (1,532); The Old Science Building (a.k.a. the Castle), 1913-25 (N/A)
First game: Dec. 12, 1913
All-time record: 1,415-958 (.596)
Total weeks in AP Top 20/25: 18
Current conference: Missouri Valley (1975-)
Conference titles:
MVC: 8 (1977 [tie], '90, '92 [tie], 2002 [tie], '03, '04, '05, '07)
Conference tournament titles:
MVC: 5 (1977, '93, '94, '95, 2006)
NCAA Tournament appearances: 10
Sweet 16s (since 1975): 3
NIT appearances: 9
Semifinals: 1
Titles: 1 (1967)

TOP 5

G **Walt Frazier** (1964-65, '66-67)
G **Charlie Vaughn** (1958-62)
G/F **Darren Brooks** (2001-05)
F **Ashraf Amaya** (1989-93)
C **Joe C. Meriweather** (1972-75)

RECORDS	GAME		SEASON		CAREER	
POINTS	46	Dick Garrett, vs. Centenary (March 1, 1968)	779	Charlie Vaughn (1959-60)	2,088	Charlie Vaughn (1958-62)
POINTS PER GAME			26.9	Charlie Vaughn (1959-60)	24.6	Charlie Vaughn (1958-62)
REBOUNDS	27	Joe C. Meriweather, vs. Indiana State (Feb. 18, 1974)	387	Joe C. Meriweather (1973-74)	1,244	Seymour Bryson (1955-59)
ASSISTS	13	Bryan Mullins, vs. Massachusetts (Nov. 12, 2008); Rob Kirsner, vs. Wichita State (March 3, 1981)	150	Darren Brooks (2004-05)	465	Wayne Abrams (1976-80)

SEASON REVIEW

EASON	W-L	CONF.	SCORING	COACH	RECORD
13-14	5-6			William McAndrew	
14-15	3-12			William McAndrew	
15-16	4-11			William McAndrew	
16-17	6-9			William McAndrew	
17-18	14-3			William McAndrew	
18-19	no team				
919-20	6-11			F. Lodge, W. Warren	6-11 .353
920-21	15-9			William McAndrew	
921-22	14-6			William McAndrew	
922-23	11-3			William McAndrew	
923-24	5-12			William McAndrew	
1924-25	12-5			William McAndrew	
1925-26	4-8			William McAndrew	
1926-27	10-5			William McAndrew	
1927-28	15-9			William McAndrew	
1928-29	10-11			William McAndrew	
1929-30	8-10			William McAndrew	
1930-31	7-13			William McAndrew	
1931-32	9-12			William McAndrew	
1932-33	18-4			William McAndrew	
1933-34	15-4			William McAndrew	
1934-35	12-5			William McAndrew	

SEAS.	W-L	CONF.	POSTSEASON	SCORING		REBOUNDS		ASSISTS		COACH	RECORD	
935-36	15-3									William McAndrew		
936-37	14-6									William McAndrew		
937-38	16-7									William McAndrew		
938-39	11-9									William McAndrew		
939-40	22-4			George Welborn	7.4					William McAndrew		
940-41	11-12			Fred Campbell	9.4					William McAndrew		
941-42	8-9			John Sebastian	12.0					William McAndrew		
942-43	9-9			John Sebastian	13.1					William McAndrew	303-216	.584
943-44	8-7			Sam Milosevich	12.1					Glenn Martin		
944-45	15-7			Sam Milosevich	12.1					Glenn Martin		
945-46	20-6		NAIB CHAMPION	Don Sheffer	14.1					Glenn Martin	43-20	.683
946-47	19-10			John Sebastian	11.8					Lynn Holder		
947-48	22-4			Bob Colborn	11.9					Lynn Holder		
948-49	13-11			Charlie Goss	11.6					Lynn Holder		
949-50	21-6			Tom Millikin	13.3					Lynn Holder		
950-51	12-14			Tom Millikin	18.7					Lynn Holder		
951-52	13-11			Tom Millikin	16.9	Charles Thate	12.0			Lynn Holder		
952-53	13-11			Ray Ripplemeyer	15.3	Ray Ripplemeyer	10.9			Lynn Holder		
953-54	12-11			Harvey Welch	12.3	Gib Kurtz	7.9			Lynn Holder		
954-55	10-13			Gib Kurtz	15.4	Gus Doss	12.0			Lynn Holder		
955-56	14-11			Rick Talley	13.6	Seymour Bryson	12.4			Lynn Holder		
956-57	12-11			Larry Whitlock	17.3	Seymour Bryson	13.9			Lynn Holder		
957-58	13-11			Seymour Bryson	16.0	Seymour Bryson	13.3			Lynn Holder	174-124	.584
958-59	17-10			Charlie Vaughn	23.8	Seymour Bryson	10.9			Harry Gallatin		
959-60	20-9			Charlie Vaughn	26.9	Charlie Vaughn	9.6			Harry Gallatin		
960-61	21-6			Charlie Vaughn	23.4	Don Hepler	10.8			Harry Gallatin		
961-62	21-10			Ed Spila	14.9	Ed Spila	10.8			Harry Gallatin	79-35	.693
962-63	20-10			Dave Henson	13.0	Lou Williams	9.2			Jack Hartman		
963-64	15-10			Joe Ramsey	16.0	Joe Ramsey	7.6			Jack Hartman		
964-65	20-6			George McNeil	17.2	Walt Frazier	9.2			Jack Hartman		
965-66	21-7			George McNeil	18.2	Boyd O'Neal	9.9			Jack Hartman		
966-67	24-2		NIT CHAMPION	Walt Frazier	18.2	Walt Frazier	11.9			Jack Hartman		
967-68	13-11			Dick Garrett	20.1	Chuck Benson	8.5			Jack Hartman		
968-69	16-8		NIT FIRST ROUND	Dick Garrett	18.5	Chuck Benson	8.4			Jack Hartman		
969-70	13-10			L.C. Brasfield	17.5	L.C. Brasfield	7.2			Jack Hartman	142-64	.689
970-71	13-10			Greg Starrick	22.4	L.C. Brasfield	11.0			Paul Lambert		
971-72	10-16			Greg Starrick	23.8	Nate Hawthorne	7.7			Paul Lambert		
972-73	11-15			Nate Hawthorne	17.3	Joe C. Meriweather	12.3			Paul Lambert		
973-74	19-7			Joe C. Meriweather	21.2	Joe C. Meriweather	14.9			Paul Lambert		
974-75	18-9		NIT FIRST ROUND	Joe C. Meriweather	20.6	Joe C. Meriweather	11.5			Paul Lambert		
975-76	16-10	9-3		Mike Glenn	19.4	Gary Wilson	7.7			Paul Lambert		
976-77	22-7	8-4	NCAA REGIONAL SEMIFINALS	Mike Glenn	21.0	Gary Wilson	7.3			Paul Lambert		
977-78	17-10	11-5		Gary Wilson	19.0	Gary Wilson	7.5	Wayne Abrams	4.4	Paul Lambert	126-84	.600
978-79	15-13	8-8		Milton Huggins	19.0	Gary Wilson	8.6	Wayne Abrams	5.1	Joe Gottfried		
979-80	9-17	5-11		Barry Smith	17.3	Charles Moore	6.2	Wayne Abrams	3.4	Joe Gottfried		
980-81	7-20	0-16		Rod Camp	15.2	Charles Nance	7.3	Rob Kirsner	3.4	Joe Gottfried	31-50	.383
981-82	11-16	7-9		Ken Byrd	11.4	Charles Nance	6.2	James Copeland	4.1	Allen Van Winkle		
982-83	9-19	5-13		Ken Byrd	11.6	Charles Nance	6.0	James Copeland	2.9	Allen Van Winkle		
983-84	15-13	7-9		Kenny Perry	13.4	Cleveland Bibbens	7.3	Bernard Campbell	3.0	Allen Van Winkle		
984-85	14-14	6-10		Kenny Perry	13.4	Cleveland Bibbens	9.3	Bernard Campbell	3.0	Allen Van Winkle	49-62	.441
985-86	8-20	4-12		Steve Middleton	16.4	Billy Ross	4.6	Steve Middleton	2.7	Rich Herrin		
986-87	12-17	5-9		Steve Middleton	19.1	Tim Richardson	6.8	Kai Nurnberger	4.2	Rich Herrin		
987-88	12-16	6-8		Steve Middleton	25.4	Rick Shipley	6.9	Kai Nurnberger	4.1	Rich Herrin		
988-89	20-14	6-8	NIT FIRST ROUND	Kai Nurnberger	16.4	Rick Shipley	7.3	Kai Nurnberger	4.0	Rich Herrin		
989-90	26-8	10-4	NIT FIRST ROUND	Freddie McSwain	17.3	Jerry Jones	10.3	Sterling Mahan	4.2	Rich Herrin		
990-91	18-14	9-7	NIT QUARTERFINALS	Sterling Mahan	17.2	Rick Shipley	9.0	Sterling Mahan	3.9	Rich Herrin		
991-92	22-8	14-4	NIT FIRST ROUND	Ashraf Amaya	19.4	Ashraf Amaya	10.3	Chris Lowery	3.9	Rich Herrin		
992-93	23-10	12-6	NCAA FIRST ROUND	Ashraf Amaya	16.5	Ashraf Amaya	10.7	Tyrone Bell	4.0	Rich Herrin		
993-94	23-7	14-4	NCAA FIRST ROUND	Paul Lusk	15.2	Marcus Timmons	9.8	Chris Lowery	4.0	Rich Herrin		
994-95	23-9	13-5	NCAA FIRST ROUND	Chris Carr	22.0	Marcus Timmons	9.3	Paul Lusk	3.4	Rich Herrin		
995-96	11-18	4-14		Troy Hudson	21.3	Jaratio Tucker	5.1	Shane Hawkins	4.5	Rich Herrin		
996-97	13-17	6-12		Troy Hudson	21.0	Rashad Tucker	8.7	Shane Hawkins	4.4	Rich Herrin		
997-98	14-16	8-10		Rashad Tucker	15.8	Chris Thunell	8.6	Shane Hawkins	3.5	Rich Herrin	225-174	.564
998-99	15-12	10-8		Monte Jenkins	14.5	Chris Thunell	6.8	Ricky Collum	2.5	Bruce Weber		
999-2000	20-13	12-6	NIT SECOND ROUND	Kent Williams	13.3	Chris Thunell	6.7	Brandon Mells	3.5	Bruce Weber		
000-01	16-14	10-8		Kent Williams	17.6	Jermaine Dearman	6.4	Kent Williams	2.8	Bruce Weber		
001-02	28-8	14-4	NCAA REGIONAL SEMIFINALS	Kent Williams	15.8	Jermaine Dearman	7.7	Marcus Belcher	3.3	Bruce Weber		
002-03	24-7	16-2	NCAA FIRST ROUND	Kent Williams	15.3	Jermaine Dearman	6.4	Darren Brooks	3.3	Bruce Weber	103-54	.656
003-04	25-5	17-1	NCAA FIRST ROUND	Darren Brooks	16.5	Darren Brooks	5.7	Darren Brooks	2.7	Matt Painter	25-5	.833
004-05	27-8	15-3	NCAA SECOND ROUND	Darren Brooks	15.0	Darren Brooks	5.2	Darren Brooks	4.3	Chris Lowery		
005-06	22-11	12-6	NCAA FIRST ROUND	Jamaal Tatum	15.0	Randal Falker	7.8	Jamaal Tatum	3.3	Chris Lowery		
006-07	29-7	15-3	NCAA REGIONAL SEMIFINALS	Jamaal Tatum	15.2	Randal Falker	7.7	Bryan Mullins	3.5	Chris Lowery		
007-08	18-15	11-7	NIT SECOND ROUND	Randal Falker	13.0	Randal Falker	7.0	Bryan Mullins	5.0	Chris Lowery		
008-09	13-18	8-10		Kevin Dillard	12.2	Tony Boyle	5.4	Bryan Mullins	5.6	Chris Lowery	109-59	.649

ESPN 92 SAGARIN

SOUTHERN METHODIST

When the good times come, they more than make up for the lean years. The squads from 1954 to '57, '64 to '67 and '83 to '88 account for nine of the school's 10 NCAA bids, both All-Americas (Jim Krebs and Jon Koncak), seven conference titles and a Final Four appearance in 1956. Let the good times roll.

BEST TEAM: 1955-56 Coach Doc Hayes' team charged to a 22–2 record and a No. 7 national ranking. Five players averaged double figures, including Krebs, guard Bobby Mills and forward Joel Krog. After squeaking past Texas Tech, 68-67, in the opening round of the NCAA Tournament, the Mustangs blew out Houston and Oklahoma City before bowing in the Final Four to defending champ San Francisco, 86-68.

BEST PLAYER: C JIM KREBS (1954-57) The 6'8" consensus All-America with a killer hook shot averaged 24.0 points and 12.0 rebounds as a senior. Krebs also led SMU to three Southwest Conference titles and a 47–8 record his last two years (23–1 in the SWC). In the 1956 NCAA national semifinal loss to San Francisco, Krebs outscored Bill Russell 24-17.

BEST COACH: E.O. "DOC" HAYES (1947-67) His teams won eight SWC titles (three shared) and went to six NCAA Tournaments, reaching the Final Four in 1956. In Hayes' first eight years, attendance at games rose 600%, forcing the school to replace Perkins Gym with SMU (now Moody) Coliseum for the 1956-57 season.

GAME FOR THE AGES: If they're playing in the NCAA Tournament, then the Mustangs must be going up against a frontcourt All-America. In its 10 Tourneys, SMU has taken on Bill Russell, Wilt Chamberlain, Wes Unseld, Elvin Hayes, Patrick Ewing and Danny Ferry. The lone victory against those six superstars: a stunning 1967 Midwest Regional semifinal upset of Unseld and No. 2-ranked Louisville, 83-81, behind 30 points from Denny Holman.

HEARTBREAKER: The Mustangs hosted a 1957 NCAA Tournament Midwest Regional semifinal at brand-new SMU Coliseum. The problem? The man opposite All-America Krebs was a Kansas Jayhawk by the name of Wilt Chamberlain. Despite shooting just 32% from the field, the Mustangs held the lead with five minutes left in regulation when Krebs fouled out. Chamberlain and the Jayhawks rallied to a 73-65 overtime win.

FIERCEST RIVAL: SMU and Texas Christian share a metro area and a rivalry that has a corporate sponsor and a name that doesn't exactly roll off the tongue: the State Farm DFW Duel. Though the Mustangs and the Horned Frogs no longer compete in the same conference, they played against each other in the SWC from 1923 to '96, then in the WAC until 2001. SMU leads the series, 101–83.

FANFARE AND HOOPLA: SMU fans hope for a little Moody Magic during every home game. And more often than not, they get it. SMU has gone 245–134 at Moody Coliseum since 1982-83.

In its 10 Tourneys, SMU has taken on Bill Russell, Wilt Chamberlain, Wes Unseld, Elvin Hayes, Patrick Ewing and Danny Ferry.

FAN FAVORITE: G JERYL SASSER (1997-2001) He was flamboyant: He wore different-size Band-Aids on different parts of his body for every game, whether he needed them or not. He was confident: When coach Mike Dement drew up a play calling for the team's best shooter in one spot, its best post-up player in another and its best passer in a third, Sasser said, "I can't be in three places at once." And he was right: In 1998-99 he led the Mustangs in scoring, rebounding, assists and steals.

CONSENSUS ALL-AMERICAS

1957 **Jim Krebs**, C

FIRST-ROUND PRO PICKS

1957 **Jim Krebs**, Minneapolis (3)
1967 **Charles Beasley**, Indiana (ABA)
1985 **Jon Koncak**, Atlanta (5)
2001 **Jeryl Sasser**, Orlando (22)

PROFILE

Southern Methodist University, University Park, TX
Founded: 1911
Enrollment: 10,901 (6,208 undergraduate)
Colors: Red and blue
Nickname: Mustangs
Current arena: Moody Coliseum, opened in 1956 as SMU Coliseum (8,998)
Previous: Perkins Gym, 1942-56 (4,000); SMU Gym 2, 1926-42 (3,500); SMU Gym, 1919-26 (500)
First game: Dec. 16, 1916
All-time record: 1,154-1,097 (.513)
Total weeks in AP Top 20/25: 41
Current conference: Conference USA (2005-)
Conference titles:
SWC: 13 (1935 [tie], '37, '55, '56, '57, '58 [tie], '62 [tie], '65 [tie], '66, '67 '72 [tie], '88, '93)
Conference tournament titles:
SWC: 1 (1988)
NCAA Tournament appearances: 10
Final Fours: 1
NIT appearances: 2

TOP 5

G **Quinton Ross** (1999-2003)
G **Jeryl Sasser** (1997-2001)
F **Larry Davis** (1981-85)
F **Gene Phillips** (1968-71)
C **Jim Krebs** (1954-57)

RECORDS	GAME		SEASON		CAREER	
POINTS	51	Gene Phillips, vs. Texas (March 2, 1971)	737	Gene Phillips (1970-71)	1,992	Jeryl Sasser (1997-2001)
POINTS PER GAME			28.5	Gene Phillips (1969-70)	26.1	Gene Phillips (1968-71)
REBOUNDS	26	Ira Terrell, vs. New Mexico State (Dec. 16, 1975)	378	Jon Koncak (1983-84)	1,169	Jon Koncak (1981-85)
ASSISTS	17	Gerald Lewis, vs. Texas (March 6, 1993)	255	Billy Allen (1979-80)	828	Butch Moore (1982-86)

SEASON REVIEW

SEASON	W-L	CONF.	SCORING	COACH	RECORD
16-17	12-2			Dale Morrison	12-2 .857
17-18	5-4			J. Burton Rix	
18-19	7-8	5-6		J. Burton Rix	
19-20	6-11	2-8		J. Burton Rix	
20-21	6-13	0-11		J. Burton Rix	24-36 .400
21-22	8-14	4-11		R.N. Blackwell	8-14 .364
922-23	10-11	4-10		H.A. Faulkner	
923-24	9-15	7-15		H.A. Faulkner	19-26 .422
924-25	5-11	4-10		J.W. St. Clair	
925-26	10-6	8-4		J.W. St. Clair	
1926-27	12-5	7-4		J.W. St. Clair	
1927-28	14-3	10-2		J.W. St. Clair	
1928-29	7-9	6-6		J.W. St. Clair	
1929-30	8-10	6-6		J.W. St. Clair	
1930-31	15-8	8-4		J.W. St. Clair	
1931-32	9-13	2-10		J.W. St. Clair	
1932-33	9-9	5-7		J.W. St. Clair	
1933-34	11-9	5-7		J.W. St. Clair	
1934-35	14-3	9-3		J.W. St. Clair	
1935-36	4-8	4-8		J.W. St. Clair	

SEAS.	W-L	CONF.	POSTSEASON	SCORING		REBOUNDS		ASSISTS		COACH	RECORD	
936-37	13-8	10-2								J.W. St. Clair		
937-38	9-6	8-4								J.W. St. Clair	140-108	.565
938-39	14-8	8-4								F.C. Baccus		
939-40	7-13	5-7								F.C. Baccus		
940-41	10-10	6-6								F.C. Baccus		
941-42	3-16	1-11								F.C. Baccus		
942-43	10-8	4-8								James Stewart		
943-44	8-9	6-6								James Stewart	18-17	.514
944-45	11-10	7-5								Roy D. Baccus	11-10	.524
945-46	7-16	0-12								F.C. Baccus		
946-47	14-8	8-4								F.C. Baccus	55-71	.437
947-48	13-10	5-7								E.O. “Doc” Hayes		
948-49	11-13	5-7								E.O. “Doc” Hayes		
949-50	10-13	7-5								E.O. “Doc” Hayes		
950-51	14-10	6-6								E.O. “Doc” Hayes		
951-52	11-13	5-7								E.O. “Doc” Hayes		
952-53	8-12	4-8								E.O. “Doc” Hayes		
953-54	13-9	6-6		Derrell Murphy	14.6					E.O. “Doc” Hayes		
954-55	15-10	9-3	NCAA REGIONAL SEMIFINALS	Jim Krebs	21.3	Joel Krog	10.8			E.O. “Doc” Hayes		
955-56	25-4	12-0	NCAA FOURTH PLACE	Jim Krebs	19.1	Jim Krebs	10.0			E.O. “Doc” Hayes		
956-57	22-4	11-1	NCAA REGIONAL SEMIFINALS	Jim Krebs	24.0	Jim Krebs	12.0			E.O. “Doc” Hayes		
957-58	15-10	9-5		Rick Herrscher	17.5	Bobby James	9.4			E.O. “Doc” Hayes		
958-59	16-8	10-4		Bobby James	16.0	Bobby James	10.0			E.O. “Doc” Hayes		
959-60	17-7	10-4		Steve Strange	17.2	Steve Strange	10.8			E.O. “Doc” Hayes		
960-61	12-12	6-8		Steve Strange	19.0	Steve Strange	8.8			E.O. “Doc” Hayes		
961-62	18-7	11-3		Jan Loudermilk	20.9	Jan Loudermilk	9.4			E.O. “Doc” Hayes		
962-63	12-12	6-8		Dave Siegmund	17.4	Dave Siegmund	6.8			E.O. “Doc” Hayes		
963-64	12-12	8-6		Gene Elmore	20.3	Gene Elmore	11.6			E.O. “Doc” Hayes		
964-65	17-10	10-4	NCAA REGIONAL SEMIFINALS	Carroll Hooser	15.8	Carroll Hooser	9.8			E.O. “Doc” Hayes		
965-66	17-9	11-3	NCAA REGIONAL SEMIFINALS	Carroll Hooser	20.1	Carroll Hooser	9.9			E.O. “Doc” Hayes		
966-67	20-6	12-2	NCAA REGIONAL FINALS	Denny Holman	16.5	Lynn Phillips	9.4			E.O. “Doc” Hayes	298-191	.609
967-68	6-18	5-9		Lynn Phillips	19.1	Bill Voight	8.8			Bob Prewitt		
968-69	12-12	8-6		Gene Phillips	21.3	Bill Voight	10.6			Bob Prewitt		
969-70	5-19	4-10		Gene Phillips	28.5	Gene Phillips	8.1			Bob Prewitt		
970-71	16-10	8-6		Gene Phillips	28.3	G. Phillips, S. Putnam	7.5			Bob Prewitt		
971-72	16-11	10-4		Ruben Triplett	18.2	Ruben Triplett	10.8	Zachary Thiel	3.4	Bob Prewitt		
972-73	10-15	7-7		Sammy Hervey	21.5	Ira Terrell	14.1	Zachary Thiel	5.6	Bob Prewitt		
973-74	15-12	10-4		Ira Terrell	22.1	Ira Terrell	13.0	Zachary Thiel	4.7	Bob Prewitt		
974-75	8-18	4-10		Rusty Bourquein	13.3	Rusty Bourquein	9.5	John Sagehorn	3.2	Bob Prewitt	88-115	.433
975-76	16-12	10-6		Ira Terrell	22.1	Ira Terrell	13.5	Mike Jaccar	7.4	Sonny Allen		
976-77	8-19	7-9		Pete Lodwick	13.6	Jeff Swanson	8.2	Mark Davis	3.5	Sonny Allen		
977-78	10-18	6-10		Jeff Swanson	13.7	Jeff Swanson	7.2	Mark Davis	3.7	Sonny Allen		
978-79	11-16	6-10		Brad Branson	17.2	Brad Branson	10.2	Billy Allen	8.9	Sonny Allen		
979-80	16-12	7-9		Brad Branson	15.7	Brad Branson	9.0	Billy Allen	9.1	Sonny Allen	61-77	.442
980-81	7-20	3-13		Dave Piehler	14.9	Johnnie James	7.7	Gordon Welch	3.1	Dave Bliss		
981-82	6-21	1-15		John Addison	12.9	Jon Koncak	5.7	John Addison	4.8	Dave Bliss		
982-83	19-11	9-7		Jon Koncak	14.6	Jon Koncak	9.4	Butch Moore	6.4	Dave Bliss		
983-84	25-8	12-4	NCAA SECOND ROUND	Jon Koncak	15.5	Jon Koncak	11.5	Carl Wright	6.2	Dave Bliss		
984-85	23-10	10-6	NCAA SECOND ROUND	Jon Koncak	17.2	Jon Koncak	10.7	Butch Moore	7.5	Dave Bliss		
985-86	18-11	10-6	NIT FIRST ROUND	Kevin Lewis	18.6	Terry Williams	7.6	Butch Moore	7.7	Dave Bliss		
986-87	16-13	7-9		Kato Armstrong	17.3	Terry Williams	7.4	Scott Johnson	5.1	Dave Bliss		
987-88	28-7	12-4	NCAA SECOND ROUND	Kato Armstrong	16.1	Terry Thomas	7.9	Kato Armstrong	6.0	Dave Bliss	142-101	.584
988-89	13-16	7-9		Eric Longino	16.6	Glenn Puddy	9.8	Rod Hampton	3.8	John Shumate		
989-90	10-18	5-11		John Colborne	18.2	John Colborne	7.3	Rod Hampton	5.4	John Shumate		
990-91	12-17	6-10		Mike Wilson	18.3	Tim Mason	7.5	Rod Hampton	5.6	John Shumate		
991-92	10-18	4-10		Mike Wilson	16.3	Greg Kinzer	7.6	Gerald Lewis	4.9	John Shumate		
992-93	20-8	12-2	NCAA FIRST ROUND	Mike Wilson	19.4	Greg Kinzer	7.6	Gerald Lewis	6.7	John Shumate		
993-94	6-21	3-11		James Gatewood	13.1	James Gatewood	7.0	Troy Matthews	4.1	John Shumate		
994-95	7-20	3-11		Troy Matthews	15.5	Matt Timme	5.5	Troy Matthews	3.9	John Shumate	78-118	.398
995-96	8-20	3-11		Jay Poerner	13.2	Mohammed Tijjani	5.5	Jemeil Rich	3.9	Mike Dement		
996-97	16-12	7-9		Jay Poerner	16.6	Jay Poerner	6.6	Stephen Woods	3.4	Mike Dement		
997-98	18-10	6-8		Jay Poerner	16.3	Jeryl Sasser	8.3	Jeryl Sasser	3.7	Mike Dement		
998-99	15-15	7-7		Jeryl Sasser	18.7	Jeryl Sasser	8.5	Jeryl Sasser	3.5	Mike Dement		
999-2000	21-9	9-5	NIT FIRST ROUND	Jeryl Sasser	17.3	Willie Davis	9.3	Jeryl Sasser	4.6	Mike Dement		
000-01	18-12	8-8		Jeryl Sasser	17.0	Jeryl Sasser	8.3	Jeryl Sasser	4.2	Mike Dement		
001-02	15-14	10-8		Damon Hancock	22.0	Patrick Simpson	6.8	Damon Hancock	3.6	Mike Dement		
002-03	17-13	11-7		Quinton Ross	20.3	Patrick Simpson	7.1	Bryan Hopkins	3.9	Mike Dement		
003-04	12-18	5-13		Bryan Hopkins	17.7	Patrick Simpson	6.0	Bryan Hopkins	3.8	Mike Dement[a]	138-120	.535
004-05	14-14	9-9		Bryan Hopkins	17.9	Eric Castro	7.3	Bryan Hopkins	3.9	Jimmy Tubbs		
005-06	13-16	4-10		Bryan Hopkins	14.5	Devon Pearson	8.3	Bryan Hopkins	3.5	Jimmy Tubbs	27-30	.474
006-07	14-17	3-13		Ike Ofoegbu	14.2	Ike Ofoegbu	7.6	Jon Killen	4.9	Matt Doherty		
007-08	10-20	4-12		Jon Killen	12.9	Papa Dia	6.5	Jon Killen	5.1	Matt Doherty		
008-09	9-21	3-13		Paul McCoy	13.4	Bamba Fall	7.1	Derek Williams	3.5	Matt Doherty	33-58	.363

[a] Mike Dement (10-15) and Robert Lineburg (2-3) both coached during the 2003-04 season.

ESPN 155 SAGARIN

SOUTHERN MISSISSIPPI

Good things seem to come in pairs for Southern Miss: successful coaches (Lee Floyd, M.K. Turk); NCAA bids (1990, '91); deep postseason runs ('52-53 NAIA, '86-87 NIT); first-round NBA picks (Randolph Keys, Clarence Weatherspoon).

BEST TEAM: 1952-53 Two of the school's three highest scorers—Nick Revon (2,135) and Tom Bishop (1,932)—led a team that was perfect at home (13–0) and 27–8 overall. Led by coach Lee Floyd, the Southerners beat Alabama, Memphis and NAIA power Evansville during the regular season, won their NAIA district title with two routs and advanced to the national elite eight before falling to three-time champ Hamline, 102-92.

BEST PLAYER: F CLARENCE WEATHERSPOON (1988-92) The 6'7", 250-pound Weatherspoon justified his nickname, Baby Barkley (after the famous Charles), finishing as the school's No. 2 scorer (2,130) and No. 1 rebounder (1,320)—making him one of just 98 D1 players with 2,000 points and 1,000 rebounds. A three-time Metro Conference Player of the Year, he was the ninth overall pick in the 1992 NBA draft (Philadelphia 76ers).

BEST COACH: M.K. TURK (1976-96) The Golden Eagles' winningest coach (300), Turk took them to six NITs (winning one), both of the school's NCAA appearances and a Top 25 AP ranking in 1991. He had four 20-win seasons and helped the program move from independent status into the Metro Conference in 1982, and then to Conference USA for the 1995-96 season.

GAME FOR THE AGES: Southern Miss went all the way to the 1987 NIT final powered by its Fab Four—juniors Casey Fisher, Derrek Hamilton, John White and tournament MVP Randolph Keys. Against La Salle, the Golden Eagles shot 11 of 24 from three-point range and withstood a late rally to win, 84-80.

FIERCEST RIVAL: Without an in-state C-USA rival, Southern Miss always gears up for its games with conference power Memphis, although the Golden Eagles trail in series, which dates back to 1938, 58–23.

SEASON REVIEW

SEAS.	W-L	CONF.	COACH	SEAS.	W-L	CONF.	COACH
1913-47	*151-139*			1960-61	23-3		Fred Lewis
1947-48	7-9		J.D. Stonestreet	1961-62	13-13		Fred Lewis
1948-49	6-10		Jess Thompson	1962-63	12-14		Lee Floyd
1949-50	19-7		Lee Floyd	1963-64	16-8		Lee Floyd
1950-51	20-15		Lee Floyd	1964-65	15-11		Lee Floyd
1951-52	29-8		Lee Floyd	1965-66	12-13		Lee Floyd
1952-53	27-8		Lee Floyd	1966-67	16-9		Lee Floyd
1953-54	23-8		Lee Floyd	1967-68	19-6		Lee Floyd
1954-55	11-17		Chuck Finley	1968-69	15-10		Lee Floyd
1955-56	16-12		Chuck Finley	1969-70	15-11		Lee Floyd
1956-57	12-13		Chuck Finley	1970-71	7-19		Lee Floyd
1957-58	18-7		Fred Lewis	1971-72	0-24		Jeep Clark
1958-59	12-13		Fred Lewis	1972-73	8-16		Jeep Clark
1959-60	23-2		Fred Lewis	1973-74	11-15		Jeep Clark

SEAS.	W-L	CONF.	SCORING		COACH	RECORD	
1974-75	11-15		Mike Coleman	28.2	Jeep Clark		
1975-76	11-15		John Prince	14.3	Jeep Clark	41-85	.325
1976-77	11-16		John Prince	20.0	M.K. Turk		
1977-78	13-12		Jerome Arnold	12.9	M.K. Turk		
1978-79	13-14		Jerome Arnold	18.2	M.K. Turk		
1979-80	17-10		Joe Dawson	18.2	M.K. Turk		
1980-81	20-7	■	Eddie Jiles	16.0	M.K. Turk		
1981-82	15-11		Joe Dawson	17.2	M.K. Turk		
1982-83	14-14	3-9	Curtis Green	16.7	M.K. Turk		
1983-84	13-15	4-10	Curtis Green	16.0	M.K. Turk		
1984-85	7-21	3-11	James Williams	16.3	M.K. Turk		
1985-86	17-12	6-6 ■	Kenny Siler	14.6	M.K. Turk		
1986-87	23-11	6-6 [1]	Randolph Keys	16.4	M.K. Turk		
1987-88	19-11	5-7 ■	Derrek Hamilton	19.1	M.K. Turk		
1988-89	10-17	2-10	Darrin Chancellor	20.6	M.K. Turk		
1989-90	20-12	9-5 ●	Darrin Chancellor	17.8	M.K. Turk		
1990-91	21-8	10-4 ●	Clarence Weatherspoon	17.8	M.K. Turk		
1991-92	13-16	5-7	Clarence Weatherspoon	22.3	M.K. Turk		
1992-93	10-17	6-6	Bernard Haslett	18.9	M.K. Turk		
1993-94	15-15	5-7 ■	Bernard Haslett	19.8	M.K. Turk		
1994-95	17-13	6-6 ■	Glen Whisby	15.2	M.K. Turk		
1995-96	12-15	6-8	Damien Smith	17.3	M.K. Turk	300-267	.529
1996-97	12-15	6-8	Damien Smith	12.0	James Green		
1997-98	22-11	9-7 ■	Kelly McCarty	14.6	James Green		
1998-99	14-16	6-10	Neil Reed	18.1	James Green		
1999-2000	17-12	7-9	David Wall	17.0	James Green		
2000-01	22-9	11-5 ■	Vandarel Jones	12.7	James Green		
2001-02	10-17	4-12	Elvin Mims	18.9	James Green		
2002-03	13-16	5-11	Charles Gaines	15.1	James Green		
2003-04	13-15	6-10	Charles Gaines	15.7	James Green	123-111	.526
2004-05	11-17	2-14	Rashaad Carruth	13.4	Larry Eustachy		
2005-06	10-21	3-11	Courtney Beasley	10.7	Larry Eustachy		
2006-07	20-11	9-7	Jeremy Wise	17.5	Larry Eustachy		
2007-08	19-14	9-7	Jeremy Wise	18.7	Larry Eustachy		
2008-09	15-17	4-12	Jeremy Wise	16.7	Larry Eustachy	75-80	.484

● NCAA Tournament appearance ■ NIT appearance [1] NIT championship

PROFILE

University of Southern Mississippi, Hattiesburg, MS
Founded: 1910
Enrollment: 15,253 (12,520 undergraduate)
Colors: Black and gold
Nickname: Golden Eagles
Current arena: Reed Green Coliseum, opened in 1965 (8,095)
Previous: The Sports Arena, 1951-65 (4,000); Hattiesburg High School Gym, 1945-51 (N/A); Demonstration School Gym, 1930-46 (N/A)
First game: Feb. 5, 1913
All-time record: 1,076-928 (.537)
Total weeks in AP Top 20/25: 19
Current conference: Conference USA (1995-)
Conference titles:
Gulf States Conference: 2 (1950, '52)
Metro Conference: 1 (1991)
C-USA: 1 (2001 [tie])
Conference tournament titles: 0
NCAA Tournament appearances: 2
NIT appearances: 8
Semifinals: 1
Titles: 1 (1987)

FIRST-ROUND PRO PICKS

1988 **Randolph Keys,** Cleveland (22)
1992 **Clarence Weatherspoon,** Philadelphia (9)

TOP 5

G **Nick Revon** (1950-54)
G **Jeremy Wise** (2006-09)
F **Tom Bishop** (1949-53)
F **Wendell Ladner** (1967-70)
F **Clarence Weatherspoon** (1988-92)

RECORDS

	GAME		SEASON		CAREER	
POINTS	45	Berlin Ladner, vs. Samford (Feb. 21, 1968)	737	Nick Revon (1953-54)	2,135	Nick Revon (1950-54)
POINTS PER GAME			28.2	Mike Coleman (1974-75)	20.5	Wendell Ladner (1967-70)
REBOUNDS	32	Wendell Ladner, vs. Texas-Pan American (Feb. 9, 1970)	436	Wendell Ladner (1969-70)	1,320	Clarence Weatherspoon (1988-92)
ASSISTS	16	Casey Fisher, vs. Oregon Tech (Dec. 18, 1985)	222	Dallas Dale (1991-92)	612	Casey Fisher (1984-88)

ESPN 271 SAGARIN

SOUTHERN UTAH

Coach Stan Jack built up the Thunderbirds in the 1970s. Bill Evans pushed them to a higher level beginning in the early '90s. And Jeff Monaco, Fred House and their 2000-01 teammates left Southern Utah fans with the most lasting memories, including an upset win for the Mid-Continent Conference tourney title and an oh-so-close near-upset in the NCAA Tournament.

BEST TEAM: 2000-01 Evans' NCAA Tourney team featured MCC Player of the Year Monaco, leading scorer and all-league pick Fred House, and the league's No. 2 rebounder, Dan Beus. The Thunderbirds won 19 of their last 21 pre-NCAA games, including the league final over favored Valparaiso. As a No. 14 seed in the Big Dance, they barely lost to No. 3-seed Boston College, 68-65.

BEST PLAYER: G Jeff Monaco (1997-2001) He never led Southern Utah in scoring. But the 2001 MCC player of the year led the school to its only NCAA Tournament—scoring a team-high 26 against Boston College All-America guard Troy Bell in the near-upset. The career leader in assists (547) and steals (225), Monaco stands second in scoring (1,568) to Davor Marcelic (1,710).

BEST COACH: Stan Jack (1971-80) He revitalized an eight-year-old NAIA program that had achieved just one winning season. He went 148–88 with two 20-win campaigns, four district tourney victories and one appearance in the NAIA national tournament.

GAME FOR THE AGES: Evans' 2000-01 Thunderbirds ended six-time defending champ Valparaiso's 17-game MCC tourney win streak with a gutty 62-59 title-game victory to earn their only NCAA Tournament bid. Monaco's 17 points and two late clutch free throws by tourney MVP House (24 points) stopped Valpo.

FIERCEST RIVAL: Westminster College was the main rival until its program was dropped in 1979 (it has since been reinstated). The Thunderbirds' D1 move ended the rivalry with Grand Canyon, which led the series, 37–15. Now SUU trails the series with its closest Summit League foe, Oral Roberts, 24–8.

SEASON REVIEW

SEAS.	W-L	CONF.		SCORING		COACH	RECORD	
1963-64	8-13			John Johnson	12.5	Boyd Adams		
1964-65	12-13			Rod Oliver	16.4	Boyd Adams		
1965-66	10-13			Rod Oliver	18.8	Boyd Adams		
1966-67	9-16			John Carey	17.4	Boyd Adams		
1967-68	10-11			Skip Mead	20.0	Boyd Adams		
1968-69	16-9			Dave Pinamonti	22.4	Boyd Adams		
1969-70	11-12			Skip Mead	27.2	Boyd Adams		
1970-71	8-11			Al Winfield	23.9	Boyd Adams	84-98	.462
1971-72	11-13			Doug Rhodus	20.7	Stan Jack		
1972-73	17-9			Kohn Smith	13.1	Stan Jack		
1973-74	18-10			Kohn Smith	17.9	Stan Jack		
1974-75	15-12			Robert Lee	15.4	Stan Jack		
1975-76	19-9			Robert Lee	20.0	Stan Jack		
1976-77	21-7			Kerry Rupp	16.6	Stan Jack		
1977-78	18-7			Marc Wilson	18.9	Stan Jack		
1978-79	20-5			Butch Douglas	16.2	Stan Jack		
1979-80	9-16			Dave Knudsen	14.6	Stan Jack	148-88	.627
1980-81	15-11			Norman Adams	12.2	Tom McCracken		
1981-82	18-10			Dean O'Driscoll	12.2	Tom McCracken		
1982-83	19-9			Karl Anderson	13.6	Tom McCracken	52-30	.634
1983-84	13-15			Shawn Daniels	18.5	Bob Schermerhorn		
1984-85	17-11			Russell Otis	19.1	Bob Schermerhorn		
1985-86	16-11			Russell Otis	20.0	Bob Schermerhorn		
1986-87	21-6			Ted Thomas	17.6	Bob Schermerhorn	67-43	.609
1987-88	16-11			Ted Thomas	22.6	Neil Roberts		
1988-89	10-18			Jerry Naulls	16.6	Neil Roberts		
1989-90	13-15			Richard Barton	15.8	Neil Roberts		
1990-91	16-12			Davor Marcelic	17.6	Neil Roberts		
1991-92	20-8			Davor Marcelic	23.5	Neil Roberts[a]	70-62	.530
1992-93	14-13			Richard Barton	20.3	Bill Evans		
1993-94	16-11			Sean Allen	16.8	Bill Evans		
1994-95	17-11	6-0		Sean Allen	15.2	Bill Evans		
1995-96	15-13	3-3		Jon Gaines	15.7	Bill Evans		
1996-97	9-17			Mark Schweigert	14.5	Bill Evans		
1997-98	7-20	4-12		Kenyatta Clyde	14.4	Bill Evans		
1998-99	13-17	6-8		Kenyatta Clyde	16.6	Bill Evans		
1999-2000	16-13	10-6		Fred House	14.8	Bill Evans		
2000-01	25-6	13-3	●	Fred House	17.8	Bill Evans		
2001-02	11-16	8-6		Dan Beus	13.5	Bill Evans		
2002-03	11-17	5-9		David Palmer	11.5	Bill Evans		
2003-04	10-18	6-10		David Palmer	15.4	Bill Evans		
2004-05	13-15	6-10		Tim Gainey	13.9	Bill Evans		
2005-06	10-20	8-8		Henry Uhegwu	13.5	Bill Evans		
2006-07	16-14	6-8		Steve Barnes	12.9	Bill Evans	209-223	.484
2007-08	11-19	9-9		Geoff Payne	20.6	Roger Reid		
2008-09	11-20	8-10		Davis Baker	17.4	Roger Reid	22-39	.361

[a] **Neil Roberts (14-6) and Bill Evans (6-2) both coached during the 1991-92 season.**

● **NCAA Tournament appearance**

PROFILE

Southern Utah University, Cedar City, UT
Founded: 1897
Enrollment: 5,093 (4,802 undergraduate)
Colors: Scarlet and white
Nickname: Thunderbirds
Current arena: Centrum Arena, opened in 1985 (5,300)
First game: 1963
All-time record: 651-583 (.528)
Total weeks in AP Top 20/25: 0

Current conference: Summit League (1997-)
Conference titles:
American West: 1 (1995)
Mid-Continent: 1 (2001 [tie])
Conference tournament titles:
American West: 2 (1995, '96)
Mid-Continent: 1 (2001)
NCAA Tournament appearances: 1
NIT appearances: 0

TOP 5

G **Skip Mead** (1967-70)
G **Jeff Monaco** (1997-2001)
G/F **Fred House** (1999-2001)
F **Davor Marcelic** (1988-92)
F **Kerry Rupp** (1975-77)

RECORDS

RECORDS	GAME		SEASON		CAREER	
POINTS	51	Skip Mead, vs. Westminster (1969-70)	659	Davor Marcelic (1991-92)	1,710	Davor Marcelic (1988-92)
POINTS PER GAME			27.2	Skip Mead (1969-70)		N/A
REBOUNDS	27	Mel Wadsworth, vs. Azusa Pacific (1965-66)	312	Eddie Owens (1969-70)	808	Gil Mullen (1965-66, '68-70)
ASSISTS	15	Jeff Monaco, vs. Western Illinois (Feb. 1, 2001)	178	Jay Collins (2002-03)	547	Jeff Monaco (1997-2001)

ESPN 128 SAGARIN

SOUTH FLORIDA

This Tampa Bay-area school has grown in basketball prowess as its enrollment has increased. A couple of NCAA Tournament appearances in the early 1990s eventually propelled the Bulls into the Big East, where they now face the challenge of reaching the level of national prominence enjoyed by Connecticut, Georgetown, Syracuse, Louisville, *et al.*

BEST TEAM: 1982-83 Though South Florida finished a victory shy of qualifying for the NCAA Tournament, falling to Alabama-Birmingham in the Sun Belt final, this squad served notice of a powerful future with a school-record 22 victories, led by the baddest Bull of them all, Charlie Bradley.

BEST PLAYER: F CHARLIE BRADLEY (1981-85) The program's first star and its all-time scoring leader, Bradley was known for his silky-smooth lefty jumper. He amassed 2,319 points, hitting double figures in 84 straight games and scoring 30 or more 24 times.

BEST COACH: BOBBY PASCHAL (1986-96) After South Florida's program first took off under Lee Rose in the 1980s, it cooled and Paschal inherited a sorry bunch. His first three teams each lost 20 or more games. But he got the Bulls to the NCAA Tournament in 1990 and '92, and also to two NITs.

GAME FOR THE AGES: It couldn't have worked out any better: Beating one of your longtime rivals to reach the NCAA Tournament for the first time in your history. That was the formula in the March 5, 1990, Sun Belt championship game. The Bulls got past Charlotte, 81-74, and into the Dance for the first time (where they lost to Arizona in the first round).

HEARTBREAKER: South Florida was still looking for its first marquee victory as a member of the Big East when No. 17 Connecticut came to town on Feb. 16, 2008. The Bulls gave the Huskies everything they could handle, with big man Kentrell Gransberry (26 points, 15 rebounds, six blocks) dominating his more heralded counterpart, Hasheem Thabeet (six points). And after Dominique Jones hit a shot with :06 left in overtime to put USF up 73-72, the Bulls could taste victory. But then UConn's Craig Austrie raced down the court and threw in a twisting line drive shot from the corner of the free throw line with 0.2 seconds on the clock. Bitter.

FIERCEST RIVAL: Alabama-Birmingham and South Florida were born of the same academic concept: commuter school in large Southern market. Though the schools are some 450 miles apart, the programs have developed quite a rivalry, with UAB holding a 37–19 lead.

FANFARE AND HOOPLA: South Florida, the current baby of the Big East, didn't have a true home court for the first nine years of its basketball program. Instead, the Bulls rotated home games among 10 different venues, including the small recreational center on campus. Finally the university opened the Sun Dome for the 1980-81 season with a game against Florida A&M, and the team has been playing there ever since.

The baddest Bull of them all, Charlie Bradley, amassed 2,319 points, hitting double figures in 84 straight games and scoring 30 or more 24 times.

FAN FAVORITE: G RADENKO DOBRAS (1988-92) The 6'7" combo guard from Yugoslavia led the Bulls to three straight postseasons. Amazingly, no one affiliated with the school had seen him play before he arrived on campus. Dobras originally committed to Kansas, but his plans fell through when Larry Brown bolted for the NBA. A neighbor recommended USF. Talk about kismet.

PROFILE

University of South Florida, Tampa, FL
Founded: 1956
Enrollment: 44,038 (34,036 undergraduate)
Colors: Green and gold
Nickname: Bulls
Current arena: The Sun Dome, opened in 1980 (10,411)
First game: Dec. 1, 1971
All-time record: 511-572 (.472)
Total weeks in AP Top 20/25: 0

Current conference: Big East (2005-)
Conference titles: 0
Conference tournament titles:
Sun Belt: 1 (1990)
NCAA Tournament appearances: 2
NIT appearances: 7

TOP 5

G **Chucky Atkins** (1992-96)
G **Radenko Dobras** (1988-92)
F **Charlie Bradley** (1981-85)
F **Altron Jackson** (1998-2002)
F **B.B. Waldon** (1998-2002)

RECORDS	GAME		SEASON		CAREER	
POINTS	42	Charlie Bradley vs. Florida State (Dec. 10, 1982)	901	Charlie Bradley (1982-83)	2,319	Charlie Bradley (1981-85)
POINTS PER GAME			28.2	Charlie Bradley (1982-83)	19.6	Charlie Bradley (1981-85)
REBOUNDS	26	Fred Gibbs vs. West Florida (Dec. 3, 1972)	383	Hakim Shahid (1989-90)	928	B.B. Waldon (1998-2002)
ASSISTS	18	Joe Coffey vs. Bowling Green (Jan. 2, 1978)	220	Reggie Kohn (2001-02)	632	Reggie Kohn (1999-2003)

EASON REVIEW

EAS.	W-L	CONF.	POSTSEASON	SCORING		REBOUNDS		ASSISTS		COACH	RECORD	
71-72	8-17			John Kiser	18.4	Arthur Jones	10.3	Tommy Davis	4.2	Don Williams		
72-73	14-11			Arthur Jones	13.2	Fred Gibbs	9.1	Jack James	5.2	Don Williams		
73-74	11-14			Jack James	13.2	Arthur Jones	7.6	Leon Smith	5.6	Don Williams	33-42	.440
74-75	15-10			Eddie Davis	17.3	Eddie Davis	8.4	Leon Smith	5.3	Bill Gibson	15-10	.600
75-76	19-8			Eddie Davis	16.8	Eddie Davis	8.4	Penny Greene	5.3	Chip Conner		
76-77	9-18	2-4		Dave Niemann	10.3	Steve Stanford	6.2	Penny Greene	3.5	Chip Conner		
977-78	13-14	2-8		Dave Niemann	15.1	Steve Stanford	7.8	Joe Coffey	5.5	Chip Conner		
978-79	14-14	6-4		Penny Greene	16.8	Willie Redden	6.0	Tony Washam	4.0	Chip Conner		
979-80	6-21	1-13		Tony Grier	19.5	Willie Redden	5.9	Tony Washam	4.3	Chip Conner[a]	59-62	.488
980-81	18-11	7-5	NIT FIRST ROUND	Tony Grier	19.2	Vince Reynolds	8.7	Tony Grier	4.4	Lee Rose		
981-82	17-11	4-6		Tony Grier	15.6	Vince Reynolds	7.9	Tony Grier	2.9	Lee Rose		
982-83	22-10	8-6	NIT SECOND ROUND	Charlie Bradley	28.2[b]	Jim Grandholm	9.2	Lewis Card	5.3	Lee Rose		
983-84	17-11	9-5		Charlie Bradley	22.3	Jim Grandholm	7.6	Tommy Tonelli	5.0	Lee Rose		
984-85	18-12	6-8	NIT SECOND ROUND	Charlie Bradley	21.7	Curtis Kitchen	7.6	Tommy Tonelli	6.0	Lee Rose		
985-86	14-14	5-9		Doug Wallace	11.6	Curtis Kitchen	8.6	Tommy Tonelli	4.6	Lee Rose	106-69	.606
986-87	8-20	3-11		Doug Wallace	13.1	Doug Wallace	7.7	Arthur Caldwell	7.3	Bobby Paschal		
987-88	6-22	3-11		Darrell Coleman	19.0	Darrell Coleman	10.8	Matt Yobe	3.7	Bobby Paschal		
988-89	7-21	2-12		Radenko Dobras	16.2	Hakim Shahid	10.8	Radenko Dobras	4.5	Bobby Paschal		
989-90	20-11	9-5	NCAA FIRST ROUND	Radenko Dobras	16.7	Hakim Shahid	12.4	Marvin Taylor	5.1	Bobby Paschal		
990-91	19-11	8-6	NIT FIRST ROUND	Radenko Dobras	16.7	Gary Alexander	10.2	Radenko Dobras	4.6	Bobby Paschal		
991-92	19-10	7-5	NCAA FIRST ROUND	Radenko Dobras	18.7	Gary Alexander	10.9	Radenko Dobras	6.0	Bobby Paschal		
992-93	8-19	2-10		Derrick Sharp	15.6	Jesse Salters	8.6	Chucky Atkins	4.0	Bobby Paschal		
993-94	10-17	2-10		Jesse Salters	13.0	Jesse Salters	7.2	Chucky Atkins	4.0	Bobby Paschal		
994-95	18-12	5-7	NIT QUARTERFINALS	Chucky Atkins	16.8	Jesse Salters	8.1	Chucky Atkins	6.4	Bobby Paschal		
995-96	12-16	2-12		Chucky Atkins	19.3	James Harper	10.4	Chucky Atkins	4.0	Bobby Paschal	127-159	.444
996-97	8-19	2-12		James Harper	17.1	James Harper	8.8	Brian Lamb	4.0	Seth Greenberg		
997-98	17-13	7-9		Scott Johnson	12.0	Shaddrick Jenkins	6.3	Brian Lamb	3.0	Seth Greenberg		
998-99	14-14	6-10		B.B. Waldon	16.2	B.B. Waldon	7.0	Cedric Smith	3.7	Seth Greenberg		
999-2000	17-14	8-8	NIT FIRST ROUND	Altron Jackson	18.2	B.B. Waldon	7.9	Reggie Kohn	3.8	Seth Greenberg		
000-01	18-13	9-7		Altron Jackson	18.9	B.B. Waldon	7.2	Reggie Kohn	3.7	Seth Greenberg		
001-02	19-13	8-8	NIT FIRST ROUND	Altron Jackson	19.1	B.B. Waldon	9.1	Reggie Kohn	6.9	Seth Greenberg		
002-03	15-14	7-9		Will McDonald	15.9	Will McDonald	8.1	Reggie Kohn	6.2	Seth Greenberg	108-100	.519
003-04	7-20	1-15		Terrence Leather	15.5	Terrence Leather	8.4	Brian Swift	4.4	Robert McCullum		
004-05	14-16	5-11		Terrence Leather	18.2	Terrence Leather	9.6	Brian Swift	5.7	Robert McCullum		
005-06	7-22	1-15		James Holmes	16.8	Solomon Jones	9.8	Chris Capko	4.4	Robert McCullum		
006-07	12-18	3-13		Kentrell Gransberry	15.6	Kentrell Gransberry	11.4	Solomon Bozeman	3.4	Robert McCullum	40-76	.345
007-08	12-19	3-15		Dominique Jones	17.1	Kentrell Gransberry	10.8	Chris Howard	4.8	Stan Heath		
008-09	9-22	4-14		Dominique Jones	18.1	Dominique Jones	5.6	Chris Howard	4.1	Stan Heath	21-41	.339

Chip Conner (4-8) and Gordon Gibbons (2-13) both coached during the 1979-80 season.
In 1982-83, the Sun Belt experimented with a three-point line; Bradley's listed ppg differs from his official NCAA average.

LATE GREAT

WASHINGTON U.
1908-50, '54-60

One of the oldest programs in the country, Washington University in St. Louis did not have much success during its time as a major college team. Even the school's field house, built in 1902 for the '04 World's Fair, conspired to keep the squad cold—it lacked hot water. Then coach Blair Gullion arrived in 1947. A disciple of the legendary Purdue coach Ward "Piggy" Lambert, Gullion manned the sidelines for 11 seasons and instilled a disciplined, methodical defense. Several of his teams were ranked among the country's top 10 scoring defenses. Although Washington U. never made it to an NIT or NCAA Tournament under Gullion (or his assistant, future NFL and AFL coach Weeb Ewbank), they just missed in 1949-50 and '55-56, when they finished their seasons 17–6 and 17–5, respectively.

NOTABLE PLAYER: F Charlie Cain (1948-52) Cain was the first player in Washington University history to surpass the 300-point mark in a single season, which he did in 1950-51, with 369. He was named a second-team All-America by the Helms Foundation following that season. Nicknamed the Hoosier Hot Shot, he finished as the school's all-time leading scorer. Cain later became a highly respected schoolteacher in his native Indiana.

ESPN 30 SAGARIN

STANFORD

For nearly half a century, the Farm lay fallow. Between Stanford's 1942 championship and the swan song of Todd Lichti in 1989, the team failed to make even one NCAA Tournament. But Mike Montgomery did harvest a winner. The coach returned Stanford to the Final Four in 1998 and laid the foundation for a program that, even after his departure in 2004, regularly competes in the postseason. In fact, the Cardinal has received a bid to either the NCAA or NIT in 15 of the past 16 seasons.

BEST TEAM: 1997-98 With a towering front line that featured eight players 6'7" or taller, including future pros Mark Madsen and Jarron Collins, the Final Four-bound Cardinal won its first 18 games, eventually finishing 30–5. The play of 6'1" point guard and leading scorer Arthur Lee (14.5 ppg) epitomized this team's grit. MVP of the Midwest Regional, Lee hit a late three-pointer that sent the Cardinal's Final Four match with Kentucky into overtime, where the team finally fell, 86-85.

BEST PLAYER: F Hank Luisetti (1935-38) A member of the Naismith Hall of Fame, Angelo Enrico Luisetti was one of the game's true pioneers. He's best known for popularizing the running one-handed jump shot, but his behind-the-back dribbling and flashy passing were equally influential. Luisetti's innovations were backed by some impressive numbers. In 1938, he put up 50 points against Duquesne, still a school record.

BEST COACH: Mike Montgomery (1986-2004) He turned the Cardinal into a Pac-10 force and guided his team to 12 NCAA Tourneys in 18 seasons, in the process proving that Stanford could be a national recruiting power despite its lofty academic standards. Meanwhile, his teams transformed the once-sleepy Maples Pavilion into Cameron West.

GAME FOR THE AGES: In 1998, Lee had a hand in 13 of Stanford's 14 points during the final minute of a 79-77 Midwest Regional final win over Rhode Island. The Cardinal trailed 74-70 before Lee completed a three-point play, then stole the inbounds pass and fed Madsen for a dunk-and-one.

HEARTBREAKER: In 2003-04, Stanford won its first 26 games, two on buzzer beaters, to earn a top seed in the NCAA Tourney. But the Cardinal's magic ran out in the second round when Dan Grunfeld missed a possible game-tying three at the horn in a 70-67 loss to Alabama. The defeat was Montgomery's last game as Stanford's head coach.

FIERCEST RIVAL: The cross-bay gridiron rivalry with Cal carries over to the hardwood. It's never been more apparent (or sillier) than when, during a February 1995 Maples Pavilion game, a fight broke out between the Stanford Tree and Oski, Cal's Golden Bear mascot. (The Tree won.) Adding to the bad blood was Cal's hiring Montgomery in 2008 as head coach.

FANFARE AND HOOPLA: The Stanford Tree became the school's ironic, Gumby-like mascot shortly after the school abolished the nickname Indians in the early 1970s. An official member of the quirky Leland Stanford Junior University Marching Band (LSJUMB), each prospective Tree must pass a rigorous audition before landing the gig. All for the right to dance in a giant green costume.

FAN FAVORITE: G Brevin Knight (1993-97) An under-six-foot guard, Knight best personified the Montgomery-era revival, leaving the Farm as the school's career leader in assists and steals and No. 4 on the all-time scoring list. He's played 12 years in the NBA for nine teams.

CONSENSUS ALL-AMERICAS

1936-38	**Hank Luisetti**, F
2001	**Casey Jacobsen**, G

FIRST-ROUND DRAFT PICK

1950	**George Yardley**, Fort Wayne (8)
1975	**Rich Kelley**, New Orleans (7)
1989	**Todd Lichti**, Denver (15)
1992	**Adam Keefe**, Atlanta (10)
1997	**Brevin Knight**, Cleveland (16)
2000	**Mark Madsen**, LA Lakers (29)
2001	**Jason Collins**, Houston (18)
2002	**Curtis Borchardt**, Orlando (18)
2002	**Casey Jacobsen**, Phoenix (22)
2004	**Josh Childress**, Atlanta (6)
2008	**Brook Lopez**, New Jersey (10)
2008	**Robin Lopez**, Phoenix (15)

PROFILE

Leland Stanford Junior University, Palo Alto, CA
Founded: 1891
Enrollment: 17,833 (6,534 undergraduate)
Colors: Cardinal red and white
Nickname: Cardinal
Current arena: Maples Pavilion, opened in 1969 (7,329)
First game: Dec. 3, 1913
All-time record: 1,345-1,013 (.571)
Total weeks in AP Top 20/25: 199

Current conference: Pacific-10 (1916-)
Conference titles:
Pacific Coast: 6 (1920, '21 [tie], '36, '37, '38, '42)
AAWU: 1 (1963 [tie])
Pac-10: 4 (1999, 2000 [tie], '01, '04)
Conference tournament titles:
Pac-10: 1 (2004)
NCAA Tournament appearances: 16
Sweet 16s (since 1975): 4
Final Fours: 2
Titles: 1 (1942)

NIT appearances: 5
Semifinals: 1
Titles: 1 (1991)

TOP 5

G	**Brevin Knight** (1993-97)
G	**Todd Lichti** (1985-89)
F	**Josh Childress** (2001-04)
F	**Adam Keefe** (1988-92)
F	**Hank Luisetti** (1935-38)

RECORDS

RECORDS	GAME		SEASON		CAREER	
POINTS	50	Hank Luisetti, vs. Duquesne (Jan. 1, 1938)	734	Adam Keefe (1991-92)	2,336	Todd Lichti (1985-89)
POINTS PER GAME			25.3	Adam Keefe (1991-92)	20.6	Claude Terry (1969-72)
REBOUNDS	27	Rich Kelley, vs. Kentucky (Dec. 22, 1973)	355	Adam Keefe (1991-92)	1,119	Adam Keefe (1988-92)
ASSISTS	16	Mitch Johnson, vs. Marquette (March 22, 2008)	234	Brevin Knight (1996-97)	780	Brevin Knight (1993-97)

SEASON REVIEW

SEASON	W-L	CONF.	SCORING	COACH	RECORD
913-16	13-19		*H.W. Maloney 11-10 in 2 seasons (1913-15)*		
916-17	8-8	0-6		Russell Wilson	
917-18	11-4			Russell Wilson	19-12 .613
918-19	9-3	0-2		Melbourne C. Evans	
919-20	12-3	8-1		Melbourne C. Evans	21-6 .778
920-21	15-3	8-3		Walter Powell	15-3 .833
921-22	8-7	4-6		Eugene Van Gent	8-7 .533
922-23	12-4	5-3		Andy Kerr	
923-24	10-5	3-5		Andy Kerr	
924-25	10-3	1-3		Andy Kerr	
925-26	10-6	3-2		Andy Kerr	42-18 .700

SEASON	W-L	CONF.	SCORING		COACH	RECORD
1926-27	9-9	3-2			E.P. "Husky" Hunt	
1927-28	8-13	1-8			E.P. "Husky" Hunt	
1928-29	13-6	6-3			E.P. "Husky" Hunt	
1929-30	10-9	2-7			E.P. "Husky" Hunt	40-37 .519
1930-31	8-9	3-6			John W. Bunn	
1931-32	6-14	2-9			John W. Bunn	
1932-33	9-18	3-8			John W. Bunn	
1933-34	8-12	5-7			John W. Bunn	
1934-35	10-17	4-8			John W. Bunn	
1935-36	22-7	8-4	Hank Luisetti	14.3	John W. Bunn	
1936-37	25-2	10-2	Hank Luisetti	17.1	John W. Bunn	

SEAS.	W-L	CONF.	POSTSEASON	SCORING		REBOUNDS		ASSISTS		COACH	RECORD
937-38	21-3	10-2		Hank Luisetti	17.2					John W. Bunn	109-82 .571
938-39	16-9	6-6								Everett S. Dean	
939-40	14-9	6-6								Everett S. Dean	
940-41	21-5	10-2								Everett S. Dean	
941-42	**28-4**	**11-1**	**NATIONAL CHAMPION**							**Everett S. Dean**	
942-43	10-11	4-4								Everett S. Dean	
943-44	no team										
944-45	no team										
945-46	6-18	0-12								Everett S. Dean	
946-47	15-16	5-7								Everett S. Dean	
947-48	15-11	3-9		Steve Stephenson	10.5					Everett S. Dean	
948-49	19-9	5-7								Everett S. Dean	
949-50	11-14	3-9								Everett S. Dean	
950-51	12-14	5-7		Ed Tucker	16.5					Everett S. Dean	167-120 .582
951-52	19-9	6-6		Ed Tucker	15.3					Robert W. Burnett	
952-53	6-17	2-10		Ron Tomsic	19.1	Don Carlson	10.6			Robert W. Burnett	
953-54	13-10	3-9		Russ Lawler	16.3	Russ Lawler	9.4			Robert W. Burnett	38-36 .514
954-55	16-8	7-5		Ron Tomsic	19.3	Russ Lawler	10.9			Howie Dallmar	
955-56	18-6	10-6		George Selleck	16.0	Barry Brown	10.8			Howie Dallmar	
956-57	11-15	7-9		Bill Bond	16.4	Dick Haga	6.5			Howie Dallmar	
957-58	12-13	7-9		John Arrillaga	12.3	Dick Haga	8.0			Howie Dallmar	
958-59	15-9	10-6		Paul Neumann	16.2	Dick Haga	7.1			Howie Dallmar	
959-60	11-14	4-7		John Arrillaga	14.2	John Windsor	6.5			Howie Dallmar	
960-61	7-17	3-9		John Windsor	13.9	John Windsor	8.4			Howie Dallmar	
961-62	16-6	8-4		Tom Dose	17.0	Tom Dose	11.5			Howie Dallmar	
962-63	16-9	7-5		Tom Dose	20.8	Tom Dose	10.8			Howie Dallmar	
963-64	15-10	9-6		Tom Dose	20.0	Clayton Raaka	10.6			Howie Dallmar	
964-65	15-8	9-5		Bob Bedell	16.2	Ray Kosanke	7.9			Howie Dallmar	
965-66	13-12	8-6		Bob Bedell	16.8	Bob Bedell	9.1			Howie Dallmar	
966-67	15-11	7-7		Don Griffin	15.6	Art Harris	7.5			Howie Dallmar	
967-68	10-15	5-9		Art Harris	20.8	Art Harris	8.1			Howie Dallmar	
968-69	8-17	4-10		Don Griffin	20.4	Bill Palmer	9.4			Howie Dallmar	
969-70	5-20	2-12		Claude Terry	19.6	Bill Palmer	8.4			Howie Dallmar	
970-71	6-20	2-12		Claude Terry	20.9	Mike Michel	8.1			Howie Dallmar	
971-72	10-15	5-9		Claude Terry	17.2	Steve Shupe	7.4			Howie Dallmar	
972-73	14-11	7-7		Rich Kelley	17.3	Rich Kelley	13.2			Howie Dallmar	
973-74	11-14	5-9		Rich Kelley	18.4	Rich Kelley	12.5			Howie Dallmar	
974-75	12-14	6-8		Rich Kelley	20.0	Rich Kelley	11.5	Melvin Arterberry	3.9	Howie Dallmar	256-264 .492
975-76	9-18 ⊗	3-11		Ed Schweitzer	15.7	Ed Schweitzer	11.2	Mike Bratz	4.9	Dick DiBiaso	
976-77	11-16	3-11		Mike Bratz	19.6	Kimberly Belton	8.4	Mike Bratz	4.2	Dick DiBiaso	
977-78	13-14	3-11		Kimberly Belton	15.0	Kimberly Belton	9.0	Paul Giovacchini	2.9	Dick DiBiaso	
978-79	12-15	6-12		Wolfe Perry	18.3	Kimberly Belton	8.7	Paul Giovacchini	3.5	Dick DiBiaso	
979-80	7-19	5-13		Kimberly Belton	18.7	Kimberly Belton	9.8	Doug Marty	3.7	Dick DiBiaso	
980-81	9-18	5-13		Brian Welch	15.7	John Revelli	7.6	Doug Marty	2.4	Dick DiBiaso	
981-82	7-20	2-16		John Revelli	16.4	John Revelli	8.6	Doug Marty	2.3	Dick DiBiaso	68-120 .362▼
982-83	14-14	6-12		Keith Jones	19.8	Hans Wichary	5.2	Keith Ramee	4.8	Tom Davis	
983-84	19-12	8-10		Keith Jones	20.0	John Revelli	7.9	Keith Ramee	2.8	Tom Davis	
984-85	11-17	3-15		Earl Koberlein	10.4	Kent Seymour	5.9	Keith Ramee	4.1	Tom Davis	
985-86	14-16	8-10		Todd Lichti	17.2	Howard Wright	6.3	Keith Ramee	5.9	Tom Davis	58-59 .496
986-87	15-13	9-9		Todd Lichti	17.6	Howard Wright	6.8	Terry Taylor	5.1	Mike Montgomery	
987-88	21-12	11-7	NIT SECOND ROUND	Todd Lichti	20.1	Howard Wright	7.7	Terry Taylor	5.0	Mike Montgomery	
988-89	26-7	15-3	NCAA FIRST ROUND	Todd Lichti	20.1	Howard Wright	6.9	Terry Taylor	4.8	Mike Montgomery	
989-90	18-12	9-9	NIT FIRST ROUND	Adam Keefe	20.0	Adam Keefe	9.1	John Patrick	4.1	Mike Montgomery	
990-91	20-13	8-10	NIT CHAMPION	Adam Keefe	21.5	Adam Keefe	9.5	John Patrick	3.8	Mike Montgomery	
991-92	18-11	10-8	NCAA FIRST ROUND	Adam Keefe	25.3	Adam Keefe	12.2	Marcus Lollie	6.5	Mike Montgomery	
992-93	7-23	2-16		Brent Williams	13.2	Brent Williams	5.8	Marcus Lollie	4.7	Mike Montgomery	
993-94	17-11	10-8	NIT FIRST ROUND	Dion Cross	15.1	Andy Poppink	7.4	Brevin Knight	5.4	Mike Montgomery	
994-95	20-9	10-8	NCAA SECOND ROUND	Dion Cross	16.8	Tim Young	8.6	Brevin Knight	6.6	Mike Montgomery	
995-96	20-9 ⊗	12-6	NCAA SECOND ROUND	Brevin Knight	15.5	Andy Poppink	8.4	Brevin Knight	7.3	Mike Montgomery	
996-97	22-8	12-6	NCAA REGIONAL SEMIFINALS	Brevin Knight	16.3	Tim Young	8.4	Brevin Knight	7.8	Mike Montgomery	
997-98	30-5	15-3	NCAA NATIONAL SEMIFINALS	Arthur Lee	14.5	Mark Madsen	8.2	Arthur Lee	4.6	Mike Montgomery	
998-99	26-7	15-3	NCAA SECOND ROUND	Arthur Lee	13.2	Mark Madsen	9.0	Arthur Lee	4.4	Mike Montgomery	
999-2000	27-4	15-3	NCAA SECOND ROUND	Casey Jacobsen	14.5	Mark Madsen	9.3	Michael McDonald	4.7	Mike Montgomery	
000-01	31-3	16-2	NCAA REGIONAL FINALS	Casey Jacobsen	18.1	Jason Collins	7.8	Michael McDonald	4.9	Mike Montgomery	
001-02	20-10	12-6	NCAA SECOND ROUND	Casey Jacobsen	21.9	Curtis Borchardt	11.4	Casey Jacobsen	3.5	Mike Montgomery	
002-03	24-9	14-4	NCAA SECOND ROUND	Julius Barnes	16.0	Josh Childress	8.1	Julius Barnes	3.9	Mike Montgomery	
003-04	30-2	17-1	NCAA SECOND ROUND	Josh Childress	15.7	Josh Childress	7.5	Chris Hernandez	4.3	Mike Montgomery	392-168 .700▼
05	18-13	11-7	NCAA FIRST ROUND	Dan Grunfeld	17.9	Matt Haryasz	9.1	Chris Hernandez	4.0	Trent Johnson	
005-06	16-14	11-7	NIT FIRST ROUND	Matt Haryasz	16.2	Matt Haryasz	8.7	Chris Hernandez	3.3	Trent Johnson	
006-07	18-13	10-8	NCAA FIRST ROUND	Lawrence Hill	15.7	Lawrence Hill	6.0	Fred Washington	3.6	Trent Johnson	
007-08	28-8	13-5	NCAA REGIONAL SEMIFINALS	Brook Lopez	19.3	Brook Lopez	8.2	Mitch Johnson	5.2	Trent Johnson	80-48 .625
008-09	20-14	6-12		Anthony Goods	16.2	Landry Fields	6.6	Mitch Johnson	4.5	Johnny Dawkins	20-14 .588

⊗ Records don't reflect games forfeited or vacated. For adjusted records, see p. 521.

▼ Coaches' records adjusted to reflect games forfeited or vacated: Dick DiBiaso, 70-118, .372; Mike Montgomery, 393-167, .702. For yearly totals, see p. 521.

ESPN 202 SAGARIN

STEPHEN F. AUSTIN

The Lumberjacks were awe-inspiring in the 1960s and early '70s under legendary coach Marshall Brown. In 1970, SFA had five players chosen in a single NBA draft—a distinction matched by only eight other schools. Fans of the old stars—James Silas, Pete Harris, George Johnson—found a new one in 2007-08 Southland Conference player of the year Josh Alexander.

BEST TEAM: 1969-70 The 29–1 Lumberjacks didn't just win, they dominated (average margin of victory: 20.1 points), notching 29 straight before a 100-94 loss to Guilford in the NAIA elite eight. NBA teams drafted George Johnson, brothers Ervin and Marvin Polnick, Surry Oliver and Narvis Anderson—and future ABA and NBA star James Silas was still a sophomore.

BEST PLAYER: G James Silas (1968-72) SFA's career scoring leader (1,884 points), Silas starred on some of the school's best teams, going 106–14 over his career and taking the Lumberjacks to three national tournaments. A two-time NAIA All-America, he holds the single-game school record of 49 points. He went on to play 10 pro seasons, nine with San Antonio.

BEST COACH: Marshall Brown (1959-78) He led SFA to its best NAIA seasons, including five national tourneys—and the 1972 final four—plus five Lone Star Conference titles. From 1967-68 to '72-73, Brown's teams went 158–20 and produced four All-Americas (Johnson, Silas, Pete Harris [NAIA] and Surry Oliver [D2]).

GAME FOR THE AGES: On Dec. 8, 2007, the Lumberjacks, led by Alexander's 19 points and a near triple-double from 5'3" point guard Eric Bell (12 points, 9 assists, 7 boards), beat NCAA Tourney-bound Oklahoma, 66-62. Danny Kaspar's team held the Sooners to 7-of-26 shooting in the first half.

FIERCEST RIVAL: It figures that schools named for rough-and-ready Texas legends would have a fierce rivalry going. Though the schools' records disagree, SFA says it has played Southland rival Sam Houston State 185 times since 1925, leading the series 98–88. (The Sam Houston folks claim the Lumberjacks only lead 91-90.)

SEASON REVIEW

SEAS.	W-L	CONF.	COACH
1924-46	*262-152*		*Van Samford, 17.3 ppg in 1940-41*
1946-47	11-13		Stan McKewen
1947-48	13-9		Stan McKewen
1948-49	15-5		Glen Rose
1949-50	8-16		Glen Rose
1950-51	13-10		Glen Rose
1951-52	20-4		Glen Rose
1952-53	15-9		John O. Stephens
1953-54	12-12		John O. Stephens
1954-55	18-6		John O. Stephens
1955-56	24-6		John O. Stephens
1956-57	23-3		John O. Stephens
1957-58	19-7		John O. Stephens
1958-59	15-7		John O. Stephens
1959-60	11-13		Marshall Brown
1960-61	19-6		Marshall Brown
1961-62	12-14		Marshall Brown
1962-63	14-11		Marshall Brown
1963-64	14-8		Marshall Brown
1964-65	19-7		Marshall Brown
1965-66	11-12		Marshall Brown
1966-67	19-7		Marshall Brown
1967-68	27-3		Marshall Brown
1968-69	22-3		Marshall Brown
1969-70	29-1		Marshall Brown
1970-71	24-7		Marshall Brown
1971-72	31-3		Marshall Brown
1972-73	25-3		Marshall Brown

SEAS.	W-L	CONF.	SCORING		COACH	RECORD	
1973-74	13-16		Archie Myers	22.2	Marshall Brown		
1974-75	19-8		Andria Brown	18.8	Marshall Brown		
1975-76	15-14		Vernon Evans	22.4	Marshall Brown		
1976-77	12-14		Mike Dukes	12.7	Marshall Brown		
1977-78	9-18		Mike Dukes	14.5	Marshall Brown	345-168	.673
1978-79	5-22		Karl Godine	20.0	Harry Miller		
1979-80	15-12		Karl Godine	16.6	Harry Miller		
1980-81	15-12		Hiram Harrison	12.3	Harry Miller		
1981-82	24-6		Hiram Harrison	14.1	Harry Miller		
1982-83	21-10		Johnny Taylor	15.7	Harry Miller		
1983-84	20-9		Johnny Taylor	14.3	Harry Miller		
1984-85	16-10	4-5	John Mouton	14.4	Harry Miller		
1985-86	22-5	7-3	Darnell Jean Louis	15.4	Harry Miller		
1986-87	22-8	10-0 ■	Eric Rhodes	14.8	Harry Miller		
1987-88	10-18	4-10	Eric Rhodes	15.9	Harry Miller	170-112	.603
1988-89	10-18	3-11	Scott Dimak	19.9	Mike Martin		
1989-90	2-25	1-13	Avery Helms	11.8	Mike Martin	12-43	.218
1990-91	11-17	6-8	Jack Little	12.3	Ned Fowler		
1991-92	15-13	10-8	Nathan Randle	19.5	Ned Fowler		
1992-93	12-14	8-10	Nathan Randle	18.2	Ned Fowler		
1993-94	9-18	6-12	Nathan Randle	14.2	Ned Fowler		
1994-95	14-14	9-9	Kevin Barker	14.1	Ned Fowler		
1995-96	17-11	11-7	Eric Leftwich	14.4	Ned Fowler	78-87	.473
1996-97	12-15	8-8	Wayne Allen	14.0	Derek Allister		
1997-98	10-16	6-10	Keith Tate	14.0	Derek Allister		
1998-99	4-22	2-16	Patrick Gusters	20.5	Derek Allister		
1999-2000	6-21	3-15	Ron Banks	14.1	Derek Allister	32-74	.302
2000-01	9-17	6-14	Skip Jackson	14.6	Danny Kaspar		
2001-02	13-15	10-10	Percy Green	14.0	Danny Kaspar		
2002-03	21-8	16-4	Percy Green	12.3	Danny Kaspar		
2003-04	21-9	10-6	Antonio Burks	15.3	Danny Kaspar		
2004-05	12-15	6-10	Marcus Clark	13.0	Danny Kaspar		
2005-06	17-12	9-7	Josh Alexander	14.2	Danny Kaspar		
2006-07	15-14	8-8	Josh Alexander	13.0	Danny Kaspar		
2007-08	26-6	13-3 ■	Josh Alexander	16.0	Danny Kaspar		
2008-09	24-8	13-3 ●	Matt Kingsley	15.8	Danny Kaspar	158-104	.603

● NCAA Tournament appearance ■ NIT appearance

PROFILE

Stephen F. Austin, Nacogdoches, TX
Founded: 1921
Enrollment: 11,990 (10,404 undergraduate)
Colors: Purple and white/red trim
Nickname: Lumberjacks
Current arena: William R. Johnson Coliseum, opened in 1974 (7,200)
Previous: Shelton Gymnasium, N/A-1974 (3,000)
First game: 1924
All-time record: 1,263-847 (.599)
Total weeks in AP Top 20/25: 0

Current conference: Southland (1987-)
Conference titles:
Gulf Star: 1 (1987)
Southland: 2 (2008 [tie], '09)
Conference tournament titles:
Southland: 1 (2009)
NCAA Tournament appearances: 1
NIT appearances: 2

CONSENSUS ALL-AMERICAS

1970 **Surry Oliver** (Little A-A), F

FIRST-ROUND PRO PICKS

1970 **George Johnson,** Baltimore (9)

TOP 5

G **Marcus Clark** (2002-06)
G **James Silas** (1968-72)
F **Josh Alexander** (2005-09)
F/C **Pete Harris** (1970-73)
C **George Johnson** (1966-70)

RECORDS

	GAME		SEASON		CAREER	
POINTS	49	James Silas, vs. Angelo State (Jan. 10, 1972)	743	Robert Gords (1971-72)	1,884	James Silas (1968-72)
POINTS PER GAME			24.5	James Silas (1970-71)	22.3	Robert Gords (1970-73)
REBOUNDS	31	Pete Harris, vs. Texas A&M-Kingsville (Jan. 22, 1973)	522	Pete Harris (1971-72)	1,566	Pete Harris (1970-73)
ASSISTS	14	Winston Harrison, vs. Abilene Christian (Feb. 8, 1982); Jimmie Weaver, vs. Angelo State (Jan. 11, 1975)	191	Winston Harrison (1981-82)	454	Marcus Clark (2002-06)

ESPN 251 SAGARIN

STETSON

Dr. Glenn Wilkes' legacy towers over Stetson like Lurch towered over *The Addams Family*. (The monster big man on the 1960s TV show was played by Ted Cassidy, a member of the early '50s Hatters.) Under Wilkes, Stetson beat many of the big programs, and several of his players went on to the NBA. The small school named after the hat manufacturer was the first Florida hoops team to reach 1,000 victories.

BEST TEAM: 1982-83 As an independent, the Hatters went 19–9 and won a handful of important games—for instance, over Charles Barkley-led Auburn and Tourney-bound West Virginia—and hung tough against Marquette and Johnny Dawkins' Duke. Led by Frank Burnell (1,491 points), Mike Reddick and Glynn Myrick, their nine losses came by a total of just 28 points.

BEST PLAYER: G Ernie Killum (1968-70) A two-time Little All-America, Killum led the Hatters to 15 straight wins in 1969-70 (including victories over Louisville and Miami), and into the College Division national tourney. After averaging a school-best 24.9 ppg for his career, he was selected by the Lakers in the 1970 NBA draft.

BEST COACH: Dr. Glenn Wilkes (1957-93) He is synonymous with Stetson basketball, having guided the NAIA team to D1 victories over national powers Duke, Florida and Auburn. Wilkes' 36-year tenure is tied for the ninth-longest at one school in NCAA history.

GAME FOR THE AGES: On Nov. 24, 1990, Stetson visited Purdue, then a perennial NCAA Tourney team that the Hatters had not beaten in three tries. With a one-point lead in the final seconds, Purdue missed a shot, Stetson got the rebound, Wilkes decided not to call a timeout to prevent Purdue from setting up its D and, at the buzzer, guard Mark Brisker sank his fifth three-pointer of the night. Final score: 58-56, Stetson.

FIERCEST RIVAL: Stetson's rivalry with Atlantic Sun foe Mercer dates to 1920, and the Hatters lead, 67–48. Since 2002-03, the Bears have been dominating with an 8–4 run. But Stetson senior Garfield Blair, a 1,000-point scorer, came up big in two 2007-08 wins.

SEASON REVIEW

SEAS.	W-L	CONF.	COACH	SEAS.	W-L	CONF.	COACH
1900-49	*303-213*	*19-0 in 1931-32*		**1962-63**	15-13		Dr. Glenn Wilkes
1949-50	8-15		Bob Trocolor	**1963-64**	16-9		Dr. Glenn Wilkes
1950-51	14-11		Loren Ellis	**1964-65**	16-10		Dr. Glenn Wilkes
1951-52	16-4		Jay Pattee	**1965-66**	13-12		Dr. Glenn Wilkes
1952-53	14-10		Dick Morland	**1966-67**	17-10		Dr. Glenn Wilkes
1953-54	10-10		Dick Morland	**1967-68**	8-18		Dr. Glenn Wilkes
1954-55	11-10		Dick Morland	**1968-69**	14-12		Dr. Glenn Wilkes
1955-56	17-6		Dick Morland	**1969-70**	22-7		Dr. Glenn Wilkes
1956-57	17-8		Dick Morland	**1970-71**	19-9		Dr. Glenn Wilkes
1957-58	14-11		Dr. Glenn Wilkes	**1971-72**	6-20		Dr. Glenn Wilkes
1958-59	17-11		Dr. Glenn Wilkes	**1972-73**	15-11		Dr. Glenn Wilkes
1959-60	16-13		Dr. Glenn Wilkes	**1973-74**	17-9		Dr. Glenn Wilkes
1960-61	20-7		Dr. Glenn Wilkes	**1974-75**	22-4		Dr. Glenn Wilkes
1961-62	16-12		Dr. Glenn Wilkes	**1975-76**	17-9		Dr. Glenn Wilkes

SEAS.	W-L	CONF.	SCORING		COACH	RECORD	
1976-77	15-12		Mel Daniels	19.9	Dr. Glenn Wilkes		
1977-78	14-13		Mel Daniels	18.8	Dr. Glenn Wilkes		
1978-79	15-12		Dirk Ewing	18.9	Dr. Glenn Wilkes		
1979-80	15-12		Dirk Ewing	14.6	Dr. Glenn Wilkes		
1980-81	18-9		Wilbur Montgomery	17.0	Dr. Glenn Wilkes		
1981-82	12-15		Frank Burnell	18.6	Dr. Glenn Wilkes		
1982-83	19-9		Frank Burnell	19.9	Dr. Glenn Wilkes		
1983-84	19-9		Glynn Myrick	14.7	Dr. Glenn Wilkes		
1984-85	12-16		Jorge Fernandez	14.1	Dr. Glenn Wilkes		
1985-86	10-18		Charles Stevenson	13.6	Dr. Glenn Wilkes		
1986-87	18-13	13-5	Randy Anderson	15.8	Dr. Glenn Wilkes		
1987-88	13-15	8-10	Randy Anderson	15.7	Dr. Glenn Wilkes		
1988-89	17-12	10-8	Randy Anderson	15.5	Dr. Glenn Wilkes		
1989-90	15-17	8-8	Maurice Cowan	18.6	Dr. Glenn Wilkes		
1990-91	15-16	9-5	Mark Brisker	19.5	Dr. Glenn Wilkes		
1991-92	11-17	6-8	Mark Brisker	22.6	Dr. Glenn Wilkes		
1992-93	13-14	6-6	Donell Grier	18.7	Dr. Glenn Wilkes	551-436	.558
1993-94	14-15	9-7	Kerry Blackshear	17.0	Dan Hipsher		
1994-95	15-12	11-5	Kerry Blackshear	20.4	Dan Hipsher	29-27	.518
1995-96	10-17	6-10	Jason Alexander	19.9	Randy Brown		
1996-97	9-18	5-11	Garrett Davis	12.7	Randy Brown	19-35	.352
1997-98	11-15	8-8	Jeff Warbritton	14.3	Murray Arnold		
1998-99	14-13	10-6	Garrett Davis	16.5	Murray Arnold		
1999-2000	13-15	8-10	Sebastian Singletary	15.3	Murray Arnold		
2000-01	17-12	11-7	Sebastian Singletary	14.4	Murray Arnold[a]	42-47	.472
2001-02	10-16	7-13	Ravii Givens	13.0	Derek Waugh		
2002-03	6-20	4-12	E.J. Gordon	14.7	Derek Waugh		
2003-04	12-15	10-10	E.J. Gordon	16.8	Derek Waugh		
2004-05	10-17	8-12	Anthony Register	16.1	Derek Waugh		
2005-06	14-18	11-9	E.J. Gordon	15.5	Derek Waugh		
2006-07	11-20	6-12	Garfield Blair	13.2	Derek Waugh		
2007-08	16-16	11-5	Garfield Blair	16.1	Derek Waugh		
2008-09	13-17	9-11	Garfield Blair	17.3	Derek Waugh	106-147	.419

[a] **Murray Arnold (4-4) and Derek Waugh (13-8) both coached during the 2000-01 season.**

PROFILE

Stetson University, DeLand, FL
Founded: 1883
Enrollment: 3,696 (2,222 undergraduate)
Colors: Hunter green and white
Nickname: Hatters
Current arena: J. Ollie Edmunds Center, opened in 1974 (4,000)
Previous: DeLand National Guard Armory, 1956-74 (600); Airport Arena, 1954-56 (800); Hulley Gymnasium, 1927-54 (500); Cummings Gymnasium, 1911-27 (250); The Gymnasium 1901, '04, '08, '10, '11 (88)
First game: Nov. 29, 1900

All-time record: 1,156-979 (.541)
Total weeks in AP Top 20/25: 0
Current conference: Atlantic Sun (1986-)
Conference titles: 0
Conference tournament titles: 0
NCAA Tournament appearances: 0
NIT appearances: 0

CONSENSUS ALL-AMERICAS

1970 **Ernie Killum** (Little A-A), G

TOP 5

G **Frank Burnell** (1979-83)
G **Ernie Killum** (1968-70)
G **Gene Wells** (1957-59)
G/F **Kerry Blackshear** (1992-96)
F **Randy Anderson** (1985-89)

RECORDS

RECORDS	GAME		SEASON		CAREER	
POINTS	48	Mel Daniels, vs. UNC Wilmington (Feb. 19, 1977)	741	Ernie Killum (1969-70)	1,826	Kerry Blackshear (1992-96)
POINTS PER GAME			25.6	Ernie Killum (1969-70)	24.9	Ernie Killum (1968-70)
REBOUNDS	25	Ralph Miller, vs. Pikeville (Dec. 9, 1957)	360	Ralph Miller (1958-59)	980	Ken Showers (1967-71)
ASSISTS	15	Brad Weston, vs. Southwestern Louisiana (Jan. 18, 1982)	179	Terry Johnson (1986-87)	526	Frank Ireland (1987-91)

ESPN 328 SAGARIN

STONY BROOK

The Seawolves joined Division I in 1999 after 39 years in D3, which included a trip to the final four in 1977-78. In 2005-06 they started building a program under coach Steve Pikiell, who had helped revive George Washington's team in the late 1990s.

BEST TEAM: 1977-78 Dr. Ron Bash's fourth and final squad went 27–4 and reached the NCAA D3 tourney. The Seawolves sank Potsdam, St. Lawrence and Brandeis before losing in the national semifinals, 48-38, to Widener. The main men were guard Larry Tillery (14.2 ppg) and forwards Earl Keith (18.0 ppg, 6.8 rpg) and Wayne Wright (14.6, 7.1).

BEST PLAYER: G D.J. MUNIR (2000-04) The Providence native finished with 1,590 career points, fourth in school history, despite a semester of academic ineligibility in 2002. He also finished third in career assists (372) and three-pointers (179).

BEST COACH: JOE CASTIGLIE (1984-91) Stony Brook's winningest coach (137–57) used an up-tempo style to ambush opponents, leading the team to the postseason in each of his seven seasons and to the 1990 ECAC D3 Metro championship. Many of Castiglie's former players consider him a strong positive influence on their lives, so it's unfortunate that he ended his career with a controversy over recruiting violations.

GAME FOR THE AGES: Boston U. had a first-round bye in the 2004 America East tourney, having won 11 straight and 23 of its last 25 games. In their second-round matchup, Stony Brook shot 54% from the field and kept it close until Munir hit a shot to make it 62-58 with :31 left. A Bobby Santiago steal iced the win.

FIERCEST RIVAL: They don't share a conference, but they do share Long Island. The fight between Hofstra and Stony Brook can get nasty, and it has a David-and-Goliath storyline—especially on the gridiron, given that Stony Brook didn't offer athletic scholarships to football players until the mid '90s. That dynamic spilled onto the hardwood; since 1998-99, SB won only three of 10 games against Hofstra.

SEASON REVIEW

SEAS.	W-L	CONF.	SCORING		COACH	RECORD	
1960-61	0-8				Dan Farrell		
1961-62	2-8				Dan Farrell		
1962-63	4-6				Dan Farrell		
1963-64	6-7				Dan Farrell	12-29	.293
1964-65	6-9				Herb Brown		
1965-66	5-14				Herb Brown		
1966-67	9-10				Herb Brown		
1967-68	7-15				Herb Brown		
1968-69	16-9				Herb Brown	43-57	.430
1969-70	18-6		Mike Kerr	19.8	Rollie Massimino		
1970-71	15-10		Billy Myrick	17.8	Rollie Massimino	33-16	.673
1971-72	16-10		Art King	19.7	Don Covaleski		
1972-73	10-11		Art King	23.2	Don Covaleski		
1973-74	12-10		Dave Stein	17.1	Don Covaleski	38-31	.551
1974-75	2-21		Earl Keith	21.7	Ron Bash		
1975-76	15-11		Earl Keith	21.6	Ron Bash		
1976-77	21-6		Wayne Wright	16.8	Ron Bash		
1977-78	27-4		Earl Keith	18.0	Ron Bash	65-42	.607
1978-79	24-3		Wayne Wright	18.0	Dick Kendall		
1979-80	19-9		Mel Walker	18.2	Dick Kendall		
1980-81	15-12		Joe Grandolfo	16.6	Dick Kendall		
1981-82	10-15		Kevin Martin	22.8	Dick Kendall		
1982-83	13-12		Kevin Martin	23.4	Dick Kendall		
1983-84	11-14		Greg Angrum	16.4	Dick Kendall	92-65	.586
1984-85	16-11		Dave Burda	17.7	Joe Castiglie		
1985-86	20-8		Tony Briscoe	12.6	Joe Castiglie		
1986-87	20-7		Charlie Bryant	18.9	Joe Castiglie		
1987-88	18-10		Tom Blumbergs	20.6	Joe Castiglie		
1988-89	16-12		Steve Hayn	18.9	Joe Castiglie		
1989-90	24-5		Emeka Smith	21.4	Joe Castiglie		
1990-91	23-4		Emeka Smith	20.3	Joe Castiglie	137-57	.706
1991-92	17-10		Emeka Smith	23.9	Bernard Tomlin		
1992-93	15-12		Ricky Wardally	14.6	Bernard Tomlin		
1993-94	12-12		Ron Duckett	15.1	Bernard Tomlin		
1994-95	13-13		Ron Duckett	18.3	Bernard Tomlin		
1995-96	9-17		Ron Duckett	17.4	Bernard Tomlin		
1996-97	10-16		Brian Hennessy	15.2	Bernard Tomlin		
1997-98	13-13		Larry Gibson, Josh Little	11.2	Bernard Tomlin		
1998-99	11-16		Achilleas Klepkos	11.4	Bernard Tomlin	100-109	.478
1999-2000	6-23		Steve Pratta	10.6	Nick Macarchuk		
2000-01	17-11		Leon Brisport	16.6	Nick Macarchuk		
2001-02	6-22	5-11	D.J. Munir	17.2	Nick Macarchuk		
2002-03	13-15	7-9	D.J. Munir	17.4	Nick Macarchuk		
2003-04	10-20	5-13	D.J. Munir	15.0	Nick Macarchuk		
2004-05	12-17	6-12	Antwan Hardy	11.0	Nick Macarchuk	64-108	.372
2005-06	4-24	2-14	Mitchell Beauford	14.1	Steve Pikiell		
2006-07	9-20	4-12	Ricky Lucas	15.2	Steve Pikiell		
2007-08	7-23	3-13	Ricky Lucas	14.3	Steve Pikiell		
2008-09	16-14	8-8	Muhammad El-Amin	15.7	Steve Pikiell	36-81	.308

PROFILE

Stony Brook University, Stony Brook, NY
Founded: 1957
Enrollment: 21,685 (13,858 undergraduate)
Colors: Red, blue and grey
Nickname: Seawolves
Current arena: Pritchard Gymnasium, 1967-89, 2008- (1,800)
Previous: Stony Brook Arena, 1990-2008 (4,000)
First game: 1960
All-time record: 620-595 (.510)
Total weeks in AP Top 20/25: 0

Current conference: America East (2001-)
Conference titles: 0
Conference tournament titles: 0
NCAA Tournament appearances: 0
NIT appearances: 0

CONSENSUS ALL-AMERICAS

1979 **Earl Keith** (Little A-A), F

TOP 5

G **Ricky Lucas** (2006-08)
G **D.J. Munir** (2000-04)
F **Mike Popko** (2003-07)
F **Earl Keith** (1974-79)
C **Leon Brisport** (2000-01)

RECORDS

RECORDS	GAME		SEASON		CAREER	
POINTS	50	Art King, vs. Pratt (Feb. 24, 1973)	645	Emeka Smith (1991-92)	1,978	Emeka Smith (1989-93)
POINTS PER GAME			23.9	Emeka Smith (1991-92)	21.3	Emeka Smith (1989-93)
REBOUNDS	25	Dave Burda, vs. New Paltz (Feb. 23, 1985); Art King, vs. Pace (Feb. 9, 1972)	413	Mike Kerr (1969-70)	905	Yves Simon (1987-91)
ASSISTS	14	D.J. Munir, vs. Northeastern (Feb. 17, 2002)	185	Stan Martin (1987-88)	433	Mel Walker (1979-83)

ESPN 23 SAGARIN

SYRACUSE

There's the indelible orange of their uniforms. There's the shaking and quaking, when Orange fans get their mojo going, of the ever-identifiable dome under which they play their home games. There's a long list of greats, from Dave Bing to Dwayne "Pearl" Washington to Derrick Coleman to Carmelo Anthony. There's the perennial Big East mayhem, the four Final Fours and the long-awaited national title in 2003. Put it all together and what do you have? Simply the most domineering program in the Northeast for the better part of three decades.

BEST TEAM: 2002-03 Freshman Carmelo Anthony led four players who averaged double figures while starting all 35 games on their way to the school's first national title. Anthony averaged 22.2 ppg, Hakim Warrick 14.8, Gerry McNamara 13.3 and Kueth Duany 11.0 to pace coach Jim Boeheim's 30–5 club. The Orange never cracked the Top 10 during the regular season but strung together six straight wins in the NCAA Tournament, including back-to-back wins over No. 1-seeds Oklahoma and Texas, and the ultimate 81-78 title win over Kansas.

BEST PLAYER: G Dave Bing (1963-66) He averaged 24.8 ppg for a career capped by his 28.4 ppg senior season—both school records. Bing was the second player chosen in the 1966 NBA draft (Detroit), after Michigan's Cazzie Russell, and he went on to be a seven-time All-Star with the Pistons and Bullets and a member of the Naismith Hall of Fame. Bing was elected mayor of Detroit in 2009.

BEST COACH: Jim Boeheim (1976-) Bing's former backcourt mate, Boeheim became a Syracuse assistant under Roy Danforth and took over as head coach in 1976. Now he's a Naismith Hall of Famer and the school's winningest coach (799), having helmed an NCAA-record 31 20-win seasons.

GAME FOR THE AGES: After going a disappointing 6–8 in the 1981 Big East season, Syracuse clawed its way to the conference tourney final on March 7 at the Carrier Dome. Villanova (8–6 in Big East play) had already beaten the Orangemen twice. But underdog Syracuse battled through three OTs and, after tourney MVP Leo Rautins tipped in a missed shot with :03 remaining in the third OT, prevailed 83-80 for its first Big East tournament title.

HEARTBREAKER: By the 1987 NCAA Tournament, Syracuse had established a reputation for raising its game in the postseason. The Orangemen plowed through the field, beating North Carolina in the East Regional final and Big East foe Providence in the Final Four to reach the school's first national title game. There, Syracuse led Indiana 73-72 when Hoosier Keith Smart nailed a baseline jumper with :04 left to crush the Orangemen—and give Indiana its fifth title.

FIERCEST RIVAL: The series with Georgetown dates back to 1930, but it only began taking shape as a life-or-death struggle in the Big East's first season, 1979-80. That's when the Hoyas upset No. 2-ranked Syracuse, 52-50, in the final regular-season game at SU's historic Manley Field House, thus ending the Orangemen's 57-game home court winning streak. Syracuse leads the series, 44–37.

FANFARE AND HOOPLA: One of the most recognizable venues in college sports, the Carrier Dome has been packing them in since it opened for the 1980-81 season, attracting the nation's top on-campus crowd each season for 29 years running. Syracuse has had home crowds of 30,000 or more 64 times.

FAN FAVORITE: G Gerry McNamara (2002-06) G-Mac started every one of his 135 games at Syracuse, where he was a crowd favorite from the very beginning for his tenacity and long-range shooting ability.

CONSENSUS ALL-AMERICAS

1912, '14	**Lewis Castle,** C
1918	**Joe Schwarzer,** C
1919	**Leon Marcus,** G
1925-27	**Vic Hanson,** F
1966	**Dave Bing,** G
1990	**Derrick Coleman,** C
1991	**Billy Owens,** F
2005	**Hakim Warrick,** F

FIRST-ROUND PRO PICKS

1966	**Dave Bing,** Detroit (2)
1978	**Marty Byrnes,** Phoenix (19)
1981	**Danny Schayes,** Utah (13)
1983	**Leo Rautins,** Philadelphia (17)
1986	**Dwayne Washington,** New Jersey (13)
1988	**Rony Seikaly,** Miami (9)
1990	**Derrick Coleman,** New Jersey (1)
1991	**Billy Owens,** Sacramento (3)
1991	**LeRon Ellis,** LA Clippers (22)
1992	**Dave Johnson,** Portland (26)
1996	**John Wallace,** New York (18)
2000	**Etan Thomas,** Dallas (12)
2003	**Carmelo Anthony,** Denver (3)
2005	**Hakim Warrick,** Memphis (19)
2008	**Donté Greene,** Memphis (28)
2009	**Jonny Flynn,** Minnesota (6)

PROFILE

Syracuse University, Syracuse, NY
Founded: 1870
Enrollment: 19,084 (13,203 undergraduate)
Colors: Orange
Nickname: Orange (formerly Orangemen)
Current arena: Carrier Dome, opened in 1980 (33,633)
Previous: Manley Field House 1962-80 (9,524); Onondaga County War Memorial, 1955-62 (N/A); Archbold Gym, 1908-47, '52-55 (N/A)
First game: Jan. 5, 1901
All-time record: 1,753-806 (.685)
Total weeks in AP Top 20/25: 444
Current conference: Big East (1979-)
Conference titles:
Big East: 8 (1980 [tie], '86 [tie], '87 [tie], '90 [tie], '91 [tie], '98, 2000 [tie], '03 [tie])
Conference tournament titles:
Big East: 5 (1981, '88, '92, 2005, '06)
NCAA Tournament appearances: 32
Sweet 16s (since 1975): 15
Final Fours: 4
Titles: 1 (2003)
NIT appearances: 12
Semifinals: 2

TOP 5

G	**Dave Bing** (1963-66)
G	**Sherman Douglas** (1985-89)
F	**Billy Owens** (1988-91)
F	**John Wallace** (1992-96)
C	**Derrick Coleman** (1986-90)

RECORDS	GAME		SEASON		CAREER	
POINTS	47	Bill Smith, vs. Lafayette (Jan. 14, 1971)	845	John Wallace (1995-96)	2,334	Lawrence Moten (1991-95)
POINTS PER GAME			28.4	Dave Bing (1965-66)	24.8	Dave Bing (1963-66)
REBOUNDS	34	Frank Reddout, vs. Temple (Feb. 9, 1952)	422	Derrick Coleman (1988-89)	1,537	Derrick Coleman (1986-90)
ASSISTS	22	Sherman Douglas, vs. Providence (Jan. 28, 1989)	326	Sherman Douglas (1988-89)	960	Sherman Douglas (1985-89)

SEASON REVIEW

SEASON	W-L	CONF.	SCORING	COACH	RECORD	SEASON	W-L	CONF.	SCORING	COACH	RECORD
1900-14	*101-73*		*John A.R. Scott became first head coach in 1903-04 (11-8)*			1924-25	15-2			Lewis Andreas	
1914-15	10-1			Edmund Dollard		1925-26	19-1			Lewis Andreas	
1915-16	9-3			Edmund Dollard		1926-27	15-4			Lewis Andreas	
1916-17	13-3			Edmund Dollard		1927-28	10-6			Lewis Andreas	
1917-18	16-1			Edmund Dollard		1928-29	11-4			Lewis Andreas	
1918-19	13-3			Edmund Dollard		1929-30	18-2			Lewis Andreas	
1919-20	15-3			Edmund Dollard		1930-31	16-4			Lewis Andreas	
1920-21	12-9			Edmund Dollard		1931-32	13-8			Lewis Andreas	
1921-22	16-8			Edmund Dollard		1932-33	14-2			Lewis Andreas	
1922-23	8-12			Edmund Dollard		1933-34	15-2			Lewis Andreas	
1923-24	8-10			Edmund Dollard	151-59 .719	1934-35	15-2			Lewis Andreas	

SEAS.	W-L	CONF.	POSTSEASON	SCORING		REBOUNDS		ASSISTS		COACH	RECORD
1935-36	12-5									Lewis Andreas	
1936-37	13-4									Lewis Andreas	
1937-38	14-5									Lewis Andreas	
1938-39	15-4									Lewis Andreas	
1939-40	10-8									Lewis Andreas	
1940-41	14-5									Lewis Andreas	
1941-42	15-6									Lewis Andreas	
1942-43	8-10									Lewis Andreas	
1943-44	no team										
1944-45	7-12									Lewis Andreas	
1945-46	23-4		NIT FIRST ROUND	Billy Gabor	14.6					Lewis Andreas	
1946-47	19-6			Billy Gabor	16.3					Lewis Andreas	
1947-48	11-13			Billy Gabor	14.4					Lewis Andreas	
1948-49	18-7			Jack Kiley	14.0					Lewis Andreas	
1949-50	18-9		NIT QUARTERFINALS	Jack Kiley	16.3					Lewis Andreas	358-135 .726
1950-51	19-9			Jack Kiley	14.4					Marc Guley	
1951-52	14-6			Ed Miller	14.0					Marc Guley	
1952-53	7-11			Frank Reddout	16.8					Marc Guley	
1953-54	10-9			Mel Besdin	16.1					Marc Guley	
1954-55	10-11			Vinnie Cohen	15.8					Marc Guley	
1955-56	14-8			Vinnie Cohen	18.2					Marc Guley	
1956-57	18-7		NCAA REGIONAL FINALS	Vinnie Cohen	24.2	Jon Cincebox	11.8			Marc Guley	
1957-58	11-10			Jon Cincebox	19.1	Jon Cincebox	16.4			Marc Guley	
1958-59	14-9			Jon Cincebox	19.0	Jon Cincebox	15.9			Marc Guley	
1959-60	13-8			Pete Chudy	15.5	Pete Chudy	9.0			Marc Guley	
1960-61	4-19			Pete Chudy	20.8	Pete Chudy	8.0			Marc Guley	
1961-62	2-22			Carl Vernick	16.5	Mannie Klutschkowski	6.8			Marc Guley	136-129 .513
1962-63	8-13			Carl Vernick	16.5	Herb Foster	8.5			Fred Lewis	
1963-64	17-8		NIT FIRST ROUND	Dave Bing	22.2	Chuck Richards	9.1			Fred Lewis	
1964-65	13-10			Dave Bing	23.2	Dave Bing	12.0			Fred Lewis	
1965-66	22-6		NCAA REGIONAL FINALS	Dave Bing	28.4	Dave Bing	10.8			Fred Lewis	
1966-67	20-6		NIT FIRST ROUND	George Hicker	18.6	Vaughn Harper	14.3			Fred Lewis	
1967-68	11-14			Vaughn Harper	15.8	Vaughn Harper	10.9			Fred Lewis	91-57 .615
1968-69	9-16			Bill Smith	19.0	Bill Smith	11.6			Roy Danforth	
1969-70	12-12			Ernie Austin	19.3	Bob McDaniel	10.6	Ernie Austin	3.9	Roy Danforth	
1970-71	19-7		NIT FIRST ROUND	Bill Smith	22.7	Bill Smith	14.5	Tom Green	5.4	Roy Danforth	
1971-72	22-6		NIT QUARTERFINALS	Greg Kohls	26.7	Bob Dooms	8.4	Dennis DuVal	3.5	Roy Danforth	
1972-73	24-5		NCAA REGIONAL SEMIFINALS	Dennis DuVal	19.5	Rudy Hackett	9.6	Dennis DuVal	4.0	Roy Danforth	
1973-74	19-7		NCAA FIRST ROUND	Dennis DuVal	22.2	Rudy Hackett	11.6	Jimmy Lee	4.1	Roy Danforth	
1974-75	23-9		NCAA FOURTH PLACE	Rudy Hackett	22.2	Rudy Hackett	12.7	Jimmy Lee	3.6	Roy Danforth	
1975-76	20-9		NCAA FIRST ROUND	James Williams	15.3	Dale Shackleford	8.8	Ross Kindel	3.3	Roy Danforth	148-71 .676
1976-77	26-4		NCAA REGIONAL SEMIFINALS	James Williams	14.1	Dale Shackleford	8.1	Ross Kindel	2.8	Jim Boeheim	
1977-78	22-6		NCAA FIRST ROUND	Marty Byrnes	16.3	Roosevelt Bouie	8.8	Dale Shackleford	3.0	Jim Boeheim	
1978-79	26-4		NCAA REGIONAL SEMIFINALS	Roosevelt Bouie	15.2	Roosevelt Bouie	8.6	Dale Shackleford	4.1	Jim Boeheim	
1979-80	26-4	5-1	NCAA REGIONAL SEMIFINALS	Roosevelt Bouie	16.1	Louis Orr	8.5	Eddie Moss	5.8	Jim Boeheim	
1980-81	22-12	6-8	NIT RUNNER-UP	Danny Schayes	14.6	Danny Schayes	8.3	Eddie Moss	5.4	Jim Boeheim	
1981-82	16-13	7-7	NIT SECOND ROUND	Erich Santifer	17.0	Erich Santifer	5.6	Leo Rautins	5.2	Jim Boeheim	
1982-83	21-10	9-7	NCAA SECOND ROUND	Erich Santifer	17.8	Leo Rautins	7.3	Leo Rautins	6.2	Jim Boeheim	
1983-84	23-9	12-4	NCAA REGIONAL SEMIFINALS	Rafael Addison	17.7	Rafael Addison	6.0	Dwayne Washington	6.2	Jim Boeheim	
1984-85	22-9	9-7	NCAA SECOND ROUND	Rafael Addison	18.4	Rony Seikaly	6.4	Dwayne Washington	6.1	Jim Boeheim	
1985-86	26-6	14-2	NCAA SECOND ROUND	Dwayne Washington	17.3	Rony Seikaly	7.8	Dwayne Washington	7.8	Jim Boeheim	
1986-87	31-7	12-4	NCAA RUNNER-UP	Sherman Douglas	17.3	Derrick Coleman	8.8	Sherman Douglas	7.6	Jim Boeheim	
1987-88	26-9	11-5	NCAA SECOND ROUND	Rony Seikaly	16.3	Derrick Coleman	11.0	Sherman Douglas	8.2	Jim Boeheim	
1988-89	30-8	10-6	NCAA REGIONAL FINALS	Sherman Douglas	18.2	Derrick Coleman	11.4	Sherman Douglas	8.6	Jim Boeheim	
1989-90	26-7	12-4	NCAA REGIONAL SEMIFINALS	Billy Owens	18.2	Derrick Coleman	12.1	Michael Edwards	5.1	Jim Boeheim	
1990-91	26-6	12-4	NCAA FIRST ROUND	Billy Owens	23.3	Billy Owens	11.6	Adrian Autry	5.3	Jim Boeheim	
1991-92	22-10	10-8	NCAA SECOND ROUND	Dave Johnson	19.8	Dave Johnson	7.0	Adrian Autry	4.0	Jim Boeheim	
1992-93	20-9	10-8		Lawrence Moten	17.9	John Wallace	7.6	Adrian Autry	5.6	Jim Boeheim	
1993-94	23-7	13-5	NCAA REGIONAL SEMIFINALS	Lawrence Moten	21.5	John Wallace	9.0	Adrian Autry	6.1	Jim Boeheim	
1994-95	20-10	12-6	NCAA SECOND ROUND	Lawrence Moten	19.6	John Wallace	8.2	Michael Lloyd	5.2	Jim Boeheim	
1995-96	29-9	12-6	NCAA RUNNER-UP	John Wallace	22.2	John Wallace	8.7	Lazarus Sims	7.4	Jim Boeheim	
1996-97	19-13	9-9	NIT FIRST ROUND	Otis Hill	15.7	Otis Hill	6.1	Jason Hart	5.8	Jim Boeheim	
1997-98	26-9	12-6	NCAA REGIONAL SEMIFINALS	Todd Burgan	17.6	Ryan Blackwell	8.2	Jason Hart	5.0	Jim Boeheim	
1998-99	21-12	10-8	NCAA FIRST ROUND	Jason Hart	13.9	Ryan Blackwell	7.8	Jason Hart	4.3	Jim Boeheim	
1999-2000	26-6	13-3	NCAA REGIONAL SEMIFINALS	Etan Thomas	13.6	Etan Thomas	9.3	Jason Hart	6.5	Jim Boeheim	
2000-01	25-9	10-6	NCAA SECOND ROUND	Preston Shumpert	19.5	Damone Brown	8.8	Allen Griffin	6.5	Jim Boeheim	
2001-02	23-13	9-7	NIT SEMIFINALS	Preston Shumpert	20.7	Preston Shumpert	6.1	James Thues	4.9	Jim Boeheim	
2002-03	**30-5**	**13-3**	**NATIONAL CHAMPION**	**Carmelo Anthony**	**22.2**	**Carmelo Anthony**	**10.0**	**Gerry McNamara**	**4.4**	**Jim Boeheim**	
2003-04	23-8	11-5	NCAA REGIONAL SEMIFINALS	Hakim Warrick	19.8	Hakim Warrick	8.6	Gerry McNamara	3.8	Jim Boeheim	
2004-05	27-7	11-5	NCAA FIRST ROUND	Hakim Warrick	21.4	Hakim Warrick	8.6	Gerry McNamara	4.9	Jim Boeheim	
2005-06	23-12	7-9	NCAA FIRST ROUND	Gerry McNamara	16.0	Terrence Roberts	7.6	Gerry McNamara	5.9	Jim Boeheim	
2006-07	24-11	10-6	NIT QUARTERFINALS	Demetris Nichols	18.9	Terrence Roberts	8.1	Eric Devendorf	4.1	Jim Boeheim	
2007-08	21-14	9-9	NIT QUARTERFINALS	Donte' Greene	17.7	Paul Harris	8.2	Jonny Flynn	5.3	Jim Boeheim	
2008-09	28-10	11-7	NCAA REGIONAL SEMIFINALS	Jonny Flynn	17.4	Paul Harris	8.1	Jonny Flynn	6.7	Jim Boeheim	799-288 .735

ESPN 31 SAGARIN

TEMPLE

Temple fielded its first basketball team in 1894, just three years after Dr. James Naismith invented the game, and the Owls' program has been powerful and prominent ever since. In 2003, Temple became the sixth team in college basketball history to win 1,600 games.

BEST TEAM: 1987-88 With John Chaney at the helm, the 1987-88 squad had the school's finest regular season, winding up 32–2 overall and a perfect 18–0 in the Atlantic 10. Led by stellar freshman guard Mark Macon and A-10 Player of the Year Tim Perry, the Owls were ranked No. 1 during the regular season for the first time and advanced as far as the NCAA Tournament Elite Eight, where they lost to Duke.

BEST PLAYER: G MARK MACON (1987-91) He was an instant success at Temple. As a freshman, this 6'5" product of Saginaw, Mich., led the Owls in scoring (as he would in every one of his four seasons under Chaney) and was named an All-America. He became the only four-time first-team all-conference player in A-10 history, Temple's all-time leading scorer (2,609 points) and all-time steals leader (281). He led the Owls to two Elite Eight appearances.

BEST COACH: JOHN CHANEY (1982-2006) To a generation of fans, admirers and even detractors, he *was* Temple basketball. The fact that his round face and those deep set eyes gave him an owl-like appearance only enhanced the image. During his Hall-of-Fame career, Chaney took Temple to 23 postseason tournaments, including 17 NCAA appearances, and he holds the record for most Atlantic 10 wins (296) and A-10 championships (six). Also a great player in the '50s at Bethune-Cookman, he was inducted into the Naismith Hall of Fame in 2001, five years before he retired with a record of 516–253 at Temple.

GAME FOR THE AGES: A No. 10 seed in the East region, Temple faced No. 3-seed Oklahoma State in the Sweet 16 at the 1991 NCAA Tournament. The game was sent into overtime by a Cowboys jumper with :02 left in regulation. Owls senior Macon dominated the extra period, scoring the first six points en route to a 72-63 victory that sent Temple to an Elite Eight showdown—and 75-72 loss—against North Carolina.

HEARTBREAKER: Heading into their second Final Four in three seasons, Temple in 1957-58 had lost just two games, including a triple-overtime loss to Kentucky on Dec. 7, 1957. Unfortunately for the Owls, their opponent in the national semifinals happened to be the Wildcats, who didn't need any extra periods this time. Kentucky's Vernon Hatton hit the game-winner with less than :20 left to squeak into the Final, 61-60.

FIERCEST RIVAL: Saint Joseph's and Temple first met during the 1901-02 season, and have tormented each other both in the Atlantic 10 and in Philadelphia's informal Big 5 ever since. The level of animosity went up a few notches after the 2005 incident known as Goongate, when John Chaney sent little-used Nehemiah Ingram in to harass a few Hawks, and Ingram fouled forward John Bryant hard enough to break his arm. Temple leads the series all-time, 83–65.

FANFARE AND HOOPLA: Playing in that loose affiliation of Philadelphia-area tribalism known (and loved) as the Big 5, Temple has consistently bested Saint Joseph's, Villanova, Pennsylvania and La Salle, winning or sharing 25 (unofficial) Big 5 titles—the most of any participant.

FAN FAVORITE: F BILL MLKVY (1949-52) To say that he had a better nickname than game is no criticism. The Owl Without a Vowel (his name is pronounced *MILK-vee)* scored a school-record 73 points against Wilkes College in 1950-51 and led the nation in scoring and rebounding that season.

THE SCHOOLS

CONSENSUS ALL-AMERICAS

1938	**Meyer Bloom,** C
1951	**Bill Mlkvy,** F
1958	**Guy Rodgers,** G

FIRST-ROUND PRO PICKS

1952	**Bill Mlkvy,** Philadelphia (4)
1958	**Guy Rogers,** Philadelphia (5)
1969	**John Baum,** LA (ABA)
1984	**Terence Stansbury,** Dallas (15)
1988	**Tim Perry,** Pheonix (7)
1990	**Duane Causwell,** Sacramento (18)
1991	**Mark Macon,** Denver (8)
1994	**Eddie Jones,** LA Lakers (10)
1994	**Aaron McKie,** Portland (17)
2006	**Mardy Collins,** New York (29)

PROFILE

Temple University, Philadelphia, PA
Founded: 1884
Enrollment: 35,489 (26,194 undergraduate)
Colors: Cherry and white
Nickname: Owls
Current arena: Liacouras Center, opened in 1997 (10,206)
First game: 1894
All-time record: 1,710-962 (.640)
Total weeks in AP Top 20/25: 132
Current conference: Atlantic 10 (1982-)

Conference titles:
East Coast: 2 (1979, 1982)
Atlantic 10: 8 (1981, '87, '88, '90, '98 [tie], '99 [tie], 2000 [tie], '02 [tie])
Conference tournament titles:
East Coast: 1 (1979)
Atlantic 10: 8 (1985, '87, '88, '90, 2000, '01, '08, '09)
NCAA Tournament appearances: 27
Sweet 16s (since 1975): 5
Final Fours: 2
NIT appearances: 17
Semifinals: 4
Titles: 2 (1938, '69)

TOP 5

G	**Mark Macon** (1987-91)
G	**Guy Rodgers** (1955-58)
F	**John Baum** (1966-69)
F	**Bill Mlkvy** (1949-52)
C	**Tim Perry** (1984-88)

RECORDS	GAME		SEASON		CAREER	
POINTS	73	Bill Mlkvy, vs. Wilkes (March 3, 1951)	745	Hal Lear (1955-56)	2,609	Mark Macon (1987-91)
POINTS PER GAME			29.2	Bill Mlkvy (1950-51)	21.1	Bill Mlkvy (1949-52)
REBOUNDS	34	Fred Cohen, vs. Connecticut (March 16, 1956)	472	Bill Mlkvy (1950-51)	1,042	John Baum (1966-69)
ASSISTS	20	Howard Evans, vs. Villanova (Feb. 18, 1988); Guy Rodgers, vs. SMU (March 23, 1956)	294	Howard Evans (1987-88)	748	Howard Evans (1984-88)

SEASON REVIEW

SEASON	W-L	CONF.	SCORING	COACH	RECORD	
1894-1915	*160-102*		*40-11 over 2 seasons (1897-99)*			
1915-16	7-6			William Nicolai		
1916-17	10-9			William Nicolai	31-26	.544
1917-18	8-7			Elwood Geiges	8-7	.533
1918-19	no team					
1919-20	9-7			Francois D'Eliscu		
1920-21	7-4			Francois D'Eliscu		
1921-22	4-8			Francois D'Eliscu		
1922-23	10-4			Francois D'Eliscu	30-23	.566
1923-24	15-5			Samuel Dienes		
1924-25	12-10			Samuel Dienes		

SEASON	W-L	CONF.	SCORING	COACH	RECORD	
1925-26	12-6			Samuel Dienes	39-21	.650
1926-27	14-5			James Usilton Sr.		
1927-28	17-5			James Usilton Sr.		
1928-29	16-4			James Usilton Sr.		
1929-30	18-3			James Usilton Sr.		
1930-31	17-4			James Usilton Sr.		
1931-32	13-7			James Usilton Sr.		
1932-33	15-6	5-3		James Usilton Sr.		
1933-34	9-12	5-5		James Usilton Sr.		
1934-35	17-7	5-3		James Usilton Sr.		
1935-36	18-6	6-4		James Usilton Sr.		

SEAS.	W-L	CONF.	POSTSEASON	SCORING		REBOUNDS		ASSISTS		COACH	RECORD	
1936-37	17-6	7-3								James Usilton Sr.		
1937-38	23-2	9-1	NIT CHAMPION							James Usilton Sr.		
1938-39	10-12	4-6								James Usilton Sr	204-79	.721
1939-40	13-10									Ernest Messikomer		
1940-41	12-9									Ernest Messikomer		
1941-42	10-8									Ernest Messikomer	35-27	.565
1942-43	11-11									Josh Cody		
1943-44	14-9		NCAA FIRST ROUND							Josh Cody		
1944-45	16-7									Josh Cody		
1945-46	12-8									Josh Cody		
1946-47	8-12									Josh Cody		
1947-48	12-11									Josh Cody		
1948-49	14-9									Josh Cody		
1949-50	14-10			Ike Borsavage	16.6					Josh Cody		
1950-51	12-13			Bill Mlkvy	29.9					Josh Cody		
1951-52	9-15			Bill Mlkvy	17.9					Josh Cody	122-104	.540
1952-53	16-10			John Kane	12.9					Harry Litwack		
1953-54	15-12			Harry Silcox	15.8					Harry Litwack		
1954-55	11-10			Hal Lear	22.2					Harry Litwack		
1955-56	27-4		NCAA THIRD PLACE	Hal Lear	24.0	Fred Cohen	9.9			Harry Litwack		
1956-57	20-9		NIT THIRD PLACE	Guy Rodgers	20.4	Jay Norman	12.8	Guy Rodgers	6.4	Harry Litwack		
1957-58	27-3		NCAA THIRD PLACE	Guy Rodgers	20.1	Jay Norman	11.9	Guy Rodgers	5.2	Harry Litwack		
1958-59	6-19	4-7		Bill Kennedy	19.5	Ophie Franklin	10.8	Bill Kennedy	5.0	Harry Litwack		
1959-60	17-9	9-2	NIT FIRST ROUND	Bill Kennedy	22.2	Russ Gordon	12.5	Bill Kennedy	3.9	Harry Litwack		
1960-61	20-8	9-1	NIT QUARTERFINALS	Bruce Drysdale	21.3	Russ Gordon	12.2	Bruce Drysdale	3.9	Harry Litwack		
1961-62	18-9	8-2	NIT QUARTERFINALS	Bruce Drysdale	17.3	Russ Gordon	12.2	Bruce Drysdale	3.6	Harry Litwack		
1962-63	15-7	6-3		Dan Fitzgerald	11.9	Dan Fitzgerald	11.5			Harry Litwack		
1963-64	17-8	6-1	NCAA FIRST ROUND	Jim Williams	18.1	Jim Williams	12.2	Bob Harrington	2.7	Harry Litwack		
1964-65	14-10			Jim Williams	14.9	Jim Williams	12.7	Chris Kefalos	3.1	Harry Litwack		
1965-66	21-7		NIT QUARTERFINALS	Jim Williams	17.8	Jim Williams	14.9	Chris Kefalos	3.4	Harry Litwack		
1966-67	20-8		NCAA FIRST ROUND	Clarence Brookins	18.1	John Baum	11.0	Chris Kefalos	2.7	Harry Litwack		
1967-68	19-9		NIT FIRST ROUND	John Baum	18.1	John Baum	11.9	Mike Kehoe	2.7	Harry Litwack		
1968-69	**22-8**		NIT CHAMPION	John Baum	19.3	John Baum	13.3	Tony Brocchi	3.1	Harry Litwack		
1969-70	15-13	2-3	NCAA FIRST ROUND	Tom Wieczerak	15.8	Lee Tress	11.2	Paul Collins	3.5	Harry Litwack		
1970-71	13-12	3-3		Ollie Johnson	13.6	Ollie Johnson	10.7	Paul Collins	3.3	Harry Litwack		
1971-72	23-8	6-0	NCAA FIRST ROUND	Ollie Johnson	16.9	Ollie Johnson	9.8	Rick Trudeau	3.3	Harry Litwack		
1972-73	17-10	5-1		John Kneib	12.0	Joe Anderson	7.9	Rick Trudeau	4.4	Harry Litwack	373-193	.659
1973-74	16-9	4-2		John Kneib	12.8	Joe Newman	8.9	Rick Trudeau	3.0	Don Casey		
1974-75	7-19	4-2		Marty Stahurski	12.8	Tim Claxton	7.1	Kevin Washington	2.5	Don Casey		
1975-76	9-18	3-2		Bruce Burnett	14.0	Bruce Burnett	7.0	Marty Stahurski	2.6	Don Casey		
1976-77	17-11	4-1		Bruce Burnett	14.0	Bruce Burnett	7.1	Rick Reed	4.4	Don Casey		
1977-78	24-5	4-1	NIT FIRST ROUND	Tim Claxton	18.6	Tim Claxton	8.8	Rick Reed	6.0	Don Casey		
1978-79	25-4	13-0	NCAA FIRST ROUND	Rick Reed	15.7	Walt Montford	5.3	Rick Reed	7.2	Don Casey		
1979-80	14-12	8-3		Keith Parham	13.2	Alton McCullough	7.2	Denny Dodds	3.6	Don Casey		
1980-81	20-8	9-2	NIT SECOND ROUND	Neal Robinson	15.5	Alton McCullough	6.6	Jim McLoughlin	3.0	Don Casey		
1981-82	19-8	11-0	NIT FIRST ROUND	Granger Hall	14.9	Granger Hall	8.6	Kevin Broadnax	3.3	Don Casey	151-94	.616
1982-83	14-15	5-9		Terence Stansbury	24.6	Charles Rayne	6.1	Jim McLoughlin	4.5	John Chaney		
1983-84	26-5	18-0	NCAA SECOND ROUND	Terence Stansbury	18.6	Granger Hall	7.1	Jim McLoughlin	5.1	John Chaney		
1984-85	25-6	15-3	NCAA SECOND ROUND	Granger Hall	18.0	Granger Hall	8.5	Nate Blackwell	4.5	John Chaney		
1985-86	25-6	15-3	NCAA SECOND ROUND	Ed Coe	15.6	Tim Perry	9.5	N. Blackwell, H. Evans	5.1	John Chaney		
1986-87	32-4	17-1	NCAA SECOND ROUND	Nate Blackwell	19.8	Tim Perry	8.6	Howard Evans	5.7	John Chaney		
1987-88	32-2	18-0	NCAA REGIONAL FINALS	Mark Macon	20.6	Tim Perry	8.0	Howard Evans	8.6	John Chaney		
1988-89	18-12	15-3	NIT FIRST ROUND	Mark Macon	18.3	Duane Causwell	8.9	Mark Macon	3.8	John Chaney		
1989-90	20-11	15-3	NCAA FIRST ROUND	Mark Macon	21.9	Donald Hodge	8.2	Michael Harden	4.6	John Chaney		
1990-91	24-10	13-5	NCAA REGIONAL FINALS	Mark Macon	22.0	Mark Strickland	6.9	Vic Carstarphen	3.5	John Chaney		
1991-92	17-13	11-5	NCAA FIRST ROUND	Mik Kilgore	14.5	Mark Strickland	6.0	Vic Carstarphen	3.4	John Chaney		
1992-93	20-13	8-6	NCAA REGIONAL FINALS	Aaron McKie	20.6	Eddie Jones	7.0	Rick Brunson	4.5	John Chaney		
1993-94	23-8	12-4	NCAA SECOND ROUND	Eddie Jones	19.2	Aaron McKie	7.2	Rick Brunson	4.6	John Chaney		
1994-95	19-11	10-6	NCAA FIRST ROUND	Rick Brunson	16.7	Rick Brunson	5.9	Rick Brunson	4.1	John Chaney		
1995-96	20-13	12-4	NCAA SECOND ROUND	Marc Jackson	15.7	Marc Jackson	9.0	Levan Alston	3.2	John Chaney		
1996-97	20-11	10-6	NCAA FIRST ROUND	Marc Jackson	16.1	Marc Jackson	9.0	Pepe Sanchez	5.3	John Chaney		
1997-98	21-9	13-3	NCAA FIRST ROUND	Lamont Barnes	13.8	Lamont Barnes	8.0	Pepe Sanchez	4.9	John Chaney		
1998-99	24-11	13-3	NCAA REGIONAL FINALS	Mark Karcher	15.8	Lamont Barnes	6.7	Pepe Sanchez	5.8	John Chaney		
1999-2000	27-6	14-2	NCAA SECOND ROUND	Mark Karcher	15.8	Kevin Lyde	7.6	Lynn Greer	1.9	John Chaney		
2000-01	24-13	12-4	NCAA REGIONAL FINALS	Lynn Greer	18.2	Kevin Lyde	8.9	Lynn Greer	5.5	John Chaney		
2001-02	19-15	12-4	NIT THIRD PLACE	Lynn Greer	23.2	Kevin Lyde	7.8	David Hawkins	2.3	John Chaney		
2002-03	18-16	10-6	NIT THIRD ROUND	David Hawkins	16.9	Alex Wesby	5.8	David Hawkins	2.8	John Chaney		
2003-04	15-14	9-7	NIT FIRST ROUND	David Hawkins	24.4	Keith Butler	5.8	Mardy Collins	2.6	John Chaney		
2004-05	16-14	11-5	NIT FIRST ROUND	Mardy Collins	17.5	Mardy Collins	5.9	Mark Tyndale	2.6	John Chaney		
2005-06	17-15	8-8	NIT OPENING ROUND	Mardy Collins	16.8	Mark Tyndale	5.1	Mardy Collins	4.0	John Chaney	516-253	.671
2006-07	12-18	6-10		Dionte Christmas	20.0	Dion Dacons	6.9	Chris Clark	2.5	Fran Dunphy		
2007-08	21-13	11-5	NCAA FIRST ROUND	Dionte Christmas	20.3	Mark Tyndale	6.8	Mark Tyndale	4.1	Fran Dunphy		
2008-09	22-12	11-5	NCAA FIRST ROUND	Dionte Christmas	19.5	Lavoy Allen	9.0	Semaj Inge	3.6	Fran Dunphy	55-43	.561

THE SCHOOLS

ESPN 33 SAGARIN

TENNESSEE

Everyone knows about the *Lady* Vols. They've long been one of the most dominant teams in college basketball. But the guys have a pretty proud hoops history of their own (even if they have zero national titles to hold up against the women's eight). Peaking with the Ernie and Bernie Show in the mid-1970s, and perking up again after the 2005 arrival of coach Bruce Pearl, Tennessee has won nine SEC championships and made 17 NCAA Tournament and 11 NIT appearances.

BEST TEAM: 2007-08 It wasn't just their school-record 31 wins, SEC title and Sweet 16 run; these Volunteers did it all with flair. On the way to the school's first No. 1 national ranking there was a 109-40 win over Middle Tennessee, a 104-82 drubbing of defending national champion Florida and a victory at Alabama for the first time in a decade. The Vols also strung together winning streaks of 12 and nine games and went undefeated at home.

BEST PLAYER: F Bernard King (1974-77) He scored 42 points in his first varsity game, a sign of the greatness that was to come. In each of his three seasons, King was chosen as the SEC's Player of the Year (sharing that honor with teammate Ernie Grunfeld in '77) and was a consensus All-America his junior year. King finished his career with averages of 25.8 ppg and 13.2 rpg, and in 2007 he became the school's first men's basketball player to have his number retired. The seventh overall pick in the 1977 NBA Draft (Nets), he went on to be a four-time All-Star and led the NBA in scoring with 32.9 ppg for the 1984-85 New York Knicks. (Grunfeld was the 11th player chosen in the 1977 draft, by Milwaukee.)

BEST COACH: Ray Mears (1962-77) During his tenure, the Vols won three SEC titles and only twice finished worse than third in the league. Mears did more than win, he established a basketball tradition at Tennessee. The orange blazer Mears always wore became a Tennessee trademark; Pearl wears an identical blazer today to honor his predecessor.

GAME FOR THE AGES: Fans throughout the state began circling the Feb. 23, 2008, Tennessee vs. Memphis matchup the moment it was scheduled. But when the clash became a No. 1 vs. No. 2 affair, just about the whole basketball world tuned in to watch the Vols gut out a 66-62 road win over the previously undefeated Tigers to take over the top spot in the polls.

HEARTBREAKER: The Ernie and Bernie Show was supposed to take Tennessee to new heights. Instead, the 1977 SEC co-champs ran into an Orange-hot Syracuse squad in the NCAA Tournament first round, and both King and Grunfeld fouled out in a 93-88 overtime loss.

FIERCEST RIVAL: Tennesseans have always enjoyed beating their more-decorated rivals from across the Kentucky border, and the Volunteers have more wins over the Wildcats (65) than any other team in the country. The bad news for the Vols is that Kentucky has prevailed in the rivalry 142 times.

Bernard King scored 42 points in his first varsity game, a sign of the greatness that was to come.

FANFARE AND HOOPLA: Just try to find a fan who doesn't know the lyrics to the bluegrass classic *Rocky Top* ("You'll always be home sweet home to me..."), which the school band first played at a 1972 football game against Alabama. It's been the Vols' unofficial anthem ever since. In basketball it gets played about 15 times per game—more if the team's doing well.

FAN FAVORITE: G/F Dane Bradshaw (2003-07) He won the hearts of fans with his hustle and hard work, then poured it out in his book *Vertical Leap: Inside the Rise of Tennessee Basketball.*

CONSENSUS ALL-AMERICAS

1977 **Bernard King,** F
1983 **Dale Ellis,** F

FIRST-ROUND PRO PICKS

1968 **Tom Boerwinkle,** Chicago (4)
1968 **Tom Boerwinkle,** Denver (ABA)
1977 **Bernard King,** Nets (7)
1977 **Ernie Grunfeld,** Milwaukee (11)
1980 **Reggie Johnson,** San Antonio (15)
1983 **Dale Ellis,** Dallas (9)
1993 **Allan Houston,** Detroit (11)
2002 **Marcus Haislip,** Milwaukee (13)

PROFILE

University of Tennessee, Knoxville, TN
Founded: 1794
Enrollment: 27,739 (20,400 undergraduate)
Colors: Orange and white
Nickname: Volunteers
Current arena: Thompson-Boling Arena, opened in 1987 (21,678)
Previous: Armory Fieldhouse (7,000), then expanded and renamed Stokely Athletic Center, 1959-87 (12,700); Alumni Gym, 1932-58 (3,200); Jefferson Hall, 1923-32 (1,500); Knoxville YMCA Gym, 1913-22 (500); UT YMCA Gym, 1909-12 (200)

First game: Jan. 22, 1909
All-time record: 1,444-921-2 (.610)
Total weeks in AP Top 20/25: 215
Current conference: Southeastern (1932-)
Conference titles:
SEC: 9 (1936, '41, '43, '67, '72 [tie], '77 [tie], '82 [tie], 2000 [tie], '08)
Conference tournament titles:
SEC: 4 (1936, '41, '43, '79)
NCAA Tournament appearances: 17
Sweet 16s (since 1975): 4
NIT appearances: 11
Semifinals: 2

TOP 5

G **Allan Houston** (1989-93)
G **Chris Lofton** (2004-08)
F **Dale Ellis** (1979-83)
G/F **Ernie Grunfeld** (1973-77)
F **Bernard King** (1974-77)

RECORDS	GAME		SEASON		CAREER	
POINTS	51	Tony White, vs. Auburn (Feb. 14, 1987)	806	Allan Houston (1990-91)	2,801	Allan Houston (1989-93)
POINTS PER GAME			26.4	Bernard King (1974-75)	25.8	Bernard King (1974-77)
REBOUNDS	36	Herb Neff, vs. Georgia Tech (Jan. 26, 1952)	384	Gene Tormohlen (1957-58)	1,113	Gene Tormohlen (1956-59)
ASSISTS	19	Bill Hann, vs. Alabama (Jan. 6, 1968)	227	Rodney Woods (1974-75)	715	Johnny Darden (1975-79)

SEASON REVIEW

SEASON	W-L	CONF.	SCORING	COACH	RECORD
1909-14	*45-34*		*Had no losing seasons under Clevenger, who started in 1911-12*		
1914-15	9-2			Zora G. Clevenger	
1915-16	12-0			Zora G. Clevenger	50-14 .781
1916-17	10-5			John R. Bender	
1917-18	3-9-1			R.H. Fitzgerald	
1918-19	2-6			R.H. Fitzgerald	5-15-1 .262
1919-20	11-3			John R. Bender	
1920-21	8-7			John R. Bender	29-15 .659
1921-22	13-7-1	1-3		M.B. Banks	
1922-23	15-2	3-1		M.B. Banks	
1923-24	10-8	5-5		M.B. Banks	
1924-25	6-8	1-5		M.B. Banks	
1925-26	9-8	1-3		M.B. Banks	53-33-1 .615
1926-27	7-12	5-4		W.H. Britton	
1927-28	0-12	0-8		W.H. Britton	
1928-29	11-5	7-4		W.H. Britton	
1929-30	13-4	7-2		W.H. Britton	
1930-31	11-10	4-8		W.H. Britton	
1931-32	8-7	5-5		W.H. Britton	
1932-33	9-11	3-7		W.H. Britton	
1933-34	10-7	3-5		W.H. Britton	
1934-35	11-5	7-4		W.H. Britton	80-73 .523

SEAS.	W-L	CONF.	POSTSEASON	SCORING		REBOUNDS		ASSISTS		COACH	RECORD	
1935-36	15-6	8-4								Blair Gullion		
1936-37	17-5	7-1								Blair Gullion		
1937-38	15-8	7-4								Blair Gullion	47-19	.712
1938-39	14-7	6-5								John Mauer		
1939-40	14-7	7-3								John Mauer		
1940-41	17-5	8-3								John Mauer		
1941-42	19-3	7-1								John Mauer		
1942-43	14-4	6-3								John Mauer		
1943-44	no team											
1944-45	18-5	8-2	NIT QUARTERFINALS							John Mauer		
1945-46	15-5	8-3								John Mauer		
1946-47	16-5	10-3								John Mauer	127-41	.756
1947-48	20-5	10-2								Emmett Lowery		
1948-49	19-7	8-3								Emmett Lowery		
1949-50	15-11	5-6								Emmett Lowery		
1950-51	10-13	5-9		Bob Garrison	13.2					Emmett Lowery		
1951-52	13-9	7-7		Herb Neff	14.1	Herb Neff	14.7			Emmett Lowery		
1952-53	13-8	7-6		Ed Wiener	17.1	Ed Wiener	9.6			Emmett Lowery		
1953-54	11-12	7-7		Carl Widseth	19.2	Carl Widseth	10.2			Emmett Lowery		
1954-55	15-7	8-6		Carl Widseth	19.9	Carl Widseth	11.2			Emmett Lowery		
1955-56	10-14	6-8		Carl Widseth	21.8	Carl Widseth	12.2			Emmett Lowery		
1956-57	13-9	5-9		Herman Thompson	19.1	Gene Tormohlen	16.2			Emmett Lowery		
1957-58	16-7	8-6		Gene Tormohlen	16.2	Gene Tormohlen	16.7			Emmett Lowery		
1958-59	14-8	8-6		Gene Tormohlen	17.8	Gene Tormohlen	17.7			Emmett Lowery	169-110	.606
1959-60	12-11	7-7		Dalen Showalter	14.7	Dalen Showalter	9.7			John Sines		
1960-61	10-15	4-10		Bobby Carter	14.4	Eddie Test	8.0			John Sines		
1961-62	4-19	2-12		Tommy Wilson	14.9	Sid Elliott	10.4			John Sines	26-45	.366
1962-63	13-11	6-8		Danny Schultz	15.9	A.W. Davis	8.2			Ray Mears		
1963-64	16-8	9-5		Danny Schultz	18.3	Sid Elliott	7.8			Ray Mears		
1964-65	20-5	12-4		A.W. Davis	19.6	Ron Widby	8.3			Ray Mears		
1965-66	18-8	10-6		Ron Widby	17.3	Red Robbins	12.6			Ray Mears		
1966-67	21-7	15-3	NCAA REGIONAL SEMIFINALS	Ron Widby	22.1	Tom Boerwinkle	10.2			Ray Mears		
1967-68	20-6	13-5		Bill Justus	18.0	Tom Boerwinkle	11.3			Ray Mears		
1968-69	21-7	13-5	NIT THIRD PLACE	Bill Justus	16.3	Bobby Croft	8.9	Bill Hann	6.2	Ray Mears		
1969-70	16-9	10-8		Jimmy England	19.4	Bobby Croft	9.6	Jimmy England	2.5	Ray Mears		
1970-71	21-7	13-5	NIT QUARTERFINALS	Jimmy England	20.6	Don Johnson	10.4	Jimmy England	5.2	Ray Mears		
1971-72	19-6	14-4		Len Kosmalski	19.5	Larry Robinson	9.0	Steve Hirschorn	3.6	Ray Mears		
1972-73	15-9	13-5		Len Kosmalski	17.0	Larry Robinson	8.5	Rodney Woods	5.9	Ray Mears		
1973-74	17-9	12-6		Ernie Grunfeld	17.4	Len Kosmalski	9.8	Rodney Woods	6.0	Ray Mears		
1974-75	18-8	12-6		Bernard King	26.4	Bernard King	12.3	Rodney Woods	8.7	Ray Mears		
1975-76	21-6	14-4	NCAA FIRST ROUND	Ernie Grunfeld	25.3	Bernard King	13.0	Johnny Darden	6.1	Ray Mears		
1976-77	22-6	16-2	NCAA FIRST ROUND	Bernard King	25.8	Bernard King	14.3	Johnny Darden	8.2	Ray Mears	278-112	.713
1977-78	11-16	6-12		Reggie Johnson	21.2	Reggie Johnson	9.6	Johnny Darden	8.3	Cliff Wettig	11-16	.407
1978-79	21-12	12-6	NCAA SECOND ROUND	Reggie Johnson	21.2	Reggie Johnson	7.7	Johnny Darden	4.2	Don DeVoe		
1979-80	18-11	12-6	NCAA SECOND ROUND	Reggie Johnson	19.4	Reggie Johnson	6.7	Bert Bertelkamp	5.3	Don DeVoe		
1980-81	21-8	12-6	NCAA REGIONAL SEMIFINALS	Dale Ellis	17.7	Howard Wood	6.9	Michael Brooks	3.1	Don DeVoe		
1981-82	20-10	13-5	NCAA SECOND ROUND	Dale Ellis	21.2	Dale Ellis	6.3	Tyrone Beaman	4.2	Don DeVoe		
1982-83	20-12	9-9	NCAA SECOND ROUND	Dale Ellis	22.6	Willie Burton	8.1	Tyrone Beaman	5.8	Don DeVoe		
1983-84	21-14	9-9	NIT QUARTERFINALS	Willie Burton	13.5	Willie Burton	7.3	Tyrone Beaman	3.9	Don DeVoe		
1984-85	22-15	8-10	NIT THIRD PLACE	Michael Brooks	17.0	Rob Jones	8.6	Michael Brooks	3.6	Don DeVoe		
1985-86	12-16	5-13		Tony White	22.2	Rob Jones	7.7	Fred Jenkins	3.9	Don DeVoe		
1986-87	14-15	7-11		Tony White	24.5	Dyron Nix	10.1	Fred Jenkins	5.5	Don DeVoe		
1987-88	16-13	9-9	NIT FIRST ROUND	Dyron Nix	22.2	Dyron Nix	9.0	Clarence Swearengen	4.4	Don DeVoe		
1988-89	19-11	11-7	NCAA FIRST ROUND	Dyron Nix	21.6	Dyron Nix	9.4	Clarence Swearengen	4.7	Don DeVoe	204-137	.598
1989-90	16-14	10-8	NIT SECOND ROUND	Allan Houston	20.3	Ian Lockhart	10.9	Allan Houston	4.2	Wade Houston		
1990-91	12-22	3-15		Allan Houston	23.7	Ronnie Reese	5.4	Allan Houston	3.9	Wade Houston		
1991-92	19-15	8-8	NIT SECOND ROUND	Allan Houston	21.1	Corey Allen	6.8	Allan Houston	3.2	Wade Houston		
1992-93	13-17	4-12		Allan Houston	22.3	Corey Allen	7.0	LaMarcus Golden	4.5	Wade Houston		
1993-94	5-22	2-14		Ed Gray	15.0	Steve Hamer	5.8	LaMarcus Golden	5.7	Wade Houston	65-90	.419
1994-95	11-16	4-12		Steve Hamer	15.0	Steve Hamer	8.8	Damon Johnson	4.7	Kevin O'Neill		
1995-96	14-15	6-10	NIT FIRST ROUND	Steve Hamer	18.2	Steve Hamer	9.4	Shane Williams	3.9	Kevin O'Neill		
1996-97	11-16	4-12		Brandon Wharton	16.8	Charles Hathaway	7.1	Cornelius Jackson	2.4	Kevin O'Neill	36-47	.434
1997-98	20-9	9-7	NCAA FIRST ROUND	Brandon Wharton	15.2	C.J. Black	6.8	Tony Harris	4.2	Jerry Green		
1998-99	21-9	12-4	NCAA SECOND ROUND	Brandon Wharton	13.0	Isiah Victor	7.3	Tony Harris	4.8	Jerry Green		
1999-2000	26-7	12-4	NCAA REGIONAL SEMIFINALS	Vincent Yarbrough	14.8	Vincent Yarbrough	6.9	Tony Harris	4.1	Jerry Green		
2000-01	22-11	8-8	NCAA FIRST ROUND	Vincent Yarbrough	13.9	Vincent Yarbrough	7.4	Tony Harris	3.6	Jerry Green	89-36	.712
2001-02	15-16	7-9		Vincent Yarbrough	18.1	Vincent Yarbrough	7.5	Jon Higgins	3.9	Buzz Peterson		
2002-03	17-12	9-7	NIT FIRST ROUND	Ron Slay	21.1	Ron Slay	7.8	C.J. Watson	5.5	Buzz Peterson		
2003-04	15-14	7-9	NIT FIRST ROUND	Scooter McFadgon	17.6	Brandon Crump	6.8	C.J. Watson	5.0	Buzz Peterson		
2004-05	14-17	6-10		Scooter McFadgon	14.3	Andre Patterson	6.2	C.J. Watson	5.0	Buzz Peterson	61-59	.508
2005-06	22-8	12-4	NCAA SECOND ROUND	Chris Lofton	17.2	Andre Patterson	6.7	C.J. Watson	3.9	Bruce Pearl		
2006-07	24-11	10-6	NCAA REGIONAL SEMIFINALS	Chris Lofton	20.8	Wayne Chism	5.2	Dane Bradshaw	4.7	Bruce Pearl		
2007-08	31-5	14-2	NCAA REGIONAL SEMIFINALS	Chris Lofton	16.1	Tyler Smith	6.8	Tyler Smith	3.5	Bruce Pearl		
2008-09	21-13	10-6	NCAA FIRST ROUND	Tyler Smith	17.4	Wayne Chism	8.0	Tyler Smith	3.4	Bruce Pearl	98-37	.726

ESPN 289 SAGARIN

TENNESSEE-MARTIN

A blessing is landing a once-in-a-program player such as Lester Hudson, who in 2007-08 received an All-America honorable mention—the school's first All-America of any stripe. A heavenly treat? Watching Hudson chase Davidson's Stephen Curry for the nation's scoring title as a senior in 2008-09. At long last, a team mostly known for its D1 futility is creating some positive vibes.

BEST TEAM: 1987-88 Go by the scoreboard and the Skyhawks' 99-77 loss to Auburn on Dec. 7, 1987, looks like a standard rout. But D2 UTM's all-out play typified what made its season so great. "I think you saw the best effort in one half by a team since I have been at Auburn," Tigers coach Sonny Smith told reporters. Led by guard Mike Meschede (23.7 ppg), the Skyhawks had the most Gulf South victories of any team in school history.

BEST PLAYER: G LESTER HUDSON (2007-09) The junior-college star became the first Division I player to record a quadruple-double with his 25 points, 12 boards, 10 assists and 10 steals against Central Baptist on Nov. 13, 2007. After finishing fifth nationally with 25.7 ppg as a junior, he scored 27.5 ppg as a senior, good for the No. 2 spot.

BEST COACH: TOM HANCOCK (1982-91) Even when his teams were taking on the D1 big boys, they usually showed signs of solid defensive organization and furious effort. Hancock led the Skyhawks to three of their five 20-win seasons and a trip to the 1983 D2 tournament.

GAME FOR THE AGES: On Dec. 12, 1981, UTM coach Art Tolis got the best of Mississippi State counterpart Bob Boyd with a shocking 65-41 win at Starkville. Boyd featured three future draft picks on his team, yet the Bulldogs still couldn't break the Skyhawks defense.

FIERCEST RIVAL: As one of the OVC's standard bearers, Austin Peay has a target on its back—one that's proven maddeningly elusive for UTM to hit. The Governors hold a 49–18 series lead, and in 2007-08 took the shine off the Skyhawks' second winning season since 1987-88 by beating them three times, including a 78-77 last-second victory in the conference tournament.

SEASON REVIEW

SEAS.	W-L	CONF.	COACH	SEAS.	W-L	CONF.	COACH
1951-52	6-12		J.C. Henson	1961-62	13-11		Floyd Burdette
1952-53	7-9		Floyd Burdette	1962-63	12-12		Floyd Burdette
1953-54	15-3		Floyd Burdette	1963-64	11-10		Floyd Burdette
1954-55	14-4		Floyd Burdette	1964-65	11-13		Floyd Burdette
1955-56	13-6		Floyd Burdette	1965-66	12-7		Floyd Burdette
1956-57	7-13		Floyd Burdette	1966-67	11-13		Floyd Burdette
1957-58	8-2		Floyd Burdette	1967-68	3-18		Floyd Burdette
1958-59	9-13		Floyd Burdette	1968-69	8-12		Floyd Burdette
1959-60	10-9		Floyd Burdette	1969-70	14-12		Floyd Burdette
1960-61	13-10		Floyd Burdette	1970-71	3-20		Floyd Burdette

SEAS.	W-L	CONF.	SCORING		COACH	RECORD
1971-72	10-16		Marcus McLemore	12.2	Bob Paynter	
1972-73	13-13		Vic Quinn	17.3	Bob Paynter	
1973-74	8-15		Jim Martin	20.9	Bob Paynter	
1974-75	11-13		Don Elliott	18.2	Bob Paynter	
1975-76	16-8		Larry Carter	19.0	Bob Paynter	
1976-77	13-9		Larry Carter	22.5	Bob Paynter	
1977-78	11-14		Joe Boddie	16.6	Bob Paynter	
1978-79	7-19		Edward Littleton	14.4	Bob Paynter	
1979-80	11-15		Don Hubbard	16.3	Bob Paynter	100-122 .450
1980-81	12-14		Don Hubbard	15.5	Art Tolis	
1981-82	20-11		Larry Brooks	12.9	Art Tolis	32-25 .561
1982-83	21-10		Jerry Davis	18.5	Tom Hancock	
1983-84	19-10		Mitch Stentiford	18.8	Tom Hancock	
1984-85	20-9		Marcus Glass	16.9	Tom Hancock	
1985-86	18-10		Marcus Glass	22.3	Tom Hancock	
1986-87	17-11		Mike Meschede	16.5	Tom Hancock	
1987-88	20-8		Mike Meschede	23.7	Tom Hancock	
1988-89	1-25		Mike Hansen	20.0	Tom Hancock	
1989-90	10-17		Shannon Redmond	16.3	Tom Hancock	
1990-91	6-21		Shannon Redmond	12.5	Tom Hancock[a]	127-106 .545
1991-92	9-19		Tim Britt	17.0	Cal Luther	
1992-93	7-19	4-12	Tim Britt	16.0	Cal Luther	
1993-94	5-22	3-13	DeWayne Powell	16.5	Cal Luther	
1994-95	7-20	5-11	Michael Hart	18.6	Cal Luther	
1995-96	13-14	9-7	Michael Hart	22.8	Cal Luther	
1996-97	11-16	8-10	B.J. Nelson	13.3	Cal Luther	
1997-98	7-20	5-13	Ryan DeMichael	14.9	Cal Luther	
1998-99	8-18	5-13	Ryan DeMichael	15.7	Cal Luther	72-163 .306
1999-2000	10-19	7-11	Byron Benton	14.3	Bret Campbell	
2000-01	10-18	5-11	Brian Foster	13.8	Bret Campbell	
2001-02	15-14	7-9	Brian Foster	14.1	Bret Campbell	
2002-03	14-14	7-9	Earl Bullock, Joey Walker	16.0	Bret Campbell	
2003-04	10-18	5-11	Justin Smith	15.9	Bret Campbell	
2004-05	6-21	3-13	Jared Newson	15.4	Bret Campbell	
2005-06	13-15	9-11	Jared Newson	18.8	Bret Campbell	
2006-07	8-23	5-15	Gerald Robinson	12.9	Bret Campbell	
2007-08	17-16	11-9	Lester Hudson	25.7	Bret Campbell	
2008-09	22-10	14-4 ■	Lester Hudson	27.5	Bret Campbell	125-168 .427

[a] Tom Hancock (1-6) and Cal Luther (5-15) both coached during the 1990-91 season.
■ NIT appearance

THE SCHOOLS

PROFILE

University of Tennessee at Martin, Martin, TN
Founded: 1900 as Hall-Moody Institute; renamed University of Tennessee Junior College in 1927; renamed University of Tennessee at Martin in 1951
Enrollment: 7,173 (6,717 undergraduate)
Colors: Navy blue and orange
Nicknames: Skyhawks
Current arena: Skyhawk Arena, opened in 1978 (5,000)
First game: 1951
All-time record: 656-793 (.453)
Total weeks in AP Top 20/25: 0

Current conference: Ohio Valley (1992-)
Conference titles:
OVC: 1 (2009)
Conference tournament titles: 0
NCAA Tournament appearances: 0
NIT appearances: 1

TOP 5

G **Lester Hudson** (2007-09)
G **Mike Meschede** (1984-88)
F **Larry Carter** (1975-77)
F **Michael Hart** (1994-96)
C **Marcus Glass** (1984-86)

RECORDS

RECORDS	GAME		SEASON		CAREER	
POINTS	44	Okechi Egbe, vs. Bethel (Tenn.) (Nov. 20, 2000)	880	Lester Hudson (2008-09)	1,729	Mike Meschede (1984-88)
POINTS PER GAME			27.5	Lester Hudson (2008-09)	26.6	Lester Hudson (2007-09)
REBOUNDS	27	Darrell Smith, vs. Maryville (Dec. 20, 1980)	320	Marcus Glass (1985-86)	794	Mike Rudolphi (1967-70)
ASSISTS	16	Kyle Herrin, vs. Miles (Dec. 17, 1986)	209	Larry Martin (1982-83)	397	Kyle Herrin (1983-87)

ESPN 137 SAGARIN

TENNESSEE STATE

Move over, Texas Western: The first all-African-American starting five to win a national title was actually coach John McLendon's Tigers, who took three straight NAIA crowns from 1957 to '59. Tennessee State (called Tennessee A&I until 1968) is arguably the best small-college program ever—NBAers Anthony Mason and Carlos Rogers don't even crack its all-time Top 5.

BEST TEAM: 1958-59 Tennessee State's best team was not the 24–0 Tigers of 1948-49, but McLendon's 1958-59 NAIA champs, which went 32–1 and made TSU the first school ever to win three straight national titles. Stars Dick Barnett, John Barnhill and Ben Warley all went on to long NBA careers.

BEST PLAYER: G/F DICK BARNETT (1955-59) A two-time first-team Little All-America, Barnett starred on all three national title teams and was twice named tourney MVP, averaging 25.1 ppg in 18 tourney games. He finished with a school-record 3,209 points and went on to win two NBA championships with the New York Knicks.

BEST COACH: JOHN MCLENDON (1954-59) Known as the Father of Black Basketball, McLendon (149–20 with three titles at TSU) learned from Dr. James Naismith himself and was a basketball pioneer in his own right. His 1954-55 squad was the first historically black college team invited to the prestigious NAIA annual pre-Christmas tipoff tournament. He was inducted into the Naismith Hall of Fame in 1978.

GAME FOR THE AGES: The 1958 title game featured two of the best teams in NAIA history: the Tigers and undefeated Western Illinois. WIU had lost to Tennessee State in the '57 tournament, but the Leathernecks were riding a 27-game winning streak that included a January victory over the Tigers. No matter: TSU won, 85-73, for their second of three consecutive titles.

FIERCEST RIVAL: Austin Peay and TSU are only 49 miles apart, so many students at one have friends at the other—except during the nip-and-tuck games. They went to the wire in 2008 OVC tournament final before APSU prevailed. Austin Peay leads the series, 39–21.

SEASON REVIEW

SEAS.	W-L	CONF.	COACH	SEAS.	W-L	CONF.	COACH
1944-50	*120-21*	*24-0 in 1948-49*		1963-64	18-8		Harold Hunter
1950-51	6-8		Henry Kean	1964-65	16-10		Harold Hunter
1951-52	19-4		Clarence Cash	1965-66	19-7		Harold Hunter
1952-53	22-4		Clarence Cash	1966-67	20-8		Harold Hunter
1953-54	18-5		Clarence Cash	1967-68	3-8		Harold Hunter
1954-55	29-4		John McLendon	1968-69	14-12		Edward Martin
1955-56	26-8		John McLendon	1969-70	21-8		Edward Martin
1956-57	31-4	◆	John McLendon	1970-71	24-3		Edward Martin
1957-58	31-3	◆	John McLendon	1971-72	26-2		Edward Martin
1958-59	32-1	◆	John McLendon	1972-73	22-8		Edward Martin
1959-60	28-5		Harold Hunter	1973-74	22-6		Edward Martin
1960-61	24-5		Harold Hunter	1974-75	19-9		Edward Martin
1961-62	16-9		Harold Hunter	1975-76	19-7		Edward Martin
1962-63	28-7		Harold Hunter	1976-77	9-16		Edward Martin

SEAS.	W-L	CONF.		SCORING		COACH	RECORD	
1977-78	11-12					Edward Martin		
1978-79	20-6					Edward Martin		
1979-80	19-7					Edward Martin		
1980-81	17-9					Edward Martin		
1981-82	13-12					Edward Martin		
1982-83	11-16					Edward Martin		
1983-84	12-15					Edward Martin		
1984-85	9-19					Edward Martin[a]	282-154	.647
1985-86	14-14					Larry Reid		
1986-87	15-12					Larry Reid		
1987-88	11-17	4-10		Anthony Mason	28.0	Larry Reid		
1988-89	4-24	2-10				Larry Reid	44-67	.396
1989-90	7-20	2-10		Darryl Brooks	28.8	Ron Abernathy		
1990-91	5-23	1-11				Ron Abernathy	12-43	.218
1991-92	4-24	2-12				Frankie Allen		
1992-93	19-10	13-3	●			Frankie Allen		
1993-94	19-12	12-4	●	Carlos Rogers	24.8	Frankie Allen		
1994-95	17-10	11-5				Frankie Allen		
1995-96	15-13	11-5				Frankie Allen		
1996-97	9-18	7-11				Frankie Allen		
1997-98	13-16	8-10				Frankie Allen		
1998-99	12-15	9-9		Jamie Roberts	17.6	Frankie Allen		
1999-2000	7-22	6-12		Jamie Roberts	16.7	Frankie Allen	115-140	.451
2000-01	10-19	7-9		Jamie Roberts	17.8	Nolan Richardson III		
2001-02	11-17	7-9		Kyle Rolston	15.9	Nolan Richardson III		
2002-03	2-25	0-16		Roshaun Bowens	15.4	Nolan Richardson III[b]	23-45	.338
2003-04	7-21	6-10		Bruce Price	17.6	Cy Alexander		
2004-05	14-17	9-7		Bruce Price	13.7	Cy Alexander		
2005-06	13-15	11-9		Kareem Grant	16.0	Cy Alexander		
2006-07	12-20	8-12		Ladarious Weaver	13.7	Cy Alexander		
2007-08	15-17	10-10		Bruce Price	17.6	Cy Alexander		
2008-09	12-18	9-9		Gerald Robinson	17.8	Cy Alexander[c]	67-106	.387

[a] Edward Martin (3-6) and Ed Meyers (6-13) both coached during the 1984-85 season.
[b] Nolan Richardson III (2-9) and Hosea Lewis (0-16) both coached during the 2002-03 season.
[c] Cy Alexander (6-16) and Mark Pittman (6-2) both coached during the 2008-09 season.
● NCAA Tournament appearance ◆ NAIA championship

PROFILE

Tennessee State University, Nashville, TN
Founded: 1912
Enrollment: 9,024 (7,132 undergraduate)
Colors: Reflex blue and white
Nickname: Tigers
Current arena: John B. McLendon Court at the Gentry Center Complex, opened in 1980 (10,500)
Previous: Kean Hall Gymnasium, a.k.a. Kean's Little Garden, 1953-80 (N/A)
First game: 1944
All-time record: 1,061-715 (.597)
Total weeks in AP Top 20/25: 0

Current conference: Ohio Valley (1986-)
Conference titles:
OVC: 2 (1993, '95 [tie])
Conference tournament titles:
OVC: 2 (1993, '94)
NCAA Tournament appearances: 2
NIT appearances: 0

CONSENSUS ALL-AMERICAS

1958, '59	**Dick Barnett** (Little A-A), G/F
1971	**Ted McClain** (Little A-A), G
1972	**Lloyd Neal** (Little A-A), F/C
1974	**Leonard "Truck" Robinson** (College Div.), F

FIRST-ROUND PRO PICKS

1959	**Dick Barnett,** Syracuse (5)
1961	**Ben Warley,** Syracuse (6)
1971	**Ted McClain,** Carolina (ABA)
1980	**Monti Davis,** Philadelphia (21)
1994	**Carlos Rogers,** Seattle (11)

TOP 5

G	**John Barnhill** (1956-59)
G/F	**Dick Barnett** (1955-59)
F	**Leonard "Truck" Robinson** (1970-74)
F/C	**Lloyd Neal** (1968-72)
C	**Ben Warley** (1957-60)

RECORDS

RECORDS	GAME		SEASON		CAREER	
POINTS	48	Dick Barnett, vs. Lincoln (Jan. 10, 1959)	783	Anthony Mason (1987-88)	3,209	Dick Barnett (1955-59)
POINTS PER GAME			29.3	Dick Barnett (1958-59)	23.6	Dick Barnett (1955-59)
REBOUNDS	30	Monti Davis, vs. Alabama A&M (Jan. 8, 1979)	528	Leonard "Truck" Robinson (1972-73)	1,667	Lloyd Neal (1968-72)
ASSISTS	14	Neil Jones, vs. Morehead State (Feb. 9, 1993)	191	Kareem Gilbert (1996-97)	451	Tremaine Smith (1985-89)

ESPN 182 SAGARIN

TENNESSEE TECH

Tech averaged 18 wins a year from 2000 to '08, recalling the glory days of coach John Oldham. Sure, the Golden Eagles' last NCAA bid came in 1963, but a shocking 1997 upset of Tennessee and an NIT elite eight run in 2002 were crowd-pleasingly good.

BEST TEAM: 2001-02 Jeff Lebo's team went 27–7, including 15–1 in the OVC, to win the regular-season title. A loss to Murray State in the conference tourney sent the Golden Eagles to the NIT, where they beat Georgia State 64-62 to notch the school's first postseason tournament victory.

BEST PLAYER: C Jim Hagan (1957-60) After installing a high-post offense, Tech plucked Hagan from nearby Kentucky and let the 6'9" sapling tear through their record books. In 1958-59 Hagan averaged 28.8 points (third in the country) and 18.2 boards a game.

BEST COACH: John Oldham (1955-64) Oldham won three OVC championships (two shared) and made two NCAA Tourney treks. He also preached, "Why win by 20 when we can win by 40?"—a message that backfired on him in the 1963 Tournament. The team ended up on the short end of the (still standing) most lopsided score in Tourney history, 111-42, to eventual champ Loyola-Chicago.

GAME FOR THE AGES: In the game before Tech's first NIT appearance in 1985, Golden Eagles fans rained toilet paper onto the court, disrupting an OVC tournament loss to Middle Tennessee State. Thirteen days later, Tech fans were ready—for 15 minutes, the Eblen Center was covered in white toilet paper falling from the stands. The shower, now known as the Blizzard, delayed Tech's 65-62 loss to Tennessee for 45 minutes.

FIERCEST RIVAL: For a long time, nothing but intense feelings of enmity have prevailed between Tech and Middle Tennessee State. The toilet paper sheets used in the Blizzard are known by Tech fans as MTSU diplomas, and players from the two schools exchanged blows in 1985 and again in 1990—leading to a total of eight ejections.

SEASON REVIEW

SEAS.	W-L	CONF.	COACH
1924-47	*170-150-1*	*44-17 over 4 seasons (1929-33)*	
1947-48	18-7		Hooper Eblen
1948-49	10-10	0-1	Raymond Brown
1949-50	9-12	1-6	Raymond Brown
1950-51	12-9	1-6	Raymond Brown
1951-52	9-13	2-10	Raymond Brown
1952-53	14-11	3-7	Raymond Brown
1953-54	12-10	4-6	Raymond Brown
1954-55	9-11	3-7	Raymond Brown
1955-56	14-7	7-3	John Oldham
1956-57	9-11	1-9	John Oldham
1957-58	17-9	8-2 ●	John Oldham
1958-59	16-9	7-5	John Oldham
1959-60	13-9	7-4	John Oldham
1960-61	6-13	3-9	John Oldham
1961-62	16-6	7-5	John Oldham
1962-63	16-8	8-4 ●	John Oldham
1963-64	11-11	7-7	John Oldham
1964-65	14-11	8-6	Kenny Sidwell
1965-66	17-8	8-6	Kenny Sidwell
1966-67	12-11	6-8	Kenny Sidwell
1967-68	10-16	4-10	Kenny Sidwell
1968-69	13-11	5-9	Kenny Sidwell
1969-70	10-15	4-10	Connie Inman
1970-71	7-17	4-10	Connie Inman
1971-72	14-11	7-7	Connie Inman
1972-73	14-11	7-7	Connie Inman
1973-74	7-18	4-10	Connie Inman

SEAS.	W-L	CONF.	SCORING		COACH	RECORD
1974-75	13-12	7-7	Frank Jones	23.3	Connie Inman	
1975-76	14-10	7-7	Tom Schmidt	23.0	Connie Inman	79-94 .457
1976-77	7-19	1-13	Bobby Porter	16.3	Cliff Malpass	
1977-78	11-15	7-7	Bobby Porter	15.8	Cliff Malpass	
1978-79	11-15	7-5	Brian Troupe	14.5	Cliff Malpass	
1979-80	5-21	1-11	Pete Abuls	12.1	Cliff Malpass	34-70 .327
1980-81	6-20	2-12	Mike Williams	14.0	Tom Deaton	
1981-82	12-14	8-8	Pete Abuls	14.5	Tom Deaton	
1982-83	16-12	9-5	Steve Taylor	13.9	Tom Deaton	
1983-84	18-10	11-3	Stephen Kite	18.0	Tom Deaton	
1984-85	19-9	11-3 ■	Stephen Kite	16.3	Tom Deaton	
1985-86	14-15	6-8	Stephen Kite	16.8	Tom Deaton	
1986-87	7-20	1-13	Earl Wise	18.6	Tom Deaton	
1987-88	12-16	5-9	Earl Wise	17.8	Tom Deaton	
1988-89	10-20	3-9	Earl Wise	21.7	Tom Deaton[a]	106-119 .471
1989-90	19-9	9-3	Earl Wise	19.5	Frank Harrell	
1990-91	12-16	6-6	John Best	13.9	Frank Harrell	
1991-92	14-15	8-6	John Best	20.0	Frank Harrell	
1992-93	15-13	9-7	John Best	28.5	Frank Harrell	
1993-94	10-21	5-11	Rob West	18.9	Frank Harrell	
1994-95	13-14	9-7	Lorenzo Coleman	15.0	Frank Harrell	
1995-96	13-15	7-9	Greg Bibb	13.5	Frank Harrell	
1996-97	15-13	10-8	Lorenzo Coleman	17.4	Frank Harrell	
1997-98	9-21	5-13	Alex Franco	11.1	Frank Harrell	128-154 .454
1998-99	12-15	8-10	Josh Heard	16.6	Jeff Lebo	
1999-2000	16-12	11-7	Josh Heard	17.5	Jeff Lebo	
2000-01	20-9	13-3	Larrie Smith	16.3	Jeff Lebo	
2001-02	27-7	15-1 ■	Damien Kinloch	16.1	Jeff Lebo	75-43 .636
2002-03	20-12	11-5	Damien Kinloch	16.3	Mike Sutton	
2003-04	13-15	7-9	Willie Jenkins	19.5	Mike Sutton	
2004-05	18-11	12-4	Willie Jenkins	19.7	Mike Sutton	
2005-06	19-12	13-7	Anthony Fisher	12.9	Mike Sutton	
2006-07	19-13	13-7	Belton Rivers	17.8	Mike Sutton	
2007-08	13-19	10-10	Anthony Fisher	17.1	Mike Sutton	
2008-09	12-18	6-13	Daniel Northern	12..6	Mike Sutton	114-100 .533

[a] Tom Deaton (2-3) and Frank Harrell (8-17) both coached during the 1988-89 season.

● NCAA Tournament appearance ■ NIT appearance

PROFILE

Tennessee Technological University, Cookeville, TN
Founded: 1915 as Tennessee Polytechnic Institute
Enrollment: 10,321 (8,060 undergraduate)
Colors: Purple and gold
Nickname: Golden Eagles
Current arena: Hooper Eblen Center, opened in 1977 (10,152)
First game: 1924
All-time record: 983-953-1 (.508)
Total weeks in AP Top 20/25: 0

Current conference: Ohio Valley (1948-)
Conference titles:
OVC: 7 (1956 [tie], '58, '63 [tie], '85, 2001, '02, '05)
Conference tournament titles:
OVC: 1 (1967)
NCAA Tournament appearances: 2
NIT appearances: 2

TOP 5

G **Kenny Sidwell** (1954-58)
G/F **Stephen Kite** (1982-86)
F **Willie Jenkins** (2003-05)
F **Earl Wise** (1986-90)
C **Jim Hagan** (1957-60)

RECORDS

RECORDS	GAME		SEASON		CAREER	
POINTS	48	Ron Filipek, vs. Middle Tennessee St. (Feb. 21, 1966); Jim Hagan, vs. East Tennessee St. (Jan. 24, 1959)	799	John Best (1992-93)	2,196	Earl Wise (1986-90)
POINTS PER GAME			28.8	Jim Hagan (1958-59)	21.1	Jim Hagan (1957-60)
REBOUNDS	30	Jim Hagan, vs. Morehead State (1958-59)	454	Jim Hagan (1958-59)	1,108	Jim Hagan (1957-60)
ASSISTS	17	Van Usher, vs. Western Kentucky (Dec. 28, 1990)	254	Van Usher (1991-92)	676	Van Usher (1989-92)

ESPN 47 SAGARIN

TEXAS

Football's still the king in Austin—always has been and always will be. But the Longhorns basketball program has converted more than a few pigskin provincialists into roundball revelers with consistent runs to the NCAA Sweet 16 during the decade of the 2000s, including a charge to the Final Four in 2003.

BEST TEAM: 2002-03 Rick Barnes' 26–7 Longhorns achieved a whole host of firsts. They were the first Texas team to be ranked in the AP Top 10 for all 20 weeks of the season; the first to earn a No. 1 seed in the NCAA Tournament; the first to go all the way to the Final Four since 1947; and sophomore guard T.J. Ford became the first male player in school history to win both the Naismith and Wooden Awards as National Player of the Year.

BEST PLAYER: F KEVIN DURANT (2006-07) Although he played just a single season in Austin, Durant instantly became a dominant figure in Longhorns hoops history as the first freshman to be honored as consensus National Player of the Year. He was the only player in the country in 2006-07 to rank in the Top 10 nationally in both scoring (25.8 ppg, fourth) and rebounding (11.1 rpg, fourth). He helped pace Texas to a 25–10 record and led the Longhorns into the second round of the Tournament (where they lost to USC).

BEST COACH: RICK BARNES (1998-) Barnes has led Texas to a school-record 11 consecutive NCAA Tourney appearances and a school-record 10 straight 20-win seasons. He stands as the Longhorns' winningest coach with a 270–105 (.720) mark in 11 campaigns, an average of 24.5 wins per season.

GAME FOR THE AGES: On March 8, 2003, for the first time in school history, Texas was involved in a matchup of two AP Top-5 teams that happened to emulate a certain annual football border war. No. 4 Texas crossed the Red River to shoot it out with No. 5 Oklahoma in Norman. After Texas fell behind by as many as 15 points, T.J. Ford drilled 14 of his 18 points in the second half to carry the Longhorns back for the 76-71 win.

HEARTBREAKER: The ecstasy and the agony of Jan. 16, 2007, will long live in Longhorns lore. At Stillwater, Texas and Oklahoma State played through three overtimes as UT's Durant and OSU's Mario Boggan each poured in 37 points. Boggan, who also grabbed 20 rebounds, had the last word, nailing a game-winning three with 3.2 seconds left in the third OT to ram the 105-103 dagger deep in the heart of Texas.

FIERCEST RIVAL: The state of Texas was one big battleground in the old Southwest Conference days, but the Longhorns always had a special enmity for Kansas, a fellow Big 12 member since 1996. The teams, which first met in the 1938-39 season (36–34, UT), are consistently at the top of the league, and in two of the five seasons from 2004-05 to '08-09 they shared the Big 12 regular-season crown. Kansas leads the series overall, 16–6.

FANFARE AND HOOPLA: The student section at Austin's Frank C. Erwin Jr. Special Events Center, the Longhorns' home court, is called the O-Zone. Its regulars camp outside the arena before home games and come rushing into each end zone 90 minutes before tip-off to claim their general admission spots. Another O-Zone must: Texas fans stand up for the opening tip and remain on their feet until UT scores its first points.

FAN FAVORITE: G ROYAL IVEY (2000-04) Though only 6'3", his wingspan was 6'11" and his teammates nicknamed him Edward Scissorfingers. He holds the Texas record for most career games started (126) and was twice selected to the Big 12 All-Defensive team.

CONSENSUS ALL-AMERICAS

1916	**Clyde Littlefield**, C
1924	**Abb Curtis**, G
1935	**Jack Gray**, F
2000	**Chris Mihm**, C
2003	**T.J. Ford**, G
2007	**Kevin Durant**, F
2008	**D.J. Augustin**, G

FIRST-ROUND PRO PICKS

1982	**LaSalle Thompson**, Kansas City (5)
1990	**Travis Mays**, Sacramento (14)
1990	**Lance Blanks**, Detroit (26)
1994	**B.J. Tyler**, Philadelphia (20)
2000	**Chris Mihm**, Cleveland (7)
2003	**T.J. Ford**, Milwaukee (8)
2006	**LaMarcus Aldridge**, Chicago (2)
2007	**Kevin Durant**, Seattle (2)
2008	**D.J. Augustin**, Charlotte (9)

PROFILE

University of Texas at Austin, Austin, TX
Founded: 1883
Enrollment: 50,006 (37,406 undergraduate)
Colors: Burnt orange and white
Nickname: Longhorns
Current arena: Frank C. Erwin Jr. Special Events Center, opened in 1977 (16,755)
Previous: Gregory Gym, 1931-77 (7,500); Men's Gym, 1917-30 (2,500); Clark Field, 1905-17 (N/A); Ben Hur Temple, 1913 (350)
First game: March 10, 1906

All-time record: 1,586-921 (.627)
Total weeks in AP Top 20/25: 191
Current conference: Big 12 (1996-)
Conference titles:
Southwest: 22 (1915, '16, '17, '19, '24, '33, '39, '43 [tie], '47, '51 [tie], '54 [tie], '60, '63, '65 [tie], '72 [tie], '74, '78 [tie], '79 [tie], '86 [tie], '92 [tie], '94, '95 [tie])
Big 12: 3 (1999, 2006 [tie], '08 [tie])
Conference tournament titles:
Southwest: 2 (1994, '95)
NCAA Tournament appearances: 27
Sweet 16s (since 1975): 7
Final Fours: 3

NIT appearances: 4
Semifinals: 1
Titles: 1 (1978)

TOP 5

G	**T.J. Ford** (2001-03)
G	**Slater Martin** (1943-44, '46-49)
F	**Raymond Downs** (1954-57)
F	**Kevin Durant** (2006-07)
C	**Chris Mihm** (1997-2000)

RECORDS

RECORDS	GAME		SEASON		CAREER	
POINTS	49	Raymond Downs, vs. Baylor (Feb. 25, 1956); Slater Martin, vs. TCU (Feb. 26, 1949)	903	Kevin Durant (2006-07)	2,306	Terrence Rencher (1991-95)
POINTS PER GAME			26.4	Raymond Downs (1955-56)	25.8	Kevin Durant (2006-07)
REBOUNDS	24	Lynn Howden, vs. Florida State (Dec. 1, 1970)	393	Damion James (2007-08)	1,077	James Thomas (2000-04)
ASSISTS	19	Johnny Moore, vs. Oklahoma State (Dec. 9, 1978); vs. Northern Montana (Nov. 27, 1978)	273	T.J. Ford (2001-02)	714	Johnny Moore (1975-79)

SEASON REVIEW

SEASON	W-L	CONF.	SCORING	COACH	RECORD	
05-15	62-24		*14-0 in 1914-15 under L. Theo Belmont*			
15-16	12-0	6-0		Roy Henderson		
16-17	13-3	7-1		Eugene Van Gent	13-3	.813
17-18	14-5	8-4		Roy Henderson		
18-19	17-3	11-2		Roy Henderson	43-8	.843
19-20	10-6	4-6		Berry M. Whitaker	10-6	.625
20-21	13-5	9-5		L. Theo Bellmont		
21-22	20-4	14-4		L. Theo Bellmont	58-9	.866
22-23	11-7	9-7		Milton Romney	11-7	.611
23-24	23-0	20-0		E.J. Stewart		
24-25	17-8	9-5		E.J. Stewart		
1925-26	12-10	6-6		E.J. Stewart		
1926-27	13-9	7-4		E.J. Stewart	65-27	.707
1927-28	12-5	7-5		Fred Walker		
1928-29	18-2	10-2		Fred Walker		
1929-30	12-8	8-4		Fred Walker		
1930-31	9-15	2-10		Fred Walker	51-30	.630
1931-32	13-9	5-7		Ed Olle		
1932-33	22-1	11-1		Ed Olle		
1933-34	14-8	6-6		Ed Olle	49-18	.731
1934-35	16-7	5-7		Marty Karow		
1935-36	15-9	8-4		Marty Karow	31-16	.660

SEAS.	W-L	CONF.	POSTSEASON	SCORING		REBOUNDS		ASSISTS		COACH	RECORD	
36-37	13-10	5-7								Jack Gray		
37-38	11-11	5-7								Jack Gray		
38-39	19-6	10-2	NCAA REGIONAL SEMIFINALS							Jack Gray		
39-40	18-5	8-4								Jack Gray		
40-41	14-10	7-5								Jack Gray		
41-42	14-9	5-7								Jack Gray		
42-43	19-7	9-3	NCAA NATIONAL SEMIFINALS							Bully Gilstrap		
43-44	14-11	6-6								Bully Gilstrap		
44-45	10-10	5-7								Bully Gilstrap	43-28	.606
45-46	16-7	7-5								Jack Gray		
46-47	26-2	12-0	NCAA THIRD PLACE							Jack Gray		
47-48	20-5	9-3	NIT QUARTERFINALS							Jack Gray		
48-49	17-7	7-5								Jack Gray		
49-50	13-11	6-6								Jack Gray		
50-51	13-14	8-4								Jack Gray	194-97	.667
51-52	16-8	8-4								Slue Hull		
52-53	12-9	8-4								Slue Hull		
53-54	16-9	9-3								Slue Hull		
54-55	4-20	3-9								Slue Hull		
55-56	12-10	5-7		Raymond Downs	26.4					Slue Hull	60-56	.517
56-57	11-13	3-9		Raymond Downs	22.2	Raymond Downs	8.3			Marshall Hughes		
57-58	10-13	5-9		Kermit Decker	12.4	Brenton Hughes	8.7			Marshall Hughes		
58-59	4-20	2-12		Jay Arnette	14.2	Al Almanza	8.0			Marshall Hughes	25-46	.352
59-60	18-8	11-3	NCAA REGIONAL SEMIFINALS	Jay Arnette	19.9	Brenton Hughes	7.3			Harold Bradley		
60-61	14-10	8-6		Donnie Lasiter	14.8	Al Almanza	9.2			Harold Bradley		
61-62	16-8	8-6		James Brown	14.1	Jack Dugan	7.3			Harold Bradley		
62-63	20-7	13-1	NCAA REGIONAL SEMIFINALS	William Humphrey	12.0	William Humphrey	7.0			Harold Bradley		
63-64	15-9	8-6		Joe Fisher	14.2	Joe Fisher	10.7			Harold Bradley		
64-65	16-9	10-4		Larry Franks	12.6	John Fultz	7.8			Harold Bradley		
65-66	12-12	7-7		Michael White	13.5	Michael White	9.0			Harold Bradley		
66-67	14-10	8-6		Robert Stout	16.0	Gary Overbeck	8.5			Harold Bradley	125-73	.631
67-68	11-13	8-6		Billy Arnold	19.9	Gary Overbeck	10.2			Leon Black		
68-69	9-15	5-9		Kurt Papp	18.0	Kurt Papp	7.4			Leon Black		
69-70	11-13	6-8		Wayne Doyal	17.3	Eric Groscurth	9.3			Leon Black		
70-71	12-12	6-8		Jimmy Blacklock	16.6	Lynn Howden	11.0			Leon Black		
71-72	19-9	10-4	NCAA REGIONAL SEMIFINALS	Larry Robinson	21.9	Larry Robinson	9.7			Leon Black		
72-73	13-12	7-7		Larry Robinson	18.1	B.G. Brosterhous	8.8			Leon Black		
73-74	12-15	11-3	NCAA FIRST ROUND	Larry Robinson	22.4	Larry Robinson	10.8			Leon Black		
74-75	10-15	6-8		Dan Krueger	13.2	Rich Parson	5.5			Leon Black		
75-76	9-17	4-12		Dan Krueger	18.9	Gary Goodner	7.6	Dan Krueger	5.8	Leon Black	106-121	.467
76-77	13-13	8-8		Jim Krivacs	18.5	Ron Baxter	8.5	Johnny Moore	5.9	Abe Lemons		
77-78	26-5	14-2	NIT CHAMPION	Jim Krivacs	21.9	Ron Baxter	8.9	Johnny Moore	5.9	Abe Lemons		
78-79	21-8	13-3	NCAA SECOND ROUND	Tyrone Branyan	18.1	Phillip Stroud	8.8	Johnny Moore	8.3	Abe Lemons		
79-80	19-11	10-6	NIT SECOND ROUND	Ron Baxter	17.8	LaSalle Thompson	9.7	Fred Carson	4.5	Abe Lemons		
80-81	15-15	7-9		LaSalle Thompson	19.2	LaSalle Thompson	12.3	Fred Carson, Ray Harper	3.9	Abe Lemons		
81-82	16-11	6-10		LaSalle Thompson	18.6	LaSalle Thompson	13.5	Jack Worthington	3.2	Abe Lemons	110-63	.636
82-83	6-22	1-15		Bill Wendlandt	15.3	Carlton Cooper	9.3	Karl Willock	3.6	Bob Weltlich		
83-84	7-21	3-13		Carlton Cooper	17.2	Carlton Cooper	8.5	Karl Willock	2.5	Bob Weltlich		
84-85	15-13	7-9		Mike Wacker	16.7	Mike Wacker	8.3	Karl Willock	3.4	Bob Weltlich		
85-86	19-12	12-4	NIT SECOND ROUND	John Brownlee	17.0	John Brownlee	8.2	Alex Broadway	5.0	Bob Weltlich		
86-87	14-17	7-9		Patrick Fairs	17.0	Patrick Fairs	5.7	Alex Broadway	4.1	Bob Weltlich		
87-88	16-13	10-6		Travis Mays	18.1	Alvin Heggs	6.5	Alex Broadway	4.9	Bob Weltlich	77-98	.440
88-89	25-9	12-4	NCAA SECOND ROUND	Travis Mays	21.9	Alvin Heggs	7.8	Lance Blanks	4.3	Tom Penders		
89-90	24-9	12-4	NCAA REGIONAL FINALS	Travis Mays	24.1	Locksley Collie	7.2	Joey Wright	3.8	Tom Penders		
90-91	23-9	13-3	NCAA SECOND ROUND	Joey Wright	21.2	Guillermo Myers	7.5	Joey Wright	3.7	Tom Penders		
91-92	23-12	11-3	NCAA FIRST ROUND	Dexter Cambridge	21.7	Albert Burditt	8.7	B.J. Tyler	6.5	Tom Penders		
92-93	11-17	4-10		Mike Richardson	20.2	Albert Burditt	14.1	B.J. Tyler	5.9	Tom Penders		
93-94	26-8	12-2	NCAA SECOND ROUND	B.J. Tyler	22.8	Albert Burditt	8.6	B.J. Tyler	6.3	Tom Penders		
94-95	23-7	11-3	NCAA SECOND ROUND	Terrence Rencher	20.8	Tremaine Wingfield	6.4	Roderick Anderson	7.0	Tom Penders		
95-96	21-10	10-4	NCAA SECOND ROUND	Reggie Freeman	22.4	Sonny Alvarado	8.2	Reggie Freeman	3.9	Tom Penders		
96-97	18-12	10-6	NCAA REGIONAL SEMIFINALS	Reggie Freeman	21.8	Reggie Freeman	7.6	Reggie Freeman	4.2	Tom Penders		
97-98	14-17	6-10		Kris Clack	17.3	Chris Mihm	8.0	Kris Clack	3.2	Tom Penders	208-110	.654
98-99	19-13	13-3	NCAA FIRST ROUND	Gabe Muoneke	16.5	Chris Mihm	11.0	Ivan Wagner	3.9	Rick Barnes		
99-2000	24-9	13-3	NCAA SECOND ROUND	Chris Mihm	17.7	Chris Mihm	10.5	Ivan Wagner	4.7	Rick Barnes		
00-01	25-9	12-4	NCAA FIRST ROUND	Maurice Evans	15.6	Chris Owens	7.9	Darren Kelly	2.9	Rick Barnes		
01-02	22-12	10-6	NCAA REGIONAL SEMIFINALS	Brandon Mouton	13.7	James Thomas	8.9	T.J. Ford	8.3	Rick Barnes		
02-03	26-7	13-3	NCAA NATIONAL SEMIFINALS	T.J. Ford	15.0	James Thomas	11.0	T.J. Ford	7.7	Rick Barnes		
03-04	25-8	12-4	NCAA REGIONAL SEMIFINALS	Brandon Mouton	13.9	P.J. Tucker	6.8	Royal Ivey	4.3	Rick Barnes		
04-05	20-11	9-7	NCAA FIRST ROUND	Daniel Gibson	14.2	Brad Buckman	8.3	Daniel Gibson	3.9	Rick Barnes		
05-06	30-7	13-3	NCAA REGIONAL FINALS	P.J. Tucker	16.1	P.J. Tucker	9.5	Daniel Gibson	3.1	Rick Barnes		
06-07	25-10	12-4	NCAA SECOND ROUND	Kevin Durant	25.8	Kevin Durant	11.1	D.J. Augustin	6.7	Rick Barnes		
07-08	31-7	13-3	NCAA REGIONAL FINALS	D.J. Augustin	19.2	Damion James	10.3	D.J. Augustin	5.8	Rick Barnes		
08-09	23-12	9-7	NCAA SECOND ROUND	A.J. Abrams	16.6	Damion James	9.2	Justin Mason	4.0	Rick Barnes	270-105	.720

THE SCHOOLS

ESPN 111 SAGARIN

TEXAS A&M

Finally. Until making the 2007 Big Dance, the Aggies had never appeared in back-to-back NCAA Tournaments. Then, in 2008, Texas A&M made the Tournament again—and returned for a fourth straight appearance in 2009. With the recent $23 million Reed Arena expansion that included a sparkling 68,000-foot practice facility, every sign indicates that an Aggies renaissance is officially under way. Who remembers that the team enjoyed just one winning season from 1989 to 2004?

BEST TEAM: 2006-07 Three years removed from a winless conference season, the Aggies established that they were a Big 12 force to be reckoned with, beating Kansas and Texas in back-to-back games in early February. That led to a second-place finish and a No. 3 seed in the Tournament. Billy Gillispie's three-point-happy crew didn't disappoint. After grinding out a victory over Penn in the first round, they rode Acie Law's 26 points to a second-round victory over Louisville before coming up just short against Memphis in the Sweet 16.

BEST PLAYER: G ACIE LAW IV (2003-07) The only consensus first team All-America in school history, Law was the cornerstone of A&M's revival. After enduring a winless Big 12 season as a freshman, Law played a key role in 70 victories over his final three years, earning the nickname Captain Clutch and ending his career fourth all-time in scoring and third in assists. His No. 1 jersey now hangs at Reed Arena, making him the first Aggie in any sport to have his number so honored.

BEST COACH: SHELBY METCALF (1963-90) The Good Doctor put up 22 winning seasons out of 27 to become the winningest coach in Southwest Conference history. Among his many highlights were six conference titles and a trip to the 1980 Sweet 16. An avid student of the game, he earned a PhD from A&M with a dissertation titled "Crowd Behavior at Southwest Conference Basketball Games."

GAME FOR THE AGES: Few folks gave Texas A&M a chance against Dean Smith and powerhouse North Carolina in the second round of the 1980 NCAA Tournament. But the Wall, as the Aggies frontcourt was known, hung tough against the Tar Heels, and A&M sent the game into overtime. In the first extra frame, both teams used a four-corners offense, resulting in zero points scored. But Texas A&M ran away with it in the second OT to win, 78-61, and advance to the Sweet 16.

HEARTBREAKER: With 26,060 people crowding the Alamodome in San Antonio on March 22, 2007, Aggies fans could taste their first Elite Eight when Law skied for a layup with under a minute to go and A&M leading Memphis, 64-63. But he missed and Tigers guard Antonio Anderson was fouled with 3.1 seconds left. Anderson hit both free throws for the win.

FIERCEST RIVAL: A key line from the Aggie War Hymn says it all: "So long to the Orange and White." There's no team in the universe that Texas A&M would rather beat in any sport than those city slickers down in Austin. True, Texas has dominated the series, 131–84, but Law put an end to the Longhorns' tyranny on March 1, 2006, with a three-pointer at the buzzer for a 46-43 win. It went down in Aggies history as simply the Shot.

Acie Law, a.k.a. Captain Clutch, played a key role in 70 victories over his final three seasons.

FANFARE AND HOOPLA: Aggies football fans are famously known as the 12th Man, in honor of E. King Gill, who came out of the stands during a 1922 game and suited up in case he was needed. What most people, including many A&M fans, don't know is that Gill no longer played football at the time; he actually was on A&M's basketball team.

FAN FAVORITE: F CHRIS WALKER (2004-06) Talk about your Aggies spirit: Walker rose from an intramural star to become a two-year starter.

CONSENSUS ALL-AMERICAS

2007 **Acie Law IV**, G

FIRST-ROUND PRO PICKS

1952 **Walt Davis**, Philadelphia (4)
1976 **Sonny Parker**, Golden State (17)
2005 **Antoine Wright**, New Jersey (15)
2007 **Acie Law IV**, Atlanta (11)

PROFILE

Texas A&M University, College Station, TX
Founded: 1872
Enrollment: 47,925 (37,357 undergraduate)
Colors: Maroon and white
Nickname: Aggies
Current arena: Reed Arena, opened in 1998 (12,989)
Previous: G. Rollie White Coliseum, 1954-97 (7,800); DeWare Fieldhouse, 1924-54 (1,000)
First game: 1912
All-time record: 1,225-1,140 (.518)
Total weeks in AP Top 20/25: 62
Current conference: Big 12 (1996-)
Conference titles:
Southwest: 11 (1920, '21, '22, '23, '51 [tie], '64, '69, '75, '76, '80, '86 [tie])
Conference tournament titles:
Southwest: 2 (1980, '87)
NCAA Tournament appearances: 10
Sweet 16s (since 1975): 2
NIT appearances: 6

TOP 5

G **Bernard King** (1999-2003)
G **Acie Law IV** (2003-07)
F **Carroll Broussard** (1959-62)
F **Vernon Smith** (1977-81)
C **John Beasley** (1963-66)

RECORDS	GAME		SEASON		CAREER	
POINTS	53	Bennie Lenox, vs. Wyoming (Dec. 28, 1963)	697	Don Marbury (1985-86)	1,990	Bernard King (1999-2003)
POINTS PER GAME			27.8	John Beasley (1965-66)	21.8	John Beasley (1963-66)
REBOUNDS	23	Cedric Joseph, vs. Angelo State (Dec. 4, 1972)	317	Claude Riley (1981-82)	978	Vernon Smith (1977-81)
ASSISTS	15	Acie Law IV, vs. Texas (Feb. 5, 2007); Kyle Kessel, vs. TCU (Feb. 26, 1996); David Edwards, vs. TCU (Jan. 25, 1994); Tony Milton, vs. Marshall (Dec. 7, 1989)	265	David Edwards (1993-94)	602	David Edwards (1991-94)

SEASON REVIEW

SEASON	W-L	CONF.	SCORING	COACH	RECORD	
912-15	*22-6*		*Two losses each year from 1912-15 under F.D. Steger (22-6 total)*			
915-16	11-2	6-2		Tubby Graves	11-2	.846
916-17	11-8	3-3		W.H.H. Morris	11-8	.579
917-18	9-9	7-7		Bill Driver		
918-19	14-4	7-3		Bill Driver		
919-20	19-0	16-0		Bill Driver	42-13	.764
920-21	16-6	10-2		D.X. Bible		
921-22	18-3	13-3		D.X. Bible		
922-23	16-4	15-3		D.X. Bible		
923-24	13-10	12-11		D.X. Bible		
924-25	9-8	6-8		D.X. Bible		
1925-26	8-9	4-8		D.X. Bible		
1926-27	10-7	4-6		D.X. Bible	90-47	.657
1927-28	4-12	1-9		Charles Bassett		
1928-29	12-6	4-6		Charles Bassett	16-18	.471
1929-30	8-10	4-6		J.B. Reid		
1930-31	14-8	5-7		J.B. Reid		
1931-32	10-9	4-8		J.B. Reid		
1932-33	9-10	8-4		J.B. Reid		
1933-34	14-6	7-5		J.B. Reid		
1934-35	10-10	4-8		J.B. Reid	65-53	.551
1935-36	9-9	3-9		H.R. McQuillan		

SEAS.	W-L	CONF.	POSTSEASON	SCORING		REBOUNDS		ASSISTS		COACH	RECORD	
1936-37	12-13	5-7								H.R. McQuillan		
1937-38	10-8	6-6								H.R. McQuillan		
1938-39	7-16	2-10								H.R. McQuillan		
1939-40	11-11	5-7								H.R. McQuillan		
1940-41	7-13	3-9								H.R. McQuillan	56-70	.444
1941-42	8-16	4-8								Marty Karow		
1942-43	11-11	4-8								Manning Smith		
1943-44	2-15	0-12								Manning Smith		
1944-45	3-18	2-10								Manning Smith	16-44	.267
1945-46	9-14	4-8		Jamie Dawson	17.0					Marty Karow		
1946-47	8-17	4-8		Bill Batey	10.5					Marty Karow		
1947-48	7-17	2-10		Bill Batey	10.4					Marty Karow		
1948-49	5-19	2-10		John DeWitt	11.9					Marty Karow		
1949-50	10-14	6-6		Jewell McDowell	13.0					Marty Karow	47-97	.326
1950-51	17-12	8-4	NCAA FIRST ROUND	Walt Davis	12.2					John Floyd		
1951-52	9-15	5-7		Walt Davis	15.1	Walt Davis	10.6			John Floyd		
1952-53	6-15	3-9		Leroy Miksch	13.1	Leroy Miksch	10.0			John Floyd		
1953-54	2-20	1-11		James Addison	14.2	James Addison	8.7			John Floyd		
1954-55	4-20	1-11		Bill Brophy	14.0	Bill Brophy	7.8			John Floyd	38-82	.317
1955-56	6-18	3-9		Ken Hutto	14.7	George Mehaffey	8.2			Ken Loeffler		
1956-57	7-17	3-9		Neil Swisher	12.6	George Mehaffey	9.9			Ken Loeffler	13-35	.271
1957-58	11-13	7-7		Neil Swisher	13.4	Archie Carroll	7.6			Bob Rogers		
1958-59	15-9	6-8		Neil Swisher	14.9	Archie Carroll	7.1			Bob Rogers		
1959-60	19-5	10-4		Carroll Broussard	17.9	Wayne Lawrence	8.3			Bob Rogers		
1960-61	16-8	10-4		Carroll Broussard	22.4	Carroll Broussard	9.1			Bob Rogers		
1961-62	15-9	9-5		Carroll Broussard	17.3	Jerry Windham	10.8			Bob Rogers		
1962-63	16-8	9-5		Bennie Lenox	23.7	Jerry Windham	10.2			Bob Rogers	92-52	.639
1963-64	18-7	13-1	NCAA FIRST ROUND	Bennie Lenox	20.8	John Beasley	9.5			Shelby Metcalf		
1964-65	14-10	7-7		John Beasley	25.8	John Beasley	10.9			Shelby Metcalf		
1965-66	15-9	10-4		John Beasley	27.8	John Beasley	11.9			Shelby Metcalf		
1966-67	6-18	5-9		Ronnie Peret	11.9	Ronnie Peret	8.5			Shelby Metcalf		
1967-68	14-10	8-6		Ronnie Peret	16.7	Ronnie Peret	11.1			Shelby Metcalf		
1968-69	18-9	12-2	NCAA REGIONAL SEMIFINALS	Billy Bob Barnett	17.6	Ronnie Peret	9.8			Shelby Metcalf		
1969-70	14-10	9-5		Mike Heitmann	19.5	Steve Niles	10.9			Shelby Metcalf		
1970-71	9-17	5-9		Steve Niles	14.0	Steve Niles	9.1			Shelby Metcalf		
971-72	16-10	9-5		Jeff Overhouse	17.2	Jeff Overhouse	10.0	Mario Brown	4.6	Shelby Metcalf		
972-73	17-9	9-5		Randy Knowles	17.4	Jeff Overhouse	9.7	Mario Brown	4.1	Shelby Metcalf		
973-74	15-11	7-7		Randy Knowles	16.8	Cedric Joseph	9.3	Mike Floyd	3.6	Shelby Metcalf		
974-75	20-7	12-2	NCAA FIRST ROUND	Sonny Parker	14.7	Barry Davis	7.3	Mike Floyd	2.4	Shelby Metcalf		
975-76	21-6	14-2		Sonny Parker	20.8	Barry Davis	9.8	Sonny Parker	3.6	Shelby Metcalf		
976-77	14-14	8-8		Steve Jones	16.9	Wally Swanson	8.7	Dave Goff	4.6	Shelby Metcalf		
977-78	12-15	5-11		Willie Foreman	15.2	Vernon Smith	8.4	Dave Goff	4.7	Shelby Metcalf		
978-79	24-9	11-5	NIT QUARTERFINALS	Vernon Smith	16.0	Rudy Woods	8.7	Dave Goff	4.5	Shelby Metcalf		
979-80	26-8	14-2	NCAA REGIONAL SEMIFINALS	Vernon Smith	15.1	Rudy Woods	7.6	Dave Goff	3.9	Shelby Metcalf		
980-81	15-12	8-8		Vernon Smith	14.7	Vernon Smith	8.9	Reggie Roberts	2.7	Shelby Metcalf		
981-82	20-11	10-6	NIT QUARTERFINALS	Claude Riley	16.3	Claude Riley	10.2	Tyren Naulls	3.1	Shelby Metcalf		
982-83	17-14	10-6		Claude Riley	14.2	Claude Riley	9.2	Tyren Naulls	4.6	Shelby Metcalf		
983-84	16-14	7-9		Todd Holloway	12.0	Jimmie Gilbert	7.6	Todd Holloway	3.5	Shelby Metcalf		
984-85	19-11	10-6	NIT FIRST ROUND	Kenny Brown	17.4	Winston Crite	8.2	Todd Holloway	4.4	Shelby Metcalf		
985-86	20-12	12-4	NIT FIRST ROUND	Don Marbury	21.8	Winston Crite	8.0	Todd Holloway	5.0	Shelby Metcalf		
986-87	17-14	6-10	NCAA FIRST ROUND	Winston Crite	16.8	Winston Crite	7.4	Todd Holloway	3.6	Shelby Metcalf		
987-88	16-15	8-8		Darryl McDonald	16.0	Donald Thompson	7.5	Darryl McDonald	6.3	Shelby Metcalf		
988-89	16-14	8-8		Donald Thompson	17.9	Donald Thompson	7.9	Tony Milton	5.3	Shelby Metcalf		
989-90	14-17	7-9		Tony Milton	20.6	David Harris	7.8	Tony Milton	6.7	Shelby Metcalf	443-313	.586
990-91	8-21	2-14		Brooks Thompson	14.5	Shedrick Anderson	6.5	Brooks Thompson	5.7	Kermit Davis	8-21	.276
991-92	6-22	2-12		David Edwards	13.8	Damon Johnson	7.7	David Edwards	5.7	Tony Barone		
992-93	10-17	5-9		Damon Johnson	15.2	Damon Johnson	6.6	David Edwards	6.6	Tony Barone		
993-94	19-11	10-4	NIT FIRST ROUND	Joe Wilbert	14.5	Brett Murry	6.6	David Edwards	8.8	Tony Barone		
994-95	14-16	7-7		Joe Wilbert	22.9	Damon Johnson	7.8	Kyle Kessel	5.4	Tony Barone		
995-96	11-16	3-11		Tracey Anderson	13.3	Dario Quesada	5.9	Kyle Kessel	6.8	Tony Barone		
996-97	9-18	3-13		Calvin Davis	13.3	Calvin Davis	7.0	Tracey Anderson	3.9	Tony Barone		
997-98	7-20	1-15		Shanne Jones	18.0	Shanne Jones	6.7	Brian Barone	4.8	Tony Barone	76-120	.388
998-99	12-15	5-11		Clifton Cook	15.6	Shanne Jones	6.0	Clifton Cook	5.8	Melvin Watkins		
999-2000	8-20	4-12		Bernard King	16.9	Aaron Jack	6.5	Bernard King	4.1	Melvin Watkins		
000-01	10-20	3-13		Bernard King	18.0	Keith Bean	5.5	Bernard King	4.8	Melvin Watkins		
001-02	9-22	3-13		Bernard King	17.2	Andy Slocum	6.4	Bernard King	4.7	Melvin Watkins		
002-03	14-14	6-10		Bernard King	17.0	Antoine Wright	6.6	Bernard King	5.6	Melvin Watkins		
003-04	7-21	0-16		Antoine Wright	13.5	Andy Slocum	8.8	Acie Law IV	3.7	Melvin Watkins	60-112	.349
004-05	21-10	8-8	NIT QUARTERFINALS	Antoine Wright	17.8	Joseph Jones	7.3	Acie Law IV	4.9	Billy Gillispie		
005-06	22-9	10-6	NCAA SECOND ROUND	Acie Law IV	16.1	Joseph Jones	6.5	Acie Law IV	4.0	Billy Gillispie		
006-07	27-7	13-3	NCAA REGIONAL SEMIFINALS	Acie Law IV	18.1	Joseph Jones	6.8	Acie Law IV	5.0	Billy Gillispie	70-26	.729
007-08	25-11	8-8	NCAA SECOND ROUND	Josh Carter	12.2	DeAndre Jordan	6.0	Dominique Kirk	3.6	Mark Turgeon		
008-09	24-10	9-7	NCAA SECOND ROUND	Josh Carter	13.8	Chinemelu Elonu	7.3	Donald Sloan	3.1	Mark Turgeon	49-21	.700

ESPN 273 SAGARIN

TEXAS A&M-CORPUS CHRISTI

Incomplete records are all that remain from Texas A&M-Corpus Christi's first, low-level go at basketball, from 1947 to '73. Now the Island University is making up for lost time. In resurrecting its program, the school jumped straight to D1 in 1999, using the campus' resort location to lure quality recruits. Eight years later, the Islanders made it to their first Big Dance.

BEST TEAM: 2006-07 Coming off consecutive 20-win seasons as an independent, the Islanders joined the Southland Conference and won the regular-season and tournament championships. The senior-laden team topped it off with an impressive performance as a No. 15 seed in the NCAA Tourney, building an 18-point lead against No. 2-seed Wisconsin before falling, 76-63.

BEST PLAYER: F MICHAEL HICKS (1999-2001) This electrifying scorer was vital to establishing the program's credibility. As a senior, he dropped 33 points in back-to-back games at Texas and Texas Tech—the latter effort resulting in the Islanders' first marquee win.

BEST COACH: RONNIE ARROW (1999-2007) The school didn't even have uniforms when it hired Arrow in 1998, never mind eligible players. By the time he left, A&M-Corpus Christi was Dancing. For much of his time there, Arrow favored an up-tempo style of play, and his 2000-01 squad averaged 85.5 ppg. For his efforts, Arrow was honored three times as Independent Coach of the Year and once more as Southland COY.

GAME FOR THE AGES: With :02 left in the 2007 Southland tournament final, Islanders guard Josh Irvin stood at the free throw line with his team hanging on to a 79-78 lead. Good and good. With that, the Islanders iced defending conference champ Northwestern State and earned their first NCAA Tourney bid.

FIERCEST RIVAL: Blood feud? Too soon for that, but there's a bit of animosity brewing between the Islanders and Texas-San Antonio. The schools, separated by a three-hour drive, routinely send fans to one another's gyms and compete for the same recruits.

SEASON REVIEW

SEAS.	W-L	CONF.	SCORING		COACH	RECORD	
1999-2000	13-13		Michael Hicks	22.2	Ronnie Arrow		
2000-01	14-14		Michael Hicks	26.7	Ronnie Arrow		
2001-02	12-15		Brian Evans	13.5	Ronnie Arrow		
2002-03	14-15		Travis Bailey	15.0	Ronnie Arrow		
2003-04	15-11		Travis Bailey	14.2	Ronnie Arrow		
2004-05	20-8		Travis Bailey	13.1	Ronnie Arrow		
2005-06	20-8		Chris Daniels	15.0	Ronnie Arrow		
2006-07	26-7	14-2 ●	Chris Daniels	15.3	Ronnie Arrow	134-91	.596
2007-08	9-20	6-10	Chris Daniels	12.4	Perry Clark		
2008-09	18-15	11-5	Kevin Palmer	18.2	Perry Clark	27-35	.435

● NCAA Tournament appearance

PROFILE

Texas A&M-Corpus Christi University, Corpus Christi, TX
Founded: 1947
Enrollment: 9,100 (7,280 undergraduate)
Colors: Blue, green and white
Nickname: Islanders
Current arena: American Bank Center, opened in 2004 (8,500)
First game: Nov. 22, 1999
All-time record: 161-126 (.561)
Total weeks in AP Top 20/25: 0

Current conference: Southland (2006-)
Conference titles:
Southland: 1 (2007)
Conference tournament titles:
Southland: 1 (2007)
NCAA Tournament appearances: 1
NIT appearances: 0

TOP 5

G **Travis Bailey** (2001-05)
G **Brian Evans** (2000-04)
F **Michael Hicks** (1999-2001)
F **Corey Lamkin** (2001-05)
C **Chris Daniels** (2004-08)

RECORDS

RECORDS	GAME		SEASON		CAREER	
POINTS	47	Michael Hicks, vs. Cal Poly (Jan. 8, 2001)	748	Michael Hicks (2000-01)	1,387	Chris Daniels (2004-08)
POINTS PER GAME			26.7	Michael Hicks (2000-01)	24.5	Michael Hicks (1999-2001)
REBOUNDS	21	Corey Lamkin, vs. Texas-Pan American (Jan. 26, 2002)	239	Michael Hicks (1999-2000)	842	Corey Lamkin (2001-05)
ASSISTS	11	Sennai Atsbeha, vs. North Texas (Dec. 2, 2000)	132	Brian Evans (2002-03)	493	Brian Evans (2000-04)

ESPN 269 SAGARIN

TEXAS-ARLINGTON

UT-Arlington had never played a better transition game than it did in 2007-08: Longtime coach Eddie McCarter turned over the Mavericks coaching reins to former player Scott Cross who, in his second season, led the team to a record 21 wins, a Southland tourney title behind tourney MVP Anthony Vereen and the team's first NCAA bid. All it took the program was 49 years.

BEST TEAM: 2007-08 Cross' second team went 21–12 in its historic run through the Southland schedule and conference tournament before a first-round NCAA loss to eventual runner-up Memphis. Four players averaged double figures (Vereen, Roge'r Guignard, Jermaine Griffin, Brandon Long). Vereen finished his career as UTA's second all-time scorer.

BEST PLAYER: G Willie Brand (1987-91) UTA's all-time leading scorer by almost 500 points (1,907), Brand carried his team from a last-place 7–22 mark his freshman year to a second-place 20–9 record his senior year. He hit 43.7% of his three-pointers, and stands fifth in career steals and sixth (tied) in assists.

BEST COACH: Eddie McCarter (1992-2006) He's the school's winningest coach (179) with the most winning seasons (four), including a share of the 2003-04 Southland regular-season title. His successor, Cross, one of only seven coaches in UTA's "senior college" era with a winning career record, may yet eclipse McCarter.

GAME FOR THE AGES: UTA had a 10-point lead with less than eight minutes left in the 2008 Southland championship against Northwestern State. NSU rallied, but tourney MVP Vereen's 25 points and clutch free throws sealed the 82-79 win and NCAA bid. Guignard (17), Rod Epps (12) and Larry Posey (11) played solid supporting roles.

FIERCEST RIVAL: North Texas (26–21 series lead) left the Southland in 1996. It was the last year the two teams met until the 2006-07 season, when UTA won, 83-81. The Mavericks won the following two contests in the renewed rivlary, including an 80-75 thriller on Dec. 29, 2008.

SEASON REVIEW

SEAS.	W-L	CONF.		SCORING		COACH	RECORD
1959-60	6-18			Jay Hawley	11.8	Tom Tinker	
1960-61	11-12			Jay Hawley	18.3	Tom Tinker	
1961-62	6-18			Noel Roberts	14.8	Tom Tinker	
1962-63	8-17			Noel Roberts	13.5	Tom Tinker	
1963-64	4-21	1-7		Bruce Tibbets	20.9	Tom Tinker	
1964-65	10-14	3-5		Bruce Tibbets	21.7	Tom Tinker	
1965-66	9-13	1-7		Mike Nau	19.6	Tom Tinker	54-113 .323
1966-67	14-12	4-4		Mike Nau	19.6	Barry Dowd	
1967-68	6-20	2-6		Eddie Stallings	20.2	Barry Dowd	
1968-69	8-18	3-5		Eddie Stallings	21.0	Barry Dowd	
1969-70	8-16	4-4		Sherman Evans	20.7	Barry Dowd	
1970-71	8-18	3-5		Sherman Evans	16.1	Barry Dowd	
1971-72	14-12	5-3		Greg Hunter	14.2	Barry Dowd	
1972-73	11-15 ⊗	8-4		Larry Moore	19.9	Barry Dowd	
1973-74	7-18	2-2		Michael Long	15.7	Barry Dowd	
1974-75	6-20	2-6		Jerry Johnson	15.8	Barry Dowd	
1975-76	6-21	1-9		Freddie Anderson	18.1	Barry Dowd	88-170 .341
1976-77	3-24	1-9		Greg Stuckey	14.2	Bob "Snake" LeGrand	
1977-78	10-17	3-7		Miles Robertson	20.8	Bob "Snake" LeGrand	
1978-79	11-16	1-9		Cal Tate	15.5	Bob "Snake" LeGrand	
1979-80	14-13	3-7		Melvin Polk	16.7	Bob "Snake" LeGrand	
1980-81	20-8	7-3	■	Ralph McPherson	15.4	Bob "Snake" LeGrand	
1981-82	16-12	6-4		Ralph McPherson	18.2	Bob "Snake" LeGrand	
1982-83	9-19	3-9		Danny Johnson	16.1	Bob "Snake" LeGrand	
1983-84	5-23	1-11		Sam Norton	21.4	Bob "Snake" LeGrand	
1984-85	12-16	3-9		Dennis Kwiecinski	12.1	Bob "Snake" LeGrand	
1985-86	12-18	2-10		Ike Mitchell	13.2	Bob "Snake" LeGrand	
1986-87	10-18			Alex Joseph	12.3	Bob "Snake" LeGrand	122-184 .399
1987-88	7-22	4-10		Willie Brand	16.3	Jerry Stone	7-22 .241
1988-89	7-21	4-10		Willie Brand	18.1	Mark Nixon	
1989-90	13-16	6-8		Willie Brand	18.0	Mark Nixon	
1990-91	20-9	11-3		Bobby Kenyon	19.8	Mark Nixon	
1991-92	16-13	11-7		Johnny McDowell	16.3	Mark Nixon	56-59 .487
1992-93	16-12	10-8		Johnny McDowell	17.6	Eddie McCarter	
1993-94	7-22	4-14		Sean Miller	13.5	Eddie McCarter	
1994-95	10-17	7-11		Keith Cornett	11.1	Eddie McCarter	
1995-96	11-15	7-11		Damon Johnson	14.5	Eddie McCarter	
1996-97	12-15	8-8		Robert Taylor	15.4	Eddie McCarter	
1997-98	13-16	8-8		Donald Harris	13.8	Eddie McCarter	
1998-99	10-16	8-10		Keith Greene	14.8	Eddie McCarter	
1999-2000	15-12	11-7		Keith Greene	17.0	Eddie McCarter	
2000-01	13-15	11-9		Jabari Johnson	17.9	Eddie McCarter	
2001-02	12-15	9-11		Steven Barber	18.8	Eddie McCarter	
2002-03	16-13	13-7		Derrick Obasohan	11.3	Eddie McCarter	
2003-04	17-12	11-5		Derrick Obasohan	16.4	Eddie McCarter	
2004-05	13-15	7-9		Steven Thomas	17.1	Eddie McCarter	
2005-06	14-16	7-9		Jarrett Howell	14.2	Eddie McCarter	179-211 .459
2006-07	13-17	8-8		Jermaine Griffin	13.2	Scott Cross	
2007-08	21-12	7-9	●	Anthony Vereen	13.6	Scott Cross	
2008-09	16-14	9-7		Anthony Vereen	17.7	Scott Cross	50-43 .538

⊗ Records don't reflect games forfeited or vacated. For adjusted record, see p. 521.
● NCAA Tournament appearance ■ NIT appearance

PROFILE

University of Texas at Arlington, Arlington, TX
Founded: 1895
Enrollment: 25,000 (19,000 undergraduate)
Colors: Royal blue and white
Nickname: Mavericks
Current arena: Texas Hall, opened in 1965 (3,600)
Previous: Arlington State College Gym, 1959-65 (1,000)
First game: Nov. 24, 1959
All-time record: 556-802 (.409)
Total weeks in AP Top 20/25: 0

Current conference: Southland (1963-)
Conference titles:
Southland: 1 (2004 [tie])
Conference tournament titles:
Southland: 1 (2008)
NCAA Tournament appearances: 1
NIT appearances: 1

TOP 5

G **Willie Brand** (1987-91)
G **Dink Ford** (1964-66)
F **Mike Nau** (1964-67)
F **Eddie Stallings** (1967-69)
F **Bruce Tibbets** (1964-65)

RECORDS

RECORDS	GAME		SEASON		CAREER	
POINTS	44	Dink Ford, vs. Texas Wesleyan (Dec. 29, 1964)	599	Sam Norton (1983-84)	1,907	Willie Brand (1987-91)
POINTS PER GAME			21.7	Bruce Tibbetts (1964-65)	20.6	Eddie Stallings (1967-69)
REBOUNDS	24	Albert Culton, vs. Northeastern (Jan. 9, 1981)	304	Sam Norton (1983-84)	857	Mack Callier (1999-2003)
ASSISTS	17	Jermaine Johnson, vs. Sam Houston State (Dec. 28, 1998)	229	Glover Cody (1990-91)	650	Ronnell Peters (1982-86)

ESPN 135 SAGARIN

TEXAS CHRISTIAN

It's been a struggle for the Horned Frogs to bring in top players since the departure of coach Billy Tubbs in 2002, surrounded as they are by fellow Texas universities with far deeper pockets. But there's at least one area where TCU can't be matched: postgame traditions. After every home game, the team stands at midcourt of Daniel-Meyer Coliseum to recite the alma mater: "Hail all hail, TCU. Memories sweet, comrades true … "

BEST TEAM: 1986-87 They had no superstar and didn't need one with the way they played defense. TCU held opponents to just 63.6 points per game—third best since 1960—to win the Southwest Conference title and earn a No. 4 seed in the NCAA Tournament. But their season ended in controversy when Jamie Dixon was called for a late foul on Notre Dame guard David Rivers, leading to a 58-57 second-round loss.

BEST PLAYER: C Kurt Thomas (1990-92, '93-95) He averaged just 3.5 ppg during his first two injury-plagued seasons, before taking a medical redshirt. As a junior, he underwent a metamorphosis and averaged 20.7 ppg. In his final season, Thomas led the country in both scoring and rebounding—only the third player in NCAA history to accomplish the feat.

BEST COACH: Billy Tubbs (1994-2002) He arrived after TCU had combined to win just 13 games over two seasons and promptly won 16. From 1996-97, Tubbs' Horned Frogs reeled off six straight winning seasons, notching a school-record 27 victories in '97-98.

GAME FOR THE AGES: Expectations were low for the 1967-68 team on the heels of eight straight losing seasons. But on March 2, the Horned Frogs played for the SWC title at Baylor. TCU pulled out a 72-65 victory to deliver the crown for rookie coach Johnny Swaim.

FIERCEST RIVAL: Located just 45 minutes apart, SMU and TCU "enjoy" a rivalry that dates back to 1919. Although the Horned Frogs trail, 102–83, the matchup picked up intensity when SMU's Matt Doherty and TCU's Neil Dougherty, once fellow Kansas assistants, were coaching the teams.

SEASON REVIEW

SEAS.	W-L	CONF.	COACH	SEAS.	W-L	CONF.	COACH
1908-49	*284-364*	*Francis Schmidt 72-24 in 5 seasons*		**1962-63**	4-20	1-13	Buster Brannon
1949-50	13-11	5-7	Buster Brannon	**1963-64**	4-20	0-14	Buster Brannon
1950-51	16-9	8-4	Buster Brannon	**1964-65**	6-18	3-11	Buster Brannon
1951-52	24-4	11-1 ●	Buster Brannon	**1965-66**	8-16	6-8	Buster Brannon
1952-53	15-8	9-3 ●	Buster Brannon	**1966-67**	10-14	8-6	Buster Brannon
1953-54	10-14	5-7	Buster Brannon	**1967-68**	15-11	9-5 ●	Johnny Swaim
1954-55	17-7	8-4	Buster Brannon	**1968-69**	12-12	5-9	Johnny Swaim
1955-56	4-20	2-10	Buster Brannon	**1969-70**	10-14	8-6	Johnny Swaim
1956-57	14-10	6-6	Buster Brannon	**1970-71**	15-12	11-3 ●	Johnny Swaim
1957-58	17-7	8-6	Buster Brannon	**1971-72**	15-9	9-5	Johnny Swaim
1958-59	20-6	12-2 ●	Buster Brannon	**1972-73**	4-21	2-12	Johnny Swaim
1959-60	7-17	4-10	Buster Brannon	**1973-74**	8-17	2-12	Johnny Swaim
1960-61	5-19	3-11	Buster Brannon	**1974-75**	9-16	4-10	Johnny Swaim
1961-62	5-19	4-10	Buster Brannon	**1975-76**	11-16	6-10	Johnny Swaim

SEAS.	W-L	CONF.	SCORING		COACH	RECORD	
1976-77	3-23	0-16	Daryl Braden	14.6	Johnny Swaim	102-151	.403
1977-78	4-22	2-14	Steve Scales	14.8	Tim Somerville		
1978-79	6-21	1-15	Jon Mansbury	11.9	Tim Somerville	10-43	.189
1979-80	7-19	2-14	Deckery Johnson	13.9	Jim Killingsworth		
1980-81	11-18	6-10	Darrell Browder	19.4	Jim Killingsworth		
1981-82	16-13	9-7	Doug Arnold	19.5	Jim Killingsworth		
1982-83	23-11	9-7 ■	Darrell Browder	17.3	Jim Killingsworth		
1983-84	11-17	4-12	Dennis Nutt	17.5	Jim Killingsworth		
1984-85	16-12	8-8	Carven Holcombe	16.5	Jim Killingsworth		
1985-86	22-9	12-4 ■	Carl Lott	15.8	Jim Killingsworth		
1986-87	24-7	14-2 ●	Carven Holcombe	17.5	Jim Killingsworth	130-106	.551
1987-88	9-19	3-13	John Lewis	13.3	Moe Iba		
1988-89	17-13	9-7	John Lewis	15.4	Moe Iba		
1989-90	16-13	9-7	Craig Sibley	13.9	Moe Iba		
1990-91	18-10	9-7	Reggie Smith	17.5	Moe Iba		
1991-92	23-11	9-5 ■	Reggie Smith	17.9	Moe Iba		
1992-93	6-22	2-12	Eric Dailey	14.9	Moe Iba		
1993-94	7-20	3-11	Kurt Thomas	20.7	Moe Iba	96-108	.471
1994-95	16-11	8-6	Kurt Thomas	28.9	Billy Tubbs		
1995-96	15-15 ⊗	6-8	Damion Walker	20.5	Billy Tubbs		
1996-97	22-13	7-9 ■	Malcolm Johnson	18.7	Billy Tubbs		
1997-98	27-6	14-0 ●	Lee Nailon	24.9	Billy Tubbs		
1998-99	21-11	7-7 ■	Lee Nailon	22.8	Billy Tubbs		
1999-2000	18-14	8-6	Marquise Gainous	20.7	Billy Tubbs		
2000-01	20-11	9-7	Ryan Carroll	17.5	Billy Tubbs		
2001-02	16-15	6-10	Junior Blount	19.5	Billy Tubbs	155-96	.618▼
2002-03	9-19	3-13	Junior Blount	17.7	Neil Dougherty		
2003-04	12-17	7-9	Corey Santee	14.5	Neil Dougherty		
2004-05	21-14	8-8 ■	Corey Santee	14.3	Neil Dougherty		
2005-06	6-25	2-14	Nile Murry	16.7	Neil Dougherty		
2006-07	13-17	4-12	Kevin Langford	13.2	Neil Dougherty		
2007-08	14-16	6-10	Kevin Langford	13.3	Neil Dougherty	75-108	.409
2008-09	14-17	5-11	Kevin Langford	13.9	Jim Christian	14-17	.452

⊗ Records don't reflect games forfeited or vacated. For adjusted records, see p. 521.

▼ Coach's record adjusted to reflect games forfeited or vacated: 156-95, .622. For yearly totals, see p. 521.

● NCAA Tournament appearance ■ NIT appearance

PROFILE

Texas Christian University, Fort Worth, TX
Founded: 1873
Enrollment: 8,696 (7,471 undergraduate)
Colors: Purple and white
Nickname: Horned Frogs
Current arena: Daniel-Meyer Coliseum, opened in 1961 (7,200)
First game: 1909
All-time record: 1,065-1,232 (.464)
Total weeks in AP Top 20/25: 33

Current conference: Mountain West (2005-)
Conference titles:
Southwest: 10 (1931, '34, '51 [tie], '52, '53, '59, '68, '71, '86 [tie], '87)
WAC: 1 (1998 [tie])
Conference tournament titles: 0
NCAA Tournament appearances: 7
NIT appearances: 6

FIRST-ROUND PRO PICKS

1995 **Kurt Thomas,** Miami (10)

TOP 5

G **Darrell Browder** (1979-83)
G **Carven Holcombe** (1983-87)
F **Lee Nailon** (1997-99)
C **Dick O'Neal** (1954-57)
C **Kurt Thomas** (1990-92, '93-95)

RECORDS

RECORDS	GAME		SEASON		CAREER	
POINTS	53	Lee Nailon, vs. Mississippi Valley State (Dec. 12, 1997)	796	Lee Nailon (1997-98)	1,886	Darrell Browder (1979-83)
POINTS PER GAME			28.9	Kurt Thomas (1994-95)	23.9	Dick O'Neal (1954-57)
REBOUNDS	28	Eugene Kennedy, vs. Arkansas (Feb. 16, 1971)	432	Eugene Kennedy (1970-71)	966	Reggie Smith (1988-92)
ASSISTS	16	Greedy Daniels, vs. Central Oklahoma (Dec. 9, 2000); Prince Fowler, vs. Wyoming (Feb. 11, 1999); vs. Central Oklahoma (Dec. 12, 1998)	234	Tony Edmond (1989-90)	575	Corey Santee (2001-05)

THE SCHOOLS

ESPN 109 SAGARIN

TEXAS-EL PASO

It was known as Texas Western in the historic 1965-66 season that was immortalized in the 2006 film *Glory Road*, but the Miners' achievement was accomplished not with Hollywood magic but with the grit, determination and imagination of legendary coach Don "The Bear" Haskins. He recruited a team of mostly African-American players—most from northern cities—to far, far West Texas, then had the temerity to beat the greatest power of the day, all-white Kentucky, for the national championship.

BEST TEAM: 1965-66 As America's racial tensions heated to a boil, Haskins' Miners worked their way to the national stage, where they would play an important supporting role in the civil rights movement. Winning every game on their schedule except for a 74-72 loss at Seattle, the Miners found themselves in the NCAA Tournament Final facing Kentucky. Haskins had overheard UK coach Adolph Rupp boasting that no black players could beat his white Wildcats. David Lattin, Bobby Joe Hill, Orsten Artis, Harry Flournoy and Willie Worsley (see Game for the Ages) proved the Baron wrong.

BEST PLAYER: G TIM HARDAWAY (1985-89) With a narrow nod over the great Nate "Tiny" Archibald, Hardaway is UTEP's No. 4 all-time scorer, a three-time All-WAC selection and the league's Player of the Year as a senior. He finished his career with 1,586 points, is the school's all-time assists (563) and steals (262) leader and led the Miners to four straight NCAA Tournaments. He went on to be a five-time NBA All-Star.

BEST COACH: DON HASKINS (1961-99) A member of the Naismith Hall of Fame, Haskins went 719–353 in a long tenure that included the 1966 title and 13 other NCAA appearances. He was the first major college coach to start a lineup of five black players.

GAME FOR THE AGES: Surely Rupp's Runts would put Texas Western in its place on March 19, 1966. But after 10 minutes the Miners took a lead they would never relinquish, though Kentucky came within a point in the second half. As time ran down, Texas Western stalled, but when the Wildcats fouled them, the Miners made their free throws—28 of 34 in all—to win 72-65. Hill led with 20 points, followed by Lattin (16) and Artis (15). Three years later, Kentucky was among the last major college teams to integrate.

HEARTBREAKER: UTEP, fresh from knocking off No.1-seed Kansas, would have made the 1992 Sweet 16 had it finished off Cincinnati after storming back from a 14-point deficit. But the Miners ran out of gas and lost, 69-67, in Haskins' last Tournament.

FIERCEST RIVAL: Separated by just 50 miles, Texas-El Paso and its I-10 rival, New Mexico State, have met almost 200 times since 1914, with NMSU holding a 103–96 lead.

FANFARE AND HOOPLA: The Don Haskins Center, named for the legendary coach who died in 2008, is one of the rowdiest home courts in all of college basketball. The Miners have won more than 75% of their home games in the 30-plus years the 12,000-seat building has been open.

> ***Don Haskins had overheard Adolph Rupp boasting that no black players could beat his white Wildcats. David Lattin, Bobby Joe Hill, Orsten Artis, Harry Flournoy and Willie Worsley proved the Baron wrong.***

FAN FAVORITE: F/C WAYNE "SOUP" CAMPBELL (1982-83, '85-88) He spent six years at UTEP because of injuries, including reconstructive knee surgery, and remains one of the best percentage shooters in school history. Though undersized down low at 6'7", Campbell was a key cog in the physical man-to-man defense that gained UTEP notoriety in the mid and late 1980s.

PROFILE

University of Texas at El Paso, El Paso, TX
Founded: 1914
Enrollment: 19,313 (15,747 undergraduate)
Colors: Dark blue, orange, silver accent
Nickname: Miners
Current arena: Don Haskins Center, opened in 1976 (12,000)
First game: 1914
All-time record: 1,211-924 (.567)
Total weeks in AP Top 20/25: 58

Current conference: Conference USA (2005-)
Conference titles:
Border: 2 (1957, '59 [tie])
WAC: 8 (1970, '83 [tie], '84, '85, '86 [tie], '87, '92 [tie], 2004 [tie])
Conference tournament titles:
WAC: 5 (1984, '86, '89, '90, 2005)
NCAA Tournament appearances: 16
Sweet 16s (since 1975): 1
Final Fours: 1
Titles: 1 (1966)
NIT appearances: 9

FIRST-ROUND PRO PICKS

1964	**Jim Barnes,** New York (1)
1967	**David Lattin,** San Francisco (10)
1970	**Nate "Tiny" Archibald,** Texas (ABA)
1989	**Tim Hardaway,** Golden State (14)

TOP 5

G	**Nate "Tiny" Archibald** (1967-70)
G	**Tim Hardaway** (1985-89)
F	**Antonio Davis** (1986-90)
F	**Brandon Wolfram** (1997-2001)
C	**Jim Barnes** (1962-64)

RECORDS	GAME		SEASON		CAREER	
POINTS	51	Jim Barnes, vs. Western New Mexico (Jan. 4, 1964)	908	Stefon Jackson (2008-09)	2,456	Stefon Jackson (2005-09)
POINTS AVERAGE			29.1	Jim Barnes (1963-64)	24.2	Jim Barnes (1962-64)
REBOUNDS	36	Jim Barnes, vs. Western New Mexico (Jan. 4, 1964)	537	Jim Barnes (1963-64)	965	Jim Barnes (1962-64)
ASSISTS	18	Filiberto Rivera, vs. Louisiana Tech (Feb. 25, 2005)	236	Julyan Stone (2008-09)	563	Tim Hardaway (1985-89)

THE SCHOOLS

SEASON REVIEW

SEASON	W-L	CONF.	SCORING	COACH	RECORD
1914-15	2-7			Tommy Dwyer	
1915-16	2-6				
1916-17	no team				
1917-18	2-6			Tommy Dwyer	
1918-19	no team				
1919-20	7-5			Tommy Dwyer	
1920-21	no team				
1921-22	no team				
1922-23	1-6			Tommy Dwyer	14-30 .318
1923-24	3-10			Jack Vowell	3-10 .231
1924-25	3-8			George Powell	
1925-26	3-5			George Powell	6-13 .316
1926-27	no team				
1927-28	6-8			E.J. Stewart	6-8 .429
1928-29	4-14			Mack Saxon	
1929-30	13-6			Mack Saxon	
1930-31	7-9			Mack Saxon	
1931-32	6-7			Mack Saxon	
1932-33	1-9			Mack Saxon	
1933-34	3-16			Mack Saxon	34-61 .358
1934-35	no team				
1935-36	0-12	0-8		J.B. Andrews	0-12 .000

SEAS.	W-L	CONF.	POSTSEASON	SCORING		REBOUNDS		ASSISTS		COACH	RECORD	
1936-37	2-16	0-10								Marshall Pennington		
1937-38	4-17	3-11								Marshall Pennington		
1938-39	6-13	6-12								Marshall Pennington		
1939-40	15-11	10-6								Marshall Pennington		
1940-41	14-9									Marshall Pennington		
1941-42	11-11	7-9								Marshall Pennington		
1942-43	11-6	4-4								Marshall Pennington	63-83	.432
1943-44	no team											
1944-45	10-12	4-11								Charles Finley	10-12	.455
1945-46	8-10	4-7								Dale Waters		
1946-47	12-8	9-7								Dale Waters		
1947-48	13-16	6-10		Mike Izquierdo	12.9					Ross Moore		
1948-49	8-12	7-9		Ventura Irrobali	9.2					Dale Waters		
1949-50	17-13	5-11		D.W. Harkins	11.2					Ross Moore	30-29	.508
1950-51	10-15	4-12		Gerald Rogers	18.0					Dale Waters		
1951-52	8-17	5-9		Gerald Rogers	15.1					Dale Waters		
1952-53	5-21	3-11		Bill Brewer	14.8	Jim Babers	3.9			Dale Waters	51-83	.381
1953-54	8-14	4-8		James Babers	9.8	Billy Gregory	5.2			George McCarty		
1954-55	14-7	8-4		Ed Haller	16.6	Ed Haller	11.2			George McCarty		
1955-56	12-10	7-5		Ed Haller	16.2	Ed Haller	12.6			George McCarty		
1956-57	15-8	8-2		Charlie Brown	21.1	Charlie Brown	10.2			George McCarty		
1957-58	14-10	5-5		Charlie Brown	15.9	Charlie Brown	8.0			George McCarty		
1958-59	14-9	7-3		Charlie Brown	15.7	Charlie Brown	7.8			George McCarty	77-58	.570
1959-60	6-19	1-9		Al Tolen	20.3	Bob Davis	8.6			Harold Davis		
1960-61	12-12	4-6		Nolan Richardson	21.0	Al Tolen	11.5			Harold Davis	18-31	.367
1961-62	18-6	5-3		Willie Brown	15.6	Bobby Joe Hill	9.0			Don Haskins		
1962-63	19-7		NCAA FIRST ROUND	Jim Barnes	18.9	Jim Barnes	16.5			Don Haskins		
1963-64	25-3		NCAA REGIONAL SEMIFINALS	Jim Barnes	29.1	Jim Barnes	19.2			Don Haskins		
1964-65	16-9		NIT FIRST ROUND	Orsten Artis	11.1	Harry Flournoy	11.8			Don Haskins		
1965-66	**28-1**		**NATIONAL CHAMPION**	**Bobby Joe Hill**	**15.0**	**Harry Flournoy**	**10.7**			**Don Haskins**		
1966-67	22-6		NCAA REGIONAL SEMIFINALS	David Lattin	15.1	David Lattin	10.1			Don Haskins		
1967-68	14-9			Nate "Tiny" Archibald	15.8	Mike Switzer	6.7			Don Haskins		
1968-69	16-9			Nate "Tiny" Archibald	22.4	Ples Vann	7.8			Don Haskins		
1969-70	17-8	10-4	NCAA FIRST ROUND	Nate "Tiny" Archibald	21.4	Dick Gibbs	8.5			Don Haskins		
1970-71	15-10	9-5		Dick Gibbs	17.5	Dick Gibbs	10.6			Don Haskins		
1971-72	20-7	9-5	NIT FIRST ROUND	Scott English	16.3	Jim Forbes	10.7			Don Haskins		
1972-73	16-10	6-8		Gus Bailey	14.4	Gus Bailey	7.0			Don Haskins		
1973-74	18-7	8-6		Gus Bailey	14.0	Jim Forbes	7.4			Don Haskins		
1974-75	20-6	10-4	NCAA FIRST ROUND	Gary Brewster	15.4	Gary Brewster	8.3			Don Haskins		
1975-76	19-7	9-5		Jake Poole	13.3	Gary Brewster	6.6			Don Haskins		
1976-77	11-15	3-11		Jake Poole	13.9	Tom Pauling	8.0			Don Haskins		
1977-78	10-16	2-12		Earl Fuller	10.5	Anthony Burns	9.4			Don Haskins		
1978-79	11-15	3-9		Anthony Burns	12.4	Anthony Burns	8.7	Gary Wilson	2.5	Don Haskins		
1979-80	20-8	10-4	NIT SECOND ROUND	Anthony Burns	11.4	Terry White	8.9	Gary Wilson	3.4	Don Haskins		
1980-81	18-12	9-7	NIT SECOND ROUND	Roshern Amie	12.7	Anthony Burns	8.1	Virgil Kennedy	2.1	Don Haskins		
1981-82	20-8	11-5		Fred Reynolds	14.5	Terry White	10.3	Byron Walker	3.8	Don Haskins		
1982-83	19-10	11-5	NIT FIRST ROUND	Luster Goodwin	12.3	Paul Cunningham	5.4	Byron Walker	5.7	Don Haskins		
1983-84	27-4	13-3	NCAA SECOND ROUND	Fred Reynolds	13.9	Kevin Hamilton	5.3	Kent Lockhart	3.6	Don Haskins		
1984-85	22-10	12-4	NCAA SECOND ROUND	Luster Goodwin	17.0	Dave Feitl	7.1	Luster Goodwin	3.4	Don Haskins		
1985-86	27-6	12-4	NCAA FIRST ROUND	Dave Feitl	16.6	Dave Feitl	6.8	Jeep Jackson	3.5	Don Haskins		
1986-87	25-7	13-3	NCAA SECOND ROUND	Jeep Jackson	12.9	Mike Richmond	6.4	Tim Hardaway	4.8	Don Haskins		
1987-88	23-10	10-6	NCAA FIRST ROUND	Chris Sandle	17.1	Antonio Davis	6.5	Tim Hardaway	5.7	Don Haskins		
1988-89	26-7	11-5	NCAA SECOND ROUND	Tim Hardaway	22.0	Antonio Davis	8.0	Tim Hardaway	5.4	Don Haskins		
1989-90	21-11	10-6	NCAA FIRST ROUND	Marlon Maxey	12.4	Marlon Maxey	7.8	Prince Stewart	5.6	Don Haskins		
1990-91	16-13	7-9		Mark McCall	13.4	David Van Dyke	5.9	Henry Hall	4.0	Don Haskins		
1991-92	27-7	12-4	NCAA REGIONAL SEMIFINALS	Marlon Maxey	15.2	Marlon Maxey	7.4	Prince Stewart	4.4	Don Haskins		
1992-93	21-13	10-8	NIT SECOND ROUND	Eddie Rivera	15.8	Ralph Davis	6.6	Eddie Rivera	5.2	Don Haskins		
1993-94	18-12	8-10		Antoine Gillespie	23.7	George Banks	8.3	Jeff Spillar	2.6	Don Haskins		
1994-95	20-10	13-5	NIT SECOND ROUND	Antoine Gillespie	20.2	George Banks	8.6	Antoine Gillespie	2.6	Don Haskins		
1995-96	13-15	4-14		Kimani Jones-Young	16.6	JoJo Garcia	5.7	Carl Davis	3.1	Don Haskins		
1996-97	13-13	6-10		Kimani Jones-Young	17.0	JoJo Garcia	9.9	Jeff Spillar	3.5	Don Haskins		
1997-98	12-14	3-11		Sharif Fajardo	15.4	Sharif Fajardo	7.4	Alton Sanders	3.4	Don Haskins		
1998-99	16-12	8-6		Sharif Fajardo	14.3	William Smith	6.3	Eggie McRae	4.2	Don Haskins	719-353	.671
1999-2000	13-15	4-10		Brandon Wolfram	20.7	Brandon Wolfram	6.8	Eggie McRae	4.8	Jason Rabedeaux		
2000-01	23-9	10-6	NIT SECOND ROUND	Brandon Wolfram	22.3	Brandon Wolfram	7.6	Eugene Costello	4.6	Jason Rabedeaux		
2001-02	10-22	3-15		Eugene Costello	13.1	Roy Smallwood	6.3	Eugene Costello	3.2	Jason Rabedeaux	46-46	.500
2002-03	6-24	3-15		Giovanni St. Amant	13.6	Justino Victoriano	8.5	Chris Craig	3.4	Billy Gillispie		
2003-04	24-8	13-5	NCAA FIRST ROUND	Omar Thomas	15.5	Jason Williams	6.1	Filiberto Rivera	4.8	Billy Gillispie	30-32	.484
2004-05	27-8	14-4	NCAA FIRST ROUND	Omar Thomas	20.5	Omar Thomas	6.7	Filiberto Rivera	7.2	Doc Sadler		
2005-06	21-10	11-3	NIT FIRST ROUND	Jason Williams	15.1	John Tofi	9.2	Edgar Moreno	3.9	Doc Sadler	48-18	.727
2006-07	14-17	6-10		Stefon Jackson	18.6	Stefon Jackson	6.4	Malik Alvin	4.4	Tony Barbee		
2007-08	19-14	8-8		Stefon Jackson	23.6	Stefon Jackson	5.7	Marvin Kilgore	5.0	Tony Barbee		
2008-09	23-14	10-6		Stefon Jackson	24.5	Arnette Moultrie	8.2	Julyan Stone	6.4	Tony Barbee	56-45	.554

ESPN 238 SAGARIN

TEXAS-PAN AMERICAN

The Broncs have given fans from different eras much to brag about: the dominating 1963 NAIA champions, for example, and coaches like the colorful Abe Lemons and long-timer Sam Williams. Throw in six NBA players—including first-round draft picks Luke Jackson and Otto Moore—and an upset of eventual 1981 NCAA champ Indiana and Isiah Thomas.

BEST TEAM: 1962-63 Sam Williams' Broncs opened up 3–4, then won 23 of 25, including 15 straight and the NAIA title after beating Willis Reed's Grambling State and Western Carolina. Jackson, Mitchell Edwards and Jim McGurk all wound up in the school's top 10 in scoring.

BEST PLAYER: C Lucious "Luke" Jackson (1961-64) Twice an NAIA All-America, the 6'9" Jackson averaged 24.1 ppg and 18.5 rpg in his career, during which the Broncs went 79–17. The fourth overall pick of the 1964 NBA draft, Jackson played eight seasons with the Philadelphia 76ers.

BEST COACH: Sam Williams (1958-73) Several big-name coaches have led UTPA (Lemons, Lon Kruger), but Williams had the most success, piling up 10 winning seasons, four 20-win years, and reaching the NAIA or College Division national tourney four times—winning the NAIA title in 1963 and finishing as runner-up in '64.

GAME FOR THE AGES: The 1963 NAIA national championship game displayed Pan American's all-around talent. Up by seven with nine minutes left, Mitchell Edwards (20 points, 12 rebounds) and Jim McGurk (12 and 10) scored 10 of the Broncs' last 13 to beat Western Carolina and All-Americas Mel Gibson and Tommy Lavelle, 73-62. Jackson had 25 points along with 25 rebounds.

FIERCEST RIVAL: An independent since leaving the Sun Belt in 1998, UTPA has no real do-or-die rivalry. Still, Texas State and Texas-Arlington will occasionally schedule the Broncs twice each season and things can get feisty. The Broncs lead both series—22–8 vs. Texas State, which dates to 1960, and 13–10 vs. Texas-Arlington, which began eight years later.

SEASON REVIEW

SEAS.	W-L	CONF.	COACH	SEAS.	W-L	CONF.	COACH
1952-53	11-10		L.A. Youngman	1962-63	26-6	◆	Sam Williams
1953-54	6-11		L.A. Youngman	1963-64	28-6		Sam Williams
1954-55	2-22		Harry Meng	1964-65	19-7		Sam Williams
1955-56	4-21		Harry Meng	1965-66	15-13		Sam Williams
1956-57	4-16		John Donnelly	1966-67	15-9		Sam Williams
1957-58	5-14		John Donnelly	1967-68	21-6		Sam Williams
1958-59	13-11		Sam Williams	1968-69	8-17		Sam Williams
1959-60	17-9		Sam Williams	1969-70	8-16		Sam Williams
1960-61	15-17		Sam Williams	1970-71	13-13		Sam Williams
1961-62	25-5		Sam Williams	1971-72	17-7		Sam Williams

SEAS.	W-L	CONF.	SCORING		COACH	RECORD
1972-73	4-22				Sam Williams	244-164 .598
1973-74	13-9		Bruce King	31.0	Abe Lemons	
1974-75	22-2		Marshall Rogers	26.7	Abe Lemons	
1975-76	20-5		Marshall Rogers	36.8	Abe Lemons	55-16 .775
1976-77	17-9				Bill White	
1977-78	22-4		Michael Edwards	24.3	Bill White	
1978-79	13-13				Bill White	
1979-80	19-9	4-2			Bill White	
1980-81	18-11	■			Bill White	
1981-82	5-20				Bill White	94-66 .588
1982-83	7-21				Lon Kruger	
1983-84	13-14				Lon Kruger	
1984-85	12-16				Lon Kruger	
1985-86	20-8				Lon Kruger	52-59 .468
1986-87	16-12				Kevin Wall	
1987-88	14-14	4-6			Kevin Wall	
1988-89	15-13	4-6			Kevin Wall	
1989-90	21-9	7-3			Kevin Wall	
1990-91	7-21	3-9			Kevin Wall	
1991-92	3-26 ⊘	1-15			Kevin Wall	76-95 .444
1992-93	2-20	2-16	Greg Guy	29.3	Mark Adams	
1993-94	16-12	9-9			Mark Adams	
1994-95	14-14	10-8			Mark Adams	
1995-96	9-19	6-12			Mark Adams	
1996-97	3-25	1-17			Mark Adams	44-90 .328
1997-98	3-24	3-15			Delray Brooks	
1998-99	5-22		Brian Merriweather	23.7	Delray Brooks	8-46 .148
1999-2000	12-16		Brian Merriweather	20.4	Bob Hoffman	
2000-01	12-17		Brian Merriweather	18.1	Bob Hoffman	
2001-02	20-10		Mire Chatman	26.2	Bob Hoffman	
2002-03	10-20		Kevin Mitchell	14.7	Bob Hoffman	
2003-04	14-14		Sergio Sanchez	12.9	Bob Hoffman	68-77 .469
2004-05	12-16		Sergio Sanchez	15.5	Robert Davenport	
2005-06	6-24		Dexter Shankle	11.0	Robert Davenport	18-40 .310
2006-07	14-15		Brian Burrell	15.6	Tom Schuberth	
2007-08	18-13		Paul Stoll	14.2	Tom Schuberth	
2008-09	10-17		Emmanuel Jones	17.7	Tom Schuberth	42-45 .483

⊘ **Records don't reflect games forfeited or vacated. For adjusted total, see p. 521.**
■ **NIT appearance** ◆ **NAIA national champion**

PROFILE

University of Texas-Pan American, Edinburg, TX
Founded: 1927
Enrollment: 19,576 (15,076 undergraduate)
Colors: Forest green, orange and white
Nickname: Broncs
Current arena: UTPA Fieldhouse, opened in 1969 (4,000)
Previous: Edinburg Fieldhouse, 1952-69 (2,000)
First game: Nov. 20, 1952
All-time record: 733-792 (.481)
Total weeks in AP Top 20/25: 5

Current conference: Great West (2009-)
Conference titles: 0
Conference tournament titles: 0
NCAA Tournament appearances: 0
NIT appearances: 1

CONSENSUS ALL-AMERICAS

1964 **Lucious "Luke" Jackson** (Little A-A), C
1968 **Otto Moore** (Little A-A), C

FIRST-ROUND PRO PICKS

1964 **Lucious "Luke" Jackson,** Philadelphia (4)
1968 **Otto Moore,** Detroit (6)

TOP 5

G **Mire Chatman** (2000-02)
G **Marshall Rogers** (1974-76)
F **Mitchell Edwards** (1962-65)
C **Lucious "Luke" Jackson** (1961-64)
C **Otto Moore** (1964-68)

RECORDS

RECORDS	GAME		SEASON		CAREER	
POINTS	58	Marshall Rogers, vs. Texas Lutheran (Feb. 16, 1976)	919	Marshall Rogers (1975-76)	1,880	Otto Moore (1964-68)
POINTS PER GAME			36.8	Marshall Rogers (1975-76)	31.8	Marshall Rogers (1974-76)
REBOUNDS	35	Otto Moore, vs. Lamar Tech (Dec. 1, 1966)	626	Luke Jackson (1962-63)	1,679	Otto Moore (1964-68)
ASSISTS	22	John Wilbanks, vs. Arkansas State (Jan. 5, 1977)	323	John Wilbanks (1977-78)	771	Jesus Guerra (1972-76)

ESPN 201 SAGARIN

TEXAS-SAN ANTONIO

Three coaches—Don Eddy, Ken Burmeister and Stu Starner—fueled UTSA's rocket-launch start: five 20-win seasons in the program's first 11 years. But even that success hardly prepared fans for the glorious chaos inside the Bird Cage in 2004, when the Roadrunners hosted and won their first nationally televised conference championship.

BEST TEAM: 2003-04 This was the first and only UTSA squad to win the Southland Conference regular-season *and* tournament titles. Coach Tim Carter's group, led by LeRoy Hurd (19.4 ppg, 8.0 rpg), Kurt Attaway, Justin Harbert and Raphael Posey, won 13 of its last 15 before an NCAA Tourney loss to No. 1-seed Stanford.

BEST PLAYER: F Derrick Gervin (1982-85) He played just three seasons but is still the school's second all-time leading scorer (1,691) and No. 4 rebounder (684). The younger brother of NBA star George Gervin, DG led UTSA in scoring and rebounding three times and guided the third-year program to 20 wins. He averaged a UTSA-record 25.6 ppg in 1984-85, before his own modest NBA career.

BEST COACH: Tim Carter (1995-2006) With almost twice as many victories (160) as any other UTSA coach, Carter won 10 or more SLC games in eight of his 11 seasons. He captured two Southland tourney titles, taking the Roadrunners to the NCAAs in 1999 and 2004.

GAME FOR THE AGES: UTSA hosted its first SLC tourney championship game in 2004 at the Convocation Center before a frenzied crowd and a national TV audience—and the Roadrunners didn't disappoint. They beat Stephen F. Austin, 74-70, for the title behind SLC Player of the Year Hurd, Attaway and shot-blocker Anthony Fuqua.

FIERCEST RIVAL: Texas State is less than an hour away in San Marcos, making Southland Conference games raucous events with no love lost between rival fans. Since their first meeting in 1985, UTSA holds the edge, 29–18, with a 4–1 record in SLC tournament games, including a 71-63 1999 SLC tourney championship victory.

SEASON REVIEW

SEAS.	W-L	CONF.		SCORING		COACH	RECORD	
1981-82	8-19			Dennis Mumford	11.4	Don Eddy		
1982-83	10-17			Derrick Gervin	13.9	Don Eddy		
1983-84	20-8			Derrick Gervin	23.2	Don Eddy		
1984-85	18-10			Derrick Gervin	25.6	Don Eddy		
1985-86	7-24			Calvin Haynes	15.3	Don Eddy[a]	60-72	.455
1986-87	13-15	7-11		Frank Hampton	18.1	Ken Burmeister		
1987-88	22-9	13-5	●	Frank Hampton	18.0	Ken Burmeister		
1988-89	15-13	8-10		Eric Cooper	18.6	Ken Burmeister		
1989-90	22-7	13-3		Darryl Eaton	15.6	Ken Burmeister	72-44	.621
1990-91	21-8	12-2		Ronnie Ellison	20.6	Stu Starner		
1991-92	21-8	15-3		Keith Horne	16.1	Stu Starner		
1992-93	15-14	10-8		Rob Wallace	13.4	Stu Starner		
1993-94	12-15	8-10		Rodney Smith	17.7	Stu Starner		
1994-95	15-13	11-7		Marlon Anderson	20.8	Stu Starner	84-58	.592
1995-96	14-14	12-6		Marlon Anderson	20.3	Tim Carter		
1996-97	9-17	4-12		Roderic Hall	14.0	Tim Carter		
1997-98	16-11	10-6		Roderic Hall	17.4	Tim Carter		
1998-99	18-11	12-6	●	Devin Brown	16.7	Tim Carter		
1999-2000	15-13	12-6		Devin Brown	18.5	Tim Carter		
2000-01	14-15	12-8		Devin Brown	19.9	Tim Carter		
2001-02	19-10	13-7		McEverett Powers	18.8	Tim Carter		
2002-03	10-17	7-13		LeRoy Hurd	17.6	Tim Carter		
2003-04	19-14	11-5	●	LeRoy Hurd	19.4	Tim Carter		
2004-05	15-13	10-6		John Millsap	13.7	Tim Carter		
2005-06	11-17	6-10		Andre Owens	17.7	Tim Carter	160-152	.513
2006-07	7-22	3-13		Melvin Smith	12.9	Brooks Thompson		
2007-08	13-17	7-9		Devin Gibson	14.1	Brooks Thompson		
2008-09	19-13	8-8		T. Gabbidon, O. Johnson	12.6	Brooks Thompson	39-52	.429

[a] **Don Eddy (4-18) and Larry Gatewood (3-6) both coached during the 1985-86 season.**

● NCAA Tournament appearance

PROFILE

University of Texas at San Antonio, San Antonio, TX
Founded: 1969
Enrollment: 28,652 (24,648 undergraduate)
Colors: Orange and white
Nickname: Roadrunners
Current arena: UTSA Convocation Center, opened in 1981, a.k.a. the Bird Cage (4,080)
First game: Nov. 30, 1981
All-time record: 418-384 (.521)
Total weeks in AP Top 20/25: 0

Current conference: Southland (1991-)
Conference titles:
Trans America Athletic: 1 (1991)
Southland: 2 (1992, 2004 [tie])
Conference tournament titles:
Trans America Atlantic: 1 (1988)
Southland: 2 (1999, 2004)
NCAA Tournament appearances: 3
NIT appearances: 0

TOP 5

G **Devin Brown** (1998-2002)
G **Lloyd Williams** (1996-2000)
F **Derrick Gervin** (1982-85)
F **LeRoy Hurd** (2002-04)
F **McEverett Powers** (1998-2002)

RECORDS

RECORDS	GAME		SEASON		CAREER	
POINTS	52	Roderic Hall, vs. Maine (Dec. 6, 1997)	718	Derrick Gervin (1984-85)	1,922	Devin Brown (1998-2002)
POINTS PER GAME			25.6	Derrick Gervin (1984-85)	21.1	Derrick Gervin (1982-85)
REBOUNDS	25	Lennell Moore, vs. Centenary (Jan. 5, 1987)	287	Bruce Wheatley (1989-90)	794	Leon Watson (1996-2000)
ASSISTS	14	Issy Washington, vs. Jarvis Christian (Nov. 29, 1986)	186	Ronnie Ellison (1991-92)	536	Lloyd Williams (1996-2000)

ESPN 207 SAGARIN

TEXAS SOUTHERN

No need for a shot clock. National scoring leaders Kevin Granger (1995-96), Harry "Machine Gun" Kelly ('81-82, '82-83) and Bennie Swain (NAIA, '57-58) typify the Tigers' high-octane approach, particularly under coach Robert Moreland. The payoff: decades of NAIA dominance (including a 1977 title) and a near-miracle upset of Arkansas in the '95 NCAA Tourney.

BEST TEAM: 1976-77 Thank-you notes went out to Utica Junior College (Miss.) immediately following the NAIA title game. That's where Moreland had coached and forward Alonzo Bradley had played in 1974-75, while TSU went 8–16, prompting Texas Southern to hire Moreland. Two years later, Moreland, Bradley and a solid crew that included Marcello Singleton, Lawrence Williams and William Caldwell, achieved a 31–5 record and were NAIA national champs.

BEST PLAYER: F/C Bennie Swain (1954-58) When it mattered most, the two-time All-America was money, scoring 302 career NAIA tournament points (20.1 per game). As an NBA rookie, Swain backed up Bill Russell during Boston's 1958-59 championship season before a knee injury cut short his career.

BEST COACH: Robert Moreland (1975-2001, '07-08) He won more conference and tourney championships than all the other Texas Southern coaches combined.

GAME FOR THE AGES: The near-defeat of No. 2-seed and defending NCAA champ Arkansas in the first round of the 1995 Tourney comes close, but Texas Southern's watershed moment came in 1977, when Bradley and Co. dominated the NAIA tournament, capping off their 31–5 season with a 71-44 title win over Campbell.

FIERCEST RIVAL: Before games against Prairie View A&M, former Tigers coach Ronnie Courtney would hide in his office to avoid alums and the media. They found him anyway. In recent years, Texas Southern has dominated, going 15–13 in the series since 1996-97. But Prairie View has taken some of the biggest matches, including the 1998 SWAC championship game, in which they overcame a 20-point deficit to win, 59-57.

SEASON REVIEW

SEAS.	W-L	CONF.	COACH
1949-52	*85-29*	*31 victories in 1951-52*	
1952-53	24-6		Edward H. Adams
1953-54	31-5		Edward H. Adams
1954-55	28-3		Edward H. Adams
1955-56	31-4		Edward H. Adams
1956-57	33-2		Edward H. Adams
1957-58	29-5		Edward H. Adams
1958-59	N/A		Stanley Y. Wright
1959-60	7-17		Isaac T. Moorehead
1960-61	14-12		Isaac T. Moorehead
1961-62	12-14		Isaac T. Moorehead
1962-63	11-12		Isaac T. Moorehead
1963-64	10-15		Isaac T. Moorehead
1964-65	9-17		Davey L. Whitney
1965-66	16-11		Davey L. Whitney
1966-67	9-12		Davey L. Whitney
1967-68	11-12		Davey L. Whitney
1968-69	12-12		Davey L. Whitney
1969-70	13-12		Lavalius Gordon
1970-71	19-9		Lavalius Gordon
1971-72	17-11		Lavalius Gordon
1972-73	14-11		Lavalius Gordon
1973-74	15-13		Kenneth McCowan
1974-75	8-16		Kenneth McCowan

SEAS.	W-L	CONF.		SCORING		COACH	RECORD
1975-76	23-10					Robert Moreland	
1976-77	31-5		◆			Robert Moreland	
1977-78	16-10	7-5				Robert Moreland	
1978-79	13-14	6-6				Robert Moreland	
1979-80	9-17	5-7		Harry Kelly	29.0	Robert Moreland	
1980-81	13-13	7-5				Robert Moreland	
1981-82	21-8	8-4		Harry Kelly	29.7	Robert Moreland	
1982-83	22-7	12-2		Harry Kelly	28.8	Robert Moreland	
1983-84	12-17	6-8				Robert Moreland	
1984-85	11-17	6-8				Robert Moreland	
1985-86	9-18	6-8				Robert Moreland	
1986-87	11-18	7-7				Robert Moreland	
1987-88	21-8	11-3				Robert Moreland	
1988-89	17-13	10-4				Robert Moreland	
1989-90	19-12	10-4	●			Robert Moreland	
1990-91	13-17	7-5				Robert Moreland	
1991-92	15-14	11-3				Robert Moreland	
1992-93	12-15	8-6				Robert Moreland	
1993-94	19-11	12-2	●			Robert Moreland	
1994-95	22-7	⊗12-2	●			Robert Moreland	
1995-96	11-15⊗	7-7		Kevin Granger	27.0	Robert Moreland	
1996-97	12-16	6-8		Randy Bolden	22.4	Robert Moreland	
1997-98	15-16	12-4		Randy Bolden	19.9	Robert Moreland	
1998-99	8-19	6-10		Ifey Anyanwu	12.1	Robert Moreland	
1999-2000	15-14	10-8		Patrick Dyse	18.0	Robert Moreland	
2000-01	7-22	5-13		Chris Miller	16.6	Robert Moreland	
2001-02	11-17	10-8		Ra'Kim Hollis	18.1	Ronnie Courtney	
2002-03	18-13	11-7	●	Ra'Kim Hollis	18.5	Ronnie Courtney	
2003-04	14-15	10-8		Allen Lovett	13.9	Ronnie Courtney	
2004-05	11-15⊗	8-9		Sean Walker	17.8	Ronnie Courtney	
2005-06	8-22	6-12		Sean Walker	13.6	Ronnie Courtney	
2006-07	14-17	9-9		Jacques Jones	14.3	Ronnie Courtney	76-99 .434▼
2007-08	7-25	6-12		Sollie Norwood	14.7	Robert Moreland	404-378 .517▼
2008-09	7-25	7-11		DeAndre Hall	13.8	Tony Harvey	7-25 .219

⊗ Records don't reflect games forfeited or vacated. For adjusted records, see p. 521.

▼ Coaches' records adjusted to reflect games forfeited or vacated: Robert Moreland, 406-376, .519; Ronnie Courtney, 73-102, .417. For yearly totals, see p. 521.

● NCAA Tournament appearance ◆ NAIA championship

PROFILE

Texas Southern University, Houston, TX
Founded: 1947 as the Texas State University for Negroes; renamed Texas Southern in 1951
Enrollment: 11,635 (9,585 undergraduate)
Colors: Maroon and gray
Nickname: Tigers
Current arena: Health and Physical Education Arena, opened in 1989 (8,100)
First game: 1949
All-time record: 945-762 (.554)
Total weeks in AP Top 20/25: 0

Current conference: Southwestern Athletic: (1954-)
Conference titles:
SWAC: 9 (1957, '58, '77, '83 [tie], '89 [tie], '92 [tie], '94, '95, '98)
Conference tournament titles:
SWAC: 4 (1990, '94, '95, 2003)
NCAA Tournament appearances: 4
NIT appearances: 0

CONSENSUS ALL-AMERICAS

1956, '57 **Bennie Swain** (Little A-A), F/C
1977 **Alonzo Bradley** (D2), F

FIRST-ROUND PRO PICK

1958 **Bennie Swain**, Boston (7)

TOP 5

G **Gaylord Davis** (1972-76)
G **Kevin Granger** (1992-96)
F **Alonzo Bradley** (1975-77)
F **Harry Kelly** (1979-83)
F/C **Bennie Swain** (1954-58)

RECORDS

RECORDS	GAME	SEASON	CAREER
POINTS	60 Harry Kelly, vs. Jarvis Christian (Feb. 23, 1983)	862 Harry Kelly (1981-82)	3,066 Harry Kelly (1979-83)
POINTS PER GAME		29.7 Harry Kelly (1981-82)	27.9 Harry Kelly (1979-83)
REBOUNDS	N/A	N/A	1,136 Fred West (1986-90)
ASSISTS	N/A	N/A	525 Gaylord Davis (1972-76)

ESPN 216 SAGARIN

TEXAS STATE

Lyndon Baines Johnson, famous alum, was the 36th president of the United States. Milton Jowers, famous coach, was really one of a kind. How so? Jowers' Bobcats, with stars such as Charles Sharp, J.C. Maze and Lewis Gilcrease, dominated the NAIA throughout the 1950s, reaching two final fours and taking the 1960 title. More recently, Texas State reached the 1979 NAIA final four and copped NCAA Tourney bids in 1994 and '97.

BEST TEAM: 1959-60 The Bobcats started the season 3–3, then won 26 of 27 behind Charles Sharp (23.9 ppg, 11.8 rpg), defensive star Rudy Davalos and all-conference pick Boonie Wilkening. They romped to the NAIA title, winning by margins of 24, 13, 8, 38 and 22 points.

BEST PLAYER: F/C CHARLES SHARP (1957-60) A two-time first-team NAIA All-America, Sharp led the team in scoring three times—twice topping 700 points—and finished as the school's all-time leading scorer. He was MVP of the 1960 NAIA tourney, in one game lighting up Wisconsin-Oshkosh for 44 points.

BEST COACH: MILTON JOWERS (1946-61) He took the Bobcats to six NAIA tourneys, four times reaching the final four and winning the title in 1960. Jowers was also versatile. Three years later he was named Lone Star Conference Coach of the Year and guided the Bobcats to the NAIA district championships—in football. The captain of his 1959-60 hoops squad, Rudy Davalos, called the tough-as-nails coach "the Bear Bryant of basketball."

GAME FOR THE AGES: On their way to the the 1960 NAIA title game, the Bobcats defeated a star-studded Grambling team that would win the 1961 title. In the final against Westminster (Pa.), which had won 16 straight, Jowers' buzzsaw of a team controlled the tempo and rolled to a 66-44 win.

FIERCEST RIVAL: SLC West Division rival Texas-San Antonio is less than an hour away on I-35. Proximity breeds intensity. The two schools battle for recruits as well as area bragging rights. UTSA leads the series, 30–18, and bumped Texas State from the conference tourney three times between 2001 and '04.

SEASON REVIEW

SEAS.	W-L	CONF.	COACH	SEAS.	W-L	CONF.	COACH
1920-48	*227-268*	*5 winning seasons in a row, '27-'32*		1961-62	15-13		Vernon McDonald
1948-49	12-11		Milton Jowers	1962-63	9-14		Vernon McDonald
1949-50	13-10		Milton Jowers	1963-64	13-10		Vernon McDonald
1950-51	21-5		Milton Jowers	1964-65	13-11		Vernon McDonald
1951-52	30-1		Milton Jowers	1965-66	16-11		Vernon McDonald
1952-53	19-3		Milton Jowers	1966-67	14-12		Vernon McDonald
1953-54	15-5		Milton Jowers	1967-68	13-10		Vernon McDonald
1954-55	18-5		Milton Jowers	1968-69	16-10		Vernon McDonald
1955-56	16-7		Milton Jowers	1969-70	12-15		Vernon McDonald
1956-57	22-7		Milton Jowers	1970-71	15-11		Vernon McDonald
1957-58	18-4		Milton Jowers	1971-72	19-9		Vernon McDonald
1958-59	27-6		Milton Jowers	1972-73	13-11		Vernon McDonald
1959-60	29-4	◆	Milton Jowers	1973-74	19-12		Vernon McDonald
1960-61	23-8		Milton Jowers	1974-75	17-10		Vernon McDonald

SEAS.	W-L	CONF.	SCORING		COACH	RECORD
1975-76	14-14		Richard Bryant	23.1	Vernon McDonald	
1976-77	8-18		Steve Frontz	17.2	Vernon McDonald	226-191 .542
1977-78	20-6		James Patrick	15.1	Dan Wall	
1978-79	29-7		James Patrick	16.7	Dan Wall	
1979-80	19-12		James Patrick	16.1	Dan Wall	
1980-81	17-10		Harold Howard	16.0	Dan Wall	85-35 .708
1981-82	16-10		Kerry Murray	18.7	Bob Derryberry	
1982-83	18-10		Kerry Murray	15.2	Bob Derryberry	
1983-84	14-12		Lonniel Blunston	17.6	Bob Derryberry	48-32 .600
1984-85	6-20	2-8	Kelvin Moore	9.5	Celester Collier	
1985-86	6-22	1-9	Kelvin Moore	11.6	Celester Collier	12-42 .222
1986-87	13-15	5-5	Eliezar Gordon	13.6	Harry Larrabee	
1987-88	9-22	6-8	Torgeir Bryn	15.1	Harry Larrabee	
1988-89	13-17	6-8	Torgeir Bryn	16.8	Harry Larrabee	
1989-90	13-15	9-5	Maxwell Curry	15.4	Harry Larrabee	
1990-91	10-17	4-10	George Conner	14.9	Harry Larrabee[a]	55-81 .404
1991-92	7-20	4-14	George Conner	20.6	Jim Wooldridge	
1992-93	14-13	9-9	Lynwood Wade	19.0	Jim Wooldridge	
1993-94	25-7	14-4 ●	Lynwood Wade	18.5	Jim Wooldridge	46-40 .535
1994-95	12-14	7-11	Tony Long	16.8	Mike Miller	
1995-96	11-15	7-11	Dameon Sansom	11.0	Mike Miller	
1996-97	16-13	10-6 ●	Dameon Sansom	13.8	Mike Miller	
1997-98	17-11	10-6	Donte Mathis	18.6	Mike Miller	
1998-99	19-9	13-5	Donte Mathis	17.6	Mike Miller	
1999-2000	12-17	8-10	Wesley Williams	14.0	Mike Miller	87-79 .524
2000-01	13-15	10-10	David Sykes	12.7	Dennis Nutt	
2001-02	12-16	10-10	Clay Click	14.7	Dennis Nutt	
2002-03	17-12	11-9	Terry Conerway	15.4	Dennis Nutt	
2003-04	13-15	8-8	Terry Conerway	13.6	Dennis Nutt	
2004-05	14-14	8-8	Anthony Dill	14.9	Dennis Nutt	
2005-06	3-24	1-15	Charles Dotson	11.8	Dennis Nutt	72-96 .429
2006-07	9-20	4-12	Brandon Bush	14.4	Doug Davalos	
2007-08	13-16	6-10	Brandon Bush	14.6	Doug Davalos	
2008-09	14-16	7-9	Brandon Bush	15.9	Doug Davalos	36-52 .409

[a] Harry Larrabee (7-12) and Jim Rosebrock (3-5) both coached during the 1990-91 season.
● NCAA Tournament appearance ◆ NAIA championship

PROFILE

Texas State University, San Marcos, TX
Founded: 1899
Enrollment: 29,125 (24,810 undergraduate)
Colors: Maroon and gold
Nickname: Bobcats
Current Arena: Strahan Coliseum, opened in 1982 (7,200)
First game: 1920
All-time record: 1,160-997 (.538)
Total weeks in AP Top 20/25: 1

Current conference: Southland (1987-)
Conference titles:
Southland: 2 (1997 [tie], '99)
Conference tournament titles:
Southland: 2 (1994, '97)
NCAA Tournament appearances: 2
NIT appearances: 0

CONSENSUS ALL-AMERICAS

1959, '60 **Charles Sharp** (Little A-A), F/C

TOP 5

G **Rudy Davalos** (1957-60)
G/F **J.C. Maze** (1948-52)
F **Jeff Foster** (1995-99)
F/C **Lewis Gilcrease** (1949-53)
F/C **Charles Sharp** (1957-60)

RECORDS

RECORDS	GAME		SEASON		CAREER	
POINTS	53	Charles Sharp, vs. Texas Wesleyan (Dec. 28, 1959)	790	Charles Sharp (1959-60)	1,984	Charles Sharp (1957-60)
POINTS PER GAME			24.7	Lewis Gilcrease (1952-53)	23.3	Charles Sharp (1957-60)
REBOUNDS	39	Joe Cole, vs. Texas Lutheran (Dec. 10, 1956)	620	J.C. Maze (1951-52)	1,960	J.C. Maze (1948-52)
ASSISTS	13	Stacy Bennett, vs. Stephen F. Austin (Feb. 17, 1990)	212	Mike Fitzhugh (1974-75)		N/A

ESPN 89 SAGARIN

TEXAS TECH

With the exception of a breakout season here and there—the brilliant 1995-96 campaign is one example—Texas Tech basketball spent decades searching for relevancy and attention in a football-loving state. The Red Raiders hit the jackpot in 2001 when they hired all-time coaching genius and human lightning rod Bob Knight. The General led the Raiders to an era of unprecedented success and, for a time at least, focused a national hoops spotlight on Lubbock.

BEST TEAM: 1995-96 Despite a stunning 28–1 record that included both the regular-season and tournament championships in the Southwest Conference, Texas Tech was still hungry for some national respect when it entered the 1996 NCAA Tournament. The No. 3-seed Red Raiders finally got some of the attention they craved by pummeling No. 6-seed North Carolina, 92-73, to advance to the school's first Sweet 16 in 20 years. Too bad soph sensation Allen Iverson and Georgetown were waiting in the next round and topped Tech, 98-90. Even worse, Tech's appearance was later vacated because of NCAA violations.

BEST PLAYER: G Andre Emmett (2000-04) His elevation to Texas Tech's basketball Pantheon came after an unspectacular freshman campaign—and just happened to coincide with Knight's first season as Tech coach. The Dallas native became the first player in conference history to be named to the All-Big 12 first team three times. He finished his career in style, displaying his superior athleticism one more time to win the 2004 New Balance College Slam Dunk Contest. He is the leading scorer (2,256) in Texas Tech and Big 12 history.

BEST COACH: Bob Knight (2001-08) He's only the coach with the second-most wins in the history of college basketball (902), and tops in Division I. So what if 662 of them came when he coached Indiana? Texas Tech raised eyebrows by hiring Knight just six months after he was dismissed for behavior that violated IU's zero-tolerance policy on misconduct, but the move certainly paid off. The Red Raiders made four NCAA Tournament appearances in Knight's six full seasons, as he passed Dean Smith's 879 wins to climb to the top of the D1 coaching heap on Jan. 1, 2007.

GAME FOR THE AGES: No Red Raiders fan will ever forget the moment Tech's Darvin Ham shattered the backboard against North Carolina on March 17, 1996, in the second round of the NCAA Tournament. After all, it ended up on the cover of *Sports Illustrated*. It also caused a 27-minute delay, but more important, the loud jam sparked a 19-point romp over the storied Tar Heels and earned Tech a Sweet 16 appearance.

HEARTBREAKER: Texas Tech faced West Virginia in the 2005 Tournament with the school's first Elite Eight appearance on the line. But Mountaineers center Kevin Pittsnogle scored 22 points and blocked a Jarrius Jackson layup try that would have tied the game at 62. Tech failed to score on several possessions thereafter and fell, 65-60.

FIERCEST RIVAL: Like the fans of almost every other school in the state, Red Raiders supporters despise no team more than the Texas Longhorns. Just as it has on the gridiron, UT has reigned supreme in the basketball rivalry, leading the series with Tech 70–53. No loss was more bitter than the 62-61 defeat in Lubbock in 2004, after UT hit a buzzer-beating trey to send the game into overtime.

FANFARE AND HOOPLA: It's a select honor to be a part of the Saddle Tramps, an all-male, spirit-service group at Texas Tech. Founded in 1936, the Tramps are required to go through rush and donate their support to the Tech community. They also have the privilege of ringing the victory bells after Red Raider wins.

FAN FAVORITE: G Ronald Ross (2001-05) A classic Bob Knight-inspired scrappy guard, Ross went from freshman walk-on to leading scorer and captain of the 2005 Sweet 16 squad.

THE SCHOOLS

CONSENSUS ALL-AMERICAS

2004 **Andre Emmett**, G

FIRST-ROUND PRO PICKS

1997 **Tony Battie**, Denver (5)

PROFILE

Texas Tech University, Lubbock, TX
Founded: 1923
Enrollment: 28,422 (23,107 undergraduate)
Colors: Scarlet and black
Nickname: Red Raiders
Current arena: United Spirit Arena, opened in 1999 (15,098)
Previous: Lubbock Municipal Coliseum, 1956-99 (8,174); Tech Gym, a.k.a. the Barn, 1926-56 (2,000); Aggie Judging Pavilion, 1926 (N/A)
First game: Jan. 25, 1926

All-time record: 1,248-950 (.568)
Total weeks in AP Top 20/25: 35
Current conference: Big 12 (1996-)
Conference titles:
Border: 6 (1933, '34, '35, '54, '55 [tie], '56)
Southwest: 6 (1961, '62 [tie],'73, '85, '95 [tie], '96)
Conference tournament titles:
Southwest: 5 (1976, '85, '86, '93, '96)
NCAA Tournament appearances: 14
Sweet 16s (since 1975): 3
NIT appearances: 3
Semifinals: 1

TOP 5

G **Andre Emmett** (2000-04)
G **Jarrius Jackson** (2003-07)
F **Jim Reed** (1952-56)
F **Jason Sasser** (1992-96)
C **Rick Bullock** (1972-76)

RECORDS	GAME		SEASON		CAREER	
POINTS	50	Dub Malaise, vs. Texas (Feb. 19, 1966)	741	Andre Emmett (2002-03)	2,256	Andre Emmett (2000-04)
POINTS PER GAME			24.5	Greg Lowery (1971-72)	21.5	Gene Knolle (1969-71)
REBOUNDS	27	Jim Reed, vs. Texas (Feb. 14, 1956); vs. Eastern New Mexico (Dec. 17, 1955)	492	Paul Nolen (1950-51)	1,333	Jim Reed (1952-56)
ASSISTS	14	Stan Bonewitz, vs. Fresno State (Dec. 21, 1996)	212	John Roberson (2008-09)	435	Stan Bonewitz (1995-99)

SEASON REVIEW

SEAS.	W-L	CONF.	POSTSEASON	SCORING		REBOUNDS		ASSISTS		COACH	RECORD	
1925-26	6-8									Grady Higgenbotham		
1926-27	8-10									Grady Higgenbotham	14-18	.438
1927-28	9-7									Victor Payne		
1928-29	9-8									Victor Payne		
1929-30	13-6									Victor Payne	31-21	.596
1930-31	11-9									W.L. Golightly	11-9	.550
1931-32	9-14									Dell Morgan		
1932-33	15-8	4-0								Dell Morgan		
1933-34	18-5	7-1								Dell Morgan	42-27	.609
1934-35	14-10	9-1								Virgil Ballard	15-9	.625
1935-36	10-10	8-6								Berl Huffman		
1936-37	18-7	11-5								Berl Huffman		
1937-38	9-13	7-7								Berl Huffman		
1938-39	13-6	13-5								Berl Huffman		
1939-40	21-7									Berl Huffman		
1940-41	19-6									Berl Huffman		
1941-42	16-11	12-4								Berl Huffman		
1942-43	13-10	7-5								Polk Robison		
1943-44	5-18	0-3								Polk Robison		
1944-45	10-14	7-6								Polk Robison		
1945-46	12-9	7-4								Polk Robison		
1946-47	10-12	8-8								Berl Huffman	116-72	.617
1947-48	16-12	10-6								Polk Robison		
1948-49	21-9	11-5								Polk Robison		
1949-50	14-12	8-8								Polk Robison		
1950-51	14-14	10-6				Paul Nolen	17.6			Polk Robison		
1951-52	14-10	9-5				Paul Nolen	13.3			Polk Robison		
1952-53	12-10	9-5				Jim Reed	13.5			Polk Robison		
1953-54	20-5	11-1	NCAA FIRST ROUND			Jim Reed	12.8			Polk Robison		
1954-55	18-7	9-3		Jim Reed	22.3	Jim Reed	16.3			Polk Robison		
1955-56	13-12	8-4	NCAA FIRST ROUND			Jim Reed	13.5			Polk Robison		
1956-57	12-11									Polk Robison		
1957-58	15-8	8-6								Polk Robison		
1958-59	15-9	8-6								Polk Robison		
1959-60	10-14	7-7								Polk Robison		
1960-61	15-10	11-3	NCAA FIRST ROUND							Polk Robison	249-194	.562
1961-62	19-8	11-3	NCAA REGIONAL SEMIFINALS							Gene Gibson		
1962-63	6-17	6-8								Gene Gibson		
1963-64	16-7	11-3								Gene Gibson		
1964-65	17-6	12-2		Dub Malaise	23.7					Gene Gibson		
1965-66	13-11	8-6		Dub Malaise	21.4					Gene Gibson		
1966-67	9-15	7-7								Gene Gibson		
1967-68	10-14	5-9								Gene Gibson		
1968-69	11-13	6-8								Gene Gibson	101-91	.526
1969-70	14-10	8-6								Bob Bass		
1970-71	16-10	9-5		Gene Knolle	22.0					Bob Bass[a]	22-15	.595
1971-72	14-12	8-6		Greg Lowery	24.5					Gerald Myers		
1972-73	19-8	12-2	NCAA FIRST ROUND							Gerald Myers		
1973-74	17-9	10-4		Rick Bullock	21.4	Rick Bullock	10.7			Gerald Myers		
1974-75	18-8	11-3				Rick Bullock	11.0			Gerald Myers		
1975-76	25-6	13-3	NCAA REGIONAL SEMIFINALS	Rick Bullock	22.8	Rick Bullock	10.4			Gerald Myers		
1976-77	20-9	12-4		Mike Russell	22.1					Gerald Myers		
1977-78	19-10	10-6								Gerald Myers		
1978-79	19-11	9-7	NIT FIRST ROUND							Gerald Myers		
1979-80	16-13	8-8								Gerald Myers		
1980-81	15-13	8-8								Gerald Myers		
1981-82	17-11	8-8								Gerald Myers		
1982-83	12-19	7-9								Gerald Myers		
1983-84	17-12	10-6								Gerald Myers		
1984-85	23-8	12-4	NCAA FIRST ROUND	Bubba Jennings	19.5					Gerald Myers		
1985-86	17-14	9-7	NCAA FIRST ROUND							Gerald Myers		
1986-87	15-14	9-7								Gerald Myers		
1987-88	9-19	4-12								Gerald Myers		
1988-89	13-15	8-8								Gerald Myers		
1989-90	5-22	0-16								Gerald Myers		
1990-91	8-23	4-12								Gerald Myers	326-261	.555
1991-92	15-14	6-8								James Dickey		
1992-93	18-12	6-8	NCAA FIRST ROUND	Will Flemons	20.2	Will Flemons	10.8			James Dickey		
1993-94	17-11	10-4		Jason Sasser	20.6					James Dickey		
1994-95	20-10	11-3	NIT FIRST ROUND	Jason Sasser	20.1					James Dickey		
1995-96	30-2 ✪	14-0	NCAA REGIONAL SEMIFINALS	Jason Sasser	19.5					James Dickey		
1996-97	19-9	10-6		Cory Carr	23.1	Tony Battie	11.8	Stan Bonewitz	5.4	James Dickey		
1997-98	13-14	7-9		Cory Carr	23.3	Cliff Owens	8.4	Rayford Young	4.3	James Dickey		
1998-99	13-17	5-11		Rayford Young	16.4	Cliff Owens	7.0	Stan Bonewitz	4.4	James Dickey		
1999-2000	12-16	3-13		Rayford Young	17.8	Brodney Kennard	7.0	Rayford Young	4.2	James Dickey		
2000-01	9-19	3-13		Andy Ellis	14.2	Cliff Owens	7.4	Jamal Brown	6.3	James Dickey	166-124	.572▼
2001-02	23-9	10-6	NCAA FIRST ROUND	Andre Emmett	18.7	Andy Ellis	7.0	Kasib Powell	3.8	Bob Knight		
2002-03	22-13	6-10	NIT THIRD PLACE	Andre Emmett	21.8	Andre Emmett	6.6	Kasib Powell	4.3	Bob Knight		
2003-04	23-11	9-7	NCAA SECOND ROUND	Andre Emmett	20.6	Andre Emmett	6.6	Ronald Ross	3.1	Bob Knight		
2004-05	22-11	10-6	NCAA REGIONAL SEMIFINALS	Ronald Ross	17.5	Devonne Giles	6.5	Jarrius Jackson	3.5	Bob Knight		
2005-06	15-17	6-10		Jarrius Jackson	20.5	Martin Zeno	5.3	Darryl Dora	3.0	Bob Knight		
2006-07	21-13	9-7	NCAA FIRST ROUND	Jarrius Jackson	19.9	Martin Zeno	5.3	Martin Zeno	3.2	Bob Knight		
2007-08	16-15	7-9		Martin Zeno	16.0	Martin Zeno	4.5	John Roberson	3.3	Bob Knight[b]	138-82	.627
2008-09	14-19	3-13		John Roberson	13.9	Mike Singletary	5.8	John Roberson	6.4	Pat Knight	18-26	.409

[a] Bob Bass (8-5) and Gerald Myers (8-5) both coached during the 1970-71 season.
[b] Bob Knight (12-8) and Pat Knight (4-7) both coached during the 2007-08 season.
✪ Records don't reflect games forfeited or vacated. For adjusted records, see p. 521.
▼ Coach's record adjusted to reflect games forfeited or vacated: 164-123, .571. For yearly totals, see p. 521.

THE SCHOOLS

ESPN 83 SAGARIN

TOLEDO

The Rockets haven't been to the NCAA Tournament since 1980, but you'll still find them atop the list of mid-majors the big boys rarely want to play. Just ask Indiana, Iowa, Michigan and Ohio State, teams that Toledo swept in a four-year span from 1976 to '79. Or ask Xavier, which lost at Savage Hall on Dec. 9, 1999, prompting fans to flood the floor. Or ask Michigan State, which the Rockets beat at the Breslin Center on Dec. 30, 2002. Or ask … well, you get the picture.

BEST TEAM: 1941-42 Led by Bob Gerber, Bart Quinn and Robert Nash, the Rockets could score from both down low and long range in what *The New York Times* called "a remarkable display of versatility." Despite having poor eyesight, Gerber excelled with his one-handed shot, leading Toledo to the NIT semifinals. Unfortunately, the All-America scored only 14 points in a 51-39 upset loss to West Virginia.

BEST PLAYER: C STEVE MIX (1966-69) The only male Rocket to have his jersey retired, Mix averaged more than 20 points and 10 rebounds each season. The lefty could score facing up, in the low post and even off the dribble. As a sophomore, he led Toledo to the NCAA Tournament and scored 18 points and grabbed 14 rebounds in a 82-76 loss to Virginia Tech. As a senior, he won MAC Player of the Year.

BEST COACH: BOB NICHOLS (1965-87) Nichols kept it simple for his players: Focus on fundamentals and don't turn the ball over. The result was 20 winning seasons out of 22, four MAC titles (one shared), three trips to the NCAA Tournament and one of the most memorable wins in Toledo history: a 59-57 upset of defending national champ Indiana to open Centennial (now Savage) Hall on Dec. 1, 1976.

GAME FOR THE AGES: Even today, most longtime Toledo fans can recount what's known as the Play in every glorious detail. In the second round of the NCAA Tournament on March 10, 1979, the Rockets trailed Big Ten power Iowa at the half, 41-29. But Toledo shot 63% over the final 20 minutes to tie it at 72, setting up the dramatic ending. Rockets point guard Jay Lehman dribbled the floor with :10 left, dished it to Dick Miller, who crossed midcourt before passing to Stan Joplin, who nailed a 20-footer at the buzzer for the win.

HEARTBREAKER: Three decades after hitting that game-winner, Joplin was on the losing end of a postseason stunner, this time as Toledo's coach. Late in the MAC quarterfinals on March 5, 2000, Joplin called a timeout with his team trailing Ball State 57-55. As he did, Chad Kamstra hit a game-winning three—which was waived off. Toledo still forced overtime, but that led to even more agony when Kamstra missed the front end of a one-and-one that could have sealed the victory. Ball State won, 64-63.

FIERCEST RIVAL: Only 25 miles apart, Bowling Green and Toledo have been heated rivals ever since coach Harold Anderson left the Rockets for the Falcons in 1942. Records mean little in the series, as the weaker team has often prevailed. "That game makes the season for players and coaches," said Mix. Toledo leads overall, 83–76.

> *The only male Rocket to have his jersey retired, Mix could score facing up, in the low post and even off the dribble.*

FANFARE AND HOOPLA: You encounter two crowds at Savage Hall—regular folks on each sideline and the student sections behind each basket. Members of the Blue Crew wear costumes, Mardi Gras masks and fake names on the back of their shirts. In case you hadn't guessed, those are the ones behind the baskets.

FAN FAVORITE: G JUSTIN INGRAM (2003-07) An early commit to Toledo, Ingram started a school-record 123 games and endeared himself to fans with his relentless, scrappy play.

PROFILE

University of Toledo, Toledo, OH
Founded: 1872
Enrollment: 20,715 (16,366 undergraduate)
Colors: Midnight blue and gold
Nickname: Rockets
Current arena: John F. Savage Hall, opened as Centennial Hall in 1976 (7,300)
Previous: The Field House, 1931-76 (4,100)
First game: Jan. 14, 1916
All-time record: 1,283-925 (.581)
Total weeks in AP Top 20/25: 22

Current conference: Mid-American (1951-)
Conference titles:
MAC: 6 (1954, '67, '79, '80, '81 [tie], 2007)
Conference tournament titles:
MAC: 1 (1980)
NCAA Tournament appearances: 4
Sweet 16s (since 1975): 1
NIT appearances: 7
Semifinals: 2

TOP 5

G **Larry Jones** (1960-64)
G **Craig Thames** (1992-96)
F **Chuck Chuckovits** (1936-39)
F **Bob Gerber** (1939-42)
C **Steve Mix** (1966-69)

RECORDS	GAME		SEASON		CAREER	
POINTS	49	Clark Pittenger, vs. Bluffton (Dec. 14, 1918)	699	Craig Thames (1995-96)	2,016	Ken Epperson (1981-85)
POINTS PER GAME			25.6	Jim Ray (1955-56)	22.9	Steve Mix (1966-69)
REBOUNDS	27	Doug Hess, vs. Marshall (Jan. 13, 1971); Ned Miklovic, at Ohio (Feb. 17, 1958)	371	Doug Hess (1969-70)	960	Ken Epperson (1981-85)
ASSISTS	14	Tim Reiser, at Kent State (Feb. 24, 1982)	210	Bill Walker (1950-51)	762	Tim Reiser (1980-84)

SEASON REVIEW

SEASON	W-L	CONF.	SCORING	COACH	RECORD	
1915-16	2-1			Harry Zimmerman	2-1	.667
1916-17	2-1			Darrell Fox		
1917-18	2-4			Darrell Fox		
1918-19	10-2			Sam Monetta	10-2	.833
1919-20	8-3			Walt Hobt	8-3	.727
1920-21	1-12			Darrell Fox		
1921-22	5-6			C.H. Watts		
1922-23	2-8			C.H. Watts	7-14	.333
1923-24	5-5			Darrell Fox		
1924-25	13-7			Darrell Fox	23-29	.442
1925-26	3-8			Louis Moorhead	3-8	.273
1926-27	6-9			Dave Connelly		
1927-28	9-7			Dave Connelly		
1928-29	6-10			Dave Connelly		
1929-30	5-9			Dave Connelly		
1930-31	5-12			Dave Connelly		
1931-32	8-9			Dave Connelly		
1932-33	3-13			Dave Connelly		
1933-34	6-9			Dave Connelly	48-78	.381
1934-35	13-3			Harold Anderson		
1935-36	12-4			Harold Anderson		
1936-37	18-4			Harold Anderson		

SEAS.	W-L	CONF.	POSTSEASON	SCORING		REBOUNDS		ASSISTS		COACH	RECORD	
1937-38	14-6									Harold Anderson		
1938-39	17-10									Harold Anderson		
1939-40	24-6									Harold Anderson		
1940-41	21-3									Harold Anderson		
1941-42	23-5		NIT FOURTH PLACE							Harold Anderson	142-41	.776
1942-43	22-4		NIT RUNNER-UP							Burl Friddle		
1943-44	5-13									Burl Friddle	27-17	.614
1944-45	9-4									Rollie Boldt		
1945-46	20-7									Rollie Boldt	29-11	.725
1946-47	18-6									Bill Orwig	18-6	.750
1947-48	21-5									Jerry Bush		
1948-49	13-12									Jerry Bush		
1949-50	22-6									Jerry Bush		
1950-51	22-7									Jerry Bush		
1951-52	20-11	8-4								Jerry Bush		
1952-53	16-7	9-3								Jerry Bush		
1953-54	13-10	10-2	NCAA FIRST ROUND							Jerry Bush	127-58	.686
1954-55	5-17	4-10		Jim Ray	17.4	Russ Bierly	6.5			Ed Melvin		
1955-56	9-13	6-6		Jim Ray	25.6	Joe Buneta	10.9			Ed Melvin		
1956-57	5-19	3-9		Murray Guttman	17.7	Ned Miklovic	9.8			Ed Melvin		
1957-58	9-14	4-8		Joe Keifer	16.5	Ned Miklovic	10.1			Ed Melvin		
1058-59	11-13	5-7		Jerry Galicki	12.0	George Patterson	10.4			Ed Melvin		
1959-60	18-6	9-3		John Papcun	11.4	George Patterson	10.0			Ed Melvin		
1960-61	15-8	8-4		Larry Jones	18.3	George Patterson	11.6			Ed Melvin		
1961-62	14-10	7-5		Larry Jones	21.1	Ray Wolford	9.9			Ed Melvin		
1962-63	13-11	8-4		Ray Wolford	21.1	Ray Wolford	13.0			Ed Melvin		
1963-64	13-11	4-8		Larry Jones	23.3	Ray Wolford	10.6			Ed Melvin		
1964-65	13-11	6-6		Bill Backensto	18.3	Bob Aston	12.5			Ed Melvin	125-133	.484
1965-66	13-11	8-4		Bob Aston	18.3	Bob Aston	13.2			Bob Nichols		
1966-67	23-2	11-1	NCAA FIRST ROUND	Steve Mix	23.0	Steve Mix	13.5			Bob Nichols		
1967-68	16-8	8-4		Steve Mix	21.8	Steve Mix	10.2			Bob Nichols		
1968-69	13-11	5-7		Steve Mix	24.1	Steve Mix	12.1			Bob Nichols		
1969-70	15-9	3-7		Mike Murnen	15.0	Doug Hess	15.4			Bob Nichols		
1970-71	13-11	4-6		Tom Kozelko	16.4	Doug Hess	13.8			Bob Nichols		
1971-72	18-7	7-3		Tom Kozelko	24.3	Tom Kozelko	11.5			Bob Nichols		
1972-73	15-11	7-5		Tom Kozelko	21.5	Tom Kozelko	9.9			Bob Nichols		
1973-74	19-9	8-4		Mike Parker	15.1	Jim Brown	12.5	Jim Kindle	3.5	Bob Nichols		
1974-75	17-9	9-5		Larry Cole	15.8	Jim Brown	10.8	Jim Kindle	3.8	Bob Nichols		
1975-76	18-7	13-3		Larry Cole	18.1	Dave Speicher	8.9	Dave Speicher	5.4	Bob Nichols		
1976-77	21-6	12-4		Ted Williams	17.2	Dick Miller	8.4	Stan Joplin	4.0	Bob Nichols		
1977-78	21-6	11-5		Ted Williams	18.3	Dick Miller	7.7	Stan Joplin	6.5	Bob Nichols		
1978-79	22-8	13-3	NCAA REGIONAL SEMIFINALS	Jim Swaney	15.9	Dick Miller	8.1	Jay Lehman	3.7	Bob Nichols		
1979-80	23-6	14-2	NCAA FIRST ROUND	Jim Swaney	19.1	Dick Miller	9.9	Tim Selgo	5.9	Bob Nichols		
1980-81	21-10	10-6	NIT SECOND ROUND	Harvey Knuckles	22.0	Mitch Adamek	8.7	Tim Reiser	6.3	Bob Nichols		
1981-82	15-11	7-9		Mitch Adamek	16.9	Mitch Adamek	9.6	Tim Reiser	7.5	Bob Nichols		
1982-83	17-12	10-8		Ken Epperson	18.1	Mitch Adamek	9.0	Tim Reiser	6.6	Bob Nichols		
1983-84	18-11	11-7		Ken Epperson	20.4	Ken Epperson	9.4	Tim Reiser	6.3	Bob Nichols		
1984-85	16-12	11-7		Jay Gast	17.1	Ken Epperson	8.0	Jay Gast	4.3	Bob Nichols		
1985-86	12-17	8-10		Blake Burnham	16.7	Blake Burnham	6.6	Gary Campbell	4.0	Bob Nichols		
1986-87	11-17	4-12		Blake Burnham	14.7	Andy Fisher	6.0	Gary Campbell	2.2	Bob Nichols	377-211	.641
1987-88	15-12	5-11		Fred King	11.8	Chad Keller	6.0	Tyrone Branch	4.6	Jay Eck		
1988-89	16-15 ⊗	11-5		A. Fisher, C. Sutters	12.9	Craig Sutters	7.8	Keith Wade	5.1	Jay Eck		
1989-90	12-16	7-9		Craig Sutters	13.8	Craig Sutters	8.7	Keith Wade	5.0	Jay Eck		
1990-91	17-16	7-9		Craig Sutters	17.3	Tom Best	8.9	Keith Wade	6.0	Jay Eck	60-59	.504▼
1991-92	7-20	3-13		J.C. Harris	14.8	J.C. Harris	7.9	Rick Rightnowar	2.3	Larry Gipson		
1992-93	12-16	9-9		Archie Fuller	14.4	Tim Schirra	8.4	S. Brown, R. Rightnowar	2.7	Larry Gipson		
1993-94	15-12	10-8		Craig Thames	15.3	Scoop Williams	7.9	Craig Thames	3.6	Larry Gipson		
1994-95	16-11	10-8		Craig Thames	18.8	Scoop Williams	8.6	C. Thames, B. Krahulik	3.7	Larry Gipson		
1995-96	18-14	9-9		Craig Thames	21.8	Craig Thames	6.1	Craig Thames	4.0	Larry Gipson	68-73	.482
1996-97	13-14	6-12		Casey Shaw	16.3	Casey Shaw	9.0	Clayton Burch	3.3	Stan Joplin		
1997-98	15-12	10-8		Casey Shaw	14.2	Casey Shaw	10.0	Clayton Burch	3.1	Stan Joplin		
1998-99	19-9	11-7	NIT FIRST ROUND	Greg Stempin	15.3	Greg Stempin	7.4	Justin Hall	2.2	Stan Joplin		
1999-2000	18-13	11-7		Greg Stempin	15.7	Greg Stempin	8.1	Justin Hall	3.1	Stan Joplin		
2000-01	22-11	12-6	NIT SECOND ROUND	Greg Stempin	18.3	Greg Stempin	8.2	Terry Reynolds	4.6	Stan Joplin		
2001-02	16-14	11-7		Nick Moore	14.3	Keith Triplett	6.0	Terry Reynolds	4.2	Stan Joplin		
2002-03	13-16	7-11		Keith Triplett	16.9	Keith Triplett	5.8	Sammy Villegas	4.2	Stan Joplin		
2003-04	20-11	12-6	NIT FIRST ROUND	Keith Triplett	19.6	Keith Triplett	4.7	Justin Ingram	3.6	Stan Joplin		
2004-05	16-13	11-7		Keith Triplett	15.1	Justin Ingram	4.0	Kashif Payne	3.4	Stan Joplin		
2005-06	20-11	10-8		Justin Ingram	14.6	Florentino Valencia	4.4	Kashif Payne	4.3	Stan Joplin		
2006-07	19-13	14-2	NIT FIRST ROUND	Keonta Howell	14.7	Florentino Valencia	4.9	Kashif Payne	4.2	Stan Joplin		
2007-08	11-19	7-8		Tyrone Kent	16.9	Jerrah Young	6.5	Tyrone Kent	3.0	Stan Joplin	202-156	.564
2008-09	7-25	5-11		Tyrone Kent	15.1	Justin Anyijong	6.4	Jonathan Amos	3.2	Gene Cross	7-25	.219

⊗ Records don't reflect games forfeited or vacated. For adjusted records, see p. 521.

▼ Coach's record adjusted to reflect games forfeited or vacated: 62-57, .521. For yearly totals, see p. 521.

ESPN 314 SAGARIN

TOWSON

We're No. 1! Even if it's in Division II. Vince Angotti's unforgettable 1976-77 Towson State D2 squad (the school dropped State from its name in '97) starred Pat McKinley, Brian Matthews and Roger Dickens. Later D1 Tigers teams won five straight Big South and East Coast Conference regular-season or tournament titles from 1989-90 to '93-94.

BEST TEAM: 1976-77 Several all-time Towson greats—including McKinley, Matthews, Dickens and Bobby Washington—led the Tigers to a 27–3 record. They won 23 straight in one stretch and were ranked No. 1 in the final Division II poll before losing in the elite eight, 85-82, to Sacred Heart.

BEST PLAYER: G KURK LEE (1988-90) In 1989-90 this transfer from Western Kentucky carried Towson to its second winning D1 campaign and its first NCAA Tournament. Lee averaged 25.7 points per game in his two seasons. He was a two-time East Coast Conference player of the year.

BEST COACH: VINCE ANGOTTI (1966-78, '79-83) The school's winningest coach is also the only one with a winning record, a robust 229–180. Angotti coached the Tigers for 12 seasons, leading them to the D2 national tournament in 1977 and '78. He took a one-year break to finish a doctoral degree and then came back to guide Towson in its first four D1 campaigns.

GAME FOR THE AGES: On Jan. 30, 1995, Towson stunned NCAA Tournament-bound Louisville, 81-69. The Tigers trailed 59-55 with 9:16 left, but outscored the Cardinals 26-10 the rest of the way, making nine of 10 late free throws. Ralph Blalock led the way for Towson with 26 points and five steals, and reserve DeRon Robinson scored 20.

FIERCEST RIVAL: Delaware is located roughly an hour's drive away from Towson and the two programs have even switched leagues together (ECC to America East to Colonial Athletic). Overall, Delaware leads the series, 36–25, and holds a 5–2 lead in conference tournament games.

SEASON REVIEW

SEAS.	W-L	CONF.	SCORING		COACH	RECORD
1958-59	1-17				Earl Killian	
1959-60	3-17				Earl Killian	
1960-61	3-12				Earl Killian	
1961-62	1-15				Earl Killian	
1962-63	1-15				Earl Killian	9-76 .106
1963-64	1-15				Ross Sachs	
1964-65	8-7				Ross Sachs	
1965-66	4-13				Ross Sachs	13-35 .271
1966-67	9-9				Vince Angotti	
1967-68	12-7				Vince Angotti	
1968-69	14-8				Vince Angotti	
1969-70	16-9				Vince Angotti	
1970-71	8-16		Mel Land	16.8	Vince Angotti	
1971-72	15-10		Mel Land	16.4	Vince Angotti	
1972-73	17-10		Larry Witherspoon	25.4	Vince Angotti	
1973-74	14-12		Larry Witherspoon	21.2	Vince Angotti	
1974-75	14-12		Pat McKinley	20.2	Vince Angotti	
1975-76	19-10		Pat McKinley	17.5	Vince Angotti	
1976-77	27-3		Brian Matthews	17.9	Vince Angotti	
1977-78	26-4		Brian Matthews	18.8	Vince Angotti	
1978-79	5-21		Michael Dukes	12.6	Mike Raudabaugh	5-21 .192
1979-80	9-17		Michael Sharpe	13.7	Vince Angotti	
1980-81	13-14		Tony Odrick	13.3	Vince Angotti	
1981-82	10-17	5-7	Tony Odrick	17.9	Vince Angotti	
1982-83	7-21	2-7	Mark Cooley	18.1	Vince Angotti	229-180 .560
1983-84	10-19	5-11	Steffan Bunsavage	12.4	Terry Truax	
1984-85	7-21	5-9	Bill Leonard	11.8	Terry Truax	
1985-86	8-20	5-9	Steffan Bunsavage	15.3	Terry Truax	
1986-87	14-16	5-9	Bill Leonard	14.9	Terry Truax	
1987-88	14-16	4-10	Marty Johnson	17.6	Terry Truax	
1988-89	19-10	10-4	Kurk Lee	25.4	Terry Truax	
1989-90	18-13	8-6 ●	Kurk Lee	26.0	Terry Truax	
1990-91	19-11	10-2 ●	Devin Boyd	20.7	Terry Truax	
1991-92	17-13	9-3	Terrance Jacobs	23.1	Terry Truax	
1992-93	18-9	14-2	Devin Boyd	23.0	Terry Truax	
1993-94	21-9	16-2	Scooter Alexander	17.4	Terry Truax	
1994-95	12-15	6-10	Ralph Blalock	17.3	Terry Truax	
1995-96	16-12	11-7	Ralph Blalock	17.1	Terry Truax	
1996-97	9-19	5-13	Ralph Biggs	18.8	Terry Truax	202-203 .499
1997-98	8-20	4-14	Ralph Biggs	18.4	Mike Jaskulski	
1998-99	6-22	4-14	Brian Barber	12.3	Mike Jaskulski	
1999-2000	11-17	7-11	Brian Barber	17.0	Mike Jaskulski	
2000-01	12-17	7-11	Brian Barber	13.8	Mike Jaskulski	37-76 .327
2001-02	11-18	7-11	Sam Sutton	12.6	Michael Hunt	
2002-03	4-24	1-17	Jamaal Gilchrist	10.6	Michael Hunt	
2003-04	8-21	4-14	Jamaal Gilchrist	12.2	Michael Hunt	23-63 .267
2004-05	5-24	2-16	Lawrence Hamm	12.0	Pat Kennedy	
2005-06	12-16	8-10	Gary Neal[a]	26.1	Pat Kennedy	
2006-07	15-17	8-10	Gary Neal	25.3	Pat Kennedy	
2007-08	13-18	7-11	Junior Hairston	12.0	Pat Kennedy	
2008-09	12-22	5-13	Junior Hairston	13.0	Pat Kennedy	57-97 .370

[a] **Gary Neal's 26.1 ppg does not qualify as Towson's season record; he only played in 17 games.**
● **NCAA Tournament appearance**

THE SCHOOLS

PROFILE

Towson University, Towson, MD
Founded: 1866 as Maryland State Normal School
Enrollment: 19,758 (16,219 undergraduate)
Colors: Gold, white and black
Nickname: Tigers
Current arena: Towson Center Arena, opened in 1976, (5,000)
First game: 1958
All-time record: 576-750 (.434)
Total weeks in AP Top 20/25: 0

Current conference: Colonial Athletic Association (2001-)
Conference titles:
East Coast: 2 (1990 [tie], '91)
Big South: 2 (1993, '94)
Conference tournament titles:
East Coast: 3 (1990, '91, '92)
NCAA Tournament appearances: 2
NIT appearances: 0

TOP 5

G **Kurk Lee** (1988-90)
G **Gary Neal** (2005-07)
G/F **Brian Matthews** (1974-78)
F **Ralph Biggs** (1994-98)
C **Pat McKinley** (1973-77)

RECORDS	GAME		SEASON		CAREER	
POINTS	51	Larry Witherspoon, vs. American (Feb. 17, 1973)	810	Gary Neal (2006-07)	2,000	Devin Boyd (1988-93)
POINTS PER GAME			26.0	Kurk Lee (1989-90)	25.7	Kurk Lee (1988-90)
REBOUNDS	30	Pat McKinley, vs. Roanoke College (Feb. 3, 1975)	396	Dan Roberts (1968-69)	1,421	Pat McKinley (1973-77)
ASSISTS	14	C.C. Williams vs. Georgia State (Feb. 10, 2007)	152	Roger Dickens (1977-1978)	438	Devin Boyd (1988-93)

ESPN 296 SAGARIN

TROY

Objective: score at will. Experience: three-time NCAA team scoring champs (1991, '92, '96); seven-time NCAA three-pointers made per game champs (1992, '94, '95, '96, 2004, '05, '06); NCAA record-holder for most points scored in a game (258). That's how Troy's hoops résumé reads. And a stretch of four regular-season conference titles in five seasons since 2000, including a trip to the Big Dance in 2003, proves all that scoring is more than just showboating.

BEST TEAM: 2002-03 In early December, Troy pulled off a 74-66 road win at Arkansas. It was just a hint of the great things to come. Led by all-conference selection Ben Fletcher, who hit a school-record 92 threes, the Trojans won the Atlantic Sun tournament title and a share of the regular-season title to earn their first NCAA Tourney trip.

BEST PLAYER: F ANTHONY REED (1986-90) Although he only shot 54.1% from the line, he still ranks as Troy's all-time leader in free throws made (363) because he never, ever stopped attacking the basket.

BEST COACH: DON MAESTRI (1982-) Mad genius. There's simply no other way to describe the coach behind Troy's up-up-up-tempo offense, which he introduced in the early 1990s and has been running at breakneck speed ever since.

GAME FOR THE AGES: On Jan. 12, 1992, the Trojans became the first and, so far, only team in NCAA history to break the 200-point barrier. Some other records Troy set in its 258-141 win over DeVry that day: 51 three-pointers made, 190 field goals attempted, 102 field goals made. The scoring pace was so insane that it took seven statisticians 57 minutes to compile the final box score.

FIERCEST RIVAL: Troy's intra-Alabama grudge match with Jacksonville State came to a close in 2003 when the Gamecocks moved to the Ohio Valley Conference. (The series ended in a 51–51 tie.) But the Trojans already have a new in-state nemesis in the making: South Alabama. The two schools have met nine times in Sun Belt play, with the Trojans winning just three games.

SEASON REVIEW

SEAS.	W-L	CONF.	COACH	SEAS.	W-L	CONF.	COACH
1950-51	3-15		Buddy Brooks	**1962-63**	20-10		John Archer
1951-52	5-20		Leonard Serfustini	**1963-64**	22-8		John Archer
1952-53	18-7		Leonard Serfustini	**1964-65**	22-8		John Archer
1953-54	22-6		Leonard Serfustini	**1965-66**	24-9		John Archer
1954-55	12-10		Leonard Serfustini	**1966-67**	26-7		John Archer
1955-56	18-9		Leonard Serfustini	**1967-68**	18-8		John Archer
1956-57	19-8		John Archer	**1968-69**	10-18		John Archer
1957-58	19-6		John Archer	**1969-70**	8-20		John Archer
1958-59	19-11		John Archer	**1970-71**	11-17		John Archer
1959-60	19-8		John Archer	**1971-72**	14-15		John Archer
1960-61	21-7		John Archer	**1972-73**	5-20		John Archer
1961-62	25-6		John Archer	**1973-74**	9-16		Wes Bizilia

SEAS.	W-L	CONF.	SCORING		COACH	RECORD
1974-75	18-8				Wes Bizilia	
1975-76	15-11				Wes Bizilia	
1976-77	15-14				Wes Bizilia	
1977-78	7-17				Wes Bizilia	
1978-79	10-16				Wes Bizilia	
1979-80	10-15				Wes Bizilia	
1980-81	13-13				Wes Bizilia	
1981-82	11-13				Wes Bizilia	108-123 .468
1982-83	15-13				Don Maestri	
1983-84	18-11				Don Maestri	
1984-85	14-13				Don Maestri	
1985-86	14-13				Don Maestri	
1986-87	12-14				Don Maestri	
1987-88	25-9				Don Maestri	
1988-89	19-8				Don Maestri	
1989-90	22-6				Don Maestri	
1990-91	23-7				Don Maestri	
1991-92	23-6				Don Maestri	
1992-93	27-5				Don Maestri	
1993-94	13-14	5-0	Cameron Boozer	18.6	Don Maestri	
1994-95	11-16	10-8	Cameron Boozer	15.2	Don Maestri	
1995-96	11-16	8-10	Rhodney Donaldson	16.3	Don Maestri	
1996-97	16-11	10-6	Jeff Black	16.3	Don Maestri	
1997-98	7-20	5-11	Terry Pickett	13.8	Don Maestri	
1998-99	9-18	6-10	Tote Christopher	17.9	Don Maestri	
1999-2000	17-11	13-5	Detric Golden	17.6	Don Maestri	
2000-01	19-12	12-6	Lamayn Wilson	14.6	Don Maestri	
2001-02	18-10	14-6	Lamayn Wilson	20.1	Don Maestri	
2002-03	26-6	14-2 ●	Ben Fletcher	13.9	Don Maestri	
2003-04	24-7	18-2 ■	Greg Davis	15.5	Don Maestri	
2004-05	12-18	10-10	Bobby Dixon	14.7	Don Maestri	
2005-06	14-15	6-9	Bobby Dixon	17.9	Don Maestri	
2006-07	13-17	8-10	O'Darien Bassett	15.1	Don Maestri	
2007-08	12-19	4-14	O'Darien Bassett	18.2	Don Maestri	
2008-09	19-13	14-4	Brandon Hazzard	16.2	Don Maestri	453-328 .580

● NCAA Tournament appearance ■ NIT appearance

PROFILE

Troy University, Troy, AL
Founded: 1887
Enrollment: 20,855 (13,253 undergraduate)
Colors: Cardinal, silver and black
Nickname: Trojans
Current arena: Trojan Arena, opened as Sartain Hall in 1962 (4,000)
Previous: Wright Hall, 1950-62 (400)
First game: Nov. 27, 1950
All-time record: 941-704 (.572)
Total weeks in AP Top 20/25: 0

Current conference: Sun Belt (2005-)
Conference titles:
East Coast: 1 (1994)
Trans America: 1 (2000 [tie])
Atlantic Sun: 3 (2002 [tie], '03 [tie], '04)
Conference tournament titles:
Atlantic Sun: 1 (2003)
NCAA Tournament appearances: 1
NIT appearances: 1

CONSENSUS ALL-AMERICAS

1993 **Terry McCord** (D2), F

TOP 5

G **Greg Davis** (2002-04)
G **Detric Golden** (1999-2000)
F **Terry McCord** (1991-93)
F **Anthony Reed** (1986-90)
F **Darryl Thomas** (1987-89)

RECORDS	GAME		SEASON		CAREER	
POINTS	45	Detric Golden, vs. Jacksonville (Feb. 5, 2000)	564	O'Darien Bassett (2007-08); Lamayn Wilson (2001-02)	1,533	Robert Rushing (1998-2002)
POINTS PER GAME			20.1	Lamayn Wilson (2001-02)	17.6	Detric Golden (1999-2000)
REBOUNDS	20	Fred Spencer, vs. Central Connecticut St. (Jan. 20, 1996)	258	Rob Lewin (2002-03)	694	Rob Lewin (2000-04)
ASSISTS	17	Mike Vogler, vs. Northwestern State (Nov. 29, 2008)	256	Greg Davis (2003-04)	408	Greg Davis (2002-04)

ESPN 123 SAGARIN

TULANE

Until the Green Wave makes that first run deep into the Tournament or turns itself into a Conference USA power, Tulane will probably be best known for one of the darkest basketball scandals of the 1980s. On March 27, 1985, star big man John "Hot Rod" Williams was arrested for allegedly manipulating point spreads. After a mistrial, he was acquitted on all counts. But in response to the initial allegations, the school disbanded the team until 1989.

BEST TEAM: 1991-92 Three seasons after returning from its self-imposed ban, the Green Wave won the Metro Conference championship and, in its NCAA Tournament debut, beat St. John's before falling to Oklahoma State in the second round. Tulane did it without a marquee show-runner, relying instead on its swarming and relentless defense. Coach Perry Clark perfected a system that kept his crew fresh: Every five minutes or so, he'd sub in a new five-man second unit (a.k.a. the Posse).

BEST PLAYER: F Phil Hicks (1973-76) The only Green Wave to average more than 20 points and 10 rebounds over a career (21.2 and 11.9), Hicks was at his best in the sweltering Fogelman Arena. It was one reason he almost led a home upset over Marquette on March 10, 1975. "It was a huge advantage for us," Hicks once said. "I remember [Marquette coach] Al McGuire talking about how hot it was in the gym."

BEST COACH: Perry Clark (1989-2000) The former Bobby Cremins assistant at Georgia Tech took over the resurrected Green Wave and led it to all of four wins in Tulane's first season back. But he had a winning team in his second season, and in year three the Wave made the Tournament. Clark ultimately coached eight winning teams in 11 seasons and won 20 games or more six times.

GAME FOR THE AGES: Before the 1992 first-round NCAA Tournament game with St. John's, the Green Wave had dropped seven of its last 12 games. But senior David Whitmore, figuring "we don't have anything to lose because we aren't expected to win," led the Wave with 15 points. Meanwhile, he and his mates clamped down hard on Lou Carnesecca's Redmen, pressuring them into 16 turnovers in a 61-57 win.

HEARTBREAKER: On Valentine's Day 1976, Tulane took No. 3-ranked North Carolina to four overtimes at the Louisiana Superdome before finally succumbing, 113-106. Four of the Green Wave's five starters fouled out trying to keep the Heels under wraps. It was a minor consolation that the Wave at least washed out Dean Smith's dinner plans. The Tar Heels coach had booked a table at the famed New Orleans joint Brennan's, but missed his reservation.

FIERCEST RIVAL: During the 1970s, LSU coach Dale Brown and Tulane coach Roy Danforth famously feuded. Brown was irked that Danforth once mocked his courtside crouch, while Danforth thought Brown often ran up scores unnecessarily. The animosity ran so deep that the Tigers dropped the series in 1980. On March 12, 1982,

Tulane took North Carolina to four overtimes before succumbing. At least the Wave washed out Dean Smith's dinner plans.

the NIT paired the two in a first-round game in Baton Rouge, which Tulane won, 83-72. The annual series finally resumed in 2002, thanks to the encouragement of LSU coach John Brady and Tulane coach Shawn Finney. LSU leads overall, 124–84.

FANFARE AND HOOPLA: For many years, Green Wave fans pelted the court with Mardi Gras beads to greet Tulane's first basket of the last game played before Fat Tuesday. Technical fouls and pleas from coaches did little to dissuade the practice, until it finally died out during the program's hiatus.

FAN FAVORITE: G Harold Sylvester (1968-71) Wave fans fondly remember Sylvester as a solid starter. TV watchers fondly remember Sylvester as a solid role player who guest starred on such shows as *Married … With Children*, *City of Angels* and *CSI: Miami*.

THE SCHOOLS

PROFILE

Tulane University, New Orleans, LA
Founded: 1834
Enrollment: 11,157 (6,749 undergraduate)
Colors: Olive green and sky blue
Nickname: Green Wave
Current arena: Avron B. Fogelman Arena, opened in 1933 (3,600)
First game: Dec. 23, 1905
All-time record: 1,093-1,105 (.497)
Total weeks in AP Top 20/25: 36

Current conference: Conference USA (1995-)
Conference titles:
Southern: 1 (1924)
Metro: 2 (1976, '92)
Conference tournament titles: 0
NCAA Tournament appearances: 3
NIT appearances: 6
Semifinals: 1

FIRST-ROUND PRO PICKS

1969 **Johnny Arthurs,** New Orleans (ABA)

TOP 5

G **Johnny Arthurs** (1966-69)
G/F **Paul Thompson** (1979-83)
F **Phil Hicks** (1973-76)
F **Anthony Reed** (1989-93)
C **John "Hot Rod" Williams** (1981-84)

RECORDS	GAME		SEASON		CAREER	
POINTS	45	Jim Kerwin, vs. Southeastern Louisiana (Feb. 1, 1961)	666	Johnny Arthurs (1968-69)	2,209	Jerald Honeycutt (1993-97)
POINTS PER GAME			25.6	Johnny Arthurs (1968-69)	22.2	Jim Kerwin (1960-63)
REBOUNDS	31	Mel Payton, vs. Mississippi State (Jan. 5, 1951)	426	Mel Payton (1950-51)	1,062	Jack Ardon (1959-62)
ASSISTS	13	Marcus Kinzer, vs. Northwestern State (Dec. 6, 2004); Tom Hicks, vs. The Citadel (Jan. 26, 1976)	208	Tom Hicks (1975-76)	419	Jerald Honeycutt (1993-97)

SEASON REVIEW

SEASON	W-L	CONF.	SCORING	COACH	RECORD	
1905-15	*43-41*		*First coach, Silas Hickey, guided team to 8-5 in only season ('05-06)*			
1915-16	10-8			Clark Shaughnessy		
1916-17	11-5			Clark Shaughnessy		
1917-18	6-2			Clark Shaughnessy	27-15	.643
1918-19	6-3			M.A. Moenck		
1919-20	5-9			M.A. Moenck	11-12	.478
1920-21	7-10			Claude Simons Sr.		
1921-22	10-11			Claude Simons Sr.		
1922-23	15-3	5-1		Claude Simons Sr.		
1923-24	21-1	10-0		Claude Simons Sr.		
1924-25	17-4	12-3		Claude Simons Sr.		
1925-26	11-7	10-7		Claude Simons Sr.		
1926-27	7-10	7-10		Claude Simons Sr.		
1927-28	3-13	3-13		Claude Simons Sr.		
1928-29	9-5	9-4		Bernie Bierman		
1929-30	16-7	7-3		Bernie Bierman	25-12	.676
1930-31	6-14	2-10		Claude Simons Sr.	97-73	.571
1931-32	6-10	5-9		George Rody		
1932-33	8-15	6-14		George Rody	14-25	.359
1933-34	10-10	8-10		Ray Dauber		
1934-35	1-16	1-16		Ray Dauber		
1935-36	2-17	1-14		Ray Dauber		

SEAS.	W-L	CONF.	POSTSEASON	SCORING		REBOUNDS		ASSISTS		COACH	RECORD	
1936-37	6-8	4-8								Ray Dauber		
1937-38	8-10	5-6								Ray Dauber	27-61	.307
1938-39	5-13	3-6								Claude Simons Jr.		
1939-40	2-13	2-8								Claude Simons Jr.		
1940-41	8-6	6-5								Claude Simons Jr.		
1941-42	4-12	3-9								Claude Simons Jr	19-44	.302
1942-43	4-9	4-8								Vernon Haynes		
1943-44	16-6									Vernon Haynes		
1944-45	6-11	3-3								Vernon Haynes	26-26	.500
1945-46	15-7	4-5								Clifford Wells		
1946-47	22-9	8-5								Clifford Wells		
1947-48	23-3	13-1								Clifford Wells		
1948-49	24-4	12-3								Clifford Wells		
1949-50	15-7	8-4								Clifford Wells		
1950-51	12-12	8-6								Clifford Wells		
1951-52	12-12	7-7								Clifford Wells		
1952-53	12-6	9-4		Fritz Schulz	13.8	Fritz Schulz	10.8			Clifford Wells		
1953-54	15-8	10-4		Hal Cervini	14.7	Pat Browne	8.2			Clifford Wells		
1954-55	14-6	9-5		Hal Cervini	16.4	Dick Brennan	8.4			Clifford Wells		
1955-56	12-12	7-7		Calvin Grosscup	18.1	Stan Stumpf	12.0			Clifford Wells		
1956-57	15-9	9-5		Calvin Grosscup	20.1	Calvin Grosscup	10.7			Clifford Wells		
1957-58	8-15	3-11		Vic Klinker	17.2	Louis Anderson	12.6			Clifford Wells		
1958-59	13-11	6-8		Vic Klinker	15.8	Vic Klinker	10.0			Clifford Wells		
1959-60	13-11	8-6		Jack Ardon	15.1	Jack Ardon	14.2			Clifford Wells		
1960-61	11-13	6-8		Jim Kerwin	20.5	Jack Ardon	16.3			Clifford Wells		
1961-62	12-10	6-8		Jim Kerwin	21.1	Jack Ardon	14.9			Clifford Wells		
1962-63	6-16	4-10		Jim Kerwin	23.0	Bob Davidson	14.0			Clifford Wells	254-171	.598
1963-64	1-22	1-13		Dale Gott	18.0	Bob Davidson	10.9			Ted Lenhardt	1-22	.043
1964-65	3-22	2-14		Al Andrews	18.9	George Fisher	7.3			Ralph Pedersen		
1965-66	9-16	5-11		Al Andrews	18.9	Craig Spitzer	8.0	O.J. Lacour	60	Ralph Pedersen		
1966-67	14-10			Al Andrews	18.3	Dan Moeser	7.4	Bill Fitzgerald	85	Ralph Pedersen		
1967-68	12-12			Johnny Arthurs	19.4	J. Arthurs, Dan Moeser	6.7	Terry Habig	34	Ralph Pedersen		
1968-69	12-14			Johnny Arthurs	25.6	Harold Sylvester	8.5	Terry Habig	39	Ralph Pedersen		
1969-70	5-18			John Sutter	24.3	John Sutter	11.8	Ned Reese	77	Ralph Pedersen		
1970-71	8-18			John Sutter	19.4	John Sutter	9.7	Rick Miller	70	Ralph Pedersen	63-110	.364
1971-72	8-18			Jeff Morris	20.0	Rick Miller	7.0	Bruce Bolyard	70	Dick Longo		
1972-73	12-14			John Kardzionak	18.4	Rick Miller	7.5	Bruce Bolyard	93	Dick Longo	20-32	.385
1973-74	12-14			Phil Hicks	20.0	Phil Hicks	12.8	T. Beaulieu, B. Bolyard	60	Charles Moir		
1974-75	16-10			Phil Hicks	22.7	Phil Hicks	12.4	Tom Hicks	101	Charles Moir		
1975-76	18-9			Phil Hicks	20.6	Jeff Cummings	11.1	Tom Hicks	208	Charles Moir	46-33	.582
1976-77	10-17	3-3		Jeff Cummings	19.2	Jeff Cummings	12.0	Pierre Gaudin	98	Roy Danforth		
1977-78	5-22	1-11		Pierre Gaudin	13.8	Carlos Zuniga	6.3	Craig Harris	95	Roy Danforth		
1978-79	8-19	2-8		Bobby Jones	12.0	Micah Blunt	6.8	Joe Holston	96	Roy Danforth		
1979-80	10-17	3-9		Paul Thompson	15.0	Paul Thompson	8.2	Joe Holston	119	Roy Danforth		
1980-81	12-15	4-8		Paul Thompson	18.7	Paul Thompson	9.4	Joe Holston	86	Roy Danforth	45-90	.333
1981-82	19-9	8-4	NIT QUARTERFINALS	John "Hot Rod" Williams	14.8	Paul Thompson	7.4	Daryl Moreau	141	Ned Fowler		
1982-83	19-12	7-5	NIT FIRST ROUND	Paul Thompson	17.5	Paul Thompson	7.4	Daryl Moreau	117	Ned Fowler		
1983-84	17-11	7-7		John "Hot Rod" Williams	19.4	John "Hot Rod" Williams	7.9	Gary Delph	82	Ned Fowler		
1984-85	15-13	6-8		John "Hot Rod" Williams	17.8	John "Hot Rod" Williams	7.8	David Dominique	91	Ned Fowler	70-45	.609
1985-86	no team											
1986-87	no team											
1987-88	no team											
1988-89	no team											
1989-90	4-24	1-13		Michael Christian	19.3	Anthony Reed	8.4	Greg Gary	158	Perry Clark		
1990-91	15-13	7-7		Anthony Reed	16.0	Anthony Reed	7.9	Greg Gary	111	Perry Clark		
1991-92	22-9	8-4	NCAA SECOND ROUND	Kim Lewis	15.4	Anthony Reed	6.5	Pointer Williams	120	Perry Clark		
1992-93	22-9	9-3	NCAA SECOND ROUND	Anthony Reed	15.7	Anthony Reed	6.8	Pointer Williams	167	Perry Clark		
1993-94	18-11	7-5	NIT SECOND ROUND	Jerald Honeycutt	15.3	Jerald Honeycutt	6.7	Pointer Williams	105	Perry Clark		
1994-95	23-10	7-5	NCAA SECOND ROUND	Jerald Honeycutt	17.3	Rayshard Allen	7.8	LeVeldro Simmons	131	Perry Clark		
1995-96	22-10	9-5	NIT THIRD PLACE	Jerald Honeycutt	18.0	Jerald Honeycutt	7.2	Jerald Honeycutt	120	Perry Clark		
1996-97	20-11	11-3	NIT FIRST ROUND	Jerald Honeycutt	19.9	Jerald Honeycutt	6.5	Jerald Honeycutt	131	Perry Clark		
1997-98	7-22	2-14		Byron Mouton	15.3	Chris Owens	5.0	P.J. Franklin	53	Perry Clark		
1998-99	12-15	6-10		Ledaryl Billingsley	11.0	Ledaryl Billingsley	6.8	Waitari Marsh	92	Perry Clark		
1999-2000	20-11	8-8	NIT FIRST ROUND	Sterling Davis	13.4	Morris Jordan	5.5	Waitari Marsh	132	Perry Clark	185-145	.561
2000-01	9-21	2-14		Ledaryl Billingsley	18.0	Ledaryl Billingsley	9.2	Brandon Spann	4.8	Shawn Finney		
2001-02	14-15	5-11		Brandon Brown	14.8	Brandon Brown	7.4	Waitari Marsh	3.6	Shawn Finney		
2002-03	16-15	8-8		Waitari Marsh	14.6	Brandon Brown	7.4	Waitari Marsh	3.3	Shawn Finney		
2003-04	11-17	4-12		Quincy Davis	10.6	Vytas Tatarunas	7.2	Wayne Tinsley	3.4	Shawn Finney		
2004-05	10-18	4-12		Quincy Davis	13.7	Quincy Davis	6.1	Marcus Kinzer	4.6	Shawn Finney	60-86	.411
2005-06	12-17	6-8		Quincy Davis	13.1	Quincy Davis	5.8	Andrew Garcia	3.2	Dave Dickerson		
2006-07	17-13	9-7		David Gomez	13.5	David Gomez	5.8	Kevin Sims	3.4	Dave Dickerson		
2007-08	17-15	6-10		David Gomez	14.4	David Gomez	6.2	Kevin Sims	3.8	Dave Dickerson		
2008-09	14-17	7-9		Kevin Sims	13.0	Robinson Louisme	6.9	Kevin Sims	4.0	Dave Dickerson	60-62	.492

Cumulative totals listed when per game averages not available.

ESPN 66 SAGARIN

TULSA

What do Nolan Richardson, Tubby Smith and Bill Self have in common? As any Golden Hurricane fan knows, they all made stops in Tulsa before winning a national title elsewhere. The Hurricane's recent coaching lineage, which also includes J.D. Barnett, Steve Robinson, Buzz Peterson, John Phillips and now Doug Wojcik, is a huge reason why Tulsa ranks among the Southwest's best teams of the past three decades, with 19 postseason trips since 1981.

BEST TEAM: 1999-2000 No pain, no gain. The Golden Hurricane's four regular-season losses (three to Fresno State) all came on the last possession, which toughened them up for a magical Tournament run. Despite starting just one player over 6'5", Self's balanced squad blew through UNLV, Cincinnati and Miami before going down in the Elite Eight to North Carolina, 59-55.

BEST PLAYER: G SHEA SEALS (1993-97) Tulsa had never won a Tournament game before Seals arrived. All the shooting guard did was lead the team to four straight Big Dances, including Sweet 16 appearances in 1994 and '95. He also finished as the school's all-time leading scorer while playing airtight defense. Almost 10 years after his final game, Seals kept his promise to his mom and received his degree from Tulsa in 2006.

BEST COACH: NOLAN RICHARDSON (1980-85) Tulsa took a chance on Richardson after he led Western Texas to a national junior college title in 1980, and reaped the benefits immediately by winning the 1981 NIT title over Syracuse. Three NCAA Tournament trips and a second NIT bid followed. Richardson donned polka-dot shirts and cowboy boots, and developed the up-tempo offense and pressure defense that would become his trademark. In 1994, he used it to guide Arkansas to the national title.

GAME FOR THE AGES: Tubby's team nearly blew its chance of making the 1994 Tournament by losing in the Missouri Valley tournament semis, but snuck in as a No. 12 seed. After beating UCLA in the first round, the Hurricane rallied from a 13-point first-half deficit to beat No. 4-seed Oklahoma State, 82-80. Point guard Alvin "Pooh" Williamson played a nearly perfect game, scoring 20 points and committing zero turnovers. Leading by one, teammate Lou Dawkins hit a three-pointer with 8.6 seconds left to seal Tulsa's first Sweet 16 appearance. The win avenged a 73-61 regular-season loss to the Cowboys.

HEARTBREAKER: In the 2003 Tournament, Tulsa appeared headed to its fourth Sweet 16 in ten seasons, leading Big Ten champion Wisconsin by 13 with 4:08 left. But the Badgers closed the game on a 16-2 run, capped by Freddie Owens' three-pointer with one tick left. The Hurricane actually had time for one more miracle play, but the game ended when Jarius Glenn stepped over the line on his inbounds pass.

FIERCEST RIVAL: In the annual battle for the Mayor's Cup, Tulsa leads crosstown foe Oral Roberts, 29–16, an edge made all the more bitter for Golden Eagles fans by the fact that their rival hired Bill Self away from ORU in 1997. Each victory invariably sets off a spirited postgame celebration by the winning team and their fans, in which the cup is hoisted high and passed proudly from player to player.

Alvin "Pooh" Williamson played a nearly perfect game, scoring 20 points and committing zero turnovers.

FANFARE AND HOOPLA: You won't find two crazier college basketball fans than Ken Penn and David Bales—better known as Mad Dog and Coach. Penn has been coming to games since 1977, and wears a rubber snout and barks at opponents. Meanwhile, Bales dresses up in a suit and tie, screams at officials and paces the Tulsa sideline.

FAN FAVORITE: G RONDIE TURNER (1981-84) He scored just 16 career points, but no one got the crowd fired up like this scrappy guard and ordained minister.

FIRST-ROUND PRO PICKS

1969	**Bobby Smith**, San Diego (6)
1971	**Dana Lewis**, Philadelphia (12)
1982	**Paul Pressey**, Milwaukee (20)
1985	**Steve Harris**, Houston (19)

PROFILE

University of Tulsa, Tulsa, OK
Founded: 1894
Enrollment: 4,192 (3,049 undergraduate)
Colors: Old gold, royal blue, crimson and yellow
Nickname: Golden Hurricane
Current arena: Donald W. Reynolds Center, opened in 1998 (8,355)
Previous: Tulsa Convention Center, 1977-98 (8,900); Fairgrounds Pavilion, 1950-77 (6,311); Fairgrounds Armory, 1948-50 (NA); Central High, Rogers High, Webster High, 1931-47 (N/A)

First game: 1907
All-time record: 1,262-1,026 (.552)
Total weeks in AP Top 20/25: 82
Current conference: Conference USA (2005-)
Conference titles:
Missouri Valley: 6 (1955 [tie], '84 [tie], '85, '87, '94, '95)
WAC: 3 (1999 [tie], 2000, '02 [tie])
Conference tournament titles:
Missouri Valley: 4 (1982, '84, '86, '96)
WAC: 1 (2003)
NCAA Tournament appearances: 14
Sweet 16s (since 1975): 3

NIT appearances: 9
Semifinals: 2
Titles: 2 (1981, 2001)

TOP 5

G	**Willie Biles** (1971-74)
G	**Steve Harris** (1981-85)
G	**Shea Seals** (1993-97)
F	**Bob Patterson** (1951-55)
F	**Paul Pressey** (1980-82)

RECORDS	GAME		SEASON		CAREER	
POINTS	48	Willie Biles, vs. St. Cloud (Dec. 13, 1973); Willie Biles, vs. Wichita State (March 3, 1973)	788	Willie Biles (1972-73)	2,288	Shea Seals (1993-97)
POINTS PER GAME			30.3	Willie Biles (1972-73)	22.7	Willie Biles (1971-74)
REBOUNDS	26	Dana Lewis, vs. MacMurray (Dec. 27, 1969)	370	Bob Patterson (1954-55)	1,211	Michael Ruffin (1995-99)
ASSISTS	15	Ricky Ross, vs. Indiana State (March 1, 1984)	201	Greg Harrington (2000-01)	551	Greg Harrington (1998-2002)

SEASON REVIEW

SEASON	W-L	CONF.	SCORING	COACH	RECORD	
1907-18	*34-26*		*No team 1909-13*			
1918-19	5-3			Francis Schmidt		
1919-20	16-3			Francis Schmidt		
1920-21	18-2			Francis Schmidt		
1921-22	14-4			Francis Schmidt	73-26	.737
1922-23	1-3			Howard Acher		
1923-24	2-1			Howard Acher		
1924-25	13-8			Howard Acher	16-12	.571
1925-26	7-10			J.B. Miller		
1926-27	3-6			J.B. Miller		
1927-28	2-12			J.B. Miller		
1928-29	2-11			J.B. Miller		
1929-30	2-6			J.B. Miller	16-45	.262
1930-31	10-4			Oliver Hodge		
1931-32	10-7			Oliver Hodge	20-11	.645
1932-33	11-6			Chet Benefiel		
1933-34	6-8			Chet Benefiel		
1934-35	6-10	4-8		Chet Benefiel		
1935-36	6-14	3-9		Chet Benefiel		
1936-37	9-9	4-8		Chet Benefiel		
1937-38	12-10	8-6		Chet Benefiel		
1938-39	15-8	8-6		Chet Benefiel	65-65	.500

SEAS.	W-L	CONF.	POSTSEASON	SCORING		REBOUNDS		ASSISTS		COACH	RECORD	
1939-40	12-15	5-7								H.B. Ryon		
1940-41	12-9	7-5								Jack Sterrett	12-9	.571
1941-42	3-13	3-7								H.B. Ryon	15-28	.349
1942-43	0-10	0-10								Mike Milligan	0-10	.000
1943-44	5-3									Woody West	5-3	.625
1944-45	4-8			Barney White	9.3					Paul Alyea	4-8	.333
1945-46	6-12	3-9								Don Shields		
1946-47	5-19	3-9								Don Shields	11-31	.262
1947-48	7-16	2-8		Gerald Carrens	8.2					John Garrison		
1948-49	4-20	0-10		Neil Ridley	10.5					John Garrison	11-36	.234
1949-50	12-11	3-9		Neil Ridley	10.3					Clarence Iba		
1950-51	10-17	4-10		Neil Ridley	10.7					Clarence Iba		
1951-52	14-10	5-5		Dick Nunneley	15.8					Clarence Iba		
1952-53	15-10	5-5	NIT FIRST ROUND	Dick Nunneley	13.1	Warren Shackelford	6.4			Clarence Iba		
1953-54	15-14	5-5		Dick Nunneley	17.3					Clarence Iba		
1954-55	21-7	8-2	NCAA REGIONAL SEMIFINALS	Bob Patterson	27.6	Bob Patterson	13.2			Clarence Iba		
1955-56	16-10	4-8		Junior Born	14.6	Clester Harrington	6.7			Clarence Iba		
1956-57	8-17	5-9		Jerry Evans	12.5	Clester Harrington	10.0			Clarence Iba		
1957-58	7-19	4-10		Roger Wendel	17.5	Bob Goodall	11.6			Clarence Iba		
1958-59	10-15	2-12		Roger Wendel	18.8	Bob Goodall	10.6			Clarence Iba		
1959-60	9-17	5-9		David Voss	15.2	Gene Estes	9.0			Clarence Iba	137-147	.482
1960-61	8-17	2-10		David Voss	16.6	Gene Estes	14.3			Joe Swank		
1961-62	7-19	4-8		Jim King	18.4	Jim King	8.5			Joe Swank		
1962-63	17-8	5-7		Bill Kusleika	17.1	Bill Kusleika	8.7			Joe Swank		
1963-64	10-15	2-10		Bill Kusleika	22.6	Bill Kusleika	9.7			Joe Swank		
1964-65	14-11	7-7		Rick Park	18.4	Herman Callands	11.2			Joe Swank		
1965-66	16-13	6-8		Julian Hammond	16.4	Julian Hammond	8.8			Joe Swank		
1966-67	19-8	10-4	NIT FIRST ROUND	Eldridge Webb	18.0	Bobby Smith	10.4			Joe Swank		
1967-68	11-12	5-11		Rob Washington	15.3	Doug Robinson	9.7			Joe Swank	102-103	.498
1968-69	19-8	11-5	NIT FIRST ROUND	Bobby Smith	24.5	Rob Washington	10.3			Ken Hayes		
1969-70	15-11	8-8		Ron Carson	20.5	Dana Lewis	11.9			Ken Hayes		
1970-71	17-9	8-6		Dana Lewis	23.3	Dana Lewis	13.5			Ken Hayes		
1971-72	15-11	5-9		Steve Bracey	24.1	Joe Voskuhl	10.4			Ken Hayes		
1972-73	18-8	10-4		Willie Biles	30.3	Joe Voskuhl	10.9			Ken Hayes		
1973-74	18-8	7-6		Willie Biles	24.7	Ken Smith	8.3			Ken Hayes		
1974-75	15-14	5-9		Ken Smith	20.9	Ken Smith	11.0			Ken Hayes	117-69	.629
1975-76	9-18	4-8		Leon Alvoid	14.9	Dan O'Leary	7.0			Jim King		
1976-77	6-21	3-9		Teko Wynder	17.7	Dan O'Leary	7.0	Jack Dobbins	3.4	Jim King		
1977-78	9-18	7-9		Terry Sims	14.7	Lester Johnson	9.0	John Gibson	2.9	Jim King		
1978-79	13-14	7-9		Terry Sims	13.7	Billy Keys	7.1	John Gibson	3.3	Jim King		
1979-80	8-19	5-11		Russell Sublet	16.6	Bob Stevenson	9.8	Russell Sublet	2.5	Jim King[a]	43-83	.341
1980-81	26-7	11-5	NIT CHAMPION	Greg Stewart	15.5	David Brown, G. Stewart	6.9	Paul Pressey	5.2	Nolan Richardson		
1981-82	24-6	12-4	NCAA SECOND ROUND	Paul Pressey	13.2	P. Pressey, G. Stewart	6.4	Mike Anderson	4.4	Nolan Richardson		
1982-83	19-12	11-7	NIT FIRST ROUND	Ricky Ross	18.5	Ricky Ross	5.6	Mike Smith	4.6	Nolan Richardson		
1983-84	27-4	13-3	NCAA SECOND ROUND	Steve Harris	21.1	Herb Johnson	7.6	Ricky Ross	6.2	Nolan Richardson		
1984-85	23-8	12-4	NCAA FIRST ROUND	Steve Harris	23.6	Herb Johnson	9.5	Herb Johnson	2.9	Nolan Richardson	119-37	.763
1985-86	23-9	10-6	NCAA FIRST ROUND	Tracy Moore	16.8	David Moss	6.4	Byron Boudreaux	4.9	J.D. Barnett		
1986-87	22-8	11-3	NCAA FIRST ROUND	David Moss	17.8	Brian Rahilly	7.3	Byron Boudreaux	5.9	J.D. Barnett		
1987-88	8-20	4-10		Tracy Moore	21.3	Ray Wingard	7.4	Tracy Moore	2.3	J.D. Barnett		
1988-89	18-13	10-4		Lamont Randolph	13.2	Ray Wingard	8.3	Jamal West	4.1	J.D. Barnett		
1989-90	17-13	9-5	NIT FIRST ROUND	Marcell Gordon	12.9	Lamont Randolph	8.0	Reggie Shields	4.9	J.D. Barnett		
1990-91	18-12	10-6	NIT FIRST ROUND	Marcell Gordon	16.7	Wade Jenkins	6.3	Reggie Shields	5.5	J.D. Barnett	106-75	.586
1991-92	17-13	12-6		Mark Morse	14.9	Gary Collier	5.6	Mark Morse	5.1	Tubby Smith		
1992-93	15-14	10-8		Mark Morse	17.4	Jeff Malham	5.8	Mark Morse	4.6	Tubby Smith		
1993-94	23-8	15-3	NCAA REGIONAL SEMIFINALS	Gary Collier	22.9	Gary Collier	6.7	Lou Dawkins	4.6	Tubby Smith		
1994-95	24-8	15-3	NCAA REGIONAL SEMIFINALS	Shea Seals	18.8	Shea Seals	6.9	Shea Seals	3.9	Tubby Smith	79-43	.648
1995-96	22-8	12-6	NCAA FIRST ROUND	Shea Seals	17.1	Michael Ruffin	7.7	Dewayne Bonner	4.9	Steve Robinson		
1996-97	24-10	12-4	NCAA SECOND ROUND	Shea Seals	20.7	Michael Ruffin	10.0	Rod Thompson	3.5	Steve Robinson	46-18	.719
1997-98	19-12	9-5		Rod Thompson	15.0	Michael Ruffin	9.5	Rod Thompson	3.7	Bill Self		
1998-99	23-10	9-5	NCAA SECOND ROUND	Brandon Kurtz	11.9	Michael Ruffin	10.4	Eric Coley	2.6	Bill Self		
1999-2000	32-5	12-2	NCAA REGIONAL FINALS	David Shelton	13.5	Brandon Kurtz	7.0	Eric Coley	3.4	Bill Self	74-27	.733
2000-01	26-11	10-6	NIT CHAMPION	Kevin Johnson	13.9	Kevin Johnson	7.0	Greg Harrington	5.4	Buzz Peterson	26-11	.703
2001-02	27-7	15-3	NCAA SECOND ROUND	Kevin Johnson	14.5	Charlie Davis	6.7	Greg Harrington	5.2	John Phillips		
2002-03	23-10	12-6	NCAA SECOND ROUND	Jason Parker	15.4	K. Johnson, C. Davis	7.0	Jason Parker	4.0	John Phillips		
2003-04	9-20	5-13		Jason Parker	16.9	Jarius Glenn	6.1	Jason Parker	2.9	John Phillips		
2004-05	9-20	5-13		Jarius Glenn	17.1	J. Glenn, G. Teichmann	6.2	Jarius Glenn	3.4	John Phillips[b]	61-42	.592
2005-06	11-17	6-8		Anthony Price	11.4	Charles Ramsdell	6.2	Brett McDade	2.6	Doug Wojcik		
2006-07	20-11	9-7		Rod Earls	11.2	Ben Uzoh	5.0	Mark Hill	3.0	Doug Wojcik		
2007-08	25-14	8-8		Ben Uzoh	15.6	Jerome Jordan	7.9	Brett McDade	3.1	Doug Wojcik		
2008-09	25-11	12-4	NIT SECOND ROUND	Ben Uzoh	14.0	Jerome Jordan	8.6	Ben Uzoh	3.6	Doug Wojcik	81-53	.604

[a] Jim King (6-12) and Bill Franey (2-7) both coached during the 1979-80 season.

[b] John Phillips (2-5) and Alvin Williamson (7-15) both coached during the 2004-05 season.

ESPN 321 SAGARIN

UC DAVIS

For eight decades, the Aggies put together just one 20-win season. Then coach Bob Williams came along in 1990 and they did it five times in eight years. He even turned UC Davis into D2 champions in his final season at the school. The Aggies, now a member of the Big West, could use another dose of that transforming magic—they have yet to achieve a winning season since officially joining D1 in 2004.

BEST TEAM: 1997-98 Behind six seniors and a swarming defense, UCD rode a 22-game winning streak to the D2 title. The Aggies held West Texas A&M to 30 points below its season scoring average in the quarterfinals, beat St. Rose (N.Y.) by 12 in the semis, then thwarted a Kentucky Wesleyan comeback in the title game, thanks to clutch play from Dante Ross and Jason Cox.

BEST PLAYER: G DANTE ROSS (1996-99) His career numbers don't scream superstar: just 12 ppg and 4.3 apg. But the two-time conference player of the year made everyone around him better, spreading the stats and playing ferocious defense. The proof is in the 1998 championship.

BEST COACH: BOB WILLIAMS (1990-98) The best testament to the power of his defensive-minded system? After Williams left UCD for the head coaching job at D1 UC Santa Barbara, the Aggies barely lost a beat under Brian Fogel, qualifying for the 1999 and 2000 D2 NCAA regional semis.

GAME FOR THE AGES: In the 1998 D2 title game, six-time champ Kentucky Wesleyan erased the Aggies' 10-point, second-half lead with less than a minute to go. But with :39 left, UCD's Jason Cox hit an uncharacteristic three from the top of the arc, giving his team the lead. Four Ross free throws later, the Aggies were celebrating their first championship, 83-77.

FIERCEST RIVAL: Even though UC Davis has a new D1 identity, its chief nemesis and tormentor remains the same: Pacific. The Tigers have beaten the Aggies 47 straight times and hold a 75–10 lead in a series that dates back to 1916-17.

SEASON REVIEW

SEAS.	W-L	CONF.	COACH	SEAS.	W-L	CONF.	COACH
1911-48	*190-326*	*9-54 between 1924-25 and '28-29*		1961-62	6-17		Jim Sells
1948-49	13-12		George Stromgren	1962-63	5-15		Jim Sells
1949-50	15-8		George Stromgren	1963-64	7-15		Joe Carlson
1950-51	2-22		George Stromgren	1964-65	13-10		Joe Carlson
1951-52	13-10		Carl Boyer	1965-66	15-7		Joe Carlson
1952-53	7-16		George Stromgren	1966-67	21-7		Joe Carlson
1953-54	3-17		George Stromgren	1967-68	16-11		Bob Hamilton
1954-55	2-16		George Stromgren	1968-69	18-10		Bob Hamilton
1955-56	3-17		George Stromgren	1969-70	15-10		Bob Hamilton
1956-57	4-18		George Stromgren	1970-71	9-16		Bob Hamilton
1957-58	5-17		H. Schmalenberger	1971-72	11-14		Bob Hamilton
1958-59	5-17		Jim Sells	1972-73	14-12		Bob Hamilton
1959-60	3-22		Jim Sells	1973-74	12-13		Bob Hamilton
1960-61	4-17		Jim Sells	1974-75	16-12		Bob Hamilton

SEAS.	W-L	CONF.	SCORING		COACH	RECORD	
1975-76	18-10		Mark Olson	543	Bob Hamilton		
1976-77	14-12		Audwin Thomas	427	Bob Hamilton		
1977-78	19-10		Audwin Thomas	557	Bob Hamilton		
1978-79	12-14		Mike Lien	529	Bob Hamilton		
1979-80	9-18		Jim Swan	418	Bob Hamilton		
1980-81	15-12		Preston Neumayr	366	Bob Hamilton		
1981-82	8-16		Preston Neumayr	413	Bob Hamilton		
1982-83	8-19		Preston Neumayr	575	Bob Hamilton		
1983-84	13-13		Angelo Rivers	21.3	Bob Hamilton		
1984-85	13-15		Robert Rose	544	Bob Hamilton		
1985-86	17-11		Pete Buchwald	380	Bob Hamilton		
1986-87	12-16		Parrish Johnson	385	Bob Hamilton		
1987-88	14-15		Randy DeBortoli	606	Bob Hamilton		
1988-89	16-13		Marc Jones	494	Bob Hamilton	299-292	.506
1989-90	11-16		Tom Neumayr	430	Lonnie Williams	11-16	.407
1990-91	20-8		Richard Saunders	453	Bob Williams		
1991-92	19-11		Richard Saunders	513	Bob Williams		
1992-93	13-14		Evan Jones	309	Bob Williams		
1993-94	11-15		Bruce Heicke	270	Bob Williams		
1994-95	20-11		Brad Foss	432	Bob Williams		
1995-96	24-6		Justis Durkee	338	Bob Williams		
1996-97	20-9		Dedrique Taylor	323	Bob Williams		
1997-98	31-2	◆	Dante Ross	397	Bob Williams	158-76	.675
1998-99	22-6		Dante Ross	14.5	Brian Fogel		
1999-2000	22-7		Jason Cox	13.9	Brian Fogel		
2000-01	18-9		Jess McElree	12.2	Brian Fogel		
2001-02	15-12		Jess McElree	15.3	Brian Fogel		
2002-03	12-15		Dominic Callori	18.5	Brian Fogel	89-49	.645
2003-04	18-9		Ryan Moore	16.3	Gary Stewart		
2004-05	11-17		Ryan Moore	15.7	Gary Stewart		
2005-06	8-20		Rommel Marentez	12.7	Gary Stewart		
2006-07	5-23		Thomas Juillerat	12.8	Gary Stewart		
2007-08	9-22	2-14	Vince Oliver	12.2	Gary Stewart		
2008-09	13-19	7-9	Vince Oliver	15.4	Gary Stewart	64-110	.368

Cumulative totals listed when per game averages not available.

◆ Division II championship

PROFILE

University of California, Davis, Davis, CA
Founded: 1908
Enrollment: 31,426 (24,209 undergraduate)
Colors: Yale blue and gold
Nickname: Aggies
Current arena: The Pavilion, opened as the Recreation Hall in 1977 (7,600)
First game: Jan. 20, 1911
All-time record: 957-1,149 (.454)
Total weeks in AP Top 20/25: 0

Current conference: Big West (2007-)
Conference titles: 0
Conference tournament titles: 0
NCAA Tournament appearances: 0
NIT appearances: 0

TOP 5

G **Dante Ross** (1996-99)
G **Audwin Thomas** (1975-79)
F **Alan Budde** (1965-68)
F/C **Jason Cox** (1996-2000)
C **Mike Lien** (1977-79)

RECORDS

	GAME		SEASON		CAREER	
POINTS	39	Mike Lien, vs. Cal State Stanislaus (Feb. 17, 1979)	606	Randy DeBortoli (1987-88)	1,821	Audwin Thomas (1975-79)
POINTS PER GAME			21.3	Preston Neumayr (1982-83)	17.8	Mike Lien (1977-79)
REBOUNDS	24	Dominic Callori, vs. Sonoma State (Feb. 16, 2001)	365	Mike Lien (1978-79)	952	Alan Budde (1965-68)
ASSISTS	13	Gus Argenal, vs. UC San Diego (Jan. 16, 2004); Matt Cordova, vs. Chico State (Feb. 15, 1991)	166	Dante Ross (1997-98)	467	Angelo Rivers (1982-86)

ESPN 176 SAGARIN

UC IRVINE

Here's a topic of discussion for your next March Madness party: the best program never to make the Big Dance. Put the Anteaters near the top of that list. Since joining D1 in 1977, they have achieved 13 winning seasons and even won back-to-back Big West regular-season titles in 2000-01 and '01-02 (the second was shared)—but have only four NIT berths to show for it.

BEST TEAM: 1981-82 Before coach Bill Mulligan and two-time All-America Kevin Magee arrived from Saddleback Junior College, the school's arena was unofficially nicknamed the Library (as in: It's a good place to get some studying done). But Magee's power game and Mulligan's fast-paced offense woke things up in a hurry. In the duo's second season, the Anteaters made the NIT for the first time in school history.

BEST PLAYER: C Kevin Magee (1980-82) How did this two-time Pacific Coast Athletic Association Player of the Year manage to shoot 65.6% while averaging 26.3 ppg during his D1 career? The big man rarely took a shot outside 10 feet, largely because he was too busy running the floor and converting easy buckets.

BEST COACH: Bill Mulligan (1980-91) The wisecracking Chicago native knew how to entertain. In his debut, the Anteaters set the school's scoring record by beating VMI, 125-96. And while the NCAA Tourney eluded him, his teams routinely ranked among the nation's top 10 in scoring.

GAME FOR THE AGES: On Feb. 15, 1986, the Anteaters became the first PCAA school to beat UNLV in the Thomas & Mack Center since it opened in 1983. Forward Johnny Rogers scored 41 points on the Armon Gilliam-led Rebels in a 99-92 victory.

FIERCEST RIVAL: When UC Irvine meets fellow Big West member Cal State Fullerton, O.C. bragging rights are on the line. Through 88 games, the Anteaters lead the series 47-41. The series was at its best in the early '80s when the media helped build up the rivalry between hotshot coaches Mulligan and George McQuarn. (Truth was, the two *liked* each other.)

SEASON REVIEW

SEAS.	W-L	CONF.		SCORING		COACH	RECORD	
1965-66	15-11			Dale Finney	15.3	Danny Rogers		
1966-67	15-11			Dale Finney	14.0	Danny Rogers	30-22	.577
1967-68	20-8			Mike Heckman	19.5	Dick Davis		
1968-69	19-9			Jeff Cunningham	21.0	Dick Davis	39-17	.696
1969-70	17-9			Jeff Cunningham	19.5	Tim Tift		
1970-71	16-10			Phil Rhyne	18.8	Tim Tift		
1971-72	16-12			Phil Rhyne	16.1	Tim Tift		
1972-73	15-13			Dave Baker	15.3	Tim Tift		
1973-74	14-12			Jerry Maras	16.5	Tim Tift		
1974-75	16-11			Jerry Maras	16.1	Tim Tift		
1975-76	14-12			Steve Cleveland	15.0	Tim Tift		
1976-77	10-17			Louis Stephens	14.4	Tim Tift		
1977-78	8-17	2-12		Wayne Smith	20.4	Tim Tift		
1978-79	9-17	3-11		Steve McGuire	14.8	Tim Tift		
1979-80	9-18	1-13		Robbie Beal	14.3	Tim Tift	144-148	.493
1980-81	17-10	9-5		Kevin Magee	27.5	Bill Mulligan		
1981-82	23-7	10-4	■	Kevin Magee	25.2	Bill Mulligan		
1982-83	16-12	8-8		George Turner	15.6	Bill Mulligan		
1983-84	19-10	14-4		Ben McDonald	15.6	Bill Mulligan		
1984-85	13-17	8-10		Johnny Rogers	21.7	Bill Mulligan		
1985-86	17-13	12-6	■	Johnny Rogers	21.2	Bill Mulligan		
1986-87	14-14	9-9		Scott Brooks	23.8	Bill Mulligan		
1987-88	16-14	9-9		Wayne Engelstad	23.6	Bill Mulligan		
1988-89	12-17	8-10		Mike Doktorczyk	15.9	Bill Mulligan		
1989-90	5-23	3-15		Ricky Butler	13.8	Bill Mulligan		
1990-91	11-19	6-12		Jeff Herdman	18.1	Bill Mulligan	163-156	.511
1991-92	7-22	3-15		Jeff Von Lutzow	12.5	Rod Baker		
1992-93	6-21	4-14		Jeff Von Lutzow	16.5	Rod Baker		
1993-94	10-20	4-14		Chris Brown	17.4	Rod Baker		
1994-95	13-16	6-12		Kevin Simmons	14.9	Rod Baker		
1995-96	15-12	11-7		Brian Keefe	16.4	Rod Baker		
1996-97	1-25	1-15		Lamarr Parker	13.4	Rod Baker	52-116	.310
1997-98	9-18	6-10		Adam Stetson	12.1	Pat Douglass		
1998-99	6-20	2-14		Jerry Green	12.8	Pat Douglass		
1999-2000	14-14	7-9		Jerry Green	15.6	Pat Douglass		
2000-01	25-5	15-1	■	Jerry Green	19.0	Pat Douglass		
2001-02	21-11	13-5	■	Jerry Green	20.3	Pat Douglass		
2002-03	20-9	13-5		Jordan Harris	12.7	Pat Douglass		
2003-04	11-17	6-12		Adam Parada	12.3	Pat Douglass		
2004-05	16-13	8-10		Ross Schraeder	12.9	Pat Douglass		
2005-06	16-13	10-4		Ross Schraeder	13.1	Pat Douglass		
2006-07	15-18	6-8		Patrick Sanders	11.9	Pat Douglass		
2007-08	18-16	9-7		Patrick Sanders	15.1	Pat Douglass		
2008-09	12-19	8-8		Eric Wise	15.5	Pat Douglass	183-173	.514

■ NIT appearance

PROFILE

University of California, Irvine, Irvine, CA
Founded: 1963
Enrollment: 27,631 (22,122 undergraduate)
Colors: Blue and gold
Nickname: Anteaters
Current arena: Bren Events Center, opened in 1987 (5,000)
First game: Dec. 1, 1965
All-time record: 611-632 (.492)
Total weeks in AP Top 20/25: 0

Current conference: Big West (1977-)
Conference titles:
Big West: 2 (2001, '02 [tie])
Conference tournament titles: 0
NCAA Tournament appearances: 0
NIT appearances: 4

TOP 5

G **Scott Brooks** (1985-87)
G **Jerry Green** (1998-2002)
F **Ben McDonald** (1980-84)
F **Tod Murphy** (1982-86)
C **Kevin Magee** (1980-82)

RECORDS

RECORDS	GAME		SEASON		CAREER	
POINTS	46	Kevin Magee, vs. Loyola Marymount (Dec. 15, 1981)	743	Kevin Magee (1980-81)	1,993	Jerry Green (1998-2002)
POINTS PER GAME			27.5	Kevin Magee (1980-81)	26.3	Kevin Magee (1980-82)
REBOUNDS	25	Kevin Magee, vs. Long Beach State (Jan. 30, 1982)	353	Kevin Magee (1981-82)	926	Dave Baker (1971-75)
ASSISTS	17	Raimonds Miglinieks, vs. UNLV (Feb. 2, 1995)	245	Raimonds Miglinieks (1994-95)	475	Raimonds Miglinieks (1994-96)

ESPN 2 SAGARIN

UCLA

The banners don't lie, and many consider the Bruins, winners of 11 national titles, the greatest program in the history of college hoops. The legacy was forged by one of the game's most influential coaches, John Wooden, and two of the best big men ever, Lew Alcindor (Kareem Abdul-Jabbar) and Bill Walton.

BEST TEAM: 1972-73 The Walton Gang went 30–0, winning 26 games by double digits. Keith Wilkes (14.8 ppg), Larry Farmer (12.2 ppg) and Greg Lee buoyed Big Bill, who averaged 20.4 points and grabbed a school-record 506 rebounds. Walton's coup de grace came in the NCAA Final, when he scored 44 points by going 21-for-22 from the floor in an 87-66 waxing of Memphis. The Bruins' seventh straight title extended their winning streak to 75 games.

BEST PLAYER: C Lew Alcindor (1966-69) The 7'2" future Kareem Abdul-Jabbar was the only man to be named Final Four Most Outstanding Player three times, leading the Bruins to three national titles. He was so a dominant under the basket that the NCAA banned the dunk before his junior season. He famously avenged a 71-69 midseason loss to Houston in 1968 by scoring 19 points in a 101-69 Final Four victory against the Cougars.

BEST COACH: John Wooden (1948-75) More high-minded philosopher than master strategist, Wooden blended talented players in a selfless, free-flowing system. The result: 10 national titles, 16 conference championships, four 30–0 seasons and the all-time record for consecutive wins at 88.

GAME FOR THE AGES: In the 1995 NCAA Tournament second round, No. 1-seed UCLA trailed No. 8-seed Missouri, 74-73, with 4.8 seconds left. That's when 5'10" Tyus Edney took the inbounds pass, drove the length of the court and banked the ball over Mizzou's 6'9" Derek Grimm at the buzzer. Four games later, the Bruins won title No. 11.

HEARTBREAKER: Three minutes and 30 seconds. That's all it took for Notre Dame to end UCLA's record 88-game winning streak on Jan. 19, 1974, in South Bend, 71-70. The Bruins led, 70-59, before the Irish forced four turnovers and hit six straight shots—the winner coming from Dwight Clay with :29 left.

FIERCEST RIVAL: While crosstown rival USC holds the upper hand in football, the Bruins have owned the Trojans on the hardwood. Competing for the same SoCal players, the rivalry heated up in the late 1960s and early '70s when USC finished second to UCLA five times in seven years. UCLA leads overall, 128–101.

FANFARE AND HOOPLA: There's more to fan tradition at Pauley Pavilion than the famed "8-clap." The student section, known as the Den, has a call and response pregame ritual called the "Frisbee Cheer" that aims at identifying the basketball ("Yes, that's a basketball!"), the court ("Yes, that's the court!") and differentiates the winning team ("Bruins!") from the "loooosing team!"

FAN FAVORITE: C Bill Walton (1971-74) Whether he was shutting down Wilshire Boulevard to protest the Vietnam War or crushing opponents inside Pauley Pavilion, Walton came to symbolize the dominant era of Bruins basketball.

CONSENSUS ALL-AMERICAS

1931-32	**Dick Linthicum,** F
1945	**Bill Putnam,** G
1947	**Don Barksdale,** C
1950	**George Stanich,** G
1952	**Don Johnson,** G
1955	**Don Bragg,** G
1955	**John Moore,** F
1956	**Willie Naulls,** C
1959	**Walt Torrence,** G
1962	**John Green,** G
1964	**Walt Hazzard,** G
1965	**Gail Goodrich,** G
1967-69	**Lew Alcindor,** C
1971	**Sidney Wicks,** F
1972-74	**Bill Walton,** C
1972	**Henry Bibby,** G
1973, '74	**Keith Wilkes,** F
1975	**Dave Meyers,** F
1976	**Richard Washington,** F/C
1977	**Marques Johnson,** F
1978, '79	**David Greenwood,** F
1995	**Ed O'Bannon,** F
2007	**Arron Afflalo,** G
2008	**Kevin Love,** C

FIRST-ROUND PRO PICKS

1964	**Walt Hazzard,** LA Lakers (5)
1965	**Gail Goodrich,** LA Lakers (10)
1969	**Lew Alcindor,** Milwaukee (1)
1969	**Lew Alcindor,** New York (ABA)
1969	**Lucius Allen,** Seattle (3)
1970	**John Vallely,** Atlanta (14)
1971	**Sidney Wicks,** Portland (2)
1971	**Curtis Rowe,** Detroit (11)
1973	**Swen Nater,** Milwaukee (16)
1973	**Bill Walton,** San Diego (ABA, 1)
1974	**Bill Walton,** Portland (1)
1974	**Keith Wilkes,** Golden State (11)
1975	**Dave Meyers,** LA Lakers (2)
1976	**Richard Washington,** Kansas City (3)
1977	**Marques Johnson,** Milwaukee (3)
1978	**Raymond Townsend,** Golden State (22)
1979	**David Greenwood,** Chicago (2)
1979	**Roy Hamilton,** Detroit (10)
1979	**Brad Holland,** LA Lakers (14)
1980	**Kiki Vandeweghe,** Dallas (11)
1984	**Kenny Fields,** Milwaukee (21)
1987	**Reggie Miller,** Indiana (11)
1989	**Jerome "Pooh" Richardson,** Minn. (10)
1992	**Tracy Murray,** San Antonio (18)
1992	**Don MacLean,** Detroit (19)
1995	**Ed O'Bannon,** New Jersey (9)
1995	**George Zidek,** Charlotte (22)
1999	**Baron Davis,** Charlotte (3)
2000	**Jerome Moiso,** Boston (11)
2006	**Jordan Farmar,** LA Lakers (26)
2007	**Arron Afflalo,** Detroit (27)
2008	**Russell Westbrook,** Seattle (4)
2008	**Kevin Love,** Memphis (5)
2009	**Jrue Holiday,** Philadelphia (17)
2009	**Darren Collison,** New Orleans (21)

PROFILE

University of California, Los Angeles, Westwood, CA
Founded: 1919
Enrollment: 38,476 (26,928 undergraduate)
Colors: Blue and gold
Nickname: Bruins
Current arena: Pauley Pavilion, opened in 1965 (12,819)
Previous: Los Angeles Memorial Sports Arena, 1959-65 (16,161); UCLA men's gymnasium, 1919-1959 (NA)
First game: 1919
All-time record: 1,675-730 (.696)
Total weeks in AP Top 20/25: 651

Current conference: Pacific-10 (1927-)
Conference titles:
Pacific Coast: 3 (1950, '52, '56)
AAWU: 6 (1962, '63 [tie], '64, '65, '67, '68)
Pac-8: 10 (1969, '70, '71, '72, '73, '74, '75, '76, '77, '78)
Pac-10: 10 ('79, '83, '87, '92, '95, '96, '97, 2006, '07, '08)
Conference tournament titles:
Pac-10: 3 (1987, 2006, '08)
NCAA Tournaments: 43 (2 appearances vacated)
Sweet 16s (since 1975): 17
Final Fours: 18
Titles: 11 (1964, '65, '67, '68, '69, '70, '71, '72, '73, '75, '95)

NIT appearances: 2
Semifinal: 1
Titles: 1 (1985)

TOP 5

G	**Gail Goodrich** (1962-65)
G	**Walt Hazzard** (1961-64)
F	**Sidney Wicks** (1969-72)
C	**Lew Alcindor** (1966-69)
C	**Bill Walton** (1971-74)

RECORDS

RECORDS	GAME		SEASON		CAREER	
POINTS	61	Lew Alcindor, vs. Washington State (Feb. 25, 1967)	870	Lew Alcindor (1966-67)	2,608	Don MacLean (1988-92)
POINTS PER GAME			29.0	Lew Alcindor (1966-67)	26.4	Lew Alcindor (1966-69)
REBOUNDS	28	Willie Naulls, vs. Arizona State (Jan. 28, 1956)	506	Bill Walton (1972-73)	1,370	Bill Walton (1971-74)
ASSISTS	16	Earl Watson, vs. Maryland (March 18, 2000)	236	Jerome "Pooh" Richardson (1985-89)	833	Jerome "Pooh" Richardson (1988-89)

SEASON REVIEW

SEASON	W-L	CONF.	SCORING	COACH	RECORD
1919-20	12-2			Fred W. Cozens	
1920-21	8-2			Fred W. Cozens	20-4 .833
1921-22	9-1			Caddy Works	
1922-23	12-4			Caddy Works	
1923-24	8-2			Caddy Works	
1924-25	11-6			Caddy Works	
1925-26	14-2			Caddy Works	
1926-27	12-4			Caddy Works	
1927-28	10-5	5-4		Caddy Works	
1928-29	7-9	1-8		Caddy Works	
1929-30	14-8	3-6		Caddy Works	
1930-31	9-6	4-5		Caddy Works	
1931-32	9-10	4-7		Caddy Works	
1932-33	10-11	1-10		Caddy Works	
1933-34	10-13	2-10		Caddy Works	
1934-35	11-12	4-8		Caddy Works	
1935-36	10-13	2-10		Caddy Works	
1936-37	6-13	2-10		Caddy Works	
1937-38	4-20	0-12		Caddy Works	
1938-39	7-20	0-12		Caddy Works	173-159 .521
1939-40	8-17	3-9		Wilbur Johns	
1940-41	6-20	2-10		Wilbur Johns	

SEAS.	W-L	CONF.	POSTSEASON	SCORING	REBOUNDS	ASSISTS	COACH	RECORD
1941-42	5-18	2-10					Wilbur Johns	
1942-43	14-7	4-4					Wilbur Johns	
1943-44	10-10	3-3					Wilbur Johns	
1944-45	12-12	3-1					Wilbur Johns	
1945-46	8-16	5-7		Chuck Clustka 8.3			Wilbur Johns	
1946-47	18-7	9-3		Don Barksdale 14.7			Wilbur Johns	
1947-48	12-13	3-9		John Stanich 9.5			Wilbur Johns	93-120 .437
1948-49	22-7	10-2		Carl Kraushaar 9.4			John Wooden	
1949-50	24-7	10-2	NCAA REGIONAL SEMIFINALS	Alan Sawyer 12.6			John Wooden	
1950-51	19-10	8-4		Dick Ridgway 16.2	Don Johnson 5.2		John Wooden	
1951-52	19-12	8-4	NCAA REGIONAL SEMIFINALS	Ron Livingston 10.1	Don Johnson 5.8		John Wooden	
1952-53	16-8	6-6		John Moore 12.2	Don Bragg 8.7		John Wooden	
1953-54	18-7	7-5		Ron Livingston 12.5	Willie Naulls 7.9		John Wooden	
1954-55	21-5	11-1		John Moore 14.6	Willie Naulls 11.3		John Wooden	
1955-56	22-6	16-0	NCAA REGIONAL SEMIFINALS	Willie Naulls 23.6	Willie Naulls 14.6		John Wooden	
1956-57	22-4	13-3		Dick Banton 14.1	Walt Torrence 7.1		John Wooden	
1957-58	16-10	10-6		Ben Rogers 12.5	Walt Torrence 6.9		John Wooden	
1958-59	16-9	10-6		Walt Torrence 21.5	Walt Torrence 11.6		John Wooden	
1959-60	14-12	7-5		John Green 10.2	John Berberich 8.5		John Wooden	
1960-61	18-8	7-5		Ron Lawson 13.7	John Berberich 11.4		John Wooden	
1961-62	18-11	10-2	NCAA FOURTH PLACE	John Green 19.3	Fred Slaughter 9.6		John Wooden	
1962-63	20-9	7-5	NCAA REGIONAL SEMIFINALS	Walt Hazzard 16.3	Fred Slaughter 9.7		John Wooden	
1963-64	**30-0**	**15-0**	**NATIONAL CHAMPION**	**Gail Goodrich 21.5**	**Keith Erickson 9.1**		**John Wooden**	
1964-65	**28-2**	**14-0**	**NATIONAL CHAMPION**	**Gail Goodrich 24.8**	**Edgar Lacey 9.8**		**John Wooden**	
1965-66	18-8	10-4		Mike Lynn 16.8	Mike Lynn 10.3		John Wooden	
1966-67	**30-0**	**14-0**	**NATIONAL CHAMPION**	**Lew Alcindor 29.0**	**Lew Alcindor 15.5**		**John Wooden**	
1967-68	**29-1**	**14-0**	**NATIONAL CHAMPION**	**Lew Alcindor 26.2**	**Lew Alcindor 16.5**		**John Wooden**	
1968-69	**29-1**	**13-1**	**NATIONAL CHAMPION**	**Lew Alcindor 24.0**	**Lew Alcindor 14.6**		**John Wooden**	
1969-70	**28-2**	**12-2**	**NATIONAL CHAMPION**	**Sidney Wicks 18.6**	**Sidney Wicks 11.9**		**John Wooden**	
1970-71	**29-1**	**14-0**	**NATIONAL CHAMPION**	**Sidney Wicks 21.3**	**Sidney Wicks 12.8**		**John Wooden**	
1971-72	**30-0**	**14-0**	**NATIONAL CHAMPION**	**Bill Walton 21.1**	**Bill Walton 15.5**		**John Wooden**	
1972-73	**30-0**	**14-0**	**NATIONAL CHAMPION**	**Bill Walton 20.4**	**Bill Walton 16.9**	**Bill Walton 5.6**	**John Wooden**	
1973-74	26-4	12-2	NCAA THIRD PLACE	Bill Walton 19.3	Bill Walton 14.7	Bill Walton 5.5	John Wooden	
1974-75	**28-3**	**12-2**	**NATIONAL CHAMPION**	**Dave Meyers 18.3**	**Dave Meyers 7.9**	**Andre McCarter 5.0**	**John Wooden**	**620-147 .808**
1975-76	27-5	⊗ 13-1	NCAA THIRD PLACE	Richard Washington 20.1	Marques Johnson 9.4	Andre McCarter 5.1	Gene Bartow	
1976-77	24-5	11-3	NCAA REGIONAL SEMIFINALS	Marques Johnson 21.4	Marques Johnson 11.1	Roy Hamilton 4.6	Gene Bartow	51-10 .836▼
1977-78	25-3	14-0	NCAA REGIONAL SEMIFINALS	David Greenwood 17.5	David Greenwood 11.4	Roy Hamilton 6.0	Gary Cunningham	
1978-79	25-5	15-3	NCAA REGIONAL FINALS	David Greenwood 19.9	David Greenwood 10.3	Roy Hamilton 6.7	Gary Cunningham	50-8 .862
1979-80	22-10	⊗ 12-6	NCAA RUNNER-UP	Kiki Vandeweghe 19.5	Kiki Vandeweghe 6.8	Rod Foster 3.2	Larry Brown	
1980-81	20-7	13-5	NCAA SECOND ROUND	Mike Sanders 15.4	Mike Sanders 6.6	Ralph Jackson 3.9	Larry Brown	42-17 .712▼
1981-82	21-6	14-4		Mike Sanders 14.4	Mike Sanders 6.4	Ralph Jackson 4.1	Larry Farmer	
1982-83	23-6	15-3	NCAA SECOND ROUND	Kenny Fields 18.0	Kenny Fields 6.6	Ralph Jackson 5.1	Larry Farmer	
1983-84	17-11	10-8		Kenny Fields 17.4	Stuart Gray 7.9	Nigel Miguel 3.0	Larry Farmer	61-23 .726
1984-85	21-12	12-6	NIT CHAMPION	Reggie Miller 15.2	Brad Wright 8.7	Nigel Miguel 3.2	Walt Hazzard	
1985-86	15-14	9-9	NIT FIRST ROUND	Reggie Miller 25.9	Jack Haley 6.3	Jerome "Pooh" Richardson 6.2	Walt Hazzard	
1986-87	25-7	14-4	NCAA SECOND ROUND	Reggie Miller 22.3	Reggie Miller 5.4	Jerome "Pooh" Richardson 6.5	Walt Hazzard	
1987-88	16-14	12-6		Trevor Wilson 15.4	Trevor Wilson 9.4	Jerome "Pooh" Richardson 7.0	Walt Hazzard	77-47 .621
1988-89	21-10	13-5	NCAA SECOND ROUND	Don MacLean 18.6	Trevor Wilson 8.7	Jerome "Pooh" Richardson 7.6	Jim Harrick	
1989-90	22-11	11-7	NCAA REGIONAL SEMIFINALS	Don MacLean 19.9	Trevor Wilson 9.1	Derrick Martin 6.0	Jim Harrick	
1990-91	23-9	11-7	NCAA FIRST ROUND	Don MacLean 23.0	Don MacLean 7.3	Derrick Martin 6.8	Jim Harrick	
1991-92	28-5	16-2	NCAA REGIONAL FINALS	Tracy Murray 21.4	Don MacLean 7.8	Derrick Martin 3.9	Jim Harrick	
1992-93	22-11	11-7	NCAA SECOND ROUND	Shon Tarver 17.2	Ed O'Bannon 7.0	Tyus Edney 5.6	Jim Harrick	
1993-94	21-7	13-5	NCAA FIRST ROUND	Ed O'Bannon 18.2	Ed O'Bannon 8.8	Tyus Edney 5.8	Jim Harrick	
1994-95	**31-2**	**⊗ 16-2**	**NATIONAL CHAMPION**	**Ed O'Bannon 20.4**	**Ed O'Bannon 8.3**	**Tyus Edney 6.8**	**Jim Harrick**	
1995-96	23-8	16-2	NCAA FIRST ROUND	Toby Bailey 14.8	Jelani McCoy 6.9	Cameron Dollar 4.5	Jim Harrick	191-63 .752▼
1996-97	24-8	15-3	NCAA REGIONAL FINALS	Charles O'Bannon 17.7	Charles O'Bannon 6.9	Toby Bailey 4.8	Steve Lavin	
1997-98	24-9	12-6	NCAA REGIONAL SEMIFINALS	J.R. Henderson 19.0	J.R. Henderson 7.8	Baron Davis 5.0	Steve Lavin	
1998-99	22-9	⊗ 12-6	NCAA FIRST ROUND	Baron Davis 15.9	JaRon Rush 7.3	Earl Watson 4.6	Steve Lavin	
1999-2000	21-12	10-8	NCAA REGIONAL SEMIFINALS	Jason Kapono 16.0	Jerome Moiso 7.6	Earl Watson 5.9	Steve Lavin	
2000-01	23-9	14-4	NCAA REGIONAL SEMIFINALS	Jason Kapono 17.2	Dan Gadzuric 8.6	Earl Watson 5.2	Steve Lavin	
2001-02	21-12	11-7	NCAA REGIONAL SEMIFINALS	Jason Kapono 16.0	Dan Gadzuric 7.7	Cedric Bozeman 3.5	Steve Lavin	
2002-03	10-19	6-12		Jason Kapono 16.8	Andre Patterson 5.5	Ryan Walcott 3.3	Steve Lavin	145-78 .650▼
2003-04	11-17	7-11		Dijon Thompson 14.4	T.J. Cummings 6.7	Cedric Bozeman 5.5	Ben Howland	
2004-05	18-11	11-7	NCAA FIRST ROUND	Dijon Thompson 18.4	Dijon Thompson 7.9	Jordan Farmar 5.3	Ben Howland	
2005-06	32-7	14-4	NCAA RUNNER-UP	Arron Afflalo 15.8	Luc Richard Mbah a Moute 8.2	Jordan Farmar 5.1	Ben Howland	
2006-07	30-6	15-3	NCAA NATIONAL SEMIFINALS	Arron Afflalo 16.9	Luc Richard Mbah a Moute 7.4	Darren Collison 5.7	Ben Howland	
2007-08	35-4	16-2	NCAA NATIONAL SEMIFINALS	Kevin Love 17.5	Kevin Love 10.6	Russell Westbrook 4.3	Ben Howland	
2008-09	26-9	13-5	NCAA SECOND ROUND	Josh Shipp 14.5	Alfred Aboya 6.3	Darren Collison 4.7	Ben Howland	152-54 .738

⊗ Records don't reflect games forfeited or vacated. For adjusted records, see p. 521.

▼ Coaches' records adjusted to reflect games forfeited or vacated: Gene Bartow, 52-9, .852; Larry Brown, 37-16, .698; Jim Harrick, 192-62, .756; Steve Lavin, 145-77, .653. For yearly totals, see p. 521.

ESPN 303 SAGARIN

UC Riverside

Humble? That would be the kind way to describe the Highlanders' eight-year D1 history, in which they've never finished higher than fourth in the Big West. But no need for euphemism to summarize UC Riverside's D2 days. Starting in the 1970s, the school routinely played in the postseason and even made a few runs at a national title.

BEST TEAM: 1972-73 Nobody expected them to be the greatest in school history, especially with the graduation of twin towers Sam Cash and Howard Lee. But thanks to coach Freddie Goss slowing the ball down and Lee McDougal's rebounding (12.5 rpg), the Highlanders went 25–5 and reached the College Division quarterfinals.

BEST PLAYER: C Sam Cash (1970-72) The 6'8", 230-pounder never met a rebound he didn't gobble up. His career rebounding average of 14.9 is especially amazing when you consider that four-year standout Lee, the UCR career boards leader, was pulling down 12.3 and 11.9 boards a game those same seasons.

BEST COACH: John Masi (1979-2005) You won't find a a better local-boy-done-good story. This UCR alum, who lived in Riverside since he was 8, led the Highlanders to a 23–5 record and a regional championship in his debut season. Over the next 17 years, UC Riverside received 10 D2 tournament bids.

GAME FOR THE AGES: The underdog Highlanders stormed out to a 28-6 lead over Southern Indiana in the 1995 D2 title game. But moxie could only take them so far, as the Screaming Eagles took the lead with 1:29 left to play and finished the game off with a jumper with :43 remaining.

FIERCEST RIVAL: Riverside and Fullerton renewed their SoCal rivalry in 2000 after a 16-year hiatus, with the Highlanders besting the Titans, 59-52, on Nov. 25. The intensity ratcheted up a notch the next season when Riverside joined Fullerton in the Big West. Since then, the Titans have owned the series, winning seven of the last 10 and ousting the Highlanders from the Big West tourney in 2008 and '09. Fullerton leads overall, 20–15.

SEASON REVIEW

SEAS.	W-L	CONF.	COACH	SEAS.	W-L	CONF.	COACH
1954-55	0-13		Franklin Lindeburg	1960-61	4-16		Franklin Lindeburg
1955-56	5-12		Franklin Lindeburg	1961-62	9-12		Franklin Lindeburg
1956-57	3-20		Franklin Lindeburg	1962-63	10-8		Franklin Lindeburg
1957-58	3-15		Franklin Lindeburg	1963-64	9-10		Franklin Lindeburg
1958-59	8-9		Franklin Lindeburg	1964-65	14-9		Franklin Lindeburg
1959-60	8-11		Franklin Lindeburg	1965-66	16-8		Franklin Lindeburg

SEAS.	W-L	CONF.	SCORING		COACH	RECORD	
1966-67	17-10				Dwain Lewis		
1967-68	13-11				Dwain Lewis		
1968-69	15-10		Dick Barton	21.4	Dwain Lewis	45-31	.592
1969-70	19-10		Mike Washington	21.1	Freddie Goss		
1970-71	14-10		Mike Washington	17.7	Freddie Goss		
1971-72	19-9		Bobby Walters	17.0	Freddie Goss		
1972-73	25-5		Bobby Walters	13.2	Freddie Goss		
1973-74	21-8		Bobby Walters	17.6	Freddie Goss		
1974-75	19-9		Larry Reynolds	13.5	Freddie Goss		
1975-76	10-16		Alvin Joseph	14.6	Freddie Goss		
1976-77	11-15		Leo Wills	11.2	Freddie Goss		
1977-78	4-23		John Green	18.5	Freddie Goss		
1978-79	21-5		John Green	13.9	Freddie Goss	163-110	.597
1979-80	23-5		Gary Pickens	15.8	John Masi		
1980-81	13-13		Teddy Morning	13.4	John Masi		
1981-82	15-11		Howard Holt	17.7	John Masi		
1982-83	14-13		Tim Bell	10.9	John Masi		
1983-84	23-5		James Fontenette	11.8	John Masi		
1984-85	20-8		Andre Greer	13.7	John Masi		
1985-86	24-7		Robert Jimerson	14.5	John Masi		
1986-87	19-9		Robert Jimerson	19.1	John Masi		
1987-88	22-8		Maurice Pullum	14.5	John Masi		
1988-89	30-4		Maurice Pullum	18.6	John Masi		
1989-90	21-10		Chris Ceballos	19.7	John Masi		
1990-91	22-7		Anthony Jenkins	14.4	John Masi		
1991-92	24-6		Gene Altamirano	12.2	John Masi		
1992-93	20-8		Charles Purdom	15.2	John Masi		
1993-94	22-7		Bob Fife	18.6	John Masi		
1994-95	26-6		William Wilson	12.2	John Masi		
1995-96	18-9		K.J. Roberts	14.8	John Masi		
1996-97	19-9		James King	13.2	John Masi		
1997-98	16-10		Erik Kennady	14.5	John Masi		
1998-99	14-13		Toby Vares	13.0	John Masi		
1999-2000	15-12		Mark Miller	16.1	John Masi		
2000-01	8-17		Mark Miller	13.2	John Masi		
2001-02	8-18	5-13	Vili Morton	10.9	John Masi		
2002-03	6-18	5-13	Nate Carter	16.4	John Masi		
2003-04	11-17	7-11	Nate Carter	15.3	John Masi		
2004-05	9-19	4-14	Vili Morton	16.5	John Masi	462-269	.632
2005-06	5-23	3-11	Rickey Porter	14.2	David Spencer	5-23	.179
2006-07	7-24	1-13	Larry Cunningham	13.7	Vonn Webb	7-24	.226
2007-08	9-21	4-12	Larry Cunningham	16.3	Jim Wooldridge		
2008-09	17-13	8-8	Kyle Austin	16.2	Jim Wooldridge	26-34	.433

PROFILE

University of California, Riverside, Riverside, CA
Founded: 1954
Enrollment: 17,187 (14,973 undergraduate)
Colors: Blue and gold
Nickname: Highlanders
Current arena: UC Riverside Student Recreation Center, opened in 1994 (3,200)
Previous: Physical Education Gym, 1954-94 (1,100)
First game: Dec. 3, 1954
All-time record: 797-634 (.557)
Total weeks in AP Top 20/25: 0

Current conference: Big West (2001-)
Conference titles: 0
Conference tournament titles: 0
NCAA Tournament appearances: 0
NIT appearances: 0

CONSENSUS ALL-AMERICAS

1989 **Maurice Pullum** (D2), G

TOP 5

G **Larry Cunningham** (2004-08)
G **Mike Washington** (1969-71)
F **Lee McDougal** (1971-73)
F/C **Howard Lee** (1969-72)
C **Sam Cash** (1970-72)

RECORDS

RECORDS	GAME		SEASON		CAREER	
POINTS	42	Dick Barton, vs. La Verne (Jan. 11, 1969)	632	Maurice Pullum (1988-89)	1,502	Larry Cunningham (2004-08)
POINTS PER GAME			21.4	Dick Barton (1968-69)	19.6	Mike Washington (1969-71)
REBOUNDS	28	Sam Cash, vs. Cal State Fullerton (Jan. 14, 1972)	428	Sam Cash (1971-72)	1,004	Howard Lee (1969-72)
ASSISTS	16	Reggie Mims, vs. Portland State (Dec. 17, 1975)	203	Brad Husen (1985-86)	403	Reggie Mims (1972-76)

ESPN 142 SAGARIN

UC Santa Barbara

Go figure. The same school that's known for tranquility, eccentricity and producing singer Jack Johnson is also responsible for the Thunderdome, one of the nation's most raucous gyms, where students used to fling tortillas as if they were frisbees. A school official gave the place its name during the 1986-87 season because it was so loud it reminded him of the Thunderdome from the *Mad Max* movies.

BEST TEAM: 1989-90 Coach Jerry Pimm boasted impressive on-court talent and an ace assistant in future UCLA coach Ben Howland. The Gauchos won the school's first NCAA Tournament game—beating Houston, 70-66—before losing to No. 1-seed Michigan State, 62-58.

BEST PLAYER: G Brian Shaw (1986-88) The Saint Mary's transfer arrived at UCSB fresh off winning a gold medal with Team USA at the 1986 World Championship. As complete a point guard as he proved to be, he was an even better leader. In fact, future Lakers teammate Shaquille O'Neal once called B-Shaw the player he respected the most.

BEST COACH: Bob Williams (1998-) Williams took over a UCSB squad that had endured five straight losing seasons. He instantly transformed the Gauchos into winners by championing the underdog—he scheduled nationally-ranked competition and rewarded walk-ons with key playing time and scholarships.

GAME FOR THE AGES: The Thunderdome fans paid the biggest dividends on Feb. 26, 1990, when Carrick DeHart and company knocked off the eventual national champion UNLV Rebels, 78-70.

FIERCEST RIVAL: UCSB vs. Cal Poly is not your typical in-state rivalry. Although the series dates back to 1938 (UCSB leads, 62–30), the most telling moment came just recently. Before the schools' Feb. 14, 2008 matchup, some Mustangs fans spray-painted "Cal Poly Rules" all over the UCSB campus—in paint that was easily washed off. That's what happens when you have two eco-conscious institutions going at it.

SEASON REVIEW

SEAS.	W-L	CONF.	COACH
1937-47	*89-66*		*All coached by Willie Wilton*
1947-48	17-8		Willie Wilton
1948-49	11-9		Willie Wilton
1949-50	14-14		Willie Wilton
1950-51	14-15		Willie Wilton
1951-52	7-20		Larry Findlay
1952-53	4-13		Willie Wilton
1953-54	13-9		Willie Wilton
1954-55	17-7		Willie Wilton
1955-56	18-8		Willie Wilton
1956-57	7-15		Willie Wilton
1957-58	15-10		Art Gallon
1958-59	4-19		Art Gallon
1959-60	17-7		Art Gallon
1960-61	20-8		Art Gallon
1961-62	12-12		Art Gallon
1962-63	16-9		Art Gallon
1963-64	18-11	9-5	Art Gallon
1964-65	12-14	7-7	Art Gallon
1965-66	10-16	5-9	Art Gallon
1966-67	10-16	8-6	Ralph Barkey
1967-68	9-17	3-11	Ralph Barkey
1968-69	17-9	8-6	Ralph Barkey
1969-70	12-14	6-4	Ralph Barkey
1970-71	20-6	8-2	Ralph Barkey
1971-72	17-9	5-7	Ralph Barkey
1972-73	17-9	8-4	Ralph Barkey
1973-74	16-10	7-5	Ralph Barkey

SEAS.	W-L	CONF.	SCORING		COACH	RECORD
1974-75	18-8		Don Ford	19.6	Ralph Barkey	
1975-76	17-9		John Service	16.1	Ralph Barkey	
1976-77	8-18	3-9	Dave Brown	18.3	Ralph Barkey	
1977-78	8-19	3-11	Matt Maderos	16.1	Ralph Barkey	169-144 .540
1978-79	12-15	6-8	Matt Maderos	14.8	Ed DeLacy	
1979-80	11-16	5-9	Richard Anderson	12.6	Ed DeLacy	
1980-81	11-16	5-9	R. Anderson, Walter Evans	15.0	Ed DeLacy	
1981-82	10-16	5-9	Richard Anderson	16.0	Ed DeLacy	
1982-83	7-20	1-15	York Gross	20.9	Ed DeLacy	51-83 .381
1983-84	10-17	5-13	Scott Fisher	14.6	Jerry Pimm	
1984-85	12-16	8-10	Scott Fisher	15.0	Jerry Pimm	
1985-86	12-15	7-11	Conner Henry	17.3	Jerry Pimm	
1986-87	16-13	10-8	Brian Vaughns	13.6	Jerry Pimm	
1987-88	22-8	13-5 ●	Brian Shaw	13.3	Jerry Pimm	
1988-89	21-9	11-7 ■	C. DeHart, Mike Doyle	16.2	Jerry Pimm	
1989-90	21-9	13-5 ●	Carrick DeHart	15.9	Jerry Pimm	
1990-91	14-15	8-10	Lucius Davis, Gary Gray	16.0	Jerry Pimm	
1991-92	20-9	13-5 ■	Lucius Davis	22.2	Jerry Pimm	
1992-93	18-11	10-8 ■	Idris Jones	12.7	Jerry Pimm	
1993-94	13-17	9-9	Doug Muse	11.2	Jerry Pimm	
1994-95	13-14	8-10	Doug Muse	13.0	Jerry Pimm	
1995-96	11-15	8-10	Lelan McDougal	18.7	Jerry Pimm	
1996-97	12-15	7-9	Raymond Tutt	24.1	Jerry Pimm	
1997-98	7-19	4-12	Raymond Tutt	18.9	Jerry Pimm	222-201 .525
1998-99	15-13	12-4	B.J. Bunton	17.5	Bob Williams	
1999-2000	14-14	10-6	Erick Ashe	12.0	Bob Williams	
2000-01	13-15	9-7	Mark Hull	13.9	Bob Williams	
2001-02	20-11	11-7 ●	Mark Hull	15.2	Bob Williams	
2002-03	18-14	14-4 ■	Branduinn Fullove	14.6	Bob Williams	
2003-04	16-12	10-8	Branduinn Fullove	10.6	Bob Williams	
2004-05	11-18	7-11	Chrismen Oliver	10.5	Bob Williams	
2005-06	15-14	6-8	Cecil Brown	13.1	Bob Williams	
2006-07	18-11	9-5	Alex Harris	21.1	Bob Williams	
2007-08	23-9	12-4 ■	Alex Harris	20.2	Bob Williams	
2008-09	16-15	8-8	Chris Devine	15.5	Bob Williams	179-146 .551

● NCAA Tournament appearance ■ NIT appearance

PROFILE

University of California, Santa Barbara, Santa Barbara, CA
Enrollment: 20,738 (18,892 undergraduate)
Founded: 1905 as Santa Barbara State College; renamed UC Santa Barbara in 1944
Colors: Blue and gold
Nickname: Gauchos
Current arena: The Thunderdome, opened as the Campus Events Center in 1979 (6,000)
Previous: Rob Gym, 1958-79 (3,100); National Armory, 1937-58 (N/A)
First game: Dec. 14, 1937

All-time record: 960-865 (.526)
Total weeks in AP Top 20/25: 0
Current conference: Big West (1969-74, '76-)
Conference titles:
Big West: 2 (2003, '08 [tie])
Conference tournament titles:
Big West: 1 (2002)
NCAA Tournament appearances: 3
NIT appearances: 5

FIRST-ROUND PRO PICKS

1988 **Brian Shaw,** Boston (24)

TOP 5

G **Carrick DeHart** (1986-90)
G **Brian Shaw** (1986-88)
F **Lucius Davis** (1988-92)
F **Tommy Guerrero** (1939-41)
F **Eric McArthur** (1986-90)

RECORDS

	GAME		SEASON		CAREER	
POINTS	39	Scott Fisher, vs. Montana State (Dec. 23, 1985)	649	Raymond Tutt (1996-97)	1,696	Alex Harris (2004-08)
POINTS PER GAME			24.1	Raymond Tutt (1996-97)	21.5	Raymond Tutt (1996-98)
REBOUNDS	28	Eric McArthur, vs. New Mexico State (Jan. 11, 1990)	377	Eric McArthur (1989-90)	904	Eric McArthur (1986-90)
ASSISTS	16	Ray Kelly, vs. UC Irvine (Feb. 15, 1993)	205	Ray Kelly (1992-93)	515	Ray Kelly (1990-93)

ESPN 19 SAGARIN

UTAH

To put Utah's success in appropriate perspective, consider this: The Utes have reached the same number of Final Fours as Syracuse, Florida and Arizona. Add in the 1944 national championship and a more recent trip to the Final, and you'll begin to understand why Utah has been such an important contributor to college basketball history.

BEST TEAM: 1943-44 Known as the Blitz Kids and led by future Utah athletic director Arnie Ferrin, the Utes (18–3 in the regular season) lost in the NIT quarterfinals to Kentucky in New York City, but then received a rare second chance for postseason glory in the NCAA Tournament. Because Arkansas had to withdraw from the Tournament after two of its players were hit by a car while changing a flat tire, Utah was invited to go to Kansas City and replace the Razorbacks in the NCAAs. With its new life, Utah beat Missouri, Iowa State and, finally, Dartmouth, 42-40 in overtime, for its only NCAA championship. To further prove its legitimacy (and its stamina), Utah *then* went back to New York's Madison Sqaure Garden and defeated NIT champion St. John's, 43-36, in a special charity event.

BEST PLAYER: C Billy McGill (1959-62) Utah boasts a long line of spectacular big men, such as Danny Vranes, Keith Van Horn, Michael Doleac and Andrew Bogut, but none was more dominant than Billy "the Hill" McGill. Averaging a school record 27.0 ppg for his career, McGill led the Utes to the 1961 Final Four. The following season he averaged a spectacular 38.8 ppg with his unstoppable jump hook. Only four players in NCAA Division I history have had a higher single-season scoring average. He scored a school-record 60 in a 1962 game against archrival BYU and topped 50 three other times.

BEST COACH: Vadal Peterson (1927-53) For all that Jack Gardner and Rick Majerus accomplished in Salt Lake City, Peterson is the man who built Utah into a national power. A strict disciplinarian, he won the 1944 NCAA and '47 NIT championships, along with 383 other games over his 26 seasons.

GAMES FOR THE AGES: After heading to overtime in the March 28, 1944, NCAA championship game, Utah and Dartmouth were knotted at 40 with just :03 left when Herb Wilkinson hit a one-hander from beyond the foul circle to secure the win. Ferrin scored 22 points and became the first freshman to be named the Tournament's Most Outstanding Player.

HEARTBREAKER: Kentucky knocked Utah out of the NCAA Tournament in 1996 and '97. In 1998, the Utes had an opportunity to get their revenge in the Final, and for a while it looked as if they were going to do just that when they got out to a 12-point lead. Uh-uh. The Wildcats prevailed yet again, 78-69.

FIERCEST RIVAL: How's this for a tight series: After 248 meetings between Utah and Brigham Young, the Utes lead 125–123. It's the 10th most-played rivalry in the country and is part of the battle for the Old Oquirrh Bucket (named for a state mountain range) that's awarded each year to the Utah college (there are six) with the best in-state basketball record.

FANFARE AND HOOPLA: If you think of Utah fans as polite and quiet, you haven't been to a game at the Huntsman Center, where the Utes have achieved eight perfect home seasons. And no crowd is louder than the 1,000-strong student fan club known as the MUSS (Mighty Utah Student Section).

FAN FAVORITE: Rick Majerus (1989-2004) With his love for sweaters and self-deprecation, the rotund coach consistently kept Utah among the nation's elite until health problems forced him to resign.

THE SCHOOLS

CONSENSUS ALL-AMERICAS

1916	**Dick Romney**, G
1936	**Bill Kinner**, C
1944, '45	**Arnie Ferrin**, G/F
1962	**Billy McGill**, C
1997	**Keith Van Horn**, F
1999	**Andre Miller**, G
2005	**Andrew Bogut**, F/C

FIRST-ROUND PRO PICKS

1949	**Vern Gardner**, Philadelphia (6)
1962	**Billy McGill**, Chicago (1)
1966	**Jerry Chambers**, LA Lakers (7)
1968	**Mervin Jackson**, LA Stars (ABA)
1974	**Mike Sojourner**, Atlanta (10)
1981	**Danny Vranes**, Seattle (5)
1981	**Tom Chambers**, San Diego (8)
1997	**Keith Van Horn**, Philadelphia (2)
1998	**Michael Doleac**, Orlando (12)
1999	**Andre Miller**, Cleveland (8)
2005	**Andrew Bogut**, Milwaukee (1)

PROFILE

University of Utah, Salt Lake City, UT
Founded: 1850
Enrollment: 24,948 (19,718 undergraduate)
Colors: Crimson and white
Nickname: Runnin' Utes
Current arena: Jon M. Huntsman Center, opened in 1969 (15,000)
Previous: Einar Neilsen Fieldhouse, 1940-69 (N/A)
First game: Dec. 10, 1908
All-time record: 1,637-858 (.656)
Total weeks in AP Top 20/25: 212

Current conference: Mountain West (1999-)
Conference titles:
Rocky Mountain: 1 (1931)
Big Seven: 1 (1938 [tie])
Mountain States: 7 (1945, '55, '56, '59, '60, '61 [tie], '62)
WAC: 12 (1966, '77, '81 [tie], '83 [tie], '86 [tie], '91, '93 [tie], '95, '96, '97 [tie], '98 [tie], '99 [tie])
Mountain West: 5 (2000 [tie], '01 [tie], '03 [tie], '05, '09 [tie])
Conference tournament titles:
WAC: 3 (1995, '97, '99); Mountain West: 2 (2004, '09)
NCAA Tournament appearances: 27
Sweet 16s (since 1975): 9
Final Fours: 4
Titles: 1 (1944)
NIT appearances: 11
Semifinals: 3
Titles: 1 (1947)

TOP 5

G	**Andre Miller** (1995-99)
G/F	**Arnie Ferrin** (1943-45, '46-48)
F	**Keith Van Horn** (1993-97)
F/C	**Andrew Bogut** (2003-05)
C	**Billy McGill** (1959-62)

RECORDS	GAME		SEASON		CAREER	
POINTS	60	Billy McGill, vs. BYU (Feb. 24, 1962)	1,009	Billy McGill (1961-62)	2,542	Keith Van Horn (1993-97)
POINTS PER GAME			38.8	Billy McGill (1961-62)	27.0	Billy McGill (1959-62)
REBOUNDS	24	Billy McGill, vs. UCLA (Dec. 29, 1961)	430	Billy McGill (1960-61)	1,106	Billy McGill (1959-62)
ASSISTS	16	Scott Jones, vs. BYU (Jan. 12, 1974); achieved 5 times by Jeff Jonas (1973-77)	309	Jeff Jonas (1976-77)	778	Jeff Jonas (1973-77)

SEASON REVIEW

SEASON	W-L	CONF.	SCORING	COACH	RECORD	
1908-15	*76-24*		*Coach Fred Bennion, 44-9 in 4 seasons (1910-14)*			
1915-16	11-0			Nelson H. Nordgren		
1916-17	3-3			Nelson H. Nordgren	26-7	.788
1917-18	5-4			Thomas Fitzpatrick		
1918-19	7-2			Thomas Fitzpatrick		
1919-20	5-1			Thomas Fitzpatrick		
1920-21	5-1			Thomas Fitzpatrick		
1921-22	8-2			Thomas Fitzpatrick		
1922-23	5-3			Thomas Fitzpatrick		
1923-24	2-6	2-6		Thomas Fitzpatrick		
1924-25	5-11	3-5		Thomas Fitzpatrick	42-30	.583
1925-26	4-8	4-8		Ike Armstrong		
1926-27	5-10	4-8		Ike Armstrong	9-18	.333
1927-28	7-10	5-7		Vadal Peterson		
1928-29	5-12	3-9		Vadal Peterson		
1929-30	15-12	4-8		Vadal Peterson		
1930-31	21-6	8-4		Vadal Peterson		
1931-32	14-9	8-4		Vadal Peterson		
1932-33	13-8	9-3		Vadal Peterson		
1933-34	14-9	7-5		Vadal Peterson		
1934-35	10-9	5-7		Vadal Peterson		
1935-36	7-15	4-8		Vadal Peterson		

SEAS.	W-L	CONF.	POSTSEASON	SCORING		REBOUNDS		ASSISTS		COACH	RECORD	
1936-37	17-7	7-5								Vadal Peterson		
1937-38	20-4	10-2								Vadal Peterson		
1938-39	13-7	7-5								Vadal Peterson		
1939-40	19-4	8-4								Vadal Peterson		
1940-41	14-7	9-3								Vadal Peterson		
1941-42	13-7	7-5								Vadal Peterson		
1942-43	10-12	1-7								Vadal Peterson		
1943-44	**22-4**		**NAT'L CHAMP, NIT QUARTERS**							**Vadal Peterson**		
1944-45	17-4	8-0	NCAA REGIONAL SEMIFINALS							Vadal Peterson		
1945-46	12-8	8-4								Vadal Peterson		
1946-47	19-5	10-2	NIT CHAMPION							Vadal Peterson		
1947-48	11-9	6-4		Arnie Ferrin	14.1					Vadal Peterson		
1948-49	24-8	14-6	NIT FIRST ROUND	Vern Gardner	15.3					Vadal Peterson		
1949-50	16-18	8-12		Glen Smith	13.0					Vadal Peterson		
1950-51	23-13	12-8		Glen Smith	15.5	Kent Bates	8.4			Vadal Peterson		
1951-52	19-9	8-6		Glen Smith	18.9	Glen Smith	7.3			Vadal Peterson		
1952-53	10-14	5-9		Bruce Goodrich	14.1	Bruce Goodrich	5.3			Vadal Peterson	385-230	.626
1953-54	12-14	7-7		Morris Buckwalter	9.5	Bill Maxwell	8.9			Jack Gardner		
1954-55	24-4	13-1	NCAA REGIONAL SEMIFINALS	Art Bunte	19.2	Gary Bergen	12.8			Jack Gardner		
1955-56	22-6	12-2	NCAA REGIONAL FINALS	Art Bunte	21.9	Gary Bergen	12.0			Jack Gardner		
1956-57	19-8	10-4	NIT FIRST ROUND	Milton Kane	16.6	Jerry McCleary	11.1			Jack Gardner		
1957-58	20-7	9-5	NIT FIRST ROUND	DeLyle Condie	10.7	DeLyle Condie	9.8			Jack Gardner		
1958-59	21-7	13-1	NCAA REGIONAL SEMIFINALS	Pearl Pollard	12.5	Pearl Pollard	7.5			Jack Gardner		
1959-60	26-3	13-1	NCAA REGIONAL SEMIFINALS	Billy McGill	15.5	Billy McGill	9.8			Jack Gardner		
1960-61	23-8	12-2	NCAA FOURTH PLACE	Billy McGill	27.8	Billy McGill	13.9			Jack Gardner		
1961-62	23-3	13-1		Billy McGill	38.8	Billy McGill	15.0			Jack Gardner		
1962-63	12-14	5-5		Bo Crain	11.6	John Allen	7.2			Jack Gardner		
1963-64	19-9	4-6		Doug Moon	17.5	George Fisher	8.7			Jack Gardner		
1964-65	17-9	3-7		Jerry Chambers	19.5	Jerry Chambers	10.6			Jack Gardner		
1965-66	23-8	7-3	NCAA FOURTH PLACE	Jerry Chambers	28.7	Jerry Chambers	11.6			Jack Gardner		
1966-67	15-11	5-5		Mervin Jackson	19.3	Dewitt Menyard	11.5			Jack Gardner		
1967-68	17-9	5-5		Mervin Jackson	23.9	Jeff Ockel	11.2			Jack Gardner		
1968-69	13-13	5-5		Mike Newlin	21.2	Ken Gardner	11.1			Jack Gardner		
1969-70	18-10	9-5	NIT SECOND ROUND	Mike Newlin	26.0	Ken Gardner	11.0			Jack Gardner		
1970-71	15-11	9-5		Mike Newlin	21.8	Ken Gardner	11.7			Jack Gardner	339-154	.688
1971-72	13-12	5-9		Eddie Trail	14.1	John Dearman	9.2			Bill Foster		
1972-73	8-19	4-10		Luther Burden	13.7	Mike Sojourner	12.2			Bill Foster		
1973-74	22-8	9-5	NIT RUNNER-UP	Luther Burden	23.7	Mike Sojourner	13.4			Bill Foster	43-39	.524
1974-75	17-9	7-7		Luther Burden	28.7	Charles Menatti	7.3	Jeff Jonas	7.8	Jerry Pimm		
1975-76	19-8	9-5		Jeff Judkins	19.4	Charles Menatti	7.4	Jeff Jonas	8.3	Jerry Pimm		
1976-77	22-7	11-3	NCAA REGIONAL SEMIFINALS	Jeff Judkins	20.6	Buster Matheney	6.7	Jeff Jonas	10.7	Jerry Pimm		
1977-78	23-6	12-2	NCAA REGIONAL SEMIFINALS	Buster Matheney	18.1	Danny Vranes	7.2	Michael Grey	4.0	Jerry Pimm		
1978-79	20-10	9-3	NCAA FIRST ROUND	Tom Chambers	16.0	Danny Vranes	10.1	Scott Martin	5.6	Jerry Pimm		
1979-80	18-10	10-4		Tom Chambers	17.2	Tom Chambers	8.7	Scott Martin	5.0	Jerry Pimm		
1980-81	25-5	13-3	NCAA REGIONAL SEMIFINALS	Tom Chambers	18.6	Tom Chambers	8.7	Scott Martin	7.4	Jerry Pimm		
1981-82	11-17	6-10		Peter Williams	13.6	Peter Williams	7.5	Pace Mannion	6.9	Jerry Pimm		
1982-83	18-14	11-5	NCAA REGIONAL SEMIFINALS	Pace Mannion	13.9	P. Williams, C. Winans	6.3	Pace Mannion	4.9	Jerry Pimm	173-86	.668
1983-84	11-19	4-12		Kelvin Upshaw	14.6	Chris Winans	8.4	Manuel Hendrix	5.1	Lynn Archibald		
1984-85	15-16	8-8		Kelvin Upshaw	17.4	Tim McLaughlin	5.9	Gale Gondrezick	4.9	Lynn Archibald		
1985-86	20-10	12-4	NCAA FIRST ROUND	Jerry Stroman	18.0	Mitch Smith	7.6	Kelvin Upshaw	4.0	Lynn Archibald		
1986-87	17-13	9-7	NIT FIRST ROUND	Mitch Smith	16.8	Mitch Smith	8.3	Gale Gondrezick	3.3	Lynn Archibald		
1987-88	19-11	11-5	NIT FIRST ROUND	Mitch Smith	14.6	Mitch Smith	9.4	Tommy Connor	3.8	Lynn Archibald		
1988-89	16-17	6-10		Mitch Smith	14.7	Mitch Smith	8.4	Mark Lenoir	3.5	Lynn Archibald	98-86	.533
1989-90	16-14	7-9		Josh Grant	16.5	Josh Grant	7.0	Tommy Connor	4.4	Rick Majerus		
1990-91	30-4	15-1	NCAA REGIONAL SEMIFINALS	Josh Grant	17.5	Josh Grant	8.0	Tyrone Tate	4.1	Rick Majerus		
1991-92	24-11	9-7	NIT THIRD PLACE	Byron Wilson	12.1	Paul Afeaki	6.1	Tyrone Tate	3.0	Rick Majerus		
1992-93	24-7	15-3	NCAA SECOND ROUND	Josh Grant	17.3	Josh Grant	10.7	Jimmy Soto	4.3	Rick Majerus		
1993-94	14-14	8-10		Keith Van Horn	18.3	Keith Van Horn	8.3	Terry Preston	4.6	Rick Majerus		
1994-95	28-6	15-3	NCAA SECOND ROUND	Keith Van Horn	21.0	Keith Van Horn	8.5	Jimmy Carroll	2.6	Rick Majerus		
1995-96	27-7	15-3	NCAA REGIONAL SEMIFINALS	Keith Van Horn	21.4	Keith Van Horn	8.8	Andre Miller	4.6	Rick Majerus		
1996-97	29-4	15-1	NCAA REGIONAL FINALS	Keith Van Horn	22.0	Keith Van Horn	9.5	Andre Miller	6.1	Rick Majerus		
1997-98	30-4	12-2	NCAA RUNNER-UP	Michael Doleac	16.1	Michael Doleac	7.1	Andre Miller	5.2	Rick Majerus		
1998-99	28-5	14-0	NCAA SECOND ROUND	Andre Miller	15.8	Alex Jensen	7.6	Andre Miller	5.6	Rick Majerus		
1999-2000	23-9	10-4	NCAA SECOND ROUND	Alex Jensen	13.1	Alex Jensen	7.5	Alex Jensen	3.1	Rick Majerus		
2000-01	19-12	10-4	NIT FIRST ROUND	Kevin Bradley	10.7	Britton Johnsen	5.4	Travis Spivey	3.6	Rick Majerus		
2001-02	21-9	10-4	NCAA FIRST ROUND	Nick Jacobson	13.0	Britton Johnsen	6.3	Travis Spivey	4.5	Rick Majerus		
2002-03	25-8	11-3	NCAA SECOND ROUND	Nick Jacobson	13.3	Britton Johnsen	6.7	Tim Drisdom	3.1	Rick Majerus		
2003-04	24-9	9-5	NCAA FIRST ROUND	Nick Jacobson	16.5	Andrew Bogut	9.9	Tim Drisdom	3.6	Rick Majerus[a]	323-95	.773
2004-05	29-6	13-1	NCAA REGIONAL SEMIFINALS	Andrew Bogut	20.4	Andrew Bogut	12.2	Marc Jackson	3.7	Ray Giacoletti		
2005-06	14-15	6-10		Johnnie Bryant	13.1	Luke Nevill	6.6	Johnnie Bryant	2.4	Ray Giacoletti		
2006-07	11-19	6-10		Luke Nevill	16.8	Luke Nevill	7.7	Johnnie Bryant	2.7	Ray Giacoletti	54-40	.574
2007-08	18-15	7-9		Luke Nevill	15.2	Luke Nevill	6.7	Luka Drca	3.8	Jim Boylen		
2008-09	24-10	12-4	NCAA FIRST ROUND	Luke Nevill	16.8	Luke Nevill	9.0	Luka Drca	3.5	Jim Boylen	42-25	.627

[a] Coaches who substituted for Rick Majerus during various seasons due to health issues: Joe Cravens (12-12 in 1989-90); Dick Hunsaker (18-12 in 2001-02); Kerry Rupp (9-4 in 2003-04).

ESPN 72 SAGARIN

UTAH STATE

Utah State has enjoyed two distinct decades of success, and in both cases great coaching and superlative defense were the program's calling cards. Simply put, the story of Aggies basketball revolves around the coaching eras of Ladell Andersen in the 1960s and Stew Morrill at the turn of the 21st century.

BEST TEAM: 1959-60 H. Cecil Baker's Aggies won on their athleticism and strong defense, so it's no surprise that the team's best player, Cornell Green (21.2 ppg), went on to become a star defensive back with the Dallas Cowboys. The Aggies went 24–5, reached No. 8 in the polls and made it to the semifinals of the NIT (see Heartbreaker).

BEST PLAYER: F Wayne Estes (1962-65) They called the 6'6" forward Baby Huey, after the popular cartoon character, because he had the power and size to do whatever he wanted on the basketball court. Estes was a prolific scorer, casually dropping 15-foot hooks to notch a 26.7 ppg career average, including 33.7 ppg in 1964-65—both school records that still stand. Tragically, the night he scored his 2,000th career point, Feb. 8, 1965, was also the night he died, accidentally walking into a downed power line while trying to help an injured motorist.

BEST COACH: Stew Morrill (1998-) He had successful stints at Colorado State and Montana, but Morrill's Utah State record is special indeed: 267–91, including 10 straight seasons of 23 wins or more. His teams have consistently ranked among the nation's leaders in defense, three-point and free throw shooting, while making six NCAA and four NIT appearances.

GAME FOR THE AGES: On March 15, 2001, against No. 5-seed Ohio State, guard Tony Brown hit the game-tying jumper with 1.8 seconds left in regulation and Curtis Bobb scored eight points in OT to give No. 12-seed Utah State its first NCAA Tournament win in 31 years. The 77-68 upset erased the pain left over from the Aggies' first-round elimination the previous year by Connecticut.

HEARTBREAKER: The great 1959-60 team made it all the way to the Mecca of basketball, Madison Square Garden, and the NIT final four, only to run into the buzz saw that was Providence's 1-3-1 zone and its brilliant lead guard, Lenny Wilkens. Cornell Green and Jerry Schofield (19 points apiece) did their best, but couldn't get enough help to counter Wilkens' 18 and Johnny Egan's 16 in the 68-62 loss.

FIERCEST RIVAL: Utah State will always have Utah and Brigham Young to spar with. But its newer rival is neighbor Nevada, which it joined in the WAC in 2005. Since then, the Aggies have won six of 11 encounters with the Wolf Pack. Nevada has been the winner (or sharer) of four conference championships, while Utah State has won or shared two WAC crowns, including 2008-09.

FANFARE AND HOOPLA: Cheer squad advisor Linda Zimmerman is the Stew Morrill of mascot coaches. She has sent four former Big Blues (he's a bull) on to do their thing for professional basketball, hockey and soccer teams.

The 6'6" Estes was nicknamed Baby Huey, because he had the power and size to do whatever he wanted on the basketball court.

FAN FAVORITE: G Jaycee Carroll (2004-08) Told that a good shooter makes 75% of his unguarded shots, Carroll charted 23,963 summertime practice attempts and hit 20,010 of them (84%). No wonder he became Utah State's all-time leading scorer (2,522), and ranks fourth in NCAA all-time three-point percentage (.465) and 18th in three-pointers made (369).

FIRST-ROUND PRO PICKS

1968 **Shaler Halimon,** Philadelphia (14)
1968 **Shaler Halimon,** Dallas (ABA)

PROFILE

Utah State University, Logan, UT
Founded: 1888
Enrollment: 24,421 (19,775 undergraduate)
Colors: Navy blue and white
Nickname: Aggies
Current arena: Dee Glen Smith Spectrum, opened in 1970 (10,270)
Previous: Nelson Fieldhouse, 1939-70 (6,500)
First game: 1903
All-time record: 1,398-997 (.584)
Total weeks in AP Top 20/25: 36

Current conference: Western Athletic (2005-)
Conference titles:
Rocky Mountain: 4 (1926, '30, '35, '36)
Pacific Coast Athletic: 1 (1980)
Big West: 6 (1995, '97 [tie] '98 [tie], 2000 [tie], '02 [tie], '04 [tie])
WAC: 2 (2008 [tie], '09)
Conference tournament titles:
Pacific Coast Athletic: 1 (1988)
Big West: 5 (1998, 2000, '01, '03, '05)
WAC: 1 (2009)

NCAA Tournament appearances: 18
NIT appearances: 9
Semifinals: 1

TOP 5

G **Jaycee Carroll** (2004-08)
G/F **Cornell Green** (1959-62)
F **Wayne Estes** (1962-65)
F **Shaler Halimon** (1966-68)
F/C **Marvin Roberts** (1968-71)

RECORDS	GAME		SEASON		CAREER	
POINTS	52	Wayne Estes, vs. Boston College (Dec. 30, 1964)	821	Wayne Estes (1963-64)	2,522	Jaycee Carroll (2004-08)
POINTS PER GAME			33.7	Wayne Estes (1964-65)	26.7	Wayne Estes (1962-65)
REBOUNDS	28	Wayne Estes, vs. Regis (Dec. 15, 1962)	403	Cornell Green (1959-60)	1,067	Cornell Green (1959-62)
ASSISTS	16	Oscar Williams, vs. Utah (Dec. 14, 1976)	224	Kris Clark (2007-08)	562	Oscar Williams (1974-78)

SEASON REVIEW

SEASON	W-L	CONF.	SCORING	COACH	RECORD
1903-16	*36-65*		*No winning seasons until 1912-13*		
1916-17	8-5			Joseph K. Jensen	
1917-18	9-0			Joseph K. Jensen	
1918-19	6-3			Joseph K. Jensen	30-17 .638
1919-20	2-0			E. Lowell "Dick" Romney	
1920-21	6-4			E. Lowell "Dick" Romney	
1921-22	8-3			E. Lowell "Dick" Romney	
1922-23	8-4			E. Lowell "Dick" Romney	
1923-24	6-6	3-5		E. Lowell "Dick" Romney	
1924-25	12-7	5-5		E. Lowell "Dick" Romney	
1925-26	13-5	8-4		E. Lowell "Dick" Romney	
1926-27	11-3	9-3		E. Lowell "Dick" Romney	
1927-28	7-7	5-7		E. Lowell "Dick" Romney	
1928-29	8-10	4-8		E. Lowell "Dick" Romney	
1929-30	15-7	7-5		E. Lowell "Dick" Romney	
1930-31	13-7	7-5		E. Lowell "Dick" Romney	
1931-32	7-15	2-10		E. Lowell "Dick" Romney	
1932-33	10-12	4-8		E. Lowell "Dick" Romney	
1933-34	14-6	7-5		E. Lowell "Dick" Romney	
1934-35	17-5	9-3		E. Lowell "Dick" Romney	
1935-36	17-9	9-3		E. Lowell "Dick" Romney	
1936-37	6-9	5-7		E. Lowell "Dick" Romney	

SEAS.	W-L	CONF.	POSTSEASON	SCORING		REBOUNDS		ASSISTS		COACH	RECORD	
1937-38	11-9	6-6								E. Lowell "Dick" Romney		
1938-39	18-6	8-4	NCAA REGIONAL SEMIFINALS							E. Lowell "Dick" Romney		
1939-40	11-7	7-5								E. Lowell "Dick" Romney		
1940-41	5-16	2-9								E. Lowell "Dick" Romney	225-157	.589
1941-42	6-10	3-9								Robert W. Burnett	6-10	.375
1942-43	14-7	4-4								D.D. Young		
1943-44	no team											
1944-45	9-10	3-7								D.D. Young	23-17	.575
1945-46	7-12	2-10								H.B. Lee		
1946-47	14-10	6-6								H.B. Lee	21-22	.488
1947-48	8-16	3-7								Joe Whitesides		
1948-49	10-21	4-16								Joe Whitesides		
1949-50	17-17	10-10								Joe Whitesides	35-54	.393
1950-51	12-22	6-14								H. Cecil Baker		
1951-52	17-14	9-5								H. Cecil Baker		
1952-53	17-13	7-7								H. Cecil Baker		
1953-54	14-13	7-7								H. Cecil Baker		
1954-55	15-7	9-5								H. Cecil Baker		
1955-56	13-13	7-7								H. Cecil Baker		
1956-57	11-13	7-7								H. Cecil Baker		
1957-58	4-20	3-11		Bob Ipsen	18.0	Harold Theus	10.2			H. Cecil Baker		
1958-59	19-7	10-4		Bob Ipsen	21.9	Jerry Schofield	12.8			H. Cecil Baker		
1959-60	24-5	12-2	NIT THIRD PLACE	Cornell Green	21.2					H. Cecil Baker		
1960-61	12-14	4-10		Cornell Green	20.4	Tyler Wilbon	13.3			H. Cecil Baker	158-141	.528
1961-62	22-7	12-2	NCAA REGIONAL SEMIFINALS	Cornell Green	25.7	Cornell Green	11.8			Ladell Andersen		
1962-63	20-7		NCAA FIRST ROUND	Wayne Estes	19.9	Troy Collier	11.0			Ladell Andersen		
1963-64	21-8		NCAA REGIONAL SEMIFINALS	Wayne Estes	28.3	Wayne Estes	13.0			Ladell Andersen		
1964-65	13-12			Wayne Estes	33.7	Wayne Estes	13.7			Ladell Andersen		
1965-66	12-14			Larry Angle	16.5	Alan Parrish	7.0			Ladell Andersen		
1966-67	20-6		NIT FIRST ROUND	Shaler Halimon	23.6	Shaler Halimon	8.7	Les Powell	3.5	Ladell Andersen		
1967-68	14-11			Shaler Halimon	26.8	Shaler Halimon	11.7			Ladell Andersen		
1968-69	9-17			Marvin Roberts	27.6	Marvin Roberts	12.5	Paul Jeppeson	2.9	Ladell Andersen		
1969-70	22-7		NCAA REGIONAL FINALS	Marvin Roberts	22.4	Marvin Roberts	13.9	Paul Jeppeson	4.0	Ladell Andersen		
1970-71	20-7		NCAA FIRST ROUND	Marvin Roberts	20.8	Marvin Roberts	11.8	Jeff Tebbs	3.7	Ladell Andersen	173-96	.643
1971-72	12-14			Bob Lauriski	17.4	Bob Lauriski	10.4	Jeff Tebbs	4.3	T.L. Plain		
1972-73	16-10			Jim Boatwright	18.7	Bob Lauriski	9.2	Ken Thompson	5.3	T.L. Plain	28-24	.538
1973-74	16-10			Jim Boatwright	18.5	Jimmy Moore	9.3	Blair Reed	3.2	Dutch Belnap		
1974-75	21-6		NCAA FIRST ROUND	Rich Haws	20.9	Jimmy Moore	9.1	Oscar Williams	4.8	Dutch Belnap		
1975-76	12-14 ⊗			Ed Gregg	22.3	Ed Gregg	11.7	Blair Reed	4.0	Dutch Belnap		
1976-77	15-12			Mike Santos	18.2	Mike Santos	11.3	Oscar Williams	7.7	Dutch Belnap		
1977-78	21-7		NIT FIRST ROUND	Mike Santos	18.3	Mike Santos	8.8	Oscar Williams	6.0	Dutch Belnap		
1978-79	19-11	9-5	NCAA FIRST ROUND	Keith McDonald	17.9	Brian Jackson	8.3	Rawlee Perkins	3.5	Dutch Belnap	104-60	.634▼
1979-80	18-9	11-2	NCAA FIRST ROUND	Dean Hunger	20.8	Dean Hunger	8.6	Rich McElrath	6.4	Rod Tueller		
1980-81	12-16	5-9		Brian Jackson	23.4	Brian Jackson	8.9	Lance Washington	3.0	Rod Tueller		
1981-82	4-23	2-12		Leo Cunningham	13.3	Leo Cunningham	9.9	Larry Bergeson	4.8	Rod Tueller		
1982-83	20-9	10-6	NCAA FIRST ROUND	Greg Grant	14.7	Greg Grant	9.1	Lance Washington	4.8	Rod Tueller		
1983-84	19-11	12-6	NIT FIRST ROUND	Greg Grant	17.4	Greg Grant	7.9	Vince Washington	3.3	Rod Tueller		
1984-85	17-11	10-8		Vince Washington	21.6	Greg Grant	9.5	Jeff J. Anderson	4.1	Rod Tueller		
1985-86	12-16	8-10		Greg Grant	22.6	Greg Grant	8.5	Kevin Nixon	3.9	Rod Tueller		
1986-87	15-16	8-10		Kevin Nixon	18.2	Dan Conway	6.6	Kevin Nixon	3.7	Rod Tueller		
1987-88	21-10	13-5	NCAA FIRST ROUND	Dan Conway	16.1	Dan Conway	5.6	Kevin Nixon	5.9	Rod Tueller	138-121	.533
1988-89	12-16	10-8		Reid Newey	19.4	Darrel White	4.8	Kendall Youngblood	4.4	Kohn Smith		
1989-90	14-16	8-10		Kendall Youngblood	15.4	Randy Funk	6.5	Allen Gordon	4.3	Kohn Smith		
1990-91	11-17	8-10		Kendall Youngblood	18.8	Kendall Youngblood	6.5	Allen Gordon	4.6	Kohn Smith		
1991-92	16-12	10-8		Kendall Youngblood	17.1	Kendall Youngblood	7.7	Malloy Nesmith	4.8	Kohn Smith		
1992-93	10-17	7-11		Jay Goodman	18.1	Rod Hay	7.9	Jay Goodman	6.9	Kohn Smith	63-78	.447
1993-94	14-13	11-7		Corwin Woodard	13.2	Eric Franson	9.1	Roddie Anderson	3.2	Larry Eustachy		
1994-95	21-8	14-4	NIT FIRST ROUND	Eric Franson	18.4	Eric Franson	9.8	Roddie Anderson	3.6	Larry Eustachy		
1995-96	18-15	10-8		Silas Mills	16.7	Eric Franson	8.5	Duane Rogers	5.2	Larry Eustachy		
1996-97	20-9	12-4		M. Spillers, M. Saxon	13.2	Maurice Spillers	8.3	Marcus Saxon	4.6	Larry Eustachy		
1997-98	25-8	13-3	NCAA FIRST ROUND	Marcus Saxon	17.4	Donnie Johnson	7.5	Marcus Saxon	4.1	Larry Eustachy	98-53	.649
1998-99	15-13	8-8		Donnie Johnson	14.3	Donnie Johnson	8.3	Rashad Elliott	4.8	Stew Morrill		
1999-2000	28-6	16-0	NCAA FIRST ROUND	S. Daniels, Troy Rolle	12.0	Shawn Daniels	7.9	Bernard Rock	4.4	Stew Morrill		
2000-01	28-6	13-3	NCAA SECOND ROUND	Shawn Daniels	11.8	Shawn Daniels	6.8	Bernard Rock	4.1	Stew Morrill		
2001-02	23-8	13-5	NIT OPENING ROUND	Desmond Penigar	17.2	Desmond Penigar	6.9	Tony Brown	4.8	Stew Morrill		
2002-03	24-9	12-6	NCAA FIRST ROUND	Desmond Penigar	15.7	Spencer Nelson	7.4	Mark Brown	4.5	Stew Morrill		
2003-04	25-4	17-1	NIT FIRST ROUND	Cardell Butler	14.0	Spencer Nelson	7.8	Mark Brown	4.9	Stew Morrill		
2004-05	24-8	13-5	NCAA FIRST ROUND	Spencer Nelson	16.0	Spencer Nelson	7.9	Spencer Nelson	4.8	Stew Morrill		
2005-06	23-9	11-5	NCAA FIRST ROUND	Nate Harris	17.3	Nate Harris	7.7	David Pak	4.6	Stew Morrill		
2006-07	23-12	9-7	NIT FIRST ROUND	Jaycee Carroll	21.3	Jaycee Carroll	6.3	Kris Clark	4.2	Stew Morrill		
2007-08	24-11	12-4	NIT FIRST ROUND	Jaycee Carroll	22.4	Gary Wilkinson	7.0	Kris Clark	6.4	Stew Morrill		
2008-09	30-5	14-2	NCAA FIRST ROUND	Gary Wilkinson	17.1	Gary Wilkinson	6.8	Jared Quayle	3.7	Stew Morrill	267-91	.746

⊗ Record doesn't reflect games forfeited or vacated. For adjusted record, see p. 521.

▼ Coach's record adjusted to reflect games forfeited or vacated: 106-58, .646. For yearly totals, see p. 521.

ESPN 172 SAGARIN

VALPARAISO

Coach Gene Bartow had success with Valparaiso when it was a College Division school, taking the Crusaders to the 1967 national quarterfinals. But it wasn't until Homer Drew inherited a losing D1 program that Valpo started to make some national noise.

BEST TEAM: 1997-98 Before the 1998 NCAA Tournament, a blizzard knocked out the power in Indiana, taking away practice time and hampering travel plans for Coach Drew's team. The No. 13-seed Crusaders still beat Mississippi and Florida State for its first two Tourney wins in school history.

BEST PLAYER: G Bryce Drew (1994-98) As Indiana's Mr. Basketball, he was recruited by many top schools, but chose to play for his father. A flurry of points, passes and pyrotechnics followed. Drew is the school's all-time leader in points, assists and threes.

BEST COACH: Homer Drew (1988-2002, '03-) His first four teams won all of 24 games. But transforming the Crusaders into three-point gunners paid off in 1992-93 when his team led the nation in three-point percentage. Valpo won 20 games in each of the next two seasons, followed by five straight NCAA Tournaments.

GAME FOR THE AGES: Valpo's first-round 1998 Tournament matchup with No. 4-seed Mississippi became an all-time classic when, with 2.5 seconds left and the Crusaders down 69-67, Coach Drew called for a set play code named Pacer. Jamie Sykes threw a long pass to just outside the three-point line, where Bill Jenkins out-jumped two Ole Miss defenders and caught the ball. In the same motion, Jenkins flipped it to Bryce Drew, who sank a 23-foot three-pointer for a 70-69 win.

FIERCEST RIVAL: Nothing captures the essence of Indiana basketball better than the Valpo-Butler series. You've got a first family of hoops in the Drews, and in Butler, you've got Hinkle Fieldhouse, the gym where the final game in *Hoosiers* was played. It's far from a bad-natured rivalry—Homer Drew is even known to come over to the Bulldogs student section to chat before each game. Butler leads overall, 64–32.

SEASON REVIEW

SEAS.	W-L	CONF.	COACH	SEAS.	W-L	CONF.	COACH
1918-49	*345-275*	*73-21 over 4 seasons (1920-24)*		1962-63	7-16		Paul Meadows
1949-50	15-8		Wilbur Allen	1963-64	9-15		Paul Meadows
1950-51	12-10		Wilbur Allen	1964-65	13-12		Gene Bartow
1951-52	12-12		Kenneth Suesens	1965-66	19-9		Gene Bartow
1952-53	9-15		Kenneth Suesens	1966-67	21-8		Gene Bartow
1953-54	10-13		Kenneth Suesens	1967-68	11-15		Gene Bartow
1954-55	13-11		Kenneth Suesens	1968-69	16-12		Gene Bartow
1955-56	12-14		Kenneth Suesens	1969-70	13-13		Gene Bartow
1956-57	11-14		Kenneth Suesens	1970-71	13-13		Bill Purden
1957-58	7-14		Kenneth Suesens	1971-72	15-11		Bill Purden
1958-59	12-11		Paul Meadows	1972-73	17-11		Bill Purden
1959-60	12-13		Paul Meadows	1973-74	15-11		Bill Purden
1960-61	7-16		Paul Meadows	1974-75	14-11		Bill Purden
1961-62	17-8		Paul Meadows	1975-76	12-14		Bill Purden

SEAS.	W-L	CONF.	SCORING		COACH	RECORD
1976-77	13-12				Ken Rochlitz	
1977-78	6-19				Ken Rochlitz	
1978-79	4-21				Ken Rochlitz	
1979-80	8-18				Ken Rochlitz	31-70 .307
1980-81	12-15				Tom Smith	
1981-82	9-18				Tom Smith	
1982-83	13-15	4-9			Tom Smith	
1983-84	9-19	3-11			Tom Smith	
1984-85	8-20	4-10			Tom Smith	
1985-86	9-19	5-9			Tom Smith	
1986-87	12-16	4-10			Tom Smith	
1987-88	12-16	3-11			Tom Smith	84-138 .378
1988-89	10-19	4-8			Homer Drew	
1989-90	4-24	1-11			Homer Drew	
1990-91	5-22	2-14			Homer Drew	
1991-92	5-22	2-14			Homer Drew	
1992-93	12-16	7-9	Tracy Gipson	21.3	Homer Drew	
1993-94	20-8	14-4			Homer Drew	
1994-95	20-8	14-4			Homer Drew	
1995-96	21-11 ⊗	13-5 ●			Homer Drew	
1996-97	24-7	13-3 ●	Bryce Drew	19.9	Homer Drew	
1997-98	23-10	13-3 ●	Bryce Drew	19.8	Homer Drew	
1998-99	23-9	10-4 ●	Lubos Barton	13.8	Homer Drew	
1999-2000	19-13	10-6 ●	Ivan Vujic	10.6	Homer Drew	
2000-01	24-8	13-3	Raitis Grafs	13.8	Homer Drew	
2001-02	25-8	12-2 ●	Lubos Barton	14.9	Homer Drew	
2002-03	20-11	12-2 ■	Raitis Grafs	16.5	Scott Drew	20-11 .645
2003-04	18-13	11-5 ●	Dan Oppland	15.7	Homer Drew	
2004-05	15-16	10-6	Dan Oppland	18.6	Homer Drew	
2005-06	17-12	8-8	Dan Oppland	19.8	Homer Drew	
2006-07	16-15	9-5	Urule Igbavboa	11.6	Homer Drew	
2007-08	22-14	9-9	Shawn Huff	12.6	Homer Drew	
2008-09	9-22	5-13	Urule Igbavboa	12.0	Homer Drew	332-277 .545▼

⊗ Records don't reflect games forfeited or vacated. For adjusted records, see p. 521.

▼ Coach's record does not reflect games forfeited or vacated: 333-276, .547. For yearly totals, see p. 521.

● NCAA Tournament appearance ■ NIT appearance

PROFILE

Valparaiso University, Valparaiso, IN
Founded: 1859
Enrollment: 3,980 (2,917 undergraduate)
Colors: Brown and gold
Nickname: Crusaders
Current arena: Athletics-Recreation Center, opened in 1984 (5,000)
Previous: Hilltop Gym, 1939-84 (3,500)
First game: 1918
All-time record: 1,156-1,101 (.512)
Total weeks in AP Top 20/25: 0

Current conference: Horizon League (2007-)
Conference titles:
Mid-Continent: 9 (1995, '96, '97, '98, '99 [tie], 2001 [tie], '02, '03, '04)
Conference tournament titles:
Mid-Continent: 8 (1995, '96, '97, '98, '99, 2000, '02, '04)
NCAA Tournament appearances: 7
Sweet 16s (since 1975): 1
NIT appearances: 1

FIRST-ROUND PRO PICKS

1998 **Bryce Drew,** Houston (16)

TOP 5

G **Bryce Drew** (1994-98)
G **Dick Jones** (1965-68)
F **Lubos Barton** (1998-2002)
F **Bob Dille** (1943-46)
F **Dan Oppland** (2002-06)

RECORDS

RECORDS	GAME		SEASON		CAREER	
POINTS	51	Bruce Lindner, vs. DePauw (Feb. 21, 1970)	725	Bruce Lindner (1969-70)	2,142	Bryce Drew (1994-98)
POINTS PER GAME			27.8	Bruce Lindner (1969-70)	19.5	Bruce Lindner (1967-70)
REBOUNDS	24	Chris Ensminger, vs. Northeastern Illinois (Jan. 4, 1996)	375	Joel Oberman (1973-74)	910	Chris Ensminger (1992-96)
ASSISTS	16	John McIlvain, vs. Illinois-Chicago (Jan. 13, 1983)	197	John McIlvain (1982-83)	626	Bryce Drew (1994-98)

ESPN 46 SAGARIN

VANDERBILT

Vanderbilt has never exactly been an SEC basketball power, but at least it has enjoyed more success than the perennial doormat football team. With several outstanding hoops teams over the years, Vandy even came close to a national title in 1965. And coach Kevin Stallings seemed to have his team on track for big things after barely missing the 2007 Elite Eight.

BEST TEAM: 1964-65 The team's 6'10" star, Clyde Lee, was built like a Clydesdale. He trampled over opponents to lead Vandy to its first SEC title, including a sweep of its series with mighty Kentucky. Vanderbilt finished off its 15–1 SEC season with a 106-69 demolition of LSU. In its first NCAA Tournament, the Commodores survived a thrilling 83-78 overtime win over DePaul, but came up short of the Final Four on a controversial call (see Heartbreaker) that allowed Michigan to advance, 87-85.

BEST PLAYER: C Clyde Lee (1963-66) The Nashville native put up impressive numbers over his three seasons and is still the No. 6 scorer (1,691) and No. 1 rebounder (1,223) in school history. He was responsible for drawing so many people to Memorial Gym that when it expanded in 1967, the two new south-side tiers instantly became known as "the balconies that Clyde Lee built." He was chosen third overall in the 1966 NBA draft (Warriors) and enjoyed a solid pro career.

BEST COACH: Roy Skinner (1958-59, '61-76) After a taste of the head coaching gig in 1958-59 when Bob Polk suffered a heart attack, Skinner took over the job permanently three years later. The winningest coach in Vandy history (278–135), Skinner was named SEC Coach of the Year four times.

GAME FOR THE AGES: As it entered the SEC Tournament final against Kentucky on March 3, 1951, Vanderbilt had already lost to the Wildcats twice that season. And Vandy fans were still licking their wounds after a profoundly humiliating 98-29 tourney loss to UK four years earlier. Legend even has it that "Kentucky" was already inscribed on the 1951 SEC trophy when the Commodores pulled off a monster 61-57 shocker over the eventual national champs.

HEARTBREAKER: With all the terrible moments Vanderbilt has experienced in its visits to Lexington, the 1965 NCAA Elite Eight loss to Michigan is the worst. Trailing by one in the final minute, Vanderbilt's John Ed Miller hit the go-ahead basket—or so it seemed. He was whistled for traveling, the basket was disallowed and Michigan prevailed, 87-85. "The referees cheated us," Skinner bluntly said afterwards.

FIERCEST RIVAL: Vanderbilt vs. Tennessee is a great rivalry in any sport, but no team has tortured the Vandy basketball program like the SEC's biggest dog, Kentucky. The Commodores were a miserable 0–28 in Rupp Arena for 32 years before a 2006 victory there. The Wildcats lead the all-time series 130–42.

FANFARE AND HOOPLA: Without a lot to cheer about during football season, Vanderbilt students have plenty of energy when basketball rolls around. Located right on top of the action, the Memorial Maniacs have easy access to opponents they love to heckle and, for even greater effect, they get to slam their feet on the elevated court, the better to make more thunderous noise.

The 1967 additions to Memorial Gym were called "the balconies that Clyde Lee built."

FAN FAVORITE: G/F Shan Foster (2004-08) Vandy's all-time leading scorer and all-around most popular Commodore, Foster's charm made his final game—a blowout loss to Siena in the 2008 NCAA Tournament—doubly depressing for fans.

CONSENSUS ALL-AMERICAS

1966 **Clyde Lee**, C

FIRST-ROUND PRO PICKS

1966 **Clyde Lee**, San Francisco (3)
1974 **Jan van Breda Kolff**, Virginia (ABA, 5)
1984 **Jeff Turner**, New Jersey (17)
1988 **Will Perdue**, Chicago (11)

PROFILE

Vanderbilt University, Nashville, TN
Founded: 1873
Enrollment: 10,893 (6,378 undergraduate)
Colors: Black and gold
Nickname: Commodores
Current arena: Memorial Gymnasium, opened in 1952 (14,316)
Previous: McQuiddy Gym, 1949-52 (3,247); Albert E. Hill Gymnasium, 1948-49 (1,900); Navy Center, 1947-48 (1,219); Father Ryan Gym, 1946-47 (N/A)
First game: Dec. 15, 1900

All-time record: 1,423-1,015 (.584)
Total weeks in AP Top 20/25: 174
Current conference: Southeastern (1932-)
Conference titles:
SEC: 3 (1965, '74 [tie], '93)
Conference tournament titles:
Southern: 1 (1927)
SEC: 1 (1951)
NCAA Tournament appearances: 10
Sweet 16s (since 1975): 4
NIT appearances: 11
Semifinals: 2
Titles: 1 (1990)

TOP 5

G **Tom Hagan** (1966-69)
G **Billy McCaffrey** (1992-94)
G/F **Shan Foster** (2004-08)
F **Billy Joe Adcock** (1946-50)
C **Clyde Lee** (1963-66)

RECORDS	GAME		SEASON		CAREER	
POINTS	44	Tom Hagan, vs. Mississippi State (March 8, 1969)	699	Billy McCaffrey (1992-93)	2,011	Shan Foster (2004-08)
POINTS PER GAME			23.4	Tom Hagan (1968-69)	21.4	Clyde Lee (1963-66)
REBOUNDS	28	Clyde Lee, vs. Mississippi (Jan. 10, 1966)	420	Clyde Lee (1964-65)	1,223	Clyde Lee (1963-66)
ASSISTS	14	Atiba Prater, vs. Wofford (Dec. 11, 1999); Billy McCaffrey, vs. Kentucky (Jan. 13, 1993)	180	Atiba Prater (1999-2000)	517	Atiba Prater (1996-2000)

THE SCHOOLS

SEASON REVIEW

SEASON	W-L	CONF.	SCORING	COACH	RECORD	
00-14	78-41		*Seven coaches in eight years from 1906-07 to 1913-14*			
14-15	6-6			G.T. Denton		
15-16	11-3			G.T. Denton		
16-17	3-8			G.T. Denton		
17-18	6-3			Ralph Palmer	6-3	.667
18-19	8-2			Ray Morrison	8-2	.800
19-20	14-4			G.T. Denton		
20-21	8-13			G.T. Denton	48-37	.565
21-22	8-8			Wallace Wade		
922-23	16-8	2-0		Wallace Wade	24-16	.600
923-24	7-15	1-3		Josh Cody		
1924-25	12-13	4-3		Josh Cody		
1925-26	8-18	2-7		Josh Cody		
1926-27	20-4	7-1		Josh Cody		
1927-28	5-7	2-5		Johnny Floyd		
1928-29	4-12	2-5		Johnny Floyd	9-19	.321
1929-30	6-16	1-9		Gus Morrow		
1930-31	16-8	7-7		Gus Morrow		
1931-32	8-11	5-7		Josh Cody		
1932-33	14-8	11-5		Josh Cody		
1933-34	11-6	8-5		Josh Cody		
1934-35	9-11	9-6		Josh Cody		

SEAS.	W-L	CONF.	POSTSEASON	SCORING		REBOUNDS		ASSISTS		COACH	RECORD	
935-36	9-14	9-4								Josh Cody	98-100	.495
936-37	6-10	3-7								Jim Buford		
937-38	9-12	4-8								Jim Buford		
938-39	14-7	7-5								Jim Buford		
939-40	10-12	5-7								Jim Buford		
940-41	8-9	3-9								Jim Buford	47-50	.485
941-42	7-9	3-8								Norm Cooper		
942-43	10-8	9-7								Norm Cooper		
943-44	12-3									Smokey Harper	12-3	.800
1944-45	6-6									Gus Morrow		
1945-46	3-10	2-5								Gus Morrow	31-40	.437
1946-47	7-8	4-7								Norm Cooper	24-25	.490
1947-48	8-14	4-11		Billy Joe Adcock	17.1					Bob Polk		
1948-49	14-8	9-5		Billy Joe Adcock	15.4					Bob Polk		
1949-50	17-8	11-3		Billy Joe Adcock	12.6					Bob Polk		
1950-51	19-8	10-4		Al Weiss	13.6					Bob Polk		
1951-52	18-9	9-5		Dave Kardokus	11.6	Dave Kardokus	8.4			Bob Polk		
1952-53	10-9	5-8		Dan Finch	20.7	Dan Finch	13.7			Bob Polk		
1953-54	12-10	5-9		Dan Finch	21.9	Dan Finch	11.3			Bob Polk		
1954-55	16-6	9-5		Al Rochelle	16.1	Charley Harrison	12.9			Bob Polk		
1955-56	19-4	11-3		Al Rochelle	18.3	Charley Harrison	14.3			Bob Polk		
1956-57	17-5	10-4		Al Rochelle	17.3	Hobby Gibbs	12.5			Bob Polk		
1957-58	14-11	7-7		Jim Henry	20.5	Don Hinton	8.9			Bob Polk		
1958-59	14-10	8-6		Jim Henry	18.8	Ben Rowan	10.7			Roy Skinner		
1959-60	14-9	7-7		Bill Johnson	15.5	Ben Rowan	11.3			Bob Polk		
1960-61	19-5	10-4		Bill Depp	17.2	Bill Depp	12.9			Bob Polk	197-106	.650
1961-62	12-12	6-8		John Russell	15.4	Ron Griffiths	10.3			Roy Skinner		
1962-63	16-7	9-5		Roger Schurig	16.8	Bob Grace	13.4			Roy Skinner		
1963-64	19-6	8-6		Clyde Lee	18.8	Clyde Lee	15.6			Roy Skinner		
1964-65	24-4	15-1	NCAA REGIONAL FINALS	Clyde Lee	22.5	Clyde Lee	15.0			Roy Skinner		
1965-66	22-4	13-3		Clyde Lee	22.6	Clyde Lee	15.8			Roy Skinner		
1966-67	21-5	14-4		Tom Hagan	17.0	Bob Warren	8.4			Roy Skinner		
1967-68	20-6	12-6		Tom Hagan	19.2	Perry Wallace	10.4			Roy Skinner		
1968-69	15-11	9-9		Tom Hagan	23.4	Perry Wallace	10.5			Roy Skinner		
1969-70	12-14	8-10		Perry Wallace	17.7	Perry Wallace	13.5			Roy Skinner		
1970-71	13-13	9-9		Thorpe Weber	16.9	Thorpe Weber	9.7	Rudy Thacker	3.1	Roy Skinner		
1971-72	16-10	10-8		Terry Compton	17.3	Ray Maddux	10.7	Jan van Breda Kolff	5.5	Roy Skinner		
1972-73	20-6	13-5		Terry Compton	17.7	Steve Turner	7.8	Jan van Breda Kolff	5.7	Roy Skinner		
1973-74	23-5	15-3	NCAA REGIONAL SEMIFINALS	Terry Compton	14.8	Jan van Breda Kolff	9.7	Jan van Breda Kolff	5.0	Roy Skinner		
1974-75	15-11	10-8		Jeff Fosnes	22.1	Jeff Fosnes	9.0	Dicky Keffer	3.8	Roy Skinner		
1975-76	16-11	12-6		Jeff Fosnes	17.9	Butch Feher	7.7	Dicky Keffer	4.0	Roy Skinner	278-135	.673
1976-77	10-16	6-12		Charles Davis	15.3	Charles Davis	7.0	Mark Elliott	3.4	Wayne Dobbs		
1977-78	10-17	6-12		Mike Rhodes	18.8	Charles Davis	7.1	Mark Elliott	3.2	Wayne Dobbs		
1978-79	18-9	11-7		Charles Davis	18.6	Charles Davis	8.6	Tommy Springer	4.3	Wayne Dobbs	38-42	.475
1979-80	13-13	7-11		Mike Rhodes	18.4	Ted Young	5.9	Tommy Springer	3.3	Richard Schmidt		
1980-81	15-14	7-11		Al Miller	14.6	Charles Davis	5.8	Jimmy Gray	3.9	Richard Schmidt	28-27	.509
1981-82	15-13	7-11		Willie Jones	15.8	Willie Jones	6.4	Al McKinney	3.2	C.M. Newton		
1982-83	19-14	9-9	NIT SECOND ROUND	Phil Cox	14.5	Ted Young	6.7	Al McKinney	3.4	C.M. Newton		
1983-84	14-15	8-10		Jeff Turner	16.8	Jeff Turner	7.3	Al McKinney	3.2	C.M. Newton		
1984-85	11-17	4-14		Phil Cox	16.5	Brett Burrow	8.0	Darrell Dulaney	3.6	C.M. Newton		
1985-86	13-15	7-11		Brett Burrow	13.2	Brett Burrow	5.8	Darrell Dulaney	3.4	C.M. Newton		
1986-87	18-16	7-11	NIT QUARTERFINALS	Will Perdue	17.4	Will Perdue	8.7	Barry Booker	2.7	C.M. Newton		
1987-88	20-11	10-8	NCAA REGIONAL SEMIFINALS	Will Perdue	18.3	Will Perdue	10.1	Barry Goheen	2.9	C.M. Newton		
1988-89	19-14	12-6	NCAA FIRST ROUND	Frank Kornet	16.8	Frank Kornet	7.1	Derrick Wilcox	5.2	C.M. Newton	129-115	.529
1989-90	21-14	7-11	NIT CHAMPION	Scott Draud	15.6	Eric Reid	5.8	Derrick Wilcox	4.5	Eddie Fogler		
1990-91	17-13	11-7	NCAA FIRST ROUND	Scott Draud	15.2	Bruce Elder	5.9	Kevin Anglin	4.1	Eddie Fogler		
1991-92	15-15	6-10	NIT FIRST ROUND	Kevin Anglin	16.9	Dan Hall	5.9	Kevin Anglin	3.8	Eddie Fogler		
1992-93	28-6	14-2	NCAA REGIONAL SEMIFINALS	Billy McCaffrey	20.6	Bruce Elder	6.1	Billy McCaffrey	3.6	Eddie Fogler	81-48	.628
1993-94	20-12	9-7	NIT RUNNER-UP	Billy McCaffrey	20.6	Chris Lawson	6.8	Billy McCaffrey	4.2	Jan van Breda Kolff		
1994-95	13-15	6-10		Ronnie McMahan	18.3	Bryan Milburn	6.3	Frank Seckar	4.1	Jan van Breda Kolff		
1995-96	18-14	7-9	NIT SECOND ROUND	Frank Seckar	16.3	Malik Evans	6.5	Frank Seckar	5.5	Jan van Breda Kolff		
1996-97	19-12	9-7	NCAA FIRST ROUND	Pax Whitehead	15.5	Billy Di Spaltro	6.3	Drew Maddux	3.7	Jan van Breda Kolff		
1997-98	20-13	7-9	NIT QUARTERFINALS	Drew Maddux	16.8	Billy Di Spaltro	5.7	Atiba Prater	4.1	Jan van Breda Kolff		
1998-99	14-15	5-11		Dan Langhi	17.7	Dan Langhi	7.3	Atiba Prater	3.4	Jan van Breda Kolff	104-81	.562
1999-2000	19-11	8-8	NIT FIRST ROUND	Dan Langhi	22.1	Anthony Williams	6.4	Atiba Prater	6.0	Kevin Stallings		
2000-01	15-15	4-12		Chuck Moore	12.0	Anthony Williams	7.9	Russell Lakey	3.1	Kevin Stallings		
2001-02	17-15	6-10	NIT SECOND ROUND	Matt Freije	15.1	Matt Freije	5.1	Brendan Plavich	3.2	Kevin Stallings		
2002-03	11-18	3-13		Matt Freije	17.9	Brian Thornton	5.7	Russell Lakey	3.4	Kevin Stallings		
2003-04	23-10	8-8	NCAA REGIONAL SEMIFINALS	Matt Freije	18.4	Matt Freije	5.4	Russell Lakey	3.9	Kevin Stallings		
2004-05	20-14	8-8	NIT QUARTERFINALS	Mario Moore	13.5	Julian Terrell	5.1	Mario Moore	3.7	Kevin Stallings		
2005-06	17-13	7-9	NIT FIRST ROUND	Shan Foster	15.9	Julian Terrell	7.2	Derrick Byars	3.2	Kevin Stallings		
2006-07	22-12	10-6	NCAA REGIONAL SEMIFINALS	Derrick Byars	17.0	Ross Neltner	5.7	Derrick Byars	3.4	Kevin Stallings		
2007-08	26-8	10-6	NCAA FIRST ROUND	Shan Foster	20.5	A.J. Ogilvy	6.8	Jermaine Beal	4.6	Kevin Stallings		
2008-09	19-12	8-8		A.J. Ogilvy	15.4	A.J. Ogilvy	7.1	Jermaine Beal	3.2	Kevin Stallings	189-128	.596

ESPN 275 SAGARIN

VERMONT

The chant of "U-V-M! U-V-M!" used to ring loudest at Vermont's hockey games, but over the past decade the basketball team has turned tiny Patrick Gym into an unmatched wall of noise. By the way, UVM—the more familiar moniker for the Catamounts—comes from the Latin phrase *Universitas Virdis Montis*, meaning the University of the Green Mountains.

BEST TEAM: 2004-05 UVM won a school-record 25 games, its first outright America East regular-season title and its third straight conference tournament crown. Advancing to the Tournament for the third straight season, the Catamounts upset Big East champ Syracuse for UVM's first postseason victory. The colorful crew was led by forward Taylor Coppenrath and coach Tom Brennan, who doubled as a morning-drive radio host.

BEST PLAYER: F Taylor Coppenrath (2001-05) His hometown of West Barnet, Vt., was so small that his parents' house didn't even have a street number. But as low-key as he was off the court, he ignited the Catamounts on it with his inside-out game. He was the nation's second-leading scorer as a senior (25.1 ppg).

BEST COACH: Tom Brennan (1986-2005) He once summed up his coaching philosophy to *ESPN The Magazine* by saying, "I know two plays. *The Producers* and 'Put the f–ing ball in the basket.'" It worked well enough. The animated Brennan guided the Catamounts to their only three Tournaments in his final three seasons.

GAME FOR THE AGES: No. 13-seed UVM stunned Syracuse with a 60-57 victory in the first round of the 2005 NCAA Tournament. Guard T.J. Sorrentine's 28-foot three-pointer with 1:10 left helped ice the win.

FIERCEST RIVAL: UVM trails Boston University, 39–51, in a series that dates back to the 1911-12 season. But two of the Catamounts' biggest wins have come against their fellow New Englanders. In 1981, they beat Rick Pitino's bunch in three overtimes in the ECAC North tournament to advance to the semifinals for the first time. In 2003, Vermont beat BU by a point in the America East finals to earn its first Tournament bid.

SEASON REVIEW

SEAS.	W-L	CONF.	COACH	SEAS.	W-L	CONF.	COACH
1900-48	*277-213*	*Thomas Keady 56-15 (1921-25)*		1961-62	12-12	3-7	John Evans
1948-49	15-5	2-1	John Evans	1962-63	10-13	2-8	John Evans
1949-50	9-11	2-3	John Evans	1963-64	11-10	4-6	John Evans
1950-51	14-6	4-1	John Evans	1964-65	7-13	1-9	John Evans
1951-52	14-6	3-1	John Evans	1965-66	12-8	3-7	Arthur Loche
1952-53	11-10	1-2	John Evans	1966-67	9-15	1-9	Arthur Loche
1953-54	13-7	1-2	John Evans	1967-68	12-12	5-5	Arthur Loche
1954-55	6-15	4-1	John Evans	1968-69	14-11	3-7	Arthur Loche
1955-56	6-12	2-3	John Evans	1969-70	8-16	3-7	Arthur Loche
1956-57	15- 5	3-2	John Evans	1970-71	9-15	1-9	Arthur Loche
1957-58	15-10	5-5	John Evans	1971-72	5-19	0-10	Arthur Loche
1958-59	12-10	4-6	John Evans	1972-73	8-16	2-10	Peter Salzberg
1959-60	9-11	2-8	John Evans	1973-74	9-17	3-9	Peter Salzberg
1960-61	9-11	3-7	John Evans	1974-75	16-10	8-4	Peter Salzberg

SEAS.	W-L	CONF.	SCORING		COACH	RECORD
1975-76	15-10	6-6			Peter Salzberg	
1976-77	8-17 ⊗				Peter Salzberg	
1977-78	11-15				Peter Salzberg	
1978-79	9-17				Peter Salzberg	
1979-80	12-15	12-14	Mike Evelti	18.2	Peter Salzberg	
1980-81	16-12	15-11	Mike Evelti	16.0	Peter Salzberg	104-129 .446▼
1981-82	10-16	2-8	Mike Evelti	18.2	Bill Whitmore	
1982-83	10-19	3-7	Peter Cole	13.2	Bill Whitmore	
1983-84	7-21	3-11	Howard Hudson	15.6	Bill Whitmore	
1984-85	9-19	5-11	Matt Thompson	15.3	Bill Whitmore	
1985-86	9-19	5-13	Howard Hudson	15.6	Bill Whitmore	45-94 .324
1986-87	5-23	3-15	Rob Zinn	20.6	Tom Brennan	
1987-88	3-24	2-16	Rahim Huland El	14.8	Tom Brennan	
1988-89	6-21	4-14	Joe Calavita	17.9	Tom Brennan	
1989-90	13-17	4-8	Kevin Roberson	14.3	Tom Brennan	
1990-91	15-13	5-5	Matt Johnson	20.7	Tom Brennan	
1991-92	16-13	7-7	Kevin Roberson	14.3	Tom Brennan	
1992-93	10-17	4-10	Eddie Benton	23.8	Tom Brennan	
1993-94	12-15	3-11	Eddie Benton	26.4	Tom Brennan	
1994-95	14-13	7-9	Eddie Benton	20.5	Tom Brennan	
1995-96	12-15	10-8	Eddie Benton	24.5	Tom Brennan	
1996-97	14-13	7-11	Craig Peper	13.0	Tom Brennan	
1997-98	16-11	11-7	Erik Nelson	16.2	Tom Brennan	
1998-99	11-16	7-11	Tony Orciari	15.6	Tom Brennan	
1999-2000	16-12	11-7	Tony Orciari	15.9	Tom Brennan	
2000-01	12-17	7-11	Tony Orciari	17.7	Tom Brennan	
2001-02	21-8	13-3	T.J. Sorrentine	18.8	Tom Brennan	
2002-03	21-12	11-5 ●	Taylor Coppenrath	20.1	Tom Brennan	
2003-04	22-9	15-3 ●	Taylor Coppenrath	24.1	Tom Brennan	
2004-05	25-7	16-2 ●	Taylor Coppenrath	25.1	Tom Brennan	264-276 .489
2005-06	13-17	7-9	Mike Trimboli	14.0	Mike Lonergan	
2006-07	25-8	15-1 ■	Mike Trimboli	15.8	Mike Lonergan	
2007-08	16-15	9-7	Marqus Blakely	19.0	Mike Lonergan	
2008-09	24-9	13-3	Marqus Blakely	16.1	Mike Lonergan	78-49 .614

⊗ Record doesn't reflect games forfeited or vacated. For adjusted record, see p. 521.
▼ Coach's record adjusted to reflect games forfeited or vacated: 105-128, .451. For yearly totals, see p. 521.
● NCAA Tournament appearance ■ NIT appearance

PROFILE

University of Vermont, Burlington, VT
Founded: 1791
Enrollment: 10,744 (9,454 undergraduate)
Colors: Green and gold
Nickname: Catamounts
Current arena: Roy L. Patrick Gym, opened in 1963 (3,226)
First game: 1900
All-time record: 1,025-1,024 (.500)
Total weeks in AP Top 20/25: 0

Current conference: America East (1979-)
Conference titles:
Yankee: 1 (1947)
America East: 4 (2002 [tie], '05, '07, '09 [tie])
Conference tournament titles:
America East: 3 (2003, '04, '05)
NCAA Tournament appearances: 3
NIT appearances: 1

FIRST-ROUND PRO PICKS

1947 **Larry Killic**, Baltimore (10)

TOP 5

G **Eddie Benton** (1992-96)
G **T.J. Sorrentine** (2000-05)
F **Taylor Coppenrath** (2001-05)
F **Clyde Lord** (1956-59)
C **Kevin Roberson** (1988-92)

RECORDS

	GAME		SEASON		CAREER	
POINTS	54	Eddie Benton, vs. Drexel (Jan. 29, 1994)	777	Taylor Coppenrath (2004-05)	2,474	Eddie Benton (1992-96)
POINTS PER GAME			26.4	Eddie Benton (1993-94)	23.8	Eddie Benton (1992-96)
REBOUNDS	29	Benny Becton, vs. Maine (Dec. 7, 1962)	401	Chris Holm (2006-07)	1,054	Kevin Roberson (1988-92)
ASSISTS	15	T.J. Sorrentine, vs. Albany (Nov. 30, 2000)	177	Howard Hudson (1985-86)	624	Mike Trimboli (2005-09)

ESPN 21 SAGARIN

VILLANOVA

This Catholic school on Philadelphia's Main Line has a basketball tradition as rich and old as its suburban setting. The Wildcats reached the Final Four in both the first NCAA Tournament in 1939 and the most recent one in 2009. The in-between wasn't bad, either: Nova is among the top 10 schools in Big Dance appearances with 30. Under Rollie Massimino in 1985, they put together perhaps the greatest Cinderella performance in the history of the game.

BEST TEAM: 1984-85 Villanova's final record of 25–10 wasn't exactly eye-popping, but the Wildcats' run through the NCAA Tournament was. The No. 8 seed won its first three games by a combined nine points and then prevailed in the title game by two over their bigger, faster, more talented Big East foe, Georgetown. How did Nova do it? By shooting a nearly impossible 78.6% from the field.

BEST PLAYER: F Paul Arizin (1947-50) Unrecruited out of high school, Arizin was discovered by coach Alexander Severance at a rec-league game. He went on to score 85 points in one game in 1949 and become Villanova's first 1,000-point scorer. Arizin finished his three-year career with 1,648 points (20.1 ppg) as Villanova went 63–17 in his three seasons. Arizin played 10 seasons with the Philadelphia Warriors and was inducted into the Naismith Hall of Fame in 1978.

BEST COACH: Rollie Massimino (1973-92) His overall winning percentage (.596) at Villanova trails that of other Wildcats coaches, but during his 19-year tenure Massimino went 20–10 in the NCAA Tournament. Between 1978 and '88, he guided five teams to the Elite Eight and took the 1984-85 squad all the way to the national title.

GAME FOR THE AGES: On April 1, 1985, before a capacity crowd at Kentucky's Rupp Arena, Villanova completed its monumental run through the NCAA Tournament by upending No. 1-seed Georgetown. Led by Ed Pinckney, Harold Jensen, Dwayne McClain and Gary McLain, the Wildcats used ferocious defense and heavenly shooting (22 of 28 from the floor, 22 of 27 from the line) to take out Patrick Ewing and the heavily favored Hoyas, 66-64.

HEARTBREAKER: Nova suffered a double whammy in 1971. The Wildcats stormed the NCAA Tournament, with a 90-47 pasting of previously unbeaten Penn followed by a double-OT 92-89 thriller over Western Kentucky, to reach the Final. There UCLA slowed the tempo to hinder Wildcat forward Howard Porter (who still scored 25), and won its seventh title in eight years. But Nova didn't just lose; the NCAA wiped its entire Tourney appearance off the books when it was disclosed that Porter had signed a pro contract before the Tournament.

FIERCEST RIVAL: Villanova plays in Philadelphia's Big 5 along with Saint Joseph's, and the two have a solid Augustinian vs. Jesuit rivalry to deepen the conflict. But the Big 5 hasn't had much impact in the upper echelon of the rankings in recent decades, and the Big East has its own Jesuit institution for Nova to clash with. Indeed, Georgetown always seems to be standing in Villanova's path when a conference or national title is in the offing. Since their first tip-off in 1922, Georgetown leads the series, 39–27.

FANFARE AND HOOPLA: Before every on-campus home game, the Wildcats take the floor via the student bleachers. Sure, as far as traditions go, it's just a baby (having begun in 2001-02), but it's got a nice We're a Team glow to it.

FAN FAVORITE: C Ed Pinckney (1981-85) He was the 1985 NCAA Tournament MOP and would play a dozen seasons in the NBA. But it was Pinckney's easygoing nature and gentle manner that made him special among Villanova fans.

CONSENSUS ALL-AMERICAS

1950	**Paul Arizin,** F
1996	**Kerry Kittles,** G
2006	**Randy Foye,** G

FIRST-ROUND PRO PICKS

1950	**Paul Arizin,** Philadelphia (3)
1963	**Tom Hoover,** Philadelphia (6)
1965	**Jim Washington,** St. Louis (8)
1972	**Chris Ford,** Utah (ABA)
1983	**Stewart Granger,** Cleveland (24)
1985	**Ed Pinckney,** Phoenix (10)
1986	**Harold Pressley,** Sacramento (17)
1996	**Kerry Kittles,** New Jersey (8)
1997	**Tim Thomas,** New Jersey (7)
2001	**Michael Bradley,** Toronto (17)
2006	**Randy Foye,** Boston (7)
2006	**Kyle Lowry,** Memphis (24)

PROFILE

Villanova University, Villanova, PA
Founded: 1842
Enrollment: 10,301 (6,335 undergraduate)
Colors: Navy blue and white
Nickname: Wildcats
Current arena: The Pavilion, opened in 1985 (6,500)
Previous: Villanova Field House, 1932-85 (N/A)
First game: 1920
All-time record: 1,508-852 (.639)
Total weeks in AP Top 20/25: 241

Current conference: Big East (1980-)
Conference titles:
Eastern 8: 2 (1978 [tie], '79)
Eastern Athletic: 1 (1980 [tie])
Big East: 4 (1982, '83 [tie],'97 [tie], 2006 [tie])
Conference tournament titles:
Eastern 8: 1 (1978)
Eastern Athletic: 1 (1980)
Big East: 1 (1995)
NCAA Tournaments: 30 (1 appearance vacated)
Sweet 16s (since 1975): 9
Final Fours: 4
Titles: 1 (1985)

NIT appearances: 17
Semifinals: 5
Titles: 1 (1994)

TOP 5

G	**Randy Foye** (2002-06)
G	**Kerry Kittles** (1992-96)
F	**Paul Arizin** (1947-50)
F	**Howard Porter** (1968-71)
C	**Ed Pinckney** (1981-85)

RECORDS	GAME		SEASON		CAREER	
POINTS	85	Paul Arizin, vs. Philadelphia NAMC (Feb. 12, 1949)	836	Bob Schafer (1953-54)	2,243	Kerry Kittles (1992-96)
POINTS PER GAME			29.2	Larry Hennessy (1952-53)	23.2	Larry Hennessy (1950-53)
REBOUNDS	30	Howard Porter, vs. Saint Peter's (Jan. 9, 1971)	503	Howard Porter (1970-71)	1,325	Howard Porter (1968-71)
ASSISTS	16	Fran O'Hanlon, vs. Toledo (Feb. 24, 1970); Jim Huggard, vs. Scranton (Dec. 4, 1959)	238	Chris Ford (1970-71)	627	Kenny Wilson (1985-89)

SEASON REVIEW

SEASON	W-L	CONF.	SCORING		COACH	RECORD	
1920-21	8-7				Michael A. Saxe		
1921-22	11-4				Michael A. Saxe		
1922-23	10-6				Michael A. Saxe		
1923-24	14-7				Michael A. Saxe		
1924-25	10-1				Michael A. Saxe		
1925-26	10-6				Michael A. Saxe	63-31	.670
1926-27	11-7				John C. Cashman		
1927-28	4-11				John C. Cashman		
1928-29	6-8				John C. Cashman	21-26	.447
1929-30	11-6		John Birmingham	136	George W. Jacobs		
1930-31	7-13		Joseph Czescik	126	George W. Jacobs		
1931-32	7-11		Joseph Czescik	123	George W. Jacobs		
1932-33	9-4		Arthur Lynch	75	George W. Jacobs		
1933-34	9-3		Benjamin Geraghy	114	George W. Jacobs		
1934-35	13-7		Michael O'Meara	136	George W. Jacobs		
1935-36	6-12		Michael O'Meara	131	George W. Jacobs	62-56	.525

SEAS.	W-L	CONF.	POSTSEASON	SCORING		REBOUNDS		ASSISTS		COACH	RECORD	
1936-37	15-8			James Montgomery	145					Alexander Severance		
1937-38	25-5			George Dusminski	213					Alexander Severance		
1938-39	20-5		NCAA NATIONAL SEMIFINALS	James Montgomery	145					Alexander Severance		
1939-40	17-2			George Dusminski	213					Alexander Severance		
1940-41	13-3			Paul Nugent	128					Alexander Severance		
1941-42	13-9			William Wood	230					Alexander Severance		
1942-43	19-2			William Wood	231					Alexander Severance		
1943-44	9-11			Frank Frascella	263					Alexander Severance		
1944-45	6-11			Lee Carter	149					Alexander Severance		
1945-46	10-13			Joseph Lord	303					Alexander Severance		
1946-47	17-7			Joseph Lord	438					Alexander Severance		
1947-48	15-9			Paul Arizin	11.1					Alexander Severance		
1948-49	23-4		NCAA REGIONAL SEMIFINALS	Paul Arizin	22.0					Alexander Severance		
1949-50	25-4			Paul Arizin	25.3					Alexander Severance		
1950-51	25-7		NCAA FIRST ROUND	Larry Hennessy	22.0	Jim Mooney	14.7			Alexander Severance		
1951-52	19-8			Larry Hennessy	21.0	Thomas Brennan	14.7			Alexander Severance		
1952-53	19-8			Larry Hennessy	29.2	Jack Devine	10.9			Alexander Severance		
1953-54	20-11			Bob Schafer	27.0	Jack Devine	12.0			Alexander Severance		
1954-55	18-10		NCAA REGIONAL SEMIFINALS	Bob Schafer	21.2	Jack Devine	12.0			Alexander Severance		
1955-56	14-12			James Smith	13.7					Alexander Severance		
1956-57	10-15			Richard Griffith	13.2					Alexander Severance		
1957-58	12-11			Jack Kelly	15.4	Tom Brennan	12.0			Alexander Severance		
1958-59	18-7		NIT FIRST ROUND	Joe Ryan	15.4	George Raveling	16.5			Alexander Severance		
1959-60	20-6		NIT QUARTERFINALS	Hubie White	19.0	George Raveling	13.1			Alexander Severance		
1960-61	11-13			Hubie White	21.2	Hubie White	9.7			Alexander Severance	413-201	.673
1961-62	21-7		NCAA REGIONAL FINALS	Hubie White	21.5	Hubie White	10.2			Jack Kraft		
1962-63	19-10		NIT FOURTH PLACE	Wally Jones	16.7	Jim Washington	12.2			Jack Kraft		
1963-64	24-4		NCAA REGIONAL SEMIFINALS	Wally Jones	16.4	Jim Washington	14.2			Jack Kraft		
1964-65	23-5		NIT RUNNER-UP	Bill Melchionni	19.4	Jim Washington	15.8			Jack Kraft		
1965-66	18-11		NIT THIRD PLACE	Bill Melchionni	27.6	Bernie Schaffer	8.2			Jack Kraft		
1966-67	17-9		NIT FIRST ROUND	Johnny Jones	18.9	Johnny Jones	9.0			Jack Kraft		
1967-68	19-9		NIT QUARTERFINALS	Johnny Jones	10.1					Jack Kraft		
1968-69	21-5		NCAA FIRST ROUND	Howard Porter	22.4	Johnny Jones	8.7			Jack Kraft		
1969-70	22-7		NCAA REGIONAL FINAL	Howard Porter	22.2	Howard Porter	15.1			Jack Kraft		
1970-71	27-7 ⊗		NCAA RUNNER-UP	Howard Porter	23.5	Howard Porter	14.8	Chris Ford	7.0	Jack Kraft		
1971-72	20-8		NCAA REGIONAL SEMIFINALS	Hank Siemiontkowski	19.1	Hank Siemiontkowski	10.4	Chris Ford	5.2	Jack Kraft		
1972-73	11-14			Tom Ingelsby	25.5	Tom Ingelsby, L. Moody	6.2	Ed Hastings	3.5	Jack Kraft	242-96	.716▼
1973-74	7-19			Chubby Cox	11.8	John Olive	6.5	Joey Rogers	2.7	Rollie Massimino		
1974-75	9-18			Larry Herron	17.9	John Olive	6.5	Joey Rogers	5.0	Rollie Massimino		
1975-76	16-11			Keith Herron	16.1	John Olive	6.8	Joey Rogers	4.4	Rollie Massimino		
1976-77	23-10	6-1	NIT THIRD PLACE	Keith Herron	19.2	John Olive	5.5	Joey Rogers	4.6	Rollie Massimino		
1977-78	23-9	7-3	NCAA REGIONAL FINALS	Keith Herron	19.8	Alex Bradley	7.2	Rory Sparrow	4.6	Rollie Massimino		
1978-79	13-13	9-1		Alex Beadley	17.3	Alex Bradley	7.5	Rory Sparrow	3.7	Rollie Massimino		
1979-80	23-8	7-3	NCAA SECOND ROUND	John Pinone	14.5	John Pinone	7.1	Rory Sparrow	4.1	Rollie Massimino		
1980-81	20-11	8-6	NCAA SECOND ROUND	John Pinone	15.8	John Pinone	7.4	Stewart Granger	5.3	Rollie Massimino		
1981-82	24-8	11-3	NCAA REGIONAL FINALS	John Pinone	17.2	Ed Pinckney	7.8	Stewart Granger	5.7	Rollie Massimino		
1982-83	24-8	12-4	NCAA REGIONAL FINALS	John Pinone	16.7	Ed Pinckney	9.7	Stewart Granger	5.5	Rollie Massimino		
1983-84	19-12	12-4	NCAA SECOND ROUND	Ed Pinckney	15.4	Ed Pinckney	7.9	Gary McLain	5.3	Rollie Massimino		
1984-85	**25-10**	**9-7**	**NATIONAL CHAMPION**	**Ed Pinckney**	**15.6**	**Ed Pinckney**	**8.9**	**Gary McLain**	**4.3**	**Rollie Massimino**		
1985-86	23-14	10-6	NCAA SECOND ROUND	Harold Pressley	16.8	Harold Pressley	10.1	Kenny Wilson	3.9	Rollie Massimino		
1986-87	15-16	6-10	NIT FIRST ROUND	Harold Jensen	15.9	Mark Plansky	5.9	Kenny Wilson	5.1	Rollie Massimino		
1987-88	24-13	9-7	NCAA REGIONAL FINALS	Doug West	15.8	Tom Greis	6.1	Kenny Wilson	4.9	Rollie Massimino		
1988-89	18-16	7-9	NIT QUARTERFINALS	Doug West	18.4	Rodney Taylor	6.3	Kenny Wilson	4.5	Rollie Massimino		
1989-90	18-15	8-8	NCAA FIRST ROUND	Tom Greis	13.4	Tom Greis	6.5	Chris Walker	3.8	Rollie Massimino		
1990-91	17-15	7-9	NCAA SECOND ROUND	Lance Miller	15.0	Lance Miller	6.8	Chris Walker	4.3	Rollie Massimino		
1991-92	14-15	11-7	NIT FIRST ROUND	Lance Miller	14.9	James Bryson	5.9	Chris Walker	3.7	Rollie Massimino	355-241	.596
1992-93	8-19	3-15		Lance Miller	13.7	James Bryson	6.8	Jonathan Haynes	5.0	Steve Lappas		
1993-94	20-12	10-8	NIT CHAMPION	Kerry Kittles	19.7	Jason Lawson	6.6	Jonathan Haynes	5.6	Steve Lappas		
1994-95	25-8	14-4	NCAA FIRST ROUND	Kerry Kittles	21.4	Jason Lawson	6.7	Alvin Williams	4.8	Steve Lappas		
1995-96	26-7	14-4	NCAA SECOND ROUND	Kerry Kittles	20.4	Kerry Kittles	7.1	Alvin Williams	5.4	Steve Lappas		
1996-97	24-10	12-6	NCAA SECOND ROUND	Alvin Williams	17.1	Jason Lawson	7.6	Alvin Williams	3.8	Steve Lappas		
1997-98	12-17	8-10		John Celestand	13.2	Malik Allen	5.8	John Celestand	5.1	Steve Lappas		
1998-99	21-11	10-8	NCAA FIRST ROUND	John Celestand	14.9	Malik Allen	6.3	John Celestand	4.4	Steve Lappas		
1999-2000	20-13	8-8	NIT SECOND ROUND	Malik Allen	14.2	Malik Allen	7.4	Brian Lynch	3.5	Steve Lappas		
2000-01	18-13	8-8	NIT FIRST ROUND	Michael Bradley	20.8	Michael Bradley	9.8	Jermaine Medley	3.6	Steve Lappas	174-110	.613
2001-02	19-13	7-9	NIT QUARTERFINALS	Gary Buchanan	17.8	Brooks Sales	9.1	Derrick Snowden	3.9	Jay Wright		
2002-03	15-16	8-8	NIT OPENING ROUND	Gary Buchanan	15.4	Ricky Wright	7.8	Derrick Snowden	3.5	Jay Wright		
2003-04	18-17	6-10	NIT QUARTERFINALS	Allan Ray	17.3	J. Fraser, Curtis Sumpter	7.1	Mike Nardi	3.7	Jay Wright		
2004-05	24-8	11-5	NCAA REGIONAL SEMIFINALS	Allan Ray	16.2	Curtis Sumpter	7.2	Mike Nardi	3.3	Jay Wright		
2005-06	28-5	14-2	NCAA REGIONAL FINALS	Randy Foye	20.5	Will Sheridan	6.3	Kyle Lowry	3.7	Jay Wright		
2006-07	22-11	9-7	NCAA FIRST ROUND	Curtis Sumpter	17.4	Curtis Sumpter	7.2	Scottie Reynolds	4.0	Jay Wright		
2007-08	22-13	9-9	NCAA REGIONAL SEMIFINALS	Scottie Reynolds	15.9	Dante Cunningham	6.5	Scottie Reynolds	3.2	Jay Wright		
2008-09	30-8	13-5	NCAA NATIONAL SEMIFINALS	Dante Cunningham	16.1	Dante Cunningham	7.5	Scottie Reynolds	3.4	Jay Wright	178-91	.662

Cumulative totals listed when per game averages not available.

⊗ Record doesn't reflect games forfeited or vacated. For adjusted record, **see p. 521.**

▼ Coach's record adjusted to reflect games forfeited or vacated: 238-95, .715. For yearly totals, **see p. 521.**

ESPN 68 SAGARIN

VIRGINIA

Ralph Sampson looms over Virginia basketball history much the way he towered over opponents during his career. He hardly stands alone, however. In fact, the first Cavaliers All-America, Wellington Stickley, played way back during the Woodrow Wilson administration.

BEST TEAM: 1980-81 The reigning NIT champion Cavs, behind sophomore Sampson and senior Jeff Lamp, raced to a 23–0 start, a No. 1 ranking, the school's only outright ACC regular-season crown, and its first NCAA Final Four appearance. But even after twice beating North Carolina in the regular season, Virginia couldn't stop the Tar Heels—or Al Wood, who scored 39—a third time.

BEST PLAYER: C RALPH SAMPSON (1979-83) For all his size, the 7'4" three-time national POY handled the ball and his lanky body with unparalleled grace. Although Sampson and his teams are remembered as big-time underachievers, they went 112–23 in his four seasons, most of which they spent ranked in the Top 5. Sampson's totals are staggering: 2,228 points, 1,511 rebounds, 462 blocks.

BEST COACH: TERRY HOLLAND (1974-90) It would be easy to credit Holland's success to Sampson, but UVa first hit it big three years earlier, when Holland guided the unranked Cavs (led by "Wonderful" Wally Walker) to the 1976 Miracle in Landover—which included upsets of No. 17 NC State, No. 9 Maryland and No. 4 UNC—to notch the school's only ACC tournament championship. Nothing validated Holland quite as much as the school's 1984 Final Four run the year *after* Sampson graduated, which prompted *Sports Illustrated* to refer to him as "the Einstein of the Pines."

GAME FOR THE AGES: Even Holland was shocked when his 1983-84 squad (6–8 in the ACC) received an NCAA bid. A year after Sampson's last NCAA title shot ended at the hands of a magical NC State team on a miraculous run, the Cavs earned an Elite Eight date with Indiana. A crucial steal and bucket by walk-on C Kenton Edelin helped seal the win and put the Cavs back in the Final Four. Into a TV camera, G Rick Carlisle said, "I'd like to say hello to ['83 NC State stars] Dereck Whittenburg, Sidney Lowe and Thurl Bailey."

HEARTBREAKER: In the 1983 NCAA Tourney, the Cavs had one last chance to realize expectations—in other words, a title—in the Sampson era. Instead, they blew a seven-point lead in the final seven minutes of their West Regional final to lose to eventual champ NC State, 63-62. The winning strategy? According to Whittenburg it was, "Four guys almost tackling Ralph, and me chasing [Virginia PG] Othell Wilson."

FIERCEST RIVAL: UVa, the genteel university founded by Thomas Jefferson, and Virginia Tech, the state's premier agricultural and engineering school, wage a traditional white collar vs. blue collar rivalry. Though the Cavaliers did put their hatred aside to leverage Virginia Tech into the ACC, sharing a conference has only ratcheted up the intensity. Virginia leads all-time, 79-50.

The 7'4" Sampson handled the ball and his lanky body with unparalleled grace.

FANFARE AND HOOPLA: Initially a heckle hurled by Washington and Lee students at rowdy Virginia baseball players, "Wahoos" (or "Hoos") has become a term of endearment in the century-plus since. True or not, common wisdom has it that the nickname refers to a fish that can drink copious amounts of liquid.

FAN FAVORITE: G JEFF LAMP (1977-81) He left UVa as the all-time scoring leader (2,317). But what most endeared the floppy-haired swingman to Wahoo-dom is that he craved the ball in the clutch. Lamp won or tied at least 14 games in the closing seconds during his four-year career.

CONSENSUS ALL-AMERICAS

1915 **Wellington Stickley**, F
1981-83 **Ralph Sampson**, C

FIRST-ROUND PRO PICKS

1973 **Barry Parkhill**, Portland (15)
1976 **Wally Walker**, Portland (5)
1981 **Jeff Lamp**, Portland (15)
1983 **Ralph Sampson**, Houston (1)
1987 **Olden Polynice**, Chicago (8)
1992 **Bryant Stith**, Denver (13)
1995 **Cory Alexander**, San Antonio (29)

PROFILE

University of Virginia, Charlottesville, VA
Founded: 1819
Enrollment: 21,057 (13,762 undergraduate)
Colors: Orange and blue
Nicknames: Cavaliers, Wahoos
Current arena: John Paul Jones Arena, opened in 2006 (14,593)
Previous: University Hall, 1965-2006 (8,392); Memorial Gymnasium, 1924-65 (2,500); Fayerweather Gymnasium, 1906-23 (N/A)
First game: Jan. 18, 1906

All-time record: 1,378-1,079-1 (.561)
Total weeks in AP Top 20/25: 182
Current conference: Atlantic Coast (1953-)
Conference titles:
Southern: 1 (1922)
ACC: 5 (1981, '82 [tie], '83 [tie], '95 [tie], 2007 [tie])
Conference tournament titles:
ACC: 1 (1976)
NCAA Tournament appearances: 16
Sweet 16s (since 1975): 7
Final Fours: 2

NIT appearances: 12
Semifinals: 2
Titles: 2 (1980, '92)

TOP 5

G **Jeff Lamp** (1977-81)
G **Barry Parkhill** (1970-73)
G **Richard "Buzzy" Wilkinson** (1952-55)
F **Bryant Stith** (1988-92)
C **Ralph Sampson** (1979-83)

RECORDS	GAME		SEASON		CAREER	
POINTS	51	Barry Parkhill, vs. Baldwin-Wallace (Dec. 11, 1971)	898	Buzzy Wilkinson (1954-55)	2,516	Bryant Stith (1988-92)
POINTS PER GAME			32.1	Buzzy Wilkinson (1954-55)	28.6	Buzzy Wilkinson (1952-55)
REBOUNDS	25	Bob Mortell, vs. Washington and Lee (Feb. 27, 1960)	386	Ralph Sampson (1982-83)	1,511	Ralph Sampson (1979-83)
ASSISTS	14	Harold Deane, vs. Maryland (March 5, 1995); Cory Alexander, vs. N.C. A&T (Nov. 30, 1994); John Crotty, vs. NC State (Jan. 29, 1991); Crotty, vs. Middle Tennessee (March 18, 1989)	214	John Crotty (1989-90)	683	John Crotty (1987-91)

SEASON REVIEW

SEASON	W-L	CONF.	SCORING	COACH	RECORD	
1906-14	*76-31-1*		*No losing seasons*			
1914-15	17-0			Henry Lannigan		
1915-16	11-2			Henry Lannigan		
1916-17	7-5			Henry Lannigan		
1917-18	7-1			Henry Lannigan		
1918-19	11-4			Henry Lannigan		
1919-20	10-3			Henry Lannigan		
1920-21	13-5			Henry Lannigan		
1921-22	17-1	5-0		Henry Lannigan		
1922-23	12-5	1-3		Henry Lannigan		
1923-24	12-3	3-2		Henry Lannigan		
1924-25	14-3	4-2		Henry Lannigan		
1925-26	9-6	4-4		Henry Lannigan		
1926-27	9-10	5-7		Henry Lannigan		
1927-28	20-6	10-5		Henry Lannigan		
1928-29	9-10	5-7		Henry Lannigan	254-95-1	.728
1929-30	3-12	2-8		Roy Randall	3-12	.200
1930-31	11-9	5-6		Gus Tebell		
1931-32	13-8	6-3		Gus Tebell		
1932-33	12-6	5-3		Gus Tebell		
1933-34	7-11	1-9		Gus Tebell		
1934-35	13-9	7-5		Gus Tebell		

SEAS.	W-L	CONF.	POSTSEASON	SCORING		REBOUNDS		ASSISTS		COACH	RECORD	
1935-36	11-13	4-8								Gus Tebell		
1936-37	9-10	6-7								Gus Tebell		
1937-38	6-10									Gus Tebell		
1938-39	15-5									Gus Tebell		
1939-40	16-5									Gus Tebell		
1940-41	18-6		NIT QUARTERFINALS							Gus Tebell		
1941-42	7-10									Gus Tebell		
1942-43	8-13									Gus Tebell		
1943-44	11-8									Gus Tebell		
1944-45	13-4									Gus Tebell		
1945-46	12-5									Gus Tebell		
1946-47	10-11									Gus Tebell		
1947-48	16-10			Chuck Noe	14.0					Gus Tebell		
1948-49	13-10			Joe Noertker	19.2					Gus Tebell		
1949-50	12-13			Joe Noertker	20.1					Gus Tebell		
1950-51	8-14			Vic Mohl	16.8					Gus Tebell	241-190	.559
1951-52	11-13			Vic Mohl	17.5					Evan Male		
1952-53	10-13			Richard "Buzzy" Wilkinson	22.7					Evan Male		
1953-54	16-11	1-4		Richard "Buzzy" Wilkinson	30.1	Charles Gamble	7.4			Evan Male		
1954-55	14-15	5-9		Richard "Buzzy" Wilkinson	32.1	Jerry Cooper	7.4			Evan Male		
1955-56	10-17	3-11		Bob McCarty	23.1	Austin Pearre	7.3			Evan Male		
1956-57	6-19	3-11		Bob Hardy	15.2	Jerry Cooper	7.0			Evan Male	67-88	.432
1957-58	10-13	6-8		Herb Busch	15.9	Herb Busch	10.1			Billy McCann		
1958-59	11-14	6-8		Paul Adkins	16.0	Herb Busch	9.1			Billy McCann		
1959-60	6-18	1-13		Paul Adkins	17.1	Bob Mortell	14.6			Billy McCann		
1960-61	3-23	2-12		Tony Laquintano	19.8	Gene Engel	9.7			Billy McCann		
1961-62	5-18	2-12		Tony Laquintano	20.4	Chip Conner	9.2			Billy McCann		
1962-63	5-20	3-11		Gene Engel	18.4	Mac Caldwell	8.2			Billy McCann	40-106	.274
1963-64	8-16	4-10		Chip Conner	18.8	Mac Caldwell	8.0			Bill Gibson		
1964-65	7-18	3-11		Jim Connelly	18.3	Mac Caldwell	7.8			Bill Gibson		
1965-66	7-15	4-10		Jim Connelly	20.5	John Naponick	6.7			Bill Gibson		
1966-67	9-17	4-10		Jim Connelly	20.0	Buddy Reams	8.6			Bill Gibson		
1967-68	9-16	5-9		Mike Katos	18.5	Norm Carmichael	12.0	Barry Koval	4.8	Bill Gibson		
1968-69	10-15	5-9		Mike Wilkes	15.7	John Gidding	11.2	Kevin Kennelly	3.8	Bill Gibson		
1969-70	10-15	3-11		Bill Gerry	17.7	Bill Gerry	11.1	Kevin Kennelly	2.9	Bill Gibson		
1970-71	15-11	6-8		Barry Parkhill	15.9	Scott McCandlish	9.9	Barry Parkhill	4.8	Bill Gibson		
1971-72	21-7	8-4	NIT FIRST ROUND	Barry Parkhill	21.6	Scott McCandlish	9.4	Barry Parkhill	4.3	Bill Gibson		
1972-73	13-12	4-8		Barry Parkhill	16.8	Gus Gerard	8.2	Barry Parkhill	5.0	Bill Gibson		
1973-74	11-16	4-8		Gus Gerard	20.8	Gus Gerard	10.2	Billy Langloh	2.8	Bill Gibson	120-158	.432
1974-75	12-13	4-8		Wally Walker	16.5	Marc Iavaroni	7.9	Andy Boninti	2.9	Terry Holland		
1975-76	18-12	4-8	NCAA FIRST ROUND	Wally Walker	22.1	Wally Walker	6.8	Billy Langloh	2.9	Terry Holland		
1976-77	12-17	2-10		Billy Langloh	13.0	Steve Castellan	7.6	Bobby Stokes	2.3	Terry Holland		
1977-78	20-8	6-6	NIT FIRST ROUND	Jeff Lamp	17.3	Steve Castellan	7.9	Tommy Hicks	2.4	Terry Holland		
1978-79	19-10	7-5	NIT SECOND ROUND	Jeff Lamp	22.9	Steve Castellan	7.1	Jeff Jones	4.9	Terry Holland		
1979-80	24-10	7-7	NIT CHAMPION	Jeff Lamp	17.4	Ralph Sampson	11.2	Jeff Jones	5.9	Terry Holland		
1980-81	29-4	13-1	NCAA THIRD PLACE	Jeff Lamp	18.2	Ralph Sampson	11.5	Jeff Jones	4.4	Terry Holland		
1981-82	30-4	12-2	NCAA REGIONAL SEMIFINALS	Ralph Sampson	15.8	Ralph Sampson	11.4	Jeff Jones	3.4	Terry Holland		
1982-83	29-5	12-2	NCAA REGIONAL FINALS	Ralph Sampson	19.1	Ralph Sampson	11.7	Othell Wilson	4.5	Terry Holland		
1983-84	21-12	6-8	NCAA NATIONAL SEMIFINALS	Othell Wilson	13.8	Kenton Edelin	6.4	Othell Wilson	4.9	Terry Holland		
1984-85	17-16	3-11	NIT QUARTERFINALS	Olden Polynice	13.0	Olden Polynice	7.6	Tim Mullen	2.6	Terry Holland		
1985-86	19-11	7-7	NCAA FIRST ROUND	Olden Polynice	16.1	Olden Polynice	8.0	John Johnson	3.1	Terry Holland		
1986-87	21-10	8-6	NCAA FIRST ROUND	Andrew Kennedy	16.5	Andrew Kennedy	7.5	John Johnson	6.3	Terry Holland		
1987-88	13-18	5-9		Mel Kennedy	19.8	Bill Batts	6.4	John Johnson	4.3	Terry Holland		
1988-89	22-11	9-5	NCAA REGIONAL FINALS	Richard Morgan	20.4	Brent Dabbs	7.3	John Crotty	6.3	Terry Holland		
1989-90	20-12	6-8	NCAA SECOND ROUND	Bryant Stith	20.8	Kenny Turner	7.0	John Crotty	6.7	Terry Holland	326-173	.653
1990-91	21-12	6-8	NCAA FIRST ROUND	Bryant Stith	19.8	Kenny Turner	7.4	John Crotty	5.1	Jeff Jones		
1991-92	20-13	8-8	NIT CHAMPION	Bryant Stith	20.7	Ted Jeffries	7.1	Cory Alexander	4.4	Jeff Jones		
1992-93	21-10	9-7	NCAA REGIONAL SEMIFINALS	Cory Alexander	18.8	Ted Jeffries	8.0	Cory Alexander	4.6	Jeff Jones		
1993-94	18-13	8-8	NCAA SECOND ROUND	Junior Burrough	15.0	Junior Burrough	7.0	Cornel Parker	3.9	Jeff Jones		
1994-95	25-9	12-4	NCAA REGIONAL FINALS	Junior Burrough	18.1	Junior Burrough	8.7	Harold Deane	4.3	Jeff Jones		
1995-96	12-15	6-10		Harold Deane	16.7	Norman Nolan	7.0	Harold Deane	3.7	Jeff Jones		
1996-97	18-13	7-9	NCAA FIRST ROUND	Courtney Alexander	14.8	Norman Nolan	7.4	Harold Deane	4.5	Jeff Jones		
1997-98	11-19	3-13		Norman Nolan	21.0	Norman Nolan	9.2	W. Dersch, D. Hand	3.3	Jeff Jones	146-104	.584
1998-99	14-16	4-12		Donald Hand	17.1	Chris Williams	7.5	Donald Hand	4.1	Pete Gillen		
1999-2000	19-12	9-7	NIT FIRST ROUND	Chris Williams	15.5	Travis Watson	8.3	Donald Hand	4.3	Pete Gillen		
2000-01	20-9	9-7	NCAA FIRST ROUND	Roger Mason Jr.	15.7	Travis Watson	9.1	Donald Hand	6.0	Pete Gillen		
2001-02	17-12	7-9	NIT FIRST ROUND	Roger Mason Jr.	18.6	Travis Watson	9.7	Roger Mason Jr.	4.1	Pete Gillen		
2002-03	16-16	6-10	NIT SECOND ROUND	Travis Watson	14.3	Travis Watson	10.4	Todd Billet	3.4	Pete Gillen		
2003-04	18-13	6-10	NIT SECOND ROUND	Elton Brown	14.8	Elton Brown	6.3	Todd Billet	3.2	Pete Gillen		
2004-05	14-15	4-12		Devin Smith	16.5	Elton Brown	8.1	Sean Singletary	3.9	Pete Gillen	118-93	.559
2005-06	15-15	7-9	NIT OPENING ROUND	Sean Singletary	17.7	Jason Cain	7.6	Sean Singletary	4.2	Dave Leitao		
2006-07	21-11	11-5	NCAA SECOND ROUND	Sean Singletary	19.0	Jason Cain	6.3	Sean Singletary	4.7	Dave Leitao		
2007-08	17-16	5-11		Sean Singletary	19.9	Adrian Joseph	6.1	Sean Singletary	6.0	Dave Leitao		
2008-09	10-18	4-12		Sylven Landesberg	16.6	Mike Scott	7.4	Sammy Zeglinsky	3.0	Dave Leitao	63-60	.512

ESPN 167 SAGARIN

VIRGINIA COMMONWEALTH

With a basketball tradition that began only in 1968, the Rams have made up for lost time by creating memories with each NCAA Tournament appearance. Highlights don't get much move vivid than VCU's 2007 first-round upset of three-time champion Duke.

BEST TEAM: 1984-85 J.D. Barnett's 26–6 Rams finished the season as the No. 11 team in the nation. Led by Rolando Lamb and Calvin Duncan, the Sun Belt champs made VCU's third straight NCAA Tournament appearance (and fifth in six years) as the No. 2 seed in the West, beating Marshall, 81-65, before falling in the second round to No. 7-seed Alabama, 63-59.

BEST PLAYER: G Gerald Henderson (1974-78) In his four seasons Henderson scored 1,542 points and VCU went 70–35. As a senior, he led the 24–5 Rams to the NIT—their first postseason appearance. A charter member of the VCU Athletic Hall of Fame, Henderson also played on four NBA championship teams (two each with Boston and Detroit).

BEST COACH: J.D. Barnett (1979-85) His six seasons at the helm were what many consider the glory days of VCU basketball. Barnett amassed a 132–48 record, won three Sun Belt tournament titles and led the program to its first five NCAA Tournament appearances.

GAME FOR THE AGES: After a great win over George Mason in the 2007 Colonial Athletic Association title game, VCU entered the NCAAs as a No. 11 seed facing none other than Duke—which was carrying a lower-than-usual No. 6 seed but also a string of nine straight Sweet 16 appearances. The lights went out for the Blue Devils when sophomore point guard Eric Maynor hit a 15-foot jumper with 1.8 seconds left to give VCU a 79-77 win, its first in the Tourney since 1985.

FIERCEST RIVAL: There's nothing like a good in-state rivalry, and VCU's with Old Dominion has gone back and forth for 40 years. The schools are located about 90 miles apart and in recent years have been among the more competitive CAA teams. VCU holds a 41–38 edge.

SEASON REVIEW

SEAS.	W-L	CONF.		SCORING		COACH	RECORD	
1968-69	12-11			Charles Wilkins	24.0	Benny Dees		
1969-70	13-10			Charles Wilkins	27.5	Benny Dees	25-21	.543
1970-71	15-9			Charles Wilkins	20.2	Chuck Noe		
1971-72	15-4			Jesse Dark	22.1	Chuck Noe		
1972-73	15-5			Bernard Harris	19.5	Chuck Noe		
1973-74	17-7			Jesse Dark	23.1	Chuck Noe		
1974-75	17-8			Richard Jones	17.6	Chuck Noe		
1975-76	16-9			Tom Motley	18.4	Chuck Noe	95-42	.693
1976-77	13-13			Gerald Henderson	20.2	Dana Kirk		
1977-78	24-5		■	Gerald Henderson	16.1	Dana Kirk		
1978-79	20-5			Lorenza Watson	15.5	Dana Kirk	57-23	.713
1979-80	18-12	8-6	●	Monty Knight	16.6	J.D. Barnett		
1980-81	24-5	9-3	●	Kenny Stancell	15.5	J.D. Barnett		
1981-82	17-11	7-3		Monty Knight	16.9	J.D. Barnett		
1982-83	24-7	12-2	●	Calvin Duncan	17.4	J.D. Barnett		
1983-84	23-7	11-3	●	Calvin Duncan	13.6	J.D. Barnett		
1984-85	26-6	12-2	●	Rolando Lamb	17.3	J.D. Barnett	132-48	.733
1985-86	12-16	6-8		Nicky Jones	15.2	Mike Pollio		
1986-87	17-14	7-7		Phil Stinnie	14.9	Mike Pollio		
1987-88	23-12	10-4	■	Phil Stinnie	23.6	Mike Pollio		
1988-89	13-15	9-5		Chris Cheeks	23.8	Mike Pollio	65-57	.533
1989-90	11-17	5-9		Elander Lewis	13.9	Sonny Smith		
1990-91	14-17	7-7		Kendrick Warren	15.7	Sonny Smith		
1991-92	14-15	5-7		Kendrick Warren	19.0	Sonny Smith		
1992-93	20-10	7-5	■	Kendrick Warren	17.6	Sonny Smith		
1993-94	14-13	5-7		Kendrick Warren	18.0	Sonny Smith		
1994-95	16-14	3-9		Tyron McCoy	15.2	Sonny Smith		
1995-96	24-9	14-2	●	Bernard Hopkins	16.3	Sonny Smith		
1996-97	14-13	9-7		Patrick Lee	16.1	Sonny Smith		
1997-98	9-19	4-12		Mylo Brooks	10.5	Sonny Smith	136-127	.517
1998-99	15-16	8-8		Bo Jones	14.3	Mack McCarthy		
1999-2000	14-14	7-9		Bo Jones	16.5	Mack McCarthy		
2000-01	16-14	9-7		Bo Jones	14.8	Mack McCarthy		
2001-02	21-11	11-7		Willie Taylor	17.1	Mack McCarthy	66-55	.545
2002-03	18-10	12-6		Willie Taylor	17.3	Jeff Capel		
2003-04	23-8	14-4	●	Domonic Jones	16.3	Jeff Capel		
2004-05	19-13	13-5	■	Nick George	16.8	Jeff Capel		
2005-06	19-10	11-7		Nick George	16.9	Jeff Capel	79-41	.658
2006-07	28-7	16-2	●	B.A. Walker	14.8	Anthony Grant		
2007-08	24-8	15-3	■	Eric Maynor	17.9	Anthony Grant		
2008-09	24-10	14-4	●	Eric Maynor	22.4	Anthony Grant	76-25	.752

● NCAA Tournament appearance ■ NIT appearance

PROFILE

Virginia Commonwealth University, Richmond, VA
Founded: 1968
Enrollment: 32,284 (22,792 undergraduate)
Colors: Black and gold
Nickname: Rams
Current arena: Alltel Pavilion at Stuart C. Siegel Center, opened in 1999 (7,500)
First game: 1968
All-time record: 731-439 (.625)
Total weeks in AP Top 20/25: 9

Current conference: Colonial Athletic Association (1995-)
Conference titles:
Sun Belt: 4 (1981 [tie], '83 [tie], '84, '85)
CAA: 5 (1996, 2004, '07, '08, '09)
Conference tournament titles:
Sun Belt: 3 (1980, '81, '85)
CAA: 4 (1996, 2004, '07, '09)
NCAA Tournament appearances: 9
NIT appearances: 5

FIRST-ROUND PRO PICKS

2009 **Eric Maynor,** Utah (20)

TOP 5

G **Calvin Duncan** (1981-85)
G **Gerald Henderson** (1974-78)
G **Eric Maynor** (2005-09)
F **Kendrick Warren** (1990-94)
C **Lorenza Watson** (1975-79)

RECORDS

RECORDS	GAME		SEASON		CAREER	
POINTS	45	Charles Wilkins, vs. West Liberty State (Dec. 20, 1968)	803	Phil Stinnie (1987-88)	1,953	Eric Maynor (2005-09)
POINTS PER GAME			27.5	Charles Wilkins (1969-70)	23.8	Charles Wilkins (1968-71)
REBOUNDS	28	Charles Wilkins, vs. Southeastern (Jan. 4, 1970)	398	Charles Wilkins (1969-70)	1,143	Lorenza Watson (1975-79)
ASSISTS	16	Kenny Harris, vs. Oklahoma (Jan. 20, 1994)	224	Eric Maynor (2006-07)	674	Eric Maynor (2005-09)

THE SCHOOLS

ESPN 297 SAGARIN

VIRGINIA MILITARY INSTITUTE

How bad were the 1970-71 Keydets? So bad that an assistant coach, Bill Blair, compiled a montage of rec-league-worthy lowlights from their 1–25 campaign, immediately dubbed the Funny Film. On the bright side, when you've had only eight winning seasons in your last 80 years, you come to appreciate any highlights you get, even when they're low.

BEST TEAM: 1976-77 Guard Will Bynum told *Sports Illustrated*, "I came to VMI because I was a basketball player, not because I had an uncontrollable urge to carry a rifle around all day." Bynum capped his hoops career in style, helping the Keydets rip off 21 straight wins, take the Southern Conference crown and beat Duquesne in the NCAA Tournament's first round.

BEST PLAYER: G RON CARTER (1974-78) Pick any scoring category and Bynum's running mate ranks among the school's all-time leaders: third in points (2,228), third in double-figure scoring games (99), fourth in single-season average (26.3 ppg in 1977-78).

BEST COACH: BILL BLAIR (1972-76) No coach since 1922 has left VMI with even a .500 mark. So Blair, the former assistant, gets the nod for notching VMI's first winning campaign in 35 years in 1975-76, crashing the Elite Eight that same season—then cashing in for a job at Colorado.

GAME FOR THE AGES: Just five seasons removed from the Funny Film, Blair's bunch was laughing all the way to the Elite Eight after upsetting Dave Corzine and DePaul in the second round of the 1976 NCAA Tournament, 71-66 in OT.

FIERCEST RIVAL: VMI is located in rural Virginia. The Citadel is located in Charleston, S.C. Both share the same educational mission (producing future military leaders) and athletic legacy (not so hot). All those factors play into the two schools' longstanding enmity. Although the two haven't played since the Keydets left the SoCon in 2002-03, you can bet that whenever they renew their series, it will all come bubbling back in an instant.

SEASON REVIEW

SEAS.	W-L	CONF.	COACH	SEAS.	W-L	CONF.	COACH
1908-47	*226-311*	*27-2 over 2 seasons, 1919-21*		1960-61	5-17	3-11	L.F. Miller
1947-48	3-17	1-12	Frank Summers	1961-62	9-11	6-8	L.F. Miller
1948-49	3-16	3-8	Frank Summers	1962-63	6-15	6-10	L.F. Miller
1949-50	4-17	2-11	Bill O'Hara	1963-64	12-12	7-7 ●	L.F. Miller
1950-51	3-18	3-11	Bill O'Hara	1964-65	8-13	5-9	Gary McPherson
1951-52	3-21	2-13	Bill O'Hara	1965-66	5-18	5-11	Gary McPherson
1952-53	5-19	1-14	Chuck Noe	1966-67	5-16	4-12	Gary McPherson
1953-54	11-12	6-7	Chuck Noe	1967-68	9-12	8-7	Gary McPherson
1954-55	8-15	4-9	Chuck Noe	1968-69	5-18	3-11	Gary McPherson
1955-56	4-19	3-11	Jack Null	1969-70	6-19	3-10	Mike Schuler
1956-57	4-22	1-13	Jack Null	1970-71	1-25	1-11	Mike Schuler
1957-58	4-17	1-12	Jack Null	1971-72	6-19	2-10	Mike Schuler
1958-59	5-13	2-11	L.F. Miller	1972-73	7-19	3-9	Bill Blair
1959-60	4-16	3-11	L.F. Miller	1973-74	6-18	3-9	Bill Blair

SEAS.	W-L	CONF.	SCORING		COACH	RECORD	
1974-75	13-13	6-6	John Krovic	15.0	Bill Blair		
1975-76	22-10	9-3 ●	Ron Carter	17.9	Bill Blair	48-60	.444
1976-77	26-4	8-2 ●	Ron Carter	20.4	Charlie Schmaus		
1977-78	21-7	7-3	Ron Carter	26.3	Charlie Schmaus		
1978-79	12-15	2-8	Andy Kolesar	14.8	Charlie Schmaus		
1979-80	11-16	6-10	Andy Kolesar	19.2	Charlie Schmaus		
1980-81	4-23	3-13	Andy Kolesar	13.9	Charlie Schmaus		
1981-82	1-25	1-15	Mark Vest	16.3	Charlie Schmaus	75-90	.455
1982-83	2-25	1-15	Darren Sawyer	15.2	Marty Fletcher		
1983-84	8-19	4-12	Gay Elmore	18.4	Marty Fletcher		
1984-85	16-14	7-9	Gay Elmore	20.0	Marty Fletcher		
1985-86	11-17	5-11	Gay Elmore	22.8	Marty Fletcher	37-75	.330
1986-87	11-17	5-11	Gay Elmore	25.5	Joe Cantafio		
1987-88	13-17	6-10	Damon Williams	16.3	Joe Cantafio		
1988-89	11-17	5-9	Ramon Williams	18.7	Joe Cantafio		
1989-90	14-15	7-7	Damon Williams	20.7	Joe Cantafio		
1990-91	10-18	5-9	Greg Fittz	17.3	Joe Cantafio		
1991-92	10-18	3-11	Jonathan Penn	19.3	Joe Cantafio		
1992-93	5-22	3-15	Lewis Preston	16.7	Joe Cantafio		
1993-94	5-23	2-16	Lawrence Gullette	11.3	Joe Cantafio	79-147	.350
1994-95	10-17	6-8	Lawrence Gullette	16.4	Bart Bellairs		
1995-96	18-10	10-4	Lawrence Gullette	15.9	Bart Bellairs		
1996-97	12-16	7-7	Maurice Spencer	15.0	Bart Bellairs		
1997-98	14-13	8-7	Jason Bell	16.3	Bart Bellairs		
1998-99	12-15	9-7	Jason Bell	18.9	Bart Bellairs		
1999-2000	6-23	1-15	Nick Richardson	12.6	Bart Bellairs		
2000-01	9-19	5-11	Eric Mann	13.5	Bart Bellairs		
2001-02	10-18	5-11	Jason Conley	29.3	Bart Bellairs		
2002-03	10-20	3-13	Radee Skipworth	18.6	Bart Bellairs		
2003-04	6-22	4-12	Radee Skipworth	16.0	Bart Bellairs		
2004-05	9-18	3-13	Reggie Williams	15.5	Bart Bellairs	116-191	.378
2005-06	7-20	2-14	Reggie Williams	19.0	Duggar Baucom		
2006-07	14-19	5-9	Reggie Williams	28.1	Duggar Baucom		
2007-08	14-15	6-8	Reggie Williams	27.8	Duggar Baucom		
2008-09	24-8	13-5	Chavis Holmes	22.0	Duggar Baucom	59-62	.488

● **NCAA Tournament appearance**

PROFILE

Virginia Military Institute, Lexington, VA
Founded: 1839
Enrollment: 1,400 (1,400 undergraduate)
Colors: Red, yellow and white
Nickname: Keydets
Current arena: Cameron Hall, opened in 1981 (5,029)
Previous: VMI Field House, 1949-81 (3,000); Cocke Hall, 1926-49 (500); J.M. Hall Gym, 1908-26 (N/A)
First game: 1908
All-time record: 778-1,353 (.365)
Total weeks in AP Top 20/25: 3

Current conference: Big South (2003-)
Conference titles:
Southern: 2 (1976, '77 [tie])
Conference tournament titles:
Southern: 3 (1964, '76, '77)
NCAA Tournament appearances: 3
Sweet 16s (since 1975): 2
NIT appearances: 0

TOP 5

G **Ron Carter** (1974-78)
G **Charlie Schmaus** (1963-66)
F **Gay Elmore** (1983-87)
F **Reggie Williams** (2004-08)
C **Bill Ralph** (1951-54)

RECORDS

RECORDS	GAME		SEASON		CAREER	
POINTS	45	Reggie Williams, vs. Virginia Intermont (Jan. 15, 2006)	928	Reggie Williams (2006-07)	2,556	Reggie Williams (2004-08)
POINTS PER GAME			29.3	Jason Conley (2001-02)	22.8	Reggie Williams (2004-08)
REBOUNDS	31	Bill Ralph, vs. Hampden-Sydney (1954)	330	Bill Ralph (1953-54)	1,068	Dave Montgomery (1974-78)
ASSISTS	14	Bobby Prince, vs. Western Carolina (Jan. 14, 1995)	216	Richard Little (2002-03)	608	Richard Little (2000-04)

ESPN 105 SAGARIN

VIRGINIA TECH

Bimbo, Ace, the Kentucky Rifle. With player nicknames like that, Virginia Tech's basketball history is as colorful as the Hokies' notorious Chicago maroon and burnt orange uniforms. Basking in the golden glow of the ACC since 2004, Tech has been looking to expand its rep beyond that of occasional NIT champ.

BEST TEAM: 1966-67 Despite losing the previous season's scoring and rebounding leader, John Wetzel, these quick-shooting Hokies opened their season by thrashing No. 4-ranked Duke. It only got more exciting from there. Deadeye shooting guard Glen "the Kentucky Rifle" Combs paved the way for Virginia Tech's first, and lengthiest, NCAA run. Tech got within an overtime of the Final Four, and three players (Combs, Ron Perry, Chris Ellis) would be drafted by the pros.

BEST PLAYER: C CHRIS SMITH (1957-61) A brilliant center, Smith outranks later Hokies greats Allan Bristow, Bimbo Coles, Dell Curry and Ace Custis. The chemical engineering major is one of only three Hokies to amass both 1,000 points and 1,000 rebounds. He averaged 20.4 boards (including 36 in one game) as a sophomore, when the Hokies as a team pulled down a staggering 57.4 rebounds per game. A year later, his 22.2 points per game powered the school's first 20-win team.

BEST COACH: CHARLES MOIR (1976-87) He won almost twice as many games as any other Tech coach and made Cassell Coliseum a feared venue for visitors. In Moir's 11 seasons, the Hokies won 20 or more games seven times and played in eight postseasons, including four NCAA Tournaments. Recruiting the likes of Curry and Coles raised Moir's profile, but his forced resignation amid an academic scandal stained his legacy.

GAME FOR THE AGES: Tech won its four games in the 1973 NIT by a total of five points, saving the biggest drama for the final. On March 25 against Notre Dame, Bobby Stevens' buzzer-beating jumper in overtime clinched the title, 92-91, and sent Stevens off the Madison Square Garden floor on the shoulders of cheering fans.

HEARTBREAKER: In its first NCAA appearance, as an independent in 1967, Tech dropped Toledo and Indiana to reach the Mideast Regional final. But the fast-paced Hokies let a 10-point lead over Dayton slip away by slowing down the game. They lost in OT, 71-66, just missing the Final Four.

FIERCEST RIVAL: If there's one thing Hokies alums can agree on, it's their wish that Thomas Jefferson had never founded that uppity school in Charlottesville. But while the University of Virginia has enjoyed more acclaim on the hardwood over the decades, leading the series 79–50, Tech has had better luck lately, winning five of 11 since joining the Cavaliers in the ACC in 2004.

FANFARE AND HOOPLA: Opened in 1961, Cassell Coliseum is a throwback on-campus fieldhouse that seats 9,847. The rackety building is perfect for amplifying the notoriously rabid spirit of Hokies fans, who have helped Tech win more than three-quarters of its games there. The crowd especially enjoys tormenting its latter-day ACC rival, Duke.

Tech won its four games in the 1973 NIT by a total of five points, saving the biggest drama for the final. On March 25 against Notre Dame, Bobby Stevens' buzzer-beating jumper in overtime clinched the title.

FAN FAVORITE: F ACE CUSTIS (1993-97) He had it all: a fun-sounding name, an ace-of-spades tattoo and personal troubles that he overcame (the loss of a brother in a car accident and his own critical crash on the same road two years later) to start 123 straight games and help Virginia Tech capture the 1995 NIT title and reach the 1996 NCAA Tourney.

PROFILE

Virginia Polytechnic Institute, Blacksburg, VA
Founded: 1872
Enrollment: 29,898 (23,041 undergraduate)
Colors: Chicago maroon and burnt orange
Nickname: Hokies
Current arena: Cassell Coliseum, opened in 1961 (9,847)
First game: 1908
All-time record: 1,279-1,072 (.544)
Total weeks in AP Top 20/25: 47
Current conference: Atlantic Coast (2004-)

Conference titles:
Southern: 1 (1960)
Atlantic 10: 1 (1996 [tie])
Conference tournament titles:
Metro: 1 (1979)
NCAA Tournament appearances: 8
NIT appearances: 10
Semifinals: 3
Titles: 2 (1973, '95)

CONSENSUS ALL-AMERICAS

1919 **George Parrish,** F

FIRST-ROUND PRO PICKS

1986 **Dell Curry,** Utah (15)

TOP 5

G **Bimbo Coles** (1986-90)
G **Dell Curry** (1982-86)
F **Allan Bristow** (1970-73)
F **Ace Custis** (1993-97)
C **Chris Smith** (1957-61)

RECORDS

	GAME		SEASON		CAREER	
POINTS	52	Allan Bristow, vs. George Washington (Feb. 21, 1973)	785	Bimbo Coles (1989-90)	2,484	Bimbo Coles (1986-90)
POINTS PER GAME			26.6	Bimbo Coles (1988-89)	23.1	Allan Bristow (1970-73)
REBOUNDS	36	Chris Smith, vs. Washington and Lee (Jan. 9, 1959)	495	Chris Smith (1959-60)	1,508	Chris Smith (1957-61)
ASSISTS	12	Troy Manns, vs. St. Bonaventure (Jan. 2, 1997); Bimbo Coles, vs. Missouri (Dec. 16, 1987); Dave Sensibaugh, vs. Oregon (Dec. 19, 1975)	192	Dave Sensibaugh (1975-76)	547	Bimbo Coles (1986-90)

SEASON REVIEW

SEASON	W-L	CONF.	SCORING	COACH	RECORD
1908-17	*89-29*		*17-2 in 1916-17 under coach H.P. Sanborn (his only season at Tech)*		
1917-18	15-5			Charles Bernier	
1918-19	18-4			Charles Bernier	
1919-20	14-4			Charles Bernier	47-13 .783
1920-21	19-5			W.L. Younger	
1921-22	14-6	2-2		W.L. Younger	
1922-23	13-6	1-2		W.L. Younger	
1923-24	5-13	0-4		B.C. Cubbage	5-13 .278
1924-25	6-9	1-4		M. Buford Blair	
1925-26	3-10	2-5		M. Buford Blair	9-19 .321
1926-27	6-8	2-6		H.B. Redd	6-8 .429
1927-28	5-11	3-7		Bud Moore	5-11 .313
1928-29	4-13	3-6		I.E. Randall	4-13 .235
1929-30	5-14	2-10		R.S. Warren	5-14 .263
1930-31	5-10	3-7		C.D. Rhodes	5-10 .333
1931-32	8-9	2-8		G.S. Proctor	
1932-33	5-10	3-7		W.L. Younger	
1933-34	1-15	1-10		W.L. Younger	
1934-35	3-16	1-11		W.L. Younger	
1935-36	5-16	1-9		W.L. Younger	
1936-37	6-11	4-9		W.L. Younger	66-85 .437
1937-38	6-8	4-5		H.M. McEver	

SEAS.	W-L	CONF.	POSTSEASON	SCORING	REBOUNDS	ASSISTS	COACH	RECORD
1938-39	3-14	2-10					H.M. McEver	
1939-40	4-15	1-9					H.M. McEver	
1940-41	8-13	4-8					H.M. McEver	
1941-42	10-10	4-8					H.M. McEver	
1942-43	7-7	3-6					H.M. McEver	
1943-44	11-4	4-1					H.M. McEver	49-71 .408
1944-45	6-8	1-3					G.S. Proctor	
1945-46	11-8	7-3					G.S. Proctor	
1946-47	13-13	4-9					G.S. Proctor	38-38 .500
1947-48	14-9	7-5					G.F. Laird	
1948-49	10-13	6-8					G.F. Laird	
1949-50	16-9	9-5					G.F. Laird	
1950-51	19-10	9-5					G.F. Laird	
1951-52	4-16	3-10					G.F. Laird	
1952-53	4-19	4-13					G.F. Laird	
1953-54	3-24	3-13					G.F. Laird	
1954-55	7-20	4-14					G.F. Laird	77-120 .391
1955-56	14-11	10-7					Charles W. Noe	
1956-57	14-8	12-5		Abe Coates 16.1	Abe Coates 14.3		Charles W. Noe	
1957-58	11-8	10-5		Bob Ayersman 20.7	Chris Smith 11.7		Charles W. Noe	
1958-59	16-5	10-2		Bob Ayersman 26.5	Chris Smith 20.4		Charles W. Noe	
1959-60	20-6	12-1		Chris Smith 22.2	Chris Smith 19.0		Charles W. Noe	
1960-61	15-7	12-3		Chris Smith 19.9	Chris Smith 16.5		Charles W. Noe	
1961-62	19-6	9-3		Bucky Keller 21.7	Howard Pardue 10.6		Charles W. Noe	109-51 .681
1962-63	12-12	6-6		Howard Pardue 18.6	Howard Pardue 9.7		William B. Matthews	
1963-64	16-7	7-3		Howard Pardue 20.5	Howard Pardue 8.9		William B. Matthews	28-19 .596
1964-65	13-10	8-3		John Wetzel 14.3	Bob King 8.6		Howard P. Shannon	
1965-66	19-5		NIT FIRST ROUND	John Wetzel 18.5	John Wetzel 8.8		Howard P. Shannon	
1966-67	20-7		NCAA REGIONAL FINALS	Glen Combs 21.3	Ken Talley 11.1		Howard P. Shannon	
1967-68	14-11			Glen Combs 20.9	Ted Ware 9.2		Howard P. Shannon	
1968-69	14-12			Chris Ellis 19.7	Dan Wetzel 8.6		Howard P. Shannon	
1969-70	10-12			Loyd King 19.3	Charlie Lipscomb 10.4		Howard P. Shannon	
1970-71	14-11			Loyd King 21.3	Allan Bristow 13.1		Howard P. Shannon	104-68 .605
1971-72	16-10			Allan Bristow 25.0	Allan Bristow 13.4		Don DeVoe	
1972-73	22-5		NIT CHAMPION	Allan Bristow 23.9	Allan Bristow 11.6		Don DeVoe	
1973-74	13-13			Craig Lieder 17.8	Craig Lieder 8.1		Don DeVoe	
1974-75	16-10			Russell Davis 18.8	Kyle McKee 8.5		Don DeVoe	
1975-76	21-7		NCAA FIRST ROUND	Russell Davis 20.1	Russell Davis 7.5		Don DeVoe	88-45 .662
1976-77	19-10		NIT QUARTERFINALS	Duke Thorpe 15.6	Duke Thorpe 8.3		Charles Moir	
1977-78	19-8			Ron Bell 16.3	Wayne Robinson 9.2		Charles Moir	
1978-79	22-9	4-6	NCAA SECOND ROUND	Dale Solomon 17.8	Wayne Robinson 9.1		Charles Moir	
1979-80	21-8	8-4	NCAA SECOND ROUND	Dale Solomon 16.7	Wayne Robinson 8.2	Dexter Reid 93	Charles Moir	
1980-81	15-13	6-6		Dale Solomon 21.0	Calvin Oldham 8.0	Jeff Schneider 70	Charles Moir	
1981-82	20-11	7-5	NIT QUATERFINALS	Dale Solomon 18.2	Calvin Oldham 7.3	Jeff Schneider 120	Charles Moir	
1982-83	23-11	7-5	NIT SECOND ROUND	Perry Young 16.1	Bobby Beecher 6.1	Al Young 138	Charles Moir	
1983-84	22-13	8-6	NIT THIRD PLACE	Dell Curry 19.3	Perry Young 6.7	Al Young 134	Charles Moir	
1984-85	20-9	10-4	NCAA FIRST ROUND	Perry Young 18.5	Perry Young 7.4	Al Young 118	Charles Moir	
1985-86	22-9	7-5	NCAA FIRST ROUND	Dell Curry 24.1	Bobby Beecher 7.9	Dell Curry 113	Charles Moir	
1986-87	10-18	5-7		Wally Lancaster 17.1	Tim Anderson 8.9	Bimbo Coles 112	Charles Moir	213-119 .642
1987-88	19-10	6-6		Bimbo Coles 24.2	Greg Brink 7.3	Bimbo Coles 172	Frankie Allen	
1988-89	11-17	2-10		Bimbo Coles 26.6	John Rivers 7.7	Bimbo Coles 141	Frankie Allen	
1989-90	13-18	5-9		Bimbo Coles 25.3	John Rivers 7.0	Bimbo Coles 122	Frankie Allen	
1990-91	13-16	6-8		Antony Moses 16.0	John Rivers 9.0	Rod Wheeler 91	Frankie Allen	56-61 .479
1991-92	10-18	3-9		Thomas Elliott 12.0	John Rivers 8.1	Jay Purcell 119	Bill Foster	
1992-93	10-18	1-11		Thomas Elliott 11.9	Thomas Elliott 6.9	Jay Purcell 101	Bill Foster	
1993-94	18-10	6-6		Jay Purcell 13.3	Ace Custis 9.1	Jay Purcell 91	Bill Foster	
1994-95	25-10	6-6	NIT CHAMPION	Shawn Smith 16.0	Ace Custis 10.5	D. Watlington, S. Good 108	Bill Foster	
1995-96	23-6	13-3	NCAA SECOND ROUND	Ace Custis 13.4	Ace Custis 9.5	Shawn Smith 81	Bill Foster	
1996-97	15-16	7-9		Ace Custis 14.7	Ace Custis 9.0	Troy Manns 138	Bill Foster	101-78 .564
1997-98	10-17	5-11		Rolan Roberts 13.6	Rolan Roberts 6.4	Jenis Grindstaff 94	Bobby Hussey	
1998-99	13-15	7-9		Eddie Lucas 14.9	Rolan Roberts 5.9	Brendan Dunlop 4.0	Bobby Hussey	23-32 .418
1999-2000	16-15	8-8		Dennis Mims 14.2	Dennis Mims 7.6	Brendan Dunlop 3.3	Ricky Stokes	
2000-01	8-19	2-14		Brian Chase 12.9	Carlton Carter 6.2	Carlos Dixon 2.9	Ricky Stokes	
2001-02	10-18	4-12		Carlos Dixon 12.2	Carlton Carter 8.2	Carlos Dixon 3.1	Ricky Stokes	
2002-03	11-18	4-12		Bryant Matthews 17.3	Terry Taylor 7.3	Carlos Dixon 2.5	Ricky Stokes	45-70 .391
2003-04	15-14	7-9		Bryant Matthews 22.1	Bryant Matthews 8.9	Jamon Gordon 4.5	Seth Greenberg	
2004-05	16-14	8-8	NIT SECOND ROUND	Zabian Dowdell 14.4	Coleman Collins 7.0	Jamon Gordon 4.1	Seth Greenberg	
2005-06	14-16	4-12		Zabian Dowdell 15.3	Coleman Collins 6.8	Jamon Gordon 4.4	Seth Greenberg	
2006-07	22-12	10-6	NCAA SECOND ROUND	Zabian Dowdell 17.4	Deron Washington 5.3	Jamon Gordon 4.5	Seth Greenberg	
2007-08	21-14	9-7	NIT QUARTERFINALS	A.D. Vassallo 16.6	Jeff Allen 7.9	Hank Thorns 3.4	Seth Greenberg	
2008-09	19-15	7-9	NIT SECOND ROUND	A.D. Vassallo 19.1	Jeff Allen 8.4	Malcolm Delaney 4.5	Seth Greenberg	107-85 .557

Cumulative totals listed when per game averages not available.

ESPN 282 SAGARIN

WAGNER

Imagine getting a chance to game-plan with legendary coach Herb Sutter. Or hearing the swish of a Terrance Bailey rainbow drop through the net. Or witnessing a string of victories for the Staten Island school over its Brooklyn archrival St. Francis—not much imagination needed there. But every Wagnerian's ultimate dream is reliving the Seahawks' unforgettable 1963 upset of NYU.

BEST TEAM: 1955-56 Herb Sutter's College Division team featured several all-time greats, including Lonny West (1,512 points), Bob Mahala Sr. (1,217) and Ed Peterson (1,172). They beat St. John's on the road and went 20-3—still Wagner's highest winning percentage. West (15.1 rpg) and Mahala (14.5 rpg) hold the top two spots for single-season rebound averages.

BEST PLAYER: G Terrance Bailey (1983-87) The 6'2" Bailey led the country in scoring in 1986 (29.4 ppg, ahead of both Reggie Miller and Len Bias) and finished as the school's and the Northeast Conference's all-time points leader. In back-to-back games against Brooklyn College and Marist, Bailey totaled 95 points and 19 boards.

BEST COACH: Herb Sutter (1937-65) He presided over Wagner's longest run of success—eight straight winning seasons and an average of 17 wins a year from 1949-56. His College Division teams routinely played—and beat—New York City powers. He was inducted into the NIT Hall of Fame in 1994.

GAME FOR THE AGES: In one of the great college upsets, on Dec. 18, 1963, College Division Wagner knocked off D1 NYU, which featured future NBAers Barry Kramer and Happy Hairston, 77-76 in overtime. The Seahawks were led by Fred Klittich (23 points), Jerry Glasser and Hank Pedro, whose last-second jumper was the game winner.

FIERCEST RIVAL: St. Francis (N.Y.) holds a 43–37 lead in the 81-year old series. However, Wagner has dominated lately, including the 2003 NEC championship game, 78-61, to reach their only NCAA Tourney.

SEASON REVIEW

SEAS.	W-L	CONF.	COACH
1920-46	*168-194*	*0-10 in 1929-30*	
1946-47	11-14		Herb Sutter
1947-48	10-10		Herb Sutter
1948-49	16-7		Herb Sutter
1949-50	19-5		Herb Sutter
1950-51	18-7		Herb Sutter
1951-52	15-12		Herb Sutter
1952-53	16-11		Herb Sutter
1953-54	18-6		Herb Sutter
1954-55	14-7		Herb Sutter
1955-56	20-3		Herb Sutter
1956-57	10-16		Herb Sutter
1957-58	18-9		Herb Sutter
1958-59	11-13		Herb Sutter
1959-60	16-8		Herb Sutter
1960-61	9-15		Herb Sutter
1961-62	12-14		Herb Sutter
1962-63	16-6		Herb Sutter
1963-64	16-8		Herb Sutter
1964-65	14-12		Herb Sutter
1965-66	14-12	1-8	Chester Sellitto
1966-67	19-9	4-5	Chester Sellitto
1967-68	21-8	5-3	Chester Sellitto
1968-69	18-10	2-6	Chester Sellitto
1969-70	11-14		Chester Sellitto
1970-71	6-19		Chester Sellitto
1971-72	8-17		Chester Sellitto
1972-73	5-19		John C. Goodwin

SEAS.	W-L	CONF.		SCORING		COACH	RECORD	
1973-74	9-16					John C. Goodwin		
1974-75	9-16					John C. Goodwin		
1975-76	2-23					John C. Goodwin	25-74	.253
1976-77	3-21					P.J. Carlesimo		
1977-78	7-19					P.J. Carlesimo		
1978-79	21-7		■			P.J. Carlesimo		
1979-80	14-13					P.J. Carlesimo		
1980-81	16-11					P.J. Carlesimo		
1981-82	4-22	1-14				P.J. Carlesimo	65-93	.411
1982-83	10-18	2-12				Neil Kennett		
1983-84	8-20	5-11				Neil Kennett		
1984-85	11-17	5-9				Neil Kennett		
1985-86	16-13	10-6		Terrance Bailey	29.4	Neil Kennett		
1986-87	16-13	8-8		Terrance Bailey	28.1	Neil Kennett		
1987-88	9-18	3-13				Neil Kennett		
1988-89	10-17	6-10				Neil Kennett	81-115	.413
1989-90	11-17	6-10				Tim Capstraw		
1990-91	4-26	2-14				Tim Capstraw		
1991-92	16-12	9-7				Tim Capstraw		
1992-93	18-12	12-6				Tim Capstraw		
1993-94	16-12	11-7				Tim Capstraw		
1994-95	10-17	9-9				Tim Capstraw		
1995-96	10-17	7-11				Tim Capstraw		
1996-97	10-17	7-11				Tim Capstraw		
1997-98	13-16	7-9				Tim Capstraw		
1998-99	9-18	7-13		Frantz Pierre-Louis	19.6	Tim Capstraw	117-164	.416
1999-2000	11-16	6-12		Jermaine Hall	16.6	Dereck Whittenburg		
2000-01	16-13	11-9		Jermaine Hall	18.4	Dereck Whittenburg		
2001-02	19-10	15-5	■	Jermaine Hall	21.0	Dereck Whittenburg		
2002-03	21-11	14-4	●	Jermaine Hall	21.4	Dereck Whittenburg	67-50	.573
2003-04	13-16	10-8		Nigel Wyatte	13.7	Mike Deane		
2004-05	13-17	10-8		Sean Munson	12.4	Mike Deane		
2005-06	13-14	6-12		Durell Vinson	15.2	Mike Deane		
2006-07	11-19	8-10		Mark Porter	13.8	Mike Deane		
2007-08	23-8	13-5		Mark Porter	16.3	Mike Deane		
2008-09	16-14	8-10		Joey Mundweiler	14.3	Mike Deane	89-88	.503

● NCAA Tournament appearance ■ NIT appearance

PROFILE

Wagner College, Staten Island, NY
Founded: 1883
Enrollment: 2,229 (1,929 undergraduate)
Colors: Green and white
Nickname: Seahawks
Current arena: Spiro Sports Center, opened in 1999 (2,000)
Previous: Sutter Gymnasium, 1951-99 (1,100); Main Hall Auditorium, 1920-55 (N/A)
First game: 1920

All-time record: 987-1,051 (.484)
Total weeks in AP Top 20/25: 0
Current conference: Northeast (1981-)
Conference titles:
Northeast: 1 (2003)
Conference tournament titles:
Northeast: 1 (2003)
NCAA Tournament appearances: 1
NIT appearances: 2

TOP 5

G **Terrance Bailey** (1983-87)
G **Ray Hodge** (1967-70)
F **Bob Bosley** (1950-54)
F **Jermaine Hall** (1999-2003)
C **Lonny West** (1953-56)

RECORDS

RECORDS	GAME		SEASON		CAREER	
POINTS	49	Terrance Bailey, vs. Brooklyn (Jan. 29, 1986); Ray Hodge, vs. Moravian (Dec. 3, 1969)	854	Terrance Bailey (1985-86)	2,591	Terrance Bailey (1983-87)
POINTS PER GAME			29.4	Terrance Bailey (1985-86)	24.5	Ray Hodge (1967-70)
REBOUNDS	24	Earl Lewis, vs. New Haven (Feb. 15, 1978); Fred Klittich, vs. Wilkes (Jan. 9, 1962) Paul Bailey, vs. Gettysburgh (Feb. 2, 1957)	382	Oliver Featherston (1968-69)	1,096	Charlie Harreus (1951-55)
ASSISTS	19	Andre Van Drost, vs. Long Island (Feb. 25, 1987)	264	Henry Dillard (1977-78)	583	Henry Dillard (1975-79)

ESPN 37 SAGARIN

WAKE FOREST

Wake Forest was one of the eight teams to make the first NCAA Tournament in 1939, losing to Ohio State, 64-52, in the East Regional semifinals. Then, for years after becoming a charter member of the ACC in 1953, Wake suffered through periods of irrelevance. But in the past two decades the program has mostly stayed near the top of the conference standings and been a consistent postseason force.

BEST TEAM: 1961-62 Horace "Bones" McKinney coached Billy Packer, Len Chappell, Bob Woollard and Co. to a 22–9 record, an ACC tournament championship (its second straight) and the school's only appearance in the Final Four, where they were ousted—again—by Ohio State.

BEST PLAYER: F TIM DUNCAN (1993-97) A native of the U.S. Virgin Islands, Duncan led Wake Forest to four straight NCAA Tournaments. He scored 2,117 points, had a school-record 87 double-doubles in 128 games and is the NCAA leader in career rebounds since 1973 with 1,570. His impact on campus was enormous; his career as a perennial NBA All-Star and four-time champion with San Antonio makes him a legend.

BEST COACH: DAVE ODOM (1989-2001) In 12 seasons in Winston-Salem, Odom guided the Demon Deacons to back-to-back ACC tournament championships in 1995 and '96, and eight NCAA Tournament appearances, including runs to the Sweet 16 in 1993 and '95 and the Elite Eight in '96.

GAME FOR THE AGES: On March 12, 1995, in the ACC tournament final, Wake Forest nipped North Carolina 82-80 in OT when Randolph Childress (37 points) hit a leaning runner with 4.6 seconds left. Childress scored all nine of WFU's points in extra time—with a dislocated pinkie on his shooting hand. He also provided the game's defining moment when he juked Jeff McInnis with a crossover move that left the future NBAer on his back. Childress looked down, motioned for McInnis to get up, then smoothly drained a three. Wake's first ACC title since 1962 was also worth a No. 1 seed in the NCAA Tournament.

HEARTBREAKER: No. 2-seed Wake Forest led No. 7-seed West Virginia by 13 at the half of their 2005 Tournament second-round matchup, but the Mountaineers stormed back to tie the game in regulation and won 111-105 in two OTs. WVU's Mike Gansey became an instant demon to the Deacons by scoring 19 points in the extra sessions (29 overall). The loss turned more poignant when sophomore star Chris Paul declared for the NBA draft.

FIERCEST RIVAL: It's tough being the smallest. Wake Forest has losing records against all three of its in-state North Carolina ACC foes. Duke has beaten WFU most often, leading their series 156–77. UNC isn't far behind with a 151–64 advantage, while NC State holds a 131–98 series edge.

FANFARE AND HOOPLA: Named for Vietnam War Congressional Medal of Honor winner Lawrence Joel, the 14,665-seat Joel Veterans Memorial Coliseum provides a true home-court advantage, thanks largely to the Screamin' Demons, a full-throated mass in black-and-gold tie-dye. Since the Joel opened in 1989, Wake has won more than 80% of its home games.

FAN FAVORITE: G TYRONE "MUGGSY" BOGUES (1983-87) He was unreal. The 5'3" Bogues could dominate at both ends of the floor. Players who dared to dribble in his vicinity—even point guards—would wind up with their pockets picked. (He's the school's all-time steals leader.) On offense, he thrived in up-tempo games. (He's the top Demon Deacon with 781 assists.) And if you guarded him soft, you discovered that Bogues could shoot, too. He went on to have a long pro career and is the shortest player in NBA history.

CONSENSUS ALL-AMERICAS

1962	**Len Chappell,** F/C
1996, '97	**Tim Duncan,** F
2003	**Josh Howard,** G/F
2005	**Chris Paul,** G

FIRST-ROUND PRO PICKS

1962	**Len Chappell,** Syracuse (5)
1971	**Charlie Davis,** New York (ABA)
1978	**Rod Griffin,** Denver (17)
1981	**Frank Johnson,** Washington (11)
1985	**Kenny Green,** Washington (12)
1987	**Tyrone Bogues,** Washington (12)
1993	**Rodney Rogers,** Denver (9)
1995	**Randolph Childress,** Detroit (19)
1997	**Tim Duncan,** San Antonio (1)
2003	**Josh Howard,** Dallas (29)
2005	**Chris Paul,** New Orleans (4)
2009	**James Johnson,** Chicago (16)
2009	**Jeff Teague,** Atlanta (19)

PROFILE

Wake Forest University, Winston-Salem, NC
Founded: 1834
Enrollment: 6,862 (4,476 undergraduate)
Colors: Old gold and black
Nickname: Demon Deacons
Current arena: Lawrence Joel Veterans Memorial Coliseum, opened in 1989 (14,665)
Previous: Greensboro Coliseum, 1960-89 (23,500); Memorial Coliseum, 1956-89 (8,200); Gore Gymnasium, opened in 1906 (2,200)
First game: Feb. 6, 1906

All-time record: 1,401-1,059 (.570)
Total weeks in AP Top 20/25: 273
Current conference: Atlantic Coast (1953-)
Conference titles:
Southern: 1 (1939)
ACC: 4 (1960 [tie], '62, '95 [tie], 2003)
Conference tournament titles:
Southern: 1 (1953)
ACC: 4 (1961, '62, '95, '96)
NCAA Tournament appearances: 21
Sweet 16s (since 1975): 6
Final Fours: 1

NIT appearances: 6
Semifinals: 2
Titles: 1 (2000)

TOP 5

G	**Randolph Childress** (1990-91, '92-95)
G	**Chris Paul** (2003-05)
F	**Tim Duncan** (1993-97)
F/C	**Len Chappell** (1959-62)
C	**Dickie Hemric** (1951-55)

RECORDS	GAME		SEASON		CAREER	
POINTS	51	Charlie Davis, vs. American (Feb. 15, 1969)	932	Len Chappell (1961-62)	2,587	Dickie Hemric (1951-55)
POINTS PER GAME			30.1	Len Chappell (1961-62)	24.9	Charlie Davis (1968-71); Len Chappell (1959-62)
REBOUNDS	36	Dickie Hemric, vs. Clemson (Feb. 4, 1955)	515	Dickie Hemric (1954-55)	1,802	Dickie Hemric (1951-55)
ASSISTS	17	Tyrone Bogues, vs. Clemson (Jan. 10, 1987); vs. North Carolina (Feb. 8, 1986)	276	Tyrone Bogues (1986-87)	781	Tyrone Bogues (1983-87)

EASON REVIEW

EASON	W-L	CONF.	SCORING	COACH	RECORD		SEASON	W-L	CONF.	SCORING	COACH	RECORD	
06-15	*70-38*		*No losing seasons*				**1925-26**	13-6			R.S. Hayes		
5-16	16-2			J.R. Crozier			**1926-27**	22-3			James Baldwin		
16-17	9-6			J.R. Crozier	95-46	.674	**1927-28**	6-14			James Baldwin	28-17	.622
17-18	4-12			E.T. MacDonnell	4-12	.250	**1928-29**	5-9			Pat Miller		
18-19	6-10			Irving Carlyle	6-10	.375	**1929-30**	2-11			Pat Miller	7-20	.259
19-20	9-4			Bill Holding			**1930-31**	8-11			R.S. Hayes	21-17	.553
0-21	7-10			J.L. White	7-10	.412	**1931-32**	4-8			Fred Emmerson		
921-22	11-6			Bill Holding	20-10	.667	**1932-33**	5-8			Fred Emmerson	9-16	.360
922-23	12-5			Phil Utley	12-5	.706	**1933-34**	5-9			Murray Greason		
923-24	18-7			Hank Garrity			**1934-35**	6-10			Murray Greason		
924-25	15-7			Hank Garrity	33-14	.702	**1935-36**	9-12			Murray Greason		

SEAS.	W-L	CONF.	POSTSEASON	SCORING		REBOUNDS		ASSISTS		COACH	RECORD	
936-37	15-6	9-4								Murray Greason		
937-38	7-12	7-8								Murray Greason		
938-39	18-6	15-3	NCAA REGIONAL SEMIFINALS							Murray Greason		
939-40	13-9	10-5								Murray Greason		
940-41	9-9	7-6								Murray Greason		
941-42	16-8	13-5								Murray Greason		
942-43	1-10	1-10								Murray Greason		
943-44	no team											
944-45	3-14	0-6								Murray Greason		
945-46	12-6	8-5								Murray Greason		
946-47	11-13	8-9								Murray Greason		
947-48	18-11	8-7		Jack Gentry	12.5					Murray Greason		
948-49	11-13	7-7		Stan Najeway	8.6					Murray Greason		
949-50	14-16	11-8		Alton McCotter	12.3					Murray Greason		
950-51	16-14	8-9		Alton McCotter	13.8					Murray Greason		
951-52	10-19	7-9		Dickie Hemric	22.4	Dickie Hemric	18.6			Murray Greason		
952-53	19-6	12-3	NCAA REGIONAL SEMIFINALS	Dickie Hemric	24.9	Dickie Hemric	16.6			Murray Greason		
953-54	17-12	8-4		Dickie Hemric	24.3	Dickie Hemric	15.1			Murray Greason		
954-55	17-10	8-6		Dickie Hemric	27.6	Dickie Hemric	19.1			Murray Greason		
955-56	19-9	10-4		Lowell Davis	19.2	Jack Williams	11.0			Murray Greason		
956-57	19-9	7-7		Jack Williams	16.2	Jim Gilley	8.0			Murray Greason	285-243	.540
957-58	6-17	3-11		Dave Budd	15.8	Dave Budd	8.5			Horace "Bones" McKinney		
958-59	10-14	5-9		Dave Budd	14.6	Dave Budd	8.6			Horace "Bones" McKinney		
959-60	21-7	12-2		Len Chappell	17.4	Len Chappell	12.5			Horace "Bones" McKinney		
960-61	19-11	11-3	NCAA REGIONAL FINALS	Len Chappell	26.6	Len Chappell	14.0			Horace "Bones" McKinney		
961-62	22-9	12-2	NCAA THIRD PLACE	Len Chappell	30.1	Len Chappell	15.2			Horace "Bones" McKinney		
962-63	16-10	11-3		Dave Wiedeman	13.9	Bob Woollard	8.7			Horace "Bones" McKinney		
963-64	16-11	9-5		Frank Christie	16.1	Ronny Watts	12.0			Horace "Bones" McKinney		
964-65	12-15	6-8		Bob Leonard	23.9	Ronny Watts	13.0			Horace "Bones" McKinney	122-94	.565
965-66	8-18	4-10		Paul Long	24.0	Bob Leonard	6.6			Jack Murdock	8-18	.308
966-67	9-18	5-9		Paul Long	22.3	David Stroupe	6.2			Jack McCloskey		
967-68	5-21	3-11		Dickie Walker	17.2	Dickie Walker	6.2			Jack McCloskey		
968-69	18-9	8-6		Charlie Davis	22.8	Gilbert McGregor	12.0			Jack McCloskey		
969-70	14-13	6-8		Charlie Davis	25.5	Gilbert McGregor	10.6			Jack McCloskey		
970-71	16-10	7-7		Charlie Davis	26.5	Gilbert McGregor	9.3			Jack McCloskey		
971-72	8-18	3-9		Willie Griffin	15.9	Rich Habegger	7.8			Jack McCloskey	70-89	.440
972-73	12-15	3-9		Tony Byers	21.7	Mike Parrish	7.5			Carl Tacy		
973-74	13-13	3-9		Tony Byers	18.0	Cal Stamp	8.6	Skip Brown	78	Carl Tacy		
974-75	13-13	2-10		Skip Brown	22.7	Rod Griffin	7.6	Skip Brown	177	Carl Tacy		
975-76	17-10	5-7		Skip Brown	20.9	Rod Griffin	9.0	Skip Brown	137	Carl Tacy		
976-77	22-8	8-4	NCAA REGIONAL FINALS	Rod Griffin	20.5	Rod Griffin	8.6	Skip Brown	187	Carl Tacy		
977-78	19-10	6-6		Rod Griffin	21.5	Rod Griffin	10.0	Frank Johnson	101	Carl Tacy		
978-79	12-15	3-9		Frank Johnson	16.1	Guy Morgan	6.3	Frank Johnson	81	Carl Tacy		
979-80	13-14	4-10		Alvis Rogers	15.4	Guy Morgan	7.3	Benny McKaig	115	Carl Tacy		
980-81	22-7	9-5	NCAA SECOND ROUND	Frank Johnson	16.2	Guy Morgan	5.7	Frank Johnson	182	Carl Tacy		
981-82	21-9	9-5	NCAA SECOND ROUND	Mike Helms	11.4	Anthony Teachey	6.1	Danny Young	132	Carl Tacy		
982-83	20-12	7-7	NIT SEMIFINALS	John Toms	13.8	Anthony Teachey	8.5	Danny Young	154	Carl Tacy		
983-84	23-9	7-7	NCAA REGIONAL FINALS	Kenny Green	17.8	Anthony Teachey	10.0	Danny Young	157	Carl Tacy		
984-85	15-14	5-9	NIT FIRST ROUND	Kenny Green	17.0	Kenny Green	8.3	Tyrone Bogues	207	Carl Tacy	222-149	.598
985-86	8-21	0-14		Rod Watson	12.8	Mark Cline	4.5	Tyrone Bogues	8.4	Bob Staak		
986-87	14-15	2-12		Tyrone Bogues	14.8	Sam Ivy	6.1	Tyrone Bogues	9.5	Bob Staak		
987-88	10-18	3-11		Sam Ivy	18.6	Sam Ivy	7.6	Cal Boyd	140	Bob Staak		
988-89	13-15	3-11		Chris King	14.4	Chris King	6.1	Derrick McQueen	147	Bob Staak	45-69	.395
989-90	12-16	3-11		Chris King	16.1	Chris King	7.4	Derrick McQueen	141	Dave Odom		
990-91	19-11	8-6	NCAA SECOND ROUND	Rodney Rogers	16.3	Rodney Rogers	7.9	Derrick McQueen	142	Dave Odom		
991-92	17-12	7-9	NCAA FIRST ROUND	Rodney Rogers	20.5	Rodney Rogers	8.5	Derrick McQueen	145	Dave Odom		
992-93	21-9	10-6	NCAA REGIONAL SEMIFINALS	Rodney Rogers	21.2	Derrick Hicks	9.0	Randolph Childress	126	Dave Odom		
993-94	21-12	9-7	NCAA SECOND ROUND	Randolph Childress	19.6	Tim Duncan	9.6	Randolph Childress	114	Dave Odom		
994-95	26-6	12-4	NCAA REGIONAL SEMIFINALS	Randolph Childress	20.1	Tim Duncan	12.5	Randolph Childress	167	Dave Odom		
995-96	26-6	12-4	NCAA REGIONAL FINALS	Tim Duncan	19.1	Tim Duncan	12.3	Tony Rutland	120	Dave Odom		
996-97	24-7	11-5	NCAA SECOND ROUND	Tim Duncan	20.8	Tim Duncan	14.7	Tim Duncan	98	Dave Odom		
997-98	16-14	7-9	NIT SECOND ROUND	Robert O'Kelley	16.6	Niki Arinze	6.1	Tony Rutland	93	Dave Odom		
998-99	17-14	7-9	NIT SECOND ROUND	Robert O'Kelley	17.5	Rafael Vidaurreta	7.3	Robert O'Kelley	2.0	Dave Odom		
999-2000	22-14	7-9	NIT CHAMPION	Darius Songaila	13.7	Rafael Vidaurreta	6.9	Robert O'Kelley	2.4	Dave Odom		
000-01	19-11	8-8	NCAA FIRST ROUND	Josh Howard	13.6	Josh Shoemaker	7.4	Ervin Murray	2.9	Dave Odom	240-132	.645
001-02	21-13	9-7	NCAA SECOND ROUND	Darius Songaila	17.9	Darius Songaila	8.1	Broderick Hicks	3.2	Skip Prosser		
002-03	25-6	13-3	NCAA SECOND ROUND	Josh Howard	19.5	Josh Howard	8.3	Taron Downey	4.2	Skip Prosser		
003-04	21-10	9-7	NCAA REGIONAL SEMIFINALS	Justin Gray	17.0	Jamaal Levy	8.4	Chris Paul	5.9	Skip Prosser		
004-05	27-6	13-3	NCAA SECOND ROUND	Eric Williams	17.0	Eric Williams	7.7	Chris Paul	6.6	Skip Prosser		
005-06	17-17	3-13	NIT FIRST ROUND	Justin Gray	18.2	Eric Williams	8.9	Justin Gray	4.3	Skip Prosser		
006-07	15-16	5-11		Kyle Visser	17.0	Kyle Visser	7.4	Ishmael Smith	6.0	Skip Prosser	126-68	.649
007-08	17-13	7-9		James Johnson	14.6	James Johnson	8.1	Ishmael Smith	4.7	Dino Gaudio		
008-09	24-7	11-5	NCAA FIRST ROUND	Jeff Teague	18.8	James Johnson	8.5	Jeff Teague	3.5	Dino Gaudio	41-20	.672

umulative totals listed when per game averages not available.

THE SCHOOLS

ESPN 35 SAGARIN

WASHINGTON

A Northwest power in the first half of the 20th century under legendary coach Clarence "Hec" Edmundson, the Huskies reached the Final Four under William H. "Tippy" Dye in 1953. The so-called German Connection—Detlef Schrempf and Chris Welp—restored Washington to Pac-10 contention in the mid-1980s, and more recently, Lorenzo Romar's Dawgs reached back-to-back Sweet 16s in 2005 and '06.

BEST TEAM: 1952-53 A year after they narrowly missed the NCAA Tournament and were forced to watch the Final Four played out in their own gym (Kansas triumphed over St. John's, 80-63), Dye's Huskies went 28–3, advancing to the NCAA semifinals (in Kansas City) before losing to Kansas, 79-53. All-America center and Helms Foundation Player of the Year Bob Houbregs (25.8 ppg, 11.5 rpg) led a starting five composed solely of in-state talent that defeated California for the Pacific Coast Conference title. At the Final Four, the Huskies beat LSU in the third-place game.

BEST PLAYER: C CHRIS WELP (1983-87) Washington's all-time leading scorer and the only Husky to top 2,000 points, the seven-footer from Delmenhorst, West Germany, was the 1984 Pac-10 Freshman of the Year as he helped lead UW to the Sweet 16. A nimble big man with a soft touch, Welp was also an outstanding defender, ranking as UW's all-time leading shot blocker (186). The Pac-10's Player of the Year as a junior piloted the Huskies to four postseason appearances, including three straight NCAA Tournaments.

BEST COACH: CLARENCE "HEC" EDMUNDSON (1920-47) The all-time winningest coach in University of Washington history (488–195), Edmundson guided the Huskies to 11 of the school's 24 20-win seasons, 12 PCC Northern Division titles and one NCAA appearance (1943). One of the game's early innovators, he advocated the fast break and the one-handed shot. The Huskies' arena bears his name.

GAME FOR THE AGES: On Feb. 22, 1975, five Huskies, led by Larry Jackson's 27 points, scored in double figures in UW's 103-81 rout of eventual NCAA champion UCLA. It turned out to be John Wooden's last coaching defeat. Before a packed home arena, the 15–7 Huskies led the 20–2, No. 2-ranked Bruins, 52-44, at the half, then went on a 16-4 run to put them away.

HEARTBREAKER: Poised for their first trip to the Elite Eight in 53 years, Washington lost a six-point lead late in their 2006 Sweet 16 clash with Connecticut. After Rashad Anderson's three-pointer tied the game with 1.8 seconds left in regulation, UConn won, 98-92, in OT while four of UW's starters fouled out.

FIERCEST RIVAL: Huskies fans often belittle Washington State as a land-grant farm school. Although UW has enjoyed considerable success over the Cougars, its biggest coup came in 1971 when the Huskies lured away longtime Wazzu coach Marv Harshman. Only 12–19 coaching against the Huskies, Harshman's record coaching *for* them against the Cougars was 21–8.

FANFARE AND HOOPLA: The only Pac-10 student section that is positioned behind the visitor's bench, UW's rowdy, 500-strong Dawg Pack is known for its, uh, wit. "Start your tractors!" is a favorite chant when Wazzu comes to town. The throng's location has drawn the ire of opposing coaches, including former Cougars head man Dick Bennett, who gave the Dawgs a single-finger salute in 2005.

FAN FAVORITE: G NATE ROBINSON (2002-05) A former UW football cornerback, the 5'9" Robinson became an Edmundson favorite with his play above the rim, made possible by his 43.5-inch vertical leap.

CONSENSUS ALL-AMERICAS

1911	**C.C. Clementson,** G
1915	**Tony Savage,** C
1920	**Irving Cook,** G
1928	**Alfred James,** G
1934	**Hal Lee,** G
1953	**Bob Houbregs,** C
2006	**Brandon Roy,** G

FIRST-ROUND PRO PICKS

1948	**Jack Nichols,** Washington (12)
1953	**Bob Houbregs,** Milwaukee (3)
1985	**Detlef Schrempf,** Dallas (8)
1987	**Chris Welp,** Philadelphia (16)
2005	**Nate Robinson,** Phoenix (21)
2006	**Brandon Roy,** Minnesota (6)
2007	**Spencer Hawes,** Sacramento (10)

PROFILE

University of Washington, Seattle, WA
Founded: 1861
Enrollment: 42,000 (27,433 undergraduate)
Colors: Purple and gold
Nickname: Huskies
Current arena: Bank of America Arena at Hec Edmundson Pavilion, opened in 1927 as the University of Washington Pavilion (10,000)
Previous: Campus Gymnasium, 1896-1927 (N/A)
First game: 1896
All-time record: 1,612-1,048 (.606)

Total weeks in AP Top 20/25: 130
Current conference: Pacific-10 (1915-)
Conference titles:
Pacific Coast: 7 (1931, '34, '43, '44 [tie], '48, '51, '53)
Pac-10: 3 (1984 [tie], '85 [tie], 2009)
Conference tournament titles:
Pac-10: 1 (2005)
NCAA Tournament appearances: 14
Sweet 16s (since 1975): 4
Final Fours: 1
NIT appearances: 5

TOP 5

G	**Eldridge Recasner** (1986-90)
G	**Brandon Roy** (2002-06)
F	**Detlef Schrempf** (1981-85)
C	**Bob Houbregs** (1950-53)
C	**Chris Welp** (1983-87)

RECORDS

RECORDS	GAME		SEASON		CAREER	
POINTS	49	Bob Houbregs, vs. Idaho (Jan. 10, 1953)	800	Bob Houbregs (1952-53)	2,073	Chris Welp (1983-87)
POINTS PER GAME			25.8	Bob Houbregs (1952-53)	20.8	Steve Hawes (1969-72)
REBOUNDS	30	Ed Corell, vs. Oregon (Feb. 24, 1962)	391	Jon Brockman (2008-09)	1,283	Jon Brockman (2005-09)
ASSISTS	16	Rafael Stone, vs. California (Feb. 20, 1970)	219	Will Conroy (2004-05)	515	Will Conroy (2001-05)

SEASON REVIEW

SEASON	W-L	CONF.	SCORING	COACH	RECORD	
96-1916	118-39		89-22 over 7 seasons (1908-15)			
16-17	9-8	7-5		John Davidson	16-15	.516
17-18	4-8			Claude J. Hunt		
18-19	6-10	5-7		Claude J. Hunt	8-19	.296
19-20	7-8	5-7		Leonard B. Allison	7-8	.467
20-21	18-4	10-4		Clarence "Hec" Edmundson		
21-22	13-5	11-5		Clarence "Hec" Edmundson		
22-23	12-4	5-3		Clarence "Hec" Edmundson		
923-24	12-4	6-2		Clarence "Hec" Edmundson		
924-25	14-7	5-5		Clarence "Hec" Edmundson		
925-26	10-6	5-5		Clarence "Hec" Edmundson		
1926-27	15-4	7-3		Clarence "Hec" Edmundson		
1927-28	22-6	9-1		Clarence "Hec" Edmundson		
1928-29	18-2	10-0		Clarence "Hec" Edmundson		
1929-30	21-7	12-4		Clarence "Hec" Edmundson		
1930-31	25-3	14-2		Clarence "Hec" Edmundson		
1931-32	19-6	12-4		Clarence "Hec" Edmundson		
1932-33	22-6	10-6		Clarence "Hec" Edmundson		
1933-34	20-5	14-2		Clarence "Hec" Edmundson		
1934-35	16-8	11-5		Clarence "Hec" Edmundson		
1935-36	25-7	13-3		Clarence "Hec" Edmundson		
1936-37	15-11	11-5		Clarence "Hec" Edmundson		

SEAS.	W-L	CONF.	POSTSEASON	SCORING		REBOUNDS		ASSISTS		COACH	RECORD	
937-38	29-7	13-7								Clarence "Hec" Edmundson		
938-39	20-5	11-5								Clarence "Hec" Edmundson		
939-40	10-15	6-10								Clarence "Hec" Edmundson		
940-41	12-13	7-9								Clarence "Hec" Edmundson		
941-42	18-7	10-6								Clarence "Hec" Edmundson		
942-43	24-7	12-4	NCAA REGIONAL SEMIFINALS							Clarence "Hec" Edmundson		
943-44	26-6	15-1								Clarence "Hec" Edmundson		
944-45	22-18	5-11								Clarence "Hec" Edmundson		
945-46	14-14	6-10								Clarence "Hec" Edmundson		
946-47	16-8	8-8								Clarence "Hec" Edmundson	488-195	.714
947-48	23-11	10-6	NCAA REGIONAL SEMIFINALS	Jack Nichols	14.8					Art McLarney		
948-49	11-15	6-10								Art McLarney		
949-50	19-10	8-8								Art McLarney	53-36	.596
950-51	24-6	11-5	NCAA REGIONAL SEMIFINALS							William H. "Tippy" Dye		
951-52	25-6	14-2		Bob Houbregs	18.6	Bob Houbregs	10.6			William H. "Tippy" Dye		
952-53	28-3	15-1	NCAA THIRD PLACE	Bob Houbregs	25.8	Bob Houbregs	11.5			William H. "Tippy" Dye		
953-54	8-18	7-9		Dean Parsons	16.5	Dean Parsons	11.9			William H. "Tippy" Dye		
954-55	13-12	7-9		Dean Parsons	19.2	Dean Parsons	13.8			William H. "Tippy" Dye		
955-56	15-11	11-5		Bruno Boin	17.2	Jim Coshow	11.0			William H. "Tippy" Dye		
956-57	17-9	13-3		Doug Smart	19.0	Doug Smart	12.7			William H. "Tippy" Dye		
957-58	8-18	5-11		Doug Smart	20.3	Doug Smart	13.4			William H. "Tippy" Dye		
958-59	18-8	11-5		Doug Smart	17.6	Doug Smart	14.3			William H. "Tippy" Dye	156-91	.632
959-60	15-13	2-9		Bill Hanson	16.4	Bill Hanson	8.1			John Grayson		
960-61	13-13	6-6		Bill Hanson	16.3	Ed Corell	7.8			John Grayson		
961-62	16-10	5-7		Bill Hanson	20.8	Ed Corell	11.4			John Grayson		
962-63	13-13	6-6		Dale Easley	15.2	Ed Corell	10.3			John Grayson	57-49	.538
963-64	9-17	5-10		Clint Peeples	12.1	Clint Peeples	7.7			Mac Duckworth		
964-65	9-16	5-9		Lynn Nance	17.5	Lynn Nance	9.4			Mac Duckworth		
965-66	10-15	4-10		Gordy Harris	17.4	Dave Hovde	8.9			Mac Duckworth		
966-67	13-12	6-8		Gordy Harris	16.8	Dave Hovde	9.6			Mac Duckworth		
967-68	12-14	4-10		Dave Carr	20.0	George Irvine	7.6			Mac Duckworth	53-74	.417
968-69	13-13	6-8		George Irvine	15.6	George Irvine	7.5			Tex Winter		
969-70	17-9	7-7		George Irvine	20.0	Steve Hawes	10.2			Tex Winter		
970-71	15-13	6-8		Steve Hawes	21.8	Steve Hawes	14.8			Tex Winter	45-35	.563
971-72	20-6	10-4		Steve Hawes	21.7	Steve Hawes	14.0			Marv Harshman		
972-73	16-11	6-8		Louie Nelson	23.0	Ray Price	9.1			Marv Harshman		
973-74	16-10	7-7		Larry Pounds	16.7	Larry Pounds	9.2			Marv Harshman		
974-75	16-10	6-8		Clarence Ramsey	17.8	James Edwards	7.5	Chester Dorsey	5.6	Marv Harshman		
975-76	22-6 ⊗	9-5	NCAA FIRST ROUND	James Edwards	17.6	Lars Hansen	7.5	Chester Dorsey	5.8	Marv Harshman		
976-77	17-10	8-6		James Edwards	20.9	James Edwards	10.4	Kim Stewart	4.2	Marv Harshman		
977-78	14-13	6-8		Mike Neill	11.5	James Woods	8.1	Kim Stewart	4.9	Marv Harshman		
978-79	11-16	6-12		Stan Walker	12.6	James Woods	7.3	Lorenzo Romar	3.0	Marv Harshman		
979-80	18-10	9-9	NIT FIRST ROUND	Stan Walker	11.6	Stan Walker	5.6	Lorenzo Romar	3.5	Marv Harshman		
980-81	14-13	8-10		Andra Griffin	19.4	Dan Caldwell	7.9	Bob Fronk	4.4	Marv Harshman		
981-82	19-10	11-7	NIT SECOND ROUND	Dan Caldwell	13.6	Dan Caldwell	6.9	Steve Burks	4.7	Marv Harshman		
982-83	16-15	7-11		Brad Watson	15.1	Darrell Tanner	7.2	Alvin Vaughn	5.6	Marv Harshman		
983-84	24-7	15-3	NCAA REGIONAL SEMIFINALS	Detlef Schrempf	16.8	Detlef Schrempf	7.4	Detlef Schrempf	3.0	Marv Harshman		
984-85	22-10	13-5	NCAA FIRST ROUND	Detlef Schrempf	15.8	Detlef Schrempf	8.0	Detlef Schrempf	4.2	Marv Harshman	245-147	.625▼
985-86	19-12	13-5	NCAA FIRST ROUND	Chris Welp	19.4	Chris Welp	8.5	Greg Hill	3.7	Andy Russo		
986-87	20-15	10-8	NIT QUARTERFINALS	Chris Welp	20.8	Chris Welp	9.0	Greg Hill	3.6	Andy Russo		
987-88	10-19	5-13		Eldridge Recasner	17.0	Mark West	6.8	Troy Morrell	3.1	Andy Russo		
988-89	12-16	8-10		Eldridge Recasner	18.1	Mark West	6.5	Eldridge Recasner	3.8	Andy Russo	61-62	.496
989-90	11-17	5-13		Eldridge Recasner	16.2	Dion Brown	6.6	Eldridge Recasner	3.4	Lynn Nance		
90-91	14-14	5-13		Doug Meekins	16.1	Dion Brown	7.9	James French	3.1	Lynn Nance		
91-92	12-17	5-13		Rich Manning	16.8	Mark Pope	8.1	Brett Pagett	2.9	Lynn Nance		
92-93	13-14	7-11		Rich Manning	17.9	Mark Pope	8.0	Prentiss Perkins	3.8	Lynn Nance	50-62	.446
93-94	5-22	3-15		Maurice Woods	12.4	Amir Rashad	5.9	Michael McClain	4.1	Bob Bender		
94-95	9-18 ⊗	5-13		Bryant Boston	14.7	Mark Sanford	5.7	Jason Hamilton	4.9	Bob Bender		
95-96	16-12	9-9	NIT FIRST ROUND	Mark Sanford	16.5	Mark Sanford	6.1	Jamie Booker	4.0	Bob Bender		
96-97	17-11	10-8	NIT FIRST ROUND	Mark Sanford	17.0	Mark Sanford	8.0	Jamie Booker	3.8	Bob Bender		
97-98	20-10	11-7	NCAA REGIONAL SEMIFINALS	Todd MacCulloch	18.6	Todd MacCulloch	9.7	Donald Watts	3.6	Bob Bender		
98-99	17-12	10-8	NCAA FIRST ROUND	Todd MacCulloch	18.7	Todd MacCulloch	11.9	Senque Carey	3.2	Bob Bender		
99-2000	10-20	5-13		Deon Luton	15.1	Will Perkins	5.9	Senque Carey	4.6	Bob Bender		
00-01	10-20	4-14		Will Perkins	12.8	Will Perkins	7.2	Bryan Brown	2.9	Bob Bender		
01-02	11-18	5-13		Doug Wrenn	19.5	David Dixon	7.6	Curtis Allen	4.3	Bob Bender	115-143	.446▼
02-03	10-17	5-13		Nate Robinson	13.0	Doug Wrenn	5.8	Will Conroy	3.2	Lorenzo Romar		
03-04	19-12	12-6	NCAA FIRST ROUND	Nate Robinson	13.2	Brandon Roy	5.3	Will Conroy	4.6	Lorenzo Romar		
04-05	29-6	14-4	NCAA REGIONAL SEMIFINALS	Nate Robinson	16.4	Bobby Jones	5.6	Will Conroy	6.4	Lorenzo Romar		
05-06	26-7	13-5	NCAA REGIONAL SEMIFINALS	Brandon Roy	20.2	Jon Brockman	6.5	Brandon Roy	4.1	Lorenzo Romar		
06-07	19-13	8-10		Spencer Hawes	14.9	Jon Brockman	9.6	Justin Dentmon	3.6	Lorenzo Romar		
07-08	16-17	7-11		Jon Brockman	17.8	Jon Brockman	11.6	Venoy Overton	3.2	Lorenzo Romar		
08-09	26-9	14-4	NCAA SECOND ROUND	Isaiah Thomas	15.3	Jon Brockman	11.5	Isaiah Thomas	2.6	Lorenzo Romar	145-81	.642

Records don't reflect games forfeited or vacated. For adjusted records, see p. 521.

Coaches' records adjusted to reflect games forfeited or vacated: Marv Harshman, 246-146, .628; Bob Bender, 116-142, .450. For yearly totals, see p. 521.

THE SCHOOLS

ESPN 70 SAGARIN

WASHINGTON STATE

A cavalcade of quality coaches has called the Palouse region home. In 1916-17, J. Fred Bohler coached Washington State (his brother, Roy, was the center) to a 25–1 record and the Helms Foundation national championship. In 1941, in the third NCAA Tournament, Jack Friel took the Cougars to the title game. Since then, Marv Harshman, George Raveling, Kelvin Sampson and the father-son duo of Dick and Tony Bennett have all run the show in the Pac-10's most remote outpost.

BEST TEAM: 1940-41 After dropping their first two Pacific Coast Conference Northern Division contests, Friel's Cougars won a then-record 13 straight league games on their way to a 26–6 season (tied for most wins in school history) and defeated Stanford for the PCC championship. Led by center Paul Lindemann and guard Ray Sundquist, the defensive-minded Cougars beat Creighton and Arkansas before falling to Wisconsin in the 1941 NCAA Tournament championship game, 39-34.

BEST PLAYER: G Isaac Fontaine (1993-97) Washington State's all-time leading career and single-season scorer, Fontaine is the only Cougar to top the 2,000-point mark (2,003). The sharpshooting guard holds the school's career record for three-point field goal percentage (.457), good for fourth all-time in the Pac-10. Twice an All-Pac-10 selection, Fontaine was a frosh on the Cougars' 1994 NCAA Tournament team; he led them to the NIT in 1995 and '96.

BEST COACH: Jack Friel (1928-58) Known alternatively as the Fox of the Palouse, the Silver Fox and, in his later years, the Prune, Friel coached 872 games (495–377) in 30 seasons. Using Friel's system of rotating two complete five-man units throughout each game, the Cougars won or shared the Pacific Coast Conference's Northern Division four times and reached the NCAA Final in 1941. Wazzu's home court is named in Friel's honor.

GAME FOR THE AGES: On March 7, 1983, Cougars fans stormed Friel Court after sophomore Bryan Pollard's tip-in at the buzzer beat No. 6-ranked UCLA. A record crowd of 12,422 saw the Cougars complete a perfect home record (15–0) for first time since 1916-17, paving their way to a second NCAA Tournament appearance in four seasons.

HEARTBREAKER: On Feb. 24, 1979, 17–7 Washington State faced off against No. 1-ranked UCLA just two days after the Cougs barely lost to Southern California, 71-69. Extra motivated to beat the Bruins, center James Donaldson and forward Don Collins led the assault that pushed the game into three overtimes before a jumper by Kiki Vandeweghe and late free throws gave UCLA a wild 110-102 win.

FIERCEST RIVAL: For the most part, cross-state foe Washington has dominated this dog vs. cat series, the basketball version of the Apple Cup. In 2007, for the first time in a rivalry that dates back to 1950, the Cougars visited Seattle as a Top-25 team. The "hayseeds" from Wazzu won seven straight between 2005-06 and '07-08, but UW leads all-time, 169-90.

Known as the Fox of the Palouse, the Silver Fox and, in his later years, the Prune, Jack Friel coached 872 games.

FANFARE AND HOOPLA: Not only does Wazzu's jaunty fight song manage to spell out W-A-S-H-I-N-G-T-O-N S-T-A-T-E C-O-U-G-S, thanks to the 1985 film *Volunteers* the ditty has achieved a unique pop culture status. In the movie, John Candy's character, WSU alum Tom Tuttle from Tacoma, teaches the song to a group of Southeast Asian villagers, who then make it their war cry.

FAN FAVORITE: G Kyle Weaver (2004-08) The popular do-it-all guy from Beloit, Wis., Weaver achieved the first triple-double in school history and helped lead the Cougs to back-to-back NCAA Tournaments.

PROFILE

Washington State University, Pullman, WA
Founded: 1890
Enrollment: 19,360 (15,147 undergraduate)
Colors: Crimson and gray
Nickname: Cougars
Current arena: Friel Court, opened in 1973 (11,671)
Previous: Bohler Gym, 1928-73 (3,000)
First game: Dec. 7, 1901
All-time record: 1,455-1,343 (.520)
Total weeks in AP Top 20/25: 37
Current conference: Pacific-10 (1916-)

Conference titles:
Pacific Coast: 2 (1917, '41)
Conference tournament titles: 0
NCAA Tournament appearances: 6
Sweet 16s (since 1975): 1
Final Fours: 1
NIT appearances: 4

CONSENSUS ALL-AMERICAS

1916 **Roy Bohler**, C
1918 **Alfred Sorenson**, G

FIRST-ROUND PRO PICKS

1980 **Don Collins**, Atlanta (18)

TOP 5

G **Isaac Fontaine** (1993-97)
G **Kyle Weaver** (2004-08)
F **Don Collins** (1976-80)
F **Mark Hendrickson** (1992-96)
C **Steve Puidokas** (1973-77)

RECORDS	GAME		SEASON		CAREER	
POINTS	45	Brian Quinnett, vs. Loyola Marymount (Dec. 5, 1986)	657	Isaac Fontaine (1996-97)	2,003	Isaac Fontaine (1993-97)
POINTS PER GAME			23.1	Don Collins (1979-80)	18.6	Steve Puidokas (1973-77)
REBOUNDS	27	Jim McKean, vs. West Virginia (Dec. 28, 1966)	323	Ted Werner (1963-64)	992	Steve Puidokas (1973-77)
ASSISTS	15	Donminic Ellison, vs. Cal State Northridge (Jan. 25, 1995)	192	Donminic Ellison (1994-95)	473	Bennie Seltzer (1989-93)

EASON REVIEW

ASON	W-L	CONF.	SCORING		COACH	RECORD	
-16	122-79		63-23 over 4 seasons (1912-16)				
16-17	25-1	8-1	Roy Bohler	12.0	J. Fred Bohler		
17-18	7-12		Milo McIver	10.7	J. Fred Bohler		
18-19	10-11	7-5	Milo McIver	10.2	J. Fred Bohler		
19-20	10-11	6-7	Bob Moss	12.9	J. Fred Bohler		
20-21	12-16	3-11	Milo McIver	8.0	J. Fred Bohler		
21-22	9-17	4-11	Jack Friel	9.0	J. Fred Bohler		
22-23	16-10	4-4	Jack Friel	7.7	J. Fred Bohler		
23-24	17-11	3-7	Hugo Schultz	7.2	J. Fred Bohler		
24-25	18-11	2-8	Wallace Kelso	8.6	J. Fred Bohler		
25-26	9-17	1-8	Walter Henry	5.5	J. Fred Bohler	226-177	.561
1926-27	11-10	3-7	Gerald Clay	5.7	Karl Schlademan		
1927-28	7-17	1-9	Erwin McDowell	7.0	Karl Schlademan	18-27	.400
1928-29	9-14	5-5	Erwin McDowell	5.5	Jack Friel		
1929-30	14-12	9-7			Jack Friel		
1930-31	18-7	10-6			Jack Friel		
1931-32	22-5	11-5	Huntly Gordon	10.4	Jack Friel		
1932-33	17-8	8-8	Huntly Gordon	6.8	Jack Friel		
1933-34	14-11	6-10	Huntley McPhee	7.9	Jack Friel		
1934-35	12-12	6-10	Ralph Rogers	6.8	Jack Friel		
1935-36	22-8	8-8	Jack Holstine	7.7	Jack Friel		
1936-37	24-8	11-5	Ivar Nelson	9.1	Jack Friel		

SEAS.	W-L	CONF.	POSTSEASON	SCORING		REBOUNDS		ASSISTS		COACH	RECORD	
937-38	19-11	12-8		Al Hooper	7.7					Jack Friel		
938-39	23-10	8-8		Al Hooper	9.2					Jack Friel		
939-40	23-10	9-7		Bud Olson	7.3					Jack Friel		
940-41	26-6	13-3	NCAA RUNNER-UP	Paul Lindemann	10.2					Jack Friel		
941-42	21-8	9-7		Marvin Gilberg	8.9					Jack Friel		
942-43	19-11	9-7		Gale Bishop	13.8					Jack Friel		
943-44	8-19	4-12		Bob Rennink	8.9					Jack Friel		
944-45	23-13	11-5								Jack Friel		
945-46	16-13	5-11								Jack Friel		
946-47	23-10	11-5		Bob Sheridan	6.2					Jack Friel		
947-48	19-10	9-7		Vince Hanson	10.4					Jack Friel		
948-49	21-9	8-8		Ed Gayda	12.7					Jack Friel		
949-50	19-13	11-5		Gene Conley	13.3					Jack Friel		
950-51	17-15	7-9		Bob Gambold	9.5					Jack Friel		
951-52	19-16	6-10		Eric Roberts	11.3					Jack Friel		
952-53	7-27	3-13		Peter Mullins	13.4					Jack Friel		
953-54	10-17	4-12		Ron Bennink	17.9	Howard McCants	7.3			Jack Friel		
954-55	11-15	5-11		Ron Bennink	16.3	Bill Rehder	8.2			Jack Friel		
955-56	4-22	2-14		Larry Beck	19.5	Larry Beck	8.2			Jack Friel		
956-57	8-18	4-12		Larry Beck	19.1	Larry Beck	7.5			Jack Friel		
957-58	7-19	3-13		John Maras	11.7	John Maras	10.0			Jack Friel	495-377	.568
958-59	10-16	3-13		John Maras	12.5	John Maras	11.0			Marv Harshman		
959-60	13-13			Terry Ball	12.3	Charlie Sells	11.8			Marv Harshman		
960-61	10-16			Terry Ball	18.5	Charlie Sells	9.9			Marv Harshman		
961-62	8-18			Terry Ball	16.6	Charlie Sells	11.0			Marv Harshman		
962-63	5-20			Byron Vadset	15.4	Ted Werner	8.7			Marv Harshman		
963-64	5-21	2-13		Byron Vadset	12.6	Ted Werner	12.4			Marv Harshman		
964-65	9-17	6-8		Ted Werner	13.4	Ted Werner	11.4			Marv Harshman		
965-66	15-11	6-8		Jim McKean	16.9	Jim McKean	10.6			Marv Harshman		
966-67	15-11	8-6		Jim McKean	18.5	Jim McKean	11.7			Marv Harshman		
967-68	16-9	8-6		Jim McKean	19.6	Jim McKean	10.6			Marv Harshman		
968-69	18-8	11-3		Ted Wierman	15.5	Ted Wierman	10.2			Marv Harshman		
969-70	19-7	9-5		Jim Meredith	14.7	Gary Elliot	9.5			Marv Harshman		
970-71	12-14	2-12		Jim Meredith	18.0	Jim Meredith	7.8			Marv Harshman	155-181	.461
971-72	11-15	3-11		Dan Steward	16.3	Rick Rawlings	8.2			Bob Greenwood	11-15	.423
972-73	6-20	2-12		Mike Dolven	14.8	Mike Dolven	8.7			George Raveling		
973-74	8-21	3-11		Steve Puidokas	16.8	Steve Puidokas	8.9			George Raveling		
974-75	10-16	1-13		Steve Puidokas	22.4	Steve Puidokas	10.4			George Raveling		
975-76	18-8 ⊗	8-6		Steve Puidokas	18.0	Steve Puidokas	10.6	Marty Giovacchini	4.1	George Raveling		
976-77	19-8	8-6		Harold Rhodes	18.1	Steve Puidokas	9.2	Marty Giovacchini	3.9	George Raveling		
977-78	16-11	7-7		Terry Kelly	13.0	James Donaldson	11.3	Ken Jones	2.9	George Raveling		
978-79	18-9	10-8		Don Collins	16.9	James Donaldson	10.8	Bryan Rison	3.2	George Raveling		
979-80	22-6	14-4	NCAA FIRST ROUND	Don Collins	23.1	Stuart House	8.4	Bryan Rison	3.6	George Raveling		
980-81	10-17	3-15		Angelo Hill	12.1	Angelo Hill	6.2	Ken McFadden	3.2	George Raveling		
981-82	16-14	10-8		Steve Harriel	12.3	Aaron Haskins	5.7	Tyrone Brown	2.9	George Raveling		
982-83	23-7	14-4	NCAA SECOND ROUND	Steve Harriel	15.0	Steve Harriel	6.3	Craig Ehlo	4.5	George Raveling	166-137	.547▼
983-84	10-18	4-14		Ricky Brown	12.8	Ricky Brown	6.4	Keith Morrison	4.1	Len Stevens		
984-85	13-15	5-13		Joe Wallace	18.1	Keith Morrison	7.1	Keith Morrison	4.9	Len Stevens		
985-86	15-16	8-10		Keith Morrison	14.4	Keith Morrison	4.9	Keith Morrison	4.3	Len Stevens		
986-87	10-18	6-12		Brian Quinnett	16.5	Dwayne Scholten	9.2	Anthony Kidd	3.8	Len Stevens	48-67	.417
987-88	13-16	7-11		David Sanders	12.9	Brian Wright	4.6	Harold Wright	3.0	Kelvin Sampson		
988-89	10-19	4-14		Brian Quinnett	18.4	Brian Quinnett	5.9	Anthony Kidd	2.7	Kelvin Sampson		
989-90	7-22	1-17		Darryl Woods	15.3	Neil Evans	4.5	Bennie Seltzer	4.1	Kelvin Sampson		
990-91	16-12	8-10		Terrence Lewis	14.8	Ken Critton	6.7	Bennie Seltzer	3.9	Kelvin Sampson		
991-92	22-11	9-9	NIT SECOND ROUND	Terrence Lewis	17.4	Ken Critton	8.2	Bennie Seltzer	3.7	Kelvin Sampson		
992-93	15-12	9-9		Bennie Seltzer	17.9	Mark Hendrickson	8.0	Bennie Seltzer	4.7	Kelvin Sampson		
993-94	20-11	10-8	NCAA FIRST ROUND	Tony Harris	13.3	Mark Hendrickson	7.9	Tony Harris	3.6	Kelvin Sampson	103-103	.500
994-95	18-12	10-8	NIT QUARTERFINALS	Isaac Fontaine	18.5	Mark Hendrickson	9.0	Donminic Ellison	6.9	Kevin Eastman		
995-96	17-12 ⊗	8-10	NIT SECOND ROUND	Isaac Fontaine	18.1	Mark Hendrickson	9.5	Donminic Ellison	5.6	Kevin Eastman		
996-97	13-17	5-13		Isaac Fontaine	21.9	Carlos Daniel	8.3	Blake Pengelly	2.7	Kevin Eastman		
997-98	10-19	3-15		Carlos Daniel	16.1	Carlos Daniel	10.1	Blake Pengelly	4.1	Kevin Eastman		
998-99	10-19	4-14		Jan-Michael Thomas	14.1	Kojo Mensah-Bonsu	6.0	Blake Pengelly	3.0	Kevin Eastman	68-79	.463▼
99-2000	6-22	1-17		Chris Crosby	15.8	Mike Bush	6.4	Mike Bush	2.4	Paul Graham		
00-01	12-16	5-13		Marcus Moore	10.4	J Locklier	6.1	Marcus Moore	3.6	Paul Graham		
001-02	6-21	1-17		Marcus Moore	16.6	J Locklier	6.5	Marcus Moore	4.9	Paul Graham		
002-03	7-20	2-16		Marcus Moore	18.2	Marcus Moore	5.4	Thomas Kelati	3.7	Paul Graham	31-79	.282
003-04	13-16	7-11		Marcus Moore	13.5	Shami Gill	5.3	Marcus Moore	2.9	Dick Bennett		
04-05	12-16	7-11		Thomas Kelati	14.3	Jeff Varem	7.8	Thomas Kelati	2.8	Dick Bennett		
005-06	11-17	4-14		Josh Akognon	10.3	Robbie Cowgill	5.1	Kyle Weaver	4.0	Dick Bennett	36-49	.424
006-07	26-8	13-5	NCAA SECOND ROUND	Derrick Low	13.7	Kyle Weaver	5.6	Kyle Weaver	4.6	Tony Bennett		
07-08	26-9	11-7	NCAA REGIONAL SEMIFINALS	Derrick Low	14.1	Aron Baynes	6.0	Taylor Rochestie	4.7	Tony Bennett		
008-09	17-16	8-10	NIT FIRST ROUND	Taylor Rochestie	13.2	Aron Baynes	7.5	Taylor Rochestie	4.5	Tony Bennett	69-33	.676

Records don't reflect games forfeited or vacated. For adjusted records, **see p. 521.**

Coaches' records adjusted to reflect games forfeited or vacated: George Raveling, 167-136, .551; Kevin Eastman, 69-78, .469. For yearly totals, **see p. 521.**

ESPN 116 SAGARIN

WEBER STATE

How do you know a program is still struggling for respect? When there's an entire page in its media guide explaining the pronunciation of the school's name (it's *WEE-ber*). But after the Wildcats managed two of the biggest NCAA Tournament upsets of the 1990s, opponents know to watch out for that team from Ogden, Utah.

BEST TEAM: 1968-69 In his first season as Weber State's coach, Phil Johnson and his star center, Willie Sojourner (18.8 ppg, 13.0 rpg), led the Wildcats to a 27–3 record and an NCAA Tournament showdown against its geographic rival Seattle. The two teams split their regular-season games, with the Chieftains trouncing WSU by 38 points in Seattle. The Wildcats took the rubber match, 75-73, but fell 63-59 in overtime to Santa Clara in the West Regional semis.

BEST PLAYER: C Willie Sojourner (1968-71) The team's success while Sojourner roamed the paint says it all: 68 wins, three Big Sky titles and three trips to the Big Dance. Still fourth in total points and tops in career rebounds at WSU, the 6'8" Philadelphia native went on to play four years in the ABA. He was a member of the Virginia Squires when he coined the famous nickname Dr. J for his teammate Julius Erving.

BEST COACH: Dick Motta (1962-68) Phil Johnson had a great three-year run (68–16, three Big Sky titles), but much of the credit belongs to the man who preceded Johnson and recruited Sojourner to WSU. Motta built the Weber State program literally from scratch. As the Wildcats' first head coach, Motta won two Big Sky titles (and shared another) in six seasons and reached the NCAA Tournament in his final year, before he moved on to a long pro coaching career that included an NBA title in 1977-78 with the Washington Bullets.

GAME FOR THE AGES: On March 11, 1999, in the first round of the NCAA Tournament, No. 3-seed North Carolina had no answer for Harold "the Show" Arceneaux in Weber State's 76-74 victory. The Show poured in 36 points, including five of the Wildcats' 14 three-pointers, handing UNC its earliest Tourney exit in 23 years.

HEARTBREAKER: Having shocked Michigan State in the first round of the 1995 Tournament, WSU was looking to slay another giant, Georgetown, which featured freshman phenom Allen Iverson. With the game tied at 51 and :07 left, the Wildcats' Ruben Nembhard missed the front end of a one-and-one. Then Iverson hoisted an air ball that his teammate Don Reid grabbed and laid in as time expired.

FIERCEST RIVAL: Where is a nose-biting wildcat (see Fanfare and Hoopla) when you need one? During a 1997 WSU home game with Big Sky foe Idaho State, the ISU coaches turned away from the court to taunt fans over recent Weber State recruiting violations. ISU lost that game, and 14 of the next 15 in the rivalry. WSU leads its oldest continual rival, 66–40.

Harold "the Show" Arceneaux poured in 36 points, handing UNC its earliest Tourney exit in 23 years.

FANFARE AND HOOPLA: Once upon a time, actual wildcats were brought to games in cages, but that tradition came to a bloody end after an unfortunate cheerleader got bitten on the nose. There was also a peacock that got roundly booed when it was tried out as mascot. But now Weber State fans rally unanimously around a grinning, white-furred, human-inhabited Waldo the Wildcat.

FAN FAVORITE: G Brad Barton (2001-03) Never a prolific scorer, Barton laid the foundations of his status as beloved when he hit a last-second trey to beat Utah State in a December 2001 game in which the Wildcats rallied from 17 down.

PROFILE

Weber State University, Ogden, UT
Founded: 1889 as Weber Academy
Enrollment: 18,498 (18,113 undergraduate)
Colors: Royal purple and white
Nickname: Wildcats
Current arena: Dee Events Center, opened in 1977 (12,000)
Previous: Swenson Gym, 1962-77 (5,500)
First game: 1962
All-time record: 852-496 (.632)
Total weeks in AP Top 20/25: 7

Current conference: Big Sky (1963-)
Conference titles:
Big Sky: 19 (1965, '66 [tie], '68, '69, '70, '71, '72, '73, '76 [tie], '79, '80, '83 [tie], '84, '94 [tie], '95 [tie], '99, 2003, '07 [tie], '09)
Conference tournament titles:
Big Sky: 8 (1978, '79, '80, '83, '95, '99, 2003, '07)
NCAA Tournament appearances: 14
NIT appearances: 2

TOP 5

G	**Jermaine Boyette** (2000-03)
G	**Bruce Collins** (1976-80)
F	**Harold Arceneaux** (1998-2000)
F	**Rico Washington** (1987-89)
C	**Willie Sojourner** (1968-71)

RECORDS

RECORDS	GAME		SEASON		CAREER	
POINTS	45	Stan Mayhew, vs. Utah State (Jan. 18, 1977)	713	Harold Arceneaux (1998-99)	2,019	Bruce Collins (1976-80)
POINTS PER GAME			23.2	Stan Rose (1992-93)	23.2	Stan Rose (1992-93)
REBOUNDS	25	Willie Sojourner, vs. West Texas A&M (Dec. 12, 1969)	411	Willie Sojourner (1969-70)	1,143	Willie Sojourner (1968-71)
ASSISTS	17	Mark Mattos, vs. Montana State (Feb. 26, 1977)	213	Mark Mattos (1979-80)	642	Mark Mattos (1976-80)

SEASON REVIEW

SEAS.	W-L	CONF.	POSTSEASON	SCORING		REBOUNDS		ASSISTS		COACH	RECORD	
62-63	22-4			Jim Lyon	20.8					Dick Motta		
63-64	17-8	7-3		Jim Lyon	20.4	Jim Lyon	11.6			Dick Motta		
64-65	22-3	8-2		Gene Visscher	18.4	Gene Visscher	11.3			Dick Motta		
65-66	20-5	8-2		Gene Visscher	21.0	Gene Visscher	14.3			Dick Motta		
66-67	18-7	5-5		Dan Sparks	15.2	Dan Sparks	11.4			Dick Motta		
67-68	21-6	12-3	NCAA FIRST ROUND	Justus Thigpen	16.4	Dan Sparks	13.7			Dick Motta	120-33	.784
968-69	27-3	15-0	NCAA REGIONAL SEMIFINALS	Willie Sojourner	18.8	Willie Sojourner	13.0			Phil Johnson		
969-70	20-7	12-3	NCAA FIRST ROUND	Willie Sojourner	21.2	Willie Sojourner	15.8			Phil Johnson		
970-71	21-6	12-2	NCAA FIRST ROUND	Willie Sojourner	17.8	Willie Sojourner	13.6			Phil Johnson	68-16	.810
971-72	18-11	10-4	NCAA REGIONAL SEMIFINALS	Bob Davis	23.1	Bob Davis	11.5			Gene Visscher		
972-73	20-7	13-1	NCAA FIRST ROUND	Rich Cooper	12.1	Rich Cooper	7.8			Gene Visscher		
973-74	14-12	8-6		Jimmie Watts	12.5	Jimmie Watts	8.4			Gene Visscher		
974-75	11-15	6-8		Jimmie Watts	16.5	Jimmie Watts	10.9			Gene Visscher[a]	58-38	.604
975-76	21-11	9-5		Jimmie Watts	19.3	Jimmie Watts	9.5			Neil McCarthy		
976-77	20-8	11-3		Stan Mayhew	22.0	Stan Mayhew	10.2	Mark Mattos	7.1	Neil McCarthy		
977-78	19-10	9-5	NCAA FIRST ROUND	Bruce Collins	18.8	Bruce Collins	8.4	Mark Mattos	5.6	Neil McCarthy		
978-79	25-9	10-4	NCAA SECOND ROUND	Bruce Collins	16.2	Richard Smith	9.1	Mark Mattos	3.5	Neil McCarthy		
979-80	26-3	13-1	NCAA FIRST ROUND	Bruce Collins	18.3	Richard Smith	7.0	Mark Mattos	7.3	Neil McCarthy		
980-81	8-19	5-9		Todd Harper	18.0	Royal Edwards	7.6	Richard Escandon	4.0	Neil McCarthy		
981-82	15-13	6-8		Todd Harper	17.9	Tom Heywood	8.1	Richard Escandon	4.9	Neil McCarthy		
982-83	23-8	10-4	NCAA FIRST ROUND	Randy Worster	12.3	Tom Heywood	6.6	John Price	4.9	Neil McCarthy		
983-84	23-8	12-2	NIT SECOND ROUND	Randy Worster	12.1	Charles Carradine	7.3	John Price	4.9	Neil McCarthy		
984-85	20-9	9-5		Shawn Campbell	16.9	Shawn Campbell	8.0	Aaron McCarthy	7.2	Neil McCarthy	205-105	.661
985-86	18-11	7-7		Walt Tyler	16.3	Harry Willis	6.9	Alan Campbell	4.7	Larry Farmer		
986-87	7-22	4-10		Harry Willis	14.6	Harry Willis	10.4	Robert Maxwell	4.8	Larry Farmer		
987-88	9-21	6-10		Rico Washington	19.9	Rico Washington	10.3	Moochie Cobb	4.7	Larry Farmer	34-54	.386
988-89	17-11	9-7		Rico Washington	22.1	Rico Washington	10.8	Moochie Cobb	4.4	Denny Huston		
989-90	14-15	8-8		Aaron Bell	11.5	Jerry McIntosh	6.5	Tony Nicholas	3.0	Denny Huston		
990-91	12-16	7-9		Aaron Bell	12.9	Dave Baldwin	7.6	Tony Nicholas	3.5	Denny Huston	43-42	.506
991-92	16-13	10-6		Al Hamilton	20.3	Al Hamilton	5.7	Anthony Steward	3.0	Ron Abegglen		
992-93	20-8	10-4		Stan Rose	23.2	Stan Rose	8.3	Robbie Johnson	4.2	Ron Abegglen		
993-94	20-10 ⊗	10-4		Robbie Johnson	15.8	Johnnie Moore	9.0	Robbie Johnson	4.7	Ron Abegglen		
994-95	21-9	11-3	NCAA SECOND ROUND	Ruben Nembhard	20.1	Kirk Smith	10.5	Ruben Nembhard	4.0	Ron Abegglen		
995-96	20-10	10-4		Jimmy DeGraffenried	21.2	Andy Smith	7.2	Ryan Cuff	5.2	Ron Abegglen		
996-97	15-13	9-7		Damien Baskerville	18.5	Damien Baskerville	6.6	Ryan Cuff	5.4	Ron Abegglen		
997-98	14-13	12-4		Damien Baskerville	15.2	Andy Jensen	7.2	Damien Baskerville	3.1	Ron Abegglen		
998-99	25-8	13-3	NCAA SECOND ROUND	Harold Arceneaux	22.3	Andy Jensen	6.5	Eddie Gill	4.5	Ron Abegglen	151-84	.643
999-2000	18-10	10-6		Harold Arceneaux	23.0	Harold Arceneaux	7.4	Eddie Gill	7.0	Joe Cravens		
000-01	15-14	8-8		Jermaine Boyette	19.1	Jake Shoff	6.0	Jermaine Boyette	4.2	Joe Cravens		
001-02	18-11	8-6		Jermaine Boyette	17.1	Chris Woods	7.1	Jermaine Boyette	3.0	Joe Cravens		
002-03	26-6	14-0	NCAA FIRST ROUND	Jermaine Boyette	20.5	Slobodan Ocokoljic	8.4	Jermaine Boyette	3.3	Joe Cravens		
003-04	15-14	7-7		Slobodan Ocokoljic	15.1	Slobodan Ocokoljic	6.4	Jamaal Jenkins	2.3	Joe Cravens		
004-05	14-16	7-7		Lance Allred	17.7	Lance Allred	12.0	Jamaal Jenkins	3.3	Joe Cravens		
005-06	10-17	4-10		Coric Riggs	14.9	Coric Riggs	6.7	Nick Covington	2.6	Joe Cravens	116-88	.569
006-07	20-12	11-5	NCAA FIRST ROUND	David Patten	14.2	David Patten	5.4	Juan Pablo Silveira	3.2	Randy Rahe		
007-08	16-14	10-6		Dezmon Harris	10.9	Arturas Valeika	10.2	Dezmon Harris	2.2	Randy Rahe		
008-09	21-10	15-1	NIT FIRST ROUND	Kellen McCoy	14.1	Kyle Bullinger	4.5	Damian Lillard	2.9	Randy Rahe	57-36	.613

Gene Visscher (6-8) and Neil McCarthy (5-7) both coached during the 1974-75 season.

⊗ Records don't reflect games forfeited or vacated. For adjusted records, see p. 521.

THE SCHOOLS

LATE GREAT

WEST TEXAS STATE
1941-86

This one-time teacher's college (now known as West Texas A&M) in the Texas Panhandle played its first season of intercollegiate basketball in 1920-21 and had a winning record in every one of its first 13 campaigns. The team made one NCAA Tournament appearance, in 1955, losing in the first round to eventual champion San Francisco, 89-66. It also went to three NITs, losing its first games of the tournament in 1942, '69 and '80.

NOTABLE PLAYERS: F Price Brookfield (1939-42), G Maurice "Mo" Cheeks (1974-78) Brookfield was one of the first big-man scoring sensations. At 6'4" and 195 pounds, local sportswriters gave Brookfield the rather distinctive nickname Sausage. His 44 points against Texas Mines in 1942 and his mark of 1,406 career points were school records that held for 64 and 34 years, respectively. The 6'1" Cheeks was a starter on the West Texas State squad in each of his four years at the school. During his senior season, Cheeks averaged 16.8 points and 5.7 assists per game, and he is still fourth in career points at the school. In a 15-year NBA career, Cheeks won one championship with the Philadelphia 76ers and was a four-time All-Star.

ESPN 36 SAGARIN

West Virginia

The golden era of West Virginia basketball spanned much of the 1940s, '50s and '60s, and produced its share of legends, including Mark Workman and the two Rods—"Hot Rod" Hundley and Rod Thorn. But its undisputed Golden Boy was Jerry West, a.k.a. Zeke from Cabin Creek. The rest of the century has been relatively quiet, but the latest coaches, John Beilein and Bob Huggins, have gotten Mountaineer fans revved for a 21st century revival.

BEST TEAM: 1958-59 Picking one squad from WVU's glory years is like choosing a dish from a dessert cart. But the slight nod goes to the crew led by junior Jerry West to the brink of an NCAA title. Coached by Fred Schaus, the Mountaineers won more games (29) than in any other season in school history, and their only losses were to Virginia (by three points), Kentucky (by six), Northwestern (in two OTs), NYU (OT) and Cal, 71-70, in the national title game. West was the Tourney's MOP, despite the loss.

BEST PLAYER: G Jerry West (1957-60) The handsome 6'3" shooting star with the bristly flattop still holds 18 Mountaineer records, including career points and rebounds. Over his three seasons, West led WVU to an 81–12 record and was twice a consensus All-America. He went on to be a 14-time All-Star with the Lakers and was inducted into the Naismith Hall of Fame in 1980. West's form was so perfect that the NBA chose him as the model that is silhouetted in the league's logo.

BEST COACH: Fred Schaus (1954-60) Between his All-America playing career and tenure as athletic director, Schaus' six years as coach at WVU were astounding. He won almost 80% of his games, five Southern Conference regular-season titles and 44 straight conference games. And he took the Mountaineers to six NCAA Tournaments, finishing two points shy of the 1959 title. No wonder Schaus left to coach the NBA Lakers in 1960: He had a rookie waiting for him there named Jerry West.

GAME FOR THE AGES: The Mountaineers barely made the 1942 NIT and a train delay almost caused them to miss their first game, but that didn't stop them from storming to the title. After upsetting Long Island and Toledo, on March 25 they toppled Western Kentucky, 47-45, for the championship.

HEARTBREAKER: West Virginia basketball peaked at the 1959 Final Four. After humbling Louisville on its home floor at Freedom Hall, the Mountaineers fell by a point to the Pete Newell-coached California Golden Bears. It remains WVU's lone Final Four.

FIERCEST RIVAL: The floorboards may not smolder the way the gridiron does for football's Backyard Brawl, but nearby Pittsburgh is also West Virginia's most hated hoops foe. In fact, WVU's very first game was a 15-12 win over Pitt (then Western University of Pennsylvania) in a low-ceiling basement gym. Overall, the Mountaineers hold a 94-84 edge in the series.

From 1957 to '63, jersey No. 44 (worn by West and Thorn) scored a combined 4,094 points.

FANFARE AND HOOPLA: West Virginia players don't get the red-carpet treatment; a blue and gold carpet is rolled out instead. Following a tradition started by Schaus in 1955, the Mountaineers take the court for warmups on a lengthy rug that says "West Virginia." When it comes to uniforms, nobody has worn No. 44 since West and Rod Thorn scored a combined 4,094 points in the jersey from 1957 to '63.

FAN FAVORITE: C Kevin Pittsnogle (2002-06) The tattooed 6'11" Pittsnogle rarely played in the paint. The three-point gunner became the Mountaineers' first All-America in 34 years and helped put them back onto the national stage with a 2005 Elite Eight run.

CONSENSUS ALL-AMERICAS

1957 **Rod Hundley,** F
1959, '60 **Jerry West,** G

FIRST-ROUND PRO PICKS

1952 **Mark Workman,** Milwaukee (1)
1957 **Rod Hundley,** Cincinnati (1)
1960 **Jerry West,** Minneapolis (2)
1963 **Rod Thorn,** Baltimore (2)
1967 **Bob Benfield,** Houston (ABA)
1968 **Ron Williams,** San Francisco (9)
2008 **Joe Alexander,** Milwaukee (8)

PROFILE

West Virginia University, Morgantown, WV
Founded: 1867
Enrollment: 21,987 (15,463 undergraduate)
Colors: Old gold and blue
Nickname: Mountaineers
Current arena: WVU Coliseum, opened in 1970 (14,000)
Previous: Stansbury Hall, 1928-70 (6,800); The Ark, 1916-27 (N/A); ROTC Armory, 1903-15 (N/A)
First game: Feb. 20, 1904
All-time record: 1,551-972 (.615)
Total weeks in AP Top 20/25: 137
Current conference: Big East (1995-)
Conference titles:
Eastern Intercollegiate: 1 (1935 [tie])
Southern: 10 (1952, '55, '56 [tie], '57, '58, '59, '61, '62, '63, '67)
Eastern Collegiate: 1 (1977 [tie])
Eastern Athletic: 1 (1982)
Atlantic 10: 3 (1983 [tie], '85, '89)
Conference tournament titles:
Southern: 10 (1955, '56, '57, '58, '59, '60, '62, '63, '65, '67)
Atlantic 10: 2 (1983, '84)
NCAA Tournament appearances: 22
Sweet 16s (since 1975): 4
Final Fours: 1
NIT appearances: 15
Semifinals: 5
Titles: 2 (1942, 2007)

TOP 5

G **Wil Robinson** (1969-72)
G **Jerry West** (1957-60)
F **Rod Hundley** (1954-57)
F **Rod Thorn** (1960-1963)
C **Mark Workman** (1949-52)

RECORDS	GAME		SEASON		CAREER	
POINTS	54	Rod Hundley, vs. Furman (Jan. 5, 1957)	908	Jerry West (1959-60)	2,309	Jerry West (1957-60)
POINTS PER GAME			29.4	Wil Robinson (1971-72)	24.8	Jerry West (1957-60)
REBOUNDS	31	Jerry West, vs. George Washington (Feb. 6, 1960); Mack Isner, vs. Virginia Tech (Feb. 14, 1952)	510	Jerry West (1959-60)	1,240	Jerry West (1957-60)
ASSISTS	16	Steve Berger, vs. Pittsburgh (Dec. 9, 1989)	197	Ron Williams (1966-67)	574	Steve Berger (1986-90)

THE SCHOOLS

EASON REVIEW

EASON	W-L	CONF.	SCORING		COACH	RECORD		SEASON	W-L	CONF.	SCORING		COACH	RECORD	
3-08	*22-31*		*Coach Anthony Chez (1904-07) also coached the football team*					1924-25	6-11		Fred Funk	7.0	Francis Stadsvold		
4-15	10-10		Eugene Kersting	9.9	George Pyle			1925-26	10-11		Wease Ashworth	7.5	Francis Stadsvold		
5-16	11-7		Ross Tuckwiller	7.5	George Pyle			1926-27	10-8		Rudolph Hagberg	7.1	Francis Stadsvold		
16-17	8-8		Frank Ice	8.1	George Pyle	29-25	.537	1927-28	13-7		Truehart Taylor	12.9	Francis Stadsvold		
17-18	4-13		Harry Whetsell	5.2	H.P. Mullenex			1928-29	16-6		Marshall Glenn	12.4	Francis Stadsvold		
18-19	8-8		Homer Martin	16.9	H.P. Mullenex	12-21	.364	1929-30	11-10		Marshall Glenn	10.3	Francis Stadsvold		
19-20	12-10		William Morrison	8.5	Francis Stadsvold			1930-31	9-11		Edwin Bartrug	6.7	Francis Stadsvold		
20-21	11-9		Homer Martin	14.6	Francis Stadsvold			1931-32	7-14		Edward Cubbon	9.6	Francis Stadsvold		
21-22	8-13		Pierre Hill	12.8	Francis Stadsvold			1932-33	10-14	1-7	Joseph Stydahar	12.5	Francis Stadsvold	149-133	.528
22-23	12-7		Pierre Hill	11.4	Francis Stadsvold			1933-34	14-5	7-3	Joseph Stydahar	10.5	Marshall Glenn		
23-24	14-2		Fred Funk	9.2	Francis Stadsvold			1934-35	16-6	6-2	Jack Gocke	10.5	Marshall Glenn		

EAS.	W-L	CONF.	POSTSEASON	SCORING		REBOUNDS		ASSISTS		COACH	RECORD	
35-36	16-8	6-4		Jack Gocke	11.1					Marshall Glenn		
36-37	9-14	3-7		Jack Gocke	11.9					Marshall Glenn		
37-38	6-13	2-8		Homer Brooks	10.6					Marshall Glenn	61-46	.570
38-39	10-9	4-6		Homer Brooks	13.2					Dyke Raese		
39-40	13-6			James Ruch	10.9					Dyke Raese		
40-41	13-10			James Ruch	12.5					Dyke Raese		
41-42	19-4		NIT CHAMPION	Rudy Baric	14.4					Dyke Raese	55-29	.655
42-43	14-7			Joseph Walthall	18.0					Rudy Baric	14-7	.667
43-44	8-11			Earl Allara	9.5					Harry Lothes	8-11	.421
44-45	12-6		NIT FIRST ROUND	Bob Carroll	12.2					John Brickels	12-6	.667
45-46	24-3		NIT THIRD PLACE	Leland Byrd	11.3					Lee Patton		
46-47	19-3		NIT FOURTH PLACE	Fred Schaus	16.9					Lee Patton		
47-48	17-3			Edward Beach	14.1					Lee Patton		
48-49	18-6			Fred Schaus	18.4					Lee Patton		
49-50	13-11			Mark Workman	11.3					Lee Patton	91-26	.778
50-51	18-9	9-3		Mark Workman	26.1					Red Brown		
51-52	23-4	15-1		Mark Workman	23.1	Mark Workman	17.5	Ralph Holmes	6.2	Red Brown		
52-53	19-7	11-3		Jim Sottile	19.3	Mack Isner	10.4			Red Brown		
53-54	12-11	6-4		Eddie Becker	18.7	Mack Isner	6.9	Ralph Holmes	4.9	Red Brown	72-31	.699
54-55	19-11	9-1	NCAA FIRST ROUND	Rod Hundley	23.7	Pete White	12.0	Rod Hundley	3.7	Fred Schaus		
55-56	21-9	10-2	NCAA FIRST ROUND	Rod Hundley	26.6	Rod Hundley	13.1	Rod Hundley	3.4	Fred Schaus		
56-57	25-5	12-0	NCAA FIRST ROUND	Rod Hundley	23.1	Lloyd Sharrar	14.8	Rod Hundley	4.3	Fred Schaus		
57-58	26-2	12-0	NCAA FIRST ROUND	Jerry West	17.8	Lloyd Sharrar	13.8	Bob Smith	3.7	Fred Schaus		
58-59	29-5	11-0	NCAA RUNNER-UP	Jerry West	26.6	Jerry West	12.3	Bob Smith	3.3	Fred Schaus		
59-60	26-5	9-2	NCAA REGIONAL SEMIFINALS	Jerry West	29.3	Jerry West	16.5	Jerry West	4.3	Fred Schaus	146-37	.798
60-61	23-4	11-1		Rod Thorn	18.5	Rod Thorn	12.5	Lee Patrone	3.5	George King		
61-62	24-6	12-1	NCAA FIRST ROUND	Rod Thorn	23.7	Rod Thorn	12.1	Rod Thorn	4.1	George King		
62-63	23-8	11-2	NCAA REGIONAL SEMIFINALS	Rod Thorn	22.5	Tom Lowry	9.6	Rod Thorn	4.2	George King		
63-64	18-10	11-3		Tom Lowry	15.6	Tom Lowry	10.5	Ricky Ray	3.4	George King		
64-65	14-15	8-6	NCAA FIRST ROUND	Robert Camp	15.9	Robert Camp	9.8	Robert Camp	2.5	George King	102-43	.703
65-66	19-9	8-2		Ron Williams	19.7	Bob Benfield	9.7	Ron Williams	5.5	Bucky Waters		
66-67	19-9	9-1	NCAA FIRST ROUND	Ron Williams	20.1	Bob Benfield	11.5	Ron Williams	7.0	Bucky Waters		
67-68	19-9	9-2	NIT FIRST ROUND	Ron Williams	20.4	Carey Bailey	10.5	Ron Williams	5.5	Bucky Waters		
68-69	12-14			Bob Hummell	15.5	Carey Bailey	10.2	Wayne Grimm	2.9	Bucky Waters	69-41	.627
69-70	11-15			Wil Robinson	20.0	Larry Woods	9.1	Bob Hummell	3.9	Sonny Moran		
70-71	13-12			Wil Robinson	25.0	Sam Oglesby	9.5	Levi Phillips	3.2	Sonny Moran		
71-72	13-11			Wil Robinson	29.4	Mike Heitz	9.0	Curt Price	3.3	Sonny Moran		
72-73	10-15			Warren Baker	16.6	Warren Baker	11.2	Jerome Anderson	3.2	Sonny Moran		
73-74	10-15			Warren Baker	17.7	Warren Baker	13.1	Levi Phillips	5.3	Sonny Moran	57-68	.456
74-75	14-13			Stan Boskovich	17.6	Warren Baker	10.4	Earnest Hall	3.4	Joedy Gardner		
75-76	15-13			Tony Robertson	17.9	Warren Baker	6.6	Tony Robertson	3.6	Joedy Gardner		
76-77	18-11	5-5		Tony Robertson	18.1	Maurice Robinson	9.8	Bob Huggins	3.8	Joedy Gardner		
77-78	12-16	3-7		Lowes Moore	21.3	Maurice Robinson	12.1	Lowes Moore	3.5	Joedy Gardner	59-53	.527
78-79	16-12	7-3		Lowes Moore	17.3	Junius Lewis	6.4	Lowes Moore	2.7	Gale Catlett		
79-80	15-14	4-6		Lowes Moore	16.4	Greg Nance	7.6	Lowes Moore	4.4	Gale Catlett		
80-81	23-10	9-4	NIT FOURTH PLACE	Greg Jones	15.5	Greg Nance	6.9	Greg Jones	4.7	Gale Catlett		
81-82	27-4	13-1	NCAA SECOND ROUND	Greg Jones	15.0	Russel Todd, Lester Rowe	5.5	Greg Jones	3.6	Gale Catlett		
82-83	23-8	10-4	NCAA FIRST ROUND	Greg Jones	22.3	Russel Todd	8.1	Greg Jones	4.1	Gale Catlett		
83-84	20-12	9-9	NCAA SECOND ROUND	Lester Rowe	15.6	Lester Rowe	6.9	Dale Blaney	3.7	Gale Catlett		
84-85	20-9	16-2	NIT FIRST ROUND	Lester Rowe	14.4	Lester Rowe	7.0	Holman Harley	3.3	Gale Catlett		
85-86	22-11	15-3	NCAA FIRST ROUND	Dale Blaney	17.0	Darrell Pinckney	6.0	Holman Harley	4.5	Gale Catlett		
86-87	23-8	15-3	NCAA FIRST ROUND	Wayne Yearwood	12.9	Darryl Prue	6.9	Steve Berger	2.5	Gale Catlett		
87-88	18-14	12-6	NIT FIRST ROUND	Chris Brooks	12.6	Darryl Prue	8.2	Steve Berger	3.8	Gale Catlett		
88-89	26-5	17-1	NCAA SECOND ROUND	Herbie Brooks	14.7	Ray Foster	6.8	Steve Berger	6.2	Gale Catlett		
89-90	16-12	11-7		Tracy Shelton	17.8	Charles Becton	7.6	Steve Berger	6.5	Gale Catlett		
90-91	17-14	10-8	NIT SECOND ROUND	Chris Brooks	16.7	Chris Brooks	8.0	Mike Boyd	5.8	Gale Catlett		
91-92	20-12	10-6	NCAA FIRST ROUND	Chris Leonard	17.2	Ricky Robinson	7.2	Marsalis Basey	5.3	Gale Catlett		
92-93	17-12	7-7	NIT SECOND ROUND	Pervires Greene	15.1	Ricky Robinson	7.7	Marsalis Basey	5.4	Gale Catlett		
93-94	17-12	8-8	NIT SECOND ROUND	Pervires Greene	18.6	Ricky Robinson	8.1	Marsalis Basey	5.1	Gale Catlett		
94-95	13-13	7-9		Seldon Jefferson	14.9	Damian Owens	7.5	Seldon Jefferson	4.3	Gale Catlett		
95-96	12-15	7-11		Seldon Jefferson	14.6	Damian Owens	8.3	Seldon Jefferson	5.1	Gale Catlett		
96-97	21-10	11-7	NIT QUARTERFINALS	Seldon Jefferson	15.6	Gordon Malone	8.6	Seldon Jefferson	4.6	Gale Catlett		
97-98	24-9	11-7	NCAA REGIONAL SEMIFINALS	Damian Owens	16.5	Brian Lewin	7.6	Jarrod West	4.1	Gale Catlett		
98-99	10-19	4-14		Marcus Goree	16.5	Marcus Goree	7.9	Jarett Kearse	4.4	Gale Catlett		
99-2000	14-14	6-10		Marcus Goree	14.5	Marcus Goree	8.2	Tim Lyles	4.5	Gale Catlett		
00-01	17-12	8-8	NIT FIRST ROUND	Calvin Bowman	17.6	Calvin Bowman	9.7	Tim Lyles	5.4	Gale Catlett		
01-02	8-20	1-15		Chris Moss	17.5	Chris Moss	8.0	Jonathan Hargett	4.6	Gale Catlett	439-276	.614
02-03	14-15	5-11		Drew Schifino	20.1	Kevin Pittsnogle	4.8	Johannes Herber	3.8	John Beilein		
03-04	17-14	7-9	NIT SECOND ROUND	D'or Fischer	10.8	D'or Fischer	6.2	Johannes Herber	3.3	John Beilein		
04-05	24-11	8-8	NCAA REGIONAL FINALS	Tyrone Sally	12.2	Mike Gansey	5.1	Jarmon Durisseau-Collins	3.3	John Beilein		
05-06	22-11	11-5	NCAA REGIONAL SEMIFINALS	Kevin Pittsnogle	19.3	Mike Gansey	5.7	Johannes Herber	4.4	John Beilein		
06-07	27-9	9-7	NIT CHAMPION	Frank Young	15.3	Rob Summers	4.6	Alex Ruoff	5.3	John Beilein	104-60	.634
07-08	26-11	11-7	NCAA REGIONAL SEMIFINALS	Joe Alexander	16.9	Joe Alexander	6.4	Darris Nichols	3.2	Bob Huggins		
08-09	23-12	10-8	NCAA FIRST ROUND	Da'Sean Butler	17.1	Devin Ebanks	7.8	Alex Ruoff	3.4	Bob Huggins	49-23	.681

ESPN 279 SAGARIN

WESTERN CAROLINA

Western Carolina was an NAIA power throughout the 1950s and '60s, winning 45 straight home games from 1962-63 to '64-65 and reaching the '63 NAIA title game. The Catamounts moved to DI in '76 and won the Southern Conference Southern Division in '96. Among notable Catamounts are NBA star Kevin Martin, ground-breaking legend Henry Logan and Ronnie Carr, who hit college basketball's very first three-point shot, in 1980.

BEST TEAM: 1962-63 Coach Jim Gudger's 28–7 NAIA runners-up fill the school's record book. All-Americas Mel Gibson and Tommy Lavelle teamed with fellow 1,000-point scorers Danny Tharpe and Charlie McConnell, plus top-10 rebounders Darrell Murray, Gaston Seal and John Brintnall. The Catamounts lost the title game, 73-62, to Texas-Pan American.

BEST PLAYER: G Henry Logan (1964-68) He was the first African-American to play at a predominantly white Southern college, a three-time NAIA All-America and a one-time Little All-America. Logan led the NAIA in scoring (36.2 ppg) as a senior, set a then-NAIA record with 1,037 career assists (9.7 apg) and amassed 3,290 points.

BEST COACH: Jim Gudger (1950-69) The school's all-time winningest coach (311–222), Gudger led the Catamounts to the 1963 NAIA title game. He had seven 20-win seasons and coached all four of WCU's All-Americas: Ronald Rogers, Gibson, Lavelle and Logan.

GAME FOR THE AGES: Davidson entered the 1996 Southern Conference tournament at 25–3 with a 19-game winning streak—and left an upset victim. Western beat them, 69-60, behind tourney MOP Anquell McCollum (13 points), Kevin Kullum (12 points, 10 rebounds), and Jarvis Graham (11, 7) earning the title and an NCAA bid. It's the school's only D1 conference tournament title.

FIERCEST RIVAL: Appalachian State has dominated the Catamounts over the last decade, winning nine straight and 22 of 26 after Western beat ASU in a first-round conference tourney game en route to the 1996 Southern title. ASU leads, 108–63 (according to them, 104–57 according to the Catamounts).

SEASON REVIEW

SEAS.	W-L	CONF.	COACH	SEAS.	W-L	CONF.	COACH
1928-47	*220-150*	*No losing seasons*		1960-61	7-20		Jim Gudger
1947-48	15-11		Tuck McConnell	1961-62	21-8		Jim Gudger
1948-49	16-13		Tuck McConnell	1962-63	28-7		Jim Gudger
1949-50	6-19		Tuck McConnell	1963-64	20-6		Jim Gudger
1950-51	6-20		Jim Gudger	1964-65	14-13		Jim Gudger
1951-52	13-14		Jim Gudger	1965-66	19-9		Jim Gudger
1952-53	22-8		Jim Gudger	1966-67	15-13		Jim Gudger
1953-54	16-9		Jim Gudger	1967-68	20-9		Jim Gudger
1954-55	11-16		Jim Gudger	1968-69	7-18		Jim Gudger
1955-56	15-14		Jim Gudger	1969-70	13-18		Jim Hartbarger
1956-57	21-11		Jim Gudger	1970-71	25-5		Jim Hartbarger
1957-58	18-10		Jim Gudger	1971-72	20-16		Jim Hartbarger
1958-59	24-4		Jim Gudger	1972-73	12-13		Jim Hartbarger
1959-60	14-13		Jim Gudger	1973-74	11-14		Jim Hartbarger

SEAS.	W-L	CONF.	SCORING		COACH	RECORD	
1974-75	15-11		Kirby Thurston	21.9	Jim Hartbarger[a]	86-73	.541
1975-76	13-12		Mike Meadows	16.9	Fred Conley		
1976-77	8-16		Ike Mims	15.0	Fred Conley	31-32	.492
1977-78	7-19	4-8	Bubba Wilson	23.5	Steve Cottrell		
1978-79	14-14	5-7	Raymond Person	17.3	Steve Cottrell		
1979-80	17-10	9-7	Greg Dennis	21.3	Steve Cottrell		
1980-81	18-10	9-7	Ronnie Carr	17.6	Steve Cottrell		
1981-82	19-8	11-5	Ronnie Carr	19.0	Steve Cottrell		
1982-83	17-12	9-7	Kenny Trimier	16.2	Steve Cottrell		
1983-84	15-13	9-7	Quinton Lytle	20.8	Steve Cottrell		
1984-85	14-14	8-8	Quinton Lytle	17.5	Steve Cottrell		
1985-86	14-14	8-8	Leroy Gasque	16.3	Steve Cottrell		
1986-87	10-19	4-12	Robert Hill	15.1	Steve Cottrell	145-133	.522
1987-88	8-19	2-14	Bennie Goettie	19.4	Herb Krusen	8-19	.296
1988-89	12-16	4-10	Bennie Goettie	19.7	Dave Possinger	12-16	.429
1989-90	10-18	3-11	Donald Donerlson	16.1	Greg Blatt		
1990-91	11-17	3-11	Terry Boyd	23.7	Greg Blatt		
1991-92	11-17	5-9	Terry Boyd	22.8	Greg Blatt		
1992-93	6-21	2-16	Robert Gaines	20.3	Greg Blatt	38-73	.342
1993-94	12-16	8-10	Frankie King	26.9	Benny Dees		
1994-95	14-14	8-6	Frankie King	26.5	Benny Dees	26-30	.464
1995-96	17-13	10-4 ●	Anquell McCollum	25.0	Phil Hopkins		
1996-97	14-13	7-7	Bobby Phillips	14.1	Phil Hopkins		
1997-98	12-15	6-9	Bobby Phillips	16.6	Phil Hopkins		
1998-99	8-21	2-14	Dondrell Whitmore	13.6	Phil Hopkins		
1999-2000	14-14	7-9	Jarvis Hayes	17.1	Phil Hopkins	65-76	.461
2000-01	6-25	3-13	Cory Largent	15.8	Steve Shurina		
2001-02	12-16	6-10	Kevin Martin	22.1	Steve Shurina		
2002-03	9-19	6-10	Kevin Martin	22.8	Steve Shurina		
2003-04	13-15	6-10	Kevin Martin	24.9	Steve Shurina		
2004-05	8-22	3-13	David Berghoefer	14.6	Steve Shurina	48-97	.331
2005-06	13-17	7-7	Antonio Russell	13.3	Larry Hunter		
2006-07	11-20	7-11	Nick Aldridge	18.3	Larry Hunter		
2007-08	10-21	6-14	Brandon Giles	15.3	Larry Hunter		
2008-09	16-15	11-9	Harouna Mutombo	14.4	Larry Hunter	50-73	.407

[a] **Jim Hartbarger (5-7) and Fred Conley (10-4) both coached during the 1974-75 season.**

● **NCAA Tournament appearance**

PROFILE

Western Carolina University, Cullowhee, NC
Founded: 1889
Enrollment: 8,396 (6,785 undergraduate)
Colors: Purple and gold
Nickname: Catamounts
Current arena: Ramsey Activity Center, opened in 1986 (7,826)
Previous: Reid Gymnasium, 1957-86 (4,000); Breese Gymnasium, 1929-56 (N/A)
First game: 1928
All-time record: 1,077-1,037 (.509)
Total weeks in AP Top 20/25: 0

Current conference: Southern (1976-)
Conference titles:
Southern: 2 (1996 [tie], 2009 [tie])
Conference tournament titles:
Southern: 1 (1996)
NCAA Tournament appearances: 1
NIT appearances: 0

CONSENSUS ALL-AMERICAS

1968 **Henry Logan** (Little A-A), G

FIRST-ROUND PRO PICKS

2004 **Kevin Martin,** Sacramento (26)

TOP 5

G **Mel Gibson** (1959-63)
G **Henry Logan** (1964-68)
G **Ronald Rogers** (1949-53)
G/F **Kevin Martin** (2001-04)
F/C **Tommy Lavelle** (1961-64)

RECORDS	GAME		SEASON		CAREER	
POINTS	60	Henry Logan, vs. Atlantic Christian (Jan. 6, 1967)	1,049	Henry Logan (1967-68)	3,290	Henry Logan (1964-68)
POINTS PER GAME			36.2	Henry Logan (1967-68)	30.7	Henry Logan (1964-68)
REBOUNDS	29	Bob Thompson, vs. Atlantic Christian (Jan. 6, 1968)	446	Greg Wittman (1967-68)	1,354	Greg Wittman (1965-69)
ASSISTS	22	Henry Logan, vs. Presbyterian (Dec. 4, 1967)	298	Henry Logan (1964-65)	1,037	Henry Logan (1964-68)

ESPN 210 SAGARIN

WESTERN ILLINOIS

Could it really be more than a half-century since Bill McAfoos beat Northern Illinois with a 25-footer to keep a perfect season alive? Since Leroy "Stix" Morley coached an All-America each year? In the 1950s, only Tennessee A&I (now Tennessee State) rivaled Western Illinois for NAIA dominance. These days the Leathernecks are still pursuing their first NCAA Tournament bid since stepping up to D1 in 1980-81.

BEST TEAM: 1957-58 The Leathernecks reached the NAIA championship game undefeated on the play of starters Jack Milam, Walt Moore, Bill McAfoos, Grady McCollum and Chuck Behrends. But in the national semis they lost Moore to an injury, then got schooled, 85-73, by defending champ Tennessee A&I, led by future NBAers Dick Barnett, John Barnhill and Ben Warley.

BEST PLAYER: F/C CHUCK SCHRAMM (1954-57) A two-time NAIA All-America, Schramm carried Western to three straight national quarterfinals and an overall 76–9 mark. The school's all-time leading rebounder (1,166) also had an 18.6 career scoring average. Schramm was drafted by the Boston Celtics, one of only two Leathernecks ever selected. (The other was Joe Dykstra in 1983.)

BEST COACH: LEROY "STIX" MORLEY (1947-69) His teams reached five straight NAIA elite eights and two championship games between 1953 and '58. Morley was the 1955 NAIA national coach of the year and was inducted into the NAIA Hall of Fame in 1963.

GAME FOR THE AGES: On March 1, 1958, the Leathernecks' perfect record was on the line when they trailed Northern Illinois, 61-60, in the regular-season finale with :02 left. But McAfoos took a pass from Moore at the free throw line and hit a long jumper for the 62-61 win.

FIERCEST RIVAL: Western has yet to make the NCAA Tournament, and Valparaiso is largely to blame. The Crusaders beat the Leathernecks three times in conference tournament finals, including an 88-85 triple-overtime heartbreaker in 1995. Valpo leads, 33–24, and with its move to the Horizon League after the 2006-07 season, Western isn't likely to get a shot at redemption any time soon.

SEASON REVIEW

SEAS.	W-L	CONF.	COACH	SEAS.	W-L	CONF.	COACH
1910-47	*301-187*		*Ray Hanson 198-95 (1926-42, '46-47)*	1960-61	12-12		Leroy "Stix" Morley
1947-48	19-7		Leroy "Stix" Morley	1961-62	21-11		Leroy "Stix" Morley
1948-49	23-7		Leroy "Stix" Morley	1962-63	19-8		Leroy "Stix" Morley
1949-50	17-6		Leroy "Stix" Morley	1963-64	13-12		Leroy "Stix" Morley
1950-51	18-9		Leroy "Stix" Morley	1964-65	11-14		Leroy "Stix" Morley
1951-52	12-10		Leroy "Stix" Morley	1965-66	16-9		Leroy "Stix" Morley
1952-53	12-10		Leroy "Stix" Morley	1966-67	7-19		Leroy "Stix" Morley
1953-54	19-9		Leroy "Stix" Morley	1967-68	3-23		Leroy "Stix" Morley
1954-55	26-3		Leroy "Stix" Morley	1968-69	7-19		Leroy "Stix" Morley
1955-56	28-3		Leroy "Stix" Morley	1969-70	14-11		Guy Ricci
1956-57	22-3		Leroy "Stix" Morley	1970-71	7-19		Guy Ricci
1957-58	27-1		Leroy "Stix" Morley	1971-72	12-14		Guy Ricci
1958-59	14-13		Leroy "Stix" Morley	1972-73	11-14		Guy Ricci
1959-60	18-7		Leroy "Stix" Morley	1973-74	17-9		Walt Moore

SEAS.	W-L	CONF.	SCORING		COACH	RECORD
1974-75	10-16				Walt Moore	
1975-76	12-14				Walt Moore	
1976-77	7-18		David Morgan	18.5	Walt Moore	46-57 .447
1977-78	12-14		David Morgan	20.8	Jack Margenthaler	
1978-79	16-11		Brad Bainter	19.9	Jack Margenthaler	
1979-80	19-10				Jack Margenthaler	
1980-81	21-8				Jack Margenthaler	
1981-82	14-13		Joe Dykstra	21.1	Jack Margenthaler	
1982-83	20-11	9-3	Joe Dykstra	21.1	Jack Margenthaler	
1983-84	17-13	6-8	Todd Hutcheson	17.9	Jack Margenthaler	
1984-85	14-14	10-4	J.D. Dykstra	18.4	Jack Margenthaler	
1985-86	13-15	7-7	Cedric Wright	12.3	Jack Margenthaler	
1986-87	12-16	2-12	Mike Ayers	15.2	Jack Margenthaler	
1987-88	15-12	6-8	Dwayne Scott	18.4	Jack Margenthaler	
1988-89	9-19	4-8	Bob Smith	11.7	Jack Margenthaler	
1989-90	16-13	6-6	Darrell Richardson	14.6	Jack Margenthaler	
1990-91	13-15	6-10	Ron Ateman	17.1	Jack Margenthaler	
1991-92	10-18	4-12	J. Forcine, Charles Turner	11.9	Jack Margenthaler	221-202 .522
1992-93	7-20	4-12	Charles Turner	17.3	Jim Kerwin	
1993-94	7-20	5-13	Garrick Vicks	15.2	Jim Kerwin	
1994-95	20-8	13-5	Garrick Vicks	17.7	Jim Kerwin	
1995-96	17-12	12-6	George Milsap	16.8	Jim Kerwin	
1996-97	19-10	11-5	Janthony Joseph	20.2	Jim Kerwin	
1997-98	16-11	11-5	Brandon Creason	11.7	Jim Kerwin	
1998-99	16-12	9-5	Shawn Doles	15.4	Jim Kerwin	
1999-2000	8-22	3-13	Juan Martinez	15.4	Jim Kerwin	
2000-01	5-23	5-11	Cory Fosdyck	10.8	Jim Kerwin	
2001-02	12-16	3-11	Quentin Mitchell	13.1	Jim Kerwin	
2002-03	7-21	3-11	J.D. Summers	12.6	Jim Kerwin	134-175 .434
2003-04	3-25	1-15	J.D. Summers	12.7	Derek Thomas	
2004-05	11-17	7-9	Eulis Baez	15.3	Derek Thomas	
2005-06	7-21	3-13	David Jackson	14.5	Derek Thomas	
2006-07	7-23	3-11	David Jackson	12.7	Derek Thomas	
2007-08	12-18	7-11	David Jackson	13.7	Derek Thomas	40-104 .278
2008-09	9-20	6-12	David DuBois	17.9	Jim Molinari	9-20 .310

PROFILE

Western Illinois University, Macomb, IL
Founded: 1899
Enrollment: 13,404 (11,147 undergraduate)
Colors: Purple and gold
Nickname: Leathernecks
Current arena: Waste Management Court at Western Hall, opened in 1964 (5,139)
First game: 1910
All-time record: 1,159-1,018 (.532)
Total weeks in AP Top 20/25: 0

Current conference: Summit League (1982-)
Conference titles:
Mid-Continent: 1 (1983)
Conference tournament titles:
Mid-Continent: 1 (1984)
NCAA Tournament appearances: 0
NIT appearances: 0

TOP 5

G **Bob Anderson** (1966-69)
G **Coleman Carrodine** (1960-64)
G **Gene Talbot** (1953-56)
F **Joe Dykstra** (1978-83)
F/C **Chuck Schramm** (1954-57)

RECORDS

	GAME		SEASON		CAREER	
POINTS	44	Dan Braun, vs. Central Missouri St. (Feb. 7, 1970)	653	Joe Dykstra (1982-83)	2,248	Joe Dykstra (1978-83)
POINTS PER GAME			23.0	Bob Anderson (1967-68)	20.2	Bob Anderson (1966-69)
REBOUNDS	24	Dan Braun, vs. Central Missouri St. (Feb. 7, 1970)	509	Dan Braun (1967-68)	1,166	Chuck Schramm (1954-57)
ASSISTS	15	John Washington, vs. St. Xavier (1979-80)	180	Ike Rudd (1972-73)	506	Dwayne Banks (1977-81)

ESPN 44 SAGARIN

WESTERN KENTUCKY

It isn't Kentucky and it isn't Louisville. But like the two major powers from the Bluegrass State, Western Kentucky has a tradition and a fan base that almost any other team in the country would envy. Having gone deep into the NCAA Tournament several times, the Hilltoppers proved their quality in 2008 with a run to the Sweet 16 and in '09 they reached the Tourney's second round.

BEST TEAM: 1970-71 Led by center Jim McDaniels, the Hilltoppers were perfect at home and claimed the Ohio Valley regular-season championship. But they were just getting warmed up. In the NCAA Tournament, WKU knocked off Artis Gilmore and Jacksonville, 74-72, pummeled Kentucky, 107-83, in the first meeting ever between the schools and survived Ohio State, 81-78, in overtime. Villanova ended the run with a 92-89 double-overtime win in the Final Four, but alas, both WKU's and Villanova's appearances were later vacated when the NCAA determined that McDaniels and Nova star Howard Porter had signed pro contracts.

BEST PLAYER: C Jim McDaniels (1968-71) With all due respect to Clem Haskins, Big Mac put the 1971 team on his back and might have taken it to the national championship. The 7-footer towered over most opponents and averaged 29.3 points and 15.1 boards that year. McDaniels was one of the early group of players tempted by the ABA-NBA bidding war, and his premature signing violated NCAA rules. He ended up a journeyman for several pro teams.

BEST COACH: E.A. Diddle (1922-64) Even after coaching 42 seasons in Bowling Green, Diddle doesn't get nearly the credit he deserves. A winner of 14 regular-season and conference tournament championships, he retired as the winningest coach in college basketball history with 759 victories (still among the all-time top 20). And WKU fans will never forget the image of him joyfully waving his red towel.

GAME FOR THE AGES: It's known at WKU simply as the Shoestring Shot. In their NCAA first-round game on March 13, 1971, the Hilltoppers climbed all the way back from 18 down to tie Gilmore's Jacksonville Dolphins. With :04 left and the score tied at 72, WKU's Clarence Glover pretended to tie his shoelace, then suddenly popped up to take a pass and hit the game-winner.

HEARTBREAKER: Many old-timers believe that WKU's loss to Michigan on March 11, 1966, in the NCAA Mideast Regional semifinal came as a result of the worst call in basketball history. Ahead 79-78 with a few seconds left, WKU forced a jump ball. After winning the tip, Hilltopper Greg Smith was called for a foul—and Michigan's Cazzie Russell dropped the two winning free throws.

FIERCEST RIVAL: Just like Kentucky, Louisville doesn't like to schedule Western Kentucky because it's afraid of being embarrassed by a country cousin. Cardinal fans *should* be worried. WKU leads the series 39–33.

FANFARE AND HOOPLA: It started with Coach Diddle being a little worried about athletic department towels being stolen; his response was to make them red and distinctive. The towels became totemic after Diddle began chewing, braiding and tossing them during games. Fans quickly followed suit. So it figures that the red towel tradition would spawn a living, breathing red towel. Designed in 1979, Big Red has been described as an "oversized cookie monster," and gained fame for appearing in ESPN *SportsCenter* commercials.

FAN FAVORITE: F Clem Haskins (1964-67) Whenever former players are honored at E.A. Diddle Arena, the three-time OVC Player of the Year and nine-year NBA star always receives the loudest ovation—despite his controversial exit as head coach from Minnesota in 1999 because of academics violations.

CONSENSUS ALL-AMERICAS

1967	**Clem Haskins,** F
1971	**Jim McDaniels,** C

FIRST-ROUND PRO PICKS

1948	**Don Ray,** Philadelphia (11)
1950	**Bob Lavoy,** Indianapolis (9)
1954	**Tom Marshall,** Rochester (7)
1954	**Jack Turner,** New York (8)
1967	**Clem Haskins,** Chicago (3)
1968	**Wayne Chapman,** Kentucky (ABA)
1971	**Clarence Glover,** Boston (10)
1987	**Tellis Frank,** Golden State (14)
2008	**Courtney Lee,** Orlando (22)

PROFILE

Western Kentucky University, Bowling Green, KY
Founded: 1906
Enrollment: 19,265 (16,508 undergraduate)
Colors: Red and white
Nickname: Hilltoppers
Current arena: E.A. Diddle Arena, opened in 1963 (7,326)
Previous Arenas: Physical Education Building, a.k.a. the Red Barn, 1931-63 (250); Resuscitation Hall (N/A)
First game: 1915
All-time record: 1,606-781 (.673)
Total weeks in AP Top 20/25: 111

Current conference: Sun Belt (1982-)
Conference titles:
Ohio Valley: 19 (1949, '50, '52, '54, '55, '56 [tie], '57 [tie], '60, '61 [tie], '62, '66, '67, '70, '71, '72 [tie], '76, '80 [tie], '81, '82 [tie])
Sun Belt: 9 (1987, '94, '95, 2001 [tie], '02 [tie], '03 [tie], '06 [tie], '08 [tie], '09 [tie])
Conference tournament titles:
Ohio Valley: 10 (1949, '52, '53, '54, '65, '66, '76, '78, '80, '81)
Sun Belt: 7 (1993, '95, 2001, '02, '03, '08, '09)

NCAA Tournaments: 21 (1 appearance vacated)
Sweet 16s (since 1975): 3
Final Fours: 1
NIT appearances: 13
Semifinals: 3

TOP 5

G	**Courtney Lee** (2004-08)
G	**Dwight Smith** (1964-67)
F	**Clem Haskins** (1964-67)
F	**Tom Marshall** (1950-54)
C	**Jim McDaniels** (1968-71)

RECORDS

RECORDS	GAME		SEASON		CAREER	
POINTS	55	Clem Haskins, vs. Middle Tenn. St. (Jan. 30, 1965)	878	Jim McDaniels (1970-71)	2,238	Courtney Lee (2004-08); Jim McDaniels (1968-71)
POINTS PER GAME			29.3	Jim McDaniels (1970-71)	27.6	Jim McDaniels (1968-71)
REBOUNDS	29	Tom Marshall, vs. Louisville (Dec. 30, 1953)	477	Tom Marshall (1953-54)	1,565	Tom Marshall (1950-54)
ASSISTS	14	Ed Gampfer, vs. Middle Tennessee St. (March 2, 1974)	202	James McNary (1986-87)	440	James McNary (1984-87)

SEASON REVIEW

SEASON	W-L	CONF.	SCORING		COACH	RECORD	
14-18	7-2		*No team 1916-18*				
18-19	no team						
19-20	no team						
20-21	no team						
21-22	3-1				L.T. Smith	3-1	.750
22-23	12-2		W.B. Owen	N/A	E.A. Diddle		
23-24	9-9		Harry "Pap" Glenn	N/A	E.A. Diddle		
924-25	8-6		Harry "Pap" Glenn	N/A	E.A. Diddle		
925-26	10-4		Ted Hornback	9.0	E.A. Diddle		
926-27	12-7		Ted Hornback	N/A	E.A. Diddle		
927-28	10-7		Ted Hornback	N/A	E.A. Diddle		
1928-29	8-10		Ted Hornback	N/A	E.A. Diddle		
1929-30	4-12		Turner Elrod	N/A	E.A. Diddle		
1930-31	11-3		Orlie Lawrence	N/A	E.A. Diddle		
1931-32	15-8		Tom Hobbs	N/A	E.A. Diddle		
1932-33	16-6		Tom Hobbs	N/A	E.A. Diddle		
1933-34	28-8		Tom Hobbs	N/A	E.A. Diddle		
1934-35	24-3		Brad Mutchler	9.6	E.A. Diddle		
1935-36	26-4		Brad Mutchler	N/A	E.A. Diddle		
1936-37	21-2		Harry Saddler	10.2	E.A. Diddle		
1937-38	30-3		Harry Saddler	11.8	E.A. Diddle		
1938-39	22-3		Harry Saddler	15.9	E.A. Diddle		

SEAS.	W-L	CONF.	POSTSEASON	SCORING		REBOUNDS		ASSISTS		COACH	RECORD	
939-40	24-6		NCAA REGIONAL SEMIFINALS	Carlisle Towery	13.8					E.A. Diddle		
940-41	22-4			Carlisle Towery	17.1					E.A. Diddle		
941-42	29-5		NIT RUNNER-UP	Buck Sydnor	10.4					E.A. Diddle		
942-43	24-3		NIT QUARTERFINALS	Don Ray	11.7					E.A. Diddle		
943-44	13-9			Lawrence Jones	9.9					E.A. Diddle		
944-45	17-10			Kenneth Sinkhorn	9.8					E.A. Diddle		
945-46	15-19			Chalmers Embry	12.5					E.A. Diddle		
946-47	25-4			Odie Spears	13.9					E.A. Diddle		
947-48	28-2		NIT THIRD PLACE	Odie Spears	14.0					E.A. Diddle		
948-49	25-4	8-2	NIT QUARTERFINALS	Bob Lavoy	12.8					E.A. Diddle		
949-50	25-6	8-0	NIT QUARTERFINALS	Bob Lavoy	21.7					E.A. Diddle		
950-51	19-10	4-4		Rip Gish	16.3	Rip Gish	15.5			E.A. Diddle		
951-52	26-5	11-1	NIT QUARTERFINALS	Art Spoelstra	15.4			Gene Rhodes	182	E.A. Diddle		
952-53	25-6	8-2	NIT QUARTERFINALS	Tom Marshall	18.5	Tom Marshall	12.8			E.A. Diddle		
953-54	29-3	9-1	NIT FOURTH PLACE	Tom Marshall	25.9	Tom Marshall	14.9			E.A. Diddle		
954-55	18-10	8-2		Lynn Cole	16.7	Ralph Crosthwaite	10.9			E.A. Diddle		
955-56	16-12	7-3		Forest Able	18.1	Bob Daniels	14.9			E.A. Diddle		
956-57	17-9	9-1		Ralph Crosthwaite	20.3	Ralph Crosthwaite	11.9			E.A. Diddle		
957-58	14-11	5-5		Ralph Crosthwaite	22.8	Ralph Crosthwaite	15.3			E.A. Diddle		
958-59	16-10	8-4		Ralph Crosthwaite	20.8	Ralph Crosthwaite	12.8			E.A. Diddle		
959-60	21-7	10-2	NCAA REGIONAL SEMIFINALS	Charlie Osborne	17.8	Harry Todd	10.6			E.A. Diddle		
960-61	18-8	9-3		Bobby Rascoe	20.1	Harry Todd	11.6			E.A. Diddle		
961-62	17-10	11-1	NCAA REGIONAL SEMIFINALS	Bobby Rascoe	25.7	Harry Todd	12.5			E.A. Diddle		
962-63	5-16	3-9		Darel Carrier	19.2	Bobby Jackson	9.4			E.A. Diddle		
963-64	5-16	3-11		Darel Carrier	26.0	Ray Keeton	12.6			E.A. Diddle	759-302	.715
964-65	18-9	10-4	NIT QUARTERFINALS	Clem Haskins	23.4	Dwight Smith	11.3			John Oldham		
965-66	25-3	14-0	NCAA REGIONAL SEMIFINALS	Clem Haskins	20.4	Greg Smith	10.3			John Oldham		
966-67	23-3	13-1	NCAA FIRST ROUND	Clem Haskins	22.6	Dwight Smith	11.9			John Oldham		
967-68	18-7	9-5		Wayne Chapman	20.8	Greg Smith	14.5			John Oldham		
968-69	16-10	9-5		Jim McDaniels	24.8	Jim McDaniels	12.5	Rich Hendrick	110	John Oldham		
969-70	22-3	14-0	NCAA FIRST ROUND	Jim McDaniels	28.6	Jim McDaniels	13.6	Gary Sundmacker	83	John Oldham		
970-71	24-6 ⊗	12-2	NCAA THIRD PLACE	Jim McDaniels	29.3	Jim McDaniels	15.1	Rex Bailey	106	John Oldham	146-41	.781▼
971-72	15-11	9-5		Jerry Dunn	19.0	Granville Bunton	11.5	Rex Bailey	72	Jim Richards		
972-73	10-16	6-8		Tony Stroud	13.0	Granville Bunton	12.1	Tony Stroud	82	Jim Richards		
973-74	15-10	8-6		Johnny Britt	18.4	Kent Allison	10.4	Calvin Wade	84	Jim Richards		
974-75	16-8	11-3		Johnny Britt	18.3	Mike Odemns	11.7	Calvin Wade	120	Jim Richards		
975-76	20-9	11-3	NCAA FIRST ROUND	Johnny Britt	19.6	James Johnson	8.8	Johnny Britt	118	Jim Richards		
976-77	10-16	6-8		Mike Prince	14.8	James Johnson	10.0	Steve Ashby	105	Jim Richards		
977-78	16-14	9-5	NCAA REGIONAL SEMIFINALS	James Johnson	18.5	James Johnson	9.7	Steve Ashby	104	Jim Richards	102-84	.548
978-79	17-11	7-5		Greg Jackson	18.2	Greg Jackson	8.8	Trey Trumbo	95	Gene Keady		
979-80	21-8	10-2	NCAA FIRST ROUND	Craig McCormick	14.6	Craig McCormick	6.7	Trey Trumbo	109	Gene Keady	38-19	.667
980-81	21-8	12-2	NCAA FIRST ROUND	Tony Wilson	14.6	Craig McCormick	6.9	Kevin Dildy	101	Clem Haskins		
981-82	19-10	13-3	NIT FIRST ROUND	Craig McCormick	14.3	Craig McCormick	6.1	Kevin Dildy	132	Clem Haskins		
982-83	12-16	4-10		Tony Wilson	14.6	Tony Wilson	6.1	Bobby Jones	111	Clem Haskins		
983-84	12-17	5-9		Bobby Jones	13.7	Gary Carver	6.5	Bobby Jones	109	Clem Haskins		
984-85	14-14	5-9		Kannard Johnson	15.0	Kannard Johnson	6.4	Dennis Johnson	88	Clem Haskins		
985-86	23-8	10-4	NCAA SECOND ROUND	Billy Gordon	14.1	Clarence Martin	6.7	James McNary	175	Clem Haskins	101-73	.580
986-87	29-9	12-2	NCAA SECOND ROUND	Tellis Frank	18.0	Kannard Johnson	8.2	James McNary	202	Murray Arnold		
987-88	15-13	6-8		Brett McNeal	20.0	Anthony Smith	10.4	Brett McNeal	112	Murray Arnold		
988-89	14-15	4-10		Brett McNeal	21.4	Anthony Smith	10.1	Brett McNeal	124	Murray Arnold		
989-90	13-17	7-7		Roland Shelton	18.2	Rodney Ross	9.5	Anthony Palm	159	Murray Arnold	71-54	.568
990-91	14-14	8-6		Jack Jennings	16.1	Jack Jennings	8.5	Anthony Palm	149	Ralph Willard		
991-92	21-11	10-6	NIT FIRST ROUND	Jack Jennings	19.1	Jack Jennings	6.6	Mark Bell	123	Ralph Willard		
992-93	26-6	14-4	NCAA REGIONAL SEMIFINALS	Darnell Mee	18.9	Darius Hall	6.1	Mark Bell	124	Ralph Willard		
993-94	20-11	14-4	NCAA FIRST ROUND	Chris Robinson	14.7	Cypheus Bunton	6.6	Michael Fraliex	107	Ralph Willard	81-42	.659
994-95	27-4	17-1	NCAA SECOND ROUND	Chris Robinson	17.0	Darius Hall	7.3	Michael Fraliex	106	Matt Kilcullen		
995-96	13-14	10-8		Chris Robinson	16.8	Tony Lovan	8.3	Rob Williams	82	Matt Kilcullen		
996-97	12-15	9-9		Tony Lovan	15.0	Tony Lovan	5.8	Rob Williams	111	Matt Kilcullen		
997-98	10-19	6-12		Steven Bides	14.1	Steven Bides	6.2	Rashon Brown	69	Matt Kilcullen[a]	59-49	.500
998-99	13-16	7-7		Joe Harney	10.2	Ravon Farris	5.1	Rashon Brown	3.0	Dennis Felton		
999-2000	11-18	8-8		Lee Lampley	14.1	Chris Marcus	9.5	Derek Robinson	4.5	Dennis Felton		
000-01	24-7	14-2	NCAA FIRST ROUND	Chris Marcus	16.7	Chris Marcus	12.1	Derek Robinson	3.9	Dennis Felton		
001-02	28-4	13-1	NCAA FIRST ROUND	David Boyden	11.3	David Boyden	6.1	Derek Robinson	4.1	Dennis Felton		
002-03	24-9	12-2	NCAA FIRST ROUND	Patrick Sparks	13.3	David Boyden	5.3	Patrick Sparks	5.9	Dennis Felton	100-54	.649
003-04	15-13	8-6		Nigel Dixon	15.9	Nigel Dixon	10.3	Antonio Haynes	4.2	Darrin Horn		
004-05	22-9	9-5	NIT FIRST ROUND	Anthony Winchester	18.2	Anthony Winchester	7.2	Antonio Haynes	4.1	Darrin Horn		
005-06	23-8	12-2	NIT FIRST ROUND	Anthony Winchester	18.6	Courtney Lee	6.3	Courtney Lee	2.9	Darrin Horn		
006-07	22-11	12-6		Courtney Lee	17.3	Jeremy Evans	5.7	Tyrone Brazelton	4.0	Darrin Horn		
007-08	29-7	16-2	NCAA REGIONAL SEMIFINALS	Courtney Lee	20.4	Courtney Lee	4.9	Tyrone Brazelton	3.7	Darrin Horn	111-48	.698
008-09	25-9	15-3	NCAA SECOND ROUND	A.J. Slaughter	16.0	Sergio Kerusch	7.4	Orlando Mendez-Valdez	4.1	Scott McDonald	25-9	.735

Cumulative totals listed when per game averages not available.

[a] Matt Kilcullen (7-16) and Al Seibert (3-3) both coached during the 1997-98 season.

⊗ Records don't reflect games forfeited or vacated. For adjusted records, see p. 521.

▼ Coach's record adjusted to reflect games forfeited or vacated: 142-40, .780. For yearly totals, see p. 521.

ESPN 120 SAGARIN

WESTERN MICHIGAN

When he became Western Michigan's coach in 2003, Steve Hawkins promised to "end the roller coaster." Hawkins knew his Broncos history—a few pinnacles of success (two NCAA and two NIT bids, some seasons of Mid-American Conference domination) punctuating decades of sustained stomach-turning seasons (the 1983-84 team went 4–22, and that wasn't even WMU's worst season). So far, Hawkins has kept his promise. The Broncos have finished first or second in the MAC West six times in as many seasons.

BEST TEAM: 1975-76 Under the steady coaching hand of Eldon Miller, the 25–3 Broncos won their first 19 games, dominated the MAC and finished the regular season ranked No. 16 in the nation. Led by MAC Player of the Year Jeff Tyson, Western Michigan beat Virginia Tech, 77-67, in overtime in the school's first NCAA Tournament game, before bowing out to Marquette.

BEST PLAYER: G MANNY NEWSOME (1961-64) He could take the ball powerfully to the basket or pull up for a midrange jumper. Opponents used double-team, triple-team, even *entire-team* defenses to try to stop Newsome. It hardly mattered. The 5'10" guard still holds the Broncos' all-time record for points (1,786), field goals (729) and scoring average (26.3 ppg).

BEST COACH: HERBERT "BUCK" READ (1922-49) An argument can be made for Eldon Miller, but longtime Broncos fans know that Read is the school's best coach. He not only holds the record for most wins (345) and highest winning percentage (.671) in the Western Michigan program's history, he was also one of the earliest teachers of the fast-break offense and up-tempo basketball.

GAME FOR THE AGES: On March 13, 1998, in the first round of the NCAA Tournament, No. 11-seed Western Michigan blew a 16-point second-half lead over No. 6-seed Clemson and fell behind by six. Then, in the last four minutes, Rashod Johnson hit four of his game-high eight three-pointers, plus a free throw, to ice the 75-72 win.

HEARTBREAKER: Western Michigan allowed TCU to reach the 2005 NIT quarterfinals—by a footstep. After sending the game into overtime with his buzzer-beating layup and now trailing by a point with 1.9 seconds left in the extra period, Broncos swingman Ben Reed was driving for what would likely be the game-winner when he slipped on a wet spot on the floor. The officials called Reed for traveling and handed the ball over to the Horned Frogs. A final TCU free throw was the dagger twist in the 78-76 killing.

FIERCEST RIVAL: Regardless of records, Western Michigan knows it will have one of its toughest games of the season whenever it plays Central Michigan, and vice versa. It's a two-and-a-half-hour drive between Kalamazoo and Mt. Pleasant, and the Broncos have gone at it with the Chippewas twice in most seasons since 1946. Western Michigan leads the series, 77–44.

Opponents used double-team, triple-team, even entire-team defenses to try to stop Newsome. It hardly mattered.

FANFARE AND HOOPLA: Known as the Zoo (as in Kalamazoo), Western Michigan's student section is one of college basketball's most raucous. When opposing players step to the free throw line, Zoo denizens spin a five-foot pinwheel behind the shooter's target. So-called "Zoo leaders" scour the Internet for embarrassing information about specific opponents—a favorite chick flick or a past legal scrape—then wait for quiet moments in the game to confront the player with some very loud public humiliation.

FAN FAVORITE: G/F BEN REED (2001-05) A native of nearby Battle Creek, Reed had the fullback-sized build of Daryl "Moose" Johnston and the three-point touch of Reggie Miller. Western Michiganders still appreciate his rare combination of talent: Reed was his team's enforcer and also its leading scorer.

PROFILE

Western Michigan University, Kalamazoo, MI
Founded: 1903
Enrollment: 24,841 (20,081 undergraduate)
Colors: Brown and gold
Nickname: Broncos
Current arena: University Arena, opened in 1957 (5,421)
First game: 1913
All-time record: 1,160-1,054 (.524)
Total weeks in AP Top 20/25: 7

Current conference: Mid-American (1947-)
Conference titles:
MAC: 5 (1952 [tie], '76, '81 [tie], '98 [tie], 2004)
Conference tournament titles:
MAC: 1 (2004)
NCAA Tournament appearances: 3
Sweet 16s (since 1975): 1
NIT appearances: 3

TOP 5

G **Manny Newsome** (1961-64)
G **Saddi Washington** (1993-98)
G/F **Ben Reed** (2001-05)
F **Paul Griffin** (1972-76)
C **Joe Reitz** (2004-08)

RECORDS	GAME		SEASON		CAREER	
POINTS	46	Gene Ford, vs. Loyola-Chicago (Feb. 4, 1969)	653	Manny Newsome (1963-64)	1,786	Manny Newsome (1961-64)
POINTS PER GAME			32.7	Manny Newsome (1963-64)	26.3	Manny Newsom (1961-64)
REBOUNDS	26	Reggie Lacefield, vs. Illinois State (Dec. 9, 1967)	324	Edgar Blair (1957-58)	1,008	Paul Griffin (1972-76)
ASSISTS	17	Todd Dietrich, vs. Bowling Green (Feb. 21, 1979)	170	Rod Brown (1999-2000)	427	Billy Stanback (1986-90)

SEASON REVIEW

SEASON	W-L	CONF.	SCORING	COACH	RECORD	
13-16	20-16		No losing seasons			
16-17	7-6			Bill Spaulding		
17-18	8-4			Bill Spaulding		
18-19	11-3			Bill Spaulding		
19-20	8-3			Bill Spaulding		
20-21	12-5			Bill Spaulding		
21-22	11-6			Bill Spaulding	77-43	.642
22-23	17-6			Herbert "Buck" Read		
23-24	13-8			Herbert "Buck" Read		
24-25	17-4			Herbert "Buck" Read		
25-26	15-4			Herbert "Buck" Read		
1926-27	16-2			Herbert "Buck" Read		
1927-28	9-8			Herbert "Buck" Read		
1928-29	10-9			Herbert "Buck" Read		
1929-30	17-0			Herbert "Buck" Read		
1930-31	14-3			Herbert "Buck" Read		
1931-32	14-5			Herbert "Buck" Read		
1932-33	14-3			Herbert "Buck" Read		
1933-34	12-5			Herbert "Buck" Read		
1934-35	11-5			Herbert "Buck" Read		
1935-36	15-3			Herbert "Buck" Read		
1936-37	13-4			Herbert "Buck" Read		

SEAS.	W-L	CONF.	POSTSEASON	SCORING		REBOUNDS		ASSISTS		COACH	RECORD	
1937-38	6-12									Herbert "Buck" Read		
1938-39	7-10									Herbert "Buck" Read		
1939-40	10-9									Herbert "Buck" Read		
1940-41	9-9									Herbert "Buck" Read		
1941-42	12-8									Herbert "Buck" Read		
1942-43	15-4									Herbert "Buck" Read		
1943-44	15-4									Herbert "Buck" Read		
1944-45	8-10									Herbert "Buck" Read		
1945-46	15-7									Herbert "Buck" Read		
1946-47	17-7									Herbert "Buck" Read		
1947-48	12-10	1-2								Herbert "Buck" Read		
1948-49	12-10	4-6								Herbert "Buck" Read	345-169	.671
1949-50	12-10	6-4								William Perigo		
1950-51	13-9	4-4								William Perigo		
1951-52	16-8	9-3								William Perigo	41-27	.603
1952-53	12-9	6-6								Joe Hoy		
1953-54	10-11	4-5								Joe Hoy		
1954-55	12-10	9-5								Joe Hoy		
1955-56	11-9	7-5				Jack Smith	13.1			Joe Hoy		
1956-57	8-13	4-8								Joe Hoy		
1957-58	5-19	1-11				Edgar Blair	13.5			Joe Hoy	58-71	.450
1958-59	2-20	1-11				Edgar Blair	12.9			Don Boven		
1959-60	12-11	5-7		Bob James	21.7	Bob Bolton	11.5			Don Boven		
1960-61	10-14	4-8				Bob Bolton	13.0			Don Boven		
1961-62	13-11	6-6		Manny Newsome	24.1					Don Boven		
1962-63	12-12	7-5		Manny Newsome	23.1					Don Boven		
1963-64	10-14	6-6		Manny Newsome	32.7	Ajac Triplett	11.5			Don Boven		
1964-65	8-16	3-9		Dave Anderson	21.6	Willie Thomas	10.8			Don Boven		
1965-66	8-14	4-8		Reggie Lacefield	18.3	Reggie Lacefield	18.3			Don Boven	75-112	.401
1966-67	10-14	4-8		Reggie Lacefield	17.1	Reggie Lacefield	10.8			Sonny Means		
1967-68	11-13	5-7		Reggie Lacefield	20.5	Reggie Lacefield	11.1			Sonny Means		
1968-69	11-13	6-6		Gene Ford	25.8	Gene Ford	9.6			Sonny Means		
1969-70	6-17	2-8		Ellis Hull	17.6	Earl Jenkins	8.9			Sonny Means	38-57	.400
1970-71	14-10	5-5		Earl Jenkins	18.8	Earl Jenkins	12.5			Eldon Miller		
1971-72	10-14	5-5		Chuck Washington	17.7	Chuck Washington	9.3			Eldon Miller		
1972-73	8-18	2-10		Mike Steele	15.4	Paul Griffin	6.4			Eldon Miller		
1973-74	13-13	5-7		Mike Steele	12.6	Paul Griffin	9.7			Eldon Miller		
1974-75	16-10	8-6		Jeff Tyson	15.3	Tom Cutter	9.1			Eldon Miller		
1975-76	25-3	15-1	NCAA REGIONAL SEMIFINALS	Jeff Tyson	17.9	Tom Cutter	10.6			Eldon Miller	86-68	.558
1976-77	14-13	8-8		Tom Cutter	12.6	Tom Cutter	10.6			Dick Shilts		
1977-78	7-20	4-12		Herman Randle	9.6	Marc Throop	5.7			Dick Shilts		
1978-79	7-23	3-13		Kenny Cunningham	19.2	Mark Weishaar	6.8			Dick Shilts	28-56	.333
1979-80	12-14	7-9		Kenny Cunningham	24.2	Mike Seberger	6.1	Todd Dietrich	4.5	Les Wothke		
1980-81	15-13	10-6		Jasper McElroy	16.9	Mike Seberger	7.1	Todd Dietrich	4.6	Les Wothke		
1981-82	15-14	8-8		Walker D. Russell	19.9	Mike Seberger	8.3	Walker D. Russell	4.2	Les Wothke	42-41	.506
1982-83	5-23	3-15		Cordell Eley	18.1	Anthony Jones	6.0	David Elliott	2.5	Vernon Payne		
1983-84	4-22	2-16		Booker James	14.3	Booker James	6.9	Cordell Eley	2.8	Vernon Payne		
1984-85	12-16	7-11		Donald Petties	19.5	Booker James	7.4	Dan Zachary	5.3	Vernon Payne		
1985-86	12-16	7-11		Donald Petties	15.7	Booker James	7.9	Dan Zachary	4.1	Vernon Payne		
1986-87	12-16	7-9		Booker James	22.1	Booker James	10.1	Billy Stanback	4.8	Vernon Payne		
1987-88	12-17	7-9		Mark Brown	19.6	Steve Riikonen	6.6	Billy Stanback	3.6	Vernon Payne		
1988-89	12-16	6-10		Tony Baumgardt	13.9	Tony Baumgardt	5.7	Billy Stanback	4.1	Vernon Payne	69-126	.354
1989-90	9-18	3-13		Jim Havrilla	20.8	Jim Havrilla	8.6	Chris Brawley	3.0	Bob Donewald		
1990-91	5-22	2-14		Jim Havrilla	17.1	Jim Havrilla	8.1	Darrick Brooks	3.5	Bob Donewald		
1991-92	21-9	11-5	NIT FIRST ROUND	Leon McGee	15.1	Virgil Grayson	6.0	Ebon Sanders	3.3	Bob Donewald		
1992-93	17-12	12-6		Leon McGee	14.3	Ben Handlogten	5.7	Ebon Sanders	2.7	Bob Donewald		
1993-94	14-14	7-11		Saddi Washington	14.0	Ben Handlogten	7.1	Saddi Washington	3.2	Bob Donewald		
1994-95	14-13	9-9		Joel Burns	15.2	Ben Handlogten	6.6	Jason Black	2.2	Bob Donewald		
1995-96	15-12 ⊗	13-5		Ben Handlogten	15.7	Ben Handlogten	8.8	Jason Black	3.0	Bob Donewald		
1996-97	14-14	9-9		Saddi Washington	16.4	Washington, Van Timmeren	4.5	Saddi Washington	2.5	Bob Donewald		
1997-98	21-8	14-4	NCAA SECOND ROUND	Saddi Washington	21.6	Shaun Jackson	7.5	Jason Kimbrough	5.7	Bob Donewald		
1998-99	11-15	6-12		Tony Barksdale	17.2	Brad Van Timmeren	6.1	Rod Brown	5.0	Bob Donewald		
1999-2000	10-18	6-12		Tony Barksdale	19.1	Brad Van Timmeren	5.9	Rod Brown	6.0	Bob Donewald	151-155	.493▼
2000-01	7-21	7-11		Jon Powell	15.9	Anthony Kann	5.6	Robby Collum	3.3	Robert McCullum		
2001-02	17-13	10-8		Steve Reynolds	16.9	Anthony Kann	7.2	Robby Collum	4.5	Robert McCullum		
2002-03	20-11	10-8	NIT FIRST ROUND	Anthony Kann	14.4	Anthony Kann	8.8	Robby Collum	4.0	Robert McCullum	44-45	.494
2003-04	26-5	15-3	NCAA FIRST ROUND	Mike Williams	18.9	Mike Williams	7.0	Brian Snider	4.8	Steve Hawkins		
2004-05	20-13	11-7	NIT SECOND ROUND	Ben Reed	17.7	Ben Reed	6.2	Ricky Willis	4.8	Steve Hawkins		
2005-06	14-17	10-8		Joe Reitz	15.5	Joe Reitz	7.4	Brian Snider	5.1	Steve Hawkins		
2006-07	16-16	9-7		David Kool	13.4	Joe Reitz	8.4	Michael Redell	4.4	Steve Hawkins		
2007-08	20-12	12-4		David Kool	16.3	Joe Reitz	7.9	Michael Redell	3.6	Steve Hawkins		
2008-09	10-21	7-9		David Kool	17.9	Donald Lawson	5.5	Michael Redell	3.2	Steve Hawkins	106-84	.558

⊗ Records don't reflect games forfeited or vacated. For adjusted records, see p. 521.

▼ Coach's record adjusted to reflect games forfeited or vacated: 152-154, .497. For yearly totals, see p. 521.

THE SCHOOLS

ESPN 81 SAGARIN

Wichita State

From X to the Rave, Cheese and the Bookend Forwards (Antoine Carr and Cliff Levingston), there's been no shortage of talent or creativity through the years at Wichita State. There's also been no dearth of enthusiasm: More than 6.5 million fans have made Charles Koch Arena—the Roundhouse—one of the destinations opposing teams least like to visit. The Shockers' 585–261 home record attests to that.

BEST TEAM: 1963-64 With two future NBA players (and New York Knicks teammates) in its frontcourt—Dave "the Rave" Stallworth (26.5 ppg) and Nate Bowman (12.8 rpg)—the 23–6 Shockers defeated nine Top-20 opponents. Entering the NCAA Tournament as the No. 5-ranked team in the nation, Wichita State beat Creighton before falling to Kansas State in the Midwest Regional final.

BEST PLAYER: F Xavier McDaniel (1981-85) Known simply as X, McDaniel was a supremely athletic 6'7" power forward. He was the first player in NCAA history to top the nation in scoring (27.2 ppg) and rebounding (14.8 rpg) in the same season, his All-America year of 1984-85. Twice the Missouri Valley's Player of the Year, McDaniel finished as the Shockers' all-time leading rebounder (1,359) and second-leading scorer (2,152).

BEST COACH: Ralph Miller (1951-64) He took over a 9–16 Wichita State team after coaching at a local high school and brought his star player, Cleo Littleton, with him. (Littleton still ranks as the program's leading scorer.) In Miller's third season, the Shockers went 27–4 and reached the NIT. Miller went 220–133 in 13 seasons at Wichita State, then won 437 more games at Iowa and Oregon State to secure his place in the Naismith Hall of Fame.

GAME FOR THE AGES: On March 15, 1981, the Shockers were trailing favored Iowa, 40-25, in a second-round NCAA Tournament game on their home floor, when a boisterous Roundhouse crowd inspired a furious rally. WSU went on a 15-0 run and tied the game at 56 with :05 left, at which point Iowa was assessed a technical for calling a timeout it didn't have. Randy Smithson's two free throws gave the crazed crowd its unforgettable victory.

HEARTBREAKER: After falling to defending champ UCLA in the 1965 Final Four, 108-89, the Shockers met Princeton and Bill Bradley in the third-place game. The outcome was shocking, indeed. Bradley hit 22 of 29 from the field and 14 of 15 from the line for 58 points in the 118-82 blowout. Wichita State did not return to the Tournament for another 11 seasons.

FIERCEST RIVAL: There are few teams Shockers fans love to hate more than Creighton. Maybe that's because the Bluejays have somehow managed to resist WSU's homecourt advantage, winning nearly half their games at the Roundhouse. They also lead the Shockers 5–1 in MVC tournament games and have won 34 of their last 41 meetings.

FANFARE AND HOOPLA: Credit much of Wichita State's home-court advantage to the creativity of fans of the yellow and black: W-shaped hand gestures made during opponents' free throws and three-point launches; shouts of "black" to punctuate the singing of the alma mater; synchronized heckles during opposing player introductions—*So what? Who's that? Big deal! Who cares?*—and so on.

Xavier McDaniel was the first player in NCAA history to top the nation in scoring (27.2 ppg) and rebounding (14.8 rpg) in the same season.

FAN FAVORITE: F Lynbert "Cheese" Johnson (1975-79) Screams of "*Cheeese!*" would greet Johnson's introduction at the Roundouse for four seasons. At 6'5", Johnson was undersized for a "big" forward, but he could shake and bake like a latter-day Earl Monroe.

CONSENSUS ALL-AMERICAS

1964 **Dave Stallworth,** F
1985 **Xavier McDaniel,** F

FIRST-ROUND PRO PICKS

1965 **Dave Stallworth,** New York (5)
1965 **Nate Bowman,** Cincinnati (9)
1982 **Cliff Levingston,** Detroit (9)
1983 **Antoine Carr,** Detroit (8)
1985 **Xavier McDaniel,** Seattle (4)

PROFILE

Wichita State University, Wichita, KS
Founded: 1895 as Fairmount College
Enrollment: 14,442 (11,323 undergraduate)
Colors: Yellow and black
Nickname: Shockers
Current arena: Charles Koch Arena, opened in 2003 (10,478)
Previous: Henry Levitt Field House, a.k.a. the Roundhouse, 1955-2003 (10,656); Henrion (Memorial) Gymnasium, 1921-55 (2,000); the Forum, 1909-21 (3,800)

First game: Jan. 31, 1906
All-time record: 1,307-1,127 (.537)
Total weeks in AP Top 20/25: 79
Current conference: Missouri Valley (1945-)
Conference titles:
Missouri Valley: 6 (1964, '65, '76, '81, '83, 2006)
Conference tournament titles:
Missouri Valley: 2 (1985, '87)
NCAA Tournament appearances: 8
Sweet 16s (since 1975): 2
Final Fours: 1
NIT appearances: 10

TOP 5

G **Warren Armstrong** (1965-68)
G **Cleo Littleton** (1951-55)
F **Xavier McDaniel** (1981-85)
F **Dave Stallworth** (1962-65)
C **Cliff Levingston** (1979-82)

RECORDS

	GAME		SEASON		CAREER	
POINTS	47	Antoine Carr, vs. Southern Illinois (March 5, 1983)	844	Xavier McDaniel (1984-85)	2,164	Cleo Littleton (1951-55)
POINTS PER GAME			27.2	Xavier McDaniel (1984-85)	24.2	Dave Stallworth (1962-65)
REBOUNDS	29	Terry Benton, vs. North Texas (Feb. 6, 1971)	460	Xavier McDaniel (1984-85)	1,359	Xavier McDaniel (1981-85)
ASSISTS	16	Joe Griffin, vs. Oral Roberts (Jan. 6, 1988)	194	Warren Armstrong (1967-68)	429	Warren Armstrong (1965-68)

SEASON REVIEW

EASON	W-L	CONF.	SCORING	COACH	RECORD	
06-14	32-61		*No winning seasons until 1910-11 (7-6); worst year in 1912-13 (1-11)*			
14-15	4-10			Harry Buck		
15-16	10-5			Harry Buck	14-15	.483
16-17	2-11			Lamar Hoover		
17-18	3-10			Lamar Hoover		
18-19	1-7			no coach		
919-20	8-8			Kenneth Cassidy	8-8	.500
920-21	16-2			Wilmer Elfrink	16-2	.889
921-22	12-4			Lamar Hoover		
922-23	13-7			Lamar Hoover	30-32	.484
923-24	10-12			Sam Hill		

SEASON	W-L	CONF.	SCORING	COACH	RECORD	
1924-25	9-9			Sam Hill	19-21	.475
1925-26	14-6			Leonard Umnus		
1926-27	19-2			Leonard Umnus		
1927-28	14-6			Leonard Umnus	47-14	.770
1928-29	16-6			Gene Johnson		
1929-30	14-4			Gene Johnson		
1930-31	18-5			Gene Johnson		
1931-32	13-7			Gene Johnson		
1932-33	14-2			Gene Johnson	75-24	.758
1933-34	no team					
1934-35	7-13			Lindsay Austin	7-13	.350

SEAS.	W-L	CONF.	POSTSEASON	SCORING		REBOUNDS		ASSISTS		COACH	RECORD	
935-36	12-12									Bill Hennigh		
936-37	9-12									Bill Hennigh		
937-38	10-13									Bill Hennigh		
938-39	9-12									Bill Hennigh		
939-40	10-8									Bill Hennigh		
940-41	9-11									Bill Hennigh	59-68	.465
1941-42	4-16									Jack Starrett	4-16	.200
1942-43	12-7									Mel Binford		
1943-44	no team											
1944-45	14-6									Mel Binford		
1945-46	14-9	6-4		Harold Beal	10.4					Mel Binford		
1946-47	8-17	2-10		Harold Beal	7.3					Mel Binford		
1947-48	12-13	1-9		Elvin Vaughn	8.6					Mel Binford	60-52	.536
1948-49	10-16	3-7		Rex McMurray	8.6					Ken Gunning		
1949-50	7-17	1-11		John Friedersdorf	13.3					Ken Gunning		
1950-51	9-16	5-9		John Friedersdorf	11.5					Ken Gunning	26-49	.347
1951-52	11-19	2-8		Cleo Littleton	18.5	Cleo Littleton	7.7	Gary Thompson	3.1	Ralph Miller		
1952-53	16-11	3-7		Cleo Littleton	18.3	Merv Carman	7.9			Ralph Miller		
1953-54	27-4	8-2	NIT FIRST ROUND	Cleo Littleton	18.2	Cleo Littleton	7.7			Ralph Miller		
1954-55	17-9	4-6		Cleo Littleton	21.2	Cleo Littleton	8.2			Ralph Miller		
1955-56	14-12	7-5		Bob Hodgson	17.5	Bob Hodgson	11.5			Ralph Miller		
1956-57	15-11	8-6		Joe Stevens	18.1	Don Woodworth	8.9			Ralph Miller		
1957-58	14-12	6-8		Joe Stevens	15.0	Al Tate	9.2			Ralph Miller		
1958-59	14-12	7-7		Al Tate	16.5	Al Tate	10.7			Ralph Miller		
1959-60	14-12	6-8		Al Tate	16.9	Ron Heller	10.9			Ralph Miller		
1960-61	18-8	6-6		Ron Heller	17.4	Gene Wiley	12.1			Ralph Miller		
1961-62	18-9	7-5	NIT FIRST ROUND	Ernie Moore	15.1	Gene Wiley	10.6			Ralph Miller		
1962-63	19-8	7-5	NIT FIRST ROUND	Dave Stallworth	22.6	Dave Stallworth	10.2			Ralph Miller		
1963-64	23-6	10-2	NCAA REGIONAL FINALS	Dave Stallworth	26.5	Dave Stallworth	10.1	Dave Stallworth	4.6	Ralph Miller	220-133	.623
1964-65	21-9	11-3	NCAA FOURTH PLACE	Dave Stallworth	25.0	Dave Stallworth	12.1	Kelly Pete	3.5	Gary Thompson		
1965-66	17-10	9-5	NIT QUARTERFINALS	Jamie Thompson	22.0	Warren Armstrong	12.0	Warren Armstrong	4.6	Gary Thompson		
1966-67	14-12	9-5		Jamie Thompson	17.8	Warren Armstrong	8.6	Warren Armstrong	4.4	Gary Thompson		
1967-68	12-14	7-9		Ron Washington	19.3	Warren Armstrong	11.6	Warren Armstrong	7.5	Gary Thompson		
1968-69	11-15	7-9		Greg Carney	21.0	Jim Givens	8.0	Ron Mendell	3.5	Gary Thompson		
1969-70	8-18	3-13		Greg Carney	23.2	Ron Harris	6.8	Preston Carrington	2.8	Gary Thompson		
1970-71	10-16	3-11		Ron Harris	18.7	Terry Benton	16.8	Preston Carrington	3.5	Gary Thompson	93-94	.497
1971-72	16-10	6-8		Ron Harris	18.3	Terry Benton	14.0	Ron Harris	3.9	Harry Miller		
1972-73	10-16	6-8		Bob Wilson	17.7	Rich Morsden	8.1	Bob Wilson	3.3	Harry Miller		
1973-74	11-15	6-7		Bob Wilson	20.0	Rich Morsden	9.2	Cal Bruton	2.9	Harry Miller		
1974-75	11-15	6-8		Robert Elmore	17.3	Robert Elmore	11.6	Cal Bruton	6.1	Harry Miller		
1975-76	18-10	10-2	NCAA FIRST ROUND	Robert Gray	13.3	Robert Elmore	10.1	Cal Bruton	5.1	Harry Miller		
1976-77	18-10	7-5		Lynbert Johnson	17.1	Robert Elmore	15.8	Bob Trogele	4.4	Harry Miller		
1977-78	13-14	8-8		Lynbert Johnson	19.0	Lynbert Johnson	10.0	Bob Trogele	3.3	Harry Miller	97-90	.519
1978-79	14-14	8-8		Lynbert Johnson	22.2	Lynbert Johnson	10.6	Ronnie Ryer	4.5	Gene Smithson		
1979-80	17-12	9-7	NIT FIRST ROUND	Cliff Levingston	15.7	Cliff Levingston	10.1	Randy Smithson	5.4	Gene Smithson		
1980-81	26-7	12-4	NCAA REGIONAL FINALS	Cliff Levingston	18.5	Cliff Levingston	11.4	Tony Martin	5.6	Gene Smithson		
1981-82	23-6	12-4		Antoine Carr	16.0	Cliff Levingston	10.2	Tony Martin	5.2	Gene Smithson		
1982-83	25-3	17-1		Antoine Carr	22.6	Xavier McDaniel	14.4	James Gibbs	3.5	Gene Smithson		
1983-84	18-12	11-5	NIT FIRST ROUND	Xavier McDaniel	20.6	Xavier McDaniel	13.1	Aubrey Sherrod	2.7	Gene Smithson		
1984-85	18-13	11-5	NCAA FIRST ROUND	Xavier McDaniel	27.2	Xavier McDaniel	14.8	Aubrey Sherrod	4.1	Gene Smithson		
1985-86	14-14	7-9		Gus Santos	15.0	Sasha Radunovich	7.3	Lew Hill	2.8	Gene Smithson	155-81	.657
1986-87	22-11	9-5	NCAA FIRST ROUND	Henry Carr	11.8	Henry Carr	7.0	Joe Griffin	3.9	Eddie Fogler		
1987-88	20-10	11-3	NCAA FIRST ROUND	Sasha Radunovich	14.1	Sasha Radunovich	7.2	Joe Griffin	6.0	Eddie Fogler		
1988-89	19-11	10-4	NIT SECOND ROUND	Steve Grayer	14.0	Steve Grayer	8.3	Paul Guffrovich	4.5	Eddie Fogler	61-32	.656
1989-90	10-19	6-8		John Cooper	17.0	John Cooper	7.2	Paul Guffrovich	3.5	Mike Cohen		
1990-91	14-17	7-9		John Cooper	20.8	Claudius Johnson	6.8	Robert George	4.2	Mike Cohen		
1991-92	8-20	6-12		John Smith	12.8	John Smith	7.4	K.C. Hunt	3.7	Mike Cohen	32-56	.364
1992-93	10-17	7-11		Jimmy Bolden	13.4	John Smith	5.8	K.C. Hunt	3.5	Scott Thompson		
1993-94	9-18	6-12		Jamie Arnold	11.7	Jamie Arnold	9.0	Keith Stricklen	4.1	Scott Thompson		
1994-95	13-14	6-12		L.D. Swanson	14.6	Jamie Arnold	9.7	L.D. Swanson	5.4	Scott Thompson		
1995-96	8-21	4-14		Darin Miller	9.7	Larry Callis	8.7	Melvin McKey	5.6	Scott Thompson	40-70	.364
1996-97	14-13	8-10		Jamie Arnold	15.0	Jamie Arnold	9.1	Terry Hankton	3.7	Randy Smithson		
1997-98	16-15	11-7		Jason Perez	13.5	Roosevelt Overstreet	5.7	Terry Hankton	4.0	Randy Smithson		
1998-99	13-17	6-12		Maurice Evans	22.6	Jason Perez	5.5	Jason Perez	3.0	Randy Smithson		
1999-2000	12-17	5-13		Jason Perez	20.2	Jason Perez	7.0	Jason Perez	3.0	Randy Smithson	55-62	.470
2000-01	9-19	4-14		Terrell Benton	12.8	O.J. Robinson	7.5	C.C. McFall	3.9	Mark Turgeon		
2001-02	15-15	9-9		Randy Burns	12.1	Troy Mack	6.9	C.C. McFall	2.8	Mark Turgeon		
2002-03	18-12	12-6	NIT OPENING ROUND	Randy Burns	15.1	Jamar Howard	5.8	Craig Steven	2.7	Mark Turgeon		
2003-04	21-11	12-6	NIT FIRST ROUND	Jamar Howard	13.8	Jamar Howard	5.8	Fridge Holman	5.8	Mark Turgeon		
2004-05	22-10	12-6	NIT SECOND ROUND	Randy Burns	12.1	Jamar Howard	5.8	Adam Liberty	2.9	Mark Turgeon		
2005-06	26-9	14-4	NCAA REGIONAL SEMIFINALS	Paul Miller	13.1	Paul Miller	6.6	P.J. Couisnard	3.0	Mark Turgeon		
2006-07	17-14	8-10		Kyle Wilson	13.7	P.J. Couisnard, R. Martin	5.8	Matt Braeuer	3.3	Mark Turgeon	128-90	.587
2007-08	11-20	4-14		P.J. Couisnard	13.4	Ramon Clemente	7.9	Gal Mekel	3.7	Gregg Marshall		
2008-09	17-17	8-10		Clevin Hannah	11.2	Ramon Clemente	7.2	Clevin Hannah	4.3	Gregg Marshall	28-37	.431

ESPN 190 SAGARIN

WILLIAM AND MARY

The Tribe boasts a century of hoops history—with zero NCAA Tournaments to show for it. At least recent seasons have provided excitement: From 2006 to '08, W&M enjoyed its first back-to-back .500-or-above teams in 23 years and made a near-miraculous run to its first CAA tournament final in '08 before losing to George Mason.

BEST TEAM: 1982-83 W&M went 9–0 in conference play to win the regular-season ECAC South crown. And even though the team lost to James Madison in a thrilling conference tournament final, the Tribe still earned its first and only postseason berth in school history—a trip to the NIT, where W&M lost by six to Virginia Tech in the first round.

BEST PLAYER: C Chet Giermak (1946-50) The two-time All-America was a scoring machine: In his final three seasons, he led the Tribe in scoring average (17.1 ppg as a sophomore, 21.8 ppg as a junior, 20.8 ppg as a senior) while guiding the school to a 60–29 record. No wonder his No. 32 hangs in the rafters of Kaplan Arena.

BEST COACH: Bill Chambers (1957-66) He's best known for holding the NCAA single-game record for rebounds (51). But Chambers also led the Tribe with 113 wins as a coach, including an upset over fourth-ranked West Virginia in 1960, ending the Mountaineers' 56-game Southern Conference winning streak.

GAME FOR THE AGES: On Dec. 7, 1977, the Tribe upset No. 2-ranked North Carolina, 78-75. Before the game, the school introduced as captain senior John Kratzer, who hadn't been able to play since his sophomore season because he was battling cancer.

FIERCEST RIVAL: Old Dominion, just 55 minutes away, was once an offshoot of W&M, but it's a stronger, dominant younger brother now: The Tribe has gone just 16–59 against the Monarchs. That includes a 5–18 record since 2000, despite William and Mary fans' recent efforts to don green-and-gold body paint and pack Kaplan Arena (5,284 seats were filled for the Jan. 26, 2008, game against ODU, the most since 1998).

SEASON REVIEW

SEAS.	W-L	CONF.	COACH	SEAS.	W-L	CONF.	COACH
1906-48	*341-314*	*0-18 in 1936-37*		**1961-62**	7-17	5-11	Bill Chambers
1948-49	24-10	10-3	Bernard E. Wilson	**1962-63**	15-9	10-5	Bill Chambers
1949-50	23-9	12-4	Bernard E. Wilson	**1963-64**	9-13	5-9	Bill Chambers
1950-51	20-11	13-6	Bernard E. Wilson	**1964-65**	12-13	6-8	Bill Chambers
1951-52	15-13	10-6	H. Lester Hooker Jr.	**1965-66**	13-12	8-3	Bill Chambers
1952-53	10-13	6-13	Boyd Baird	**1966-67**	14-11	8-5	Warren Mitchell
1953-54	9-14	6-5	Boyd Baird	**1967-68**	6-18	4-10	Warren Mitchell
1954-55	11-14	7-5	Boyd Baird	**1968-69**	6-20	3-8	Warren Mitchell
1955-56	12-14	9-7	Boyd Baird	**1969-70**	11-16	5-7	Warren Mitchell
1956-57	9-18	7-11	Boyd Baird	**1970-71**	11-16	7-3	Warren Mitchell
1957-58	15-14	9-9	Bill Chambers	**1971-72**	10-17	6-4	Warren Mitchell
1958-59	13-11	7-7	Bill Chambers	**1972-73**	10-17	5-6	Ed Ashnault
1959-60	15-11	10-5	Bill Chambers	**1973-74**	9-18	5-6	Ed Ashnault[a]
1960-61	14-10	9-6	Bill Chambers	**1974-75**	16-12	6-5	George Balanis

SEAS.	W-L	CONF.	SCORING		COACH	RECORD	
1975-76	15-13	8-3	John Lowenhaupt	16.0	George Balanis		
1976-77	16-14	7-4	John Lowenhaupt	17.3	George Balanis	50-43	.538
1977-78	16-10		John Lowenhaupt	19.4	Bruce Parkhill		
1978-79	9-17		Scott Whitley	12.4	Bruce Parkhill		
1979-80	12-15		Scott Whitley	13.4	Bruce Parkhill		
1980-81	16-12		Scott Whitley	10.6	Bruce Parkhill		
1981-82	16-12		Keith Cieplicki	12.6	Bruce Parkhill		
1982-83	20-9	9-0 ■	Keith Cieplicki	16.0	Bruce Parkhill	89-75	.543
1983-84	14-14	6-4	Keith Cieplicki	15.3	Barry Parkhill		
1984-85	16-12	9-5	Keith Cieplicki	20.2	Barry Parkhill		
1985-86	8-20	3-11	Scott Coval	12.2	Barry Parkhill		
1986-87	5-22	2-12	Tim Trout	12.8	Barry Parkhill	43-68	.387
1987-88	10-19	5-9	Tim Trout	16.9	Chuck Swenson		
1988-89	5-23	2-12	Tom Bock	16.3	Chuck Swenson		
1989-90	6-22	2-12	Scott Smith	14.6	Chuck Swenson		
1990-91	13-15	6-8	Thomas Roberts	16.8	Chuck Swenson		
1991-92	10-19	3-11	Thomas Roberts	15.5	Chuck Swenson		
1992-93	14-13	6-8	Thomas Roberts	17.4	Chuck Swenson		
1993-94	4-23	2-12	Kurt Small	15.7	Chuck Swenson	62-134	.316
1994-95	8-19	6-8	Kurt Small	17.9	Charlie Woollum		
1995-96	10-16	6-10	Carl Parker	15.2	Charlie Woollum		
1996-97	12-16	8-8	Bobby Fitzgibbons	14.6	Charlie Woollum		
1997-98	20-7	13-3	Randy Bracy	17.2	Charlie Woollum		
1998-99	8-19	3-13	Jim Moran	13.2	Charlie Woollum		
1999-2000	11-17	6-10	Jim Moran	14.1	Charlie Woollum	69-94	.423
2000-01	11-17	7-9	Jim Moran	13.6	Rick Boyages		
2001-02	10-19	7-11	Mike Johnson	11.5	Rick Boyages		
2002-03	12-16	7-11	Adam Hess	20.1	Rick Boyages	33-52	.388
2003-04	7-21	4-14	Adam Hess	20.3	Tony Shaver		
2004-05	8-21	3-15	Corey Cofield	13.2	Tony Shaver		
2005-06	8-20	3-15	Calvin Baker	11.6	Tony Shaver		
2006-07	15-15	8-10	Adam Payton	13.8	Tony Shaver		
2007-08	17-16	10-8	Laimis Kisielius	11.3	Tony Shaver		
2008-09	10-20	5-13	David Schneider	14.1	Tony Shaver	65-113	.365

[a] **Ed Ashnault (6-14) and George Balanis (3-4) both coached during the 1973-74 season.**

■ **NIT appearance**

PROFILE

The College of William and Mary, Williamsburg, VA
Founded: 1693
Enrollment: 7,741 (5,792 undergraduate)
Colors: Green, gold and silver
Nickname: Tribe
Current arena: Kaplan Arena at William and Mary Hall, opened in 2005 (8,600)
Previous: William & Mary Hall, 1970-2005 (8,600); Blow Gym, 1924-70 (2,500); Old Gymnasium, 1905-24 (N/A)
First game: 1906
All-time record: 1,072-1,248 (.462)
Total weeks in AP Top 20/25: 0

Current conference: Colonial Athletic Association (1982-)
Conference titles:
Eastern Collegiate Athletic South: 1 (1983)
CAA: 1 (1998 [tie])
Conference tournament titles: 0
NCAA Tournament appearances: 0
NIT appearances: 1

TOP 5

G **Randy Bracy** (1995-99)
G **Keith Cieplicki** (1981-85)
F **Bill Chambers** (1950-53)
F **Adam Hess** (2001-04)
C **Chet Giermak** (1946-50)

RECORDS

	GAME		SEASON		CAREER	
POINTS	49	Jeff Cohen, vs. Richmond (Feb. 25, 1961)	740	Chet Giermak (1948-49)	2,052	Chet Giermak (1946-50)
POINTS PER GAME			27.3	John Mahoney (1954-55)	20.6	Bob Sherwood (1967-68, '69-70)
REBOUNDS	51	Bill Chambers, vs. Virginia (Feb. 14, 1953)	509	Bill Chambers (1951-52)	1,679	Jeff Cohen (1957-61)
ASSISTS	15	Scott Coval, vs. George Mason (Feb. 23, 1985)	168	Scott Coval (1984-85)	409	Scott Coval (1982-86)

ESPN 261 SAGARIN

WINTHROP

The Eagles played their first home game in 1978 at a junior high gym. It was just a few years after Winthrop first admitted men, after nearly a century as an all-girls school. If that sounds like a tough way to start, wait until you hear where the story leads: nine conference tourney crowns, eight NCAA Tournaments and one luck-of-the-Irish slice of March Madness.

BEST TEAM: 2006-07 In coach Gregg Marshall's final season, the self-proclamed Junkyard Dogs won 29 games, and went undefeated both at home and in the Big South. They took hustle to a new level: Marshall rewarded the hardest worker in each game with an action figure of the '80s wrestler Junkyard Dog.

BEST PLAYER: G TYSON WATERMAN (1995-97, 1998-2000) His passing and three-point touch made the Eagles' balanced offense hum, while his quick hands and smarts fueled the defense. He ranks fourth on Winthrop's all-time list in points (1,461), steals (186) and assists (469), and was a two-time first-team All-Big South selection.

BEST COACH: GREGG MARSHALL (1998-2007) With an emphasis on defense, rebounding and strong point-guard play, Marshall transformed a fledgling program into a mid-major powerhouse. He inherited a team that had endured eight straight losing seasons and led it to six 20-win seasons, seven NCAA Tournament appearances and a 112–18 home record.

GAME FOR THE AGES: In the first round of the 2007 NCAA Tournament, a day before St. Patrick's Day, the No. 11-seed Eagles squandered an 18-point second-half lead over No. 6-seed Notre Dame, but rode a late rally and Craig Bradshaw's 24 points to pull off a 74-64 upset. Afterward, Marshall gave every member of the team a Junkyard Dog.

FIERCEST RIVAL: It's no coincidence that the Eagles' first sellout at the Winthrop Coliseum came against Coastal Carolina on Jan. 27, 2007. The two teams have battled for Big South supremacy since 1985-86, with the Chanticleers winning four regular-season crowns and the Eagles seven. Coastal Carolina leads the series, 35–32.

SEASON REVIEW

SEAS.	W-L	CONF.		SCORING		COACH	RECORD	
1978-79	25-10					Nield Gordon		
1979-80	17-13					Nield Gordon		
1980-81	31-8					Nield Gordon		
1981-82	21-12					Nield Gordon		
1982-83	14-21					Nield Gordon		
1983-84	21-11					Nield Gordon		
1984-85	11-16					Nield Gordon		
1985-86	20-9	5-3				Nield Gordon	160-100	.615
1986-87	8-20	7-7		Ted Houpt	17.6	Steve Vacendak		
1987-88	17-13	5-7		Greg Washington	12.9	Steve Vacendak		
1988-89	16-13	5-7		Greg Washington	15.2	Steve Vacendak		
1989-90	19-10	6-6		Shaun Wise	16.6	Steve Vacendak		
1990-91	8-20	5-9		George Henson	12.3	Steve Vacendak		
1991-92	6-22	2-12		Mark Hailey	15.1	Steve Vacendak	74-98	.430
1992-93	14-16	5-11		Eddie Gay	17.2	Dan Kenney		
1993-94	4-23	3-15		LaShawn Coulter	16.9	Dan Kenney		
1994-95	7-20	4-12		David McMahan	15.5	Dan Kenney		
1995-96	7-19	6-8		David McMahan	14.5	Dan Kenney		
1996-97	12-15	5-9		Tyson Waterman	16.1	Dan Kenney		
1997-98	7-20	4-8		Marcus Laster	10.8	Dan Kenney	51-113	.311
1998-99	21-8	9-1	●	Heson Groves	11.9	Gregg Marshall		
1999-2000	21-9	11-3	●	Greg Lewis	15.7	Gregg Marshall		
2000-01	18-13	11-3	●	Marcus Stewart	12.2	Gregg Marshall		
2001-02	19-12	10-4	●	Greg Lewis	15.4	Gregg Marshall		
2002-03	20-10	11-3		Tyrone Walker	13.2	Gregg Marshall		
2003-04	16-12	10-6		Tyrone Walker	12.9	Gregg Marshall		
2004-05	27-6	15-1	●	Torrell Martin	13.1	Gregg Marshall		
2005-06	23-8	13-3	●	Torrell Martin	13.8	Gregg Marshall		
2006-07	29-5	14-0	●	Michael Jenkins	14.8	Gregg Marshall	194-83	.700
2007-08	22-12	10-4	●	Michael Jenkins	13.9	Randy Peele		
2008-09	11-19	9-9		Charles Corbin	9.5	Randy Peele	33-31	.516

● NCAA Tournament appearance

PROFILE

Winthrop University, Rock Hill, SC
Founded: 1886
Enrollment: 6,400 (5,120 undergraduate)
Colors: Garnet and gold
Nickname: Eagles
Current arena: Winthrop Coliseum, opened in 1982 (6,100)
Previous: Sullivan Jr. High School, 1978-82 (N/A)
First game: 1978
All-time record: 512-425 (.546)
Total weeks in AP Top 20/25: 2

Current conference: Big South (1985-)
Conference titles:
Big South: 7 (1999, 2002 [tie], '03, '05, '06, '07, '08 [tie])
Conference tournament titles:
Big South: 9 (1988, '99, 2000, '01, '02, '05, '06, '07, '08)
NCAA Tournament appearances: 8
NIT appearances: 0

TOP 5

G **Torrell Martin** (2003-07)
G **Tyson Waterman** (1995-97, 1998-2000)
F **Charles Brunson** (1979-82)
F **Greg Lewis** (1999-2002)
C **Craig Bradshaw** (2003-07)

RECORDS

RECORDS	GAME		SEASON		CAREER	
POINTS	45	Melvin Branham, vs. Charleston Southern (Jan. 10, 1994)	875	Charles Brunson (1980-81)	1,850	Charles Brunson (1979-82)
POINTS PER GAME			22.4	Charles Brunson (1980-81)	20.1	Charles Brunson (1979-82)
REBOUNDS	23	Allen Washington, vs. Piedmont (Nov. 30, 1985)	453	Charles Brunson (1980-81)	913	Charles Brunson (1979-82)
ASSISTS	17	Rick Riese, vs. Limestone (Feb. 12, 1981)	317	Rick Riese (1980-81)	656	Rick Riese (1978-81)

ESPN 28 SAGARIN

WISCONSIN

Wisconsin was an NCAA champion before Kansas, Kentucky, UCLA or North Carolina ever was. Okay, so 1941 was a while ago. In more recent years, 1941 legends Gene Englund and John Kotz have been joined by Badgers heroes such as Michael Finley, Devin Harris and Alando Tucker. And UW has appeared in the Tournament every year from 1999 through 2009.

BEST TEAM: 1940-41 The Badgers' only national championship came after an inauspicious start to the season. UW dropped three of its first eight games, including a 44-27 defeat at the hands of Big Ten archrival Minnesota. But that turned out to be Wisconsin's last loss. The Badgers were led by All-America captain Gene Englund, who set a Big Ten scoring record with 162 points in UW's 12 conference games, and NCAA Tournament MOP John Kotz, only a sophomore at the time.

BEST PLAYER: F ALANDO TUCKER (2002-07) Although he tops Wisconsin's all-time scoring list with 2,217 points, the Illinois native did a lot more than score. He was the leader—and a first-team All-America—of the first Badgers team to reach No. 1 in the AP poll. During his time in Madison the Badgers made two strong Tournament runs, reaching the Sweet 16 in 2003 and the Elite Eight in '05. By the time his college career was done, Tucker had scored in double figures for 43 straight games.

BEST COACH: BO RYAN (2001-) He continued reawakening memories of 1941 when he took his first Badgers team—expected to finish near the bottom of the Big Ten—to the Big Dance instead. Wisconsin has been a postseason powerhouse ever since, topping out at No. 1 for a spell during the 2006-07 season. Through 2008-09, Ryan's career winning percentage of .726 ranked second only to UNC's Roy Williams among coaches with at least 500 victories.

GAME FOR THE AGES: In front of a sellout crowd in its home arena on March 5, 2003, Wisconsin denied Illinois its third straight Big Ten regular-season title when, with 0.4 seconds left and the game tied 59-59, Devin Harris missed the first of two free throws—then canned the game-winner. It was the Badgers' first outright conference championship since 1947.

HEARTBREAKER: The No. 8-seed Badgers were the story of the 2000 NCAA Tournament, as they clawed their way to the Final Four by beating three higher-seeded teams: Arizona (1), LSU (4) and Purdue (6). In the national semis against Big Ten rival Michigan State (another No. 1 seed), Wisconsin had Mateen Cleaves stymied with a 1-for-7 shooting night, but Mo Peterson stepped up with 20 points and the Spartans beat the Badgers for the fourth time that season, 53-41, to claim a spot in the Final.

FIERCEST RIVAL: Minnesota has always been Wisconsin's nemesis, even beyond their annual football fight for Paul Bunyan's axe. The rivalry got especially heated after 1997, when Ty Calderwood hit two free throws to upset the No. 2-ranked Gophers, 66-65, and snap their 12-game winning streak. Minnesota leads the series all-time, 99–88.

FANFARE AND HOOPLA: Meet one of America's best-named student sections—the Grateful Red. Decked out in tie-dyed T's, they've been described by coach Ryan as "hearty." That's like describing the Grand Canyon as "deep." Former Michigan State star Cleaves might use a less printable word, after Red fans serenaded him with "Ninety-Nine Bottles of Beer" following his 1998 bust for underage drinking.

FAN FAVORITE: G TANNER BRONSON (2004-08) Bronson worked his tail off to get promoted from student team manager to scholarship benchwarmer. The fans would call for their beloved T-Bron during blowouts.

CONSENSUS ALL-AMERICAS

1905	**C.D. McLees**, G
1905	**Chris Steinmetz**, F
1907	**Arthur Frank**, G
1908	**Hugh Harper**, G
1908, '09	**Helmer Swenholt**, F
1911	**Walter Scoville**, G/F
1912	**Otto Stangel**, F
1913	**Allen Johnson**, F
1914	**Carl Harper**, G
1914	**Eugene Van Gent**, C
1915, '16	**George Levis**, F
1916, '18	**Bill Chandler**, C
1917	**Harold G. Olsen**, G
1918	**Eber Simpson**, G
1941	**Gene Englund**, C
1942	**John Kotz**, F
2007	**Alando Tucker**, F

FIRST-ROUND PRO PICKS

1947	**Glen Selbo**, Toronto (2)
1950	**Don Rehfeldt**, Baltimore (2)
1970	**Al Henry**, Philadelphia (12)
1980	**Wes Matthews**, Washington (14)
1995	**Michael Finley**, Phoenix (21)
1997	**Paul Grant**, Minnesota (20)
2004	**Devin Harris**, Washington (5)
2007	**Alando Tucker**, Phoenix (29)

PROFILE

University of Wisconsin-Madison, Madison, WI
Founded: 1848
Enrollment: 39,672 (27,375 undergraduate)
Colors: Cardinal and white
Nickname: Badgers
Current arena: Kohl Center, opened in 1998 (17,190)
Previous: UW Field House, 1930-98 (12,000), Old Red Gym, 1904-30 (N/A)
First game: Jan. 21, 1899
All-time record: 1,363-1,110 (.551)
Total weeks in AP Top 20/25: 141

Current conference: Big Ten (1905-)
Conference titles:
Big Ten: 17 (1907 [tie], '08 [tie], '12 [tie], '13, '14, '16, '18, '21 [tie], '23 [tie], '24[tie], '29 [tie], '35 [tie], '41, '47, 2002 [tie], '03, '08)
Conference tournament titles:
Big Ten: 2 (2004, '08)
NCAA Tournament appearances: 15
Sweet 16s (since 1975): 4
Final Fours: 2
Titles: 1 (1941)
NIT appearances: 4

TOP 5

G	**Devin Harris** (2001-04)
G/F	**Michael Finley** (1991-95)
F	**Chris Steinmetz** (1902-05)
F	**Alando Tucker** (2002-07)
C	**Don Rehfeldt** (1946-50)

RECORDS

RECORDS	GAME		SEASON		CAREER	
POINTS	42	Michael Finley, vs. Eastern Michigan (Dec. 10, 1994); Ken Barnes, vs. Indiana (March 8, 1965)	716	Alando Tucker (2006-07)	2,217	Alando Tucker (2002-07)
POINTS PER GAME			23.8	Clarence Sherrod (1970-71)	19.6	Clarence Sherrod (1968-71)
REBOUNDS	30	Paul Morrow, vs. Purdue (Jan. 3, 1953)	344	Jim Clinton (1950-51)	904	Claude Gregory (1977-81)
ASSISTS	13	Tracy Webster, vs. Michigan (Feb. 26, 1992); Wes Matthews, vs. Army (Dec. 30, 1979)	179	Tracy Webster (1992-93)	501	Tracy Webster (1991-94)

EASON REVIEW

EASON	W-L	CONF.	SCORING	COACH	RECORD	SEASON	W-L	CONF.	SCORING		COACH	RECORD
99-1918	*200-56*		*Undefeated (15-0) in 1911-12, Walter "Doc" Meanwell's first year.*			1928-29	15-2	10-2			Walter "Doc" Meanwell	
8-19	5-11	3-9		Guy Lowman		1929-30	15-2	8-2			Walter "Doc" Meanwell	
9-20	15-5	7-5		Guy Lowman	34-19 .642	1930-31	8-9	4-8			Walter "Doc" Meanwell	
20-21	13-4	8-4		Walter "Doc" Meanwell		1931-32	8-10	3-9			Walter "Doc" Meanwell	
21-22	14-5	8-4		Walter "Doc" Meanwell		1932-33	7-13	4-8			Walter "Doc" Meanwell	
22-23	12-3	11-1		Walter "Doc" Meanwell		1933-34	14-6	8-4			W. "Doc" Meanwell	246-99-1 .712
23-24	11-5-1	8-4		Walter "Doc" Meanwell		1934-35	15-5	9-3			Harold Foster	
24-25	6-11	3-9		Walter "Doc" Meanwell		1935-36	11-9	4-8			Harold Foster	
25-26	8-9	4-8		Walter "Doc" Meanwell		1936-37	8-12	3-9			Harold Foster	
26-27	10-7	7-5		Walter "Doc" Meanwell		1937-38	10-10	5-7			Harold Foster	
27-28	13-4	9-3		Walter "Doc" Meanwell		1938-39	10-10	4-8	Dave Dupee	7.7	Harold Foster	

EAS.	W-L	CONF.	POSTSEASON	SCORING		REBOUNDS		ASSISTS		COACH	RECORD	
39-40	5-15	3-9		Gene Englund	10.0					Harold Foster		
40-41	**20-3**	**11-1**	**NATIONAL CHAMPION**	**Gene Englund**	**13.2**					**Harold Foster**		
41-42	14-7	10-5		John Kotz	15.5					Harold Foster		
42-43	12-9	6-6		John Kotz	14.7					Harold Foster		
43-44	12-9	9-3		Ray Patterson	14.0					Harold Foster		
44-45	10-11	4-8		Ray Patterson	10.7					Harold Foster		
945-46	4-17	1-11		Bob Cook	13.8					Harold Foster		
946-47	16-6	9-3	NCAA REGIONAL SEMIFINALS	Bob Cook	14.7					Harold Foster		
947-48	12-8	7-5		Bob Cook	12.4					Harold Foster		
948-49	12-10	5-7		Don Rehfeldt	17.3					Harold Foster		
949-50	17-5	9-3		Don Rehfeldt	19.8					Harold Foster		
950-51	10-12	7-7		Ab Nicholas	16.6	Jim Clinton	15.6			Harold Foster		
951-52	10-12	5-9		Ab Nicholas	16.4	Paul Morrow	13.2			Harold Foster		
952-53	13-9	10-8		Paul Murrow	16.0					Harold Foster		
953-54	12-10	6-8		Dick Cable	13.7	Paul Morrow	9.6			Harold Foster		
954-55	10-12	5-9		Dick Cable	20.1	Curt Mueller	5.8			Harold Foster		
955-56	6-16	4-10		Dick Miller	19.5	Curt Mueller	9.4			Harold Foster		
956-57	5-17	3-11		Bob Litzow	16.1	Ray Gross	7.9			Harold Foster		
957-58	8-14	3-11		Bob Litzow	14.7	Ray Gross	7.1			Harold Foster		
958-59	3-19	1-13		Bob Barneson	12.3	Bob Barneson	7.2			Harold Foster	265-267	.498
959-60	8-16	4-10		Tom Hughbanks	13.0	Fred Clow	9.8			John Erickson		
960-61	7-17	4-10		Tom Hughbanks	13.1	Tom Hughbanks	8.6			John Erickson		
961-62	17-7	10-4		Ken Siebel	16.3	Tom Gwyn	8.0			John Erickson		
962-63	14-10	7-7		Jack Brens	17.8	Jack Brens	12.8			John Erickson		
963-64	8-16	2-12		Ken Gustafson	14.9	Ken Gustafson	9.8			John Erickson		
964-65	9-13	4-10		Mark Zubor	15.7	Ken Barnes	8.8			John Erickson		
965-66	11-13	6-8		Ken Gustafson	13.8	Joe Franklin	9.8			John Erickson		
966-67	13-11	8-6		Chuck Nagle	19.3	Joe Franklin	12.0			John Erickson		
967-68	13-11	7-7		Joe Franklin	22.7	Joe Franklin	13.9			John Erickson	100-114	.467
968-69	11-13	5-9		James Johnson	19.2	James Johnson	8.8			John Powless		
969-70	10-14	5-9		Clarence Sherrod	22.4	Albert Henry	11.0			John Powless		
970-71	9-15	4-10		Clarence Sherrod	23.8	Glen Richgels	10.6			John Powless		
971-72	13-11	6-8		Leon Howard	16.4	Kim Hughes	10.0			John Powless		
972-73	11-13	5-9		Leon Howard	18.0	Kim Hughes	12.5			John Powless		
973-74	16-8	8-6		Kim Hughes	15.3	Kim Hughes	11.1	Marcus McCoy	3.1	John Powless		
974-75	8-18	5-13		Bruce McCauley	16.7	Dale Koehler	10.1	Bruce McCauley	3.5	John Powless		
975-76	10-16	4-14		Dale Koehler	19.4	Dale Koehler	10.1	James Smith	3.3	John Powless	88-108	.449
976-77	9-18 ⊗	7-11		James Gregory	15.9	James Gregory	10.0	Bob Falk, Arnold Gaines	3.4	Bill Cofield		
977-78	8-19	4-14		Wes Matthews	14.5	Joe Chrnelich	6.7	Arnold Gaines	3.1	Bill Cofield		
978-79	12-15	6-12		Wes Matthews	18.5	Claude Gregory	8.7	Wes Matthews	3.9	Bill Cofield		
979-80	15-14	7-11		Wes Matthews	19.6	Claude Gregory	8.8	Wes Matthews	4.2	Bill Cofield		
980-81	11-16	5-13		Claude Gregory	20.4	Claude Gregory	9.2	Dan Hastings	3.1	Bill Cofield		
981-82	6-21 ⊗	3-15		Brad Sellers	14.0	Brad Sellers	9.4	Carl Golston	3.4	Bill Cofield	61-103	.372▼
982-83	8-20 ⊗	3-15		Cory Blackwell	18.3	Brad Sellers	7.8	Rick Olson	3.0	Steve Yoder		
983-84	8-20 ⊗	4-14		Cory Blackwell	18.9	Cory Blackwell	8.7	Scott Roth	3.1	Steve Yoder		
984-85	14-14	5-13		Scott Roth	18.3	J.J. Weber	5.8	Mike Heineman	4.4	Steve Yoder		
985-86	12-16	4-14		Rick Olson	20.4	Rod Ripley	6.9	Mike Heineman	4.5	Steve Yoder		
986-87	14-17	4-14		J.J. Weber	15.1	J.J. Weber	8.1	Mike Heineman	4.9	Steve Yoder		
987-88	12-16	6-12		Trent Jackson	19.5	Danny Jones	4.7	Tom Molaski	3.7	Steve Yoder		
988-89	18-12	8-10	NIT SECOND ROUND	Danny Jones	20.4	Danny Jones	4.7	Tom Molaski	3.6	Steve Yoder		
989-90	14-17	4-14		Danny Jones	17.7	Patrick Tompkins	6.4	Willie Simms	3.2	Steve Yoder		
990-91	15-15	8-10	NIT SECOND ROUND	Willie Simms	14.5	Patrick Tompkins	8.8	Willie Simms	3.4	Steve Yoder		
991-92	13-18	4-14		Tracy Webster	17.3	Michael Finley	4.9	Tracy Webster	4.9	Steve Yoder	128-165	.437
992-93	14-14	7-11	NIT FIRST ROUND	Michael Finley	22.1	Michael Finley	5.8	Tracy Webster	6.4	Stu Jackson		
993-94	18-11	8-10	NCAA SECOND ROUND	Michael Finley	20.4	Rashard Griffith	8.5	Tracy Webster	5.9	Stu Jackson	32-25	.561
994-95	13-14	7-11		Michael Finley	20.5	Rashard Griffith	10.8	Michael Finley	4.0	Stan Van Gundy	13-14	.481
995-96	17-15 ⊗	8-10	NIT SECOND ROUND	Sam Okey	13.2	Sam Okey	6.8	Sam Okey	3.1	Dick Bennett		
996-97	18-10	11-7	NCAA FIRST ROUND	Paul Grant	12.5	Sam Okey	8.5	Ty Calderwood	3.7	Dick Bennett		
997-98	12-19	3-13		Sean Mason	15.5	Sean Daugherty	6.2	Hennssy Auriantal	2.2	Dick Bennett		
998-99	22-10	9-7	NCAA FIRST ROUND	Sean Mason	16.8	Andy Kowske	4.9	Ty Calderwood	3.3	Dick Bennett		
999-2000	22-14	8-8	NCAA NATIONAL SEMIFINALS	Mark Vershaw	11.8	Andy Kowske	6.2	Mark Vershaw	3.3	Dick Bennett		
000-01	18-11	9-7	NCAA FIRST ROUND	Roy Boone	12.8	Andy Kowske	5.4	Mike Kelley	3.1	Dick Bennett[a]	93-69	.574▼
001-02	19-13	11-5	NCAA SECOND ROUND	Kirk Penney	15.1	Mike Wilkinson	5.3	Travon Davis	3.9	Bo Ryan		
002-03	24-8	12-4	NCAA REGIONAL SEMIFINALS	Kirk Penney	16.2	Mike Wilkinson	6.8	Kirk Penney	3.1	Bo Ryan		
003-04	25-7	12-4	NCAA SECOND ROUND	Devin Harris	19.5	Mike Wilkinson	6.8	Devin Harris	4.4	Bo Ryan		
004-05	25-9	11-5	NCAA REGIONAL FINALS	Mike Wilkinson	14.3	Mike Wilkinson	7.4	Sharif Chambliss	2.8	Bo Ryan		
005-06	19-12	9-7	NCAA FIRST ROUND	Alando Tucker	19.0	Brian Butch	6.0	Kammron Taylor	2.4	Bo Ryan		
006-07	30-6	13-3	NCAA SECOND ROUND	Alando Tucker	19.9	Brian Butch	5.9	Michael Flowers	2.9	Bo Ryan		
007-08	31-5	16-2	NCAA REGIONAL SEMIFINALS	Brian Butch	12.4	Brian Butch	6.6	Michael Flowers	2.7	Bo Ryan		
008-09	20-13	10-8	NCAA SECOND ROUND	Marcus Landry	12.7	Joe Krabbenhoft	6.7	Trevon Hughes	2.8	Bo Ryan	193-73	.726

[a] Dick Bennett (2-1) and Brad Soderberg (16-10) both coached during the 2000-01 season.

⊗ Records don't reflect games forfeited or vacated. For adjusted records, see p. 521.

▼ Coaches' records adjusted to reflect games forfeited or vacated: Bill Cofield, 63-101, .384; Dick Bennett, 94-68, .580. For yearly totals, see p. 521.

ESPN 134 SAGARIN

WISCONSIN-GREEN BAY

Was there ever a bad time to follow the Phoenix? In the 1970s, coach Dave Buss started the program by stockpiling 20-win seasons. In the 1980s and '90s, the father-and-son act of Dick and Tony Bennett took Wisconsin-Green Bay to the NCAAs, and Jeff Nordgaard got them to even greater heights—ask Jason Kidd and Cal just how high.

BEST TEAM: 1993-94 During the regular season, Nordgaard, John Martinez, Logan Vander Velden and the rest of the Phoenix almost beat Glenn Robinson's Purdue (74-69) and Tim Duncan's Wake Forest (61-58 OT), before reeling off quality wins against NCAA-bound Marquette, NC State and Oregon. In the Tourney, they ambushed Kidd's California team, 61-57, in the first round before losing by five to No. 15-ranked Syracuse.

BEST PLAYER: G TONY BENNETT (1988-92) Coach Dick Bennett's son ended his career as the UWGB and Mid-Continent Conference leader in points (2,285) and assists (601) and tops in the NCAA in three-point percentage (.497). Tony played briefly in the NBA and went on to coach at Washington State and Virginia.

BEST COACH: DICK BENNETT (1985-95) A master program builder (he also upgraded UW-Stevens Point and Wisconsin), Bennett inherited a 4–24 team barely four seasons into D1 play and in time created a Mid-Con giant. He had five 20-win seasons and coached the Phoenix to two NITs and three NCAA Tournaments.

GAME FOR THE AGES: Cal entered the 1994 Tourney with a No. 16 ranking and T-shirts that read "In It to Win It." Instead, it was one-and-done for the Golden Bears courtesy of the Phoenix. Nordgaard (24 points) and Martinez (13) paced Green Bay to a 19-point lead. Cal fought back, gaining the lead with 2:44 left, but missed their last five shots. The Phoenix held Kidd and Lamond Murray to a combined 10 of 38 from the floor in the 61-57 win.

FIERCEST RIVAL: The Phoenix used to dominate the rivalry with UW-Milwaukee, going 17–4 until a blowout loss in 2000. The Panthers have gone 13–7 since.

SEASON REVIEW

SEAS.	W-L	CONF.	SCORING		COACH	RECORD
1969-70	16-8		Ray Willis	24.5	Dave Buss	
1970-71	23-5		Ray Willis	28.6	Dave Buss	
1971-72	21-7		Dennis Woelffer	20.3	Dave Buss	
1972-73	28-4		Tom Jones	15.3	Dave Buss	
1973-74	20-8		Tom Jones	18.9	Dave Buss	
1974-75	10-15		Bryan Boettcher	14.9	Dave Buss	
1975-76	21-8		Ron Ripley	14.8	Dave Buss	
1976-77	26-3		Ron Ripley	14.2	Dave Buss	
1977-78	30-2		Tom Anderson	14.8	Dave Buss	
1978-79	24-8		Ron Ripley	15.5	Dave Buss	
1979-80	15-12		Joe Mauel	15.7	Dave Buss	
1980-81	23-9		Joe Mauel	14.5	Dave Buss	
1981-82	14-13		Tom Brown	10.7	Dave Buss	271-102 .727
1982-83	9-19	2-11	Tom Brown	12.6	Dick Lien	
1983-84	9-19	5-9	Richard Sims	16.8	Dick Lien	
1984-85	4-24	1-13	Richard Sims	13.8	Dick Lien	22-62 .262
1985-86	5-23	3-11	Alonzo Skanes	13.3	Dick Bennett	
1986-87	15-14	8-6	Richard Sims	14.3	Dick Bennett	
1987-88	18-9	9-5	Frank Nardi	13.0	Dick Bennett	
1988-89	14-14	6-6	Tony Bennett	19.1	Dick Bennett	
1989-90	24-8	9-3 ■	Tony Bennett	16.6	Dick Bennett	
1990-91	24-7	13-3 ●	Tony Bennett	21.5	Dick Bennett	
1991-92	25-5	14-2 ■	Tony Bennett	20.2	Dick Bennett	
1992-93	13-14	9-7	Dean Rondorf	14.2	Dick Bennett	
1993-94	27-7	15-3 ●	Jeff Nordgaard	15.6	Dick Bennett	
1994-95	22-8	11-4 ●	Jeff Nordgaard	18.6	Dick Bennett	187-109 .632
1995-96	25-4	16-0 ●	Jeff Nordgaard	22.6	Mike Heideman	
1996-97	14-14	10-6	Matt Hill	9.5	Mike Heideman	
1997-98	17-12	7-7	Wayne Walker	13.0	Mike Heideman	
1998-99	20-11	9-5	B.J. LaRue	13.2	Mike Heideman	
1999-2000	14-16	6-8	Jerry Carstensen	13.9	Mike Heideman	
2000-01	11-17	4-10	Chris Sager	11.8	Mike Heideman	
2001-02	9-21	4-12	DeVante Blanks	12.7	Mike Heideman	110-95 .537
2002-03	10-20	4-12	Matt Rohde	12.8	Tod Kowalczyk	
2003-04	17-11	11-5	Brandon Morris, M. King	10.9	Tod Kowalczyk	
2004-05	17-11	10-6	Benito Flores	13.4	Tod Kowalczyk	
2005-06	15-16	8-8	Ryan Evanochko	15.8	Tod Kowalczyk	
2006-07	18-15	7-9	Ryan Evanochko	15.0	Tod Kowalczyk	
2007-08	15-15	9-9	Mike Schachtner	15.8	Tod Kowalczyk	
2008-09	22-11	13-5	Ryan Tillema	17.2	Tod Kowalczyk	114-99 .535

● NCAA Tournament appearance ■ NIT appearance

PROFILE

University of Wisconsin-Green Bay, Green Bay, WI
Founded: 1965
Enrollment: 4,357 (4,013 undergraduate)
Colors: Green, white and red
Nickname: Phoenix
Current arena: Resch Center, opened in 2002 (9,279)
Previous: Brown County Veterans Memorial Arena, 1969-2002 (5,248)
First game: Dec. 3, 1969
All-time record: 704-467 (.601)
Total weeks in AP Top 20/25: 3

Current conference: Horizon League (1994-)
Conference titles:
Mid-Continent: 2 (1992, '94)
Midwestern Collegiate: 1 (1996)
Conference tournament titles:
Mid-Continent: 2 (1991, '94)
Midwestern Collegiate: 1 (1995)
NCAA Tournament appearances: 4
NIT appearances: 2

CONSENSUS ALL-AMERICAS

1978 **Tom Anderson** (D2), G
1979 **Ron Ripley** (D2), F/C

TOP 5

G **Tom Anderson** (1974-78)
G **Tony Bennett** (1988-92)
F **Jeff Nordgaard** (1992-96)
F **Ray Willis** (1969-71)
F/C **Ron Ripley** (1975-79)

RECORDS

RECORDS	GAME		SEASON		CAREER	
POINTS	45	Ray Willis, vs. Wisconsin-Parkside (Feb. 9, 1971)	802	Ray Willis (1970-71)	2,285	Tony Bennett (1988-92)
POINTS PER GAME			28.6	Ray Willis (1970-71)	26.8	Ray Willis (1969-71)
REBOUNDS	21	Nate Barnes, vs. Central Michigan (Nov. 26, 1982)	373	Nate Barnes (1980-81)	947	Dennis Woelffer (1969-73)
ASSISTS	19	Frank Nardi, vs. Northern Iowa (Feb. 24, 1986)	193	Tom Anderson (1976-77)	601	Tony Bennett (1988-92)

ESPN 209 SAGARIN

WISCONSIN-MILWAUKEE

A small college until the 1970s, UWM tried Division I briefly (1973-80) before moving up permanently in 1990-91. After several seasons as a doormat, UWM was catapulted into the national spotlight during the successive coaching regimes of Bo Ryan and Bruce Pearl.

BEST TEAM: 2004-05 Pearl's Panthers regularly wore down opponents with a high-energy three-guard offense and a quick trapping defense, to go 26–6, win the Horizon League and notch the school's first two NCAA Tourney wins. Winning 19 of their last 21, the Panthers leaned on go-to scorers Ed McCants (17.4 ppg) and Joah Tucker (16.2).

BEST PLAYER: G/F Clay Tucker (1999-2003) His team's best defender, Tucker (no relation to Joah Tucker) became the program's all-time leading scorer (1,788 points) with his ability to penetrate or pull up for the quick jumper. Sometimes listed as a forward, Tucker was the main ball handler, especially in clutch time: His 2002 buzzer-beater three against Butler gave UWM its first win over a ranked opponent. The next season he scored 23 to beat Butler again, this time for the Horizon title, and lead the Panthers to their first NCAA Tournament.

BEST COACH: Bruce Pearl (2001-05) After Bo Ryan resuscitated the program (1999-2001), Pearl brought the team national acclaim. With an up-tempo offense and zone press, his Eagles went 86–38 (51–13 in conference), nabbed an NIT berth and two NCAA Tournament bids.

GAME FOR THE AGES: Facing the co-Big East regular-season champ, Boston College, in the second round of the 2005 NCAA Tournament, the Panthers fell behind 11-0. But they turned up the defensive heat—and hit 20 of 22 from the charity stripe—to stun the Eagles, 83-75, and advance to the Sweet 16. There UWM lost to Illinois, 77-63, but got a taste of the big time.

FIERCEST RIVAL: Wisconsin-Green Bay is the top in-state rival, but matchups with Butler have provided more drama. The two programs are the only ones to win Horizon League regular-season titles since 2002, with WMU winning in 2004, '05 and '06.

SEASON REVIEW

SEAS.	W-L	CONF.	COACH	SEAS.	W-L	CONF.	COACH
1896-47	*399-325*	*16-0 in '40-41 under Guy Penwell*		1960-61	8-12		Russ Rebholz
1947-48	13-8		Guy Penwell	1961-62	4-17		Russ Rebholz
1948-49	10-12		Guy Penwell	1962-63	4-17		Ray Krzoska
1949-50	20-7		Guy Penwell	1963-64	3-18		Ray Krzoska
1950-51	6-15		Guy Penwell	1964-65	9-14		Ray Krzoska
1951-52	5-15		Guy Penwell	1965-66	15-10		Ray Krzoska
1952-53	9-12		Russ Rebholz	1966-67	14-11		Ray Krzoska
1953-54	14-7		Russ Rebholz	1967-68	16-11		Ray Krzoska
1954-55	11-10		Russ Rebholz	1968-69	15-11		Ray Krzoska
1955-56	13-8		Russ Rebholz	1969-70	14-12		Ray Krzoska
1956-57	12-7		Russ Rebholz	1970-71	13-10		Charles Parsley
1957-58	13-7		Russ Rebholz	1971-72	15-11		Charles Parsley
1958-59	17-4		Russ Rebholz	1972-73	18-8		Charles Parsley
1959-60	18-4		Russ Rebholz	1973-74	14-12		Bill Klucas

SEAS.	W-L	CONF.	SCORING		COACH	RECORD	
1974-75	8-18		Raymond Nixon	14.7	Bill Klucas	22-30	.423
1975-76	11-15		Glen Allen	12.8	Bob Gottlieb		
1976-77	19-8		Gerald Hardnett	17.1	Bob Gottlieb		
1977-78	15-12		Gerald Hardnett	20.6	Bob Gottlieb		
1978-79	8-18		Gerald Hardnett	14.7	Bob Gottlieb		
1979-80	9-17		Bob Flood	16.3	Bob Gottlieb	62-70	.470
1980-81	13-13		Ricky Trotter	18.5	Bob Voight		
1981-82	20-6		Kevin Jones	25.4	Bob Voight		
1982-83	18-6		Kevin Jones	26.1	Bob Voight	51-25	.671
1983-84	6-20		Steve Pitrof	19.2	Ray Swetalla		
1984-85	9-17		John Smilanich	16.0	Ray Swetalla		
1985-86	10-17		Erik Schten	13.9	Ray Swetalla		
1986-87	8-20		Erik Schten	16.8	Ray Swetalla	33-74	.308
1987-88	16-12		Clarence Wright	20.0	Steve Antrim		
1988-89	24-7		Andy Ronan	17.5	Steve Antrim		
1989-90	10-18		Andy Ronan	17.2	Steve Antrim		
1990-91	18-10		Von McDade	29.6	Steve Antrim		
1991-92	20-8		Craig Greene	16.9	Steve Antrim		
1992-93	23-4		C. Greene, Marc Mitchell	17.3	Steve Antrim		
1993-94	10-17	7-11	Michael Hughes	20.1	Steve Antrim		
1994-95	3-24	2-13	Shannon Smith	24.5	Steve Antrim	124-100	.554
1995-96	9-18	5-11	Roderick Johnson	14.5	Ric Cobb		
1996-97	8-20	4-12	Pat McCabe	12.4	Ric Cobb		
1997-98	3-24	2-12	Pat McCabe	9.9	Ric Cobb		
1998-99	8-19	5-9	Chad Angeli	14.9	Ric Cobb	28-81	.257
1999-2000	15-14	6-8	Chad Angeli	16.6	Bo Ryan		
2000-01	15-13	7-7	Clay Tucker	13.9	Bo Ryan	30-27	.526
2001-02	16-13	11-5	Clay Tucker	17.6	Bruce Pearl		
2002-03	24-8	13-3 ●	Clay Tucker	18.3	Bruce Pearl		
2003-04	20-11	13-3 ■	Dylan Page	20.9	Bruce Pearl		
2004-05	26-6	14-2 ●	Ed McCants	17.4	Bruce Pearl	86-38	.694
2005-06	22-9	12-4 ●	Joah Tucker	16.5	Rob Jeter		
2006-07	9-22	6-10	Avery Smith	15.5	Rob Jeter		
2007-08	14-16	9-9	Paige Paulsen	13.3	Rob Jeter		
2008-09	17-14	11-7	Tone Boyle	13.2	Rob Jeter	62-61	.504

● NCAA Tournament appearance ■ NIT appearance

PROFILE

University of Wisconsin-Milwaukee, Milwaukee, WI
Founded: 1885
Enrollment: 29,358 (24,414 undergraduate)
Colors: Black and gold
Nickname: Panthers
Current arena: U.S. Cellular Arena, opened in 1950 (12,700)
Previous: Wisconsin Center Arena, 1995-98 (12,700); MECCA, 1992-95 (12,700); Klotsche Center, 1977-92, 1998-2003 (5,000)
First game: 1896
All-time record: 1,206-1,109 (.521)

Total weeks in AP Top 20/25: 0
Current conference: Horizon League (1994-)
Conference titles:
Horizon: 3 (2004, '05, '06)
Conference tournament titles:
Horizon: 3 (2003, '05, '06)
NCAA Tournament appearances: 3
Sweet 16s (since 1975): 1
NIT appearances: 1

TOP 5

G **Gerald Hardnett** (1975-79)
G **Ed McCants** (2003-05)
G/F **Clay Tucker** (1999-2003)
F **Dylan Page** (2000-04)
F/C **Adrian Tigert** (2001-02, '03-06)

RECORDS

	GAME		SEASON		CAREER	
POINTS	50	Von McDade, vs. Illinois (Dec. 3, 1990)	830	Von McDade (1990-91)	1,788	Clay Tucker (1999-2003)
POINTS PER GAME			29.6	Von McDade (1990-91)	29.6	Von McDade (1990-91)
REBOUNDS	18	Nathan Schrameyer, vs. Southeast Missouri St. (1994-95)	462	Larry Reed (1966-67)	1,529	Larry Reed (1959-60, '64-67)
ASSISTS	13	Marc Mitchell, vs. Northeast Illinois (1992-93); vs. Wisconsin-Parkside (1991-92)	189	Marc Mitchell (1992-93)	448	Gerald Hardnett (1975-79)

ESPN 323 SAGARIN

WOFFORD

Wofford has a steep hill to climb. One of the smallest institutions in Division I (1,400 students), it's predominantly a football school that plays its basketball in the tough Southern Conference. The tension shows: The Terriers have not achieved a winning record since joining D1 in 1995-96.

BEST TEAM: 1993-94 Playing as an independent back in 1991-92, Wofford went 21–7 but was snubbed by the D2 tournament committee. In 1993-94, led by Matt Allen and three other senior starters, the Terriers again won 21, highlighted by a win over D1 rival Furman. This time, the selection committee rewarded the team with its first D2 tournament bid.

BEST PLAYER: C Ellerbe "Daddy" Neal (1949-53) The first dominant big man in South Carolina, Neal, a shade under seven feet, set school records that are considered untouchable: 57 points in a single game, 32.6 ppg and 26.5 rpg in 1952-53, a 22.0 career rebounding average. To this day, Wofford post players are compared to Neal—and they never measure up.

BEST COACH: Gene Alexander (1958-77) He was a tough, old-school coach (283-268) who was loved by all and is revered still. In 1975 Alexander was inducted into the NAIA Hall of Fame.

GAME FOR THE AGES: Playing in just its second Southern Conference tournament, Wofford was a big underdog heading into its March 3, 2000, quarterfinal game against Davidson, but the Terriers kept it close. With a couple of ticks left on the clock, Ian Chadwick hit a 15-footer to seal the Terriers' 65-64 win and their first (and only) semifinals appearance. (They lost to the College of Charleston, 74-64.)

FIERCEST RIVAL: Wofford, an affiliate of the Methodist church, and Furman, originally affiliated with the Baptists, are separated by less than 40 miles. They played in South Carolina's first intercollegiate football game in 1889, so it's only fitting that the rivalry would carry to other sports. On the court, Furman leads the series, 81–42.

SEASON REVIEW

SEAS.	W-L	CONF.	COACH	SEAS.	W-L	CONF.	COACH
1906-48	*229-198*	*18-6 in '47-48, J. Robertson's second*		1961-62	11-15		Gene Alexander
1948-49	11-8		Joel Robertson	1962-63	14-14		Gene Alexander
1949-50	10-13		Joel Robertson	1963-64	24-9		Gene Alexander
1950-51	14-8		Joel Robertson	1964-65	22-8		Gene Alexander
1951-52	16-8		Joel Robertson	1965-66	17-8		Gene Alexander
1952-53	14-9		Joel Robertson	1966-67	21-10		Gene Alexander
1953-54	8-16		Joel Robertson	1967-68	12-17		Gene Alexander
1954-55	15-12		Joel Robertson	1968-69	2-28		Gene Alexander
1955-56	13-13		Joel Robertson	1969-70	10-18		Gene Alexander
1956-57	10-15		Joel Robertson	1970-71	18-13		Gene Alexander
1957-58	13-10		Joel Robertson	1971-72	14-16		Gene Alexander
1958-59	10-14		Gene Alexander	1972-73	12-15		Gene Alexander
1959-60	25-6		Gene Alexander	1973-74	19-14		Gene Alexander
1960-61	9-18		Gene Alexander	1974-75	22-11		Gene Alexander

SEAS.	W-L	CONF.	SCORING		COACH	RECORD
1975-76	15-13		Collie Feemster	563	Gene Alexander	
1976-77	6-21		Reggie Gosnell	489	Gene Alexander	283-268 .514
1977-78	8-24		Ronnie Howard	474	Wayne Earhardt	
1978-79	14-17		Ronnie Harris	674	Wayne Earhardt	
1979-80	7-25		Mike Howard	543	Wayne Earhardt	
1980-81	19-12		Mike Howard	621	Wayne Earhardt	
1981-82	12-18		James Blair	596	Wayne Earhardt	
1982-83	14-15		James Blair	609	Wayne Earhardt	
1983-84	11-17		Robert Mickle	415	Wayne Earhardt	
1984-85	21-11		Robert Mickle	509	Wayne Earhardt	106-139 .433
1985-86	15-12		John McGinnis	463	Richard Johnson	
1986-87	17-10		Matt Mayes	488	Richard Johnson	
1987-88	10-17		Stephon Blanding	384	Richard Johnson	
1988-89	17-11		Greg O'Dell	624	Richard Johnson	
1989-90	17-11		Stephon Blanding	399	Richard Johnson	
1990-91	16-12		Greg O'Dell	621	Richard Johnson	
1991-92	21-7		Greg O'Dell	569	Richard Johnson	
1992-93	17-9		John McGinnis	340	Richard Johnson	
1993-94	21-6		Matt Allen	490	Richard Johnson	
1994-95	17-9		Two Morton	470	Richard Johnson	
1995-96	4-22		Terry Gilyard	411	Richard Johnson	
1996-97	7-20		Seth Chadwick	376	Richard Johnson	
1997-98	9-18	6-8	Ian Chadwick	323	Richard Johnson	
1998-99	11-16	8-8	Ian Chadwick	16.8	Richard Johnson	
1999-2000	14-16	8-8	Ian Chadwick	16.8	Richard Johnson	
2000-01	12-16	7-9	Ian Chadwick	20.4	Richard Johnson	
2001-02	11-18	5-11	Mike Lenzly	14.4	Richard Johnson	236-230 .506
2002-03	14-15	8-8	Mike Lenzly	15.7	Mike Young	
2003-04	9-20	4-12	Howard Wilkerson	13.8	Mike Young	
2004-05	14-14	7-9	Adrien Borders	12.6	Mike Young	
2005-06	11-18	6-9	Howard Wilkerson	13.9	Mike Young	
2006-07	10-20	5-13	Shane Nichols	15.6	Mike Young	
2007-08	16-16	8-12	Shane Nichols	13.5	Mike Young	
2008-09	16-14	12-8	Noah Dahlman	17.8	Mike Young	90-117 .435

Cumulative totals listed when per game averages not available.

PROFILE

Wofford College, Spartanburg, SC
Founded: 1854
Enrollment: 1,400 undergraduates
Colors: Old gold and black
Nickname: Terriers
Current arena: Benjamin Johnson Arena, opened in 1981 (3,500)
Previous: Andrews Fieldhouse, 1930-80 (2,200)
First game: 1906
All-time record: 1,068-1,064 (.501)
Total weeks in AP Top 20/25: 0

Current conference: Southern (1997-)
Conference titles: 0
Conference tournament titles: 0
NCAA Tournament appearances: 0
NIT appearances: 0

FIRST-ROUND PRO PICKS

1953 **Ellerbe "Daddy" Neal,** Syracuse (7)

TOP 5

G **Ian Chadwick** (1997-2001)
G **Greg O'Dell** (1988-92)
F **James Blair** (1980-83)
F **George Lyons** (1961-65)
C **Ellerbe "Daddy" Neal** (1949-53)

RECORDS

RECORDS	GAME		SEASON		CAREER	
POINTS	57	Ellerbe "Daddy" Neal, vs. Erskine (Feb. 10, 1953)	750	Ellerbe "Daddy" Neal (1952-53)	2,521	George Lyons (1961-65)
POINTS PER GAME			32.6	Ellerbe "Daddy" Neal (1952-53)	23.3	Ellerbe "Daddy" Neal (1949-53)
REBOUNDS	40	Don Fowler, vs. Mercer (Jan. 22, 1955); Ellerbe "Daddy" Neal, vs. Piedmont (Dec. 9, 1952)	609	Ellerbe "Daddy" Neal (1952-53)	1,500	Ellerbe "Daddy" Neal (1949-53)
ASSISTS	15	Antoine Saunders, vs. Allen (Feb. 18, 1987)	210	Antoine Saunders (1986-87)	582	Antoine Saunders (1983-87)

ESPN 170 SAGARIN

WRIGHT STATE

Appropriately for a school named after the Wright brothers, Raiders fans have enjoyed moments when their team has soared. NCAA Tournament appearances in 1993 and 2007 qualify. But even in less successful years, any team that can inspire the Raider Rowdies who fill the Ervin J. Nutter Center—a.k.a. the Nut House—is surely doing a few things right.

BEST TEAM: 1992-93 In just their sixth D1 season, the Raiders, led by Bill Edwards (25.2 ppg), won the Mid-Continent crown. WSU fans were so elated that they stormed the court and joined a player pileup that left guard Chris McGuire unconscious (he was okay later). Wright State made the NCAA Tournament as a No. 16 seed (and promptly lost, 97-54, to Indiana).

BEST PLAYER: F Bill Edwards (1989-93) His career numbers were 20.2 ppg and 8.0 rpg, and he was named the team's MVP in all four of his seasons. WSU made his legacy official when it retired his No. 42 jersey in 1997.

BEST COACH: Ralph Underhill (1978-96) A winning coach with a winning sense of humor, upon being inducted into Wright's Hall of Fame in 2003 Underhill said, "It's kinda nice being in before you're dead." He compiled a 356–162 record with the Raiders, including a 1983 upset of the University of the District of Columbia to win the D2 national championship.

GAME FOR THE AGES: On Dec. 30, 1999, unranked Wright State faced No. 8 Michigan State at the Nutter Center. WSU was coming off three straight losing seasons. But Kevin Melson scored 16 points and Marcus May hit 14, including two free throws with :13 left that sealed a 53-49 win. That victory looked even better after MSU beat Florida for the NCAA championship.

FIERCEST RIVAL: It's not that Wright State fans are jealous of Butler, exactly. But every now and then one holds up a "We hate Butler" sign. Why? Well, Butler *is* just two hours west on I-70, and the teams *have* been playing each other since 1994-95 (Butler leads 20–15). And Butler *did* go to the Big Dance eight times between 1997 and 2009. But it's not jealousy. Is it?

SEASON REVIEW

SEAS.	W-L	CONF.		SCORING		COACH	RECORD	
1970-71	7-17			Dave Magill	16.8	John Ross		
1971-72	9-14			Tim Walker	17.1	John Ross		
1972-73	17-5			Lyle Falknor	15.7	John Ross		
1973-74	17-8			Bob Grote	14.2	John Ross		
1974-75	15-10			Bob Grote	17.1	John Ross	65-54	.546
1975-76	20-8			Bob Grote	17.1	Marcus Jackson		
1976-77	11-16			Bob Schaefer	16.9	Marcus Jackson		
1977-78	14-13			Bob Schaefer	17.5	Marcus Jackson	45-37	.549
1978-79	20-8			Bob Schaefer	14.1	Ralph Underhill		
1979-80	25-3			Roman Welch	17.9	Ralph Underhill		
1980-81	25-4			Rodney Benson	21.9	Ralph Underhill		
1981-82	22-7			Stan Hearns	17.8	Ralph Underhill		
1982-83	28-4		◆	Gary Monroe	18.7	Ralph Underhill		
1983-84	19-9			Fred Moore	19.5	Ralph Underhill		
1984-85	22-7			Mark Vest	18.4	Ralph Underhill		
1985-86	28-3			Andy Warner	17.8	Ralph Underhill		
1986-87	20-8			Joe Jackson	16.5	Ralph Underhill		
1987-88	16-11			Joe Jackson	15.9	Ralph Underhill		
1988-89	17-11			Brad Smith	21.7	Ralph Underhill		
1989-90	21-7			Bill Edwards	15.4	Ralph Underhill		
1990-91	19-9			Bill Edwards	18.9	Ralph Underhill		
1991-92	15-13	9-7		Bill Edwards	20.9	Ralph Underhill		
1992-93	20-10	10-6	●	Bill Edwards	25.2	Ralph Underhill		
1993-94	12-18	9-9		Mike Nahar	15.4	Ralph Underhill		
1994-95	13-17	6-8		Vitaly Potapenko	19.2	Ralph Underhill		
1995-96	14-13	8-8		Vitaly Potapenko	20.7	Ralph Underhill	356-162	.687
1996-97	7-20	5-11		Keion Brooks	14.6	Jim Brown	7-20	.259
1997-98	10-18	3-11		Keion Brooks	17.1	Ed Schilling		
1998-99	9-18	4-10		Keion Brooks	20.7	Ed Schilling		
1999-2000	11-17	6-8		Kevin Melson	18.6	Ed Schilling		
2000-01	18-11	8-6		Kevin Melson	15.0	Ed Schilling		
2001-02	17-11	9-7		Cain Doliboa	16.8	Ed Schilling		
2002-03	10-18	4-12		Seth Doliboa	22.3	Ed Schilling	75-93	.446
2003-04	14-14	10-6		Vernard Hollins	16.3	Paul Biancardi		
2004-05	15-15	8-8		DaShaun Wood	15.2	Paul Biancardi		
2005-06	13-15	8-8		DaShaun Wood	17.9	Paul Biancardi	42-44	.488
2006-07	23-10	13-3	●	DaShaun Wood	19.6	Brad Brownell		
2007-08	21-10	12-6		Vaughn Duggins	13.8	Brad Brownell		
2008-09	20-13	12-6		Todd Brown	11.7	Brad Brownell	64-33	.660

● NCAA Tournament appearance ◆ Division II championship

PROFILE

Wright State University, Dayton, OH
Founded: 1964 as the Dayton Branch Campus of Miami and the Ohio State Universities
Enrollment: 17,074 (12,938 undergraduate)
Colors: Hunter green and gold
Nickname: Raiders
Current arena: Ervin J. Nutter Center, opened in 1990 (11,019)
Previous: Wright State PE Building, 1973-90 (3,200); Stebbins High School, 1970-72 (500)
First game: Nov. 20, 1970
All-time record: 654-443 (.596)

Total weeks in AP Top 20/25: 0
Current conference: Horizon League (1994-)
Conference titles:
Horizon: 1 (2007 [tie])
Conference tournament titles:
Mid-Continent: 1 (1993)
Horizon: 1 (2007)
NCAA Tournament appearances: 2
NIT appearances: 0

CONSENSUS ALL-AMERICAS

1981 **Rodney Benson** (D2), F
1986 **Mark Vest** (D2), F

FIRST-ROUND PRO PICKS

1996 **Vitaly Potapenko,** Cleveland (12)

TOP 5

G **Vernard Hollins** (2000-04)
G **DaShaun Wood** (2003-07)
F **Bill Edwards** (1989-93)
F **Bob Schaefer** (1975-79)
C **Vitaly Potapenko** (1994-96)

RECORDS

RECORDS	GAME		SEASON		CAREER	
POINTS	45	Bill Edwards, vs. Morehead State (Dec. 12, 1992)	757	Bill Edwards (1992-93)	2,303	Bill Edwards (1989-93)
POINTS PER GAME			25.2	Bill Edwards (1992-93)	20.2	Bill Edwards (1989-93)
REBOUNDS	22	Thad Burton, vs. Old Dominion (Nov. 18, 1997)	305	Thad Burton (1997-98)	907	Bill Edwards (1989-93)
ASSISTS	15	Lenny Lyons, vs. Kentucky State (Feb. 27, 1986); vs. Kentucky Wesleyan (Feb. 8, 1986)	259	Lenny Lyons (1985-86)	744	Mark Woods (1988-91, '92-93)

THE SCHOOLS

ESPN 63 SAGARIN

WYOMING

What is the story of Wyoming basketball? It's Ev Shelton's team winning the 1943 national championship; Kenny Sailors "inventing" the jump shot; Cowboy Fennis Dembo showing up UCLA superstar Reggie Miller; 6'7", 230-pound Reginald Slater playing like a seven-footer; Eric Leckner dominating in the post; Flynn Robinson dazzling at the point. In short, it's a history every bit as colorful as the state that has long defined the wild, wild West.

BEST TEAM: 1986-87 These 24–10 Cowboys edge out the 1943 national champions because they faced much tougher competition. Coach Jim Brandenburg's WAC champs took out Virginia in their NCAA Tournament opener, then knocked off UCLA, 78-68, as Dembo outgunned Miller, 41 points to 24. The Cowboys then lost to UNLV, but Dembo's performance (67 points in three Tourney games) landed him, in full cowboy regalia, on the cover of *Sports Illustrated*'s college hoops preview issue the following season.

BEST PLAYER: F FENNIS DEMBO (1984-88) His one-year career in the NBA was forgettable, but his college career was anything but. Wyoming's all-time leading scorer also ranks third in rebounds, fourth in assists and second in steals. In the 1986 NIT, he sat atop the rim after finishing with 19 points and 16 rebounds in a win over Clemson that sent Wyoming to the NIT semifinals. In his senior season he averaged 20.4 ppg, and scored 14 in the Cowboys' 119-115 first-round NCAA loss to high-rolling Loyola Marymount.

BEST COACH: EVERETT SHELTON (1939-59) Most eastern basketball fans knew cowboys only from the movies, before Shelton's posse thrilled the Madison Square Garden crowd by beating Georgetown for the 1943 NCAA championship. Shelton (328–201) had eight 20-plus-win seasons, and five of his teams won at least 25.

GAME FOR THE AGES: The NCAA championship was big, but in 1943 it was the NIT champ that was considered king of the sport—and that was St. John's. After the two tournaments (both of which culminated at Madison Square Garden), a special charity event, dubbed the World's Championship, was played, also at the Garden. Wyoming, led by Kenny Sailors—with his innovative jump shot—and Milo Komenich, beat the Johnnies, 52-47 in overtime.

HEARTBREAKER: In the 1986 WAC tournament final, host Wyoming faced Texas-El Paso with an NCAA berth at stake. The Cowboys led, 64-63, as UTEP missed its final shot—or so it seemed. Wyoming allowed UTEP's Juden Smith to get the rebound and his putback killed the Cowboys, 65-64.

FIERCEST RIVAL: The Border War between Colorado State and Wyoming—just 65 miles apart—has seen many great battles, none better than Wyoming's 81-78 triple-overtime victory at Fort Collins on Feb. 14, 1987. A three by Cowboy Reggie Fox forced a second overtime, and another by Turk Boyd forced the third OT. Wyoming leads the series, 127–83.

Fennis Dembo's one-year career in the NBA was forgettable, but his college career was anything but.

FANFARE AND HOOPLA: Wyoming has the highest university campus in the country—7,220 feet above sea level—and students like to brag about it. The Arena-Auditorium is sometimes referred to as the Dome of Doom, while a sign in the visitor's locker room asks, "How's your oxygen?"

FAN FAVORITE: G CHARLES "TUB" BRADLEY (1977-81) He led the Cowboys to an NCAA appearance that included a heartbreaking second-round loss to Illinois in 1981. The Wyoming faithful loved Bradley's outgoing personality; they could always trust Tub to be at games early to press the flesh and sign autographs.

CONSENSUS ALL-AMERICAS

1932, '34	**Les Witte**, F
1943	**Kenny Sailors**, G

FIRST-ROUND PRO PICKS

1949	**Ron Livingstone**, Baltimore (7)
1970	**Carl Ashley**, Utah (ABA)
1981	**Charles Bradley**, Boston (23)
1982	**Bill Garnett**, Dallas (4)
1988	**Eric Leckner**, Utah (17)
1995	**Theo Ratliff**, Detroit (18)

PROFILE

University of Wyoming, Laramie, WY
Founded: 1886
Enrollment: 12,067 (9,544 undergraduate)
Colors: Brown and gold
Nickname: Cowboys
Current arena: Arena-Auditorium, opened in 1982 (15,028)
Previous: War Memorial Fieldhouse, 1951-82 (10,580); Half Acre Gym, 1924-51 (4,000); Little Red Gym, 1904-24 (1,000)
First game: April 21, 1905
All-time record: 1,368-1,021 (.573)
Total weeks in AP Top 20/25: 38

Current conference: Mountain West (1999-)
Conference titles:
Rocky Mountain: 2 (1932, '34 [tie])
Big Seven: 4 (1941, '43, '46, '47)
Skyline Six: 1 (1949)
Skyline Eight: 3 (1952, '53, '58)
WAC: 5 (1967 [tie], '69 [tie], '81 [tie], '82, '86 [tie])
MWC: 2 (2001 [tie], '02)
Conference tournament titles:
WAC: 2 (1987, '88)
NCAA Tournament appearances: 14
Sweet 16s (since 1975): 1
Final Fours: 1
Titles: 1 (1943)

NIT appearances: 8
Semifinals: 1

TOP 5

G	**Charles Bradley** (1977-81)
G	**Flynn Robinson** (1962-65)
G	**Kenny Sailors** (1940-1943, '45-46)
F	**Fennis Dembo** (1984-88)
F	**Reginald Slater** (1988-92)

RECORDS

	GAME		SEASON		CAREER	
POINTS	51	Joe Capua, vs. Montana (Feb. 3, 1956)	701	Flynn Robinson (1964-65)	2,311	Fennis Dembo (1984-88)
POINTS PER GAME			27.0	Flynn Robinson (1964-65)	26.3	Flynn Robinson (1962-65)
REBOUNDS	27	Reginald Slater, vs. Troy (Dec. 14, 1991)	331	Reginald Slater (1990-91)	1,197	Reginald Slater (1988-92)
ASSISTS	15	Jay Straight, vs. Winthrop (Dec. 20, 2003)	183	Sean Dent (1986-87)	502	Sean Dent (1983-84, '85-88)

EASON REVIEW

EASON	W-L	CONF.	SCORING		COACH	RECORD	
5-14	24-33		*Oscar Prestegard averaged 15.2 ppg in 1909-10*				
4-15	2-4		Fulton Bellamy	21.0	Ralph Thacker	3-7	.300
5-16	3-2		Fulton Bellamy	20.0	John Corbett		
6-17	4-4		Harry Craig	14.6	John Corbett		
7-18	4-2		Milward Simpson	11.6	John Corbett		
8-19	7-2		Bob Burns	8.3	John Corbett		
9-20	10-1		Bob Burns	11.2	John Corbett		
20-21	3-4		Robert Fitske	9.4	John Corbett		
21-22	2-7		William Smyth	7.7	John Corbett		
22-23	2-6	0-6	Don Thompson	6.4	John Corbett		
23-24	2-13	1-7	Bill Lester	7.1	John Corbett	37-41	.474
1924-25	9-6	5-3	Cyril Fox	4.6	Stewart Clark		
1925-26	12-5	6-6	O.B. Koerfer	7.5	Stewart Clark		
1926-27	9-5	8-4	Don Harkins	11.2	Stewart Clark		
1927-28	13-8	9-3	O.B. Koerfer	8.0	Stewart Clark	43-24	.642
1928-29	15-4	11-3	Bob Outsen	11.7	George McLaren		
1929-30	13-6	7-3	Jim Jiacoletti	10.1	George McLaren	28-10	.737
1930-31	19-4	11-1	Les Witte	11.9	Willard Witte		
1931-32	18-2	12-0	Les Witte	11.9	Willard Witte		
1932-33	18-5	12-2	Les Witte	10.2	Willard Witte		
1933-34	26-3	14-0	Les Witte	12.0	Willard Witte		
1934-35	11-5	10-4	Willard West	7.8	Willard Witte		

SEAS.	W-L	CONF.	POSTSEASON	SCORING		REBOUNDS		ASSISTS		COACH	RECORD	
935-36	12-7	11-3		Lew Young	10.2					Willard Witte		
936-37	8-9	7-7		John Winterholler	8.2					Willard Witte		
937-38	12-5	8-4		Lew Young	13.5					Willard Witte		
938-39	10-11	7-5		Lew Young	11.0					Willard Witte	134-51	.724
939-40	6-10	3-9		Willie Rothman	10.5					Everett Shelton		
940-41	14-6	10-2	NCAA REGIONAL SEMIFINALS	Bill Strannigan	10.5					Everett Shelton		
941-42	15-5	9-3		Milo Komenich	11.7					Everett Shelton		
942-43	**31-2**	**4-0**	**NATIONAL CHAMPION**	**Milo Komenich**	**16.7**					**Everett Shelton**		
943-44	no team									Everett Shelton		
944-45	10-18	7-5		George Nostrand	9.9					Everett Shelton		
945-46	22-4	10-2		Milo Komenich	14.3					Everett Shelton		
946-47	22-6	11-1	NCAA REGIONAL SEMIFINALS	Jimmy Reese	11.7					Everett Shelton		
947-48	18-9	6-4	NCAA REGIONAL SEMIFINALS	John Pilch	9.7					Everett Shelton		
948-49	25-10	15-5	NCAA REGIONAL SEMIFINALS	John Pilch	10.8					Everett Shelton		
949-50	25-11	13-7		John Pilch	11.5					Everett Shelton		
950-51	26-11	13-7		George Radovich	13.6					Everett Shelton		
951-52	28-7	13-1	NCAA REGIONAL FINALS	George Radovich	12.9	Dick Haag	9.2	George Radovich	3.2	Everett Shelton		
952-53	20-10	12-2	NCAA REGIONAL SEMIFINALS	Bill Sharp	14.3	Ron Rivers	10.5			Everett Shelton		
953-54	19-9	10-4		Bill Sharp	12.3	Ron Rivers	7.8			Everett Shelton		
954-55	17-9	9-5		Harry Jorgensen	14.5	Harry Jorgensen	9.9			Everett Shelton		
955-56	7-19	5-9		Joe Capua	24.5	Dave Bradley	9.5			Everett Shelton		
956-57	6-19	4-10		Tony Windis	19.0	Dave Bradley	9.2			Everett Shelton		
957-58	13-14	10-4	NCAA FIRST ROUND	Tony Windis	20.9	John Bertolero	9.5			Everett Shelton		
958-59	4-22	1-13		Tony Windis	24.3	Clarence Lively	9.6			Everett Shelton	328-201	.620
959-60	5-19	2-12		Terry Happel	17.2	Clarence Lively	9.3			Bill Strannigan		
960-61	7-18	3-11		Earl Nau	16.8	Ron Bostick	5.8			Bill Strannigan		
961-62	9-17	3-11		Curt Jimerson	17.5	Bob Hanson	3.5			Bill Strannigan		
962-63	11-15	3-7		Flynn Robinson	26.2	Randy Richardson	7.7			Bill Strannigan		
963-64	12-14	3-7		Flynn Robinson	25.6	Leon Clark	10.5			Bill Strannigan		
964-65	16-10	5-5		Flynn Robinson	27.0	Leon Clark	12.1			Bill Strannigan		
965-66	17-9	5-5		Leon Clark	22.4	Leon Clark	11.6			Bill Strannigan		
966-67	15-14	8-2	NCAA REGIONAL SEMIFINALS	Harry Hall	18.4	Tom Asbury	9.0			Bill Strannigan		
967-68	18-9	5-5	NIT FIRST ROUND	Harry Hall	20.1	Carl Ashley	10.3			Bill Strannigan		
968-69	19-9	6-4	NIT FIRST ROUND	Carl Ashley	21.0	Carl Ashley	9.6			Bill Strannigan		
969-70	19-7	9-5		Carl Ashley	21.3	Carl Ashley	10.9			Bill Strannigan		
970-71	10-15	6-8		Willie Roberson	20.1	Jerry Brucks	8.2			Bill Strannigan		
971-72	12-14	3-11		Rod Penner	16.8	Rod Penner	9.7			Bill Strannigan		
972-73	9-17	4-10		Ron Crowell	12.0	Ken Morgan Clark	8.1			Bill Strannigan	179-187	.489
973-74	4-22	0-14		Ron Crowell	17.7	Stan Boyer	10.5			George "Moe" Radovich		
974-75	10-16	3-11		Stan Boyer	15.6	Stan Boyer	10.3			George "Moe" Radovich		
975-76	10-17	2-12		Pat Flanigin	12.6	Craig Shanor	8.0			George "Moe" Radovich	24-55	.304
976-77	17-10	8-6		Joe Fazekas	13.5	Doug Bessert	7.2	Gary Phillips	3.9	Don DeVoe		
977-78	12-15	3-11		Charles Bradley	13.7	Charles Bradley	6.2	Tony Barnett	3.0	Don DeVoe	29-25	.537
978-79	15-12	5-7		Charles Bradley	15.7	Kenneth Ollie	8.5	Charles Bradley	2.6	Jim Brandenburg		
979-80	18-10	8-6		Charles Bradley	19.1	Kenneth Ollie	8.0	Anthony Johnson	3.4	Jim Brandenburg		
980-81	24-6	13-3	NCAA SECOND ROUND	Charles Bradley	19.2	Kenneth Ollie	8.6	Mike Jackson	3.0	Jim Brandenburg		
981-82	23-7	14-2	NCAA SECOND ROUND	Bill Garnett	18.1	Bill Garnett	8.1	Mike Jackson	3.0	Jim Brandenburg		
982-83	16-13	8-8		Anthony Martin	13.0	Mark Wrapp	6.9	Mike Jackson	5.2	Jim Brandenburg		
983-84	17-13	9-7		Anthony Martin	14.5	Anthony Martin	8.6	Rodney Gowens	2.3	Jim Brandenburg		
984-85	15-14	7-9		Rodney Gowens	14.4	Jamal Hosey	8.0	Jamal Hosey	2.8	Jim Brandenburg		
985-86	24-12	12-4	NIT RUNNER-UP	Fennis Dembo	17.0	Fennis Dembo	6.7	Sean Dent	4.6	Jim Brandenburg		
986-87	24-10	11-5	NCAA REGIONAL SEMIFINALS	Fennis Dembo	20.3	Fennis Dembo	8.3	Sean Dent	5.5	Jim Brandenburg	176-97	.645
987-88	26-6	11-5	NCAA FIRST ROUND	Fennis Dembo	20.4	Fennis Dembo	7.2	Sean Dent	4.1	Benny Dees		
988-89	14-17	6-10		Robyn Davis	19.5	Reggie Fox	6.8	Kenny Smith	3.6	Benny Dees		
989-90	15-14	7-9		Reginald Slater	16.7	Reginald Slater	11.3	Kenny Smith	3.7	Benny Dees		
990-91	20-12	8-8	NIT SECOND ROUND	Reginald Slater	19.2	Reginald Slater	10.3	Maurice Alexander	3.9	Benny Dees		
991-92	16-13	8-8		Reginald Slater	17.9	Reginald Slater	11.3	Maurice Alexander	5.1	Benny Dees		
992-93	13-15	7-11		David Murray	13.7	Brian Rewers	7.8	David Murray	4.6	Benny Dees	104-77	.575
993-94	14-14	7-11		David Murray	16.9	Theo Ratliff	7.8	David Murray	4.1	Joby Wright		
994-95	13-15	9-9		LaDrell Whitehead	14.9	H.L. Coleman	7.8	LaDrell Whitehead	3.5	Joby Wright		
995-96	14-15	8-10		LaDrell Whitehead	17.7	H.L. Coleman	10.4	LaDrell Whitehead	4.0	Joby Wright		
996-97	12-16	8-8		LaDrell Whitehead	21.7	H.L. Coleman	10.8	Andy Young	2.3	Joby Wright	53-60	.469
997-98	19-9	9-5	NIT FIRST ROUND	Jeron Roberts	19.0	Jeron Roberts	5.9	Andy Young	2.1	Larry Shyatt	19-9	.679
998-99	18-10	7-7	NIT SECOND ROUND	Ugo Udezue	20.5	Ugo Udezue, A. Blakes	7.4	Chris McMillian	4.6	Steve McClain		
999-2000	19-12	8-6		Josh Davis	14.3	Josh Davis	8.7	Chris McMillian	3.7	Steve McClain		
2000-01	20-10	10-4	NIT FIRST ROUND	Marcus Bailey	17.4	Josh Davis	9.4	Chris McMillian	4.2	Steve McClain		
2001-02	22-9	11-3	NCAA SECOND ROUND	Marcus Bailey	14.6	Uche Nsonwu-Amadi	8.2	Jay Straight	3.3	Steve McClain		
2002-03	21-11	8-6	NIT SECOND ROUND	Donta Richardson	18.1	Uche Nsonwu-Amadi	9.6	Jay Straight	3.1	Steve McClain		
2003-04	11-17	4-10		Jay Straight	15.7	Alex Dunn	5.6	Jay Straight	3.8	Steve McClain		
2004-05	15-13	7-7		Jay Straight	18.0	Alex Dunn	8.6	Jay Straight	5.3	Steve McClain		
2005-06	14-18	5-11		Brandon Ewing	13.2	Justin Williams	11.0	Brad Jones	3.5	Steve McClain		
2006-07	17-15	7-9		Brandon Ewing	19.9	Daaron Brown	6.9	Brad Jones	4.5	Steve McClain	157-115	.577
2007-08	12-18	5-11		Brandon Ewing	17.2	Joseph Taylor	6.8	Brandon Ewing	4.0	Heath Schroyer		
2008-09	19-14	7-9		Brandon Ewing	18.5	Tyson Johnson	7.5	Brandon Ewing	5.0	Heath Schroyer	31-32	.492

THE SCHOOLS

ESPN 59 SAGARIN

XAVIER

For a school of less than 4,000 undergraduates, undersized Xavier in Cincinnati has certainly managed to create a lot of oversized basketball memories. Ever since the mid-1980s, when coach Pete Gillen first started taking the Musketeers on almost annual trips to the NCAA Tournament, the X-men have represented their tiny school like true giants.

BEST TEAM: 2007-08 The Musketeers won a school-record 30 games under the direction of head coach Sean Miller, reached the Elite Eight for the second time in five years and further solidified a decade of success—they appeared in all but one NCAA Tournament between 2001 and '09. Senior Josh Duncan (12.4 ppg) led a balanced attack that had four players average double figures in scoring and two others top 9.7 ppg.

BEST PLAYER: F David West (1999-2003) Xavier's first national Player of the Year (2002-03) is also the school's No. 2 career scorer (2,132 points), its all-time blocked shots leader (228) and No. 3 all-time rebounder (1,309). He is the first Musketeer to have his number retired while still an active player. West was chosen by New Orleans as the 18th overall pick in the 2003 draft. Since then, he's been one of the top power forwards in the NBA.

BEST COACH: Pete Gillen (1985-94) The school's all-time winningest coach, Gillen led Xavier to seven NCAA Tournaments—including six straight from 1986 to '91—in which the X-men compiled a 5–7 record. In 1987, as a No. 13 seed, Gillen's Musketeers upset No. 4-seed Missouri, 70-69, in the Tournament's first round. All but one of Gillen's Xavier squads won 19 or more games in his nine seasons on the bench.

GAME FOR THE AGES: The Musketeers earned their first trip to the Sweet 16 in 1990. To arrive there, they had to get past a powerful Georgetown crew that had as its centerpiece the twin towers combination of Alonzo Mourning and Dikembe Mutumbo. Gillen mapped out a stifling defense that held the Hoyas to 33% shooting from the field in the first half. Xavier center Derek Strong's 19 points and 12 rebounds, combined with Georgetown's poor free throw shooting down the stretch, led to Xavier's 74-71 upset victory. The Musketeers were then taken out by Texas, 102-89.

HEARTBREAKER: During the 2004 Atlantic 10 tournament, Xavier destroyed previously undefeated, No. 1-ranked Saint Joseph's, 87-67, en route to the title. The team carried that momentum into the NCAA Tourney and all the way to the Elite Eight, before meeting a Duke team that was one of coach Mike Krzyzewski's all-time favorites. The teams set the tough tone early; 4:20 into the game, Duke led by only 3-0. Neither team led by more than six at any point, but Xavier was felled by its inability to hit three-pointers (Chris Duhon kept Romain Sato, Xavier's all-time three-point leader, from hitting any treys) and its inability to stop Duke freshman Luol Deng (19 points).

FIERCEST RIVAL: Once upon a time (back in the '90s, that is), their coaches would refuse to shake hands after games. Xavier and Cincinnati have faced off in the Crosstown Shootout 76 times since 1927-28. The Musketeers have won seven of the last 10, but the Bearcats lead overall, 47–29. Each year, a week-long run-up to the game features events like eating and shooting contests, and plenty of obligatory trash talk. Here's hoping the new sponsor, the local restaurant chain Skyline Chili, can restore some of the rivalry's spice.

FANFARE AND HOOPLA: There's no consensus about the origin of the Blue Blob, Xavier's secondary mascot. One tale has it that the furry beastie was introduced because D'Artagnan, the gun-toting Musketeer, was scary to younger fans. Slightly older children—members of a school club called X-treme Fans, who meet at pregame parties and then, during the action, dispense creative heckles—often paint themselves blue in homage.

FAN FAVORITE: G Jamal Walker (1987-91) As the point guard on XU's 1989-90 team that made a run to the Sweet 16, Jumpin' Jamal demonstrated a natural flair for exciting plays and dramatic finishes.

CONSENSUS ALL-AMERICAS

2003	**David West,** F

FIRST-ROUND PRO PICKS

1969	**Luther Rackley,** Minnesota (ABA)
1990	**Tyrone Hill,** Golden State (11)
1994	**Brian Grant,** Sacramento (8)
1999	**James Posey,** Denver (18)
2003	**David West,** New Orleans (18)

PROFILE

Xavier University, Cincinnati, OH
Founded: 1831
Enrollment: 6,646 (3,961 undergraduate)
Colors: Navy blue, gray and white
Nickname: Musketeers
Current arena: Cintas Center, opened in 2000 (10,250)
Previous: Cincinnati Gardens, 1983-99 (10,100); Schmidt Fieldhouse, 1927-82 (2,900)
First game: 1919
All-time record: 1,256-891 (.585)
Total weeks in AP Top 20/25: 108

Current conference: Atlantic 10 (1995-)
Conference titles:
Midwestern City: 1 (1981)
Midwestern Collegiate: 7 (1986, '88, '90, '91, '93 [tie], '94, '95)
Atlantic 10: 7 (1997 [tie], '98 [tie], 2002 [tie], '03 [tie], '07 [tie], '08, '09)
Conference tournament titles:
Midwestern City: 1 (1983)
Midwestern Collegiate: 5 (1986, '87, '88, '89, '91)
Atlantic 10: 4 (1998, 2002, '04, '06)
NCAA Tournament appearances: 20
Sweet 16s (since 1975): 4

NIT appearances: 7
Semifinals: 2
Titles: 1 (1958)

TOP 5

G	**Byron Larkin** (1984-88)
G	**Romain Sato** (2000-04)
F	**Tyrone Hill** (1986-90)
F	**David West** (1999-2003)
C	**Brian Grant** (1990-94)

RECORDS

	GAME		SEASON		CAREER	
POINTS	50	Steve Thomas, vs. Detroit (Jan. 6, 1964)	792	Byron Larkin (1986-87)	2,696	Bryon Larkin (1984-88)
POINTS PER GAME			30.0	Steve Thomas (1963-64)	23.6	Steve Thomas (1962-66)
REBOUNDS	31	Bob Pelkington, vs. Saint Francis (Pa.), (Feb. 18, 1964)	567	Bob Pelkington (1963-64)	1,380	Tyrone Hill (1986-90)
ASSISTS	18	Keith Walker, vs. Detroit (Feb. 7, 1980)	251	Ralph Lee (1985-86)	699	Ralph Lee (1982-86)

THE SCHOOLS

EASON REVIEW

ASON	W-L	CONF.	SCORING	COACH	RECORD		SEASON	W-L	CONF.	SCORING	COACH	RECORD	
-20	0-1			Harry Gilligan	0-1	.000	1927-28	8-1			Joe Meyer		
-21	1-2			Joe Meyer			1928-29	9-6			Joe Meyer		
-22	2-4			Joe Meyer			1929-30	8-8			Joe Meyer		
-23	2-0			Joe Meyer			1930-31	10-3			Joe Meyer		
3-24	12-4			Joe Meyer			1931-32	10-3			Joe Meyer		
4-25	6-7			Joe Meyer			1932-33	5-3			Joe Meyer	94-52	.644
5-26	10-8			Joe Meyer			1933-34	9-1			Clem Crowe		
6-27	11-3			Joe Meyer			1934-35	14-4			Clem Crowe		

EAS.	W-L	CONF.	POSTSEASON	SCORING		REBOUNDS		ASSISTS		COACH	RECORD	
5-36	8-7									Clem Crowe		
6-37	7-7									Clem Crowe		
7-38	10-9									Clem Crowe		
8-39	13-6									Clem Crowe		
9-40	6-17									Clem Crowe		
0-41	13-9									Clem Crowe		
1-42	10-8									Clem Crowe		
2-43	6-10									Clem Crowe	96-78	.552
3-44	no team											
4-45	no team											
5-46	3-16									Ed Burns	3-16	.158
6-47	8-17									Lew Hirt		
7-48	24-8			Art Morthorst	10.1					Lew Hirt		
8-49	16-10			Malcolm McMullen	12.0					Lew Hirt		
9-50	12-16			Gene Smith	15.8					Lew Hirt		
0-51	16-10			Gene Smith	13.9					Lew Hirt	76-61	.555
1-52	10-14			Gene Smith	20.6					Ned Wulk		
2-53	11-12			Huck Budde	21.8	Huck Budde	10.1			Ned Wulk		
3-54	18-12			Dave Piontek	14.6	Chuck Holmann	11.0			Ned Wulk		
4-55	13-13			Dave Piontek	16.9	Dave Piontek	11.3			Ned Wulk		
5-56	17-11		NIT QUARTERFINALS	Jim Boothe	16.5	Dave Piontek	15.3	Jim Boothe	3.7	Ned Wulk		
6-57	20-8		NIT QUARTERFINALS	Corny Freeman	15.5	Corny Freeman	18.8	Jim Boothe	2.2	Ned Wulk	89-70	.560
7-58	19-11		NIT CHAMPION	Joe Viviano	18.1	Joe Viviano	12.6			Jim McCafferty		
8-59	12-13			Joe Viviano	17.0	Rich Piontek	10.5			Jim McCafferty		
9-60	17-9			Jack Thobe	18.4	Jack Thobe	10.0			Jim McCafferty		
0-61	17-10		NCAA FIRST ROUND	Jack Thobe	17.5	Jack Thobe	10.7	Bill Kirvin	4.7	Jim McCafferty		
1-62	14-12			Jack Thobe	14.6	Bob Pelkington	11.7	Bill Kirvin	4.0	Jim McCafferty		
2-63	12-16			Steve Thomas	16.1	Bob Pelkington	16.2	Bob Pelkington	3.4	Jim McCafferty	91-71	.562
3-64	16-10			Steve Thomas	30.0	Bob Pelkington	21.8	Bob Pelkington	3.4	Don Ruberg		
4-65	10-15			Steve Thomas	28.9	Ben Cooper	13.1	Joe McNeil	2.5	Don Ruberg		
5-66	13-13			Bob Quick	20.0	Bob Quick	11.6	Bryan Williams	2.8	Don Ruberg		
6-67	13-13			Bob Quick	19.3	Luther Rackley	12.6	Joe Pangrazio	2.3	Don Ruberg	52-51	.505
7-68	10-16			Bob Quick	23.7	Bob Quick	14.0	Joe Pangrazio	3.2	George Krajack		
8-69	10-16			Luther Rackley	17.5	Luther Rackley	14.0	Chris Hall	2.7	George Krajack		
9-70	5-20			Jerry Helmers	17.5	Jerry Helmers	8.4			George Krajack		
0-71	9-17			Jerry Helmers	19.4	Conny Warren	6.3	Doug Alt	1.7	George Krajack	34-69	.330
1-72	12-14			Bob Fullarton	14.8	Conny Warren	10.9	Tom Binegar	2.0	Dick Campbell		
2-73	3-23			Conny Warren	15.0	Conny Warren	11.4	Jim Rippe	3.0	Dick Campbell	15-37	.289
3-74	8-18			Mike Plunkett	14.0	Mike Plunkett	7.0	Ron Laker	2.5	Tay Baker		
4-75	11-15			Mike Plunkett	15.9	Mike Plunkett	8.3	Jim Rippe	2.2	Tay Baker		
5-76	14-12			Garry Whitfield	16.3	N. Daniels, D.Haarman	7.1	Garry Whitfield	2.9	Tay Baker		
6-77	10-17			Dale Haarman	13.3	Steve Spivery	7.9	Dale Haarman	2.6	Tay Baker		
7-78	13-14			Nick Daniels	16.7	Steve Spivery	8.0	Keith Walker	5.3	Tay Baker		
8-79	14-13			Nick Daniels	21.2	Joe Sunderman	8.6	Keith Walker	5.4	Tay Baker	70-89	.440
9-80	8-18	0-5		Jon Hanley	18.4	David Anderson	7.6	Keith Walker	6.4	Bob Staak		
0-81	12-16	8-3		Anthony Hicks	16.7	Dwight Hollins	5.0	Anthony Hicks	4.0	Bob Staak		
1-82	8-20	1-11		Anthony Hicks	20.4	Dexter Bailey	7.5	Anthony Hicks	4.3	Bob Staak		
2-83	22-8	10-4	NCAA OPENING ROUND	Anthony Hicks	14.9	Dexter Bailey	6.7	Anthony Hicks	4.0	Bob Staak		
3-84	22-11	9-5	NIT THIRD ROUND	Jeff Jenkins	17.0	Dexter Bailey	5.8	Ralph Lee	4.9	Bob Staak		
4-85	16-13	7-7		Byron Larkin	17.0	Walt McBride	5.5	Ralph Lee	6.9	Bob Staak	88-86	.506
5-86	25-5	10-2	NCAA FIRST ROUND	Byron Larkin	21.8	Eddie Johnson	6.7	Ralph Lee	8.4	Pete Gillen		
6-87	19-13	7-5	NCAA SECOND ROUND	Byron Larkin	24.8	Tyrone Hill	8.4	Stan Kimbrough	3.3	Pete Gillen		
7-88	26-4	9-1	NCAA FIRST ROUND	Byron Larkin	25.3	Tyrone Hill	10.5	Stan Kimbrough	3.6	Pete Gillen		
8-89	21-12	7-5	NCAA FIRST ROUND	Tyrone Hill	18.9	Tyrone Hill	12.2	Jamal Walker	7.1	Pete Gillen		
9-90	28-5	12-2	NCAA REGIONAL SEMIFINALS	Tyrone Hill	20.2	Tyrone Hill	12.6	Jamal Walker	5.9	Pete Gillen		
0-91	22-10	11-3	NCAA SECOND ROUND	Jamie Gladden	15.2	Brian Grant	8.5	Jamal Walker	5.1	Pete Gillen		
1-92	15-12	7-3		Jamie Gladden	19.4	Brian Grant	9.1	Michael Hawkins	4.4	Pete Gillen		
2-93	24-6	12-2	NCAA SECOND ROUND	Brian Grant	18.5	Brian Grant	9.4	Michael Hawkins	3.7	Pete Gillen		
3-94	22-8	8-2	NIT THIRD ROUND	Brian Grant	16.7	Brian Grant	9.9	Steve Gentry	6.1	Pete Gillen	202-75	.729
4-95	23-5	14-0	NCAA FIRST ROUND	Jeff Massey	18.9	Larry Sykes	10.8	Michael Hawkins	5.8	Skip Prosser		
5-96	13-15	8-8		Lenny Brown	12.5	T.J. Johnson	6.8	Gary Lumpkin	3.2	Skip Prosser		
6-97	23-6	13-3	NCAA SECOND ROUND	Lenny Brown	15.6	James Posey	7.8	Gary Lumpkin	4.3	Skip Prosser		
7-98	22-8	11-5	NCAA FIRST ROUND	Darnell Williams	17.3	James Posey	8.4	Gary Lumpkin	4.5	Skip Prosser		
8-99	25-11	12-4	NIT THIRD PLACE	Lenny Brown	18.1	James Posey	8.9	Gary Lumpkin	3.4	Skip Prosser		
9-2000	21-12	9-7	NIT SECOND ROUND	Maurice McAfee	15.1	David West	9.1	Maurice McAfee	4.2	Skip Prosser		
0-01	21-8	12-4	NCAA FIRST ROUND	David West	17.8	David West	10.9	Maurice McAfee	4.8	Skip Prosser	148-65	.695
1-02	26-6	14-2	NCAA SECOND ROUND	David West	18.3	David West	9.8	Lionel Chalmers	4.2	Thad Matta		
2-03	26-6	15-1	NCAA SECOND ROUND	David West	20.1	David West	11.8	Dedrick Finn	4.3	Thad Matta		
3-04	26-11	10-6	NCAA REGIONAL FINAL	Lionel Chalmers	16.6	Romain Sato	8.0	Dedrick Finn	3.4	Thad Matta	78-23	.772
4-05	17-12	10-6		Stanley Burrell	12.7	Justin Doellman	6.0	Dedrick Finn	4.2	Sean Miller		
5-06	21-11	8-8	NCAA FIRST ROUND	Brian Thornton	15.3	Justin Doellman	6.7	Stanley Burrell	3.2	Sean Miller		
6-07	25-9	13-3	NCAA SECOND ROUND	Justin Doellman	13.7	Justin Doellman	5.5	Drew Lavender	4.8	Sean Miller		
7-08	30-7	14-2	NCAA REGIONAL FINAL	Josh Duncan	12.4	Derrick Brown	6.5	Drew Lavender	4.5	Sean Miller		
8-09	27-8	12-4	NCAA REGIONAL SEMIFINALS	B.J. Raymond	14.1	Derrick Brown	6.1	Dante' Jackson	2.7	Sean Miller	120-47	.719

ESPN 185 SAGARIN

YALE

History, tradition—these words have deeper meaning at Yale than at other schools. The Bulldogs dominated the first years of the 20th century and remained an Ivy League power into the 1960s. But the distant past may be so important in New Haven because recent decades have been scant on highlights: The Bulldogs haven't won an Ivy League title since 1961-62.

BEST TEAM: 1961-62 Led by sharpshooter Bill Madden (15.9 ppg), the Elis finished 13–1 in the Ivy to earn an NCAA bid. In the first round they faced a powerful Wake Forest crew headlined by Billy Packer. The game was tied with :02 left as Yale center Dave Schumacher stepped to the free throw line. He missed the front end of a one-and-one; Wake dominated the overtime to win, 92-82.

BEST PLAYER: F Tony Lavelli (1945-49) A musician by training and inclination, Lavelli took up basketball mostly to impress his friends. It worked. He led the Elis in scoring four years, was a three-time All-America, was the 1949 Helms national player of the year and still holds the school record for points in a game (52). Lavelli went on to play for the Celtics, where he would leave halftime pep talks to entertain the Boston Garden crowd with his accordion.

BEST COACH: Joseph Vancisin (1956-75) He took the Elis to two of the program's three NCAA Tournaments, the first time in 1957, when they lost in the first round to North Carolina. The coach with the most career wins at Yale, he has attended 62 straight Final Fours—one as a player (with Dartmouth in 1944), 61 as a spectator.

GAME FOR THE AGES: The Elis had never won a post-season game when they finished in a three-way tie for the 2001-02 Ivy title. They lost out on the NCAA bid but earned a first-round NIT match at Rutgers. Yale had a deep bench (26.6 ppg) led by junior guard Chris Leanza, and hung tough to win a back-and-forth affair, 67-65.

FIERCEST RIVAL: Harvard vs. Yale extends from the gridiron to the basketball court to claims on intellectual superiority. The Elis dominate both on the gridiron (65–52–8) and the hardwood (113–66), but we are not making a call on the intellectual superiority question.

SEASON REVIEW

SEAS.	W-L	CONF.	COACH
1895-1948	*592-498*	*Helms champion, '00-01 and '02-03*	
1948-49	22-8	9-3 ●	Howard Hobson
1949-50	17-9	7-5	Howard Hobson
1950-51	14-13	4-8	Howard Hobson
1951-52	13-14	4-8	Howard Hobson
1952-53	10-15	6-6	Howard Hobson
1953-54	12-14	7-7	Howard Hobson
1954-55	3-21	3-11	Howard Hobson
1955-56	15-11	7-7	Howard Hobson
1956-57	18-8	12-2 ●	Joseph Vancisin
1957-58	14-10	9-5	Joseph Vancisin
1958-59	10-13	9-5	Joseph Vancisin
1959-60	6-17	3-11	Joseph Vancisin
1960-61	12-12	8-6	Joseph Vancisin
1961-62	18-6	13-1 ●	Joseph Vancisin
1962-63	13-10	11-3	Joseph Vancisin
1963-64	16-8	11-3	Joseph Vancisin
1964-65	10-12	7-7	Joseph Vancisin
1965-66	9-12	6-8	Joseph Vancisin
1966-67	14-7	11-3	Joseph Vancisin
1967-68	15-9	8-6	Joseph Vancisin
1968-69	9-16	6-8	Joseph Vancisin
1969-70	11-13	7-7	Joseph Vancisin
1970-71	4-20	2-12	Joseph Vancisin
1971-72	7-17	5-9	Joseph Vancisin
1972-73	9-16	6-8	Joseph Vancisin
1973-74	8-16	5-9	Joseph Vancisin
1974-75	3-20	2-12	Joseph Vancisin

SEAS.	W-L	CONF.	SCORING		COACH	RECORD
1975-76	7-21	5-9	Steve Switchenko	398	Ray Carazo	
1976-77	6-20	4-10	Carnell Cooper	315	Ray Carazo	
1977-78	8-16	3-11	Joe Jolson	249	Ray Carazo	
1978-79	11-15	5-9	Frank Maturo	399	Ray Carazo	
1979-80	16-10	8-6	Steve Leondis	398	Ray Carazo	
1980-81	7-19	4-10	Butch Graves	411	Ray Carazo	
1981-82	13-13	7-7	Butch Graves	464	Ray Carazo	68-114 .374
1982-83	12-14	7-7	Butch Graves	606	Tom Brennan	
1983-84	7-19	4-10	Butch Graves	609	Tom Brennan	
1984-85	14-12	7-7	Brian Fitzpatrick	360	Tom Brennan	
1985-86	13-13	7-7	Chris Dudley	422	Tom Brennan	46-58 .442
1986-87	14-12	7-7	Paul Maley	452	Dick Kuchen	
1987-88	12-14	8-6	Paul Maley	524	Dick Kuchen	
1988-89	11-17	6-8	Ed Petersen	458	Dick Kuchen	
1989-90	19-7	10-4	Dean Campbell	385	Dick Kuchen	
1990-91	15-11	9-5	Ed Petersen	364	Dick Kuchen	
1991-92	17-9	7-7	Ed Petersen	427	Dick Kuchen	
1992-93	10-16	6-8	Rob Connolly	297	Dick Kuchen	
1993-94	10-16	7-7	Damon Franklin	324	Dick Kuchen	
1994-95	9-17	5-9	Gabe Hunterton	335	Dick Kuchen	
1995-96	8-18	3-11	Daniel Okonkwo	275	Dick Kuchen	
1996-97	10-16	3-11	Daniel Okonkwo	421	Dick Kuchen	
1997-98	12-14	7-7	Emerson Whitley	419	Dick Kuchen	
1998-99	4-22	2-12	David Tompkins	16.2	Dick Kuchen	151-189 .444
1999-2000	7-20	5-9	Onaje Woodbine	14.7	James Jones	
2000-01	10-17	7-7	Chris Leanza	13.3	James Jones	
2001-02	21-11	11-3 ■	Edwin Draughan	11.5	James Jones	
2002-03	14-13	8-6	Edwin Draughan	11.4	James Jones	
2003-04	12-15	7-7	Edwin Draughan	11.6	James Jones	
2004-05	11-16	7-7	Edwin Draughan	15.8	James Jones	
2005-06	15-14	7-7	Dominick Martin	13.7	James Jones	
2006-07	14-13	10-4	Eric Flato	15.3	James Jones	
2007-08	13-15	7-7	Eric Flato	11.9	James Jones	
2008-09	13-15	8-6	Ross Morin	13.6	James Jones	130-149 .466

Cumulative totals listed when per game averages not available.
● NCAA Tournament appearance ■ NIT appearance

PROFILE

Yale University, New Haven, CT
Founded: 1701
Enrollment: 11,416 (5,247 undergraduate)
Colors: Yale blue and white
Nicknames: Bulldogs, Elis
Current arena: John J. Lee Amphitheater, opened in 1932 (2,532)
First game: Dec. 7, 1895
All-time record: 1,299-1,355 (.489)
Total weeks in AP Top 20/25: 4
Current conference: Ivy League (1901-)

Conference titles:
Ivy: 10 (1902, '03, '07, '15, '17, '23, '33, '49, '57, '62)
NCAA Tournament appearances: 3
NIT appearances: 1

CONSENSUS ALL-AMERICAS

1905	**Willard Hyatt,** C
1905, '07	**Gilmore Kinney,** F
1908	**Haskell Noyes,** G
1915	**W.P. Arnold,** G
1917	**Orson Kinney,** F
1917	**Charles Taft,** G
1949	**Tony Lavelli,** F

FIRST-ROUND PRO PICKS

1949 **Tony Lavelli,** Boston (4)

TOP 5

G	**Butch Graves** (1980-84)
G	**Ed Petersen** (1988-92)
F	**Tony Lavelli** (1945-49)
F	**John Lee** (1955-58)
C	**Chris Dudley** (1983-87)

RECORDS

	GAME		SEASON		CAREER	
POINTS	52	Tony Lavelli, vs. Williams (Feb. 26, 1949)	671	Tony Lavelli (1948-49)	2,090	Butch Graves (1980-84)
POINTS PER GAME			24.9	Rick Kaminsky (1963-64)	20.7	Jim Morgan (1968-71)
REBOUNDS	32	Ed Robinson, vs. Harvard (March 10, 1956)	433	Ed Robinson (1955-56)	1,182	Ed Robinson (1954-57)
ASSISTS	17	Peter White, vs. Harvard (Feb. 7, 1987)	225	Larry Zigerelli (1979-80)	611	Peter White (1984-87)

ESPN 222 SAGARIN

YOUNGSTOWN STATE

Since joining D1 in 1981, the Penguins have never reached the NCAA tournament, though they did reach conference tourney finals in 1984, '85 and '98. But recent frustrations can't diminish the glorious decades of coach Dom Rosselli's legacy—midnight packed-house OVC games, deep runs into the NAIA tournament and the domination of Jeff Covington.

BEST TEAM: 1957-58 The 23–7 Penguins reached the NAIA national tournament quarterfinals for the second straight season, behind all-time leading rebounder (1,848) and two-time NAIA All-America Herb Lake, and Mickey Yugovich, the school's No. 4 all-time scorer (1,917). They lost, 70-67, to unbeaten Western Illinois.

BEST PLAYER: F Jeff Covington (1974-78) A three-time D2 All-America, Covington was *Basketball Weekly*'s Player of the Year in 1978, when he averaged 26.4 ppg and 15.5 rpg. He led the Penguins in scoring and rebounding all four of his years (22.9 career ppg), hitting 30 points or more 14 times.

BEST COACH: Dom Rosselli (1940-42, '46-82) Few coaches have had a more profound impact on their school than Rosselli. He won 589 games over 38 seasons; he also was the baseball coach for 31 years and an assistant football coach for 21. He had 24 winning hoops seasons—eight with at least 20 wins—and reached the NAIA national tourney four times.

GAME FOR THE AGES: YSU's only win over a ranked team, on Feb. 5, 1952, was a stunner: the 68-57 victory over that year's NIT champ (and 1954 NCAA champ) La Salle, which was led by freshman and eventual three-time consensus All-America Tom Gola. Sam Jankovich scored a career-high 22 for Rosselli's team, led that season by Mike Magula (21.0 ppg.).

FIERCEST RIVAL: Pre-D1, Youngstown State battled Gannon yearly, including a dramatic six-overtime 71-69 YSU loss in 1966. The Penguins' 2001 move to the Horizon League has renewed a rivalry with Cleveland State, a former Mid-Continent Conference foe. YSU leads the series, 36–35, but has won just three of the last nine.

SEASON REVIEW

SEAS.	W-L	CONF.	COACH	SEAS.	W-L	CONF.	COACH
1927-47	*129-147*	*Only six winning seasons*		1960-61	21-7		Dom Rosselli
1947-48	10-14		Dom Rosselli	1961-62	16-12		Dom Rosselli
1948-49	9-14		Dom Rosselli	1962-63	18-9		Dom Rosselli
1949-50	3-20		Dom Rosselli	1963-64	24-3		Dom Rosselli
1950-51	16-7		Dom Rosselli	1964-65	20-6		Dom Rosselli
1951-52	16-7		Dom Rosselli	1965-66	19-7		Dom Rosselli
1952-53	10-14		Dom Rosselli	1966-67	18-7		Dom Rosselli
1953-54	11-16		Dom Rosselli	1967-68	17-8		Dom Rosselli
1954-55	10-17		Dom Rosselli	1968-69	19-7		Dom Rosselli
1955-56	12-14		Dom Rosselli	1969-70	22-5		Dom Rosselli
1956-57	23-4		Dom Rosselli	1970-71	19-6		Dom Rosselli
1957-58	23-7		Dom Rosselli	1971-72	22-7		Dom Rosselli
1958-59	19-9		Dom Rosselli	1972-73	10-13		Dom Rosselli
1959-60	11-14		Dom Rosselli	1973-74	10-16		Dom Rosselli

SEAS.	W-L	CONF.	SCORING		COACH	RECORD	
1974-75	19-9		Jeff Covington	543	Dom Rosselli		
1975-76	17-9		Jeff Covington	542	Dom Rosselli		
1976-77	22-7		Jeff Covington	679	Dom Rosselli		
1977-78	16-9		Jeff Covington	26.4	Dom Rosselli		
1978-79	13-13		Dave Zeigler	623	Dom Rosselli		
1979-80	17-10		Dave Zeigler	665	Dom Rosselli		
1980-81	13-13		Bruce Alexander	450	Dom Rosselli		
1981-82	8-18	5-11	Art McCullough	450	Dom Rosselli	589-388	.603
1982-83	15-12	5-9	Ricky Tunstall	299	Mike Rice		
1983-84	18-11	9-5	Ray Robinson	359	Mike Rice		
1984-85	19-11	9-5	John Keshock	455	Mike Rice		
1985-86	12-16	8-6	Garry Robinson	413	Mike Rice		
1986-87	11-17	4-10	Tilman Bevely	662	Mike Rice	75-67	.528
1987-88	7-21	2-12	Tilman Bevely	414	Jim Cleamons		
1988-89	5-23		Shane Johnson	381	Jim Cleamons	12-44	.214
1989-90	8-20		Reggie Kemp	564	John Stroia		
1990-91	12-16		Reggie Kemp	589	John Stroia		
1991-92	6-22		Mike Alcorn	392	John Stroia		
1992-93	3-23	1-15	Reggie Kemp	413	John Stroia	29-81	.264
1993-94	5-21	3-15	Andre Smith	371	Dan Peters		
1994-95	18-10	10-8	Andre Smith	441	Dan Peters		
1995-96	12-15	7-11	Marcus Culbreth	348	Dan Peters		
1996-97	9-18	4-12	Anthony Hunt	332	Dan Peters		
1997-98	20-9	11-5	Anthony Hunt	418	Dan Peters		
1998-99	14-14	9-5	DeVon Lewis	9.8	Dan Peters	78-87	.473
1999-2000	12-16	9-7	Elmer Brown	12.0	John Robic		
2000-01	19-11	11-5	Craig Haese	14.1	John Robic		
2001-02	5-23	2-14	Ryan Patton	14.6	John Robic		
2002-03	9-20	4-12	Doug Underwood	14.7	John Robic		
2003-04	8-20	4-12	Doug Underwood	12.2	John Robic		
2004-05	5-23	2-14	Quin Humphrey	14.4	John Robic	58-113	.339
2005-06	7-21	4-12	Quin Humphrey	19.2	Jerry Slocum		
2006-07	14-17	7-9	Quin Humphrey	18.8	Jerry Slocum		
2007-08	9-21	5-13	Byron Davis	15.5	Jerry Slocum		
2008-09	11-19	7-11	Kelvin Bright	11.4	Jerry Slocum	41-78	.345

Cumulative totals listed when per game averages not available.

PROFILE

Youngstown State University, Youngstown, OH
Founded: 1908
Enrollment: 13,497 (11,564 undergraduate)
Colors: Red and white
Nickname: Penguins
Current arena: Beeghly Center, opened in 1972 (6,300)
First game: Dec. 14, 1927
All-time record: 975-975 (.500)
Total weeks in AP Top 20/25: 0

Current conference: Horizon League (2001-)
Conference titles: 0
Conference tournament titles: 0
NCAA Tournament appearances: 0
NIT appearances: 0

CONSENSUS ALL-AMERICAS

1977, '78 **Jeff Covington** (D2), F

TOP 5

G **Quin Humphrey** (2003-07)
G **John McElroy** (1965-69)
F **Jeff Covington** (1974-78)
F/C **Leo Mogus** (1939-43)
C **Herb Lake** (1955-59)

RECORDS	GAME		SEASON		CAREER	
POINTS	72	John McElroy, vs. Wayne State (Feb. 26, 1969)	729	John McElroy (1968-69)	2,424	Jeff Covington (1974-78)
POINTS PER GAME			28.0	John McElroy (1968-69)	26.3	Dave Zeigler (1978-80)
REBOUNDS	33	Herb Lake, vs. Westminster (Feb. 12, 1958)	555	Herb Lake (1956-57)	1,848	Herb Lake (1955-59)
ASSISTS	26	Bill Eckert, vs. Wayne State (Feb. 26, 1969)	239	Billy Johnson (1971-72)	619	Terry Moore (1973-77)

KENNESAW STATE

This suburban Atlanta school is a Division I newcomer, but State is determined to become a significant achiever after years of success at the lower collegiate levels. The Owls were Division II national champions in 2004, two seasons before they jumped to the underrated Atlantic Sun Conference.
BEST TEAM: 2003-04 (35–4, Division II championship)
BEST PLAYER: G TERRENCE HILL (2002-04)
BEST COACH: TONY INGLE (2000-)

PROFILE
Kennesaw State University, Kennesaw, GA
Founded: 1963
Enrollment: 21,449 (19,171 undergraduate)
Colors: Black and gold
Nickname: Owls
Arena: KSU Convocation Center, opened in 2005 (4,483)
All-time record: 385-323 (.544)
First game: 1985
Current conference: Atlantic Sun (2005-)

RECORDS	GAME		SEASON		CAREER	
POINTS	55	Taylor Patterson, vs. Carver (Dec. 15, 2003)	652	Herman Smith (1988-89)	1683	Herman Smith (1986-90)
POINTS PER GAME			21.0	Herman Smith (1988-89)	17.7	Scott Tapp (1988-90)
REBOUNDS	27	Reggie McKoy, vs. Augusta State (Jan. 24, 2004)	363	Reggie McKoy (2003-04)	734	Israel Brown (1989-93)
ASSISTS	16	Alex Guilford, vs. LaGrange (Feb. 24, 1989)	256	Daniel Dunlap (1992-93)	483	Golden Ingle (2001-02, '05-07)

NJIT

In just its third season in the reclassification process, the New Jersey Institute of Technology made D1 history—as the worst team in college hoops history. The Highlanders came out of the gate in 2007-08 with a 42-point loss to Manhattan and went straight downhill, finishing 0–29. But NJIT's basketball story dates back to the 1922-23 season, and it isn't all bad. A D3 power in the 1990s, the Highlanders advanced to five NCAA tournaments, and in 1995 they reached the D3 final eight.
BEST TEAM: 1994-95 (28–2, Division III tournament elite eight)
BEST PLAYER: G CLARENCE PIERCE (1992-96)
BEST COACH: JAMES CATALANO (1979-2001)

PROFILE
New Jersey Institute of Technology, Newark, NJ
Founded: 1881
Enrollment: 8,209 (5,380 undergraduate)
Colors: Red and white with blue accents
Nickname: Highlanders
Arena: Estelle and Zoom Fleisher Athletic Center, opened in 1965 (1,500)
All-time record: 796-718 (.526)
First game: 1922
Current conference: Great West (2009-)

RECORDS	GAME		SEASON		CAREER	
POINTS	45	Clayton Barker, vs. Post (Conn.), (Feb. 25, 2006)	624	Clarence Pierce (1994-95)	2,028	Clarence Pierce (1992-96)
POINTS PER GAME			24.3	Clarence Pierce (1993-94)	24.5	Larry Tosato (1952-56)
REBOUNDS	23	Andrew South, vs. NY Maritime (March 7, 1994); Vic Foster, vs. William Paterson (Jan. 18, 1988)	402	Joe Galvao (1968-69)	1,191	Rich Olsen (1964-68)
ASSISTS	17	Clarence Pierce, vs. Centenary (N.J.), (Jan. 18, 1995); Joe Marcotte, vs. Southern Vermont (Feb. 26, 1994); vs. Yeshiva (Jan. 25, 1994)	292	Joe Marcotte (1994-95)	611	Lance Andrews (1989-93)

NORTH FLORIDA

North Florida's program is no older than many of the university's students, which explains why the Ospreys and their fans have so much fun. The 2002-03 squad had the best time of all, with winning records overall (15–14) and in-conference (11–8), plus a Peach Belt Conference tournament victory. The team featured Donny Lotz, the school's No. 2 scorer (1,412) and rebounder (660), all-time assist leader Joe Gaetano (449) and the top three-point shooter (44.1%) Michael Drayton.
BEST TEAM: 2002-03 (15–14, third winning season in program history)
BEST PLAYER: G/F KORAN GODWIN (1999-2002)
BEST COACH: MATT KILCULLEN (1999-2009)

PROFILE
University of North Florida, Jacksonville, FL
Founded: 1965
Enrollment: 16,561 (13,934 undergraduate)
Colors: Navy blue and gray
Nickname: Ospreys
Arena: UNF Arena, opened in 1993 (5,800)
First game: Nov. 28, 1992
All-time record: 172-303 (.362)
Current conference: Atlantic Sun (2005-)

RECORDS	GAME		SEASON		CAREER	
POINTS	42	Ian Foster, vs. Florida Tech (Feb. 27, 1997)	601	Brian Sitter (1993-94)	1,513	Koran Godwin (1999-2002)
POINTS PER GAME			29.0	Darrin Jackson (1994-95)	21.5	Brian Sitter (1993-94)
REBOUNDS	20	Chris Sneed, vs. Edward Waters (Jan. 18, 1993)	264	Chris Sneed (1993-94)	889	Chris Sneed (1992-96)
ASSISTS	12	Pershin Williams, vs. USC Aiken (Feb. 21, 2004)	161	Pershin Williams (2003-04)	449	Joe Gaetano (1999-2003)

UTAH VALLEY

In leaving the junior college ranks, UVU bypassed D3 and even D2, leaping directly to provisional Division I competition in 2003-04. Success came quickly. Led by guards Ronnie Price (who went on to the NBA) and Ryan Toolson, at the end of that season the Wolverines won an unofficial tournament for provisional teams hosted by Florida Gulf Coast. They went 16–12 the following season. After five seasons of playing a catch-as-catch-can schedule, Utah Valley calls the new Great West Conference home.
BEST TEAM: 2006-07 (22–7, best record by a D1 independent since 1992-93)
BEST PLAYER: G RONNIE PRICE (2002-05)
BEST COACH: DICK HUNSAKER (2002-)

PROFILE
Utah Valley University, Orem, UT
Founded: 1941
Enrollment: 23,214 (23,214 undergraduate)
Colors: Forest green, gold and white
Nickname: Wolverines
Arena: The McKay Events Center, opened in 1996 (8,500)
All-time record: 687-422 (.619)
First game: 1972
Current conference: Great West (2009-)

RECORDS	GAME		SEASON		CAREER	
POINTS	63	Ryan Toolson, vs. Chicago State (Jan. 29, 2009)	680	Ronnie Price (2004-05)	2,163	Ryan Toolson (2003-04, '06-09)
POINTS PER GAME			24.3	Ronnie Price (2004-05)	19.6	Ronnie Price (2002-05)
REBOUNDS	18	Jon Bell, vs. Florida Gulf Coast (March 5, 2004)	243	Jordan Brady (2007-08)	475	David Heck (2003-07)
ASSISTS	11	Ryan Toolson, vs. NJIT (Feb. 28, 2009)	97	Chris Bailey (2006-07)	282	Ryan Toolson (2003-04, '06-09)

FORFEITED OR VACATED GAMES

V = vacated; F = forfeited; CF = conference forfeit

Note: A **forfeited** game changes a sanctioned team's victory into a loss and its opponent's loss into a win. A **vacated** game, regardless of outcome, is eliminated from the sanctioned team's record. The opponent's record is unchanged. For example, in 1995-96, Purdue played to a 26–6 record, including its NCAA Tournament appearance, but after the season it was penalized by the NCAA. It forfeited 18 of its 25 regular-season wins, all of which became losses, changing its record to 8–24. (Purdue's opponents had their records adjusted as well. Big Ten rival Ohio State picked up two victories, going from 10–17 to 12–15.) The Boilermakers also had two Tournament games—a win over Western Carolina and a loss to Georgia—vacated. Both games were erased from Purdue's final record, which was adjusted to 7–23. (The records of Western Carolina and Georgia remained unchanged.) NCAA forfeits in conference play affect overall and conference records. **Conference forfeits** affect a team's conference record, but not its overall record.

Team	Coach	Season	Orig. W-L (Conf.)	Adj. W-L (Conf.)	Type	Games Affected
Alabama	Wimp Sanderson	1986-87	28-5	**26-4**	V	3 NCAA Tournament games
American	Jeff Jones	2004-05	(8-6)	**(9-5)**	CF	1 conference game (by opp.)
Arizona	Lute Olson	1994-95	23-8 (13-5)	**24-7 (14-4)**	F	1 game (by opp.)
Arizona	Lute Olson	1995-96	26-7 (13-5)	**27-6 (14-4)**	F	1 game (by opp.)
Arizona	Lute Olson	1998-99	22-7	**22-6**	V	1 NCAA Tournament game
Arizona State	Ned Wulk	1975-76	16-11	**17-10**	F	1 game (by opp.)
Arizona State	Bill Frieder	1994-95	24-9	**22-8**	V	3 NCAA Tournament games
Arizona State	Bill Frieder	1995-96	11-16 (6-12)	**12-15 (7-11)**	F	1 game (by opp.)
Arkansas-Little Rock	Jim Platt	1991-92	(8-8)	**(9-7)**	CF	1 conference game (by opp.)
Arkansas-Pine Bluff	Van Holt	2004-05	(5-13)	**(6-12)**	CF	1 conference game (by opp.)
Arkansas State	John Rose	1972-73	(2-10)	**(4-8)**	CF	2 conference games (by opp.)
Army	Jim Crews	2004-05	(1-13)	**(2-12)**	CF	1 conference game (by opp.)
Austin Peay	Lake Kelly	1972-73	22-7	**21-5**	V	3 NCAA Tournament games
Boise State	Bobby Dye	1993-94	(7-7)	**(8-6)**	CF	1 conference game (by opp.)
Bowling Green	Jim Larranaga	1988-89	12-16 (6-10)	**13-15 (7-9)**	F	1 game (by opp.)
Bucknell	Pat Flannery	2004-05	(10-4)	**(11-3)**	CF	1 conference game (by opp.)
California	Dick Edwards	1975-76	12-14	**13-13**	F	1 game (by opp.)
California	Todd Bozeman	1994-95	13-14 (5-13)	**0-27 (0-18)**	F	13 games
California	Todd Bozeman	1995-96	17-11 (11-7)	**2-25 (2-16)**	F V	15 games (15-0) 1 NCAA Tournament game (0-1)
Cal State Northridge	Pete Cassidy	1994-95	8-20	**9-19**	F	1 game (by opp.)
Central Michigan	Charlie Coles	1988-89	12-16 (6-8)	**13-15 (7-9)**	F	1 game (by opp.)
Charlotte	Roy Thomas	1995-96	14-15	**15-14**	F	1 game (by opp.)
Cincinnati	Bob Huggins	1994-95	22-12	**23-11**	F	1 game (by opp.)
Clemson	Cliff Ellis	1989-90	26-9	**24-8**	V	3 NCAA Tournament games
Colgate	Emmett Davis	2004-05	(7-7)	**(8-6)**	CF	1 conference game (by opp.)
Colorado	Russell "Sox" Walseth	1960-61	(7-7)	**(1-13)**	CF	6 conference games
Columbia	Jack Rohan	1994-95	4-22	**5-21**	F	1 game (by opp.)
Connecticut	Jim Calhoun	1995-96	32-3	**30-2**	V	3 NCAA Tournament games
Cornell	Ben Bluitt	1976-77	8-18	**9-17**	F	1 game (by opp.)
Davidson	Bobby Hussey	1988-89	7-24	**8-23**	F	1 game (by opp.)
DePaul	Joey Meyer	1985-86	18-13	**16-12**	V	3 NCAA Tournament games
DePaul	Joey Meyer	1986-87	28-3	**26-2**	V	3 NCAA Tournament games
DePaul	Joey Meyer	1987-88	22-8	**21-7**	V	2 NCAA Tournament games
DePaul	Joey Meyer	1988-89	21-12	**20-11**	V	2 NCAA Tournament games
DePaul	Joey Meyer	1995-96	11-18	**12-17**	F	1 game (by opp.)
Detroit	Dick Vitale	1976-77	25-4	**26-3**	F	1 game (by opp.)
Eastern Michigan	Ben Braun	1988-89	16-13 (7-9)	**17-12 (8-8)**	F	1 game (by opp.)
Eastern Washington	John Wade	1993-94	(0-14)	**(2-12)**	CF	2 conference games (by opp.)
Florida	Norm Sloan	1986-87	23-11	**21-10**	V	3 NCAA Tournament games
Florida	Norm Sloan	1987-88	23-12	**22-11**	V	2 NCAA Tournament games
Florida International	Donnie Marsh	2002-03	8-21	**1-21**	V	7 games
Florida International	Donnie Marsh	2003-04	5-22	**0-22**	V	5 games
Florida International	Sergio Rouco	2004-05	13-17	**0-17**	V	13 games
Florida International	Sergio Rouco	2005-06	8-20	**1-20**	V	7 games
Florida State	Hugh Durham	1975-76	21-6	**22-5**	F	1 game (by opp.)
Fresno State	Jerry Tarkanian	1998-99	21-12	**1-12**	V	20 games
Fresno State	Jerry Tarkanian	1999-2000	24-10	**12-9**	V	12 games (12-0); 1 NCAA Tournament game (0-1)
Fresno State	Jerry Tarkanian	2000-01	26-7	**9-7**	V	17 games
Georgia	Hugh Durham	1984-85	22-9	**21-8**	V	2 NCAA Tournament games
Georgia	Jim Harrick	2001-02	22-10	**21-9**	V	2 NCAA Tournament games
Gonzaga	Dan Fitzgerald	1979-80	(8-8)	**(10-6)**	CF	2 conference games (by opp.)
Holy Cross	Bill Raynor	1995-96	16-13	**17-12**	F	1 game (by opp.)
Idaho	Joe Cravens	1993-94	(9-5)	**(10-4)**	CF	1 conference game (by opp.)
Idaho State	Herb Williams	1993-94	(9-5)	**(10-4)**	CF	1 conference game (by opp.)
Illinois	Lou Henson	1976-77	14-16 (6-12)	**16-14 (8-10)**	F	2 games (by opp.)
Illinois-Chicago	Bob Hallberg	1995-96	10-18	**11-17**	F	1 game (by opp.)
Indiana	Bob Knight	1976-77	14-13 (11-7)	**16-11 (13-5)**	F	2 games (by opp.)
Indiana	Bob Knight	1995-96	19-12	**20-11**	F	1 game (by opp.)
Iona	Jim Valvano	1979-80	29-5	**28-4**	V	2 NCAA Tournament games
Iowa	Lute Olson	1976-77	18-9 (10-8)	**20-7 (12-6)**	F	2 games (by opp.)
Iowa	Tom Davis	1995-96	23-9	**24-8**	F	1 game (by opp.)
Iowa State	Glenn Anderson	1960-61	(6-8)	**(8-6)**	CF	2 conference games (by opp.)

Team	Coach	Season	Orig. W-L (Conf.)	Adj. W-L (Conf.)	Type	Games Affected
Iowa State	Tim Floyd	1995-96	24-9	**25-8**	F	1 game (by opp.)
Jackson State	Tevester Anderson	2004-05	(10-8)	**(11-7)**	CF	1 conference game (by opp.)
Kansas State	Tex Winter	1960-61	(12-2)	**(13-1)**	CF	1 conference game (by opp.)
Kansas State	Jack Hartman	1976-77	23-8	**24-7**	F	1 game (by opp.)
Kent State	Jim McDonald	1988-89	20-11 (11-5)	**21-10 (12-4)**	F	1 game (by opp.)
Kentucky	Eddie Sutton	1987-88	27-6	**25-5**	V	3 NCAA Tournament games
Lafayette	Fran O'Hanlon	2004-05	(5-9)	**(6-8)**	CF	1 conference game (by opp.)
Lamar	Jack Martin	1972-73	(4-8)	**(6-6)**	CF	2 conference games (by opp.)
Lehigh	Billy Taylor	2004-05	(7-7)	**(1-13)**	CF	6 conference games
Long Beach State	Jerry Tarkanian	1970-71	24-5	**22-4**	V	3 NCAA Tournament games
Long Beach State	Jerry Tarkanian	1971-72	25-4	**23-3**	V	3 NCAA Tournament games
Long Beach State	Jerry Tarkanian	1972-73	26-3	**24-2**	V	3 NCAA Tournament games
Long Beach State	Larry Reynolds	2005-06	18-12	**0-12**	V	18 games
Louisiana-Lafayette	Beryl Shipley	1971-72	25-4 (8-0)	**23-3** **(6-2)**	V CF	3 NCAA Tournament games 2 conference games
Louisiana-Lafayette	Beryl Shipley	1972-73	24-5 (12-0)	**23-3** **(0-12)**	V CF	3 NCAA Tournament games 12 conference games
Louisiana-Lafayette	Jessie Evans	2003-04	20-9	**6-8**	V	14 games (14-0); 1 NCAA Tournament game (0-1)
Louisiana-Lafayette	Robert Lee	2004-05	20-11	**3-10**	V	17 games (17-0); 1 NCAA Tournament game (0-1)
Louisiana Tech	Scotty Robertson	1971-72	(6-2)	**(8-0)**	CF	2 conference games (by opp.)
Louisiana Tech	Scotty Robertson	1972-73	(8-4)	**(10-2)**	CF	2 conference games (by opp.)
Louisiana Tech	Jerry Loyd	1991-92	(12-4)	**(13-3)**	CF	1 conference game (by opp.)
Loyola Marymount	Ron Jacobs	1979-80	14-14 (10-6)	**14-13** **(2-14)**	V CF	1 NCAA Tournament game 8 conference games
Marquette	Al McGuire	1976-77	25-7	**26-6**	F	1 game (by opp.)
Marshall	Ricky Huckabay	1986-87	25-6	**25-5**	V	1 NCAA Tournament game
Maryland	Bob Wade	1987-88	18-13	**17-12**	V	2 NCAA Tournament games
Massachusetts	John Calipari	1995-96	35-2	**31-1**	V	5 NCAA Tournament games
McNeese State	Bill Reigel	1972-73	(8-4)	**(10-2)**	CF	2 conference games (by opp.)
Memphis	Dana Kirk	1981-82	24-5	**23-4**	V	2 NCAA Tournament games
Memphis	Dana Kirk	1982-83	23-8	**22-7**	V	2 NCAA Tournament games
Memphis	Dana Kirk	1983-84	26-7	**24-6**	V	3 NCAA Tournament games
Memphis	Dana Kirk	1984-85	31-4	**27-3**	V	5 NCAA Tournament games
Memphis	Dana Kirk	1985-86	28-6	**27-5**	V	2 NCAA Tournament games
Miami (OH)	Jerry Peirson	1988-89	13-15 (8-8)	**5-23 (1-15)**	F	8 games
Michigan	Steve Fisher	1991-92	25-9	**24-9**	V	1 NCAA Tournament game
Michigan	Steve Fisher	1992-93	31-5	**0-4**	V	26 games (26-0); 6 NCAA Tournament games (5-1)
Michigan	Steve Fisher	1995-96	20-12	**1-10**	V F	20 games (20-0); 1 NCAA Tournament game (0-1) 1 game (by opp.)
Michigan	Steve Fisher	1996-97	24-11	**0-11**	V	24 games
Michigan	Brian Ellerbe	1997-98	25-9	**0-8**	V	24 games (24-0); 2 NCAA Tournament games (1-1)
Michigan	Brian Ellerbe	1998-99	12-19	**0-19**	V	12 games
Michigan State	Jud Heathcote	1976-77	10-17 (7-11)	**12-15 (9-9)**	F	2 games (by opp.)
Minnesota	Bill Musselman	1971-72	18-7	**17-6**	V	2 NCAA Tournament games
Minnesota	Jim Dutcher	1976-77	24-3 (15-3)	**0-27 (0-18)**	F	24 games
Minnesota	Clem Haskins	1993-94	22-13	**21-12**	V	2 NCAA Tournament games
Minnesota	Clem Haskins	1994-95	19-13	**20-11**	F V	1 game (by opp.) 1 NCAA Tournament game (0-1)
Minnesota	Clem Haskins	1995-96	19-13	**20-10**	F V	2 games (by opp.) (0-2) 2 NIT games (1-1)
Minnesota	Clem Haskins	1996-97	35-5	**31-4**	V	5 NCAA Tournament games
Minnesota	Clem Haskins	1997-98	20-15	**15-15**	V	5 NIT games
Missouri	Wilbur Stalcup	1960-61	(7-7)	**(8-6)**	CF	1 conference game (by opp.)
Missouri	Norm Stewart	1993-94	28-4	**25-3**	V	4 NCAA Tournament games
Montana	Jim Brandenburg	1976-77	18-8	**19-7**	F	1 game (by opp.)
Montana	Blaine Taylor	1993-94	(6-8)	**(7-7)**	CF	1 conference game (by opp.)
Montana State	Mick Durham	1993-94	(8-6)	**(0-14)**	CF	8 conference games
Murray State	Mark Gottfried	1995-96	19-10	**20-9**	F	1 game (by opp.)
Navy	Billy Lange	2004-05	(5-9)	**(6-8)**	CF	1 conference game (by opp.)
Nebraska	Jerry Bush	1960-61	(4-10)	**(5-9)**	CF	1 conference game (by opp.)
Nebraska	Joe Cipriano	1976-77	15-14	**16-13**	F	1 game (by opp.)
New Mexico State	Neil McCarthy	1991-92	25-8	**23-7**	V	3 NCAA Tournament games
New Mexico State	Neil McCarthy	1992-93	26-8	**25-7**	V	2 NCAA Tournament games
New Mexico State	Neil McCarthy	1993-94	23-8	**23-7**	V	1 NCAA Tournament game
New Mexico State	Neil McCarthy	1996-97	19-9	**0-0**	V	28 games
New Mexico State	Lou Henson	1997-98	18-12	**0-0**	V	30 games
New Orleans	Tim Floyd	1991-92	(9-7)	**(8-8)**	CF	1 conference game
North Carolina State	Jim Valvano	1986-87	20-14	**20-13**	V	1 NCAA Tournament game
North Carolina State	Jim Valvano	1987-88	24-7	**24-6**	V	1 NCAA Tournament game
Northern Arizona	Harold Merritt	1993-94	(6-8)	**(7-7)**	CF	1 conference game (by opp.)
Northern Arizona	Ben Howland	1994-95	8-18	**9-17**	F	1 game (by opp.)
Northern Arizona	Ben Howland	1995-96	6-20	**7-19**	F	1 game (by opp.)
Northern Michigan	Glenn Brown	1976-77	15-12	**16-11**	F	1 game (by opp.)
Northwestern	Tex Winter	1976-77	7-20 (5-13)	**9-18 (7-11)**	F	2 games (by opp.)

Team	Coach	Season	Orig. W-L (Conf.)	Adj. W-L (Conf.)	Type	Games Affected
Northwestern	Ricky Byrdsong	1995-96	7-20	**9-19**	F	2 games (by opp.)
Ohio	Billy Hahn	1988-89	12-17 (5-11)	**13-16 (6-10)**	F	1 game (by opp.)
Ohio State	Eldon Miller	1976-77	9-18 (4-14)	**11-16 (6-12)**	F	2 games (by opp.)
Ohio State	Randy Ayers	1995-96	10-17	**12-15**	F	2 games (by opp.)
Ohio State	Jim O'Brien	1998-99	27-9	**1-1**	V	29 games (22-7); 5 NCAA Tournament games (4-1)
Ohio State	Jim O'Brien	1999-00	23-7	**11-3**	V	14 games (11-3); 2 NCAA Tournament games (1-1)
Ohio State	Jim O'Brien	2000-01	20-11	**0-0**	V	30 games (20-10); 1 NCAA Tournament game (0-1)
Ohio State	Jim O'Brien	2001-02	24-8	**0-0**	V	30 games (23-7); 2 NCAA Tournament games (1-1)
Oklahoma	Doyle Parrack	1960-61	(2-12)	**(3-11)**	CF	1 conference game (by opp.)
Oklahoma	Kelvin Sampson	1995-96	17-13	**18-12**	F	1 game (by opp.)
Oklahoma State	Hank Iba	1960-61	(8-6)	**(9-5)**	CF	1 conference game (by opp.)
Oregon	Dick Harter	1975-76	19-11	**20-10**	F	1 game (by opp.)
Oregon	Jerry Green	1995-96	16-13 (9-9)	**17-12 (10-8)**	F	1 game (by opp.)
Oregon State	Ralph Miller	1975-76	18-9	**3-24**	F	15 games
Oregon State	Ralph Miller	1979-80	26-4	**26-3**	V	1 NCAA Tournament game
Oregon State	Ralph Miller	1980-81	26-2	**26-1**	V	1 NCAA Tournament game
Oregon State	Ralph Miller	1981-82	25-5	**23-4**	V	3 NCAA Tournament games
Oregon State	Eddie Payne	1995-96	4-23 (2-16)	**6-21 (4-14)**	F	2 games (by opp.)
Pacific	Bob Thomason	1994-95	14-13	**15-12**	F	1 game (by opp.)
Portland	Jack Avina	1975-76	9-18	**10-17**	F	1 game (by opp.)
Portland State	Ken Edwards	1975-76	17-10	**18-9**	F	1 game (by opp.)
Prairie View A&M	Jerry Francis	2004-05	(5-13)	**(6-12)**	CF	1 conference game (by opp.)
Purdue	Fred Schaus	1976-77	19-9 (13-5)	**20-8 (14-4)**	F	1 game (by opp.)
Purdue	Gene Keady	1995-96	26-6	**7-23**	F V	18 games (18-0) 2 NCAA Tournament games (1-1)
Radford	Dr. Ron Bradley	1992-93	(8-8)	**(9-7)**	CF	1 conference game (by opp.)
St. Bonaventure	Jan van Breda Kolff	2002-03	13-14	**1-14**	V	12 games
St. John's	Mike Jarvis	2000-01	14-15	**5-15**	V	9 games
St. John's	Mike Jarvis	2001-02	20-12	**7-11**	V	13 games (13-0); 1 NCAA Tournament game (0-1)
St. John's	Mike Jarvis	2002-03	21-13	**1-13**	V	20 games
St. John's	Mike Jarvis	2003-04	6-21	**2-21**	V	4 games
Saint Joseph's	Jack Ramsay	1960-61	25-5	**22-4**	V	4 NCAA Tournament games
Saint Mary's (CA)	Bill Oates	1979-80	(9-7)	**(11-5)**	CF	2 conference games (by opp.)
San Diego	Jim Brovelli	1979-80	(1-15)	**(2-14)**	CF	1 conference game (by opp.)
San Francisco	Jim Brovelli	1994-95	10-19	**11-18**	F	1 game (by opp.)
San Francisco	Philip Mathews	1995-96	15-12	**16-11**	F	1 game (by opp.)
Santa Clara	Carroll Williams	1979-80	(8-8)	**(10-6)**	CF	2 conference games (by opp.)
Seattle	Bill O'Connor	1975-76	11-16	**12-15**	F	1 game (by opp.)
Seton Hall	George Blaney	1995-96	12-16	**13-15**	F	1 game (by opp.)
Southern California	Bob Boyd	1975-76	11-16	**12-15**	F	1 game (by opp.)
Southern California	Charlie Parker	1994-95	7-21 (2-16)	**9-19 (4-14)**	F	2 games (by opp.)
Southern California	Henry Bibby (1-8 adj.); Charlie Parker (12-9)	1995-96	11-19 (4-14)	**13-17 (6-12)**	F	2 games (by opp.)
Stanford	Dick DiBiaso	1975-76	9-18	**11-16**	F	2 games (by opp.)
Stanford	Mike Montgomery	1995-96	20-9 (12-6)	**21-8 (13-5)**	F	1 game (by opp.)
Texas-Arlington	Barry Dowd	1972-73	(6-6)	**(8-4)**	CF	2 conference games (by opp.)
Texas Christian	Billy Tubbs	1995-96	15-15	**16-14**	F	1 game (by opp.)
Texas-Pan American	Kevin Wall	1991-92	1-15	**0-16**	F	1 conference game
Texas Southern	Robert Moreland	1993-94	22-7	**23-6**	F	1 game (by opp.)
Texas Southern	Robert Moreland	1995-96	11-15	**12-14**	F	1 game (by opp.)
Texas Southern	Ronnie Courtney	2004-05	(8-9)	**(5-12)**	CF	3 conference games
Texas Tech	James Dickey	1995-96	30-2	**28-1**	V	3 NCAA Tournament games
Toledo	Jay Eck	1988-89	16-15 (9-7)	**18-13 (11-5)**	F	2 games (by opp.)
UCLA	Gene Bartow	1975-76	27-5	**28-4**	F	1 game (by opp.)
UCLA	Larry Brown	1979-80	22-10	**17-9**	V	6 NCAA Tournament games
UCLA	Jim Harrick	1994-95	31-2 (16-2)	**32-1 (17-1)**	F	1 game (by opp.)
UCLA	Steve Lavin	1998-99	22-9	**22-8**	V	1 NCAA Tournament game
Utah State	Dutch Belnap	1975-76	12-14	**14-12**	F	2 games (by opp.)
Valparaiso	Homer Drew	1995-96	21-11	**22-10**	F	1 game (by opp.)
Vermont	Peter Salzberg	1976-77	8-17	**9-16**	F	1 game (by opp.)
Villanova	Jack Kraft	1970-71	27-7	**23-6**	V	5 NCAA Tournament games
Washington	Marv Harshman	1975-76	22-6	**23-5**	F	1 game (by opp.)
Washington	Bob Bender	1994-95	9-18 (5-13)	**10-17 (6-12)**	F	1 game (by opp.)
Washington State	George Raveling	1975-76	18-8	**19-7**	F	1 game (by opp.)
Washington State	Kevin Eastman	1995-96	17-12	**18-11**	F	1 game (by opp.)
Weber State	Ron Abegglen	1993-94	(10-4)	**(11-3)**	CF	1 conference game (by opp.)
Western Kentucky	John Oldham	1970-71	24-6	**20-5**	V	5 NCAA Tournament games
Western Michigan	Bob Donewald	1995-96	15-12	**16-11**	F	1 game (by opp.)
Wisconsin	Bill Cofield	1976-77	9-18 (5-13)	**11-16 (7-11)**	F	2 games (by opp.)
Wisconsin	Bill Cofield	1981-82	(3-15)	**(0-18)**	CF	3 conference games
Wisconsin	Steve Yoder	1982-83	(3-15)	**(0-18)**	CF	3 conference games
Wisconsin	Steve Yoder	1983-84	(4-14)	**(0-18)**	CF	4 conference games
Wisconsin	Dick Bennett	1995-96	17-15	**18-14**	F	1 game (by opp.)

ANNUAL REVIEW

Annual Review

What follows is a year-by-year rundown of 114 seasons of college basketball, incorporating an in-depth look at every NCAA Tournament (with annotated brackets, box scores and statistics) along with conference standings, consensus All-America teams, award winners, postseason NIT results, NCAA individual and team statistical leaders, polls and top recruits.

THE EARLY YEARS: The Premo-Porretta Polls (1895-96 through 1947-48 seasons) provide a rare snapshot of the sport's hierarchy in the years before national polling. Pat Premo, a professor emeritus at St. Bonaventure University, and Phil Porretta, a former computer programmer, have 40 years' experience each researching college basketball games. Their archival work, first published in 1995, has helped them retroactively determine rankings, because they often uncover game results that were not reported in record books or media guides, including competition against YMCA, club and AAU teams.

CONFERENCE STANDINGS: The standings begin with the 1901-02 season. Any discrepancies between the schools' archives and records kept by the NCAA have been resolved by Gary Johnson, the NCAA's associate director for statistics. The NCAA, for example, will consider a game against a military base in the 1950s an exhibition, while a school may count the match as part of its official record.

Throughout their history, conferences have changed the way their regular-season champions are determined if they have multiple divisions or in the case of a tie at the top of the standings.

- **Big East** 1995-96 through '97-98 and 2000-01 through '02-03: The winners of the East and West Divisions were considered conference co-champions.
- **Conference USA** From 1995-96 through 2002-03: The title went to the division winner with the best conference record.
- **Ivy League** If the top teams had the same conference record, a one-game playoff determined the champion.
- **Mid-American** Through 1997-98: If the top teams had the same conference record, a playoff determined the champion. Starting in 1998-99: The title went to the division winner with the highest conference winning percentage.
- **Missouri Valley** For 1907-08 through '09-10 and '12-13: A playoff between division winners determined the champion. 1911-12, '13-14: Each division leader was considered co-champion. 1943-44, '44-45: With no conference play due to WWII, the champion (Oklahoma State both years) was chosen by a vote of the teams. 1961-62, '63-64, '68-69, '70-71, '71-72: If the top teams had the same conference record, a playoff determined the champion.
- **Pacific-10 (PCC)** 1922-23 through '54-55: A playoff between division winners determined the champion.
- **Southeastern** There was no conference tournament to determine the 1934-35 SEC champion. LSU and Kentucky shared the title.
- **Sun Belt** Starting in 2000-01: Division winners were considered conference co-champions.
- **Western Athletic** 1996-97 through '98-99: Each division winner was considered co-champion.

CONSENSUS ALL-AMERICAS: The NCAA recognizes certain selectors every year—predominantly media outlets—and assigns points to each of their All-America choices based on whether they were named to first, second or third teams. The players with the most total points are named to the consensus first or second teams. We have included the Helms Athletic Foundation's retroactive consensus All-Americas from the 1904-05 season to '27-28 and its national champions from 1900-01 through '37-38.

NATIONAL STATISTICS: Individual and team statistical leaders, beginning with the 1947-48 season, come from the NCAA archives and were supplemented by the *ESPN College Basketball Encyclopedia* research staff. The NCAA began recording weekly scoring and shooting statistics in 1947-48. It added modern rebounding statistics in '62-63, assists in '83-84, blocked shots and steals in '85-86, and three-point field goals in '86-87. In some seasons, however, a full listing of certain individual or team statistics may not be available.

RECRUITING: The listings of top high school seniors are based on *Bob Gibbons All-Star Report* (1979-2006) and on the ESPNU 150 by Scouts Inc. (2007-09). Gibbons has been rating the nation's top 150 high school seniors for more than 30 years. High school rankings are subjective; both the Gibbons and the Scouts Inc. staffs watch players in action (sometimes several times) to evaluate them fairly. Scouts Inc. grades each player according to his potential. A grade of 98-100 (high-major-plus prospect) means he should have an immediate impact at a national program with the potential for early entry into the NBA. A 94-97 grade (high-major prospect) means a player could be a three- or four-year starter and have an opportunity for all-league honors.

POLL PROGRESSIONS: For each season beginning in 1948-49, readers can track a team's movement from week to week in the Associated Press poll. Each team's weekly record corresponds to the day of the poll's release. The coaches' poll—usually released a day later—accompanies the AP's for comparison. An arrow followed by a number (↓4) indicates the team's upward or downward movement in the polls and the number of places it moved. Teams that were unranked the previous week are marked ↥. Teams that dropped from the AP poll but still appeared in the coaches' poll are marked Ր. Each poll is annotated with several historical notes, each note labeled by a letter (Ⓒ). A letter appearing on a poll's date line is not associated with a specific team but is of general historical interest. Some team records in final polls may not reflect postseason tournament results.

RPI: The Ratings Percentage Index was devised in 1981 to help the NCAA Tournament Selection Committee evaluate teams for possible at-large bids. As currently calculated, a school's RPI is 25% of the team's D1 winning percentage, 50% of the team's opponents' D1 winning percentage and 25% the team's opponents' opponents' D1 winning percentage. Jim Sukup of *Collegiate Basketball News* began publishing his RPI in 1992, and the NCAA started releasing its own listing in 2005-06.

NCAA TOURNAMENT BRACKETS, BOX SCORES AND STATISTICAL LEADERS: Each Tournament bracket includes notations highlighting compelling games or significant moments. The box scores for Tournaments from 1939 through '92 were provided by Jim Savage, author of *The Encyclopedia of the NCAA Basketball Tournament.* The ESPN Stats & Information Group in Bristol, Conn., gathered box scores for 1993-2009. The *College Basketball Encyclopedia* includes box scores for each Tournamet from the Round of 16 through the national championship game. Individual and team statistical leaders from the Tournament, along with statistics for consensus and All-Tournament teams, were generated from a database of all Tournament box scores, which is accessible via ESPN.com.

Readers reviewing box scores from NIT or NCAA Tournaments before 1945 should note that the 1944-45 season was the first in which five personal fouls disqualified a player. Before that, players fouled out with four (five in overtime games). From 1951-52 to '53-54, games consisted of four 10-minute quarters. For those Tournaments, we have combined the quarters into first- and second-half totals. In some box scores, a player with statistics might show zero minutes played; in fact, he played less than one minute.

IN THE BEGINNING

With all the splendor and spectacle that now defines college basketball—especially during that wonderful season of the year known as March Madness—it is difficult to imagine a time when the game was played with nine players to a side shooting at peach baskets hung in small, musty gyms. Games were composed of two 15-minute halves and went into sudden death overtime to resolve ties. Very little of what happened in those games looked anything like the high-flying, (mostly) fast-paced battles that take place at the domes, fancy arenas and even asphalt courts of today. But at its core, the modern game is still firmly rooted in the 13 original rules of "basket ball" set out by Dr. James Naismith, a physical education instructor in Springfield, Mass., in December 1891—rules that were originally published in the Springfield College newspaper, *The Triangle*, in 1892.

The first known public basketball game was played on March 11, 1892, at the Springfield YMCA Training School. (A team of students beat the faculty, 5-1.) It took a while for basketball to catch on and propagate throughout the college ranks; most early games were confined to YMCA teams. But catch on it did. On Feb. 9, 1895, the Minnesota School of Agriculture defeated Hamline in the first game between two colleges. It was played on a handball court in the basement of the Hamline science building. With nine players to a side, defense trumped offense. The final score was 9-3.

After that, college basketball began to evolve quickly. In 1896, a team of Yale students helped elevate the sport's profile by playing against many of the East's top YMCA teams. The first known women's intercollegiate game took place on April 4, 1896, at the San Francisco Armory, with Stanford beating Cal, 2-1. The first game of five-on-five between two true college squads was played in New Haven, Conn., in 1897, with Yale defeating Penn, 32-10.

That year the YMCA ceded oversight of basketball to the Amateur Athletic Union (AAU)—an arrangement that didn't last a decade. In April 1905, representatives of 15 colleges met in Philadelphia and, led by Penn's Ralph Morgan, created the Basket Ball Rules Committee. Within three months they had drawn up a set of rules that allowed for rougher play than the AAU did. Later that year, concerned about the increasing number of injuries in college football, President Theodore Roosevelt called together the presidents of Harvard, Yale and Princeton for a series of meetings at the White House. One result of those meetings was the formation in 1906 of the Intercollegiate Athletic Association of the United States (IAAUS), which was charged with establishing rules for football, and eventually all amateur sports. In 1909, the Basket Ball Rules Committee was absorbed by the IAAUS, which a year later was renamed the National Collegiate Athletic Association.

Yale was an early power—and also an early rules violator: The 1898 squad was suspended by the AAU, though reinstated a week later, for playing against an unsanctioned team (a National Guard unit from Yonkers). But such minor transgressions weren't enough to hold the game back. It spread to clusters of schools along the East Coast, the West Coast and in middle America. Basketball thrived at the University of Minnesota, and at Bucknell, too. Columbia established its team in the 20th century's first decade, as did Wisconsin, Chicago, Washington State and Navy.

In 1906, nets began to replace the peach baskets. A five-minute overtime period to decide tied games was introduced in 1908. The rules of basketball for colleges, YMCAs and AAU games were unified in 1914. The first major college tournament was held from Feb. 25 to March 2, 1921, by the Southern Conference; it was won by Kentucky. The tournament format would catch on—to a greater extent than anyone could have predicted—spread to other conferences and, in the 1930s, serve as a model for national tournaments.

One of the stars of the early era was Wisconsin's Chris Steinmetz (1902-05), a Naismith Hall of Famer and a three-time All-America who, in his senior season, scored 25.7 ppg for a team that averaged only 37.8 a game. John Schommer led the University of Chicago to three straight Big Ten championships (1907-09) and led the conference in scoring four times. In the 1920s, future Hall of Fame forward Vic Hanson helped establish Syracuse's basketball tradition by guiding the Orangemen to a three-year record of 48–7 and the 1926 national championship (as retroactively determined in 1941 by the Helms Athletic Foundation). Hanson is the only athlete to be inducted into both the College Football Hall of Fame and the Naismith Memorial Basketball Hall of Fame.

Charles "Stretch" Murphy, at 6'6" one of the sport's first great big men, helped pioneer a revolutionary running game at Purdue between 1927 and '30. A dominant rebounder, Murphy uncorked outlet passes that created easy baskets for teammates (such as the future legendary UCLA coach John Wooden). Around that same time, forward Charley Hyatt was making his mark at Pittsburgh, scoring 880 points in three seasons and leading the Panthers to the 1928 and 1930 Helms Foundation national championships. Perhaps the biggest win of Pitt's 1929-30 campaign came against Montana State. Hyatt scored 27 points against Hall of Famer John "Cat" Thompson, including a last-second basket, in the Panthers' 37-36 victory.

The list of teams with the most wins in the 1930s shows the game's national appeal: Washington (206), Long Island (198), Western Kentucky (197), St. John's (181) and Notre Dame (170). On Dec. 30, 1936, Stanford traveled cross-country to play Long Island, the presumed No. 1 team in the nation and owner of a 43-game winning streak. Before 17,623 fans at New York City's Madison Square Garden, the hometown favorites fell 45-31, thanks largely to Stanford forward Hank Luisetti—a three-time All-America and future Hall of Famer—who showed off his running one-hander to great effect. Players at the time were still taking mostly two-handed set shots and occasional one-handed hook shots. In the years that followed, Luisetti's shot caught on in the East and helped speed up play. On Jan. 1, 1938, Luisetti became the first player to score 50 points in a game, during a 92-27 win over Duquesne.

The days of 5-1 and 6-4 final scores were truly dead. College basketball was poised to expand in appeal with the birth of the national tournaments. The first was Naismith's own National Association of Intercollegiate Basketball (today's NAIA), which held an eight-team tourney in Kansas City in 1937; Central Missouri State beat Morningside College (Iowa), 35-24. The following year, the more prestigious National Invitational Tournament began; on March 16, 1938, Temple beat Colorado, 60-36 at Madison Square Garden, in the first NIT championship game. In 1939, another upstart tournament began, organized by the National Association of Basketball Coaches, with Oregon beating Ohio State, 46-33, in the final at Evanston, Ill. In 1940, that upstart would take on the name by which we know it today: the NCAA Tournament. —David Scott

1895-1896

The first college game with five players on each side was played on Jan. 16, 1896, when the University of Chicago beat Iowa, 15-12, in Iowa City. Iowa's starters were students who happened to be a YMCA team. The athletic director at Chicago, Amos Alonzo Stagg, had been the football coach at the Springfield, Mass., YMCA Training School, where one of his players was James Naismith.

PREMO-PORRETTA POWER POLL

	SCHOOL	RECORD
1	**Yale**	8-5
2	**Minnesota School of Agriculture**	10-2
3	**Temple**	15-7
4	**Bloomsburg**	6-1
5	**Chicago❖**	5-2
6	**Wesleyan (CT)❖**	1-0
7	**Savage School of Phys. Ed. (NY)**	0-1
8	**Iowa❖**	2-5
9	**Bucknell**	1-3
10	**Mount Union**	3-1
11	**Minnesota**	3-5
12	**Allegheny**	1-1
13	**Central Pennsylvania**	0-2
14	**Washington**	1-1
15	**Macalester❖**	0-4

1896-97

Yale's 32-10 defeat of Penn is considered the first intercollegiate game between two "true" college teams. It was also the first time Yale sold tickets—25 cents for general admission and 35 cents for a reserved seat—to a basketball game.

PREMO-PORRETTA POWER POLL

	SCHOOL	RECORD
1	**Yale**	11-6#
2	**Bucknell**	4-1
3	**Chicago❖**	5-2
4	**Trinity (CT)**	8-5
5	**Minnesota School of Agriculture**	6-0
6	**Notre Dame❖**	2-1
7	**Wabash**	1-0
8	**Nebraska**	2-0
9	**Temple**	10-11
10	**Purdue**	1-1
11	**Penn State**	1-1
12	**Central Pennsylvania**	1-1
13	**Minnesota**	3-6-1
14	**Butler**	1-0
15	**Penn**	2-4#
16	**Bloomsburg**	6-3
17	**Iowa❖**	2-4
18	**Springfield (MA)❖**	0-2
19	**Mount Union**	1-1
20	**Macalester❖**	0-3

1897-98

Backboards were first installed behind baskets, although it wasn't until 1921 that the backboards were moved away from the wall of the gym. There were still very few intercollegiate games; school teams mainly played against AAU squads or in YMCA leagues. This was the first year in which YMCA league rules called for five men per side.

PREMO-PORRETTA POWER POLL

	SCHOOL	RECORD
1	**Mount Union**	8-1
2	**Westminster (PA)**	4-2
3	**Yale**	12-9#
4	**Bloomsburg**	5-1
5	**Chicago❖**	1-0
6	**Temple**	22-5
7	**Minnesota School of Agriculture**	1-0
8	**Penn State**	2-1
9	**Bucknell**	4-4
10	**Western Reserve**	4-1
11	**Hiram**	3-2
12	**Allegheny**	2-2
13	**Savage School of Phys. Ed. (NY)**	6-1
14	**Central Pennsylvania**	0-1
15	**Nebraska**	1-3
16	**Iowa❖**	0-1
17	**Notre Dame**	1-2
18	**Minnesota**	2-4
19	**Macalester❖**	1-3
20	**Rose-Hulman**	2-2

1898-99

Yale captain John Kirkland Clark would soon bring the game of basketball to rival Harvard when he began attending law school there in 1900.

PREMO-PORRETTA POWER POLL

	SCHOOL	RECORD
1	**Yale**	9-2
2	**Bloomsburg**	10-0
3	**Nebraska**	4-0
4	**Allegheny**	8-1
5	**Macalester❖**	7-3
6	**Wabash**	2-0
7	**Temple**	18-6
8	**Minnesota**	5-4
9	**Ohio State**	12-4
10	**Hiram**	4-1
11	**Stevens Point (WI)**	6-2
12	**Notre Dame**	2-0
13	**Kansas**	7-4
14	**Penn Military College**	1-0
15	**West Chester**	11-1
16	**Penn State**	2-3
17	**Mount Union**	2-3
18	**Geneva College (PA)**	3-6
19	**Bucknell**	3-5
20	**Illinois State**	2-0

1899-1900

Basketball was still very much a contact sport. The players on Yale's squad—who called themselves the Bruisers—wore padded pants.

PREMO-PORRETTA POWER POLL

	SCHOOL	RECORD
1	**Yale**	9-6
2	**Nebraska**	5-0
3	**Dartmouth❖**	22-4-1
4	**Penn State**	7-1
5	**Geneva College (PA)**	8-3#
6	**Minnesota**	10-2
7	**Allegheny**	10-4
8	**Illinois State**	5-0
9	**Hiram**	7-1
10	**Bucknell**	6-3
11	**Ohio State**	8-4
12	**Wisconsin**	1-1
13	**Drexel Institute (PA)**	2-0
14	**Mount Union**	4-3
15	**Superior State College (WI)**	2-2
16	**Central Pennsylvania**	1-0
17	**Bloomsburg**	12-2
18	**Trenton State**	3-2
19	**Westminster (PA)**	4-5
20	**Trinity (CT)**	2-0

1900-01

At Bucknell, future baseball Hall of Fame pitcher Christy Mathewson also excelled in basketball and football (as a kicker and a fullback). Yale became a member of the New England Inter-collegiate Basketball League, precursor to the Ivy League.

PREMO-PORRETTA POWER POLL

	SCHOOL	RECORD
1	**Bucknell**	12-1
2	**Purdue**	12-0
3	**Yale (Helms champion)**	10-6
4	**Allegheny**	14-2
5	**Amherst❖**	4-0
6	**Penn State**	5-1
7	**Minnesota**	11-3#
8	**Williams**	9-2#
9	**Geneva College (PA)**	10-2
10	**Hiram**	9-2#
11	**Superior State College (WI)**	8-2
12	**Dartmouth**	13-11#
13	**Western Reserve**	5-3#
14	**Princeton**	7-5
15	**Michigan State**	3-0
16	**Harvard**	11-8
17	**Mount Union**	10-6#
18	**Rensselaer Polytechnic❖**	4-4
19	**Butler**	2-1
20	**Lafayette**	4-3

1901-02

East met West (as defined at the time) as Yale lost to Minnesota. East Coast teams played a more physical style of basketball, while Western teams were known for their more up-tempo approach.

PREMO-PORRETTA POWER POLL

	SCHOOL	RECORD
1	**Minnesota (Helms champion)**	15-0
2	**Allegheny**	12-1
3	**Amherst❖**	8-0
4	**Purdue**	10-3
5	**Bucknell**	13-2#
6	**Mount Union**	11-3
7	**Williams**	13-4#
8	**Ripon❖**	4-0
9	**Yale**	13-8
10	**Dartmouth**	11-5
11	**Michigan State**	5-0
12	**Iowa**	10-2
13	**St. Lawrence**	6-1
14	**Wisconsin**	7-3
15	**Penn State**	8-3#
16	**Geneva College (PA)**	7-4
17	**Hiram**	7-4#
18	**Harvard**	9-5
19	**Washington**	7-0
20	**Rensselaer Polytechnic❖**	3-4

CONFERENCE STANDINGS

IVY	Conference			Overall		
	W	L	PCT	W	L	PCT
Yale	5	3	.625	13	8	.619
Princeton	4	4	.500	10	10	.500
Columbia	3	3	.500	4	3	.571
Harvard	3	5	.375	9	5	.643
Cornell	2	4	.333	5	5	.500

1902-1903

Minnesota's players were known as the Invincible Five for their pressure defense. They held three opponents to zero field goals, an amazing achievement even then.

PREMO-PORRETTA POWER POLL

	SCHOOL	RECORD
1	**Minnesota**	13-0
2	**Yale (Helms champion)**	15-1
3	**Bucknell**	10-0
4	**Purdue**	8-0
5	**Colgate**	7-1
6	**Williams**	18-2#
7	**Grove City (PA)**	13-1
8	**Geneva College (PA)**	10-1
9	**Allegheny**	10-2-1
10	**Michigan State**	6-0
11	**Minnesota School of Agriculture**	10-1
12	**Vanderbilt**	6-0
13	**Ohio State**	5-2
14	**Columbia**	10-6
15	**Wheaton**	14-3#
16	**Princeton**	8-7
17	**Cheyenne Business College**	1-0
18	**Haskell Indian Institute (KS)**	3-1
19	**Nebraska**	7-5
20	**Latter Day Saints (UT)**	15-1

CONFERENCE STANDINGS

IVY	Conference			Overall		
	W	L	PCT	W	L	PCT
Yale	7	1	.875	15	1	.938
Columbia	5	3	.625	10	6	.625
Princeton	4	4	.500	8	7	.533
Cornell	2	6	.250	6	6	.500
Harvard	2	6	.250	5	8	.385

❖ Record for a club team that featured student players, but not an official part of the program's history
Record differs from the school's and/or the NCAA's because it includes noncollegiate competition or because the outcome of some games is in dispute

1903-04

Harry Fisher, Columbia's leading scorer from 1902 to '05 (6.7 ppg in 1903-04), went on to coach four schools in his career, including his alma mater, and to edit the *Collegiate Guide*, the official basketball rulebook.

PREMO-PORRETTA POWER POLL

	SCHOOL	RECORD
1	Columbia (Helms champion)	17-1
2	Minnesota	10-2
3	Allegheny	13-2
4	Holy Cross	10-2
5	Chicago	7-0
6	Penn	10-4
7	Princeton	10-5
8	Purdue	11-2
9	Hiram	10-3#
10	Cumberland (TN)	4-0
11	Williams	15-7#
12	Ohio State	10-4
13	Wisconsin	11-4
14	Washington	5-1
15	Colgate	12-5
16	Dartmouth	10-7#
17	Iowa	6-2
18	Nebraska	9-5
19	Vanderbilt	6-1
20	Lehigh	5-2

CONFERENCE STANDINGS

IVY	Conference			Overall		
	W	L	PCT	W	L	PCT
Columbia	10	0	1.000	17	1	.944
Penn	6	4	.600	10	4	.714
Princeton	5	5	.500	10	5	.667
Yale	5	5	.500	10	12	.455
Harvard	1	6	.143	1	7	.125
Cornell	1	7	.125	6	13	.316

1904-05

Columbia was able to get past Minnesota, 27-15, and Wisconsin, 21-15, in New York City. Minnesota had been dubbed the champions of the West, allowing Columbia to claim national superiority.

PREMO-PORRETTA POWER POLL

	SCHOOL	RECORD
1	Columbia (Helms champion)	19-1
2	Williams	20-2#
3	Wabash	8-0
4	Allegheny	10-2
5	Ohio State	12-2
6	Syracuse	16-7#
7	Harvard	11-5
8	Bucknell	8-1
9	Colgate	10-7
10	Holy Cross	6-4
11	Brown	13-6#
12	Yale	22-13
13	Muskingum (OH)	8-0
14	Butler	16-2#
15	Augustana (IL)	9-0#
16	Dartmouth	20-10-1
17	Princeton	8-5
18	Lewis (IL)❖	20-5
19	Nebraska	11-5
20	Oberlin	7-4

CONFERENCE STANDINGS

IVY	Conference			Overall		
	W	L	PCT	W	L	PCT
Columbia	8	0	1.000	19	1	.950
Yale	5	3	.625	22	13	.629
Princeton	4	4	.500	8	5	.615
Cornell	3	7	.300	5	17	.227
Penn	1	7	.125	8	15	.348

CONSENSUS ALL-AMERICAS

PLAYER	POS	SCHOOL
Oliver DeGray Vanderbilt	G	Princeton
Harry Fisher	F	Columbia
Marcus Hurley	G	Columbia
Willard Hyatt	C	Yale
Gilmore Kinney	F	Yale
C.D. McLees	G	Wisconsin
James Ozanne	F	Chicago
Walter Runge	F	Colgate
Chris Steinmetz	F	Wisconsin
George Tuck	C	Minnesota

Selector: Helms Foundation

1905-06

Five of the six Wabash players were local kids from the same town as the school—Crawfordsville, Ind. Dartmouth was named Helms champion after posting a 16–2 record that included two two-point victories and a 2–1 record against Wesleyan. Former Yale guard Mike Donahue brought the game to Auburn as the school's first head coach. Iron Mike believed basketball was a contact sport; he didn't bother to call fouls during scrimmages because it slowed the pace of the game.

PREMO-PORRETTA POWER POLL

	SCHOOL	RECORD
1	Wabash	17-1
2	Dartmouth (Helms champion)	16-2
3	Minnesota	13-2
4	Williams	14-3-1#
5	Wisconsin	12-2
6	Penn	16-4
7	Columbia	12-4
8	Syracuse	9-3
9	Harvard	12-4
10	Westminster (PA)	13-5
11	Oregon State	10-0
12	Holy Cross	12-3
13	Colgate	7-6
14	Bucknell	10-2
15	Lowell Tech	16-1
16	Nebraska	12-3
17	Wesleyan	12-8#
18	Allegheny	12-5
19	Swarthmore	11-4
20	BYU	11-1

CONFERENCE STANDINGS

BIG TEN	Conference			Overall		
	W	L	PCT	W	L	PCT
Minnesota	6	1	.857	13	2	.867
Wisconsin	6	2	.750	12	2	.857
Indiana	2	2	.500	7	9	.438
Chicago	3	5	.375	5	5	.500
Purdue	3	6	.333	4	7	.364
Illinois	3	7	.300	6	8	.429
Iowa	-	-	-	11	5	.686

IVY	Conference			Overall			
	W	L	PCT	W	L	T	PCT
Penn	9	1	.900	16	4	-	.800
Columbia	7	3	.700	12	4	-	.750
Harvard	6	4	.600	12	4	-	.750
Yale	4	6	.400	11	17	2	.400
Princeton	3	7	.300	5	10	-	.333
Cornell	1	9	.100	2	10	1	.192

CONSENSUS ALL-AMERICAS

PLAYER	POS	SCHOOL
Harold Amberg	C	Harvard
Garfield Brown	G	Minnesota
Eugene Cowell	G	Williams
George M. Flint	F	Penn
George Grebenstein	F	Dartmouth
Ralph Griffiths	G	Harvard
Marcus Hurley	G/F	Columbia
Charles Keinath	F	Penn
James McKeag	G/F	Chicago
John Schommer	C	Chicago

Selector: Helms Foundation

1906-07

Williams captain Oswald Tower would become a major influence on basketball as a longtime member of the official rules committee. Chicago guard Harlan O. "Pat" Page was also an end on the 1907 football team that, in 1908, would execute the Statue of Liberty play 21 times in an 18-12 win over Wisconsin. A sportswriter gave the play its name that day.

PREMO-PORRETTA POWER POLL

	SCHOOL	RECORD
1	Williams	15-1
2	Chicago (Helms champion)	21-2#
3	Dartmouth	13-4
4	Yale	30-7-1
5	Columbia	15-4
6	Wabash	17-2
7	Baker (KS)	13-0
8	Allegheny	10-1
9	Minnesota	10-2
10	Wisconsin	11-3
11	Oregon State	17-1
12	Concordia Seminary (MO)	5-0
13	Bucknell	10-1
14	Dayton	15-0#
15	Penn	15-8
16	North Dakota State	11-1
17	Lehigh	9-2
18	Westminster (PA)	7-1
19	Michigan State	14-2
20	Grinnell	9-2

CONFERENCE STANDINGS

BIG TEN	Conference			Overall		
	W	L	PCT	W	L	PCT
Chicago	6	2	.750	22	2	.917
Minnesota	6	2	.750	10	2	.833
Wisconsin	6	2	.750	11	3	.786
Purdue	2	6	.250	7	8	.467
Illinois	0	8	.000	1	10	.091
Indiana	-	-	-	9	5	.643
Iowa	-	-	-	5	5	.500
Northwestern	-	-	-	1	5	.167

IVY	Conference			Overall			
	W	L	PCT	W	L	T	PCT
Yale	9	1	.900	30	7	1	.803
Columbia	8	2	.800	15	4	-	.789
Penn	6	4	.600	15	8	-	.652
Harvard	4	6	.400	7	9	-	.438
Princeton	2	8	.200	4	10	-	.286
Cornell	1	9	.100	1	11	-	.083

CONSENSUS ALL-AMERICAS

PLAYER	POS	SCHOOL
Arthur Frank	G	Wisconsin
George M. Flint	F	Penn
Albert Houghton	G	Chicago
Marcus Hurley	G	Columbia
Charles Keinath	F	Penn
Gilmore Kinney	F	Yale
John Ryan	C	Columbia
John Schommer	C	Chicago
Oswald Tower	F	Williams
L. Parson Warren	F	Williams

Selector: Helms Foundation

❖ Record for a club team that featured student players, but not an official part of the program's history

Record differs from the school's and/or the NCAA's because it includes noncollegiate competition or because the outcome of some games is in dispute

ANNUAL REVIEW

1907-08

All five starters on the Wabash team—now collectively known as the First Wonder 5 (there would be four future Wonder 5s)—were named first-team all-state by the *Indianapolis News*.

PREMO-PORRETTA POWER POLL

	SCHOOL	RECORD
1	Wabash	24-0
2	Chicago (Helms champion)	24-2
3	Penn	24-4
4	Wisconsin	10-2
5	Allegheny	12-0
6	Bucknell	12-0
7	Grinnell	14-3
8	Syracuse	10-3
9	Colorado Mines❖	5-0
10	Lehigh	6-1
11	Notre Dame	12-4
12	Brigham Young College-Logan	10-1
13	CCNY	9-2
14	Army	9-3
15	Williams	10-4
16	Penn State	10-4
17	Cincinnati	9-0
18	Illinois	20-6
19	Michigan State	15-5
20	Dartmouth	11-4

CONFERENCE STANDINGS

BIG TEN	Conference			Overall		
	W	L	PCT	W	L	PCT
Chicago	7	1	.875	24	2	.923
Wisconsin	7	1	.875	10	2	.833
Illinois	4	4	.500	20	6	.769
Minnesota	2	6	.250	11	7	.611
Purdue	0	8	.000	5	9	.357
Indiana	-	-	-	9	6	.600
Iowa	-	-	-	10	6	.625
Northwestern	-	-	-	2	7	.222

Playoff: **Chicago d. Wisconsin 18-16**

IVY	Conference			Overall		
	W	L	PCT	W	L	PCT
Penn	8	0	1.000	24	4	.857
Yale	5	3	.625	20	9	.690
Columbia	5	3	.625	12	13	.480
Princeton	1	7	.125	7	10	.412
Cornell	1	7	.125	5	8	.385

MISSOURI VALLEY	Conference			Overall		
	W	L	PCT	W	L	PCT
NORTH						
Iowa State	1	0	1.000	1	1	.500
Nebraska	0	0	.000	9	10	.474
Drake	0	1	.000	1	4	.200
SOUTH						
Kansas	4	0	1.000	18	6	.750
Wash.-St. Louis	1	0	1.000	4	2	.667
Missouri	0	5	.000	8	10	.444

CONSENSUS ALL-AMERICAS

PLAYER	POS	SCHOOL
Hugh Harper	G	Wisconsin
Julian Hayward	G	Wesleyan
Charles Keinath	F	Penn
Haskell Noyes	G	Yale
Harlan O. "Pat" Page	G	Chicago
Don Pryor	F/C	Brown
John Ryan	C	Columbia
Raymond Scanlon	G	Notre Dame
John Schommer	C	Chicago
Ira Streusand	F	CCNY
Helmer Swenholt	F	Wisconsin

SELECTOR: HELMS FOUNDATION

1908-09

Chicago center John Schommer became the first player to lead the Big Ten (then the Western Conference) in scoring for three consecutive seasons (1906-07 to '08-09)—a feat that would not be matched until the early 1950s. Schommer was a four-sport varsity athlete, and he is often credited with inventing the glass backboard.

PREMO-PORRETTA POWER POLL

	SCHOOL	RECORD
1	Chicago (Helms champion)	12-0
2	NYU	13-0
3	Swarthmore	12-0
4	Columbia	16-1
5	Williams	13-1
6	Ohio State	11-1
7	Grinnell	12-1
8	Allegheny	11-2
9	Notre Dame	33-7
10	Army	9-2
11	California	10-0#
12	Oregon State	10-1
13	Kansas	25-3
14	Hope (MI)	8-1
15	Wooster	10-2
16	Whittier	14-0
17	Illinois State	9-0
18	Penn	19-6
19	Wisconsin	8-4
20	Vanderbilt	11-4

CONFERENCE STANDINGS

BIG TEN	Conference			Overall		
	W	L	PCT	W	L	PCT
Chicago	12	0	1.000	12	0	1.000
Purdue	6	4	.600	8	4	.667
Wisconsin	5	4	.556	8	4	.667
Illinois	5	6	.455	7	6	.538
Minnesota	3	6	.333	8	6	.571
Indiana	2	6	.250	5	9	.357
Northwestern	1	4	.200	1	7	.125
Iowa	1	5	.167	8	7	.533

MISSOURI VALLEY	Conference			Overall		
	W	L	PCT	W	L	PCT
NORTH						
Nebraska	5	3	.625	8	15	.348
Iowa State	4	4	.500	4	10	.286
Drake	3	5	.375	3	8	.273
SOUTH						
Kansas	6	2	.750	25	3	.893
Missouri	3	5	.375	11	5	.688
Wash.-St. Louis	3	5	.375	6	5	.545

CONSENSUS ALL-AMERICAS

PLAYER	POS	SCHOOL
Biaggio Gerussi	G	Columbia
Julian Hayward	G	Wesleyan
Tommy Johnson	F	Kansas
Charles Keinath	F	Penn
Ted Kiendl	F	Columbia
Harlan O. "Pat" Page	G	Chicago
John Ryan	C	Columbia
Raymond Scanlon	G	Notre Dame
John Schommer	C	Chicago
Helmer Swenholt	F	Wisconsin

SELECTOR: HELMS FOUNDATION

1909-10

Williams College captured the New England League for the fourth straight year. Columbia boasted victories over quality teams, including a 40-9 rout of Princeton.

PREMO-PORRETTA POWER POLL

	SCHOOL	RECORD
1	Williams	11-0
2	Columbia (Helms champion)	11-1
3	Kansas	18-1
4	Army	14-1
5	Chicago	10-3
6	Minnesota	10-3
7	Virginia Tech	11-0
8	Navy	10-1
9	Oklahoma	8-0
10	Grinnell	12-1
11	Centre (KY)	20-3
12	Kansas State	11-3
13	Rochester	17-2
14	Ohio State	11-1
15	Cotner (NE)	11-1
16	NYU	13-4
17	Iowa	11-3
18	Allegheny	8-3
19	Wisconsin	9-5
20	Whittier	8-0
21	Niagara	13-3
22	Colgate	9-5
23	Oberlin	10-3
24	Purdue	8-5
25	Illinois	5-4

CONFERENCE STANDINGS

BIG TEN	Conference			Overall		
	W	L	PCT	W	L	PCT
Chicago	9	3	.750	10	3	.769
Minnesota	7	3	.700	10	3	.769
Wisconsin	7	5	.583	9	5	.643
Illinois	5	4	.556	5	4	.556
Iowa	2	2	.500	11	3	.786
Purdue	5	5	.500	8	5	.615
Indiana	3	7	.300	5	8	.385
Northwestern	0	9	.000	0	9	.000

MISSOURI VALLEY	Conference			Overall		
	W	L	PCT	W	L	PCT
NORTH						
Iowa State	6	2	.750	9	7	.563
Nebraska	6	2	.750	6	10	.375
Drake	0	8	.000	0	12	.000
SOUTH						
Kansas	7	1	.875	18	1	.947
Wash.-St. Louis	3	5	.375	7	5	.583
Missouri	2	6	.250	8	10	.444

Note: Iowa State and Nebraska conceded the MVC title to Kansas

CONSENSUS ALL-AMERICAS

PLAYER	POS	SCHOOL
William Broadhead	C	NYU
Leon Campbell	G	Colgate
Dave Charters	C	Purdue
William Copthorne	G	Army
Charles Eberle	G	Swarthmore
Samuel Harman	F	Rochester
Ted Kiendl	F	Columbia
Ernest Lambert	F	Oklahoma
W. Vaughn Lewis	F	Williams
Harlan O. "Pat" Page	G	Chicago

SELECTOR: HELMS FOUNDATION

1910-11

St. John's dominated the opposition with a 21-point average margin of victory. The impressive résumé included a road victory over Penn and an 11-point defeat of traditional power Yale.

PREMO-PORRETTA POWER POLL

	SCHOOL	RECORD
1	St. John's (Helms champion)	14-0
2	Columbia	13-1
3	Navy	10-1
4	Oberlin	10-2
5	Dayton	10-0
6	Wabash	10-1
7	Allegheny	9-2
8	Ohio State	6-3
9	Wesleyan	11-4#
10	Virginia Tech	11-1
11	Army	9-3
12	Swarthmore	9-3
13	Notre Dame	7-3
14	Washington	11-1
15	Minnesota	10-4
16	Purdue	12-4
17	North Dakota State	14-0
18	North Central (IL)	14-2
19	Cotner (NE)	13-2
20	Grinnell	13-1
21	Williams	8-2
22	Augustana (IL)	10-0
23	Penn	15-8
24	Chicago	13-6#
25	CCNY	7-2

CONFERENCE STANDINGS

BIG TEN	Conference			Overall		
	W	L	PCT	W	L	PCT
Purdue	8	4	.667	12	4	.750
Minnesota	8	4	.667	10	4	.714
Chicago	7	5	.583	13	5	.722
Illinois	6	5	.545	6	6	.500
Iowa	2	2	.500	9	4	.692
Indiana	5	5	.500	11	5	.686
Wisconsin	6	6	.500	9	6	.600
Northwestern	1	12	.077	3	15	.167

IVY	Conference			Overall		
	W	L	PCT	W	L	PCT
Columbia	7	1	.875	13	1	.929
Penn	5	3	.625	15	8	.652
Cornell	4	4	.500	7	6	.538
Yale	3	5	.375	10	11	.476
Princeton	1	7	.125	4	9	.308

MISSOURI VALLEY	Conference			Overall		
	W	L	PCT	W	L	PCT
Kansas	9	3	.750	12	6	.667
Nebraska	6	6	.500	9	9	.500
Iowa State	6	8	.429	6	11	.353
Missouri	5	7	.417	5	7	.417
Drake	0	2	.000	0	6	.000

CONSENSUS ALL-AMERICAS

PLAYER	POS	SCHOOL
A.D. Alexander	C	Columbia
Dave Charters	C	Purdue
C.C. Clementson	G	Washington
Harry Hill	F	Navy
John Keenan	F	St. John's
Ted Kiendl	F	Columbia
Frank Lawler	F	Minnesota
W.M. Lee	G	Columbia
Walter Scoville	G/F	Wisconsin
Lewis Walton	G	Penn

SELECTOR: HELMS FOUNDATION

1911-12

Led by coach Walter "Doc" Meanwell and Big Ten scoring leader Otto Stangel, Wisconsin won the school's third Big Ten title. Meanwell was born in Leeds, England, and doubled as a physician during his coaching tenure.

PREMO-PORRETTA POWER POLL

	SCHOOL	RECORD
1	Wisconsin (Helms champion)	15-0
2	Purdue	12-0
3	Wesleyan	13-0
4	Swarthmore	11-1
5	Allegheny	11-1
6	Grove City (PA)	12-0
7	Navy	8-1
8	Columbia	10-2
9	Notre Dame	16-2
10	Syracuse	11-3
11	St. Lawrence	12-3
12	Beloit	6-2
13	Dayton	13-0
14	CCNY	9-2
15	Dartmouth	9-5
16	Chicago	12-6
17	Baylor	13-0
18	Nebraska	14-1
19	Oregon State	16-3
20	BYU	7-0
21	Washington	12-4
22	Oregon	12-2
23	Kentucky	9-0
24	Mississippi State	9-0
25	Georgia	6-1

CONFERENCE STANDINGS

BIG TEN	Conference			Overall		
	W	L	PCT	W	L	PCT
Wisconsin	12	0	1.000	15	0	1.000
Purdue	10	0	1.000	12	0	1.000
Chicago	7	5	.583	12	6	.667
Minnesota	6	6	.500	7	6	.538
Illinois	4	8	.333	8	8	.500
Indiana	1	9	.100	6	11	.353
Iowa	0	4	.000	6	8	.429
Northwestern	0	8	.000	4	9	.308

IVY	Conference			Overall		
	W	L	PCT	W	L	PCT
Columbia	8	2	.800	10	2	.833
Dartmouth	7	3	.700	9	5	.643
Penn	6	4	.600	10	7	.588
Cornell	5	5	.500	6	7	.462
Princeton	3	7	.300	8	8	.500
Yale	1	9	.100	1	9	.100

MISSOURI VALLEY	Conference			Overall		
	W	L	PCT	W	L	PCT
NORTH						
Nebraska	12	0	1.000	14	1	.933
Iowa State	7	6	.538	8	7	.533
Drake	0	6	.000	2	7	.222
SOUTH						
Kansas	6	6	.500	11	7	.611
Wash.-St. Louis	5	5	.500	8	5	.615
Missouri	4	9	.308	5	10	.333

CONSENSUS ALL-AMERICAS

PLAYER	POS	SCHOOL
Claus D. Benson	G	Columbia
Thomas Canfield	G	St. Lawrence
Lewis Castle	C	Syracuse
Fred Gieg	G	Swarthmore
Ernst Mensel	G	Dartmouth
Emil Schradieck	F	Colgate
Alphonse Schumacher	C	Dayton
Rufus Sisson	F	Dartmouth
Otto Stangel	F	Wisconsin
William Turner	F	Penn

SELECTOR: HELMS FOUNDATION

1912-13

Navy capitalized on a schedule full of home games, including victories in Annapolis over highly-rated Lehigh and Catholic.

PREMO-PORRETTA POWER POLL

	SCHOOL	RECORD
1	Navy (Helms champion)	9-0
2	Denison	13-1
3	Wisconsin	14-1
4	Grinnell	11-0
5	Union (NY)	11-1
6	Dayton	11-0
7	Army	11-2
8	Wesleyan	14-2
9	Detroit	13-0
10	Georgia	10-1
11	Lehigh	12-2
12	Penn State	8-3
13	Akron	7-1
14	Allegheny	9-2
15	Syracuse	8-3
16	Nebraska	17-2
17	Cornell	11-4
18	Chicago	20-6
19	Catholic (DC)	14-3
20	Northwestern	14-4
21	St. Lawrence	12-5
22	Notre Dame	13-2
23	Utah	21-3
24	Potsdam State	11-1
25	Virginia	11-4

CONFERENCE STANDINGS

BIG TEN	Conference			Overall		
	W	L	PCT	W	L	PCT
Wisconsin	11	1	.917	14	1	.933
Northwestern	7	2	.778	14	4	.778
Chicago	8	4	.667	20	6	.769
Purdue	6	5	.545	7	5	.583
Illinois	7	6	.538	10	6	.625
Ohio State	4	5	.444	13	7	.650
Minnesota	2	8	.200	3	8	.273
Iowa	1	5	.167	9	13	.409
Indiana	0	10	.000	5	11	.313

IVY	Conference			Overall		
	W	L	PCT	W	L	PCT
Cornell	7	1	.875	11	4	.733
Princeton	4	4	.500	11	9	.550
Columbia	3	5	.375	8	6	.571
Penn	3	5	.375	6	12	.333
Dartmouth	3	5	.375	4	8	.333

MISSOURI VALLEY	Conference			Overall		
	W	L	PCT	W	L	PCT
NORTH						
Nebraska	10	1	.909	17	2	.895
Iowa State	3	9	.250	3	13	.188
Drake	0	6	.000	1	8	.111
SOUTH						
Kansas	8	3	.727	16	6	.727
Missouri	8	4	.667	13	5	.722
Wash.-St. Louis	2	8	.200	4	8	.333

CONSENSUS ALL-AMERICAS

PLAYER	POS	SCHOOL
Eddie Calder	F	St. Lawrence
Sam Carrier	G	Nebraska
Gil Halstead	G	Cornell
Edward Hayward	G	Wesleyan
Allen Johnson	F	Wisconsin
William Roberts	C	Army
Hamilton Salmon	F	Princeton
Alphonse Schumacher	C	Dayton
Larry Teeple	C	Purdue
Laurence Wild	F	Navy

SELECTOR: HELMS FOUNDATION

Record differs from the school's and/or the NCAA's because it includes noncollegiate competition or because the outcome of some games is in dispute

1913-14

On Jan. 6, 1914, Wisconsin accomplished a feat that would never be matched in Big Ten history: a shutout, over Parsons College. The Badgers beat the small Iowa school, 50-0.

PREMO-PORRETTA POWER POLL

	SCHOOL	RECORD
1	Wisconsin (Helms champion)	15-0
2	Syracuse	12-0
3	Navy	10-0
4	Denison	15-1
5	Cornell	14-2
6	Lehigh	12-2
7	Georgia	9-1
8	Rochester	14-2
9	Virginia	12-1-1
10	Kansas	17-1
11	Union (NY)	11-3
12	Grinnell	10-1
13	Oberlin	7-3
14	Columbia	9-4
15	Saint Mary's (CA)	16-2
16	Texas	11-0
17	Chicago	19-9
18	Princeton	12-6
19	Nebraska Wesleyan	19-2#
20	Yale	11-7
21	Nebraska	15-3
22	Illinois	10-5#
23	Washington	12-2
24	BYU	10-2
25	Ohio State	11-5#

CONFERENCE STANDINGS

BIG TEN	CONFERENCE			OVERALL		
	W	L	PCT	W	L	PCT
Wisconsin	12	0	1.000	15	0	1.000
Ohio State	5	1	.833	10	4	.714
Chicago	8	4	.667	19	9	.679
Illinois	7	4	.636	9	4	.692
Northwestern	6	5	.545	11	6	.647
Minnesota	4	8	.333	4	11	.267
Purdue	3	9	.250	5	9	.357
Iowa	1	5	.167	9	7	.563
Indiana	1	11	.083	2	12	.143

IVY	CONFERENCE			OVERALL		
	W	L	PCT	W	L	PCT
Cornell	8	2	.800	14	2	.875
Columbia	8	2	.800	9	4	.692
Yale	6	4	.600	11	7	.611
Princeton	5	5	.500	12	6	.667
Penn	2	8	.200	4	12	.250
Dartmouth	1	9	.100	4	13	.235

MISSOURI VALLEY	CONFERENCE			OVERALL		
	W	L	PCT	W	L	PCT
NORTH						
Nebraska	7	0	1.000	15	3	.833
Iowa State	4	10	.286	4	13	.235
Drake	0	5	.000	1	9	.100
SOUTH						
Kansas	13	1	.929	17	1	.944
Kansas State	7	5	.583	10	7	.588
Wash.-St. Louis	4	6	.400	7	6	.538
Missouri	4	12	.250	4	12	.250

CONSENSUS ALL-AMERICAS

PLAYER	POS	SCHOOL
Lewis Castle	C	Syracuse
Gil Halstead	G	Cornell
Carl Harper	G	Wisconsin
Ernest Houghton	G	Union (NY)
Walter Lunden	F	Cornell
Dan Meenan	F	Columbia
Nelson Norgren	F	Chicago
Elmer Oliphant	G	Purdue
Everett Southwick	F	CCNY
Eugene Van Gent	C	Wisconsin

SELECTOR: HELMS FOUNDATION

1914-15

The Fighting Illini were led by three-time Helms All-America Ray Woods and his twin brother, Ralf—who is remembered today because the school's award for free throw shooting excellence is named for him.

PREMO-PORRETTA POWER POLL

	SCHOOL	RECORD
1	Illinois (Helms champion)	16-0
2	Virginia	17-0
3	Navy	9-2
4	Yale	14-3
5	Army	11-2
6	Union (NY)	13-1
7	Chicago	20-5
8	Syracuse	10-1
9	Cornell	12-4
10	Allegheny	11-1
11	Kansas	16-1
12	Texas	14-0
13	Denison	12-2
14	Penn State	10-3
15	Wisconsin	13-4
16	Pittsburgh	14-4
17	Washington	17-2#
18	Santa Clara	9-1
19	Notre Dame	14-3
20	Whittier	16-3-1
21	Columbia	12-5
22	Wabash	7-2
23	Princeton	13-5
24	Lake Forest (IL)	12-1
25	California	8-3#

CONFERENCE STANDINGS

BIG TEN	CONFERENCE			OVERALL		
	W	L	PCT	W	L	PCT
Illinois	12	0	1.000	16	0	1.000
Chicago	9	3	.750	20	5	.800
Wisconsin	8	4	.667	13	4	.765
Minnesota	6	6	.500	11	6	.647
Northwestern	5	5	.500	11	8	.579
Purdue	4	8	.333	5	8	.385
Iowa	2	6	.250	9	8	.529
Ohio State	3	9	.250	6	10	.375
Indiana	1	9	.100	4	9	.308

IVY	CONFERENCE			OVERALL		
	W	L	PCT	W	L	PCT
Yale	8	2	.800	14	3	.824
Cornell	7	3	.700	12	4	.750
Princeton	6	4	.600	13	5	.722
Columbia	6	4	.600	12	5	.706
Penn	3	7	.300	9	10	.474
Dartmouth	0	10	.000	6	11	.353

MISSOURI VALLEY	CONFERENCE			OVERALL		
	W	L	PCT	W	L	PCT
Kansas	13	1	.929	16	1	.941
Nebraska	8	4	.667	10	8	.556
Missouri	6	6	.500	8	6	.571
Iowa State	5	5	.500	6	7	.462
Kansas State	4	10	.286	6	12	.333
Drake	1	5	.167	5	6	.455
Wash.-St. Louis	1	7	.125	6	7	.462

SWC	CONFERENCE			OVERALL		
	W	L	PCT	W	L	PCT
Texas	5	0	1.000	14	0	1.000
Rice	5	1	.833	8	1	.889
Texas A&M	4	1	.800	13	2	.867
Southwestern (TX)	1	5	.167	1	5	.167
Baylor	0	7	.000	1	10	.091

CONSENSUS ALL-AMERICAS

PLAYER	POS	SCHOOL
W.P. Arnold	G	Yale
Leslie Brown	F	Cornell
Ernest Houghton	G	Union (NY)
Charlie Lee	G/F	Columbia
George Levis	F	Wisconsin
Elmer Oliphant	G	Army
Tony Savage	C	Washington
Ralph Sproull	F	Kansas
Wellington Stickley	F	Virginia
Ray Woods	G	Illinois

SELECTOR: HELMS FOUNDATION

1915-16

Wisconsin's George Levis starred on a team that was the first in Big Ten history to win 20 games. Levis scored 109 points in 12 conference games.

PREMO-PORRETTA POWER POLL

	SCHOOL	RECORD
1	Wisconsin (Helms champion)	20-1
2	Allegheny	10-1
3	Utah	11-0
4	Illinois	13-3
5	Marietta (OH)	18-1#
6	Navy	12-2
7	Pittsburgh	16-2#
8	Swarthmore	10-2
9	Texas	12-0
10	Nebraska	13-2#
11	Princeton	16-4
12	North Dakota State	18-0
13	Roanoke	9-0
14	Northwestern	14-5
15	Nebraska Wesleyan	20-2
16	Missouri	13-3
17	Colgate	14-4
18	Kansas State	13-3
19	Virginia	11-2
20	Syracuse	9-3
21	Penn	11-7
22	Wabash	17-4
23	Washington State	18-3
24	Carleton	15-0
25	Cornell	13-5

CONFERENCE STANDINGS

BIG TEN	CONFERENCE			OVERALL		
	W	L	PCT	W	L	PCT
Wisconsin	11	1	.917	20	1	.952
Illinois	9	3	.750	13	3	.813
Northwestern	9	3	.750	14	5	.737
Minnesota	6	6	.500	10	6	.625
Indiana	3	5	.375	6	7	.462
Iowa	2	4	.333	11	4	.733
Chicago	4	8	.333	15	11	.577
Ohio State	2	8	.200	9	13	.409
Purdue	2	10	.167	4	10	.286

IVY	CONFERENCE			OVERALL		
	W	L	PCT	W	L	PCT
Penn	8	2	.800	11	7	.611
Princeton	8	2	.800	16	4	.800
Cornell	5	5	.500	13	5	.722
Yale	5	5	.500	12	8	.600
Dartmouth	3	7	.300	11	12	.478
Columbia	1	9	.100	3	9	.250

Playoff: **Penn d. Princeton 16-14**

MISSOURI VALLEY	CONFERENCE			OVERALL		
	W	L	PCT	W	L	PCT
Nebraska	12	0	1.000	13	1	.929
Missouri	10	2	.833	13	3	.813
Kansas State	9	3	.750	13	3	.813
Kansas	5	11	.313	6	12	.333
Iowa State	2	8	.200	4	12	.250
Drake	1	5	.167	3	9	.250
Wash.-St. Louis	1	11	.083	6	11	.353

PACIFIC COAST	CONFERENCE			OVERALL		
	W	L	PCT	W	L	PCT
Oregon State	5	3	.625	16	5	.762
California	5	3	.625	11	5	.688
Washington	2	6	.250	7	7	.500

SWC	CONFERENCE			OVERALL		
	W	L	PCT	W	L	PCT
Texas	6	0	1.000	12	0	1.000
Texas A&M	6	2	.750	11	2	.846
Rice	5	3	.625	12	5	.706
Southwestern (TX)	0	4	.000	0	4	.000
Baylor	0	8	.000	8	9	.471

CONSENSUS ALL-AMERICAS

PLAYER	POS	SCHOOL
Roy Bohler	C	Washington State
Bill Chandler	C	Wisconsin
Cyril Haas	G/F	Princeton
George Levis	F	Wisconsin
Clyde Littlefield	C	Texas
Edward McNichol	G	Penn
E. Lowell "Dick" Romney	G	Utah
Adolph "Ade" Sieberts	F	Oregon State
Fred Williams	G	Missouri
Ray Woods	G	Illinois

SELECTOR: HELMS FOUNDATION

1916-17

Washington State's coach was J. Fred Bohler; the team captain was his younger brother, Roy. The Crimson and Gray—the school's nickname back then—were true road warriors, playing 18 of 26 games away from home.

PREMO-PORRETTA POWER POLL

	SCHOOL	RECORD
1	Washington State (Helms champion)	25-1
2	Wabash	19-2
3	Minnesota	17-2
4	Illinois	13-3
5	Navy	11-0
6	Wisconsin	15-3
7	Washington and Lee	13-0
8	Kansas State	15-2
9	CCNY	15-3
10	California	16-2#
11	Georgia	8-1
12	Yale	19-5
13	Penn State	12-2
14	BYU	14-2
15	Lehigh	15-4
16	Purdue	11-3
17	Montana State	19-1
18	Syracuse	13-3
19	Kalamazoo	14-1#
20	Princeton	15-5
21	Virginia Tech	17-2
22	NYU	9-3
23	LSU	20-2
24	Colgate	15-4
25	Colorado College	10-1

CONFERENCE STANDINGS

BIG TEN	Conference			Overall		
	W	L	PCT	W	L	PCT
Minnesota	10	2	.833	17	2	.895
Illinois	10	2	.833	13	3	.813
Purdue	7	2	.778	11	3	.786
Wisconsin	9	3	.750	15	3	.833
Indiana	3	5	.375	13	6	.684
Chicago	4	8	.333	13	15	.464
Ohio State	3	9	.250	15	11	.577
Northwestern	2	10	.167	3	11	.214
Iowa	1	8	.111	7	9	.438

IVY	Conference			Overall		
	W	L	PCT	W	L	PCT
Yale	9	1	.900	19	5	.792
Princeton	8	2	.800	15	5	.750
Penn	5	5	.500	11	7	.611
Dartmouth	4	6	.400	10	12	.455
Columbia	3	7	.300	6	8	.429
Cornell	1	9	.100	6	10	.375

MISSOURI VALLEY	Conference			Overall		
	W	L	PCT	W	L	PCT
Kansas State	10	2	.833	15	2	.882
Missouri	10	4	.714	12	4	.750
Iowa State	6	4	.600	12	6	.667
Kansas	9	7	.563	12	8	.600
Nebraska	4	8	.333	12	10	.545
Wash.-St. Louis	1	11	.083	7	12	.368
Drake	0	4	.000	5	7	.417

PACIFIC COAST	Conference			Overall		
	W	L	PCT	W	L	PCT
Washington State	8	1	.889	25	1	.962
California	5	1	.833	15	1	.938
Washington	7	5	.583	9	8	.529
Oregon State	7	6	.538	11	7	.611
Stanford	0	6	.000	8	8	.500
Oregon	0	8	.000	0	11	.000

SWC	Conference			Overall		
	W	L	PCT	W	L	PCT
Texas	7	1	.875	13	3	.813
Texas A&M	3	3	.500	11	8	.579
Baylor	0	6	.000	7	10	.412

CONSENSUS ALL-AMERICAS

PLAYER	POS	SCHOOL
Clyde Alwood	C	Illinois
Cyril Haas	G/F	Princeton
George Hjelte	G	California
Orson Kinney	F	Yale
Harold G. Olsen	G	Wisconsin
F.I. Reynolds	F	Kansas State
Francis Stadsvold	F	Minnesota
Charles Taft	G	Yale
Ray Woods	G	Illinois
Harry "Cy" Young	F	Washington and Lee

SELECTOR: HELMS FOUNDATION

1917-18

Syracuse captain and center Joe Schwarzer was an All-America in both basketball and football, and he also played baseball. The Orangemen's only loss was to Penn, a team they had beaten earlier in the season.

PREMO-PORRETTA POWER POLL

	SCHOOL	RECORD
1	Syracuse (Helms champion)	16-1
2	Oregon State	15-0
3	Penn	18-2
4	Stevens Tech	14-0#
5	Penn State	12-1
6	Creighton	14-0#
7	Saint Mary's (CA)	15-0#
8	Navy	14-2
9	Missouri	17-1
10	Princeton	12-3
11	Union (NY)	14-1
12	Wisconsin	14-3
13	Geneva	13-2
14	CCNY	8-3
15	Minnesota	13-3
16	Miami (OH)	10-0
17	Washington and Jefferson	10-2
18	Centre (KY)	10-1
19	Virginia	7-1
20	Cornell	11-4
21	LSU	12-1
22	Northwestern	7-4
23	North Dakota	15-0
24	Purdue	11-5
25	Illinois	9-6

CONFERENCE STANDINGS

BIG TEN	Conference			Overall		
	W	L	PCT	W	L	PCT
Wisconsin	9	3	.750	14	3	.824
Minnesota	7	3	.700	13	3	.813
Northwestern	5	3	.625	7	4	.636
Indiana	3	3	.500	10	4	.714
Purdue	5	5	.500	11	5	.688
Ohio State	5	5	.500	13	7	.650
Illinois	6	6	.500	9	6	.600
Chicago	6	6	.500	11	8	.579
Iowa	4	6	.400	6	8	.429
Michigan	0	10	.000	6	12	.333

IVY	Conference			Overall		
	W	L	PCT	W	L	PCT
Penn	9	1	.900	18	2	.900
Princeton	8	2	.800	12	3	.800
Cornell	7	3	.700	11	4	.733
Yale	4	6	.400	7	14	.333
Columbia	2	8	.200	4	9	.308
Dartmouth	0	10	.000	0	26	.000

MISSOURI VALLEY	Conference			Overall		
	W	L	PCT	W	L	PCT
Missouri	15	1	.938	17	1	.944
Kansas State	10	5	.667	12	5	.706
Kansas	9	8	.529	10	8	.556
Nebraska	4	5	.444	7	7	.500
Wash.-St. Louis	4	8	.333	9	8	.529
Iowa State	1	6	.143	6	9	.400
Drake	0	10	.000	2	17	.105

SWC	Conference			Overall		
	W	L	PCT	W	L	PCT
Rice	7	3	.700	10	4	.714
Texas	8	4	.667	14	5	.737
Texas A&M	7	7	.500	9	9	.500
Baylor	2	7	.222	2	15	.118
Oklahoma A&M	1	4	.200	6	10	.375

CONSENSUS ALL-AMERICAS

PLAYER	POS	SCHOOL
Earl Anderson	F	Illinois
Bill Chandler	C	Wisconsin
Harold Gillen	F	Minnesota
Hubert Peck	G	Penn
J. Craig Ruby	F	Missouri
Joe Schwarzer	C	Syracuse
Eber Simpson	G	Wisconsin
Alfred Sorenson	G	Washington State
George Sweeney	F	Penn
Gene Vidal	C	Army

SELECTOR: HELMS FOUNDATION

1918-19

Navy—led by All-America Knight Farwell—had an undefeated season (with only four of its games being decided by less than 10 points) despite fielding an entirely new starting lineup as a result of WWI commitments. Minnesota guard Erling Platou (11.6 ppg) went on to become a doctor and teach at the university's medical school.

PREMO-PORRETTA POWER POLL

	SCHOOL	RECORD
1	Navy	16-0
2	Minnesota (Helms champion)	13-0
3	Penn	15-1
4	Georgetown	9-1
5	Creighton	14-0#
6	Penn State	11-2
7	Kansas State	17-2
8	Oklahoma	12-0
9	Yale	7-2
10	Cornell	11-3
11	Oregon	13-4
12	Missouri	14-3
13	Akron	14-0
14	Centre (KY)	11-0
15	Syracuse	13-3
16	Idaho	14-4#
17	Colorado	8-1
18	Texas	17-3
19	DePauw	12-3
20	Virginia Tech	18-4
21	Chicago	21-6
22	CCNY	8-4
23	Wabash	13-4
24	Washington and Jefferson	7-3
25	Utah	7-2

CONFERENCE STANDINGS

BIG TEN	Conference			Overall		
	W	L	PCT	W	L	PCT
Minnesota	10	0	1.000	13	0	1.000
Chicago	10	2	.833	21	6	.778
Northwestern	6	4	.600	7	6	.538
Michigan	5	5	.500	16	8	.667
Illinois	5	7	.417	6	8	.429
Indiana	4	6	.400	10	7	.588
Iowa	4	7	.364	8	7	.533
Purdue	4	7	.364	6	8	.429
Ohio State	2	6	.250	7	12	.368
Wisconsin	3	9	.250	5	11	.313

IVY	Conference			Overall		
	W	L	PCT	W	L	PCT
Penn	7	1	.875	15	1	.938
Yale	4	2	.667	7	2	.778
Cornell	2	3	.400	11	3	.786
Princeton	2	5	.286	5	5	.500
Columbia	2	6	.250	3	7	.300

Note: Dartmouth couldn't field a team, so conference play was informal without a declared champion

MISSOURI VALLEY	Conference			Overall		
	W	L	PCT	W	L	PCT
Kansas State	10	2	.833	17	2	.895
Missouri	11	3	.786	14	3	.824
Nebraska	10	6	.625	10	6	.625
Grinnell	5	3	.625	6	5	.545
Kansas	5	9	.357	7	9	.438
Iowa State	3	8	.273	5	11	.313
Wash.-St. Louis	2	8	.200	9	9	.500
Drake	2	9	.182	10	18	.357

PACIFIC COAST	Conference			Overall		
	W	L	PCT	W	L	PCT
Oregon	11	3	.786	13	4	.765
Washington State	7	5	.583	10	11	.476
California	2	2	.500	6	3	.667
Washington	5	7	.417	6	10	.375
Oregon State	3	9	.250	3	13	.188
Stanford	0	2	.000	9	3	.750

SWC	Conference			Overall		
	W	L	PCT	W	L	PCT
Texas	11	2	.846	17	3	.850
Texas A&M	7	3	.700	14	4	.778
SMU	5	6	.455	7	8	.467
Rice	2	8	.200	4	10	.286
Baylor	2	8	.200	2	11	.154

Record differs from the school's and/or the NCAA's because it includes noncollegiate competition or because the outcome of some games is in dispute

CONSENSUS ALL-AMERICAS

PLAYER	POS	SCHOOL
Knight Farwell	G	Navy
Paul D. "Tony" Hinkle	G	Chicago
Arthur "Dutch" Lonborg	G	Kansas
Leon Marcus	G/C	Syracuse
Dan McNichol	G	Penn
Arnold Oss	F	Minnesota
George Parrish	C	Virginia Tech
Erling Platou	G	Minnesota
J. Craig Ruby	F	Missouri
Andrew Stannard	F	Penn

Selector: Helms Foundation

1919-20

Penn extended a challenge to Western Conference (Big Ten) champion Chicago. After each team beat the other on its home court, the deciding game was played at neutral Princeton, where Penn won, 23-21.

PREMO-PORRETTA POWER POLL

	SCHOOL	RECORD
1	Penn (Helms champion)	22-1
2	Missouri	17-1
3	NYU	16-1
4	Penn State	12-1
5	Texas A&M	19-0
6	Georgetown	13-1
7	Purdue	16-4
8	Chicago	27-8
9	Delaware	13-2
10	Southwestern (KS)	20-0
11	Navy	14-3
12	VMI	11-1
13	Westminster (MO)	17-0
14	Army	12-2
15	Montana State	13-0
16	Nebraska	22-2
17	Buffalo	9-1
18	Syracuse	15-3
19	DePauw	13-3
20	Nevada	7-2#
21	North Dakota	16-0
22	CCNY	13-3
23	Millikin	24-1
24	Stevens Tech	12-3
25	Worcester Polytechnic (MA)	14-2

CONFERENCE STANDINGS

BIG TEN	Conference W	L	Pct	Overall W	L	Pct
Chicago	10	2	.833	27	8	.771
Purdue	8	2	.800	16	4	.800
Illinois	8	4	.667	9	4	.692
Indiana	6	4	.600	13	8	.619
Wisconsin	7	5	.583	15	5	.750
Iowa	6	6	.500	9	10	.474
Ohio State	3	9	.250	17	10	.630
Minnesota	3	9	.250	7	9	.438
Michigan	3	9	.250	10	13	.435
Northwestern	2	6	.250	3	7	.300

IVY	Conference W	L	Pct	Overall W	L	Pct
Penn	10	0	1.000	22	1	.957
Princeton	6	4	.600	16	6	.727
Yale	6	4	.600	16	9	.640
Cornell	4	6	.400	14	6	.700
Columbia	3	7	.300	4	10	.286
Dartmouth	1	9	.100	5	20	.200

MISSOURI VALLEY	Conference W	L	Pct	Overall W	L	Pct
Missouri	17	1	.944	17	1	.944
Wash.-St. Louis	11	5	.688	13	5	.722
Kansas	9	7	.563	11	7	.611
Kansas State	8	8	.500	10	8	.556
Oklahoma	3	7	.300	9	7	.563
Drake	3	7	.300	12	11	.522
Iowa State	2	10	.167	6	12	.333
Grinnell	1	9	.100	4	10	.286

PACIFIC COAST	Conference W	L	Pct	Overall W	L	Pct
Stanford	8	1	.900	12	3	.800
California	5	5	.500	8	5	.615
Washington State	6	7	.462	10	11	.476
Washington	5	7	.417	7	8	.467
Oregon State	5	7	.417	7	12	.368
Oregon	5	8	.385	8	9	.471

SWC	Conference W	L	Pct	Overall W	L	Pct
Texas A&M	16	0	1.000	19	0	1.000
Phillips	2	1	.667	2	1	.667
Texas	4	6	.400	10	6	.625
Rice	2	5	.286	6	6	.500
SMU	2	8	.200	6	11	.353
Baylor	1	7	.125	8	13	.381

CONSENSUS ALL-AMERICAS

PLAYER	POS	SCHOOL
Howard Cann	F	NYU
Charles Carney	F	Illinois
Irving Cook	G	Washington
Forrest DeBernardi	C	Westminster (MO)
George Gardner	F	Southwestern (KS)
Paul D. "Tony" Hinkle	G	Chicago
Dan McNichol	G	Penn
Hubert Peck	G	Penn
George Sweeney	F	Penn
George Williams	C	Missouri

Selector: Helms Foundation

1920-21

Missouri center George Williams averaged 17.2 points a game. J. Craig Ruby was the new head coach—a year after being team captain. Another first-year coach, Edward McNichol of Penn, was the Quaker captain from 1915-17. McNichol's younger brother, Dan, was the current captain and the team's leading scorer, as well as a Helms All-America. Penn's two losses came by a combined three points.

PREMO-PORRETTA POWER POLL

	SCHOOL	RECORD
1	Missouri	17-1
2	Penn (Helms champion)	21-2
3	Navy	18-1
4	NYU	12-1
5	Penn State	14-2
6	VMI	16-1
7	Grove City (PA)	16-1
8	Stanford	15-3
9	Nebraska	15-3
10	Wisconsin	13-4
11	Wabash	22-4
12	Washington	18-4
13	Michigan	16-4
14	Colorado	8-0
15	DePauw	15-3
16	Ohio	17-2#
17	Kentucky	13-1
18	California	19-4
19	St. John's College (OH)	15-0
20	Wichita State	16-2
21	Centre (KY)	11-2
22	Arizona	7-0
23	North Dakota	14-1
24	Southwestern (KS)	19-7
25	Army	18-5

CONFERENCE STANDINGS

BIG TEN	Conference W	L	Pct	Overall W	L	Pct
Michigan	8	4	.667	18	4	.818
Wisconsin	8	4	.667	13	4	.765
Purdue	8	4	.667	13	7	.650
Minnesota	7	5	.583	10	5	.667
Illinois	7	5	.583	11	7	.611
Indiana	6	5	.545	15	6	.714
Iowa	6	5	.545	9	9	.500
Chicago	6	6	.500	12	6	.667
Ohio State	2	10	.167	4	13	.235
Northwestern	1	11	.083	2	12	.143

IVY	Conference W	L	Pct	Overall W	L	Pct
Penn	9	1	.900	21	2	.913
Dartmouth	7	3	.700	13	9	.591
Cornell	6	4	.600	14	8	.636
Princeton	4	6	.400	14	9	.609
Columbia	3	7	.300	7	9	.438
Yale	1	9	.100	9	17	.346

MISSOURI VALLEY	Conference W	L	Pct	Overall W	L	Pct
Missouri	17	1	.944	17	1	.944
Nebraska	9	1	.900	15	3	.833
Kansas State	11	5	.688	14	5	.737
Kansas	10	8	.556	10	8	.556
Iowa State	6	8	.429	10	8	.556
Drake	5	8	.385	10	8	.556
Oklahoma	5	9	.357	8	10	.444
Grinnell	2	12	.143	6	12	.333
Wash.-St. Louis	2	16	.111	3	15	.167

PACIFIC COAST	Conference W	L	Pct	Overall W	L	Pct
Stanford	8	3	.727	15	3	.833
California	8	3	.727	19	4	.826
Washington	10	4	.714	18	4	.818
Oregon	8	4	.667	15	5	.750
Washington State	3	11	.214	12	16	.429
Oregon State	2	14	.125	6	17	.261

SOUTHERN	Overall W	L	Pct
Kentucky	13	1	.929
Georgia	13	4	.765
Clemson	10	4	.714
Millsaps	9	4	.692
Mississippi State	10	6	.625
Tennessee	8	7	.533
Newberry	2	2	.500
Tulane	7	10	.412
South Carolina	7	11	.389
Auburn	5	8	.385
Birmingham Southern	5	8	.385
Georgia Tech	4	10	.286
Furman	1	12	.077

Tournament: **Kentucky d. Georgia 20-19**
Note: Conference did not play a formal schedule

SWC	Conference W	L	Pct	Overall W	L	Pct
Texas A&M	10	2	.833	16	6	.727
Baylor	8	4	.667	13	11	.542
Texas	9	5	.643	13	5	.722
Rice	4	9	.308	5	10	.333
SMU	0	11	.000	6	13	.316

CONSENSUS ALL-AMERICAS

PLAYER	POS	SCHOOL
R.D. Birkhoff	F	Chicago
Herbert Bunker	G	Missouri
Everett Dean	C	Indiana
Forrest DeBernardi	F/C	Westminster (MO)
Eddie Durno	F	Oregon
Basil Hayden	G/F	Kentucky
Dan McNichol	G	Penn
Arnold Oss	F	Minnesota
Donald White	G	Purdue
George Williams	C	Missouri

Selector: Helms Foundation

1921-22

Missouri and Phog Allen-coached Kansas finished with identical Missouri Valley Conference records, each suffering its only league loss to the other by 10 points.

PREMO-PORRETTA POWER POLL

	SCHOOL	RECORD
1	Missouri	16-1
2	Kansas (Helms champion)	16-2
3	Army	17-2
4	CCNY	10-2
5	Wabash	21-3
6	Purdue	15-3
7	Penn	24-3
8	Princeton	20-5
9	Navy	16-3
10	Holy Cross	14-3
11	Michigan	15-4
12	DePauw	17-3
13	Wooster	14-1
14	Texas A&M	18-3
15	Oregon State	21-2
16	Idaho	19-2
17	Texas	20-4
18	Kalamazoo	22-3
19	Rutgers	10-2
20	Wisconsin	14-5
21	Butler	24-6#
22	Beloit	12-0
23	Colorado College	13-2#
24	Illinois	14-5
25	Southwestern (KS)	19-5

CONFERENCE STANDINGS

BIG TEN	Conference W	L	Pct	Overall W	L	Pct
Purdue	8	1	.889	15	3	.833
Michigan	8	4	.667	15	4	.789
Wisconsin	8	4	.667	14	5	.737
Illinois	7	5	.583	14	5	.737
Iowa	5	6	.455	11	7	.611
Ohio State	5	7	.417	8	10	.444
Chicago	5	7	.417	8	11	.421
Minnesota	4	7	.364	5	8	.385
Indiana	3	7	.300	10	10	.500
Northwestern	3	9	.250	7	11	.389

IVY	Conference W	L	PCT	Overall W	L	PCT
Princeton	8	2	.800	20	5	.800
Penn	8	3	.727	24	3	.889
Dartmouth	6	4	.600	13	7	.650
Cornell	5	5	.500	14	5	.737
Columbia	2	8	.200	6	13	.316
Yale	1	9	.100	6	21	.222

MISSOURI VALLEY	Conference W	L	PCT	Overall W	L	PCT
Missouri	15	1	.938	16	1	.941
Kansas	15	1	.938	16	2	.889
Drake	12	4	.750	14	4	.778
Iowa State	8	8	.500	10	8	.556
Oklahoma	8	8	.500	9	9	.500
Nebraska	8	8	.500	8	9	.471
Kansas State	3	13	.188	3	14	.176
Grinnell	2	14	.125	5	14	.263
Wash.-St. Louis	1	15	.063	1	18	.053

PACIFIC COAST	Conference W	L	PCT	Overall W	L	PCT
Idaho	7	0	1.000	19	2	.905
Oregon State	10	2	.833	21	2	.913
California	10	4	.714	19	6	.760
Washington	11	5	.688	13	5	.722
Stanford	4	6	.400	8	7	.533
Washington State	4	11	.267	9	17	.346
Southern California	1	3	.250	7	5	.583
Oregon	0	16	.000	7	24	.226

SOUTHERN	Conference W	L	PCT	Overall W	L	T	PCT
Virginia	5	0	1.000	17	1	-	.944
Alabama	6	1	.857	15	4	-	.789
Georgia	4	1	.800	10	5	-	.667
Washington and Lee	6	2	.750	11	3	-	.786
Kentucky	3	1	.750	10	6	-	.625
Auburn	2	1	.667	5	8	-	.385
North Carolina	3	3	.500	15	6	-	.714
Virginia Tech	2	2	.500	14	6	-	.700
Georgia Tech	2	3	.400	11	6	-	.647
Tennessee	1	3	.250	13	7	1	.643
NC State	1	5	.167	6	13	-	.316
Clemson	0	3	.000	8	13	-	.381
Mississippi State	0	4	.000	12	10	-	.545

All-Comers' Tournament: **North Carolina d. Mercer 40-25**

SWC	Conference W	L	PCT	Overall W	L	PCT
Texas A&M	13	3	.813	18	3	.857
Texas	14	4	.778	20	4	.833
Baylor	8	8	.500	10	8	.556
Rice	1	1	.500	2	12	.143
SMU	4	11	.267	8	14	.364
Oklahoma State	1	4	.200	6	15	.286

CONSENSUS ALL-AMERICAS

PLAYER	POS	SCHOOL
Arthur Browning	F	Missouri
Herb Bunker	G	Missouri
Charles Carney	G	Illinois
Paul Endacott	G	Kansas
George Gardner	C	Southwestern (KS)
William Graves	C	Penn
Marshall Hjelte	C	Oregon State
Arthur Loeb	G	Princeton
Ira McKee	G	Navy
Ray Miller	G	Purdue

Selector: Helms Foundation

1922-23

Johnny Roosma was Army's top scorer despite playing only nine games. Kansas went 16–0 in Missouri Valley play and earned back-to-back Helms championships.

PREMO-PORRETTA POWER POLL

	SCHOOL	RECORD
1	Army	17-0
2	Kansas (Helms champion)	17-1
3	Missouri	15-3
4	Penn State	13-1
5	Springfield (MA)	17-1#
6	Franklin (IN)	17-1#
7	Butler	17-3
8	Marquette	19-2
9	Iowa	13-2
10	DePauw	15-3
11	Wisconsin	12-3
12	Yale	16-3
13	CCNY	12-1
14	Grove City (PA)	19-4
15	Michigan	11-4
16	Akron	12-1
17	Princeton	16-4
18	Navy	14-4
19	Concordia Seminary (MO)	9-2
20	Denison	12-1
21	Duquesne	16-2
22	Cornell	15-6
23	Idaho	15-3
24	Washington (MD)	21-2
25	North Carolina	15-1

CONFERENCE STANDINGS

BIG TEN	Conference W	L	PCT	Overall W	L	PCT
Iowa	11	1	.917	13	2	.867
Wisconsin	11	1	.917	12	3	.800
Michigan	8	4	.667	11	4	.733
Illinois	7	5	.583	9	6	.600
Purdue	7	5	.583	9	6	.600
Chicago	6	6	.500	7	7	.500
Indiana	5	7	.417	8	7	.533
Northwestern	3	9	.250	5	11	.313
Ohio State	1	11	.083	4	11	.267
Minnesota	1	11	.083	2	13	.133

IVY	Conference W	L	PCT	Overall W	L	PCT
Yale	7	3	.700	16	3	.842
Princeton	6	4	.600	16	4	.800
Cornell	6	4	.600	15	6	.714
Columbia	5	5	.500	9	7	.563
Dartmouth	3	7	.300	14	7	.667
Penn	3	7	.300	14	11	.560

MISSOURI VALLEY	Conference W	L	PCT	Overall W	L	PCT
Kansas	16	0	1.000	17	1	.944
Missouri	14	2	.875	15	3	.833
Drake	10	6	.625	10	6	.625
Iowa State	9	7	.563	10	8	.556
Wash.-St. Louis	8	8	.500	8	10	.444
Nebraska	5	11	.313	6	12	.333
Oklahoma	5	11	.313	6	12	.333
Grinnell	3	13	.188	3	13	.188
Kansas State	2	14	.125	2	14	.125

PACIFIC COAST	Conference W	L	PCT	Overall W	L	PCT
North						
Idaho	5	3	.625	15	3	.833
Washington	5	3	.625	12	4	.750
Oregon State	4	4	.500	19	7	.731
Washington State	4	4	.500	16	10	.615
Oregon	2	6	.250	15	10	.600
South						
California	5	3	.625	12	6	.667
Stanford	5	3	.625	12	4	.750
Southern California	2	6	.250	5	12	.294

Playoff: Idaho d. Washington 24-21 to win the North; California won the South based on head-to-head record vs. Stanford (3-1); **Idaho d. California 2-0** in a best-of-three series for the PCC title

ROCKY MOUNTAIN	Conference W	L	PCT	Overall W	L	PCT
Colorado College	7	1	.875	9	1	.900
Colorado Mines	6	2	.750	7	3	.700
Denver	4	4	.500	5	4	.556
Colorado	1	5	.167	1	7	.125
Wyoming	0	6	.000	2	6	.250

SOUTHERN	Conference W	L	PCT	Overall W	L	PCT
North Carolina	5	0	1.000	15	1	.938
Vanderbilt	2	0	1.000	16	8	.667
Tulane	5	1	.833	15	3	.833
Tennessee	3	1	.750	15	2	.882
Mississippi State	8	3	.727	15	4	.789
Washington and Lee	4	2	.667	7	8	.467
Georgia Tech	5	3	.625	9	9	.500
Alabama	3	3	.500	20	5	.800
Clemson	3	3	.500	11	6	.647
Georgia	3	3	.500	11	8	.579
Auburn	2	3	.400	7	7	.500
Virginia Tech	1	2	.333	13	6	.684
Mississippi	2	4	.333	8	7	.533
NC State	1	2	.333	5	8	.385
Virginia	1	3	.250	12	5	.706
Florida	0	3	.000	2	5	.286
South Carolina	0	3	.000	6	13	.235
Kentucky	0	5	.000	3	10	.231
LSU	0	6	.000	10	10	.500

All-Comers' Tournament: **Mississippi State d. Chattanooga 31-21**

SWC	Conference W	L	PCT	Overall W	L	PCT
Texas A&M	15	3	.833	16	4	.800
Texas	9	7	.563	11	7	.611
Rice	7	8	.467	10	9	.526
Oklahoma State	7	8	.467	12	11	.522
Baylor	7	13	.350	7	16	.304
SMU	4	10	.286	10	11	.476

CONSENSUS ALL-AMERICAS

PLAYER	POS	SCHOOL
Charlie T. Black	G/F	Kansas
Arthur Browning	F	Missouri
Herb Bunker	G	Missouri
Cartwright Carmichael	G/F	North Carolina
Paul Endacott	G	Kansas
Al Fox	F	Idaho
Ira McKee	G	Navy
Arthur Loeb	G	Princeton
Jimmy Lovley	F	Creighton
John Luther	C	Cornell

Selector: Helms Foundation

1923-24

Forward Jack Cobb, who averaged 15.0 ppg over his career, led North Carolina to its first national championship. A 26-18 win over Alabama capped an undefeated season and a Southern Conference title for the Tar Heels. Cobb became the first UNC player to have his jersey retired.

PREMO-PORRETTA POWER POLL

	SCHOOL	RECORD
1	North Carolina (Helms champion)	26-0
2	Kansas	16-3
3	Texas	23-0
4	Penn State	13-2
5	Franklin (IN)	19-1
6	Oklahoma	15-3
7	Cornell	13-3
8	Columbia	15-4
9	DePauw	14-3-1#
10	Creighton	15-2#
11	Navy	15-3
12	Princeton	11-6
13	Vermont	15-2
14	Illinois	11-6
15	Butler	12-7
16	Army	16-2
17	Wisconsin	11-5-1
18	CCNY	12-1
19	Carleton	14-0
20	Beloit	14-0
21	Chicago	10-7#
22	Rensselaer Polytechnic	11-1
23	Alabama	13-4#
24	Tulane	22-1#
25	Springfield (MA)	13-3

Record differs from the school's and/or the NCAA's because it includes noncollegiate competition or because the outcome of some games is in dispute

CONFERENCE STANDINGS

BIG TEN	Conference W	L	Pct	Overall W	L	T	Pct
Wisconsin	8	4	.667	11	5	1	.676
Illinois	8	4	.667	11	6	-	.647
Chicago	8	4	.667	9	7	-	.563
Ohio State	7	5	.583	12	5	-	.706
Purdue	7	5	.583	12	5	-	.706
Indiana	7	5	.583	11	6	-	.647
Michigan	6	6	.500	10	7	-	.588
Minnesota	5	7	.417	9	8	-	.529
Iowa	4	8	.333	7	10	-	.412
Northwestern	0	12	.000	0	16	-	.000

IVY	Conference W	L	Pct	Overall W	L	Pct
Cornell	8	2	.800	13	3	.813
Columbia	6	4	.600	15	4	.789
Princeton	6	4	.600	11	6	.647
Dartmouth	4	6	.400	12	9	.571
Penn	3	7	.300	18	8	.692
Yale	3	7	.300	12	10	.545

MISSOURI VALLEY	Conference W	L	Pct	Overall W	L	Pct
Kansas	15	1	.938	16	3	.842
Oklahoma	13	3	.813	15	3	.833
Nebraska	10	6	.625	11	7	.611
Wash.-St. Louis	8	8	.500	12	7	.632
Drake	8	8	.500	9	9	.500
Kansas State	8	8	.500	8	8	.500
Grinnell	4	12	.250	4	14	.222
Missouri	4	12	.250	4	14	.222
Iowa State	2	14	.125	2	16	.111

PACIFIC COAST	Conference W	L	Pct	Overall W	L	Pct
North						
Washington	6	2	.750	12	4	.750
Oregon State	6	2	.750	20	5	.800
Oregon	4	4	.500	15	5	.750
Idaho	4	6	.400	10	8	.556
Washington State	3	7	.300	17	11	.607
Montana	1	4	.200	7	8	.467
South						
California	5	3	.625	14	4	.778
Southern California	4	4	.500	15	4	.789
Stanford	3	5	.375	10	5	.667

Playoff: **California d. Washington 2-0** in a best-of-three series for the title

ROCKY MOUNTAIN	Conference W	L	Pct	Overall W	L	Pct
Colorado Division						
Colorado College	9	1	.900	15	2	.882
Colorado Mines	8	4	.667	8	4	.667
Colorado State	6	4	.600	6	5	.545
Denver	3	7	.300	3	8	.273
Wyoming	1	7	.125	2	13	.133
Utah Division						
BYU	7	1	.875	14	4	.778
Utah State	3	5	.375	6	6	.500
Utah	2	6	.250	2	6	.250

Playoff: **BYU d. Colorado College 2-1** in a best-of-three series for the title

SOUTHERN	Conference W	L	Pct	Overall W	L	Pct
Tulane	10	0	1.000	21	1	.955
North Carolina	7	0	1.000	26	0	1.000
Georgia	7	0	1.000	16	5	.762
Alabama	5	1	.833	12	4	.750
Kentucky	6	2	.750	13	3	.813
Mississippi State	8	4	.667	13	8	.619
Virginia	3	2	.600	12	3	.800
Tennessee	5	5	.500	10	8	.556
South Carolina	2	2	.500	11	9	.550
Georgia Tech	4	5	.444	9	13	.409
Mississippi	2	4	.333	16	6	.727
Washington and Lee	2	4	.333	9	5	.643
Maryland	1	2	.333	5	7	.417
NC State	2	4	.333	7	16	.304
Vanderbilt	1	3	.250	7	15	.318
Florida	0	2	.000	5	10	.333
Sewanee	0	2	.000	2	7	.222
Virginia Tech	0	4	.000	5	13	.278
Auburn	0	6	.000	4	9	.308
Clemson	0	6	.000	2	14	.125
LSU	0	7	.000	8	12	.400

Tournament: **North Carolina d. Alabama 26-18**

SWC	Conference W	L	Pct	Overall W	L	Pct
Texas	20	0	1.000	23	0	1.000
TCU	15	4	.789	16	4	.800
Oklahoma State	10	4	.714	14	6	.700
Texas A&M	12	11	.522	13	10	.565
SMU	7	15	.318	9	15	.375
Baylor	7	17	.292	11	23	.324
Arkansas	3	9	.250	17	11	.607
Rice	3	17	.150	3	17	.150

CONSENSUS ALL-AMERICAS

PLAYER	POS	SCHOOL
Arthur Ackerman	F/C	Kansas
Charlie T. Black	G/F	Kansas
Cartwright Carmichael	G/F	North Carolina
Jack Cobb	F	North Carolina
Abb Curtis	G	Texas
Slats Gill	F	Oregon State
Harry Kipke	G	Michigan
Hugh Latham	C	Oregon
Jimmy Lovley	F	Creighton
Hugh Middlesworth	G	Butler

Selector: Helms Foundation

1924-25

Coached by its 1921-22 captain, Albert Wittmer, Princeton's 21–2 record included a five-point win in Columbus over Big Ten champ Ohio State.

PREMO-PORRETTA POWER POLL

	SCHOOL	RECORD
1	Princeton (Helms champion)	21-2
2	Wabash	18-1
3	Kansas	17-1
4	Ohio State	14-2
5	Fordham	18-1
6	Syracuse	15-2
7	Butler	20-4
8	Washburn	19-4#
9	Franklin	17-4
10	Oklahoma State	15-3
11	Washington (MD)	20-0
12	Penn State	12-2
13	Army	12-3
14	CCNY	12-2
15	Nebraska	14-4
16	Penn	17-5
17	Dartmouth	12-5
18	Creighton	14-2#
19	Harvard	11-2
20	Grove City (PA)	16-2
21	Union (NY)	12-2
22	Navy	18-5
23	Mount Union	14-3
24	TCU	14-5
25	North Carolina	20-5

CONFERENCE STANDINGS

BIG TEN	Conference W	L	Pct	Overall W	L	Pct
Ohio State	11	1	.917	14	2	.875
Indiana	8	4	.667	12	5	.706
Illinois	8	4	.667	11	6	.647
Purdue	7	4	.636	9	5	.643
Michigan	6	5	.545	8	6	.571
Minnesota	6	6	.500	9	7	.563
Iowa	5	7	.417	6	10	.375
Northwestern	4	8	.333	6	10	.375
Wisconsin	3	9	.250	6	11	.353
Chicago	1	11	.083	1	13	.071

IVY	Conference W	L	Pct	Overall W	L	Pct
Princeton	9	1	.900	21	2	.913
Penn	6	4	.600	17	5	.773
Dartmouth	6	4	.600	12	5	.706
Columbia	6	4	.600	10	7	.588
Cornell	3	7	.300	7	8	.467
Yale	0	10	.000	3	16	.158

MISSOURI VALLEY	Conference W	L	Pct	Overall W	L	Pct
Kansas	15	1	.938	17	1	.944
Nebraska	13	3	.813	14	4	.778
Kansas State	10	6	.625	10	8	.556
Wash.-St. Louis	10	6	.625	10	8	.556
Oklahoma	9	7	.563	10	8	.556
Missouri	6	10	.375	7	11	.389
Drake	4	12	.250	4	13	.235
Grinnell	4	12	.250	4	13	.235
Iowa State	1	15	.063	2	15	.118

PACIFIC COAST	Conference W	L	Pct	Overall W	L	Pct
North						
Oregon State	7	2	.778	29	8	.784
Oregon	7	2	.778	15	5	.750
Idaho	5	5	.500	11	5	.688
Washington	5	5	.500	14	7	.667
Montana	2	6	.250	9	10	.474
Washington State	2	8	.200	18	11	.621
South						
California	3	1	.750	11	4	.733
Stanford	1	3	.250	10	3	.769

Playoff: Oregon State d. Oregon 2-1 in a best-of-three seires to win the North; **California d. Oregon State 2-1** in a best-of-three series for the PCC title

ROCKY MOUNTAIN	Conference W	L	Pct	Overall W	L	Pct
Eastern Division						
Colorado College	10	3	.769	13	3	.813
Northern Colorado	9	3	.750	12	4	.750
Colorado	7	4	.636	9	5	.643
Wyoming	5	3	.625	9	6	.600
Denver	5	6	.455	5	6	.455
Colorado Mines	4	7	.364	4	7	.364
Colorado State	2	9	.182	2	10	.167
Western State	0	6	.000	3	6	.333
Western Division						
BYU	5	3	.625	10	6	.625
Montana State	1	1	.500	20	4	.833
Utah State	5	5	.500	12	7	.632
Utah	3	5	.375	5	11	.313

Playoff: **Colorado College d. BYU 3-0** in a best-of-three series for the title

SOUTHERN	Conference W	L	Pct	Overall W	L	Pct
North Carolina	8	0	1.000	20	5	.800
Tulane	12	3	.800	17	4	.810
Maryland	3	1	.750	12	5	.706
Kentucky	6	2	.750	13	8	.619
Alabama	5	2	.714	15	4	.789
Virginia	4	2	.667	14	3	.824
South Carolina	4	2	.667	10	7	.588
Washington and Lee	3	2	.600	8	5	.615
Clemson	3	2	.600	4	14	.222
Vanderbilt	4	3	.571	12	13	.480
Mississippi State	4	4	.500	14	9	.609
Georgia	4	4	.500	9	11	.450
Georgia Tech	2	7	.222	4	12	.250
NC State	1	4	.200	11	7	.611
LSU	1	4	.200	10	7	.588
Virginia Tech	1	4	.200	6	9	.400
Tennessee	1	5	.167	6	8	.429
Auburn	1	5	.167	3	11	.214
Mississippi	1	6	.143	17	8	.680
Florida	0	0	.000	2	7	.222
Sewanee	0	0	.000	2	7	.222

Tournament: **North Carolina d. Tulane 36-28**

SWC	Conference W	L	Pct	Overall W	L	Pct
Oklahoma State	12	2	.857	15	3	.833
TCU	11	3	.786	14	5	.737
Arkansas	10	4	.714	21	5	.808
Texas	9	5	.643	17	8	.680
Texas A&M	6	8	.429	9	8	.529
SMU	4	10	.286	5	11	.313
Baylor	2	12	.143	3	12	.200
Rice	2	12	.143	2	12	.143

CONSENSUS ALL-AMERICAS

PLAYER	POS	SCHOOL
Arthur Ackerman	F/C	Kansas
Burgess Carey	G	Kentucky
Jack Cobb	F	North Carolina
Emanuel Goldblatt	G	Penn
Vic Hanson	F	Syracuse
Noble Kizer	G	Notre Dame
Johnny Miner	F	Ohio State
Earl Mueller	C	Colorado College
Gerald Spohn	C	Washburn
Carlos Steele	G	Oregon State

Selector: Helms Foundation

1925-26

Syracuse's captain, the 5'10" All-America forward Vic Hanson, was also a football All-America and even went on to play baseball for several years in the Yankees organization.

PREMO-PORRETTA POWER POLL

	SCHOOL	RECORD
1	Syracuse (Helms champion)	19-1
2	Notre Dame	19-1
3	California	17-0#
4	Columbia	16-2
5	Kansas	16-2
6	Lehigh	13-1
7	Purdue	13-4
8	Michigan	12-5
9	Indiana	12-5
10	Arkansas	23-2
11	Iowa	12-5
12	Cincinnati	17-2
13	Oregon	18-4
14	Butler	16-5
15	Oklahoma	11-5#
16	Manchester (IN)	15-1
17	Dickinson (PA)	15-2
18	North Carolina	20-5
19	North Dakota State	22-3
20	Duquesne	15-4
21	Mount Union	10-0
22	Saint Louis	9-4
23	Muskingum	17-2
24	Maryland	14-3
25	Massachusetts	12-2

CONFERENCE STANDINGS

BIG TEN	Conference			Overall		
	W	L	PCT	W	L	PCT
Purdue	8	4	.667	13	4	.765
Indiana	8	4	.667	12	5	.706
Iowa	8	4	.667	12	5	.706
Michigan	8	4	.667	12	5	.706
Ohio State	6	6	.500	10	7	.588
Illinois	6	6	.500	9	8	.529
Minnesota	5	7	.417	7	10	.412
Wisconsin	4	8	.333	8	9	.471
Chicago	4	8	.333	5	11	.313
Northwestern	3	9	.250	5	12	.294

IVY	Conference			Overall		
	W	L	PCT	W	L	PCT
Columbia	9	1	.900	16	2	.889
Dartmouth	6	4	.600	11	7	.611
Penn	5	5	.500	14	7	.667
Princeton	5	5	.500	9	13	.409
Cornell	5	5	.500	8	12	.400
Yale	0	10	.000	6	15	.286

MISSOURI VALLEY	Conference			Overall		
	W	L	PCT	W	L	PCT
Kansas	16	2	.889	16	2	.889
Oklahoma	9	3	.750	11	4	.733
Kansas State	9	3	.750	11	7	.611
Missouri	8	8	.500	8	10	.444
Nebraska	7	7	.500	8	10	.444
Drake	7	9	.438	9	9	.500
Wash.-St. Louis	7	9	.438	7	9	.438
Oklahoma State	5	7	.417	9	9	.500
Iowa State	3	11	.214	4	14	.222
Grinnell	1	13	.071	1	14	.067

PACIFIC COAST	Conference			Overall		
	W	L	PCT	W	L	PCT
North						
Oregon	10	0	1.000	18	4	.818
Oregon State	6	4	.600	18	6	.750
Idaho	5	4	.556	14	10	.583
Washington	5	5	.500	10	6	.625
Montana	2	8	.200	5	10	.333
Washington State	1	8	.111	9	17	.346
South						
California	5	0	1.000	14	0	1.000
Stanford	3	2	.600	10	6	.625
Southern California	0	6	.000	4	8	.333

Playoff: **California d. Oregon 2-0** in a best-of-three series for the title

ROCKY MOUNTAIN	Conference			Overall		
	W	L	PCT	W	L	PCT
Eastern Division						
Northern Colorado	13	1	.929	13	5	.722
Colorado College	9	4	.692	9	4	.692
Colorado	7	5	.583	8	5	.615
Wyoming	6	6	.500	12	5	.706
Denver	5	7	.417	5	7	.417
Colorado Mines	3	7	.300	3	7	.300
Colorado State	2	10	.167	2	11	.154
Western State	0	5	.000	5	9	.357
Western Division						
Utah State	8	4	.667	13	5	.722
BYU	7	5	.583	11	5	.688
Montana State	5	7	.417	20	12	.625
Utah	4	8	.333	4	8	.333

Playoff: **Utah State d. Northern Colorado 3-0** in a best-of-three series for the title

SOUTHERN	Conference			Overall		
	W	L	PCT	W	L	PCT
Kentucky	8	0	1.000	15	3	.833
North Carolina	7	0	1.000	20	5	.800
Mississippi	8	1	.889	16	2	.889
Maryland	7	1	.875	14	3	.824
Georgia	9	4	.692	18	6	.750
South Carolina	4	2	.667	9	5	.643
NC State	5	3	.625	20	4	.833
Mississippi State	5	3	.625	14	8	.636
Tulane	10	7	.588	11	7	.611
Virginia	4	4	.500	9	6	.600
Alabama	6	6	.500	10	11	.476
LSU	4	5	.444	9	9	.500
VMI	3	5	.375	7	8	.467
Georgia Tech	4	10	.286	6	11	.353
Virginia Tech	2	5	.286	3	10	.231
Washington and Lee	2	6	.250	9	7	.563
Tennessee	1	3	.250	9	8	.529
Vanderbilt	2	7	.222	8	18	.308
Auburn	1	7	.125	5	10	.333
Clemson	1	7	.125	4	17	.190
Sewanee	0	2	.000	4	6	.400
Florida	0	3	.000	7	7	.500

Tournament: **North Carolina d. Mississippi State 37-23**

SWC	Conference			Overall		
	W	L	PCT	W	L	PCT
Arkansas	11	1	.917	23	2	.920
SMU	8	4	.667	10	6	.625
TCU	7	5	.583	13	9	.545
Texas	6	6	.500	12	10	.545
Baylor	5	7	.417	7	8	.467
Texas A&M	4	8	.333	8	9	.471
Rice	1	11	.083	1	13	.071

CONSENSUS ALL-AMERICAS

PLAYER	POS	SCHOOL
Jack Cobb	F	North Carolina
George Dixon	G	California
Richard Doyle	C	Michigan
Emanuel Goldblatt	G	Penn
Gale Gordon	C	Kansas
Vic Hanson	F	Syracuse
Carl Loeb	G/F	Princeton
Albert Petersen	C	Kansas
George Spradling	F	Purdue
Algot Westergren	G	Oregon

SELECTOR: HELMS FOUNDATION

1926-27

Cal was led by guard George Dixon, a member of the 1924 gold-medal-winning U.S. Olympic rugby team. Notre Dame coach George Keogan guided the Irish to their second straight 19–1 record. Keogan never had a losing season at Notre Dame; when he died of a heart attack during the 1942-43 season, the Irish were 12–1.

PREMO-PORRETTA POWER POLL

	SCHOOL	RECORD
1	California	17-0#
2	Notre Dame (Helms champion)	19-1
3	Fordham	20-2
4	Kansas	15-2
5	Michigan	14-3
6	Springfield (MA)	13-1
7	Indiana	13-4
8	Navy	15-2
9	Butler	17-4
10	Arkansas	14-2
11	New Hampshire	14-1
12	Oregon	24-4
13	Syracuse	15-4
14	Colgate	17-3
15	Montana State	32-7#
16	Western Michigan	16-2
17	Vanderbilt	20-4
18	Pittsburg State (KS)	16-2
19	Creighton	14-5
20	Wichita State	19-2
21	Dartmouth	17-6
22	Evansville	16-4
23	West Texas A&M	23-3
24	Northern Illinois	20-2#
25	Muskingum	19-2

CONFERENCE STANDINGS

BIG TEN	Conference			Overall		
	W	L	PCT	W	L	PCT
Michigan	10	2	.833	14	3	.824
Indiana	9	3	.750	13	4	.765
Purdue	9	3	.750	12	5	.706
Illinois	7	5	.583	10	7	.588
Wisconsin	7	5	.583	10	7	.588
Iowa	7	5	.583	9	8	.529
Ohio State	6	6	.500	11	6	.647
Chicago	3	9	.250	4	11	.267
Minnesota	1	11	.083	3	13	.188
Northwestern	1	11	.083	3	14	.176

IVY	Conference			Overall		
	W	L	PCT	W	L	PCT
Dartmouth	7	3	.700	17	6	.739
Princeton	7	3	.700	11	11	.500
Penn	5	5	.500	16	10	.615
Columbia	5	5	.500	9	9	.500
Cornell	4	6	.400	5	13	.278
Yale	2	8	.200	11	12	.478

Playoff: **Dartmouth d. Princeton 26-24**

MISSOURI VALLEY	Conference			Overall		
	W	L	PCT	W	L	PCT
Kansas	11	2	.846	15	2	.882
Oklahoma	8	4	.667	12	5	.706
Nebraska	7	5	.583	12	6	.667
Kansas State	6	6	.500	10	8	.556
Missouri	6	6	.500	9	8	.529
Oklahoma State	6	6	.500	8	9	.471
Drake	7	7	.500	8	10	.444
Iowa State	7	8	.467	9	9	.500
Wash.-St. Louis	2	10	.167	5	10	.333
Grinnell	2	13	.133	2	15	.118

PACIFIC COAST	Conference			Overall		
	W	L	PCT	W	L	PCT
North						
Oregon	8	2	.800	24	4	.857
Washington	7	3	.700	15	4	.789
Idaho	7	3	.700	10	4	.714
Oregon State	4	6	.400	14	11	.560
Washington State	3	7	.300	11	10	.524
Montana	1	9	.100	5	11	.313
South						
California	5	0	1.000	17	0	1.000
Stanford	3	2	.600	9	9	.500
Southern California	0	6	.000	10	8	.556

Playoff: **California d. Oregon 2-0** in a best-of-three series for the title

Record differs from the school's and/or the NCAA's because it includes noncollegiate competition or because the outcome of some games is in dispute

ROCKY MOUNTAIN

	Conference W	L	PCT	Overall W	L	PCT
Eastern Division						
Colorado College	12	2	.857	12	4	.750
Northern Colorado	10	4	.714	10	4	.714
Wyoming	8	4	.667	9	5	.643
Colorado	7	5	.583	7	5	.583
Denver	5	7	.417	5	7	.417
Colorado State	4	8	.333	4	8	.333
Colorado Mines	2	10	.167	3	10	.231
Western State	0	7	.000	5	7	.417
Western Division						
Montana State	10	2	.833	30	7	.811
Utah State	9	3	.750	11	3	.786
Utah	4	8	.333	5	10	.333
BYU	1	11	.083	5	14	.263

SOUTHERN

	Conference W	L	PCT	Overall W	L	PCT
South Carolina	9	1	.900	14	4	.778
Vanderbilt	7	1	.875	20	4	.833
Georgia Tech	8	2	.800	17	10	.630
Auburn	12	4	.750	13	6	.684
Washington and Lee	6	2	.750	10	6	.625
Mississippi	10	4	.714	13	5	.722
NC State	5	2	.714	12	5	.706
North Carolina	7	3	.700	17	7	.708
Maryland	6	4	.600	10	10	.500
Mississippi State	7	5	.583	17	7	.708
Tennessee	5	4	.556	7	12	.368
Alabama	4	5	.444	5	8	.385
Virginia	5	7	.417	9	10	.474
Tulane	7	10	.412	7	10	.412
LSU	3	5	.375	7	9	.438
Georgia	3	6	.333	14	8	.636
Virginia Tech	2	6	.250	6	8	.429
Kentucky	1	6	.143	3	13	.188
Clemson	1	7	.125	2	13	.133
Florida	1	8	.111	6	20	.231
VMI	0	7	.000	3	12	.167
Sewanee	0	10	.000	3	11	.214

Tournament: **Vanderbilt d. Georgia 46-44**

SWC

	Conference W	L	PCT	Overall W	L	PCT
Arkansas	8	2	.800	14	2	.875
SMU	7	4	.636	12	5	.706
Texas	7	4	.636	13	9	.591
TCU	6	4	.600	9	8	.529
Texas A&M	4	6	.400	10	7	.588
Baylor	0	3	.000	8	4	.667
Rice	0	9	.000	0	9	.000

CONSENSUS ALL-AMERICAS

PLAYER	POS	SCHOOL
Sidney Corenman	G	Creighton
George Dixon	G	California
Vic Hanson	F	Syracuse
Jack Lorch	G	Columbia
Ross McBurney	C	Wichita State
John Nyikos	C	Notre Dame
Bennie Oosterbaan	F	Michigan
Gerald Spohn	C	Washburn
John "Cat" Thompson	G	Montana State
Harry Wilson	G	Army

Selector: Helms Foundation

1927-28

Charley "Chuck" Hyatt averaged 13.1 ppg over his career, during which Pittsburgh had a 60–7 record and won two national titles. He is one of only 19 players in Division I/Major College history to earn All-America honors three times.

PREMO-PORRETTA POWER POLL

	SCHOOL	RECORD
1	Pittsburgh (Helms champion)	21-0
2	Oklahoma	18-0
3	Montana State	36-2
4	Indiana	15-2
5	Purdue	15-2
6	Arkansas	19-1
7	Butler	19-3
8	Fordham	15-1#
9	Notre Dame	18-4
10	Georgetown	12-1
11	Springfield (MA)	18-2
12	Auburn	20-2
13	Penn	22-5
14	Evansville	14-3
15	Wisconsin	13-4
16	Westminster (PA)	17-3
17	Northwestern	12-5
18	Illinois Wesleyan	13-1
19	St. John's	18-4
20	Wayne State (MI)	18-1
21	Southern California	23-4#
22	Michigan	10-7
23	Oregon	18-3
24	Michigan State	11-4
25	Washington	22-6

CONFERENCE STANDINGS

BIG TEN

	Conference W	L	PCT	Overall W	L	PCT
Indiana	10	2	.833	15	2	.882
Purdue	10	2	.833	15	2	.882
Wisconsin	9	3	.750	13	4	.765
Northwestern	9	3	.750	12	5	.706
Michigan	7	5	.583	10	7	.588
Chicago	5	7	.417	7	8	.467
Iowa	3	9	.250	6	11	.353
Ohio State	3	9	.250	5	12	.294
Illinois	2	10	.167	5	12	.294
Minnesota	2	10	.167	4	12	.250

IVY

	Conference W	L	PCT	Overall W	L	PCT
Penn	7	3	.700	22	5	.815
Princeton	7	3	.700	14	10	.583
Dartmouth	6	4	.600	19	8	.704
Cornell	5	5	.500	7	11	.389
Yale	3	7	.300	12	9	.571
Columbia	2	8	.200	4	14	.222

Playoff: **Penn d. Princeton 24-22**

MISSOURI VALLEY

	Conference W	L	PCT	Overall W	L	PCT
Oklahoma	18	0	1.000	18	0	1.000
Missouri	13	5	.722	13	5	.722
Oklahoma State	11	7	.611	11	7	.611
Kansas	9	9	.500	9	9	.500
Washington-St. Louis	8	10	.444	10	12	.455
Kansas State	8	10	.444	8	10	.444
Nebraska	7	11	.389	7	11	.389
Drake	7	11	.389	7	13	.350
Grinnell	6	12	.333	6	13	.316
Iowa State	3	15	.167	3	15	.167

PACIFIC COAST

	Conference W	L	PCT	Overall W	L	PCT
North						
Washington	9	1	.900	22	6	.786
Oregon	8	2	.800	18	3	.857
Idaho	4	6	.400	7	7	.500
Oregon State	4	6	.400	15	16	.484
Montana	4	6	.400	6	8	.429
Washington State	1	9	.100	7	17	.292
South						
Southern California	6	3	.667	22	4	.846
California	6	3	.667	9	6	.600
UCLA	5	4	.556	10	5	.667
Stanford	1	8	.111	8	13	.381

Playoff: Southern California won the South based on head-to-head record vs. California (2-1); **Southern California d. Washington 2-0** in a best-of-three series for the PCC title

ROCKY MOUNTAIN

	Conference W	L	PCT	Overall W	L	PCT
Eastern Division						
Wyoming	9	3	.750	13	8	.619
Colorado College	9	5	.643	10	7	.588
Denver	8	6	.571	8	6	.571
Northern Colorado	8	6	.571	8	6	.571
Colorado	5	7	.417	5	7	.417
Colorado Mines	5	7	.417	5	7	.417
Colorado State	5	7	.417	5	7	.417
Western State	1	9	.100	1	9	.100
Western Division						
Montana State	11	1	.917	36	2	.947
Utah State	5	7	.417	7	7	.500
Utah	5	7	.417	7	10	.412
BYU	3	9	.250	13	10	.565

Playoff: **Montana State d. Wyoming 3-0** in a best-of-three series for the title

SOUTHERN

	Conference W	L	PCT	Overall W	L	PCT
Auburn	12	1	.923	20	2	.909
Mississippi State	10	1	.909	13	7	.650
North Carolina	8	1	.889	17	2	.895
Maryland	8	1	.889	14	4	.778
Kentucky	8	1	.889	12	6	.667
LSU	7	3	.700	14	4	.778
Virginia	10	5	.667	20	6	.769
Georgia Tech	8	4	.667	10	7	.588
Georgia	8	5	.615	12	10	.545
VMI	5	5	.500	7	6	.538
Alabama	5	5	.500	10	10	.500
Clemson	5	7	.417	9	14	.391
South Carolina	4	7	.364	8	12	.400
Mississippi	5	9	.357	10	9	.526
NC State	3	6	.333	10	8	.556
Virginia Tech	3	7	.300	5	11	.313
Washington and Lee	3	7	.300	5	12	.294
Vanderbilt	2	5	.286	5	7	.417
Florida	2	10	.167	5	16	.238
Sewanee	1	5	.167	2	7	.222
Tulane	3	13	.188	3	13	.188
Tennessee	0	8	.000	0	12	.000

Tournament: **Mississippi d. Auburn 31-30**

SWC

	Conference W	L	PCT	Overall W	L	PCT
Arkansas	12	0	1.000	19	1	.950
SMU	10	2	.833	14	3	.824
Texas	7	5	.583	12	5	.706
TCU	5	7	.417	9	8	.529
Rice	3	9	.250	3	9	.250
Baylor	2	8	.200	9	9	.500
Texas A&M	1	9	.100	4	12	.250

CONSENSUS ALL-AMERICAS

PLAYER	POS	SCHOOL
Victor Holt	C	Oklahoma
Charley "Chuck" Hyatt	F	Pittsburgh
Alfred James	G	Washington
Charles "Stretch" Murphy	C	Purdue
Bennie Oosterbaan	F	Michigan
Wallace Reed	G	Pittsburgh
Glen Rose	C	Arkansas
Joe Schaaf	G/F	Penn
Ernest Simpson	F	Colorado College
John "Cat" Thompson	G	Montana State

Selector: Helms Foundation

1928-29

Montana State ruled the Rocky Mountains with a fast-break offense. The Bobcats' John "Cat" Thompson used his lightning quickness to set picks on opponents and set up shots for his teammates. He also scored plenty himself—1,539 points in four seasons.

PREMO-PORRETTA POWER POLL

	SCHOOL	RECORD
1	Montana State (Helms champion)	36-2
2	Arkansas	19-1
3	Fordham	18-1#
4	Michigan	13-3
5	Wisconsin	15-2
6	Butler	17-2
7	Texas	18-2
8	Oklahoma	13-2
9	Purdue	13-4
10	Loyola-Chicago	16-0
11	San Francisco	22-2#
12	California	17-3
13	Northwestern	12-5
14	St. John's	23-2
15	Washington	18-2
16	Notre Dame	15-5
17	Westminster (PA)	15-2
18	Washington and Lee	16-2
19	Pittsburgh	16-5
20	Ohio Wesleyan	18-3
21	Colgate	16-4
22	Creighton	13-4
23	East Central Oklahoma	21-2
24	Saint Louis	14-4
25	Michigan State	11-5

CONFERENCE STANDINGS

BIG SIX	CONFERENCE			OVERALL		
	W	L	PCT	W	L	PCT
Oklahoma	10	0	1.000	13	2	.867
Missouri	7	3	.700	11	7	.611
Nebraska	5	5	.500	11	5	.688
Iowa State	4	6	.400	8	7	.533
Kansas State	2	8	.200	6	10	.375
Kansas	2	8	.200	3	15	.167

BIG TEN	CONFERENCE			OVERALL		
	W	L	PCT	W	L	PCT
Wisconsin	10	2	.833	15	2	.882
Michigan	10	2	.833	13	3	.813
Purdue	9	3	.750	13	4	.765
Northwestern	7	5	.583	12	5	.706
Illinois	6	6	.500	10	7	.588
Ohio State	6	6	.500	9	8	.529
Iowa	5	7	.417	9	8	.529
Indiana	4	8	.333	7	10	.412
Chicago	2	10	.167	3	12	.200
Minnesota	1	11	.083	4	13	.235

IVY	CONFERENCE			OVERALL		
	W	L	PCT	W	L	PCT
Penn	8	2	.800	20	6	.769
Dartmouth	7	3	.700	13	6	.684
Columbia	5	5	.500	10	9	.526
Cornell	5	5	.500	9	11	.450
Yale	4	6	.400	11	9	.550
Princeton	1	9	.100	9	15	.375

MISSOURI VALLEY	CONFERENCE			OVERALL		
	W	L	PCT	W	L	PCT
Wash.-St. Louis	7	0	1.000	11	7	.611
Creighton	4	1	.800	13	4	.765
Drake	3	4	.429	6	13	.316
Oklahoma State	0	4	.000	1	14	.067
Grinnell	0	5	.000	6	11	.353

PACIFIC COAST	CONFERENCE			OVERALL		
	W	L	PCT	W	L	PCT
NORTH						
Washington	10	0	1.000	18	2	.900
Idaho	6	4	.600	11	10	.524
Washington State	5	5	.500	9	14	.391
Oregon State	4	6	.400	12	8	.600
Oregon	3	7	.300	10	8	.556
Montana	2	8	.200	9	11	.450
SOUTH						
California	9	0	1.000	17	3	.850
Stanford	6	3	.667	13	6	.684
Southern California	3	6	.333	16	6	.727
UCLA	1	8	.111	7	9	.438

Playoff: **California d. Washington 2-0** in a best-of-three series for the title

ROCKY MOUNTAIN	CONFERENCE			OVERALL		
	W	L	PCT	W	L	PCT
EASTERN DIVISION						
Colorado	10	2	.833	10	2	.833
Wyoming	11	3	.786	15	4	.789
Northern Colorado	8	6	.571	8	6	.571
Denver	7	7	.500	12	8	.600
Colorado State	6	6	.500	6	6	.500
Colorado College	6	6	.500	8	9	.471
Western State	1	9	.100	1	9	.100
Colorado Mines	1	11	.083	1	11	.083
WESTERN DIVISION						
Montana State	11	1	.917	36	2	.947
BYU	6	6	.500	20	10	.667
Utah State	4	8	.333	8	10	.444
Utah	3	9	.250	5	12	.294

SOUTHERN	CONFERENCE			OVERALL		
	W	L	PCT	W	L	PCT
Washington and Lee	7	1	.875	16	2	.889
North Carolina	12	2	.857	17	8	.680
Georgia Tech	10	2	.833	15	6	.714
Georgia	13	4	.765	18	6	.750
Tulane	9	4	.692	9	5	.643
Kentucky	7	4	.636	12	5	.706
Tennessee	7	4	.636	11	5	.688
Alabama	10	6	.625	16	10	.615
Clemson	6	4	.600	15	12	.556
Duke	5	4	.556	12	8	.600
NC State	6	5	.545	15	6	.714
Mississippi	7	8	.467	9	9	.500
Virginia	5	7	.417	9	10	.474
Mississippi State	5	8	.385	8	15	.348
LSU	5	9	.357	8	13	.381
Virginia Tech	3	6	.333	4	13	.235
South Carolina	4	9	.308	8	13	.381
Vanderbilt	2	5	.286	4	12	.250
Florida	4	11	.267	7	13	.350
Maryland	2	6	.250	7	9	.438
Auburn	3	9	.250	6	15	.286
VMI	1	7	.125	6	7	.462
Sewanee	0	7	.000	3	8	.273

Tournament: **NC State d. Duke 44-35**

SWC	CONFERENCE			OVERALL		
	W	L	PCT	W	L	PCT
Arkansas	11	1	.917	19	1	.950
Texas	10	2	.833	18	2	.900
SMU	6	6	.500	7	9	.438
TCU	5	7	.417	10	7	.588
Texas A&M	4	6	.400	12	6	.667
Baylor	2	8	.200	7	9	.438
Rice	2	10	.167	2	10	.167

CONSENSUS ALL-AMERICAS

PLAYER	CL	POS	HT	SCHOOL	PPG
Vern Corbin	SR	C	6-0	California	10.0*
Thomas Churchill	JR	F	6-2	Oklahoma	12.4*
Charley Hyatt	JR	F	6-0	Pittsburgh	14.3
Stretch Murphy	JR	C	6-6	Purdue	12.1
Joe Schaaf	SR	G/F	5-11	Penn	10.5
Cat Thompson	JR	G	5-9	Montana State	15.7

*Conference games only

SELECTORS: CHRISTY WALSH SYNDICATE, COLLEGE HUMOR MAGAZINE, HELMS FOUNDATION

1929-30

Alabama relied on its center, James "Lindy" Hood, who first played basketball during his freshman year, to win the Southern Conference tournament.

PREMO-PORRETTA POWER POLL

	SCHOOL	RECORD
1	Alabama	20-0
2	St. John's	23-1
3	Syracuse	18-2
4	Pittsburgh (Helms champion)	23-2
5	NYU	13-3
6	Duke	18-2
7	Wisconsin	15-2
8	Purdue	13-2
9	CCNY	12-3#
10	Missouri	15-3
11	Temple	18-3
12	Western Michigan	17-0
13	Northwest Missouri State	31-0
14	Pittsburg State (KS)	20-0
15	Furman	16-1
16	Kansas	14-4
17	East Central Oklahoma	23-2
18	Southern California	15-5
19	Buffalo	15-1
20	Columbia	17-5
21	Michigan State	12-4
22	Loyola-Chicago	13-5
23	Fordham	13-5
24	Notre Dame	14-6
25	Rider (NJ)	17-3

CONFERENCE STANDINGS

BIG SIX	CONFERENCE			OVERALL		
	W	L	PCT	W	L	PCT
Missouri	8	2	.800	15	3	.833
Kansas	7	3	.700	14	4	.778
Nebraska	6	4	.600	9	9	.500
Iowa State	5	5	.500	9	8	.529
Kansas State	4	6	.400	9	7	.563
Oklahoma	0	10	.000	6	12	.333

BIG TEN	CONFERENCE			OVERALL		
	W	L	PCT	W	L	PCT
Purdue	10	0	1.000	13	2	.867
Wisconsin	8	2	.800	15	2	.882
Michigan	6	4	.600	9	5	.643
Illinois	7	5	.583	8	8	.500
Indiana	7	5	.583	8	9	.471
Northwestern	6	6	.500	8	8	.500
Minnesota	3	9	.250	8	9	.471
Chicago	2	10	.167	3	11	.214
Ohio State	1	9	.100	4	11	.267
Iowa	-	-	-	4	13	.235

IVY	CONFERENCE			OVERALL		
	W	L	PCT	W	L	PCT
Columbia	9	1	.900	17	5	.773
Penn	7	3	.700	20	6	.769
Yale	4	6	.400	13	8	.619
Dartmouth	4	6	.400	11	9	.550
Princeton	3	7	.300	13	12	.520
Cornell	3	7	.300	6	12	.333

MISSOURI VALLEY	CONFERENCE			OVERALL		
	W	L	PCT	W	L	PCT
Creighton	6	2	.750	12	7	.632
Wash.-St. Louis	6	2	.750	8	8	.500
Drake	4	4	.500	10	9	.526
Grinnell	4	4	.500	6	9	.400
Oklahoma State	0	8	.000	1	15	.063

PACIFIC COAST	CONFERENCE			OVERALL		
	W	L	PCT	W	L	PCT
NORTH						
Washington	12	4	.750	21	7	.750
Washington State	9	7	.563	14	12	.538
Oregon	8	8	.500	14	12	.538
Oregon State	7	9	.438	14	13	.519
Idaho	4	12	.250	7	18	.280
SOUTH						
Southern California	7	2	.778	15	5	.750
California	6	3	.667	9	8	.529
UCLA	3	6	.333	14	8	.636
Stanford	2	7	.222	10	9	.526

Playoff: **Southern California d. Washington 2-1** in a best-of-three series for the title

Record differs from the school's and/or the NCAA's because it includes noncollegiate competition or because the outcome of some games is in dispute

ROCKY MOUNTAIN	Conference W	L	Pct	Overall W	L	Pct
Eastern Division						
Colorado	11	3	.786	11	6	.647
Wyoming	7	3	.700	13	6	.684
Colorado College	9	5	.643	20	11	.645
Western State	6	6	.500	9	6	.600
Denver	7	7	.500	10	7	.588
Northern Colorado	7	7	.500	7	7	.500
Colorado State	4	10	.286	4	10	.286
Colorado Mines	1	11	.083	1	11	.083
Western Division						
Utah State	7	5	.583	15	7	.682
Montana State	7	5	.583	21	10	.677
BYU	6	6	.500	23	7	.767
Utah	4	8	.333	15	12	.556

Playoff: Colorado refused to participate in a playoff; **Utah State d. Montana State 2-1** in a best-of-three series for the RMC title

SOUTHERN	Conference W	L	Pct	Overall W	L	Pct
Alabama	10	0	1.000	20	0	1.000
Duke	9	1	.900	18	2	.900
Kentucky	9	1	.900	16	3	.842
Washington and Lee	9	2	.818	16	4	.800
Tennessee	7	2	.778	13	4	.765
Georgia	7	3	.700	17	6	.739
Tulane	7	3	.700	16	7	.696
Clemson	8	4	.667	16	9	.640
Sewanee	5	3	.625	9	11	.450
Maryland	8	5	.615	16	6	.727
NC State	7	5	.583	11	6	.647
Mississippi	6	6	.500	6	7	.462
LSU	6	7	.462	10	11	.476
Florida	2	3	.400	10	4	.714
Georgia Tech	5	8	.385	10	13	.438
North Carolina	4	7	.364	14	11	.560
VMI	2	6	.250	4	10	.286
Mississippi State	2	7	.222	5	8	.385
Virginia	2	8	.200	3	12	.200
Virginia Tech	2	10	.167	5	14	.263
Vanderbilt	1	9	.100	6	16	.273
Auburn	1	10	.091	1	10	.091
South Carolina	0	6	.000	6	10	.375

Tournament: **Alabama d. Duke 31-24**

SWC	Conference W	L	Pct	Overall W	L	Pct
Arkansas	10	2	.833	16	7	.696
Texas	8	4	.667	12	8	.600
SMU	6	6	.500	8	10	.444
Baylor	4	6	.400	10	6	.625
Texas A&M	4	6	.400	8	10	.444
Rice	4	8	.333	7	9	.438
TCU	4	8	.333	7	10	.412

CONSENSUS ALL-AMERICAS

PLAYER	CL	POS	HT	SCHOOL	PPG
Charley Hyatt	SR	F	6-0	Pittsburgh	N/A
Branch McCracken	SR	F	6-4	Indiana	12.3
Stretch Murphy	SR	C	6-6	Purdue	13.7
Cat Thompson	SR	G	5-9	Montana State	N/A
Frank Ward	SR	C	6-2	Montana State	14.9
John Wooden	SO	G	5-10	Purdue	8.9

Selectors: Christy Walsh Syndicate, College Humor Magazine, Helms Foundation

1930-31

Northwestern sophomore All-America Joseph Reiff was so committed to the team that he supposedly helped pay his way through college by sweeping up the lobby of Patten Gymnasium for 40 cents an hour. Pitt coach Henry Clifford Carlson—the inventor of the figure 8 offense, in which players take turns cutting to the basket on give-and-gos—became the first coach to take an Eastern team on a West Coast road trip.

PREMO-PORRETTA POWER POLL

	SCHOOL	RECORD
1	Northwestern (Helms champion)	16-1
2	St. John's	21-1
3	Columbia	21-2
4	Washington	25-3
5	Manhattan	17-2
6	Michigan	13-4
7	Georgia	23-2
8	Pittsburg State (KS)	21-0
9	Pittsburgh	20-4
10	Michigan State	16-1
11	Syracuse	16-4
12	Kansas	15-3
13	Buffalo	15-0
14	Minnesota	13-4
15	Utah	21-6
16	Wittenberg (OH)	18-2
17	East Central Oklahoma	22-4
18	Butler	17-2
19	Purdue	12-5
20	Wyoming	19-4
21	Illinois	12-5
22	Central Normal (IN)	19-0
23	Wooster (OH)	16-2
24	Loyola (MD)	15-1#
25	Maryland	18-4

CONFERENCE STANDINGS

BIG SIX	Conference W	L	Pct	Overall W	L	Pct
Kansas	7	3	.700	15	3	.833
Nebraska	6	4	.600	9	9	.500
Kansas State	5	5	.500	11	6	.647
Missouri	5	5	.500	8	9	.471
Iowa State	4	6	.400	8	8	.500
Oklahoma	3	7	.300	10	8	.556

BIG TEN	Conference W	L	Pct	Overall W	L	Pct
Northwestern	11	1	.917	16	1	.941
Michigan	8	4	.667	13	4	.765
Minnesota	8	4	.667	13	4	.765
Purdue	8	4	.667	12	5	.706
Illinois	7	5	.583	12	5	.706
Indiana	5	7	.417	9	8	.529
Wisconsin	4	8	.333	8	9	.471
Chicago	4	8	.333	6	8	.429
Ohio State	3	9	.250	4	13	.235
Iowa	2	10	.167	5	12	.294

IVY	Conference W	L	Pct	Overall W	L	Pct
Columbia	10	0	1.000	21	2	.913
Dartmouth	6	4	.600	14	7	.667
Yale	6	4	.600	15	8	.652
Cornell	4	6	.400	10	9	.526
Penn	3	7	.300	9	17	.346
Princeton	1	9	.100	9	13	.409

MISSOURI VALLEY	Conference W	L	Pct	Overall W	L	Pct
Creighton	5	3	.625	8	10	.444
Oklahoma State	5	3	.625	7	9	.438
Wash.-St. Louis	5	3	.625	6	12	.333
Grinnell	3	5	.375	7	8	.467
Drake	2	6	.250	4	15	.211

PACIFIC COAST	Conference W	L	Pct	Overall W	L	Pct
North						
Washington	14	2	.875	25	3	.893
Washington State	10	6	.625	18	7	.720
Oregon State	9	7	.563	19	9	.679
Oregon	6	10	.375	12	10	.545
Idaho	1	15	.063	3	16	.158
South						
California	6	3	.667	12	10	.545
Southern California	5	4	.556	8	8	.500
UCLA	4	5	.444	9	6	.600
Stanford	3	6	.333	8	9	.471

Playoff: **Washington d. California 2-1** in a best-of-three series for the title

ROCKY MOUNTAIN	Conference W	L	Pct	Overall W	L	Pct
Eastern Division						
Wyoming	11	1	.917	19	4	.826
Northern Colorado	10	4	.714	11	5	.688
Colorado	8	4	.667	8	7	.533
Denver	7	7	.500	10	8	.556
Western State	5	4	.556	8	5	.615
Colorado College	5	9	.357	14	15	.483
Colorado State	4	8	.333	4	8	.333
Colorado Mines	0	12	.000	0	12	.000
Western Division						
Utah	8	4	.667	21	6	.778
Utah State	7	5	.583	13	7	.650
BYU	7	5	.583	20	13	.606
Montana State	2	10	.167	9	13	.409

Playoff: **Utah d. Wyoming 2-1** in a best-of-three series for the title

SOUTHERN	Conference W	L	Pct	Overall W	L	Pct
Georgia	15	1	.938	23	2	.920
Maryland	8	1	.889	18	4	.818
Alabama	11	2	.846	14	6	.700
Kentucky	8	2	.800	15	3	.833
Auburn	7	4	.636	9	6	.600
Washington and Lee	4	3	.571	11	7	.611
Duke	5	4	.556	14	7	.667
Georgia Tech	8	7	.533	11	13	.458
Vanderbilt	7	7	.500	16	8	.667
North Carolina	6	6	.500	15	9	.625
NC State	5	5	.500	8	8	.500
LSU	4	4	.500	7	8	.467
Virginia	5	6	.455	11	9	.550
Florida	5	7	.417	10	9	.526
Clemson	3	5	.375	6	7	.462
Sewanee	3	5	.375	5	9	.357
Tennessee	4	8	.333	11	10	.524
Mississippi	2	4	.333	6	9	.400
Virginia Tech	3	7	.300	5	10	.333
VMI	2	8	.200	4	12	.250
Tulane	2	10	.167	6	14	.300
South Carolina	1	12	.077	1	17	.056

Tournament: **Maryland d. Kentucky 29-27**

SWC	Conference W	L	Pct	Overall W	L	Pct
TCU	9	3	.750	18	4	.818
SMU	8	4	.667	15	8	.652
Arkansas	7	5	.583	14	9	.609
Baylor	7	5	.583	12	8	.600
Texas A&M	5	7	.417	14	8	.636
Rice	4	8	.333	8	9	.471
Texas	2	10	.167	9	15	.375

CONSENSUS ALL-AMERICAS

PLAYER	CL	POS	HT	SCHOOL	PPG
Wesley Fesler	SR	G/C	5-11	Ohio State	5.4
George Gregory	SR	C	6-4	Columbia	7.7
Joseph Reiff	SO	F/C	6-2	Northwestern	8.7
Elwood Romney	SO	F	N/A	BYU	15.0
John Wooden	JR	G	5-10	Purdue	8.2

Selectors: College Humor Magazine, Helms Foundation

1931-32

Purdue wore out its opponents with a revolutionary fast-break offense. Only two years after the departure of their Hall of Fame big man, Charles "Stretch" Murphy, senior guard John Wooden led the Boilermakers to their only national championship. Wooden averaged 12.2 ppg during the campaign—good enough to be named Helms Foundation Player of the Year—and went on to have a bit of success as a head coach.

PREMO-PORRETTA POWER POLL

	SCHOOL	RECORD
1	**Purdue (Helms champion)**	17-1
2	**Notre Dame**	18-2
3	**CCNY**	16-1
4	**Northwest Missouri State**	26-2
5	**Minnesota**	15-3
6	**Kentucky**	15-2
7	**St. John's**	22-4
8	**Wyoming**	18-2
9	**Princeton**	18-4
10	**Northwestern**	13-5
11	**Creighton**	17-4
12	**Butler**	14-5
13	**Carleton**	17-1
14	**DePauw**	14-2
15	**Columbia**	17-6
16	**Westminster (PA)**	22-2#
17	**North Carolina**	16-5
18	**Michigan**	11-6
19	**Mount Union (OH)**	16-1
20	**Loyola-Chicago**	15-2
21	**Maryland**	16-4
22	**Illinois**	11-6
23	**Dakota Wesleyan**	19-1
24	**Georgia**	19-7
25	**West Texas A&M**	20-3

CONFERENCE STANDINGS

BIG SIX	Conference W	L	PCT	Overall W	L	PCT
Kansas	7	3	.700	13	5	.722
Oklahoma	6	4	.600	9	5	.643
Missouri	6	4	.600	9	9	.500
Kansas State	5	5	.500	7	8	.467
Iowa State	4	6	.400	9	6	.600
Nebraska	2	8	.200	3	17	.150

BIG TEN	Conference W	L	PCT	Overall W	L	PCT
Purdue	11	1	.917	17	1	.944
Minnesota	9	3	.750	15	3	.833
Northwestern	9	3	.750	13	5	.722
Michigan	8	4	.667	11	6	.647
Illinois	7	5	.583	11	6	.647
Ohio State	5	7	.417	9	9	.500
Indiana	4	8	.333	8	10	.444
Wisconsin	3	9	.250	8	10	.444
Iowa	3	9	.250	5	12	.294
Chicago	1	11	.083	1	13	.071

BORDER	Conference W	L	PCT	Overall W	L	PCT
Arizona	8	2	.800	18	2	.900
Northern Arizona	8	4	.667	9	8	.529
New Mexico	5	5	.500	10	6	.625
Arizona State	4	8	.333	7	12	.368
New Mexico State	1	7	.125	9	10	.474

IVY	Conference W	L	PCT	Overall W	L	PCT
Princeton	8	2	.800	18	4	.818
Columbia	8	2	.800	17	6	.739
Cornell	6	4	.600	10	10	.500
Dartmouth	5	5	.500	15	6	.714
Penn	2	8	.200	10	11	.476
Yale	1	9	.100	10	12	.455

Playoff: **Princeton d. Columbia 38-35**

MISSOURI VALLEY	Conference W	L	PCT	Overall W	L	PCT
Creighton	8	0	1.000	17	4	.810
Grinnell	5	3	.625	8	8	.500
Wash.-St. Louis	3	5	.375	10	9	.526
Oklahoma State	2	6	.250	4	16	.200
Drake	2	6	.250	2	17	.105

PACIFIC COAST	Conference W	L	PCT	Overall W	L	PCT
NORTH						
Washington	12	4	.750	19	6	.760
Washington State	11	5	.688	22	5	.815
Oregon State	8	8	.500	12	12	.500
Oregon	7	9	.438	13	11	.542
Idaho	2	14	.125	8	16	.333
SOUTH						
California	8	3	.727	16	8	.667
Southern California	8	3	.727	10	12	.455
UCLA	4	7	.364	9	10	.474
Stanford	2	9	.182	6	14	.300

Playoff: California d. Southern California 26-22 to win the South; **California d. Washington 2-0** in a best-of-three series for the PCC title

ROCKY MOUNTAIN	Conference W	L	PCT	Overall W	L	PCT
EASTERN DIVISION						
Wyoming	12	0	1.000	18	2	.900
Northern Colorado	10	4	.714	10	4	.714
Colorado College	10	4	.714	14	6	.700
Colorado	9	5	.643	10	7	.588
Colorado State	4	8	.333	4	8	.333
Western State	2	8	.200	3	8	.273
Denver	2	12	.143	3	15	.167
Colorado Mines	1	9	.100	1	9	.100
WESTERN DIVISION						
BYU	8	4	.667	20	12	.625
Utah	8	4	.667	14	9	.609
Montana State	6	6	.500	14	15	.483
Utah State	2	10	.167	7	15	.318

Playoff: BYU d. Utah 35-33 to win the Western Division; **Wyoming d. BYU 2-1** in a best-of-three series for the RMC title

SOUTHERN	Conference W	L	PCT	Overall W	L	PCT
Kentucky	9	1	.900	15	2	.882
Maryland	9	1	.900	16	4	.800
Auburn	9	2	.818	12	3	.800
Alabama	11	3	.786	16	4	.800
North Carolina	6	3	.667	16	5	.762
Virginia	6	3	.667	13	8	.619
Georgia	7	4	.636	19	7	.731
Georgia Tech	5	3	.625	7	6	.538
Mississippi	8	5	.615	9	6	.600
NC State	6	4	.600	10	6	.625
Duke	6	5	.545	14	11	.560
South Carolina	2	2	.500	9	7	.563
LSU	8	8	.500	11	9	.550
Tennessee	5	5	.500	8	7	.533
Vanderbilt	5	7	.417	8	11	.421
Mississippi State	4	7	.364	5	10	.333
Tulane	5	9	.357	6	10	.375
Florida	4	10	.286	8	12	.400
Washington and Lee	3	8	.273	9	10	.474
Virginia Tech	2	8	.200	8	9	.471
Clemson	2	9	.182	7	13	.350
Sewanee	1	7	.125	3	9	.250
VMI	0	9	.000	0	14	.000

Tournament: **Georgia d. North Carolina 26-24**

SWC	Conference W	L	PCT	Overall W	L	PCT
Baylor	10	2	.833	14	4	.778
TCU	9	3	.750	18	4	.818
Arkansas	8	4	.667	18	6	.750
Texas	5	7	.417	13	9	.591
Texas A&M	4	8	.333	10	9	.526
Rice	4	8	.333	5	9	.357
SMU	2	10	.167	9	13	.409

CONSENSUS ALL-AMERICAS

PLAYER	CL	POS	HT	SCHOOL	PPG
Louis Berger	SR	G	6-2	Maryland	6.9
Edward Krause	SO	C	6-3	Notre Dame	7.7
Forest Sale	JR	F/C	6-4	Kentucky	13.8
Les Witte	SO	F	6-0	Wyoming	11.9
John Wooden	SR	G	5-10	Purdue	12.2

SELECTORS: COLLEGE HUMOR MAGAZINE, CONVERSE YEARBOOK, HELMS FOUNDATION

1932-33

Texas sensation Jack Gray led the Southwest Conference in scoring in his first season on the varsity squad. Gray used a one-handed push shot that was unique at the time. Kentucky's Forest Sale, who averaged 13.8 ppg, was the Helms Player of the Year.

PREMO-PORRETTA POWER POLL

	SCHOOL	RECORD
1	**Texas**	22-1
2	**Duquesne**	15-1
3	**South Carolina**	21-2#
4	**Ohio State**	17-3
5	**Kentucky (Helms champion)**	21-3
6	**CCNY**	13-1
7	**Navy**	14-2
8	**Princeton**	19-3
9	**Yale**	19-3
10	**Northwestern**	15-4
11	**Syracuse**	14-2
12	**St. John's**	23-4
13	**Pittsburgh**	17-5
14	**Marquette**	14-3
15	**Kansas**	13-4
16	**TCU**	16-4
17	**Notre Dame**	16-6
18	**Eastern Michigan**	15-2#
19	**Providence**	13-3
20	**Butler**	16-5
21	**Dartmouth**	12-6
22	**Oregon State**	21-6
23	**West Texas A&M**	20-4
24	**Penn**	12-6
25	**Creighton**	12-5

CONFERENCE STANDINGS

BIG SIX	Conference W	L	PCT	Overall W	L	PCT
Kansas	8	2	.800	13	4	.765
Oklahoma	7	3	.700	12	5	.706
Missouri	6	4	.600	10	8	.556
Kansas State	4	6	.400	9	9	.500
Iowa State	2	8	.200	6	10	.375
Nebraska	2	8	.200	3	13	.188

BIG TEN	Conference W	L	PCT	Overall W	L	PCT
Ohio State	10	2	.833	17	3	.850
Northwestern	10	2	.833	15	4	.789
Iowa	8	4	.667	15	5	.750
Michigan	8	4	.667	10	8	.556
Illinois	6	6	.500	11	7	.611
Purdue	6	6	.500	11	7	.611
Indiana	6	6	.500	10	8	.556
Wisconsin	4	8	.333	7	13	.350
Minnesota	1	11	.083	5	15	.250
Chicago	1	11	.083	1	14	.067

BORDER	Conference W	L	PCT	Overall W	L	PCT
Texas Tech	4	0	1.000	15	8	.652
Arizona	7	3	.700	19	5	.792
Northern Arizona	7	5	.583	9	5	.643
New Mexico	8	6	.571	13	6	.684
Arizona State	7	9	.438	13	12	.520
New Mexico State	2	10	.167	7	11	.389

EAST. INTERCOLL.	Conference W	L	PCT	Overall W	L	PCT
Pittsburgh	7	1	.875	17	5	.773
Temple	5	3	.625	15	6	.714
Carnegie Mellon	4	4	.500	9	10	.474
Georgetown	3	5	.375	6	11	.353
West Virginia	1	7	.125	10	14	.417

IVY	Conference W	L	PCT	Overall W	L	PCT
Yale	8	2	.800	19	3	.864
Princeton	7	3	.700	19	3	.864
Penn	6	4	.600	12	6	.667
Dartmouth	5	5	.500	12	6	.667
Columbia	3	7	.300	9	10	.474
Cornell	1	9	.100	6	11	.353

MISSOURI VALLEY	Conference W	L	PCT	Overall W	L	PCT
Butler	9	1	.900	16	5	.762
Creighton	8	2	.800	12	5	.706
Wash.-St. Louis	5	5	.500	11	6	.647
Grinnell	3	7	.300	5	11	.313
Oklahoma State	3	7	.300	5	12	.294
Drake	2	8	.200	4	12	.250

Record differs from the school's and/or the NCAA's because it includes noncollegiate competition or because the outcome of some games is in dispute

ANNUAL REVIEW

PACIFIC COAST

	Conference W	L	PCT	Overall W	L	PCT
North						
Oregon State	12	4	.750	21	6	.778
Washington	10	6	.625	22	6	.786
Washington State	8	8	.500	17	8	.680
Idaho	8	8	.500	8	8	.500
Oregon	2	14	.125	8	19	.296
South						
Southern California	10	1	.909	18	5	.783
California	8	3	.727	18	7	.720
Stanford	3	8	.273	9	18	.333
UCLA	1	10	.091	10	11	.476

Playoff: **Oregon State d. Southern California 2-1** in a best-of-three series for the title

ROCKY MOUNTAIN

	Conference W	L	PCT	Overall W	L	PCT
Eastern Division						
Wyoming	12	2	.857	18	5	.783
Northern Colorado	12	2	.857	13	7	.650
Colorado State	7	5	.583	7	5	.583
Western State	6	6	.500	8	6	.571
Colorado	7	7	.500	8	8	.500
Colorado College	6	8	.429	7	12	.368
Denver	4	10	.286	7	12	.368
Colorado Mines	0	14	.000	0	14	.000
Western Division						
BYU	9	3	.750	20	7	.741
Utah	9	3	.750	13	8	.619
Utah State	4	8	.333	10	12	.455
Montana State	2	10	.167	9	18	.333

Playoff: BYU d. Utah 43-26 to win the Western Division; Wyoming d. Northern Colorado 44-34 to win the Eastern Division; **BYU d. Wyoming 2-1** in a best-of-three series for the RMC title

SEC

	Conference W	L	PCT	Overall W	L	PCT
Kentucky	8	0	1.000	21	3	.875
Alabama	12	3	.800	14	5	.737
Vanderbilt	11	5	.688	14	8	.636
LSU	13	7	.650	15	8	.652
Georgia Tech	7	5	.583	9	6	.600
Florida	4	4	.500	9	5	.643
Georgia	5	6	.455	9	10	.474
Mississippi	5	7	.417	6	12	.333
Auburn	4	7	.364	4	9	.308
Tennessee	3	7	.300	9	11	.450
Tulane	6	14	.300	8	15	.348
Mississippi State	3	9	.250	6	13	.316
Sewanee	0	7	.000	1	10	.091

Tournament: **Kentucky d. Mississippi State 46-27**

SOUTHERN

	Conference W	L	PCT	Overall W	L	PCT
South Carolina	4	0	1.000	17	2	.895
Duke	7	3	.700	17	5	.773
Maryland	7	3	.700	11	9	.550
NC State	6	3	.667	11	8	.579
North Carolina	5	3	.625	12	5	.706
Virginia	5	3	.625	12	6	.667
Virginia Tech	3	7	.300	5	10	.333
VMI	2	8	.200	4	11	.267
Washington and Lee	1	8	.111	6	10	.375
Clemson	0	2	.000	10	9	.526

Tournament: **South Carolina d. Duke 33-21**

SWC

	Conference W	L	PCT	Overall W	L	PCT
Texas	11	1	.917	22	1	.957
TCU	9	3	.750	16	4	.800
Texas A&M	8	4	.667	9	10	.474
Arkansas	6	6	.500	14	7	.667
SMU	5	7	.417	9	9	.500
Rice	2	10	.167	8	10	.444
Baylor	1	11	.083	4	13	.235

CONSENSUS ALL-AMERICAS

PLAYER	CL	POS	HT	SCHOOL	PPG
Edward Krause	JR	C	6-3	Notre Dame	8.5
Elliott Loughlin	SR	G	5-11	Navy	14.9
Jerry Nemer	SR	F	6-0	USC	9.0*
Joseph Reiff	SR	F/C	6-2	Northwestern	13.9
Forest Sale	SR	F/C	6-4	Kentucky	13.8
Don Smith	SR	G	6-0	Pittsburgh	N/A

*Conference games only

Selectors: College Humor Magazine, Converse Yearbook, Helms Foundation

1933-34

Kentucky—undefeated in Southeastern Conference play—was upset in the first game of the SEC tournament by Florida, despite 16 points from senior center John DeMoisey. Wyoming senior Les Witte, a forward, was the younger brother of the team's coach, Willard "Dutch" Witte.

PREMO-PORRETTA POWER POLL

	SCHOOL	RECORD
1	Kentucky	16-1
2	NYU	16-0
3	Duquesne	19-2
4	CCNY	14-1
5	South Carolina	18-2#
6	Wyoming (Helms champion)	26-4#
7	Purdue	17-3
8	Pittsburgh	19-4#
9	Alabama	16-2
10	Long Island	27-1#
11	Notre Dame	20-4
12	DePaul	17-0
13	Syracuse	15-2
14	Penn	16-3
15	Navy	11-2
16	Westminster (PA)	24-5#
17	Kansas	16-1
18	Akron	15-1
19	St. John's	16-3
20	Washington	20-5
21	Marquette	15-4
22	Xavier	9-1
23	Creighton	14-3
24	TCU	13-2
25	Emporia State (KS)	17-1

CONFERENCE STANDINGS

BIG SIX

	Conference W	L	PCT	Overall W	L	PCT
Kansas	9	1	.900	16	1	.941
Missouri	6	4	.600	10	8	.556
Oklahoma	6	4	.600	10	8	.556
Nebraska	5	5	.500	7	11	.389
Iowa State	2	8	.200	6	11	.353
Kansas State	2	8	.200	3	15	.167

BIG TEN

	Conference W	L	PCT	Overall W	L	PCT
Purdue	10	2	.833	17	3	.850
Wisconsin	8	4	.667	14	6	.700
Northwestern	8	4	.667	11	8	.579
Illinois	7	5	.583	13	6	.684
Iowa	6	6	.500	13	6	.684
Indiana	6	6	.500	13	7	.650
Minnesota	5	7	.417	9	11	.450
Ohio State	4	8	.333	8	12	.400
Michigan	4	8	.333	6	14	.300
Chicago	2	10	.167	4	14	.222

BORDER

	Conference W	L	PCT	Overall W	L	PCT
Texas Tech	7	1	.875	18	5	.783
Arizona	9	3	.750	18	9	.667
New Mexico	6	4	.600	16	4	.800
Arizona State	8	10	.444	9	11	.450
Northern Arizona	6	10	.375	9	14	.391
New Mexico State	2	6	.250	10	9	.526

EAST. INTERCOLL.

	Conference W	L	PCT	Overall W	L	PCT
Pittsburgh	8	0	1.000	18	4	.818
West Virginia	7	3	.700	14	5	.737
Georgetown	5	5	.500	12	11	.522
Temple	5	5	.500	9	12	.429
Carnegie Mellon	2	7	.222	4	12	.250
Bucknell	0	7	.000	2	16	.111

IVY

	Conference W	L	PCT	Overall W	L	PCT
Penn	10	2	.833	16	3	.842
Cornell	9	3	.750	11	5	.688
Princeton	7	5	.583	13	8	.619
Yale	7	5	.583	14	9	.609
Dartmouth	6	6	.500	13	7	.650
Columbia	3	9	.250	6	14	.300
Harvard	0	12	.000	3	19	.136

Note: Columbia also played in the Metro

METRO

	Conference W	L	PCT	Overall W	L	PCT
NYU	9	0	1.000	16	0	1.000
Long Island	4	0	1.000	26	1	.963
St. John's	3	4	.429	16	3	.842
Fordham	1	4	.200	11	5	.688
Brooklyn	1	6	.143	14	7	.667
CCNY	4	1	.667	14	1	.625
Pratt Institute	0	0	.000	8	6	.571
St. Francis (NY)	3	8	.273	13	11	.542
Manhattan	4	4	.500	8	10	.444
Columbia	1	2	.333	6	14	.300

Note: Teams did not play an official conference schedule

MISSOURI VALLEY

	Conference W	L	PCT	Overall W	L	PCT
Butler	9	1	.900	14	7	.667
Creighton	7	3	.700	14	3	.824
Grinnell	5	5	.500	8	7	.533
Wash.-St. Louis	4	6	.400	7	11	.389
Drake	4	6	.400	6	12	.333
Oklahoma State	1	9	.100	4	14	.222

PACIFIC COAST

	Conference W	L	PCT	Overall W	L	PCT
North						
Washington	14	2	.875	20	5	.800
Oregon	9	7	.563	17	8	.680
Oregon State	7	9	.438	14	10	.583
Washington State	6	10	.375	14	11	.560
Idaho	4	12	.250	4	12	.250
South						
Southern California	9	3	.750	16	8	.667
California	8	4	.667	19	7	.731
Stanford	5	7	.417	8	12	.400
UCLA	2	10	.167	10	13	.435

Playoff: **Washington d. Southern California 2-1** in a best-of-three series for the title

ROCKY MOUNTAIN

	Conference W	L	PCT	Overall W	L	PCT
Eastern Division						
Wyoming	14	0	1.000	26	3	.897
Colorado	7	5	.583	9	8	.529
Colorado College	8	6	.571	10	11	.476
Denver	7	7	.500	8	9	.471
Northern Colorado	6	8	.429	13	14	.481
Colorado State	5	7	.417	5	7	.417
Western State	4	6	.400	9	8	.529
Colorado Mines	1	13	.071	1	13	.071
Western Division						
BYU	9	3	.750	18	12	.600
Utah State	7	5	.583	14	6	.700
Utah	7	5	.583	14	9	.609
Montana State	1	11	.083	5	22	.185

Playoff: **Wyoming d. BYU 3-0** in a best-of-three series for the RMC title

SEC

	Conference W	L	PCT	Overall W	L	PCT
Kentucky	11	0	1.000	16	1	.941
Alabama	13	2	.867	16	2	.889
LSU	13	3	.813	13	4	.765
Florida	4	2	.667	11	7	.611
Vanderbilt	8	5	.615	11	6	.647
Tulane	8	10	.444	10	10	.500
Georgia Tech	5	8	.385	6	12	.333
Tennessee	3	5	.375	10	7	.588
Georgia	3	6	.333	10	9	.526
Mississippi State	4	8	.333	8	11	.421
Mississippi	2	8	.200	7	9	.438
Auburn	2	9	.182	2	11	.154
Sewanee	0	10	.000	0	13	.000

Tournament: **Alabama d. Florida 41-25**

SOUTHERN

	Conference W	L	PCT	Overall W	L	PCT
South Carolina	6	0	1.000	18	1	.947
North Carolina	12	2	.857	18	4	.818
Maryland	6	1	.857	11	8	.579
Duke	9	4	.692	18	6	.750
NC State	6	5	.545	11	6	.647
Washington and Lee	4	5	.444	10	6	.625
VMI	3	6	.333	4	10	.286
Virginia	1	9	.100	7	11	.389
Virginia Tech	1	10	.091	1	15	.063
Clemson	0	6	.000	7	12	.368

Tournament: **Washington and Lee d. Duke 30-29**

ANNUAL REVIEW

SWC

	Conference W	L	Pct	Overall W	L	Pct
TCU	10	2	.833	13	2	.867
Texas A&M	7	5	.583	14	6	.700
Arkansas	6	6	.500	16	8	.667
Texas	6	6	.500	14	8	.636
Rice	6	6	.500	6	6	.500
SMU	5	7	.417	11	9	.550
Baylor	2	10	.167	8	10	.444

CONSENSUS ALL-AMERICAS

PLAYER	CL	POS	HT	SCHOOL	PPG
Norman Cottom	JR	F	6-0	Purdue	9.0
Claire Cribbs	JR	G	6-0	Pittsburgh	N/A
Edward Krause	SR	C	6-3	Notre Dame	8.5
Hal Lee	SR	G	6-3	Washington	6.9*
Les Witte	SR	F	6-0	Wyoming	12.0

*Conference games only

SELECTORS: CONVERSE YEARBOOK, HELMS FOUNDATION, LITERARY DIGEST MAGAZINE

1934-35

On Jan. 5, 1935, the largest crowd for a college basketball game at the time (16,559) saw NYU nip Kentucky, 23-22, at Madison Square Garden. The Violets used a quick-cutting, fast-breaking offense.

PREMO-PORRETTA POWER POLL

	SCHOOL	RECORD
1	NYU (Helms champion)	19-1#
2	Richmond	20-0
3	Duquesne	18-1
4	Kentucky	19-2
5	LSU	14-1
6	North Carolina	23-2
7	Purdue	17-3
8	Long Island	24-2
9	DePaul	15-1
10	SMU	14-3
11	Rice	20-3
12	Navy	13-3
13	Arkansas	14-5
14	Penn	16-4
15	Syracuse	15-2
16	Pittsburgh	18-6
17	Wisconsin	15-5
18	Southern California	20-6
19	Ohio Wesleyan	17-2
20	Westminster (PA)	22-5#
21	West Virginia	16-6
22	Cincinnati	16-3
23	Illinois	15-5
24	Temple	17-7
25	Utah State	17-5

CONFERENCE STANDINGS

BIG SIX

	Conference W	L	Pct	Overall W	L	Pct
Iowa State	8	2	.800	13	3	.813
Kansas	12	4	.750	15	5	.750
Oklahoma	8	8	.500	9	9	.500
Missouri	7	9	.438	7	11	.389
Nebraska	3	7	.300	6	12	.333
Kansas State	4	12	.250	5	15	.250

BIG TEN

	Conference W	L	Pct	Overall W	L	Pct
Purdue	9	3	.750	17	3	.850
Illinois	9	3	.750	15	5	.750
Wisconsin	9	3	.750	15	5	.750
Indiana	8	4	.667	14	6	.700
Ohio State	8	4	.667	12	7	.632
Iowa	6	6	.500	10	9	.526
Minnesota	5	7	.417	11	9	.550
Northwestern	3	9	.250	10	10	.500
Michigan	2	10	.167	8	12	.400
Chicago	1	11	.083	1	15	.063

BORDER

	Conference W	L	Pct	Overall W	L	Pct
Texas Tech	9	1	.900	14	10	.583
Northern Arizona	10	4	.714	12	8	.600
New Mexico	7	9	.438	10	10	.500
Arizona	5	7	.417	11	8	.579
New Mexico State	4	6	.400	12	6	.667
Arizona State	3	9	.250	8	11	.421

EAST. INTERCOLL.

	Conference W	L	Pct	Overall W	L	Pct
Pittsburgh	6	2	.750	18	6	.750
West Virginia	6	2	.750	16	6	.727
Temple	5	3	.625	17	7	.708
Carnegie Mellon	2	6	.250	7	10	.412
Georgetown	1	7	.125	6	13	.316

Playoff: **Pittsburgh d. West Virginia 35-22**

IVY

	Conference W	L	Pct	Overall W	L	Pct
Penn	10	2	.833	16	4	.800
Columbia	10	2	.833	13	6	.684
Dartmouth	7	5	.583	12	9	.571
Yale	5	7	.417	11	10	.524
Princeton	4	8	.333	6	14	.300
Harvard	3	9	.250	7	12	.368
Cornell	3	9	.250	5	15	.250

Playoff: **Penn d. Columbia 35-34**

MISSOURI VALLEY

	Conference W	L	Pct	Overall W	L	Pct
Creighton	8	4	.667	12	8	.600
Drake	8	4	.667	14	11	.560
Grinnell	7	5	.583	11	8	.579
Wash.-St. Louis	6	6	.500	7	11	.389
Oklahoma State	5	7	.417	9	9	.500
Washburn	5	7	.417	7	13	.350
Tulsa	4	8	.333	6	10	.375

PACIFIC COAST

	Conference W	L	Pct	Overall W	L	Pct
NORTH						
Oregon State	12	4	.750	19	9	.679
Washington	11	5	.688	16	8	.667
Oregon	7	9	.438	16	12	.571
Washington State	6	10	.375	12	12	.500
Idaho	4	12	.250	4	12	.250
SOUTH						
Southern California	11	1	.917	20	6	.769
California	5	7	.417	11	14	.440
UCLA	4	8	.333	11	12	.478
Stanford	4	8	.333	10	17	.370

Playoff: **Southern California d. Oregon State 2-1** in a best-of-three series for the title

ROCKY MOUNTAIN

	Conference W	L	Pct	Overall W	L	Pct
EASTERN DIVISION						
Northern Colorado	9	3	.750	12	14	.462
Wyoming	10	4	.714	11	5	.688
Colorado College	9	5	.643	13	10	.565
Denver	7	5	.583	13	7	.650
Colorado State	6	6	.500	6	6	.500
Western State	3	7	.300	3	7	.300
Colorado	3	9	.250	3	9	.250
Colorado Mines	3	11	.214	3	11	.214
WESTERN DIVISION						
Utah State	9	3	.750	17	5	.773
BYU	6	6	.500	18	10	.643
Utah	5	7	.417	10	9	.526
Montana State	4	8	.333	16	13	.552

Playoff: **Utah State d. Northern Colorado 2-1** in a best-of-three series for the title

SEC

	Conference W	L	Pct	Overall W	L	Pct
LSU	12	0	1.000	14	1	.933
Kentucky	11	0	1.000	19	2	.905
Tennessee	7	4	.636	11	5	.688
Vanderbilt	9	6	.600	9	11	.450
Florida	4	3	.571	8	7	.533
Alabama	8	7	.533	9	8	.529
Mississippi State	5	5	.500	12	6	.667
Georgia Tech	5	6	.455	6	8	.429
Georgia	4	5	.444	12	8	.600
Mississippi	5	7	.417	8	10	.444
Auburn	3	9	.250	4	13	.235
Sewanee	1	7	.125	2	12	.143
Tulane	1	16	.059	1	16	.059

SOUTHERN

	Conference W	L	Pct	Overall W	L	Pct
North Carolina	12	1	.923	23	2	.920
Clemson	3	1	.750	15	3	.833
Duke	10	4	.714	18	8	.692
Virginia	7	5	.583	13	9	.591
Maryland	4	3	.571	8	10	.444
NC State	6	5	.545	10	9	.526
South Carolina	5	7	.417	15	9	.625
Washington and Lee	4	8	.333	10	10	.500
VMI	2	9	.182	3	14	.176
Virginia Tech	1	11	.083	3	16	.158

Tournament: **North Carolina d. Washington and Lee 35-27**

SWC

	Conference W	L	Pct	Overall W	L	Pct
Rice	9	3	.750	20	3	.870
SMU	9	3	.750	14	3	.824
Arkansas	9	3	.750	14	5	.737
Texas	5	7	.417	16	7	.696
Texas A&M	4	8	.333	10	10	.500
Baylor	4	8	.333	8	9	.471
TCU	2	10	.167	6	13	.316

CONSENSUS ALL-AMERICAS

PLAYER	CL	POS	HT	SCHOOL	PPG
Bud Browning	SR	G	N/A	Oklahoma	9.7
Claire Cribbs	SR	G	6-0	Pittsburgh	N/A
LeRoy Edwards	SO	C	6-4	Kentucky	16.3
Jack Gray	SR	F	6-2	Texas	13.4
Lee Guttero	SR	C	6-2	USC	13.7

SELECTORS: CONVERSE YEARBOOK, HELMS FOUNDATION

1935-36

Guard/forward Jules Bender was LIU's leading scorer for the second of three straight seasons. In Bender's time, coach Clair Bee's team went 103–6. In a Notre Dame-Northwestern game, the scorekeeper failed to record an Irish free throw in what was at first a 20-19 Northwestern victory. The teams later agreed to call it a tie.

PREMO-PORRETTA POWER POLL

	SCHOOL	RECORD
1	Long Island	26-0#
2	Notre Dame (Helms champion)	22-2-1
3	Indiana	18-2
4	Kansas	21-2
5	Arkansas	24-3
6	Manhattan	17-3
7	Duquesne	14-3
8	Washington	25-7
9	NYU	15-4#
10	Purdue	16-4
11	Washington and Lee	19-2
12	Stanford	22-7
13	St. John's	18-4
14	Columbia	19-3
15	George Washington	16-3
16	DePaul	18-4
17	North Carolina	21-4
18	Illinois Wesleyan	20-0
19	Western Kentucky	26-4
20	Springfield (MA)	17-4
21	Murray State	23-2
22	Michigan	15-5
23	NC State	15-4
24	Temple	18-6
25	Northwestern	13-7-1#

CONFERENCE STANDINGS

BIG SIX

	Conference W	L	Pct	Overall W	L	Pct
Kansas	10	0	1.000	21	2	.913
Nebraska	7	3	.700	13	8	.619
Oklahoma	5	5	.500	9	8	.529
Kansas State	3	7	.300	9	9	.500
Iowa State	3	7	.300	8	8	.500
Missouri	2	8	.200	5	12	.294

BIG TEN

	Conference W	L	Pct	Overall W	L	T	Pct
Indiana	11	1	.917	18	2	-	.900
Purdue	11	1	.917	16	4	-	.800
Michigan	7	5	.583	15	5	-	.750
Illinois	7	5	.583	13	6	-	.684
Northwestern	7	5	.583	13	6	1	.675
Ohio State	5	7	.417	12	8	-	.600
Iowa	5	7	.417	9	10	-	.474
Wisconsin	4	8	.333	11	9	-	.550
Minnesota	3	9	.250	7	17	-	.292
Chicago	0	12	.000	4	12	-	.250

BORDER

	Conference W	L	Pct	Overall W	L	Pct
Arizona	11	5	.688	16	7	.696
Arizona State	11	7	.611	12	14	.462
Texas Tech	8	6	.571	10	10	.500
New Mexico	11	9	.550	16	10	.615
Northern Arizona	7	7	.500	15	9	.625
New Mexico State	8	8	.500	10	9	.526
UTEP	0	8	.000	0	12	.000

EAST. INTERCOLL.

	Conference W	L	Pct	Overall W	L	Pct
Carnegie Mellon	7	3	.700	15	8	.652
Pittsburgh	7	3	.700	18	9	.667
Temple	6	4	.600	18	6	.750
West Virginia	6	4	.600	16	8	.667
Georgetown	4	6	.400	7	11	.389
Penn State	0	10	.000	6	11	.353

Playoff: **Carnegie Mellon d. Pittsburgh 32-27**

Record differs from the school's and/or the NCAA's because it includes noncollegiate competition or because the outcome of some games is in dispute

IVY

	Conference W	L	PCT	Overall W	L	PCT
Columbia	12	0	1.000	19	3	.864
Penn	7	5	.583	12	9	.571
Dartmouth	6	6	.500	11	10	.524
Yale	6	6	.500	8	16	.333
Princeton	5	7	.417	9	14	.391
Harvard	3	9	.250	7	15	.318
Cornell	3	9	.250	5	12	.294

Note: Columbia also played in the Metro

METRO

	Conference W	L	PCT	Overall W	L	PCT
Long Island	3	0	1.000	25	0	1.000
Columbia	0	3	.000	19	3	.864
Manhattan	5	1	.833	17	3	.850
St. John's	4	3	.571	18	4	.818
NYU	7	1	.875	14	4	.778
Fordham	2	4	.333	11	4	.733
CCNY	3	3	.500	10	4	.714
Brooklyn	0	7	.000	18	9	.667
St. Francis (NY)	4	6	.400	15	8	.652

Note: Teams did not play an official conference schedule

MISSOURI VALLEY

	Conference W	L	PCT	Overall W	L	PCT
Creighton	8	4	.667	13	6	.684
Oklahoma State	8	4	.667	16	8	.667
Drake	8	4	.667	16	12	.571
Washburn	6	6	.500	7	14	.333
Grinnell	4	8	.333	7	11	.389
Wash.-St. Louis	3	9	.250	6	13	.316
Tulsa	3	9	.250	6	14	.300

PACIFIC COAST

	Conference W	L	PCT	Overall W	L	PCT
North						
Washington	13	3	.813	25	7	.781
Oregon State	10	6	.625	16	9	.640
Washington State	8	8	.500	22	8	.733
Oregon	7	9	.438	20	11	.645
Idaho	4	12	.333	4	12	.333
South						
Stanford	8	4	.667	21	8	.724
Southern California	8	4	.667	14	12	.538
California	6	6	.500	13	16	.448
UCLA	2	10	.167	10	13	.435

Playoff: Stanford d. Southern California 39-36 to win the South; **Stanford d. Washington 2-0** in a best-of-three series for the PCC title

ROCKY MOUNTAIN

	Conference W	L	PCT	Overall W	L	PCT
Eastern Division						
Wyoming	11	3	.786	12	7	.632
Northern Colorado	10	4	.714	14	6	.700
Denver	8	4	.667	11	5	.688
Colorado College	9	5	.643	14	9	.609
Western State	5	5	.500	13	7	.650
Colorado	6	8	.429	6	8	.429
Colorado State	3	9	.250	3	9	.250
Colorado Mines	0	14	.000	0	14	.000
Western Division						
Utah State	9	3	.750	17	9	.654
BYU	6	6	.500	16	9	.640
Montana State	5	7	.417	11	8	.579
Utah	4	8	.333	7	15	.318

Playoff: **Utah State d. Wyoming 2-1** in a best-of-three series for the title

SEC

	Conference W	L	PCT	Overall W	L	PCT
Kentucky	6	2	.750	15	6	.714
Vanderbilt	9	4	.692	9	14	.391
Tennessee	8	4	.667	15	6	.714
Mississippi State	9	5	.643	11	6	.647
Auburn	7	4	.636	10	7	.588
Alabama	9	6	.600	15	9	.625
LSU	9	6	.600	10	10	.500
Georgia Tech	7	5	.583	10	8	.556
Mississippi	7	5	.583	11	9	.550
Georgia	6	7	.462	9	11	.450
Florida	2	8	.200	4	11	.267
Tulane	1	14	.067	2	17	.105
Sewanee	0	10	.000	2	13	.133

Tournament: **Tennessee d. Alabama 29-25**

SOUTHERN

	Conference W	L	PCT	Overall W	L	PCT
Washington and Lee	10	1	.909	19	2	.905
North Carolina	13	3	.813	21	4	.840
NC State	10	3	.769	15	4	.789
Maryland	4	3	.571	14	6	.700
Clemson	5	5	.500	15	7	.682
Duke	4	5	.444	20	6	.769
Virginia	4	8	.333	11	13	.458
South Carolina	1	6	.143	11	8	.579
Virginia Tech	1	9	.100	5	16	.238
VMI	0	10	.000	3	14	.176

Tournament: **North Carolina d. Washington and Lee 50-45**

SWC

	Conference W	L	PCT	Overall W	L	PCT
Arkansas	11	1	.917	24	3	.889
Texas	8	4	.667	15	9	.625
Rice	8	4	.667	12	10	.545
Baylor	6	6	.500	12	13	.480
SMU	4	8	.333	4	8	.333
Texas A&M	3	9	.250	9	9	.500
TCU	2	10	.167	3	11	.214

INDEPENDENTS

	Overall W	L	T	PCT
Notre Dame	22	2	1	.900
Western Kentucky	26	4	-	.867
George Washington	16	3	-	.842
Western Michigan	15	3	-	.833
Duquesne	14	3	-	.824
DePaul	18	4	-	.818
Indiana State	11	3	-	.786
St. Bonaventure	7	2	-	.778
Bucknell	13	4	-	.765
Colgate	12	4	-	.750
Furman	12	4	-	.750
Toledo	12	4	-	.750
Niagara	17	6	-	.739
Saint Joseph's	14	5	-	.737
Rhode Island	13	5	-	.722
Detroit	12	5	-	.706
Syracuse	12	5	-	.706
Richmond	14	6	-	.700
Loyola (MD)	13	6	-	.684
Saint Mary's (CA)	14	7	-	.667
Santa Clara	12	6	-	.667
Ohio	13	7	-	.650
William and Mary	11	6	-	.647
Canisius	10	7	-	.588
Cincinnati	10	7	-	.588
Kent State	10	7	-	.588
The Citadel	7	5	-	.583
Louisville	14	11	-	.560
San Francisco	11	9	-	.550
Montana	13	11	-	.542
Rutgers	8	7	-	.533
Xavier	8	7	-	.533
Miami (OH)	9	8	-	.529
Army	7	7	-	.500
Brown	8	8	-	.500
Loyola-Chicago	8	8	-	.500
Navy	7	7	-	.500
Valparaiso	8	8	-	.500
Wichita State	12	12	-	.500
Michigan State	8	9	-	.471
Bowling Green	7	8	-	.467
Saint Louis	9	11	-	.450
Lafayette	7	9	-	.438
Wake Forest	9	12	-	.429
Lehigh	5	7	-	.417
Bradley	6	10	-	.375
Marshall	6	10	-	.375
Marquette	7	12	-	.368
Villanova	6	12	-	.333
Butler	6	15	-	.286
Seton Hall	4	11	-	.267
Muhlenberg	5	16	-	.238
La Salle	4	13	-	.235
Connecticut	3	11	-	.214
Davidson	4	15	-	.211
Dayton	3	13	-	.188
Boston U.	1	13	-	.071

CONSENSUS ALL-AMERICAS

PLAYER	CL	POS	HT	SCHOOL	PPG
Vern Huffman	JR	G	6-2	Indiana	4.6
Bob Kessler	SR	F	6-0	Purdue	13.0
Bill Kinner	SR	C	6-3	Utah	13.1
Hank Luisetti	SO	F	6-2	Stanford	14.3
John Moir	SO	F	6-2	Notre Dame	11.3
Paul Nowak	SO	C	6-6	Notre Dame	7.0
Ike Poole	SR	C	6-4	Arkansas	N/A

Selectors: College Humor Magazine, Converse Yearbook, Helms Foundation

1936-37

Stanford made a wildly successful cross-country trip, beating Temple in Philadelphia and snapping LIU's 43-game winning streak in front of 18,000 fans at Madison Square Garden. Throughout the season, Hank Luisetti used his innovative running one-handed shot to average 15.2 ppg.

PREMO-PORRETTA POWER POLL

	SCHOOL	RECORD
1	Stanford (Helms champion)	25-2
2	Notre Dame	20-3
3	Long Island	28-3
4	Michigan	16-4
5	Penn	17-3
6	Purdue	15-5
7	Illinois	14-4
8	George Washington	16-4
9	Western Kentucky	21-2
10	Loyola-Chicago	16-3
11	Hardin-Simmons	16-1
12	Springfield (MA)	18-3
13	Rhode Island	18-3
14	Oklahoma State	20-3#
15	Georgia Tech	13-2
16	Southern California	19-6
17	Temple	17-6
18	Syracuse	13-4
19	Rutgers	13-2
20	Amherst	11-2
21	Kentucky	17-5
22	Fordham	13-3
23	Minnesota	14-6
24	Washington State	24-8
25	Murray State	22-3

CONFERENCE STANDINGS

BIG SIX

	Conference W	L	PCT	Overall W	L	PCT
Kansas	8	2	.800	15	4	.789
Nebraska	8	2	.800	13	7	.650
Oklahoma	7	3	.700	12	4	.750
Kansas State	5	5	.500	9	9	.500
Missouri	2	8	.200	7	9	.438
Iowa State	0	10	.000	3	15	.167

BIG TEN

	Conference W	L	PCT	Overall W	L	PCT
Illinois	10	2	.833	14	4	.778
Minnesota	10	2	.833	14	6	.700
Michigan	9	3	.750	16	4	.800
Purdue	8	4	.667	15	5	.750
Ohio State	7	5	.583	13	7	.650
Indiana	6	6	.500	13	7	.650
Northwestern	4	8	.333	11	9	.550
Iowa	3	9	.250	11	9	.550
Wisconsin	3	9	.250	8	12	.400
Chicago	0	12	.000	1	15	.063

BORDER

	Conference W	L	PCT	Overall W	L	PCT
New Mexico State	15	3	.833	22	5	.815
Texas Tech	11	5	.688	18	7	.720
Arizona	9	7	.563	14	11	.560
New Mexico	10	10	.500	12	14	.462
Northern Arizona	6	10	.375	11	13	.458
Arizona State	7	11	.389	8	12	.400
UTEP	0	10	.000	2	16	.111

EAST. INTERCOLL.

	Conference W	L	PCT	Overall W	L	PCT
Pittsburgh	7	3	.700	14	7	.667
Temple	7	3	.700	17	6	.739
Penn State	6	4	.600	10	7	.588
Carnegie Mellon	4	6	.400	9	11	.450
Georgetown	3	7	.300	9	8	.529
West Virginia	3	7	.300	9	14	.391

Playoff: **Pittsburgh d. Temple 35-29**

IVY

	Conference W	L	PCT	Overall W	L	PCT
Penn	12	0	1.000	17	3	.850
Dartmouth	8	4	.667	14	8	.636
Columbia	7	5	.583	17	6	.739
Yale	7	5	.583	12	8	.600
Harvard	6	6	.500	10	8	.556
Princeton	2	10	.167	6	14	.300
Cornell	0	12	.000	3	14	.176

Note: Columbia also played in the Metro

METRO

	Conference W	L	PCT	Overall W	L	PCT
Long Island	2	0	1.000	28	3	.903
Fordham	5	1	.833	13	3	.813
Manhattan	5	2	.714	14	4	.778
Columbia	1	0	1.000	17	6	.739
St. John's	1	4	.200	12	7	.632
NYU	4	2	.667	10	6	.625
CCNY	3	3	.500	10	6	.625
St. Francis (NY)	1	5	.167	13	8	.619
Brooklyn	1	6	.143	11	8	.579

Note: Teams did not play an official conference schedule

MISSOURI VALLEY

	Conference W	L	PCT	Overall W	L	PCT
Oklahoma State	11	1	.917	19	3	.864
Creighton	8	4	.667	11	9	.550
Drake	7	5	.583	13	10	.565
Grinnell	7	5	.583	8	10	.444
Tulsa	4	8	.333	9	9	.500
Wash.-St. Louis	3	9	.250	6	12	.333
Washburn	2	10	.167	4	17	.190

PACIFIC COAST

	Conference W	L	PCT	Overall W	L	PCT
North						
Washington State	11	5	.688	24	8	.750
Oregon	11	5	.688	20	9	.690
Washington	11	5	.688	15	11	.577
Oregon State	5	11	.313	11	15	.423
Idaho	2	14	.125	2	14	.125
South						
Stanford	10	2	.833	25	2	.926
Southern California	8	4	.667	19	6	.760
California	4	8	.333	17	10	.630
UCLA	2	10	.167	6	13	.316

Playoff: Washington State d. Oregon 42-25 and Washington 36-33 to win the North; **Stanford d. Washington State 2-0** in a best-of-three series for the PCC title

ROCKY MOUNTAIN

	Conference W	L	PCT	Overall W	L	PCT
Eastern Division						
Denver	10	2	.833	14	6	.700
Colorado	10	2	.833	10	5	.667
Western State	5	3	.625	10	7	.588
Colorado State	7	5	.583	7	6	.538
Northern Colorado	8	6	.571	9	8	.529
Wyoming	7	7	.500	8	9	.471
Colorado College	3	11	.214	4	14	.222
Colorado Mines	0	14	.000	0	14	.000
Western Division						
Montana State	7	5	.583	17	10	.630
Utah	7	5	.583	17	7	.708
BYU	5	7	.417	17	10	.630
Utah State	5	7	.417	6	9	.400

Playoff: Montana State d. Utah 56-37 to win the Western Division; **Montana State d. Denver 2-1** in a best-of-three series for the PCC title

SEC

	Conference W	L	PCT	Overall W	L	PCT
Georgia Tech	10	0	1.000	13	2	.867
Tennessee	7	1	.875	17	5	.773
Mississippi	7	3	.700	20	6	.769
Auburn	7	4	.636	11	4	.733
Kentucky	5	3	.625	17	5	.773
Georgia	5	3	.625	10	6	.625
LSU	7	6	.538	13	7	.650
Alabama	7	8	.467	11	10	.524
Mississippi State	6	7	.462	15	9	.625
Tulane	4	8	.333	6	8	.429
Vanderbilt	3	7	.300	6	10	.375
Florida	1	9	.100	5	13	.278
Sewanee	0	10	.000	1	15	.063

Tournament: **Kentucky d. Tennessee 39-25**

SOUTHERN

	Conference W	L	PCT	Overall W	L	PCT
Washington and Lee	11	1	.917	17	4	.810
North Carolina	14	3	.824	18	5	.783
Wake Forest	9	4	.692	15	6	.714
NC State	14	7	.667	15	9	.625
Duke	11	6	.647	15	8	.652
South Carolina	7	4	.636	13	7	.650
Richmond	6	4	.600	13	7	.650
Virginia	6	7	.462	9	10	.474
Furman	3	4	.429	8	7	.533
Davidson	5	8	.385	13	10	.565
Maryland	5	8	.385	8	12	.400
VMI	5	11	.313	6	11	.353
Virginia Tech	4	9	.308	6	11	.353
Clemson	2	7	.222	6	15	.286
The Citadel	0	5	.000	7	12	.368
William and Mary	0	13	.000	0	18	.000

Tournament: **Washington and Lee d. North Carolina 44-33**

SWC

	Conference W	L	PCT	Overall W	L	PCT
SMU	10	2	.833	13	8	.619
Arkansas	8	4	.667	12	6	.667
Rice	7	5	.583	6	10	.375
Baylor	6	6	.500	11	9	.550
Texas	5	7	.417	13	10	.565
Texas A&M	5	7	.417	12	13	.480
TCU	1	11	.083	1	13	.071

INDEPENDENTS

	Overall W	L	PCT
Western Kentucky	21	2	.913
Notre Dame	20	3	.870
Rutgers	13	2	.867
Ohio	18	3	.857
Rhode Island	18	3	.857
Loyola-Chicago	16	3	.842
Toledo	18	4	.818
George Washington	16	4	.800
Bradley	15	4	.789
Saint Joseph's	15	4	.789
Syracuse	13	4	.765
Western Michigan	13	4	.765
Marshall	21	8	.724
DePaul	15	6	.714
Detroit	11	5	.688
Duquesne	13	6	.684
Kent State	15	7	.682
Villanova	15	8	.652
Santa Clara	13	7	.650
Navy	9	5	.643
La Salle	12	7	.632
Connecticut	11	7	.611
Saint Mary's (CA)	14	9	.609
Boston U.	9	6	.600
Colgate	9	6	.600
San Francisco	10	7	.588
Bucknell	9	7	.563
Canisius	9	7	.563
Niagara	12	10	.545
Army	7	6	.538
Indiana State	7	6	.538
Montana	14	12	.538
Marquette	8	8	.500
Muhlenberg	9	9	.500
Valparaiso	9	9	.500
Xavier	7	7	.500
Cincinnati	9	10	.474
Wichita State	9	12	.429
Dayton	7	12	.368
St. Bonaventure	4	7	.364
Lehigh	5	10	.333
Louisville	4	8	.333
Seton Hall	5	10	.333
Lafayette	6	13	.316
Brown	5	11	.313
Miami (OH)	5	11	.313
Butler	6	14	.300
Michigan State	5	12	.294
Saint Louis	6	15	.286
Bowling Green	4	11	.267
Loyola (MD)	4	12	.250

CONSENSUS ALL-AMERICAS

PLAYER	CL	POS	HT	SCHOOL	PPG
Jules Bender	SR	G/F	5-11	Long Island	9.1
Hank Luisetti	JR	F	6-2	Stanford	17.1
John Moir	JR	F	6-2	Notre Dame	13.2
Paul Nowak	JR	C	6-6	Notre Dame	7.2
Jewell Young	JR	F	6-0	Purdue	12.1

Selectors: Converse Yearbook, Helms Foundation, Madison Square Garden, Omaha World Newspaper

1937-38

The season marks the birth of modern college basketball, with two important changes introduced to the game. For the first time, the ball was put into play by the defending team from under its own basket after every score (previously, a center jump was contested after every field goal). This change drew immediate raves because it increased the action on the court and sped up the pace of play. But the second innovation had an even greater impact on the sport: New York City's Metropolitan Basketball Writers Association inaugurated the National Invitation Tournament, held in Madison Square Garden after each season, for the nation's top teams. The first official national championship was claimed by Temple—20–2 in the regular season with a victory over West Coast power Stanford—after beating Bradley, Oklahoma State and, finally, Colorado, 60-36. The Owls co-captain, 6'6½" center Meyer Bloom, led both Temple (10.6 ppg) and the NIT (24 points in three games) in scoring.

PREMO-PORRETTA POWER POLL

	SCHOOL	RECORD
1	Temple (NIT, Helms champion)	23-2
2	Stanford	21-3
3	Purdue	18-2
4	Oklahoma State	25-3
5	Notre Dame	20-3
6	Bradley	18-2
7	Western Kentucky	30-3
8	Kansas	18-2
9	Minnesota	16-4
10	Georgia Tech	18-2
11	Arkansas	19-3
12	Central Missouri State	24-3
13	Rhode Island	19-2
14	Oklahoma	14-4
15	Roanoke	19-2
16	Army	12-2
17	Long Island	23-5
18	Oregon	25-8
19	Southwestern (KS)	21-6
20	Murray State	27-4
21	New Mexico State	22-3
22	Villanova	25-5
23	Marshall	28-4
24	CCNY	13-3
25	Colorado	15-6

CONFERENCE STANDINGS

BIG SEVEN

	Conference W	L	PCT	Overall W	L	PCT
Colorado□	10	2	.833	15	6	.714
Utah	10	2	.833	20	4	.833
Wyoming	8	4	.667	12	5	.706
Utah State	6	6	.500	11	9	.550
BYU	4	8	.333	8	13	.381
Colorado State	3	9	.250	7	9	.438
Denver	1	11	.083	2	16	.111

BIG SIX

	Conference W	L	PCT	Overall W	L	PCT
Kansas	9	1	.900	18	2	.900
Oklahoma	8	2	.800	14	4	.778
Missouri	4	6	.400	9	9	.500
Nebraska	4	6	.400	9	11	.450
Kansas State	3	7	.300	7	11	.389
Iowa State	2	8	.200	6	9	.400

BIG TEN

	Conference W	L	PCT	Overall W	L	PCT
Purdue	10	2	.833	18	2	.900
Minnesota	9	3	.750	16	4	.800
Ohio State	7	5	.583	12	8	.600
Northwestern	7	5	.583	10	10	.500
Michigan	6	6	.500	12	8	.600
Iowa	6	6	.500	11	9	.550
Wisconsin	5	7	.417	10	10	.500
Indiana	4	8	.333	10	10	.500
Illinois	4	8	.333	9	9	.500
Chicago	2	10	.167	6	12	.333

BORDER

	Conference W	L	PCT	Overall W	L	PCT
New Mexico State	18	0	1.000	22	3	.880
Arizona	9	7	.563	13	8	.619
Arizona State	9	9	.500	11	12	.478
Texas Tech	7	7	.500	9	13	.409
New Mexico	6	10	.375	9	16	.360
Northern Arizona	4	12	.250	6	15	.286
UTEP	3	11	.214	4	17	.190

EAST. INTERCOLL.

	Conference W	L	PCT	Overall W	L	PCT
Temple□	9	1	.900	23	2	.920
Penn State	6	4	.600	13	5	.722
Pittsburgh	5	5	.500	9	12	.429
Georgetown	5	5	.500	7	11	.389
Carnegie Mellon	3	7	.300	12	9	.571
West Virginia	2	8	.200	6	13	.316

IVY

	Conference W	L	PCT	Overall W	L	PCT
Dartmouth	8	4	.667	20	5	.800
Harvard	7	5	.583	13	5	.722
Penn	7	5	.583	8	10	.444
Cornell	6	6	.500	11	7	.611
Columbia	6	6	.500	11	8	.579
Princeton	5	7	.417	10	10	.500
Yale	3	9	.250	7	12	.368

Note: Columbia also played in the Metro

Record differs from the school's and/or the NCAA's because it includes noncollegiate competition or because the outcome of some games is in dispute

□ NIT appearance

METRO	Conf W	Conf L	Conf Pct	Overall W	Overall L	Overall Pct
Long Island□	3	0	1.000	23	5	.821
CCNY	4	2	.667	13	3	.813
St. John's	4	2	.667	15	4	.789
NYU□	6	0	1.000	16	8	.667
Manhattan	2	4	.333	12	6	.667
St. Francis (NY)	1	5	.167	14	8	.636
Columbia	1	0	1.000	11	8	.579
Fordham	0	6	.000	10	10	.500
Brooklyn	2	4	.333	7	8	.467

Note: Teams did not play an official conference schedule

MISSOURI VALLEY	Conf W	Conf L	Conf Pct	Overall W	Overall L	Overall Pct
Oklahoma State□	13	1	.929	25	3	.893
Drake	10	4	.714	14	6	.700
Tulsa	8	6	.571	12	10	.545
Grinnell	7	7	.500	10	9	.526
Creighton	7	7	.500	11	14	.440
Washburn	6	8	.429	9	13	.409
Wash.-St. Louis	3	11	.214	4	17	.190
Saint Louis	2	12	.143	8	21	.276

NEW ENGLAND	Conf W	Conf L	Conf Pct	Overall W	Overall L	Overall Pct
Rhode Island	8	0	1.000	19	2	.905
Connecticut	4	4	.500	13	5	.722
New Hampshire	4	4	.500	11	6	.647
Northeastern	3	5	.375	6	12	.333
Maine	1	7	.125	4	9	.308

NORTHERN CALIF.	Conf W	Conf L	Conf Pct	Overall W	Overall L	Overall Pct
San Jose State	6	2	.750	19	4	.826
Santa Clara	6	2	.750	12	6	.667
Saint Mary's (CA)	5	3	.625	10	9	.526
San Francisco	3	5	.375	10	12	.455
Pacific	0	8	.000	6	13	.316

PACIFIC COAST	Conf W	Conf L	Conf Pct	Overall W	Overall L	Overall Pct
North						
Oregon	14	6	.700	25	8	.758
Washington	13	7	.650	29	7	.806
Washington State	12	8	.600	19	11	.633
Idaho	11	9	.550	11	9	.550
Oregon State	6	14	.300	17	16	.515
Montana	3	17	.150	10	19	.345
South						
Stanford	10	2	.833	21	3	.875
California	8	4	.667	18	11	.621
Southern California	6	6	.500	17	9	.654
UCLA	0	12	.000	4	20	.167

Playoff: **Stanford d. Oregon 2-0** in a best-of-three series for the title

SEC	Conf W	Conf L	Conf Pct	Overall W	Overall L	Overall Pct
Kentucky	6	0	1.000	13	5	.722
Mississippi	11	2	.846	22	12	.647
Georgia Tech	9	2	.818	18	2	.900
Auburn	6	3	.667	14	5	.737
Tennessee	7	4	.636	15	8	.652
LSU	7	6	.538	10	10	.500
Tulane	5	6	.455	8	10	.444
Mississippi State	7	9	.438	9	12	.429
Georgia	4	6	.400	12	10	.545
Vanderbilt	4	8	.333	9	12	.429
Florida	3	7	.300	11	9	.550
Alabama	4	12	.250	4	13	.235
Sewanee	2	10	.167	4	13	.235

Tournament: **Georgia Tech d. Mississippi 58-47**

SOUTHERN	Conf W	Conf L	Conf Pct	Overall W	Overall L	Overall Pct
North Carolina	13	3	.813	16	5	.762
NC State	10	3	.769	13	6	.684
The Citadel	7	3	.700	13	5	.722
Clemson	9	4	.692	16	7	.696
Richmond	8	4	.667	15	5	.750
Duke	9	5	.643	15	9	.625 #
Maryland	6	4	.600	15	9	.625
Washington and Lee	6	5	.545	12	9	.571
Wake Forest	7	8	.467	7	12	.368
Virginia Tech	4	5	.444	6	8	.429
Davidson	4	11	.267	10	12	.455
Furman	2	6	.250	6	13	.316
VMI	2	7	.222	4	11	.267
South Carolina	1	13	.071	3	21	.125
William and Mary	0	8	.000	2	10	.167

Tournament: **Duke d. Clemson 40-30**

SWC	Conf W	Conf L	Conf Pct	Overall W	Overall L	Overall Pct
Arkansas	11	1	.917	19	3	.864
Baylor	9	3	.750	10	6	.625
SMU	8	4	.667	9	6	.600
Texas A&M	6	6	.500	10	8	.556
Texas	5	7	.417	11	11	.500
Rice	2	10	.167	6	17	.261
TCU	1	11	.083	8	15	.348

INDEPENDENTS	Overall W	Overall L	Overall Pct
St. Bonaventure	9	0	1.000
Western Kentucky	30	3	.909
Bradley□	18	2	.900
Marshall	28	4	.875
Notre Dame	20	3	.870
Army	12	2	.857
Villanova	25	5	.833
Montana State	22	5	.815

INDEPENDENTS (CONT.)	Overall W	Overall L	Overall Pct
Bowling Green	16	4	.800
Detroit	16	4	.800
Navy	11	3	.786
George Washington	13	4	.765
Marquette	14	5	.737
Syracuse	14	5	.737
Rutgers	11	4	.733
Saint Joseph's	13	5	.722
Toledo	14	6	.700
Miami (OH)	11	5	.688
Valparaiso	13	6	.684
Santa Clara	12	6	.667
Loyola-Chicago	12	8	.600
Ohio	12	8	.600
Loyola (MD)	9	7	.563
Seton Hall	10	8	.556
DePaul	12	10	.545
Bucknell	7	6	.538
Lafayette	9	8	.529
La Salle	9	8	.529
Michigan State	9	8	.529
Colgate	10	9	.526
Xavier	10	9	.526
Boston U.	9	9	.500
Butler	11	12	.478
Canisius	8	9	.471
Lehigh	7	8	.467
Muhlenberg	9	11	.450
Kent State	10	13	.435
Wichita State	10	13	.435
Brown	7	11	.389
Niagara	8	13	.381
Virginia	6	10	.375
Cincinnati	6	11	.353
Dayton	6	11	.353
Duquesne	6	11	.353
Western Michigan	6	12	.333
Louisville	4	11	.267
Indiana State	1	17	.056

CONSENSUS ALL-AMERICAS

PLAYER	CL	POS	HT	SCHOOL	PPG
Meyer Bloom	SR	C	6-6½	Temple	10.6
Hank Luisetti	SR	F	6-2	Stanford	17.2
John Moir	SR	F	6-2	Notre Dame	10.5
Paul Nowak	SR	C	6-6	Notre Dame	7.5
Fred Pralle	SR	G	6-3	Kansas	10.7
Jewell Young	SR	F	6-0	Purdue	14.5

Selectors: Converse Yearbook, Helms Foundation, Madison Square Garden, Newspaper Enterprises Association

1938 National Invitation Tournament

Round 1

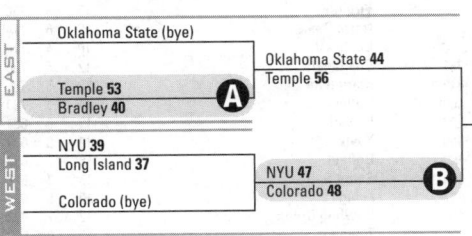

East:
- Oklahoma State (bye)
- Temple **53**, Bradley **40** (A)

West:
- NYU **39**, Long Island **37**
- Colorado (bye)

Round 2

- Oklahoma State **44**, Temple **56**
- NYU **47**, Colorado **48** (B)

Championship — New York City

Temple 60, Colorado 36

Temple breezes as Colorado succumbs to the Owls' stout zone. After the game, Oklahoma A&M (today's Oklahoma State), impressed by Temple's style and prowess, invites the boys from Philadelphia to play the inaugural home game in its new field house in Stillwater.

Third Place Oklahoma State d. NYU 37-24

A Bradley faces a zone for the first time this season. Tempers flare when a Temple defender tries to pry the ball from Dar Hutchins, and the players square off before the refs intervene.

B Colorado defeats NYU on Don Hendricks' game-winning shot. The Buffs use only five players, one of whom is Byron "Whizzer" White, a future U.S. Supreme Court justice.

NIT Final 1938 — 60-36

	1H	2H
Temple	33	27
Colorado	18	18

TEMPLE	FG	FT	TP
Don Shields	8	0	16
Howard Black	7	0	14
Jim Boyle	7	0	14
Meyer Bloom	2	2	6
Robert Nicol	1	1	3
Albert Freiberg	1	0	2
Edward McDermott	1	0	2
James Usilton Jr.	1	0	2
Donald Henderson	0	1	1
TOTALS	28	4	60

Coach: James Usilton

COLORADO	FG	FT	TP
Jack Harvey	3	5	11
Byron White	5	0	10
Jim Schwartz	1	5	7
Don Hendrick	2	1	5
Jim Wilcoxon	1	1	3
TOTALS	12	12	36

Coach: Frosty Cox

Officials: Pat Kennedy, Pete Sinnott
Attendance: 14,487

Tournament MVP: **Don Shields**, Temple

ANNUAL REVIEW

1938-39: And So It Begins

The NCAA Tournament started out as the ugly sister. The annual National Invitation Tournament in New York's Madison Square Garden, the sport's mecca, was the more prestigious event and it would remain so for more than a decade. LIU went undefeated (21–0) during the regular season and, of course, chose to play in—and won—the NIT. Still, let the record show that Oregon (29–5) downed Ohio State, 46-33, to win the first (eight-team) NCAA championship on March 27, 1939, at Patten Gymnasium in Evanston, Ill. The Ducks—with their Tall Firs front line of 6'8" center Urgel "Slim" Wintermute and 6'4" forwards Lauren "Laddie" Gale and John Dick—played a fierce, hand-waving zone defense. The game's total of 79 points is the second-lowest in NCAA Final history (73 were scored in the 1941 Final). Ohio State's Jimmy Hull was named Most Outstanding Player after scoring 58 points in three games. Oh, and it wasn't technically the NCAA Tournament. The event was sponsored by the National Association of Basketball Coaches; the NCAA took it over the following season.

Major Conference Standings

BIG SEVEN	Conference			Overall		
	W	L	PCT	W	L	PCT
Colorado	10	2	.833	14	4	.778
Utah State○	8	4	.667	18	6	.750
Utah	7	5	.583	13	7	.650
Wyoming	7	5	.583	10	11	.476
BYU	4	8	.333	12	12	.500
Denver	4	8	.333	5	13	.278
Colorado State	2	10	.167	2	14	.125

BIG SIX	Conference			Overall		
	W	L	PCT	W	L	PCT
Missouri	7	3	.700	12	6	.667
Oklahoma○	7	3	.700	12	9	.571
Kansas	6	4	.600	13	7	.650
Iowa State	5	5	.500	8	9	.471
Nebraska	3	7	.300	7	13	.350
Kansas State	2	8	.200	5	13	.278

BIG TEN	Conference			Overall		
	W	L	PCT	W	L	PCT
Ohio State○	10	2	.833	16	7	.696
Indiana	9	3	.750	17	3	.850
Illinois	8	4	.667	14	5	.737
Minnesota	7	5	.583	14	6	.700
Purdue	6	6	.500	12	7	.632
Northwestern	5	7	.417	7	13	.350
Michigan	4	8	.333	11	9	.550
Wisconsin	4	8	.333	10	10	.500
Chicago	4	8	.333	9	11	.450
Iowa	3	9	.250	8	11	.421

BORDER	Conference			Overall		
	W	L	PCT	W	L	PCT
New Mexico State□	14	2	.875	20	4	.833
Texas Tech	13	5	.722	13	6	.684
Northern Arizona	12	6	.667	13	11	.542
Arizona State	11	11	.500	13	13	.500
Arizona	8	10	.444	12	11	.522
Texas Western	6	12	.333	6	13	.316
New Mexico	4	16	.200	4	21	.160

EAST. INTERCOLL.	Conference			Overall		
	W	L	PCT	W	L	PCT
Carnegie Mellon	6	4	.600	12	7	.632
Georgetown	6	4	.600	13	9	.591
Penn State	5	5	.500	13	10	.565
Pittsburgh	5	5	.500	10	8	.556
West Virginia	4	6	.400	10	9	.526
Temple	4	6	.400	10	12	.455

IVY	Conference			Overall		
	W	L	PCT	W	L	PCT
Dartmouth	10	2	.833	18	5	.783
Columbia	9	3	.750	12	5	.706
Cornell	7	5	.583	12	12	.500
Princeton	6	6	.500	10	9	.526
Penn	6	6	.500	7	11	.389
Yale	3	9	.250	4	16	.200
Harvard	1	11	.083	5	14	.263

Note: Columbia also played in the Metro

METRO	Conference			Overall		
	W	L	PCT	W	L	PCT
Long Island□	21	0	1.000	24	0	1.000
St. John's□	17	2	.895	18	4	.818
Manhattan	12	5	.706	12	5	.706
Columbia	11	5	.688	12	5	.706
St. Francis (NY)	15	7	.682	15	7	.682
CCNY	11	6	.647	11	6	.647
Fordham	10	8	.556	10	8	.556
Brooklyn	9	8	.529	9	8	.529
NYU	11	11	.500	11	11	.500

MISSOURI VALLEY	Conference			Overall		
	W	L	PCT	W	L	PCT
Oklahoma A&M	11	3	.786	19	8	.704
Drake	11	3	.786	14	7	.667
Grinnell	8	6	.571	14	7	.667
Tulsa	8	6	.571	15	8	.652
Creighton	7	7	.500	11	12	.478
Wash.-St. Louis	6	8	.429	11	10	.524
Saint Louis	3	11	.214	5	16	.238
Washburn	2	12	.143	4	18	.182

NEW ENGLAND	Conference			Overall		
	W	L	PCT	W	L	PCT
Rhode Island	7	1	.875	17	4	.810
Connecticut	6	2	.750	12	6	.667
Maine	4	4	.500	8	4	.667
Northeastern	3	5	.375	6	12	.333
New Hampshire	0	8	.000	3	14	.176

NORTHERN CALIF.	Conference			Overall		
	W	L	PCT	W	L	PCT
Santa Clara	7	1	.875	15	5	.750
San Jose State	5	3	.625	11	7	.611
San Francisco	4	4	.500	7	10	.412
Saint Mary's (CA)	3	5	.375	20	11	.645
Pacific	1	7	.125	5	14	.263

PACIFIC COAST	Conference			Overall		
	W	L	PCT	W	L	PCT
North						
Oregon○	14	2	.875	29	5	.853
Washington	11	5	.688	20	5	.800
Washington State	8	8	.500	23	10	.697
Oregon State	6	10	.375	13	11	.542
Idaho	1	15	.063	12	19	.387
South						
California	9	3	.750	24	8	.750
Southern California	9	3	.750	20	5	.800
Stanford	6	6	.500	16	9	.640
UCLA	0	12	.000	7	20	.259

Playoff: California d. Southern California 42-36 to win the South; **Oregon d. California 2-0** in a best-of-three series for the PCC title

SEC	Conference			Overall		
	W	L	PCT	W	L	PCT
Alabama	13	4	.765	16	5	.762
Georgia	8	3	.727	11	6	.647
Kentucky	5	2	.714	16	4	.800
Auburn	8	4	.667	16	6	.727
LSU	10	5	.667	13	7	.650
Vanderbilt	7	5	.583	14	7	.667
Florida	5	4	.556	9	6	.600
Tennessee	6	5	.545	14	7	.667
Georgia Tech	4	7	.364	6	9	.400
Mississippi State	5	10	.333	8	12	.400
Tulane	3	6	.333	5	13	.278
Mississippi	4	10	.286	10	16	.385
Sewanee	0	13	.000	1	16	.059

Tournament: **Kentucky d. Tennessee 46-38**

SOUTHERN	Conference			Overall		
	W	L	PCT	W	L	PCT
Wake Forest○	15	3	.833	18	6	.750
Maryland	8	3	.727	15	9	.625
Washington and Lee	8	3	.727	13	9	.591
The Citadel	7	3	.700	14	5	.737
Davidson	9	7	.563	19	10	.655
NC State	7	6	.538	10	7	.588
North Carolina	8	7	.533	10	11	.476
Clemson	6	6	.500	16	8	.667
Richmond	5	5	.500	10	10	.500
Duke	8	8	.500	10	12	.455
VMI	6	6	.500	7	10	.412
William and Mary	4	9	.308	9	12	.429
South Carolina	2	8	.200	5	18	.217
Virginia Tech	2	10	.167	3	14	.176
Furman	0	10	.000	6	16	.273

Tournament: **Clemson d. Maryland 39-27**

SOUTHWEST	Conference			Overall		
	W	L	PCT	W	L	PCT
Texas○	10	2	.833	19	6	.760
Arkansas	9	3	.750	18	5	.783
SMU	8	4	.667	14	8	.636
Baylor	7	5	.583	15	6	.714
Rice	6	6	.500	10	11	.476
Texas A&M	2	10	.167	7	16	.304
TCU	0	12	.000	2	17	.105

INDEPENDENTS	Overall		
	W	L	PCT
Loyola-Chicago□	21	1	.955
Western Kentucky	22	3	.880
Roanoke□	21	3	.875
Army	13	2	.867
Bradley□	19	3	.864
Marshall	22	5	.815
Villanova○	20	5	.800
Brown○	16	4	.800
Siena	8	2	.800
Syracuse	15	4	.789
Duquesne	14	4	.778
Detroit	15	5	.750
Virginia	15	5	.750
Notre Dame	15	6	.714
Boston U.	10	4	.714
Cincinnati	12	5	.706
Marquette	12	5	.706
Butler	14	6	.700
La Salle	13	6	.684
Xavier	13	6	.684
DePaul	15	7	.682
Seton Hall	15	7	.682
Lehigh	10	5	.667
Bowling Green	12	7	.632
Toledo	17	10	.630
Montana State	18	11	.621
George Washington	13	8	.619
Muhlenberg	13	8	.619
Ohio	12	8	.600
St. Bonaventure	10	7	.588
Niagara	11	8	.579
Navy	8	6	.571
Rutgers	8	6	.571
Montana	17	13	.567
Michigan State	9	8	.529
Indiana State	10	9	.526
Kent State	12	11	.522
Bucknell	8	8	.500
Loyola (MD)	10	13	.435
Saint Joseph's	9	12	.429
Wichita State	9	12	.429
Western Michigan	7	10	.412
Lafayette	6	11	.353

⊛ Automatic NCAA Tournament bid ○ At-large NCAA Tournament bid □ NIT appearance ⊗ Team record doesn't reflect games forfeited or vacated. For adjusted record, see p. 521.

INDEPENDENTS (CONT.)

	Overall W	L	Pct
Valparaiso	5	10	.333
Colgate	6	13	.316
Miami (OH)	5	13	.278
Dayton	2	12	.143
Louisville	1	15	.063
Canisius	0	13	.000

PREMO-PORRETTA POWER POLL

	School	Record
1	Long Island (NIT champion)	24-0
2	Loyola-Chicago	21-1
3	Bradley	19-3
4	Oregon (NCAA champion)	29-5
5	Indiana	17-3
6	St. John's	18-4
7	Southern California	20-5
8	California	24-8
9	New Mexico State	20-4
10	Ohio State	16-7
11	Colorado	14-4
12	Army	13-2
13	Washington	20-5
14	Villanova	20-5
15	Kentucky	16-4
16	Illinois	14-5
17	Roanoke	21-3
18	Marquette	12-5
19	Panzer (NJ)	20-1
20	Duquesne	14-4
21	Southwestern (KS)	21-2
22	Waynesburg (PA)	18-4
23	Dartmouth	18-5
24	Notre Dame	15-6
25	Santa Clara	15-5

CONSENSUS ALL-AMERICAS

FIRST TEAM

PLAYER	CL	POS	HT	SCHOOL	PPG
Ernie Andres	SR	G	6-1	Indiana	13.5
Chet Jaworski	SR	G	5-11	Rhode Island	22.6
Jimmy Hull	SR	F	6-1	Ohio State	11.3
Irving Torgoff	SR	F	6-3	Long Island	9.5
Urgel "Slim" Wintermute	SR	C	6-8	Oregon	8.0

SECOND TEAM

PLAYER	CL	POS	HT	SCHOOL	PPG
Bobby Anet	SR	G	5-8	Oregon	5.6
Bernard Opper	SR	G	5-10	Kentucky	4.7
Bob Calihan	JR	C	6-3	Detroit	13.3
Bob Hassmiller	SR	C	6-1	Fordham	10.1
Michael Novak	SR	C	6-9	Loyola-Chicago	11.4

Selectors: Collier's (Basketball Coaches), Converse Yearbook, Helms Foundation, Madison Square Garden

1939 NCAA Tournament (A)

Regional Semifinals

EAST
- Villanova **42**, Brown **30**
- Ohio State **64**, Wake Forest **52**

WEST
- Oregon **56**, Texas **41**
- Oklahoma **50**, Utah State **39**

Regional Finals

- EAST: Ohio State **53**, Villanova **36**
- WEST: Oregon **55**, Oklahoma **37** (B)

National Final — Evanston, IL

Oregon 46, Ohio State 33

Oregon's Tall Firs whip Ohio State with a controlled fast break and taking no timeouts, holding Big Ten scoring leader Jimmy Hull to 12 points. Diving for a loose ball, Oregon's Bobby Anet breaks the championship trophy in two. That's how the Ducks cart it home ... For the pregame, Northwestern students play using original rules, with peach baskets and 12-man teams ... Dr. James Naismith attends.

Regional Third Place Utah State d. Texas 51-49

(A) The first NCAA Tournament, with an average attendance of 3,005, nets a $2,531 loss. In 1940, the NCAA takes over the event from the National Association of Basketball Coaches.

(B) Kansas coach Phog Allen, concerned about the prevalence of big men—particularly at Oregon, whose center Urgel "Slim" Wintermute is 6'8"—recommends the hoop be raised to 12 feet. (There is also talk of using convex curved backboards.)

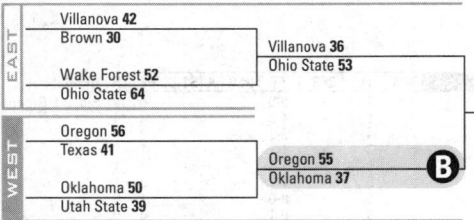

Tournament Leaders

INDIVIDUAL LEADERS

Scoring	CL	POS	G	PTS	PPG
1 **Jimmy Hull**, Ohio State	SR	F	3	58	19.3
2 **John Dick**, Oregon	JR	F	3	40	13.3
3 **Delbert Bingham**, Utah State	JR	F	2	25	12.5
4 **James McNatt**, Oklahoma	JR	F	2	24	12.0
5 **Floyd Morris**, Utah State	JR	F	2	23	11.5
6 **Richard Baker**, Ohio State	SR	F	3	29	9.7
7 **John Krutulis**, Villanova	SR	G	2	19	9.5
8 **Lauren "Laddie" Gale**, Oregon	SR	F	3	28	9.3
Urgel "Slim" Wintermute, Oregon	SR	C	3	28	9.3
10 **Paul Nugent**, Villanova	SO	G	2	18	9.0

Minimum: 2 games

Field Goals Per Game	CL	POS	G	FG	FGPG
1 **Jimmy Hull**, Ohio State	SR	F	3	22	7.3
2 **John Dick**, Oregon	JR	F	3	16	5.3
3 **Delbert Bingham**, Utah State	JR	F	2	10	5.0
James McNatt, Oklahoma	JR	F	2	10	5.0
5 **Floyd Morris**, Utah State	JR	F	2	9	4.5

Minimum: 2 games

Free Throws Per Game	CL	POS	G	FT	FTPG
1 **Jimmy Hull**, Ohio State	SR	F	3	14	4.7
2 **Lauren "Laddie" Gale**, Oregon	SR	F	3	12	4.0
Thurman Hull, Texas	SO	F	2	8	4.0
4 **Bobby Anet**, Oregon	SR	G	3	8	2.7
John Dick, Oregon	JR	F	3	8	2.7

Minimum: 2 games

TEAM LEADERS

Scoring	G	PTS	PPG
1 **Oregon**	3	157	52.3
2 **Ohio State**	3	150	50.0
3 **Utah State**	2	90	45.0
Texas	2	90	45.0
5 **Oklahoma**	2	87	43.5
6 **Villanova**	2	78	39.0

FT per game	G	FT	FTPG
1 **Texas**	2	30	15.0
2 **Wake Forest**	1	14	14.0
3 **Oregon**	3	39	13.0
4 **Oklahoma**	2	21	10.5
5 **Ohio State**	3	30	10.0
Utah State	2	20	10.0

Minimum: 2 games

FG per game	G	FG	FGPG
1 **Ohio State**	3	60	20.0
2 **Oregon**	3	59	19.7
3 **Wake Forest**	1	19	19.0
4 **Utah State**	2	35	17.5
5 **Villanova**	2	34	17.0

TOURNAMENT MOP

PLAYER	CL	POS	HT	SCHOOL	FG	FT	PPG
Jimmy Hull	SR	F	6-1	Ohio State	22	14	19.3

1939 NCAA TOURNAMENT BOX SCORES

42-30 (Elite 8) — 1H: Villanova 17, Brown 7; 2H: Villanova 25, Brown 23

VILLANOVA	MIN	FG	3FG	FT	REB	A	ST	BL	PF	TP
John Krutulis	-	6	-	2-3	-	-	-	-	0	14
James Montgomery	-	5	-	2-3	-	-	-	-	0	12
Michael Lazorchak	-	3	-	0-1	-	-	-	-	2	6
Louis Dubino	-	2	-	0-0	-	-	-	-	1	4
Paul Nugent	-	1	-	0-0	-	-	-	-	3	2
William Sinnott	-	1	-	0-0	-	-	-	-	1	2
Arthur Vigilante	-	1	-	0-0	-	-	-	-	0	2
Lloyd Rice	-	0	-	0-0	-	-	-	-	1	0
Ernest Robinson	-	0	-	0-1	-	-	-	-	0	0
Charles Yung	-	0	-	0-0	-	-	-	-	2	0
TOTALS	**-**	**19**	**-**	**4-8**	**-**	**-**	**-**	**-**	**10**	**42**
Percentages				50.0						

Coach: Alexander Severance

BROWN	MIN	FG	3FG	FT	REB	A	ST	BL	PF	TP
Robert Person	-	3	-	2-3	-	-	-	-	0	8
Harry Platt	-	3	-	1-2	-	-	-	-	3	7
John Padden	-	2	-	2-2	-	-	-	-	3	6
Francis Wilson	-	2	-	1-4	-	-	-	-	0	5
G.W. Fisher	-	1	-	0-0	-	-	-	-	0	2
W.B. Mullen	-	0	-	1-1	-	-	-	-	0	1
George Truman	-	0	-	1-1	-	-	-	-	1	1
Leonard Campbell	-	0	-	0-0	-	-	-	-	0	0
TOTALS	**-**	**11**	**-**	**8-13**	**-**	**-**	**-**	**-**	**7**	**30**
Percentages				61.5						

Coach: George E. Allen

Officials: Kearney, Schoenfeld

64-52 (Elite 8) — 1H: Ohio State 23, Wake Forest 29; 2H: Ohio State 41, Wake Forest 23

OHIO STATE	MIN	FG	3FG	FT	REB	A	ST	BL	PF	TP
Richard Baker	-	10	-	5-7	-	-	-	-	1	25
Jimmy Hull	-	7	-	4-5	-	-	-	-	2	18
Robert Lynch	-	2	-	3-3	-	-	-	-	1	7
Jack Dawson	-	2	-	0-1	-	-	-	-	4	4
Gilbert Mickelson	-	1	-	2-2	-	-	-	-	3	4
William Sattler	-	2	-	0-4	-	-	-	-	3	4
John Schick	-	1	-	0-1	-	-	-	-	3	2
Richard Boughner	-	0	-	0-0	-	-	-	-	2	0
Charles Maag	-	0	-	0-0	-	-	-	-	0	0
Jed Mees	-	0	-	0-0	-	-	-	-	0	0
Don Scott	-	0	-	0-0	-	-	-	-	0	0
TOTALS	**-**	**25**	**-**	**14-23**	**-**	**-**	**-**	**-**	**19**	**64**
Percentages				60.9						

Coach: Harold Olsen

WAKE FOREST	MIN	FG	3FG	FT	REB	A	ST	BL	PF	TP
Boyd Owen	-	7	-	5-9	-	-	-	-	0	19
Jim Waller	-	5	-	4-5	-	-	-	-	4	14
Stanley Apple	-	4	-	2-2	-	-	-	-	3	10
Vince Convery	-	3	-	1-1	-	-	-	-	1	7
Bill Sweel	-	0	-	1-3	-	-	-	-	4	1
Smith Young	-	0	-	1-1	-	-	-	-	3	1
Rex Carter	-	0	-	0-0	-	-	-	-	1	0
Dave Fuller	-	0	-	0-1	-	-	-	-	0	0
TOTALS	**-**	**19**	**-**	**14-22**	**-**	**-**	**-**	**-**	**16**	**52**
Percentages				63.6						

Coach: Murray Greason

Officials: Sinnott, Brennan

56-41 (Elite 8) — 1H: Oregon 19, Texas 16; 2H: Oregon 37, Texas 25

OREGON	MIN	FG	3FG	FT	REB	A	ST	BL	PF	TP
Urgel "Slim" Wintermute	-	7	-	0	-	-	-	-	0	14
John Dick	-	6	-	1	-	-	-	-	3	13
Lauren "Laddie" Gale	-	2	-	3	-	-	-	-	1	7
Wally Johansen	-	3	-	1	-	-	-	-	2	7
Bobby Anet	-	1	-	2	-	-	-	-	0	4
Ford Mullen	-	1	-	1	-	-	-	-	0	3
Matt Pavalunas	-	1	-	1	-	-	-	-	1	3
Robert Hardy	-	1	-	0	-	-	-	-	1	2
Earl Sandness	-	1	-	0	-	-	-	-	2	2
Ted Sarpola	-	0	-	1	-	-	-	-	1	1
TOTALS	**-**	**23**	**-**	**10**	**-**	**-**	**-**	**-**	**11**	**56**

Coach: Howard "Hobby" Hobson

TEXAS	MIN	FG	3FG	FT	REB	A	ST	BL	PF	TP
Willie Tate	-	3	-	1	-	-	-	-	3	7
Elmer Finley	-	2	-	2	-	-	-	-	0	6
Thurman Hull	-	1	-	4	-	-	-	-	4	6
Bobby Moers	-	3	-	0	-	-	-	-	4	6
Oran Spears	-	2	-	1	-	-	-	-	4	5
Warren Wiggins	-	1	-	2	-	-	-	-	0	4
Denton Cooley	-	1	-	1	-	-	-	-	0	3
Chester Granville	-	0	-	2	-	-	-	-	2	2
Tommie Nelms	-	1	-	0	-	-	-	-	0	2
TOTALS	**-**	**14**	**-**	**13**	**-**	**-**	**-**	**-**	**17**	**41**

Coach: Jack Gray

Officials: Leith, DeGroot

OKLAHOMA	MIN	FG	3FG	FT	REB	A	ST	BL	PF	TP
Garnett Corbin	-	5	-	2-3	-	-	-	-	2	12
James McNatt	-	5	-	2-3	-	-	-	-	3	12
Marvin Mesch	-	3	-	1-1	-	-	-	-	2	7
Marvin Snodgrass	-	3	-	0-0	-	-	-	-	1	6
Gene Roop	-	1	-	3-4	-	-	-	-	1	5
Herb Scheffler	-	1	-	3-4	-	-	-	-	3	5
Matthew Zoller	-	1	-	0-1	-	-	-	-	1	2
Ben Kerr	-	0	-	1-1	-	-	-	-	1	1
Vernon Mullen	-	0	-	0-0	-	-	-	-	1	0
Roscoe Walker	-	0	-	0-0	-	-	-	-	0	0
TOTALS	-	19	-	12-17	-	-	-	-	15	50
Percentages				70.6						
Coach: Bruce Drake										

50-39

25	1H	14
25	2H	25

ELITE 8

UTAH STATE	MIN	FG	3FG	FT	REB	A	ST	BL	PF	TP
Floyd Morris	-	6	-	3-5	-	-	-	-	3	15
Roland Reading	-	4	-	1-2	-	-	-	-	1	9
Delbert Bingham	-	1	-	4-5	-	-	-	-	3	6
Leonard James	-	1	-	1-1	-	-	-	-	0	3
Calvin Agricola	-	0	-	2-3	-	-	-	-	4	2
Ray Lindquist	-	1	-	0-0	-	-	-	-	0	2
Clyde Morris	-	1	-	0-1	-	-	-	-	1	2
Lloyd Jacobsen	-	0	-	0-0	-	-	-	-	0	0
TOTALS	-	14	-	11-17	-	-	-	-	12	39
Percentages				64.7						
Coach: Ernest Lowell "Dick" Romney										

Officials: Bailey, Hubbard

OHIO STATE	MIN	FG	3FG	FT	REB	A	ST	BL	PF	TP
Jimmy Hull	-	10-0	-	8-8	-	-	-	-	1	28
William Sattler	-	3	-	2-3	-	-	-	-	1	8
John Schick	-	3	-	1-1	-	-	-	-	3	7
Richard Baker	-	2	-	0-0	-	-	-	-	2	4
Jack Dawson	-	1	-	0-2	-	-	-	-	1	2
Gilbert Mickelson	-	1	-	0-0	-	-	-	-	0	2
Robert Stafford	-	1	-	0-0	-	-	-	-	0	2
Richard Boughner	-	0	-	0-0	-	-	-	-	0	0
Robert Lynch	-	0	-	0-1	-	-	-	-	3	0
Charles Maag	-	0	-	0-0	-	-	-	-	0	0
Jed Mees	-	0	-	0-0	-	-	-	-	0	0
Don Scott	-	0	-	0-0	-	-	-	-	0	0
TOTALS	-	21	-	11-15	-	-	-	-	11	53
Percentages				73.3						
Coach: Harold Olsen										

53-36

25	1H	10
28	2H	26

FINAL 4

VILLANOVA	MIN	FG	3FG	FT	REB	A	ST	BL	PF	TP
Paul Nugent	-	7	-	2-3	-	-	-	-	2	16
George Duzminski	-	2	-	2-3	-	-	-	-	3	6
John Krutulis	-	2	-	1-1	-	-	-	-	2	5
Michael Lazorchak	-	2	-	0-0	-	-	-	-	1	4
James Montgomery	-	1	-	1-3	-	-	-	-	4	3
Louis Dubino	-	1	-	0-3	-	-	-	-	3	2
Lloyd Rice	-	0	-	0-0	-	-	-	-	0	0
Ernest Robinson	-	0	-	0-0	-	-	-	-	0	0
William Sinnott	-	0	-	0-0	-	-	-	-	0	0
Charles Yung	-	0	-	0-0	-	-	-	-	0	0
TOTALS	-	15	-	6-13	-	-	-	-	15	36
Percentages				46.2						
Coach: Alexander Severance										

Officials: Kennedy, Walsh

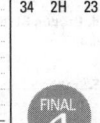

OREGON	MIN	FG	3FG	FT	REB	A	ST	BL	PF	TP
John Dick	-	6	-	2-2	-	-	-	-	1	14
Laddie Gale	-	3	-	5-7	-	-	-	-	4	11
Slim Wintermute	-	4	-	2-2	-	-	-	-	1	10
Wally Johansen	-	4	-	0-1	-	-	-	-	3	8
Bobby Anet	-	1	-	4-5	-	-	-	-	2	6
Robert Hardy	-	0	-	3-3	-	-	-	-	1	3
Matt Pavalunas	-	1	-	0-0	-	-	-	-	1	2
Ford Mullen	-	0	-	1-2	-	-	-	-	0	1
Ted Sarpola	-	0	-	0-0	-	-	-	-	0	0
TOTALS	-	19	-	17-22	-	-	-	-	13	55
Percentages				77.3						
Coach: Howard "Hobby" Hobson										

55-37

21	1H	14
34	2H	23

FINAL 4

OKLAHOMA	MIN	FG	3FG	FT	REB	A	ST	BL	PF	TP
James McNatt	-	5	-	2-3	-	-	-	-	1	12
Ben Kerr	-	3	-	3-3	-	-	-	-	0	9
Garnett Corbin	-	2	-	0-0	-	-	-	-	3	4
Herb Scheffler	-	1	-	2-2	-	-	-	-	4	4
Gene Roop	-	1	-	1-2	-	-	-	-	2	3
Marvin Mesch	-	1	-	0-1	-	-	-	-	4	2
Roscoe Walker	-	1	-	0-1	-	-	-	-	0	2
Marvin Snodgrass	-	0	-	1-1	-	-	-	-	1	1
Vernon Mullen	-	0	-	0-0	-	-	-	-	1	0
Matthew Zoller	-	0	-	0-0	-	-	-	-	2	0
TOTALS	-	14	-	9-13	-	-	-	-	18	37
Percentages				69.2						
Coach: Bruce Drake										

Officials: Leith, Bailey

OREGON	MIN	FG	3FG	FT	REB	A	ST	BL	PF	TP
John Dick	-	4	-	5-5	-	-	-	-	3	13
Bobby Anet	-	4	-	2-3	-	-	-	-	3	10
Lauren "Laddie" Gale	-	3	-	4-5	-	-	-	-	0	10
Wally Johansen	-	4	-	1-2	-	-	-	-	1	9
Urgel "Slim" Wintermute	-	2	-	0-1	-	-	-	-	1	4
Ford Mullen	-	0	-	0-0	-	-	-	-	0	0
Matt Pavalunas	-	0	-	0-0	-	-	-	-	0	0
TOTALS	-	17	-	12-16	-	-	-	-	8	46
Percentages				75.0						
Coach: Howard "Hobby" Hobson										

46-33

21	1H	16
25	2H	17

NCAA FINAL 1939

OHIO STATE	MIN	FG	3FG	FT	REB	A	ST	BL	PF	TP
Jimmy Hull	-	5	-	2-4	-	-	-	-	2	12
Robert Lynch	-	3	-	1-3	-	-	-	-	3	7
William Sattler	-	3	-	1-2	-	-	-	-	0	7
Richard Boughner	-	1	-	0-0	-	-	-	-	0	2
Jack Dawson	-	1	-	0-0	-	-	-	-	4	2
John Schick	-	1	-	0-0	-	-	-	-	1	2
Don Scott	-	0	-	1-1	-	-	-	-	1	1
Richard Baker	-	0	-	0-0	-	-	-	-	0	0
Charles Maag	-	0	-	0-0	-	-	-	-	0	0
Gilbert Mickelson	-	0	-	0-0	-	-	-	-	2	0
Robert Stafford	-	0	-	0-0	-	-	-	-	0	0
TOTALS	-	14	-	5-10	-	-	-	-	13	33
Percentages				50.0						
Coach: Harold Olsen										

Officials: Getchell, Clarno
Attendance: 5,500

National Invitation Tournament (NIT)

Quarterfinals: Long Island d. New Mexico St. 52-45, St. John's d. Roanoke 71-47
Semifinals: Long Island d. Bradley 36-32, Loyola-Chicago d. St. John's 51-46 (OT)
Third place: Bradley d. St. John's 40-35
Championship: Long Island d. Loyola-Chicago 44-32
MVP: Bill Lloyd, St. John's

1939-40: Hurryin' Hoosiers

Dr. James Naismith died on Nov. 28, 1939, at age 78. On Feb. 28, 1940, the first basketball game to be televised aired from Madison Square Garden on W2XBS, with Pittsburgh beating Fordham, 57-37. But it was 20–3 Indiana that put an indelible mark on the season. Branch McCracken broke with the prevailing tradition of ball control and let his players run. The Hurryin' Hoosiers sprinted all the way to the national title game, where they jumped out to a 32-19 halftime lead over Kansas (where Naismith had reigned as coach) and never looked back, closing out the Jayhawks, 60-42. MOP Marv Huffman scored 12 points—he averaged just 4.3 ppg during the regular season. The game took place before a standing-room-only crowd of 10,000 at Kansas City's Municipal Auditorium. It was the first of nine title games played there, still the most for any venue. (Madison Square Garden in New York City is second with seven.)

Major Conference Standings

BIG SEVEN	Conference W	L	Pct	Overall W	L	Pct
Colorado○□	11	1	.917	17	4	.810
Utah	8	4	.667	19	4	.826
BYU	7	5	.583	17	8	.680
Utah State	7	5	.583	11	7	.611
Wyoming	3	9	.250	6	10	.375
Colorado State	3	9	.250	6	12	.333
Denver	3	9	.250	6	15	.286

BIG SIX	Conference W	L	Pct	Overall W	L	Pct
Kansas○	8	2	.800	19	6	.760
Oklahoma	8	2	.800	12	7	.632
Missouri	8	2	.800	13	6	.684
Iowa State	2	8	.200	9	9	.500
Kansas State	2	8	.200	6	12	.333
Nebraska	2	8	.200	6	12	.333

BIG TEN	Conference W	L	Pct	Overall W	L	Pct
Purdue	10	2	.833	16	4	.800
Indiana○	9	3	.750	20	3	.870
Ohio State	8	4	.667	13	7	.650
Illinois	7	5	.583	14	6	.700
Northwestern	7	5	.583	13	7	.650
Michigan	6	6	.500	13	7	.650
Minnesota	5	7	.417	12	8	.600
Iowa	4	8	.333	9	12	.429
Wisconsin	3	9	.250	5	15	.250
Chicago	1	11	.083	5	14	.263

BORDER	Conference W	L	Pct	Overall W	L	Pct
New Mexico State	12	4	.750	16	7	.696
Arizona	12	4	.750	15	10	.600
Texas Western	10	6	.625	15	11	.577
Northern Arizona	7	9	.438	8	12	.400
Arizona State	7	11	.389	8	13	.381
New Mexico	1	15	.063	3	22	.120

IVY	Conference W	L	Pct	Overall W	L	Pct
Dartmouth	11	1	.917	15	6	.714
Princeton	8	4	.667	14	8	.636
Yale	7	5	.583	13	6	.684
Cornell	7	5	.583	10	13	.435
Columbia	4	8	.333	6	12	.333
Harvard	3	9	.250	5	14	.263
Penn	2	10	.167	5	13	.278

MISSOURI VALLEY	Conference W	L	Pct	Overall W	L	Pct
Oklahoma A&M□	12	0	1.000	26	3	.897
Creighton	8	4	.667	11	9	.550
Drake	7	5	.583	13	12	.520
Washburn	6	6	.500	8	8	.500
Tulsa	5	7	.417	12	15	.444
Wash.-St. Louis	2	10	.167	7	13	.350
Saint Louis	2	10	.167	4	14	.222

NEW ENGLAND	Conference W	L	Pct	Overall W	L	Pct
Rhode Island	8	0	1.000	19	3	.864
Connecticut	6	2	.750	9	7	.563
New Hampshire	3	5	.375	5	10	.333
Northeastern	3	5	.375	4	13	.235
Maine	0	8	.000	3	9	.250

PACIFIC COAST	Conference W	L	Pct	Overall W	L	Pct
North						
Oregon State	12	4	.750	27	11	.711
Oregon	10	6	.625	19	12	.613
Washington State	9	7	.563	23	10	.697
Washington	6	10	.375	10	15	.400
Idaho	3	13	.188	11	15	.423
South						
Southern California○	10	2	.833	20	3	.870
Stanford	6	6	.500	14	9	.609
California	5	7	.417	15	17	.469
UCLA	3	9	.250	8	17	.320

Playoff: **Southern California d. Oregon State 2-0** in a best-of-three series for the title.

SEC	Conference W	L	Pct	Overall W	L	Pct
Alabama	14	4	.778	18	5	.783
Tennessee	7	3	.700	14	7	.667
Georgia	9	4	.692	20	6	.769
LSU	8	4	.667	10	8	.556
Florida	5	4	.556	13	9	.591
Kentucky	4	4	.500	15	6	.714
Georgia Tech	6	6	.500	7	8	.467
Auburn	6	7	.462	7	10	.412
Mississippi State	4	5	.444	9	6	.600
Vanderbilt	5	7	.417	10	12	.455
Mississippi	3	8	.273	9	10	.474
Tulane	2	8	.200	2	13	.133
Sewanee	0	9	.000	2	13	.133

Tournament: **Kentucky d. Georgia 51-43**

SOUTHERN	Conference W	L	Pct	Overall W	L	Pct
Duke	13	2	.867	19	7	.731
North Carolina	11	2	.846	23	3	.885
Washington and Lee	7	3	.700	13	5	.722
Wake Forest	10	5	.667	13	9	.591
Maryland	7	5	.583	14	9	.609
Clemson	9	7	.563	9	12	.429
Richmond	6	5	.545	11	6	.647
William and Mary	6	5	.545	13	10	.565
The Citadel	6	5	.545	8	9	.471
Furman	4	6	.400	11	11	.500
NC State	5	10	.333	8	11	.421
Davidson	4	11	.267	8	13	.381
South Carolina	3	10	.231	5	13	.278
VMI	2	9	.182	3	12	.200
Virginia Tech	1	9	.100	4	15	.211

Tournament: **North Carolina d. Duke 43-23**

SOUTHWEST	Conference W	L	Pct	Overall W	L	Pct
Rice○	10	2	.833	25	4	.862
Texas	8	4	.667	18	5	.783
Baylor	7	5	.583	12	9	.571
Arkansas	6	6	.500	12	10	.545
Texas A&M	5	7	.417	11	11	.500
SMU	5	7	.417	7	13	.350
TCU	1	11	.083	7	16	.304

INDEPENDENTS	Overall W	L	Pct
Seton Hall	19	0	1.000
NYU	18	1	.947
Marshall	26	3	.897
Villanova	17	2	.895
Duquesne○□	20	3	.870
Santa Clara	17	3	.850
Springfield○	16	3	.842
Indiana State	15	3	.833
Long Island□	19	4	.826
Toledo	24	6	.800
Western Kentucky○	24	6	.800
DePaul□	22	6	.786
Bowling Green	16	5	.762
Virginia	16	5	.762
Ohio	19	6	.760
St. John's□	15	5	.750
Butler	17	6	.739
Army	11	4	.733
St. Francis (NY)	13	5	.722
Notre Dame	15	6	.714
Bradley	14	6	.700
Michigan State	14	6	.700
Brown	13	6	.684
George Washington	13	6	.684
West Virginia	13	6	.684
Montana	17	8	.680
Colgate	12	6	.667
Miami (OH)	12	6	.667
Saint Joseph's	10	5	.667
Penn State	15	8	.652
Bucknell	13	7	.650
St. Bonaventure	11	6	.647
Loyola (MD)	14	8	.636
Niagara	12	7	.632
Siena	12	7	.632
Detroit	14	9	.609
Manhattan	14	9	.609
La Salle	12	8	.600
Fordham	11	8	.579
Lafayette	11	8	.579
Kent State	13	10	.565
Temple	13	10	.565
Syracuse	10	8	.556
Wichita State	10	8	.556
Muhlenberg	11	9	.550
San Francisco	9	8	.529
Western Michigan	10	9	.526
Brooklyn	9	9	.500
CCNY	8	8	.500
Canisius	8	9	.471
Cincinnati	8	9	.471
Pittsburgh	8	9	.471
Boston U.	6	7	.462
Georgetown	8	10	.444
Marquette	7	9	.438
Holy Cross	2	3	.400
Montana State	10	16	.385
Saint Mary's (CA)	7	12	.368
Lehigh	5	10	.333
Valparaiso	6	14	.300
Loyola-Chicago	5	14	.263
Rutgers	5	14	.263
Xavier	6	17	.261
Navy	3	11	.214
Dayton	4	17	.190
Louisville	1	18	.053

⊕ Automatic NCAA Tournament bid ○ At-large NCAA Tournament bid □ NIT appearance ✪ Team record doesn't reflect games forfeited or vacated. For adjusted record, see p. 521.

PREMO-PORRETTA POWER POLL

	SCHOOL	RECORD
1	**Indiana (NCAA champion)**	20-3
2	**Southern California**	20-3
3	**Colorado (NIT champion)**	17-4
4	**Purdue**	16-4
5	**Duquesne**	20-3
6	**Rice**	25-4
7	**Oklahoma A&M**	26-3
8	**NYU**	18-1
9	**Kansas**	19-6
10	**DePaul**	22-6
11	**Seton Hall**	19-0
12	**Long Island**	20-4#
13	**Utah**	19-4
14	**St. John's**	15-5
15	**Santa Clara**	17-3
16	**Villanova**	17-2
17	**Texas**	18-5
18	**Marshall**	26-3
19	**Notre Dame**	15-6
20	**Panzer (NJ)**	22-0
21	**Illinois**	14-6
22	**Oklahoma**	12-7
23	**Rhode Island**	19-3
24	**Springfield (MA)**	16-3
25	**Missouri**	13-6

CONSENSUS ALL-AMERICAS

FIRST TEAM

PLAYER	CL	POS	HT	SCHOOL	PPG
Gus Broberg	JR	G/F	6-1	Dartmouth	14.9
John Dick	SR	F	6-4	Oregon	11.5
George Glamack	JR	F/C	6-6	North Carolina	17.6
Bill Hapac	SR	F	6-2	Illinois	12.2
Ralph Vaughn	SR	F	6-0	Southern California	11.5

SECOND TEAM

PLAYER	CL	POS	HT	SCHOOL	PPG
Jack Harvey	SR	F/C	6-3	Colorado	10.1*
Marv Huffman	SR	G	6-2	Indiana	4.3
James McNatt	SR	F	6-0	Oklahoma	12.6
Jesse Renick	SR	G	6-2	Oklahoma A&M	7.7

SELECTORS: CONVERSE YEARBOOK, HELMS FOUNDATION, MADISON SQUARE GARDEN

*Conference games only

1940 NCAA TOURNAMENT

Regional Semifinals — East
- Indiana **48**, Springfield (MA) **24** (A)
- Duquesne **30**, Western Kentucky **29**

Regional Semifinals — West
- USC **38**, Colorado **32**
- Rice **44**, Kansas **50**

Regional Finals
- Indiana **39**, Duquesne **30**
- USC **42**, Kansas **43** (B)

National Final — Kansas City

Indiana 60
Kansas 42

Flashing the up-tempo game for which they were called the Hurryin' Hoosiers, Indiana easily dispatches KU in Kansas City. Thirty fouls are called and three players foul out. Jay McCreary, described by the AP as a "gum-chewing, blond midget in a forest of physical giants," comes off the bench to score 12 points. The 5'10" McCreary will later coach at LSU.

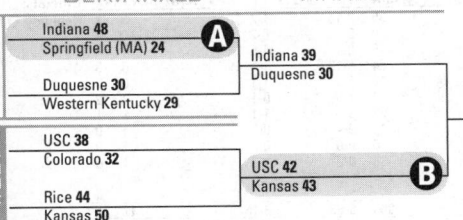

Regional Third Place Rice d. Colorado 60-56 (OT)

A IU Coach Branch McCracken attends a pregame late-night meeting with a faculty athletics committee that fears participation will pre-empt players' classroom time. McCracken prevails.

B Phog Allen's son, Bob, steals the ball and dishes to Howard Engleman, whose corner shot with :16 left caps a Jayhawks comeback.

Record differs from the school's and/or the NCAA's because it includes noncollegiate competition or because the outcome of some games is in dispute.

Tournament Leaders

Individual Leaders

Scoring	CL	POS	G	PTS	PPG
1 **Howard Engleman**, Kansas	JR	F	3	39	13.0
Bob Kinney, Rice	SO	C	2	26	13.0
3 **Frank Carswell**, Rice	JR	G	2	25	12.5
4 **Dale Sears**, Southern California	SR	C	2	23	11.5
5 **Herman Schaefer**, Indiana	JR	F	3	31	10.3
6 **Levi Craddock**, Rice	SR	F	2	20	10.0
Don Thurman, Colorado	SR	G	2	20	10.0
8 **Don Hendricks**, Colorado	SR	F	2	19	9.5
9 **Dick Harp**, Kansas	SR	G	3	27	9.0
10 **Bob Doll**, Colorado	SO	C	2	17	8.5

Minimum: 2 games

Free Throw Pct	CL	POS	G	FT	FTA	PCT
1 **Marv Huffman**, Indiana	SR	G	3	6	8	75.0
Don Thurman, Colorado	SR	G	2	6	8	75.0
3 **Bob Allen**, Kansas	JR	C	3	5	7	71.4
Jack Harvey, Colorado	SR	F/C	2	5	7	71.4
5 **Herman Schaefer**, Indiana	JR	F	3	7	10	70.0

Minimum: 5 made

Field Goals Per Game	CL	POS	G	FG	FGPG
1 **Howard Engleman**, Kansas	JR	F	3	18	6.0
Bob Kinney, Rice	SO	C	2	12	6.0
3 **Frank Carswell**, Rice	JR	G	2	11	5.5
4 **Levi Craddock**, Rice	SR	F	2	10	5.0
Dale Sears, Southern California	SR	C	2	10	5.0

Minimum: 2 games

Team Leaders

Scoring	G	PTS	PPG
1 **Rice**	2	104	52.0
2 **Indiana**	3	147	49.0
3 **Kansas**	3	135	45.0
4 **Colorado**	2	88	44.0
5 **Southern California**	2	80	40.0
6 **Duquesne**	2	60	30.0

Minimum: 2 games

FT Pct	G	FT	FTA	PCT
1 **Colorado**	2	20	29	69.0
2 **Indiana**	3	31	51	60.8
3 **Kansas**	3	31	54	57.4
4 **Southern California**	2	14	27	51.8
5 **Duquesne**	2	12	28	42.9

Minimum: 2 games

FG Per Game	G	FG	FGPG
1 **Rice**	2	48	24.0
2 **Indiana**	3	58	19.3
3 **Kansas**	3	52	17.3
4 **Colorado**	2	34	17.0
5 **Southern California**	2	33	16.5

All-Tournament Team

Player	CL	POS	HT	School	PPG
Marv Huffman*	SR	G	6-2	Indiana	8.0
Bob Allen	JR	C	6-0	Kansas	7.0
Howard Engleman	JR	F	6-2	Kansas	13.0
Jay McCreary	JR	G	5-10	Indiana	5.3
Bill Menke	JR	C	6-3	Indiana	6.3

* Most outstanding player

1940 NCAA Tournament Box Scores

INDIANA	MIN	FG	3FG	FT	REB	A	ST	BL	PF	TP
Herman Schaefer	24	6-15	-	2-5	-	-	-	-	0	14
Marv Huffman	26	2-5	-	2-3	-	-	-	-	1	6
Paul Armstrong	16	2-10	-	2-5	-	-	-	-	1	6
Bob Dro	18	2-7	-	1-1	-	-	-	-	2	5
Jay McCreary	17	2-5	-	0-1	-	-	-	-	0	4
Bill Menke	17	2-3	-	0-0	-	-	-	-	2	4
Ralph Dorsey	15	1-6	-	2-3	-	-	-	-	2	4
James Gridley	16	1-4	-	0-0	-	-	-	-	1	2
Chester Francis	14	1-5	-	0-0	-	-	-	-	2	2
Bob Menke	17	0-1	-	1-2	-	-	-	-	0	1
William Frey	12	0-3	-	0-0	-	-	-	-	0	0
Andrew Zimmer	8	0-5	-	0-1	-	-	-	-	1	0
TOTALS	**200**	**19-69**	**-**	**10-21**	**-**	**-**	**-**	**-**	**12**	**48**
Percentages		27.5		47.6						

Coach: Branch McCracken

48-24

30 1H 11
18 2H 13

ELITE 8

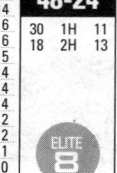

SPRINGFIELD (MA)	MIN	FG	3FG	FT	REB	A	ST	BL	PF	TP
Richard Redding	35	3-15	-	1-2	-	-	-	-	3	7
Ray Schmidt	40	2-12	-	0-2	-	-	-	-	0	4
Bruce Munro	15	0-1	-	4-5	-	-	-	-	4	4
Percy MacVean	24	1-13	-	1-1	-	-	-	-	0	3
Robert Mortenson	16	1-8	-	1-1	-	-	-	-	0	3
Alfred Werner	24	1-5	-	0-1	-	-	-	-	4	2
Bud Gray	21	0-3	-	1-1	-	-	-	-	3	1
Charles Kistner	13	0-4	-	0-3	-	-	-	-	1	0
Leo Nover	6	0-0	-	0-0	-	-	-	-	1	0
John Panatier	6	0-2	-	0-0	-	-	-	-	1	0
TOTALS	**200**	**8-63**	**-**	**8-16**	**-**	**-**	**-**	**-**	**17**	**24**
Percentages		12.7		50.0						

Coach: Edward J. Hickox

Officials: Kennedy, Clamo

DUQUESNE	MIN	FG	3FG	FT	REB	A	ST	BL	PF	TP
Bill Lacey	-	4	-	0-4	-	-	-	-	2	8
Rudy Debnar	-	3	-	1-2	-	-	-	-	3	7
Ed Milkovich	-	2	-	2-3	-	-	-	-	2	6
Paul Widowitz	-	2	-	1-1	-	-	-	-	3	5
Moe Becker	-	1	-	0-1	-	-	-	-	3	2
Lou Kasperik	-	1	-	0-0	-	-	-	-	0	2
TOTALS	**-**	**13**	**-**	**4-11**	**-**	**-**	**-**	**-**	**13**	**30**
Percentages				36.4						

Coach: Charles "Chick" Davies

30-29

14 1H 12
16 2H 17

ELITE 8

WESTERN KENTUCKY	MIN	FG	3FG	FT	REB	A	ST	BL	PF	TP
Carlisle Towery	-	6	-	1-5	-	-	-	-	4	13
Jed Walters	-	4	-	4-5	-	-	-	-	0	12
Herb Ball	-	1	-	2-3	-	-	-	-	4	4
Alec Downing	-	0	-	0-0	-	-	-	-	0	0
Howard Downing	-	0	-	0-1	-	-	-	-	1	0
Kendrick Fulks	-	0	-	0-0	-	-	-	-	2	0
Earl Shelton	-	0	-	0-0	-	-	-	-	0	0
Roger Woodward	-	0	-	0-0	-	-	-	-	0	0
TOTALS	**-**	**11**	**-**	**7-14**	**-**	**-**	**-**	**-**	**11**	**29**
Percentages				50.0						

Coach: E.A. Diddle

Officials: Feezle, Burt

USC	MIN	FG	3FG	FT	REB	A	ST	BL	PF	TP
Jack Morrison	-	3	-	4-4	-	-	-	-	2	10
Ralph Vaughn	-	5	-	0-1	-	-	-	-	0	10
Jack Lippert	-	2	-	2-3	-	-	-	-	1	6
Joesph Reising	-	2	-	1-2	-	-	-	-	2	5
Dale Sears	-	2	-	0-1	-	-	-	-	4	4
John Luber	-	1	-	0-0	-	-	-	-	2	2
Keith Lambert	-	0	-	1-2	-	-	-	-	2	1
Tom McGarvin	-	0	-	0-1	-	-	-	-	3	0
TOTALS	**-**	**15**	**-**	**8-14**	**-**	**-**	**-**	**-**	**16**	**38**
Percentages				57.1						

Coach: Sam Barry

38-32

20 1H 20
18 2H 12

ELITE 8

COLORADO	MIN	FG	3FG	FT	REB	A	ST	BL	PF	TP
Bob Doll	-	2	-	3-5	-	-	-	-	2	7
Don Hendricks	-	3	-	1-2	-	-	-	-	1	7
Don Thurman	-	2	-	2-3	-	-	-	-	0	6
Jack Harvey	-	1	-	3-4	-	-	-	-	4	5
George Hamburg	-	2	-	0-0	-	-	-	-	4	4
Leason McCloud	-	1	-	1-1	-	-	-	-	0	3
Gene Grove	-	0	-	0-1	-	-	-	-	0	0
TOTALS	**-**	**11**	**-**	**10-16**	**-**	**-**	**-**	**-**	**11**	**32**
Percentages				62.5						

Coach: Forrest B. "Frosty" Cox

Officials: O'Sullivan, Curtis

50-44 (ELITE 8)

	1H	2H
Kansas	24	26
Rice	14	30

KANSAS	MIN	FG	3FG	FT	REB	A	ST	BL	PF	TP
Howard Engleman	-	10	-	1-1	-	-	-	-	1	21
Donald Ebling	-	4	-	2-3	-	-	-	-	0	10
Ralph Miller	-	3	-	4-8	-	-	-	-	2	10
Dick Harp	-	3	-	1-1	-	-	-	-	1	7
John Kline	-	1	-	0-1	-	-	-	-	4	2
Bob Allen	-	0	-	0-1	-	-	-	-	0	0
Bill Hogben	-	0	-	0-0	-	-	-	-	0	0
Thomas Hunter	-	0	-	0-0	-	-	-	-	1	0
Wallace Johnson	-	0	-	0-0	-	-	-	-	0	0
Bruce Voran	-	0	-	0-0	-	-	-	-	0	0
TOTALS	**-**	**21**	**-**	**8-15**	**-**	**-**	**-**	**-**	**9**	**50**
Percentages				53.3						

Coach: Forrest "Phog" Allen

RICE	MIN	FG	3FG	FT	REB	A	ST	BL	PF	TP
Bob Kinney	-	8	-	2-6	-	-	-	-	3	18
Frank Carswell	-	4	-	1-1	-	-	-	-	1	9
Chester Palmer	-	3	-	0-0	-	-	-	-	3	6
Placido Gomez	-	2	-	1-2	-	-	-	-	1	5
Fred Pepper	-	2	-	0-0	-	-	-	-	0	4
Levi Craddock	-	1	-	0-0	-	-	-	-	2	2
Bert Selman	-	0	-	0-0	-	-	-	-	3	0
Whitlock Zander	-	0	-	0-0	-	-	-	-	0	0
TOTALS	**-**	**20**	**-**	**4-9**	**-**	**-**	**-**	**-**	**13**	**44**
Percentages				44.4						

Coach: Buster Brannon

Officials: DeGroot, Vidal

39-30 (FINAL 4)

	1H	2H
Indiana	25	14
Duquesne	13	17

INDIANA	MIN	FG	3FG	FT	REB	A	ST	BL	PF	TP
Bill Menke	33	4-11	-	2-3	-	-	-	-	4	10
Herman Schaefer	34	2-8	-	4-4	-	-	-	-	3	8
Paul Armstrong	20	2-11	-	3-4	-	-	-	-	0	7
Marv Huffman	26	2-8	-	2-2	-	-	-	-	3	6
Bob Dro	40	2-9	-	1-3	-	-	-	-	2	5
Andrew Zimmer	12	1-3	-	1-1	-	-	-	-	0	3
Jay McCreary	34	0-6	-	0-2	-	-	-	-	3	0
Ralph Dorsey	1	0-0	-	0-0	-	-	-	-	0	0
TOTALS	**200**	**13-56**	**-**	**13-19**	**-**	**-**	**-**	**-**	**15**	**39**
Percentages		23.2		68.4						

Coach: Branch McCracken

DUQUESNE	MIN	FG	3FG	FT	REB	A	ST	BL	PF	TP
Ed Milkovich	39	4-11	-	2-4	-	-	-	-	4	10
Paul Widowitz	40	3-13	-	1-1	-	-	-	-	3	7
Moe Becker	38	2-14	-	2-4	-	-	-	-	4	6
Lou Kasperik	23	1-2	-	1-4	-	-	-	-	1	3
Rudy Debnar	40	0-1	-	2-2	-	-	-	-	2	2
Bill Lacey	19	1-6	-	0-2	-	-	-	-	3	2
George Reiber	1	0-0	-	0-0	-	-	-	-	0	0
TOTALS	**200**	**11-47**	**-**	**8-17**	**-**	**-**	**-**	**-**	**17**	**30**
Percentages		23.4		47.1						

Coach: Charles "Chick" Davies

Officials: Kennedy, Adams

43-42 (FINAL 4)

	1H	2H
Kansas	20	23
USC	21	21

KANSAS	MIN	FG	3FG	FT	REB	A	ST	BL	PF	TP
Dick Harp	-	6	-	3-4	-	-	-	-	3	15
Bob Allen	-	3	-	2-2	-	-	-	-	2	8
Donald Ebling	-	2	-	4-8	-	-	-	-	1	8
Howard Engleman	-	3	-	0-0	-	-	-	-	1	6
Ralph Miller	-	2	-	2-4	-	-	-	-	2	6
John Kline	-	0	-	0-0	-	-	-	-	0	0
Bruce Voran	-	0	-	0-1	-	-	-	-	0	0
TOTALS	**-**	**16**	**-**	**11-19**	**-**	**-**	**-**	**-**	**9**	**43**
Percentages				57.9						

Coach: Forrest "Phog" Allen

USC	MIN	FG	3FG	FT	REB	A	ST	BL	PF	TP
Dale Sears	-	8	-	3-4	-	-	-	-	2	19
Jack Lippert	-	4	-	0-1	-	-	-	-	3	8
Tom McGarvin	-	3	-	0-0	-	-	-	-	4	6
Ralph Vaughn	-	2	-	2-5	-	-	-	-	2	6
John Luber	-	1	-	0-1	-	-	-	-	2	2
Keith Lambert	-	0	-	1-2	-	-	-	-	2	1
Jack Morrison	-	0	-	0-0	-	-	-	-	3	0
TOTALS	**-**	**18**	**-**	**6-13**	**-**	**-**	**-**	**-**	**18**	**42**
Percentages				46.2						

Coach: Sam Barry

Officials: Curtis, Vidal

60-42 (NCAA FINAL 1940)

	1H	2H
Indiana	32	28
Kansas	19	23

INDIANA	MIN	FG	3FG	FT	REB	A	ST	BL	PF	TP
Marv Huffman	-	5	-	2-3	-	-	-	-	4	12
Jay McCreary	-	6	-	0-0	-	-	-	-	2	12
Paul Armstrong	-	4	-	2-3	-	-	-	-	3	10
Herman Schaefer	-	4	-	1-1	-	-	-	-	1	9
Bob Dro	-	3	-	1-1	-	-	-	-	4	7
Bill Menke	-	2	-	1-2	-	-	-	-	3	5
Andrew Zimmer	-	2	-	1-1	-	-	-	-	1	5
Ralph Dorsey	-	0	-	0-0	-	-	-	-	0	0
Chester Francis	-	0	-	0-0	-	-	-	-	1	0
James Gridley	-	0	-	0-0	-	-	-	-	0	0
Bob Menke	-	0	-	0-0	-	-	-	-	0	0
TOTALS	**-**	**26**	**-**	**8-11**	**-**	**-**	**-**	**-**	**19**	**60**
Percentages				72.7						

Coach: Branch McCracken

KANSAS	MIN	FG	3FG	FT	REB	A	ST	BL	PF	TP
Bob Allen	-	5	-	3-4	-	-	-	-	3	13
Howard Engleman	-	5	-	2-3	-	-	-	-	3	12
Dick Harp	-	2	-	1-3	-	-	-	-	1	5
Donald Ebling	-	1	-	2-5	-	-	-	-	0	4
Bill Hogben	-	2	-	0-0	-	-	-	-	0	4
Ralph Miller	-	0	-	2-2	-	-	-	-	4	2
Thomas Hunter	-	0	-	1-1	-	-	-	-	0	1
Bruce Voran	-	0	-	1-2	-	-	-	-	0	1
Wallace Johnson	-	0	-	0-0	-	-	-	-	0	0
John Kline	-	0	-	0-0	-	-	-	-	0	0
Jack Sands	-	0	-	0-0	-	-	-	-	0	0
TOTALS	**-**	**15**	**-**	**12-20**	**-**	**-**	**-**	**-**	**11**	**42**
Percentages				60.0						

Coach: Forrest "Phog" Allen

Officials: O'Sullivan, McDonald
Technicals: Indiana (McCreary)
Attendance: 10,000

National Invitation Tournament (NIT)

Quarterfinals: DePaul d. Long Island 45-38, Duquesne d. St. John's 38-31
Semifinals: Colorado d. DePaul 52-37, Duquesne d. Oklahoma A&M 34-30
Third place: Oklahoma A&M d. DePaul 23-22
Championship: Colorado d. Duquesne 51-40
MVP: Bob Doll, Colorado

1940-41: Badgers of Honor

Harold "Bud" Foster's Wisconsin squad, coming off a dismal 5–15 season in 1939-40, lost its first Big Ten game to Minnesota, 44-27. But the Badgers turned their season around in a big way, ending up 17–3 and in the NCAA Tournament. In their East Regional games, Wisconsin came back from halftime deficits to edge Dartmouth, 51-50, and then Pittsburgh, 36-30. Washington State and its 6'7", 230-pound star center, Paul Lindeman, had an easier run through its regional, but in the Final, Gene Englund (13 points) led the Badgers to a 39-34 win. The two teams combined to shoot 23.4% from the field and their total of 73 points is the lowest in championship game history.

North Carolina's George Glamack, on the other hand, scored 31 against Dartmouth in the East Regional third-place game—although the Tar Heels lost the game, 60-59. Glamack was the only player to score more than 30 points in a game in the first 11 years of the NCAA Tournament.

Major Conference Standings

BIG SEVEN	Conference W	L	Pct	Overall W	L	Pct
Wyoming○	10	2	.833	14	6	.700
Utah	9	3	.750	14	7	.667
Colorado	7	5	.583	10	6	.625
BYU	6	6	.500	14	9	.609
Colorado State	4	8	.333	10	9	.526
Denver	4	8	.333	8	9	.471
Utah State	2	9	.182	5	16	.238

BIG SIX	Conference W	L	Pct	Overall W	L	Pct
Kansas	7	3	.700	12	6	.667
Iowa State	7	3	.700	15	4	.789
Nebraska	6	4	.600	8	10	.444
Oklahoma	5	5	.500	6	12	.333
Kansas State	3	7	.300	6	12	.333
Missouri	2	8	.200	6	10	.375

BIG TEN	Conference W	L	Pct	Overall W	L	Pct
Wisconsin○	11	1	.917	20	3	.870
Indiana	10	2	.833	17	3	.850
Illinois	7	5	.583	13	7	.650
Minnesota	7	5	.583	11	9	.550
Ohio State	7	5	.583	10	10	.500
Purdue	6	6	.500	13	7	.650
Michigan	5	7	.417	9	10	.474
Iowa	4	8	.333	12	8	.600
Northwestern	3	9	.250	7	11	.389
Chicago	0	12	.000	4	16	.200

IVY	Conference W	L	Pct	Overall W	L	Pct
Dartmouth○	10	2	.833	19	5	.792
Cornell	9	3	.750	17	6	.739
Columbia	8	4	.667	12	5	.706
Harvard	4	8	.333	10	9	.526
Yale	4	8	.333	10	12	.455
Princeton	4	8	.333	10	13	.435
Penn	3	9	.250	5	12	.294

MISSOURI VALLEY	Conference W	L	Pct	Overall W	L	Pct
Creighton○	9	3	.750	18	7	.720
Oklahoma A&M	8	4	.667	18	7	.720
Tulsa	7	5	.583	12	9	.571
Wash.-St. Louis	6	6	.500	9	8	.529
Drake	6	6	.500	9	11	.450
Washburn	4	8	.333	7	12	.368
Saint Louis	2	10	.167	3	14	.176

NEW ENGLAND	Conference W	L	Pct	Overall W	L	Pct
Rhode Island□	7	1	.875	21	4	.840
Connecticut	7	1	.875	14	2	.875
New Hampshire	3	5	.375	9	8	.529
Maine	2	6	.250	4	8	.333
Northeastern	1	7	.125	3	13	.188

PACIFIC COAST	Conference W	L	Pct	Overall W	L	Pct
North						
Washington State○	13	3	.813	26	6	.813
Oregon State	9	7	.563	19	9	.679
Oregon	7	9	.438	18	18	.500
Washington	7	9	.438	12	13	.480
Idaho	4	12	.250	14	15	.483
South						
Stanford	10	2	.833	21	5	.808
Southern California	6	6	.500	15	10	.600
California	6	6	.500	15	12	.556
UCLA	2	10	.167	6	20	.231

Playoff: **Washington State d. Stanford 2-0** in a best-of-three series for the title

SEC	Conference W	L	Pct	Overall W	L	Pct
Kentucky	8	1	.889	17	8	.680
Florida	6	2	.750	15	3	.833
Tennessee	8	3	.727	17	5	.773
Alabama	11	7	.611	14	8	.636
LSU	7	5	.583	9	9	.500
Auburn	6	5	.545	13	6	.684
Tulane	6	5	.545	8	6	.571
Mississippi State	6	6	.500	12	10	.545
Georgia	6	7	.462	13	11	.542
Georgia Tech	4	8	.333	8	11	.421
Vanderbilt	3	9	.250	8	9	.471
Mississippi	2	15	.118	2	18	.100

Tournament: **Tennessee d. Kentucky 36-33**

SOUTHERN	Conference W	L	Pct	Overall W	L	Pct
North Carolina○	14	1	.933	19	9	.679
South Carolina	8	3	.727	15	9	.625
William and Mary	8	3	.727	15	10	.600
Washington and Lee	9	4	.692	11	11	.500
Duke	8	4	.667	14	8	.636
VMI	8	4	.667	10	6	.625
Richmond	7	6	.583	11	10	.524
Wake Forest	7	6	.538	9	9	.500
Clemson	7	8	.467	8	14	.364
Davidson	5	7	.417	11	12	.478
NC State	6	9	.400	6	9	.400
Virginia Tech	4	8	.333	8	13	.381
The Citadel	1	8	.111	6	12	.333
Furman	1	10	.091	4	13	.235
Maryland	0	13	.000	1	21	.045

Tournament: **Duke d. South Carolina 53-30**

SOUTHWEST	Conference W	L	Pct	Overall W	L	Pct
Arkansas○	12	0	1.000	20	3	.870
Rice	8	4	.667	18	6	.750
Texas	7	5	.583	14	10	.583
Baylor	6	6	.500	11	11	.500
SMU	6	6	.500	10	10	.500
Texas A&M	3	9	.250	7	13	.350
TCU	0	12	.000	5	16	.238

INDEPENDENTS	Overall W	L	Pct
Long Island□	25	2	.926
Seton Hall□	20	2	.909
Westminster (PA)□	20	2	.909
Toledo	21	3	.875
Duquesne□	17	3	.850
Western Kentucky	22	4	.846
George Washington	18	4	.818
Loyola (MD)	18	4	.818

INDEPENDENTS (CONT.)	Overall W	L	Pct
Ohio□	18	4	.818
Boston U.	13	3	.813
Villanova	13	3	.813
Bradley	16	4	.800
Georgetown	16	4	.800
CCNY□	17	5	.773
Notre Dame	17	5	.773
Virginia□	18	6	.750
Penn State	15	5	.750
Syracuse	14	5	.737
St. Bonaventure	12	5	.706
NYU	13	6	.684
Pittsburgh○	13	6	.684
Santa Clara	15	7	.682
Saint Joseph's	12	6	.667
Niagara	13	7	.650
Brooklyn	11	6	.647
Michigan State	11	6	.647
St. John's	11	6	.647
Navy	9	5	.643
Fordham	14	8	.636
DePaul	13	8	.619
Loyola-Chicago	13	8	.619
Arizona	11	7	.611
Manhattan	11	7	.611
Marshall	14	9	.609
Colgate	9	6	.600
Butler	13	9	.591
Xavier	13	9	.591
Bucknell	10	7	.588
Miami (OH)	10	7	.588
Indiana State	11	8	.579
La Salle	11	8	.579
Temple	12	9	.571
Muhlenberg	13	10	.565
West Virginia	13	10	.565
Kent State	12	10	.545
Canisius	10	9	.526
Detroit	11	10	.524
Montana State	13	12	.520
Brown	10	10	.500
St. Francis (NY)	9	9	.500
Siena	9	9	.500
Western Michigan	9	9	.500
Montana	13	14	.481
Bowling Green	10	11	.476
Wichita State	9	11	.450
Lafayette	8	10	.444
Rutgers	8	10	.444
Arizona State	8	11	.421
Dayton	9	14	.391
Holy Cross	4	7	.364
Cincinnati	6	12	.333
Saint Mary's (CA)	6	13	.316
Army	5	11	.313
Lehigh	5	12	.294
Valparaiso	4	12	.250
Marquette	2	13	.133
San Francisco	2	13	.133
Louisville	2	14	.125
Sewanee	1	14	.067

⊛ Automatic NCAA Tournament bid ○ At-large NCAA Tournament bid □ NIT appearance ● Team record doesn't reflect games forfeited or vacated. For adjusted record, see p. 521.

PREMO-PORRETTA POWER POLL

	SCHOOL	RECORD
1	**Long Island (NIT champion)**	25-2
2	**Wisconsin (NCAA champion)**	20-3
3	**Toledo**	21-3
4	**Washington State**	26-6
5	**Indiana**	17-3
6	**Arkansas**	20-3
7	**Ohio**	18-4
8	**Stanford**	21-5
9	**Duquesne**	17-3
10	**Western Kentucky**	22-4
11	**Westminster (PA)**	20-2
12	**Dartmouth**	19-5
13	**CCNY**	17-5
14	**Seton Hall**	20-2
15	**Washington and Jefferson (PA)**	15-3
16	**Penn State**	15-5
17	**Indiana Central**	17-1
18	**Georgetown**	16-4
19	**Santa Clara**	15-7
20	**Bradley**	16-4
21	**Oregon State**	19-9
22	**Creighton**	18-7
23	**Illinois**	13-7
24	**Rice**	18-6
25	**Pittsburgh**	13-6

CONSENSUS ALL-AMERICAS

FIRST TEAM

PLAYER	CL	POS	HT	SCHOOL	PPG
John Adams	SR	F	6-3	Arkansas	N/A
Gus Broberg	SR	G/F	6-1	Dartmouth	14.9
Howard Engleman	SR	F	6-2	Kansas	16.1
Gene Englund	SR	C	6-4	Wisconsin	13.2
George Glamack	SR	F/C	6-6	North Carolina	20.6

SECOND TEAM

PLAYER	CL	POS	HT	SCHOOL	PPG
Frank Baumholtz	SR	G	5-10	Ohio	17.5
Bob Kinney	JR	C	6-6	Rice	14.7
Paul Lindeman	SR	C	6-7	Washington State	10.2
Stan Modzelewski	JR	G	5-10	Rhode Island	19.2
Ossie Schechtman	SR	G/F	6-0	Long Island	5.0

SELECTORS: CONVERSE YEARBOOK, HELMS FOUNDATION, MADISON SQUARE GARDEN

1941 NCAA TOURNAMENT

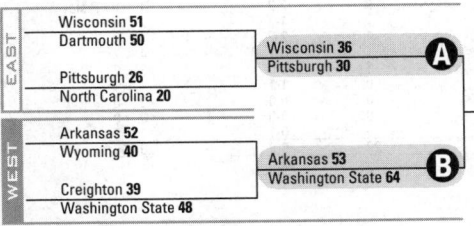

REGIONAL SEMIFINALS — REGIONAL FINALS — NATIONAL FINAL

EAST

Wisconsin **51**
Dartmouth **50**

Pittsburgh **26**
North Carolina **20**

Wisconsin **36** (A)
Pittsburgh **30**

WEST

Arkansas **52**
Wyoming **40**

Creighton **39**
Washington State **48**

Arkansas **53** (B)
Washington State **64**

NATIONAL FINAL

Wisconsin 39
Washington State 34

KANSAS CITY

The Badgers complete a 15-game winning streak by double-teaming 6'7" WSU center Paul Lindeman, holding him to just three points. As many as 12,000 Wisconsin fans meet the team's train when it pulls into Madison after 1 a.m. "House mothers even suspended rules and allowed female students to stay out for the event," according to the school archives.

East Regional Third Place Dartmouth d. North Carolina 60-59
West Regional Third Place Creighton d. Wyoming 45-44

A Despite its home-court advantage, Wisconsin struggles and trails by four at halftime. But the Badgers pull out the win thanks to double-digit efforts from Gene Englund, the Big Ten MVP, and John Kotz, who wins the Tourney MOP award.

B The Cougars lead by as many as 20 points in the second half, mainly on the strength of their one-handed shots (popularized in the 1930s by Stanford's Hank Luisetti) instead of the customary two-handed set shots that most coaches still prefer.

Tournament Leaders

Individual Leaders

Scoring	CL	POS	G	PTS	PPG
1 **John Adams**, Arkansas	SR	F	2	48	24.0
2 **George Glamack**, North Carolina	SR	F/C	2	40	20.0
3 **Gus Broberg**, Dartmouth	SR	G/F	2	38	19.0
4 **George Munroe**, Dartmouth	SO	F	2	33	16.5
5 **Paul Lindeman**, Washington State	SR	C	3	43	14.3
6 **Gene Englund**, Wisconsin	SR	C	3	42	14.0
7 **Kirk Gebert**, Washington State	JR	G	3	37	12.3
John Kotz, Wisconsin	SO	F	3	37	12.3
9 **Don Fleming**, Creighton	SR	F	2	24	12.0
Kenny Sailors, Wyoming	FR	G	2	24	12.0

Minimum: 2 games

Free Throw Pct	CL	POS	G	FT	FTA	PCT
1 **Fred Rehm**, Wisconsin	SO	G	3	7	8	87.5
2 **Gene Englund**, Wisconsin	SR	C	3	16	19	84.2
3 **George Glamack**, North Carolina	SR	F/C	2	12	16	75.0
John Freiberger, Arkansas	SR	C	2	6	8	75.0
Kenny Sailors, Wyoming	FR	G	2	6	8	75.0

Minimum: 5 made

Field Goals Per Game	CL	POS	G	FG	FGPG
1 **John Adams**, Arkansas	SR	F	2	21	10.5
2 **Gus Broberg**, Dartmouth	SR	G/F	2	17	8.5
3 **George Munroe**, Dartmouth	SO	F	2	15	7.5
4 **George Glamack**, North Carolina	SR	F/C	2	14	7.0
5 **Kirk Gebert**, Washington State	JR	G	3	17	5.7

Minimum: 2 games

Team Leaders

Scoring	G	PTS	PPG
1 **Dartmouth**	2	110	55.0
2 **Arkansas**	2	105	52.5
3 **Washington State**	3	146	48.7
4 **Wisconsin**	3	126	42.0
Creighton	2	84	42.0
Wyoming	2	84	42.0
7 **North Carolina**	2	79	39.5
8 **Pittsburgh**	2	56	28.0

Minimum: 2 games

FT Pct	G	FT	FTA	PCT
1 **Wisconsin**	3	40	55	72.7
2 **Pittsburgh**	2	14	20	70.0
3 **Creighton**	2	14	22	63.6
4 **Dartmouth**	2	16	26	61.5
5 **Arkansas**	2	21	35	60.0
North Carolina	2	15	25	60.0

Minimum: 2 games

FG Per Game	G	FG	FGPG
1 **Dartmouth**	2	47	23.5
2 **Arkansas**	2	42	21.0
3 **Washington State**	3	62	20.7
4 **Creighton**	2	35	17.5
5 **Wyoming**	2	34	17.0

Tournament MOP

PLAYER	CL	POS	HT	SCHOOL	FG	FT	PPG
John Kotz	SO	F	6-3	Wisconsin	13	11-16	12.3

1941 NCAA Tournament Box Scores

51-50 (Elite 8)

	Wisconsin	Dartmouth
1H	22	24
2H	29	26

WISCONSIN	MIN	FG	3FG	FT	REB	A	ST	BL	PF	TP
Gene Englund	-	6	-	6-7	-	-	-	-	3	18
John Kotz	-	5	-	5-9	-	-	-	-	0	15
Fred Rehm	-	2	-	5-5	-	-	-	-	2	9
Charles Epperson	-	4	-	0-0	-	-	-	-	0	8
Wililam Strain	-	0	-	1-3	-	-	-	-	4	1
Bob Alwin	-	0	-	0-0	-	-	-	-	1	0
Donald Timmerman	-	0	-	0-0	-	-	-	-	1	0
TOTALS	-	17	-	17-24	-	-	-	-	11	51
Percentages				70.8						

Coach: Harold Foster

DARTMOUTH	MIN	FG	3FG	FT	REB	A	ST	BL	PF	TP
Gus Broberg	-	9	-	2-2	-	-	-	-	1	20
George Munroe	-	7	-	1-2	-	-	-	-	2	15
Stanley Skaug	-	4	-	2-2	-	-	-	-	3	10
James Olsen	-	1	-	0-1	-	-	-	-	4	2
William Parmer	-	1	-	0-0	-	-	-	-	3	2
Charles Pearson	-	0	-	1-1	-	-	-	-	4	1
Vincent Else	-	0	-	0-0	-	-	-	-	2	0
John Horner	-	0	-	0-0	-	-	-	-	0	0
Conor Shaw	-	0	-	0-1	-	-	-	-	1	0
TOTALS	-	22	-	6-9	-	-	-	-	20	50
Percentages				66.7						

Coach: Osborne Cowles

Officials: Chest, Risley

26-20 (Elite 8)

	Pittsburgh	North Carolina
1H	8	12
2H	18	8

PITTSBURGH	MIN	FG	3FG	FT	REB	A	ST	BL	PF	TP
Tay Malarkey	-	3	-	1-1	-	-	-	-	0	7
George Kocheran	-	2	-	2-2	-	-	-	-	1	6
Eddie Straloski	-	3	-	0-2	-	-	-	-	1	6
Samuel Milanovich	-	1	-	2-2	-	-	-	-	1	4
Melvin Port	-	0	-	3-6	-	-	-	-	2	3
James Klein	-	0	-	0-0	-	-	-	-	1	0
Lawrence Paffrath	-	0	-	0-0	-	-	-	-	3	0
TOTALS	-	9	-	8-13	-	-	-	-	9	26
Percentages				61.5						

Coach: Henry "Doc" Carlson

NORTH CAROLINA	MIN	FG	3FG	FT	REB	A	ST	BL	PF	TP
George Glamack	-	4	-	1-2	-	-	-	-	4	9
Paul Severin	-	1	-	1-1	-	-	-	-	0	3
Jimmy Howard	-	1	-	0-0	-	-	-	-	2	2
Hank Pessar	-	1	-	0-1	-	-	-	-	0	2
Bob Rose	-	1	-	0-1	-	-	-	-	1	2
Reid Suggs	-	1	-	0-1	-	-	-	-	0	2
Bobby Gersten	-	0	-	0-1	-	-	-	-	0	0
George Paine	-	0	-	0-1	-	-	-	-	2	0
TOTALS	-	9	-	2-8	-	-	-	-	9	20
Percentages				25.0						

Coach: Bill Lange

Officials: Haarlow, Boyle

52-40 (Elite 8)

	Arkansas	Wyoming
1H	29	18
2H	23	22

ARKANSAS	MIN	FG	3FG	FT	REB	A	ST	BL	PF	TP
John Adams	-	11	-	4-4	-	-	-	-	0	26
Gordon Carpenter	-	3	-	2-3	-	-	-	-	2	8
R.C. Pitts	-	4	-	0-0	-	-	-	-	4	8
John Freiberger	-	2	-	3-4	-	-	-	-	2	7
Howard Hickey	-	1	-	1-2	-	-	-	-	4	3
O'neal Adams	-	0	-	0-0	-	-	-	-	0	0
Clayton Wynne	-	0	-	0-0	-	-	-	-	2	0
TOTALS	-	21	-	10-13	-	-	-	-	14	52
Percentages				76.9						

Coach: Glen Rose

WYOMING	MIN	FG	3FG	FT	REB	A	ST	BL	PF	TP
Kenny Sailors	-	6	-	5-5	-	-	-	-	2	17
Willie Rothman	-	3	-	2-3	-	-	-	-	2	8
Bill Strannigan	-	3	-	2-2	-	-	-	-	0	8
Jim Weir	-	2	-	0-1	-	-	-	-	2	4
Charles Bentson	-	1	-	0-0	-	-	-	-	2	2
Nick Krpan	-	0	-	1-2	-	-	-	-	2	1
Clinton Butcher	-	0	-	0-0	-	-	-	-	0	0
Curt Gowdy	-	0	-	0-2	-	-	-	-	4	0
Lou Muir	-	0	-	0-0	-	-	-	-	0	0
TOTALS	-	15	-	10-15	-	-	-	-	14	40
Percentages				66.7						

Coach: Everett Shelton

Officials: O'Sullivan, Cameron

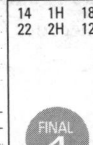

48-39 — 25 1H 14 / 23 2H 25 — ELITE 8

WASHINGTON STATE	MIN	FG	3FG	FT	REB	A	ST	BL	PF	TP
Paul Lindeman	-	12	-	2-6	-	-	-	-	3	26
Vern Butts	-	4	-	1-2	-	-	-	-	1	9
Kirk Gebert	-	2	-	0-1	-	-	-	-	3	4
Ray Sundquist	-	2	-	0-3	-	-	-	-	1	4
Dale Gentry	-	1	-	1-2	-	-	-	-	1	3
Jim Zimmerman	-	1	-	0-0	-	-	-	-	0	2
Marvin Gilberg	-	0	-	0-0	-	-	-	-	0	0
John Hooper	-	0	-	0-0	-	-	-	-	0	0
Owen Hunt	-	0	-	0-0	-	-	-	-	0	0
Phil Mahan	-	0	-	0-0	-	-	-	-	1	0
TOTALS	-	22	-	4-14	-	-	-	-	10	48
Percentages				28.6						

Coach: Jack Friel

CREIGHTON	MIN	FG	3FG	FT	REB	A	ST	BL	PF	TP
Dick Nolan	-	5	-	4-5	-	-	-	-	2	14
Ed Beisser	-	4	-	0-0	-	-	-	-	3	8
Don Fleming	-	3	-	1-2	-	-	-	-	1	7
Arthur Jaquay	-	3	-	1-2	-	-	-	-	0	7
James Thynne	-	1	-	1-1	-	-	-	-	1	3
Gene Haldeman	-	0	-	0-1	-	-	-	-	3	0
Ralph Langer	-	0	-	0-1	-	-	-	-	2	0
TOTALS	-	16	-	7-12	-	-	-	-	12	39
Percentages				58.3						

Coach: Eddie S. Hickey

Officials: Curtis, Herigstad

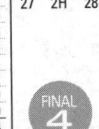

36-30 — 14 1H 18 / 22 2H 12 — FINAL 4

WISCONSIN	MIN	FG	3FG	FT	REB	A	ST	BL	PF	TP
Gene Englund	-	2	-	7-8	-	-	-	-	4	11
John Kotz	-	3	-	4-4	-	-	-	-	1	10
Charles Epperson	-	2	-	3-4	-	-	-	-	0	7
Fred Rehm	-	1	-	2-2	-	-	-	-	0	4
Wililam Strain	-	2	-	0-2	-	-	-	-	3	4
Donald Timmerman	-	0	-	0-1	-	-	-	-	0	0
TOTALS	-	10	-	16-21	-	-	-	-	8	36
Percentages				76.2						

Coach: Harold Foster

PITTSBURGH	MIN	FG	3FG	FT	REB	A	ST	BL	PF	TP
Eddie Straloski	-	6	-	0-0	-	-	-	-	4	12
George Kocheran	-	1	-	2-2	-	-	-	-	0	4
Samuel Milanovich	-	2	-	0-0	-	-	-	-	3	4
Melvin Port	-	1	-	2-3	-	-	-	-	4	4
Tay Malarkey	-	1	-	1-1	-	-	-	-	3	3
Lawrence Paffrath	-	1	-	1-1	-	-	-	-	0	3
James Klein	-	0	-	0-0	-	-	-	-	1	0
Lefty Ziolkauiski	-	0	-	0-0	-	-	-	-	2	0
TOTALS	-	12	-	6-7	-	-	-	-	17	30
Percentages				85.7						

Coach: Henry "Doc" Carlson

Officials: Boyle, Chest

64-53 — 37 1H 25 / 27 2H 28 — FINAL 4

WASHINGTON STATE	MIN	FG	3FG	FT	REB	A	ST	BL	PF	TP
Paul Lindeman	-	4	-	6-9	-	-	-	-	2	14
Kirk Gebert	-	5	-	2-2	-	-	-	-	1	12
Vern Butts	-	5	-	1-1	-	-	-	-	1	11
Dale Gentry	-	4	-	1-2	-	-	-	-	2	9
Marvin Gilberg	-	3	-	0-3	-	-	-	-	4	6
Ray Sundquist	-	2	-	2-2	-	-	-	-	2	6
John Hooper	-	2	-	0-0	-	-	-	-	4	4
Owen Hunt	-	1	-	0-0	-	-	-	-	3	2
Frank Akins	-	0	-	0-0	-	-	-	-	0	0
Jim Zimmerman	-	0	-	0-0	-	-	-	-	2	0
TOTALS	-	26	-	12-19	-	-	-	-	21	64
Percentages				63.2						

Coach: Jack Friel

ARKANSAS	MIN	FG	3FG	FT	REB	A	ST	BL	PF	TP
John Adams	-	10	-	2-5	-	-	-	-	1	22
R.C. Pitts	-	5	-	2-4	-	-	-	-	2	12
O'neal Adams	-	2	-	2-3	-	-	-	-	0	6
Gordon Carpenter	-	2	-	1-3	-	-	-	-	2	5
John Freiberger	-	1	-	3-4	-	-	-	-	3	5
Howard Hickey	-	1	-	1-2	-	-	-	-	2	3
Nobel Robbins	-	0	-	0-1	-	-	-	-	3	0
Clayton Wynne	-	0	-	0-0	-	-	-	-	2	0
TOTALS	-	21	-	11-22	-	-	-	-	15	53
Percentages				50.0						

Coach: Glen Rose

Officials: Herigstad, O'Sullivan

39-34 — 21 1H 17 / 18 2H 17 — NCAA FINAL 1941

WISCONSIN	MIN	FG	3FG	FT	REB	A	ST	BL	PF	TP
Gene Englund	-	5	-	3-4	-	-	-	-	2	13
John Kotz	-	5	-	2-3	-	-	-	-	2	12
Charles Epperson	-	2	-	0-0	-	-	-	-	3	4
Fred Rehm	-	2	-	0-1	-	-	-	-	2	4
Bob Alwin	-	1	-	0-0	-	-	-	-	0	2
Wililam Strain	-	0	-	2-2	-	-	-	-	1	2
Donald Timmerman	-	1	-	0-0	-	-	-	-	1	2
Warren Schrage	-	0	-	0-0	-	-	-	-	1	0
TOTALS	-	16	-	7-10	-	-	-	-	12	39
Percentages				70.0						

Coach: Harold Foster

WASHINGTON STATE	MIN	FG	3FG	FT	REB	A	ST	BL	PF	TP
Kirk Gebert	-	10-24	-	1-2	-	-	-	-	1	21
Ray Sundquist	-	2	-	0-1	-	-	-	-	3	4
Vern Butts	-	1	-	1-1	-	-	-	-	1	3
Paul Lindeman	-	0	-	3-4	-	-	-	-	1	3
Marvin Gilberg	-	1	-	0-2	-	-	-	-	1	2
Dale Gentry	-	0	-	1-2	-	-	-	-	1	1
John Hooper	-	0	-	0-0	-	-	-	-	0	0
Owen Hunt	-	0	-	0-0	-	-	-	-	0	0
Jim Zimmerman	-	0	-	0-0	-	-	-	-	0	0
TOTALS	-	14	-	6-12	-	-	-	-	8	34
Percentages				50.0						

Coach: Jack Friel

Officials: Haarlow, Cameron
Attendance: 7,219

NATIONAL INVITATION TOURNAMENT (NIT)

Quarterfinals: CCNY d. Virginia 64-35, Ohio d. Duquesne 55-40, Seton Hall d. Rhode Island 70-54, Long Island d. Westminster 48-36
Semifinals: Long Island d. Seton Hall 49-26, Ohio d. CCNY 45-43
Third place: CCNY d. Seton Hall 42-27
Championship: Long Island d. Ohio 56-42
MVP: Frank Baumholtz, Ohio

1941-42: Mentor vs. Pupil

Osborne "Ozzie" Cowles guided his Dartmouth squad into the NCAA title game with a 47-28 win over first-time participant Kentucky and coach Adolph Rupp. In the West Regional final, Stanford, coached by Cowles' mentor, the legendary Everett Dean, beat Colorado, 46-35. During the NCAA Final in Kansas City's Municipal Auditorium, Dean used his athletic big men—Stanford had what was considered a lineup of giants, with no starter shorter than 6'3"—to pressure Dartmouth and earn Stanford (28–4) a 53-38 win. Forward Howie Dallmar scored 15 points and was named MOP. Of all the men who have coached in the NCAA Tournament, Dean is the only one who has never lost a Tourney game.

But the 1942 title seems to have carried a curse. Stanford went 46 years before returning to the Big Dance, while Dartmouth—though back in the championship game in 1944 and in the field three times in the '50s—then went five decades (and counting) without a Tournament appearance.

Major Conference Standings

BIG SIX

	Conference			Overall		
	W	L	Pct	W	L	Pct
Kansas○	8	2	.800	17	5	.773
Oklahoma	8	2	.800	11	7	.611
Iowa State	5	5	.500	11	6	.647
Nebraska	4	6	.400	6	13	.316
Kansas State	3	7	.300	8	10	.444
Missouri	2	8	.200	6	12	.333

BIG TEN

	Conference			Overall		
	W	L	Pct	W	L	Pct
Illinois○	13	2	.867	18	5	.783
Indiana	10	5	.667	15	6	.714
Wisconsin	10	5	.667	14	7	.667
Iowa	10	5	.667	12	8	.600
Minnesota	9	6	.600	15	6	.714
Purdue	9	6	.600	14	7	.667
Northwestern	5	10	.333	8	13	.381
Michigan	5	10	.333	6	14	.300
Ohio State	4	11	.267	6	14	.300
Chicago	0	15	.000	2	19	.095

BORDER

	Conference			Overall		
	W	L	Pct	W	L	Pct
West Texas A&M□	16	0	1.000	28	3	.903
Texas Tech	12	4	.750	16	11	.593
Arizona State	10	6	.625	10	10	.500
Northern Arizona	8	9	.471	11	10	.524
Texas Western	7	9	.438	11	11	.500
Arizona	6	10	.375	9	13	.409
Hardin-Simmons	6	10	.375	6	10	.375
New Mexico	5	11	.313	9	13	.409
New Mexico State	4	10	.286	8	18	.308

IVY

	Conference			Overall		
	W	L	Pct	W	L	Pct
Dartmouth○	10	2	.833	22	4	.846
Princeton	10	2	.833	16	5	.762
Cornell	7	5	.583	9	12	.429
Penn	5	7	.417	9	9	.500
Harvard	5	7	.417	8	16	.333
Yale	3	9	.250	7	12	.368
Columbia	2	10	.167	2	13	.133

MISSOURI VALLEY

	Conference			Overall		
	W	L	Pct	W	L	Pct
Creighton□	9	1	.900	18	5	.783
Oklahoma A&M	9	1	.900	20	6	.769
Wash.-St. Louis	4	6	.400	10	13	.435
Saint Louis	4	6	.400	8	12	.400
Tulsa	3	7	.300	3	13	.188
Drake	1	9	.100	2	13	.133

MOUNTAIN STATES

	Conference			Overall		
	W	L	Pct	W	L	Pct
Colorado○	11	1	.917	16	2	.889
BYU	9	3	.750	17	3	.850
Wyoming	9	3	.750	15	5	.750
Utah	7	5	.583	13	7	.650
Utah State	3	9	.250	6	10	.375
Denver	2	10	.167	4	16	.200
Colorado State	1	11	.083	3	16	.158

NEW ENGLAND

	Conference			Overall		
	W	L	Pct	W	L	Pct
Rhode Island□	8	0	1.000	18	4	.818
Connecticut	6	2	.750	12	5	.706
Northeastern	4	4	.500	6	9	.400
Maine	2	6	.250	7	7	.500
New Hampshire	0	8	.000	4	15	.211

PACIFIC COAST

	Conference			Overall		
	W	L	Pct	W	L	Pct
North						
Oregon State	11	5	.688	18	9	.667
Washington	10	6	.625	18	7	.720
Washington State	9	7	.563	21	8	.724
Oregon	7	9	.438	12	15	.444
Idaho	3	13	.188	12	16	.429
South						
Stanford○	11	1	.917	28	4	.875
Southern California	7	5	.583	12	8	.600
California	4	8	.333	11	19	.367
UCLA	2	10	.167	5	18	.217

Playoff: **Stanford d. Oregon State 2-1** in a best of three series for the title

SEC

	Conference			Overall		
	W	L	Pct	W	L	Pct
Tennessee	7	1	.875	19	3	.864
Alabama	13	4	.765	18	6	.750
Kentucky○	6	2	.750	19	6	.760
LSU	8	3	.727	8	7	.533
Auburn	9	5	.643	11	6	.647
Mississippi State	9	6	.600	13	7	.650
Georgia	5	8	.385	7	10	.412
Georgia Tech	4	7	.364	8	8	.500
Florida	3	8	.273	8	9	.471
Vanderbilt	3	8	.273	7	9	.438
Tulane	3	9	.250	4	12	.250
Mississippi	3	12	.200	4	15	.211

Tournament: **Kentucky d. Alabama 36-34**

SOUTHERN

	Conference			Overall		
	W	L	Pct	W	L	Pct
Duke	15	1	.938	22	2	.917
George Washington	8	3	.727	11	9	.550
Wake Forest	13	5	.722	16	8	.667
NC State	9	4	.692	15	7	.682
William and Mary	8	4	.667	15	9	.625
South Carolina	8	4	.667	12	9	.571
North Carolina	9	5	.643	14	9	.609
Washington and Lee	7	7	.500	10	15	.400
Furman	7	8	.467	10	9	.526
VMI	5	9	.357	7	11	.389
Virginia Tech	4	8	.333	10	10	.500
Richmond	4	8	.333	9	10	.474
Davidson	3	8	.273	12	13	.480
Maryland	3	8	.273	7	15	.318
Clemson	2	10	.167	3	14	.176
The Citadel	1	12	.077	2	14	.125

Tournament: **Duke d. North Carolina 45-34**

SOUTHWEST

	Conference			Overall		
	W	L	Pct	W	L	Pct
Rice○	10	2	.833	22	5	.815
Arkansas	10	2	.833	19	4	.826
TCU	6	6	.500	13	10	.565
Baylor	6	6	.500	11	9	.550
Texas	5	7	.417	14	9	.609
Texas A&M	4	8	.333	8	16	.333
SMU	1	11	.083	3	16	.158

INDEPENDENTS

	Overall		
	W	L	Pct
Long Island□	25	3	.893
St. Francis (NY)	16	2	.889
Penn State○	18	3	.857
Western Kentucky□	29	5	.853
CCNY□	16	3	.842
Seton Hall	16	3	.842
West Virginia□	19	4	.826
Toledo□	23	5	.821
Loyola (MD)	18	4	.818
Indiana State	17	4	.810
Saint Mary's (CA)	20	5	.800
St. John's	16	5	.762
Bradley	15	5	.750
Loyola-Chicago	17	6	.739
Niagara	16	6	.727
Notre Dame	16	6	.727
Duquesne	15	6	.714
Michigan State	15	6	.714
Syracuse	15	6	.714
Muhlenberg	17	7	.708
Canisius	12	6	.667
Dayton	12	6	.667
Saint Joseph's	12	6	.667
Boston U.	9	5	.643
Montana State	14	8	.636
Fordham	12	7	.632
NYU	12	7	.632
Marshall	15	9	.625
Army	10	6	.625
Detroit	13	8	.619
Brown	11	7	.611
St. Bonaventure	12	8	.600
Western Michigan	12	8	.600
Butler	13	9	.591
Villanova	13	9	.591
Montana	14	10	.583
San Francisco	14	10	.583
Ohio	12	9	.571
Navy	8	6	.571
Siena	9	7	.563
Kent State	14	11	.560
Brooklyn	10	8	.556
Temple	10	8	.556
Xavier	10	8	.556
Holy Cross	5	4	.556
Santa Clara	10	9	.526
La Salle	12	11	.522
Cincinnati	10	10	.500
Manhattan	10	10	.500
Bucknell	9	9	.500
Lehigh	7	8	.467
DePaul	10	12	.455
Georgetown	9	11	.450
Louisville	7	10	.412
Virginia	7	10	.412
Bowling Green	8	12	.400
Rutgers	8	12	.400
Miami (OH)	6	9	.400
Colgate	5	9	.357
Marquette	6	11	.353
Pittsburgh	5	10	.333
Lafayette	4	12	.250
Valparaiso	4	13	.235
Wichita State	4	16	.200

⊕ Automatic NCAA Tournament bid ○ At-large NCAA Tournament bid □ NIT appearance ✪ Team record doesn't reflect games forfeited or vacated. For adjusted record, see p. 521.

PREMO-PORRETTA POWER POLL

	SCHOOL	RECORD
1	Stanford (NCAA champion)	28-4
2	Colorado	16-2
3	Rice	22-5
4	Long Island	25-4#
5	Dartmouth	22-4
6	West Virginia (NIT champion)	19-4
7	Western Kentucky	29-5
8	Penn State	18-3
9	West Texas A&M	28-3
10	Duke	22-2
11	Tennessee	19-3
12	Kansas	17-5
13	Toledo	23-5
14	CCNY	16-3
15	Creighton	19-5#
16	Arkansas	19-4
17	Kentucky	19-6
18	Illinois	18-5
19	Oklahoma A&M	20-6
20	East Stroudsburg State (PA)	18-1
21	Rhode Island	18-4
22	Seton Hall	16-3
23	St. Francis (NY)	17-2#
24	BYU	17-3
25	Indiana Central	16-0

CONSENSUS ALL-AMERICAS

FIRST TEAM

PLAYER	CL	POS	HT	SCHOOL	PPG
Price Brookfield	JR	C	6-4	West Texas A&M	16.8
Bob Davies	SR	G	6-1	Seton Hall	11.8
Bob Kinney	SR	C	6-6	Rice	13.7
John Kotz	JR	F	6-3	Wisconsin	15.5
Andrew Phillip	SO	G	6-2	Illinois	10.1

SECOND TEAM

PLAYER	CL	POS	HT	SCHOOL	PPG
Donald Burness	SR	F	6-3	Stanford	8.8*
Gus Doerner	JR	F	6-3	Evansville	24.4
Bob Doll	SR	C	6-5	Colorado	9.3
John Mandic	SR	C	6-4	Oregon State	10.0
Stan Modzelewski	SR	G	5-10	Rhode Island	19.7
George Munroe	JR	F	5-11	Dartmouth	14.6

SELECTORS: CONVERSE YEARBOOK, HELMS FOUNDATION, MADISON SQUARE GARDEN, PIC MAGAZINE

*Conference games only

1942 NCAA TOURNAMENT

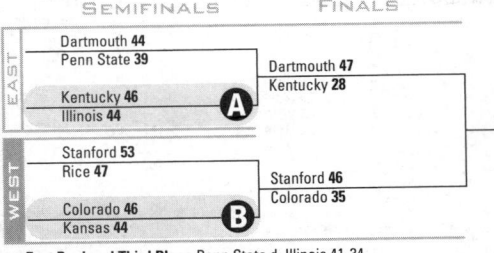

REGIONAL SEMIFINALS

EAST
- Dartmouth **44**, Penn State **39**
- Kentucky **46**, Illinois **44** (A)

WEST
- Stanford **53**, Rice **47**
- Colorado **46**, Kansas **44** (B)

REGIONAL FINALS

- Dartmouth **47**, Kentucky **28**
- Stanford **46**, Colorado **35**

NATIONAL FINAL

Stanford 53
Dartmouth 38

KANSAS CITY

After scoring 43 points in Stanford's first two games, Jim Pollard, known as the Kangaroo Kid because he's one of the few players who can dunk, sits out the title game with the flu. Sophomore forward Howie Dallmar steps in and scores a game-high 15 to win MOP honors. Dallmar would later coach Stanford for 21 seasons.

East Regional Third Place Penn State d. Illinois 41-34
West Regional Third Place Kansas d. Rice 55-53

(A) Kentucky wins its Tournament debut under Adolph Rupp, but is no match for Dartmouth.

(B) Three Colorado players pile up eight fouls trying to stop Charlie B. "Hawk" Black, a tenacious defender who would become the first 1,000-point scorer in Kansas history. He would go to war as a pilot after the next season, returning to Kansas in 1946.

Record differs from the school's and/or the NCAA's because it includes noncollegiate competition or because the outcome of some games is in dispute.

Tournament Leaders

Individual Leaders

Scoring

	CL	POS	G	PTS	PPG
1 **Chester Palmer**, Rice	SR	G	2	43	21.5
Jim Pollard, Stanford	SO	F	2	43	21.5
3 **Charlie B. Black**, Kansas	FR	F	2	34	17.0
4 **George Munroe**, Dartmouth	JR	F	3	41	13.7
5 **James Olsen**, Dartmouth	JR	C	3	38	12.7
Ed Voss, Stanford	JR	C	3	38	12.7
7 **Lawrence Gent**, Penn State	SO	F	2	23	11.5
Ken Menke, Illinois	SO	F	2	23	11.5
9 **Ray Evans**, Kansas	SO	G	2	22	11.0
Leason McCloud, Colorado	SR	F	2	22	11.0

Minimum: 2 games

Free Throw Pct

	CL	POS	G	FT	FTA	PCT
1 **Bob Doll**, Colorado	SR	C	2	7	7	100.0
Art Mathisen, Illinois	JR	C	2	5	5	100.0
Chester Palmer, Rice	SR	G	2	5	5	100.0
4 **Charles Pearson**, Dartmouth	SR	G	3	6	7	85.7
5 **George Munroe**, Dartmouth	JR	F	3	5	6	83.3

Minimum: 5 made

Field Goals Per Game

	CL	POS	G	FG	FGPG
1 **Jim Pollard**, Stanford	SO	F	2	20	10.0
2 **Chester Palmer**, Rice	SR	G	2	19	9.5
3 **George Munroe**, Dartmouth	JR	F	3	18	6.0
Charlie B. Black, Kansas	FR	F	2	12	6.0
5 **James Olsen**, Dartmouth	JR	C	3	17	5.7

Minimum: 2 games

Team Leaders

Scoring

		G	PTS	PPG
1	**Stanford**	3	152	50.7
2	**Rice**	2	100	50.0
3	**Kansas**	2	99	49.5
4	**Dartmouth**	3	130	43.3
5	**Colorado**	2	81	40.5
6	**Penn State**	2	80	40.0
7	**Illinois**	2	78	39.0
8	**Kentucky**	2	74	37.0

Minimum: 2 games

FT Pct

		G	FT	FTA	PCT
1	**Colorado**	2	17	22	77.3
2	**Illinois**	2	18	26	69.2
3	**Rice**	2	20	29	69.0
4	**Kentucky**	2	16	25	64.0
5	**Stanford**	3	24	38	63.2

Minimum: 2 games

FG Per Game

		G	FG	FGPG
1	**Stanford**	3	64	21.3
2	**Kansas**	2	40	20.0
	Rice	2	40	20.0
4	**Dartmouth**	3	55	18.3
5	**Colorado**	2	32	16.0

Tournament MOP

PLAYER	CL	POS	HT	SCHOOL	FG	FT	PPG
Howie Dallmar	SO	F	6-4	Stanford	11	4-6	8.7

1942 NCAA Tournament Box Scores

44-39 (Elite 8)

	Dartmouth	Penn State
1H	22	16
2H	22	23

DARTMOUTH	MIN	FG	3FG	FT	REB	A	ST	BL	PF	TP
James Olsen	-	8	-	3-4	-	-	-	-	4	19
George Munroe	-	4	-	0-0	-	-	-	-	1	8
Robert Myers	-	3	-	1-1	-	-	-	-	3	7
Stanley Skaug	-	2	-	3-4	-	-	-	-	2	7
Charles Pearson	-	1	-	1-2	-	-	-	-	4	3
William Parmer	-	0	-	0-1	-	-	-	-	0	0
Conor Shaw	-	0	-	0-0	-	-	-	-	0	0
TOTALS	**-**	**18**	**-**	**8-12**	**-**	**-**	**-**	**-**	**14**	**44**
Percentages				66.7						

Coach: Osborne Cowles

PENN STATE	MIN	FG	3FG	FT	REB	A	ST	BL	PF	TP
John Egli	-	5	-	2-4	-	-	-	-	4	12
David Hornstein	-	3	-	3-4	-	-	-	-	2	9
Herschel Baltimore	-	3	-	1-1	-	-	-	-	0	7
Elmer Gross	-	2	-	3-3	-	-	-	-	1	7
Lawrence Gent	-	1	-	0-0	-	-	-	-	0	2
R.F. Ramin	-	0	-	2-3	-	-	-	-	1	2
Dick Grimes	-	0	-	0-1	-	-	-	-	3	0
TOTALS	**-**	**14**	**-**	**11-16**	**-**	**-**	**-**	**-**	**11**	**39**
Percentages				68.8						

Coach: John Lawther

Officials: Adams, Pailet

46-44 (Elite 8)

	Kentucky	Illinois
1H	20	22
2H	26	22

KENTUCKY	MIN	FG	3FG	FT	REB	A	ST	BL	PF	TP
Milton Ticco	-	6	-	1-2	-	-	-	-	0	13
Carl Staker	-	4	-	1-2	-	-	-	-	3	9
Marvin Akers	-	4	-	0-0	-	-	-	-	0	8
James King	-	2	-	2-4	-	-	-	-	1	6
Ermal Allen	-	2	-	0-0	-	-	-	-	2	4
Kenneth England	-	1	-	2-2	-	-	-	-	3	4
Melvin Brewer	-	0	-	1-1	-	-	-	-	3	1
Waller White	-	0	-	1-1	-	-	-	-	2	1
TOTALS	**-**	**19**	**-**	**8-12**	**-**	**-**	**-**	**-**	**14**	**46**
Percentages				66.7						

Coach: Adolph Rupp

ILLINOIS	MIN	FG	3FG	FT	REB	A	ST	BL	PF	TP
Ken Menke	-	7	-	1-1	-	-	-	-	2	15
Jack Smiley	-	5	-	3-3	-	-	-	-	2	13
Andy Phillip	-	2	-	2-4	-	-	-	-	0	6
Henry Sachs	-	2	-	1-2	-	-	-	-	2	5
Victor Wukovits	-	2	-	0-4	-	-	-	-	3	4
Art Mathisen	-	0	-	1-1	-	-	-	-	0	1
Charles Fowler	-	0	-	0-0	-	-	-	-	1	0
William Hocking	-	0	-	0-0	-	-	-	-	0	0
Gene Vance	-	0	-	0-0	-	-	-	-	3	0
TOTALS	**-**	**18**	**-**	**8-15**	**-**	**-**	**-**	**-**	**13**	**44**
Percentages				53.3						

Coach: Douglas R. Mills

Officials: Coogan, Snyder

53-47 (Elite 8)

	Stanford	Rice
1H	33	21
2H	20	26

STANFORD	MIN	FG	3FG	FT	REB	A	ST	BL	PF	TP
Jim Pollard	-	12	-	2-4	-	-	-	-	1	26
Ed Voss	-	4	-	7-8	-	-	-	-	3	15
Bill Cowden	-	2	-	2-4	-	-	-	-	3	6
Howie Dallmar	-	3	-	0-0	-	-	-	-	0	6
Jack Dana	-	0	-	0-1	-	-	-	-	0	0
Freddie Linari	-	0	-	0-0	-	-	-	-	0	0
Leo McCaffrey	-	0	-	0-0	-	-	-	-	0	0
TOTALS	**-**	**21**	**-**	**11-17**	**-**	**-**	**-**	**-**	**7**	**53**
Percentages				64.7						

Coach: Everett S. Dean

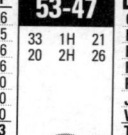

RICE	MIN	FG	3FG	FT	REB	A	ST	BL	PF	TP
Chester Palmer	-	8	-	2-2	-	-	-	-	3	18
Bill Tom Closs	-	3	-	2-3	-	-	-	-	4	8
Bob Kinney	-	3	-	2-3	-	-	-	-	4	8
Harold Lambert	-	4	-	0-0	-	-	-	-	0	8
Placido Gomez	-	2	-	0-0	-	-	-	-	3	4
John McDonald	-	0	-	1-2	-	-	-	-	0	1
Whitlock Zander	-	0	-	0-0	-	-	-	-	1	0
TOTALS	**-**	**20**	**-**	**7-10**	**-**	**-**	**-**	**-**	**15**	**47**
Percentages				70.0						

Coach: Buster Brannon

Officials: House, Herigstad

46-44 (ELITE 8)

COLORADO	MIN	FG	3FG	FT	REB	A	ST	BL	PF	TP
Leason McCloud	-	8	-	3-4	-	-	-	-	0	19
George Hamburg	-	4	-	1-3	-	-	-	-	1	9
Bob Doll	-	2	-	2-2	-	-	-	-	4	6
Horace Huggins	-	2	-	1-1	-	-	-	-	4	5
Bob Kirchner	-	2	-	0-0	-	-	-	-	3	4
Heath Nuckolls	-	1	-	1-1	-	-	-	-	2	3
Donald Putnam	-	0	-	0-0	-	-	-	-	0	0
TOTALS	**-**	**19**	**-**	**8-11**	**-**	**-**	**-**	**-**	**14**	**46**
Percentages				72.7						

Coach: Forrest B. "Frosty" Cox

	1H	2H
Colorado	27	19
Kansas	20	24

KANSAS	MIN	FG	3FG	FT	REB	A	ST	BL	PF	TP
Charlie B. Black	-	6	-	6-8	-	-	-	-	2	18
Ray Evans	-	5	-	0-0	-	-	-	-	2	10
John Buescher	-	1	-	3-4	-	-	-	-	2	5
Ralph Miller	-	2	-	1-2	-	-	-	-	4	5
Vance Hall	-	1	-	0-0	-	-	-	-	1	2
Thomas Hunter	-	1	-	0-2	-	-	-	-	1	2
Marvin Sollenberger	-	1	-	0-0	-	-	-	-	0	2
John Ballard	-	0	-	0-0	-	-	-	-	0	0
TOTALS	**-**	**17**	**-**	**10-16**	**-**	**-**	**-**	**-**	**12**	**44**
Percentages				62.5						

Coach: Forrest "Phog" Allen

Officials: Curtis, Piluso

47-28 (FINAL 4)

DARTMOUTH	MIN	FG	3FG	FT	REB	A	ST	BL	PF	TP
George Munroe	-	9	-	2-4	-	-	-	-	2	20
James Olsen	-	5	-	1-4	-	-	-	-	2	11
Robert Myers	-	4	-	1-3	-	-	-	-	2	9
Charles Pearson	-	0	-	3-3	-	-	-	-	1	3
Conor Shaw	-	1	-	0-0	-	-	-	-	0	2
Stanley Skaug	-	1	-	0-1	-	-	-	-	4	2
William Parmer	-	0	-	0-1	-	-	-	-	2	0
TOTALS	**-**	**20**	**-**	**7-16**	**-**	**-**	**-**	**-**	**13**	**47**
Percentages				43.8						

Coach: Osborne Cowles

	1H	2H
Dartmouth	23	24
Kentucky	13	15

KENTUCKY	MIN	FG	3FG	FT	REB	A	ST	BL	PF	TP
Marvin Akers	-	5	-	1-2	-	-	-	-	3	11
Ermal Allen	-	2	-	2-4	-	-	-	-	2	6
Melvin Brewer	-	1	-	2-4	-	-	-	-	1	4
James King	-	1	-	2-2	-	-	-	-	0	4
Kenneth England	-	1	-	0-0	-	-	-	-	0	2
Milton Ticco	-	0	-	1-1	-	-	-	-	1	1
Lloyd Ramsey	-	0	-	0-0	-	-	-	-	0	0
William Smith	-	0	-	0-0	-	-	-	-	2	0
Carl Staker	-	0	-	0-0	-	-	-	-	4	0
TOTALS	**-**	**10**	**-**	**8-13**	**-**	**-**	**-**	**-**	**13**	**28**
Percentages				61.5						

Coach: Adolph Rupp

Officials: Snyder, Adams

46-35 (FINAL 4)

STANFORD	MIN	FG	3FG	FT	REB	A	ST	BL	PF	TP
Jim Pollard	-	8	-	1-1	-	-	-	-	2	17
Ed Voss	-	4	-	2-5	-	-	-	-	3	10
Bill Cowden	-	2	-	3-5	-	-	-	-	2	7
Jack Dana	-	3	-	1-1	-	-	-	-	1	7
Howie Dallmar	-	2	-	1-1	-	-	-	-	0	5
John Eikelman	-	0	-	0-0	-	-	-	-	1	0
Freddie Linari	-	0	-	0-0	-	-	-	-	0	0
Morris Madden	-	0	-	0-0	-	-	-	-	0	0
Leo McCaffrey	-	0	-	0-0	-	-	-	-	0	0
Fred Oliver	-	0	-	0-0	-	-	-	-	0	0
TOTALS	**-**	**19**	**-**	**8-13**	**-**	**-**	**-**	**-**	**9**	**46**
Percentages				61.5						

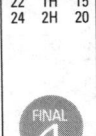

Coach: Everett S. Dean

	1H	2H
Stanford	22	24
Colorado	15	20

COLORADO	MIN	FG	3FG	FT	REB	A	ST	BL	PF	TP
Bob Doll	-	3	-	5-5	-	-	-	-	3	11
George Hamburg	-	3	-	2-2	-	-	-	-	2	8
Bob Kirchner	-	3	-	1-1	-	-	-	-	0	7
Donald Putnam	-	3	-	0-0	-	-	-	-	1	6
Leason McCloud	-	1	-	1-2	-	-	-	-	2	3
Horace Huggins	-	0	-	0-0	-	-	-	-	0	0
Heath Nuckolls	-	0	-	0-1	-	-	-	-	3	0
TOTALS	**-**	**13**	**-**	**9-11**	**-**	**-**	**-**	**-**	**11**	**35**
Percentages				81.8						

Coach: Forrest B. "Frosty" Cox

Officials: Curtis, House

53-38 (NCAA FINAL 1942)

STANFORD	MIN	FG	3FG	FT	REB	A	ST	BL	PF	TP
Howie Dallmar	40	6	-	3-5	-	-	-	-	0	15
Jack Dana	40	7	-	0-0	-	-	-	-	0	14
Ed Voss	40	6	-	1-2	-	-	-	-	2	13
Freddie Linari	31	3	-	0-0	-	-	-	-	0	6
Bill Cowden	40	2	-	1-1	-	-	-	-	3	5
Don Burness	9	0	-	0-0	-	-	-	-	0	0
TOTALS	**200**	**24**	**-**	**5-8**	**-**	**-**	**-**	**-**	**5**	**53**
Percentages				62.5						

Coach: Everett S. Dean

	1H	2H
Stanford	24	29
Dartmouth	22	16

DARTMOUTH	MIN	FG	3FG	FT	REB	A	ST	BL	PF	TP
George Munroe	40	5	-	2-2	-	-	-	-	1	12
James Olsen	40	4	-	0-1	-	-	-	-	0	8
Robert Myers	29	4	-	0-1	-	-	-	-	1	8
Charles Pearson	40	2	-	2-2	-	-	-	-	3	6
Stanley Skaug	40	1	-	0-0	-	-	-	-	2	2
William Parmer	11	1	-	0-0	-	-	-	-	0	2
TOTALS	**200**	**17**	**-**	**4-6**	**-**	**-**	**-**	**-**	**7**	**38**
Percentages				66.7						

Coach: Osborne Cowles

Officials: Curtis, Adams
Attendance: 6,500

National Invitation Tournament (NIT)

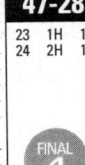

Quarterfinals: West Virginia d. Long Island 58-49, Creighton d. West Texas A&M 59-58, Western Kentucky d. CCNY 49-46, Toledo d. Rhode Island 82-71
Semifinals: West Virginia d. Toledo 51-39, Western Kentucky d. Creighton 49-36
Third place: Creighton d. Toledo 48-46
Championship: West Virginia d. Western Kentucky, 47-45
MVP: Rudy Baric, West Virginia

1942-43: The Birth of the J

NCAA champions of the era usually thrived on innovation, extreme size or some combination of the two. The teams in the 1943 title game both had height: Wyoming center Milo Komenich was 6'7" and Georgetown's 6'8" John Mahnken scored 37 points in Tournament wins over NYU and DePaul (which featured 6'9" George Mikan). But the Cowboys—who at one point in the season reeled off 23 straight wins—also had innovation on their side: While most players relied on two-handed set shots with their feet on the floor, Wyoming guard Kenny Sailors would elevate and dominate with his jump shots. In the championship match (the first to be played in Madison Square Garden), Komenich held Mahnken to six points—while Sailors scored 16 and earned MOP honors in Wyoming's 46-34 victory.

In the first of three annual Red Cross benefit games—a sort of collegiate Super Bowl between the winners of the NCAA Tournament and the NIT—Wyoming beat St. John's, 52-47, in overtime at Madison Square Garden. The winner of the NCAA Tourney won the game all three years.

Major Conference Standings

BIG SIX	Conference W	L	Pct	Overall W	L	Pct
Kansas	10	0	1.000	22	6	.786
Oklahoma○	7	3	.700	18	9	.667
Missouri	5	5	.500	7	10	.412
Nebraska	5	5	.500	6	10	.375
Iowa State	2	8	.200	7	9	.438
Kansas State	1	9	.100	6	14	.300

BIG TEN	Conference W	L	Pct	Overall W	L	Pct
Illinois	12	0	1.000	17	1	.944
Indiana	11	2	.846	18	2	.900
Northwestern	7	5	.583	8	9	.471
Wisconsin	6	6	.500	12	9	.571
Purdue	6	6	.500	9	11	.450
Minnesota	5	7	.417	10	9	.526
Ohio State	5	7	.417	8	9	.471
Michigan	4	8	.333	10	8	.556
Iowa	3	9	.250	7	10	.412
Chicago	0	9	.000	0	18	.000

BORDER	Conference W	L	Pct	Overall W	L	Pct
West Texas A&M	10	0	1.000	15	7	.682
Arizona	11	1	.917	22	2	.917
Texas Tech	7	5	.583	13	10	.565
Texas Western	4	4	.500	11	6	.647
Arizona State	6	6	.500	10	9	.526
Northern Arizona	1	7	.125	4	8	.333
New Mexico	1	11	.083	3	17	.150
Hardin-Simmons	0	6	.000	1	9	.100

IVY	Conference W	L	Pct	Overall W	L	Pct
Dartmouth○	11	1	.917	20	3	.870
Princeton	9	3	.750	14	6	.700
Penn	6	6	.500	14	7	.667
Cornell	6	6	.500	7	15	.318
Columbia	5	7	.417	10	8	.556
Harvard	4	8	.333	12	14	.462
Yale	1	11	.083	6	17	.261

METRO NY	Conference W	L	Pct	Overall W	L	Pct
St. John's□	6	1	.857	21	3	.875
Manhattan□	5	2	.714	18	3	.857
Fordham□	4	2	.667	16	6	.727
NYU○	3	2	.600	16	6	.727
Hofstra	3	2	.600	15	6	.714
CCNY	2	5	.286	8	10	.444
St. Francis (NY)	1	5	.167	13	7	.650
Brooklyn	0	5	.000	6	11	.353

MIDDLE THREE	Conference W	L	Pct	Overall W	L	Pct
Rutgers	3	1	.750	7	9	.438
Lafayette	2	2	.500	7	6	.538
Lehigh	1	3	.250	5	10	.333

MISSOURI VALLEY	Conference W	L	Pct	Overall W	L	Pct
Creighton□	10	0	1.000	16	1	.941
Oklahoma A&M	7	3	.700	14	10	.583
Wash.-St. Louis	7	3	.700	9	10	.474
Saint Louis	3	7	.300	11	10	.524
Drake	3	7	.300	8	9	.471
Tulsa	0	10	.000	0	10	.000

BIG SEVEN	Conference W	L	Pct	Overall W	L	Pct
Wyoming○	4	0	1.000	31	2	.939
BYU	7	1	.875	15	7	.682
Utah State	4	4	.500	14	7	.667
Utah	1	7	.125	10	12	.455
Colorado State	0	4	.000	7	9	.438

NEW ENGLAND	Conference W	L	Pct	Overall W	L	Pct
Rhode Island	7	1	.875	16	3	.842
Connecticut	5	3	.625	8	7	.533
Maine	4	4	.500	9	6	.600
Northeastern	2	6	.250	7	12	.368
New Hampshire	2	6	.250	4	14	.222

PACIFIC COAST	Conference W	L	Pct	Overall W	L	Pct
North						
Washington○	12	4	.750	24	7	.774
Oregon	10	6	.625	19	10	.655
Washington State	9	7	.563	19	11	.633
Oregon State	8	8	.500	19	9	.679
Idaho	1	15	.063	14	20	.412
South						
Southern California	7	1	.875	23	5	.821
UCLA	4	4	.500	14	7	.667
Stanford	4	4	.500	10	11	.476
California	1	7	.125	9	15	.375

Playoff: **Washington d. Southern California 2-0** in a best-of-three series for the title

SEC	Conference W	L	Pct	Overall W	L	Pct
Kentucky	8	1	.889	17	6	.739
LSU	11	2	.846	18	4	.818
Tennessee	6	3	.667	14	4	.778
Mississippi State	13	7	.650	14	8	.636
Georgia Tech	7	4	.636	11	5	.688
Vanderbilt	9	7	.563	10	8	.556
Alabama	9	9	.500	10	10	.500
Mississippi	6	8	.429	8	10	.444
Tulane	4	8	.333	4	9	.308
Georgia	1	8	.111	4	13	.235
Auburn	1	12	.077	1	14	.067
Florida	0	6	.000	8	7	.533

Tournament: **Tennessee d. Kentucky 33-30**

SOUTHERN	Conference W	L	Pct	Overall W	L	Pct
Duke	12	1	.923	20	6	.769
George Washington	8	2	.800	17	6	.739
South Carolina	6	3	.667	13	6	.684
Davidson	7	4	.636	18	6	.750
The Citadel	5	3	.625	8	6	.571
William and Mary	6	4	.600	11	10	.524
VMI	7	5	.583	8	8	.500
NC State	7	5	.583	7	9	.438
Richmond	4	4	.500	11	5	.688
Maryland	5	5	.500	8	8	.500
North Carolina	8	9	.471	12	10	.545
Virginia Tech	3	6	.333	7	7	.500
Washington and Lee	2	10	.167	7	12	.368
Wake Forest	1	10	.091	1	10	.091
Clemson	0	10	.000	3	13	.188

Tournament: **George Washington d. Duke 56-40**

SOUTHWEST	Conference W	L	Pct	Overall W	L	Pct
Texas○	9	3	.750	19	7	.731
Rice□	9	3	.750	17	9	.654
Arkansas	8	4	.667	19	7	.731
TCU	5	7	.417	18	9	.667
SMU	4	8	.333	10	8	.556
Texas A&M	4	8	.333	11	11	.500
Baylor	3	9	.250	6	14	.300

INDEPENDENTS	Overall W	L	Pct
Villanova	19	2	.905
Notre Dame	18	2	.900
Western Kentucky□	24	3	.889
Seton Hall	16	2	.889
Rochester (NY)	12	2	.857
Toledo□	22	4	.846
Akron	18	4	.818
Saint Joseph's	18	4	.818
Georgetown○	22	5	.815
DePaul○	19	5	.792
Penn State	15	4	.789
Western Michigan	15	4	.789
Bowling Green	18	5	.783
Washington and Jefferson□	18	5	.783
Nevada	14	4	.778
Montana State	17	5	.773
Valparaiso	17	5	.773
Niagara	20	6	.769
Indiana State	13	4	.765
Detroit	15	5	.750
Denver	19	8	.704
Long Island	13	6	.684
Siena	13	6	.684
West Virginia	14	7	.667
Pittsburgh	10	5	.667
Duquesne	12	7	.632
Wichita State	12	7	.632
Miami (OH)	10	6	.625
Montana	15	9	.625
Muhlenberg	13	8	.619
Ohio	11	7	.611
San Francisco	13	9	.591
Marshall	10	7	.588
Saint Mary's (CA)	12	9	.571
La Salle	13	10	.565
Santa Clara	10	9	.526
Canisius	11	9	.550
Loyola-Chicago	12	10	.545
Dayton	9	8	.529
Kent State	12	12	.500
Temple	11	11	.500
Cincinnati	9	10	.474
Marquette	9	10	.474
St. Bonaventure	8	9	.471
Brown	9	11	.450
Syracuse	8	10	.444
Rutgers	7	9	.438
Geneva	9	12	.429
Navy	6	8	.429
Bradley	8	11	.421
Colgate	5	7	.417
Bucknell	5	8	.385
Virginia	8	13	.381
Xavier	6	10	.375
Army	5	10	.333
Loyola (MD)	7	14	.333
Butler	4	9	.308
Boston U.	3	10	.231
Loyola Marymount	3	13	.188
Holy Cross	1	5	.167
Michigan State	2	14	.125

⊛ Automatic NCAA Tournament bid ○ At-large NCAA Tournament bid □ NIT appearance ❍ Team record doesn't reflect games forfeited or vacated. For adjusted record, see p. 521.

PREMO-PORRETTA POWER POLL

	SCHOOL	RECORD
1	**Illinois**	17-1
2	**Wyoming (NCAA champion)**	31-2
3	**Notre Dame**	18-2
4	**St. John's (NIT champion)**	21-3
5	**Indiana**	18-2
6	**Creighton**	19-2#
7	**Georgetown**	22-5
8	**DePaul**	19-5
9	**Dartmouth**	20-3
10	**Western Kentucky**	24-3
11	**Manhattan**	18-3
12	**Toledo**	22-4
13	**Penn State**	15-4
14	**Kansas**	22-6
15	**Fordham**	16-6
16	**Washington and Jefferson**	18-5
17	**Villanova**	19-2
18	**Seton Hall**	16-2
19	**Kentucky**	17-6
20	**Niagara**	20-6
21	**Tennessee**	14-5#
22	**NYU**	17-6#
23	**Saint Joseph's**	18-4
24	**Washington**	24-7
25	**Rice**	17-9

CONSENSUS ALL-AMERICAS

FIRST TEAM

PLAYER	CL	POS	HT	SCHOOL	PPG
Ed Beisser	SR	C	6-6½	Creighton	10.9
Charlie B. Black	SO	F	6-4	Kansas	11.4
Harry Boykoff	SO	C	6-9	St. John's	16.6
Bill Tom Closs	SR	C	6-5	Rice	17.0
Andrew Phillip	JR	G	6-2	Illinois	16.9
Kenny Sailors	JR	G	5-10	Wyoming	15.0
George Senesky	SR	G/F	6-2	Saint Joseph's	23.4

SECOND TEAM

PLAYER	CL	POS	HT	SCHOOL	PPG
Gale Bishop	SO	F	6-3	Washington State	13.8
Otto Graham	JR	F	6-0	Northwestern	13.9
John Kotz	SR	F	6-3	Wisconsin	14.7
Bob Rensberger	SR	G	6-1	Notre Dame	9.3
Gene Rock	JR	F	5-9	Southern California	12.6
Gerald Tucker	JR	C	6-4	Oklahoma	14.3

SELECTORS: CONVERSE YEARBOOK, HELMS FOUNDATION, PIC MAGAZINE, SPORTING NEWS

1943 NCAA TOURNAMENT

EAST

REGIONAL SEMIFINALS
- Georgetown **55**, NYU **36** (A)
- DePaul **46**, Dartmouth **35**

REGIONAL FINALS
- Georgetown **53**, DePaul **49** (B)

WEST

REGIONAL SEMIFINALS
- Texas **59**, Washington **55**
- Wyoming **53**, Oklahoma **50**

REGIONAL FINALS
- Texas **54**, Wyoming **58**

NATIONAL FINAL — NEW YORK CITY

Wyoming 46
Georgetown 34

Kenny Sailors, the Cowboys' junior guard and a pioneer of the modern-day jump shot, scores a game-high 16 against Georgetown. He would soon join the Marines. In a post-NCAA Tournament Red Cross charity event at Madison Square Garden, Wyoming beats NIT champ St. John's, 52-47, in overtime.

East Regional Third Place Dartmouth d. NYU 51-49
West Regional Third Place Oklahoma d. Washington 48-43

A NYU's Sam Mele (five points) is the first man to appear in the Tournament and go on to play Major League Baseball (10 years with four AL teams and Twins manager, 1961-67).

B Ray Meyer coaches DePaul to the regional finals in his first of 42 seasons at the school. George Mikan, in his only NCAA Tournament, totals 31 points in two games for the Blue Demons.

Record differs from the school's and/or the NCAA's because it includes noncollegiate competition or because the outcome of some games is in dispute.

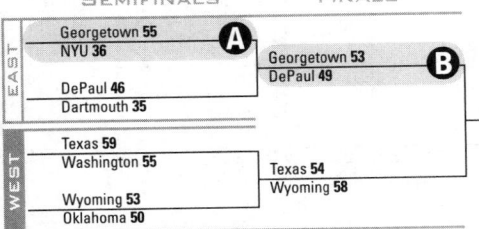

Tournament Leaders

INDIVIDUAL LEADERS

Scoring

	CL	POS	G	PTS	PPG
1 **John Hargis**, Texas	JR	F	2	59	29.5
2 **Milo Komenich**, Wyoming	JR	C	3	48	16.0
3 **George Mikan**, DePaul	FR	C	2	31	15.5
4 **Dick Reich**, Oklahoma	SO	F	2	30	15.0
5 **V.C. Overall**, Texas	SR	F	2	29	14.5
Gerald Tucker, Oklahoma	JR	C	2	29	14.5
7 **John Mahnken**, Georgetown	FR	C	3	43	14.3
8 **Bill Morris**, Washington	JR	G	2	27	13.5
Robert Myers, Dartmouth	JR	F	2	27	13.5
10 **Kenny Sailors**, Wyoming	JR	G	3	36	12.0

Minimum: 2 games

Free Throw Pct

	CL	POS	G	FT	FTA	PCT
1 **Alva Paine**, Oklahoma	SO	G	2	5	5	100.0
2 **Sam Mele**, NYU	SO	G	2	6	7	85.7
3 **Gerald Tucker**, Oklahoma	JR	C	2	7	9	77.8
4 **Bill Hassett**, Georgetown	SO	G	3	10	13	76.9
5 **Al Grenert**, NYU	JR	F	2	6	8	75.0

Minimum: 5 made

Field Goals Per Game

	CL	POS	G	FG	FGPG
1 **John Hargis**, Texas	JR	F	2	21	10.5
2 **Milo Komenich**, Wyoming	JR	C	3	22	7.3
3 **John Mahnken**, Georgetown	FR	C	3	20	6.7
4 **Robert Myers**, Dartmouth	JR	F	2	12	6.0
5 **John Jorgensen**, DePaul	SO	F	2	11	5.5
Dick Reich, Oklahoma	SO	F	2	11	5.5
Gerald Tucker, Oklahoma	JR	C	2	11	5.5

Minimum: 2 games

TEAM LEADERS

Scoring

	G	PTS	PPG
1 **Texas**	2	113	56.5
2 **Wyoming**	3	157	52.3
3 **Washington**	2	98	49.0
Oklahoma	2	98	49.0
5 **DePaul**	2	95	47.5
6 **Georgetown**	3	142	47.3
7 **Dartmouth**	2	86	43.0
8 **NYU**	2	85	42.5

Minimum: 2 games

FG Per Game

	G	FG	FGPG
1 **Wyoming**	3	67	22.3
2 **Texas**	2	41	20.5
3 **Washington**	2	40	20.0
4 **Georgetown**	3	58	19.3
5 **Oklahoma**	2	37	18.5

FT Pct

	G	FT	FTA	PCT
1 **Oklahoma**	2	24	34	70.6
2 **DePaul**	2	23	33	69.7
3 **Texas**	2	31	45	68.9
4 **NYU**	2	19	29	65.5
5 **Georgetown**	3	26	40	65.0

Minimum: 2 games

TOURNAMENT MOP

PLAYER	CL	POS	HT	SCHOOL	FG	FT	PPG
Kenny Sailors	JR	G	5-10	Wyoming	14	8-13	12.0

1943 NCAA TOURNAMENT BOX SCORES

55-36 (Elite 8)

	1H	2H
Georgetown	32	23
NYU	19	17

GEORGETOWN	MIN	FG	3FG	FT	REB	A	ST	BL	PF	TP
John Mahnken	-	10	-	0-1	-	-	-	-	1	20
Danny Kraus	-	4	-	0-0	-	-	-	-	1	8
Bill Hassett	-	2	-	3-3	-	-	-	-	1	7
Lloyd Potolicchio	-	3	-	0-0	-	-	-	-	0	6
Dan Gabbianelli	-	2	-	1-1	-	-	-	-	3	5
Jim Reilly	-	1	-	2-3	-	-	-	-	2	4
Bob Duffey	-	1	-	1-1	-	-	-	-	0	3
Bill Feeney	-	1	-	0-0	-	-	-	-	0	2
Frank Finnerty	-	0	-	0-0	-	-	-	-	0	0
Henry Hyde	-	0	-	0-0	-	-	-	-	0	0
TOTALS	-	**24**	-	**7-9**	-	-	-	-	**8**	**55**
Percentages				77.8						

Coach: Elmer Ripley

NYU	MIN	FG	3FG	FT	REB	A	ST	BL	PF	TP
Stanley Danto	-	5	-	1-2	-	-	-	-	1	11
Bob Maher	-	4	-	1-2	-	-	-	-	3	9
Sam Mele	-	2	-	1-1	-	-	-	-	0	5
Al Grenert	-	1	-	2-4	-	-	-	-	1	4
John Simmons	-	1	-	1-3	-	-	-	-	0	3
Jerome Fleishman	-	1	-	0-0	-	-	-	-	1	2
Harry Leggat	-	1	-	0-0	-	-	-	-	1	2
Charles Heiser	-	0	-	0-0	-	-	-	-	0	0
TOTALS	-	**15**	-	**6-12**	-	-	-	-	**7**	**36**
Percentages				50.0						

Coach: Howard Cann

Officials: Burns, Nucatola

46-35 (Elite 8)

	1H	2H
DePaul	26	20
Dartmouth	14	21

DEPAUL	MIN	FG	3FG	FT	REB	A	ST	BL	PF	TP
George Mikan	-	7	-	6-8	-	-	-	-	3	20
John Jorgensen	-	5	-	0-0	-	-	-	-	3	10
Jimmy Cominsky	-	3	-	3-4	-	-	-	-	3	9
Tony Kelly	-	1	-	2-2	-	-	-	-	2	4
Billy Ryan	-	1	-	1-2	-	-	-	-	2	3
Ray Crowley	-	0	-	0-0	-	-	-	-	0	0
Billy Donato	-	0	-	0-0	-	-	-	-	0	0
Mel Frailey	-	0	-	0-0	-	-	-	-	1	0
Richard Starzyk	-	0	-	0-1	-	-	-	-	4	0
Dick Triptow	-	0	-	0-0	-	-	-	-	0	0
Frank Wiscons	-	0	-	0-0	-	-	-	-	0	0
TOTALS	-	**17**	-	**12-17**	-	-	-	-	**18**	**46**
Percentages				70.6						

Coach: Ray Meyer

DARTMOUTH	MIN	FG	3FG	FT	REB	A	ST	BL	PF	TP
Aud Brindley	-	5	-	0-3	-	-	-	-	1	10
George Munroe	-	3	-	2-4	-	-	-	-	0	8
James Olsen	-	2	-	3-3	-	-	-	-	4	7
Robert Myers	-	1	-	3-5	-	-	-	-	4	5
James Coleman	-	1	-	1-1	-	-	-	-	1	3
Stanley Skaug	-	0	-	2-3	-	-	-	-	3	2
James Briggs	-	0	-	0-0	-	-	-	-	0	0
John Carroll	-	0	-	0-0	-	-	-	-	0	0
James Monahan	-	0	-	0-0	-	-	-	-	0	0
TOTALS	-	**12**	-	**11-19**	-	-	-	-	**13**	**35**
Percentages				57.9						

Coach: Osborne Cowles

Officials: Kennedy, Litwack

59-55 (Elite 8)

	1H	2H
Texas	28	31
Washington	33	22

TEXAS	MIN	FG	3FG	FT	REB	A	ST	BL	PF	TP
John Hargis	-	10	-	10-12	-	-	-	-	3	30
V.C. Overall	-	5	-	5-6	-	-	-	-	4	15
Roy Cox	-	3	-	0-0	-	-	-	-	0	6
Frank Brahaney	-	1	-	2-3	-	-	-	-	4	4
Jack Fitzgerald	-	1	-	0-1	-	-	-	-	4	2
John Langdon	-	1	-	0-0	-	-	-	-	4	2
Atwell Goss	-	0	-	0-0	-	-	-	-	0	0
Edward Kemp	-	0	-	0-0	-	-	-	-	1	0
Dudley Wright	-	0	-	0-0	-	-	-	-	1	0
TOTALS	-	**21**	-	**17-22**	-	-	-	-	**21**	**59**
Percentages				77.3						

Coach: Bully Gilstrap

WASHINGTON	MIN	FG	3FG	FT	REB	A	ST	BL	PF	TP
Bill Morris	-	8	-	6-9	-	-	-	-	2	22
Doug Ford	-	3	-	4-5	-	-	-	-	2	10
Bob Bird	-	3	-	0-0	-	-	-	-	2	6
Bill Gissberg	-	2	-	2-2	-	-	-	-	2	6
Chuck Gilmur	-	2	-	1-3	-	-	-	-	4	5
Merlin Gilbertson	-	2	-	0-0	-	-	-	-	4	4
Bill Taylor	-	1	-	0-3	-	-	-	-	1	2
Webster Brown	-	0	-	0-0	-	-	-	-	0	0
Dale Grondsdahl	-	0	-	0-0	-	-	-	-	0	0
Harry Nelson	-	0	-	0-3	-	-	-	-	1	0
Chuck Sheaffer	-	0	-	0-0	-	-	-	-	4	0
TOTALS	-	**21**	-	**13-25**	-	-	-	-	**22**	**55**
Percentages				52.0						

Coach: Clarence "Hec" Edmundson

Officials: Doubenmeier, O'Sullivan

53-50 (ELITE 8)

	1H	2H
Wyoming	22	31
Oklahoma	25	25

WYOMING	MIN	FG	3FG	FT	REB	A	ST	BL	PF	TP
Milo Komenich	-	10	-	2-3	-	-	-	-	2	22
Jim Weir	-	6	-	2-2	-	-	-	-	3	14
Kenny Sailors	-	4	-	0-1	-	-	-	-	2	8
Floyd Volker	-	3	-	0-0	-	-	-	-	4	6
James Collins	-	1	-	0-0	-	-	-	-	1	2
Lewis Roney	-	0	-	1-1	-	-	-	-	2	1
Earl Ray	-	0	-	0-0	-	-	-	-	0	0
Jim Reese	-	0	-	0-0	-	-	-	-	0	0
Don Waite	-	0	-	0-0	-	-	-	-	0	0
TOTALS	**-**	**24**	**-**	**5-7**	**-**	**-**	**-**	**-**	**14**	**53**
Percentages				71.4						

Coach: Everett Shelton

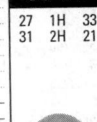

OKLAHOMA	MIN	FG	3FG	FT	REB	A	ST	BL	PF	TP
Dick Reich	-	5	-	7-12	-	-	-	-	1	17
Allie Paine	-	5	-	1-1	-	-	-	-	4	11
Gerald Tucker	-	5	-	1-1	-	-	-	-	4	11
Paul Heap	-	1	-	1-1	-	-	-	-	0	3
James Marteney	-	1	-	0-0	-	-	-	-	0	2
Simon Mitchell	-	1	-	0-0	-	-	-	-	0	2
Charles Pugsley	-	1	-	0-0	-	-	-	-	0	2
Tom Rousey	-	0	-	2-4	-	-	-	-	0	2
Bob McCurdy	-	0	-	0-0	-	-	-	-	0	0
TOTALS	**-**	**19**	**-**	**12-19**	**-**	**-**	**-**	**-**	**9**	**50**
Percentages				63.2						

Coach: Bruce Drake

Officials: Curtis, Leith

53-49 (FINAL 4)

	1H	2H
Georgetown	23	30
DePaul	28	21

GEORGETOWN	MIN	FG	3FG	FT	REB	A	ST	BL	PF	TP
John Mahnken	-	8	-	1-2	-	-	-	-	4	17
Bill Hassett	-	2	-	7-7	-	-	-	-	0	11
Lloyd Potolicchio	-	5	-	1-2	-	-	-	-	1	11
Dan Gabbianelli	-	3	-	0-0	-	-	-	-	1	6
Danny Kraus	-	1	-	4-6	-	-	-	-	3	6
Henry Hyde	-	1	-	0-0	-	-	-	-	2	2
Bob Duffey	-	0	-	0-0	-	-	-	-	0	0
Bill Feeney	-	0	-	0-0	-	-	-	-	2	0
Jim Reilly	-	0	-	0-0	-	-	-	-	0	0
TOTALS	**-**	**20**	**-**	**13-17**	**-**	**-**	**-**	**-**	**13**	**53**
Percentages				76.5						

Coach: Elmer Ripley

DEPAUL	MIN	FG	3FG	FT	REB	A	ST	BL	PF	TP
John Jorgensen	-	6	-	2-3	-	-	-	-	2	14
Jimmy Cominsky	-	5	-	1-3	-	-	-	-	2	11
George Mikan	-	3	-	5-7	-	-	-	-	1	11
Richard Starzyk	-	3	-	1-1	-	-	-	-	3	7
Tony Kelly	-	2	-	2-2	-	-	-	-	4	6
Mel Frailey	-	0	-	0-0	-	-	-	-	0	0
Billy Ryan	-	0	-	0-0	-	-	-	-	3	0
TOTALS	**-**	**19**	**-**	**11-16**	**-**	**-**	**-**	**-**	**15**	**49**
Percentages				68.8						

Coach: Ray Meyer

Officials: Kennedy, Nucatola

58-54 (FINAL 4)

	1H	2H
Wyoming	27	31
Texas	33	21

WYOMING	MIN	FG	3FG	FT	REB	A	ST	BL	PF	TP
Milo Komenich	-	8	-	1-4	-	-	-	-	2	17
Jim Weir	-	6	-	1-1	-	-	-	-	3	13
Kenny Sailors	-	4	-	4-6	-	-	-	-	3	12
Floyd Volker	-	3	-	1-3	-	-	-	-	4	7
James Collins	-	2	-	1-2	-	-	-	-	2	5
Lewis Roney	-	1	-	2-3	-	-	-	-	3	4
Don Waite	-	0	-	0-0	-	-	-	-	1	0
TOTALS	**-**	**24**	**-**	**10-19**	**-**	**-**	**-**	**-**	**18**	**58**
Percentages				52.6						

Coach: Everett Shelton

TEXAS	MIN	FG	3FG	FT	REB	A	ST	BL	PF	TP
John Hargis	-	11	-	7-12	-	-	-	-	3	29
V.C. Overall	-	5	-	4-7	-	-	-	-	3	14
John Langdon	-	1	-	2-3	-	-	-	-	2	4
Dudley Wright	-	1	-	1-1	-	-	-	-	2	3
Frank Brahaney	-	1	-	0-0	-	-	-	-	3	2
Jack Fitzgerald	-	1	-	0-0	-	-	-	-	4	2
Roy Cox	-	0	-	0-0	-	-	-	-	3	0
TOTALS	**-**	**20**	**-**	**14-23**	**-**	**-**	**-**	**-**	**20**	**54**
Percentages				60.9						

Coach: Bully Gilstrap

Officials: O'Sullivan, Leith
Attendance: 13,300

46-34 (NCAA FINAL 1943)

	1H	2H
Wyoming	13	33
Georgetown	16	18

WYOMING	MIN	FG	3FG	FT	REB	A	ST	BL	PF	TP
Kenny Sailors	-	6	-	4-6	-	-	-	-	2	16
Milo Komenich	-	4	-	1-4	-	-	-	-	2	9
James Collins	-	4	-	0-1	-	-	-	-	1	8
Floyd Volker	-	2	-	1-2	-	-	-	-	3	5
Jim Weir	-	2	-	1-3	-	-	-	-	2	5
Jim Reese	-	1	-	0-0	-	-	-	-	0	2
Lewis Roney	-	0	-	1-2	-	-	-	-	1	1
Don Waite	-	0	-	0-0	-	-	-	-	0	0
TOTALS	**-**	**19**	**-**	**8-18**	**-**	**-**	**-**	**-**	**11**	**46**
Percentages				44.4						

Coach: Everett Shelton

GEORGETOWN	MIN	FG	3FG	FT	REB	A	ST	BL	PF	TP
Bill Feeney	-	4	-	0-0	-	-	-	-	1	8
Bill Hassett	-	3	-	0-3	-	-	-	-	4	6
John Mahnken	-	2	-	2-3	-	-	-	-	2	6
Dan Gabbianelli	-	1	-	2-3	-	-	-	-	3	4
Danny Kraus	-	2	-	0-1	-	-	-	-	3	4
Lloyd Potolicchio	-	1	-	2-3	-	-	-	-	1	4
Jim Reilly	-	1	-	0-0	-	-	-	-	0	2
Bob Duffey	-	0	-	0-1	-	-	-	-	0	0
Henry Hyde	-	0	-	0-0	-	-	-	-	0	0
TOTALS	**-**	**14**	**-**	**6-14**	**-**	**-**	**-**	**-**	**14**	**34**
Percentages				42.9						

Coach: Elmer Ripley

Officials: Kennedy, Begovich
Attendance: 13,300

National Invitation Tournament (NIT)

Quarterfinals: St. John's d. Rice 51-49, Fordham d. Western Kentucky 60-58, Toledo d. Manhattan 54-47, Washington and Jefferson d. Creighton 43-42
Semifinals: Toledo d. Washington and Jefferson 46-39, St. John's d. Fordham 69-43
Third place: Washington and Jefferson d. Fordham 39-34
Championship: St. John's d. Toledo, 48-27
MVP: Harry Boykoff, St. John's

Red Cross Benefit

Wyoming (NCAA champ) vs. St. John's (NIT champ), April 1, 1943

52-47

	1H	2H	OT
Wyoming	30	16	6
St. John's	23	23	1

WYOMING	FG	FT	TP
Milo Komenich	8	4	20
Jim Weir	5	3	13
Kenny Sailors	5	1	11
Floyd Volker	3	1	7
James Collins	0	1	1
Jim Reese	0	0	0
Lewis Roney	0	0	0
Don Waite	0	0	0
TOTALS	**21**	**10**	**52**

Coach: Everett Shelton

ST. JOHN'S	FG	FT	TP
Harry Boykoff	6	5	17
Larry Baxter	5	5	15
Al Moschetti	4	0	8
Andrew Levane	2	1	5
Hy Gotkin	1	0	2
Frank Plantamura	0	0	0
Ray Wertis	0	0	0
TOTALS	**18**	**11**	**47**

Coach: Joe Lapchick

Officials: Pat Kennedy, Joe Burns
Attendance: 18,316

1943-44: War Spoils

So many players on defending champ Wyoming's squad enlisted in the military or were drafted that the Cowboys could not field a team. Dartmouth benefited from the war effort when New York-area players Dick McGuire, Bob Gale, Harry Leggat and Walter Mercer were stationed at the Navy training base in Hanover, N.H. The quartet helped take the Big Green back to the NCAA Final.

Southwest Conference co-champion Rice had to decline an NCAA Tournament invitation because of players' military commitments; the other co-champ, Arkansas, had to withdraw after two players were struck by a car while changing a tire.

Utah at first declined an NCAA invitation in favor of the NIT, but after its first-round loss to Kentucky the team was asked to replace Arkansas in the NCAA field. With their new life, the Utes managed to wind up in the NCAA Final, where a long jumper by Herb Wilkinson in overtime enabled them to squeak past Dartmouth, 42-40. Coach Vadal Peterson's team is the only NCAA champion to have started five freshmen.

Major Conference Standings

BIG SIX	Conference			Overall		
	W	L	PCT	W	L	PCT
Iowa State○	9	1	.900	14	4	.778
Oklahoma	9	1	.900	15	8	.652
Kansas	5	5	.500	17	9	.654
Missouri○	5	5	.500	10	9	.526
Kansas State	1	9	.100	7	15	.318
Nebraska	1	9	.100	2	13	.133

BIG TEN	Conference			Overall		
	W	L	PCT	W	L	PCT
Ohio State○	10	2	.833	15	6	.714
Iowa	9	3	.750	14	4	.778
Wisconsin	9	3	.750	12	9	.571
Northwestern	8	4	.667	12	7	.632
Purdue	8	4	.667	11	10	.524
Illinois	5	7	.417	11	9	.550
Michigan	5	7	.417	8	10	.444
Minnesota	2	10	.167	7	14	.333
Indiana	2	10	.167	7	15	.318
Chicago	0	8	.000	1	19	.050

BORDER	Conference			Overall		
	W	L	PCT	W	L	PCT
New Mexico	3	0	1.000	11	2	.846
Texas Tech	0	3	.000	5	18	.217
Northern Arizona	-	-	-	2	0	1.000
Arizona	-	-	-	12	2	.857

IVY	Conference			Overall		
	W	L	PCT	W	L	PCT
Dartmouth○	8	0	1.000	19	2	.905
Penn	6	2	.750	10	4	.714
Columbia	2	6	.250	9	10	.474
Cornell	2	6	.250	9	11	.450
Princeton	2	6	.250	6	12	.333

PACIFIC COAST	Conference			Overall		
	W	L	PCT	W	L	PCT
North						
Washington	15	1	.938	26	6	.813
Oregon	11	5	.688	16	10	.615
Oregon State	5	11	.313	8	16	.333
Idaho	5	11	.313	7	16	.304
Washington State	4	12	.250	8	19	.296
South						
California	4	0	1.000	7	3	.700
UCLA	3	3	.500	10	10	.500
Southern California	1	5	.167	8	12	.400

Note: No playoff was held; Washington and California shared title

SEC	Conference			Overall		
	W	L	PCT	W	L	PCT
Tulane	4	0	1.000	16	6	.727
Georgia Tech	2	0	1.000	14	4	.778
Georgia	0	2	.000	7	10	.412
LSU	0	4	.000	10	15	.400
Kentucky□	-	-	-	19	2	.905
Vanderbilt	-	-	-	12	3	.800

Tournament: **Kentucky d. Tulane 62-46**

SOUTHERN	Conference			Overall		
	W	L	PCT	W	L	PCT
North Carolina	9	1	.900	17	10	.630
Virginia Tech	4	1	.800	11	4	.733
Duke	4	2	.667	13	13	.500
Maryland	2	1	.667	4	14	.222
Richmond	3	2	.600	7	6	.538
Davidson	3	4	.429	16	7	.696
South Carolina	1	2	.333	13	2	.867
Clemson	1	2	.333	1	10	.091
NC State	2	5	.286	5	13	.278
William and Mary	1	3	.250	10	11	.476
The Citadel	0	1	.000	2	3	.400
VMI	0	5	.000	0	14	.000

Tournament: **Duke d. North Carolina 44-27**

SOUTHWEST	Conference			Overall		
	W	L	PCT	W	L	PCT
Arkansas	11	1	.917	16	8	.667
Rice	11	1	.917	15	5	.750
Texas	6	6	.500	14	11	.560
SMU	6	6	.500	8	9	.471
TCU	6	6	.500	9	12	.429
Baylor	2	10	.167	6	12	.333
Texas A&M	0	12	.000	2	15	.118

INDEPENDENTS	Overall		
	W	L	PCT
Army	15	0	1.000
Bowling Green□	22	4	.846
DePaul□	22	4	.846
Gonzaga	22	4	.846
Utah○	22	4	.846
Miami (OH)	10	2	.833
Oklahoma A&M□	27	6	.818
Indiana State	17	4	.810
Muhlenberg□	20	5	.800
Long Island	12	3	.800
Loyola Marymount	4	1	.800
Western Michigan	15	4	.789
St. John's□	18	5	.783
Bucknell	9	3	.750
Rochester (NY)	11	4	.733
Tulane	16	6	.727
Saint Joseph's	18	7	.720
Canisius□	15	6	.714
Navy	10	4	.714
Catholic○	17	7	.708
Wash.-St. Louis	12	5	.706
Rhode Island	14	6	.700
Yale	14	6	.700
Lafayette	7	3	.700
Colgate	11	5	.688
Pacific	13	6	.684
Valparaiso	17	8	.680
Marshall	15	7	.682
Detroit	13	7	.650
Washington and Jefferson□	11	6	.647
Temple○	14	9	.609
St. Francis (NY)	10	6	.625
Tulsa	5	3	.625
BYU	3	2	.600
Pepperdine○	20	14	.588
Western Kentucky	13	9	.591
Virginia	11	8	.579
Marquette	8	6	.571
Ohio	9	7	.563
Loyola (MD)	15	12	.556
Cincinnati	6	5	.545
Penn State	8	7	.533
Connecticut	10	9	.526
Notre Dame	10	9	.526
Louisville	10	10	.500
La Salle	8	8	.500
Northeastern	8	8	.500
NYU	7	7	.500
Pittsburgh	7	7	.500
Villanova	9	11	.450
Delaware	7	9	.438
Holy Cross	6	8	.429
San Francisco	8	11	.421
West Virginia	8	11	.421
Brown	10	14	.417
Maine	4	6	.400
Georgia	5	9	.357
CCNY	6	11	.353
Drake	7	13	.350
Denver	6	18	.333
Brooklyn	6	14	.300
Toledo	5	13	.278
Lehigh	4	12	.250
Rider	3	12	.200
Tennessee Tech	3	13	.188
Montana	2	10	.167
Harvard	2	12	.143
Northern Colorado	1	13	.071

⊛ Automatic NCAA Tournament bid ○ At-large NCAA Tournament bid □ NIT appearance ⊗ Team record doesn't reflect games forfeited or vacated. For adjusted record, see p. 521.

PREMO-PORRETTA POWER POLL

	SCHOOL	RECORD
1	**Army**	15-0
2	**Utah (NCAA champion)**	22-4
3	**Kentucky**	19-2
4	**Dartmouth**	19-2
5	**DePaul**	22-4
6	**St. John's (NIT champion)**	18-5
7	**Oklahoma A&M**	27-6
8	**Bowling Green**	22-4
9	**Gonzaga**	21-2#
10	**Ohio State**	14-7#
11	**Western Michigan**	15-4
12	**Iowa State**	14-4
13	**Denison**	18-2
14	**Rice**	15-5
15	**Muhlenberg**	20-5
16	**Washington**	26-6
17	**Penn**	10-4
18	**Navy**	10-4
19	**Northwestern**	12-7
20	**Iowa**	14-4
21	**Illinois**	11-9
22	**Saint Joseph's**	18-7
23	**Miami (OH)**	10-2
24	**Temple**	14-9
25	**Notre Dame**	10-9

CONSENSUS ALL-AMERICAS

FIRST TEAM

PLAYER	CL	POS	HT	SCHOOL	PPG
Bob Brannum	FR	C	6-5	Kentucky	12.1
Aud Brindley	JR	F/C	6-4	Dartmouth	16.1
Otto Graham	SR	F	6-0	Northwestern	11.0
Leo Klier	JR	F	6-1	Notre Dame	15.4
Bob Kurland	SO	C	7-0	Oklahoma A&M	13.5
George Mikan	SO	C	6-9	DePaul	18.6
Alva Paine	JR	G	6-0	Oklahoma	11.0*

SECOND TEAM

PLAYER	CL	POS	HT	SCHOOL	PPG
Bob Dille	SO	F	6-3	Valparaiso	16.9
Arnie Ferrin	FR	G/F	6-4	Utah	12.5
Don Grate	JR	G	6-2	Ohio State	12.9
Dale Hall	SO	G/F	5-11	Army	18.2
Bill Henry	SO	C	6-8	Rice	17.6
Dick Triptow	SR	G/F	6-0	DePaul	11.3

SELECTORS: CONVERSE YEARBOOK, HELMS FOUNDATION, PIC MAGAZINE, SPORTING NEWS

*Conference games only

1944 NCAA TOURNAMENT

Regional Semifinals

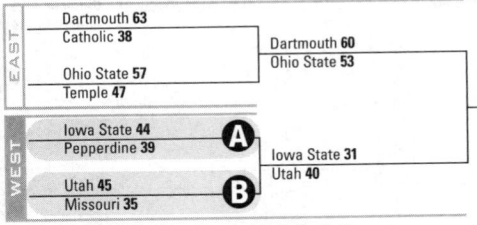

EAST
- Dartmouth **63**, Catholic **38**
- Ohio State **57**, Temple **47**

WEST
- Iowa State **44**, Pepperdine **39** (A)
- Utah **45**, Missouri **35** (B)

Regional Finals
- Dartmouth **60**, Ohio State **53**
- Iowa State **31**, Utah **40**

National Final — New York City

Utah 42 (OT)
Dartmouth 40

The lead changes six times in the last two minutes of regulation and the game goes into overtime. Arnie Ferrin—one of Utah's five freshman starters known as the Blitz Kids—scores four points in the OT and 22 in the game. The Utes claim the title when another Blitz Kid, guard Herb Wilkinson, hits the buzzer-beater from well beyond the top of the key.

East Regional Third Place Temple d. Catholic 55-35
West Regional Third Place Missouri d. Pepperdine 61-46

A Wyoming and Georgetown, the 1943 finalists, don't field teams because of WWII. Price Brookfield, an Ames-based naval cadet from West Texas A&M, leads Iowa State.

B First-round NIT losers transformed into New York City sightseers, Utah gets an NCAA invitation only when Arkansas is forced to pull out after two players are seriously injured in a car accident.

Record differs from the school's and/or the NCAA's because it includes noncollegiate competition or because the outcome of some games is in dispute.

Tournament Leaders

Individual Leaders

Scoring	CL	POS	G	PTS	PPG
1 **Nick Buzolich**, Pepperdine	SO	C	2	45	22.5
2 **Aud Brindley**, Dartmouth	JR	F/C	3	52	17.3
3 **Jim Joyce**, Temple	FR	F	2	31	15.5
4 **Arnold Risen**, Ohio State	SO	C	2	28	14.0
5 **Arnie Ferrin**, Utah	FR	G/F	3	40	13.3
6 **Charles Minx**, Missouri	SR	F	2	26	13.0
7 **Don Grate**, Ohio State	JR	G	2	24	12.0
8 **Harry Leggat**, Dartmouth	JR	F	3	35	11.7
9 **Paul Huston**, Ohio State	FR	G	2	23	11.5
Dick Scanlon, Catholic	SR	C	2	23	11.5

Minimum: 2 games

Field Goals Per Game	CL	POS	G	FG	FGPG
1 **Nick Buzolich**, Pepperdine	SO	C	2	17	8.5
2 **Aud Brindley**, Dartmouth	JR	F/C	3	24	8.0
3 **Jim Joyce**, Temple	FR	F	2	14	7.0
4 **Don Grate**, Ohio State	JR	G	2	11	5.5
Arnold Risen, Ohio State	SO	C	2	11	5.5

Minimum: 2 games

Free Throws Per Game	CL	POS	G	FT	FTPG
1 **Nick Buzolich**, Pepperdine	SO	C	2	11	5.5
2 **Dick Scanlon**, Catholic	SR	C	2	7	3.5
3 **Charles Minx**, Missouri	SR	F	2	6	3.0
Arnold Risen, Ohio State	SO	C	2	6	3.0
5 **Arnie Ferrin**, Utah	FR	G/F	3	8	2.7

Minimum: 2 games

Team Leaders

Scoring	G	PTS	PPG
1 **Ohio State**	2	110	55.0
2 **Dartmouth**	3	163	54.3
3 **Temple**	2	102	51.0
4 **Missouri**	2	96	48.0
5 **Pepperdine**	2	46	46.0
6 **Utah**	3	127	42.3
7 **Catholic**	2	73	36.5
8 **Iowa State**	2	31	31.0

Minimum: 2 games

FG Per Game	G	FG	FGPG
1 **Dartmouth**	3	76	25.3
2 **Ohio State**	2	47	23.5
3 **Temple**	2	44	22.0
4 **Missouri**	2	38	19.0
5 **Utah**	3	52	17.3

FT Per Game	G	FT	FTPG
1 **Missouri**	2	20	10.0
2 **Catholic**	2	17	8.5
3 **Pepperdine**	2	17	8.5
4 **Ohio State**	2	16	8.0
5 **Utah**	3	23	7.7

Tournament MOP

PLAYER	CL	POS	HT	SCHOOL	FG	FT	PPG
Arnie Ferrin	FR	G/F	6-4	Utah	16	8	13.3

1944 NCAA Tournament Box Scores

Dartmouth 63-38 Catholic (Elite 8)

	1H	2H
Dartmouth	28	35
Catholic	12	26

DARTMOUTH	MIN	FG	3FG	FT	REB	A	ST	BL	PF	TP
Bob Gale	40	8	-	1-1	-	-	-	-	1	17
Harry Leggat	27	7	-	1-5	-	-	-	-	4	15
Aud Brindley	34	6	-	1-1	-	-	-	-	2	13
Dick McGuire	40	4	-	0-0	-	-	-	-	2	8
Joseph Vancisin	17	3	-	0-0	-	-	-	-	2	6
Walter Mercer	13	1	-	0-0	-	-	-	-	1	2
Vincent Goering	9	1	-	0-0	-	-	-	-	0	2
James Monahan	14	0	-	0-2	-	-	-	-	0	0
Franklin Murphy	5	0	-	0-0	-	-	-	-	0	0
Floyd Wilson	1	0	-	0-0	-	-	-	-	0	0
TOTALS	**200**	**30**	**-**	**3-9**	**-**	**-**	**-**	**-**	**12**	**63**
Percentages				33.3						

Coach: Earl M. Brown

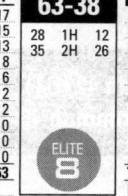

CATHOLIC	MIN	FG	3FG	FT	REB	A	ST	BL	PF	TP
John Mercak	40	5	-	2-3	-	-	-	-	0	12
Dick Scanlon	40	4	-	3-5	-	-	-	-	4	11
Fred Rice	31	3	-	1-3	-	-	-	-	0	7
Gene Szklarz	40	2	-	2-5	-	-	-	-	1	6
Ed Carlin	40	1	-	0-0	-	-	-	-	1	2
Alan Kingsbury	9	0	-	0-0	-	-	-	-	0	0
TOTALS	**200**	**15**	**-**	**8-16**	**-**	**-**	**-**	**-**	**6**	**38**
Percentages				50.0						

Coach: John Long

Officials: Adams, DeGroot

Ohio State 57-47 Temple (Elite 8)

	1H	2H
Ohio State	26	31
Temple	23	24

OHIO STATE	MIN	FG	3FG	FT	REB	A	ST	BL	PF	TP
Don Grate	-	8	-	1-2	-	-	-	-	3	17
Paul Huston	-	5	-	2-2	-	-	-	-	2	12
Robert Bowen	-	4	-	2-5	-	-	-	-	3	10
Arnold Risen	-	3	-	1-3	-	-	-	-	3	7
Rodney Caudill	-	3	-	0-1	-	-	-	-	0	6
John Dugger	-	2	-	0-0	-	-	-	-	0	4
Ollie Fink	-	0	-	1-4	-	-	-	-	0	1
Bill Gunton	-	0	-	0-0	-	-	-	-	0	0
Ernie Plank	-	0	-	0-0	-	-	-	-	0	0
TOTALS	**-**	**25**	**-**	**7-17**	**-**	**-**	**-**	**-**	**11**	**57**
Percentages				41.2						

Coach: Harold Olsen

TEMPLE	MIN	FG	3FG	FT	REB	A	ST	BL	PF	TP
Jim Joyce	-	7	-	2-6	-	-	-	-	0	16
Richard Koecher	-	5	-	2-3	-	-	-	-	4	12
Dave Fox	-	2	-	5-6	-	-	-	-	3	9
Charley Bramble	-	3	-	0-0	-	-	-	-	0	6
Bill Budd	-	2	-	0-0	-	-	-	-	3	4
Jack Burns	-	0	-	0-0	-	-	-	-	0	0
Collins	-	0	-	0-0	-	-	-	-	0	0
TOTALS	**-**	**19**	**-**	**9-15**	**-**	**-**	**-**	**-**	**10**	**47**
Percentages				60.0						

Coach: Josh Cody

Officials: Dissinger, Menton

Iowa State 44-39 Pepperdine (Elite 8)

	1H	2H
Iowa State	26	18
Pepperdine	21	18

IOWA STATE	MIN	FG	3FG	FT	REB	A	ST	BL	PF	TP
Roy Wehde	-	5	-	2-5	-	-	-	-	-	12
James Myers	-	5	-	1-1	-	-	-	-	-	11
Price Brookfield	-	4	-	2-2	-	-	-	-	-	10
Ray Wehde	-	1	-	2-3	-	-	-	-	-	4
Robert Sauer	-	0	-	3-3	-	-	-	-	-	3
William Block	-	1	-	0-1	-	-	-	-	-	2
Gene Oulman	-	1	-	0-0	-	-	-	-	-	2
TOTALS	**-**	**17**	**-**	**10-15**	**-**	**-**	**-**	**-**	**-**	**44**
Percentages				66.7						

Coach: Louis Menze

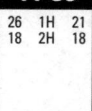

PEPPERDINE	MIN	FG	3FG	FT	REB	A	ST	BL	PF	TP
Nick Buzolich	-	9	-	4-7	-	-	-	-	-	22
Lowery Ruby	-	2	-	1-2	-	-	-	-	-	5
Bill Whaley	-	2	-	1-2	-	-	-	-	-	5
Warren Nunn	-	2	-	0-2	-	-	-	-	-	4
Joe Witeck	-	1	-	1-1	-	-	-	-	-	3
Reggie Asher	-	0	-	0-0	-	-	-	-	-	0
Les Wandell	-	0	-	0-0	-	-	-	-	-	0
TOTALS	**-**	**16**	**-**	**7-14**	**-**	**-**	**-**	**-**	**-**	**39**
Percentages				50.0						

Coach: Al O. Duer

Officials: Gibbs, Hess

ELITE 8 — **45-35** (1H: 27-14; 2H: 18-21)

UTAH	MIN	FG	3FG	FT	REB	A	ST	BL	PF	TP
Arnie Ferrin	-	5	-	2-2	-	-	-	-	1	12
Herb Wilkinson	-	3	-	2-3	-	-	-	-	1	8
Fred Sheffield	-	3	-	1-1	-	-	-	-	1	7
Dick Smuin	-	3	-	1-2	-	-	-	-	3	7
Bob Lewis	-	3	-	0-1	-	-	-	-	2	6
Wat Misaka	-	2	-	1-1	-	-	-	-	4	5
Ray Kingston	-	0	-	0-0	-	-	-	-	0	0
Fred Lewis	-	0	-	0-1	-	-	-	-	1	0
James Nance	-	0	-	0-0	-	-	-	-	0	0
TOTALS	-	19	-	7-11	-	-	-	-	13	45
Percentages				63.6						

Coach: Vadal Peterson

MISSOURI	MIN	FG	3FG	FT	REB	A	ST	BL	PF	TP
Paul Collins	35	4	-	2-7	-	-	-	-	3	10
Dale Crowder	36	3	-	1-1	-	-	-	-	3	7
Dan Pippin	38	3	-	0-1	-	-	-	-	0	6
Beauford Minx	40	2	-	1-2	-	-	-	-	3	5
Charles Minx	40	2	-	1-3	-	-	-	-	2	5
Leonard Brown	4	1	-	0-0	-	-	-	-	0	2
Robert Heinsohn	5	0	-	0-0	-	-	-	-	0	0
Robert Toal	2	0	-	0-1	-	-	-	-	0	0
TOTALS	200	15	-	5-15	-	-	-	-	11	35
Percentages				33.3						

Coach: George Edwards

Officials: Curtis, Piluso

FINAL 4 — **60-53** (1H: 31-28; 2H: 29-25)

DARTMOUTH	MIN	FG	3FG	FT	REB	A	ST	BL	PF	TP
Aud Brindley	40	13	-	2-3	-	-	-	-	3	28
Harry Leggat	40	5	-	2-4	-	-	-	-	2	12
Dick McGuire	40	4	-	1-3	-	-	-	-	1	9
Bob Gale	40	3	-	1-1	-	-	-	-	2	7
James Monahan	15	2	-	0-0	-	-	-	-	1	4
Joseph Vancisin	25	0	-	0-0	-	-	-	-	2	0
TOTALS	200	27	-	6-11	-	-	-	-	11	60
Percentages				54.5						

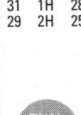

Coach: Earl M. Brown

OHIO STATE	MIN	FG	3FG	FT	REB	A	ST	BL	PF	TP
Arnold Risen	35	8	-	5-6	-	-	-	-	0	21
Paul Huston	40	5	-	1-1	-	-	-	-	3	11
John Dugger	29	3	-	2-6	-	-	-	-	4	8
Don Grate	40	3	-	1-2	-	-	-	-	2	7
Robert Bowen	34	3	-	0-0	-	-	-	-	1	6
Bill Gunton	11	0	-	0-0	-	-	-	-	0	0
Ollie Fink	6	0	-	0-0	-	-	-	-	0	0
Rodney Caudill	5	0	-	0-0	-	-	-	-	1	0
TOTALS	200	22	-	9-15	-	-	-	-	11	53
Percentages				60.0						

Coach: Harold Olsen

Officials: Menton, DeGroot

FINAL 4 — **40-31** (1H: 19-16; 2H: 21-15)

UTAH	MIN	FG	3FG	FT	REB	A	ST	BL	PF	TP
Wat Misaka	-	4	-	1	-	-	-	-	-	9
Fred Sheffield	-	4	-	1	-	-	-	-	-	9
Bob Lewis	-	3	-	1	-	-	-	-	-	7
Arnie Ferrin	-	3	-	0	-	-	-	-	-	6
Dick Smuin	-	2	-	1	-	-	-	-	-	5
Herb Wilkinson	-	1	-	2	-	-	-	-	-	4
TOTALS	-	17	-	6	-	-	-	-	-	40
Percentages				0.0						

Coach: Vadal Peterson

IOWA STATE	MIN	FG	3FG	FT	REB	A	ST	BL	PF	TP
Price Brookfield	-	3	-	0	-	-	-	-	-	6
William Block	-	2	-	1	-	-	-	-	-	5
Gene Oulman	-	2	-	1	-	-	-	-	-	5
Ray Wehde	-	2	-	1	-	-	-	-	-	5
James Myers	-	2	-	0	-	-	-	-	-	4
Roy Wehde	-	2	-	0	-	-	-	-	-	4
Robert Sauer	-	0	-	2	-	-	-	-	-	2
Roy Ewoldt	-	0	-	0	-	-	-	-	-	0
TOTALS	-	13	-	5	-	-	-	-	-	31
Percentages				0.0						

Coach: Louis Menze

Officials: Curtis, Gibbs
Attendance: 15,000

NCAA FINAL 1944 — **42-40** (1H: 17-18; 2H: 19-18; OT1: 6-4)

UTAH	MIN	FG	3FG	FT	REB	A	ST	BL	PF	TP
Arnie Ferrin	45	8	-	6-7	-	-	-	-	0	22
Bob Lewis	45	2	-	3-3	-	-	-	-	2	7
Herb Wilkinson	45	3	-	1-4	-	-	-	-	0	7
Wat Misaka	41	2	-	0-0	-	-	-	-	1	4
Fred Sheffield	4	1	-	0-0	-	-	-	-	1	2
Dick Smuin	45	0	-	0-0	-	-	-	-	2	0
TOTALS	225	16	-	10-14	-	-	-	-	6	42
Percentages				71.4						

Coach: Vadal Peterson

DARTMOUTH	MIN	FG	3FG	FT	REB	A	ST	BL	PF	TP
Aud Brindley	39	5	-	1-1	-	-	-	-	3	11
Bob Gale	37	5	-	0-2	-	-	-	-	1	10
Harry Leggat	34	4	-	0-0	-	-	-	-	1	8
Dick McGuire	38	3	-	0-1	-	-	-	-	3	6
Joseph Vancisin	19	2	-	0-0	-	-	-	-	3	4
Walter Mercer	19	0	-	1-1	-	-	-	-	3	1
Franklin Murphy	17	0	-	0-0	-	-	-	-	0	0
Vincent Goering	14	0	-	0-0	-	-	-	-	0	0
Everett Nordstrom	8	0	-	0-0	-	-	-	-	0	0
TOTALS	225	19	-	2-5	-	-	-	-	14	40
Percentages				40.0						

Coach: Earl M. Brown

Officials: Osborne, Menton
Attendance: 15,000

National Invitation Tournament (NIT)

Quarterfinals: Oklahoma A&M d. Canisius 43-29, Kentucky d. Utah 46-38, St. John's d. Bowling Green 44-40. DePaul d. Muhlenberg 68-45
Semifinals: St. John's d. Kentucky 48-45, DePaul d. Oklahoma A&M 41-38
Third place: Kentucky d. Oklahoma A&M 45-29
Championship: St. John's d. DePaul 47-39
MVP: Bill Kotsores, St. John's

Red Cross Benefit

1944: Utah (NCAA champ) vs. St. John's (NIT champ)
March 30, 1944

43-36 (1H: 19-19; 2H: 24-17)

UTAH	FG	FT	TP
Arnie Ferrin	6	5	17
Herb Wilkinson	4	3	11
Bob Lewis	4	0	8
Wat Misaka	2	1	5
Dick Smuin	1	0	2
Fred Sheffield	0	0	0
TOTAL:	17	9	43

Coach: Vadal Peterson

ST. JOHN'S	FG	FT	TP
Hy Gotkin	4	3	11
Sonny Wertis	5	0	10
Ivy Summer	3	1	7
Bill Kotsores	2	1	5
Wade Duym	1	0	2
Tom Larkin	0	1	1
Norman Mager	0	0	0
Murray Robinson	0	0	0
Don Wehr	0	0	0
TOTAL	15	6	36

Coach: Joe Lapchick

Officials: Joe Burns, Hagan Anderson
Attendance: 18,125

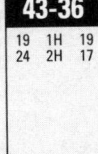

1944-45: Giants Rule

Iowa went 17–1 and won the Big Ten, led by co-captains Herb Wilkinson (a transfer from Utah who had been the Utes' 1944 Tournament hero) and Ned Postels, but the Hawkeyes declined to play in the postseason for academic reasons. Oklahoma A&M (today's Oklahoma State), which finished with a 27–4 mark under coach Hank Iba, accepted an NCAA bid and beat Utah and Arkansas, then NYU, 49-45, in the Final.

In the last American Red Cross benefit game between the NCAA and NIT champions, a crowd of more than 18,000 packed New York's Madison Square Garden to witness the battle of the standout centers—Oklahoma A&M's 7-foot Bob Kurland vs. DePaul's 6'9" George Mikan. Mikan fouled out after just 14 minutes, finishing with only nine points to Kurland's 14, and A&M won, 52-44. Even so, the era of the dominant big men had officially begun.

Four rules changes took effect at the beginning of the season: A player deflecting a shot on its descent would be called for goaltending and the basket would count for the team that shot; a player's personal foul quota would increase from four to five before he was disqualified; a coach could make an unlimited number of substitutions; and three seconds in the lane would be a violation for an offensive player.

Major Conference Standings

BIG SIX	Conference W	L	Pct	Overall W	L	Pct
Iowa State	8	2	.800	11	5	.688
Kansas	8	4	.667	12	5	.706
Missouri	6	5	.545	8	10	.444
Oklahoma	5	5	.500	12	13	.480
Kansas State	5	7	.417	10	13	.435
Nebraska	1	9	.100	2	17	.105

BIG TEN	Conference W	L	Pct	Overall W	L	Pct
Iowa	11	1	.917	17	1	.944
Ohio State○	10	2	.833	15	5	.750
Illinois	7	5	.583	13	7	.650
Purdue	6	6	.500	9	11	.450
Michigan	5	7	.417	12	7	.632
Wisconsin	4	8	.333	10	11	.476
Minnesota	4	8	.333	8	13	.381
Northwestern	4	8	.333	7	12	.368
Indiana	3	9	.250	10	11	.476
Chicago	-	-	-	7	8	.467

BORDER	Conference W	L	Pct	Overall W	L	Pct
New Mexico	12	0	1.000	14	2	.875
West Texas A&M	9	3	.750	16	10	.615
Northern Arizona	4	2	.667	5	6	.455
New Mexico State	4	3	.571	9	5	.643
Texas Tech	7	6	.538	10	14	.417
Arizona	3	4	.429	7	11	.389
Arizona State	3	5	.375	5	9	.357
Texas Western	4	11	.267	10	12	.455
Hardin-Simmons	2	14	.125	7	23	.233

IVY	Conference W	L	Pct	Overall W	L	Pct
Penn	5	1	.833	12	5	.706
Cornell	4	2	.667	12	5	.706
Dartmouth	2	4	.333	6	8	.429
Columbia	1	5	.167	9	11	.450

BIG SEVEN	Conference W	L	Pct	Overall W	L	Pct
Utah○	8	0	1.000	17	4	.810
Colorado	9	1	.900	13	3	.813
Wyoming	7	5	.583	10	18	.357
BYU	5	5	.500	11	12	.478
Utah State	3	7	.300	9	10	.474
Colorado State	1	5	.167	7	11	.389
Denver	1	11	.083	7	16	.304

PACIFIC COAST	Conference W	L	Pct	Overall W	L	Pct
North						
Oregon○	11	5	.688	30	15	.667
Washington State	11	5	.688	23	13	.639
Oregon State	10	6	.625	20	8	.714
Washington	5	11	.313	22	18	.550
Idaho	3	13	.188	13	20	.394
South						
UCLA	3	1	.750	12	12	.500
Southern California	3	3	.500	15	9	.625
California	1	3	.250	7	8	.467

Playoff: **Oregon d. Washington State 2-1** in a best of three series to win the North; no division playoffs were held and Oregon was awarded the PCC title

SEC	Conference W	L	Pct	Overall W	L	Pct
Tennessee□	8	2	.800	18	5	.783
Kentucky○	4	1	.800	22	4	.846
Mississippi	3	1	.750	15	8	.652
Florida	4	2	.667	7	12	.368
Georgia Tech	7	4	.636	11	6	.647
Alabama	5	3	.625	10	5	.667
LSU	3	3	.500	15	9	.625
Tulane	3	3	.500	6	11	.353
Auburn	2	6	.250	3	14	.176
Mississippi State	2	9	.182	5	13	.278
Georgia	2	9	.182	5	16	.238
Vanderbilt	-	-	-	6	6	.500

Tournament: **Kentucky d. Tennessee 39-35**

SOUTHERN	Conference W	L	Pct	Overall W	L	Pct
South Carolina	9	0	1.000	19	3	.864
Richmond	2	0	1.000	3	4	.429
Duke	6	1	.857	13	9	.591
North Carolina	11	3	.786	22	6	.786
The Citadel	8	4	.667	16	7	.696
NC State	7	5	.583	10	11	.476
William and Mary	3	4	.429	7	10	.412
Clemson	3	5	.375	8	8	.500
Davidson	3	6	.333	9	9	.500
Maryland	2	5	.286	2	14	.125
Virginia Tech	1	3	.250	6	8	.429
VMI	1	4	.200	2	10	.167
Wake Forest	0	6	.000	3	14	.176
Furman	0	8	.000	2	15	.118

Tournament: **North Carolina d. Duke 49-38**

SOUTHWEST	Conference W	L	Pct	Overall W	L	Pct
Rice	12	0	1.000	20	1	.952
Arkansas○	9	3	.750	17	9	.654
SMU	7	5	.583	11	10	.524
TCU	7	5	.583	9	20	.310
Texas	5	7	.417	10	10	.500
Texas A&M	2	10	.167	3	18	.143
Baylor	0	12	.000	0	17	.000

INDEPENDENTS	Overall W	L	Pct
Army	14	1	.933
Rensselaer Poly□	13	1	.929
Lafayette	16	2	.889
DePaul□	21	3	.875
St. John's□	21	3	.875
Valparaiso	21	3	.875
Oklahoma A&M○	27	4	.871
Bowling Green□	24	4	.857
Muhlenberg□	24	4	.857
Navy	12	2	.857
Louisville	16	3	.842
Rhode Island□	20	5	.800
Brown	15	4	.789
Rutgers	11	3	.786
Yale	14	4	.778
Virginia	13	4	.765
Indiana State	18	6	.750
Notre Dame	15	5	.750
CCNY	12	4	.750
Long Island	14	5	.737
Saint Louis	10	4	.714
Butler	14	6	.700
Wichita State	14	6	.700
Temple	16	7	.696
Toledo	9	4	.692
NYU○	14	7	.667
West Virginia□	12	6	.667
Pittsburgh	8	4	.667
Marshall	17	9	.654
Western Kentucky	17	10	.630
Bucknell	10	7	.588
Penn State	10	7	.588
La Salle	11	8	.579
Ohio	11	8	.579
Michigan State	9	7	.563
Tufts○	10	8	.556
Niagara	7	6	.538
Miami (OH)	8	7	.533
Wash.-St. Louis	10	9	.526
Canisius	12	11	.522
Saint Joseph's	12	11	.522
St. Francis (NY)	9	9	.500
Cincinnati	8	9	.471
Chicago	7	8	.467
Drake	11	13	.458
Loyola (MD)	10	12	.455
Western Michigan	8	10	.444
Montana State	10	14	.417
Marquette	7	10	.412
Detroit	8	12	.400
Boston U.	4	6	.400
Princeton	7	12	.368
Syracuse	7	12	.368
Tulane	6	11	.353
Villanova	6	11	.353
Fordham	7	13	.350
Colgate	5	10	.333
Tulsa	4	8	.333
Connecticut	5	11	.313
Holy Cross	4	9	.308
St. Bonaventure	3	7	.300
Montana	7	22	.241
Kent State	3	11	.214
Brooklyn	3	15	.167
Harvard	2	13	.133
Lehigh	2	16	.111
Santa Clara	0	11	.000

⊛ Automatic NCAA Tournament bid ○ At-large NCAA Tournament bid □ NIT appearance ⊗ Team record doesn't reflect games forfeited or vacated. For adjusted record, see p. 521.

PREMO-PORRETTA POWER POLL

	SCHOOL	RECORD
1	**Iowa**	17-1
2	**Oklahoma A&M (NCAA champion)**	27-4
3	**DePaul (NIT champion)**	21-3
4	**Rice**	20-1
5	**Army**	14-1
6	**Navy**	12-2
7	**Ohio State**	15-5
8	**Bowling Green**	24-4
9	**Notre Dame**	15-5
10	**Kentucky**	22-4
11	**St. John's**	21-3
12	**Rensselaer Poly**	13-1
13	**Akron**	21-2
14	**NYU**	16-8 #
15	**Muhlenberg**	24-4
16	**South Carolina**	19-3
17	**Valparaiso**	21-3
18	**Tennessee**	18-5
19	**Rhode Island**	20-5
20	**Hamline**	20-4
21	**North Carolina**	22-6
22	**Temple**	16-7
23	**Illinois**	13-7
24	**Penn**	12-5
25	**Yale**	14-4

CONSENSUS ALL-AMERICAS

FIRST TEAM

PLAYER	CL	POS	HT	SCHOOL	PPG
Howie Dallmar	JR	F	6-4	Penn	10.5
Arnie Ferrin	SO	G/F	6-4	Utah	17.5
Wyndol Gray	JR	F	6-1	Bowling Green	14.6
Bill Hassett	JR	G	5-10	Notre Dame	8.6
Bill Henry	JR	C	6-8	Rice	20.7
Walton Kirk	JR	G	6-3	Illinois	10.6
Bob Kurland	JR	C	7-0	Oklahoma A&M	17.1
George Mikan	JR	C	6-9	DePaul	23.3

SECOND TEAM

PLAYER	CL	POS	HT	SCHOOL	PPG
Don Grate	SR	G	6-2	Ohio State	N/A
Dale Hall	JR	G/F	5-11	Army	23.0
Vince Hanson	SO	C	6-8	Washington State	15.6
Dick Ives	SO	F	6-2	Iowa	12.1
Max Morris	SO	F	6-2	Northwestern	15.4
Herb Wilkinson	SO	G	6-4	Iowa	9.6

SELECTORS: ARGOSY MAGAZINE, CONVERSE YEARBOOK, HELMS FOUNDATION, SPORTING NEWS

1945 NCAA TOURNAMENT

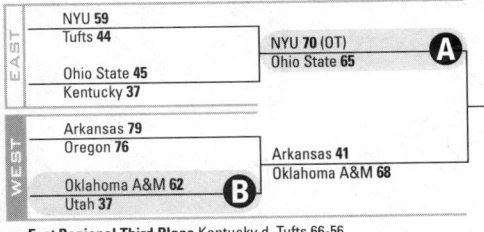

Regional Semifinals

EAST
- NYU **59**, Tufts **44**
- Ohio State **45**, Kentucky **37**

WEST
- Arkansas **79**, Oregon **76**
- Oklahoma A&M **62**, Utah **37** (B)

Regional Finals
- NYU **70** (OT), Ohio State **65** (A)
- Arkansas **41**, Oklahoma A&M **68**

National Final (New York City)

Oklahoma A&M 49, NYU 45

East Regional Third Place: **East Regional Third Place** Kentucky d. Tufts 66-56

West Regional Third Place Oregon d. Utah 69-66

(A) Led by 16-year-old Dolph Schayes (14 points), NYU overcomes a 10-point deficit in the last two minutes to force OT. OSU star Arnie Risen (26) fouls out late in regulation.

Coach Hank Iba's slow-motion offense opens up lanes or puts Bob "Foothills" Kurland in position for lobs, and the big man scores 22 to give the Aggies their first title. In a subsequent Red Cross benefit game against NIT champ DePaul, the Aggies win but the Kurland-Mikan matchup fizzles.

(B) Despite a no-goaltending rule aimed at neutralizing oversized centers, Bob Kurland helps Oklahoma A&M dominate defending champion Utah. The Utes do well to return to the Tournament, having lost top scorers Arnie Ferrin and Fred Sheffield to the military after the regular season.

Record differs from the school's and/or the NCAA's because it includes noncollegiate competition or because the outcome of some games is in dispute.

Tournament Leaders

Individual Leaders

Scoring

	CL	POS	G	PTS	PPG
1 **Dick Wilkins**, Oregon	FR	F	2	44	22.0
2 **Bob Kurland**, Oklahoma A&M	JR	C	3	65	21.7
3 **Arnold Risen**, Ohio State	JR	C	2	35	17.5
Bob Skarda, Tufts	JR	F	2	35	17.5
5 **George Kok**, Arkansas	SO	C	2	34	17.0
Murray Satterfield, Utah	FR	C	2	34	17.0
7 **Cecil Hankins**, Oklahoma A&M	SR	G/F	3	48	16.0
Bob Hamilton, Oregon	JR	G	2	32	16.0
9 **Don Dorton**, Utah	FR	G	2	31	15.5
10 **Wilber Schu**, Kentucky	JR	F	2	29	14.5

Minimum: 2 games

Free Throws Per Game

	CL	POS	G	FT	FTPG
1 **Arnold Risen**, Ohio State	JR	C	2	11	5.5
2 **Bob Hamilton**, Oregon	JR	G	2	8	4.0
George Kok, Arkansas	SO	C	2	8	4.0
Murray Satterfield, Utah	FR	C	2	8	4.0
Mike Schumchyk, Arkansas	SR	F	2	8	4.0

Minimum: 2 games

Field Goals Per Game

	CL	POS	G	FG	FGPG
1 **Bob Kurland**, Oklahoma A&M	JR	C	3	30	10.0
2 **Dick Wilkins**, Oregon	FR	F	2	19	9.5
3 **Bob Skarda**, Tufts	JR	F	2	15	7.5
4 **Don Dorton**, Utah	FR	G	2	14	7.0
5 **George Kok**, Arkansas	SO	C	2	13	6.5
Murray Satterfield, Utah	FR	C	2	13	6.5

Minimum: 2 games

Team Leaders

Scoring

	G	PTS	PPG
1 **Oregon**	2	145	72.5
2 **Arkansas**	2	120	60.0
3 **Oklahoma A&M**	3	179	59.7
4 **NYU**	3	174	58.0
5 **Ohio State**	2	110	55.0
6 **Utah**	2	103	51.5
Kentucky	2	103	51.5
8 **Tufts**	2	100	50.0

Minimum: 2 games

FT Per Game

	G	FT	FTPG
1 **Ohio State**	2	30	15.0
2 **Oregon**	2	29	14.5
3 **Kentucky**	2	27	13.5
4 **Arkansas**	2	26	13.0
5 **NYU**	3	38	12.7

FG Per Game

	G	FG	FGPG
1 **Oregon**	2	58	29.0
2 **Oklahoma A&M**	3	78	26.0
3 **Arkansas**	2	47	23.5
4 **NYU**	3	68	22.7
5 **Utah**	2	41	20.5

Tournament MOP

PLAYER	CL	POS	HT	SCHOOL	FG	FT	PPG
Bob Kurland	JR	C	7-0	Oklahoma A&M	30	5	21.7

1945 NCAA Tournament Box Scores

59-44 (Elite 8)

	1H	2H
NYU	27	32
Tufts	22	22

NYU	MIN	FG	3FG	FT	REB	A	ST	BL	PF	TP
Sid Tanenbaum	-	7	-	3-4	-	-	-	-	3	17
Dolph Schayes	-	6	-	1-3	-	-	-	-	1	13
Al Grenert	-	5	-	2-4	-	-	-	-	0	12
Don Forman	-	3	-	0-2	-	-	-	-	1	6
Frank Mangiapane	-	2	-	2-5	-	-	-	-	3	6
Alvin Most	-	0	-	3-3	-	-	-	-	1	3
Herbert Walsh	-	1	-	0-1	-	-	-	-	1	2
Frank Benanti	-	0	-	0-0	-	-	-	-	0	0
Howard Sarath	-	0	-	0-1	-	-	-	-	2	0
TOTALS	**-**	**24**	**-**	**11-23**	**-**	**-**	**-**	**-**	**12**	**59**
Percentages				47.8						

Coach: Howard Cann

TUFTS	MIN	FG	3FG	FT	REB	A	ST	BL	PF	TP
Bob Skarda	-	7	-	1-3	-	-	-	-	5	15
Jim Cumiskey	-	6	-	2-4	-	-	-	-	3	14
Robert Burgbacher	-	3	-	2-2	-	-	-	-	1	8
Richard Walz	-	2	-	0-0	-	-	-	-	1	4
Roger Johnson	-	1	-	1-5	-	-	-	-	3	3
Bob Cooney	-	0	-	0-0	-	-	-	-	4	0
Bob Moran	-	0	-	0-0	-	-	-	-	3	0
TOTALS	**-**	**19**	**-**	**6-14**	**-**	**-**	**-**	**-**	**20**	**44**
Percentages				42.9						

Coach: Dick Cochran

Officials: Beiersdorfer, Adams

45-37 (Elite 8)

	1H	2H
Ohio State	21	24
Kentucky	15	22

OHIO STATE	MIN	FG	3FG	FT	REB	A	ST	BL	PF	TP
Don Grate	-	5	-	5-9	-	-	-	-	3	15
Rodney Caudill	-	5	-	4-6	-	-	-	-	5	14
Arnold Risen	-	4	-	1-3	-	-	-	-	5	9
Paul Huston	-	2	-	1-1	-	-	-	-	2	5
James Sims	-	1	-	0-0	-	-	-	-	0	2
Warren Amling	-	0	-	0-4	-	-	-	-	4	0
John Dugger	-	0	-	0-1	-	-	-	-	2	0
Ray Snyder	-	0	-	0-0	-	-	-	-	0	0
TOTALS	**-**	**17**	**-**	**11-24**	**-**	**-**	**-**	**-**	**21**	**45**
Percentages				45.8						

Coach: Harold Olsen

KENTUCKY	MIN	FG	3FG	FT	REB	A	ST	BL	PF	TP
Jack Tingle	-	5	-	1-2	-	-	-	-	0	11
Wilber Schu	-	2	-	4-5	-	-	-	-	4	8
Jack Parkinson	-	1	-	5-6	-	-	-	-	4	7
Kenton Campbell	-	2	-	2-5	-	-	-	-	4	6
Johnny Strogh	-	1	-	1-3	-	-	-	-	4	3
George Vulich	-	0	-	2-3	-	-	-	-	0	2
Edward Parker	-	0	-	0-3	-	-	-	-	0	0
William Sturgill	-	0	-	0-0	-	-	-	-	3	0
TOTALS	**-**	**11**	**-**	**15-27**	**-**	**-**	**-**	**-**	**19**	**37**
Percentages				55.6						

Coach: Adolph Rupp

Officials: Boyle, Melman

79-76 (Elite 8)

	1H	2H
Arkansas	47	32
Oregon	34	42

ARKANSAS	MIN	FG	3FG	FT	REB	A	ST	BL	PF	TP
George Kok	-	9	-	4-5	-	-	-	-	2	22
Mike Schumchyk	-	7	-	6-9	-	-	-	-	4	20
Ocie Richie	-	6	-	1-1	-	-	-	-	2	13
Earl Wheeler	-	5	-	2-3	-	-	-	-	0	12
Bill Flynt	-	4	-	3-4	-	-	-	-	3	11
Frank Schumchyk	-	0	-	1-1	-	-	-	-	0	1
Charles Jollif	-	0	-	0-1	-	-	-	-	2	0
Ken Kearns	-	0	-	0-0	-	-	-	-	1	0
TOTALS	**-**	**31**	**-**	**17-24**	**-**	**-**	**-**	**-**	**14**	**79**
Percentages				70.8						

Coach: Eugene Lambert

OREGON	MIN	FG	3FG	FT	REB	A	ST	BL	PF	TP
Dick Wilkins	-	10	-	3-3	-	-	-	-	2	23
Bob Hamilton	-	9	-	2-3	-	-	-	-	2	20
Del Smith	-	4	-	3-4	-	-	-	-	3	11
Raymond Berg	-	3	-	2-3	-	-	-	-	4	8
Jim Bartelt	-	3	-	1-1	-	-	-	-	5	7
Ken Hays	-	3	-	1-2	-	-	-	-	3	7
Charles Stamper	-	0	-	0-0	-	-	-	-	2	0
TOTALS	**-**	**32**	**-**	**12-16**	**-**	**-**	**-**	**-**	**21**	**76**
Percentages				75.0						

Coach: John A. Warren

Officials: Lance, Smith

OKLAHOMA A&M	MIN	FG	3FG	FT	REB	A	ST	BL	PF	TP
Bob Kurland	-	14	-	0	-	-	-	-	2	28
Cecil Hankins	-	5	-	1	-	-	-	-	3	11
Blake Williams	-	4	-	0	-	-	-	-	3	8
Weldon Kern	-	2	-	3	-	-	-	-	2	7
Doyle Parrack	-	3	-	0	-	-	-	-	2	6
J.L. Parks	-	1	-	0	-	-	-	-	1	2
Joe Halbert	-	0	-	0	-	-	-	-	1	0
Bill Johnson	-	0	-	0	-	-	-	-	0	0
John Wylie	-	0	-	0	-	-	-	-	1	0
TOTALS	-	**29**	-	**4**	-	-	-	-	**15**	**62**
Percentages										
Coach: Hank Iba										

62-37

	1H	2H
Oklahoma A&M	22	40
Utah	12	25

ELITE 8

UTAH	MIN	FG	3FG	FT	REB	A	ST	BL	PF	TP
Murray Satterfield	-	4	-	6	-	-	-	-	2	14
Dave Howard	-	4	-	3	-	-	-	-	2	11
Don Dorton	-	3	-	1	-	-	-	-	0	7
Lee Hamblin	-	2	-	1	-	-	-	-	3	5
Ray Barnes	-	0	-	0	-	-	-	-	0	0
George Keil	-	0	-	0	-	-	-	-	1	0
TOTALS	-	**13**	-	**11**	-	-	-	-	**8**	**37**
Percentages										
Coach: Vadal Peterson										

Officials: Curtis, McLarney

NYU	MIN	FG	3FG	FT	REB	A	ST	BL	PF	TP
Frank Mangiapane	-	7	-	3-5	-	-	-	-	4	17
Dolph Schayes	-	5	-	4-8	-	-	-	-	4	14
Sid Tanenbaum	-	5	-	3-3	-	-	-	-	2	13
Don Forman	-	4	-	2-2	-	-	-	-	2	10
Al Grenert	-	2	-	2-5	-	-	-	-	3	6
Herbert Walsh	-	2	-	2-3	-	-	-	-	5	6
Marty Goldstein	-	1	-	0-0	-	-	-	-	2	2
Alvin Most	-	1	-	0-1	-	-	-	-	2	2
Frank Benanti	-	0	-	0-0	-	-	-	-	1	0
TOTALS	-	**27**	-	**16-27**	-	-	-	-	**25**	**70**
Percentages				59.3						
Coach: Howard Cann										

70-65

	1H	2H	OT1
NYU	34	28	8
Ohio State	36	26	3

FINAL 4

OHIO STATE	MIN	FG	3FG	FT	REB	A	ST	BL	PF	TP
Arnold Risen	-	8	-	10-13	-	-	-	-	5	26
Warren Amling	-	5	-	0-2	-	-	-	-	1	10
Rodney Caudill	-	3	-	1-1	-	-	-	-	3	7
James Sims	-	2	-	3-4	-	-	-	-	3	7
Don Grate	-	2	-	2-3	-	-	-	-	4	6
Paul Huston	-	2	-	1-3	-	-	-	-	5	5
John Dugger	-	1	-	2-5	-	-	-	-	5	4
Ray Snyder	-	0	-	0-0	-	-	-	-	0	0
TOTALS	-	**23**	-	**19-31**	-	-	-	-	**26**	**65**
Percentages				61.3						
Coach: Harold Olsen										

Officials: Boyle, Beiersdorfer

OKLAHOMA A&M	MIN	FG	3FG	FT	REB	A	ST	BL	PF	TP
Cecil Hankins	-	8	-	6	-	-	-	-	1	22
Doyle Parrack	-	7	-	2	-	-	-	-	1	16
Bob Kurland	-	6	-	3	-	-	-	-	3	15
Blake Williams	-	2	-	3	-	-	-	-	2	7
Weldon Kern	-	3	-	0	-	-	-	-	2	6
J.L. Parks	-	1	-	0	-	-	-	-	1	2
Joe Halbert	-	0	-	0	-	-	-	-	1	0
John Wylie	-	0	-	0	-	-	-	-	0	0
TOTALS	-	**27**	-	**14**	-	-	-	-	**11**	**68**
Percentages										
Coach: Hank Iba										

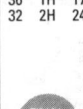

68-41

	1H	2H
Oklahoma A&M	36	32
Arkansas	17	24

FINAL 4

ARKANSAS	MIN	FG	3FG	FT	REB	A	ST	BL	PF	TP
George Kok	-	4	-	4	-	-	-	-	2	12
Bill Flynt	-	5	-	1	-	-	-	-	2	11
Ocie Richie	-	2	-	0	-	-	-	-	0	4
Mike Schumchyk	-	1	-	2	-	-	-	-	3	4
Earl Wheeler	-	2	-	0	-	-	-	-	3	4
Ken Kearns	-	1	-	1	-	-	-	-	2	3
T.B. Byles	-	1	-	0	-	-	-	-	1	2
Jody Copeland	-	0	-	1	-	-	-	-	0	1
Charles Jollif	-	0	-	0	-	-	-	-	3	0
Frank Schumchyk	-	0	-	0	-	-	-	-	1	0
TOTALS	-	**16**	-	**9**	-	-	-	-	**17**	**41**
Percentages										
Coach: Eugene Lambert										

Officials: McLarney, Smith
Attendance: 18,035

OKLAHOMA A&M	MIN	FG	3FG	FT	REB	A	ST	BL	PF	TP
Bob Kurland	-	10	-	2-3	-	-	-	-	3	22
Cecil Hankins	-	6	-	3-6	-	-	-	-	3	15
Weldon Kern	-	3	-	0-4	-	-	-	-	3	6
Doyle Parrack	-	2	-	0-1	-	-	-	-	3	4
Blake Williams	-	1	-	0-1	-	-	-	-	1	2
J.L. Parks	-	0	-	0-0	-	-	-	-	3	0
John Wylie	-	0	-	0-0	-	-	-	-	0	0
TOTALS	-	**22**	-	**5-15**	-	-	-	-	**16**	**49**
Percentages				33.3						
Coach: Hank Iba										

49-45

	1H	2H
Oklahoma A&M	26	23
NYU	21	24

NCAA FINAL 1945

NYU	MIN	FG	3FG	FT	REB	A	ST	BL	PF	TP
Al Grenert	-	5	-	2-3	-	-	-	-	3	12
Don Forman	-	5	-	1-1	-	-	-	-	1	11
Frank Mangiapane	-	2	-	2-2	-	-	-	-	3	6
Dolph Schayes	-	2	-	2-6	-	-	-	-	2	6
Alvin Most	-	1	-	2-3	-	-	-	-	2	4
Sid Tanenbaum	-	2	-	0-0	-	-	-	-	2	4
Marty Goldstein	-	0	-	2-2	-	-	-	-	0	2
Herbert Walsh	-	0	-	0-0	-	-	-	-	2	0
TOTALS	-	**17**	-	**11-17**	-	-	-	-	**15**	**45**
Percentages				64.7						
Coach: Howard Cann										

Officials: Curtis, Adams
Attendance: 18,035

National Invitation Tournament (NIT)

Quarterfinals: Rhode Island d. Tennessee 51-44, Bowling Green d. Rensselaer Polytechnic Institute 60-45, DePaul d. West Virginia 76-52, St. John's d. Muhlenberg 34-33
Semifinals: DePaul d. Rhode Island 97-53, Bowling Green d. St. John's 57-44
Third place: St. John's d. Rhode Island 64-57
Championship: DePaul d. Bowling Green 71-54
MVP: George Mikan, DePaul

Red Cross Benefit

Oklahoma A&M (NCAA champ) vs. DePaul (NIT champ), March 29, 1945

OKLAHOMA A&M	FG	FT	TP
Cecil Hankins	8	4	20
Bob Kurland	4	6	14
J.L. Parks	3	0	6
Doyle Parrack	3	0	6
Weldon Kern	0	5	5
Blake Williams	0	1	1
Joe Halbert	0	0	0
TOTAL	**18**	**16**	**52**
Coach: Hank Iba			

52-44

	1H	2H
Oklahoma A&M	28	24
DePaul	21	23

DEPAUL	FG	FT	TP
Ernest DiBenedetto	5	2	12
Gene Stump	5	2	12
George Mikan	2	5	9
Edwin Kachan	2	0	4
Ted Furman	1	1	3
John Phelan	1	0	2
Jack Allen	0	1	1
Gene LaRochelle	0	1	1
Nick Comerford	0	0	0
Tom Niemara	0	0	0
TOTAL	**16**	**12**	**44**
Coach: Ray Meyer			

Officials: Pat Kennedy, Hagan Anderson
Attendance: 18,158

1945-46: THE FIRST DYNASTY

Oklahoma A&M (today's Oklahoma State) became the first team to win two NCAA championships, and the (31–2) Aggies won them back to back. In the NCAA Final—the first one to be televised, on New York's WCBW—the Aggies beat North Carolina, 43-40. Bob Kurland, the Tournament's Most Outstanding Player, scored 23 points in the Final and accounted for 51.8% of the Aggies' total offense during the Tournament (72 of 139 points). This year's Tournament also featured the first national third-place game, in which Ohio State beat California, 63-45.

A college basketball record crowd of 22,822 watched a Feb. 23, 1946, doubleheader in Chicago Stadium, where Ohio State beat Northwestern, 53-46, and DePaul dumped Notre Dame, 63-47. After a fifth consecutive winless record in conference play, the University of Chicago dropped out of the Big Ten at the end of the season.

MAJOR CONFERENCE STANDINGS

BIG SIX	Conference			Overall		
	W	L	PCT	W	L	PCT
Kansas	10	0	1.000	19	2	.905
Oklahoma	7	3	.700	11	10	.524
Iowa State	5	5	.500	8	8	.500
Missouri	3	7	.300	6	11	.353
Nebraska	3	7	.300	7	13	.350
Kansas State	2	8	.200	4	20	.167

BIG TEN	Conference			Overall		
	W	L	PCT	W	L	PCT
Ohio State○	10	2	.833	16	5	.762
Indiana	9	3	.750	18	3	.857
Iowa	8	4	.667	14	4	.778
Northwestern	8	4	.667	15	5	.750
Illinois	7	5	.583	14	7	.667
Minnesota	7	5	.583	14	7	.667
Michigan	6	6	.500	12	7	.632
Purdue	4	8	.333	10	11	.476
Wisconsin	1	11	.083	4	17	.190
Chicago	0	12	.000	6	14	.300

BORDER	Conference			Overall		
	W	L	PCT	W	L	PCT
Arizona□	13	2	.867	25	5	.833
West Texas A&M	9	2	.818	19	8	.704
Texas Tech	7	4	.636	12	9	.571
New Mexico	13	8	.619	16	9	.640
Arizona State	6	8	.429	12	16	.429
Northern Arizona	4	6	.400	12	8	.600
Texas Western	4	7	.364	8	10	.444
New Mexico State	2	12	.143	5	16	.238
Hardin-Simmons	0	10	.000	2	10	.167

IVY	Conference			Overall		
	W	L	PCT	W	L	PCT
Dartmouth	7	1	.875	10	3	.769
Cornell	6	2	.750	12	5	.706
Penn	4	4	.500	7	10	.412
Columbia	3	5	.375	11	9	.550
Princeton	0	8	.000	7	12	.368

METRO NY	Conference			Overall		
	W	L	PCT	W	L	PCT
NYU○	5	1	.833	19	3	.864
St. John's□	5	1	.833	17	6	.739
CCNY	4	1	.800	14	4	.778
St. Francis (NY)	3	2	.600	12	6	.667
Manhattan	2	4	.333	15	8	.652
Brooklyn	1	5	.167	8	9	.471
Fordham	0	6	.000	5	16	.238

MISSOURI VALLEY	Conference			Overall		
	W	L	PCT	W	L	PCT
Oklahoma A&M○	12	0	1.000	31	2	.939
Wichita State	6	4	.600	14	9	.609
Saint Louis	6	5	.545	13	11	.542
Drake	5	7	.417	10	16	.385
Wash.-St. Louis	3	6	.333	10	17	.370
Creighton	3	7	.300	9	10	.474
Tulsa	3	9	.250	6	12	.333

BIG SEVEN	Conference			Overall		
	W	L	PCT	W	L	PCT
Wyoming	10	2	.833	22	4	.846
Colorado○	9	3	.750	12	6	.667
Utah	8	4	.667	12	8	.600
Colorado State	6	6	.500	15	9	.625
BYU	6	6	.500	12	13	.480
Utah State	2	10	.167	7	12	.368
Denver	1	11	.083	9	15	.375

NEW ENGLAND	Conference			Overall		
	W	L	PCT	W	L	PCT
Rhode Island□	4	0	1.000	21	3	.875
Connecticut	4	2	.667	11	6	.647
Maine	4	4	.500	10	4	.714
Northeastern	2	4	.333	4	13	.235
New Hampshire	0	4	.000	3	11	.214

PACIFIC COAST	Conference			Overall		
	W	L	PCT	W	L	PCT
North Division						
Idaho	11	5	.688	23	11	.676
Oregon State	10	6	.625	13	11	.542
Oregon	8	8	.500	16	17	.485
Washington	6	10	.375	14	14	.500
Washington State	5	11	.313	16	13	.552
South Division						
California○	11	1	.917	30	6	.833
Southern California	8	4	.667	14	7	.667
UCLA	5	7	.417	8	16	.333
Stanford	0	12	.000	6	18	.250

Playoff: **California d. Idaho 2-1** in a best-of-three series to win the title

SEC	Conference			Overall		
	W	L	PCT	W	L	PCT
LSU	8	0	1.000	18	3	.857
Kentucky□	6	0	1.000	28	2	.933
Tennessee	8	3	.727	15	5	.750
Alabama	8	4	.667	11	5	.688
Auburn	7	6	.538	7	9	.438
Georgia	6	6	.500	12	9	.571
Georgia Tech	7	7	.500	10	11	.476
Tulane	4	5	.444	15	7	.682
Vanderbilt	2	5	.286	3	10	.231
Florida	2	6	.250	7	14	.333
Mississippi	2	8	.200	8	11	.421
Mississippi State	3	13	.188	5	14	.263

Tournament: **Kentucky d. LSU 59-36**

SOUTHERN	Conference			Overall		
	W	L	PCT	W	L	PCT
North Carolina○	13	1	.929	30	5	.857
Duke	12	2	.857	21	6	.778
Virginia Tech	7	3	.700	11	8	.579
Wake Forest	8	5	.615	12	6	.667
Maryland	5	4	.556	9	12	.429
Furman	4	4	.500	16	3	.842
William and Mary	5	5	.500	10	10	.500
George Washington	4	5	.444	7	8	.467
Clemson	5	7	.417	9	11	.450
NC State	5	7	.417	6	12	.333
South Carolina	4	7	.364	9	11	.450
Davidson	5	9	.357	13	12	.520
Richmond	3	7	.300	8	12	.400
The Citadel	1	6	.143	7	11	.389
VMI	1	6	.143	1	10	.091
Washington and Lee	0	4	.000	2	11	.154

Tournament: **Duke d. Wake Forest 49-30**

SOUTHWEST	Conference			Overall		
	W	L	PCT	W	L	PCT
Baylor○	11	1	.917	25	5	.833
Arkansas	9	3	.750	16	7	.696
Texas	7	5	.583	16	7	.696
TCU	6	6	.500	13	11	.911
Rice	5	7	.417	10	11	.476
Texas A&M	4	8	.333	9	14	.391
SMU	0	12	.000	7	16	.304

INDEPENDENTS	Overall		
	W	L	PCT
Yale	14	1	.933
West Virginia□	24	3	.889
Harvard○	20	3	.870
Boston U.	12	2	.857
Loyola-Chicago	23	4	.852
Syracuse□	23	4	.852
Lafayette	17	3	.850
Bowling Green□	27	5	.844
Muhlenberg□	23	5	.821
Holy Cross	12	3	.800
Notre Dame	17	4	.810
Navy	12	3	.800
St. Bonaventure	12	3	.800
DePaul	19	5	.792
Louisville	22	6	.786
Indiana State	21	7	.750
Ohio	15	5	.750
Toledo	20	7	.741
Marshall	25	10	.714
Virginia	12	5	.706
Loyola (MD)	18	8	.692
Western Michigan	15	7	.682
Colgate	12	6	.667
Saint Mary's (CA)	10	5	.667
Detroit	15	8	.652
Rutgers	13	7	.650
Montana State	17	10	.630
Marquette	11	7	.611
Long Island	14	9	.609
Valparaiso	17	11	.607
Butler	12	8	.600
Temple	12	8	.600
Army	9	6	.600
Niagara	11	8	.579
Michigan State	12	9	.571
Santa Clara	8	6	.571
Georgetown	11	9	.550
Miami (OH)	10	9	.526
Kent State	10	10	.500
Pittsburgh	7	7	.500
Bradley	11	12	.478
Saint Joseph's	9	11	.450
Montana	13	16	.448
Western Kentucky	15	19	.441
Penn State	7	9	.438
Villanova	10	13	.435
San Francisco	9	12	.429
Canisius	8	11	.421
La Salle	9	14	.391
Cincinnati	8	13	.381
Bucknell	6	11	.353
Merchant Marine	5	10	.333
Brown	5	15	.250
Boston College	3	11	.214
Dayton	3	13	.188
Lehigh	3	13	.188
Xavier	3	16	.158

⊛ Automatic NCAA Tournament bid ○ At-large NCAA Tournament bid □ NIT appearance ❷ Team record doesn't reflect games forfeited or vacated. For adjusted record, see p. 521.

PREMO-PORRETTA POWER POLL

	SCHOOL	RECORD
1	Oklahoma A&M (NCAA champion)	31-2
2	Kentucky (NIT champion)	28-2
3	North Carolina	30-5
4	Indiana	18-3
5	Rhode Island	21-3
6	DePaul	19-5
7	West Virginia	24-3
8	Ohio State	16-5
9	Bowling Green	27-5
10	Notre Dame	17-4
11	Yale	14-1
12	Kansas	19-2
13	NYU	19-3
14	Illinois	14-7
15	Northwestern	15-5
16	Holy Cross	12-3
17	Wyoming	22-4
18	Iowa	14-4
19	Dartmouth	13-3#
20	Michigan	12-7
21	Harvard	20-3
22	Muhlenberg	23-5
23	Syracuse	23-4
24	Lafayette	17-3
25	Minnesota	14-7

CONSENSUS ALL-AMERICAS

FIRST TEAM

PLAYER	CL	POS	HT	SCHOOL	PPG
Leo Klier	SR	F	6-2	Notre Dame	16.9
Bob Kurland	SR	C	7-0	Oklahoma A&M	19.5
George Mikan	SR	C	6-9	DePaul	23.1
Max Morris	JR	F	6-2	Northwestern	17.2
Sid Tanenbaum	JR	G	6-0	NYU	12.9

SECOND TEAM

PLAYER	CL	POS	HT	SCHOOL	PPG
Charlie B. Black	JR	F	6-4	Kansas	16.3
John Dillon	SO	F	6-3	North Carolina	12.9
Bill Hassett	SR	G	5-10	Notre Dame	8.0
Tony Lavelli	FR	F	6-3	Yale	21.3
Jack Parkinson	JR	G	6-0	Kentucky	11.3
Kenny Sailors	SR	G	5-10	Wyoming	9.2

SELECTORS: CONVERSE YEARBOOK, HELMS FOUNDATION, SPORTING NEWS, TRUE MAGAZINE

1946 NCAA TOURNAMENT

REGIONAL SEMIFINALS | REGIONAL FINALS (A)

EAST

Ohio State **46**
Harvard **38**

North Carolina **57**
NYU **49**

Ohio State **57** (OT)
North Carolina **60** (B)

WEST

Oklahoma A&M **44**
Baylor **29**

California **50**
Colorado **44**

Oklahoma A&M **52**
California **35**

NATIONAL FINAL

Oklahoma A&M 43
North Carolina 40

NEW YORK CITY

Bob Kurland brings his Oklahoma A&M career to a close with two dunks and 23 points. UNC's 6'6" Horace "Bones" McKinney fouls out early in the second half trying to guard him. The game is televised for the first time, but only in the New York City area. The viewing audience is estimated at 500,000.

National Third Place Ohio State d. California 63-45
East Regional Third Place NYU d. Harvard 67-61
West Regional Third Place Colorado d. Baylor 59-44

(A) This is the first Tournament in which four teams advance to the Final site. With only East and West divisions, the two regional champs play for the title while the losers vie for third place.

(B) UNC's Bob Paxton hits a 35-foot one-hander with :10 left to send the game into overtime. Bones McKinney, who would later coach Wake Forest, scores nine points for the Tar Heels.

Record differs from the school's and/or the NCAA's because it includes noncollegiate competition or because the outcome of some games is in dispute.

TOURNAMENT LEADERS

INDIVIDUAL LEADERS

SCORING

	CL	POS	G	PTS	PPG
1 **Bob Kurland**, Oklahoma A&M	SR	C	3	72	24.0
2 **Jack Underman**, Ohio State	JR	C	3	56	18.7
3 **Wyndol Gray**, Harvard	SR	F	2	33	16.5
4 **John Dillon**, North Carolina	SO	F	3	47	15.7
5 **Joseph DeBonis**, NYU	SO	G/F	2	28	14.0
6 **Merv Lafaille**, California	SR	F	3	40	13.3
7 **Frank Mangiapane**, NYU	JR	G	2	26	13.0
8 **Andy Wolfe**, California	SO	F	3	37	12.3
9 **Robert Bowen**, Ohio State	JR	F	3	34	11.3
10 **Tommy Kelly**, NYU	SO	F	2	22	11.0

MINIMUM: 2 GAMES

FIELD GOALS PER GAME

	CL	POS	G	FG	FGPG
1 **Bob Kurland**, Oklahoma A&M	SR	C	3	28	9.3
2 **Jack Underman**, Ohio State	JR	C	3	19	6.3
3 **Andy Wolfe**, California	SO	F	3	18	6.0
Joseph DeBonis, NYU	SO	G/F	2	12	6.0
5 **John Dillon**, North Carolina	SO	F	3	17	5.7

MINIMUM: 2 GAMES

FREE THROW PCT

	CL	POS	G	FT	FTA	PCT
1 **Robert Bowen**, Ohio State	JR	F	3	10	10	100.0
Merv Lafaille, California	SR	F	3	8	8	100.0
Sid Tanenbaum, NYU	JR	G	2	7	7	100.0
Eugene Bell, Oklahoma A&M	SR	G	3	6	6	100.0
5 **Jack Underman**, Ohio State	JR	C	3	18	21	85.7
Bob Hogeboom, California	JR	G	3	6	7	85.7

MINIMUM: 5 MADE

TEAM LEADERS

SCORING

	G	PTS	PPG
1 **NYU**	2	116	58.0
2 **Ohio State**	3	166	55.3
3 **North Carolina**	3	157	52.3
4 **Colorado**	2	103	51.5
5 **Harvard**	2	99	49.5
6 **Oklahoma A&M**	3	139	46.3
7 **California**	3	130	43.3
8 **Baylor**	2	73	36.5

MINIMUM: 2 GAMES

FT PCT

	G	FT	FTA	PCT
1 **Baylor**	2	23	33	69.7
2 **NYU**	2	30	45	66.7
3 **Ohio State**	3	48	74	64.9
4 **Oklahoma A&M**	3	37	61	60.7
5 **Harvard**	2	33	55	60.0

MINIMUM: 2 GAMES

FG PER GAME

	G	FG	FGPG
1 **NYU**	2	43	21.5
2 **North Carolina**	3	60	20.0
3 **Ohio State**	3	59	19.7
4 **Colorado**	2	39	19.5
5 **California**	3	53	17.7

TOURNAMENT MOP

PLAYER	CL	POS	HT	SCHOOL	FG	FT	PPG
Bob Kurland	SR	C	7-0	Oklahoma A&M	28	16-27	24.0

1946 NCAA TOURNAMENT BOX SCORES

46-38 (ELITE 8)

	1H	2H
Ohio State	26	20
Harvard	20	18

OHIO STATE	MIN	FG	3FG	FT	REB	A	ST	BL	PF	TP
Jack Underman	-	5	-	4-5	-	-	-	-	5	14
Paul Huston	-	3	-	6-9	-	-	-	-	3	12
Warren Amling	-	3	-	0-2	-	-	-	-	3	6
Robert Bowen	-	3	-	0-0	-	-	-	-	4	6
Wayne Wells	-	2	-	0-2	-	-	-	-	2	4
Ray Snyder	-	1	-	1-2	-	-	-	-	4	3
Clark Elliott	-	0	-	1-2	-	-	-	-	4	1
Charles Kuhn	-	0	-	0-0	-	-	-	-	0	0
TOTALS	**-**	**17**	**-**	**12-22**	**-**	**-**	**-**	**-**	**25**	**46**
Percentages				54.5						

Coach: Harold Olsen

HARVARD	MIN	FG	3FG	FT	REB	A	ST	BL	PF	TP
Wyndol Gray	-	2	-	7-9	-	-	-	-	3	11
Saul Mariaschin	-	5	-	1-2	-	-	-	-	2	11
Louis Decsi	-	1	-	5-8	-	-	-	-	4	7
John Gantt	-	1	-	2-2	-	-	-	-	1	4
Paul Champion	-	0	-	2-6	-	-	-	-	4	2
Donald Swegan	-	1	-	0-1	-	-	-	-	3	2
Ralph Petrillo	-	0	-	1-2	-	-	-	-	1	1
John Clark	-	0	-	0-0	-	-	-	-	0	0
Stephen Davis	-	0	-	0-0	-	-	-	-	0	0
William McDaniel	-	0	-	0-0	-	-	-	-	0	0
TOTALS	**-**	**10**	**-**	**18-30**	**-**	**-**	**-**	**-**	**18**	**38**
Percentages				60.0						

Coach: Floyd S. Stahl

Officials: Orwig, Nucatola

57-49 (ELITE 8)

	1H	2H
North Carolina	29	28
NYU	22	27

NORTH CAROLINA	MIN	FG	3FG	FT	REB	A	ST	BL	PF	TP
John Dillon	-	7	-	1-4	-	-	-	-	5	15
Bob Paxton	-	6	-	1-4	-	-	-	-	1	13
Bones McKinney	-	4	-	3-4	-	-	-	-	4	11
Jim Jordan	-	4	-	2-2	-	-	-	-	5	10
Don Anderson	-	1	-	2-4	-	-	-	-	2	4
Taylor Thorne	-	2	-	0-0	-	-	-	-	1	4
Roger Scholbe	-	0	-	0-0	-	-	-	-	0	0
Jim White	-	0	-	0-0	-	-	-	-	5	0
TOTALS	**-**	**24**	**-**	**9-18**	**-**	**-**	**-**	**-**	**23**	**57**
Percentages				50.0						

Coach: Ben Carnevale

NYU	MIN	FG	3FG	FT	REB	A	ST	BL	PF	TP
Joseph Debonis	-	5	-	3-4	-	-	-	-	4	13
Frank Mangiapane	-	4	-	3-6	-	-	-	-	4	11
Dolph Schayes	-	2	-	5-6	-	-	-	-	1	9
Don Forman	-	1	-	3-4	-	-	-	-	2	5
Sid Tanenbaum	-	1	-	3-3	-	-	-	-	3	5
Howard Sarath	-	2	-	0-2	-	-	-	-	1	4
Joseph Dolhon	-	1	-	0-0	-	-	-	-	0	2
Frank Benanti	-	0	-	0-0	-	-	-	-	0	0
Marty Goldstein	-	0	-	0-0	-	-	-	-	0	0
Tommy Kelly	-	0	-	0-0	-	-	-	-	3	0
TOTALS	**-**	**16**	**-**	**17-25**	**-**	**-**	**-**	**-**	**18**	**49**
Percentages				68.0						

Coach: Howard Cann

Officials: Kennedy, Collins

44-29 (ELITE 8)

	1H	2H
Oklahoma A&M	22	22
Baylor	17	12

OKLAHOMA A&M	MIN	FG	3FG	FT	REB	A	ST	BL	PF	TP
Bob Kurland	-	7	-	6-12	-	-	-	-	2	20
J.L. Parks	-	4	-	1-2	-	-	-	-	0	9
Joe Bradley	-	3	-	1-2	-	-	-	-	1	7
Eugene Bell	-	0	-	3-3	-	-	-	-	1	3
Weldon Kern	-	0	-	3-5	-	-	-	-	2	3
Blake Williams	-	1	-	0-1	-	-	-	-	5	2
Sam Aubrey	-	0	-	0-0	-	-	-	-	0	0
A.L. Bennett	-	0	-	0-0	-	-	-	-	0	0
Joe Halbert	-	0	-	0-0	-	-	-	-	0	0
TOTALS	**-**	**15**	**-**	**14-25**	**-**	**-**	**-**	**-**	**11**	**44**
Percentages				56.0						

Coach: Hank Iba

BAYLOR	MIN	FG	3FG	FT	REB	A	ST	BL	PF	TP
Bill Johnson	-	4	-	2-3	-	-	-	-	4	10
Bill Hailey	-	3	-	1-1	-	-	-	-	2	7
Jackie Robinson	-	1	-	3-4	-	-	-	-	4	5
Mark Belew	-	2	-	0-1	-	-	-	-	3	4
Charles Devereaux	-	1	-	0-0	-	-	-	-	1	2
Len McCormick	-	0	-	1-2	-	-	-	-	1	1
Frankie Edwards	-	0	-	0-0	-	-	-	-	5	0
Dickie Gonzales	-	0	-	0-0	-	-	-	-	0	0
George Shearin	-	0	-	0-0	-	-	-	-	5	0
TOTALS	**-**	**11**	**-**	**7-11**	**-**	**-**	**-**	**-**	**25**	**29**
Percentages				63.6						

Coach: Bill Henderson

Officials: Oberhelman, Baker

50-44 (Elite 8)

CALIFORNIA	MIN	FG	3FG	FT	REB	A	ST	BL	PF	TP
Andy Wolfe	-	8	-	1-2	-	-	-	-	0	17
Bob Hogeboom	-	3	-	2-2	-	-	-	-	0	8
Merv Lafaille	-	3	-	2-2	-	-	-	-	4	8
Jim Wray	-	4	-	0-2	-	-	-	-	2	8
George Walker	-	2	-	1-6	-	-	-	-	3	5
Jim Smith	-	2	-	0-3	-	-	-	-	4	4
TOTALS	-	**22**	-	**6-17**	-	-	-	-	**13**	**50**
Percentages				35.3						

Coach: Clarence "Nibs" Price

23	1H	18
27	2H	26

COLORADO	MIN	FG	3FG	FT	REB	A	ST	BL	PF	TP
Hank Knocke	-	4	-	1-1	-	-	-	-	2	9
Horace Huggins	-	2	-	4-5	-	-	-	-	3	8
Russell Walseth	-	3	-	1-1	-	-	-	-	0	7
Clarence Ellis	-	3	-	0-0	-	-	-	-	0	6
Harold Beattie	-	2	-	1-1	-	-	-	-	0	5
Donald Putnam	-	2	-	1-2	-	-	-	-	3	5
Ernie Fuller	-	1	-	0-0	-	-	-	-	2	2
Lee Robbins	-	1	-	0-3	-	-	-	-	5	2
Bill Allen	-	0	-	0-0	-	-	-	-	0	0
Jack Hunt	-	0	-	0-0	-	-	-	-	0	0
TOTALS	-	**18**	-	**8-13**	-	-	-	-	**15**	**44**
Percentages				61.5						

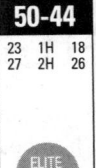

Coach: Forrest B. "Frosty" Cox

Officials: Curtis, VanReen

60-57 (Final 4)

NORTH CAROLINA	MIN	FG	3FG	FT	REB	A	ST	BL	PF	TP
John Dillon	-	5	-	6-13	-	-	-	-	4	16
Jim Jordan	-	4	-	4-5	-	-	-	-	3	12
Bones McKinney	-	4	-	1-3	-	-	-	-	5	9
Bob Paxton	-	4	-	0-2	-	-	-	-	3	8
Jim White	-	2	-	3-4	-	-	-	-	4	7
Don Anderson	-	3	-	0-1	-	-	-	-	2	6
Taylor Thorne	-	1	-	0-1	-	-	-	-	1	2
Roger Scholbe	-	0	-	0-0	-	-	-	-	1	0
TOTALS	-	**23**	-	**14-29**	-	-	-	-	**23**	**60**
Percentages				48.3						

Coach: Ben Carnevale

19	1H	20
35	2H	34
6	OT1	3

OHIO STATE	MIN	FG	3FG	FT	REB	A	ST	BL	PF	TP
Jack Underman	-	8	-	7-8	-	-	-	-	4	23
Robert Bowen	-	3	-	6-6	-	-	-	-	4	12
Ray Snyder	-	4	-	3-7	-	-	-	-	3	11
Paul Huston	-	3	-	3-6	-	-	-	-	5	9
Warren Amling	-	1	-	0-1	-	-	-	-	5	2
Wilbur Johnston	-	0	-	0-0	-	-	-	-	0	0
Wayne Wells	-	0	-	0-2	-	-	-	-	4	0
TOTALS	-	**19**	-	**19-30**	-	-	-	-	**25**	**57**
Percentages				63.3						

Coach: Harold Olsen

Officials: Nucatola, Orwig

52-35 (Final 4)

OKLAHOMA A&M	MIN	FG	3FG	FT	REB	A	ST	BL	PF	TP
Bob Kurland	-	12	-	5-6	-	-	-	-	3	29
J.L. Parks	-	2	-	1-1	-	-	-	-	1	5
Eugene Bell	-	1	-	2-2	-	-	-	-	2	4
A.L. Bennett	-	1	-	2-2	-	-	-	-	1	4
Weldon Kern	-	2	-	0-0	-	-	-	-	1	4
Joe Bradley	-	1	-	1-2	-	-	-	-	1	3
Blake Williams	-	1	-	1-1	-	-	-	-	0	3
Sam Aubrey	-	0	-	0-0	-	-	-	-	0	0
Paul Geymann	-	0	-	0-0	-	-	-	-	0	0
Joe Halbert	-	0	-	0-0	-	-	-	-	0	0
Lou Steinmeir	-	0	-	0-0	-	-	-	-	0	0
TOTALS	-	**20**	-	**12-14**	-	-	-	-	**9**	**52**
Percentages				85.7						

Coach: Hank Iba

26	1H	21
26	2H	14

CALIFORNIA	MIN	FG	3FG	FT	REB	A	ST	BL	PF	TP
Andy Wolfe	-	7	-	0-1	-	-	-	-	2	14
Merv Lafaille	-	4	-	2-2	-	-	-	-	4	10
George Walker	-	2	-	2-3	-	-	-	-	2	6
Bob Hogeboom	-	0	-	2-3	-	-	-	-	0	2
Jim Wray	-	1	-	0-0	-	-	-	-	2	2
Jim Smith	-	0	-	1-3	-	-	-	-	3	1
Les Dean	-	0	-	0-0	-	-	-	-	0	0
Dick Larner	-	0	-	0-0	-	-	-	-	0	0
TOTALS	-	**14**	-	**7-12**	-	-	-	-	**13**	**35**
Percentages				58.3						

Coach: Clarence "Nibs" Price

Officials: Baker, Curtis

63-45 (3rd Place)

OHIO STATE	MIN	FG	3FG	FT	REB	A	ST	BL	PF	TP
Jack Underman	-	6	-	7-8	-	-	-	-	4	19
Robert Bowen	-	6	-	4-4	-	-	-	-	2	16
Warren Amling	-	5	-	0-1	-	-	-	-	4	10
Ray Snyder	-	3	-	4-5	-	-	-	-	2	10
Paul Huston	-	2	-	1-2	-	-	-	-	3	5
Clark Elliott	-	1	-	1-1	-	-	-	-	1	3
Wilbur Johnston	-	0	-	0-0	-	-	-	-	0	0
Charles Kuhn	-	0	-	0-0	-	-	-	-	0	0
John Lovett	-	0	-	0-1	-	-	-	-	0	0
Wayne Wells	-	0	-	0-0	-	-	-	-	0	0
TOTALS	-	**23**	-	**17-22**	-	-	-	-	**16**	**63**
Percentages				77.3						

Coach: Harold Olsen

22	1H	21
41	2H	24

CALIFORNIA	MIN	FG	3FG	FT	REB	A	ST	BL	PF	TP
Merv Lafaille	-	9	-	4-4	-	-	-	-	2	22
Bob Hogeboom	-	2	-	2-2	-	-	-	-	1	6
Andy Wolfe	-	3	-	0-0	-	-	-	-	1	6
Jim Smith	-	2	-	0-0	-	-	-	-	4	4
George Walker	-	1	-	2-7	-	-	-	-	4	4
Lowell Holcombe	-	0	-	1-1	-	-	-	-	1	1
Art Mower	-	0	-	1-1	-	-	-	-	2	1
Jim Wray	-	0	-	1-2	-	-	-	-	1	1
Bob Anderson	-	0	-	0-0	-	-	-	-	0	0
Les Dean	-	0	-	0-0	-	-	-	-	0	0
Dick Larner	-	0	-	0-0	-	-	-	-	0	0
Cal Remke	-	0	-	0-0	-	-	-	-	1	0
TOTALS	-	**17**	-	**11-17**	-	-	-	-	**17**	**45**
Percentages				64.7						

Coach: Clarence "Nibs" Price

Officials: Orwig, Nucatola

43-40 (NCAA Final 1946)

OKLAHOMA A&M	MIN	FG	3FG	FT	REB	A	ST	BL	PF	TP
Bob Kurland	-	9	-	5-9	-	-	-	-	5	23
Weldon Kern	-	3	-	1-3	-	-	-	-	2	7
A.L. Bennett	-	3	-	0-0	-	-	-	-	4	6
Joe Bradley	-	1	-	1-2	-	-	-	-	1	3
Blake Williams	-	0	-	2-4	-	-	-	-	2	2
Sam Aubrey	-	0	-	1-2	-	-	-	-	1	1
Eugene Bell	-	0	-	1-1	-	-	-	-	1	1
Joe Halbert	-	0	-	0-0	-	-	-	-	0	0
J.L. Parks	-	0	-	0-1	-	-	-	-	2	0
TOTALS	-	**16**	-	**11-22**	-	-	-	-	**18**	**43**
Percentages				50.0						

Coach: Hank Iba

23	1H	17
20	2H	23

NORTH CAROLINA	MIN	FG	3FG	FT	REB	A	ST	BL	PF	TP
John Dillon	-	5	-	6-6	-	-	-	-	5	16
Don Anderson	-	3	-	2-3	-	-	-	-	3	8
Bones McKinney	-	2	-	1-3	-	-	-	-	5	5
Jim Jordan	-	0	-	4-8	-	-	-	-	3	4
Bob Paxton	-	2	-	0-0	-	-	-	-	4	4
Taylor Thorne	-	1	-	0-0	-	-	-	-	2	2
Jim White	-	0	-	1-1	-	-	-	-	0	1
TOTALS	-	**13**	-	**14-21**	-	-	-	-	**22**	**40**
Percentages			-	66.7						

Coach: Ben Carnevale

Officials: Kennedy, Collins
Attendance: 18,479

NATIONAL INVITATION TOURNAMENT (NIT)

Quarterfinals: Rhode Island d. Bowling Green 82-79 (OT), West Virginia d. St. John's 70-58, Kentucky d. Arizona 77-53, Muhlenberg d. Syracuse 47-41
Semifinals: Rhode Island d. Muhlenberg 59-49, Kentucky d. West Virginia 59-51
Third place: West Virginia d. Muhlenberg 65-40,
Championship: Kentucky d. Rhode Island 46-45
MVP: Ernie Calverley, Rhode Island

1946-47: Doggie Days

Texas and its Mighty Mice—three starters 5'10" or shorter—amassed a 25–1 record before falling to Oklahoma 55-54 in the NCAA Tournament West Regional finals Both of the Longhorns losses came by a single point. Holy Cross (24–3), coached by Alvin "Doggie" Julian, won 20 consecutive games entering the Tournament, but the Crusaders had to battle back from early deficits in all three of their games, beating Navy, CCNY and finally Oklahoma, 58-47, in the championship game at New York's Madison Square Garden.

Before the season, the NCAA announced that transparent backboards could be used in games. UCLA's Don Barksdale became the second African-American player to be chosen as a consensus All-America, after George Gregory of Columbia in 1930-31. And, in an accomplishment certain to never be equaled, 27-year-old Seton Hall coach Bob Davies led the Pirates to a 24–3 record while also earning National Basketball League Most Valuable Player honors for the Rochester Royals. Davies is also credited as the inventor of the behind-the-back dribble.

Major Conference Standings

BIG SIX	Conference W	L	Pct	Overall W	L	Pct
Oklahoma○	8	2	.800	24	7	.774
Missouri	6	4	.600	15	10	.600
Kansas	5	5	.500	16	11	.593
Iowa State	5	5	.500	7	14	.333
Kansas State	3	7	.300	14	10	.583
Nebraska	3	7	.300	10	14	.417

BIG TEN	Conference W	L	Pct	Overall W	L	Pct
Wisconsin○	9	3	.750	16	6	.727
Illinois	8	4	.667	14	6	.700
Indiana	8	4	.667	12	8	.600
Minnesota	7	5	.583	14	7	.667
Michigan	6	6	.500	12	8	.600
Iowa	5	7	.417	12	7	.632
Ohio State	5	7	.417	7	13	.350
Purdue	4	8	.333	9	11	.450
Northwestern	2	10	.167	7	13	.350

BORDER	Conference W	L	Pct	Overall W	L	Pct
Arizona	14	2	.875	21	3	.875
Northern Arizona	11	5	.688	20	7	.741
New Mexico	10	6	.625	11	8	.579
Texas Western	9	7	.563	12	8	.600
West Texas A&M	8	8	.500	12	12	.500
Texas Tech	8	8	.500	10	12	.455
Arizona State	6	11	.352	7	13	.350
Hardin-Simmons	5	11	.313	8	21	.276
New Mexico State	2	14	.125	8	17	.320

IVY	Conference W	L	Pct	Overall W	L	Pct
Columbia	11	1	.917	15	5	.750
Cornell	8	4	.667	14	8	.636
Penn	7	5	.583	14	8	.636
Harvard	5	7	.417	16	9	.640
Dartmouth	5	7	.417	9	15	.375
Yale	4	8	.333	7	18	.280
Princeton	2	10	.167	7	16	.304

METRO NY	Conference W	L	Pct	Overall W	L	Pct
St. John's□	6	0	1.000	16	7	.696
CCNY○	4	1	.800	17	6	.739
Fordham	4	2	.667	19	5	.792
NYU	3	3	.500	12	9	.571
St. Francis (NY)	2	3	.400	14	7	.667
Manhattan	1	5	.167	13	13	.500
Brooklyn	0	6	.000	12	8	.600

MID-AMERICAN	Conference W	L	Pct	Overall W	L	Pct
Butler	6	2	.750	16	7	.696
Cincinnati	6	2	.750	17	9	.654
Ohio	5	3	.625	13	10	.565
Western Reserve	2	6	.250	7	11	.389
Wayne State (MI)	1	7	.125	3	15	.167

MISSOURI VALLEY	Conference W	L	Pct	Overall W	L	Pct
Saint Louis	11	1	.917	18	11	.621
Oklahoma A&M	8	4	.667	24	8	.750
Drake	8	4	.667	18	11	.621
Creighton	7	5	.583	17	8	.680
Wash.-St. Louis	3	9	.250	11	14	.440
Tulsa	3	9	.250	5	19	.208
Wichita State	2	10	.167	8	17	.320

BIG SEVEN	Conference W	L	Pct	Overall W	L	Pct
Wyoming○	11	1	.917	22	6	.786
Utah□	10	2	.833	19	5	.792
Denver	6	6	.500	16	10	.615
Utah State	6	6	.500	14	10	.583
Colorado	5	7	.417	7	11	.389
BYU	3	9	.250	9	16	.360
Colorado State	1	11	.083	3	18	.143

PACIFIC COAST	Conference W	L	Pct	Overall W	L	Pct
North						
Oregon State○	13	3	.813	28	5	.848
Washington State	11	5	.688	23	10	.697
Washington	8	8	.500	16	8	.667
Oregon	7	9	.438	18	9	.667
Idaho	1	15	.063	4	24	.143
South						
UCLA	9	3	.750	18	7	.720
California	8	4	.667	20	11	.645
Stanford	5	7	.417	15	16	.484
Southern California	2	10	.167	10	14	.417

Playoff: **Oregon State d. UCLA 2-0** in a best-of-three series to win the title

SEC	Conference W	L	Pct	Overall W	L	Pct
Kentucky□	11	0	1.000	34	3	.919
LSU	8	2	.800	17	4	.810
Tennessee	10	3	.769	16	5	.762
Alabama	13	5	.722	16	6	.727
Tulane	8	5	.615	22	9	.710
Florida	4	4	.500	17	9	.654
Georgia Tech	6	6	.500	12	11	.522
Vanderbilt	4	7	.364	7	8	.467
Mississippi State	4	9	.308	10	11	.476
Georgia	4	9	.308	5	14	.263
Mississippi	2	11	.154	7	14	.333
Auburn	1	15	.063	3	18	.143

Tournament: **Kentucky d. Tulane 55-38**

SOUTHERN	Conference W	L	Pct	Overall W	L	Pct
NC State□	11	2	.846	26	5	.839
North Carolina	10	2	.833	19	8	.704
Duke	10	4	.714	19	8	.704
George Washington	9	4	.692	21	7	.750
Maryland	9	5	.643	14	10	.583
Richmond	8	5	.615	17	9	.654
South Carolina	7	5	.583	16	9	.640
Washington and Lee	7	6	.538	16	7	.696
Davidson	7	7	.500	17	8	.680
William and Mary	6	6	.500	14	12	.538
Wake Forest	8	9	.471	11	13	.458
Furman	5	7	.417	9	10	.474
Virginia Tech	4	9	.308	13	13	.500
Clemson	2	12	.143	7	13	.350
The Citadel	1	11	.083	5	11	.313
VMI	1	11	.083	4	15	.211

Tournament: **NC State d. North Carolina 50-48**

SOUTHWEST	Conference W	L	Pct	Overall W	L	Pct
Texas○	12	0	1.000	26	2	.929
SMU	8	4	.667	14	8	.636
Arkansas	8	4	.667	14	10	.583
Baylor	6	6	.500	11	11	.500
Texas A&M	4	8	.333	8	17	.320
Rice	3	9	.250	7	17	.292
TCU	1	11	.083	1	22	.043

WNY LITTLE THREE	Conference W	L	Pct	Overall W	L	Pct
Canisius	3	0	1.000	18	13	.581
Niagara	2	2	.500	13	8	.619
St. Bonaventure	0	3	.000	10	11	.476

YANKEE	Conference W	L	Pct	Overall W	L	Pct
Vermont	1	0	1.000	19	3	.864
Connecticut	6	1	.857	16	2	.889
Rhode Island	4	1	.800	17	3	.850
Maine	2	4	.333	9	8	.529
New Hampshire	0	5	.000	6	11	.353
Massachusetts	0	2	.000	4	12	.250

⊛ Automatic NCAA Tournament bid ○ At-large NCAA Tournament bid □ NIT appearance ❂ Team record doesn't reflect games forfeited or vacated. For adjusted record, see p. 521.

INDEPENDENTS

	Overall W	L	Pct
Duquesne□	20	2	.909
Holy Cross○	27	3	.900
Seton Hall	24	3	.889
West Virginia□	19	3	.864
Western Kentucky	25	4	.862
Navy○	16	3	.842
Santa Clara	21	4	.840
Notre Dame	20	4	.833
Bowling Green	28	7	.800
Bradley□	25	7	.781
Long Island□	17	5	.773
Syracuse	19	6	.760
Georgetown	19	7	.731
Saint Joseph's	16	6	.727
Villanova	17	7	.708
Western Michigan	17	7	.708
Loyola-Chicago	20	9	.690
Boston U.	14	7	.667
Colgate	11	6	.647
DePaul	16	9	.640
Nevada	19	13	.594
Army	9	7	.563
Penn State	10	8	.556
Boston College	12	10	.545
Michigan State	11	10	.524
Siena	12	11	.522
San Francisco	13	14	.481
Virginia	10	11	.476
Detroit	11	13	.458
Pittsburgh	8	10	.444
Saint Mary's (CA)	13	17	.433
Montana	12	16	.429
Brown	8	12	.400
Temple	8	12	.400
Marquette	9	14	.391
Rutgers	7	12	.368
Merchant Marine	8	16	.333

PREMO-PORRETTA POWER POLL

	School	Record
1	Kentucky	34-3
2	Holy Cross (NCAA champion)	27-3
3	Texas	26-2
4	Utah (NIT champion)	19-5
5	Duquesne	21-2
6	NC State	26-5
7	Oklahoma	24-7
8	Western Kentucky	25-4
9	Oregon State	28-5
10	Navy	16-3
11	Notre Dame	20-4
12	West Virginia	19-3
13	CCNY	17-6
14	Wyoming	22-6
15	Oklahoma A&M	24-8
16	Seton Hall	24-3
17	Long Island	18-5#
18	Wisconsin	16-6
19	Bowling Green	28-7
20	Santa Clara	21-4
21	Washington State	23-10
22	Illinois	14-6
23	Syracuse	19-6
24	St. John's	16-7
25	Washington	16-8

CONSENSUS ALL-AMERICAS

FIRST TEAM

PLAYER	CL	POS	HT	SCHOOL	PPG
Ralph Beard	SO	G	5-10	Kentucky	10.6
Ralph Hamilton	SR	F	6-1	Indiana	13.4
Alex Groza	SO	C	6-7	Kentucky	10.6
Sid Tanenbaum	SR	G	6-0	NYU	13.2
Gerald Tucker	SR	C	6-6	Oklahoma	10.5

SECOND TEAM

PLAYER	CL	POS	HT	SCHOOL	PPG
Don Barksdale	SR	C	6-6	UCLA	14.7
Arnie Ferrin	JR	G/F	6-4	Utah	11.4
Vern Gardner	SO	C	6-5	Utah	14.5
John Hargis	SR	F	6-2	Texas	N/A
George Kaftan	SO	C	6-3	Holy Cross	11.1
Ed Koffenberger	JR	C	6-2	Duke	15.4
Andrew Phillip	SR	G	6-2	Illinois	9.6

SELECTORS: CONVERSE YEARBOOK, HELMS FOUNDATION, TRUE MAGAZINE

1947 NCAA TOURNAMENT

Regional Semifinals

EAST
- Holy Cross **55**, Navy **47**
- CCNY **70**, Wisconsin **56**

WEST
- Texas **42**, Wyoming **40**
- Oklahoma **56**, Oregon State **54**

Regional Finals
- Holy Cross **60**, CCNY **45** (A)
- Texas **54**, Oklahoma **55** (B)

National Final — New York City
- **Holy Cross 58, Oklahoma 47**

Holy Cross shuts down Oklahoma's 6'6" center, Gerald Tucker, in the second half and becomes the first Eastern school to win the Tournament. It wasn't easy: The Crusaders practiced in a barn and played home games 45 miles away at the Boston Garden.

A Holy Cross has talented scorers in George Kaftan and Joe Mullaney while future star Bob Cousy rides the bench. Kaftan scores 30 to break open a close game late in the second half.

B Texas has a one-point lead with :10 left but Ken Pryor, a little-used reserve, sinks the game-winner from 40 feet for his only points of the game. The teams play in Kansas City, but both ride the same train to New York City for the title and third-place games.

National Third Place Texas d. CCNY 54-50
East Regional Third Place Wisconsin d. Navy 50-49
West Regional Third Place Oregon State d. Wyoming 63-46

\# Record differs from the school's and/or the NCAA's because it includes noncollegiate competition or because the outcome of some games is in dispute.

TOURNAMENT LEADERS

INDIVIDUAL LEADERS

SCORING

	CL	POS	G	PTS	PPG
1 **George Kaftan**, Holy Cross	SO	C	3	63	21.0
2 **Lew Beck**, Oregon State	SR	G	2	40	20.0
3 **Gerald Tucker**, Oklahoma	SR	C	3	54	18.0
4 **Bob Cook**, Wisconsin	JR	F	2	34	17.0
5 **Irwin Dambrot**, CCNY	FR	F/C	3	43	14.3
6 **Slater Martin**, Texas	SO	G	3	41	13.7
7 **Jim Reese**, Wyoming	SR	F	2	27	13.5
8 **Floyd Waldrop**, Navy	JR	C	2	26	13.0
9 **John Hargis**, Texas	SR	F	3	35	11.7
10 **Paul Courty**, Oklahoma	SO	G	3	33	11.0

MINIMUM: 2 GAMES

FIELD GOALS PER GAME

	CL	POS	G	FG	FGPG
1 **George Kaftan**, Holy Cross	SO	C	3	25	8.3
2 **Lew Beck**, Oregon State	SR	G	2	16	8.0
3 **Bob Cook**, Wisconsin	JR	F	2	15	7.5
4 **Slater Martin**, Texas	SO	G	3	19	6.3
Gerald Tucker, Oklahoma	SR	C	3	19	6.3

MINIMUM: 2 GAMES

FREE THROW PCT

	CL	POS	G	FT	FTA	PCT
1 **Dick Reich**, Oklahoma	SR	F	3	8	8	100.0
2 **Frank Oftring**, Holy Cross	FR	F	3	6	7	85.7
Cliff Crandall, Oregon State	SO	G/F	2	6	7	85.7
4 **Gerald Tucker**, Oklahoma	SR	C	3	16	19	84.2
5 **John Langdon**, Texas	JR	C	3	5	6	83.3
Ken Shugart, Navy	SR	G	2	5	6	83.3

MINIMUM: 5 MADE

TEAM LEADERS

SCORING

	G	PTS	PPG
1 **Oregon State**	2	117	58.5
2 **Holy Cross**	3	173	57.7
3 **CCNY**	3	165	55.0
4 **Wisconsin**	2	106	53.0
5 **Oklahoma**	3	158	52.7
6 **Texas**	3	150	50.0
7 **Navy**	2	96	48.0
8 **Wyoming**	2	86	43.0

MINIMUM: 2 GAMES

FT PCT

	G	FT	FTA	PCT
1 **Oklahoma**	3	46	61	75.4
2 **Oregon State**	2	23	35	65.7
3 **Wisconsin**	2	22	35	62.9
4 **Texas**	3	32	51	62.7
5 **Holy Cross**	3	37	60	61.7

MINIMUM: 2 GAMES

FG PER GAME

	G	FG	FGPG
1 **Oregon State**	2	47	23.5
2 **Holy Cross**	3	68	22.7
3 **CCNY**	3	65	21.7
4 **Wisconsin**	2	42	21.0
5 **Texas**	3	59	19.7

TOURNAMENT MOP

PLAYER	CL	POS	HT	SCHOOL	FG	FT	PPG
George Kaftan	SO	C	6-3	Holy Cross	25	13-24	21.0

1947 NCAA TOURNAMENT BOX SCORES

55-47 (ELITE 8)

	1H	2H
Holy Cross	29	26
Navy	27	20

HOLY CROSS	MIN	FG	3FG	FT	REB	A	ST	BL	PF	TP
Joe Mullaney	-	9	-	0-0	-	-	-	-	4	18
George Kaftan	-	7	-	1-7	-	-	-	-	2	15
Ken Haggerty	-	3	-	1-1	-	-	-	-	0	7
Bob Cousy	-	3	-	0-0	-	-	-	-	2	6
Frank Oftring	-	2	-	1-1	-	-	-	-	1	5
Robert Curran	-	0	-	2-2	-	-	-	-	4	2
Dermott O'Connell	-	1	-	0-0	-	-	-	-	1	2
Andrew Laska	-	0	-	0-0	-	-	-	-	0	0
Robert McMullan	-	0	-	0-1	-	-	-	-	1	0
TOTALS	-	**25**	-	**5-12**	-	-	-	-	**15**	**55**
Percentages				41.7						

Coach: Alvin "Doggie" Julian

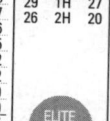

NAVY	MIN	FG	3FG	FT	REB	A	ST	BL	PF	TP
Floyd Waldrop	-	6	-	3-4	-	-	-	-	3	15
John Barrow	-	5	-	1-1	-	-	-	-	4	11
Ken Shugart	-	3	-	3-4	-	-	-	-	0	9
Charley Sheehan	-	2	-	1-3	-	-	-	-	0	5
Robert Searle	-	1	-	2-3	-	-	-	-	0	4
Jack Robbins	-	1	-	1-1	-	-	-	-	0	3
Donald Dick	-	0	-	0-1	-	-	-	-	2	0
James Durham	-	0	-	0-0	-	-	-	-	1	0
Lee Rensberger	-	0	-	0-1	-	-	-	-	0	0
TOTALS	-	**18**	-	**11-18**	-	-	-	-	**10**	**47**
Percentages				61.1						

Coach: Ben Carnevale

Officials: Orwig, Haarlow

70-56 (ELITE 8)

	1H	2H
CCNY	27	43
Wisconsin	37	19

CCNY	MIN	FG	3FG	FT	REB	A	ST	BL	PF	TP
Irwin Dambrot	-	6	-	4-5	-	-	-	-	1	16
Lionel Malamed	-	6	-	1-1	-	-	-	-	3	13
Sonny Jameson	-	5	-	0-0	-	-	-	-	1	10
Everett Finestone	-	4	-	1-1	-	-	-	-	1	9
Paul Schmones	-	3	-	1-2	-	-	-	-	3	7
Phil Farbman	-	2	-	2-3	-	-	-	-	1	6
Sidney Finger	-	2	-	0-0	-	-	-	-	1	4
Joe Galiber	-	0	-	4-6	-	-	-	-	4	4
Hilton Shapiro	-	0	-	1-2	-	-	-	-	2	1
Morris Brickman	-	0	-	0-0	-	-	-	-	0	0
Sidney Trubowitz	-	0	-	0-0	-	-	-	-	1	0
TOTALS	-	**28**	-	**14-20**	-	-	-	-	**18**	**70**
Percentages				70.0						

Coach: Nat Holman

WISCONSIN	MIN	FG	3FG	FT	REB	A	ST	BL	PF	TP
Exner Menzel	-	5	-	5-8	-	-	-	-	3	15
Bob Cook	-	5	-	3-4	-	-	-	-	4	13
Glen Selbo	-	6	-	0-0	-	-	-	-	3	12
Edward Mills	-	2	-	2-3	-	-	-	-	4	6
Don Rehfeldt	-	2	-	0-2	-	-	-	-	1	4
Gilman Hertz	-	1	-	0-0	-	-	-	-	0	2
Walt Lautenbach	-	1	-	0-0	-	-	-	-	2	2
Robert Haarlow	-	0	-	1-1	-	-	-	-	1	1
Robert Krueger	-	0	-	1-1	-	-	-	-	0	1
Richard Falls	-	0	-	0-0	-	-	-	-	0	0
Robert Mader	-	0	-	0-0	-	-	-	-	0	0
Larry Pokrzywinski	-	0	-	0-0	-	-	-	-	0	0
TOTALS	-	**22**	-	**12-19**	-	-	-	-	**18**	**56**
Percentages				63.2						

Coach: Harold Foster

Officials: Kennedy, Andersen

42-40 (ELITE 8)

	1H	2H
Texas	24	18
Wyoming	27	13

TEXAS	MIN	FG	3FG	FT	REB	A	ST	BL	PF	TP
John Langdon	-	4	-	3-3	-	-	-	-	3	11
John Hargis	-	3	-	3-4	-	-	-	-	1	9
Slater Martin	-	4	-	1-4	-	-	-	-	4	9
Dan Wagner	-	3	-	0-0	-	-	-	-	4	6
Al Madsen	-	1	-	3-4	-	-	-	-	3	5
Roy Cox	-	1	-	0-1	-	-	-	-	4	2
Tom Hamilton	-	0	-	0-0	-	-	-	-	1	0
TOTALS	-	**16**	-	**10-16**	-	-	-	-	**20**	**42**
Percentages				62.5						

Coach: Jack Gray

WYOMING	MIN	FG	3FG	FT	REB	A	ST	BL	PF	TP
Floyd Volker	40	5	-	1-3	-	-	-	-	3	11
Jim Reese	40	3	-	4-7	-	-	-	-	4	10
Mike Todorovich	30	3	-	3-4	-	-	-	-	3	9
James Collins	40	2	-	2-2	-	-	-	-	4	6
Mack Peyton	32	1	-	0-2	-	-	-	-	2	2
John Pilch	10	1	-	0-1	-	-	-	-	1	2
Ted Rogers	8	0	-	0-0	-	-	-	-	0	0
TOTALS	**200**	**15**	-	**10-19**	-	-	-	-	**17**	**40**
Percentages				52.6						

Coach: Everett Shelton

Officials: Ogden, Leith

56-54 — 32 1H 27 / 24 2H 27 — ELITE 8

OKLAHOMA	MIN	FG	3FG	FT	REB	A	ST	BL	PF	TP
Paul Courty	-	5	-	7-8	-	-	-	-	4	17
Gerald Tucker	-	7	-	3-3	-	-	-	-	2	17
Dick Reich	-	4	-	3-3	-	-	-	-	3	11
Bill Waters	-	2	-	1-4	-	-	-	-	0	5
Allie Paine	-	2	-	0-1	-	-	-	-	4	4
Jack Landon	-	0	-	2-4	-	-	-	-	3	2
Bob Jones	-	0	-	0-0	-	-	-	-	0	0
Paul Merchant	-	0	-	0-0	-	-	-	-	0	0
TOTALS	-	20	-	16-23	-	-	-	-	16	56
Percentages				69.6						

Coach: Bruce Drake

OREGON STATE	MIN	FG	3FG	FT	REB	A	ST	BL	PF	TP
Lew Beck	-	8	-	4-5	-	-	-	-	2	20
Red Rocha	-	5	-	2-4	-	-	-	-	3	12
Cliff Crandall	-	3	-	2-2	-	-	-	-	5	8
Dan Torrey	-	3	-	0-1	-	-	-	-	1	6
Alex Petersen	-	2	-	1-2	-	-	-	-	4	5
Morris Silver	-	1	-	0-0	-	-	-	-	1	2
Erland Anderson	-	0	-	1-4	-	-	-	-	2	1
Norm Carey	-	0	-	0-0	-	-	-	-	0	0
Frank Roelandt	-	0	-	0-0	-	-	-	-	1	0
Don Samuel	-	0	-	0-0	-	-	-	-	1	0
TOTALS	-	22	-	10-18	-	-	-	-	20	54
Percentages				55.6						

Coach: Slats Gill

Officials: Curtis, Shields

60-45 — 27 1H 25 / 33 2H 20 — FINAL 4

HOLY CROSS	MIN	FG	3FG	FT	REB	A	ST	BL	PF	TP
George Kaftan	-	11	-	8-12	-	-	-	-	2	30
Frank Oftring	-	2	-	3-3	-	-	-	-	3	7
Bob Cousy	-	2	-	1-2	-	-	-	-	3	5
Dermott O'Connell	-	2	-	1-2	-	-	-	-	1	5
Ken Haggerty	-	2	-	0-0	-	-	-	-	3	4
Robert McMullan	-	1	-	1-3	-	-	-	-	2	3
Joe Mullaney	-	0	-	3-5	-	-	-	-	2	3
Andrew Laska	-	1	-	0-0	-	-	-	-	1	2
Robert Curran	-	0	-	1-2	-	-	-	-	2	1
TOTALS	-	21	-	18-29	-	-	-	-	19	60
Percentages				62.1						

Coach: Alvin "Doggie" Julian

CCNY	MIN	FG	3FG	FT	REB	A	ST	BL	PF	TP
Irwin Dambrot	-	5	-	4-7	-	-	-	-	3	14
Everett Finestone	-	4	-	1-2	-	-	-	-	4	9
Joe Galiber	-	1	-	3-5	-	-	-	-	3	5
Hilton Shapiro	-	2	-	1-1	-	-	-	-	3	5
Sidney Trubowitz	-	2	-	0-1	-	-	-	-	1	4
Sonny Jameson	-	1	-	1-1	-	-	-	-	5	3
Lionel Malamed	-	1	-	1-1	-	-	-	-	2	3
Phil Farbman	-	0	-	1-1	-	-	-	-	1	1
Paul Schmones	-	0	-	1-1	-	-	-	-	1	1
Mason Benson	-	0	-	0-0	-	-	-	-	1	0
TOTALS	-	16	-	13-20	-	-	-	-	24	45
Percentages				65.0						

Coach: Nat Holman

Officials: Haarlow, Orwig

55-54 — 22 1H 29 / 33 2H 25 — FINAL 4

OKLAHOMA	MIN	FG	3FG	FT	REB	A	ST	BL	PF	TP
Gerald Tucker	-	6	-	3-4	-	-	-	-	0	15
Dick Reich	-	4	-	3-3	-	-	-	-	4	11
Paul Courty	-	3	-	2-4	-	-	-	-	4	8
Allie Paine	-	4	-	0-0	-	-	-	-	4	8
Jack Landon	-	2	-	2-3	-	-	-	-	4	6
Bill Waters	-	1	-	2-2	-	-	-	-	0	4
Ken Pryor	-	1	-	0-0	-	-	-	-	0	2
Paul Merchant	-	0	-	1-1	-	-	-	-	2	1
TOTALS	-	21	-	13-17	-	-	-	-	18	55
Percentages				76.5						

Coach: Bruce Drake

TEXAS	MIN	FG	3FG	FT	REB	A	ST	BL	PF	TP
Slater Martin	-	8	-	2-2	-	-	-	-	2	18
Dan Wagner	-	5	-	1-1	-	-	-	-	3	11
John Hargis	-	3	-	3-4	-	-	-	-	5	9
John Langdon	-	3	-	1-1	-	-	-	-	4	7
Al Madsen	-	1	-	4-5	-	-	-	-	1	6
Roy Cox	-	1	-	0-0	-	-	-	-	0	2
Tom Hamilton	-	0	-	1-1	-	-	-	-	4	1
TOTALS	-	21	-	12-14	-	-	-	-	19	54
Percentages				85.7						

Coach: Jack Gray

Officials: Leith, Ogden

54-50 — 32 1H 28 / 22 2H 22 — 3RD PLACE

TEXAS	MIN	FG	3FG	FT	REB	A	ST	BL	PF	TP
John Hargis	-	7	-	3-6	-	-	-	-	3	17
Slater Martin	-	7	-	0-2	-	-	-	-	2	14
John Langdon	-	4	-	1-2	-	-	-	-	4	9
Roy Cox	-	2	-	4-6	-	-	-	-	2	8
Al Madsen	-	2	-	2-4	-	-	-	-	3	6
Tom Hamilton	-	0	-	0-1	-	-	-	-	0	0
Dan Wagner	-	0	-	0-0	-	-	-	-	1	0
TOTALS	-	22	-	10-21	-	-	-	-	15	54
Percentages				47.6						

Coach: Jack Gray

CCNY	MIN	FG	3FG	FT	REB	A	ST	BL	PF	TP
Everett Finestone	-	6	-	2-4	-	-	-	-	3	14
Irwin Dambrot	-	5	-	3-5	-	-	-	-	3	13
Sonny Jameson	-	4	-	2-3	-	-	-	-	2	10
Lionel Malamed	-	3	-	0-3	-	-	-	-	3	6
Joe Galiber	-	1	-	0-1	-	-	-	-	3	2
Paul Schmones	-	1	-	0-0	-	-	-	-	1	2
Hilton Shapiro	-	1	-	0-0	-	-	-	-	0	2
Phil Farbman	-	0	-	1-2	-	-	-	-	3	1
Sidney Trubowitz	-	0	-	0-0	-	-	-	-	1	0
TOTALS	-	21	-	8-18	-	-	-	-	19	50
Percentages				44.4						

Coach: Nat Holman

Officials: Orwig, Haarlow
Attendance: 18,445

58-47 — 28 1H 31 / 30 2H 16 — NCAA FINAL 1947

HOLY CROSS	MIN	FG	3FG	FT	REB	A	ST	BL	PF	TP
George Kaftan	-	7	-	4-5	-	-	-	-	4	18
Dermott O'Connell	-	7	-	2-4	-	-	-	-	3	16
Frank Oftring	-	6	-	2-3	-	-	-	-	5	14
Robert McMullan	-	2	-	4-4	-	-	-	-	0	8
Bob Cousy	-	0	-	2-2	-	-	-	-	1	2
Charles Bollinger	-	0	-	0-0	-	-	-	-	0	0
Robert Curran	-	0	-	0-1	-	-	-	-	2	0
Charles Graver	-	0	-	0-0	-	-	-	-	0	0
Ken Haggerty	-	0	-	0-0	-	-	-	-	0	0
Andrew Laska	-	0	-	0-0	-	-	-	-	0	0
Joe Mullaney	-	0	-	0-0	-	-	-	-	2	0
James Riley	-	0	-	0-0	-	-	-	-	1	0
TOTALS	-	22	-	14-19	-	-	-	-	18	58
Percentages				73.7						

Coach: Alvin "Doggie" Julian

OKLAHOMA	MIN	FG	3FG	FT	REB	A	ST	BL	PF	TP
Gerald Tucker	-	6	-	10-12	-	-	-	-	3	22
Paul Courty	-	3	-	2-3	-	-	-	-	4	8
Dick Reich	-	3	-	2-2	-	-	-	-	3	8
Allie Paine	-	2	-	2-2	-	-	-	-	0	6
Jack Landon	-	1	-	0-1	-	-	-	-	4	2
Ken Pryor	-	0	-	1-1	-	-	-	-	1	1
Harley Day	-	0	-	0-0	-	-	-	-	0	0
Paul Merchant	-	0	-	0-0	-	-	-	-	1	0
Bill Waters	-	0	-	0-0	-	-	-	-	0	0
TOTALS	-	15	-	17-21	-	-	-	-	16	47
Percentages				81.0						

Coach: Bruce Drake

Officials: Andersen, Kennedy
Attendance: 18,445

National Invitation Tournament (NIT)

Quarterfinals: Utah d. Duquesne 45-44, Kentucky d. Long Island 66-62, NC State d. St. John's 61-55, West Virginia d. Bradley 69-60
Semifinals: Utah d. West Virginia 64-62, Kentucky d. NC State 60-42
Third place: NC State d. West Virginia 64-52
Championship: Utah d. Kentucky 49-45
MVP: Vern Gardner, Utah

1947-48: Kentucky Gold

Kentucky (36–3) had only one senior on its roster but still managed to win its first NCAA championship, beating Baylor, 58-42, in the Final at Madison Square Garden. Alex Groza earned Most Outstanding Player honors after scoring 14 points against the Bears. The season didn't really end in New York City for the Wildcats. Adolph Rupp's entire starting five joined nine other players to form the U.S. Olympic team that went on to win the gold medal in London that summer.

Arkansas (16–8) had its 25th consecutive winning season. Kansas (9–15) had its streak of 18 consecutive seasons with a winning record come to an end, but this was the Jayhawks' only losing season in a 29-year span. The NCAA changed a rule governing timing in the last three minutes of the second half and overtime: The clock would stop on every dead ball, including after each field goal. The rule was rescinded in 1951.

Major Conference Standings

BIG SEVEN	Conference			Overall		
	W	L	PCT	W	L	PCT
Kansas State○	9	3	.750	22	6	.786
Oklahoma	7	5	.583	13	9	.591
Missouri	7	5	.583	14	10	.583
Iowa State	6	6	.500	14	9	.609
Nebraska	5	7	.417	11	13	.458
Kansas	4	8	.333	9	15	.375
Colorado	4	8	.333	7	14	.333

BIG NINE	Conference			Overall		
	W	L	PCT	W	L	PCT
Michigan○	10	2	.833	16	6	.727
Iowa	8	4	.667	15	4	.789
Illinois	7	5	.583	15	5	.750
Wisconsin	7	5	.583	12	8	.600
Purdue	6	6	.500	11	9	.550
Minnesota	5	7	.417	10	10	.500
Ohio State	5	7	.417	10	10	.500
Indiana	3	9	.250	8	12	.400
Northwestern	3	9	.250	6	14	.300

BORDER	Conference			Overall		
	W	L	PCT	W	L	PCT
Arizona	12	4	.750	19	10	.655
Texas Tech	10	6	.625	16	12	.571
Arizona State	9	7	.563	13	11	.542
Northern Arizona	8	8	.500	13	8	.619
New Mexico	8	8	.500	14	15	.483
West Texas A&M	7	9	.438	11	13	.458
New Mexico State	6	10	.375	13	11	.542
Texas Western	6	10	.375	13	16	.448
Hardin-Simmons	6	10	.375	6	10	.375

IVY	Conference			Overall		
	W	L	PCT	W	L	PCT
Columbia○	11	1	.917	21	3	.875
Cornell	9	3	.750	16	9	.640
Princeton	6	6	.500	12	11	.522
Dartmouth	6	6	.500	12	12	.500
Penn	5	7	.417	10	14	.417
Yale	4	8	.333	14	13	.519
Harvard	1	11	.083	5	20	.200

METRO NY	Conference			Overall		
	W	L	PCT	W	L	PCT
NYU□	5	1	.833	22	4	.846
CCNY	4	1	.800	18	3	.857
Fordham	4	2	.667	20	4	.833
Manhattan	3	3	.500	22	6	.786
St. John's	3	3	.500	12	11	.522
St. Francis (NY)	2	3	.400	16	9	.640
Brooklyn	0	6	.000	10	10	.500

MID-AMERICAN	Conference			Overall		
	W	L	PCT	W	L	PCT
Cincinnati	7	2	.778	17	7	.708
Butler	4	2	.667	14	7	.667
Ohio	4	4	.500	10	10	.500
Miami (OH)	3	5	.375	13	15	.464
Western Michigan	1	2	.333	12	10	.545
Western Reserve	2	6	.250	14	10	.583

MISSOURI VALLEY	Conference			Overall		
	W	L	PCT	W	L	PCT
Oklahoma A&M	10	0	1.000	27	4	.871
Saint Louis□	8	2	.800	24	3	.889
Drake	5	5	.500	14	12	.538
Creighton	4	6	.400	10	13	.435
Tulsa	2	8	.200	7	16	.304
Wichita State	1	9	.100	12	13	.480

BIG SEVEN	Conference			Overall		
	W	L	PCT	W	L	PCT
BYU	8	2	.800	16	11	.593
Wyoming○	6	4	.600	18	9	.667
Denver	6	4	.600	18	11	.621
Utah	6	4	.600	11	9	.550
Utah State	3	7	.300	8	16	.333
Colorado State	1	9	.100	6	15	.286

PACIFIC COAST	Conference			Overall		
	W	L	PCT	W	L	PCT
North						
Washington○	10	6	.625	23	11	.676
Oregon State	10	6	.625	21	13	.618
Washington State	9	7	.563	19	10	.655
Oregon	8	8	.500	18	11	.621
Idaho	3	13	.188	12	18	.400
South						
California	11	1	.917	25	9	.735
Southern California	7	5	.583	14	10	.583
Stanford	3	9	.250	15	11	.577
UCLA	3	9	.250	12	13	.480

Playoff: Washington d. Oregon State 59-42 to win the North; **Washington d. California 2-1** in a best of three series to win the title

SEC	Conference			Overall		
	W	L	PCT	W	L	PCT
Kentucky○	9	0	1.000	36	3	.923
Tulane	13	1	.929	23	3	.885
Tennessee	10	2	.833	20	5	.800
Alabama	8	8	.500	15	12	.556
Auburn	7	7	.500	12	10	.545
Georgia	6	8	.429	18	10	.643
Florida	5	7	.417	15	10	.600
Georgia Tech	6	10	.375	12	16	.429
Mississippi State	6	10	.375	6	12	.333
Mississippi	5	9	.357	11	12	.478
LSU	4	10	.286	8	18	.308
Vanderbilt	4	11	.267	8	14	.364

Tournament: **Kentucky d. Georgia Tech 54-43**

SOUTHERN	Conference			Overall		
	W	L	PCT	W	L	PCT
NC State□	12	0	1.000	29	3	.906
George Washington	13	3	.813	19	7	.731
North Carolina	11	4	.733	20	7	.741
Maryland	9	6	.600	11	14	.440
Davidson	10	7	.588	19	9	.679
Virginia Tech	7	5	.583	14	9	.609
Duke	8	6	.571	17	12	.586
Wake Forest	8	7	.533	18	11	.621
William and Mary	8	7	.533	13	10	.565
South Carolina	8	7	.533	12	11	.522
Washington and Lee	5	9	.357	7	17	.292
The Citadel	4	8	.333	8	9	.471
Richmond	4	9	.308	8	14	.364
Furman	3	10	.231	11	15	.423
Clemson	3	14	.176	6	17	.261
VMI	1	12	.077	3	17	.150

Tournament: **NC State d. Duke 58-50**
Tournament MOP: **Jere Bunting**, William and Mary

SOUTHWEST	Conference			Overall		
	W	L	PCT	W	L	PCT
Baylor○	11	1	.917	24	8	.750
Texas□	9	3	.750	20	5	.800
Arkansas	8	4	.667	16	8	.667
Rice	6	6	.500	10	14	.417
SMU	5	7	.417	13	10	.565
Texas A&M	2	10	.167	7	17	.292
TCU	1	11	.083	3	20	.130

WNY LITTLE THREE	Conference			Overall		
	W	L	PCT	W	L	PCT
Niagara	3	1	.750	15	9	.625
Canisius	2	2	.500	10	15	.400
St. Bonaventure	1	3	.250	12	10	.545

YANKEE	Conference			Overall		
	W	L	PCT	W	L	PCT
Connecticut	6	1	.857	17	6	.739
Rhode Island	5	1	.833	17	6	.739
Vermont	2	1	.667	14	6	.700
Maine	2	5	.286	11	7	.611
New Hampshire	2	5	.286	5	12	.294
Massachusetts	0	4	.000	2	14	.125

INDEPENDENTS	Overall		
	W	L	PCT
Western Kentucky□	28	2	.933
Bradley	28	3	.903
Holy Cross○	26	4	.867
West Virginia	17	3	.850
Muhlenberg	21	4	.840
La Salle□	20	4	.833
Louisville	29	6	.829
Bowling Green□	27	6	.818
Seton Hall	18	4	.818
Long Island	17	4	.810
Lawrence Tech	22	6	.786
Siena	22	6	.786
Xavier	24	8	.750
Loyola-Chicago	26	9	.743
Duquesne	17	6	.739
Colgate	14	5	.737
DePaul□	22	8	.733
Notre Dame	17	7	.708
Montana	21	11	.656
Akron	15	9	.625
Villanova	15	9	.625
Virginia	16	10	.615
Rutgers	14	9	.609
Navy	10	7	.588
Boston College	13	10	.565
Michigan State	12	10	.545
Saint Joseph's	13	11	.542
San Francisco	13	11	.542
Boston U.	10	9	.526
Temple	12	11	.522
Santa Clara	11	11	.500
Pittsburgh	10	11	.476
Penn State	9	10	.474
Army	8	9	.471
Georgetown	13	15	.464
Dayton	12	14	.462
Saint Mary's (CA)	11	13	.458
Syracuse	11	13	.458
Youngstown State	10	14	.417
Marquette	9	15	.375
Nevada	9	16	.360
Detroit	7	15	.318
Brown	6	14	.300

⊛ Automatic NCAA Tournament bid ○ At-large NCAA Tournament bid □ NIT appearance ⊗ Team record doesn't reflect games forfeited or vacated. For adjusted record, see p. 521.

Premo-Porretta Power Poll

School	Record
1 Kentucky (NCAA champion)	36-3
2 Saint Louis (NIT champion)	24-3
3 Western Kentucky	28-2
4 Holy Cross	26-4
5 NC State	29-3
6 NYU	22-4
7 Oklahoma A&M	27-4
8 DePaul	22-8
9 CCNY	18-3
10 Baylor	24-8
11 Michigan	16-6
12 West Virginia	17-3
13 Bowling Green	27-6

Premo-Porretta Poll (cont.)

School	Record
14 Columbia	21-3
15 Iowa	15-4
16 Texas	20-5
17 Kansas State	22-6
18 Bradley	28-3
19 Tulane	23-3
20 Illinois	15-5
21 Long Island	18-4
22 La Salle	20-4
23 Muhlenberg	21-4
24 Louisville	29-6
25 Loyola-Chicago	26-9

Individual Leaders—Season

Scoring

Scoring	CL	POS	G	FG	FT	PTS	PPG
1 **Murray Wier**, Iowa	SR	G	19	152	95	399	**21.0**
2 **Tony Lavelli**, Yale	JR	F	27	196	162	554	**20.5**
3 **Frank Kudelka**, Saint Mary's (CA)	SO	F	24	193	103	489	**20.4**
4 **Ernie Vandeweghe**, Colgate	JR	F	19	134	117	385	**20.3**
5 **George Kok**, Arkansas	SR	C	24	192	85	469	**19.5**
6 **Hal Haskins**, Hamline	SO	F	31	234	137	605	**19.5**
7 **Jim McIntyre**, Minnesota	JR	C	19	125	110	360	**18.9**
8 **William Hatchett**, Rutgers	SO	F	11	84	33	201	**18.3**
9 **Gene Berce**, Marquette	SR	F	22	146	98	390	**17.7**
10 **Duane Klueh**, Indiana State	JR	G	34	220	157	597	**17.6**

Field Goal Pct

Field Goal Pct	CL	POS	G	FG	FGA	PCT
1 **Alex Petersen**, Oregon State	JR	F	27	89	187	**47.6**
2 **Dan Mackin**, Muhlenberg	SO	G	25	158	338	**46.7**
3 **Jack Coleman**, Louisville	JR	F/C	28	136	292	**46.6**
4 **Dee Compton**, Louisville	SR	F	28	109	241	**45.2**
5 **Harry Karpiak**, Colorado State	JR	G	21	77	176	**43.8**

Minimum: 75 made

Free Throw Pct

Free Throw Pct	CL	POS	G	FT	FTA	PCT
1 **Sam Urzetta**, St. Bonaventure	SO	G	22	59	64	**92.2**
2 **Eddie Sterling**, West Virginia	SO	F	11	40	45	**88.9**
3 **Howie Shannon**, Kansas State	SR	G	28	58	66	**87.9**
4 **Bill Sharman**, Southern California	SO	F	24	38	44	**86.4**
5 **Mark Wylie**, Ohio	JR	G	18	88	102	**86.3**

Minimum: 35 made

Individual Leaders—Game

Points

Points	CL	POS	OPP	DATE	PTS
1 **Jim Lacy**, Loyola (MD)	JR	F	Western Maryland	F14	**44**
2 **Hal Haskins**, Hamline	SO	F	Saint Mary's (MN)	F17	**42**
3 **William Hatchett**, Rutgers	SO	F	Bucknell	M10	**40**
Bob Cope, Montana	SO	C	Gonzaga	F20	**40**
Norm Hankins, Lawrence Tech (MI)	JR	G	Selfridge Field	F17	**40**

Free Throws Made

Free Throws Made	CL	POS	OPP	DATE	FT	FTA	PCT
1 **Tony Lavelli**, Yale	JR	F	Dartmouth	F18	17	18	**94.4**
2 **Mac Otten**, Bowling Green	JR	F	CCNY	D13	15	17	**88.2**
3 **Bob Cope**, Montana	SO	C	Gonzaga	F20	14	16	**87.5**
Jim Graham, Montana	SO	C	Nevada	J14	14	17	**82.4**
5 **Ed Lerner**, Temple	JR	G	Kentucky	D20	12	12	**100.0**
Mark Wylie, Ohio	JR	G	Cincinnati	F17	12	12	**100.0**
Dick Dickey, NC State	SO	F	St. John's	D20	12	14	**85.7**
Vern Mikkelsen, Hamline	JR	F	Mankato State	M4	12	14	**85.7**
Bob Brannum, Michigan State	JR	F	Missouri	J5	12	16	**75.0**
Jim McIntyre, Minnesota	JR	C	Indiana	J24	12	17	**70.6**

Team Leaders—Season

Scoring Offense

Scoring Offense	G	W-L	PTS	PPG
1 **Rhode Island**	23	17-6	1,755	**76.3**
2 **NC State**	32	29-3	2,409	**75.3**
3 **Bowling Green**	33	27-6	2,327	**70.5**
4 **Bradley**	31	28-3	2,157	**69.6**
5 **Kentucky**	39	36-3	2,690	**69.0**

Field Goal Pct

Field Goal Pct	G	W-L	FG	FGA	PCT
1 **Oregon State**	34	21-13	668	1,818	**36.7**
2 **Muhlenberg**	25	21-4	655	1,822	**35.9**
3 **Akron**	24	15-9	571	1,617	**35.3**
4 **Louisville**	35	29-6	709	2,028	**35.0**
5 **Bowling Green**	33	27-6	918	2,639	**34.8**

Free Throw Pct

Free Throw Pct	G	W-L	FT	FTA	PCT
1 **Texas**	25	20-5	351	481	**73.0**
2 **Michigan**	22	16-6	280	411	**68.1**
3 **St. Bonaventure**	22	12-10	286	421	**67.9**
4 **DePaul**	30	22-8	468	698	**67.0**
5 **NYU**	26	22-4	433	646	**67.0**

Scoring Defense

Scoring Defense	G	W-L	OPP PTS	OPP PPG
1 **Oklahoma A&M**	31	27-4	1,006	**32.5**
2 **Alabama**	27	15-12	1,070	**39.6**
3 **Creighton**	23	10-13	925	**40.2**
4 **Wyoming**	27	18-9	1,101	**40.8**
5 **Siena**	28	22-6	1,161	**41.5**

Consensus All-Americas

First Team

Player	CL	POS	HT	School	PPG
Ralph Beard	JR	G	5-10	Kentucky	12.5
Ed Macauley	JR	F/C	6-8	Saint Louis	13.4
Jim McIntyre	JR	C	6-10	Minnesota	18.9
Kevin O'Shea	SO	G	6-1	Notre Dame	11.5
Murray Wier	SR	G	5-9	Iowa	21.0

Second Team

Player	CL	POS	HT	School	PPG
Dick Dickey	SO	F	6-1	NC State	15.5
Arnie Ferrin	SR	G/F	6-1	Utah	14.1
Alex Groza	JR	C	6-7	Kentucky	12.5
Hal Haskins	SO	F	6-3	Hamline	19.5
George Kaftan	JR	C	6-3	Holy Cross	15.6
Duane Klueh	JR	G	6-3	Indiana State	17.6
Tony Lavelli	JR	F	6-3	Yale	20.5
Jack Nichols	SR	C	6-7	Washington	14.8
Andy Wolfe	SR	F/G	6-1	California	12.1

Selectors: AP, Converse Yearbook, Helms Foundation

Annual Review

1948 NCAA Tournament

Regional Semifinals

East:
- Kentucky **76**, Columbia **53**
- Holy Cross **63**, Michigan **45**

West:
- Kansas State **58**, Wyoming **48** (B)
- Baylor **64**, Washington **62**

Regional Finals

- East: Kentucky **60**, Holy Cross **52** (A)
- West: Kansas State **52**, Baylor **60**

National Final — New York City

Kentucky 58, Baylor 42

The Fabulous Five—Alex Groza, Ralph Beard, Kenny Rollins, Cliff Barker and Wallace "Wah Wah" Jones—win their first title. The team includes just one senior but several war veterans, including ex-POW Barker. Coach Adolph Rupp, who played for Phog Allen at Kansas, uses a fast-break offense and a man-to-man defense that's unique for the time.

A Bob Cousy runs up against Kentucky's tenacious Ralph Beard, netting just a single field goal as the defending champions are ousted.

B The FBI starts a crackdown on ticket scalping. Kansas State students are demanding $7.50 to $25 for tickets that ordinarily have a face value of less than $2.

National Third Place Holy Cross d. Kansas State 60-54
East Regional Third Place Michigan d. Columbia 66-49
West Regional Third Place Washington d. Wyoming 57-47

Tournament Leaders

INDIVIDUAL LEADERS

Scoring	CL	POS	G	PTS	PPG
1 **Jack Nichols**, Washington	SR	C	2	39	19.5
2 **Alex Groza**, Kentucky	JR	C	3	54	18.0
3 **John Pilch**, Wyoming	SO	C	2	31	15.5
4 **Bill Johnson**, Baylor	JR	G	3	43	14.3
5 **Wallace Jones**, Kentucky	JR	F	3	42	14.0
Mack Suprunowicz, Michigan	SO	F	2	28	14.0
7 **George Kaftan**, Holy Cross	JR	C	3	41	13.7
8 **Mack Peyton**, Wyoming	JR	F	2	27	13.5
9 **Ralph Beard**, Kentucky	JR	G	3	40	13.3
10 **Walter Budko**, Columbia	SR	C	2	26	13.0

Minimum: 2 games

Free Throw Pct	CL	POS	G	FT	FTA	PCT
1 **Howie Shannon**, Kansas State	SR	G	3	15	15	100.0
Ward Clark, Kansas State	SO	C	3	5	5	100.0
3 **Jack Nichols**, Washington	SR	C	2	13	14	92.9
4 **Frank Oftring**, Holy Cross	SO	F	3	7	8	87.5
5 **Pete Elliott**, Michigan	JR	G	2	5	6	83.3

Minimum: 5 made

Field Goals Per Game	CL	POS	G	FG	FGPG
1 **Alex Groza**, Kentucky	JR	C	3	23	7.7
2 **Mack Suprunowicz**, Michigan	SO	F	2	14	7.0
3 **Jack Nichols**, Washington	SR	C	2	13	6.5
4 **Loy Doty**, Wyoming	SO	F	2	12	6.0
Mack Peyton, Wyoming	JR	F	2	12	6.0

Minimum: 2 games

TEAM LEADERS

Scoring	G	PTS	PPG
1 **Kentucky**	3	194	64.7
2 **Washington**	2	119	59.5
3 **Holy Cross**	3	175	58.3
4 **Michigan**	2	111	55.5
5 **Baylor**	3	166	55.3
6 **Kansas State**	3	164	54.7
7 **Columbia**	2	102	51.0
8 **Wyoming**	2	95	47.5

Minimum: 2 games

FT Pct	G	FT	FTA	PCT
1 **Washington**	2	33	40	82.5
2 **Kansas State**	3	50	71	70.4
3 **Baylor**	3	50	74	67.6
4 **Holy Cross**	3	31	48	64.6
5 **Columbia**	2	28	44	63.6

Minimum: 2 games

FG Per Game	G	FG	FGPG
1 **Kentucky**	3	79	26.3
2 **Holy Cross**	3	72	24.0
3 **Michigan**	2	44	22.0
4 **Washington**	2	43	21.5
5 **Baylor**	3	58	19.3

TOURNAMENT MOP

PLAYER	CL	POS	HT	SCHOOL	FG	FT	PPG
Alex Groza	JR	C	6-7	Kentucky	23	8-12	18.0

1948 NCAA Tournament Box Scores

76-53 (Elite 8)

	Kentucky	Columbia
1H	38	28
2H	38	25

KENTUCKY	MIN	FG	3FG	FT	REB	A	ST	BL	PF	TP
Wallace Jones	-	9	-	3-5	-	-	-	-	5	21
Alex Groza	-	7	-	3-3	-	-	-	-	2	17
Ralph Beard	-	6	-	3-5	-	-	-	-	1	15
Dale Barnstable	-	2	-	1-3	-	-	-	-	0	5
Jim Line	-	2	-	1-1	-	-	-	-	1	5
Roger Day	-	2	-	0-0	-	-	-	-	1	4
Joe Holland	-	2	-	0-0	-	-	-	-	4	4
Cliff Barker	-	1	-	0-1	-	-	-	-	3	2
Kenneth Rollins	-	0	-	2-2	-	-	-	-	3	2
Jim Jordan	-	0	-	1-1	-	-	-	-	0	1
Johnny Strogh	-	0	-	0-1	-	-	-	-	0	0
Garland Townes	-	0	-	0-0	-	-	-	-	0	0
TOTALS	**-**	**31**	**-**	**14-22**	**-**	**-**	**-**	**-**	**20**	**76**
Percentages				63.6						

Coach: Adolph Rupp

COLUMBIA	MIN	FG	3FG	FT	REB	A	ST	BL	PF	TP
Walter Budko	-	7	-	3-4	-	-	-	-	5	17
Alex Kaplan	-	5	-	2-5	-	-	-	-	2	12
Norman Skinner	-	2	-	5-6	-	-	-	-	2	9
Al Vogel	-	2	-	2-4	-	-	-	-	2	6
Bruce Gehrke	-	2	-	1-2	-	-	-	-	5	5
Sherrod Marshall	-	1	-	2-3	-	-	-	-	0	4
Stanley Harwood	-	0	-	0-0	-	-	-	-	2	0
William Lockwood	-	0	-	0-0	-	-	-	-	0	0
Monroe Moss	-	0	-	0-0	-	-	-	-	0	0
Gunnar Olsen	-	0	-	0-0	-	-	-	-	1	0
TOTALS	**-**	**19**	**-**	**15-24**	**-**	**-**	**-**	**-**	**19**	**53**
Percentages				62.5						

Coach: Gordon Ridings

Officials: Begovich, Osborne

63-45 (Elite 8)

	Holy Cross	Michigan
1H	34	27
2H	29	18

HOLY CROSS	MIN	FG	3FG	FT	REB	A	ST	BL	PF	TP
Bob Cousy	-	9	-	5-9	-	-	-	-	3	23
George Kaftan	-	7	-	1-4	-	-	-	-	3	15
Frank Oftring	-	5	-	0-0	-	-	-	-	1	10
Robert Curran	-	2	-	1-1	-	-	-	-	1	5
Joe Mullaney	-	2	-	1-1	-	-	-	-	0	5
Charles Bollinger	-	1	-	0-0	-	-	-	-	0	2
Robert McMullan	-	1	-	0-0	-	-	-	-	1	2
Dermott O'Connell	-	0	-	1-1	-	-	-	-	1	1
Bert Dolan	-	0	-	0-0	-	-	-	-	0	0
Matthew Formon	-	0	-	0-1	-	-	-	-	0	0
Charles Graver	-	0	-	0-1	-	-	-	-	0	0
Andrew Laska	-	0	-	0-0	-	-	-	-	0	0
TOTALS	**-**	**27**	**-**	**9-18**	**-**	**-**	**-**	**-**	**10**	**63**
Percentages				50.0						

Coach: Alvin "Doggie" Julian

MICHIGAN	MIN	FG	3FG	FT	REB	A	ST	BL	PF	TP
Mack Suprunowicz	-	7	-	0-0	-	-	-	-	1	14
Don McIntosh	-	4	-	2-2	-	-	-	-	1	10
Bill Roberts	-	3	-	4-4	-	-	-	-	3	10
Bob Harrison	-	2	-	3-5	-	-	-	-	0	7
Pete Elliott	-	2	-	0-0	-	-	-	-	5	4
Bill Bauerle	-	0	-	0-0	-	-	-	-	0	0
Boyd McCaslin	-	0	-	0-0	-	-	-	-	1	0
Bill Mikulich	-	0	-	0-0	-	-	-	-	0	0
Hal Morrill	-	0	-	0-2	-	-	-	-	2	0
Joseph Stottlebauer	-	0	-	0-0	-	-	-	-	0	0
Gerritt Wierda	-	0	-	0-0	-	-	-	-	0	0
Irv Wisniewski	-	0	-	0-0	-	-	-	-	2	0
TOTALS	**-**	**18**	**-**	**9-13**	**-**	**-**	**-**	**-**	**15**	**45**
Percentages				69.2						

Coach: Osborne Cowles

Officials: Begovich, Osborne

58-48 (Elite 8)

	Kansas State	Wyoming
1H	23	15
2H	35	33

KANSAS STATE	MIN	FG	3FG	FT	REB	A	ST	BL	PF	TP
Howie Shannon	-	4	-	6-6	-	-	-	-	2	14
Jack Dean	-	5	-	2-3	-	-	-	-	2	12
Rick Harman	-	5	-	2-3	-	-	-	-	2	12
Clarence Brannum	-	3	-	2-3	-	-	-	-	5	8
Ward Clark	-	3	-	2-2	-	-	-	-	0	8
Harold Howey	-	1	-	0-0	-	-	-	-	0	2
Dave Weatherby	-	1	-	0-0	-	-	-	-	2	2
Lloyd Krone	-	0	-	0-1	-	-	-	-	0	0
Al Langton	-	0	-	0-1	-	-	-	-	0	0
Ken Mahoney	-	0	-	0-0	-	-	-	-	1	0
Joe Thornton	-	0	-	0-0	-	-	-	-	1	0
William Thuston	-	0	-	0-0	-	-	-	-	0	0
TOTALS	**-**	**22**	**-**	**14-19**	**-**	**-**	**-**	**-**	**15**	**58**
Percentages				73.7						

Coach: Jack Gardner

WYOMING	MIN	FG	3FG	FT	REB	A	ST	BL	PF	TP
Mack Peyton	40	9	-	2-2	-	-	-	-	2	20
Loy Doty	20	6	-	1-3	-	-	-	-	3	13
John Pilch	40	1	-	5-7	-	-	-	-	5	7
Gerald Reed	30	1	-	1-2	-	-	-	-	5	3
Leonard Larson	20	1	-	1-2	-	-	-	-	1	3
Keith Bloom	30	1	-	0-0	-	-	-	-	2	2
James Collins	10	0	-	0-0	-	-	-	-	1	0
Jack Cotton	10	0	-	0-0	-	-	-	-	0	0
TOTALS	**200**	**19**	**-**	**10-16**	**-**	**-**	**-**	**-**	**19**	**48**
Percentages				62.5						

Coach: Everett Shelton

Officials: Curtis, Ferguson

ANNUAL REVIEW

64-62 — ELITE 8

	1H	2H
Baylor	26	38
Washington	37	25

BAYLOR	MIN	FG	3FG	FT	REB	A	ST	BL	PF	TP
Bill Johnson	-	9	-	2-2	-	-	-	-	0	20
Don Heathington	-	4	-	4-8	-	-	-	-	4	12
James Owens	-	3	-	6-7	-	-	-	-	3	12
Jackie Robinson	-	3	-	6-6	-	-	-	-	3	12
Bill Hickman	-	3	-	0-2	-	-	-	-	2	6
Odell Preston	-	1	-	0-0	-	-	-	-	1	2
Bill Dewitt	-	0	-	0-0	-	-	-	-	2	0
Ralph Pulley	-	0	-	0-0	-	-	-	-	0	0
TOTALS	**-**	**23**	**-**	**18-25**	**-**	**-**	**-**	**-**	**15**	**64**
Percentages				72.0						

Coach: Bill Henderson

WASHINGTON	MIN	FG	3FG	FT	REB	A	ST	BL	PF	TP
Jack Nichols	-	6	-	5-5	-	-	-	-	5	17
Bill Vandenburgh	-	6	-	2-2	-	-	-	-	5	14
Sammy White	-	4	-	3-5	-	-	-	-	3	11
Bill Taylor	-	3	-	2-2	-	-	-	-	2	8
Bob Jorgenson	-	3	-	0-0	-	-	-	-	1	6
Andy Opacich	-	1	-	4-4	-	-	-	-	3	6
Hal Arnason	-	0	-	0-0	-	-	-	-	1	0
George Bird	-	0	-	0-0	-	-	-	-	1	0
Bob Engstrom	-	0	-	0-0	-	-	-	-	1	0
Jim Mallory	-	0	-	0-0	-	-	-	-	1	0
Jim Millikan	-	0	-	0-0	-	-	-	-	0	0
TOTALS	**-**	**23**	**-**	**16-18**	**-**	**-**	**-**	**-**	**23**	**62**
Percentages				88.9						

Coach: Art McLarney

Officials: Herigstad, Ogden

60-52 — FINAL 4

	1H	2H
Kentucky	36	24
Holy Cross	28	24

KENTUCKY	MIN	FG	3FG	FT	REB	A	ST	BL	PF	TP
Alex Groza	-	10	-	3-5	-	-	-	-	4	23
Ralph Beard	-	6	-	1-5	-	-	-	-	1	13
Wallace Jones	-	4	-	4-4	-	-	-	-	3	12
Kenneth Rollins	-	3	-	2-2	-	-	-	-	3	8
Cliff Barker	-	2	-	0-0	-	-	-	-	4	4
Dale Barnstable	-	0	-	0-0	-	-	-	-	2	0
Joe Holland	-	0	-	0-0	-	-	-	-	0	0
Jim Line	-	0	-	0-0	-	-	-	-	1	0
TOTALS	**-**	**25**	**-**	**10-16**	**-**	**-**	**-**	**-**	**18**	**60**
Percentages				62.5						

Coach: Adolph Rupp

HOLY CROSS	MIN	FG	3FG	FT	REB	A	ST	BL	PF	TP
George Kaftan	-	6	-	3-4	-	-	-	-	2	15
Frank Oftring	-	4	-	4-4	-	-	-	-	2	12
Dermott O'Connell	-	3	-	3-4	-	-	-	-	2	9
Bob Cousy	-	1	-	4-5	-	-	-	-	5	6
Robert Curran	-	3	-	0-0	-	-	-	-	5	6
Charles Bollinger	-	1	-	0-0	-	-	-	-	0	2
Andrew Laska	-	1	-	0-0	-	-	-	-	1	2
Matthew Formon	-	0	-	0-0	-	-	-	-	1	0
Robert McMullan	-	0	-	0-0	-	-	-	-	3	0
Joe Mullaney	-	0	-	0-0	-	-	-	-	0	0
TOTALS	**-**	**19**	**-**	**14-17**	**-**	**-**	**-**	**-**	**21**	**52**
Percentages				82.4						

Coach: Alvin "Doggie" Julian

Officials: Begovich, Osborne

60-52 — FINAL 4

	1H	2H
Baylor	28	32
Kansas State	32	20

BAYLOR	MIN	FG	3FG	FT	REB	A	ST	BL	PF	TP
Don Heathington	-	3	-	9-10	-	-	-	-	2	15
Bill Johnson	-	4	-	5-6	-	-	-	-	3	13
Jackie Robinson	-	5	-	1-1	-	-	-	-	4	11
James Owens	-	3	-	2-3	-	-	-	-	5	8
Bill Dewitt	-	3	-	0-1	-	-	-	-	5	6
Odell Preston	-	1	-	3-4	-	-	-	-	1	5
Ralph Pulley	-	1	-	0-0	-	-	-	-	0	2
Bill Hickman	-	0	-	0-0	-	-	-	-	2	0
TOTALS	**-**	**20**	**-**	**20-25**	**-**	**-**	**-**	**-**	**22**	**60**
Percentages				80.0						

Coach: Bill Henderson

KANSAS STATE	MIN	FG	3FG	FT	REB	A	ST	BL	PF	TP
Rick Harman	-	3	-	6-10	-	-	-	-	4	12
Harold Howey	-	3	-	3-3	-	-	-	-	5	9
Jack Dean	-	3	-	2-2	-	-	-	-	4	8
Clarence Brannum	-	3	-	1-1	-	-	-	-	5	7
Howie Shannon	-	1	-	4-4	-	-	-	-	1	6
Ward Clark	-	1	-	3-3	-	-	-	-	5	5
Al Langton	-	1	-	1-1	-	-	-	-	3	3
Lloyd Krone	-	0	-	2-2	-	-	-	-	0	2
Dave Weatherby	-	0	-	0-0	-	-	-	-	2	0
TOTALS	**-**	**15**	**-**	**22-26**	**-**	**-**	**-**	**-**	**29**	**52**
Percentages				84.6						

Coach: Jack Gardner

Officials: Curtis, Ogden

60-54 — 3RD PLACE

	1H	2H
Holy Cross	36	24
Kansas State	24	30

HOLY CROSS	MIN	FG	3FG	FT	REB	A	ST	BL	PF	TP
George Kaftan	-	4	-	3-6	-	-	-	-	3	11
Frank Oftring	-	4	-	3-4	-	-	-	-	2	11
Dermott O'Connell	-	5	-	0-0	-	-	-	-	2	10
Robert McMullan	-	3	-	0-0	-	-	-	-	2	6
Joe Mullaney	-	3	-	0-0	-	-	-	-	2	6
Bob Cousy	-	2	-	1-1	-	-	-	-	2	5
Robert Curran	-	2	-	1-2	-	-	-	-	4	5
Andrew Laska	-	2	-	0-0	-	-	-	-	0	4
Charles Bollinger	-	1	-	0-0	-	-	-	-	3	2
Bert Dolan	-	0	-	0-0	-	-	-	-	0	0
Matthew Formon	-	0	-	0-0	-	-	-	-	1	0
TOTALS	**-**	**26**	**-**	**8-13**	**-**	**-**	**-**	**-**	**21**	**60**
Percentages				61.5						

Coach: Alvin "Doggie" Julian

KANSAS STATE	MIN	FG	3FG	FT	REB	A	ST	BL	PF	TP
Howie Shannon	-	6	-	5-5	-	-	-	-	1	17
Jack Dean	-	5	-	2-3	-	-	-	-	2	12
Harold Howey	-	4	-	2-6	-	-	-	-	1	10
Rick Harman	-	3	-	3-6	-	-	-	-	3	9
Clarence Brannum	-	1	-	2-6	-	-	-	-	3	4
Lloyd Krone	-	1	-	0-0	-	-	-	-	0	2
Ward Clark	-	0	-	0-0	-	-	-	-	0	0
Al Langton	-	0	-	0-0	-	-	-	-	0	0
Ken Mahoney	-	0	-	0-0	-	-	-	-	0	0
Joe Thornton	-	0	-	0-0	-	-	-	-	0	0
Dave Weatherby	-	0	-	0-0	-	-	-	-	2	0
TOTALS	**-**	**20**	**-**	**14-26**	**-**	**-**	**-**	**-**	**12**	**54**
Percentages				53.8						

Coach: Jack Gardner

Officials: Begovich, Osborne
Attendance: 16,174

58-42 — NCAA FINAL 1948

	1H	2H
Kentucky	29	29
Baylor	16	26

KENTUCKY	MIN	FG	3FG	FT	REB	A	ST	BL	PF	TP
Alex Groza	-	6	-	2-4	-	-	-	-	4	14
Ralph Beard	-	4	-	4-4	-	-	-	-	1	12
Wallace Jones	-	4	-	1-1	-	-	-	-	3	9
Kenneth Rollins	-	3	-	3-5	-	-	-	-	3	9
Jim Line	-	3	-	1-1	-	-	-	-	3	7
Cliff Barker	-	2	-	1-3	-	-	-	-	4	5
Joe Holland	-	1	-	0-0	-	-	-	-	1	2
Dale Barnstable	-	0	-	0-1	-	-	-	-	0	0
TOTALS	**-**	**23**	**-**	**12-19**	**-**	**-**	**-**	**-**	**19**	**58**
Percentages				63.2						

Coach: Adolph Rupp

BAYLOR	MIN	FG	3FG	FT	REB	A	ST	BL	PF	TP
Bill Johnson	-	3	-	4-7	-	-	-	-	5	10
Bill Dewitt	-	3	-	2-4	-	-	-	-	3	8
Don Heathington	-	3	-	2-4	-	-	-	-	5	8
Jackie Robinson	-	3	-	2-4	-	-	-	-	4	8
James Owens	-	2	-	1-2	-	-	-	-	0	5
Bill Hickman	-	1	-	0-0	-	-	-	-	0	2
Ralph Pulley	-	0	-	1-1	-	-	-	-	0	1
Odell Preston	-	0	-	0-2	-	-	-	-	2	0
Bill Srack	-	0	-	0-0	-	-	-	-	0	0
TOTALS	**-**	**15**	**-**	**12-24**	**-**	**-**	**-**	**-**	**19**	**42**
Percentages				50.0						

Coach: Bill Henderson

Officials: Haarlow, McDonald
Attendance: 16,174

National Invitation Tournament (NIT)

Quarterfinals: Western Kentucky d. La Salle 68-61, Saint Louis d. Bowling Green 69-53, NYU d. Texas 45-43, DePaul d. NC State 75-64
Semifinals: NYU d. DePaul 72-59, Saint Louis d. Western Kentucky 60-53
Third place: Western Kentucky d. DePaul 61-59
Championship: Saint Louis d. NYU 65-52
MVP: Ed Macauley, Saint Louis

1948-49: Glory and Shame

On Jan. 18, 1949, the Associated Press released its first basketball poll and almost nailed it: No. 2 Kentucky—returning six of its eight top scorers from the 1948 championship team—went on to win another NCAA title, beating Oklahoma A&M, 46-36, in the Final at the Hec Edmundson Pavilion in Seattle. Alex Groza scored 25 points and was named MOP for the second straight year. But there was a taint on those Wildcats. In the years that followed, Groza, Ralph Beard and Dale Barnstable admitted in sworn testimony to having taken $1,500 in bribes to throw their quarterfinal game in the NIT, a 61-56 loss to Loyola-Chicago, and to have shaved points in other games during the season. (Kentucky was banned from playing in 1952-53.)

Before the season, the NCAA reversed a longstanding policy and began allowing coaches to talk to players during timeouts. As a result, these would come to be used mainly as strategy discussions rather than as rest periods for players.

Major Conference Standings

BIG SEVEN

	Conference			Overall		
	W	L	PCT	W	L	PCT
Nebraska	9	3	.750	16	10	.615
Oklahoma	9	3	.750	14	10	.583
Kansas State	8	4	.667	13	11	.542
Missouri	6	6	.500	11	13	.458
Colorado	4	8	.333	6	12	.333
Kansas	3	9	.250	12	12	.500
Iowa State	3	9	.250	7	14	.333

BIG TEN

	Conference			Overall		
	W	L	PCT	W	L	PCT
Illinois○	10	2	.833	21	4	.840
Minnesota	9	3	.750	18	3	.857
Michigan	7	5	.583	15	6	.714
Ohio State	6	6	.500	14	7	.667
Indiana	6	6	.500	14	8	.636
Purdue	6	6	.500	13	9	.591
Wisconsin	5	7	.417	12	10	.545
Iowa	3	9	.250	10	10	.500
Northwestern	2	10	.167	5	16	.238

BORDER

	Conference			Overall		
	W	L	PCT	W	L	PCT
Arizona	13	3	.813	17	11	.607
Texas Tech	11	5	.688	21	9	.700
Hardin-Simmons	10	6	.625	13	15	.464
West Texas A&M	9	7	.563	16	8	.667
Northern Arizona	7	9	.438	11	10	.524
New Mexico	7	9	.438	11	12	.478
Texas Western	7	9	.438	8	12	.400
Arizona State	4	12	.250	12	17	.414
New Mexico State	4	12	.250	9	15	.375

IVY

	Conference			Overall		
	W	L	PCT	W	L	PCT
Yale○	9	3	.750	22	8	.733
Columbia	8	4	.667	13	5	.722
Penn	8	4	.667	15	8	.652
Princeton	8	4	.667	13	9	.591
Cornell	5	7	.417	11	15	.423
Dartmouth	4	8	.333	15	11	.577
Harvard	0	12	.000	3	20	.130

METRO NY

	Conference			Overall		
	W	L	PCT	W	L	PCT
Manhattan□	5	1	.833	18	8	.692
St. John's□	5	1	.833	15	9	.625
CCNY□	3	2	.600	17	8	.680
NYU□	3	2	.600	12	8	.600
St. Francis (NY)	2	2	.500	20	13	.606
Fordham	1	5	.167	11	15	.423
Brooklyn	0	6	.000	8	14	.364

MID-AMERICAN

	Conference			Overall		
	W	L	PCT	W	L	PCT
Cincinnati	9	1	.900	23	5	.821
Butler	8	2	.800	18	5	.783
Western Michigan	4	6	.400	12	10	.545
Western Reserve	4	6	.400	9	15	.375
Miami (OH)	3	7	.300	8	13	.381
Ohio	2	8	.200	6	16	.273

MASC-N

	Conference			Overall		
	W	L	PCT	W	L	PCT
Lafayette	6	2	.750	20	9	.690
Muhlenberg	6	2	.750	17	8	.680
Gettysburg	5	3	.625	16	10	.615
Lehigh	3	5	.375	7	11	.389
Bucknell	0	8	.000	2	18	.100

Note: Lafayette and Lehigh were also in the Middle Three

MIDDLE THREE

	Conference			Overall		
	W	L	PCT	W	L	PCT
Lafayette	3	1	.750	20	9	.690
Rutgers	3	1	.750	14	12	.538
Lehigh	0	4	.000	7	11	.389

MISSOURI VALLEY

	Conference			Overall		
	W	L	PCT	W	L	PCT
Oklahoma A&M○	9	1	.900	23	5	.821
Saint Louis□	8	2	.800	22	4	.846
Bradley□	6	4	.600	27	8	.771
Drake	4	6	.400	13	13	.500
Wichita State	3	7	.300	10	16	.385
Tulsa	0	10	.000	4	20	.167

SKYLINE 6

	Conference			Overall		
	W	L	PCT	W	L	PCT
Wyoming○	15	5	.750	25	10	.714
Utah□	14	6	.700	24	8	.750
Denver	13	7	.650	18	15	.545
BYU	11	9	.550	21	13	.618
Utah State	4	16	.200	10	21	.323
Colorado State	3	17	.150	14	21	.400

OHIO VALLEY

	Conference			Overall		
	W	L	PCT	W	L	PCT
Western Kentucky□	8	2	.800	25	4	.862
Eastern Kentucky	7	3	.700	16	4	.800
Louisville	6	3	.667	23	10	.697
Marshall	2	2	.500	16	12	.571
Evansville	4	5	.444	14	11	.560
Murray State	3	9	.250	13	12	.520
Morehead State	2	7	.222	14	9	.609
Tennessee Tech	0	1	.000	10	10	.500

Tournament: **Western Kentucky d. Louisville 74-68**

PACIFIC COAST

	Conference			Overall		
	W	L	PCT	W	L	PCT
North						
Oregon State○	12	4	.750	24	12	.667
Washington State	8	8	.500	21	9	.700
Idaho	7	9	.438	17	15	.531
Oregon	7	9	.438	12	18	.400
Washington	6	10	.375	11	15	.423
South						
UCLA	10	2	.833	22	7	.759
Southern California	8	4	.667	14	10	.583
Stanford	5	7	.417	19	9	.679
California	1	11	.083	14	19	.424

Playoff: **Oregon State d. UCLA 2-1** in a best of three series for the title

SEC

	Conference			Overall		
	W	L	PCT	W	L	PCT
Kentucky○□	13	0	1.000	32	2	.941
Tulane	12	3	.800	24	4	.857
Tennessee	8	3	.727	19	7	.731
Vanderbilt	9	5	.643	14	8	.636
LSU	7	6	.538	15	10	.600
Alabama	9	9	.500	13	12	.520
Georgia Tech	7	9	.438	11	13	.458
Georgia	6	9	.400	17	13	.567
Florida	4	8	.333	11	16	.407
Auburn	5	11	.313	9	15	.375
Mississippi	4	12	.250	8	13	.381
Mississippi State	3	12	.200	4	13	.235

Tournament: **Kentucky d. Tulane 68-52**

SOUTHERN

	Conference			Overall		
	W	L	PCT	W	L	PCT
NC State	14	1	.933	25	8	.758
William and Mary	10	3	.769	24	10	.706
North Carolina	13	5	.722	20	8	.714
George Washington	9	4	.692	18	8	.692
Davidson	11	6	.647	18	8	.692
Wake Forest	7	7	.500	11	13	.458
South Carolina	7	6	.538	10	12	.455
Maryland	7	7	.500	9	17	.346
Virginia Tech	6	8	.429	10	13	.435
Duke	5	7	.417	13	9	.591
Clemson	6	9	.400	10	11	.476
Washington and Lee	5	9	.357	10	12	.455
Richmond	5	10	.333	8	15	.348
VMI	3	8	.273	3	16	.158
Furman	4	11	.267	8	14	.364
The Citadel	0	11	.000	1	17	.056

Tournament: **NC State d. George Washington 55-39**
Tournament MOP: **Chet Giermak**, William and Mary

SOUTHWEST

	Conference			Overall		
	W	L	PCT	W	L	PCT
Arkansas○	9	3	.750	15	11	.577
Baylor	9	3	.750	14	10	.583
Rice	9	3	.750	13	11	.542
Texas	7	5	.583	17	7	.708
SMU	5	7	.417	11	13	.458
Texas A&M	2	10	.167	5	19	.208
TCU	1	11	.083	4	20	.167

WNY LITTLE THREE

	Conference			Overall		
	W	L	PCT	W	L	PCT
Niagara	3	1	.750	24	7	.774
Canisius	2	2	.500	16	12	.571
St. Bonaventure	1	3	.250	18	8	.692

YANKEE

	Conference			Overall		
	W	L	PCT	W	L	PCT
Connecticut	7	1	.875	19	6	.760
Rhode Island	5	1	.833	16	6	.727
Vermont	2	1	.667	15	5	.750
Massachusetts	2	2	.500	6	12	.333
New Hampshire	2	6	.250	7	10	.412
Maine	0	7	.000	4	14	.222

⊛ Automatic NCAA Tournament bid ○ At-large NCAA Tournament bid □ NIT appearance ❂ Team record doesn't reflect games forfeited or vacated. For adjusted record, see p. 521.

INDEPENDENTS

	Overall W	L	Pct
Villanova○	23	4	.852
San Francisco□	25	5	.833
Loyola-Chicago□	25	6	.806
Bowling Green□	24	7	.774
Duquesne	17	5	.773
Siena	22	7	.759
La Salle	21	7	.750
West Virginia	18	6	.750
Syracuse	18	7	.720
Notre Dame	17	7	.708
Holy Cross	19	8	.704
Miami (FL)	19	8	.704
Seton Hall	16	8	.667
DePaul	16	9	.640
Brown	13	8	.619
Xavier	16	10	.615
Colgate	11	7	.611
Temple	14	9	.609
Long Island	18	12	.600

INDEPENDENTS (cont.)

	Overall W	L	Pct
Baldwin-Wallace	13	9	.591
Navy	12	9	.571
Virginia	13	10	.565
Detroit	12	10	.545
Dayton	16	14	.533
Saint Joseph's	12	11	.522
Toledo	13	12	.520
Boston College	9	9	.500
Pittsburgh	12	13	.480
Saint Mary's (CA)	13	17	.433
Michigan State	9	12	.429
Army	7	10	.412
Penn State	7	10	.412
Marquette	8	13	.381
Georgetown	9	15	.375
Santa Clara	8	15	.348
Boston U.	6	12	.333
Providence	7	19	.269

INDIVIDUAL LEADERS—SEASON

Scoring

Scoring	CL	POS	G	FG	FT	PTS	PPG
1 **Tony Lavelli**, Yale	SR	F	30	228	215	671	**22.4**
2 **Paul Arizin**, Villanova	JR	F	27	210	174	594	**22.0**
3 **Chet Giermak**, William and Mary	JR	C	34	301	138	740	**21.8**
4 **Paul Senesky**, Saint Joseph's	JR	F	23	192	99	483	**21.0**
5 **Ernie Vandeweghe**, Colgate	SR	F	18	152	93	397	**20.9**
6 **Alex Groza**, Kentucky	SR	C	34	259	180	698	**20.5**
7 **Ken Goodwin**, Rhode Island	SR	C	22	145	143	433	**19.7**
8 **Joe Noertker**, Virginia	JR	C	23	183	76	442	**19.2**
9 **Vince Boryla**, Denver	JR	F	33	212	200	624	**18.9**
10 **Fred Schaus**, West Virginia	SR	F	24	154	134	442	**18.4**

Field Goal Pct

Field Goal Pct	CL	POS	G	FG	FGA	PCT
1 **Ed Macauley**, Saint Louis	SR	F/C	26	144	275	**52.4**
2 **Ken Goodwin**, Rhode Island	SR	C	22	145	291	**49.8**
3 **Lee Brawley**, Maryland	FR	F/C	26	78	161	**48.4**
4 **Tom LeVerte**, Seton Hall	SR	F	23	101	210	**48.1**
5 **Don Boven**, Western Michigan	SR	F	22	123	257	**47.9**

Minimum 75 made

Free Throw Pct

Free Throw Pct	CL	POS	G	FT	FTA	PCT
1 **Bill Schroer**, Valparaiso	SO	F	24	59	68	**86.8**
2 **Jim Line**, Kentucky	JR	F	32	43	51	**84.3**
3 **Frank Oftring**, Holy Cross	JR	F	25	47	56	**83.9**
4 **Julius Dolnics**, TCU	SR	C	24	99	119	**83.2**
5 **Ken Goodwin**, Rhode Island	SR	C	22	143	172	**83.1**

Minimum 40 made

INDIVIDUAL LEADERS—GAME

Points

Points	CL	POS	OPP	DATE	PTS
1 **Paul Arizin**, Villanova	JR	F	Philadelphia NAMC	F12	**85**
2 **Tony Lavelli**, Yale	SR	F	Williams	F26	**52**
3 **Slater Martin**, Texas	SR	G	TCU	F26	**49**
4 **Chet Giermak**, William and Mary	JR	C	Baltimore	J11	**45**
5 **Tony Lavelli**, Yale	SR	F	Princeton	F5	**40**

Free Throws Made

Free Throws Made	CL	POS	OPP	DATE	FT	FTA	PCT
1 **Hillary Chollet**, Cornell	SR	F	Syracuse	F23	**19**	24	79.2
2 **Tony Lavelli**, Yale	SR	F	Penn	J8	**15**	19	78.9
Paul Arizin, Villanova	JR	F	Philadelphia NAMC	F12	**15**	22	68.2
4 **Alex Groza**, Kentucky	SR	C	Georgia	F21	**14**	20	70.0
5 **Vince Boryla**, Denver	JR	F	BYU	F7	**13**	14	92.9
Ken Goodwin, Rhode Island	SR	C	Providence	F28	**13**	13	100.0
Ed Gayda, Washington State	JR	G	Idaho	J22	**13**	15	86.7
Bob Anderson, Loyola (MD)	JR	C	St. Benedict	M26	**13**	16	81.3
Chet Giermak, William and Mary	JR	C	The Citadel	F18	**13**	16	81.3
Bill Stephenson, Stanford	SR	C	California	J14	**13**	17	76.5

TEAM LEADERS—SEASON

Scoring Offense

Scoring Offense	G	W-L	PTS	PPG
1 **Rhode Island**	22	16-6	1,575	**71.6**
2 **Western Kentucky**	29	25-4	2,028	**69.9**
3 **Yale**	30	22-8	2,089	**69.6**
4 **Bowling Green**	31	24-7	2,139	**69.0**
5 **Kentucky**	34	32-2	2,320	**68.2**

Scoring Margin

Scoring Margin	G	W-L	PPG	OPP PPG	MAR
1 **Kentucky**	34	32-2	68.2	43.9	**24.3**
2 **Tulane**	28	24-4	65.6	48.8	**16.8**
3 **Rhode Island**	22	16-6	71.6	56.0	**15.6**
Loyola-Chicago	31	25-6	61.3	45.7	**15.6**
5 **Western Kentucky**	29	25-4	69.9	54.4	**15.5**

Field Goal Pct

Field Goal Pct	G	W-L	FG	FGA	PCT
1 **Muhlenberg**	25	17-8	593	1,512	**39.2**
2 **Wyoming**	35	25-10	674	1,777	**37.9**
3 **Loyola-Chicago**	31	25-6	720	1,918	**37.5**
4 **Seton Hall**	24	16-8	566	1,509	**37.5**
5 **Bradley**	35	27-8	889	2,372	**37.5**

Free Throw Pct

Free Throw Pct	G	W-L	FT	FTA	PCT
1 **Davidson**	26	18-8	347	489	**71.0**
2 **Kentucky**	34	32-2	514	728	**70.6**
3 **Utah**	32	24-8	489	704	**69.5**
4 **Denver**	33	18-15	505	730	**69.2**
5 **Texas**	24	17-7	302	440	**68.6**

Scoring Defense

Scoring Defense	G	W-L	OPP PTS	OPP PPG
1 **Oklahoma A&M**	28	23-5	985	**35.2**
2 **Siena**	29	22-7	1,215	**41.9**
3 **Wyoming**	35	25-10	1,509	**43.1**
4 **Minnesota**	21	18-3	912	**43.4**
5 **St. Bonaventure**	26	18-8	1,137	**43.7**

CONSENSUS ALL-AMERICAS

First Team

PLAYER	CL	POS	HT	SCHOOL	PPG
Ralph Beard	SR	G	5-10	Kentucky	10.9
Vince Boryla	JR	F	6-5	Denver	18.9
Alex Groza	SR	C	6-7	Kentucky	20.5
Tony Lavelli	SR	F	6-3	Yale	22.4
Ed Macauley	SR	F/C	6-8	Saint Louis	15.5

Second Team

PLAYER	CL	POS	HT	SCHOOL	PPG
Bill Erickson	JR	G	6-1	Illinois	10.4
Vern Gardner	SR	C	6-4	Utah	15.3
Wallace Jones	SR	F	6-4	Kentucky	9.7
Jim McIntyre	SR	C	6-10	Minnesota	16.9
Ernie Vandeweghe	SR	F	6-3	Colgate	20.9

Selectors: AP, Colliers (Basketball Coaches), Look Magazine, UP

Poll Progression

Week of Jan 18

AP	School	
1	**Saint Louis** (11-0)	(A)
2	**Kentucky** (11-1)	(A)
3	**Western Kentucky** (12-0)	
4	**Minnesota** (12-0)	
5	**Oklahoma A&M** (9-2)	
6	**San Francisco** (13-1)	
7	**Illinois** (12-1)	
8	**Hamline** (11-0)	
9	**Villanova** (11-0)	
10	**Utah** (10-2)	
11	**Tulane** (13-2)	
12	**Loyola-Chicago** (11-2)	
13	**Cincinnati** (8-1)	
14	**Holy Cross** (8-5)	
15	**Bowling Green** (9-6)	
16	**Bradley** (15-3)	
17	**Stanford** (11-2)	
18	**Washington State** (17-1)	
19	**Butler** (9-2)	
20	**NYU** (7-3)	

Week of Jan 25

AP	School	AP↓↑
1	**Saint Louis** (12-1) (B)	
2	**Kentucky** (12-1)	
3	**Oklahoma A&M** (10-2) (B)	↑2
4	**Western Kentucky** (15-0)	↓1
5	**Minnesota** (13-0)	↓1
6	**Illinois** (12-1)	↑1
7	**Hamline** (13-0)	↑1
8	**Villanova** (11-0)	↑1
9	**San Francisco** (15-2)	↓3
10	**Utah** (13-2)	
11	**Stanford** (15-2)	↑6
12	**Tulane** (15-2)	↓1
13	**Loyola-Chicago** (13-2)	↓1
14	**Washington State** (18-1)	↑4
15	**NC State** (11-7)	⤴
16	**DePaul** (10-6)	⤴
17	**Butler** (11-3)	↑2
18	**Baylor** (10-6)	⤴
19	**Bradley** (18-3)	↓3
20	**Holy Cross** (9-5)	↓6

Week of Feb 1

AP	School	AP↓↑
1	**Kentucky** (13-1)	↑1
2	**Saint Louis** (13-1)	↓1
3	**Oklahoma A&M** (11-2)	
4	**Illinois** (13-1)	↑2
5	**Minnesota** (13-1)	
6	**Western Kentucky** (16-1)	↓2
7	**Villanova** (12-1)	↑1
8	**Hamline** (14-0)	↓1
9	**Stanford** (17-2)	↑2
10	**San Francisco** (16-2)	↓1
11	**Tulane** (15-2)	↑1
12	**Utah** (14-3)	↓2
13	**Loyola-Chicago** (14-2)	
14	**Bowling Green** (10-6)	⤴
15	**NYU** (7-3)	⤴
16	**Butler** (12-3)	↑1
17	**NC State** (14-7)	↓2
18	**Bradley** (19-3)	↑1
19	**Holy Cross** (9-5)	↑1
20	**Eastern Kentucky** (12-3)	⤴

Week of Feb 8

AP	School	AP↓↑
1	**Kentucky** (17-1)	
2	**Saint Louis** (15-1)	
3	**Oklahoma A&M** (13-2)	
4	**Illinois** (14-2)	
5	**Hamline** (15-0) (C)	↑3
6	**Western Kentucky** (17-2)	
7	**Minnesota** (14-2)	↓2
8	**Tulane** (18-2)	↑3
9	**San Francisco** (18-3)	↑1
10	**Stanford** (17-3)	↓1
11	**Loyola-Chicago** (16-3)	↑2
12	**Utah** (16-4)	
13	**Villanova** (13-3)	↓6
14	**Bowling Green** (12-6)	
15	**Holy Cross** (12-5)	↑4
16	**Butler** (13-3)	
17	**Washington State** (18-2)	⤴
18	**Ohio State** (9-4)	⤴
19	**Wyoming** (17-6)	⤴
20	**Duquesne** (13-2)	⤴

Week of Feb 15

AP	School	AP↓↑
1	**Kentucky** (20-1)	
2	**Saint Louis** (16-2)	
3	**Oklahoma A&M** (16-3)	
4	**Illinois** (16-2)	
5	**Tulane** (19-2)	↑3
6	**Minnesota** (15-2)	↑1
7	**Western Kentucky** (20-3)	↓1
8	**San Francisco** (19-4)	↑1
9	**Hamline** (17-1)	↓4
10	**Bowling Green** (16-6)	↑4
11	**Butler** (15-3)	↑5
12	**Bradley** (22-4)	⤴
13	**Loyola-Chicago** (16-4)	↓2
14	**Utah** (18-5)	↓2
15	**Villanova** (15-3)	↓2
16	**Oklahoma** (11-5)	⤴
17	**DePaul** (14-7)	⤴
18	**NC State** (17-8)	⤴
19	**Wyoming** (20-6)	
20	**Duquesne** (15-3)	
20	**Stanford** (17-5)	↓10
20	**Yale** (15-4)	⤴

Week of Feb 22

AP	School	AP↓↑
1	**Kentucky** (22-1)	
2	**Saint Louis** (18-2)	
3	**Oklahoma A&M** (17-3)	
4	**Illinois** (16-2)	
5	**Minnesota** (16-2)	↑1
6	**Tulane** (20-2)	↓1
7	**Western Kentucky** (22-3)	
8	**San Francisco** (20-5)	
9	**Bowling Green** (18-6)	↑1
10	**Bradley** (23-4)	↑2
11	**Butler** (17-3)	
12	**Loyola-Chicago** (18-4)	↑1
13	**Yale** (18-4)	⤴
14	**Wyoming** (22-6)	↑5
15	**Hamline** (19-3)	↓6
16	**Utah** (20-6)	↓2
17	**Duquesne** (15-4)	↑3
18	**Ohio State** (11-6)	⤴
19	**USC** (12-8)	⤴
20	**Texas** (16-5)	⤴

Week of Mar 1

AP	School	AP↓↑
1	**Kentucky** (25-1)	
2	**Oklahoma A&M** (19-4)	↑1
3	**Saint Louis** (19-3)	↓1
4	**Illinois** (19-2)	
5	**Minnesota** (18-2)	
6	**Western Kentucky** (25-3)	↑1
7	**Tulane** (21-3)	↓1
8	**San Francisco** (21-5)	
9	**Bowling Green** (20-6)	
10	**Bradley** (25-5)	
11	**Butler** (18-5)	
12	**Wyoming** (22-8)	↑2
13	**Utah** (23-6)	↑3
14	**Loyola-Chicago** (21-5)	↓2
15	**NC State** (22-8)	⤴
16	**Hamline** (23-3)	↓1
17	**Villanova** (18-3)	⤴
18	**Yale** (19-5) (D)	↓5
19	**Ohio State** (13-7)	↓1
20	**Arkansas** (12-10)	⤴

Week of Mar 8

AP	School	AP↓↑
1	**Kentucky** (29-1) (E)	
2	**Oklahoma A&M** (20-4)	
3	**Saint Louis** (20-3)	
4	**Illinois** (19-2)	
5	**Western Kentucky** (25-3)	↑1
6	**Minnesota** (18-3)	↓1
7	**Bradley** (25-6)	↑3
8	**San Francisco** (21-5)	
9	**Tulane** (24-4)	↓2
10	**Bowling Green** (21-6)	↓1
11	**Yale** (21-5)	↑7
12	**Utah** (24-7)	↑1
13	**NC State** (25-8)	↑2
14	**Villanova** (20-3)	↑3
15	**UCLA** (21-5) (F)	⤴
16	**Loyola-Chicago** (22-5)	↓2
17	**Wyoming** (24-8)	↓5
18	**Butler** (18-5)	↓7
19	**Hamline** (23-3)	↓3
20	**Ohio State** (14-7)	↓1

(A) The Associated Press starts a college basketball poll modeled after its football poll, which began in 1934. Saint Louis claims the No. 1 spot, having upset defending NCAA champion Kentucky, 42-40, on Dec. 30 in the Sugar Bowl tournament in New Orleans.

(B) Oklahoma A&M upsets Saint Louis, 29-27, on Jan. 20. The 29 points still are the fewest ever by a team defeating a No. 1.

(C) Little Hamline College of St. Paul, Minn., climbs to No. 5 behind F Vern Mikkelsen, later an NBA star on the Minneapolis Lakers alongside George Mikan. Hamline's previous claim to fame was as host of the first intercollegiate basketball game, a 9-3 loss to the Minnesota School of Agriculture on Feb. 9, 1895.

(D) The nation's leading scorer, Yale's 6'3" Tony Lavelli, pours in a school-record 52 points in a victory over Williams College.

(E) Kentucky defeats Tulane in the SEC tournament final and rolls into the NIT on a 21-game winning streak. This is the second edition of the Fabulous Five. The previous year's crew—Ralph Beard, Alex Groza, Wallace "Wah Wah" Jones, Cliff Barker and Kenny Rollins—posted a 36–3 record and, after winning the 1948 NCAA title, joined the U.S. Olympic team as a group and won a gold medal in London. Only Rollins graduated, and he was replaced in the starting lineup by Dale Barnstable.

(F) UCLA concludes its first season under coach John Wooden with a 22–7 record.

1949 NCAA Tournament

Regional Semifinals

EAST
- Illinois **71**, Yale **67** (A)
- Kentucky **85**, Villanova **72** (B)

WEST
- Oklahoma A&M **40**, Wyoming **39**
- Oregon State **56**, Arkansas **38**

Regional Finals
- Illinois **47**, Kentucky **76**
- Oklahoma A&M **55**, Oregon State **30**

National Final (Seattle)

Kentucky 46
Oklahoma A&M 36

Alex Groza, the brother of NFL placekicker Lou, pours in 25 points as Kentucky takes back-to-back titles. No other Wildcat scores more than five points. But two years later, Groza and two other players would admit to accepting bribes to shave points in their 1949 NIT game against Loyola-Chicago.

(A) The nation's top scorer in ppg, Yale's Tony Lavelli, a music student with a deadly hook shot, scores 27 points. He is drafted by Boston, where he plays accordion during Celtics halftimes.

(B) Paul Arizin scores 30 for Villanova but only one other teammate hits double figures (Brooks Ricca, 14). Meanwhile, Alex Groza's 30 leads Kentucky's balanced attack in the highest-scoring game by a team yet.

National Third Place Illinois d. Oregon State 57-53
East Regional Third Place Villanova d. Yale 78-67
West Regional Third Place Arkansas d. Wyoming 61-48

TOURNAMENT LEADERS

INDIVIDUAL LEADERS

SCORING

	CL	POS	G	PTS	PPG
1 **Alex Groza**, Kentucky	SR	C	3	82	27.3
2 **Paul Arizin**, Villanova	JR	F	2	52	26.0
3 **Tony Lavelli**, Yale	SR	F	2	35	17.5
4 **Joseph Hannan**, Villanova	SO	G	2	32	16.0
5 **Ted Anderson**, Yale	JR	F	2	31	15.5
6 **Cliff Crandall**, Oregon State	SR	G/F	3	42	14.0
Cliff Horton, Arkansas	SR	F	2	28	14.0
8 **Jim Line**, Kentucky	JR	F	3	41	13.7
Jack Shelton, Oklahoma A&M	JR	C	3	41	13.7
10 **Brooks Ricca**, Villanova	JR	C	2	27	13.5

MINIMUM: 2 GAMES

FIELD GOALS PER GAME

	CL	POS	G	FG	FGPG
1 **Alex Groza**, Kentucky	SR	C	3	31	10.3
2 **Paul Arizin**, Villanova	JR	F	2	18	9.0
3 **Joseph Hannan**, Villanova	SO	G	2	15	7.5
4 **Ted Anderson**, Yale	JR	F	2	12	6.0
5 **Jim Line**, Kentucky	JR	F	3	17	5.7

MINIMUM: 2 GAMES

FREE THROWS PER GAME

	CL	POS	G	FT	FTPG
1 **Paul Arizin**, Villanova	JR	F	2	16	8.0
2 **Alex Groza**, Kentucky	SR	C	3	20	6.7
3 **Tony Lavelli**, Yale	SR	F	2	13	6.5
4 **Jack Shelton**, Oklahoma A&M	JR	C	3	19	6.3
5 **Cliff Crandall**, Oregon State	SR	G/F	3	16	5.3

MINIMUM: 5 MADE

TEAM LEADERS

SCORING

	G	PTS	PPG
1 **Villanova**	2	150	75.0
2 **Kentucky**	3	207	69.0
3 **Yale**	2	134	67.0
4 **Illinois**	3	175	58.3
5 **Arkansas**	2	99	49.5
6 **Oregon State**	3	139	46.3
7 **Oklahoma A&M**	3	131	43.7
8 **Wyoming**	2	87	43.5

MINIMUM: 2 GAMES

FT PCT

	G	FT	FTA	PCT
1 **Oklahoma A&M**	3	49	64	76.6
2 **Kentucky**	3	51	71	71.8
3 **Oregon State**	3	43	67	64.2
4 **Illinois**	3	33	58	56.9
5 **Wyoming**	2	23	42	54.8

MINIMUM: 2 GAMES

FG PER GAME

	G	FG	FGPG
1 **Villanova**	2	59	29.5
2 **Yale**	2	52	26.0
3 **Kentucky**	3	78	26.0
4 **Illinois**	3	71	23.7
5 **Arkansas**	2	40	20.0

TOURNAMENT MOP

PLAYER	CL	POS	HT	SCHOOL	FG	FT	PPG
Alex Groza	SR	C	6-7	Kentucky	31	20	27.3

1949 NCAA TOURNAMENT BOX SCORES

71-67 (ELITE 8)

	1H	2H
Illinois	31	40
Yale	35	32

ILLINOIS	MIN	FG	3FG	FT	REB	A	ST	BL	PF	TP
Walter Osterkorn	-	5	-	5-8	-	-	-	-	3	15
Don Sunderlage	-	7	-	1-3	-	-	-	-	5	15
Dwight Eddleman	-	5	-	1-1	-	-	-	-	4	11
Fred Green	-	4	-	2-2	-	-	-	-	2	10
Walt Kersulis	-	3	-	1-1	-	-	-	-	3	7
William Erickson	-	1	-	3-6	-	-	-	-	3	5
Van Anderson	-	2	-	0-0	-	-	-	-	1	4
Richard Foley	-	2	-	0-0	-	-	-	-	1	4
Ted Beach	-	0	-	0-0	-	-	-	-	0	0
Jim Cottrell	-	0	-	0-0	-	-	-	-	0	0
Roy Gatewood	-	0	-	0-0	-	-	-	-	0	0
John Marks	-	0	-	0-0	-	-	-	-	1	0
TOTALS	**-**	**29**	**-**	**13-21**	**-**	**-**	**-**	**-**	**23**	**71**
Percentages				61.9						

Coach: Harry Combes

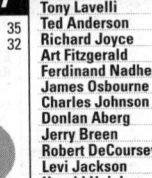

YALE	MIN	FG	3FG	FT	REB	A	ST	BL	PF	TP
Tony Lavelli	-	10	-	7-7	-	-	-	-	3	27
Ted Anderson	-	7	-	5-8	-	-	-	-	4	19
Richard Joyce	-	4	-	1-1	-	-	-	-	5	9
Art Fitzgerald	-	1	-	3-5	-	-	-	-	3	5
Ferdinand Nadherny	-	2	-	0-2	-	-	-	-	2	4
James Osbourne	-	1	-	0-0	-	-	-	-	0	2
Charles Johnson	-	0	-	1-4	-	-	-	-	1	1
Donlan Aberg	-	0	-	0-0	-	-	-	-	0	0
Jerry Breen	-	0	-	0-0	-	-	-	-	0	0
Robert DeCoursey	-	0	-	0-0	-	-	-	-	0	0
Levi Jackson	-	0	-	0-0	-	-	-	-	0	0
Harold Upjohn	-	0	-	0-0	-	-	-	-	0	0
TOTALS	**-**	**25**	**-**	**17-27**	**-**	**-**	**-**	**-**	**18**	**67**
Percentages				63.0						

Coach: Howard "Hobby" Hobson

Officials: Begovich, Chest

85-72 (ELITE 8)

	1H	2H
Kentucky	48	37
Villanova	37	35

KENTUCKY	MIN	FG	3FG	FT	REB	A	ST	BL	PF	TP
Alex Groza	-	12	-	6-7	-	-	-	-	4	30
Jim Line	-	9	-	3-4	-	-	-	-	5	21
Cliff Barker	-	6	-	6-6	-	-	-	-	3	18
Dale Barnstable	-	2	-	1-1	-	-	-	-	2	5
Wallace Jones	-	0	-	4-4	-	-	-	-	5	4
Ralph Beard	-	0	-	3-5	-	-	-	-	3	3
Roger Day	-	1	-	0-3	-	-	-	-	1	2
Wah Hirsch	-	1	-	0-0	-	-	-	-	3	2
TOTALS	**-**	**31**	**-**	**23-30**	**-**	**-**	**-**	**-**	**26**	**85**
Percentages				76.7						

Coach: Adolph Rupp

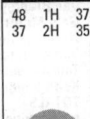

VILLANOVA	MIN	FG	3FG	FT	REB	A	ST	BL	PF	TP
Paul Arizin	-	11	-	8-11	-	-	-	-	5	30
Brooks Ricca	-	6	-	2-5	-	-	-	-	5	14
Joseph Hannan	-	3	-	1-3	-	-	-	-	2	7
Frederick Raiken	-	3	-	0-0	-	-	-	-	5	6
John Weglicki	-	2	-	1-5	-	-	-	-	2	5
Perry Delpurgatorio	-	2	-	0-0	-	-	-	-	2	4
John Crossin	-	0	-	2-2	-	-	-	-	1	2
Thomas Dolan	-	1	-	0-0	-	-	-	-	0	2
Leo Wolf	-	0	-	2-4	-	-	-	-	3	2
Sidney Gecker	-	0	-	0-0	-	-	-	-	0	0
TOTALS	**-**	**28**	**-**	**16-30**	**-**	**-**	**-**	**-**	**25**	**72**
Percentages				53.3						

Coach: Alexander Severance

Officials: McDonald, Gentile

40-39 (ELITE 8)

	1H	2H
Oklahoma A&M	22	18
Wyoming	25	14

OKLAHOMA A&M	MIN	FG	3FG	FT	REB	A	ST	BL	PF	TP
Jack Shelton	-	5	-	6-7	-	-	-	-	3	16
Joe Bradley	-	3	-	2-4	-	-	-	-	2	8
J.L. Parks	-	2	-	2-3	-	-	-	-	4	6
Bob Harris	-	2	-	0-1	-	-	-	-	4	4
Tom Jacquet	-	1	-	0-0	-	-	-	-	5	2
Gale McArthur	-	1	-	0-0	-	-	-	-	0	2
Vernon Yates	-	1	-	0-0	-	-	-	-	0	2
Jack Hobbs	-	0	-	0-0	-	-	-	-	1	0
Norman Pilgrim	-	0	-	0-1	-	-	-	-	1	0
TOTALS	**-**	**15**	**-**	**10-16**	**-**	**-**	**-**	**-**	**20**	**40**
Percentages				62.5						

Coach: Hank Iba

WYOMING	MIN	FG	3FG	FT	REB	A	ST	BL	PF	TP
John Pilch	-	6	-	2-4	-	-	-	-	5	14
Keith Bloom	-	3	-	3-5	-	-	-	-	1	9
Ron Livingston	-	4	-	0-1	-	-	-	-	3	8
Loy Doty	-	1	-	4-10	-	-	-	-	4	6
Mack Peyton	-	1	-	0-1	-	-	-	-	1	2
Gerald Reed	-	0	-	0-0	-	-	-	-	0	0
TOTALS	**-**	**15**	**-**	**9-21**	**-**	**-**	**-**	**-**	**14**	**39**
Percentages				42.9						

Coach: Everett Shelton

Officials: Curtis, Leith

ANNUAL REVIEW

OREGON STATE	MIN	FG	3FG	FT	REB	A	ST	BL	PF	TP
Dick Ballantyne	-	2	-	9-11	-	-	-	-	1	13
Cliff Crandall	-	3	-	7-7	-	-	-	-	4	13
Alex Petersen	-	5	-	0-1	-	-	-	-	1	10
Bill Harper	-	2	-	3-4	-	-	-	-	2	7
Dan Torrey	-	3	-	0-2	-	-	-	-	4	6
Ed Fleming	-	1	-	0-1	-	-	-	-	3	2
Paul Sliper	-	1	-	0-0	-	-	-	-	0	2
Harvey Watt	-	1	-	0-0	-	-	-	-	2	2
Len Rinearson	-	0	-	1-1	-	-	-	-	2	1
Jim Catterall	-	0	-	0-0	-	-	-	-	1	0
Tom Holman	-	0	-	0-0	-	-	-	-	0	0
Ray Snyder	-	0	-	0-0	-	-	-	-	1	0
TOTALS	-	18	-	20-27	-	-	-	-	21	56
Percentages				74.1						

Coach: Slats Gill

56-38
21 1H 17
35 2H 21
ELITE 8

ARKANSAS	MIN	FG	3FG	FT	REB	A	ST	BL	PF	TP
Cliff Horton	-	4	-	4-6	-	-	-	-	5	12
James Cathcart	-	2	-	2-4	-	-	-	-	5	6
Johnny Campbell	-	2	-	1-3	-	-	-	-	3	5
Robert Ambler	-	2	-	0-5	-	-	-	-	1	4
Roxie Rankin	-	2	-	0-0	-	-	-	-	0	4
Ken Kearns	-	1	-	1-1	-	-	-	-	4	3
Paul Coleman	-	0	-	2-2	-	-	-	-	0	2
Robert Williams	-	0	-	2-2	-	-	-	-	2	2
Johnny Adams	-	0	-	0-0	-	-	-	-	0	0
Gerald Hudspeth	-	0	-	0-0	-	-	-	-	2	0
Norman Price	-	0	-	0-0	-	-	-	-	2	0
TOTALS	-	13	-	12-23	-	-	-	-	24	38
Percentages				52.2						

Coach: Eugene Lambert

Officials: Ogden, Ball

KENTUCKY	MIN	FG	3FG	FT	REB	A	ST	BL	PF	TP
Alex Groza	-	10	-	7-10	-	-	-	-	4	27
Jim Line	-	6	-	3-4	-	-	-	-	0	15
Ralph Beard	-	4	-	1-3	-	-	-	-	3	9
Wallace Jones	-	4	-	1-2	-	-	-	-	3	9
Cliff Barker	-	3	-	2-3	-	-	-	-	2	8
Wah Hirsch	-	3	-	0-0	-	-	-	-	1	6
Dale Barnstable	-	1	-	0-0	-	-	-	-	1	2
Roger Day	-	0	-	0-0	-	-	-	-	0	0
Johnny Strogh	-	0	-	0-0	-	-	-	-	0	0
TOTALS	-	31	-	14-22	-	-	-	-	14	76
Percentages				63.6						

Coach: Adolph Rupp

76-47
39 1H 22
37 2H 25
FINAL 4

ILLINOIS	MIN	FG	3FG	FT	REB	A	ST	BL	PF	TP
Walt Kersulis	-	3	-	3-3	-	-	-	-	2	9
Fred Green	-	3	-	1-1	-	-	-	-	2	7
Dwight Eddleman	-	3	-	0-2	-	-	-	-	1	6
Roy Gatewood	-	3	-	0-0	-	-	-	-	0	6
William Erickson	-	2	-	1-3	-	-	-	-	2	5
Walter Osterkorn	-	2	-	1-2	-	-	-	-	5	5
Richard Foley	-	1	-	1-1	-	-	-	-	1	3
Ted Beach	-	1	-	0-0	-	-	-	-	0	2
John Marks	-	1	-	0-0	-	-	-	-	2	2
Don Sunderlage	-	0	-	2-2	-	-	-	-	2	2
Van Anderson	-	0	-	0-0	-	-	-	-	1	0
Jim Cottrell	-	0	-	0-0	-	-	-	-	1	0
TOTALS	-	19	-	9-14	-	-	-	-	19	47
Percentages				64.3						

Coach: Harry Combes

Officials: Begovich, Gentile

OKLAHOMA A&M	MIN	FG	3FG	FT	REB	A	ST	BL	PF	TP
Bob Harris	-	8	-	7-7	-	-	-	-	1	23
Jack Shelton	-	3	-	7-8	-	-	-	-	3	13
J.L. Parks	-	2	-	4-6	-	-	-	-	2	8
Joe Bradley	-	3	-	1-1	-	-	-	-	1	7
Keith Smith	-	1	-	2-2	-	-	-	-	1	4
Frank Allen	-	0	-	0-0	-	-	-	-	1	0
Larry Hayes	-	0	-	0-0	-	-	-	-	1	0
Jack Hobbs	-	0	-	0-0	-	-	-	-	0	0
Tom Jacquet	-	0	-	0-0	-	-	-	-	0	0
Gale McArthur	-	0	-	0-0	-	-	-	-	2	0
Norman Pilgrim	-	0	-	0-0	-	-	-	-	4	0
Vernon Yates	-	0	-	0-0	-	-	-	-	0	0
TOTALS	-	17	-	21-24	-	-	-	-	16	55
Percentages				87.5						

Coach: Hank Iba

55-30
21 1H 11
34 2H 19
FINAL 4

OREGON STATE	MIN	FG	3FG	FT	REB	A	ST	BL	PF	TP
Cliff Crandall	-	4	-	3-4	-	-	-	-	3	11
Tom Holman	-	1	-	2-2	-	-	-	-	1	4
Alex Petersen	-	2	-	0-3	-	-	-	-	5	4
Dick Ballantyne	-	1	-	1-1	-	-	-	-	2	3
Ed Fleming	-	1	-	0-1	-	-	-	-	0	2
Bill Harper	-	1	-	0-1	-	-	-	-	1	2
Ray Snyder	-	1	-	0-0	-	-	-	-	1	2
Jim Catterall	-	0	-	1-2	-	-	-	-	1	1
Dan Torrey	-	0	-	1-1	-	-	-	-	0	1
Len Rinearson	-	0	-	0-0	-	-	-	-	2	0
Paul Sliper	-	0	-	0-0	-	-	-	-	1	0
Harvey Watt	-	0	-	0-0	-	-	-	-	1	0
TOTALS	-	11	-	8-15	-	-	-	-	18	30
Percentages				53.3						

Coach: Slats Gill

Officials: Curtis, Ball

ILLINOIS	MIN	FG	3FG	FT	REB	A	ST	BL	PF	TP
Walter Osterkorn	-	6	-	5-8	-	-	-	-	5	17
Dwight Eddleman	-	5	-	1-2	-	-	-	-	5	11
Richard Foley	-	2	-	3-6	-	-	-	-	4	7
Fred Green	-	3	-	1-1	-	-	-	-	5	7
Walt Kersulis	-	3	-	1-4	-	-	-	-	2	7
William Erickson	-	3	-	0-2	-	-	-	-	4	6
Don Sunderlage	-	1	-	0-0	-	-	-	-	0	2
Van Anderson	-	0	-	0-0	-	-	-	-	1	0
Ted Beach	-	0	-	0-0	-	-	-	-	0	0
Jim Cottrell	-	0	-	0-0	-	-	-	-	0	0
Roy Gatewood	-	0	-	0-0	-	-	-	-	0	0
John Marks	-	0	-	0-0	-	-	-	-	0	0
TOTALS	-	23	-	11-23	-	-	-	-	26	57
Percentages				47.8						

Coach: Harry Combes

57-53
28 1H 19
29 2H 34
3RD PLACE

OREGON STATE	MIN	FG	3FG	FT	REB	A	ST	BL	PF	TP
Cliff Crandall	-	6	-	6-8	-	-	-	-	4	18
Dick Ballantyne	-	3	-	2-3	-	-	-	-	4	8
Alex Petersen	-	3	-	2-2	-	-	-	-	1	8
Harvey Watt	-	3	-	0-5	-	-	-	-	2	6
Ed Fleming	-	1	-	3-4	-	-	-	-	4	5
Ray Snyder	-	1	-	2-2	-	-	-	-	2	4
Bill Harper	-	1	-	0-1	-	-	-	-	3	2
Len Rinearson	-	1	-	0-0	-	-	-	-	1	2
Jim Catterall	-	0	-	0-0	-	-	-	-	0	0
Tom Holman	-	0	-	0-0	-	-	-	-	0	0
Paul Sliper	-	0	-	0-0	-	-	-	-	0	0
Dan Torrey	-	0	-	0-0	-	-	-	-	1	0
TOTALS	-	19	-	15-25	-	-	-	-	22	53
Percentages				60.0						

Coach: Slats Gill

Officials: Ogden, Curtis
Attendance: 10,600

KENTUCKY	MIN	FG	3FG	FT	REB	A	ST	BL	PF	TP
Alex Groza	-	9	-	7-8	-	-	-	-	5	25
Cliff Barker	-	1	-	3-3	-	-	-	-	4	5
Jim Line	-	2	-	1-2	-	-	-	-	3	5
Dale Barnstable	-	1	-	1-1	-	-	-	-	1	3
Ralph Beard	-	1	-	1-2	-	-	-	-	4	3
Wallace Jones	-	1	-	1-3	-	-	-	-	3	3
Wah Hirsch	-	1	-	0-0	-	-	-	-	1	2
TOTALS	-	16	-	14-19	-	-	-	-	21	46
Percentages				73.7						

Coach: Adolph Rupp

46-36
25 1H 20
21 2H 16
NCAA FINAL 1949

OKLAHOMA A&M	MIN	FG	3FG	FT	REB	A	ST	BL	PF	TP
Jack Shelton	-	3	-	6-7	-	-	-	-	4	12
Bob Harris	-	3	-	1-1	-	-	-	-	5	7
J.L. Parks	-	2	-	3-4	-	-	-	-	5	7
Joe Bradley	-	0	-	3-6	-	-	-	-	3	3
Gale McArthur	-	0	-	2-2	-	-	-	-	1	2
Norman Pilgrim	-	0	-	2-2	-	-	-	-	1	2
Vernon Yates	-	1	-	0-0	-	-	-	-	1	2
Tom Jacquet	-	0	-	1-2	-	-	-	-	0	1
Keith Smith	-	0	-	0-0	-	-	-	-	1	0
TOTALS	-	9	-	18-24	-	-	-	-	21	36
Percentages				75.0						

Coach: Hank Iba

Officials: Lee, McCullough
Attendance: 10,600

National Invitation Tournament (NIT)

First Round: Bowling Green d. St. John's 77-64, San Francisco d. Manhattan 68-43, Bradley d. NYU 89-67, Loyola-Chicago d. CCNY 62-47
Quarterfinals: Loyola-Chicago d. Kentucky 61-56, Bradley d. Western Kentucky 95-86, San Francisco d. Utah 64-63, Bowling Green d. Saint Louis 80-74
Semifinals: San Francisco d. Bowling Green 49-39, Loyola-Chicago d. Bradley 55-50
Third place: Bowling Green d. Bradley 82-77
Championship: San Francisco d. Loyola-Chicago 48-47
MVP: Don Lofgran, San Francisco

1949-50: Double, Trouble

March Madness has produced a slew of Cinderella stories, but none tops that of CCNY. During the NCAA Tournament, the unranked Beavers (24–5) defeated three Top 5 teams—including No. 1 Bradley, 71-68, in the championship game at Madison Square Garden. Coach Nat Holman's squad was also notable because it was one of the first teams with African-American starters (Floyd Layne and Ed Warner) to win a high-profile championship. But that's just the half of it. The Beavers also beat Bradley, 69-61, to win the NIT—remaining now, and certainly forever, the only team to win both tournaments in the same season.

Sadly, CCNY's dream season devolved into a nightmare the following season when charges were made—and evidence was revealed—of point shaving by several of its players. In 1953, another investigation uncovered scholastic records that had been doctored to admit basketball recruits. It would prove to be the final nail. The school suspended Holman for "conduct unbecoming a teacher" until an investigation could be completed (it showed he had no knowledge of the point shaving) and dropped to the College Division before the 1953-54 season. Also, Madison Square Garden never hosted another NCAA championship game.

Major Conference Standings

BIG SEVEN	Conference			Overall		
	W	L	Pct	W	L	Pct
Kansas	8	4	.667	14	11	.560
Kansas State	8	4	.667	17	7	.708
Nebraska	8	4	.667	16	7	.696
Colorado	6	6	.500	14	8	.636
Oklahoma	6	6	.500	12	10	.545
Missouri	4	8	.333	14	10	.583
Iowa State	2	10	.167	6	17	.261

BIG TEN	Conference			Overall		
	W	L	Pct	W	L	Pct
Ohio State○	11	1	.917	22	4	.846
Wisconsin	9	3	.750	17	5	.773
Indiana	7	5	.583	17	5	.773
Illinois	7	5	.583	14	8	.636
Iowa	6	6	.500	15	7	.682
Minnesota	4	8	.333	13	9	.591
Michigan	4	8	.333	11	11	.500
Northwestern	3	9	.250	10	12	.455
Purdue	3	9	.250	9	13	.409

BORDER	Conference			Overall		
	W	L	Pct	W	L	Pct
Arizona□	14	2	.875	26	5	.839
Hardin-Simmons	12	4	.750	15	10	.600
West Texas A&M	10	6	.625	18	10	.643
Arizona State	10	6	.625	12	14	.462
Texas Tech	8	8	.500	14	12	.538
New Mexico State	7	11	.389	17	13	.567
Texas Western	5	11	.313	17	13	.567
New Mexico	4	12	.250	5	19	.208
Northern Arizona	2	14	.125	3	19	.136

IVY	Conference			Overall		
	W	L	Pct	W	L	Pct
Princeton	11	1	.917	14	9	.609
Columbia	9	3	.750	21	7	.750
Cornell	7	5	.583	18	7	.720
Yale	7	5	.583	17	9	.654
Penn	4	8	.333	11	14	.440
Harvard	3	9	.250	9	15	.375
Dartmouth	1	11	.083	8	17	.320

METRO NY	Conference			Overall		
	W	L	Pct	W	L	Pct
CCNY○□	6	0	1.000	24	5	.828
Fordham	3	2	.600	16	12	.571
St. John's□	3	3	.500	24	5	.828
Manhattan	3	3	.500	14	11	.560
Brooklyn	2	2	.500	24	5	.828
NYU	1	4	.200	8	11	.421
St. Francis (NY)	0	4	.000	6	18	.250

MID-AMERICAN	Conference			Overall		
	W	L	Pct	W	L	Pct
Cincinnati	10	0	1.000	20	6	.769
Western Michigan	6	4	.600	12	10	.545
Butler	6	4	.600	12	12	.500
Ohio	3	7	.300	6	14	.300
Miami (OH)	3	7	.300	5	15	.250
Western Reserve	2	8	.200	7	17	.292

MIDDLE THREE	Conference			Overall		
	W	L	Pct	W	L	Pct
Lafayette	3	1	.750	18	6	.750
Rutgers	3	1	.750	13	15	.464
Lehigh	0	4	.000	4	14	.222

MISSOURI VALLEY	Conference			Overall		
	W	L	Pct	W	L	Pct
Bradley○□	11	1	.917	32	5	.865
Saint Louis	8	4	.667	17	9	.654
Detroit	7	5	.583	20	6	.769
Oklahoma A&M	7	5	.583	18	9	.667
Drake	5	7	.417	14	12	.538
Tulsa	3	9	.250	12	11	.522
Wichita State	1	11	.083	7	17	.292

SKYLINE 6	Conference			Overall		
	W	L	Pct	W	L	Pct
BYU○	14	6	.700	22	12	.647
Wyoming	13	7	.650	25	11	.694
Denver	13	7	.650	18	13	.581
Utah State	10	10	.500	17	17	.500
Utah	8	12	.400	16	18	.471
Colorado State	2	18	.100	7	23	.233

OHIO VALLEY	Conference			Overall		
	W	L	Pct	W	L	Pct
Western Kentucky□	8	0	1.000	25	6	.806
Eastern Kentucky	7	3	.700	16	6	.727
Marshall	5	4	.556	15	9	.625
Morehead State	5	6	.455	12	10	.545
Murray State	5	7	.417	18	13	.581
Evansville	2	7	.222	14	14	.500
Tennessee Tech	1	6	.143	9	12	.429

Tournament: **Eastern Kentucky d. Western Kentucky 62-50**

PACIFIC COAST	Conference			Overall		
	W	L	Pct	W	L	Pct
North						
Washington State	11	5	.688	19	13	.594
Washington	8	8	.500	19	10	.655
Oregon State	8	8	.500	13	14	.481
Idaho	7	9	.438	15	17	.469
Oregon	6	10	.375	9	19	.321
South						
UCLA○	10	2	.833	24	7	.774
Southern California	7	5	.583	16	8	.667
California	4	8	.333	10	17	.370
Stanford	3	9	.250	11	14	.440

Playoff: **UCLA d. Washington State 2-0** in a best of three series for the title

SEC	Conference			Overall		
	W	L	Pct	W	L	Pct
Kentucky□	11	2	.846	25	5	.833
Vanderbilt	11	3	.786	17	8	.680
Auburn	12	6	.667	17	7	.708
Tulane	8	4	.667	15	7	.682
Alabama	8	9	.471	9	12	.429
Georgia	6	7	.462	15	9	.625
Tennessee	5	6	.455	15	11	.577
Georgia Tech	7	9	.438	14	13	.519
LSU	5	8	.385	13	12	.520
Mississippi State	6	10	.375	7	11	.389
Florida	4	10	.286	9	14	.391
Mississippi	4	13	.235	8	17	.320

Tournament: **Kentucky d. Tennessee 95-58**

SOUTHERN	Conference			Overall		
	W	L	Pct	W	L	Pct
NC State○	12	2	.857	27	6	.818
William and Mary	12	4	.750	23	9	.719
George Washington	12	4	.750	17	8	.680
South Carolina	12	5	.706	13	9	.591
North Carolina	13	6	.684	17	12	.586
Virginia Tech	9	5	.643	16	9	.640
Wake Forest	11	8	.579	14	16	.467
Duke	9	7	.563	15	15	.500
Clemson	8	8	.500	10	10	.500
Davidson	6	12	.333	10	16	.385
Furman	4	8	.333	9	12	.429
Washington and Lee	4	9	.308	8	12	.400
Maryland	5	13	.278	7	18	.280
Richmond	4	13	.235	8	16	.333
The Citadel	2	10	.167	4	16	.200
VMI	2	11	.154	4	17	.190

Tournament: **NC State d. Duke 67-47**
Tournament MOP: **Sam Ranzino**, NC State

SOUTHWEST	Conference			Overall		
	W	L	Pct	W	L	Pct
Baylor○	8	4	.667	14	13	.519
Arkansas	8	4	.667	12	12	.500
SMU	7	5	.583	10	13	.435
Texas	6	6	.500	13	11	.542
Texas A&M	6	6	.500	10	14	.417
TCU	5	7	.417	13	11	.542
Rice	2	10	.167	8	15	.348

WNY LITTLE THREE	Conference			Overall		
	W	L	Pct	W	L	Pct
St. Bonaventure	2	2	.500	17	5	.773
Niagara□	2	2	.500	20	7	.741
Canisius	2	2	.500	17	8	.680

YANKEE	Conference			Overall		
	W	L	Pct	W	L	Pct
Rhode Island	6	1	.857	18	8	.692
Connecticut	5	2	.714	17	8	.680
Vermont	2	3	.400	9	11	.450
Massachusetts	2	3	.400	8	11	.421
Maine	3	5	.375	13	6	.684
New Hampshire	1	5	.167	4	11	.267

Conference Standings Continue →

⊕ Automatic NCAA Tournament bid ○ At-large NCAA Tournament bid □ NIT appearance ❶ Team record doesn't reflect games forfeited or vacated. For adjusted record, see p. 521.

INDEPENDENTS

	Overall W	L	Pct
Holy Cross○	27	4	.871
Villanova	25	4	.862
La Salle□	21	4	.840
Long Island□	20	5	.800
Duquesne□	23	6	.793
Toledo	22	6	.786
Dayton	24	8	.750
Muhlenberg	17	6	.739
Wash.-St. Louis	17	6	.739
San Francisco□	19	7	.731
Syracuse□	18	9	.667
Navy	14	7	.667
Louisville	21	11	.656
Valparaiso	15	8	.652
Akron	16	9	.640
Santa Clara	14	8	.636
Bowling Green	19	11	.633
Notre Dame	15	9	.625
Miami (FL)	14	9	.609
Temple	14	10	.583
Loyola-Chicago	17	13	.567
Penn State	13	10	.565

INDEPENDENTS (CONT.)

	Overall W	L	Pct
Colgate	10	8	.556
Boston College	11	9	.550
West Virginia	13	11	.542
Army	9	8	.529
Creighton	13	13	.500
Georgetown	12	12	.500
DePaul	12	13	.480
Virginia	12	13	.480
John Carroll	9	11	.450
Brown	11	14	.440
Baldwin-Wallace	12	16	.429
Xavier	12	16	.429
Seton Hall	11	15	.423
Saint Joseph's	10	15	.400
Loyola Marymount	9	17	.346
Wayne State (MI)	7	15	.318
Marquette	6	17	.261
Bucknell	5	16	.238
Pittsburgh	4	14	.222
Michigan State	4	18	.182
Saint Mary's (CA)	3	22	.120

INDIVIDUAL LEADERS—SEASON

Scoring

	CL	POS	G	FG	FT	PTS	PPG
1 **Paul Arizin**, Villanova	SR	F	29	260	215	735	**25.3**
2 **Paul Senesky**, Saint Joseph's	SR	F	24	216	105	537	**22.4**
3 **Sherman White**, Long Island	JR	F	25	210	131	551	**22.0**
4 **Clyde Lovellette**, Kansas	SO	C	25	214	117	545	**21.8**
5 **Bob Lavoy**, Western Kentucky	SR	C	31	271	129	671	**21.6**
6 **Dick Schnittker**, Ohio State	SR	F	22	158	153	469	**21.3**
7 **Chet Giermak**, William and Mary	SR	C	31	258	130	646	**20.8**
8 **Jay Handlan**, Washington and Lee	SO	F	20	165	76	406	**20.3**
9 **Bob Zawoluk**, St. John's	SO	C	29	222	144	588	**20.3**
10 **Joe Noertker**, Virginia	SR	C	25	210	83	503	**20.1**

Field Goal Pct

	CL	POS	G	FG	FGA	PCT
1 **Jim Moran**, Niagara	JR	F	27	98	185	**53.0**
2 **Dale Toft**, Denver	SO	C	29	146	281	**52.0**
3 **Bob McDonald**, Toledo	JR	F	27	102	200	**51.0**
4 **Paul Arizin**, Villanova	SR	F	29	260	527	**49.3**
5 **Steve Skendrovich**, Duquesne	SR	G	29	108	220	**49.1**

Minimum: 75 made

Free Throw Pct

	CL	POS	G	FT	FTA	PCT
1 **Sam Urzetta**, St. Bonaventure	SR	G	22	54	61	**88.5**
2 **Hal Morrill**, Michigan	SR	G	22	41	48	**85.4**
3 **John Ballots**, Temple	SR	F	24	73	86	**84.9**
4 **John Popp**, Baldwin-Wallace	SR	C	25	69	83	**83.1**
5 **Mickey Sermersheim**, Georgia Tech	JR	G	27	68	82	**82.9**

Minimum: 40 made

INDIVIDUAL LEADERS—GAME

Points

	CL	POS	OPP	DATE	PTS
1 **Bob Zawoluk**, St. John's	SO	C	Saint Peter's	M3	**65**
2 **Sherman White**, Long Island	JR	F	John Marshall	F28	**63**
3 **Ike Borsavage**, Temple	SR	C	West Virginia	F18	**42**
Curt Norris, Colgate	SR	F	Alfred	J14	**42**
5 **Paul Arizin**, Villanova	SR	F	Seton Hall	F8	**41**

Free Throws Made

	CL	POS	OPP	DATE	FT	FTA	PCT
1 **Jay Handlan**, Washington and Lee	SO	F	Virginia	F24	**18**	18	100.0
2 **Bob Zawoluk**, St. John's	SO	C	Saint Peter's	M3	**15**	19	78.9
Francis Miller, Creighton	JR	C	Phillips Oilers (OK)	F21	**15**	20	75.0
4 **Bob Cousy**, Holy Cross	SR	G	Boston College	F21	**14**	14	100.0
Ed Dahler, Duquesne	SR	F	Indiana State	F20	**14**	15	93.3
Curt Norris, Colgate	SR	F	Alfred	J14	**14**	16	87.5
Bob Zawoluk, St. John's	SO	C	Saint Joseph's	J7	**14**	18	77.8

TEAM LEADERS—SEASON

Scoring Offense

	G	W-L	PTS	PPG
1 Villanova	29	25-4	2,111	**72.8**
2 Holy Cross	31	27-4	2,251	**72.6**
3 St. John's	29	24-5	2,093	**72.2**
4 Muhlenberg	23	17-6	1,651	**71.8**
5 Western Kentucky	31	25-6	2,216	**71.5**

Scoring Margin

	G	W-L	PPG	OPP PPG	MAR
1 Holy Cross	31	27-4	72.6	55.4	**17.2**
2 Villanova	29	25-4	72.8	55.7	**17.1**
3 St. John's	29	24-5	72.2	56.7	**15.5**
4 La Salle	25	21-4	69.8	54.8	**15.0**
5 NC State	33	27-6	65.3	51.7	**13.6**

Field Goal Pct

	G	W-L	FG	FGA	PCT
1 TCU	24	13-11	476	1,191	**40.0**
2 Bowling Green	30	19-11	808	2,070	**39.0**
3 Toledo	28	22-6	633	1,631	**38.8**
4 Bradley	37	32-5	999	2,588	**38.6**
5 Akron	25	16-9	676	1,752	**38.6**

Free Throw Pct

	G	W-L	FT	FTA	PCT
1 Temple	24	14-10	342	483	**70.8**
2 Colorado	22	14-8	395	576	**68.6**
3 Auburn	24	17-7	390	574	**67.9**
4 Duquesne	29	23-6	418	616	**67.9**
5 Washington State	32	19-13	456	673	**67.8**

Scoring Defense

	G	W-L	OPP PTS	OPP PPG
1 Oklahoma A&M	27	18-9	1,059	**39.2**
2 Wyoming	36	25-11	1,491	**41.4**
3 Tulsa	23	12-11	1,027	**44.7**
4 Wash.-St. Louis	23	17-6	1,066	**46.3**
5 San Francisco	26	19-7	1,237	**47.6**

CONSENSUS ALL-AMERICAS

FIRST TEAM

PLAYER	CL	POS	HT	SCHOOL	PPG
Paul Arizin	SR	F	6-3	Villanova	25.3
Bob Cousy	SR	G	6-1	Holy Cross	19.4
Dick Schnittker	SR	F	6-5	Ohio State	21.3
Bill Sharman	SR	F	6-2	Southern California	18.6
Paul Unruh	SR	C	6-4	Bradley	12.8

SECOND TEAM

PLAYER	CL	POS	HT	SCHOOL	PPG
Chuck Cooper	SR	C	6-5	Duquesne	12.0
Don Lofgran	SR	F/C	6-6	San Francisco	14.7
Kevin O'Shea	SR	G	6-1	Notre Dame	14.9
Don Rehfeldt	SR	C	6-6	Wisconsin	19.8
Sherman White	JR	F	6-8	Long Island	22.0

Selectors: AP, Colliers (Basketball Coaches), International News Service, Look Magazine, UP

National Invitation Tournament (NIT)

First round: Western Kentucky d. Niagara 79-72, CCNY d. San Francisco 65-46, Syracuse d. LIU 80-52, La Salle d. Arizona 72-66
Quarterfinals: St. John's d. Western Kentucky 69-60, Bradley d. Syracuse 78-66, Duquesne d. La Salle 49-47, CCNY d. Kentucky 89-50
Semifinals: CCNY d. Duquesne 62-52, Bradley d. St. John's 83-72
Third place: St. John's d. Duquesne 69-67 (OT)
Championship: CCNY d. Bradley 69-61
MVP: Ed Warner, CCNY

POLL PROGRESSION

WEEK OF JAN 5

AP	SCHOOL
1	**St. John's** (12-1)
2	**Kentucky** (7-1)
3	**Bradley** (10-2)
4	**Long Island** (10-1)
5	**Indiana** (9-0)
6	**Holy Cross** (9-0)
7	**NC State** (9-1)
8	**Duquesne** (9-0)
9	**UCLA** (8-3)
10	**Minnesota** (7-1)
11	**Saint Louis** (6-1)
12	**Missouri** (8-1)
13	**Villanova** (7-2)
14	**CCNY** (7-2)
15	**Wisconsin** (8-2)
16	**Illinois** (7-3)
17	**Oklahoma** (5-2)
18	**La Salle** (6-2)
19	**Bowling Green** (10-4)
20	**Kansas State** (9-3)

WEEK OF JAN 10

AP	SCHOOL	AP↓↑
1	**St. John's** (13-1)	
2	**Kentucky** (8-1)	
3	**Long Island** (11-1)	↑1
4	**Indiana** (10-0)	↑1
5	**Holy Cross** (11-0)	↑1
6	**Bradley** (11-2)	↓3
7	**CCNY** (8-2)	↑7
8	**Duquesne** (9-0)	
9	**NC State** (9-2)	↓2
10	**UCLA** (10-3)	↓1
11	**Minnesota** (8-1)	↓1
12	**Cincinnati** (6-0)	⤴
13	**La Salle** (7-2)	↑5
14	**Western Kentucky** (6-4)	⤴
15	**Ohio State** (6-2)	⤴
16	**Missouri** (9-1)	↓4
17	**Villanova** (8-2)	↓4
18	**Siena** (14-0)	⤴
19	**Oklahoma** (5-3)	↓2
20	**Washington** (12-1)	⤴

WEEK OF JAN 17

AP	SCHOOL	AP↓↑
1	**Holy Cross** (13-0) Ⓐ	↑4
2	**St. John's** (14-1)	↓1
3	**Long Island** (12-1)	
4	**Bradley** (14-2)	↑2
5	**Kentucky** (9-2)	↓3
6	**Duquesne** (12-0)	↑2
7	**CCNY** (9-2)	
8	**Indiana** (10-2)	↓4
9	**UCLA** (11-4)	↑1
10	**La Salle** (9-2)	↑3
11	**Ohio State** (8-2)	↑4
12	**NC State** (11-3)	↓3
13	**Kansas State** (10-3)	⤴
14	**Western Kentucky** (9-4)	
15	**Tulane** (11-2)	⤴
16	**Minnesota** (9-2)	↓5
17	**Tennessee** (7-5)	⤴
18	**Villanova** (10-2)	↓1
19	**Louisville** (14-2)	⤴
20	**Cincinnati** (7-1)	↓8

WEEK OF JAN 24

AP	SCHOOL	AP↓↑
1	**Holy Cross** (14-0)	
2	**Duquesne** (13-0)	↑4
3	**Long Island** (13-2)	
4	**Kentucky** (11-4)	↑1
5	**St. John's** (15-2)	↓3
6	**Bradley** (15-3)	↓2
7	**La Salle** (11-2)	↑3
8	**CCNY** (9-2)	↓1
9	**Indiana** (12-2)	↓1
10	**NC State** (13-3)	↑2
11	**UCLA** (11-4)	↓2
12	**Kansas State** (12-3)	↑1
13	**Ohio State** (9-3)	↓2
14	**Wyoming** (17-4)	⤴
15	**Wisconsin** (10-3)	⤴
16	**Washington** (12-2)	⤴
17	**Western Kentucky** (12-4)	↓3
18	**Minnesota** (9-2)	↓2
19	**Villanova** (11-2)	↓1
20	**Illiinois** (10-4)	⤴

WEEK OF JAN 31

AP	SCHOOL	AP↓↑
1	**Holy Cross** (14-0)	
2	**Duquesne** (14-0)	
3	**Bradley** (17-3)	↑3
4	**Long Island** (14-2)	↓1
5	**St. John's** (16-2)	
6	**Kentucky** (13-4)	↓2
7	**Ohio State** (11-3)	↑6
8	**La Salle** (12-2)	↓1
9	**NC State** (15-3)	↑1
10	**CCNY** (10-2)	↓2
11	**Kansas State** (12-3)	↑1
12	**Indiana** (12-2)	↓3
13	**UCLA** (13-4)	↓2
14	**Western Kentucky** (14-4)	↑3
15	**Louisville** (19-5)	⤴
16	**Notre Dame** (9-5)	⤴
17	**Wisconsin** (10-3)	↓2
18	**Vanderbilt** (11-5)	⤴
19	**Oklahoma A&M** (11-4)	⤴
20	**Wyoming** (18-5)	↓6

WEEK OF FEB 7

AP	SCHOOL	AP↓↑
1	**Holy Cross** (17-0)	
2	**Bradley** (19-3)	↑1
3	**Duquesne** (16-1) Ⓑ	↓1
4	**St. John's** (18-2)	↑1
4	**Ohio State** (14-3)	↑3
6	**Long Island** (15-2)	↓2
7	**Kentucky** (16-4)	↓1
8	**NC State** (17-3)	↑1
9	**La Salle** (14-2)	↓1
10	**Kansas State** (13-4)	↑1
11	**Western Kentucky** (16-4)	↑3
12	**UCLA** (15-4)	↑1
13	**Louisville** (20-6) Ⓑ	↑2
14	**CCNY** (12-2)	↓4
15	**San Francisco** (12-5)	⤴
16	**Indiana** (13-3)	↓4
17	**Washington State** (14-8)	⤴
18	**Arizona** (17-2)	⤴
19	**Saint Louis** (12-5)	⤴
20	**Hamline** (20-1)	⤴

WEEK OF FEB 14

AP	SCHOOL	AP↓↑
1	**Holy Cross** (20-0)	
2	**Bradley** (21-3)	
3	**Ohio State** (15-3)	↑1
4	**St. John's** (20-2)	
5	**Kentucky** (17-4)	↑2
6	**Long Island** (17-2)	
7	**Duquesne** (18-1)	↓4
8	**NC State** (18-4)	
9	**Western Kentucky** (19-4)	↑2
10	**UCLA** (17-4)	↑2
11	**La Salle** (14-3)	↓2
12	**San Francisco** (14-5)	↑3
13	**CCNY** (13-3)	↑1
14	**Kansas State** (13-5)	↓4
15	**Villanova** (18-3)	⤴
16	**Washington State** (15-9)	↑1
17	**Arizona** (20-2)	↑1
18	**Saint Louis** (13-5)	↑1
19	**USC** (13-5)	⤴
20	**Vanderbilt** (14-6)	⤴

WEEK OF FEB 21

AP	SCHOOL	AP↓↑
1	**Bradley** (24-3) Ⓒ	↑1
2	**Holy Cross** (22-0)	↓1
3	**Ohio State** (18-3)	
4	**Duquesne** (21-1)	↑3
5	**Kentucky** (20-4)	
6	**St. John's** (20-3)	↓2
7	**UCLA** (19-4)	↑3
8	**Western Kentucky** (22-4)	↑1
9	**NC State** (20-4)	↓1
10	**Long Island** (17-3)	↓4
11	**San Francisco** (15-6)	↑1
12	**La Salle** (16-3)	↓1
13	**Kansas State** (16-5)	↑1
14	**Toledo** (19-4)	⤴
15	**Saint Louis** (14-6)	↑3
16	**USC** (18-5)	↑3
17	**Indiana** (16-4)	⤴
18	**San Jose State** (17-6)	⤴
19	**Arizona** (23-2)	↓2
20	**CCNY** (14-4)	↓7

WEEK OF FEB 28

AP	SCHOOL	AP↓↑
1	**Bradley** (25-3)	
2	**Ohio State** (18-3)	↑1
3	**Holy Cross** (24-0)	↓1
4	**Kentucky** (22-4)	↑1
5	**Duquesne** (22-1)	↓1
6	**UCLA** (21-4) Ⓓ	↑1
7	**Western Kentucky** (24-5)	↑1
8	**NC State** (21-5)	↑1
9	**La Salle** (18-3)	↑3
10	**St. John's** (21-4)	↓4
11	**Villanova** (22-4)	⤴
12	**Kansas State** (16-5)	↑1
13	**San Francisco** (16-6)	↓2
14	**Long Island** (18-4)	↓4
15	**Arizona** (24-3)	↑4
16	**Nebraska** (16-5)	⤴
17	**Toledo** (21-5)	↓3
18	**Wyoming** (24-5)	⤴
19	**San Jose State** (18-7)	↓1
20	**Vanderbilt** (17-7)	⤴

WEEK OF MAR 7 Ⓔ

AP	SCHOOL	AP↓↑
1	**Bradley** (27-3)	
2	**Ohio State** (19-3)	
3	**Kentucky** (24-5)	↑1
4	**Holy Cross** (26-1)	↓1
5	**NC State** (24-5)	↑3
6	**Duquesne** (22-3)	↓1
7	**UCLA** (22-5)	↓1
8	**Western Kentucky** (24-5)	↓1
9	**St. John's** (22-4)	↑1
10	**La Salle** (20-3)	↓1
11	**Villanova** (23-4)	
12	**San Francisco** (19-6)	↑1
13	**Long Island** (20-4)	↑1
14	**Kansas State** (16-6)	↓2
15	**Arizona** (25-4)	
16	**Wisconsin** (16-6)	⤴
17	**San Jose State** (21-7)	↑2
18	**Washington State** (19-11)	⤴
19	**Kansas** (13-9)	⤴
20	**Indiana** (18-4)	⤴

Ⓐ Led by ball-handling wizard Bob Cousy, Holy Cross defeats Saint Louis, 69-55, to begin a five-week run at No. 1. Cousy, now a senior, had teamed as a freshman with All-America George Kaftan and future coach Joe Mullaney to win the 1947 NCAA championship.

Ⓑ Making its first national splash under coach Peck Hickman, Louisville upsets Duquesne at home, 64-58, on Feb. 4. After the season, Duquesne's Chuck Cooper becomes the first African-American player drafted by the NBA.

Ⓒ Bradley is voted No. 1 and will remain there through the final poll. The team is led by 5'8" forward Gene "Squeaky" Melchiorre. *Time* magazine enthuses: "Crowds ... expect him to be reduced to a puddle of watery chowder within minutes. Instead, he makes all but the cleverest of his tall opponents look like croupy giraffes."

Ⓓ Coach John Wooden's second UCLA team wraps up the Pacific Coast title by sweeping two playoff games against Washington State, 60-58 and 52-49. The Cougars are led by 6'8" Gene Conley, who will go on to become the only man to play for championship teams in both the MLB (1957 Braves) and NBA (1959 Celtics).

Ⓔ Late in the season, CCNY loses three times in a five-game stretch and drops out of the Top 20. Coach Nat Holman's team ends the regular season 17–5, however, and receives one of the last bids to the NIT.

1950 NCAA Tournament

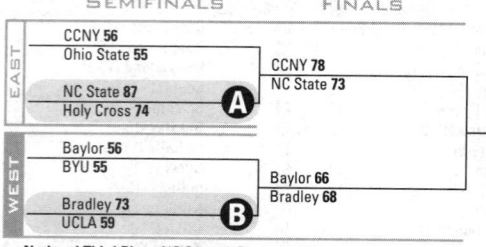

Regional Semifinals / **Regional Finals**

EAST

- CCNY **56** / Ohio State **55**
- NC State **87** / Holy Cross **74** (A)
- Regional Final: CCNY **78** / NC State **73**

WEST

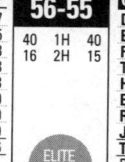

- Baylor **56** / BYU **55**
- Bradley **73** / UCLA **59** (B)
- Regional Final: Baylor **66** / Bradley **68**

National Final

CCNY 71
Bradley 68

New York City

CCNY's Cinderella Kids, unranked most of the season, live up to their nickname and become the only school to win NCAA and NIT titles in the same year. CCNY is also the first integrated champion, with starter Ed Warner and two other African-American players. But the accomplishments are tarnished when it's later learned that CCNY players were involved in point-shaving scandals.

A NC State players cut down the nets—something never done after a Tourney game. Coach Everett Case brought the tradition from Indiana, where it began in the state's high school championship.

B UCLA, coached by 39-year-old former Purdue All-America guard John Wooden, makes its first appearance in the Tournament. The defeat is the first of Wooden's 10, against 47 future Tourney victories in his 27 seasons with the Bruins.

National Third Place NC State d. Baylor 53-41
East Regional Third Place Ohio State d. Holy Cross 72-52
West Regional Third Place BYU d. UCLA 83-62

Tournament Leaders

Individual Leaders

Scoring

		CL	POS	G	PTS	PPG
1	**Sam Ranzino**, NC State	JR	G	3	77	25.7
2	**Joe Nelson**, BYU	SR	F	2	43	21.5
	Dick Schnittker, Ohio State	SR	F	2	43	21.5
4	**Mel Hutchins**, BYU	JR	C	2	40	20.0
5	**Bob Cousy**, Holy Cross	SR	G	2	38	19.0
6	**Don Heathington**, Baylor	SR	F/C	3	54	18.0
7	**Roland Minson**, BYU	JR	F	2	32	16.0
	Eddie Sheldrake, UCLA	JR	G	2	32	16.0
9	**Dick Dickey**, NC State	SR	F	3	47	15.7
10	**Gene Melchiorre**, Bradley	JR	G	3	46	15.3

Minimum: 2 games

Field Goal Pct

		CL	POS	G	FG	FGA	PCT
1	**Aaron Preece**, Bradley	JR	G/F	3	11	20	55.0
2	**Dick Schnittker**, Ohio State	SR	F	2	15	29	51.7
3	**George Chianakas**, Bradley	SR	F	3	8	16	50.0
4	**Gerald Cobb**, Baylor	JR	G	3	8	18	44.4
5	**Ed Roman**, CCNY	SO	C	3	19	43	44.2

Minimum: 8 made

Free Throw Pct

		CL	POS	G	FT	FTA	PCT
1	**Joe Harand**, NC State	SR	G	3	7	8	87.5
	Matthew Formon, Holy Cross	SR	C	2	7	8	87.5
3	**Bob Burkholder**, Ohio State	SR	G	2	6	7	85.7
4	**Joe Nelson**, BYU	SR	F	2	9	11	81.8
5	**Floyd Layne**, CCNY	SO	G	3	12	15	80.0
	Gene Melchiorre, Bradley	JR	G	3	12	15	80.0
	Norm Mager, CCNY	SR	G/F	3	8	10	80.0

Minimum: 5 made

Team Leaders

Scoring

		G	PTS	PPG
1	**NC State**	3	213	71.0
2	**Bradley**	3	209	69.7
3	**BYU**	2	138	69.0
4	**CCNY**	3	205	68.3
5	**Ohio State**	2	127	63.5
6	**Holy Cross**	2	126	63.0
7	**UCLA**	2	121	60.5
8	**Baylor**	3	163	54.3

Minimum: 2 games

FT Pct

		G	FT	FTA	PCT
1	**Bradley**	3	53	76	69.7
2	**Holy Cross**	2	24	37	64.9
3	**Ohio State**	2	35	54	64.8
4	**NC State**	3	67	104	64.4
5	**Baylor**	3	45	71	63.4

Minimum: 2 games

FG Pct

		G	FG	FGA	PCT
1	**Ohio State**	2	46	115	40.0
2	**CCNY**	3	80	208	38.5
3	**BYU**	2	56	148	37.8
4	**Bradley**	3	78	210	37.1
5	**Baylor**	3	59	173	34.1

Tournament MOP

Player	CL	POS	HT	School	FG	FT	PPG
Irwin Dambrot	SR	F/C	6-4	CCNY	15-34	6-12	12.0

All-Regional Teams

East

Player	CL	POS	HT	School	PPG
Dick Dickey	SR	F	6-1	NC State	25.0
Norm Mager	SR	G/F	6-5	CCNY	15.0
Sam Ranzino	JR	G	6-2	NC State	32.0
Ed Roman	SO	C	6-6	CCNY	8.0
Dick Schnittker	SR	F	6-5	Ohio State	21.5

West

Player	CL	POS	HT	School	PPG
Don Heathington	SR	F/C	6-3	Baylor	21.0
Gene Melchiorre	JR	G	5-8	Bradley	19.0
Joe Nelson	SR	F	6-3	BYU	21.5
George Stanich	SR	G	6-3	UCLA	9.5
Paul Unruh	SR	C	6-4	Bradley	13.0

1950 NCAA Tournament Box Scores

Elite 8 — 56-55

	1H	2H
CCNY	40	16
Ohio State	40	15

CCNY	MIN	FG	3FG	FT	REB	A	ST	BL	PF	TP
Floyd Layne	-	7-11	-	3-4	-	4	-	-	2	17
Norm Mager	-	7-16	-	1-2	-	3	-	-	5	15
Irwin Dambrot	-	3-6	-	2-4	-	5	-	-	2	8
Ed Roman	-	4-9	-	0-2	-	2	-	-	5	8
Ed Warner	-	3-16	-	2-3	-	1	-	-	1	8
Joe Galiber	-	0-4	-	0-0	-	0	-	-	1	0
Alvin Roth	-	0-1	-	0-0	-	1	-	-	2	0
Leroy Watkins	-	0-0	-	0-0	-	0	-	-	1	0
TOTALS	**-**	**24-63**	**-**	**8-15**	**-**	**16**	**-**	**-**	**19**	**56**
Percentages		38.1	-	53.3						

Coach: Nat Holman

Ohio State	MIN	FG	3FG	FT	REB	A	ST	BL	PF	TP
Dick Schnittker	36	9-19	-	8-11	-	1	-	-	5	26
Bob Donham	35	4-9	-	1-3	-	5	-	-	5	9
Fred Taylor	40	4-11	-	0-2	-	0	-	-	0	8
Ted Jacobs	11	2-5	-	2-3	-	0	-	-	2	6
Harvey Brown	40	1-4	-	1-1	-	2	-	-	1	3
Bob Burkholder	36	1-1	-	1-2	-	6	-	-	1	3
Ralph Armstrong	1	0-1	-	0-0	-	0	-	-	1	0
James Remington	1	0-1	-	0-0	-	0	-	-	0	0
TOTALS	**200**	**21-51**	**-**	**13-22**	**-**	**14**	**-**	**-**	**15**	**55**
Percentages		41.2	-	59.1						

Coach: William H. "Tippy" Dye

Officials: Boyle, Heft

Elite 8 — 87-74

	1H	2H
NC State	44	43
Holy Cross	29	45

NC State	MIN	FG	3FG	FT	REB	A	ST	BL	PF	TP
Sam Ranzino	-	12-30	-	8-10	-	2	-	-	4	32
Dick Dickey	-	8-17	-	9-13	-	2	-	-	3	25
Warren Cartier	-	5-9	-	2-4	-	5	-	-	4	12
Vic Bubas	-	3-3	-	0-0	-	1	-	-	2	6
Joe Harand	-	1-3	-	3-4	-	7	-	-	2	5
Lee Terrill	-	2-6	-	0-4	-	3	-	-	1	4
Bob Cook	-	1-3	-	0-2	-	0	-	-	0	2
Paul Horvath	-	0-2	-	1-1	-	1	-	-	1	1
TOTALS	**-**	**32-73**	**-**	**23-38**	**-**	**21**	**-**	**-**	**17**	**87**
Percentages		43.8	-	60.5						

Coach: Everett Case

Holy Cross	MIN	FG	3FG	FT	REB	A	ST	BL	PF	TP
Bob Cousy	-	11-38	-	2-3	-	5	-	-	3	24
Matthew Formon	-	7-10	-	5-6	-	2	-	-	1	19
Robert McLarnon	-	6-15	-	0-1	-	1	-	-	4	12
James Dilling	-	2-6	-	2-2	-	2	-	-	2	6
Andrew Laska	-	2-17	-	2-2	-	2	-	-	1	6
Robert McDonough	-	2-3	-	0-1	-	0	-	-	3	4
Frank Oftring	-	1-3	-	1-2	-	2	-	-	5	3
Russ Dieffenbach	-	0-4	-	0-0	-	0	-	-	2	0
Eugene Mann	-	0-1	-	0-0	-	1	-	-	0	0
Robert McMullan	-	0-4	-	0-2	-	2	-	-	5	0
James O'Neil	-	0-0	-	0-0	-	0	-	-	2	0
Dennis O'Shea	-	0-0	-	0-0	-	0	-	-	4	0
TOTALS	**-**	**31-101**	**-**	**12-19**	**-**	**17**	**-**	**-**	**32**	**74**
Percentages		30.7	-	63.2						

Coach: Lester Sheary

Officials: Meyer, Eisenstein

56-55 | 25 1H 26 | 31 2H 29 | ELITE 8

BAYLOR	MIN	FG	3FG	FT	REB	A	ST	BL	PF	TP
Don Heathington	-	7-16	-	7-12	-	-	-	-	3	21
Bill Srack	-	6-14	-	2-4	-	-	-	-	1	14
Gerald Cobb	-	4-9	-	4-4	-	-	-	-	3	12
Bill Dewitt	-	2-4	-	3-3	-	-	-	-	5	7
Bill Hickman	-	0-2	-	2-2	-	-	-	-	4	2
Gordon Carrington	-	0-0	-	0-2	-	-	-	-	0	0
Howard Hovde	-	0-0	-	0-0	-	-	-	-	1	0
Ralph Johnson	-	0-0	-	0-0	-	-	-	-	0	0
Norman Mullins	-	0-0	-	0-0	-	-	-	-	0	0
Odell Preston	-	0-7	-	0-3	-	-	-	-	1	0
TOTALS	-	**19-52**	-	**18-30**	-	-	-	-	**18**	**56**
Percentages		36.5	-	60.0						

Coach: Bill Henderson

BYU	MIN	FG	3FG	FT	REB	A	ST	BL	PF	TP
Mel Hutchins	-	8-22	-	3-5	-	-	-	-	3	19
Roland Minson	-	8-23	-	3-8	-	-	-	-	2	19
Joe Nelson	-	5-23	-	3-4	-	-	-	-	4	13
Dick Jones	-	1-4	-	0-1	-	-	-	-	2	2
Jerry Romney	-	1-4	-	0-1	-	-	-	-	3	2
Bob Craig	-	0-4	-	0-0	-	-	-	-	5	0
Russ Hillman	-	0-0	-	0-0	-	-	-	-	2	0
Jack Whipple	-	0-2	-	0-1	-	-	-	-	4	0
TOTALS	-	**23-82**	-	**9-20**	-	-	-	-	**25**	**55**
Percentages		28.0	-	45.0						

Coach: Stan Watts

Officials: Lee, Gibbs

73-59 | 33 1H 33 | 40 2H 26 | ELITE 8

BRADLEY	MIN	FG	3FG	FT	REB	A	ST	BL	PF	TP
Gene Melchiorre	-	6-12	-	7-8	-	-	-	-	4	19
Charley Grover	-	7-14	-	2-3	-	-	-	-	2	16
Paul Unruh	-	5-14	-	3-4	-	-	-	-	1	13
Elmer Behnke	-	3-13	-	4-7	-	-	-	-	2	10
Bill Mann	-	2-6	-	3-4	-	-	-	-	3	7
George Chianakas	-	2-4	-	0-0	-	-	-	-	4	4
Aaron Preece	-	1-3	-	1-2	-	-	-	-	1	3
Fred Schlichtman	-	0-1	-	1-2	-	-	-	-	1	1
Jim Kelley	-	0-1	-	0-0	-	-	-	-	1	0
TOTALS	-	**26-68**	-	**21-30**	-	-	-	-	**19**	**73**
Percentages		38.2	-	70.0						

Coach: Forrest "Forddy" Anderson

UCLA	MIN	FG	3FG	FT	REB	A	ST	BL	PF	TP
Alan Sawyer	-	7-21	-	0-2	-	-	-	-	1	14
George Stanich	-	6-12	-	2-6	-	-	-	-	5	14
Ralph Joeckel	-	5-13	-	3-5	-	-	-	-	2	13
Eddie Sheldrake	-	4-14	-	3-5	-	-	-	-	5	11
Carl Kraushaar	-	2-4	-	1-1	-	-	-	-	5	5
Don Seidel	-	1-3	-	0-0	-	-	-	-	2	2
Ray Alba	-	0-8	-	0-2	-	-	-	-	2	0
Art Alper	-	0-0	-	0-0	-	-	-	-	1	0
Don Johnson	-	0-0	-	0-0	-	-	-	-	0	0
John Matulich	-	0-0	-	0-0	-	-	-	-	0	0
Jerry Norman	-	0-6	-	0-0	-	-	-	-	3	0
Paul Saunders	-	0-0	-	0-1	-	-	-	-	1	0
TOTALS	-	**25-81**	-	**9-22**	-	-	-	-	**27**	**59**
Percentages		30.9	-	40.9						

Coach: John Wooden

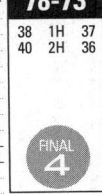

Officials: Morrow, Herigstad

78-73 | 38 1H 37 | 40 2H 36 | FINAL 4

CCNY	MIN	FG	3FG	FT	REB	A	ST	BL	PF	TP
Ed Roman	-	9-17	-	3-4	-	1	-	-	5	21
Ed Warner	-	5-18	-	7-11	-	2	-	-	3	17
Irwin Dambrot	-	5-14	-	3-6	-	3	-	-	3	13
Floyd Layne	-	3-13	-	4-5	-	9	-	-	2	10
Norm Mager	-	4-11	-	1-2	-	3	-	-	5	9
Ronald Nadell	-	2-2	-	0-1	-	0	-	-	2	4
Alvin Roth	-	2-6	-	0-0	-	2	-	-	5	4
Herb Cohen	-	0-0	-	0-2	-	0	-	-	0	0
Joe Galiber	-	0-0	-	0-0	-	0	-	-	1	0
TOTALS	-	**30-81**	-	**18-31**	-	**20**	-	-	**26**	**78**
Percentages		37.0	-	58.1						

Coach: Nat Holman

NC STATE	MIN	FG	3FG	FT	REB	A	ST	BL	PF	TP
Sam Ranzino	-	9-30	-	6-9	-	0	-	-	5	24
Dick Dickey	-	7-19	-	2-6	-	6	-	-	5	16
Paul Horvath	-	4-4	-	6-8	-	1	-	-	4	14
Warren Cartier	-	4-8	-	3-4	-	4	-	-	5	11
Vic Bubas	-	0-2	-	2-2	-	0	-	-	4	2
Bob Cook	-	1-3	-	0-0	-	0	-	-	0	2
Joe Harand	-	0-0	-	2-2	-	5	-	-	2	2
Charles Stine	-	1-2	-	0-0	-	0	-	-	0	2
Joe Stoll	-	0-0	-	0-0	-	0	-	-	0	0
TOTALS	-	**26-68**	-	**21-31**	-	**16**	-	-	**25**	**73**
Percentages		38.2	-	67.7						

Coach: Everett Case

Officials: Meyer, Boyle

68-66 | 35 1H 32 | 33 2H 34 | FINAL 4

BRADLEY	MIN	FG	3FG	FT	REB	A	ST	BL	PF	TP
Charley Grover	-	6-14	-	1-1	-	-	-	-	2	13
Bill Mann	-	4-7	-	5-8	-	-	-	-	4	13
Aaron Preece	-	4-6	-	4-6	-	-	-	-	3	12
Gene Melchiorre	-	4-11	-	3-3	-	-	-	-	4	11
Jim Kelley	-	3-7	-	2-2	-	-	-	-	2	8
Paul Unruh	-	2-11	-	3-4	-	-	-	-	2	7
Elmer Behnke	-	1-7	-	0-1	-	-	-	-	0	2
George Chianakas	-	1-5	-	0-0	-	-	-	-	0	2
Fred Schlichtman	-	0-0	-	0-0	-	-	-	-	0	0
TOTALS	-	**25-68**	-	**18-25**	-	-	-	-	**17**	**68**
Percentages		36.8	-	72.0						

Coach: Forrest "Forddy" Anderson

BAYLOR	MIN	FG	3FG	FT	REB	A	ST	BL	PF	TP
Don Heathington	-	10-20	-	6-6	-	-	-	-	5	26
Odell Preston	-	4-11	-	6-7	-	-	-	-	4	14
Bill Srack	-	3-7	-	3-3	-	-	-	-	3	9
Gerald Cobb	-	3-8	-	1-2	-	-	-	-	3	7
Bill Hickman	-	3-7	-	0-0	-	-	-	-	3	6
Bill Dewitt	-	1-6	-	2-3	-	-	-	-	5	4
Bill Fleetwood	-	0-0	-	0-0	-	-	-	-	0	0
Howard Hovde	-	0-0	-	0-0	-	-	-	-	0	0
Ralph Johnson	-	0-2	-	0-0	-	-	-	-	0	0
TOTALS	-	**24-61**	-	**18-21**	-	-	-	-	**23**	**66**
Percentages		39.3	-	85.7						

Coach: Bill Henderson

Officials: Lee, Herigstad

53-41 | 21 1H 20 | 32 2H 21 | 3RD PLACE

NC STATE	MIN	FG	3FG	FT	REB	A	ST	BL	PF	TP
Sam Ranzino	-	5-25	-	11-15	-	0	-	-	2	21
Warren Cartier	-	3-11	-	3-4	-	0	-	-	3	9
Vic Bubas	-	1-7	-	4-6	-	5	-	-	4	6
Dick Dickey	-	2-14	-	2-3	-	2	-	-	3	6
Paul Horvath	-	2-8	-	1-3	-	0	-	-	2	5
Joe Harand	-	1-3	-	2-2	-	0	-	-	1	4
Lee Terrill	-	1-9	-	0-2	-	2	-	-	0	2
TOTALS	-	**15-77**	-	**23-35**	-	**9**	-	-	**15**	**53**
Percentages		19.5	-	65.7						

Coach: Everett Case

BAYLOR	MIN	FG	3FG	FT	REB	A	ST	BL	PF	TP
Bill Srack	-	5-17	-	1-3	-	3	-	-	3	11
Bill Hickman	-	4-14	-	0-0	-	1	-	-	1	8
Don Heathington	-	3-14	-	1-5	-	2	-	-	5	7
Bill Dewitt	-	2-7	-	2-3	-	0	-	-	5	6
Odell Preston	-	1-7	-	3-5	-	3	-	-	3	5
Gerald Cobb	-	1-1	-	1-2	-	0	-	-	5	3
Ralph Johnson	-	0-0	-	1-2	-	0	-	-	0	1
Gordon Carrington	-	0-0	-	0-0	-	0	-	-	1	0
Bill Fleetwood	-	0-0	-	0-0	-	0	-	-	1	0
William Harris	-	0-0	-	0-0	-	0	-	-	2	0
Howard Hovde	-	0-0	-	0-0	-	0	-	-	0	0
Norman Mullins	-	0-0	-	0-0	-	0	-	-	1	0
TOTALS	-	**16-60**	-	**9-20**	-	**9**	-	-	**27**	**41**
Percentages		26.7	-	45.0						

Coach: Bill Henderson

Officials: Meyer, Morrow

71-68 | 39 1H 32 | 32 2H 36 | NCAA FINAL 1950

CCNY	MIN	FG	3FG	FT	REB	A	ST	BL	PF	TP
Irwin Dambrot	-	7-14	-	1-2	-	2	-	-	0	15
Norm Mager	-	4-10	-	6-6	-	2	-	-	3	14
Ed Warner	-	4-9	-	6-14	-	3	-	-	2	14
Ed Roman	-	6-17	-	0-2	-	1	-	-	5	12
Floyd Layne	-	3-7	-	5-6	-	4	-	-	3	11
Alvin Roth	-	2-7	-	1-5	-	3	-	-	2	5
Joe Galiber	-	0-0	-	0-0	-	0	-	-	1	0
Ronald Nadell	-	0-0	-	0-0	-	1	-	-	1	0
TOTALS	-	**26-64**	-	**19-35**	-	**16**	-	-	**17**	**71**
Percentages		40.6	-	54.3						

Coach: Nat Holman

BRADLEY	MIN	FG	3FG	FT	REB	A	ST	BL	PF	TP
Gene Melchiorre	-	7-16	-	2-4	-	5	-	-	4	16
Aaron Preece	-	6-11	-	0-0	-	0	-	-	5	12
George Chianakas	-	5-7	-	1-3	-	1	-	-	4	11
Elmer Behnke	-	3-10	-	3-3	-	2	-	-	4	9
Bill Mann	-	2-7	-	5-5	-	1	-	-	5	9
Paul Unruh	-	4-9	-	0-0	-	2	-	-	5	8
Charley Grover	-	0-10	-	2-3	-	3	-	-	3	2
Joe Stowell	-	0-0	-	1-1	-	0	-	-	0	1
Jim Kelley	-	0-1	-	0-2	-	0	-	-	0	0
Deno Melchiorre	-	0-0	-	0-0	-	0	-	-	0	0
Fred Schlichtman	-	0-3	-	0-0	-	0	-	-	2	0
TOTALS	-	**27-74**	-	**14-21**	-	**14**	-	-	**32**	**68**
Percentages		36.5	-	66.7						

Coach: Forrest "Forddy" Anderson

Officials: Eisenstein, Gibbs

Attendance: 18,142

ANNUAL REVIEW

1950-51: The First Sweet 16

The NCAA Tournament field expanded from eight to 16 teams as champions from 10 conferences—the Big Seven, Big Ten, Border, Eastern (today's Ivy), Missouri Valley, Pacific Coast, Skyline, Southeastern, Southern and Southwest—became automatic qualifiers. But even with more competition and an extra round of games, the Tournament was still Kentucky's domain: The Wildcats won their third national title in four years. They survived a scare in the East Regional final, beating Illinois, 76-74, in the closing seconds on a layup by Shelby Linville. In the 68-58 Final over Kansas State, Cliff Hagan sparked a comeback from seven down. Seven-foot senior Bill Spivey was named Most Outstanding Player with 50 points and 37 rebounds in Kentucky's final two games. Alas, Spivey was later accused of point-shaving; he claimed innocence but the NCAA banned the Wildcats from competing in the 1952-53 season.

Major Conference Standings

BIG SEVEN	Conference W	L	Pct	Overall W	L	Pct
Kansas State ⊕	11	1	.917	25	4	.862
Kansas	8	4	.667	16	8	.667
Missouri	8	4	.667	16	8	.667
Oklahoma	6	6	.500	14	10	.583
Nebraska	4	8	.333	9	14	.391
Iowa State	3	9	.250	9	12	.429
Colorado	2	10	.167	4	20	.167

BIG TEN	Conference W	L	Pct	Overall W	L	Pct
Illinois ⊕	13	1	.929	22	5	.815
Indiana	12	2	.857	19	3	.864
Iowa	9	5	.643	15	7	.682
Minnesota	7	7	.500	13	9	.591
Northwestern	7	7	.500	12	10	.545
Wisconsin	7	7	.500	10	12	.455
Michigan State	5	9	.357	10	11	.476
Purdue	4	10	.286	8	14	.364
Michigan	3	11	.214	7	15	.318
Ohio State	3	11	.214	6	16	.273

BORDER	Conference W	L	Pct	Overall W	L	Pct
Arizona ⊕□	15	1	.938	24	6	.800
New Mexico State	11	6	.647	19	14	.576
Texas Tech	10	6	.625	14	14	.500
New Mexico	9	7	.563	13	11	.542
West Texas A&M	9	7	.563	14	12	.538
Hardin-Simmons	6	10	.375	13	15	.464
Arizona State	6	10	.375	8	16	.333
Texas Western	4	12	.250	10	15	.400
Northern Arizona	3	13	.188	8	19	.296

IVY	Conference W	L	Pct	Overall W	L	Pct
Columbia ⊕	12	0	1.000	23	1	.958
Cornell	10	2	.833	20	5	.800
Penn	7	5	.583	19	8	.704
Princeton	5	7	.417	15	7	.682
Yale	4	8	.333	14	13	.519
Harvard	3	9	.250	8	18	.308
Dartmouth	1	11	.083	3	23	.115

METRO NY	Conference W	L	Pct	Overall W	L	Pct
St. John's ○□	6	0	1.000	26	5	.839
Fordham	4	2	.667	20	8	.714
NYU	3	2	.600	12	4	.750
Manhattan	3	2	.600	16	6	.727
CCNY	2	2	.500	12	7	.632
St. Francis (NY)	1	5	.167	19	11	.633
Brooklyn	1	5	.167	11	9	.550

MID-AMERICAN	Conference W	L	Pct	Overall W	L	Pct
Cincinnati □	7	1	.875	18	4	.818
Western Michigan	4	4	.500	13	9	.591
Ohio	4	4	.500	13	11	.542
Miami (OH)	4	4	.500	10	13	.435
Western Reserve	1	7	.125	3	18	.143

MIDDLE THREE	Conference W	L	Pct	Overall W	L	Pct
Rutgers	3	1	.750	7	14	.333
Lafayette	2	2	.500	14	11	.560
Lehigh	1	3	.250	6	13	.333

MISSOURI VALLEY	Conference W	L	Pct	Overall W	L	Pct
Oklahoma A&M ⊕	12	2	.857	29	6	.829
Bradley	11	3	.786	32	6	.842
Saint Louis □	11	3	.786	22	8	.733
Detroit	7	7	.500	17	14	.548
Wichita State	5	9	.357	9	16	.360
Drake	4	10	.286	11	14	.440
Tulsa	4	10	.286	10	17	.370
Houston	2	12	.143	11	17	.393

SKYLINE 6	Conference W	L	Pct	Overall W	L	Pct
BYU ⊕□	15	5	.750	28	9	.757
Wyoming	13	7	.650	26	11	.703
Utah	12	8	.600	23	13	.639
Denver	8	12	.400	14	16	.467
Colorado State	6	14	.300	13	20	.394
Utah State	6	14	.300	12	22	.353

OHIO VALLEY	Conference W	L	Pct	Overall W	L	Pct
Murray State	9	3	.750	21	6	.778
Eastern Kentucky	8	3	.727	18	8	.692
Evansville	5	4	.556	23	7	.767
Western Kentucky	4	4	.500	19	10	.655
Morehead State	4	7	.364	14	12	.538
Marshall	2	6	.250	13	13	.500
Tennessee Tech	1	6	.143	12	9	.571

Tournament: **Murray State d. Eastern Kentucky 92-60**

PACIFIC COAST	Conference W	L	Pct	Overall W	L	Pct
North						
Washington ⊕	11	5	.688	24	6	.800
Oregon	10	6	.625	18	13	.581
Washington State	7	9	.438	17	15	.531
Idaho	6	10	.375	15	14	.517
Oregon State	6	10	.375	14	18	.438
South						
UCLA	8	4	.667	19	10	.655
Southern California	8	4	.667	21	6	.778
Stanford	5	7	.417	12	14	.462
California	3	9	.250	16	16	.500

Playoff: UCLA d. Southern California 49-41 to win the South; **Washington d. UCLA 2-0** in a best-of-three series for the PCC title

SEC	Conference W	L	Pct	Overall W	L	Pct
Kentucky ⊕	14	0	1.000	32	2	.941
Vanderbilt	10	4	.714	19	8	.704
Alabama	10	4	.714	15	8	.652
Tulane	8	6	.571	12	12	.500
Auburn	6	8	.429	12	10	.545
Georgia	6	8	.429	13	11	.542
Florida	6	8	.429	11	12	.478
LSU	6	8	.429	10	14	.417
Georgia Tech	6	8	.429	8	19	.296
Mississippi	5	9	.357	12	12	.500
Tennessee	5	9	.357	10	13	.435
Mississippi State	2	12	.143	3	16	.158

Tournament: **Vanderbilt d. Kentucky 61-57**

SOUTHERN	Conference W	L	Pct	Overall W	L	Pct
NC State ⊕□	13	1	.929	30	7	.811
West Virginia	9	3	.750	18	9	.667
Clemson	9	4	.692	11	7	.611
William and Mary	13	6	.684	20	11	.645
Duke	13	6	.684	20	13	.606
Virginia Tech	9	5	.643	19	10	.655
South Carolina	12	7	.632	13	12	.520
Maryland	11	8	.579	15	10	.600
North Carolina	9	8	.529	12	15	.444
Wake Forest	8	9	.471	16	14	.533
George Washington	8	9	.471	12	12	.500
Richmond	5	10	.333	7	14	.333
Washington and Lee	5	13	.278	8	17	.320
Davidson	5	15	.250	7	19	.269
The Citadel	2	7	.222	6	11	.353
VMI	3	11	.214	3	18	.143
Furman	1	13	.071	3	20	.130

Tournament: **NC State d. Duke 67-63**
Tournament MOP: **Dick Groat**, Duke

SOUTHWEST	Conference W	L	Pct	Overall W	L	Pct
Texas A&M ⊕	8	4	.667	17	12	.586
TCU	8	4	.667	16	9	.640
Texas	8	4	.667	13	14	.481
Arkansas	7	5	.583	13	11	.542
SMU	6	6	.500	14	10	.583
Baylor	3	9	.250	8	16	.333
Rice	2	10	.167	8	15	.348

WNY LITTLE THREE	Conference W	L	Pct	Overall W	L	Pct
St. Bonaventure □	3	1	.750	19	6	.760
Niagara	2	2	.500	18	10	.643
Canisius	1	3	.250	15	10	.600

YANKEE	Conference W	L	Pct	Overall W	L	Pct
Connecticut ○	6	1	.857	22	4	.846
Vermont	4	1	.800	14	6	.700
Rhode Island	5	2	.714	13	15	.464
Maine	2	5	.286	5	13	.278
Massachusetts	1	3	.250	6	14	.300
New Hampshire	2	6	.250	4	12	.250

⊕ Automatic NCAA Tournament bid ○ At-large NCAA Tournament bid □ NIT appearance ✪ Team record doesn't reflect games forfeited or vacated. For adjusted record, see p. 521.

INDEPENDENTS

	Overall W	L	Pct
Dayton□	27	5	.844
Long Island	20	4	.833
Holy Cross	20	5	.800
Villanova○	25	7	.781
Seton Hall□	24	7	.774
La Salle□	22	7	.759
Toledo	22	7	.759
Baldwin-Wallace	19	7	.731
Louisville○	19	7	.731
Navy	16	6	.727
Siena	19	8	.704
Syracuse	19	9	.679
Montana State○	24	12	.667
Xavier	16	10	.615
Penn State	14	9	.609
Boston College	17	11	.607
San Jose State○	18	12	.600
Duquesne	16	11	.593
Loyola Marymount	14	11	.560
Bowling Green	15	12	.556
Colgate	12	10	.545
Valparaiso	12	10	.545

INDEPENDENTS (CONT.)

	Overall W	L	Pct
Notre Dame	13	11	.542
Oklahoma City	16	14	.533
Army	9	8	.529
DePaul	13	12	.520
Loyola-Chicago	15	14	.517
Saint Joseph's	13	14	.481
Temple	12	13	.480
Miami (FL)	10	12	.455
Saint Mary's (CA)	9	11	.450
Muhlenberg	11	14	.440
Brown	8	11	.421
Bucknell	9	13	.409
Santa Clara	9	15	.375
Georgetown	8	14	.364
Marquette	8	14	.364
Virginia	8	14	.364
Pittsburgh	9	17	.346
San Francisco	9	17	.346
Creighton	9	18	.333
Butler	5	19	.208
John Carroll	2	21	.087

INDIVIDUAL LEADERS—SEASON

Scoring

	CL	POS	G	FG	FT	PTS	PPG
1 **Bill Mlkvy**, Temple	JR	F	25	303	125	731	**29.2**
2 **Jay Handlan**, Washington and Lee	JR	F	25	249	158	656	**26.2**
3 **Mark Workman**, West Virginia	JR	C	27	273	159	705	**26.1**
4 **Dick Groat**, Duke	JR	G	33	285	261	831	**25.2**
5 **Clyde Lovellette**, Kansas	JR	C	24	245	58	548	**22.8**
6 **Jim Slaughter**, South Carolina	SR	C	25	222	125	569	**22.8**
7 **Larry Hennessy**, Villanova	SO	F	32	306	91	703	**22.0**
8 **Jim Ove**, Valparaiso	SR	C	22	158	153	469	**21.3**
9 **Bob Zawoluk**, St. John's	JR	C	31	223	208	654	**21.1**
10 **Sam Ranzino**, NC State	SR	G	34	241	224	706	**20.8**

Field Goal Pct

	CL	POS	G	FG	FGA	PCT
1 **Don Meineke**, Dayton	JR	C	32	240	469	**51.2**
2 **Nicholas Maguire**, Villanova	SO	F	31	86	170	**50.6**
3 **Mark Workman**, West Virginia	JR	C	27	273	558	**48.9**
4 **Gerald Rogers**, Texas Western	JR	C	25	154	317	**48.6**
5 **Jim Slaughter**, South Carolina	SR	C	25	222	458	**48.5**

Minimum: 80 made

Free Throw Pct

	CL	POS	G	FT	FTA	PCT
1 **Jay Handlan**, Washington and Lee	JR	F	25	158	184	**85.9**
2 **Rex McMurray**, Wichita State	SR	C	25	81	95	**85.3**
3 **Aaron Preece**, Bradley	SR	G/F	35	67	79	**84.8**
4 **Stan Gordon**, Temple	SR	F	25	53	63	**84.1**
5 **Whitey Skoog**, Minnesota	SR	G	22	52	63	**82.5**

Minimum: 50 made

Assists Per Game

	CL	POS	G	AST	APG
1 **Bill Walker**, Toledo	SR	G	29	210	**7.2**
2 **Bill Mlkvy**, Temple	JR	F	25	176	**7.0**
3 **Tom Birch**, Niagara	SR	G	28	193	**6.9**
4 **Roger Chadwick**, Cornell	JR	G	25	170	**6.8**
5 **Richie Regan**, Seton Hall	SO	G	28	158	**5.6**
6 **Dan Markham**, Wisconsin	SR	F	18	99	**5.5**
7 **Abe Becker**, NYU	SR	G/F	16	87	**5.4**
8 **Walter Baird**, Holy Cross	SR	G	21	114	**5.4**
9 **Joe Stratton**, Colgate	JR	F	22	119	**5.4**
10 **Don Cox**, South Carolina	JR	G	25	135	**5.4**

Rebounds Per Game

	CL	POS	G	REB	RPG
1 **Ernie Beck**, Penn	SO	C	27	556	**20.6**
2 **Bill Mlkvy**, Temple	JR	F	25	472	**18.9**
3 **Fred Christ**, Fordham	JR	F	27	493	**18.3**
4 **Mel Payton**, Tulane	SR	F	24	426	**17.8**
5 **Chuck Darling**, Iowa	JR	C	22	387	**17.6**
6 **Paul Nolen**, Texas Tech	SO	C	28	492	**17.6**
7 **Howard Deasy**, North Carolina	JR	G	23	399	**17.3**
8 **Bill Spivey**, Kentucky	JR	C	33	567	**17.2**
9 **Jim Slaughter**, South Carolina	SR	C	25	413	**16.5**
10 **Harold Corizzi**, Rutgers	JR	C	21	339	**16.1**

INDIVIDUAL LEADERS—GAME

Points

	CL	POS	OPP	DATE	PTS
1 **Bill Mlkvy**, Temple	JR	F	Wilkes	M3	**73**
2 **Jay Handlan**, Washington and Lee	JR	F	Furman	F17	**66**
3 **Mark Workman**, West Virginia	JR	C	Salem	J27	**50**
4 **Don Meineke**, Dayton	JR	C	Muskingum	J13	**49**
5 **Sam Ranzino**, NC State	SR	G	Virginia Tech	J23	**47**

Free Throws Made

	CL	POS	OPP	DATE	FT	FTA	PCT
1 **Dick Groat**, Duke	JR	G	Davidson	J29	**17**	17	100.0
2 **Bob Zawoluk**, St. John's	JR	C	Saint Joseph's	J27	**16**	17	94.1
Jim Ove, Valparaiso	SR	C	Butler	F10	**16**	22	92.7
4 **Ralph Carroll**, Toledo	JR	C	Western Michigan	F28	**15**	15	100.0
Francis Miller, Creighton	SR	C	Cornell College	F8	**15**	16	93.8
Glen Smith, Utah	JR	F	BYU	M3	**15**	18	83.3
Sumner Tilson, Virginia Tech	SR	C	Norfolk NAS	D2	**15**	18	83.3
Don Meineke, Dayton	JR	C	Arizona	M13	**15**	21	81.4

TEAM LEADERS—SEASON

Scoring Offense

	G	W-L	PTS	PPG
1 **Cincinnati**	22	18-4	1,694	**77.0**
2 **NC State**	37	30-7	2,842	**76.8**
3 **Columbia**	24	23-1	1,676	**76.2**
4 **Kentucky**	34	32-2	2,540	**74.7**
5 **Virginia Tech**	29	19-10	2,149	**74.1**

Scoring Margin

	G	W-L	PPG	OPP PPG	MAR
1 **Columbia**	24	23-1	76.2	52.7	**23.5**
2 **Kentucky**	34	32-2	74.7	52.5	**22.2**
3 **Cincinnati**	22	18-4	77.0	58.1	**18.9**
4 **Arizona**	30	24-6	69.5	55.4	**14.1**
5 **Kansas State**	29	25-4	68.8	55.1	**13.7**

Field Goal Pct

	G	W-L	FG	FGA	PCT
1 **Maryland**	25	15-10	481	1,210	**39.8**
2 **Virginia Tech**	29	19-10	805	2,029	**39.7**
3 **Washington and Lee**	25	8-17	639	1,613	**39.6**
4 **Toledo**	29	22-7	725	1,852	**39.1**
5 **Bradley**	38	32-6	941	2,427	**38.8**

Free Throw Pct

	G	W-L	FT	FTA	PCT
1 **Minnesota**	22	13-9	287	401	**71.6**
2 **Virginia Tech**	29	19-10	539	756	**71.3**
3 **Oklahoma**	24	14-10	383	547	**70.0**
4 **Duke**	33	20-13	619	888	**69.7**
5 **Baylor**	24	8-16	371	533	**69.6**

Scoring Defense

	G	W-L	OPP PTS	OPP PPG
1 **Texas A&M**	29	17-12	1,275	**44.0**
2 **Arkansas**	24	13-11	1,101	**45.9**
3 **Oklahoma A&M**	35	29-6	1,616	**46.2**
4 **Texas**	27	13-14	1,258	**46.6**
5 **Oklahoma City**	30	16-14	1,423	**47.4**

CONSENSUS ALL-AMERICAS

FIRST TEAM

PLAYER	CL	POS	HT	SCHOOL	RPG	PPG
Clyde Lovellette	JR	C	6-9	Kansas	9.9	22.8
Gene Melchiorre	SR	G	5-8	Bradley	N/A	11.3
Bill Mlkvy	JR	F	6-4	Temple	18.9	29.2
Sam Ranzino	SR	G	6-2	NC State	6.5	20.8
Bill Spivey	JR	C	7-0	Kentucky	17.2	19.2

SECOND TEAM

PLAYER	CL	POS	HT	SCHOOL	RPG	PPG
Ernie Barrett	SR	G	6-3	Kansas State	N/A	10.3
Bill Garrett	SR	F	6-3	Indiana	8.5	13.1
Dick Groat	JR	G	6-0	Duke	N/A	25.2
Mel Hutchins	SR	C	6-5	BYU	12.7	15.4
Gale McArthur	SR	G	6-2	Oklahoma A&M	N/A	11.6

Selectors: AP, Colliers (coaches), International News Service, Look Magazine, UP

Poll Progression

Preseason Poll

UP	School
1	**CCNY**
2	**Bradley**
3	**Kentucky**
4	**NC State**
5	**Kansas**
6	**Oklahoma A&M**
7	**Long Island**
8	**Iowa**
9	**St. John's**
10	**Indiana**
11	**UCLA**
12	**Kansas State**
13	**Arkansas**
13	**Syracuse**
13	**Western Kentucky**
16	**Washington**
17	**DePaul**
17	**Illinois**
17	**Ohio State**
20	**BYU**

Week of Dec 12

UP	School
1	**Kentucky** (2-0)
2	**Bradley** (4-0)
3	**NC State** (4-0)
4	**Kansas** (3-0)
5	**Oklahoma A&M** (3-0)
6	**CCNY** (3-1)
7	**Long Island** (2-0)
8	**St. John's** (4-0)
9	**Kansas State** (3-1)
10	**Indiana** (2-0)
11	**Missouri** (2-1)
12	**BYU** (5-1)
13	**Washington** (2-0)
14	**UCLA** (2-1)
14	**Minnesota** (2-1)
16	**Syracuse** (3-1)
17	**DePaul** (3-2)
18	**Iowa** (1-2)
19	**Saint Louis** (4-0)
20	**Illinois** (2-1)
20	**Holy Cross** (1-0)

Week of Dec 19

AP	UP	School
1	1	**Kentucky** (5-0) (A)
2	2	**Bradley** (6-0)
3	3	**NC State** (6-0)
4	5	**Indiana** (4-0)
5	4	**Oklahoma A&M** (5-0)
6	6	**CCNY** (4-1)
7	7	**Long Island** (3-0)
8	9	**Missouri** (3-1)
9	16	**UCLA** (4-1)
10	16	**Toledo** (7-0)
11	10	**Kansas** (4-1)
12	11	**Washington** (4-0)
13	8	**St. John's** (5-1)
14	—	**Notre Dame** (4-0)
15	15	**BYU** (5-1)
16	14	**Oklahoma** (3-0)
17	18	**Cincinnati** (3-0)
18	—	**Villanova** (4-0)
19	—	**Cornell** (5-0)
20	19	**Kansas State** (4-2)
—	12	**Duquesne** (5-0)
—	13	**Saint Louis** (6-0)
—	20	**Illinois** (3-1)

Week of Dec 26

AP	UP	School	AP↓↑
1	1	**Kentucky** (6-0)	
2	2	**Bradley** (9-0)	
3	3	**Oklahoma A&M** (9-0)	↑2
4	4	**Long Island** (6-0)	↑3
5	5	**Indiana** (6-0)	↓1
6	6	**NC State** (7-1)	↓3
7	12	**Villanova** (6-0)	↑11
8	—	**Columbia** (7-0)	⤴
9	7	**Missouri** (4-1)	↓1
10	10	**Kansas** (5-1)	↑1
11	9	**CCNY** (6-2)	↓5
12	8	**St. John's** (7-2)	↑1
13	18	**Toledo** (8-1)	↓3
14	14	**Wyoming** (9-0)	⤴
15	11	**Washington** (6-0)	↓3
16	20	**La Salle** (6-1)	⤴
17	17	**Cincinnati** (5-0)	
18	—	**Cornell** (6-0)	↑1
19	—	**West Virginia** (6-0)	⤴
20	—	**Illinois** (5-1)	⤴
—	13	**BYU** (7-1)	⤵
—	15	**Kansas State** (6-2)	⤵
—	16	**Duquesne** (6-0)	
—	19	**Saint Louis** (7-1)	

Week of Jan 3

AP	UP	School	AP↓↑
1	1	**Bradley** (13-0) (B)	↑1
2	3	**Oklahoma A&M** (12-0)	↑1
3	2	**Kentucky** (7-1)	↓2
4	4	**Long Island** (8-0)	
5	7	**Saint Louis** (9-2)	⤴
6	5	**Indiana** (7-1)	↓1
7	6	**NC State** (11-1)	↓1
8	11	**Villanova** (8-0)	↓1
9	8	**Kansas State** (9-2)	⤴
10	10	**Wyoming** (12-0)	↑4
11	9	**St. John's** (9-2)	↑1
12	11	**Washington** (7-0)	↑3
13	19	**Duquesne** (9-0)	⤴
14	14	**Columbia** (7-0)	↓6
14	—	**Cornell** (9-0)	↑4
16	18	**Arizona** (8-2)	⤴
17	13	**Cincinnati** (6-0)	
18	—	**Princeton** (7-0)	⤴
19	—	**Toledo** (9-1)	↓6
20	15	**Kansas** (7-2)	↓10
—	16	**CCNY** (6-4)	⤵
—	17	**Oklahoma** (4-3)	
—	19	**Missouri** (5-3)	⤵

Week of Jan 9

AP	UP	School	AP↓↑
1	1	**Bradley** (15-0)	
2	2	**Oklahoma A&M** (13-0)	
3	3	**Kentucky** (9-1)	
4	4	**Long Island** (9-0)	
5	6	**Saint Louis** (11-2)	
6	5	**Indiana** (8-1)	
7	7	**NC State** (13-1)	
8	9	**Columbia** (8-0)	↑6
9	8	**Kansas State** (10-2)	
10	11	**Wyoming** (12-1)	
11	10	**St. John's** (10-2)	
12	12	**Washington** (9-0)	
13	19	**USC** (10-1)	⤴
14	—	**Illinois** (9-2)	⤴
15	15	**Duquesne** (10-1)	↓2
16	13	**Villanova** (10-1)	↓8
17	14	**Kansas** (9-2)	↑3
18	—	**Toledo** (11-1)	↑1
19	16	**La Salle** (9-1)	⤴
20	—	**Princeton** (8-0)	↓2
—	16	**Arizona** (9-2)	⤵
—	16	**Cincinnati** (8-1)	⤵
—	19	**Iowa** (6-2)	

Week of Jan 16

AP	UP	School	AP↓↑
1	1	**Oklahoma A&M** (15-0)	↑1
2	2	**Kentucky** (10-1)	↑1
3	4	**Bradley** (16-2)	↓2
4	3	**Long Island** (11-0)	
5	6	**St. John's** (11-2)	↑6
6	5	**Indiana** (9-1)	
7	10	**Columbia** (10-0)	↑1
8	8	**Saint Louis** (12-3)	↓3
9	9	**NC State** (15-2)	↓2
10	7	**Kansas State** (11-2)	↓1
11	11	**Villanova** (12-1)	↑5
12	—	**Toledo** (12-2)	↑6
13	13	**Wyoming** (14-1)	↓3
14	11	**Illinois** (10-2)	
15	16	**Washington** (10-1)	↓3
16	14	**Cincinnati** (9-1)	⤴
17	—	**St. Bonaventure** (10-0)	⤴
18	—	**Siena** (13-1)	⤴
19	17	**USC** (12-2)	↓6
20	18	**Duquesne** (11-1)	↓5
—	15	**Kansas** (10-2)	⤵
—	19	**Arizona** (12-2)	
—	19	**BYU** (12-4)	

Week of Jan 23

AP	UP	School	AP↓↑
1	1	**Kentucky** (13-1)	↑1
2	2	**Long Island** (15-0)	↑2
3	3	**Oklahoma A&M** (16-1)	↓2
4	5	**Bradley** (18-2)	↓1
5	4	**Indiana** (12-1)	↑1
6	6	**St. John's** (12-2)	↓1
7	8	**Columbia** (12-0)	
8	9	**NC State** (17-2)	↑1
9	7	**Kansas State** (12-2)	↑1
10	10	**Saint Louis** (13-4)	↓2
11	14	**Villanova** (13-1)	
12	15	**USC** (14-2)	↑7
13	—	**Siena** (13-1)	↑5
14	16	**Arizona** (13-2)	⤴
15	13	**Cincinnati** (10-1)	↑1
16	12	**Illinois** (11-3)	↓2
17	—	**La Salle** (12-3)	⤴
18	—	**Oklahoma** (9-5)	⤴
19	11	**BYU** (14-4)	⤴
20	18	**Wyoming** (15-4)	↓7
—	17	**NYU** (6-2)	
—	19	**Kansas** (10-3)	
—	19	**Washington State** (13-8)	

Week of Jan 30

AP	UP	School	AP↓↑
1	1	**Kentucky** (14-1)	
2	2	**Oklahoma A&M** (16-1)	↑1
3	4	**Indiana** (13-1)	↑2
4	3	**Long Island** (16-1)	↓2
5	6	**Bradley** (18-3)	↓1
6	8	**Columbia** (12-0)	↑1
7	5	**Kansas State** (13-2)	↑2
8	9	**NC State** (19-2)	
9	7	**St. John's** (13-2)	↓3
10	10	**Saint Louis** (14-4)	
11	12	**Villanova** (14-1)	
12	11	**BYU** (16-4)	↑7
13	13	**USC** (14-2)	↓1
14	14	**Illinois** (11-3)	↑2
15	20	**Arizona** (14-3)	↓1
16	14	**Cincinnati** (10-1)	↓1
17	16	**Kansas** (11-3)	⤴
18	—	**Oklahoma** (9-6)	
19	18	**UCLA** (9-7)	⤴
20	—	**Toledo** (14-3)	⤴
—	17	**Washington State** (14-8)	
—	19	**NYU** (7-2)	

Week of Feb 6

AP	UP	School	AP↓↑
1	1	**Kentucky** (18-1)	
2	2	**Oklahoma A&M** (19-1)	
3	3	**Indiana** (13-1)	
4	4	**Kansas State** (16-2)	↑3
5	5	**Bradley** (20-3)	
6	6	**Columbia** (12-0)	
7	7	**St. John's** (15-2)	↑2
8	8	**Saint Louis** (16-4)	↑2
9	12	**Villanova** (16-1)	↑2
10	10	**NC State** (19-4)	↓2
11	15	**Cincinnati** (11-1)	↑5
12	14	**Long Island** (16-4) (C)	↓8
13	18	**Arizona** (16-3)	↑2
14	9	**BYU** (18-4)	↓2
15	11	**USC** (16-2)	↓2
16	13	**Illinois** (11-3)	↓2
17	—	**Louisville** (14-2)	⤴
18	—	**Dayton** (15-3)	⤴
19	—	**Siena** (15-2)	⤴
20	17	**Kansas** (11-5)	↓3
—	16	**Washington** (13-4)	
—	19	**NYU** (9-2)	
—	20	**Holy Cross** (12-3)	
—	20	**Texas A&M** (10-7)	
—	20	**Washington State** (15-9)	

Week of Feb 13

AP	UP	School	AP↓↑
1	1	**Kentucky** (19-1)	
2	2	**Oklahoma A&M** (21-1)	
3	3	**Kansas State** (17-2)	↑1
4	4	**Columbia** (15-0)	↑2
5	7	**Saint Louis** (18-4)	↑3
6	5	**Indiana** (13-2)	↓3
7	6	**St. John's** (18-2)	
8	9	**Bradley** (21-4)	↓3
9	10	**NC State** (21-4)	↑1
10	13	**Villanova** (18-2)	↓1
11	12	**Illinois** (13-3)	↑5
12	8	**BYU** (20-4)	↑2
13	11	**USC** (18-2)	↑2
14	—	**Louisville** (17-2)	↑3
15	14	**Cincinnati** (12-2)	↓4
16	17	**Arizona** (18-3)	↓3
17	—	**Dayton** (18-4)	↑1
18	—	**Beloit** (14-3)	⤴
19	15	**Long Island** (17-4)	↓7
20	—	**Seattle** (27-2)	⤴
—	16	**Washington** (15-4)	
—	18	**NYU** (10-3)	
—	19	**Kansas** (12-5)	⤵
—	20	**Oklahoma** (11-7)	

Week of Feb 20

AP	UP	School	AP↓↑
1	1	**Kentucky** (22-1)	
2	2	**Oklahoma A&M** (23-1)	
3	4	**Columbia** (17-0)	↑1
4	3	**Indiana** (15-3)	↑2
5	5	**Kansas State** (17-3)	↓2
6	6	**Saint Louis** (19-5)	↓1
7	7	**Bradley** (24-4)	↑1
8	9	**St. John's** (19-3)	↓1
9	8	**NC State** (23-4)	
10	11	**Illinois** (16-3)	↑1
11	18	**Arizona** (21-4)	↑5
12	10	**BYU** (21-5)	
13	13	**USC** (19-3)	
14	—	**Dayton** (20-4)	↑3
15	17	**Villanova** (20-4)	↓5
16	12	**Long Island** (20-4)	↑3
17	19	**Oklahoma** (13-7)	⤴
18	15	**Cincinnati** (13-2)	↓3
19	14	**Washington** (17-4)	⤴
20	20	**Beloit** (15-3)	↓2
—	16	**Oregon** (16-11)	

WEEK OF FEB 27

AP	UP	SCHOOL	AP↓↑
1	1	**Kentucky** (24-1)	
2	2	**Oklahoma A&M** (25-1)	
3	4	**Columbia** (19-0)	
4	3	**Kansas State** (18-3)	↑1
5	8	**Bradley** (26-4)	↑2
6	5	**Illinois** (17-3)	↑4
7	6	**Indiana** (16-3)	↓3
8	9	**NC State** (25-4)	↑1
9	7	**St. John's** (20-3)	↓1
10	11	**Saint Louis** (20-6)	↓4
11	10	**BYU** (23-5)	↑1
12	13	**Arizona** (22-4)	↓1
13	—	**Toledo** (20-6)	⤴
14	—	**Dayton** (23-4)	
15	15	**Villanova** (22-4)	
16	17	**Beloit** (17-4)	↑4
17	—	**UCLA** (16-8)	⤴
18	12	**USC** (20-4)	↓5
19	13	**Washington** (18-5)	
20	—	**Murray State** (21-6)	⤴
—	16	**Oregon** (17-12)	
—	18	**Cincinnati** (14-3)	↱
—	19	**St. Bonaventure** (17-4)	

FINAL POLL

AP	UP	SCHOOL	AP↓↑
1	2	**Kentucky** (27-2) Ⓓ	
2	1	**Oklahoma A&M** (26-3) Ⓓ	
3	5	**Columbia** (21-0) Ⓔ	
4	3	**Kansas State** (21-3)	
5	4	**Illinois** (19-3)	↑1
6	7	**Bradley** (28-4)	↓1
7	8	**Indiana** (19-3)	
8	6	**NC State** (28-4)	
9	9	**St. John's** (22-3)	
10	11	**Saint Louis** (21-7)	
11	10	**BYU** (24-7)	
12	13	**Arizona** (24-4)	
13	19	**Dayton** (23-4)	↑1
14	—	**Toledo** (23-6)	↓1
15	12	**Washington** (20-5)	↑4
16	—	**Murray State** (21-6)	↑4
17	—	**Cincinnati** (17-3)	⤴
18	17	**Siena** (18-6)	⤴
19	15	**USC** (21-5)	↓1
20	17	**Villanova** (23-5)	↓5
—	14	**Beloit** (18-5)	↱
—	16	**Vanderbilt** (19-8)	
—	19	**St. Bonaventure** (18-5)	

Ⓐ AP rival United Press starts its own poll with selected coaches voting instead of sportswriters. On Dec. 16, Kentucky impresses all voters with a 68-39 victory over Kansas in the Wildcats' new Memorial Coliseum.
Ⓑ After Saint Louis hands Kentucky its first loss, Bradley rises to No. 1. Two weeks later it will become the first top-ranked team to lose twice in one week, falling to St. John's and Detroit.
Ⓒ Long Island loses four straight after allegations of point-shaving involving LIU and CCNY players appear in the press. On Feb. 18, after a road victory against Temple, City College upperclassmen Ed Warner, Ed Roman and Al Roth are arrested in Penn Station. The next day, police pick up LIU's Adolph Bigos, Leroy Smith and the nation's leading scorer, Sherman White (27.7 ppg). After the season, Blackbirds coach Clair Bee retires and the university will not field a varsity basketball team for six years.
Ⓓ Two polls, two No. 1s. The AP and UP split their decision on which team is the best. Kentucky's Adolph Rupp turns down the NIT—where his Wildcats had been humiliated in 1950 by CCNY, 89-50—and accepts a bid to the NCAA Tournament, setting up a potential showdown with Oklahoma A&M.
Ⓔ Coached by Lou Rossini, Columbia finishes the season as the only unbeaten team in the nation, but they lose to Illinois in the first round of the NCAAs. Two other Ivies, Cornell and Princeton, are also ranked at one time or another during the season.

1951 NCAA TOURNAMENT

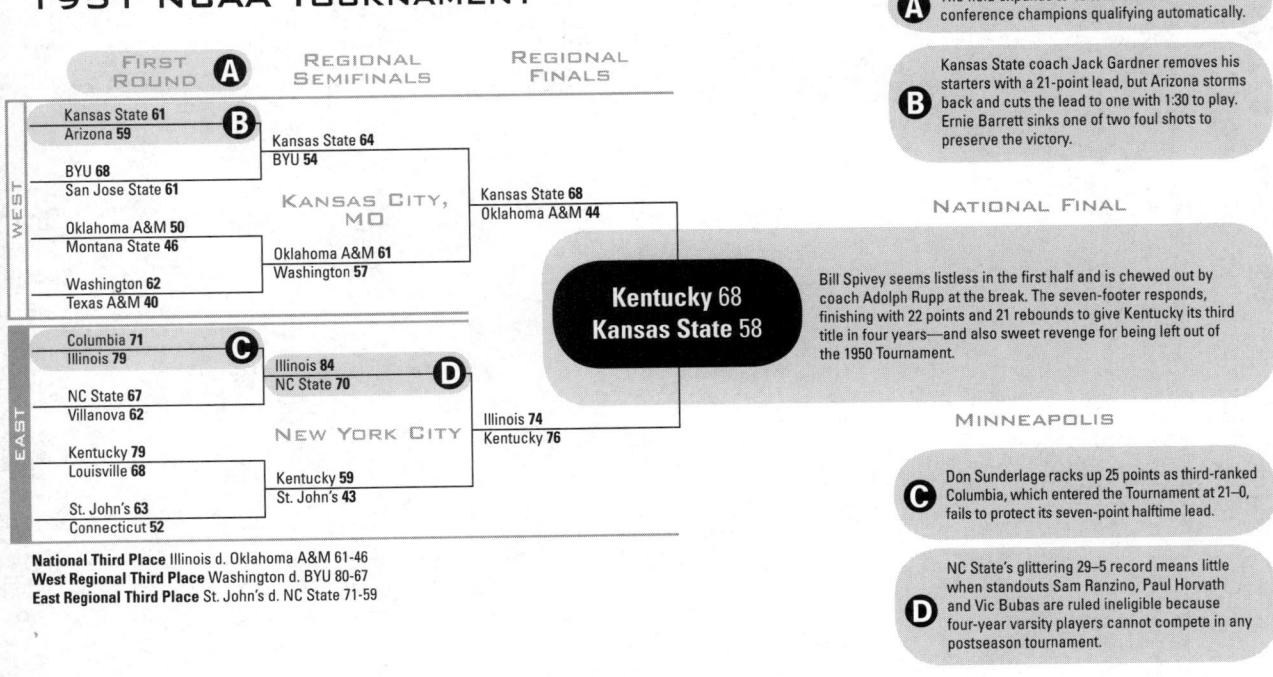

FIRST ROUND Ⓐ | **REGIONAL SEMIFINALS** | **REGIONAL FINALS**

WEST — KANSAS CITY, MO

First Round:
- Kansas State **61**, Arizona **59** Ⓑ
- BYU **68**, San Jose State **61**
- Oklahoma A&M **50**, Montana State **46**
- Washington **62**, Texas A&M **40**

Regional Semifinals:
- Kansas State **64**, BYU **54**
- Oklahoma A&M **61**, Washington **57**

Regional Final:
- Kansas State **68**, Oklahoma A&M **44**

EAST — NEW YORK CITY

First Round:
- Columbia **71**, Illinois **79** Ⓒ
- NC State **67**, Villanova **62**
- Kentucky **79**, Louisville **68**
- St. John's **63**, Connecticut **52**

Regional Semifinals:
- Illinois **84**, NC State **70** Ⓓ
- Kentucky **59**, St. John's **43**

Regional Final:
- Illinois **74**, Kentucky **76**

NATIONAL FINAL — MINNEAPOLIS

Kentucky 68
Kansas State 58

Bill Spivey seems listless in the first half and is chewed out by coach Adolph Rupp at the break. The seven-footer responds, finishing with 22 points and 21 rebounds to give Kentucky its third title in four years—and also sweet revenge for being left out of the 1950 Tournament.

National Third Place Illinois d. Oklahoma A&M 61-46
West Regional Third Place Washington d. BYU 80-67
East Regional Third Place St. John's d. NC State 71-59

Ⓐ The field expands to 16 teams with 10 conference champions qualifying automatically.

Ⓑ Kansas State coach Jack Gardner removes his starters with a 21-point lead, but Arizona storms back and cuts the lead to one with 1:30 to play. Ernie Barrett sinks one of two foul shots to preserve the victory.

Ⓒ Don Sunderlage racks up 25 points as third-ranked Columbia, which entered the Tournament at 21–0, fails to protect its seven-point halftime lead.

Ⓓ NC State's glittering 29–5 record means little when standouts Sam Ranzino, Paul Horvath and Vic Bubas are ruled ineligible because four-year varsity players cannot compete in any postseason tournament.

Tournament Leaders

INDIVIDUAL LEADERS

Scoring	CL	POS	G	PTS	PPG
1 **Bill Kukoy**, NC State	SO	F	3	69	23.0
2 **Don Sunderlage**, Illinois	SR	G	4	83	20.8
3 **Bill Spivey**, Kentucky	JR	C	4	72	18.0
4 **Bob Houbregs**, Washington	SO	C	3	53	17.7
5 **Rod Fletcher**, Illinois	JR	G	4	67	16.8
6 **Bobby Speight**, NC State	SO	F	3	45	15.0
7 **Ted Beach**, Illinois	SR	G	4	58	14.5
8 **Bob Zawoluk**, St. John's	JR	C	3	42	14.0
9 **Mel Hutchins**, BYU	SR	C	3	41	13.7
Jack McMahon, St. John's	JR	G	3	41	13.7

Minimum: 2 games

Field Goal Pct	CL	POS	G	FG	FGA	PCT
1 **Lucian Whitaker**, Kentucky	JR	G	4	18	35	51.4
2 **Don Sunderlage**, Illinois	SR	G	4	28	62	45.2
3 **Lew Hitch**, Kansas State	SR	C	4	18	40	45.0
4 **Rod Fletcher**, Illinois	JR	G	4	28	66	42.4
5 **Mike McCutchen**, Washington	SO	F	3	11	26	42.3

Minimum: 8 made

Free Throw Pct	CL	POS	G	FT	FTA	PCT
1 **Ted Beach**, Illinois	SR	G	4	10	10	100.0
Louie Soriano, Washington	SR	G	3	6	6	100.0
3 **Bobby Speight**, NC State	SO	F	3	13	14	92.9
4 **Doug McClary**, Washington	SO	F	3	8	9	88.9
5 **Ray Dombrosky**, St. John's	SR	G/F	3	7	8	87.5

Minimum: 5 made

TEAM LEADERS

Scoring	G	PTS	PPG
1 **Illinois**	4	298	74.5
2 **Kentucky**	4	282	70.5
3 **Washington**	3	199	66.3
4 **NC State**	3	196	65.3
5 **BYU**	3	189	63.0
6 **Kansas State**	4	251	62.8
7 **St. John's**	3	177	59.0
8 **Oklahoma A&M**	4	201	50.3

Minimum: 2 games

FT Pct	G	FT	FTA	PCT
1 **Oklahoma A&M**	4	49	67	73.1
2 **NC State**	3	48	66	72.7
3 **Illinois**	4	78	109	71.6
4 **St. John's**	3	39	58	67.2
5 **Kentucky**	4	56	90	62.2

Minimum: 2 games

FG Pct	G	FG	FGA	PCT
1 **Illinois**	4	110	293	37.5
2 **Kansas State**	4	99	266	37.2
3 **Washington**	3	80	216	37.0
4 **Kentucky**	4	113	321	35.2
5 **St. John's**	3	69	199	34.7

TOURNAMENT MOP

PLAYER	CL	POS	HT	SCHOOL	FG	FT	PPG
Bill Spivey	JR	C	7-0	Kentucky	27-68	18-25	18.0

ALL-REGIONAL TEAMS

WEST

PLAYER	CL	POS	HT	SCHOOL	PPG
Ed Head	SR	F	6-0	Kansas State	12.0
Bob Houbregs	SO	C	6-7	Washington	17.7
Don Johnson	JR	F	6-2	Oklahoma A&M	13.0
Gale McArthur	SR	G	6-2	Oklahoma A&M	14.0
Jack Stone	SR	F	6-3	Kansas State	8.5

1951 NCAA TOURNAMENT BOX SCORES

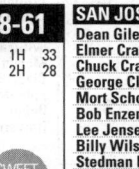

KANSAS STATE	MIN	FG	3FG	FT	REB	A	ST	BL	PF	TP
Ed Head	-	6-13	-	1-2	9	-	-	-	1	13
Lew Hitch	-	5-8	-	2-6	7	-	-	-	2	12
Jim Iverson	-	4-11	-	1-3	5	-	-	-	1	9
Robert Rousey	-	3-10	-	2-3	2	-	-	-	1	8
Ernie Barrett	-	3-13	-	1-1	8	-	-	-	1	7
Jack Stone	-	2-8	-	2-3	3	-	-	-	3	6
Richard Peck	-	1-2	-	1-1	4	-	-	-	2	3
Dick Knostman	-	0-7	-	2-3	2	-	-	-	1	2
John Gibson	-	0-0	-	1-1	1	-	-	-	0	1
Dan Schuyler	-	0-0	-	0-1	1	-	-	-	1	0
Don Upson	-	0-1	-	0-0	0	-	-	-	1	0
TOTALS	-	24-73	-	13-24	42	-	-	-	14	61
Percentages		32.9	-	54.2						

Coach: Jack Gardner

61-59
36 1H 20
25 2H 39

ARIZONA	MIN	FG	3FG	FT	REB	A	ST	BL	PF	TP
Robert Honea	-	7-19	-	1-1	5	-	-	-	4	15
Roger Johnson	-	6-17	-	3-4	8	-	-	-	4	15
Leo Johnson	-	3-9	-	3-3	2	-	-	-	4	9
David Schuff	-	3-5	-	2-3	4	-	-	-	5	8
Jerome Dillon	-	2-8	-	0-4	3	-	-	-	3	4
Jack Howell	-	2-8	-	0-0	5	-	-	-	3	4
William Kemmeries	-	2-4	-	0-0	0	-	-	-	0	4
Arthur Carroll	-	0-0	-	0-0	1	-	-	-	3	0
TOTALS	-	25-70	-	9-15	28	-	-	-	26	59
Percentages		35.7	-	60.0						

Coach: Fred A. Enke

BYU	MIN	FG	3FG	FT	REB	A	ST	BL	PF	TP
Mel Hutchins	-	10-23	-	2-4	12	-	-	-	1	22
Joe Richey	-	9-21	-	0-3	8	-	-	-	3	18
Roland Minson	-	5-11	-	2-4	4	-	-	-	5	12
Harold Christensen	-	3-11	-	1-2	4	-	-	-	3	7
Jerry Romney	-	1-11	-	3-4	7	-	-	-	2	5
Russ Hillman	-	0-3	-	2-5	1	-	-	-	1	2
Boyd Jarman	-	1-1	-	0-0	0	-	-	-	0	2
Dick Jones	-	0-1	-	0-0	0	-	-	-	0	0
TOTALS	-	29-82	-	10-22	36	-	-	-	15	68
Percentages		35.4	-	45.5						

Coach: Stan Watts

68-61
43 1H 33
25 2H 28

SAN JOSE STATE	MIN	FG	3FG	FT	REB	A	ST	BL	PF	TP
Dean Giles	-	7-23	-	4-5	10	-	-	-	2	18
Elmer Craig	-	5-9	-	1-1	2	-	-	-	4	11
Chuck Crampton	-	5-11	-	0-0	7	-	-	-	1	10
George Clark	-	3-11	-	2-2	6	-	-	-	2	8
Mort Schorr	-	2-4	-	1-1	0	-	-	-	1	5
Bob Enzensperger	-	2-5	-	0-1	1	-	-	-	5	4
Lee Jensen	-	1-5	-	0-0	3	-	-	-	2	2
Billy Wilson	-	1-3	-	0-1	7	-	-	-	2	2
Stedman Prescott	-	0-0	-	1-1	0	-	-	-	0	1
Duane Baptiste	-	0-1	-	0-1	1	-	-	-	0	0
Lee Deming	-	0-3	-	0-1	2	-	-	-	1	0
TOTALS	-	26-75	-	9-14	39	-	-	-	20	61
Percentages		34.7	-	64.3						

Coach: Walt McPherson

OKLAHOMA A&M	MIN	FG	3FG	FT	REB	A	ST	BL	PF	TP
Gale McArthur	-	5-12	-	1-3	0	-	-	-	2	11
Don Johnson	-	4-22	-	1-2	6	-	-	-	1	9
Bob Pager	-	3-9	-	3-3	5	-	-	-	3	9
Keith Smith	-	3-6	-	2-4	6	-	-	-	5	8
Harold Rogers	-	1-5	-	2-2	4	-	-	-	4	4
Pete Darcey	-	1-2	-	1-1	6	-	-	-	4	3
Louis Amaya	-	1-1	-	0-0	0	-	-	-	1	2
John Miller	-	1-1	-	0-0	1	-	-	-	0	2
Gerald Stockton	-	1-3	-	0-0	0	-	-	-	1	2
Kendall Sheets	-	0-4	-	0-0	1	-	-	-	1	0
TOTALS	-	20-65	-	10-15	29	-	-	-	22	50
Percentages		30.8	-	66.7						

Coach: Hank Iba

50-46
25 1H 21
25 2H 25

MONTANA STATE	MIN	FG	3FG	FT	REB	A	ST	BL	PF	TP
Joe McKethen	-	3-5	-	9-14	2	-	-	-	3	15
Leslie Curry	-	5-13	-	1-3	0	-	-	-	0	11
Bob Miller	-	4-9	-	0-0	3	-	-	-	2	8
Jerry Gleason	-	2-7	-	1-1	2	-	-	-	0	5
Ray Johnson	-	0-3	-	5-6	6	-	-	-	5	5
Jim Ward	-	1-5	-	0-1	2	-	-	-	5	2
Perry McCahill	-	0-3	-	0-0	5	-	-	-	1	0
Bob Saunders	-	0-0	-	0-0	0	-	-	-	0	0
TOTALS	-	15-45	-	16-25	20	-	-	-	16	46
Percentages		33.3	-	64.0						

Coach: Brick Breeden

WASHINGTON	MIN	FG	3FG	FT	REB	A	ST	BL	PF	TP
Frank Guisness	-	6-12	-	4-8	1	-	-	-	3	16
LaDon Henson	-	5-6	-	2-3	1	-	-	-	3	12
Bob Houbregs	-	5-18	-	1-2	13	-	-	-	3	11
Doug McClary	-	4-14	-	2-3	13	-	-	-	2	10
Louie Soriano	-	2-8	-	3-3	3	-	-	-	5	7
Mike McCutchen	-	2-7	-	0-1	6	-	-	-	3	4
Duane Enochs	-	1-1	-	0-0	5	-	-	-	1	2
Joe Cipriano	-	0-1	-	0-0	1	-	-	-	1	0
Bill Ward	-	0-0	-	0-0	0	-	-	-	0	0
TOTALS	-	25-67	-	12-20	43	-	-	-	21	62
Percentages		37.3	-	60.0						

Coach: William H. "Tippy" Dye

62-40
27 1H 15
35 2H 25

TEXAS A&M	MIN	FG	3FG	FT	REB	A	ST	BL	PF	TP
John Dewitt	-	6-16	-	2-2	8	-	-	-	3	14
Walter Davis	-	4-8	-	1-4	4	-	-	-	5	9
Marvin Martin	-	3-8	-	0-0	3	-	-	-	2	6
Leroy Miksch	-	2-7	-	1-4	7	-	-	-	2	5
Raymond Walker	-	1-13	-	1-1	3	-	-	-	3	3
Don Heft	-	1-1	-	0-0	0	-	-	-	0	2
Jewell McDowell	-	0-11	-	1-1	0	-	-	-	5	1
William Carpenter	-	0-1	-	0-0	1	-	-	-	2	0
Robert Farmer	-	0-0	-	0-0	1	-	-	-	0	0
Glen Williams	-	0-0	-	0-1	1	-	-	-	0	0
TOTALS	-	17-65	-	6-13	28	-	-	-	22	40
Percentages		26.2	-	46.2						

Coach: John Floyd

ILLINOIS	MIN	FG	3FG	FT	REB	A	ST	BL	PF	TP
Don Sunderlage	-	9-19	-	7-10	9	4	-	-	1	25
Ted Beach	-	10-17	-	2-2	2	3	-	-	1	22
Rod Fletcher	-	6-18	-	1-4	12	5	-	-	3	13
Irv Bemoras	-	2-7	-	4-5	8	4	-	-	2	8
Bob Peterson	-	1-8	-	3-3	8	0	-	-	5	5
Max Baumgardner	-	1-4	-	1-1	2	1	-	-	0	3
Clive Follmer	-	1-6	-	1-3	3	3	-	-	3	3
TOTALS	-	30-79	-	19-28	44	20	-	-	15	79
Percentages		38.0	-	67.9						

Coach: Harry Combes

79-71
38 1H 45
41 2H 26

COLUMBIA	MIN	FG	3FG	FT	REB	A	ST	BL	PF	TP
Jack Molinas	-	8-19	-	4-4	15	0	-	-	4	20
John Azary	-	5-14	-	3-3	9	6	-	-	2	13
Thomas Powers	-	4-12	-	1-1	1	3	-	-	5	9
Robert Reiss	-	4-9	-	1-1	2	2	-	-	3	9
Alan Stein	-	4-21	-	1-1	4	4	-	-	4	9
Frank Lewis	-	2-6	-	4-5	7	2	-	-	4	8
Leroy Guittar	-	1-1	-	0-0	0	0	-	-	1	2
Paul Brandt	-	0-2	-	1-2	1	0	-	-	1	1
Stanley Maratos	-	0-1	-	0-0	1	0	-	-	0	0
John Rohan	-	0-1	-	0-0	0	0	-	-	0	0
TOTALS	-	28-86	-	15-17	40	17	-	-	24	71
Percentages		32.6	-	88.2						

Coach: Lou Rossini

NC STATE	MIN	FG	3FG	FT	REB	A	ST	BL	PF	TP
Bill Kukoy	-	12-31	-	3-4	10	-	-	-	3	27
Bobby Speight	-	5-16	-	6-6	7	-	-	-	3	16
Paul Brandenburg	-	3-6	-	2-2	3	-	-	-	2	8
Lee Terrill	-	3-8	-	1-4	8	-	-	-	2	7
Bob Goss	-	1-12	-	3-7	17	-	-	-	5	5
Bernie Yurin	-	1-8	-	2-3	9	-	-	-	2	4
Bob Cook	-	0-2	-	0-0	2	-	-	-	1	0
TOTALS	-	25-83	-	17-26	56	-	-	-	18	67
Percentages		30.1	-	65.4						

Coach: Everett Case

67-62
32 1H 38
35 2H 24

VILLANOVA	MIN	FG	3FG	FT	REB	A	ST	BL	PF	TP
Ben Stewart	-	8-21	-	3-4	15	-	-	-	5	19
Larry Hennessy	-	6-19	-	4-5	6	-	-	-	4	16
Thomas Brennan	-	4-12	-	1-1	6	-	-	-	5	9
James Mooney	-	2-13	-	4-4	9	-	-	-	3	8
Samuel Glassmire	-	3-7	-	1-3	5	-	-	-	5	7
Stephan Gepp	-	1-3	-	1-1	7	-	-	-	3	3
Joseph Maguire	-	0-2	-	0-0	0	-	-	-	0	0
Nicholas Maguire	-	0-1	-	0-0	1	-	-	-	1	0
George Stanko	-	0-0	-	0-0	0	-	-	-	0	0
TOTALS	-	24-78	-	14-18	49	-	-	-	26	62
Percentages		30.8	-	77.8						

Coach: Alexander Severance

ANNUAL REVIEW

KENTUCKY	MIN	FG	3FG	FT	REB	A	ST	BL	PF	TP
Shelby Linville	-	9-26	-	4-4	10	-	-	-	5	22
Lucian Whitaker	-	8-15	-	0-3	1	-	-	-	2	16
Frank Ramsey	-	4-17	-	7-11	15	-	-	-	3	15
Bill Spivey	-	2-9	-	6-6	7	-	-	-	5	10
Cliff Hagan	-	2-8	-	4-4	12	-	-	-	4	8
Bobby Watson	-	3-9	-	0-0	2	-	-	-	1	6
Lou Tsioropoulos	-	1-5	-	0-0	9	-	-	-	1	2
TOTALS	-	29-89	-	21-28	56	-	-	-	21	79
Percentages		32.6	-	75.0						

Coach: Adolph Rupp

79-68

	1H	2H
Kentucky	44	35
Louisville	40	28

SWEET 16

LOUISVILLE	MIN	FG	3FG	FT	REB	A	ST	BL	PF	TP
Bob Brown	-	7-26	-	1-1	11	-	-	-	3	15
Bob Naber	-	6-8	-	3-5	3	-	-	-	5	15
Bob Lochmueller	-	6-23	-	2-7	18	-	-	-	4	14
Dick Robison	-	5-10	-	0-3	3	-	-	-	5	10
Bill Sullivan	-	3-6	-	0-0	4	-	-	-	2	6
Wayne Larrabee	-	2-5	-	0-1	6	-	-	-	3	4
Roy Rubin	-	2-5	-	0-1	2	-	-	-	4	4
Bob Dunbar	-	0-1	-	0-0	1	-	-	-	0	0
Leon Ford	-	0-0	-	0-0	0	-	-	-	0	0
Bob Wellman	-	0-1	-	0-0	0	-	-	-	1	0
TOTALS	-	31-85	-	6-18	48	-	-	-	27	68
Percentages		36.5	-	33.3						

Coach: Bernard "Peck" Hickman

ST. JOHN'S	MIN	FG	3FG	FT	REB	A	ST	BL	PF	TP
Bob Zawoluk	-	7-18	-	4-5	18	2	-	-	3	18
Ray Dombrosky	-	6-13	-	5-5	10	1	-	-	0	17
Jack McMahon	-	5-12	-	0-0	5	2	-	-	3	10
Ron MacGilvray	-	2-8	-	5-8	13	1	-	-	3	9
Frank Mulzoff	-	2-7	-	1-1	3	5	-	-	5	5
Don Dunn	-	2-4	-	0-0	3	2	-	-	2	4
Frank Giancontieri	-	0-0	-	0-0	0	0	-	-	1	0
John McAndrew	-	0-0	-	0-0	0	0	-	-	0	0
Hugh McCool	-	0-1	-	0-0	0	0	-	-	0	0
Al McGuire	-	0-0	-	0-1	4	1	-	-	2	0
Don Noonan	-	0-0	-	0-0	0	1	-	-	0	0
Tom O'Shea	-	0-0	-	0-0	0	0	-	-	0	0
TOTALS	-	24-63	-	15-20	56	15	-	-	19	63
Percentages		38.1	-	75.0						

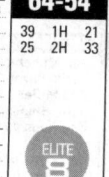

Coach: Frank McGuire

63-52

	1H	2H
St. John's	34	29
Connecticut	19	33

SWEET 16

CONNECTICUT	MIN	FG	3FG	FT	REB	A	ST	BL	PF	TP
Vince Yokabaskas	-	7-15	-	8-11	3	3	-	-	2	22
William Ebel	-	5-12	-	2-3	4	0	-	-	1	12
Ernest Gates	-	3-17	-	1-3	1	3	-	-	2	7
Wallace Widholm	-	2-5	-	3-3	6	3	-	-	5	7
William Clark	-	1-6	-	0-1	3	2	-	-	3	2
Melvin Kleckner	-	1-3	-	0-0	3	4	-	-	1	2
Clyde Brouker	-	0-2	-	0-0	1	0	-	-	1	0
Pete Demir	-	0-0	-	0-0	0	0	-	-	1	0
Robert Fleischman	-	0-2	-	0-0	0	0	-	-	0	0
Howard Silverstein	-	0-1	-	0-0	0	0	-	-	0	0
TOTALS	-	19-63	-	14-21	21	15	-	-	16	52
Percentages		30.2	-	66.7						

Coach: Hugh Greer

KANSAS STATE	MIN	FG	3FG	FT	REB	A	ST	BL	PF	TP
Robert Rousey	-	5-9	-	3-3	3	-	-	-	2	13
Ed Head	-	5-11	-	1-2	12	-	-	-	3	11
Jack Stone	-	4-13	-	3-9	6	-	-	-	1	11
Ernie Barrett	-	4-9	-	2-2	4	-	-	-	5	10
Jim Iverson	-	3-9	-	1-2	2	-	-	-	0	7
Lew Hitch	-	3-6	-	0-1	11	-	-	-	2	6
John Gibson	-	1-1	-	1-1	4	-	-	-	4	3
Dick Knostman	-	1-1	-	1-1	1	-	-	-	0	3
TOTALS	-	26-59	-	12-21	43	-	-	-	17	64
Percentages		44.1	-	57.1						

Coach: Jack Gardner

64-54

	1H	2H
Kansas State	39	25
BYU	21	33

ELITE 8

BYU	MIN	FG	3FG	FT	REB	A	ST	BL	PF	TP
Roland Minson	-	5-17	-	2-3	4	-	-	-	4	12
Joe Richey	-	6-15	-	0-2	7	-	-	-	3	12
Mel Hutchins	-	5-13	-	0-1	7	-	-	-	4	10
Russ Hillman	-	4-10	-	1-3	1	-	-	-	5	9
Jerry Romney	-	1-9	-	6-8	5	-	-	-	4	8
Dick Jones	-	1-2	-	0-0	1	-	-	-	2	2
Boyd Jarman	-	0-2	-	1-1	1	-	-	-	0	1
Harold Christensen	-	0-0	-	0-0	1	-	-	-	3	0
TOTALS	-	22-68	-	10-18	27	-	-	-	25	54
Percentages		32.4	-	55.6						

Coach: Stan Watts

OKLAHOMA A&M	MIN	FG	3FG	FT	REB	A	ST	BL	PF	TP
Don Johnson	-	7-11	-	3-4	5	-	-	-	5	17
Gale McArthur	-	6-8	-	5-6	0	-	-	-	3	17
Keith Smith	-	4-6	-	4-5	1	-	-	-	2	12
Bob Pager	-	3-5	-	1-1	3	-	-	-	4	7
John Miller	-	1-4	-	2-4	6	-	-	-	5	4
Pete Darcey	-	1-2	-	1-1	1	-	-	-	5	3
Gerald Stockton	-	0-1	-	1-1	4	-	-	-	1	1
Louis Amaya	-	0-2	-	0-0	2	-	-	-	2	0
Harold Rogers	-	0-1	-	0-0	0	-	-	-	0	0
Kendall Sheets	-	0-0	-	0-0	0	-	-	-	3	0
TOTALS	-	22-40	-	17-22	22	-	-	-	30	61
Percentages		55.0	-	77.3						

Coach: Hank Iba

61-57

	1H	2H
Oklahoma A&M	36	25
Washington	23	34

ELITE 8

WASHINGTON	MIN	FG	3FG	FT	REB	A	ST	BL	PF	TP
Bob Houbregs	-	6-18	-	7-7	9	-	-	-	5	19
Doug McClary	-	2-7	-	4-4	10	-	-	-	3	8
Mike McCutchen	-	3-7	-	2-3	5	-	-	-	2	8
Joe Cipriano	-	3-8	-	0-2	0	-	-	-	4	6
Duane Enochs	-	3-6	-	0-0	1	-	-	-	2	6
Frank Guisness	-	1-5	-	2-3	0	-	-	-	5	4
Louie Soriano	-	1-4	-	1-1	1	-	-	-	4	3
LaDon Henson	-	1-7	-	0-2	1	-	-	-	3	2
Bill Ward	-	0-0	-	1-1	0	-	-	-	1	1
Don Stewart	-	0-0	-	0-0	0	-	-	-	0	0
TOTALS	-	20-62	-	17-23	27	-	-	-	29	57
Percentages		32.3	-	73.9						

Coach: William H. "Tippy" Dye

ILLINOIS	MIN	FG	3FG	FT	REB	A	ST	BL	PF	TP
Don Sunderlage	-	9-17	-	3-3	0	10	-	-	1	21
Rod Fletcher	-	9-18	-	1-2	9	6	-	-	3	19
Ted Beach	-	8-20	-	1-1	5	3	-	-	1	17
Bob Peterson	-	5-11	-	0-1	10	2	-	-	5	10
Irv Bemoras	-	3-10	-	1-1	12	2	-	-	2	7
Clive Follmer	-	2-8	-	2-2	4	1	-	-	2	6
Max Baumgardner	-	2-3	-	0-0	3	1	-	-	3	4
TOTALS	-	38-87	-	8-10	43	25	-	-	17	84
Percentages		43.7	-	80.0						

Coach: Harry Combes

84-70

	1H	2H
Illinois	40	44
NC State	29	41

ELITE 8

NC STATE	MIN	FG	3FG	FT	REB	A	ST	BL	PF	TP
Bill Kukoy	-	7-19	-	6-8	5	3	-	-	2	20
Bobby Speight	-	7-20	-	3-4	10	5	-	-	2	17
Paul Brandenburg	-	4-5	-	1-4	3	1	-	-	0	9
Bob Goss	-	3-11	-	2-3	10	0	-	-	3	8
Lee Terrill	-	4-14	-	0-1	4	3	-	-	0	8
Peter Jackmowski	-	2-2	-	0-0	4	5	-	-	2	4
Bob Cook	-	1-4	-	0-0	2	0	-	-	0	2
Eddie Morris	-	1-4	-	0-0	9	2	-	-	1	2
Bernie Yurin	-	0-1	-	0-0	1	0	-	-	0	0
TOTALS	-	29-80	-	12-20	48	19	-	-	10	70
Percentages		36.2	-	60.0						

Coach: Everett Case

KENTUCKY	MIN	FG	3FG	FT	REB	A	ST	BL	PF	TP
Frank Ramsey	-	4-12	-	5-5	12	4	-	-	5	13
Bill Spivey	-	5-9	-	2-3	11	1	-	-	4	12
Bobby Watson	-	6-23	-	0-0	3	4	-	-	0	12
Shelby Linville	-	4-9	-	1-2	5	3	-	-	2	9
Cliff Hagan	-	1-8	-	2-4	11	1	-	-	3	4
Lucian Whitaker	-	2-4	-	0-0	2	1	-	-	1	4
Lou Tsioropoulos	-	1-5	-	1-2	4	1	-	-	2	3
Roger Layne	-	1-2	-	0-1	1	1	-	-	1	2
TOTALS	-	24-72	-	11-17	49	16	-	-	18	59
Percentages		33.3	-	64.7						

Coach: Adolph Rupp

59-43

	1H	2H
Kentucky	23	36
St. John's	23	20

ELITE 8

ST. JOHN'S	MIN	FG	3FG	FT	REB	A	ST	BL	PF	TP
Bob Zawoluk	-	6-24	-	3-5	10	3	-	-	3	15
Ron MacGilvray	-	4-11	-	2-4	11	1	-	-	2	10
Jack McMahon	-	2-16	-	3-3	5	2	-	-	1	7
Al McGuire	-	2-7	-	1-4	2	2	-	-	3	5
Ray Dombrosky	-	1-5	-	2-3	5	1	-	-	4	4
Frank Giancontieri	-	1-3	-	0-0	1	0	-	-	0	2
Don Dunn	-	0-0	-	0-0	0	0	-	-	0	0
John McAndrew	-	0-0	-	0-0	0	0	-	-	0	0
Hugh McCool	-	0-0	-	0-0	0	0	-	-	0	0
Frank Mulzoff	-	0-4	-	0-0	4	2	-	-	3	0
Tom O'Shea	-	0-0	-	0-0	0	0	-	-	0	0
TOTALS	-	16-70	-	11-19	38	11	-	-	16	43
Percentages		22.9	-	57.9						

Coach: Frank McGuire

Attendance: 14,214

68-44

	1H	2H
Kansas State	37	31
Oklahoma A&M	14	30

FINAL 4

KANSAS STATE	MIN	FG	3FG	FT	REB	A	ST	BL	PF	TP
Lew Hitch	-	4-11	-	4-6	8	-	-	-	2	12
Dick Knostman	-	4-8	-	3-6	3	-	-	-	0	11
Jack Stone	-	5-5	-	0-0	1	-	-	-	2	10
Ed Head	-	4-9	-	1-1	5	-	-	-	3	9
Jim Iverson	-	3-4	-	3-3	2	-	-	-	0	9
Don Upson	-	3-4	-	0-0	1	-	-	-	2	6
Ernie Barrett	-	1-7	-	3-3	4	-	-	-	4	5
Dan Schuyler	-	2-4	-	0-1	0	-	-	-	1	4
Richard Peck	-	0-1	-	1-1	1	-	-	-	2	1
Robert Rousey	-	0-1	-	1-4	0	-	-	-	2	1
John Gibson	-	0-0	-	0-2	3	-	-	-	0	0
TOTALS	-	**26-54**	-	**16-27**	**28**	-	-	-	**18**	**68**
Percentages		48.1	-	59.3						

Coach: Jack Gardner

OKLAHOMA A&M	MIN	FG	3FG	FT	REB	A	ST	BL	PF	TP
Bob Pager	-	5-10	-	1-2	2	-	-	-	3	11
Don Johnson	-	2-10	-	3-3	5	-	-	-	4	7
Gale McArthur	-	1-11	-	5-5	2	-	-	-	2	7
Kendall Sheets	-	2-4	-	1-1	0	-	-	-	1	5
Pete Darcey	-	2-5	-	0-1	1	-	-	-	4	4
Harold Rogers	-	2-5	-	0-0	0	-	-	-	2	4
Louis Amaya	-	1-2	-	0-0	1	-	-	-	0	2
Maurice Ward	-	1-2	-	0-0	0	-	-	-	1	2
Keith Smith	-	0-0	-	1-1	1	-	-	-	2	1
Gerald Stockton	-	0-0	-	1-1	1	-	-	-	0	1
Emmett McAfee	-	0-1	-	0-0	0	-	-	-	3	0
John Miller	-	0-2	-	0-0	2	-	-	-	3	0
TOTALS	-	**16-52**	-	**12-14**	**15**	-	-	-	**25**	**44**
Percentages		30.8	-	85.7						

Coach: Hank Iba

76-74

	1H	2H
Kentucky	32	44
Illinois	39	35

FINAL 4

KENTUCKY	MIN	FG	3FG	FT	REB	A	ST	BL	PF	TP
Bill Spivey	-	11-21	-	6-10	16	2	-	-	5	28
Shelby Linville	-	7-12	-	0-0	4	4	-	-	4	14
Bobby Watson	-	5-17	-	0-0	8	3	-	-	4	10
Lucian Whitaker	-	4-11	-	2-4	4	6	-	-	5	10
Cliff Hagan	-	3-9	-	2-2	4	3	-	-	5	8
Frank Ramsey	-	2-19	-	1-3	12	7	-	-	2	5
Lou Tsioropoulos	-	0-2	-	1-2	1	0	-	-	1	1
C.M. Newton	-	0-0	-	0-0	0	0	-	-	1	0
TOTALS	-	**32-91**	-	**12-21**	**49**	**25**	-	-	**27**	**76**
Percentages		35.2	-	57.1						

Coach: Adolph Rupp

ILLINOIS	MIN	FG	3FG	FT	REB	A	ST	BL	PF	TP
Rod Fletcher	-	8-19	-	5-11	10	1	-	-	0	21
Don Sunderlage	-	6-15	-	8-11	3	5	-	-	2	20
Irv Bemoras	-	5-8	-	2-3	7	2	-	-	2	12
Bob Peterson	-	3-11	-	2-3	5	0	-	-	5	8
Ted Beach	-	2-12	-	3-3	6	4	-	-	1	7
Clive Follmer	-	2-3	-	2-3	5	3	-	-	2	6
Max Baumgardner	-	0-2	-	0-1	1	0	-	-	4	0
TOTALS	-	**26-70**	-	**22-35**	**37**	**15**	-	-	**16**	**74**
Percentages		37.1	-	62.9						

Coach: Harry Combes

Attendance: 16,425

61-46

	1H	2H
Illinois	31	30
Oklahoma A&M	22	24

3RD PLACE

ILLINOIS	MIN	FG	3FG	FT	REB	A	ST	BL	PF	TP
Don Sunderlage	-	4-11	-	9-10	6	-	-	-	4	17
Rod Fletcher	-	5-11	-	4-8	9	-	-	-	2	14
Ted Beach	-	4-12	-	4-4	4	-	-	-	2	12
Clive Follmer	-	0-2	-	6-6	3	-	-	-	4	6
Irv Bemoras	-	2-7	-	1-2	5	-	-	-	0	5
Bob Peterson	-	0-10	-	4-5	7	-	-	-	5	4
Herb Gerecke	-	1-1	-	1-1	0	-	-	-	0	3
Max Baumgardner	-	0-2	-	0-0	0	-	-	-	2	0
James Bredar	-	0-0	-	0-0	0	-	-	-	0	0
Mack Follmer	-	0-0	-	0-0	0	-	-	-	0	0
John Marks	-	0-1	-	0-0	0	-	-	-	0	0
Jim Schuldt	-	0-0	-	0-0	0	-	-	-	0	0
TOTALS	-	**16-57**	-	**29-36**	**34**	-	-	-	**19**	**61**
Percentages		28.1	-	80.6						

Coach: Harry Combes

OKLAHOMA A&M	MIN	FG	3FG	FT	REB	A	ST	BL	PF	TP
Gale McArthur	-	7-16	-	3-4	2	-	-	-	4	17
Don Johnson	-	4-20	-	3-6	7	-	-	-	3	11
John Miller	-	2-7	-	2-3	7	-	-	-	4	6
Bob Pager	-	2-8	-	2-4	5	-	-	-	1	6
Harold Rogers	-	2-7	-	0-0	7	-	-	-	4	4
Pete Darcey	-	1-10	-	0-1	10	-	-	-	4	2
Louis Amaya	-	0-0	-	0-0	0	-	-	-	3	0
Emmett McAfee	-	0-0	-	0-0	0	-	-	-	0	0
Kendall Sheets	-	0-0	-	0-1	0	-	-	-	4	0
Gerald Stockton	-	0-3	-	0-1	0	-	-	-	3	0
Maurice Ward	-	0-0	-	0-0	0	-	-	-	1	0
TOTALS	-	**18-71**	-	**10-20**	**38**	-	-	-	**31**	**46**
Percentages		25.4	-	50.0						

Coach: Hank Iba

Officials: Ogden, Wilson

68-58

	1H	2H
Kentucky	27	41
Kansas State	29	29

NCAA FINAL 1951

KENTUCKY	MIN	FG	3FG	FT	REB	A	ST	BL	PF	TP
Bill Spivey	-	9-29	-	4-6	21	-	-	-	2	22
Cliff Hagan	-	5-6	-	0-2	4	-	-	-	5	10
Frank Ramsey	-	4-10	-	1-3	4	-	-	-	5	9
Lucian Whitaker	-	4-5	-	1-1	2	-	-	-	2	9
Shelby Linville	-	2-7	-	4-8	8	-	-	-	5	8
Bobby Watson	-	3-8	-	2-4	3	-	-	-	3	8
Lou Tsioropoulos	-	1-4	-	0-0	3	-	-	-	1	2
C.M. Newton	-	0-0	-	0-0	0	-	-	-	0	0
TOTALS	-	**28-69**	-	**12-24**	**45**	-	-	-	**23**	**68**
Percentages		40.6	-	50.0						

Coach: Adolph Rupp

KANSAS STATE	MIN	FG	3FG	FT	REB	A	ST	BL	PF	TP
Lew Hitch	-	6-15	-	1-1	9	-	-	-	3	13
Jack Stone	-	3-8	-	6-8	6	-	-	-	2	12
Ed Head	-	3-11	-	2-2	3	-	-	-	2	8
Jim Iverson	-	3-12	-	1-2	0	-	-	-	3	7
Ernie Barrett	-	2-12	-	0-2	3	-	-	-	1	4
Richard Peck	-	2-3	-	0-0	0	-	-	-	0	4
Robert Rousey	-	2-10	-	0-0	2	-	-	-	3	4
Dick Knostman	-	1-4	-	1-2	3	-	-	-	1	3
Dan Schuyler	-	1-2	-	0-0	1	-	-	-	2	2
John Gibson	-	0-2	-	1-1	1	-	-	-	5	1
Don Upson	-	0-1	-	0-0	2	-	-	-	1	0
TOTALS	-	**23-80**	-	**12-18**	**30**	-	-	-	**23**	**58**
Percentages		28.7	-	66.7						

Coach: Jack Gardner

Officials: Conway, Leith

Attendance: 15,348

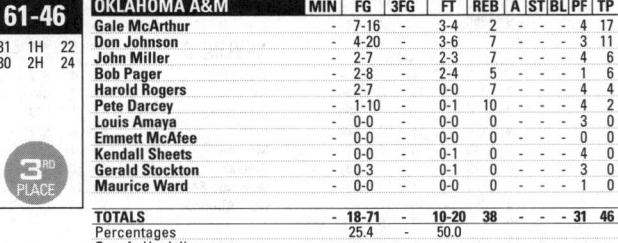

NATIONAL INVITATION TOURNAMENT (NIT)

First round: Dayton d. Lawrence Tech 77-71, Seton Hall d. Beloit 71-57, Saint Louis d. La Salle 73-61, St. Bonaventure d. Cincinnati 70-67 (2OT)

Quarterfinals: BYU d. Saint Louis 75-68, St. John's d. St. Bonaventure 60-58, Dayton d. Arizona 74-68, Seton Hall d. NC State 71-59

Semifinals: Dayton d. St. John's 69-62 (OT), BYU d. Seton Hall 69-59

Third place: St. John's d. Seton Hall 70-68 (2OT)

Championship: BYU d. Dayton 62-43

MVP: Roland Minson, BYU

1951-52: The Phog Lifts

Kansas' Clyde Lovellette had 33 points and 17 rebounds in the NCAA Final, an 80-63 win over St. John's at Seattle's Hec Edmundson Pavilion. At last coach Phog Allen had his NCAA championship. The Tournament was the first to use the Final Four format—the winners of four regional finals advancing to a single site for the national semis and the Final.

St. John's stunned pre-Tournament favorite Kentucky, 64-57, in the East Regional final. It was revenge for an 81-40 debacle in December, when Solly Walker of St. John's became the first black player to play in a game in Lexington. Adolph Rupp wrote a letter to *The Lexington Herald* urging fans to treat Walker with respect, which they did. Seattle's Johnny O'Brien became the first player to score 1,000 points in a season (1,051). With many players fighting in the Korean War, schools were given exemptions allowing them to put freshmen on varsity squads. The NCAA altered the format of games from two 20-minute halves to four 10-minute quarters. After three seasons, the 20-minute halves would be reinstated.

Major Conference Standings

BIG SEVEN	Conference			Overall		
	W	L	PCT	W	L	PCT
Kansas ⊕	11	1	.917	28	3	.903
Kansas State	10	2	.833	19	5	.792
Missouri	6	6	.500	14	10	.583
Iowa State	4	8	.333	10	11	.476
Colorado	4	8	.333	8	16	.333
Oklahoma	4	8	.333	7	17	.292
Nebraska	3	9	.250	7	17	.292

BIG TEN	Conference			Overall		
	W	L	PCT	W	L	PCT
Illinois ⊕	12	2	.857	22	4	.846
Iowa	11	3	.786	19	3	.864
Minnesota	10	4	.714	15	7	.682
Indiana	9	5	.643	16	6	.727
Michigan State	6	8	.429	13	9	.591
Ohio State	6	8	.429	8	14	.364
Wisconsin	5	9	.357	10	12	.455
Michigan	4	10	.286	7	15	.318
Northwestern	4	10	.286	7	15	.318
Purdue	3	11	.214	8	14	.364

BORDER	Conference			Overall		
	W	L	PCT	W	L	PCT
West Texas A&M	12	2	.857	19	9	.679
New Mexico State ⊕	14	4	.778	22	11	.667
Texas Tech	9	5	.643	14	10	.583
Arizona	6	8	.429	11	16	.407
Arizona State	6	8	.429	8	16	.333
Hardin-Simmons	5	9	.357	17	15	.531
Texas Western	5	9	.357	8	17	.320
Northern Arizona	1	13	.071	4	23	.148

IVY	Conference			Overall		
	W	L	PCT	W	L	PCT
Princeton ⊕	10	2	.833	16	11	.593
Penn	9	3	.750	21	8	.724
Cornell	8	4	.667	16	9	.640
Columbia	7	5	.583	12	10	.545
Yale	4	8	.333	13	14	.481
Dartmouth	4	8	.333	11	19	.367
Harvard	0	12	.000	5	17	.227

METRO NY	Conference			Overall		
	W	L	PCT	W	L	PCT
St. John's ○ □	6	0	1.000	25	6	.806
St. Francis (NY)	4	2	.667	20	8	.714
Manhattan	4	2	.667	12	9	.571
Fordham	3	3	.500	20	8	.714
NYU □	2	3	.400	18	8	.692
CCNY	1	5	.167	9	11	.450
Brooklyn	0	5	.000	9	7	.563

MID-AMERICAN	Conference			Overall		
	W	L	PCT	W	L	PCT
Miami (OH)	9	3	.750	19	6	.760
Western Michigan	9	3	.750	16	8	.667
Toledo	8	4	.667	20	11	.645
Ohio	6	6	.500	12	12	.500
Cincinnati	5	5	.500	11	16	.407
Kent State	3	7	.300	14	10	.583
Western Reserve	0	12	.000	1	23	.042

MIDDLE THREE	Conference			Overall		
	W	L	PCT	W	L	PCT
Lafayette	3	0	1.000	15	9	.625
Rutgers	1	2	.333	6	13	.316
Lehigh	1	3	.250	7	12	.368

MISSOURI VALLEY	Conference			Overall		
	W	L	PCT	W	L	PCT
Saint Louis ⊕ □	9	1	.900	23	8	.742
Oklahoma A&M	7	3	.700	19	8	.704
Tulsa	5	5	.500	14	10	.583
Detroit	4	6	.400	14	12	.538
Houston	3	7	.300	7	14	.333
Wichita State	2	8	.200	11	19	.367

SKYLINE 8	Conference			Overall		
	W	L	PCT	W	L	PCT
Wyoming ⊕	13	1	.929	28	7	.800
BYU	9	5	.643	14	10	.583
Utah State	9	5	.643	17	14	.548
Utah	8	6	.571	19	9	.679
Montana	7	7	.500	12	14	.462
Denver	6	8	.429	11	15	.423
Colorado State	3	11	.214	13	15	.464
New Mexico	1	13	.071	6	19	.240

OHIO VALLEY	Conference			Overall		
	W	L	PCT	W	L	PCT
Western Kentucky □	11	1	.900	26	5	.839
Eastern Kentucky	10	2	.833	13	11	.542
Murray State	9	3	.750	24	10	.706
Marshall	5	7	.417	15	11	.577
Morehead State	3	9	.250	11	14	.440
Tennessee Tech	2	10	.167	9	13	.409
Evansville	2	10	.167	7	20	.259

Tournament: **Western Kentucky d. Murray State 47-45**

PACIFIC COAST	Conference			Overall		
	W	L	PCT	W	L	PCT
North						
Washington	14	2	.875	25	6	.806
Idaho	9	7	.563	19	13	.594
Oregon	8	8	.500	14	16	.467
Washington State	6	10	.375	19	16	.543
Oregon State	3	13	.188	9	19	.321
South						
UCLA ⊕	8	4	.667	19	12	.613
Stanford	6	6	.500	19	9	.679
California	6	6	.500	17	13	.567
Southern California	4	8	.333	16	14	.533

Playoff: **UCLA defeated Washington 2-1** in a best of three series for the PCC title

SEC	Conference			Overall		
	W	L	PCT	W	L	PCT
Kentucky ⊕	14	0	1.000	29	3	.906
LSU	9	5	.643	17	7	.708
Vanderbilt	9	5	.643	18	9	.667
Alabama	9	5	.643	13	9	.591
Mississippi	8	6	.571	15	11	.577
Florida	7	7	.500	15	9	.625
Tennessee	7	7	.500	13	9	.591
Tulane	7	7	.500	12	12	.500
Auburn	6	8	.429	14	12	.538
Mississippi State	4	10	.286	12	11	.522
Georgia Tech	2	12	.143	7	15	.318
Georgia	2	12	.143	3	22	.120

Tournament: **Kentucky d. LSU 44-43**

SOUTHERN	Conference			Overall		
	W	L	PCT	W	L	PCT
West Virginia	15	1	.938	23	4	.852
NC State ⊕	12	2	.857	24	10	.706
Duke	13	3	.813	24	6	.800
Clemson	11	4	.733	17	7	.708
George Washington	12	6	.667	15	9	.625
Furman	9	5	.643	18	6	.750
Maryland	9	5	.643	13	9	.591
William and Mary	10	6	.625	15	13	.536
South Carolina	8	7	.533	14	10	.583
Wake Forest	7	9	.438	10	19	.345
North Carolina	8	11	.421	12	15	.444
Virginia Tech	3	10	.231	4	16	.200
Richmond	3	11	.214	7	15	.318
Washington and Lee	3	11	.214	6	21	.222
Davidson	4	15	.211	7	18	.280
VMI	2	13	.133	3	21	.125
The Citadel	1	11	.083	8	20	.286

Tournament: **NC State d. Duke 77-68**
Tournament MOP: **Dick Groat**, Duke

SOUTHWEST	Conference			Overall		
	W	L	PCT	W	L	PCT
TCU ⊕	11	1	.917	24	4	.857
Texas	8	4	.667	16	8	.667
SMU	5	7	.417	11	13	.458
Texas A&M	5	7	.417	9	15	.375
Baylor	5	7	.417	6	18	.250
Arkansas	4	8	.333	10	14	.417
Rice	4	8	.333	9	15	.375

WNY LITTLE THREE	Conference			Overall		
	W	L	PCT	W	L	PCT
St. Bonaventure □	3	1	.750	21	6	.778
Canisius	3	1	.750	15	9	.625
Niagara	0	4	.000	8	21	.276

YANKEE	Conference			Overall		
	W	L	PCT	W	L	PCT
Connecticut	6	1	.857	20	7	.741
Vermont	3	1	.750	14	6	.700
Rhode Island	6	2	.750	10	13	.435
New Hampshire	4	5	.444	11	9	.550
Maine	2	6	.250	7	12	.368
Massachusetts	0	6	.000	4	17	.190

⊕ Automatic NCAA Tournament bid ○ At-large NCAA Tournament bid □ NIT appearance ✪ Team record doesn't reflect games forfeited or vacated. For adjusted record, see p. 521.

INDEPENDENTS

	Overall W	L	Pct
Seton Hall□	25	3	.893
Holy Cross□	24	4	.857
Duquesne○□	23	4	.852
Dayton○□	28	5	.848
La Salle□	24	5	.828
Boston College	22	5	.815
Siena	24	6	.800
Louisville□	20	6	.769
Penn State○	20	6	.769
Saint Joseph's	20	7	.741
DePaul	19	8	.704
Oklahoma City○	19	8	.704
Villanova	19	8	.704
Syracuse	14	6	.700
Navy	16	7	.696
Loyola-Chicago	17	8	.680
Miami (FL)	14	8	.636
Bowling Green	17	10	.630
Notre Dame	16	10	.615
Saint Mary's (CA)	16	10	.615
Georgetown	15	10	.600

INDEPENDENTS (CONT.)

	Overall W	L	Pct
Loyola (LA)	20	14	.588
Bradley	17	12	.586
Santa Clara○	17	12	.586
Drake	13	12	.520
Butler	12	12	.500
Valparaiso	12	12	.500
Army	8	9	.471
Loyola Marymount	12	14	.462
Marquette	12	14	.462
San Francisco	11	13	.458
Virginia	11	13	.458
Colgate	10	12	.455
Pittsburgh	10	12	.455
John Carroll	11	14	.440
Muhlenberg	10	13	.435
Baldwin-Wallace	9	12	.429
Xavier	10	14	.417
Temple	9	15	.375
Bucknell	8	16	.333
Creighton	6	15	.286
Brown	5	15	.250

INDIVIDUAL LEADERS—SEASON

Scoring	CL	POS	G	FG	FT	PTS	PPG
1 **Clyde Lovellette**, Kansas	SR	C	31	352	182	886	**28.6**
2 **Dick Groat**, Duke	SR	G	30	288	204	780	**26.0**
3 **Bob Pettit**, LSU	SO	F/C	24	247	118	612	**25.5**
Chuck Darling, Iowa	SR	C	22	204	153	561	**25.5**
5 **Frank Selvy**, Furman	SO	G	24	223	145	591	**24.6**
6 **Mark Workman**, West Virginia	SR	C	25	207	163	577	**23.1**
7 **Dickie Hemric**, Wake Forest	FR	C	29	218	193	629	**21.7**
8 **Cliff Hagan**, Kentucky	JR	F/C	32	264	164	692	**21.6**
9 **John Clune**, Navy	SO	G/F	23	191	105	487	**21.2**
10 **Jay Handlan**, Washington and Lee	SR	F	27	218	134	570	**21.1**

Field Goal Pct	CL	POS	G	FG	FGA	PCT
1 **Art Spoelstra**, Western Kentucky	SO	C	31	178	345	**51.6**
2 **Gerald Rogers**, Texas Western	SR	C	25	136	270	**50.4**
3 **Norm Swanson**, Detroit	SR	C	26	172	342	**50.3**
4 **Karl Klinar**, VMI	SO	C	21	98	199	**49.2**
5 **Tom Marshall**, Western Kentucky	SO	F	24	189	385	**49.1**

Minimum: 90 made

Free Throw Pct	CL	POS	G	FT	FTA	PCT
1 **Sy Chadroff**, Miami (FL)	SR	F	22	99	123	**80.5**
2 **Bob Kenney**, Kansas	SR	G	27	110	137	**80.3**
3 **Drew Turner**, Saint Mary's (CA)	SR	F	27	81	101	**80.2**
4 **Tommy Bartlett**, Tennessee	SR	G	21	93	116	**80.2**
5 **Russ Rerucha**, Colorado State	JR	F	28	76	95	**80.0**
Harry Moore, West Virginia	SR	G/F	26	68	85	**80.0**

Minimum: 65 made

Assists Per Game	CL	POS	G	AST	APG
1 **Tom O'Toole**, Boston College	SR	G	27	213	**7.9**
2 **Dick Groat**, Duke	SR	G	30	229	**7.6**
3 **Malcolm McLean**, Davidson	SR	G	25	187	**7.5**
4 **Larry Friedman**, Muhlenberg	SO	G/F	23	168	**7.3**
5 **Roger Chadwick**, Cornell	SR	G	25	171	**6.8**

Rebounds Per Game	CL	POS	G	REB	RPG
1 **Bill Hannon**, Army	SO	C	17	355	**20.9**
2 **Walter Dukes**, Seton Hall	JR	C	26	513	**19.7**
3 **Ernie Beck**, Penn	JR	C	29	551	**19.0**
4 **Elton Tuttle**, Creighton	SO	F	21	396	**18.9**
5 **Bill Chambers**, William and Mary	JR	F	28	509	**18.2**

INDIVIDUAL LEADERS—GAME

Points	CL	POS	OPP	DATE	PTS
1 **Bob Pettit**, LSU	[illegible]	F/C	Georgia	J18	**50**
2 **Frank Selvy**, Furman	SO	G	Wofford	F20	**49**
3 **Dick Groat**, Duke	SR	[illegible]	North Carolina	F29	**48**
4 **Sy Chadroff**, Miami (FL)	SR	F	Rollins	F14	**47**
5 **Dick Groat**, Duke	SR	G	George Washington	F2	**46**
Mark Workman, West Virginia	SR	C	VMI	F1	**46**
Bill Mlkvy, Temple	SR	F	Muhlenberg	F20	**46**

Free Throws Made	CL	POS	OPP	DATE	FT	FTA	PCT
1 **Dick Walls**, Miami (OH)	JR	C	Cincinnati	M4	**18**	23	78.3
2 **Cliff Hagan**, Kentucky	JR	F/C	Mississippi	[illegible]	**17**	18	94.4
Ernie Beck, Penn	JR	C	Harvard	[illegible]	**17**	19	89.5
Mark Workman, West Virginia	SR	C	Bethany (WV)	[illegible]	[illegible]	19	89.5
5 **Chuck Darling**, Iowa	SR	C	Minnesota	J19	[illegible]	21	76.2

TEAM LEADERS—SEASON

Scoring Offense	G	W-L	PTS	PPG
1 **Kentucky**	32	29-3	2,635	**82.3**
2 **West Virginia**	27	23-4	2,172	**80.4**
3 **Louisville**	26	20-6	2,080	**80.0**
4 **Duke**	30	24-6	2,320	**77.3**
5 **Western Kentucky**	31	26-5	2,388	**77.0**

Field Goal Pct	G	W-L	FG	FGA	PCT
1 **Boston College**	27	22-5	787	1,893	**41.6**
2 **Western Kentucky**	31	26-5	959	2,339	**41.0**
3 **Seton Hall**	28	25-3	783	1,941	**40.3**
4 **Stanford**	28	19-9	743	1,889	**39.3**
5 **Kansas**	31	28-3	748	1,906	**39.2**

Free Throw Pct	G	W-L	FT	FTA	PCT
1 **Kansas**	31	28-3	491	707	**69.4**
2 **Penn**	29	21-8	454	654	**69.4**
3 **Kansas State**	24	19-5	473	684	**69.2**
4 **South Carolina**	24	14-10	400	582	**68.7**
5 **Syracuse**	20	14-6	430	626	**68.7**

Scoring Defense	G	W-L	OPP PTS	OPP PPG
1 **Oklahoma A&M**	27	19-8	1,228	**45.5**
2 **Oklahoma City**	27	19-8	1,287	**47.7**
3 **Texas A&M**	24	9-15	1,159	**48.3**
4 **TCU**	28	24-4	1,395	**49.8**
5 **New Mexico State**	33	22-11	1,642	**49.8**

CONSENSUS ALL-AMERICAS

FIRST TEAM

PLAYER	CL	POS	HT	SCHOOL	RPG	PPG
Chuck Darling	SR	C	6-8	Iowa	N/A	25.5
Rod Fletcher	SR	G	6-4	Illinois	N/A	11.1
Dick Groat	SR	G	6-0	Duke	7.6	26.0
Cliff Hagan	JR	F/C	6-4	Kentucky	16.5	21.6
Clyde Lovellette	SR	C	6-9	Kansas	12.8	28.6

SECOND TEAM

PLAYER	CL	POS	HT	SCHOOL	RPG	PPG
Bob Houbregs	JR	C	6-7	Washington	10.6	18.6
Don Meineke	SR	C	6-7	Dayton	11.8	21.1
Johnny O'Brien	JR	C	5-9	Seattle	N/A	28.4*
Mark Workman	SR	C	6-8	West Virginia	17.5	23.1
Bob Zawoluk	SR	C	6-7	St. John's	12.8	18.9

Selectors: AP, Collier's (Basketball Coaches), International News Service, Look Magazine, UP

* O'Brien wasn't eligible for scoring title because Seattle wasn't considered a major college

Poll Progression

Week of Dec 6

UP	School
1	**Kentucky** (0-0)
2	**Illinois** (0-0)
3	**Washington** (1-1)
4	**Oklahoma A&M** (0-0)
5	**St. John's** (1-0)
6	**Saint Louis** (0-0)
7	**NC State** (3-0)
8	**Kansas** (1-0)
9	**Wyoming** (1-0)
10	**Kansas State** (2-0)
11	**Indiana** (1-0)
12	**BYU** (1-2)
13	**UCLA** (1-0)
14	**Dayton** (3-0)
15	**Seton Hall** (3-0)
16	**La Salle** (3-0)
17	**Villanova** (0-0)
18	**Columbia** (2-0)
19	**Holy Cross** (0-0)
20	**Texas A&M** (0-1)

Week of Dec 10

AP	UP	School	
1	1	**Kentucky** (1-0)	
2	3	**St. John's** (3-0)	
3	2	**Illinois** (1-0)	
4	6	**Saint Louis** (1-0)	
5	5	**Kansas State** (3-0)	
6	4	**Washington** (1-1)	
7	17	**Seton Hall** (4-0)	
8	8	**Kansas** (2-0)	
9	12	**La Salle** (4-0)	
10	9	**NC State** (3-0)	
11	11	**Indiana** (2-0)	
12	—	**Duke** (4-0)	Ⓐ
13	7	**Oklahoma A&M** (1-0)	
14	14	**Notre Dame** (3-0)	
15	13	**Villanova** (2-0)	
16	—	**Stanford** (3-0)	
17	14	**Louisville** (3-0)	
18	—	**Vanderbilt** (3-0)	
19	—	**Eastern Kentucky** (4-0)	
20	18	**NYU** (7-0)	
—	10	**Wyoming** (3-0)	
—	16	**UCLA** (1-2)	
—	18	**Western Kentucky** (4-0)	
—	20	**Dayton** (4-0)	

Week of Dec 17

AP	UP	School	AP↓↑
1	2	**St. John's** (5-0)	↑1
2	3	**Kentucky** (2-1)	↓1
3	1	**Illinois** (2-0)	
4	6	**Saint Louis** (3-1)	
5	7	**Kansas State** (5-1)	
6	8	**Indiana** (4-0)	↑5
7	4	**Kansas** (5-0)	↑1
8	5	**Washington** (5-1)	↓2
9	10	**NC State** (4-1)	↑1
10	15	**Seton Hall** (5-0)	↓3
11	14	**NYU** (10-0)	↑9
12	17	**La Salle** (5-0)	↓3
13	9	**Oklahoma A&M** (4-0)	
14	13	**Wyoming** (4-1)	⤴
15	17	**Minnesota** (2-2)	⤴
16	16	**Western Kentucky** (6-0)	⤴
17	—	**Holy Cross** (3-0)	⤴
18	19	**Villanova** (3-0)	↓3
19	—	**Duke** (5-1)	↓7
20	12	**Notre Dame** (4-0)	↓6
—	11	**Utah** (7-1)	
—	20	**Iowa** (3-0)	

Week of Dec 25

AP	UP	School	AP↓↑
1	2	**Kentucky** (4-1)	Ⓑ ↑1
2	1	**Illinois** (5-0)	↑1
3	4	**Washington** (7-1)	↑5
4	3	**Kansas** (7-0)	↑3
5	5	**Indiana** (5-0)	↑1
6	7	**NYU** (11-0)	↑5
7	8	**St. John's** (6-1)	Ⓑ ↓6
8	6	**Kansas State** (6-2)	↓3
9	12	**Notre Dame** (6-0)	↑11
10	17	**Seton Hall** (6-0)	
11	17	**Western Kentucky** (8-0)	↑5
12	9	**Saint Louis** (4-2)	↓8
13	13	**Stanford** (9-1)	⤴
14	—	**Villanova** (5-0)	↑4
15	10	**Utah** (9-1)	⤴
16	—	**UCLA** (5-2)	⤴
17	20	**La Salle** (6-0)	↓5
18	—	**Murray State** (10-0)	⤴
19	16	**NC State** (5-2)	↓10
20	15	**Syracuse** (5-0)	⤴
—	11	**Oklahoma A&M** (5-1)	⤵
—	14	**Iowa** (3-0)	
—	19	**Wyoming** (6-2)	⤵
—	20	**St. Bonaventure** (4-0)	

Week of Jan 1

AP	UP	School	AP↓↑
1	3	**Kansas** (10-0)	Ⓒ ↑3
2	1	**Illinois** (6-0)	
3	5	**Washington** (10-1)	
4	2	**Kentucky** (6-2)	↓3
5	4	**Indiana** (7-0)	
6	7	**NYU** (12-0)	
7	6	**Saint Louis** (7-2)	↑5
8	9	**St. John's** (8-1)	↓1
9	8	**Kansas State** (8-3)	↓1
10	16	**St. Bonaventure** (6-0)	⤴
11	14	**Seton Hall** (7-0)	↓1
12	13	**Iowa** (7-0)	⤴
13	22	**La Salle** (7-0)	↑4
14	15	**Notre Dame** (7-1)	↓5
15	17	**Oklahoma City** (7-1)	⤴
16	—	**Murray State** (10-0)	↑2
17	10	**NC State** (8-2)	↑2
18	11	**Utah** (11-2)	↓3
19	22	**Syracuse** (5-0)	↑1
20	—	**Michigan State** (6-0)	⤴
—	12	**Villanonva** (5-1)	
—	18	**Minnesota** (4-3)	
—	18	**Duquesne** (5-0)	
—	18	**Louisville** (7-1)	
—	18	**Arkansas** (5-6)	
—	24	**Stanford** (11-1)	⤵
—	26	**Tulane** (5-6)	
—	27	**Texas A&M** (3-6)	

Week of Jan 8

AP	UP	School	AP↓↑
1	2	**Kansas** (11-0)	
2	1	**Illinois** (8-0)	
3	3	**Kentucky** (8-2)	↑1
4	4	**Indiana** (8-0)	↑1
5	5	**Saint Louis** (9-2)	↑2
6	6	**Washington** (10-2)	↓3
7	7	**Kansas State** (9-3)	Ⓓ ↑2
8	12	**St. Bonaventure** (7-0)	↑2
9	16	**Seton Hall** (10-0)	↑2
10	10	**Iowa** (8-0)	↑2
11	20	**West Virginia** (8-1)	⤴
12	8	**St. John's** (9-1)	↓4
13	9	**NYU** (13-1)	↓7
14	15	**Syracuse** (6-0)	↑5
15	13	**Louisville** (9-2)	⤴
16	—	**Duquesne** (8-0)	⤴
17	—	**Siena** (12-2)	⤴
18	—	**Oklahoma City** (7-2)	↓3
19	—	**Michigan State** (6-0)	↑1
20	—	**Dayton** (10-2)	⤴
—	11	**NC State** (9-3)	⤵
—	14	**Utah** (13-3)	⤵
—	17	**Minnesota** (5-4)	
—	18	**Notre Dame** (7-3)	⤵
—	19	**Oklahoma A&M** (8-2)	

Week of Jan 15

AP	UP	School	AP↓↑
1	2	**Kansas** (12-0)	
2	1	**Illinois** (10-0)	
3	3	**Kentucky** (10-2)	
4	6	**Iowa** (10-0)	↑6
5	5	**Saint Louis** (10-3)	
6	9	**St. Bonaventure** (9-0)	↑2
7	10	**Duquesne** (10-0)	↑9
8	4	**Washington** (12-2)	↓2
9	7	**Kansas State** (10-3)	↓2
10	20	**West Virginia** (9-1)	↑1
11	—	**Siena** (12-2)	↑6
12	13	**Seton Hall** (12-1)	↓3
13	17	**Louisville** (11-2)	↑2
14	8	**Indiana** (8-2)	↓10
15	16	**La Salle** (10-1)	⤴
16	19	**TCU** (14-1)	⤴
17	12	**NC State** (11-3)	⤴
18	—	**Oklahoma City** (9-3)	
19	—	**Dayton** (12-2)	↑1
20	—	**Holy Cross** (8-1)	⤴
—	11	**St. John's** (10-2)	⤵
—	14	**Oklahoma A&M** (10-2)	
—	15	**NYU** (15-1)	⤵
—	18	**Wyoming** (12-3)	

Week of Jan 22

AP	UP	School	AP↓↑
1	1	**Illinois** (11-0)	↑1
2	2	**Kansas** (13-0)	↓1
3	3	**Kentucky** (12-2)	
4	4	**Iowa** (12-0)	
5	8	**St. Bonaventure** (10-0)	↑1
6	5	**Washington** (14-2)	↑2
7	6	**Kansas State** (12-3)	↑2
8	7	**Saint Louis** (11-4)	↓3
9	17	**West Virginia** (11-1)	↑1
10	9	**Duquesne** (11-0)	↓3
11	12	**Holy Cross** (11-2)	↑9
12	14	**TCU** (14-1)	↑3
13	15	**Seton Hall** (14-1)	↓1
14	13	**Louisville** (14-2)	↓1
15	16	**St. John's** (12-2)	⤴
16	—	**Dayton** (14-2)	↑3
17	—	**Utah** (16-4)	⤴
18	—	**La Salle** (12-1)	↓3
19	—	**Siena** (12-3)	↓8
20	10	**Indiana** (9-3)	↓6
—	11	**Oklahoma A&M** (11-2)	
—	17	**NC State** (11-5)	⤵
—	19	**NYU** (16-1)	
—	19	**Villanova** (9-3)	

Week of Jan 29

AP	UP	School	AP↓↑
1	2	**Kentucky** (14-2)	Ⓔ ↑2
2	3	**Kansas State** (13-3)	↑5
3	1	**Illinois** (11-1)	↓2
4	4	**Kansas** (13-1)	↓2
5	5	**St. Bonaventure** (12-4)	
6	5	**Saint Louis** (12-4)	↑2
7	9	**Duquesne** (11-0)	↑3
8	8	**Iowa** (12-1)	↓4
9	7	**Washington** (15-3)	↓3
10	12	**West Virginia** (12-1)	↓1
11	11	**Seton Hall** (15-1)	↑2
12	14	**Louisville** (15-2)	↑2
13	10	**Indiana** (10-3)	↑7
14	—	**Dayton** (16-2)	↑2
15	18	**St. John's** (13-2)	
16	16	**Oklahoma City** (10-4)	⤴
17	—	**Holy Cross** (11-2)	↓6
18	—	**Siena** (13-3)	↑1
19	14	**DePaul** (15-4)	⤴
20	—	**Fordham** (12-2)	⤴
—	13	**NC State** (13-5)	
—	17	**Wyoming** (16-4)	
—	19	**La Salle** (13-2)	⤵
—	19	**Notre Dame** (11-4)	

Week of Feb 5

AP	UP	School	AP↓↑
1	1	**Kentucky** (18-2)	
2	3	**Kansas State** (13-3)	
3	2	**Illinois** (13-1)	
4	5	**St. Bonaventure** (13-0)	↑1
5	8	**Duquesne** (15-0)	↑2
6	6	**Kansas** (14-2)	↓2
7	4	**Saint Louis** (15-5)	↓1
8	7	**Washington** (17-3)	↑1
9	9	**Iowa** (13-1)	↓1
10	12	**St. John's** (13-2)	↑5
11	20	**Dayton** (17-2)	↑3
12	14	**West Virginia** (14-2)	↓2
13	12	**Louisville** (16-2)	↓1
14	—	**Penn State** (13-1)	⤴
15	18	**Oklahoma City** (12-4)	↑1
16	10	**Oklahoma A&M** (12-4)	⤴
17	11	**Seton Hall** (17-1)	↓6
18	19	**Indiana** (10-4)	↓5
19	—	**La Salle** (14-2)	⤴
20	20	**Western Kentucky** (15-3)	⤴
—	15	**Wyoming** (19-4)	
—	16	**NC State** (16-7)	
—	17	**DePaul** (16-4)	⤵

Week of Feb 12

AP	UP	School	AP↓↑
1	1	**Kentucky** (21-2)	
2	2	**Kansas State** (15-3)	
3	6	**Duquesne** (16-0)	↑2
4	5	**St. Bonaventure** (16-0)	
5	4	**Iowa** (14-1)	↑4
6	3	**Illinois** (13-2)	↓3
7	7	**Saint Louis** (16-6)	
8	9	**Washington** (19-3)	
9	8	**Kansas** (15-2)	↓3
10	10	**St. John's** (17-2)	
11	13	**Dayton** (18-2)	
12	14	**Seton Hall** (18-1)	↑5
13	17	**Oklahoma City** (13-4)	↑2
14	17	**West Virginia** (15-2)	↓2
15	15	**Louisville** (17-3)	↓2
16	—	**Siena** (14-3)	⤴
17	—	**Penn State** (15-1)	↓3
18	20	**DePaul** (18-4)	⤴
19	—	**Holy Cross** (14-2)	⤴
20	11	**Indiana** (10-4)	↓2
—	12	**Wyoming** (20-4)	
—	16	**NC State** (16-7)	
—	19	**NYU** (17-1)	

Week of Feb 19

AP	UP	School	AP↓↑
1	1	**Kentucky** (22-2)	
2	2	**Kansas State** (16-3)	
3	4	**Duquesne** (17-0)	
4	5	**Iowa** (16-1)	↑1
5	3	**Illinois** (15-2)	↑1
6	6	**Washington** (21-3)	↑2
7	7	**Kansas** (17-2)	↑2
8	9	**St. John's** (18-2)	↑2
9	8	**Saint Louis** (17-6)	↓2
10	10	**St. Bonaventure** (17-2)	↓6
11	14	**Dayton** (21-2)	
12	13	**West Virginia** (19-2)	↑2
13	—	**Penn State** (17-1)	↑4
14	12	**Seton Hall** (21-1)	↓2
15	14	**Louisville** (18-4)	
16	—	**Seattle** (26-5)	⤴
17	—	**Holy Cross** (17-2)	↑2
18	—	**Siena** (16-3)	↓2
19	11	**Wyoming** (21-4)	⤴
20	—	**La Salle** (18-4)	⤴
—	14	**Indiana** (12-5)	⤵
—	17	**TCU** (17-3)	
—	18	**NC State** (17-8)	
—	18	**NYU** (18-1)	
—	20	**Villanova** (14-7)	

Week of Feb 26

AP	UP	School	AP↓↑
1	1	**Kentucky** (24-2)	
2	2	**Illinois** (17-2)	↑3
3	3	**Kansas State** (16-3)	↓1
4	4	**Duquesne** (19-1)	↓1
5	6	**Saint Louis** (19-6)	↑4
6	7	**Washington** (22-4)	
7	9	**Iowa** (18-2)	↓3
8	5	**Kansas** (19-2)	↓1
9	8	**St. John's** (20-3)	↓1
10	12	**West Virginia** (21-2)	↑2
11	16	**Dayton** (23-2)	
12	11	**St. Bonaventure** (18-3)	↓2
13	15	**Louisville** (19-4)	↑2
14	13	**Seton Hall** (22-2)	
15	—	**Duke** (20-5)	⤴
16	10	**Wyoming** (23-5)	↑3
17	—	**Holy Cross** (19-2)	
18	16	**Western Kentucky** (23-4)	⤴
19	—	**Villanova** (16-7)	⤴
20	—	**Siena** (18-4)	↓2
—	14	**Indiana** (13-6)	
—	18	**La Salle** (18-5)	⤵
—	19	**Minnesota** (15-6)	
—	19	**NYU** (19-1)	

Week of Mar 4

AP	UP	School	AP↓↑
1	1	**Kentucky** (28-2)	
2	2	**Illinois** (19-2)	
3	3	**Kansas State** (18-4)	
4	5	**Duquesne** (21-1)	
5	6	**Saint Louis** (20-7)	
6	7	**Washington** (24-4)	
7	8	**Iowa** (19-3)	
8	4	**Kansas** (20-2)	
9	18	**West Virginia** (22-3)	↑1
10	9	**St. John's** (21-3)	↓1
11	14	**Dayton** (24-2)	
12	—	**Duke** (22-5)	↑3
13	18	**Holy Cross** (21-3)	↑4
14	12	**Seton Hall** (25-2)	
15	11	**St. Bonaventure** (19-3)	↓3
16	10	**Wyoming** (23-6)	
17	13	**Louisville** (20-5)	↓4
18	—	**Seattle** (29-7)	⤴
19	—	**UCLA** (17-9)	⤴
20	—	**Texas State** (24-0)	⤴
—	14	**TCU** (21-3)	
—	16	**Western Kentucky** (24-4)	⤵
—	16	**Villanova** (17-8)	⤵
—	20	**Indiana** (15-6)	

Final Poll

UP	School
1	**Kentucky** (28-2) Ⓕ
2	**Illinois** (19-3)
3	**Kansas** (21-2)
4	**Duquesne** (21-1)
5	**Washington** (25-6)
6	**Kansas State** (18-5)
7	**Saint Louis** (21-7)
8	**Iowa** (19-3)
9	**St. John's** (22-3)
10	**Wyoming** (27-6)
11	**St. Bonaventure** (19-5)
12	**Seton Hall** (25-3)
13	**TCU** (21-3)
14	**West Virginia** (23-4)
15	**Holy Cross** (24-3)
16	**Western Kentucky** (26-4)
17	**La Salle** (21-5)
18	**Dayton** (25-2)
19	**Louisville** (21-5)
19	**UCLA** (19-10)
19	**Indiana** (16-6)

Ⓐ Dick Groat enters his senior year at Duke as one of the nation's top pro prospects. He does not disappoint, averaging 26.0 ppg. He will turn pro—not in basketball, but in baseball. In 1960, as shortstop and captain of the World Series-champion Pittsburgh Pirates, Groat is named NL MVP.

Ⓑ On Dec. 17, the day Kentucky drops to the No. 2 spot, the Wildcats stun St. John's, 81-40—still the biggest margin of defeat for a No. 1 team. On Christmas Eve, it's Kentucky's turn to be shocked. Seven-foot center Bill Spivey leaves the team because his name surfaces in the ongoing point-shaving investigation. Spivey hopes to be cleared in time to play in the SEC tournament.

Ⓒ Kansas becomes No. 1 behind 6'9" Clyde Lovellette, who will lead the country with 28.6 ppg but still doesn't make New York-based *Look* magazine's All-America team—prompting Phog Allen to observe, "New Yorkers are taller and fairer [in appearance] than the Chinese, but not nearly as progressive."

Ⓓ Arizona's 81-game home winning streak is snapped by Kansas State, 76-57.

Ⓔ Kentucky reclaims the top spot in the AP poll, thanks in part to Bill Spivey's replacement, the 6'4" hook shot specialist Cliff Hagan.

Ⓕ Kentucky's Athletics Board suspends Bill Spivey's eligibility, ending his college career. Persisting in his claim of innocence, Spivey is tried in January 1953 on perjury charges. The trial ends in a hung jury, but he is barred from playing in the NBA. Instead, Spivey plays in the ABL and on various barnstorming teams.

1952 NCAA Tournament

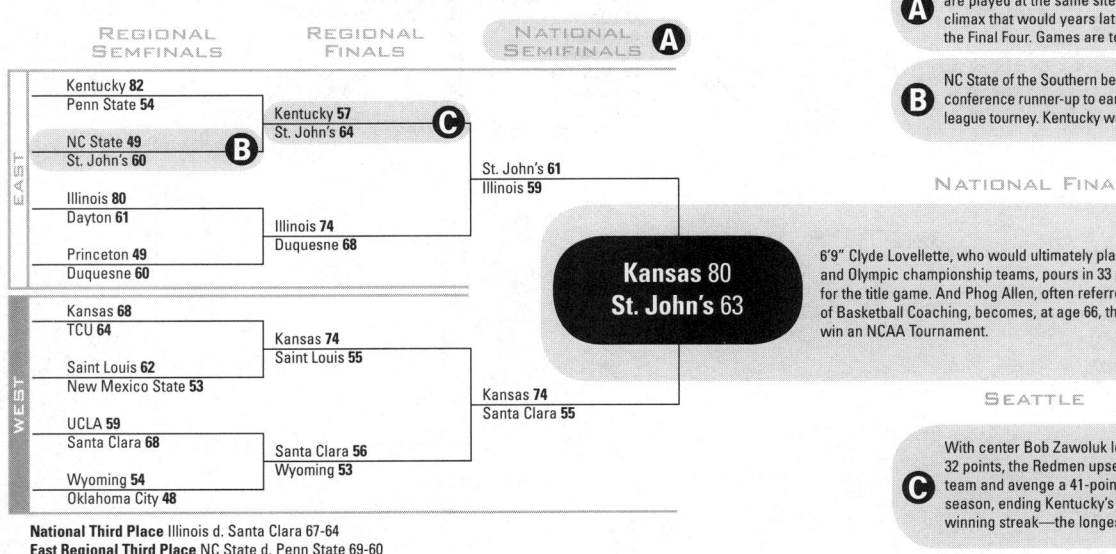

Regional Semifinals — Regional Finals — National Semifinals Ⓐ

EAST

Regional Semifinals:
- Kentucky **82**, Penn State **54**
- NC State **49**, St. John's **60** Ⓑ
- Illinois **80**, Dayton **61**
- Princeton **49**, Duquesne **60**

Regional Finals:
- Kentucky **57**, St. John's **64** Ⓒ
- Illinois **74**, Duquesne **68**

National Semifinal:
- St. John's **61**, Illinois **59**

WEST

Regional Semifinals:
- Kansas **68**, TCU **64**
- Saint Louis **62**, New Mexico State **53**
- UCLA **59**, Santa Clara **68**
- Wyoming **54**, Oklahoma City **48**

Regional Finals:
- Kansas **74**, Saint Louis **55**
- Santa Clara **56**, Wyoming **53**

National Semifinal:
- Kansas **74**, Santa Clara **55**

National Final

Kansas 80
St. John's 63

6'9" Clyde Lovellette, who would ultimately play on NCAA, NBA and Olympic championship teams, pours in 33 points—a record for the title game. And Phog Allen, often referred to as the Father of Basketball Coaching, becomes, at age 66, the oldest coach to win an NCAA Tournament.

Seattle

National Third Place Illinois d. Santa Clara 67-64
East Regional Third Place NC State d. Penn State 69-60
East Regional Third Place Dayton d. Princeton 77-61
West Regional Third Place TCU d. New Mexico State 61-44
West Regional Third Place Oklahoma City d. UCLA 55-53 Ⓓ

Ⓐ For the first time, both semifinals and the Final are played at the same site, in a three-game climax that would years later become known as the Final Four. Games are televised regionally.

Ⓑ NC State of the Southern becomes the second conference runner-up to earn a bid by winning its league tourney. Kentucky was the first, in 1942.

Ⓒ With center Bob Zawoluk leading the way with 32 points, the Redmen upset the nation's No. 1 team and avenge a 41-point loss earlier in the season, ending Kentucky's 11-game Tourney winning streak—the longest at the time.

Ⓓ Down by two with :02 left, UCLA coach John Wooden tries to call timeout. No referee sees or hears him and time expires. Wooden is now 0–4 in Tournament games.

Tournament Leaders

INDIVIDUAL LEADERS

Scoring	CL	POS	G	PTS	PPG
1 **Clyde Lovellette**, Kansas	SR	C	4	141	35.3
2 **Bob Zawoluk**, St. John's	SR	C	4	88	22.0
Jesse Arnelle, Penn State	FR	F/C	2	44	22.0
Don Meineke, Dayton	SR	C	2	44	22.0
5 **Cliff Hagan**, Kentucky	JR	F/C	2	42	21.0
6 **Jim Tucker**, Duquesne	SO	C	2	40	20.0
7 **Dick Ricketts**, Duquesne	FR	F	2	36	18.0
8 **Chuck Grigsby**, Dayton	SR	F	2	35	17.5
Jim Tackett, New Mexico State	SR	F	2	35	17.5
10 **Lou McKenna**, Saint Louis	SR	G	2	33	16.5

Minimum: 2 games

Field Goals Per Game	CL	POS	G	FG	FGPG
1 **Clyde Lovellette**, Kansas	SR	C	4	53	13.3
2 **Cliff Hagan**, Kentucky	JR	F/C	2	18	9.0
3 **Bob Zawoluk**, St. John's	SR	C	4	33	8.3
4 **Jesse Arnelle**, Penn State	FR	F/C	2	16	8.0
5 **Jim Tucker**, Duquesne	SO	C	2	15	7.5

Minimum: 8 made

Free Throw Pct	CL	POS	G	FT	FTA	PCT
1 **Ken Sears**, Santa Clara	FR	F/C	4	10	10	100.0
Jim Tucker, Duquesne	SO	C	2	10	10	100.0
3 **Ron Livingston**, UCLA	SO	G	2	9	10	90.0
4 **Jim Walsh**, St. John's	SO	F	4	6	7	85.7
Cliff Hagan, Kentucky	JR	F/C	2	6	7	85.7

Minimum: 5 made

TEAM LEADERS

Scoring	G	PTS	PPG
1 **Kansas**	4	296	74.0
2 **Illinois**	4	280	70.0
3 **Kentucky**	2	139	69.5
4 **Dayton**	2	138	69.0
5 **Duquesne**	2	128	64.0
6 **TCU**	2	125	62.5
7 **St. John's**	4	248	62.0
8 **Santa Clara**	4	243	60.8
9 **NC State**	2	118	59.0
10 **Saint Louis**	2	117	58.5

Minimum: 2 games

FT Pct	G	FT	FTA	PCT
1 **Duquesne**	2	30	38	79.0
2 **Dayton**	2	36	50	72.0
3 **Kansas**	4	78	112	69.6
4 **UCLA**	2	34	49	69.4
5 **Oklahoma City**	2	27	39	69.2

Minimum: 2 games

Fg Per Game	G	FG	FGPG
1 **Kentucky**	2	56	28.0
2 **Kansas**	4	109	27.3
3 **Dayton**	2	51	25.5
4 **Illinois**	4	100	25.0
5 **Duquesne**	2	49	24.5
TCU	2	49	24.5

ALL-TOURNAMENT TEAM

PLAYER	CL	POS	HT	SCHOOL	PPG
Clyde Lovellette*	SR	C	6-9	Kansas	35.3
James Bredar	JR	G	5-11	Illinois	12.8
Dean Kelley	JR	G	5-11	Kansas	7.8
John Kerr	SO	C	6-8	Illinois	13.5
Ron MacGilvray	SR	G	6-1	St. John's	6.5
Bob Zawoluk	SR	C	6-7	St. John's	22.0

ALL-REGIONAL TEAMS

East (Raleigh, NC)

PLAYER	CL	POS	HT	SCHOOL	PPG
Jesse Arnelle	FR	F/C	6-5	Penn State	22.0
Cliff Hagan	JR	F/C	6-4	Kentucky	21.0
Ron MacGilvray	SR	G	6-1	St. John's	6.0
Jack McMahon	SR	G	6-1	St. John's	14.5
Bob Zawoluk	SR	C	6-7	St. John's	22.0

East (Chicago)

PLAYER	CL	POS	HT	SCHOOL	PPG
N/A					

West (Corvallis, OR)

PLAYER	CL	POS	HT	SCHOOL	PPG
Ron Livingston	SO	G	5-10	UCLA	13.5
Don Penwell	SR	C	6-7	Oklahoma City	14.5
George Radovich	SR	G	6-0	Wyoming	15.5
Herbert Schoenstein	SO	C	6-11	Santa Clara	15.0
Ken Sears	FR	F/C	6-9	Santa Clara	11.5
Arnold Short	SO	G	6-2	Oklahoma City	15.0

West (Kansas City, MO)

PLAYER	CL	POS	HT	SCHOOL	PPG
Bob Kenney	SR	G	6-2	Kansas	11.5
Clyde Lovellette	SR	C	6-9	Kansas	37.5
Lou McKenna	SR	G	6-0	Saint Louis	16.5
Ray Steiner	SR	G	5-10	Saint Louis	6.0
Jim Tackett	SR	F	6-2	New Mexico State	17.5

* Most outstanding player

1952 NCAA TOURNAMENT BOX SCORES

82-54 (SWEET 16)

	Kentucky	Penn State
1H	43	25
2H	39	29

KENTUCKY	MIN	FG	3FG	FT	REB	A	ST	BL	PF	TP
Cliff Hagan	-	9	-	2-2	-	-	-	-	3	20
Shelby Linville	-	6	-	0-0	-	-	-	-	1	12
Frank Ramsey	-	4	-	3-3	-	-	-	-	3	11
Lucian Whitaker	-	5	-	0-0	-	-	-	-	5	10
Bobby Watson	-	4	-	0-1	-	-	-	-	0	8
Lou Tsioropoulos	-	2	-	3-6	-	-	-	-	5	7
Gayle Rose	-	2	-	2-2	-	-	-	-	0	6
Bill Evans	-	2	-	1-2	-	-	-	-	2	5
Gene Neff	-	1	-	0-0	-	-	-	-	0	2
Willie Rouse	-	0	-	1-2	-	-	-	-	2	1
Ronald Clark	-	0	-	0-2	-	-	-	-	0	0
TOTALS	**-**	**35**	**-**	**12-20**	**-**	**-**	**-**	**-**	**21**	**82**
Percentages				60.0						

Coach: Adolph Rupp

PENN STATE	MIN	FG	3FG	FT	REB	A	ST	BL	PF	TP
Jesse Arnelle	-	8	-	6-10	-	-	-	-	5	22
Herm Sledzik	-	4	-	4-7	-	-	-	-	5	12
Jack Sherry	-	4	-	2-4	-	-	-	-	3	10
Ed Haag	-	1	-	1-2	-	-	-	-	1	3
Jay McMahan	-	1	-	0-0	-	-	-	-	2	2
Ron Weidenhammer	-	1	-	0-1	-	-	-	-	1	2
Hardy Williams	-	0	-	2-5	-	-	-	-	0	2
Joe Piorkowski	-	0	-	1-1	-	-	-	-	3	1
TOTALS	**-**	**19**	**-**	**16-30**	**-**	**-**	**-**	**-**	**20**	**54**
Percentages				53.3						

Coach: Elmer Gross

Attendance: 11,000

60-49 (SWEET 16)

	St. John's	NC State
1H	28	25
2H	32	24

ST. JOHN'S	MIN	FG	3FG	FT	REB	A	ST	BL	PF	TP
Bob Zawoluk	-	5	-	2-2	-	-	-	-	3	12
Dick Duckett	-	5	-	1-4	-	-	-	-	3	11
Jack McMahon	-	3	-	5-8	-	-	-	-	5	11
Jim Davis	-	5	-	0-2	-	-	-	-	4	10
Ron MacGilvray	-	1	-	5-6	-	-	-	-	3	7
Jim Walsh	-	1	-	4-4	-	-	-	-	3	6
Solly Walker	-	1	-	0-0	-	-	-	-	4	2
Frank Giancontieri	-	0	-	1-2	-	-	-	-	0	1
Jim McMorrow	-	0	-	0-0	-	-	-	-	0	0
Carl Peterson	-	0	-	0-0	-	-	-	-	0	0
TOTALS	**-**	**21**	**-**	**18-28**	**-**	**-**	**-**	**-**	**25**	**60**
Percentages				64.3						

Coach: Frank McGuire

NC STATE	MIN	FG	3FG	FT	REB	A	ST	BL	PF	TP
Dave Gotkin	-	5	-	3-3	-	-	-	-	1	13
Lee Terrill	-	4	-	0-1	-	-	-	-	4	8
Dick Tyler	-	3	-	2-3	-	-	-	-	5	8
Mel Thompson	-	3	-	0-1	-	-	-	-	3	6
Bobby Speight	-	1	-	3-3	-	-	-	-	3	5
Dan Knapp	-	1	-	1-2	-	-	-	-	1	3
Bill Kukoy	-	1	-	1-2	-	-	-	-	5	3
Bob Cook	-	1	-	0-0	-	-	-	-	2	2
Paul Brandenburg	-	0	-	1-2	-	-	-	-	0	1
Herb Applebaum	-	0	-	0-0	-	-	-	-	1	0
Bob Goss	-	0	-	0-0	-	-	-	-	1	0
Bernie Yurin	-	0	-	0-2	-	-	-	-	1	0
TOTALS	**-**	**19**	**-**	**11-19**	**-**	**-**	**-**	**-**	**27**	**49**
Percentages				57.9						

Coach: Everett Case

80-61 (SWEET 16)

	Illinois	Dayton
1H	36	37
2H	44	24

ILLINOIS	MIN	FG	3FG	FT	REB	A	ST	BL	PF	TP
James Bredar	-	5	-	9-11	-	-	-	-	2	19
John Kerr	-	5	-	3-9	-	-	-	-	2	13
Rod Fletcher	-	4	-	4-7	-	-	-	-	2	12
Irv Bemoras	-	4	-	3-3	-	-	-	-	4	11
Clive Follmer	-	4	-	3-5	-	-	-	-	1	11
Bob Peterson	-	1	-	4-5	-	-	-	-	5	6
Ed Makovsky	-	0	-	4-4	-	-	-	-	2	4
Mack Follmer	-	0	-	2-3	-	-	-	-	0	2
Max Hooper	-	1	-	0-0	-	-	-	-	0	2
Dick Christiansen	-	0	-	0-0	-	-	-	-	0	0
Herb Gerecke	-	0	-	0-0	-	-	-	-	1	0
Jim Wright	-	0	-	0-0	-	-	-	-	1	0
TOTALS	**-**	**24**	**-**	**32-47**	**-**	**-**	**-**	**-**	**20**	**80**
Percentages				68.1						

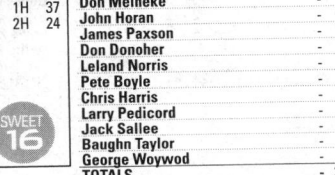

Coach: Harry Combes

DAYTON	MIN	FG	3FG	FT	REB	A	ST	BL	PF	TP
Chuck Grigsby	-	8	-	5-6	-	-	-	-	5	21
Don Meineke	-	6	-	6-8	-	-	-	-	5	18
John Horan	-	4	-	0-0	-	-	-	-	5	8
James Paxson	-	3	-	0-1	-	-	-	-	2	6
Don Donoher	-	2	-	0-0	-	-	-	-	3	4
Leland Norris	-	1	-	1-1	-	-	-	-	5	3
Pete Boyle	-	0	-	1-2	-	-	-	-	5	1
Chris Harris	-	0	-	0-0	-	-	-	-	3	0
Larry Pedicord	-	0	-	0-0	-	-	-	-	1	0
Jack Sallee	-	0	-	0-0	-	-	-	-	1	0
Baughn Taylor	-	0	-	0-0	-	-	-	-	2	0
George Woywod	-	0	-	0-0	-	-	-	-	4	0
TOTALS	**-**	**24**	**-**	**13-18**	**-**	**-**	**-**	**-**	**41**	**61**
Percentages				72.2						

Coach: Tom S. Blackburn

60-49 (SWEET 16)

	Duquesne	Princeton
1H	28	24
2H	32	25

DUQUESNE	MIN	FG	3FG	FT	REB	A	ST	BL	PF	TP
Jim Kennedy	-	8	-	0-0	-	-	-	-	3	16
Dick Ricketts	-	6	-	2-4	-	-	-	-	2	14
Jim Tucker	-	4	-	3-3	-	-	-	-	3	11
Carl Pacacha	-	3	-	4-5	-	-	-	-	0	10
Hal Cerra	-	2	-	0-0	-	-	-	-	0	4
Steve Garay	-	1	-	2-2	-	-	-	-	1	4
Al Bailey	-	0	-	1-1	-	-	-	-	4	1
TOTALS	**-**	**24**	**-**	**12-15**	**-**	**-**	**-**	**-**	**13**	**60**
Percentages				80.0						

Coach: Dudey Moore

PRINCETON	MIN	FG	3FG	FT	REB	A	ST	BL	PF	TP
Charles Devoe	-	9	-	5-8	-	-	-	-	2	23
Philip Zuravleff	-	5	-	1-2	-	-	-	-	5	11
David Sisler	-	3	-	1-1	-	-	-	-	2	7
Foster Cooper	-	1	-	2-3	-	-	-	-	4	4
Frederic Tritschler	-	1	-	2-2	-	-	-	-	2	4
John Emery	-	0	-	0-0	-	-	-	-	0	0
TOTALS	**-**	**19**	**-**	**11-16**	**-**	**-**	**-**	**-**	**15**	**49**
Percentages				68.8						

Coach: Frankin "Cappy" Cappon

68-64 (SWEET 16)

	Kansas	TCU
1H	34	24
2H	34	40

KANSAS	MIN	FG	3FG	FT	REB	A	ST	BL	PF	TP
Clyde Lovellette	-	13-33	-	5-7	-	-	-	-	4	31
Bob Kenney	-	7-12	-	3-7	-	-	-	-	2	17
Charlie Hoag	-	2-8	-	0-1	-	-	-	-	0	4
Dean Kelley	-	1-4	-	2-2	-	-	-	-	2	4
John Keller	-	1-7	-	1-2	-	-	-	-	1	3
William Lienhard	-	1-3	-	1-1	-	-	-	-	5	3
B.H. Born	-	1-1	-	0-0	-	-	-	-	2	2
William Hougland	-	1-1	-	0-0	-	-	-	-	1	2
Dean Smith	-	1-1	-	0-0	-	-	-	-	2	2
Larry Davenport	-	0-2	-	0-0	-	-	-	-	0	0
Bill Heitholt	-	0-3	-	0-1	-	-	-	-	0	0
Allen Kelley	-	0-0	-	0-1	-	-	-	-	0	0
TOTALS	**-**	**28-75**	**-**	**12-22**	**-**	**-**	**-**	**-**	**19**	**68**
Percentages		37.3		54.5						

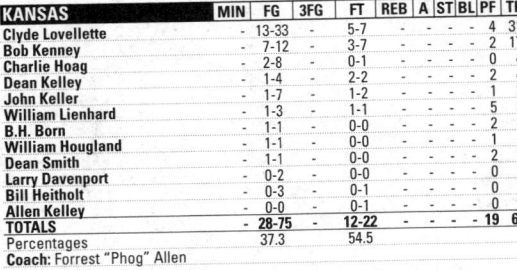

Coach: Forrest "Phog" Allen

TCU	MIN	FG	3FG	FT	REB	A	ST	BL	PF	TP
Henry Ohlen	-	8-20	-	4-6	-	-	-	-	2	20
John Ethridge	-	4-13	-	2-2	-	-	-	-	1	10
Ted Reynolds	-	3-12	-	2-6	-	-	-	-	1	8
George Mcleod	-	3-7	-	1-1	-	-	-	-	5	7
Johnny Swaim	-	3-5	-	1-1	-	-	-	-	2	7
Jim Knox	-	2-5	-	0-0	-	-	-	-	1	4
Harvey Fromme	-	1-7	-	1-3	-	-	-	-	5	3
J. Bryan Kilpatrick	-	1-7	-	1-1	-	-	-	-	5	3
Richard Allen	-	1-2	-	0-2	-	-	-	-	2	2
John Campbell	-	0-0	-	0-0	-	-	-	-	0	0
TOTALS	**-**	**26-78**	**-**	**12-22**	**-**	**-**	**-**	**-**	**24**	**64**
Percentages		33.3		54.5						

Coach: Buster Brannon

62-53 (SWEET 16)

	Saint Louis	New Mexico State
1H	35	26
2H	27	27

SAINT LOUIS	MIN	FG	3FG	FT	REB	A	ST	BL	PF	TP
Lou McKenna	-	9	-	4-6	-	-	-	-	3	22
Ray Steiner	-	4	-	2-3	-	-	-	-	2	10
Dick Boushka	-	2	-	4-5	-	-	-	-	2	8
Tom Lillis	-	3	-	1-2	-	-	-	-	5	7
Jack Shockley	-	2	-	1-1	-	-	-	-	1	5
Bob Koch	-	1	-	2-3	-	-	-	-	5	4
Jerry Koch	-	1	-	0-0	-	-	-	-	3	2
Fred Kovar	-	1	-	0-1	-	-	-	-	3	2
Ray Sonnenberg	-	1	-	0-1	-	-	-	-	4	2
Bob Klostermeyer	-	0	-	0-0	-	-	-	-	0	0
Helm Lillis	-	0	-	0-0	-	-	-	-	1	0
Pat Partington	-	0	-	0-0	-	-	-	-	0	0
TOTALS	**-**	**24**	**-**	**14-22**	**-**	**-**	**-**	**-**	**29**	**62**
Percentages				63.6						

Coach: Eddie Hickey

NEW MEXICO STATE	MIN	FG	3FG	FT	REB	A	ST	BL	PF	TP
Jim Tackett	-	8	-	5-9	-	-	-	-	2	21
Mike Svilar	-	3	-	3-4	-	-	-	-	5	9
Jim Crouch	-	2	-	2-2	-	-	-	-	3	6
Bob Priddy	-	2	-	2-4	-	-	-	-	3	6
Charles Clement	-	2	-	1-1	-	-	-	-	5	5
Jim Blevins	-	1	-	1-2	-	-	-	-	5	3
Bill Dunn	-	1	-	0-0	-	-	-	-	1	2
Bo Coats	-	0	-	1-1	-	-	-	-	1	1
Ray Apodaca	-	0	-	0-0	-	-	-	-	0	0
TOTALS	**-**	**19**	**-**	**15-23**	**-**	**-**	**-**	**-**	**25**	**53**
Percentages				65.2						

Coach: George McCarty

Santa Clara 68, UCLA 59 — Sweet 16

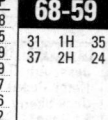

	1H	2H
Santa Clara	31	37
UCLA	35	24

SANTA CLARA	MIN	FG	3FG	FT	REB	A	ST	BL	PF	TP
Herb Schoenstein	-	7-16	-	4-8	11	1	-	-	4	18
Jim Young	-	7-16	-	1-2	5	2	-	-	1	15
Dick Garibaldi	-	4-10	-	1-4	9	4	-	-	2	9
Ken Sears	-	3-12	-	3-3	11	3	-	-	4	9
Bob Peters	-	3-7	-	1-2	7	0	-	-	5	7
Dal Brock	-	3-11	-	0-1	4	4	-	-	2	6
Don Benedetti	-	1-5	-	0-1	2	0	-	-	0	2
Dick Soares	-	1-3	-	0-0	0	0	-	-	2	2
TOTALS	-	29-80	-	10-21	49	14	-	-	20	68
Percentages		36.2		47.6						

Coach: Bob Feerick

UCLA	MIN	FG	3FG	FT	REB	A	ST	BL	PF	TP
Ron Livingston	-	4-16	-	6-6	4	3	-	-	1	14
Ron Bane	-	3-6	-	7-8	2	0	-	-	1	13
Mike Hibler	-	3-8	-	2-4	8	0	-	-	5	8
Don Bragg	-	3-10	-	1-1	11	0	-	-	4	7
John Moore	-	2-7	-	2-2	3	0	-	-	5	6
Don Johnson	-	2-16	-	1-1	4	3	-	-	2	5
Jerry Norman	-	2-12	-	0-0	6	2	-	-	2	4
Mark Costello	-	1-1	-	0-0	1	0	-	-	0	2
Jack Davidson	-	0-1	-	0-0	0	0	-	-	1	0
Jerry Evans	-	0-0	-	0-0	0	0	-	-	0	0
Barry Porter	-	0-6	-	0-0	2	1	-	-	0	0
Bobby Pounds	-	0-2	-	0-0	0	0	-	-	1	0
TOTALS	-	20-85	-	19-22	41	9	-	-	22	59
Percentages		23.5		86.4						

Coach: John Wooden

Technicals: Santa Clara (Soares), UCLA (Norman, Livingston)

Wyoming 54, Oklahoma City 48 — Sweet 16

	1H	2H
Wyoming	29	25
Oklahoma City	21	27

WYOMING	MIN	FG	3FG	FT	REB	A	ST	BL	PF	TP
George Radovich	-	4	-	5-6	-	-	-	-	2	13
Ron Rivers	-	4	-	3-4	-	-	-	-	2	11
Leroy Esau	-	4	-	1-1	-	-	-	-	2	9
Pete Fowler	-	4	-	0-0	-	-	-	-	2	8
John Hughes	-	1	-	5-6	-	-	-	-	3	7
Morris Samuelson	-	2	-	0-0	-	-	-	-	4	4
Richard Haag	-	1	-	0-1	-	-	-	-	0	2
Robert Burns	-	0	-	0-0	-	-	-	-	0	0
Nick Eliopulos	-	0	-	0-0	-	-	-	-	0	0
TOTALS	-	20	-	14-18	-	-	-	-	15	54
Percentages				77.8						

Coach: Everett Shelton

OKLAHOMA CITY	MIN	FG	3FG	FT	REB	A	ST	BL	PF	TP
Don Penwell	-	8	-	2-4	-	-	-	-	3	18
Andy Likens	-	4	-	2-2	-	-	-	-	3	10
Arnold Short	-	3	-	2-3	-	-	-	-	0	8
Ken Rose	-	3	-	0-0	-	-	-	-	3	6
Doyle Mayfield	-	2	-	0-2	-	-	-	-	3	4
Bill Couts	-	1	-	0-1	-	-	-	-	3	2
Jim Thompson	-	0	-	0-0	-	-	-	-	3	0
TOTALS	-	21	-	6-12	-	-	-	-	18	48
Percentages				50.0						

Coach: Doyle Parrack

St. John's 64, Kentucky 57 — Elite 8

	1H	2H
St. John's	34	30
Kentucky	28	29

ST. JOHN'S	MIN	FG	3FG	FT	REB	A	ST	BL	PF	TP
Bob Zawoluk	-	12	-	8-9	-	-	-	-	4	32
Jack McMahon	-	8	-	2-5	-	-	-	-	2	18
Ron MacGilvray	-	1	-	3-4	-	-	-	-	1	5
Jim Walsh	-	1	-	2-2	-	-	-	-	5	4
Dick Duckett	-	1	-	1-3	-	-	-	-	5	3
Jim Davis	-	1	-	0-1	-	-	-	-	2	2
Solly Walker	-	0	-	0-1	-	-	-	-	4	0
TOTALS	-	24	-	16-25	-	-	-	-	23	64
Percentages				64.0						

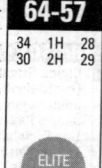

Coach: Frank McGuire

KENTUCKY	MIN	FG	3FG	FT	REB	A	ST	BL	PF	TP
Cliff Hagan	-	9	-	4-5	-	-	-	-	5	22
Frank Ramsey	-	5	-	4-6	-	-	-	-	5	14
Lucian Whitaker	-	3	-	3-4	-	-	-	-	3	9
Shelby Linville	-	1	-	2-3	-	-	-	-	3	4
Bobby Watson	-	1	-	2-2	-	-	-	-	3	4
Bill Evans	-	1	-	0-0	-	-	-	-	5	2
Gayle Rose	-	1	-	0-0	-	-	-	-	3	2
Willie Rouse	-	0	-	0-0	-	-	-	-	0	0
Lou Tsioropoulos	-	0	-	0-0	-	-	-	-	5	0
TOTALS	-	21	-	15-20	-	-	-	-	32	57
Percentages				75.0						

Coach: Adolph Rupp

Attendance: 11,200

Illinois 74, Duquesne 68 — Elite 8

	1H	2H
Illinois	37	37
Duquesne	34	34

ILLINOIS	MIN	FG	3FG	FT	REB	A	ST	BL	PF	TP
Irv Bemoras	-	7	-	2-3	-	-	-	-	4	16
James Bredar	-	8	-	0-1	-	-	-	-	1	16
Rod Fletcher	-	5	-	5-6	-	-	-	-	5	15
Clive Follmer	-	2	-	8-9	-	-	-	-	4	12
Bob Peterson	-	4	-	0-2	-	-	-	-	3	8
John Kerr	-	3	-	1-1	-	-	-	-	3	7
Ed Makovsky	-	0	-	0-0	-	-	-	-	1	0
TOTALS	-	29	-	16-22	-	-	-	-	21	74
Percentages				72.7						

Coach: Harry Combes

DUQUESNE	MIN	FG	3FG	FT	REB	A	ST	BL	PF	TP
Jim Tucker	-	11	-	7-7	-	-	-	-	5	29
Dick Ricketts	-	7	-	8-9	-	-	-	-	4	22
Jim Kennedy	-	3	-	2-2	-	-	-	-	5	8
Hal Cerra	-	2	-	0-2	-	-	-	-	5	4
John Nosworthy	-	1	-	1-1	-	-	-	-	0	3
Carl Pacacha	-	1	-	0-1	-	-	-	-	3	2
Al Bailey	-	0	-	0-1	-	-	-	-	1	0
Milo Ringer	-	0	-	0-0	-	-	-	-	3	0
TOTALS	-	25	-	18-23	-	-	-	-	26	68
Percentages				78.3						

Coach: Dudey Moore

Kansas 74, Saint Louis 55 — Elite 8

	1H	2H
Kansas	27	47
Saint Louis	27	28

KANSAS	MIN	FG	3FG	FT	REB	A	ST	BL	PF	TP
Clyde Lovellette	-	16	-	12-14	-	-	-	-	3	44
Dean Kelley	-	4	-	2-3	-	-	-	-	5	10
Charlie Hoag	-	2	-	3-3	-	-	-	-	2	7
Bob Kenney	-	2	-	2-3	-	-	-	-	4	6
William Hougland	-	2	-	1-1	-	-	-	-	1	5
B.H. Born	-	0	-	1-1	-	-	-	-	0	1
John Keller	-	0	-	1-2	-	-	-	-	1	1
Larry Davenport	-	0	-	0-0	-	-	-	-	0	0
Bill Heitholt	-	0	-	0-0	-	-	-	-	0	0
William Lienhard	-	0	-	0-0	-	-	-	-	1	0
Dean Smith	-	0	-	0-0	-	-	-	-	0	0
Lavannes Squires	-	0	-	0-0	-	-	-	-	0	0
TOTALS	-	26	-	22-27	-	-	-	-	17	74
Percentages				81.5						

Coach: Forrest "Phog" Allen

SAINT LOUIS	MIN	FG	3FG	FT	REB	A	ST	BL	PF	TP
Tom Lillis	-	7	-	0-2	-	-	-	-	5	14
Lou McKenna	-	4	-	3-3	-	-	-	-	4	11
Fred Kovar	-	3	-	4-5	-	-	-	-	2	10
Ray Sonnenberg	-	3	-	2-3	-	-	-	-	2	8
Jerry Koch	-	2	-	0-0	-	-	-	-	2	4
Bob Koch	-	1	-	1-1	-	-	-	-	5	3
Pat Partington	-	1	-	0-0	-	-	-	-	0	2
Ray Steiner	-	1	-	0-1	-	-	-	-	3	2
Dick Boushka	-	0	-	1-1	-	-	-	-	2	1
Bob Klostermeyer	-	0	-	0-0	-	-	-	-	1	0
Helm Lillis	-	0	-	0-0	-	-	-	-	0	0
Jack Shockley	-	0	-	0-0	-	-	-	-	1	0
TOTALS	-	22	-	11-16	-	-	-	-	27	55
Percentages				68.8						

Coach: Eddie Hickey

Santa Clara 56, Wyoming 53 — Elite 8

	1H	2H
Santa Clara	24	32
Wyoming	27	26

SANTA CLARA	MIN	FG	3FG	FT	REB	A	ST	BL	PF	TP
Ken Sears	-	5	-	4-4	-	-	-	-	5	14
Jim Young	-	5	-	4-5	-	-	-	-	2	14
Herb Schoenstein	-	5	-	2-4	-	-	-	-	1	12
Dick Garibaldi	-	2	-	1-2	-	-	-	-	3	5
Don Benedetti	-	2	-	0-1	-	-	-	-	2	4
Dick Soares	-	1	-	2-2	-	-	-	-	1	4
Bob Peters	-	1	-	1-1	-	-	-	-	5	3
Dal Brock	-	0	-	0-3	-	-	-	-	3	0
TOTALS	-	21	-	14-22	-	-	-	-	22	56
Percentages				63.6						

Coach: Bob Feerick

WYOMING	MIN	FG	3FG	FT	REB	A	ST	BL	PF	TP
George Radovich	-	7	-	4-5	-	-	-	-	2	18
Leroy Esau	-	6	-	1-3	-	-	-	-	5	13
Ron Rivers	-	2	-	2-6	-	-	-	-	1	6
Morris Samuelson	-	1	-	3-3	-	-	-	-	3	5
Robert Burns	-	1	-	2-2	-	-	-	-	3	4
Richard Haag	-	2	-	0-0	-	-	-	-	5	4
Pete Fowler	-	1	-	0-1	-	-	-	-	4	2
John Hughes	-	0	-	1-2	-	-	-	-	2	1
Nick Eliopulos	-	0	-	0-0	-	-	-	-	0	0
LeRoy Rutz	-	0	-	0-0	-	-	-	-	1	0
TOTALS	-	20	-	13-22	-	-	-	-	26	53
Percentages				59.1						

Coach: Everett Shelton

61-59 — 1H: St. John's 33, Illinois 27; 2H: St. John's 28, Illinois 32 — FINAL 4

ST. JOHN'S	MIN	FG	3FG	FT	REB	A	ST	BL	PF	TP
Bob Zawoluk	-	9	-	6-7	-	-	-	-	4	24
Dick Duckett	-	4	-	3-4	-	-	-	-	5	11
Jack McMahon	-	3	-	3-3	-	-	-	-	3	9
Ron MacGilvray	-	2	-	2-3	-	-	-	-	2	6
Solly Walker	-	2	-	1-1	-	-	-	-	1	5
Jim Walsh	-	2	-	0-1	-	-	-	-	4	4
Jim Davis	-	1	-	0-1	-	-	-	-	3	2
Carl Peterson	-	0	-	0-0	-	-	-	-	0	0
TOTALS	-	**23**	-	**15-20**	-	-	-	-	**22**	**61**
Percentages				75.0						

Coach: Frank McGuire

ILLINOIS	MIN	FG	3FG	FT	REB	A	ST	BL	PF	TP
James Bredar	-	7	-	0-1	-	-	-	-	1	14
Rod Fletcher	-	5	-	4-7	-	-	-	-	3	14
Clive Follmer	-	4	-	2-4	-	-	-	-	3	10
John Kerr	-	3	-	2-5	-	-	-	-	1	8
Herb Gerecke	-	3	-	0-1	-	-	-	-	3	6
Bob Peterson	-	2	-	0-3	-	-	-	-	4	4
Irv Bemoras	-	1	-	1-3	-	-	-	-	5	3
Jim Wright	-	0	-	0-0	-	-	-	-	2	0
TOTALS	-	**25**	-	**9-24**	-	-	-	-	**22**	**59**
Percentages				37.5						

Coach: Harry Combes

74-55 — 1H: Kansas 38, Santa Clara 25; 2H: Kansas 36, Santa Clara 30 — FINAL 4

KANSAS	MIN	FG	3FG	FT	REB	A	ST	BL	PF	TP
Clyde Lovellette	-	12-22	-	9-12	-	-	-	-	3	33
Charlie Hoag	-	4-5	-	2-2	-	-	-	-	0	10
Dean Kelley	-	4-9	-	2-4	-	-	-	-	0	10
Bob Kenney	-	3-11	-	1-1	-	-	-	-	0	7
B.H. Born	-	1-1	-	2-3	-	-	-	-	1	4
Bill Heitholt	-	2-4	-	0-1	-	-	-	-	4	4
John Keller	-	1-1	-	2-2	-	-	-	-	2	4
Larry Davenport	-	0-2	-	2-3	-	-	-	-	1	2
Allen Kelley	-	0-0	-	0-0	-	-	-	-	0	0
William Lienhard	-	0-1	-	0-0	-	-	-	-	1	0
Dean Smith	-	0-0	-	0-0	-	-	-	-	0	0
TOTALS	-	**27-56**	-	**20-28**	-	-	-	-	**12**	**74**
Percentages				71.4						

Coach: Forrest "Phog" Allen

SANTA CLARA	MIN	FG	3FG	FT	REB	A	ST	BL	PF	TP
Dick Soares	-	7-12	-	2-2	-	-	-	-	3	16
Herb Schoenstein	-	6-18	-	1-1	-	-	-	-	4	13
Jim Young	-	3-9	-	2-3	-	-	-	-	1	8
Dal Brock	-	3-6	-	1-1	-	-	-	-	2	7
Gary Gatzert	-	1-2	-	1-2	-	-	-	-	2	3
Bob Peters	-	1-4	-	1-1	-	-	-	-	1	3
Don Benedetti	-	1-6	-	0-0	-	-	-	-	1	2
Dick Garibaldi	-	1-5	-	0-0	-	-	-	-	4	2
Ken Sears	-	0-3	-	1-1	-	-	-	-	5	1
Dick Simoni	-	0-0	-	0-1	-	-	-	-	0	0
TOTALS	-	**23-65**	-	**9-12**	-	-	-	-	**23**	**55**
Percentages				75.0						

Coach: Bob Feerick

67-64 — 1H: Illinois 32, Santa Clara 28; 2H: Illinois 35, Santa Clara 36 — 3RD PLACE

ILLINOIS	MIN	FG	3FG	FT	REB	A	ST	BL	PF	TP
John Kerr	-	10	-	6-7	-	-	-	-	3	26
Clive Follmer	-	6	-	5-5	-	-	-	-	1	17
Herb Gerecke	-	2	-	3-4	-	-	-	-	1	7
Bob Peterson	-	1	-	3-5	-	-	-	-	0	5
Rod Fletcher	-	1	-	2-6	-	-	-	-	4	4
Irv Bemoras	-	0	-	3-4	-	-	-	-	0	3
Max Hooper	-	1	-	1-1	-	-	-	-	3	3
James Bredar	-	1	-	0-0	-	-	-	-	5	2
Jim Wright	-	0	-	0-0	-	-	-	-	0	0
TOTALS	-	**22**	-	**23-32**	-	-	-	-	**17**	**67**
Percentages				71.9						

Coach: Harry Combes

SANTA CLARA	MIN	FG	3FG	FT	REB	A	ST	BL	PF	TP
Jim Young	-	6	-	6-6	-	-	-	-	4	18
Bob Peters	-	4	-	5-7	-	-	-	-	2	13
Ken Sears	-	4	-	2-2	-	-	-	-	4	10
Herb Schoenstein	-	2	-	4-4	-	-	-	-	3	8
Dal Brock	-	2	-	1-1	-	-	-	-	2	5
Gary Gatzert	-	1	-	2-2	-	-	-	-	4	4
Dick Soares	-	2	-	0-0	-	-	-	-	2	4
Don Benedetti	-	1	-	0-0	-	-	-	-	0	2
Dick Garibaldi	-	0	-	0-0	-	-	-	-	0	0
TOTALS	-	**22**	-	**20-22**	-	-	-	-	**21**	**64**
Percentages				90.9						

Coach: Bob Feerick

80-63 — 1H: Kansas 41, St. John's 27; 2H: Kansas 39, St. John's 36 — NCAA FINAL 1952

KANSAS	MIN	FG	3FG	FT	REB	A	ST	BL	PF	TP
Clyde Lovellette	-	12-25	-	9-11	17	-	-	-	4	33
Bob Kenney	-	4-11	-	4-6	4	-	-	-	2	12
William Lienhard	-	5-8	-	2-2	4	-	-	-	4	12
Charlie Hoag	-	2-6	-	5-7	4	-	-	-	5	9
Dean Kelley	-	2-5	-	3-6	3	-	-	-	5	7
William Hougland	-	2-5	-	1-3	6	-	-	-	2	5
John Keller	-	1-1	-	0-0	4	-	-	-	2	2
B.H. Born	-	0-0	-	0-0	0	-	-	-	0	0
Larry Davenport	-	0-0	-	0-0	0	-	-	-	1	0
Allen Kelley	-	0-2	-	0-0	1	-	-	-	0	0
Dean Smith	-	0-0	-	0-0	0	-	-	-	0	0
TOTALS	-	**28-63**	-	**24-35**	**43**	-	-	-	**25**	**80**
Percentages		44.4		68.6						

Coach: Forrest "Phog" Allen

ST. JOHN'S	MIN	FG	3FG	FT	REB	A	ST	BL	PF	TP
Bob Zawoluk	-	7-12	-	6-11	9	-	-	-	5	20
Jack McMahon	-	6-12	-	1-4	2	-	-	-	4	13
Ron MacGilvray	-	3-8	-	2-5	10	-	-	-	3	8
Dick Duckett	-	2-5	-	2-2	2	-	-	-	4	6
Jim Walsh	-	3-6	-	0-0	4	-	-	-	3	6
Jim Davis	-	1-4	-	2-3	2	-	-	-	4	4
Philip Sagona	-	2-2	-	0-0	0	-	-	-	5	4
Jim McMorrow	-	1-3	-	0-0	0	-	-	-	3	2
Frank Giancontieri	-	0-0	-	0-2	1	-	-	-	0	0
Carl Peterson	-	0-1	-	0-0	0	-	-	-	0	0
Solly Walker	-	0-2	-	0-0	2	-	-	-	4	0
TOTALS	-	**25-55**	-	**13-27**	**32**	-	-	-	**35**	**63**
Percentages		45.5		48.1						

Coach: Frank McGuire

Officials: Eisenstein, Ogden
Attendance: 11,302

National Invitation Tournament (NIT)

First round: Dayton d. NYU 81-66, Western Kentucky d. Louisville 62-59, La Salle d. Seton Hall 80-76, Holy Cross d. Seattle, 77-72
Quarterfinals: St. Bonaventure d. Western Kentucky 70-69, La Salle d. St. John's 51-45, Duquesne d. Holy Cross 78-68, Dayton d. Saint Louis 68-58
Semifinals: La Salle d. Duquesne 59-46, Dayton d. St. Bonaventure 69-62,
Third place: St. Bonaventure d. Duquesne 48-34
Championship: La Salle d. Dayton 75-64
MVP: Tom Gola, La Salle & Norm Grekin, La Salle

1952-53: IU Gets No. 2

Indiana was close to perfect, achieving a record of 23–3 with its three losses coming by a total of just five points. After trouncing LSU in the national semifinals, 80-67, the Hoosiers won their last game by a single point—a Bobby Leonard free throw with :27 remaining—over defending champion Kansas, 69-68, for their second NCAA title, at Kansas City's Municipal Auditorium. The NCAA field was expanded from 16 to 22 teams, and one of those was Lebanon Valley (Pa.). With only 425 students, it was the smallest school ever to compete in the Tournament. The Flying Dutchmen didn't have a player taller than 6'1", but the so-called Seven Dwarfs trounced Fordham, 80-67, in the first round.

The NCAA began to define intercollegiate competition as taking place between varsity teams representing four-year schools that grant degrees—thus eliminating junior colleges, freshman squads, military base teams, and AAU teams from the NCAA record book. It also continued to exclude what are known today as historically black colleges and universities. Teams were no longer allowed to waive free throws and take the ball out of bounds instead.

Major Conference Standings

BIG SEVEN

	Conference			Overall		
	W	L	Pct	W	L	Pct
Kansas⊛	10	2	.833	19	6	.760
Kansas State	9	3	.750	17	4	.810
Missouri	6	6	.500	11	9	.550
Iowa State	5	7	.417	10	11	.476
Oklahoma	5	7	.417	8	13	.381
Nebraska	4	8	.333	9	11	.450
Colorado	3	9	.250	10	11	.476

BIG TEN

	Conference			Overall		
	W	L	Pct	W	L	Pct
Indiana⊛	17	1	.944	23	3	.885
Illinois	14	4	.778	18	4	.818
Minnesota	11	7	.611	14	8	.636
Michigan State	11	7	.611	13	9	.591
Wisconsin	10	8	.556	13	9	.591
Iowa	9	9	.500	12	10	.545
Ohio State	7	11	.389	10	12	.455
Northwestern	5	13	.278	6	16	.273
Michigan	3	15	.167	6	16	.273
Purdue	3	15	.167	4	18	.182

BORDER

	Conference			Overall		
	W	L	Pct	W	L	Pct
Hardin-Simmons⊛	11	3	.786	19	12	.613
Arizona	11	3	.786	13	11	.542
Arizona State	10	4	.714	12	7	.632
Texas Tech	9	5	.643	12	10	.545
West Texas A&M	5	9	.357	8	13	.381
New Mexico State	5	9	.357	7	17	.292
Northern Arizona	3	11	.214	5	18	.217
Texas Western	3	11	.214	5	21	.192

CBA

	Conference			Overall		
	W	L	Pct	W	L	Pct
Santa Clara○	6	2	.750	20	7	.741
San Francisco	6	2	.750	10	11	.476
San Jose State	4	4	.500	15	8	.652
Saint Mary's (CA)	4	4	.500	9	11	.450
Pacific	0	8	.000	2	18	.100

IVY

	Conference			Overall		
	W	L	Pct	W	L	Pct
Penn⊛	10	2	.833	22	5	.815
Columbia	8	4	.667	17	6	.739
Cornell	6	6	.500	9	12	.429
Yale	6	6	.500	10	15	.400
Dartmouth	5	7	.417	12	14	.462
Princeton	5	7	.417	9	14	.391
Harvard	2	10	.167	7	16	.304

METRO NY

	Conference			Overall		
	W	L	Pct	W	L	Pct
Manhattan□	6	0	1.000	20	6	.769
St. John's□	5	1	.833	17	6	.739
Fordham○	5	1	.833	19	8	.704
St. Francis (NY)	2	3	.400	20	7	.741
NYU	1	3	.250	9	11	.450
CCNY	1	5	.167	10	6	.625
Brooklyn	0	5	.000	6	11	.353

MID-AMERICAN

	Conference			Overall		
	W	L	Pct	W	L	Pct
Miami (OH)⊛	10	2	.833	17	6	.739
Toledo	9	3	.750	16	7	.696
Cincinnati	9	3	.750	11	13	.458
Western Michigan	6	6	.500	12	9	.571
Ohio	4	8	.333	9	13	.409
Kent State	3	9	.250	7	15	.318
Western Reserve	1	11	.083	5	17	.227

MISSOURI VALLEY

	Conference			Overall		
	W	L	Pct	W	L	Pct
Oklahoma A&M⊛	8	2	.800	23	7	.767
Tulsa□	5	5	.500	15	10	.600
Saint Louis□	5	5	.500	16	11	.593
Houston	5	5	.500	9	13	.409
Detroit	4	6	.400	12	14	.462
Wichita State	3	7	.300	16	11	.593

SKYLINE 8

	Conference			Overall		
	W	L	Pct	W	L	Pct
Wyoming⊛	12	2	.857	20	10	.667
BYU□	11	3	.786	22	8	.733
Utah State	7	7	.500	17	13	.567
Montana	6	8	.429	14	11	.560
Colorado State	5	9	.357	12	14	.462
New Mexico	5	9	.357	10	14	.417
Utah	5	9	.357	10	14	.417
Denver	5	9	.357	9	16	.360

OHIO VALLEY

	Conference			Overall		
	W	L	Pct	W	L	Pct
Eastern Kentucky○	9	1	.900	16	9	.640
Western Kentucky□	8	2	.800	25	6	.806
Murray State	7	3	.700	18	9	.667
Tennessee Tech	3	7	.300	14	11	.560
Morehead State	3	7	.300	13	12	.520
Middle Tennessee St.	0	10	.000	7	16	.304

Tournament: **Western Kentucky d. Eastern Kentucky 70-60**

PACIFIC COAST

	Conference			Overall		
	W	L	Pct	W	L	Pct
North						
Washington⊛	15	1	.938	28	3	.903
Idaho	8	8	.500	14	11	.560
Oregon	8	8	.500	14	14	.500
Oregon State	6	10	.375	11	18	.379
Washington State	3	13	.188	7	27	.206
South						
California	9	3	.750	15	10	.600
Southern California	7	5	.583	17	5	.773
UCLA	6	6	.500	16	8	.667
Stanford	2	10	.167	6	17	.261

Playoff: **Washington defeated California 2-0** in a best of three series for the title

SEC

	Conference			Overall		
	W	L	Pct	W	L	Pct
LSU⊛	13	0	1.000	22	3	.880
Tulane	9	4	.692	12	6	.667
Florida	8	5	.615	13	6	.684
Tennessee	7	6	.538	13	8	.619
Auburn	6	7	.462	13	8	.619
Alabama	6	7	.462	12	9	.571
Mississippi	5	8	.385	14	11	.560
Vanderbilt	5	8	.385	10	9	.526
Mississippi State	5	8	.385	9	10	.474
Georgia Tech	4	9	.308	5	17	.227
Georgia	3	10	.231	7	18	.280

SOUTHERN

	Conference			Overall		
	W	L	Pct	W	L	Pct
NC State	13	3	.813	26	6	.813
Wake Forest⊛	12	3	.800	19	6	.760
Maryland	12	3	.800	15	8	.652
West Virginia	11	3	.786	19	7	.731
Furman	10	3	.769	21	6	.778
Duke	12	4	.750	17	8	.680
Richmond	13	5	.722	20	7	.741
North Carolina	15	6	.714	17	10	.630
George Washington	12	6	.667	15	7	.682
Clemson	6	8	.429	8	10	.444
South Carolina	7	12	.368	11	13	.458
William and Mary	6	13	.316	10	13	.435
Virginia Tech	4	13	.235	4	19	.174
Davidson	3	14	.176	4	16	.200
VMI	1	14	.067	5	19	.208
Washington and Lee	1	17	.056	2	20	.091
The Citadel	0	11	.000	4	14	.222

Tournament: **Wake Forest d. NC State 71-70**
Tournament MOP: **Gene Shue**, Maryland

SOUTHWEST

	Conference			Overall		
	W	L	Pct	W	L	Pct
TCU⊛	9	3	.750	15	8	.652
Rice	8	4	.667	15	6	.714
Texas	8	4	.667	12	9	.571
Baylor	6	6	.500	10	11	.476
Arkansas	4	8	.333	10	11	.476
SMU	4	8	.333	8	12	.400
Texas A&M	3	9	.250	6	15	.286

WNY LITTLE THREE

	Conference			Overall		
	W	L	Pct	W	L	Pct
Niagara□	4	0	1.000	22	6	.786
St. Bonaventure	1	3	.250	10	11	.476
Canisius	1	3	.250	9	14	.391

YANKEE

	Conference			Overall		
	W	L	Pct	W	L	Pct
Connecticut	5	1	.833	17	4	.810
Rhode Island	6	2	.750	13	10	.565
Maine	3	4	.429	7	10	.412
Vermont	1	2	.333	11	10	.524
New Hampshire	2	5	.286	8	10	.444
Massachusetts	1	4	.200	4	15	.211

⊛ Automatic NCAA Tournament bid ○ At-large NCAA Tournament bid □ NIT appearance ⊗ Team record doesn't reflect games forfeited or vacated. For adjusted record, see p. 521.

INDEPENDENTS

	Overall W	L	Pct
Seton Hall□	31	2	.939
Seattle○	29	3	.906
Lebanon Valley○	19	2	.905
La Salle□	25	3	.893
Notre Dame○	19	5	.792
Louisville□	22	6	.786
Holy Cross⊕	20	6	.769
Navy○	16	5	.762
Oklahoma City○	18	6	.750
Duquesne□	21	8	.724
Idaho State○	18	7	.720
Villanova	19	8	.704
DePaul○	19	9	.679
Georgetown□	13	7	.650
Penn State	15	9	.625
Temple	16	10	.615
Butler	14	9	.609
Lehigh	12	8	.600
Baldwin-Wallace	13	9	.591
Army	11	8	.579
Colgate	12	9	.571
Muhlenberg	13	10	.565
Saint Joseph's	14	11	.560

INDEPENDENTS (CONT.)

	Overall W	L	Pct
Bradley	15	12	.556
Dayton	16	13	.552
Marquette	13	11	.542
Pittsburgh	12	11	.522
Drake	13	12	.520
Lafayette	13	12	.520
Loyola (LA)	14	13	.519
Gonzaga	15	14	.517
Loyola Marymount	14	14	.500
John Carroll	13	14	.481
Xavier	11	12	.478
Siena	10	11	.476
Bowling Green	12	15	.444
Creighton	11	14	.440
Virginia	10	13	.435
Miami (FL)	8	12	.400
Syracuse	7	11	.389
Rutgers	8	13	.381
Valparaiso	9	15	.375
Loyola-Chicago	8	15	.348
Boston College	7	15	.318
Brown	5	14	.263
Bucknell	3	16	.158

INDIVIDUAL LEADERS—SEASON

Scoring

	CL	POS	G	FG	FT	PTS	PPG
1 **Frank Selvy**, Furman	JR	G	25	272	194	738	**29.5**
2 **Larry Hennessy**, Villanova	SR	F	15	173	92	438	**29.2**
3 **Johnny O'Brien**, Seattle	SR	C	31	276	332	884	**28.5**
4 **Walter Dukes**, Seton Hall	SR	C	33	272	317	861	**26.1**
5 **Ernie Beck**, Penn	SR	C	26	245	183	673	**25.9**
6 **Bob Houbregs**, Washington	SR	C	31	306	188	800	**25.8**
7 **Don Schlundt**, Indiana	SO	C	26	206	249	661	**25.4**
8 **Dickie Hemric**, Wake Forest	SO	C	25	212	199	623	**24.9**
9 **George Dalton**, John Carroll	SO	F	27	230	209	669	**24.8**
10 **Bob Pettit**, LSU	JR	F/C	21	193	133	519	**24.7**

Field Goal Pct

	CL	POS	G	FG	FGA	PCT
1 **Vernon Stokes**, St. Francis (NY)	SR	F	24	147	247	**59.5**
2 **Bob Houbregs**, Washington	SR	C	31	306	564	**54.3**
3 **Eddie O'Brien**, Seattle	SR	G	31	176	325	**54.2**
4 **Johnny O'Brien**, Seattle	SR	C	31	276	518	**53.3**
5 **Charlie Hoxie**, Niagara	SO	F	28	125	235	**53.2**

Minimum: 100 made

Free Throw Pct

	CL	POS	G	FT	FTA	PCT
1 **John Weber**, Yale	SR	F	24	117	141	**83.0**
2 **Jake Dohner**, Virginia	SR	G	23	96	117	**82.1**
3 **Bill Sharp**, Wyoming	JR	G	27	163	200	**81.5**
4 **Kendall Sheets**, Oklahoma A&M	SR	G	30	87	107	**81.3**
5 **Bob Matheny**, California	JR	G	25	101	125	**80.8**

Minimum: 75 made

Rebounds Per Game

	CL	POS	G	REB	RPG
1 **Ed Conlin**, Fordham	SO	F	26	612	**23.5**
2 **Walter Dukes**, Seton Hall	SR	C	33	734	**22.2**
3 **Bill Chambers**, William and Mary	SR	F	22	480	**21.8**
4 **Art Quimby**, Connecticut	SO	C	21	430	**20.5**
5 **Don Virostek**, Pittsburgh	SR	C	21	424	**20.2**

INDIVIDUAL LEADERS—GAME

Points

	CL	POS	OPP	DATE	PTS
1 **Frank Selvy**, Furman	JR	G	Mercer	F11	**63**
2 **Nield Gordon**, Furman	SR	C	Charleston	J17	**52**
3 **Jerry Varn**, Citadel	SR	C	Piedmont	F1	**51**
Johnny O'Brien, Seattle	SR	C	Gonzaga	F15	**51**
5 **Bob Houbregs**, Washington	SR	C	Idaho	J10	**49**

Free Throws Made

	CL	POS	OPP	DATE	FT	FTA	PCT
1 **Frank Selvy**, Furman	JR	G	Mercer	F11	**21**	27	77.8
2 **Harry Sacks**, Harvard	SO	F	Army	F21	**20**	25	80.0
3 **George Dalton**, John Carroll	SO	F	Seton Hall	M4	**19**	22	86.4
Ray Burrus, West Texas A&M	FR	F	New Mexico St.	F14	**19**	23	82.6
5 **Huck Budde**, Xavier	SR	F	Minnesota	D8	**18**	21	85.7
Johnny O'Brien, Seattle	SR	C	Wyoming	M14	**18**	22	81.8
Dick Knostman, Kansas State	SR	C	Oklahoma	F14	**18**	26	69.2

TEAM LEADERS—SEASON

Scoring Offense

	G	W-L	PTS	PPG
1 **Furman**	27	21-6	2,435	**90.2**
2 **Seattle**	32	29-3	2,818	**88.1**
3 **George Washington**	22	15-7	1,890	**85.9**
4 **Duke**	25	17-8	2,093	**83.7**
5 **Miami (OH)**	23	17-6	1,916	**83.3**

Field Goal Pct

	G	W-L	FG	FGA	PCT
1 **Furman**	27	21-6	936	2,106	**44.4**
2 **Niagara**	28	22-6	718	1,640	**43.8**
3 **Seattle**	32	29-3	1,019	2,350	**43.4**
4 **Seton Hall**	33	31-2	914	2,129	**42.9**
5 **William and Mary**	23	10-13	603	1,410	**42.8**

Free Throw Pct

	G	W-L	FT	FTA	PCT
1 **George Washington**	22	15-7	502	696	**72.1**
2 **Penn**	27	22-5	502	702	**71.5**
3 **Oklahoma City**	24	18-6	548	771	**71.1**
4 **Loyola-Chicago**	23	8-15	525	743	**70.7**
5 **Fordham**	27	19-8	493	699	**70.5**

Scoring Defense

	G	W-L	OPP PTS	OPP PPG
1 **Oklahoma A&M**	30	23-7	1,614	**53.8**
2 **Maryland**	23	15-8	1,256	**54.6**
3 **Oklahoma City**	24	18-6	1,338	**55.8**
4 **Wyoming**	30	20-10	1,676	**55.9**
5 **San Jose State**	23	15-8	1,293	**56.2**

CONSENSUS ALL-AMERICAS

First Team

PLAYER	CL	POS	HT	SCHOOL	RPG	PPG
Ernie Beck	SR	C	6-4	Penn	17.3	25.9
Walter Dukes	SR	C	6-11	Seton Hall	22.2	26.1
Tom Gola	SO	C	6-6	La Salle	15.5	18.5
Bob Houbregs	SR	C	6-7	Washington	11.5	25.8
Johnny O'Brien	SR	C	5-9	Seattle	5.4	28.5

Second Team

PLAYER	CL	POS	HT	SCHOOL	RPG	PPG
Dick Knostman	SR	C	6-6	Kansas State	11.9	22.7
Bob Pettit	JR	F/C	6-9	LSU	11.9	24.7
Joe Richey	SR	F	6-1	BYU	7.5	17.6
Don Schlundt	SO	C	6-9	Indiana	8.5	25.4
Frank Selvy	JR	G	6-3	Furman	N/A	29.5

Selectors: AP, Collier's (Basketball Coaches), International News Service, Look Magazine, Newspaper Enterprises Assn., UP

Poll Progression

Preseason Poll

UP	School
1	Illinois
2	Kansas State
3	La Salle
4	Washington
5	NC State
6	Oklahoma A&M
7	UCLA
8	Indiana
9	Seton Hall
10	Saint Louis
11	Holy Cross
12	Santa Clara
13	Notre Dame
14	Duquesne
15	Wyoming
16	St. John's
17	BYU
17	Minnesota
19	Kansas
20	St. Bonaventure

Week of Dec 9

UP	School
1	Illinois (0-0)
2	La Salle (2-0)
3	Kansas State (1-0)
4	Washington (2-0)
5	Oklahoma A&M (3-0)
6	NC State (3-0)
7	UCLA (2-0)
8	Seton Hall (3-0)
9	Minnesota (1-0)
10	Holy Cross (0-0)
11	Notre Dame (2-0)
12	Ohio State (1-0)
13	St. Bonaventure (3-0)
14	Indiana (1-1)
15	LSU (2-0)
16	Saint Louis (0-1)
17	BYU (4-0)
18	NYU (4-0)
18	Santa Clara (2-0)
18	St. John's (1-0)

Week of Dec 16

AP	UP	School
1	2	La Salle (6-0) (A)
2	3	Kansas State (3-0)
3	1	Illinois (2-0)
4	6	Seton Hall (6-0)
5	5	Oklahoma A&M (4-0)
6	8	NC State (5-1)
7	10	Notre Dame (3-0)
8	11	Holy Cross (2-0)
9	4	Washington (3-1)
10	13	LSU (4-0)
11	—	Western Kentucky (3-0) (B)
12	7	UCLA (3-1)
13	—	Oklahoma City (4-2)
14	17	St. Bonaventure (4-0)
15	—	Tulsa (3-0)
16	9	Minnesota (3-0)
17	14	Saint Louis (1-1)
18	16	California (4-0)
19	12	Indiana (1-2)
20	15	Navy (4-0)
20	—	Kansas (1-1)
—	17	BYU (5-0)
—	19	DePaul (5-0)
—	20	Missouri (1-0)
—	20	NYU (5-0)

Week of Dec 23

AP	UP	School	AP↓↑
1	2	La Salle (8-0)	
2	1	Illinois (3-0)	↑1
3	5	Seton Hall (9-0)	↑1
4	8	Holy Cross (4-0)	↑4
5	3	Kansas State (4-1)	↓3
6	6	NC State (7-1)	
7	4	Washington (3-1)	↑2
8	13	LSU (5-0)	↑2
9	7	Oklahoma A&M (6-1)	↓4
10	—	Western Kentucky (5-1)	↑1
11	12	Notre Dame (5-1)	↓4
12	15	St. Bonaventure (5-0)	↑2
13	16	Navy (6-0)	↑7
14	—	Tulsa (5-0)	↑1
15	10	Indiana (3-2)	↑4
15	—	Seattle (2-2)	⤴
17	9	Minnesota (3-0)	↓1
18	11	Colorado (4-0)	⤴
19	—	Oklahoma City (6-0)	↓6
20	14	UCLA (4-2)	↓8
20	—	Idaho (4-1)	⤴
—	16	Saint Louis (2-1)	⤵
—	18	Michigan State (2-1)	
—	18	Missouri (3-1)	
—	20	Vanderbilt (3-1)	

Week of Dec 30

AP	UP	School	AP↓↑
1	3	Kansas State (6-1)	↑4
2	5	Seton Hall (9-0)	↑1
3	2	La Salle (9-1)	↓2
4	1	Illinois (4-1)	↓2
5	4	Washington (7-1)	↑2
6	10	Holy Cross (5-0)	↓2
7	7	Oklahoma A&M (9-1)	↑2
8	12	Tulsa (7-1)	↑6
9	6	Minnesota (4-0)	↑8
10	—	Western Kentucky (5-2)	
11	9	NC State (9-2)	↓5
12	8	Indiana (3-2)	↑3
13	—	Seattle (8-2)	↑2
14	15	DePaul (8-2)	⤴
15	14	St. Bonaventure (5-1)	↓3
16	—	Oklahoma City (7-0)	↑3
17	20	LSU (6-1)	↓9
18	—	Toledo (5-0)	⤴
19	13	Notre Dame (5-1)	↓8
20	—	Wayne State (7-0)	⤴
—	11	UCLA (7-2)	⤵
—	16	Navy (6-0)	⤵
—	17	Michigan State (3-1)	
—	18	BYU (8-2)	
—	19	Fordham (7-0)	
—	20	Saint Louis (2-4)	

Week of Jan 6

AP	UP	School	AP↓↑
1	2	Kansas State (7-1)	
2	5	Seton Hall (13-0)	
3	3	La Salle (11-1)	
4	1	Illinois (5-1)	
5	6	Oklahoma A&M (10-1)	↑2
6	4	Washington (9-1)	↓1
7	8	Indiana (5-2)	↑5
8	14	Fordham (9-0)	⤴
9	7	NC State (12-2)	↑2
10	16	Western Kentucky (9-2)	
11	10	LSU (7-1)	↑6
12	17	USC (10-0)	⤴
13	10	Notre Dame (8-1)	↑6
14	13	Holy Cross (5-3)	↓8
15	19	Navy (6-0)	⤴
16	—	Seattle (9-1)	↓3
17	—	Tulsa (9-2)	↓9
18	—	Idaho (8-4)	⤴
19	9	Minnesota (5-2)	↓10
20	12	California (6-4)	⤴
—	14	BYU (11-3)	
—	18	Saint Louis (4-5)	
—	19	UCLA (7-4)	

Week of Jan 13

AP	UP	School	AP↓↑
1	1	Kansas State (8-1)	
2	5	Seton Hall (15-0)	
3	3	La Salle (13-1)	
4	2	Illinois (8-1)	
5	4	Washington (11-1)	↑1
6	6	Indiana (7-2)	↑1
7	12	Fordham (11-0)	↑1
8	7	NC State (14-2)	↑1
9	8	Oklahoma A&M (10-2)	↓4
10	15	Western Kentucky (11-2)	
11	9	Notre Dame (9-1)	↑2
12	10	USC (11-1)	
13	17	Tulsa (11-2)	↑4
14	11	LSU (10-1)	↓3
15	—	Kansas (8-3)	⤴
16	—	Seattle (11-2)	
17	16	Holy Cross (7-3)	↓3
18	—	Oklahoma City (10-1)	⤴
19	19	UCLA (8-5)	⤴
20	—	Georgetown (6-1)	⤴
—	13	BYU (13-3)	
—	14	Minnesota (6-3)	⤵
—	18	California (7-5)	⤵
—	19	Michigan State (5-3)	

Week of Jan 20

AP	UP	School	AP↓↑
1	1	Seton Hall (18-0) (C)	↑1
2	2	Indiana (8-2)	↑4
3	3	Washington (13-1)	↑2
4	4	Kansas State (8-2)	↓3
5	6	La Salle (14-2)	↓2
6	5	Illinois (8-2)	↓2
7	7	Oklahoma A&M (12-2)	↑2
8	8	NC State (16-2)	
9	9	Kansas (9-3)	↑6
10	13	Fordham (12-1)	↓3
11	14	Tulsa (12-2)	↑2
12	18	Western Kentucky (12-3)	↓2
13	—	Seattle (13-2)	↑3
14	11	LSU (11-1)	
15	12	California (9-5)	⤴
16	10	Notre Dame (10-2)	↓5
17	—	Oklahoma City (11-2)	↑1
18	—	Eastern Kentucky (9-2)	⤴
19	18	Minnesota (7-4)	⤴
20	—	Manhattan (8-2)	⤴
—	15	Holy Cross (7-4)	⤵
—	16	Saint Louis (6-7)	
—	17	USC (11-3)	⤵
—	20	DePaul (12-4)	
—	20	UCLA (10-5)	⤵

Week of Jan 27

AP	UP	School	AP↓↑
1	1	Seton Hall (19-0)	
2	2	Indiana (9-2)	
3	3	Washington (15-1)	
4	6	La Salle (15-2)	↑1
5	4	Kansas State (9-2)	↓1
6	5	Illinois (9-2)	
7	13	Fordham (13-2)	↑3
8	7	Oklahoma A&M (12-3)	↓1
9	—	Western Kentucky (15-3)	↑3
10	11	DePaul (14-4)	⤴
11	12	LSU (13-1)	↑3
12	8	NC State (16-3)	↓4
13	—	Seattle (15-2)	
14	10	Kansas (9-4)	↓5
15	—	Eastern Kentucky (11-3)	↑3
16	—	Navy (9-2)	⤴
17	9	Notre Dame (11-2)	↓1
18	17	North Carolina (13-3)	⤴
19	—	Manhattan (10-2)	↑1
20	—	Tulsa (13-4)	↓9
—	14	California (9-5)	⤵
—	15	BYU (15-4)	
—	16	Saint Louis (7-7)	
—	18	USC (11-3)	
—	19	Minnesota (8-4)	⤵
—	20	Holy Cross (7-4)	

Week of Feb 3

AP	UP	School	AP↓↑
1	1	Seton Hall (21-0)	
2	2	Indiana (10-2)	
3	3	Washington (18-1)	
4	6	La Salle (16-2)	
5	5	Kansas State (10-2)	
6	4	Illinois (9-2)	
7	8	DePaul (15-4)	↑3
8	15	Western Kentucky (16-3)	↑1
9	7	Oklahoma A&M (14-3)	↓1
10	10	LSU (14-1)	↑1
11	—	Seattle (15-2)	↑2
12	16	North Carolina (15-3)	↑6
13	12	Fordham (14-2)	↓6
14	11	California (11-5)	⤴
15	9	NC State (17-4)	↓3
16	—	Oklahoma City (11-3)	⤴
17	18	Holy Cross (8-4)	⤴
18	13	Kansas (9-4)	↓4
19	—	Manhattan (12-2)	
20	—	Niagara (15-2)	⤴
—	14	Notre Dame (11-3)	⤵
—	16	BYU (17-4)	
—	19	Minnesota (9-5)	
—	20	Oklahoma (6-5)	
—	20	Saint Louis (8-8)	

Week of Feb 10

AP	UP	School	AP↓↑
1	2	Seton Hall (22-0)	
2	1	Indiana (12-2)	
3	3	Washington (20-1)	
4	5	La Salle (18-2)	
5	4	Illinois (12-2)	↑1
6	6	Oklahoma A&M (16-3)	↑3
7	8	DePaul (17-4)	
8	10	LSU (15-1)	↑2
9	12	Western Kentucky (20-3)	↓1
10	7	Kansas State (11-3)	↓5
11	—	Seattle (19-2)	
12	9	NC State (19-4)	↑3
13	—	Oklahoma City (13-3)	↑3
14	11	Kansas (10-4)	↑4
15	—	Manhattan (14-2)	↑4
16	—	Fordham (15-3)	↓3
17	—	Louisville (16-3)	⤴
17	—	Niagara (17-3)	↑3
19	13	California (12-6)	↓5
19	19	Tulsa (14-5)	⤴
—	14	Notre Dame (12-3)	
—	15	BYU (18-5)	
—	16	UCLA (13-5)	
—	17	Minnesota (11-5)	
—	18	Saint Louis (10-8)	
—	19	Wyoming (15-6)	

Week of Feb 17

AP	UP	School	AP↓↑
1	2	Seton Hall (24-0)	
2	1	Indiana (13-2)	
3	3	Washington (22-1)	
4	5	La Salle (20-2)	
5	4	Illinois (13-2)	
6	8	LSU (17-1)	↑2
7	7	Oklahoma A&M (17-4)	↓1
8	6	Kansas State (12-3)	↑2
9	14	Western Kentucky (20-4)	
10	9	Kansas (12-4)	↑4
11	—	Seattle (20-3) (D)	
12	20	Oklahoma City (14-3)	↑1
13	—	Manhattan (16-2)	↑2
14	10	DePaul (17-6)	↓7
15	11	NC State (20-5)	↓3
16	—	Louisville (18-4)	↑1
17	—	Murray State (17-5)	⤴
18	17	Duke (15-6)	⤴
19	12	California (13-7)	
19	—	Villanova (13-7)	⤴
—	13	BYU (19-5)	
—	15	Saint Louis (12-8)	
—	16	Notre Dame (14-4)	
—	17	Duquesne (15-7)	
—	17	UCLA (14-6)	

Week of Feb 24

AP	UP	SCHOOL	AP↓↑
1	2	**Seton Hall** (26-0)	
2	1	**Indiana** (16-2)	
3	3	**Washington** (24-1)	
4	4	**La Salle** (22-2)	
5	5	**Kansas** (13-5)	↑5
6	7	**LSU** (19-1)	
7	8	**Oklahoma A&M** (19-5)	
8	12	**Western Kentucky** (22-5)	↑1
9	10	**Kansas State** (13-4)	↓1
10	6	**Illinois** (15-3)	↓5
11	—	**Oklahoma City** (15-4)	↑1
12	—	**Miami (OH)** (16-3)	⤴
13	9	**NC State** (22-5)	↑2
14	19	**Seattle** (22-3)	↓3
15	11	**DePaul** (19-6)	↓1
16	17	**Manhattan** (18-2)	↓3
17	15	**Notre Dame** (16-4)	⤴
18	—	**Louisville** (20-4)	↓2
19	18	**Duquesne** (15-7)	⤴
20	—	**Eastern Kentucky** (15-6)	⤴
—	13	**BYU** (20-5)	
—	14	**California** (14-8)	⤵
—	16	**Saint Louis** (13-10)	
—	19	**USC** (15-5)	

Week of Mar 3

AP	UP	SCHOOL	AP↓↑
1	1	**Indiana** (17-2)	↑1
2	4	**La Salle** (24-2)	↑2
3	2	**Seton Hall** (27-1)	↓2
4	3	**Washington** (25-2)	↓1
5	6	**LSU** (20-1)	↑1
6	5	**Kansas** (13-5)	↓1
7	7	**Oklahoma A&M** (19-6)	
8	9	**Kansas State** (15-4)	↑1
9	11	**Western Kentucky** (22-5)	↓1
10	10	**Illinois** (15-4)	
11	18	**Oklahoma City** (17-4)	
12	8	**NC State** (25-5)	↑1
13	13	**Notre Dame** (17-4)	↑4
14	23	**Louisville** (20-5)	↑4
15	21	**Seattle** (26-3)	↓1
16	27	**Miami (OH)** (17-4)	↓4
17	25	**Eastern Kentucky** (16-8)	↑3
18	20	**Duquesne** (18-7)	↑1
18	25	**Navy** (16-4)	⤴
20	17	**Holy Cross** (18-5)	⤴
—	12	**California** (16-8)	
—	14	**DePaul** (19-7)	⤵
—	14	**Wyoming** (19-8)	
—	16	**Saint Louis** (15-10)	
—	19	**BYU** (20-7)	
—	21	**Manhattan** (18-4)	⤵
—	23	**Niagara** (19-5)	
—	27	**Villanova** (16-8)	
—	27	**USC** (17-5)	
—	30	**Fordham** (17-7)	
—	30	**St. John's** (14-5)	
—	30	**Tulane** (14-5)	

Week of Mar 10

AP	UP	SCHOOL	AP↓↑
1	—	**Indiana** (19-3)	
2	—	**Washington** (27-2)	↑2
3	—	**La Salle** (24-2)	↓1
4	—	**Seton Hall** (28-2) Ⓔ	↓1
5	—	**Kansas** (16-5)	↑1
6	—	**Oklahoma A&M** (22-6)	↑1
7	—	**LSU** (20-1)	↓2
8	—	**Kansas State** (16-4)	
9	—	**Western Kentucky** (24-5)	
10	—	**Oklahoma City** (18-4)	↑1
11	—	**Duquesne** (19-7)	↑7
12	—	**Wake Forest** (23-6)	⤴
13	—	**Illinois** (18-4)	↓3
14	—	**Louisville** (22-6) Ⓔ	
14	—	**Seattle** (27-3)	↑1
16	—	**Wyoming** (23-8)	⤴
17	—	**Notre Dame** (17-4)	↓4
18	—	**NC State** (26-6)	↓6
19	—	**Navy** (16-4)	↓1
20	—	**Manhattan** (20-4)	⤴
20	—	**St. John's** (15-5)	⤴

Final Poll

AP	SCHOOL	AP↓↑
1	**Indiana** (23-3)	
2	**Seton Hall** (31-2)	↑2
3	**Kansas** (19-6)	↑2
4	**Washington** (29-3)	↓2
5	**LSU** (22-3)	↑2
6	**La Salle** (25-3)	↓3
7	**St. John's** (17-6)	↑13
8	**Oklahoma A&M** (23-7)	↓2
9	**Duquesne** (21-8)	↑2
10	**Notre Dame** (19-5)	↑7
11	**Illinois** (18-4)	↑2
12	**Kansas State** (17-4)	↓4
13	**Holy Cross** (20-6)	⤴
14	**Seattle** (29-4)	
15	**Wake Forest** (22-7)	↓3
16	**Santa Clara** (20-7)	⤴
17	**Western Kentucky** (25-6)	↓8
18	**NC State** (26-6)	
19	**DePaul** (19-9)	⤴
20	**Missouri State** (21-4)	⤴

Ⓐ A year after winning the NIT behind 6'6" freshman Tom Gola, La Salle becomes the first of Philadelphia's Big 5 to receive a No. 1 ranking. (St. Joseph's and Temple eventually attain top spots, but not Penn or Villanova.)

Ⓑ Which is the better band of Hilltoppers: the Western Kentucky squad coached by "Uncle Ed" Diddle, or the musical group that made the charts with "Trying"? The singing quartet (all current or former Western students) appears on the *Ed Sullivan Show*, which gives them one more national TV appearance than the basketball quintet led by forward Tom Marshall and center Art Spoelstra.

Ⓒ Seton Hall takes over the top spot, riding the play of 6'11" Walter Dukes, an African-American player and therefore an NCAA rarity, who will average 26.1 points and 22.2 rebounds a game. Dukes' 734 rebounds is still the NCAA D1 record for a single season.

Ⓓ On Feb. 15, Seattle's consensus All-America, Johnny O'Brien, scores 51 points in a 109-68 win over Gonzaga, becoming the first player to score 3,000 points in his college career (although the NCAA does not recognize 596 points he scored while on the Seattle freshman team). He and his twin brother, Eddie, a Seattle teammate, skip the NBA and sign bonus contracts with baseball's Pittsburgh Pirates.

Ⓔ Seton Hall loses back-to-back games at Dayton, 70-65, and Louisville, 73-67. A riot breaks out at the end of the Louisville game, but all parties deny it has anything to do with Walter Dukes, who scores 35 points and becomes one of the first African-Americans to play South of the Mason-Dixon Line.

1953 NCAA Tournament

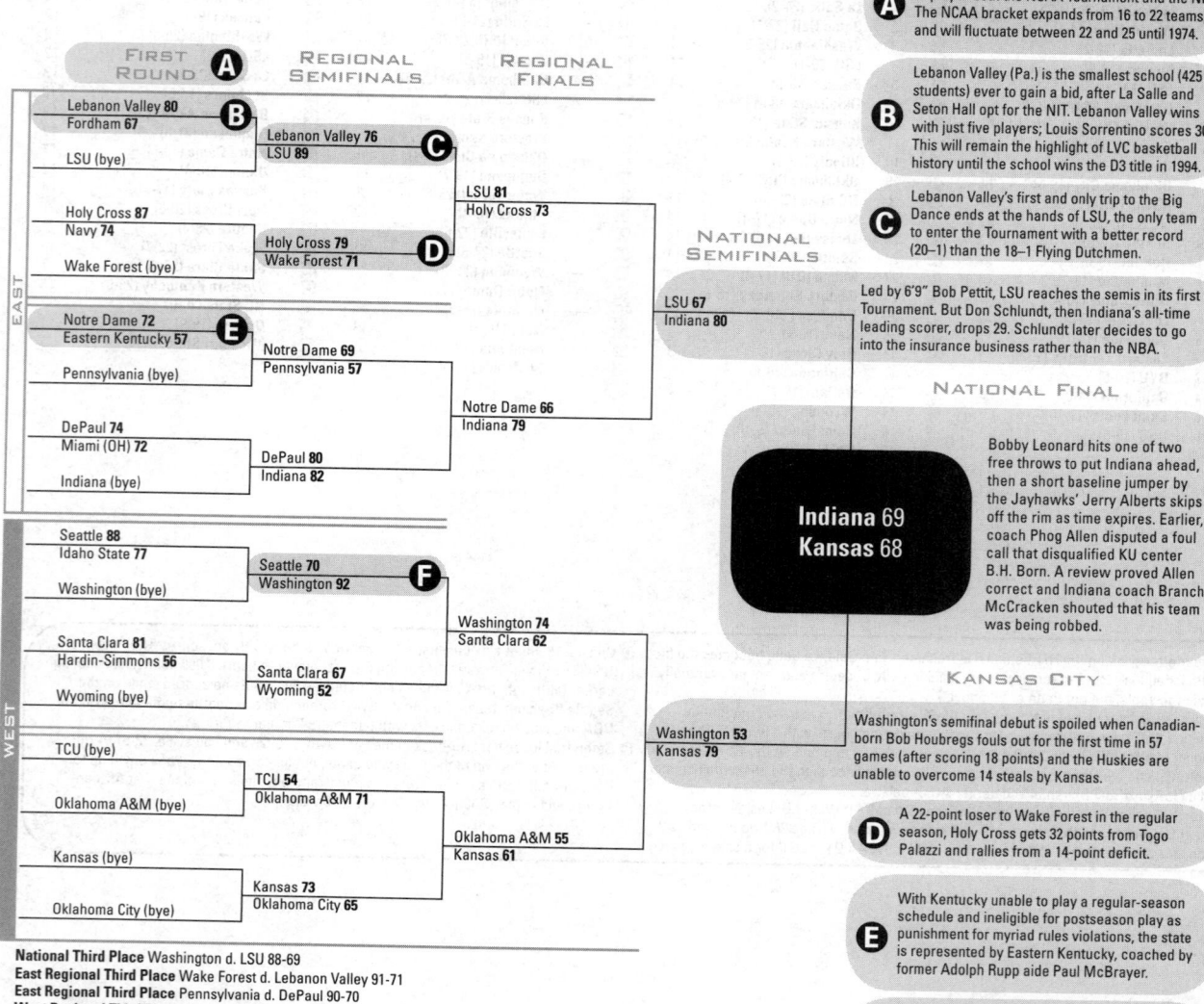

East

First Round (A)
- Lebanon Valley **80**, Fordham **67** (B)
- LSU (bye)
- Holy Cross **87**, Navy **74**
- Wake Forest (bye)
- Notre Dame **72**, Eastern Kentucky **57** (E)
- Pennsylvania (bye)
- DePaul **74**, Miami (OH) **72**
- Indiana (bye)

Regional Semifinals
- Lebanon Valley **76**, LSU **89** (C)
- Holy Cross **79**, Wake Forest **71** (D)
- Notre Dame **69**, Pennsylvania **57**
- DePaul **80**, Indiana **82**

Regional Finals
- LSU **81**, Holy Cross **73**
- Notre Dame **66**, Indiana **79**

West

First Round
- Seattle **88**, Idaho State **77**
- Washington (bye)
- Santa Clara **81**, Hardin-Simmons **56**
- Wyoming (bye)
- TCU (bye)
- Oklahoma A&M (bye)
- Kansas (bye)
- Oklahoma City (bye)

Regional Semifinals
- Seattle **70**, Washington **92** (F)
- Santa Clara **67**, Wyoming **52**
- TCU **54**, Oklahoma A&M **71**
- Kansas **73**, Oklahoma City **65**

Regional Finals
- Washington **74**, Santa Clara **62**
- Oklahoma A&M **55**, Kansas **61**

National Semifinals
- LSU **67**, Indiana **80**
- Washington **53**, Kansas **79**

National Final

Kansas City

Indiana 69
Kansas 68

National Third Place Washington d. LSU 88-69
East Regional Third Place Wake Forest d. Lebanon Valley 91-71
East Regional Third Place Pennsylvania d. DePaul 90-70
West Regional Third Place Seattle d. Wyoming 80-64
West Regional Third Place TCU d. Oklahoma City 58-56

A For the first time, teams are no longer permitted to play in both the NCAA Tournament and the NIT. The NCAA bracket expands from 16 to 22 teams, and will fluctuate between 22 and 25 until 1974.

B Lebanon Valley (Pa.) is the smallest school (425 students) ever to gain a bid, after La Salle and Seton Hall opt for the NIT. Lebanon Valley wins with just five players; Louis Sorrentino scores 30. This will remain the highlight of LVC basketball history until the school wins the D3 title in 1994.

C Lebanon Valley's first and only trip to the Big Dance ends at the hands of LSU, the only team to enter the Tournament with a better record (20–1) than the 18–1 Flying Dutchmen.

Led by 6'9" Bob Pettit, LSU reaches the semis in its first Tournament. But Don Schlundt, then Indiana's all-time leading scorer, drops 29. Schlundt later decides to go into the insurance business rather than the NBA.

Bobby Leonard hits one of two free throws to put Indiana ahead, then a short baseline jumper by the Jayhawks' Jerry Alberts skips off the rim as time expires. Earlier, coach Phog Allen disputed a foul call that disqualified KU center B.H. Born. A review proved Allen correct and Indiana coach Branch McCracken shouted that his team was being robbed.

Washington's semifinal debut is spoiled when Canadian-born Bob Houbregs fouls out for the first time in 57 games (after scoring 18 points) and the Huskies are unable to overcome 14 steals by Kansas.

D A 22-point loser to Wake Forest in the regular season, Holy Cross gets 32 points from Togo Palazzi and rallies from a 14-point deficit.

E With Kentucky unable to play a regular-season schedule and ineligible for postseason play as punishment for myriad rules violations, the state is represented by Eastern Kentucky, coached by former Adolph Rupp aide Paul McBrayer.

F In a battle of crosstown rivals and consensus All-Americas (Washington's Bob Houbregs vs. Seattle's Johnny O'Brien), the Huskies win as Houbregs scores 45—a Tournament record at the time.

Tournament Leaders

INDIVIDUAL LEADERS

Scoring

		CL	POS	G	PTS	PPG
1	**Bob Houbregs**, Washington	SR	C	4	139	34.8
2	**Johnny O'Brien**, Seattle	SR	C	3	96	32.0
3	**Don Schlundt**, Indiana	SO	C	4	123	30.8
4	**Bob Pettit**, LSU	JR	F/C	4	122	30.5
5	**Dickie Hemric**, Wake Forest	SO	C	2	58	29.0
6	**Bob Mattick**, Oklahoma A&M	JR	C	2	57	28.5
7	**Ernie Beck**, Penn	SR	C	2	47	23.5
8	**Togo Palazzi**, Holy Cross	JR	F	3	70	23.3
9	**Jack Williams**, Wake Forest	SO	F	2	42	21.0
10	**Ron Feiereisel**, DePaul	SR	G	3	61	20.3

Minimum: 2 games

Field Goals Per Game

		CL	POS	G	FG	FGPG
1	**Bob Houbregs**, Washington	SR	C	4	57	14.3
2	**Bob Pettit**, LSU	JR	F/C	4	49	12.3
3	**Dickie Hemric**, Wake Forest	SO	C	2	20	10.0
	Bob Mattick, Oklahoma A&M	JR	C	2	20	10.0
5	**Johnny O'Brien**, Seattle	SR	C	3	29	9.7

Minimum: 8 made

Free Throws Per Game

		CL	POS	G	FT	FTPG
1	**Johnny O'Brien**, Seattle	SR	C	3	38	12.7
2	**Don Schlundt**, Indiana	SO	C	4	49	12.3
3	**Dickie Hemric**, Wake Forest	SO	C	2	18	9.0
4	**Bob Mattick**, Oklahoma A&M	JR	C	2	17	8.5
	Bill Sharp, Wyoming	JR	G	2	17	8.5

Minimum: 5 made

TEAM LEADERS

Scoring

		G	PTS	PPG
1	**Wake Forest**	2	162	81.0
2	**Holy Cross**	3	239	79.7
3	**Seattle**	3	238	79.3
4	**Indiana**	4	310	77.5
5	**Washington**	4	307	76.8
6	**LSU**	4	306	76.5
7	**NYU**	3	227	75.7
8	**DePaul**	3	224	74.7
9	**Penn**	2	147	73.5
10	**Kansas**	4	281	70.2

Minimum: 2 games

FT Per Game

		G	FT	FTPG
1	**Indiana**	4	108	27.0
2	**NYU**	3	79	26.3
3	**Seattle**	3	70	23.3
4	**Wake Forest**	2	46	23.0
	Idaho State	1	23	23.0
	Notre Dame	3	69	23.0
	Holy Cross	3	69	23.0

Fg Per Game

		G	FG	FGPG
1	**Fordham**	1	31	31.0
2	**Navy**	1	30	30.0
3	**Washington**	4	118	29.5
4	**LSU**	4	117	29.3
5	**Wake Forest**	2	58	29.0

ALL-TOURNAMENT TEAM

PLAYER	CL	POS	HT	SCHOOL	PPG
B.H. Born*	JR	C	6-9	Kansas	20.0
Bob Houbregs	SR	C	6-7	Washington	34.8
Dean Kelley	SR	G	5-11	Kansas	11.8
Bobby Leonard	JR	G	6-3	Indiana	16.8
Don Schlundt	SO	C	6-9	Indiana	30.8

ALL-REGIONAL TEAMS

EAST (Chicago)

PLAYER	CL	POS	HT	SCHOOL	PPG
Ernie Beck	SR	C	6-4	Penn	23.5
Ron Feiereisel	SR	G	6-3	DePaul	20.3
Bobby Leonard	JR	G	6-3	Indiana	16.5
Dick Rosenthal	JR	F/C	6-5	Notre Dame	18.0
Don Schlundt	SO	C	6-9	Indiana	32.0

EAST (Raleigh, NC)

PLAYER	CL	POS	HT	SCHOOL	PPG
Dickie Hemric	SO	C	6-6	Wake Forest	29.0
Howard Landa	SO	G	5-9	Lebanon Valley	17.3
Earle Markey	SR	G	6-1	Holy Cross	15.7
Togo Palazzi	JR	F	6-4	Holy Cross	23.3
Bob Pettit	JR	F/C	6-9	LSU	28.5

WEST (Corvallis, OR)

PLAYER	CL	POS	HT	SCHOOL	PPG
Joe Cipriano	SR	G	5-11	Washington	13.5
Bob Houbregs	SR	C	6-7	Washington	39.5
Doug McClary	SR	F	6-8	Washington	8.5
Johnny O'Brien	SR	C	5-9	Seattle	32.0
Ken Sears	SO	F/C	6-9	Santa Clara	16.3

WEST (Manhattan, KS)

PLAYER	CL	POS	HT	SCHOOL	PPG
Dean Kelley*	SR	G	5-11	Kansas	11.5
B.H. Born	JR	C	6-9	Kansas	14.5
Bob Mattick	JR	C	6-11	Oklahoma A&M	28.5
Gilbert Reich	JR	G	6-1	Kansas	14.0
Arnold Short	JR	G	6-2	Oklahoma City	16.0

* Most outstanding player

1953 NCAA TOURNAMENT BOX SCORES

89-76 (SWEET 16)

	1H	2H
LSU	49	40
Lebanon Valley	43	33

LSU	MIN	FG	3FG	FT	REB	A	ST	BL	PF	TP
Bob Pettit	-	13	-	2-7	-	-	-	-	4	28
Norman Magee	-	8	-	7-8	-	-	-	-	5	23
Don Belcher	-	8	-	1-3	-	-	-	-	2	17
Benny McArdle	-	6	-	1-4	-	-	-	-	3	13
Kenny Bridges	-	1	-	2-3	-	-	-	-	4	4
Ned Clark	-	2	-	0-2	-	-	-	-	5	4
Bob Freshley	-	0	-	0-0	-	-	-	-	4	0
TOTALS	-	**38**	-	**13-27**	-	-	-	-	**27**	**89**
Percentages				48.1						

Coach: Harry Rabenhorst

LEBANON VALLEY	MIN	FG	3FG	FT	REB	A	ST	BL	PF	TP
Leon Miller	-	7	-	12-17	-	-	-	-	3	26
Howard Landa	-	5	-	8-10	-	-	-	-	5	18
Herb Finkelstein	-	7	-	3-7	-	-	-	-	4	17
Louis Sorrentino	-	3	-	5-6	-	-	-	-	3	11
William Vought	-	1	-	2-3	-	-	-	-	3	4
Robert Blakeney	-	0	-	0-0	-	-	-	-	0	0
Martin Gluntz	-	0	-	0-0	-	-	-	-	0	0
TOTALS	-	**23**	-	**30-43**	-	-	-	-	**18**	**76**
Percentages				69.8						

Coach: George "Rinso" Marquette

79-71 (SWEET 16)

	1H	2H
Holy Cross	43	36
Wake Forest	32	39

HOLY CROSS	MIN	FG	3FG	FT	REB	A	ST	BL	PF	TP
Togo Palazzi	40	14-28	-	4-6	12	1	-	-	4	32
Ronald Perry	36	5-7	-	6-8	5	4	-	-	2	16
Earle Markey	29	5-15	-	4-8	11	1	-	-	4	14
Robert Magilligan	38	2-3	-	3-7	3	6	-	-	4	7
David Nangle	16	2-8	-	2-4	5	0	-	-	4	6
James Kielley	24	2-5	-	0-0	1	1	-	-	5	4
Walter Suprunowicz	17	0-2	-	0-0	4	0	-	-	3	0
TOTALS	**200**	**30-68**	-	**19-33**	**41**	**13**	-	-	**26**	**79**
Percentages		44.1		57.6						

Coach: Lester Sheary

WAKE FOREST	MIN	FG	3FG	FT	REB	A	ST	BL	PF	TP
Dickie Hemric	40	9-22	-	11-16	17	1	-	-	1	29
Jack Williams	40	6-14	-	7-9	14	2	-	-	4	19
Ray Lipstas	32	4-12	-	3-10	5	6	-	-	3	11
Billy Lyles	40	2-17	-	1-1	4	5	-	-	3	5
Al Deporter	34	1-4	-	3-3	5	1	-	-	5	5
Maurice George	13	1-3	-	0-0	0	0	-	-	5	2
Joe Koch	1	0-0	-	0-0	0	0	-	-	0	0
TOTALS	**200**	**23-72**	-	**25-39**	**45**	**15**	-	-	**21**	**71**
Percentages		31.9		64.1						

Coach: Murray Greason

69-57 (SWEET 16)

	1H	2H
Notre Dame	30	39
Penn	31	26

NOTRE DAME	MIN	FG	3FG	FT	REB	A	ST	BL	PF	TP
Jack Stephens	-	8	-	3-3	-	-	-	-	3	19
Dick Rosenthal	-	3	-	12-14	-	-	-	-	3	18
Joe Bertrand	-	5	-	7-9	-	-	-	-	3	17
Norbert Lewinski	-	3	-	4-4	-	-	-	-	2	10
William Sullivan	-	1	-	1-1	-	-	-	-	0	3
Jim Gibbons	-	0	-	2-2	-	-	-	-	2	2
Edward McGinn	-	0	-	0-0	-	-	-	-	0	0
TOTALS	-	**20**	-	**29-33**	-	-	-	-	**13**	**69**
Percentages				87.9						

Coach: John Jordan

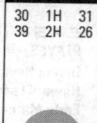

PENN	MIN	FG	3FG	FT	REB	A	ST	BL	PF	TP
Ernie Beck	-	9	-	7-9	-	-	-	-	2	25
Richard Heylmun	-	5	-	3-6	-	-	-	-	4	13
Karl Hoagland	-	4	-	1-1	-	-	-	-	5	9
Thomas Holt	-	2	-	4-5	-	-	-	-	4	8
Barton Leach	-	1	-	0-0	-	-	-	-	4	2
Edward Gramigna	-	0	-	0-0	-	-	-	-	1	0
Richard Harter	-	0	-	0-0	-	-	-	-	0	0
John Lavin	-	0	-	0-0	-	-	-	-	3	0
Lawrence Masters	-	0	-	0-0	-	-	-	-	0	0
Francis Vitetta	-	0	-	0-0	-	-	-	-	0	0
TOTALS	-	**21**	-	**15-21**	-	-	-	-	**23**	**57**
Percentages				71.4						

Coach: Howie Dallmar

82-80 (SWEET 16)

	1H	2H
Indiana	42	40
DePaul	33	47

INDIANA	MIN	FG	3FG	FT	REB	A	ST	BL	PF	TP
Don Schlundt	-	5-16	-	13-17	-	-	-	-	3	23
Bobby Leonard	-	9-30	-	4-9	-	-	-	-	1	22
Richard Farley	-	2-6	-	8-11	-	-	-	-	4	12
Richard White	-	3-9	-	4-5	-	-	-	-	4	10
Charles Kraak	-	3-4	-	0-0	-	-	-	-	5	6
Burke Scott	-	3-11	-	0-0	-	-	-	-	5	6
James Deakyne	-	1-3	-	0-0	-	-	-	-	0	2
Paul Poff	-	0-2	-	1-2	-	-	-	-	3	1
TOTALS	-	**26-81**	-	**30-44**	-	-	-	-	**25**	**82**
Percentages		32.1		68.2						

Coach: Branch McCracken

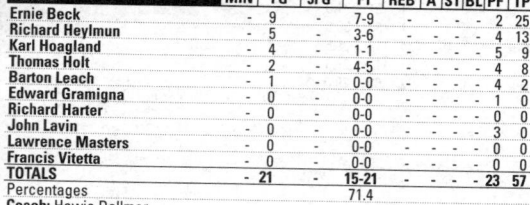

DEPAUL	MIN	FG	3FG	FT	REB	A	ST	BL	PF	TP
Ron Feiereisel	-	9-14	-	9-12	-	-	-	-	4	27
Bill Schyman	-	4-9	-	9-13	-	-	-	-	5	17
Jim Lamkin	-	6-20	-	3-4	-	-	-	-	5	15
Frank Blum	-	4-12	-	2-4	-	-	-	-	2	10
Russ Johnson	-	4-7	-	1-1	-	-	-	-	5	9
Dan Kieres	-	0-1	-	2-2	-	-	-	-	0	2
Dan Lecos	-	0-5	-	0-0	-	-	-	-	5	0
Donald Rose	-	0-0	-	0-0	-	-	-	-	0	0
Earl Wylder	-	0-0	-	0-0	-	-	-	-	0	0
TOTALS	-	**27-68**	-	**26-36**	-	-	-	-	**26**	**80**
Percentages		39.7		72.2						

Coach: Ray Meyer

92-70 (SWEET 16)

	1H	2H
Washington	47	45
Seattle	32	38

WASHINGTON	MIN	FG	3FG	FT	REB	A	ST	BL	PF	TP
Bob Houbregs	-	20	-	5-10	-	-	-	-	2	45
Charlie Koon	-	6	-	1-2	-	-	-	-	1	13
Joe Cipriano	-	4	-	4-6	-	-	-	-	3	12
Doug McClary	-	5	-	0-2	-	-	-	-	3	10
Mike McCutchen	-	3	-	4-4	-	-	-	-	3	10
Dean Parsons	-	1	-	0-2	-	-	-	-	3	2
Don Apeland	-	0	-	0-0	-	-	-	-	0	0
Will Elliott	-	0	-	0-0	-	-	-	-	1	0
Roland Halle	-	0	-	0-0	-	-	-	-	0	0
Bill Ward	-	0	-	0-0	-	-	-	-	0	0
TOTALS	-	**39**	-	**14-26**	-	-	-	-	**16**	**92**
Percentages				53.8						

Coach: William H. "Tippy" Dye

SEATTLE	MIN	FG	3FG	FT	REB	A	ST	BL	PF	TP
Johnny O'Brien	-	6	-	12-14	-	-	-	-	2	24
Stan Glowaski	-	10	-	2-4	-	-	-	-	1	22
Eddie O'Brien	-	3	-	3-4	-	-	-	-	4	9
John Kelly	-	2	-	1-1	-	-	-	-	2	5
Jack Johansen	-	2	-	0-0	-	-	-	-	1	4
Ray Moscatel	-	1	-	0-0	-	-	-	-	3	2
Joe Pehanick	-	0	-	2-3	-	-	-	-	2	2
Larry Sanford	-	1	-	0-2	-	-	-	-	0	2
Jack Doherty	-	0	-	0-0	-	-	-	-	1	0
TOTALS	-	**25**	-	**20-28**	-	-	-	-	**16**	**70**
Percentages				71.4						

Coach: H. Albert Brightman

67-52 (SWEET 16)

	1H	2H
Santa Clara	26	41
Wyoming	24	28

SANTA CLARA	MIN	FG	3FG	FT	REB	A	ST	BL	PF	TP
Ken Sears	-	8	-	3-4	-	-	-	-	3	19
Herb Schoenstein	-	4	-	2-2	-	-	-	-	1	10
Gary Gatzert	-	4	-	1-2	-	-	-	-	3	9
Don Benedetti	-	1	-	6-6	-	-	-	-	3	8
Dick Garibaldi	-	1	-	6-6	-	-	-	-	1	8
Mickey Mount	-	2	-	4-7	-	-	-	-	3	8
Jim Young	-	0	-	3-5	-	-	-	-	3	3
Dick Soares	-	1	-	0-0	-	-	-	-	3	2
TOTALS	-	**21**	-	**25-32**	-	-	-	-	**20**	**67**
Percentages				78.1						

Coach: Bob Feerick

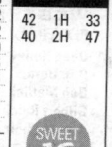

WYOMING	MIN	FG	3FG	FT	REB	A	ST	BL	PF	TP
Bill Sharp	-	7	-	9-9	-	-	-	-	5	23
Harry Jorgensen	-	4	-	5-8	-	-	-	-	2	13
Robert Burns	-	3	-	1-1	-	-	-	-	5	7
Ron Rivers	-	2	-	0-2	-	-	-	-	1	4
Robert Moore	-	1	-	0-2	-	-	-	-	0	2
Charles Wing	-	0	-	2-2	-	-	-	-	4	2
Jim Milvehal	-	0	-	1-1	-	-	-	-	2	1
Dan Kuska	-	0	-	0-0	-	-	-	-	1	0
TOTALS	-	**17**	-	**18-25**	-	-	-	-	**20**	**52**
Percentages				72.0						

Coach: Everett Shelton

71-54

	1H	2H
Oklahoma A&M	28	43
TCU	29	25

SWEET 16

OKLAHOMA A&M	MIN	FG	3FG	FT	REB	A	ST	BL	PF	TP
Bob Mattick	-	13	-	9-14	-	-	-	-	2	35
Kendall Sheets	-	6	-	3-5	-	-	-	-	3	15
Harold Rogers	-	3	-	4-5	-	-	-	-	3	10
Ken Hicks	-	1	-	2-2	-	-	-	-	0	4
Gerald Stockton	-	1	-	2-2	-	-	-	-	3	4
Dale Roark	-	1	-	1-1	-	-	-	-	5	3
Tom Fuller	-	0	-	0-0	-	-	-	-	4	0
Don Haskins	-	0	-	0-0	-	-	-	-	0	0
Bob Hendrick	-	0	-	0-0	-	-	-	-	1	0
Tom Maloney	-	0	-	0-0	-	-	-	-	0	0
TOTALS	-	25	-	21-29	-	-	-	-	21	71
Percentages				72.4						

Coach: Hank Iba

TCU	MIN	FG	3FG	FT	REB	A	ST	BL	PF	TP
Ray Warren	-	7	-	8-10	-	-	-	-	1	22
Richard Allen	-	2	-	7-9	-	-	-	-	0	11
Henry Ohlen	-	3	-	2-3	-	-	-	-	5	8
Tommy Hill	-	1	-	2-4	-	-	-	-	2	4
Johnny Swaim	-	1	-	1-1	-	-	-	-	3	3
Charles Brown	-	1	-	0-0	-	-	-	-	1	2
Buddy Brumbley	-	1	-	0-2	-	-	-	-	3	2
Albert Lampkin	-	0	-	1-2	-	-	-	-	1	1
Charles White	-	0	-	1-3	-	-	-	-	2	1
Ross Hoyt	-	0	-	0-0	-	-	-	-	0	0
TOTALS	-	16	-	22-34	-	-	-	-	18	54
Percentages				64.7						

Coach: Buster Brannon

73-65

	1H	2H
Kansas	47	26
Oklahoma City	26	39

SWEET 16

KANSAS	MIN	FG	3FG	FT	REB	A	ST	BL	PF	TP
Gilbert Reich	-	8	-	4-6	-	-	-	-	4	20
Allen Kelley	-	7	-	3-4	-	-	-	-	4	17
B.H. Born	-	4	-	3-4	-	-	-	-	4	11
Hal Patterson	-	1	-	7-8	-	-	-	-	1	9
Larry Davenport	-	4	-	0-0	-	-	-	-	1	8
Dean Kelley	-	2	-	3-5	-	-	-	-	5	7
Dean Smith	-	0	-	1-1	-	-	-	-	0	1
John Anderson	-	0	-	0-0	-	-	-	-	0	0
Lavannes Squires	-	0	-	0-0	-	-	-	-	1	0
TOTALS	-	26	-	21-28	-	-	-	-	20	73
Percentages				75.0						

Coach: Forrest "Phog" Allen

OKLAHOMA CITY	MIN	FG	3FG	FT	REB	A	ST	BL	PF	TP
Arnold Short	-	7	-	3-3	-	-	-	-	1	17
Andy Likens	-	5	-	4-4	-	-	-	-	4	14
Jack Key	-	2	-	8-10	-	-	-	-	2	12
Ken Rose	-	3	-	5-7	-	-	-	-	3	11
Clyde Nath	-	2	-	0-0	-	-	-	-	2	4
Gerald Bullard	-	1	-	1-1	-	-	-	-	1	3
Don Rich	-	1	-	1-1	-	-	-	-	3	3
Bill Couts	-	0	-	1-1	-	-	-	-	3	1
Tom Bolin	-	0	-	0-2	-	-	-	-	1	0
Don Jones	-	0	-	0-0	-	-	-	-	1	0
TOTALS	-	21	-	23-29	-	-	-	-	21	65
Percentages				79.3						

Coach: Doyle Parrack

81-73

	1H	2H
LSU	41	40
Holy Cross	33	40

ELITE 8

LSU	MIN	FG	3FG	FT	REB	A	ST	BL	PF	TP
Bob Pettit	-	12	-	5-7	-	-	-	-	3	29
Don Belcher	-	6	-	5-7	-	-	-	-	4	17
Norman Magee	-	5	-	5-7	-	-	-	-	3	15
Benny McArdle	-	4	-	5-8	-	-	-	-	5	13
Ned Clark	-	2	-	0-0	-	-	-	-	5	4
Kenny Bridges	-	1	-	0-2	-	-	-	-	2	2
Bob Freshley	-	0	-	1-3	-	-	-	-	0	1
Darrell Schultz	-	0	-	0-0	-	-	-	-	0	0
TOTALS	-	30	-	21-34	-	-	-	-	22	81
Percentages				61.8						

Coach: Harry Rabenhorst

HOLY CROSS	MIN	FG	3FG	FT	REB	A	ST	BL	PF	TP
Ronald Perry	-	6	-	5-5	-	-	-	-	4	17
Earle Markey	-	5	-	6-14	-	-	-	-	2	16
David Nangle	-	2	-	4-4	-	-	-	-	2	8
Togo Palazzi	-	1	-	6-9	-	-	-	-	2	8
James Kielley	-	3	-	1-2	-	-	-	-	3	7
Joe Early	-	3	-	0-0	-	-	-	-	4	6
Robert Magilligan	-	2	-	1-2	-	-	-	-	3	5
Walter Suprunowicz	-	2	-	0-1	-	-	-	-	1	4
James Lewis	-	1	-	0-0	-	-	-	-	0	2
John Carroll	-	0	-	0-0	-	-	-	-	0	0
Robert Casey	-	0	-	0-0	-	-	-	-	0	0
Frank Kasprzak	-	0	-	0-0	-	-	-	-	2	0
TOTALS	-	25	-	23-37	-	-	-	-	23	73
Percentages				62.2						

Coach: Lester Sheary

79-66

	1H	2H
Indiana	42	37
Notre Dame	32	34

ELITE 8

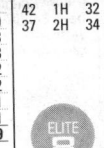

INDIANA	MIN	FG	3FG	FT	REB	A	ST	BL	PF	TP
Don Schlundt	-	13-24	-	15-18	-	-	-	-	5	41
Bobby Leonard	-	4-12	-	3-4	-	-	-	-	4	11
Burke Scott	-	4-8	-	2-2	-	-	-	-	5	10
Charles Kraak	-	2-6	-	4-5	-	-	-	-	3	8
Paul Poff	-	1-3	-	1-1	-	-	-	-	1	3
Phil Byers	-	1-1	-	0-2	-	-	-	-	1	2
Richard Farley	-	0-3	-	2-2	-	-	-	-	4	2
James Deakyne	-	0-0	-	1-2	-	-	-	-	0	1
Richard White	-	0-5	-	1-1	-	-	-	-	2	1
TOTALS	-	25-62	-	29-37	-	-	-	-	25	79
Percentages		40.3		78.4						

Coach: Branch McCracken

NOTRE DAME	MIN	FG	3FG	FT	REB	A	ST	BL	PF	TP
Norbert Lewinski	-	8-21	-	3-3	-	-	-	-	5	19
Richard Rosenthal	-	6-17	-	7-8	-	-	-	-	4	19
Jack Stephens	-	5-15	-	4-11	-	-	-	-	2	14
Joe Bertrand	-	3-9	-	2-4	-	-	-	-	4	8
William Sullivan	-	1-2	-	1-4	-	-	-	-	3	3
Jim Gibbons	-	0-6	-	2-3	-	-	-	-	5	2
Jack Reynolds	-	0-1	-	1-2	-	-	-	-	1	1
Richard Wise	-	0-3	-	0-0	-	-	-	-	1	0
TOTALS	-	23-74	-	20-35	-	-	-	-	25	66
Percentages		31.1		57.1						

Coach: John Jordan

74-62

	1H	2H
Washington	28	46
Santa Clara	30	32

ELITE 8

WASHINGTON	MIN	FG	3FG	FT	REB	A	ST	BL	PF	TP
Bob Houbregs	-	12	-	10-13	-	-	-	-	3	34
Joe Cipriano	-	6	-	3-5	-	-	-	-	3	15
Charlie Koon	-	3	-	3-4	-	-	-	-	1	9
Doug McClary	-	2	-	3-6	-	-	-	-	4	7
Mike McCutchen	-	2	-	1-1	-	-	-	-	3	5
Dean Parsons	-	1	-	2-7	-	-	-	-	0	4
TOTALS	-	26	-	22-36	-	-	-	-	14	74
Percentages				61.1						

Coach: William H. "Tippy" Dye

SANTA CLARA	MIN	FG	3FG	FT	REB	A	ST	BL	PF	TP
Ken Sears	-	7	-	9-11	-	-	-	-	5	23
Gary Gatzert	-	4	-	0-0	-	-	-	-	3	8
Jim Young	-	3	-	2-2	-	-	-	-	5	8
Dick Garibaldi	-	3	-	0-0	-	-	-	-	2	6
Herb Schoenstein	-	2	-	2-2	-	-	-	-	3	6
Mickey Mount	-	1	-	3-4	-	-	-	-	4	5
Dick Soares	-	2	-	1-2	-	-	-	-	1	5
Don Benedetti	-	0	-	1-1	-	-	-	-	1	1
TOTALS	-	22	-	18-22	-	-	-	-	24	62
Percentages				81.8						

Coach: Bob Feerick

61-55

	1H	2H
Kansas	30	31
Oklahoma A&M	28	27

ELITE 8

KANSAS	MIN	FG	3FG	FT	REB	A	ST	BL	PF	TP
B.H. Born	-	6	-	6-6	-	-	-	-	5	18
Dean Kelley	-	6	-	4-7	-	-	-	-	2	16
Allen Kelley	-	4	-	5-8	-	-	-	-	4	13
Gilbert Reich	-	2	-	4-4	-	-	-	-	3	8
Hal Patterson	-	0	-	4-6	-	-	-	-	5	4
Jerry Alberts	-	0	-	1-1	-	-	-	-	1	1
Larry Davenport	-	0	-	1-1	-	-	-	-	1	1
Dean Smith	-	0	-	0-0	-	-	-	-	0	0
TOTALS	-	18	-	25-33	-	-	-	-	21	61
Percentages				75.8						

Coach: Forrest "Phog" Allen

OKLAHOMA A&M	MIN	FG	3FG	FT	REB	A	ST	BL	PF	TP
Bob Mattick	-	7	-	8-16	-	-	-	-	3	22
Chester Reams	-	4	-	4-4	-	-	-	-	5	12
Dale Roark	-	3	-	2-3	-	-	-	-	2	8
Tom Fuller	-	1	-	4-5	-	-	-	-	2	6
Ken Hicks	-	2	-	2-2	-	-	-	-	5	6
Bob Hendrick	-	0	-	1-1	-	-	-	-	0	1
Don Haskins	-	0	-	0-0	-	-	-	-	0	0
Tom Maloney	-	0	-	0-0	-	-	-	-	0	0
Kendall Sheets	-	0	-	0-0	-	-	-	-	5	0
Gerald Stockton	-	0	-	0-0	-	-	-	-	0	0
TOTALS	-	17	-	21-31	-	-	-	-	22	55
Percentages				67.7						

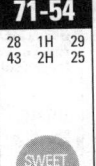

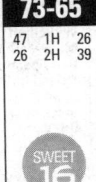

Coach: Hank Iba

80-67 — 1H: Indiana 49, LSU 41; 2H: Indiana 31, LSU 26 — FINAL 4

INDIANA	MIN	FG	3FG	FT	REB	A	ST	BL	PF	TP
Don Schlundt	-	8-15	-	13-17	5	-	-	-	4	29
Bobby Leonard	-	9-12	-	4-5	1	-	-	-	4	22
Richard Farley	-	4-5	-	2-5	7	-	-	-	4	10
Charles Kraak	-	2-6	-	5-7	9	-	-	-	4	9
Burke Scott	-	2-7	-	3-4	2	-	-	-	4	7
Richard White	-	0-6	-	3-4	8	-	-	-	2	3
Phil Byers	-	0-0	-	0-0	0	-	-	-	3	0
James Deakyne	-	0-0	-	0-0	0	-	-	-	0	0
Paul Poff	-	0-2	-	0-0	1	-	-	-	2	0
TOTALS	-	25-53	-	30-42	33	-	-	-	27	80
Percentages		47.2		71.4						

Coach: Branch McCracken

LSU	MIN	FG	3FG	FT	REB	A	ST	BL	PF	TP
Bob Pettit	-	10-24	-	9-18	15	-	-	-	4	29
Norman Magee	-	6-15	-	5-8	2	-	-	-	3	17
Don Belcher	-	4-15	-	2-3	6	-	-	-	3	10
Kenny Bridges	-	1-2	-	3-6	0	-	-	-	2	5
Benny McArdle	-	1-6	-	1-3	1	-	-	-	5	3
Ned Clark	-	0-7	-	2-2	10	-	-	-	5	2
Bob Freshley	-	0-1	-	1-4	0	-	-	-	4	1
TOTALS	-	22-70	-	23-44	34	-	-	-	26	67
Percentages		31.4		52.3						

Coach: Harry Rabenhorst

Officials: Ogde
Lightner

79-53 — 1H: Kansas 45, Washington 34; 2H: Kansas 34, Washington 19 — FINAL 4

KANSAS	MIN	FG	3FG	FT	REB	A	ST	BL	PF	TP
B.H. Born	-	9-17	-	7-9	-	-	-	-	4	25
Dean Kelley	-	7-17	-	2-4	-	-	-	-	4	16
Hal Patterson	-	6-11	-	4-7	-	-	-	-	2	16
Allen Kelley	-	5-16	-	1-2	-	-	-	-	3	11
Gilbert Reich	-	2-5	-	2-2	-	-	-	-	3	6
Larry Davenport	-	0-1	-	2-2	-	-	-	-	0	2
Bill Heitholt	-	1-2	-	0-0	-	-	-	-	0	2
Ken Buller	-	0-0	-	1-4	-	-	-	-	1	1
Jerry Alberts	-	0-0	-	0-0	-	-	-	-	0	0
John Anderson	-	0-0	-	0-0	-	-	-	-	1	0
Dean Smith	-	0-1	-	0-0	-	-	-	-	1	0
Lavannes Squires	-	0-0	-	0-0	-	-	-	-	0	0
TOTALS	-	30-70	-	19-30	-	-	-	-	19	79
Percentages		42.9		63.3						

Coach: Forrest "Phog" Allen

WASHINGTON	MIN	FG	3FG	FT	REB	A	ST	BL	PF	TP
Bob Houbregs	-	8-13	-	2-2	-	-	-	-	5	18
Joe Cipriano	-	4-14	-	3-5	-	-	-	-	1	11
Charlie Koon	-	3-12	-	2-3	-	-	-	-	4	8
Doug McClary	-	2-8	-	1-1	-	-	-	-	4	5
Will Elliott	-	1-3	-	1-1	-	-	-	-	0	3
Mike McCutchen	-	0-6	-	3-6	-	-	-	-	2	3
Don Apeland	-	1-2	-	0-0	-	-	-	-	1	2
Roland Halle	-	0-0	-	2-6	-	-	-	-	0	2
Dean Parsons	-	0-3	-	1-4	-	-	-	-	3	1
Steve Roake	-	0-1	-	0-0	-	-	-	-	3	0
Bill Ward	-	0-0	-	0-0	-	-	-	-	0	0
TOTALS	-	19-62	-	15-28	-	-	-	-	23	53
Percentages		30.6		53.6						

Coach: William H. "Tippy" Dye

Officials: Conway, George

88-69 — 1H: Washington 39, LSU 26; 2H: Washington 49, LSU 43 — 3RD PLACE

WASHINGTON	MIN	FG	3FG	FT	REB	A	ST	BL	PF	TP
Bob Houbregs	-	17	-	8-10	-	-	-	-	0	42
Joe Cipriano	-	11	-	2-4	-	-	-	-	3	24
Dean Parsons	-	2	-	2-3	-	-	-	-	5	6
Steve Roake	-	0	-	4-4	-	-	-	-	0	4
Roland Halle	-	1	-	1-1	-	-	-	-	1	3
Doug McClary	-	1	-	1-1	-	-	-	-	2	3
Mike McCutchen	-	1	-	1-1	-	-	-	-	0	3
Charlie Koon	-	1	-	0-0	-	-	-	-	2	2
Will Elliott	-	0	-	1-2	-	-	-	-	0	1
Bill Ward	-	0	-	0-2	-	-	-	-	0	0
TOTALS	-	34	-	20-28	-	-	-	-	13	88
Percentages				71.4						

Coach: William H. "Tippy" Dye

LSU	MIN	FG	3FG	FT	REB	A	ST	BL	PF	TP
Bob Pettit	-	14	-	8-10	-	-	-	-	5	36
Ned Clark	-	5	-	4-5	-	-	-	-	5	14
Benny McArdle	-	3	-	1-1	-	-	-	-	1	7
Don Belcher	-	2	-	2-2	-	-	-	-	1	6
Darrell Schultz	-	2	-	0-0	-	-	-	-	0	4
Kenny Bridges	-	1	-	0-0	-	-	-	-	2	2
Bob Freshley	-	0	-	0-0	-	-	-	-	1	0
Don Loughmiller	-	0	-	0-0	-	-	-	-	0	0
Norman Magee	-	0	-	0-0	-	-	-	-	4	0
Jim McNeilly	-	0	-	0-0	-	-	-	-	0	0
Charley Robert	-	0	-	0-0	-	-	-	-	0	0
TOTALS	-	27	-	15-18	-	-	-	-	19	69
Percentages				83.3						

Coach: Harry Rabenhorst

Attendance: 10,500

69-68 — 1H: Indiana 41, Kansas 41; 2H: Indiana 28, Kansas 27 — NCAA FINAL 1953

INDIANA	MIN	FG	3FG	FT	REB	A	ST	BL	PF	TP
Don Schlundt	-	11-26	-	8-11	-	-	-	-	3	30
Charles Kraak	-	5-8	-	7-10	-	-	-	-	5	17
Bobby Leonard	-	5-15	-	2-4	-	-	-	-	2	12
Burke Scott	-	2-4	-	2-3	-	-	-	-	3	6
Richard Farley	-	1-8	-	0-0	-	-	-	-	5	2
Richard White	-	1-5	-	0-0	-	-	-	-	2	2
Phil Byers	-	0-2	-	0-0	-	-	-	-	0	0
James Deakyne	-	0-0	-	0-0	-	-	-	-	1	0
Paul Poff	-	0-1	-	0-0	-	-	-	-	0	0
TOTALS	-	25-69	-	19-28	-	-	-	-	21	69
Percentages		36.2		67.9						

Coach: Branch McCracken

KANSAS	MIN	FG	3FG	FT	REB	A	ST	BL	PF	TP
B.H. Born	-	8-27	-	10-12	-	-	-	-	5	26
Allen Kelley	-	7-20	-	6-8	-	-	-	-	3	20
Hal Patterson	-	1-3	-	7-8	-	-	-	-	3	9
Dean Kelley	-	3-4	-	2-4	-	-	-	-	2	8
Gilbert Reich	-	2-9	-	0-0	-	-	-	-	2	4
Dean Smith	-	0-0	-	1-1	-	-	-	-	1	1
Jerry Alberts	-	0-1	-	0-0	-	-	-	-	1	0
Larry Davenport	-	0-1	-	0-0	-	-	-	-	0	0
TOTALS	-	21-65	-	26-33	-	-	-	-	17	68
Percentages		32.3		78.8						

Coach: Forrest "Phog" Allen

Officials: Lightner, Shaw
Technicals: Indiana (Kraak, Leonard, Schlundt)
Attendance: 10,500

National Invitation Tournament (NIT)

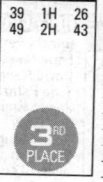

First round: Duquesne d. Tulsa 88-69, Louisville d. Georgetown 92-79, St. John's d. Saint Louis 81-66, Niagara d. BYU 82-76 (OT)
Quarterfinals: St. John's d. La Salle 75-74, Manhattan d. Louisville 79-66, Seton Hall d. Niagara 79-74, Duquesne d. Western Kentucky 69-61
Semifinals: Seton Hall d. Manhattan 74-56, St. John's d. Duquesne 64-55
Third place: Duquesne d. Manhattan 81-67
Championship: Seton Hall d. St. John's 58-46
MVP: Walter Dukes, Seton Hall

1953-54: THE EXPLORERS

Because three of its fifth-year players were declared ineligible, No. 1-ranked Kentucky turned down the NCAA Tournament, and 26–4 La Salle—which lost to the Wildcats by 13 points on Dec. 22, 1953—took advantage, beating Bradley, 92-76, for the championship. Explorers center Tom Gola was Most Outstanding Player after scoring 19 points in the Final. He's the only player to win both that award and MVP of the NIT (1952). Hoping to improve radio ratings and attract a younger fan base, the national semifinals and the Final were moved from a Tuesday-Wednesday to a Friday-Saturday schedule.

Unhappy about the Southern Conference's ban on postseason play, seven schools—Clemson, Duke, Maryland, North Carolina, North Carolina State, South Carolina and Wake Forest—split off to form the Atlantic Coast Conference (Virginia, an independent, also joined the ACC). Furman guard Frank "the Corbin Comet" Selvy scored 100 points against Newberry on Feb. 13, 1954, becoming the only NCAA Division I player ever to hit the century mark. Selvy made 41 of 66 shots from the field and 18 of 22 from the line. He played every minute of every game during the season.

MAJOR CONFERENCE STANDINGS

ACC	Conference			Overall		
	W	L	PCT	W	L	PCT
Duke	9	1	.900	21	6	.777
Maryland	7	2	.778	23	7	.767
Wake Forest	8	4	.667	17	12	.586
NC State⊕	5	3	.625	26	7	.788
North Carolina	5	6	.455	11	10	.524
South Carolina	2	8	.200	10	16	.385
Virginia	1	4	.200	16	11	.593
Clemson	0	9	.000	5	18	.217

Tournament: **NC State d. Wake Forest 82-80 (OT)**
Tournament MVP: **Dickie Hemric**, Wake Forest

BIG SEVEN	Conference			Overall		
	W	L	PCT	W	L	PCT
Kansas	10	2	.833	16	5	.762
Colorado○	10	2	.833	11	11	.500
Missouri	6	6	.500	11	10	.524
Kansas State	5	7	.417	11	10	.524
Nebraska	5	7	.417	8	13	.381
Oklahoma	4	8	.333	8	13	.381
Iowa State	2	10	.167	6	15	.286

BIG TEN	Conference			Overall		
	W	L	PCT	W	L	PCT
Indiana⊕	12	2	.857	20	4	.833
Iowa	11	3	.786	17	5	.773
Illinois	10	4	.714	17	5	.773
Minnesota	10	4	.714	17	5	.773
Wisconsin	6	8	.429	12	10	.545
Northwestern	6	8	.429	9	13	.409
Ohio State	5	9	.357	11	11	.500
Michigan State	4	10	.286	9	13	.409
Michigan	3	11	.214	9	13	.409
Purdue	3	11	.214	9	13	.409

BORDER	Conference			Overall		
	W	L	PCT	W	L	PCT
Texas Tech⊕	11	1	.917	20	5	.800
West Texas A&M	9	3	.750	13	7	.650
Arizona	8	4	.667	14	10	.583
Texas Western	4	8	.333	8	14	.364
Hardin-Simmons	4	8	.333	7	17	.292
New Mexico State	3	9	.250	6	12	.333
Arizona State	3	9	.250	5	18	.217

CBA	Conference			Overall		
	W	L	PCT	W	L	PCT
Santa Clara○	9	3	.750	20	7	.741
San Francisco	8	4	.667	14	7	.667
San Jose State	6	6	.500	12	15	.444
Saint Mary's (CA)	4	8	.333	10	14	.417
Pacific	3	9	.250	9	17	.346

IVY	Conference			Overall		
	W	L	PCT	W	L	PCT
Cornell⊕	12	3	.800	17	7	.708
Princeton	11	4	.733	16	9	.640
Penn	10	4	.714	17	8	.680
Yale	7	7	.500	12	14	.462
Columbia	6	8	.429	11	13	.458
Dartmouth	5	9	.357	13	13	.500
Brown	4	10	.286	13	11	.542
Harvard	2	12	.143	9	16	.360

METRO NY	Conference			Overall		
	W	L	PCT	W	L	PCT
St. Francis (NY)□	5	0	1.000	23	5	.808
Fordham○	3	1	.750	18	6	.750
Manhattan□	3	3	.500	15	11	.577
NYU	2	2	.500	9	9	.500
St. John's	2	3	.400	9	11	.450
CCNY	2	4	.333	10	8	.556
Brooklyn	0	4	.000	6	11	.353

MID-AMERICAN	Conference			Overall		
	W	L	PCT	W	L	PCT
Toledo⊕	10	2	.833	13	10	.565
Bowling Green□	10	3	.769	17	7	.708
Miami (OH)	7	5	.583	12	10	.545
Marshall	6	7	.462	12	9	.571
Western Michigan	4	5	.444	10	11	.476
Ohio	5	7	.417	12	10	.545
Kent State	3	9	.250	8	13	.381
Western Reserve	2	9	.182	7	17	.292

MISSOURI VALLEY	Conference			Overall		
	W	L	PCT	W	L	PCT
Oklahoma A&M⊕	9	1	.900	24	5	.828
Wichita State□	8	2	.800	27	4	.871
Tulsa	5	5	.500	15	14	.517
Saint Louis	4	6	.400	14	12	.538
Houston	3	7	.300	11	15	.423
Detroit	1	9	.100	11	17	.393

SKYLINE 8	Conference			Overall		
	W	L	PCT	W	L	PCT
Colorado State⊕	12	2	.857	22	7	.759
Wyoming	10	4	.714	19	9	.679
BYU□	9	5	.643	18	11	.621
Utah State	7	7	.500	14	13	.519
Utah	7	7	.500	12	14	.462
New Mexico	5	9	.357	11	11	.500
Montana	3	11	.214	8	19	.296
Denver	3	11	.214	6	21	.222

OHIO VALLEY	Conference			Overall		
	W	L	PCT	W	L	PCT
Western Kentucky□	9	1	.900	29	3	.906
Morehead State	6	4	.600	16	8	.667
Murray State	6	4	.600	15	16	.484
Tennessee Tech	4	6	.400	12	10	.545
Eastern Kentucky	4	6	.400	7	16	.304
Middle Tenn State	1	9	.100	12	17	.414

Tournament: **Western Kentucky d. Eastern Kent. 85-69**

PACIFIC COAST	Conference			Overall		
	W	L	PCT	W	L	PCT
NORTH						
Oregon State	11	5	.688	19	10	.655
Idaho	9	7	.563	15	8	.652
Oregon	9	7	.563	17	10	.630
Washington	7	9	.438	8	18	.308
Washington State	4	12	.250	10	17	.370
SOUTH						
Southern California⊕	8	4	.667	19	14	.576
UCLA	7	5	.583	18	7	.720
California	6	6	.500	17	7	.708
Stanford	3	9	.250	13	10	.565

Playoff: **Southern California defeated Oregon State 2-1** in a best of three series for the title

SEC	Conference			Overall		
	W	L	PCT	W	L	PCT
Kentucky	14	0	1.000	25	0	1.000
LSU⊕	14	0	1.000	20	5	.800
Alabama	10	4	.714	16	8	.667
Tulane	10	4	.714	15	8	.652
Auburn	8	6	.571	16	8	.667
Mississippi	7	7	.500	12	12	.500
Tennessee	7	7	.500	11	12	.478
Vanderbilt	5	9	.357	12	10	.545
Mississippi State	5	9	.357	11	10	.524
Florida	3	11	.214	7	15	.318
Georgia	2	12	.143	7	18	.280
Georgia Tech	0	14	.000	2	22	.083

SOUTHERN	Conference			Overall		
	W	L	PCT	W	L	PCT
George Washington⊕	10	0	1.000	23	3	.885
Furman	6	1	.857	20	9	.690
Richmond	10	3	.769	23	8	.742
West Virginia	6	4	.600	12	11	.522
William and Mary	6	5	.545	9	14	.391
VMI	6	7	.462	11	12	.478
Davidson	3	5	.375	7	15	.318
Washington and Lee	3	9	.250	6	17	.261
Virginia Tech	3	13	.188	3	24	.111
The Citadel	1	7	.125	1	18	.053

Tournament: **George Washington d. Richmond 83-70**
Tournament MOP: **Joe Holup**, George Washington

SOUTHWEST	Conference			Overall		
	W	L	PCT	W	L	PCT
Rice⊕	9	3	.750	23	5	.821
Texas	9	3	.750	16	9	.640
Arkansas	6	6	.500	13	9	.591
SMU	6	6	.500	13	9	.591
Baylor	6	6	.500	12	11	.522
TCU	5	7	.417	10	14	.417
Texas A&M	1	11	.083	2	20	.091

WNY LITTLE THREE	Conference			Overall		
	W	L	PCT	W	L	PCT
Niagara□	3	1	.750	24	6	.800
St. Bonaventure	2	2	.500	12	11	.522
Canisius	1	3	.250	9	14	.391

YANKEE	Conference			Overall		
	W	L	PCT	W	L	PCT
Connecticut⊕	7	0	1.000	23	3	.885
Massachusetts	5	1	.833	13	9	.591
Rhode Island	5	4	.556	8	13	.381
New Hampshire	2	6	.250	8	10	.444
Maine	1	7	.125	6	12	.333
Vermont	1	2	.333	13	7	.650

Conference Standings Continue →

⊕ Automatic NCAA Tournament bid ○ At-large NCAA Tournament bid □ NIT appearance ⊗ Team record doesn't reflect games forfeited or vacated. For adjusted record, see p. 521.

INDEPENDENTS

	Overall W	L	Pct
Holy Cross□	26	2	.929
Seattle○	26	2	.929
Duquesne□	26	3	.897
Notre Dame○	22	3	.880
La Salle⊛	26	4	.867
Idaho State○	22	5	.815
Saint Francis (PA)□	21	5	.808
Dayton□	25	7	.781
Louisville□	22	7	.759
Penn State○	18	6	.750
Oklahoma City○	18	7	.720
Navy○	18	8	.692
Army	15	7	.682
Villanova	20	11	.645
Loyola (LA)○	16	9	.640
Lafayette	17	10	.630
Saint Joseph's	14	9	.609
Xavier	18	12	.600
Bradley○	19	13	.594
John Carroll	15	11	.577
Seton Hall	13	10	.565
Temple	15	12	.556
Muhlenberg	12	10	.545

INDEPENDENTS (cont.)

	Overall W	L	Pct
Wash.-St. Louis	12	10	.545
Syracuse	10	9	.526
Cincinnati	11	10	.524
DePaul	11	10	.524
Iona	11	10	.524
Butler	13	12	.520
Boston College	11	11	.500
Loyola Marymount	14	16	.467
Rutgers	11	13	.458
Creighton	14	17	.452
Valparaiso	10	13	.435
Gonzaga	12	16	.429
Marquette	11	15	.423
Lehigh	8	12	.400
Pittsburgh	9	14	.391
Georgetown	11	18	.379
Loyola-Chicago	8	15	.348
Siena	7	14	.333
Portland	9	19	.321
Drake	7	16	.304
Colgate	5	12	.294
Bucknell	4	16	.200

INDIVIDUAL LEADERS—SEASON

Scoring

	CL	POS	G	FG	FT	PTS	PPG
1 **Frank Selvy**, Furman	SR	G	29	427	355	1,209	**41.7**
2 **Bob Pettit**, LSU	SR	F/C	25	281	223	785	**31.4**
3 **Buzzy Wilkinson**, Virginia	JR	G	27	288	238	814	**30.1**
4 **Arnold Short**, Oklahoma City	SR	G	25	232	232	696	**27.8**
5 **Bob Schafer**, Villanova	JR	G	31	287	262	836	**27.0**
6 **Walt Walowac**, Marshall	SR	F	21	208	132	548	**26.1**
7 **Tom Marshall**, Western Kentucky	SR	F	32	282	265	829	**25.9**
8 **John Kerr**, Illinois	SR	C	22	210	136	556	**25.3**
9 **Al Bianchi**, Bowling Green	SR	F	24	226	148	600	**25.0**
10 **Togo Palazzi**, Holy Cross	SR	F	27	255	160	670	**24.8**

Field Goal Pct

	CL	POS	G	FG	FGA	PCT
1 **Joe Holup**, George Washington	SO	C	26	179	313	**57.2**
2 **Elliott Karver**, George Washington	SR	G	25	124	221	**56.1**
3 **Bob Mattick**, Oklahoma A&M	SR	C	29	199	358	**55.6**
4 **Charlie Hoxie**, Niagara	JR	F	28	115	211	**54.5**
5 **Art Spoelstra**, Western Kentucky	SR	C	32	202	381	**53.0**

Minimum: 100 made

Free Throw Pct

	CL	POS	G	FT	FTA	PCT
1 **Dick Daugherty**, Arizona State	SO	F/G	23	75	86	**87.2**
2 **Allen Kelley**, Kansas	SR	G	21	75	87	**86.2**
3 **Sonny Powell**, Florida	JR	G	22	166	195	**85.1**
4 **George Dalton**, John Carroll	JR	F	26	189	225	**84.0**
5 **Russ Nystedt**, New Mexico	SR	C	22	98	118	**83.1**

Minimum: 75 made

Rebounds Per Game

	CL	POS	G	REB	RPG
1 **Art Quimby**, Connecticut	JR	C	26	588	**22.6**
2 **Charlie Slack**, Marshall	SO	C	21	466	**22.2**
3 **Tom Gola**, La Salle	JR	C	30	652	**21.7**
4 **George Sundstrom**, Rutgers	SR	C	24	494	**20.6**
5 **Jerry Koch**, Saint Louis	JR	F	25	502	**20.1**

INDIVIDUAL LEADERS—GAME

Points

	CL	POS	OPP	DATE	PTS
1 **Frank Selvy**, Furman	SR	G	Newberry	F13	**100**
2 **Bob Pettit**, LSU	SR	F/C	Louisiana College	D7	**60**
3 **Frank Selvy**, Furman	SR	G	Wofford	F23	**58**
4 **Frank Selvy**, Furman	SR	G	Wofford	F16	**57**
Bob Pettit, LSU	SR	F/C	Georgia	J9	**57**

TEAM LEADERS—SEASON

Scoring Offense

	G	W-L	PTS	PPG
1 **Furman**	29	20-9	2,658	**91.7**
2 **Kentucky**	25	25-0	2,187	**87.5**
3 **Western Kentucky**	32	29-3	2,730	**85.3**
4 **Duke**	27	21-6	2,250	**83.3**
5 **Holy Cross**	28	26-2	2,329	**83.2**

Field Goal Pct

	G	W-L	FG	FGA	PCT
1 **George Washington**	26	23-3	744	1,632	**45.6**
2 **Holy Cross**	28	26-2	871	2,018	**43.2**
3 **Niagara**	30	24-6	778	1,817	**42.8**
4 **Maryland**	30	23-7	669	1,564	**42.8**
5 **Furman**	29	20-9	990	2,370	**41.8**

Free Throw Pct

	G	W-L	FT	FTA	PCT
1 **Wake Forest**	29	17-12	734	1,010	**72.7**
2 **Florida**	22	7-15	540	746	**72.4**
3 **Tulane**	23	15-8	422	583	**72.4**
4 **New Mexico**	22	11-11	444	614	**72.3**
5 **Niagara**	30	24-6	667	929	**71.8**

Scoring Defense

	G	W-L	OPP PTS	OPP PPG
1 **Oklahoma A&M**	29	24-5	1,539	**53.1**
2 **Duquesne**	29	26-3	1,551	**53.5**
3 **Wyoming**	28	19-9	1,522	**54.4**
4 **Oregon State**	29	19-10	1,585	**54.7**
5 **Oklahoma City**	25	18-7	1,370	**54.8**

CONSENSUS ALL-AMERICAS

First Team

PLAYER	CL	POS	HT	SCHOOL	RPG	PPG
Tom Gola	JR	C	6-6	La Salle	21.7	23.0
Cliff Hagan	SR	F/C	6-4	Kentucky	13.5	24.0
Bob Pettit	SR	F/C	6-9	LSU	17.3	31.4
Don Schlundt	JR	C	6-9	Indiana	11.1	24.3
Frank Selvy	SR	G	6-3	Furman	13.8	41.7

Second Team

PLAYER	CL	POS	HT	SCHOOL	RPG	PPG
Bobby Leonard	SR	G	6-3	Indiana	N/A	15.4
Tom Marshall	SR	F	6-4	Western Kentucky	14.9	25.9
Bob Mattick	SR	C	6-11	Oklahoma A&M	11.2	20.7
Frank Ramsey	SR	G	6-3	Kentucky	8.8	19.6
Dick Ricketts	JR	F	6-7	Duquesne	10.4	17.2

Selectors: AP, Colliers (Basketball Coaches), International News Service, Look Magazine, Newspaper Enterprises Assn., UP

Poll Progression

Preseason Poll

AP	UP	School
1	1	Indiana
2	2	Kentucky
3	3	Duquesne
4	5	Oklahoma A&M
5	4	Kansas
6	6	La Salle
7	8	NC State
8	12	Kansas State
9	11	Illinois
10	7	LSU
11	—	Western Kentucky
12	9	Minnesota
13	15	Oregon State
14	17	Wyoming
15	16	Dayton
16	18	Santa Clara
17	10	California
18	13	Saint Louis
19	14	Holy Cross
19	—	Oklahoma City
—	19	Notre Dame
—	20	UCLA

Week of Dec 15

AP	UP	School	AP↓↑
1	1	Indiana (3-0)	
2	2	Kentucky (2-0) (A)	
3	3	Duquesne (4-0)	
4	4	Illinois (4-0)	↑5
5	5	LSU (3-0)	↑5
6	6	Minnesota (3-0)	↑6
7	7	Oklahoma A&M (4-1)	↓3
8	8	NC State (3-1)	↓1
9	10	Fordham (4-0)	⤴
10	18	Western Kentucky (6-0)	↑1
11	15	Oregon State (6-1)	↑2
12	—	Oklahoma City (4-0)	↑7
13	—	Duke (3-1)	⤴
14	17	Holy Cross (2-0)	↑5
15	12	California (3-1)	↑2
16	14	Notre Dame (3-1)	⤴
17	9	UCLA (3-0)	⤴
18	—	Niagara (4-1)	⤴
19	—	Siena (3-1)	⤴
20	11	La Salle (3-1)	↓14
—	13	Kansas (0-2)	⤵
—	16	Ohio State (3-0)	
—	18	Saint Louis (4-1)	⤵
—	20	Kansas State (2-1)	⤵
—	20	Wyoming (4-1)	⤵

Week of Dec 22

AP	UP	School	AP↓↑
1	1	Indiana (6-0)	
2	2	Kentucky (5-0)	
3	3	Duquesne (7-0)	
4	4	Illinois (5-1)	
5	6	Oklahoma A&M (8-1)	↑2
6	14	Western Kentucky (9-0)	↑4
7	9	Fordham (6-0)	↑2
8	5	Minnesota (5-0)	↓2
9	7	NC State (6-1)	↓1
10	19	Holy Cross (3-0)	↑4
11	17	Rice (6-0)	⤴
12	11	Oregon State (6-1)	↓1
13	8	UCLA (6-1)	↑4
14	12	LSU (4-1)	↓9
15	—	Oklahoma City (5-0)	↓3
16	10	La Salle (6-1)	↑4
16	—	Dayton (6-1)	⤴
18	15	Wisconsin (5-1)	⤴
19	20	Notre Dame (4-1)	↓3
20	—	Idaho (5-0)	⤴
20	—	Vanderbilt (5-0)	⤴
—	12	California (5-1)	⤵
—	16	Wyoming (6-1)	
—	17	Kansas (1-2)	

Week of Dec 29

AP	UP	School	AP↓↑
1	1	Kentucky (6-0)	↑1
2	3	Duquesne (8-0)	↑1
3	2	Indiana (6-1)	↓2
4	4	Oregon State (6-1)	↑8
5	5	Oklahoma A&M (9-1)	
6	6	Minnesota (7-0)	↑2
7	11	Western Kentucky (9-0)	↓1
8	7	Illinois (5-1)	↓4
9	8	NC State (7-1)	
10	9	Fordham (6-0)	↓3
11	—	Oklahoma City (6-0)	↑4
12	16	Holy Cross (5-0)	↓2
13	12	La Salle (7-2)	↑3
14	14	UCLA (8-1)	↓1
15	—	Seattle (8-1)	⤴
16	14	Rice (7-0)	↓5
17	—	Idaho (5-0)	↑3
18	13	LSU (5-1)	↓4
19	10	BYU (8-0)	⤴
20	17	Wyoming (6-1)	⤴
20	—	Vanderbilt (5-1)	
—	18	California (9-1)	
—	19	Kansas State (5-2)	
—	20	Navy (6-0)	

Week of Jan 5

AP	UP	School	AP↓↑
1	1	Kentucky (7-0)	
2	3	Duquesne (11-0)	
3	2	Indiana (7-1)	
4	4	Oklahoma A&M (12-1)	↑1
5	7	Western Kentucky (12-0)	↑2
6	5	Minnesota (8-1)	
7	6	Holy Cross (8-0)	↑5
8	13	Duke (9-3)	⤴
9	19	Oklahoma City (8-1)	↑2
10	11	Oregon State (7-3)	↓6
11	10	Rice (10-0)	↑5
12	14	Niagara (8-2)	⤴
12	—	George Washington (6-0)	⤴
14	—	Dayton (9-2)	⤴
15	9	Illinois (6-2)	↓7
16	8	Kansas (4-2)	⤴
16	—	Seattle (9-1)	↓1
18	18	Navy (7-2)	⤴
19	—	Vanderbilt (7-1)	↑1
20	16	NC State (9-3)	↓11
—	12	LSU (6-2)	⤵
—	15	UCLA (9-2)	⤵
—	16	La Salle (9-3) (B)	⤵
—	20	California (9-1)	

Week of Jan 12

AP	UP	School	AP↓↑
1	1	Kentucky (9-0)	
2	3	Duquesne (13-0)	
3	2	Indiana (9-1)	
4	4	Oklahoma A&M (13-1)	
5	6	Western Kentucky (14-0)	
6	5	Holy Cross (10-0)	↑1
7	—	George Washington (10-0)	↑5
8	18	Oklahoma City (9-1)	↑1
9	9	Duke (12-3)	↓1
10	8	Minnesota (8-2)	↓4
11	7	Kansas (6-2)	↑5
11	20	Wichita State (14-1)	⤴
13	11	Niagara (10-2)	↓1
14	—	Seattle (12-1)	↑2
15	14	Rice (11-1)	↓4
16	12	LSU (10-2)	⤴
17	—	Dayton (11-2)	↓3
18	—	Colorado State (11-1)	⤴
19	15	Illinois (8-3)	↓4
20	—	Idaho (8-3)	⤴
—	9	California (12-1)	
—	13	La Salle (11-3)	
—	16	NC State (10-3)	⤵
—	17	Notre Dame (7-2)	
—	19	Wyoming (10-3)	
—	20	Oregon State (8-4)	⤵

Week of Jan 19

AP	UP	School	AP↓↑
1	1	Kentucky (11-0)	
2	3	Duquesne (15-0)	
3	2	Indiana (12-1)	
4	5	Western Kentucky (16-0)	↑1
5	4	Oklahoma A&M (15-1)	↓1
6	9	Notre Dame (9-2)	⤴
7	12	Oklahoma City (11-1)	↑1
8	12	Holy Cross (12-1)	↓2
9	6	Minnesota (9-2)	↑1
10	—	George Washington (11-1)	↓3
11	14	Wichita State (15-1)	
12	10	LSU (11-2)	↑4
13	11	Duke (12-4)	↓4
14	—	Maryland (13-4)	⤴
15	7	California (14-2)	⤴
16	—	Seattle (14-1)	↓2
17	8	Kansas (8-3)	↓6
18	18	Niagara (10-3)	↓5
19	19	La Salle (14-3)	⤴
20	16	Illinois (9-4)	↓1
—	15	NC State (11-4)	
—	16	Oregon State (10-4)	
—	19	Wyoming (13-3)	

Week of Jan 26

AP	UP	School	AP↓↑
1	1	Kentucky (12-0)	
2	3	Duquesne (15-0)	
3	2	Indiana (12-1)	
4	4	Oklahoma A&M (16-1)	↑1
5	5	Western Kentucky (18-0)	
6	8	Notre Dame (10-2)	
7	10	Holy Cross (13-1)	↑1
8	6	Minnesota (10-2)	↑1
9	16	Oklahoma City (11-2)	↓2
10	—	George Washington (12-1)	
11	—	Seattle (16-1)	↑5
12	11	La Salle (15-3)	↑7
13	—	Maryland (13-4)	↑1
14	7	California (14-2)	↑1
15	12	LSU (11-2)	↓2
16	9	Kansas (8-3)	↑1
16	—	Wichita State (16-2)	↓5
18	—	Connecticut (14-0)	⤴
18	—	Dayton (14-4)	⤴
20	14	Duke (12-4)	↓7
—	13	Wyoming (14-3)	
—	15	Iowa (10-3)	
—	17	Oregon State (11-5)	
—	18	Texas (9-4)	
—	19	Bradley (11-4)	
—	20	NC State (12-5)	

Week of Feb 2

AP	UP	School	AP↓↑
1	1	Kentucky (13-0)	
2	3	Duquesne (17-0)	
3	2	Indiana (12-1)	
4	5	Western Kentucky (19-0)	
5	4	Oklahoma A&M (17-1)	↓1
6	—	Seattle (20-1)	↑5
7	9	Notre Dame (10-2)	↓1
8	13	Duke (13-4)	↑12
9	12	La Salle (15-3)	↑3
10	8	Holy Cross (14-1)	↓3
11	—	George Washington (12-1)	↓1
12	6	Minnesota (12-2)	↓4
13	—	Maryland (15-4)	
14	18	Wichita State (19-2)	↑2
15	7	California (16-2)	↓1
16	—	Oklahoma City (11-4)	↓7
17	11	LSU (13-2)	↓3
18	17	Bradley (11-5)	⤴
19	10	Kansas (8-3)	↓3
20	18	Louisville (14-5)	⤴
—	14	Iowa (11-3)	
—	14	NC State (12-5)	
—	16	Wyoming (15-4)	
—	18	Illinois (9-4)	

Week of Feb 9 (C)

AP	UP	School	AP↓↑
1	3	Kentucky (16-0)	
2	2	Duquesne (18-0)	
3	1	Indiana (14-1)	
4	4	Oklahoma A&M (18-1)	↑1
5	6	Western Kentucky (21-1)	↓1
6	8	Notre Dame (12-2)	↑1
7	10	La Salle (17-3)	↑2
8	14	Seattle (23-1)	↓2
9	8	Holy Cross (16-1)	↑1
10	20	George Washington (13-1)	↑1
11	—	Maryland (17-4)	↑2
12	5	Minnesota (13-2)	
13	—	Oklahoma City (12-4)	↑3
14	7	California (16-2)	↑1
15	13	Duke (14-5)	↓7
16	—	Navy (14-4)	⤴
17	12	LSU (14-2)	
18	—	Wichita State (20-3)	↓4
19	16	NC State (15-5)	⤴
20	11	Kansas (9-4)	↓1
—	14	Iowa (12-3)	
—	17	Colorado State (15-4)	
—	17	Oregon State (14-6)	
—	19	Fordham (14-2)	

Week of Feb 16

AP	UP	School	AP↓↑
1	1	Duquesne (19-0) (D)	↑1
2	2	Kentucky (18-0)	↓1
3	3	Indiana (15-2)	
4	5	Western Kentucky (23-1)	↑1
5	4	Oklahoma A&M (20-2)	↓1
6	8	Notre Dame (13-2)	
7	16	Seattle (24-1)	↑1
8	15	George Washington (16-1)	↑2
9	6	Holy Cross (17-1)	
10	7	Iowa (14-3)	⤴
11	—	Maryland (20-4)	
12	11	La Salle (18-4)	↓5
13	9	LSU (15-2)	↑4
14	13	Duke (16-5)	↑1
15	19	Wichita State (22-3)	↑3
16	—	Oklahoma City (13-5)	↓3
17	—	Dayton (20-5)	⤴
18	12	Minnesota (14-4)	↓6
19	18	Colorado State (17-4)	⤴
20	—	Navy (15-5)	↓4
—	10	Kansas (12-4)	⤵
—	13	California (16-4)	⤵
—	17	UCLA (13-5)	
—	20	NC State (16-6)	⤵

Week of Feb 23

AP	UP	School	AP↓↑
1	1	Duquesne (21-0)	
2	3	Kentucky (21-0)	
3	2	Indiana (17-2)	
4	5	Western Kentucky (25-1)	
5	4	Oklahoma A&M (21-2)	
6	7	Notre Dame (16-2)	
7	6	Holy Cross (20-1)	↑2
8	13	George Washington (18-1)	
9	15	Seattle (24-1)	↓2
10	14	Duke (19-5)	↑4
11	—	Maryland (21-5)	
12	8	LSU (17-2)	↑1
13	10	La Salle (20-4)	↓1
14	17	Wichita State (23-3)	↑1
15	—	Oklahoma City (14-5)	↑1
16	—	Dayton (22-5)	↑1
17	9	Kansas (13-4)	⤴
18	16	Colorado State (20-4)	↑1
19	11	UCLA (18-5)	⤴
20	11	Illinois (16-4)	⤴
20	18	Iowa (16-5)	↓10
—	18	Rice (18-3)	
—	20	NC State (16-6)	

Poll Progression Continues →

Week of Mar 2

AP	UP	SCHOOL	AP↓↑
1	1	**Kentucky** (23-0)	↑1
2	2	**Indiana** (18-3)	↑1
3	4	**Western Kentucky** (28-1)	↑1
4	3	**Duquesne** (22-2)	↓3
5	6	**Notre Dame** (19-2)	↑1
6	5	**Oklahoma A&M** (21-4)	↓1
7	9	**LSU** (19-2)	↑5
8	10	**La Salle** (21-4)	↑5
9	—	**George Washington** (20-2)	↓1
10	16	**Seattle** (26-1)	↓1
11	12	**Duke** (21-5)	↓1
12	15	**Wichita State** (25-3)	↑2
13	8	**Holy Cross** (22-2)	↓6
14	18	**Dayton** (24-6)	↑2
15	7	**Kansas** (15-4)	↑2
16	11	**Iowa** (16-5)	↑4
17	—	**Maryland** (22-6)	↓6
18	17	**NC State** (19-6)	⤴
19	—	**Connecticut** (21-2)	⤴
20	—	**Louisville** (21-6)	⤴
—	13	**Colorado State** (22-4)	⤵
—	14	**Illinois** (16-4)	⤵
—	18	**Minnesota** (16-5)	
—	20	**Oregon State** (18-8)	
—	20	**UCLA** (18-7)	⤵
—	20	**USC** (15-11)	

Week of Mar 9

AP	UP	SCHOOL	AP↓↑
1	2	**Kentucky** (24-0)	
2	1	**Indiana** (19-3)	
3	3	**Duquesne** (24-2)	↑1
4	6	**Western Kentucky** (28-1)	↓1
5	4	**Oklahoma A&M** (23-4)	↑1
6	5	**Notre Dame** (20-2)	↓1
7	—	**George Washington** (23-2)	↑2
8	8	**LSU** (20-2)	↓1
9	9	**Holy Cross** (23-2)	↑4
10	—	**NC State** (24-6)	↑8
11	—	**Seattle** (26-1)	↓1
12	—	**La Salle** (21-4)	↓4
13	7	**Kansas** (16-4)	↑2
14	—	**Maryland** (23-7)	↑3
15	—	**Dayton** (25-6)	↓1
16	10	**Iowa** (17-5)	
16	—	**Oregon State** (18-10)	⤴
18	—	**Duke** (22-6)	↓7
19	—	**Colorado State** (22-5)	⤴
20	—	**Wichita State** (27-4)	↓8

FINAL POLL

AP	SCHOOL	AP↓↑
1	**Kentucky** (25-0) Ⓔ	
2	**La Salle** (26-4)	↑10
3	**Holy Cross** (26-2)	↑6
4	**Indiana** (20-4)	↓2
5	**Duquesne** (26-3)	↓2
6	**Notre Dame** (22-3)	
7	**Bradley** (19-13)	⤴
8	**Western Kentucky** (29-3)	↓4
9	**Penn State** (18-6)	⤴
10	**Oklahoma A&M** (24-5)	↓5
11	**USC** (20-11)	⤴
12	**George Washington** (23-3)	↓5
13	**Iowa** (17-5)	↑3
14	**LSU** (20-5) Ⓔ	↓6
15	**Duke** (22-6)	↑3
16	**Niagara** (24-6)	⤴
17	**Seattle** (26-2)	↓6
18	**Kansas** (16-5)	↓5
19	**Illinois** (17-5)	⤴
20	**Maryland** (28-7)	↓6

Ⓐ With a roster featuring the Big Three—Cliff Hagan, Frank Ramsey and Lou Tsioropoulos—Kentucky adds a third digit to its scoreboards. "By Gawd," says coach Adolph Rupp, "nobody's going to accuse us of shaving points this season." The Wildcats will break the century mark four times at home.

Ⓑ After losing its third game, La Salle seems headed for a fifth straight NIT instead of the increasingly important NCAA. "We don't have any business being in any tournament," coach Ken Loeffler says. The team will become known as Tom Gola and the Eight Garbage Men.

Ⓒ On Feb. 2, Clarence "Bevo" Francis of Rio Grande, an NAIA school in Ohio, scores 113 points in a 134-91 win over Hillsdale (Mich.) College, still the single-game collegiate record. Eleven days later, Furman's Frank Selvy sets the NCAA record against Newberry by scoring 100 in a 149-95 victory. Selvy will win the national scoring title with a phenomenal 41.7 ppg.

Ⓓ Duquesne rides junior Dick Ricketts and sophomore Sihugo Green to No. 1. The Dukes hang on to the top spot for two weeks before losing back-to-back games at Cincinnati and Dayton. It's Dayton's second victory over a top-ranked team in two years.

Ⓔ Unable to settle on a venue, Kentucky and LSU avoid playing during the regular season but wind up in a playoff when they finish tied atop the SEC. The Wildcats win the game (which takes place in Nashville), 63-56, and the conference's automatic NCAA bid. But when Adolph Rupp decides not to accept, LSU and the great Bob Petit wind up in the Tournament anyway.

1954 NCAA Tournament

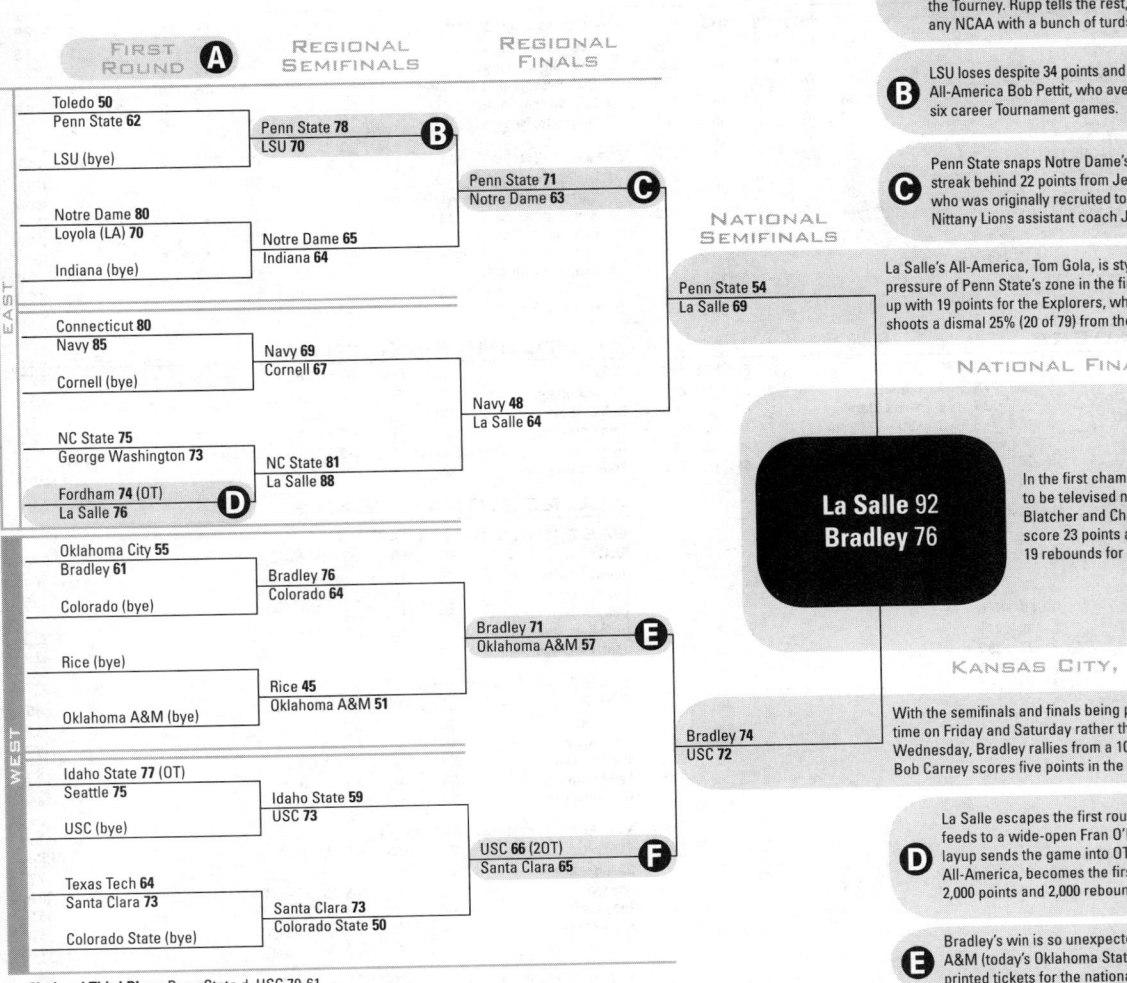

First Round (A)

East

- Toledo **50**, Penn State **62**
- LSU (bye)
- Notre Dame **80**, Loyola (LA) **70**
- Indiana (bye)
- Connecticut **80**, Navy **85**
- Cornell (bye)
- NC State **75**, George Washington **73**
- Fordham **74** (OT), La Salle **76** (D)

West

- Oklahoma City **55**, Bradley **61**
- Colorado (bye)
- Rice (bye)
- Oklahoma A&M (bye)
- Idaho State **77** (OT), Seattle **75**
- USC (bye)
- Texas Tech **64**, Santa Clara **73**
- Colorado State (bye)

Regional Semifinals

- Penn State **78**, LSU **70** (B)
- Notre Dame **65**, Indiana **64**
- Navy **69**, Cornell **67**
- NC State **81**, La Salle **88**
- Bradley **76**, Colorado **64**
- Rice **45**, Oklahoma A&M **51**
- Idaho State **59**, USC **73**
- Santa Clara **73**, Colorado State **50**

Regional Finals

- Penn State **71**, Notre Dame **63** (C)
- Navy **48**, La Salle **64**
- Bradley **71**, Oklahoma A&M **57** (E)
- USC **66** (2OT), Santa Clara **65** (F)

National Semifinals

- Penn State **54**, La Salle **69**
- Bradley **74**, USC **72**

National Final

La Salle 92
Bradley 76

Kansas City, MO

National Third Place Penn State d. USC 70-61
East Regional Third Place Indiana d. LSU 73-62
East Regional Third Place NC State d. Cornell 65-54
West Regional Third Place Rice d. Colorado 78-55
West Regional Third Place Idaho State d. Colorado State 62-57

A Notably absent from the Tournament is Adolph Rupp's only unbeaten Kentucky team, which went 25–0, but Cliff Hagan, Frank Ramsey and Lou Tsioropoulos are grad students, ineligible for the Tourney. Rupp tells the rest, "I'm not going to any NCAA with a bunch of turds like you."

B LSU loses despite 34 points and 24 rebounds from All-America Bob Pettit, who averages 30.5 ppg in six career Tournament games.

C Penn State snaps Notre Dame's 18-game winning streak behind 22 points from Jesse Arnelle, who was originally recruited to play football by Nittany Lions assistant coach Joe Paterno.

La Salle's All-America, Tom Gola, is stymied by the pressure of Penn State's zone in the first half, but ends up with 19 points for the Explorers, while Penn State shoots a dismal 25% (20 of 79) from the floor.

In the first championship game to be televised nationally, Frank Blatcher and Charles Singley each score 23 points and Tom Gola grabs 19 rebounds for La Salle.

With the semifinals and finals being played for the first time on Friday and Saturday rather than Tuesday and Wednesday, Bradley rallies from a 10-point deficit as Bob Carney scores five points in the final 65 seconds.

D La Salle escapes the first round when Tom Gola feeds to a wide-open Fran O'Malley, whose layup sends the game into OT. Gola, a three-time All-America, becomes the first player to amass 2,000 points and 2,000 rebounds.

E Bradley's win is so unexpected that Oklahoma A&M (today's Oklahoma State) is on the pre-printed tickets for the national semifinals.

F The only score in the second overtime is a single free throw by USC's Dick Welsh.

Tournament Leaders

INDIVIDUAL LEADERS

Scoring	CL	POS	G	PTS	PPG
1 **Bob Pettit**, LSU	SR	F/C	2	61	30.5
2 **John Clune**, Navy	SR	G/F	3	79	26.3
3 **Dick Rosenthal**, Notre Dame	SR	F/C	3	76	25.3
4 **Tom Gola**, La Salle	JR	C	5	114	22.8
5 **Lee Morton**, Cornell	SR	G	2	45	22.5
6 **Bob Carney**, Bradley	SR	G	5	107	21.4
7 **Jesse Arnelle**, Penn State	JR	F/C	5	102	20.4
8 **Mel Thompson**, NC State	SR	C	3	59	19.7
9 **Don Schlundt**, Indiana	JR	C	2	39	19.5
10 **Roy Irvin**, Southern California	JR	C	4	75	18.8

Minimum: 2 games

Field Goals Per Game	CL	POS	G	FG	FGPG
1 **Bob Pettit**, LSU	SR	F/C	2	23	11.5
2 **John Clune**, Navy	SR	G/F	3	30	10.0
3 **Dick Rosenthal**, Notre Dame	SR	F/C	3	29	9.7
4 **Lee Morton**, Cornell	SR	G	2	17	8.5
5 **Tom Gola**, La Salle	JR	C	5	38	7.6

Free Throw Pct	CL	POS	G	FT	FTA	PCT
1 **Lee Morton**, Cornell	SR	G	2	11	11	100.0
Corky Devlin, George Washington	JR	F	1	8	8	100.0
Bob Jeangerard, Colorado	JR	F	2	7	7	100.0
Don Lance, Rice	SR	F	2	6	6	100.0
Earl Fields, Penn State	SO	F	5	5	5	100.0
Benny McArdle, LSU	SR	G	2	5	5	100.0
Arnold Short, Oklahoma City	SR	G	1	5	5	100.0

Minimum: 5 made

TEAM LEADERS

Scoring	G	PTS	PPG
1 **La Salle**	5	389	77.8
2 **NC State**	3	221	73.7
3 **Bradley**	5	358	71.6
4 **Santa Clara**	3	208	69.3
Notre Dame	3	208	69.3
6 **Indiana**	2	137	68.5
7 **Southern California**	4	272	68.0
8 **Navy**	3	202	67.3
9 **Penn State**	5	335	67.0
10 **LSU**	2	132	66.0

Minimum: 2 games

FT Pct	G	FT	FTA	PCT
1 **Cornell**	2	31	38	81.6
2 **Santa Clara**	3	57	72	79.2
3 **LSU**	2	40	52	76.9
4 **Bradley**	5	146	194	75.3
5 **Southern California**	4	84	117	71.8

Minimum: 2 games

FG Per Game	G	FG	FGPG
1 **La Salle**	5	138	27.6
2 **Santa Clara**	3	77	25.7
3 **NC State**	3	76	25.3
4 **Rice**	2	50	25.0
5 **Penn State**	5	122	24.4

ALL-TOURNAMENT TEAM

PLAYER	CL	POS	HT	SCHOOL	PPG
Jesse Arnelle	JR	F/C	6-5	Penn State	20.4
Bob Carney	SR	G	6-3	Bradley	21.4
Tom Gola	JR	C	6-6	La Salle	22.8
Roy Irvin	JR	C	6-5	Southern California	18.8
Charles Singley	SO	F	6-3	La Salle	17.2

ALL-REGIONAL TEAMS

East (Iowa City, IA)

PLAYER	CL	POS	HT	SCHOOL	PPG
Jesse Arnelle	JR	F/C	6-5	Penn State	19.7
Bobby Leonard	SR	G	6-3	Indiana	9.5
Bob Pettit	SR	F/C	6-9	LSU	30.5
Dick Rosenthal	SR	F/C	6-5	Notre Dame	25.3
Jack Stephens	JR	G	6-3	Notre Dame	12.7

East (Philadelphia)

PLAYER	CL	POS	HT	SCHOOL	PPG
Tom Gola*	JR	C	6-6	La Salle	25.3
Don Lange	SR	F	6-4	Navy	16.7
Vic Molodet	SO	G	5-11	NC State	15.0
Lee Morton	SR	G	6-2	Cornell	22.5
Mel Thompson	SR	C	6-4	NC State	19.7

West (Corvallis, OR)

PLAYER	CL	POS	HT	SCHOOL	PPG
Sam Beckham	SR	G	5-10	Idaho State	17.7
Roy Irvin	JR	C	6-5	Southern California	20.0
Tony Psaltis	SO	G	6-3	Southern California	15.5
Ken Sears	JR	F/C	6-9	Santa Clara	16.0
Jim Young	SR	F	6-3	Santa Clara	17.3

West (Stillwater, OK)

PLAYER	CL	POS	HT	SCHOOL	PPG
Bob Carney	SR	G	6-3	Bradley	23.3
Dick Estergard	SR	F	6-4	Bradley	11.0
Don Lance	SR	F	6-4	Rice	16.0
Bob Mattick	SR	C	6-11	Oklahoma A&M	15.0
Gene Schwinger	SR	F	6-5	Rice	12.5

* Most outstanding player

1954 NCAA TOURNAMENT BOX SCORES

78-70 (SWEET 16)

	1H	2H
Penn State	34	44
LSU	32	38

PENN STATE	MIN	FG	3FG	FT	REB	A	ST	BL	PF	TP
Jesse Arnelle	-	10-25	-	4-6	14	-	-	-	2	24
Jack Sherry	-	1-10	-	9-11	2	-	-	-	3	11
Jim Blocker	-	4-5	-	1-1	6	-	-	-	2	9
Earl Fields	-	4-5	-	1-1	3	-	-	-	2	9
Ed Haag	-	4-10	-	1-4	2	-	-	-	2	9
Ron Weidenhammer	-	4-12	-	1-4	4	-	-	-	2	9
Jim Brewer	-	2-11	-	1-2	4	-	-	-	2	5
Bob Rohland	-	0-4	-	2-3	2	-	-	-	4	2
Rudy Marisa	-	0-0	-	0-0	0	-	-	-	0	0
TOTALS	-	**29-82**	-	**20-32**	**37**	-	-	-	**19**	**78**
Percentages		35.4		62.5						

Coach: Elmer Gross

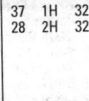

LSU	MIN	FG	3FG	FT	REB	A	ST	BL	PF	TP
Bob Pettit	-	13-21	-	8-9	24	-	-	-	3	34
Ned Clark	-	4-12	-	2-5	13	-	-	-	2	10
Norman Magee	-	3-7	-	3-3	3	-	-	-	3	9
Benny McArdle	-	2-10	-	5-5	3	-	-	-	4	9
Don Belcher	-	3-12	-	0-0	6	-	-	-	4	6
Jim McNeilly	-	0-1	-	2-2	1	-	-	-	0	2
Bob Freshley	-	0-0	-	0-0	1	-	-	-	1	0
Leslie Jones	-	0-0	-	0-0	0	-	-	-	1	0
Don Sebastian	-	0-4	-	0-0	0	-	-	-	3	0
TOTALS	-	**25-67**	-	**20-24**	**51**	-	-	-	**21**	**70**
Percentages		37.3		83.3						

Coach: Harry Rabenhorst

65-64 (SWEET 16)

	1H	2H
Notre Dame	37	28
Indiana	32	32

NOTRE DAME	MIN	FG	3FG	FT	REB	A	ST	BL	PF	TP
Dick Rosenthal	-	9-29	-	7-8	15	-	-	-	3	25
Jack Stephens	-	2-6	-	8-18	4	-	-	-	3	12
Joe Bertrand	-	4-14	-	3-5	6	-	-	-	4	11
William Sullivan	-	4-10	-	2-3	8	-	-	-	2	10
John Fannon	-	2-7	-	0-0	9	-	-	-	5	4
Edward McGinn	-	1-3	-	1-3	2	-	-	-	3	3
William Weiman	-	0-1	-	0-0	0	-	-	-	4	0
TOTALS	-	**22-70**	-	**21-37**	**44**	-	-	-	**24**	**65**
Percentages		31.4		56.8						

Coach: John Jordan

INDIANA	MIN	FG	3FG	FT	REB	A	ST	BL	PF	TP
Burke Scott	-	9-16	-	2-5	9	-	-	-	5	20
Richard Farley	-	2-6	-	9-13	3	-	-	-	5	13
Bobby Leonard	-	5-20	-	1-2	4	-	-	-	4	11
Don Schlundt	-	1-4	-	8-8	6	-	-	-	4	10
Charles Kraak	-	2-5	-	3-6	8	-	-	-	3	7
Wally Choice	-	1-6	-	1-2	5	-	-	-	1	3
Phil Byers	-	0-0	-	0-0	0	-	-	-	1	0
Richard White	-	0-2	-	0-2	4	-	-	-	1	0
TOTALS	-	**20-59**	-	**24-38**	**39**	-	-	-	**24**	**64**
Percentages		33.9		63.2						

Coach: Branch McCracken

69-67 (SWEET 16)

	1H	2H
Navy	40	29
Cornell	32	35

NAVY	MIN	FG	3FG	FT	REB	A	ST	BL	PF	TP
Don Lange	40	11	-	7-11	-	-	-	-	2	29
John Clune	40	7	-	7-8	-	-	-	-	1	21
William Hoover	31	2	-	1-1	-	-	-	-	3	5
Ed Hogan	38	2	-	0-0	-	-	-	-	1	4
Tom Wells	9	1	-	2-5	-	-	-	-	5	4
Larry Wigley	28	0	-	2-2	-	-	-	-	5	2
Doral Sandlin	8	1	-	0-0	-	-	-	-	0	2
Ken McCally	4	1	-	0-0	-	-	-	-	0	2
William Slattery	2	0	-	0-0	-	-	-	-	0	0
TOTALS	**200**	**25**	-	**19-27**	-	-	-	-	**17**	**69**
Percentages				70.4						

Coach: Ben Carnevale

CORNELL	MIN	FG	3FG	FT	REB	A	ST	BL	PF	TP
Lee Morton	-	12	-	10-10	-	-	-	-	4	34
David Bradfield	-	5	-	0-0	-	-	-	-	4	10
Raymond Zelek	-	4	-	0-2	-	-	-	-	3	8
Max Mattes	-	2	-	3-3	-	-	-	-	3	7
Martin Wilens	-	1	-	3-5	-	-	-	-	1	5
Charles Rolles	-	0	-	2-3	-	-	-	-	1	2
Henry Buncom	-	0	-	1-1	-	-	-	-	2	1
Richard Coddington	-	0	-	0-0	-	-	-	-	0	0
Wendell MacPhee	-	0	-	0-0	-	-	-	-	0	0
TOTALS	-	**24**	-	**19-24**	-	-	-	-	**18**	**67**
Percentages				79.2						

Coach: Royner C. Green

88-81 (SWEET 16)

	1H	2H
La Salle	36	52
NC State	35	46

LA SALLE	MIN	FG	3FG	FT	REB	A	ST	BL	PF	TP
Tom Gola	-	6	-	14-18	-	-	-	-	3	26
Charles Singley	-	9	-	8-10	-	-	-	-	4	26
Fran O'Malley	-	5	-	3-5	-	-	-	-	4	13
Frank Blatcher	-	4	-	2-2	-	-	-	-	1	10
Francis O'Hara	-	3	-	3-4	-	-	-	-	2	9
Bob Maples	-	2	-	0-0	-	-	-	-	4	4
Charles Greenberg	-	0	-	0-0	-	-	-	-	0	0
TOTALS	-	**29**	-	**30-39**	-	-	-	-	**18**	**88**
Percentages				76.9						

Coach: Ken Loeffler

NC STATE	MIN	FG	3FG	FT	REB	A	ST	BL	PF	TP
Ronnie Shavlik	-	10	-	4-4	-	-	-	-	3	24
Mel Thompson	-	5	-	9-16	-	-	-	-	1	19
Vic Molodet	-	6	-	3-4	-	-	-	-	2	15
Herb Applebaum	-	4	-	1-1	-	-	-	-	4	9
Dick Tyler	-	3	-	1-1	-	-	-	-	5	7
Phil Dinardo	-	2	-	1-2	-	-	-	-	2	5
Ronnie Scheffel	-	0	-	2-2	-	-	-	-	2	2
William Bell	-	0	-	0-0	-	-	-	-	3	0
TOTALS	-	**30**	-	**21-30**	-	-	-	-	**22**	**81**
Percentages				70.0						

Coach: Everett Case

76-64 (SWEET 16)

	1H	2H
Bradley	36	40
Colorado	35	29

BRADLEY	MIN	FG	3FG	FT	REB	A	ST	BL	PF	TP
Bob Carney	-	7	-	23-26	-	-	-	-	4	37
John Kent	-	7	-	3-4	-	-	-	-	2	17
Eddie King	-	3	-	3-3	-	-	-	-	4	9
Dick Estergard	-	1	-	5-7	-	-	-	-	3	7
Harvey Babetch	-	0	-	2-2	-	-	-	-	1	2
Dick Petersen	-	1	-	0-0	-	-	-	-	5	2
Jerry Hansen	-	0	-	1-1	-	-	-	-	0	1
Barney Kilcullen	-	0	-	1-1	-	-	-	-	5	1
Jack Gower	-	0	-	0-0	-	-	-	-	2	0
Lee O'Connell	-	0	-	0-0	-	-	-	-	1	0
John Riley	-	0	-	0-0	-	-	-	-	0	0
TOTALS	-	**19**	-	**38-44**	-	-	-	-	**27**	**76**
Percentages				86.4						

Coach: Forrest "Forddy" Anderson

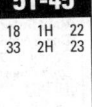

COLORADO	MIN	FG	3FG	FT	REB	A	ST	BL	PF	TP
Charley Mock	-	7	-	3-4	-	-	-	-	5	17
Tom Harrold	-	6	-	1-2	-	-	-	-	5	13
Burdette Haldorson	-	2	-	7-13	-	-	-	-	5	11
George Hannah	-	2	-	3-3	-	-	-	-	4	7
Jim Ranglos	-	1	-	3-5	-	-	-	-	3	5
Bob Jeangerard	-	0	-	4-4	-	-	-	-	3	4
Wilbert Walter	-	1	-	2-3	-	-	-	-	2	4
Mel Coffman	-	0	-	2-2	-	-	-	-	5	2
Bill Peterson	-	0	-	1-1	-	-	-	-	2	1
Merle Abrames	-	0	-	0-2	-	-	-	-	0	0
TOTALS	-	**19**	-	**26-39**	-	-	-	-	**34**	**64**
Percentages				66.7						

Coach: H.B. Lee

51-45 (SWEET 16)

	1H	2H
Oklahoma A&M	18	33
Rice	22	23

OKLAHOMA A&M	MIN	FG	3FG	FT	REB	A	ST	BL	PF	TP
Frank Bigham	-	5	-	2-3	-	-	-	-	0	12
Bob Mattick	-	5	-	1-4	-	-	-	-	4	11
Fred Babb	-	2	-	5-6	-	-	-	-	0	9
Clayton Carter	-	2	-	3-8	-	-	-	-	2	7
V.R. Barnhouse	-	2	-	2-4	-	-	-	-	2	6
Tom Fuller	-	2	-	2-2	-	-	-	-	1	6
Bob Hendrick	-	0	-	0-2	-	-	-	-	0	0
Tom Maloney	-	0	-	0-0	-	-	-	-	1	0
TOTALS	-	**18**	-	**15-29**	-	-	-	-	**10**	**51**
Percentages				51.7						

Coach: Hank Iba

RICE	MIN	FG	3FG	FT	REB	A	ST	BL	PF	TP
Gene Schwinger	-	4	-	3-4	-	-	-	-	1	11
Joe Durrenberger	-	3	-	4-8	-	-	-	-	5	10
Don Lance	-	4	-	1-1	-	-	-	-	5	9
Bobby Brashear	-	3	-	1-2	-	-	-	-	3	7
Monte Robicheaux	-	3	-	0-0	-	-	-	-	3	6
Charles Christensen	-	1	-	0-0	-	-	-	-	0	2
James Beavers	-	0	-	0-0	-	-	-	-	2	0
Oree Bryan	-	0	-	0-0	-	-	-	-	1	0
TOTALS	-	**18**	-	**9-15**	-	-	-	-	**20**	**45**
Percentages				60.0						

Coach: Don Suman

USC 73-59 Idaho State (SWEET 16)

	1H	2H
USC	33	40
Idaho State	25	34

USC	MIN	FG	3FG	FT	REB	A	ST	BL	PF	TP
Roy Irvin	-	9-19	-	7-8	3	-	-	-	2	25
Chet Carr	-	5-12	-	1-3	4	-	-	-	2	11
Tony Psaltis	-	4-8	-	3-4	6	-	-	-	3	11
Jack Dunne	-	3-7	-	1-2	3	-	-	-	0	7
Dick Hammer	-	3-10	-	1-1	8	-	-	-	2	7
Ralph Pausig	-	3-13	-	0-0	6	-	-	-	1	6
Dick Welsh	-	3-8	-	0-0	1	-	-	-	4	6
Jack Findlay	-	0-0	-	0-0	0	-	-	-	0	0
Jack Lovrich	-	0-1	-	0-0	0	-	-	-	1	0
Al Ludecke	-	0-0	-	0-0	2	-	-	-	3	0
Dick Nagai	-	0-1	-	0-0	0	-	-	-	1	0
Walter Thompson	-	0-1	-	0-0	1	-	-	-	0	0
TOTALS	-	30-80	-	13-18	34	-	-	-	19	73
Percentages		37.5		72.2						

Coach: Forrest Twogood

IDAHO STATE	MIN	FG	3FG	FT	REB	A	ST	BL	PF	TP
Les Roh	-	3-13	-	7-8	6	-	-	-	3	13
Sam Beckham	-	4-11	-	4-5	2	-	-	-	3	12
Roy Dakich	-	4-9	-	2-3	0	-	-	-	0	10
Bus Connor	-	3-7	-	3-6	5	-	-	-	1	9
Rick Bauer	-	3-5	-	2-3	12	-	-	-	3	8
Jerry Belkow	-	2-6	-	2-2	1	-	-	-	1	6
Bill Hays	-	0-2	-	1-2	3	-	-	-	0	1
Bryce Dethlefs	-	0-0	-	0-2	1	-	-	-	1	0
TOTALS	-	19-53	-	21-31	30	-	-	-	12	59
Percentages		35.8		67.7						

Coach: Steve Belko

Santa Clara 73-50 Colorado State (SWEET 16)

	1H	2H
Santa Clara	44	29
Colorado State	27	23

SANTA CLARA	MIN	FG	3FG	FT	REB	A	ST	BL	PF	TP
Jim Young	-	9	-	2-2	-	-	-	-	2	20
Herb Schoenstein	-	4	-	5-5	-	-	-	-	2	13
Ken Sears	-	5	-	1-2	-	-	-	-	2	11
Gary Gatzert	-	3	-	4-5	-	-	-	-	4	10
Don Benedetti	-	3	-	2-3	-	-	-	-	2	8
John Boudreau	-	2	-	0-0	-	-	-	-	0	4
Dick Simoni	-	2	-	0-0	-	-	-	-	2	4
Danny Ball	-	0	-	2-2	-	-	-	-	1	2
Mickey Mount	-	0	-	1-1	-	-	-	-	3	1
Dean Robinson	-	0	-	0-0	-	-	-	-	0	0
TOTALS	-	28	-	17-20	-	-	-	-	18	73
Percentages				85.0						

Coach: Bob Feerick

COLORADO STATE	MIN	FG	3FG	FT	REB	A	ST	BL	PF	TP
Dennis Stuehm	-	6	-	6-19	-	-	-	-	4	18
Ronald Caylor	-	5	-	1-1	-	-	-	-	3	11
Robert Betz	-	2	-	2-2	-	-	-	-	2	6
Jack Bryant	-	2	-	2-2	-	-	-	-	0	6
Harold Kinard	-	1	-	2-2	-	-	-	-	2	4
James Savioni	-	1	-	0-0	-	-	-	-	0	2
Clark Vanderhoff	-	1	-	0-0	-	-	-	-	0	2
Stanley Pivic	-	0	-	1-2	-	-	-	-	1	1
William Bartran	-	0	-	0-0	-	-	-	-	1	0
Bob Cates	-	0	-	0-0	-	-	-	-	0	0
Leonard Gregory	-	0	-	0-2	-	-	-	-	1	0
Gary Hibbard	-	0	-	0-0	-	-	-	-	2	0
TOTALS	-	18	-	14-30	-	-	-	-	16	50
Percentages				46.7						

Coach: Bill Strannigan

Penn State 71-63 Notre Dame (ELITE 8)

	1H	2H
Penn State	31	40
Notre Dame	28	35

PENN STATE	MIN	FG	3FG	FT	REB	A	ST	BL	PF	TP
Jesse Arnelle	-	7	-	8-9	-	-	-	-	0	22
Jack Sherry	-	4	-	6-7	-	-	-	-	5	14
Jim Blocker	-	5	-	3-6	-	-	-	-	3	13
Ed Haag	-	4	-	4-5	-	-	-	-	5	12
Jim Brewer	-	3	-	1-1	-	-	-	-	1	7
Ron Weidenhammer	-	1	-	1-2	-	-	-	-	3	3
Earl Fields	-	0	-	0-0	-	-	-	-	1	0
Bob Rohland	-	0	-	0-0	-	-	-	-	1	0
TOTALS	-	24	-	23-30	-	-	-	-	19	71
Percentages				76.7						

Coach: Elmer Gross

NOTRE DAME	MIN	FG	3FG	FT	REB	A	ST	BL	PF	TP
Richard Rosenthal	-	8	-	4-5	-	-	-	-	4	20
Jack Stephens	-	4	-	8-12	-	-	-	-	3	16
Joe Bertrand	-	3	-	4-6	-	-	-	-	5	10
William Sullivan	-	3	-	3-4	-	-	-	-	3	9
John Fannon	-	3	-	2-3	-	-	-	-	4	8
Edward McGinn	-	0	-	0-0	-	-	-	-	1	0
William Weiman	-	0	-	0-0	-	-	-	-	0	0
TOTALS	-	21	-	21-30	-	-	-	-	20	63
Percentages				70.0						

Coach: John Jordan

La Salle 64-48 Navy (ELITE 8)

	1H	2H
La Salle	21	43
Navy	21	27

LA SALLE	MIN	FG	3FG	FT	REB	A	ST	BL	PF	TP
Tom Gola	-	8	-	6-11	-	-	-	-	3	22
Charles Singley	-	5	-	6-7	-	-	-	-	2	16
Bob Maples	-	5	-	3-9	-	-	-	-	3	13
Frank Blatcher	-	2	-	1-1	-	-	-	-	1	5
Fran O'Malley	-	1	-	3-4	-	-	-	-	2	5
Francis O'Hara	-	0	-	3-3	-	-	-	-	2	3
Bob Ames	-	0	-	0-0	-	-	-	-	0	0
Charles Greenberg	-	0	-	0-0	-	-	-	-	0	0
John Yodsnukis	-	0	-	0-0	-	-	-	-	0	0
TOTALS	-	21	-	22-35	-	-	-	-	13	64
Percentages				62.9						

Coach: Ken Loeffler

NAVY	MIN	FG	3FG	FT	REB	A	ST	BL	PF	TP
John Clune	35	7	-	2-3	-	-	-	-	4	16
Ed Hogan	34	3	-	1-3	-	-	-	-	3	7
William Hoover	34	3	-	1-1	-	-	-	-	0	7
Doral Sandlin	10	2	-	2-2	-	-	-	-	1	6
Larry Wigley	28	0	-	4-5	-	-	-	-	3	4
Don Lange	25	1	-	1-2	-	-	-	-	5	3
Ben Thompson	16	1	-	1-2	-	-	-	-	2	3
Tom Wells	7	0	-	2-2	-	-	-	-	1	2
William Slattery	4	0	-	0-0	-	-	-	-	0	0
Ken McCally	3	0	-	0-0	-	-	-	-	3	0
Jim Degroff	2	0	-	0-0	-	-	-	-	0	0
John McDonnell	2	0	-	0-0	-	-	-	-	0	0
TOTALS	200	17	-	14-20	-	-	-	-	22	48
Percentages				70.0						

Coach: Ben Carnevale

Bradley 71-57 Oklahoma A&M (ELITE 8)

	1H	2H
Bradley	31	40
Oklahoma A&M	28	29

BRADLEY	MIN	FG	3FG	FT	REB	A	ST	BL	PF	TP
Eddie King	-	5	-	13-16	-	-	-	-	1	23
Dick Estergard	-	5	-	5-7	-	-	-	-	3	15
John Kent	-	6	-	0-1	-	-	-	-	3	12
Bob Carney	-	1	-	4-4	-	-	-	-	5	6
Jack Gower	-	2	-	2-2	-	-	-	-	1	6
Dick Petersen	-	1	-	2-4	-	-	-	-	5	4
Barney Kilcullen	-	0	-	2-4	-	-	-	-	5	2
Lee O'Connell	-	1	-	0-0	-	-	-	-	0	2
Harvey Babetch	-	0	-	1-1	-	-	-	-	0	1
Jerry Hansen	-	0	-	0-0	-	-	-	-	0	0
John Riley	-	0	-	0-0	-	-	-	-	0	0
Lee Utt	-	0	-	0-0	-	-	-	-	0	0
TOTALS	-	21	-	29-39	-	-	-	-	23	71
Percentages				74.4						

Coach: Forrest "Forddy" Anderson

OKLAHOMA A&M	MIN	FG	3FG	FT	REB	A	ST	BL	PF	TP
Bob Mattick	-	6	-	7-11	-	-	-	-	5	19
Frank Bigham	-	5	-	2-4	-	-	-	-	1	12
V.R. Barnhouse	-	3	-	4-5	-	-	-	-	5	10
Tom Maloney	-	2	-	2-4	-	-	-	-	2	6
Clayton Carter	-	1	-	3-3	-	-	-	-	5	5
Bob Hendrick	-	0	-	3-3	-	-	-	-	4	3
Tom Fuller	-	1	-	0-0	-	-	-	-	5	2
Fred Babb	-	0	-	0-0	-	-	-	-	3	0
Chester Reams	-	0	-	0-0	-	-	-	-	0	0
TOTALS	-	18	-	21-30	-	-	-	-	30	57
Percentages				70.0						

Coach: Hank Iba

USC 66-65 Santa Clara (ELITE 8)

	1H	2H	OT1	OT2
USC	28	29	8	1
Santa Clara	26	31	8	0

USC	MIN	FG	3FG	FT	REB	A	ST	BL	PF	TP
Tony Psaltis	-	6-9	-	8-12	2	-	-	-	2	20
Roy Irvin	-	6-14	-	3-3	4	-	-	-	4	15
Dick Welsh	-	3-11	-	7-10	8	-	-	-	2	13
Chet Carr	-	2-8	-	5-7	2	-	-	-	5	9
Dick Hammer	-	2-8	-	1-1	5	-	-	-	3	5
Al Ludecke	-	1-1	-	0-0	1	-	-	-	0	2
Ralph Pausig	-	0-1	-	2-3	4	-	-	-	3	2
TOTALS	-	20-52	-	26-36	26	-	-	-	19	66
Percentages		38.5		72.2						

Coach: Forrest Twogood

SANTA CLARA	MIN	FG	3FG	FT	REB	A	ST	BL	PF	TP
Jim Young	-	8-13	-	4-5	4	-	-	-	5	20
Ken Sears	-	6-16	-	4-4	8	-	-	-	4	16
Mickey Mount	-	4-6	-	7-10	7	-	-	-	3	15
Herb Schoenstein	-	3-6	-	1-3	2	-	-	-	5	7
Gary Gatzert	-	1-6	-	2-3	4	-	-	-	5	4
Don Benedetti	-	1-7	-	1-1	1	-	-	-	1	3
Danny Ball	-	0-0	-	0-0	0	-	-	-	1	0
Dick Simoni	-	0-0	-	0-0	0	-	-	-	1	0
TOTALS	-	23-54	-	19-26	26	-	-	-	25	65
Percentages		42.6		73.1						

Coach: Bob Feerick

Technicals: Santa Clara (Mount)

LA SALLE	MIN	FG	3FG	FT	REB	A	ST	BL	PF	TP
Frank Blatcher	-	7	-	5-7	-	-	-	-	2	19
Tom Gola	-	5	-	9-12	-	-	-	-	4	19
Charles Singley	-	4	-	2-3	-	-	-	-	4	10
Fran O'Malley	-	3	-	3-6	-	-	-	-	4	9
Bob Maples	-	3	-	1-1	-	-	-	-	1	7
Francis O'Hara	-	2	-	1-3	-	-	-	-	0	5
TOTALS	**-**	**24**	**-**	**21-32**	**-**	**-**	**-**	**-**	**15**	**69**
Percentages				65.6						

Coach: Ken Loeffler

69-54

33	1H	22
36	2H	32

FINAL 4

PENN STATE	MIN	FG	3FG	FT	REB	A	ST	BL	PF	TP
Jesse Arnelle	-	5	-	8-10	-	-	-	-	2	18
Jim Brewer	-	3	-	0-0	-	-	-	-	2	6
Jack Sherry	-	1	-	4-7	-	-	-	-	4	6
Earl Fields	-	2	-	1-1	-	-	-	-	4	5
Jim Blocker	-	2	-	0-2	-	-	-	-	1	4
Dave Edwards	-	2	-	0-0	-	-	-	-	1	4
Ed Haag	-	2	-	0-0	-	-	-	-	4	4
Bob Rohland	-	2	-	0-2	-	-	-	-	1	4
Ron Weidenhammer	-	1	-	1-2	-	-	-	-	2	3
TOTALS	**-**	**20-79**	**-**	**14-24**	**-**	**-**	**-**	**-**	**21**	**54**
Percentages		25.3		58.3						

Coach: Elmer Gross

Officials: Enright, Ball

BRADLEY	MIN	FG	3FG	FT	REB	A	ST	BL	PF	TP
Dick Estergard	-	7	-	7-7	-	-	-	-	2	21
Bob Carney	-	6	-	8-9	-	-	-	-	4	20
Eddie King	-	6	-	5-7	-	-	-	-	3	17
John Kent	-	3	-	1-5	-	-	-	-	3	7
Dick Petersen	-	1	-	3-4	-	-	-	-	1	5
Harvey Babetch	-	1	-	0-0	-	-	-	-	0	2
Jack Gower	-	1	-	0-0	-	-	-	-	3	2
Barney Kilcullen	-	0	-	0-0	-	-	-	-	0	0
Lee O'Connell	-	0	-	0-0	-	-	-	-	0	0
Lee Utt	-	0	-	0-0	-	-	-	-	0	0
TOTALS	**-**	**25**	**-**	**24-32**	**-**	**-**	**-**	**-**	**16**	**74**
Percentages				75.0						

Coach: Forrest "Forddy" Anderson

74-72

36	1H	42
38	2H	30

FINAL 4

USC	MIN	FG	3FG	FT	REB	A	ST	BL	PF	TP
Roy Irvin	-	9	-	5-6	-	-	-	-	5	23
Dick Welsh	-	6	-	7-11	-	-	-	-	2	19
Ralph Pausig	-	5	-	2-2	-	-	-	-	3	12
Dick Hammer	-	2	-	3-3	-	-	-	-	5	7
Tony Psaltis	-	2	-	0-2	-	-	-	-	4	4
Chet Carr	-	1	-	1-2	-	-	-	-	1	3
Jack Dunne	-	1	-	0-0	-	-	-	-	0	2
Al Ludecke	-	1	-	0-0	-	-	-	-	0	2
TOTALS	**-**	**27**	**-**	**18-26**	**-**	**-**	**-**	**-**	**20**	**72**
Percentages				69.2						

Coach: Forrest Twogood

Officials: Andersen, Dean

PENN STATE	MIN	FG	3FG	FT	REB	A	ST	BL	PF	TP
Jesse Arnelle	-	10	-	5-6	-	-	-	-	5	25
Ron Weidenhammer	-	4	-	4-4	-	-	-	-	1	12
Ed Haag	-	4	-	1-2	-	-	-	-	1	9
Jim Brewer	-	4	-	0-0	-	-	-	-	3	8
Jack Sherry	-	2	-	3-3	-	-	-	-	5	7
Earl Fields	-	2	-	0-0	-	-	-	-	1	4
Bob Rohland	-	1	-	1-2	-	-	-	-	3	3
Jim Blocker	-	0	-	2-3	-	-	-	-	3	2
Dave Edwards	-	0	-	0-0	-	-	-	-	1	0
TOTALS	**-**	**27**	**-**	**16-20**	**-**	**-**	**-**	**-**	**23**	**70**
Percentages				80.0						

Coach: Elmer Gross

70-61

44	1H	26
26	2H	35

3RD PLACE

USC	MIN	FG	3FG	FT	REB	A	ST	BL	PF	TP
Dick Welsh	-	3	-	12-14	-	-	-	-	0	18
Roy Irvin	-	5	-	2-3	-	-	-	-	4	12
Tony Psaltis	-	4	-	3-3	-	-	-	-	1	11
Dick Hammer	-	2	-	4-7	-	-	-	-	3	8
Ralph Pausig	-	2	-	1-3	-	-	-	-	3	5
Chet Carr	-	1	-	2-2	-	-	-	-	3	4
Walter Thompson	-	0	-	2-2	-	-	-	-	0	2
Al Ludecke	-	0	-	1-3	-	-	-	-	0	1
Jack Dunne	-	0	-	0-0	-	-	-	-	0	0
TOTALS	**-**	**17**	**-**	**27-37**	**-**	**-**	**-**	**-**	**14**	**61**
Percentages				73.0						

Coach: Forrest Twogood

Officials: Ball, Enright
Attendance: 10,500

LA SALLE	MIN	FG	3FG	FT	REB	A	ST	BL	PF	TP
Frank Blatcher	-	11	-	1-2	-	-	-	-	4	23
Charles Singley	-	8	-	7-10	-	-	-	-	4	23
Tom Gola	-	7	-	5-5	-	-	-	-	5	19
Fran O'Malley	-	5	-	1-1	-	-	-	-	4	11
Francis O'Hara	-	2	-	3-4	-	-	-	-	1	7
Charles Greenberg	-	2	-	1-2	-	-	-	-	1	5
Bob Maples	-	2	-	0-0	-	-	-	-	4	4
John Yodasnukis	-	0	-	0-0	-	-	-	-	5	0
TOTALS	**-**	**37**	**-**	**18-24**	**-**	**-**	**-**	**-**	**28**	**92**
Percentages				75.0						

Coach: Ken Loeffler

92-76

42	1H	43
50	2H	33

NCAA FINAL 1954

BRADLEY	MIN	FG	3FG	FT	REB	A	ST	BL	PF	TP
Bob Carney	-	3	-	11-17	-	-	-	-	4	17
Dick Estergard	-	3	-	11-12	-	-	-	-	1	17
John Kent	-	8	-	0-2	-	-	-	-	2	16
Eddie King	-	3	-	6-7	-	-	-	-	4	12
Dick Petersen	-	4	-	2-2	-	-	-	-	2	10
John Riley	-	1	-	1-2	-	-	-	-	1	3
Jack Gower	-	0	-	1-2	-	-	-	-	1	1
Harvey Babetch	-	0	-	0-0	-	-	-	-	0	0
Lee Utt	-	0	-	0-0	-	-	-	-	1	0
TOTALS	**-**	**22**	**-**	**32-44**	**-**	**-**	**-**	**-**	**16**	**76**
Percentages				72.7						

Coach: Forrest "Forddy" Anderson

Officials: Andersen, Dean
Attendance: 10,500

National Invitation Tournament (NIT)

First round: St. Francis (NY) d. Louisville 60-55, Dayton d. Manhattan 90-79, Bowling Green d. Wichita State 88-64, Saint Francis (PA) d. BYU 81-68
Quarterfinals: Western Kentucky d. Bowling Green 95-81, Niagara d. Dayton 77-74, Duquesne d. Saint Francis (PA) 69-63. Holy Cross d. St. Francis (NY) 93-69
Semifinals: Duquesne d. Niagara 66-51, Holy Cross d. Western Kentucky 75-69
Third place: Niagara d. Western Kentucky 71-65
Championship: Holy Cross d. Duquesne 71-62
MVP: Togo Palazzi, Holy Cross

1954-55: Russell Rules I

One streak was just beginning as another came to an end. On Dec. 17, 1954, San Francisco (28–1) began a string that would reach to 60 consecutive victories. (The record stood until UCLA's 88-game run from 1971 to '74.) The 26th of those wins, a 77-63 victory over La Salle—which had won its first three Tournament games by an average of 32 points before edging Iowa, 76-73, in the national semifinal—earned the Dons the NCAA championship. All-America center Bill Russell scored 23 points and pulled down 25 rebounds in the title game and was named the Tournament's Most Outstanding Player.

On Jan. 8, 1955, Georgia Tech beat Kentucky, 59-58, ending the Wildcats' record string of 129 home wins, spanning 13 seasons. The 1954-55 season marked the return of two 20-minute halves. The Wildcats were ranked No. 2 in the country entering the Tourney, but were upset by Marquette in their first game, 79-71.

Major Conference Standings

ACC	Conference			Overall		
	W	L	Pct	W	L	Pct
NC State	12	2	.857	28	4	.875
Duke⊛	11	3	.786	20	8	.714
Maryland	10	4	.714	17	7	.708
Wake Forest	8	6	.571	17	10	.630
North Carolina	8	6	.571	10	11	.476
Virginia	5	9	.357	14	15	.483
South Carolina	2	12	.143	10	17	.370
Clemson	0	14	.000	2	21	.087

Tournament: **NC State d. Duke 87-77**
Tournament MVP: **Ron Shavlik**, NC State
Note: NC State was banned from postseason play due to recruiting violations

Big Seven	Conference			Overall		
	W	L	Pct	W	L	Pct
Colorado⊛	11	1	.917	19	6	.760
Missouri	9	3	.750	16	5	.762
Kansas State	6	6	.500	11	10	.524
Nebraska	6	6	.500	9	12	.429
Kansas	5	7	.417	11	10	.524
Iowa State	4	8	.333	11	10	.524
Oklahoma	1	11	.083	3	18	.143

Big Ten	Conference			Overall		
	W	L	Pct	W	L	Pct
Iowa⊛	11	3	.786	19	7	.731
Illinois	10	4	.714	17	5	.773
Minnesota	10	4	.714	15	7	.682
Michigan State	8	6	.571	13	9	.591
Northwestern	7	7	.500	12	10	.545
Purdue	5	9	.357	12	10	.545
Michigan	5	9	.357	11	11	.500
Wisconsin	5	9	.357	10	12	.455
Indiana	5	9	.357	8	14	.364
Ohio State	4	10	.286	10	12	.455

Border	Conference			Overall		
	W	L	Pct	W	L	Pct
West Texas A&M⊛	9	3	.750	15	7	.682
Texas Tech	9	3	.750	18	7	.720
Texas Western	8	4	.667	14	7	.667
Arizona State	8	4	.667	9	13	.409
Hardin-Simmons	4	8	.333	9	15	.375
Arizona	3	9	.250	8	17	.320
New Mexico State	1	11	.083	6	13	.316

CBA	Conference			Overall		
	W	L	Pct	W	L	Pct
San Francisco○	12	0	1.000	28	1	.966
San Jose State	7	5	.583	16	9	.640
Santa Clara	6	6	.500	13	11	.542
Pacific	4	8	.333	11	15	.423
Saint Mary's (CA)	1	11	.083	6	19	.240

Ivy	Conference			Overall		
	W	L	Pct	W	L	Pct
Princeton⊛	10	4	.714	13	12	.520
Penn	10	4	.714	19	6	.760
Columbia	10	4	.714	17	8	.680
Dartmouth	9	5	.643	18	7	.720
Cornell	8	6	.571	10	13	.435
Brown	3	11	.214	7	16	.304
Harvard	3	11	.214	7	16	.304
Yale	3	11	.214	3	21	.125

Metro NY	Conference			Overall		
	W	L	Pct	W	L	Pct
Manhattan□	6	0	1.000	18	5	.783
St. John's	5	1	.833	11	9	.550
Fordham	3	2	.600	18	9	.667
St. Francis (NY)	2	3	.400	21	8	.724
Brooklyn	1	3	.250	7	11	.389
NYU	1	3	.250	7	13	.350
CCNY	0	6	.000	8	10	.444

Mid-American	Conference			Overall		
	W	L	Pct	W	L	Pct
Miami (OH)⊛	11	3	.786	14	9	.609
Marshall	10	4	.714	17	4	.810
Ohio	9	5	.643	16	5	.762
Western Michigan	9	5	.643	12	10	.545
Kent State	5	9	.357	8	14	.364
Bowling Green	5	9	.357	6	16	.273
Toledo	4	10	.286	5	17	.227
Western Reserve	3	11	.214	8	14	.364

Missouri Valley	Conference			Overall		
	W	L	Pct	W	L	Pct
Tulsa⊛	8	2	.800	21	7	.750
Saint Louis□	8	2	.800	20	8	.714
Oklahoma A&M	5	5	.500	12	13	.480
Wichita State	4	6	.400	17	9	.654
Houston	3	7	.300	15	10	.600
Detroit	2	8	.200	15	11	.577

Skyline 8	Conference			Overall		
	W	L	Pct	W	L	Pct
Utah⊛	13	1	.929	24	4	.857
BYU	10	4	.714	13	13	.500
Utah State	9	5	.643	15	7	.682
Wyoming	9	5	.643	17	9	.654
Colorado State	5	9	.357	11	12	.478
Montana	4	10	.286	12	14	.462
Denver	4	10	.286	9	14	.391
New Mexico	2	12	.143	7	17	.292

Ohio Valley	Conference			Overall		
	W	L	Pct	W	L	Pct
Western Kentucky	8	2	.800	18	10	.643
Eastern Kentucky	6	4	.600	15	8	.652
Murray State	6	4	.600	11	15	.423
Morehead State	5	5	.500	14	10	.583
Tennessee Tech	3	7	.300	9	11	.450
Middle Tennessee St.	2	8	.200	11	16	.407

Tournament: **Eastern Kentucky d. Murray State 76-59**

Pacific Coast	Conference			Overall		
	W	L	Pct	W	L	Pct
North						
Oregon State⊛	15	1	.938	22	8	.733
Oregon	8	8	.500	13	13	.500
Washington	7	9	.438	13	12	.520
Washington State	5	11	.313	11	15	.423
Idaho	5	11	.313	8	18	.308
South						
UCLA	11	1	.917	21	5	.808
Stanford	7	5	.583	16	8	.667
Southern California	5	7	.417	14	11	.560
California	1	11	.083	9	16	.360

Playoff: **Oregon State d. UCLA 2-0** in a best of three series for the title

SEC	Conference			Overall		
	W	L	Pct	W	L	Pct
Kentucky⊛	12	2	.857	23	3	.885
Alabama	11	3	.786	19	5	.792
Vanderbilt	9	5	.643	16	6	.727
Tulane	9	5	.643	14	6	.700
Tennessee	8	6	.571	15	7	.682
Georgia Tech	7	7	.500	12	13	.480
Georgia	7	7	.500	9	16	.360
Auburn	6	8	.429	11	9	.550
Florida	5	9	.357	12	10	.545
Mississippi	5	9	.357	8	15	.348
LSU	3	11	.214	6	18	.250
Mississippi State	2	12	.143	6	17	.261

Southern	Conference			Overall		
	W	L	Pct	W	L	Pct
West Virginia⊛	9	1	.900	19	11	.633
George Washington	8	2	.800	24	6	.800
Richmond	9	4	.692	19	9	.679
Washington and Lee	8	5	.615	16	13	.552
Furman	6	4	.600	17	10	.630
William and Mary	7	5	.583	11	14	.440
Davidson	4	6	.400	8	13	.381
VMI	4	9	.308	8	15	.348
Virginia Tech	4	14	.222	7	20	.259
The Citadel	0	10	.000	0	17	.000

Tournament: **West Virginia d. George Washington 58-48**
Tournament MOP: **Rod Hundley**, West Virginia

Southwest	Conference			Overall		
	W	L	Pct	W	L	Pct
SMU⊛	9	3	.750	15	10	.600
TCU	8	4	.667	17	7	.708
Arkansas	8	4	.667	14	9	.609
Baylor	7	5	.583	13	11	.542
Rice	6	6	.500	10	12	.455
Texas	3	9	.250	4	20	.167
Texas A&M	1	11	.083	4	20	.167

WNY Little Three	Conference			Overall		
	W	L	Pct	W	L	Pct
Niagara□	3	1	.750	20	6	.769
Canisius○	2	2	.500	18	7	.720
St. Bonaventure	1	3	.250	13	10	.565

Yankee	Conference			Overall		
	W	L	Pct	W	L	Pct
Connecticut□	7	0	1.000	20	5	.800
Vermont	4	1	.800	6	15	.286
Massachusetts	4	2	.667	10	14	.417
Rhode Island	5	3	.625	17	10	.630
Maine	1	7	.125	4	13	.235
New Hampshire	1	9	.100	4	14	.222

⊛ Automatic NCAA Tournament bid ○ At-large NCAA Tournament bid □ NIT appearance ⊗ Team record doesn't reflect games forfeited or vacated. For adjusted record, see p. 521.

INDEPENDENTS

INDEPENDENTS	Overall W	L	Pct
Williams○	17	2	.895
Marquette○	24	3	.889
Lafayette□	23	3	.885
Dayton□	25	4	.862
Duquesne□	22	4	.846
La Salle⊛	26	5	.839
Memphis○	17	5	.773
Seattle○	22	7	.759
Saint Francis (PA)□	21	7	.750
Holy Cross□	19	7	.731
DePaul	16	6	.727
Cincinnati□	21	8	.724
Louisville□	19	8	.704
Idaho State○	18	8	.692
Seton Hall□	17	9	.654
Penn State○	18	10	.643
Villanova○	18	10	.643
Loyola Marymount	16	9	.640
John Carroll	14	9	.609
Notre Dame	14	10	.583
Gonzaga	15	11	.577
Loyola (LA)	13	10	.565
Muhlenberg	14	11	.560
Colgate	11	9	.550

INDEPENDENTS (cont.)	Overall W	L	Pct
Navy	11	9	.550
Loyola-Chicago	13	11	.542
Valparaiso	13	11	.542
Temple	11	10	.524
Xavier	13	13	.500
Army	9	9	.500
Georgetown	12	13	.480
Iona	10	11	.476
Lehigh	10	11	.476
Syracuse	10	11	.476
Saint Joseph's	12	14	.462
Miami (FL)	9	11	.450
Drake	9	12	.429
Butler	10	14	.417
Portland	9	13	.409
Pittsburgh	10	16	.385
Wash.-St. Louis	8	14	.364
Oklahoma City○	9	18	.333
Bradley○	9	20	.310
Boston College	8	18	.308
Creighton	5	14	.263
Siena	3	13	.188
Bucknell	3	18	.143
Rutgers	2	22	.083

INDIVIDUAL LEADERS—SEASON

Scoring	CL	POS	G	FG	FT	PTS	PPG
1 Darrell Floyd, Furman	JR	G	25	344	209	897	**35.9**
2 Buzzy Wilkinson, Virginia	SR	G	28	308	282	898	**32.1**
3 Robin Freeman, Ohio State	JR	G	13	149	111	409	**31.5**
4 Bill Yarborough, Clemson	SR	G	23	247	157	651	**28.3**
5 Dick O'Neal, TCU	SO	C	24	223	230	676	**28.2**
6 Dickie Hemric, Wake Forest	SR	C	27	222	302	746	**27.6**
7 Bob Patterson, Tulsa	SR	F	28	272	229	773	**27.6**
8 John Mahoney, William and Mary	SR	F	24	220	216	656	**27.3**
9 Denver Brackeen, Mississippi	SR	C	22	203	193	599	**27.2**
10 Jesse Arnelle, Penn State	SR	F/C	28	244	243	731	**26.1**

Field Goal	CL	POS	G	FG	FGA	PCT
1 Ed O'Connor, Manhattan	SR	C	23	147	243	**60.5**
2 Joe Holup, George Washington	JR	C	30	223	373	**59.8**
3 Stan Glowaski, Seattle	SR	G/F	23	144	245	**58.8**
4 Jim Francis, Dartmouth	SO	C	24	117	204	**57.4**
5 Gene Carpenter, Texas Tech	JR	C	25	129	227	**56.8**

Minimum: 100 made

Free Throw Pct	CL	POS	G	FT	FTA	PCT
1 James Scott, West Texas A&M	SR	F	22	153	171	**89.5**
2 Bob Walczak, Marquette	SO	G	27	104	118	**88.1**
3 Carroll Williams, San Jose State	SR	G	25	181	214	**84.6**
4 Chet Forte, Columbia	SO	G	25	187	222	**84.2**
5 Ronnie Ryan, Hardin-Simmons	JR	G	25	105	125	**84.0**

Minimum: 80 made

Rebounds Per Game	CL	POS	G	REB	RPG
1 Charlie Slack, Marshall	JR	C	21	538	**25.6**
2 Art Quimby, Connecticut	SR	C	25	611	**24.4**
3 Ed Conlin, Fordham	SR	F	27	578	**21.4**
4 Bill Russell, San Francisco	JR	C	29	594	**20.5**
5 Wally McCarvill, Iona	SR	C	21	422	**20.1**

INDIVIDUAL LEADERS—GAME

Points	CL	POS	OPP	DATE	PTS
1 Darrell Floyd, Furman	JR	G	Morehead State	J22	**67**
2 Ronnie Shavlik, NC State	JR	F/C	William and Mary	F9	**55**
3 Darrell Floyd, Furman	JR	G	William and Mary	D4	**53**
4 Don Boldebuck, Houston	JR	C	Sam Houston State	F7	**50**
Darrell Floyd, Furman	JR	G	The Citadel	J8	**50**

TEAM LEADERS—SEASON

Scoring Offense	G	W-L	PTS	PPG
1 Furman	27	17-10	2,572	**95.3**
2 Connecticut	25	20-5	2,252	**90.1**
3 Virginia	29	14-15	2,605	**89.8**
4 NC State	32	28-4	2,839	**88.7**
5 Marshall	21	17-4	1,834	**87.3**

Field Goal Pct	G	W-L	FG	FGA	PCT
1 George Washington	30	24-6	867	1,822	**47.6**
2 Wake Forest	27	17-10	803	1,745	**46.0**
3 Lafayette	26	23-3	760	1,700	**44.7**
4 Manhattan	23	18-5	604	1,351	**44.7**
5 Virginia	29	14-15	935	2,115	**44.2**

Free Throw Pct	G	W-L	FT	FTA	PCT
1 Wake Forest	27	17-10	709	938	**75.6**
2 Arizona State	22	9-13	627	832	**75.4**
3 George Washington	30	24-6	615	819	**75.1**
4 Missouri	21	16-5	550	747	**73.6**
5 Richmond	28	19-9	641	879	**72.9**

Scoring Defense	G	W-L	OPP PTS	OPP PPG
1 San Francisco	29	28-1	1,511	**52.1**
2 Oklahoma A&M	25	12-13	1,333	**53.3**
3 Oregon State	30	22-8	1,660	**55.3**
4 Duquesne	26	22-4	1,512	**58.2**
5 Santa Clara	24	13-11	1,427	**59.5**

CONSENSUS ALL-AMERICAS

FIRST TEAM

PLAYER	CL	POS	HT	SCHOOL	RPG	PPG
Sihugo Green	JR	G	6-2	Duquesne	13.6	22.0
Dick Garmaker	SR	F	6-3	Minnesota	8.4	24.2
Tom Gola	SR	C	6-6	La Salle	19.9	24.2
Dick Ricketts	SR	F	6-7	Duquesne	17.3	20.1
Bill Russell	JR	C	6-9	San Francisco	20.5	21.4

SECOND TEAM

PLAYER	CL	POS	HT	SCHOOL	RPG	PPG
Darrell Floyd	JR	G	6-1	Furman	8.3	35.9
Robin Freeman	JR	G	5-11	Ohio State	N/A	31.5
Dickie Hemric	SR	C	6-6	Wake Forest	19.1	27.6
Ronnie Shavlik	JR	F/C	6-9	NC State	18.2	22.1
Don Schlundt	SR	C	6-9	Indiana	9.8	26.0

Selectors: AP, Colliers (coaches), International News Service, Look Magazine, Newspaper Enterprises Assn., UP

AWARD WINNERS

PLAYER OF THE YEAR

PLAYER	CL	POS	HT	SCHOOL	AWARDS
Tom Gola	SR	C	6-6	La Salle	UP

COACH OF THE YEAR

COACH	SCHOOL	REC	AWARDS
Phil Woolpert	San Francisco	28-1	UP

Poll Progression

Week of Dec 7

AP	UP	School
1	1	La Salle (2-0)
2	4	Kentucky (1-0)
3	3	Duquesne (1-0)
4	2	Iowa (2-0)
5	8	Holy Cross (1-0)
6	5	Indiana (0-0)
7	12	Dayton (2-0)
8	10	Niagara (3-0)
9	11	Notre Dame (1-0)
10	7	NC State (2-0)
11	17	Oklahoma A&M (2-0)
12	13	Saint Louis (1-0)
13	9	UCLA (1-0)
14	6	Illinois (2-0)
15	20	Wichita State (0-0)
16	13	Utah (2-0)
17	—	Duke (1-0)
17	—	Wake Forest (2-0)
19	—	Penn State (1-0)
20	—	Western Kentucky (1-1)
—	15	USC (1-0)
—	16	DePaul (2-0)
—	17	Oregon State (2-1)
—	19	Cincinnati (2-0)

Week of Dec 14

AP	UP	School	AP↓↑
1	1	La Salle (4-0)	
2	2	Kentucky (2-0)	
3	3	Illinois (3-0)	↑11
4	4	NC State (3-0)	↑6
5	12	Dayton (4-0)	↑2
6	9	Missouri (3-1)	⤴
7	5	Indiana (2-2)	↓1
8	6	UCLA (3-0)	↑5
9	7	Duquesne (2-1)	↓6
10	10	Niagara (3-1)	↓2
11	19	George Washington (3-0)	⤴
12	—	Louisville (6-0)	⤴
13	10	Iowa (4-1)	↓9
14	13	Ohio State (3-0)	⤴
15	8	Utah (6-0)	↑1
16	—	St. John's (3-0)	⤴
17	—	Wake Forest (4-1)	
17	—	Wichita State (2-0)	↓2
19	16	Holy Cross (2-1)	↓14
20	15	Notre Dame (3-1)	↓11
—	14	USC (3-1)	
—	17	Saint Louis (2-1)	↱
—	18	Oklahoma A&M (3-1)	↱
—	19	Cincinnati (4-0)	
—	21	Colorado (3-0)	
—	21	Minnesota (1-1)	

Week of Dec 21

AP	UP	School	AP↓↑
1	3	Kentucky (3-0)	↑1
2	2	Utah (7-0)	↑13
3	1	Illinois (5-0)	
4	4	La Salle (5-1)	↓3
5	5	NC State (8-0)	↓1
6	6	Dayton (6-0)	↓1
7	8	Missouri (4-1)	↓1
8	—	George Washington (4-1)	↑3
9	10	Duquesne (4-1)	
10	9	Niagara (6-1)	
11	7	Ohio State (4-0)	↑3
12	—	West Virginia (4-1)	⤴
13	12	USC (5-1)	⤴
14	17	Louisville (7-1)	↓2
14	19	Wichita State (3-0)	↑3
16	—	Penn (6-0)	⤴
17	11	UCLA (5-1)	↓9
17	—	San Francisco (4-1) Ⓐ	⤴
19	19	Alabama (4-1)	⤴
20	14	Iowa (5-2)	↓7
20	16	Kansas (4-0)	⤴
—	13	Cincinnati (6-1)	
—	15	Wyoming (5-2)	
—	18	Holy Cross (4-1)	↱

Week of Dec 28

AP	UP	School	AP↓↑
1	1	Kentucky (5-0)	
2	2	NC State (10-0)	↑3
3	3	La Salle (6-2)	↑1
4	5	Dayton (7-0)	↑2
5	6	San Francisco (7-1)	↑12
6	4	Illinois (6-1)	↓3
7	7	Utah (7-2)	↓5
8	8	Duquesne (4-1)	↑1
9	—	George Washington (5-2)	↓1
10	11	Niagara (6-1)	
11	10	Missouri (4-2)	↓4
12	16	Alabama (5-1)	↑7
13	20	Louisville (8-1)	↑1
14	12	USC (6-3)	↓1
15	9	UCLA (6-1)	↑2
16	14	Kansas (4-0)	↑4
17	—	Penn (6-0)	↓1
18	—	Duke (5-1)	⤴
19	19	Iowa (5-2)	↑1
20	20	Ohio State (4-2)	↓9
—	13	Cincinnati (7-1)	
—	15	California (7-1)	
—	17	Seton Hall (7-0)	
—	18	Holy Cross (5-1)	
—	20	Minnesota (4-2)	

Week of Jan 4

AP	UP	School	AP↓↑
1	1	Kentucky (7-0)	
2	2	Duquesne (8-1)	↑6
3	3	NC State (12-1)	↓1
4	4	La Salle (9-3)	↓1
5	5	San Francisco (8-1)	
6	13	George Washington (8-2)	↑3
7	9	UCLA (9-2)	↑8
8	7	Utah (7-2)	↓1
9	6	Missouri (7-2)	↑2
10	11	Dayton (8-2)	↓6
11	14	Maryland (7-2)	⤴
12	8	Illinois (6-2)	↓6
13	10	Minnesota (5-4)	⤴
14	14	Iowa (6-2)	↑5
15	12	Niagara (7-3)	↓5
16	—	Louisville (10-2)	↓3
17	—	Duke (6-3)	↑1
17	—	Villanova (5-2)	⤴
19	—	Penn (6-1)	↓2
20	16	Notre Dame (5-4)	⤴
20	20	Alabama (7-2)	↓8
20	—	Seton Hall (8-1)	⤴
—	17	Cincinnati (9-2)	
—	17	Holy Cross (6-2)	
—	19	Wisconsin (5-4)	

Week of Jan 11

AP	UP	School	AP↓↑
1	1	Kentucky (7-1) Ⓑ	
2	4	NC State (13-1)	↑1
3	2	Duquesne (9-2)	↓1
4	3	La Salle (10-3)	
5	5	San Francisco (9-1)	
6	8	Missouri (9-2)	↑3
7	6	Illinois (7-2)	↑5
8	19	George Washington (9-3)	↓2
9	7	Utah (9-2)	↓1
10	9	UCLA (10-3)	↓3
11	14	Maryland (10-2)	
12	11	Dayton (8-3)	↓2
13	—	Richmond (8-3)	⤴
14	10	Minnesota (7-4)	↓1
15	13	Niagara (8-3)	
16	—	Alabama (9-2)	↑4
17	14	Purdue (8-1)	⤴
18	12	USC (9-4)	⤴
19	17	Iowa (7-3)	↓5
20	19	Louisville (11-3)	↓4
20	—	Auburn (6-0)	⤴
—	16	Wichita State (9-1)	
—	17	Xavier (7-3) Ⓑ	

Week of Jan 18

AP	UP	School	AP↓↑
1	1	Kentucky (9-1)	
2	5	NC State (15-2)	
3	4	San Francisco (12-1)	↑2
4	2	La Salle (12-3)	
5	6	Duquesne (10-3)	↓2
6	11	Maryland (12-2)	↑5
7	3	Illinois (9-2)	
8	8	Missouri (10-2)	↓2
9	18	George Washington (11-3)	↓1
10	7	Utah (11-2)	↓1
10	10	UCLA (11-3)	
12	19	Alabama (11-2)	↑4
13	—	Richmond (12-3)	
14	9	Minnesota (8-4)	
15	14	Marquette (13-1)	⤴
16	13	Holy Cross (10-2)	⤴
17	—	Vanderbilt (8-1)	⤴
18	15	Dayton (11-3)	↓6
19	12	Iowa (8-3)	
20	16	Niagara (11-3)	↓5
20	19	TCU (11-3)	⤴
—	17	Cincinnati (11-3)	
—	19	Oregon State (8-6)	
—	19	Saint Louis (8-5)	

Week of Jan 25

AP	UP	School	AP↓↑
1	1	Kentucky (11-1)	
2	3	San Francisco (12-1)	↑1
3	2	NC State (16-3)	↓1
4	5	Duquesne (11-3)	↑1
5	6	La Salle (13-4)	↓1
6	8	George Washington (13-3)	↑3
7	4	Utah (13-2)	↑3
8	12	Maryland (13-3)	↓2
9	7	UCLA (11-3)	↑1
10	9	Illinois (9-3)	↓3
11	13	Marquette (13-1)	↑4
12	11	Missouri (10-3)	↓4
13	14	Holy Cross (11-2)	↑3
14	—	Alabama (11-2)	↓2
15	17	Dayton (13-3)	↑3
16	9	Northwestern (8-4)	⤴
17	—	Richmond (12-3)	↓4
18	—	Vanderbilt (10-2)	↓1
19	—	Iowa (9-4)	
20	14	Niagara (12-3)	
—	14	Minnesota (8-5)	↱
—	18	Stanford (10-3)	
—	19	Oregon State (10-6)	
—	20	Saint Louis (9-5)	

Week of Feb 1

AP	UP	School	AP↓↑
1	1	Kentucky (12-1)	
2	2	San Francisco (14-1)	
3	4	La Salle (14-4)	↑2
4	5	Duquesne (11-3)	
5	3	Utah (14-2)	↑2
6	6	NC State (16-4)	↓3
7	8	George Washington (13-3)	↓1
8	7	UCLA (13-3)	↑1
9	10	Marquette (15-1)	↑2
10	11	Illinois (10-3)	
11	9	Minnesota (10-5)	⤴
12	14	Maryland (13-3)	↓4
13	—	Alabama (12-2)	↑1
14	15	Holy Cross (11-2)	↓1
15	17	Dayton (14-3)	
16	13	Niagara (13-3)	↑4
17	12	Missouri (10-3)	↓5
17	17	Villanova (11-4)	⤴
19	15	Oregon State (12-6)	⤴
20	—	Vanderbilt (10-3)	↓2
—	19	Saint Louis (10-5)	
—	20	Cincinnati (15-3)	

Week of Feb 8

AP	UP	School	AP↓↑
1	1	San Francisco (16-1) Ⓒ	↑1
2	2	Kentucky (14-2) Ⓒ	↓1
3	3	La Salle (16-4)	
4	5	Duquesne (12-3)	
5	4	Utah (17-2)	
6	8	George Washington (15-3)	↑1
7	6	NC State (18-4)	↓1
8	7	UCLA (15-3)	
9	11	Marquette (16-1)	
10	10	Illinois (11-3)	
11	18	Maryland (14-3)	↑1
12	9	Minnesota (11-5)	↓1
13	—	Alabama (13-3)	
14	13	Missouri (12-3)	↑3
15	12	Iowa (11-4)	⤴
16	14	Dayton (16-3)	↓1
17	15	Cincinnati (17-3)	⤴
18	15	Oregon State (14-6)	↑1
19	16	Villanova (12-4)	↓2
20	—	Vanderbilt (11-3)	
—	18	Niagara (15-3)	↱
—	20	Stanford (14-4)	

Week of Feb 15

AP	UP	School	AP↓↑
1	1	San Francisco (18-1)	
2	2	Kentucky (16-2)	
3	3	La Salle (18-4)	
4	4	Duquesne (15-3)	
5	9	George Washington (18-3)	↑1
6	10	Marquette (18-1)	↑3
7	7	NC State (21-4) Ⓓ	
8	8	Minnesota (12-5)	↑4
9	6	UCLA (16-3)	↓1
10	5	Utah (18-3)	↓5
11	17	Maryland (15-4)	
12	16	Cincinnati (19-3)	↑5
13	15	Dayton (18-3)	↑3
14	11	Illinois (12-4)	↓4
15	13	Iowa (12-4)	
16	14	Oregon State (14-6)	↑2
17	—	Alabama (14-4)	↓4
18	—	Tennessee (13-3)	⤴
19	—	Tulsa (12-6)	⤴
20	—	Vanderbilt (13-4)	
—	12	Missouri (12-4)	↱
—	18	Holy Cross (14-4)	
—	18	Saint Louis (13-6)	
—	20	Colorado (11-5)	

Week of Feb 22

AP	UP	School	AP↓↑
1	1	San Francisco (20-1)	
2	2	Kentucky (18-2)	
3	3	La Salle (20-4)	
4	5	Duquesne (17-3)	
5	9	Marquette (20-1)	↑1
6	7	NC State (23-4)	↑1
7	4	Minnesota (14-5)	↑1
8	8	Utah (19-3)	↑2
9	6	UCLA (19-3)	
10	10	George Washington (19-4)	↓5
11	13	Dayton (20-3)	↑2
12	—	Alabama (16-4)	↑5
13	11	Illinois (14-4)	↑1
14	—	Vanderbilt (14-5)	↑6
15	—	Memphis (17-3)	⤴
16	12	Iowa (14-4)	↓1
17	—	Cincinnati (19-5)	↓5
17	—	Maryland (16-5)	↓6
19	—	Tulsa (17-6)	
20	15	Missouri (15-3)	⤴
—	14	Oregon State (17-7)	↱
—	16	Saint Louis (16-6)	
—	17	TCU (17-5)	
—	18	Colorado (12-5)	
—	18	Wyoming (16-7)	
—	20	Niagara (18-5)	

EEK OF MAR 1 (E)

AP	UP	SCHOOL	AP↓↑
1	1	**San Francisco** (21-1)	
2	2	**Kentucky** (20-2)	
3	3	**La Salle** (22-4)	
4	8	**Marquette** (22-1)	↑1
5	4	**NC State** (25-4)	↑1
6	4	**Minnesota** (15-6)	↑1
7	6	**Utah** (21-3)	↑1
8	9	**Duquesne** (19-4)	↓4
9	7	**UCLA** (21-4)	
10	11	**Dayton** (22-3)	↑1
11	19	**Alabama** (18-4)	↑1
12	10	**Iowa** (14-4)	↑4
13	14	**George Washington** (21-5)	↓3
14	12	**Oregon State** (19-7)	↑
15	17	**Tulsa** (14-6)	↑4
16	—	**Vanderbilt** (15-6)	↓2
17	16	**Illinois** (15-5)	↓4
18	—	**Maryland** (17-6)	↓1
19	—	**Memphis** (18-3)	↓4
20	13	**Missouri** (15-4)	
—	15	**Colorado** (14-5)	
—	18	**Niagara** (19-5)	
—	20	**Cincinnati** (19-6)	↓
—	20	**Holy Cross** (19-6)	
—	20	**Louisville** (19-7)	
—	20	**Villanova** (16-8)	

FINAL POLL

AP	UP	SCHOOL	AP↓↑
1	1	**San Francisco** (23-1)	
2	2	**Kentucky** (22-2)	
3	3	**La Salle** (22-4) (F)	
4	6	**NC State** (28-4)	↑1
5	5	**Iowa** (17-4)	↑7
6	7	**Duquesne** (19-4)	↑2
7	4	**Utah** (23-3)	
8	9	**Marquette** (22-2)	↓4
9	10	**Dayton** (23-3)	↑1
10	8	**Oregon State** (21-7)	↑4
11	13	**Minnesota** (15-7)	↓5
12	—	**Alabama** (19-5)	↓1
13	12	**UCLA** (21-5)	↓4
14	15	**George Washington** (24-6)	↓1
15	11	**Colorado** (16-5)	↑
16	14	**Tulsa** (20-6)	↓1
17	—	**Vanderbilt** (16-6)	↓1
18	16	**Illinois** (17-5)	↓1
19	—	**West Virginia** (19-10)	↑
20	18	**Saint Louis** (19-7)	↑
—	16	**Niagara** (20-5)	
—	19	**Holy Cross** (19-6)	
—	20	**Cincinnati** (19-7)	
—	20	**SMU** (15-8)	

(A) San Francisco, led by its 6'9" junior center Bill Russell, wins the All-College Tournament in Oklahoma City, trouncing favorite Wichita State, 94-75. Unlike previous dominant big men, the quick, agile Russell is as much a force on defense as he is on offense.

(B) On Jan. 8, Georgia Tech beats top-ranked Kentucky, 59-58, snapping the Wildcats' 129-game home winning streak, the longest streak among major colleges. Kentucky's previous home loss had been to Ohio State on Jan. 2, 1943. Coach Adolph Rupp later tells radio announcer Cawood Ledford that the worst two disasters in his lifetime were "Pearl Harbor and the night we lost to Georgia Tech." On Jan. 10, Xavier ends Western Kentucky's 67-game home winning streak, 82-80, in two overtimes.

(C) After Kentucky loses a second time to Georgia Tech, San Francisco is voted No. 1 in both polls and stays there for the rest of the season.

(D) Two weeks after hauling down 35 rebounds against Villanova, junior Ronnie Shavlik of NC State grabs 34 against South Carolina on Feb. 11. Shavlik will lose the rebounding title to Marshall's Charlie Slack, whose 25.6 rpg is still the NCAA single-season high.

(E) Kansas dedicates Allen Fieldhouse, named for longtime coach Forrest "Phog" Allen, on March 1 with a 77-67 victory over Kansas State.

(F) La Salle's Tom Gola, Dickie Hemric of Wake Forest and Penn State's Jesse Arnelle end their careers with at least 2,000 points and 1,000 rebounds—the first players to do so at the major college level.

1955 NCAA Tournament

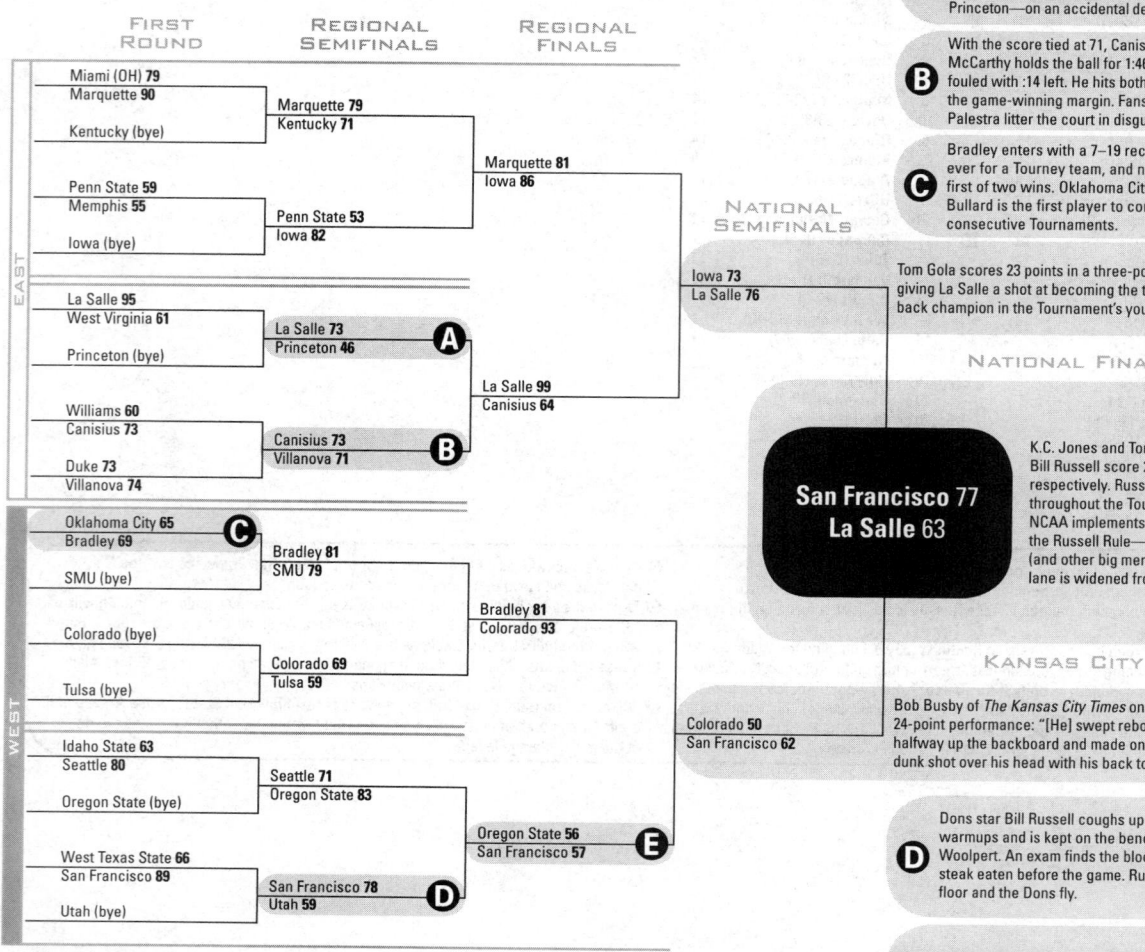

East

First Round
- Miami (OH) 79, Marquette 90
- Kentucky (bye)
- Penn State 59, Memphis 55
- Iowa (bye)
- La Salle 95, West Virginia 61
- Princeton (bye)
- Williams 60, Canisius 73
- Duke 73, Villanova 74

Regional Semifinals
- Marquette 79, Kentucky 71
- Penn State 53, Iowa 82
- La Salle 73, Princeton 46 (A)
- Canisius 73, Villanova 71 (B)

Regional Finals
- Marquette 81, Iowa 86
- La Salle 99, Canisius 64

West

First Round
- Oklahoma City 65, Bradley 69 (C)
- SMU (bye)
- Colorado (bye)
- Tulsa (bye)
- Idaho State 63, Seattle 80
- Oregon State (bye)
- West Texas State 66, San Francisco 89
- Utah (bye)

Regional Semifinals
- Bradley 81, SMU 79
- Colorado 69, Tulsa 59
- Seattle 71, Oregon State 83
- San Francisco 78, Utah 59 (D)

Regional Finals
- Bradley 81, Colorado 93
- Oregon State 56, San Francisco 57 (E)

National Semifinals
- Iowa 73, La Salle 76
- Colorado 50, San Francisco 62

National Final
San Francisco 77
La Salle 63

Kansas City

National Third Place Colorado d. Iowa 75-54
East Regional Third Place Kentucky d. Penn State 84-59
East Regional Third Place Villanova d. Princeton 64-57
West Regional Third Place Tulsa d. SMU 68-67
West Regional Third Place Utah d. Seattle 108-85

A Two days after beating Columbia for the Ivy League title, Princeton runs out of gas in its fourth game in seven days. Tom Gola gets 24 points and 24 rebounds for La Salle also scoring two for Princeton—on an accidental defensive tip-in.

B With the score tied at 71, Canisius' John McCarthy holds the ball for 1:46 before getting fouled with :14 left. He hits both free throws for the game-winning margin. Fans in Philadelphia's Palestra litter the court in disgust.

C Bradley enters with a 7–19 record, the worst ever for a Tourney team, and notches the first of two wins. Oklahoma City guard Gerald Bullard is the first player to compete in four consecutive Tournaments.

Tom Gola scores 23 points in a three-point squeaker, giving La Salle a shot at becoming the third back-to-back champion in the Tournament's young history.

K.C. Jones and Tournament MOP Bill Russell score 24 and 23 points, respectively. Russell is so dominant throughout the Tournament that the NCAA implements a rule change—the Russell Rule—to lessen his (and other big men's) impact: The lane is widened from 6 to 12 feet.

Bob Busby of *The Kansas City Times* on Bill Russell's 24-point performance: "[He] swept rebounds from levels halfway up the backboard and made one two-handed dunk shot over his head with his back to the basket."

D Dons star Bill Russell coughs up blood during warmups and is kept on the bench by coach Phil Woolpert. An exam finds the blood is from raw steak eaten before the game. Russell hits the floor and the Dons fly.

E Oregon State, playing on its home court, falls just shy of an upset win when Ron Robins' shot from the corner hits the back rim in the final seconds.

Tournament Leaders

Individual Leaders

Scoring	CL	POS	G	PTS	PPG
1 **Bob Patterson**, Tulsa	SR	F	2	57	28.5
2 **Terry Rand**, Marquette	JR	C	3	73	24.3
3 **Bill Russell**, San Francisco	JR	C	5	118	23.6
4 **Art Bunte**, Utah	JR	C	2	47	23.5
5 **Tom Gola**, La Salle	SR	C	5	115	23.0
6 **John McCarthy**, Canisius	JR	G	3	64	21.3
Bob Schafer, Villanova	SR	G	3	64	21.3
8 **Bob Burrow**, Kentucky	JR	C	2	41	20.5
9 **Harvey Babetch**, Bradley	SR	G	3	61	20.3
10 **Swede Halbrook**, Oregon State	SR	C	2	39	19.5

Minimum: 2 games

Field Goals Per Game	CL	POS	G	FG	FGPG
1 **Terry Rand**, Marquette	JR	C	3	31	10.3
2 **Bob Patterson**, Tulsa	SR	F	2	20	10.0
3 **Bill Russell**, San Francisco	JR	C	5	49	9.8
4 **Art Bunte**, Utah	JR	C	2	17	8.5
5 **Harold Haabestad**, Princeton	SR	F	2	16	8.0
Swede Halbrook, Oregon State	SR	C	2	16	8.0

Free Throw Pct	CL	POS	G	FT	FTA	PCT
1 **Stan Buchanan**, San Francisco	SR	F	5	13	13	100.0
Cal Bauer, Seattle	JR	G	3	12	12	100.0
Tom Cox, Seattle	JR	G	3	6	6	100.0
Bill Peterson, Colorado	JR	G	3	6	6	100.0
5 **Jerry Hopfensperger**, Marquette	SO	F	3	13	14	92.9

Minimum: 5 made

Team Leaders

Scoring	G	PTS	PPG
1 **Utah**	2	167	83.5
2 **Marquette**	3	250	83.3
3 **La Salle**	5	406	81.2
4 **Seattle**	3	236	78.7
5 **Kentucky**	2	155	77.5
6 **Bradley**	3	231	77.0
7 **Iowa**	4	295	73.8
8 **SMU**	2	146	73.0
9 **San Francisco**	5	363	72.6
10 **Colorado**	4	287	71.8

Minimum: 2 games

FG Per Game	G	FG	FGPG
1 **Miami (OH)**	1	33	33.0
2 **Kentucky**	2	64	32.0
3 **Utah**	2	62	31.0
4 **La Salle**	5	148	29.6
5 **Marquette**	3	86	28.7

FT Pct	G	FT	FTA	PCT
1 **Tulsa**	2	45	58	77.6
2 **Villanova**	3	75	100	75.0
3 **Penn State**	3	51	69	73.9
4 **La Salle**	5	110	150	73.3
5 **Bradley**	3	67	92	72.8

Minimum: 2 games

All-Tournament Team

PLAYER	CL	POS	HT	SCHOOL	PPG
Bill Russell*	JR	C	6-9	San Francisco	23.6
Carl Cain	JR	F	6-3	Iowa	15.5
Tom Gola	SR	C	6-6	La Salle	23.0
K.C. Jones	JR	G	6-1	San Francisco	13.6
Jim Ranglos	JR	F	6-4	Colorado	9.8

All-Regional Teams

East (Evanston, IL)

PLAYER	CL	POS	HT	SCHOOL	PPG
N/A					

East (Philadelphia)

PLAYER	CL	POS	HT	SCHOOL	PPG
Jack Devine	SR	C	6-4	Villanova	19.3
Tom Gola	SR	C	6-6	La Salle	25.3
Harold Haabestad	SR	F	6-1	Princeton	19.0
John McCarthy	JR	G	6-1	Canisius	21.3
Bob Schafer	SR	G	6-2	Villanova	21.3

West (Corvallis, OR)

PLAYER	CL	POS	HT	SCHOOL	PPG
Art Bunte	JR	C	6-3	Utah	23.5
Swede Halbrook	SR	C	7-3	Oregon State	19.5
K.C. Jones	JR	G	6-1	San Francisco	12.0
Jerry Mullen	SR	F	6-4	San Francisco	15.3
Bill Russell	JR	C	6-9	San Francisco	23.7

West (Manhattan, KS)

PLAYER	CL	POS	HT	SCHOOL	PPG
Stan Albeck	SR	G	5-9	Bradley	13.7
Burdette Haldorson	SR	C	6-7	Colorado	25.5
Tom Harrold	SR	G	5-11	Colorado	14.0
Bob Jeangerard	SR	F	6-3	Colorado	18.0
Bob Patterson	SR	F	6-4	Tulsa	28.5

* Most outstanding player

1955 NCAA TOURNAMENT BOX SCORES

Sweet 16: Marquette 79-71 Kentucky

	Marquette	Kentucky
1H	36	38
2H	43	33

MARQUETTE	MIN	FG	3FG	FT	REB	A	ST	BL	PF	TP
Terry Rand	-	8	-	3-5	-	-	-	-	4	19
Russell Wittberger	-	4	-	10-12	-	-	-	-	1	18
Don Bugalski	-	6	-	3-4	-	-	-	-	3	15
Jerry Hopfensperger	-	3	-	7-8	-	-	-	-	5	13
Rueben Schulz	-	5	-	0-2	-	-	-	-	1	10
Bob Walczak	-	2	-	0-0	-	-	-	-	1	4
TOTALS	-	**28**	-	**23-31**	-	-	-	-	**15**	**79**
Percentages				74.2						

Coach: Jack Nagle

KENTUCKY	MIN	FG	3FG	FT	REB	A	ST	BL	PF	TP
Gayle Rose	-	8	-	4-6	-	-	-	-	3	20
Bob Burrow	-	6	-	7-13	-	-	-	-	1	19
John Brewer	-	7	-	2-3	-	-	-	-	2	16
Gerry Calvert	-	4	-	0-1	-	-	-	-	5	8
Jerry Bird	-	2	-	0-1	-	-	-	-	2	4
Ray Mills	-	2	-	0-1	-	-	-	-	5	4
Earl Adkins	-	0	-	0-0	-	-	-	-	1	0
Harry Gorum	-	0	-	0-0	-	-	-	-	0	0
TOTALS	-	**29**	-	**13-25**	-	-	-	-	**19**	**71**
Percentages				52.0						

Coach: Adolph Rupp

Attendance: 9,700

Sweet 16: Iowa 82-53 Penn State

	Iowa	Penn State
1H	39	25
2H	43	28

IOWA	MIN	FG	3FG	FT	REB	A	ST	BL	PF	TP
Carl Cain	-	8-13	-	5-6	9	-	-	-	3	21
McKinley Davis	-	6-13	-	7-9	6	-	-	-	2	19
Bill Seaberg	-	6-8	-	1-2	2	-	-	-	1	13
Bill Logan	-	4-14	-	0-0	5	-	-	-	1	8
Robert George	-	3-5	-	1-3	4	-	-	-	1	7
Bill Schoof	-	2-4	-	2-2	5	-	-	-	0	6
Lester Hawthorne	-	1-3	-	1-2	1	-	-	-	0	3
Gerald Ridley	-	1-4	-	0-2	4	-	-	-	1	2
Milton Scheuerman	-	1-3	-	0-0	3	-	-	-	1	2
Augustine Martel	-	0-3	-	1-2	1	-	-	-	0	1
Douglas Duncan	-	0-0	-	0-1	1	-	-	-	1	0
Roy Johnson	-	0-1	-	0-0	1	-	-	-	0	0
TOTALS	-	**32-71**	-	**18-29**	**42**	-	-	-	**11**	**82**
Percentages		45.1		62.1						

Coach: Bucky O'Connor

PENN STATE	MIN	FG	3FG	FT	REB	A	ST	BL	PF	TP
Bob Hoffman	-	6-18	-	2-2	3	-	-	-	1	14
Jesse Arnelle	-	3-15	-	5-6	10	-	-	-	2	11
Rudy Marisa	-	3-7	-	2-4	6	-	-	-	2	8
Jim Blocker	-	2-9	-	1-2	7	-	-	-	0	5
Ron Weidenhammer	-	2-7	-	0-0	1	-	-	-	2	4
Earl Fields	-	1-6	-	1-1	5	-	-	-	1	3
Bob Ramsay	-	1-3	-	1-2	2	-	-	-	4	3
Bob Rohland	-	0-0	-	2-2	0	-	-	-	0	2
Clarence Watts	-	1-3	-	0-0	1	-	-	-	2	2
Norm Hall	-	0-1	-	1-2	0	-	-	-	0	1
Dave Edwards	-	0-0	-	0-0	1	-	-	-	0	0
Joe Hartnett	-	0-3	-	0-0	2	-	-	-	2	0
TOTALS	-	**19-72**	-	**15-21**	**38**	-	-	-	**16**	**53**
Percentages		26.4		71.4						

Coach: John S. Egli

Sweet 16: La Salle 73-46 Princeton

	La Salle	Princeton
1H	33	22
2H	40	24

LA SALLE	MIN	FG	3FG	FT	REB	A	ST	BL	PF	TP
Tom Gola	-	9	-	6-8	-	-	-	-	3	24
Charles Greenberg	-	4	-	2-2	-	-	-	-	1	10
Alonzo Lewis	-	4	-	1-5	-	-	-	-	2	9
Charles Singley	-	4	-	1-2	-	-	-	-	1	9
Frank Blatcher	-	2	-	3-4	-	-	-	-	0	7
Bob Maples	-	1	-	4-4	-	-	-	-	0	6
Fran O'Malley	-	2	-	2-3	-	-	-	-	3	6
Bob Ames	-	1	-	0-0	-	-	-	-	0	2
Walt Fredricks	-	0	-	0-0	-	-	-	-	1	0
John Gola	-	0	-	0-0	-	-	-	-	1	0
Bob Kraemer	-	0	-	0-0	-	-	-	-	0	0
TOTALS	-	**27**	-	**19-28**	-	-	-	-	**12**	**73**
Percentages				67.9						

Coach: Ken Loeffler

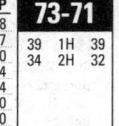

PRINCETON	MIN	FG	3FG	FT	REB	A	ST	BL	PF	TP
Harold Haabestad	-	6	-	3-6	-	-	-	-	2	15
John Devoe	-	3	-	5-7	-	-	-	-	2	11
Donald Davidson	-	3	-	2-3	-	-	-	-	3	8
John Easton	-	2	-	2-4	-	-	-	-	4	6
Richard Batt	-	1	-	0-0	-	-	-	-	5	2
Kenneth Mackenzie	-	1	-	0-0	-	-	-	-	1	2
Walter Blankley	-	0	-	0-0	-	-	-	-	0	0
Thomas Dailey	-	0	-	0-0	-	-	-	-	0	0
TOTALS	-	**16**	-	**12-20**	-	-	-	-	**17**	**44***
Percentages				60.0						

Coach: Franklin "Cappy" Cappon

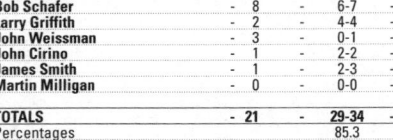

* La Salle's Tom Gola scored a field goal for Princeton.

Sweet 16: Canisius 73-71 Villanova

	Canisius	Villanova
1H	39	39
2H	34	32

CANISIUS	MIN	FG	3FG	FT	REB	A	ST	BL	PF	TP
John McCarthy	-	7	-	14-15	-	-	-	-	4	28
Hank Nowak	-	8	-	11-15	-	-	-	-	3	27
Robert Adams	-	4	-	2-3	-	-	-	-	3	10
Robert Kelly	-	2	-	0-0	-	-	-	-	4	4
Joseph Leone	-	1	-	2-8	-	-	-	-	4	4
Frank Corcoran	-	0	-	0-0	-	-	-	-	0	0
James McCarthy	-	0	-	0-0	-	-	-	-	1	0
John Zatorski	-	0	-	0-0	-	-	-	-	1	0
TOTALS	-	**22**	-	**29-41**	-	-	-	-	**20**	**73**
Percentages				70.7						

Coach: Joseph Curran

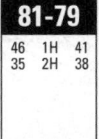

VILLANOVA	MIN	FG	3FG	FT	REB	A	ST	BL	PF	TP
Jack Devine	-	6	-	15-17	-	-	-	-	5	27
Bob Schafer	-	8	-	6-7	-	-	-	-	2	22
Larry Griffith	-	2	-	4-4	-	-	-	-	3	8
John Weissman	-	3	-	0-1	-	-	-	-	3	6
John Cirino	-	1	-	2-2	-	-	-	-	5	4
James Smith	-	1	-	2-3	-	-	-	-	4	4
Martin Milligan	-	0	-	0-0	-	-	-	-	1	0
TOTALS	-	**21**	-	**29-34**	-	-	-	-	**23**	**71**
Percentages				85.3						

Coach: Alexander Severance

Sweet 16: Bradley 81-79 SMU

	Bradley	SMU
1H	46	41
2H	35	38

BRADLEY	MIN	FG	3FG	FT	REB	A	ST	BL	PF	TP
Lee Utt	-	8-14	-	6-7	7	-	-	-	3	22
Harvey Babetch	-	6-16	-	6-11	11	-	-	-	3	18
Stan Albeck	-	5-12	-	6-7	4	-	-	-	2	16
Jack Gower	-	3-9	-	2-3	8	-	-	-	5	8
Dick Petersen	-	2-7	-	4-5	5	-	-	-	5	8
Jerry Hansen	-	3-11	-	0-0	12	-	-	-	4	6
John Kent	-	1-4	-	1-2	3	-	-	-	1	3
Fred Dickman	-	0-1	-	0-2	2	-	-	-	0	0
TOTALS	-	**28-74**	-	**25-37**	**52**	-	-	-	**23**	**81**
Percentages		37.8		67.6						

Coach: Bob Vanatta

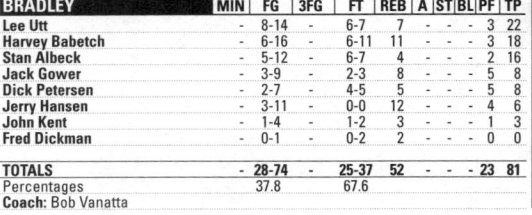

SMU	MIN	FG	3FG	FT	REB	A	ST	BL	PF	TP
Arthur Barnes Jr.	-	8-20	-	4-4	4	-	-	-	2	20
Jim Krebs	-	5-16	-	9-11	15	-	-	-	4	19
Joel Krog	-	5-17	-	2-5	11	-	-	-	4	12
Ronnie Morris	-	3-7	-	3-5	1	-	-	-	3	9
Bobby Mills	-	2-5	-	3-4	4	-	-	-	4	7
Carl Scharffenberger	-	1-3	-	2-6	0	-	-	-	1	4
Larry Showalter	-	2-9	-	0-0	10	-	-	-	0	4
Bob McGregor	-	1-1	-	0-0	0	-	-	-	3	2
Tom Miller	-	0-4	-	2-3	0	-	-	-	1	2
TOTALS	-	**27-82**	-	**25-38**	**45**	-	-	-	**22**	**79**
Percentages		32.9		65.8						

Coach: E.O. "Doc" Hayes

Sweet 16: Colorado 69-59 Tulsa

	Colorado	Tulsa
1H	34	33
2H	35	26

COLORADO	MIN	FG	3FG	FT	REB	A	ST	BL	PF	TP
Burdette Haldorson	-	9-20	-	10-12	14	-	-	-	3	28
Charley Mock	-	4-7	-	3-6	5	-	-	-	1	11
Tom Harrold	-	2-5	-	6-9	5	-	-	-	2	10
Bob Jeangerard	-	3-15	-	1-2	5	-	-	-	4	7
Jim Ranglos	-	3-5	-	1-2	6	-	-	-	3	7
Mel Coffman	-	3-5	-	0-0	5	-	-	-	2	6
George Hannah	-	0-0	-	0-0	0	-	-	-	0	0
Mick Mansfield	-	0-1	-	0-0	0	-	-	-	1	0
TOTALS	-	**24-58**	-	**21-31**	**40**	-	-	-	**16**	**69**
Percentages		41.4		67.7						

Coach: H.B. Lee

TULSA	MIN	FG	3FG	FT	REB	A	ST	BL	PF	TP
Bob Patterson	-	7-19	-	7-8	9	-	-	-	2	21
Jerry Hacker	-	3-9	-	7-8	6	-	-	-	3	13
Junior Born	-	3-10	-	4-4	2	-	-	-	2	10
Dick Courter	-	2-9	-	6-7	10	-	-	-	2	10
Jim Duncan	-	1-1	-	1-2	3	-	-	-	5	3
Ernie Stewart	-	1-2	-	0-0	2	-	-	-	3	2
Jerry Evans	-	0-1	-	0-0	0	-	-	-	1	0
John Jobe	-	0-0	-	0-0	0	-	-	-	0	0
Melvin Johnston	-	0-0	-	0-0	1	-	-	-	0	0
Jim Krouse	-	0-0	-	0-0	0	-	-	-	0	0
John Stob	-	0-0	-	0-0	0	-	-	-	0	0
John Yates	-	0-0	-	0-0	0	-	-	-	0	0
TOTALS	-	**17-51**	-	**25-29**	**33**	-	-	-	**18**	**59**
Percentages		33.3		86.2						

Coach: Clarence Iba

83-71

50	1H	36
33	2H	35

SWEET 16

OREGON STATE	MIN	FG	3FG	FT	REB	A	ST	BL	PF	TP
Swede Halbrook	-	9	-	3-6	-	-	-	-	3	21
Tony Vlastelica	-	7	-	0-0	-	-	-	-	0	14
Phil Shadoin	-	5	-	0-6	-	-	-	-	4	10
Bill Toole	-	4	-	2-3	-	-	-	-	3	10
Tex Whiteman	-	3	-	3-3	-	-	-	-	3	9
Jay Dean	-	2	-	3-4	-	-	-	-	2	7
Reggie Halligan	-	1	-	2-2	-	-	-	-	2	4
Johnny Jarboe	-	0	-	4-4	-	-	-	-	3	4
Bob Allord	-	1	-	0-1	-	-	-	-	0	2
Ron Fundingsland	-	1	-	0-0	-	-	-	-	0	2
Larry Paulus	-	0	-	0-1	-	-	-	-	3	0
TOTALS	-	**33**	-	**17-30**	-	-	-	-	**23**	**83**
Percentages				56.7						

Coach: Slats Gill

SEATTLE	MIN	FG	3FG	FT	REB	A	ST	BL	PF	TP
Bob Godes	-	6	-	4-6	-	-	-	-	3	16
Dick Stricklin	-	3	-	8-11	-	-	-	-	1	14
Stan Glowaski	-	4	-	3-5	-	-	-	-	4	11
Cal Bauer	-	3	-	2-2	-	-	-	-	2	8
Ken Fuhrer	-	2	-	3-7	-	-	-	-	3	7
Bob Malone	-	3	-	1-2	-	-	-	-	3	7
John Kelly	-	3	-	0-1	-	-	-	-	2	6
Jerry Vaughan	-	1	-	0-0	-	-	-	-	1	2
Tom Cox	-	0	-	0-0	-	-	-	-	0	0
TOTALS	-	**25**	-	**21-34**	-	-	-	-	**19**	**71**
Percentages				61.8						

Coach: H. Albert Brightman

78-59

41	1H	20
37	2H	39

SWEET 16

SAN FRANCISCO	MIN	FG	3FG	FT	REB	A	ST	BL	PF	TP
Jerry Mullen	-	7	-	10-14	-	-	-	-	3	24
Hal Perry	-	6	-	2-3	-	-	-	-	1	14
K.C. Jones	-	4	-	5-13	-	-	-	-	2	13
Bill Russell	-	5	-	3-5	-	-	-	-	3	13
Warren Baxter	-	1	-	2-2	-	-	-	-	1	4
Dick Lawless	-	0	-	4-4	-	-	-	-	1	4
Bob Wiebusch	-	2	-	0-1	-	-	-	-	2	4
Stan Buchanan	-	1	-	0-0	-	-	-	-	1	2
Bill Bush	-	0	-	0-0	-	-	-	-	0	0
Jack King	-	0	-	0-0	-	-	-	-	0	0
Gordon Kirby	-	0	-	0-0	-	-	-	-	0	0
Rudy Zannini	-	0	-	0-0	-	-	-	-	1	0
TOTALS	-	**26**	-	**26-42**	-	-	-	-	**15**	**78**
Percentages				61.9						

Coach: Phil Woolpert

UTAH	MIN	FG	3FG	FT	REB	A	ST	BL	PF	TP
Gary Bergen	-	5	-	2-2	-	-	-	-	5	12
Art Bunte	-	4	-	4-5	-	-	-	-	1	12
Morris Buckwalter	-	1	-	6-6	-	-	-	-	5	8
Ted Berner	-	3	-	0-0	-	-	-	-	2	6
Curt Jenson	-	3	-	0-2	-	-	-	-	2	6
Jerry McCleary	-	1	-	4-5	-	-	-	-	1	6
Alden Lewis	-	1	-	1-2	-	-	-	-	1	3
Delyle Condie	-	1	-	0-0	-	-	-	-	2	2
John Crowe	-	1	-	0-0	-	-	-	-	4	2
Roger Tonnesen	-	0	-	2-2	-	-	-	-	2	2
Eddie Pepple	-	0	-	0-0	-	-	-	-	1	0
TOTALS	-	**20**	-	**19-24**	-	-	-	-	**26**	**59**
Percentages				79.2						

Coach: Jack Gardner

86-81

46	1H	33
40	2H	48

ELITE 8

IOWA	MIN	FG	3FG	FT	REB	A	ST	BL	PF	TP
Bill Logan	-	11-20	-	9-14	15	-	-	-	5	31
Bill Seaberg	-	5-8	-	2-4	5	-	-	-	5	12
Milton Scheuerman	-	3-8	-	5-6	7	-	-	-	2	11
Carl Cain	-	5-14	-	0-1	8	-	-	-	4	10
Bill Schoof	-	3-8	-	2-5	7	-	-	-	5	8
McKinley Davis	-	2-11	-	3-5	4	-	-	-	2	7
Robert George	-	1-1	-	1-2	0	-	-	-	1	3
Roy Johnson	-	1-1	-	1-2	0	-	-	-	0	3
Lester Hawthorne	-	0-0	-	1-2	0	-	-	-	0	1
TOTALS	-	**31-71**	-	**24-41**	**46**	-	-	-	**24**	**86**
Percentages		43.7		58.5						

Coach: Bucky O'Connor

MARQUETTE	MIN	FG	3FG	FT	REB	A	ST	BL	PF	TP
Rueben Schulz	-	5-11	-	12-18	9	-	-	-	4	22
Terry Rand	-	7-11	-	3-3	12	-	-	-	5	17
Jerry Hopfensperger	-	5-11	-	6-6	0	-	-	-	4	16
Russell Wittberger	-	7-14	-	2-3	6	-	-	-	5	16
Don Bugalski	-	0-5	-	7-12	6	-	-	-	4	7
Bob Walczak	-	1-7	-	1-2	3	-	-	-	3	3
Pat O'Keefe	-	0-1	-	0-0	2	-	-	-	0	0
Dale Sevcik	-	0-0	-	0-0	1	-	-	-	1	0
Robert Van Vooren	-	0-0	-	0-0	0	-	-	-	0	0
TOTALS	-	**25-60**	-	**31-44**	**39**	-	-	-	**26**	**81**
Percentages		41.7		70.5						

Coach: Jack Nagle

99-64

43	1H	30
56	2H	34

ELITE 8

LA SALLE	MIN	FG	3FG	FT	REB	A	ST	BL	PF	TP
Tom Gola	-	9	-	12-12	25	-	-	-	4	30
Alonzo Lewis	-	7	-	4-5	0	-	-	-	2	18
Charles Singley	-	5	-	6-9	0	-	-	-	2	16
Charles Greenberg	-	5	-	4-4	0	-	-	-	1	14
Bob Maples	-	1	-	7-8	0	-	-	-	0	9
Bob Ames	-	1	-	2-2	0	-	-	-	0	4
Fran O'Malley	-	2	-	0-1	0	-	-	-	5	4
Frank Blatcher	-	1	-	0-0	0	-	-	-	4	2
John Gola	-	1	-	0-0	0	-	-	-	2	2
Walt Fredricks	-	0	-	0-0	0	-	-	-	1	0
Bob Kraemer	-	0	-	0-0	0	-	-	-	0	0
TOTALS	-	**32**	-	**35-41**	**25**	-	-	-	**21**	**99**
Percentages				85.4						

Coach: Ken Loeffler

CANISIUS	MIN	FG	3FG	FT	REB	A	ST	BL	PF	TP
John McCarthy	-	5	-	7-9	-	-	-	-	3	17
David Markey	-	2	-	11-13	-	-	-	-	2	15
Hank Nowak	-	3	-	4-5	-	-	-	-	3	10
Robert Adams	-	4	-	0-1	-	-	-	-	0	8
John Coogan	-	2	-	0-3	-	-	-	-	2	4
James McCarthy	-	1	-	2-2	-	-	-	-	1	4
John Flynn	-	1	-	1-2	-	-	-	-	1	3
Robert Kelly	-	0	-	2-2	-	-	-	-	5	2
Frank Corcoran	-	0	-	1-1	-	-	-	-	3	1
Joseph Leone	-	0	-	0-0	-	-	-	-	2	0
John Zatorski	-	0	-	0-0	-	-	-	-	0	0
TOTALS	-	**18**	-	**28-38**	-	-	-	-	**22**	**64**
Percentages				73.7						

Coach: Joseph Curran

93-81

49	1H	41
44	2H	40

ELITE 8

COLORADO	MIN	FG	3FG	FT	REB	A	ST	BL	PF	TP
Bob Jeangerard	-	12-24	-	5-6	4	-	-	-	3	29
Burdette Haldorson	-	7-14	-	9-12	10	-	-	-	3	23
Tom Harrold	-	4-10	-	10-15	3	-	-	-	1	18
Jim Ranglos	-	3-8	-	4-5	19	-	-	-	4	10
Charley Mock	-	2-7	-	2-4	1	-	-	-	0	6
Mick Mansfield	-	1-1	-	2-3	2	-	-	-	1	4
Bob Yardley	-	1-1	-	0-0	1	-	-	-	0	2
George Hannah	-	0-0	-	1-2	1	-	-	-	0	1
Mel Coffman	-	0-0	-	0-0	0	-	-	-	1	0
Jamie Grant	-	0-0	-	0-0	0	-	-	-	0	0
Dave Mowbray	-	0-0	-	0-0	0	-	-	-	0	0
Bill Peterson	-	0-0	-	0-0	0	-	-	-	0	0
TOTALS	-	**30-65**	-	**33-47**	**41**	-	-	-	**13**	**93**
Percentages		46.2		70.2						

Coach: H.B. Lee

BRADLEY	MIN	FG	3FG	FT	REB	A	ST	BL	PF	TP
Harvey Babetch	-	7-9	-	8-9	3	-	-	-	5	22
Stan Albeck	-	6-15	-	4-6	3	-	-	-	5	16
Lee Utt	-	6-18	-	3-4	11	-	-	-	2	15
Dick Petersen	-	5-12	-	2-2	10	-	-	-	5	12
Jack Gower	-	3-6	-	0-2	4	-	-	-	1	6
Jerry Hansen	-	2-6	-	0-0	3	-	-	-	5	4
John Kent	-	2-6	-	0-0	3	-	-	-	1	4
Fred Dickman	-	1-4	-	0-0	1	-	-	-	2	2
Jon Burnham	-	0-0	-	0-0	1	-	-	-	1	0
TOTALS	-	**32-76**	-	**17-23**	**39**	-	-	-	**27**	**81**
Percentages		42.1		73.9						

Coach: Bob Vanatta

57-56

30	1H	27
27	2H	29

ELITE 8

SAN FRANCISCO	MIN	FG	3FG	FT	REB	A	ST	BL	PF	TP
Bill Russell	-	11	-	7-11	-	-	-	-	2	29
K.C. Jones	-	2	-	7-10	-	-	-	-	3	11
Bob Wiebusch	-	1	-	4-5	-	-	-	-	0	6
Stan Buchanan	-	2	-	0-0	-	-	-	-	3	4
Hal Perry	-	2	-	0-0	-	-	-	-	1	4
Jerry Mullen	-	0	-	2-6	-	-	-	-	3	2
Warren Baxter	-	0	-	1-2	-	-	-	-	0	1
Rudy Zannini	-	0	-	0-0	-	-	-	-	0	0
TOTALS	-	**18**	-	**21-34**	-	-	-	-	**12**	**57**
Percentages				61.8						

Coach: Phil Woolpert

OREGON STATE	MIN	FG	3FG	FT	REB	A	ST	BL	PF	TP
Swede Halbrook	-	7	-	4-6	-	-	-	-	4	18
Tony Vlastelica	-	6	-	0-1	-	-	-	-	3	12
Tex Whiteman	-	2	-	7-8	-	-	-	-	2	11
Bill Toole	-	2	-	2-6	-	-	-	-	2	6
Reggie Halligan	-	2	-	1-2	-	-	-	-	3	5
Ron Robins	-	2	-	0-0	-	-	-	-	3	4
Johnny Jarboe	-	0	-	0-0	-	-	-	-	2	0
Phil Shadoin	-	0	-	0-0	-	-	-	-	0	0
TOTALS	-	**21**	-	**14-23**	-	-	-	-	**19**	**56**
Percentages				60.9						

Coach: Slats Gill

ANNUAL REVIEW

76-73 — FINAL 4

LA SALLE	MIN	FG	3FG	FT	REB	A	ST	BL	PF	TP
Tom Gola	-	8	-	7-7	-	-	-	-	4	23
Charles Singley	-	5	-	6-6	-	-	-	-	2	16
Alonzo Lewis	-	5	-	4-4	-	-	-	-	3	14
Charles Greenberg	-	4	-	0-2	-	-	-	-	4	8
Fran O'Malley	-	1	-	4-6	-	-	-	-	1	6
Frank Blatcher	-	2	-	1-2	-	-	-	-	5	5
Bob Maples	-	1	-	2-2	-	-	-	-	0	4
TOTALS	-	26	-	24-29	-	-	-	-	19	76
Percentages				82.8						

Coach: Ken Loeffler

	1H	2H
La Salle	45	31
Iowa	36	37

IOWA	MIN	FG	3FG	FT	REB	A	ST	BL	PF	TP
Bill Logan	-	7	-	6-7	-	-	-	-	3	20
Carl Cain	-	8	-	1-3	-	-	-	-	3	17
Bill Seaberg	-	5	-	5-8	-	-	-	-	2	15
Milton Scheuerman	-	1	-	11-13	-	-	-	-	3	13
Bill Schoof	-	3	-	0-1	-	-	-	-	4	6
McKinley Davis	-	1	-	0-0	-	-	-	-	2	2
TOTALS	-	25	-	23-32	-	-	-	-	17	73
Percentages				71.9						

Coach: Bucky O'Connor

Officials: Milner, Ogden

62-50 — FINAL 4

SAN FRANCISCO	MIN	FG	3FG	FT	REB	A	ST	BL	PF	TP
Bill Russell	-	10-14	-	4-10	9	-	-	-	4	24
Hal Perry	-	5-8	-	0-0	4	-	-	-	1	10
K.C. Jones	-	3-9	-	2-3	5	-	-	-	3	8
Warren Baxter	-	2-2	-	3-5	1	-	-	-	0	7
Stan Buchanan	-	0-4	-	6-6	1	-	-	-	2	6
Jack King	-	1-1	-	2-2	0	-	-	-	0	4
Bob Wiebusch	-	1-2	-	0-0	3	-	-	-	2	2
Bill Bush	-	0-0	-	1-2	0	-	-	-	0	1
Gordon Kirby	-	0-0	-	0-0	0	-	-	-	1	0
Jerry Mullen	-	0-2	-	0-0	4	-	-	-	0	0
Rudy Zannini	-	0-1	-	0-0	1	-	-	-	1	0
TOTALS	-	22-43	-	18-28	28	-	-	-	14	62
Percentages		51.2		64.3						

Coach: Phil Woolpert

	1H	2H
San Francisco	25	37
Colorado	19	31

COLORADO	MIN	FG	3FG	FT	REB	A	ST	BL	PF	TP
Burdette Haldorson	-	3-11	-	3-4	6	-	-	-	5	9
George Hannah	-	2-6	-	5-7	3	-	-	-	2	9
Bill Peterson	-	2-3	-	2-2	3	-	-	-	1	6
Mel Coffman	-	1-1	-	2-2	1	-	-	-	2	4
Bob Jeangerard	-	1-12	-	2-3	4	-	-	-	0	4
Mick Mansfield	-	0-3	-	4-6	1	-	-	-	1	4
Charley Mock	-	2-6	-	0-0	6	-	-	-	5	4
Jim Ranglos	-	1-3	-	2-2	8	-	-	-	1	4
Bob Yardley	-	1-2	-	2-4	1	-	-	-	0	4
Jamie Grant	-	1-2	-	0-0	0	-	-	-	0	2
TOTALS	-	14-49	-	22-30	33	-	-	-	17	50
Percentages		28.6		73.3						

Coach: H.B. Lee

Officials: Fox, Mohr

75-54 — 3RD PLACE

COLORADO	MIN	FG	3FG	FT	REB	A	ST	BL	PF	TP
Jim Ranglos	-	6	-	6-9	-	-	-	-	4	18
Bob Jeangerard	-	5	-	4-7	-	-	-	-	3	14
Charley Mock	-	3	-	7-9	-	-	-	-	3	13
Burdette Haldorson	-	4	-	4-5	-	-	-	-	4	12
Bill Peterson	-	3	-	4-4	-	-	-	-	2	10
George Hannah	-	1	-	4-6	-	-	-	-	1	6
Jamie Grant	-	1	-	0-0	-	-	-	-	0	2
Mick Mansfield	-	0	-	0-0	-	-	-	-	0	0
Wilbert Walter	-	0	-	0-0	-	-	-	-	0	0
Bob Yardley	-	0	-	0-0	-	-	-	-	0	0
TOTALS	-	23	-	29-40	-	-	-	-	17	75
Percentages				72.5						

Coach: H.B. Lee

	1H	2H
Colorado	35	40
Iowa	28	26

IOWA	MIN	FG	3FG	FT	REB	A	ST	BL	PF	TP
Bill Logan	-	5	-	7-10	-	-	-	-	1	17
Carl Cain	-	4	-	6-6	-	-	-	-	2	14
Milton Scheuerman	-	2	-	2-2	-	-	-	-	3	6
Bill Schoof	-	2	-	2-3	-	-	-	-	3	6
Bill Seaberg	-	1	-	2-2	-	-	-	-	1	4
Robert George	-	0	-	3-4	-	-	-	-	3	3
McKinley Davis	-	1	-	0-2	-	-	-	-	3	2
Augustine Martel	-	1	-	0-0	-	-	-	-	2	2
Douglas Duncan	-	0	-	0-0	-	-	-	-	1	0
Lester Hawthorne	-	0	-	0-0	-	-	-	-	1	0
Roy Johnson	-	0	-	0-0	-	-	-	-	3	0
Gerald Ridley	-	0	-	0-0	-	-	-	-	0	0
TOTALS	-	16	-	22-29	-	-	-	-	23	54
Percentages				75.9						

Coach: Bucky O'Connor

Attendance: 10,500

77-63 — NCAA FINAL 1955

SAN FRANCISCO	MIN	FG	3FG	FT	REB	A	ST	BL	PF	TP
K.C. Jones	-	10-23	-	4-4	-	-	-	-	2	24
Bill Russell	-	9-22	-	5-7	-	-	-	-	1	23
Jerry Mullen	-	4-0	-	2-5	-	-	-	-	5	10
Stan Buchanan	-	3-0	-	2-2	-	-	-	-	1	8
Hal Perry	-	1-0	-	2-2	-	-	-	-	4	4
Bob Wiebusch	-	2-0	-	0-0	-	-	-	-	0	4
Dick Lawless	-	1-0	-	0-0	-	-	-	-	0	2
Rudy Zannini	-	1-0	-	0-0	-	-	-	-	0	2
Gordon Kirby	-	0-0	-	0-0	-	-	-	-	1	0
TOTALS	-	31-45	-	15-20	-	-	-	-	14	77
Percentages		68.9		75.0						

Coach: Phil Woolpert

	1H	2H
San Francisco	35	42
La Salle	24	39

LA SALLE	MIN	FG	3FG	FT	REB	A	ST	BL	PF	TP
Charles Singley	-	8	-	4-4	-	-	-	-	1	20
Tom Gola	-	6	-	4-5	-	-	-	-	4	16
Fran O'Malley	-	4	-	2-3	-	-	-	-	1	10
Frank Blatcher	-	4	-	0-0	-	-	-	-	1	8
Alonzo Lewis	-	1	-	4-9	-	-	-	-	1	6
Charles Greenberg	-	1	-	1-2	-	-	-	-	4	3
Walt Fredricks	-	0	-	0-0	-	-	-	-	0	0
Bob Maples	-	0	-	0-0	-	-	-	-	0	0
TOTALS	-	24	-	15-23	-	-	-	-	12	63
Percentages				65.2						

Coach: Ken Loeffler

Officials: Mohr, Ogden
Attendance: 10,500

National Invitation Tournament (NIT)

First round: Louisville d. Manhattan 91-86, Niagara d. Lafayette, 83-70, Saint Francis (PA) d. Seton Hall 89-78, Saint Louis d. Connecticut 110-103
Quarterfinals: Duquesne d. Louisville 74-66, Cincinnati d. Niagara 85-83 (2OT), Saint Francis (PA) d. Holy Cross 68-64, Dayton d. Saint Louis, 97-81
Semifinals: Dayton d. Saint Francis (PA), 79-73 (OT), Duquesne d. Cincinnati 65-51
Third place: Cincinnati d. Saint Francis (PA) 96-91 (OT)
Championship: Duquesne d. Dayton 70-58
MVP: Maurice Stokes, Saint Francis (PA)

1955-56: Russell Rules II

Led by the great Bill Russell, San Francisco (29–0) cruised to its second consecutive NCAA championship with an 83-71 win over Iowa at McGaw Hall in Evanston, Ill. The All-America center scored 26 points and pulled down 27 rebounds—a Final Four record that has never been seriously challenged. The Dons were the first team since the inception of the NCAA tournament to go undefeated. Iowa lost five of eight games at the start of the season, but its Fabulous Five starters all averaged double figures in scoring and reeled off 17 straight wins to reach the Final. Despite Russell's performance, Temple's Hal Lear—who averaged 32 ppg in five Tournament games, including 48 against SMU in the third-place game—was named Tournament MOP. The 1956 Tournament was the first to be laid out in four regions that each had a distinct name: East, Midwest, West and Far West. The one-and-one free throw rule (make the first, get a second) was now in effect the entire game. The two-shot penalty that had been used in the final three minutes was eliminated.

Major Conference Standings

ACC	Conference			Overall		
	W	L	Pct	W	L	Pct
NC State ⊛	11	3	.786	24	4	.857
North Carolina	11	3	.786	18	5	.783
Duke	10	4	.714	19	7	.731
Wake Forest	10	4	.714	19	9	.679
Maryland	7	7	.500	14	10	.583
South Carolina	3	11	.214	9	14	.391
Virginia	3	11	.214	10	17	.370
Clemson	1	13	.071	9	17	.346

Tournament: **NC State d. Wake Forest 76-64**
Tournament MVP: **Vic Molodet**, NC State

BIG SEVEN	Conference			Overall		
	W	L	Pct	W	L	Pct
Kansas State ⊛	9	3	.750	17	8	.680
Iowa State	8	4	.667	18	5	.783
Missouri	8	4	.667	15	7	.682
Colorado	7	5	.583	11	10	.524
Kansas	6	6	.500	14	9	.609
Nebraska	3	9	.250	7	16	.304
Oklahoma	1	11	.083	4	19	.174

BIG TEN	Conference			Overall		
	W	L	Pct	W	L	Pct
Iowa ⊛	13	1	.929	20	6	.769
Illinois	11	3	.786	18	4	.818
Ohio State	9	5	.643	16	6	.727
Purdue	9	5	.643	16	6	.727
Michigan State	7	7	.500	13	9	.591
Indiana	6	8	.429	13	9	.591
Minnesota	6	8	.429	11	11	.500
Michigan	4	10	.286	9	13	.409
Wisconsin	4	10	.286	6	16	.273
Northwestern	1	13	.071	2	20	.091

BORDER	Conference			Overall		
	W	L	Pct	W	L	Pct
Texas Tech ⊛	8	4	.667	13	12	.520
New Mexico State	7	5	.583	16	7	.696
Texas Western	7	5	.583	12	10	.545
West Texas A&M	6	6	.500	12	10	.545
Arizona	6	6	.500	11	15	.423
Arizona State	5	7	.417	11	15	.423
Hardin-Simmons	3	9	.250	7	18	.280

CBA	Conference			Overall		
	W	L	Pct	W	L	Pct
San Francisco ⊛	14	0	1.000	29	0	1.000
Pacific	9	5	.643	15	11	.577
Loyola Marymount	9	5	.643	13	12	.520
Saint Mary's (CA)	8	6	.571	16	10	.615
San Jose State	8	6	.571	15	10	.600
Santa Clara	6	8	.429	8	16	.333
Fresno State	2	12	.143	9	17	.346
Pepperdine	0	14	.000	2	23	.080

IVY	Conference			Overall		
	W	L	Pct	W	L	Pct
Dartmouth ⊛	10	4	.714	18	11	.621
Columbia	9	5	.643	15	9	.625
Penn	9	5	.643	12	13	.480
Cornell	8	6	.571	11	13	.458
Yale	7	7	.500	15	11	.577
Princeton	7	7	.500	11	13	.458
Harvard	3	11	.214	8	16	.333
Brown	3	11	.214	7	18	.280

METRO NY	Conference			Overall		
	W	L	Pct	W	L	Pct
St. Francis (NY) □	4	0	1.000	21	4	.840
Manhattan ○	4	1	.800	16	8	.667
Brooklyn	2	2	.500	11	7	.611
NYU	2	2	.500	10	8	.556
St. John's	3	3	.500	12	12	.500
Fordham	2	2	.500	11	14	.440
CCNY	0	7	.000	4	14	.222

MID-AMERICAN	Conference			Overall		
	W	L	Pct	W	L	Pct
Marshall ⊛	10	2	.833	18	5	.783
Miami (OH)	8	4	.667	12	8	.600
Western Michigan	7	5	.583	11	9	.550
Toledo	6	6	.500	9	13	.409
Ohio	5	7	.417	13	11	.542
Kent State	5	7	.417	10	11	.476
Bowling Green	1	11	.083	4	19	.174

MISSOURI VALLEY	Conference			Overall		
	W	L	Pct	W	L	Pct
Houston ⊛	9	3	.750	19	7	.731
Saint Louis □	8	4	.667	18	7	.720
Oklahoma A&M □	8	4	.667	18	9	.667
Wichita State	7	5	.583	14	12	.538
Tulsa	4	8	.333	16	10	.615
Detroit	3	9	.250	13	12	.520
Bradley	3	9	.250	13	13	.500

SKYLINE 8	Conference			Overall		
	W	L	Pct	W	L	Pct
Utah ⊛	12	2	.857	22	6	.786
BYU	10	4	.714	18	8	.692
Utah State	7	7	.500	13	13	.500
Colorado State	7	7	.500	12	13	.480
Denver	6	8	.429	13	12	.520
New Mexico	5	9	.357	6	16	.273
Wyoming	5	9	.357	7	19	.269
Montana	4	10	.286	14	12	.538

OHIO VALLEY	Conference			Overall		
	W	L	Pct	W	L	Pct
Morehead State ⊛	7	3	.700	19	10	.655
Tennessee Tech	7	3	.700	14	7	.667
Western Kentucky	7	3	.700	16	12	.571
Murray State	6	4	.600	15	10	.600
Eastern Kentucky	3	7	.300	9	16	.360
Middle Tennessee St.	0	10	.000	6	15	.286

PACIFIC COAST	Conference			Overall		
	W	L	Pct	W	L	Pct
UCLA ⊛	16	0	1.000	22	6	.786
Washington	11	5	.688	15	11	.577
Stanford	10	6	.625	18	6	.750
California	10	6	.625	17	8	.680
Southern California	9	7	.563	14	12	.538
Oregon	5	11	.313	11	15	.423
Oregon State	5	11	.313	8	18	.308
Idaho	4	12	.250	6	19	.240
Washington State	2	14	.125	4	22	.154

SEC	Conference			Overall		
	W	L	Pct	W	L	Pct
Alabama	14	0	1.000	21	3	.875
Kentucky ⊛	12	2	.857	20	6	.769
Vanderbilt	11	3	.786	19	4	.826
Auburn	8	6	.571	11	10	.524
Tulane	7	7	.500	12	12	.500
Georgia Tech	6	8	.429	12	11	.522
Mississippi State	6	8	.429	12	12	.500
Tennessee	6	8	.429	10	14	.417
LSU	5	9	.357	7	17	.292
Florida	4	10	.286	11	12	.478
Mississippi	4	10	.286	10	13	.435
Georgia	1	13	.071	3	21	.125

SOUTHERN	Conference			Overall		
	W	L	Pct	W	L	Pct
George Washington	10	2	.833	19	7	.731
West Virginia ⊛	10	2	.833	21	9	.700
Virginia Tech	10	7	.588	14	11	.560
Richmond	8	6	.571	16	13	.552
William and Mary	9	7	.563	12	14	.462
Furman	7	7	.500	12	16	.429
Davidson	5	7	.417	10	15	.400
Washington and Lee	5	8	.385	12	16	.429
VMI	3	11	.214	4	19	.174
The Citadel	0	10	.000	2	19	.095

Tournament: **West Virginia d. Richmond 58-56**
Tournament MOP: **Rod Hundley**, West Virginia

SOUTHWEST	Conference			Overall		
	W	L	Pct	W	L	Pct
SMU ⊛	12	0	1.000	25	4	.862
Arkansas	9	3	.750	11	12	.478
Rice	8	4	.667	19	5	.792
Texas	5	7	.417	12	10	.545
Baylor	3	9	.250	6	17	.261
Texas A&M	3	9	.250	6	18	.250
TCU	2	10	.167	4	20	.167

WNY LITTLE THREE	Conference			Overall		
	W	L	Pct	W	L	Pct
Canisius ○	4	0	1.000	19	7	.731
Niagara □	2	2	.500	20	7	.741
St. Bonaventure	0	4	.000	11	12	.478

YANKEE	Conference			Overall		
	W	L	Pct	W	L	Pct
Connecticut ⊛	6	1	.857	17	11	.607
Massachusetts	5	1	.833	17	6	.739
Rhode Island	6	2	.750	11	14	.440
Vermont	2	3	.400	6	12	.333
Maine	3	5	.375	6	12	.333
New Hampshire	0	10	.000	2	15	.118

Conference Standings Continue →

⊛ Automatic NCAA Tournament bid ○ At-large NCAA Tournament bid □ NIT appearance ⊗ Team record doesn't reflect games forfeited or vacated. For adjusted record, see p. 521.

INDEPENDENTS

	Overall W	L	PCT
Louisville□	26	3	.897
Temple⊕	27	4	.871
Dayton□	25	4	.862
Wayne State (MI)○	18	3	.857
Holy Cross○	22	5	.815
Seton Hall□	20	5	.800
Saint Joseph's□	23	6	.793
Wash.-St. Louis	17	5	.773
Lafayette□	20	7	.741
Memphis○	20	7	.741
Oklahoma City○	20	7	.741
Portland	20	8	.714
Cincinnati	17	7	.708
Idaho State	18	8	.692
DePaul○	16	8	.667
Colgate	17	9	.654
Syracuse	14	8	.636
Duquesne□	17	10	.630
Seattle○	18	11	.621
Butler	14	9	.609
Xavier□	17	11	.607
La Salle	15	10	.600
Muhlenberg	15	10	.600

INDEPENDENTS (CONT.)

	Overall W	L	PCT
Pittsburgh	15	10	.600
Georgetown	13	11	.542
Marquette□	13	11	.542
Miami (FL)	14	12	.538
Villanova	14	12	.538
Navy	10	9	.526
Creighton	11	12	.478
Gonzaga	13	15	.464
Penn State	12	14	.462
Valparaiso	12	14	.462
Loyola (LA)	11	14	.440
Army	10	13	.435
Bucknell	10	14	.417
Drake	10	14	.417
Loyola-Chicago	10	14	.417
Saint Francis (PA)	10	14	.417
Lehigh	7	11	.389
Notre Dame	9	15	.375
Iona	8	14	.364
Siena	7	13	.350
Boston College	6	17	.261
Rutgers	3	15	.167

INDIVIDUAL LEADERS—SEASON

Scoring

	CL	POS	G	FG	FT	PTS	PPG
1 **Darrell Floyd**, Furman	SR	G	28	339	268	946	**33.8**
2 **Robin Freeman**, Ohio State	SR	G	22	259	205	723	**32.9**
3 **Dan Swartz**, Morehead State	SR	F	29	282	264	828	**28.6**
4 **Tom Heinsohn**, Holy Cross	SR	F	27	254	232	740	**27.4**
5 **Julius McCoy**, Michigan State	SR	F	22	228	144	600	**27.3**
6 **Lennie Rosenbluth**, North Carolina	JR	F	23	227	160	614	**26.7**
7 **Rod Hundley**, West Virginia	JR	F	30	290	218	798	**26.6**
8 **Raymond Downs**, Texas	JR	F	22	167	246	580	**26.4**
9 **Jim Ray**, Toledo	SR	G	22	171	221	563	**25.6**
10 **Roger Sigler**, LSU	JR	F	20	175	151	501	**25.1**

Field Goal Pct

	CL	POS	G	FG	FGA	PCT
1 **Joe Holup**, George Washington	SR	C	26	200	309	**64.7**
2 **Hal Greer**, Marshall	SO	G	23	128	213	**60.1**
3 **Odell Johnson**, Saint Mary's (CA)	JR	G	26	134	238	**56.3**
4 **Raymond Downs**, Texas	JR	F	22	167	309	**54.0**
5 **Angelo Lombardo**, Manhattan	JR	C	24	172	322	**53.4**

Minimum: 100 made

Free Throw Pct

	CL	POS	G	FT	FTA	PCT
1 **Bill Von Weyhe**, Rhode Island	JR	F	25	180	208	**86.5**
2 **Jackie Murdock**, Wake Forest	JR	G	28	203	237	**85.7**
3 **Vic Molodet**, NC State	SR	G	27	167	196	**85.2**
4 **Dick Miani**, Miami (FL)	SR	G	26	139	166	**83.7**
5 **Bob McCarty**, Virginia	SR	F	27	163	196	**83.2**

Minimum: 85 made

INDIVIDUAL LEADERS—GAME

Points

	CL	POS	OPP	DATE	PTS
1 **Darrell Floyd**, Furman	SR	G	The Citadel	J14	**62**
2 **Joe Capua**, Wyoming	SR	G	Montana	F3	**51**
Tom Heinsohn, Holy Cross	SR	F	Boston College	M1	**51**
4 **Mark Binstein**, Army	SR	G	Rhode Island	D29	**50**
Bob Burrow, Kentucky	SR	C	LSU	J14	**50**
Jim Krebs, SMU	JR	C	Texas	F7	**50**

Free Throws Made

	CL	POS	OPP	DATE	FT	FTA	PCT
1 **Jim Ray**, Toledo	SR	G	Ohio	F27	**22**	24	91.7
2 **Jim Babers**, Texas Western	SR	F	Arizona State	F11	**21**	23	91.3
3 **Chet Forte**, Columbia	JR	G	Yale	J18	**20**	21	95.2
Jim Winters, Portland	SR	G	Seattle	F12	**20**	23	87.0
Tom Hemans, Niagara	SR	F	Fordham	D2	**20**	26	76.9

TEAM LEADERS—SEASON

Scoring Offense

	G	W-L	PTS	PPG
1 **Morehead State**	29	19-10	2,782	**95.9**
2 **Marshall**	23	18-5	2,145	**93.3**
3 **Illinois**	22	18-4	1,996	**90.7**
4 **Furman**	28	12-16	2,492	**89.0**
5 **Memphis**	27	20-7	2,385	**88.3**

Field Goal Pct

	G	W-L	FG	FGA	PCT
1 **George Washington**	26	19-7	725	1,415	**51.2**
2 **Manhattan**	24	16-8	698	1,519	**46.0**
3 **DePaul**	24	16-8	659	1,456	**45.3**
4 **Niagara**	27	20-7	739	1,653	**44.7**
5 **Wake Forest**	28	19-9	777	1,754	**44.3**

Free Throw Pct

	G	W-L	FT	FTA	PCT
1 **SMU**	29	25-4	701	917	**76.4**
2 **Murray State**	25	15-10	590	791	**74.6**
3 **Texas Western**	22	12-10	517	698	**74.1**
4 **Illinois**	22	18-4	534	725	**73.7**
5 **NC State**	28	24-4	639	869	**73.5**

Scoring Defense

	G	W-L	OPP PTS	OPP PPG
1 **San Francisco**	29	29-0	1,514	**52.2**
2 **Oklahoma A&M**	27	18-9	1,428	**52.9**
3 **New Mexico State**	23	16-7	1,358	**59.0**
4 **Tulsa**	26	16-10	1,537	**59.1**
5 **San Jose State**	25	15-10	1,485	**59.4**

CONSENSUS ALL-AMERICAS

First Team

PLAYER	CL	POS	HT	SCHOOL	RPG	PPG
Robin Freeman	SR	G	5-11	Ohio State	N/A	32.9
Sihugo Green	SR	G	6-2	Duquesne	13.2	24.5
Tom Heinsohn	SR	F	6-7	Holy Cross	21.1	27.4
Bill Russell	SR	C	6-9	San Francisco	21.0	20.5
Ronnie Shavlik	SR	F/C	6-9	NC State	19.5	18.2

Second Team

PLAYER	CL	POS	HT	SCHOOL	RPG	PPG
Bob Burrow	SR	C	6-7	Kentucky	14.6	21.1
Darrell Floyd	SR	G	6-1	Furman	9.4	33.8
Rod Hundley	JR	F	6-4	West Virginia	13.1	26.6
K.C. Jones	SR	G	6-1	San Francisco	5.2	9.8
Willie Naulls	SR	C	6-6	UCLA	14.6	23.6
Bill Uhl	SR	C	7-0	Dayton	14.7	18.4

Selectors: AP, Colliers (coaches), International News Service, Look Magazine, Newspaper Enterprises Assn., UP

AWARD WINNERS

Player of the Year

PLAYER	CL	POS	HT	SCHOOL	AWARDS
Bill Russell	SR	C	6-9	San Francisco	UP

Coach of the Year

COACH	SCHOOL	REC	AWARDS
Phil Woolpert	San Francisco	29-0	UP

Poll Progression

Preseason Poll

UP	SCHOOL
1	San Francisco (A)
2	Kentucky
3	Utah
4	NC State
5	Iowa
6	Dayton
7	Illinois
7	UCLA
9	Duquesne
10	George Washington
11	Holy Cross
12	Marquette
13	Fordham
14	Washington
15	Alabama
16	Indiana
16	Saint Louis
18	Oregon State
18	SMU
20	Kansas

Week of Dec 6

AP	UP	SCHOOL
1	1	San Francisco (2-0)
2	2	Kentucky (1-0)
3	3	NC State (2-0)
4	5	Iowa (1-0)
5	4	Utah (1-0)
6	18	Alabama (2-0)
7	6	Dayton (2-0)
8	7	Illinois (0-0)
9	8	Duquesne (1-0)
10	10	BYU (2-0)
11	9	Holy Cross (1-0)
12	—	Oklahoma City (2-0)
13	11	George Washington (1-0)
14	15	Marquette (1-0)
14	—	West Virginia (1-0)
16	14	UCLA (0-2)
16	—	Ohio State (1-1)
18	—	La Salle (1-1)
19	16	Stanford (2-0)
20	—	Minnesota (1-0)
—	12	Indiana (1-0)
—	13	Saint Louis (1-0)
—	17	Kansas (0-0)
—	19	Seton Hall (2-0)
—	20	Louisville (1-0)

Week of Dec 13

AP	UP	SCHOOL	AP↓↑
1	1	San Francisco (3-0)	
2	2	NC State (4-0)	↑1
3	3	Utah (3-0)	↑2
4	4	Iowa (2-0)	
5	5	Alabama (4-0)	↑1
6	6	Duquesne (3-0)	↑3
7	7	Dayton (4-0)	
8	8	BYU (4-0)	↑2
9	9	Vanderbilt (4-0)	⤴
10	10	Holy Cross (3-0)	↑1
11	11	Temple (3-0)	⤴
12	12	Kentucky (1-1)	↓10
13	13	George Washington (3-0)	
14	14	Cincinnati (3-0)	⤴
15	15	West Virginia (3-0)	↓1
16	16	North Carolina (3-0)	⤴
17	17	Saint Louis (3-0)	⤴
18	18	Kansas (3-0)	⤴
19	19	Indiana (2-0)	⤴
20	20	Oklahoma City (2-1)	↓8

Week of Dec 20

AP	UP	SCHOOL	AP↓↑
1	1	San Francisco (5-0)	
2	3	NC State (7-0)	
3	2	Utah (5-0)	
4	4	Dayton (6-0)	↑3
5	5	BYU (6-0)	↑3
6	8	North Carolina (6-0)	↑10
7	7	Holy Cross (5-0)	↑3
8	19	Vanderbilt (4-0)	↑1
9	9	Kentucky (4-1)	↑3
10	6	Iowa (3-1)	↓6
11	11	George Washington (6-0)	↑2
12	16	Temple (5-0)	↓1
13	10	Marquette (5-1)	⤴
14	—	Duke (5-0)	⤴
15	—	Oklahoma City (4-0)	↑5
16	—	Alabama (4-2)	↓11
17	13	Illinois (3-1)	⤴
18	20	Indiana (3-1)	↑1
18	—	Memphis (5-0)	⤴
20	16	Duquesne (4-2)	↓14
—	12	SMU (6-1)	
—	13	Saint Louis (4-1)	⤵
—	15	Louisville (6-0)	
—	16	Ohio State (5-1)	

Week of Dec 27

AP	UP	SCHOOL	AP↓↑
1	1	San Francisco (7-0)	
2	2	Dayton (8-0)	↑2
3	3	NC State (8-0)	↓1
4	4	North Carolina (5-0)	↑2
5	13	Vanderbilt (6-1)	↑3
6	5	Iowa (3-1)	↑4
7	6	Utah (5-2)	↓4
8	15	Duke (6-0)	↑6
9	8	Illinois (5-1)	↑8
10	—	Oklahoma City (6-0)	↑5
11	8	Louisville (7-0)	⤴
12	19	George Washington (6-1)	↓1
13	12	Kentucky (5-2)	↓4
14	7	Holy Cross (5-1)	↓7
15	—	Ohio State (6-1)	⤴
16	—	Michigan State (4-0)	⤴
17	14	Rice (8-0)	⤴
17	—	Temple (5-0)	↓5
19	18	Alabama (5-2)	↓3
20	11	BYU (6-2)	↓15
—	10	Marquette (5-2)	⤵
—	16	Saint Louis (6-2)	
—	17	Indiana (5-1)	⤵
—	19	SMU (7-1)	

Week of Jan 3

AP	UP	SCHOOL	AP↓↑
1	1	San Francisco (10-0)	
2	3	NC State (11-0)	↑1
3	2	Dayton (9-0)	↓1
4	—	Vanderbilt (7-1)	↑1
5	4	North Carolina (7-1)	↓1
6	6	Kentucky (6-2)	↑7
7	10	George Washington (9-1)	↑5
8	7	Iowa State (9-1)	⤴
9	5	Illinois (6-1)	
10	21	Ohio State (7-1)	↑5
11	18	Duke (8-1)	↓3
12	—	Memphis (7-0)	⤴
13	14	Indiana (6-1)	⤴
14	9	Holy Cross (7-2)	
15	17	Tulsa (10-1)	⤴
16	19	Temple (6-0)	↑1
17	—	Alabama (6-3)	↑2
18	13	Rice (9-1)	↓1
19	—	West Virginia (7-2)	⤴
20	—	Michigan State (5-1)	↓4
20	—	Cincinnati (7-2)	⤴
—	8	Utah (6-3)	⤵
—	10	SMU (10-2)	
—	12	Louisville (9-1)	⤵
—	14	UCLA (4-5)	
—	16	Iowa (3-4)	⤵
—	20	Stanford (6-0)	

Week of Jan 10

AP	UP	SCHOOL	AP↓↑
1	1	San Francisco (11-0)	
2	2	Dayton (11-0)	↑1
3	3	NC State (11-1)	↓1
4	8	Vanderbilt (8-2)	
5	4	Kentucky (7-2)	↑1
6	8	Duke (9-2)	↑5
7	15	Ohio State (8-1)	↑3
8	5	Illinois (7-1)	↑1
9	10	North Carolina (8-2)	↓4
10	14	Temple (8-0)	↑6
11	11	Holy Cross (9-2)	↑3
12	6	Indiana (8-1)	↑1
13	13	Louisville (10-1)	⤴
14	—	George Washington (9-3)	↓7
15	16	Iowa State (8-2)	↓7
16	—	Oklahoma City (9-1)	⤴
17	—	Memphis (9-1)	↓5
18	—	Wake Forest (8-5)	⤴
19	—	Alabama (7-3)	↓2
20	12	Utah (8-3)	⤴
20	—	Cincinnati (8-2)	
—	7	SMU (12-2)	
—	17	UCLA (6-5)	
—	18	Marquette (8-4)	
—	18	Saint Louis (8-2)	
—	20	Michigan (5-4)	

Week of Jan 17

AP	UP	SCHOOL	AP↓↑
1	1	San Francisco (13-0)	
2	2	Dayton (12-0)	
3	3	NC State (12-1)	
4	5	Kentucky (9-2)	↑1
5	6	Vanderbilt (12-1)	↓1
6	4	Illinois (10-1)	↑2
7	7	Duke (12-2)	↓1
8	9	Temple (10-0)	↑2
9	11	North Carolina (12-2)	
10	10	Louisville (13-1)	↑3
11	15	Ohio State (9-2)	↓4
12	13	Holy Cross (11-2)	↓1
13	—	Alabama (9-3)	↑6
14	17	Oklahoma City (10-2)	↑2
15	—	Memphis (11-1)	↑2
16	12	Utah (11-3)	↑4
17	20	Saint Louis (10-2)	⤴
18	14	UCLA (8-5)	⤴
19	7	SMU (13-2)	⤴
20	—	Iowa (5-5)	⤴
20	—	Oklahoma A&M (11-3)	⤴
—	16	BYU (11-3)	
—	17	Iowa State (9-3)	⤵
—	17	Stanford (10-1)	
—	20	Marquette (10-4)	

Week of Jan 24

AP	UP	SCHOOL	AP↓↑
1	1	San Francisco (13-0)	
2	2	Dayton (14-0)	
3	4	Kentucky (10-2)	↑1
4	5	NC State (13-2)	↓1
5	3	Illinois (10-1)	↑1
6	7	Temple (11-0)	↑2
7	8	Vanderbilt (13-1)	↓2
8	6	North Carolina (13-2)	↑1
9	10	Louisville (15-1)	↑1
10	11	Duke (12-2)	↓3
11	13	Holy Cross (13-2)	↑1
12	18	Alabama (10-3)	↑1
13	13	Iowa (6-5)	↑7
14	16	Cincinnati (12-3)	⤴
15	—	St. Francis (NY) (11-0)	⤴
16	—	Oklahoma City (12-4)	↓2
17	17	Saint Louis (11-2)	
18	9	SMU (13-2)	↑1
19	—	Memphis (12-2)	↓4
20	—	Oklahoma A&M (11-2)	
—	12	Utah (12-3)	⤵
—	15	UCLA (8-5)	⤵
—	18	Marquette (10-4)	
—	20	Stanford (11-2)	

Week of Jan 31

AP	UP	SCHOOL	AP↓↑
1	1	San Francisco (14-0)	
2	2	Dayton (14-1) (B)	
3	5	Vanderbilt (14-1)	↑4
4	4	NC State (14-2)	
5	6	Louisville (16-1) (B)	↑4
6	3	Illinois (11-1)	↓1
7	7	Temple (13-0)	↓1
8	9	Kentucky (10-3)	↓5
9	8	North Carolina (13-2)	↓1
10	11	Duke (12-2)	
11	14	Saint Louis (12-2)	↑6
12	17	Alabama (11-3)	
13	18	St. Francis (NY) (13-0)	↑2
14	15	Holy Cross (13-2)	↓3
15	—	Oklahoma City (13-4)	↑1
16	—	Memphis (13-2)	↑3
17	10	SMU (14-2)	↑1
18	—	Marshall (13-2)	⤴
19	12	Iowa (7-5)	↓6
20	13	UCLA (9-5)	⤴
—	16	Utah (14-3)	
—	19	BYU (11-5)	
—	20	Canisius (9-5)	
—	20	Cincinnati (12-3)	⤵

Week of Feb 7

AP	UP	SCHOOL	AP↓↑
1	1	San Francisco (15-0)	
2	2	Dayton (16-1)	
3	6	Vanderbilt (15-1)	
4	4	NC State (16-2)	
5	5	Louisville (18-1)	
6	3	Illinois (12-1)	
7	7	Kentucky (13-3)	↑1
8	10	Duke (13-3)	↑2
9	8	Temple (14-1)	↓2
10	14	Alabama (12-3)	↑2
11	11	Saint Louis (14-2)	
12	12	North Carolina (13-3)	↓3
13	14	Holy Cross (16-2)	↑1
14	—	Oklahoma City (15-4)	↑1
15	9	SMU (16-2)	↑2
16	18	St. Francis (NY) (15-0)	↓3
17	16	Iowa (8-5)	↑2
18	13	UCLA (11-5)	↑2
19	—	George Washington (12-4)	⤴
20	—	Cincinnati (13-3)	⤴
—	17	BYU (13-5)	
—	19	Utah (14-5)	
—	20	Stanford (13-2)	

Week of Feb 14

AP	UP	SCHOOL	AP↓↑
1	1	San Francisco (18-0)	
2	2	Dayton (18-1)	
3	3	Illinois (14-1)	↑3
4	5	Louisville (19-2)	↑1
5	4	NC State (18-2)	↓1
6	6	Vanderbilt (16-2)	↓3
7	7	Kentucky (15-3)	
8	11	Alabama (14-3)	↑2
9	9	Temple (17-1)	
10	10	North Carolina (15-3)	↑2
11	14	Duke (15-4)	↓3
12	8	SMU (17-2)	↑3
13	—	St. Francis (NY) (16-0)	↑3
14	—	Oklahoma City (16-4)	
15	13	Iowa (10-5)	↑2
16	16	Holy Cross (17-3)	↓3
17	15	Saint Louis (14-4)	↓6
18	19	Houston (17-3)	⤴
19	—	Memphis (17-3)	⤴
20	12	UCLA (13-5)	↓2
—	17	BYU (14-6)	
—	17	Utah (16-5)	
—	20	Cincinnati (14-4) (C)	⤵
—	20	Iowa State (15-3)	
—	20	Xavier (12-7)	

Poll Progression Continues →

Week of Feb 21

AP	UP	School	AP↓↑
1	1	**San Francisco** (20-0)	
2	2	**Illinois** (16-1)	↑1
3	4	**Louisville** (21-2)	↑1
4	3	**Dayton** (20-2)	↓2
5	6	**Vanderbilt** (18-2)	↑1
6	5	**NC State** (19-3)	↓1
7	11	**Alabama** (16-3)	↑1
8	10	**Kentucky** (16-4)	↓1
9	9	**North Carolina** (16-3)	↑1
10	8	**Temple** (19-1)	↓1
11	—	**Duke** (16-5)	
12	7	**SMU** (19-2)	
13	12	**Iowa** (12-5)	↑2
14	14	**Houston** (18-3)	↑4
15	13	**UCLA** (15-5)	↑5
16	17	**St. Francis (NY)** (18-1)	↓3
17	15	**Holy Cross** (19-4)	↓1
18	—	**Oklahoma City** (16-5)	↓4
19	—	**George Washington** (17-5)	⤴
20	18	**Iowa State** (16-3)	⤴
—	15	**Utah** (17-5)	
—	19	**Cincinnati** (15-4)	
—	19	**Xavier** (13-9)	

Week of Feb 28

AP	UP	School	AP↓↑
1	1	**San Francisco** (21-0)	
2	3	**Illinois** (17-2)	
3	2	**Dayton** (22-2)	↑1
4	6	**Alabama** (18-3)	↑3
5	4	**NC State** (21-3)	↑1
6	5	**Louisville** (22-3)	↓3
7	11	**Vanderbilt** (19-3)	↓2
8	8	**North Carolina** (17-4)	↑1
9	7	**SMU** (21-2)	↑3
10	9	**Iowa** (14-5)	↑3
11	15	**Duke** (18-6)	
12	13	**Kentucky** (17-5)	↓4
13	10	**UCLA** (17-5)	↑2
14	12	**Temple** (20-3)	↓4
15	20	**Holy Cross** (21-4)	↑2
16	—	**Oklahoma City** (17-6)	↑2
17	19	**Kansas State** (15-6)	⤴
18	18	**Houston** (19-4)	↓4
19	15	**Saint Louis** (17-5)	⤴
20	—	**Wake Forest** (17-8)	⤴
—	14	**Utah** (19-5)	
—	15	**Cincinnati** (16-5)	
—	20	**Ohio State** (15-5)	

Week of Mar 6

AP	UP	School	AP↓↑
1	1	**San Francisco** (24-0)	
2	2	**NC State** (24-3)	↑3
3	3	**Dayton** (23-3)	
4	5	**Alabama** (20-3)	
5	4	**Iowa** (16-5)	↑5
6	7	**Louisville** (26-3)	
7	8	**Illinois** (18-3)	↓5
8	6	**SMU** (22-2)	↑1
9	12	**Kentucky** (19-5)	↑3
10	9	**UCLA** (19-5)	↑3
11	10	**Vanderbilt** (19-4)	↓4
12	15	**Holy Cross** (22-4)	↑3
13	14	**Temple** (21-3)	↑1
14	—	**West Virginia** (21-8)	⤴
15	11	**North Carolina** (18-5)	↓7
16	16	**Oklahoma City** (18-6)	
17	—	**Houston** (19-5)	↑1
18	—	**Wake Forest** (19-9)	↑2
19	18	**Duke** (19-7)	↓8
20	13	**Utah** (21-5)	⤴
—	16	**Saint Louis** (17-6)	⤵
—	18	**Canisius** (17-6)	
—	18	**Seattle** (17-9)	

Final Poll

AP	School	AP↓↑
1	**San Francisco** (25-0)	
2	**NC State** (24-3)	
3	**Dayton** (23-3) Ⓓ	
4	**Iowa** (17-5)	↑1
5	**Alabama** (21-3)	↓1
6	**Louisville** (26-3) Ⓓ	
7	**SMU** (22-2)	↑1
8	**UCLA** (21-5)	↑2
9	**Kentucky** (19-5)	
10	**Illinois** (18-4)	↓3
11	**Oklahoma City** (18-6)	↑5
12	**Vanderbilt** (19-4)	↓1
13	**North Carolina** (18-5)	↑2
14	**Holy Cross** (22-4)	↓2
15	**Temple** (23-3)	↓2
16	**Wake Forest** (19-9)	↑2
17	**Duke** (19-7)	↑2
18	**Utah** (21-5)	↑2
19	**Oklahoma A&M** (18-8)	⤴
20	**West Virginia** (21-8)	↓6
—	**George Washington** (19-7)	

Ⓐ Before the start of the season, the NCAA adopts what will become known as the Russell Rule, widening the lane by six feet to move big men like San Francisco's Bill Russell farther away from the basket. Even so, defending NCAA champ USF opens the season ranked first in both polls and will become the first team to go wire-to-wire as No. 1.

Ⓑ On Jan. 28, Louisville upsets Dayton, 66-64, in OT. Charlie Tyra, a 6'8" center, leads the winners with 30 points. Says Louisville coach Peck Hickman, "Is it okay to vote my boys No. 1 now since we just beat No. 2?" Not quite. The Cardinals jump four places to No. 5.

Ⓒ On Feb. 11, Cincinnati and Morehead State combine to make 88 free throws (35 for Cincy, 53 for Morehead) in 111 attempts, both totals being NCAA records. Led by lefty forward Steve Hamilton, Morehead State winds up setting the single-season NCAA record with 28.9 free throws made per game. Hamilton goes on to have a 12-year MLB career as a pitcher.

Ⓓ With undefeated San Francisco headed to the NCAA Tourney, both No. 3 Dayton and No. 6 Louisville opt for the NIT, where they wind up playing one another for the championship on March 24. With Charlie Tyra getting 27 points and nine boards against Dayton's seven-footer, Bill Uhl, Louisville wins, 93-80.

1956 NCAA TOURNAMENT (A)

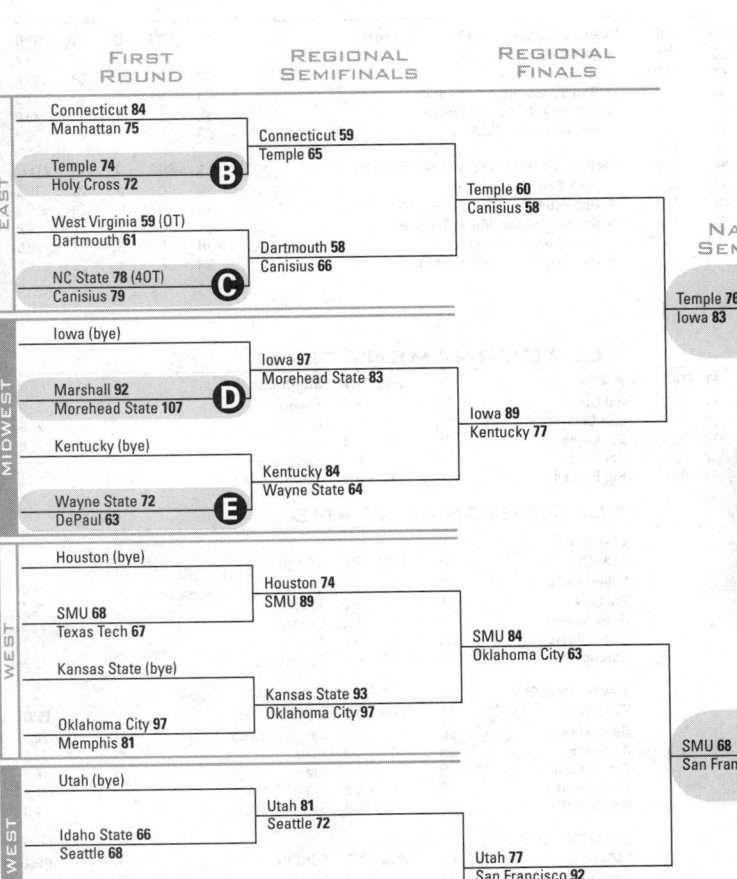

First Round / Regional Semifinals / Regional Finals / National Semifinals / National Final

EAST

First Round
- Connecticut **84**, Manhattan **75**
- Temple **74**, Holy Cross **72** (B)
- West Virginia **59** (OT), Dartmouth **61**
- NC State **78** (4OT), Canisius **79** (C)

Regional Semifinals
- Connecticut **59**, Temple **65**
- Dartmouth **58**, Canisius **66**

Regional Finals
- Temple **60**, Canisius **58**

MIDWEST

First Round
- Iowa (bye)
- Marshall **92**, Morehead State **107** (D)
- Kentucky (bye)
- Wayne State **72**, DePaul **63** (E)

Regional Semifinals
- Iowa **97**, Morehead State **83**
- Kentucky **84**, Wayne State **64**

Regional Finals
- Iowa **89**, Kentucky **77**

WEST

First Round
- Houston (bye)
- SMU **68**, Texas Tech **67**
- Kansas State (bye)
- Oklahoma City **97**, Memphis **81**

Regional Semifinals
- Houston **74**, SMU **89**
- Kansas State **93**, Oklahoma City **97**

Regional Finals
- SMU **84**, Oklahoma City **63**

FAR WEST

First Round
- Utah (bye)
- Idaho State **66**, Seattle **68**
- San Francisco (bye)
- UCLA (bye)

Regional Semifinals
- Utah **81**, Seattle **72**
- San Francisco **72**, UCLA **61**

Regional Finals
- Utah **77**, San Francisco **92**

NATIONAL SEMIFINALS

- Temple **76**, Iowa **83**
- SMU **68**, San Francisco **86**

NATIONAL FINAL

San Francisco 83
Iowa 71

EVANSTON, IL

National Third Place Temple d. SMU 90-81
East Regional Third Place Dartmouth d. Connecticut 85-64
Midwest Regional Third Place Morehead State d. Wayne State 95-84
West Regional Third Place Kansas State d. Houston 89-70
Far West Regional Third Place UCLA d. Seattle 94-70 (F)

(A) The rival NIT lures No. 3 Dayton and No. 6 Louisville, and the Cardinals beat the Flyers for the championship. Louisville is led by 6'8" junior center Charlie Tyra, who averages 23.8 points and 22.2 rebounds for the season.

(B) Future Celtics star (and coach) Tom Heinsohn scores 26 points and grabs 20 rebounds for Holy Cross in his lone Tournament game. But his last-second field goal is disallowed, starting a melee in which referee John Stevens is roughed up by a group of fans.

(C) Canisius and NC State play to a record four overtimes, after neither team scores in the third OT. Fran Corcoran's only shot of the contest proves to be the game-winner.

Temple's Hal "King" Lear and Guy Rodgers combine for 60 points. Lear is nearly unstoppable in the second half, scoring 24 of his 32. He then hits 48 in the consolation game, becoming the first MOP not to make the final.

San Francisco is the first team to win the Tournament with an undefeated record (29-0), and stretches its unbeaten streak to 55 games behind Bill Russell's 26 points and 27 rebounds.

Mike Farmer scores 26 points for the Dons, who jump to a 40-19 lead and are never threatened. Bill Russell scores just 17 points against constant double-teaming, but pulls down 23 rebounds.

(D) Steve Hamilton scores 23 points for Morehead State. He will become one of only two men to play in both the NBA Finals (1958, with the Lakers) and the World Series (1963 and '64, as a Yankees reliever). The other is Gene Conley (1959-61 Celtics and '57 Milwaukee Braves).

(E) After sitting out a week because of an infection on his face, DePaul starter Ed Curtin returns to the lineup. However, his five-point contribution does not make a dent in Wayne State's offense and the Blue Demons lose.

(F) UCLA's Bill Eblen nearly comes to blows with Seattle's Ken Fuhrer while attempting to corral a rebound. Eblen is ejected from the game and a bench-clearing brawl is barely averted.

Tournament Leaders

INDIVIDUAL LEADERS

Scoring

	CL	POS	G	PTS	PPG
1 **Hal Lear**, Temple	SR	G	5	160	32.0
Bob Burrow, Kentucky	SR	C	2	64	32.0
3 **Dan Swartz**, Morehead State	SR	F	3	91	30.3
4 **Carl Cain**, Iowa	SR	F	4	99	24.8
5 **Willie Naulls**, UCLA	SR	C	2	49	24.5
6 **Art Bunte**, Utah	SR	C	2	47	23.5
7 **Bill Russell**, San Francisco	SR	C	4	91	22.8
8 **Hank Nowak**, Canisius	JR	F	3	67	22.3
9 **Jim Krebs**, SMU	JR	C	5	109	21.8
10 **Hub Reed**, Oklahoma City	SO	C	3	63	21.0

Minimum: 2 games

Field Goals Per Game

	CL	POS	G	FG	FGPG
1 **Bob Burrow**, Kentucky	SR	C	2	27	13.5
2 **Hal Lear**, Temple	SR	G	5	63	12.6
3 **Dan Swartz**, Morehead State	SR	F	3	33	11.0
4 **Bill Russell**, San Francisco	SR	C	4	40	10.0
Willie Naulls, UCLA	SR	C	2	20	10.0

Free Throws Per Game

	CL	POS	G	FT	FTPG
1 **Jack Parr**, Kansas State	SO	C	2	20	10.0
2 **Bob Kendrick**, Wayne State (MI)	SO	G/F	3	29	9.7
3 **Donnie Gaunce**, Morehead State	SR	G	3	27	9.0
Hank Nowak, Canisius	JR	F	3	27	9.0
5 **Dan Swartz**, Morehead State	SR	F	3	25	8.3

TEAM LEADERS

Scoring

	G	PTS	PPG
1 **Morehead State**	3	285	95.0
2 **Kansas State**	2	182	91.0
3 **Oklahoma City**	3	257	85.7
4 **Iowa**	4	340	85.0
5 **San Francisco**	4	333	83.3
6 **Kentucky**	2	161	80.5
7 **Utah**	2	158	79.0
8 **SMU**	5	390	78.0
9 **UCLA**	2	155	77.5
10 **Wayne State**	3	220	73.3

Minimum: 2 games

FG Per Game

	G	FG	FGPG
1 **San Francisco**	4	136	34.0
2 **Kentucky**	2	66	33.0
3 **Morehead State**	3	97	32.3
4 **Kansas State**	2	61	30.5
5 **Oklahoma City**	3	91	30.3

FT Per Game

	G	FT	FTPG
1 **Morehead State**	3	91	30.3
2 **Kansas State**	2	60	30.0
3 **SMU**	5	130	26.0
4 **Iowa**	4	102	25.5
UCLA	2	51	25.5

ALL-TOURNAMENT TEAM

PLAYER	CL	POS	HT	SCHOOL	PPG
Hal Lear*	SR	G	6-0	Temple	32.0
Carl Cain	SR	F	6-3	Iowa	24.8
Bill Logan	SR	C	6-7	Iowa	19.8
Hal Perry	SR	G	5-11	San Francisco	10.5
Bill Russell	SR	C	6-9	San Francisco	22.8

ALL-REGIONAL TEAMS

EAST

PLAYER	CL	POS	HT	SCHOOL	PPG
Robert Kelly	SR	G	6-1	Canisius	12.0
Hal Lear	SR	G	6-0	Temple	26.7
Hank Nowak	JR	F	6-3	Canisius	22.3
Guy Rodgers	SO	G	6-0	Temple	15.7
Gordon Ruddy	SR	F/G	6-1	Connecticut	15.7

FAR WEST

PLAYER	CL	POS	HT	SCHOOL	PPG
Gene Brown	SO	G	6-3	San Francisco	20.5
Art Bunte	SR	C	6-3	Utah	23.5
Curt Jenson	JR	G	5-10	Utah	16.5
Willie Naulls	SR	C	6-6	UCLA	24.5
Bill Russell	SR	C	6-9	San Francisco	24.0

MIDWEST

PLAYER	CL	POS	HT	SCHOOL	PPG
Jerry Bird	SR	F	6-6	Kentucky	16.5
Bob Burrow	SR	C	6-7	Kentucky	32.0
Carl Cain	SR	F	6-3	Iowa	31.0
Sharm Scheuerman	SR	G	6-2	Iowa	18.0
Bill Seaberg	SR	G	6-0	Iowa	9.0
Dan Swartz	SR	F	6-4	Morehead State	30.3

WEST

PLAYER	CL	POS	HT	SCHOOL	PPG
Jim Krebs	JR	C	6-8	SMU	18.7
Joel Krog	SR	F	6-3	SMU	16.3
Bobby Mills	JR	G	6-0	SMU	12.7
Hub Reed	SO	C	6-10	Oklahoma City	21.0
Eddie Wallace	JR	G	5-10	Kansas State	19.5

* Most outstanding player

1956 NCAA TOURNAMENT BOX SCORES

65-59 (SWEET 16)

	Temple	Connecticut
1H	38	27
2H	27	32

TEMPLE	MIN	FG	3FG	FT	REB	A	ST	BL	PF	TP
Hal Lear	-	18-27	-	4-5	9	1	-	-	2	40
Fred Cohen	-	5-21	-	0-1	34	3	-	-	3	10
Guy Rodgers	-	1-15	-	5-7	5	13	-	-	3	7
Jay Norman	-	2-6	-	2-4	10	1	-	-	5	6
Hal Reinfeld	-	1-7	-	0-1	6	0	-	-	1	2
Dan Fleming	-	0-4	-	0-1	9	0	-	-	2	0
Tink Van Patton	-	0-1	-	0-0	3	0	-	-	0	0
TOTALS	-	27-81	-	11-19	76	18	-	-	16	65
Percentages		33.3		57.9						

Coach: Harry Litwack

CONNECTICUT	MIN	FG	3FG	FT	REB	A	ST	BL	PF	TP
Gordon Ruddy	-	8-23	-	3-5	9	0	-	-	1	19
Fran Quinn	-	6-15	-	4-5	5	3	-	-	4	16
Bob Osborne	-	4-14	-	3-4	15	2	-	-	0	11
Ron Bushwell	-	2-14	-	1-3	7	1	-	-	2	5
Paul Kaspar	-	1-8	-	2-5	6	3	-	-	3	4
Donald Burns	-	1-5	-	0-1	0	1	-	-	0	2
Robert Cherepy	-	1-2	-	0-1	1	0	-	-	1	2
Jim O'Connor	-	0-1	-	0-0	1	0	-	-	1	0
William O'Leary	-	0-1	-	0-0	2	0	-	-	1	0
TOTALS	-	23-83	-	13-24	46	10	-	-	13	59
Percentages		27.7		54.2						

Coach: Hugh S. Greer

66-58 (SWEET 16)

	Canisius	Dartmouth
1H	33	30
2H	33	28

CANISIUS	MIN	FG	3FG	FT	REB	A	ST	BL	PF	TP
Hank Nowak	-	9-15	-	11-15	16	3	-	-	2	29
Robert Kelly	-	6-10	-	0-0	7	2	-	-	3	12
John McCarthy	-	2-18	-	5-7	5	7	-	-	0	9
Fran Corcoran	-	4-10	-	0-2	5	0	-	-	1	8
Joseph Leone	-	2-7	-	0-1	4	0	-	-	4	4
David Markey	-	2-10	-	0-0	5	2	-	-	1	4
Eugene Bartkowski	-	0-0	-	0-0	0	0	-	-	1	0
Gregory Britz	-	0-0	-	0-0	0	0	-	-	0	0
John Coogan	-	0-0	-	0-0	0	0	-	-	0	0
James McCarthy	-	0-0	-	0-0	0	0	-	-	0	0
James McMullen	-	0-1	-	0-0	0	0	-	-	0	0
TOTALS	-	25-71	-	16-25	42	14	-	-	12	66
Percentages		35.2		64.0						

Coach: Joseph Curran

DARTMOUTH	MIN	FG	3FG	FT	REB	A	ST	BL	PF	TP
Jim Francis	-	7-10	-	5-6	11	1	-	-	2	19
M. David Carruthers	-	7-19	-	0-0	3	2	-	-	2	14
Tom Donahoe	-	2-5	-	3-5	5	1	-	-	3	7
Eugene Booth	-	3-5	-	0-0	5	2	-	-	3	6
Ronald Judson	-	0-7	-	6-6	5	2	-	-	2	6
Larry Blades	-	1-2	-	0-1	0	0	-	-	2	2
F. Tobias Julian	-	1-6	-	0-0	3	5	-	-	1	2
Herbert Markman	-	0-0	-	2-2	1	0	-	-	1	2
Harold Douglas	-	0-0	-	0-0	0	0	-	-	0	0
Hugh Erwin	-	0-1	-	0-0	1	0	-	-	0	0
Ronald Fraser	-	0-0	-	0-0	1	0	-	-	0	0
John Jones	-	0-0	-	0-0	0	0	-	-	0	0
TOTALS	-	21-55	-	16-20	35	13	-	-	16	58
Percentages		38.2		80.0						

Coach: Alvin "Doggie" Julian

97-83 (SWEET 16)

	Iowa	Morehead State
1H	54	35
2H	43	48

IOWA	MIN	FG	3FG	FT	REB	A	ST	BL	PF	TP
Carl Cain	-	8-25	-	12-13	14	-	-	-	3	28
Bill Logan	-	6-21	-	5-8	11	-	-	-	2	17
Bill Schoof	-	5-13	-	5-8	11	-	-	-	3	15
Sharm Scheuerman	-	6-10	-	2-3	5	-	-	-	5	14
Bill Seaberg	-	4-12	-	1-1	7	-	-	-	5	9
Lester Hawthorne	-	0-7	-	4-4	0	-	-	-	4	4
Robert George	-	0-4	-	3-8	3	-	-	-	4	3
Norman Paul	-	1-1	-	1-2	1	-	-	-	0	3
Augustine Martel	-	1-4	-	0-2	4	-	-	-	3	2
Gregg Schroeder	-	0-0	-	2-2	2	-	-	-	1	2
Jim McConnell	-	0-2	-	0-0	1	-	-	-	2	0
Frank Sebolt	-	0-1	-	0-1	1	-	-	-	3	0
TOTALS	-	31-100	-	35-52	60	-	-	-	35	97
Percentages		31.0		67.3						

Coach: Bucky O'Connor

MOREHEAD STATE	MIN	FG	3FG	FT	REB	A	ST	BL	PF	TP
Donnie Gaunce	-	5-14	-	14-24	8	-	-	-	3	24
Dan Swartz	-	8-23	-	4-6	12	-	-	-	5	20
Steve Hamilton	-	7-18	-	5-6	16	-	-	-	5	19
Harlan Tolle	-	2-8	-	2-4	4	-	-	-	4	6
Ken Thompson	-	1-2	-	2-3	3	-	-	-	1	4
Dave Keleher	-	0-4	-	3-4	3	-	-	-	5	3
Bernie Shimfessel	-	1-4	-	1-3	2	-	-	-	5	3
Gene Carroll	-	1-3	-	0-0	1	-	-	-	2	2
Jim Jewell	-	0-2	-	2-3	4	-	-	-	1	2
Bob Richards	-	0-2	-	0-0	1	-	-	-	2	0
TOTALS	-	25-80	-	33-53	54	-	-	-	33	83
Percentages		31.2		62.3						

Coach: Bobby Laughlin

84-64 (SWEET 16)

	Kentucky	Wayne State
1H	32	34
2H	52	30

KENTUCKY	MIN	FG	3FG	FT	REB	A	ST	BL	PF	TP
Bob Burrow	-	14	-	5-6	-	-	-	-	5	33
Gerry Calvert	-	5	-	4-6	-	-	-	-	1	14
Jerry Bird	-	5	-	0-2	-	-	-	-	5	10
Vernon Hatton	-	4	-	2-2	-	-	-	-	2	10
Phil Grawemeyer	-	3	-	1-3	-	-	-	-	4	7
Billy Cassady	-	1	-	1-4	-	-	-	-	2	3
Ed Beck	-	1	-	0-0	-	-	-	-	0	2
John Brewer	-	1	-	0-0	-	-	-	-	2	2
Phil Johnson	-	0	-	2-2	-	-	-	-	1	2
Ray Mills	-	0	-	1-2	-	-	-	-	1	1
TOTALS	-	34	-	16-27	-	-	-	-	23	84
Percentages				59.3						

Coach: Adolph Rupp

WAYNE STATE	MIN	FG	3FG	FT	REB	A	ST	BL	PF	TP
George Brown	-	5	-	4-6	-	-	-	-	5	14
Bob Kendrick	-	2	-	10-18	-	-	-	-	3	14
Tom Keller	-	5	-	3-5	-	-	-	-	2	13
George Duncan	-	4	-	1-3	-	-	-	-	0	9
Clarence Straughn	-	3	-	0-5	-	-	-	-	3	6
Tarpon London	-	2	-	0-0	-	-	-	-	0	4
Ron Porter	-	2	-	0-0	-	-	-	-	1	4
Jerry Greenberg	-	0	-	0-0	-	-	-	-	0	0
Donald Halverson	-	0	-	0-0	-	-	-	-	2	0
Ulysses Harvey	-	0	-	0-0	-	-	-	-	0	0
TOTALS	-	23	-	18-37	-	-	-	-	16	64
Percentages				48.6						

Coach: Joel G. Mason

Attendance: 14,600

89-74 (SWEET 16)

	SMU	Houston
1H	47	31
2H	42	43

SMU	MIN	FG	3FG	FT	REB	A	ST	BL	PF	TP
Jim Krebs	-	11-28	-	5-7	14	-	-	-	3	27
Ronnie Morris	-	4-10	-	5-6	6	-	-	-	2	13
Bobby Mills	-	3-10	-	5-6	7	-	-	-	3	11
Larry Showalter	-	4-8	-	1-4	9	-	-	-	4	9
Rick Herrscher	-	0-3	-	8-10	3	-	-	-	0	8
Joel Krog	-	0-7	-	8-10	9	-	-	-	3	8
Tom Miller	-	3-3	-	1-2	2	-	-	-	3	7
Carl Scharffenberger	-	2-2	-	0-0	2	-	-	-	0	4
Bob McGregor	-	1-1	-	0-1	2	-	-	-	1	2
William Eldridge	-	0-1	-	0-0	1	-	-	-	1	0
George Lee	-	0-0	-	0-0	0	-	-	-	0	0
Herschel O'Kelley	-	0-1	-	0-0	0	-	-	-	1	0
TOTALS	-	28-74	-	33-46	54	-	-	-	21	89
Percentages		37.8		71.7						

Coach: E.O. "Doc" Hayes

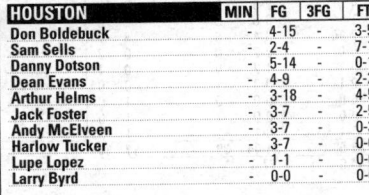

HOUSTON	MIN	FG	3FG	FT	REB	A	ST	BL	PF	TP
Don Boldebuck	-	4-15	-	3-5	7	-	-	-	5	11
Sam Sells	-	2-4	-	7-11	5	-	-	-	2	11
Danny Dotson	-	5-14	-	0-1	6	-	-	-	4	10
Dean Evans	-	4-9	-	2-2	3	-	-	-	1	10
Arthur Helms	-	3-18	-	4-5	10	-	-	-	5	10
Jack Foster	-	3-7	-	2-5	5	-	-	-	2	8
Andy McElveen	-	3-7	-	0-3	2	-	-	-	3	6
Harlow Tucker	-	3-7	-	0-0	8	-	-	-	3	6
Lupe Lopez	-	1-1	-	0-0	0	-	-	-	2	2
Larry Byrd	-	0-0	-	0-0	1	-	-	-	0	0
TOTALS	-	28-82	-	18-32	47	-	-	-	27	74
Percentages		34.1		56.2						

Coach: Alden Pasche

97-93 (SWEET 16)

	Oklahoma City	Kansas State
1H	47	43
2H	50	50

OKLAHOMA CITY	MIN	FG	3FG	FT	REB	A	ST	BL	PF	TP
Leon Griffin	-	6-14	-	8-9	5	-	-	-	2	20
Lyndon Lee	-	5-13	-	10-15	9	-	-	-	2	20
Roger Holloway	-	5-9	-	7-9	7	-	-	-	5	17
Cecil Magana	-	5-9	-	6-6	6	-	-	-	1	16
Hub Reed	-	6-11	-	3-4	4	-	-	-	5	15
Larry Bradshaw	-	3-7	-	1-3	9	-	-	-	5	7
Bill Juby	-	1-2	-	0-1	0	-	-	-	2	2
Fred Dunbar	-	0-0	-	0-1	1	-	-	-	1	0
Dennis Jeter	-	0-0	-	0-0	1	-	-	-	0	0
TOTALS	-	31-65	-	35-48	42	-	-	-	23	97
Percentages		47.7		72.9						

Coach: Abe Lemons

KANSAS STATE	MIN	FG	3FG	FT	REB	A	ST	BL	PF	TP
Eddie Wallace	-	9-18	-	5-6	5	-	-	-	4	23
Jack Parr	-	3-12	-	13-19	17	-	-	-	4	19
Juan Vicens	-	4-10	-	7-8	3	-	-	-	5	15
Francis Stone	-	6-15	-	2-2	7	-	-	-	1	14
Fritz Schneider	-	4-13	-	2-2	8	-	-	-	5	10
Clyde Kiddoo	-	3-4	-	3-4	0	-	-	-	2	9
James Abbott	-	1-4	-	0-0	2	-	-	-	5	2
Larry Powell	-	0-2	-	1-3	2	-	-	-	1	1
Larry Fischer	-	0-1	-	0-0	1	-	-	-	1	0
TOTALS	-	30-79	-	33-44	45	-	-	-	28	93
Percentages		38.0		75.0						

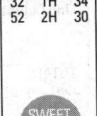

Coach: Tex Winter

81-72 (Sweet 16)

	1H	2H
Utah	44	37
Seattle	38	34

UTAH	MIN	FG	3FG	FT	REB	A	ST	BL	PF	TP
Art Bunte	-	8	-	8	-	-	-	-	3	24
Gary Bergen	-	6	-	4	-	-	-	-	4	16
Curt Jenson	-	6	-	0	-	-	-	-	3	12
Morris Buckwalter	-	3	-	4	-	-	-	-	1	10
Gary Hale	-	3	-	4	-	-	-	-	3	10
John Crowe	-	2	-	1	-	-	-	-	1	5
Jerry McCleary	-	1	-	2	-	-	-	-	3	4
Dick Eiler	-	0	-	0	-	-	-	-	1	0
Edward Gaythwaite	-	0	-	0	-	-	-	-	0	0
William Koncor	-	0	-	0	-	-	-	-	1	0
Darrell Pastrell	-	0	-	0	-	-	-	-	0	0
TOTALS	**-**	**29**	**-**	**23**	**-**	**-**	**-**	**-**	**20**	**81**
Percentages										

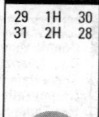

Coach: Jack Gardner

SEATTLE	MIN	FG	3FG	FT	REB	A	ST	BL	PF	TP
Dick Stricklin	-	7	-	2	-	-	-	-	2	16
Ken Fuhrer	-	5	-	5	-	-	-	-	3	15
Cal Bauer	-	3	-	7	-	-	-	-	2	13
Jerry Frizzell	-	5	-	0	-	-	-	-	2	10
Bob Godes	-	4	-	1	-	-	-	-	4	9
Clair Markey	-	1	-	2	-	-	-	-	0	4
Larry Sanford	-	1	-	1	-	-	-	-	4	3
Fred Gockel	-	0	-	2	-	-	-	-	0	2
Tom Cox	-	0	-	0	-	-	-	-	1	0
Jim Harney	-	0	-	0	-	-	-	-	0	0
Bill Rajcich	-	0	-	0	-	-	-	-	2	0
TOTALS	**-**	**26**	**-**	**20**	**-**	**-**	**-**	**-**	**20**	**72**
Percentages										

Coach: H. Albert Brightman

72-61 (Sweet 16)

	1H	2H
San Francisco	39	33
UCLA	21	40

SAN FRANCISCO	MIN	FG	3FG	FT	REB	A	ST	BL	PF	TP
Gene Brown	-	9-16	-	5-11	5	-	-	-	3	23
Bill Russell	-	9-15	-	3-4	23	-	-	-	4	21
Mike Farmer	-	4-13	-	7-8	15	-	-	-	2	15
Hal Perry	-	4-17	-	2-2	0	-	-	-	2	10
Mike Preaseau	-	1-6	-	1-4	1	-	-	-	5	3
Warren Baxter	-	0-0	-	0-0	0	-	-	-	1	0
Carl Boldt	-	0-4	-	0-0	3	-	-	-	4	0
TOTALS	**-**	**27-71**	**-**	**18-29**	**47**	**-**	**-**	**-**	**21**	**72**
Percentages		38.0		62.1						

Coach: Phil Woolpert

UCLA	MIN	FG	3FG	FT	REB	A	ST	BL	PF	TP
Willie Naulls	-	6-18	-	4-4	8	-	-	-	4	16
Morris Taft	-	6-23	-	4-8	12	-	-	-	2	16
Dick Banton	-	3-10	-	7-7	3	-	-	-	2	13
Al Herring	-	2-5	-	3-6	11	-	-	-	4	7
Jim Halsten	-	1-3	-	4-6	2	-	-	-	1	6
Connie Burke	-	0-5	-	2-2	3	-	-	-	1	2
Nolan Johnson	-	0-1	-	1-2	1	-	-	-	1	1
Carroll Adams	-	0-0	-	0-0	0	-	-	-	1	0
Jack Arnold	-	0-1	-	0-0	0	-	-	-	0	0
Art Hutchins	-	0-0	-	0-0	0	-	-	-	0	0
TOTALS	**-**	**18-66**	**-**	**25-35**	**40**	**-**	**-**	**-**	**16**	**61**
Percentages		27.3		71.4						

Coach: John Wooden

60-58 (Elite 8)

	1H	2H
Temple	29	31
Canisius	30	28

TEMPLE	MIN	FG	3FG	FT	REB	A	ST	BL	PF	TP
Guy Rodgers	-	9-22	-	4-8	8	4	-	-	3	22
Hal Lear	-	4-14	-	6-6	3	3	-	-	2	14
Jay Norman	-	3-5	-	7-8	10	2	-	-	4	13
Fred Cohen	-	2-3	-	0-0	5	1	-	-	4	4
Dan Fleming	-	2-8	-	0-0	6	0	-	-	0	4
Tink Van Patton	-	1-5	-	0-1	5	0	-	-	3	2
Hal Reinfeld	-	0-7	-	1-2	7	1	-	-	3	1
TOTALS	**-**	**21-64**	**-**	**18-25**	**44**	**11**	**-**	**-**	**19**	**60**
Percentages		32.8		72.0						

Coach: Harry Litwack

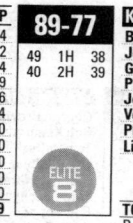

CANISIUS	MIN	FG	3FG	FT	REB	A	ST	BL	PF	TP
David Markey	-	7-7	-	3-5	5	5	-	-	4	17
Joseph Leone	-	5-10	-	2-5	9	0	-	-	3	12
Robert Kelly	-	5-11	-	0-0	8	2	-	-	2	10
John McCarthy	-	2-12	-	6-9	9	3	-	-	2	10
Hank Nowak	-	3-11	-	3-9	9	4	-	-	2	9
Fran Corcoran	-	0-1	-	0-0	0	0	-	-	1	0
TOTALS	**-**	**22-52**	**-**	**14-28**	**40**	**14**	**-**	**-**	**14**	**58**
Percentages		42.3		50.0						

Coach: Joseph Curran

89-77 (Elite 8)

	1H	2H
Iowa	49	40
Kentucky	38	39

IOWA	MIN	FG	3FG	FT	REB	A	ST	BL	PF	TP
Carl Cain	-	12-21	-	10-11	9	-	-	-	2	34
Sharm Scheuerman	-	8-13	-	6-9	5	-	-	-	4	22
Bill Logan	-	6-18	-	2-6	13	-	-	-	3	14
Bill Seaberg	-	2-12	-	5-5	11	-	-	-	1	9
Robert George	-	3-10	-	0-1	11	-	-	-	3	6
Bill Schoof	-	2-6	-	0-0	3	-	-	-	3	4
Lester Hawthorne	-	0-0	-	0-0	0	-	-	-	0	0
Augustine Martel	-	0-0	-	0-0	0	-	-	-	0	0
Jim McConnell	-	0-1	-	0-0	1	-	-	-	2	0
Norman Paul	-	0-2	-	0-0	2	-	-	-	0	0
Frank Sebolt	-	0-0	-	0-0	0	-	-	-	0	0
TOTALS	**-**	**33-83**	**-**	**23-32**	**55**	**-**	**-**	**-**	**18**	**89**
Percentages		39.8		71.9						

Coach: Bucky O'Connor

KENTUCKY	MIN	FG	3FG	FT	REB	A	ST	BL	PF	TP
Bob Burrow	-	13-23	-	5-8	12	-	-	-	3	31
Jerry Bird	-	9-21	-	5-9	24	-	-	-	1	23
Gerry Calvert	-	3-10	-	1-1	6	-	-	-	3	7
Phil Grawemeyer	-	2-10	-	1-1	7	-	-	-	4	5
John Brewer	-	2-5	-	0-0	1	-	-	-	4	4
Vernon Hatton	-	2-4	-	0-3	1	-	-	-	2	4
Phil Johnson	-	1-9	-	1-3	6	-	-	-	1	3
Linc Collinsworth	-	0-0	-	0-0	0	-	-	-	1	0
TOTALS	**-**	**32-82**	**-**	**13-25**	**57**	**-**	**-**	**-**	**19**	**77**
Percentages		39.0		52.0						

Coach: Adolph Rupp

Attendance: 15,375

84-63 (Elite 8)

	1H	2H
SMU	46	38
Oklahoma City	34	29

SMU	MIN	FG	3FG	FT	REB	A	ST	BL	PF	TP
Joel Krog	-	6-16	-	10-13	12	-	-	-	2	22
Larry Showalter	-	8-15	-	4-4	6	-	-	-	1	20
Bobby Mills	-	4-6	-	6-7	2	-	-	-	2	14
Ronnie Morris	-	4-5	-	2-3	5	-	-	-	3	10
Tom Miller	-	1-1	-	6-8	3	-	-	-	2	8
Jim Krebs	-	2-10	-	3-4	8	-	-	-	4	7
Rick Herrscher	-	0-0	-	2-2	0	-	-	-	0	2
George Lee	-	0-1	-	1-2	0	-	-	-	0	1
William Eldridge	-	0-1	-	0-0	1	-	-	-	0	0
Bob McGregor	-	0-0	-	0-0	0	-	-	-	1	0
Herschel O'Kelley	-	0-0	-	0-0	1	-	-	-	1	0
Carl Scharffenberger	-	0-1	-	0-1	1	-	-	-	1	0
TOTALS	**-**	**25-56**	**-**	**34-44**	**39**	**-**	**-**	**-**	**17**	**84**
Percentages		44.6		77.3						

Coach: E.O. "Doc" Hayes

OKLAHOMA CITY	MIN	FG	3FG	FT	REB	A	ST	BL	PF	TP
Hub Reed	-	7-20	-	7-8	9	-	-	-	4	21
Leon Griffin	-	7-14	-	0-1	3	-	-	-	3	14
Larry Bradshaw	-	4-8	-	0-0	5	-	-	-	2	8
Lyndon Lee	-	2-11	-	4-7	4	-	-	-	3	8
Roger Holloway	-	3-7	-	0-0	5	-	-	-	1	6
Ray Bilber	-	1-1	-	2-2	1	-	-	-	0	4
Charles Wheeler	-	1-3	-	0-0	0	-	-	-	2	2
Fred Dunbar	-	0-2	-	0-0	0	-	-	-	2	0
Dennis Jeter	-	0-4	-	0-3	2	-	-	-	3	0
Bill Juby	-	0-1	-	0-0	2	-	-	-	1	0
Cecil Magana	-	0-1	-	0-0	7	-	-	-	3	0
TOTALS	**-**	**25-72**	**-**	**13-21**	**38**	**-**	**-**	**-**	**24**	**63**
Percentages		34.7		61.9						

Coach: Abe Lemons

92-77 (Elite 8)

	1H	2H
San Francisco	44	48
Utah	41	36

SAN FRANCISCO	MIN	FG	3FG	FT	REB	A	ST	BL	PF	TP
Bill Russell	-	12	-	3	-	-	-	-	4	27
Gene Brown	-	7	-	4	-	-	-	-	3	18
Mike Farmer	-	5	-	4	-	-	-	-	3	14
Mike Preaseau	-	3	-	8	-	-	-	-	3	14
Carl Boldt	-	6	-	1	-	-	-	-	3	13
Hal Perry	-	2	-	0	-	-	-	-	0	4
Warren Baxter	-	1	-	0	-	-	-	-	2	2
Steve Balchios	-	0	-	0	-	-	-	-	0	0
Bill Bush	-	0	-	0	-	-	-	-	1	0
Jack King	-	0	-	0	-	-	-	-	0	0
Tom Nelson	-	0	-	0	-	-	-	-	1	0
Harold Payne	-	0	-	0	-	-	-	-	0	0
TOTALS	**-**	**36**	**-**	**20**	**-**	**-**	**-**	**-**	**20**	**92**
Percentages										

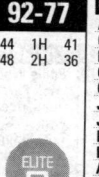

Coach: Phil Woolpert

UTAH	MIN	FG	3FG	FT	REB	A	ST	BL	PF	TP
Art Bunte	-	8	-	7	-	-	-	-	2	23
Curt Jenson	-	9	-	3	-	-	-	-	3	21
Morris Buckwalter	-	2	-	7	-	-	-	-	4	11
Gary Hale	-	1	-	6	-	-	-	-	3	8
Gary Bergen	-	2	-	2	-	-	-	-	3	6
Jerry McCleary	-	2	-	0	-	-	-	-	3	4
John Crowe	-	1	-	0	-	-	-	-	2	2
Edward Gaythwaite	-	1	-	0	-	-	-	-	1	2
Dick Eiler	-	0	-	0	-	-	-	-	0	0
Angelo Mitaritonna	-	0	-	0	-	-	-	-	0	0
Darrell Pastrell	-	0	-	0	-	-	-	-	0	0
TOTALS	**-**	**26**	**-**	**25**	**-**	**-**	**-**	**-**	**21**	**77**
Percentages										

Coach: Jack Gardner

83-76 — 1H: Iowa 39, Temple 36; 2H: Iowa 44, Temple 40 — FINAL 4

IOWA	MIN	FG	3FG	FT	REB	A	ST	BL	PF	TP
Bill Logan	-	13-21	-	10-15	8	-	-	-	2	36
Carl Cain	-	8-20	-	4-9	15	-	-	-	1	20
Bill Schoof	-	5-15	-	8-9	18	-	-	-	4	18
Sharm Scheuerman	-	1-3	-	2-2	2	-	-	-	4	4
Augustine Martel	-	1-4	-	1-3	2	-	-	-	0	3
Bill Seaberg	-	1-7	-	0-0	6	-	-	-	4	2
TOTALS	**-**	**29-70**	**-**	**25-38**	**51**	**-**	**-**	**-**	**15**	**83**
Percentages		41.4		65.8						

Coach: Bucky O'Connor

TEMPLE	MIN	FG	3FG	FT	REB	A	ST	BL	PF	TP
Hal Lear	-	15-30	-	2-4	2	-	-	-	4	32
Guy Rodgers	-	12-29	-	4-9	7	-	-	-	3	28
Fred Cohen	-	3-7	-	0-1	12	-	-	-	5	6
Dan Fleming	-	2-4	-	0-0	2	-	-	-	1	4
Jay Norman	-	1-8	-	0-2	17	-	-	-	4	2
Hal Reinfeld	-	1-6	-	0-0	2	-	-	-	2	2
Tink Van Patton	-	1-4	-	0-1	5	-	-	-	4	2
TOTALS	**-**	**35-88**	**-**	**6-17**	**47**	**-**	**-**	**-**	**23**	**76**
Percentages		39.8		35.3						

Coach: Harry Litwack

Attendance: 10,525

86-68 — 1H: San Francisco 44, SMU 32; 2H: San Francisco 42, SMU 36 — FINAL 4

SAN FRANCISCO	MIN	FG	3FG	FT	REB	A	ST	BL	PF	TP
Mike Farmer	-	11	-	4-6	10	-	-	-	4	26
Bill Russell	-	8	-	1-2	23	-	-	-	3	17
Hal Perry	-	6	-	2-3	0	-	-	-	1	14
Gene Brown	-	5	-	2-5	0	-	-	-	1	12
Warren Baxter	-	4	-	0-0	0	-	-	-	2	8
Carl Boldt	-	3	-	1-2	0	-	-	-	3	7
Mike Preaseau	-	1	-	0-0	0	-	-	-	2	2
Bill Bush	-	0	-	0-0	0	-	-	-	0	0
Jack King	-	0	-	0-0	0	-	-	-	0	0
TOTALS	**-**	**38**	**-**	**10-18**	**33**	**-**	**-**	**-**	**16**	**86**
Percentages				55.6						

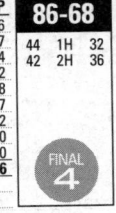

Coach: Phil Woolpert

SMU	MIN	FG	3FG	FT	REB	A	ST	BL	PF	TP
Jim Krebs	-	10	-	4-7	-	-	-	-	1	24
Bobby Mills	-	1	-	9-12	-	-	-	-	0	11
Ronnie Morris	-	4	-	2-3	-	-	-	-	4	10
Larry Showalter	-	4	-	0-0	-	-	-	-	1	8
Joel Krog	-	3	-	0-1	-	-	-	-	3	6
Rick Herrscher	-	1	-	2-3	-	-	-	-	1	4
Bob McGregor	-	1	-	1-2	-	-	-	-	0	3
Tom Miller	-	1	-	0-0	-	-	-	-	2	2
TOTALS	**-**	**25**	**-**	**18-28**	**-**	**-**	**-**	**-**	**12**	**68**
Percentages				64.3						

Coach: E.O. "Doc" Hayes

90-81 — 1H: Temple 41, SMU 38; 2H: Temple 49, SMU 43 — 3RD PLACE

TEMPLE	MIN	FG	3FG	FT	REB	A	ST	BL	PF	TP
Hal Lear	-	17	-	14-17	-	-	-	-	4	48
Jay Norman	-	8	-	1-2	-	-	-	-	3	17
Guy Rodgers	-	6	-	2-2	-	-	-	-	4	14
Tink Van Patton	-	2	-	2-2	-	-	-	-	4	6
Dan Fleming	-	2	-	1-2	-	-	-	-	1	5
Fred Cohen	-	0	-	0-0	-	-	-	-	1	0
Hal Reinfeld	-	0	-	0-0	-	-	-	-	0	0
TOTALS	**-**	**35**	**-**	**20-25**	**-**	**-**	**-**	**-**	**17**	**90**
Percentages				80.0						

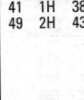

Coach: Harry Litwack

SMU	MIN	FG	3FG	FT	REB	A	ST	BL	PF	TP
Jim Krebs	-	9	-	11-12	-	-	-	-	1	29
Bobby Mills	-	6	-	7-9	-	-	-	-	4	19
Ronnie Morris	-	2	-	8-8	-	-	-	-	4	12
Joel Krog	-	4	-	0-0	-	-	-	-	1	8
Larry Showalter	-	4	-	0-0	-	-	-	-	2	8
Rick Herrscher	-	2	-	1-3	-	-	-	-	0	5
Tom Miller	-	0	-	0-0	-	-	-	-	1	0
TOTALS	**-**	**27**	**-**	**27-32**	**-**	**-**	**-**	**-**	**13**	**81**
Percentages				84.4						

Coach: E.O. "Doc" Hayes

Attendance: 10,600

83-71 — 1H: San Francisco 38, Iowa 33; 2H: San Francisco 45, Iowa 38 — NCAA FINAL 1956

SAN FRANCISCO	MIN	FG	3FG	FT	REB	A	ST	BL	PF	TP
Bill Russell	-	11-24	-	4-5	27	-	-	-	2	26
Carl Boldt	-	7-0	-	2-2	0	-	-	-	4	16
Gene Brown	-	6-0	-	4-4	0	-	-	-	0	16
Hal Perry	-	6-0	-	2-2	0	-	-	-	2	14
Mike Preaseau	-	3-0	-	1-2	0	-	-	-	3	7
Warren Baxter	-	2-0	-	0-0	0	-	-	-	0	4
Mike Farmer	-	0-0	-	0-0	12	-	-	-	2	0
Tom Nelson	-	0-0	-	0-0	0	-	-	-	0	0
TOTALS	**-**	**35-24**	**-**	**13-15**	**39**	**-**	**-**	**-**	**13**	**83**
Percentages		145.8		86.7						

Coach: Phil Woolpert

IOWA	MIN	FG	3FG	FT	REB	A	ST	BL	PF	TP
Carl Cain	-	7	-	3-4	12	-	-	-	1	17
Bill Seaberg	-	5	-	7-10	0	-	-	-	1	17
Bill Schoof	-	5	-	4-4	0	-	-	-	3	14
Bill Logan	-	5	-	2-2	15	-	-	-	3	12
Sharm Scheuerman	-	4	-	3-4	0	-	-	-	2	11
Robert George	-	0	-	0-0	0	-	-	-	0	0
Augustine Martel	-	0	-	0-0	0	-	-	-	0	0
Jim McConnell	-	0	-	0-0	0	-	-	-	0	0
TOTALS	**-**	**26**	**-**	**19-24**	**27**	**-**	**-**	**-**	**10**	**71**
Percentages				79.2						

Coach: Bucky OConner

Officials: Bell, Mihalik
Attendance: 10,600

National Invitation Tournament (NIT)

First round: St. Francis (NY) d. Lafayette 85-74, Duquesne d. Oklahoma A&M 69-61, Seton Hall d. Marquette, 96-78, Xavier d. Saint Louis, 84-80
Quarterfinals: Louisville d. Duquesne 84-72, St. Francis (NY) d. Niagara 74-72, Saint Joseph's d. Seton Hall 74-65, Dayton d. Xavier 72-68
Semifinals: Dayton d. St. Francis (NY) 89-58, Louisville d. Saint Joseph's 89-79
Third place: Saint Joseph's d. St. Francis (NY) 93-82
Championship: Louisville d. Dayton 93-80
MVP: Charlie Tyra, Louisville

1956-57: Double Triple

No 1. North Carolina (32–0) won 22 games by nine points or more, but their last two games in the NCAA Tournament went on ... and on ... and on. The Tar Heels needed three overtimes to beat Michigan State in the semifinals, 74-70, on Friday, March 22, and another three OTs the next night to beat Wilt Chamberlain and No. 2-ranked Kansas in the Final, 54-53. (No other team has played back-to-back triple-overtime games in an NCAA Tournament.) It took two free throws by UNC's Joe Quigg with :06 remaining to end it. Chamberlain had 23 points and 14 rebounds and was named the Tournament's Most Outstanding Player. Lennie Rosenbluth scored 20 for UNC.

At the end of the regular season, a number of players were fighting for the scoring title. South Carolina's Grady Wallace emerged as the first ACC player to lead the nation in scoring (31.2 ppg), beating out Mississippi's Joe Gibbon, Seattle's Elgin Baylor, Kansas' Chamberlain and Columbia's Chet Forte.

Major Conference Standings

ACC	Conference			Overall		
	W	L	PCT	W	L	PCT
North Carolina⊕	14	0	1.000	32	0	1.000
Maryland	9	5	.643	16	10	.615
Duke	8	6	.571	13	11	.542
Wake Forest	7	7	.500	19	9	.679
NC State	7	7	.500	15	11	.577
South Carolina	5	9	.357	17	12	.586
Clemson	3	11	.214	7	17	.292
Virginia	3	11	.214	6	19	.240

Tournament: **North Carolina d. South Carolina 95-75**
Tournament MVP: **Lennie Rosenbluth**, North Carolina

BIG SEVEN	Conference			Overall		
	W	L	PCT	W	L	PCT
Kansas⊕	11	1	.917	24	3	.889
Kansas State	8	4	.667	15	8	.652
Iowa State	6	6	.500	16	7	.696
Colorado	5	7	.417	14	9	.609
Nebraska	5	7	.417	11	12	.478
Missouri	4	8	.333	10	13	.435
Oklahoma	3	9	.250	8	15	.348

BIG TEN	Conference			Overall		
	W	L	PCT	W	L	PCT
Indiana	10	4	.714	14	8	.636
Michigan State⊕	10	4	.714	16	10	.615
Minnesota	9	5	.643	14	8	.636
Ohio State	9	5	.643	14	8	.636
Purdue	8	6	.571	15	7	.682
Michigan	8	6	.571	13	9	.591
Illinois	7	7	.500	14	8	.636
Iowa	4	10	.286	8	14	.364
Wisconsin	3	11	.214	5	17	.227
Northwestern	2	12	.143	6	16	.273

BORDER	Conference			Overall		
	W	L	PCT	W	L	PCT
Texas Western	8	2	.800	15	8	.652
Hardin-Simmons⊕	7	3	.700	17	9	.654
Arizona	5	5	.500	13	13	.500
Arizona State	4	6	.400	10	15	.400
West Texas A&M	3	7	.300	6	14	.300
New Mexico State	3	7	.300	6	18	.250

CBA	Conference			Overall		
	W	L	PCT	W	L	PCT
San Francisco⊕	12	2	.857	21	7	.750
Santa Clara	10	4	.714	15	7	.682
Saint Mary's (CA)	10	4	.714	17	9	.654
Fresno State	7	7	.500	16	10	.615
San Jose State	7	7	.500	13	12	.520
Loyola Marymount	5	9	.357	11	16	.407
Pacific	3	11	.214	9	17	.346
Pepperdine	2	12	.143	7	18	.280

IVY	Conference			Overall		
	W	L	PCT	W	L	PCT
Yale○	12	2	.857	18	8	.692
Dartmouth	10	4	.714	18	7	.720
Columbia	9	5	.643	18	6	.750
Princeton	9	5	.643	14	9	.609
Harvard	7	7	.500	12	9	.571
Brown	4	10	.286	8	16	.333
Penn	3	11	.214	7	19	.269
Cornell	2	12	.143	4	19	.174

METRO NY	Conference			Overall		
	W	L	PCT	W	L	PCT
NYU	3	1	.750	8	13	.381
St. John's	4	2	.667	14	9	.609
Manhattan□	2	2	.500	15	9	.625
Fordham	2	2	.500	16	10	.615
CCNY	3	4	.429	11	8	.579
St. Francis (NY)	1	2	.333	12	14	.462
Brooklyn	1	3	.250	11	7	.611

MID-AMERICAN	Conference			Overall		
	W	L	PCT	W	L	PCT
Miami (OH)⊕	11	1	.917	17	8	.680
Marshall	8	4	.667	15	9	.625
Ohio	7	5	.583	15	8	.652
Bowling Green	7	5	.583	14	9	.609
Western Michigan	4	8	.333	8	13	.381
Toledo	3	9	.250	5	19	.208
Kent State	2	10	.167	5	18	.217

MISSOURI VALLEY	Conference			Overall		
	W	L	PCT	W	L	PCT
Saint Louis⊕	12	2	.857	19	9	.679
Bradley□	9	5	.643	22	7	.759
Oklahoma A&M	8	6	.571	17	9	.654
Wichita State	8	6	.571	15	11	.577
Detroit	5	9	.357	11	15	.423
Houston	5	9	.357	10	16	.385
Tulsa	5	9	.357	8	17	.320
Drake	4	10	.286	8	16	.333

SKYLINE 8	Conference			Overall		
	W	L	PCT	W	L	PCT
BYU⊕	11	3	.786	19	9	.679
Utah□	10	4	.714	19	8	.704
Montana	9	5	.643	13	9	.591
Denver	8	6	.571	11	12	.478
Utah State	7	7	.500	11	13	.458
Colorado State	6	8	.429	9	16	.360
Wyoming	4	10	.286	6	19	.240
New Mexico	1	13	.071	5	21	.192

OHIO VALLEY	Conference			Overall		
	W	L	PCT	W	L	PCT
Morehead State⊕	9	1	.900	19	8	.704
Western Kentucky	9	1	.900	17	9	.654
Murray State	5	5	.500	11	13	.458
Eastern Kentucky	4	6	.400	6	15	.286
Middle Tenn. State	2	8	.200	12	13	.480
Tennessee Tech	1	9	.100	9	11	.450

PACIFIC COAST	Conference			Overall		
	W	L	PCT	W	L	PCT
California⊕	14	2	.875	21	5	.808
UCLA	13	3	.813	22	4	.846
Washington	13	3	.813	17	9	.654
Southern California	9	7	.563	16	12	.571
Stanford	7	9	.438	11	15	.423
Oregon State	6	10	.375	11	15	.423
Idaho	4	12	.250	10	16	.385
Washington State	4	12	.250	8	18	.308
Oregon	2	14	.125	4	21	.160

SEC	Conference			Overall		
	W	L	PCT	W	L	PCT
Kentucky⊕	12	2	.857	23	5	.821
Vanderbilt	10	4	.714	17	5	.773
Georgia Tech	9	5	.643	18	8	.692
Mississippi State	9	5	.643	17	8	.680
Tulane	9	5	.643	15	9	.625
Auburn	8	6	.571	13	8	.619
Alabama	7	7	.500	15	11	.577
Florida	6	8	.429	14	10	.583
Tennessee	5	9	.357	13	9	.591
Mississippi	4	10	.286	9	13	.409
Georgia	4	10	.286	8	16	.333
LSU	1	13	.071	6	19	.240

SOUTHERN	Conference			Overall		
	W	L	PCT	W	L	PCT
West Virginia⊕	12	0	1.000	25	5	.833
Washington and Lee	10	3	.769	20	7	.741
Virginia Tech	12	5	.706	14	8	.636
Richmond	9	7	.563	15	11	.577
Furman	7	5	.583	10	17	.370
William and Mary	7	11	.389	9	18	.333
The Citadel	5	9	.357	11	14	.440
Davidson	4	8	.333	7	20	.259
George Washington	3	9	.250	3	21	.125
VMI	1	13	.071	4	22	.154

Tournament: **West Virginia d. Washington and Lee 67-52**
Tournament MOP: **Lloyd Sharrar**, West Virginia

SOUTHWEST	Conference			Overall		
	W	L	PCT	W	L	PCT
SMU⊕	11	1	.917	22	4	.846
Rice	8	4	.667	16	8	.667
TCU	6	6	.500	14	10	.583
Baylor	6	6	.500	9	15	.375
Arkansas	5	7	.417	11	12	.478
Texas	3	9	.250	11	13	.458
Texas A&M	3	9	.250	7	17	.292

WNY LITTLE THREE	Conference			Overall		
	W	L	PCT	W	L	PCT
Canisius○	3	1	.750	22	6	.786
St. Bonaventure□	3	1	.750	17	7	.708
Niagara	0	4	.000	12	13	.480

YANKEE	Conference			Overall		
	W	L	PCT	W	L	PCT
Connecticut⊕	8	0	1.000	17	8	.680
Rhode Island	6	3	.667	11	11	.500
Vermont	3	2	.600	15	5	.750
Massachusetts	4	4	.500	13	11	.542
Maine	2	6	.250	6	14	.300
New Hampshire	1	9	.100	3	16	.158

⊕ Automatic NCAA Tournament bid ○ At-large NCAA Tournament bid □ NIT appearance ⊗ Team record doesn't reflect games forfeited or vacated. For adjusted record, see p. 521.

INDEPENDENTS

	Overall W	L	PCT
Seattle□	22	3	.880
Idaho State○	25	4	.862
Saint Peter's□	18	4	.818
Lafayette⊕	22	5	.815
Louisville	21	5	.808
Memphis□	24	6	.800
Syracuse○	18	7	.720
Notre Dame○	20	8	.714
Xavier□	20	8	.714
St. Joseph's	17	7	.708
Duquesne	16	7	.696
Temple□	20	9	.690
Dayton□	19	9	.679
Oklahoma City○	19	9	.679
Bucknell	16	8	.667
La Salle	17	9	.654
Muhlenberg	17	9	.654
Navy	15	8	.652
Iona	12	7	.632
Seton Hall□	17	10	.630
Cincinnati□	15	9	.625
Portland	18	12	.600

INDEPENDENTS (CONT.)

	Overall W	L	PCT
Penn State	15	10	.600
Pittsburgh○	16	11	.593
Colgate	14	10	.583
Loyola-Chicago	14	10	.583
Wash.-St. Louis	12	9	.571
Loyola (LA)○	14	12	.538
Boston College	12	11	.522
Miami (FL)	13	13	.500
Saint Francis (PA)	12	12	.500
Georgetown	11	11	.500
Holy Cross	11	12	.478
Lehigh	8	10	.444
Butler	11	14	.440
Valparaiso	11	14	.440
Gonzaga	11	16	.407
Marquette	10	15	.400
Villanova	10	15	.400
DePaul	8	14	.364
Army	7	13	.350
Rutgers	8	15	.348
Siena	5	15	.250

INDIVIDUAL LEADERS—SEASON

Scoring

	CL	POS	G	FG	FT	PTS	PPG
1 **Grady Wallace**, South Carolina	SR	F	29	336	234	906	**31.2**
2 **Joe Gibbon**, Mississippi	SR	F	21	227	177	631	**30.0**
3 **Elgin Baylor**, Seattle	SO	F/C	25	271	201	743	**29.7**
4 **Wilt Chamberlain**, Kansas	SO	C	27	275	250	800	**29.6**
5 **Chet Forte**, Columbia	SR	G	24	235	224	694	**28.9**
6 **Jim Ashmore**, Mississippi State	SR	G	25	270	168	708	**28.3**
7 **Lennie Rosenbluth**, North Carolina	SR	F	32	305	285	895	**28.0**
8 **Bill Ebben**, Detroit	SR	F	26	263	198	724	**27.8**
9 **Bailey Howell**, Mississippi State	SO	C	25	217	213	647	**25.9**
10 **Archie Dees**, Indiana	JR	C	22	187	176	550	**25.0**

Field Goal Pct

	CL	POS	G	FG	FGA	PCT
1 **Bailey Howell**, Mississippi State	SO	C	25	217	382	**56.8**
2 **Alvin Innis**, St. Francis (NY)	JR	C	26	189	337	**56.1**
3 **Dennis Roth**, Muhlenberg	SR	F/C	26	162	298	**54.4**
4 **Bob Hoitsma**, William and Mary	SR	F	27	117	216	**54.2**
5 **Alex "Boo" Ellis**, Niagara	JR	C	25	209	389	**53.7**

Minimum: 100 made

Free Throw Pct

	CL	POS	G	FT	FTA	PCT
1 **Ernie Wiggins**, Wake Forest	SR	G	28	93	106	**87.7**
2 **Jackie Murdock**, Wake Forest	SR	G	28	161	184	**87.5**
3 **Bob Seitz**, NC State	SR	C	26	95	109	**87.2**
4 **Dave Ricketts**, Duquesne	SR	G	23	150	174	**86.2**
5 **Bobby Plump**, Butler	JR	G	25	160	186	**86.0**

Minimum: 90 made

INDIVIDUAL LEADERS—GAME

Points

	CL	POS	OPP	DATE	PTS
1 **Grady Wallace**, South Carolina	SR	F	Georgia	D21	**54**
Rod Hundley, West Virginia	SR	F	Furman	J5	**54**
3 **Wilt Chamberlain**, Kansas	SO	C	Northwestern	D3	**52**
4 **Steve Hamilton**, Morehead State	JR	F	Ohio	J5	**51**
Elgin Baylor, Seattle	SO	F/C	Portland	F26	**51**

Free Throws Made

	CL	POS	OPP	DATE	FT	FTA	PCT
1 **Win Wilfong**, Memphis	SR	G/F	Oklahoma City	F18	**22**	23	95.7
2 **Grady Wallace**, South Carolina	SR	F	Duke	F23	**21**	23	91.3
Larry Beck, Washington State	SR	F	Oregon	J26	**21**	26	80.8
4 **Terry Penn**, Virginia Tech	SO	G	The Citadel	J10	**20**	21	95.2
Bucky Allen, Duke	JR	G	NC State	J15	**20**	23	87.0

TEAM LEADERS—SEASON

Scoring Offense

	G	W-L	PTS	PPG
1 **Connecticut**	25	17-8	2,183	**87.3**
2 **Ohio**	23	15-8	2,004	**87.1**
3 **Marshall**	24	15-9	2,070	**86.3**
4 **Memphis**	30	24-6	2,562	**85.4**
5 **Morehead State**	27	19-8	2,301	**85.2**

Field Goal Pct

	G	W-L	FG	FGA	PCT
1 **Manhattan**	24	15-9	679	1,489	**45.6**
2 **Seattle**	25	22-3	742	1,644	**45.1**
3 **Western Kentucky**	26	17-9	802	1,788	**44.9**
4 **Lafayette**	27	22-5	776	1,736	**44.7**
5 **Niagara**	25	12-13	756	1,693	**44.7**

Free Throw Pct

	G	W-L	FT	FTA	PCT
1 **Oklahoma A&M**	26	17-9	569	752	**75.7**
2 **Auburn**	21	13-8	479	648	**73.9**
3 **Tulane**	24	15-9	459	622	**73.8**
4 **Wake Forest**	28	19-9	610	827	**73.8**
5 **Memphis**	30	24-6	714	971	**73.5**

Scoring Defense

	G	W-L	OPP PTS	OPP PPG
1 **Oklahoma A&M**	26	17-9	1,420	**54.6**
2 **San Francisco**	28	21-7	1,560	**55.7**
3 **California**	26	21-5	1,484	**57.1**
4 **Santa Clara**	22	15-7	1,260	**57.3**
5 **Kansas**	27	24-3	1,583	**58.6**

CONSENSUS ALL-AMERICAS

First Team

PLAYER	CL	POS	HT	SCHOOL	RPG	PPG
Wilt Chamberlain	SO	C	7-1	Kansas	18.9	29.6
Chet Forte	SR	G	5-9	Columbia	4.5	28.9
Rod Hundley	SR	F	6-4	West Virginia	10.5	23.1
Jim Krebs	SR	C	6-8	SMU	12.0	24.0
Lennie Rosenbluth	SR	F	6-5	North Carolina	8.8	28.0
Charlie Tyra	SR	C	6-8	Louisville	20.0	21.4

Second Team

PLAYER	CL	POS	HT	SCHOOL	RPG	PPG
Elgin Baylor	SO	F/C	6-5	Seattle	20.3	29.7
Frank Howard	JR	F	6-6	Ohio State	15.3	20.1
Guy Rodgers	JR	G	6-0	Temple	7.0	20.4
Gary Thompson	SR	G	5-10	Iowa State	4.0	20.7
Grady Wallace	SR	F	6-4	South Carolina	14.4	31.2

Selectors: AP, International News Service, Look Magazine, NABC, Newspaper Enterprises Assn., UP

AWARD WINNERS

Player of the Year

PLAYER	CL	POS	HT	SCHOOL	AWARDS
Chet Forte	SR	G	5-9	Columbia	UP

Coach of the Year

COACH	SCHOOL	REC	AWARDS
Frank McGuire	North Carolina	32-0	UP

Poll Progression

Preseason Poll

UP	School
1	Kansas
2	Louisville
3	North Carolina
4	Illinois
5	SMU
6	Dayton
7	Temple
8	San Francisco
9	Saint Louis
10	Western Kentucky
11	West Virginia
12	Oklahoma City
13	Oregon State
14	Kentucky
15	Washington
16	St. John's
16	NC State
18	Kansas State
19	Vanderbilt
20	Wyoming

Week of Dec 11

AP	UP	School	
1	1	Kansas (2-0)	(A)
2	5	San Francisco (4-0)	
3	7	Kentucky (3-0)	
4	6	Louisville (3-1)	
5	4	SMU (2-0)	
6	2	North Carolina (2-0)	
7	3	Illinois (2-0)	
8	12	NC State (3-0)	
9	—	Alabama (3-0)	
10	11	Canisius (4-0)	
11	8	Ohio State (3-0)	
12	12	Western Kentucky (1-0)	
13	16	West Virginia (3-0)	
14	9	Kansas State (2-0)	
15	10	Dayton (2-1)	
16	18	Niagara (2-1)	
17	12	Iowa State (3-0)	
18	—	Oklahoma City (1-1)	
19	—	Oklahoma A&M (3-1)	
20	—	Seattle (3-1)	
—	15	UCLA (3-0)	
—	17	Indiana (2-0)	
—	18	St. John's (2-0)	
—	18	Temple (2-1)	

Week of Dec 18

AP	UP	School	AP↓↑
1	1	Kansas (4-0)	
2	4	San Francisco (5-0)	
3	2	North Carolina (4-0)	↑3
4	5	SMU (5-0)	↑1
5	3	Illinois (3-0)	↑2
6	6	Louisville (4-1)	↓2
7	7	Kentucky (4-1)	↓4
8	13	West Virginia (6-0)	↑5
9	9	Saint Louis (4-1)	⤴
10	8	Kansas State (4-0)	↑4
11	11	Ohio State (3-0)	
12	10	Oklahoma A&M (6-1)	↑7
13	16	Duke (4-1)	⤴
14	12	Iowa State (5-0)	↑3
15	14	St. John's (2-1)	⤴
16	—	Oklahoma City (2-1)	↑3
17	—	Alabama (4-1)	↓8
18	15	Canisius (4-1)	↓8
19	—	NC State (4-2)	↓11
20	17	Western Kentucky (3-1)	↓8
—	18	UCLA (4-1)	
—	19	Rice (4-2)	
—	19	Washington (1-4)	

Week of Dec 26

AP	UP	School	AP↓↑
1	1	Kansas (6-0)	
2	2	North Carolina (8-0)	↑1
3	3	Kentucky (6-2)	↑4
4	8	West Virginia (8-0)	↑4
5	5	Saint Louis (6-1)	↑4
6	6	Illinois (5-1)	↓1
7	4	SMU (7-1)	↓3
8	7	Louisville (5-2)	(B) ↓2
9	12	Duke (5-1)	↑4
10	9	Oklahoma A&M (7-1)	↑2
11	—	Oklahoma City (5-1)	↑4
12	13	Vanderbilt (5-1)	⤴
12	—	Tennessee (6-0)	⤴
14	9	Iowa State (6-0)	
15	—	Western Kentucky (6-1)	↑5
16	18	Tulane (6-1)	⤴
17	15	Canisius (6-1)	↑1
18	—	Seattle (7-2)	⤴
19	17	San Francisco (6-2)	(C) ↓17
20	—	Idaho State (8-0)	⤴
—	11	Kansas State (4-2)	Γ
—	13	UCLA (6-1)	
—	16	Utah (7-1)	
—	19	Ohio State (3-1)	Γ
—	20	California (4-2)	
—	20	Colorado (6-1)	
—	20	Iowa (3-1)	

Week of Jan 2

AP	UP	School	AP↓↑
1	1	Kansas (9-0)	
2	2	North Carolina (11-0)	
3	3	Kentucky (8-2)	
4	4	SMU (10-1)	↑3
5	6	Illinois (6-1)	↑1
6	5	Louisville (7-2)	↑2
7	7	Iowa State (8-1)	↑7
8	7	UCLA (8-1)	⤴
9	11	Vanderbilt (6-1)	↑3
10	17	Seattle (10-2)	↑8
11	9	Oklahoma A&M (7-1)	↓1
12	—	Tennessee (7-0)	
13	10	Manhattan (7-2)	⤴
14	—	Western Kentucky (6-2)	↑1
15	13	Canisius (8-1)	↑2
16	14	Saint Louis (6-4)	↓11
17	—	Oklahoma City (5-2)	↓6
18	15	Wake Forest (8-3)	⤴
19	12	West Virginia (8-3)	↓15
20	—	Memphis (9-1)	⤴
—	16	California (6-2)	
—	18	Utah (9-2)	
—	19	Kansas State (5-4)	
—	20	NC State (7-5)	

Week of Jan 8

AP	UP	School	AP↓↑
1	1	Kansas (10-0)	
2	2	North Carolina (11-0)	
3	3	Kentucky (9-2)	
4	4	SMU (11-1)	
5	5	Louisville (8-2)	↑1
6	9	Vanderbilt (8-1)	↑3
7	7	Iowa State (8-1)	
8	6	UCLA (11-1)	
9	12	Seattle (11-2)	↑1
10	10	Illinois (6-2)	↓5
11	19	Oklahoma City (8-2)	↑6
12	8	Oklahoma A&M (7-1)	↓1
13	14	Wake Forest (10-3)	↑5
14	11	Canisius (10-1)	↑1
15	18	Duke (7-3)	⤴
16	—	Tennessee (8-1)	↓4
17	15	Saint Louis (7-4)	↓1
18	—	West Virginia (9-3)	↑1
19	13	Minnesota (5-3)	⤴
20	—	Western Kentucky (6-2)	↓6
—	15	Manhattan (7-3)	Γ
—	17	BYU (7-5)	
—	19	California (8-2)	
—	19	San Francisco (7-4)	

Week of Jan 15

AP	UP	School	AP↓↑
1	1	Kansas (12-0)	
2	2	North Carolina (14-0)	
3	4	SMU (13-1)	↑1
4	3	Kentucky (11-2)	↓1
5	6	Louisville (9-2)	
6	5	UCLA (13-1)	↑2
7	9	Seattle (13-2)	↑2
8	7	Illinois (8-2)	↑2
9	8	Iowa State (9-2)	↓2
10	10	Vanderbilt (9-2)	↓4
11	11	Wake Forest (12-3)	↑2
12	14	Bradley (10-2)	⤴
13	19	Oklahoma City (9-3)	↓2
14	12	Canisius (11-2)	
15	18	West Virginia (11-3)	↑3
16	—	Duke (8-4)	↓1
17	15	Ohio State (7-3)	⤴
18	—	Western Kentucky (7-4)	↑2
19	13	California (10-2)	⤴
19	19	Oklahoma A&M (7-3)	↓7
—	16	BYU (9-5)	
—	17	Saint Louis (8-5)	Γ

Week of Jan 22

AP	UP	School	AP↓↑
1	1	North Carolina (15-0)	(D) ↑1
2	2	Kansas (12-1)	(E) ↓1
3	4	Iowa State (11-2)	(E) ↑6
4	6	Louisville (11-2)	↑1
5	3	Kentucky (12-3)	↓1
6	5	SMU (14-2)	↓3
7	7	UCLA (13-1)	↓1
8	9	Seattle (14-2)	↓1
9	8	Illinois (9-2)	↓1
10	11	Bradley (12-2)	↑2
11	14	Wake Forest (12-3)	
12	10	Ohio State (9-3)	↑5
13	15	Vanderbilt (10-3)	↓3
14	13	Canisius (12-2)	
15	17	Duke (8-4)	↑1
16	—	Oklahoma City (9-3)	↓3
17	—	West Virginia (12-3)	↓2
18	18	Tulane (10-5)	⤴
19	12	California (10-2)	
20	—	Western Kentucky (8-4)	↓2
—	16	BYU (9-6)	
—	18	Oklahoma A&M (8-3)	Γ
—	18	Saint Louis (10-5)	

Week of Jan 29

AP	UP	School	AP↓↑
1	1	North Carolina (16-0)	
2	2	Kansas (12-1)	
3	6	Louisville (12-2)	↑1
4	3	Kentucky (13-3)	↑1
5	5	UCLA (13-1)	↑2
6	4	SMU (14-2)	
7	7	Illinois (10-2)	↑2
8	9	Iowa State (11-3)	↓5
9	10	Seattle (17-2)	↓1
10	11	Bradley (13-2)	
11	8	Ohio State (11-3)	↑1
12	12	Canisius (14-2)	↑2
13	14	Wake Forest (12-3)	↓2
14	—	Tulane (10-5)	↑4
15	12	California (11-2)	↑4
16	—	Oklahoma City (10-5)	
17	—	Idaho State (13-3)	⤴
18	—	West Virginia (13-3)	↓1
19	19	Duke (8-4)	↓4
20	20	Oklahoma A&M (9-4)	⤴
—	15	Vanderbilt (10-4)	Γ
—	16	BYU (11-6)	
—	16	Saint Louis (11-5)	
—	18	Washington (10-7)	
—	20	Syracuse (10-3)	

Week of Feb 5

AP	UP	School	AP↓↑
1	1	North Carolina (16-0)	
2	2	Kansas (13-1)	
3	3	Kentucky (16-3)	↑1
4	4	SMU (15-2)	↑2
5	5	UCLA (15-1)	
6	6	Louisville (14-3)	↓3
7	7	Seattle (17-2)	↑2
8	8	Bradley (13-2)	↑2
9	10	Iowa State (12-4)	↓1
10	15	Wake Forest (15-3)	↑3
11	27	West Virginia (15-3)	↑7
12	9	Ohio State (11-4)	↓1
13	21	Oklahoma City (12-6)	↑3
14	11	Canisius (15-2)	↓2
15	12	Illinois (10-3)	↓8
16	25	Memphis (17-3)	⤴
17	14	Purdue (12-2)	⤴
18	25	Vanderbilt (11-4)	⤴
19	12	California (11-2)	↓4
20	28	Idaho State (17-2)	↓3
—	16	BYU (12-6)	
—	17	Syracuse (11-3)	
—	17	Washington (11-7)	
—	19	Saint Louis (12-6)	
—	20	Western Kentucky (11-4)	
—	21	Dayton (10-5)	
—	21	Oklahoma A&M (10-5)	Γ
—	24	Temple (11-5)	
—	28	Nebraska (8-7)	
—	28	San Francisco (10-5)	
—	28	Xavier (12-4)	

Week of Feb 12

AP	UP	School	AP↓↑
1	1	North Carolina (18-0)	
2	2	Kansas (14-1)	
3	3	Kentucky (17-3)	
4	7	Seattle (18-2)	↑3
5	5	Bradley (15-2)	↑3
6	4	SMU (16-3)	↓2
7	6	UCLA (16-2)	↓2
8	8	Louisville (15-4)	↓2
9	10	Iowa State (14-4)	
10	—	West Virginia (18-3)	↑1
11	14	Wake Forest (16-4)	↓1
12	9	California (13-2)	↑7
13	18	Oklahoma City (12-6)	
14	11	Canisius (16-3)	
15	—	West Virginia Tech (15-1)	⤴
16	12	Illinois (11-4)	↓1
17	—	Duke (10-7)	⤴
18	13	Indiana (9-6)	⤴
19	20	Vanderbilt (13-4)	
20	—	Saint Louis (14-6)	⤴
—	15	BYU (14-6)	
—	15	Ohio State (11-6)	Γ
—	17	Syracuse (13-3)	
—	19	Dayton (12-5)	
—	20	Temple (13-5)	

Week of Feb 19

AP	UP	School	AP↓↑
1	1	North Carolina (20-0)	
2	2	Kansas (16-1)	
3	3	Kentucky (18-4)	
4	7	Seattle (19-2)	
5	5	Bradley (17-3)	
6	4	SMU (17-3)	
7	8	Louisville (17-4)	↑1
8	5	UCLA (18-2)	↓1
9	10	Iowa State (15-5)	
10	13	Vanderbilt (15-4)	↑8
11	11	Indiana (11-6)	↑7
12	—	Wake Forest (16-6)	↓1
13	—	Oklahoma City (15-7)	
14	16	West Virginia (19-4)	↓4
15	9	California (15-2)	↓3
16	—	Duke (11-8)	↑1
17	19	Kansas State (12-6)	⤴
18	—	West Virginia Tech (21-1)	↓3
19	—	Mississippi State (13-7)	⤴
20	—	Memphis (19-4)	⤴
—	12	BYU (16-6)	
—	14	Dayton (14-5)	
—	14	Ohio State (12-6)	
—	17	Canisius (16-5)	Γ
—	18	Michigan State (12-7)	
—	20	Saint Louis (15-7)	Γ

Week of Feb 26

AP	UP	SCHOOL	AP↓↑
1	1	**North Carolina** (22-0)	
2	2	**Kansas** (18-2)	
3	3	**Kentucky** (20-4)	
4	4	**SMU** (19-3)	↑2
5	6	**Seattle** (20-2)	↓1
6	5	**UCLA** (20-2)	↑2
7	8	**Bradley** (18-4)	↓2
8	10	**Louisville** (18-5)	↓1
9	15	**Vanderbilt** (16-5)	↑1
10	7	**Indiana** (13-6)	↑1
11	15	**West Virginia** (20-4)	↑3
12	12	**Kansas State** (14-6)	↑5
13	—	**Wake Forest** (18-6)	↓1
14	12	**Saint Louis** (16-7)	⤴
15	—	**Idaho State** (23-2)	⤴
16	14	**Iowa State** (15-6)	↓7
17	—	**Oklahoma A&M** (13-8)	⤴
18	19	**Oklahoma City** (16-8)	↓5
19	—	**Memphis** (20-5)	↑1
20	—	**Mississippi State** (13-8)	↓1
—	9	**California** (17-3)	⤵
—	11	**Michigan State** (12-7)	
—	17	**BYU** (16-8)	
—	18	**Dayton** (15-6)	
—	19	**Notre Dame** (15-7)	
—	19	**Ohio** (13-8)	

Week of Mar 5

AP	UP	SCHOOL	AP↓↑
1	1	**North Carolina** (24-0)	
2	2	**Kansas** (19-2)	
3	3	**Kentucky** (22-4)	
4	4	**SMU** (21-3)	
5	6	**Seattle** (22-2)	
6	9	**Louisville** (20-5)	↑2
7	5	**UCLA** (21-4)	↓1
8	8	**Michigan State** (14-7)	⤴
9	15	**Vanderbilt** (17-5)	
10	—	**Oklahoma City** (17-8)	↑8
11	12	**West Virginia** (22-4)	
12	11	**Saint Louis** (18-7)	↑2
13	10	**Bradley** (19-5)	↓6
14	7	**California** (18-4)	⤴
15	—	**Idaho State** (23-3)	
16	—	**Oklahoma A&M** (16-8)	↑1
17	19	**Iowa State** (16-6)	↓1
18	—	**Mississippi State** (17-8)	↑2
19	—	**Memphis** (21-5)	
20	—	**Wake Forest** (18-8)	↓7
—	12	**Dayton** (17-6)	
—	12	**Indiana** (13-8)	⤵
—	15	**BYU** (18-8)	
—	17	**Kansas State** (15-7)	⤵
—	17	**Notre Dame** (18-7)	
—	20	**Ohio State** (14-7)	

Final Poll

AP	UP	SCHOOL	AP↓↑
1	1	**North Carolina** (27-0)	
2	2	**Kansas** (21-2)	
3	3	**Kentucky** (22-4)	
4	4	**SMU** (21-3)	
5	5	**Seattle** (22-2)	
6	8	**Louisville** (21-5)	
7	11	**West Virginia** (25-4)	↑4
8	16	**Vanderbilt** (17-5)	↑1
9	16	**Oklahoma City** (17-8)	↑1
10	9	**Saint Louis** (19-7)	↑2
11	7	**Michigan State** (14-8)	↓3
12	—	**Memphis** (21-5)	↑7
13	6	**California** (20-4)	↑1
14	9	**UCLA** (22-4)	↓7
15	—	**Mississippi State** (17-8) **F**	↑3
16	—	**Idaho State** (24-2)	↓1
17	19	**Notre Dame** (18-7)	⤴
18	—	**Wake Forest** (19-9)	↑2
19	13	**Bradley** (19-7)	↓6
20	—	**Canisius** (20-5)	⤴
20	—	**Oklahoma A&M** (17-9)	↓4
—	12	**Dayton** (17-6)	
—	14	**BYU** (18-8)	
—	15	**Indiana** (14-8)	
—	16	**Xavier** (19-6)	
—	20	**Kansas State** (15-8)	

A Kansas' 7'1" sophomore, Wilt Chamberlain, makes his debut on Dec. 3 with a 52-point, 31-rebound explosion against Northwestern. Phog Allen, who recruited him out of Philadelphia's Overbrook High, reached the university's mandatory retirement age of 70 during the previous season and the administration refused to waive the rules. The new Jayhawks coach is Dick Harp.

B Louisville plays three December home games in Freedom Hall. With a capacity of 16,600, the new arena is the biggest basketball venue south of the Mason-Dixon Line. It will host the NCAA Final Four six times between 1958 and '69.

C San Francisco's 60-game winning streak, the longest in NCAA history at the time, is snapped by Illinois, 62-33. The Dons lose again two days later, to Western Kentucky.

D North Carolina climbs to No. 1 with New York-area talents Lennie Rosenbluth, Pete Brennan, Joe Quigg, Tommy Kearns and Bob Cunningham. Frank McGuire, who previously coached St. John's, funnels so many N.Y. players to Chapel Hill that his recruiting is jokingly known as the Underground Railroad.

E The Jayhawks lose to Iowa State, 39-37, in Ames. Through 2008-09, it's the only time that the Cyclones have defeated a No. 1 team.

F Mississippi State's Jim Ashmore (28.3 ppg) and Bailey Howell (25.9 ppg) become the first teammates to average more than 25 ppg in the same season. The Bulldogs stars don't get any postseason exposure, though, because of an unwritten Mississippi policy prohibiting schools receiving state funds from competing against integrated teams.

ANNUAL REVIEW

1957 NCAA Tournament

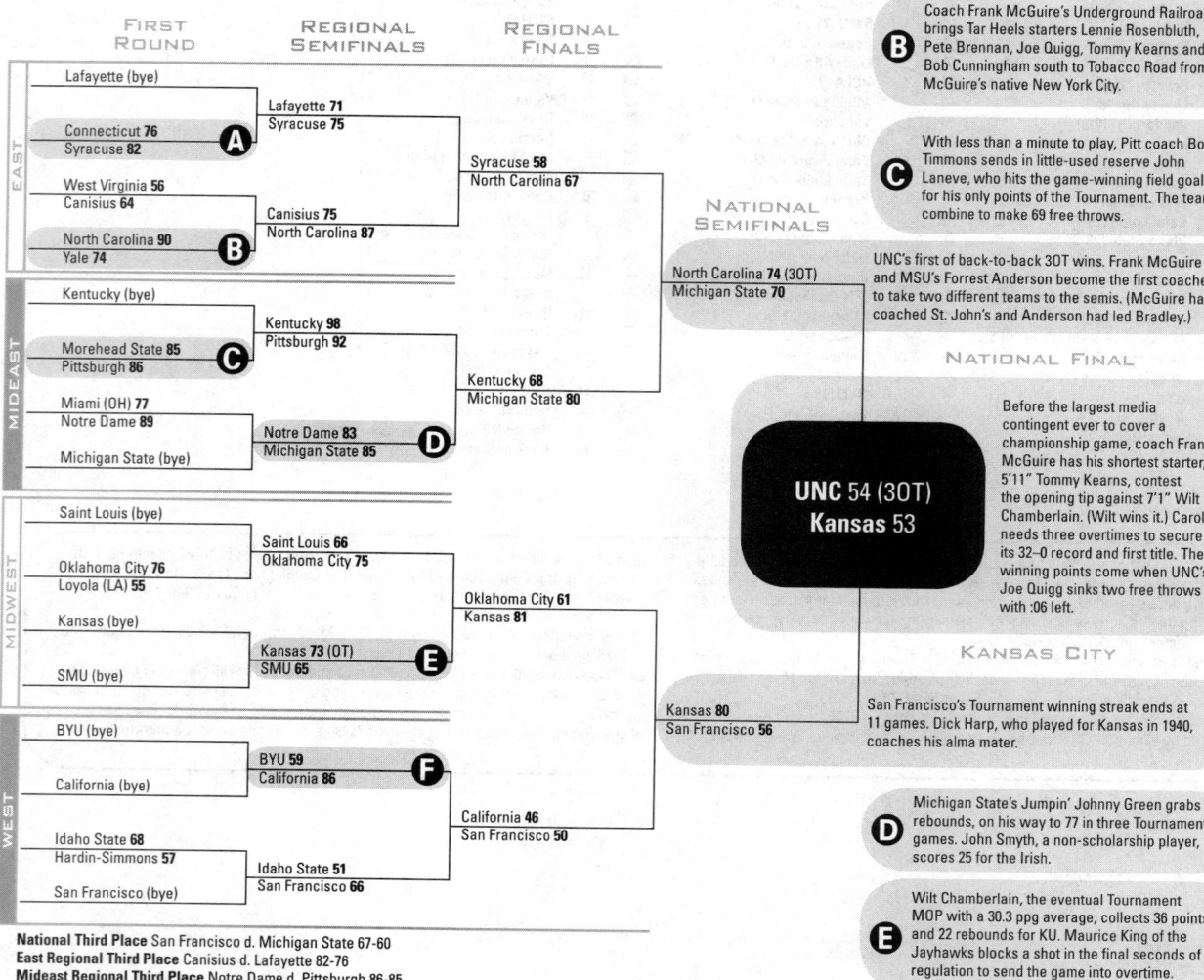

East

First Round
- Lafayette (bye)
- Connecticut 76, Syracuse 82 (A)
- West Virginia 56, Canisius 64
- North Carolina 90, Yale 74 (B)

Regional Semifinals
- Lafayette 71, Syracuse 75
- Canisius 75, North Carolina 87

Regional Finals
- Syracuse 58, North Carolina 67

Mideast

First Round
- Kentucky (bye)
- Morehead State 85, Pittsburgh 86 (C)
- Miami (OH) 77, Notre Dame 89
- Michigan State (bye)

Regional Semifinals
- Kentucky 98, Pittsburgh 92
- Notre Dame 83, Michigan State 85 (D)

Regional Finals
- Kentucky 68, Michigan State 80

Midwest

First Round
- Saint Louis (bye)
- Oklahoma City 76, Loyola (LA) 55
- Kansas (bye)
- SMU (bye)

Regional Semifinals
- Saint Louis 66, Oklahoma City 75
- Kansas 73 (OT), SMU 65 (E)

Regional Finals
- Oklahoma City 61, Kansas 81

West

First Round
- BYU (bye)
- California (bye)
- Idaho State 68, Hardin-Simmons 57
- San Francisco (bye)

Regional Semifinals
- BYU 59, California 86 (F)
- Idaho State 51, San Francisco 66

Regional Finals
- California 46, San Francisco 50

National Semifinals

- North Carolina 74 (3OT), Michigan State 70

UNC's first of back-to-back 3OT wins. Frank McGuire and MSU's Forrest Anderson become the first coaches to take two different teams to the semis. (McGuire had coached St. John's and Anderson had led Bradley.)

- Kansas 80, San Francisco 56

San Francisco's Tournament winning streak ends at 11 games. Dick Harp, who played for Kansas in 1940, coaches his alma mater.

National Final

UNC 54 (3OT)
Kansas 53

Before the largest media contingent ever to cover a championship game, coach Frank McGuire has his shortest starter, 5'11" Tommy Kearns, contest the opening tip against 7'1" Wilt Chamberlain. (Wilt wins it.) Carolina needs three overtimes to secure its 32–0 record and first title. The winning points come when UNC's Joe Quigg sinks two free throws with :06 left.

Kansas City

National Third Place San Francisco d. Michigan State 67-60
East Regional Third Place Canisius d. Lafayette 82-76
Mideast Regional Third Place Notre Dame d. Pittsburgh 86-85
Midwest Regional Third Place SMU d. Saint Louis 78-68
West Regional Third Place BYU d. Idaho State 65-54

A Trailing by 10 with 11 minutes to go, Syracuse goes into a full-court press that yields a 22-3 run.

B Coach Frank McGuire's Underground Railroad brings Tar Heels starters Lennie Rosenbluth, Pete Brennan, Joe Quigg, Tommy Kearns and Bob Cunningham south to Tobacco Road from McGuire's native New York City.

C With less than a minute to play, Pitt coach Bob Timmons sends in little-used reserve John Laneve, who hits the game-winning field goal for his only points of the Tournament. The teams combine to make 69 free throws.

D Michigan State's Jumpin' Johnny Green grabs 27 rebounds, on his way to 77 in three Tournament games. John Smyth, a non-scholarship player, scores 25 for the Irish.

E Wilt Chamberlain, the eventual Tournament MOP with a 30.3 ppg average, collects 36 points and 22 rebounds for KU. Maurice King of the Jayhawks blocks a shot in the final seconds of regulation to send the game into overtime.

F Coach Pete Newell makes his first Tournament appearance. One of his reserves is Joe Kapp, a future Super Bowl QB (Vikings) and Cal football coach.

Tournament Leaders

INDIVIDUAL LEADERS

Scoring	CL	POS	G	PTS	PPG
1 **Wilt Chamberlain**, Kansas	SO	C	4	121	30.3
2 **Lennie Rosenbluth**, North Carolina	SR	F	5	140	28.0
John Riser, Pittsburgh	SR	C	3	84	28.0
4 **Jim Krebs**, SMU	SR	C	2	51	25.5
5 **Don Hennon**, Pittsburgh	SO	G	3	75	25.0
Hub Reed, Oklahoma City	JR	C	3	75	25.0
7 **Gary Clark**, Syracuse	SR	F	3	71	23.7
8 **Stu Murray**, Lafayette	SR	G	2	47	23.5
9 **John Smyth**, Notre Dame	SR	F	3	70	23.3
10 **John McCarthy**, Notre Dame	JR	F	3	66	22.0

Minimum: 2 games

Field Goals Per Game	CL	POS	G	FG	FGPG
1 **Hub Reed**, Oklahoma City	JR	C	3	33	11.0
2 **Lennie Rosenbluth**, North Carolina	SR	F	5	53	10.6
3 **Stu Murray**, Lafayette	SR	G	2	21	10.5
4 **Wilt Chamberlain**, Kansas	SO	C	4	40	10.0
Gary Clark, Syracuse	SR	F	3	30	10.0

Free Throw Pct	CL	POS	G	FT	FTA	PCT
1 **Rick Herrscher**, SMU	JR	F	2	12	12	100.0
Rod Hundley, West Virginia	SR	F	1	9	9	100.0
John Lee, Yale	JR	F	1	9	9	100.0
John Brewer, Kentucky	SR	G	1	8	8	100.0
Earl Robinson, California	JR	G	2	6	6	100.0
Dave Keleher, Morehead State	JR	F/C	1	6	6	100.0

Minimum: 5 made

TEAM LEADERS

Scoring	G	PTS	PPG
1 **Pittsburgh**	3	263	87.7
2 **Notre Dame**	3	258	86.0
3 **Kentucky**	2	166	83.0
4 **North Carolina**	5	372	74.4
5 **Michigan State**	4	295	73.8
6 **Canisius**	3	221	73.7
7 **Lafayette**	2	147	73.5
8 **Kansas**	4	287	71.8
9 **Syracuse**	3	215	71.7
10 **SMU**	2	143	71.5

Minimum: 2 games

FG Per Game	G	FG	FGPG
1 **Pittsburgh**	3	93	31.0
2 **Notre Dame**	3	88	29.3
3 **Kentucky**	2	58	29.0
Syracuse	3	87	29.0
4 **Oklahoma City**	3	83	27.7
Canisius	3	83	27.7

FT Pct	G	FT	FTA	PCT
1 **Notre Dame**	3	82	103	79.6
2 **BYU**	2	36	47	76.6
3 **Pittsburgh**	3	77	101	76.2
4 **SMU**	2	37	50	74.0
5 **Kentucky**	2	50	70	71.4

Minimum: 2 games

ALL-TOURNAMENT TEAM

PLAYER	CL	POS	HT	SCHOOL	PPG
Wilt Chamberlain*	SO	C	7-1	Kansas	30.3
Pete Brennan	JR	F	6-6	North Carolina	12.8
Gene Brown	JR	G	6-3	San Francisco	17.5
Johnny Green	SO	F	6-5	Michigan State	13.5
Lennie Rosenbluth	SR	F	6-5	North Carolina	28.0

ALL-REGIONAL TEAMS

EAST

PLAYER	CL	POS	HT	SCHOOL	PPG
Pete Brennan	JR	F	6-6	North Carolina	13.0
Gary Clark	SR	F	6-5	Syracuse	23.7
Tommy Kearns	JR	G	5-11	North Carolina	19.0
Stu Murray	SR	G	6-1	Lafayette	23.5
Hank Nowak	SR	F	6-3	Canisius	19.3
Lennie Rosenbluth	SR	F	6-5	North Carolina	30.3

MIDEAST

PLAYER	CL	POS	HT	SCHOOL	PPG
Gerry Calvert	SR	G	5-11	Kentucky	18.0
Johnny Cox	SO	F	6-4	Kentucky	21.5
Johnny Green	SO	F	6-5	Michigan State	17.0
Jack Quiggle	JR	G/F	6-3	Michigan State	20.0
John Riser	SR	C	6-4	Pittsburgh	28.0

MIDWEST

PLAYER	CL	POS	HT	SCHOOL	PPG
Harold Alcorn	SR	G	6-1	Saint Louis	18.0
Wilt Chamberlain	SO	C	7-1	Kansas	33.0
Maurice King	SR	G	6-2½	Kansas	8.5
Jim Krebs	SR	C	6-8	SMU	25.5
Hub Reed	JR	C	6-10	Oklahoma City	25.0

WEST

PLAYER	CL	POS	HT	SCHOOL	PPG
John Benson	SR	F	6-6	BYU	19.5
Gene Brown	JR	G	6-3	San Francisco	19.0
Mike Farmer	JR	F	6-7	San Francisco	11.0
Larry Friend	SR	F	6-4	California	18.5
Earl Robinson	JR	G	6-1	California	17.0

* Most outstanding player

1957 NCAA TOURNAMENT BOX SCORES

SYRACUSE	MIN	FG	3FG	FT	REB	A	ST	BL	PF	TP
Gary Clark	-	13-20	-	8-10	13	-	-	-	3	34
James Snyder	-	6-10	-	2-5	14	-	-	-	4	14
Vincent Albanese	-	5-14	-	2-3	4	-	-	-	3	12
Vince Cohen	-	3-15	-	2-3	4	-	-	-	3	8
W. Jon Cincebox	-	3-9	-	1-4	9	-	-	-	0	7
Emanuel Breland	-	0-7	-	0-2	7	-	-	-	3	0
Larry Loudis	-	0-0	-	0-0	2	-	-	-	1	0
TOTALS	-	30-75	-	15-27	53	-	-	-	17	75
Percentages		40.0		55.6						

Coach: Marcel Guley

75-71

	1H	2H
Syracuse	42	33
Lafayette	40	31

SWEET 16

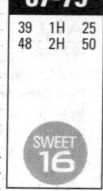

LAFAYETTE	MIN	FG	3FG	FT	REB	A	ST	BL	PF	TP
Stu Murray	-	14-25	-	2-5	6	-	-	-	0	30
Bob Mantz	-	5-11	-	6-7	17	-	-	-	2	16
Gordon Galtere	-	1-9	-	6-8	11	-	-	-	3	8
Anthony Mack	-	1-8	-	6-9	3	-	-	-	5	8
Joe Sterlein	-	2-6	-	0-1	11	-	-	-	4	4
Dick Kohler	-	1-4	-	1-2	0	-	-	-	2	3
David Jones	-	1-2	-	0-0	0	-	-	-	1	2
TOTALS	-	25-65	-	21-32	48	-	-	-	17	71
Percentages		38.5		65.6						

Coach: George E. Davidson

Officials: MacPherson, Filippi

NORTH CAROLINA	MIN	FG	3FG	FT	REB	A	ST	BL	PF	TP
Lennie Rosenbluth	-	15-30	-	9-11	10	-	-	-	2	39
Tommy Kearns	-	8-11	-	3-5	4	-	-	-	2	19
Bob Cunningham	-	2-5	-	11-15	8	-	-	-	4	15
Joe Quigg	-	4-5	-	0-2	9	-	-	-	4	8
Pete Brennan	-	1-8	-	4-4	13	-	-	-	5	6
Danny Lotz	-	0-0	-	0-0	0	-	-	-	0	0
Roy Searcy	-	0-0	-	0-0	0	-	-	-	0	0
Bob Young	-	0-1	-	0-0	1	-	-	-	2	0
TOTALS	-	30-60	-	27-37	45	-	-	-	19	87
Percentages		50.0		73.0						

Coach: Frank McGuire

87-75

	1H	2H
North Carolina	39	48
Canisius	25	50

SWEET 16

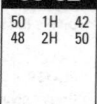

CANISIUS	MIN	FG	3FG	FT	REB	A	ST	BL	PF	TP
Hank Nowak	-	8-11	-	8-12	9	-	-	-	4	24
Joseph Leone	-	3-10	-	7-9	6	-	-	-	5	13
David Markey	-	5-11	-	2-2	6	-	-	-	3	12
Gregory Britz	-	2-15	-	7-7	5	-	-	-	4	11
John Coogan	-	5-11	-	0-2	6	-	-	-	3	10
James Springer	-	2-4	-	0-0	1	-	-	-	1	4
Tom Rojek	-	0-0	-	1-2	0	-	-	-	2	1
Jim MacKinnon	-	0-0	-	0-0	0	-	-	-	0	0
John Ruska	-	0-0	-	0-0	1	-	-	-	0	0
James Shea	-	0-0	-	0-0	0	-	-	-	0	0
TOTALS	-	25-62	-	25-34	34	-	-	-	22	75
Percentages		40.3		73.5						

Coach: Joseph Curran

Officials: Conway, Pace

KENTUCKY	MIN	FG	3FG	FT	REB	A	ST	BL	PF	TP
Johnny Cox	-	7	-	12-14	-	-	-	-	2	26
Vernon Hatton	-	10	-	4-5	-	-	-	-	1	24
Gerry Calvert	-	9	-	0-0	-	-	-	-	0	18
John Brewer	-	1	-	8-8	-	-	-	-	1	10
Ed Beck	-	3	-	3-6	-	-	-	-	5	9
Ray Mills	-	4	-	1-3	-	-	-	-	4	9
John Crigler	-	0	-	2-3	-	-	-	-	5	2
TOTALS	-	34	-	30-39	-	-	-	-	18	98
Percentages				76.9						

Coach: Adolph Rupp

98-92

	1H	2H
Kentucky	50	48
Pittsburgh	42	50

SWEET 16

PITTSBURGH	MIN	FG	3FG	FT	REB	A	ST	BL	PF	TP
John Riser	-	7-13	-	16-17	13	-	-	-	5	30
Don Hennon	-	11-29	-	2-2	5	-	-	-	4	24
Julius Pegues	-	7-15	-	1-1	7	-	-	-	4	15
Barry Brautigam	-	4-11	-	5-6	5	-	-	-	1	13
Dennis Dorman	-	2-3	-	0-0	2	-	-	-	5	4
Milan Markovich	-	1-2	-	1-2	4	-	-	-	0	3
Dave Sawyer	-	1-1	-	0-0	1	-	-	-	0	2
Chuck Hursh	-	0-2	-	1-2	7	-	-	-	5	1
John Laneve	-	0-0	-	0-1	1	-	-	-	0	0
TOTALS	-	33-76	-	26-31	45	-	-	-	24	92
Percentages		43.4		83.9						

Coach: Robert Timmons

Officials: Mihalik, Andersen
Attendance: 11,000

MICHIGAN STATE	MIN	FG	3FG	FT	REB	A	ST	BL	PF	TP
Johnny Green	-	8-21	-	4-7	27	-	-	-	3	20
Jack Quiggle	-	8-22	-	2-3	7	-	-	-	3	18
George Ferguson	-	8-20	-	0-0	10	-	-	-	4	16
Bob Anderegg	-	4-8	-	6-8	5	-	-	-	2	14
Larry Hedden	-	4-16	-	5-12	11	-	-	-	3	13
Dave Scott	-	1-2	-	2-4	3	-	-	-	0	4
Pat Wilson	-	0-2	-	0-0	3	-	-	-	1	0
TOTALS	-	33-91	-	19-34	66	-	-	-	16	85
Percentages		36.3		55.9						

Coach: Forrest "Forddy" Anderson

85-83

	1H	2H
Michigan State	37	48
Notre Dame	36	47

SWEET 16

NOTRE DAME	MIN	FG	3FG	FT	REB	A	ST	BL	PF	TP
John Smyth	-	11-22	-	3-3	14	-	-	-	4	25
John McCarthy	-	5-13	-	11-12	11	-	-	-	3	21
Tom Hawkins	-	6-14	-	7-7	11	-	-	-	3	19
Robert Devine	-	3-14	-	4-5	5	-	-	-	2	10
Eugene Duffy	-	3-4	-	0-0	1	-	-	-	5	6
Edward Gleason	-	1-3	-	0-1	0	-	-	-	3	2
Joseph Morelli	-	0-3	-	0-0	0	-	-	-	0	0
Thomas Sullivan	-	0-0	-	0-0	2	-	-	-	1	0
TOTALS	-	29-73	-	25-28	44	-	-	-	21	83
Percentages		39.7		89.3						

Coach: John Jordan

Officials: Fox, DiGravio
Attendance: 11,000

OKLAHOMA CITY	MIN	FG	3FG	FT	REB	A	ST	BL	PF	TP
Hub Reed	-	12-26	-	1-5	12	-	-	-	3	25
Lyndon Lee	-	7-19	-	10-14	12	-	-	-	1	24
Roger Holloway	-	4-11	-	5-5	14	-	-	-	1	13
Cecil Magana	-	4-13	-	2-2	6	-	-	-	3	10
Larry Bradshaw	-	0-9	-	2-3	5	-	-	-	3	2
Troy Hill	-	0-0	-	1-4	1	-	-	-	0	1
Leon Griffin	-	0-1	-	0-0	0	-	-	-	0	0
Dennis Jeter	-	0-0	-	0-0	1	-	-	-	0	0
TOTALS	-	27-79	-	21-33	51	-	-	-	11	75
Percentages		34.2		63.6						

Coach: Abe Lemons

75-66

	1H	2H
Oklahoma City	37	38
Saint Louis	32	34

SWEET 16

SAINT LOUIS	MIN	FG	3FG	FT	REB	A	ST	BL	PF	TP
Jack Mimlitz	-	9-21	-	2-3	10	-	-	-	3	20
Harold Alcorn	-	4-13	-	8-9	6	-	-	-	4	16
Joe Todd	-	6-14	-	2-2	2	-	-	-	2	14
Robert Ferry	-	3-5	-	0-0	3	-	-	-	0	6
Al Serkin	-	3-9	-	0-1	11	-	-	-	5	6
Cal Burnett	-	0-4	-	2-2	11	-	-	-	3	2
Rich Rogers	-	1-2	-	0-0	0	-	-	-	1	2
Ron Flood	-	0-1	-	0-0	0	-	-	-	0	0
Larry Smith	-	0-0	-	0-1	0	-	-	-	1	0
TOTALS	-	26-69	-	14-18	43	-	-	-	19	66
Percentages		37.7		77.8						

Coach: Eddie Hickey

KANSAS	MIN	FG	3FG	FT	REB	A	ST	BL	PF	TP
Wilt Chamberlain	-	14-26	-	8-13	22	-	-	-	4	36
Donald Elstun	-	4-12	-	1-2	8	-	-	-	1	9
Ron Loneski	-	4-8	-	0-0	7	-	-	-	0	8
John Parker	-	4-7	-	0-0	1	-	-	-	2	8
Lew Johnson	-	3-3	-	0-0	2	-	-	-	2	6
Maurice King	-	1-7	-	2-4	4	-	-	-	2	4
Bob Billings	-	0-3	-	2-2	0	-	-	-	0	2
TOTALS	-	30-66	-	13-21	44	-	-	-	11	73
Percentages		45.5		61.9						

Coach: Dick Harp

73-65

	1H	2H	OT1
Kansas	33	26	14
SMU	32	27	6

SWEET 16

SMU	MIN	FG	3FG	FT	REB	A	ST	BL	PF	TP
Jim Krebs	-	8-28	-	2-2	6	-	-	-	5	18
Rick Herrscher	-	3-14	-	6-6	14	-	-	-	3	12
Bob McGregor	-	5-9	-	1-2	7	-	-	-	0	11
Bobby Mills	-	5-11	-	0-2	2	-	-	-	0	10
Larry Showalter	-	4-9	-	0-1	5	-	-	-	4	8
Ned Duncan	-	1-10	-	4-4	0	-	-	-	1	6
TOTALS	-	26-81	-	13-17	34	-	-	-	13	65
Percentages		32.1		76.5						

Coach: E.O. "Doc" Hayes

CALIFORNIA	MIN	FG	3FG	FT	REB	A	ST	BL	PF	TP
Larry Friend	-	11-25	-	3-6	7	-	-	-	1	25
Earl Robinson	-	8-14	-	2-2	4	-	-	-	2	18
Al Buch	-	5-8	-	2-3	3	-	-	-	1	12
Joe Hagler	-	3-8	-	3-4	5	-	-	-	3	9
Gabe Arrillaga	-	3-6	-	0-1	4	-	-	-	1	6
Jack Grout	-	3-4	-	0-0	3	-	-	-	0	6
Everett McKeen	-	2-6	-	1-2	6	-	-	-	0	5
Don McIntosh	-	2-4	-	0-0	5	-	-	-	0	4
George Sterling	-	0-0	-	1-2	0	-	-	-	0	1
Mike Diaz	-	0-4	-	0-0	0	-	-	-	1	0
Joe Kapp	-	0-0	-	0-0	1	-	-	-	0	0
Bernie Simpson	-	0-2	-	0-0	1	-	-	-	0	0
TOTALS	-	37-81	-	12-20	39	-	-	-	9	86
Percentages		45.7		60.0						

Coach: Pete Newell

86-59
40 1H 35
46 2H 24
SWEET 16

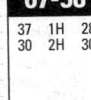

BYU	MIN	FG	3FG	FT	REB	A	ST	BL	PF	TP
John Benson	-	7-15	-	3-4	6	-	-	-	1	17
Tom Steinke	-	6-17	-	2-2	6	-	-	-	1	14
Lynn Rowe	-	3-7	-	2-2	5	-	-	-	0	8
Harry Anderson	-	2-7	-	1-3	8	-	-	-	2	5
Roy Thacker	-	2-4	-	1-2	7	-	-	-	4	5
John Gustin	-	1-3	-	2-2	3	-	-	-	1	4
Russ Jones	-	2-3	-	0-0	3	-	-	-	1	4
Mel Wilkes	-	0-0	-	2-2	0	-	-	-	0	2
Hal Jensen	-	0-0	-	0-0	0	-	-	-	0	0
Russ Peterson	-	0-1	-	0-0	0	-	-	-	1	0
TOTALS	-	23-57	-	13-17	38	-	-	-	11	59
Percentages		40.4		76.5						

Coach: Stan Watts

Officials: Williamson, Morrow
Attendance: 4,688

SAN FRANCISCO	MIN	FG	3FG	FT	REB	A	ST	BL	PF	TP
Gene Brown	-	6-14	-	6-8	8	-	-	-	3	18
Art Day	-	4-13	-	5-6	7	-	-	-	4	13
Mike Preaseau	-	4-8	-	4-4	3	-	-	-	2	12
Mike Farmer	-	5-13	-	1-1	8	-	-	-	4	11
Bill Mallen	-	3-6	-	0-0	3	-	-	-	3	6
Al Dunbar	-	2-4	-	1-3	5	-	-	-	0	5
John Koljian	-	0-3	-	1-3	2	-	-	-	1	1
Jack King	-	0-0	-	0-0	0	-	-	-	0	0
Dave Lillevand	-	0-3	-	0-0	0	-	-	-	0	0
Ron Mancasola	-	0-1	-	0-0	1	-	-	-	1	0
Bob Radanovich	-	0-2	-	0-0	2	-	-	-	0	0
Charles Russell	-	0-1	-	0-0	2	-	-	-	0	0
TOTALS	-	24-68	-	18-25	41	-	-	-	18	66
Percentages		35.3		72.0						

Coach: Phil Woolpert

66-51
36 1H 15
30 2H 36
SWEET 16

IDAHO STATE	MIN	FG	3FG	FT	REB	A	ST	BL	PF	TP
Jack Allain	-	4-10	-	4-8	15	-	-	-	5	12
Conrad Wells	-	5-10	-	1-2	3	-	-	-	3	11
Gale Siemen	-	4-8	-	2-2	10	-	-	-	0	10
Jerry Hicks	-	1-7	-	4-4	4	-	-	-	5	6
Ron Adlehardt	-	2-2	-	1-5	3	-	-	-	0	5
Fred Easterbrooks	-	1-11	-	3-6	2	-	-	-	2	5
Steve Detmer	-	0-1	-	2-4	1	-	-	-	1	2
Ray Cheney	-	0-0	-	0-0	0	-	-	-	0	0
Bob Hoge	-	0-1	-	0-0	2	-	-	-	0	0
Ron Manley	-	0-0	-	0-0	0	-	-	-	0	0
TOTALS	-	17-50	-	17-31	40	-	-	-	16	51
Percentages		34.0		54.8						

Coach: John Grayson

Officials: Ogden, Pryor
Attendance: 4,688

NORTH CAROLINA	MIN	FG	3FG	FT	REB	A	ST	BL	PF	TP
Lennie Rosenbluth	-	8-18	-	7-11	9	-	-	-	2	23
Tommy Kearns	-	4-11	-	14-19	4	-	-	-	3	22
Pete Brennan	-	3-9	-	7-9	15	-	-	-	4	13
Joe Quigg	-	1-3	-	4-4	8	-	-	-	4	6
Bob Cunningham	-	1-4	-	0-0	5	-	-	-	3	2
Danny Lotz	-	0-2	-	1-2	6	-	-	-	0	1
TOTALS	-	17-47	-	33-45	47	-	-	-	16	67
Percentages		36.2		73.3						

Coach: Frank McGuire

67-58
37 1H 28
30 2H 30
ELITE 8

SYRACUSE	MIN	FG	3FG	FT	REB	A	ST	BL	PF	TP
Vince Cohen	-	9-23	-	7-11	13	-	-	-	3	25
Gary Clark	-	5-13	-	1-2	12	-	-	-	5	11
James Snyder	-	5-19	-	0-2	12	-	-	-	4	10
Larry Loudis	-	3-6	-	0-0	2	-	-	-	3	6
Vincent Albanese	-	1-2	-	0-0	0	-	-	-	0	2
W. Jon Cincebox	-	0-5	-	2-6	15	-	-	-	5	2
Bruce Schmeizer	-	1-1	-	0-0	0	-	-	-	2	2
Emanuel Breland	-	0-6	-	0-2	2	-	-	-	5	0
Maury Youmans	-	0-0	-	0-0	1	-	-	-	0	0
TOTALS	-	24-75	-	10-23	57	-	-	-	27	58
Percentages		32.0		43.5						

Coach: Marcel Guley

Officials: Conway, MacPherson

MICHIGAN STATE	MIN	FG	3FG	FT	REB	A	ST	BL	PF	TP
Jack Quiggle	-	9-22	-	4-4	4	-	-	-	4	22
George Ferguson	-	5-15	-	5-6	12	-	-	-	3	15
Johnny Green	-	5-11	-	4-6	18	-	-	-	5	14
Larry Hedden	-	4-16	-	2-6	7	-	-	-	2	10
Dave Scott	-	1-3	-	4-5	0	-	-	-	0	6
Pat Wilson	-	3-10	-	0-0	3	-	-	-	0	6
Chuck Bencie	-	2-5	-	1-2	5	-	-	-	1	5
Bob Anderegg	-	1-4	-	0-0	1	-	-	-	2	2
Harry Lux	-	0-1	-	0-0	0	-	-	-	0	0
Tom Markovich	-	0-0	-	0-0	1	-	-	-	1	0
TOTALS	-	30-87	-	20-29	51	-	-	-	18	80
Percentages		34.5		69.0						

Coach: Forrest "Forddy" Anderson

80-68
35 1H 47
45 2H 21
ELITE 8

KENTUCKY	MIN	FG	3FG	FT	REB	A	ST	BL	PF	TP
Gerry Calvert	-	8-18	-	2-4	6	-	-	-	4	18
Johnny Cox	-	3-12	-	11-12	4	-	-	-	5	17
Vernon Hatton	-	6-13	-	3-5	7	-	-	-	1	15
John Crigler	-	5-11	-	0-1	9	-	-	-	2	10
Ed Beck	-	2-10	-	0-2	16	-	-	-	2	4
Ray Mills	-	0-2	-	2-4	4	-	-	-	2	2
Adrian Smith	-	0-1	-	2-3	1	-	-	-	0	2
Earl Adkins	-	0-0	-	0-0	0	-	-	-	2	0
Linc Collinsworth	-	0-0	-	0-0	0	-	-	-	0	0
TOTALS	-	24-67	-	20-31	47	-	-	-	18	68
Percentages		35.8		64.5						

Coach: Adolph Rupp

Officials: Andersen, Mihalik
Attendance: 12,300

KANSAS	MIN	FG	3FG	FT	REB	A	ST	BL	PF	TP
Wilt Chamberlain	-	8-17	-	14-22	15	-	-	-	2	30
Ron Loneski	-	3-8	-	8-9	4	-	-	-	0	14
Maurice King	-	5-12	-	3-4	3	-	-	-	3	13
John Parker	-	4-4	-	2-2	4	-	-	-	0	10
Donald Elstun	-	2-7	-	2-3	10	-	-	-	0	6
Eddie Dater	-	2-3	-	0-0	2	-	-	-	2	4
Lew Johnson	-	1-5	-	0-0	9	-	-	-	1	2
Lynn Kindred	-	0-3	-	2-2	1	-	-	-	0	2
Bob Billings	-	0-0	-	0-0	0	-	-	-	0	0
Lee Green	-	0-0	-	0-0	2	-	-	-	1	0
Blaine Hollinger	-	0-3	-	0-0	1	-	-	-	1	0
Monte Johnson	-	0-0	-	0-0	0	-	-	-	0	0
TOTALS	-	25-62	-	31-42	51	-	-	-	10	81
Percentages		40.3		73.8						

Coach: Dick Harp

81-61
27 1H 24
54 2H 37
ELITE 8

OKLAHOMA CITY	MIN	FG	3FG	FT	REB	A	ST	BL	PF	TP
Hub Reed	-	12-34	-	2-3	13	-	-	-	3	26
Lyndon Lee	-	5-12	-	9-12	4	-	-	-	4	19
Leon Griffin	-	3-8	-	0-0	1	-	-	-	1	6
Bill Hanson	-	3-4	-	0-0	2	-	-	-	4	6
Roger Holloway	-	1-7	-	0-0	10	-	-	-	5	2
Cecil Magana	-	1-10	-	0-0	5	-	-	-	3	2
Larry Bradshaw	-	0-5	-	0-0	3	-	-	-	3	0
Gary Gardner	-	0-4	-	0-2	3	-	-	-	1	0
Troy Hill	-	0-1	-	0-1	2	-	-	-	0	0
Mike Kelley	-	0-0	-	0-0	0	-	-	-	0	0
James Wallace	-	0-1	-	0-0	0	-	-	-	1	0
TOTALS	-	25-86	-	11-18	43	-	-	-	25	61
Percentages		29.1		61.1						

Coach: Abe Lemons

Officials: Haggerty, Lightner

SAN FRANCISCO	MIN	FG	3FG	FT	REB	A	ST	BL	PF	TP
Gene Brown	-	8-16	-	4-5	4	-	-	-	3	20
Mike Farmer	-	4-12	-	3-4	8	-	-	-	3	11
Art Day	-	4-9	-	1-5	9	-	-	-	4	9
Al Dunbar	-	0-3	-	5-8	3	-	-	-	1	5
Mike Preaseau	-	0-7	-	5-6	6	-	-	-	2	5
Bill Mallen	-	0-0	-	0-0	0	-	-	-	0	0
TOTALS	-	16-47	-	18-28	30	-	-	-	13	50
Percentages		34.0		64.3						

Coach: Phil Woolpert

50-46
27 1H 22
23 2H 24
ELITE 8

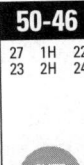

CALIFORNIA	MIN	FG	3FG	FT	REB	A	ST	BL	PF	TP
Earl Robinson	-	6-13	-	4-4	6	-	-	-	3	16
Larry Friend	-	5-13	-	2-3	6	-	-	-	1	12
Everett McKeen	-	3-5	-	0-1	6	-	-	-	4	6
Mike Diaz	-	0-1	-	4-5	2	-	-	-	3	4
Don McIntosh	-	1-3	-	2-2	2	-	-	-	2	4
Al Buch	-	0-2	-	2-2	1	-	-	-	1	2
Jack Grout	-	1-3	-	0-1	2	-	-	-	0	2
Gabe Arrillaga	-	0-2	-	0-0	1	-	-	-	1	0
Joe Hagler	-	0-1	-	0-2	2	-	-	-	1	0
Joe Kapp	-	0-0	-	0-0	0	-	-	-	1	0
TOTALS	-	16-43	-	14-20	28	-	-	-	17	46
Percentages		37.2		70.0						

Coach: Pete Newell

Officials: Pryor, Ogden
Attendance: 6,070

ANNUAL REVIEW

Final 4 — 74-70

NORTH CAROLINA	MIN	FG	3FG	FT	REB	A	ST	BL	PF	TP
Lennie Rosenbluth	-	11-42	-	7-9	3	-	-	-	1	29
Bob Cunningham	-	9-18	-	3-5	12	-	-	-	5	21
Pete Brennan	-	6-16	-	2-4	17	-	-	-	5	14
Tommy Kearns	-	1-8	-	4-5	6	-	-	-	4	6
Joe Quigg	-	0-1	-	2-3	4	-	-	-	5	2
Bob Young	-	1-3	-	0-1	2	-	-	-	1	2
Danny Lotz	-	0-0	-	0-1	4	-	-	-	1	0
Roy Searcy	-	0-0	-	0-0	1	-	-	-	0	0
TOTALS	-	28-88	-	18-28	49	-	-	-	22	74
Percentages		31.8		64.3						

Coach: Frank McGuire

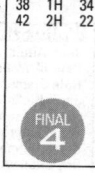

29	1H	29
29	2H	29
6	OT1	6
2	OT2	2
8	OT3	4

MICHIGAN STATE	MIN	FG	3FG	FT	REB	A	ST	BL	PF	TP
Jack Quiggle	-	6-21	-	8-10	10	-	-	-	1	20
Larry Hedden	-	4-20	-	6-7	15	-	-	-	5	14
Johnny Green	-	4-12	-	3-6	19	-	-	-	2	11
George Ferguson	-	4-8	-	2-3	1	-	-	-	5	10
Bob Anderegg	-	2-7	-	3-6	3	-	-	-	2	7
Dave Scott	-	2-3	-	0-2	3	-	-	-	1	4
Chuck Bencie	-	1-6	-	0-0	2	-	-	-	1	2
Pat Wilson	-	0-3	-	2-2	5	-	-	-	1	2
TOTALS	-	23-80	-	24-36	58	-	-	-	18	70
Percentages		28.7		66.7						

Coach: Forrest "Forddy" Anderson

Officials: Ogden, Lightner

Final 4 — 80-56

KANSAS	MIN	FG	3FG	FT	REB	A	ST	BL	PF	TP
Wilt Chamberlain	-	12-22	-	8-11	11	-	-	-	0	32
Donald Elstun	-	8-12	-	0-0	6	-	-	-	3	16
Maurice King	-	6-8	-	1-1	4	-	-	-	1	13
Ron Loneski	-	2-6	-	3-4	1	-	-	-	2	7
Eddie Dater	-	1-1	-	0-0	0	-	-	-	2	2
Lee Green	-	1-1	-	0-0	2	-	-	-	1	2
Blaine Hollinger	-	1-1	-	0-1	0	-	-	-	0	2
Lew Johnson	-	1-3	-	0-0	8	-	-	-	0	2
Monte Johnson	-	1-1	-	0-0	0	-	-	-	0	2
John Parker	-	1-1	-	0-0	3	-	-	-	0	2
Bob Billings	-	0-1	-	0-0	0	-	-	-	0	0
Lynn Kindred	-	0-0	-	0-2	2	-	-	-	0	0
TOTALS	-	34-57	-	12-19	37	-	-	-	9	80
Percentages		59.6		63.2						

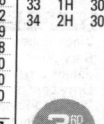

Coach: Dick Harp

38	1H	34
42	2H	22

SAN FRANCISCO	MIN	FG	3FG	FT	REB	A	ST	BL	PF	TP
Mike Farmer	-	6-15	-	2-2	4	-	-	-	2	14
Mike Preaseau	-	5-8	-	2-2	2	-	-	-	2	12
Gene Brown	-	5-14	-	0-0	2	-	-	-	2	10
Art Day	-	3-14	-	3-8	7	-	-	-	2	9
Al Dunbar	-	2-8	-	0-0	4	-	-	-	1	4
John Koljian	-	0-1	-	3-4	0	-	-	-	0	3
Dave Lillevand	-	1-3	-	0-0	0	-	-	-	1	2
Ron Mancasola	-	1-2	-	0-0	0	-	-	-	1	2
Jack King	-	0-3	-	0-0	0	-	-	-	1	0
Bill Mallen	-	0-2	-	0-0	1	-	-	-	1	0
Bob Radanovich	-	0-1	-	0-0	0	-	-	-	0	0
Charles Russell	-	0-0	-	0-0	5	-	-	-	0	0
TOTALS	-	23-71	-	10-16	25	-	-	-	13	56
Percentages		32.4		62.5						

Coach: Phil Woolpert

Officials: Conway, Andersen

3rd Place — 67-60

SAN FRANCISCO	MIN	FG	3FG	FT	REB	A	ST	BL	PF	TP
Gene Brown	-	8-18	-	6-11	7	-	-	-	3	22
Mike Farmer	-	4-12	-	8-9	2	-	-	-	1	16
Art Day	-	6-14	-	0-3	6	-	-	-	3	12
Al Dunbar	-	4-9	-	1-4	3	-	-	-	4	9
Mike Preaseau	-	2-6	-	4-4	6	-	-	-	4	8
Jack King	-	0-2	-	0-0	0	-	-	-	2	0
Dave Lillevand	-	0-1	-	0-0	1	-	-	-	0	0
Bill Mallen	-	0-0	-	0-0	1	-	-	-	0	0
TOTALS	-	24-62	-	19-31	26	-	-	-	17	67
Percentages		38.7		61.3						

Coach: Phil Woolpert

33	1H	30
34	2H	30

MICHIGAN STATE	MIN	FG	3FG	FT	REB	A	ST	BL	PF	TP
George Ferguson	-	4-11	-	6-9	11	-	-	-	2	14
Johnny Green	-	4-9	-	1-1	13	-	-	-	5	9
Larry Hedden	-	4-10	-	1-2	5	-	-	-	5	9
Bob Anderegg	-	2-8	-	3-4	4	-	-	-	5	7
Jack Quiggle	-	2-6	-	2-2	4	-	-	-	1	6
Pat Wilson	-	3-6	-	0-1	0	-	-	-	1	6
Harry Lux	-	2-2	-	1-1	3	-	-	-	2	5
Dave Scott	-	2-6	-	0-1	3	-	-	-	1	4
Chuck Bencie	-	0-5	-	0-0	4	-	-	-	1	0
TOTALS	-	23-63	-	14-21	47	-	-	-	23	60
Percentages		36.5		66.7						

Coach: Forrest "Forddy" Anderson

Officials: Ogden, Lightner
Attendance: 10,500

NCAA Final 1957 — 54-53

NORTH CAROLINA	MIN	FG	3FG	FT	REB	A	ST	BL	PF	TP
Lennie Rosenbluth	-	8-15	-	4-4	5	-	-	-	5	20
Pete Brennan	-	4-8	-	3-7	11	-	-	-	3	11
Tommy Kearns	-	4-8	-	3-7	1	-	-	-	4	11
Joe Quigg	-	4-10	-	2-3	9	-	-	-	4	10
Bob Young	-	1-1	-	0-0	3	-	-	-	1	2
Bob Cunningham	-	0-3	-	0-1	5	-	-	-	4	0
Danny Lotz	-	0-0	-	0-0	2	-	-	-	0	0
TOTALS	-	21-45	-	12-22	36	-	-	-	21	54
Percentages		46.7		54.5						

Coach: Frank McGuire

29	1H	22
17	2H	24
2	OT1	2
0	OT2	0
6	OT3	5

KANSAS	MIN	FG	3FG	FT	REB	A	ST	BL	PF	TP
Wilt Chamberlain	-	6-13	-	11-16	14	-	-	-	3	23
Donald Elstun	-	4-12	-	3-6	4	-	-	-	2	11
Maurice King	-	3-12	-	5-6	4	-	-	-	4	11
John Parker	-	2-4	-	0-0	0	-	-	-	0	4
Lew Johnson	-	0-1	-	2-2	0	-	-	-	1	2
Ron Loneski	-	0-5	-	2-3	3	-	-	-	2	2
Bob Billings	-	0-0	-	0-0	0	-	-	-	2	0
TOTALS	-	15-47	-	23-33	25	-	-	-	14	53
Percentages		31.9		69.7						

Coach: Dick Harp

Officials: Conway, Andersen
Attendance: 10,500

National Invitation Tournament (NIT)

First round: Memphis d. Utah, 77-75, Xavier d. Seton Hall 85-79, Dayton d. Saint Peter's 79-71, St. Bonaventure d. Cincinnati 90-72

Quarterfinals: Memphis d. Manhattan 85-73, St. Bonaventure d. Seattle 85-68, Bradley d. Xavier 116-81, Temple d. Dayton 77-66

Semifinals: Memphis d. St. Bonaventure 80-78, Bradley d. Temple 94-66

Third place: Temple d. St. Bonaventure 67-50

Championship: Bradley d. Memphis 84-83

MVP: Win Wilfong, Memphis

1957-58: Fiddlin' Five

Three men who were eventually named to the NBA's 50 Greatest Players list each averaged more than 30 points and 15 rebounds per game: Kansas' Wilt Chamberlain, Cincinnati's Oscar Robertson and Seattle's Elgin Baylor. Meanwhile, Adolph Rupp was leading a middling Kentucky squad he dubbed the Fiddlin' Five to a 19–6 regular-season record and into the NCAA Tournament.

With the Mideast Regional held in Lexington and the Final Four in Louisville, the Wildcats had a distinct home-state advantage in their run to the championship game. There they faced Seattle, which had drubbed Kansas State, 73-51, in the semis behind Baylor's 23 points and 22 rebounds. Baylor scored 25 points and grabbed 19 rebounds against Kentucky and was named the Tournament's Most Outstanding Player. But the Wildcats, with guard Vernon Hatton scoring 30, won the championship, 84-72. Baylor was selected by Minneapolis as the No. 1 pick in the 1958 NBA draft.

Major Conference Standings

ACC	Conference W	L	Pct	Overall W	L	Pct
Duke	11	3	.786	18	7	.720
NC State	10	4	.714	18	6	.750
North Carolina	10	4	.714	19	7	.731
Maryland⊕	9	5	.643	22	7	.759
Virginia	6	8	.429	10	13	.435
Clemson	4	10	.286	8	16	.333
Wake Forest	3	11	.214	6	17	.261
South Carolina	3	11	.214	5	19	.208

Tournament: **Maryland d. North Carolina 86-74**
Tournament MVP: **Nick Davis**, Maryland

Big Eight	Conference W	L	Pct	Overall W	L	Pct
Kansas State⊕	10	2	.833	22	5	.815
Kansas	8	4	.667	18	5	.783
Iowa State	8	4	.667	15	8	.652
Oklahoma	5	7	.417	13	10	.565
Nebraska	5	7	.417	10	13	.435
Missouri	3	9	.250	9	13	.409
Colorado	3	9	.250	8	15	.348
Oklahoma State○	-	-	-	21	8	.724

Big Ten	Conference W	L	Pct	Overall W	L	Pct
Indiana⊕	10	4	.714	13	11	.542
Michigan State	9	5	.643	16	6	.727
Purdue	9	5	.643	14	8	.636
Northwestern	8	6	.571	13	9	.591
Ohio State	8	6	.571	9	13	.409
Iowa	7	7	.500	13	9	.591
Michigan	6	8	.429	11	11	.500
Illinois	5	9	.357	11	11	.500
Minnesota	5	9	.357	9	12	.429
Wisconsin	3	11	.214	8	14	.364

Border	Conference W	L	Pct	Overall W	L	Pct
Arizona State⊕	8	2	.800	13	13	.500
New Mexico State	7	3	.700	14	9	.609
Texas Western	5	5	.500	14	10	.583
Hardin-Simmons	4	6	.400	11	14	.440
Arizona	4	6	.400	10	15	.400
West Texas A&M	2	8	.200	3	15	.167

Ivy	Conference W	L	Pct	Overall W	L	Pct
Dartmouth○	11	3	.786	22	5	.815
Princeton	9	5	.643	15	8	.652
Yale	9	5	.643	14	10	.583
Penn	8	6	.571	13	12	.520
Harvard	7	7	.500	16	9	.640
Cornell	5	9	.357	11	11	.500
Brown	5	9	.357	10	15	.400
Columbia	2	12	.143	6	18	.250

Metro NY	Conference W	L	Pct	Overall W	L	Pct
St. John's□	6	0	1.000	18	8	.692
Manhattan○	3	1	.750	16	10	.615
St. Francis (NY)	2	1	.667	14	9	.609
NYU	2	2	.500	10	11	.476
CCNY	2	5	.286	9	8	.529
Fordham□	1	3	.250	16	9	.640
Brooklyn	0	4	.000	11	7	.611

Mid-American	Conference W	L	Pct	Overall W	L	Pct
Miami (OH)⊕	12	0	1.000	18	9	.667
Marshall	9	3	.750	17	7	.708
Ohio	7	5	.583	16	8	.667
Bowling Green	6	6	.500	15	8	.652
Toledo	4	8	.333	9	14	.391
Kent State	3	9	.250	9	14	.391
Western Michigan	1	11	.083	5	19	.208

Skyline 8	Conference W	L	Pct	Overall W	L	Pct
Cincinnati⊕	13	1	.929	25	3	.893
Bradley□	12	2	.857	20	7	.741
Saint Louis	9	5	.643	16	10	.615
Drake	7	7	.500	13	12	.520
Wichita State	6	8	.429	14	12	.538
Houston	4	10	.286	9	16	.360
Tulsa	4	10	.286	7	19	.269
North Texas	1	13	.071	3	18	.143

Mountain States	Conference W	L	Pct	Overall W	L	Pct
Wyoming⊕	10	4	.714	13	14	.481
Utah□	9	5	.643	20	7	.741
Colorado State	9	5	.643	14	11	.560
BYU	9	5	.643	13	13	.500
Montana	8	6	.571	12	10	.545
Denver	8	6	.571	13	12	.520
Utah State	3	11	.214	4	20	.167
New Mexico	0	14	.000	3	21	.125

Ohio Valley	Conference W	L	Pct	Overall W	L	Pct
Tennessee Tech⊕	8	2	.800	17	9	.654
Morehead State	6	4	.600	13	10	.565
Western Kentucky	5	5	.500	14	11	.560
Middle Tennessee St.	4	6	.400	11	10	.524
Murray State	4	6	.400	8	16	.333
Eastern Kentucky	3	7	.300	8	11	.421
East Tennessee St.	-	-	-	6	19	.240

Pacific Coast	Conference W	L	Pct	Overall W	L	Pct
Oregon State	12	4	.750	20	6	.769
California⊕	12	4	.750	19	9	.679
UCLA	10	6	.625	16	10	.615
Idaho	9	7	.563	17	9	.654
Southern California	8	8	.500	12	13	.480
Stanford	7	9	.438	12	13	.480
Oregon	6	10	.375	13	11	.542
Washington	5	11	.313	8	18	.308
Washington State	3	13	.188	7	19	.269

SEC	Conference W	L	Pct	Overall W	L	Pct
Kentucky⊕	12	2	.857	23	6	.793
Auburn	11	3	.786	16	6	.727
Mississippi State	9	5	.643	20	5	.800
Alabama	9	5	.643	17	9	.654
Tennessee	8	6	.571	16	7	.696
Georgia Tech	8	6	.571	15	11	.577
Vanderbilt	7	7	.500	14	11	.560
Mississippi	6	8	.429	12	12	.500
Florida	5	9	.357	12	9	.571
Tulane	3	11	.214	8	15	.348
LSU	3	11	.214	7	18	.280
Georgia	3	11	.214	7	19	.269

Southern	Conference W	L	Pct	Overall W	L	Pct
West Virginia⊕	12	0	1.000	26	2	.929
Virginia Tech	10	5	.667	11	8	.579
George Washington	8	4	.667	12	11	.522
The Citadel	9	6	.600	16	11	.593
William and Mary	9	9	.500	15	14	.517
Richmond	7	8	.467	14	12	.538
Furman	4	8	.333	10	16	.385
Davidson	4	8	.333	9	15	.375
Washington and Lee	4	9	.308	9	16	.360
VMI	1	12	.077	4	17	.190

Tournament: **West Virginia d. William and Mary 74-58**
Tournament MOP: **Jerry West**, West Virginia

Southwest	Conference W	L	Pct	Overall W	L	Pct
Arkansas⊕	9	5	.643	17	10	.630
SMU	9	5	.643	15	10	.600
TCU	8	6	.571	17	7	.708
Texas Tech	8	6	.571	15	8	.652
Rice	7	7	.500	13	11	.542
Texas A&M	7	7	.500	11	13	.458
Texas	5	9	.357	10	13	.435
Baylor	3	11	.214	5	19	.208

WCAC	Conference W	L	Pct	Overall W	L	Pct
San Francisco⊕	12	0	1.000	25	2	.926
Saint Mary's (CA)	8	4	.667	11	15	.423
Santa Clara	6	6	.500	13	11	.542
Pepperdine	5	7	.417	15	11	.577
San Jose State	5	7	.417	13	13	.500
Pacific	5	7	.417	9	15	.375
Loyola Marymount	1	11	.083	6	18	.250

WNY Little Three	Conference W	L	Pct	Overall W	L	Pct
St. Bonaventure□	4	0	1.000	21	5	.808
Niagara□	0	2	.000	18	7	.720
Canisius	0	2	.000	2	19	.095

Yankee	Conference W	L	Pct	Overall W	L	Pct
Connecticut⊕	9	1	.900	17	10	.630
Vermont	5	5	.500	15	10	.600
Massachusetts	5	5	.500	13	12	.520
Maine	4	6	.400	8	12	.400
New Hampshire	3	7	.300	10	12	.455
Rhode Island	3	7	.300	4	17	.190

Conference Standings Continue →

⊕ Automatic NCAA Tournament bid ○ At-large NCAA Tournament bid □ NIT appearance ⊗ Team record doesn't reflect games forfeited or vacated. For adjusted record, see p. 521.

INDEPENDENTS	W	L	PCT
Temple⊕	27	3	.900
Dayton□	25	4	.862
Notre Dame○	24	5	.828
Saint Francis (PA)□	20	5	.800
Seattle○	23	6	.793
Idaho State○	22	6	.786
Iona	18	6	.750
Providence	18	6	.750
Boston U.	15	5	.750
Air Force	17	6	.739
Pittsburgh○	18	7	.720
Boston College○	15	6	.714
Saint Joseph's□	18	9	.667
Bucknell	16	8	.667
Loyola-Chicago	16	8	.667
Holy Cross	16	9	.640
La Salle	16	9	.640
Loyola (LA)○	16	9	.640
Miami (FL)	14	8	.636
Xavier□	19	11	.633
Portland	18	11	.621
Gonzaga	16	10	.615

INDEPENDENTS (CONT.)	W	L	PCT
Lafayette	16	10	.615
Butler□	15	10	.600
Oklahoma City	14	12	.538
Syracuse	11	10	.524
Wash.-St. Louis	11	10	.524
Villanova	12	11	.522
Army	13	12	.520
Detroit	13	12	.520
Louisville	13	12	.520
Muhlenberg	12	12	.500
Marquette	11	11	.500
Navy	10	10	.500
Georgetown	10	11	.476
Duquesne	10	12	.455
Lehigh	8	10	.444
Penn State	8	11	.421
DePaul	8	12	.400
Valparaiso	7	14	.333
Rutgers	7	15	.318
Colgate	6	16	.273
Seton Hall	7	19	.269
Siena	5	15	.250

INDIVIDUAL LEADERS—SEASON

SCORING	CL	POS	G	FG	FT	PTS	PPG
1 **Oscar Robertson**, Cincinnati	SO	G/F	28	352	280	984	**35.1**
2 **Elgin Baylor**, Seattle	JR	F/C	29	353	237	943	**32.5**
3 **Wilt Chamberlain**, Kansas	JR	C	21	228	177	633	**30.1**
4 **Bailey Howell**, Mississippi State	JR	C	25	226	243	695	**27.8**
5 **Red Murrell**, Drake	SR	F	25	254	160	668	**26.7**
6 **"King" Kelly Coleman**, Kentucky Wesleyan	SO	G	24	264	111	639	**26.6**
7 **Don Hennon**, Pittsburgh	JR	G	25	267	117	651	**26.0**
8 **Hub Reed**, Oklahoma City	SR	C	26	230	206	666	**25.6**
9 **Archie Dees**, Indiana	SR	C	24	230	153	613	**25.5**
10 **Dom Flora**, Washington and Lee	SR	G/F	25	233	168	634	**25.4**

FIELD GOAL PCT	CL	POS	G	FG	FGA	PCT
1 **Ralph Crosthwaite**, Western Kentucky	JR	C	25	202	331	**61.0**
2 **Oscar Robertson**, Cincinnati	SO	G/F	28	352	617	**57.1**
3 **Pete Brunone**, Manhattan	SO	C	26	100	178	**56.2**
4 **Bob Goodall**, Tulsa	SO	C	26	108	194	**55.7**
5 **Hal Greer**, Marshall	SR	G	24	236	432	**54.6**

MINIMUM: 100 MADE

FREE THROW PCT	CL	POS	G	FT	FTA	PCT
1 **Semi Mintz**, Davidson	JR	G	24	105	119	**88.2**
2 **Gerald Myers**, Texas Tech	JR	G	23	107	123	**87.0**
3 **Arlen Clark**, Oklahoma State	JR	C	29	160	185	**86.5**
4 **Joe Hobbs**, Florida	SR	G	21	98	114	**86.0**
5 **Hub Reed**, Oklahoma City	SR	C	26	206	242	**85.1**

MINIMUM: 90 MADE

INDIVIDUAL LEADERS—GAME

POINTS	CL	POS	OPP	DATE	PTS
1 **Elgin Baylor**, Seattle	JR	F/C	Portland	J30	**60**
2 **Oscar Robertson**, Cincinnati	SO	G/F	Seton Hall	J9	**56**
Oscar Robertson, Cincinnati	SO	G/F	Arkansas	M15	**56**
4 **Elgin Baylor**, Seattle	JR	F/C	Montana State	J15	**53**
5 **Elgin Baylor**, Seattle	JR	F/C	Pacific Lutheran	F28	**51**
Red Murrell, Drake	SR	F	Houston	M3	**51**

FREE THROWS MADE	CL	POS	OPP	DATE	FT	FTA	PCT
1 **John Lee**, Yale	SR	F	Oregon State	D27	**21**	21	100.0
2 **Oscar Robertson**, Cincinnati	SO	G/F	Wichita State	M1	**20**	21	95.2
Roger Wendel, Tulsa	JR	G	Arkansas	D7	**20**	22	90.9
4 **Bailey Howell**, Mississippi State	JR	C	Murray State	D19	**19**	21	90.5
5 **Jim McClellan**, Saint Francis (PA)	SR	F	Saint Joseph's	D11	**18**	19	94.7
Hub Reed, Oklahoma City	SR	C	Canisius	J18	**18**	19	94.7

TEAM LEADERS—SEASON

SCORING OFFENSE	G	W-L	PTS	PPG
1 **Marshall**	24	17-7	2,113	**88.0**
2 **West Virginia**	28	26-2	2,433	**86.9**
3 **Cincinnati**	28	25-3	2,422	**86.5**
4 **Kentucky Wesleyan**	24	14-10	1,993	**83.0**
5 **Notre Dame**	29	24-5	2,374	**81.9**

FIELD GOAL PCT	G	W-L	FG	FGA	PCT
1 **Fordham**	25	16-9	693	1,440	**48.1**
2 **Cincinnati**	28	25-3	910	1,895	**48.0**
3 **Marshall**	24	17-7	817	1,740	**47.0**
4 **Seattle**	29	23-6	938	2,014	**46.6**
5 **Oklahoma State**	29	21-8	620	1,346	**46.1**

FREE THROW PCT	G	W-L	FT	FTA	PCT
1 **Oklahoma State**	29	21-8	488	617	**79.1**
2 **Marshall**	24	17-7	479	608	**78.8**
3 **Oklahoma City**	26	14-12	503	667	**75.4**
4 **Stanford**	25	12-13	448	603	**74.3**
5 **Kentucky**	29	23-6	502	680	**73.8**

SCORING DEFENSE	G	W-L	OPP PTS	OPP PPG
1 **San Francisco**	27	25-2	1,363	**50.5**
2 **Oklahoma State**	29	21-8	1,500	**51.7**
3 **Kansas**	23	18-5	1,273	**55.3**
4 **Providence**	24	18-6	1,332	**55.5**
5 **Oregon State**	26	20-6	1,449	**55.7**

CONSENSUS ALL-AMERICAS

FIRST TEAM

PLAYER	CL	POS	HT	SCHOOL	RPG	PPG
Elgin Baylor	JR	F/C	6-5	Seattle	19.3	32.5
Bob Boozer	JR	F	6-8	Kansas State	10.4	20.1
Wilt Chamberlain	JR	C	7-1	Kansas	17.5	30.1
Don Hennon	JR	G	5-9	Pittsburgh	4.7	26.0
Oscar Robertson	SO	G/F	6-5	Cincinnati	15.2	35.1
Guy Rodgers	SR	G	6-0	Temple	6.6	20.1

SECOND TEAM

PLAYER	CL	POS	HT	SCHOOL	RPG	PPG
Pete Brennan	SR	F	6-6	North Carolina	11.7	21.3
Archie Dees	SR	C	6-8	Indiana	14.4	25.5
Mike Farmer	SR	F	6-7	San Francisco	8.2	11.3
Dave Gambee	SR	F	6-6	Oregon State	11.0	18.3
Bailey Howell	JR	C	6-7	Mississippi State	16.2	27.8

SELECTORS: AP, INTERNATIONAL NEWS SERVICE, LOOK MAGAZINE, NABC, NEWSPAPER ENTERPRISES ASSN., UP

AWARD WINNERS

PLAYER OF THE YEAR

PLAYER	CL	POS	HT	SCHOOL	AWARDS
Oscar Robertson	SO	G/F	6-5	Cincinnati	UP

COACH OF THE YEAR

COACH	SCHOOL	REC	AWARDS
Tex Winter	Kansas State	22-5	UP

Poll Progression

Week of Dec 10

AP	UP	School
1	1	North Carolina (1-0)
2	2	Kansas (3-0)
3	3	Kentucky (3-0)
4	4	Bradley (1-0)
5	6	Kansas State (2-0)
6	5	San Francisco (2-0)
7	7	Michigan State (2-0)
8	16	West Virginia (3-0)
9	12	Saint Louis (1-0)
10	8	Temple (1-1)
11	15	Minnesota (3-0)
12	—	NC State (2-0)
13	9	UCLA (2-0)
14	13	Seattle (0-0)
15	10	Notre Dame (2-0)
16	11	Rice (2-0)
17	—	Syracuse (1-0)
18	—	Oklahoma State (1-1)
19	17	Cincinnati (2-0)
20	—	Memphis (2-0)
—	14	Utah (2-0)
—	18	Ohio State (0-2)
—	19	Illinois (2-0)
—	20	Washington (1-1)

Week of Dec 17

AP	UP	School	AP↓↑
1	1	North Carolina (4-0)	
2	2	Kansas (5-0)	
3	3	Kansas State (4-0)	↑2
4	7	Cincinnati (4-0)	↑15
5	6	Kentucky (4-1)	↓2
6	9	Maryland (4-0)	⤴
7	4	San Francisco (3-0)	↓1
8	14	West Virginia (5-0)	
9	5	Michigan State (3-0)	↓2
10	16	Minnesota (3-0)	↑1
11	11	Bradley (2-1)	↓7
12	8	Seattle (3-0)	↑2
13	10	UCLA (4-0)	
14	12	Rice (3-0)	↑2
15	15	Utah (4-0)	⤴
16	—	Oklahoma State (3-1)	↑2
17	16	Oregon State (5-0)	⤴
18	—	Mississippi State (6-0)	⤴
19	—	Richmond (5-0)	⤴
20	—	NC State (5-1)	↓8
—	13	Temple (2-2)	⤵
—	18	Iowa State (3-1)	
—	19	Duke (2-1)	
—	19	Michigan (3-1)	
—	19	Notre Dame (3-1)	⤵

Week of Dec 24

AP	UP	School	AP↓↑
1	3	West Virginia (8-0) Ⓐ	↑7
2	1	Kansas (7-0)	
3	2	Kansas State (7-0)	
4	4	North Carolina (5-1)	↓3
5	7	Cincinnati (6-0)	↓1
6	9	Maryland (6-0)	
7	5	San Francisco (6-1)	
8	6	Michigan State (4-0)	↑1
9	11	Kentucky (5-3)	↓4
10	—	Mississippi State (7-0)	↑8
11	8	Bradley (3-1)	
12	10	Utah (6-0)	↑3
13	—	NC State (6-1)	↑7
14	16	Oklahoma State (6-1)	↑2
15	13	Seattle (3-2)	↓3
16	—	Western Kentucky (4-1)	⤴
17	—	Richmond (5-2)	↑2
18	15	Saint Louis (2-1)	⤴
19	19	St. John's (6-0)	⤴
20	14	Iowa State (4-2)	⤴
—	12	Temple (4-2)	
—	17	Oregon State (5-1)	⤵
—	18	Illinois (5-1)	
—	20	Louisville (5-3)	
—	20	Wichita State (6-1)	
—	20	Yale (3-1)	

Week of Dec 31

AP	UP	School	AP↓↑
1	4	West Virginia (8-0)	
2	1	Kansas (9-0)	
3	2	Kansas State (9-0)	
4	3	North Carolina (8-1)	
5	8	Cincinnati (7-1)	
6	5	San Francisco (8-1)	↑1
7	7	Maryland (6-0)	↓1
8	6	Michigan State (7-0)	
9	24	Mississippi State (9-0)	↑1
10	15	Kentucky (6-3)	↓1
11	—	NC State (8-2)	↑2
12	9	Bradley (5-1)	↓1
13	10	Temple (6-2)	⤴
14	14	Oklahoma State (6-1)	
15	12	Utah (8-1)	↓3
16	13	TCU (9-1)	⤴
17	21	St. John's (6-0)	↑2
18	11	Oregon State (8-1)	⤴
19	17	California (3-4)	⤴
20	—	La Salle (6-2)	⤴
—	16	Seattle (4-3)	⤵
—	18	Notre Dame (6-2)	
—	19	UCLA (5-4)	
—	20	Iowa State (6-3)	⤵
—	21	Louisville (5-3)	
—	21	Illinois (6-1)	
—	24	Dartmouth (8-1)	

Week of Jan 7

AP	UP	School	AP↓↑
1	1	West Virginia (10-0)	
2	2	Kansas (10-1)	
3	3	North Carolina (9-1)	↑1
4	5	Kansas State (9-1)	↓1
5	11	Mississippi State (10-0)	↑4
6	4	San Francisco (10-1)	
7	6	Cincinnati (8-1)	↓2
8	9	Oklahoma State (8-1)	↑6
9	15	Kentucky (8-3)	↑1
10	7	Bradley (6-1)	↑2
11	12	Maryland (7-2)	↓4
12	7	Temple (8-2)	↑1
13	18	NC State (9-2)	↓2
14	12	Michigan State (7-2)	↓6
15	10	Oregon State (10-1)	↑3
16	—	St. John's (7-0)	↑1
17	—	Illinois (7-1)	⤴
18	—	Memphis (4-3)	⤴
19	16	Utah (9-2)	↓4
20	—	Seattle (4-4)	⤴
20	—	Wichita State (9-1)	⤴
—	12	TCU (10-1)	⤵
—	17	Minnesota (5-2)	
—	18	California (5-2)	⤵
—	18	Iowa State (5-2)	

Week of Jan 14

AP	UP	School	AP↓↑
1	1	West Virginia (12-0)	
2	4	Kansas State (11-1)	↑2
3	3	Kansas (10-2)	↓1
4	2	San Francisco (12-1)	↑2
5	6	Cincinnati (10-2) Ⓑ	↑2
6	5	North Carolina (11-2)	↓3
7	9	Oklahoma State (10-1)	↑1
8	7	Maryland (9-2)	↑3
9	13	Kentucky (10-3)	
10	8	Bradley (8-1)	
11	15	Mississippi State (11-1)	↓6
12	10	Temple (10-2)	
13	16	Tennessee (8-2)	⤴
14	—	Oklahoma (9-2)	⤴
15	—	St. John's (8-0)	↑1
16	11	Oregon State (10-1)	↓1
17	—	Wichita State (10-1)	↑3
18	12	Michigan State (8-2)	↓4
19	—	Dartmouth (11-1)	⤴
20	—	NC State (9-3)	↓7
—	14	Utah (10-2)	⤵
—	16	Notre Dame (9-2)	
—	18	Dayton (11-2)	
—	19	Illinois (7-3)	⤵
—	19	Minnesota (5-3)	
—	19	Seattle (6-4)	⤵

Week of Jan 21

AP	UP	School	AP↓↑
1	1	West Virginia (13-0)	
2	2	Kansas (12-2)	↑1
3	4	Kansas State (12-1)	↓1
4	5	Cincinnati (12-2)	↑1
5	3	San Francisco (12-1)	↓1
6	7	Maryland (10-2)	↑2
7	6	Oklahoma State (11-1)	
8	8	North Carolina (12-3)	↓2
9	12	Kentucky (12-3)	
10	10	Bradley (10-2)	
11	9	Temple (12-2)	↑1
12	14	NC State (11-3)	↑8
13	17	St. John's (8-0)	↑2
14	15	Mississippi State (11-3)	↓3
15	11	Michigan State (9-2)	↑3
16	18	Tennessee (8-4)	↓3
17	16	Dayton (13-2)	⤴
18	—	Dartmouth (13-1)	↑1
19	—	Wichita State (11-2)	↓2
20	—	Arkansas (10-3)	⤴
—	13	Oregon State (10-2)	⤵
—	18	Notre Dame (10-3)	
—	18	Xavier (10-2)	

Week of Jan 28

AP	UP	School	AP↓↑
1	1	West Virginia (14-0)	
2	2	Kansas (12-2)	
3	4	Cincinnati (13-2)	↑1
4	5	Kansas State (13-1)	↓1
5	3	San Francisco (13-1)	
6	6	Oklahoma State (12-1)	↑1
7	7	North Carolina (12-3)	↑1
8	10	Kentucky (12-3)	↑1
9	11	Maryland (10-3)	↓3
10	12	NC State (11-3)	↑2
11	7	Temple (13-2)	
12	9	Bradley (11-3)	↓2
13	17	St. John's (9-0)	
14	—	Mississippi State (12-3)	
15	13	Michigan State (10-3)	
16	15	Dayton (14-2)	↑1
17	16	Arkansas (11-3)	↑3
18	—	Wichita State (11-4)	↑1
19	—	Dartmouth (13-1)	↓1
20	14	Oregon State (12-3)	⤴
—	18	California (9-5)	
—	19	BYU (6-9)	
—	19	Notre Dame (12-3)	
—	19	Seattle (9-4)	

Week of Feb 4

AP	UP	School	AP↓↑
1	2	West Virginia (15-1)	
2	1	Kansas (12-2)	
3	5	Cincinnati (15-2)	
4	4	Kansas State (14-1)	
5	3	San Francisco (15-1)	
6	7	Oklahoma State (13-2)	
7	6	North Carolina (13-3)	
8	10	Maryland (11-3)	↑1
9	14	NC State (12-3)	↑1
10	8	Temple (14-2)	↑1
11	9	Bradley (12-3)	↑1
12	12	Kentucky (14-4)	↓4
13	18	Duke (9-5)	⤴
14	13	Dayton (16-2)	↑2
15	11	Michigan State (11-3)	
16	15	Seattle (10-4)	⤴
17	—	Mississippi State (14-3)	↓3
18	16	Arkansas (12-4)	↓1
19	—	Georgia Tech (12-7)	⤴
20	—	Dartmouth (14-1)	↓1
—	16	Oregon State (13-4)	⤵
—	18	Notre Dame (13-4)	
—	20	BYU (8-9)	

Week of Feb 11

AP	UP	School	AP↓↑
1	1	Kansas State (16-1)	↑3
2	2	West Virginia (17-1)	↓1
3	4	Cincinnati (16-2)	
4	5	Kansas (13-3)	↓2
5	3	San Francisco (16-1)	
6	6	Oklahoma State (15-2)	
7	7	Temple (16-2)	↑3
8	13	Duke (12-5)	↑5
9	8	Maryland (13-3)	↓1
10	9	NC State (14-3)	↓1
11	10	North Carolina (13-4)	↓4
12	10	Kentucky (15-4)	
13	14	Bradley (13-4)	↓2
14	12	Dayton (18-2)	
15	19	Tennessee (15-3)	⤴
16	20	Seattle (12-4)	
17	15	Notre Dame (13-4)	⤴
18	—	Mississippi State (15-4)	↓1
19	16	Michigan State (11-4)	↓4
20	—	Oklahoma (11-4)	⤴
—	17	Michigan (9-5)	
—	18	California (11-6)	
—	20	BYU (10-9)	

Week of Feb 18

AP	UP	School	AP↓↑
1	1	Kansas State (17-1)	
2	3	Cincinnati (18-2)	↑1
3	2	West Virginia (20-1)	↓1
4	5	Kansas (15-3) Ⓒ	
5	4	San Francisco (19-1)	
6	6	Temple (18-2)	↑1
7	9	Duke (14-5)	↑1
8	7	Oklahoma State (16-3)	↓2
9	8	NC State (15-4)	↑1
10	13	Notre Dame (15-4)	↑7
11	12	Dayton (20-2)	↑3
12	10	Michigan State (14-4)	↑7
13	16	Kentucky (16-5) Ⓓ	↓1
14	11	Maryland (14-4)	↓5
15	15	Bradley (14-4)	↓2
16	14	North Carolina (15-5)	↓5
17	17	Seattle (15-5)	↓1
18	—	Mississippi State (16-5)	
19	—	Dartmouth (17-2)	⤴
20	—	Tennessee (11-7)	↓5
—	18	BYU (11-9)	
—	19	St. Bonaventure (15-3)	
—	20	California (12-6)	
—	20	Purdue (11-7)	
—	20	Saint Louis (12-7)	

Week of Feb 25

AP	UP	School	AP↓↑
1	1	Kansas State (18-1)	
2	2	West Virginia (22-1)	↑1
3	3	Cincinnati (20-2)	↓1
4	4	San Francisco (21-1)	↑1
5	5	Temple (20-2)	↑1
6	6	Duke (16-5)	↑1
7	7	Kansas (16-4)	↓3
8	10	Notre Dame (17-4)	↑2
9	11	North Carolina (17-5)	↑7
10	13	Dayton (20-2)	↑1
11	9	NC State (16-5)	↓2
12	15	Kentucky (18-5)	↑1
13	12	Oklahoma State (18-5)	↓5
14	14	Bradley (17-5)	↑1
15	8	Michigan State (15-4)	↓3
16	—	Mississippi State (18-5)	↑2
17	15	Maryland (15-6)	↓3
18	18	Seattle (16-5)	↓1
19	17	California (15-6)	⤴
20	25	Auburn (14-6)	⤴
—	19	St. Bonaventure (17-3)	
—	20	Purdue (12-7)	
—	21	Oregon State (17-4)	
—	21	Saint Louis (13-8)	
—	21	Idaho State (18-3)	
—	21	Michigan (9-9)	
—	25	Indiana (8-10)	

Poll Progression Continues →

Week of Mar 4

AP	UP	SCHOOL	AP↓↑
1	1	**Kansas State** (20-1)	
2	3	**West Virginia** (23-1)	
3	2	**Cincinnati** (22-2)	
4	4	**San Francisco** (23-1)	
5	5	**Temple** (22-2)	
6	6	**Duke** (17-6)	
7	8	**Notre Dame** (21-4)	↑1
8	10	**Dayton** (22-2)	↑2
9	14	**Kentucky** (19-6)	↑3
10	9	**Kansas** (17-5)	↓3
11	11	**Bradley** (18-5)	↑3
12	7	**Michigan State** (16-5)	↑3
13	15	**North Carolina** (17-6)	↓4
14	13	**NC State** (17-5)	↓3
15	—	**Mississippi State** (20-5)	↑1
16	—	**Auburn** (16-6)	↑4
17	17	**Maryland** (17-6)	
18	12	**Oklahoma State** (18-6)	↓5
19	—	**Seattle** (17-5) [E]	↓1
20	18	**St. Bonaventure** (19-3)	↥
—	16	**Indiana** (11-10)	
—	18	**California** (17-7)	↧
—	20	**Oregon State** (18-4)	

Final Poll

AP	UP	SCHOOL	AP↓↑
1	1	**West Virginia** (26-1) [F]	↑1
2	2	**Cincinnati** (24-2)	↑1
3	4	**Kansas State** (20-3)	↓2
4	3	**San Francisco** (24-1)	
5	5	**Temple** (24-2)	
6	6	**Maryland** (20-6)	↑11
7	8	**Kansas** (18-5)	↑3
8	7	**Notre Dame** (22-4)	↓1
9	14	**Kentucky** (19-6)	
10	13	**Duke** (18-7)	↓4
11	9	**Dayton** (23-3)	↓3
12	10	**Indiana** (12-10)	↥
13	12	**North Carolina** (19-7)	
14	11	**Bradley** (20-5)	↓3
15	—	**Mississippi State** (20-5)	
16	—	**Auburn** (16-6)	
17	19	**Michigan State** (16-6)	↓5
18	19	**Seattle** (19-5)	↑1
19	15	**Oklahoma State** (19-7)	↓1
20	16	**NC State** (18-6)	↓6
—	16	**Oregon State** (20-5)	
—	18	**St. Bonaventure** (19-4)	↧
—	19	**Wyoming** (13-13)	
—	22	**Arkansas** (16-8)	
—	22	**Idaho State** (21-4)	
—	22	**Utah** (20-6)	
—	25	**SMU** (15-9)	

[A] On back-to-back nights at the Kentucky Invitational, No. 8-ranked West Virginia—led by the brilliant sophomore guard Jerry West—shoots down the host Wildcats, 77-70, then whips No. 1 North Carolina, 75-64. Those victories catapult the Mountaineers to No. 1, the biggest leap to the top spot in AP poll history.

[B] Making his Madison Square Garden debut, 6'5" Cincinnati sophomore Oscar Robertson electrifies the New York crowd with 56 points, an arena record at the time, in a victory over Seton Hall.

[C] On Feb. 15, Wilt Chamberlain hauls in a career-best 36 rebounds against Iowa State. After the season, Chamberlain announces he is bypassing his senior year to play for the Harlem Globetrotters. "The game I was playing at KU wasn't basketball," he says later. "It was hurting my chances of ever developing into a successful professional player."

[D] A 57-56 loss to Loyola-Chicago on Feb. 15 gives Kentucky five losses. Before the season, Adolph Rupp said of his squad, "We're just fiddlers, that's all ... pretty good fiddlers—be right entertaining at a barn dance—but you need violinists to play at Carnegie Hall. We don't have any violinists."

[E] On Feb. 28, Seattle's Elgin Baylor hauls down 37 rebounds against Pacific Lutheran. Baylor will end the season with a 32.5 ppg scoring average, second only to Oscar Robertson's 35.1 ppg at Cincinnati.

[F] On the day the final polls come out, West Virginia loses to Manhattan, 89-84. The Mountaineers are the first No. 1 team to reach 80 points in a losing effort.

1958 NCAA Tournament (A)

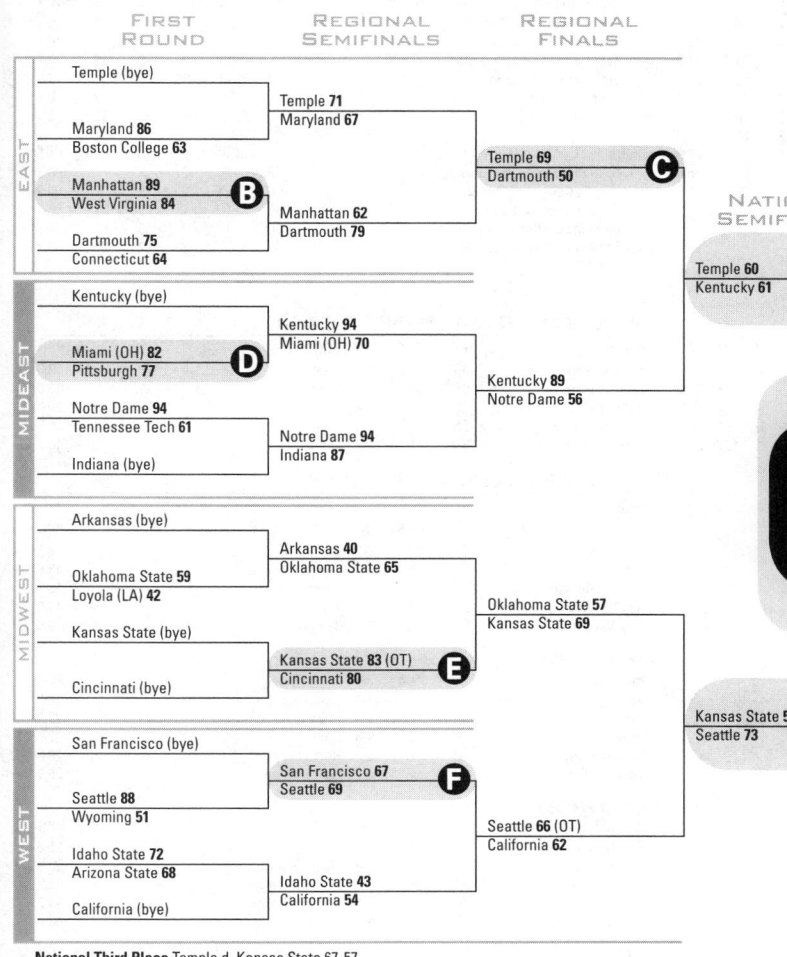

East

First Round
- Temple (bye)
- Maryland **86**, Boston College **63**
- Manhattan **89**, West Virginia **84** (B)
- Dartmouth **75**, Connecticut **64**

Regional Semifinals
- Temple **71**, Maryland **67**
- Manhattan **62**, Dartmouth **79**

Regional Finals
- Temple **69**, Dartmouth **50** (C)

Mideast

First Round
- Kentucky (bye)
- Miami (OH) **82**, Pittsburgh **77** (D)
- Notre Dame **94**, Tennessee Tech **61**
- Indiana (bye)

Regional Semifinals
- Kentucky **94**, Miami (OH) **70**
- Notre Dame **94**, Indiana **87**

Regional Finals
- Kentucky **89**, Notre Dame **56**

Midwest

First Round
- Arkansas (bye)
- Oklahoma State **59**, Loyola (LA) **42**
- Kansas State (bye)
- Cincinnati (bye)

Regional Semifinals
- Arkansas **40**, Oklahoma State **65**
- Kansas State **83** (OT), Cincinnati **80** (E)

Regional Finals
- Oklahoma State **57**, Kansas State **69**

West

First Round
- San Francisco (bye)
- Seattle **88**, Wyoming **51**
- Idaho State **72**, Arizona State **68**
- California (bye)

Regional Semifinals
- San Francisco **67**, Seattle **69** (F)
- Idaho State **43**, California **54**

Regional Finals
- Seattle **66** (OT), California **62**

National Semifinals

- Temple **60**, Kentucky **61**

Temple's Guy Rodgers misses the first of a one-and-one with :27 left and Vernon Hatton hits the game-winner. It's a near repeat of an early-season finish, when Hatton's buzzer-beater forced a third OT and eventual UK win.

- Kansas State **51**, Seattle **73**

Kansas State can't stop Elgin Baylor, who has 23 points and 22 rebounds, but also shoots itself in the foot with a 9½-minute scoring drought in the second half.

National Final

Kentucky 84
Seattle 72

Louisville, KY

Before a decidedly pro-Kentucky, championship-game record crowd of 18,803 in Louisville's Freedom Hall, the Wildcats' hyperactive forward, John Crigler, gets Elgin Baylor in early foul trouble and UK hangs on to give coach Adolph Rupp his fourth and last title. Vernon Hatton scores 30 and Johnny Cox 24 for the Fiddlin' Five.

National Third Place Temple d. Kansas State 67-57
East Regional Third Place Maryland d. Manhattan 59-55
Mideast Regional Third Place Indiana d Miami (OH) 98-91
Midwest Regional Third Place Cincinnati d. Arkansas 97-62
West Regional Third Place San Francisco d. Idaho State 57-51

A The old brown ball is replaced by an orange one in a test by Spalding for the title game. Butler coach Tony Hinkle believes that players and fans can more easily see the brighter ball. It would become the standard by the early 1960s.

B The Jaspers score a stunning upset over West Virginia, which gets only 10 points from sophomore Jerry West, who is saddled with four fouls most of the game.

C Temple's athletic director threatens to move his team, which includes two black starters, to the NIT in New York City to avoid potential "embarrassing team arrangements" in North Carolina and Kentucky on the way to the finals.

D First team All-America Don Hennon scores 28 points despite playing with a severe charley horse that requires a heavy bandage on his left leg.

E After missing the second of two free throws in the final seconds of regulation, Oscar Robertson fouls out in the overtime period, opening the way for Kansas State. Roy DeWitz, better known for his defense, scores seven of the nine overtime points, including three straight free throws, to decide the game.

F Seattle's Elgin Baylor, who will be the top pick in the upcoming NBA draft, scores 35 points, including the game-winning 35-foot shot in the final seconds. Baylor will rack up 91 rebounds in five Tournament games.

Tournament Leaders

Individual Leaders

Scoring	CL	POS	G	PTS	PPG
1 **Oscar Robertson**, Cincinnati	SO	G/F	2	86	43.0
2 **Wayne Embry**, Miami (OH)	SR	C	3	83	27.7
3 **Elgin Baylor**, Seattle	JR	F/C	5	135	27.0
4 **Archie Dees**, Indiana	SR	C	2	53	26.5
5 **Tom Hawkins**, Notre Dame	JR	F	3	76	25.3
6 **Arlen Clark**, Oklahoma State	JR	C	3	70	23.3
7 **John McCarthy**, Notre Dame	SR	F	3	66	22.0
8 **Bob Boozer**, Kansas State	JR	F	4	84	21.0
9 **Johnny Cox**, Kentucky	JR	F	4	83	20.8
Vernon Hatton, Kentucky	SR	G	4	83	20.8

Minimum: 2 games

Field Goals Per Game	CL	POS	G	FG	FGPG
1 **Oscar Robertson**, Cincinnati	SO	G/F	2	33	16.5
2 **Wayne Embry**, Miami (OH)	SR	C	3	32	10.7
3 **Tom Hawkins**, Notre Dame	JR	F	3	29	9.7
4 **Elgin Baylor**, Seattle	JR	F/C	5	48	9.6
5 **Archie Dees**, Indiana	SR	C	2	17	8.5
Peter Obremskey, Indiana	SO	F	2	17	8.5

Free Throw Pct	CL	POS	G	FT	FTA	PCT
1 **Gale Siemen**, Idaho State	JR	F	3	7	7	100.0
Fred LaCour, San Francisco	SO	G/F	2	5	5	100.0
3 **Archie Dees**, Indiana	SR	C	2	19	20	95.0
4 **John McCarthy**, Notre Dame	SR	F	3	16	17	94.1
5 **Mike Mendenhall**, Cincinnati	JR	G/F	2	12	13	92.3

Minimum: 5 made

Team Leaders

Scoring	G	PTS	PPG
1 **Indiana**	2	185	92.5
2 **Cincinnati**	2	177	88.5
3 **Kentucky**	4	328	82.0
4 **Notre Dame**	3	244	81.3
5 **Miami (OH)**	3	243	81.0
6 **Seattle**	5	368	73.6
7 **Maryland**	3	212	70.7
8 **Manhattan**	3	206	68.7
9 **Dartmouth**	3	204	68.0
10 **Temple**	4	267	66.8

Minimum: 2 games

FG Per Game	G	FG	FGPG
1 **Indiana**	2	75	37.5
2 **Cincinnati**	2	62	31.0
3 **Miami (OH)**	3	92	30.7
4 **Notre Dame**	3	89	29.7
6 **Kentucky**	4	116	29.0

FT Pct	G	FT	FTA	PCT
1 **Oklahoma State**	3	69	81	85.2
2 **Kentucky**	4	96	124	77.4
3 **Notre Dame**	3	66	86	76.7
4 **San Francisco**	2	32	42	76.2
5 **Maryland**	3	76	101	75.3

Minimum: 2 games

All-Tournament Team

PLAYER	CL	POS	HT	SCHOOL	PPG
Elgin Baylor*	JR	F/C	6-5	Seattle	27.0
Charlie Brown	JR	F	6-2	Seattle	13.0
Johnny Cox	JR	F	6-4	Kentucky	20.8
Vernon Hatton	SR	G	6-3	Kentucky	20.8
Guy Rodgers	SR	G	6-0	Temple	18.0

All-Regional Teams

East

PLAYER	CL	POS	HT	SCHOOL	PPG
Nick Davis	SR	F	6-2	Maryland	18.3
Bill Kennedy	SO	G	5-11	Temple	15.5
Rudy LaRusso	JR	C	6-7	Dartmouth	18.7
Jay Norman	SR	F	6-3	Temple	14.0
Guy Rodgers	SR	G	6-0	Temple	16.5

Mideast

PLAYER	CL	POS	HT	SCHOOL	PPG
Johnny Cox	JR	F	6-4	Kentucky	18.5
Archie Dees	SR	C	6-8	Indiana	26.5
Wayne Embry	SR	C	6-8	Miami (OH)	27.7
Vernon Hatton	SR	G	6-3	Kentucky	20.0
Tom Hawkins	JR	F	6-5	Notre Dame	25.3

Midwest

PLAYER	CL	POS	HT	SCHOOL	PPG
Bob Boozer	JR	F	6-8	Kansas State	25.0
Arlen Clark	JR	C	6-8	Oklahoma State	23.3
Roy DeWitz	SR	G/F	6-3	Kansas State	10.5
Jack Parr	SR	C	6-9	Kansas State	15.0
Oscar Robertson	SO	G/F	6-5	Cincinnati	43.0

West

PLAYER	CL	POS	HT	SCHOOL	PPG
Elgin Baylor	JR	F/C	6-5	Seattle	29.0
Charlie Brown	JR	F	6-2	Seattle	11.3
Don McIntosh	SR	C	6-6	California	13.0
Earl Robinson	SR	G	6-1	California	14.0
Gale Siemen	SR	F	6-4	Idaho State	16.3

* Most outstanding player

1958 NCAA TOURNAMENT BOX SCORES

71-67 — 39 1H 32 / 32 2H 35

TEMPLE	MIN	FG	3FG	FT	REB	A	ST	BL	PF	TP
Bill Kennedy	-	8-11	-	2-2	5	-	-	-	3	18
Guy Rodgers	-	7-25	-	2-11	6	-	-	-	3	16
Jay Norman	-	6-12	-	2-4	14	-	-	-	3	14
Mel Brodsky	-	4-8	-	1-1	5	-	-	-	3	9
Dan Fleming	-	4-7	-	0-0	4	-	-	-	2	8
Tink Van Patton	-	3-10	-	0-3	11	-	-	-	4	6
TOTALS	-	32-73	-	7-21	45	-	-	-	18	71
Percentages		43.8		33.3						

Coach: Harry Litwack

MARYLAND	MIN	FG	3FG	FT	REB	A	ST	BL	PF	TP
Charles McNeil	-	8-19	-	8-9	13	-	-	-	2	24
Nick Davis	-	8-15	-	2-2	2	-	-	-	1	18
Gene Danko	-	2-3	-	5-6	2	-	-	-	2	9
Tom Young	-	1-5	-	6-8	5	-	-	-	2	8
Al Bunge	-	2-8	-	1-2	6	-	-	-	3	5
John Nacincik	-	1-4	-	1-1	2	-	-	-	3	3
Jim Halleck	-	0-1	-	0-0	4	-	-	-	2	0
Bill Murphy	-	0-2	-	0-0	0	-	-	-	2	0
TOTALS	-	22-57	-	23-28	34	-	-	-	17	67
Percentages		38.6		82.1						

Coach: Bud Millikan

79-62 — 38 1H 27 / 41 2H 35

DARTMOUTH	MIN	FG	3FG	FT	REB	A	ST	BL	PF	TP
Chuck Kaufman	-	8-20	-	6-6	2	-	-	-	1	22
Rudy LaRusso	-	4-15	-	5-6	15	-	-	-	4	13
Walt Sosnowski	-	6-14	-	1-5	7	-	-	-	2	13
M. David Carruthers	-	6-12	-	0-0	7	-	-	-	2	12
David Farnsworth	-	3-5	-	0-1	8	-	-	-	2	6
Tom Aley	-	2-8	-	0-0	3	-	-	-	3	4
Gary Vandeweghe	-	1-5	-	2-2	2	-	-	-	2	4
Harold Douglas	-	0-0	-	2-2	0	-	-	-	0	2
A. Stuart Hanson	-	0-2	-	2-2	1	-	-	-	1	2
David Gavitt	-	0-1	-	1-2	5	-	-	-	1	1
Edward Hobbie	-	0-0	-	0-0	0	-	-	-	0	0
John Jones	-	0-0	-	0-0	0	-	-	-	0	0
TOTALS	-	30-82	-	19-26	50	-	-	-	18	79
Percentages		36.6		73.1						

Coach: Alvin "Doggie" Julian

MANHATTAN	MIN	FG	3FG	FT	REB	A	ST	BL	PF	TP
Don McGorty	-	6-16	-	0-3	6	-	-	-	3	12
John Powers	-	4-13	-	4-7	6	-	-	-	3	12
Mickey Burkoski	-	3-7	-	3-3	3	-	-	-	1	9
Peter Brunone	-	3-8	-	2-3	8	-	-	-	2	8
Bob Mealy	-	3-15	-	1-5	21	-	-	-	4	7
Charley Koenig	-	3-4	-	0-1	1	-	-	-	3	6
Dick Wilbur	-	2-8	-	2-3	4	-	-	-	1	6
Frank Quarto	-	1-1	-	0-0	1	-	-	-	1	2
Joseph Dougherty	-	0-3	-	0-0	1	-	-	-	1	0
John Schoenberger	-	0-1	-	0-0	0	-	-	-	0	0
TOTALS	-	25-76	-	12-25	51	-	-	-	19	62
Percentages		32.9		48.0						

Coach: Kenneth Norton

94-70 — 50 1H 35 / 44 2H 35

KENTUCKY	MIN	FG	3FG	FT	REB	A	ST	BL	PF	TP
Johnny Cox	-	9-25	-	5-5	15	-	-	-	0	23
Adrian Smith	-	6-16	-	6-8	3	-	-	-	1	18
Vernon Hatton	-	5-16	-	4-5	4	-	-	-	3	14
Don Mills	-	4-14	-	3-5	12	-	-	-	4	11
Linc Collinsworth	-	2-4	-	4-4	5	-	-	-	0	8
John Crigler	-	4-10	-	0-0	10	-	-	-	4	8
Ed Beck	-	2-7	-	2-2	8	-	-	-	5	6
Earl Adkins	-	1-2	-	0-0	0	-	-	-	0	2
Billy Cassady	-	1-1	-	0-0	1	-	-	-	0	2
Phil Johnson	-	1-4	-	0-0	3	-	-	-	2	2
Dick Howe	-	0-0	-	0-0	0	-	-	-	0	0
Bill Smith	-	0-0	-	0-0	0	-	-	-	0	0
TOTALS	-	35-99	-	24-29	61	-	-	-	19	94
Percentages		35.4		82.8						

Coach: Adolph Rupp

MIAMI (OH)	MIN	FG	3FG	FT	REB	A	ST	BL	PF	TP
Wayne Embry	-	8-22	-	10-13	15	-	-	-	4	26
John Powell	-	5-16	-	2-3	11	-	-	-	3	12
Jim Thomas	-	5-17	-	1-1	8	-	-	-	2	11
Jim Hamilton	-	3-7	-	2-4	1	-	-	-	2	8
Bill Brown	-	3-9	-	1-1	9	-	-	-	4	7
Jerry Higgins	-	2-3	-	0-0	0	-	-	-	2	4
Eddie Wingard	-	0-2	-	2-2	6	-	-	-	2	2
Kenneth Babbs	-	0-0	-	0-0	0	-	-	-	0	0
Larry Crist	-	0-1	-	0-1	0	-	-	-	0	0
Bob Miller	-	0-0	-	0-0	0	-	-	-	1	0
Herb Rowan	-	0-1	-	0-0	1	-	-	-	0	0
TOTALS	-	26-78	-	18-25	51	-	-	-	20	70
Percentages		33.3		72.0						

Coach: Richard Shrider

Officials: Mihalik, Mills
Attendance: 11,600

94-87 — 48 1H 37 / 46 2H 50

NOTRE DAME	MIN	FG	3FG	FT	REB	A	ST	BL	PF	TP
Tom Hawkins	-	10-24	-	11-14	11	-	-	-	3	31
John McCarthy	-	12-26	-	5-6	11	-	-	-	1	29
Robert Devine	-	4-9	-	6-8	6	-	-	-	0	14
Eugene Duffy	-	2-4	-	5-6	2	-	-	-	4	9
Thomas Reinhart	-	3-4	-	2-2	5	-	-	-	5	8
Michael Graney	-	1-9	-	0-0	10	-	-	-	5	2
Michael Ireland	-	0-2	-	1-1	5	-	-	-	3	1
James Williams	-	0-0	-	0-0	0	-	-	-	0	0
TOTALS	-	32-78	-	30-37	50	-	-	-	21	94
Percentages		41.0		81.1						

Coach: John Jordan

INDIANA	MIN	FG	3FG	FT	REB	A	ST	BL	PF	TP
Archie Dees	-	9-27	-	10-11	15	-	-	-	2	28
Peter Obremskey	-	7-15	-	4-6	7	-	-	-	4	18
Robert Wilkinson	-	7-14	-	3-7	3	-	-	-	5	17
Jerry Thompson	-	4-7	-	1-1	3	-	-	-	4	9
James Hinds	-	3-4	-	0-0	6	-	-	-	3	6
Samuel Gee	-	2-5	-	0-0	2	-	-	-	3	4
Allen Schlegelmilch	-	1-1	-	1-2	0	-	-	-	1	3
Frank Radovich	-	1-7	-	0-1	6	-	-	-	4	2
TOTALS	-	34-80	-	19-28	42	-	-	-	26	87
Percentages		42.5		67.9						

Coach: Branch McCracken

Officials: Meyer, Lannon
Attendance: 11,600

65-40 — 37 1H 23 / 28 2H 17

OKLAHOMA STATE	MIN	FG	3FG	FT	REB	A	ST	BL	PF	TP
Arlen Clark	-	4-7	-	12-15	13	-	-	-	2	20
Jerry Adair	-	5-11	-	1-1	5	-	-	-	2	11
Roy Carberry	-	3-8	-	5-7	8	-	-	-	3	11
Jerry Hale	-	3-8	-	4-4	4	-	-	-	3	10
Eddie Sutton	-	3-5	-	2-2	5	-	-	-	1	8
Larry Deutschendorf	-	1-2	-	0-0	0	-	-	-	0	2
Don Heffington	-	1-1	-	0-0	0	-	-	-	0	2
Joe Crutchfield	-	0-2	-	1-1	1	-	-	-	1	1
Jim Fleming	-	0-1	-	0-0	0	-	-	-	0	0
Dick Soergel	-	0-0	-	0-0	0	-	-	-	0	0
Lew Wade	-	0-0	-	0-0	0	-	-	-	0	0
Dennis Walker	-	0-0	-	0-0	0	-	-	-	0	0
TOTALS	-	20-45	-	25-30	36	-	-	-	12	65
Percentages		44.4		83.3						

Coach: Hank Iba

ARKANSAS	MIN	FG	3FG	FT	REB	A	ST	BL	PF	TP
Fred Grim	-	5-16	-	3-5	5	-	-	-	2	13
Wayne Dunn	-	3-9	-	2-3	4	-	-	-	4	8
Harry Thompson	-	3-9	-	1-1	6	-	-	-	1	7
Larry Grisham	-	3-13	-	0-1	7	-	-	-	4	6
Jay Carpenter	-	2-2	-	0-1	2	-	-	-	5	4
Lawrence Stolzer	-	1-2	-	0-2	2	-	-	-	1	2
Ora Lee Boss	-	0-1	-	0-0	0	-	-	-	0	0
Zane Hankins	-	0-1	-	0-0	1	-	-	-	0	0
Tommy Rankin	-	0-5	-	0-0	2	-	-	-	2	0
Richard Rittman	-	0-2	-	0-0	0	-	-	-	1	0
TOTALS	-	17-60	-	6-13	29	-	-	-	20	40
Percentages		28.3		46.2						

Coach: Glen Rose

Officials: Mercer, Milner

83-80 — 39 1H 40 / 35 2H 34 / 9 OT1 6

KANSAS STATE	MIN	FG	3FG	FT	REB	A	ST	BL	PF	TP
Bob Boozer	-	9-25	-	6-11	14	-	-	-	4	24
Jack Parr	-	7-22	-	3-4	12	-	-	-	4	17
Roy DeWitz	-	4-10	-	7-10	9	-	-	-	1	15
Wally Frank	-	5-10	-	2-2	5	-	-	-	5	12
Don Matuszak	-	2-6	-	5-7	4	-	-	-	5	9
Larry Fischer	-	1-1	-	3-4	2	-	-	-	2	5
Jim Holwerda	-	0-0	-	1-2	0	-	-	-	0	1
James Abbott	-	0-1	-	0-0	2	-	-	-	3	0
TOTALS	-	28-75	-	27-40	48	-	-	-	24	83
Percentages		37.3		67.5						

Coach: Tex Winter

CINCINNATI	MIN	FG	3FG	FT	REB	A	ST	BL	PF	TP
Oscar Robertson	-	12-20	-	6-8	14	-	-	-	5	30
Connie Dierking	-	4-17	-	10-13	5	-	-	-	5	18
Wayne Stevens	-	4-15	-	5-7	6	-	-	-	5	13
Ralph Davis	-	4-12	-	2-4	2	-	-	-	3	10
Mike Mendenhall	-	3-10	-	3-3	3	-	-	-	2	9
Ron Dykes	-	0-2	-	0-2	1	-	-	-	4	0
Spud Hornsby	-	0-0	-	0-0	0	-	-	-	0	0
Rod Nall	-	0-0	-	0-0	0	-	-	-	1	0
Bill Whitaker	-	0-0	-	0-0	0	-	-	-	1	0
Larry Willey	-	0-0	-	0-1	2	-	-	-	0	0
TOTALS	-	27-76	-	26-38	33	-	-	-	26	80
Percentages		35.5		68.4						

Coach: George Smith

Officials: Batmale, Kobe

Seattle 69, San Francisco 67 (Sweet 16)

	1H	2H	Final
Seattle	31	38	69
San Francisco	33	34	67

SEATTLE	MIN	FG	3FG	FT	REB	A	ST	BL	PF	TP
Elgin Baylor	-	11-20	-	13-14	14	-	-	-	3	35
Charlie Brown	-	5-9	-	3-7	7	-	-	-	3	13
Jerry Frizzell	-	4-8	-	0-0	7	-	-	-	2	8
Don Ogorek	-	2-10	-	3-6	8	-	-	-	4	7
Don Piasecki	-	2-2	-	0-0	5	-	-	-	0	4
Jim Harney	-	1-3	-	0-0	2	-	-	-	0	2
TOTALS	-	25-52	-	19-27	43	-	-	-	12	69
Percentages		48.1		70.4						

Coach: John Castellani

SAN FRANCISCO	MIN	FG	3FG	FT	REB	A	ST	BL	PF	TP
Fred LaCour	-	8-16	-	4-4	4	-	-	-	4	20
Gene Brown	-	7-18	-	5-6	10	-	-	-	5	19
Art Day	-	4-14	-	5-6	10	-	-	-	1	13
Mike Farmer	-	5-14	-	0-1	7	-	-	-	5	10
Dave Lillevand	-	1-2	-	1-1	1	-	-	-	0	3
Al Dunbar	-	1-7	-	0-0	2	-	-	-	1	2
John Cunningham	-	0-1	-	0-1	1	-	-	-	1	0
Charles Russell	-	0-2	-	0-0	0	-	-	-	1	0
TOTALS	-	26-74	-	15-19	35	-	-	-	18	67
Percentages		35.1		78.9						

Coach: Phil Woolpert

Attendance: 16,034

California 54, Idaho State 43 (Sweet 16)

	1H	2H	Final
California	24	30	54
Idaho State	20	23	43

CALIFORNIA	MIN	FG	3FG	FT	REB	A	ST	BL	PF	TP
Earl Robinson	-	5-11	-	3-5	9	-	-	-	2	13
Bob Dalton	-	4-7	-	2-4	8	-	-	-	0	10
Don McIntosh	-	4-11	-	2-2	14	-	-	-	3	10
George Sterling	-	2-7	-	2-3	6	-	-	-	1	6
Al Buch	-	2-11	-	1-3	0	-	-	-	0	5
Earle Schneider	-	1-1	-	2-2	0	-	-	-	0	4
Denny Fitzpatrick	-	1-3	-	1-1	1	-	-	-	2	3
Darrall Imhoff	-	1-2	-	1-1	2	-	-	-	2	3
Jack Grout	-	0-1	-	0-0	1	-	-	-	0	0
Joe Kapp	-	0-0	-	0-1	0	-	-	-	0	0
TOTALS	-	20-54	-	14-22	41	-	-	-	10	54
Percentages		37.0		63.6						

Coach: Pete Newell

IDAHO STATE	MIN	FG	3FG	FT	REB	A	ST	BL	PF	TP
Gale Siemen	-	7-14	-	0-0	9	-	-	-	2	14
LeRoy Bacher	-	5-13	-	1-5	10	-	-	-	4	11
Joe Germaine	-	3-5	-	4-6	2	-	-	-	4	10
Roy Christian	-	0-2	-	2-2	7	-	-	-	4	2
Jerry Griffin	-	1-2	-	0-0	0	-	-	-	0	2
Alan Morris	-	1-2	-	0-0	0	-	-	-	2	2
Jim Rodgers	-	1-16	-	0-0	7	-	-	-	2	2
Ron Adelhardt	-	0-1	-	0-0	0	-	-	-	1	0
Don Kugler	-	0-0	-	0-0	0	-	-	-	0	0
TOTALS	-	18-55	-	7-13	35	-	-	-	19	43
Percentages		32.7		53.8						

Coach: John Grayson

Attendance: 16,034

Temple 69, Dartmouth 50 (Elite 8)

	1H	2H	Final
Temple	32	37	69
Dartmouth	22	28	50

TEMPLE	MIN	FG	3FG	FT	REB	A	ST	BL	PF	TP
Guy Rodgers	-	8-20	-	1-6	9	-	-	-	2	17
Mel Brodsky	-	6-12	-	4-4	8	-	-	-	4	16
Jay Norman	-	6-14	-	2-6	9	-	-	-	3	14
Bill Kennedy	-	6-10	-	1-1	3	-	-	-	3	13
Dan Fleming	-	3-6	-	1-1	4	-	-	-	2	7
Tink Van Patton	-	0-1	-	2-3	9	-	-	-	4	2
Ophie Franklin	-	0-0	-	0-0	0	-	-	-	0	0
Joe Goldenberg	-	0-0	-	0-0	0	-	-	-	0	0
Pete Goss	-	0-0	-	0-0	0	-	-	-	0	0
Jack Peepe	-	0-0	-	0-0	0	-	-	-	1	0
TOTALS	-	29-63	-	11-21	42	-	-	-	19	69
Percentages		46.0		52.4						

Coach: Harry Litwack

DARTMOUTH	MIN	FG	3FG	FT	REB	A	ST	BL	PF	TP
Rudy LaRusso	-	7-22	-	5-7	21	-	-	-	5	19
Gary Vandeweghe	-	4-12	-	2-7	6	-	-	-	3	10
Chuck Kaufman	-	2-14	-	5-6	5	-	-	-	3	9
David Gavitt	-	2-6	-	0-0	2	-	-	-	1	4
Walt Sosnowski	-	1-10	-	1-1	3	-	-	-	0	3
Tom Aley	-	1-2	-	0-0	2	-	-	-	2	2
David Farnsworth	-	1-7	-	0-3	10	-	-	-	0	2
M. David Carruthers	-	0-3	-	1-2	1	-	-	-	2	1
Harold Douglas	-	0-0	-	0-0	1	-	-	-	0	0
A. Stuart Hanson	-	0-0	-	0-0	0	-	-	-	0	0
Edward Hobbie	-	0-0	-	0-0	0	-	-	-	0	0
John Jones	-	0-1	-	0-1	1	-	-	-	0	0
TOTALS	-	18-77	-	14-27	52	-	-	-	16	50
Percentages		23.4		51.9						

Coach: Alvin "Doggie" Julian

Kentucky 89, Notre Dame 56 (Elite 8)

	1H	2H	Final
Kentucky	43	46	89
Notre Dame	31	25	56

KENTUCKY	MIN	FG	3FG	FT	REB	A	ST	BL	PF	TP
Vernon Hatton	-	11-22	-	4-5	9	-	-	-	2	26
Adrian Smith	-	4-10	-	8-8	3	-	-	-	3	16
Johnny Cox	-	6-18	-	2-3	13	-	-	-	2	14
Ed Beck	-	4-8	-	3-5	12	-	-	-	3	11
John Crigler	-	4-10	-	3-3	15	-	-	-	1	11
Don Mills	-	1-1	-	1-2	0	-	-	-	0	3
Billy Cassady	-	0-1	-	2-3	1	-	-	-	1	2
Linc Collinsworth	-	1-3	-	0-0	1	-	-	-	1	2
Harold Ross	-	0-0	-	2-2	1	-	-	-	1	2
Bill Smith	-	1-2	-	0-0	1	-	-	-	0	2
Earl Adkins	-	0-1	-	0-0	1	-	-	-	0	0
Phil Johnson	-	0-2	-	0-0	3	-	-	-	0	0
TOTALS	-	32-78	-	25-31	60	-	-	-	14	89
Percentages		41.0		80.6						

Coach: Adolph Rupp

NOTRE DAME	MIN	FG	3FG	FT	REB	A	ST	BL	PF	TP
John McCarthy	-	7-18	-	3-3	8	-	-	-	2	17
Tom Hawkins	-	7-24	-	1-4	16	-	-	-	4	15
Robert Devine	-	3-9	-	1-1	1	-	-	-	1	7
Thomas Reinhart	-	3-13	-	0-0	10	-	-	-	4	6
Edward Gleason	-	1-4	-	2-3	0	-	-	-	0	4
Michael Graney	-	1-6	-	2-3	5	-	-	-	4	4
Robert Bradtke	-	0-0	-	2-2	1	-	-	-	1	2
Eugene Duffy	-	0-3	-	1-2	0	-	-	-	4	1
Lee Ayotte	-	0-0	-	0-0	0	-	-	-	1	0
Michael Ireland	-	0-0	-	0-0	0	-	-	-	1	0
James Williams	-	0-1	-	0-0	0	-	-	-	0	0
TOTALS	-	22-78	-	12-18	41	-	-	-	22	56
Percentages		28.2		66.7						

Coach: John Jordan

Officials: Mihalik, Mills
Attendance: 12,000

Kansas State 69, Oklahoma State 57 (Elite 8)

	1H	2H	Final
Kansas State	38	31	69
Oklahoma State	31	26	57

KANSAS STATE	MIN	FG	3FG	FT	REB	A	ST	BL	PF	TP
Bob Boozer	-	12-16	-	2-5	9	-	-	-	3	26
Don Matuszak	-	6-7	-	2-2	5	-	-	-	4	14
Jack Parr	-	5-14	-	3-5	10	-	-	-	4	13
Wally Frank	-	4-11	-	2-2	8	-	-	-	4	10
Roy DeWitz	-	3-6	-	0-2	2	-	-	-	4	6
James Abbott	-	0-1	-	0-0	0	-	-	-	0	0
Sonny Ballard	-	0-0	-	0-0	0	-	-	-	0	0
Larry Fischer	-	0-0	-	0-0	0	-	-	-	0	0
Jim Holwerda	-	0-0	-	0-1	0	-	-	-	0	0
Glen Long	-	0-0	-	0-0	0	-	-	-	0	0
TOTALS	-	30-55	-	9-17	34	-	-	-	19	69
Percentages		54.5		52.9						

Coach: Tex Winter

OKLAHOMA STATE	MIN	FG	3FG	FT	REB	A	ST	BL	PF	TP
Arlen Clark	-	8-22	-	8-12	8	-	-	-	4	24
Jerry Hale	-	4-9	-	3-4	5	-	-	-	3	11
Jerry Adair	-	2-10	-	3-4	5	-	-	-	0	7
Joe Crutchfield	-	2-8	-	2-2	1	-	-	-	3	6
Eddie Sutton	-	2-2	-	1-1	0	-	-	-	1	5
Roy Carberry	-	0-3	-	2-2	0	-	-	-	2	2
Dick Soergel	-	0-1	-	2-2	0	-	-	-	0	2
Don Heffington	-	0-0	-	0-0	1	-	-	-	1	0
Dennis Walker	-	0-0	-	0-0	0	-	-	-	0	0
TOTALS	-	18-55	-	21-27	20	-	-	-	14	57
Percentages		32.7		77.8						

Coach: Hank Iba

Officials: Batmale, Mercer

Seattle 66, California 62 (Elite 8)

	1H	2H	OT1	Final
Seattle	29	31	6	66
California	37	23	2	62

SEATTLE	MIN	FG	3FG	FT	REB	A	ST	BL	PF	TP
Elgin Baylor	-	9-25	-	8-8	18	-	-	-	3	26
Charlie Brown	-	5-11	-	0-0	5	-	-	-	2	10
Francis Saunders	-	4-7	-	2-3	8	-	-	-	1	10
Jim Harney	-	2-7	-	5-5	1	-	-	-	2	9
Don Ogorek	-	3-9	-	2-2	7	-	-	-	4	8
Jerry Frizzell	-	1-2	-	1-1	1	-	-	-	3	3
Don Piasecki	-	0-2	-	0-0	0	-	-	-	1	0
TOTALS	-	24-63	-	18-19	40	-	-	-	16	66
Percentages		38.1		94.7						

Coach: John Castellani

CALIFORNIA	MIN	FG	3FG	FT	REB	A	ST	BL	PF	TP
Don McIntosh	-	7-14	-	2-3	10	-	-	-	1	16
Earl Robinson	-	6-18	-	3-6	6	-	-	-	2	15
George Sterling	-	7-10	-	1-2	3	-	-	-	4	15
Al Buch	-	4-10	-	2-4	7	-	-	-	2	10
Bob Dalton	-	1-6	-	1-2	4	-	-	-	5	3
Jack Grout	-	1-1	-	0-0	2	-	-	-	0	2
Denny Fitzpatrick	-	0-3	-	1-1	0	-	-	-	0	1
TOTALS	-	26-62	-	10-18	32	-	-	-	14	62
Percentages		41.9		55.6						

Coach: Pete Newell

Officials: Lichty, Morrow
Attendance: 16,034

KENTUCKY	MIN	FG	3FG	FT	REB	A	ST	BL	PF	TP
Johnny Cox	-	6-17	-	10-11	13	-	-	-	4	22
Vernon Hatton	-	5-16	-	3-4	2	-	-	-	3	13
Adrian Smith	-	2-10	-	8-9	5	-	-	-	3	12
Ed Beck	-	3-9	-	2-2	15	-	-	-	2	8
John Crigler	-	3-11	-	0-2	9	-	-	-	4	6
Linc Collinsworth	-	0-0	-	0-0	0	-	-	-	1	0
TOTALS	-	19-63	-	23-28	44	-	-	-	17	61
Percentages		30.2		82.1						

Coach: Adolph Rupp

61-60

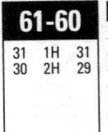

31 1H 31
30 2H 29

FINAL 4

TEMPLE	MIN	FG	3FG	FT	REB	A	ST	BL	PF	TP
Guy Rodgers	-	9-24	-	4-6	5	-	-	-	4	22
Jay Norman	-	7-17	-	2-3	6	-	-	-	3	16
Dan Fleming	-	3-7	-	3-6	5	-	-	-	1	9
Bill Kennedy	-	3-7	-	0-1	3	-	-	-	4	6
Mel Brodsky	-	2-5	-	0-2	14	-	-	-	2	4
Tink Van Patton	-	1-1	-	1-2	3	-	-	-	4	3
TOTALS	-	25-61	-	10-20	36	-	-	-	18	60
Percentages		41.0		50.0						

Coach: Harry Litwack

Officials: Morrow, Mercer
Attendance: 18,586

SEATTLE	MIN	FG	3FG	FT	REB	A	ST	BL	PF	TP
Elgin Baylor	-	9-21	-	5-7	22	-	-	-	3	23
Charlie Brown	-	5-6	-	4-5	13	-	-	-	2	14
Francis Saunders	-	5-11	-	2-3	8	-	-	-	1	12
Jerry Frizzell	-	2-4	-	6-7	2	-	-	-	2	10
Don Ogorek	-	3-9	-	1-2	4	-	-	-	4	7
Don Piasecki	-	1-1	-	3-4	0	-	-	-	1	5
John Kootnekoff	-	1-1	-	0-0	0	-	-	-	0	2
Jim Harney	-	0-4	-	0-0	2	-	-	-	1	0
Thornton Humphries	-	0-0	-	0-0	0	-	-	-	0	0
Jack Petrie	-	0-0	-	0-0	0	-	-	-	0	0
TOTALS	-	26-57	-	21-28	51	-	-	-	14	73
Percentages		45.6		75.0						

Coach: John Castellani

73-51

37 1H 32
36 2H 19

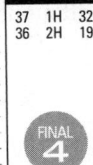

FINAL 4

KANSAS STATE	MIN	FG	3FG	FT	REB	A	ST	BL	PF	TP
Bob Boozer	-	6-15	-	3-5	4	-	-	-	4	15
Wally Frank	-	6-12	-	3-4	7	-	-	-	4	15
Don Matuszak	-	3-8	-	1-3	7	-	-	-	1	7
Roy DeWitz	-	2-7	-	2-3	0	-	-	-	2	6
Glen Long	-	2-6	-	0-1	4	-	-	-	2	4
Jack Parr	-	2-11	-	0-1	8	-	-	-	1	4
James Abbott	-	0-4	-	0-0	2	-	-	-	1	0
Larry Fischer	-	0-1	-	0-0	0	-	-	-	1	0
Jim Holwerda	-	0-2	-	0-0	1	-	-	-	2	0
TOTALS	-	21-66	-	9-17	33	-	-	-	18	51
Percentages		31.8		52.9						

Coach: Tex Winter

Officials: Conway, Mihalik
Attendance: 18,586

TEMPLE	MIN	FG	3FG	FT	REB	A	ST	BL	PF	TP
Bill Kennedy	-	8-16	-	7-9	0	-	-	-	0	23
Guy Rodgers	-	7-17	-	3-3	4	-	-	-	2	17
Mel Brodsky	-	4-13	-	2-5	12	-	-	-	3	10
Dan Fleming	-	2-3	-	3-3	6	-	-	-	4	7
Jay Norman	-	1-11	-	5-8	13	-	-	-	3	7
Tink Van Patton	-	1-6	-	1-3	12	-	-	-	5	3
TOTALS	-	23-66	-	21-31	47	-	-	-	17	67
Percentages		34.8		67.7						

Coach: Harry Litwack

67-57

28 1H 39
39 2H 18

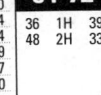

3RD PLACE

KANSAS STATE	MIN	FG	3FG	FT	REB	A	ST	BL	PF	TP
Bob Boozer	-	6-19	-	7-9	12	-	-	-	4	19
James Abbott	-	6-11	-	2-2	3	-	-	-	3	14
Wally Frank	-	3-9	-	2-3	11	-	-	-	2	8
Jack Parr	-	1-13	-	5-8	10	-	-	-	2	7
Roy DeWitz	-	3-12	-	0-1	4	-	-	-	1	6
Don Matuszak	-	1-4	-	1-3	2	-	-	-	4	3
Sonny Ballard	-	0-1	-	0-0	0	-	-	-	1	0
Steve Douglas	-	0-1	-	0-0	1	-	-	-	3	0
Jim Holwerda	-	0-1	-	0-0	0	-	-	-	2	0
TOTALS	-	20-71	-	17-26	43	-	-	-	22	57
Percentages		28.2		65.4						

Coach: Tex Winter

Attendance: 18,803

KENTUCKY	MIN	FG	3FG	FT	REB	A	ST	BL	PF	TP
Vernon Hatton	-	9-20	-	12-15	3	-	-	-	3	30
Johnny Cox	-	10-23	-	4-4	16	-	-	-	3	24
John Crigler	-	5-12	-	4-7	14	-	-	-	4	14
Don Mills	-	4-9	-	1-4	5	-	-	-	3	9
Adrian Smith	-	2-8	-	3-5	6	-	-	-	4	7
Ed Beck	-	0-1	-	0-1	3	-	-	-	4	0
TOTALS	-	30-73	-	24-36	47	-	-	-	21	84
Percentages		41.1		66.7						

Coach: Adolph Rupp

84-72

36 1H 39
48 2H 33

NCAA FINAL 1958

SEATTLE	MIN	FG	3FG	FT	REB	A	ST	BL	PF	TP
Elgin Baylor	-	9-32	-	7-9	19	-	-	-	4	25
Charlie Brown	-	6-17	-	5-7	5	-	-	-	5	17
Jerry Frizzell	-	4-6	-	8-11	5	-	-	-	3	16
Don Ogorek	-	4-7	-	2-2	11	-	-	-	5	10
Jim Harney	-	2-5	-	0-1	1	-	-	-	1	4
Don Piasecki	-	0-0	-	0-0	0	-	-	-	0	0
Francis Saunders	-	0-2	-	0-0	2	-	-	-	3	0
TOTALS	-	25-69	-	22-30	43	-	-	-	21	72
Percentages		36.2		73.3						

Coach: John Castellani

Officials: Conway, Unknown
Attendance: 18,803

NATIONAL INVITATION TOURNAMENT (NIT)

First round: St. John's d. Butler 76-69, Saint Joseph's d. Saint Peter's 83-76, Xavier d. Niagara 95-86, Fordham d. Saint Francis (PA) 83-59
Quarterfinals: St. John's d. Utah 71-70, St. Bonaventure d. Saint Joseph's 79-75, Xavier d. Bradley 72-62, Dayton d. Fordham 74-70
Semifinals: Dayton d. St. John's 80-56, Xavier d. St. Bonaventure 72-53
Third place: St. Bonaventure d. St. John's 84-69
Championship: Xavier d. Dayton 78-74 (OT)
MVP: Hank Stein, Xavier

1958-59: Bear Claws

California's defensive-minded coach, Pete Newell, faced consecutive Final Four games against Cincinnati's Oscar Robertson and West Virginia's Jerry West. During the regular season, Robertson averaged 32.6 points per game along with 16.3 rpg and 6.9 apg—the first player to lead the nation in scoring as both a sophomore and a junior. In the semis, Cal and Newell limited the Big O to 19 points. West fared better against the Golden Bears in the Final, scoring 28 (his average was 26.6) in the back-and-forth contest. But with :17 left, Darrall Imhoff tipped in the winning bucket to give Cal (25–4) the 71-70 victory and its first national title. West was the fourth consecutive MOP from a nonchampionship team.

The Pacific Coast Conference disbanded after the season, following revelations of athletes receiving slush-fund payments from booster clubs. Five schools, including Cal, went on to form the Athletic Association of Western Universities, the forerunner of today's Pac-10. Kansas State's Bob Boozer, the No. 1 pick in the NBA draft, decided to put off his pro career to be part of the gold-medal-winning 1960 U.S. Olympic team.

Major Conference Standings

ACC

	Conference			Overall		
	W	L	Pct	W	L	Pct
NC State	12	2	.857	22	4	.846
North Carolina⊕	12	2	.857	20	5	.800
Duke	7	7	.500	13	12	.520
Maryland	7	7	.500	10	13	.435
Virginia	6	8	.429	11	14	.440
Wake Forest	5	9	.357	10	14	.417
Clemson	5	9	.357	8	16	.333
South Carolina	2	12	.143	4	20	.167

Tournament: **NC State d. North Carolina 80-56**
Tournament MVP: **Lou Pucillo**, NC State

Big Eight

	Conference			Overall		
	W	L	Pct	W	L	Pct
Kansas State⊕	14	0	1.000	25	2	.926
Oklahoma	9	5	.643	15	10	.600
Colorado	8	6	.571	14	10	.583
Kansas	8	6	.571	11	14	.440
Nebraska	5	9	.357	12	13	.480
Oklahoma State	5	9	.357	11	14	.440
Iowa State	4	10	.286	9	16	.360
Missouri	3	11	.214	6	19	.240

Big Ten

	Conference			Overall		
	W	L	Pct	W	L	Pct
Michigan State⊕	12	2	.857	19	4	.826
Michigan	8	6	.571	15	7	.682
Northwestern	8	6	.571	15	7	.682
Purdue	8	6	.571	15	7	.682
Illinois	7	7	.500	12	10	.545
Indiana	7	7	.500	11	11	.500
Ohio State	7	7	.500	11	11	.500
Iowa	7	7	.500	10	12	.455
Minnesota	5	9	.357	8	14	.364
Wisconsin	1	13	.071	3	19	.136

Border

	Conference			Overall		
	W	L	Pct	W	L	Pct
New Mexico State⊕	7	3	.700	17	11	.607
Arizona State	7	3	.700	17	9	.654
Texas Western	7	3	.700	14	9	.609
West Texas A&M	5	5	.500	6	16	.273
Hardin-Simmons	3	7	.300	14	12	.538
Arizona	1	9	.100	4	22	.154

Ivy

	Conference			Overall		
	W	L	Pct	W	L	Pct
Dartmouth○	13	1	.929	22	6	.786
Princeton	13	1	.929	19	5	.792
Yale	9	5	.643	10	13	.435
Brown	6	8	.429	11	13	.458
Penn	5	9	.357	12	14	.462
Harvard	4	10	.286	10	15	.400
Cornell	4	10	.286	8	15	.348
Columbia	2	12	.143	3	21	.125

Metro NY

	Conference			Overall		
	W	L	Pct	W	L	Pct
Manhattan□	4	0	1.000	15	6	.714
Brooklyn	3	1	.750	8	10	.444
St. John's□	4	2	.667	20	6	.769
Fordham□	2	2	.500	17	8	.680
NYU□	2	2	.500	15	8	.652
CCNY	1	6	.143	6	12	.333
St. Francis (NY)	0	3	.000	5	18	.217

Mid-American

	Conference			Overall		
	W	L	Pct	W	L	Pct
Bowling Green⊕	9	3	.750	18	8	.692
Miami (OH)	9	3	.750	14	11	.560
Ohio	6	6	.500	14	10	.583
Marshall	6	6	.500	12	12	.500
Kent State	6	6	.500	11	13	.458
Toledo	5	7	.417	11	13	.458
Western Michigan	1	11	.083	2	20	.091

Middle Atlantic

	Conference			Overall		
	W	L	Pct	W	L	Pct
Saint Joseph's⊕	7	0	1.000	22	5	.815
La Salle	5	2	.714	16	7	.696
Muhlenberg	8	6	.571	13	9	.591
Bucknell	6	5	.545	16	7	.696
Lafayette	7	6	.538	13	8	.619
Gettysburg	4	5	.444	13	13	.500
Delaware	4	6	.400	9	13	.409
Rutgers	3	5	.375	9	15	.375
Temple	4	7	.364	6	19	.240
Lehigh	4	10	.286	6	16	.273

Missouri Valley

	Conference			Overall		
	W	L	Pct	W	L	Pct
Cincinnati⊕	13	1	.929	26	4	.867
Bradley□	12	2	.857	25	4	.862
Saint Louis□	10	4	.714	20	6	.769
Wichita State	7	7	.500	14	12	.538
Houston	6	8	.429	12	14	.462
Drake	4	10	.286	9	15	.375
Tulsa	2	12	.143	10	15	.400
North Texas	2	12	.143	6	18	.250

Skyline 8

	Conference			Overall		
	W	L	Pct	W	L	Pct
Utah⊕	13	1	.929	21	7	.750
Utah State	10	4	.714	19	7	.731
Denver□	10	4	.714	14	10	.583
BYU	8	6	.571	15	11	.577
Montana	7	7	.500	10	14	.417
Colorado State	6	8	.429	8	14	.364
Wyoming	1	13	.071	4	22	.154
New Mexico	1	13	.071	3	19	.136

Ohio Valley

	Conference			Overall		
	W	L	Pct	W	L	Pct
Eastern Kentucky⊕	10	2	.833	16	6	.727
Western Kentucky	8	4	.667	16	10	.615
Tennessee Tech	7	5	.583	16	9	.640
East Tennessee State	5	7	.417	13	10	.565
Morehead State	5	7	.417	11	12	.478
Middle Tenn State	4	8	.333	9	17	.346
Murray State	3	9	.250	10	15	.400

Pacific Coast

	Conference			Overall		
	W	L	Pct	W	L	Pct
California⊕	14	2	.875	25	4	.862
Washington	11	5	.688	18	8	.692
UCLA	10	6	.625	16	9	.640
Stanford	10	6	.625	15	9	.625
Southern California	8	8	.500	15	11	.577
Oregon State	7	9	.438	13	13	.500
Idaho	6	10	.375	11	15	.423
Washington State	3	13	.188	10	16	.385
Oregon	3	13	.188	9	16	.360

SEC

	Conference			Overall		
	W	L	Pct	W	L	Pct
Mississippi State	13	1	.929	24	1	.960
Auburn	12	2	.857	20	2	.909
Kentucky⊕	12	2	.857	24	3	.889
Georgia Tech	9	5	.643	17	9	.654
Tennessee	8	6	.571	14	8	.636
Vanderbilt	8	6	.571	14	10	.583
Tulane	6	8	.429	13	11	.542
Alabama	6	8	.429	10	12	.455
Georgia	5	9	.357	11	15	.423
LSU	2	12	.143	10	15	.400
Florida	2	12	.143	8	15	.348
Mississippi	1	13	.071	7	17	.292

Southern

	Conference			Overall		
	W	L	Pct	W	L	Pct
West Virginia⊕	11	0	1.000	29	5	.853
Virginia Tech	10	2	.833	16	5	.762
The Citadel	7	4	.636	15	5	.750
William and Mary	7	7	.500	13	11	.542
Richmond	6	8	.429	11	11	.500
Furman	5	7	.417	14	12	.538
George Washington	4	7	.364	14	11	.560
Davidson	2	8	.200	9	15	.375
VMI	2	11	.154	5	13	.278

Tournament: **West Virginia d. The Citadel 85-66**
Tournament MOP: **Jerry West**, West Virginia

Southwest

	Conference			Overall		
	W	L	Pct	W	L	Pct
TCU⊕	12	2	.857	20	6	.769
SMU	10	4	.714	16	8	.667
Texas Tech	8	6	.571	15	9	.625
Baylor	7	7	.500	11	13	.458
Texas A&M	6	8	.429	15	9	.625
Arkansas	6	8	.429	9	14	.391
Rice	5	9	.357	11	13	.458
Texas	2	12	.143	4	20	.167

WCAC

	Conference			Overall		
	W	L	Pct	W	L	Pct
Saint Mary's (CA)⊕	11	1	.917	19	6	.760
Santa Clara	9	3	.750	16	9	.640
Pepperdine	8	4	.667	16	8	.667
Pacific	6	6	.500	11	15	.423
Loyola Marymount	4	8	.333	8	15	.348
San Francisco	3	9	.250	6	20	.231
San Jose State	1	11	.083	5	19	.208

Yankee

	Conference			Overall		
	W	L	Pct	W	L	Pct
Connecticut⊕	8	2	.800	17	7	.708
Maine	7	3	.700	15	7	.682
Massachusetts	5	5	.500	11	13	.458
Rhode Island	5	5	.500	8	12	.400
Vermont	4	6	.400	12	10	.545
New Hampshire	1	9	.100	9	14	.391

⊕ Automatic NCAA Tournament bid ○ At-large NCAA Tournament bid □ NIT appearance ⊗ Team record doesn't reflect games forfeited or vacated. For adjusted record, see p. 521.

INDEPENDENTS

	Overall W	L	Pct
St. Bonaventure□	20	3	.870
Saint Francis (PA)	20	5	.800
Marquette○	23	6	.793
Seattle	21	6	.778
Idaho State○	21	7	.750
Navy○	18	6	.750
Boston U.○	20	7	.741
Oklahoma City□	20	7	.741
Providence□	20	7	.741
Miami (FL)	18	7	.720
Villanova□	18	7	.720
Portland○	19	8	.704
Memphis	15	7	.682
Niagara	15	7	.682
Butler□	19	9	.679
Iona	14	7	.667
Boston College	17	9	.654
Louisville○	19	12	.613
Air Force	14	9	.609
Syracuse	14	9	.609
Army	14	10	.583

INDEPENDENTS (CONT.)

	Overall W	L	Pct
Seton Hall	13	10	.565
Holy Cross	14	11	.560
Penn State	11	9	.550
DePaul○	13	11	.542
Duquesne	13	11	.542
Dayton	14	12	.538
Notre Dame	12	13	.480
Xavier	12	13	.480
Loyola-Chicago	11	13	.458
Detroit	11	14	.440
Gonzaga	11	15	.423
Pittsburgh	10	14	.417
Wash.-St. Louis	9	13	.409
Loyola (LA)	10	16	.385
Colgate	7	12	.368
Florida State	8	15	.348
Georgetown	8	15	.348
Canisius	7	16	.304
Siena	3	16	.158
Washington and Lee	1	15	.063

INDIVIDUAL LEADERS—SEASON

Scoring

	CL	POS	G	FG	FT	PTS	PPG
1 **Oscar Robertson**, Cincinnati	JR	G/F	30	331	316	978	**32.6**
2 **Leo Byrd**, Marshall	SR	G	24	242	220	704	**29.3**
3 **Jim Hagan**, Tennessee Tech	JR	C	25	254	212	720	**28.8**
4 **Bailey Howell**, Mississippi State	SR	C	25	231	226	688	**27.5**
5 **Jerry West**, West Virginia	JR	G	34	340	223	903	**26.6**
6 **Bob Ayersman**, Virginia Tech	SO	F	21	204	148	556	**26.5**
7 **Don Hennon**, Pittsburgh	SR	G	24	231	155	617	**25.7**
8 **Bob Boozer**, Kansas State	SR	F	27	247	197	691	**25.6**
9 **Tony Windis**, Wyoming	SR	G	19	178	107	463	**24.4**
10 **Tom Hawkins**, Notre Dame	SR	F	22	197	120	514	**23.4**

Field Goal Pct

	CL	POS	G	FG	FGA	PCT
1 **Ralph Crosthwaite**, Western Kentucky	SR	C	26	191	296	**64.5**
2 **George Carter**, Iona	SR	F	21	137	225	**60.9**
3 **Mel Kessler**, Muhlenberg	SR	F	22	153	271	**56.5**
4 **Bob Herdelin**, La Salle	SO	F	22	144	256	**56.3**
5 **Tom Sanders**, NYU	JR	C	23	131	236	**55.5**

Minimum: 100 made

Free Throw Pct

	CL	POS	G	FT	FTA	PCT
1 **Arlen Clark**, Oklahoma State	SR	C	25	201	236	**85.2**
2 **Frank Burgess**, Gonzaga	SO	G	26	151	178	**84.8**
3 **Paul Neumann**, Stanford	SR	G	24	127	150	**84.7**
4 **Roger Kaiser**, Georgia Tech	SO	G	26	106	127	**83.5**
5 **Roger Wendel**, Tulsa	SR	G	25	185	222	**83.3**

Minimum: 90 made

INDIVIDUAL LEADERS—GAME

Points

	CL	POS	OPP	DATE	PTS
1 **Bob Beckel**, Air Force	SR	G	Arizona	F29	**50**
Tom Harrington, Rhode Island	JR	G	Brandeis	F4	**50**
3 **Jim Hagan**, Tennessee Tech	JR	C	East Tennessee State	F16	**48**
4 **Bailey Howell**, Mississippi St.	SR	C	Union	D4	**47**
Bob Ayersman, Virginia Tech	SO	F	Richmond	F10	**47**

Free Throws Made

	CL	POS	OPP	DATE	FT	FTA	PCT
1 **Arlen Clark**, Oklahoma State	SR	C	Colorado	M7	**24**	24	100.0
2 **Bob Boozer**, Kansas State	SR	F	Purdue	D1	**23**	26	88.5
3 **Oscar Robertson**, Cincinnati	JR	G/F	North Texas	J12	**22**	25	88.0
4 **Tom Harrington**, Rhode Island	JR	G	Brandeis	F4	**20**	23	87.0
5 **Arlen Clark**, Oklahoma State	SR	C	Oklahoma	J24	**19**	20	95.0

TEAM LEADERS-SEASON

Scoring Offense

	G	W-L	PTS	PPG
1 **Miami (FL)**	25	18-7	2,190	**87.6**
2 **West Virginia**	34	29-5	2,884	**84.8**
3 **Cincinnati**	30	26-4	2,519	**84.0**
4 **Virginia Tech**	21	16-5	1,758	**83.7**
5 **Illinois**	22	12-10	1,815	**82.5**

Scoring Defense

	G	W-L	OPP PTS	OPP PPG
1 **California**	29	25-4	1,480	**51.0**
2 **Oklahoma State**	25	11-14	1,319	**52.8**
3 **Idaho State**	28	21-7	1,504	**53.7**
4 **San Jose State**	24	5-19	1,352	**56.3**
5 **Maryland**	23	10-13	1,296	**56.4**

Field Goal Pct

	G	W-L	FG	FGA	PCT
1 **Auburn**	22	20-2	593	1,216	**48.8**
2 **Cincinnati**	30	26-4	970	2,062	**47.0**
3 **Oklahoma City**	27	20-7	769	1,680	**45.8**
4 **St. Bonaventure**	23	20-3	724	1,584	**45.7**
5 **West Virginia**	34	29-5	1075	2,355	**45.6**

Free Throw Pct

	G	W-L	FT	FTA	PCT
1 **Tulsa**	25	10-15	446	586	**76.1**
2 **Mississippi State**	25	24-1	532	700	**76.0**
3 **George Washington**	25	14-11	402	534	**75.3**
4 **Kentucky**	27	24-3	570	758	**75.2**
5 **Marshall**	24	12-12	472	631	**74.8**

CONSENSUS ALL-AMERICAS

First Team

PLAYER	CL	POS	HT	SCHOOL	RPG	PPG
Bob Boozer	SR	F	6-8	Kansas State	11.3	25.6
Johnny Cox	SR	F	6-4	Kentucky	12.2	18.0
Bailey Howell	SR	C	6-7	Mississippi State	15.2	27.5
Oscar Robertson	JR	G/F	6-5	Cincinnati	16.3	32.6
Jerry West	JR	G	6-3	West Virginia	12.3	26.6

Second Team

PLAYER	CL	POS	HT	SCHOOL	RPG	PPG
Leo Byrd	SR	G	6-1	Marshall	5.3	29.3
Johnny Green	SR	F	6-5	Michigan State	16.6	18.5
Tom Hawkins	SR	F	6-5	Notre Dame	15.2	23.4
Don Hennon	SR	G	5-9	Pittsburgh	4.4	25.7
Alan Seiden	SR	G	5-11	St. John's	3.9	21.9

Selectors: AP, Look Magazine, NABC, Newspaper Enterprises Assn., UPI

AWARD WINNERS

Player of the Year

PLAYER	CL	POS	HT	SCHOOL	AWARDS
Oscar Robertson	JR	G/F	6-5	Cincinnati	UPI, USBWA

Coach of the Year

COACH	SCHOOL	REC	AWARDS
Adolph Rupp	Kentucky	24-3	UPI
Eddie Hickey	Marquette	23-6	USBWA

ANNUAL REVIEW

Poll Progression

Preseason Poll

UPI	SCHOOL
1	**Cincinnati** Ⓐ
2	**Kansas State**
3	**Notre Dame**
4	**Kentucky**
5	**Michigan State**
6	**Washington**
7	**West Virginia**
8	**Xavier**
9	**Oklahoma State**
10	**St. John's**
11	**Maryland**
12	**NC State**
13	**Northwestern**
14	**North Carolina**
15	**Saint Joseph's**
16	**Saint Louis**
17	**Mississippi State**
18	**Purdue**
19	**Louisville**
20	**Iowa**

Week of Dec 9

AP	UPI	SCHOOL
1	1	**Cincinnati** (2-0)
2	3	**Kentucky** (2-0)
3	2	**Kansas State** (2-0)
4	7	**West Virginia** (3-0)
5	6	**NC State** (3-0)
6	16	**Tennessee** (3-0)
7	12	**Kansas** (2-0)
8	17	**Mississippi State** (3-0)
9	9	**Saint Louis** (2-0)
10	7	**Northwestern** (2-0)
11	5	**Notre Dame** (1-0)
12	—	**Auburn** (2-0)
13	19	**North Carolina** (2-0)
14	11	**Saint Mary's (CA)** (2-0)
15	4	**Michigan State** (1-0)
16	13	**Xavier** (2-0)
17	19	**Marquette** (2-0)
18	—	**SMU** (1-1)
19	—	**Indiana** (4-1)
20	10	**St. John's** (1-0)
20	18	**Oklahoma State** (1-0)
—	13	**Utah** (2-0)
—	15	**TCU** (2-0)
—	19	**Texas Tech** (3-0)

Week of Dec 16

AP	UPI	SCHOOL	AP↓↑
1	1	**Cincinnati** (3-0)	
2	3	**Kentucky** (5-0)	
3	2	**Kansas State** (4-0)	
4	4	**NC State** (4-0)	↑1
5	12	**Tennessee** (4-0)	↑1
6	5	**Northwestern** (3-0)	↑4
7	7	**West Virginia** (5-1)	↓3
8	17	**Mississippi State** (5-0)	
9	8	**Xavier** (4-0)	↑7
10	14	**North Carolina** (2-0)	↑3
11	6	**Michigan State** (2-0)	↑4
11	16	**Bradley** (4-0)	⤴
13	—	**Auburn** (2-0)	↓1
14	9	**Saint Joseph's** (4-0)	⤴
15	—	**California** (3-1)	⤴
16	—	**Seattle** (4-0)	⤴
17	—	**Saint Louis** (2-1)	↓8
18	—	**Pittsburgh** (3-1)	⤴
19	18	**UCLA** (1-2)	⤴
20	—	**SMU** (3-2)	↓2
—	10	**TCU** (4-1)	
—	11	**Indiana** (4-1)	⤵
—	13	**Utah** (4-1)	
—	14	**USC** (3-0)	
—	19	**Purdue** (3-1)	
—	20	**Kansas** (2-3)	⤵

Week of Dec 23

AP	UPI	SCHOOL	AP↓↑
1	2	**Kentucky** (8-0)	↑1
2	1	**Cincinnati** (5-0)	↓1
3	5	**North Carolina** (5-0)	↑7
4	3	**Kansas State** (6-1)	↓1
5	7	**West Virginia** (7-2)	↑2
6	6	**NC State** (6-1)	↓2
7	14	**Mississippi State** (7-0)	↑1
8	9	**Auburn** (5-0)	↑5
9	4	**Michigan State** (4-0)	↑2
10	8	**Xavier** (5-0)	↓1
11	—	**Tennessee** (5-1)	↓6
12	10	**Northwestern** (4-1)	↓6
13	12	**Bradley** (5-0)	↓2
14	10	**California** (5-1)	↑1
15	—	**Villanova** (6-0)	⤴
16	—	**Saint Louis** (3-2)	↑1
17	—	**Marquette** (7-1)	⤴
18	—	**Memphis** (5-0)	⤴
19	18	**Washington** (5-2)	⤴
20	—	**Dayton** (4-0)	⤴
—	13	**TCU** (5-1)	
—	15	**St. John's** (5-1)	
—	16	**Purdue** (5-1)	
—	17	**St. Bonaventure** (4-0)	
—	18	**Utah** (4-2)	
—	20	**Saint Joseph's** (6-1)	⤵

Week of Dec 30

AP	UPI	SCHOOL	AP↓↑
1	2	**Kentucky** (8-0)	
2	1	**Cincinnati** (5-0)	
3	3	**Kansas State** (7-1)	↑1
4	5	**North Carolina** (5-0)	↓1
5	6	**NC State** (6-1)	↑1
6	7	**Northwestern** (6-1)	↑6
7	4	**Michigan State** (4-0)	↑2
8	16	**Mississippi State** (7-0)	↓1
9	10	**Auburn** (6-0)	↓1
10	8	**Bradley** (7-0)	↑3
11	14	**West Virginia** (7-3)	↓6
12	13	**Saint Joseph's** (8-1)	⤴
13	12	**St. John's** (7-1)	⤴
14	—	**Tennessee** (6-1)	↓3
15	19	**Marquette** (9-1)	↑2
16	17	**Saint Louis** (3-3)	
17	—	**Oklahoma City** (7-1)	⤴
18	11	**Purdue** (7-1)	⤴
19	9	**TCU** (7-1)	⤴
20	15	**California** (6-2)	↓6
—	18	**Xavier** (6-2)	⤵
—	20	**Washington** (6-3)	⤵

Week of Jan 6

AP	UPI	SCHOOL	AP↓↑
1	1	**Kentucky** (11-0)	
2	2	**NC State** (9-1)	↑3
3	4	**North Carolina** (8-1)	↑1
4	3	**Kansas State** (9-1)	↓1
5	5	**Michigan State** (7-1)	↑2
6	9	**Auburn** (8-0)	↑3
7	6	**Cincinnati** (6-2)	↓5
8	7	**Northwestern** (8-1)	↓2
9	8	**Bradley** (8-0)	↑1
10	10	**St. John's** (9-1)	↑3
11	11	**West Virginia** (9-3)	
12	15	**Mississippi State** (10-1)	↓4
13	19	**Oklahoma City** (8-1)	↑4
14	—	**Saint Louis** (5-3)	↑2
15	18	**Marquette** (10-1)	
16	—	**Seattle** (8-2)	⤴
17	—	**Tennessee** (7-2)	↓3
18	—	**Villanova** (7-0)	⤴
19	12	**Texas A&M** (9-1)	⤴
20	—	**Illinois** (6-2)	⤴
—	13	**TCU** (8-2)	⤵
—	14	**California** (7-3)	⤵
—	15	**Purdue** (7-3)	⤵
—	17	**St. Bonaventure** (6-0)	
—	19	**Utah State** (9-3)	

Week of Jan 13

AP	UPI	SCHOOL	AP↓↑
1	2	**NC State** (11-1)	↑1
2	1	**Kentucky** (12-1)	↓1
3	4	**North Carolina** (9-1)	
4	3	**Kansas State** (11-1)	
5	7	**Auburn** (10-0)	↑1
6	5	**Cincinnati** (8-2)	↑1
7	8	**Bradley** (9-1)	↑2
8	6	**Michigan State** (8-2)	↓3
9	10	**St. John's** (10-1)	↑1
10	12	**West Virginia** (12-3)	↑1
11	9	**Northwestern** (9-2)	↓3
12	17	**Mississippi State** (11-1)	
13	14	**Marquette** (12-1)	↑2
14	13	**St. Bonaventure** (7-0)	⤴
15	16	**Saint Louis** (7-3)	↓1
16	—	**Seattle** (9-3)	
17	—	**Oklahoma City** (10-1)	↓4
18	—	**Portland** (10-2)	⤴
19	18	**Indiana** (5-5)	⤴
20	15	**California** (9-3)	⤴
—	11	**TCU** (10-2)	
—	19	**Utah** (9-4)	
—	19	**Vanderbilt** (7-5)	

Week of Jan 20

AP	UPI	SCHOOL	AP↓↑
1	1	**Kentucky** (14-1)	↑1
2	2	**North Carolina** (10-1) Ⓑ	↑1
3	3	**Kansas State** (13-1)	↑1
4	4	**NC State** (12-2)	↓3
5	6	**Auburn** (11-0)	
6	5	**Cincinnati** (10-2)	
7	7	**St. John's** (11-1)	↑2
8	7	**Michigan State** (8-2)	
9	9	**Bradley** (11-2)	↓2
10	10	**West Virginia** (13-3)	
11	12	**Mississippi State** (13-1)	↑1
12	13	**Marquette** (13-1)	↑1
13	16	**St. Bonaventure** (9-0)	↑1
14	16	**Saint Louis** (7-4)	↑1
15	26	**Oklahoma City** (11-2)	↑2
16	—	**Seattle** (11-3)	
17	—	**Portland** (12-2)	↑1
18	15	**Northwestern** (9-3)	↓7
19	—	**Villanova** (10-1)	⤴
20	18	**Utah** (11-4)	⤴
—	11	**TCU** (11-3)	
—	13	**California** (10-4)	⤵
—	19	**Illinois** (8-3)	
—	19	**Michigan** (9-2)	
—	21	**Iowa** (5-7)	
—	21	**UCLA** (10-5)	
—	21	**Utah State** (10-4)	
—	24	**BYU** (9-6)	
—	25	**Texas A&M** (11-3)	

Week of Jan 27

AP	UPI	SCHOOL	AP↓↑
1	1	**Kentucky** (14-1)	
2	2	**North Carolina** (10-1)	
3	3	**Kansas State** (13-1)	
4	6	**Auburn** (12-0)	↑1
5	5	**Cincinnati** (11-2)	↑1
6	4	**NC State** (12-2)	↓2
7	8	**St. John's** (12-1)	
8	7	**Michigan State** (10-2)	
9	9	**Bradley** (11-2)	
10	10	**West Virginia** (14-3)	
11	13	**Mississippi State** (18-1)	
12	12	**Marquette** (13-1)	
13	—	**Seattle** (12-3)	↑3
14	20	**Oklahoma City** (12-2)	↑1
15	11	**Saint Louis** (9-4)	↓1
16	—	**St. Bonaventure** (9-1)	↓3
17	—	**Louisville** (9-8)	⤴
18	—	**Illinois** (8-4)	⤴
19	17	**TCU** (11-4)	⤴
20	13	**California** (10-4)	⤴
—	13	**Utah** (12-4)	⤵
—	16	**Northwestern** (10-4)	⤵
—	17	**UCLA** (10-5)	
—	19	**Utah State** (12-4)	

Week of Feb 3

AP	UPI	SCHOOL	AP↓↑
1	1	**Kentucky** (17-1)	
2	2	**North Carolina** (12-1)	
3	3	**Kansas State** (15-1)	
4	7	**Auburn** (14-0)	
5	4	**Cincinnati** (13-2)	
6	5	**NC State** (14-2)	
7	6	**Michigan State** (11-2)	↑1
8	8	**Bradley** (14-2)	↑1
9	9	**Saint Louis** (12-4)	↑6
10	10	**West Virginia** (16-3)	
11	17	**Mississippi State** (18-1)	
12	13	**Marquette** (14-1)	
13	15	**Oklahoma City** (15-2)	↑1
14	—	**Seattle** (15-3)	↓1
15	11	**St. John's** (12-3)	↓8
16	14	**Utah** (13-4)	⤴
17	16	**TCU** (12-4)	↑2
18	—	**St. Bonaventure** (11-1)	↓2
19	12	**California** (11-4)	↑1
20	—	**Saint Joseph's** (12-3)	⤴
—	18	**Memphis** (12-4)	
—	19	**Northwestern** (10-5)	
—	19	**UCLA** (10-5)	

Week of Feb 10

AP	UPI	SCHOOL	AP↓↑
1	1	**Kentucky** (18-1)	
2	2	**North Carolina** (14-1)	
3	3	**Kansas State** (17-1)	
4	6	**Auburn** (16-0)	
5	4	**Cincinnati** (16-2)	
6	5	**NC State** (16-2)	
7	8	**Bradley** (17-2)	↑1
8	9	**Saint Louis** (12-4)	↑1
9	10	**West Virginia** (18-3)	↑1
10	15	**Mississippi State** (18-1)	↑1
11	11	**Marquette** (17-1)	↑1
12	7	**Michigan State** (12-3)	↓5
13	19	**Seattle** (15-3)	↑1
14	19	**Oklahoma City** (16-4)	↓1
15	16	**Indiana** (9-6)	⤴
16	14	**TCU** (14-4)	↑1
17	13	**Utah** (15-4)	↓1
18	12	**California** (13-4)	↑1
19	23	**St. John's** (13-3)	↓4
20	—	**Purdue** (11-4)	⤴
—	16	**Memphis** (12-5)	
—	16	**Tennessee State** (N/A)	
—	19	**Notre Dame** (9-10)	
—	19	**St. Bonaventure** (13-1)	⤵

Week of Feb 17

AP	UPI	SCHOOL	AP↓↑
1	1	**North Carolina** (16-1)	↑1
2	6	**Auburn** (18-0)	↑2
3	3	**Kentucky** (19-2)	↓2
4	2	**Kansas State** (19-1)	↓1
5	10	**Mississippi State** (20-1)	↑5
6	4	**Cincinnati** (16-2)	↓1
6	5	**NC State** (18-2)	
8	8	**Saint Louis** (14-5)	
9	7	**Michigan State** (13-3)	↑3
10	12	**Bradley** (17-3)	↓3
11	14	**West Virginia** (19-4)	↓2
12	—	**Seattle** (16-5)	↑1
13	15	**Marquette** (17-3)	↓2
14	18	**St. Bonaventure** (17-3)	⤴
15	9	**California** (15-4)	↑3
16	11	**TCU** (16-4)	
17	13	**Utah** (16-4)	
18	19	**Oklahoma City** (17-5)	↓4
19	—	**Indiana** (10-7)	↓4
20	—	**Purdue** (12-5)	
—	16	**Louisville** (13-9)	
—	16	**St. John's** (13-5)	⤵
—	19	**Saint Mary's (CA)** (14-4)	

Week of Feb 24

AP	UPI	SCHOOL	AP↓↑
1	1	**Kentucky** (21-2) Ⓒ	↑2
2	2	**Kansas State** (21-1)	↑2
3	4	**North Carolina** (17-2)	↓2
4	3	**Cincinnati** (18-2)	↑2
5	7	**Mississippi State** (22-1)	
6	8	**Auburn** (19-1) Ⓒ	↓4
7	5	**NC State** (19-3)	↓1
8	6	**Michigan State** (15-3)	↑1
9	10	**Bradley** (19-3)	↑1
10	13	**West Virginia** (22-4)	↑1
11	12	**Saint Louis** (14-6)	↓3
12	9	**California** (17-4)	↑3
13	15	**Marquette** (18-3)	
14	11	**TCU** (18-4)	↑2
15	—	**Oklahoma City** (19-5)	↑3
16	—	**Seattle** (17-5)	↓4
17	—	**St. John's** (14-5)	⤴
18	18	**St. Bonaventure** (17-2)	↓4
19	—	**Portland** (17-7)	⤴
20	20	**Saint Mary's (CA)** (17-4)	⤴
—	14	**Utah** (17-5)	⌐
—	16	**Maryland** (8-12) Ⓓ	
—	17	**Navy** (14-5)	
—	19	**Louisville** (14-10)	

Week of Mar 2

AP	UPI	SCHOOL	AP↓↑
1	2	**Kentucky** (23-2)	
2	1	**Kansas State** (22-1)	
3	3	**Cincinnati** (21-2)	↑1
4	6	**Mississippi State** (24-1)	↑1
5	5	**North Carolina** (18-3)	↓2
6	4	**Michigan State** (16-3)	↑2
7	10	**Auburn** (20-2)	↓1
8	11	**West Virginia** (25-4)	↑2
9	9	**Bradley** (21-3)	
10	7	**NC State** (19-4)	↓3
11	8	**California** (20-4)	↑1
12	12	**Saint Louis** (15-6)	↓1
13	15	**Marquette** (21-3)	
14	18	**Oklahoma City** (20-5)	↑1
15	13	**TCU** (18-5)	↓1
16	14	**Utah** (19-5)	⤴
17	16	**Saint Mary's (CA)** (18-4)	↑3
18	17	**St. John's** (15-6)	↓1
19	18	**St. Bonaventure** (18-2)	↓1
20	—	**Saint Joseph's** (20-3)	⤴
—	18	**Louisville** (16-10)	
—	21	**Utah State** (17-7)	
—	22	**Eastern Kentucky** (15-5)	
—	22	**Washington** (18-6)	

Final Poll

AP	UPI	SCHOOL	AP↓↑
1	1	**Kansas State** (24-1)	↑1
2	2	**Kentucky** (23-2)	↓1
3	6	**Mississippi St.** (24-1) Ⓔ	↑1
4	8	**Bradley** (23-3)	↑5
5	4	**Cincinnati** (23-3)	↓2
6	5	**NC State** (22-4)	↑4
7	3	**Michigan State** (18-3)	↓1
8	10	**Auburn** (20-2)	↓1
9	6	**North Carolina** (20-4)	↓4
10	11	**West Virginia** (25-4)	↓2
11	9	**California** (21-4)	
12	13	**Saint Louis** (17-7)	
13	—	**Seattle** (22-6)	⤴
14	20	**Saint Joseph's** (22-3)	↑6
15	18	**Saint Mary's (CA)** (19-6)	⤴
16	12	**TCU** (19-5)	↓1
17	—	**Oklahoma City** (20-5)	↓3
18	14	**Utah** (21-5)	↓2
19	21	**St. Bonaventure** (20-2)	
20	15	**Marquette** (22-4)	↓7
—	16	**Tennessee State A&I** (27-1)	
—	17	**St. John's** (16-6)	⌐
—	18	**Navy** (16-5)	

Ⓐ Cincinnati is the preseason No. 1 based mainly on Oscar Robertson's impressive performance as a sophomore. His junior season will turn out even better, when he sets an NCAA record (since broken) with 28 double-doubles and becomes the first player to lead the nation in scoring in his sophomore and junior campaigns.

Ⓑ On Jan. 14, North Carolina upsets NC State, 72-68, the first of the Tar Heels' all-time NCAA record of 12 victories over No. 1 teams. UNC's 28-year-old assistant coach, Dean Smith—a benchwarmer on Phog Allen's 1952 NCAA championship team at Kansas—creates a stir by joining a protest of a popular Chapel Hill restaurant that refuses to serve African-Americans.

Ⓒ Auburn, coached by Joel Eaves, plays an offense known as the Shuffle, designed to generate easy buckets on backdoor cuts. The Shuffle works to perfection until Feb. 21, when the undefeated Tigers are clobbered, 75-56, by Kentucky in Lexington. On the strength of that win, the Wildcats take over the No. 1 ranking.

Ⓓ With a 69-51 victory over top-ranked North Carolina, Maryland becomes the first unranked team to defeat a No. 1 by more than 15 points. With their unsightly 8–12 record, the Terps become the first ranked team with a losing record that's played more than six games.

Ⓔ SEC champion Mississippi State again declines a bid to the NCAA Tournament because of its state's policy forbidding competition against teams with black players. It's replaced in the Tournament by No. 2 Kentucky.

1959 NCAA Tournament

East

First Round
- Saint Joseph's (bye)
- West Virginia **82** / Dartmouth **68** (A)
- Boston U. **60** / Connecticut **58** (C)
- Navy **76** / North Carolina **63**

Regional Semifinals
- Saint Joseph's **92** / West Virginia **95** (B)
- Boston U. **62** / Navy **55**

Regional Finals
- West Virginia **86** / Boston U. **82**

Mideast

First Round
- Kentucky (bye)
- Louisville **77** / Eastern Kentucky **63**
- Marquette **89** / Bowling Green **71** (E)
- Michigan State (bye)

Regional Semifinals
- Kentucky **61** / Louisville **76** (D)
- Marquette **69** / Michigan State **74**

Regional Finals
- Lousiville **88** / Michigan State **81**

Midwest

First Round
- Kansas State (bye)
- DePaul **57** / Portland **56**
- Cincinnati (bye)
- TCU (bye)

Regional Semifinals
- Kansas State **102** / DePaul **70**
- Cincinnati **77** / TCU **73**

Regional Finals
- Kansas State **75** / Cincinnati **85** (F)

West

First Round
- St. Mary's (CA) (bye)
- Idaho State **62** / New Mexico State **61**
- California (bye)
- Utah (bye)

Regional Semifinals
- St. Mary's (CA) **80** / Idaho State **71**
- California **71** / Utah **53**

Regional Finals
- St. Mary's (CA) **46** / California **66**

National Semifinals

West Virginia **94** / Louisville **79**

Jerry West overcomes early foul trouble to get 38 points and 15 rebounds. The Mountaineers eliminate the Cardinals (the first team to play a national semifinal on its home court) by shooting 53% from the floor.

Cincinnati **58** / California **64**

California triple-teams Oscar Robertson, holding him to 19 points, and dictates the game's tempo. To condition his players for their famous full-court zone press, coach Pete Newell had them run the Berkeley hills every day.

National Final

California 71
West Virginia 70

6'10" Darrall Imhoff taps in the game-clinching basket with :17 seconds left, enabling Cal to overcome a 28-point effort by Tournament MOP Jerry West. Imhoff almost becomes the goat when he's called for goaltending a West shot with :50 left and is tied up for a jump ball seconds later.

Louisville, KY

National Third Place Cincinnati d. Louisville 98-85
East Regional Third Place Navy d. Saint Joseph's 70-56
Mideast Regional Third Place Kentucky d. Marquette 98-69
Midwest Regional Third Place TCU d. DePaul 71-65
West Regional Third Place Idaho State d. Utah 71-65

A Captain Ronnie Retton, the Mountaineers' shortest player at 5'7", scores seven points. At the 1984 Olympic Games, his daughter, Mary Lou Retton, will win one gold and five overall medals in gymnastics.

B West Virginia fans storm the court and carry off Jerry West after the 6'3" sharpshooter's 36-point outburst triggers the Mountaineers' comeback from 18 points down, in the Tournament's highest-scoring game to date.

C Connecticut leads by 10 and begins to stall, but the plan backfires. Coach Hugh Greer claims the tactic was concocted by his players. One possible reason: Top rebounder Ed Martin was hospitalized before the game with appendicitis.

D Although Kentucky (ranked No. 1 nationally) finished tied with Auburn for second in the SEC behind Mississippi State, it gets the league's automatic berth when the Bulldogs pass because of an unwritten state policy prohibiting games against teams with black players.

E Marquette's Eddie Hickey, nicknamed the Little General for his military strictness, becomes the first coach to take three schools to the NCAA Tournament (Creighton in 1941 and St. Louis in 1952).

F Cincinnati's Oscar Robertson, the two-time national scoring leader, achieves the second triple-double in a Tournament game as the Bearcats oust the nation's top-ranked team. Robertson has 24 points, 17 boards and 13 assists.

Tournament Leaders

INDIVIDUAL LEADERS

Scoring

		CL	POS	G	PTS	PPG
1	**Jerry West**, West Virginia	JR	G	5	160	32.0
2	**Oscar Robertson**, Cincinnati	JR	G/F	4	116	29.0
3	**Jim Rodgers**, Idaho State	SR	G	3	80	26.7
4	**H.E. Kirchner**, TCU	SR	C	2	49	24.5
5	**Bob Boozer**, Kansas State	SR	F	2	48	24.0
6	**Bob Anderegg**, Michigan State	SR	F	2	45	22.5
7	**Johnny Green**, Michigan State	SR	F	2	43	21.5
8	**Don Goldstein**, Louisville	SR	F	5	107	21.4
9	**Howie Carl**, DePaul	SO	G	3	62	20.7
10	**Bennie Coffman**, Kentucky	JR	G	2	41	20.5

Minimum: 2 games

Field Goals Per Game

		CL	POS	G	FG	FGPG
1	**Jerry West**, West Virginia	JR	G	5	57	11.4
2	**H.E. Kirchner**, TCU	SR	C	2	21	10.5
3	**Jim Rodgers**, Idaho State	SR	G	3	30	10.0
4	**Oscar Robertson**, Cincinnati	JR	G/F	4	37	9.3
5	**Bob Anderegg**, Michigan State	SR	F	2	18	9.0
	Bob Boozer, Kansas State	SR	F	2	18	9.0

Free Throw Pct

		CL	POS	G	FT	FTA	PCT
1	**LaRoy Doss**, Saint Mary's (CA)	SR	F	2	7	7	100.0
	Joe Gallo, Saint Joseph's	JR	G	2	6	6	100.0
	Dave Van Wagenen, Utah	JR	G	2	5	5	100.0
4	**Johnny Cox**, Kentucky	SR	F	2	9	10	90.0
5	**Howie Carl**, DePaul	SO	G	3	16	18	88.9
	Joe Kitchen, Louisville	JR	F	5	8	9	88.9

Minimum: 5 made

TEAM LEADERS

Scoring

		G	PTS	PPG
1	**Kansas State**	2	177	88.5
2	**West Virginia**	5	427	85.4
3	**Louisville**	5	405	81.0
4	**Kentucky**	2	159	79.5
	Cincinnati	4	318	79.5
6	**Michigan State**	2	155	77.5
7	**Marquette**	3	227	75.7
8	**Saint Joseph's**	2	148	74.0
9	**TCU**	2	144	72.0
10	**California**	4	272	68.0

Minimum: 2 games

FG Per Game

		G	FG	FGPG
1	**Kansas State**	2	65	32.5
	Kentucky	2	65	32.5
3	**Michigan State**	2	61	30.5
4	**Marquette**	3	91	30.3
5	**Cincinnati**	4	120	30.0

FT Pct

		G	FT	FTA	PCT
1	**Kentucky**	2	29	37	78.4
2	**Kansas State**	2	47	61	77.0
3	**Saint Joseph's**	2	34	45	75.6
4	**Louisville**	5	109	145	75.2
5	**DePaul**	3	44	60	73.3

Minimum: 2 games

ALL-TOURNAMENT TEAM

PLAYER	CL	POS	HT	SCHOOL	PPG
Jerry West*	JR	G	6-3	West Virginia	32.0
Denny Fitzpatrick	SR	G	6-0	California	14.3
Don Goldstein	SR	F	6-5	Louisville	21.4
Darrall Imhoff	JR	C	6-10	California	12.8
Oscar Robertson	JR	G/F	6-5	Cincinnati	29.0

ALL-REGIONAL TEAMS

EAST

PLAYER	CL	POS	HT	SCHOOL	PPG
Bob Cumings	SR	F	6-6	Boston U.	17.0
Jack Egan	SO	F	6-6	Saint Joseph's	19.0
Jay Metzler	JR	C	6-6	Navy	18.0
Joe Spratt	SR	F	6-1	Saint Joseph's	14.5
Jerry West	JR	G	6-3	West Virginia	31.3

MIDEAST

PLAYER	CL	POS	HT	SCHOOL	PPG
Bob Anderegg	SR	F	6-3	Michigan State	22.5
Bennie Coffman	JR	G	6-3	Kentucky	20.5
Don Goldstein	SR	F	6-5	Louisville	21.7
Johnny Green	SR	F	6-5	Michigan State	21.5
Don Kojis	SO	F	6-3	Marquette	15.0

MIDWEST

PLAYER	CL	POS	HT	SCHOOL	PPG
Bob Boozer	SR	F	6-8	Kansas State	24.0
Howie Carl	SO	G	5-9	DePaul	20.7
H.E. Kirchner	SR	C	6-10	TCU	24.5
Don Matuszak	SR	G	6-0	Kansas State	7.0
Oscar Robertson	JR	G/F	6-5	Cincinnati	29.0

WEST

PLAYER	CL	POS	HT	SCHOOL	PPG
Al Buch	SR	G	6-2	California	9.5
LaRoy Doss	SR	F	6-5	Saint Mary's (CA)	17.5
Denny Fitzpatrick	SR	G	6-0	California	16.5
Darrall Imhoff	JR	C	6-10	California	9.5
Jim Rodgers	SR	G	5-10	Idaho State	26.7

* Most outstanding player

1959 NCAA TOURNAMENT BOX SCORES

95-92 (SWEET 16)

42	1H	48
53	2H	44

WEST VIRGINIA	MIN	FG	3FG	FT	REB	A	ST	BL	PF	TP
Jerry West	-	12-22	-	12-18	15	1	-	-	1	36
Willie Akers	-	3-10	-	7-8	6	0	-	-	4	13
Lee Patrone	-	5-16	-	3-7	8	3	-	-	1	13
Bucky Bolyard	-	4-10	-	2-4	5	4	-	-	3	10
Jim Ritchie	-	2-11	-	4-7	8	0	-	-	1	8
Bob Smith	-	2-11	-	3-4	5	1	-	-	2	7
Bob Clousson	-	2-7	-	0-0	7	0	-	-	4	4
Ronnie Retton	-	1-4	-	2-2	2	1	-	-	2	4
Joe Posch	-	0-1	-	0-0	0	0	-	-	2	0
TOTALS	-	31-92	-	33-50	56	10	-	-	20	95
Percentages		33.7		66.0						

Coach: Fred Schaus

SAINT JOSEPH'S	MIN	FG	3FG	FT	REB	A	ST	BL	PF	TP
Joe Gallo	-	9-22	-	4-4	4	4	-	-	4	22
Jack Egan	-	9-13	-	2-2	8	0	-	-	5	20
Joe Spratt	-	6-10	-	5-7	10	1	-	-	5	17
Bob Clarke	-	6-9	-	3-4	13	1	-	-	5	15
Bob McNeill	-	1-8	-	5-6	5	4	-	-	5	7
Frank Majewski	-	2-4	-	0-2	1	2	-	-	5	4
Jared Reilly	-	1-4	-	2-2	3	0	-	-	2	4
Al Cooke	-	1-1	-	0-0	0	0	-	-	0	2
John Hoffacker	-	0-0	-	1-2	0	0	-	-	1	1
TOTALS	-	35-71	-	22-29	44	12	-	-	32	92
Percentages		49.3		75.9						

Coach: Jack Ramsay

62-55 (SWEET 16)

32	1H	30
30	2H	25

BOSTON U.	MIN	FG	3FG	FT	REB	A	ST	BL	PF	TP
Bob Cumings	-	6-15	-	2-3	6	-	-	-	1	14
Edward Washington	-	4-13	-	6-7	19	-	-	-	3	14
John Leaman	-	5-16	-	3-4	2	-	-	-	4	13
William Gates	-	3-9	-	3-4	3	-	-	-	2	9
Tom Stagis	-	3-13	-	2-2	5	-	-	-	0	8
Dick O'Connell	-	1-3	-	0-0	0	-	-	-	1	2
Harold Supriano	-	0-0	-	2-2	0	-	-	-	0	2
TOTALS	-	22-69	-	18-22	35	-	-	-	11	62
Percentages		31.9		81.8						

Coach: Matt Zunic

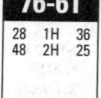

NAVY	MIN	FG	3FG	FT	REB	A	ST	BL	PF	TP
Jay Metzler	38	8-14	-	0-0	8	-	-	-	5	16
Gary Bagnard	24	4-6	-	3-3	1	-	-	-	2	11
Dick Brown	45	4-10	-	0-0	14	-	-	-	1	8
Jim Bower	43	1-11	-	6-6	10	-	-	-	1	8
Frank Delano	22	2-2	-	4-6	2	-	-	-	4	8
Ronnie Doyle	23	1-3	-	0-0	2	-	-	-	2	2
Dick Johnson	18	1-4	-	0-0	1	-	-	-	0	2
Walt Land	7	0-1	-	0-0	1	-	-	-	1	0
Henry Egan	5	0-0	-	0-0	1	-	-	-	0	0
TOTALS	225	21-51	-	13-15	40	-	-	-	16	55
Percentages		41.2		86.7						

Coach: Ben Carnevale

76-61 (SWEET 16)

28	1H	36
48	2H	25

LOUISVILLE	MIN	FG	3FG	FT	REB	A	ST	BL	PF	TP
Don Goldstein	-	7-12	-	5-7	13	-	-	-	4	19
Harold Andrews	-	5-9	-	5-5	5	-	-	-	2	15
Roger Tieman	-	5-8	-	3-4	1	-	-	-	3	13
John Turner	-	4-10	-	5-7	8	-	-	-	2	13
Joe Kitchen	-	1-2	-	5-5	2	-	-	-	2	7
Fred Sawyer	-	2-10	-	3-5	10	-	-	-	2	7
Buddy Leathers	-	1-4	-	0-0	7	-	-	-	1	2
TOTALS	-	25-55	-	26-33	46	-	-	-	16	76
Percentages		45.5		78.8						

Coach: Bernard "Peck" Hickman

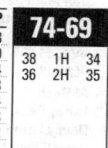

KENTUCKY	MIN	FG	3FG	FT	REB	A	ST	BL	PF	TP
Bill Lickert	-	7-11	-	2-3	7	-	-	-	1	16
Bennie Coffman	-	4-12	-	5-6	3	-	-	-	5	13
Johnny Cox	-	3-15	-	4-5	7	-	-	-	5	10
Don Mills	-	1-3	-	4-5	7	-	-	-	4	6
Sid Cohen	-	2-7	-	1-1	4	-	-	-	1	5
Phil Johnson	-	2-4	-	0-0	4	-	-	-	0	4
Dick Parsons	-	2-9	-	0-0	2	-	-	-	3	4
Bobby Slusher	-	1-6	-	1-1	3	-	-	-	3	3
TOTALS	-	22-67	-	17-21	37	-	-	-	22	61
Percentages		32.8		81.0						

Coach: Adolph Rupp

74-69 (SWEET 16)

38	1H	34
36	2H	35

MICHIGAN STATE	MIN	FG	3FG	FT	REB	A	ST	BL	PF	TP
Bob Anderegg	-	10-19	-	3-7	8	-	-	-	1	23
Horace Walker	-	9-21	-	2-3	8	-	-	-	2	20
Johnny Green	-	6-18	-	2-4	18	-	-	-	5	14
Lance Olson	-	1-7	-	6-8	4	-	-	-	4	8
David Fahs	-	2-6	-	0-1	1	-	-	-	0	4
Thomas Rand	-	1-5	-	1-2	5	-	-	-	2	3
Art Gowens	-	1-1	-	0-0	1	-	-	-	0	2
TOTALS	-	30-77	-	14-25	45	-	-	-	14	74
Percentages		39.0		56.0						

Coach: Forrest "Forddy" Anderson

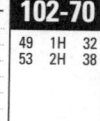

MARQUETTE	MIN	FG	3FG	FT	REB	A	ST	BL	PF	TP
Don Kojis	-	7-17	-	3-6	21	-	-	-	3	17
Walt Mangham	-	6-17	-	3-7	9	-	-	-	3	15
Jim Kollar	-	6-11	-	1-1	5	-	-	-	4	13
James McCoy	-	6-18	-	1-1	10	-	-	-	2	13
Mike Moran	-	3-15	-	3-4	5	-	-	-	4	9
Joel Plinska	-	1-1	-	0-0	0	-	-	-	1	2
James Kersten	-	0-0	-	0-0	0	-	-	-	0	0
Greg Ripp	-	0-2	-	0-0	1	-	-	-	0	0
TOTALS	-	29-81	-	11-19	51	-	-	-	17	69
Percentages		35.8		57.9						

Coach: Eddie Hickey

102-70 (SWEET 16)

49	1H	32
53	2H	38

KANSAS STATE	MIN	FG	3FG	FT	REB	A	ST	BL	PF	TP
Wally Frank	-	9-13	-	5-6	4	-	-	-	2	23
Bob Boozer	-	7-21	-	2-3	12	-	-	-	1	16
Steve Douglas	-	7-8	-	1-1	6	-	-	-	3	15
Cedric Price	-	3-13	-	8-10	8	-	-	-	2	14
Jim Holwerda	-	5-8	-	1-1	2	-	-	-	3	11
Mickie Heinz	-	1-5	-	4-4	4	-	-	-	1	6
Don Matuszak	-	2-6	-	2-3	4	-	-	-	3	6
William Guthridge	-	2-4	-	0-0	1	-	-	-	1	4
Jerry Johnson	-	2-2	-	0-0	3	-	-	-	1	4
Robert Graham	-	1-1	-	0-0	0	-	-	-	1	2
Glen Long	-	0-2	-	1-2	1	-	-	-	1	1
Gary Balding	-	0-0	-	0-0	2	-	-	-	0	0
TOTALS	-	39-83	-	24-30	47	-	-	-	19	102
Percentages		47.0		80.0						

Coach: Tex Winter

DEPAUL	MIN	FG	3FG	FT	REB	A	ST	BL	PF	TP
Howie Carl	-	7-23	-	8-10	6	-	-	-	2	22
Paul Ruddy	-	6-10	-	6-7	6	-	-	-	5	18
Bill Haig	-	3-11	-	3-4	5	-	-	-	2	9
Jim Flemming	-	3-7	-	2-4	11	-	-	-	4	8
Mack Cowsen	-	3-18	-	1-3	9	-	-	-	4	7
Mike Salzinski	-	2-4	-	2-2	1	-	-	-	3	6
TOTALS	-	24-73	-	22-30	38	-	-	-	20	70
Percentages		32.9		73.3						

Coach: Ray Meyer

Officials: Haggerty, Hayes

77-73 (SWEET 16)

38	1H	37
39	2H	36

CINCINNATI	MIN	FG	3FG	FT	REB	A	ST	BL	PF	TP
Oscar Robertson	40	12-24	-	10-13	10	7	-	-	4	34
Bob Wiesenhahn	40	5-8	-	2-2	14	0	-	-	3	12
Ralph Davis	36	5-14	-	0-3	2	5	-	-	0	10
Bill Whitaker	16	3-8	-	0-1	3	1	-	-	1	6
Mel Landfried	13	3-5	-	0-0	4	0	-	-	1	6
Carl Bouldin	27	2-4	-	1-1	6	2	-	-	3	5
Dave Tenwick	19	2-7	-	0-0	1	0	-	-	4	4
Larry Willey	9	0-1	-	0-0	3	0	-	-	3	0
TOTALS	200	32-71	-	13-20	43	15	-	-	19	77
Percentages		45.1		65.0						

Coach: George Smith

TCU	MIN	FG	3FG	FT	REB	A	ST	BL	PF	TP
H.E. Kirchner	-	11-23	-	3-7	18	-	-	-	0	25
Ronny Stevenson	-	4-16	-	7-8	12	-	-	-	5	15
Kenneth Brunson	-	5-14	-	0-0	2	-	-	-	1	10
Derrill Nippert	-	2-11	-	5-5	5	-	-	-	0	9
Bobby Tyler	-	3-8	-	2-2	1	-	-	-	3	8
Jerry Cobb	-	2-5	-	0-0	2	-	-	-	1	4
Kenneth King	-	1-6	-	0-0	1	-	-	-	5	2
TOTALS	-	28-83	-	17-22	41	-	-	-	15	73
Percentages		33.7		77.3						

Coach: Buster Brannon

Officials: Lightner, Bussenius

SAINT MARY'S (CA)	MIN	FG	3FG	FT	REB	A	ST	BL	PF	TP
LaRoy Doss	-	8-12	-	5-5	5	-	-	-	1	21
Tom Meschery	-	8-14	-	3-4	13	-	-	-	3	19
Joe Barry	-	4-6	-	5-7	2	-	-	-	2	13
Bob Dold	-	4-10	-	3-3	2	-	-	-	4	11
Larry Brennan	-	3-3	-	0-1	0	-	-	-	0	6
Dick Sigaty	-	3-11	-	0-2	12	-	-	-	5	6
Al Claiborne	-	1-3	-	0-0	3	-	-	-	1	2
Gene Womack	-	0-1	-	2-2	1	-	-	-	0	2
Jack Dold	-	0-0	-	0-0	0	-	-	-	0	0
Wes Tamm	-	0-1	-	0-1	1	-	-	-	0	0
TOTALS	**-**	**31-61**	**-**	**18-25**	**39**	**-**	**-**	**-**	**16**	**80**
Percentages		50.8		72.0						

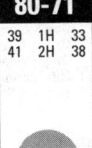

Coach: James Weaver

80-71

39 1H 33
41 2H 38

SWEET 16

IDAHO STATE	MIN	FG	3FG	FT	REB	A	ST	BL	PF	TP
Jim Rodgers	-	12-27	-	5-6	0	-	-	-	3	29
Homer Watkins	-	5-7	-	1-2	4	-	-	-	5	11
Alan Morris	-	4-9	-	2-2	5	-	-	-	3	10
Jerry Griffin	-	4-9	-	0-2	3	-	-	-	2	8
Nick Clock	-	1-6	-	3-3	2	-	-	-	2	5
Raymond Griffith	-	1-2	-	2-3	5	-	-	-	2	4
Dennis Moulton	-	2-3	-	0-0	5	-	-	-	1	4
Ray Cheney	-	0-0	-	0-1	1	-	-	-	0	0
Jim Link	-	0-0	-	0-2	1	-	-	-	0	0
TOTALS	**-**	**29-63**	**-**	**13-21**	**26**	**-**	**-**	**-**	**18**	**71**
Percentages		46.0		61.9						

Coach: John Grayson

CALIFORNIA	MIN	FG	3FG	FT	REB	A	ST	BL	PF	TP
Al Buch	-	7	-	1-2	-	-	-	-	1	15
Bob Dalton	-	6	-	1-1	-	-	-	-	2	13
Denny Fitzpatrick	-	4	-	4-4	-	-	-	-	3	12
Darrall Imhoff	-	3	-	3-4	-	-	-	-	4	9
Bill McClintock	-	4	-	1-3	-	-	-	-	1	9
Dick Doughty	-	3	-	0-0	-	-	-	-	1	6
Tandy Gillis	-	1	-	0-0	-	-	-	-	0	2
Jack Grout	-	1	-	0-0	-	-	-	-	2	2
Bernie Simpson	-	1	-	0-0	-	-	-	-	1	2
Earl Schultz	-	0	-	1-2	-	-	-	-	3	1
Jim Langley	-	0	-	0-0	-	-	-	-	0	0
Jerry Mann	-	0	-	0-0	-	-	-	-	0	0
TOTALS	**-**	**30**	**-**	**11-16**	**-**	**-**	**-**	**-**	**18**	**71**
Percentages				68.8						

Coach: Pete Newell

71-53

42 1H 27
29 2H 26

SWEET 16

UTAH	MIN	FG	3FG	FT	REB	A	ST	BL	PF	TP
Gary Chestang	-	3	-	3-4	-	-	-	-	2	9
Carney Crisler	-	3	-	3-5	-	-	-	-	2	9
Pearl Pollard	-	4	-	1-1	-	-	-	-	2	9
Delyle Condie	-	4	-	0-1	-	-	-	-	0	8
Richard Ruffell	-	4	-	0-0	-	-	-	-	1	8
Joe Morton	-	1	-	2-2	-	-	-	-	1	4
Dave Van Wagenen	-	0	-	3-3	-	-	-	-	0	3
Dick Shores	-	0	-	2-3	-	-	-	-	3	2
Jim Rhead	-	0	-	1-2	-	-	-	-	0	1
Keith Ancell	-	0	-	0-0	-	-	-	-	1	0
Ben Cutler	-	0	-	0-0	-	-	-	-	1	0
TOTALS	**-**	**19**	**-**	**15-21**	**-**	**-**	**-**	**-**	**13**	**53**
Percentages				71.4						

Coach: Jack Gardner

WEST VIRGINIA	MIN	FG	3FG	FT	REB	A	ST	BL	PF	TP
Jerry West	-	12-24	-	9-12	17	3	-	-	4	33
Jim Ritchie	-	2-5	-	8-10	9	0	-	-	4	12
Bob Smith	-	6-11	-	0-1	1	2	-	-	0	12
Willie Akers	-	3-13	-	5-5	8	0	-	-	4	11
Bob Clousson	-	2-4	-	4-5	6	0	-	-	4	8
Bucky Bolyard	-	2-11	-	1-1	0	3	-	-	3	5
Lee Patrone	-	1-4	-	2-5	5	3	-	-	1	4
Ronnie Retton	-	0-0	-	1-3	0	0	-	-	2	1
Joe Posch	-	0-0	-	0-0	0	0	-	-	2	0
TOTALS	**-**	**28-72**	**-**	**30-42**	**46**	**11**	**-**	**-**	**24**	**86**
Percentages		38.9		71.4						

Coach: Fred Schaus

86-82

45 1H 45
41 2H 37

ELITE 8

BOSTON U.	MIN	FG	3FG	FT	REB	A	ST	BL	PF	TP
Bob Cumings	-	9-17	-	4-7	13	1	-	-	1	22
William Gates	-	7-14	-	4-6	8	0	-	-	4	18
Tom Stagis	-	5-15	-	3-6	7	5	-	-	5	13
John Leaman	-	3-9	-	4-4	3	3	-	-	4	10
Harold Supriano	-	3-7	-	2-5	3	3	-	-	2	8
Edward Washington	-	2-5	-	2-4	10	1	-	-	5	6
Dick O'Connell	-	1-7	-	3-3	4	0	-	-	3	5
Tom Chamberlain	-	0-0	-	0-0	0	0	-	-	2	0
TOTALS	**-**	**30-74**	**-**	**22-35**	**48**	**13**	**-**	**-**	**26**	**82**
Percentages		40.5		62.9						

Coach: Matt Zunic

LOUISVILLE	MIN	FG	3FG	FT	REB	A	ST	BL	PF	TP
John Turner	-	10-19	-	2-3	6	-	-	-	4	22
Don Goldstein	-	7-15	-	7-7	7	-	-	-	4	21
Fred Sawyer	-	6-12	-	2-5	15	-	-	-	4	14
Harold Andrews	-	5-9	-	3-4	4	-	-	-	5	13
Buddy Leathers	-	3-10	-	4-5	3	-	-	-	3	10
Joe Kitchen	-	2-4	-	1-1	4	-	-	-	1	5
Roger Tieman	-	0-6	-	3-3	4	-	-	-	2	3
TOTALS	**-**	**33-75**	**-**	**22-28**	**43**	**-**	**-**	**-**	**23**	**88**
Percentages		44.0		78.6						

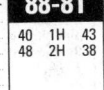

Coach: Bernard "Peck" Hickman

88-81

40 1H 43
48 2H 38

ELITE 8

MICHIGAN STATE	MIN	FG	3FG	FT	REB	A	ST	BL	PF	TP
Johnny Green	-	11-21	-	7-12	23	-	-	-	3	29
Bob Anderegg	-	8-21	-	6-10	3	-	-	-	5	22
Lance Olson	-	6-15	-	4-4	3	-	-	-	3	16
James Stouffer	-	3-5	-	0-0	1	-	-	-	0	6
Art Gowens	-	1-1	-	1-2	0	-	-	-	0	3
Horace Walker	-	1-9	-	1-1	9	-	-	-	5	3
Thomas Rand	-	1-7	-	0-0	2	-	-	-	3	2
David Fahs	-	0-5	-	0-1	1	-	-	-	2	0
TOTALS	**-**	**31-84**	**-**	**19-30**	**42**	**-**	**-**	**-**	**21**	**81**
Percentages		36.9		63.3						

Coach: Forrest "Forddy" Anderson

Officials: Mihalik, Andersen

CINCINNATI	MIN	FG	3FG	FT	REB	A	ST	BL	PF	TP
Oscar Robertson	40	8-19	-	8-9	17	13	-	-	4	24
Dave Tenwick	40	5-16	-	12-15	9	0	-	-	4	22
Ralph Davis	40	6-16	-	1-2	2	2	-	-	3	13
Bob Wiesenhahn	21	6-12	-	0-1	9	0	-	-	5	12
Mel Landfried	19	4-5	-	2-3	10	1	-	-	1	10
Bill Whitaker	32	1-4	-	2-3	0	2	-	-	3	4
Carl Bouldin	8	0-1	-	0-0	0	2	-	-	0	0
TOTALS	**200**	**30-73**	**-**	**25-33**	**47**	**20**	**-**	**-**	**20**	**85**
Percentages		41.1		75.8						

Coach: George Smith

85-75

39 1H 41
46 2H 34

ELITE 8

KANSAS STATE	MIN	FG	3FG	FT	REB	A	ST	BL	PF	TP
Bob Boozer	-	11-26	-	10-13	13	-	-	-	5	32
Cedric Price	-	1-6	-	9-10	5	-	-	-	5	11
Wally Frank	-	4-16	-	2-4	3	-	-	-	3	10
Don Matuszak	-	4-7	-	0-0	4	-	-	-	2	8
Jim Holwerda	-	3-11	-	0-0	3	-	-	-	2	6
Steve Douglas	-	1-5	-	1-1	4	-	-	-	5	3
William Guthridge	-	1-3	-	1-2	2	-	-	-	0	3
Mickie Heinz	-	1-6	-	0-1	8	-	-	-	1	2
Jerry Johnson	-	0-2	-	0-0	0	-	-	-	0	0
TOTALS	**-**	**26-82**	**-**	**23-31**	**42**	**-**	**-**	**-**	**23**	**75**
Percentages		31.7		74.2						

Coach: Tex Winter

Officials: Lightner, Bussenius

CALIFORNIA	MIN	FG	3FG	FT	REB	A	ST	BL	PF	TP
Denny Fitzpatrick	-	9	-	3-3	0	-	-	-	2	21
Bob Dalton	-	3	-	7-7	0	-	-	-	3	13
Darrall Imhoff	-	4	-	2-2	15	-	-	-	1	10
Bill McClintock	-	4	-	2-3	0	-	-	-	4	10
Al Buch	-	2	-	0-0	0	-	-	-	1	4
Jack Grout	-	2	-	0-0	0	-	-	-	1	4
Earl Schultz	-	0	-	2-2	0	-	-	-	0	2
Bernie Simpson	-	0	-	2-3	0	-	-	-	0	2
Dick Doughty	-	0	-	0-0	0	-	-	-	0	0
Tandy Gillis	-	0	-	0-0	0	-	-	-	1	0
Jim Langley	-	0	-	0-0	0	-	-	-	0	0
Jerry Mann	-	0	-	0-0	0	-	-	-	1	0
TOTALS	**-**	**24**	**-**	**18-20**	**15**	**-**	**-**	**-**	**14**	**66**
Percentages				90.0						

Coach: Pete Newell

66-46

31 1H 18
35 2H 28

ELITE 8

SAINT MARY'S (CA)	MIN	FG	3FG	FT	REB	A	ST	BL	PF	TP
Joe Barry	-	6	-	2-2	-	-	-	-	4	14
LaRoy Doss	-	6	-	2-2	-	-	-	-	1	14
Larry Brennan	-	2	-	2-3	-	-	-	-	2	6
Tom Meschery	-	2	-	1-3	-	-	-	-	2	5
Dick Sigaty	-	2	-	0-1	-	-	-	-	2	4
Bob Dold	-	1	-	1-1	-	-	-	-	3	3
Al Claiborne	-	0	-	0-0	-	-	-	-	0	0
Jack Dold	-	0	-	0-0	-	-	-	-	0	0
Wes Tamm	-	0	-	0-2	-	-	-	-	0	0
Gene Womack	-	0	-	0-1	-	-	-	-	0	0
TOTALS	**-**	**19**	**-**	**8-15**	**-**	**-**	**-**	**-**	**14**	**46**
Percentages				53.3						

Coach: James Weaver

94-79 (FINAL 4)

	1H	2H
West Virginia	48	46
Louisville	32	47

WEST VIRGINIA	MIN	FG	3FG	FT	REB	A	ST	BL	PF	TP
Jerry West	-	12-21	-	14-20	15	-	-	-	3	38
Bucky Bolyard	-	4-10	-	5-7	3	-	-	-	1	13
Bob Clousson	-	5-5	-	2-2	4	-	-	-	4	12
Bob Smith	-	5-9	-	2-4	5	-	-	-	0	12
Ronnie Retton	-	3-4	-	0-0	0	-	-	-	1	6
Willie Akers	-	2-5	-	1-2	8	-	-	-	5	5
Jim Ritchie	-	2-6	-	0-2	5	-	-	-	1	4
Lee Patrone	-	1-4	-	0-0	1	-	-	-	0	2
Joe Posch	-	1-2	-	0-0	0	-	-	-	0	2
Butch Goode	-	0-0	-	0-0	0	-	-	-	0	0
Howie Schertzinger	-	0-0	-	0-0	0	-	-	-	0	0
Nick Visnic	-	0-0	-	0-0	0	-	-	-	0	0
TOTALS	**-**	**35-66**	**-**	**24-37**	**41**	**-**	**-**	**-**	**15**	**94**
Percentages		53.0		64.9						

Coach: Fred Schaus

LOUISVILLE	MIN	FG	3FG	FT	REB	A	ST	BL	PF	TP
Don Goldstein	-	6-10	-	9-9	9	-	-	-	4	21
Harold Andrews	-	9-15	-	1-1	2	-	-	-	3	19
John Turner	-	8-16	-	2-5	7	-	-	-	4	18
Fred Sawyer	-	2-6	-	3-4	2	-	-	-	5	7
Joe Kitchen	-	3-7	-	0-0	5	-	-	-	4	6
Buddy Leathers	-	2-8	-	1-1	3	-	-	-	3	5
Roger Tieman	-	1-7	-	1-1	0	-	-	-	0	3
Bill Geiling	-	0-0	-	0-0	0	-	-	-	0	0
Howard Stacey	-	0-0	-	0-0	2	-	-	-	1	0
TOTALS	**-**	**31-69**	**-**	**17-21**	**30**	**-**	**-**	**-**	**24**	**79**
Percentages		44.9		81.0						

Coach: Bernard "Peck" Hickman

Attendance: 18,619

64-58 (FINAL 4)

	1H	2H
California	29	35
Cincinnati	33	25

CALIFORNIA	MIN	FG	3FG	FT	REB	A	ST	BL	PF	TP
Darrall Imhoff	-	10-25	-	2-5	16	-	-	-	4	22
Al Buch	-	7-15	-	4-6	6	-	-	-	2	18
Bob Dalton	-	2-4	-	3-4	7	-	-	-	5	7
Bill McClintock	-	2-11	-	2-4	11	-	-	-	1	6
Jack Grout	-	2-7	-	1-2	2	-	-	-	1	5
Denny Fitzpatrick	-	2-9	-	0-0	3	-	-	-	4	4
Bernie Simpson	-	1-2	-	0-0	3	-	-	-	0	2
TOTALS	**-**	**26-73**	**-**	**12-21**	**48**	**-**	**-**	**-**	**17**	**64**
Percentages		35.6		57.1						

Coach: Pete Newell

CINCINNATI	MIN	FG	3FG	FT	REB	A	ST	BL	PF	TP
Oscar Robertson	40	5-16	-	9-11	19	9	-	-	4	19
Ralph Davis	40	6-15	-	1-2	2	2	-	-	2	13
Bob Wiesenhahn	25	5-11	-	0-0	3	0	-	-	1	10
Bill Whitaker	36	4-7	-	0-2	3	0	-	-	3	8
Dave Tenwick	27	2-6	-	1-1	4	0	-	-	1	5
Mel Landfried	28	0-1	-	3-5	4	2	-	-	3	3
Carl Bouldin	4	0-0	-	0-1	0	1	-	-	1	0
TOTALS	**200**	**22-56**	**-**	**14-22**	**35**	**14**	**-**	**-**	**15**	**58**
Percentages		39.3		63.6						

Coach: George Smith

Attendance: 18,619

98-85 (3RD PLACE)

	1H	2H
Cincinnati	49	49
Louisville	53	32

CINCINNATI	MIN	FG	3FG	FT	REB	A	ST	BL	PF	TP
Oscar Robertson	39	12-26	-	15-19	17	10	-	-	3	39
Ralph Davis	39	11-25	-	2-3	3	6	-	-	3	24
Bill Whitaker	35	6-8	-	3-6	2	3	-	-	2	15
Bob Wiesenhahn	33	4-9	-	4-5	10	1	-	-	3	12
Dave Tenwick	36	2-8	-	2-4	6	1	-	-	2	6
Mel Landfried	8	1-1	-	0-1	5	1	-	-	2	2
Carl Bouldin	5	0-0	-	0-0	1	2	-	-	0	0
Rod Nall	2	0-0	-	0-0	0	0	-	-	1	0
Larry Willey	2	0-0	-	0-0	1	0	-	-	1	0
Dick Cetrone	1	0-0	-	0-0	0	0	-	-	1	0
TOTALS	**200**	**36-77**	**-**	**26-38**	**45**	**24**	**-**	**-**	**18**	**98**
Percentages		46.8		68.4						

Coach: George Smith

LOUISVILLE	MIN	FG	3FG	FT	REB	A	ST	BL	PF	TP
Roger Tieman	-	10-18	-	3-4	1	-	-	-	4	23
Don Goldstein	-	8-15	-	5-6	8	-	-	-	4	21
Harold Andrews	-	6-15	-	6-6	4	-	-	-	3	18
John Turner	-	4-11	-	1-2	12	-	-	-	4	9
Buddy Leathers	-	2-4	-	2-2	3	-	-	-	4	6
Fred Sawyer	-	0-5	-	5-5	9	-	-	-	4	5
Joe Kitchen	-	1-2	-	0-0	3	-	-	-	2	2
Bill Geiling	-	0-2	-	1-1	0	-	-	-	0	1
Alex Mantel	-	0-0	-	0-0	0	-	-	-	0	0
Howard Stacey	-	0-0	-	0-0	0	-	-	-	0	0
Jerry Watkins	-	0-0	-	0-0	0	-	-	-	0	0
TOTALS	**-**	**31-72**	**-**	**23-26**	**40**	**-**	**-**	**-**	**25**	**85**
Percentages		43.1		88.5						

Coach: Bernard "Peck" Hickman

Attendance: 18,498

71-70 (NCAA FINAL 1959)

	1H	2H
California	39	32
West Virginia	33	37

CALIFORNIA	MIN	FG	3FG	FT	REB	A	ST	BL	PF	TP
Denny Fitzpatrick	-	8-13	-	4-7	2	-	-	-	1	20
Bob Dalton	-	6-11	-	3-4	2	-	-	-	4	15
Jack Grout	-	4-5	-	2-2	3	-	-	-	1	10
Darrall Imhoff	-	4-13	-	2-2	9	-	-	-	3	10
Bill McClintock	-	4-13	-	0-1	10	-	-	-	1	8
Dick Doughty	-	3-6	-	0-0	1	-	-	-	3	6
Al Buch	-	0-4	-	2-2	2	-	-	-	3	2
Bernie Simpson	-	0-1	-	0-0	2	-	-	-	2	0
TOTALS	**-**	**29-66**	**-**	**13-18**	**31**	**-**	**-**	**-**	**18**	**71**
Percentages		43.9		72.2						

Coach: Pete Newell

WEST VIRGINIA	MIN	FG	3FG	FT	REB	A	ST	BL	PF	TP
Jerry West	-	10-21	-	8-12	11	-	-	-	4	28
Willie Akers	-	5-8	-	0-1	6	-	-	-	0	10
Bob Clousson	-	4-7	-	2-3	4	-	-	-	4	10
Bucky Bolyard	-	1-4	-	4-4	3	-	-	-	4	6
Lee Patrone	-	2-6	-	1-2	4	-	-	-	1	5
Bob Smith	-	2-5	-	1-1	2	-	-	-	3	5
Jim Ritchie	-	1-4	-	2-2	4	-	-	-	0	4
Ronnie Retton	-	0-0	-	2-2	0	-	-	-	0	2
TOTALS	**-**	**25-55**	**-**	**20-27**	**34**	**-**	**-**	**-**	**16**	**70**
Percentages		45.5		74.1						

Coach: Fred Schaus

Officials: Bell, Mihalik
Attendance: 18,498

National Invitational Tournament (NIT)

First round: Butler d. Fordham 94-80, NYU d. Denver 90-81, Providence d. Manhattan 68-66, St. John's d. Villanova 75-67
Quarterfinals: Bradley d. Butler 83-77, NYU d. Oklahoma City 63-48, Providence d. Saint Louis 75-72 (2OT), St. John's d. St. Bonaventure 82-74
Semifinals: Bradley d. NYU 59-57, St. John's d. Providence 76-55
Third place: NYU d. Providence 71-57
Championship: St. John's d. Bradley 76-71 (OT)
MVP: Tony Jackson, St. John's

1959-60: Buckeye Power

With the Final Four slated for San Francisco's Cow Palace, California seemed a shoo-in to repeat as NCAA champion. Too bad Ohio State ruined the party. The young Buckeyes led the nation in scoring offense (90.4 ppg) and held NYU to 39% shooting in their national semifinal en route to a 76-54 win. In the Final, the Buckeyes slashed the Golden Bears, 75-55, led by Tournament MOP Jerry Lucas' 16 points and 10 rebounds. Ohio State made an astounding 31 of 46 shots from the field (67.4%) and all five starters hit double figures. The 20-point rout was the biggest win in an NCAA title game in the first 22 years of the Tournament. The Buckeyes (25–3) were the first team to lead the country in scoring and win the NCAA championship.

One of the Buckeyes reserves was future coaching legend Bob Knight. California coach Pete Newell retired after the season with a 234–123 record. Cincinnati's Oscar Robertson was UPI's National Player of the Year for the third straight season. He was the No. 1 pick (Cincinnati Royals) in the 1960 NBA draft.

Major Conference Standings

ACC	Conference			Overall		
	W	L	Pct	W	L	Pct
North Carolina	12	2	.857	18	6	.750
Wake Forest	12	2	.857	21	7	.750
Maryland	9	5	.643	15	8	.652
Duke⊕	7	7	.500	17	11	.607
South Carolina	6	8	.429	10	16	.385
NC State	5	9	.357	11	15	.423
Clemson	4	10	.286	10	16	.385
Virginia	1	13	.071	6	18	.250

Tournament: **Duke d. Wake Forest 63-59**
Tournament MVP: **Doug Kistler**, Duke

Big Eight	Conference			Overall		
	W	L	Pct	W	L	Pct
Kansas⊕	10	4	.714	19	9	.679
Kansas State	10	4	.714	16	10	.615
Oklahoma	9	5	.643	14	11	.560
Colorado	9	7	.563	13	11	.542
Iowa State	7	7	.500	15	9	.625
Missouri	5	9	.357	12	13	.480
Oklahoma State	4	10	.286	10	15	.400
Nebraska	4	10	.286	7	17	.292

AAWU	Conference			Overall		
	W	L	Pct	W	L	Pct
California○	11	1	.917	28	2	.933
UCLA	7	5	.583	14	12	.538
Southern California○	5	7	.417	16	11	.593
Stanford	4	7	.364	11	14	.440
Washington	2	9	.182	15	13	.536

Big Ten	Conference			Overall		
	W	L	Pct	W	L	Pct
Ohio State⊕	13	1	.929	25	3	.893
Indiana	11	3	.786	20	4	.833
Illinois	8	6	.571	16	7	.696
Minnesota	8	6	.571	12	12	.500
Northwestern	8	6	.571	11	12	.478
Iowa	6	8	.429	14	10	.583
Purdue	6	8	.429	11	12	.478
Michigan State	5	9	.357	10	11	.476
Wisconsin	4	10	.286	8	16	.333
Michigan	1	13	.071	4	20	.167

Border	Conference			Overall		
	W	L	Pct	W	L	Pct
New Mexico State⊕	8	2	.800	20	7	.741
Arizona State	7	3	.700	16	7	.696
West Texas A&M	7	3	.700	11	9	.550
Arizona	4	6	.400	10	14	.417
Hardin-Simmons	3	7	.300	8	18	.308
Texas Western	1	9	.100	6	19	.240

Ivy	Conference			Overall		
	W	L	Pct	W	L	Pct
Princeton○	11	3	.786	15	9	.625
Dartmouth	10	4	.714	14	9	.609
Cornell	8	6	.571	13	10	.565
Penn	8	6	.571	14	11	.560
Brown	8	6	.571	13	12	.520
Harvard	6	8	.429	12	11	.522
Yale	3	11	.214	6	17	.261
Columbia	2	12	.143	9	14	.391

Metro NY	Conference			Overall		
	W	L	Pct	W	L	Pct
NYU○	4	0	1.000	22	5	.815
St. John's□	5	1	.833	17	8	.680
St. Francis (NY)	2	1	.667	13	8	.619
Manhattan	2	2	.500	13	11	.542
Fordham	1	3	.250	8	18	.308
CCNY	1	5	.167	4	14	.222
Brooklyn	0	3	.000	5	13	.278

Mid-American	Conference			Overall		
	W	L	Pct	W	L	Pct
Ohio⊕	10	2	.833	16	8	.667
Toledo	9	3	.750	18	6	.750
Bowling Green	6	6	.500	10	14	.417
Miami (OH)	6	6	.500	8	16	.333
Western Michigan	5	7	.417	12	11	.522
Marshall	4	8	.333	10	13	.435
Kent State	2	10	.167	7	16	.304

Middle Atlantic	Conference			Overall		
	W	L	Pct	W	L	Pct
Saint Joseph's⊕	7	1	.875	20	7	.741
La Salle	6	1	.857	16	6	.727
Temple□	9	2	.818	17	9	.654
Gettysburg	7	3	.700	15	11	.577
Bucknell	6	5	.545	10	11	.476
Rutgers	4	4	.500	11	14	.440
Lafayette	6	7	.462	12	13	.480
Lehigh	4	10	.286	6	16	.273
Muhlenberg	3	11	.214	8	18	.308
Delaware	1	9	.100	7	16	.304

Missouri Valley	Conference			Overall		
	W	L	Pct	W	L	Pct
Cincinnati⊕	13	1	.929	28	2	.933
Bradley□	12	2	.857	27	2	.931
Saint Louis□	9	5	.643	19	8	.704
Wichita State	6	8	.429	14	12	.538
Houston	6	8	.429	13	12	.520
Tulsa	5	9	.357	9	17	.346
Drake	4	10	.286	11	14	.440
North Texas	1	13	.071	7	19	.269

Skyline 8	Conference			Overall		
	W	L	Pct	W	L	Pct
Utah⊕	13	1	.929	26	3	.897
Utah State□	12	2	.857	24	5	.828
Colorado State	10	4	.714	13	10	.565
Denver	8	6	.571	13	11	.542
BYU	5	9	.357	8	17	.320
Montana	3	11	.214	7	17	.292
New Mexico	3	11	.214	6	19	.240
Wyoming	2	12	.143	5	19	.208

Ohio Valley	Conference			Overall		
	W	L	Pct	W	L	Pct
Western Kentucky⊕	10	2	.833	21	7	.750
Eastern Kentucky	9	3	.750	14	8	.636
Tennessee Tech	7	4	.636	13	9	.591
Murray State	7	4	.636	12	11	.522
Morehead State	3	7	.300	5	14	.263
Middle Tennessee St.	2	10	.167	9	14	.391
East Tennessee St.	2	10	.167	9	14	.391

SEC	Conference			Overall		
	W	L	Pct	W	L	Pct
Auburn	12	2	.857	19	3	.864
Georgia Tech⊕	11	3	.786	22	6	.786
Kentucky	10	4	.714	18	7	.720
Mississippi	8	6	.571	15	9	.625
Tulane	8	6	.571	13	11	.542
Vanderbilt	7	7	.500	14	9	.609
Tennessee	7	7	.500	12	11	.522
Georgia	6	8	.429	12	13	.480
Mississippi State	5	9	.357	12	13	.480
Alabama	4	10	.286	7	17	.292
Florida	3	11	.214	6	16	.273
LSU	3	11	.214	5	18	.217

Southern	Conference			Overall		
	W	L	Pct	W	L	Pct
Virginia Tech	12	1	.923	20	6	.769
West Virginia⊕	9	2	.818	26	5	.839
William and Mary	10	5	.667	15	11	.577
The Citadel	8	4	.667	15	8	.652
George Washington	7	5	.583	15	11	.577
Furman	6	7	.462	9	16	.360
VMI	3	11	.214	4	16	.200
Richmond	2	12	.143	7	18	.280
Davidson	0	10	.000	5	19	.208

Tournament: **West Virginia d. Virginia Tech 82-72**
Tournament MOP: **Jerry West**, West Virginia

Southwest	Conference			Overall		
	W	L	Pct	W	L	Pct
Texas⊕	11	3	.786	18	8	.692
Texas A&M	10	4	.714	19	5	.792
SMU	10	4	.714	17	7	.708
Arkansas	7	7	.500	12	11	.522
Texas Tech	7	7	.500	10	14	.417
Baylor	6	8	.429	12	12	.500
TCU	4	10	.286	7	17	.292
Rice	1	13	.071	4	20	.167

WCAC	Conference			Overall		
	W	L	Pct	W	L	Pct
Santa Clara⊕	9	3	.750	21	10	.677
Loyola Marymount	9	3	.750	19	8	.704
Pepperdine	8	4	.667	14	11	.560
Saint Mary's (CA)	7	5	.583	15	11	.577
San Francisco	5	7	.417	9	16	.360
Pacific	2	10	.167	9	17	.346
San Jose State	2	10	.167	6	19	.240

Yankee	Conference			Overall		
	W	L	Pct	W	L	Pct
Connecticut⊕	8	2	.800	17	9	.654
Maine	6	4	.600	19	4	.826
Massachusetts	6	4	.600	14	10	.583
Rhode Island	6	4	.600	12	14	.462
Vermont	2	8	.200	9	11	.450
New Hampshire	2	8	.200	9	14	.391

Conference Standings Continue →

⊕ Automatic NCAA Tournament bid ○ At-large NCAA Tournament bid □ NIT appearance ⊗ Team record doesn't reflect games forfeited or vacated. For adjusted record, see p. 521.

INDEPENDENTS

	Overall W	L	Pct
Miami (FL)○	23	4	.852
Providence□	24	5	.828
Idaho State○	21	5	.808
St. Bonaventure□	21	5	.808
Memphis□	18	5	.783
Holy Cross□	20	6	.769
Villanova□	20	6	.769
Dayton□	21	7	.750
Detroit□	20	7	.741
Navy○	16	6	.727
Iona	13	5	.722
DePaul○	17	7	.708
Seton Hall	16	7	.696
Oregon○	19	10	.655
Notre Dame○	17	9	.654
Xavier	17	9	.654
Syracuse	13	8	.619
Seattle	16	10	.615
Army	14	9	.609
Saint Francis (PA)	14	9	.609
Boston U.	14	10	.583
Butler	15	11	.577
Louisville	15	11	.577
Oregon State	15	11	.577

INDEPENDENTS (CONT.)

	Overall W	L	Pct
Air Force○	12	10	.545
Creighton	13	11	.542
Gonzaga	14	12	.538
Marquette	13	12	.520
Niagara	13	12	.520
Washington State	13	13	.500
Centenary	12	12	.500
Penn State	11	11	.500
Loyola (LA)	12	13	.480
Oklahoma City	12	13	.480
Colgate	11	12	.478
Georgetown	11	12	.478
Wash.-St. Louis	11	13	.458
Loyola-Chicago	10	12	.455
Boston College	11	14	.440
Montana State	11	14	.440
Pittsburgh	11	14	.440
Canisius	10	13	.435
Idaho	11	15	.423
Portland	11	15	.423
Florida State	10	15	.400
Duquesne	8	15	.348
Siena	3	18	.143

INDIVIDUAL LEADERS—SEASON

Scoring

	CL	POS	G	FG	FT	PTS	PPG
1 **Oscar Robertson**, Cincinnati	SR	G/F	30	369	273	1,011	**33.7**
2 **Tom Stith**, St. Bonaventure	JR	F	26	318	183	819	**31.5**
3 **Jim Darrow**, Bowling Green	SR	G	24	289	127	705	**29.4**
4 **Jerry West**, West Virginia	SR	G	31	325	258	908	**29.3**
5 **Frank Burgess**, Gonzaga	JR	G	26	270	211	751	**28.9**
6 **Al Butler**, Niagara	JR	G	25	278	158	714	**28.6**
7 **Terry Dischinger**, Purdue	SO	C	23	201	203	605	**26.3**
8 **Jerry Lucas**, Ohio State	SO	C	27	283	144	710	**26.3**
9 **Dave DeBusschere**, Detroit	SO	F	27	288	115	691	**25.6**
10 **Jim Mudd**, North Texas	SR	F	24	212	181	605	**25.2**

Field Goal Pct

	CL	POS	G	FG	FGA	PCT
1 **Jerry Lucas**, Ohio State	SO	C	27	283	444	**63.7**
2 **Paul Hogue**, Cincinnati	SO	C	30	152	264	**57.6**
3 **Hank Gunter**, Seton Hall	SO	C	22	128	224	**57.1**
4 **Chet Walker**, Bradley	SO	F	29	244	436	**56.0**
5 **Bob Nordmann**, Saint Louis	JR	C	27	173	310	**55.8**

Minimum: 100 made

Free Throw Pct

	CL	POS	G	FT	FTA	PCT
1 **Jack Waters**, Mississippi	JR	F	24	103	118	**87.3**
2 **York Larese**, North Carolina	JR	G	24	131	151	**86.8**
3 **Roger Kaiser**, Georgia Tech	JR	G	28	164	190	**86.3**
4 **Howie Carl**, DePaul	JR	G	24	135	158	**85.4**
5 **Don Smith**, Middle Tenn. State	SR	G/F	23	144	170	**84.7**

Minimum: 90 made

INDIVIDUAL LEADERS—GAME

Points

	CL	POS	OPP	DATE	PTS
1 **Oscar Robertson**, Cincinnati	SR	G/F	North Texas	F8	**62**
2 **Jack Foley**, Holy Cross	SO	F	Colgate	M5	**55**
3 **Jim Darrow**, Bowling Green	SR	G	Marshall	F27	**52**
Jim Darrow, Bowling Green	SR	G	Toledo	J13	**52**
5 **Bob Mealy**, Manhattan	SR	F	CCNY	F24	**51**

Free Throws Made

	CL	POS	OPP	DATE	FT	FTA	PCT
1 **Ron Godfrey**, Miami (FL)	JR	F	Oklahoma City	J29	**22**	26	84.6
2 **York Larese**, North Carolina	JR	G	Duke	D29	**21**	21	100.0
3 **Mike Callahan**, South Carolina	SR	F	Tennessee	D17	**20**	23	87.0
Larry Chanay, Montana State	SR	F	Oregon	D11	**20**	27	74.1
5 **Oscar Robertson**, Cincinnati	SR	G/F	St. Bonaventure	D26	**19**	25	76.0

TEAM LEADERS—SEASON

Scoring Offense

	G	W-L	PTS	PPG
1 **Ohio State**	28	25-3	2,532	**90.4**
2 **Miami (FL)**	27	23-4	2,427	**89.9**
3 **West Virginia**	31	26-5	2,775	**89.5**
4 **Cincinnati**	30	28-2	2,602	**86.7**
5 **Arizona State**	23	16-7	1,930	**83.9**

Field Goal Pct

	G	W-L	FG	FGA	PCT
1 **Auburn**	22	19-3	532	1,022	**52.1**
2 **Cincinnati**	30	28-2	1,035	2,025	**51.1**
3 **Ohio State**	28	25-3	1,044	2,101	**49.7**
4 **Texas**	26	18-8	713	1,503	**47.4**
5 **Bradley**	29	27-2	921	1,969	**46.8**

Free Throw Pct

	G	W-L	FT	FTA	PCT
1 **Auburn**	22	19-3	424	549	**77.2**
2 **Tulane**	24	13-11	438	573	**76.4**
3 **North Carolina**	24	18-6	542	715	**75.8**
4 **Mississippi**	24	15-9	451	600	**75.2**
5 **East Tennessee State**	23	9-14	438	585	**74.9**

Scoring Defense

	G	W-L	OPP PTS	OPP PPG
1 **California**	30	28-2	1,480	**49.3**
2 **Oklahoma State**	25	10-15	1,304	**52.2**
3 **Stanford**	25	11-14	1,376	**55.0**
4 **Oregon State**	26	15-11	1,458	**56.1**
5 **Providence**	29	24-5	1,632	**56.3**

CONSENSUS ALL-AMERICAS

First Team

PLAYER	CL	POS	HT	SCHOOL	RPG	PPG
Darrall Imhoff	SR	C	6-10	California	12.4	13.7
Jerry Lucas	SO	C	6-8	Ohio State	16.4	26.3
Oscar Robertson	SR	G/F	6-5	Cincinnati	14.1	33.7
Tom Stith	JR	F	6-5	St. Bonaventure	10.6	31.5
Jerry West	SR	G	6-3	West Virginia	16.5	29.3

Second Team

PLAYER	CL	POS	HT	SCHOOL	RPG	PPG
Terry Dischinger	SO	C	6-7	Purdue	14.3	26.3
Tony Jackson	JR	F	6-4	St. John's	12.9	21.2
Roger Kaiser	JR	G	6-1	Georgia Tech	5.5	22.8
Lee Shaffer	SR	F	6-7	North Carolina	11.2	18.2
Lenny Wilkens	SR	G	6-0	Providence	7.1	14.2

Selectors: AP, Look Magazine, NABC, Newspaper Enterprises Assn., UPI, USBWA

AWARD WINNERS

Player of the Year

PLAYER	CL	POS	HT	SCHOOL	AWARDS
Oscar Robertson	SR	G/F	6-5	Cincinnati	UPI, USBWA

Coach of the Year

COACH	SCHOOL	REC	AWARDS
Pete Newell	California	28-2	UPI, USBWA

Poll Progression

Week of Dec 8

UPI	School
1	Cincinnati (2-0)
2	California (1-0)
3	West Virginia (3-0)
4	Ohio State (3-0)
5	North Carolina (1-0)
6	Kentucky (2-1)
7	Saint Louis (3-0)
8	Indiana (1-0)
9	Kansas (1-0)
10	Utah (1-0)
11	Saint Joseph's (2-0)
12	Bradley (1-0)
13	Louisville (2-1)
14	Kansas State (1-1)
15	USC (3-0)
15	Georgia Tech (3-0)
17	Wake Forest (1-1)
18	Villanova (2-0)
18	St. John's (2-1)
20	UCLA (2-1)
20	NC State (1-1)

Week of Dec 14

UPI	School
1	Cincinnati (4-0)
2	Ohio State (5-0)
3	West Virginia (5-0)
4	California (3-0)
5	North Carolina (3-0)
6	Saint Louis (4-1)
7	Utah (4-0)
8	Bradley (3-0)
9	Kansas (3-1)
10	USC (3-2)
11	Indiana (2-1)
12	Georgia Tech (5-0)
13	Kentucky (2-2)
14	Iowa (4-0)
15	Villanova (4-0)
16	Illinois (2-0)
16	NC State (2-3)
18	NYU (4-0)
18	Texas A&M (4-0)
18	Louisville (4-1)

Week of Dec 22

AP	UPI	School
1	1	Cincinnati (5-0)
2	2	West Virginia (8-0)
3	3	Ohio State (6-0)
4	4	California (5-0)
5	7	Bradley (6-0)
6	6	Utah (6-0)
7	5	Saint Louis (6-2)
8	8	Georgia Tech (6-0)
9	10	Indiana (4-1)
10	17	Illinois (4-0)
11	19	Michigan State (4-0)
12	13	NYU (5-0)
13	12	Kentucky (4-3)
14	—	La Salle (6-0)
15	14	Villanova (6-0)
16	—	Duke (4-1)
17	—	Detroit (6-1)
18	16	Texas A&M (5-0)
19	17	Iowa (5-1)
20	15	USC (3-2)
—	9	Kansas (5-3)
—	11	North Carolina (3-2)
—	20	Notre Dame (6-1)

Week of Dec 29

AP	UPI	School	AP↑↓
1	1	Cincinnati (7-0)	
2	2	West Virginia (8-0)	
3	3	California (6-0)	↑1
4	5	Utah (8-0)	↑2
5	4	Ohio State (7-1) Ⓐ	↓2
6	6	Saint Louis (8-2)	↑1
7	8	Indiana (6-1)	↑2
8	9	Illinois (5-0)	↑2
9	7	Bradley (6-1)	↓4
10	17	Georgia Tech (7-1)	↓2
11	—	Detroit (7-1)	↑6
12	10	NYU (6-0)	
13	14	Kentucky (5-3) Ⓐ	
14	13	Iowa (7-1)	↑5
15	—	Miami (FL) (6-0)	⤴
16	—	Toledo (4-1)	⤴
17	16	Villanova (6-0)	↓2
18	18	Duke (8-1)	↓2
19	—	Wake Forest (4-1)	⤴
20	—	DePaul (6-0)	⤴
—	11	North Carolina (4-2)	
—	12	Texas A&M (5-0)	⤵
—	15	Kansas (5-3)	
—	18	USC (6-2)	⤵
—	20	Michigan State (4-2)	⤵

Week of Jan 5

AP	UPI	School	AP↑↓
1	1	Cincinnati (10-0)	
2	2	California (9-1) Ⓑ	↑1
3	3	West Virginia (10-1) Ⓑ	↓1
4	4	Bradley (8-1)	↑5
5	6	Utah (10-1)	↓1
6	8	Georgia Tech (9-1)	↑4
7	5	Ohio State (7-2)	↓2
8	11	Wake Forest (7-2)	↑11
9	20	Illinois (7-1)	↓1
10	7	USC (8-3)	⤴
11	13	Indiana (8-2)	↓4
12	9	Saint Louis (8-3)	↓6
13	10	Texas A&M (8-0)	⤴
14	—	Miami (FL) (11-1)	↑1
15	—	Detroit (9-1)	↓4
16	14	Villanova (7-0)	↑1
17	17	Utah State (10-2)	⤴
18	—	Western Kentucky (7-1)	⤴
19	12	North Carolina (6-3)	⤴
20	—	Toledo (7-1)	↓4
—	15	Iowa (8-3)	⤵
—	16	Iowa State (8-2)	
—	18	SMU (7-3)	
—	19	Saint Joseph's (8-2)	
—	20	Kentucky (6-4)	⤵

Week of Jan 12

AP	UPI	School	AP↑↓
1	1	Cincinnati (12-0)	
2	2	California (12-1)	
3	3	West Virginia (12-1)	
4	5	Bradley (10-1)	
5	4	Ohio State (9-2)	↑2
6	6	Georgia Tech (10-1)	
7	9	Utah (11-2)	↓2
8	7	Texas A&M (10-0)	↑5
9	12	Villanova (9-0)	↑7
10	8	USC (10-4)	
11	10	Saint Louis (10-3)	↑1
12	13	Utah State (11-2)	↑5
13	17	Wake Forest (8-3)	↓5
14	16	Illinois (8-2)	↓5
15	—	Miami (FL) (12-1)	↓1
16	11	North Carolina (7-3)	↑3
17	18	Kentucky (8-4)	⤴
18	—	Toledo (8-1)	↑2
19	—	La Salle (8-0)	⤴
20	—	Detroit (10-2)	↓5
—	14	Iowa (10-3)	
—	15	Iowa State (9-3)	
—	18	Indiana (8-4)	⤵
—	20	Kansas (8-4)	
—	20	Notre Dame (11-5)	

Week of Jan 19

AP	UPI	School	AP↑↓
1	1	Cincinnati (13-1)	
2	4	Bradley (12-1) Ⓒ	↑2
3	2	California (14-1)	↓1
4	3	West Virginia (15-1)	↓1
5	5	Ohio State (11-2)	
6	6	Georgia Tech (13-1)	
7	7	Utah (13-2)	
8	9	Villanova (10-1)	↑1
9	12	Utah State (13-2)	↑3
10	8	Texas A&M (11-1)	↓2
11	—	Miami (FL) (15-1)	↑4
12	11	North Carolina (9-3)	↑4
13	16	Illinois (10-2)	↑1
14	10	USC (11-5)	↓4
15	13	Iowa (12-3)	⤴
16	15	Kentucky (10-4)	↑1
17	—	Toledo (10-2)	↑1
18	14	Saint Louis (10-5)	↓7
19	—	Dayton (12-3)	⤴
20	—	Detroit (12-2)	
—	17	Notre Dame (13-5)	
—	18	Kansas (9-5)	
—	19	Indiana (9-4)	
—	20	NYU (9-2)	
—	20	SMU (10-4)	
—	20	Saint Joseph's (11-3)	

Week of Jan 26

AP	UPI	School	AP↑↓
1	1	Cincinnati (14-1)	
2	4	Bradley (13-1)	
3	2	California (14-1)	
4	3	West Virginia (15-1)	
5	5	Ohio State (12-2)	
6	6	Georgia Tech (14-2)	
7	8	Utah (14-2)	
8	7	Villanova (12-1)	
9	10	Utah State (14-2)	
10	9	Texas A&M (12-1)	
11	—	Miami (FL) (15-2)	
12	11	North Carolina (9-3)	
13	—	Toledo (11-2)	↑4
14	—	Detroit (13-2)	↑6
15	14	Kentucky (10-4)	↑1
16	13	Saint Louis (10-5)	↑2
17	—	Virginia Tech (11-2)	⤴
18	12	USC (11-5)	↓4
19	18	Dayton (13-3)	
20	19	Wake Forest (11-4)	⤴
20	—	Providence (10-3)	⤴
—	14	Iowa State (9-6)	
—	16	Kansas State (10-5)	
—	17	Iowa (13-3)	⤵
—	20	Indiana (9-4)	
—	20	Saint Joseph's (11-4)	

Week of Feb 2

AP	UPI	School	AP↑↓
1	2	Cincinnati (15-1)	
2	3	Bradley (14-1)	
3	1	California (16-1)	
4	4	Ohio State (13-2)	↑1
5	5	West Virginia (16-2)	↓1
6	6	Georgia Tech (16-2)	
7	8	Utah (15-2)	
8	7	Villanova (14-1)	
9	10	Utah State (15-2)	
10	9	Texas A&M (12-1)	
11	—	Miami (FL) (16-2)	
12	—	Toledo (13-2)	↑1
13	12	Dayton (15-3)	↑6
14	—	Detroit (14-2) Ⓓ	
15	14	Kansas State (11-5)	⤴
16	—	Providence (10-3)	↑4
17	11	North Carolina (9-3)	↓5
18	15	Saint Louis (11-5)	↓2
19	16	St. Bonaventure (11-3)	⤴
19	—	Illinois (11-3)	⤴
—	13	USC (11-5)	⤵
—	16	Saint Joseph's (12-4)	
—	16	Indiana (10-4)	
—	16	Kentucky (12-5)	⤵
—	16	Iowa State (12-6)	
—	16	SMU (10-4)	

Week of Feb 9

AP	UPI	School	AP↑↓
1	2	Cincinnati (17-1) Ⓔ	
2	3	Bradley (17-1)	
3	1	California (17-1)	
4	4	Ohio State (15-2)	
5	5	West Virginia (18-2)	
6	8	Georgia Tech (17-3)	
7	9	Utah State (17-2)	↑2
8	6	Villanova (16-1)	
9	7	Utah (17-2)	↓2
10	—	Miami (FL) (20-2)	↑1
11	—	Toledo (15-2)	↑1
12	10	Texas A&M (14-2)	↓2
13	11	North Carolina (10-3)	↑4
14	—	Providence (13-3)	↑2
15	12	Dayton (16-3)	↓2
16	—	Holy Cross (13-2)	⤴
17	—	Auburn (13-3)	⤴
18	13	Saint Louis (13-5)	
19	—	Detroit (15-3)	↓5
20	14	Illinois (12-3)	↓1
—	14	Kentucky (13-5)	
—	16	St. Bonaventure (11-3)	⤵
—	16	USC (11-7)	
—	18	Saint Joseph's (12-5)	
—	18	Louisville (12-6)	
—	18	Kansas State (11-6)	⤵
—	18	Wake Forest (13-6)	

Week of Feb 16

AP	UPI	School	AP↑↓
1	2	Cincinnati (19-1)	
2	4	Bradley (19-1)	
3	1	California (19-1)	
4	3	Ohio State (17-2)	
5	5	West Virginia (20-3)	
6	8	Georgia Tech (19-3)	
7	7	Utah State (18-2)	
8	6	Utah (18-2)	↑1
9	9	Villanova (17-2)	↓1
10	—	Miami (FL) (20-3)	
11	10	Texas A&M (16-2)	↑1
12	—	Toledo (17-2)	↓1
13	—	Holy Cross (15-2)	↑3
14	16	St. Bonaventure (13-3)	⤴
15	13	St. John's (14-5)	⤴
16	—	Providence (14-4)	↓2
17	—	Auburn (15-3)	
18	—	Ohio (13-4)	⤴
19	11	North Carolina (12-4)	↓6
20	18	Illinois (13-4)	
—	12	Saint Louis (14-6)	⤵
—	14	Dayton (16-4)	⤵
—	15	Kentucky (15-5)	
—	16	NYU (13-3)	
—	18	Wake Forest (15-6)	
—	20	Kansas State (12-7)	

Week of Feb 23

AP	UPI	School	AP↑↓
1	2	Cincinnati (20-1)	
2	3	Ohio State (19-2)	↑2
3	4	Bradley (21-1)	↓1
4	1	California (20-1)	↓1
5	5	Utah (20-2)	↑3
6	8	Georgia Tech (20-4)	
7	6	West Virginia (21-4)	↓2
8	7	Utah State (19-3)	↓1
9	—	Miami (FL) (21-3)	↑1
10	13	St. Bonaventure (15-3)	↑4
11	11	St. John's (16-5)	↑4
12	9	Villanova (17-3)	↓3
13	16	Auburn (17-3)	↑4
14	15	NYU (15-3)	⤴
15	—	Providence (18-4)	↑1
16	14	Saint Louis (17-6)	⤴
17	—	Holy Cross (17-3)	↓4
18	10	Texas A&M (17-3)	↓7
19	—	Toledo (17-4)	↓7
20	—	Indiana (16-4)	⤴
—	12	North Carolina (14-5)	⤵
—	17	Wake Forest (17-6)	
—	18	Dayton (16-6)	
—	19	Texas (15-5)	
—	20	Kentucky (16-6)	

Poll Progression Continues →

ANNUAL REVIEW

WEEK OF MAR 1

AP	UPI	SCHOOL	AP↓↑
1	2	**Cincinnati** (22-1)	
2	3	**Ohio State** (20-2)	
3	1	**California** (22-1)	↑1
4	4	**Bradley** (22-2)	↓1
5	6	**West Virginia** (24-4)	↑2
6	5	**Utah** (22-2)	↓1
7	8	**Georgia Tech** (21-5)	↓1
8	—	**Miami (FL)** (23-3)	↑1
9	11	**St. Bonaventure** (17-3)	↑1
10	7	**Utah State** (20-4)	↓2
11	16	**Auburn** (19-3)	↑2
12	—	**Indiana** (18-4)	↑8
13	12	**Saint Louis** (17-6)	↑3
14	13	**NYU** (17-3)	
15	20	**Providence** (19-4)	
16	9	**North Carolina** (17-5)	⤴
17	10	**Villanova** (18-5)	↓5
18	17	**Wake Forest** (19-6)	⤴
19	13	**St. John's** (17-6)	↓8
20	—	**Holy Cross** (17-5)	↓3
—	15	**Texas** (18-5)	
—	18	**Texas A&M** (17-5)	⤵
—	19	**Dayton** (17-6)	
—	20	**Kansas** (15-8)	

FINAL POLL

AP	UPI	SCHOOL	AP↓↑
1	2	**Cincinnati** (24-1) Ⓕ	
2	1	**California** (24-1)	↑1
3	3	**Ohio State** (21-3)	↓1
4	4	**Bradley** (24-2)	
5	6	**West Virginia** (24-4)	
6	5	**Utah** (24-2)	
7	10	**Indiana** (20-4)	↑5
8	7	**Utah State** (22-5)	↑2
9	11	**St. Bonaventure** (19-3) Ⓖ	
10	—	**Miami (FL)** (23-3)	↓2
11	17	**Auburn** (19-3)	
12	12	**NYU** (19-3)	↑2
13	8	**Georgia Tech** (21-5)	↓6
14	18	**Providence** (21-4)	↑1
15	19	**Saint Louis** (18-7)	↓2
16	—	**Holy Cross** (20-5)	↑4
17	9	**Villanova** (19-5)	
18	15	**Duke** (15-10)	⤴
19	—	**Wake Forest** (21-7) Ⓗ	↓1
20	—	**St. John's** (17-7)	↓1
—	13	**Texas** (18-6)	
—	14	**North Carolina** (18-6)	⤵
—	16	**Kansas State** (16-9)	
—	20	**Dayton** (19-6)	

Ⓐ Trailing 59-49 at halftime, Kentucky roars back to defeat Ohio State 96-93 in Lexington. Sophomore stars Jerry Lucas and John Havlicek score 34 and 16, respectively, for the Buckeyes, but they're offset by Billy Ray Lickert's 29 and Bennie Coffman's 26.

Ⓑ Cal beats West Virginia, 65-45, holding Jerry West to six points, the lowest output of his college career.

Ⓒ On Jan. 16, Bradley becomes the first team to score 90 points or more against a No. 1 team, squeaking past Cincinnati, 91-90.

Ⓓ Dave DeBusschere grabs a career-high 39 rebounds in a Jan. 30 victory over Central Michigan. The 6'8" Detroit forward will win two NBA championships with the New York Knicks, in addition to pitching for the Chicago White Sox.

Ⓔ Oscar Robertson scores a career-high 62 points against North Texas. On Feb. 20, Robertson will score 29 in a 67-55 win over Houston, breaking Dickie Hemric's NCAA career scoring record of 2,587 points.

Ⓕ Cincinnati becomes the second team to go wire-to-wire as No. 1 in the AP Poll.

Ⓖ Tom and Sam Stith combine to average 52 points a game for St. Bonaventure, an NCAA record for brothers on the same team.

Ⓗ Future broadcaster Billy Packer leads Wake Forest to the ACC tournament, where he shoots only six for 35 from the floor in three games.

1960 NCAA Tournament

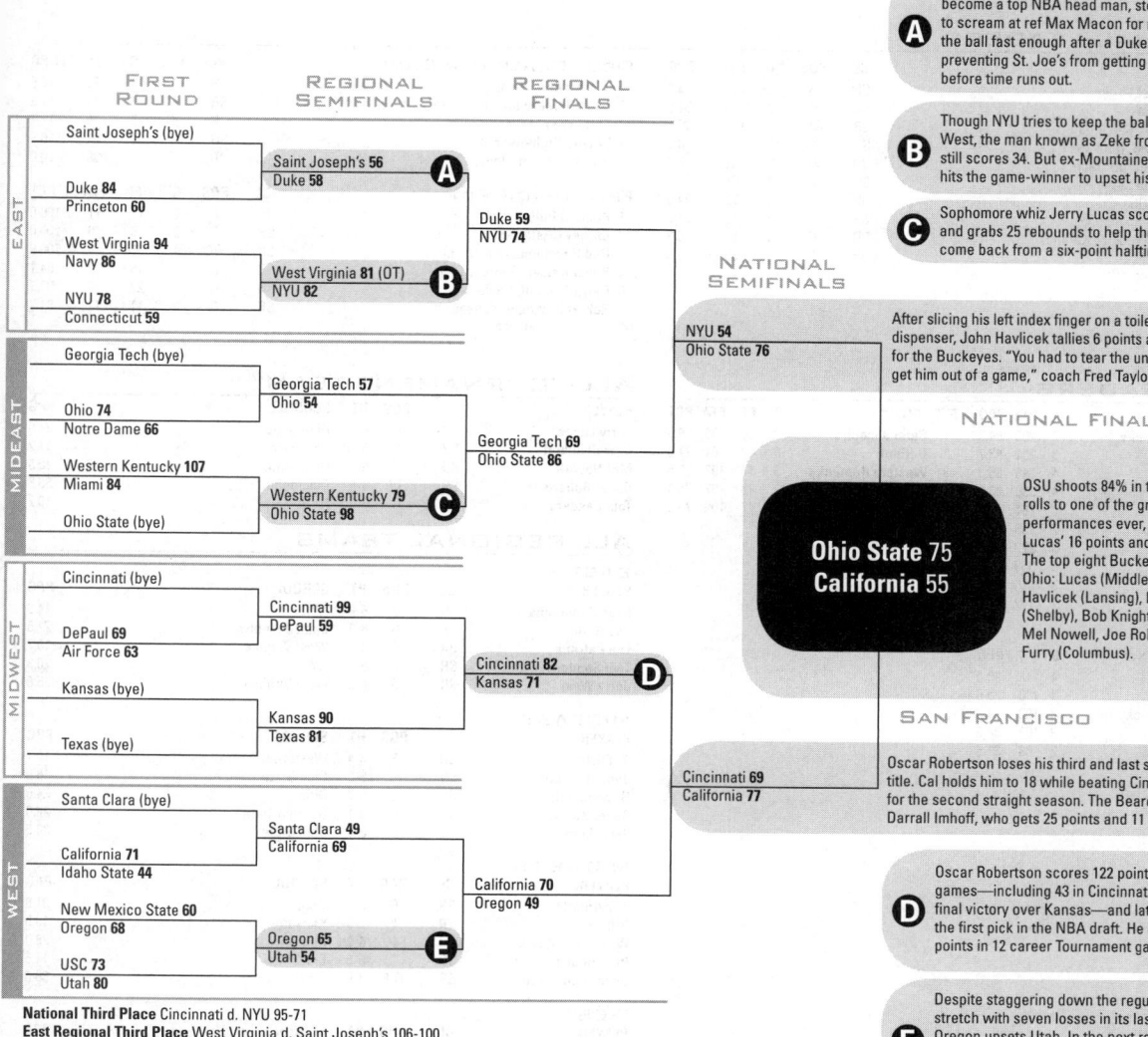

First Round | Regional Semifinals | Regional Finals | National Semifinals | National Final

EAST

First Round:
Saint Joseph's (bye)
Duke **84**
Princeton **60**
West Virginia **94**
Navy **86**
NYU **78**
Connecticut **59**

Regional Semifinals:
Saint Joseph's **56**
Duke **58** (A)
West Virginia **81** (OT)
NYU **82** (B)

Regional Finals:
Duke **59**
NYU **74**

MIDEAST

First Round:
Georgia Tech (bye)
Ohio **74**
Notre Dame **66**
Western Kentucky **107**
Miami **84**
Ohio State (bye)

Regional Semifinals:
Georgia Tech **57**
Ohio **54**
Western Kentucky **79**
Ohio State **98** (C)

Regional Finals:
Georgia Tech **69**
Ohio State **86**

MIDWEST

First Round:
Cincinnati (bye)
DePaul **69**
Air Force **63**
Kansas (bye)
Texas (bye)

Regional Semifinals:
Cincinnati **99**
DePaul **59**
Kansas **90**
Texas **81**

Regional Finals:
Cincinnati **82**
Kansas **71** (D)

WEST

First Round:
Santa Clara (bye)
California **71**
Idaho State **44**
New Mexico State **60**
Oregon **68**
USC **73**
Utah **80**

Regional Semifinals:
Santa Clara **49**
California **69**
Oregon **65**
Utah **54** (E)

Regional Finals:
California **70**
Oregon **49**

National Semifinals

NYU **54**
Ohio State **76**

After slicing his left index finger on a toilet paper dispenser, John Havlicek tallies 6 points and 10 rebounds for the Buckeyes. "You had to tear the uniform off him to get him out of a game," coach Fred Taylor says.

Cincinnati **69**
California **77**

Oscar Robertson loses his third and last shot at an NCAA title. Cal holds him to 18 while beating Cincy in the semis for the second straight season. The Bearcats can't stop Darrall Imhoff, who gets 25 points and 11 rebounds.

National Final

Ohio State 75
California 55

OSU shoots 84% in the first half and rolls to one of the greatest title-game performances ever, led by Jerry Lucas' 16 points and 10 rebounds. The top eight Buckeyes are all from Ohio: Lucas (Middletown), John Havlicek (Lansing), Larry Siegfried (Shelby), Bob Knight (Orrville) and Mel Nowell, Joe Roberts and Richard Furry (Columbus).

San Francisco

National Third Place Cincinnati d. NYU 95-71
East Regional Third Place West Virginia d. Saint Joseph's 106-100
Mideast Regional Third Place Western Kentucky d. Ohio 97-87
Midwest Regional Third Place DePaul d. Texas 67-61
West Regional Third Place Utah d. Santa Clara 89-81 (F)

A Saint Joseph's coach Jack Ramsay, who will become a top NBA head man, storms the court to scream at ref Max Macon for not retrieving the ball fast enough after a Duke basket, preventing St. Joe's from getting a final shot before time runs out.

B Though NYU tries to keep the ball from Jerry West, the man known as Zeke from Cabin Creek still scores 34. But ex-Mountaineer Jimmy Reiss hits the game-winner to upset his former team.

C Sophomore whiz Jerry Lucas scores 36 points and grabs 25 rebounds to help the Buckeyes come back from a six-point halftime deficit.

D Oscar Robertson scores 122 points in four games—including 43 in Cincinnati's regional final victory over Kansas—and later becomes the first pick in the NBA draft. He averages 32.4 points in 12 career Tournament games.

E Despite staggering down the regular-season stretch with seven losses in its last 12 games, Oregon upsets Utah. In the next round, however, the Ducks get cooked by defending NCAA champ California, which rolls to a 21-point win.

F Utah sinks 41 free throws—a Tournament record that would not be broken for 41 years—on 48 attempts. Richard Ruffell goes a perfect 11 for 11, scoring a game-high 25 points.

Tournament Leaders

Individual Leaders

Scoring

	CL	POS	G	PTS	PPG
1 **Jerry West**, West Virginia	SR	G	3	105	35.0
2 **Jay Arnette**, Texas	SR	G	2	63	31.5
3 **Oscar Robertson**, Cincinnati	SR	G/F	4	122	30.5
4 **Wayne Hightower**, Kansas	SO	F	2	56	28.0
5 **Roger Kaiser**, Georgia Tech	JR	G	2	52	26.0
6 **Jerry Lucas**, Ohio State	SO	C	4	96	24.0
Howard Jolliff, Ohio	JR	C	3	72	24.0
8 **Joe Gallo**, Saint Joseph's	SR	G	2	43	21.5
9 **Bobby Rascoe**, Western Kentucky	SO	G	3	61	20.3
10 **Bill Bridges**, Kansas	JR	F	2	39	19.5

Minimum: 2 games

Field Goals Per Game

	CL	POS	G	FG	FGPG
1 **Jay Arnette**, Texas	SR	G	2	29	14.5
2 **Oscar Robertson**, Cincinnati	SR	G/F	4	47	11.8
3 **Jerry West**, West Virginia	SR	G	3	35	11.7
4 **Wayne Hightower**, Kansas	SO	F	2	21	10.5
5 **Howard Jolliff**, Ohio	JR	C	3	30	10.0

Free Throw Pct

	CL	POS	G	FT	FTA	PCT
1 **Richard Ruffell**, Utah	JR	F	3	11	11	100.0
Carney Crisler, Utah	SR	C	2	6	6	100.0
Dod Hammond, Miami (FL)	SR	F/C	1	5	5	100.0
4 **Roger Kaiser**, Georgia Tech	JR	G	2	16	17	94.1
5 **Darrall Imhoff**, California	SR	C	5	22	24	91.7
Robert Hickman, Kansas	SR	G	2	11	12	91.7

Minimum: 5 made

Team Leaders

Scoring

	G	PTS	PPG
1 **Western Kentucky**	3	283	94.3
2 **West Virginia**	3	281	93.7
3 **Cincinnati**	4	345	86.3
4 **Ohio State**	4	335	83.8
5 **Kansas**	2	161	80.5
6 **Saint Joseph's**	2	156	78.0
7 **Utah**	3	223	74.3
8 **NYU**	5	359	71.8
9 **Ohio**	3	215	71.7
10 **Texas**	2	142	71.0

Minimum: 2 games

FG per Game

	G	FG	FGPG
1 **Cincinnati**	4	143	35.8
2 **Ohio State**	4	140	35.0
3 **Western Kentucky**	3	103	34.3
4 **West Virginia**	3	102	34.0
5 **Saint Joseph's**	2	63	31.5

FT Pct

	G	FT	FTA	PCT
1 **Saint Joseph's**	2	30	38	79.0
2 **DePaul**	3	47	61	77.0
3 **Western Kentucky**	3	77	102	75.5
4 **Kansas**	2	43	57	75.4
5 **West Virginia**	3	77	105	73.3

Minimum: 2 games

All-Tournament Team

PLAYER	CL	POS	HT	SCHOOL	PPG
Jerry Lucas*	SO	C	6-8	Ohio State	24.0
Darrall Imhoff	SR	C	6-10	California	17.2
Mel Nowell	SO	G	6-2	Ohio State	10.8
Oscar Robertson	SR	G/F	6-5	Cincinnati	30.5
Tom Sanders	SR	C	6-6	NYU	19.2

All-Regional Teams

East

PLAYER	CL	POS	HT	SCHOOL	PPG
Russ Cunningham	SR	G	5-8	NYU	14.3
Joe Gallo	SR	G	6-2	Saint Joseph's	21.5
Lee Patrone	JR	G	6-1	West Virginia	16.7
Tom Sanders	SR	C	6-6	NYU	20.3
Jerry West	SR	G	6-3	West Virginia	35.0

Mideast

PLAYER	CL	POS	HT	SCHOOL	PPG
Al Ellison	SR	F	6-4	Western Kentucky	16.7
John Havlicek	SO	F	6-5	Ohio State	16.0
Howard Jolliff	JR	C	6-7	Ohio	24.0
Roger Kaiser	JR	G	6-1	Georgia Tech	26.0
Jerry Lucas	SO	C	6-8	Ohio State	30.5

Midwest

PLAYER	CL	POS	HT	SCHOOL	PPG
Jay Arnette	SR	G	6-2	Texas	31.5
Bill Bridges	JR	F	6-5½	Kansas	19.5
Wayne Hightower	SO	F	6-8½	Kansas	28.0
Paul Hogue	SO	C	6-9	Cincinnati	14.5
Oscar Robertson	SR	G/F	6-5	Cincinnati	36.0

West

PLAYER	CL	POS	HT	SCHOOL	PPG
Darrall Imhoff	SR	C	6-10	California	17.7
Bill McClintock	JR	F	6-4	California	13.3
Chuck Rask	SR	G	6-1	Oregon	15.3
Jim Russi	SR	G	6-3	Santa Clara	19.5
Earl Shultz	JR	G	6-4	California	4.0

* Most outstanding player

1960 NCAA TOURNAMENT BOX SCORES

SWEET 16 — Duke 58, Saint Joseph's 56 (1H: 27–20; 2H: 31–36)

DUKE	MIN	FG	3FG	FT	REB	A	ST	BL	PF	TP
Carroll Youngkin	-	9-15	-	4-6	12	-	-	-	5	22
Howard Hurt	-	7-14	-	1-2	6	-	-	-	2	15
John Frye	-	2-9	-	2-4	3	-	-	-	0	6
Doug Kistler	-	2-11	-	2-4	8	-	-	-	2	6
Jack Mullen	-	0-1	-	5-7	2	-	-	-	0	5
Buzzy Mewhort	-	1-1	-	2-3	2	-	-	-	2	4
TOTALS	-	21-51	-	16-26	33	-	-	-	11	58
Percentages		41.2		61.5						

Coach: Vic Bubas

SAINT JOSEPH'S	MIN	FG	3FG	FT	REB	A	ST	BL	PF	TP
Bob Clarke	-	7-15	-	8-11	15	-	-	-	4	22
Joe Gallo	-	6-20	-	2-2	5	-	-	-	5	14
Bob McNeill	-	4-12	-	0-0	5	-	-	-	1	8
Jack Egan	-	2-12	-	0-3	6	-	-	-	2	4
Jared Reilly	-	2-5	-	0-0	1	-	-	-	1	4
Vincent Kempton	-	0-7	-	2-2	14	-	-	-	2	2
Paul Westhead	-	1-1	-	0-0	1	-	-	-	3	2
Harry Booth	-	0-0	-	0-0	0	-	-	-	0	0
Frank Majewski	-	0-2	-	0-0	0	-	-	-	0	0
TOTALS	-	22-74	-	12-18	47	-	-	-	18	56
Percentages		29.7		66.7						

Coach: Jack Ramsay

Officials: Macon

SWEET 16 — NYU 82, West Virginia 81 (1H: 40–41; 2H: 36–37; OT: 5–4)

NYU	MIN	FG	3FG	FT	REB	A	ST	BL	PF	TP
Tom Sanders	-	12-21	-	4-7	19	-	-	-	3	28
Russ Cunningham	-	6-16	-	4-8	2	-	-	-	4	16
Ray Paprocky	-	5-13	-	5-7	5	-	-	-	2	15
Al Filardi	-	4-20	-	5-9	21	-	-	-	4	13
Mike Dinapoli	-	1-6	-	3-3	1	-	-	-	1	5
Al Barden	-	1-4	-	1-2	6	-	-	-	5	3
Jimmy Reiss	-	1-2	-	0-0	0	-	-	-	1	2
Art Loche	-	0-2	-	0-0	1	-	-	-	0	0
TOTALS	-	30-84	-	22-36	55	-	-	-	20	82
Percentages		35.7		61.1						

Coach: Lou Rossini

WEST VIRGINIA	MIN	FG	3FG	FT	REB	A	ST	BL	PF	TP
Jerry West	-	11-28	-	12-13	16	-	-	-	2	34
Lee Patrone	-	8-13	-	3-5	10	-	-	-	4	19
Paul Popovich	-	5-6	-	0-0	3	-	-	-	2	10
Willie Akers	-	2-11	-	4-5	12	-	-	-	3	8
Jim Ritchie	-	1-6	-	3-6	7	-	-	-	5	5
Paul Miller	-	1-3	-	1-4	1	-	-	-	4	3
Jim Warren	-	1-4	-	0-0	2	-	-	-	2	2
Joe Posch	-	0-1	-	0-0	0	-	-	-	1	0
TOTALS	-	29-72	-	23-33	51	-	-	-	23	81
Percentages		40.3		69.7						

Coach: Fred Schaus

SWEET 16 — Georgia Tech 57, Ohio 54 (1H: 23–33; 2H: 34–21)

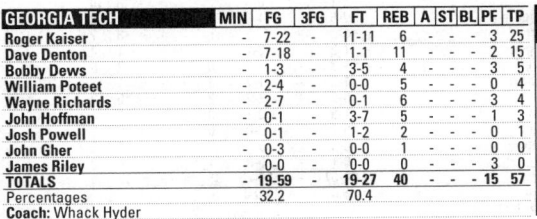

GEORGIA TECH	MIN	FG	3FG	FT	REB	A	ST	BL	PF	TP
Roger Kaiser	-	7-22	-	11-11	6	-	-	-	3	25
Dave Denton	-	7-18	-	1-1	11	-	-	-	2	15
Bobby Dews	-	1-3	-	3-5	4	-	-	-	3	5
William Poteet	-	2-4	-	0-0	5	-	-	-	0	4
Wayne Richards	-	2-7	-	0-1	6	-	-	-	3	4
John Hoffman	-	0-1	-	3-7	5	-	-	-	1	3
Josh Powell	-	0-1	-	1-2	2	-	-	-	0	1
John Gher	-	0-3	-	0-0	1	-	-	-	0	0
James Riley	-	0-0	-	0-0	0	-	-	-	3	0
TOTALS	-	19-59	-	19-27	40	-	-	-	15	57
Percentages		32.2		70.4						

Coach: Whack Hyder

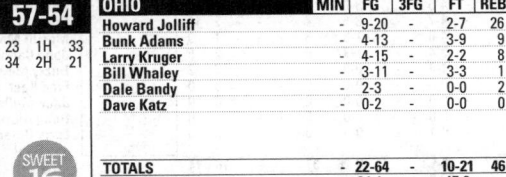

OHIO	MIN	FG	3FG	FT	REB	A	ST	BL	PF	TP
Howard Jolliff	-	9-20	-	2-7	26	-	-	-	4	20
Bunk Adams	-	4-13	-	3-9	9	-	-	-	3	11
Larry Kruger	-	4-15	-	2-2	8	-	-	-	3	10
Bill Whaley	-	3-11	-	3-3	1	-	-	-	1	9
Dale Bandy	-	2-3	-	0-0	2	-	-	-	5	4
Dave Katz	-	0-2	-	0-0	0	-	-	-	2	0
TOTALS	-	22-64	-	10-21	46	-	-	-	18	54
Percentages		34.4		47.6						

Coach: Jim Snyder

Attendance: 16,524

SWEET 16 — Ohio State 98, Western Kentucky 79 (1H: 37–43; 2H: 61–36)

OHIO STATE	MIN	FG	3FG	FT	REB	A	ST	BL	PF	TP
Jerry Lucas	-	14-25	-	8-10	25	-	-	-	4	36
John Havlicek	-	7-15	-	3-4	8	-	-	-	1	17
Mel Nowell	-	6-11	-	3-5	0	-	-	-	2	15
Larry Siegfried	-	6-15	-	0-1	7	-	-	-	2	12
Bob Knight	-	3-7	-	0-0	1	-	-	-	2	6
Gary Gearhart	-	2-4	-	0-0	3	-	-	-	5	4
Joe Roberts	-	2-4	-	0-0	3	-	-	-	1	4
Richard Furry	-	1-4	-	0-0	2	-	-	-	2	2
Howard Nourse	-	1-1	-	0-0	0	-	-	-	0	2
David Barker	-	0-0	-	0-0	1	-	-	-	0	0
Richie Hoyt	-	0-0	-	0-0	0	-	-	-	0	0
TOTALS	-	42-86	-	14-20	50	-	-	-	19	98
Percentages		48.8		70.0						

Coach: Fred R. Taylor

WESTERN KENTUCKY	MIN	FG	3FG	FT	REB	A	ST	BL	PF	TP
Charlie Osborne	-	6-11	-	6-7	9	-	-	-	1	18
Al Ellison	-	8-21	-	1-2	7	-	-	-	4	17
Don Parsons	-	6-11	-	5-6	6	-	-	-	2	17
Bobby Rascoe	-	4-9	-	8-11	6	-	-	-	3	16
Harry Todd	-	3-8	-	0-0	7	-	-	-	4	6
Bob Cole	-	1-2	-	0-0	0	-	-	-	0	2
Panny Sarakatsannie	-	1-4	-	0-0	0	-	-	-	3	2
Jude Talbott	-	0-2	-	1-1	2	-	-	-	0	1
TOTALS	-	29-68	-	21-27	37	-	-	-	17	79
Percentages		42.6		77.8						

Coach: E.A. Diddle

Attendance: 16,524

SWEET 16 — Cincinnati 99, DePaul 59 (1H: 53–23; 2H: 46–36)

CINCINNATI	MIN	FG	3FG	FT	REB	A	ST	BL	PF	TP
Oscar Robertson	-	12-25	-	5-7	9	-	-	-	2	29
Paul Hogue	-	9-12	-	0-3	15	-	-	-	3	18
Ralph Davis	-	7-13	-	0-0	2	-	-	-	0	14
Carl Bouldin	-	4-6	-	3-3	1	-	-	-	1	11
Bob Wiesenhahn	-	4-8	-	1-3	10	-	-	-	1	9
Tom Sizer	-	2-2	-	2-2	0	-	-	-	1	6
Larry Willey	-	2-2	-	2-3	5	-	-	-	3	6
Sandy Pomerantz	-	2-7	-	0-2	3	-	-	-	1	4
Jim Calhoun	-	1-2	-	0-0	1	-	-	-	0	2
John Bryant	-	0-0	-	0-0	0	-	-	-	0	0
Fred Dierking	-	0-1	-	0-0	0	-	-	-	0	0
Ron Reis	-	0-0	-	0-0	0	-	-	-	1	0
TOTALS	-	43-78	-	13-23	46	-	-	-	13	99
Percentages		55.1		56.5						

Coach: George Smith

DEPAUL	MIN	FG	3FG	FT	REB	A	ST	BL	PF	TP
Mack Cowsen	-	4-11	-	7-8	6	-	-	-	4	15
Howie Carl	-	5-16	-	2-5	3	-	-	-	1	12
Paul Ruddy	-	4-12	-	2-2	6	-	-	-	2	10
John Bagley	-	3-3	-	0-0	1	-	-	-	1	6
Jim Flemming	-	3-7	-	0-0	3	-	-	-	5	6
Bill Haig	-	3-7	-	0-1	2	-	-	-	0	6
Mike Salzinski	-	2-6	-	0-1	4	-	-	-	3	4
Jerry Meier	-	0-0	-	0-2	0	-	-	-	1	0
TOTALS	-	24-62	-	11-19	25	-	-	-	17	59
Percentages		38.7		57.9						

Coach: Ray Meyer

Officials: Overstreet, Murdock

SWEET 16 — Kansas 90, Texas 81 (1H: 36–42; 2H: 54–39)

KANSAS	MIN	FG	3FG	FT	REB	A	ST	BL	PF	TP
Wayne Hightower	-	13-26	-	8-12	9	-	-	-	3	34
Bill Bridges	-	7-10	-	3-7	14	-	-	-	4	17
Jerry Gardner	-	6-13	-	1-2	7	-	-	-	4	13
Robert Hickman	-	0-4	-	11-11	6	-	-	-	2	11
Richard Gisel	-	2-6	-	3-3	2	-	-	-	1	7
Allen Correll	-	2-3	-	2-2	2	-	-	-	1	6
Jim Myers	-	1-1	-	0-0	0	-	-	-	1	2
James Hoffman	-	0-0	-	0-0	1	-	-	-	0	0
TOTALS	-	31-63	-	28-37	41	-	-	-	16	90
Percentages		49.2		75.7						

Coach: Dick Harp

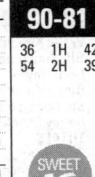

TEXAS	MIN	FG	3FG	FT	REB	A	ST	BL	PF	TP
Jay Arnette	-	16-31	-	2-3	7	-	-	-	4	34
Albert Almanza	-	7-13	-	3-5	6	-	-	-	3	17
Donnie Lasiter	-	6-12	-	2-3	2	-	-	-	1	14
Wayne Clark	-	2-6	-	2-2	3	-	-	-	5	6
Donald Wilson	-	1-1	-	3-3	2	-	-	-	2	5
Brenton Hughes	-	0-6	-	2-3	8	-	-	-	2	2
Butch Skeete	-	1-3	-	0-1	4	-	-	-	1	2
James Brown	-	0-2	-	1-1	4	-	-	-	5	1
Jerry Graham	-	0-2	-	0-0	0	-	-	-	3	0
TOTALS	-	33-76	-	15-21	36	-	-	-	26	81
Percentages		43.4		71.4						

Coach: Harold Bradley

Officials: Fouts, Kellogg

69-49 (Sweet 16)

	California	Santa Clara
1H	31	22
2H	38	27

CALIFORNIA	MIN	FG	3FG	FT	REB	A	ST	BL	PF	TP
Darrall Imhoff	-	7-12	-	2-2	12	-	-	-	2	16
Earl Schultz	-	6-13	-	4-5	5	-	-	-	3	16
Bill McClintock	-	6-12	-	1-2	6	-	-	-	3	13
Tandy Gillis	-	4-12	-	3-3	3	-	-	-	2	11
Bob Wendell	-	2-3	-	1-1	2	-	-	-	3	5
Stan Morrison	-	1-1	-	1-4	1	-	-	-	1	3
Dick Doughty	-	0-2	-	2-2	0	-	-	-	1	2
Dave Stafford	-	1-1	-	0-0	1	-	-	-	0	2
Ed Pearson	-	0-0	-	1-2	0	-	-	-	3	1
Bill Alexander	-	0-0	-	0-0	0	-	-	-	0	0
Ned Averbuck	-	0-0	-	0-0	0	-	-	-	0	0
Jerry Mann	-	0-0	-	0-0	0	-	-	-	0	0
TOTALS	**-**	**27-56**	**-**	**15-21**	**30**	**-**	**-**	**-**	**18**	**69**
Percentages		48.2		71.4						

Coach: Pete Newell

SANTA CLARA	MIN	FG	3FG	FT	REB	A	ST	BL	PF	TP
Jim Russi	-	7-18	-	6-6	4	-	-	-	2	20
Ron McGee	-	2-8	-	3-4	2	-	-	-	2	7
Pete Lillevand	-	1-3	-	3-4	3	-	-	-	1	5
Joe Sheaff	-	2-5	-	1-3	6	-	-	-	3	5
Frank Sobrero	-	2-8	-	1-1	4	-	-	-	3	5
Jerry Bachich	-	2-3	-	0-1	3	-	-	-	1	4
Gary Keister	-	1-2	-	1-3	0	-	-	-	0	3
Adrian Buonocristiani	-	0-1	-	0-0	0	-	-	-	0	0
Barry Cristina	-	0-3	-	0-2	0	-	-	-	0	0
John Marshall	-	0-0	-	0-0	0	-	-	-	2	0
David Ramm	-	0-1	-	0-0	0	-	-	-	1	0
TOTALS	**-**	**17-52**	**-**	**15-24**	**22**	**-**	**-**	**-**	**15**	**49**
Percentages		32.7		62.5						

Coach: Bob Feerick

Attendance: 5,000

65-54 (Sweet 16)

	Oregon	Utah
1H	26	19
2H	39	35

OREGON	MIN	FG	3FG	FT	REB	A	ST	BL	PF	TP
Glenn Moore	-	7-13	-	5-9	5	-	-	-	3	19
Chuck Rask	-	6-13	-	6-8	8	-	-	-	4	18
Dale Herron	-	3-6	-	2-5	5	-	-	-	4	8
Denny Strickland	-	3-7	-	1-1	2	-	-	-	4	7
Butch Kimpton	-	0-2	-	5-6	2	-	-	-	0	5
Charlie Warren	-	2-3	-	1-2	1	-	-	-	2	5
Bill Simmons	-	0-1	-	3-6	4	-	-	-	3	3
Jim Granata	-	0-0	-	0-1	0	-	-	-	0	0
Leon Hayes	-	0-0	-	0-0	0	-	-	-	0	0
Wally Knecht	-	0-0	-	0-0	0	-	-	-	1	0
Stu Robertson	-	0-0	-	0-0	0	-	-	-	0	0
TOTALS	**-**	**21-45**	**-**	**23-38**	**27**	**-**	**-**	**-**	**21**	**65**
Percentages		46.7		60.5						

Coach: Steve Belko

UTAH	MIN	FG	3FG	FT	REB	A	ST	BL	PF	TP
Richard Ruffell	-	5-8	-	0-0	4	-	-	-	4	10
Jim Rhead	-	2-5	-	5-8	6	-	-	-	4	9
Bill Cowan	-	3-7	-	2-2	1	-	-	-	1	8
Allen Holmes	-	1-2	-	5-8	1	-	-	-	3	7
Carney Crisler	-	2-6	-	2-2	1	-	-	-	4	6
Billy McGill	-	2-3	-	2-3	6	-	-	-	5	6
Gary Chestang	-	2-6	-	0-0	2	-	-	-	3	4
Joe Morton	-	0-1	-	4-6	0	-	-	-	2	4
Keith Ancell	-	0-2	-	0-0	0	-	-	-	0	0
Joe Aufderheide	-	0-1	-	0-0	2	-	-	-	1	0
Gary Lambert	-	0-0	-	0-0	0	-	-	-	0	0
TOTALS	**-**	**17-41**	**-**	**20-29**	**23**	**-**	**-**	**-**	**27**	**54**
Percentages		41.5		69.0						

Coach: Jack Gardner

Officials: McAlister, Lawson
Attendance: 5,000

74-59 (Elite 8)

	NYU	Duke
1H	35	26
2H	39	33

NYU	MIN	FG	3FG	FT	REB	A	ST	BL	PF	TP
Tom Sanders	-	6-14	-	10-12	16	-	-	-	2	22
Al Barden	-	7-11	-	0-0	5	-	-	-	3	14
Al Filardi	-	4-6	-	3-3	8	-	-	-	2	11
Ray Padrocky	-	4-7	-	3-5	4	-	-	-	2	11
Russ Cunningham	-	4-6	-	1-3	3	-	-	-	1	9
Art Loche	-	2-4	-	1-3	0	-	-	-	2	5
Jimmy Reiss	-	1-4	-	0-0	1	-	-	-	3	2
Mike Dinapoli	-	0-0	-	0-0	0	-	-	-	0	0
Bernie Mlodinoff	-	0-0	-	0-0	0	-	-	-	0	0
Leo Murphy	-	0-0	-	0-0	0	-	-	-	1	0
Bob Regan	-	0-1	-	0-0	0	-	-	-	0	0
TOTALS	**-**	**28-53**	**-**	**18-26**	**37**	**-**	**-**	**-**	**16**	**74**
Percentages		52.8		69.2						

Coach: Lou Rossini

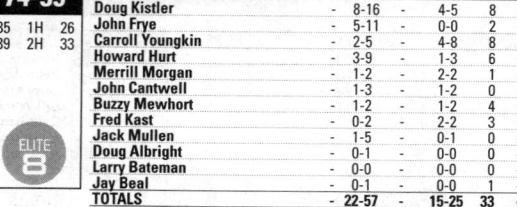

DUKE	MIN	FG	3FG	FT	REB	A	ST	BL	PF	TP
Doug Kistler	-	8-16	-	4-5	8	-	-	-	4	20
John Frye	-	5-11	-	0-0	2	-	-	-	3	10
Carroll Youngkin	-	2-5	-	4-8	8	-	-	-	2	8
Howard Hurt	-	3-9	-	1-3	6	-	-	-	3	7
Merrill Morgan	-	1-2	-	2-2	1	-	-	-	1	4
John Cantwell	-	1-3	-	1-2	0	-	-	-	2	3
Buzzy Mewhort	-	1-2	-	1-2	4	-	-	-	1	3
Fred Kast	-	0-2	-	2-2	3	-	-	-	0	2
Jack Mullen	-	1-5	-	0-1	0	-	-	-	3	2
Doug Albright	-	0-1	-	0-0	0	-	-	-	0	0
Larry Bateman	-	0-0	-	0-0	0	-	-	-	0	0
Jay Beal	-	0-1	-	0-0	1	-	-	-	0	0
TOTALS	**-**	**22-57**	**-**	**15-25**	**33**	**-**	**-**	**-**	**19**	**59**
Percentages		38.6		60.0						

Coach: Vic Bubas

Attendance: 11,666

86-69 (Elite 8)

	Ohio State	Georgia Tech
1H	41	35
2H	45	34

OHIO STATE	MIN	FG	3FG	FT	REB	A	ST	BL	PF	TP
Jerry Lucas	-	9-12	-	7-10	16	-	-	-	2	25
Joe Roberts	-	8-13	-	3-4	9	-	-	-	2	19
John Havlicek	-	7-14	-	1-3	10	-	-	-	3	15
Larry Siegfried	-	6-11	-	2-2	4	-	-	-	4	14
Mel Nowell	-	3-6	-	1-1	2	-	-	-	4	7
Gary Gearhart	-	2-4	-	0-3	3	-	-	-	3	4
David Barker	-	1-2	-	0-0	0	-	-	-	0	2
John Cedargren	-	0-0	-	0-0	1	-	-	-	0	0
Richard Furry	-	0-1	-	0-0	0	-	-	-	0	0
Richie Hoyt	-	0-1	-	0-0	0	-	-	-	2	0
Bob Knight	-	0-0	-	0-0	1	-	-	-	0	0
Howard Nourse	-	0-1	-	0-0	1	-	-	-	0	0
TOTALS	**-**	**36-65**	**-**	**14-23**	**47**	**-**	**-**	**-**	**20**	**86**
Percentages		55.4		60.9						

Coach: Fred R. Taylor

GEORGIA TECH	MIN	FG	3FG	FT	REB	A	ST	BL	PF	TP
Roger Kaiser	-	11-24	-	5-6	5	-	-	-	2	27
Dave Denton	-	5-17	-	5-6	6	-	-	-	4	15
Bobby Dews	-	3-6	-	3-6	2	-	-	-	2	9
James Riley	-	2-5	-	4-4	15	-	-	-	4	8
Wayne Richards	-	2-8	-	1-1	3	-	-	-	5	5
John Hoffman	-	1-5	-	1-4	2	-	-	-	0	3
John Gher	-	1-1	-	0-0	1	-	-	-	0	2
William Poteet	-	0-2	-	0-0	0	-	-	-	0	0
Josh Powell	-	0-0	-	0-0	1	-	-	-	0	0
TOTALS	**-**	**25-68**	**-**	**19-27**	**35**	**-**	**-**	**-**	**17**	**69**
Percentages		36.8		70.4						

Coach: Whack Hyder

82-71 (Elite 8)

	Cincinnati	Kansas
1H	40	42
2H	42	29

CINCINNATI	MIN	FG	3FG	FT	REB	A	ST	BL	PF	TP
Oscar Robertson	-	19-30	-	5-10	14	-	-	-	2	43
Paul Hogue	-	5-10	-	1-2	10	-	-	-	4	11
Ralph Davis	-	4-9	-	0-1	3	-	-	-	0	8
Larry Willey	-	4-7	-	0-0	6	-	-	-	4	8
Bob Wiesenhahn	-	1-6	-	5-5	8	-	-	-	3	7
Carl Bouldin	-	0-5	-	2-3	7	-	-	-	3	2
Sandy Pomerantz	-	1-1	-	0-0	1	-	-	-	0	2
Tom Sizer	-	0-0	-	1-1	0	-	-	-	0	1
TOTALS	**-**	**34-68**	**-**	**14-22**	**49**	**-**	**-**	**-**	**16**	**82**
Percentages		50.0		63.6						

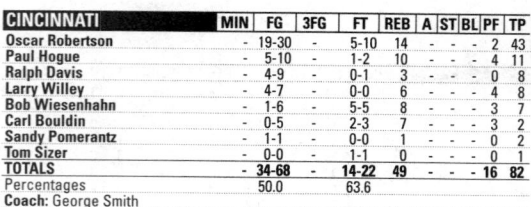

Coach: George Smith

KANSAS	MIN	FG	3FG	FT	REB	A	ST	BL	PF	TP
Bill Bridges	-	8-14	-	6-7	9	-	-	-	4	22
Wayne Hightower	-	8-24	-	6-7	9	-	-	-	3	22
Jerry Gardner	-	6-15	-	0-1	6	-	-	-	3	12
Allen Correll	-	4-5	-	3-4	3	-	-	-	5	11
Richard Gisel	-	1-8	-	0-0	3	-	-	-	0	2
Robert Hickman	-	1-5	-	0-1	3	-	-	-	3	2
TOTALS	**-**	**28-71**	**-**	**15-20**	**33**	**-**	**-**	**-**	**18**	**71**
Percentages		39.4		75.0						

Coach: Dick Harp

Officials: Fouts, Kellogg

70-49 (Elite 8)

	California	Oregon
1H	32	21
2H	38	28

CALIFORNIA	MIN	FG	3FG	FT	REB	A	ST	BL	PF	TP
Darrall Imhoff	-	5-12	-	8-9	12	-	-	-	2	18
Bill McClintock	-	5-15	-	2-6	15	-	-	-	1	12
Earl Schultz	-	5-6	-	1-2	7	-	-	-	3	11
Dick Doughty	-	3-4	-	4-5	5	-	-	-	3	10
Dave Stafford	-	0-2	-	5-9	2	-	-	-	5	5
Tandy Gillis	-	2-6	-	0-0	1	-	-	-	4	4
Jerry Mann	-	2-3	-	0-0	1	-	-	-	1	4
Bob Wendell	-	1-6	-	2-3	3	-	-	-	2	4
Stan Morrison	-	1-1	-	0-0	1	-	-	-	0	2
Bill Alexander	-	0-0	-	0-0	0	-	-	-	0	0
TOTALS	**-**	**24-55**	**-**	**22-34**	**47**	**-**	**-**	**-**	**21**	**70**
Percentages		43.6		64.7						

Coach: Pete Newell

OREGON	MIN	FG	3FG	FT	REB	A	ST	BL	PF	TP
Chuck Rask	-	7-10	-	1-4	4	-	-	-	4	15
Dale Herron	-	3-12	-	8-11	6	-	-	-	4	14
Glenn Moore	-	3-9	-	3-3	1	-	-	-	3	9
Charlie Warren	-	1-7	-	4-5	8	-	-	-	4	6
Wally Knecht	-	0-0	-	3-5	0	-	-	-	1	3
Bill Simmons	-	1-3	-	0-1	2	-	-	-	3	2
Leon Hayes	-	0-0	-	0-0	0	-	-	-	0	0
Butch Kimpton	-	0-1	-	0-0	0	-	-	-	1	0
Stu Robertson	-	0-0	-	0-0	1	-	-	-	1	0
Denny Strickland	-	0-6	-	0-0	4	-	-	-	2	0
TOTALS	**-**	**15-48**	**-**	**19-29**	**26**	**-**	**-**	**-**	**23**	**49**
Percentages		31.2		65.5						

Coach: Steve Belko

Officials: George, Ryan
Attendance: 7,000

76-54

	1H	2H
Ohio State	37	39
NYU	28	26

FINAL 4

OHIO STATE	MIN	FG	3FG	FT	REB	A	ST	BL	PF	TP
Jerry Lucas	-	9-15	-	1-1	13	-	-	-	2	19
Larry Siegfried	-	7-11	-	5-5	3	-	-	-	3	19
Richard Furry	-	4-7	-	2-3	7	-	-	-	2	10
Joe Roberts	-	3-6	-	1-2	7	-	-	-	0	7
John Havlicek	-	2-8	-	2-2	10	-	-	-	0	6
Mel Nowell	-	3-8	-	0-0	0	-	-	-	4	6
Gary Gearhart	-	1-3	-	1-1	1	-	-	-	3	3
David Barker	-	1-1	-	0-0	0	-	-	-	0	2
John Cedargren	-	1-1	-	0-0	1	-	-	-	0	2
Richie Hoyt	-	0-0	-	2-2	0	-	-	-	0	2
Bob Knight	-	0-0	-	0-0	1	-	-	-	0	0
Howard Nourse	-	0-0	-	0-0	0	-	-	-	0	0
TOTALS	**-**	**31-60**	**-**	**14-16**	**43**	**-**	**-**	**-**	**14**	**76**
Percentages		51.7		87.5						

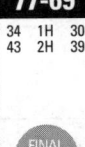

Coach: Fred R. Taylor

NYU	MIN	FG	3FG	FT	REB	A	ST	BL	PF	TP
Russ Cunningham	-	4-14	-	6-8	3	-	-	-	2	14
Al Filardi	-	6-12	-	0-1	6	-	-	-	3	12
Ray Paprocky	-	4-17	-	1-2	0	-	-	-	3	9
Al Barden	-	2-11	-	4-4	8	-	-	-	2	8
Tom Sanders	-	4-13	-	0-3	22	-	-	-	2	8
Leo Murphy	-	1-1	-	0-1	0	-	-	-	0	2
Art Loche	-	0-3	-	1-1	0	-	-	-	0	1
Mike Dinapoli	-	0-0	-	0-0	1	-	-	-	0	0
Richard Keith	-	0-1	-	0-0	0	-	-	-	0	0
Bernie Mlodinoff	-	0-1	-	0-0	0	-	-	-	0	0
Bob Regan	-	0-1	-	0-0	0	-	-	-	1	0
Jimmy Reiss	-	0-0	-	0-0	1	-	-	-	1	0
TOTALS	**-**	**21-74**	**-**	**12-20**	**41**	**-**	**-**	**-**	**14**	**54**
Percentages		28.4		60.0						

Coach: Lou Rossini

77-69

	1H	2H
California	34	43
Cincinnati	30	39

FINAL 4

CALIFORNIA	MIN	FG	3FG	FT	REB	A	ST	BL	PF	TP
Darrall Imhoff	-	10-21	-	5-5	11	-	-	-	4	25
Bill McClintock	-	5-12	-	8-10	10	-	-	-	3	18
Tandy Gillis	-	5-10	-	3-3	4	-	-	-	4	13
Earl Schultz	-	4-7	-	3-5	3	-	-	-	1	11
Dave Stafford	-	1-4	-	2-2	0	-	-	-	2	4
Bob Wendell	-	0-4	-	4-7	3	-	-	-	2	4
Dick Doughty	-	1-3	-	0-0	2	-	-	-	1	2
TOTALS	**-**	**26-61**	**-**	**25-32**	**33**	**-**	**-**	**-**	**17**	**77**
Percentages		42.6		78.1						

Coach: Pete Newell

CINCINNATI	MIN	FG	3FG	FT	REB	A	ST	BL	PF	TP
Oscar Robertson	-	4-16	-	10-12	10	-	-	-	4	18
Paul Hogue	-	5-9	-	4-6	11	-	-	-	5	14
Ralph Davis	-	4-8	-	2-2	2	-	-	-	1	10
Bob Wiesenhahn	-	5-8	-	0-0	9	-	-	-	3	10
Larry Willey	-	4-9	-	1-2	4	-	-	-	4	9
Carl Bouldin	-	4-7	-	0-0	0	-	-	-	4	8
John Bryant	-	0-1	-	0-0	1	-	-	-	3	0
Sandy Pomerantz	-	0-0	-	0-0	0	-	-	-	0	0
Tom Sizer	-	0-0	-	0-1	1	-	-	-	0	0
TOTALS	**-**	**26-58**	**-**	**17-23**	**38**	**-**	**-**	**-**	**24**	**69**
Percentages		44.8		73.9						

Coach: George Smith

95-71

	1H	2H
Cincinnati	39	56
NYU	25	46

3RD PLACE

CINCINNATI	MIN	FG	3FG	FT	REB	A	ST	BL	PF	TP
Oscar Robertson	-	12-23	-	8-11	14	-	-	-	4	32
Paul Hogue	-	7-9	-	1-5	19	-	-	-	2	15
Carl Bouldin	-	7-11	-	0-1	3	-	-	-	2	14
Bob Wiesenhahn	-	4-4	-	2-2	2	-	-	-	1	10
Larry Willey	-	5-8	-	0-0	5	-	-	-	4	10
Ralph Davis	-	3-9	-	3-3	1	-	-	-	0	9
John Bryant	-	1-2	-	0-0	1	-	-	-	0	2
Sandy Pomerantz	-	1-2	-	0-0	0	-	-	-	0	2
Tom Sizer	-	0-4	-	1-2	4	-	-	-	2	1
Fred Dierking	-	0-2	-	0-0	2	-	-	-	0	0
Ron Reis	-	0-1	-	0-0	1	-	-	-	0	0
TOTALS	**-**	**40-75**	**-**	**15-24**	**52**	**-**	**-**	**-**	**15**	**95**
Percentages		53.3		62.5						

Coach: George Smith

NYU	MIN	FG	3FG	FT	REB	A	ST	BL	PF	TP
Tom Sanders	-	11-23	-	5-6	11	-	-	-	4	27
Ray Paprocky	-	6-13	-	3-4	1	-	-	-	3	15
Russ Cunningham	-	4-9	-	2-3	0	-	-	-	2	10
Al Barden	-	3-12	-	1-2	13	-	-	-	4	7
Jimmy Reiss	-	2-4	-	1-2	2	-	-	-	3	5
Art Loche	-	1-2	-	2-2	0	-	-	-	0	4
Al Filardi	-	1-4	-	1-1	4	-	-	-	0	3
Leo Murphy	-	0-4	-	0-0	2	-	-	-	0	0
TOTALS	**-**	**28-71**	**-**	**15-20**	**33**	**-**	**-**	**-**	**16**	**71**
Percentages		39.4		75.0						

Coach: Lou Rossini

Attendance: 14,500

75-55

	1H	2H
Ohio State	37	38
California	19	36

NCAA FINAL 1960

OHIO STATE	MIN	FG	3FG	FT	REB	A	ST	BL	PF	TP
Jerry Lucas	-	7-9	-	2-2	10	-	-	-	2	16
Mel Nowell	-	6-7	-	3-3	4	-	-	-	2	15
Larry Siegfried	-	5-6	-	3-6	1	-	-	-	2	13
John Havlicek	-	4-8	-	4-5	6	-	-	-	2	12
Joe Roberts	-	5-6	-	0-1	5	-	-	-	1	10
Richard Furry	-	2-4	-	0-0	3	-	-	-	1	4
Howard Nourse	-	2-3	-	0-0	3	-	-	-	1	4
John Cedargren	-	0-0	-	1-2	1	-	-	-	1	1
David Barker	-	0-0	-	0-0	0	-	-	-	0	0
Gary Gearhart	-	0-1	-	0-0	1	-	-	-	0	0
Richie Hoyt	-	0-1	-	0-0	0	-	-	-	0	0
Bob Knight	-	0-1	-	0-0	0	-	-	-	1	0
TOTALS	**-**	**31-46**	**-**	**13-19**	**34**	**-**	**-**	**-**	**13**	**75**
Percentages		67.4		68.4						

Coach: Fred R. Taylor

CALIFORNIA	MIN	FG	3FG	FT	REB	A	ST	BL	PF	TP
Dick Doughty	-	4-5	-	3-3	6	-	-	-	1	11
Bill McClintock	-	4-15	-	2-3	3	-	-	-	3	10
Tandy Gillis	-	4-9	-	0-0	1	-	-	-	1	8
Darrall Imhoff	-	3-9	-	2-2	5	-	-	-	2	8
Jerry Mann	-	3-5	-	1-1	0	-	-	-	0	7
Earl Schultz	-	2-8	-	2-2	4	-	-	-	4	6
Bob Wendell	-	0-6	-	4-4	0	-	-	-	2	4
Dave Stafford	-	0-1	-	1-2	0	-	-	-	1	1
Bill Alexander	-	0-0	-	0-0	0	-	-	-	0	0
Ned Averbuck	-	0-0	-	0-1	1	-	-	-	0	0
Stan Morrison	-	0-0	-	0-0	1	-	-	-	1	0
Ed Pearson	-	0-1	-	0-0	0	-	-	-	0	0
TOTALS	**-**	**20-59**	**-**	**15-18**	**21**	**-**	**-**	**-**	**15**	**55**
Percentages		33.9		83.3						

Coach: Pete Newell

Officials: George, unknown
Attendance: 14,500

National Invitation Tournament (NIT)

First round: Villanova d. Detroit 88-86, Providence d. Memphis 71-70, St. Bonaventure d. Holy Cross 94-81, Dayton d. Temple 72-51
Quarterfinals: Utah State d. Villanova 73-72 (OT), Providence d. Saint Louis 64-53, Bradley d. Dayton 78-64, St. Bonaventure d. St. John's 106-71
Semifinals: Bradley d. St. Bonaventure 82-71, Providence d. Utah State 68-62
Third place: Utah State d. St. Bonaventure 99-83
Championship: Bradley d. Providence 88-72
MVP: Lenny Wilkens, Providence

1960-61: Oscar Who?

It was a clean break. In the previous three seasons under coach George Smith, Cincinnati's offense had run through the incomparable Oscar Robertson. As a result, the Bearcats went 79–9, made three NCAA Tourneys and twice reached the Final Four, only to walk away with third-place finishes. Now, with the Big O lighting up the NBA, Smith's assistant, Ed Jucker, took over and instituted a team approach that brought the 27–3 Bearcats to a level they hadn't been able to reach under Smith: the NCAA Final. There, Cincy faced Ohio State, the undefeated and heavily favored defending champ and in-state rival. The Bearcats' balanced scoring—four players hit double figures—gave Cincinnati a 70-65 win even though the Buckeyes' Bob Knight made a layup to force overtime. OSU center Jerry Lucas (27 points, 12 boards in the Final) was Tournament MOP and a consensus selection for national POY, having averaged 24.9 ppg and 17.4 rpg.

Major Conference Standings

ACC	Conference			Overall		
	W	L	PCT	W	L	PCT
North Carolina	12	2	.857	19	4	.826
Wake Forest ⊕	11	3	.786	19	11	.633
Duke	10	4	.714	22	6	.786
NC State	8	6	.571	16	9	.640
Maryland	6	8	.429	14	12	.538
Clemson	5	9	.357	10	16	.385
South Carolina	2	12	.143	9	17	.346
Virginia	2	12	.143	3	23	.115

Tournament: **Wake Forest d. Duke 96-81**
Tournament MVP: **Len Chappell**, Wake Forest

Big Eight	Conference			Overall		
	W	L	PCT	W	L	PCT
Kansas State ⊕ ✪	13	1	.929	22	5	.815
Kansas	10	4	.714	17	8	.680
Oklahoma State ✪	8	6	.571	14	11	.560
Colorado ✪	7	7	.500	15	10	.600
Missouri ✪	7	7	.500	9	15	.375
Iowa State ✪	6	8	.429	13	12	.520
Nebraska ✪	4	10	.286	10	14	.417
Oklahoma ✪	2	12	.143	10	15	.400

AAWU	Conference			Overall		
	W	L	PCT	W	L	PCT
USC ⊕	9	3	.750	21	8	.724
UCLA	7	5	.583	18	8	.692
Washington	6	6	.500	13	13	.500
California	5	7	.417	13	9	.591
Stanford	3	9	.250	7	17	.292

Big Ten	Conference			Overall		
	W	L	PCT	W	L	PCT
Ohio State ⊕	14	0	1.000	27	1	.964
Iowa	10	4	.714	18	6	.750
Purdue	10	4	.714	16	7	.696
Indiana	8	6	.571	15	9	.625
Minnesota	8	6	.571	10	13	.435
Northwestern	6	8	.429	10	12	.455
Illinois	5	9	.357	9	15	.375
Wisconsin	4	10	.286	7	17	.292
Michigan State	3	11	.214	7	17	.292
Michigan	2	12	.143	6	18	.250

Border	Conference			Overall		
	W	L	PCT	W	L	PCT
Arizona State ⊕	9	1	.900	23	6	.793
New Mexico St.	9	1	.900	19	5	.792
Arizona	5	5	.500	11	15	.423
Texas Western	4	6	.400	12	12	.500
Hardin-Simmons	2	8	.200	12	14	.462
West Texas A&M	1	9	.100	7	16	.304

Ivy	Conference			Overall		
	W	L	PCT	W	L	PCT
Princeton ○	11	3	.786	18	8	.692
Penn	10	4	.714	16	9	.640
Yale	8	6	.571	12	12	.500
Brown	8	6	.571	11	14	.440
Cornell	7	7	.500	14	10	.583
Harvard	4	10	.286	11	13	.458
Columbia	4	10	.286	8	15	.348
Dartmouth	4	10	.286	5	19	.208

Metro NY	Conference			Overall		
	W	L	PCT	W	L	PCT
St. John's ○	4	0	1.000	20	5	.800
NYU	2	1	.667	12	11	.522
St. Francis (NY)	2	1	.667	10	10	.500
CCNY	1	1	.500	7	10	.412
Manhattan	1	2	.333	8	11	.421
Fordham	0	3	.000	7	16	.304
Brooklyn	0	2	.000	4	14	.222

Mid-American	Conference			Overall		
	W	L	PCT	W	L	PCT
Ohio ⊕	10	2	.833	17	7	.708
Toledo	8	4	.667	15	8	.652
Miami (OH)	7	5	.583	12	12	.500
Marshall	5	7	.417	11	13	.458
Bowling Green	4	8	.333	10	14	.417
Western Michigan	4	8	.333	10	14	.417
Kent State	4	8	.333	9	14	.391

Middle Atlantic	Conference			Overall		
	W	L	PCT	W	L	PCT
Saint Joseph's ⊕ ✪	8	0	1.000	25	5	.833
Temple □	9	1	.900	20	8	.714
La Salle	7	2	.778	15	7	.682
Gettysburg	8	4	.667	19	6	.760
Lafayette	6	6	.500	16	8	.667
Bucknell	5	6	.455	12	11	.522
Rutgers	3	6	.333	11	10	.524
Lehigh	4	10	.286	5	16	.238
Delaware	2	7	.222	8	11	.421
Muhlenberg	2	12	.143	5	20	.200

Missouri Valley	Conference			Overall		
	W	L	PCT	W	L	PCT
Cincinnati ⊕	10	2	.833	27	3	.900
Bradley	9	3	.750	21	5	.808
Drake	7	5	.583	19	7	.731
Saint Louis □	7	5	.583	21	9	.700
Wichita State	6	6	.500	18	8	.692
Tulsa	2	10	.167	8	17	.320
North Texas	1	11	.083	2	22	.083

Skyline 8	Conference			Overall		
	W	L	PCT	W	L	PCT
Utah ⊕	12	2	.857	23	8	.742
Colorado State □	12	2	.857	17	9	.654
BYU	9	5	.643	15	11	.577
Montana	7	7	.500	14	9	.609
Denver	6	8	.429	12	14	.462
Utah State	4	10	.286	12	14	.462
Wyoming	3	11	.214	7	18	.280
New Mexico	3	11	.214	6	17	.261

Ohio Valley	Conference			Overall		
	W	L	PCT	W	L	PCT
Morehead State ⊕	9	3	.750	19	12	.613
Western Kentucky	9	3	.750	18	8	.692
Eastern Kentucky	9	3	.750	15	9	.625
Murray State	7	5	.583	13	10	.565
Middle Tenn. State	4	8	.333	9	14	.391
Tennessee Tech	3	9	.250	6	13	.316
East Tenn. State	1	11	.083	9	15	.375

SEC	Conference			Overall		
	W	L	PCT	W	L	PCT
Mississippi State	11	3	.786	19	6	.760
Vanderbilt	10	4	.714	19	5	.792
Kentucky ⊕	10	4	.714	19	9	.679
Florida	9	5	.643	15	11	.577
Auburn	8	6	.571	15	7	.682
Georgia Tech	6	8	.429	13	13	.500
Tulane	6	8	.429	11	13	.458
LSU	6	8	.429	11	14	.440
Mississippi	5	9	.357	10	14	.417
Alabama	5	9	.357	7	18	.280
Tennessee	4	10	.286	10	15	.400
Georgia	4	10	.286	8	18	.308

Southern	Conference			Overall		
	W	L	PCT	W	L	PCT
West Virginia	11	1	.917	23	4	.852
Virginia Tech	12	3	.800	15	7	.682
The Citadel	10	3	.769	17	8	.680
William and Mary	9	6	.600	14	10	.583
Furman	6	7	.462	15	11	.577
Richmond	5	11	.313	9	14	.391
George Washington ⊕	3	9	.250	9	17	.346
VMI	3	11	.214	5	17	.227
Davidson	2	10	.167	9	14	.391

Tournament: **George Washington d. Wm and Mary 93-82**
Tournament MOP: **Jon Feldman**, George Washington

Southwest	Conference			Overall		
	W	L	PCT	W	L	PCT
Texas Tech ⊕	11	3	.786	15	10	.600
Texas A&M	10	4	.714	16	8	.667
Arkansas	9	5	.643	16	7	.696
Texas	8	6	.571	14	10	.583
Rice	7	7	.500	11	12	.478
SMU	6	8	.429	12	12	.500
TCU	3	11	.214	5	19	.208
Baylor	2	12	.143	4	20	.167

WCAC	Conference			Overall		
	W	L	PCT	W	L	PCT
Loyola Marymount ⊕	10	2	.833	20	7	.741
Saint Mary's (CA)	8	4	.667	19	7	.731
Santa Clara	8	4	.667	18	9	.667
San Francisco	8	4	.667	17	11	.607
San Jose State	5	7	.417	11	14	.440
Pepperdine	3	9	.250	9	16	.360
Pacific	0	12	.000	5	21	.192

Yankee	Conference			Overall		
	W	L	PCT	W	L	PCT
Rhode Island ⊕	9	1	.900	18	9	.667
Maine	7	3	.700	18	5	.783
Connecticut	6	4	.600	11	13	.458
Massachusetts	4	6	.400	16	10	.615
Vermont	3	7	.300	9	11	.450
New Hampshire	1	9	.100	6	18	.250

Independents	Overall		
	W	L	PCT
Memphis □	20	3	.870
St. Bonaventure ○	24	4	.857
Providence □	24	5	.828
Holy Cross □	21	5	.808
Niagara □	16	5	.762
Miami (FL) □	20	7	.741
Louisville ○	21	8	.724
Army □	17	7	.708
Seattle ○	18	8	.692
Dayton □	20	9	.690
Duquesne	15	7	.682
DePaul □	17	8	.680
Detroit □	18	9	.667
Loyola-Chicago	15	8	.652
Portland	16	9	.640
Xavier ○	17	10	.630
Seton Hall	15	9	.625
Boston College	14	9	.609
Houston ○	17	11	.607
Marquette ○	16	11	.593
Florida State	14	10	.583
Butler	15	11	.577
Canisius	13	10	.565
Oregon ○	15	12	.556
Centenary	14	12	.538
Colgate	14	12	.538
Oklahoma City	14	12	.538
Oregon State	14	12	.538

⊕ Automatic NCAA Tournament bid ○ At-large NCAA Tournament bid □ NIT appearance ✪ Team record doesn't reflect games forfeited or vacated. For adjusted record, see p. 521.

INDEPENDENTS (CONT.)

	OVERALL W	L	PCT
Navy	10	9	.526
Georgetown	11	10	.524
Pittsburgh	12	11	.522
Idaho State	13	12	.520
Air Force	12	12	.500
Iona	10	11	.476
Notre Dame	12	14	.462
Penn State	11	13	.458
Villanova	11	13	.458
Gonzaga	11	15	.423
Montana State	10	15	.400
Boston U.	9	14	.391
Idaho	10	16	.385
Washington State	10	16	.385
Creighton	8	17	.320
Loyola (LA)	6	18	.250
Saint Francis (PA)	6	19	.240
Syracuse	4	19	.174

INDIVIDUAL LEADERS—SEASON

SCORING	CL	POS	G	FG	FT	PTS	PPG
1 **Frank Burgess**, Gonzaga	SR	G	26	304	234	842	**32.4**
2 **Tom Chilton**, East Tennessee State	SR	F	24	295	181	771	**32.1**
3 **Tom Stith**, St. Bonaventure	SR	F	28	327	176	830	**29.6**
4 **Terry Dischinger**, Purdue	JR	C	23	215	218	648	**28.2**
5 **Billy McGill**, Utah	JR	C	31	342	178	862	**27.8**
6 **Len Chappell**, Wake Forest	JR	F/C	28	271	203	745	**26.6**
7 **Jack Foley**, Holy Cross	JR	F	26	266	156	688	**26.5**
8 **Chet Walker**, Bradley	JR	F	26	238	180	656	**25.2**
9 **Art Heyman**, Duke	SO	F/G	25	229	171	629	**25.2**
10 **Ronald Warner**, Gettysburg	JR	G	25	227	169	623	**24.9**

FIELD GOAL PCT	CL	POS	G	FG	FGA	PCT
1 **Jerry Lucas**, Ohio State	JR	C	27	256	411	**62.3**
2 **Hank Gunter**, Seton Hall	JR	C	24	200	325	**61.5**
3 **Carroll Youngkin**, Duke	SR	C	28	146	253	**57.7**
4 **Terry Dischinger**, Purdue	JR	C	23	215	373	**57.6**
5 **Harold Lundy**, Lafayette	JR	C	24	174	303	**57.4**

MINIMUM: 100 MADE

FREE THROW PCT	CL	POS	G	FT	FTA	PCT
1 **Stew Sherard**, Army	JR	G	24	135	154	**87.7**
2 **Howie Carl**, DePaul	SR	G	25	161	184	**87.5**
3 **Roger Kaiser**, Georgia Tech	SR	G	26	176	203	**86.7**
4 **Henderson Thompson**, Morehead State	SR	F	31	180	208	**86.5**
5 **Jerry Carlton**, Arkansas	JR	G	23	101	117	**86.3**

MINIMUM: 90 MADE

INDIVIDUAL LEADERS—GAME

POINTS	CL	POS	OPP	DATE	PTS
1 **Frank Burgess**, Gonzaga	SR	G	UC Davis	J26	**52**
Tom Chilton, East Tennessee State	SR	F	Austin Peay	F4	**52**
Terry Dischinger, Purdue	JR	C	Michigan State	D25	**52**
4 **Chet Walker**, Bradley	JR	F	UC Davis	D5	**50**
5 **Jeff Cohen**, William and Mary	SR	C	Richmond	F25	**49**

FREE THROWS MADE	CL	POS	OPP	DATE	FT	FTA	PCT
1 **Howie Carl**, DePaul	SR	G	Marquette	F9	**23**	27	85.2
2 **Terry Dischinger**, Purdue	JR	C	Iowa	F27	**21**	24	87.5
Jerry Graves, Mississippi State	SR	F	Vanderbilt	J14	**21**	27	77.8
4 **Jerry Graves**, Mississippi State	SR	F	Spring Hill	D13	**20**	22	90.9
Tom Chilton, East Tennessee State	SR	F	Austin Peay	F4	**20**	23	87.0

TEAM LEADERS—SEASON

SCORING OFFENSE	G	W-L	PTS	PPG
1 **St. Bonaventure**	28	24-4	2,479	**88.5**
2 **Loyola-Chicago**	23	15-8	1,989	**86.5**
3 **West Virginia**	27	23-4	2,325	**86.1**
4 **Virginia Tech**	22	15-7	1,874	**85.2**
5 **Ohio State**	28	27-1	2,383	**85.1**

FIELD GOAL PCT	G	W-L	FG	FGA	PCT
1 **Ohio State**	28	27-1	939	1,886	**49.8**
2 **St. Bonaventure**	28	24-4	1,010	2,041	**49.5**
3 **Bradley**	26	21-5	798	1,622	**49.2**
4 **Auburn**	22	15-7	500	1,018	**49.1**
5 **Utah**	31	23-8	1,008	2,069	**48.7**

FREE THROW PCT	G	W-L	FT	FTA	PCT
1 **Tulane**	24	11-13	459	604	**76.0**
2 **Ohio State**	28	27-1	505	671	**75.3**
3 **West Texas A&M**	31	23-8	421	561	**75.0**
4 **Western Kentucky**	26	18-8	554	742	**74.7**
5 **Arkansas**	23	16-7	428	574	**74.6**

SCORING DEFENSE	G	W-L	OPP PTS	OPP PPG
1 **Santa Clara**	27	18-9	1,314	**48.7**
2 **San Jose State**	25	11-14	1,254	**50.2**
3 **San Francisco**	28	17-11	1,440	**51.4**
4 **California**	22	13-9	1,192	**54.2**
5 **Portland**	25	16-9	1,415	**56.6**

CONSENSUS ALL-AMERICAS

FIRST TEAM

PLAYER	CL	POS	HT	SCHOOL	RPG	PPG
Terry Dischinger	JR	C	6-7	Purdue	13.4	28.2
Roger Kaiser	SR	G	6-1	Georgia Tech	4.1	23.4
Jerry Lucas	JR	C	6-8	Ohio State	17.4	24.9
Tom Stith	SR	F	6-5	St. Bonaventure	6.8	29.6
Chet Walker	JR	F	6-6	Bradley	12.3	25.2

SECOND TEAM

PLAYER	CL	POS	HT	SCHOOL	RPG	PPG
Walt Bellamy	SR	C	6-11	Indiana	17.8	21.8
Frank Burgess	SR	G	6-1	Gonzaga	N/A	32.4
Tony Jackson	SR	F	6-4	St. John's	10.7	22.0
Billy McGill	JR	C	6-9	Utah	13.9	27.8
Larry Siegfried	SR	G	6-4	Ohio State	9.6	15.2

SELECTORS: AP, LOOK MAGAZINE, NABC, NEWSPAPER ENTERPRISES ASSN., UPI, USBWA

AWARD WINNERS

PLAYER OF THE YEAR

PLAYER	CL	POS	HT	SCHOOL	AWARDS
Jerry Lucas	JR	C	6-8	Ohio State	AP, UPI, USBWA

COACH OF THE YEAR

COACH	SCHOOL	REC	AWARDS
Fred Taylor	Ohio State	27-1	UPI, USBWA

Poll Progression

Week of Dec 5

UPI	School
1	**Ohio State** (1-0)
2	**Bradley** (1-0)
3	**Indiana** (1-0)
4	**Kansas** (1-0)
5	**North Carolina** (1-0)
6	**St. Bonaventure** (2-0)
6	**Utah State** (1-0)
8	**Cincinnati** (2-0)
9	**Detroit** (1-0)
10	**St. John's** (1-0)
11	**Kansas State** (1-0)
12	**Georgia Tech** (2-0)
13	**Providence** (1-0)
14	**Auburn** (2-0)
15	**Utah** (0-2) Ⓐ
16	**Duke** (1-0)
17	**California** (1-0)
18	**Washington** (1-1)
19	**Western Kentucky** (2-0)
20	**Dayton** (0-0)

Week of Dec 13

AP	UPI	School
1	1	**Ohio State** (3-0)
2	2	**Bradley** (3-0)
3	5	**Detroit** (3-0)
4	4	**Indiana** (2-1)
5	3	**North Carolina** (2-0)
6	7	**St. Bonaventure** (4-0)
7	6	**St. John's** (3-0)
8	13	**Duke** (3-0)
9	—	**Louisville** (5-0)
10	—	**NC State** (4-0)
11	14	**Auburn** (3-0)
12	15	**Maryland** (4-0)
13	11	**UCLA** (3-1)
14	17	**Utah State** (2-2)
15	12	**Georgia Tech** (3-0)
16	8	**Kansas** (2-1)
16	—	**Wichita State** (4-0)
18	18	**Utah** (3-2)
19	19	**Illinois** (2-0)
20	—	**Dayton** (4-0)
20	—	**Kansas State** (2-2)
20	—	**Kentucky** (2-1)
—	9	**Providence** (3-0)
—	10	**Cincinnati** (3-1)
—	16	**California** (3-0)
—	20	**Washington** (2-1)

Week of Dec 20

AP	UPI	School	AP↓↑
1	1	**Ohio State** (4-0)	
2	2	**Bradley** (6-0)	
3	5	**St. Bonaventure** (6-0)	↑3
4	3	**Indiana** (4-1)	
5	9	**Louisville** (8-0)	↑4
6	4	**St. John's** (4-0)	↑1
7	12	**Duke** (5-0)	↑1
8	6	**Detroit** (4-1)	↓5
9	16	**Auburn** (5-0)	↑2
10	7	**North Carolina** (3-2)	↓5
10	18	**NC State** (5-1)	
12	11	**Kansas State** (5-2)	↑8
13	17	**Providence** (6-0)	⤴
14	8	**UCLA** (5-1)	↓1
15	15	**Colorado** (7-0)	⤴
16	13	**Saint Louis** (4-1)	⤴
17	20	**Vanderbilt** (5-0)	⤴
18	—	**Utah** (4-2)	
19	19	**Wake Forest** (5-2)	⤴
20	10	**Kansas** (3-2)	↓4
20	—	**Drake** (5-0)	⤴
—	14	**California** (4-0)	
—	20	**Utah State** (4-3)	⤵

Week of Dec 27

AP	UPI	School	AP↓↑
1	1	**Ohio State** (6-0)	
2	2	**Bradley** (8-0)	
3	5	**St. Bonaventure** (7-0)	
4	4	**Indiana** (5-1)	
5	9	**Louisville** (9-0)	
6	10	**Duke** (7-0)	↑1
7	3	**St. John's** (6-0)	↓1
8	6	**Saint Louis** (7-1)	↑8
9	13	**Auburn** (5-0)	
10	20	**NC State** (6-1)	
11	11	**North Carolina** (4-2)	↓1
12	12	**Kansas State** (6-2)	
13	8	**Detroit** (5-2)	↓5
14	—	**Drake** (6-0)	↑6
15	16	**Providence** (7-0)	↓2
16	7	**UCLA** (5-1)	↓2
16	16	**Vanderbilt** (7-0)	↑1
18	—	**Wichita State** (7-2)	⤴
19	19	**Memphis** (7-0)	⤴
19	—	**Kentucky** (4-3)	⤴
—	13	**Kansas** (4-3)	⤵
—	15	**California** (6-1)	
—	18	**Utah** (6-2)	⤵

Week of Jan 3

AP	UPI	School	AP↓↑
1	1	**Ohio State** (9-0)	
2	2	**Bradley** (10-0)	
3	3	**St. Bonaventure** (9-1)	
4	6	**Louisville** (11-0)	↑1
5	4	**St. John's** (8-1)	↑2
6	5	**North Carolina** (7-2)	↑5
7	9	**Iowa** (8-1)	⤴
8	10	**Duke** (9-1)	↓2
9	8	**UCLA** (7-2)	↑7
10	19	**Auburn** (6-0)	↓1
—	7	**Kansas State** (9-2)	⤵
—	11	**Detroit** (7-2)	⤵
—	12	**Saint Louis** (8-2)	⤵
—	13	**Indiana** (6-3) Ⓑ	⤵
—	14	**Vanderbilt** (8-2)	⤵
—	14	**Utah** (7-4)	
—	14	**West Virginia** (6-2)	
—	17	**Wichita State** (10-2)	⤵
—	18	**Kansas** (6-4)	
—	20	**Memphis** (8-1)	⤵
—	20	**Providence** (7-2)	⤵
—	20	**NC State** (8-2)	⤵
—	20	**USC** (8-2)	
—	20	**Iowa State** (5-4)	

Week of Jan 10

AP	UPI	School	AP↓↑
1	1	**Ohio State** (10-0)	
2	2	**Bradley** (12-0)	
3	3	**St. Bonaventure** (11-1)	
4	4	**Louisville** (13-0)	
5	5	**St. John's** (9-1)	
6	8	**Iowa** (9-1)	↑1
7	7	**North Carolina** (8-2)	↓1
8	9	**Duke** (11-1)	
9	6	**Kansas State** (10-2)	⤴
10	10	**UCLA** (8-3)	↓1
—	11	**Indiana** (7-3)	
—	12	**Utah** (8-4)	
—	13	**USC** (10-2)	
—	14	**Detroit** (9-3)	
—	15	**Memphis** (9-1)	
—	15	**Vanderbilt** (10-0)	
—	17	**Wichita State** (11-3)	
—	18	**DePaul** (9-0)	
—	18	**Kansas** (7-4)	
—	20	**West Virginia** (8-2)	

Week of Jan 17

AP	UPI	School	AP↓↑
1	1	**Ohio State** (12-0)	
2	2	**St. Bonaventure** (13-1)	↑1
3	3	**Bradley** (13-1)	↓1
4	4	**Iowa** (11-1)	↑2
5	9	**Louisville** (13-1)	↓1
6	6	**North Carolina** (10-2)	↑1
7	10	**DePaul** (11-0)	⤴
8	8	**Duke** (13-1)	
9	7	**St. John's** (10-2)	↓4
10	5	**Kansas State** (11-2)	↓1
—	11	**UCLA** (10-3)	⤵
—	12	**USC** (12-2)	
—	13	**Kansas** (9-4)	
—	14	**Indiana** (8-3)	
—	15	**Utah** (10-4)	
—	16	**Memphis** (11-1)	
—	17	**Wake Forest** (9-5)	
—	18	**Cincinnati** (11-3)	
—	19	**Wichita State** (12-4)	
—	20	**Detroit** (9-5)	

Week of Jan 24

AP	UPI	School	AP↓↑
1	1	**Ohio State** (13-0)	
2	2	**St. Bonaventure** (14-1)	
3	3	**Bradley** (13-1)	
4	4	**North Carolina** (12-2)	↑2
5	6	**Duke** (13-1)	↑3
6	8	**Iowa** (12-2)	↓2
7	5	**St. John's** (10-2)	↑2
8	7	**Louisville** (14-2)	↓3
9	9	**USC** (12-2)	⤴
10	—	**Purdue** (9-3)	⤴
—	10	**Kansas State** (11-3)	⤵
—	11	**UCLA** (10-3)	
—	12	**Kansas** (10-5)	
—	13	**Indiana** (8-3)	
—	13	**Memphis** (13-1)	
—	15	**DePaul** (11-2)	⤵
—	16	**Cincinnati** (13-3)	
—	17	**Utah** (11-5)	
—	18	**Xavier** (11-3)	
—	19	**West Virginia** (12-3)	
—	20	**Wake Forest** (10-5)	
—	20	**Wichita State** (13-4)	

Week of Jan 31

AP	UPI	School	AP↓↑
1	1	**Ohio State** (14-0)	
2	3	**St. Bonaventure** (14-1)	
3	2	**Bradley** (14-2)	
4	5	**Duke** (14-1)	↑1
5	4	**North Carolina** (12-2)	↓1
6	7	**Iowa** (12-2)	
7	9	**St. John's** (10-3)	
8	7	**Louisville** (15-2)	
9	6	**USC** (14-2)	
10	10	**Kansas State** (12-3)	⤴
—	11	**UCLA** (12-3)	
—	12	**Kansas** (10-5)	
—	13	**Indiana** (9-3)	
—	14	**Cincinnati** (14-3)	
—	15	**Memphis** (14-1)	
—	16	**Utah** (12-5)	
—	17	**Wake Forest** (11-5)	
—	18	**Detroit** (11-5)	
—	19	**West Virginia** (13-3)	
—	20	**Wichita State** (14-4)	

Week of Feb 7

AP	UPI	School	AP↓↑
1	1	**Ohio State** (16-0)	
2	2	**St. Bonaventure** (16-1)	
3	3	**Duke** (16-1)	↑1
4	4	**Bradley** (14-3) Ⓒ	↓1
5	9	**Cincinnati** (16-3)	⤴
6	5	**North Carolina** (14-3)	↓1
7	7	**Kansas State** (14-3)	↑3
8	6	**USC** (15-3)	↑1
9	8	**Iowa** (12-3)	↓3
10	9	**Louisville** (17-2)	↓2
—	11	**Kansas** (11-5)	
—	12	**UCLA** (13-4)	
—	13	**St. John's** (11-4)	⤵
—	14	**Indiana** (10-5)	
—	15	**Utah** (14-5)	
—	16	**West Virginia** (16-3)	
—	17	**Wichita State** (15-4)	
—	18	**Mississippi State** (14-3)	
—	19	**Saint Louis** (12-5)	
—	19	**Oregon** (12-5)	

Week of Feb 14

AP	UPI	School	AP↓↑
1	1	**Ohio State** (18-0)	
2	2	**St. Bonaventure** (18-1)	
3	3	**Duke** (17-2)	
4	6	**Cincinnati** (17-3)	↑1
5	5	**Bradley** (16-4)	↓1
6	8	**Kansas State** (15-3)	↑1
7	7	**North Carolina** (15-4)	↓1
8	4	**USC** (16-3)	
9	11	**Iowa** (13-3)	
10	15	**West Virginia** (18-3)	⤴
—	9	**St. John's** (13-4)	
—	10	**Louisville** (17-4)	⤵
—	12	**Kansas** (13-5)	
—	13	**Utah** (15-5)	
—	14	**UCLA** (13-5)	
—	16	**Memphis** (17-2)	
—	17	**Wichita State** (16-4)	
—	18	**Indiana** (10-7)	
—	18	**Saint Joseph's** (16-4)	
—	20	**Ohio** (15-4)	
—	20	**Providence** (16-3)	

Week of Feb 21

AP	UPI	School	AP↓↑
1	1	**Ohio State** (20-0)	
2	2	**St. Bonaventure** (20-1)	
3	4	**Cincinnati** (19-3)	↑1
4	3	**Bradley** (19-4)	↑1
5	9	**Iowa** (14-4)	↑4
6	8	**Duke** (18-4)	↓3
7	5	**North Carolina** (18-4)	
8	7	**Kansas State** (16-4)	↓2
9	14	**West Virginia** (20-3)	↑1
10	6	**USC** (16-4)	↓2
—	10	**St. John's** (15-4)	
—	11	**Kansas** (15-5)	
—	12	**Utah** (17-5)	
—	13	**Louisville** (18-5)	
—	15	**UCLA** (14-6)	
—	16	**Dayton** (15-7)	
—	17	**Memphis** (19-2)	
—	18	**Kentucky** (13-7)	
—	18	**Wichita State** (16-7)	
—	20	**Saint Louis** (14-7)	

WEEK OF FEB 28

AP	UPI	SCHOOL	AP↓↑
1	1	**Ohio State** (22-0)	
2	2	**St. Bonaventure** (21-2)	
3	3	**Cincinnati** (21-3)	
4	4	**Bradley** (21-4)	
5	6	**North Carolina** (19-4)	↑2
6	8	**Iowa** (16-4)	↓1
7	5	**Kansas State** (18-4)	↑1
8	11	**West Virginia** (22-3)	↑1
9	7	**Duke** (20-5)	↓3
10	10	**USC** (17-5)	
—	9	**St. John's** (17-4)	
—	12	**Utah** (19-5)	
—	13	**Louisville** (18-6)	
—	14	**Dayton** (17-7)	
—	15	**UCLA** (15-6)	
—	16	**Memphis** (20-2)	
—	17	**Kentucky** (15-7)	
—	18	**Vanderbilt** (18-4)	
—	18	**Wichita State** (16-8)	
—	20	**Texas Tech** (13-8)	

FINAL POLL

AP	UPI	SCHOOL	AP↓↑
1	1	**Ohio State** (23-0)	
2	2	**Cincinnati** (23-3)	↑1
3	3	**St. Bonaventure** (22-3) D	↓1
4	4	**Kansas State** (20-4)	↑3
5	6	**North Carolina** (19-4)	
6	7	**Bradley** (21-5)	↓2
7	5	**USC** (19-5)	↑3
8	10	**Iowa** (17-5)	↓2
9	12	**West Virginia** (23-4)	↓1
10	9	**Duke** (22-6)	↓1
—	8	**St. John's** (19-4)	
—	10	**Wake Forest** (17-10)	
—	13	**Utah** (20-6)	
—	14	**Saint Louis** (20-7)	
—	15	**Louisville** (18-7)	
—	16	**Saint Joseph's** (22-4)	
—	17	**Dayton** (19-7)	
—	18	**Kentucky** (17-7) E	
—	19	**Texas Tech** (14-9)	
—	20	**Memphis** (20-2)	
—	21	**Kansas** (16-7)	
—	22	**UCLA** (18-8)	
—	23	**Niagara** (16-4)	
—	24	**Indiana** (13-9) F	
—	25	**Mississippi State** (19-6) E	
—	26	**Duquesne** (12-7)	
—	27	**Houston** (16-9)	
—	27	**William and Mary** (14-10)	

A Utah drops its first two games, including a 59-56 heartbreaker at Stanford during which Utes coach Jack Gardner, protesting a foul call with his team down by one, shoves referee Bill Bissinius with :15 left and gets called for a technical.

B Indiana suffers back-to-back road losses to UCLA (94-72) and USC (90-71). The Hoosiers, 6–1 going into Los Angeles, will stumble to a 15–9 record.

C Four days after St. Bonaventure beats Bradley, 76-61, at Madison Square Garden, Drake stuns the Braves, 86-76, in Peoria, snapping a 46-game home-court winning streak.

D In the upset of the season, Niagara beats St. Bonaventure at home, 87-77, to snap the Bonnies' 99-game home winning streak. The last team to have beaten the Bonnies at home? Niagara, 13 years and 13 days earlier.

E After SEC champ Mississippi State again declines to participate in the integrated NCAA Tournament, Kentucky crushes Vanderbilt, 85-67, in a playoff to represent the conference. It was the 12th time the Wildcats were making an NCAA appearance, the most of any school at the time.

F Indiana center Walt Bellamy pulls down 33 rebounds, snapping his own Big Ten record, in IU's 82-67 win over Michigan in the Big Ten finale. The Hoosiers and Wolverines combine for an NCAA-record 152 boards.

1961 NCAA Tournament

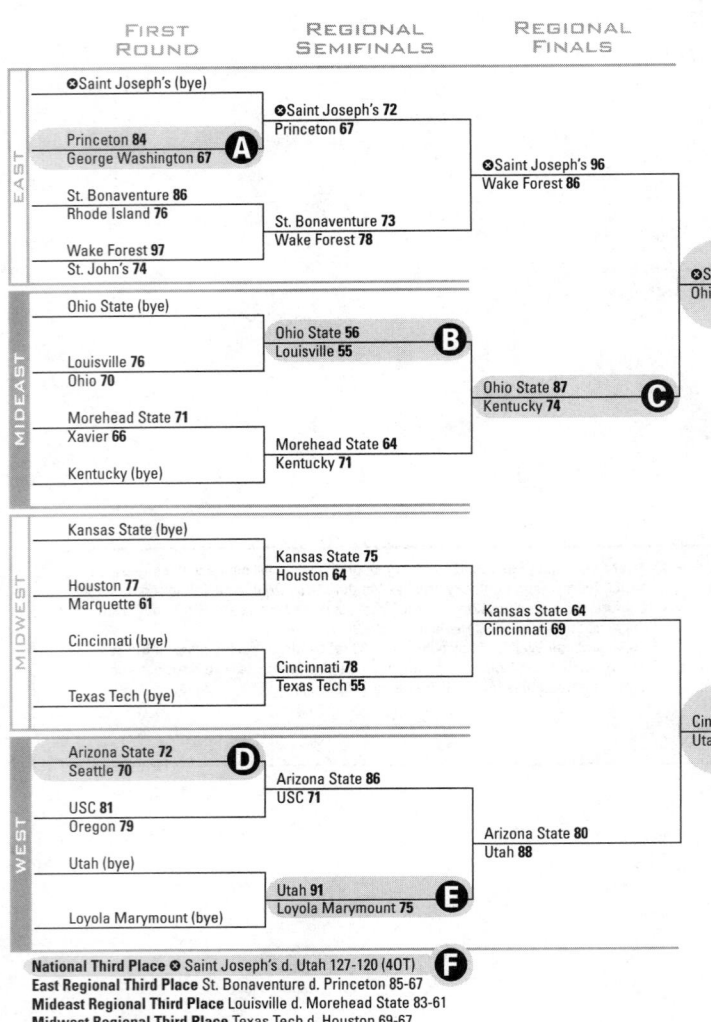

East

First Round
- ⊗Saint Joseph's (bye)
- Princeton **84**, George Washington **67** (A)
- St. Bonaventure **86**, Rhode Island **76**
- Wake Forest **97**, St. John's **74**

Regional Semifinals
- ⊗Saint Joseph's **72**, Princeton **67**
- St. Bonaventure **73**, Wake Forest **78**

Regional Finals
- ⊗Saint Joseph's **96**, Wake Forest **86**

Mideast

First Round
- Ohio State (bye)
- Louisville **76**, Ohio **70**
- Morehead State **71**, Xavier **66**
- Kentucky (bye)

Regional Semifinals
- Ohio State **56**, Louisville **55** (B)
- Morehead State **64**, Kentucky **71**

Regional Finals
- Ohio State **87**, Kentucky **74** (C)

Midwest

First Round
- Kansas State (bye)
- Houston **77**, Marquette **61**
- Cincinnati (bye)
- Texas Tech (bye)

Regional Semifinals
- Kansas State **75**, Houston **64**
- Cincinnati **78**, Texas Tech **55**

Regional Finals
- Kansas State **64**, Cincinnati **69**

West

First Round
- Arizona State **72**, Seattle **70** (D)
- USC **81**, Oregon **79**
- Utah (bye)
- Loyola Marymount (bye)

Regional Semifinals
- Arizona State **86**, USC **71**
- Utah **91**, Loyola Marymount **75** (E)

Regional Finals
- Arizona State **80**, Utah **88**

National Semifinals
- ⊗Saint Joseph's **69**, Ohio State **95**
- Cincinnati **82**, Utah **67**

National Final

Cincinnati 70 (OT)
Ohio State 65

Kansas City, MO

National Third Place ⊗ Saint Joseph's d. Utah 127-120 (4OT) (F)
East Regional Third Place St. Bonaventure d. Princeton 85-67
Mideast Regional Third Place Louisville d. Morehead State 83-61
Midwest Regional Third Place Texas Tech d. Houston 69-67
West Regional Third Place Loyola Marymount d. USC 69-67

⊗ Team participation later vacated.

A By winning its conference tournament, George Washington (9–16) becomes the third team with a sub-.500 record to qualify for the NCAAs. The first two were Bradley (7–19) and Oklahoma City (9–17), both in 1955.

B The unbeaten defending national champs get a big scare but survive when John Havlicek hits the game-winner with :06 left. With :01 left, Louisville's John Turner misses the back end of a one-and-one that would have tied the game.

C Kentucky's Roger Newman knocks down 17 free throws and scores 31 points, but Ohio State wins behind Jerry Lucas' 33 points and 30 rebounds (then a Tournament record and four more than the entire Wildcats team).

Jerry Lucas, called by *The New York Times* "6 feet 9 inches of basketball perfection," almost lives up to the billing, scoring 29 points on 10 of 11 field goals and 9 of 10 free throws. As a team, the Buckeyes shoot 63%.

In the first game between the two schools since the 1921-22 season and the first title matchup between teams from the same state, the Bearcats notch their 22nd consecutive win while also snapping Ohio State's 32-game win streak. Bob Wiesenhahn leads Cincy with 17 points, as Ed Jucker becomes the first coach to win a title in his first year at a school.

Cincinnati does what it couldn't do in the Oscar Robertson era—reach the Final—by holding Utah scoring machine Billy "the Hill" McGill (29.8 ppg in the Tournament) to just 11-for-31 shooting.

D Jerry Hahn, a 6'6" ASU center, hits the tying free throw with :16 left and the game-winning shot as time expires.

E Utah's R Boys, Richard Ruffell and Jim Rhead, combine for 43 points to give the Utes an overwhelming win. Rhead is known for his physical play—not surprising, considering that he also plays for the Utah football team.

F In a four-overtime shootout, the teams combine for 247 points, a record that will stand for 29 years. In August, St. Joe's is stripped of its third-place title after Jack Egan, Vince Kempton and Frank Majewski are declared retroactively ineligible because of their involvement in a point-shaving scandal.

Tournament Leaders

INDIVIDUAL LEADERS

Scoring	CL	POS	G	PTS	PPG
1 **Billy McGill**, Utah	JR	C	4	119	29.8
2 **Len Chappell**, Wake Forest	JR	F/C	3	87	29.0
Tom Stith, St. Bonaventure	SR	F	3	87	29.0
4 **John Turner**, Louisville	SR	F	3	77	25.7
5 **Peter Campbell**, Princeton	JR	F	3	75	25.0
Harold Hudgens, Texas Tech	JR	C	2	50	25.0
7 **Jerry Lucas**, Ohio State	JR	C	4	98	24.5
8 **Ed Bento**, Loyola Marymount	JR	C	2	47	23.5
9 **Fred Crawford**, St. Bonaventure	SO	G	3	69	23.0
John Rudometkin, Southern California	JR	C	3	69	23.0

Minimum: 2 games

Field Goals Per Game	CL	POS	G	FG	FGPG
1 **Billy McGill**, Utah	JR	C	4	49	12.3
2 **Fred Crawford**, St. Bonaventure	SO	G	3	32	10.7
3 **Larry Armstrong**, Arizona State	JR	G	3	31	10.3
4 **Harold Hudgens**, Texas Tech	JR	C	2	20	10.0
5 **Tom Stith**, St. Bonaventure	SR	F	3	29	9.7
John Turner, Louisville	SR	F	3	29	9.7

Free Throw Pct	CL	POS	G	FT	FTA	PCT
1 **Tony Jackson**, St. John's	SR	F	1	8	8	100.0
David Nelson, Kansas State	SO	F	2	6	6	100.0
Dick Parsons, Kentucky	SR	G	2	5	5	100.0
Tom Ryan, Loyola Marymount	SR	F	2	5	5	100.0
Charlie Lee, Rhode Island	SO	G	1	5	5	100.0
Barry Multer, Rhode Island	SR	G	1	5	5	100.0

Minimum: 5 made

TEAM LEADERS

Scoring	G	PTS	PPG
1 **Utah**	4	366	91.5
2 **Saint Joseph's**	4	364	91.0
3 **Wake Forest**	3	261	87.0
4 **St. Bonaventure**	3	244	81.3
5 **Arizona State**	3	238	79.3
6 **Ohio State**	4	303	75.8
7 **Cincinnati**	4	299	74.8
8 **Southern California**	3	219	73.0
9 **Princeton**	3	218	72.7
10 **Kentucky**	2	145	72.5

Minimum: 2 games

FG Per Game	G	FG	FGPG
1 **Utah**	4	148	37.0
2 **Arizona State**	3	103	34.3
3 **St. Bonaventure**	3	99	33.0
4 **Saint Joseph's**	4	128	32.0
5 **Wake Forest**	3	94	31.3

FT Pct	G	FT	FTA	PCT
1 **Saint Joseph's**	4	108	135	80.0
2 **Kansas State**	2	45	59	76.3
3 **Kentucky**	2	53	71	74.7
4 **Wake Forest**	3	73	103	70.9
5 **Utah**	4	70	99	70.7

Minimum: 2 games

ALL-TOURNAMENT TEAM

PLAYER	CL	POS	HT	SCHOOL	PPG
Jerry Lucas*	JR	C	6-8	Ohio State	24.5
Carl Bouldin	SR	G	6-2	Cincinnati	14.8
Jack Egan†	SR	F	6-6	Saint Joseph's	20.8
Larry Siegfried	SR	G	6-4	Ohio State	17.3
Bob Wiesenhahn	SR	F	6-4	Cincinnati	18.5

ALL-REGIONAL TEAMS

EAST

PLAYER	CL	POS	HT	SCHOOL	PPG
Peter Campbell	JR	F	6-1	Princeton	25.0
Len Chappell	JR	F/C	6-8	Wake Forest	29.0
Jack Egan	SR	F	6-6	Saint Joseph's	16.5
Jim Lynam	SO	G	5-8	Saint Joseph's	13.0
Tom Stith	SR	F	6-5	St. Bonaventure	29.0

MIDEAST

PLAYER	CL	POS	HT	SCHOOL	PPG
John Havlicek	JR	F	6-5	Ohio State	12.5
Bill Lickert	SR	F/G	6-3	Kentucky	22.5
Jerry Lucas	JR	C	6-8	Ohio State	21.0
Larry Siegfried	SR	G	6-4	Ohio State	17.0
John Turner	SR	F	6-5	Louisville	25.7

MIDWEST

PLAYER	CL	POS	HT	SCHOOL	PPG
Larry Comley*	JR	G/F	6-5	Kansas State	17.0
Bob Wiesenhahn*	SR	F	6-4	Cincinnati	21.5
Harold Hudgens	JR	C	6-10	Texas Tech	25.0
Gary Phillips	SR	G	6-3	Houston	20.3
Tom Thacker	SO	G/F	6-2	Cincinnati	11.0

WEST

PLAYER	CL	POS	HT	SCHOOL	PPG
Larry Armstrong	JR	G	5-9	Arizona State	22.0
Ed Bento	JR	C	6-6	Loyola Marymount	23.5
Billy McGill	JR	C	6-9	Utah	30.0
Jim Rhead	SR	F	6-4	Utah	20.0
John Rudometkin	JR	C	6-6	Southern California	23.0

* Most outstanding player
† Honor later vacated

1961 NCAA TOURNAMENT BOX SCORES

72-67 (SWEET 16)

	Team	1H	2H
	Saint Joseph's	29	43
	Princeton	28	39

SAINT JOSEPH'S	MIN	FG	3FG	FT	REB	A	ST	BL	PF	TP
Vincent Kempton	-	9-15	-	3-4	10	1	-	-	3	21
Jack Egan	-	7-21	-	5-7	13	2	-	-	0	19
James Lynam	-	4-9	-	3-4	7	1	-	-	3	11
Bill Hoy	-	2-5	-	6-8	4	0	-	-	3	10
Bob Gormley	-	2-3	-	0-0	3	0	-	-	2	4
Tom Wynne	-	1-10	-	1-2	10	1	-	-	5	3
Harry Booth	-	0-1	-	2-3	1	0	-	-	0	2
Frank Majewski	-	0-10	-	2-2	8	1	-	-	5	2
TOTALS	-	25-74	-	22-30	56	6	-	-	21	72
Percentages		33.8		73.3						

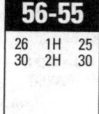

Coach: Jack Ramsay

PRINCETON	MIN	FG	3FG	FT	REB	A	ST	BL	PF	TP
Peter Campbell	-	6-15	-	12-13	2	0	-	-	5	24
Alfred Kaemmerlen	-	7-11	-	4-5	9	0	-	-	3	18
Jack Whitehouse	-	3-10	-	2-7	13	1	-	-	0	8
Arthur Hyland	-	3-9	-	1-1	7	0	-	-	5	7
Drew Hyland	-	2-4	-	1-2	1	0	-	-	1	5
Michael Burton	-	2-4	-	0-0	2	0	-	-	2	4
Thomas Adams	-	0-6	-	1-3	4	0	-	-	2	1
William Haarlow	-	0-0	-	0-0	0	0	-	-	0	0
Andrew Higgins	-	0-2	-	0-0	0	0	-	-	3	0
TOTALS	-	23-61	-	21-31	38	1	-	-	21	67
Percentages		37.7		67.7						

Coach: Jake L. McCandless

78-73 (SWEET 16)

	Team	1H	2H
	Wake Forest	36	42
	St. Bonaventure	37	36

WAKE FOREST	MIN	FG	3FG	FT	REB	A	ST	BL	PF	TP
Len Chappell	40	7-20	-	10-12	15	1	-	-	4	24
Dave Wiedeman	39	4-14	-	6-9	7	1	-	-	4	14
Alley Hart	33	5-11	-	0-1	2	0	-	-	2	10
Bob Woollard	19	2-4	-	6-7	11	3	-	-	4	10
Billy Packer	25	3-8	-	1-1	0	5	-	-	3	7
Bill Hull	21	3-5	-	0-0	6	0	-	-	4	6
Thomas McCoy	20	1-4	-	3-4	4	1	-	-	0	5
Albert Koehler	3	1-1	-	0-0	0	1	-	-	2	2
TOTALS	200	26-67	-	26-34	45	12	-	-	23	78
Percentages		38.8		76.5						

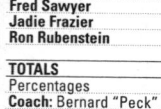

Coach: Horace McKinney

ST. BONAVENTURE	MIN	FG	3FG	FT	REB	A	ST	BL	PF	TP
Tom Stith	40	8-21	-	13-16	12	5	-	-	2	29
Fred Crawford	40	9-20	-	1-6	10	1	-	-	4	19
Whitey Martin	26	3-10	-	1-1	6	1	-	-	5	7
Orrie Jirele	37	2-4	-	1-1	3	2	-	-	4	5
Tom Fitzmorris	9	1-2	-	3-4	3	0	-	-	5	5
Bob McCully	31	1-7	-	2-6	8	1	-	-	2	4
Tom Hannon	17	2-3	-	0-0	1	2	-	-	1	4
TOTALS	200	26-67	-	21-34	43	12	-	-	23	73
Percentages		38.8		61.8						

Coach: Eddie Donovan

56-55 (SWEET 16)

	Team	1H	2H
	Ohio State	26	30
	Louisville	25	30

OHIO STATE	MIN	FG	3FG	FT	REB	A	ST	BL	PF	TP
John Havlicek	-	8-13	-	1-2	8	-	-	-	4	17
Larry Siegfried	-	6-12	-	2-2	5	-	-	-	1	14
Jerry Lucas	-	2-7	-	5-7	18	-	-	-	1	9
Bob Knight	-	4-8	-	0-0	3	-	-	-	3	8
Gary Gearhart	-	2-4	-	0-0	2	-	-	-	3	4
Richie Hoyt	-	1-4	-	0-0	0	-	-	-	1	2
Melvyn Nowell	-	1-8	-	0-1	5	-	-	-	4	2
TOTALS	-	24-56	-	8-12	41	-	-	-	17	56
Percentages		42.9		66.7						

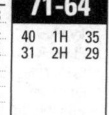

Coach: Fred R. Taylor

LOUISVILLE	MIN	FG	3FG	FT	REB	A	ST	BL	PF	TP
John Turner	-	9-20	-	7-8	15	-	-	-	1	25
Howard Stacey	-	6-15	-	3-6	1	-	-	-	2	15
Bud Olsen	-	2-12	-	2-3	9	-	-	-	2	6
Fred Sawyer	-	1-6	-	2-5	7	-	-	-	4	4
Jadie Frazier	-	1-7	-	1-3	3	-	-	-	0	3
Ron Rubenstein	-	1-3	-	0-0	2	-	-	-	1	2
TOTALS	-	20-63	-	15-25	37	-	-	-	10	55
Percentages		31.7		60.0						

Coach: Bernard "Peck" Hickman

71-64 (SWEET 16)

	Team	1H	2H
	Kentucky	40	31
	Morehead State	35	29

KENTUCKY	MIN	FG	3FG	FT	REB	A	ST	BL	PF	TP
Bill Lickert	-	11-23	-	6-7	16	-	-	-	1	28
Roger Newman	-	5-14	-	4-10	8	-	-	-	4	14
Carroll Burchett	-	2-7	-	8-10	7	-	-	-	1	12
Dick Parsons	-	2-7	-	3-3	4	-	-	-	5	7
Larry Pursiful	-	2-10	-	2-2	7	-	-	-	3	6
Ned Jennings	-	2-8	-	0-0	1	-	-	-	5	4
Scotty Baesler	-	0-0	-	0-0	0	-	-	-	1	0
Allen Feldhaus	-	0-0	-	0-0	0	-	-	-	0	0
TOTALS	-	24-69	-	23-32	43	-	-	-	20	71
Percentages		34.8		71.9						

Coach: Adolph Rupp

MOREHEAD STATE	MIN	FG	3FG	FT	REB	A	ST	BL	PF	TP
Granny Williams	-	7-22	-	6-7	4	-	-	-	4	20
John Gibson	-	4-8	-	6-7	4	-	-	-	3	14
Ed Noe	-	4-10	-	5-5	11	-	-	-	5	13
Hecky Thompson	-	3-15	-	4-5	4	-	-	-	4	10
Norm Pokley	-	2-2	-	1-3	15	-	-	-	3	5
Arthur Cole	-	1-1	-	0-0	1	-	-	-	2	2
TOTALS	-	21-58	-	22-27	39	-	-	-	21	64
Percentages		36.2		81.5						

Coach: Bobby Laughlin

75-64 (SWEET 16)

	Team	1H	2H
	Kansas State	33	42
	Houston	29	35

KANSAS STATE	MIN	FG	3FG	FT	REB	A	ST	BL	PF	TP
Larry Comley	-	7-15	-	4-5	12	-	-	-	3	18
Cedric Price	-	2-6	-	8-11	12	-	-	-	3	12
Patrick McKenzie	-	3-7	-	1-3	4	-	-	-	1	7
Mike Wroblewski	-	3-4	-	1-2	3	-	-	-	3	7
Warren Brown	-	1-2	-	4-4	1	-	-	-	1	6
George Davidson	-	2-2	-	2-2	1	-	-	-	4	6
David Nelson	-	1-5	-	4-4	4	-	-	-	1	6
J.P. Heitmeyer	-	2-3	-	1-1	3	-	-	-	2	5
Richard Ewy	-	2-3	-	0-1	0	-	-	-	4	4
Allen Peithman	-	1-8	-	2-2	1	-	-	-	3	4
Jim Baxter	-	0-0	-	0-0	1	-	-	-	0	0
Jerry Roy	-	0-0	-	0-0	0	-	-	-	1	0
TOTALS	-	24-55	-	27-35	42	-	-	-	26	75
Percentages		43.6		77.1						

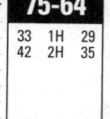

Coach: Tex Winter

HOUSTON	MIN	FG	3FG	FT	REB	A	ST	BL	PF	TP
Gary Phillips	-	6-14	-	10-11	6	-	-	-	2	22
Tom Thomson	-	5-12	-	4-5	5	-	-	-	2	14
Jack Thompson	-	1-5	-	6-9	0	-	-	-	1	8
Lyle Harger	-	2-5	-	1-4	6	-	-	-	4	5
Ted Luckenbill	-	1-7	-	3-3	7	-	-	-	5	5
Richard Thurman	-	2-4	-	0-2	2	-	-	-	2	4
Richard Molchany	-	1-1	-	1-1	1	-	-	-	3	3
Jim Lemmon	-	1-2	-	0-0	0	-	-	-	0	2
Norm Tuffli	-	0-0	-	1-1	2	-	-	-	2	1
Denny Bishop	-	0-0	-	0-0	0	-	-	-	1	0
Bill Brown	-	0-0	-	0-0	0	-	-	-	0	0
Bob Pollan	-	0-1	-	0-0	1	-	-	-	0	0
TOTALS	-	19-51	-	26-36	30	-	-	-	22	64
Percentages		37.3		72.2						

Coach: Guy V. Lewis

Attendance: 8,500

78-55 (SWEET 16)

	Team	1H	2H
	Cincinnati	37	41
	Texas Tech	20	35

CINCINNATI	MIN	FG	3FG	FT	REB	A	ST	BL	PF	TP
Paul Hogue	-	10-17	-	4-5	8	-	-	-	3	24
Bob Wiesenhahn	-	9-21	-	3-5	18	-	-	-	2	21
Carl Bouldin	-	6-12	-	0-0	0	-	-	-	3	12
Tom Thacker	-	3-10	-	0-2	14	-	-	-	2	6
Dale Heidotting	-	2-5	-	0-0	3	-	-	-	3	4
Tom Sizer	-	2-3	-	0-1	2	-	-	-	1	4
Tony Yates	-	2-4	-	0-0	5	-	-	-	0	4
Larry Shingleton	-	1-2	-	0-0	1	-	-	-	0	2
Fred Dierking	-	0-3	-	1-1	2	-	-	-	1	1
Mark Altenau	-	0-1	-	0-1	0	-	-	-	2	0
Jim Calhoun	-	0-2	-	0-0	1	-	-	-	0	0
Ron Reis	-	0-0	-	0-1	0	-	-	-	1	0
TOTALS	-	35-80	-	8-16	54	-	-	-	18	78
Percentages		43.8		50.0						

Coach: Ed L. Jucker

TEXAS TECH	MIN	FG	3FG	FT	REB	A	ST	BL	PF	TP
Harold Hudgens	-	9-20	-	8-10	6	-	-	-	1	26
Roger Hennig	-	3-11	-	1-3	2	-	-	-	2	7
Del Ray Mounts	-	2-11	-	3-5	2	-	-	-	0	7
Mac Percival	-	3-7	-	0-3	9	-	-	-	4	6
John Lemmons	-	2-2	-	1-1	0	-	-	-	1	5
Mickey Milton	-	0-0	-	2-3	0	-	-	-	0	2
Don Perkins	-	1-2	-	0-0	1	-	-	-	0	2
Bobby Gindorf	-	0-1	-	0-0	2	-	-	-	1	0
Tom Patty	-	0-5	-	0-0	3	-	-	-	3	0
Gilbert Vernell	-	0-1	-	0-0	0	-	-	-	1	0
TOTALS	-	20-60	-	15-25	25	-	-	-	13	55
Percentages		33.3		60.0						

Coach: Polk Robison

Officials: Filiberti, Bycort
Attendance: 8,500

ARIZONA STATE	MIN	FG	3FG	FT	REB	A	ST	BL	PF	TP
Larry Armstrong	-	12-27	-	3-6	4	-	-	-	1	27
Jerry Hahn	-	9-17	-	2-4	14	-	-	-	3	20
Mike McConnell	-	4-7	-	1-1	8	-	-	-	2	9
Ollie Payne	-	4-11	-	1-3	6	-	-	-	4	9
Tony Cerkvenik	-	2-6	-	3-3	18	-	-	-	4	7
Bill Pryor	-	3-6	-	1-3	6	-	-	-	2	7
Raul Disarufino	-	3-11	-	0-1	5	-	-	-	3	6
Rex Dernovich	-	0-0	-	1-2	1	-	-	-	1	1
Jerry Daugherty	-	0-1	-	0-0	0	-	-	-	0	0
Lee Engbretston	-	0-0	-	0-0	0	-	-	-	0	0
TOTALS	-	37-86	-	12-23	62	-	-	-	20	86
Percentages		43.0		52.2						

Coach: Ned Wulk

86-71
42 1H 32
44 2H 39
SWEET 16

USC	MIN	FG	3FG	FT	REB	A	ST	BL	PF	TP
John Rudometkin	-	7-23	-	7-8	13	-	-	-	2	21
Gordon Martin	-	7-17	-	1-1	6	-	-	-	4	15
Ken Stanley	-	4-12	-	3-6	8	-	-	-	1	11
Chris Appel	-	4-11	-	2-2	4	-	-	-	4	10
Neil Edwards	-	3-5	-	0-4	5	-	-	-	1	6
Wells Sloniger	-	0-5	-	4-4	2	-	-	-	2	4
Robert Benedetti	-	1-1	-	0-0	0	-	-	-	0	2
Peter Hillman	-	1-1	-	0-0	0	-	-	-	2	2
Vern Ashby	-	0-2	-	0-0	1	-	-	-	1	0
Will Carleton	-	0-1	-	0-0	0	-	-	-	1	0
Bill Ledger	-	0-0	-	0-0	1	-	-	-	0	0
Bill Parsons	-	0-0	-	0-0	0	-	-	-	0	0
TOTALS	-	27-78	-	17-25	40	-	-	-	18	71
Percentages		34.6		68.0						

Coach: Forrest Twogood

Officials: Lichty, Glennon
Attendance: 3,332

UTAH	MIN	FG	3FG	FT	REB	A	ST	BL	PF	TP
Billy McGill	-	12-21	-	5-8	13	-	-	-	3	29
Jim Rhead	-	8-12	-	7-7	20	-	-	-	2	23
Richard Ruffell	-	7-15	-	6-8	8	-	-	-	3	20
Joe Morton	-	3-7	-	2-2	3	-	-	-	3	8
Bo Crain	-	2-3	-	1-2	2	-	-	-	0	5
Joe Aufderheide	-	2-2	-	0-0	5	-	-	-	0	4
Ed Rowe	-	1-7	-	0-0	2	-	-	-	0	2
Bob Cozby	-	0-0	-	0-0	0	-	-	-	0	0
Neil Jenson	-	0-0	-	0-0	0	-	-	-	0	0
Jim Thomas	-	0-1	-	0-0	1	-	-	-	0	0
TOTALS	-	35-68	-	21-27	54	-	-	-	11	91
Percentages		51.5		77.8						

Coach: Jack Gardner

91-75
49 1H 42
42 2H 33
SWEET 16

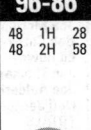

LOYOLA MARYMOUNT	MIN	FG	3FG	FT	REB	A	ST	BL	PF	TP
Brian Quinn	-	8-20	-	1-1	3	-	-	-	0	17
Ed Bento	-	7-11	-	1-2	3	-	-	-	5	15
Tom Ryan	-	6-15	-	3-3	9	-	-	-	3	15
Jerry Grote	-	5-11	-	0-2	5	-	-	-	2	10
Tony Krallman	-	4-10	-	1-2	5	-	-	-	4	9
Bernie Bowler	-	3-4	-	1-2	0	-	-	-	3	7
Omar Simeon	-	1-4	-	0-1	3	-	-	-	0	2
Jim Senske	-	0-1	-	0-0	0	-	-	-	0	0
TOTALS	-	34-76	-	7-13	28	-	-	-	17	75
Percentages		44.7		53.8						

Coach: William Donovan

Officials: Shelton, Gebhardt
Attendance: 3,332

SAINT JOSEPH'S	MIN	FG	3FG	FT	REB	A	ST	BL	PF	TP
Bill Hoy	39	6-13	-	8-11	6	1	-	-	1	20
Frank Majewski	39	8-13	-	3-4	9	2	-	-	4	19
Tom Wynne	22	7-10	-	2-2	4	0	-	-	4	16
James Lynam	39	3-11	-	9-12	2	5	-	-	4	15
Jack Egan	35	6-15	-	2-3	9	3	-	-	4	14
Vincent Kempton	22	6-11	-	0-1	2	1	-	-	5	12
Harry Booth	2	0-0	-	0-0	1	0	-	-	0	0
Paul Westhead	2	0-0	-	0-0	0	0	-	-	0	0
TOTALS	200	36-73	-	24-33	33	12	-	-	22	96
Percentages		49.3		72.7						

Coach: Jack Ramsay

96-86
48 1H 28
48 2H 58
ELITE 8

WAKE FOREST	MIN	FG	3FG	FT	REB	A	ST	BL	PF	TP
Len Chappell	40	11-18	-	10-14	16	3	-	-	3	32
Alley Hart	33	5-11	-	6-6	3	4	-	-	5	16
Thomas McCoy	20	6-6	-	2-2	3	3	-	-	3	14
Dave Wiedeman	35	5-13	-	1-4	5	0	-	-	3	11
Bill Hull	32	4-10	-	1-2	12	2	-	-	2	9
Billy Packer	24	2-6	-	0-1	1	1	-	-	5	4
Albert Koehler	7	0-2	-	0-0	3	0	-	-	1	0
Bob Woollard	5	0-1	-	0-0	0	0	-	-	0	0
Bill Fennell	3	0-0	-	0-0	0	0	-	-	0	0
Paul Caldwell	1	0-1	-	0-0	0	0	-	-	1	0
TOTALS	200	33-68	-	20-29	43	13	-	-	23	86
Percentages		48.5		69.0						

Coach: Bones McKinney

OHIO STATE	MIN	FG	3FG	FT	REB	A	ST	BL	PF	TP
Jerry Lucas	-	14-18	-	5-12	30	-	-	-	4	33
Larry Siegfried	-	8-14	-	4-7	3	-	-	-	3	20
Melvyn Nowell	-	5-7	-	3-5	1	-	-	-	3	13
John Havlicek	-	2-10	-	4-5	10	-	-	-	2	8
Bob Knight	-	3-4	-	1-1	1	-	-	-	4	7
Gary Gearhart	-	1-2	-	0-0	0	-	-	-	2	2
Richie Hoyt	-	1-3	-	0-0	2	-	-	-	2	2
Nelson Miller	-	1-1	-	0-0	0	-	-	-	1	2
Kenneth Lee	-	0-0	-	0-0	0	-	-	-	0	0
Douglas McDonald	-	0-0	-	0-1	2	-	-	-	2	0
Richard Reasbeck	-	0-0	-	0-0	0	-	-	-	1	0
TOTALS	-	35-59	-	17-31	49	-	-	-	24	87
Percentages		59.3		54.8						

Coach: Fred R. Taylor

87-74
36 1H 28
51 2H 46
ELITE 8

KENTUCKY	MIN	FG	3FG	FT	REB	A	ST	BL	PF	TP
Roger Newman	-	7-12	-	17-22	7	-	-	-	1	31
Bill Lickert	-	6-16	-	5-6	3	-	-	-	1	17
Larry Pursiful	-	4-16	-	2-2	2	-	-	-	5	10
Dick Parsons	-	2-10	-	2-2	3	-	-	-	3	6
Ned Jennings	-	1-3	-	2-2	4	-	-	-	5	4
Allen Feldhaus	-	1-3	-	1-2	1	-	-	-	2	3
Carroll Burchett	-	1-4	-	0-0	2	-	-	-	5	2
Jim McDonald	-	0-3	-	1-2	4	-	-	-	1	1
Scotty Baesler	-	0-2	-	0-1	0	-	-	-	0	0
TOTALS	-	22-69	-	30-39	26	-	-	-	23	74
Percentages		31.9		76.9						

Coach: Adolph Rupp

Attendance: 17,494

CINCINNATI	MIN	FG	3FG	FT	REB	A	ST	BL	PF	TP
Bob Wiesenhahn	-	8-12	-	6-9	12	-	-	-	2	22
Tom Thacker	-	5-11	-	6-10	12	-	-	-	4	16
Carl Bouldin	-	4-16	-	2-4	2	-	-	-	0	10
Paul Hogue	-	3-6	-	2-6	7	-	-	-	5	8
Tony Yates	-	1-5	-	6-7	4	-	-	-	1	8
Dale Heidotting	-	2-4	-	1-1	5	-	-	-	5	5
Fred Dierking	-	0-1	-	0-0	1	-	-	-	0	0
Tom Sizer	-	0-0	-	0-0	0	-	-	-	0	0
TOTALS	-	23-55	-	23-37	43	-	-	-	17	69
Percentages		41.8		62.2						

Coach: Ed L. Jucker

69-64
33 1H 33
36 2H 31
ELITE 8

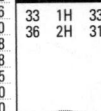

KANSAS STATE	MIN	FG	3FG	FT	REB	A	ST	BL	PF	TP
Larry Comley	-	7-19	-	2-2	9	-	-	-	4	16
Mike Wroblewski	-	3-7	-	5-5	2	-	-	-	2	11
Allen Peithman	-	5-11	-	0-0	1	-	-	-	4	10
Cedric Price	-	3-8	-	4-6	6	-	-	-	4	10
Richard Ewy	-	3-5	-	1-4	1	-	-	-	5	7
David Nelson	-	1-5	-	2-2	3	-	-	-	0	4
Patrick McKenzie	-	1-4	-	1-1	5	-	-	-	5	3
George Davidson	-	0-0	-	2-2	0	-	-	-	0	2
J.P. Heitmeyer	-	0-1	-	1-2	1	-	-	-	2	1
Edwin Matuszak	-	0-0	-	0-0	0	-	-	-	0	0
TOTALS	-	23-60	-	18-24	28	-	-	-	26	64
Percentages		38.3		75.0						

Coach: Tex Winter

Officials: Filiberti, Lightner
Attendance: 10,000

UTAH	MIN	FG	3FG	FT	REB	A	ST	BL	PF	TP
Billy McGill	-	12-27	-	7-8	18	-	-	-	3	31
Richard Ruffell	-	12-17	-	0-0	8	-	-	-	1	24
Jim Rhead	-	5-10	-	7-9	10	-	-	-	3	17
Joe Morton	-	4-15	-	1-2	6	-	-	-	0	9
Joe Aufderheide	-	1-4	-	1-1	2	-	-	-	1	3
Bo Crain	-	1-4	-	0-0	2	-	-	-	0	2
Ed Rowe	-	1-3	-	0-0	4	-	-	-	2	2
Bob Cozby	-	0-1	-	0-0	1	-	-	-	1	0
Jim Thomas	-	0-1	-	0-0	2	-	-	-	0	0
TOTALS	-	36-82	-	16-20	53	-	-	-	11	88
Percentages		43.9		80.0						

Coach: Jack Gardner

88-80
46 1H 28
42 2H 52
ELITE 8

ARIZONA STATE	MIN	FG	3FG	FT	REB	A	ST	BL	PF	TP
Larry Armstrong	-	13-23	-	1-2	6	-	-	-	4	27
Jerry Hahn	-	6-15	-	2-3	11	-	-	-	5	14
Raul Disarufino	-	5-12	-	2-4	4	-	-	-	1	12
Ollie Payne	-	6-17	-	0-0	4	-	-	-	2	12
Mike McConnell	-	4-10	-	0-0	6	-	-	-	3	8
Tony Cerkvenik	-	3-6	-	1-3	7	-	-	-	0	7
Bill Pryor	-	0-1	-	0-1	3	-	-	-	0	0
TOTALS	-	37-84	-	6-13	41	-	-	-	15	80
Percentages		44.0		46.2						

Coach: Ned Wulk

Officials: Glennon, Gebhardt
Attendance: 5,059

ANNUAL REVIEW

95-69 — FINAL 4

	1H	2H
Ohio State	45	50
Saint Joseph's	28	41

OHIO STATE	MIN	FG	3FG	FT	REB	A	ST	BL	PF	TP
Jerry Lucas	-	10-11	-	9-10	13	-	-	-	2	29
Larry Siegfried	-	8-11	-	5-7	9	-	-	-	4	21
Melvyn Nowell	-	7-11	-	1-1	0	-	-	-	2	15
John Havlicek	-	5-6	-	1-2	9	-	-	-	2	11
Bob Knight	-	2-5	-	1-2	3	-	-	-	2	5
Richie Hoyt	-	2-6	-	0-0	1	-	-	-	3	4
J.T. Landes	-	2-2	-	0-0	0	-	-	-	1	4
Gary Gearhart	-	0-2	-	2-2	1	-	-	-	2	2
Kenneth Lee	-	1-1	-	0-0	2	-	-	-	0	2
Douglas McDonald	-	1-4	-	0-0	2	-	-	-	1	2
Nelson Miller	-	0-0	-	0-0	0	-	-	-	0	0
Richard Reasbeck	-	0-1	-	0-1	1	-	-	-	1	0
TOTALS	-	**38-60**	-	**19-25**	**41**	-	-	-	**20**	**95**
Percentages		63.3		76.0						

Coach: Fred R. Taylor

SAINT JOSEPH'S	MIN	FG	3FG	FT	REB	A	ST	BL	PF	TP
Vincent Kempton	-	5-9	-	8-8	8	-	-	-	3	18
Bill Hoy	-	6-17	-	1-1	2	-	-	-	2	13
Frank Majewski	-	4-12	-	5-7	4	-	-	-	1	13
Jack Egan	-	3-15	-	2-3	5	-	-	-	2	8
James Lynam	-	2-5	-	3-4	0	-	-	-	0	7
Bob Gormley	-	1-5	-	2-2	1	-	-	-	3	4
Tom Wynne	-	1-9	-	2-2	2	-	-	-	4	4
Harry Booth	-	0-3	-	2-2	2	-	-	-	3	2
Dan Bugey	-	0-0	-	0-0	1	-	-	-	0	0
Bob Dickey	-	0-0	-	0-0	0	-	-	-	0	0
Paul Westhead	-	0-1	-	0-1	2	-	-	-	0	0
TOTALS	-	**22-76**	-	**25-30**	**27**	-	-	-	**18**	**69**
Percentages		28.9		83.3						

Coach: Jack Ramsay

Officials: Glennon, Filiber
Attendance: 10,700

82-67 — FINAL 4

	1H	2H
Cincinnati	35	47
Utah	20	47

CINCINNATI	MIN	FG	3FG	FT	REB	A	ST	BL	PF	TP
Carl Bouldin	-	7-14	-	7-8	3	-	-	-	0	21
Paul Hogue	-	9-16	-	0-4	14	-	-	-	4	18
Bob Wiesenhahn	-	5-7	-	4-6	5	-	-	-	4	14
Tony Yates	-	4-6	-	5-7	5	-	-	-	2	13
Dale Heidotting	-	3-8	-	1-1	6	-	-	-	1	7
Tom Thacker	-	1-7	-	5-6	6	-	-	-	3	7
Tom Sizer	-	1-1	-	0-0	0	-	-	-	0	2
Mark Altenau	-	0-0	-	0-0	0	-	-	-	0	0
Jim Calhoun	-	0-0	-	0-0	0	-	-	-	0	0
Fred Dierking	-	0-0	-	0-0	1	-	-	-	1	0
Larry Shingleton	-	0-0	-	0-0	0	-	-	-	0	0
TOTALS	-	**30-59**	-	**22-32**	**40**	-	-	-	**15**	**82**
Percentages		50.8		68.8						

Coach: Ed L. Jucker

UTAH	MIN	FG	3FG	FT	REB	A	ST	BL	PF	TP
Billy McGill	-	11-31	-	3-4	8	-	-	-	4	25
Richard Ruffell	-	6-11	-	2-2	5	-	-	-	4	14
Jim Rhead	-	2-5	-	4-6	10	-	-	-	4	8
Joe Morton	-	3-9	-	1-1	1	-	-	-	4	7
Joe Aufderheide	-	2-3	-	2-2	3	-	-	-	1	6
Bo Crain	-	2-5	-	0-1	5	-	-	-	4	4
Ed Rowe	-	1-3	-	0-0	1	-	-	-	2	2
Jim Thomas	-	0-0	-	1-2	0	-	-	-	0	1
Bob Cozby	-	0-0	-	0-0	0	-	-	-	0	0
Neil Jenson	-	0-0	-	0-0	0	-	-	-	0	0
TOTALS	-	**27-67**	-	**13-18**	**33**	-	-	-	**23**	**67**
Percentages		40.3		72.2						

Coach: Jack Gardner

Officials: Wirtz, Fox
Attendance: 10,700

127-120 — 3RD PLACE

	1H	2H	OT1	OT2	OT3	OT4
Saint Joseph's	48	41	8	4	11	15
Utah	41	48	8	4	11	8

SAINT JOSEPH'S	MIN	FG	3FG	FT	REB	A	ST	BL	PF	TP
Jack Egan	-	17-33	-	8-8	16	-	-	-	5	42
James Lynam	-	9-18	-	13-14	2	-	-	-	2	31
Vincent Kempton	-	7-12	-	2-3	10	-	-	-	5	16
Tom Wynne	-	4-12	-	7-9	10	-	-	-	5	15
Frank Majewski	-	5-9	-	1-2	11	-	-	-	3	11
Bill Hoy	-	3-14	-	4-4	3	-	-	-	1	10
Harry Booth	-	0-0	-	2-2	1	-	-	-	0	2
Bob Dickey	-	0-1	-	0-0	2	-	-	-	3	0
Bob Gormley	-	0-2	-	0-0	1	-	-	-	0	0
Paul Westhead	-	0-0	-	0-0	0	-	-	-	0	0
TOTALS	-	**45-101**	-	**37-42**	**56**	-	-	-	**24**	**127**
Percentages		44.6		88.1						

Coach: Jack Ramsay

UTAH	MIN	FG	3FG	FT	REB	A	ST	BL	PF	TP
Billy McGill	-	14-23	-	6-9	14	-	-	-	5	34
Jim Rhead	-	12-20	-	4-10	11	-	-	-	4	28
Richard Ruffell	-	7-14	-	0-0	5	-	-	-	3	14
Bo Crain	-	5-13	-	3-3	8	-	-	-	5	13
Joe Morton	-	3-11	-	5-9	6	-	-	-	3	11
Bob Cozby	-	2-3	-	2-2	3	-	-	-	1	6
Ed Rowe	-	3-8	-	0-0	3	-	-	-	4	6
Jim Thomas	-	3-7	-	0-0	3	-	-	-	0	6
Joe Aufderheide	-	1-4	-	0-1	3	-	-	-	3	2
Neil Jenson	-	0-0	-	0-0	0	-	-	-	0	0
TOTALS	-	**50-103**	-	**20-34**	**56**	-	-	-	**28**	**120**
Percentages		48.5		58.8						

Coach: Jack Gardner

Officials: Wirtz, Glennon
Attendance: 10,700

70-65 — NCAA FINAL 1961

	1H	2H	OT1
Cincinnati	38	23	9
Ohio State	39	22	4

CINCINNATI	MIN	FG	3FG	FT	REB	A	ST	BL	PF	TP
Bob Wiesenhahn	-	8-15	-	1-1	9	-	-	-	3	17
Carl Bouldin	-	7-12	-	2-3	4	-	-	-	4	16
Tom Thacker	-	7-21	-	1-4	7	-	-	-	0	15
Tony Yates	-	4-8	-	5-5	2	-	-	-	3	13
Paul Hogue	-	3-8	-	3-6	7	-	-	-	3	9
Dale Heidotting	-	0-0	-	0-0	0	-	-	-	0	0
Tom Sizer	-	0-0	-	0-0	1	-	-	-	0	0
TOTALS	-	**29-64**	-	**12-19**	**30**	-	-	-	**13**	**70**
Percentages		45.3		63.2						

Coach: Ed L. Jucker

OHIO STATE	MIN	FG	3FG	FT	REB	A	ST	BL	PF	TP
Jerry Lucas	-	10-17	-	7-7	12	-	-	-	4	27
Larry Siegfried	-	6-10	-	2-3	3	-	-	-	2	14
Melvyn Nowell	-	3-9	-	3-3	3	-	-	-	1	9
Richie Hoyt	-	3-5	-	1-1	1	-	-	-	3	7
John Havlicek	-	1-5	-	2-2	4	-	-	-	2	4
Gary Gearhart	-	1-1	-	0-0	0	-	-	-	1	2
Bob Knight	-	1-3	-	0-0	1	-	-	-	1	2
TOTALS	-	**25-50**	-	**15-16**	**24**	-	-	-	**14**	**65**
Percentages		50.0		93.8						

Coach: Fred R. Taylor

Officials: Fox, Filiberti
Attendance: 10,700

National Invitation Tournament (NIT)

First round: Saint Louis d. Miami (FL) 58-56, Holy Cross d. Detroit 86-82, Temple d. Army 79-66, Providence d. DePaul 73-67
Quarterfinals: Saint Louis d. Colorado State 59-53, Holy Cross d. Memphis 81-69, Dayton d. Temple 62-60, Providence d. Niagara 71-68
Semifinals: Saint Louis d. Dayton 67-60, Providence d. Holy Cross 90-83 (OT)
Third place: Holy Cross d. Dayton 85-67
Championship: Providence d. Saint Louis 62-59
MVP: Vinnie Ernst, Providence

1961-62: Cincy Repeat

Coach John Wooden took UCLA to the Final Four. (Get used to that sentence. You'll be seeing it often in the pages that follow.) And, in their national semifinal, the Bruins nearly ruined what most people had expected all season: a championship rematch between in-state rivals Ohio State and Cincinnati. The Bruins staged a late comeback to tie the reigning champ Bearcats at 70 before a broken-play, 25-footer by Tom Thacker—who had not scored all game—with :03 left gave Cincy the 72-70 win.

But the championship may actually have been determined in the other semifinal, when OSU's Jerry Lucas injured his left knee during an 84-68 romp over Wake Forest. Nothing short of amputation would have kept Lucas from playing in the Final, but he was ineffective, scoring 11 points (less than half his season average) as Cincinnati was led by MOP Paul Hogue's 22 points and 19 boards. Still, Lucas earned his second straight consensus national POY.

Major Conference Standings

ACC	Conference			Overall		
	W	L	Pct	W	L	Pct
Wake Forest⊛	12	2	.857	22	9	.710
Duke	11	3	.786	20	5	.800
NC State	10	4	.714	11	6	.647
South Carolina	7	7	.500	15	12	.556
North Carolina	7	7	.500	8	9	.471
Clemson	4	10	.286	12	15	.444
Maryland	3	11	.214	8	17	.320
Virginia	2	12	.143	5	18	.217

Tournament: **Wake Forest d. Clemson 77-66**
Tournament MVP: **Len Chappell**, Wake Forest

BIG EIGHT	Conference			Overall		
	W	L	Pct	W	L	Pct
Colorado⊛	13	1	.929	19	7	.731
Kansas State	12	2	.857	22	3	.880
Iowa State	8	6	.571	13	12	.520
Oklahoma State	7	7	.500	14	11	.560
Nebraska	5	9	.357	9	16	.360
Oklahoma	5	9	.357	7	17	.292
Missouri	3	11	.214	9	16	.360
Kansas	3	11	.214	7	18	.280

AAWU	Conference			Overall		
	W	L	Pct	W	L	Pct
UCLA⊛	10	2	.833	18	11	.621
Stanford	8	4	.667	16	6	.727
Washington	5	7	.417	16	10	.615
Southern California	5	7	.417	14	11	.560
California	2	10	.167	8	17	.320

BIG TEN	Conference			Overall		
	W	L	Pct	W	L	Pct
Ohio State⊛	13	1	.929	26	2	.929
Wisconsin	10	4	.714	17	7	.708
Purdue	9	5	.643	17	7	.708
Illinois	7	7	.500	15	8	.652
Indiana	7	7	.500	13	11	.542
Iowa	7	7	.500	13	11	.542
Minnesota	6	8	.429	10	14	.417
Michigan	5	9	.357	7	17	.292
Michigan State	3	11	.214	8	14	.364
Northwestern	3	11	.214	8	15	.348

BORDER	Conference			Overall		
	W	L	Pct	W	L	Pct
Arizona State⊛	10	0	1.000	23	4	.852
Texas Western	5	3	.625	18	6	.750
New Mexico State	3	5	.375	10	14	.417
West Texas A&M	3	5	.375	5	18	.217
Hardin-Simmons	1	7	.125	8	17	.320

IVY	Conference			Overall		
	W	L	Pct	W	L	Pct
Yale○	13	1	.929	18	6	.750
Penn	11	3	.786	17	8	.680
Princeton	10	4	.714	13	10	.565
Cornell	9	5	.643	18	7	.720
Brown	6	8	.429	11	14	.440
Harvard	3	11	.214	10	14	.417
Dartmouth	3	11	.214	6	18	.250
Columbia	1	13	.071	3	21	.125

METRO NY	Conference			Overall		
	W	L	Pct	W	L	Pct
St. John's□	5	0	1.000	21	5	.808
CCNY	2	1	.667	9	9	.500
NYU○	3	2	.600	20	5	.800
St. Francis (NY)	2	3	.400	8	15	.348
Manhattan	1	3	.250	12	10	.545
Fordham	1	3	.250	10	14	.417
Brooklyn	0	2	.000	4	13	.235

MID-AMERICAN	Conference			Overall		
	W	L	Pct	W	L	Pct
Bowling Green⊛	11	1	.917	21	4	.840
Ohio	8	4	.667	13	10	.565
Toledo	7	5	.583	14	10	.583
Western Michigan	6	6	.500	13	11	.542
Marshall	6	6	.500	10	13	.435
Miami (OH)	3	9	.250	7	17	.292
Kent State	1	11	.083	2	19	.095

MIDDLE ATLANTIC	Conference			Overall		
	W	L	Pct	W	L	Pct
Saint Joseph's⊛	9	1	.900	18	10	.643
Temple□	8	2	.800	18	9	.667
Delaware	9	3	.750	18	5	.783
Lafayette	9	3	.750	18	6	.750
La Salle	5	3	.625	16	9	.640
Gettysburg	7	5	.583	18	8	.692
Lehigh	4	10	.286	7	12	.368
Rutgers	2	8	.200	10	13	.435
Bucknell	2	9	.182	7	15	.318
Muhlenberg	1	12	.077	5	17	.227

MISSOURI VALLEY	Conference			Overall		
	W	L	Pct	W	L	Pct
Cincinnati⊛	10	2	.833	29	2	.935
Bradley□	10	2	.833	21	7	.750
Wichita State□	7	5	.583	18	9	.667
Drake	6	6	.500	16	8	.667
Saint Louis	5	7	.417	11	15	.423
Tulsa	4	8	.333	7	19	.269
North Texas	0	12	.000	3	23	.115

SKYLINE 8	Conference			Overall		
	W	L	Pct	W	L	Pct
Utah	13	1	.929	23	3	.885
Utah State⊛	12	2	.857	22	7	.759
Colorado State□	10	4	.714	18	9	.667
Montana	5	9	.357	10	14	.417
BYU	5	9	.357	10	16	.385
Denver	5	9	.357	8	17	.320
Wyoming	3	11	.214	9	17	.346
New Mexico	3	11	.214	6	20	.231

OHIO VALLEY	Conference			Overall		
	W	L	Pct	W	L	Pct
Western Kentucky⊛	11	1	.917	17	10	.630
Tennessee Tech	7	5	.583	16	6	.727
Morehead State	7	5	.583	14	8	.636
Eastern Kentucky	7	5	.583	10	6	.625
Murray State	5	7	.417	13	12	.520
East Tennessee St.	3	9	.250	11	14	.440
Middle Tennessee St.	2	10	.167	6	12	.333

SEC	Conference			Overall		
	W	L	Pct	W	L	Pct
Mississippi State	13	1	.929	24	1	.960
Kentucky⊛	13	1	.929	23	3	.885
Auburn	11	3	.786	18	6	.750
Florida	8	6	.571	12	11	.522
LSU	7	7	.500	13	11	.542
Tulane	6	8	.429	12	10	.545
Vanderbilt	6	8	.429	12	12	.500
Alabama	6	8	.429	11	15	.423
Mississippi	5	9	.357	12	13	.480
Georgia Tech	4	10	.286	10	16	.385
Georgia	3	11	.214	8	16	.333
Tennessee	2	12	.143	4	19	.174

SOUTHERN	Conference			Overall		
	W	L	Pct	W	L	Pct
West Virginia⊛	12	1	.923	24	6	.800
Virginia Tech	9	3	.750	19	6	.760
Furman	8	5	.615	15	12	.556
George Washington	6	7	.462	9	15	.375
Davidson	5	6	.455	14	11	.560
VMI	6	8	.429	9	11	.450
Citadel	4	8	.333	8	15	.348
William and Mary	5	11	.313	7	17	.292
Richmond	5	11	.313	6	21	.222

Tournament: **West Virginia d. Virginia Tech 88-72**
Tournament MOP: **Rod Thorn**, West Virginia

SOUTHWEST	Conference			Overall		
	W	L	Pct	W	L	Pct
SMU	11	3	.786	18	7	.720
Texas Tech⊛	11	3	.786	19	8	.704
Texas A&M	9	5	.643	15	9	.625
Texas	8	6	.571	16	8	.667
Rice	7	7	.500	12	11	.522
Arkansas	5	9	.357	14	10	.583
TCU	4	10	.286	5	19	.208
Baylor	1	13	.071	4	20	.167

WCAC	Conference			Overall		
	W	L	Pct	W	L	Pct
Pepperdine⊛	11	1	.917	20	7	.741
Santa Clara	8	4	.667	19	6	.760
Saint Mary's (CA)	8	4	.667	13	11	.542
Loyola Marymount	6	6	.500	18	9	.667
San Jose State	6	6	.500	13	11	.542
Pacific	5	7	.417	10	16	.385
San Francisco	4	8	.333	10	15	.400

YANKEE	Conference			Overall		
	W	L	Pct	W	L	Pct
Massachusetts⊛	8	2	.800	15	9	.625
Connecticut	7	3	.700	16	8	.667
Rhode Island	7	3	.700	14	12	.538
Maine	4	6	.400	11	13	.458
Vermont	3	7	.300	12	12	.500
New Hampshire	1	9	.100	3	20	.130

Conference Standings Continue →

⊛ Automatic NCAA Tournament bid ○ At-large NCAA Tournament bid □ NIT appearance ✪ Team record doesn't reflect games forfeited or vacated. For adjusted record, see p. 521.

INDEPENDENTS

	Overall W	L	Pct
Loyola-Chicago□	23	4	.852
Oregon State○	24	5	.828
Creighton○	21	5	.808
Dayton□	24	6	.800
Butler○	22	6	.786
Houston□	21	6	.778
Holy Cross□	20	6	.769
Providence□	20	6	.769
Duquesne□	22	7	.759
Villanova○	21	7	.750
Air Force○	16	7	.696
Boston College	15	7	.682
Memphis○	15	7	.682
Seattle○	18	9	.667
Niagara	16	8	.667
St. Bonaventure	14	7	.667
Centenary	17	9	.654
Idaho State	17	9	.654
Florida State	15	8	.652
Saint Francis (PA)	14	8	.636
Seton Hall	15	9	.625
Navy□	13	8	.619
Georgetown	14	9	.609
Louisville	15	10	.600

INDEPENDENTS (CONT.)

	Overall W	L	Pct
Marquette	15	11	.577
Canisius	12	9	.571
DePaul	13	10	.565
Detroit○	15	12	.556
Gonzaga	14	12	.538
Miami (FL)	14	12	.538
Oklahoma City	14	12	.538
Xavier	14	12	.538
Penn State	12	11	.522
Pittsburgh	12	11	.522
Idaho	13	13	.500
Loyola (LA)	11	12	.478
Army	10	11	.476
Regis (CO)	10	11	.476
Montana State	10	13	.435
Iona	8	11	.421
Colgate	8	15	.348
Oregon	9	17	.346
Portland	8	18	.308
Washington State	8	18	.308
Notre Dame	7	16	.304
Boston U.	5	15	.250
Syracuse	2	22	.083

INDIVIDUAL LEADERS—SEASON

Scoring

	CL	POS	G	FG	FT	PTS	PPG
1 **Billy McGill**, Utah	SR	C	26	394	221	1,009	**38.8**
2 **Jack Foley**, Holy Cross	SR	F	26	322	222	866	**33.3**
3 **Nick Werkman**, Seton Hall	SO	F	24	271	251	793	**33.0**
4 **Terry Dischinger**, Purdue	SR	C	24	217	292	726	**30.3**
5 **Len Chappell**, Wake Forest	SR	F/C	31	327	278	932	**30.1**
6 **Jimmy Rayl**, Indiana	JR	G	24	254	206	714	**29.8**
7 **Jerry Smith**, Furman	JR	G/F	27	261	206	728	**27.0**
8 **Dave DeBusschere**, Detroit	SR	F	26	267	162	696	**26.8**
9 **Bob Duffy**, Colgate	SR	G	23	235	141	611	**26.6**
10 **Chet Walker**, Bradley	SR	F	26	268	151	687	**26.4**

Field Goal Pct

	CL	POS	G	FG	FGA	PCT
1 **Jerry Lucas**, Ohio State	SR	C	28	237	388	**61.1**
2 **Layton Johns**, Auburn	JR	C	24	129	221	**58.4**
3 **Bill Green**, Colorado State	JR	C	27	203	348	**58.3**
4 **Ray Swain**, Florida State	SR	F	23	157	274	**57.3**
5 **Hunter Beckman**, Memphis	JR	F	22	206	361	**57.1**

Minimum: 100 made

Free Throw Pct

	CL	POS	G	FT	FTA	PCT
1 **Tommy Boyer**, Arkansas	JR	G	23	125	134	**93.3**
2 **Jerry Carlton**, Arkansas	SR	G	24	140	159	**88.1**
3 **Skip Chappelle**, Maine	SR	G	20	132	151	**87.4**
4 **Jack Foley**, Holy Cross	SR	F	26	222	256	**86.7**
5 **Granville Williams**, Morehead State	SR	F	22	138	160	**86.3**

Minimum: 90 made

INDIVIDUAL LEADERS—GAME

Points

	CL	POS	OPP	DATE	PTS
1 **Billy McGill**, Utah	SR	C	BYU	F24	**60**
2 **Jack Foley**, Holy Cross	SR	F	Connecticut	F17	**56**
Jimmy Rayl, Indiana	JR	G	Minnesota	J27	**56**
4 **Billy McGill**, Utah	SR	C	Montana	F10	**53**
5 **Billy McGill**, Utah	SR	C	West Texas State	D6	**51**

Free Throws Made

	CL	POS	OPP	DATE	FT	FTA	PCT
1 **Bill Jarman**, Davidson	JR	C	George Washington	D11	**23**	27	85.2
2 **Ronald Warner**, Gettysburg	SR	G	Saint Joseph's	F13	**22**	22	100.0
Jan Loudermilk, SMU	SR	F/C	TCU	F24	**22**	24	91.7
Gary Daniels, The Citadel	SR	F	Toledo	D21	**22**	29	75.9
5 **Don Nelson**, Iowa	SR	F	Indiana	F17	**21**	25	84.0
John Green, UCLA	SR	G	Washington	J6	**21**	26	80.8

TEAM LEADERS—SEASON

Scoring Offense

	G	W-L	PTS	PPG
1 **Loyola-Chicago**	27	23-4	2,436	**90.2**
2 **Arizona State**	27	23-4	2,434	**90.1**
3 **Seton Hall**	24	15-9	2,115	**88.1**
4 **Indiana**	24	13-11	2,089	**87.0**
5 **West Virginia**	30	24-6	2,562	**85.4**

Field Goal Pct

	G	W-L	FG	FGA	PCT
1 **Florida State**	23	15-8	709	1,386	**51.2**
2 **Utah**	26	23-3	883	1,812	**48.7**
3 **Ohio State**	28	26-2	952	1,961	**48.5**
4 **Memphis**	22	15-7	736	1,530	**48.1**
5 **Bradley**	28	21-7	887	1,849	**48.0**

Free Throw Pct

	G	W-L	FT	FTA	PCT
1 **Arkansas**	24	14-10	502	647	**77.6**
2 **SMU**	25	18-7	552	718	**76.9**
3 **Holy Cross**	26	20-6	497	650	**76.5**
4 **Memphis**	22	15-7	367	482	**76.1**
5 **Western Kentucky**	27	17-10	538	713	**75.5**

Scoring Defense

	G	W-L	OPP PTS	OPP PPG
1 **Santa Clara**	25	19-6	1,302	**52.1**
2 **Auburn**	24	18-6	1,254	**52.3**
3 **San Jose State**	24	13-11	1,262	**52.6**
4 **Cincinnati**	31	29-2	1,707	**55.1**
5 **Texas Western**	24	18-6	1,348	**56.2**

CONSENSUS ALL-AMERICAS

First Team

PLAYER	CL	POS	HT	SCHOOL	RPG	PPG
Len Chappell	SR	F/C	6-8	Wake Forest	15.2	30.1
Terry Dischinger	SR	C	6-7	Purdue	13.4	30.3
Jerry Lucas	SR	C	6-8	Ohio State	17.8	21.8
Billy McGill	SR	C	6-9	Utah	15.0	38.8
Chet Walker	SR	F	6-6	Bradley	12.3	26.4

Second Team

PLAYER	CL	POS	HT	SCHOOL	RPG	PPG
Jack Foley	SR	F	6-5	Holy Cross	8.3	33.3
John Havlicek	SR	F	6-5	Ohio State	9.7	17.0
Art Heyman	JR	F/G	6-5	Duke	11.2	25.3
Cotton Nash	SO	F	6-5	Kentucky	13.3	23.4
John Rudometkin	SR	C	6-6	Southern California	11.6	21.0
Rod Thorn	JR	F	6-4	West Virginia	12.1	23.7

Selectors: AP, Look Magazine, NABC, Newspaper Enterprises Assn., UPI, USBWA

AWARD WINNERS

Player of the Year

PLAYER	CL	POS	HT	SCHOOL	AWARDS
Jerry Lucas	SR	C	6-8	Ohio State	AP, UPI, USBWA

Coach of the Year

COACH	SCHOOL	REC	AWARDS
Fred Taylor	Ohio State	26-2	UPI, USBWA

Poll Progression

Preseason Poll

AP	SCHOOL
1	Ohio State
2	Cincinnati
3	Wake Forest
4	USC
5	Providence
6	Purdue
7	Duke
8	Kansas State
9	St. John's
10	Seattle

Week of Dec 12

UPI	SCHOOL	
1	**Ohio State** (4-0)	
2	**Cincinnati** (3-0)	
3	**Kansas State** (3-0)	
4	**Providence** (3-0)	
5	**Duke** (3-0)	Ⓐ
6	**Purdue** (2-0)	
7	**USC** (3-1)	
8	**Arizona State** (3-0)	
9	**West Virginia** (4-0)	
10	**Wake Forest** (2-1)	

Week of Dec 19

AP	UPI	SCHOOL
1	1	**Ohio State** (5-0)
2	2	**Cincinnati** (5-0)
3	4	**Providence** (5-0)
4	3	**Kansas State** (5-0)
5	6	**West Virginia** (6-0)
6	5	**USC** (5-1)
7	12	**Duquesne** (5-0)
8	9	**Purdue** (3-1)
9	15	**St. Bonaventure** (6-0)
10	7	**Arizona State** (5-0)
10	—	**Seattle** (5-0)
—	8	**Duke** (6-1)
—	10	**Wichita State** (5-1)
—	11	**Utah** (5-1)
—	13	**St. John's** (3-1)
—	14	**Kentucky** (3-1)
—	16	**Drake** (3-1)
—	17	**Dayton** (5-0)
—	18	**NYU** (5-0)
—	18	**Texas Tech** (3-1)
—	20	**Illinois** (5-0)

Week of Dec 26

AP	UPI	SCHOOL	AP↓↑
1	1	**Ohio State** (7-0) Ⓑ	
2	2	**Cincinnati** (6-1) Ⓒ	
3	7	**Duquesne** (6-0)	↑4
4	4	**USC** (7-1)	↑2
5	3	**Kansas State** (7-1)	↓1
6	6	**Kentucky** (6-1)	⤴
7	9	**West Virginia** (6-1)	↓2
8	5	**Wichita State** (7-1) Ⓒ	⤴
9	12	**Purdue** (5-1)	↓1
10	8	**Duke** (7-1)	⤴
—	10	**Utah** (8-1)	
—	11	**Providence** (5-2)	⤵
—	13	**NYU** (6-0)	
—	14	**St. John's** (4-1)	
—	15	**Texas Tech** (4-1)	
—	16	**Seattle** (5-0)	⤵
—	17	**Santa Clara** (8-1)	
—	17	**Villanova** (9-0)	
—	19	**Mississippi State** (7-0)	
—	20	**Washington** (5-1)	
—	21	**St. Bonaventure** (6-1)	⤵
—	22	**DePaul** (6-0)	
—	22	**Utah State** (8-1)	
—	24	**Oregon State** (4-1)	
—	24	**Pittsburgh** (4-3)	
—	26	**Bradley** (5-2)	

Week of Jan 2

AP	UPI	SCHOOL	AP↓↑
1	1	**Ohio State** (10-0)	
2	2	**Cincinnati** (10-1)	
3	5	**Kentucky** (8-1)	↑3
4	3	**Kansas State** (10-1)	↑1
5	6	**Villanova** (11-0)	⤴
6	4	**USC** (9-2)	↓2
7	8	**Duquesne** (9-1)	↓4
8	7	**Duke** (8-1)	↑2
9	14	**Mississippi State** (9-0)	⤴
10	14	**Bowling Green** (8-1)	⤴
—	9	**Wichita State** (9-2)	⤵
—	10	**Oregon State** (7-1)	
—	11	**Purdue** (7-2)	⤵
—	12	**West Virginia** (7-3)	⤵
—	13	**Texas Tech** (6-1)	
—	16	**Utah** (10-2)	
—	17	**Santa Clara** (11-1)	
—	17	**Temple** (7-1)	
—	19	**Illinois** (7-1)	
—	19	**St. John's** (6-2)	

Week of Jan 9

AP	UPI	SCHOOL	AP↓↑
1	1	**Ohio State** (11-0)	
2	2	**Cincinnati** (11-1)	
3	4	**Kentucky** (10-1)	
4	3	**USC** (11-2)	↑2
5	5	**Kansas State** (10-2)	↓1
6	6	**Villanova** (12-1)	↓1
7	11	**Mississippi State** (10-0)	↑2
8	7	**Duquesne** (9-1)	↓1
9	16	**Bowling Green** (10-1)	↑1
10	8	**Duke** (9-2)	↓2
—	9	**Oregon State** (9-1)	
—	10	**West Virginia** (9-3)	
—	12	**Utah** (11-2)	
—	13	**Bradley** (8-2)	
—	14	**Wichita State** (11-3)	
—	15	**Santa Clara** (12-1)	
—	17	**Illinois** (8-1)	
—	18	**Purdue** (7-3)	
—	18	**Temple** (9-1)	
—	20	**Colorado State** (8-3)	

Week of Jan 16

AP	UPI	SCHOOL	AP↓↑
1	1	**Ohio State** (12-0)	
2	3	**Kentucky** (12-1)	↑1
3	2	**Cincinnati** (11-2)	↓1
4	4	**Kansas State** (12-2)	↑1
5	6	**Duquesne** (11-1)	↑3
6	5	**USC** (12-3)	↓2
7	8	**Duke** (11-2)	↑3
8	14	**Bowling Green** (12-1)	↑1
9	7	**Bradley** (10-2)	⤴
10	13	**Mississippi State** (11-1)	↓3
—	9	**Villanova** (13-2)	⤵
—	10	**Oregon State** (11-1)	
—	10	**Wichita State** (13-3)	
—	12	**West Virginia** (11-3)	
—	15	**Utah** (13-2)	
—	16	**Stanford** (7-2)	
—	17	**Purdue** (10-3)	
—	18	**St. John's** (9-3)	
—	19	**Illinois** (9-2)	
—	19	**Santa Clara** (12-3)	

Week of Jan 23

AP	UPI	SCHOOL	AP↓↑
1	1	**Ohio State** (13-0)	
2	3	**Kentucky** (13-1)	
3	2	**Cincinnati** (13-2)	
4	5	**Kansas State** (13-2)	
5	4	**USC** (12-3)	↑1
6	6	**Duquesne** (12-2)	↓1
7	9	**Duke** (11-2)	
8	12	**Bowling Green** (14-1)	
9	7	**Bradley** (11-3)	
10	13	**Mississippi State** (13-1)	
—	8	**Villanova** (14-2)	
—	10	**Oregon State** (13-1)	
—	11	**Wichita State** (14-4)	
—	14	**West Virginia** (13-3)	
—	15	**Utah** (15-2)	
—	16	**Stanford** (8-2)	
—	17	**Colorado** (8-5)	
—	18	**St. John's** (10-3)	
—	19	**Arizona State** (13-3)	
—	20	**Santa Clara** (12-3)	

Week of Jan 30

AP	UPI	SCHOOL	AP↓↑
1	1	**Ohio State** (14-0)	
2	3	**Kentucky** (13-1)	
3	2	**Cincinnati** (14-2)	
4	4	**Kansas State** (14-2)	
5	5	**USC** (12-3)	
6	6	**Duke** (12-2)	↑1
7	7	**Duquesne** (14-2)	↓1
8	11	**Bowling Green** (16-1)	
9	8	**Bradley** (12-3)	
10	13	**Mississippi State** (16-1)	
—	9	**Oregon State** (14-1)	
—	10	**Villanova** (15-2)	
—	12	**West Virginia** (14-3)	
—	14	**Utah** (15-2)	
—	15	**Loyola-Chicago** (12-2)	
—	16	**Colorado** (9-5)	
—	17	**Arizona State** (13-3)	
—	17	**Wichita State** (14-5)	
—	19	**Houston** (14-3)	
—	19	**North Carolina** (6-2)	
—	19	**Santa Clara** (12-3)	

Week of Feb 6

AP	UPI	SCHOOL	AP↓↑
1	1	**Ohio State** (16-0)	
2	3	**Kentucky** (16-1)	
3	2	**Cincinnati** (17-2)	
4	4	**Kansas State** (15-2)	
5	5	**Duke** (11-2)	↑1
6	6	**Duquesne** (16-2)	↑1
7	8	**Bradley** (14-3)	↑2
8	10	**Bowling Green** (16-1)	
9	11	**Mississippi State** (16-1)	↑1
10	9	**Oregon State** (16-1)	⤴
—	7	**USC** (12-4)	⤵
—	12	**Villanova** (15-4)	
—	13	**Colorado** (10-5)	
—	13	**Utah** (16-3)	
—	13	**West Virginia** (16-4)	
—	16	**Arizona State** (14-3)	
—	17	**Loyola-Chicago** (14-2)	
—	18	**St. John's** (13-4)	
—	19	**Stanford** (10-4)	
—	20	**Loyola Marymount** (14-3)	
—	20	**UCLA** (10-7)	
—	20	**Utah State** (15-4)	

Week of Feb 13

AP	UPI	SCHOOL	AP↓↑
1	1	**Ohio State** (18-0)	
2	3	**Kentucky** (17-1)	
3	2	**Cincinnati** (19-2)	
4	4	**Kansas State** (17-2)	
5	5	**Bradley** (16-3)	↑2
6	6	**Oregon State** (17-1)	↑4
7	7	**Duke** (15-3)	↓2
8	8	**Mississippi State** (18-1)	↑1
9	9	**Duquesne** (16-3)	↓3
10	12	**Bowling Green** (16-2)	↓2
—	10	**USC** (13-5)	
—	11	**Villanova** (16-5)	
—	12	**St. John's** (15-4)	
—	14	**Utah** (17-3)	
—	15	**UCLA** (11-7)	
—	16	**Loyola-Chicago** (15-2)	
—	17	**Arizona State** (18-3)	
—	18	**Colorado** (12-5)	
—	19	**West Virginia** (18-4)	
—	20	**Washington** (11-8)	

Week of Feb 20

AP	UPI	SCHOOL	AP↓↑
1	1	**Ohio State** (20-0)	
2	2	**Cincinnati** (21-2)	↑1
3	3	**Kentucky** (17-2)	↓1
4	4	**Kansas State** (18-2)	
5	5	**Mississippi State** (20-1)	↑3
6	6	**Bradley** (18-3)	↓1
7	10	**Bowling Green** (18-2)	↑3
8	7	**Duke** (17-4) Ⓓ	↓1
9	13	**Colorado** (14-5)	⤴
10	8	**Oregon State** (17-3)	↓4
—	9	**St. John's** (15-4)	
—	10	**Loyola-Chicago** (16-2)	
—	10	**USC** (14-6)	
—	14	**Duquesne** (16-5)	⤵
—	14	**Utah** (19-3) Ⓔ	
—	16	**West Virginia** (19-5)	
—	17	**Utah State** (18-4)	
—	18	**UCLA** (12-8)	
—	19	**Wake Forest** (13-8) Ⓓ	
—	20	**Arizona State** (20-3)	
—	20	**North Carolina State** (11-4)	

Poll Progression Continues →

Week of Feb 27

AP	UPI	SCHOOL	AP↓↑
1	1	**Ohio State** (21-0)	
2	2	**Cincinnati** (23-2)	
3	3	**Kansas State** (19-2)	↑1
4	4	**Kentucky** (19-2)	↓1
5	5	**Mississippi State** (22-1)	
6	7	**Bradley** (19-4)	
7	8	**Bowling Green** (20-2)	
8	6	**Duke** (19-4)	
9	10	**Colorado** (15-5)	
10	15	**Utah** (21-3)	⤴
—	9	**Loyola-Chicago** (18-2)	
—	11	**Oregon State** (18-4)	⤵
—	12	**UCLA** (14-8)	
—	13	**St. John's** (16-4)	
—	14	**Duquesne** (18-5)	
—	16	**Houston** (21-5)	
—	16	**Wake Forest** (15-8)	
—	18	**Arizona State** (21-3)	
—	19	**Villanova** (17-6)	
—	20	**West Virginia** (21-5)	
—	20	**USC** (14-8) (F)	

Week of Mar 6

AP	UPI	SCHOOL	AP↓↑
1	1	**Ohio State** (22-1) (G)	
2	2	**Cincinnati** (24-2)	
3	3	**Kansas State** (21-2)	
4	4	**Kentucky** (20-2)	
5	5	**Mississippi State** (24-1)	
6	6	**Bradley** (21-4)	
7	7	**Utah** (22-3)	↑3
8	10	**Bowling Green** (21-3)	↓1
9	11	**Duke** (20-5)	↓1
10	9	**Loyola-Chicago** (21-2)	⤴
—	8	**Wake Forest** (18-8)	
—	12	**UCLA** (15-8)	
—	13	**Oregon State** (20-4)	
—	14	**West Virginia** (24-5)	
—	15	**St. John's** (17-4)	
—	16	**Wisconsin** (18-6) (G)	
—	17	**Arizona State** (22-3)	
—	18	**Villanova** (18-6)	
—	19	**Colorado** (16-6)	⤵
—	20	**NYU** (17-3)	

Final Poll

AP	UPI	SCHOOL	AP↓↑
1	1	**Ohio State** (23-1)	
2	2	**Cincinnati** (24-2)	
3	3	**Kentucky** (22-2)	↑1
4	4	**Mississippi State** (24-1)	↑1
5	6	**Bradley** (21-5)	↑1
6	5	**Kansas State** (22-3)	↓3
7	10	**Utah** (23-3)	
8	9	**Bowling Green** (21-3)	
9	8	**Colorado** (18-5)	⤴
10	13	**Duke** (20-5)	↓1
—	7	**Wake Forest** (18-8)	
—	11	**Oregon State** (22-4)	
—	12	**St. John's** (19-4)	
—	13	**Loyola-Chicago** (21-3)	⤵
—	15	**Arizona State** (22-3)	
—	16	**West Virginia** (24-5)	
—	17	**UCLA** (16-9)	
—	18	**Duquesne** (22-5)	
—	19	**Utah State** (21-5)	
—	20	**Villanova** (19-6)	
—	21	**Texas Tech** (18-6)	
—	22	**Dayton** (20-6)	
—	22	**Stanford** (16-6)	
—	24	**NYU** (18-4)	
—	25	**Houston** (21-6)	
—	25	**Pepperdine** (19-6)	
—	25	**Saint Joseph's** (18-8)	

(A) Taking the floor for an 85-56 rout of Louisville, Duke becomes the first college team to apply player names to the backs of its jerseys. Coach Vic Bubas says the new uniforms will be a "big help to the fans."

(B) Jerry Lucas is named 1961 *Sports Illustrated* Sportsman of the Year. Lucas "has remained as imperturbable as a Mount Rushmore face, behaving in a studied, discerning and appealing fashion both on and off the basketball court," the magazine observes.

(C) Wichita State beats Cincinnati, 52-51, to snap a 27-game winning streak. The Bearcats will lose just once more in the 1961-62 season—to Bradley in a two-point, overtime heartbreaker on Jan. 10.

(D) Wake Forest beats Duke, 97-79, as consensus All-America forward Len Chappell scores 37 points. Chappell will lead Wake to its first ACC title and a surprise berth in the Final Four.

(E) Utah's Billy "the Hill" McGill drops a school-record 60 points on archrival BYU in a 106-101 victory in Provo. The 6'9" McGill is still the only Ute to top 50 (four times).

(F) USC's free fall accelerates with back-to-back losses to Houston. The Trojans, 9–1 on Dec. 28, will lose 11 of their last 15, including six straight to end the season.

(G) Wisconsin blows past Ohio State, 86-67, in Madison, snapping the Buckeyes' 27-game Big Ten winning streak.

1962 NCAA Tournament

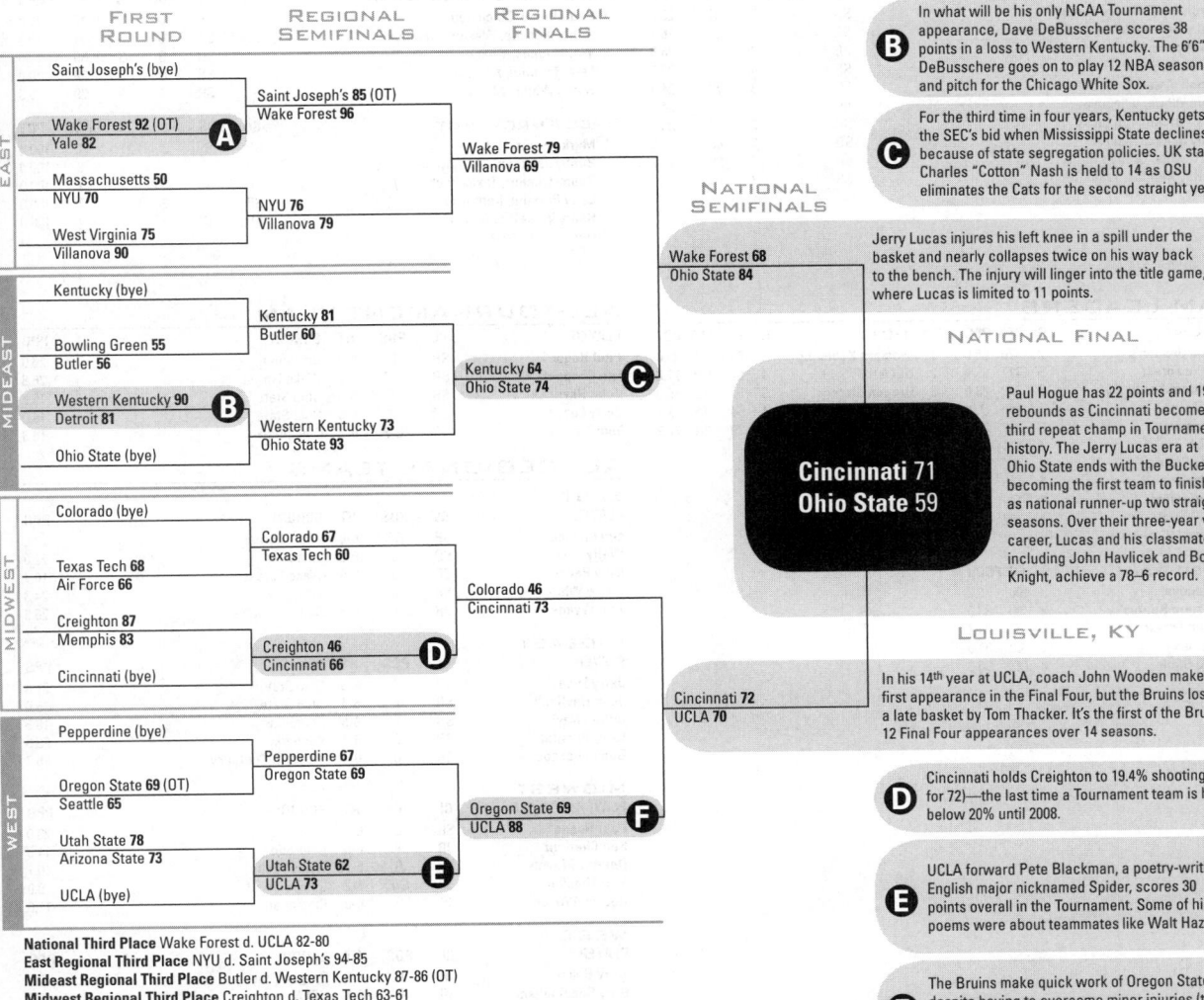

East

First Round
- Saint Joseph's (bye)
- Wake Forest **92** (OT), Yale **82** (A)
- Massachusetts **50**, NYU **70**
- West Virginia **75**, Villanova **90**

Regional Semifinals
- Saint Joseph's **85** (OT), Wake Forest **96**
- NYU **76**, Villanova **79**

Regional Finals
- Wake Forest **79**, Villanova **69**

Mideast

First Round
- Kentucky (bye)
- Bowling Green **55**, Butler **56**
- Western Kentucky **90**, Detroit **81** (B)
- Ohio State (bye)

Regional Semifinals
- Kentucky **81**, Butler **60**
- Western Kentucky **73**, Ohio State **93**

Regional Finals
- Kentucky **64**, Ohio State **74** (C)

Midwest

First Round
- Colorado (bye)
- Texas Tech **68**, Air Force **66**
- Creighton **87**, Memphis **83**
- Cincinnati (bye)

Regional Semifinals
- Colorado **67**, Texas Tech **60**
- Creighton **46**, Cincinnati **66** (D)

Regional Finals
- Colorado **46**, Cincinnati **73**

West

First Round
- Pepperdine (bye)
- Oregon State **69** (OT), Seattle **65**
- Utah State **78**, Arizona State **73**
- UCLA (bye)

Regional Semifinals
- Pepperdine **67**, Oregon State **69**
- Utah State **62**, UCLA **73** (E)

Regional Finals
- Oregon State **69**, UCLA **88** (F)

National Semifinals
- Wake Forest **68**, Ohio State **84**
- Cincinnati **72**, UCLA **70**

National Final

Cincinnati 71
Ohio State 59

Louisville, KY

National Third Place Wake Forest d. UCLA 82-80
East Regional Third Place NYU d. Saint Joseph's 94-85
Mideast Regional Third Place Butler d. Western Kentucky 87-86 (OT)
Midwest Regional Third Place Creighton d. Texas Tech 63-61
West Regional Third Place Pepperdine d. Utah State 75-71

A Senior Wake Forest guard Billy Packer scores 89 Tournament points before embarking on a career in coaching, sales and eventually, broadcasting. He will call 34 NCAA Tournaments on television between 1974 and 2008.

B In what will be his only NCAA Tournament appearance, Dave DeBusschere scores 38 points in a loss to Western Kentucky. The 6'6" DeBusschere goes on to play 12 NBA seasons and pitch for the Chicago White Sox.

C For the third time in four years, Kentucky gets the SEC's bid when Mississippi State declines because of state segregation policies. UK star Charles "Cotton" Nash is held to 14 as OSU eliminates the Cats for the second straight year.

Jerry Lucas injures his left knee in a spill under the basket and nearly collapses twice on his way back to the bench. The injury will linger into the title game, where Lucas is limited to 11 points.

Paul Hogue has 22 points and 19 rebounds as Cincinnati becomes the third repeat champ in Tournament history. The Jerry Lucas era at Ohio State ends with the Buckeyes becoming the first team to finish as national runner-up two straight seasons. Over their three-year varsity career, Lucas and his classmates, including John Havlicek and Bob Knight, achieve a 78–6 record.

In his 14th year at UCLA, coach John Wooden makes his first appearance in the Final Four, but the Bruins lose on a late basket by Tom Thacker. It's the first of the Bruins' 12 Final Four appearances over 14 seasons.

D Cincinnati holds Creighton to 19.4% shooting (14 for 72)—the last time a Tournament team is held below 20% until 2008.

E UCLA forward Pete Blackman, a poetry-writing English major nicknamed Spider, scores 30 points overall in the Tournament. Some of his poems were about teammates like Walt Hazzard.

F The Bruins make quick work of Oregon State despite having to overcome minor injuries (to Gary Cunningham and John Green) and illness (Walt Hazzard's upset stomach).

Tournament Leaders

Individual Leaders

Scoring

	CL	POS	G	PTS	PPG
1 **Len Chappell**, Wake Forest	SR	F/C	5	134	26.8
2 **Bobby Rascoe**, Western Kentucky	SR	G	3	80	26.7
3 **Tom Wynne**, Saint Joseph's	JR	F	2	53	26.5
4 **Paul Hogue**, Cincinnati	SR	C	4	104	26.0
5 **Cornell Green**, Utah State	SR	G/F	3	73	24.3
Hubie White, Villanova	SR	F	3	73	24.3
7 **Larry Pursiful**, Kentucky	SR	G	2	47	23.5
8 **Wally Jones**, Villanova	SO	G	3	66	22.0
9 **Mel Counts**, Oregon State	SO	C	3	59	19.7
Del Ray Mounts, Texas Tech	SR	G	3	59	19.7

Minimum: 2 games

Field Goals Per Game

	CL	POS	G	FG	FGPG
1 **Paul Hogue**, Cincinnati	SR	C	4	42	10.5
2 **Bobby Rascoe**, Western Kentucky	SR	G	3	31	10.3
3 **Wally Jones**, Villanova	SO	G	3	30	10.0
Larry Pursiful, Kentucky	SR	G	2	20	10.0
5 **Hubie White**, Villanova	SR	F	3	28	9.3

Free Throw Pct

	CL	POS	G	FT	FTA	PCT
1 **Mark Reiner**, NYU	SR	G	3	11	11	100.0
Bobby Jackson, Western Kentucky	JR	F	3	9	9	100.0
Bobby Gindorf, Texas Tech	JR	G	3	7	7	100.0
Larry Pursiful, Kentucky	SR	G	2	7	7	100.0
Henry Viccellio, Air Force	SR	C	1	7	7	100.0

Minimum: 5 made

Team Leaders

Scoring

		G	PTS	PPG
1	**Saint Joseph's**	2	170	85.0
2	**Wake Forest**	5	417	83.4
3	**Western Kentucky**	3	249	83.0
4	**NYU**	3	240	80.0
5	**Villanova**	3	238	79.3
6	**UCLA**	4	311	77.8
7	**Ohio State**	4	310	77.5
8	**Kentucky**	2	145	72.5
9	**Pepperdine**	2	142	71.0
10	**Cincinnati**	4	282	70.5

Minimum: 2 games

FT Pct

		G	FT	FTA	PCT
1	**Western Kentucky**	3	51	61	83.6
2	**UCLA**	4	87	113	77.0
3	**Oregon State**	3	51	68	75.0
4	**Ohio State**	4	64	88	72.7
5	**Butler**	3	39	54	72.2

Minimum: 2 games

FG Per Game

		G	FG	FGPG
1	**Villanova**	3	100	33.3
2	**Western Kentucky**	3	99	33.0
3	**Wake Forest**	5	157	31.4
4	**Kentucky**	2	62	31.0
5	**Ohio State**	4	123	30.8

All-Tournament Team

PLAYER	CL	POS	HT	SCHOOL	PPG
Paul Hogue*	SR	C	6-9	Cincinnati	26.0
Len Chappell	SR	F/C	6-8	Wake Forest	26.8
John Havlicek	SR	F	6-5	Ohio State	16.5
Jerry Lucas	SR	C	6-8	Ohio State	18.0
Tom Thacker	JR	G/F	6-2	Cincinnati	10.3

All-Regional Teams

East

PLAYER	CL	POS	HT	SCHOOL	PPG
Len Chappell*	SR	F/C	6-8	Wake Forest	27.0
Wally Jones	SO	G	6-2	Villanova	22.0
Billy Packer	SR	G	5-9	Wake Forest	16.7
Hubie White	SR	F	6-3	Villanova	24.3
Tom Wynne	JR	F	6-5	Saint Joseph's	26.5

Mideast

PLAYER	CL	POS	HT	SCHOOL	PPG
Jerry Lucas*	SR	C	6-8	Ohio State	21.0
John Havlicek	SR	F	6-5	Ohio State	15.0
Cotton Nash	SO	F	6-5	Kentucky	18.5
Larry Pursiful	SR	G	6-1	Kentucky	23.5
Bobby Rascoe	SR	G	6-4	Western Kentucky	26.7

Midwest

PLAYER	CL	POS	HT	SCHOOL	PPG
Paul Hogue*	SR	C	6-9	Cincinnati	23.0
Ken Charlton	JR	F	6-6	Colorado	14.5
Del Ray Mounts	SR	G	5-10	Texas Tech	19.7
Tom Thacker	JR	G/F	6-2	Cincinnati	9.0
George Wilson	SO	F	6-8	Cincinnati	11.0

West

PLAYER	CL	POS	HT	SCHOOL	PPG
Terry Baker	JR	G	6-3	Oregon State	8.3
Gary Cunningham	SR	F	6-6	UCLA	16.5
Cornell Green	SR	G/F	6-4	Utah State	24.3
John Green	SR	G	6-2	UCLA	17.0
Walt Hazzard	SO	G	6-2	UCLA	15.0
Bob Warlick	JR	F	6-5	Pepperdine	17.0

* Most outstanding player

1962 NCAA TOURNAMENT BOX SCORES

WAKE FOREST	MIN	FG	3FG	FT	REB	A	ST	BL	PF	TP
Len Chappell	-	9-17	-	16-20	18	4	-	-	4	34
Billy Packer	-	8-14	-	1-2	1	2	-	-	2	17
Dave Wiedeman	-	5-12	-	5-6	4	1	-	-	3	15
Bob Woollard	-	4-8	-	4-4	11	0	-	-	5	12
Frank Christie	-	5-10	-	0-1	10	0	-	-	3	10
Thomas McCoy	-	3-5	-	2-2	4	1	-	-	1	8
Richard Carmichael	-	0-0	-	0-0	0	0	-	-	0	0
Butch Hassell	-	0-0	-	0-0	0	0	-	-	0	0
Bill Hull	-	0-3	-	0-0	4	0	-	-	1	0
TOTALS	-	34-69	-	28-35	52	8	-	-	19	96
Percentages		49.3		80.0						

Coach: Horace "Bones" McKinney

96-85

36	1H	41
38	2H	33
22	OT1	11

SWEET 16

SAINT JOSEPH'S	MIN	FG	3FG	FT	REB	A	ST	BL	PF	TP
Tom Wynne	-	10-26	-	9-9	7	0	-	-	2	29
Jim Boyle	-	6-13	-	4-4	7	0	-	-	4	16
James Lynam	-	6-12	-	3-3	3	0	-	-	2	15
Bob Gormley	-	5-6	-	0-0	0	0	-	-	3	10
Bill Hoy	-	1-6	-	4-5	9	1	-	-	3	6
Bob Dickey	-	2-8	-	1-2	4	1	-	-	5	5
Larry Hoffman	-	0-1	-	3-6	5	0	-	-	5	3
Harry Booth	-	0-2	-	1-2	1	0	-	-	1	1
Steve Courtin	-	0-0	-	0-0	0	0	-	-	0	0
John Tiller	-	0-0	-	0-0	0	0	-	-	0	0
TOTALS	-	30-74	-	25-31	36	2	-	-	25	85
Percentages		40.5		80.6						

Coach: Jack Ramsay

Attendance: 11,700

VILLANOVA	MIN	FG	3FG	FT	REB	A	ST	BL	PF	TP
Hubie White	-	11-19	-	9-12	6	1	-	-	4	31
Wally Jones	-	6-15	-	2-3	4	0	-	-	1	14
Jim McMonagle	-	5-10	-	3-3	8	0	-	-	3	13
Joseph O'Brien	-	6-13	-	0-0	10	2	-	-	5	12
George Leftwich	-	3-13	-	3-5	2	1	-	-	2	9
Joseph Walsh	-	0-1	-	0-0	1	0	-	-	1	0
TOTALS	-	31-71	-	17-23	31	4	-	-	16	79
Percentages		43.7		73.9						

Coach: Jack Kraft

79-76

40	1H	42
39	2H	34

SWEET 16

NYU	MIN	FG	3FG	FT	REB	A	ST	BL	PF	TP
Barry Kramer	-	10-15	-	6-6	10	1	-	-	4	26
Happy Hairston	-	7-14	-	7-9	12	0	-	-	4	21
Mark Reiner	-	5-8	-	2-2	5	4	-	-	4	12
Tom Boose	-	4-6	-	3-4	4	0	-	-	4	11
Neil O'Neill	-	3-5	-	0-2	1	2	-	-	1	6
Don Blaha	-	0-0	-	0-0	0	0	-	-	0	0
Al Filardi	-	0-1	-	0-0	0	0	-	-	0	0
Steve Jordan	-	0-0	-	0-0	1	0	-	-	0	0
Bob Williams	-	0-0	-	0-0	0	0	-	-	0	0
TOTALS	-	29-49	-	18-23	33	7	-	-	17	76
Percentages		59.2		78.3						

Coach: Lou Rossini

Attendance: 11,700

KENTUCKY	MIN	FG	3FG	FT	REB	A	ST	BL	PF	TP
Larry Pursiful	-	12-21	-	2-2	6	-	-	-	1	26
Cotton Nash	-	11-24	-	1-1	10	-	-	-	5	23
Carroll Burchett	-	6-11	-	0-0	9	-	-	-	4	12
Roy Roberts	-	2-4	-	3-5	6	-	-	-	2	7
Scotty Baesler	-	3-9	-	0-1	4	-	-	-	1	6
Allen Feldhaus	-	2-4	-	1-2	3	-	-	-	3	5
Charles Ishmael	-	1-1	-	0-0	1	-	-	-	1	2
Ted Deeken	-	0-1	-	0-0	0	-	-	-	0	0
Jim McDonald	-	0-2	-	0-0	0	-	-	-	0	0
Adolph Rupp	-	0-1	-	0-0	0	-	-	-	0	0
TOTALS	-	37-78	-	7-11	39	-	-	-	17	81
Percentages		47.4		63.6						

Coach: Adolph Rupp

81-60

37	1H	36
44	2H	24

SWEET 16

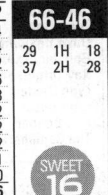

BUTLER	MIN	FG	3FG	FT	REB	A	ST	BL	PF	TP
Jerry Williams	-	9-20	-	2-3	3	-	-	-	2	20
Jeff Blue	-	7-14	-	5-8	11	-	-	-	2	19
Tom Bowman	-	4-11	-	1-1	2	-	-	-	1	9
Earl Engle	-	1-8	-	3-3	2	-	-	-	4	5
Ken Freeman	-	2-3	-	0-0	3	-	-	-	1	4
Dick Haslam	-	1-9	-	1-1	6	-	-	-	3	3
Larry Shook	-	0-1	-	0-1	1	-	-	-	0	0
TOTALS	-	24-66	-	12-17	28	-	-	-	13	60
Percentages		36.4		70.6						

Coach: Paul D. "Tony" Hinkle

Officials: Honzo, Eckman
Attendance: 8,300

OHIO STATE	MIN	FG	3FG	FT	REB	A	ST	BL	PF	TP
Douglas McDonald	-	9-14	-	3-6	5	-	-	-	0	21
John Havlicek	-	7-9	-	3-3	5	-	-	-	4	17
Richard Reasbeck	-	6-11	-	0-0	1	-	-	-	3	12
Gary Bradds	-	3-7	-	4-5	7	-	-	-	0	10
Melvyn Nowell	-	3-9	-	4-6	4	-	-	-	2	10
Jerry Lucas	-	4-13	-	1-1	13	-	-	-	4	9
Gary Gearhart	-	3-7	-	1-2	2	-	-	-	2	7
James Doughty	-	1-4	-	1-2	1	-	-	-	0	3
Bob Knight	-	1-6	-	0-0	1	-	-	-	2	2
Richard Taylor	-	1-2	-	0-0	0	-	-	-	0	2
Donald Flatt	-	0-0	-	0-0	1	-	-	-	0	0
Leroy Frazier	-	0-1	-	0-1	0	-	-	-	1	0
Gene Lane	-	0-0	-	0-0	0	-	-	-	0	0
TOTALS	-	38-83	-	17-26	40	-	-	-	18	93
Percentages		45.8		65.4						

Coach: Fred R. Taylor

93-73

43	1H	30
50	2H	43

SWEET 16

WESTERN KENTUCKY	MIN	FG	3FG	FT	REB	A	ST	BL	PF	TP
Bobby Rascoe	-	8-23	-	10-12	7	-	-	-	3	26
Jim Dunn	-	5-13	-	2-2	11	-	-	-	3	12
Harry Todd	-	4-9	-	4-7	8	-	-	-	3	12
Bobby Jackson	-	4-9	-	3-3	7	-	-	-	4	11
Darel Carrier	-	4-13	-	0-0	2	-	-	-	3	8
Mike Ridley	-	1-1	-	0-0	2	-	-	-	0	2
Jim Smith	-	1-1	-	0-0	0	-	-	-	1	2
Warner Caines	-	0-0	-	0-0	0	-	-	-	1	0
Larry Castle	-	0-0	-	0-0	0	-	-	-	0	0
Danny Day	-	0-0	-	0-0	0	-	-	-	1	0
TOTALS	-	27-69	-	19-24	37	-	-	-	19	73
Percentages		39.1		79.2						

Coach: E.A. Diddle

Officials: Bello, Eisenstein
Technicals: Ohio State 1
Attendance: 8,300

COLORADO	MIN	FG	3FG	FT	REB	A	ST	BL	PF	TP
Ken Charlton	-	9-21	-	0-0	6	-	-	-	0	18
Jim Davis	-	8-11	-	1-5	9	-	-	-	4	17
Wilky Gilmore	-	4-8	-	3-4	9	-	-	-	2	11
Eric Lee	-	3-7	-	2-4	8	-	-	-	3	8
Milt Mueller	-	2-5	-	1-1	5	-	-	-	2	5
Gil Whissen	-	2-4	-	1-3	4	-	-	-	2	5
Lonnie Melton	-	1-4	-	0-0	1	-	-	-	0	2
Gene Sparks	-	0-1	-	1-2	1	-	-	-	1	1
TOTALS	-	29-61	-	9-19	43	-	-	-	14	67
Percentages		47.5		47.4						

Coach: Russell "Sox" Walseth

67-60

43	1H	32
24	2H	28

SWEET 16

TEXAS TECH	MIN	FG	3FG	FT	REB	A	ST	BL	PF	TP
Del Ray Mounts	-	7-20	-	5-6	3	-	-	-	2	19
Harold Hudgens	-	5-13	-	2-3	10	-	-	-	1	12
Bobby Gindorf	-	4-7	-	3-3	1	-	-	-	3	11
Mac Percival	-	3-6	-	1-2	5	-	-	-	3	7
Sid Wall	-	3-6	-	0-0	0	-	-	-	2	6
Roger Hennig	-	1-6	-	3-3	5	-	-	-	5	5
TOTALS	-	23-58	-	14-17	24	-	-	-	16	60
Percentages		39.7		82.4						

Coach: Gene Gibson

Attendance: 8,000

CINCINNATI	MIN	FG	3FG	FT	REB	A	ST	BL	PF	TP
Paul Hogue	-	10-14	-	4-5	19	-	-	-	4	24
Ron Bonham	-	4-10	-	6-7	5	-	-	-	2	14
Tom Thacker	-	5-8	-	2-3	13	-	-	-	1	12
Tom Sizer	-	1-3	-	4-6	1	-	-	-	3	6
George Wilson	-	0-3	-	3-6	1	-	-	-	4	3
Jim Calhoun	-	1-1	-	0-0	1	-	-	-	0	2
Fred Dierking	-	1-3	-	0-0	2	-	-	-	1	2
Tony Yates	-	0-7	-	2-3	5	-	-	-	1	2
Larry Shingleton	-	0-1	-	1-2	1	-	-	-	0	1
Dale Heidotting	-	0-1	-	0-2	1	-	-	-	1	0
TOTALS	-	22-51	-	22-34	49	-	-	-	17	66
Percentages		43.1		64.7						

Coach: Ed L. Jucker

66-46

29	1H	18
37	2H	28

SWEET 16

CREIGHTON	MIN	FG	3FG	FT	REB	A	ST	BL	PF	TP
Paul Silas	-	3-14	-	9-12	7	-	-	-	4	15
Jim Bakos	-	2-14	-	3-4	12	-	-	-	5	7
Larry Wagner	-	2-11	-	3-4	3	-	-	-	4	7
Herb Millard	-	2-13	-	1-2	4	-	-	-	4	5
Pete McManamon	-	1-8	-	2-4	8	-	-	-	5	4
Chuck Officer	-	2-9	-	0-0	1	-	-	-	1	4
Carl Silvestrini	-	2-3	-	0-0	3	-	-	-	1	4
TOTALS	-	14-72	-	18-26	38	-	-	-	24	46
Percentages		19.4		69.2						

Coach: John J. McManus

Attendance: 8,000

ANNUAL REVIEW

OREGON STATE	MIN	FG	3FG	FT	REB	A	ST	BL	PF	TP
Terry Baker	-	6-14	-	3-5	3	-	-	-	4	15
Mel Counts	-	4-18	-	7-8	21	-	-	-	5	15
Steve Pauly	-	7-18	-	1-2	7	-	-	-	1	15
Jay Carty	-	4-15	-	6-6	6	-	-	-	1	14
Bob Jacobson	-	4-9	-	2-2	6	-	-	-	5	10
Tim Campbell	-	0-0	-	0-0	0	-	-	-	0	0
Dave Hayward	-	0-2	-	0-0	0	-	-	-	0	0
Ray Torgerson	-	0-0	-	0-1	4	-	-	-	1	0
TOTALS	-	25-76	-	19-24	47	-	-	-	17	69
Percentages		32.9		79.2						

Coach: Slats Gill

69-67

35 1H 30
34 2H 37

SWEET 16

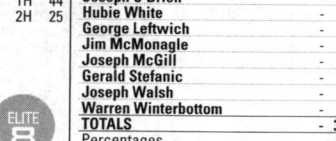

PEPPERDINE	MIN	FG	3FG	FT	REB	A	ST	BL	PF	TP
Bob Warlick	-	9-21	-	5-6	13	-	-	-	4	23
Tim Tift	-	6-11	-	3-7	9	-	-	-	3	15
Lee Tinsley	-	6-15	-	1-2	3	-	-	-	3	13
Harry Dinnel	-	3-10	-	2-8	9	-	-	-	4	8
Noel Smith	-	4-9	-	0-0	4	-	-	-	3	8
Ted Bridges	-	0-1	-	0-0	2	-	-	-	0	0
Dave Dougan	-	0-1	-	0-1	1	-	-	-	3	0
TOTALS	-	28-68	-	11-24	41	-	-	-	20	67
Percentages		41.2		45.8						

Coach: Robert Dowell

Attendance: 9,816

UCLA	MIN	FG	3FG	FT	REB	A	ST	BL	PF	TP
Gary Cunningham	-	9-18	-	3-4	7	-	-	-	4	21
Walt Hazzard	-	4-12	-	5-8	8	-	-	-	0	13
John Green	-	3-15	-	5-8	7	-	-	-	2	11
Fred Slaughter	-	5-7	-	0-0	9	-	-	-	5	10
Pete Blackman	-	3-8	-	2-2	2	-	-	-	4	8
Kim Stewart	-	2-5	-	4-6	7	-	-	-	4	8
Bill Hicks	-	1-2	-	0-0	0	-	-	-	2	2
Jim Rosvall	-	0-0	-	0-0	0	-	-	-	0	0
Dave Waxman	-	0-2	-	0-0	1	-	-	-	1	0
TOTALS	-	27-69	-	19-28	41	-	-	-	22	73
Percentages		39.1		67.9						

Coach: John Wooden

73-62

43 1H 30
30 2H 32

SWEET 16

UTAH STATE	MIN	FG	3FG	FT	REB	A	ST	BL	PF	TP
Cornell Green	-	9-20	-	8-12	16	-	-	-	4	26
Darnell Haney	-	4-16	-	4-9	14	-	-	-	4	12
Mark Hasen	-	5-15	-	0-1	0	-	-	-	4	10
Phil Johnson	-	4-9	-	2-6	15	-	-	-	2	10
Reid Goldsberry	-	1-3	-	0-0	2	-	-	-	4	2
Don Holman	-	1-6	-	0-1	0	-	-	-	2	2
Dennis Nate	-	0-0	-	0-0	0	-	-	-	2	0
TOTALS	-	24-69	-	14-29	47	-	-	-	22	62
Percentages		34.8		48.3						

Coach: Ladell Andersen

Attendance: 10,186

WAKE FOREST	MIN	FG	3FG	FT	REB	A	ST	BL	PF	TP
Len Chappell	-	9-23	-	4-6	21	0	-	-	2	22
Bob Woollard	-	9-15	-	1-1	18	2	-	-	1	19
Billy Packer	-	7-15	-	4-4	1	0	-	-	2	18
Dave Wiedeman	-	5-12	-	2-4	3	1	-	-	2	12
Frank Christie	-	2-4	-	2-3	3	0	-	-	2	6
Thomas McCoy	-	1-2	-	0-0	2	0	-	-	1	2
Bill Hull	-	0-0	-	0-0	0	0	-	-	0	0
TOTALS	-	33-71	-	13-18	48	3	-	-	10	79
Percentages		46.5		72.2						

Coach: Horace "Bones" McKinney

79-69

42 1H 44
37 2H 25

ELITE 8

VILLANOVA	MIN	FG	3FG	FT	REB	A	ST	BL	PF	TP
Wally Jones	-	11-18	-	3-3	5	0	-	-	2	25
Joseph O'Brien	-	7-10	-	0-0	10	0	-	-	3	14
Hubie White	-	6-25	-	2-4	14	1	-	-	2	14
George Leftwich	-	4-13	-	2-6	8	0	-	-	2	10
Jim McMonagle	-	3-11	-	0-1	6	0	-	-	4	6
Joseph McGill	-	0-0	-	0-0	0	0	-	-	0	0
Gerald Stefanic	-	0-0	-	0-0	0	0	-	-	0	0
Joseph Walsh	-	0-0	-	0-0	0	0	-	-	1	0
Warren Winterbottom	-	0-0	-	0-0	0	0	-	-	0	0
TOTALS	-	31-77	-	7-14	43	1	-	-	14	69
Percentages		40.3		50.0						

Coach: Jack Kraft

Attendance: 12,500

OHIO STATE	MIN	FG	3FG	FT	REB	A	ST	BL	PF	TP
Jerry Lucas	-	12-21	-	9-10	15	-	-	-	3	33
John Havlicek	-	5-15	-	3-4	10	-	-	-	3	13
James Doughty	-	4-12	-	0-0	2	-	-	-	2	8
Richard Reasbeck	-	4-11	-	0-0	3	-	-	-	3	8
Gary Gearhart	-	1-1	-	5-7	4	-	-	-	0	7
Melvyn Nowell	-	1-5	-	3-4	3	-	-	-	2	5
Gary Bradds	-	0-0	-	0-1	0	-	-	-	0	0
Donald Flatt	-	0-0	-	0-0	0	-	-	-	0	0
Bob Knight	-	0-0	-	0-0	0	-	-	-	0	0
Douglas McDonald	-	0-0	-	0-0	0	-	-	-	1	0
Richard Taylor	-	0-0	-	0-0	0	-	-	-	0	0
TOTALS	-	27-65	-	20-26	37	-	-	-	14	74
Percentages		41.5		76.9						

Coach: Fred R. Taylor

74-64

41 1H 37
33 2H 27

ELITE 8

KENTUCKY	MIN	FG	3FG	FT	REB	A	ST	BL	PF	TP
Larry Pursiful	-	8-17	-	5-5	4	-	-	-	4	21
Cotton Nash	-	5-19	-	4-6	9	-	-	-	1	14
Carroll Burchett	-	3-9	-	2-4	3	-	-	-	5	8
Roy Roberts	-	4-8	-	0-0	0	-	-	-	5	8
Scotty Baesler	-	2-10	-	3-4	9	-	-	-	4	7
Jim McDonald	-	2-2	-	0-0	1	-	-	-	0	4
Allen Feldhaus	-	1-4	-	0-2	2	-	-	-	2	2
Ted Deeken	-	0-0	-	0-0	0	-	-	-	0	0
TOTALS	-	25-69	-	14-21	28	-	-	-	21	64
Percentages		36.2		66.7						

Coach: Adolph Rupp

Officials: Eckman, Honzo
Attendance: 14,500

CINCINNATI	MIN	FG	3FG	FT	REB	A	ST	BL	PF	TP
Paul Hogue	-	9-17	-	4-4	12	-	-	-	3	22
George Wilson	-	7-12	-	5-8	7	-	-	-	2	19
Ron Bonham	-	8-20	-	1-2	7	-	-	-	3	17
Tom Thacker	-	3-8	-	0-1	4	-	-	-	0	6
Tony Yates	-	1-8	-	3-3	6	-	-	-	1	5
Jim Calhoun	-	1-1	-	0-0	0	-	-	-	1	2
Tom Sizer	-	1-1	-	0-0	1	-	-	-	2	2
Fred Dierking	-	0-0	-	0-0	0	-	-	-	0	0
Dale Heidotting	-	0-0	-	0-0	0	-	-	-	1	0
Ron Reis	-	0-0	-	0-0	1	-	-	-	0	0
Larry Shingleton	-	0-1	-	0-0	1	-	-	-	0	0
TOTALS	-	30-68	-	13-18	39	-	-	-	13	73
Percentages		44.1		72.2						

Coach: Ed L. Jucker

73-46

41 1H 29
32 2H 17

ELITE 8

COLORADO	MIN	FG	3FG	FT	REB	A	ST	BL	PF	TP
Wilky Gilmore	-	5-6	-	5-6	7	-	-	-	3	15
Ken Charlton	-	4-16	-	3-6	7	-	-	-	3	11
Jim Davis	-	3-8	-	0-0	4	-	-	-	2	6
Eric Lee	-	2-5	-	0-0	1	-	-	-	4	4
Wayne Millies	-	2-4	-	0-1	4	-	-	-	1	4
Gil Whissen	-	2-6	-	0-0	0	-	-	-	0	4
Milt Mueller	-	0-1	-	2-2	2	-	-	-	1	2
Tom McCann	-	0-0	-	0-0	0	-	-	-	0	0
Lonnie Melton	-	0-0	-	0-0	0	-	-	-	0	0
Gene Sparks	-	0-1	-	0-1	1	-	-	-	0	0
Terry Woodward	-	0-0	-	0-2	0	-	-	-	0	0
Gene Zyzda	-	0-0	-	0-0	0	-	-	-	0	0
TOTALS	-	18-47	-	10-18	26	-	-	-	14	46
Percentages		38.3		55.6						

Coach: Russell "Sox" Walseth

Attendance: 9,000

UCLA	MIN	FG	3FG	FT	REB	A	ST	BL	PF	TP
John Green	-	5-16	-	13-16	3	-	-	-	3	23
Walt Hazzard	-	6-9	-	5-5	4	-	-	-	5	17
Gary Cunningham	-	4-9	-	4-4	11	-	-	-	4	12
Dave Waxman	-	5-8	-	2-2	5	-	-	-	0	12
Pete Blackman	-	3-9	-	1-1	5	-	-	-	1	7
Fred Slaughter	-	2-8	-	3-5	10	-	-	-	0	7
Bill Hicks	-	2-2	-	0-1	2	-	-	-	0	4
Larry Gower	-	0-0	-	2-2	1	-	-	-	0	2
Jim Rosvall	-	1-2	-	0-0	0	-	-	-	0	2
Kim Stewart	-	1-2	-	0-0	1	-	-	-	1	2
Mike Huggins	-	0-0	-	0-1	0	-	-	-	0	0
Jim Milhorn	-	0-1	-	0-0	0	-	-	-	0	0
TOTALS	-	29-66	-	30-37	42	-	-	-	14	88
Percentages		43.9		81.1						

Coach: John Wooden

88-69

44 1H 30
44 2H 39

ELITE 8

OREGON STATE	MIN	FG	3FG	FT	REB	A	ST	BL	PF	TP
Mel Counts	-	11-25	-	2-2	17	-	-	-	2	24
Steve Pauly	-	4-8	-	2-5	2	-	-	-	3	10
Jay Carty	-	4-8	-	1-5	5	-	-	-	2	9
Terry Baker	-	2-10	-	2-3	2	-	-	-	4	6
Dave Hayward	-	3-9	-	0-0	2	-	-	-	1	6
Bob Jacobson	-	2-3	-	1-2	5	-	-	-	1	5
Ray Torgerson	-	2-3	-	0-0	2	-	-	-	0	4
Lynn Baxter	-	1-3	-	1-1	0	-	-	-	2	3
Gary Rossi	-	1-4	-	0-0	2	-	-	-	3	2
Rex Benner	-	0-3	-	0-0	3	-	-	-	2	0
Tim Campbell	-	0-1	-	0-0	2	-	-	-	1	0
TOTALS	-	30-77	-	9-18	42	-	-	-	21	69
Percentages		39.0		50.0						

Coach: Slats Gill

Attendance: 9,816

84-68 — 46 1H 34 / 38 2H 34 — FINAL 4

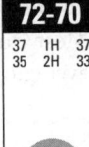

OHIO STATE	MIN	FG	3FG	FT	REB	A	ST	BL	PF	TP
John Havlicek	-	9-16	-	7-9	16	-	-	-	3	25
Jerry Lucas	-	8-16	-	3-4	16	-	-	-	1	19
Douglas McDonald	-	5-10	-	1-2	5	-	-	-	3	11
Richard Reasbeck	-	5-7	-	0-0	3	-	-	-	4	10
James Doughty	-	2-4	-	4-4	5	-	-	-	1	8
Gary Gearhart	-	2-5	-	0-0	0	-	-	-	4	4
Melvyn Nowell	-	2-11	-	0-0	2	-	-	-	2	4
Leroy Frazier	-	1-1	-	0-0	0	-	-	-	0	2
Donald Flatt	-	0-0	-	1-2	0	-	-	-	0	1
Gary Bradds	-	0-0	-	0-1	4	-	-	-	3	0
Bob Knight	-	0-2	-	0-0	2	-	-	-	2	0
Richard Taylor	-	0-0	-	0-0	0	-	-	-	1	0
TOTALS	-	34-72	-	16-22	53	-	-	-	24	84
Percentages		47.2		72.7						

Coach: Fred R. Taylor

WAKE FOREST	MIN	FG	3FG	FT	REB	A	ST	BL	PF	TP
Len Chappell	-	10-24	-	7-11	18	-	-	-	5	27
Billy Packer	-	8-14	-	1-2	5	-	-	-	3	17
Dave Wiedeman	-	5-16	-	3-6	8	-	-	-	0	13
Bob Woollard	-	1-3	-	1-2	3	-	-	-	2	3
Brad Brooks	-	0-1	-	2-2	1	-	-	-	1	2
Butch Hassell	-	1-2	-	0-0	0	-	-	-	0	2
Thomas McCoy	-	0-1	-	2-2	1	-	-	-	1	2
Frank Christie	-	0-2	-	1-1	4	-	-	-	2	1
Ted Zawacki	-	0-0	-	1-3	0	-	-	-	0	1
Richard Carmichael	-	0-0	-	0-0	1	-	-	-	1	0
Bill Hull	-	0-2	-	0-0	2	-	-	-	2	0
Albert Koehler	-	0-1	-	0-0	0	-	-	-	0	0
TOTALS	-	25-66	-	18-29	43	-	-	-	17	68
Percentages		37.9		62.1						

Coach: Horace "Bones" McKinney

Attendance: 18,274

72-70 — 37 1H 37 / 35 2H 33 — FINAL 4

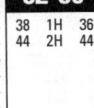

CINCINNATI	MIN	FG	3FG	FT	REB	A	ST	BL	PF	TP
Paul Hogue	-	12-18	-	12-17	19	-	-	-	3	36
Ron Bonham	-	8-14	-	3-6	2	-	-	-	4	19
Tony Yates	-	4-10	-	2-3	3	-	-	-	3	10
George Wilson	-	1-6	-	1-2	4	-	-	-	1	3
Tom Sizer	-	1-3	-	0-0	1	-	-	-	3	2
Tom Thacker	-	1-7	-	0-0	4	-	-	-	3	2
TOTALS	-	27-58	-	18-28	33	-	-	-	17	72
Percentages		46.6		64.3						

Coach: Ed L. Jucker

UCLA	MIN	FG	3FG	FT	REB	A	ST	BL	PF	TP
John Green	-	9-16	-	9-11	7	-	-	-	1	27
Gary Cunningham	-	8-14	-	3-3	9	-	-	-	2	19
Walt Hazzard	-	5-10	-	2-3	6	-	-	-	2	12
Dave Waxman	-	2-3	-	2-3	3	-	-	-	1	6
Pete Blackman	-	2-3	-	0-0	2	-	-	-	5	4
Fred Slaughter	-	1-4	-	0-0	7	-	-	-	5	2
Kim Stewart	-	0-0	-	0-0	1	-	-	-	2	0
TOTALS	-	27-50	-	16-20	35	-	-	-	18	70
Percentages		54.0		80.0						

Coach: John Wooden

Attendance: 18,274

82-80 — 38 1H 36 / 44 2H 44 — 3RD PLACE

WAKE FOREST	MIN	FG	3FG	FT	REB	A	ST	BL	PF	TP
Len Chappell	-	9-13	-	8-10	11	-	-	-	5	26
Billy Packer	-	10-19	-	2-2	5	-	-	-	1	22
Dave Wiedeman	-	7-13	-	4-6	1	-	-	-	4	18
Bob Woollard	-	4-6	-	1-3	12	-	-	-	3	9
Thomas McCoy	-	0-1	-	3-3	2	-	-	-	3	3
Frank Christie	-	1-8	-	0-0	2	-	-	-	3	2
Butch Hassell	-	1-1	-	0-0	0	-	-	-	0	2
Brad Brooks	-	0-0	-	0-0	0	-	-	-	0	0
Bill Hull	-	0-0	-	0-1	2	-	-	-	1	0
TOTALS	-	32-61	-	18-25	35	-	-	-	20	82
Percentages		52.5		72.0						

Coach: Horace "Bones" McKinney

UCLA	MIN	FG	3FG	FT	REB	A	ST	BL	PF	TP
Gary Cunningham	-	5-17	-	7-8	11	-	-	-	5	17
Fred Slaughter	-	8-11	-	1-1	10	-	-	-	1	17
Walt Hazzard	-	5-17	-	5-5	10	-	-	-	3	15
Pete Blackman	-	4-10	-	3-4	8	-	-	-	2	11
John Green	-	3-12	-	1-3	4	-	-	-	5	7
Dave Waxman	-	1-3	-	5-6	8	-	-	-	0	7
Bill Hicks	-	2-4	-	0-1	3	-	-	-	1	4
Kim Stewart	-	1-2	-	0-0	1	-	-	-	2	2
Jim Milhorn	-	0-1	-	0-0	0	-	-	-	0	0
TOTALS	-	29-77	-	22-28	55	-	-	-	19	80
Percentages		37.7		78.6						

Coach: John Wooden

Attendance: 18,469

71-59 — 37 1H 29 / 34 2H 30 — NCAA FINAL 1962

CINCINNATI	MIN	FG	3FG	FT	REB	A	ST	BL	PF	TP
Paul Hogue	-	11-18	-	0-2	19	-	-	-	2	22
Tom Thacker	-	6-14	-	9-11	6	-	-	-	2	21
Tony Yates	-	4-8	-	4-7	1	-	-	-	1	12
Ron Bonham	-	3-12	-	4-4	6	-	-	-	3	10
George Wilson	-	1-6	-	4-4	11	-	-	-	2	6
Tom Sizer	-	0-0	-	0-0	0	-	-	-	0	0
TOTALS	-	25-58	-	21-28	43	-	-	-	10	71
Percentages		43.1		75.0						

Coach: Ed L. Jucker

OHIO STATE	MIN	FG	3FG	FT	REB	A	ST	BL	PF	TP
Gary Bradds	-	5-7	-	5-6	4	-	-	-	2	15
John Havlicek	-	5-14	-	1-2	9	-	-	-	1	11
Jerry Lucas	-	5-17	-	1-2	16	-	-	-	3	11
Melvyn Nowell	-	4-16	-	1-1	6	-	-	-	2	9
Richard Reasbeck	-	4-6	-	0-0	0	-	-	-	4	8
Douglas McDonald	-	0-1	-	3-3	1	-	-	-	2	3
Gary Gearhart	-	1-4	-	0-0	4	-	-	-	3	2
James Doughty	-	0-1	-	0-0	2	-	-	-	2	0
TOTALS	-	24-66	-	11-14	42	-	-	-	19	59
Percentages		36.4		78.6						

Coach: Fred R. Taylor

Officials: Eckman, Marick
Attendance: 18,469

National Invitation Tournament (NIT)

First round: Dayton d. Wichita State 79-71, Temple d. Providence 80-78, Holy Cross d. Colorado State 72-71, Duquesne d. Navy, 70-58
Quarterfinals: Dayton d. Houston 94-77, Loyola-Chicago d. Temple 75-64, Duquesne d. Bradley 88-85, St. John's d. Holy Cross 80-74
Semifinals: Dayton d. Loyola-Chicago 98-82, St. John's d. Duquesne 75-65
Third place: Loyola-Chicago d. Duquesne 95-84
Championship: Dayton d. St. John's 73-67
MVP: Bill Chmielewski, Dayton

1962-63: Times Change

As the civil rights movement gained momentum and racial tensions increased across America, Loyola-Chicago brought four African-American starters to its first NCAA Tournament and the nation took notice. The Ramblers handily defeated Mississippi State (which had turned down NCAA bids in previous years to abide by an unwritten state policy forbidding interracial competition) on their way to the Final, which is also where Cincinnati, with three African-American starters of its own, found itself for the third straight year.

Loyola trailed by 15 late in the second half at Louisville's Freedom Hall, but coach George Ireland's stifling full-court press sparked a comeback. A Jerry Harkness basket with :06 left forced overtime, and then a put-back at the buzzer by Vic Rouse gave the Ramblers a 60-58 win. Ireland's starting five played all 45 minutes; Cincinnati had five players play all but four minutes of the game.

Duke's Art Heyman was named the Tournament's Most Outstanding Player and was the national POY after averaging 24.9 ppg and 10.8 rpg.

Major Conference Standings

AAWU	Conference W	L	Pct	Overall W	L	Pct
UCLA⊕	7	5	.583	20	9	.690
Stanford	7	5	.583	16	9	.640
Southern California	6	6	.500	20	9	.690
Washington	6	6	.500	13	13	.500
California	4	8	.333	13	11	.542

ACC	Conference W	L	Pct	Overall W	L	Pct
Duke⊕	14	0	1.000	27	3	.900
Wake Forest	11	3	.786	16	10	.615
North Carolina	10	4	.714	15	6	.714
Clemson	5	9	.357	12	13	.480
NC State	5	9	.357	10	11	.476
Maryland	4	10	.286	8	13	.381
South Carolina	4	10	.286	9	15	.375
Virginia	3	11	.214	5	20	.200

Tournament: **Duke d. Wake Forest 68-57**
Tournament MVP: **Art Heyman**, Duke

Big Eight	Conference W	L	Pct	Overall W	L	Pct
Colorado⊕	11	3	.786	19	7	.731
Kansas State	11	3	.786	16	9	.640
Iowa State	8	6	.571	14	11	.560
Oklahoma	8	6	.571	12	13	.480
Oklahoma State	7	7	.500	16	9	.640
Kansas	5	9	.357	12	13	.480
Missouri	5	9	.357	10	15	.400
Nebraska	1	13	.071	6	19	.240

Big Ten	Conference W	L	Pct	Overall W	L	Pct
Ohio State	11	3	.786	20	4	.833
Illinois⊕	11	3	.786	20	6	.769
Indiana	9	5	.643	13	11	.542
Michigan	8	6	.571	16	8	.667
Minnesota	8	6	.571	12	12	.500
Wisconsin	7	7	.500	14	10	.583
Northwestern	6	8	.429	9	15	.375
Iowa	5	9	.357	9	15	.375
Michigan State	3	11	.214	4	16	.200
Purdue	2	12	.143	7	17	.292

Ivy	Conference W	L	Pct	Overall W	L	Pct
Princeton⊕	11	3	.786	19	6	.760
Yale	11	3	.786	13	10	.565
Penn	10	4	.714	19	6	.760
Cornell	6	7	.462	12	12	.500
Brown	6	8	.429	11	13	.458
Harvard	5	9	.357	6	15	.286
Columbia	4	9	.308	10	12	.455
Dartmouth	2	12	.143	7	18	.280

Metro NY	Conference W	L	Pct	Overall W	L	Pct
Fordham□	4	1	.800	18	8	.692
NYU○	3	1	.750	18	5	.783
St. Francis (NY)□	4	2	.667	16	7	.696
St. John's	2	2	.500	9	15	.375
CCNY	1	2	.333	8	10	.444
Manhattan	0	4	.000	9	14	.391
Brooklyn	0	2	.000	6	12	.333

Mid-American	Conference W	L	Pct	Overall W	L	Pct
Bowling Green⊕	9	3	.750	19	8	.704
Ohio	8	4	.667	13	11	.542
Toledo	8	4	.667	13	11	.542
Miami (OH)	8	4	.667	12	12	.500
Western Michigan	7	5	.583	12	12	.500
Marshall	1	11	.083	7	16	.304
Kent State	1	11	.083	3	18	.143

Middle Atlantic	Conference W	L	Pct	Overall W	L	Pct
Saint Joseph's⊕	8	0	1.000	23	5	.821
La Salle□	7	1	.875	16	8	.667
Delaware	7	3	.700	14	8	.636
Temple	6	3	.667	15	7	.682
Lafayette	6	4	.600	13	11	.542
Gettysburg	6	5	.545	16	9	.640
Lehigh	3	10	.231	6	19	.240
Bucknell	2	8	.200	7	16	.304
Muhlenberg	0	11	.000	4	17	.235

Missouri Valley	Conference W	L	Pct	Overall W	L	Pct
Cincinnati⊕	11	1	.917	26	2	.929
Wichita State□	7	5	.583	19	8	.704
Bradley	6	6	.500	17	9	.654
Saint Louis□	6	6	.500	16	12	.571
Tulsa	5	7	.417	17	8	.680
North Texas	4	8	.333	10	14	.417
Drake	3	9	.250	11	14	.440

Ohio Valley	Conference W	L	Pct	Overall W	L	Pct
Tennessee Tech⊕	8	4	.667	16	8	.667
Morehead State	8	4	.667	13	7	.650
East Tennessee St.	7	5	.583	14	8	.636
Murray State	6	6	.500	13	9	.591
Eastern Kentucky	6	6	.500	9	12	.429
Middle Tennessee St.	4	8	.333	9	15	.375
Western Kentucky	3	9	.250	5	16	.238

SEC	Conference W	L	Pct	Overall W	L	Pct
Mississippi State⊕	12	2	.857	22	6	.786
Auburn	10	4	.714	18	4	.818
Georgia Tech	10	4	.714	21	5	.808
Vanderbilt	9	5	.643	16	7	.696
Kentucky	8	6	.571	16	9	.640
Alabama	7	7	.500	14	11	.560
Tennessee	6	8	.429	13	11	.542
LSU	5	9	.357	12	12	.500
Florida	5	9	.357	12	14	.462
Georgia	4	10	.286	9	17	.346
Mississippi	4	10	.286	7	17	.292
Tulane	4	10	.286	6	16	.273

Southern	Conference W	L	Pct	Overall W	L	Pct
West Virginia⊕	11	2	.846	23	8	.742
Davidson	8	3	.727	20	7	.741
William and Mary	10	5	.667	15	9	.625
Furman	9	6	.600	14	14	.500
Virginia Tech	6	6	.500	12	12	.500
George Washington	6	6	.500	8	15	.348
VMI	6	10	.375	6	15	.286
Richmond	3	13	.188	7	18	.280
The Citadel	2	10	.167	3	20	.130

Tournament: **West Virginia d. Davidson 79-74**
Tournament MOP: **Rod Thorn**, West Virginia

Southwest	Conference W	L	Pct	Overall W	L	Pct
Texas⊕	13	1	.929	20	7	.741
Texas A&M	9	5	.643	16	8	.667
Rice	9	5	.643	12	11	.522
Arkansas	8	6	.571	13	11	.542
SMU	6	8	.429	12	12	.500
Texas Tech	6	8	.429	6	17	.261
Baylor	4	10	.286	7	17	.292
TCU	1	13	.071	4	20	.167

WCAC	Conference W	L	Pct	Overall W	L	Pct
San Francisco⊕	10	2	.833	18	9	.667
Santa Clara	9	3	.750	16	9	.640
Saint Mary's (CA)	8	4	.667	14	11	.560
San Jose State	6	6	.500	14	10	.583
Pepperdine	6	6	.500	14	11	.560
Loyola Marymount	3	9	.250	9	17	.346
Pacific	0	12	.000	4	22	.154

WAC	Conference W	L	Pct	Overall W	L	Pct
Arizona State⊕	9	1	.900	26	3	.897
BYU	6	4	.600	12	14	.462
Utah	5	5	.500	12	14	.462
New Mexico	4	6	.400	16	9	.640
Arizona	3	7	.300	13	13	.500
Wyoming	3	7	.300	11	15	.423

Yankee	Conference W	L	Pct	Overall W	L	Pct
Connecticut⊕	9	1	.900	18	7	.720
Rhode Island	8	2	.800	15	11	.577
Massachusetts	6	4	.600	12	12	.500
Maine	3	7	.300	8	15	.348
Vermont	2	8	.200	10	13	.435
New Hampshire	2	8	.200	7	17	.292

⊕ Automatic NCAA Tournament bid ○ At-large NCAA Tournament bid □ NIT appearance ❂ Team record doesn't reflect games forfeited or vacated. For adjusted record, see p. 521.

INDEPENDENTS

	Overall W	L	Pct
Loyola-Chicago○	29	2	.935
Providence□	24	4	.857
Miami (FL)□	23	5	.821
Colorado State○	18	5	.783
Seattle○	21	6	.778
Niagara	14	4	.778
Idaho	20	6	.769
Pittsburgh○	19	6	.760
Penn State	15	5	.750
Utah State○	20	7	.741
Canisius□	19	7	.731
Memphis□	19	7	.731
Texas Western○	19	7	.731
Oregon State○	22	9	.710
Seton Hall	16	7	.696
Marquette□	20	9	.690
Oklahoma City○	19	10	.655
Villanova□	19	10	.655
Notre Dame○	17	9	.654
DePaul□	15	8	.652
Holy Cross	16	9	.640
Iona	12	7	.632
Regis (CO)	15	9	.625
Butler	16	10	.615
Dayton	16	10	.615
Florida State	15	10	.600
Duquesne	13	9	.591
Houston	15	11	.577

INDEPENDENTS (CONT.)

	Overall W	L	Pct
Louisville	14	11	.560
Detroit	14	12	.538
Gonzaga	14	12	.538
Boston U.	10	9	.526
Loyola (LA)	12	11	.522
St. Bonaventure	13	12	.520
Creighton	14	13	.519
Georgetown	13	13	.500
Montana State	13	13	.500
Navy	9	9	.500
Centenary	12	14	.462
Air Force	10	12	.455
Saint Francis (PA)	10	12	.455
Xavier	12	16	.429
Oregon	11	15	.423
Army	8	11	.421
Boston College	10	16	.385
Hardin-Simmons	10	16	.385
Syracuse	8	13	.381
Idaho State	9	15	.375
Portland	8	18	.308
Rutgers	7	16	.304
Colgate	5	13	.278
Montana	6	18	.250
West Texas	6	18	.250
Denver	6	19	.240
Washington State	5	20	.200
New Mexico State	4	17	.190

INDIVIDUAL LEADERS—SEASON

Scoring

	CL	POS	G	FG	FT	PTS	PPG
1 **Nick Werkman**, Seton Hall	JR	F	22	221	208	650	**29.5**
2 **Barry Kramer**, NYU	JR	F	23	220	235	675	**29.3**
3 **Bill Green**, Colorado State	SR	C	23	215	219	649	**28.2**
4 **Gary Bradds**, Ohio State	JR	C	24	237	198	672	**28.0**
5 **Bill Bradley**, Princeton	SO	F	25	212	258	682	**27.3**
6 **Flynn Robinson**, Wyoming	SO	G	26	255	172	682	**26.2**
7 **Eddie Miles**, Seattle	SR	G	27	282	133	697	**25.8**
8 **Jimmy Rayl**, Indiana	SR	G	24	215	178	608	**25.3**
9 **Art Heyman**, Duke	SR	F/G	30	265	217	747	**24.9**
10 **Art Crump**, Idaho State	JR	G	24	208	179	595	**24.8**

Field Goal Pct

	CL	POS	G	FG	FGA	PCT
1 **Lyle Harger**, Houston	SR	C	26	193	294	**65.6**
2 **James Raftery**, St. Francis (NY)	SR	F	23	115	186	**61.8**
3 **Jay Buckley**, Duke	JR	C	30	130	217	**59.9**
4 **Bill Green**, Colorado State	SR	C	23	215	371	**58.0**
5 **Ollie Johnson**, San Francisco	SO	C	27	178	314	**56.7**

Minimum: 100 made

Free Throw Pct

	CL	POS	G	FT	FTA	PCT
1 **Tommy Boyer**, Arkansas	SR	G	24	147	161	**91.3**
2 **Bill Bradley**, Princeton	SO	F	25	258	289	**89.3**
3 **Ron Bonham**, Cincinnati	JR	F	28	173	194	**89.2**
4 **Gary Batchelor**, BYU	SR	G	26	104	119	**87.4**
5 **Jimmy Rayl**, Indiana	SR	G	24	178	204	**87.3**

Minimum: 90 made

Rebounds Per Game

	CL	POS	G	REB	RPG
1 **Paul Silas**, Creighton	JR	F/C	27	557	**20.6**
2 **Gus Johnson**, Idaho	SO	F	23	466	**20.3**
3 **Norm Pokley**, Morehead State	SR	F	19	323	**17.0**
4 **Don Petersen**, Rutgers	SR	F	23	389	**16.9**
5 **Walter Sahm**, Notre Dame	SO	C	26	438	**16.8**

INDIVIDUAL LEADERS—GAME

Points

	CL	POS	OPP	DATE	PTS
1 **Jimmy Rayl**, Indiana	SR	G	Michigan State	F23	**56**
2 **Dave Downey**, Illinois	SR	F	Indiana	F16	**53**
3 **Lyle Harger**, Houston	SR	C	Trinity (TX)	F16	**50**
4 **Don Kessinger**, Mississippi	JR	G	Tulane	F2	**49**
5 **Mike McCoy**, Miami (FL)	SR	C	Rollins	F12	**48**
Bill Green, Colorado State	SR	C	Denver	F9	**48**

Free Throws Made

	CL	POS	OPP	DATE	FT	FTA	PCT
1 **Bill Bradley**, Princeton	SO	F	Cornell	J19	**21**	21	100.0
2 **Bill Green**, Colorado State	SR	C	Denver	F9	**18**	20	90.0
Dave Stallworth, Wichita State	SO	F	Cincinnati	F16	**18**	23	78.3
Barry Kramer, NYU	JR	F	Georgetown	D7	**18**	25	72.0
Randy Cross, Boston U.	SO	G/F	Rutgers	D7	**18**	25	72.0

TEAM LEADERS—SEASON

Scoring Offense

	G	W-L	PTS	PPG
1 **Loyola-Chicago**	31	29-2	2,847	**91.8**
2 **Miami (FL)**	28	23-5	2,509	**89.6**
3 **Indiana**	24	13-11	2,032	**84.7**
4 **Illinois**	26	20-6	2,201	**84.7**
5 **Duke**	30	27-3	2,496	**83.2**

Field Goal Pct

	G	W-L	FG	FGA	PCT
1 **Duke**	30	27-3	984	1,926	**51.1**
2 **Auburn**	22	18-4	601	1,188	**50.6**
3 **St. Francis (NY)**	23	16-7	553	1,109	**49.9**
4 **Memphis**	26	19-7	773	1,553	**49.8**
5 **Colorado State**	23	18-5	593	1,193	**49.7**

Free Throw Pct

	G	W-L	FT	FTA	PCT
1 **Tulane**	22	6-16	390	492	**79.3**
2 **Furman**	28	14-14	539	708	**76.1**
3 **Princeton**	25	19-6	531	699	**76.0**
4 **Cornell**	24	12-12	378	498	**75.9**
5 **Florida**	26	12-14	533	703	**75.8**

Scoring Defense

	G	W-L	OPP PTS	OPP PPG
1 **Cincinnati**	28	26-2	1,480	**52.9**
2 **Oklahoma State**	25	16-9	1,328	**53.1**
3 **Texas Western**	26	19-7	1,419	**54.6**
4 **San Jose State**	24	14-10	1,383	**57.6**
5 **New Mexico**	25	16-9	1,447	**57.9**

CONSENSUS ALL-AMERICAS

First Team

PLAYER	CL	POS	HT	SCHOOL	RPG	PPG
Ron Bonham	JR	F	6-5	Cincinnati	6.4	21.0
Jerry Harkness	SR	F	6-3	Loyola-Chicago	7.6	21.4
Art Heyman	SR	F/G	6-5	Duke	10.8	24.9
Barry Kramer	JR	F	6-4	NYU	12.0	29.3
Tom Thacker	SR	G/F	6-2	Cincinnati	10.0	15.8

Second Team

PLAYER	CL	POS	HT	SCHOOL	RPG	PPG
Gary Bradds	JR	C	6-8	Ohio State	13.0	28.0
Bill Green	SR	C	6-6	Colorado State	9.2	28.2
Cotton Nash	JR	F	6-5	Kentucky	12.0	20.6
Rod Thorn	SR	F	6-4	West Virginia	9.0	22.5
Nate Thurmond	SR	C	6-11	Bowling Green	16.7	19.9

Selectors: AP, Look Magazine, NABC, Newspaper Enterprises Assn., UPI, USBWA

AWARD WINNERS

Player of the Year

PLAYER	CL	POS	HT	SCHOOL	AWARDS
Art Heyman	SR	F/G	6-5	Duke	AP, UPI, USBWA

Coach of the Year

COACH	SCHOOL	REC	AWARDS
Ed Jucker	Cincinnati	26-2	UPI, USBWA

Poll Progression

Preseason Poll

AP	UPI	School
1	1	Cincinnati
2	2	Duke
3	3	Kentucky
4	5	Loyola-Chicago
5	4	West Virginia
6	7	Mississippi State
7	6	Oregon State
8	13	Illinois
9	8	St. Bonaventure
10	9	Wisconsin
—	10	Bowling Green
—	10	Stanford
—	12	Dayton
—	14	Kansas State
—	15	Arizona State
—	16	NYU
—	17	UCLA
—	18	Colorado State
—	19	Creighton
—	20	Indiana

Week of Dec 4

AP	UPI	School	AP↓↑
1	1	Cincinnati (1-0)	
2	2	Duke (1-0)	
3	4	West Virginia (1-0)	↑2
4	3	Loyola-Chicago (1-0)	
5	6	Mississippi State (0-0)	↑1
6	8	Wisconsin (1-0)	↑4
7	5	Oregon State (0-0)	
8	18	Indiana (1-0)	⤴
9	14	Kentucky (0-1)	↓6
10	—	Wichita State (1-0)	⤴
—	7	Illinois (1-0)	⤵
—	9	Kansas State (1-0)	
—	10	Bowling Green (1-0)	
—	11	Stanford (2-0)	
—	12	Creighton (1-0)	
—	12	UCLA (2-0)	
—	15	NYU (1-0) Ⓐ	
—	16	Arizona State (2-0)	
—	17	Ohio State (1-0)	
—	19	Dayton (1-0)	
—	20	USC (2-0)	

Week of Dec 11

AP	UPI	School	AP↓↑
1	1	Cincinnati (4-0)	
2	2	Duke (3-0)	
3	4	Ohio State (4-0)	⤴
4	3	Loyola-Chicago (2-0)	
5	5	Mississippi State (3-0)	
6	10	West Virginia (2-1)	↓3
7	12	Wisconsin (2-1)	↓1
8	11	Colorado (3-0)	⤴
9	6	Oregon State (1-1)	↓2
10	8	Illinois (2-0)	⤴
—	7	Stanford (2-0)	
—	9	Bowling Green (1-0)	
—	13	Arizona State (3-0)	
—	14	Drake (3-0)	
—	15	Kentucky (1-1)	⤵
—	16	Minnesota (2-0)	
—	17	NYU (2-0)	
—	18	St. Bonaventure (2-1)	
—	19	Seattle	
—	20	Iowa State (2-1)	
—	20	Texas (3-1)	

Week of Dec 18

AP	UPI	School	AP↓↑
1	1	Cincinnati (6-0)	
2	2	Duke (6-0)	
3	4	Ohio State (5-0)	
4	3	Loyola-Chicago (4-0)	
5	5	Mississippi State (5-0)	
6	11	Colorado (4-0)	↑2
7	10	West Virginia (3-1)	↓1
8	7	Illinois (3-0)	↑2
9	12	Kentucky (3-1)	⤴
10	14	Seattle (4-0)	⤴
—	6	Bowling Green (4-0)	
—	8	Stanford (3-0)	
—	9	Arizona State (5-0)	
—	13	Oregon State (2-2)	⤵
—	15	Minnesota (3-1)	
—	16	Notre Dame (6-0)	
—	16	UCLA (4-2)	
—	18	Wisconsin (3-2)	⤵
—	19	Marquette (4-0)	
—	20	Princeton (5-0)	

Week of Dec 25

AP	UPI	School	AP↓↑
1	1	Cincinnati (8-0)	
2	3	Ohio State (6-0)	↑1
3	2	Loyola-Chicago (7-0)	↑1
4	5	Illinois (5-0)	↑4
5	8	Kentucky (5-2)	↑4
6	6	Arizona State (7-1)	⤴
7	15	USC (9-0)	⤴
8	10	Duke (6-2)	↓6
9	4	Stanford (7-0)	⤴
10	9	Mississippi State (6-1)	↓5
—	7	Bowling Green (4-0)	
—	11	UCLA (7-2)	
—	12	West Virginia (4-2)	⤵
—	13	Seattle (5-1)	⤵
—	14	Virginia Tech (4-1)	
—	16	Wichita State (7-2)	
—	17	Colorado (5-2)	⤵
—	18	Georgia Tech (5-0)	
—	19	Princeton (6-0)	
—	20	North Carolina (4-1)	

Week of Jan 1

AP	UPI	School	AP↓↑
1	1	Cincinnati (9-0)	
2	2	Loyola-Chicago (11-0)	↑1
3	3	Illinois (8-1)	↑1
4	4	Arizona State (10-1)	↑2
5	6	Ohio State (8-1)	↓3
6	7	Kentucky (7-3)	↓1
7	9	Duke (8-2)	↑1
8	8	Wichita State (9-2)	⤴
9	5	UCLA (10-2)	⤴
10	12	Auburn (8-0)	⤴
—	10	Oregon State (6-3)	
—	11	Mississippi State (7-2)	⤵
—	13	Georgia Tech (7-0)	
—	14	North Carolina (4-1)	
—	15	Miami (FL) (8-0)	
—	16	Colorado State (7-3)	
—	17	Saint Joseph's (8-2)	
—	17	Stanford (9-2)	⤵
—	19	Kansas (7-4)	
—	20	West Virginia (6-3)	

Week of Jan 8

AP	UPI	School	AP↓↑
1	1	Cincinnati (11-0)	
2	2	Loyola-Chicago (13-0)	
3	4	Arizona State (12-1)	↑1
4	5	Ohio State (9-1)	↑1
5	3	Illinois (9-1)	↓2
6	6	Duke (10-2)	↑1
7	7	Georgia Tech (9-0)	⤴
8	9	Wichita State (9-3)	
9	13	West Virginia (8-3)	⤴
10	12	North Carolina (6-1)	⤴
—	8	Mississippi State (9-2)	
—	10	UCLA (10-4)	⤵
—	11	Oregon State (8-3)	
—	13	Colorado State (9-3)	
—	15	Kentucky (7-4)	⤵
—	16	Auburn (8-1)	⤵
—	17	Colorado (8-3)	
—	18	Saint Joseph's (9-2)	
—	19	California (10-2)	
—	19	Stanford (9-2)	
—	19	Utah State (11-3)	
—	19	Wisconsin (7-3)	

Week of Jan 15

AP	UPI	School	AP↓↑
1	1	Cincinnati (13-0)	
2	2	Loyola-Chicago (15-0)	
3	3	Illinois (11-1)	↑2
4	4	Arizona State (14-1)	↓1
5	5	Duke (12-2)	↑1
6	6	Georgia Tech (11-1)	↑1
7	7	Wichita State (11-3)	↑1
8	8	Ohio State (10-2)	↓4
9	9	Mississippi State (10-3)	⤴
10	10	Oregon State (9-4)	⤴
—	11	Colorado State (9-3)	
—	12	Colorado (10-3)	
—	13	UCLA (11-4)	
—	14	West Virginia (10-3)	⤵
—	14	Notre Dame (12-3)	
—	16	Stanford (10-3)	
—	17	Kentucky (10-4)	
—	18	Niagara (8-0)	
—	18	Texas (8-5)	
—	20	Utah State (12-3)	

Week of Jan 22

AP	UPI	School	AP↓↑
1	1	Cincinnati (14-0)	
2	2	Loyola-Chicago (16-0)	
3	3	Illinois (12-1)	
4	4	Duke (12-2)	↑1
5	5	Arizona State (15-2)	↓1
6	10	West Virginia (12-3)	⤴
7	6	Georgia Tech (12-1)	↓1
8	8	Wichita State (12-4)	↓1
9	7	Mississippi State (12-3)	
10	9	Stanford (12-3)	⤴
—	11	Colorado (11-3)	
—	12	Oregon State (10-4)	⤵
—	13	Ohio State (10-3)	⤵
—	14	UCLA (11-4)	
—	15	Utah State (13-3)	
—	16	Auburn (11-1)	
—	16	Colorado State (9-3)	
—	16	DePaul (9-2)	
—	19	Miami (FL) (12-2)	
—	19	Niagara (9-0)	

Week of Jan 29

AP	UPI	School	AP↓↑
1	1	Cincinnati (15-0)	
2	2	Loyola-Chicago (18-0)	
3	3	Duke (13-2)	↑1
4	4	Illinois (12-2)	↓1
5	5	Arizona State (15-2)	
6	6	Georgia Tech (14-1)	↑1
7	7	Stanford (12-3)	↑3
8	8	Colorado (11-3)	⤴
9	11	Mississippi State (12-4)	
10	10	Wichita State (13-5)	↓2
—	9	Oregon State (11-4)	
—	12	UCLA (13-4)	
—	13	Utah State (15-3)	
—	14	Ohio State (11-4)	
—	15	Niagara (10-0)	
—	16	Colorado State (11-4)	
—	17	West Virginia (12-4)	⤵
—	18	Miami (FL) (13-2)	
—	19	Texas (8-5)	
—	19	Saint Louis (11-5)	
—	19	Indiana (7-6)	
—	19	Oregon (6-8)	

Week of Feb 5

AP	UPI	School	AP↓↑
1	1	Cincinnati (17-0)	
2	2	Loyola-Chicago (20-0)	
3	3	Duke (15-2)	
4	4	Illinois (12-2)	
5	5	Arizona State (16-2)	
6	6	Georgia Tech (16-1)	
7	7	Colorado (12-3)	↑1
8	9	Mississippi State (14-4)	↑1
9	11	Wichita State (14-5)	↑1
10	8	Stanford (12-4)	↓3
—	10	Oregon State (12-4)	
—	12	Utah (8-11)	
—	13	UCLA (13-4)	
—	14	Ohio State (12-4)	
—	15	Colorado State (12-4)	
—	16	Notre Dame (13-4)	
—	16	Texas (10-5)	
—	18	DePaul (11-3)	
—	19	Auburn (13-2)	
—	19	West Virginia (14-5)	

Week of Feb 12

AP	UPI	School	AP↓↑
1	1	Cincinnati (19-0)	
2	2	Loyola-Chicago (20-0)	
3	3	Duke (17-2)	
4	4	Illinois (14-2)	
5	5	Arizona State (18-2)	
6	7	Mississippi State (16-4)	↑2
7	6	Colorado (13-4)	
8	8	Stanford (13-5)	↑2
9	12	Ohio State (14-3)	⤴
10	9	Georgia Tech (17-3)	↓4
—	10	Oregon State (13-5)	
—	11	Utah State (17-3)	
—	13	Texas (12-5)	
—	14	UCLA (13-5)	
—	15	Oklahoma State (14-4)	
—	16	Colorado State (14-4)	
—	17	Wichita State (14-6)	⤵
—	18	Bradley (12-7)	
—	18	NYU (12-2)	
—	20	Saint Joseph's (16-3)	

Week of Feb 19

AP	UPI	SCHOOL	AP↓↑
1	1	**Cincinnati** (19-1) Ⓑ	
2	2	**Duke** (19-2)	↑1
3	3	**Loyola-Chicago** (21-1) Ⓒ	↓1
4	4	**Arizona State** (20-2)	↑1
5	7	**Ohio State** (15-3)	↑4
6	5	**Illinois** (14-4) Ⓓ	↓2
7	6	**Wichita State** (16-6) Ⓑ	⤴
8	11	**Mississippi State** (17-5)	↓2
9	15	**Auburn** (16-2)	⤴
10	12	**NYU** (13-2)	⤴
—	7	**Stanford** (14-6)	⤵
—	9	**Colorado** (14-5)	⤵
—	10	**Georgia Tech** (18-4)	⤵
—	13	**Oregon State** (14-6)	
—	14	**Texas** (14-5)	
—	16	**Oklahoma State** (15-4)	
—	17	**Utah State** (19-5)	
—	18	**Colorado State** (16-4)	
—	19	**UCLA** (13-5)	
—	20	**Providence** (15-4)	
—	20	**Texas Western** (15-5)	

Week of Feb 26

AP	UPI	SCHOOL	AP↓↑
1	1	**Cincinnati** (21-1)	
2	2	**Duke** (21-2)	
3	3	**Loyola-Chicago** (23-1)	
4	4	**Arizona State** (22-2)	
5	6	**Ohio State** (17-3)	
6	5	**Illinois** (16-4)	
7	7	**Mississippi State** (19-5)	↑1
8	9	**Wichita State** (16-7)	↓1
9	10	**NYU** (15-2)	↑1
10	12	**Georgia Tech** (10-4)	⤴
—	8	**Stanford** (15-6)	
—	11	**Texas** (16-5)	
—	13	**Colorado** (15-6)	
—	14	**Colorado State** (17-4)	
—	15	**Texas Western** (17-5)	
—	16	**UCLA** (14-6)	
—	17	**Auburn** (17-3)	⤵
—	17	**Providence** (17-4) Ⓔ	
—	19	**Oregon State** (15-7)	
—	20	**Saint Joseph's** (20-3)	

Week of Mar 5

AP	UPI	SCHOOL	AP↓↑
1	1	**Cincinnati** (23-1)	
2	2	**Duke** (24-2)	
3	4	**Ohio State** (19-3)	↑2
4	3	**Arizona State** (23-2)	
5	5	**Loyola-Chicago** (24-2)	↓2
6	6	**Wichita State** (19-7)	↑2
7	7	**Mississippi St.** (21-5) Ⓕ	
8	8	**Illinois** (17-5)	↓2
9	9	**Stanford** (18-6)	⤴
10	13	**Providence** (19-4)	⤴
—	10	**NYU** (15-3)	⤵
—	11	**Texas** (18-5)	
—	12	**Colorado State** (18-4)	
—	13	**Kansas State** (15-8)	
—	15	**Oregon State** (17-7)	
—	16	**Texas Western** (19-6)	
—	17	**Bowling Green** (17-7)	
—	18	**Saint Joseph's** (21-4)	
—	19	**Seattle** (20-5)	
—	20	**West Virginia** (21-7)	

Final Poll

AP	UPI	SCHOOL	AP↓↑
1	1	**Cincinnati** (23-1)	
2	2	**Duke** (24-2)	
3	4	**Loyola-Chicago** (24-2)	↑2
4	3	**Arizona State** (24-2) Ⓖ	
5	6	**Wichita State** (19-7)	↑1
6	7	**Mississippi State** (21-5)	↑1
7	8	**Ohio State** (20-4)	↓4
8	5	**Illinois** (19-5)	
9	11	**NYU** (17-3)	⤴
10	9	**Colorado** (17-6)	⤴
—	10	**Stanford** (18-6)	⤵
—	12	**Texas** (19-6)	
—	13	**Providence** (21-4)	⤵
—	14	**Oregon State** (19-7)	
—	15	**UCLA** (19-7)	
—	16	**Saint Joseph's** (21-4)	
—	16	**West Virginia** (21-7)	
—	18	**Bowling Green** (18-7)	
—	19	**Kansas State** (17-8)	
—	19	**Seattle** (21-6)	

Ⓐ Barry Kramer scores 42 to lead NYU past Georgetown, 85-65, at Madison Square Garden. The 6'4" junior forward finishes the season second in the nation with 29.3 ppg.

Ⓑ Wichita State upsets Cincinnati for the second straight season, this time snapping a 37-game Bearcats winning streak with a 65-64 victory. The Shockers' Dave "the Rave" Stallworth scores 46.

Ⓒ Bowling Green beats Loyola-Chicago, 92-75, holding the nation's top-scoring team to its second-lowest point total of the season. Center Nate Thurmond scores 24 for the Falcons.

Ⓓ Indiana outguns Illinois, 103-100, despite 53 points—a national best for the season—by the Illini's Dave Downey. The Hoosiers' Jimmy Rayl will hang 56 on Michigan State just a week later.

Ⓔ Providence whips Saint Joseph's, 83-64. The Friars will go on to win the NIT behind 6'10" center and future Georgetown coach John Thompson Jr., and guard Ray Flynn, who will go on to become mayor of Boston.

Ⓕ Mississippi State announces it will accept a bid to the NCAA Tournament, flouting the unwritten rule that Mississippi college teams do not compete against teams with black players. The Bulldogs then clinch their third straight SEC title with a 75-72 win at Ole Miss.

Ⓖ Arizona State wins its fourth straight road game, 58-53 at Arizona, to clinch the inaugural WAC championship. The '63 Sun Devils go on to win 26 games—the most in school history.

1963 NCAA Tournament

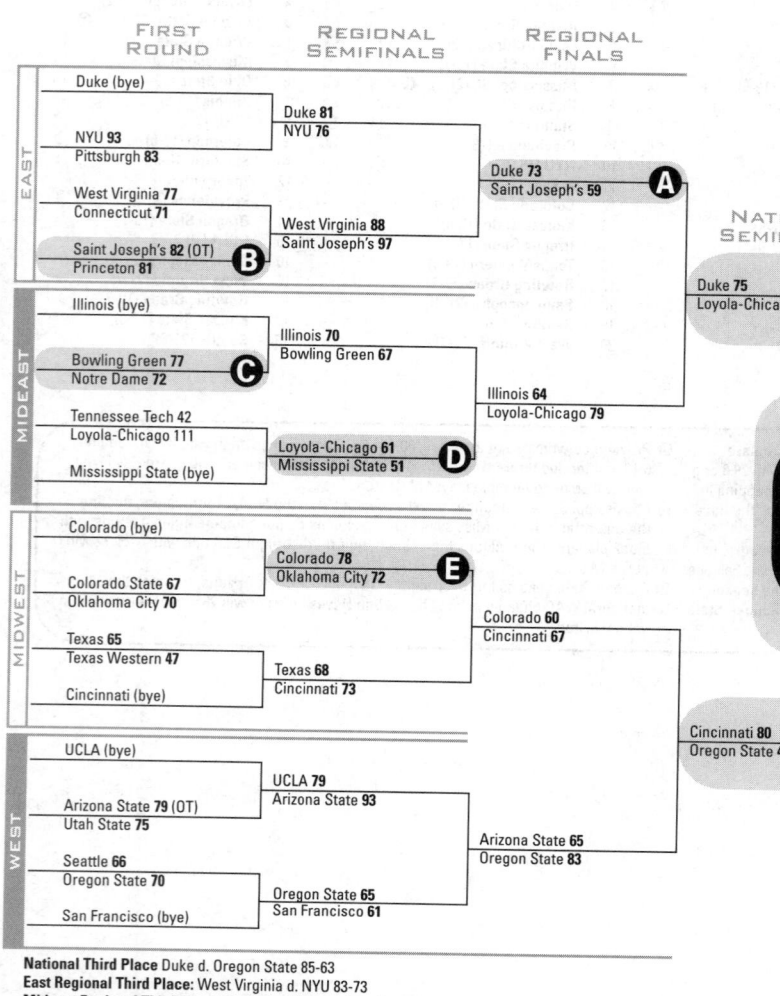

First Round | Regional Semifinals | Regional Finals | National Semifinals | National Final

East

First Round
- Duke (bye)
- NYU **93**, Pittsburgh **83**
- West Virginia **77**, Connecticut **71**
- Saint Joseph's **82** (OT), Princeton **81** (B)

Regional Semifinals
- Duke **81**, NYU **76**
- West Virginia **88**, Saint Joseph's **97**

Regional Finals
- Duke **73**, Saint Joseph's **59** (A)

Mideast

First Round
- Illinois (bye)
- Bowling Green **77**, Notre Dame **72** (C)
- Tennessee Tech 42, Loyola-Chicago 111
- Mississippi State (bye)

Regional Semifinals
- Illinois **70**, Bowling Green **67**
- Loyola-Chicago **61**, Mississippi State **51** (D)

Regional Finals
- Illinois **64**, Loyola-Chicago **79**

Midwest

First Round
- Colorado (bye)
- Colorado State **67**, Oklahoma City **70**
- Texas **65**, Texas Western **47**
- Cincinnati (bye)

Regional Semifinals
- Colorado **78**, Oklahoma City **72** (E)
- Texas **68**, Cincinnati **73**

Regional Finals
- Colorado **60**, Cincinnati **67**

West

First Round
- UCLA (bye)
- Arizona State **79** (OT), Utah State **75**
- Seattle **66**, Oregon State **70**
- San Francisco (bye)

Regional Semifinals
- UCLA **79**, Arizona State **93**
- Oregon State **65**, San Francisco **61**

Regional Finals
- Arizona State **65**, Oregon State **83**

National Semifinals

- Duke **75**, Loyola-Chicago **94**
- Cincinnati **80**, Oregon State **46**

National Final

Loyola-Chicago 60 (OT)
Cincinnati 58

Louisville, KY

National Third Place Duke d. Oregon State 85-63
East Regional Third Place: West Virginia d. NYU 83-73
Mideast Regional Third Place Mississippi State d. Bowling Green 65-60
Midwest Regional Third Place Texas d. Oklahoma City 90-83
West Regional Third Place San Francisco d. UCLA 76-75 (F)

A With the win, Duke's Vic Bubas becomes one of only six coaches who also appeared in the Final Four as a player. Bubas was a guard on NC State's third-place team in 1950.

B Sophomore Bill Bradley, who, as a Missouri schoolboy, turned down scholarship offers from virtually every major power to attend an Ivy League school, hits 16 of 16 free throws.

C Bowling Green's Howard Komives scores 34 points and Nate Thurmond pulls down 20 rebounds to defeat the Fighting Irish. The following year, Komives will lead the NCAA in scoring (36.7 ppg), becoming the first player from the MAC to do so.

Before their regional final, Loyola and Illinois split the cost of a scouting film that shows how to beat Duke: Let Art Heyman and Jeff Mullins score; stop the others. Sure enough, Heyman gets 29 and Mullins 21; Loyola prevails.

Loyola denies Cincinnati a third straight title, rallying from 15 points down to win in overtime on a putback by Vic Rouse. It was, said Rouse, "like a blessing." If so, credit an assist to Loyola coach George Ireland's daughter, cheerleader Kathy, who is photographed praying on the court.

OSU's Terry Baker, the only Heisman Trophy winner to play in the Final Four, is 0 for 9 from the field. The LA Rams send an exec to Louisville to sign the QB before the AFL Raiders can, but Baker ends up an NFL bust.

D Defying both unwritten policy and a court injunction to keep its teams from leaving the state to play integrated squads, Mississippi State coach Babe McCarthy takes the Bulldogs to their first Tournament. Jerry Harkness, one of four African-American starters for Loyola, later refers to the event as "the beginning of the end of segregation."

E After Colorado's Eric Lee misses a second-half layup, a scramble results in a fight between the Buffs' Gene Sparks and two OCU players, Jim Miller and Bill Johnston. Spectators and coaches join the fray before order is restored and the three players are ejected. Colorado holds on to win.

F John Wooden's Tournament record drops to 3–9.

TOURNAMENT LEADERS

INDIVIDUAL LEADERS

SCORING

	CL	POS	G	PTS	PPG
1 **Barry Kramer**, NYU	JR	F	3	100	33.3
2 **Rod Thorn**, West Virginia	SR	F	3	94	31.3
3 **Howard Komives**, Bowling Green	JR	G	3	79	26.3
4 **Mel Counts**, Oregon State	JR	C	5	123	24.6
5 **Ken Charlton**, Colorado	SR	F	2	49	24.5
6 **Joe Caldwell**, Arizona State	JR	F	3	70	23.3
7 **Bud Koper**, Oklahoma City	JR	G	3	68	22.7
8 **Art Heyman**, Duke	SR	F/G	4	89	22.3
9 **Tom Wynne**, Saint Joseph's	SR	F	3	66	22.0
10 **Happy Hairston**, NYU	JR	F	3	64	21.3

MINIMUM: 2 GAMES

FIELD GOAL PCT

	CL	POS	G	FG	FGA	PCT
1 **Mike Humphrey**, Texas	JR	C	3	16	22	72.7
2 **John Fultz**, Texas	SO	F	3	17	25	68.0
3 **Larry Franks**, Texas	SO	F	3	17	27	63.0
4 **Jim Davis**, Colorado	JR	C	2	13	22	59.1
5 **Fred Schmidt**, Duke	SR	G	4	25	43	58.1

MINIMUM: 10 MADE

FREE THROW PCT

	CL	POS	G	FT	FTA	PCT
1 **Bill Bradley**, Princeton	SO	F	1	16	16	100.0
2 **Howard Komives**, Bowling Green	JR	G	3	29	32	90.6
3 **Les Hunter**, Loyola-Chicago	SR	F	5	26	29	89.7
4 **Frank Peters**, Oregon State	JR	G	5	17	19	89.5
5 **Ron Miller**, Loyola-Chicago	JR	G	5	13	15	86.7
Ken Charlton, Colorado	SR	F	2	13	15	86.7

MINIMUM: 10 MADE

REBOUNDS PER GAME

	CL	POS	G	REB	RPG
1 **Nate Thurmond**, Bowling Green	SR	C	3	70	23.3
2 **Art Becker**, Arizona State	JR	C	3	48	16.0
3 **Ollie Johnson**, San Francisco	SO	C	2	30	15.0
4 **Jim Davis**, Colorado	JR	C	2	29	14.5
5 **Vic Rouse**, Loyola-Chicago	JR	F	5	70	14.0

MINIMUM: 2 GAMES

TEAM LEADERS

SCORING

	G	PTS	PPG
1 **West Virginia**	3	248	82.7
2 **Loyola-Chicago**	5	405	81.0
3 **NYU**	3	242	80.7
4 **Saint Joseph's**	3	238	79.3
5 **Arizona State**	3	237	79.0
6 **Duke**	4	314	78.5
7 **UCLA**	2	154	77.0
8 **Oklahoma City**	3	225	75.0
9 **Texas**	3	223	74.3
10 **Cincinnati**	4	278	69.5

MINIMUM: 2 GAMES

FG PCT

	G	FG	FGA	PCT
1 **Texas**	3	84	152	55.3
2 **NYU**	3	85	181	47.0
3 **Colorado**	2	55	118	46.6
4 **West Virginia**	3	92	198	46.5
5 **Cincinnati**	4	100	216	46.3

FT PCT

	G	FT	FTA	PCT
1 **Bowling Green**	3	58	71	81.7
2 **West Virginia**	3	64	84	76.2
3 **Loyola-Chicago**	5	101	134	75.4
4 **Oregon State**	5	71	95	74.7
5 **San Francisco**	2	47	64	73.4

MINIMUM: 2 GAMES

REBOUNDS

	G	REB	RPG
1 **Bowling Green**	3	145	48.3
2 **Loyola-Chicago**	5	241	48.2
3 **Arizona State**	3	133	44.3
4 **Duke**	4	174	43.5
5 **Colorado**	2	84	42.0

MINIMUM: 2 GAMES

ALL-TOURNAMENT TEAM

PLAYER	CL	POS	HT	SCHOOL	RPG	PPG
Art Heyman*	SR	F/G	6-5	Duke	10.5	22.3
Ron Bonham	JR	F	6-5	Cincinnati	3.8	20.5
Les Hunter	JR	C	6-7	Loyola-Chicago	12.0	17.2
Tom Thacker	SR	G/F	6-2	Cincinnati	11.5	14.8
George Wilson	JR	F	6-8	Cincinnati	12.0	18.5

ALL-REGIONAL TEAMS

EAST

PLAYER	CL	POS	HT	SCHOOL	RPG	PPG
Art Heyman	SR	F/G	6-5	Duke	11.5	19.0
Barry Kramer	JR	F	6-4	NYU	9.0	33.3
Jeff Mullins	JR	G/F	6-4	Duke	6.0	24.5
Rod Thorn	SR	F	6-4	West Virginia	7.3	31.3
Tom Wynne	SR	F	6-5	Saint Joseph's	7.7	22.0

MIDEAST

PLAYER	CL	POS	HT	SCHOOL	RPG	PPG
Jerry Harkness*	SR	F	6-3	Loyola-Chicago	9.3	24.0
Dave Downey	SR	F	6-4	Illinois	9.0	20.0
Howard Komives	JR	G	6-1	Bowling Green	5.7	26.3
Leland Mitchell	SR	G	6-4	Mississippi State	9.5	18.5
Nate Thurmond	SR	C	6-11	Bowling Green	23.3	16.3

MIDWEST

PLAYER	CL	POS	HT	SCHOOL	RPG	PPG
Ken Charlton*	SR	F	6-6	Colorado	12.0	24.5
Ron Bonham	JR	F	6-5	Cincinnati	3.0	23.0
Bud Koper	JR	G	6-5	Oklahoma City	4.0	22.7
Tom Thacker	SR	G/F	6-2	Cincinnati	10.0	16.0
George Wilson	JR	F	6-8	Cincinnati	11.0	20.0

WEST

PLAYER	CL	POS	HT	SCHOOL	RPG	PPG
Terry Baker	SR	G	6-3	Oregon State	1.3	15.0
Art Becker	JR	C	6-8	Arizona State	16.0	17.7
Joe Caldwell	JR	F	6-5	Arizona State	9.3	23.3
Mel Counts	JR	C	7-0	Oregon State	9.3	26.0
Ollie Johnson	SO	C	6-8	San Francisco	15.0	17.5

* MOST OUTSTANDING PLAYER

1963 NCAA TOURNAMENT BOX SCORES

DUKE	MIN	FG	3FG	FT	REB	A	ST	BL	PF	TP
Jeff Mullins	-	10-16	-	5-7	7	-	-	-	0	25
Art Heyman	-	6-21	-	10-14	13	-	-	-	2	22
Fred Schmidt	-	6-10	-	0-0	0	-	-	-	3	12
Jay Buckley	-	4-8	-	2-5	16	-	-	-	5	10
Ron Herbster	-	3-3	-	0-0	1	-	-	-	2	6
Buzzy Harrison	-	2-2	-	0-0	0	-	-	-	4	4
Hack Tison	-	1-2	-	0-0	4	-	-	-	3	2
Dennis Ferguson	-	0-2	-	0-0	1	-	-	-	0	0
TOTALS	**-**	**32-64**	**-**	**17-26**	**42**	**-**	**-**	**-**	**19**	**81**
Percentages		50.0		65.4						

Coach: Vic Bubas

81-76

32 1H 27
49 2H 49

SWEET 16

NYU	MIN	FG	3FG	FT	REB	A	ST	BL	PF	TP
Barry Kramer	-	12-26	-	10-11	4	-	-	-	4	34
Happy Hairston	-	8-13	-	2-4	11	-	-	-	4	18
Don Blaha	-	3-9	-	3-6	4	-	-	-	1	9
Neil O'Neill	-	3-9	-	0-0	4	-	-	-	3	6
Bob Williams	-	2-4	-	1-2	3	-	-	-	2	5
Bob Patton	-	2-5	-	0-1	5	-	-	-	4	4
Steve Jordan	-	0-1	-	0-0	1	-	-	-	0	0
TOTALS	**-**	**30-67**	**-**	**16-24**	**32**	**-**	**-**	**-**	**18**	**76**
Percentages		44.8		66.7						

Coach: Lou Rossini

SAINT JOSEPH'S	MIN	FG	3FG	FT	REB	A	ST	BL	PF	TP
Jim Boyle	-	9-11	-	5-6	8	7	-	-	4	23
Tom Wynne	-	10-19	-	3-5	7	2	-	-	3	23
Jim Lynam	-	6-8	-	8-12	1	3	-	-	3	20
Steve Courtin	-	7-13	-	3-4	4	2	-	-	5	17
Larry Hoffman	-	4-9	-	1-7	11	0	-	-	3	9
John Tiller	-	2-3	-	1-2	1	0	-	-	1	5
Bill Hoy	-	0-0	-	0-1	1	1	-	-	1	0
Joe Kelly	-	0-0	-	0-0	1	0	-	-	0	0
TOTALS	**-**	**38-63**	**-**	**21-37**	**34**	**15**	**-**	**-**	**20**	**97**
Percentages		60.3		56.8						

Coach: Jack Ramsay

97-88

58 1H 37
39 2H 51

SWEET 16

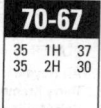

WEST VIRGINIA	MIN	FG	3FG	FT	REB	A	ST	BL	PF	TP
Rod Thorn	-	16-28	-	12-15	6	1	-	-	3	44
Jim McCormick	-	10-18	-	3-5	2	2	-	-	3	23
Gale Catlett	-	2-5	-	1-1	2	1	-	-	5	5
Mike Wolfe	-	2-5	-	1-1	7	0	-	-	5	5
Ricky Ray	-	1-2	-	2-2	2	0	-	-	3	4
Tom Lowry	-	1-3	-	1-1	5	0	-	-	3	3
Bill Maphis	-	1-6	-	0-0	3	1	-	-	2	2
Dave Shuck	-	1-1	-	0-0	3	0	-	-	1	2
Don Weir	-	0-1	-	0-0	0	0	-	-	1	0
TOTALS	**-**	**34-69**	**-**	**20-25**	**30**	**5**	**-**	**-**	**26**	**88**
Percentages		49.3		80.0						

Coach: George S. King

ILLINOIS	MIN	FG	3FG	FT	REB	A	ST	BL	PF	TP
Bill Burwell	-	8-16	-	5-9	11	-	-	-	1	21
Dave Downey	-	7-20	-	6-9	12	-	-	-	4	20
Bill Small	-	4-14	-	5-5	2	-	-	-	1	13
Skip Thoren	-	5-9	-	0-0	12	-	-	-	2	10
Tal Brody	-	1-2	-	1-1	0	-	-	-	4	3
Bob Starnes	-	1-7	-	1-2	2	-	-	-	1	3
Bill Edwards	-	0-0	-	0-0	1	-	-	-	2	0
TOTALS	**-**	**26-68**	**-**	**18-26**	**40**	**-**	**-**	**-**	**15**	**70**
Percentages		38.2		69.2						

Coach: Harry Combes

70-67

35 1H 37
35 2H 30

SWEET 16

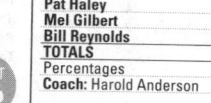

BOWLING GREEN	MIN	FG	3FG	FT	REB	A	ST	BL	PF	TP
Howard Komives	-	8-21	-	9-10	8	-	-	-	5	25
Wayne Junior	-	6-17	-	2-2	8	-	-	-	4	14
Nate Thurmond	-	6-19	-	2-3	19	-	-	-	3	14
Elijah Chatman	-	2-5	-	1-1	3	-	-	-	3	5
Pat Haley	-	1-3	-	3-3	4	-	-	-	3	5
Mel Gilbert	-	2-8	-	0-0	6	-	-	-	4	4
Bill Reynolds	-	0-1	-	0-0	0	-	-	-	0	0
TOTALS	**-**	**25-74**	**-**	**17-19**	**48**	**-**	**-**	**-**	**22**	**67**
Percentages		33.8		89.5						

Coach: Harold Anderson

Officials: Fox, Mills

LOYOLA-CHICAGO	MIN	FG	3FG	FT	REB	A	ST	BL	PF	TP
Jerry Harkness	-	7-11	-	6-7	9	-	-	-	1	20
Vic Rouse	-	8-24	-	0-0	19	-	-	-	4	16
Les Hunter	-	3-13	-	6-7	10	-	-	-	3	12
Ron Miller	-	5-9	-	1-1	4	-	-	-	1	11
John Egan	-	1-9	-	0-1	1	-	-	-	5	2
Chuck Wood	-	0-0	-	0-0	1	-	-	-	3	0
TOTALS	**-**	**24-66**	**-**	**13-16**	**44**	**-**	**-**	**-**	**17**	**61**
Percentages		36.4		81.2						

Coach: George Ireland

61-51

26 1H 19
35 2H 32

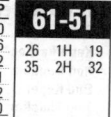

SWEET 16

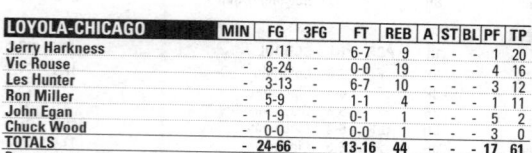

MISSISSIPPI STATE	MIN	FG	3FG	FT	REB	A	ST	BL	PF	TP
Leland Mitchell	-	6-10	-	2-5	11	-	-	-	5	14
Joe Gold	-	3-9	-	5-7	3	-	-	-	3	11
Doug Hutton	-	5-9	-	0-2	1	-	-	-	0	10
Stan Brinker	-	3-6	-	3-5	7	-	-	-	4	9
W.D. Stroud	-	3-15	-	1-1	3	-	-	-	2	7
Aubrey Nichols	-	0-0	-	0-0	0	-	-	-	0	0
TOTALS	**-**	**20-49**	**-**	**11-20**	**25**	**-**	**-**	**-**	**14**	**51**
Percentages		40.8		55.0						

Coach: Babe McCarthy

Officials: Fox, Stevens

COLORADO	MIN	FG	3FG	FT	REB	A	ST	BL	PF	TP
Ken Charlton	-	9-14	-	8-10	12	-	-	-	0	26
Eric Lee	-	8-19	-	1-4	6	-	-	-	0	17
Jim Davis	-	8-13	-	0-4	17	-	-	-	3	16
Milt Mueller	-	4-6	-	3-5	5	-	-	-	3	11
George Parsons	-	0-6	-	5-7	5	-	-	-	2	5
Lonnie Melton	-	1-3	-	1-2	1	-	-	-	1	3
Bob Joyce	-	0-0	-	0-0	0	-	-	-	1	0
Gene Sparks	-	0-1	-	0-0	0	-	-	-	1	0
TOTALS	**-**	**30-62**	**-**	**18-32**	**46**	**-**	**-**	**-**	**11**	**78**
Percentages		48.4		56.2						

Coach: Russell "Sox" Walseth

78-72

37 1H 34
41 2H 38

SWEET 16

OKLAHOMA CITY	MIN	FG	3FG	FT	REB	A	ST	BL	PF	TP
Bud Koper	-	11-28	-	4-4	1	-	-	-	2	26
Gary Hill	-	7-15	-	1-1	2	-	-	-	5	15
Eddie Jackson	-	5-11	-	1-2	11	-	-	-	3	11
Gary White	-	4-10	-	0-0	2	-	-	-	0	8
Manuel Housman	-	2-3	-	0-0	2	-	-	-	2	4
Bill Johnston	-	1-3	-	2-3	6	-	-	-	2	4
Jim Miller	-	0-3	-	2-2	2	-	-	-	2	2
Eddie Stephens	-	0-2	-	2-3	4	-	-	-	4	2
Joe Gibbon	-	0-0	-	0-0	0	-	-	-	0	0
Ray Snider	-	0-1	-	0-0	0	-	-	-	0	0
TOTALS	**-**	**30-76**	**-**	**12-15**	**30**	**-**	**-**	**-**	**20**	**72**
Percentages		39.5		80.0						

Coach: Abe Lemons

Officials: Bussenius, Soriano
Attendance: 5,500

CINCINNATI	MIN	FG	3FG	FT	REB	A	ST	BL	PF	TP
George Wilson	-	8-20	-	9-12	12	-	-	-	2	25
Ron Bonham	-	9-23	-	6-11	4	-	-	-	1	24
Tom Thacker	-	5-11	-	4-7	7	-	-	-	1	14
Tony Yates	-	2-6	-	3-3	2	-	-	-	4	7
Dale Heidotting	-	1-1	-	0-0	0	-	-	-	1	2
Larry Shingleton	-	0-3	-	1-2	4	-	-	-	2	1
TOTALS	**-**	**25-64**	**-**	**23-35**	**29**	**-**	**-**	**-**	**11**	**73**
Percentages		39.1		65.7						

Coach: Ed L. Jucker

73-68

36 1H 34
37 2H 34

SWEET 16

TEXAS	MIN	FG	3FG	FT	REB	A	ST	BL	PF	TP
Larry Franks	-	8-13	-	2-2	6	-	-	-	5	18
John Fultz	-	6-9	-	1-2	8	-	-	-	4	13
Jimmy Gilbert	-	4-10	-	5-5	1	-	-	-	2	13
Mike Humphrey	-	4-4	-	1-1	5	-	-	-	4	9
James Puryear	-	4-8	-	1-1	5	-	-	-	1	9
Joe Fisher	-	2-6	-	0-0	3	-	-	-	2	4
James Clark	-	0-0	-	1-1	0	-	-	-	0	1
Jack Dugan	-	0-0	-	1-1	2	-	-	-	3	1
John Heller	-	0-1	-	0-0	0	-	-	-	1	0
James Smith	-	0-0	-	0-0	0	-	-	-	1	0
Ronald Weaks	-	0-0	-	0-0	0	-	-	-	0	0
TOTALS	**-**	**28-51**	**-**	**12-13**	**30**	**-**	**-**	**-**	**23**	**68**
Percentages		54.9		92.3						

Coach: Harold Bradley

93-79

62	1H	31
31	2H	48

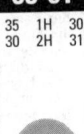

SWEET 16

ARIZONA STATE	MIN	FG	3FG	FT	REB	A	ST	BL	PF	TP
Art Becker	-	9-14	-	5-6	13	-	-	-	3	23
Joe Caldwell	-	10-18	-	2-3	12	-	-	-	2	22
Tony Cerkvenik	-	9-12	-	0-1	13	-	-	-	2	18
Dennis Dairman	-	6-10	-	1-4	3	-	-	-	3	13
Gary Senitza	-	5-7	-	3-4	1	-	-	-	3	13
Bob Howard	-	1-5	-	0-1	1	-	-	-	2	2
Gerald Jones	-	1-6	-	0-0	0	-	-	-	2	2
Raul Disarufino	-	0-4	-	0-0	2	-	-	-	4	0
Harry Orr	-	0-1	-	0-2	2	-	-	-	2	0
Tom Owens	-	0-1	-	0-0	1	-	-	-	1	0
Jim Sturgeon	-	0-1	-	0-0	0	-	-	-	1	0
TOTALS	**-**	**41-79**	**-**	**11-21**	**48**	**-**	**-**	**-**	**25**	**93**
Percentages		51.9		52.4						
Coach: Ned Wulk										

UCLA	MIN	FG	3FG	FT	REB	A	ST	BL	PF	TP
Jack Hirsch	-	8-17	-	3-4	4	-	-	-	5	19
Fred Slaughter	-	4-9	-	6-7	5	-	-	-	4	14
Walt Hazzard	-	4-11	-	5-7	5	-	-	-	2	13
Kim Stewart	-	5-15	-	3-4	11	-	-	-	2	13
Fred Goss	-	3-10	-	2-3	5	-	-	-	0	8
Dave Waxman	-	2-5	-	1-3	1	-	-	-	2	5
Gail Goodrich	-	1-8	-	1-2	1	-	-	-	0	3
Keith Erickson	-	0-6	-	2-2	2	-	-	-	0	2
Jim Milhorn	-	1-5	-	0-0	3	-	-	-	3	2
TOTALS	**-**	**28-86**	**-**	**23-32**	**37**	**-**	**-**	**-**	**18**	**79**
Percentages		32.6		71.9						
Coach: John Wooden										

65-61

35	1H	30
30	2H	31

SWEET 16

OREGON STATE	MIN	FG	3FG	FT	REB	A	ST	BL	PF	TP
Mel Counts	-	9-22	-	4-5	4	-	-	-	5	22
Terry Baker	-	10-17	-	1-1	0	-	-	-	0	21
Frank Peters	-	2-4	-	5-7	3	-	-	-	2	9
Jim Jarvis	-	3-5	-	2-2	3	-	-	-	2	8
Jim Kraus	-	1-3	-	1-2	9	-	-	-	4	3
Steve Pauly	-	1-3	-	0-2	4	-	-	-	2	2
Tim Campbell	-	0-1	-	0-0	0	-	-	-	1	0
TOTALS	**-**	**26-55**	**-**	**13-19**	**23**	**-**	**-**	**-**	**16**	**65**
Percentages		47.3		68.4						
Coach: Slats Gill										

SAN FRANCISCO	MIN	FG	3FG	FT	REB	A	ST	BL	PF	TP
Ed Thomas	-	8-10	-	5-7	8	-	-	-	4	21
Ollie Johnson	-	5-11	-	5-6	10	-	-	-	3	15
Dave Lee	-	4-14	-	4-4	9	-	-	-	4	12
Jim Brovelli	-	3-7	-	1-2	4	-	-	-	5	7
Lloyd Moffatt	-	2-4	-	0-1	1	-	-	-	1	4
Dick Brainard	-	1-4	-	0-0	1	-	-	-	1	2
Dan Belluomini	-	0-0	-	0-0	1	-	-	-	0	0
Ed Thomas	-	0-1	-	0-2	0	-	-	-	0	0
TOTALS	**-**	**23-51**	**-**	**15-22**	**34**	**-**	**-**	**-**	**18**	**61**
Percentages		45.1		68.2						
Coach: Peter P. Peletta										

73-59

34	1H	33
39	2H	26

ELITE 8

DUKE	MIN	FG	3FG	FT	REB	A	ST	BL	PF	TP
Jeff Mullins	-	10-16	-	4-4	5	2	-	-	1	24
Fred Schmidt	-	9-16	-	2-2	5	0	-	-	0	20
Art Heyman	-	3-14	-	10-15	10	3	-	-	2	16
Jay Buckley	-	4-9	-	2-3	18	0	-	-	2	10
Ron Herbster	-	0-2	-	2-2	0	0	-	-	1	2
Buzzy Harrison	-	0-3	-	1-2	2	0	-	-	0	1
Hack Tison	-	0-1	-	0-0	1	0	-	-	0	0
TOTALS	**-**	**26-61**	**-**	**21-28**	**41**	**5**	**-**	**-**	**6**	**73**
Percentages		42.6		75.0						
Coach: Vic Bubas										

SAINT JOSEPH'S	MIN	FG	3FG	FT	REB	A	ST	BL	PF	TP
Tom Wynne	-	13-23	-	3-3	9	0	-	-	2	29
Steve Courtin	-	7-16	-	0-0	4	0	-	-	1	14
Jim Lynam	-	4-7	-	0-1	5	1	-	-	4	8
Jim Boyle	-	2-17	-	0-1	10	2	-	-	5	4
Larry Hoffman	-	1-5	-	0-0	4	0	-	-	4	2
John Tiller	-	0-2	-	2-2	5	0	-	-	3	2
Joe Kelly	-	0-2	-	0-0	1	0	-	-	1	0
TOTALS	**-**	**27-72**	**-**	**5-7**	**38**	**3**	**-**	**-**	**20**	**59**
Percentages		37.5		71.4						
Coach: Jack Ramsay										

79-64

38	1H	30
41	2H	34

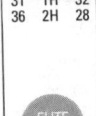

ELITE 8

LOYOLA-CHICAGO	MIN	FG	3FG	FT	REB	A	ST	BL	PF	TP
Jerry Harkness	40	13-23	-	7-11	7	-	-	-	3	33
Ron Miller	40	6-15	-	3-4	11	-	-	-	2	15
John Egan	39	3-11	-	7-8	4	-	-	-	3	13
Les Hunter	40	4-9	-	4-4	15	-	-	-	4	12
Vic Rouse	40	3-17	-	0-0	19	-	-	-	2	6
Chuck Wood	1	0-1	-	0-0	1	-	-	-	0	0
TOTALS	**200**	**29-76**	**-**	**21-27**	**57**	**-**	**-**	**-**	**14**	**79**
Percentages		38.2		77.8						
Coach: George Ireland										

ILLINOIS	MIN	FG	3FG	FT	REB	A	ST	BL	PF	TP
Dave Downey	31	9-22	-	2-5	6	-	-	-	4	20
Bill Burwell	37	5-15	-	0-1	7	-	-	-	4	10
Bill Small	37	3-9	-	3-3	4	-	-	-	3	9
Skip Thoren	23	4-11	-	0-2	7	-	-	-	3	8
Tal Brody	22	3-8	-	0-1	5	-	-	-	3	6
Bill Edwards	12	2-4	-	1-2	0	-	-	-	2	5
Bill McKeown	9	1-4	-	2-3	0	-	-	-	1	4
Bob Starnes	20	1-6	-	0-0	4	-	-	-	2	2
Bogie Redmon	9	0-1	-	0-0	2	-	-	-	1	0
TOTALS	**200**	**28-80**	**-**	**8-17**	**35**	**-**	**-**	**-**	**23**	**64**
Percentages		35.0		47.1						
Coach: Harry Combes										

Officials: Stevens, Lennon

67-60

31	1H	32
36	2H	28

ELITE 8

CINCINNATI	MIN	FG	3FG	FT	REB	A	ST	BL	PF	TP
Ron Bonham	-	8-18	-	6-7	2	-	-	-	3	22
Tom Thacker	-	7-13	-	4-5	13	-	-	-	1	18
George Wilson	-	6-11	-	3-7	10	-	-	-	3	15
Tony Yates	-	2-11	-	1-3	4	-	-	-	4	5
Larry Shingleton	-	1-2	-	2-4	0	-	-	-	1	4
Dale Heidotting	-	1-1	-	1-1	1	-	-	-	3	3
TOTALS	**-**	**25-56**	**-**	**17-27**	**30**	**-**	**-**	**-**	**15**	**67**
Percentages		44.6		63.0						
Coach: Ed L. Jucker										

COLORADO	MIN	FG	3FG	FT	REB	A	ST	BL	PF	TP
Ken Charlton	-	9-17	-	5-5	12	-	-	-	3	23
Jim Davis	-	5-9	-	1-4	12	-	-	-	3	11
Milt Mueller	-	3-10	-	3-6	14	-	-	-	4	9
George Parsons	-	4-11	-	1-5	0	-	-	-	3	9
Eric Lee	-	2-7	-	0-1	0	-	-	-	2	4
Lonnie Melton	-	2-2	-	0-0	0	-	-	-	2	4
Bob Joyce	-	0-0	-	0-0	0	-	-	-	1	0
Ed Price	-	0-0	-	0-0	0	-	-	-	0	0
Norm Saunders	-	0-0	-	0-0	0	-	-	-	0	0
Gene Sparks	-	0-0	-	0-0	0	-	-	-	1	0
Glenn Sponholtz	-	0-0	-	0-0	0	-	-	-	0	0
Terry Woodward	-	0-0	-	0-0	0	-	-	-	0	0
TOTALS	**-**	**25-56**	**-**	**10-21**	**38**	**-**	**-**	**-**	**19**	**60**
Percentages		44.6		47.6						
Coach: Russell "Sox" Walseth										

Officials: Soriano, Bussenius
Attendance: 8,500

83-65

43	1H	38
40	2H	27

ELITE 8

OREGON STATE	MIN	FG	3FG	FT	REB	A	ST	BL	PF	TP
Mel Counts	-	11-20	-	4-4	13	-	-	-	3	26
Steve Pauly	-	9-14	-	3-6	6	-	-	-	3	21
Terry Baker	-	6-9	-	3-3	1	-	-	-	4	15
Frank Peters	-	4-7	-	6-6	5	-	-	-	4	14
Jim Jarvis	-	1-3	-	3-3	1	-	-	-	5	5
Gary Rossi	-	0-1	-	2-3	0	-	-	-	3	2
Jim Kraus	-	0-0	-	0-0	2	-	-	-	2	0
Ray Torgerson	-	0-0	-	0-2	0	-	-	-	0	0
TOTALS	**-**	**31-54**	**-**	**21-27**	**28**	**-**	**-**	**-**	**24**	**83**
Percentages		57.4		77.8						
Coach: Slats Gill										

ARIZONA STATE	MIN	FG	3FG	FT	REB	A	ST	BL	PF	TP
Joe Caldwell	-	6-19	-	5-10	7	-	-	-	3	17
Tony Cerkvenik	-	5-12	-	6-10	7	-	-	-	5	16
Art Becker	-	6-16	-	1-3	16	-	-	-	3	13
Gary Senitza	-	4-15	-	0-2	1	-	-	-	3	8
Dennis Dairman	-	2-4	-	2-3	2	-	-	-	2	6
Bob Howard	-	0-2	-	3-3	4	-	-	-	3	3
Raul Disarufino	-	1-1	-	0-0	0	-	-	-	3	2
TOTALS	**-**	**24-69**	**-**	**17-31**	**37**	**-**	**-**	**-**	**22**	**65**
Percentages		34.8		54.8						
Coach: Ned Wulk										

LOYOLA-CHICAGO	MIN	FG	3FG	FT	REB	A	ST	BL	PF	TP
Les Hunter	-	11-20	-	7-9	18	-	-	-	3	29
Jerry Harkness	-	7-18	-	6-9	11	-	-	-	3	20
Ron Miller	-	8-11	-	2-2	5	-	-	-	4	18
John Egan	-	4-9	-	6-7	3	-	-	-	2	14
Vic Rouse	-	6-12	-	1-2	6	-	-	-	4	13
Dan Connaughton	-	0-0	-	0-0	0	-	-	-	0	0
Jim Reardon	-	0-0	-	0-0	0	-	-	-	0	0
Rich Rochelle	-	0-0	-	0-0	0	-	-	-	0	0
Chuck Wood	-	0-1	-	0-0	3	-	-	-	0	0
TOTALS	-	**36-71**	-	**22-29**	**46**	-	-	-	**16**	**94**
Percentages		50.7		75.9						

Coach: George Ireland

94-75

44 1H 31
50 2H 44

FINAL 4

DUKE	MIN	FG	3FG	FT	REB	A	ST	BL	PF	TP
Art Heyman	-	11-30	-	7-9	12	-	-	-	5	29
Jeff Mullins	-	10-20	-	1-3	9	-	-	-	4	21
Hack Tison	-	5-12	-	1-3	8	-	-	-	3	11
Jay Buckley	-	4-10	-	2-4	13	-	-	-	3	10
Dennis Ferguson	-	1-2	-	0-0	0	-	-	-	1	2
Buzzy Harrison	-	0-3	-	2-3	3	-	-	-	0	2
Ray Cox	-	0-0	-	0-0	0	-	-	-	0	0
Ron Herbster	-	0-2	-	0-0	0	-	-	-	1	0
Bob Jamieson	-	0-0	-	0-0	0	-	-	-	0	0
Ted Mann	-	0-1	-	0-0	0	-	-	-	0	0
Fred Schmidt	-	0-2	-	0-0	2	-	-	-	3	0
TOTALS	-	**31-82**	-	**13-22**	**47**	-	-	-	**20**	**75**
Percentages		37.8		59.1						

Coach: Vic Bubas

CINCINNATI	MIN	FG	3FG	FT	REB	A	ST	BL	PF	TP
George Wilson	34	8-9	-	8-12	13	0	-	-	2	24
Tom Thacker	35	5-8	-	4-8	11	1	-	-	3	14
Ron Bonham	30	3-12	-	8-9	5	0	-	-	3	14
Tony Yates	32	5-9	-	2-3	5	3	-	-	1	12
Ken Cunningham	8	2-3	-	0-0	0	0	-	-	1	4
Fritz Meyer	8	1-1	-	1-2	1	1	-	-	1	3
Larry Shingleton	32	1-2	-	0-0	2	0	-	-	1	2
Gene Smith	6	1-3	-	0-2	1	0	-	-	1	2
Larry Elsasser	5	1-2	-	0-1	1	0	-	-	0	2
Bill Abernethy	2	1-2	-	0-0	3	0	-	-	0	2
Dale Heidotting	8	0-0	-	1-2	2	0	-	-	1	1
TOTALS	**200**	**28-51**	-	**24-39**	**44**	**5**	-	-	**14**	**80**
Percentages		54.9		61.5						

Coach: Ed L. Jucker

80-46

30 1H 27
50 2H 19

FINAL 4

OREGON STATE	MIN	FG	3FG	FT	REB	A	ST	BL	PF	TP
Mel Counts	27	8-14	-	4-4	9	0	-	-	5	20
Jim Jarvis	27	1-6	-	3-4	0	0	-	-	3	5
Frank Peters	29	1-5	-	2-2	4	1	-	-	4	4
Steve Pauly	26	2-8	-	0-1	3	0	-	-	5	4
Rex Benner	10	2-2	-	0-0	1	0	-	-	0	4
Jim Kraus	22	1-6	-	1-1	3	0	-	-	3	3
Gary Rossi	13	1-3	-	0-0	0	0	-	-	1	2
Ray Torgerson	1	1-2	-	0-0	0	0	-	-	0	2
Dave Hayward	12	0-2	-	1-1	2	0	-	-	3	1
Tim Campbell	6	0-2	-	1-1	2	0	-	-	2	1
Terry Baker	27	0-9	-	0-1	2	0	-	-	0	0
TOTALS	**200**	**17-59**	-	**12-15**	**26**	**1**	-	-	**26**	**46**
Percentages		28.8		80.0						

Coach: Slats Gill

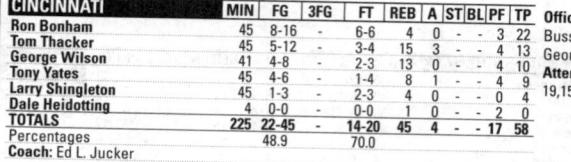

DUKE	MIN	FG	3FG	FT	REB	A	ST	BL	PF	TP
Art Heyman	-	7-14	-	8-13	7	-	-	-	3	22
Fred Schmidt	-	10-15	-	0-0	4	-	-	-	1	20
Jeff Mullins	-	4-13	-	6-8	10	-	-	-	2	14
Hack Tison	-	4-9	-	3-5	11	-	-	-	3	11
Buzzy Harrison	-	4-8	-	1-2	5	-	-	-	1	9
Jay Buckley	-	2-5	-	2-5	7	-	-	-	4	6
Dennis Ferguson	-	1-1	-	0-0	0	-	-	-	0	2
Ron Herbster	-	0-0	-	1-2	0	-	-	-	0	1
Ray Cox	-	0-0	-	0-0	0	-	-	-	0	0
Bob Jamieson	-	0-0	-	0-0	0	-	-	-	2	0
Brent Kitching	-	0-0	-	0-0	0	-	-	-	0	0
Ted Mann	-	0-0	-	0-0	0	-	-	-	0	0
TOTALS	-	**32-65**	-	**21-35**	**44**	-	-	-	**16**	**85**
Percentages		49.2		60.0						

Coach: Vic Bubas

85-63

34 1H 23
51 2H 40

3RD PLACE

OREGON STATE	MIN	FG	3FG	FT	REB	A	ST	BL	PF	TP
Mel Counts	-	9-30	-	7-10	18	-	-	-	2	25
Steve Pauly	-	5-15	-	2-2	11	-	-	-	4	12
Frank Peters	-	3-9	-	2-2	6	-	-	-	4	8
Terry Baker	-	3-11	-	1-1	3	-	-	-	2	7
Jim Jarvis	-	3-12	-	1-1	6	-	-	-	5	7
Dave Hayward	-	2-6	-	0-0	1	-	-	-	3	4
Rex Benner	-	0-1	-	0-0	0	-	-	-	1	0
Jim Kraus	-	0-3	-	0-1	8	-	-	-	3	0
Ray Torgerson	-	0-0	-	0-0	1	-	-	-	0	0
TOTALS	-	**25-87**	-	**13-17**	**54**	-	-	-	**24**	**63**
Percentages		28.7		76.5						

Coach: Slats Gill

Attendance: 19,153

LOYOLA-CHICAGO	MIN	FG	3FG	FT	REB	A	ST	BL	PF	TP
Les Hunter	45	6-22	-	4-4	11	1	-	-	3	16
Vic Rouse	45	6-22	-	3-4	12	0	-	-	4	15
Jerry Harkness	45	5-18	-	4-8	6	0	-	-	4	14
John Egan	45	3-8	-	3-5	3	0	-	-	3	9
Ron Miller	45	3-14	-	0-0	2	0	-	-	3	6
TOTALS	**225**	**23-84**	-	**14-21**	**34**	**1**	-	-	**17**	**60**
Percentages		27.4		66.7						

Coach: George Ireland

60-58

21 1H 29
33 2H 25
6 OT1 4

NCAA FINAL 1963

CINCINNATI	MIN	FG	3FG	FT	REB	A	ST	BL	PF	TP
Ron Bonham	45	8-16	-	6-6	4	0	-	-	3	22
Tom Thacker	45	5-12	-	3-4	15	3	-	-	4	13
George Wilson	41	4-8	-	2-3	13	0	-	-	4	10
Tony Yates	45	4-6	-	1-4	8	1	-	-	4	9
Larry Shingleton	45	1-3	-	2-3	4	0	-	-	0	4
Dale Heidotting	4	0-0	-	0-0	1	0	-	-	2	0
TOTALS	**225**	**22-45**	-	**14-20**	**45**	**4**	-	-	**17**	**58**
Percentages		48.9		70.0						

Coach: Ed L. Jucker

Officials: Bussenius, George
Attendance: 19,153

National Invitation Tournament (NIT)

First round: Villanova d. DePaul 63-51, Memphis d. Fordham 70-49, Saint Louis d. La Salle 63-61, Miami (FL) d. St. Francis (NY) 71-70

Quarterfinals: Villanova d. Wichita State 54-53, Canisius d. Memphis 76-67, Marquette d. Saint Louis 84-49, Providence d. Miami (FL) 106-96

Semifinals: Providence d. Marquette 70-64, Canisius d. Villanova 61-46

Third place: Marquette d. Villanova 66-58

Championship: Providence d. Canisius 81-66

MVP: Ray Flynn, Providence

1963-64: First of Many

It may have been perfect, but it sure wasn't easy. UCLA rolled to a 30–0 season and its first NCAA title. Eight of those games were decided by seven points or fewer, including three of four Tournament matches. Against San Francisco in the West Regional final, John Wooden's crew overcame a 13-point deficit to win. But the championship game against Duke—the ACC champ and odds-on favorite—was never close. A swarming pack of Bruins assailed the Blue Devils from the start, and UCLA led, 50-38, at halftime. Behind Gail Goodrich (27 points) and Kenny Washington (26 points, 12 rebounds), UCLA cruised to a 98-83 win. With a total of 30 points and 10 rebounds, Walt Hazzard was named Tournament MOP despite being UCLA's fourth-best scorer in the two Final Four games.

In a 102-59 thrashing of Ole Miss on Feb. 8, Kentucky set an NCAA record by grabbing 108 boards. Five Wildcats wound up with double digits in rebounds that game, led by Cotton Nash with 30.

Major Conference Standings

AAWU	Conference			Overall		
	W	L	Pct	W	L	Pct
UCLA ⊛	15	0	1.000	30	0	1.000
Stanford	9	6	.600	15	10	.600
California	8	7	.533	11	13	.458
Southern California	6	9	.400	10	16	.385
Washington	5	10	.333	9	17	.346
Washington State	2	13	.133	5	21	.192

ACC	Conference			Overall		
	W	L	Pct	W	L	Pct
Duke ⊛	13	1	.929	26	5	.839
Wake Forest	9	5	.643	16	11	.593
Clemson	8	6	.571	13	12	.520
South Carolina	7	7	.500	10	14	.417
North Carolina	6	8	.429	12	12	.500
Maryland	5	9	.357	9	17	.346
NC State	4	10	.286	8	11	.421
Virginia	4	10	.286	8	16	.333

Tournament: **Duke d. Wake Forest 80-59**
Tournament MVP: **Jeff Mullins**, Duke

Big Eight	Conference			Overall		
	W	L	Pct	W	L	Pct
Kansas State ⊛	12	2	.857	22	7	.759
Colorado	9	5	.643	15	10	.600
Kansas	8	6	.571	13	12	.520
Oklahoma State	7	7	.500	15	10	.600
Missouri	7	7	.500	13	11	.542
Iowa State	5	9	.357	9	16	.360
Nebraska	5	9	.357	7	18	.280
Oklahoma	3	11	.214	7	18	.280

Big Sky	Conference			Overall		
	W	L	Pct	W	L	Pct
Montana State	8	2	.800	16	9	.640
Weber State	7	3	.700	17	8	.680
Idaho State	5	5	.500	11	13	.458
Gonzaga	5	5	.500	10	15	.400
Idaho	4	6	.400	7	19	.269
Montana	1	9	.100	6	17	.261

Big Ten	Conference			Overall		
	W	L	Pct	W	L	Pct
Michigan ⊛	11	3	.786	23	5	.821
Ohio State	11	3	.786	16	8	.667
Minnesota	10	4	.714	17	7	.708
Michigan State	8	6	.571	14	10	.583
Purdue	8	6	.571	12	12	.500
Illinois	6	8	.429	13	11	.542
Northwestern	6	8	.429	8	13	.381
Indiana	5	9	.357	9	15	.375
Iowa	3	11	.214	8	15	.348
Wisconsin	2	12	.143	8	16	.333

Ivy	Conference			Overall		
	W	L	Pct	W	L	Pct
Princeton ⊛	12	2	.857	20	9	.690
Yale	11	3	.786	16	8	.667
Penn	10	4	.714	14	10	.583
Cornell	9	5	.643	15	10	.600
Harvard	6	8	.429	12	10	.545
Columbia	6	8	.429	11	12	.478
Brown	2	12	.143	6	19	.240
Dartmouth	0	14	.000	2	23	.080

Mid-American	Conference			Overall		
	W	L	Pct	W	L	Pct
Ohio ⊛	10	2	.833	21	6	.778
Miami (OH)	9	3	.750	17	7	.708
Bowling Green	7	5	.583	14	9	.609
Western Michigan	6	6	.500	10	14	.417
Kent State	5	7	.417	11	13	.458
Toledo	4	8	.333	13	11	.542
Marshall	1	11	.083	6	17	.261

Middle Atlantic	Conference			Overall		
	W	L	Pct	W	L	Pct
Temple ⊛	6	1	.857	17	8	.680
Saint Joseph's □	5	1	.833	18	10	.643
La Salle	5	1	.833	16	9	.640
Delaware	4	3	.571	13	10	.565
Lafayette	4	4	.500	15	8	.652
Gettysburg	4	5	.444	15	9	.625
Bucknell	3	7	.300	8	13	.381
Lehigh	1	10	.091	5	17	.227

Missouri Valley	Conference			Overall		
	W	L	Pct	W	L	Pct
Wichita State ⊛	10	2	.833	23	6	.793
Drake □	10	2	.833	21	7	.750
Bradley □	7	5	.583	23	6	.793
Cincinnati	6	6	.500	17	9	.654
Saint Louis	6	6	.500	13	12	.520
Tulsa	2	10	.167	10	15	.400
North Texas	1	11	.083	7	17	.292

Ohio Valley	Conference			Overall		
	W	L	Pct	W	L	Pct
Murray State ⊛	11	3	.786	16	9	.640
Eastern Kentucky	9	5	.643	15	9	.625
East Tennessee St.	8	6	.571	12	10	.545
Austin Peay	7	7	.500	14	9	.609
Tennessee Tech	7	7	.500	11	11	.500
Morehead State	6	8	.429	10	11	.476
Middle Tennessee St.	5	9	.357	11	10	.524
Western Kentucky	3	11	.214	5	16	.238

Tournament: **Murray State d. Western Kentucky 77-68**

SEC	Conference			Overall		
	W	L	Pct	W	L	Pct
Kentucky ⊛	11	3	.786	21	6	.778
Tennessee	9	5	.643	16	8	.667
Georgia Tech	9	5	.643	17	9	.654
Vanderbilt	8	6	.571	19	6	.760
LSU	8	6	.571	12	13	.480
Georgia	8	6	.571	12	14	.462
Alabama	7	7	.500	14	12	.538
Mississippi	7	7	.500	10	12	.455
Florida	6	8	.429	12	10	.545
Auburn	6	8	.429	11	12	.478
Mississippi State	4	10	.286	9	17	.346
Tulane	1	13	.071	1	22	.043

Southern	Conference			Overall		
	W	L	Pct	W	L	Pct
Davidson	9	2	.818	22	4	.846
West Virginia	11	3	.786	18	10	.643
Virginia Tech	7	3	.700	16	7	.696
VMI ⊛	7	7	.500	12	12	.500
Furman	7	8	.467	11	15	.423
George Washington	5	7	.417	11	15	.423
William and Mary	5	9	.357	9	13	.409
The Citadel	4	8	.333	11	10	.524
Richmond	4	12	.250	6	16	.273

Tournament: **VMI d. George Washington 61-56**
Tournament MOP: **Fred Hetzel**, Davidson

Southland	Conference			Overall		
	W	L	Pct	W	L	Pct
Lamar	7	1	.875	19	6	.760
Abilene Christian	6	2	.750	18	9	.667
Arkansas State	5	3	.625	16	9	.640
Texas-Arlington	1	7	.125	4	21	.160
Trinity (TX)	1	7	.125	3	21	.125

Southwest	Conference			Overall		
	W	L	Pct	W	L	Pct
Texas A&M ⊛	13	1	.929	18	7	.720
Texas Tech	11	3	.786	16	7	.696
Rice	8	6	.571	15	9	.625
Texas	8	6	.571	15	9	.625
SMU	8	6	.571	12	12	.500
Arkansas	6	8	.429	9	14	.391
Baylor	2	12	.143	7	17	.292
TCU	0	14	.000	4	20	.167

WCAC	Conference			Overall		
	W	L	Pct	W	L	Pct
San Francisco ⊛	12	0	1.000	23	5	.821
Pacific	7	5	.583	15	11	.577
San Jose State	6	6	.500	14	10	.583
Loyola Marymount	6	6	.500	12	13	.480
Saint Mary's (CA)	5	7	.417	7	19	.269
Pepperdine	3	9	.250	6	19	.240
Santa Clara	3	9	.250	6	20	.231

WAC	Conference			Overall		
	W	L	Pct	W	L	Pct
New Mexico □	7	3	.700	23	6	.793
Arizona State ⊛	7	3	.700	16	11	.593
BYU	5	5	.500	13	12	.520
Utah	4	6	.400	19	9	.679
Arizona	4	6	.400	15	11	.577
Wyoming	3	7	.300	12	14	.462

Yankee	Conference			Overall		
	W	L	Pct	W	L	Pct
Connecticut ⊛	8	2	.800	16	11	.593
Rhode Island	8	2	.800	19	8	.704
Massachusetts	5	5	.500	15	9	.625
Vermont	4	6	.400	11	10	.524
Maine	2	8	.200	12	11	.522
New Hampshire	2	8	.200	8	15	.348

Conference Standings Continue →

⊛ Automatic NCAA Tournament bid ○ At-large NCAA Tournament bid □ NIT appearance ⊗ Team record doesn't reflect games forfeited or vacated. For adjusted record, see p. 521.

INDEPENDENTS

	Overall W	L	Pct
Texas Western○	25	3	.893
Oregon State○	25	4	.862
Villanova○	24	4	.857
DePaul□	21	4	.840
Loyola-Chicago○	22	6	.786
Seattle○	22	6	.786
Providence○	20	6	.769
Creighton○	22	7	.759
Iona	15	5	.750
Miami (FL)□	20	7	.741
Army□	19	7	.731
Utah State○	21	8	.724
Boston U.	16	7	.696
Duquesne□	16	7	.696
Penn State	16	7	.696
Pittsburgh□	17	8	.680
Syracuse□	17	8	.680
Centenary	16	8	.667
St. Bonaventure□	16	8	.667
Portland	17	9	.654
Holy Cross	15	8	.652
Colorado State	16	9	.640
NYU□	17	10	.630
Houston	16	10	.615
Xavier	16	10	.615
Dayton	15	10	.600
Georgetown	15	10	.600

INDEPENDENTS (CONT.)

	Overall W	L	Pct
Louisville○	15	10	.600
West Texas	13	9	.591
Oklahoma City○	15	11	.577
Regis (CO)	12	9	.571
Detroit	14	11	.560
Memphis	14	11	.560
St. John's	14	11	.560
Oregon	14	12	.538
Seton Hall	13	12	.520
Butler	13	13	.500
Loyola (LA)	12	12	.500
Manhattan	11	11	.500
Air Force	11	12	.478
Boston College	10	11	.476
Navy	10	12	.455
Fordham	9	11	.450
Florida State	11	14	.440
Canisius	10	14	.417
Notre Dame	10	14	.417
Saint Francis (PA)	10	14	.417
Niagara	8	12	.400
St. Francis (NY)	10	16	.385
New Mexico State	8	15	.348
Colgate	7	16	.304
Denver	6	20	.231
Rutgers	5	17	.227
Marquette	5	21	.192

INDIVIDUAL LEADERS—SEASON

Scoring

	CL	POS	G	FG	FT	PTS	PPG
1 **Howard Komives**, Bowling Green	SR	G	23	292	260	844	**36.7**
2 **Nick Werkman**, Seton Hall	SR	F	25	320	190	830	**33.2**
3 **Manny Newsome**, Western Michigan	SR	G	20	262	129	653	**32.7**
4 **Bill Bradley**, Princeton	JR	F	29	338	260	936	**32.3**
5 **Rick Barry**, Miami (FL)	JR	F	27	314	242	870	**32.2**
6 **Gary Bradds**, Ohio State	SR	C	24	276	183	735	**30.6**
7 **Steve Thomas**, Xavier	SO	G	26	302	175	779	**30.0**
8 **John Austin**, Boston College	SO	G	21	235	144	614	**29.2**
9 **Jim Barnes**, Texas Western	SR	C	28	299	218	816	**29.1**
10 **Wayne Estes**, Utah State	JR	F	29	309	203	821	**28.3**

Field Goal Pct

	CL	POS	G	FG	FGA	PCT
1 **Terry Holland**, Davidson	SR	F	26	135	214	**63.1**
2 **Gene DeBerardinis**, Saint Francis (PA)	SR	F	21	112	181	**61.9**
3 **Joe Fisher**, Texas	SR	F	24	136	222	**61.3**
4 **Frank Nightingale**, Rhode Island	JR	C	26	139	229	**60.7**
5 **Ollie Johnson**, San Francisco	JR	C	28	206	346	**59.5**

Minimum: 100 made

Free Throw Pct

	CL	POS	G	FT	FTA	PCT
1 **Rick Park**, Tulsa	JR	G	25	121	134	**90.3**
2 **Danny Schultz**, Tennessee	SR	G	24	101	113	**89.4**
3 **Dave Lee**, San Francisco	SR	F	28	108	121	**89.3**
4 **Chuck Izor**, Dayton	SR	G	25	95	107	**88.8**
5 **Garland Bailey**, North Texas	SR	G	23	136	156	**87.2**

Minimum: 85 made

Rebounds Per Game

	CL	POS	G	REB	RPG
1 **Bob Pelkington**, Xavier	SR	C	26	567	**21.8**
2 **Paul Silas**, Creighton	SR	F/C	29	631	**21.8**
3 **Dick Dzik**, Detroit	SR	F	25	521	**20.8**
4 **Warren Isaac**, Iona	JR	F	20	403	**20.2**
5 **Jim Barnes**, Texas Western	SR	C	28	537	**19.2**

INDIVIDUAL LEADERS—GAME

Points

	CL	POS	OPP	DATE	PTS
1 **Bennie Lenox**, Texas A&M	SR	G	Wyoming	D28	**53**
2 **Nick Werkman**, Seton Hall	SR	F	Scranton	J22	**52**
Rick Barry, Miami (FL)	JR	F	Jacksonville	F4	**52**
4 **Jim Barnes**, Texas Western	SR	C	Western New Mexico	J4	**51**
Cozel Walker, Regis (CO)	SO	F/C	St. Joseph's (NM)	F28	**51**
Bill Bradley, Princeton	JR	F	Harvard	F15	**51**

Free Throws Made

	CL	POS	OPP	DATE	FT	FTA	PCT
1 **Sandy Williams**, Saint Francis (PA)	SR	F/C	Kent State	D28	**24**	25	96.0
2 **Rick Park**, Tulsa	JR	G	Arkansas	J25	**23**	24	95.8
3 **Howard Komives**, Bowling Green	SR	G	Marshall	M7	**21**	22	95.5
4 **Cozel Walker**, Regis (CO)	SO	F/C	N.M. Highlands	J25	**20**	24	83.3
5 **Dave Schellhase**, Purdue	SO	G/F	Notre Dame	J21	**19**	21	90.5
Steve Thomas, Xavier	SO	G	Cincinnati	M4	**19**	21	90.5

TEAM LEADERS—SEASON

Scoring Offense

	G	W-L	PTS	PPG
1 **Detroit**	25	14-11	2,402	**96.1**
2 **Miami (FL)**	27	20-7	2,575	**95.4**
3 **Michigan State**	24	14-10	2,211	**92.1**
4 **Weber State**	25	17-8	2,288	**91.5**
5 **Loyola-Chicago**	28	22-6	2,556	**91.3**

Field Goal Pct

	G	W-L	FG	FGA	PCT
1 **Davidson**	26	22-4	894	1,644	**54.4**
2 **Texas State**	23	13-10	681	1,356	**50.2**
3 **Rhode Island**	27	19-8	910	1,854	**49.1**
4 **Wichita State**	29	23-6	817	1,688	**48.4**
5 **San Francisco**	28	23-5	764	1,581	**48.3**

Free Throw Pct

	G	W-L	FT	FTA	PCT
1 **Miami (FL)**	27	20-7	593	780	**76.0**
2 **Bowling Green**	23	14-9	430	571	**75.3**
3 **Utah**	28	19-9	578	769	**75.2**
4 **Kentucky**	27	21-6	454	605	**75.0**
5 **Lafayette**	23	15-8	454	608	**74.7**

Scoring Defense

	G	W-L	OPP PTS	OPP PPG
1 **San Jose State**	24	14-10	1,307	**54.5**
2 **Texas Western**	28	25-3	1,548	**55.3**
3 **Gettysburg**	24	15-9	1,363	**56.8**
4 **New Mexico**	29	23-6	1,660	**57.2**
5 **Oklahoma State**	25	15-10	1,449	**58.0**

CONSENSUS ALL-AMERICAS

First Team

PLAYER	CL	POS	HT	SCHOOL	RPG	PPG
Bill Bradley	JR	F	6-5	Princeton	12.4	32.3
Gary Bradds	SR	C	6-8	Ohio State	13.4	30.6
Walt Hazzard	SR	G	6-2	UCLA	4.7	18.6
Cotton Nash	SR	F	6-5	Kentucky	11.7	24.0
Dave Stallworth	JR	F	6-7	Wichita State	10.1	26.5

Second Team

PLAYER	CL	POS	HT	SCHOOL	RPG	PPG
Ron Bonham	SR	F	6-5	Cincinnati	6.0	24.4
Mel Counts	SR	C	7-0	Oregon State	16.9	26.7
Fred Hetzel	JR	F/C	6-8	Davidson	13.5	27.3
Jeff Mullins	SR	F	6-4	Duke	6.8	24.2
Cazzie Russell	SO	G/F	6-5	Michigan	9.0	24.8

Selectors: AP, NABC, UPI, USBWA

AWARD WINNERS

Player of the Year

PLAYER	CL	POS	HT	SCHOOL	AWARDS
Gary Bradds	SR	C	6-8	Ohio State	AP, UPI
Walt Hazzard	SR	G	6-2	UCLA	USBWA

Coach of the Year

COACH	SCHOOL	REC	AWARDS
John Wooden	UCLA	30-0	UPI, USBWA, Sporting News

Poll Progression

Preseason Poll

AP	UPI	SCHOOL
1	1	Loyola-Chicago
2	3	NYU
3	2	Cincinnati
4	3	Duke
5	5	Wichita State
6	6	Arizona State
7	7	Ohio State
8	8	Michigan
9	11	Kentucky
10	9	Oregon State
—	10	Texas
—	12	Providence
—	13	San Francisco
—	13	UCLA
—	15	Villanova
—	16	Kansas State
—	16	Stanford
—	18	Minnesota
—	19	Oklahoma State
—	20	Bradley

Week of Dec 10

AP	UPI	SCHOOL		AP↓↑
1	1	Loyola-Chicago (2-0)		
2	3	NYU (2-0)		
3	2	Duke (3-0)		↑1
4	4	Arizona State (2-0)		↑2
5	7	Kentucky (3-0)		↑4
6	6	Cincinnati (2-1)	(A)	↓3
7	5	Michigan (3-0)		↑1
8	10	Ohio State (3-1)		↓1
9	7	Oregon State (4-0)		↑1
10	11	Kansas (2-0)	(A)	⤴
—	9	Texas (3-0)		
—	12	Wichita State (2-2)		⤵
—	13	San Francisco (3-0)		
—	14	UCLA (2-0)		
—	15	Villanova (2-0)		
—	16	Vanderbilt (3-0)		
—	17	Minnesota (3-0)		
—	18	Stanford (2-0)		
—	19	Kansas State (2-1)		
—	20	Oklahoma State (2-0)		

Week of Dec 17

AP	UPI	SCHOOL	AP↓↑
1	1	Loyola-Chicago (4-0)	
2	3	Kentucky (5-0)	↑3
3	2	Michigan (5-0)	↑4
4	5	Cincinnati (3-1)	↑2
5	4	Duke (4-1)	↓2
6	6	UCLA (4-0)	⤴
7	7	NYU (4-1)	↓5
8	9	Vanderbilt (5-0)	⤴
9	10	Toledo (6-0)	⤴
10	10	Davidson (6-0)	⤴
—	8	Texas (5-0)	
—	10	Oregon State (5-1)	⤵
—	13	Minnesota (4-0)	
—	14	Wichita State (4-2)	
—	15	Arizona State (2-4)	⤵
—	16	Oklahoma City (5-1)	
—	17	Kansas State (4-2)	
—	18	Creighton (6-0)	
—	19	Bradley (5-1)	
—	20	Georgia Tech (2-0)	
—	20	Villanova (4-1)	

Week of Dec 24

AP	UPI	SCHOOL		AP↓↑
1	1	Loyola-Chicago (6-0)		
2	3	Kentucky (7-0)	(B)	
3	2	Michigan (6-0)		
4	5	UCLA (6-0)		↑2
5	4	Cincinnati (5-1)		↓1
6	6	Vanderbilt (7-0)		↑2
7	8	Davidson (7-0)		↑3
8	9	Duke (6-2)	(B)	↓3
9	7	Oregon State (7-1)		⤴
10	10	NYU (4-2)		↓3
—	11	Villanova (6-1)		
—	12	Creighton (9-1)		
—	12	Toledo (6-2)		⤵
—	14	Texas Western (10-1)		
—	15	Minnesota (5-2)		
—	16	Bradley (5-2)		
—	17	Kansas State (5-2)		
—	18	St. Bonaventure (6-0)		
—	19	Stanford (4-0)		
—	20	Arizona State (4-4)		

Week of Dec 31

AP	UPI	SCHOOL		AP↓↑
1	1	Kentucky (8-0)		↑1
2	2	UCLA (9-0)	(C)	↑2
3	3	Loyola-Chicago (8-1)		↓2
4	5	Cincinnati (7-1)		↑1
5	4	Michigan (8-1)	(C)	↓2
6	6	Vanderbilt (9-0)		
7	7	Davidson (7-0)		
8	8	Oregon State (9-1)		↑1
9	9	Duke (6-2)		↓1
10	10	Villanova (8-1)		⤴
—	11	Wichita State (9-3)		
—	12	Stanford (6-0)		
—	13	Minnesota (7-3)		
—	14	Kansas State (7-3)		
—	15	Texas Western (12-1)		
—	16	St. Bonaventure (8-1)		
—	17	NYU (7-2)		⤵
—	17	Utah (9-1)		
—	19	North Carolina (5-2)		
—	19	Oklahoma State (8-3)		

Week of Jan 7

AP	UPI	SCHOOL		AP↓↑
1	1	UCLA (11-0)	(D)	↑1
2	2	Kentucky (10-2)		↓1
3	3	Loyola-Chicago (10-1)		
4	4	Michigan (10-1)		↑1
5	5	Davidson (10-0)	(E)	↑2
6	6	Oregon State (11-2)		↑2
7	7	Vanderbilt (10-1)		↓1
8	8	Cincinnati (8-3)		↓4
9	10	Villanova (9-1)		↑1
10	9	Duke (8-3)		↓1
—	11	Wichita State (10-3)		
—	12	Utah (11-1)		
—	13	Texas Western (13-1)		
—	14	Kansas State (8-3)		
—	15	Saint Louis (11-3)		
—	16	St. Bonaventure (10-1)		
—	16	Stanford (7-2)		
—	18	Bradley (8-3)		
—	19	Illinois (7-3)		
—	20	La Salle (8-2)		
—	20	Minnesota (8-3)		

Week of Jan 14

AP	UPI	SCHOOL	AP↓↑
1	1	UCLA (13-0)	
2	2	Loyola-Chicago (11-1)	↑1
3	3	Michigan (11-1)	↑1
4	4	Kentucky (12-2)	↓2
5	5	Davidson (12-0)	
6	6	Vanderbilt (12-1)	↑1
7	7	Oregon State (13-2)	↓1
8	8	Cincinnati (9-3)	
9	10	Villanova (11-1)	
10	9	Duke (10-3)	
—	11	Texas Western (15-1)	
—	12	Wichita State (11-3)	
—	13	DePaul (10-0)	
—	13	Utah (13-2)	
—	15	Illinois (8-3)	
—	16	Stanford (9-2)	
—	17	Utah State (9-2)	
—	18	Creighton (12-2)	
—	18	New Mexico (11-2)	
—	18	St. Bonaventure (10-1)	

Week of Jan 21

AP	UPI	SCHOOL	AP↓↑
1	1	UCLA (15-0)	
2	3	Michigan (12-1)	↑1
3	2	Loyola-Chicago (11-1)	↓1
4	5	Davidson (14-0)	↑1
5	4	Kentucky (13-2)	↓1
6	6	Vanderbilt (13-1)	
7	7	Villanova (12-1)	↑2
8	9	Duke (10-3)	↑2
9	12	DePaul (12-0)	⤴
10	8	Wichita State (13-3)	⤴
10	10	Oregon State (14-3)	↓3
—	11	Texas Western (15-1)	
—	13	Oklahoma State (11-3)	
—	14	Cincinnati (9-5)	⤵
—	15	Utah (14-3)	
—	16	Bradley (10-4)	
—	17	Utah State (10-2)	
—	18	Illinois (8-3)	
—	19	New Mexico (14-2)	
—	20	Stanford (9-4)	

Week of Jan 28

AP	UPI	SCHOOL	AP↓↑
1	1	UCLA (15-0)	
2	2	Michigan (14-1)	
3	4	Davidson (15-0)	↑1
4	3	Kentucky (14-2)	↑1
5	5	Vanderbilt (13-1)	↑1
6	7	Villanova (14-1)	↑1
7	6	Wichita State (14-3)	↑3
8	8	Duke (11-3)	
9	12	DePaul (12-0)	
10	9	Loyola-Chicago (11-3)	↓7
—	10	Oregon State (16-3)	⤵
—	11	Texas Western (16-1)	
—	13	Illinois (9-3)	
—	14	Utah State (12-2)	
—	15	Cincinnati (9-6)	
—	16	Creighton (15-2)	
—	17	New Mexico (14-2)	
—	17	Utah (15-3)	
—	19	Oklahoma State (11-3)	
—	20	Tennessee (10-4)	

Week of Feb 4

AP	UPI	SCHOOL		AP↓↑
1	1	UCLA (17-0)		
2	2	Michigan (15-1)		
3	3	Kentucky (15-2)	(F)	↑1
4	4	Wichita State (16-3)		↑3
5	5	Davidson (16-1)		↓2
6	6	Villanova (16-1)		
7	7	Duke (13-3)		↑1
8	8	Vanderbilt (14-2)		↓3
9	9	Loyola-Chicago (14-3)		↑1
10	13	DePaul (12-1)		↓1
—	10	Oregon State (18-3)		
—	11	Texas Western (17-2)		
—	12	Oklahoma State (12-4)		
—	14	Illinois (10-3)		
—	15	Utah (17-3)		
—	16	New Mexico (16-2)		
—	17	Drake (13-3)		
—	17	Ohio (13-3)		
—	19	Tennessee (11-5)		
—	19	Utah State (13-3)		

Week of Feb 11

AP	UPI	SCHOOL	AP↓↑
1	1	UCLA (19-0)	
2	3	Michigan (16-2)	
3	2	Kentucky (17-2)	
4	4	Davidson (18-1)	↑1
5	5	Duke (15-3)	↑2
6	6	Wichita State (17-4)	↓2
7	7	Vanderbilt (17-2)	↑1
8	9	Villanova (17-2)	↓2
9	8	Oregon State (20-3)	⤴
10	14	DePaul (14-2)	
—	10	Texas Western (18-2)	
—	11	Loyola-Chicago (14-5)	⤵
—	12	Oklahoma State (13-5)	
—	13	Utah (18-3)	
—	15	Drake (14-4)	
—	15	Ohio State (11-7)	
—	17	Illinois (10-6)	
—	18	New Mexico (16-3)	
—	19	Bradley (13-5)	
—	19	Texas A&M (11-6)	
—	19	Utah State (16-3)	

Week of Feb 18

AP	UPI	SCHOOL	AP↓↑
1	1	UCLA (21-0)	
2	2	Michigan (17-2)	
3	3	Kentucky (18-2)	
4	4	Duke (17-3)	↑1
5	5	Villanova (19-2)	↑3
6	7	Wichita State (18-5)	
7	6	Oregon State (21-3)	↑2
8	8	Davidson (19-3)	↓4
9	13	DePaul (16-2)	↑1
10	12	Drake (17-4)	⤴
—	9	Vanderbilt (17-4)	⤵
—	10	Loyola-Chicago (15-5)	
—	11	Texas Western (19-2)	
—	14	Ohio State (12-7)	
—	15	San Francisco (15-4)	
—	15	Utah (18-5)	
—	17	Tennessee (15-5)	
—	17	Texas A&M (12-6)	
—	19	New Mexico (18-3)	
—	20	Utah State (17-3)	

Poll Progression Continues →

Week of Feb 25

AP	UPI	SCHOOL	AP↓↑
1	1	**UCLA** (23-0)	
2	2	**Kentucky** (20-3)	↑1
3	3	**Michigan** (18-3)	↓1
4	4	**Duke** (20-4)	
5	6	**Wichita State** (19-5)	↑1
6	5	**Oregon State** (23-3)	↑1
7	8	**Davidson** (21-3)	↑1
8	7	**Villanova** (19-3)	↓3
9	11	**DePaul** (18-2)	
10	9	**Loyola-Chicago** (17-5)	↑
—	10	**Texas Western** (22-2) Ⓖ	
—	11	**Ohio State** (14-7)	
—	13	**Drake** (18-5)	↓
—	13	**Vanderbilt** (18-5)	
—	15	**San Francisco** (17-4)	
—	16	**Utah State** (18-4)	
—	17	**Kansas State** (16-5)	
—	18	**New Mexico** (18-5)	
—	18	**Providence** (17-4)	
—	20	**Seattle** (17-4)	
—	20	**St. Bonaventure** (15-5)	
—	20	**Texas A&M** (14-6)	

Week of Mar 3

AP	UPI	SCHOOL	AP↓↑
1	1	**UCLA** (25-0)	
2	3	**Michigan** (19-3)	↑1
3	2	**Kentucky** (21-4)	↓1
4	4	**Duke** (20-4)	
5	6	**Wichita State** (21-5)	
6	5	**Oregon State** (25-3)	
7	7	**Villanova** (21-3)	↑1
8	12	**DePaul** (20-2)	↑1
9	8	**Loyola-Chicago** (19-5)	↑1
10	9	**Davidson** (22-4)	↓3
—	10	**Texas Western** (23-2)	
—	11	**Drake** (20-5)	
—	13	**Ohio State** (15-7)	
—	14	**Vanderbilt** (19-6)	
—	15	**Arizona State** (15-10)	
—	15	**Kansas State** (17-5)	
—	17	**New Mexico** (20-5)	
—	18	**Providence** (18-5)	
—	18	**San Francisco** (19-4)	
—	20	**Texas A&M** (16-6)	
—	20	**Utah State** (20-5)	

FINAL POLL

AP	UPI	SCHOOL	AP↓↑
1	1	**UCLA** (26-0)	
2	2	**Michigan** (20-4)	
3	4	**Duke** (23-4)	↑1
4	3	**Kentucky** (21-4)	↓1
5	6	**Wichita State** (22-5)	
6	5	**Oregon State** (25-3)	
7	7	**Villanova** (22-3)	
8	8	**Loyola-Chicago** (20-5)	↑1
9	11	**DePaul** (21-2)	↓1
10	10	**Davidson** (22-4)	
—	9	**Texas Western** (23-2)	
—	12	**Kansas State** (19-5)	
—	13	**Drake** (20-6)	
—	13	**San Francisco** (22-4)	
—	15	**Utah State** (20-6)	
—	16	**New Mexico** (22-5)	
—	16	**Ohio State** (17-7)	
—	18	**Texas A&M** (18-6)	
—	19	**Arizona State** (16-10)	
—	19	**Providence** (20-5)	

Ⓐ Kansas shocks Cincinnati, 51-47, ending the Bearcats' homecourt winning streak at 72. It is Cincy's first loss at home since losing to Dayton on March 1, 1957.

Ⓑ Kentucky rallies from a 10-point halftime deficit to edge Duke, 81-79, and win the Sugar Bowl Classic in New Orleans. The Wildcats' Cotton Nash scores 20 of his 30 points in the second half.

Ⓒ Michigan's effort to be ranked "first by the first [of the year]" is derailed by UCLA, 98-80.

Ⓓ Georgia Tech's 76-67 victory over SEC rival Kentucky allows UCLA to rise to No. 1 in the polls for the first time in its history. It won't be the last.

Ⓔ Davidson weathers a 30-point performance by Princeton's Bill Bradley to win the Charlotte Invitational, 102-68. The Wildcats' Terry Holland, who will later coach Davidson and Virginia, scores 13 on six-for-six shooting.

Ⓕ Kentucky grabs an NCAA-record 108 rebounds in a 102-59 rout of Mississippi and holds Ole Miss guard Don Kessinger (23.5 ppg) to just five points. Kessinger will later become an All-Star shortstop for the Chicago Cubs.

Ⓖ Texas Western grinds out a 62-56 win over North Texas as Miners center Jim "Bad News" Barnes, the school's first All-America, scores a game-high 22 points. The Miners finish second in the nation in defense, allowing only 55.3 ppg.

1964 NCAA Tournament

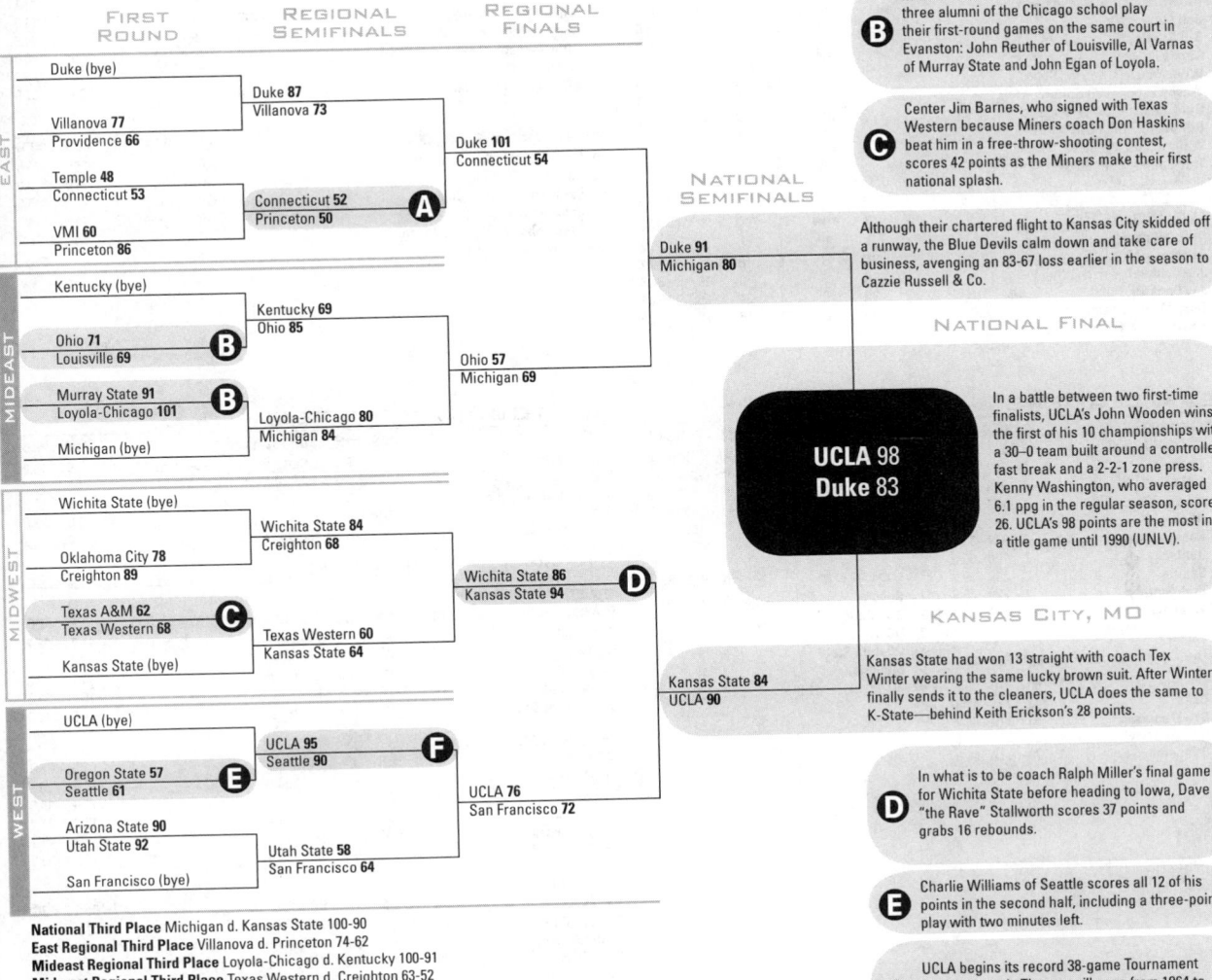

East

First Round
- Duke (bye)
- Villanova **77**, Providence **66**
- Temple **48**, Connecticut **53**
- VMI **60**, Princeton **86**

Regional Semifinals
- Duke **87**, Villanova **73**
- Connecticut **52**, Princeton **50** (A)

Regional Finals
- Duke **101**, Connecticut **54**

Mideast

First Round
- Kentucky (bye)
- Ohio **71**, Louisville **69** (B)
- Murray State **91**, Loyola-Chicago **101** (B)
- Michigan (bye)

Regional Semifinals
- Kentucky **69**, Ohio **85**
- Loyola-Chicago **80**, Michigan **84**

Regional Finals
- Ohio **57**, Michigan **69**

Midwest

First Round
- Wichita State (bye)
- Oklahoma City **78**, Creighton **89**
- Texas A&M **62**, Texas Western **68** (C)
- Kansas State (bye)

Regional Semifinals
- Wichita State **84**, Creighton **68**
- Texas Western **60**, Kansas State **64**

Regional Finals
- Wichita State **86**, Kansas State **94** (D)

West

First Round
- UCLA (bye)
- Oregon State **57**, Seattle **61** (E)
- Arizona State **90**, Utah State **92**
- San Francisco (bye)

Regional Semifinals
- UCLA **95**, Seattle **90** (F)
- Utah State **58**, San Francisco **64**

Regional Finals
- UCLA **76**, San Francisco **72**

National Semifinals

- Duke **91**, Michigan **80**

Although their chartered flight to Kansas City skidded off a runway, the Blue Devils calm down and take care of business, avenging an 83-67 loss earlier in the season to Cazzie Russell & Co.

- Kansas State **84**, UCLA **90**

Kansas State had won 13 straight with coach Tex Winter wearing the same lucky brown suit. After Winter finally sends it to the cleaners, UCLA does the same to K-State—behind Keith Erickson's 28 points.

National Final

UCLA 98
Duke 83

In a battle between two first-time finalists, UCLA's John Wooden wins the first of his 10 championships with a 30–0 team built around a controlled fast break and a 2-2-1 zone press. Kenny Washington, who averaged 6.1 ppg in the regular season, scores 26. UCLA's 98 points are the most in a title game until 1990 (UNLV).

Kansas City, MO

National Third Place Michigan d. Kansas State 100-90
East Regional Third Place Villanova d. Princeton 74-62
Mideast Regional Third Place Loyola-Chicago d. Kentucky 100-91
Midwest Regional Third Place Texas Western d. Creighton 63-52
West Regional Third Place Seattle d. Utah State 88-78

A Connecticut secures the win by stealing the ball from Princeton star Bill Bradley in the game's final seconds. Bradley hits 10 of 11 free throws, but none of his teammates get to the line.

B In what is deemed the St. Rita's High reunion, three alumni of the Chicago school play their first-round games on the same court in Evanston: John Reuther of Louisville, Al Varnas of Murray State and John Egan of Loyola.

C Center Jim Barnes, who signed with Texas Western because Miners coach Don Haskins beat him in a free-throw-shooting contest, scores 42 points as the Miners make their first national splash.

D In what is to be coach Ralph Miller's final game for Wichita State before heading to Iowa, Dave "the Rave" Stallworth scores 37 points and grabs 16 rebounds.

E Charlie Williams of Seattle scores all 12 of his points in the second half, including a three-point play with two minutes left.

F UCLA begins its record 38-game Tournament winning streak. The run will span from 1964 to 1974—not including 1966, when the Bruins failed to make the Tournament.

Tournament Leaders

INDIVIDUAL LEADERS

Scoring

		CL	POS	G	PTS	PPG
1	**Dave Stallworth**, Wichita State	JR	F	2	59	29.5
2	**Jeff Mullins**, Duke	SR	G/F	4	116	29.0
3	**Bill Bradley**, Princeton	JR	F	3	86	28.7
4	**Cazzie Russell**, Michigan	SO	G/F	3	77	25.7
5	**Willie Murrell**, Kansas State	SR	F	4	101	25.3
6	**Wayne Estes**, Utah State	JR	F	3	73	24.3
7	**Ollie Johnson**, San Francisco	JR	C	2	48	24.0
8	**Bill Buntin**, Michigan	JR	C	4	93	23.3
9	**Wally Jones**, Villanova	SR	G	3	69	23.0
10	**Troy Collier**, Utah State	SR	C	3	66	22.0

Minimum: 2 games

Field Goal Pct

		CL	POS	G	FG	FGA	PCT
1	**Ollie Johnson**, San Francisco	JR	C	2	15	22	68.2
2	**Al Varnas**, Murray State	SR	G	1	10	15	66.7
3	**Joe Caldwell**, Arizona State	SR	F	1	10	16	62.5
4	**Jay Buckley**, Duke	SR	C	4	24	39	61.5
	Terry Mobley, Kentucky	JR	G	2	16	26	61.5

Minimum: 10 made

Free Throw Pct

		CL	POS	G	FT	FTA	PCT
1	**Wayne Estes**, Utah State	JR	F	3	21	23	91.3
2	**Andy Stoglin**, Texas Western	JR	F	3	10	11	90.9
3	**Ollie Johnson**, San Francisco	JR	C	2	18	20	90.0
4	**Jeff Mullins**, Duke	SR	G/F	4	16	18	88.9
5	**Bill Buntin**, Michigan	JR	C	4	29	33	87.9

Minimum: 10 made

Rebounds Per Game

		CL	POS	G	REB	RPG
1	**Dave Stallworth**, Wichita State	JR	F	2	39	19.5
2	**Paul Silas**, Creighton	SR	F/C	3	57	19.0
3	**Les Hunter**, Loyola-Chicago	SR	C	3	46	15.3
	John Tresvant, Seattle	SR	F	3	46	15.3
5	**Ollie Johnson**, San Francisco	JR	C	2	30	15.0

Minimum: 2 games

TEAM LEADERS

Scoring

		G	PTS	PPG
1	**Loyola-Chicago**	3	281	93.7
2	**Duke**	4	362	90.5
3	**UCLA**	4	359	89.8
4	**Wichita State**	2	170	85.0
5	**Michigan**	4	333	83.3
6	**Kansas State**	4	332	83.0
7	**Kentucky**	2	160	80.0
8	**Seattle**	3	239	79.7
9	**Utah State**	3	228	76.0
10	**Villanova**	3	224	74.7

Minimum: 2 games

FG Pct

		G	FG	FGA	PCT
1	**Wichita State**	2	60	119	50.4
2	**Duke**	4	145	291	49.8
3	**San Francisco**	2	53	110	48.2
4	**Kansas State**	4	131	276	47.5
5	**Princeton**	3	79	172	45.9

FT Pct

		G	FT	FTA	PCT
1	**Princeton**	3	40	49	81.6
2	**Michigan**	4	75	94	79.8
3	**Wichita State**	2	50	63	79.4
4	**Texas Western**	3	47	65	72.3
5	**Loyola-Chicago**	3	75	106	70.8

Minimum: 2 games

Rebounds

		G	REB	RPG
1	**Seattle**	3	153	51.0
2	**Creighton**	3	141	47.0
3	**UCLA**	4	183	45.8
4	**Wichita State**	2	90	45.0
5	**Michigan**	4	174	43.5

Minimum: 2 games

ALL-TOURNAMENT TEAM

PLAYER	CL	POS	HT	SCHOOL	RPG	PPG
Walt Hazzard*	SR	G	6-2	UCLA	5.0	19.8
Bill Buntin	JR	C	6-7	Michigan	11.5	23.3
Gail Goodrich	JR	G	6-1	UCLA	4.8	18.8
Jeff Mullins	SR	G/F	6-4	Duke	8.0	29.0
Willie Murrell	SR	F	6-6	Kansas State	11.0	25.3

ALL-REGIONAL TEAMS

East

PLAYER	CL	POS	HT	SCHOOL	RPG	PPG
Bill Bradley	JR	F	6-5	Princeton	11.7	28.7
Wally Jones	SR	G	6-2	Villanova	6.3	23.0
Toby Kimball	JR	C	6-8	Connecticut	14.7	15.3
Jeff Mullins	SR	G/F	6-4	Duke	10.0	36.5
Steve Vacendak	SO	G	6-1	Duke	4.5	11.0

Mideast

PLAYER	CL	POS	HT	SCHOOL	RPG	PPG
Bill Buntin	JR	C	6-7	Michigan	11.5	20.5
Don Hilt	JR	F	6-4	Ohio	11.0	15.3
Les Hunter	SR	C	6-7	Loyola-Chicago	15.3	21.7
Jerry Jackson	SR	G/F	6-3	Ohio	7.3	17.7
Cazzie Russell	SO	G/F	6-5	Michigan	6.5	23.0

Midwest

PLAYER	CL	POS	HT	SCHOOL	RPG	PPG
Bobby Dibler	JR	G	5-10	Texas Western	2.7	9.0
Willie Murrell	SR	F	6-6	Kansas State	10.5	26.0
Paul Silas	SR	F/C	6-7	Creighton	19.0	17.0
Dave Stallworth	JR	F	6-7	Wichita State	19.5	29.5
Roger Suttner	SR	C	7-0	Kansas State	9.5	16.0

West

PLAYER	CL	POS	HT	SCHOOL	RPG	PPG
Walt Hazzard*	SR	G	6-2	UCLA	5.0	24.5
Troy Collier	SR	C	6-9	Utah State	11.7	22.0
Gail Goodrich	JR	G	6-1	UCLA	5.0	17.0
Ollie Johnson	JR	C	6-8	San Francisco	15.0	24.0
John Tresvant	SR	F	6-7	Seattle	15.3	14.3

* Most outstanding player

1964 NCAA TOURNAMENT BOX SCORES

87-73 (SWEET 16)

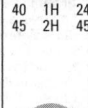

DUKE	MIN	FG	3FG	FT	REB	A	ST	BL	PF	TP
Jeff Mullins	40	19-28	-	5-6	12	1	-	-	1	43
Hack Tison	31	3-6	-	7-8	6	3	-	-	5	13
Jay Buckley	40	3-8	-	3-6	12	2	-	-	0	9
Steve Vacendak	25	3-5	-	2-3	6	2	-	-	0	8
Jack Marin	9	2-5	-	4-6	5	0	-	-	1	8
Ron Herbster	10	2-3	-	0-0	0	0	-	-	0	4
Buzzy Harrison	13	1-8	-	0-0	1	1	-	-	2	2
Dennis Ferguson	32	0-3	-	0-0	2	1	-	-	4	0
TOTALS	200	33-66	-	21-29	44	10	-	-	13	87
Percentages		50.0		72.4						

Coach: Vic Bubas

49	1H	33
38	2H	40

VILLANOVA	MIN	FG	3FG	FT	REB	A	ST	BL	PF	TP
Wally Jones	40	6-20	-	6-7	6	3	-	-	3	18
Bill Melchionni	36	9-17	-	0-2	3	1	-	-	4	18
Eric Erickson	12	5-7	-	0-2	2	0	-	-	2	10
Richie Moore	35	4-12	-	0-0	3	2	-	-	3	8
Jim Washington	27	2-7	-	4-4	11	0	-	-	5	8
Al Sallee	34	3-7	-	0-0	6	1	-	-	1	6
Bernie Schaffer	14	2-4	-	1-1	4	0	-	-	3	5
George Leftwich	2	0-1	-	0-0	0	0	-	-	1	0
TOTALS	200	31-75	-	11-16	35	7	-	-	22	73
Percentages		41.3		68.8						

Coach: Jack Kraft

Officials: Mihalik, Machock
Attendance: 12,400

52-50 (SWEET 16)

CONNECTICUT	MIN	FG	3FG	FT	REB	A	ST	BL	PF	TP
Toby Kimball	40	6-11	-	4-8	13	0	-	-	2	16
Dominic Perno	40	4-15	-	4-5	3	3	-	-	2	12
Alan Ritter	37	5-9	-	0-0	0	0	-	-	1	10
Ed Slomcenski	40	1-4	-	5-5	8	1	-	-	1	7
William Dellasala	16	2-3	-	0-0	3	0	-	-	1	4
Daniel Hesford	27	1-2	-	1-1	1	0	-	-	4	3
TOTALS	200	19-44	-	14-19	28	4	-	-	11	52
Percentages		43.2		73.7						

Coach: Fred A. Shabel

27	1H	28
25	2H	22

PRINCETON	MIN	FG	3FG	FT	REB	A	ST	BL	PF	TP
Bill Bradley	40	6-15	-	10-11	10	1	-	-	3	22
Robert Haarlow	40	5-13	-	0-0	7	0	-	-	0	10
Don Rodenbach	25	3-6	-	0-0	0	0	-	-	0	6
Walter Uhle	30	2-5	-	0-0	4	1	-	-	1	4
Donald Niemann	21	1-1	-	0-0	1	1	-	-	2	2
Bill Howard	19	1-3	-	0-0	3	0	-	-	3	2
Edward Steube	13	1-4	-	0-0	0	0	-	-	2	2
William Kingston	2	1-1	-	0-0	0	0	-	-	1	2
Don Roth	10	0-0	-	0-0	0	0	-	-	1	0
TOTALS	200	20-48	-	10-11	25	3	-	-	13	50
Percentages		41.7		90.9						

Coach: Butch van Breda Kolff

Officials: Tanksley, Scobey
Attendance: 12,400

85-69 (SWEET 16)

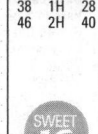

OHIO	MIN	FG	3FG	FT	REB	A	ST	BL	PF	TP
Jerry Jackson	-	11-22	-	3-5	11	-	-	-	1	25
Paul Storey	-	8-15	-	3-6	9	-	-	-	0	19
Mike Haley	-	7-14	-	1-1	7	-	-	-	1	15
Don Hilt	-	4-9	-	6-7	9	-	-	-	4	14
Tom Davis	-	1-5	-	5-7	3	-	-	-	2	7
Charles Gill	-	1-1	-	1-3	5	-	-	-	3	3
Dave Brown	-	1-2	-	0-0	1	-	-	-	0	2
Joe Barry	-	0-0	-	0-0	0	-	-	-	0	0
Lloyd Buck	-	0-0	-	0-0	0	-	-	-	0	0
Tom Weirich	-	0-0	-	0-0	0	-	-	-	0	0
TOTALS	-	33-68	-	19-29	45	-	-	-	11	85
Percentages		48.5		65.5						

Coach: Jim Snyder

40	1H	24
45	2H	45

KENTUCKY	MIN	FG	3FG	FT	REB	A	ST	BL	PF	TP
Larry Conley	-	7-16	-	3-3	5	-	-	-	5	17
Terry Mobley	-	8-13	-	1-1	5	-	-	-	3	17
Randy Embry	-	5-12	-	1-3	2	-	-	-	2	11
Ted Deeken	-	5-17	-	0-1	14	-	-	-	4	10
Cotton Nash	-	4-14	-	2-3	9	-	-	-	3	10
Sam Harper	-	1-2	-	0-1	1	-	-	-	1	2
Charles Ishmael	-	1-5	-	0-0	1	-	-	-	1	2
John Adams	-	0-0	-	0-0	0	-	-	-	1	0
Tommy Kron	-	0-1	-	0-0	1	-	-	-	0	0
TOTALS	-	31-80	-	7-12	38	-	-	-	20	69
Percentages		38.8		58.3						

Coach: Adolph Rupp

Officials: Eisenstein, Honzo
Attendance: 9,948

84-80 (SWEET 16)

MICHIGAN	MIN	FG	3FG	FT	REB	A	ST	BL	PF	TP
Bill Buntin	-	9-23	-	8-10	13	-	-	-	4	26
Cazzie Russell	-	8-15	-	5-8	7	-	-	-	2	21
Larry Tregoning	-	7-15	-	0-0	14	-	-	-	5	14
Bob Cantrell	-	3-6	-	6-8	3	-	-	-	2	12
Oliver Darden	-	4-10	-	1-1	6	-	-	-	4	9
Jim Myers	-	1-4	-	0-0	3	-	-	-	1	2
George Pomey	-	0-0	-	0-0	1	-	-	-	1	0
TOTALS	-	32-73	-	20-27	47	-	-	-	19	84
Percentages		43.8		74.1						

Coach: Dave Strack

43	1H	36
41	2H	44

LOYOLA-CHICAGO	MIN	FG	3FG	FT	REB	A	ST	BL	PF	TP
Les Hunter	-	11-18	-	3-6	6	-	-	-	5	25
Jim Coleman	-	7-14	-	3-4	6	-	-	-	3	17
Ron Miller	-	7-26	-	2-5	7	-	-	-	2	16
Vic Rouse	-	5-13	-	2-3	14	-	-	-	2	12
John Egan	-	3-15	-	4-5	3	-	-	-	5	10
Eddie Manzke	-	0-1	-	0-0	0	-	-	-	0	0
Chuck Wood	-	0-1	-	0-0	1	-	-	-	1	0
TOTALS	-	33-88	-	14-23	37	-	-	-	18	80
Percentages		37.5		60.9						

Coach: George Ireland

Officials: Bello, Fox
Attendance: 9,948

84-68 (SWEET 16)

WICHITA STATE	MIN	FG	3FG	FT	REB	A	ST	BL	PF	TP
Dave Stallworth	-	7-17	-	8-9	23	-	-	-	3	22
Nate Bowman	-	5-10	-	6-9	8	-	-	-	4	16
Dave Leach	-	3-5	-	8-10	3	-	-	-	3	14
Kelly Pete	-	4-7	-	3-4	7	-	-	-	5	11
Vernon Smith	-	1-5	-	7-7	5	-	-	-	3	9
Larry Nosich	-	4-5	-	0-1	2	-	-	-	3	8
John Criss	-	1-6	-	0-0	1	-	-	-	5	2
Gerald Davis	-	1-1	-	0-0	0	-	-	-	1	2
Gerard Reimond	-	0-0	-	0-1	1	-	-	-	0	0
Donny Rowland	-	0-0	-	0-0	0	-	-	-	0	0
TOTALS	-	26-56	-	32-41	50	-	-	-	27	84
Percentages		46.4		78.0						

Coach: Ralph Miller

38	1H	28
46	2H	40

CREIGHTON	MIN	FG	3FG	FT	REB	A	ST	BL	PF	TP
Paul Silas	-	5-12	-	12-15	17	-	-	-	2	22
Chuck Officer	-	10-25	-	1-3	3	-	-	-	4	21
Bob Miles	-	3-6	-	1-2	4	-	-	-	3	7
Fritz Pointer	-	3-10	-	1-1	5	-	-	-	5	7
Elton McGriff	-	1-7	-	4-9	6	-	-	-	5	6
Charlie Brown	-	1-8	-	1-3	2	-	-	-	2	3
Harry Forehand	-	1-2	-	0-0	0	-	-	-	2	2
Tom Apke	-	0-1	-	0-1	3	-	-	-	4	0
Loren James	-	0-0	-	0-2	0	-	-	-	1	0
TOTALS	-	24-71	-	20-36	40	-	-	-	28	68
Percentages		33.8		55.6						

Coach: John J. McManus

Officials: Marick, Lloyd
Attendance: 10,811

64-60 (SWEET 16)

KANSAS STATE	MIN	FG	3FG	FT	REB	A	ST	BL	PF	TP
Willie Murrell	-	9-24	-	6-8	11	1	-	-	2	24
Roger Suttner	-	5-10	-	6-8	13	0	-	-	4	16
Sammy Robinson	-	5-6	-	4-6	4	1	-	-	1	14
Jeff Simons	-	2-7	-	2-3	4	4	-	-	2	6
Max Moss	-	0-3	-	2-2	4	4	-	-	0	2
Gary Williams	-	1-2	-	0-0	0	0	-	-	2	2
TOTALS	-	22-52	-	20-27	36	10	-	-	11	64
Percentages		42.3		74.1						

Coach: Tex Winter

23	1H	21
41	2H	39

TEXAS WESTERN	MIN	FG	3FG	FT	REB	A	ST	BL	PF	TP
Charlie Banks	-	8-16	-	4-6	6	1	-	-	2	20
Bobby Dibler	-	6-15	-	1-1	4	3	-	-	1	13
Andy Stoglin	-	5-12	-	2-2	5	1	-	-	5	12
Harry Flournoy	-	3-5	-	1-1	5	3	-	-	3	7
Jim Barnes	-	1-5	-	2-3	9	1	-	-	5	4
Orsten Artis	-	1-12	-	0-1	4	4	-	-	2	2
Ron Shockley	-	1-2	-	0-0	0	0	-	-	1	2
Steve Tredennick	-	0-1	-	0-0	0	0	-	-	0	0
TOTALS	-	25-68	-	10-14	33	13	-	-	19	60
Percentages		36.8		71.4						

Coach: Don Haskins

Officials: Filiberti, Fouts
Attendance: 10,811

UCLA 95-90 Seattle (Sweet 16)

	1H	2H
UCLA	49	46
Seattle	39	51

UCLA	MIN	FG	3FG	FT	REB	A	ST	BL	PF	TP
Walt Hazzard	-	9-14	-	8-11	7	-	-	-	3	26
Jack Hirsch	-	8-12	-	5-5	13	-	-	-	5	21
Gail Goodrich	-	6-22	-	7-11	6	-	-	-	4	19
Fred Slaughter	-	6-10	-	1-3	13	-	-	-	5	13
Keith Erickson	-	3-13	-	1-4	13	-	-	-	5	7
Kenny Washington	-	3-4	-	1-4	3	-	-	-	4	7
Doug McIntosh	-	1-1	-	0-1	1	-	-	-	1	2
Chuck Darrow	-	0-0	-	0-0	0	-	-	-	0	0
Vaughn Hoffman	-	0-0	-	0-0	0	-	-	-	0	0
Mike Huggins	-	0-0	-	0-0	0	-	-	-	0	0
Kim Stewart	-	0-1	-	0-0	0	-	-	-	2	0
TOTALS	-	**36-77**	-	**23-39**	**56**	-	-	-	**29**	**95**
Percentages		46.8		59.0						

Coach: John Wooden

SEATTLE	MIN	FG	3FG	FT	REB	A	ST	BL	PF	TP
John Tresvant	-	5-15	-	10-16	20	-	-	-	3	20
L.J. Wheeler	-	7-16	-	6-11	8	-	-	-	4	20
Greg Vermillion	-	6-9	-	3-3	5	-	-	-	5	15
Charlie Williams	-	5-20	-	2-4	13	-	-	-	5	12
Ralph Heyward	-	3-8	-	3-5	4	-	-	-	4	9
Rich Turney	-	2-6	-	4-4	2	-	-	-	5	8
Peller Phillips	-	2-8	-	2-2	4	-	-	-	4	6
Jack Tebbs	-	0-0	-	0-0	0	-	-	-	1	0
TOTALS	-	**30-82**	-	**30-45**	**56**	-	-	-	**31**	**90**
Percentages		36.6		66.7						

Coach: Bob Boyd

Officials: George, Magnusson
Attendance: 9,661

San Francisco 64-58 Utah State (Sweet 16)

	1H	2H
San Francisco	29	35
Utah State	25	33

SAN FRANCISCO	MIN	FG	3FG	FT	REB	A	ST	BL	PF	TP
Ollie Johnson	-	9-13	-	8-9	17	-	-	-	3	26
Joe Ellis	-	6-13	-	3-4	4	-	-	-	1	15
Jim Brovelli	-	4-8	-	0-0	1	-	-	-	0	8
Erwin Mueller	-	4-8	-	0-2	4	-	-	-	5	8
Dave Lee	-	1-3	-	1-1	2	-	-	-	5	3
Dick Brainard	-	1-4	-	0-2	4	-	-	-	1	2
Ed Thomas	-	1-4	-	0-2	1	-	-	-	3	2
Russ Gumina	-	0-0	-	0-0	0	-	-	-	0	0
TOTALS	-	**26-53**	-	**12-20**	**33**	-	-	-	**18**	**64**
Percentages		49.1		60.0						

Coach: Peter P. Peletta

UTAH STATE	MIN	FG	3FG	FT	REB	A	ST	BL	PF	TP
Troy Collier	-	9-18	-	4-6	14	-	-	-	3	22
Wayne Estes	-	6-19	-	9-9	11	-	-	-	4	21
Leroy Walker	-	7-16	-	1-2	4	-	-	-	3	15
Mickey Dittebrand	-	0-2	-	0-0	3	-	-	-	0	0
Myron Long	-	0-6	-	0-0	3	-	-	-	0	0
Gary Watts	-	0-4	-	0-0	1	-	-	-	5	0
TOTALS	-	**22-65**	-	**14-17**	**36**	-	-	-	**15**	**58**
Percentages		33.8		82.4						

Coach: Ladell Andersen

Officials: Glennon, Watson
Attendance: 9,500

Duke 101-54 Connecticut (Elite 8)

	1H	2H
Duke	62	39
Connecticut	27	27

DUKE	MIN	FG	3FG	FT	REB	A	ST	BL	PF	TP
Jeff Mullins	33	14-23	-	2-2	8	5	-	-	1	30
Hack Tison	27	4-8	-	6-7	8	2	-	-	3	14
Steve Vacendak	16	7-7	-	0-0	3	1	-	-	1	14
Jay Buckley	30	5-7	-	2-3	6	2	-	-	3	12
Dennis Ferguson	22	3-4	-	0-0	1	6	-	-	1	6
Buzzy Harrison	23	2-6	-	1-1	2	1	-	-	0	5
Frank Harscher	6	2-3	-	1-1	3	0	-	-	2	5
Ron Herbster	14	2-3	-	0-1	2	2	-	-	3	4
Jack Marin	9	2-3	-	0-0	0	1	-	-	5	4
Ray Cox	5	1-2	-	1-2	1	2	-	-	1	3
Brent Kitching	9	1-6	-	0-1	2	0	-	-	1	2
Ted Mann	6	0-3	-	2-3	5	0	-	-	0	2
TOTALS	**200**	**43-75**	-	**15-21**	**41**	**22**	-	-	**21**	**101**
Percentages		57.3		71.4						

Coach: Vic Bubas

CONNECTICUT	MIN	FG	3FG	FT	REB	A	ST	BL	PF	TP
Toby Kimball	36	6-21	-	6-8	14	1	-	-	3	18
Alan Ritter	25	4-8	-	0-0	0	0	-	-	1	8
Daniel Hesford	22	3-6	-	1-1	3	1	-	-	2	7
William Dellasala	12	3-5	-	1-1	1	2	-	-	3	7
Dominic Perno	32	2-7	-	1-3	3	3	-	-	2	5
Ed Slomcenski	25	1-5	-	1-2	6	1	-	-	1	3
Chris Witcomb	12	1-4	-	0-1	1	0	-	-	0	2
Thomas Capiga	8	1-4	-	0-0	1	0	-	-	3	2
Kenneth Whitney	12	0-3	-	1-3	0	0	-	-	1	1
Kenneth Libertoff	9	0-5	-	1-3	2	1	-	-	2	1
Charles Talbott	4	0-1	-	0-0	1	0	-	-	0	0
Dennis Stanek	3	0-0	-	0-1	0	0	-	-	0	0
TOTALS	**200**	**21-69**	-	**12-23**	**32**	**9**	-	-	**18**	**54**
Percentages		30.4		52.2						

Coach: Fred A. Shabel

Officials: Mihalik, Machock
Attendance: 12,400

Michigan 69-57 Ohio (Elite 8)

	1H	2H
Michigan	32	37
Ohio	27	30

MICHIGAN	MIN	FG	3FG	FT	REB	A	ST	BL	PF	TP
Cazzie Russell	-	9-20	-	7-7	6	-	-	-	0	25
Bill Buntin	-	6-17	-	3-3	10	-	-	-	4	15
Bob Cantrell	-	2-2	-	2-2	1	-	-	-	2	6
Oliver Darden	-	3-5	-	0-0	7	-	-	-	3	6
Jim Myers	-	2-10	-	2-2	7	-	-	-	1	6
George Pomey	-	3-7	-	0-0	2	-	-	-	1	6
Larry Tregoning	-	1-3	-	1-2	3	-	-	-	2	3
Doug Herner	-	0-1	-	2-3	0	-	-	-	0	2
TOTALS	-	**26-65**	-	**17-19**	**36**	-	-	-	**13**	**69**
Percentages		40.0		89.5						

Coach: Dave Strack

OHIO	MIN	FG	3FG	FT	REB	A	ST	BL	PF	TP
Don Hilt	-	8-15	-	2-3	9	-	-	-	1	18
Jerry Jackson	-	6-14	-	1-2	7	-	-	-	2	13
Paul Storey	-	6-12	-	0-0	3	-	-	-	2	12
Mike Haley	-	4-16	-	2-6	11	-	-	-	3	10
Joe Barry	-	0-0	-	2-2	0	-	-	-	0	2
Charles Gill	-	1-5	-	0-0	3	-	-	-	4	2
Lloyd Buck	-	0-0	-	0-0	0	-	-	-	0	0
Tom Davis	-	0-1	-	0-0	0	-	-	-	0	0
Gary Lashley	-	0-0	-	0-0	0	-	-	-	1	0
James Schoon	-	0-0	-	0-0	0	-	-	-	1	0
Tom Weirich	-	0-2	-	0-0	0	-	-	-	1	0
TOTALS	-	**25-65**	-	**7-13**	**33**	-	-	-	**15**	**57**
Percentages		38.5		53.8						

Coach: Jim Snyder

Officials: Bello, Honzo
Attendance: 8,706

Kansas State 94-86 Wichita State (Elite 8)

	1H	2H
Kansas State	46	48
Wichita State	33	53

KANSAS STATE	MIN	FG	3FG	FT	REB	A	ST	BL	PF	TP
Willie Murrell	-	11-24	-	6-10	10	2	-	-	1	28
Roger Suttner	-	7-11	-	2-4	6	1	-	-	5	16
Jeff Simons	-	6-14	-	2-3	6	3	-	-	5	14
Max Moss	-	4-8	-	3-5	2	2	-	-	1	11
Sammy Robinson	-	2-7	-	7-10	7	5	-	-	3	11
Gary Williams	-	3-3	-	2-2	6	1	-	-	4	8
Ron Paradis	-	2-2	-	2-3	1	0	-	-	1	6
TOTALS	-	**35-69**	-	**24-37**	**38**	**14**	-	-	**20**	**94**
Percentages		50.7		64.9						

Coach: Tex Winter

WICHITA STATE	MIN	FG	3FG	FT	REB	A	ST	BL	PF	TP
Dave Stallworth	-	14-22	-	9-12	16	1	-	-	3	37
Kelly Pete	-	7-12	-	3-3	5	2	-	-	2	17
Nate Bowman	-	4-6	-	4-5	8	1	-	-	5	12
John Criss	-	4-9	-	1-1	1	6	-	-	5	9
Dave Leach	-	3-10	-	1-1	5	3	-	-	5	7
Vernon Smith	-	2-3	-	0-0	3	1	-	-	4	4
Gerald Davis	-	0-1	-	0-0	2	0	-	-	1	0
Larry Nosich	-	0-0	-	0-0	0	0	-	-	0	0
Donny Rowland	-	0-0	-	0-0	0	0	-	-	0	0
TOTALS	-	**34-63**	-	**18-22**	**40**	**14**	-	-	**25**	**86**
Percentages		54.0		81.8						

Coach: Ralph Miller

Officials: Filiberti, Fouts
Attendance: 10,815

UCLA 76-72 San Francisco (Elite 8)

	1H	2H
UCLA	28	48
San Francisco	36	36

UCLA	MIN	FG	3FG	FT	REB	A	ST	BL	PF	TP
Walt Hazzard	-	9-19	-	5-5	3	-	-	-	3	23
Gail Goodrich	-	6-18	-	3-5	4	-	-	-	1	15
Jack Hirsch	-	5-11	-	4-5	7	-	-	-	3	14
Fred Slaughter	-	4-9	-	1-4	8	-	-	-	4	9
Keith Erickson	-	3-10	-	1-6	10	-	-	-	4	7
Kenny Washington	-	2-4	-	1-4	3	-	-	-	1	5
Doug McIntosh	-	0-1	-	3-5	4	-	-	-	1	3
TOTALS	-	**29-72**	-	**18-34**	**39**	-	-	-	**17**	**76**
Percentages		40.3		52.9						

Coach: John Wooden

SAN FRANCISCO	MIN	FG	3FG	FT	REB	A	ST	BL	PF	TP
Ollie Johnson	-	6-9	-	10-11	13	-	-	-	2	22
Erwin Mueller	-	6-12	-	3-5	7	-	-	-	4	15
Jim Brovelli	-	5-8	-	1-1	2	-	-	-	4	11
Joe Ellis	-	5-14	-	1-2	10	-	-	-	3	11
Dave Lee	-	2-5	-	2-2	4	-	-	-	4	6
Dick Brainard	-	2-8	-	1-2	4	-	-	-	5	5
Russ Gumina	-	1-1	-	0-0	1	-	-	-	1	2
Ed Thomas	-	0-0	-	0-0	2	-	-	-	2	0
TOTALS	-	**27-57**	-	**18-23**	**43**	-	-	-	**25**	**72**
Percentages		47.4		78.3						

Coach: Peter P. Peletta

Officials: Glennon, Watson
Technicals: San Francisco (Brovelli)
Attendance: 9,416

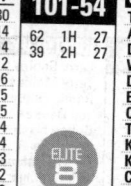

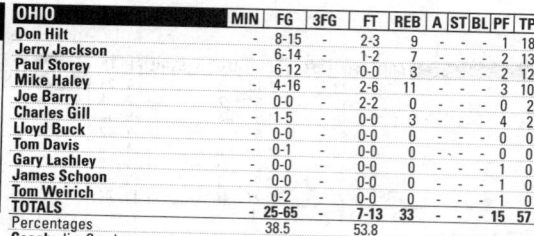

DUKE	MIN	FG	3FG	FT	REB	A	ST	BL	PF	TP
Jay Buckley	-	11-16	-	3-5	14	-	-	-	4	25
Jeff Mullins	-	8-19	-	5-6	8	-	-	-	1	21
Buzzy Harrison	-	6-15	-	2-3	2	-	-	-	2	14
Dennis Ferguson	-	6-11	-	0-1	0	-	-	-	0	12
Hack Tison	-	3-10	-	6-10	13	-	-	-	4	12
Steve Vacendak	-	2-5	-	1-2	2	-	-	-	1	5
Jack Marin	-	1-2	-	0-0	2	-	-	-	1	2
Ron Herbster	-	0-0	-	0-0	0	-	-	-	0	0
TOTALS	**-**	**37-78**	**-**	**17-27**	**41**	**-**	**-**	**-**	**13**	**91**
Percentages		47.4		63.0						
Coach: Vic Bubas										

91-80

48	1H	39
43	2H	41

FINAL 4

MICHIGAN	MIN	FG	3FG	FT	REB	A	ST	BL	PF	TP
Cazzie Russell	-	13-19	-	5-6	8	-	-	-	5	31
Bill Buntin	-	8-18	-	3-3	9	-	-	-	5	19
Bob Cantrell	-	6-10	-	0-0	4	-	-	-	2	12
Larry Tregoning	-	3-11	-	2-2	6	-	-	-	4	8
Oliver Darden	-	2-6	-	1-1	9	-	-	-	5	5
Jim Myers	-	2-5	-	0-0	5	-	-	-	2	4
George Pomey	-	0-1	-	1-2	0	-	-	-	0	1
Doug Herner	-	0-1	-	0-0	0	-	-	-	0	0
TOTALS	**-**	**34-71**	**-**	**12-14**	**41**	**-**	**-**	**-**	**23**	**80**
Percentages		47.9		85.7						
Coach: Dave Strack										

Officials: Fouts, Glennon
Attendance: 10,731

UCLA	MIN	FG	3FG	FT	REB	A	ST	BL	PF	TP
Keith Erickson	-	10-21	-	8-9	10	1	-	-	2	28
Walt Hazzard	-	7-10	-	5-7	7	9	-	-	2	19
Gail Goodrich	-	7-18	-	0-0	6	2	-	-	3	14
Kenny Washington	-	5-11	-	3-4	6	0	-	-	1	13
Doug McIntosh	-	3-5	-	2-3	10	1	-	-	3	8
Jack Hirsch	-	2-11	-	0-0	1	0	-	-	4	4
Fred Slaughter	-	2-6	-	0-0	5	0	-	-	4	4
TOTALS	**-**	**36-82**	**-**	**18-23**	**45**	**13**	**-**	**-**	**19**	**90**
Percentages		43.9		78.3						
Coach: John Wooden										

90-84

43	1H	41
47	2H	43

FINAL 4

KANSAS STATE	MIN	FG	3FG	FT	REB	A	ST	BL	PF	TP
Willie Murrell	-	13-22	-	3-5	13	2	-	-	3	29
Jeff Simons	-	10-17	-	4-6	7	2	-	-	3	24
Ron Paradis	-	5-9	-	0-0	1	2	-	-	0	10
Max Moss	-	3-9	-	1-1	5	4	-	-	3	7
Roger Suttner	-	3-9	-	0-5	10	0	-	-	2	6
Sammy Robinson	-	2-7	-	0-1	5	2	-	-	4	4
Gary Williams	-	1-1	-	2-3	1	1	-	-	2	4
Dick Barnard	-	0-1	-	0-0	0	1	-	-	0	0
Joe Gottfrid	-	0-0	-	0-0	0	0	-	-	1	0
David Nelson	-	0-1	-	0-0	0	0	-	-	1	0
TOTALS	**-**	**37-76**	**-**	**10-21**	**42**	**14**	**-**	**-**	**19**	**84**
Percentages		48.7		47.6						
Coach: Tex Winter										

Officials: Mihalik, Honzo
Attendance: 10,731

MICHIGAN	MIN	FG	3FG	FT	REB	A	ST	BL	PF	TP
Bill Buntin	-	9-18	-	15-17	14	1	-	-	2	33
Bob Cantrell	-	8-17	-	4-5	3	2	-	-	2	20
Oliver Darden	-	8-16	-	1-3	14	2	-	-	3	17
Larry Tregoning	-	6-13	-	4-5	8	1	-	-	1	16
Jim Myers	-	3-10	-	1-2	6	2	-	-	1	7
George Pomey	-	2-4	-	0-0	2	0	-	-	1	4
John Clawson	-	1-3	-	1-2	2	0	-	-	0	3
Doug Herner	-	0-3	-	0-0	1	10	-	-	3	0
TOTALS	**-**	**37-84**	**-**	**26-34**	**50**	**18**	**-**	**-**	**13**	**100**
Percentages		44.0		76.5						
Coach: Dave Strack										

100-90

52	1H	47
48	2H	43

3RD PLACE

KANSAS STATE	MIN	FG	3FG	FT	REB	A	ST	BL	PF	TP
Willie Murrell	-	10-19	-	0-0	10	1	-	-	2	20
Roger Suttner	-	7-15	-	6-8	5	6	-	-	4	20
Sammy Robinson	-	6-11	-	0-0	6	1	-	-	2	12
Max Moss	-	4-9	-	3-3	3	6	-	-	5	11
Jeff Simons	-	4-8	-	3-3	3	5	-	-	3	11
David Nelson	-	2-6	-	1-1	2	0	-	-	2	5
Ron Paradis	-	1-4	-	3-4	0	0	-	-	0	5
Gary Williams	-	2-4	-	0-1	2	0	-	-	0	4
Joe Gottfrid	-	1-1	-	0-0	2	1	-	-	3	2
Dick Barnard	-	0-1	-	0-0	3	0	-	-	1	0
James Hoffman	-	0-0	-	0-0	0	0	-	-	0	0
Lou Poma	-	0-1	-	0-0	1	0	-	-	1	0
TOTALS	**-**	**37-79**	**-**	**16-20**	**37**	**20**	**-**	**-**	**23**	**90**
Percentages		46.8		80.0						
Coach: Tex Winter										

Officials: Fouts, Honzo
Attendance: 10,864

UCLA	MIN	FG	3FG	FT	REB	A	ST	BL	PF	TP
Gail Goodrich	-	9-18	-	9-9	3	1	-	-	1	27
Kenny Washington	-	11-16	-	4-4	12	1	-	-	4	26
Jack Hirsch	-	5-9	-	3-5	6	6	-	-	3	13
Walt Hazzard	-	4-10	-	3-5	3	8	-	-	5	11
Keith Erickson	-	2-7	-	4-4	5	1	-	-	5	8
Doug McIntosh	-	4-9	-	0-0	11	1	-	-	2	8
Chuck Darrow	-	0-1	-	3-4	1	0	-	-	2	3
Vaughn Hoffman	-	1-2	-	0-0	0	0	-	-	0	2
Mike Huggins	-	0-1	-	0-1	1	2	-	-	2	0
Richard Levin	-	0-1	-	0-0	0	0	-	-	0	0
Fred Slaughter	-	0-1	-	0-0	1	2	-	-	0	0
Kim Stewart	-	0-1	-	0-0	0	0	-	-	1	0
TOTALS	**-**	**36-76**	**-**	**26-32**	**43**	**22**	**-**	**-**	**25**	**98**
Percentages		47.4		81.2						
Coach: John Wooden										

98-83

50	1H	38
48	2H	45

NCAA FINAL 1964

DUKE	MIN	FG	3FG	FT	REB	A	ST	BL	PF	TP
Jeff Mullins	-	9-21	-	4-4	4	1	-	-	5	22
Jay Buckley	-	5-8	-	8-12	9	0	-	-	4	18
Jack Marin	-	8-16	-	0-1	10	1	-	-	3	16
Hack Tison	-	3-8	-	1-1	1	2	-	-	2	7
Steve Vacendak	-	2-7	-	3-3	6	0	-	-	4	7
Dennis Ferguson	-	2-6	-	0-1	1	4	-	-	3	4
Ted Mann	-	0-0	-	3-4	2	0	-	-	1	3
Buzzy Harrison	-	1-1	-	0-0	1	1	-	-	2	2
Ron Herbster	-	1-4	-	0-2	0	0	-	-	0	2
Brent Kitching	-	1-1	-	0-0	1	0	-	-	0	2
Ray Cox	-	0-0	-	0-0	0	0	-	-	0	0
Frank Harscher	-	0-0	-	0-0	0	0	-	-	0	0
TOTALS	**-**	**32-72**	**-**	**19-28**	**35**	**9**	**-**	**-**	**24**	**83**
Percentages		44.4		67.9						
Coach: Vic Bubas										

Officials: Mihalik, Glennon
Attendance: 10,864

National Invitation Tournament (NIT)

First round: Saint Joseph's d. Miami (FL) 86-76, NYU d. Syracuse 77-68, Army d. St. Bonaventure 64-62, Drake d. Pittsburgh 87-82
Quarterfinals: Bradley d. Saint Joseph's 83-81, NYU d. DePaul 79-66, New Mexico d. Drake 65-60, Army d. Duquesne 67-65 (OT)
Semifinals: New Mexico d. NYU 72-65, Bradley d. Army 67-52
Third place: Army d. NYU 60-59
Championship: Bradley d. New Mexico 86-54
MVP: Lavern Tart, Bradley

1964-65: Twice Is Nice, Too

With a significant part of its championship squad graduated, UCLA (28–2) reloaded instead of rebuilt. But its second consecutive NCAA title was nearly overshadowed by superstar forward Bill Bradley, who carried Princeton to the Final Four. There the Tigers lost to a bigger, faster Michigan team that "held" Bradley to 29 points (just below his season average)—but the future New York Knick and U.S. senator scored 58 in the national third-place game to set a Tournament record (eclipsed in 1970 by Notre Dame's Austin Carr). Against Michigan, UCLA standout Gail Goodrich set two championship-game scoring records: most points (42) and free throws made (18)—the latter still a record. The Bruins became the first team to average triple digits in scoring (100.0) for a Tournament.

Bradley earned Tourney MOP honors and was the unanimous choice for national player of the year after averaging 30.5 ppg. The San Francisco Warriors used their first two picks in the NBA draft to select Davidson's Fred Hetzel and Miami's Rick Barry, who led the nation with 37.4 ppg. Barry became the only man ever to lead the NCAA, NBA and ABA in scoring.

Major Conference Standings

AAWU

	Conference W	L	Pct	Overall W	L	Pct
UCLA⊕	14	0	1.000	28	2	.933
Stanford	9	5	.643	15	8	.652
Southern California	8	6	.571	14	12	.538
Oregon State	7	7	.500	16	10	.615
Washington State	6	8	.429	9	17	.346
Washington	5	9	.357	9	16	.360
California	4	10	.286	8	15	.348
Oregon	3	11	.214	9	17	.346

ACC

	Conference W	L	Pct	Overall W	L	Pct
Duke	11	3	.786	20	5	.800
NC State⊕	10	4	.714	21	5	.808
Maryland	10	4	.714	18	8	.692
North Carolina	10	4	.714	15	9	.625
Wake Forest	6	8	.429	12	15	.444
Clemson	4	10	.286	8	15	.348
Virginia	3	11	.214	7	18	.280
South Carolina	2	12	.143	6	17	.261

Tournament: **NC State d. Duke 91-85**
Tournament MVP: **Larry Worsley**, NC State

Big Eight

	Conference W	L	Pct	Overall W	L	Pct
Oklahoma State⊕	12	2	.857	20	7	.741
Kansas	9	5	.643	17	8	.680
Missouri	8	6	.571	13	11	.542
Colorado	8	6	.571	13	12	.520
Iowa State	6	8	.429	9	16	.360
Kansas State	5	9	.357	12	13	.480
Nebraska	5	9	.357	10	15	.400
Oklahoma	3	11	.214	8	17	.320

Big Sky

	Conference W	L	Pct	Overall W	L	Pct
Weber State	8	2	.800	22	3	.880
Gonzaga	6	4	.600	18	8	.692
Montana State	6	4	.600	15	10	.600
Idaho State	4	6	.400	7	19	.269
Idaho	4	6	.400	6	19	.240
Montana	2	8	.200	11	15	.423

Big Ten

	Conference W	L	Pct	Overall W	L	Pct
Michigan⊕	13	1	.929	24	4	.857
Minnesota	11	3	.786	19	5	.792
Illinois	10	4	.714	18	6	.750
Indiana	9	5	.643	19	5	.792
Iowa	8	6	.571	14	10	.583
Ohio State	6	8	.429	12	12	.500
Purdue	5	9	.357	12	12	.500
Wisconsin	4	10	.286	9	13	.429
Northwestern	3	11	.214	7	17	.292
Michigan State	1	13	.071	5	18	.217

Ivy

	Conference W	L	Pct	Overall W	L	Pct
Princeton⊕	13	1	.929	23	6	.793
Cornell	11	3	.786	19	5	.792
Penn	10	4	.714	15	10	.600
Yale	7	7	.500	10	12	.455
Harvard	6	8	.429	11	12	.478
Columbia	5	9	.357	7	15	.318
Brown	3	11	.214	7	17	.292
Dartmouth	1	13	.071	4	21	.160

Mid-American

	Conference W	L	Pct	Overall W	L	Pct
Ohio⊕	11	1	.917	19	7	.731
Miami (OH)	11	1	.917	20	5	.800
Toledo	6	6	.500	13	11	.542
Bowling Green	6	6	.500	9	15	.375
Kent State	4	8	.333	9	11	.450
Western Michigan	3	9	.250	8	16	.333
Marshall	1	11	.083	4	20	.167

Middle Atlantic

	Conference W	L	Pct	Overall W	L	Pct
Saint Joseph's⊕	-	-	-	26	3	.897
La Salle□	-	-	-	15	8	.652
Lafayette	-	-	-	12	8	.600
Temple	-	-	-	14	10	.583
Gettysburg	-	-	-	12	11	.522
Bucknell	-	-	-	11	13	.458
Lehigh	-	-	-	7	13	.350
Delaware	-	-	-	3	17	.150

Missouri Valley

	Conference W	L	Pct	Overall W	L	Pct
Wichita State⊕	11	3	.786	21	9	.700
Bradley□	9	5	.643	18	9	.667
Saint Louis□	9	5	.643	18	9	.667
Louisville	8	6	.571	15	10	.600
Tulsa	7	7	.500	14	11	.560
Drake	6	8	.429	15	10	.600
Cincinnati	5	9	.357	14	12	.538
North Texas	1	13	.071	7	19	.269

Ohio Valley

	Conference W	L	Pct	Overall W	L	Pct
Eastern Kentucky⊕	13	1	.929	19	6	.760
Western Kentucky□	10	4	.714	18	9	.667
Murray State	9	5	.643	19	7	.731
Tennessee Tech	8	6	.571	14	11	.560
Morehead State	6	8	.429	13	10	.565
East Tennessee St.	4	10	.286	6	17	.261
Middle Tennessee St.	4	10	.286	6	18	.250
Austin Peay	2	12	.143	4	17	.190

Tournament: **Western Kentucky d. Eastern Kentucky 83-67**

SEC

	Conference W	L	Pct	Overall W	L	Pct
Vanderbilt⊕	15	1	.938	24	4	.857
Tennessee	12	4	.750	20	5	.800
Florida	11	5	.688	18	7	.720
Auburn	11	5	.688	16	9	.640
Kentucky	10	6	.625	15	10	.600
Alabama	9	7	.563	17	9	.654
LSU	7	9	.438	12	14	.462
Mississippi State	6	10	.375	10	16	.385
Georgia	4	12	.250	8	18	.308
Tulane	2	14	.125	3	22	.120
Mississippi	1	15	.063	4	21	.160

Southern

	Conference W	L	Pct	Overall W	L	Pct
Davidson	12	0	1.000	24	2	.923
Virginia Tech	8	3	.727	13	10	.565
Citadel	8	5	.615	13	11	.542
West Virginia⊕	8	6	.571	14	15	.483
George Washington	6	7	.462	10	13	.435
William and Mary	6	8	.429	12	13	.480
Richmond	6	10	.375	10	16	.385
VMI	5	9	.357	8	13	.381
Furman	1	13	.071	6	19	.240
East Carolina	-	-	-	12	10	.545

Tournament: **W. Virginia d. William and Mary 70-67 (2OT)**
Tournament MOP: **Fred Hetzel**, Davidson

Southland

	Conference W	L	Pct	Overall W	L	Pct
Abilene Christian	6	2	.750	17	9	.654
Arkansas State	6	2	.750	13	9	.591
Lamar	5	3	.625	18	6	.750
Texas-Arlington	3	5	.375	10	14	.417
Trinity (TX)	0	8	.000	2	21	.087

Southwest

	Conference W	L	Pct	Overall W	L	Pct
Texas Tech	12	2	.857	17	6	.739
Texas	10	4	.714	16	9	.640
SMU⊕	10	4	.714	17	10	.630
Baylor	8	6	.571	15	9	.625
Texas A&M	7	7	.500	14	10	.583
Arkansas	5	9	.357	9	14	.391
TCU	3	11	.214	6	18	.250
Rice	1	13	.071	2	22	.083

Note: Texas Tech was stripped of the conference title after players were declared ineligible. The title was awarded to SMU and Texas.

WCAC

	Conference W	L	Pct	Overall W	L	Pct
San Francisco⊕	13	1	.929	24	5	.828
San Jose St.	9	5	.643	14	10	.583
Santa Clara	9	5	.643	14	12	.538
Pacific	8	6	.571	13	12	.520
UC Santa Barbara	7	7	.500	12	14	.462
Saint Mary's (CA)	5	9	.357	8	18	.308
Pepperdine	3	11	.214	6	19	.240
Loyola Marymount	2	12	.143	6	20	.231

WAC

	Conference W	L	Pct	Overall W	L	Pct
BYU⊕	8	2	.800	21	7	.750
New Mexico□	5	5	.500	19	8	.704
Arizona	5	5	.500	17	9	.654
Wyoming	5	5	.500	16	10	.615
Arizona State	4	6	.400	13	14	.481
Utah	3	7	.300	17	9	.654

Yankee

	Conference W	L	Pct	Overall W	L	Pct
Connecticut⊕	10	0	1.000	23	3	.885
Massachusetts	8	2	.800	13	11	.542
Rhode Island	6	4	.600	15	11	.577
Maine	4	6	.400	13	10	.565
Vermont	1	9	.100	7	13	.350
New Hampshire	1	9	.100	2	19	.095

⊕ Automatic NCAA Tournament bid ○ At-large NCAA Tournament bid □ NIT appearance ⊗ Team record doesn't reflect games forfeited or vacated. For adjusted record, see p. 521.

INDEPENDENTS

	Overall W	L	PCT
Providence○	24	2	.923
Miami (FL)	22	4	.846
Penn State○	20	4	.833
Villanova□	23	5	.821
Dayton○	22	7	.759
Boston College□	21	7	.750
Seattle	19	7	.731
Army□	21	8	.724
St. John's□	21	8	.724
Detroit□	20	8	.714
Oklahoma City○	21	10	.677
Colorado State○	16	8	.667
Fairfield	14	7	.667
Houston○	19	10	.655
St. Bonaventure	15	8	.652
Texas Western□	16	9	.640
West Texas	16	9	.640
DePaul○	17	10	.630
Florida State	16	10	.615
NYU□	16	10	.615
Hardin-Simmons	12	8	.600
Manhattan□	13	9	.591
Duquesne	14	10	.583
Creighton	13	10	.565
Georgetown	13	10	.565
Holy Cross	13	10	.565
Syracuse	13	10	.565

INDEPENDENTS (CONT.)

	Overall W	L	PCT
Georgia Tech	14	11	.560
Fordham□	15	12	.556
Notre Dame○	15	12	.556
St. Francis (NY)	11	9	.550
Centenary	13	11	.542
Iona	12	11	.522
Utah State	13	12	.520
Rutgers	12	12	.500
Boston U.	10	10	.500
Navy	10	10	.500
Portland	12	13	.480
Seton Hall	12	13	.480
Canisius	10	12	.455
Denver	11	14	.440
Loyola-Chicago	11	14	.440
Butler	11	15	.423
Memphis	10	14	.417
Saint Francis (PA)	10	15	.400
Xavier	10	15	.400
Air Force	9	14	.391
Loyola (LA)	8	16	.333
Marquette	8	18	.308
New Mexico State	8	18	.308
Colgate	7	16	.304
Pittsburgh	7	16	.304
Niagara	4	17	.190

INDIVIDUAL LEADERS—SEASON

Scoring

	CL	POS	G	FG	FT	PTS	PPG
1 **Rick Barry**, Miami (FL)	SR	F	26	340	293	973	**37.4**
2 **Wayne Estes**, Utah State	SR	F	19	252	137	641	**33.7**
3 **Bill Bradley**, Princeton	SR	F	29	306	273	885	**30.5**
4 **Dave Schellhase**, Purdue	JR	G/F	24	249	206	704	**29.3**
5 **Steve Thomas**, Xavier	JR	G	14	166	73	405	**28.9**
6 **Flynn Robinson**, Wyoming	SR	G	26	267	167	701	**27.0**
7 **John Austin**, Boston College	JR	G	25	231	211	673	**26.9**
8 **Fred Hetzel**, Davidson	SR	F/C	26	273	143	689	**26.5**
9 **John Beasley**, Texas A&M	JR	C	24	250	119	619	**25.8**
10 **Cazzie Russell**, Michigan	JR	G/F	27	271	152	694	**25.7**

Field Goal Pct

	CL	POS	G	FG	FGA	PCT
1 **Tim Kehoe**, Saint Peter's	SR	G	19	138	209	**66.0**
2 **Henry Finkel**, Dayton	JR	C	29	293	450	**65.1**
3 **Doug McKendrick**, Rice	JR	F	24	152	250	**60.8**
4 **Joe Newton**, Auburn	SR	C	24	126	208	**60.6**
5 **Ollie Johnson**, San Francisco	SR	C	29	242	405	**59.8**

Minimum: 125 made

Free Throw Pct

	CL	POS	G	FT	FTA	PCT
1 **Bill Bradley**, Princeton	SR	F	29	273	308	**88.6**
2 **Russ Banko**, UC Santa Barbara	JR	F	26	156	177	**88.1**
3 **Rick Park**, Tulsa	SR	G	25	145	165	**87.9**
4 **Wayne Estes**, Utah State	SR	F	19	137	156	**87.8**
5 **Ken McIntyre**, St. John's	SR	G	27	144	164	**87.8**

Minimum: 95 made

Rebounds Per Game

	CL	POS	G	REB	RPG
1 **Toby Kimball**, Connecticut	SR	C	23	483	**21.0**
2 **Warren Isaac**, Iona	SR	F	23	480	**20.9**
3 **Tommy Woods**, East Tenn. State	SO	F	23	450	**19.6**
4 **Rick Barry**, Miami (FL)	SR	F	26	475	**18.3**
5 **Keith Swagerty**, Pacific	SO	F	25	449	**18.0**

INDIVIDUAL LEADERS—GAME

Points

	CL	POS	OPP	DATE	PTS
1 **Rick Barry**, Miami (FL)	SR	F	Rollins	F23	**59**
2 **Bill Bradley**, Princeton	SR	F	Wichita State	M20	**58**
3 **Rick Barry**, Miami (FL)	SR	F	Tampa	D1	**55**
Clem Haskins, Western Kentucky	SO	F	Middle Tenn. State	J30	**55**
5 **Rick Barry**, Miami (FL)	SR	F	Florida Southern	J13	**54**

Free Throws Made

	CL	POS	OPP	DATE	FT	FTA	PCT
1 **Rick Barry**, Miami (FL)	SR	F	Florida Southern	J13	**22**	24	91.7
2 **Bill Bradley**, Princeton	SR	F	Saint Louis	D17	**20**	21	95.2
3 **Fred Hetzel**, Davidson	SR	F/C	George Washington	F5	**19**	21	90.5
4 **Dave Anderson**, Western Michigan	SR	G	Marshall	F27	**18**	19	94.7
Gail Goodrich, UCLA	SR	G	Michigan	M20	**18**	20	90.0
Lonnie Wright, Colorado State	JR	G	Wyoming	F6	**18**	20	90.0
Dave Schellhase, Purdue	JR	G/F	Iowa	F27	**18**	23	78.3

TEAM LEADERS-SEASON

Scoring Offense

	G	W-L	PTS	PPG
1 **Miami (FL)**	26	22-4	2,558	**98.4**
2 **BYU**	28	21-7	2,639	**94.3**
3 **Duke**	25	20-5	2,310	**92.4**
4 **Illinois**	24	18-6	2,213	**92.2**
5 **Indiana**	24	19-5	2,200	**91.7**

Field Goal Pct

	G	W-L	FG	FGA	PCT
1 **Saint Peter's**	20	10-10	579	1,089	**53.2**
2 **Davidson**	26	24-2	908	1,784	**50.9**
3 **San Francisco**	29	24-5	931	1,893	**49.2**
4 **Duke**	25	20-5	942	1,921	**49.0**
5 **Manhattan**	22	13-9	677	1,382	**49.0**

Free Throw Pct

	G	W-L	FT	FTA	PCT
1 **Miami (FL)**	26	22-4	642	807	**79.6**
2 **Morehead State**	23	13-10	487	620	**78.5**
3 **Indiana**	24	19-5	464	604	**76.8**
4 **Kentucky**	25	15-10	517	675	**76.6**
5 **UC Santa Barbara**	26	12-14	482	633	**76.1**

Scoring Defense

	G	W-L	OPP PTS	OPP PPG
1 **Tennessee**	25	20-5	1,391	**55.6**
2 **Oklahoma State**	27	20-7	1,503	**55.7**
3 **New Mexico**	27	19-8	1,504	**55.7**
4 **Texas Western**	25	16-9	1,419	**56.8**
5 **Oregon State**	26	16-10	1,525	**58.7**

CONSENSUS ALL-AMERICAS

First Team

PLAYER	CL	POS	HT	SCHOOL	RPG	PPG
Rick Barry	SR	F	6-7	Miami (FL)	18.3	37.4
Bill Bradley	SR	F	6-5	Princeton	11.8	30.5
Gail Goodrich	SR	G	6-1	UCLA	5.3	24.8
Fred Hetzel	SR	F/C	6-8	Davidson	14.8	26.5
Cazzie Russell	JR	G/F	6-5	Michigan	7.9	25.7

Second Team

PLAYER	CL	POS	HT	SCHOOL	RPG	PPG
Bill Buntin	SR	C	6-7	Michigan	11.5	20.1
Wayne Estes	SR	F	6-6	Utah State	13.7	33.7
Clyde Lee	JR	C	6-10	Vanderbilt	15.0	22.5
Dave Schellhase	JR	G/F	6-4	Purdue	8.0	29.3
Dave Stallworth	SR	F	6-7	Wichita State	12.1	25.0

Selectors: AP, NABC, UPI, USBWA

AWARD WINNERS

Player of the Year

PLAYER	CL	POS	HT	SCHOOL	AWARDS
Bill Bradley	SR	F	6-5	Princeton	AP, UPI, USBWA, Sullivan‡

‡ Top amateur athlete in U.S.

Coach of the Year

COACH	SCHOOL	REC	AWARDS
Dave Strack	Michigan	24-4	UPI
Butch van Breda Kolff	Princeton	23-6	USBWA

Poll Progression

Preseason Poll

AP	UPI	School
1	1	Michigan
2	2	UCLA
3	4	Wichita State
4	3	Davidson
5	5	Duke
6	6	Vanderbilt
7	12	Syracuse
8	14	Kansas State
9	7	San Francisco
10	15	St. John's
11	10	Minnesota
11	15	Kentucky
13	8	North Carolina
14	—	Bradley
15	9	Seattle
16	13	Villanova
17	19	Notre Dame
18	11	Kansas
19	17	BYU
20	20	DePaul
—	18	Saint Louis

Week of Dec 8

AP	UPI	School	AP↓↑
1	1	Michigan (3-0)	
2	3	Wichita State (1-0)	↑1
3	2	Vanderbilt (2-0)	↑3
4	4	Saint Louis (3-0)	⤴
5	6	San Francisco (2-0)	↑4
6	5	Minnesota (3-0)	↑5
7	8	UCLA (1-1) (A)	↓5
8	7	Duke (1-1)	↓3
9	10	Kentucky (1-1)	↑2
10	13	St. John's (1-0)	
—	9	BYU (2-0)	⤵
—	11	Davidson (1-1)	⤵
—	12	Villanova (2-0)	⤵
—	14	Illinois (1-1) (A)	
—	15	Saint Joseph's (2-0)	
—	16	Miami (FL) (3-0)	
—	17	Notre Dame (2-0)	⤵
—	18	Kansas (2-1)	⤵
—	19	North Carolina (3-1)	
—	20	Utah State (3-0) (B)	

Week of Dec 15

AP	UPI	School	AP↓↑
1	1	Wichita State (4-0)	↑1
2	2	Michigan (4-1)	↓1
3	3	San Francisco (4-0)	↑2
4	4	Minnesota (4-0)	↑2
5	5	UCLA (3-1)	↑2
6	6	Duke (3-1)	↑2
7	11	St. John's (3-0)	↑3
8	9	Kentucky (3-1)	↑1
9	6	Vanderbilt (3-1)	↓6
10	8	Saint Louis (3-1)	↓6
—	10	Indiana (4-0)	
—	12	Saint Joseph's (4-0)	
—	13	Davidson (3-1)	
—	14	Penn State (3-1)	
—	15	Illinois (3-1)	
—	16	Villanova (4-0)	
—	17	Nebraska (3-1)	
—	18	Bradley (4-0)	
—	19	Notre Dame (4-1)	
—	20	BYU (2-2)	

Week of Dec 22

AP	UPI	School	AP↓↑
1	1	Michigan (5-1)	↑1
2	2	Wichita State (5-1)	↓1
3	3	Minnesota (5-0)	↑1
4	5	UCLA (5-1)	↑1
5	4	San Francisco (5-0)	↓2
6	6	Duke (5-1)	
7	9	Illinois (6-1)	⤴
8	8	Indiana (6-0)	⤴
9	7	Saint Louis (5-1)	↑1
10	10	Davidson (5-1)	⤴
—	11	Vanderbilt (5-2)	⤵
—	12	St. John's (4-1)	⤵
—	12	Saint Joseph's (6-0)	
—	12	Villanova (5-0)	
—	15	Tennessee (4-0)	
—	16	Kentucky (4-2)	⤵
—	16	Utah (6-0)	
—	18	BYU (4-2)	
—	18	Colorado State (5-2)	
—	18	New Mexico (6-1)	

Week of Dec 29

AP	UPI	School	AP↓↑
1	1	Michigan (6-1) (C)	
2	2	Wichita State (6-1)	
3	3	Minnesota (6-0)	
4	5	UCLA (6-1)	
5	4	San Francisco (6-0)	
6	8	Illinois (7-1)	↑1
7	6	Indiana (7-0)	↑1
8	7	Duke (5-1)	↓2
9	9	Saint Louis (6-1)	
10	11	Saint Joseph's (6-0)	⤴
—	10	Davidson (6-1)	⤵
—	12	Vanderbilt (6-2)	
—	13	Villanova (8-0)	
—	14	Tennessee (5-0)	
—	15	Utah (8-0)	
—	16	Kansas (6-3)	
—	17	BYU (5-2)	
—	18	Kansas State (6-3)	
—	19	Kentucky (4-3)	
—	19	New Mexico (7-1)	
—	19	Seattle (6-4)	

Week of Jan 5

AP	UPI	School	AP↓↑
1	1	UCLA (9-1) (D)	↑3
2	3	Indiana (9-1)	↑5
3	2	Michigan (8-2)	↓2
4	6	Saint Joseph's (10-1)	↑6
5	3	Wichita State (9-2)	↓3
6	5	Duke (7-1)	↑2
7	8	St. John's (7-2)	⤴
8	7	San Francisco (8-1)	↓3
9	12	Providence (9-0)	⤴
10	10	Davidson (10-1)	⤴
—	9	Illinois (7-2)	⤵
—	11	Minnesota (7-2)	⤵
—	12	Vanderbilt (9-2)	
—	14	Utah (10-1) (D)	
—	15	Saint Louis (8-2)	⤵
—	16	Kansas (8-3)	
—	17	New Mexico (10-1)	
—	18	DePaul (9-2)	
—	18	Kentucky (5-4)	
—	20	Bradley (8-3)	
—	20	BYU (7-3)	

Week of Jan 12

AP	UPI	School	AP↓↑
1	1	UCLA (11-1)	
2	2	Michigan (9-2)	↑1
3	3	Wichita State (10-2)	↑2
4	5	Saint Joseph's (12-1)	
5	4	Indiana (10-1)	↓3
6	6	Providence (11-0)	↑3
7	8	St. John's (9-2)	
8	9	Davidson (11-1)	↑2
9	7	San Francisco (10-1)	↓1
10	11	Duke (8-2)	↓4
—	10	Vanderbilt (11-2)	
—	12	Illinois (9-3)	
—	13	New Mexico (12-1)	
—	14	Kansas (10-3)	
—	15	Minnesota (9-2)	
—	16	BYU (9-3)	
—	17	Saint Louis (11-3)	
—	18	Kentucky (6-5)	
—	19	Miami (OH) (10-1)	
—	20	Tennessee (8-2)	

Week of Jan 19

AP	UPI	School	AP↓↑
1	1	UCLA (13-1)	
2	2	Michigan (10-2)	
3	4	Saint Joseph's (14-1)	↑1
4	3	Wichita State (12-2)	↓1
5	5	Indiana (12-2)	
6	7	Providence (11-0)	
7	8	Davidson (14-1)	↑1
8	9	St. John's (11-2)	↓1
9	6	San Francisco (12-1)	
10	10	Duke (10-2)	
—	11	Vanderbilt (12-2)	
—	12	Illinois (10-3)	
—	13	Tennessee (10-2)	
—	14	DePaul (12-2)	
—	15	Kansas (11-4)	
—	15	New Mexico (12-2)	
—	17	Oklahoma State (10-4)	
—	18	NC State (10-1)	
—	19	Miami (FL) (11-3)	
—	19	St. Bonaventure (9-2)	

Week of Jan 26

AP	UPI	School	AP↓↑
1	1	UCLA (14-1)	
2	2	Michigan (11-2)	
3	4	Saint Joseph's (15-1)	
4	5	Providence (12-0)	↑2
5	3	Wichita State (12-2)	↓1
6	7	Davidson (14-1)	↑1
7	8	St. John's (12-2)	↑1
8	6	San Francisco (12-1)	↑1
9	10	Indiana (12-2)	↓4
10	9	Duke (10-2)	
—	11	Vanderbilt (12-2)	
—	12	Illinois (10-3)	
—	13	Tennessee (12-2)	
—	13	New Mexico (12-2)	
—	15	Minnesota (11-3)	
—	15	NC State (11-1)	
—	15	Oklahoma State (11-4)	
—	18	BYU (11-4)	
—	18	DePaul (13-3)	
—	20	Miami (Ohio) (13-1)	

Week of Feb 2

AP	UPI	School	AP↓↑
1	1	Michigan (13-2)	↑1
2	2	UCLA (14-2) (E)	↓1
3	3	Saint Joseph's (17-1)	
4	4	Providence (14-0)	
5	6	Davidson (16-1)	↑1
6	8	Duke (10-2)	↑4
7	10	Indiana (12-2)	↑2
8	5	Wichita State (13-3) (E)	↓3
9	7	Vanderbilt (14-2)	⤴
10	9	San Francisco (13-2)	↓2
—	11	St. John's (12-3)	⤵
—	12	Illinois (11-3)	
—	13	Iowa (10-5) (E)	
—	14	Arizona (14-4)	
—	14	New Mexico (14-2)	
—	14	Oklahoma State (13-4)	
—	17	Tennessee (13-2)	
—	18	NC State (12-1)	
—	19	BYU (13-4)	
—	20	DePaul (14-3)	
—	20	St. Bonaventure (10-4)	

Week of Feb 9

AP	UPI	School	AP↓↑
1	1	Michigan (13-2)	
2	2	UCLA (15-2)	
3	3	Saint Joseph's (19-1)	
4	4	Providence (16-0)	
5	6	Davidson (18-1)	
6	7	Duke (13-2)	
7	5	Vanderbilt (15-2)	↑2
8	9	Indiana (13-2)	↓1
9	8	Wichita State (14-3)	↓1
10	10	Illinois (12-3)	⤴
—	11	Iowa (11-5)	
—	12	San Francisco (15-3)	⤵
—	13	New Mexico (16-2)	
—	14	BYU (15-4)	
—	15	Tennessee (15-2)	
—	16	St. John's (13-4)	
—	17	Villanova (15-3)	
—	18	Miami (FL) (16-4)	
—	18	Minnesota (13-3)	
—	18	NC State (13-2)	

Week of Feb 16

AP	UPI	School	AP↓↑
1	1	Michigan (15-2)	
2	2	UCLA (18-2)	
3	4	Providence (18-0)	↑1
4	3	Saint Joseph's (19-1)	↓1
5	6	Davidson (21-1)	
6	5	Duke (16-2)	
7	9	Indiana (15-2)	↑1
8	10	Tennessee (17-2)	⤴
9	11	Minnesota (14-3)	⤴
10	7	Wichita State (15-4)	↓1
—	8	Vanderbilt (16-3)	⤵
—	12	San Francisco (17-3)	
—	13	New Mexico (18-2)	
—	14	Illinois (13-4)	⤵
—	15	BYU (16-5)	
—	16	Villanova (17-3)	
—	17	Oklahoma State (15-5)	
—	18	NC State (14-3)	
—	19	Arizona (15-6)	
—	19	Kansas (14-6)	
—	19	Miami (FL) (18-4)	

EEK OF FEB 23

AP	UPI	SCHOOL	AP↓↑
1	1	**Michigan** (17-2)	
2	2	**UCLA** (20-2)	
3	3	**Saint Joseph's** (23-1)	↑1
4	4	**Providence** (19-0)	↓1
5	5	**Duke** (18-2)	↑1
6	6	**Davidson** (23-1)	↓1
7	9	**Indiana** (16-3)	
8	7	**Minnesota** (16-3)	↑1
9	8	**Vanderbilt** (18-3)	⤴
10	14	**New Mexico** (19-3)	⤴
—	10	**Wichita State** (17-5)	⤵
—	11	**San Francisco** (19-3)	
—	12	**Tennessee** (17-3)	⤵
—	13	**Illinois** (15-4)	
—	15	**BYU** (17-5)	
—	16	**St. John's** (15-6)	
—	17	**Miami (FL)** (20-4) Ⓕ	
—	18	**Kansas** (17-7)	
—	18	**Oklahoma State** (15-6)	
—	18	**Villanova** (17-4)	

WEEK OF MAR 2

AP	UPI	SCHOOL	AP↓↑
1	1	**Michigan** (19-2) Ⓖ	
2	2	**UCLA** (22-2)	
3	3	**Saint Joseph's** (24-1)	
4	4	**Providence** (20-1)	
5	5	**Vanderbilt** (20-3)	↑4
6	8	**Minnesota** (17-4)	↑2
7	7	**Davidson** (24-2)	↓1
8	6	**Duke** (18-4)	↓3
9	12	**Villanova** (19-4)	⤴
10	9	**BYU** (19-5)	⤴
—	10	**San Francisco** (21-4)	
—	11	**Illinois** (16-5)	
—	13	**Wichita State** (17-6)	
—	14	**Indiana** (17-5)	⤵
—	14	**New Mexico** (19-5)	⤵
—	16	**Connecticut** (21-2)	
—	17	**Tennessee** (18-4)	
—	18	**Oklahoma State** (17-6)	
—	18	**Penn State** (19-3)	
—	20	**Kansas** (18-7)	
—	20	**NC State** (17-4)	

FINAL POLL

AP	UPI	SCHOOL	AP↓↑
1	1	**Michigan** (21-2)	
2	2	**UCLA** (24-2)	
3	3	**Saint Joseph's** (25-1)	
4	4	**Providence** (22-1)	
5	5	**Vanderbilt** (22-3)	
6	7	**Davidson** (24-2)	↑1
7	8	**Minnesota** (18-5)	↓1
8	11	**Villanova** (21-4)	↑1
9	6	**BYU** (21-5)	↑1
10	9	**Duke** (20-5)	↓2
—	10	**San Francisco** (23-4)	
—	12	**NC State** (21-5)	
—	13	**Oklahoma State** (19-6)	
—	14	**Wichita State** (18-7)	
—	15	**Connecticut** (23-2)	
—	16	**Illinois** (17-6)	
—	17	**Tennessee** (19-5)	
—	18	**Indiana** (18-5)	
—	19	**Miami (OH)** (20-5)	
—	20	**Dayton** (20-6)	

Ⓐ Illinois ends UCLA's 30-game winning streak, 110-83, in Assembly Hall. The 110 points is an Illinois homecourt record that will last 18 years.

Ⓑ Utah State routs Loyola Marymount, 97-69, as 6'6" forward Wayne Estes scores 37 points. On Feb. 8, the 21-year-old Estes will be electrocuted at the scene of a traffic accident. The AP will name him its first posthumous All-America.

Ⓒ In the ECAC Holiday Festival final in New York's Madison Square Garden, Princeton's Bill Bradley scores 41 against Michigan before fouling out with 4:37 left to play and the Tigers up 76-63. The Wolverines go on a 17-3 run to win, 80-78.

Ⓓ UCLA routs Utah, 104-74, on Dec. 30, sending the previously undefeated Utes into a second-half tailspin. Utah will finish last in the WAC despite a 17–9 overall record.

Ⓔ A doubleheader at Chicago Stadium on Jan. 29 reshuffles the Top 10: Iowa upends UCLA, 87-82, and Loyola-Chicago takes out No. 5 Wichita State, 93-92 in overtime.

Ⓕ Rick Barry explodes for 59 points as Miami (FL) blitzes Rollins, 148-79. Barry will finish the season the nation's top scorer (37.4 ppg).

Ⓖ Wracked with a 101-degree fever, Michigan's Cazzie Russell watches from the bench as Ohio State wrecks the Wolverines' perfect Big Ten season with a 93-85 victory in Columbus.

1965 NCAA Tournament

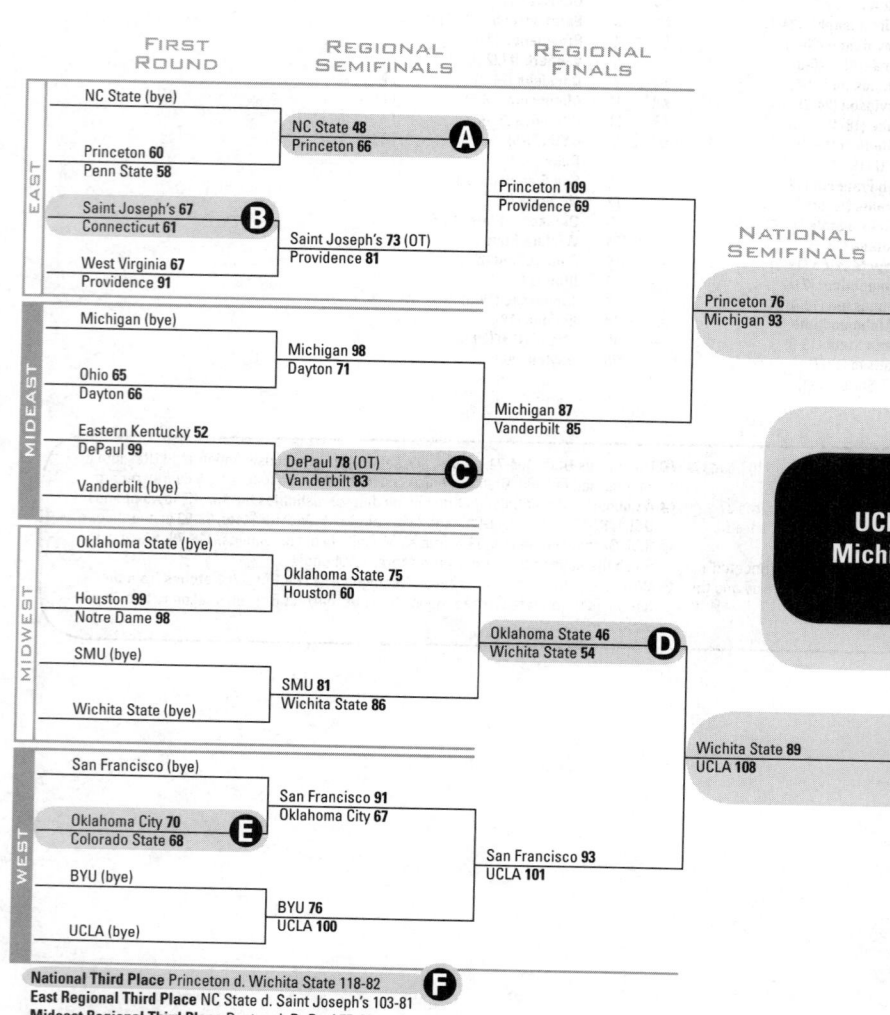

East

First Round
- NC State (bye)
- Princeton **60**, Penn State **58**
- Saint Joseph's **67**, Connecticut **61** (B)
- West Virginia **67**, Providence **91**

Regional Semifinals
- NC State **48**, Princeton **66** (A)
- Saint Joseph's **73** (OT), Providence **81**

Regional Finals
- Princeton **109**, Providence **69**

Mideast

First Round
- Michigan (bye)
- Ohio **65**, Dayton **66**
- Eastern Kentucky **52**, DePaul **99**
- Vanderbilt (bye)

Regional Semifinals
- Michigan **98**, Dayton **71**
- DePaul **78** (OT), Vanderbilt **83** (C)

Regional Finals
- Michigan **87**, Vanderbilt **85**

Midwest

First Round
- Oklahoma State (bye)
- Houston **99**, Notre Dame **98**
- SMU (bye)
- Wichita State (bye)

Regional Semifinals
- Oklahoma State **75**, Houston **60**
- SMU **81**, Wichita State **86**

Regional Finals
- Oklahoma State **46**, Wichita State **54** (D)

West

First Round
- San Francisco (bye)
- Oklahoma City **70**, Colorado State **68** (E)
- BYU (bye)
- UCLA (bye)

Regional Semifinals
- San Francisco **91**, Oklahoma City **67**
- BYU **76**, UCLA **100**

Regional Finals
- San Francisco **93**, UCLA **101**

National Semifinals

- Princeton **76**, Michigan **93**

Some 2,000 Princeton students sign a six-word telegram wishing their team good luck. Michigan's Cazzie Russell obviously doesn't get the message, amassing 28 points and 10 boards to offset Bill Bradley's 29 points.

- Wichita State **89**, UCLA **108**

UCLA shocks the Shockers, scoring 65 points in the first half to open a 27-point lead. Gail Goodrich has 28 points and Edgar Lacey 24 as the Bruins reach 100 points for the third straight Tournament game.

National Final

Portland

UCLA 91
Michigan 80

After the Bruins fall behind in the early going, coach John Wooden subs Kenny Washington for the gimpy Keith Erickson and tweaks his press to cut off the passing lanes to Michigan's Cazzie Russell. Gail Goodrich pours in 42 points—then a championship-game record—as UCLA wins its second straight title and becomes the first team to average 100 points for the Tournament.

National Third Place Princeton d. Wichita State 118-82 (F)
East Regional Third Place NC State d. Saint Joseph's 103-81
Mideast Regional Third Place Dayton d. DePaul 75-69
Midwest Regional Third Place SMU d. Houston 89-87
West Regional Third Place Oklahoma City d. BYU 112-102

A Future NBA star and U.S. Senator Bill Bradley scores 27 points for Princeton against a Wolfpack team coached by Press Maravich, whose teenage son, Pete, is already drawing raves from recruiters.

B Despite Toby Kimball's 21 points and 29 rebounds (then a record for the opening round), Connecticut falls to Saint Joseph's, which entered the Tournament with just one loss.

C Errol Palmer stars in defeat, scoring 28 points and grabbing 19 rebounds before fouling out. As Palmer leaves the floor, even several sportswriters join in a standing ovation.

D Hank Iba, nicknamed the Iron Duke, becomes the only coach to reach the regional final in every one of his eight Tournament appearances. This will be Iba's last NCAA Tournament.

E After Gary Hape and Dick Bagby are declared academically ineligible, Oklahoma City, already reeling from the mid-semester graduation of Eddie Jackson and Joe Biggon, is left with only eight players. Fortunately, they still have Charlie Hunter, whose last-second jump shot gives OCU the victory.

F Bill Bradley scores 58 points, a single-game Final Four record, and 177 for the Tournament, a record that will stand for 24 years. After making 22 of 29 field goal attempts and 14 of 15 free throws, Bradley gets a minute-long standing ovation when he's removed from the game.

Tournament Leaders

INDIVIDUAL LEADERS

Scoring	CL	POS	G	PTS	PPG
1 **Ollie Johnson**, San Francisco	SR	C	2	72	36.0
2 **Bill Bradley**, Princeton	SR	F	5	177	35.4
3 **Gail Goodrich**, UCLA	SR	G	4	140	35.0
4 **Clyde Lee**, Vanderbilt	JR	C	2	52	26.0
5 **Henry Finkel**, Dayton	JR	C	3	75	25.0
6 **Cazzie Russell**, Michigan	JR	G/F	4	96	24.0
Gary Gray, Oklahoma City	SO	G	3	72	24.0
8 **Carroll Hooser**, SMU	JR	F	2	47	23.5
9 **Bill Buntin**, Michigan	SR	C	4	88	22.0
Kelly Pete, Wichita State	JR	G	4	88	22.0

Minimum: 2 games

Field Goal Pct	CL	POS	G	FG	FGA	PCT
1 **Dave Mills**, DePaul	JR	C	3	16	21	76.2
2 **Steve Kramer**, BYU	JR	F	2	13	18	72.2
3 **Henry Finkel**, Dayton	JR	C	3	32	47	68.1
Ollie Johnson, San Francisco	SR	C	2	32	47	68.1
5 **Kelly Pete**, Wichita State	JR	G	4	30	47	63.8

Minimum: 10 made

Free Throw Pct	CL	POS	G	FT	FTA	PCT
1 **Jim Murphy**, DePaul	SR	G/F	3	12	13	92.3
2 **Bill Bradley**, Princeton	SR	F	5	47	51	92.2
3 **Dennis Papp**, Dayton	JR	G	3	11	12	91.7
Charles Beasley, SMU	SO	G	2	11	12	91.7
5 **Mike Gardner**, BYU	SR	G	2	10	11	90.9

Minimum: 10 made

Rebounds Per Game	CL	POS	G	REB	RPG
1 **Ollie Johnson**, San Francisco	SR	C	2	37	18.5
2 **Jim Ware**, Oklahoma City	JR	C	3	55	18.3
3 **Clyde Lee**, Vanderbilt	JR	C	2	35	17.5
4 **John Fairchild**, BYU	SR	C	2	34	17.0
5 **Errol Palmer**, DePaul	SO	F	3	50	16.7

Minimum: 2 games

TEAM LEADERS

Scoring	G	PTS	PPG
1 **UCLA**	4	400	100.0
2 **San Francisco**	2	184	92.0
3 **Michigan**	4	358	89.5
4 **BYU**	2	178	89.0
5 **Princeton**	5	429	85.8
6 **SMU**	2	170	85.0
7 **Vanderbilt**	2	168	84.0
8 **Oklahoma City**	3	249	83.0
9 **Houston**	3	246	82.0
DePaul	3	246	82.0

Minimum: 2 games

FG Pct	G	FG	FGA	PCT
1 **Princeton**	5	169	328	51.5
2 **San Francisco**	2	79	155	51.0
3 **UCLA**	4	162	323	50.1
4 **Michigan**	4	144	296	48.6
5 **Oklahoma State**	2	48	101	47.5
6 **Wichita State**	4	115	242	47.5

FT Pct	G	FT	FTA	PCT
1 **Dayton**	3	46	57	80.7
2 **Oklahoma City**	3	61	77	79.2
3 **DePaul**	3	50	65	76.9
4 **Princeton**	5	91	120	75.8
5 **Oklahoma State**	2	25	33	75.8

Minimum: 2 games

Rebounds	G	REB	RPG
1 **BYU**	2	104	52.0
2 **San Francisco**	2	96	48.0
3 **SMU**	2	92	46.0
4 **Vanderbilt**	2	91	45.5
5 **Michigan**	4	179	44.8

Minimum: 2 games

ALL-TOURNAMENT TEAM

PLAYER	CL	POS	HT	SCHOOL	RPG	PPG
Bill Bradley*	SR	F	6-5	Princeton	11.4	35.4
Gail Goodrich	SR	G	6-1	UCLA	4.3	35.0
Edgar Lacey	SO	F	6-6	UCLA	10.0	16.3
Cazzie Russell	JR	G/F	6-5	Michigan	8.0	24.0
Kenny Washington	JR	F	6-3	UCLA	4.3	7.5

ALL-REGIONAL TEAMS

EAST

PLAYER	CL	POS	HT	SCHOOL	RPG	PPG
Cliff Anderson	SO	F/C	6-4	Saint Joseph's	15.7	17.7
Bill Bradley	SR	F	6-5	Princeton	11.0	30.0
Robinson Brown	SO	C	6-9	Princeton	9.7	6.0
Larry Lakins	SR	C	6-6	NC State	11.0	30.0
Jimmy Walker	SO	G	6-3	Providence	3.3	20.3

MIDEAST

PLAYER	CL	POS	HT	SCHOOL	RPG	PPG
Clyde Lee*	JR	C	6-10	Vanderbilt	17.5	26.0
Bill Buntin	SR	C	6-7	Michigan	12.5	26.0
Errol Palmer	SO	F	6-5	DePaul	16.7	17.3
Cazzie Russell	JR	G/F	6-5	Michigan	8.5	20.0
Keith Thomas	JR	G	6-3	Vanderbilt	4.5	19.5

MIDWEST

PLAYER	CL	POS	HT	SCHOOL	RPG	PPG
Carroll Hooser	JR	F	6-7	SMU	15.5	23.5
James King	SR	F	6-5	Oklahoma State	8.0	8.0
Dave Leach	SR	F	6-5	Wichita State	5.0	11.0
Kelly Pete	JR	G	6-1	Wichita State	10.5	25.0
Vernon Smith	SR	F	6-4	Wichita State	4.0	10.5

WEST

PLAYER	CL	POS	HT	SCHOOL	RPG	PPG
Ollie Johnson*	SR	C	6-8	San Francisco	18.5	36.0
Joe Ellis	JR	F	6-6	San Francisco	12.5	14.0
Keith Erickson	SR	F	6-5	UCLA	10.0	28.5
Gail Goodrich	SR	G	6-1	UCLA	4.0	35.0
Gary Gray	SO	G	6-1	Oklahoma City	1.3	24.0

* Most outstanding player

1965 NCAA TOURNAMENT BOX SCORES

Princeton 66, NC State 48 — Sweet 16

	1H	2H
Princeton	27	39
NC State	16	32

PRINCETON	MIN	FG	3FG	FT	REB	A	ST	BL	PF	TP
Bill Bradley	-	10-18	-	7-9	14	8	-	-	4	27
Edward Hummer	-	5-12	-	3-4	10	1	-	-	3	13
Robert Haarlow	-	4-9	-	2-2	3	2	-	-	4	10
Don Rodenbach	-	3-6	-	2-2	4	0	-	-	2	8
Robinson Brown	-	2-6	-	0-2	13	0	-	-	3	4
William Koch	-	1-4	-	0-2	3	0	-	-	0	2
Don Roth	-	1-1	-	0-0	2	0	-	-	0	2
Allen Adler	-	0-0	-	0-0	1	0	-	-	0	0
William Kingston	-	0-0	-	0-0	0	0	-	-	0	0
Kenneth Shank	-	0-1	-	0-1	2	0	-	-	0	0
Gary Walters	-	0-3	-	0-0	2	1	-	-	2	0
TOTALS	-	26-60	-	14-22	54	12	-	-	18	66
Percentages		43.3		63.6						

Coach: Butch van Breda Kolff

NC STATE	MIN	FG	3FG	FT	REB	A	ST	BL	PF	TP
Larry Worsley	-	5-15	-	4-5	13	0	-	-	2	14
Pete Coker	-	4-10	-	0-3	8	0	-	-	3	8
Larry Lakins	-	2-10	-	3-5	2	0	-	-	5	7
Tom Mattocks	-	3-14	-	1-2	4	1	-	-	2	7
Billy Moffitt	-	0-2	-	4-6	3	3	-	-	3	4
Eddie Biedenbach	-	1-7	-	0-2	3	1	-	-	1	2
Hal Blondeau	-	1-3	-	0-0	1	0	-	-	1	2
Gary Hale	-	1-1	-	0-0	0	0	-	-	0	2
Jerry Moore	-	0-3	-	2-2	2	0	-	-	3	2
Sam Gealy	-	0-0	-	0-0	1	0	-	-	0	0
Ray Hodgdon	-	0-0	-	0-0	0	0	-	-	0	0
Phil Taylor	-	0-1	-	0-0	1	0	-	-	0	0
TOTALS	-	17-66	-	14-25	38	5	-	-	20	48
Percentages		25.8		56.0						

Coach: Press Maravich

Providence 81, Saint Joseph's 73 — Sweet 16

	1H	2H	OT
Providence	34	27	20
Saint Joseph's	40	21	12

PROVIDENCE	MIN	FG	3FG	FT	REB	A	ST	BL	PF	TP
Jim Benedict	-	11-17	-	0-0	3	-	-	-	2	22
Jimmy Walker	-	6-16	-	8-10	3	-	-	-	2	20
Mike Riordan	-	5-11	-	6-8	6	-	-	-	4	16
Dexter Westbrook	-	6-13	-	4-10	17	-	-	-	5	16
William Blair	-	3-9	-	1-1	7	-	-	-	3	7
William Lasher	-	0-1	-	0-0	0	-	-	-	0	0
TOTALS	-	31-67	-	19-29	36	-	-	-	16	81
Percentages		46.3		65.5						

Coach: Joseph Mullaney

SAINT JOSEPH'S	MIN	FG	3FG	FT	REB	A	ST	BL	PF	TP
Clifford Anderson	-	5-14	-	5-6	12	-	-	-	5	15
Matt Guokas	-	7-11	-	0-1	6	-	-	-	4	14
Marty Ford	-	5-14	-	3-5	12	-	-	-	2	13
William Oakes	-	6-17	-	0-2	4	-	-	-	3	12
Tom Duff	-	3-10	-	5-6	11	-	-	-	5	11
Chuck McKenna	-	4-10	-	0-3	10	-	-	-	1	8
Steve Chapman	-	0-0	-	0-0	0	-	-	-	2	0
TOTALS	-	30-76	-	13-23	55	-	-	-	22	73
Percentages		39.5		56.5						

Coach: Jack Ramsay

Michigan 98, Dayton 71 — Sweet 16

	1H	2H
Michigan	44	54
Dayton	27	44

MICHIGAN	MIN	FG	3FG	FT	REB	A	ST	BL	PF	TP
Bill Buntin	-	12-21	-	2-5	11	-	-	-	1	26
Oliver Darden	-	7-12	-	3-3	9	-	-	-	0	17
Cazzie Russell	-	5-14	-	4-4	9	-	-	-	2	14
Larry Tregoning	-	6-10	-	0-0	7	-	-	-	1	12
George Pomey	-	4-7	-	3-3	4	-	-	-	1	11
Craig Dill	-	4-9	-	0-1	2	-	-	-	1	8
Jim Myers	-	1-2	-	3-4	4	-	-	-	0	5
John Clawson	-	1-6	-	1-1	4	-	-	-	0	3
John Thompson	-	1-2	-	0-0	2	-	-	-	1	2
Dennis Bankey	-	0-0	-	0-0	0	-	-	-	0	0
Dan Brown	-	0-1	-	0-0	1	-	-	-	0	0
Tom Ludwig	-	0-3	-	0-0	3	-	-	-	1	0
TOTALS	-	41-87	-	16-21	56	-	-	-	8	98
Percentages		47.1		76.2						

Coach: Dave Strack

DAYTON	MIN	FG	3FG	FT	REB	A	ST	BL	PF	TP
Henry Finkel	-	11-18	-	0-2	12	-	-	-	4	22
Dennis Papp	-	7-16	-	1-1	4	-	-	-	0	15
Bob Sullivan	-	6-14	-	1-1	3	-	-	-	2	13
Bill Cassidy	-	4-15	-	2-2	8	-	-	-	4	10
Jim Wannemacher	-	2-4	-	0-0	2	-	-	-	2	4
Fred Johnston	-	1-2	-	0-0	1	-	-	-	0	2
Gene Klaus	-	1-3	-	0-0	0	-	-	-	1	2
Jack Warrell	-	1-3	-	0-0	0	-	-	-	2	2
Tom Brooks	-	0-0	-	1-1	0	-	-	-	0	1
Dennis Hrcka	-	0-0	-	0-0	0	-	-	-	0	0
Dave Inderrieden	-	0-0	-	0-0	0	-	-	-	0	0
John Samanich	-	0-0	-	0-0	0	-	-	-	0	0
TOTALS	-	33-75	-	5-7	30	-	-	-	15	71
Percentages		44.0		71.4						

Coach: Don Donoher

Vanderbilt 83, DePaul 78 — Sweet 16

	1H	2H	OT1
Vanderbilt	39	37	7
DePaul	32	44	2

VANDERBILT	MIN	FG	3FG	FT	REB	A	ST	BL	PF	TP
Clyde Lee	-	8-20	-	8-10	15	-	-	-	5	24
Keith Thomas	-	7-10	-	4-4	6	-	-	-	0	18
John Miller	-	5-13	-	6-10	1	-	-	-	1	16
Wayne Calvert	-	6-8	-	0-1	4	-	-	-	3	12
Bob Grace	-	4-9	-	3-3	4	-	-	-	5	11
Wayne Taylor	-	0-2	-	2-3	7	-	-	-	1	2
Kenny Gibbs	-	0-0	-	0-0	0	-	-	-	0	0
Ron Green	-	0-2	-	0-0	5	-	-	-	3	0
TOTALS	-	30-64	-	23-31	42	-	-	-	18	83
Percentages		46.9		74.2						

Coach: Roy Skinner

DEPAUL	MIN	FG	3FG	FT	REB	A	ST	BL	PF	TP
Errol Palmer	-	10-18	-	8-11	19	-	-	-	5	28
Jim Murphy	-	9-25	-	3-4	7	-	-	-	2	21
Tom Meyer	-	5-11	-	1-3	4	-	-	-	2	11
Don Swanson	-	4-8	-	1-1	8	-	-	-	5	9
Dave Mills	-	3-4	-	1-2	5	-	-	-	5	7
Ed Birgells	-	1-3	-	0-0	2	-	-	-	1	2
Terry Flanagan	-	0-3	-	0-0	1	-	-	-	4	0
Mike Norris	-	0-3	-	0-0	1	-	-	-	0	0
TOTALS	-	32-75	-	14-21	47	-	-	-	24	78
Percentages		42.7		66.7						

Coach: Ray Meyer

Oklahoma State 75, Houston 60 — Sweet 16

	1H	2H
Oklahoma State	33	42
Houston	22	38

OKLAHOMA STATE	MIN	FG	3FG	FT	REB	A	ST	BL	PF	TP
Gene Johnson	-	11-17	-	3-5	13	-	-	-	4	25
Gary Hassmann	-	9-20	-	0-0	7	-	-	-	3	18
James King	-	3-6	-	4-4	11	-	-	-	2	10
Skip Iba	-	2-3	-	3-5	3	-	-	-	4	7
Larry Hawk	-	2-9	-	2-3	6	-	-	-	3	6
Paul LaBrue	-	2-2	-	2-2	0	-	-	-	0	6
Freddie Moulder	-	1-2	-	1-1	1	-	-	-	0	3
Jim Feamster	-	0-0	-	0-0	1	-	-	-	0	0
TOTALS	-	30-59	-	15-20	42	-	-	-	16	75
Percentages		50.8		75.0						

Coach: Hank Iba

HOUSTON	MIN	FG	3FG	FT	REB	A	ST	BL	PF	TP
Joe Hamood	-	8-24	-	1-1	7	-	-	-	1	17
Richard Apolskis	-	3-5	-	2-5	1	-	-	-	3	8
Jack Margenthaler	-	3-8	-	1-1	1	-	-	-	1	7
Wayne Ballard	-	3-12	-	0-1	5	-	-	-	4	6
Jim Jones	-	2-8	-	2-4	8	-	-	-	3	6
Leary Lentz	-	3-9	-	0-0	9	-	-	-	1	6
Ed Winch	-	2-4	-	1-1	0	-	-	-	2	5
Gary Grider	-	0-1	-	2-3	1	-	-	-	0	2
Lou Perry	-	1-1	-	0-0	2	-	-	-	1	2
Tim Palmquist	-	0-1	-	1-3	2	-	-	-	0	1
Ben Arning	-	0-0	-	0-0	0	-	-	-	1	0
TOTALS	-	25-73	-	10-19	36	-	-	-	17	60
Percentages		34.2		52.6						

Coach: Guy V. Lewis

Officials: Filiberti, Sorian
Attendance: 10,500

Wichita State 86, SMU 81 — Sweet 16

	1H	2H
Wichita State	43	43
SMU	41	40

WICHITA STATE	MIN	FG	3FG	FT	REB	A	ST	BL	PF	TP
Kelly Pete	-	12-16	-	7-12	12	-	-	-	4	31
Jamie Thompson	-	8-22	-	2-3	7	-	-	-	3	18
Dave Leach	-	4-13	-	3-6	8	-	-	-	4	11
John Criss	-	4-6	-	1-1	2	-	-	-	4	9
Vernon Smith	-	3-9	-	3-3	4	-	-	-	4	9
Melvin Reed	-	2-4	-	3-5	7	-	-	-	3	7
Gerald Davis	-	0-0	-	1-1	0	-	-	-	0	1
Larry Nosich	-	0-2	-	0-0	1	-	-	-	1	0
TOTALS	-	33-72	-	20-31	41	-	-	-	23	86
Percentages		45.8		64.5						

Coach: Gary Thompson

SMU	MIN	FG	3FG	FT	REB	A	ST	BL	PF	TP
Carroll Hooser	-	9-16	-	2-3	9	-	-	-	5	20
Charles Beasley	-	7-16	-	4-4	6	-	-	-	3	18
Bob Begert	-	5-8	-	6-10	9	-	-	-	4	16
Bill Ward	-	3-6	-	4-7	5	-	-	-	5	10
Denny Holman	-	3-10	-	2-2	5	-	-	-	5	8
Jim Smith	-	3-6	-	0-0	3	-	-	-	0	6
Hank Wendorf	-	1-3	-	1-2	2	-	-	-	3	3
Bobby Carpenter	-	0-0	-	0-0	1	-	-	-	0	0
TOTALS	-	31-65	-	19-28	40	-	-	-	25	81
Percentages		47.7		67.9						

Coach: E.O. "Doc" Hayes

SWEET 16 — 91-67

SAN FRANCISCO	MIN	FG	3FG	FT	REB	A	ST	BL	PF	TP
Ollie Johnson	-	17-27	-	1-2	16	-	-	-	0	35
Larry Blum	-	7-11	-	1-2	1	-	-	-	0	15
Erwin Mueller	-	5-14	-	3-4	12	-	-	-	4	13
Joe Ellis	-	6-18	-	0-0	14	-	-	-	3	12
Russ Gumina	-	6-10	-	0-2	5	-	-	-	5	12
Huey Thomas	-	1-4	-	1-1	2	-	-	-	4	3
Rich Gale	-	0-1	-	1-1	1	-	-	-	0	1
Clarence Esters	-	0-2	-	0-0	0	-	-	-	1	0
Charles James	-	0-3	-	0-0	2	-	-	-	2	0
TOTALS	-	42-90	-	7-12	53	-	-	-	19	91
Percentages		46.7		58.3						

Coach: Peter P. Peletta

29	1H	29
62	2H	38

OKLAHOMA CITY	MIN	FG	3FG	FT	REB	A	ST	BL	PF	TP
Gary Gray	-	8-15	-	4-6	0	-	-	-	5	20
Jim Ware	-	6-18	-	5-6	22	-	-	-	3	17
Jerry Wells	-	4-15	-	5-7	6	-	-	-	3	13
Charlie Hunter	-	5-16	-	2-2	3	-	-	-	1	12
John Hopkins	-	2-6	-	1-1	8	-	-	-	1	5
Ron Bolen	-	0-1	-	0-0	1	-	-	-	0	0
Joe Castleberry	-	0-1	-	0-0	0	-	-	-	0	0
Gene Morrison	-	0-0	-	0-0	0	-	-	-	0	0
TOTALS	-	25-72	-	17-22	40	-	-	-	13	67
Percentages		34.7		77.3						

Coach: Abe Lemons

SWEET 16 — 100-76

UCLA	MIN	FG	3FG	FT	REB	A	ST	BL	PF	TP
Gail Goodrich	-	16-27	-	8-9	5	-	-	-	2	40
Keith Erickson	-	14-22	-	0-1	9	-	-	-	4	28
Edgar Lacey	-	7-11	-	1-3	13	-	-	-	3	15
Mike Lynn	-	3-9	-	2-2	10	-	-	-	3	8
Fred Goss	-	2-10	-	0-0	2	-	-	-	5	4
John Lyons	-	1-2	-	0-0	0	-	-	-	0	2
Doug McIntosh	-	1-6	-	0-2	9	-	-	-	3	2
Kenny Washington	-	0-5	-	1-1	4	-	-	-	5	1
Brice Chambers	-	0-1	-	0-0	1	-	-	-	0	0
Vaughn Hoffman	-	0-1	-	0-1	2	-	-	-	0	0
Richard Levin	-	0-0	-	0-0	0	-	-	-	1	0
TOTALS	-	44-94	-	12-19	55	-	-	-	26	100
Percentages		46.8		63.2						

Coach: John Wooden

51	1H	40
49	2H	36

BYU	MIN	FG	3FG	FT	REB	A	ST	BL	PF	TP
John Fairchild	-	8-17	-	7-8	13	-	-	-	2	23
Mike Gardner	-	5-10	-	4-4	4	-	-	-	4	14
Steve Kramer	-	5-7	-	0-1	4	-	-	-	2	10
Neil Roberts	-	2-11	-	3-4	6	-	-	-	0	7
Dick Nemelka	-	2-11	-	1-5	1	-	-	-	2	5
Jeff Congdon	-	2-5	-	0-1	1	-	-	-	1	4
Gary Hill	-	2-5	-	0-3	7	-	-	-	4	4
Bob Quinney	-	1-5	-	2-2	4	-	-	-	0	4
Jon Stanley	-	2-3	-	0-1	4	-	-	-	0	4
Craig Raymond	-	0-2	-	1-2	4	-	-	-	1	1
Ken James	-	0-3	-	0-1	1	-	-	-	0	0
Jimas Jimas	-	0-1	-	0-0	0	-	-	-	0	0
TOTALS	-	29-80	-	18-32	49	-	-	-	16	76
Percentages		36.2		56.2						

Coach: Stan Watts

Attendance: 10,766

ELITE 8 — 109-69

PRINCETON	MIN	FG	3FG	FT	REB	A	ST	BL	PF	TP
Bill Bradley	-	14-20	-	13-13	10	-	-	-	3	41
Robert Haarlow	-	7-10	-	4-5	7	-	-	-	2	18
Robinson Brown	-	5-10	-	4-5	11	-	-	-	3	14
Edward Hummer	-	4-4	-	5-5	9	-	-	-	3	13
Don Rodenbach	-	3-4	-	0-0	1	-	-	-	4	6
Donald Niemann	-	2-2	-	0-0	0	-	-	-	0	4
Gary Walters	-	2-4	-	0-0	0	-	-	-	3	4
William Kingston	-	1-2	-	1-3	1	-	-	-	1	3
William Koch	-	1-1	-	0-0	2	-	-	-	0	2
Don Roth	-	1-1	-	0-0	0	-	-	-	0	2
Kenneth Shank	-	1-2	-	0-0	1	-	-	-	1	2
Allen Adler	-	0-0	-	0-0	0	-	-	-	0	0
TOTALS	-	41-60	-	27-31	42	-	-	-	20	109
Percentages		68.3		87.1						

Coach: Butch van Breda Kolff

47	1H	34
62	2H	35

PROVIDENCE	MIN	FG	3FG	FT	REB	A	ST	BL	PF	TP
Jimmy Walker	-	8-19	-	11-13	4	-	-	-	5	27
Dexter Westbrook	-	6-12	-	1-5	8	-	-	-	4	13
Jim Benedict	-	4-17	-	2-2	3	-	-	-	1	10
Mike Riordan	-	4-8	-	1-2	5	-	-	-	2	9
William Lasher	-	1-4	-	4-4	3	-	-	-	1	6
James Ahern	-	1-4	-	0-1	0	-	-	-	0	2
Steve Sarantopoulos	-	1-2	-	0-0	0	-	-	-	0	2
William Blair	-	0-0	-	0-0	1	-	-	-	5	0
James Cox	-	0-0	-	0-0	1	-	-	-	0	0
Donald Dutton	-	0-3	-	0-0	1	-	-	-	1	0
Noel Kinski	-	0-0	-	0-0	0	-	-	-	2	0
Peter McLaughlin	-	0-0	-	0-0	0	-	-	-	0	0
TOTALS	-	25-69	-	19-27	26	-	-	-	21	69
Percentages		36.2		70.4						

Coach: Joseph Mullaney

ELITE 8 — 87-85

MICHIGAN	MIN	FG	3FG	FT	REB	A	ST	BL	PF	TP
Bill Buntin	-	11-25	-	4-7	14	-	-	-	5	26
Cazzie Russell	-	9-19	-	8-10	8	-	-	-	2	26
Oliver Darden	-	6-14	-	2-6	12	-	-	-	4	14
Larry Tregoning	-	5-9	-	1-3	6	-	-	-	1	11
George Pomey	-	3-4	-	0-2	3	-	-	-	4	6
Jim Myers	-	2-3	-	0-0	2	-	-	-	1	4
Craig Dill	-	0-0	-	0-1	0	-	-	-	0	0
TOTALS	-	36-74	-	15-29	45	-	-	-	17	87
Percentages		48.6		51.7						

Coach: Dave Strack

38	1H	39
49	2H	46

VANDERBILT	MIN	FG	3FG	FT	REB	A	ST	BL	PF	TP
Clyde Lee	-	11-22	-	6-7	20	-	-	-	4	28
Keith Thomas	-	9-18	-	3-3	3	-	-	-	5	21
John Miller	-	8-16	-	1-2	3	-	-	-	2	17
Bob Grace	-	2-4	-	3-5	12	-	-	-	4	7
Wayne Taylor	-	3-7	-	0-1	6	-	-	-	3	6
Ron Green	-	1-2	-	2-2	3	-	-	-	0	4
Wayne Calvert	-	1-2	-	0-0	0	-	-	-	3	2
Kenny Gibbs	-	0-2	-	0-1	2	-	-	-	2	0
TOTALS	-	35-73	-	15-21	49	-	-	-	23	85
Percentages		47.9		71.4						

Coach: Roy Skinner

Officials: Lennon, Grossman
Attendance: 11,800

ELITE 8 — 54-46

WICHITA STATE	MIN	FG	3FG	FT	REB	A	ST	BL	PF	TP
Kelly Pete	40	6-9	-	7-9	9	-	-	-	0	19
Vernon Smith	40	2-2	-	8-9	4	-	-	-	4	12
Dave Leach	40	5-8	-	1-3	2	-	-	-	4	11
Jamie Thompson	40	2-4	-	3-3	2	-	-	-	2	7
John Criss	40	2-6	-	1-1	3	-	-	-	3	5
TOTALS	200	17-29	-	20-25	20	-	-	-	13	54
Percentages		58.6		80.0						

Coach: Gary Thompson

31	1H	22
23	2H	24

OKLAHOMA STATE	MIN	FG	3FG	FT	REB	A	ST	BL	PF	TP
Gary Hassmann	-	4-9	-	1-1	1	-	-	-	5	9
Gene Johnson	-	3-8	-	3-3	3	-	-	-	3	9
Larry Hawk	-	2-6	-	3-4	4	-	-	-	1	7
James King	-	2-3	-	2-2	5	-	-	-	2	6
Freddie Moulder	-	3-10	-	0-1	4	-	-	-	2	6
Skip Iba	-	2-2	-	1-2	2	-	-	-	3	5
Paul LaBrue	-	2-4	-	0-0	1	-	-	-	1	4
TOTALS	-	18-42	-	10-13	20	-	-	-	17	46
Percentages		42.9		76.9						

Coach: Hank Iba

Officials: Soriano, Korte
Attendance: 12,500

ELITE 8 — 101-93

UCLA	MIN	FG	3FG	FT	REB	A	ST	BL	PF	TP
Gail Goodrich	-	10-18	-	10-11	3	-	-	-	3	30
Keith Erickson	-	13-26	-	3-6	11	-	-	-	4	29
Edgar Lacey	-	7-13	-	1-2	7	-	-	-	4	15
Fred Goss	-	6-15	-	1-1	0	-	-	-	1	13
Mike Lynn	-	2-3	-	3-4	1	-	-	-	4	7
Doug McIntosh	-	2-3	-	1-1	6	-	-	-	1	5
Ken Washington	-	1-4	-	0-1	1	-	-	-	2	2
TOTALS	-	41-82	-	19-26	29	-	-	-	19	101
Percentages		50.0		73.1						

Coach: John Wooden

51	1H	46
50	2H	47

SAN FRANCISCO	MIN	FG	3FG	FT	REB	A	ST	BL	PF	TP
Ollie Johnson	-	15-20	-	7-10	21	-	-	-	4	37
Joe Ellis	-	7-13	-	2-4	11	-	-	-	3	16
Russ Gumina	-	6-12	-	4-5	4	-	-	-	2	16
Erwin Mueller	-	4-6	-	4-5	4	-	-	-	5	12
Huey Thomas	-	3-4	-	2-2	0	-	-	-	1	8
Larry Blum	-	1-4	-	0-0	1	-	-	-	2	2
Charles James	-	1-5	-	0-0	0	-	-	-	2	2
Clarence Esters	-	0-1	-	0-1	2	-	-	-	1	0
TOTALS	-	37-65	-	19-27	43	-	-	-	20	93
Percentages		56.9		70.4						

Coach: Peter P. Peletta

Attendance: 10,515

93-76 — 40 1H 36; 53 2H 40 — FINAL 4

MICHIGAN	MIN	FG	3FG	FT	REB	A	ST	BL	PF	TP
Cazzie Russell	-	10-21	-	8-9	10	-	-	-	0	28
Bill Buntin	-	7-13	-	8-10	14	-	-	-	4	22
Oliver Darden	-	6-13	-	1-3	9	-	-	-	3	13
Larry Tregoning	-	6-9	-	1-1	10	-	-	-	2	13
George Pomey	-	2-8	-	2-2	3	-	-	-	4	6
John Clawson	-	2-2	-	0-1	1	-	-	-	0	4
Craig Dill	-	0-0	-	3-4	1	-	-	-	2	3
Jim Myers	-	1-4	-	0-0	4	-	-	-	1	2
John Thompson	-	0-1	-	2-2	0	-	-	-	0	2
Tom Ludwig	-	0-0	-	0-0	0	-	-	-	1	0
TOTALS	-	34-71	-	25-32	52	-	-	-	17	93
Percentages		47.9		78.1						

Coach: Dave Strack

PRINCETON	MIN	FG	3FG	FT	REB	A	ST	BL	PF	TP
Bill Bradley	-	12-25	-	5-5	7	-	-	-	5	29
Edward Hummer	-	4-10	-	4-5	9	-	-	-	4	12
Gary Walters	-	5-10	-	1-2	3	-	-	-	1	11
Robert Haarlow	-	4-10	-	1-4	3	-	-	-	1	9
Don Rodenbach	-	2-5	-	2-2	1	-	-	-	3	6
Robinson Brown	-	2-6	-	0-0	3	-	-	-	5	4
William Koch	-	1-4	-	1-2	4	-	-	-	1	3
William Kingston	-	0-1	-	2-2	2	-	-	-	1	2
TOTALS	-	30-71	-	16-22	32	-	-	-	21	76
Percentages		42.3		72.7						

Coach: Butch van Breda Kolff

Officials: Korte, Magnusson

108-89 — 65 1H 38; 43 2H 51 — FINAL 4

UCLA	MIN	FG	3FG	FT	REB	A	ST	BL	PF	TP
Gail Goodrich	-	11-21	-	6-8	5	-	-	-	2	28
Edgar Lacey	-	9-13	-	6-10	13	-	-	-	2	24
Fred Goss	-	8-13	-	3-3	9	-	-	-	2	19
Doug McIntosh	-	4-5	-	3-4	4	-	-	-	2	11
Mike Lynn	-	5-9	-	0-0	8	-	-	-	2	10
Kenny Washington	-	4-13	-	2-4	7	-	-	-	1	10
John Lyons	-	2-3	-	0-0	1	-	-	-	2	4
Keith Erickson	-	1-6	-	0-0	5	-	-	-	2	2
Brice Chambers	-	0-5	-	0-0	2	-	-	-	1	0
John Galbraith	-	0-0	-	0-0	0	-	-	-	1	0
Vaughn Hoffman	-	0-0	-	0-0	0	-	-	-	0	0
Richard Levin	-	0-1	-	0-0	1	-	-	-	1	0
TOTALS	-	44-89	-	20-29	55	-	-	-	18	108
Percentages		49.4		69.0						

Coach: John Wooden

WICHITA STATE	MIN	FG	3FG	FT	REB	A	ST	BL	PF	TP
Jamie Thompson	-	13-19	-	10-11	6	-	-	-	2	36
Kelly Pete	-	6-11	-	5-5	6	-	-	-	5	17
Dave Leach	-	6-14	-	0-1	10	-	-	-	3	12
John Criss	-	4-13	-	0-0	4	-	-	-	4	8
Vernon Smith	-	4-11	-	0-1	2	-	-	-	3	8
Melvin Reed	-	2-3	-	1-1	4	-	-	-	4	5
Gerald Davis	-	1-2	-	0-0	1	-	-	-	0	2
Larry Nosich	-	0-0	-	1-3	0	-	-	-	0	1
Gerard Reimond	-	0-1	-	0-0	1	-	-	-	0	0
Al Trope	-	0-1	-	0-0	0	-	-	-	0	0
TOTALS	-	36-75	-	17-22	34	-	-	-	21	89
Percentages		48.0		77.3						

Coach: Gary Thompson

Officials: Mihalik, Honzo
Attendance: 13,197

118-82 — 53 1H 39; 65 2H 43 — 3RD PLACE

PRINCETON	MIN	FG	3FG	FT	REB	A	ST	BL	PF	TP
Bill Bradley	-	22-29	-	14-15	17	4	-	-	4	58
Don Rodenbach	-	7-14	-	2-2	1	0	-	-	2	16
Robert Haarlow	-	4-7	-	2-3	0	1	-	-	3	10
William Koch	-	5-6	-	0-3	3	1	-	-	1	10
Edward Hummer	-	3-4	-	3-3	4	2	-	-	3	9
Robinson Brown	-	3-5	-	1-1	11	0	-	-	4	7
Gary Walters	-	3-5	-	0-0	3	2	-	-	1	6
Kenneth Shank	-	1-2	-	0-0	2	0	-	-	0	2
Allen Adler	-	0-1	-	0-0	0	0	-	-	0	0
William Kingston	-	0-1	-	0-1	1	0	-	-	1	0
Donald Niemann	-	0-1	-	0-0	1	0	-	-	2	0
Don Roth	-	0-0	-	0-0	2	0	-	-	0	0
TOTALS	-	48-75	-	22-28	45	10	-	-	21	118
Percentages		64.0		78.6						

Coach: Butch van Breda Kolff

WICHITA STATE	MIN	FG	3FG	FT	REB	A	ST	BL	PF	TP
Kelly Pete	-	6-11	-	9-13	8	0	-	-	2	21
Jamie Thompson	-	6-15	-	6-7	3	0	-	-	4	18
Vernon Smith	-	3-6	-	7-9	5	0	-	-	4	13
John Criss	-	5-9	-	0-0	1	1	-	-	5	10
Dave Leach	-	5-10	-	0-0	2	0	-	-	5	10
Larry Nosich	-	1-3	-	2-2	1	0	-	-	0	4
Melvin Reed	-	2-7	-	0-0	3	0	-	-	1	4
Gerald Davis	-	1-4	-	0-1	0	0	-	-	0	2
Gerard Reimond	-	0-0	-	0-0	0	0	-	-	0	0
Al Trope	-	0-0	-	0-0	0	0	-	-	0	0
Manny Zafiros	-	0-1	-	0-0	0	0	-	-	0	0
TOTALS	-	29-66	-	24-32	23	1	-	-	21	82
Percentages		43.9		75.0						

Coach: Gary Thompson

Officials: Korte, Magnusson
Attendance: 13,204

91-80 — 47 1H 34; 44 2H 46 — NCAA FINAL 1965

UCLA	MIN	FG	3FG	FT	REB	A	ST	BL	PF	TP
Gail Goodrich	-	12-22	-	18-20	4	1	-	-	4	42
Kenny Washington	-	7-9	-	3-4	5	0	-	-	2	17
Edgar Lacey	-	5-7	-	1-2	7	0	-	-	3	11
Fred Goss	-	4-12	-	0-0	3	0	-	-	1	8
Mike Lynn	-	2-3	-	1-2	6	2	-	-	1	5
Keith Erickson	-	1-1	-	1-2	1	1	-	-	1	3
Doug McIntosh	-	1-2	-	1-2	0	0	-	-	2	3
Vaughn Hoffman	-	1-1	-	0-0	1	0	-	-	0	2
Brice Chambers	-	0-0	-	0-1	0	0	-	-	0	0
John Galbraith	-	0-0	-	0-0	0	0	-	-	0	0
Richard Levin	-	0-1	-	0-0	1	0	-	-	0	0
John Lyons	-	0-0	-	0-0	0	0	-	-	1	0
TOTALS	-	33-58	-	25-33	28	4	-	-	15	91
Percentages		56.9		75.8						

Coach: John Wooden

MICHIGAN	MIN	FG	3FG	FT	REB	A	ST	BL	PF	TP
Cazzie Russell	-	10-16	-	8-9	5	1	-	-	2	28
Oliver Darden	-	8-10	-	1-1	4	0	-	-	5	17
Bill Buntin	-	6-14	-	2-4	6	1	-	-	5	14
John Clawson	-	3-4	-	0-0	0	0	-	-	2	6
Larry Tregoning	-	2-7	-	1-1	5	0	-	-	5	5
Craig Dill	-	1-2	-	2-2	1	0	-	-	1	4
George Pomey	-	2-5	-	0-0	2	0	-	-	2	4
Tom Ludwig	-	1-2	-	0-0	0	0	-	-	0	2
Dan Brown	-	0-0	-	0-0	0	0	-	-	0	0
Jim Myers	-	0-4	-	0-0	3	0	-	-	2	0
John Thompson	-	0-0	-	0-0	0	0	-	-	0	0
TOTALS	-	33-64	-	14-17	26	2	-	-	24	80
Percentages		51.6		82.4						

Coach: Dave Strack

Officials: Mihalik, Honzo
Attendance: 13,204

National Invitation Tournament (NIT)

First round: St. John's d. Boston College 114-92, Manhattan d. Texas Western 71-53, Western Kentucky d. Fordham 57-53, Army d. Saint Louis 70-66, NYU d. Bradley 71-70, Detroit d. La Salle 93-86

Quarterfinals: St. John's d. New Mexico 61-54, Villanova d. Manhattan 73-71, NYU d. Detroit 87-76, Army d. Western Kentucky 58-54

Semifinals: Villanova d. NYU 91-69, St. John's d. Army 67-60

Third place: Army d. NYU 75-74

Championship: St. John's d. Villanova 55-51

MVP: Ken McIntyre, St. John's

1965-66: Miner Miracle

Don Haskins, the coach of Texas Western (now UTEP), changed college basketball, and the country at large, when he started an all African-American lineup against heavily favored Kentucky in the NCAA championship game. The Wildcats, who had no black players, were competing in their 15th Tournament and seeking a record fifth title—while the Miners had won only two Tourney games before 1966. But with tenacious defense and 20 points from guard Bobby Joe Hill, Texas Western won, 72-65, at Cole Field House in College Park, Md. And it really wasn't as close as the score suggests. It was an inglorious last trip to the Final Four for coach Adolph Rupp.

Jerry Chambers of Utah, which lost in the national third-place game to Duke, was named Most Outstanding Player—the only player in NCAA history to earn the honor from a fourth-place team. Michigan's Cazzie Russell was the unanimous National Player of the Year and was chosen as the No. 1 overall pick in the NBA draft (New York Knicks).

Major Conference Standings

AAWU	Conference			Overall		
	W	L	Pct	W	L	Pct
Oregon State⊕	12	2	.857	21	7	.750
UCLA	10	4	.714	18	8	.692
Stanford	8	6	.571	13	12	.520
Washington State	6	8	.429	15	11	.577
Oregon	6	8	.429	13	13	.500
Southern California	6	8	.429	13	13	.500
Washington	4	10	.286	10	15	.400
California	4	10	.286	9	16	.360

ACC	Conference			Overall		
	W	L	Pct	W	L	Pct
Duke⊕	12	2	.857	26	4	.867
NC State	9	5	.643	18	9	.667
Clemson	8	6	.571	15	10	.600
North Carolina	8	6	.571	16	11	.593
Maryland	7	7	.500	14	11	.560
South Carolina	4	10	.286	11	13	.458
Virginia	4	10	.286	7	15	.318
Wake Forest	4	10	.286	8	18	.308

Tournament: **Duke d. NC State 71-66**
Tournament MVP: **Steve Vacendak**, Duke

Big Eight	Conference			Overall		
	W	L	Pct	W	L	Pct
Kansas⊕	13	1	.929	23	4	.852
Nebraska	12	2	.857	20	5	.800
Kansas State	9	5	.643	14	11	.560
Oklahoma	7	7	.500	11	14	.440
Colorado	6	8	.429	12	13	.480
Iowa State	6	8	.429	11	14	.440
Oklahoma State	2	12	.143	4	21	.160
Missouri	1	13	.071	3	21	.125

Big Sky	Conference			Overall		
	W	L	Pct	W	L	Pct
Weber State	8	2	.800	20	5	.800
Gonzaga	8	2	.800	19	7	.731
Montana	6	4	.600	14	10	.583
Montana State	5	5	.500	7	17	.292
Idaho	2	8	.200	12	14	.462
Idaho State	1	9	.100	7	19	.269

Big Ten	Conference			Overall		
	W	L	Pct	W	L	Pct
Michigan⊕	11	3	.786	18	8	.692
Michigan State	10	4	.714	15	7	.682
Iowa	8	6	.571	17	7	.708
Illinois	8	6	.571	12	12	.500
Minnesota	7	7	.500	14	10	.583
Northwestern	7	7	.500	12	12	.500
Wisconsin	6	8	.429	11	13	.458
Ohio State	5	9	.357	11	13	.458
Indiana	4	10	.286	8	16	.333
Purdue	4	10	.286	8	16	.333

Ivy	Conference			Overall		
	W	L	Pct	W	L	Pct
Penn	12	2	.857	19	6	.760
Columbia	10	4	.714	18	6	.750
Cornell	10	4	.714	15	9	.625
Princeton	9	5	.643	16	7	.696
Yale	6	8	.429	9	12	.429
Harvard	6	8	.429	10	14	.417
Brown	3	11	.214	9	17	.346
Dartmouth	0	14	.000	3	21	.125

Metro	Conference			Overall		
	W	L	Pct	W	L	Pct
Manhattan□	8	1	.889	13	9	.591
Long Island	7	2	.778	22	4	.846
NYU□	7	2	.778	18	10	.643
Hofstra	6	3	.667	16	10	.615
Fairleigh Dickinson	5	4	.556	15	10	.600
Saint Peter's	5	4	.556	11	12	.478
Seton Hall	3	6	.333	6	18	.250
Iona	3	6	.333	5	16	.238
Wagner	1	8	.111	14	12	.538
St. Francis (NY)	0	9	.000	5	17	.227

Note: Hofstra also played in the Middle Atlantic

Mid-American	Conference			Overall		
	W	L	Pct	W	L	Pct
Miami (OH)⊕	11	1	.917	18	7	.720
Toledo	8	4	.667	13	11	.542
Ohio	6	6	.500	13	10	.565
Bowling Green	6	6	.500	9	15	.375
Marshall	4	8	.333	12	12	.500
Western Michigan	4	8	.333	8	14	.364
Kent State	3	9	.250	8	16	.333

Middle Atlantic	Conference			Overall		
	W	L	Pct	W	L	Pct
Saint Joseph's⊕	-	-	-	24	5	.828
Temple□	-	-	-	21	7	.750
Hofstra	-	-	-	16	10	.615
Bucknell	-	-	-	15	10	.600
Lafayette	-	-	-	9	11	.450
La Salle	-	-	-	10	15	.400
Delaware	-	-	-	9	15	.375
Gettysburg	-	-	-	9	15	.375
West Chester	-	-	-	6	17	.261
Lehigh	-	-	-	4	17	.190

Missouri Valley	Conference			Overall		
	W	L	Pct	W	L	Pct
Cincinnati⊕	10	4	.714	21	7	.750
Bradley	9	5	.643	20	6	.769
Wichita State□	9	5	.643	17	10	.630
Louisville□	8	6	.571	16	10	.615
Saint Louis	8	6	.571	16	10	.615
Tulsa	6	8	.429	16	13	.552
Drake	6	8	.429	13	12	.520
North Texas	0	14	.000	5	20	.200

Ohio Valley	Conference			Overall		
	W	L	Pct	W	L	Pct
Western Kentucky⊕	14	0	1.000	25	3	.893
Eastern Kentucky	9	5	.643	16	9	.640
Tennessee Tech	8	6	.571	17	8	.680
Murray State	8	6	.571	13	12	.520
Morehead State	8	6	.571	12	12	.500
Austin Peay	3	11	.214	7	14	.333
East Tennessee St.	3	11	.214	7	14	.333
Middle Tennessee St.	3	11	.214	7	17	.292

Tournament: **Western Kentucky d. East Tenn. St. 72-59**

SEC	Conference			Overall		
	W	L	Pct	W	L	Pct
Kentucky⊕	15	1	.938	27	2	.931
Vanderbilt	13	3	.813	22	4	.846
Tennessee	10	6	.625	18	8	.692
Mississippi State	10	6	.625	14	11	.560
Alabama	9	7	.563	16	10	.615
Florida	9	7	.563	16	10	.615
Auburn	8	8	.500	16	10	.615
Georgia	5	11	.313	10	15	.400
Tulane	5	11	.313	9	16	.360
LSU	2	14	.125	6	20	.231
Mississippi	2	14	.125	5	18	.217

Southern	Conference			Overall		
	W	L	Pct	W	L	Pct
Davidson⊕	11	1	.917	21	7	.750
West Virginia	8	2	.800	19	9	.679
William and Mary	8	3	.727	13	12	.520
Richmond	9	7	.563	12	13	.480
East Carolina	5	7	.417	11	15	.423
Furman	4	8	.333	9	17	.346
VMI	5	11	.313	5	18	.217
The Citadel	4	9	.308	7	16	.304
George Washington	3	9	.250	3	18	.143

Tournament: **Davidson d. West Virginia 80-69**
Tournament MOP: **Dick Snyder**, Davidson

Southland	Conference			Overall		
	W	L	Pct	W	L	Pct
Abilene Christian	8	0	1.000	21	7	.750
Arkansas State	4	4	.500	17	9	.654
Lamar	4	4	.500	17	9	.654
Trinity (TX)	3	5	.375	12	10	.545
Texas-Arlington	1	7	.125	9	13	.409

Southwest	Conference			Overall		
	W	L	Pct	W	L	Pct
SMU⊕	11	3	.786	17	9	.654
Texas A&M	10	4	.714	15	9	.625
Texas Tech	8	6	.571	13	11	.542
Arkansas	7	7	.500	13	10	.565
Texas	7	7	.500	12	12	.500
Baylor	6	8	.429	8	16	.333
TCU	6	8	.429	8	16	.333
Rice	1	13	.071	1	22	.043

WCAC	Conference			Overall		
	W	L	Pct	W	L	Pct
Pacific⊕	13	1	.929	22	6	.786
San Francisco□	11	3	.786	22	6	.786
Santa Clara	8	6	.571	16	11	.593
San Jose State	7	7	.500	11	13	.458
Loyola Marymount	7	7	.500	11	15	.423
UC Santa Barbara	5	9	.357	10	16	.385
Saint Mary's (CA)	4	10	.286	8	17	.320
Pepperdine	1	13	.071	2	24	.077

WAC	Conference			Overall		
	W	L	Pct	W	L	Pct
Utah⊕	7	3	.700	23	8	.742
BYU□	6	4	.600	20	5	.800
Wyoming	5	5	.500	17	9	.654
Arizona	5	5	.500	15	11	.577
New Mexico	4	6	.400	16	8	.667
Arizona State	3	7	.300	12	14	.462

Yankee	Conference			Overall		
	W	L	Pct	W	L	Pct
Rhode Island⊕	9	1	.900	20	8	.714
Connecticut	9	1	.900	16	8	.667
Massachusetts	5	5	.500	11	13	.458
Maine	4	6	.400	9	13	.409
Vermont	3	7	.300	12	8	.600
New Hampshire	0	10	.000	3	21	.125

Conference Standings Continue →

⊕ Automatic NCAA Tournament bid ○ At-large NCAA Tournament bid □ NIT appearance ⊗ Team record doesn't reflect games forfeited or vacated. For adjusted record, see p. 521.

ANNUAL REVIEW

INDEPENDENTS

	Overall W	L	Pct
Texas Western○	28	1	.966
Loyola-Chicago○	22	3	.880
Oklahoma City○	24	5	.828
Providence○	22	5	.815
Boston College□	21	5	.808
Dayton○	23	6	.793
Houston○	23	6	.793
Fairfield	19	5	.792
Virginia Tech□	19	5	.792
Syracuse○	22	6	.786
Hardin-Simmons	20	6	.769
Penn State□	18	6	.750
Rutgers	17	7	.708
St. Bonaventure	16	7	.696
Army□	18	8	.692
DePaul□	18	8	.692
St. John's□	18	8	.692
Detroit	17	8	.680
Georgetown	16	8	.667
Colorado State○	14	8	.636
Villanova□	18	11	.621
Butler	16	10	.615
Seattle	16	10	.615
Duquesne	14	9	.609
Miami (FL)	15	11	.577

INDEPENDENTS (CONT.)

	Overall W	L	Pct
Denver	14	11	.560
Florida State	14	11	.560
Air Force	14	12	.538
Creighton	14	12	.538
Marquette	14	12	.538
Georgia Tech	13	13	.500
Xavier	13	13	.500
Centenary	12	14	.462
Utah State	12	14	.462
Niagara	11	13	.458
Holy Cross	10	13	.435
Fordham	10	15	.400
Memphis	10	15	.400
Navy	7	12	.368
Colgate	8	14	.364
Loyola (LA)	9	17	.346
Canisius	7	15	.318
Saint Francis (PA)	8	18	.308
West Texas	6	17	.261
Portland	6	19	.240
Pittsburgh	5	17	.227
Notre Dame	5	21	.192
Boston U.	4	19	.174
New Mexico State	4	22	.154

INDIVIDUAL LEADERS—SEASON

Scoring

	CL	POS	G	FG	FT	PTS	PPG
1 **Dave Schellhase**, Purdue	SR	G/F	24	284	213	781	**32.5**
2 **Dave Wagnon**, Idaho State	SR	G	26	312	221	845	**32.5**
3 **Cazzie Russell**, Michigan	SR	G/F	26	308	184	800	**30.8**
4 **Jerry Chambers**, Utah	SR	F/C	31	343	206	892	**28.8**
5 **Dave Bing**, Syracuse	SR	G	28	308	178	794	**28.4**
6 **Tom Kerwin**, Centenary	SR	F	26	282	162	726	**27.9**
7 **Don Freeman**, Illinois	SR	F	24	258	152	668	**27.8**
8 **John Beasley**, Texas A&M	SR	C	24	246	176	668	**27.8**
9 **Bill Melchionni**, Villanova	SR	G	29	321	159	801	**27.6**
10 **Bob Lewis**, North Carolina	SR	F/G	27	259	222	740	**27.4**

Field Goal Pct

	CL	POS	G	FG	FGA	PCT
1 **Julian Hammond**, Tulsa	SR	F	29	172	261	**65.9**
2 **Doug McKendrick**, Rice	SR	F	23	168	265	**63.4**
3 **Henry Finkel**, Dayton	SR	C	29	248	397	**62.5**
4 **Mike Lewis**, Duke	SO	C	30	161	271	**59.4**
5 **Art Stephenson**, Rhode Island	SO	F	27	128	216	**59.3**

Minimum: 125 made

Free Throw Pct

	CL	POS	G	FT	FTA	PCT
1 **Bill Blair**, Providence	SR	F	27	101	112	**90.2**
2 **Terry Morawski**, Seton Hall	SR	F	21	136	153	**88.9**
3 **Bob Lloyd**, Rutgers	JR	G	24	161	183	**88.0**
4 **Rick Jones**, Miami (FL)	JR	G	26	134	153	**87.6**
5 **Paul Long**, Wake Forest	JR	G	26	153	176	**86.9**

Minimum: 95 made

Rebounds

	CL	POS	G	REB	RPG
1 **Jim Ware**, Oklahoma City	SR	C	29	607	**20.9**
2 **Wes Unseld**, Louisville	SO	C	26	505	**19.4**
3 **Keith Swagerty**, Pacific	JR	F	28	514	**18.4**
4 **Tommy Woods**, East Tennessee State	JR	F	21	361	**17.2**
5 **Elvin Hayes**, Houston	SO	F/C	29	490	**16.9**

INDIVIDUAL LEADERS—GAME

Points

	CL	POS	OPP	DATE	PTS
1 **Dave Schellhase**, Purdue	SR	G/F	Michigan	F19	**57**
2 **Elvin Hayes**, Houston	SO	F/C	Southwestern Texas	F12	**55**
3 **Bob Lloyd**, Rutgers	JR	G	Delaware	D8	**51**
4 **Jimmy Walker**, Providence	JR	G	Boston College	D30	**50**
Dub Malaise, Texas Tech	SR	G	Texas	F19	**50**

Free Throws Made

	CL	POS	OPP	DATE	FT	FTA	PCT
1 **Dave Brown**, Lafayette	SR	F	Gettysburg	F12	**22**	24	91.7
2 **John Block**, Southern California	SR	F/C	Washington	F11	**21**	21	100.0
3 **Tom Workman**, Seattle	JR	F	UC Santa Barbara	D13	**20**	24	83.3
4 **Hal Jackson**, Austin Peay	SR	F	Tennessee-Martin	J12	**19**	21	90.5
Bob Lloyd, Rutgers	JR	G	Delaware	D8	**19**	22	86.4
Dave Wagnon, Idaho State	SR	G	Seattle	F4	**19**	24	79.2

TEAM LEADERS—SEASON

Scoring Offense

	G	W-L	PTS	PPG
1 **Syracuse**	28	22-6	2,773	**99.0**
2 **Houston**	29	23-6	2,845	**98.1**
3 **Oklahoma City**	29	24-5	2,829	**97.6**
4 **Loyola-Chicago**	25	22-3	2,438	**97.5**
5 **BYU**	25	20-5	2,388	**95.5**

Field Goal Pct

	G	W-L	FG	FGA	PCT
1 **North Carolina**	27	16-11	838	1,620	**51.7**
2 **Davidson**	28	21-7	877	1,713	**51.2**
3 **Syracuse**	28	22-6	1,132	2,271	**49.8**
4 **BYU**	25	20-5	946	1,898	**49.8**
5 **Seattle**	26	16-10	849	1,722	**49.3**

Free Throw Pct

	G	W-L	FT	FTA	PCT
1 **Auburn**	26	16-10	476	601	**79.2**
2 **Austin Peay**	21	7-14	463	591	**78.3**
3 **Rhode Island**	28	20-8	596	770	**77.4**
4 **Murray State**	25	13-12	488	640	**76.3**
5 **Davidson**	28	21-7	563	739	**76.2**

Scoring Defense

	G	W-L	OPP PTS	OPP PPG
1 **Oregon State**	28	21-7	1,527	**54.5**
2 **Tennessee**	26	18-8	1,499	**57.7**
3 **Oklahoma State**	25	4-21	1,523	**60.9**
4 **Princeton**	23	16-7	1,425	**62.0**
5 **Texas Western**	29	28-1	1,817	**62.7**

CONSENSUS ALL-AMERICAS

First Team

PLAYER	CL	POS	HT	SCHOOL	RPG	PPG
Dave Bing	SR	G	6-3	Syracuse	10.8	28.4
Clyde Lee	SR	C	6-9	Vanderbilt	15.8	22.7
Cazzie Russell	SR	G/F	6-5	Michigan	8.4	30.8
Dave Schellhase	SR	G/F	6-4	Purdue	10.6	32.5
Jimmy Walker	JR	G	6-3	Providence	6.7	24.5

Second Team

PLAYER	CL	POS	HT	SCHOOL	RPG	PPG
Louie Dampier	JR	G	6-0	Kentucky	5.0	21.1
Matt Guokas Jr.	SR	G	6-5	Saint Joseph's	2.5	17.5
Jack Marin	SR	F	6-6	Duke	9.7	18.9
Dick Snyder	SR	F	6-5	Davidson	9.2	26.9
Bob Verga	JR	G	6-0	Duke	4.0	18.5
Walt Wesley	SR	C	6-11	Kansas	9.3	20.7

Selectors: AP, NABC, UPI, USBWA

AWARD WINNERS

Player of the Year

PLAYER	CL	POS	HT	SCHOOL	AWARDS
Cazzie Russell	SR	G/F	6-5	Michigan	AP, UPI, USBWA

Coach of the Year

COACH	SCHOOL	REC	AWARDS
Adolph Rupp	Kentucky	27-2	UPI, USBWA, Sporting News

Poll Progression

Preseason Poll

AP	UPI	School
1	1	UCLA Ⓐ
2	2	Michigan
3	5	Duke
4	4	Saint Joseph's
5	6	Vanderbilt
6	7	Providence
7	3	Minnesota
8	8	Kansas
9	9	Bradley
10	12	Kansas State
—	10	BYU
—	11	San Francisco
—	13	NC State
—	14	Dayton
—	15	Boston College
—	15	St. John's
—	17	Louisville
—	17	Tennessee
—	17	West Virginia
—	20	Iowa
—	20	New Mexico
—	20	Princeton

Week of Dec 7

AP	UPI	School	AP↓↑
1	1	UCLA (2-0)	
2	2	Michigan (3-0)	
3	3	Saint Joseph's (2-0)	↑1
4	6	Vanderbilt (1-0)	↑1
5	5	Minnesota (2-0)	↑2
6	4	Duke (2-0)	↓3
7	7	Kansas (2-0)	↑1
8	8	Providence (1-0)	↓2
9	10	Bradley (1-0)	
10	—	South Carolina (2-0)	⤴
—	9	BYU (1-0)	
—	11	San Francisco (2-1)	
—	12	Iowa (3-0)	
—	13	Kentucky (2-0)	
—	14	Louisville (2-0)	
—	15	NC State (1-0)	
—	16	New Mexico (2-0)	
—	16	Ohio State (1-2)	
—	18	Boston College (1-0)	
—	18	Tennessee (0-1)	
—	20	Dayton (2-0)	

Week of Dec 14

AP	UPI	School	AP↓↑
1	1	Duke (4-1) Ⓑ	↑5
2	2	Saint Joseph's (4-0)	↑1
3	5	Michigan (4-1) Ⓒ	↓1
4	4	Kansas (5-0)	↑3
5	3	Vanderbilt (4-0)	↓1
6	6	Minnesota (3-0)	↓1
7	7	Providence (3-0)	↑1
8	8	UCLA (2-2) Ⓑ	↓7
9	11	Bradley (6-0)	
10	10	Wichita State (3-0)	⤴
—	9	BYU (2-0)	
—	12	Iowa (5-0)	
—	13	Kentucky (4-0)	
—	14	South Carolina (4-0)	⤵
—	15	Oklahoma City (5-0)	
—	16	New Mexico (3-1)	
—	16	Saint Louis (4-0)	
—	18	Florida (3-0)	
—	19	NC State (1-1)	
—	19	Utah (4-0)	

Week of Dec 21

AP	UPI	School	AP↓↑
1	1	Duke (6-1)	
2	2	Saint Joseph's (6-0)	
3	5	Michigan (4-1)	
4	3	Vanderbilt (6-0)	↑1
5	11	Bradley (8-0)	↑4
6	4	Minnesota (4-0)	
7	6	Providence (5-0)	
8	7	Wichita State (4-0)	↑2
9	9	Iowa (7-0)	⤴
10	9	Kentucky (6-0)	⤴
—	8	BYU (4-0)	
—	12	Kansas (5-2)	⤵
—	13	UCLA (3-3)	⤵
—	14	Syracuse (7-0)	
—	15	Cincinnati (5-1)	
—	15	Utah (6-0)	
—	17	Dayton (6-0)	
—	17	NC State (2-1)	
—	19	Colorado State (5-0)	
—	19	San Francisco (5-2)	

Week of Dec 28

AP	UPI	School	AP↓↑
1	1	Duke (7-1)	
2	2	Vanderbilt (8-0)	↑2
3	4	Bradley (10-0)	↑2
4	6	Iowa (7-0)	↑5
5	5	Kentucky (7-0)	↑5
6	3	BYU (6-0)	⤴
7	9	Michigan (4-3)	↓4
8	7	Saint Joseph's (6-2)	↓6
9	10	Minnesota (5-1)	↓3
10	8	Providence (5-1)	↓3
—	11	UCLA (5-3)	
—	12	Kansas (6-2)	
—	13	Syracuse (7-0)	
—	14	NC State (3-2)	
—	14	Utah (7-0)	
—	16	Cincinnati (6-1)	
—	16	Wichita State (4-2)	⤵
—	18	Dayton (7-0)	
—	19	New Mexico (6-1)	
—	20	North Carolina (6-2)	

Week of Jan 4

AP	UPI	School	AP↓↑
1	1	Duke (9-1)	
2	2	Kentucky (8-0)	↑3
3	3	Vanderbilt (10-1)	↓1
4	4	Saint Joseph's (9-2)	↑4
5	7	Bradley (10-1)	↓2
6	6	Providence (8-1)	↑4
7	9	Iowa (8-1)	↓3
8	5	BYU (8-1)	↓2
9	11	Texas Western (10-0)	⤴
10	8	UCLA (7-3)	⤴
—	9	Kansas (9-2)	
—	12	Cincinnati (8-1)	
—	13	Syracuse (9-2)	
—	14	Loyola-Chicago (9-1)	
—	15	Minnesota (7-3)	⤵
—	16	Michigan (6-4)	⤵
—	17	Utah (8-2)	
—	18	DePaul (8-1)	
—	18	New Mexico (9-1)	
—	20	Oregon State (6-3)	

Week of Jan 11

AP	UPI	School	AP↓↑
1	1	Duke (11-1)	
2	2	Kentucky (10-0)	
3	3	Vanderbilt (12-1)	
4	4	Saint Joseph's (10-2)	
5	5	Bradley (13-1)	
6	7	Providence (10-1)	
7	6	BYU (10-1)	↑1
8	9	Texas Western (12-0)	↑1
9	8	UCLA (9-3)	↑1
10	10	Kansas (11-2)	⤴
—	11	Loyola-Chicago (11-1)	
—	12	Iowa (8-2)	⤵
—	13	New Mexico (10-1)	
—	14	Dayton (10-1)	
—	15	Tulsa (12-3)	
—	15	Utah (10-3)	
—	17	Louisville (9-3)	
—	18	Western Kentucky (10-1)	
—	19	Temple (12-1)	
—	19	Texas A&M (7-4)	

Week of Jan 18

AP	UPI	School	AP↓↑
1	1	Duke (14-1)	
2	2	Kentucky (12-0)	
3	3	Saint Joseph's (11-2)	↑1
4	4	Providence (12-1)	↑2
5	5	Vanderbilt (14-2)	↓2
6	7	Kansas (13-2)	↑4
7	6	Bradley (14-2)	↓2
8	8	Texas Western (12-0)	
9	9	Loyola-Chicago (13-1)	⤴
10	12	UCLA (10-4)	↓1
—	10	Utah (12-3)	
—	11	BYU (10-3)	⤵
—	13	Michigan (9-4)	
—	14	Cincinnati (11-2)	
—	15	New Mexico (11-2)	
—	15	San Francisco (12-2)	
—	17	Michigan State (10-3)	
—	18	Nebraska (12-2)	
—	19	Iowa (9-3)	
—	20	NC State (8-4)	

Week of Jan 25

AP	UPI	School	AP↓↑
1	1	Duke (14-1)	
2	2	Kentucky (12-0)	
3	3	Providence (12-1)	↑1
4	4	Vanderbilt (14-2)	↑1
5	5	Saint Joseph's (13-3)	↓2
6	6	Texas Western (12-0)	↑2
7	7	Loyola-Chicago (13-1)	↑2
8	10	Cincinnati (13-2)	⤴
9	9	Kansas (14-3)	↓3
10	14	UCLA (10-4)	
—	8	Bradley (14-3)	⤵
—	11	Michigan State (10-4)	
—	12	Utah (13-3)	
—	13	Nebraska (13-2)	
—	15	St. John's (10-3)	
—	16	San Francisco (12-2)	
—	17	BYU (11-3)	
—	18	Dayton (13-3)	
—	18	Tulsa (13-4)	
—	20	Iowa (10-3)	
—	20	Syracuse (11-3)	

Week of Feb 1

AP	UPI	School	AP↓↑
1	1	Duke (15-1)	
2	2	Kentucky (14-0)	
3	3	Vanderbilt (15-2)	↑1
4	4	Providence (13-1)	↓1
5	5	Loyola-Chicago (15-1)	↑2
6	6	Texas Western (14-0)	
7	7	Kansas (14-3)	↑2
8	8	Saint Joseph's (13-4)	↓3
9	9	Michigan (11-4)	⤴
10	10	Cincinnati (14-3)	↓2
—	11	Utah (14-3)	
—	12	Nebraska (13-2)	
—	13	Bradley (14-4)	
—	13	St. John's (11-3)	
—	15	Dayton (14-3)	
—	16	San Francisco (13-2)	
—	17	BYU (11-3)	
—	18	New Mexico (12-2)	
—	19	Oklahoma City (9-4)	
—	19	Tulsa (13-6)	

Week of Feb 8

AP	UPI	School	AP↓↑
1	1	Kentucky (17-0)	↑1
2	2	Duke (15-1)	↓1
3	3	Loyola-Chicago (16-1)	↑2
4	5	Texas Western (16-0)	↑2
5	7	Vanderbilt (16-3)	↓2
6	4	Providence (15-1)	↓2
7	6	Kansas (15-3)	
8	8	Saint Joseph's (15-4)	
9	9	Nebraska (14-2)	⤴
10	10	Michigan (12-5)	↓1
—	11	Cincinnati (14-5)	⤵
—	11	San Francisco (15-2)	
—	13	Utah (14-4)	
—	14	Dayton (15-3)	
—	15	St. John's (12-4)	
—	15	Syracuse (13-3)	
—	17	BYU (12-3)	
—	18	Illinois (9-7)	
—	19	Bradley (15-4)	
—	20	Michigan State (13-4)	

Week of Feb 15

AP	UPI	School	AP↓↑
1	1	Kentucky (19-0)	
2	2	Duke (17-2)	
3	3	Texas Western (18-0)	↑1
4	5	Loyola-Chicago (17-2)	↓1
5	8	Vanderbilt (17-3)	
6	4	Providence (17-2)	
7	7	Kansas (16-3)	
8	6	Saint Joseph's (17-4)	
9	9	Nebraska (16-3)	
10	10	Michigan (13-5)	
—	11	San Francisco (16-3)	
—	12	Cincinnati (16-5)	
—	13	Syracuse (15-3)	
—	14	BYU (14-3)	
—	14	Utah (17-4)	
—	16	Houston (17-4) Ⓓ	
—	17	St. John's (14-4)	
—	18	Oklahoma City (12-4)	
—	19	Western Kentucky (17-2)	
—	20	Dayton (17-3)	

Poll Progression Continues →

Week of Feb 22

AP	UPI	SCHOOL	AP↓↑
1	1	**Kentucky** (21-0)	
2	2	**Duke** (19-2)	
3	3	**Texas Western** (20-0)	
4	4	**Loyola-Chicago** (20-2)	
5	6	**Vanderbilt** (19-3)	
6	5	**Kansas** (18-3)	↑1
7	7	**Saint Joseph's** (19-4)	↑1
8	10	**Nebraska** (17-3)	↑1
9	8	**Providence** (19-3)	↓3
10	9	**Michigan** (14-5)	
—	11	**Cincinnati** (18-5)	
—	12	**Utah** (18-5)	
—	13	**San Francisco** (18-3)	
—	14	**Western Kentucky** (19-2)	
—	15	**Houston** (18-4)	
—	16	**Syracuse** (18-4)	
—	17	**St. John's** (16-4)	
—	18	**Oklahoma City** (15-5)	
—	19	**Oregon State** (16-6)	
—	20	**Boston College** (16-4)	
—	20	**Tennessee** (17-6)	

Week of Mar 1

AP	UPI	SCHOOL	AP↓↑
1	1	**Kentucky** (23-0)	
2	3	**Texas Western** (22-0)	↑1
3	2	**Duke** (20-3)	↓1
4	4	**Loyola-Chicago** (21-2)	
5	7	**Vanderbilt** (21-3)	
6	5	**Kansas** (20-3)	
7	6	**Saint Joseph's** (21-4)	
8	8	**Providence** (21-3)	↑1
9	13	**Nebraska** (18-4)	↓1
10	10	**Cincinnati** (20-5)	⤴
—	9	**Michigan** (15-6)	⤵
—	11	**Utah** (20-5) Ⓔ	
—	12	**San Francisco** (20-4)	
—	14	**Oregon State** (17-6)	
—	15	**Syracuse** (19-5)	
—	16	**Dayton** (21-4)	
—	17	**Western Kentucky** (21-2)	
—	18	**Pacific** (20-4)	
—	19	**Oklahoma City** (17-5)	
—	20	**Boston College** (19-4)	
—	20	**Michigan State** (16-6)	

Final Poll

AP	UPI	SCHOOL	AP↓↑
1	1	**Kentucky** (23-1) Ⓕ	
2	2	**Duke** (23-3)	↑1
3	3	**Texas Western** (23-1) Ⓕ	↓1
4	4	**Kansas** (21-3)	↑2
5	6	**Saint Joseph's** (22-4)	↑2
6	5	**Loyola-Chicago** (21-2)	↓2
7	9	**Cincinnati** (21-5)	↑3
8	8	**Vanderbilt** (22-4)	↓3
9	7	**Michigan** (17-6)	⤴
10	—	**Western Kentucky** (24-2)	⤴
—	10	**Providence** (22-4)	⤵
—	11	**Nebraska** (20-5)	⤵
—	12	**Utah** (21-6)	
—	13	**Oklahoma City** (18-5)	
—	14	**Houston** (21-5)	
—	15	**Oregon State** (20-6)	
—	16	**Syracuse** (21-5)	
—	17	**Pacific** (22-4)	
—	18	**Davidson** (20-5)	
—	19	**BYU** (17-5)	
—	19	**Dayton** (23-4)	

Ⓐ No. 1 in the polls, No. 2 on campus: The defending NCAA champion UCLA varsity squad is beaten by the school's freshman team, 75-60, led by 7'2" Lew Alcindor's 31 points. Seven years before freshmen could play varsity ball, the Brubabes will go 21–0 and outscore opponents by 50 points a game.

Ⓑ Duke hammers UCLA, 94-75, in Charlotte. The previous night, the Blue Devils beat the Bruins, 82-66, in Durham behind Mike Lewis' 16 points and 21 rebounds. UCLA will finish 18–8 and miss the postseason.

Ⓒ Michigan rebounds from a 100-94 upset at Wichita State to defeat San Francisco, 94-78, in Chicago. Windy City native Cazzie Russell has 45 points and 10 rebounds.

Ⓓ Sophomore big man Elvin Hayes scores 55 points and grabs 37 rebounds in Houston's 140-87 rout of Southwestern Texas. The future NBA star and Hall of Famer will go on to score 40 or more points 18 times as a Cougar, including four games of 50 or more.

Ⓔ With team captain and top rebounder George Fisher on the sideline with a broken leg, Jerry Chambers scores 47 to carry Utah to a 116-103 victory over Seattle. Despite Fisher's injury, the Utes will reach the Final Four.

Ⓕ The last two undefeated teams in the nation fall. Tennessee stops Kentucky's 25-game regular-season win streak, 69-62, in Knoxville, and Seattle hands Texas Western its first (and only) loss of the season, edging the Miners 74-72.

1966 NCAA Tournament (A)

(A) Net income for the Tournament exceeds $500,000 for the first time. A local-market television blackout provision requiring a 48-hour advance sellout is adopted.

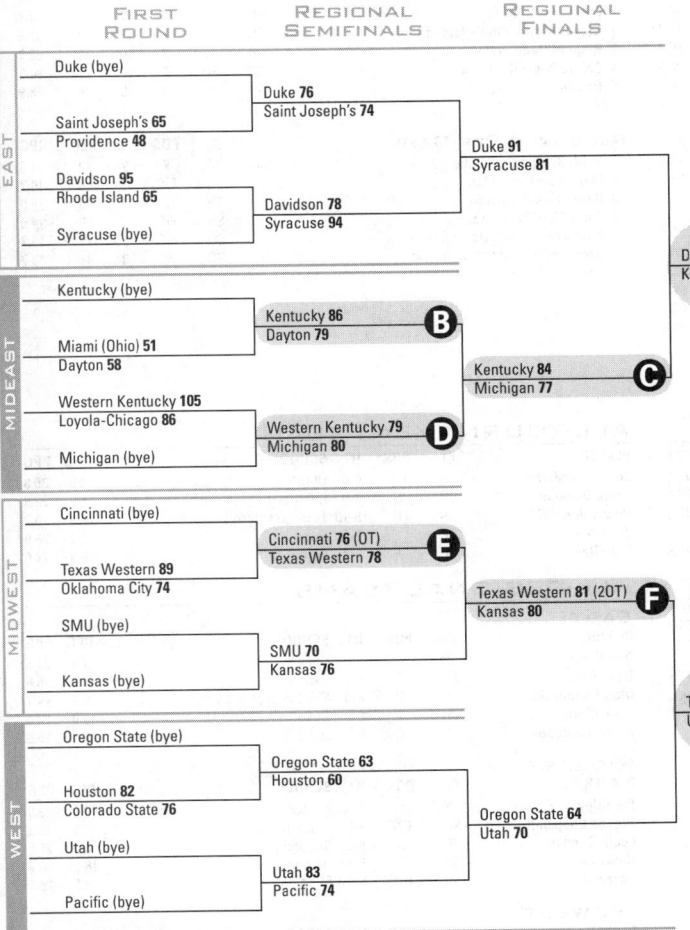

East

First Round
- Duke (bye)
- Saint Joseph's **65**, Providence **48**
- Davidson **95**, Rhode Island **65**
- Syracuse (bye)

Regional Semifinals
- Duke **76**, Saint Joseph's **74**
- Davidson **78**, Syracuse **94**

Regional Finals
- Duke **91**, Syracuse **81**

Mideast

First Round
- Kentucky (bye)
- Miami (Ohio) **51**, Dayton **58**
- Western Kentucky **105**, Loyola-Chicago **86**
- Michigan (bye)

Regional Semifinals
- Kentucky **86**, Dayton **79** (B)
- Western Kentucky **79**, Michigan **80** (D)

Regional Finals
- Kentucky **84**, Michigan **77** (C)

Midwest

First Round
- Cincinnati (bye)
- Texas Western **89**, Oklahoma City **74**
- SMU (bye)
- Kansas (bye)

Regional Semifinals
- Cincinnati **76** (OT), Texas Western **78** (E)
- SMU **70**, Kansas **76**

Regional Finals
- Texas Western **81** (2OT), Kansas **80** (F)

West

First Round
- Oregon State (bye)
- Houston **82**, Colorado State **76**
- Utah (bye)
- Pacific (bye)

Regional Semifinals
- Oregon State **63**, Houston **60**
- Utah **83**, Pacific **74**

Regional Finals
- Oregon State **64**, Utah **70**

National Semifinals

Duke **79**
Kentucky **83**

In a game many consider the "real" championship, Kentucky and Duke slug it out down the stretch. KU's Louie Dampier steals an inbounds pass that leads to a game-icing layup by Pat Riley.

Texas Western **85**
Utah **78**

The Final Four's shortest player, 5'6" Willie Worsley, scores 10 straight points in the second half for Texas Western. Utah's Jerry Chambers is the only player from a fourth-place team ever to be Tournament MOP.

National Final

Texas Western 72
Kentucky 65

Either Kentucky or Duke would have filled the role of "all-white team" against Texas Western's five African-American starters—a Final first—in a game that becomes a civil rights morality play. The Miners set the tone early when Dave "Big Daddy D" Lattin dunks over Pat Riley and guard Bobby Joe Hill makes back-to-back steals. "They were just better than we were tonight," says coach Adolph Rupp.

College Park, MD

National Third Place Duke d. Utah 79-77
East Regional Third Place Saint Joseph's d. Davidson 92-76
Mideast Regional Third Place Western Kentucky d. Dayton 82-62
Midwest Regional Third Place SMU d. Cincinnati 89-84
West Regional Third Place Houston d. Pacific 102-91

(B) With no starter over 6'5", No. 1 Kentucky is known as Rupp's Runts. UK's Pat Riley, 6'4", who jumps center against 6'11" Henry Finkel, posts the first of back-to-back 29-point performances.

(C) Members of Western Kentucky's official party are angry because Kentucky coach Adolph Rupp "crashed" a 71st birthday party for retired Hilltoppers coach E.A. Diddle. But Western still "donates" its pep band and cheerleaders to help root Kentucky past Michigan.

(D) WKU leads with seconds left when a jump ball is called between Michigan's Cazzie Russell and Western's Greg Smith. On a crooked toss, Smith fouls Russell, who then hits two free throws to deny Western the chance to play Kentucky in the regional final.

(E) Even though Nevil "the Shadow" Shed gets ejected in the first half for throwing a punch, Texas Western survives. The wonderfully named Willie Cager scores five straight points for the Miners in overtime.

(F) Kansas' Jo Jo White hits what appears to be a game-winning 25-footer in the first OT, but is ruled to have stepped out of bounds as he released the shot. Willie Cager tips in the game-winner with :32 left in the second OT.

Tournament Leaders

INDIVIDUAL LEADERS

Scoring

	CL	POS	G	PTS	PPG
1 **Jerry Chambers**, Utah	SR	F/C	4	143	35.8
2 **Henry Finkel**, Dayton	SR	C	3	92	30.7
Rodney Knowles, Davidson	SO	F/C	3	92	30.7
4 **Cazzie Russell**, Michigan	SR	G/F	2	53	26.5
5 **Pat Riley**, Kentucky	JR	F	4	96	24.0
6 **Walt Wesley**, Kansas	SR	C	2	47	23.5
7 **Jack Marin**, Duke	SR	F	4	92	23.0
8 **Louie Dampier**, Kentucky	JR	G	4	91	22.8
9 **Carroll Hooser**, SMU	SR	F	2	43	21.5
10 **Elvin Hayes**, Houston	SO	F/C	3	63	21.0

Minimum: 2 games

Field Goal Pct

	CL	POS	G	FG	FGA	PCT
1 **Ron Krick**, Cincinnati	SR	C	2	10	13	76.9
2 **Denny Holman**, SMU	JR	G	2	15	21	71.4
3 **Jim Boeheim**, Syracuse	SR	G	2	13	19	68.4
4 **Thad Jaracz**, Kentucky	SO	C	4	19	30	63.3
5 **Ron Franz**, Kansas	JR	F	2	14	23	60.9

Minimum: 10 made

Free Throw Pct

	CL	POS	G	FT	FTA	PCT
1 **Mike Lewis**, Duke	SO	C	4	17	18	94.4
2 **Steve Chubin**, Rhode Island	SR	G	1	13	14	92.9
3 **Richard Dean**, Syracuse	JR	C	2	10	11	90.9
4 **Cazzie Russell**, Michigan	SR	G/F	2	19	21	90.5
5 **Orsten Artis**, Texas Western	SR	F	5	16	18	88.9

Minimum: 10 made

Rebounds Per Game

	CL	POS	G	REB	RPG
1 **Keith Swagerty**, Pacific	JR	F	2	42	21.0
2 **Elvin Hayes**, Houston	SO	F/C	3	50	16.7
3 **Henry Finkel**, Dayton	SR	C	3	48	16.0
4 **Jerry Chambers**, Utah	SR	F/C	4	56	14.0
5 **Rodney Knowles**, Davidson	SO	F/C	3	41	13.7
Greg Smith, Western Kentucky	SO	F	3	41	13.7

Minimum: 2 games

TEAM LEADERS

Scoring

	G	PTS	PPG
1 **Western Kentucky**	3	266	88.7
2 **Syracuse**	2	175	87.5
3 **Davidson**	3	249	83.0
4 **Pacific**	2	165	82.5
5 **Houston**	3	244	81.3
6 **Duke**	4	325	81.3
7 **Texas Western**	5	405	81.0
8 **Cincinnati**	2	160	80.0
9 **SMU**	2	159	79.5
Kentucky	4	318	79.5

Minimum: 2 games

FG Pct

	G	FG	FGA	PCT
1 **SMU**	2	62	123	50.4
2 **Cincinnati**	2	66	136	48.5
3 **Kentucky**	4	130	274	47.4
4 **Syracuse**	2	72	154	46.8
5 **Duke**	4	125	274	45.6

FT Pct

	G	FT	FTA	PCT
1 **Syracuse**	2	31	40	77.5
Michigan	2	31	40	77.5
3 **Kentucky**	4	58	76	76.3
4 **SMU**	2	35	46	76.1
5 **Davidson**	3	63	83	75.9

Minimum: 2 games

Rebounds

	G	REB	RPG
1 **Pacific**	2	112	56.0
2 **Western Kentucky**	3	144	48.0
3 **Houston**	3	141	47.0
4 **Saint Joseph's**	3	137	45.7
5 **Kansas**	2	91	45.5

Minimum: 2 games

ALL-TOURNAMENT TEAM

PLAYER	CL	POS	HT	SCHOOL	RPG	PPG
Jerry Chambers*	SR	F/C	6-4	Utah	14.0	35.8
Louie Dampier	JR	G	6-0	Kentucky	6.3	22.8
Bobby Joe Hill	JR	G	5-10	Texas Western	5.4	20.2
Jack Marin	SR	F	6-6	Duke	9.8	23.0
Pat Riley	JR	F	6-4	Kentucky	6.3	24.0

ALL-REGIONAL TEAMS

EAST

PLAYER	CL	POS	HT	SCHOOL	RPG	PPG
Bob Verga*	JR	G	6-0	Duke	2.5	21.5
Dave Bing	SR	G	6-3	Syracuse	10.0	15.0
Matt Guokas Jr.	SR	G	6-5	Saint Joseph's	6.0	14.7
Jack Marin	SR	F	6-6	Duke	12.0	20.0
Steve Vacendak	SR	G	6-1	Duke	5.0	16.0

MIDEAST

PLAYER	CL	POS	HT	SCHOOL	RPG	PPG
Pat Riley*	JR	F	6-4	Kentucky	6.5	29.0
Wayne Chapman	SO	G/F	6-6	Western Kentucky	6.3	15.3
Louie Dampier	JR	G	6-0	Kentucky	6.0	24.5
Henry Finkel	SR	C	6-11	Dayton	16.0	30.7
Cazzie Russell	SR	G/F	6-5	Michigan	8.5	26.5

MIDWEST

PLAYER	CL	POS	HT	SCHOOL	RPG	PPG
Bobby Joe Hill*	JR	G	5-10	Texas Western	4.3	21.0
Denny Holman	JR	G	6-3	SMU	6.0	15.5
Carroll Hooser	SR	F	6-7	SMU	7.5	21.5
David Lattin	SO	F	6-6	Texas Western	13.3	21.3
Walt Wesley	SR	C	6-11	Kansas	13.5	23.5

WEST

PLAYER	CL	POS	HT	SCHOOL	RPG	PPG
Jerry Chambers*	SR	F/C	6-4	Utah	10.5	36.5
Elvin Hayes	SO	F/C	6-8	Houston	16.7	21.0
Mervin Jackson	SO	G	6-2	Utah	7.5	10.0
Richard Tate	SR	G	5-11	Utah	8.0	11.5
Rick Whelan	SR	G	6-0	Oregon State	3.5	17.0
Charlie White	SR	G/F	6-4	Oregon State	11.0	15.0

* Most outstanding player

1966 NCAA TOURNAMENT BOX SCORES

SWEET 16 — Duke 76, Saint Joseph's 74

	1H	2H	Final
Duke	37	39	76
Saint Joseph's	33	41	74

DUKE	MIN	FG	3FG	FT	REB	A	ST	BL	PF	TP
Bob Verga	-	8-17	-	6-6	4	0	-	-	1	22
Jack Marin	-	6-16	-	6-8	15	0	-	-	2	18
Mike Lewis	-	6-12	-	2-2	15	0	-	-	4	14
Steve Vacendak	-	6-14	-	1-2	7	2	-	-	2	13
Bob Reidy	-	1-5	-	3-5	5	1	-	-	3	5
Warren Chapman	-	1-3	-	2-3	5	0	-	-	4	4
Ron Wendelin	-	0-0	-	0-0	0	0	-	-	1	0
TOTALS	-	28-67	-	20-26	51	3	-	-	17	76
Percentages		41.8		76.9						

Coach: Vic Bubas

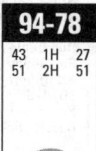

SAINT JOSEPH'S	MIN	FG	3FG	FT	REB	A	ST	BL	PF	TP
Clifford Anderson	-	6-15	-	8-10	15	1	-	-	4	20
Matt Guokas	-	7-15	-	5-5	4	2	-	-	5	19
Tom Duff	-	7-22	-	3-5	8	1	-	-	3	17
William Oakes	-	4-18	-	0-0	1	0	-	-	1	8
Marty Ford	-	2-5	-	2-4	6	0	-	-	1	6
Chuck McKenna	-	1-8	-	2-2	13	0	-	-	3	4
Steve Chapman	-	0-1	-	0-0	0	0	-	-	0	0
TOTALS	-	27-84	-	20-26	47	4	-	-	17	74
Percentages		32.1		76.9						

Coach: Jack Ramsay

Officials: MacPherson, Wirtz

SWEET 16 — Syracuse 94, Davidson 78

	1H	2H	Final
Syracuse	43	51	94
Davidson	27	51	78

SYRACUSE	MIN	FG	3FG	FT	REB	A	ST	BL	PF	TP
George Hicker	-	9-14	-	4-6	8	-	-	-	2	22
Dave Bing	-	9-20	-	2-2	12	-	-	-	2	20
Jim Boeheim	-	7-9	-	0-0	3	-	-	-	3	14
Richard Dean	-	5-13	-	2-2	12	-	-	-	4	12
Richard Cornwall	-	4-7	-	1-1	3	-	-	-	1	9
Sam Penceal	-	4-5	-	0-1	0	-	-	-	0	8
Norman Goldsmith	-	2-4	-	0-0	2	-	-	-	3	4
Valentine Reid	-	1-3	-	0-3	5	-	-	-	1	2
Rex Trobridge	-	0-1	-	2-2	2	-	-	-	2	2
Vaughn Harper	-	0-2	-	1-2	2	-	-	-	4	1
Richard Ableman	-	0-1	-	0-0	0	-	-	-	1	0
Frank Nicoletti	-	0-0	-	0-0	3	-	-	-	2	0
TOTALS	-	41-79	-	12-19	52	-	-	-	25	94
Percentages		51.9		63.2						

Coach: Fred Lewis

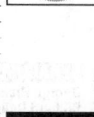

DAVIDSON	MIN	FG	3FG	FT	REB	A	ST	BL	PF	TP
Rodney Knowles	-	9-24	-	7-9	11	-	-	-	3	25
Dick Snyder	-	9-22	-	7-9	8	-	-	-	4	25
Tom Youngdale	-	3-9	-	4-6	9	-	-	-	5	10
Sam Hatcher	-	2-4	-	2-4	5	-	-	-	1	6
Bobby Lane	-	1-7	-	3-3	3	-	-	-	3	5
Phil Squier	-	2-11	-	1-1	3	-	-	-	1	5
George Leight	-	1-4	-	0-1	4	-	-	-	1	2
TOTALS	-	27-81	-	24-33	43	-	-	-	18	78
Percentages		33.3		72.7						

Coach: Lefty Driesell

SWEET 16 — Kentucky 86, Dayton 79

	1H	2H	Final
Kentucky	38	48	86
Dayton	40	39	79

KENTUCKY	MIN	FG	3FG	FT	REB	A	ST	BL	PF	TP
Louie Dampier	-	14-23	-	6-7	6	-	-	-	1	34
Pat Riley	-	11-18	-	7-8	8	-	-	-	3	29
Thad Jaracz	-	7-9	-	3-3	7	-	-	-	3	17
Tommy Kron	-	1-6	-	1-1	6	-	-	-	3	3
Cliff Berger	-	1-3	-	0-0	0	-	-	-	4	2
Larry Conley	-	0-5	-	1-1	3	-	-	-	1	1
Jim LeMaster	-	0-2	-	0-0	1	-	-	-	0	0
TOTALS	-	34-66	-	18-20	31	-	-	-	15	86
Percentages		51.5		90.0						

Coach: Adolph Rupp

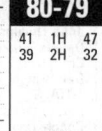

DAYTON	MIN	FG	3FG	FT	REB	A	ST	BL	PF	TP
Henry Finkel	-	15-26	-	6-7	13	-	-	-	4	36
Don May	-	6-16	-	4-5	3	-	-	-	3	16
Rudy Waterman	-	6-13	-	2-4	9	-	-	-	3	14
Glinder Torain	-	2-10	-	2-2	4	-	-	-	3	6
Bobby Joe Hooper	-	2-7	-	1-2	7	-	-	-	3	5
Gene Klaus	-	1-1	-	0-0	0	-	-	-	1	2
Bill Cassidy	-	0-0	-	0-0	0	-	-	-	0	0
TOTALS	-	32-73	-	15-20	36	-	-	-	17	79
Percentages		43.8		75.0						

Coach: Don Donoher

Officials: Allmond, Eckman
Attendance: 11,500

SWEET 16 — Michigan 80, Western Kentucky 79

	1H	2H	Final
Michigan	41	39	80
Western Kentucky	47	32	79

MICHIGAN	MIN	FG	3FG	FT	REB	A	ST	BL	PF	TP
Cazzie Russell	-	7-15	-	10-12	6	-	-	-	3	24
John Clawson	-	8-12	-	2-2	2	-	-	-	2	18
Oliver Darden	-	7-16	-	4-5	12	-	-	-	1	18
Jim Myers	-	4-15	-	2-3	10	-	-	-	3	10
John Thompson	-	4-9	-	0-0	5	-	-	-	3	8
Craig Dill	-	1-2	-	0-0	1	-	-	-	1	2
Dennis Bankey	-	0-0	-	0-0	0	-	-	-	0	0
TOTALS	-	31-69	-	18-22	36	-	-	-	13	80
Percentages		44.9		81.8						

Coach: Dave Strack

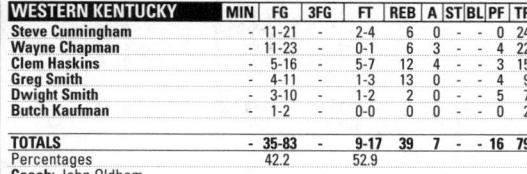

WESTERN KENTUCKY	MIN	FG	3FG	FT	REB	A	ST	BL	PF	TP
Steve Cunningham	-	11-21	-	2-4	6	0	-	-	0	24
Wayne Chapman	-	11-23	-	0-1	6	3	-	-	4	22
Clem Haskins	-	5-16	-	5-7	12	4	-	-	3	15
Greg Smith	-	4-11	-	1-3	13	0	-	-	4	9
Dwight Smith	-	3-10	-	1-2	2	0	-	-	5	7
Butch Kaufman	-	1-2	-	0-0	0	0	-	-	0	2
TOTALS	-	35-83	-	9-17	39	7	-	-	16	79
Percentages		42.2		52.9						

Coach: John Oldham

Officials: Eisenstein, Honzo

SWEET 16 — Texas Western 78, Cincinnati 76

	1H	2H	OT1	Final
Texas Western	36	33	9	78
Cincinnati	42	27	7	76

TEXAS WESTERN	MIN	FG	3FG	FT	REB	A	ST	BL	PF	TP
David Lattin	-	10-15	-	9-10	8	0	-	-	3	29
Bobby Joe Hill	-	7-18	-	3-6	5	1	-	-	1	17
Willie Cager	-	5-5	-	5-6	2	0	-	-	2	15
Orsten Artis	-	4-8	-	3-3	1	1	-	-	4	11
Willie Worsley	-	1-10	-	2-2	2	3	-	-	3	4
Harry Flournoy	-	1-5	-	0-0	7	0	-	-	2	2
Nevil Shed	-	0-2	-	0-0	2	0	-	-	0	0
TOTALS	-	28-63	-	22-27	27	5	-	-	15	78
Percentages		44.4		81.5						

Coach: Don Haskins

CINCINNATI	MIN	FG	3FG	FT	REB	A	ST	BL	PF	TP
Roland West	-	7-12	-	5-6	11	0	-	-	5	19
Ron Krick	-	9-12	-	0-0	9	0	-	-	4	18
Dean Foster	-	5-9	-	1-2	2	6	-	-	2	11
Don Rolfes	-	3-9	-	4-6	4	1	-	-	2	10
Mike Rolf	-	4-8	-	1-1	7	0	-	-	1	9
John Howard	-	1-9	-	3-3	6	4	-	-	4	5
Ken Calloway	-	2-3	-	0-0	1	0	-	-	0	4
Paul Weidner	-	0-0	-	0-0	1	0	-	-	0	0
TOTALS	-	31-62	-	14-18	41	11	-	-	18	76
Percentages		50.0		77.8						

Coach: Tay Baker

Officials: Filiberti, Bussenius

SWEET 16 — Kansas 76, SMU 70

	1H	2H	Final
Kansas	46	30	76
SMU	46	24	70

KANSAS	MIN	FG	3FG	FT	REB	A	ST	BL	PF	TP
Walt Wesley	-	9-17	-	5-8	12	-	-	-	2	23
Ron Franz	-	9-15	-	1-2	5	-	-	-	5	19
Albert Lopes	-	4-10	-	3-3	5	-	-	-	5	11
Jo Jo White	-	4-17	-	2-2	7	-	-	-	4	10
Delvin Lewis	-	4-12	-	1-1	7	-	-	-	1	9
Rodger Bohnenstiehl	-	1-6	-	0-0	7	-	-	-	1	2
Riney Lochmann	-	1-4	-	0-1	6	-	-	-	2	2
TOTALS	-	32-81	-	12-17	49	-	-	-	20	76
Percentages		39.5		70.6						

Coach: Ted Owens

SMU	MIN	FG	3FG	FT	REB	A	ST	BL	PF	TP
Carroll Hooser	-	10-20	-	2-4	7	-	-	-	4	22
Charles Beasley	-	5-13	-	7-9	9	-	-	-	2	17
Bob Begert	-	4-10	-	4-7	9	-	-	-	4	12
Denny Holman	-	3-8	-	0-1	10	-	-	-	1	6
John Ramsay	-	2-5	-	1-1	3	-	-	-	2	5
John Higginbotham	-	1-2	-	2-2	1	-	-	-	0	4
Robert Jones	-	2-3	-	0-0	0	-	-	-	1	4
TOTALS	-	27-61	-	16-24	39	-	-	-	14	70
Percentages		44.3		66.7						

Coach: E.O. "Doc" Hayes

Officials: Varnell, Marick
Attendance: 8,000

63-60 — SWEET 16

	1H	2H
Oregon State	28	35
Houston	30	30

OREGON STATE	MIN	FG	3FG	FT	REB	A	ST	BL	PF	TP
Rick Whelan	-	11-14	-	2-5	6	-	-	-	3	24
Eric Petersen	-	6-8	-	1-2	10	-	-	-	5	13
Ed Fredenburg	-	3-6	-	4-7	5	-	-	-	2	10
Charlie White	-	4-9	-	2-4	8	-	-	-	1	10
Scott Eaton	-	2-5	-	2-2	1	-	-	-	1	6
Harry Gunner	-	0-0	-	0-0	2	-	-	-	2	0
TOTALS	-	26-42	-	11-20	32	-	-	-	14	63
Percentages		61.9		55.0						

Coach: Paul Valenti

HOUSTON	MIN	FG	3FG	FT	REB	A	ST	BL	PF	TP
Joe Hamood	40	6-18	-	6-8	4	3	-	-	3	18
Elvin Hayes	40	6-13	-	2-4	10	0	-	-	4	14
Don Kruse	17	4-10	-	0-2	2	1	-	-	2	8
Don Chaney	34	2-8	-	2-2	9	1	-	-	3	6
Gary Grider	20	2-5	-	2-2	6	2	-	-	2	6
Leary Lentz	20	1-7	-	1-1	3	1	-	-	2	3
Richard Apolskis	9	0-1	-	3-3	1	1	-	-	2	3
Wayne Ballard	20	1-8	-	0-0	2	1	-	-	1	2
TOTALS	200	22-70	-	16-22	37	10	-	-	19	60
Percentages		31.4		72.7						

Coach: Guy V. Lewis

83-74 — SWEET 16

	1H	2H
Utah	49	34
Pacific	41	33

UTAH	MIN	FG	3FG	FT	REB	A	ST	BL	PF	TP
Jerry Chambers	-	17-30	-	6-8	11	-	-	-	1	40
Mervin Jackson	-	5-9	-	0-2	4	-	-	-	4	10
Lyndon Mackay	-	4-8	-	2-5	9	-	-	-	3	10
Jeff Ockel	-	3-6	-	4-7	10	-	-	-	4	10
Richard Tate	-	3-12	-	1-3	9	-	-	-	1	7
Eugene Lake	-	1-4	-	2-2	1	-	-	-	1	4
Leonard Black	-	1-3	-	0-0	1	-	-	-	0	2
TOTALS	-	34-72	-	15-27	45	-	-	-	14	83
Percentages		47.2		55.6						

Coach: Jack Gardner

PACIFIC	MIN	FG	3FG	FT	REB	A	ST	BL	PF	TP
Bob Krulish	-	8-18	-	3-4	10	-	-	-	5	19
Bruce Parsons	-	7-13	-	3-5	9	-	-	-	3	17
Keith Swagerty	-	6-22	-	4-6	19	-	-	-	3	16
David Fox	-	5-16	-	1-2	6	-	-	-	4	11
Don Odale	-	3-9	-	1-2	4	-	-	-	3	7
Ron Seum	-	2-4	-	0-0	1	-	-	-	0	4
Art Gilbert	-	0-0	-	0-0	0	-	-	-	1	0
TOTALS	-	31-82	-	12-19	49	-	-	-	19	74
Percentages		37.8		63.2						

Coach: Dick Edwards

Officials: Watson, Laws
Attendance: 8,846

91-81 — ELITE 8

	1H	2H
Duke	44	47
Syracuse	37	44

DUKE	MIN	FG	3FG	FT	REB	A	ST	BL	PF	TP
Jack Marin	40	7-14	-	8-10	9	1	-	-	1	22
Bob Verga	40	10-13	-	1-3	1	1	-	-	2	21
Steve Vacendak	40	7-15	-	5-7	3	3	-	-	3	19
Mike Lewis	31	4-10	-	8-8	13	0	-	-	3	16
Bob Riedy	30	3-6	-	6-8	10	1	-	-	4	12
Warren Chapman	10	0-0	-	1-1	2	0	-	-	2	1
Jim Liccardo	9	0-2	-	0-0	0	0	-	-	0	0
TOTALS	200	31-60	-	29-37	38	6	-	-	15	91
Percentages		51.7		78.4						

Coach: Vic Bubas

SYRACUSE	MIN	FG	3FG	FT	REB	A	ST	BL	PF	TP
George Hicker	30	7-20	-	3-3	7	0	-	-	4	17
Richard Dean	39	4-8	-	8-9	7	1	-	-	4	16
Jim Boeheim	34	6-10	-	3-4	1	1	-	-	3	15
Vaughn Harper	33	5-12	-	3-3	10	3	-	-	5	13
Dave Bing	36	4-14	-	2-2	8	3	-	-	4	10
Richard Cornwall	18	5-10	-	0-0	1	1	-	-	1	10
Sam Penceal	6	0-1	-	0-0	0	0	-	-	0	0
Norman Goldsmith	3	0-0	-	0-0	0	0	-	-	0	0
Frank Nicoletti	1	0-0	-	0-0	0	0	-	-	2	0
TOTALS	200	31-75	-	19-21	34	9	-	-	23	81
Percentages		41.3		90.5						

Coach: Fred Lewis

Officials: Wir
Stout

84-77 — ELITE 8

	1H	2H
Kentucky	42	42
Michigan	32	45

KENTUCKY	MIN	FG	3FG	FT	REB	A	ST	BL	PF	TP
Pat Riley	-	13-27	-	3-4	5	-	-	-	2	29
Louie Dampier	-	6-12	-	3-4	6	-	-	-	3	15
Larry Conley	-	6-11	-	2-6	8	-	-	-	4	14
Tommy Kron	-	6-14	-	2-5	9	-	-	-	4	14
Thad Jaracz	-	6-8	-	0-0	7	-	-	-	2	12
Tommy Porter	-	0-0	-	0-0	0	-	-	-	0	0
TOTALS	-	37-72	-	10-19	35	-	-	-	15	84
Percentages		51.4		52.6						

Coach: Adolph Rupp

MICHIGAN	MIN	FG	3FG	FT	REB	A	ST	BL	PF	TP
Cazzie Russell	-	10-25	-	9-9	11	-	-	-	2	29
Oliver Darden	-	8-16	-	1-3	12	-	-	-	5	17
John Clawson	-	5-14	-	1-2	5	-	-	-	3	11
Jim Myers	-	5-19	-	0-0	11	-	-	-	3	10
John Thompson	-	2-6	-	2-4	3	-	-	-	2	6
Dennis Bankey	-	1-1	-	0-0	0	-	-	-	1	2
Craig Dill	-	1-3	-	0-0	0	-	-	-	0	2
Dan Brown	-	0-1	-	0-0	0	-	-	-	1	0
TOTALS	-	32-85	-	13-18	42	-	-	-	17	77
Percentages		37.6		72.2						

Coach: Dave Strack

Officials: Eckman, Honz
Attendance: 11,500

81-80 — ELITE 8

	1H	2H	OT1	OT2
Texas Western	38	31	2	10
Kansas	35	34	2	9

TEXAS WESTERN	MIN	FG	3FG	FT	REB	A	ST	BL	PF	TP
Bobby Joe Hill	-	7-20	-	8-13	4	-	-	-	3	22
David Lattin	-	7-16	-	1-2	17	-	-	-	4	15
Orsten Artis	-	5-12	-	2-3	7	-	-	-	3	12
Nevil Shed	-	3-5	-	6-9	4	-	-	-	2	12
Harry Flournoy	-	3-7	-	5-6	8	-	-	-	5	11
Willie Cager	-	3-7	-	0-1	4	-	-	-	4	6
Willie Worsley	-	1-4	-	1-1	1	-	-	-	0	3
Jerry Armstrong	-	0-0	-	0-0	1	-	-	-	0	0
TOTALS	-	29-71	-	23-35	46	-	-	-	21	81
Percentages		40.8		65.7						

Coach: Don Haskins

KANSAS	MIN	FG	3FG	FT	REB	A	ST	BL	PF	TP
Walt Wesley	-	9-23	-	6-12	15	-	-	-	5	24
Jo Jo White	-	7-14	-	5-6	11	-	-	-	4	19
Albert Lopes	-	7-15	-	3-4	6	-	-	-	4	17
Ron Franz	-	5-8	-	2-3	4	-	-	-	5	12
Delvin Lewis	-	1-3	-	4-4	1	-	-	-	5	6
Rodger Bohnenstiehl	-	1-3	-	0-0	2	-	-	-	1	2
Riney Lochmann	-	0-0	-	0-0	3	-	-	-	1	0
Robert Wilson	-	0-0	-	0-0	0	-	-	-	0	0
TOTALS	-	30-66	-	20-29	42	-	-	-	25	80
Percentages		45.5		69.0						

Coach: Ted Owens

Officials: Marick, Bussenius
Technicals: Texas Wester (Lattin)
Attendance: 8,200

70-64 — ELITE 8

	1H	2H
Utah	41	29
Oregon State	24	40

UTAH	MIN	FG	3FG	FT	REB	A	ST	BL	PF	TP
Jerry Chambers	-	13-31	-	7-8	10	-	-	-	4	33
Richard Tate	-	5-14	-	6-10	7	-	-	-	0	16
Mervin Jackson	-	5-10	-	0-1	11	-	-	-	3	10
Jeff Ockel	-	2-6	-	1-2	14	-	-	-	1	5
Lyndon Mackay	-	1-8	-	2-2	9	-	-	-	0	4
Leonard Black	-	1-2	-	0-0	3	-	-	-	1	2
TOTALS	-	27-71	-	16-23	54	-	-	-	9	70
Percentages		38.0		69.6						

Coach: Jack Gardner

OREGON STATE	MIN	FG	3FG	FT	REB	A	ST	BL	PF	TP
Charlie White	-	9-18	-	2-2	14	-	-	-	4	20
Ed Fredenburg	-	7-14	-	1-1	9	-	-	-	2	15
Scott Eaton	-	6-13	-	1-1	5	-	-	-	3	13
Rick Whelan	-	5-14	-	0-0	1	-	-	-	1	10
Loy Peterson	-	2-13	-	1-1	4	-	-	-	4	5
Harry Gunner	-	0-4	-	1-2	3	-	-	-	2	1
Ray Carlile	-	0-4	-	0-0	2	-	-	-	2	0
TOTALS	-	29-80	-	6-7	38	-	-	-	18	64
Percentages		36.2		85.7						

Coach: Paul Valenti

Officials: Jenkins, Over
Attendance: 10,365

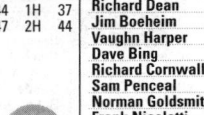

83-79 (1H: 41-42; 2H: 42-37) — FINAL 4

KENTUCKY	MIN	FG	3FG	FT	REB	A	ST	BL	PF	TP
Louie Dampier	-	11-20	-	1-2	4	-	-	-	3	23
Pat Riley	-	8-17	-	3-4	8	-	-	-	5	19
Tommy Kron	-	5-13	-	2-2	10	-	-	-	1	12
Larry Conley	-	3-5	-	4-4	1	-	-	-	0	10
Thad Jaracz	-	3-5	-	2-3	4	-	-	-	5	8
Cliff Berger	-	1-4	-	5-6	5	-	-	-	1	7
Bob Tallent	-	1-2	-	2-2	1	-	-	-	0	4
Gary Gamble	-	0-0	-	0-1	0	-	-	-	1	0
TOTALS	**-**	**32-66**	**-**	**19-24**	**33**	**-**	**-**	**-**	**16**	**83**
Percentages		48.5		79.2						

Coach: Adolph Rupp

DUKE	MIN	FG	3FG	FT	REB	A	ST	BL	PF	TP
Jack Marin	-	11-18	-	7-10	7	-	-	-	2	29
Mike Lewis	-	9-13	-	3-3	6	-	-	-	3	21
Steve Vacendak	-	7-16	-	3-3	3	-	-	-	5	17
Bob Riedy	-	2-7	-	2-2	8	-	-	-	3	6
Bob Verga	-	2-7	-	0-0	3	-	-	-	1	4
Ron Wendelin	-	1-4	-	0-1	2	-	-	-	4	2
Tony Barone	-	0-0	-	0-0	0	-	-	-	1	0
Jim Liccardo	-	0-1	-	0-0	0	-	-	-	0	0
TOTALS	**-**	**32-66**	**-**	**15-19**	**29**	**-**	**-**	**-**	**19**	**79**
Percentages		48.5		78.9						

Coach: Vic Bubas

Officials: Honzo, Jenkins
Attendance: 14,253

85-78 (1H: 42-39; 2H: 43-39) — FINAL 4

TEXAS WESTERN	MIN	FG	3FG	FT	REB	A	ST	BL	PF	TP
Orsten Artis	-	10-20	-	2-3	5	-	-	-	2	22
Bobby Joe Hill	-	5-20	-	8-10	11	-	-	-	4	18
Willie Worsley	-	5-8	-	2-3	5	-	-	-	3	12
David Lattin	-	5-7	-	1-1	4	-	-	-	3	11
Nevil Shed	-	2-3	-	5-6	3	-	-	-	5	9
Harry Flournoy	-	3-6	-	2-2	9	-	-	-	5	8
Willie Cager	-	2-5	-	1-1	0	-	-	-	3	5
Jerry Armstrong	-	0-2	-	0-1	3	-	-	-	2	0
TOTALS	**-**	**32-71**	**-**	**21-27**	**40**	**-**	**-**	**-**	**27**	**85**
Percentages		45.1		77.8						

Coach: Don Haskins

UTAH	MIN	FG	3FG	FT	REB	A	ST	BL	PF	TP
Jerry Chambers	-	14-31	-	10-12	17	-	-	-	3	38
Lyndon Mackay	-	4-10	-	6-9	7	-	-	-	2	14
Leonard Black	-	3-8	-	2-4	2	-	-	-	3	8
Mervin Jackson	-	3-9	-	2-2	2	-	-	-	1	8
Jeff Ockel	-	1-1	-	3-3	9	-	-	-	3	5
Joseph Day	-	1-2	-	0-0	0	-	-	-	0	2
Eugene Lake	-	1-1	-	0-0	0	-	-	-	3	2
Richard Tate	-	0-4	-	1-3	2	-	-	-	5	1
TOTALS	**-**	**27-66**	**-**	**24-33**	**39**	**-**	**-**	**-**	**20**	**78**
Percentages		40.9		72.7						

Coach: Jack Gardner

Officials: Bussenius, Wirtz
Attendance: 14,253

79-77 (1H: 41-37; 2H: 38-40) — 3RD PLACE

DUKE	MIN	FG	3FG	FT	REB	A	ST	BL	PF	TP
Jack Marin	-	9-26	-	5-5	8	-	-	-	4	23
Bob Verga	-	7-13	-	1-1	3	-	-	-	2	15
Mike Lewis	-	5-7	-	4-5	11	-	-	-	1	14
Steve Vacendak	-	5-13	-	1-4	4	-	-	-	3	11
Warren Chapman	-	2-8	-	0-1	4	-	-	-	1	4
Bob Riedy	-	2-5	-	0-0	2	-	-	-	5	4
Ron Wendelin	-	2-4	-	0-2	0	-	-	-	1	4
Tony Barone	-	1-2	-	0-0	1	-	-	-	1	2
Tim Kolodziej	-	1-1	-	0-0	0	-	-	-	1	2
Joe Kennedy	-	0-0	-	0-0	1	-	-	-	0	0
Jim Liccardo	-	0-2	-	0-2	3	-	-	-	0	0
TOTALS	**-**	**34-81**	**-**	**11-20**	**37**	**-**	**-**	**-**	**19**	**79**
Percentages		42.0		55.0						

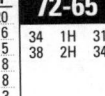

Coach: Vic Bubas

UTAH	MIN	FG	3FG	FT	REB	A	ST	BL	PF	TP
Jerry Chambers	-	11-16	-	10-12	18	-	-	-	3	32
Mervin Jackson	-	6-12	-	2-2	5	-	-	-	0	14
Lyndon Mackay	-	4-10	-	5-6	8	-	-	-	4	13
Jeff Ockel	-	5-9	-	0-0	5	-	-	-	3	10
Leonard Black	-	2-5	-	0-1	3	-	-	-	3	4
Richard Tate	-	1-8	-	2-5	2	-	-	-	1	4
Joseph Day	-	0-1	-	0-0	0	-	-	-	0	0
TOTALS	**-**	**29-61**	**-**	**19-26**	**41**	**-**	**-**	**-**	**14**	**77**
Percentages		47.5		73.1						

Coach: Jack Gardner

Officials: Bussenius, Wirtz
Attendance: 14,253

72-65 (1H: 34-31; 2H: 38-34) — NCAA FINAL 1966

TEXAS WESTERN	MIN	FG	3FG	FT	REB	A	ST	BL	PF	TP
Bobby Joe Hill	-	7-17	-	6-9	3	-	-	-	3	20
David Lattin	-	5-10	-	6-6	9	-	-	-	4	16
Orsten Artis	-	5-13	-	5-5	8	-	-	-	1	15
Willie Cager	-	1-3	-	6-7	6	-	-	-	3	8
Willie Worsley	-	2-4	-	4-6	4	-	-	-	0	8
Nevil Shed	-	1-1	-	1-1	3	-	-	-	1	3
Harry Flournoy	-	1-1	-	0-0	2	-	-	-	0	2
TOTALS	**-**	**22-49**	**-**	**28-34**	**35**	**-**	**-**	**-**	**12**	**72**
Percentages		44.9		82.4						

Coach: Don Haskins

KENTUCKY	MIN	FG	3FG	FT	REB	A	ST	BL	PF	TP
Louie Dampier	-	7-18	-	5-5	9	-	-	-	4	19
Pat Riley	-	8-22	-	3-4	4	-	-	-	4	19
Larry Conley	-	4-9	-	2-2	8	-	-	-	5	10
Thad Jaracz	-	3-8	-	1-2	5	-	-	-	5	7
Tommy Kron	-	3-6	-	0-0	7	-	-	-	2	6
Cliff Berger	-	2-3	-	0-0	0	-	-	-	0	4
Gary Gamble	-	0-0	-	0-0	0	-	-	-	1	0
Jim LeMaster	-	0-1	-	0-0	0	-	-	-	1	0
Bob Tallent	-	0-3	-	0-0	0	-	-	-	1	0
TOTALS	**-**	**27-70**	**-**	**11-13**	**33**	**-**	**-**	**-**	**23**	**65**
Percentages		38.6		84.6						

Coach: Adolph Rupp

Officials: Honzo, Jenkins
Attendance: 14,253

National Invitation Tournament (NIT)

First round: Temple d. Virginia Tech 88-73, NYU d. DePaul 68-65, San Francisco d. Penn State 89-77, Villanova d. St. John's 63-61, Army d. Manhattan 71-66, Boston College d. Louisville, 96-90 (3OT)
Quarterfinals: BYU d. Temple 90-78, NYU d. Wichita State 90-84 (OT), Army d. San Francisco 80-63, Villanova d. Boston College 86-85
Semifinals: BYU d. Army 66-60, NYU d. Villanova 69-63,
Third place: Villanova d. Army 76-65
Championship: BYU d. NYU 97-84
MVP: Bill Melchionni, Villanova

1966-67: Super Soph

With four sophomore starters and nary a senior on its roster come Tournament time, UCLA completed its second 30–0 season in four years with a 79-64 win over Dayton at Louisville's Freedom Hall. Of course, one of those sophs was 7'2" Lew Alcindor, playing in the rookie season of what has been hailed as the greatest career in the history of college basketball.

Dayton reached the Final Four in dramatic fashion, with two overtime wins against Western Kentucky and Virginia Tech, and a one-point victory over Tennessee. Then the Flyers convincingly defeated North Carolina behind 34 points from forward Don May. May had 21 points and 17 rebounds for Dayton in the Final, but got no help; and the Flyers had no answer for Alcindor, who scored 20 points and grabbed 18 rebounds. The Bruins won four Tournament games by an average margin of 23.8 points, an NCAA record.

Alcindor was named Tournament MOP and was the unanimous national Player of the Year after averaging 29.0 ppg and 15.5 rpg. The No. 1 pick in the draft, Providence's Jimmy Walker (Detroit Pistons), led Division I with an impressive 30.4 ppg. The second pick (Baltimore Bullets) had even gaudier numbers: Winston-Salem's Earl "Black Jesus" Monroe led the College Division with a fantastic 41.5 ppg.

Major Conference Standings

AAWU	Conference			Overall		
	W	L	PCT	W	L	PCT
UCLA ⊛	14	0	1.000	30	0	1.000
Washington State	8	6	.571	15	11	.577
Oregon State	8	6	.571	14	14	.500
Stanford	7	7	.500	15	11	.577
California	6	8	.429	15	10	.600
Southern California	6	8	.429	13	12	.520
Washington	6	8	.429	13	12	.520
Oregon	1	13	.071	9	17	.346

ACC	Conference			Overall		
	W	L	PCT	W	L	PCT
North Carolina ⊛	12	2	.857	26	6	.813
Duke □	9	3	.750	18	9	.667
South Carolina	8	4	.667	16	7	.696
Clemson	9	5	.643	17	8	.680
Maryland	5	9	.357	11	14	.440
Wake Forest	5	9	.357	9	18	.333
Virginia	4	10	.286	9	17	.346
NC State	2	12	.143	7	19	.269

Tournament: **North Carolina d. Duke 82-73**
Tournament MVP: **Larry Miller**, North Carolina

BIG EIGHT	Conference			Overall		
	W	L	PCT	W	L	PCT
Kansas ⊛	13	1	.929	23	4	.852
Colorado	10	4	.714	17	8	.680
Nebraska □	10	4	.714	16	9	.640
Kansas State	9	5	.643	17	8	.680
Iowa State	6	8	.429	13	12	.520
Oklahoma	5	9	.357	8	17	.320
Oklahoma State	2	12	.143	7	18	.280
Missouri	1	13	.071	3	22	.120

BIG SKY	Conference			Overall		
	W	L	PCT	W	L	PCT
Gonzaga	7	3	.700	21	6	.778
Montana State	7	3	.700	14	11	.560
Weber State	5	5	.500	18	7	.720
Idaho	5	5	.500	14	11	.560
Idaho State	5	5	.500	10	15	.400
Montana	1	9	.100	6	18	.250

BIG TEN	Conference			Overall		
	W	L	PCT	W	L	PCT
Indiana ⊛	10	4	.714	18	8	.692
Michigan State	10	4	.714	16	7	.696
Iowa	9	5	.643	16	8	.667
Wisconsin	8	6	.571	13	11	.542
Purdue	7	7	.500	15	9	.625
Northwestern	7	7	.500	11	11	.500
Ohio State	6	8	.429	13	11	.542
Illinois	6	8	.429	12	12	.500
Minnesota	5	9	.357	9	15	.375
Michigan	2	12	.143	8	16	.333

IVY	Conference			Overall		
	W	L	PCT	W	L	PCT
Princeton ⊛	13	1	.929	25	3	.893
Cornell	11	3	.786	19	5	.792
Yale	11	3	.786	14	7	.667
Penn	7	7	.500	11	14	.440
Columbia	6	8	.429	11	14	.440
Harvard	4	10	.286	10	14	.417
Brown	3	11	.214	10	16	.385
Dartmouth	1	13	.071	7	17	.292

METRO	Conference			Overall		
	W	L	PCT	W	L	PCT
Saint Peter's □	7	2	.778	18	6	.750
St. Francis (NY)	7	2	.778	15	8	.652
Manhattan	7	2	.778	13	8	.619
NYU	6	3	.667	10	16	.385
Long Island	5	4	.556	22	7	.759
Wagner	4	5	.444	19	9	.679
Iona	4	5	.444	11	10	.524
Seton Hall	3	6	.333	7	17	.292
Hofstra	2	7	.222	12	13	.480
Fairleigh Dickinson	0	9	.000	4	19	.174

Note: Hofstra also played in the Middle Atlantic

MID-AMERICAN	Conference			Overall		
	W	L	PCT	W	L	PCT
Toledo ⊛	11	1	.917	23	2	.920
Marshall □	10	2	.833	20	8	.714
Miami (OH)	7	5	.583	14	10	.583
Bowling Green	5	7	.417	11	13	.458
Western Michigan	4	8	.333	10	14	.417
Ohio	4	8	.333	8	15	.348
Kent State	1	11	.083	5	18	.217

MIDDLE ATLANTIC	Conference			Overall		
	W	L	PCT	W	L	PCT
Temple ⊛	-	-	-	20	8	.714
American	-	-	-	16	8	.667
Delaware	-	-	-	15	9	.625
Saint Joseph's	-	-	-	16	10	.615
Gettysburg	-	-	-	12	10	.545
La Salle	-	-	-	14	12	.538
Bucknell	-	-	-	11	11	.500
Hofstra	-	-	-	12	13	.480
Lehigh	-	-	-	11	12	.478
Rider	-	-	-	11	12	.478
West Chester	-	-	-	8	15	.348
Lafayette	-	-	-	4	21	.160

MISSOURI VALLEY	Conference			Overall		
	W	L	PCT	W	L	PCT
Louisville ⊛	12	2	.857	23	5	.821
Tulsa □	10	4	.714	19	8	.704
Wichita State	9	5	.643	14	12	.538
Bradley	6	8	.429	17	9	.654
Cincinnati	6	8	.429	17	9	.654
Saint Louis	5	9	.357	13	13	.500
North Texas	4	10	.286	12	13	.480
Drake	4	10	.286	9	16	.360

OHIO VALLEY	Conference			Overall		
	W	L	PCT	W	L	PCT
Western Kentucky ⊛	13	1	.929	23	3	.885
East Tenn. St.	8	6	.571	17	9	.654
Morehead State	8	6	.571	16	8	.667
Murray State	8	6	.571	14	9	.609
Austin Peay	7	7	.500	14	9	.609
Tennessee Tech	6	8	.429	12	11	.522
Middle Tenn. St.	4	10	.286	10	15	.400
Eastern Kentucky	2	12	.143	5	18	.217

Tournament: **Tennessee Tech d. Murray State 67-60**

SEC	Conference			Overall		
	W	L	PCT	W	L	PCT
Tennessee ⊛	15	3	.833	21	7	.750
Florida	14	4	.778	21	4	.840
Vanderbilt	14	4	.778	21	5	.808
Auburn	12	6	.667	17	8	.680
Mississippi State	8	10	.444	14	11	.560
Kentucky	8	10	.444	13	13	.500
Mississippi	7	11	.389	13	12	.520
Alabama	6	12	.333	13	13	.500
Georgia	5	13	.278	9	17	.346
LSU	1	17	.056	3	23	.115

SOUTHERN	Conference			Overall		
	W	L	PCT	W	L	PCT
West Virginia ⊛	9	1	.900	19	9	.679
Davidson	8	4	.667	15	12	.556
William and Mary	8	5	.615	14	11	.560
Richmond	9	7	.563	11	12	.478
The Citadel	6	7	.462	8	16	.333
George Washington	5	7	.417	6	18	.250
Furman	4	6	.400	9	15	.375
East Carolina	4	8	.333	7	17	.292
VMI	4	12	.250	5	16	.238

Tournament: **West Virginia d. Davidson 81-65**
Tournament MOP: **Johnny Moates**, Richmond

SOUTHLAND	Conference			Overall		
	W	L	PCT	W	L	PCT
Arkansas State	8	0	1.000	17	7	.708
Trinity (TX)	4	4	.500	16	6	.727
Texas-Arlington	4	4	.500	14	12	.538
Abilene Christian	4	4	.500	11	11	.500
Lamar	0	8	.000	5	19	.208

SOUTHWEST	Conference			Overall		
	W	L	PCT	W	L	PCT
SMU ⊛	12	2	.857	20	6	.769
Baylor	8	6	.571	14	10	.583
Texas	8	6	.571	14	10	.583
TCU	8	6	.571	10	14	.417
Texas Tech	7	7	.500	9	15	.375
Texas A&M	5	9	.357	6	18	.250
Rice	4	10	.286	7	17	.292
Arkansas	4	10	.286	6	17	.261

WCAC	Conference			Overall		
	W	L	PCT	W	L	PCT
Pacific ⊛	14	0	1.000	24	4	.857
Loyola Marymount	10	4	.714	16	10	.615
Santa Clara	8	6	.571	13	13	.500
UC Santa Barbara	8	6	.571	10	16	.385
San Francisco	7	7	.500	13	12	.520
Pepperdine	5	9	.357	9	17	.346
San Jose St.	4	10	.286	9	15	.375
Saint Mary's (CA)	2	12	.143	4	21	.160

WAC	Conference			Overall		
	W	L	PCT	W	L	PCT
BYU	8	2	.800	14	10	.583
Wyoming ⊛	8	2	.800	15	14	.517
New Mexico □	5	5	.500	19	8	.704
Utah	5	5	.500	15	11	.577
Arizona	3	7	.300	8	17	.320
Arizona State	1	9	.100	5	21	.192

⊛ Automatic NCAA Tournament bid ○ At-large NCAA Tournament bid □ NIT appearance ❶ Team record doesn't reflect games forfeited or vacated. For adjusted record, see p. 521.

YANKEE

	Conference W	L	Pct	Overall W	L	Pct
Connecticut⊕	9	1	.900	17	7	.708
Rhode Island	8	2	.800	14	12	.538
Massachusetts	7	3	.700	11	14	.440
New Hampshire	4	6	.400	10	12	.455
Maine	1	9	.100	8	12	.400
Vermont	1	9	.100	9	15	.375

INDEPENDENTS

	Overall W	L	Pct
Southern Illinois□	24	2	.923
Boston College○	21	3	.875
Houston○	27	4	.871
St. John's○	23	5	.821
Dayton○	25	6	.806
UTEP○	22	6	.786
Saint Francis (PA)	20	6	.769
Syracuse□	20	6	.769
Utah State□	20	6	.769
Rutgers□	22	7	.759
Providence□	21	7	.750
Virginia Tech○	20	7	.741
Marquette□	21	9	.700
Seattle○	18	8	.692
DePaul	17	8	.680
Georgia Tech	17	9	.654
Hardin-Simmons	17	9	.654
Memphis□	17	9	.654
Villanova□	17	9	.654
Holy Cross	16	9	.640
Southern Mississippi	16	9	.640
Army	13	8	.619
Oklahoma City	16	10	.615
Loyola-Chicago	13	9	.591
St. Bonaventure	13	9	.591
Canisius	14	10	.583
Tulane	14	10	.583

INDEPENDENTS (CONT.)

	Overall W	L	Pct
Miami (FL)	15	11	.577
New Mexico State○	15	11	.577
Fairfield	12	9	.571
Colorado State	13	10	.565
Fordham	14	11	.560
Loyola (LA)	12	10	.545
Georgetown	12	11	.522
Denver	13	12	.520
Notre Dame	14	14	.500
Xavier	13	13	.500
Creighton	12	13	.480
Niagara	12	13	.480
Navy	8	10	.444
Colgate	10	13	.435
Florida State	11	15	.423
Penn State	10	14	.417
Detroit	10	15	.400
Portland	10	16	.385
Butler	9	17	.346
Centenary	9	17	.346
Jacksonville	8	17	.320
Duquesne	7	15	.318
Air Force	6	18	.250
Pittsburgh	6	19	.240
Boston U.	4	18	.182
West Texas	1	18	.053

INDIVIDUAL LEADERS—SEASON

Scoring

	CL	POS	G	FG	FT	PTS	PPG
1 **Jimmy Walker**, Providence	SR	G	28	323	205	851	**30.4**
2 **Lew Alcindor**, UCLA	SO	C	30	346	178	870	**29.0**
3 **Mal Graham**, NYU	SR	G	24	250	188	688	**28.7**
4 **Elvin Hayes**, Houston	JR	F/C	31	373	135	881	**28.4**
5 **Wes Bialosuknia**, Connecticut	SR	G	24	257	159	673	**28.0**
6 **Bob Lloyd**, Rutgers	SR	G	29	277	255	809	**27.9**
7 **Gary Gray**, Oklahoma City	SR	G	26	298	119	715	**27.5**
8 **Cliff Anderson**, Saint Joseph's	SR	C	26	243	204	690	**26.5**
9 **Bob Verga**, Duke	SR	G	27	283	139	705	**26.1**
10 **Jim Tillman**, Loyola-Chicago	JR	C	22	219	115	553	**25.1**

Field Goal Pct

	CL	POS	G	FG	FGA	PCT
1 **Lew Alcindor**, UCLA	SO	C	30	346	519	**66.7**
2 **Joe Allen**, Bradley	JR	C	26	232	373	**62.2**
3 **Gary Lechman**, Gonzaga	SR	C	25	196	316	**62.0**
4 **Larry Lewis**, Saint Francis (PA)	SO	C	26	181	295	**61.4**
5 **Jim Youngblood**, Georgia	JR	F	26	140	237	**59.1**

Minimum: 125 made

Free Throw Pct

	CL	POS	G	FT	FTA	PCT
1 **Bob Lloyd**, Rutgers	SR	G	29	255	277	**92.1**
2 **Jim Sandfoss**, Morehead State	SR	G	24	106	117	**90.6**
3 **Jamie Thompson**, Wichita State	SR	F	26	124	137	**90.5**
4 **Jim Sutherland**, Clemson	SR	G	25	104	116	**89.7**
5 **Richard Cornwall**, Syracuse	JR	G	26	103	117	**88.0**

Minimum: 90 made

Rebounds Per Game

	CL	POS	G	REB	RPG
1 **Dick Cunningham**, Murray State	JR	C	22	479	**21.8**
2 **Art Beatty**, American	SO	F	24	458	**19.1**
3 **Wes Unseld**, Louisville	JR	C	28	533	**19.0**
4 **Keith Swagerty**, Pacific	SR	F	28	518	**18.5**
5 **Don May**, Dayton	JR	F	31	519	**16.7**

INDIVIDUAL LEADERS—GAME

Points

	CL	POS	OPP	DATE	PTS
1 **Lew Alcindor**, UCLA	SO	C	Washington State	F25	**61**
2 **Lew Alcindor**, UCLA	SO	C	Southern California	D4	**56**
3 **Gary Gray**, Oklahoma City	SR	G	Texas State	J20	**55**
Bud Ogden, Santa Clara	SO	F	Pepperdine	M3	**55**
5 **Mike Nordholz**, Alabama	JR	G	Southern Miss	D12	**50**
Wes Bialosuknia, Connecticut	SR	G	Maine	F4	**50**
Ron Widby, Tennessee	SR	F	LSU	M4	**50**

Free Throws Made

	CL	POS	OPP	DATE	FT	FTA	PCT
1 **Bob Lloyd**, Rutgers	SR	G	NYU	F2	19	19	**100.0**
2 **Jim Sandfoss**, Morehead State	SR	G	Marshall	F6	17	17	**100.0**
Mal Graham, NYU	SR	G	St. Francis (NY)	F11	17	18	**94.4**
Don Sidle, Oklahoma	JR	C	Nebraska	J9	17	20	**85.0**
Jimmy Walker, Providence	SR	G	Holy Cross	F25	17	21	**81.0**
Don Smith, Iowa State	JR	C	Kansas State	J14	17	24	**70.8**

Rebounds

	CL	POS	OPP	DATE	REB
1 **Dick Cunningham**, Murray State	JR	C	MacMurray	J2	**36**
2 **Gary Gregor**, South Carolina	JR	F/C	Elon	D19	**35**
3 **Dick Cunningham**, Murray State	JR	C	Eastern Kentucky	J2	**34**
4 **Art Beatty**, American	SO	F	La Salle	J10	**33**
5 **Cliff Anderson**, Saint Joseph's	SR	C	La Salle	F26	**32**
Keith Swagerty, Pacific	SR	F	Loyola-Marymount	F23	**32**

TEAM LEADERS—SEASON

Scoring Offense

	G	W-L	PTS	PPG
1 **Oklahoma City**	26	16-10	2,496	**96.0**
2 **Northwestern**	22	11-11	2,009	**91.3**
3 **UCLA**	30	30-0	2,687	**89.6**
4 **Murray State**	23	14-9	2,058	**89.5**
5 **Houston**	31	27-4	2,765	**89.2**

Field Goal Pct

	G	W-L	FG	FGA	PCT
1 **UCLA**	30	30-0	1,082	2,081	**52.0**
2 **Saint Peter's**	24	18-6	773	1,498	**51.6**
3 **Bradley**	26	17-9	832	1,641	**50.7**
4 **Vanderbilt**	26	21-5	834	1,654	**50.4**
5 **Tulane**	24	14-10	843	1,679	**50.2**

Free Throw Pct

	G	W-L	FT	FTA	PCT
1 **West Texas A&M**	26	14-12	400	518	**77.2**
2 **Santa Clara**	26	13-13	571	742	**77.0**
3 **Kentucky**	26	13-13	429	559	**76.7**
4 **Rice**	24	7-17	493	648	**76.1**
5 **Georgia**	26	9-17	454	598	**75.9**

Scoring Defense

	G	W-L	OPP PTS	OPP PPG
1 **Tennessee**	28	21-7	1,511	**54.0**
2 **Memphis**	26	17-9	1,470	**56.5**
3 **Army**	21	13-8	1,206	**57.4**
4 **Princeton**	28	25-3	1,619	**57.8**
5 **Kansas**	27	23-4	1,607	**59.5**

CONSENSUS ALL-AMERICAS

First Team

PLAYER	CL	POS	HT	SCHOOL	RPG	PPG
Lew Alcindor	SO	C	7-2	UCLA	15.5	29.0
Clem Haskins	SR	F	6-3	Western Kentucky	11.2	22.6
Elvin Hayes	JR	F/C	6-8	Houston	15.7	28.4
Bob Lloyd	SR	G	6-1	Rutgers	3.3	27.9
Wes Unseld	JR	C	6-8	Louisville	19.0	18.7
Bob Verga	SR	G	6-0	Duke	3.8	26.1
Jimmy Walker	SR	G	6-3	Providence	6.0	30.4

Second Team

PLAYER	CL	POS	HT	SCHOOL	RPG	PPG
Louie Dampier	SR	G	6-0	Kentucky	5.5	20.7
Mel Daniels	SR	C	6-9	New Mexico	11.6	21.5
Sonny Dove	SR	F	6-7	St. John's	14.8	22.4
Don May	JR	F	6-4	Dayton	16.7	22.2
Larry Miller	JR	G/F	6-4	North Carolina	9.3	21.9

Selectors: AP, NABC, UPI, USBWA

AWARD WINNERS

Player of the Year

PLAYER	CL	POS	HT	SCHOOL	AWARDS
Lew Alcindor	SO	C	7-2	UCLA	AP, UPI, USBWA

Coach of the Year

COACH	SCHOOL	REC	AWARDS
John Wooden	UCLA	30-0	AP, UPI, USBWA
Jack Hartman	Southern Illinois	24-2	Sporting News

Poll Progression

Preseason Poll

AP	UPI	School
1	1	**UCLA**
2	2	**UTEP**
3	3	**Kentucky**
4	4	**Duke**
5	7	**Louisville**
6	16	**New Mexico**
7	6	**Houston**
8	9	**Western Kentucky**
9	15	**North Carolina**
10	18	**Cincinnati**
—	5	**Michigan State**
—	8	**BYU**
—	10	**Providence**
—	11	**Nebraska**
—	12	**Boston College**
—	13	**Dayton**
—	13	**Kansas**
—	16	**Loyola-Chicago**
—	19	**Colorado State**
—	20	**St. John's**

Week of Dec 6

AP	UPI	School	AP↓↑
1	1	**UCLA** (1-0)	
2	2	**UTEP** (2-0)	
3	3	**Kentucky** (1-0)	
4	6	**Louisville** (1-0)	↑1
5	5	**Houston** (2-0)	↑2
6	7	**New Mexico** (2-0)	
7	11	**Duke** (1-1)	↓3
8	9	**North Carolina** (2-0)	↑1
9	8	**BYU** (1-0)	⤴
10	12	**Cincinnati** (2-0)	
—	4	**Michigan State** (2-0)	
—	10	**Virginia Tech** (2-0)	
—	12	**Nebraska** (1-0)	
—	14	**Kansas** (2-0)	
—	15	**Providence** (1-0)	
—	16	**Boston College** (2-0)	
—	17	**Loyola-Chicago** (1-0)	
—	18	**Vanderbilt** (2-0)	
—	19	**Colorado State** (2-0)	
—	20	**Dayton** (2-0)	

Week of Dec 13

AP	UPI	School		AP↓↑
1	1	**UCLA** (3-0)	A	
2	2	**UTEP** (5-0)		
3	5	**Louisville** (3-0)		↑1
4	4	**Kentucky** (2-1)	B	↓1
5	7	**New Mexico** (4-0)		↑1
6	8	**North Carolina** (3-0)		↑2
7	6	**BYU** (3-0)		↑2
8	3	**Michigan State** (4-0)		⤴
9	13	**Houston** (4-1)		↓4
10	10	**Cincinnati** (3-0)	C	
—	9	**Kansas** (5-0)		
—	11	**Vanderbilt** (4-0)		
—	12	**Boston College** (4-0)		
—	14	**Illinois** (2-1)		
—	15	**West Virginia** (4-0)		
—	16	**Loyola-Chicago** (3-0)		
—	17	**Virginia Tech** (2-1)		
—	18	**Providence** (3-0)		
—	18	**St. John's** (2-0)		
—	20	**Seattle** (3-0)		

Week of Dec 20

AP	UPI	School	AP↓↑
1	1	**UCLA** (3-0)	
2	3	**Louisville** (6-0)	↑1
3	2	**North Carolina** (5-0)	↑3
4	4	**UTEP** (6-1)	↓2
5	5	**Michigan State** (4-0)	↑3
6	6	**New Mexico** (5-1)	↓1
7	7	**Cincinnati** (5-0)	↑3
8	8	**Houston** (8-1)	↑1
9	9	**Kansas** (6-1)	⤴
10	11	**Vanderbilt** (6-1)	⤴
—	10	**Boston College** (6-0)	
—	12	**BYU** (3-2)	⤵
—	13	**Illinois** (2-1)	
—	14	**St. John's** (4-0)	
—	15	**Tennessee** (4-0)	
—	16	**Florida** (4-0)	
—	17	**West Virginia** (5-0)	
—	18	**Bradley** (5-1)	
—	19	**Colorado** (5-1)	
—	19	**Western Kentucky** (4-1)	

Week of Dec 27

AP	UPI	School	AP↓↑
1	1	**UCLA** (5-0)	
2	2	**Louisville** (8-0)	
3	3	**North Carolina** (7-0)	
4	4	**UTEP** (7-1)	
5	5	**New Mexico** (7-1)	↑1
6	8	**Houston** (9-1)	↑2
7	6	**Cincinnati** (7-0)	
8	11	**St. John's** (5-0)	⤴
9	9	**Vanderbilt** (8-1)	↑1
10	7	**Michigan State** (5-1)	↓5
—	10	**Boston College** (8-0)	
—	12	**Kansas** (6-2)	⤵
—	13	**Tennessee** (4-0)	
—	14	**West Virginia** (5-0)	
—	15	**Princeton** (6-0)	
—	16	**Seattle** (7-1)	
—	17	**Western Kentucky** (7-1)	
—	18	**Kentucky** (4-3)	
—	18	**Virginia Tech** (4-1)	
—	20	**Colorado State** (4-3)	
—	20	**Mississippi State** (7-0)	

Week of Jan 3

AP	UPI	School	AP↓↑
1	1	**UCLA** (8-0)	
2	2	**Louisville** (11-0)	
3	3	**North Carolina** (9-0)	
4	4	**New Mexico** (9-1)	↑1
5	6	**Houston** (11-1)	↑1
6	7	**UTEP** (8-2)	↓2
7	8	**Providence** (8-2)	⤴
8	5	**Cincinnati** (8-1)	↓1
9	9	**Kansas** (9-2)	⤴
10	13	**Bradley** (9-2)	⤴
—	10	**Vanderbilt** (8-2)	⤵
—	11	**Western Kentucky** (9-1)	
—	12	**Boston College** (9-1)	
—	14	**St. John's** (7-1)	⤵
—	15	**Michigan State** (5-3)	⤵
—	16	**Seattle** (9-1)	
—	17	**Utah State** (7-2)	
—	18	**Dayton** (10-1)	
—	18	**Princeton** (8-1)	
—	20	**Florida** (7-1)	

Week of Jan 10

AP	UPI	School		AP↓↑
1	1	**UCLA** (9-0)		
2	2	**Louisville** (13-0)		
3	4	**New Mexico** (11-1)		↑1
4	5	**Houston** (13-1)		↑1
5	3	**North Carolina** (11-1)	D	↓2
6	6	**UTEP** (10-2)		
7	9	**Princeton** (11-1)	D	⤴
8	7	**Kansas** (10-2)		↑1
9	11	**Providence** (9-3)		↓2
10	14	**Florida** (9-1)		⤴
—	8	**Cincinnati** (9-2)		⤵
—	10	**Vanderbilt** (10-2)		
—	12	**Western Kentucky** (10-1)		
—	13	**Boston College** (10-1)		
—	15	**Dayton** (11-1)		
—	15	**Seattle** (10-2)		
—	17	**Mississippi State** (9-1)		
—	17	**St. John's** (9-1)		
—	17	**Tennessee** (6-2)		
—	20	**Iowa** (8-2)		
—	20	**SMU** (8-3)		

Week of Jan 17

AP	UPI	School	AP↓↑
1	1	**UCLA** (12-0)	
2	2	**Louisville** (14-1)	
3	4	**Houston** (14-1)	↑1
4	3	**North Carolina** (12-1)	↑1
5	7	**Princeton** (13-1)	↑2
6	5	**UTEP** (11-2)	
7	6	**Kansas** (11-2)	↑1
8	9	**Florida** (11-1)	↑2
9	8	**New Mexico** (11-3)	↓6
10	13	**Providence** (11-3)	↓1
—	10	**Vanderbilt** (12-2)	
—	12	**Boston College** (12-1)	
—	14	**Western Kentucky** (12-1)	
—	15	**St. John's** (11-1)	
—	16	**Dayton** (12-2)	
—	17	**Tennessee** (7-3)	
—	17	**Toledo** (9-0)	
—	17	**Syracuse** (11-2)	
—	19	**Mississippi State** (11-1)	
—	20	**Utah State** (10-3)	
—	20	**Tulsa** (11-3)	

Week of Jan 24

AP	UPI	School	AP↓↑
1	1	**UCLA** (14-0)	
2	2	**North Carolina** (12-1)	↑2
3	3	**Houston** (14-1)	
4	4	**Louisville** (15-2)	↓2
5	6	**Princeton** (13-1)	
6	5	**UTEP** (12-2)	
7	7	**Kansas** (12-3)	
8	9	**Western Kentucky** (14-1)	⤴
9	10	**Vanderbilt** (13-2)	⤴
10	11	**Providence** (11-3)	
—	8	**Cincinnati** (12-3)	
—	12	**St. John's** (12-1)	
—	13	**Boston College** (12-1)	
—	14	**Utah State** (11-3)	
—	15	**New Mexico** (11-5)	⤵
—	15	**Tennessee** (9-3)	
—	17	**Mississippi State** (11-1)	
—	18	**BYU** (10-5)	
—	19	**Florida** (11-3)	⤵
—	19	**Northwestern** (7-4)	

Week of Jan 31

AP	UPI	School	AP↓↑
1	1	**UCLA** (15-0)	
2	2	**North Carolina** (13-1)	
3	3	**Louisville** (16-2)	↑1
4	4	**UTEP** (14-2)	↑2
5	6	**Princeton** (14-1)	
6	5	**Houston** (14-2)	↓3
7	7	**Kansas** (12-3)	
8	9	**Western Kentucky** (14-1)	
9	8	**Vanderbilt** (14-2)	
10	10	**Providence** (13-3)	
—	11	**Cincinnati** (11-6)	
—	12	**Boston College** (12-1)	
—	13	**Tennessee** (11-3)	
—	14	**Tulsa** (13-3)	
—	15	**Toledo** (13-0)	
—	16	**St. John's** (12-2)	
—	16	**Syracuse** (12-2)	
—	18	**Utah** (11-6)	
—	19	**New Mexico** (11-5)	
—	20	**Duke** (8-5)	

Week of Feb 7

AP	UPI	School	AP↓↑
1	1	**UCLA** (17-0)	
2	2	**North Carolina** (14-1)	
3	3	**Louisville** (18-2)	
4	4	**Princeton** (17-1)	↑1
5	5	**Houston** (15-2)	↑1
6	8	**Western Kentucky** (16-1)	↑2
7	7	**Kansas** (13-3)	
8	6	**UTEP** (15-3)	↓4
9	9	**Providence** (14-3)	↑1
10	11	**Boston College** (12-1)	⤴
	10	**Vanderbilt** (15-3)	⤵
	12	**Syracuse** (15-2)	
	13	**Toledo** (14-1)	
	14	**Duke** (10-5)	
	14	**Utah State** (14-3)	
	16	**Tennessee** (13-4)	
	17	**Cincinnati** (12-7)	
	18	**Northwestern** (9-5)	
	19	**Tulsa** (14-4)	
	20	**St. John's** (13-3)	

Week of Feb 14

AP	UPI	School		AP↓↑
1	1	**UCLA** (19-0)		
2	2	**Louisville** (20-2)		↑1
3	4	**Princeton** (19-1)		↑1
4	3	**North Carolina** (16-2)		↓2
5	6	**Western Kentucky** (18-1)		↑1
6	5	**Kansas** (15-3)		↑1
7	8	**Houston** (16-3)	E	↓2
8	7	**UTEP** (16-4)		
9	9	**Vanderbilt** (17-3)		⤴
10	12	**Syracuse** (17-2)		⤴
—	10	**Utah State** (17-3)		
—	11	**Boston College** (13-2)		⤵
—	13	**Tennessee** (15-4)		
—	14	**Duke** (12-5)		
—	15	**Providence** (15-4)		⤵
—	16	**Toledo** (16-1)		
—	17	**Florida** (17-4)		
—	18	**Cincinnati** (12-9)		
—	19	**St. John's** (16-3)		
—	20	**Tulsa** (15-5)		

EEK OF FEB 21

P	UPI	SCHOOL	AP↓↑
1	1	**UCLA** (21-0)	
2	2	**Louisville** (22-2)	
3	5	**Western Kentucky** (20-1)	↑2
4	4	**Kansas** (17-3)	↑2
5	3	**North Carolina** (18-3)	↓1
6	6	**Princeton** (20-2)	↓3
7	7	**Houston** (19-3)	
8	11	**Syracuse** (19-2)	↑2
9	8	**Tennessee** (17-4)	⤴
10	9	**UTEP** (17-5)	↓2
—	10	**Boston College** (15-2)	
—	12	**Utah State** (18-3)	
—	13	**Vanderbilt** (17-4)	⤵
—	14	**Providence** (16-5)	
—	15	**Duke** (13-6)	
—	16	**Toledo** (18-1)	
—	17	**St. John's** (18-3)	
—	18	**BYU** (12-7)	
—	19	**Florida** (18-4)	
—	20	**Virginia Tech** (16-4)	

WEEK OF FEB 28

AP	UPI	SCHOOL	AP↓↑
1	1	**UCLA** (23-0)	
2	2	**Louisville** (23-3)	
3	3	**North Carolina** (20-3)	↑2
4	4	**Kansas** (19-3)	
5	5	**Princeton** (22-2)	↑1
6	7	**Western Kentucky** (21-2)	↓3
7	6	**Houston** (21-3)	
8	8	**Tennessee** (18-4)	↑1
9	9	**UTEP** (19-5)	↑1
10	10	**Boston College** (17-2)	⤴
—	11	**Vanderbilt** (19-4)	
—	12	**St. John's** (20-3)	
—	13	**Providence** (18-6)	
—	14	**Duke** (13-6)	
—	15	**Toledo** (21-1)	
—	16	**Tulsa** (18-6)	
—	17	**Dayton** (21-4)	
—	18	**Florida** (20-4)	
—	19	**Syracuse** (19-4)	⤵
—	20	**Utah State** (18-5)	

FINAL POLL

AP	UPI	SCHOOL	AP↓↑
1	1	**UCLA** (25-0)	
2	2	**Louisville** (23-3)	
3	4	**Kansas** (20-3)	↑1
4	3	**North Carolina** (21-4) (F)	↓1
5	5	**Princeton** (23-2)	
6	7	**Western Kentucky** (23-2)	
7	6	**Houston** (23-3)	
8	9	**Tennessee** (20-5)	
9	10	**Boston College** (19-2)	↑1
10	8	**UTEP** (20-5)	↓1
—	11	**Toledo** (23-1)	
—	12	**St. John's** (22-3)	
—	13	**Tulsa** (19-7)	
—	14	**Utah State** (20-5)	
—	14	**Vanderbilt** (20-5)	
—	16	**Pacific** (21-3)	
—	17	**Providence** (20-6)	
—	18	**New Mexico** (18-7)	
—	19	**Duke** (13-7) (F)	
—	20	**Florida** (21-4)	

(A) What a difference a year and Lew Alcindor make. In 1965-66 Duke routed UCLA on consecutive nights on Tobacco Road. This season the Bruins torch the Blue Devils, 88-54 and 107-87, in Westwood, with Alcindor scoring 57 in the two routs. (In his varsity debut against USC, the 7'2" sophomore scored 56 on 23-of-32 shooting.) "He destroys you, that's what he does," Duke coach Vic Bubas says.

(B) Losses to North Carolina on Dec. 13 and unranked Florida four days later send Kentucky into a tailspin. They end up 13–13, the only non-winning record in Adolph Rupp's 41 seasons at the helm.

(C) Cincinnati edges visiting Miami of Ohio, 45-44 in overtime, the first of five home OT wins for the Bearcats during the season.

(D) Princeton shoots 65% from the floor to beat North Carolina, 91-81. The two will face off again in an NCAA East Regional semifinal, with the Tar Heels winning the rematch, 78-70 in OT.

(E) Notre Dame roars to a 42-18 first half lead and holds on to beat Houston, 87-78, in South Bend, Ind. Elvin Hayes misses his first eight shots but still ends up netting 30.

(F) Duke upsets North Carolina, 21-20, in an ACC tournament semifinal as the two teams take a combined paltry 36 shots from the field. The Blue Devils led at halftime, 7-5.

1967 NCAA Tournament

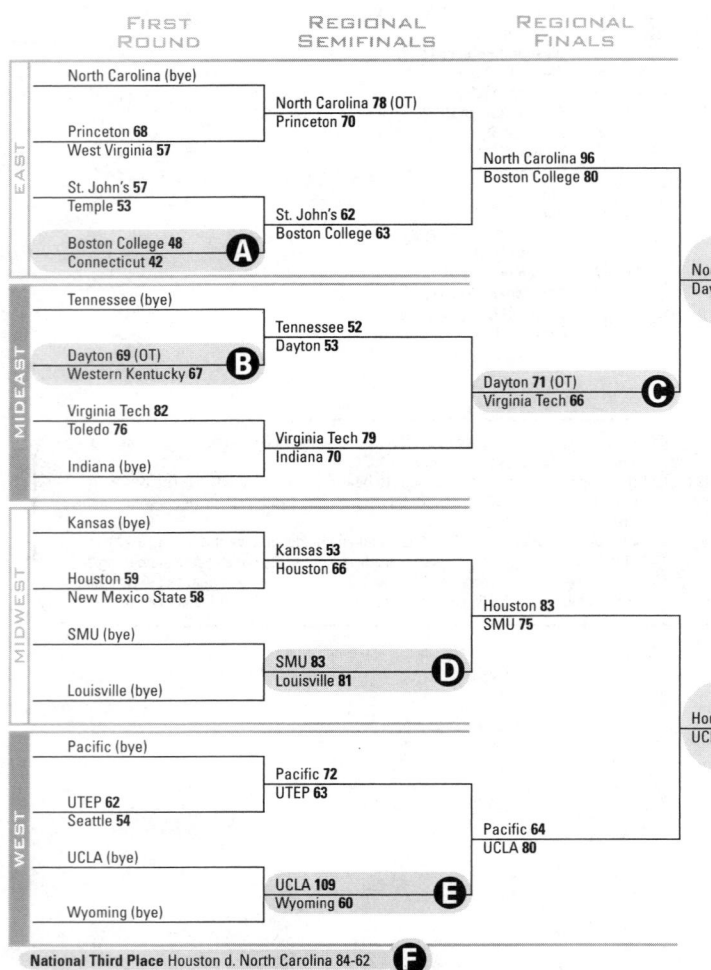

East

First Round
- North Carolina (bye)
- Princeton **68**, West Virginia **57**
- St. John's **57**, Temple **53**
- Boston College **48**, Connecticut **42** (A)

Regional Semifinals
- North Carolina **78** (OT), Princeton **70**
- St. John's **62**, Boston College **63**

Regional Finals
- North Carolina **96**, Boston College **80**

Mideast

First Round
- Tennessee (bye)
- Dayton **69** (OT), Western Kentucky **67** (B)
- Virginia Tech **82**, Toledo **76**
- Indiana (bye)

Regional Semifinals
- Tennessee **52**, Dayton **53**
- Virginia Tech **79**, Indiana **70**

Regional Finals
- Dayton **71** (OT), Virginia Tech **66** (C)

Midwest

First Round
- Kansas (bye)
- Houston **59**, New Mexico State **58**
- SMU (bye)
- Louisville (bye)

Regional Semifinals
- Kansas **53**, Houston **66**
- SMU **83**, Louisville **81** (D)

Regional Finals
- Houston **83**, SMU **75**

West

First Round
- Pacific (bye)
- UTEP **62**, Seattle **54**
- UCLA (bye)
- Wyoming (bye)

Regional Semifinals
- Pacific **72**, UTEP **63**
- UCLA **109**, Wyoming **60** (E)

Regional Finals
- Pacific **64**, UCLA **80**

National Semifinals
- North Carolina **62**, Dayton **76**
- Houston **58**, UCLA **73**

National Final
UCLA 79
Dayton 64

Louisville, KY

National Third Place Houston d. North Carolina 84-62 (F)
East Regional Third Place Princeton d. St. John's 78-58
Mideast Regional Third Place Indiana d. Tennessee 51-44
Midwest Regional Third Place Kansas d. Louisville 70-68
West Regional Third Place UTEP d. Wyoming 69-67

A Former Holy Cross and Boston Celtics star Bob Cousy makes his first Tournament appearance as a coach. Cousy will win 114 games in six seasons on the BC bench and compile a 2–2 Tournament record before becoming coach of the NBA Cincinnati Royals.

B Bobby Joe Hooper of Dayton hits the game-winning 25-foot jumper with :01 left, the first of three straight nail-biters the Flyers will win in the Tournament.

C Virginia Tech tries to stall long enough to take the final shot, but instead is called for lack of ball movement and loses the game in overtime.

UNC's Dean Smith appears in his first Final Four. It's UNC's first-ever matchup with Dayton. But UNC won't get revenge for four decades, when it beats Dayton by 30 at the Dean Dome in 2006.

With Lew Alcindor getting 20 points and 18 rebounds, UCLA (30–0) becomes John Wooden's second unbeaten team and third national champion. One of the game's referees, Mike DiTomasso, will become a broadcaster for the New York/New Jersey Nets in the 1970s.

A year after missing the Tournament, UCLA is back with a young team built around 7'2" sophomore Lew Alcindor. The Bruins overcome a 25-point, 24-rebound effort by Elvin Hayes, who had called Alcindor "overrated."

D Underdog SMU rallies from an eight-point deficit in the final minute and goes ahead for good when Denny Holman sinks a layup following a jump ball. The Cardinals are led by 6'8" All-America junior center Wes Unseld.

E UCLA rolls to an easy victory, one of many in the Tournament. The Bruins outscore their four opponents by a record average margin of 23.8 points. Wyoming, using its "Oklahoma State Shuffle"—an offense built on merry-go-round passing and cutting with little shooting—is unable to dance around the mighty Bruins.

F Dubbed "the disappointment of the Tourney" by *The Los Angeles Times*, North Carolina finishes in fourth place overall after being heavily favored to win the national title. Houston's Ken Spain and Elvin Hayes stick the Heels for 24 and 23 points, respectively.

Tournament Leaders

Individual Leaders

Scoring	CL	POS	G	PTS	PPG
1 **Lew Alcindor**, UCLA	SO	C	4	106	26.5
2 **Elvin Hayes**, Houston	JR	F/C	5	128	25.6
3 **Don May**, Dayton	JR	F	5	118	23.6
4 **Denny Holman**, SMU	SR	G	2	46	23.0
5 **Ron Widby**, Tennessee	SR	F	2	43	21.5
6 **David Lattin**, UTEP	JR	F	3	64	21.3
7 **Glen Combs**, Virginia Tech	JR	G	3	63	21.0
8 **Harry Hall**, Wyoming	SO	G	2	40	20.0
Jo Jo White, Kansas	SO	G	2	40	20.0
10 **Bob Lewis**, North Carolina	SR	F	4	79	19.8

Minimum: 2 games

Field Goal Pct	CL	POS	G	FG	FGA	PCT
1 **Ken Talley**, Virginia Tech	SO	C	3	20	30	66.7
2 **Fred Holden**, Louisville	JR	G	2	17	26	65.4
3 **Lew Alcindor**, UCLA	SO	C	4	39	60	65.0
4 **Jerry King**, Louisville	SO	F	2	16	25	64.0
5 **Ken Spain**, Houston	SO	C	5	14	24	58.3

Minimum: 10 made

Free Throw Pct	CL	POS	G	FT	FTA	PCT
1 **Gene Klaus**, Dayton	SR	G	5	12	13	92.3
2 **Denny Holman**, SMU	SR	G	2	10	11	90.9
3 **Steve Adelman**, Boston College	JR	F	3	14	16	87.5
4 **Jim Kissane**, Boston College	JR	F	3	12	14	85.7
5 **Chris Thomforde**, Princeton	SO	C	3	16	19	84.2

Minimum: 10 made

Rebounds Per Game	CL	POS	G	REB	RPG
1 **Don May**, Dayton	JR	F	5	82	16.4
2 **Elvin Hayes**, Houston	JR	F/C	5	79	15.8
3 **Lew Alcindor**, UCLA	SO	C	4	62	15.5
4 **Wes Unseld**, Louisville	JR	C	2	29	14.5
5 **William DeHeer**, Indiana	SO	C	2	27	13.5

Minimum: 2 games

Team Leaders

Scoring	G	PTS	PPG
1 **UCLA**	4	341	85.3
2 **SMU**	2	158	79.0
3 **Virginia Tech**	3	227	75.7
4 **Louisville**	2	149	74.5
North Carolina	4	298	74.5
6 **Princeton**	3	216	72.0
7 **Houston**	5	350	70.0
8 **Pacific**	2	136	68.0
9 **Dayton**	5	333	66.6
10 **UTEP**	3	194	64.7

Minimum: 2 games

FG Pct	G	FG	FGA	PCT
1 **Louisville**	2	66	125	52.8
2 **UCLA**	4	139	267	52.1
3 **SMU**	2	63	134	47.0
4 **Virginia Tech**	3	90	201	44.8
5 **Pacific**	2	52	118	44.1

FT Pct	G	FT	FTA	PCT
1 **Kansas**	2	17	22	77.3
2 **Tennessee**	2	28	37	75.7
3 **Boston College**	3	61	81	75.3
4 **St. John's**	3	43	58	74.1
5 **North Carolina**	4	82	112	73.2

Minimum: 2 games

Rebounds	G	REB	RPG
1 **Houston**	5	241	48.2
2 **Virginia Tech**	3	138	46.0
3 **Indiana**	2	89	44.5
4 **Princeton**	3	131	43.7
5 **North Carolina**	4	172	43.0

Minimum: 2 games

All-Tournament Team

PLAYER	CL	POS	HT	SCHOOL	RPG	PPG
Lew Alcindor*	SO	C	7-2	UCLA	15.5	26.5
Lucius Allen	SO	G	6-2	UCLA	7.3	16.0
Elvin Hayes	JR	F/C	6-8	Houston	15.8	25.6
Don May	JR	F	6-4	Dayton	16.4	23.6
Mike Warren	JR	G	5-10	UCLA	5.8	13.3

All-Regional Teams

East

PLAYER	CL	POS	HT	SCHOOL	RPG	PPG
Bobby Lewis*	SR	F	6-3	North Carolina	6.5	22.5
Rudy Bogad	JR	F	6-7	St. John's	11.0	17.3
Terry Driscoll	SO	F	6-7	Boston College	6.7	8.0
Larry Miller	JR	G/F	6-4	North Carolina	7.5	19.0
Chris Thomforde	SO	C	6-9	Princeton	9.3	16.7

Mideast

PLAYER	CL	POS	HT	SCHOOL	RPG	PPG
Don May*	JR	F	6-4	Dayton	16.7	21.0
Glen Combs	JR	G	6-2	Virginia Tech	5.0	21.0
Bobby Joe Hooper	JR	G	6-0	Dayton	1.3	11.7
Vernon Payne	JR	G	5-10	Indiana	3.0	13.0
Ron Widby	SR	F	6-4	Tennessee	6.5	21.5

Midwest

PLAYER	CL	POS	HT	SCHOOL	RPG	PPG
Elvin Hayes*	JR	F/C	6-8	Houston	13.0	26.7
Don Chaney	JR	G	6-5	Houston	5.3	13.7
Denny Holman	SR	G	6-3	SMU	2.5	23.0
Wes Unseld	JR	C	6-8	Louisville	14.5	17.0
Jo Jo White	SO	G	6-3	Kansas	4.0	20.0

West

PLAYER	CL	POS	HT	SCHOOL	RPG	PPG
Lew Alcindor*	SO	C	7-2	UCLA	12.0	33.5
Lucius Allen	SO	G	6-2	UCLA	5.5	14.0
David Fox	SR	G	6-2	Pacific	5.0	15.5
David Lattin	JR	F	6-6	UTEP	10.7	21.3
Mike Warren	JR	G	5-10	UCLA	3.5	11.0

* Most outstanding player

1967 NCAA TOURNAMENT BOX SCORES

North Carolina 78-70 Princeton (Sweet 16)

29	1H	28
34	2H	35
15	OT1	7

NORTH CAROLINA	MIN	FG	3FG	FT	REB	A	ST	BL	PF	TP
Larry Miller	44	7-17	-	2-2	10	3	-	-	4	16
Dick Grubar	43	2-5	-	12-16	7	3	-	-	4	16
Bob Lewis	43	4-17	-	6-9	10	1	-	-	3	14
Rusty Clark	28	3-10	-	7-9	9	0	-	-	5	13
Bill Bunting	35	4-8	-	1-2	9	1	-	-	0	9
Joe Brown	8	2-4	-	1-1	5	1	-	-	0	5
Gerald Tuttle	19	0-0	-	3-4	0	1	-	-	1	3
Tom Gauntlett	5	1-3	-	0-0	2	0	-	-	0	2
TOTALS	**225**	**23-64**	**-**	**32-43**	**52**	**10**	**-**	**-**	**17**	**78**
Percentages		35.9		74.4						

Coach: Dean Smith

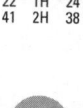

PRINCETON	MIN	FG	3FG	FT	REB	A	ST	BL	PF	TP
Joe Heiser	45	8-20	-	2-3	8	1	-	-	4	18
Edward Hummer	45	6-18	-	2-5	9	1	-	-	4	14
Chris Thomforde	24	6-17	-	2-2	7	1	-	-	5	14
David Lawyer	23	3-9	-	2-2	4	1	-	-	5	8
Robinson Brown	20	3-8	-	2-4	7	0	-	-	2	8
Larry Lucchino	20	2-4	-	0-0	1	0	-	-	2	4
Gary Walters	31	1-5	-	0-4	4	4	-	-	5	2
John Haarlow	17	1-4	-	0-1	2	1	-	-	1	2
TOTALS	**225**	**30-85**	**-**	**10-21**	**42**	**9**	**-**	**-**	**28**	**70**
Percentages		35.3		47.6						

Coach: Butch van Breda Kolff

Boston College 63-62 St. John's (Sweet 16)

22	1H	24
41	2H	38

BOSTON COLLEGE	MIN	FG	3FG	FT	REB	A	ST	BL	PF	TP
Steve Adelman	-	5-14	-	7-7	4	-	-	-	1	17
Billy Evans	-	2-7	-	6-9	3	-	-	-	0	10
Willie Wolters	-	2-9	-	5-5	7	-	-	-	3	9
Jim Kissane	-	1-8	-	5-6	5	-	-	-	3	7
Jack Kvancz	-	2-7	-	3-3	1	-	-	-	1	7
Doug Hice	-	1-1	-	4-4	1	-	-	-	3	6
Terry Driscoll	-	2-8	-	1-2	8	-	-	-	3	5
Steve Kelleher	-	1-1	-	0-0	0	-	-	-	1	2
TOTALS	**-**	**16-55**	**-**	**31-36**	**29**	**-**	**-**	**-**	**15**	**63**
Percentages		29.1		86.1						

Coach: Bob Cousy

ST. JOHN'S	MIN	FG	3FG	FT	REB	A	ST	BL	PF	TP
Rudy Bogad	-	7-16	-	7-8	16	-	-	-	4	21
Sonny Dove	-	6-11	-	3-4	10	-	-	-	5	15
Carmine Calzonetti	-	5-9	-	2-2	4	-	-	-	1	12
Jack Brunner	-	2-3	-	0-0	3	-	-	-	2	4
Albie Swartz	-	2-5	-	0-1	3	-	-	-	3	4
John Warren	-	2-8	-	0-0	4	-	-	-	4	4
Brian Hill	-	1-1	-	0-0	0	-	-	-	5	2
TOTALS	**-**	**25-53**	**-**	**12-15**	**40**	**-**	**-**	**-**	**24**	**62**
Percentages		47.2		80.0						

Coach: Lou Carnesecca

Dayton 53-52 Tennessee (Sweet 16)

36	1H	25
17	2H	27

DAYTON	MIN	FG	3FG	FT	REB	A	ST	BL	PF	TP
Bobby Joe Hooper	-	6-7	-	2-2	2	-	-	-	0	14
Gene Klaus	-	5-7	-	2-2	0	-	-	-	0	12
Dan Sadlier	-	4-4	-	2-2	1	-	-	-	4	10
Don May	-	2-10	-	5-5	14	-	-	-	2	9
Rudy Waterman	-	2-3	-	0-0	0	-	-	-	0	4
Dan Obrovac	-	1-2	-	1-2	4	-	-	-	2	3
Glinder Torain	-	0-2	-	1-1	3	-	-	-	2	1
TOTALS	**-**	**20-35**	**-**	**13-14**	**24**	**-**	**-**	**-**	**10**	**53**
Percentages		57.1		92.9						

Coach: Don Donoher

TENNESSEE	MIN	FG	3FG	FT	REB	A	ST	BL	PF	TP
Ron Widby	-	7-20	-	6-7	4	-	-	-	2	20
Tom Boerwinkle	-	4-7	-	2-3	9	-	-	-	5	10
Tom Hendrix	-	5-11	-	0-0	1	-	-	-	2	10
Bill Justus	-	4-9	-	2-3	5	-	-	-	2	10
David Bell	-	0-1	-	1-2	2	-	-	-	0	1
Bill Hann	-	0-4	-	1-1	2	-	-	-	0	1
Wes Coffman	-	0-0	-	0-0	0	-	-	-	0	0
TOTALS	**-**	**20-52**	**-**	**12-16**	**23**	**-**	**-**	**-**	**11**	**52**
Percentages		38.5		75.0						

Coach: Ray Mears

Virginia Tech 79-70 Indiana (Sweet 16)

35	1H	31
44	2H	39

VIRGINIA TECH	MIN	FG	3FG	FT	REB	A	ST	BL	PF	TP
Glen Combs	-	11-24	-	7-10	4	-	-	-	2	29
Ken Talley	-	6-10	-	4-4	11	-	-	-	2	16
Don Brown	-	2-4	-	4-4	7	-	-	-	4	8
Chris Ellis	-	4-9	-	0-0	7	-	-	-	5	8
Ron Perry	-	2-12	-	3-5	13	-	-	-	5	7
Ted Ware	-	1-4	-	5-8	8	-	-	-	4	7
Wayne Mallard	-	1-1	-	2-2	0	-	-	-	0	4
TOTALS	**-**	**27-64**	**-**	**25-33**	**50**	**-**	**-**	**-**	**22**	**79**
Percentages		42.2		75.8						

Coach: Howie Shannon

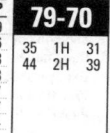

INDIANA	MIN	FG	3FG	FT	REB	A	ST	BL	PF	TP
Vernon Payne	-	7-19	-	4-8	4	-	-	-	5	18
Jack Johnson	-	6-15	-	3-4	14	-	-	-	3	15
Harry Joyner	-	6-18	-	2-7	10	-	-	-	4	14
William Russell	-	4-17	-	3-7	7	-	-	-	3	11
William DeHeer	-	2-5	-	1-1	11	-	-	-	3	5
Vernon Pfaff	-	2-3	-	0-1	0	-	-	-	3	4
William Stenberg	-	1-1	-	1-1	0	-	-	-	1	3
Gabriel Oliverio	-	0-3	-	0-0	2	-	-	-	0	0
Earl Schneider	-	0-3	-	0-0	2	-	-	-	3	0
Larry Turpen	-	0-0	-	0-0	0	-	-	-	0	0
TOTALS	**-**	**28-84**	**-**	**14-29**	**50**	**-**	**-**	**-**	**25**	**70**
Percentages		33.3		48.3						

Coach: Lou Watson

Houston 66-53 Kansas (Sweet 16)

32	1H	29
34	2H	24

HOUSTON	MIN	FG	3FG	FT	REB	A	ST	BL	PF	TP
Don Chaney	40	8-16	-	4-4	5	-	-	-	0	20
Elvin Hayes	40	9-18	-	1-2	14	-	-	-	3	19
Melvin Bell	31	5-11	-	1-4	8	-	-	-	0	11
Leary Lentz	22	2-6	-	2-3	4	-	-	-	0	6
Don Kruse	20	2-4	-	2-3	7	-	-	-	4	6
Gary Grider	36	1-2	-	2-5	5	-	-	-	0	4
Ken Spain	7	0-1	-	0-0	1	-	-	-	0	0
Vern Lewis	4	0-3	-	0-0	0	-	-	-	0	0
TOTALS	**200**	**27-61**	**-**	**12-21**	**44**	**-**	**-**	**-**	**7**	**66**
Percentages		44.3		57.1						

Coach: Guy V. Lewis

KANSAS	MIN	FG	3FG	FT	REB	A	ST	BL	PF	TP
Jo Jo White	-	9-24	-	0-0	3	-	-	-	4	18
Vernon Vanoy	-	4-5	-	5-6	9	-	-	-	1	13
Rodger Bohnenstiehl	-	5-13	-	2-3	8	-	-	-	1	12
Ron Franz	-	3-11	-	0-0	2	-	-	-	4	6
Phillip Harmon	-	2-9	-	0-0	3	-	-	-	4	4
Howard Arndt	-	0-0	-	0-0	0	-	-	-	0	0
Bruce Sloan	-	0-1	-	0-0	0	-	-	-	2	0
TOTALS	**-**	**23-63**	**-**	**7-9**	**25**	**-**	**-**	**-**	**16**	**53**
Percentages		36.5		77.8						

Coach: Ted Owens

SMU 83-81 Louisville (Sweet 16)

44	1H	45
39	2H	36

SMU	MIN	FG	3FG	FT	REB	A	ST	BL	PF	TP
Denny Holman	-	13-21	-	4-4	5	-	-	-	2	30
Lynn Phillips	-	8-14	-	2-8	6	-	-	-	0	18
Bob Begert	-	7-10	-	2-2	9	-	-	-	2	16
Charles Beasley	-	4-13	-	1-2	4	-	-	-	3	9
Robert Jones	-	3-6	-	0-0	1	-	-	-	2	6
Bill Voight	-	2-6	-	0-0	4	-	-	-	2	4
TOTALS	**-**	**37-70**	**-**	**9-16**	**29**	**-**	**-**	**-**	**11**	**83**
Percentages		52.9		56.2						

Coach: E.O. "Doc" Hayes

LOUISVILLE	MIN	FG	3FG	FT	REB	A	ST	BL	PF	TP
Fred Holden	-	11-17	-	1-2	3	-	-	-	2	23
Jerry King	-	10-13	-	0-2	8	-	-	-	3	20
Wes Unseld	-	8-14	-	2-2	12	-	-	-	4	18
Butch Beard	-	6-15	-	2-7	9	-	-	-	2	14
Dave Gilbert	-	2-8	-	0-0	3	-	-	-	1	4
Dennis Deeken	-	1-1	-	0-1	1	-	-	-	0	2
Joe Liedtke	-	0-0	-	0-0	0	-	-	-	1	0
TOTALS	**-**	**38-68**	**-**	**5-14**	**36**	**-**	**-**	**-**	**13**	**81**
Percentages		55.9		35.7						

Coach: Bernard "Peck" Hickman

72-63 — 36 1H 33, 36 2H 30 — SWEET 16

PACIFIC	MIN	FG	3FG	FT	REB	A	ST	BL	PF	TP
Bob Krulish	-	10-14	-	4-5	3	-	-	-	2	24
Keith Swagerty	-	5-9	-	9-12	8	-	-	-	4	19
David Fox	-	7-15	-	0-2	4	-	-	-	3	14
Bruce Parsons	-	4-9	-	2-4	4	-	-	-	2	10
Pat Foley	-	1-6	-	3-5	8	-	-	-	2	5
Robby Dewitt	-	0-0	-	0-0	1	-	-	-	1	0
Bob Jones	-	0-1	-	0-0	1	-	-	-	1	0
TOTALS	-	27-54	-	18-28	29	-	-	-	15	72
Percentages		50.0		64.3						

Coach: Dick Edwards

UTEP	MIN	FG	3FG	FT	REB	A	ST	BL	PF	TP
Willie Cager	-	5-15	-	3-3	10	-	-	-	3	13
David Lattin	-	6-13	-	1-1	5	-	-	-	5	13
Willie Worsley	-	6-22	-	1-4	4	-	-	-	4	13
Fred Carr	-	5-8	-	2-6	12	-	-	-	0	12
Phil Harris	-	3-4	-	2-2	9	-	-	-	4	8
Dick Myers	-	1-1	-	0-0	2	-	-	-	2	2
David Palacio	-	1-7	-	0-0	3	-	-	-	1	2
Kenny John	-	0-1	-	0-0	0	-	-	-	0	0
TOTALS	-	27-71	-	9-16	45	-	-	-	19	63
Percentages		38.0		56.2						

Coach: Don Haskins

Technicals: UTEP (bench)

109-60 — 55 1H 18, 54 2H 42 — SWEET 16

UCLA	MIN	FG	3FG	FT	REB	A	ST	BL	PF	TP
Lew Alcindor	-	12-17	-	5-5	10	-	-	-	1	29
Lucius Allen	-	6-11	-	3-3	5	-	-	-	1	15
Lynn Shackelford	-	5-8	-	0-0	7	-	-	-	2	10
Mike Warren	-	4-11	-	2-4	5	-	-	-	0	10
Jim Nielsen	-	4-6	-	0-0	5	-	-	-	1	8
Don Saffer	-	4-6	-	0-0	2	-	-	-	0	8
Bill Sweek	-	4-6	-	0-2	5	-	-	-	2	8
Joe Chrisman	-	2-2	-	2-3	0	-	-	-	3	6
Kenny Heitz	-	3-3	-	0-0	0	-	-	-	5	6
Gene Sutherland	-	2-4	-	1-2	1	-	-	-	1	5
Neville Saner	-	2-3	-	0-0	4	-	-	-	1	4
Dick Lynn	-	0-1	-	0-0	0	-	-	-	1	0
TOTALS	-	48-78	-	13-19	44	-	-	-	18	109
Percentages		61.5		68.4						

Coach: John Wooden

WYOMING	MIN	FG	3FG	FT	REB	A	ST	BL	PF	TP
Tom Asbury	-	8-20	-	4-6	10	-	-	-	2	20
Harry Hall	-	6-16	-	7-11	5	-	-	-	2	19
Mike Eberle	-	6-12	-	0-1	5	-	-	-	4	12
Bob Wilson	-	2-6	-	1-1	3	-	-	-	3	5
Gary Von Krosigk	-	1-7	-	2-4	8	-	-	-	4	4
Clifford Nelson	-	0-2	-	0-0	2	-	-	-	1	0
TOTALS	-	23-63	-	14-23	33	-	-	-	16	60
Percentages		36.5		60.9						

Coach: Bill Strannigan

96-80 — 44 1H 42, 52 2H 38 — ELITE 8

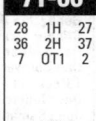

NORTH CAROLINA	MIN	FG	3FG	FT	REB	A	ST	BL	PF	TP
Bob Lewis	-	11-18	-	9-10	3	-	-	-	1	31
Larry Miller	-	6-16	-	10-12	5	-	-	-	2	22
Rusty Clark	-	7-10	-	4-5	18	-	-	-	3	18
Bill Bunting	-	5-10	-	2-3	4	-	-	-	4	12
Joe Brown	-	2-4	-	0-0	3	-	-	-	2	4
Dick Grubar	-	1-2	-	1-1	3	-	-	-	3	3
Jim Frye	-	1-1	-	0-1	0	-	-	-	0	2
Tom Gauntlett	-	1-1	-	0-0	0	-	-	-	0	2
Gerald Tuttle	-	1-1	-	0-0	0	-	-	-	1	2
Jim Bostick	-	0-0	-	0-0	0	-	-	-	0	0
Ralph Fletcher	-	0-0	-	0-0	0	-	-	-	0	0
Donnie Moe	-	0-0	-	0-0	0	-	-	-	0	0
TOTALS	-	35-63	-	26-32	36	-	-	-	16	96
Percentages		55.6		81.2						

Coach: Dean Smith

BOSTON COLLEGE	MIN	FG	3FG	FT	REB	A	ST	BL	PF	TP
Terry Driscoll	-	7-17	-	3-4	10	-	-	-	2	17
Jim Kissane	-	5-15	-	5-5	10	-	-	-	3	15
Jack Kvancz	-	5-8	-	1-1	1	-	-	-	4	11
Steve Adelman	-	4-12	-	1-2	6	-	-	-	2	9
Billy Evans	-	3-8	-	2-5	3	-	-	-	2	8
Doug Hice	-	3-7	-	0-1	2	-	-	-	4	6
Tom Pacynski	-	3-3	-	0-0	2	-	-	-	1	6
Willie Wolters	-	2-8	-	2-2	7	-	-	-	4	6
Jim King	-	1-2	-	0-0	1	-	-	-	1	2
Barry Gallup	-	0-0	-	0-0	0	-	-	-	1	0
Steve Kelleher	-	0-1	-	0-0	0	-	-	-	0	0
Ed Rooney	-	0-1	-	0-0	0	-	-	-	0	0
TOTALS	-	33-82	-	14-20	42	-	-	-	24	80
Percentages		40.2		70.0						

Coach: Bob Cousy

71-66 — 28 1H 27, 36 2H 37, 7 OT1 2 — ELITE 8

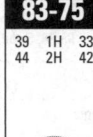

DAYTON	MIN	FG	3FG	FT	REB	A	ST	BL	PF	TP
Don May	-	9-24	-	10-11	16	-	-	-	1	28
Glinder Torain	-	5-11	-	3-3	9	-	-	-	4	13
Bobby Joe Hooper	-	5-10	-	2-2	1	-	-	-	0	12
Rudy Waterman	-	4-12	-	1-2	4	-	-	-	2	9
Dan Sadlier	-	3-6	-	0-1	7	-	-	-	4	6
Dan Obrovac	-	1-2	-	1-1	0	-	-	-	3	3
Gene Klaus	-	0-1	-	0-0	0	-	-	-	1	0
TOTALS	-	27-66	-	17-20	37	-	-	-	15	71
Percentages		40.9		85.0						

Coach: Don Donoher

VIRGINIA TECH	MIN	FG	3FG	FT	REB	A	ST	BL	PF	TP
Glen Combs	-	7-23	-	2-3	8	-	-	-	0	16
Ron Perry	-	6-12	-	2-5	2	-	-	-	5	14
Chris Ellis	-	5-11	-	1-1	4	-	-	-	4	11
Ken Talley	-	4-5	-	1-1	10	-	-	-	4	9
Ted Ware	-	3-7	-	2-3	8	-	-	-	4	8
Don Brown	-	2-4	-	0-0	3	-	-	-	1	4
Wayne Mallard	-	1-2	-	2-2	2	-	-	-	0	4
TOTALS	-	28-64	-	10-15	37	-	-	-	18	66
Percentages		43.8		66.7						

Coach: Howie Shannon

83-75 — 39 1H 33, 44 2H 42 — ELITE 8

HOUSTON	MIN	FG	3FG	FT	REB	A	ST	BL	PF	TP
Elvin Hayes	39	14-27	-	3-6	11	2	-	-	3	31
Melvin Bell	25	5-11	-	1-2	8	2	-	-	4	11
Don Chaney	40	3-15	-	4-4	10	9	-	-	2	10
Ken Spain	14	4-4	-	2-3	6	0	-	-	3	10
Gary Grider	35	3-4	-	3-5	2	8	-	-	2	9
Leary Lentz	27	3-5	-	2-4	10	3	-	-	3	8
Don Kruse	15	1-1	-	2-2	1	2	-	-	3	4
Vern Lewis	5	0-1	-	0-0	0	1	-	-	0	0
TOTALS	200	33-68	-	17-26	48	27	-	-	20	83
Percentages		48.5		65.4						

Coach: Guy V. Lewis

SMU	MIN	FG	3FG	FT	REB	A	ST	BL	PF	TP
Charles Beasley	-	8-16	-	2-2	4	-	-	-	3	18
Denny Holman	-	5-14	-	6-7	0	-	-	-	4	16
Bill Voight	-	4-10	-	6-8	4	-	-	-	2	14
Bob Begert	-	3-11	-	5-5	15	-	-	-	3	11
Robert Jones	-	5-9	-	0-0	1	-	-	-	1	10
Lynn Phillips	-	1-4	-	4-7	7	-	-	-	4	6
John Higginbotham	-	0-0	-	0-1	0	-	-	-	0	0
TOTALS	-	26-64	-	23-30	31	-	-	-	17	75
Percentages		40.6		76.7						

Coach: E.O. "Doc" Hayes

80-64 — 37 1H 27, 43 2H 37 — ELITE 8

UCLA	MIN	FG	3FG	FT	REB	A	ST	BL	PF	TP
Lew Alcindor	-	13-20	-	12-14	14	-	-	-	4	38
Lucius Allen	-	5-8	-	3-6	6	-	-	-	3	13
Mike Warren	-	4-8	-	4-6	2	-	-	-	1	12
Kenny Heitz	-	4-6	-	1-1	3	-	-	-	3	9
Lynn Shackelford	-	3-12	-	0-1	4	-	-	-	2	6
Bill Sweek	-	1-4	-	0-0	0	-	-	-	4	2
Don Saffer	-	0-0	-	0-0	0	-	-	-	0	0
TOTALS	-	30-58	-	20-28	29	-	-	-	17	80
Percentages		51.7		71.4						

Coach: John Wooden

PACIFIC	MIN	FG	3FG	FT	REB	A	ST	BL	PF	TP
David Fox	-	6-18	-	5-7	6	-	-	-	4	17
Bob Krulish	-	5-12	-	2-2	7	-	-	-	3	12
Keith Swagerty	-	5-12	-	1-5	8	-	-	-	4	11
Pat Foley	-	4-6	-	1-2	4	-	-	-	4	9
Bruce Parsons	-	1-3	-	5-6	6	-	-	-	2	7
Robby Dewitt	-	3-9	-	0-3	13	-	-	-	2	6
Joe Ferguson	-	1-3	-	0-0	0	-	-	-	1	2
Bob Jones	-	0-1	-	0-0	0	-	-	-	1	0
TOTALS	-	25-64	-	14-25	44	-	-	-	21	64
Percentages		39.1		56.0						

Coach: Dick Edwards

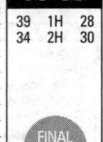

76-62 — 29 1H 23 · 47 2H 39 — FINAL 4

DAYTON	MIN	FG	3FG	FT	REB	A	ST	BL	PF	TP
Don May	39	16-22	-	2-6	15	3	-	-	2	34
Gene Klaus	40	3-6	-	9-10	8	2	-	-	4	15
Glinder Torain	34	4-14	-	6-8	11	4	-	-	5	14
Dan Sadlier	40	4-7	-	0-1	0	0	-	-	0	8
Bobby Joe Hooper	40	1-7	-	3-4	4	3	-	-	1	5
Dan Obrovac	4	0-0	-	0-0	1	0	-	-	1	0
Jim Wannemacher	2	0-0	-	0-2	0	0	-	-	0	0
Rudy Waterman	1	0-0	-	0-0	0	0	-	-	0	0
TOTALS	200	28-56	-	20-31	39	12	-	-	13	76
Percentages		50.0		64.5						
Coach: Don Donoher										

NORTH CAROLINA	MIN	FG	3FG	FT	REB	A	ST	BL	PF	TP
Rusty Clark	37	8-14	-	3-5	11	0	-	-	4	19
Larry Miller	40	6-18	-	1-1	13	0	-	-	4	13
Bob Lewis	37	5-18	-	1-1	3	0	-	-	3	11
Dick Grubar	36	2-7	-	3-3	2	2	-	-	4	7
Gerald Tuttle	14	3-5	-	1-1	1	3	-	-	3	7
Bill Bunting	22	1-3	-	1-1	5	2	-	-	4	3
Tom Gauntlett	8	1-4	-	0-0	3	0	-	-	0	2
Joe Brown	6	0-3	-	0-0	0	0	-	-	0	0
TOTALS	200	26-72	-	10-12	38	7	-	-	22	62
Percentages		36.1		83.3						
Coach: Dean Smith										

73-58 — 39 1H 28 · 34 2H 30 — FINAL 4

UCLA	MIN	FG	3FG	FT	REB	A	ST	BL	PF	TP
Lynn Shackelford	40	11-19	-	0-1	8	1	-	-	1	22
Lew Alcindor	40	6-11	-	7-13	20	0	-	-	1	19
Lucius Allen	40	6-15	-	5-5	9	1	-	-	2	17
Mike Warren	40	4-10	-	6-7	9	1	-	-	0	14
Kenny Heitz	7	0-0	-	1-1	0	0	-	-	1	1
Jim Nielsen	19	0-3	-	0-0	3	0	-	-	5	0
Bill Sweek	12	0-4	-	0-0	1	0	-	-	2	0
Don Saffer	2	0-0	-	0-0	0	0	-	-	0	0
TOTALS	200	27-62	-	19-27	50	3	-	-	12	73
Percentages		43.5		70.4						
Coach: John Wooden										

HOUSTON	MIN	FG	3FG	FT	REB	A	ST	BL	PF	TP
Elvin Hayes	40	12-31	-	1-2	24	1	-	-	4	25
Melvin Bell	30	3-11	-	4-7	11	1	-	-	4	10
Don Chaney	40	3-11	-	0-2	4	1	-	-	4	6
Don Kruse	14	2-5	-	1-1	0	0	-	-	2	5
Gary Grider	32	2-7	-	0-0	2	2	-	-	2	4
Theodis Lee	6	2-3	-	0-0	1	0	-	-	0	4
Leary Lentz	18	1-2	-	0-3	4	0	-	-	1	2
Ken Spain	12	1-5	-	0-0	4	0	-	-	2	2
Vern Lewis	8	0-0	-	0-1	0	0	-	-	1	0
TOTALS	200	26-75	-	6-16	50	5	-	-	20	58
Percentages		34.7		37.5						
Coach: Guy V. Lewis										

84-62 — 42 1H 23 · 42 2H 39 — 3RD PLACE

HOUSTON	MIN	FG	3FG	FT	REB	A	ST	BL	PF	TP
Ken Spain	26	9-14	-	6-9	14	1	-	-	3	24
Elvin Hayes	38	10-23	-	3-5	16	1	-	-	3	23
Don Chaney	38	6-13	-	7-8	8	0	-	-	0	19
Leary Lentz	33	3-10	-	0-1	17	1	-	-	3	6
Gary Grider	30	2-6	-	2-3	3	2	-	-	1	6
Don Kruse	7	2-5	-	0-0	2	1	-	-	5	4
Niemer Hamood	2	1-1	-	0-0	0	0	-	-	0	2
Vern Lewis	9	0-1	-	0-0	0	0	-	-	1	0
Melvin Bell	8	0-2	-	0-2	7	0	-	-	2	0
Theodis Lee	6	0-1	-	0-1	5	0	-	-	1	0
Andrew Benson	2	0-1	-	0-0	0	0	-	-	0	0
Elliott McVey	1	0-1	-	0-0	0	0	-	-	0	0
TOTALS	200	33-78	-	18-29	72	6	-	-	19	84
Percentages		42.3		62.1						
Coach: Guy V. Lewis										

NORTH CAROLINA	MIN	FG	3FG	FT	REB	A	ST	BL	PF	TP
Bob Lewis	35	9-23	-	5-6	11	2	-	-	3	23
Larry Miller	36	5-20	-	2-4	11	1	-	-	0	12
Rusty Clark	23	3-6	-	3-4	10	2	-	-	5	9
Tom Gauntlett	18	2-7	-	2-3	1	1	-	-	2	6
Bill Bunting	24	1-8	-	2-7	4	1	-	-	2	4
Dick Grubar	27	1-7	-	0-0	4	1	-	-	2	2
Gerald Tuttle	9	1-4	-	0-0	1	1	-	-	2	2
Ralph Fletcher	4	1-3	-	0-0	2	0	-	-	1	2
Jim Bostick	2	1-1	-	0-0	1	0	-	-	0	2
Joe Brown	16	0-5	-	0-1	1	0	-	-	2	0
Donnie Moe	4	0-0	-	0-0	0	1	-	-	0	0
Jim Frye	2	0-1	-	0-0	0	0	-	-	0	0
TOTALS	200	24-85	-	14-25	46	10	-	-	19	62
Percentages		28.2		56.0						
Coach: Dean Smith										

Attendance: 18,892

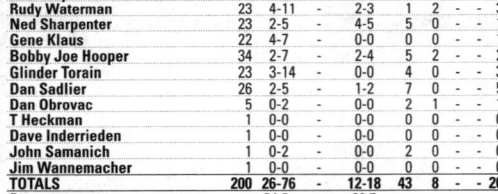

79-64 — 38 1H 20 · 41 2H 44 — NCAA FINAL 1967

UCLA	MIN	FG	3FG	FT	REB	A	ST	BL	PF	TP
Lew Alcindor	35	8-12	-	4-11	18	3	-	-	0	20
Lucius Allen	36	7-15	-	5-8	9	2	-	-	2	19
Mike Warren	35	8-16	-	1-1	7	0	-	-	1	17
Lynn Shackelford	35	5-10	-	0-2	3	1	-	-	1	10
Kenny Heitz	27	2-7	-	0-0	6	1	-	-	2	4
Don Saffer	5	2-5	-	0-0	0	0	-	-	1	4
Bill Sweek	8	1-1	-	0-0	0	0	-	-	1	2
Neville Saner	5	1-1	-	0-0	2	0	-	-	2	2
Joe Chrisman	4	0-0	-	1-2	1	0	-	-	2	1
Jim Nielsen	4	0-1	-	0-1	1	0	-	-	3	0
Gene Sutherland	4	0-0	-	0-0	0	0	-	-	0	0
Dick Lynn	2	0-1	-	0-0	0	0	-	-	0	0
TOTALS	200	34-69	-	11-25	47	7	-	-	15	79
Percentages		49.3		44.0						
Coach: John Wooden										

DAYTON	MIN	FG	3FG	FT	REB	A	ST	BL	PF	TP
Don May	40	9-23	-	3-4	17	3	-	-	4	21
Rudy Waterman	23	4-11	-	2-3	1	2	-	-	3	10
Ned Sharpenter	23	2-5	-	4-5	5	0	-	-	1	8
Gene Klaus	22	4-7	-	0-0	0	0	-	-	1	8
Bobby Joe Hooper	34	2-7	-	2-4	5	2	-	-	2	6
Glinder Torain	23	3-14	-	0-0	4	0	-	-	3	6
Dan Sadlier	26	2-5	-	1-2	7	0	-	-	5	5
Dan Obrovac	5	0-2	-	0-0	2	1	-	-	1	0
T Heckman	1	0-0	-	0-0	0	0	-	-	0	0
Dave Inderrieden	1	0-0	-	0-0	0	0	-	-	0	0
John Samanich	1	0-2	-	0-0	2	0	-	-	0	0
Jim Wannemacher	1	0-0	-	0-0	0	0	-	-	0	0
TOTALS	200	26-76	-	12-18	43	8	-	-	20	64
Percentages		34.2		66.7						
Coach: Don Donoher										

Officials: Wirtz, DiTomasso
Attendance: 18,892

National Invitation Tournament (NIT)

First round: Marshall d. Villanova 70-68 (OT), Southern Illinois d. Saint Peter's 103-58, Providence d. Memphis 77-68, New Mexico d. Syracuse 66-64, Marquette d. Tulsa 64-60, Rutgers d. Utah State 78-76
Quarterfinals: Southern Illinois d. Duke 72-63, Marshall d. Nebraska 119-88, Rutgers d. New Mexico 65-60, Marquette d. Providence 81-80 (OT)
Semifinals: Marquette d. Marshall 83-78, Southern Illinois d. Rutgers 79-70
Third place: Rutgers d. Marshall 93-76
Championship: Southern Illinois d. Marquette 71-56
MVP: Walt Frazier, Southern Illinois

1967-68: Big A vs. Big E

It was an event more typical of heavyweight boxing: No. 1 vs. No. 2 in front of 52,693 frenzied fans at Houston's Astrodome and millions more watching on national primetime television. In the Game of the Century, on Jan. 20, John Wooden's defending champion UCLA Bruins had their 47-game winning streak snapped, 71-69, by Elvin Hayes and the undefeated Houston Cougars. Hayes scored 39 points and grabbed 15 rebounds against Lew Alcindor, who was limited by a severe eye injury.

Of course, there had to be a rematch, and it happened in the Final Four at the Los Angeles Sports Arena. Now healthy, Alcindor (19 points, 18 rebounds) and the Bruins held Hayes to a mere 10 points and UCLA unleashed a merciless 101-69 beating. The Final was another cakewalk for UCLA, a 78-55 win over North Carolina. Alcindor won his second consecutive MOP award after scoring 34 points and grabbing 16 rebounds in the title game.

The NCAA may have encouraged big spectacles like the Astrodome game, but before this season began it banned its big men from the spectacle of dunking—the shot was declared illegal, both in games and in pregame warmups. The rule was reversed for the 1976-77 season.

Major Conference Standings

AAWU	Conference			Overall		
	W	L	Pct	W	L	Pct
UCLA⊕	14	0	1.000	29	1	.967
Southern California	11	3	.786	18	8	.692
Washington State	8	6	.571	16	9	.640
California	7	7	.500	15	9	.625
Oregon State	5	9	.357	12	13	.480
Stanford	5	9	.357	10	15	.400
Washington	4	10	.286	12	14	.462
Oregon	2	12	.143	7	19	.269

ACC	Conference			Overall		
	W	L	Pct	W	L	Pct
North Carolina⊕	12	2	.857	28	4	.875
Duke□	11	3	.786	22	6	.786
South Carolina	9	5	.643	15	7	.682
NC State	9	5	.643	16	10	.615
Virginia	5	9	.357	9	16	.360
Maryland	4	10	.286	8	16	.333
Wake Forest	3	11	.214	5	21	.192
Clemson	3	11	.214	4	20	.167

Tournament: **North Carolina d. NC State 87-50**
Tournament MVP: **Larry Miller**, North Carolina

Big Eight	Conference			Overall		
	W	L	Pct	W	L	Pct
Kansas State⊕	11	3	.786	19	9	.679
Kansas□	10	4	.714	22	8	.733
Nebraska	8	6	.571	15	10	.600
Oklahoma	8	6	.571	13	13	.500
Iowa State	8	6	.571	12	13	.480
Missouri	5	9	.357	10	16	.385
Oklahoma State	3	11	.214	10	16	.385
Colorado	3	11	.214	9	16	.360

Big Sky	Conference			Overall		
	W	L	Pct	W	L	Pct
Weber State⊕	12	3	.800	21	6	.778
Idaho	9	6	.600	15	11	.577
Idaho State	7	8	.467	13	13	.500
Montana State	6	9	.400	10	15	.400
Gonzaga	6	9	.400	9	17	.346
Montana	5	10	.333	8	17	.320

Big Ten	Conference			Overall		
	W	L	Pct	W	L	Pct
Ohio State⊕	10	4	.714	21	8	.724
Iowa	10	4	.714	16	9	.640
Purdue	9	5	.643	15	9	.625
Northwestern	8	6	.571	13	10	.565
Wisconsin	7	7	.500	13	11	.542
Michigan State	6	8	.429	12	12	.500
Illinois	6	8	.429	11	13	.458
Michigan	6	8	.429	11	13	.458
Indiana	4	10	.286	10	14	.417
Minnesota	4	10	.286	7	17	.292

Ivy	Conference			Overall		
	W	L	Pct	W	L	Pct
Columbia○	12	2	.857	23	5	.821
Princeton	12	2	.857	20	6	.769
Yale	8	6	.571	15	9	.625
Cornell	6	8	.429	14	11	.560
Dartmouth	6	8	.429	8	18	.308
Brown	4	10	.286	9	16	.360
Penn	4	10	.286	9	17	.346
Harvard	4	10	.286	7	14	.333

Metro	Conference			Overall		
	W	L	Pct	W	L	Pct
Saint Peter's□	8	0	1.000	24	4	.857
Long Island□	7	1	.875	22	2	.917
Wagner	5	3	.625	21	8	.724
Iona	4	4	.500	13	9	.591
Fairleigh Dickinson	4	4	.500	10	12	.455
Seton Hall	4	4	.500	9	15	.375
Manhattan	3	5	.375	8	14	.364
Hofstra	1	7	.125	13	12	.520
St. Francis (NY)	0	8	.000	7	16	.304

Note: Hofstra also played in the Middle Atlantic

Mid-American	Conference			Overall		
	W	L	Pct	W	L	Pct
Bowling Green⊕	10	2	.833	18	7	.720
Marshall□	9	3	.750	17	8	.680
Toledo	8	4	.667	16	8	.667
Western Michigan	5	7	.417	11	13	.458
Miami (OH)	4	8	.333	11	12	.478
Kent State	3	9	.250	9	15	.375
Ohio	3	9	.250	7	16	.304

Middle Atlantic	Conference			Overall		
	W	L	Pct	W	L	Pct
La Salle⊕	-	-	-	20	8	.714
Delaware	-	-	-	16	7	.696
Temple□	-	-	-	19	9	.679
Saint Joseph's	-	-	-	17	9	.654
Gettysburg	-	-	-	14	11	.560
American	-	-	-	14	12	.538
Bucknell	-	-	-	12	11	.522
Lehigh	-	-	-	12	11	.522
Hofstra	-	-	-	13	12	.520
Rider	-	-	-	9	15	.375
Lafayette	-	-	-	5	19	.208

Missouri Valley	Conference			Overall		
	W	L	Pct	W	L	Pct
Louisville⊕	14	2	.875	21	7	.750
Bradley□	12	4	.750	19	9	.679
Cincinnati	11	5	.688	18	8	.692
Drake	9	7	.563	18	8	.692
Saint Louis	9	7	.563	15	11	.577
Wichita State	7	9	.438	12	14	.462
Tulsa	5	11	.313	11	12	.478
North Texas	3	13	.188	8	18	.308
Memphis	2	14	.125	8	17	.320

Ohio Valley	Conference			Overall		
	W	L	Pct	W	L	Pct
East Tennessee St.⊕	10	4	.714	19	8	.704
Murray State	10	4	.714	16	8	.667
Western Kentucky	9	5	.643	18	7	.720
Morehead State	8	6	.571	12	9	.571
Middle Tennessee St.	7	7	.500	15	9	.625
Eastern Kentucky	6	8	.429	10	14	.417
Tennessee Tech	4	10	.286	10	16	.385
Austin Peay	4	10	.286	8	16	.333

SEC	Conference			Overall		
	W	L	Pct	W	L	Pct
Kentucky⊕	15	3	.833	22	5	.815
Tennessee	13	5	.722	20	6	.769
Vanderbilt	12	6	.667	20	6	.769
Georgia	11	7	.611	17	8	.680
Florida	11	7	.611	15	10	.600
LSU	8	10	.444	14	12	.538
Auburn	8	10	.444	13	13	.500
Mississippi State	5	13	.278	9	17	.346
Mississippi	4	14	.222	7	17	.292
Alabama	3	15	.167	10	16	.385

Southern	Conference			Overall		
	W	L	Pct	W	L	Pct
Davidson⊕	9	1	.900	24	5	.828
West Virginia□	9	2	.818	19	9	.679
The Citadel	6	5	.545	11	14	.440
VMI	8	7	.533	9	12	.429
Furman	6	6	.500	13	14	.481
Richmond	8	8	.500	12	13	.480
East Carolina	6	7	.462	9	16	.360
William and Mary	4	10	.286	6	18	.250
George Washington	2	12	.143	5	19	.208

Tournament: **Davidson d. West Virginia 87-70**
Tournament MOP: **Mike Maloy**, Davidson

Southland	Conference			Overall		
	W	L	Pct	W	L	Pct
Abilene Christian	6	2	.750	11	13	.458
Trinity (TX)	5	3	.625	23	7	.767
Arkansas State	4	4	.500	6	17	.261
Lamar	3	5	.375	8	17	.320
Texas-Arlington	2	6	.250	6	20	.231

Southwest	Conference			Overall		
	W	L	Pct	W	L	Pct
TCU⊕	9	5	.643	15	11	.577
Baylor	8	6	.571	15	9	.625
Texas A&M	8	6	.571	14	10	.583
Texas	8	6	.571	11	13	.458
Arkansas	7	7	.500	10	14	.417
Rice	6	8	.429	8	16	.333
Texas Tech	5	9	.357	10	14	.417
SMU	5	9	.357	6	18	.250

WCAC	Conference			Overall		
	W	L	Pct	W	L	Pct
Santa Clara⊕	13	1	.929	22	4	.846
Loyola Marymount	11	3	.786	19	6	.760
San Francisco	10	4	.714	16	10	.615
San Jose State	8	6	.571	13	12	.520
Pacific	6	8	.429	17	9	.654
UC Santa Barbara	3	11	.214	9	17	.346
Saint Mary's (CA)	3	11	.214	4	20	.167
Pepperdine	2	12	.143	9	17	.346

WAC	Conference			Overall		
	W	L	Pct	W	L	Pct
New Mexico⊕	8	2	.800	23	5	.821
Wyoming□	5	5	.500	18	9	.667
Utah	5	5	.500	17	9	.654
BYU	4	6	.400	13	12	.520
Arizona	4	6	.400	11	13	.458
Arizona State	4	6	.400	11	17	.393

Conference Standings Continue →

⊕ Automatic NCAA Tournament bid ○ At-large NCAA Tournament bid □ NIT appearance ❂ Team record doesn't reflect games forfeited or vacated. For adjusted record, see p. 521.

YANKEE

	Conference W	L	Pct	Overall W	L	Pct
Rhode Island	8	2	.800	15	11	.577
Massachusetts	8	2	.800	14	11	.560
Connecticut	7	3	.700	11	13	.458
Vermont	5	5	.500	12	12	.500
Maine	2	8	.200	7	17	.292
New Hampshire	0	10	.000	1	22	.043

INDEPENDENTS

	Overall W	L	Pct
Houston○	31	2	.939
St. Bonaventure○	23	2	.920
Army□	20	5	.800
Marquette○	23	6	.793
New Mexico State○	23	6	.793
Saint Francis (PA)	19	6	.760
Oklahoma City□	20	7	.741
Duquesne□	18	7	.720
Florida State○	19	8	.704
Fordham□	19	8	.704
St. John's○	19	8	.704
Dayton□	21	9	.700
Notre Dame□	21	9	.700

INDEPENDENTS (CONT.)

	Overall W	L	Pct
Boston College○	17	8	.680
Villanova□	19	9	.679
Holy Cross	15	8	.652
Loyola-Chicago○	15	9	.625
Fairfield	16	10	.615
UTEP	14	9	.609
Miami (FL)	17	11	.607
Rutgers	14	10	.583
Utah State	14	11	.560
Virginia Tech	14	11	.560
Southern Illinois	13	11	.542
DePaul	13	12	.520
Detroit	13	12	.520
Seattle	14	13	.519
Jacksonville	13	13	.500
Niagara	12	12	.500
Tulane	12	12	.500
Penn State	10	10	.500
Georgia Tech	12	13	.480
Georgetown	11	12	.478
West Texas	10	11	.476
Colorado State	11	13	.458

INDEPENDENTS (CONT.)

	Overall W	L	Pct
Navy	9	11	.450
Butler	11	14	.440
Denver	11	14	.440
Loyola (LA)	11	14	.440
Providence	11	14	.440
Syracuse	11	14	.440
Boston U.	10	14	.417
Northern Illinois	10	14	.417
Colgate	10	16	.385
Hardin-Simmons	10	16	.385
Xavier	10	16	.385
Air Force	9	15	.375
NYU	8	16	.333
Creighton	8	17	.320
Pittsburgh	7	15	.318
Canisius	7	17	.292
Portland	5	21	.192
Centenary	3	23	.115

INDIVIDUAL LEADERS—SEASON

Scoring

	CL	POS	G	FG	FT	PTS	PPG
1 **Pete Maravich**, LSU	SO	G	26	432	274	1,138	**43.8**
2 **Calvin Murphy**, Niagara	SO	G	24	337	242	916	**38.2**
3 **Elvin Hayes**, Houston	SR	F/C	33	519	176	1,214	**36.8**
4 **Rich Travis**, Oklahoma City	JR	G	27	324	160	808	**29.9**
5 **Bob Portman**, Creighton	JR	F	25	303	132	738	**29.5**
6 **Rick Mount**, Purdue	SO	G	24	259	165	683	**28.5**
7 **Jimmy Hill**, West Texas A&M	JR	F	21	237	99	573	**27.3**
8 **Shaler Halimon**, Utah State	SR	G/F	25	256	159	671	**26.8**
9 **Fred Foster**, Miami (OH)	SR	F	23	230	157	617	**26.8**
10 **Neal Walk**, Florida	JR	C	25	239	185	663	**26.5**

Field Goal Pct

	CL	POS	G	FG	FGA	PCT
1 **Joe Allen**, Bradley	SR	C	28	258	394	**65.5**
2 **Steve Hunt**, Army	SR	C	22	154	248	**62.1**
3 **Wes Unseld**, Louisville	SR	C	28	234	382	**61.3**
4 **Lew Alcindor**, UCLA	JR	C	28	294	480	**61.3**
5 **Dave Sorenson**, Ohio State	SO	C	29	196	329	**59.6**

Minimum: 130 made

Free Throw Pct

	CL	POS	G	FT	FTA	PCT
1 **Joe Heiser**, Princeton	SR	G	26	117	130	**90.0**
2 **Larry Ward**, Centenary	JR	G	26	94	106	**88.7**
3 **Fred Carpenter**, Pacific	SO	G	26	96	109	**88.1**
4 **Brad Luchini**, Marquette	SR	G	29	107	124	**86.3**
5 **Greg Williams**, Rice	JR	G	24	113	131	**86.3**

Minimum: 90 made

Rebounds Per Game

	CL	POS	G	REB	RPG
1 **Neal Walk**, Florida	JR	C	25	494	**19.8**
2 **Garfield Smith**, Eastern Kentucky	SR	C	24	472	**19.7**
3 **Elvin Hayes**, Houston	SR	F/C	33	624	**18.9**
4 **Dick Cunningham**, Murray State	SR	C	23	423	**18.4**
5 **Wes Unseld**, Louisville	SR	C	28	513	**18.3**

INDIVIDUAL LEADERS—GAME

Points

	CL	POS	OPP	DATE	PTS
1 **Elvin Hayes**, Houston	SR	F/C	Valparaiso	F24	**62**
2 **Pete Maravich**, LSU	SO	G	Alabama	F17	**59**
3 **Pete Maravich**, LSU	SO	G	Mississippi State	D22	**58**
4 **Calvin Murphy**, Niagara	SO	G	Villa Madonna	D6	**57**
5 **Pete Maravich**, LSU	SO	G	Auburn	J3	**55**
Pete Maravich, LSU	SO	G	Tulane	F21	**55**

Free Throws Made

	CL	POS	OPP	DATE	FT	FTA	PCT
1 **Bob Quick**, Xavier	SR	F	Marquette	F26	**22**	24	91.7
2 **Ron Moore**, Montana	JR	F	Gonzaga	J12	**20**	23	87.0
Calvin Murphy, Niagara	SO	G	Syracuse	J31	**20**	23	87.0
4 **Larry Miller**, North Carolina	SR	G/F	Oregon State	D30	**19**	22	86.4
5 **Bob Portman**, Creighton	JR	F	Milwaukee	D16	**19**	23	82.6

Rebounds

	CL	POS	OPP	DATE	REB
1 **Elvin Hayes**, Houston	SR	F/C	Centenary	F10	**37**
2 **Dick Cunningham**, Murray State	SR	C	Western Kentucky	D2	**34**
3 **Neal Walk**, Florida	JR	C	Alabama	J27	**31**
Dave Cowens, Florida State	SO	C	LSU	D16	**31**
5 **Ed Wilson**, Idaho State	SR	F	Tex.-Pan American	D16	**30**
Rusty Clark, North Carolina	JR	C	Maryland	F21	**30**

TEAM LEADERS—SEASON

Win-Loss Pct

	W	L	PCT
1 **UCLA**	29	1	**.967**
2 **Houston**	31	2	**.939**
3 **St. Bonaventure**	23	2	**.920**
4 **North Carolina**	28	4	**.875**
5 **Saint Peter's**	24	4	**.857**

Scoring Offense

	G	W-L	PTS	PPG
1 **Houston**	33	31-2	3,226	**97.8**
2 **Saint Peter's**	28	24-4	2,630	**93.9**
3 **UCLA**	30	29-1	2,802	**93.4**
4 **Oklahoma City**	27	20-7	2,492	**92.3**
5 **Florida State**	27	19-8	2,438	**90.3**

Scoring Margin

	G	W-L	PPG	OPP PPG	MAR
1 **UCLA**	30	29-1	93.4	67.2	**26.2**
2 **Houston**	33	31-2	97.8	72.5	**25.3**
3 **Saint Peter's**	28	24-4	93.9	76.1	**17.8**
4 **Columbia**	28	23-5	78.8	61.7	**17.1**
5 **Boston College**	25	17-8	88.8	74.9	**13.9**

Field Goal Pct

	G	W-L	FG	FGA	PCT
1 **Bradley**	28	19-9	927	1,768	**52.4**
2 **Saint Peter's**	28	24-4	1,019	1,953	**52.2**
3 **St. Bonaventure**	25	23-2	875	1,732	**50.5**
4 **UCLA**	30	29-1	1,161	2,321	**50.0**
5 **Louisville**	28	21-7	881	1,770	**49.8**

Rebounds Per Game

	G	W-L	REB	RPG
1 **Houston**	33	31-2	2,074	**62.8**
2 **Northern Illinois**	24	10-14	1,383	**57.6**
3 **Saint Francis (PA)**	25	19-6	1,434	**57.4**
4 **Eastern Kentucky**	24	10-14	1,348	**56.2**
5 **American**	26	14-12	1,459	**56.1**

Scoring Defense

	G	W-L	OPP PTS	OPP PPG
1 **Army**	25	20-5	1,448	**57.9**
2 **Oklahoma State**	26	10-16	1,528	**58.8**
3 **Tennessee**	26	20-6	1,548	**59.5**
4 **Princeton**	26	20-6	1,579	**60.7**
5 **Villanova**	28	19-9	1,705	**60.9**

CONSENSUS ALL-AMERICAS

FIRST TEAM

PLAYER	CL	POS	HT	SCHOOL	RPG	PPG
Lew Alcindor	JR	C	7-2	UCLA	16.5	26.2
Elvin Hayes	SR	F/C	6-8	Houston	18.9	36.8
Pete Maravich	SO	G	6-5	LSU	7.5	43.8
Larry Miller	SR	G/F	6-4	North Carolina	8.1	22.4
Wes Unseld	SR	C	6-8	Louisville	18.3	23.0

SECOND TEAM

PLAYER	CL	POS	HT	SCHOOL	RPG	PPG
Lucius Allen	JR	G	6-2	UCLA	6.0	15.1
Bob Lanier	SO	C	6-11	St. Bonaventure	15.6	26.2
Don May	SR	F	6-4	Dayton	15.0	23.4
Calvin Murphy	SO	G	5-9	Niagara	4.9	38.2
Jo Jo White	JR	G	6-3	Kansas	3.6	15.3

Selectors: AP, NABC, UPI, USBWA

AWARD WINNERS

PLAYER OF THE YEAR

PLAYER	CL	POS	HT	SCHOOL	AWARDS
Elvin Hayes	SR	F/C	6-8	Houston	AP, UPI, USBWA

COACH OF THE YEAR

COACH	SCHOOL	REC	AWARDS
Guy V. Lewis	Houston	31-2	AP, UPI, USBWA, Sporting News

Poll Progression

Preseason Poll

AP	UPI	School
1	1	UCLA
2	2	Houston
3	4	Louisville
4	5	North Carolina
5	3	Kansas
6	6	Dayton
7	7	Boston College
8	8	Princeton
9	9	Vanderbilt
10	12	Davidson
—	9	Tennessee
—	11	Indiana
—	13	Cincinnati
—	14	UTEP
—	15	Loyola-Chicago
—	15	St. John's
—	15	Wyoming
—	18	Marquette
—	19	Duke
—	19	Niagara

Week of Dec 5

AP	UPI	School	AP↓↑
1	1	UCLA (1-0) Ⓐ	
2	3	Houston (1-0)	
3	2	Louisville (1-0)	
4	4	Kansas (1-0)	↑1
5	5	North Carolina (1-0)	↓1
6	6	Dayton (1-0)	
7	8	Purdue (0-1)	⤴
8	11	Vanderbilt (1-0) Ⓑ	↑1
9	13	Kentucky (1-0)	⤴
10	9	Boston College (0-0)	↓3
—	7	Princeton (1-0)	⤵
—	10	Tennessee (1-0)	
—	12	Davidson (2-0)	⤵
—	14	Cincinnati (1-0)	
—	15	St. John's (1-0)	
—	16	Indiana (2-0)	
—	17	Syracuse (1-0)	
—	18	Utah (2-0)	
—	19	BYU (2-0)	
—	19	Loyola-Chicago (1-0)	
—	19	Wyoming (2-0)	

Week of Dec 12

AP	UPI	School	AP↓↑
1	1	UCLA (3-0)	
2	2	Houston (4-0)	
3	3	Vanderbilt (3-0)	↑5
4	6	Kentucky (4-0)	↑5
5	4	Louisville (2-1)	↓2
6	5	Boston College (2-0)	↑4
7	8	North Carolina (2-1) Ⓒ	↓2
8	9	Davidson (4-0)	⤴
9	12	Indiana (3-0)	⤴
10	7	Princeton (4-0)	⤴
—	10	Tennessee (1-0)	
—	11	Kansas (1-2)	⤵
—	13	Wyoming (4-0)	
—	14	Loyola-Chicago (3-0)	
—	15	Purdue (2-2)	⤵
—	16	Dayton (1-2)	⤵
—	17	Cincinnati (3-0)	
—	18	St. John's (2-1)	
—	19	Bradley (5-0)	
—	19	Duke (3-0)	

Week of Dec 19

AP	UPI	School	AP↓↑
1	1	UCLA (3-0)	
2	2	Houston (7-0)	
3	3	Vanderbilt (5-0)	
4	4	North Carolina (4-1)	↑3
5	6	Indiana (5-0)	↑4
6	10	Davidson (5-1)	↑2
7	8	Kentucky (4-1)	↓3
8	5	Boston College (3-0)	↓2
9	7	Tennessee (3-0)	⤴
10	13	Bradley (7-0)	⤴
—	9	Louisville (2-2)	⤵
—	10	Princeton (5-1)	⤵
—	12	Wyoming (5-1)	
—	13	Kansas (3-2)	
—	15	Dayton (3-2)	
—	16	Utah (6-0)	
—	17	St. John's (5-1)	
—	18	Wisconsin (4-1)	
—	19	Duke (4-1)	
—	19	Purdue (4-3)	

Week of Dec 26

AP	UPI	School	AP↓↑
1	1	UCLA (5-0)	
2	2	Houston (10-0)	
3	5	Indiana (6-0)	↑2
4	6	Tennessee (4-0)	↑5
5	4	North Carolina (4-1)	↓1
6	7	Kentucky (6-1)	↑1
7	13	Utah (8-0)	⤴
8	11	Davidson (7-1)	↓2
9	3	Vanderbilt (7-1)	↓6
10	8	Boston College (5-1)	↓2
—	9	St. John's (6-1)	
—	10	Kansas (6-2)	
—	12	Louisville (3-3)	
—	14	New Mexico (8-0)	
—	14	Wisconsin (5-1)	
—	16	Duke (4-1)	
—	17	Bradley (8-1)	⤵
—	17	Princeton (5-2)	
—	19	Florida (4-2)	
—	20	California (6-0)	
—	20	Tulsa (7-1)	

Week of Jan 2

AP	UPI	School	AP↓↑
1	1	UCLA (8-0)	
2	2	Houston (13-0)	
3	4	North Carolina (7-1)	↑2
4	3	Vanderbilt (9-1)	↑5
5	5	Kentucky (7-1)	↑1
6	6	Tennessee (6-1)	↓2
7	6	Utah (10-1)	
8	8	Oklahoma City (8-0)	⤴
9	17	St. Bonaventure (9-0)	⤴
10	15	New Mexico (10-0)	⤴
—	9	Columbia (7-3)	
—	10	Davidson (8-2)	⤵
—	11	St. John's (8-2)	
—	12	Duke (5-1)	
—	13	Wyoming (8-3)	
—	14	Indiana (6-3)	⤵
—	15	Louisville (5-4)	
—	18	Tulsa (7-1)	
—	19	Temple (8-2)	
—	20	Western Kentucky (7-2)	

Week of Jan 9

AP	UPI	School	AP↓↑
1	1	UCLA (10-0)	
2	2	Houston (15-0)	
3	3	North Carolina (9-1)	
4	4	Kentucky (8-1)	↑1
5	5	Tennessee (7-1)	↑1
6	7	Utah (11-1)	↑1
7	9	St. Bonaventure (11-0)	↑2
8	6	Vanderbilt (10-2)	↓4
9	8	New Mexico (13-0)	↑1
10	11	Columbia (9-3)	⤴
—	10	Davidson (9-3)	
—	12	Louisville (7-4)	
—	13	Kansas (10-3)	
—	14	Wyoming (9-3)	
—	15	St. John's (9-3)	
—	16	Princeton (9-3)	
—	17	Boston College (7-3)	
—	17	Western Kentucky (8-3)	
—	19	Oklahoma City (8-2)	⤵
—	19	UTEP (9-2)	

Week of Jan 16

AP	UPI	School	AP↓↑
1	1	UCLA (12-0)	
2	2	Houston (16-0)	
3	3	North Carolina (11-1)	
4	4	Tennessee (9-1)	↑1
5	5	Utah (13-1)	↑1
6	6	New Mexico (14-0)	↑3
7	8	St. Bonaventure (12-0)	
8	7	Kentucky (9-2)	↓4
9	9	Vanderbilt (11-3)	↓1
10	10	Columbia (10-3)	
—	11	Kansas (11-4)	
—	12	UTEP (10-2)	
—	13	Duke (9-2)	
—	14	Davidson (10-4)	
—	14	Louisville (8-5)	
—	14	Princeton (11-3)	
—	17	Cincinnati (9-3)	
—	18	Tulsa (9-2)	
—	19	Marquette (12-2)	
—	19	Oklahoma City (9-3)	
—	19	St. John's (11-3)	

Week of Jan 23

AP	UPI	School	AP↓↑
1	1	Houston (17-0) Ⓓ	↑1
2	2	UCLA (13-1) Ⓓ	↓1
3	3	North Carolina (11-1)	
4	4	New Mexico (16-0)	↑2
5	5	St. Bonaventure (13-0)	↑2
6	6	Tennessee (10-2)	↓2
7	10	Vanderbilt (12-3)	↑2
8	7	Columbia (11-3)	↑2
9	9	Kentucky (10-3)	↓1
10	8	Utah (13-3)	↓5
—	11	Cincinnati (12-3)	
—	12	Marquette (12-2)	
—	13	Duke (9-2)	
—	14	Davidson (10-4)	
—	15	Tulsa (10-3)	
—	16	New Mexico State (15-2)	
—	16	Princeton (11-3)	
—	16	UTEP (10-3)	
—	19	Wyoming (11-4)	
—	20	St. John's (12-3)	

Week of Jan 30

AP	UPI	School	AP↓↑
1	1	Houston (18-0)	
2	2	UCLA (15-1)	
3	3	North Carolina (12-1)	
4	4	New Mexico (16-0)	
5	5	St. Bonaventure (15-0)	
6	6	Tennessee (13-2)	
7	8	Vanderbilt (13-3)	
8	7	Columbia (11-3)	
9	10	Duke (10-2)	⤴
10	9	Kentucky (11-4)	↓1
—	11	Utah (13-6)	⤵
—	12	Boston College (9-4)	
—	12	New Mexico State (15-2)	
—	14	Cincinnati (12-4)	
—	15	Wyoming (13-4)	
—	16	Drake (14-2)	
—	16	Marquette (13-3)	
—	18	Davidson (11-4)	
—	19	Northwestern (9-5)	
—	19	Princeton (12-3)	

Week of Feb 6

AP	UPI	School	AP↓↑
1	1	Houston (20-0)	
2	2	UCLA (16-1)	
3	3	North Carolina (14-1)	
4	6	St. Bonaventure (16-0)	↑1
5	4	Tennessee (14-2)	↑1
6	5	New Mexico (17-1)	↓2
7	7	Columbia (13-3)	↑1
8	8	Kentucky (13-4)	↑2
9	9	Vanderbilt (14-4)	↓2
10	12	New Mexico State (17-2)	⤴
—	10	Duke (11-3)	⤵
—	11	Louisville (12-6)	
—	13	Boston College (10-5)	
—	13	Davidson (13-4)	
—	15	Wyoming (14-5)	
—	16	Ohio State (12-4)	
—	17	Drake (15-3)	
—	18	Florida (14-6)	
—	19	Utah State (10-10)	
—	20	Kansas (13-5)	

Week of Feb 13

AP	UPI	School	AP↓↑
1	1	Houston (21-0)	
2	2	UCLA (17-1)	
3	3	North Carolina (17-1)	
4	4	St. Bonaventure (17-0)	
5	5	New Mexico (19-1)	↑1
6	7	Columbia (15-3)	↑1
7	6	Tennessee (15-3)	↓2
8	8	Kentucky (15-4)	
9	9	Vanderbilt (16-4)	
10	10	Duke (14-3)	⤴
—	11	Louisville (14-6)	
—	12	New Mexico State (17-4)	⤵
—	13	Ohio State (13-5) Ⓔ	
—	14	Army (17-3)	
—	14	Princeton (15-4)	
—	16	Marquette (16-3)	
—	17	Fordham (14-4)	
—	18	Loyola-Chicago (12-5)	
—	18	Wyoming (15-5)	
—	20	Davidson (14-4)	

Poll Progression Continues →

Week of Feb 20

AP	UPI	SCHOOL	AP↓↑
1	1	**Houston** (23-0)	
2	2	**UCLA** (20-1)	
3	3	**North Carolina** (20-1)	
4	4	**St. Bonaventure** (18-0)	
5	5	**Kentucky** (17-4)	↑3
6	6	**Columbia** (17-3)	
7	7	**New Mexico** (20-2)	↓2
8	9	**Duke** (16-3)	↑2
9	8	**Vanderbilt** (17-4)	
10	15	**Marquette** (18-3)	⤴
—	10	**Louisville** (16-6)	
—	11	**Tennessee** (15-5)	⤵
—	12	**Kansas** (15-5)	
—	13	**New Mexico State** (17-4)	
—	14	**Princeton** (17-4)	
—	15	**Utah** (17-6)	
—	17	**Davidson** (16-4)	
—	18	**Army** (18-4)	
—	19	**Wyoming** (15-7)	
—	20	**USC** (15-6)	

Week of Feb 27

AP	UPI	SCHOOL	AP↓↑
1	1	**Houston** (25-0)	
2	2	**UCLA** (21-1)	
3	3	**North Carolina** (22-1)	
4	4	**St. Bonaventure** (19-0)	
5	5	**Kentucky** (19-4)	
6	6	**Columbia** (19-3)	
7	7	**New Mexico** (22-2)	
8	10	**Marquette** (20-3)	↑2
9	8	**Louisville** (18-6)	⤴
10	9	**Duke** (18-4)	↓2
—	11	**Vanderbilt** (19-5)	⤵
—	12	**New Mexico State** (19-4)	
—	13	**Tennessee** (17-6)	
—	14	**USC** (17-6)	
—	15	**Davidson** (17-4)	
—	15	**Utah** (17-7)	
—	17	**Kansas State** (16-7)	
—	18	**Princeton** (18-5)	
—	19	**Western Kentucky** (17-7)	
—	20	**West Virginia** (17-7)	

Week of Mar 5

AP	UPI	SCHOOL	AP↓↑
1	1	**Houston** (27-0)	
2	2	**UCLA** (24-1)	
3	3	**St. Bonaventure** (21-0)	↑1
4	5	**Kentucky** (21-4)	↑1
5	4	**North Carolina** (22-3)	↓2
6	7	**Duke** (20-4)	↑4
7	6	**New Mexico** (23-3)	
8	9	**Columbia** (20-4)	↓2
9	8	**Louisville** (19-6)	
10	11	**Davidson** (20-4)	⤴
—	10	**Vanderbilt** (19-6)	
—	12	**Princeton** (20-5)	
—	13	**New Mexico State** (20-5)	
—	14	**Marquette** (21-5)	⤵
—	15	**Tennessee** (19-6) Ⓕ	
—	16	**Western Kentucky** (18-7)	
—	17	**Iowa** (16-7)	
—	18	**Santa Clara** (19-3)	
—	19	**Kansas State** (18-7)	
—	19	**Utah** (17-9)	

Final Poll

AP	UPI	SCHOOL	AP↓↑
1	1	**Houston** (29-0)	
2	2	**UCLA** (25-1)	
3	3	**St. Bonaventure** (23-0)	
4	4	**North Carolina** (25-3)	↑1
5	5	**Kentucky** (21-4)	↓1
6	7	**New Mexico** (23-3)	↑1
7	6	**Columbia** (22-4)	↑1
8	9	**Davidson** (23-4)	↑2
9	8	**Louisville** (20-6)	
10	11	**Duke** (21-5) Ⓖ	↓4
—	10	**Marquette** (22-5)	
—	12	**New Mexico State** (22-5)	
—	13	**Vanderbilt** (20-6)	
—	14	**Kansas State** (19-7)	
—	15	**Princeton** (20-6)	
—	16	**Army** (20-4)	
—	17	**Santa Clara** (21-3)	
—	18	**Utah** (17-9)	
—	19	**Bradley** (19-9)	
—	20	**Iowa State** (12-13)	

Ⓐ Playing his first game under the NCAA's new no-dunk (a.k.a. Stop Alcindor) rule, Lew Alcindor scores 17 in UCLA's 73-71 win at Purdue.

Ⓑ Vanderbilt forward Perry Wallace, the SEC's first African-American player, debuts with six points in the Commodores' 88-84 win over SMU. Wallace will be named all-conference in 1969-70 and will go on to become a law professor at American University.

Ⓒ North Carolina routs Kent State, 107-83, despite 41 points by the Golden Flash's Doug Grayson, who sets an NCAA record by hitting 16 consecutive shots.

Ⓓ In the first nationally televised regular-season game, Houston snaps UCLA's 47-game winning streak with a 71-69 victory in front of 52,693 fans at the Astrodome.

Ⓔ Wisconsin beats Big Ten leader Ohio State, 86-78, in Madison, tightening the conference race. The Buckeyes will recover to take the conference title, then make a surprise trip to the Final Four.

Ⓕ In a 74-71 win over LSU, Tennessee holds Pete Maravich to 17 points. Pistol Pete, who will become college basketball's all-time leading scorer with a 44.8 ppg career average, will average just 23.0 in six games against the Vols.

Ⓖ NC State upsets Duke, 12-10, in the ACC tournament semifinals—the lowest-scoring game in the modern era, at least for the next five years, until Dec. 15, 1973, when Tennessee beats Temple, 11-6.

1968 NCAA Tournament

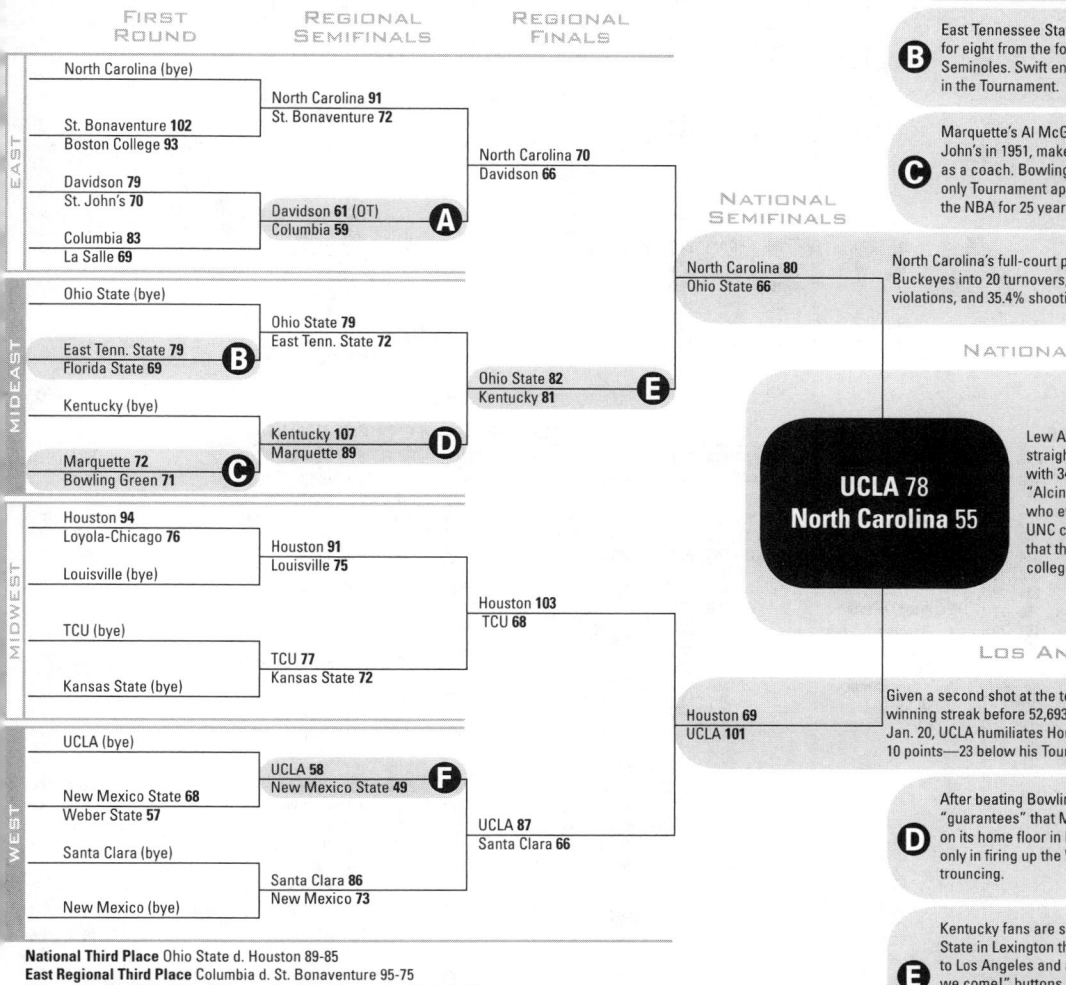

East

First Round
- North Carolina (bye)
- St. Bonaventure **102**, Boston College **93**
- Davidson **79**, St. John's **70**
- Columbia **83**, La Salle **69**

Regional Semifinals
- North Carolina **91**, St. Bonaventure **72**
- Davidson **61** (OT), Columbia **59** (A)

Regional Finals
- North Carolina **70**, Davidson **66**

Mideast

First Round
- Ohio State (bye)
- East Tenn. State **79**, Florida State **69** (B)
- Kentucky (bye)
- Marquette **72**, Bowling Green **71** (C)

Regional Semifinals
- Ohio State **79**, East Tenn. State **72**
- Kentucky **107**, Marquette **89** (D)

Regional Finals
- Ohio State **82**, Kentucky **81** (E)

Midwest

First Round
- Houston **94**, Loyola-Chicago **76**
- Louisville (bye)
- TCU (bye)
- Kansas State (bye)

Regional Semifinals
- Houston **91**, Louisville **75**
- TCU **77**, Kansas State **72**

Regional Finals
- Houston **103**, TCU **68**

West

First Round
- UCLA (bye)
- New Mexico State **68**, Weber State **57**
- Santa Clara (bye)
- New Mexico (bye)

Regional Semifinals
- UCLA **58**, New Mexico State **49** (F)
- Santa Clara **86**, New Mexico **73**

Regional Finals
- UCLA **87**, Santa Clara **66**

National Semifinals

- North Carolina **80**, Ohio State **66**

North Carolina's full-court pressure harasses the Buckeyes into 20 turnovers, including two 10-second violations, and 35.4% shooting.

- Houston **69**, UCLA **101**

Given a second shot at the team that ended its 47-game winning streak before 52,693 fans in the Astrodome on Jan. 20, UCLA humiliates Houston, holding Elvin Hayes to 10 points—23 below his Tourney average.

National Final

UCLA 78
North Carolina 55

Lew Alcindor wins his second straight Tournament MOP award with 34 points and 16 rebounds. "Alcindor is the greatest player who ever played the game," says UNC coach Dean Smith, who adds that the Bruins are the greatest college basketball team of all time.

Los Angeles

National Third Place Ohio State d. Houston 89-85
East Regional Third Place Columbia d. St. Bonaventure 95-75
Mideast Regional Third Place Marquette d. East Tennessee State 69-57
Midwest Regional Third Place Louisville d. Kansas State 93-63
West Regional Third Place New Mexico State d. New Mexico 62-58

A Davidson coach Lefty Driesell calls back-to-back timeouts as Columbia's Bruce Metz prepares to shoot a one-and-one with the score knotted at 55 and :02 left. The tactic works: Metz misses the front end and Davidson wins in overtime.

B East Tennessee State's Harley Swift goes eight for eight from the foul line as his team upsets the Seminoles. Swift ends up 18 for 18 from the line in the Tournament.

C Marquette's Al McGuire, who played for St. John's in 1951, makes his NCAA Tourney debut as a coach. Bowling Green's Bill Fitch makes his only Tournament appearance before coaching in the NBA for 25 years.

D After beating Bowling Green, coach Al McGuire "guarantees" that Marquette will beat Kentucky on its home floor in Lexington. But he succeeds only in firing up the Wildcats for an 18-point trouncing.

E Kentucky fans are so confident of beating Ohio State in Lexington that many have booked flights to Los Angeles and are wearing "California, here we come!" buttons. But the Buckeyes shock the Dan Issel-led Wildcats when David Sorenson hits a short jumper with :03 remaining.

F Starting guard Mike Warren, who later stars in the popular TV series *Hill Street Blues*, scores 10 points for the Bruins.

Tournament Leaders

INDIVIDUAL LEADERS

Scoring

	Player	CL	POS	G	PTS	PPG
1	**Elvin Hayes**, Houston	SR	F/C	5	167	33.4
2	**Dan Issel**, Kentucky	SO	C	2	55	27.5
3	**Lew Alcindor**, UCLA	JR	C	4	103	25.8
4	**Bill Butler**, St. Bonaventure	SR	G/F	3	73	24.3
	Bob Lanier, St. Bonaventure	SO	C	3	73	24.3
6	**Wes Unseld**, Louisville	SR	C	2	48	24.0
7	**Ron Nelson**, New Mexico	SR	G	2	46	23.0
8	**Heyward Dotson**, Columbia	SO	G	3	67	22.3
9	**George Thompson**, Marquette	JR	G	3	66	22.0
10	**Butch Beard**, Louisville	JR	G	2	42	21.0

Minimum: 2 games

Field Goal Pct

	Player	CL	POS	G	FG	FGA	PCT
1	**Heyward Dotson**, Columbia	SO	G	3	22	28	78.6
2	**Terry O'Brien**, Santa Clara	SO	G	2	10	13	76.9
3	**Lew Alcindor**, UCLA	JR	C	4	37	56	66.1
4	**Bud Ogden**, Santa Clara	JR	F	2	13	20	65.0
5	**Mike Kretzer**, East Tenn. State	SO	F	3	25	40	62.5

Minimum: 10 made

Free Throw Pct

	Player	CL	POS	G	FT	FTA	PCT
1	**Harley Swift**, East Tenn. St.	JR	G	3	18	18	100.0
2	**Lynn Shackelford**, UCLA	JR	F	4	10	11	90.9
	Ron Nelson, New Mexico	SR	G	2	10	11	90.9
4	**Dick Grubar**, North Carolina	JR	G	4	10	12	83.3
5	**Mike Maloy**, Davidson	SO	F	3	14	17	82.3

Minimum: 10 made

Rebounds Per Game

	Player	CL	POS	G	REB	RPG
1	**Wes Unseld**, Louisville	SR	C	2	41	20.5
2	**Elvin Hayes**, Houston	SR	F/C	5	97	19.4
3	**Lew Alcindor**, UCLA	JR	C	4	75	18.8
4	**Bill Hosket**, Ohio State	SR	F/C	4	58	14.5
5	**Ken Spain**, Houston	JR	C	5	67	13.4

Minimum: 2 games

TEAM LEADERS

Scoring

	Team	G	PTS	PPG
1	**Kentucky**	2	188	94.0
2	**Houston**	5	442	88.4
3	**Louisville**	2	168	84.0
4	**St. Bonaventure**	3	249	83.0
5	**UCLA**	4	324	81.0
6	**Ohio State**	4	316	79.0
	Columbia	3	237	79.0
8	**Marquette**	3	230	76.7
9	**Santa Clara**	2	152	76.0
10	**North Carolina**	4	296	74.0

Minimum: 2 games

FG Pct

	Team	G	FG	FGA	PCT
1	**Kentucky**	2	79	149	53.0
2	**Marquette**	3	83	162	51.2
3	**Columbia**	3	85	166	51.2
4	**Santa Clara**	2	58	121	47.9
5	**UCLA**	4	127	269	47.2

FT Pct

	Team	G	FT	FTA	PCT
1	**East Tenn. State**	3	46	60	76.7
2	**Davidson**	3	60	79	75.9
3	**UCLA**	4	70	94	74.5
4	**Columbia**	3	67	90	74.4
5	**TCU**	2	33	45	73.3

Minimum: 2 games

Rebounds

	Team	G	REB	RPG
1	**Houston**	5	265	53.0
2	**Louisville**	2	96	48.0
3	**TCU**	2	94	47.0
4	**Kansas State**	2	89	44.5
5	**UCLA**	4	177	44.3

Minimum: 2 games

ALL-TOURNAMENT TEAM

PLAYER	CL	POS	HT	SCHOOL	RPG	PPG
Lew Alcindor*	JR	C	7-2	UCLA	18.8	25.8
Lucius Allen	JR	G	6-2	UCLA	6.3	14.3
Larry Miller	SR	G/F	6-4	North Carolina	8.5	19.3
Lynn Shackelford	JR	F	6-5	UCLA	4.3	8.5
Mike Warren	SR	G	5-10	UCLA	4.0	11.5

ALL-REGIONAL TEAMS

EAST

PLAYER	CL	POS	HT	SCHOOL	RPG	PPG
Rusty Clark*	JR	C	6-10	North Carolina	13.5	20.0
Mike Maloy	SO	F	6-7	Davidson	11.0	17.3
Jim McMillian	SO	F	6-5	Columbia	11.3	16.7
Larry Miller	SR	G/F	6-4	North Carolina	11.0	21.5
Charlie Scott	SO	G/F	6-5	North Carolina	4.5	19.5

MIDEAST

PLAYER	CL	POS	HT	SCHOOL	RPG	PPG
Dave Sorenson*	SO	C	6-7	Ohio State	6.5	19.0
Mike Casey	SO	G	6-4	Kentucky	7.0	17.5
Bill Hosket	SR	F/C	6-7	Ohio State	16.0	19.5
Dan Issel	SO	C	6-8	Kentucky	10.5	27.5
Brad Luchini	SR	G	6-2	Marquette	4.0	15.0

MIDWEST

PLAYER	CL	POS	HT	SCHOOL	RPG	PPG
Elvin Hayes*	SR	F/C	6-8	Houston	25.3	41.0
Butch Beard	JR	G	6-3	Louisville	6.0	21.0
Don Chaney	SR	G	6-5	Houston	4.0	13.7
Theodis Lee	JR	F	6-7	Houston	7.3	15.7
Wes Unseld	SR	C	6-8	Louisville	20.5	24.0

WEST

PLAYER	CL	POS	HT	SCHOOL	RPG	PPG
Lew Alcindor*	JR	C	7-2	UCLA	20.5	25.0
Lucius Allen	JR	G	6-2	UCLA	5.5	13.5
Ron Nelson	SR	G	6-2	New Mexico	1.5	23.0
Bud Ogden	JR	F	6-6	Santa Clara	8.0	17.5
Mike Warren	SR	G	5-10	UCLA	4.0	12.5

* Most outstanding player

1968 NCAA TOURNAMENT BOX SCORES

North Carolina 91, St. Bonaventure 72 (1H: 40–30; 2H: 51–42) — SWEET 16

NORTH CAROLINA	MIN	FG	3FG	FT	REB	A	ST	BL	PF	TP
Larry Miller	37	9-18	-	9-14	16	2	-	-	4	27
Charlie Scott	35	9-13	-	3-4	3	2	-	-	3	21
Rusty Clark	34	9-13	-	0-0	10	2	-	-	3	18
Dick Grubar	26	4-7	-	1-1	3	2	-	-	4	9
Bill Bunting	27	1-5	-	2-3	8	1	-	-	2	4
Joe Brown	15	2-5	-	0-1	5	1	-	-	4	4
Eddie Fogler	13	2-5	-	0-0	0	2	-	-	0	4
Ralph Fletcher	2	1-3	-	2-3	2	0	-	-	0	4
Gerald Tuttle	8	0-2	-	0-0	0	1	-	-	1	0
Jim Delany	1	0-0	-	0-0	0	1	-	-	0	0
Jim Frye	1	0-0	-	0-0	1	0	-	-	1	0
Gra Whitehead	1	0-0	-	0-0	0	0	-	-	0	0
TOTALS	**200**	**37-71**	**-**	**17-26**	**48**	**14**	**-**	**-**	**22**	**91**
Percentages		52.1		65.4						

Coach: Dean Smith

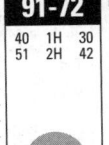

ST. BONAVENTURE	MIN	FG	3FG	FT	REB	A	ST	BL	PF	TP
Bill Butler	40	10-22	-	3-5	12	1	-	-	3	23
Bob Lanier	39	10-24	-	3-5	9	2	-	-	5	23
John Hayes	35	4-8	-	2-2	7	1	-	-	4	10
Jim Satalin	31	2-11	-	3-4	5	1	-	-	5	7
Gene Fahey	1	1-3	-	2-2	1	0	-	-	0	4
Bill Kalbaugh	40	1-3	-	1-2	1	5	-	-	3	3
Vinnie Martin	14	0-1	-	2-5	4	2	-	-	1	2
TOTALS	**200**	**28-72**	**-**	**16-25**	**39**	**12**	**-**	**-**	**21**	**72**
Percentages		38.9		64.0						

Coach: Larry Weise

Officials: Fouty, Stout
Attendance: 12,600

Davidson 61, Columbia 59 (1H: 32–28; 2H: 23–27; OT1: 6–4) — SWEET 16

DAVIDSON	MIN	FG	3FG	FT	REB	A	ST	BL	PF	TP
Rodney Knowles	22	7-13	-	0-0	7	1	-	-	5	14
Mike Maloy	45	4-8	-	3-4	10	1	-	-	1	11
Wayne Huckel	37	3-14	-	4-5	2	1	-	-	4	10
Mike O'Neill	31	3-7	-	3-6	8	1	-	-	2	9
Dave Moser	45	4-8	-	0-0	8	3	-	-	0	8
Jerry Kroll	30	2-7	-	1-4	4	1	-	-	3	5
Doug Cook	10	1-2	-	2-2	2	0	-	-	1	4
Jim Youngsdale	5	0-0	-	0-0	0	0	-	-	1	0
TOTALS	**225**	**24-59**	**-**	**13-21**	**41**	**8**	**-**	**-**	**17**	**61**
Percentages		40.7		61.9						

Coach: Lefty Driesell

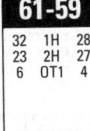

COLUMBIA	MIN	FG	3FG	FT	REB	A	ST	BL	PF	TP
David Newmark	44	8-20	-	3-3	9	2	-	-	1	19
Heyward Dotson	38	4-6	-	7-7	3	0	-	-	5	15
Jim McMillian	44	6-15	-	2-3	12	1	-	-	4	14
Bill Ames	28	2-4	-	0-2	1	0	-	-	4	4
Larry Borger	15	2-2	-	0-0	2	0	-	-	1	4
Bruce Metz	24	1-1	-	0-1	2	0	-	-	0	2
Roger Walaszek	32	0-5	-	1-3	3	1	-	-	2	1
TOTALS	**225**	**23-53**	**-**	**13-19**	**32**	**4**	**-**	**-**	**17**	**59**
Percentages		43.4		68.4						

Coach: John Rohan

Officials: Allen, Wirtz
Attendance: 12,600

Ohio State 79, East Tennessee State 72 (1H: 37–27; 2H: 42–45) — SWEET 16

OHIO STATE	MIN	FG	3FG	FT	REB	A	ST	BL	PF	TP
Steve Howell	-	10-17	-	2-3	8	-	-	-	2	22
Bill Hosket	-	7-13	-	4-7	20	-	-	-	5	18
David Sorenson	-	7-9	-	0-0	6	-	-	-	4	14
Denny Meadors	-	4-11	-	4-7	3	-	-	-	3	12
Bruce Schnabel	-	4-8	-	1-1	1	-	-	-	3	9
Edward Smith	-	2-5	-	0-0	5	-	-	-	0	4
Daniel Andreas	-	0-0	-	0-0	0	-	-	-	0	0
Jody Finney	-	0-0	-	0-0	1	-	-	-	0	0
TOTALS	**-**	**34-63**	**-**	**11-18**	**44**	**-**	**-**	**-**	**17**	**79**
Percentages		54.0		61.1						

Coach: Fred R. Taylor

EAST TENNESSEE STATE	MIN	FG	3FG	FT	REB	A	ST	BL	PF	TP
Mike Kretzer	-	10-15	-	3-4	9	-	-	-	3	23
Harley Swift	-	7-21	-	7-7	6	-	-	-	4	21
Leroy Fisher	-	6-16	-	1-1	4	-	-	-	1	13
Richard Arnold	-	2-10	-	2-2	1	-	-	-	3	6
Ernie Sims	-	2-9	-	1-7	18	-	-	-	1	5
George Walling	-	1-2	-	0-0	0	-	-	-	0	2
Larry Woods	-	0-1	-	2-2	2	-	-	-	1	2
Tim Fleming	-	0-1	-	0-0	0	-	-	-	1	0
Bobby Hall	-	0-1	-	0-0	0	-	-	-	1	0
Worley Ward	-	0-2	-	0-0	3	-	-	-	1	0
TOTALS	**-**	**28-78**	**-**	**16-23**	**43**	**-**	**-**	**-**	**16**	**72**
Percentages		35.9		69.6						

Coach: Madison Brooks

Officials: Honzo, Allmond
Attendance: 11,500

Kentucky 107, Marquette 89 (1H: 53–40; 2H: 54–49) — SWEET 16

KENTUCKY	MIN	FG	3FG	FT	REB	A	ST	BL	PF	TP
Dan Issel	-	14-18	-	8-10	13	-	-	-	2	36
Mike Casey	-	8-19	-	3-4	6	-	-	-	2	19
Mike Pratt	-	8-13	-	2-2	6	-	-	-	3	18
Gary Gamble	-	3-3	-	2-3	1	-	-	-	4	8
Tommy Porter	-	4-5	-	0-2	3	-	-	-	0	8
Steve Clevenger	-	2-4	-	2-2	1	-	-	-	3	6
Jim LeMaster	-	2-3	-	2-3	2	-	-	-	2	6
Phil Argento	-	0-0	-	2-2	0	-	-	-	1	2
Thad Jaracz	-	1-4	-	0-0	2	-	-	-	1	2
Randy Pool	-	1-1	-	0-0	2	-	-	-	3	2
Bill Busey	-	0-0	-	0-0	0	-	-	-	0	0
Art Laib	-	0-0	-	0-0	0	-	-	-	1	0
TOTALS	**-**	**43-70**	**-**	**21-28**	**36**	**-**	**-**	**-**	**22**	**107**
Percentages		61.4		75.0						

Coach: Adolph Rupp

MARQUETTE	MIN	FG	3FG	FT	REB	A	ST	BL	PF	TP
Brian Brunkhorst	-	6-14	-	11-12	7	-	-	-	2	23
Brad Luchini	-	6-11	-	7-8	1	-	-	-	5	19
James Burke	-	7-13	-	2-2	1	-	-	-	1	16
George Thompson	-	4-7	-	5-5	2	-	-	-	5	13
Joe Thomas	-	5-10	-	0-2	7	-	-	-	3	10
Ron Rahn	-	2-5	-	0-0	3	-	-	-	2	4
Jeff Sewell	-	1-1	-	2-2	0	-	-	-	0	4
Mike Curran	-	0-1	-	0-1	1	-	-	-	0	0
Pat Smith	-	0-0	-	0-2	5	-	-	-	4	0
TOTALS	**-**	**31-62**	**-**	**27-34**	**27**	**-**	**-**	**-**	**22**	**89**
Percentages		50.0		79.4						

Coach: Al McGuire

Officials: DiTomasso, Fox
Attendance: 11,500

Houston 91, Louisville 75 (1H: 45–32; 2H: 46–43) — SWEET 16

HOUSTON	MIN	FG	3FG	FT	REB	A	ST	BL	PF	TP
Elvin Hayes	40	16-31	-	3-8	24	1	-	-	1	35
Theodis Lee	40	9-21	-	0-2	9	2	-	-	4	18
Don Chaney	40	7-12	-	3-6	3	3	-	-	4	17
Ken Spain	40	4-15	-	4-5	11	3	-	-	2	12
Vern Lewis	38	4-7	-	1-1	3	10	-	-	3	9
Niemer Hamood	2	0-0	-	0-0	0	0	-	-	0	0
TOTALS	**200**	**40-86**	**-**	**11-22**	**50**	**19**	**-**	**-**	**14**	**91**
Percentages		46.5		50.0						

Coach: Guy V. Lewis

LOUISVILLE	MIN	FG	3FG	FT	REB	A	ST	BL	PF	TP
Wes Unseld	-	9-16	-	5-9	22	3	-	-	4	23
Butch Beard	-	9-23	-	3-5	7	6	-	-	5	21
Jerry King	-	5-13	-	0-1	1	3	-	-	2	10
Fred Holden	-	4-11	-	1-1	1	4	-	-	2	9
Mike Grosso	-	2-7	-	1-1	12	3	-	-	3	5
Bob Gorius	-	2-2	-	0-0	2	0	-	-	0	4
Dennis Deeken	-	1-2	-	0-0	0	0	-	-	0	2
Ed Linonis	-	0-4	-	1-2	4	0	-	-	0	1
Gordon Minner	-	0-0	-	0-0	0	0	-	-	0	0
Marv Selvy	-	0-2	-	0-0	1	0	-	-	0	0
TOTALS	**-**	**32-80**	**-**	**11-19**	**50**	**19**	**-**	**-**	**16**	**75**
Percentages		40.0		57.9						

Coach: John Dromo

Officials: Brown, Filiberti
Attendance: 10,938

TCU 77, Kansas State 72 (1H: 37–41; 2H: 40–31) — SWEET 16

TCU	MIN	FG	3FG	FT	REB	A	ST	BL	PF	TP
Rick Wittenbraker	-	6-14	-	6-8	6	4	-	-	1	18
Mickey McCarty	-	8-23	-	1-1	15	1	-	-	3	17
Tom Swift	-	6-12	-	1-1	4	1	-	-	5	13
Jeff Harp	-	3-5	-	5-6	1	0	-	-	2	11
James Cash	-	5-9	-	0-0	5	2	-	-	2	10
Carey Sloan	-	0-2	-	5-5	3	2	-	-	2	5
Mike Sechrist	-	1-3	-	0-1	6	0	-	-	1	2
Bill Swanson	-	0-4	-	1-2	5	4	-	-	0	1
Randy Kerth	-	0-3	-	0-1	1	0	-	-	2	0
TOTALS	**-**	**29-75**	**-**	**19-25**	**46**	**14**	**-**	**-**	**18**	**77**
Percentages		38.7		76.0						

Coach: Johnny Swaim

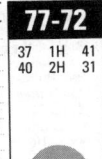

KANSAS STATE	MIN	FG	3FG	FT	REB	A	ST	BL	PF	TP
Steven Honeycutt	-	7-17	-	5-5	4	1	-	-	5	19
Nick Pino	-	7-21	-	1-5	8	1	-	-	2	15
Eugene Williams	-	5-9	-	2-2	10	4	-	-	1	12
Jeff Webb	-	4-12	-	3-6	12	4	-	-	4	11
Earl Seyfert	-	4-9	-	2-5	9	2	-	-	3	10
Kent Lifton	-	2-3	-	1-1	2	0	-	-	1	5
Frederick Arnold	-	0-1	-	0-0	0	0	-	-	1	0
George Shupe	-	0-0	-	0-0	0	0	-	-	0	0
Ray Wills	-	0-2	-	0-0	2	0	-	-	0	0
TOTALS	**-**	**29-74**	**-**	**14-24**	**47**	**12**	**-**	**-**	**17**	**72**
Percentages		39.2		58.3						

Coach: Tex Winter

Officials: Bussenius, Wader
Attendance: 10,938

UCLA 58-49 New Mexico State (Sweet 16)

	1H	2H
UCLA	28	30
New Mexico State	28	21

UCLA	MIN	FG	3FG	FT	REB	A	ST	BL	PF	TP
Lew Alcindor	-	9-13	-	10-16	23	-	-	-	3	28
Mike Warren	-	4-6	-	2-2	3	-	-	-	1	10
Lynn Shackelford	-	2-7	-	3-3	6	-	-	-	3	7
Lucius Allen	-	3-11	-	0-0	3	-	-	-	5	6
Mike Lynn	-	2-7	-	0-0	4	-	-	-	3	4
Kenny Heitz	-	1-7	-	1-3	2	-	-	-	4	3
Jim Nielsen	-	0-1	-	0-0	0	-	-	-	0	0
Bill Sweek	-	0-0	-	0-0	0	-	-	-	1	0
TOTALS	-	21-52	-	16-24	41	-	-	-	20	58
Percentages		40.4		66.7						

Coach: John Wooden

NEW MEXICO STATE	MIN	FG	3FG	FT	REB	A	ST	BL	PF	TP
Jimmy Collins	-	7-16	-	2-5	6	-	-	-	1	16
Bob Evans	-	4-13	-	6-10	3	-	-	-	4	14
Sam Lacey	-	3-12	-	0-0	5	-	-	-	5	6
Richard Collins	-	2-6	-	1-2	11	-	-	-	5	5
John Burgess	-	2-5	-	0-3	5	-	-	-	4	4
Paul Landis	-	1-4	-	2-5	3	-	-	-	0	4
Tom Las	-	0-0	-	0-0	1	-	-	-	2	0
Wes Morehead	-	0-1	-	0-1	1	-	-	-	0	0
Hardy Murphy	-	0-1	-	0-0	0	-	-	-	0	0
TOTALS	-	19-58	-	11-26	35	-	-	-	21	49
Percentages		32.8		42.3						

Coach: Lou Henson

Officials: Jenkins, Smith
Attendance: 15,345

Santa Clara 86-73 New Mexico (Sweet 16)

	1H	2H
Santa Clara	45	41
New Mexico	34	39

SANTA CLARA	MIN	FG	3FG	FT	REB	A	ST	BL	PF	TP
Bud Ogden	-	9-13	-	4-7	7	-	-	-	4	22
Terry O'Brien	-	7-7	-	4-5	10	-	-	-	3	18
Dennis Awtrey	-	5-11	-	3-5	5	-	-	-	5	13
Ralph Ogden	-	5-9	-	1-3	7	-	-	-	3	11
Chris Dempsey	-	4-5	-	0-0	3	-	-	-	2	8
Joe Diffley	-	1-2	-	5-9	5	-	-	-	2	7
Bob Heaney	-	3-7	-	1-1	6	-	-	-	1	7
Kevin Eagleson	-	0-2	-	0-2	1	-	-	-	4	0
TOTALS	-	34-56	-	18-32	44	-	-	-	24	86
Percentages		60.7		56.2						

Coach: Dick Garibaldi

NEW MEXICO	MIN	FG	3FG	FT	REB	A	ST	BL	PF	TP
Ron Nelson	-	9-19	-	2-3	1	-	-	-	5	20
Ron Becker	-	7-15	-	4-5	4	-	-	-	5	18
Ron Sanford	-	3-9	-	2-3	3	-	-	-	5	8
Dave Culver	-	1-2	-	5-7	6	-	-	-	3	7
Leonard Lopez	-	2-4	-	3-5	4	-	-	-	3	7
Howard Grimes	-	3-7	-	0-3	7	-	-	-	4	6
Keith Griffith	-	1-4	-	0-0	1	-	-	-	1	2
Larry Jones	-	1-3	-	0-1	3	-	-	-	1	2
George Maes	-	1-1	-	0-0	0	-	-	-	1	2
Steve Shropshire	-	0-2	-	1-2	0	-	-	-	0	1
Terry Schaafsma	-	0-2	-	0-0	0	-	-	-	1	0
TOTALS	-	28-68	-	17-29	29	-	-	-	29	73
Percentages		41.2		58.6						

Coach: Bob King

Officials: Overby, Dreight
Attendance: 15,345

North Carolina 70-66 Davidson (Elite 8)

	1H	2H
North Carolina	28	42
Davidson	34	32

NORTH CAROLINA	MIN	FG	3FG	FT	REB	A	ST	BL	PF	TP
Rusty Clark	37	8-17	-	6-7	17	3	-	-	3	22
Charlie Scott	39	8-15	-	2-2	6	0	-	-	2	18
Larry Miller	40	7-14	-	2-5	6	4	-	-	2	16
Dick Grubar	36	3-8	-	5-6	1	1	-	-	5	11
Bill Bunting	20	1-4	-	0-0	4	0	-	-	4	2
Eddie Fogler	10	0-3	-	1-2	0	3	-	-	0	1
Gerald Tuttle	13	0-0	-	0-1	2	1	-	-	0	0
Joe Brown	5	0-1	-	0-0	1	0	-	-	0	0
TOTALS	200	27-62	-	16-23	37	12	-	-	16	70
Percentages		43.5		69.6						

Coach: Dean Smith

DAVIDSON	MIN	FG	3FG	FT	REB	A	ST	BL	PF	TP
Mike Maloy	40	6-13	-	6-6	13	2	-	-	1	18
Jerry Kroll	28	5-13	-	6-6	5	1	-	-	5	16
Wayne Huckel	31	4-8	-	4-5	5	0	-	-	0	12
Rodney Knowles	39	5-17	-	1-2	12	0	-	-	4	11
Mike O'Neill	22	3-7	-	1-1	5	0	-	-	2	7
Dave Moser	40	0-7	-	2-2	7	2	-	-	4	2
TOTALS	200	23-65	-	20-22	47	5	-	-	16	66
Percentages		35.4		90.9						

Coach: Lefty Driesell

Officials: Allen, Fouty
Attendance: 12,500

Ohio State 82-81 Kentucky (Elite 8)

	1H	2H
Ohio State	44	38
Kentucky	40	41

OHIO STATE	MIN	FG	3FG	FT	REB	A	ST	BL	PF	TP
David Sorenson	-	11-17	-	2-5	7	-	-	-	1	24
Bill Hosket	-	8-14	-	5-5	12	-	-	-	4	21
Steve Howell	-	8-16	-	2-2	7	-	-	-	2	18
Jody Finney	-	4-9	-	1-1	7	-	-	-	2	9
Denny Meadors	-	3-6	-	0-0	2	-	-	-	1	6
Edward Smith	-	2-5	-	0-1	4	-	-	-	0	4
Bruce Schnabel	-	0-0	-	0-0	0	-	-	-	0	0
TOTALS	-	36-67	-	10-14	39	-	-	-	10	82
Percentages		53.7		71.4						

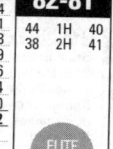

Coach: Fred R. Taylor

KENTUCKY	MIN	FG	3FG	FT	REB	A	ST	BL	PF	TP
Dan Issel	-	7-18	-	5-6	8	-	-	-	2	19
Mike Casey	-	8-18	-	0-0	8	-	-	-	4	16
Steve Clevenger	-	7-12	-	1-2	3	-	-	-	1	15
Mike Pratt	-	6-18	-	2-3	7	-	-	-	2	14
Thad Jaracz	-	6-8	-	1-1	7	-	-	-	3	13
Gary Gamble	-	1-1	-	0-0	1	-	-	-	0	2
Jim LeMaster	-	1-4	-	0-1	0	-	-	-	0	2
TOTALS	-	36-79	-	9-13	34	-	-	-	12	81
Percentages		45.6		69.2						

Coach: Adolph Rupp

Officials: Honzo, Fox
Attendance: 11,500

Houston 103-68 TCU (Elite 8)

	1H	2H
Houston	59	44
TCU	26	42

HOUSTON	MIN	FG	3FG	FT	REB	A	ST	BL	PF	TP
Elvin Hayes	38	17-34	-	5-10	25	0	-	-	2	39
Ken Spain	38	5-11	-	6-7	16	3	-	-	2	16
Theodis Lee	31	7-14	-	2-3	7	3	-	-	2	16
Don Chaney	29	4-11	-	4-5	6	1	-	-	4	12
Carlos Bell	9	2-4	-	3-4	3	0	-	-	0	7
Tom Gribben	11	2-6	-	2-2	5	0	-	-	4	6
Niemer Hamood	9	2-4	-	0-0	2	1	-	-	1	4
Vern Lewis	31	0-5	-	3-5	3	2	-	-	1	3
Larry Cooper	2	0-0	-	0-0	0	0	-	-	0	0
Kent Taylor	2	0-0	-	0-0	0	0	-	-	1	0
TOTALS	200	39-89	-	25-36	67	10	-	-	17	103
Percentages		43.8		69.4						

Coach: Guy V. Lewis

TCU	MIN	FG	3FG	FT	REB	A	ST	BL	PF	TP
Tommy Gowan	-	5-9	-	1-1	2	0	-	-	1	11
Tom Swift	-	3-14	-	3-3	7	1	-	-	4	9
James Cash	-	4-8	-	0-0	14	3	-	-	3	8
Jeff Harp	-	4-11	-	0-0	1	0	-	-	2	8
Mickey McCarty	-	3-12	-	2-4	7	2	-	-	2	8
Rick Wittenbraker	-	2-12	-	3-5	6	3	-	-	3	7
Randy Kerth	-	2-2	-	1-1	2	1	-	-	0	5
Carey Sloan	-	1-7	-	2-3	4	0	-	-	1	4
Bill Swanson	-	2-10	-	0-1	3	0	-	-	3	4
Robert Nees	-	1-4	-	0-0	1	0	-	-	1	2
Jerry Chambers	-	0-1	-	1-1	0	0	-	-	0	1
Mike Sechrist	-	0-1	-	1-1	1	0	-	-	3	1
TOTALS	-	27-91	-	14-20	48	10	-	-	23	68
Percentages		29.7		70.0						

Coach: Johnny Swaim

Officials: Brown, Bussenius
Attendance: 11,004

UCLA 87-66 Santa Clara (Elite 8)

	1H	2H
UCLA	51	36
Santa Clara	34	32

UCLA	MIN	FG	3FG	FT	REB	A	ST	BL	PF	TP
Lew Alcindor	-	6-8	-	10-17	18	-	-	-	2	22
Lucius Allen	-	7-15	-	7-7	8	-	-	-	3	21
Mike Warren	-	6-14	-	3-3	5	-	-	-	3	15
Mike Lynn	-	5-9	-	0-1	5	-	-	-	4	10
Kenny Heitz	-	3-8	-	1-1	3	-	-	-	1	7
Jim Nielsen	-	2-4	-	0-0	3	-	-	-	4	4
Lynn Shackelford	-	1-8	-	2-2	6	-	-	-	0	4
Neville Saner	-	1-3	-	0-0	1	-	-	-	3	2
Bill Sweek	-	1-2	-	0-0	1	-	-	-	3	2
Gene Sutherland	-	0-3	-	0-0	1	-	-	-	0	0
TOTALS	-	32-74	-	23-31	51	-	-	-	23	87
Percentages		43.2		74.2						

Coach: John Wooden

SANTA CLARA	MIN	FG	3FG	FT	REB	A	ST	BL	PF	TP
Dennis Awtrey	-	7-12	-	3-4	10	-	-	-	4	17
Bud Ogden	-	4-7	-	5-10	9	-	-	-	3	13
Ralph Ogden	-	5-11	-	1-1	3	-	-	-	2	11
Terry O'Brien	-	3-6	-	1-1	2	-	-	-	3	7
Bob Stuckey	-	1-5	-	3-4	2	-	-	-	0	5
Bob Heaney	-	2-10	-	0-1	1	-	-	-	2	4
Ray Thomas	-	2-3	-	0-1	2	-	-	-	2	4
Joe Diffley	-	0-3	-	2-2	0	-	-	-	2	2
Kevin Eagleson	-	0-1	-	2-3	0	-	-	-	4	2
Chris Dempsey	-	0-4	-	1-2	4	-	-	-	1	1
Kevin Donahue	-	0-0	-	0-0	1	-	-	-	0	0
Keith Paulson	-	0-3	-	0-0	1	-	-	-	1	0
TOTALS	-	24-65	-	18-29	35	-	-	-	24	66
Percentages		36.9		62.1						

Coach: Dick Garibaldi

Officials: Overby, Jenkins
Attendance: 15,010

FINAL 4: North Carolina 80, Ohio State 66

	1H	2H
North Carolina	34	46
Ohio State	27	39

NORTH CAROLINA	MIN	FG	3FG	FT	REB	A	ST	BL	PF	TP
Larry Miller	-	10-23	-	0-1	6	-	-	-	2	20
Bill Bunting	-	4-7	-	9-10	12	-	-	-	2	17
Rusty Clark	-	7-9	-	1-1	11	-	-	-	4	15
Charlie Scott	-	6-16	-	1-4	5	-	-	-	3	13
Dick Grubar	-	4-9	-	3-3	6	-	-	-	0	11
Eddie Fogler	-	1-2	-	0-0	0	-	-	-	1	2
Gerald Tuttle	-	1-1	-	0-1	0	-	-	-	0	2
Joe Brown	-	0-4	-	0-0	4	-	-	-	2	0
TOTALS	-	33-71	-	14-20	44	-	-	-	14	80
Percentages		46.5		70.0						

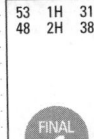

Coach: Dean Smith

OHIO STATE	MIN	FG	3FG	FT	REB	A	ST	BL	PF	TP
Jody Finney	-	8-13	-	0-2	4	-	-	-	2	16
Bill Hosket	-	4-11	-	6-9	9	-	-	-	5	14
Steve Howell	-	6-17	-	1-2	3	-	-	-	2	13
David Sorenson	-	5-17	-	1-3	11	-	-	-	3	11
Denny Meadors	-	3-13	-	2-2	3	-	-	-	3	8
Edward Smith	-	2-6	-	0-0	5	-	-	-	1	4
Daniel Andreas	-	0-0	-	0-0	0	-	-	-	0	0
Craig Barclay	-	0-1	-	0-0	0	-	-	-	0	0
James Geddes	-	0-0	-	0-0	1	-	-	-	1	0
Bruce Schnabel	-	0-1	-	0-0	2	-	-	-	1	0
TOTALS	-	28-79	-	10-18	38	-	-	-	18	66
Percentages		35.4		55.6						

Coach: Fred R. Taylor

Officials: Bussenius, Jenkins
Attendance: 15,742

FINAL 4: UCLA 101, Houston 69

	1H	2H
UCLA	53	48
Houston	31	38

UCLA	MIN	FG	3FG	FT	REB	A	ST	BL	PF	TP
Lew Alcindor	38	7-14	-	5-6	18	0	-	-	3	19
Lucius Allen	35	9-18	-	1-2	9	12	-	-	1	19
Mike Lynn	30	8-10	-	3-3	8	2	-	-	4	19
Lynn Shackelford	24	6-10	-	5-5	3	0	-	-	4	17
Mike Warren	33	7-18	-	0-0	5	9	-	-	3	14
Kenny Heitz	12	3-6	-	1-1	1	1	-	-	1	7
Jim Nielsen	12	2-3	-	0-0	1	0	-	-	4	4
Bill Sweek	7	1-1	-	0-1	0	0	-	-	0	2
Gene Sutherland	5	0-1	-	0-0	0	2	-	-	1	0
Neville Saner	4	0-2	-	0-0	1	0	-	-	2	0
TOTALS	200	43-83	-	15-18	46	26	-	-	23	101
Percentages		51.8		83.3						

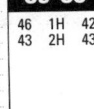

Coach: John Wooden

HOUSTON	MIN	FG	3FG	FT	REB	A	ST	BL	PF	TP
Ken Spain	39	4-12	-	7-10	13	2	-	-	1	15
Don Chaney	33	5-13	-	5-7	7	2	-	-	2	15
Elvin Hayes	39	3-10	-	4-7	5	0	-	-	4	10
Niemer Hamood	14	3-5	-	4-6	0	0	-	-	2	10
Carlos Bell	7	3-8	-	3-4	5	0	-	-	0	9
Vern Lewis	33	2-8	-	2-2	5	3	-	-	0	6
Theodis Lee	21	2-15	-	0-0	4	2	-	-	4	4
Tom Gribben	12	0-5	-	0-1	5	3	-	-	1	0
Larry Cooper	1	0-2	-	0-0	1	0	-	-	0	0
Kent Taylor	1	0-0	-	0-0	0	0	-	-	0	0
TOTALS	200	22-78	-	25-37	45	12	-	-	14	69
Percentages		28.2		67.6						

Coach: Guy V. Lewis

Officials: Honzo, Fouty
Attendance: 15,742

3RD PLACE: Ohio State 89, Houston 85

	1H	2H
Ohio State	46	43
Houston	42	43

OHIO STATE	MIN	FG	3FG	FT	REB	A	ST	BL	PF	TP
Steve Howell	40	12-26	-	2-2	13	2	-	-	4	26
David Sorenson	39	8-13	-	3-4	9	3	-	-	2	19
Bill Hosket	38	5-11	-	9-11	17	5	-	-	4	19
Jody Finney	28	5-11	-	3-3	3	5	-	-	3	13
Denny Meadors	40	3-11	-	3-4	5	4	-	-	0	9
Mike Swain	12	1-3	-	0-0	2	1	-	-	1	2
Edward Smith	3	0-2	-	1-2	1	0	-	-	0	1
TOTALS	200	34-77	-	21-26	50	20	-	-	14	89
Percentages		44.2		80.8						

Coach: Fred R. Taylor

HOUSTON	MIN	FG	3FG	FT	REB	A	ST	BL	PF	TP
Elvin Hayes	39	14-34	-	6-8	16	1	-	-	4	34
Theodis Lee	40	13-26	-	1-2	8	4	-	-	0	27
Ken Spain	40	4-12	-	2-4	12	1	-	-	4	10
Don Chaney	39	4-15	-	0-1	8	1	-	-	5	8
Vern Lewis	35	3-7	-	0-1	3	14	-	-	3	6
Niemer Hamood	5	0-1	-	0-0	0	1	-	-	1	0
Carlos Bell	1	0-0	-	0-0	0	0	-	-	1	0
Tom Gribben	1	0-0	-	0-0	0	0	-	-	1	0
TOTALS	200	38-95	-	9-16	47	22	-	-	19	85
Percentages		40.0		56.2						

Coach: Guy V. Lewis

Officials: Bussenius, Jenkins
Attendance: 14,438

NCAA FINAL 1968: UCLA 78, North Carolina 55

	1H	2H
UCLA	32	46
North Carolina	22	33

UCLA	MIN	FG	3FG	FT	REB	A	ST	BL	PF	TP
Lew Alcindor	37	15-21	-	4-4	16	1	-	-	3	34
Lucius Allen	35	3-7	-	5-7	5	5	-	-	0	11
Mike Warren	35	3-7	-	1-1	3	1	-	-	2	7
Mike Lynn	22	1-7	-	5-7	6	4	-	-	3	7
Kenny Heitz	20	3-6	-	1-1	2	2	-	-	3	7
Lynn Shackelford	26	3-5	-	0-1	2	4	-	-	0	6
Jim Nielsen	10	1-1	-	0-0	1	0	-	-	1	2
Neville Saner	5	1-3	-	0-0	2	1	-	-	2	2
Gene Sutherland	5	1-2	-	0-0	2	1	-	-	1	2
Bill Sweek	5	0-1	-	0-0	0	0	-	-	1	0
TOTALS	200	31-60	-	16-21	39	19	-	-	16	78
Percentages		51.7		76.2						

Coach: John Wooden

NORTH CAROLINA	MIN	FG	3FG	FT	REB	A	ST	BL	PF	TP
Larry Miller	37	5-13	-	4-6	6	3	-	-	3	14
Charlie Scott	35	6-17	-	0-1	3	2	-	-	3	12
Rusty Clark	37	4-12	-	1-3	8	1	-	-	3	9
Joe Brown	13	2-5	-	2-2	5	0	-	-	1	6
Dick Grubar	35	2-5	-	1-2	0	1	-	-	2	5
Eddie Fogler	16	1-4	-	2-2	0	2	-	-	0	4
Bill Bunting	15	1-3	-	1-2	2	1	-	-	5	3
Jim Frye	3	1-2	-	0-1	1	0	-	-	0	2
Jim Delany	3	0-1	-	0-0	0	0	-	-	0	0
Ralph Fletcher	3	0-1	-	0-0	0	0	-	-	0	0
Gerald Tuttle	2	0-0	-	0-0	0	1	-	-	0	0
Gra Whitehead	1	0-0	-	0-0	0	0	-	-	0	0
TOTALS	200	22-63	-	11-19	25	11	-	-	17	55
Percentages		34.9		57.9						

Coach: Dean Smith

Officials: Honzo, Fouty
Attendance: 14,438

National Invitation Tournament (NIT)

First round: Saint Peter's d. Marshall 102-93 (2OT), Duke d. Oklahoma City 97-81, Kansas d. Temple 82-76, Villanova d. Wyoming 77-66, Notre Dame d. Army 62-58, Long Island d. Bradley 80-77, Fordham d. Duquesne 69-60, Dayton d. West Virginia, 87-68
Quarterfinals: Kansas d. Villanova 55-49, Saint Peter's d. Duke 100-71, Dayton d. Fordham 61-60, Notre Dame d. Long Island 62-60
Semifinals: Dayton d. Notre Dame 76-74 (OT), Kansas d. Saint Peter's 58-46
Third place: Notre Dame d. Saint Peter's 81-78
Championship: Dayton d. Kansas 61-48
MVP: Don May, Dayton

1968-69: King Lewis

The season wasn't so much about a chase for the national title as it was a coronation of one of the most remarkable players the game has ever seen. Lew Alcindor ended his college career by leading UCLA to an otherworldly three-year record of 88–2 and its third consecutive NCAA title. The Bruins' biggest Tournament challenge was a hard-fought 85-82 national semifinal win over scrappy Drake. North Carolina made its third straight Final Four and its third straight exit from contention via a double-digit loss, this time to Purdue, 92-65. The Bruins beat the Boilermakers in the Final, 92-72, at Louisville's Freedom Hall. Purdue's Rick Mount set a title game record by hoisting 36 field goal attempts—but made only 12. Alcindor became the only player to win the MOP award three years in a row, and was named the inaugural Naismith National Player of the Year. After converting to Islam, he changed his name to Kareem Abdul-Jabbar and went on to win six NBA titles and score 38,387 points—more than any other NBA player.

Major Conference Standings

ACC	Conference W	L	Pct	Overall W	L	Pct
North Carolina⊛	12	2	.857	27	5	.844
South Carolina□	11	3	.786	21	7	.750
Wake Forest	8	6	.571	18	9	.667
NC State	8	6	.571	15	10	.600
Duke	8	6	.571	15	13	.536
Virginia	5	9	.357	10	15	.400
Maryland	2	12	.143	8	18	.308
Clemson	2	12	.143	6	19	.240

Tournament: **North Carolina d. Duke 85-74**
Tournament MVP: **Charlie Scott**, North Carolina

BIG EIGHT	Conference W	L	Pct	Overall W	L	Pct
Colorado⊛	10	4	.714	21	7	.750
Kansas□	9	5	.643	20	7	.741
Kansas State	9	5	.643	14	12	.538
Iowa State	8	6	.571	14	12	.538
Missouri	7	7	.500	14	11	.560
Oklahoma State	5	9	.357	12	13	.480
Nebraska	5	9	.357	12	14	.462
Oklahoma	3	11	.214	7	19	.269

BIG SKY	Conference W	L	Pct	Overall W	L	Pct
Weber State⊛	15	0	1.000	27	3	.900
Montana State	11	4	.733	17	8	.680
Gonzaga	6	9	.400	11	15	.423
Idaho	6	9	.400	11	15	.423
Montana	4	11	.267	9	17	.346
Idaho State	3	12	.200	8	18	.308

BIG TEN	Conference W	L	Pct	Overall W	L	Pct
Purdue⊛	13	1	.929	23	5	.821
Illinois	9	5	.643	19	5	.792
Ohio State	9	5	.643	17	7	.708
Michigan	7	7	.500	13	11	.542
Northwestern	6	8	.429	14	10	.583
Minnesota	6	8	.429	12	12	.500
Michigan State	6	8	.429	11	12	.478
Iowa	5	9	.357	12	12	.500
Wisconsin	5	9	.357	11	13	.458
Indiana	4	10	.286	9	15	.375

IVY	Conference W	L	Pct	Overall W	L	Pct
Princeton⊛	14	0	1.000	19	7	.731
Columbia	11	3	.786	20	4	.833
Penn	10	4	.714	15	10	.600
Cornell	7	7	.500	12	13	.480
Yale	6	8	.429	9	16	.360
Dartmouth	4	10	.286	10	15	.400
Harvard	3	11	.214	7	18	.280
Brown	1	13	.071	3	23	.115

METRO	Conference W	L	Pct	Overall W	L	Pct
Saint Peter's□	7	1	.875	21	7	.750
Manhattan	7	1	.875	13	9	.591
Long Island	6	2	.750	17	6	.739
Iona	4	4	.500	11	11	.500
Hofstra	4	4	.500	12	13	.480
Seton Hall	4	4	.500	9	16	.360
Wagner	2	6	.250	18	10	.643
Fairleigh Dickinson	2	6	.250	9	13	.409

Note: Hofstra also played in the Middle Atlantic

MID-AMERICAN	Conference W	L	Pct	Overall W	L	Pct
Miami (OH)⊛	10	2	.833	15	12	.556
Ohio□	9	3	.750	17	9	.654
Kent State	6	6	.500	14	10	.583
Western Michigan	6	6	.500	11	13	.458
Toledo	5	7	.417	13	11	.542
Bowling Green	3	9	.250	9	15	.375
Marshall	3	9	.250	9	15	.375

MIDDLE ATLANTIC	Conference W	L	Pct	Overall W	L	Pct
La Salle	-	-	-	23	1	.958
Temple□	-	-	-	22	8	.733
Saint Joseph's⊛	-	-	-	17	11	.607
Gettysburg	-	-	-	14	10	.583
Bucknell	-	-	-	13	11	.542
Delaware	-	-	-	11	10	.524
Hofstra	-	-	-	12	13	.480
West Chester	-	-	-	12	13	.480
Rider	-	-	-	11	14	.440
Lafayette	-	-	-	9	17	.346
Lehigh	-	-	-	7	17	.292
American	-	-	-	4	19	.174

MISSOURI VALLEY	Conference W	L	Pct	Overall W	L	Pct
Drake⊛	13	3	.813	26	5	.839
Louisville□	13	3	.813	21	6	.778
Tulsa□	11	5	.688	19	8	.704
Cincinnati	8	8	.500	17	9	.654
North Texas	8	8	.500	15	10	.600
Bradley	7	9	.438	14	12	.538
Wichita State	7	9	.438	11	15	.423
Saint Louis	5	11	.313	6	20	.231
Memphis	0	16	.000	6	19	.240

OHIO VALLEY	Conference W	L	Pct	Overall W	L	Pct
Murray State⊛	11	3	.786	22	6	.786
Morehead State	11	3	.786	18	9	.667
Western Kentucky	9	5	.643	16	10	.615
Eastern Kentucky	7	7	.500	13	9	.591
East Tennessee St.	6	8	.429	15	11	.577
Tennessee Tech	5	9	.357	13	11	.542
Middle Tennessee St.	4	10	.286	13	13	.500
Austin Peay	3	11	.214	10	14	.417

PAC-8	Conference W	L	Pct	Overall W	L	Pct
UCLA⊛	13	1	.929	29	1	.967
Washington State	11	3	.786	18	8	.692
Southern California	8	6	.571	15	11	.577
Washington	6	8	.429	13	13	.500
Oregon	5	9	.357	13	13	.500
Oregon State	5	9	.357	12	14	.462
California	4	10	.286	12	13	.480
Stanford	4	10	.286	8	17	.320

SEC	Conference W	L	Pct	Overall W	L	Pct
Kentucky⊛	16	2	.889	23	5	.821
Tennessee□	13	5	.722	21	7	.750
Florida□	12	6	.667	18	9	.667
Auburn	10	8	.556	15	10	.600
Vanderbilt	9	9	.500	15	11	.577
Georgia	9	9	.500	13	12	.520
LSU	7	11	.389	13	13	.500
Mississippi	7	11	.389	10	14	.417
Mississippi State	6	12	.333	8	17	.320
Alabama	1	17	.056	4	20	.167

SOUTHERN	Conference W	L	Pct	Overall W	L	Pct
Davidson⊛	9	0	1.000	27	3	.900
East Carolina	9	2	.818	17	11	.607
George Washington	7	5	.583	14	11	.560
Richmond	6	7	.462	13	14	.481
Furman	5	6	.455	9	17	.346
The Citadel	5	8	.385	13	12	.520
William and Mary	3	8	.273	6	20	.231
VMI	3	11	.214	5	18	.217

Tournament: **Davidson d. East Carolina 102-76**
Tournament MOP: **Doug Cook**, Davidson

SOUTHLAND	Conference W	L	Pct	Overall W	L	Pct
Trinity (TX)○	7	1	.875	19	5	.792
Lamar	6	2	.750	20	4	.833
Texas-Arlington	3	5	.375	8	18	.308
Arkansas State	3	5	.375	6	16	.273
Abilene Christian	1	7	.125	5	20	.200

SOUTHWEST	Conference W	L	Pct	Overall W	L	Pct
Texas A&M⊛	12	2	.857	18	9	.667
Baylor	10	4	.714	18	6	.750
SMU	8	6	.571	12	12	.500
Texas Tech	6	8	.429	11	13	.458
Rice	6	8	.429	10	14	.417
TCU	5	9	.357	12	12	.500
Texas	5	9	.357	9	15	.375
Arkansas	4	10	.286	10	14	.417

WCAC	Conference W	L	Pct	Overall W	L	Pct
Santa Clara⊛	13	1	.929	27	2	.931
San Jose State	11	3	.786	16	8	.667
Pacific	9	5	.643	17	9	.654
UC Santa Barbara	8	6	.571	17	9	.654
Pepperdine	6	8	.429	14	12	.538
San Francisco	3	11	.214	7	18	.280
Loyola Marymount	3	11	.214	6	19	.240
Saint Mary's (CA)	3	11	.214	6	19	.240

WAC	Conference W	L	Pct	Overall W	L	Pct
Wyoming□	6	4	.600	19	9	.679
BYU⊛	6	4	.600	16	12	.571
Arizona	5	5	.500	17	10	.630
Utah	5	5	.500	13	13	.500
New Mexico	4	6	.400	17	9	.654
Arizona State	4	6	.400	11	15	.423

YANKEE	Conference W	L	Pct	Overall W	L	Pct
Massachusetts	9	1	.900	17	7	.708
Rhode Island	7	3	.700	10	15	.400
Maine	5	5	.500	10	13	.435
Vermont	3	7	.300	14	11	.560
New Hampshire	3	7	.300	9	15	.375
Connecticut	3	7	.300	5	19	.208

INDEPENDENTS	Overall W	L	Pct
Boston College□	24	4	.857
Rutgers□	21	4	.840
Marquette○	24	5	.828
New Mexico State○	24	5	.828
Duquesne○	21	5	.808
Villanova○	21	5	.808
St. John's○	23	6	.793
Dayton○	20	7	.741
Notre Dame○	20	7	.741
Seattle○	20	8	.714
Colorado State○	17	7	.708
Jacksonville	17	7	.708
St. Bonaventure	17	7	.708

⊛ Automatic NCAA Tournament bid ○ At-large NCAA Tournament bid □ NIT appearance ⊗ Team record doesn't reflect games forfeited or vacated. For adjusted record, see p. 521.

INDEPENDENTS (CONT.)

	Overall W	L	Pct
Florida State	18	8	.692
West Texas□	18	8	.692
Holy Cross	16	8	.667
Oklahoma City	18	9	.667
Saint Francis (PA)	16	8	.667
Southern Illinois□	16	8	.667
Fordham□	17	9	.654
Army□	18	10	.643
UTEP	16	9	.640
Houston	16	10	.615
Penn State	13	9	.591
Boston U.	14	10	.583
Detroit	14	10	.583
Miami (FL)	14	10	.583
Providence	14	10	.583

INDEPENDENTS (CONT.)

	Overall W	L	Pct
NYU	12	9	.571
DePaul	14	11	.560
Northern Illinois	13	11	.542
Virginia Tech	14	12	.538
Creighton	13	13	.500
Georgetown	12	12	.500
Hardin-Simmons	13	13	.500
Georgia Tech	12	13	.480
Tulane	12	14	.462
West Virginia	12	14	.462
Air Force	11	13	.458
Niagara	11	13	.458
Colgate	11	14	.440
Butler	11	15	.423
Loyola-Chicago	9	14	.391

INDEPENDENTS (CONT.)

	Overall W	L	Pct
Fairfield	10	16	.385
Xavier	10	16	.385
Syracuse	9	16	.360
Utah State	9	17	.346
Centenary	9	18	.333
Navy	7	14	.333
Texas-Pan American	8	17	.320
Canisius	7	16	.304
Loyola (LA)	5	19	.208
Pittsburgh	4	20	.167
Portland	3	23	.115
Denver	2	24	.077

INDIVIDUAL LEADERS—SEASON

Scoring

	CL	POS	G	FG	FT	PTS	PPG
1 **Pete Maravich**, LSU	JR	G	26	433	282	1,148	**44.2**
2 **Rick Mount**, Purdue	JR	G	28	366	200	932	**33.3**
3 **Calvin Murphy**, Niagara	JR	G	24	294	190	778	**32.4**
4 **Spencer Haywood**, Detroit	SO	F	24	288	195	771	**32.1**
5 **Bob Tallent**, George Washington	SR	G	25	284	155	723	**28.9**
6 **Marvin Roberts**, Utah State	SO	F	26	271	176	718	**27.6**
7 **Don Curnutt**, Miami (FL)	JR	G	24	262	137	661	**27.5**
8 **Bob Lanier**, St. Bonaventure	JR	C	24	270	114	654	**27.3**
9 **Rich Travis**, Oklahoma City	SR	G	27	286	157	729	**27.0**
10 **Rex Morgan**, Jacksonville	JR	G	23	199	215	613	**26.7**

Field Goal Pct

	CL	POS	G	FG	FGA	PCT
1 **Lew Alcindor**, UCLA	SR	C	30	303	477	**63.5**
2 **Bill Bunting**, North Carolina	SR	F	32	217	363	**59.8**
3 **Mike Wilkes**, Virginia	SR	F	24	153	256	**59.8**
4 **Dennis Awtrey**, Santa Clara	JR	F	29	240	406	**59.1**
5 **Bob Lanier**, St. Bonaventure	JR	C	24	270	460	**58.7**

Minimum: 140 made

Free Throw Pct

	CL	POS	G	FT	FTA	PCT
1 **Bill Justus**, Tennessee	SR	G	28	133	147	**90.5**
2 **Jody Finney**, Ohio State	JR	G	24	99	110	**90.0**
3 **Chris Thomforde**, Princeton	SR	C	26	123	137	**89.8**
4 **Larry Ward**, Centenary	SR	G	27	99	112	**88.4**
5 **Charlie Davis**, Wake Forest	SO	G	27	194	220	**88.2**

Minimum: 95 made

Rebounds Per Game

	CL	POS	G	REB	RPG
1 **Spencer Haywood**, Detroit	SO	F	24	530	**22.1**
2 **Larry Lewis**, Saint Francis (PA)	SR	C	24	495	**20.6**
3 **Lamar Green**, Morehead State	SR	F/C	27	483	**17.9**
4 **Neal Walk**, Florida	SR	C	27	481	**17.8**
5 **Terry Driscoll**, Boston College	SR	F	28	498	**17.8**

INDIVIDUAL LEADERS—GAME

Points

	CL	POS	OPP	DATE	PTS
1 **Calvin Murphy**, Niagara	JR	G	Syracuse	D7	**68**
2 **Pete Maravich**, LSU	JR	G	Tulane	F10	**66**
3 **Pete Maravich**, LSU	JR	G	Georgia	M8	**58**
4 **Pete Maravich**, LSU	JR	G	Tulane	D14	**55**
Pete Maravich, LSU	JR	G	Mississippi State	M3	**55**

Free Throws Made

	CL	POS	OPP	DATE	FT	FTA	PCT
1 **Bill Justus**, Tennessee	SR	G	Ohio	M17	**22**	23	95.7
Pete Maravich, LSU	JR	G	Florida	F12	**22**	27	81.5
3 **Calvin Murphy**, Niagara	JR	G	Columbia	J16	**21**	22	95.5
4 **Don Tomlinson**, Missouri	JR	F/C	Iowa State	J18	**20**	22	90.9
Calvin Murphy, Niagara	JR	G	Syracuse	D7	**20**	23	87.0

Rebounds

	CL	POS	OPP	DATE	REB
1 **Spencer Haywood**, Detroit	SO	F	La Salle	F22	**32**
Willie Watson, Oklahoma City	JR	C	Denver	F8	**32**
3 **Spencer Haywood**, Detroit	SO	F	Aquinas	N30	**31**
4 **Willie Brown**, Middle Tenn. St.	SR	G/F	Austin Peay	J25	**30**
Lamar Green, Morehead State	SR	F/C	Middle Tennessee St.	F10	**30**
Wendell Ladner, Southern Miss	JR	F	Louisville	D7	**30**
Rudy Tomjanovich, Michigan	JR	C	Loyola-Chicago	F1	**30**

TEAM LEADERS—SEASON

Win-Loss Pct

	W	L	PCT
1 **UCLA**	29	1	**.967**
2 **La Salle**	23	1	**.958**
3 **Santa Clara**	27	2	**.931**
4 **Weber State**	27	3	**.900**
Davidson	27	3	**.900**

Scoring Offense

	G	W-L	PTS	PPG
1 **Purdue**	28	23-5	2,605	**93.0**
2 **Hardin-Simmons**	26	13-13	2,387	**91.8**
3 **Kentucky**	28	23-5	2,542	**90.8**
4 **Michigan**	24	13-11	2,153	**89.7**
5 **LSU**	26	13-13	2,316	**89.1**

Scoring Margin

	G	W-L	PPG	OPP PPG	MAR
1 **UCLA**	30	29-1	84.7	63.8	**20.9**
2 **La Salle**	24	23-1	89.0	70.9	**18.1**
3 **Columbia**	24	20-4	77.0	61.3	**15.7**
Santa Clara	29	27-2	77.0	61.3	**15.7**
5 **Purdue**	28	23-5	93.0	79.1	**13.9**

Field Goal Pct

	G	W-L	FG	FGA	PCT
1 **UCLA**	30	29-1	1,027	1,999	**51.4**
2 **Auburn**	25	15-10	734	1,461	**50.2**
3 **Southern Miss**	25	15-10	855	1,710	**50.0**
4 **Columbia**	24	20-4	689	1,380	**49.9**
5 **Saint Peter's**	28	21-7	913	1,847	**49.4**

Rebounds Per Game

	G	W-L	REB	RPG
1 **Middle Tennessee State**	26	13-13	1,685	**64.8**
2 **Saint Francis (PA)**	24	16-8	1,411	**58.8**
3 **Morehead State**	27	18-9	1,583	**58.6**
4 **Indiana**	24	9-15	1,354	**56.4**
5 **Maine**	23	10-13	1,286	**55.9**

Scoring Defense

	G	W-L	OPP PTS	OPP PPG
1 **Army**	28	18-10	1,498	**53.5**
2 **Tennessee**	28	21-7	1,651	**59.0**
3 **Oklahoma State**	25	12-13	1,481	**59.2**
4 **Long Island**	23	17-6	1,372	**59.7**
5 **Kansas**	27	20-7	1,625	**60.2**

CONSENSUS ALL-AMERICAS

First Team

PLAYER	CL	POS	HT	SCHOOL	RPG	PPG
Lew Alcindor	SR	C	7-2	UCLA	14.7	24.0
Spencer Haywood	SO	F	6-8	Detroit	22.1	32.1
Pete Maravich	JR	G	6-5	LSU	6.5	44.2
Rick Mount	JR	G	6-4	Purdue	3.2	33.3
Calvin Murphy	JR	G	5-9	Niagara	3.6	32.4

Second Team

PLAYER	CL	POS	HT	SCHOOL	RPG	PPG
Dan Issel	JR	C	6-8	Kentucky	13.6	26.6
Mike Maloy	JR	F	6-7	Davidson	14.3	24.6
Bud Ogden	SR	F	6-6	Santa Clara	8.5	16.1
Charlie Scott	JR	G/F	6-5	North Carolina	7.1	22.3
Jo Jo White	SR	G	6-3	Kansas	4.7	18.1

Selectors: AP, NABC, UPI, USBWA

AWARD WINNERS

Player of the Year

PLAYER	CL	POS	HT	SCHOOL	AWARDS
Lew Alcindor	SR	C	7-2	UCLA	Naismith, AP, UPI, USBWA
Bill Keller	SR	G	5-10	Purdue	Frances Pomeroy Naismith*

* For the most outstanding senior player who is 6 feet or under.

Coach of the Year

COACH	SCHOOL	REC	AWARDS
John Wooden	UCLA	29-1	AP, UPI, NABC, Sporting News
Maury John	Drake	26-5	USBWA

Poll Progression

Preseason Poll

AP	School
1	UCLA
2	North Carolina
3	Kentucky
4	Notre Dame
5	Kansas
6	Davidson
7	St. Bonaventure
8	Houston
9	New Mexico
10	Purdue
11	Villanova
12	Ohio State
13	Vanderbilt
14	Cincinnati
15	Marquette
16	Western Kentucky
17	Duke
18	Detroit
19	Florida
20	Tennessee

Week of Dec 3

AP	UPI	School	AP↓↑
1	1	UCLA (1-0)	
2	2	North Carolina (0-0)	
3	3	Kentucky (1-0)	
4	5	Kansas (1-0)	↑1
5	4	Notre Dame (0-0)	↓1
6	6	Houston (1-0)	↑2
6	7	Davidson (1-0)	
8	8	New Mexico (1-0)	↑1
9	10	Cincinnati (1-0)	↑5
10	9	Villanova (1-0)	↑1
11	12	St. Bonaventure (0-0)	↓4
12	—	Vanderbilt (0-0)	↑1
13	14	Ohio State (1-0)	↓1
14	11	Purdue (0-1)	↓4
15	—	Detroit (1-0)	↑3
16	15	Duke (1-0)	↑1
17	15	Western Kentucky (1-0)	↓1
18	17	Santa Clara (1-0)	⤴
19	20	California (0-0)	⤴
20	—	Iowa (1-0)	⤴
20	—	Marquette (0-0)	↓5
20	—	Tennessee (1-0)	
—	13	New Mexico State (1-0)	
—	18	USC (0-2)	
—	19	Florida (0-0)	⤵

Week of Dec 10

AP	UPI	School	AP↓↑
1	1	UCLA (3-0)	
2	2	North Carolina (3-0)	
3	3	Davidson (3-0)	↑3
4	4	Kentucky (2-1)	↓1
5	5	New Mexico (3-0)	↑3
6	8	Cincinnati (3-0)	↑3
7	7	Notre Dame (1-1)	↓2
8	6	Villanova (3-0)	↑2
9	12	Duke (3-0)	↑7
10	11	St. Bonaventure (2-0)	↑1
11	10	Kansas (3-1)	↓7
12	13	Houston (3-1)	↓6
13	9	Purdue (2-1)	↑1
14	17	Detroit (4-0)	↑1
15	14	Western Kentucky (4-0)	↑2
16	15	Santa Clara (3-0)	↑2
17	18	Ohio State (1-1)	↓4
18	—	California (2-0)	↑1
19	—	Iowa (3-0)	↑1
20	—	La Salle (1-0)	⤴
—	16	New Mexico State (3-0)	
—	18	Dayton (4-0)	
—	20	USC (2-2)	

Week of Dec 17

AP	UPI	School	AP↓↑
1	1	UCLA (3-0)	
2	2	North Carolina (4-0)	
3	3	Davidson (3-0)	
4	5	Kentucky (3-1)	
5	6	New Mexico (5-0)	
6	4	Cincinnati (4-0)	
7	8	Notre Dame (3-1)	
8	7	Villanova (4-0)	
9	11	St. Bonaventure (4-0)	↑1
10	10	Santa Clara (5-0)	↑6
11	9	Kansas (5-1)	
12	12	Purdue (4-1)	↑1
13	—	Detroit (6-0)	↑1
14	13	New Mexico State (5-0)	⤴
15	—	California (3-0)	↑3
16	14	La Salle (4-0) (A)	↑4
17	—	Ohio State (2-1)	
18	19	Western Kentucky (6-1)	↓3
19	—	Louisville (5-0)	⤴
20	15	Houston (4-2)	↓8
—	16	Illinois (4-0)	
—	17	Columbia (4-0)	
—	18	Tulsa (5-1)	
—	20	USC (4-2)	

Week of Dec 24

AP	UPI	School	AP↓↑
1	1	UCLA (5-0)	
2	2	North Carolina (6-0)	
3	3	Davidson (5-0)	
4	4	Kentucky (5-1)	
5	5	Villanova (5-0)	↑3
6	8	New Mexico (8-1)	↓1
7	7	Notre Dame (5-1)	
8	9	Kansas (8-1)	↑3
9	6	Santa Clara (6-0)	↑1
10	10	Cincinnati (6-1)	↓4
11	15	Detroit (8-0)	↑2
12	11	Illinois (7-0)	⤴
13	13	St. Bonaventure (5-1)	↓4
14	16	Louisville (7-0)	↑5
15	12	New Mexico State (7-0)	↓1
16	18	Ohio State (4-1)	↑1
17	—	La Salle (6-0)	↓1
18	19	Purdue (5-2)	↓6
19	14	Wyoming (7-0)	⤴
20	—	Tennessee (5-1)	⤴
—	17	Dayton (6-1)	
—	20	USC (5-3)	

Week of Dec 31

AP	UPI	School	AP↓↑
1	1	UCLA (7-0)	
2	3	Davidson (7-0)	↑1
3	4	Kentucky (6-1)	↑1
4	2	North Carolina (7-1)	↓2
5	6	Kansas (10-1)	↑3
6	5	Santa Clara (9-0)	↑3
7	13	Detroit (10-0)	↑4
8	8	Illinois (9-0)	↑4
9	7	Villanova (6-1)	↓4
10	9	Cincinnati (7-1)	
11	16	La Salle (8-0)	↑6
12	15	New Mexico State (9-0)	↑3
13	—	Ohio State (6-1)	↑3
14	18	Louisville (7-0)	
15	11	Duquesne (9-0)	⤴
16	—	Notre Dame (5-2)	↓9
17	10	St. John's (8-1)	⤴
18	12	New Mexico (8-2)	↓12
19	—	Northwestern (8-1)	⤴
20	—	St. Bonaventure (6-2)	↓7
—	14	Columbia (8-0)	
—	17	Purdue (7-3)	⤵
—	18	Vanderbilt (6-2)	
—	18	Wyoming (8-1)	⤵

Week of Jan 7

AP	UPI	School	AP↓↑
1	1	UCLA (9-0)	
2	2	North Carolina (8-1)	↑2
3	3	Santa Clara (12-0)	↑3
4	5	Illinois (10-0)	↑4
5	6	Kansas (12-1)	
6	4	Davidson (8-1)	↓4
7	7	Kentucky (7-2)	↓4
8	8	St. John's (8-2)	↑9
9	9	Villanova (8-1)	
10	10	New Mexico State (11-0)	↑2
11	—	La Salle (9-1)	
12	19	Northwestern (9-1)	↑7
13	19	Detroit (10-2)	↓6
14	16	Louisville (9-1)	
15	14	Duquesne (9-1)	
16	—	Ohio State (7-2)	↓3
17	12	Notre Dame (7-2)	↓1
18	17	Drake (10-1) (B)	⤴
19	—	Cincinnati (7-3)	↓9
20	—	Marquette (8-2)	⤴
—	11	New Mexico (10-3)	⤵
—	13	Purdue (8-3)	
—	15	Columbia (9-1)	
—	18	Tulsa (10-2)	

Week of Jan 14

AP	UPI	School	AP↓↑
1	1	UCLA (11-0)	
2	2	North Carolina (11-1)	
3	3	Santa Clara (14-0)	
4	4	Davidson (10-1)	↑2
5	6	Kentucky (9-2)	↑2
6	8	St. John's (9-2)	↑2
7	7	New Mexico State (14-0)	↑3
8	5	Illinois (11-1)	↓4
9	10	Villanova (10-1)	
10	9	Kansas (13-2)	↓5
11	—	La Salle (11-1)	
12	14	Duquesne (10-1)	↑3
13	—	Ohio State (8-2)	↑3
14	11	Tulsa (11-2)	⤴
15	—	Marquette (11-2)	↑5
16	13	Notre Dame (10-2)	↑1
17	—	Northwestern (9-2)	↓5
18	—	Baylor (9-2)	⤴
19	19	Cincinnati (9-3)	
20	17	Colorado (13-2)	⤴
—	12	New Mexico (11-4)	
—	14	Wyoming (9-2)	
—	16	Purdue (9-3)	
—	17	St. Bonaventure (7-5)	
—	19	Columbia (11-1)	
—	19	Louisville (10-2)	⤵

Week of Jan 21

AP	UPI	School	AP↓↑
1	1	UCLA (12-0)	
2	2	North Carolina (13-1)	
3	3	Santa Clara (16-0)	
4	4	Davidson (12-1)	
5	5	Kentucky (11-2) (C)	
6	7	St. John's (11-2)	
7	6	New Mexico State (15-0)	
8	8	Illinois (11-1)	
9	16	La Salle (12-1)	↑2
10	13	Duquesne (11-1)	↑2
11	9	Villanova (11-2)	↓2
12	15	Ohio State (9-2)	↑1
13	11	Kansas (14-3)	↓3
14	10	Tulsa (13-2)	
15	13	Notre Dame (12-2)	↑1
16	—	Marquette (12-2)	↓1
17	12	Colorado (14-2)	↑3
18	—	Purdue (9-3)	⤴
19	17	Columbia (13-1)	⤴
20	19	Dayton (12-2)	⤴
—	18	St. Bonaventure (7-5)	
—	19	New Mexico (11-6)	

Week of Jan 28

AP	UPI	School	AP↓↑
1	1	UCLA (14-0)	
2	2	North Carolina (13-1)	
3	3	Santa Clara (16-0)	
4	4	Davidson (14-1)	
5	5	Kentucky (12-2)	
6	7	St. John's (12-2)	
7	8	Illinois (12-1)	↑1
8	6	New Mexico State (16-0)	↓1
9	10	La Salle (14-1)	
10	9	Villanova (13-2)	↑1
11	11	Duquesne (11-1)	↓1
12	17	Ohio State (11-2)	
13	12	Tulsa (14-2)	↑1
14	20	Purdue (10-3)	↑4
15	13	Kansas (14-3)	↓2
16	—	Marquette (13-2)	
17	14	Colorado (14-2)	
18	15	Columbia (13-1)	↑1
19	—	South Carolina (10-2)	⤴
20	18	Dayton (13-3)	
—	16	Notre Dame (13-3)	⤵
—	18	New Mexico (11-6)	
—	20	Wyoming (10-3)	

Week of Feb 4

AP	UPI	School	AP↓↑
1	1	UCLA (16-0)	
2	2	North Carolina (14-1)	
3	3	Santa Clara (17-0)	
4	4	Kentucky (14-2)	↑1
5	5	St. John's (13-2)	↑1
6	6	Davidson (15-2)	↓2
7	9	La Salle (16-1)	↑2
8	7	Villanova (15-2)	↑2
9	12	Purdue (11-3)	↑5
10	8	Illinois (13-2)	↓3
11	11	Tulsa (16-2)	↑2
12	18	Ohio State (12-3)	
13	10	Kansas (15-3)	↑2
14	14	Columbia (15-1)	↑4
15	16	Duquesne (12-2)	↓4
16	13	New Mexico State (16-2)	↓8
17	—	Marquette (14-3)	↓1
18	15	New Mexico (13-6)	⤴
19	—	Dayton (15-3)	↑1
20	20	Colorado (14-3)	↓3
—	17	Iowa (19-4)	
—	18	Lamar (15-0)	

Week of Feb 11

AP	UPI	School	AP↓↑
1	1	UCLA (18-0)	
2	2	North Carolina (17-1)	
3	3	Santa Clara (20-0)	
4	4	Kentucky (16-2)	
5	7	La Salle (18-1)	↑2
6	5	Davidson (18-2)	
7	11	Tulsa (18-2)	↑4
8	8	Purdue (13-3)	↑1
9	6	St. John's (16-3)	↓4
10	9	Illinois (14-2)	
11	10	Villanova (16-3)	↓3
12	12	Kansas (17-3)	↑1
13	15	Duquesne (14-2)	↑2
14	13	Colorado (16-3)	↑6
15	—	New Mexico State (19-2)	↑1
16	—	Ohio State (12-4)	↓4
17	—	Dayton (16-4)	↑2
18	—	Marquette (16-3)	↓1
19	—	Baylor (14-3)	⤴
20	16	Louisville (14-3)	⤴
—	14	New Mexico (13-7)	⤵
—	16	Wyoming (14-5)	
—	18	Columbia (15-3)	⤵
—	18	South Carolina (14-3)	
—	20	Notre Dame (15-4)	
—	20	Boston College (15-3)	

Week of Feb 18

AP	UPI	SCHOOL	AP↓↑
1	1	**UCLA** (19-0)	
2	2	**Santa Clara** (21-0)	↑1
3	3	**North Carolina** (19-2)	↓1
4	5	**La Salle** (20-1)	↑1
5	4	**Davidson** (20-2)	↑1
6	6	**Kentucky** (17-3)	↓2
7	7	**St. John's** (18-3)	↑2
8	10	**Duquesne** (16-2)	↑5
9	8	**Purdue** (14-4)	↓1
10	15	**Ohio State** (14-4)	↑6
11	9	**Villanova** (17-4)	
12	11	**South Carolina** (17-3)	⤴
13	14	**Louisville** (16-3)	↑7
14	12	**Tulsa** (18-4)	↓7
15	13	**New Mexico State** (21-2)	
16	19	**Kansas** (18-4)	↓4
17	—	**Tennessee** (15-3)	⤴
18	—	**Colorado** (17-4)	↓4
19	16	**Illinois** (14-4)	↓9
20	—	**Marquette** (17-4)	↓2
—	17	**New Mexico** (15-7)	
—	17	**Wyoming** (15-5)	
—	19	**Columbia** (17-3)	

Week of Feb 25

AP	UPI	SCHOOL	AP↓↑
1	1	**UCLA** (22-0)	
2	2	**North Carolina** (21-2)	↑1
3	4	**La Salle** (22-1) Ⓓ	↑1
4	3	**Santa Clara** (22-1) Ⓔ	↓2
5	5	**Davidson** (22-2)	
6	6	**Kentucky** (19-3)	
7	8	**St. John's** (20-3)	
8	12	**South Carolina** (19-3)	↑4
9	7	**Purdue** (16-4)	
10	10	**Duquesne** (17-3)	↓2
11	11	**Louisville** (17-3)	↑2
12	9	**Villanova** (19-4)	↓1
13	14	**Kansas** (19-4)	↑3
14	15	**Ohio State** (15-5)	↓4
15	20	**Illinois** (16-4)	↑4
16	13	**New Mexico State** (21-3)	↓1
17	—	**Tennessee** (16-4)	
18	—	**Marquette** (19-4)	↑2
19	20	**Tulsa** (18-5)	↓5
20	18	**Boston College** (19-3)	⤴
—	16	**Wyoming** (16-8)	
—	17	**Drake** (19-4)	
—	18	**New Mexico** (16-8)	

Week of Mar 4

AP	UPI	SCHOOL	AP↓↑
1	1	**UCLA** (24-0)	
2	5	**La Salle** (23-1)	↑1
3	2	**Santa Clara** (24-1)	↑1
4	3	**North Carolina** (22-3)	↓2
5	4	**Davidson** (24-2)	
6	6	**Purdue** (18-4)	↑3
7	7	**Kentucky** (20-4)	↓1
8	8	**St. John's** (22-4)	↓1
9	9	**Duquesne** (19-3)	↑1
10	10	**Villanova** (21-4)	↑2
11	11	**Drake** (21-4)	⤴
12	12	**New Mexico State** (23-3)	↑4
13	16	**South Carolina** (19-5)	↓5
14	17	**Marquette** (21-4)	↑4
15	—	**Louisville** (18-4)	↓4
16	19	**Boston College** (20-3)	↑4
17	14	**Notre Dame** (20-5)	⤴
18	14	**Colorado** (19-6)	⤴
19	18	**Kansas** (20-5)	↓6
20	—	**Illinois** (17-5)	↓5
—	12	**Wyoming** (19-7)	
—	20	**Princeton** (19-6)	

Final Poll

UPI	SCHOOL
1	**UCLA** (25-1) Ⓕ
2	**North Carolina** (25-3)
3	**Davidson** (26-2)
4	**Santa Clara** (26-1)
5	**Kentucky** (22-4)
6	**La Salle** (23-1)
7	**Purdue** (20-4)
8	**St. John's** (23-5)
9	**New Mexico State** (24-3)
10	**Duquesne** (20-4)
11	**Drake** (22-4)
12	**Colorado** (20-6)
13	**Louisville** (20-4)
14	**Marquette** (23-4)
15	**Boston College** (21-3)
15	**Villanova** (21-5)
17	**Weber State** (26-2)
17	**Wyoming** (19-8)
19	**Colorado State** (17-6)
20	**Kansas** (20-6)
20	**South Carolina** (21-6)

Ⓐ La Salle beats Niagara 88-73, holding 5'9" guard Calvin Murphy to 24 points. The week before, Murphy set an NCAA record by ripping Syracuse for 68.

Ⓑ An on-court fight with three minutes left punctuates Drake's 73-71 win over Memphis State. The Bulldogs will battle their way to the MVC title and a berth in the Final Four.

Ⓒ Adolph Rupp is forced out of his beloved man-to-man D and into a zone to contain Tennessee's Bill Justus (25 points), as the Wildcats edge the Vols, 69-66, in Knoxville to become the first college program to win 1,000 games.

Ⓓ La Salle nips Detroit, 98-96, at the Palestra in Philadelphia, surviving a 41-point outburst by 1968 Olympic hero Spencer Haywood. Afterward, Tom Gola, star of La Salle's 1954 NCAA championship squad, calls this Explorers team the best in school history. NCAA sanctions for recruiting violations will prevent the players from proving him right.

Ⓔ San Jose State snaps WCAC rival Santa Clara's 21-game winning streak, beating the Broncos, 73-69 in double OT. Spartans coach Dan Glines is carried off the San Jose Civic Auditorium floor in triumph.

Ⓕ One night after losing to UCLA in double overtime, USC halts the Bruins' 41-game winning streak when Ernie Powell connects on a 15-footer with :06 remaining to seal a 46-44 victory. It's UCLA's first loss at Pauley Pavilion.

1969 NCAA Tournament (A)

EAST

First Round	Regional Semifinals	Regional Finals
North Carolina (bye)	North Carolina **79**	North Carolina **87** (B)
Duquesne **74** / Saint Joseph's **52**	Duquesne **78**	Davidson **85**
Davidson **75** / Villanova **61**	Davidson **79**	
St. John's **72** / Princeton **63**	St. John's **69**	

MIDEAST

First Round	Regional Semifinals	Regional Finals
Purdue (bye)	Purdue **91**	Purdue **75** (OT) (E)
Miami (OH) **63** / Notre Dame **60** (C)	Miami (OH) **71**	Marquette **73**
Marquette **82** / Murray State **62**	Marquette **81** (D)	
Kentucky (bye)	Kentucky **74**	

MIDWEST

First Round	Regional Semifinals	Regional Finals
Drake (bye)	Drake **81**	Drake **84**
Texas A&M **81** / Trinity (Texas) **66**	Texas A&M **63**	Colorado State **77**
Colorado State **52** / Dayton **50** (F)	Colorado State **64**	
Colorado (bye)	Colorado **56**	

WEST

First Round	Regional Semifinals	Regional Finals
UCLA (bye)	UCLA **53**	UCLA **90**
New Mexico State **74** / BYU **62**	New Mexico State **38**	Santa Clara **52**
Santa Clara (bye)	Santa Clara **63** (OT)	
Weber State **75** / Seattle **73**	Weber State **59**	

National Semifinals

North Carolina **65**
Purdue **92**

With guards Rick Mount and Bill Keller bombing away for a combined 56 points, Purdue never trails and hands North Carolina its third double-digit Final Four loss in as many years.

Drake **82**
UCLA **85**

Cheered on by an underdog-loving crowd in Freedom Hall, Drake scores eight straight points in the final :55 to cut UCLA's lead to a single point, but the Bruins hold on to win.

National Final

UCLA 92
Purdue 72

With Lew Alcindor pouring in 37 points and grabbing 20 rebounds in his final college game, UCLA becomes the first team to win three consecutive national championships. While Alcindor is making shots, his father, Ferdinand, is making music, playing trombone with the UCLA band in the stands.

LOUISVILLE, KY

National Third Place Drake d. North Carolina 104-84
East Regional Third Place Duquesne d. St. John's 75-72
Mideast Regional Third Place Kentucky d. Miami (OH) 72-71
Midwest Regional Third Place Colorado d. Texas A&M 97-82
West Regional Third Place Weber State d. New Mexico State 58-56

A Net income for the Tournament tops the million-dollar mark ($1,032,915) for the first time.

B Charlie Scott, the first African-American to play for North Carolina, hits a 20-footer with :03 left to seal the Tar Heels' two-point win over Davidson. It's the second straight year that UNC has eliminated coach Lefty Driesell's Wildcats.

C Irish eyes are *not* smiling when scoring machine Austin Carr, who gets six early points, sprains his ankle and misses the rest of the game. After sustaining a gash across the bridge of his nose, Miami's Mike Wren wipes away the blood and knocks down four free throws to secure the win.

D Marquette's Al McGuire plays the race card to psyche up his players for their revenge game against all-white Kentucky, and the crowd also gets stirred up. One Kentucky player describes his fear by saying, "Somebody could have gotten killed." McGuire later apologizes.

E Purdue's Rick Mount has a rare off game, making only 11 of 32 shots from the floor, but comes off a double screen to hit the game-winning jumper as time expires.

F Twin guards Lloyd and Floyd Kerr spark the upset for Colorado State. Lloyd has 17 points and Floyd, whose late steal leads to the game-winning free throw, has 11.

TOURNAMENT LEADERS

INDIVIDUAL LEADERS

SCORING	CL	POS	G	PTS	PPG
1 **Rick Mount**, Purdue	JR	G	4	122	30.5
2 **Mike Maloy**, Davidson	JR	F	3	91	30.3
3 **Cliff Meely**, Colorado	SO	F	2	58	29.0
4 **Charlie Scott**, North Carolina	JR	G/F	4	105	26.3
5 **Dan Issel**, Kentucky	JR	C	2	49	24.5
6 **George Thompson**, Marquette	SR	G	3	73	24.3
7 **Willie McCarter**, Drake	SR	G	4	97	24.3
8 **Lew Alcindor**, UCLA	SR	C	4	95	23.8
9 **Jarrett Durham**, Duquesne	SO	G	3	64	21.3
10 **Mike Wren**, Miami (OH)	SO	G	3	54	18.0

MINIMUM: 2 GAMES

FIELD GOAL PCT	CL	POS	G	FG	FGA	PCT
1 **George Faerber**, Purdue	SO	F	4	15	18	83.3
2 **John Hummer**, Princeton	JR	F	1	13	16	81.3
3 **Jarrett Durham**, Duquesne	SO	G	3	26	38	68.4
4 **Dan Issel**, Kentucky	JR	C	2	16	25	64.0
5 **John Vallely**, UCLA	JR	G	4	23	37	62.2

MINIMUM: 10 MADE

FREE THROW PCT	CL	POS	G	FT	FTA	PCT
1 **Mike Casey**, Kentucky	JR	G	2	13	14	92.9
2 **Cliff Shegogg**, Colorado State	JR	F	3	12	13	92.3
3 **Willie McCarter**, Drake	SR	G	4	11	12	91.7
Glen Pryor, Miami (OH)	JR	F	3	11	12	91.7
5 **Jim Delany**, North Carolina	JR	G	4	10	11	90.9
Ralph Abraham, St. John's	JR	F	3	10	11	90.9
Jerry Kroll, Davidson	JR	F	3	10	11	90.9

MINIMUM: 10 MADE

REBOUNDS PER GAME	CL	POS	G	REB	RPG
1 **Lew Alcindor**, UCLA	SR	C	4	64	16.0
2 **Mike Maloy**, Davidson	JR	F	3	42	14.0
3 **Willie Sojourner**, Weber State	SO	C	3	41	13.7
4 **Dan Issel**, Kentucky	JR	C	2	26	13.0
5 **Mike Davis**, Colorado State	SR	F	3	38	12.7

MINIMUM: 2 GAMES

TEAM LEADERS

SCORING	G	PTS	PPG
1 **Drake**	4	351	87.8
2 **Purdue**	4	330	82.5
3 **UCLA**	4	320	80.0
4 **Davidson**	3	239	79.7
5 **North Carolina**	4	315	78.8
6 **Marquette**	3	236	78.7
7 **Colorado**	2	153	76.5
8 **Duquesne**	3	227	75.7
9 **Texas A&M**	3	226	75.3
10 **Kentucky**	2	146	73.0

MINIMUM: 2 GAMES

FG PCT	G	FG	FGA	PCT
1 **UCLA**	4	122	231	52.8
2 **Duquesne**	3	91	186	48.9
Marquette	3	91	186	48.9
4 **North Carolina**	4	120	256	46.9
5 **St. John's**	3	83	180	46.1

FT PCT	G	FT	FTA	PCT
1 **St. John's**	3	47	54	87.0
2 **Kentucky**	2	46	54	85.2
3 **Davidson**	3	69	88	78.4
4 **Purdue**	4	66	86	76.7
5 **Miami (OH)**	3	51	67	76.1

MINIMUM: 2 GAMES

REBOUNDS	G	REB	RPG
1 **Texas A&M**	3	141	47.0
2 **Purdue**	4	173	43.3
3 **New Mexico State**	3	127	42.3
4 **UCLA**	4	168	42.0
5 **Duquesne**	3	120	40.0

MINIMUM: 2 GAMES

ALL-TOURNAMENT TEAM

PLAYER	CL	POS	HT	SCHOOL	RPG	PPG
Lew Alcindor*	SR	C	7-2	UCLA	16.0	23.8
Willie McCarter	SR	G	6-3	Drake	3.8	24.3
Rick Mount	JR	G	6-4	Purdue	2.0	30.5
Charlie Scott	JR	G/F	6-5	North Carolina	6.3	26.3
John Vallely	JR	G	6-2	UCLA	4.5	16.3

ALL-REGIONAL TEAMS

EAST

PLAYER	CL	POS	HT	SCHOOL	RPG	PPG
Charlie Scott*	JR	G/F	6-5	North Carolina	7.5	27.0
Bill Bunting	SR	F	6-9	North Carolina	8.5	18.0
Doug Cook	JR	F	6-6	Davidson	5.3	17.7
Jarrett Durham	SO	G	6-5	Duquesne	5.3	21.3
Mike Maloy	JR	F	6-7	Davidson	14.0	30.3

MIDEAST

PLAYER	CL	POS	HT	SCHOOL	RPG	PPG
Rick Mount*	JR	G	6-4	Purdue	1.5	29.0
Dan Issel	JR	C	6-8	Kentucky	13.0	24.5
Bill Keller	SR	G	5-10	Purdue	4.0	18.0
Dean Meminger	SO	G	6-0	Marquette	8.3	15.7
George Thompson	SR	G	6-2	Marquette	5.7	24.3

MIDWEST

PLAYER	CL	POS	HT	SCHOOL	RPG	PPG
Willie McCarter*	SR	G	6-3	Drake	4.0	22.5
Floyd Kerr	SR	G	6-2	Colorado State	5.7	15.3
Cliff Meely	SO	F	6-7	Colorado	8.0	29.0
Dolph Pulliam	SR	F	6-4	Drake	4.5	11.0
Willie Wise	SR	F	6-5	Drake	11.5	13.0

WEST

PLAYER	CL	POS	HT	SCHOOL	RPG	PPG
Lew Alcindor*	SR	C	7-2	UCLA	11.5	16.5
Jimmy Collins	JR	G	6-2	New Mexico State	4.3	16.0
Kenny Heitz	SR	G/F	6-3	UCLA	2.5	7.5
Bud Ogden	SR	F	6-6	Santa Clara	9.0	13.5
Justus Thigpen	SR	G	6-0	Weber State	2.0	14.7
John Vallely	JR	G	6-2	UCLA	4.0	10.5

* MOST OUTSTANDING PLAYER

1969 NCAA TOURNAMENT BOX SCORES

Sweet 16: North Carolina 79, Duquesne 78

	1H	2H
North Carolina	48	31
Duquesne	41	37

NORTH CAROLINA	MIN	FG	3FG	FT	REB	A	ST	BL	PF	TP
Charlie Scott	40	9-19	-	4-7	9	6	-	-	2	22
Rusty Clark	38	5-9	-	5-6	8	1	-	-	2	15
Bill Bunting	28	6-8	-	2-2	9	1	-	-	5	14
Lee Dedmon	27	4-10	-	2-5	6	1	-	-	3	10
Eddie Fogler	31	3-8	-	3-3	2	4	-	-	2	9
Jim Delany	13	0-1	-	5-5	0	0	-	-	1	5
Joe Brown	14	1-4	-	2-4	2	0	-	-	0	4
Gerald Tuttle	9	0-2	-	0-1	1	1	-	-	0	0
TOTALS	200	28-61	-	23-33	37	14	-	-	15	79
Percentages		45.9		69.7						

Coach: Dean Smith

DUQUESNE	MIN	FG	3FG	FT	REB	A	ST	BL	PF	TP
Jarrett Durham	-	9-16	-	3-3	5	6	-	-	3	21
Moe Barr	-	8-16	-	1-3	9	3	-	-	1	17
Bill Zopf	-	6-11	-	1-2	5	3	-	-	3	13
Garry Nelson	-	5-9	-	2-2	5	1	-	-	5	12
Barry Nelson	-	3-8	-	0-0	5	0	-	-	3	6
Gary Major	-	2-5	-	1-6	5	1	-	-	4	5
Willie Hines	-	2-4	-	0-1	3	2	-	-	1	4
TOTALS	-	35-69	-	8-17	37	16	-	-	20	78
Percentages		50.7		47.1						

Coach: Red Manning

Officials: Lawson, Overb
Attendance: 13,166

Sweet 16: Davidson 79, St. John's 69

	1H	2H
Davidson	44	35
St. John's	43	26

DAVIDSON	MIN	FG	3FG	FT	REB	A	ST	BL	PF	TP
Mike Maloy	-	11-19	-	13-13	12	-	-	-	3	35
Doug Cook	-	6-10	-	7-9	5	-	-	-	3	19
Jerry Kroll	-	3-8	-	5-6	10	-	-	-	3	11
Dave Moser	-	2-7	-	5-6	7	-	-	-	2	9
Mike O'Neill	-	1-2	-	1-2	1	-	-	-	1	3
Wayne Huckel	-	1-3	-	0-2	0	-	-	-	0	2
Steve Kirley	-	0-0	-	0-0	0	-	-	-	0	0
TOTALS	-	24-49	-	31-38	35	-	-	-	12	79
Percentages		49.0		81.6						

Coach: Lefty Driesell

ST. JOHN'S	MIN	FG	3FG	FT	REB	A	ST	BL	PF	TP
John Warren	-	9-20	-	0-1	5	-	-	-	4	18
Joe Depre	-	8-15	-	0-0	1	-	-	-	4	16
Jim Smyth	-	4-10	-	0-0	2	-	-	-	2	8
Ralph Abraham	-	2-7	-	3-3	9	-	-	-	4	7
Dan Cornelius	-	2-4	-	3-3	5	-	-	-	4	7
Rich Gilkes	-	2-2	-	2-2	2	-	-	-	2	6
Bill Paultz	-	2-3	-	0-1	4	-	-	-	5	4
Carmine Calzonetti	-	1-4	-	1-1	0	-	-	-	2	3
TOTALS	-	30-65	-	9-11	28	-	-	-	27	69
Percentages		46.2		81.8						

Coach: Lou Carnesecca

Officials: Dreith, Jeter
Attendance: 13,166

Sweet 16: Purdue 91, Miami (OH) 71

	1H	2H
Purdue	49	42
Miami (OH)	34	37

PURDUE	MIN	FG	3FG	FT	REB	A	ST	BL	PF	TP
Rick Mount	-	12-20	-	8-8	1	-	-	-	0	32
Bill Keller	-	9-15	-	1-1	6	-	-	-	2	19
George Faerber	-	8-8	-	0-2	14	-	-	-	1	16
Larry Weatherford	-	3-9	-	1-2	7	-	-	-	1	7
Jerry Johnson	-	2-2	-	1-1	5	-	-	-	4	5
Tyrone Bedford	-	2-5	-	0-0	5	-	-	-	3	4
Frank Kaufman	-	0-1	-	3-4	4	-	-	-	0	3
Chuck Bavis	-	1-1	-	0-0	1	-	-	-	4	2
Steve Longfellow	-	1-1	-	0-0	1	-	-	-	0	2
Ted Reasoner	-	0-0	-	1-2	0	-	-	-	0	1
Ralph Taylor	-	0-0	-	0-0	0	-	-	-	0	0
TOTALS	-	38-62	-	15-20	44	-	-	-	15	91
Percentages		61.3		75.0						

Coach: George King

MIAMI (OH)	MIN	FG	3FG	FT	REB	A	ST	BL	PF	TP
Terry Martin	-	8-15	-	2-4	10	-	-	-	2	18
Mike Wren	-	6-13	-	4-4	1	-	-	-	2	16
Walt Williams	-	4-15	-	3-3	5	-	-	-	1	11
Glen Pryor	-	4-5	-	1-1	2	-	-	-	1	9
Frank Lukacas	-	4-10	-	0-0	2	-	-	-	3	8
Gerald Sears	-	2-8	-	0-0	0	-	-	-	0	4
Ron Snyder	-	0-3	-	3-4	2	-	-	-	3	3
George Burkhart	-	0-2	-	1-2	2	-	-	-	1	1
Ray Loucks	-	0-3	-	1-1	3	-	-	-	1	1
Tom Slater	-	0-1	-	0-0	0	-	-	-	0	0
Bill Strauch	-	0-0	-	0-0	0	-	-	-	1	0
TOTALS	-	28-75	-	15-19	27	-	-	-	15	71
Percentages		37.3		78.9						

Coach: Taylor "Tates" Locke

Officials: Filiberti, Bussenius
Attendance: 12,725

Sweet 16: Marquette 81, Kentucky 74

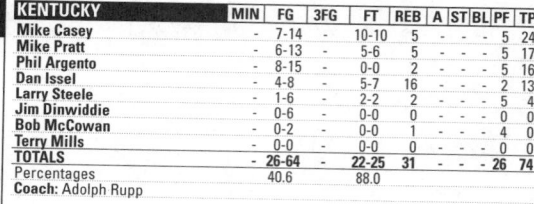

	1H	2H
Marquette	36	45
Kentucky	33	41

MARQUETTE	MIN	FG	3FG	FT	REB	A	ST	BL	PF	TP
George Thompson	-	7-16	-	8-13	4	-	-	-	1	22
Dean Meminger	-	6-15	-	8-13	6	-	-	-	2	20
Ric Cobb	-	7-8	-	3-7	14	-	-	-	1	17
Jeff Sewell	-	7-9	-	1-2	3	-	-	-	5	15
Joe Thomas	-	3-6	-	0-0	2	-	-	-	5	6
Jack Burke	-	0-1	-	1-2	0	-	-	-	2	1
Ron Rahn	-	0-1	-	0-0	1	-	-	-	1	0
Pat Smith	-	0-1	-	0-1	1	-	-	-	2	0
TOTALS	-	30-57	-	21-38	31	-	-	-	19	81
Percentages		52.6		55.3						

Coach: Al McGuire

KENTUCKY	MIN	FG	3FG	FT	REB	A	ST	BL	PF	TP
Mike Casey	-	7-14	-	10-10	5	-	-	-	5	24
Mike Pratt	-	6-13	-	5-6	5	-	-	-	5	17
Phil Argento	-	8-15	-	0-0	2	-	-	-	5	16
Dan Issel	-	4-8	-	5-7	16	-	-	-	2	13
Larry Steele	-	1-6	-	2-2	2	-	-	-	5	4
Jim Dinwiddie	-	0-6	-	0-0	0	-	-	-	0	0
Bob McCowan	-	0-2	-	0-0	1	-	-	-	4	0
Terry Mills	-	0-0	-	0-0	0	-	-	-	0	0
TOTALS	-	26-64	-	22-25	31	-	-	-	26	74
Percentages		40.6		88.0						

Coach: Adolph Rupp

Officials: Herrold, Brown
Attendance: 12,725

Sweet 16: Drake 81, Texas A&M 63

	1H	2H
Drake	32	49
Texas A&M	26	37

DRAKE	MIN	FG	3FG	FT	REB	A	ST	BL	PF	TP
Willie McCarter	-	12-24	-	0-0	3	-	-	-	1	24
Don Draper	-	6-16	-	1-1	3	-	-	-	2	13
Willie Wise	-	2-15	-	6-9	16	-	-	-	3	10
Dolph Pulliam	-	4-8	-	1-1	6	-	-	-	4	9
Garry Odom	-	2-2	-	4-8	12	-	-	-	2	8
Gary Zeller	-	3-6	-	2-2	0	-	-	-	3	8
Al Williams	-	1-3	-	3-4	3	-	-	-	4	5
Rob Gwyn	-	2-2	-	0-0	1	-	-	-	1	4
Bob Mast	-	0-0	-	0-0	0	-	-	-	0	0
Al Sakys	-	0-0	-	0-0	0	-	-	-	0	0
Rick Wanamaker	-	0-0	-	0-0	0	-	-	-	0	0
TOTALS	-	32-76	-	17-25	44	-	-	-	20	81
Percentages		42.1		68.0						

Coach: Maury John

TEXAS A&M	MIN	FG	3FG	FT	REB	A	ST	BL	PF	TP
Mike Heitman	-	3-12	-	6-8	4	-	-	-	1	12
Steve Niles	-	5-10	-	2-3	9	-	-	-	5	12
Bill Cooksey	-	4-8	-	3-4	6	-	-	-	2	11
Chuck Smith	-	5-12	-	0-1	11	-	-	-	4	10
Sonny Benefield	-	2-14	-	4-4	2	-	-	-	1	8
Billy Bob Barnett	-	2-8	-	2-4	11	-	-	-	2	6
Ronnie Paret	-	1-5	-	2-4	9	-	-	-	5	4
Harry Bostic	-	0-0	-	0-0	0	-	-	-	1	0
Bill Brown	-	0-2	-	0-0	0	-	-	-	0	0
TOTALS	-	22-71	-	19-28	52	-	-	-	21	63
Percentages		31.0		67.9						

Coach: Shelby Metcalf

Officials: Stout, Bushkar
Attendance: 5,500

Sweet 16: Colorado State 64, Colorado 56

	1H	2H
Colorado State	28	36
Colorado	27	29

COLORADO STATE	MIN	FG	3FG	FT	REB	A	ST	BL	PF	TP
Cliff Shegogg	-	9-18	-	2-3	9	-	-	-	4	20
Floyd Kerr	-	4-6	-	6-9	3	-	-	-	1	14
Lloyd Kerr	-	4-17	-	4-8	9	-	-	-	1	12
Mike Davis	-	3-5	-	4-6	13	-	-	-	5	10
Charles Meeker	-	1-3	-	1-3	3	-	-	-	1	3
James Stockham	-	1-1	-	1-2	0	-	-	-	2	3
William Peden	-	0-0	-	2-3	0	-	-	-	0	2
Joseph Weems	-	0-2	-	0-0	4	-	-	-	4	0
TOTALS	-	22-52	-	20-34	41	-	-	-	18	64
Percentages		42.3		58.8						

Coach: Jim Williams

COLORADO	MIN	FG	3FG	FT	REB	A	ST	BL	PF	TP
Cliff Meely	-	11-26	-	10-14	11	-	-	-	4	32
Dudley Mitchell	-	5-16	-	0-0	2	-	-	-	3	10
Ted Erfert	-	2-4	-	0-0	4	-	-	-	2	4
Tim Wedgeworth	-	1-9	-	2-2	10	-	-	-	2	4
Gordon Tope	-	1-6	-	1-1	0	-	-	-	5	3
Tim Richardson	-	1-3	-	0-0	3	-	-	-	3	2
Mike Coleman	-	0-5	-	1-7	9	-	-	-	0	1
Lloyd Hutchinson	-	0-0	-	0-0	0	-	-	-	0	0
Terry Jameson	-	0-1	-	0-0	0	-	-	-	0	0
Mickey Kern	-	0-0	-	0-0	1	-	-	-	4	0
Ron Maulsby	-	0-0	-	0-0	0	-	-	-	0	0
Scoopy Smith	-	0-0	-	0-0	0	-	-	-	1	0
TOTALS	-	21-70	-	14-24	40	-	-	-	24	56
Percentages		30.0		58.3						

Coach: Russell "Sox" Walseth

Officials: Honzo, DiTomasso
Attendance: 5,500

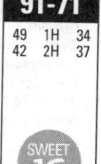

53-38 (SWEET 16)

UCLA	MIN	FG	3FG	FT	REB	A	ST	BL	PF	TP
Lew Alcindor	-	8-15	-	0-5	16	-	-	-	3	16
John Vallely	-	5-12	-	0-0	5	-	-	-	1	10
Kenny Heitz	-	4-6	-	1-1	4	-	-	-	3	9
Curtis Rowe	-	3-12	-	2-2	7	-	-	-	2	8
Lynn Shackelford	-	4-10	-	0-0	3	-	-	-	0	8
Bill Sweek	-	1-1	-	0-2	0	-	-	-	1	2
Steve Patterson	-	0-0	-	0-0	0	-	-	-	1	0
Terry Schofield	-	0-0	-	0-0	0	-	-	-	0	0
Sidney Wicks	-	0-2	-	0-0	0	-	-	-	0	0
TOTALS	-	25-58	-	3-10	35	-	-	-	11	53
Percentages		43.1		30.0						

Coach: John Wooden

21	1H	17
32	2H	21

NEW MEXICO STATE	MIN	FG	3FG	FT	REB	A	ST	BL	PF	TP
Jimmy Collins	-	4-17	-	3-3	4	-	-	-	1	11
Sam Lacey	-	5-16	-	1-1	11	-	-	-	4	11
Jeff Smith	-	2-4	-	3-3	8	-	-	-	3	7
Chito Reyes	-	2-5	-	1-2	2	-	-	-	0	5
Heris Bowen	-	1-1	-	0-0	0	-	-	-	0	2
Hardy Murphy	-	1-2	-	0-0	1	-	-	-	1	2
John Burgess	-	0-3	-	0-1	2	-	-	-	0	0
TOTALS	-	15-48	-	8-10	28	-	-	-	9	38
Percentages		31.2		80.0						

Coach: Lou Henson

Officials: Wirtz, Fouty
Attendance: 12,817

63-59 (SWEET 16)

SANTA CLARA	MIN	FG	3FG	FT	REB	A	ST	BL	PF	TP
Dennis Awtrey	-	9-17	-	1-1	7	-	-	-	5	19
Bud Ogden	-	7-13	-	4-7	13	-	-	-	2	18
Ralph Ogden	-	4-13	-	1-1	6	-	-	-	3	9
Chris Dempsey	-	1-2	-	3-5	8	-	-	-	0	5
Kevin Eagleson	-	2-2	-	1-3	2	-	-	-	4	5
Terry O'Brien	-	1-3	-	3-3	1	-	-	-	4	5
Joe Diffley	-	1-5	-	0-1	5	-	-	-	0	2
TOTALS	-	25-55	-	13-21	42	-	-	-	18	63
Percentages		45.5		61.9						

Coach: Dick Garibaldi

29	1H	19
26	2H	36
8	OT1	4

WEBER STATE	MIN	FG	3FG	FT	REB	A	ST	BL	PF	TP
Justice Thigpen	-	7-16	-	2-4	2	-	-	-	1	16
Willie Sojourner	-	2-14	-	8-9	18	-	-	-	3	12
Sessions Harlan	-	4-10	-	3-4	5	-	-	-	1	11
Larry Bergh	-	3-5	-	2-2	1	-	-	-	5	8
Gary Strong	-	4-10	-	0-2	6	-	-	-	1	8
Dave Sackolwitz	-	1-2	-	2-5	3	-	-	-	5	4
Gus Chatmon	-	0-1	-	0-0	3	-	-	-	3	0
Richard Nielsen	-	0-2	-	0-0	0	-	-	-	0	0
TOTALS	-	21-60	-	17-26	38	-	-	-	19	59
Percentages		35.0		65.4						

Coach: Phil Johnson

Officials: MacPherson, Payak
Attendance: 12,817

87-85 (ELITE 8)

NORTH CAROLINA	MIN	FG	3FG	FT	REB	A	ST	BL	PF	TP
Charlie Scott	40	14-21	-	4-5	6	4	-	-	1	32
Bill Bunting	39	7-12	-	8-9	8	4	-	-	2	22
Rusty Clark	26	8-9	-	0-1	6	2	-	-	4	16
Eddie Fogler	31	4-8	-	0-1	1	3	-	-	2	8
Jim Delany	33	0-6	-	3-4	2	2	-	-	2	3
Lee Dedmon	12	1-2	-	0-0	3	0	-	-	5	2
Joe Brown	10	0-4	-	2-2	4	1	-	-	0	2
Gerald Tuttle	9	1-3	-	0-0	2	0	-	-	2	2
TOTALS	200	35-65	-	17-22	32	16	-	-	18	87
Percentages		53.8		77.3						

Coach: Dean Smith

47	1H	46
40	2H	39

DAVIDSON	MIN	FG	3FG	FT	REB	A	ST	BL	PF	TP
Mike Maloy	40	10-23	-	5-7	13	0	-	-	3	25
Doug Cook	25	7-13	-	4-4	6	2	-	-	5	18
Jerry Kroll	23	6-15	-	4-4	2	0	-	-	5	16
Mike O'Neill	30	3-9	-	4-7	1	2	-	-	2	10
Wayne Huckel	27	3-10	-	1-1	8	5	-	-	1	7
Dave Moser	37	2-6	-	0-0	3	5	-	-	3	4
Steve Kirley	15	2-3	-	0-0	5	0	-	-	2	4
Ron Stelzer	3	0-0	-	1-2	1	0	-	-	0	1
TOTALS	200	33-79	-	19-25	39	14	-	-	21	85
Percentages		41.8		76.0						

Coach: Lefty Driesell

Officials: Dreith, Jeter
Attendance: 13,166

75-73 (ELITE 8)

PURDUE	MIN	FG	3FG	FT	REB	A	ST	BL	PF	TP
Rick Mount	-	11-32	-	4-5	2	-	-	-	2	26
Bill Keller	-	6-11	-	5-5	2	-	-	-	5	17
Larry Weatherford	-	5-14	-	3-3	3	-	-	-	0	13
George Faerber	-	3-5	-	2-3	8	-	-	-	4	8
Herman Gilliam	-	2-3	-	3-3	3	-	-	-	2	7
Jerry Johnson	-	2-6	-	0-1	16	-	-	-	3	4
Tyrone Bedford	-	0-1	-	0-0	3	-	-	-	2	0
Frank Kaufman	-	0-0	-	0-0	0	-	-	-	3	0
TOTALS	-	29-72	-	17-20	37	-	-	-	21	75
Percentages		40.3		85.0						

Coach: George King

35	1H	30
28	2H	33
12	OT	10

MARQUETTE	MIN	FG	3FG	FT	REB	A	ST	BL	PF	TP
George Thompson	-	9-17	-	10-11	8	-	-	-	1	28
Dean Meminger	-	5-14	-	2-6	14	-	-	-	1	12
Joe Thomas	-	5-13	-	1-2	13	-	-	-	3	11
Jeff Sewell	-	3-9	-	2-2	2	-	-	-	4	8
Jack Burke	-	3-5	-	1-1	2	-	-	-	3	7
Ric Cobb	-	2-10	-	3-7	9	-	-	-	4	7
TOTALS	-	27-68	-	19-29	48	-	-	-	16	73
Percentages		39.7		65.5						

Coach: Al McGuire

Officials: Brown, Bussenius
Attendance: 13,025

84-77 (ELITE 8)

DRAKE	MIN	FG	3FG	FT	REB	A	ST	BL	PF	TP
Willie McCarter	-	9-23	-	3-3	5	-	-	-	4	21
Willie Wise	-	4-11	-	8-12	7	-	-	-	4	16
Dolph Pulliam	-	5-14	-	3-4	3	-	-	-	4	13
Don Draper	-	5-11	-	1-1	4	-	-	-	4	11
Garry Odom	-	4-5	-	2-3	6	-	-	-	1	10
Gary Zeller	-	4-5	-	1-2	3	-	-	-	2	9
Al Williams	-	2-8	-	0-0	5	-	-	-	3	4
Rob Gwyn	-	0-1	-	0-0	1	-	-	-	0	0
TOTALS	-	33-78	-	18-25	34	-	-	-	22	84
Percentages		42.3		72.0						

Coach: Maury John

38	1H	37
46	2H	40

COLORADO STATE	MIN	FG	3FG	FT	REB	A	ST	BL	PF	TP
Floyd Kerr	-	8-17	-	5-7	6	-	-	-	4	21
William Peden	-	7-10	-	5-6	1	-	-	-	2	19
Mike Davis	-	2-4	-	9-10	16	-	-	-	4	13
Lloyd Kerr	-	5-15	-	2-2	8	-	-	-	2	12
Cliff Shegogg	-	1-7	-	6-6	2	-	-	-	5	8
Joseph Weems	-	2-7	-	0-0	9	-	-	-	4	4
Charles Meeker	-	0-0	-	0-0	0	-	-	-	1	0
James Stockham	-	0-0	-	0-0	0	-	-	-	0	0
TOTALS	-	25-60	-	27-31	42	-	-	-	22	77
Percentages		41.7		87.1						

Coach: Jim Williams

Officials: Honzo, DiTomasso
Attendance: 7,000

90-52 (ELITE 8)

UCLA	MIN	FG	3FG	FT	REB	A	ST	BL	PF	TP
Lew Alcindor	-	8-14	-	1-3	7	-	-	-	2	17
Bill Sweek	-	4-7	-	4-5	1	-	-	-	1	12
John Vallely	-	5-5	-	1-2	3	-	-	-	2	11
Sidney Wicks	-	3-4	-	5-8	2	-	-	-	1	11
Steve Patterson	-	4-6	-	1-1	5	-	-	-	4	9
Curtis Rowe	-	3-6	-	1-2	5	-	-	-	1	7
Kenny Heitz	-	3-6	-	0-0	1	-	-	-	2	6
Lynn Shackelford	-	3-7	-	0-1	3	-	-	-	1	6
John Ecker	-	2-2	-	1-1	1	-	-	-	0	5
George Farmer	-	1-2	-	0-0	0	-	-	-	0	2
Terry Schofield	-	1-6	-	0-0	2	-	-	-	0	2
Bill Seibert	-	0-0	-	2-2	3	-	-	-	1	2
TOTALS	-	37-65	-	16-25	33	-	-	-	15	90
Percentages		56.9		64.0						

Coach: John Wooden

46	1H	25
44	2H	27

SANTA CLARA	MIN	FG	3FG	FT	REB	A	ST	BL	PF	TP
Dennis Awtrey	-	5-9	-	4-6	8	-	-	-	4	14
Bud Ogden	-	3-10	-	3-3	5	-	-	-	4	9
Chris Dempsey	-	2-3	-	1-1	2	-	-	-	2	5
Keith Paulson	-	2-4	-	1-3	1	-	-	-	0	5
Mitch Champi	-	2-3	-	0-0	2	-	-	-	3	4
Ralph Ogden	-	1-13	-	2-4	7	-	-	-	2	4
Tom Scherer	-	2-5	-	0-0	1	-	-	-	0	4
Gary Graves	-	1-1	-	1-1	1	-	-	-	1	3
Joe Diffley	-	1-4	-	0-0	2	-	-	-	2	2
Bob Tobin	-	1-2	-	0-0	4	-	-	-	2	2
Kevin Eagleson	-	0-0	-	0-1	3	-	-	-	3	0
Terry O'Brien	-	0-2	-	0-1	1	-	-	-	2	0
TOTALS	-	20-56	-	12-20	37	-	-	-	25	52
Percentages		35.7		60.0						

Coach: Dick Garibaldi

Officials: Fouty, Payak
Attendance: 12,812

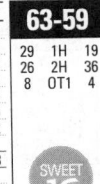

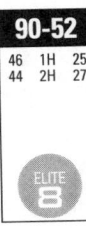

92-65 — 39 1H 35 / 53 2H 30 — FINAL 4

PURDUE	MIN	FG	3FG	FT	REB	A	ST	BL	PF	TP
Rick Mount	33	14-28	-	8-9	4	3	-	-	0	36
Bill Keller	32	9-19	-	2-3	5	5	-	-	3	20
George Faerber	31	3-3	-	2-2	9	0	-	-	3	8
Larry Weatherford	11	3-6	-	1-1	2	0	-	-	1	7
Herman Gilliam	27	3-11	-	0-0	8	7	-	-	0	6
Tyrone Bedford	17	3-3	-	0-0	5	1	-	-	4	6
Jerry Johnson	13	2-5	-	1-3	5	0	-	-	4	5
Frank Kaufman	26	0-1	-	2-3	6	1	-	-	4	2
Ralph Taylor	2	1-1	-	0-1	3	0	-	-	0	2
Steve Longfellow	4	0-1	-	0-0	2	0	-	-	0	0
Ted Reasoner	2	0-0	-	0-0	0	0	-	-	1	0
Glenn Young	2	0-0	-	0-0	0	0	-	-	0	0
TOTALS	**200**	**38-78**	**-**	**16-22**	**49**	**17**	**-**	**-**	**20**	**92**
Percentages		48.7		72.7						

Coach: George King

NORTH CAROLINA	MIN	FG	3FG	FT	REB	A	ST	BL	PF	TP
Rusty Clark	37	7-9	-	6-10	9	1	-	-	2	20
Bill Bunting	37	7-13	-	5-7	7	2	-	-	2	19
Charlie Scott	36	6-19	-	4-6	6	6	-	-	3	16
Gerald Tuttle	20	2-4	-	0-1	3	1	-	-	3	4
Eddie Fogler	27	1-4	-	0-0	2	1	-	-	2	2
Joe Brown	6	1-4	-	0-0	1	0	-	-	0	2
Dave Chadwick	2	1-2	-	0-0	2	0	-	-	0	2
Lee Dedmon	16	0-1	-	0-1	4	2	-	-	2	0
Jim Delany	13	0-2	-	0-0	1	2	-	-	4	0
Dale Gipple	4	0-3	-	0-0	1	0	-	-	0	0
Don Eggleston	1	0-0	-	0-0	0	0	-	-	0	0
Richard Tuttle	1	0-1	-	0-0	0	0	-	-	0	0
TOTALS	**200**	**25-62**	**-**	**15-25**	**36**	**15**	**-**	**-**	**18**	**65**
Percentages		40.3		60.0						

Coach: Dean Smith

Officials: Overby, Brown
Attendance: 18,435

85-82 — 41 1H 39 / 44 2H 43 — FINAL 4

UCLA	MIN	FG	3FG	FT	REB	A	ST	BL	PF	TP
John Vallely	-	9-11	-	11-14	6	5	-	-	5	29
Lew Alcindor	-	8-14	-	9-16	21	3	-	-	3	25
Curtis Rowe	-	6-9	-	2-2	13	3	-	-	2	14
Kenny Heitz	-	3-6	-	1-3	1	3	-	-	5	7
Lynn Shackelford	-	2-5	-	2-3	2	3	-	-	4	6
Steve Patterson	-	0-0	-	2-2	0	0	-	-	0	2
Terry Schofield	-	0-3	-	2-4	0	1	-	-	0	2
Bill Sweek	-	0-0	-	0-0	0	0	-	-	1	0
Sidney Wicks	-	0-2	-	0-0	1	0	-	-	1	0
TOTALS	**-**	**28-50**	**-**	**29-44**	**44**	**18**	**-**	**-**	**21**	**85**
Percentages		56.0		65.9						

Coach: John Wooden

DRAKE	MIN	FG	3FG	FT	REB	A	ST	BL	PF	TP
Willie McCarter	-	10-27	-	4-4	1	2	-	-	3	24
Willie Wise	-	5-7	-	3-4	16	1	-	-	3	13
Don Draper	-	5-13	-	2-2	1	1	-	-	2	12
Dolph Pulliam	-	4-14	-	4-5	5	6	-	-	4	12
Gary Zeller	-	4-12	-	4-6	3	1	-	-	3	12
Rick Wanamaker	-	4-7	-	1-1	7	1	-	-	4	9
Rob Gwyn	-	0-0	-	0-1	1	0	-	-	3	0
Garry Odom	-	0-2	-	0-1	2	0	-	-	4	0
Al Williams	-	0-1	-	0-0	1	0	-	-	4	0
TOTALS	**-**	**32-83**	**-**	**18-24**	**37**	**12**	**-**	**-**	**30**	**82**
Percentages		38.6		75.0						

Coach: Maury John

Officials: Fouty, DiTomasso
Attendance: 18,435

104-84 — 50 1H 39 / 54 2H 45 — 3RD PLACE

DRAKE	MIN	FG	3FG	FT	REB	A	ST	BL	PF	TP
Willie McCarter	39	12-20	-	4-5	6	11	-	-	3	28
Al Williams	34	8-13	-	0-1	8	1	-	-	4	16
Willie Wise	29	6-9	-	4-4	9	0	-	-	3	16
Rick Wanamaker	11	5-6	-	1-2	4	0	-	-	2	11
Dolph Pulliam	32	4-10	-	2-3	3	1	-	-	4	10
Gary Zeller	20	3-9	-	1-1	3	1	-	-	0	7
Don Draper	19	3-8	-	0-0	0	2	-	-	1	6
Garry Odom	11	2-2	-	0-0	3	0	-	-	3	4
Rob Gwyn	2	1-2	-	2-2	0	0	-	-	1	4
Dale Teeter	1	1-1	-	0-0	0	0	-	-	0	2
Bob Mast	1	0-0	-	0-0	0	0	-	-	1	0
Jim O'Dea	1	0-0	-	0-0	0	0	-	-	0	0
TOTALS	**200**	**45-80**	**-**	**14-18**	**36**	**16**	**-**	**-**	**22**	**104**
Percentages		56.2		77.8						

Coach: Maury John

NORTH CAROLINA	MIN	FG	3FG	FT	REB	A	ST	BL	PF	TP
Charlie Scott	35	16-26	-	3-6	4	1	-	-	2	35
Rusty Clark	39	2-9	-	8-10	12	3	-	-	1	12
Lee Dedmon	31	5-10	-	1-2	10	2	-	-	3	11
Bill Bunting	33	3-6	-	1-2	9	0	-	-	5	7
Eddie Fogler	32	3-7	-	1-3	4	5	-	-	1	7
Gerald Tuttle	6	1-3	-	2-2	0	0	-	-	1	4
Richard Tuttle	1	1-1	-	1-2	1	0	-	-	0	3
Jim Delany	10	0-2	-	2-2	1	1	-	-	2	2
Dave Chadwick	1	1-2	-	0-0	2	0	-	-	0	2
Dale Gipple	2	0-0	-	1-2	0	0	-	-	1	1
Joe Brown	9	0-2	-	0-0	2	0	-	-	1	0
Don Eggleston	1	0-0	-	0-0	0	0	-	-	0	0
TOTALS	**200**	**32-68**	**-**	**20-31**	**45**	**12**	**-**	**-**	**17**	**84**
Percentages		47.1		64.5						

Coach: Dean Smith

Officials: Overby, Fouty
Attendance: 18,669

92-72 — 42 1H 31 / 50 2H 41 — NCAA FINAL 1969

UCLA	MIN	FG	3FG	FT	REB	A	ST	BL	PF	TP
Lew Alcindor	36	15-20	-	7-9	20	0	-	-	2	37
John Vallely	31	4-9	-	7-10	4	0	-	-	3	15
Curtis Rowe	37	4-10	-	4-4	12	3	-	-	2	12
Lynn Shackelford	35	3-8	-	5-8	9	0	-	-	3	11
Bill Sweek	10	3-3	-	0-1	1	0	-	-	3	6
Steve Patterson	5	1-1	-	2-2	2	0	-	-	0	4
Sidney Wicks	6	0-1	-	3-6	4	1	-	-	1	3
Terry Schofield	3	1-2	-	0-0	0	0	-	-	0	2
John Ecker	1	1-1	-	0-0	0	0	-	-	0	2
Kenny Heitz	34	0-3	-	0-1	3	4	-	-	4	0
George Farmer	1	0-0	-	0-0	0	0	-	-	1	0
Bill Seibert	1	0-0	-	0-0	1	0	-	-	0	0
TOTALS	**200**	**32-58**	**-**	**28-41**	**56**	**8**	**-**	**-**	**19**	**92**
Percentages		55.2		68.3						

Coach: John Wooden

PURDUE	MIN	FG	3FG	FT	REB	A	ST	BL	PF	TP
Rick Mount	37	12-36	-	4-5	1	0	-	-	3	28
Bill Keller	32	4-17	-	3-4	4	3	-	-	5	11
Jerry Johnson	27	4-9	-	3-4	9	0	-	-	2	11
Herman Gilliam	32	2-14	-	3-3	11	3	-	-	2	7
Tyrone Bedford	25	3-8	-	1-3	8	0	-	-	3	7
Larry Weatherford	15	1-5	-	2-2	1	0	-	-	3	4
George Faerber	17	1-2	-	0-0	3	0	-	-	5	2
Frank Kaufman	13	0-0	-	2-2	5	0	-	-	5	2
Ted Reasoner	1	0-1	-	0-1	1	0	-	-	2	0
Ralph Taylor	1	0-0	-	0-0	0	0	-	-	0	0
TOTALS	**200**	**27-92**	**-**	**18-24**	**43**	**6**	**-**	**-**	**30**	**72**
Percentages		29.3		75.0						

Coach: George King

Officials: DiTomasso, Brown
Attendance: 18,669

National Invitation Tournament (NIT)

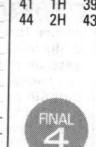

First round: Temple d. Florida 82-66, Saint Peter's d. Tulsa 75-71, Ohio d. West Texas A&M 82-80, Tennessee d. Rutgers 67-51, Army d. Wyoming 51-49, South Carolina d. Southern Illinois 72-63, Boston College d. Kansas 78-62, Louisville d. Fordham 73-70
Quarterfinals: Temple d. Saint Peter's 94-78, Tennessee d. Ohio, 75-64, Army d. South Carolina 59-45, Boston College d. Louisville 88-83
Semifinals: Temple d. Tennessee 63-58, Boston College d. Army 73-61
Third place: Tennessee d. Army 64-52
Championship: Temple d. Boston College 89-76
MVP: Terry Driscoll, Boston College

1969-70: FOUR FOR FOUR

The Final Four was more notable for who *wasn't* there. Lew Alcindor was in the NBA and LSU's Pete Maravich was in the NIT. During the season, Pistol Pete set NCAA Division I single-season records for most points (1,381) highest scoring average (44.5 ppg), career points (3,667) and scoring average (44.2 ppg), and was named Naismith National POY. He also secured a more dubious distinction: Maravich is the only three-time first-team All-America never to appear in the NCAA Tournament.

Even making the Final Four was no guarantee of getting to play in it. St. Bonaventure's 6'11" center, Bob Lanier, had to sit out the Bonnies' national semifinal game with Jacksonville, and the third-place game, because of a torn knee ligament. The Dolphins' 7'2" center, Artis Gilmore, took advantage of Lanier's absence, scoring 29 points and grabbing 21 rebounds.

In the championship game, UCLA used a balanced attack—four players scored 15 or more—and a remarkable performance by Sidney Wicks to win its fourth straight title, 80-69. Wicks scored 17 points and pulled down 18 rebounds and, despite giving up six inches to Gilmore, forced the Jacksonville giant into 9-for-29 shooting. The more things change, the more they stay the same—for UCLA, that is.

MAJOR CONFERENCE STANDINGS

ACC

	Conference			Overall		
	W	L	PCT	W	L	PCT
South Carolina	14	0	1.000	25	3	.893
NC State⊕	9	5	.643	23	7	.767
North Carolina□	9	5	.643	18	9	.667
Duke□	8	6	.571	17	9	.654
Wake Forest	6	8	.429	14	13	.519
Maryland	5	9	.357	13	13	.500
Virginia	3	11	.214	10	15	.400
Clemson	2	12	.143	7	19	.269

Tournament: **NC State d. South Carolina 42-39 (2OT)**
Tournament MVP: **Vann Williford**, NC State

BIG EIGHT

	Conference			Overall		
	W	L	PCT	W	L	PCT
Kansas State⊕	10	4	.714	20	8	.714
Kansas	8	6	.571	17	9	.654
Oklahoma□	7	7	.500	19	9	.679
Nebraska	7	7	.500	16	9	.640
Missouri	7	7	.500	15	11	.577
Colorado	7	7	.500	14	12	.538
Oklahoma State	5	9	.357	14	12	.538
Iowa State	5	9	.357	12	14	.462

BIG SKY

	Conference			Overall		
	W	L	PCT	W	L	PCT
Weber State⊕	12	3	.800	20	7	.741
Idaho State	11	4	.733	13	11	.542
Gonzaga	7	8	.467	10	16	.385
Idaho	6	9	.400	10	15	.400
Montana	5	10	.333	8	18	.308
Montana State	4	11	.267	4	22	.154

BIG TEN

	Conference			Overall		
	W	L	PCT	W	L	PCT
Iowa⊕	14	0	1.000	20	5	.800
Purdue	11	3	.786	18	6	.750
Ohio State	8	6	.571	17	7	.708
Illinois	8	6	.571	15	9	.625
Minnesota	7	7	.500	13	11	.542
Michigan	5	9	.357	10	14	.417
Wisconsin	5	9	.357	10	14	.417
Michigan State	5	9	.357	9	15	.375
Northwestern	4	10	.286	9	15	.375
Indiana	3	11	.214	7	17	.292

IVY

	Conference			Overall		
	W	L	PCT	W	L	PCT
Penn⊕	14	0	1.000	25	2	.926
Columbia	11	3	.786	20	5	.800
Princeton	9	5	.643	16	9	.640
Dartmouth	7	7	.500	13	12	.520
Yale	7	7	.500	11	13	.458
Cornell	4	10	.286	7	16	.304
Brown	3	11	.214	6	20	.231
Harvard	1	13	.071	7	19	.269

MID-AMERICAN

	Conference			Overall		
	W	L	PCT	W	L	PCT
Ohio⊕	9	1	.900	20	5	.800
Miami (OH)□	7	3	.700	16	8	.667
Bowling Green	7	3	.700	15	9	.625
Toledo	3	7	.300	15	9	.625
Kent State	2	8	.200	7	17	.292
Western Michigan	2	8	.200	6	17	.261

MIDDLE ATLANTIC

	Conference			Overall		
	W	L	PCT	W	L	PCT
Eastern						
Saint Joseph's	5	0	1.000	15	12	.556
La Salle	3	2	.600	14	12	.538
Temple⊕	2	3	.400	15	13	.536
Hofstra	2	3	.400	13	13	.500
American	2	3	.400	11	12	.478
West Chester	1	4	.200	11	15	.423
Western						
Rider	7	3	.700	16	10	.615
Lehigh	7	3	.700	13	14	.481
Lafayette	7	3	.700	12	14	.462
Delaware	6	4	.600	16	9	.640
Bucknell	3	7	.300	6	17	.261
Gettysburg	0	10	.000	8	18	.308

MISSOURI VALLEY

	Conference			Overall		
	W	L	PCT	W	L	PCT
Drake⊕	14	2	.875	22	7	.759
Cincinnati□	12	4	.750	21	6	.778
North Texas	11	5	.688	18	8	.692
Louisville□	11	5	.688	18	9	.667
Tulsa	8	8	.500	15	11	.577
Bradley	7	9	.438	14	12	.538
Saint Louis	5	11	.313	9	17	.346
Wichita State	3	13	.188	8	18	.308
Memphis	1	15	.063	6	20	.231

OHIO VALLEY

	Conference			Overall		
	W	L	PCT	W	L	PCT
Western Kentucky⊕	14	0	1.000	22	3	.880
Murray State	9	5	.643	17	9	.654
East Tennessee St.	8	6	.571	15	11	.577
Eastern Kentucky	8	6	.571	12	10	.545
Middle Tennessee St.	6	8	.429	15	11	.577
Morehead State	5	9	.357	13	11	.542
Tennessee Tech	4	10	.286	10	15	.400
Austin Peay	2	12	.143	5	21	.192

PCAA

	Conference			Overall		
	W	L	PCT	W	L	PCT
Long Beach State○	10	0	1.000	24	5	.828
Cal State LA	6	4	.600	18	8	.692
UC Santa Barbara	6	4	.600	12	14	.462
Fresno State	5	5	.500	14	12	.538
San Diego State	3	7	.300	13	13	.500
San Jose State	0	10	.000	3	21	.125

PAC-8

	Conference			Overall		
	W	L	PCT	W	L	PCT
UCLA⊕	12	2	.857	28	2	.933
Washington State	9	5	.643	19	7	.731
Southern California	9	5	.643	18	8	.692
Oregon	8	6	.571	17	9	.654
Washington	7	7	.500	17	9	.654
California	5	9	.357	11	15	.423
Oregon State	4	10	.286	10	16	.385
Stanford	2	12	.143	5	20	.200

SEC

	Conference			Overall		
	W	L	PCT	W	L	PCT
Kentucky⊕	17	1	.944	26	2	.929
LSU□	13	5	.722	22	10	.688
Auburn	11	7	.611	15	11	.577
Georgia	11	7	.611	13	12	.520
Tennessee	10	8	.556	16	9	.640
Vanderbilt	8	10	.444	12	14	.462
Mississippi	6	12	.333	10	15	.400
Florida	6	12	.333	9	17	.346
Alabama	5	13	.278	8	18	.308
Mississippi State	3	15	.167	6	18	.250

SOUTHERN

	Conference			Overall		
	W	L	PCT	W	L	PCT
Davidson⊕	10	0	1.000	22	5	.815
East Carolina	9	2	.818	16	10	.615
George Washington	6	4	.600	12	15	.444
Furman	5	6	.455	13	13	.500
William and Mary	5	7	.417	11	16	.407
The Citadel	4	8	.333	8	16	.333
Richmond	4	9	.308	9	18	.333
VMI	3	10	.231	6	19	.240

Tournament: **Davidson d. Richmond 81-61**
Tournament MOP: **Doug Cook**, Davidson

SOUTHLAND

	Conference			Overall		
	W	L	PCT	W	L	PCT
Lamar	7	1	.875	15	9	.625
Trinity (TX)	4	4	.500	16	8	.667
Arkansas State	4	4	.500	14	9	.609
Texas-Arlington	4	4	.500	8	16	.333
Abilene Christian	1	7	.125	10	16	.385

SOUTHWEST

	Conference			Overall		
	W	L	PCT	W	L	PCT
Rice⊕	10	4	.714	14	11	.560
Texas A&M	9	5	.643	14	10	.583
Baylor	8	6	.571	15	9	.625
Texas Tech	8	6	.571	14	10	.583
TCU	8	6	.571	10	14	.417
Texas	6	8	.429	11	13	.458
SMU	4	10	.286	5	19	.208
Arkansas	3	11	.214	5	19	.208

WCAC

	Conference			Overall		
	W	L	PCT	W	L	PCT
Santa Clara⊕	11	3	.786	23	6	.793
Pacific	11	3	.786	21	6	.778
UNLV	9	5	.643	17	9	.654
San Francisco	9	5	.643	15	11	.577
Pepperdine	7	7	.500	14	12	.538
Loyola Marymount	7	7	.500	13	13	.500
Nevada	2	12	.143	5	17	.227
Saint Mary's (CA)	0	14	.000	3	22	.120

WAC

	Conference			Overall		
	W	L	PCT	W	L	PCT
UTEP⊕	10	4	.714	17	8	.680
Wyoming	9	5	.643	19	7	.731
Utah□	9	5	.643	18	10	.643
Arizona	8	6	.571	12	14	.462
Colorado State	7	7	.500	14	9	.609
New Mexico	7	7	.500	13	13	.500
BYU	4	10	.286	8	18	.308
Arizona State	2	12	.143	4	22	.154

Conference Standings Continue →

⊕ Automatic NCAA Tournament bid ○ At-large NCAA Tournament bid □ NIT appearance ✪ Team record doesn't reflect games forfeited or vacated. For adjusted record, see p. 521.

YANKEE

	Conference W	L	Pct	Overall W	L	Pct
Massachusetts□	8	2	.800	18	7	.720
Connecticut	8	2	.800	14	9	.609
Rhode Island	7	3	.700	16	10	.615
New Hampshire	3	7	.300	12	11	.522
Vermont	3	7	.300	8	16	.333
Maine	1	9	.100	7	17	.292

INDEPENDENTS

	Overall W	L	Pct
Jacksonville○	27	2	.931
New Mexico State ○	27	3	.900
Marquette□	26	3	.897
St. Bonaventure○	25	3	.893
Florida State	23	3	.885
Houston○	25	5	.833
Army□	22	6	.786
Niagara○	22	7	.759
Utah State○	22	7	.759
Villanova○	22	7	.759
Notre Dame○	21	8	.724
St. John's□	21	8	.724
Georgetown□	18	7	.720
Duquesne□	17	7	.708
Dayton○	19	8	.704
Manhattan□	18	8	.692
Hardin-Simmons	17	9	.654
Holy Cross	16	9	.640
Long Island	16	9	.640
Georgia Tech□	17	10	.630
Creighton	15	10	.600
Seattle	15	10	.600
Boston U.	14	10	.583
Butler	15	11	.577
Oklahoma City	17	13	.567
Fairleigh Dickinson	13	10	.565
Southern Illinois	13	10	.565
Colgate	14	11	.560
Providence	14	11	.560
Denver	13	11	.542

INDEPENDENTS (CONT.)

	Overall W	L	Pct
Loyola-Chicago	13	11	.542
Penn State	13	11	.542
Rutgers	13	11	.542
Saint Peter's	13	11	.542
Northern Illinois	13	12	.520
Fairfield	13	13	.500
Air Force	12	12	.500
Iona	12	12	.500
NYU	12	12	.500
Pittsburgh	12	12	.500
Saint Francis (PA)	12	12	.500
Syracuse	12	12	.500
DePaul	12	13	.480
Loyola (LA)	12	14	.462
Boston College	11	13	.458
Virginia Tech	10	12	.455
St. Francis (NY)	9	12	.429
West Virginia	11	15	.423
Canisius	9	13	.409
Fordham	10	15	.400
Seton Hall	10	15	.400
Marshall	9	14	.391
Miami (FL)	9	17	.346
Centenary	8	16	.333
Texas-Pan American	8	16	.333
Detroit	7	18	.280
Tulane	5	18	.217
Xavier	5	20	.200
Navy	4	19	.174

INDIVIDUAL LEADERS—SEASON

Scoring

	CL	POS	G	FG	FT	PTS	PPG
1 **Pete Maravich**, LSU	SR	G	31	522	337	1,381	**44.5**
2 **Austin Carr**, Notre Dame	JR	G	29	444	218	1,106	**38.1**
3 **Rick Mount**, Purdue	SR	G	20	285	138	708	**35.4**
4 **Dan Issel**, Kentucky	SR	C	28	369	210	948	**33.9**
5 **Willie Humes**, Idaho State	JR	G	24	278	177	733	**30.5**
6 **Rich Yunkus**, Georgia Tech	JR	G	27	317	180	814	**30.1**
7 **Rudy Tomjanovich**, Michigan	SR	C	24	286	150	722	**30.1**
8 **Calvin Murphy**, Niagara	SR	G	29	316	222	854	**29.4**
9 **Bob Lanier**, St. Bonaventure	SR	C	26	308	141	757	**29.1**
10 **Ralph Simpson**, Michigan State	SO	G	23	264	139	667	**29.0**

Field Goal Pct

	CL	POS	G	FG	FGA	PCT
1 **Willie Williams**, Florida State	SR	F	26	185	291	**63.6**
2 **Bob Lienhard**, Georgia	SR	C	25	215	340	**63.2**
3 **Vic Bartolome**, Oregon State	SR	C	26	178	286	**62.2**
4 **William Chatmon**, Baylor	JR	F/C	24	207	345	**60.0**
5 **Jim Cleamons**, Ohio State	JR	G	24	211	353	**59.8**

Minimum: 140 made

Free Throw Pct

	CL	POS	G	FT	FTA	PCT
1 **Steve Kaplan**, Rutgers	SO	F	23	102	110	**92.7**
2 **Jimmy England**, Tennessee	JR	G	25	131	146	**89.7**
3 **Jody Finney**, Ohio State	SR	G	23	119	134	**88.8**
4 **Calvin Murphy**, Niagara	SR	G	29	222	252	**88.1**
5 **Charlie Davis**, Wake Forest	JR	G	26	196	224	**87.5**
Glenn Vidnovic, Iowa	SR	G	25	133	152	**87.5**

Minimum: 100 made

Rebounds Per Game

	CL	POS	G	REB	RPG
1 **Artis Gilmore**, Jacksonville	JR	C	28	621	**22.2**
2 **Julius Erving**, Massachusetts	SO	F	25	522	**20.9**
3 **Pete Cross**, San Francisco	SR	C	26	467	**18.0**
4 **Dave Cowens**, Florida State	SR	C	26	447	**17.2**
5 **Gordon Stiles**, American	SR	C	22	378	**17.2**

INDIVIDUAL LEADERS—GAME

Points

	CL	POS	OPP	DATE	PTS
1 **Pete Maravich**, LSU	SR	G	Alabama	F7	**69**
2 **Pete Maravich**, LSU	SR	G	Kentucky	F21	**64**
3 **Austin Carr**, Notre Dame	JR	G	Ohio	M7	**61**
Pete Maravich, LSU	SR	G	Vanderbilt	D11	**61**
Rick Mount, Purdue	SR	G	Iowa	F2	**61**

TEAM LEADERS—SEASON

Win-Loss Pct

	W	L	PCT
1 **UCLA**	28	2	**.933**
2 **Jacksonville**	27	2	**.931**
3 **Kentucky**	26	2	**.929**
4 **Penn**	25	2	**.926**
5 **New Mexico State**	27	3	**.900**

Scoring Offense

	G	W-L	PTS	PPG
1 **Iowa**	25	20-5	2,467	**98.7**
2 **Jacksonville**	29	27-2	2,809	**96.9**
3 **Kentucky**	28	26-2	2,709	**96.8**
4 **Saint Peter's**	24	13-11	2,247	**93.6**
5 **Notre Dame**	29	21-8	2,711	**93.5**

Scoring Margin

	G	W-L	PPG	OPP PPG	MAR
1 **St. Bonaventure**	28	25-3	88.4	65.9	**22.5**
2 **Jacksonville**	29	27-2	100.3	78.5	**21.8**
3 **UCLA**	30	28-2	92.0	73.4	**18.6**
4 **South Carolina**	28	25-3	74.0	57.4	**16.6**
5 **Florida State**	26	23-3	91.7	75.2	**16.5**

Field Goal Pct

	G	W-L	FG	FGA	PCT
1 **Ohio State**	24	17-7	831	1,527	**54.4**
2 **Jacksonville**	29	27-2	1,118	2,137	**52.3**
3 **Iowa**	25	20-5	959	1,834	**52.3**
4 **Georgia Tech**	27	17-10	841	1,647	**51.1**
5 **Columbia**	25	20-5	748	1,481	**50.5**

Rebounds Per Game

	G	W-L	G	REB	RPG
1 **Florida State**	26	23-3	26	1,451	**55.8**
2 **Western Kentucky**	25	22-3	25	1,386	**55.4**
3 **UNLV**	26	17-9	26	1,421	**54.7**
4 **New Mexico State**	30	27-3	30	1,632	**54.4**
5 **Seton Hall**	25	10-15	25	1,356	**54.2**

Scoring Defense

	G	W-L	OPP PTS	OPP PPG
1 **Army**	28	22-6	1,515	**54.1**
2 **South Carolina**	28	25-3	1,606	**57.4**
3 **Fairleigh Dickinson**	23	13-10	1,409	**61.3**
4 **Long Island**	25	16-9	1,532	**61.3**
5 **Miami (OH)**	24	16-8	1,497	**62.4**

CONSENSUS ALL-AMERICAS

FIRST TEAM

PLAYER	CL	POS	HT	SCHOOL	RPG	PPG
Dan Issel	SR	C	6-8	Kentucky	13.2	33.9
Bob Lanier	SR	C	6-11	St. Bonaventure	16.0	29.1
Pete Maravich	SR	G	6-5	LSU	5.3	44.5
Rick Mount	SR	G	6-4	Purdue	2.7	35.4
Calvin Murphy	SR	G	5-9	Niagara	3.6	29.4

SECOND TEAM

PLAYER	CL	POS	HT	SCHOOL	RPG	PPG
Austin Carr	JR	G	6-3	Notre Dame	8.3	38.1
Jimmy Collins	SR	G	6-2	New Mexico State	4.6	24.3
John Roche	JR	G	6-3	South Carolina	2.5	22.3
Charlie Scott	SR	G/F	6-5	North Carolina	7.1	27.1
Sidney Wicks	JR	F	6-8	UCLA	11.9	18.6

Selectors: AP, UPI, NABC, USBWA

AWARD WINNERS

PLAYER OF THE YEAR

PLAYER	CL	POS	HT	SCHOOL	AWARDS
Pete Maravich	SR	G	6-5	LSU	Naismith, AP, UPI, USBWA
John Rinka	SR	G	5-9	Kenyon	Frances Pomeroy Naismith*

* For the most outstanding senior player who is 6 feet or under

COACH OF THE YEAR

COACH	SCHOOL	REC	AWARDS
John Wooden	UCLA	28-2	AP, UPI, USBWA, NABC
Adolph Rupp	Kentucky	26-2	Sporting News

Poll Progression

Preseason Poll

AP	UPI	SCHOOL
1	2	South Carolina
2	3	Kentucky
3	4	Purdue
4	1	UCLA
5	8	Davidson
6	5	New Mexico State
7	7	North Carolina
8	13	Marquette
9	15	Villanova
10	6	Colorado
11	10	Duquesne
12	11	Santa Clara
13	—	Notre Dame
14	14	St. John's
15	19	Louisville
16	9	USC
17	16	St. Bonaventure
18	—	Ohio State
19	—	Drake
20	—	Houston
—	12	Kansas
—	17	Arizona
—	17	New Mexico
—	20	La Salle

Week of Dec 9

AP	UPI	SCHOOL	AP↓↑
1	1	Kentucky (2-0)	↑1
2	2	UCLA (2-0)	↑2
3	3	New Mexico State (3-0)	↑3
4	7	Davidson (2-0)	↑1
5	8	North Carolina (2-0)	↑2
6	5	USC (2-0)	↑10
7	5	Duquesne (3-0)	↑4
8	4	South Carolina (1-1) Ⓐ	↓7
9	9	Tennessee (1-0)	⤴
10	16	Notre Dame (3-0)	↑3
11	12	Louisville (1-0)	↑4
12	10	Villanova (2-0)	↓3
12	14	Marquette (2-0)	↓4
14	15	Purdue (1-1)	↓11
15	12	Santa Clara (2-0)	↓3
16	10	Ohio State (2-0)	↑2
17	18	Colorado (3-1)	↓7
18	20	Jacksonville (2-0) Ⓑ	⤴
19	—	Ohio (2-0)	⤴
20	20	St. Bonaventure (1-0)	↓3
—	17	Illinois (2-0)	
—	19	Western Kentucky (2-3)	

Week of Dec 16

AP	UPI	SCHOOL	AP↓↑
1	1	Kentucky (4-0)	
2	2	UCLA (4-0)	
3	3	New Mexico State (6-0)	
4	6	Davidson (2-0)	
5	4	South Carolina (4-1)	↑3
6	7	Notre Dame (5-0)	↑4
7	9	North Carolina (3-1)	↓2
8	11	Tennessee (2-0)	↑1
9	10	Villanova (3-0)	↑3
10	12	Ohio (3-0)	↑9
11	8	Santa Clara (4-0)	↑4
12	—	Purdue (3-1)	↑2
13	4	USC (3-1)	↓7
14	—	Louisville (2-1)	↓3
15	17	LSU (4-0)	⤴
16	13	Colorado (5-1)	↑1
17	—	Marquette (4-1)	↓5
18	19	Jacksonville (4-0)	
19	20	Houston (5-0)	⤴
20	15	Washington (4-0)	⤴
—	14	Illinois (4-0)	
—	16	St. Bonaventure (2-0)	⤵
—	18	Dayton (3-0)	

Week of Dec 23

AP	UPI	SCHOOL	AP↓↑
1	1	Kentucky (6-0)	
2	2	UCLA (4-0)	
3	3	South Carolina (6-1)	↑2
4	4	North Carolina (5-1)	↑3
5	8	Ohio (6-0)	↑5
6	6	Tennessee (4-0)	↑2
7	7	New Mexico State (8-1)	↓4
8	5	Houston (8-0)	↑11
9	16	Davidson (3-1)	↓5
10	11	Washington (6-0)	↑10
11	13	Notre Dame (6-1)	↓5
12	14	USC (4-2)	↑1
13	19	Jacksonville (5-0)	↑5
14	—	Louisville (3-1)	
15	12	Illinois (6-0)	⤴
16	9	Kansas (6-1)	⤴
17	—	Penn (6-0)	⤴
18	—	Purdue (5-2)	↓6
19	10	St. Bonaventure (4-0)	⤴
20	15	Villanova (3-1)	↓11
—	17	St. John's (5-1)	
—	18	Wyoming (7-0)	
—	19	Marquette (5-1)	⤵

Week of Dec 30

AP	UPI	SCHOOL	AP↓↑
1	1	Kentucky (7-0)	
2	2	UCLA (6-0)	
3	3	South Carolina (6-1)	
4	4	North Carolina (6-1)	
5	5	Ohio (7-0)	
6	11	Tennessee (5-0)	
7	8	New Mexico State (10-1)	
8	9	Houston (9-0)	
9	6	Washington (7-0)	↑1
10	10	Jacksonville (8-0)	↑3
11	16	Davidson (4-1)	↓2
12	7	St. Bonaventure (5-0)	↑7
13	12	Notre Dame (6-2)	↓2
14	13	Penn (7-0)	↑3
15	—	Columbia (8-0)	⤴
15	—	NC State (9-0)	⤴
17	18	Purdue (6-2)	↑1
18	17	Marquette (8-1)	⤴
19	18	USC (5-3)	↓7
20	20	Colorado (6-3)	⤴
—	14	Wyoming (7-0)	
—	15	Kansas (6-2)	⤵

Week of Jan 6

AP	UPI	SCHOOL	AP↓↑
1	1	UCLA (8-0)	↑1
2	2	Kentucky (9-0)	↓1
3	3	South Carolina (8-1)	
4	5	North Carolina (9-1)	
5	4	St. Bonaventure (8-0)	↑7
6	6	New Mexico State (12-1)	↑1
7	7	Jacksonville (9-0)	↑3
8	14	Davidson (7-1)	↑3
9	9	Ohio (9-1)	↓4
10	12	NC State (10-0)	↑5
11	8	Houston (11-1)	↓3
12	10	Tennessee (7-1)	↓6
13	13	Marquette (9-1)	↑5
14	11	Washington (9-2)	↓5
15	—	Niagara (10-0)	⤴
16	16	Oklahoma (10-1)	⤴
17	15	Columbia (11-1)	↓2
18	—	Penn (8-1)	↓4
19	—	Duke (8-1)	⤴
20	—	Louisville (5-2)	⤴
—	17	Oregon (7-2)	
—	17	Santa Clara (8-2)	
—	17	Utah (9-3)	
—	20	Washington State (9-2)	
—	20	Wyoming (8-1)	

Week of Jan 13

AP	UPI	SCHOOL	AP↓↑
1	1	UCLA (10-0)	
2	2	Kentucky (11-0)	
3	3	South Carolina (10-1)	
4	4	St. Bonaventure (10-0)	↑1
5	5	New Mexico State (14-1)	↑1
6	7	Jacksonville (12-0)	↑1
7	6	North Carolina (11-2)	↓3
8	9	Davidson (10-1)	
9	8	Houston (12-1)	↑2
10	10	Marquette (11-1)	↑3
11	—	NC State (11-1)	↓1
12	20	Niagara (11-0)	↑3
13	14	Columbia (13-1)	↑4
14	11	Ohio (9-2)	↓5
15	13	Washington (10-2)	↓1
16	16	Penn (11-1)	↑3
17	12	Illinois (10-2)	⤴
18	—	Louisville (7-2)	↑2
19	—	Duke (9-2)	
20	16	USC (10-3)	⤴
—	15	UTEP (9-2)	
—	18	Utah (11-3)	
—	18	Wyoming (9-2)	

Week of Jan 20

AP	UPI	SCHOOL	AP↓↑
1	1	UCLA (12-0)	
2	2	Kentucky (13-0)	
3	3	South Carolina (12-1)	
4	4	St. Bonaventure (10-0)	
5	5	New Mexico State (15-1)	
6	6	Jacksonville (13-0)	
7	7	Houston (12-1)	↑2
8	8	Marquette (12-1)	↑2
9	10	North Carolina (12-3)	↓2
10	19	NC State (12-1)	↑1
11	11	Davidson (11-2)	↓3
12	9	Illinois (12-2)	↑5
13	12	Ohio (11-2)	↑1
14	16	Penn (12-1)	↑1
15	15	USC (10-3)	↑5
16	—	Duke (9-2)	↑3
17	—	Kansas State (12-3)	⤴
18	—	Iowa (8-3)	⤴
18	—	Louisville (7-4)	
20	—	Notre Dame (11-4)	⤴
—	13	UTEP (11-2)	
—	14	Columbia (13-2)	⤵
—	16	Santa Clara (12-2)	
—	18	Wyoming (11-2)	
—	20	Drake (12-4)	
—	20	Utah (11-4)	

Week of Jan 27

AP	UPI	SCHOOL	AP↓↑
1	1	UCLA (14-0)	
2	2	Kentucky (14-0)	
3	3	St. Bonaventure (12-0)	↑1
4	4	South Carolina (12-1)	↓1
5	5	New Mexico State (16-1)	
6	6	Jacksonville (13-0)	
7	7	Marquette (13-1)	↑1
8	12	NC State (13-1)	↑2
9	8	North Carolina (12-3)	
10	9	Illinois (12-2)	↑2
11	11	Davidson (13-2)	
12	10	Houston (12-2)	↓5
13	15	Ohio (12-2)	
14	16	Penn (14-1)	
15	14	USC (11-3)	
16	18	Drake (13-4)	⤴
17	—	Columbia (13-2)	⤴
18	—	Florida State (14-2)	⤴
19	—	Kansas State (12-3)	↓2
20	—	Iowa (8-4)	↓2
—	13	Utah (12-4)	
—	16	UTEP (11-3)	
—	19	Santa Clara (13-2)	
—	20	Western Kentucky (12-2)	

Week of Feb 3

AP	UPI	SCHOOL	AP↓↑
1	1	UCLA (16-0)	
2	2	South Carolina (15-1)	↑2
3	3	Kentucky (15-1)	↓1
4	4	St. Bonaventure (13-1) Ⓒ	↓1
5	7	NC State (15-1)	↑3
6	5	New Mexico State (17-2)	↓1
7	6	North Carolina (13-3)	↑2
8	8	Jacksonville (14-1)	↓2
9	10	Marquette (14-2)	↓2
10	14	Penn (16-1)	↑4
11	13	USC (13-3)	↑4
12	17	Florida State (16-2)	↑6
13	11	Drake (15-4)	↑3
14	9	Illinois (12-3)	↓4
15	16	Davidson (14-3)	↓4
16	20	Houston (14-3)	↓4
17	20	Columbia (14-2)	
18	15	Kansas State (14-3)	↑1
19	—	Villanova (12-5) Ⓒ	⤴
20	—	Iowa (9-4)	
—	12	Utah (14-4)	
—	18	Santa Clara (14-2)	
—	18	Utah State (13-3)	

Week of Feb 10

AP	UPI	SCHOOL	AP↓↑
1	1	UCLA (17-0)	
2	2	South Carolina (17-1)	
3	3	Kentucky (17-1)	
4	4	St. Bonaventure (15-1)	
5	6	NC State (17-1)	
6	5	New Mexico State (18-2)	
7	7	Jacksonville (17-1)	↑1
8	9	Penn (19-1)	↑2
9	19	Florida State (18-2)	↑3
10	8	North Carolina (14-4)	↓3
11	10	Drake (16-4)	↑2
12	15	Marquette (14-3)	↓3
13	11	Davidson (16-3)	↑2
14	11	Iowa (11-4)	↑6
15	13	Houston (16-3)	↑1
16	15	Notre Dame (14-5)	⤴
17	18	Western Kentucky (15-2)	⤴
18	—	USC (13-4)	↓7
19	—	Columbia (16-3)	↓2
20	—	Georgia (11-6)	⤴
—	14	Wyoming (15-4)	
—	17	Santa Clara (15-3)	
—	20	Illinois (12-5)	⤵
—	20	Ohio (15-3)	

Week of Feb 17

AP	UPI	SCHOOL	AP↓↑
1	1	UCLA (20-0)	
2	2	Kentucky (19-1)	↑1
3	4	St. Bonaventure (17-1)	↑1
4	3	South Carolina (19-2)	↓2
5	5	New Mexico State (20-2)	↑1
6	6	Jacksonville (19-1)	↑1
7	7	Penn (21-1)	↑1
8	11	Florida State (20-2)	↑1
9	10	Davidson (18-3)	↑4
10	15	Marquette (17-3)	↑2
11	9	Iowa (13-4)	↑3
12	8	NC State (18-3)	↓7
13	13	North Carolina (16-5)	↓3
14	16	Notre Dame (16-5)	↑2
15	14	Houston (18-3)	
16	18	Western Kentucky (17-2)	↑1
17	12	Drake (17-5)	↓6
18	—	Kansas State (16-5)	⤴
19	—	Louisville (15-4)	⤴
20	—	Santa Clara (17-3)	⤴
—	16	Utah (16-6)	
—	19	Utah State (15-4)	
—	20	Columbia (18-3)	⤵

Poll Progression Continues →

Week of Feb 24

AP	UPI	SCHOOL		AP↓↑
1	2	**Kentucky** (21-1)	Ⓓ	↑1
2	1	**UCLA** (21-1)	Ⓔ	↓1
3	4	**St. Bonaventure** (19-1)		
4	3	**South Carolina** (21-2)		
5	5	**New Mexico State** (21-2)		
6	6	**Jacksonville** (21-1)		
7	7	**Penn** (23-1)		
8	10	**Marquette** (18-3)		↑2
9	8	**Iowa** (15-4)		↑2
10	9	**Florida State** (21-3)		↓2
11	13	**Davidson** (19-4)		↓2
12	16	**Western Kentucky** (19-2)		↑4
13	15	**Notre Dame** (19-5)		↑1
14	11	**NC State** (19-4)		↓2
15	11	**Houston** (20-3)		
16	14	**Drake** (19-5)		↑1
17	20	**Kansas State** (18-5)		↑1
18	16	**Columbia** (20-3)		⤴
19	16	**North Carolina** (17-6)		↓6
20	—	**Utah State** (17-5)		⤴
—	19	**Utah** (17-7)		

Week of Mar 3

AP	UPI	SCHOOL		AP↓↑
1	1	**UCLA** (23-1)		↑1
2	2	**Kentucky** (23-1)	Ⓕ	↓1
3	3	**South Carolina** (23-2)		↑1
4	4	**St. Bonaventure** (20-1)		↓1
5	5	**New Mexico State** (23-2)		
6	6	**Jacksonville** (22-1)		
7	8	**Penn** (25-1)		
8	7	**Iowa** (17-4)	Ⓖ	↑1
9	10	**Marquette** (20-3)		↓1
10	13	**Davidson** (22-4)		↑1
11	12	**Florida State** (23-3)		↓1
12	15	**Western Kentucky** (21-2)		
13	11	**Houston** (22-3)		↑2
14	9	**Drake** (20-6)		↑2
15	18	**Notre Dame** (20-6)		↓2
16	—	**Kansas State** (19-6)		↑1
17	—	**Ohio** (20-4)		⤴
18	—	**Utah State** (19-6)		↑2
19	16	**NC State** (19-6)		↓5
19	17	**Cincinnati** (20-4)		⤴
—	14	**UTEP** (17-6)		
—	19	**North Carolina** (18-7)		⤵
—	20	**Villanova** (19-6)		

Final Poll

AP	UPI	SCHOOL	AP↓↑
1	1	**Kentucky** (25-1)	↑1
2	2	**UCLA** (24-2)	↓1
3	3	**St. Bonaventure** (23-1)	↑1
4	5	**Jacksonville** (24-1)	↑2
5	4	**New Mexico State** (24-2)	
6	6	**South Carolina** (25-3)	↓3
7	7	**Iowa** (19-4)	↑1
8	10	**Marquette** (22-3)	↑1
9	8	**Notre Dame** (21-6)	↑6
10	12	**NC State** (22-6)	↑9
11	14	**Florida State** (23-3)	
12	11	**Houston** (25-3)	↑1
13	13	**Penn** (25-2)	↓6
14	9	**Drake** (21-6)	
15	—	**Davidson** (22-5)	↓5
16	17	**Utah State** (21-6)	↑2
17	17	**Niagara** (22-5)	⤴
18	17	**Western Kentucky** (22-3)	↓6
19	15	**Long Beach State** (24-3)	⤴
20	—	**USC** (18-8)	⤴
—	15	**Villanova** (21-6)	
—	20	**Cincinnati** (21-5)	⤵
—	20	**UTEP** (17-7)	

Ⓐ South Carolina falls to No. 8 after losing to Tennessee, 55-54, and goes on to become the first team ranked No. 1 in the preseason AP to never reach the top spot again during the season. (In 1977-78, UNC will double South Carolina's dubious feat by being ranked No. 1 in both preseason polls and not returning to the top spot in either.)

Ⓑ Jacksonville, with 7-footers Artis Gilmore and Pembrook Burrows, demolishes Mercer 102-62. The Dolphins will lose only once before the NCAA Final and become the first team in NCAA history to average more than 100 points a game for the season.

Ⓒ Villanova beats St. Bonaventure, 64-62, as Bob Lanier manages just six first-half points. The Bonnies will not lose again until the Final Four.

Ⓓ In Pete Maravich's final home game, LSU falls to Kentucky, 121-105. Maravich and Wildcat Dan Issel light up the scoreboard for 64 and 51, respectively. Their combined 115 is the highest total scored by two opposing players in a matchup of D1 teams.

Ⓔ UCLA falls to Oregon, with Rusty Blair's five straight field goals helping to seal the upset. It's only the third loss in 110 games for the Bruins.

Ⓕ Kentucky's Dan Issel becomes the first Wildcat to score 2,000 career points during a 90-86 victory over Vanderbilt.

Ⓖ Purdue's Rick Mount sets a Big Ten record by pouring in 61 points against Iowa on 27-of-47 shooting. The Hawkeyes nevertheless hold on for a 108-107 victory.

1970 NCAA Tournament

East

First Round (A)
- St. Bonaventure **85**, Davidson **72**
- NC State (bye)
- Villanova **77**, Temple **69**
- Niagara **79**, Pennsylvania **69**

Regional Semifinals
- St. Bonaventure **80**, NC State **68**
- Villanova **98**, Niagara **73**

Regional Finals
- St. Bonaventure **97**, Villanova **74** (B)

Mideast

First Round
- Jacksonville **109**, Western Kentucky **96**
- Iowa (bye)
- Kentucky (bye)
- Notre Dame **112**, Ohio **82** (C)

Regional Semifinals
- Jacksonville **104**, Iowa **103**
- Kentucky **109**, Notre Dame **99** (D)

Regional Finals
- Jacksonville **106**, Kentucky **100** (E)

Midwest

First Round
- New Mexico State **101**, Rice **77**
- Kansas State (bye)
- Drake (bye)
- Houston **71**, Dayton **64**

Regional Semifinals
- New Mexico State **70**, Kansas State **66**
- Drake **92**, Houston **87**

Regional Finals
- New Mexico State **87**, Drake **78**

West

First Round
- UCLA (bye)
- Long Beach State **92**, Weber State **73**
- Utah State **91**, UTEP **81** (F)
- Santa Clara (bye)

Regional Semifinals
- UCLA **88**, Long Beach State **65**
- Utah State **69**, Santa Clara **68**

Regional Finals
- UCLA **101**, Utah State **79**

National Semifinals
- St. Bonaventure **83**, Jacksonville **91**
- New Mexico State **77**, UCLA **93**

National Final
UCLA 80
Jacksonville 69

College Park, MD

National Third Place New Mexico State d. St. Bonaventure 79-73
East Regional Third Place NC State d. Niagara 108-88
Mideast Regional Third Place Iowa d. Notre Dame 121-106
Midwest Regional Third Place Kansas State d. Houston 107-98
West Regional Third Place Santa Clara d. Long Beach State 89-86

A Angry because the NCAA would have placed Marquette in the Midwest rather than the Mideast region, coach Al McGuire takes his Warriors to the NIT, where Dean "the Dream" Meminger leads them to the championship over St. John's.

B The win is costly for the Bonnies as star center Bob Lanier tears a knee ligament in a collision with the Wildcats' Chris Ford. Lanier is forced to sit out St. Bonaventure's next two games.

C Notre Dame's Austin Carr sets the Tournament single-game record with 61 points. In three games, Carr scores 158 points (52.7 ppg), blowing by Jerry Chambers' 1966 single-Tournament scoring average of 35.8 ppg.

Artis Gilmore, Jacksonville's 7'2" center, dominates the Lanier-less Bonnies with 29 points and 21 rebounds. Four players foul out trying to stop Gilmore and 7-foot teammate Pembrook Burrows.

Sidney Wicks scores 17 points and grabs 18 rebounds as well as the Tournament MOP award. The 6'8" Wicks also does a great job defending the much taller Gilmore; although he starts the game fronting Jacksonville's star, Wicks moves behind him halfway through the first half and ends up blocking four of Gilmore's shots.

John Wooden brings his Bruins to College Park a day earlier than the other Final Four teams to acclimate them to the time difference from LA. It works (as if they really need the help): UCLA shoots 55.6% from the floor.

D At a press gathering, a Chicago sportswriter questions both coaches on whether Kentucky played a "patsy" regular-season schedule. After beating Notre Dame, Adolph Rupp says of the sportswriter, "I might point out to him how our patsy schedule proved a little tough on us tonight."

E As 6'8" Kentucky center Dan Issel is trotting up the floor looking backwards after a Jacksonville basket, the Dolphins' 5'10" Vaughn Wedeking plants himself in Issel's path and gets run over. Issel is whistled for his fifth foul, ending the career of Kentucky's all-time leading scorer.

F With Utah State's lead cut to four, UTEP coach Don Haskins draws two technical fouls. Utah State converts both free throws and scores on the next possession, icing the win. UTEP's Nate Archibald scores 36 points in his only Tournament game.

Tournament Leaders

INDIVIDUAL LEADERS

Scoring

		CL	POS	G	PTS	PPG
1	**Austin Carr**, Notre Dame	JR	G	3	158	52.7
2	**Dan Issel**, Kentucky	SR	C	2	72	36.0
3	**Vann Williford**, NC State	SR	F	2	71	35.5
4	**Dennis Awtrey**, Santa Clara	SR	F	2	61	30.5
5	**Calvin Murphy**, Niagara	SR	G	3	88	29.3
6	**Artis Gilmore**, Jacksonville	JR	C	5	132	26.4
7	**Marvin Roberts**, Utah State	JR	F/C	3	79	26.3
8	**Bob Lanier**, St. Bonaventure	SR	C	3	78	26.0
	Chad Calabria, Iowa	SR	G	2	52	26.0
10	**John Johnson**, Iowa	SR	F	2	50	25.0

Minimum: 2 games

Field Goal Pct

		CL	POS	G	FG	FGA	PCT
1	**Pembrook Burrows**, Jacksonville	JR	F/C	5	24	33	72.7
	Dennis Awtrey, Santa Clara	SR	F	2	24	33	72.7
3	**Rick Anheuser**, NC State	JR	F	2	15	21	71.4
4	**Sidney Wicks**, UCLA	JR	F	4	33	49	67.3
5	**Terry Mills**, Kentucky	JR	G	2	12	18	66.7

Minimum: 10 made

Free Throw Pct

		CL	POS	G	FT	FTA	PCT
1	**Chip Dublin**, Jacksonville	JR	G	5	19	20	95.0
2	**Bill Kalbaugh**, St. Bonaventure	SR	G	5	13	14	92.9
	Jeff Halliburton, Drake	JR	G/F	2	13	14	92.9
4	**Calvin Murphy**, Niagara	SR	G	3	20	22	90.9
	Paul Jeppesen, Utah State	SR	G	3	10	11	90.9
	Nate Archibald, UTEP	SR	G	1	10	11	90.9

Minimum: 10 made

Rebounds Per Game

		CL	POS	G	REB	RPG
1	**David Hall**, Kansas State	SO	F/C	2	40	20.0
2	**Artis Gilmore**, Jacksonville	JR	C	5	93	18.6
3	**Sam Lacey**, New Mexico State	SR	C	5	90	18.0
4	**Bob Lanier**, St. Bonaventure	SR	C	3	48	16.0
5	**Marvin Roberts**, Utah State	JR	F/C	3	47	15.7

Minimum: 2 games

TEAM LEADERS

Scoring

		G	PTS	PPG
1	**Iowa**	2	224	112.0
2	**Notre Dame**	3	317	105.7
3	**Kentucky**	2	209	104.5
4	**Jacksonville**	5	479	95.8
5	**UCLA**	4	362	90.5
6	**NC State**	2	176	88.0
7	**Kansas State**	2	173	86.5
8	**Houston**	3	256	85.3
9	**Drake**	2	170	85.0
10	**St. Bonaventure**	5	418	83.6

Minimum: 2 games

FG Pct

		G	FG	FGA	PCT
1	**Iowa**	2	94	181	51.9
2	**Kentucky**	2	83	161	51.5
3	**Jacksonville**	5	180	358	50.3
4	**Notre Dame**	3	130	262	49.6
5	**UCLA**	4	135	273	49.5

FT Pct

		G	FT	FTA	PCT
1	**Long Beach State**	3	49	62	79.0
2	**Niagara**	3	56	72	77.8
3	**Utah State**	3	55	72	76.4
4	**Notre Dame**	3	57	76	75.0
5	**Kentucky**	2	43	58	74.1

Minimum: 2 games

Rebounds

		G	REB	RPG
1	**Kansas State**	2	123	61.5
2	**New Mexico State**	5	243	48.6
3	**UCLA**	4	193	48.3
4	**Villanova**	3	140	46.7
5	**Utah State**	3	139	46.3

Minimum: 2 games

ALL-TOURNAMENT TEAM

PLAYER	CL	POS	HT	SCHOOL	RPG	PPG
Sidney Wicks*	JR	F	6-8	UCLA	13.3	21.3
Jimmy Collins	SR	G	6-2	New Mexico State	2.8	23.4
Artis Gilmore	JR	C	7-2	Jacksonville	18.6	26.4
Curtis Rowe	JR	F	6-6	UCLA	12.5	18.8
John Vallely	SR	G	6-2	UCLA	4.8	16.5

ALL-REGIONAL TEAMS

EAST

PLAYER	CL	POS	HT	SCHOOL	RPG	PPG
Bob Lanier*	SR	C	6-11	St. Bonaventure	16.0	26.0
Matt Gantt	SO	F	6-5	St. Bonaventure	15.0	17.7
Calvin Murphy	SR	G	5-9	Niagara	6.3	29.3
Howard Porter	JR	F	6-8	Villanova	13.7	20.3
Vann Williford	SR	F	6-6	NC State	11.5	35.5

MIDEAST

PLAYER	CL	POS	HT	SCHOOL	RPG	PPG
Austin Carr*	JR	G	6-3	Notre Dame	8.0	52.7
Fred Brown	JR	G	6-3	Iowa	5.0	21.5
Artis Gilmore	JR	C	7-2	Jacksonville	18.7	28.0
Dan Issel	SR	C	6-8	Kentucky	10.5	36.0
Rex Morgan	SR	G	6-5	Jacksonville	4.3	25.0

MIDWEST

PLAYER	CL	POS	HT	SCHOOL	RPG	PPG
Jimmy Collins*	SR	G	6-2	New Mexico State	3.7	23.7
David Hall	SO	C/F	6-7	Kansas State	20.0	20.5
Sam Lacey	SR	C	6-9	New Mexico State	18.3	18.0
Jerry Venable	SR	F	6-5	Kansas State	12.0	25.0
Al Williams	SR	C	6-6	Drake	15.5	16.5

WEST

PLAYER	CL	POS	HT	SCHOOL	RPG	PPG
Sidney Wicks*	JR	F	6-8	UCLA	9.5	23.0
Dennis Awtrey	SR	F	6-10	Santa Clara	12.0	30.5
Henry Bibby	SO	G	6-1	UCLA	6.5	17.5
Marvin Roberts	JR	F/C	6-8	Utah State	15.7	26.3
Curtis Rowe	JR	F	6-6	UCLA	13.5	20.5
Nate Williams	JR	F	6-5	Utah State	8.3	23.0

* Most outstanding player

1970 NCAA TOURNAMENT BOX SCORES

St. Bonaventure 80-68 NC State

	1H	2H
St. Bonaventure	41	39
NC State	31	37

SWEET 16

ST. BONAVENTURE	MIN	FG	3FG	FT	REB	A	ST	BL	PF	TP
Bob Lanier	39	10-23	-	4-5	19	0	-	-	4	24
Matt Gantt	36	7-18	-	1-4	11	0	-	-	5	15
Bill Kalbaugh	37	4-8	-	5-6	2	1	-	-	3	13
Greg Gary	36	6-11	-	0-1	11	1	-	-	0	12
Paul Hoffman	33	6-9	-	0-1	9	0	-	-	1	12
Mike Kull	16	1-4	-	2-3	0	2	-	-	2	4
Tom Baldwin	3	0-1	-	0-0	0	0	-	-	1	0
TOTALS	200	34-74	-	12-20	52	4	-	-	16	80
Percentages		45.9		60.0						

Coach: Larry Weise

NC STATE	MIN	FG	3FG	FT	REB	A	ST	BL	PF	TP
Vann Williford	40	13-22	-	9-13	12	3	-	-	3	35
Paul Coder	40	8-14	-	0-1	6	0	-	-	3	16
Ed Leftwich	35	4-13	-	0-1	5	0	-	-	3	8
Rick Anheuser	40	3-6	-	1-2	10	5	-	-	4	7
Joe Dunning	36	0-7	-	2-2	3	4	-	-	3	2
Alfred Heartey	9	0-1	-	0-1	1	0	-	-	0	0
TOTALS	200	28-63	-	12-20	37	12	-	-	16	68
Percentages		44.4		60.0						

Coach: Norm Sloan

Officials: Jenkins, Shosid
Attendance: 12,316

Villanova 98-73 Niagara

	1H	2H
Villanova	46	52
Niagara	29	44

SWEET 16

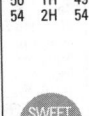

VILLANOVA	MIN	FG	3FG	FT	REB	A	ST	BL	PF	TP
Howard Porter	38	13-22	-	3-3	18	0	-	-	3	29
Sammy Sims	27	8-15	-	3-5	14	0	-	-	1	19
Fran O'Hanlon	34	5-11	-	4-4	7	4	-	-	4	14
Clarence Smith	37	6-9	-	1-1	12	1	-	-	1	13
Chris Ford	31	3-8	-	5-8	2	6	-	-	4	11
Hank Siemiontkowski	13	2-6	-	0-0	1	0	-	-	1	4
John Fox	6	1-3	-	0-0	2	0	-	-	0	2
Bob Gohl	6	1-1	-	0-3	1	1	-	-	0	2
Mike Daly	3	1-1	-	0-0	0	0	-	-	1	2
Joe McDowell	3	1-1	-	0-0	0	0	-	-	1	2
Leon Wojnowski	2	0-1	-	0-0	0	0	-	-	0	0
TOTALS	200	41-78	-	16-24	57	12	-	-	16	98
Percentages		52.6		66.7						

Coach: Jack Kraft

NIAGARA	MIN	FG	3FG	FT	REB	A	ST	BL	PF	TP
Calvin Murphy	39	8-22	-	2-3	7	1	-	-	4	18
Wayne Jones	38	7-19	-	3-3	8	1	-	-	3	17
Marshall Wingate	17	3-9	-	5-7	7	1	-	-	0	11
Bob Churchwell	36	2-9	-	6-6	4	0	-	-	3	10
Michael Brown	31	3-6	-	1-2	1	1	-	-	3	7
Steve Schafer	22	3-9	-	0-0	7	1	-	-	2	6
Mike Samuel	13	1-5	-	0-0	2	0	-	-	1	2
Joe Adomanis	1	1-1	-	0-0	0	0	-	-	0	2
Peter Aiello	1	0-0	-	0-0	0	0	-	-	0	0
Orlander Harrison	1	0-0	-	0-0	0	0	-	-	0	0
Paul Thornton	1	0-0	-	0-0	0	0	-	-	0	0
TOTALS	200	28-80	-	17-21	36	5	-	-	16	73
Percentages		35.0		81.0						

Coach: Frank Layden

Officials: Scott, Jeter
Attendance: 12,316

Jacksonville 104-103 Iowa

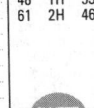

	1H	2H
Jacksonville	50	54
Iowa	49	54

SWEET 16

JACKSONVILLE	MIN	FG	3FG	FT	REB	A	ST	BL	PF	TP
Artis Gilmore	-	13-24	-	4-7	17	-	-	-	5	30
Pembrook Burrows	-	11-12	-	1-2	9	-	-	-	3	23
Rex Morgan	-	9-14	-	5-9	4	-	-	-	4	23
Greg Nelson	-	6-7	-	6-6	9	-	-	-	1	18
Vaughn Wedeking	-	2-8	-	1-3	4	-	-	-	1	5
Chip Dublin	-	2-8	-	0-0	2	-	-	-	5	4
Rod McIntyre	-	0-1	-	1-2	1	-	-	-	0	1
Rusty Baldwin	-	0-1	-	0-0	0	-	-	-	1	0
Mike Blevins	-	0-1	-	0-0	1	-	-	-	3	0
TOTALS	-	43-76	-	18-29	47	-	-	-	23	104
Percentages		56.6		62.1						

Coach: Joe Williams

IOWA	MIN	FG	3FG	FT	REB	A	ST	BL	PF	TP
Fred Brown	-	13-23	-	1-2	4	-	-	-	3	27
Glenn Vidnovic	-	8-13	-	8-11	8	-	-	-	3	24
Chad Calabria	-	7-12	-	7-8	8	-	-	-	4	21
John Johnson	-	9-19	-	1-3	8	-	-	-	3	19
Ben McGilmer	-	4-8	-	0-2	3	-	-	-	4	8
Dick Jensen	-	1-8	-	2-3	4	-	-	-	3	4
Ken Grabinski	-	0-0	-	0-2	2	-	-	-	0	0
TOTALS	-	42-83	-	19-31	37	-	-	-	20	103
Percentages		50.6		61.3						

Coach: Ralph Miller

Officials: Bussenius, Vidal
Attendance: 13,937

Kentucky 109-99 Notre Dame

	1H	2H
Kentucky	48	61
Notre Dame	53	46

SWEET 16

KENTUCKY	MIN	FG	3FG	FT	REB	A	ST	BL	PF	TP
Dan Issel	-	17-28	-	10-14	11	-	-	-	4	44
Mike Pratt	-	7-15	-	0-2	4	-	-	-	5	14
Terry Mills	-	5-7	-	3-5	5	-	-	-	3	13
Tom Parker	-	4-7	-	4-5	6	-	-	-	4	12
Jim Dinwiddie	-	5-7	-	1-1	2	-	-	-	1	11
Larry Steele	-	2-3	-	4-4	6	-	-	-	4	8
Kent Hollenbeck	-	3-5	-	1-3	4	-	-	-	3	7
Stan Key	-	0-0	-	0-0	0	-	-	-	0	0
TOTALS	-	43-72	-	23-34	38	-	-	-	24	109
Percentages		59.7		67.6						

Coach: Adolph Rupp

NOTRE DAME	MIN	FG	3FG	FT	REB	A	ST	BL	PF	TP
Austin Carr	-	22-35	-	8-8	8	-	-	-	2	52
Collis Jones	-	9-17	-	4-10	9	-	-	-	5	22
Jackie Meehan	-	3-6	-	1-2	0	-	-	-	0	7
Michael O'Connell	-	1-3	-	4-5	0	-	-	-	2	6
John Gallagher	-	2-7	-	1-2	5	-	-	-	2	5
Tom Sinnott	-	1-2	-	2-2	4	-	-	-	5	4
Jay Ziznewski	-	1-3	-	1-1	6	-	-	-	4	3
Sid Catlett	-	0-2	-	0-1	5	-	-	-	5	0
James Hinga	-	0-0	-	0-1	0	-	-	-	1	0
TOTALS	-	39-75	-	21-32	37	-	-	-	26	99
Percentages		52.0		65.6						

Coach: Johnny Dee

Officials: Filiberti, Marick
Attendance: 13,937

New Mexico State 70-66 Kansas State

	1H	2H
New Mexico State	35	35
Kansas State	27	39

SWEET 16

NEW MEXICO STATE	MIN	FG	3FG	FT	REB	A	ST	BL	PF	TP
Jimmy Collins	-	8-19	-	7-9	6	-	-	-	2	23
Sam Lacey	-	5-12	-	5-7	11	-	-	-	3	15
Charley Criss	-	4-9	-	5-7	4	-	-	-	3	13
Jeff Smith	-	3-10	-	2-3	7	-	-	-	4	8
Chito Reyes	-	2-3	-	2-2	2	-	-	-	1	6
John Burgess	-	0-4	-	3-3	10	-	-	-	3	3
Roy Neal	-	1-1	-	0-1	2	-	-	-	5	2
Milton Horne	-	0-0	-	0-0	1	-	-	-	1	0
Bill Moore	-	0-0	-	0-0	1	-	-	-	0	0
TOTALS	-	23-58	-	24-32	44	-	-	-	22	70
Percentages		39.7		75.0						

Coach: Lou Henson

KANSAS STATE	MIN	FG	3FG	FT	REB	A	ST	BL	PF	TP
Jerry Venable	-	12-30	-	2-8	14	-	-	-	3	26
David Hall	-	5-16	-	6-11	21	-	-	-	5	16
Jeff Webb	-	4-17	-	0-0	1	-	-	-	4	8
Robert Zender	-	3-10	-	1-2	9	-	-	-	2	7
Wheeler Hughes	-	2-7	-	2-4	3	-	-	-	4	6
Terry Snider	-	1-4	-	0-0	6	-	-	-	4	2
David Lawrence	-	0-1	-	1-3	4	-	-	-	0	1
Eddie Smith	-	0-0	-	0-0	0	-	-	-	0	0
Jack Thomas	-	0-0	-	0-1	0	-	-	-	0	0
TOTALS	-	27-85	-	12-29	58	-	-	-	22	66
Percentages		31.8		41.4						

Coach: Cotton Fitzsimmons

Officials: Cooper, Wirtz
Attendance: 10,200

Drake 92-87 Houston

	1H	2H
Drake	45	47
Houston	32	55

SWEET 16

DRAKE	MIN	FG	3FG	FT	REB	A	ST	BL	PF	TP
Al Williams	-	10-19	-	4-7	17	-	-	-	3	24
Gary Zeller	-	7-16	-	5-7	3	-	-	-	3	19
Bobby Jones	-	7-15	-	1-2	5	-	-	-	2	15
Jeff Halliburton	-	3-8	-	5-6	7	-	-	-	4	11
Carl Salyers	-	4-4	-	0-1	0	-	-	-	3	8
Rick Wanamaker	-	4-10	-	0-1	10	-	-	-	0	8
Tom Bush	-	3-6	-	1-2	7	-	-	-	4	7
TOTALS	-	38-78	-	16-26	49	-	-	-	19	92
Percentages		48.7		61.5						

Coach: Maury John

HOUSTON	MIN	FG	3FG	FT	REB	A	ST	BL	PF	TP
Dwight Davis	-	9-19	-	6-8	10	1	-	-	4	24
Poo Welch	-	9-18	-	4-4	3	3	-	-	3	22
Jeff Hickman	-	7-11	-	2-3	4	5	-	-	3	16
Ollie Taylor	-	6-12	-	3-5	9	2	-	-	3	15
Tom Gribben	-	2-9	-	1-2	7	1	-	-	5	5
Mars Evans	-	1-1	-	1-2	2	0	-	-	1	3
Bob Hall	-	1-2	-	0-0	2	0	-	-	2	2
Melvin Bell	-	0-0	-	0-1	0	0	-	-	0	0
Sonny Willis	-	0-3	-	0-1	2	0	-	-	1	0
TOTALS	-	35-75	-	17-26	39	12	-	-	22	87
Percentages		46.7		65.4						

Coach: Guy V. Lewis

Officials: DiTomasso, Rooney
Attendance: 10,200

UCLA	MIN	FG	3FG	FT	REB	A	ST	BL	PF	TP
Henry Bibby	-	8-13	-	4-5	6	3	-	-	2	20
Sidney Wicks	-	8-14	-	4-7	11	3	-	-	3	20
Curtis Rowe	-	5-11	-	5-9	11	6	-	-	1	15
John Vallely	-	6-15	-	2-5	5	4	-	-	2	14
Steve Patterson	-	6-14	-	1-1	12	4	-	-	4	13
Jon Chapman	-	1-1	-	0-0	1	1	-	-	0	2
John Ecker	-	1-2	-	0-0	1	0	-	-	0	2
Terry Schofield	-	1-2	-	0-0	1	1	-	-	0	2
Kenny Booker	-	0-1	-	0-0	0	1	-	-	1	0
Bill Seibert	-	0-1	-	0-0	0	0	-	-	0	0
TOTALS	-	36-74	-	16-27	48	23	-	-	13	88
Percentages		48.6		59.3						

Coach: John Wooden

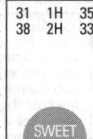

88-65
42 1H 29
46 2H 36
SWEET 16

LONG BEACH STATE	MIN	FG	3FG	FT	REB	A	ST	BL	PF	TP
George Trapp	-	10-18	-	0-1	4	3	-	-	3	20
Sam Robinson	-	7-13	-	4-6	7	4	-	-	2	18
Shawn Johnson	-	5-12	-	3-3	4	1	-	-	0	13
Arthur Montgomery	-	3-4	-	0-0	1	0	-	-	5	6
Billy Jankans	-	2-10	-	1-3	7	2	-	-	5	5
Dwight Taylor	-	1-7	-	1-2	0	1	-	-	3	3
Ray Gritton	-	0-2	-	0-0	1	4	-	-	1	0
Dave Mclucas	-	0-0	-	0-0	1	0	-	-	0	0
Bernard Williams	-	0-1	-	0-0	1	0	-	-	2	0
TOTALS	-	28-67	-	9-15	26	15	-	-	21	65
Percentages		41.8		60.0						

Coach: Jerry Tarkanian

Officials: Stou Huiot
Attendance: 5,500

UTAH STATE	MIN	FG	3FG	FT	REB	A	ST	BL	PF	TP
Nate Williams	-	10-22	-	4-5	4	1	-	-	3	24
Marvin Roberts	-	5-14	-	6-9	16	0	-	-	1	16
Ed Epps	-	3-5	-	3-3	2	1	-	-	1	9
Paul Jeppesen	-	2-8	-	4-4	3	2	-	-	5	8
Tim Tollestrup	-	3-11	-	1-2	13	2	-	-	5	7
Jeff Tebbs	-	1-8	-	1-1	4	3	-	-	2	3
Ron Hatch	-	1-4	-	0-0	3	1	-	-	3	2
Chris Bean	-	0-1	-	0-0	0	0	-	-	0	0
John Erickson	-	0-0	-	0-0	1	0	-	-	1	0
TOTALS	-	25-73	-	19-24	46	10	-	-	21	69
Percentages		34.2		79.2						

Coach: Ladell Andersen

69-68
31 1H 35
38 2H 33
SWEET 16

SANTA CLARA	MIN	FG	3FG	FT	REB	A	ST	BL	PF	TP
Dennis Awtrey	-	9-16	-	6-8	11	3	-	-	4	24
Jolly Spight	-	8-16	-	5-7	9	7	-	-	4	21
Ralph Ogden	-	5-15	-	2-7	4	2	-	-	3	12
Kevin Eagleson	-	2-5	-	1-2	3	7	-	-	2	5
Bruce Bochte	-	1-3	-	2-4	8	1	-	-	4	4
Mart Petersen	-	1-3	-	0-0	2	0	-	-	3	2
Keith Paulson	-	0-1	-	0-0	0	2	-	-	0	0
TOTALS	-	26-59	-	16-28	37	22	-	-	20	68
Percentages		44.1		57.1						

Coach: Dick Garibaldi

Officials: MacPherson, Scott
Attendance: 5,500

ST. BONAVENTURE	MIN	FG	3FG	FT	REB	A	ST	BL	PF	TP
Bob Lanier	31	11-22	-	4-4	14	0	-	-	2	26
Greg Gary	36	10-17	-	0-1	11	0	-	-	1	20
Matt Gantt	40	7-20	-	5-8	18	1	-	-	3	19
Bill Kalbaugh	40	5-9	-	5-5	3	3	-	-	1	15
Mike Kull	30	4-6	-	3-3	2	2	-	-	2	11
Paul Hoffman	23	3-6	-	0-1	4	0	-	-	3	6
TOTALS	200	40-80	-	17-22	52	6	-	-	12	97
Percentages		50.0		77.3						

Coach: Larry Weise

97-74
46 1H 30
51 2H 44
ELITE 8

VILLANOVA	MIN	FG	3FG	FT	REB	A	ST	BL	PF	TP
Fran O'Hanlon	36	10-15	-	0-2	4	3	-	-	5	20
Chris Ford	34	7-14	-	1-2	4	1	-	-	3	15
Howard Porter	33	6-14	-	2-2	9	0	-	-	5	14
Hank Siemiontkowski	28	3-13	-	4-4	3	0	-	-	2	10
Joe McDowell	14	3-7	-	0-1	3	1	-	-	2	6
Sammy Sims	24	1-5	-	3-5	7	0	-	-	1	5
Clarence Smith	19	1-8	-	0-0	4	0	-	-	1	2
John Fox	6	1-2	-	0-0	0	0	-	-	0	2
Bob Gohl	4	0-1	-	0-0	0	0	-	-	1	0
Leon Wojnowski	2	0-0	-	0-0	0	0	-	-	0	0
TOTALS	200	32-79	-	10-16	34	5	-	-	20	74
Percentages		40.5		62.5						

Coach: Jack Kraft

Officials: Shosid, Scott
Attendance: 10,981

JACKSONVILLE	MIN	FG	3FG	FT	REB	A	ST	BL	PF	TP
Rex Morgan	-	10-14	-	8-9	3	-	-	-	4	28
Artis Gilmore	-	10-20	-	4-7	20	-	-	-	4	24
Chip Dublin	-	6-8	-	7-8	2	-	-	-	4	19
Greg Nelson	-	5-7	-	3-5	6	-	-	-	1	13
Vaughn Wedeking	-	4-13	-	4-5	3	-	-	-	0	12
Pembrook Burrows	-	3-4	-	2-2	4	-	-	-	3	8
Rod McIntyre	-	1-2	-	0-0	3	-	-	-	2	2
Mike Blevins	-	0-1	-	0-0	3	-	-	-	2	0
TOTALS	-	39-69	-	28-36	44	-	-	-	20	106
Percentages		56.5		77.8						

Coach: Joe Williams

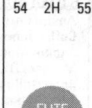

106-100
52 1H 45
54 2H 55
ELITE 8

KENTUCKY	MIN	FG	3FG	FT	REB	A	ST	BL	PF	TP
Dan Issel	-	13-25	-	2-2	10	-	-	-	5	28
Tom Parker	-	8-18	-	5-5	4	-	-	-	2	21
Terry Mills	-	7-11	-	4-4	3	-	-	-	5	18
Mike Pratt	-	4-13	-	6-9	13	-	-	-	5	14
Kent Hollenbeck	-	4-8	-	2-2	7	-	-	-	3	10
Mark Soderberg	-	2-5	-	0-0	3	-	-	-	0	4
Larry Steele	-	1-4	-	1-1	2	-	-	-	5	3
Jim Dinwiddie	-	1-2	-	0-1	0	-	-	-	0	2
Stan Key	-	0-2	-	0-0	1	-	-	-	1	0
Randy Noll	-	0-1	-	0-0	0	-	-	-	0	0
TOTALS	-	40-89	-	20-24	43	-	-	-	26	100
Percentages		44.9		83.3						

Coach: Adolph Rupp

Officials: Maic Bussenius
Attendance: 13,865

NEW MEXICO STATE	MIN	FG	3FG	FT	REB	A	ST	BL	PF	TP
Jimmy Collins	-	9-18	-	8-10	3	-	-	-	3	26
Sam Lacey	-	7-12	-	6-10	24	-	-	-	2	20
Charley Criss	-	5-10	-	4-7	0	-	-	-	4	14
Milton Horne	-	3-6	-	7-9	0	-	-	-	4	13
Roy Neal	-	2-2	-	3-4	4	-	-	-	1	7
Jeff Smith	-	2-4	-	1-3	3	-	-	-	5	5
Chito Reyes	-	0-1	-	2-2	5	-	-	-	1	2
John Burgess	-	0-0	-	0-0	7	-	-	-	2	0
TOTALS	-	28-53	-	31-45	46	-	-	-	22	87
Percentages		52.8		68.9						

Coach: Lou Henson

87-78
47 1H 35
40 2H 43
ELITE 8

DRAKE	MIN	FG	3FG	FT	REB	A	ST	BL	PF	TP
Jeff Halliburton	-	8-18	-	8-8	9	-	-	-	3	24
Tom Bush	-	6-8	-	1-6	7	-	-	-	5	13
Bobby Jones	-	5-8	-	0-0	1	-	-	-	5	10
Al Williams	-	4-15	-	1-3	14	-	-	-	5	9
Gary Zeller	-	4-15	-	1-1	1	-	-	-	5	9
Carl Salyers	-	3-5	-	0-0	0	-	-	-	1	6
Rick Wanamaker	-	1-4	-	1-2	3	-	-	-	3	3
Lee Allen	-	1-3	-	0-0	0	-	-	-	2	2
Al Sakys	-	0-2	-	2-4	1	-	-	-	3	2
Dale Teeter	-	0-1	-	0-0	1	-	-	-	0	0
TOTALS	-	32-79	-	14-24	37	-	-	-	32	78
Percentages		40.5		58.3						

Coach: Maury John

Officials: DiTomasso, Wirtz
Attendance: 8,400

UCLA	MIN	FG	3FG	FT	REB	A	ST	BL	PF	TP
Curtis Rowe	-	9-17	-	8-8	16	4	-	-	3	26
Sidney Wicks	-	10-14	-	6-7	8	3	-	-	4	26
Henry Bibby	-	4-8	-	7-9	7	5	-	-	4	15
John Vallely	-	5-13	-	4-7	3	3	-	-	1	14
Steve Patterson	-	4-12	-	1-2	9	6	-	-	2	9
Kenny Booker	-	2-4	-	0-1	1	0	-	-	2	4
Bill Seibert	-	1-1	-	2-2	1	0	-	-	1	4
Rick Betchley	-	1-2	-	0-0	0	0	-	-	0	2
John Ecker	-	0-0	-	1-2	2	1	-	-	1	1
Jon Chapman	-	0-2	-	0-0	3	0	-	-	0	0
Andy Hill	-	0-0	-	0-0	0	0	-	-	0	0
Terry Schofield	-	0-0	-	0-0	0	0	-	-	0	0
TOTALS	-	36-73	-	29-38	50	22	-	-	18	101
Percentages		49.3		76.3						

Coach: John Wooden

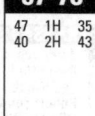

101-79
51 1H 44
50 2H 35
ELITE 8

UTAH STATE	MIN	FG	3FG	FT	REB	A	ST	BL	PF	TP
Marvin Roberts	-	14-35	-	5-7	15	0	-	-	4	33
Nate Williams	-	7-24	-	0-0	11	3	-	-	4	14
Ed Epps	-	6-13	-	0-1	6	2	-	-	3	12
Paul Jeppesen	-	4-6	-	4-4	1	0	-	-	4	12
Tim Tollestrup	-	1-4	-	4-6	10	3	-	-	4	6
Ron Hatch	-	0-4	-	2-2	2	0	-	-	2	2
Chris Bean	-	0-0	-	0-0	1	0	-	-	0	0
John Erickson	-	0-0	-	0-0	0	0	-	-	0	0
Jeff Tebbs	-	0-4	-	0-0	2	4	-	-	4	0
Dick Wade	-	0-1	-	0-0	1	1	-	-	0	0
Terry Wakefield	-	0-0	-	0-0	0	0	-	-	1	0
TOTALS	-	32-91	-	15-20	49	13	-	-	26	79
Percentages		35.2		75.0						

Coach: Ladell Andersen

Officials: Huiot, White
Attendance: 4,200

91-83 | 42 1H 34 | 49 2H 49 | FINAL 4

JACKSONVILLE	MIN	FG	3FG	FT	REB	A	ST	BL	PF	TP
Artis Gilmore	-	9-14	-	11-15	21	-	-	-	2	29
Rex Morgan	-	6-15	-	5-6	5	-	-	-	3	17
Vaughn Wedeking	-	7-15	-	1-1	6	-	-	-	4	15
Greg Nelson	-	1-7	-	10-12	7	-	-	-	3	12
Chip Dublin	-	1-3	-	9-9	2	-	-	-	2	11
Pembrook Burrows	-	2-4	-	1-1	4	-	-	-	4	5
Mike Blevins	-	1-1	-	0-0	0	-	-	-	1	2
Rusty Baldwin	-	0-1	-	0-1	0	-	-	-	1	0
Rod McIntyre	-	0-3	-	0-0	3	-	-	-	1	0
TOTALS	**-**	**27-63**	**-**	**37-45**	**48**	**-**	**-**	**-**	**21**	**91**
Percentages		42.9		82.2						
Coach: Joe Williams										

ST. BONAVENTURE	MIN	FG	3FG	FT	REB	A	ST	BL	PF	TP
Matt Gantt	-	8-17	-	0-0	8	-	-	-	5	16
Vic Thomas	-	7-17	-	1-2	4	-	-	-	3	15
Bill Kalbaugh	-	5-8	-	2-2	4	-	-	-	3	12
Paul Hoffman	-	4-14	-	2-4	6	-	-	-	3	10
Greg Gary	-	2-7	-	5-8	13	-	-	-	5	9
Mike Kull	-	4-7	-	0-0	0	-	-	-	5	8
Tom Baldwin	-	2-10	-	1-2	4	-	-	-	5	5
Paul Grys	-	1-5	-	2-2	1	-	-	-	2	4
Gene Fahey	-	1-1	-	0-0	0	-	-	-	1	2
Dale Tepas	-	0-0	-	2-2	1	-	-	-	0	2
TOTALS	**-**	**34-86**	**-**	**15-22**	**41**	**-**	**-**	**-**	**32**	**83**
Percentages		39.5		68.2						
Coach: Larry Weise										

Officials: Scott, Marick
Attendance: 14,380

93-77 | 48 1H 41 | 45 2H 36 | FINAL 4

UCLA	MIN	FG	3FG	FT	REB	A	ST	BL	PF	TP
John Vallely	35	7-19	-	9-10	4	1	-	-	3	23
Sidney Wicks	39	10-12	-	2-5	16	2	-	-	3	22
Henry Bibby	34	8-13	-	3-3	2	0	-	-	5	19
Curtis Rowe	39	4-7	-	7-11	15	1	-	-	0	15
Steve Patterson	38	5-9	-	2-2	6	7	-	-	3	12
Jon Chapman	1	1-1	-	0-0	1	0	-	-	0	2
Kenny Booker	7	0-1	-	0-0	0	0	-	-	2	0
John Ecker	3	0-0	-	0-0	0	0	-	-	0	0
Rick Betchley	1	0-0	-	0-0	0	0	-	-	0	0
Andy Hill	1	0-0	-	0-1	0	0	-	-	1	0
Terry Schofield	1	0-0	-	0-0	0	0	-	-	1	0
Bill Seibert	1	0-1	-	0-0	1	1	-	-	0	0
TOTALS	**200**	**35-63**	**-**	**23-32**	**45**	**12**	**-**	**-**	**18**	**93**
Percentages		55.6		71.9						
Coach: John Wooden										

NEW MEXICO STATE	MIN	FG	3FG	FT	REB	A	ST	BL	PF	TP
Jimmy Collins	35	13-23	-	2-3	0	2	-	-	3	28
Charley Criss	33	6-16	-	7-9	2	1	-	-	5	19
Jeff Smith	28	4-11	-	2-3	7	0	-	-	5	10
Sam Lacey	31	3-9	-	2-3	16	0	-	-	3	8
Roy Neal	19	2-4	-	0-0	6	0	-	-	2	4
John Burgess	25	1-6	-	0-0	2	0	-	-	2	2
Chito Reyes	14	1-6	-	0-0	4	0	-	-	2	2
Milton Horne	7	0-4	-	2-2	1	2	-	-	2	2
Bill Moore	5	1-1	-	0-0	1	0	-	-	0	2
Rudy Franco	1	0-0	-	0-0	0	0	-	-	0	0
Lonnie Lefevre	1	0-0	-	0-0	1	0	-	-	0	0
Tom McCarthy	1	0-0	-	0-0	0	0	-	-	0	0
TOTALS	**200**	**31-80**	**-**	**15-20**	**40**	**5**	**-**	**-**	**24**	**77**
Percentages		38.8		75.0						
Coach: Lou Henson										

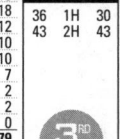

Officials: White, Wirtz
Attendance: 14,380

79-73 | 36 1H 30 | 43 2H 43 | 3RD PLACE

NEW MEXICO STATE	MIN	FG	3FG	FT	REB	A	ST	BL	PF	TP
Jimmy Collins	-	9-22	-	0-0	3	2	-	-	2	18
Sam Lacey	-	7-17	-	4-6	19	1	-	-	0	18
Roy Neal	-	5-7	-	2-2	7	0	-	-	1	12
Charley Criss	-	4-16	-	2-2	7	4	-	-	3	10
Chito Reyes	-	4-7	-	2-2	5	2	-	-	0	10
Jeff Smith	-	2-5	-	3-6	5	1	-	-	4	7
John Burgess	-	1-2	-	0-0	9	0	-	-	1	2
Milton Horne	-	1-1	-	0-0	0	2	-	-	1	2
Bill Moore	-	0-0	-	0-0	0	0	-	-	0	0
TOTALS	**-**	**33-77**	**-**	**13-18**	**55**	**12**	**-**	**-**	**12**	**79**
Percentages		42.9		72.2						
Coach: Lou Henson										

ST. BONAVENTURE	MIN	FG	3FG	FT	REB	A	ST	BL	PF	TP
Greg Gary	-	8-14	-	6-7	11	2	-	-	4	22
Matt Gantt	-	6-16	-	2-5	10	0	-	-	2	14
Mike Kull	-	7-17	-	0-0	2	2	-	-	2	14
Vic Thomas	-	3-7	-	2-2	1	0	-	-	2	8
Bill Kalbaugh	-	3-9	-	0-0	3	5	-	-	1	6
Paul Hoffman	-	2-5	-	0-1	4	2	-	-	3	4
Tom Baldwin	-	1-1	-	1-1	0	1	-	-	0	3
Paul Grys	-	1-1	-	0-0	1	0	-	-	0	2
Dale Tepas	-	0-1	-	0-0	0	0	-	-	0	0
TOTALS	**-**	**31-71**	**-**	**11-16**	**32**	**12**	**-**	**-**	**14**	**73**
Percentages		43.7		68.8						
Coach: Larry Weise										

Officials: White, Marick, Allmond
Attendance: 14,380

80-69 | 41 1H 36 | 39 2H 33 | NCAA FINAL 1970

UCLA	MIN	FG	3FG	FT	REB	A	ST	BL	PF	TP
Curtis Rowe	38	7-15	-	5-5	8	1	-	-	4	19
Steve Patterson	38	8-15	-	1-4	11	2	-	-	1	17
Sidney Wicks	38	5-9	-	7-10	18	3	-	-	3	17
John Vallely	38	5-10	-	5-7	7	5	-	-	2	15
Henry Bibby	38	2-11	-	4-4	4	2	-	-	1	8
John Ecker	2	1-1	-	0-0	0	0	-	-	0	2
Kenny Booker	1	0-0	-	2-3	0	0	-	-	0	2
Jon Chapman	2	0-1	-	0-0	1	0	-	-	0	0
Bill Seibert	2	0-1	-	0-0	1	0	-	-	1	0
Rick Betchley	1	0-0	-	0-1	0	0	-	-	0	0
Andy Hill	1	0-0	-	0-1	0	0	-	-	0	0
Terry Schofield	1	0-0	-	0-0	0	0	-	-	0	0
TOTALS	**200**	**28-63**	**-**	**24-35**	**50**	**13**	**-**	**-**	**12**	**80**
Percentages		44.4		68.6						
Coach: John Wooden										

JACKSONVILLE	MIN	FG	3FG	FT	REB	A	ST	BL	PF	TP
Artis Gilmore	38	9-29	-	1-1	16	1	-	-	5	19
Vaughn Wedeking	37	6-11	-	0-0	2	3	-	-	2	12
Pembrook Burrows	24	6-9	-	0-0	6	0	-	-	1	12
Rex Morgan	37	5-11	-	0-0	4	11	-	-	5	10
Greg Nelson	16	3-9	-	2-2	5	0	-	-	1	8
Mike Blevins	19	1-2	-	1-2	0	1	-	-	1	3
Chip Dublin	18	0-5	-	2-2	1	1	-	-	4	2
Rod McIntyre	6	1-3	-	0-0	3	0	-	-	3	2
Dan Hawkins	2	0-1	-	1-1	1	0	-	-	1	1
Rusty Baldwin	2	0-0	-	0-0	0	0	-	-	0	0
Ken Selke	1	0-0	-	0-0	0	0	-	-	0	0
TOTALS	**200**	**31-80**	**-**	**7-8**	**38**	**17**	**-**	**-**	**23**	**69**
Percentages		38.8		87.5						
Coach: Joe Williams										

Officials: Scott, Wirtz
Attendance: 14,380

National Invitation Tournament (NIT)

First round: Georgia Tech d. Duquesne 78-68, St. John's d. Miami (OH) 70-57, Manhattan d. North Carolina 95-90, Army d. Cincinnati 72-67, Utah d. Duke 78-75, Marquette d. Massachusetts 62-55, LSU d. Georgetown 83-82, Oklahoma d. Louisville, 74-73
Quarterfinals: Army d. Manhattan 77-72, St. John's d. Georgia Tech 56-55, Marquette d. Utah 83-63, LSU d. Oklahoma 97-94
Semifinals: St. John's d. Army 60-59, Marquette d. LSU 101-79,
Third place: Army d. LSU 75-68
Championship: Marquette d. St. John's 65-53
MVP: Dean Meminger, Marquette

1970-71: Make It Five

UCLA lost to Notre Dame, 89-82, on Jan. 23, 1971—and the Bruins would not lose another game until Jan. 19, 1974 (again to Notre Dame, 71-70). At the Astrodome, UCLA (29–1) battled its way to a fifth straight national title with a 68-62 win over Villanova. But the best game of the Final Four was Nova's semifinal, which went to double OT before the Wildcats topped Western Kentucky, 92-89. Officially, though, that game never happened. Tournament MOP Howard Porter and Hilltoppers center Jim McDaniels had prematurely signed pro contracts, causing the NCAA to wipe both teams' appearances off the books. If not for that, the two teams would have set a national semifinal record for most combined field goal attempts (178) and most attempted by one team (Western Kentucky with 105).

Will Robinson became the first African-American to coach a Division I team, Illinois State, where he would compile a 78–51 record over the next five seasons. The spectacular Notre Dame guard Austin Carr was the Naismith National POY, averaging 38.0 ppg and finishing as the all-time leading scorer in Irish history.

Major Conference Standings

ACC

	Conference			Overall		
	W	L	PCT	W	L	PCT
North Carolina □	11	3	.786	26	6	.813
South Carolina ⊛	10	4	.714	23	6	.793
Duke □	9	5	.643	20	10	.667
Wake Forest	7	7	.500	16	10	.615
Virginia	6	8	.429	15	11	.577
Maryland	5	9	.357	14	12	.538
NC State	5	9	.357	13	14	.481
Clemson	3	11	.214	9	17	.346

Tournament: **South Carolina d. North Carolina 52-51**
Tournament MVPs: **Lee Dedmon**, North Carolina and **John Roche**, South Carolina

Big Eight

	Conference			Overall		
	W	L	PCT	W	L	PCT
Kansas ⊛	14	0	1.000	27	3	.900
Oklahoma □	9	5	.643	19	8	.704
Missouri	9	5	.643	17	9	.654
Nebraska	8	6	.571	18	8	.692
Colorado	6	8	.429	14	12	.538
Kansas State	6	8	.429	11	15	.423
Oklahoma State	2	12	.143	7	19	.269
Iowa State	2	12	.143	5	21	.192

Big Sky

	Conference			Overall		
	W	L	PCT	W	L	PCT
Weber State ⊛	12	2	.857	21	6	.778
Idaho	8	6	.571	14	12	.538
Montana State	8	6	.571	12	13	.480
Idaho State	7	7	.500	9	15	.375
Gonzaga	6	8	.429	13	13	.500
Montana	6	8	.429	9	15	.375
Boise State	5	9	.357	10	16	.385
Northern Arizona	4	10	.286	6	19	.240

Big Ten

	Conference			Overall		
	W	L	PCT	W	L	PCT
Ohio State ⊛	13	1	.929	20	6	.769
Michigan □	12	2	.857	19	7	.731
Purdue □	11	3	.786	18	7	.720
Indiana	9	5	.643	17	7	.708
Illinois	5	9	.357	11	12	.478
Minnesota	5	9	.357	11	13	.458
Michigan State	4	10	.286	10	14	.417
Iowa	4	10	.286	9	15	.375
Wisconsin	4	10	.286	9	15	.375
Northwestern	3	11	.214	7	17	.292

Ivy

	Conference			Overall		
	W	L	PCT	W	L	PCT
Penn ⊛	14	0	1.000	28	1	.966
Harvard	11	3	.786	16	10	.615
Columbia	9	5	.643	15	9	.625
Princeton	9	5	.643	14	11	.560
Brown	5	9	.357	10	15	.400
Dartmouth	5	9	.357	10	16	.385
Yale	2	12	.143	4	20	.167
Cornell	1	13	.071	5	21	.192

Mid-American

	Conference			Overall		
	W	L	PCT	W	L	PCT
Miami (OH) ⊛	9	1	.900	20	5	.800
Ohio	6	4	.600	17	7	.708
Western Michigan	5	5	.500	14	10	.583
Kent State	4	6	.400	13	11	.542
Toledo	4	6	.400	13	11	.542
Bowling Green	2	8	.200	7	18	.280

Middle Atlantic

	Conference			Overall		
	W	L	PCT	W	L	PCT
Eastern						
Saint Joseph's ⊛	6	0	1.000	19	9	.679
La Salle □	5	1	.833	20	7	.741
Hofstra	4	2	.667	16	8	.667
Temple	3	3	.500	13	12	.520
American	2	4	.333	13	12	.520
West Chester	1	5	.167	7	18	.280
Drexel	0	6	.000	7	17	.292
Western						
Lafayette	9	1	.900	17	9	.654
Rider	8	2	.800	20	6	.769
Delaware	5	5	.500	11	14	.440
Bucknell	4	6	.400	9	14	.391
Lehigh	4	6	.400	10	16	.385
Gettysburg	0	10	.000	4	21	.160

Missouri Valley

	Conference			Overall		
	W	L	PCT	W	L	PCT
Drake ⊛	9	5	.643	21	8	.724
Louisville □	9	5	.643	20	9	.690
Saint Louis	9	5	.643	17	12	.586
Memphis	8	6	.571	18	8	.692
Tulsa	8	6	.571	17	9	.654
Bradley	6	8	.429	13	12	.520
North Texas	4	10	.286	10	15	.400
Wichita State	3	11	.214	10	16	.385
West Texas A&M	-	-	-	19	7	.731
New Mexico State ○	-	-	-	19	8	.704

Ohio Valley

	Conference			Overall		
	W	L	PCT	W	L	PCT
Western Kentucky ⊛ ⊗	12	2	.857	24	6	.800
Murray State	10	4	.714	19	5	.792
Eastern Kentucky	10	4	.714	16	8	.667
East Tennessee St.	8	6	.571	12	12	.500
Austin Peay	5	9	.357	10	14	.417
Morehead State	4	10	.286	8	17	.320
Tennessee Tech	4	10	.286	7	17	.292
Middle Tennessee St.	3	11	.214	11	15	.423

PCAA

	Conference			Overall		
	W	L	PCT	W	L	PCT
Long Beach State ○ ⊗	10	0	1.000	24	5	.828
UC Santa Barbara	8	2	.800	20	6	.769
Cal State LA	5	5	.500	15	11	.577
Fresno State	4	6	.400	15	11	.577
San Diego State	3	7	.300	12	14	.462
San Jose State	0	10	.000	2	24	.077

Pac-8

	Conference			Overall		
	W	L	PCT	W	L	PCT
UCLA ⊛	14	0	1.000	29	1	.967
Southern California	12	2	.857	24	2	.923
Oregon	8	6	.571	17	9	.654
California	8	6	.571	16	9	.640
Washington	6	8	.429	15	13	.536
Oregon State	4	10	.286	12	14	.462
Washington State	2	12	.143	12	14	.462
Stanford	2	12	.143	6	20	.231

SEC

	Conference			Overall		
	W	L	PCT	W	L	PCT
Kentucky ⊛	16	2	.889	22	6	.786
Tennessee □	13	5	.722	21	7	.750
LSU	10	8	.556	14	12	.538
Mississippi State	9	9	.500	15	10	.600
Vanderbilt	9	9	.500	13	13	.500
Auburn	8	10	.444	11	15	.423
Florida	8	10	.444	11	15	.423
Mississippi	6	12	.333	11	15	.423
Alabama	6	12	.333	10	16	.385
Georgia	5	13	.278	6	19	.240

Southern

	Conference			Overall		
	W	L	PCT	W	L	PCT
Davidson	9	1	.900	15	11	.577
William and Mary	7	3	.700	11	16	.407
East Carolina	7	4	.636	13	12	.520
The Citadel	6	5	.545	13	12	.520
Furman ⊛	5	5	.500	15	12	.556
Richmond	3	9	.250	7	21	.250
VMI	1	11	.083	1	25	.038

Tournament: **Furman d. Richmond 68-61**
Tournament MOP: **Jerry Martin**, Furman

Southland

	Conference			Overall		
	W	L	PCT	W	L	PCT
Arkansas State	6	2	.750	15	9	.625
Abilene Christian	5	3	.625	15	9	.625
Lamar	5	3	.625	11	13	.458
Texas-Arlington	3	5	.375	8	18	.308
Trinity (TX)	1	7	.125	7	16	.304

Southwest

	Conference			Overall		
	W	L	PCT	W	L	PCT
TCU ⊛	11	3	.786	15	12	.556
Baylor	10	4	.714	18	8	.692
Texas Tech	9	5	.643	16	10	.615
SMU	8	6	.571	16	10	.615
Rice	6	8	.429	14	12	.538
Texas	6	8	.429	12	12	.500
Texas A&M	5	9	.357	9	17	.346
Arkansas	1	13	.071	5	21	.192

WCAC

	Conference			Overall		
	W	L	PCT	W	L	PCT
Pacific ⊛	12	2	.857	22	6	.786
Loyola Marymount	10	4	.714	15	10	.600
UNLV	9	5	.643	16	10	.615
Santa Clara	8	6	.571	11	15	.423
San Francisco	8	6	.571	10	16	.385
Pepperdine	4	10	.286	12	13	.480
Saint Mary's (CA)	4	10	.286	10	16	.385
Nevada	1	13	.071	3	23	.115

WAC

	Conference			Overall		
	W	L	PCT	W	L	PCT
BYU ⊛	10	4	.714	18	11	.621
UTEP	9	5	.643	15	10	.600
Utah	9	5	.643	15	11	.577
Arizona State	8	6	.571	16	10	.615
Colorado State	7	7	.500	15	10	.600
Wyoming	6	8	.429	10	15	.400
New Mexico	4	10	.286	14	12	.538
Arizona	3	11	.214	10	16	.385

⊛ Automatic NCAA Tournament bid ○ At-large NCAA Tournament bid □ NIT appearance ⊗ Team record doesn't reflect games forfeited or vacated. For adjusted record, see p. 521.

YANKEE

	Conference W	Conference L	Conference Pct	Overall W	Overall L	Overall Pct
Massachusetts□	10	0	1.000	23	4	.852
Rhode Island	8	2	.800	10	17	.370
Connecticut	5	5	.500	10	14	.417
New Hampshire	3	7	.300	11	12	.478
Maine	3	7	.300	8	16	.333
Vermont	1	9	.100	9	15	.375

INDEPENDENTS

	Overall W	Overall L	Overall Pct
Marquette○	28	1	.966
Fordham○	26	3	.897
Jacksonville○	22	4	.846
Duquesne○	21	4	.840
Hawaii□	23	5	.821
Villanova○⊗	27	7	.794
St. Bonaventure□	21	6	.778
Houston○	22	7	.759
Utah State○	20	7	.741
Syracuse□	19	7	.731
Georgia Tech□	23	9	.719
Providence□	20	8	.714
Fairleigh Dickinson	16	7	.696
Rutgers	16	7	.696
Holy Cross	18	8	.692

INDEPENDENTS (CONT.)

	Overall W	Overall L	Overall Pct
Notre Dame○	20	9	.690
Dayton□	18	9	.667
St. John's□	18	9	.667
Denver	17	9	.654
Florida State	17	9	.654
Loyola (LA)	16	10	.615
Marshall	16	10	.615
Colgate	15	10	.600
Saint Francis (PA)	15	10	.600
Pittsburgh	14	10	.583
Boston College	15	11	.577
Northern Illinois	13	10	.565
Southern Illinois	13	10	.565
Creighton	14	11	.560
Virginia Tech	14	11	.560
Manhattan	13	11	.542
Cincinnati	14	12	.538
Detroit	14	12	.538
Niagara	14	12	.538
West Virginia	13	12	.520
Centenary	13	13	.500
Texas-Pan American	13	13	.500
Navy	12	12	.500
Air Force	12	14	.462

INDEPENDENTS (CONT.)

	Overall W	Overall L	Overall Pct
Georgetown	12	14	.462
Seattle	12	14	.462
Army	11	13	.458
Saint Peter's	11	13	.458
Iona	10	12	.455
Penn State	10	12	.455
George Washington	11	14	.440
Seton Hall	11	15	.423
Long Island	10	15	.400
Butler	10	16	.385
Canisius	8	13	.381
Fairfield	9	15	.375
Hardin-Simmons	9	16	.360
Oklahoma City	9	16	.360
Xavier	9	17	.346
DePaul	8	17	.320
St. Francis (NY)	8	17	.320
Tulane	8	18	.308
Boston U.	7	18	.280
Miami (FL)	7	19	.269
NYU	5	20	.200
Portland	5	21	.192
Loyola-Chicago	4	20	.167

INDIVIDUAL LEADERS—SEASON

Scoring

	CL	POS	G	FG	FT	PTS	PPG
1 **Johnny Neumann**, Mississippi	SO	G/F	23	366	191	923	**40.1**
2 **Austin Carr**, Notre Dame	SR	G	29	430	241	1,101	**38.0**
3 **Willie Humes**, Idaho State	SR	G	24	287	203	777	**32.4**
4 **George McGinnis**, Indiana	SO	F/C	24	283	153	719	**30.0**
5 **Jim McDaniels**, Western Kentucky	SR	C	30	357	164	878	**29.3**
6 **Rich Rinaldi**, Saint Peter's	SR	G	24	260	167	687	**28.6**
7 **John Mengelt**, Auburn	SR	G	26	265	208	738	**28.4**
8 **Gene Phillips**, SMU	SR	F	26	262	213	737	**28.3**
9 **Cliff Meely**, Colorado	SR	F	26	282	165	729	**28.0**
10 **Fred Brown**, Iowa	SR	G	24	268	126	662	**27.6**

Field Goal Pct

	CL	POS	G	FG	FGA	PCT
1 **John Belcher**, Arkansas State	JR	F/C	24	174	275	**63.3**
2 **Dennis Wuycik**, North Carolina	JR	F	29	182	300	**60.7**
3 **Bill Smith**, Syracuse	SR	C	26	222	366	**60.7**
4 **Eugene Kennedy**, TCU	SR	F	25	202	340	**59.4**
5 **Walt Szczerbiak**, George Washington	SR	F	25	225	379	**59.4**

Minimum: 140 made

Free Throw Pct

	CL	POS	G	FT	FTA	PCT
1 **Greg Starrick**, Southern Illinois	JR	G	23	119	132	**90.2**
2 **Rusty Tyler**, Brown	SR	G	25	128	147	**87.1**
3 **Jimmy England**, Tennessee	SR	G	28	143	165	**86.7**
4 **Steve Kaplan**, Rutgers	JR	F	23	102	118	**86.4**
5 **Charlie Davis**, Wake Forest	SR	G	26	188	218	**86.2**

Minimum: 100 made

Rebounds Per Game

	CL	POS	G	REB	RPG
1 **Artis Gilmore**, Jacksonville	SR	C	26	603	**23.2**
2 **Kermit Washington**, American	SO	C	25	512	**20.5**
3 **Julius Erving**, Massachusetts	JR	F	27	527	**19.5**
4 **John Gianelli**, Pacific	JR	F	28	509	**18.2**
5 **Mel Davis**, St. John's	SO	F	27	479	**17.7**

INDIVIDUAL LEADERS—GAME

Points

	CL	POS	OPP	DATE	PTS
1 **Johnny Neumann**, Mississippi	SO	G/F	LSU	J30	**63**
2 **Johnny Neumann**, Mississippi	SO	G/F	Baylor	D29	**60**
3 **Johnny Neumann**, Mississippi	SO	G/F	Southern Miss	D15	**57**
4 **John Roche**, South Carolina	SR	G	Furman	F4	**56**
5 **Austin Carr**, Notre Dame	SR	G	Indiana	D15	**54**
Rich Rinaldi, Saint Peter's	SR	G	St. Francis (NY)	F13	**54**

TEAM LEADERS-SEASON

Win-Loss Pct

	W	L	PCT
1 **UCLA**	29	1	**.967**
2 **Marquette**	28	1	**.966**
Penn	28	1	**.966**
4 **Southern California**	24	2	**.923**
5 **Kansas**	27	3	**.900**

Scoring Offense

	G	W-L	PTS	PPG
1 **Jacksonville**	26	22-4	2,598	**99.9**
2 **Kentucky**	28	22-6	2,670	**95.4**
3 **Northern Illinois**	23	13-10	2,132	**92.7**
4 **Saint Peter's**	24	11-13	2,221	**92.5**
5 **Loyola (LA)**	26	16-10	2,394	**92.1**

Scoring Margin

	G	W-L	PPG	OPP PPG	MAR
1 **Jacksonville**	26	22-4	99.9	79.0	**20.9**
2 **Marquette**	29	28-1	81.7	62.8	**18.9**
3 **UCLA**	30	29-1	83.5	68.5	**15.0**
4 **Penn**	29	28-1	81.4	66.8	**14.6**
Massachusetts	27	23-4	79.7	65.1	**14.6**

Field Goal Pct

	G	W-L	FG	FGA	PCT
1 **Jacksonville**	26	22-4	1,077	2,008	**53.6**
2 **North Carolina**	32	26-6	1,010	1,935	**52.2**
3 **LSU**	26	14-12	897	1,725	**52.0**
4 **Loyola (LA)**	26	16-10	956	1,880	**50.9**
5 **Kentucky**	28	22-6	1,077	2,129	**50.6**

Rebounds Per Game

	G	W-L	REB	RPG
1 **Pacific**	28	22-6	1,643	**58.7**
2 **West Texas A&M**	26	19-7	1,502	**57.8**
3 **Hawaii**	28	23-5	1,596	**57.0**
4 **Arizona State**	26	16-10	1,477	**56.8**
5 **Cal State LA**	26	15-11	1,458	**56.1**

Scoring Defense

	G	W-L	OPP PTS	OPP PPG
1 **Fairleigh Dickinson**	23	16-7	1,236	**53.7**
2 **Army**	24	11-13	1,403	**58.5**
3 **Marquette**	29	28-1	1,820	**62.8**
4 **Miami (OH)**	25	20-5	1,591	**63.6**
5 **Temple**	25	13-12	1,614	**64.6**

CONSENSUS ALL-AMERICAS

First Team

PLAYER	CL	POS	HT	SCHOOL	RPG	PPG
Austin Carr	SR	G	6-3	Notre Dame	7.4	38.0
Artis Gilmore	SR	C	7-2	Jacksonville	23.2	21.9
Jim McDaniels	SR	C	7-0	Western Kentucky	15.1	29.3
Dean Meminger	SR	G	6-1	Marquette	4.0	21.2
Sidney Wicks	SR	F	6-8	UCLA	12.8	21.3

Second Team

PLAYER	CL	POS	HT	SCHOOL	RPG	PPG
Ken Durrett	SR	F	6-7	La Salle	12.0	27.0
Johnny Neumann	SO	G/F	6-6	Mississippi	6.6	40.1
Howard Porter	SR	F	6-8	Villanova	14.8	23.5
John Roche	SR	G	6-3	South Carolina	2.3	21.6
Curtis Rowe	SR	F	6-6	UCLA	9.9	17.5

Selectors: AP, NABC, UPI, USBWA

AWARD WINNERS

Player of the Year

PLAYER	CL	POS	HT	SCHOOL	AWARDS
Austin Carr	SR	G	6-3	Notre Dame	Naismith, AP, UPI
Sidney Wicks	SR	F	6-8	UCLA	USBWA
Charlie Johnson	SR	G	6-0	California	Frances Pomeroy Naismith*

* For the most outstanding senior player who is 6 feet or under

Coach of the Year

COACH	SCHOOL	REC	AWARDS
Al McGuire	Marquette	28-1	AP, UPI, USBWA, Sporting News
Jack Kraft	Villanova	27-7	NABC

Poll Progression

Preseason Poll

AP	UPI	School
1	1	UCLA
2	2	South Carolina
3	4	Kentucky
4	3	Jacksonville
5	6	Notre Dame
6	5	Marquette
7	10	USC
8	13	Villanova
9	8	Western Kentucky
10	16	Drake
11	7	Penn
12	9	Utah State
13	19	Duke
14	11	Kansas
15	—	New Mexico State
16	12	Indiana
17	—	Houston
18	15	Long Beach State
19	—	NC State
20	—	St. Bonaventure
—	14	Florida State
—	16	Utah
—	18	Kansas State
—	20	Illinois

Week of Dec 8

AP	UPI	School	AP↓↑
1	1	UCLA (2-0)	
2	2	South Carolina (2-0)	
3	4	Jacksonville (2-0) Ⓐ	↑1
4	5	Marquette (2-0)	↑2
5	3	Kentucky (2-0)	↓2
6	6	Notre Dame (1-1)	↓1
7	14	Drake (2-0)	↑3
8	10	Penn (2-0)	↑3
9	7	USC (2-0)	↓2
10	12	Villanova (2-0)	↓2
11	9	Kansas (2-0)	↑3
11	11	Indiana (2-0)	↑5
13	8	Western Kentucky (2-0)	↓4
14	—	Army (2-0) Ⓑ	⤴
15	—	New Mexico State (2-0)	
16	13	Utah State (2-1)	↓4
17	18	Tennessee (2-0)	⤴
18	—	Oregon (3-0)	⤴
19	—	St. Bonaventure (2-0)	↑1
20	15	Louisville (2-0)	⤴
—	16	Florida State (3-0)	
—	17	Long Beach State (1-1)	⤵
—	18	New Mexico (2-0)	
—	20	North Carolina (2-0)	

Week of Dec 15

AP	UPI	School	AP↓↑
1	1	UCLA (4-0)	
2	2	South Carolina (3-0)	
3	4	Kentucky (4-0)	↑2
4	5	Marquette (4-0)	
5	3	Jacksonville (5-0)	↓2
6	7	Penn (4-0)	↑2
7	9	Notre Dame (3-1)	↓1
8	6	USC (4-0)	↑1
9	12	Drake (4-0)	↓2
10	10	Villanova (4-0)	
11	11	Western Kentucky (4-0)	↑2
12	8	Kansas (4-0)	↓1
13	15	Indiana (3-1)	↓2
14	—	Tennessee (3-0)	↑3
15	13	Utah State (5-1)	↑1
16	—	Oregon (4-1)	↑2
17	16	New Mexico State (6-0)	↓2
17	18	Florida State (5-1)	⤴
19	—	St. Bonaventure (3-0)	
20	14	North Carolina (3-0)	⤴
—	17	Colorado State (5-0)	
—	19	Long Beach State (4-1)	
—	20	St. John's (3-0)	

Week of Dec 22

AP	UPI	School	AP↓↑
1	1	UCLA (4-0)	
2	2	South Carolina (5-0)	
3	4	Marquette (5-0)	↑1
4	3	Jacksonville (5-0)	↑1
5	6	Penn (5-0)	↑1
6	5	USC (6-0)	↑2
7	7	Kentucky (5-1)	↓4
8	8	Kansas (6-0)	↑4
9	10	Drake (6-0)	
10	11	Western Kentucky (5-0)	↑1
11	12	Indiana (5-1)	↑2
12	17	Tennessee (5-0)	↑2
13	13	Villanova (6-1)	↓3
14	14	Notre Dame (3-2)	↓7
15	—	St. Bonaventure (5-0)	↑4
16	—	Purdue (5-2)	⤴
17	15	Oregon (5-1)	↓1
17	16	North Carolina (5-1)	↑3
19	9	St. John's (6-0)	⤴
20	—	New Mexico State (6-1)	↓3
—	17	Utah State (5-2)	⤵
—	19	Colorado State (6-1)	
—	19	New Mexico (8-1)	

Week of Dec 29

AP	UPI	School	AP↓↑
1	1	UCLA (6-0)	
2	2	South Carolina (6-0)	
3	3	Marquette (6-0)	
4	4	USC (7-0)	↑2
5	5	Western Kentucky (7-0)	↑5
6	6	Penn (6-0)	↓1
7	9	Drake (8-0)	↑2
8	7	Kentucky (6-1)	↓1
9	8	Jacksonville (5-1)	↓5
10	12	Tennessee (6-0)	↑2
11	10	Villanova (8-1)	↑2
12	11	Kansas (7-1)	↓4
13	—	St. Bonaventure (6-0)	↑2
14	18	Indiana (6-2)	↓3
15	—	Notre Dame (3-2)	↓1
16	17	Oregon (6-1)	↑1
17	14	Louisville (5-1)	⤴
18	18	LSU (5-0)	⤴
19	18	Utah State (5-2)	⤴
20	—	Purdue (5-3)	↓4
—	13	St. John's (7-1)	⤵
—	15	Colorado State (7-1)	
—	15	New Mexico (9-1)	

Week of Jan 5

AP	UPI	School	AP↓↑
1	1	UCLA (9-0)	
2	2	South Carolina (9-0)	
3	4	Marquette (9-0)	
4	3	USC (10-0)	
5	5	Penn (8-0)	↑1
6	6	Western Kentucky (9-1)	↓1
7	9	Jacksonville (7-2)	↑2
8	7	Kansas (9-1)	↑4
9	10	Notre Dame (6-2)	↑6
10	11	St. Bonaventure (8-0)	↑3
11	8	Kentucky (7-2)	↓3
12	13	Indiana (8-2)	↑2
13	14	Louisville (8-1)	↑4
14	12	Villanova (8-2)	↓3
15	17	Utah State (9-2)	↑4
16	19	Drake (8-2)	↓9
17	—	Tennessee (7-2)	↓7
18	16	Fordham (11-0)	⤴
19	18	North Carolina (8-2)	⤴
19	—	Purdue (6-5)	↑1
—	14	Oregon (7-2)	⤵
—	19	New Mexico (9-2)	

Week of Jan 12

AP	UPI	School	AP↓↑
1	1	UCLA (11-0)	
2	3	Marquette (11-0)	↑1
3	2	USC (12-0)	↑1
4	4	Penn (11-0)	↑1
5	5	Western Kentucky (11-1)	↑1
6	6	South Carolina (10-2) Ⓒ	↓4
7	7	Jacksonville (8-2)	
8	8	Kansas (9-1)	
9	10	Notre Dame (7-2)	
10	9	Kentucky (9-2)	↑1
11	14	Indiana (9-2)	↑1
12	12	St. Bonaventure (9-1)	↓2
13	13	Villanova (11-3)	↑1
14	11	Fordham (12-0)	↑4
15	15	North Carolina (10-2)	↑4
16	19	Louisville (10-2)	↓3
17	18	Utah State (10-2)	↓2
18	—	Tennessee (9-2)	↓1
19	—	Memphis (11-2)	⤴
20	—	Oregon State (9-2)	⤴
—	16	Oregon (9-2)	
—	17	Weber State (9-1)	
—	19	New Mexico (10-3)	

Week of Jan 19

AP	UPI	School	AP↓↑
1	1	UCLA (13-0)	
2	3	Marquette (13-0)	
3	2	USC (14-0)	
4	4	Penn (13-0)	
5	5	Kansas (11-1)	↑3
6	6	Jacksonville (10-2)	↑1
7	7	Western Kentucky (12-2)	↓2
8	9	Tennessee (11-2)	↑10
9	13	Notre Dame (8-3)	
10	12	St. Bonaventure (9-1)	↑2
11	8	South Carolina (10-3)	↓5
12	17	Kentucky (10-3)	↓2
13	11	Utah State (12-2)	↑4
14	10	Villanova (13-3)	↓1
15	14	La Salle (10-1)	⤴
16	15	Oregon (9-2)	⤴
17	16	Fordham (12-1)	↓3
18	—	Indiana (9-3)	↓7
19	—	Virginia (11-2)	⤴
20	20	North Carolina (11-3)	↓5
—	17	Weber State (10-1)	
—	19	Illinois (8-2)	

Week of Jan 26

AP	UPI	School	AP↓↑
1	3	Marquette (14-0)	↑1
2	2	UCLA (14-1)	↓1
3	1	USC (14-0)	
4	4	Penn (15-0)	
5	5	Kansas (13-1)	
6	6	Jacksonville (12-2)	
7	7	Notre Dame (9-4) Ⓓ	↑2
8	8	Tennessee (12-2)	
9	11	Utah State (15-2)	↑4
10	9	South Carolina (10-3)	↑1
11	13	Kentucky (11-3)	↑1
12	10	Western Kentucky (12-3)	↓5
13	12	Oregon (10-2)	↑3
14	14	La Salle (12-1)	↑1
15	—	Virginia (11-2)	↑4
16	17	Villanova (14-4)	↓2
17	18	Duquesne (10-2)	⤴
18	16	Illinois (8-2)	⤴
19	—	Murray State (13-2)	⤴
20	18	North Carolina (11-3)	
—	15	Fordham (12-1)	⤵
—	18	Memphis (12-3)	

Week of Feb 2

AP	UPI	School	AP↓↑
1	3	Marquette (16-0)	
2	1	USC (16-0)	↑1
3	2	UCLA (15-1)	↓1
4	4	Penn (16-0)	
5	5	Kansas (14-1)	
6	6	Jacksonville (14-2)	
7	7	South Carolina (11-3)	↑3
8	10	Kentucky (13-3)	↑3
9	8	Western Kentucky (14-3)	↑3
10	12	La Salle (14-1)	↑4
11	9	Tennessee (13-3)	↓3
12	13	Notre Dame (10-5)	↓5
13	16	Utah State (15-3)	↓4
14	18	Duquesne (12-2)	↑3
15	11	Illinois (9-3)	↑3
16	15	North Carolina (12-3)	↑4
17	19	Villanova (15-4)	↓1
18	—	Houston (15-3)	⤴
19	—	Murray State (14-2)	
20	17	Michigan (10-4)	⤴
—	14	Fordham (13-1)	
—	19	Nebraska (12-3)	

Week of Feb 9

AP	UPI	School	AP↓↑
1	1	UCLA (16-1)	↑2
2	2	Marquette (18-0)	↓1
3	3	USC (16-1)	↓1
4	4	Penn (18-0)	
5	5	Kansas (16-1)	
6	6	Jacksonville (16-2)	
7	7	Western Kentucky (15-3)	↑2
8	8	Kentucky (15-3) Ⓔ	
9	10	Notre Dame (11-5)	↑3
10	9	South Carolina (13-4)	↓3
11	11	North Carolina (13-3)	↑5
12	13	Duquesne (15-2)	↑2
13	15	La Salle (15-2)	↓3
14	15	Tennessee (14-4)	↓3
15	17	Houston (17-3)	↑3
16	12	Michigan (12-4)	↑4
17	—	Murray State (15-2)	↑2
18	—	Villanova (16-4)	↓1
19	—	Utah State (17-4)	↓6
20	14	Fordham (16-1)	⤴
—	17	Illinois (10-4)	⤵
—	17	Oregon (12-4)	
—	20	Louisville (15-4)	

Week of Feb 16

AP	UPI	School	AP↓↑
1	1	UCLA (18-1)	
2	2	Marquette (20-0)	
3	3	USC (18-1)	
4	4	Penn (20-0)	
5	5	Kansas (18-1)	
6	6	Jacksonville (18-2)	
7	9	South Carolina (14-4)	↑3
8	10	North Carolina (16-3)	↑3
9	7	Western Kentucky (16-4)	↓2
10	12	Duquesne (17-2)	↑2
11	11	La Salle (17-2)	↑2
12	14	Kentucky (16-4)	↓4
13	15	Tennessee (16-4)	↑1
14	20	Notre Dame (13-6)	↓5
15	16	Utah State (19-4)	↑4
16	8	Michigan (13-4)	
17	—	Murray State (17-2)	
18	13	Fordham (18-1)	↑2
19	17	Louisville (16-4)	⤴
20	—	Ohio State (12-5)	⤴
—	18	Houston (17-4)	⤵
—	18	Villanova (18-6)	⤵

eek of Feb 23

AP	UPI	SCHOOL	AP↓↑
1	1	**UCLA** (20-1)	
2	2	**Marquette** (21-0)	
3	3	**USC** (20-1)	
4	4	**Penn** (22-0)	
5	5	**Kansas** (20-1)	
6	6	**Jacksonville** (21-2)	
7	7	**South Carolina** (16-4)	
8	11	**Duquesne** (19-2)	↑2
9	8	**Western Kentucky** (18-4)	
10	12	**Kentucky** (18-4)	↑2
11	9	**Fordham** (20-1)	↑7
12	10	**Michigan** (14-4)	↑4
13	13	**North Carolina** (17-4)	↓5
14	13	**La Salle** (18-3)	↓3
15	13	**Louisville** (17-4)	↑4
16	18	**Utah State** (19-5)	↓1
17	16	**Tennessee** (17-5)	↓4
18	—	**Ohio State** (14-5)	↑2
19	—	**Notre Dame** (15-7)	↓5
20	—	**Long Beach State** (20-4)	⤴
—	17	**Villanova** (20-6)	
—	18	**Arizona State** (15-7)	
—	18	**Hawaii** (21-3)	

Week of Mar 2

AP	UPI	SCHOOL	AP↓↑
1	1	**UCLA** (21-1)	
2	2	**Marquette** (23-0)	
3	3	**USC** (21-1)	
4	5	**Kansas** (22-1)	↑1
5	4	**Penn** (24-0)	↓1
6	6	**South Carolina** (19-4)	↑1
7	7	**Western Kentucky** (20-4)	↑2
8	10	**Kentucky** (20-4)	↑2
9	8	**Jacksonville** (21-3)	↓3
10	9	**Fordham** (21-2)	↑1
11	12	**Duquesne** (19-3)	↓3
12	11	**North Carolina** (19-4)	↑1
13	13	**Ohio State** (16-5)	↑5
14	—	**Tennessee** (19-5)	↑3
15	14	**Houston** (20-5)	⤴
16	—	**Notre Dame** (17-7)	↑3
17	—	**Long Beach State** (21-4)	↑3
18	16	**La Salle** (19-4)	↓4
18	—	**Indiana** (16-4)	⤴
20	17	**Utah State** (20-6)	↓4
—	15	**Louisville** (17-6)	↱
—	18	**Hawaii** (22-4)	
—	18	**Villanova** (22-6)	
—	18	**Weber State** (20-5)	

Week of Mar 9

AP	UPI	SCHOOL	AP↓↑
1	1	**UCLA** (24-1)	
2	2	**Marquette** (26-0)	
3	3	**USC** (24-1)	
4	4	**Penn** (26-0)	↑1
5	5	**Kansas** (23-1)	↓1
6	7	**South Carolina** (20-4)	
7	8	**Western Kentucky** (20-5)	
8	9	**Kentucky** (22-4)	
9	6	**Jacksonville** (22-3)	
10	10	**Fordham** (23-2)	
11	12	**Duquesne** (21-3)	
12	11	**Ohio State** (18-5)	↑1
13	14	**North Carolina** (20-5) (F)	↓1
14	18	**Notre Dame** (19-7)	↑2
15	—	**Tennessee** (20-6)	↓1
16	18	**Utah State** (20-6)	↑4
17	—	**Long Beach State** (22-4)	
18	15	**Houston** (20-6)	↓3
19	—	**Duke** (18-7)	⤴
20	—	**Miami (Ohio)** (20-4)	⤴
—	13	**BYU** (18-9)	
—	15	**Drake** (19-7)	
—	15	**Hawaii** (22-4)	
—	18	**La Salle** (20-6)	↱
—	18	**Louisville** (19-7)	
—	18	**Weber State** (21-5)	

Final Poll

AP	UPI	SCHOOL	AP↓↑
1	1	**UCLA** (25-1)	
2	2	**Marquette** (27-0)	
3	3	**Penn** (27-0)	↑1
4	4	**Kansas** (25-1)	↑1
5	5	**USC** (24-2)	↓2
6	6	**South Carolina** (23-4)	
7	7	**Western Kentucky** (21-5)	
8	8	**Kentucky** (22-4)	
9	9	**Fordham** (25-2)	↑1
10	10	**Ohio State** (19-5)	↑2
11	11	**Jacksonville** (22-4)	↓2
12	14	**Notre Dame** (20-7)	↑2
13	13	**North Carolina** (22-6)	
14	18	**Houston** (21-6)	↑4
15	18	**Duquesne** (21-4)	↓4
16	14	**Long Beach State** (23-4)	↑1
17	—	**Tennessee** (20-6)	↓2
18	16	**Drake** (20-7)	⤴
19	17	**Villanova** (24-6)	⤴
20	11	**BYU** (19-9)	⤴
—	20	**Weber State** (21-6)	

(A) Jacksonville scores 152 points in a Dec. 3 victory over Saint Peter's at New York's Madison Square Garden, setting a single-game scoring record (broken in 1992 by Troy, with 258 points against DeVry). Ernie Fleming leads the Dolphins with 30 points, while Artis Gilmore gets 28 with 34 rebounds.

(B) Coming off a third-place finish in the 1970 NIT, Bob Knight's last Army team opens up with back-to-back wins of 25 and 35 points over Lehigh and VMI, respectively, holding each opponent to 47 points. The Cadets lose five of their next six and finish 11–13, out of the polls for good. Knight will move to Indiana for the 1971-72 season.

(C) Maryland connects on 15 of 18 field goals against South Carolina to eke out a 31-30 overtime upset. The Terps set the record for highest team field-goal percentage with at least 15 shots attempted (83.3%).

(D) Notre Dame defeats top-ranked UCLA, 89-82, as Irish guard Austin Carr racks up 46 points, the most scored by an individual against a John Wooden-coached team.

(E) Mississippi's Johnny Neumann pours in 46 points (on a school-record 50 field goal attempts), but six Wildcats score in double figures at Memorial Coliseum in a 121-86 Kentucky win on Feb 6.

(F) North Carolina achieves the first of 31 consecutive 20-win seasons. Dean Smith and the Tar Heels will ride the stellar play of 6'10" center Lee Dedmon to the NIT championship.

1971 NCAA Tournament

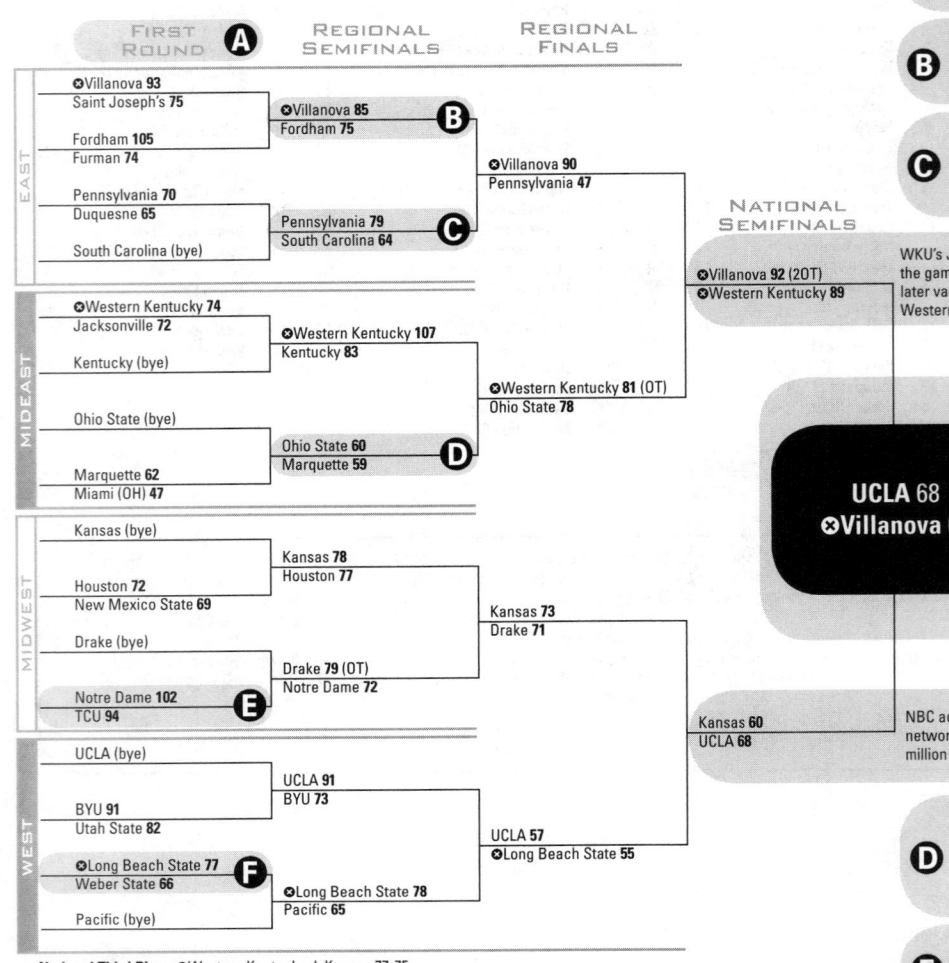

First Round (A)

East
- ⊗Villanova **93**, Saint Joseph's **75**
- Fordham **105**, Furman **74**
- Pennsylvania **70**, Duquesne **65**
- South Carolina (bye)

Mideast
- ⊗Western Kentucky **74**, Jacksonville **72**
- Kentucky (bye)
- Ohio State (bye)
- Marquette **62**, Miami (OH) **47**

Midwest
- Kansas (bye)
- Houston **72**, New Mexico State **69**
- Drake (bye)
- Notre Dame **102**, TCU **94** (E)

West
- UCLA (bye)
- BYU **91**, Utah State **82**
- ⊗Long Beach State **77**, Weber State **66** (F)
- Pacific (bye)

Regional Semifinals

- ⊗Villanova **85**, Fordham **75** (B)
- Pennsylvania **79**, South Carolina **64** (C)
- ⊗Western Kentucky **107**, Kentucky **83**
- Ohio State **60**, Marquette **59** (D)
- Kansas **78**, Houston **77**
- Drake **79** (OT), Notre Dame **72**
- UCLA **91**, BYU **73**
- ⊗Long Beach State **78**, Pacific **65**

Regional Finals

- ⊗Villanova **90**, Pennsylvania **47**
- ⊗Western Kentucky **81** (OT), Ohio State **78**
- Kansas **73**, Drake **71**
- UCLA **57**, ⊗Long Beach State **55**

National Semifinals

- ⊗Villanova **92** (2OT), ⊗Western Kentucky **89**
- Kansas **60**, UCLA **68**

National Final

UCLA 68
⊗Villanova 62

Houston

A No. 5-ranked USC (24–2) misses the Tournament because only the Pac-8's champion, UCLA, can qualify. Worse still, the Trojans can't play in the NIT either because of the conference's one postseason team per year rule.

B Fordham falls after star guard Charlie Yelverton gets into early foul trouble. After the season, first-year Fordham coach Digger Phelps takes over as head coach at Notre Dame.

C Penn, which entered the Tournament with a 26–0 record, gets three rebounds from forward Craig Littlepage who, 35 years later, will become chairman of the NCAA Men's Basketball Committee.

WKU's Jerry Dunn misses a FT that would have won the game in regulation. Both teams' appearances are later vacated because Villanova's Howard Porter and Western's Jim McDaniels had signed ABA contracts.

Steve Patterson (the answer to the trivia question "Who was UCLA's center between Lew Alcindor and Bill Walton?") stuns Villanova with 20 first-half points and a career-high 29 for the game. The championship is the Bruins' fifth in a row and seventh in eight years.

NBC accumulates the largest audience to date for a network basketball telecast during the seminfinals: 9.3 million households.

D A key turnover dooms Marquette. After Al McGuire's son, Allie, inbounds the ball, teammate Mike Mills passes it back to McGuire before he has stepped inbounds. OSU's Allan Hornyak makes two free throws for the win.

E Notre Dame's Austin Carr scores 52 points to become the only player with three Tournament games of 50 or more points. In seven career Tourney games, Carr averages a record 41.3 ppg.

F Officials call a foul on Weber State center Willie Sojourner—later famous for giving his ABA teammate Julius Erving the nickname Dr. J—and rule that he has fouled out. Sojourner protests that it's only foul No. 4. Several sportswriters in attendance later agree that the refs miscounted.

National Third Place ⊗Western Kentucky d. Kansas 77-75
East Regional Third Place Fordham d. South Carolina 100-90
Mideast Regional Third Place Marquette d. Kentucky 91-74
Midwest Regional Third Place Houston d. Notre Dame 119-106
West Regional Third Place Pacific d. BYU 84-81

⊗Team participation later vacated

Tournament Leaders

INDIVIDUAL LEADERS

Scoring

	CL	POS	G	PTS	PPG
1 **Austin Carr**, Notre Dame	SR	G	3	125	41.7
2 **Poo Welch**, Houston	SR	G	3	89	29.7
3 **Jim McDaniels**, Western Kentucky	SR	C	5	147	29.4
4 **Charlie Yelverton**, Fordham	SR	G	3	87	29.0
5 **Howard Porter**, Villanova	SR	F	5	133	26.6
6 **Tom Riker**, South Carolina	JR	C	2	49	24.5
7 **Dave Robisch**, Kansas	SR	F	4	96	24.0
8 **Collis Jones**, Notre Dame	SR	F	3	70	23.3
9 **Hank Siemiontkowski**, Villanova	JR	F	5	112	22.4
10 **Dwight Davis**, Houston	JR	F	3	67	22.3

Minimum: 2 games

Field Goal Pct

	CL	POS	G	FG	FGA	PCT
1 **Tom Bush**, Drake	SR	C	2	13	20	65.0
2 **Jim Chones**, Marquette	SO	C	3	29	48	60.4
3 **Alex Scott**, New Mexico State	JR	G	1	13	22	59.1
4 **Bob Hall**, Houston	JR	C	3	18	31	58.1
5 **John Gianelli**, Pacific	JR	F	2	15	26	57.7

Minimum: 10 made

Free Throw Pct

	CL	POS	G	FT	FTA	PCT
1 **Henry Bibby**, UCLA	JR	G	4	17	17	100.0
Kevin Joyce, South Carolina	SO	G	2	10	10	100.0
3 **Hank Siemiontkowski**, Villanova	JR	F	5	20	22	90.9
William Mainor, Fordham	SR	G	3	10	11	90.9
5 **Collis Jones**, Notre Dame	SR	F	3	20	24	83.3

Minimum: 10 made

Rebounds Per Game

	CL	POS	G	REB	RPG
1 **Clarence Glover**, Western Kentucky	SR	F	5	89	17.8
2 **Collis Jones**, Notre Dame	SR	F	3	49	16.3
3 **Kresimir Cosic**, BYU	SO	C	3	47	15.7
4 **Tom Bush**, Drake	SR	C	2	31	15.5
5 **Bob Hall**, Houston	JR	C	3	45	15.0
John Gianelli, Pacific	JR	F	2	30	15.0

Minimum: 2 games

TEAM LEADERS

Scoring

	G	PTS	PPG
1 **Notre Dame**	3	280	93.3
Fordham	3	280	93.3
3 **Houston**	3	268	89.3
4 **Western Kentucky**	5	428	85.6
5 **Villanova**	5	422	84.4
6 **Kentucky**	2	157	78.5
7 **South Carolina**	2	154	77.0
8 **Drake**	2	150	75.0
9 **Pacific**	2	149	74.5
10 **Kansas**	4	286	71.5

Minimum: 2 games

FG Pct

	G	FG	FGA	PCT
1 **Villanova**	5	167	328	50.9
2 **Marquette**	3	81	164	49.4
3 **Houston**	3	103	216	47.7
4 **Kentucky**	2	61	129	47.3
5 **BYU**	3	92	198	46.5

FT Pct

	G	FT	FTA	PCT
1 **Penn**	3	56	69	81.2
2 **Fordham**	3	60	79	75.9
3 **Notre Dame**	3	66	88	75.0
South Carolina	2	36	48	75.0
5 **Ohio State**	2	32	43	74.4

Minimum: 2 games

Rebounds

	G	REB	RPG
1 **Western Kentucky**	5	260	52.0
2 **Drake**	2	102	51.0
3 **Notre Dame**	3	151	50.3
4 **Houston**	3	135	45.0
UCLA	4	180	45.0

Minimum: 2 games

ALL-TOURNAMENT TEAM

PLAYER	CL	POS	HT	SCHOOL	RPG	PPG
Howard Porter*†	SR	F	6-8	Villanova	13.0	26.6
Jim McDaniels†	SR	C	7-0	Western Kentucky	13.2	29.4
Steve Patterson	SR	C	6-9	UCLA	7.5	13.3
Hank Siemiontkowski†	JR	F	6-7	Villanova	9.4	22.4
Sidney Wicks	SR	F	6-8	UCLA	13.0	15.0

ALL-REGIONAL TEAMS

EAST

PLAYER	CL	POS	HT	SCHOOL	RPG	PPG
Howard Porter*	SR	F	6-8	Villanova	13.7	28.7
Chris Ford	JR	G	6-5	Villanova	6.3	9.3
Tom Riker	JR	C	6-10	South Carolina	10.0	24.5
Hank Siemiontkowski	JR	F	6-7	Villanova	8.7	20.7
Charlie Yelverton	SR	G	6-2	Fordham	12.7	29.0

MIDEAST

PLAYER	CL	POS	HT	SCHOOL	RPG	PPG
Jim McDaniels*	SR	C	7-0	Western Kentucky	10.0	29.7
Jim Chones	SO	C	6-11	Marquette	12.0	22.0
Allan Hornyak	SO	G	6-1	Ohio State	3.5	18.5
Dean Meminger	SR	G	6-0	Marquette	3.0	20.7
Luke Witte	SO	C	7-0	Ohio State	14.0	18.0

MIDWEST

PLAYER	CL	POS	HT	SCHOOL	RPG	PPG
Dave Robisch*	SR	F	6-10	Kansas	13.0	28.0
Austin Carr	SR	G	6-3	Notre Dame	8.7	41.7
Jeff Halliburton	SR	G/F	6-5	Drake	9.0	14.5
Bud Stallworth	JR	F	6-5	Kansas	5.5	19.0
Poo Welch	SR	G	6-0	Houston	4.3	29.7

WEST

PLAYER	CL	POS	HT	SCHOOL	RPG	PPG
Sidney Wicks*	SR	F	6-8	UCLA	17.5	16.0
John Gianelli	JR	F	6-9	Pacific	15.0	20.0
Ed Ratleff	SO	G/F	6-6	Long Beach State	9.0	20.7
Curtis Rowe	SR	F	6-6	UCLA	10.5	12.5
George Trapp	SR	F/C	6-8½	Long Beach State	9.0	19.7

* Most outstanding player
† Honor later vacated

1971 NCAA TOURNAMENT BOX SCORES

Villanova 85, Fordham 75 (Sweet 16)

	Villanova	Fordham
1H	47	36
2H	38	39

VILLANOVA	MIN	FG	3FG	FT	REB	A	ST	BL	PF	TP
Howard Porter	-	11-17	-	3-3	8	0	-	-	5	25
Hank Siemiontkowski	-	7-9	-	5-5	8	0	-	-	3	19
Chris Ford	-	5-10	-	2-4	5	9	-	-	3	12
Tom Ingelsby	-	4-9	-	4-4	8	6	-	-	2	12
Clarence Smith	-	5-11	-	1-1	10	0	-	-	4	11
Joe McDowell	-	3-4	-	0-0	0	0	-	-	0	6
Mike Daly	-	0-0	-	0-0	0	0	-	-	0	0
John Fox	-	0-0	-	0-0	0	0	-	-	0	0
Bob Gohl	-	0-1	-	0-0	0	0	-	-	0	0
TOTALS	**-**	**35-61**	**-**	**15-17**	**39**	**15**	**-**	**-**	**17**	**85**
Percentages		57.4		88.2						

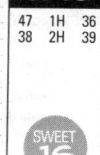

Coach: Jack Kraft

FORDHAM	MIN	FG	3FG	FT	REB	A	ST	BL	PF	TP
Charlie Yelverton	-	12-28	-	8-8	9	1	-	-	3	32
Bart Woytowicz	-	5-17	-	5-6	8	0	-	-	0	15
William Mainor	-	4-15	-	2-2	2	0	-	-	4	10
John Burik	-	2-6	-	2-2	5	2	-	-	1	6
Ken Charles	-	2-8	-	2-2	8	0	-	-	3	6
Thomas Sullivan	-	2-5	-	2-7	6	1	-	-	3	6
Steven Cain	-	0-0	-	0-0	0	0	-	-	0	0
Peter Carlesimo	-	0-0	-	0-0	0	0	-	-	0	0
Paul Griswold	-	0-0	-	0-0	1	0	-	-	0	0
Robert Larbes	-	0-0	-	0-0	0	0	-	-	0	0
Thomas Pipich	-	0-1	-	0-0	0	0	-	-	0	0
George Zambetti	-	0-0	-	0-0	0	0	-	-	0	0
TOTALS	**-**	**27-80**	**-**	**21-27**	**39**	**4**	**-**	**-**	**14**	**75**
Percentages		33.8		77.8						

Coach: Digger Phelps

Officials: Lawson, Bain
Attendance: 12,400

Penn 79, South Carolina 64 (Sweet 16)

	Penn	South Carolina
1H	36	37
2H	43	27

PENN	MIN	FG	3FG	FT	REB	A	ST	BL	PF	TP
Bob Morse	39	10-18	-	8-10	5	0	-	-	3	28
Dave Wohl	39	5-15	-	10-11	3	2	-	-	3	20
Corky Calhoun	39	3-8	-	4-4	7	1	-	-	3	10
Steve Bilsky	16	3-8	-	2-2	1	1	-	-	1	8
James Wolf	29	1-2	-	4-4	10	1	-	-	4	6
Phillip Hankinson	23	2-6	-	2-2	7	0	-	-	1	6
Al Cotler	1	0-0	-	1-2	0	0	-	-	0	1
Craig Littlepage	11	0-0	-	0-0	3	0	-	-	2	0
James Haney	1	0-0	-	0-0	0	0	-	-	0	0
John Koller	1	0-1	-	0-0	0	0	-	-	0	0
Bill Walters	1	0-0	-	0-0	0	0	-	-	0	0
TOTALS	**200**	**24-58**	**-**	**31-35**	**36**	**5**	**-**	**-**	**17**	**79**
Percentages		41.4		88.6						

Coach: Dick Harter

SOUTH CAROLINA	MIN	FG	3FG	FT	REB	A	ST	BL	PF	TP
Tom Owens	39	6-14	-	4-7	10	1	-	-	2	16
John Roche	39	5-18	-	4-5	5	6	-	-	2	14
Tom Riker	20	3-15	-	4-4	9	0	-	-	2	10
Kevin Joyce	30	3-8	-	2-2	9	1	-	-	4	8
Rick Aydlett	24	3-5	-	2-2	3	1	-	-	5	8
Bob Carver	13	2-5	-	0-0	1	0	-	-	1	4
John Ribock	20	1-2	-	0-1	3	0	-	-	5	2
Danny Traylor	12	1-2	-	0-0	3	0	-	-	1	2
Casey Manning	1	0-0	-	0-0	1	0	-	-	0	0
Dennis Powell	1	0-0	-	0-0	0	0	-	-	0	0
Jimmy Powell	1	0-0	-	0-0	0	0	-	-	0	0
TOTALS	**200**	**24-69**	**-**	**16-21**	**44**	**9**	**-**	**-**	**22**	**64**
Percentages		34.8		76.2						

Coach: Frank McGuire

Officials: Dreith, Wilcoxen
Attendance: 12,400

Western Kentucky 107, Kentucky 83 (Sweet 16)

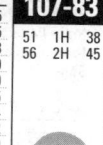

	Western Kentucky	Kentucky
1H	51	38
2H	56	45

WESTERN KENTUCKY	MIN	FG	3FG	FT	REB	A	ST	BL	PF	TP
Jim McDaniels	-	12-21	-	11-11	11	1	-	-	4	35
Jim Rose	-	12-21	-	1-1	3	3	-	-	3	25
Clarence Glover	-	8-16	-	2-5	17	8	-	-	2	18
Rex Bailey	-	3-10	-	3-4	2	3	-	-	2	9
Jerry Dunn	-	3-8	-	3-5	7	4	-	-	4	9
Gary Sundmacker	-	2-2	-	1-2	1	1	-	-	3	5
Chuck Witt	-	2-4	-	0-0	1	0	-	-	0	4
Danny Johnson	-	0-0	-	2-2	0	3	-	-	1	2
Terry Davis	-	0-0	-	0-0	0	0	-	-	0	0
Steve Eaton	-	0-1	-	0-0	0	1	-	-	0	0
Ray Kleykamp	-	0-0	-	0-0	0	0	-	-	0	0
TOTALS	**-**	**42-83**	**-**	**23-30**	**42**	**24**	**-**	**-**	**19**	**107**
Percentages		50.6		76.7						

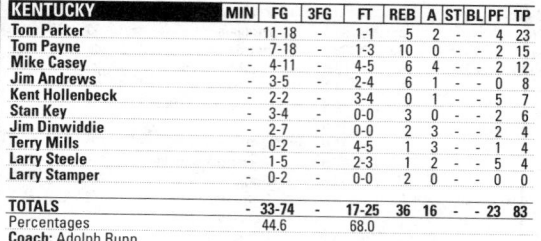

Coach: John Oldham

KENTUCKY	MIN	FG	3FG	FT	REB	A	ST	BL	PF	TP
Tom Parker	-	11-18	-	1-1	5	2	-	-	4	23
Tom Payne	-	7-18	-	1-3	10	0	-	-	2	15
Mike Casey	-	4-11	-	4-5	6	4	-	-	2	12
Jim Andrews	-	3-5	-	2-4	6	1	-	-	0	8
Kent Hollenbeck	-	2-2	-	3-4	0	1	-	-	5	7
Stan Key	-	3-4	-	0-0	3	0	-	-	2	6
Jim Dinwiddie	-	2-7	-	0-0	2	3	-	-	2	4
Terry Mills	-	0-2	-	4-5	1	3	-	-	1	4
Larry Steele	-	1-5	-	2-3	1	2	-	-	5	4
Larry Stamper	-	0-2	-	0-0	2	0	-	-	0	0
TOTALS	**-**	**33-74**	**-**	**17-25**	**36**	**16**	**-**	**-**	**23**	**83**
Percentages		44.6		68.0						

Coach: Adolph Rupp

Officials: Evans, Brown
Attendance: 10,615

Ohio State 60, Marquette 59 (Sweet 16)

	Ohio State	Marquette
1H	27	31
2H	33	28

OHIO STATE	MIN	FG	3FG	FT	REB	A	ST	BL	PF	TP
James Cleamons	-	7-13	-	7-8	4	4	-	-	2	21
Luke Witte	-	5-13	-	3-4	11	1	-	-	3	13
Allan Hornyak	-	4-15	-	3-3	4	1	-	-	4	11
Robert Siekmann	-	4-5	-	2-2	4	4	-	-	4	10
David Merchant	-	1-3	-	0-0	1	0	-	-	1	2
Mark Minor	-	1-5	-	0-2	3	3	-	-	2	2
Mark Wagar	-	0-2	-	1-3	2	0	-	-	1	1
TOTALS	**-**	**22-56**	**-**	**16-22**	**29**	**13**	**-**	**-**	**17**	**60**
Percentages		39.3		72.7						

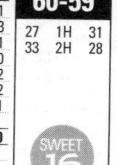

Coach: Fred R. Taylor

MARQUETTE	MIN	FG	3FG	FT	REB	A	ST	BL	PF	TP
Jim Chones	-	9-19	-	0-2	10	0	-	-	3	18
Allie McGuire	-	5-11	-	2-3	0	0	-	-	4	12
Dean Meminger	-	4-11	-	3-7	3	5	-	-	5	11
Gary Brell	-	5-10	-	0-0	8	8	-	-	0	10
Bob Lackey	-	1-9	-	6-8	9	1	-	-	4	8
George Frazier	-	0-1	-	0-1	0	0	-	-	0	0
Gary Grzesk	-	0-0	-	0-0	1	0	-	-	0	0
Hugh McMahon	-	0-1	-	0-0	2	0	-	-	3	0
TOTALS	**-**	**24-62**	**-**	**11-21**	**33**	**14**	**-**	**-**	**19**	**59**
Percentages		38.7		52.4						

Coach: Al McGuire

Officials: Herrold, Ross
Attendance: 10,615

Kansas 78, Houston 77 (Sweet 16)

	Kansas	Houston
1H	36	37
2H	42	40

KANSAS	MIN	FG	3FG	FT	REB	A	ST	BL	PF	TP
Dave Robisch	-	10-23	-	9-14	16	2	-	-	3	29
Bud Stallworth	-	10-21	-	5-7	8	1	-	-	2	25
Aubrey Nash	-	4-7	-	1-3	1	3	-	-	4	9
Pierre Russell	-	3-10	-	0-0	4	2	-	-	3	6
Randy Canfield	-	2-3	-	0-0	4	0	-	-	3	4
Roger Brown	-	1-9	-	1-2	7	1	-	-	4	3
Bob Kivisto	-	0-1	-	2-3	0	2	-	-	0	2
Greg Douglas	-	0-1	-	0-0	1	0	-	-	0	0
TOTALS	**-**	**30-75**	**-**	**18-29**	**41**	**11**	**-**	**-**	**19**	**78**
Percentages		40.0		62.1						

Coach: Ted Owens

HOUSTON	MIN	FG	3FG	FT	REB	A	ST	BL	PF	TP
Poo Welch	-	13-22	-	2-2	5	3	-	-	4	28
Dwight Davis	-	5-18	-	9-14	10	3	-	-	5	19
Bob Hall	-	5-8	-	3-5	17	1	-	-	2	13
Steve Newsome	-	4-13	-	2-2	11	0	-	-	4	10
Jerry Bonney	-	1-2	-	2-2	1	1	-	-	2	4
Sonny Willis	-	1-3	-	0-1	1	1	-	-	2	2
Gene Bodden	-	0-1	-	1-3	3	0	-	-	2	1
Larry Brown	-	0-1	-	0-0	0	0	-	-	1	0
TOTALS	**-**	**29-68**	**-**	**19-29**	**48**	**9**	**-**	**-**	**22**	**77**
Percentages		42.6		65.5						

Coach: Guy V. Lewis

Officials: Honzo, Woolridge
Attendance: 10,550

Drake 79, Notre Dame 72 (Sweet 16)

	Drake	Notre Dame
1H	39	32
2H	23	30
OT1	17	10

DRAKE	MIN	FG	3FG	FT	REB	A	ST	BL	PF	TP
Tom Bush	-	7-11	-	5-10	16	3	-	-	4	19
Leon Huff	-	7-19	-	1-3	12	2	-	-	5	15
Al Sakys	-	7-13	-	1-1	8	1	-	-	5	15
Jeff Halliburton	-	5-21	-	2-3	11	3	-	-	5	12
Bobby Jones	-	5-16	-	1-2	9	3	-	-	0	11
Carl Salyers	-	1-2	-	2-2	0	0	-	-	0	4
Jim Nordrum	-	1-3	-	1-3	5	0	-	-	0	3
Tony Johnson	-	0-1	-	0-2	2	0	-	-	0	0
Dave Wicklund	-	0-0	-	0-0	1	0	-	-	0	0
TOTALS	**-**	**33-86**	**-**	**13-26**	**63**	**12**	**-**	**-**	**19**	**79**
Percentages		38.4		50.0						

Coach: Maury John

NOTRE DAME	MIN	FG	3FG	FT	REB	A	ST	BL	PF	TP
Austin Carr	-	11-27	-	4-5	8	0	-	-	4	26
Collis Jones	-	7-26	-	5-7	16	1	-	-	4	19
Jackie Meehan	-	4-8	-	3-4	4	6	-	-	5	11
Sid Catlett	-	2-11	-	3-3	17	4	-	-	2	7
John Pleick	-	2-4	-	0-0	4	1	-	-	5	4
Tom Sinnott	-	1-2	-	1-2	2	0	-	-	1	3
Doug Gemmell	-	1-4	-	0-1	6	2	-	-	2	2
TOTALS	**-**	**28-82**	**-**	**16-22**	**57**	**14**	**-**	**-**	**23**	**72**
Percentages		34.1		72.7						

Coach: Johnny Dee

Officials: Diehl, Hermjack
Attendance: 10,550

UCLA	MIN	FG	3FG	FT	REB	A	ST	BL	PF	TP
Henry Bibby	-	6-13	-	3-3	9	4	-	-	3	15
Sidney Wicks	-	6-16	-	2-5	20	1	-	-	1	14
Steve Patterson	-	6-13	-	1-3	11	4	-	-	4	13
Curtis Rowe	-	5-11	-	3-6	9	6	-	-	0	13
Terry Schofield	-	6-13	-	0-2	6	3	-	-	3	12
Larry Farmer	-	5-9	-	1-3	6	1	-	-	0	11
Rick Betchley	-	3-4	-	1-1	0	0	-	-	0	7
Kenny Booker	-	2-6	-	0-0	1	1	-	-	2	4
John Ecker	-	1-3	-	0-0	0	0	-	-	0	2
TOTALS	-	40-88	-	11-23	62	20	-	-	13	91
Percentages		45.5		47.8						

Coach: John Wooden

91-73

41	1H	32
50	2H	41

SWEET 16

BYU	MIN	FG	3FG	FT	REB	A	ST	BL	PF	TP
Steve Kelly	-	9-16	-	6-6	5	2	-	-	1	24
Kresimir Cosic	-	8-18	-	2-2	23	5	-	-	3	18
Bernie Fryer	-	8-19	-	2-6	4	6	-	-	3	18
Jim Miller	-	4-11	-	2-5	5	1	-	-	3	10
Joe Bunker	-	1-3	-	0-0	5	4	-	-	4	2
Phil Tollestrup	-	0-3	-	1-2	1	2	-	-	2	1
Dave Bailey	-	0-1	-	0-0	0	0	-	-	1	0
Craig Jorgensen	-	0-1	-	0-0	1	0	-	-	0	0
Kalevi Sarkalahti	-	0-0	-	0-0	0	0	-	-	0	0
TOTALS	-	30-72	-	13-21	44	20	-	-	17	73
Percentages		41.7		61.9						

Coach: Stan Watts

Officials: White, Strauthers
Attendance: 15,032

LONG BEACH STATE	MIN	FG	3FG	FT	REB	A	ST	BL	PF	TP
George Trapp	-	8-18	-	7-10	6	4	-	-	3	23
Chuck Terry	-	9-19	-	0-0	9	1	-	-	3	18
Ed Ratleff	-	5-13	-	3-5	10	6	-	-	2	13
Dwight Taylor	-	3-5	-	5-6	3	7	-	-	2	11
Eric McWilliams	-	3-6	-	1-1	2	1	-	-	5	7
Bob Lynn	-	3-9	-	0-1	7	1	-	-	4	6
Bernard Williams	-	0-3	-	0-2	4	3	-	-	2	0
TOTALS	-	31-73	-	16-25	41	23	-	-	21	78
Percentages		42.5		64.0						

Coach: Jerry Tarkanian

78-65

31	1H	44
47	2H	21

SWEET 16

PACIFIC	MIN	FG	3FG	FT	REB	A	ST	BL	PF	TP
Bob Thomason	-	7-22	-	5-6	3	7	-	-	2	19
John Gianelli	-	5-9	-	6-8	17	1	-	-	4	16
Robbie Sperring	-	4-4	-	5-6	4	6	-	-	2	13
Jim McCargo	-	3-9	-	5-9	10	0	-	-	5	11
Bernard Dulaney	-	2-9	-	0-1	6	3	-	-	3	4
Paul Scheidegger	-	1-3	-	0-0	2	0	-	-	1	2
Pat Douglass	-	0-1	-	0-0	0	0	-	-	1	0
Pete Jensen	-	0-0	-	0-0	1	0	-	-	2	0
Jonh Joshua	-	0-0	-	0-0	1	1	-	-	0	0
Ozzie Noble	-	0-0	-	0-0	0	0	-	-	0	0
TOTALS	-	22-57	-	21-30	44	18	-	-	20	65
Percentages		38.6		70.0						

Coach: Dick Edwards

Officials: Jones, Stout
Attendance: 15,032

VILLANOVA	MIN	FG	3FG	FT	REB	A	ST	BL	PF	TP
Howard Porter	39	16-24	-	3-4	15	0	-	-	2	35
Hank Siemiontkowski	38	10-15	-	0-0	7	1	-	-	3	20
Clarence Smith	36	7-11	-	1-2	8	1	-	-	0	15
Chris Ford	35	2-4	-	5-9	5	4	-	-	0	9
Tom Ingelsby	37	1-3	-	6-7	4	7	-	-	2	8
Bob Gohl	3	1-1	-	0-0	1	0	-	-	1	2
John Fox	5	0-1	-	1-1	0	0	-	-	0	1
Joe McDowell	6	0-1	-	0-0	1	1	-	-	0	0
Mike Daly	1	0-0	-	0-0	0	0	-	-	0	0
TOTALS	200	37-60	-	16-23	41	14	-	-	8	90
Percentages		61.7		69.6						

Coach: Jack Kraft

90-47

43	1H	22
47	2H	25

ELITE 8

PENN	MIN	FG	3FG	FT	REB	A	ST	BL	PF	TP
Phillip Hankinson	26	4-9	-	0-0	4	-	-	-	1	8
James Wolf	19	3-8	-	1-1	8	-	-	-	3	7
Dave Wohl	33	3-10	-	0-0	0	-	-	-	2	6
Bob Morse	22	2-8	-	2-2	2	-	-	-	1	6
Craig Littlepage	20	1-7	-	3-5	4	-	-	-	2	5
John Koller	13	2-4	-	0-0	1	-	-	-	0	4
Al Cotler	8	2-7	-	0-0	2	-	-	-	2	4
Bill Walters	1	1-1	-	1-1	1	-	-	-	1	3
Corky Calhoun	38	1-7	-	0-0	5	-	-	-	2	2
Steve Bilsky	14	1-4	-	0-0	0	-	-	-	2	2
James Haney	6	0-2	-	0-0	2	-	-	-	0	0
TOTALS	200	20-67	-	7-9	29	-	-	-	16	47
Percentages		29.9		77.8						

Coach: Dick Harter

Officials: Wilcoxen, Bain
Attendance: 12,400

WESTERN KENTUCKY	MIN	FG	3FG	FT	REB	A	ST	BL	PF	TP
Jim McDaniels	-	14-35	-	3-6	6	0	-	-	4	31
Rex Bailey	-	7-9	-	0-1	0	4	-	-	2	14
Jim Rose	-	6-13	-	1-1	6	3	-	-	4	13
Jerry Dunn	-	5-14	-	2-5	15	3	-	-	4	12
Clarence Glover	-	2-9	-	7-9	22	2	-	-	2	11
Danny Johnson	-	0-1	-	0-0	0	1	-	-	1	0
Chuck Witt	-	0-1	-	0-0	1	0	-	-	0	0
TOTALS	-	34-82	-	13-22	50	13	-	-	17	81
Percentages		41.5		59.1						

Coach: John Oldham

81-78

34	1H	40
35	2H	29
12	OT1	9

ELITE 8

OHIO STATE	MIN	FG	3FG	FT	REB	A	ST	BL	PF	TP
Allan Hornyak	-	11-21	-	4-4	3	2	-	-	1	26
Luke Witte	-	10-19	-	3-5	17	1	-	-	4	23
James Cleamons	-	4-9	-	4-6	7	4	-	-	4	12
Mark Minor	-	3-8	-	1-1	3	6	-	-	4	7
Mark Wagar	-	2-6	-	3-4	3	3	-	-	5	7
Robert Siekmann	-	1-2	-	1-1	2	0	-	-	0	3
David Merchant	-	0-2	-	0-0	0	0	-	-	0	0
TOTALS	-	31-67	-	16-21	35	16	-	-	18	78
Percentages		46.3		76.2						

Coach: Fred R. Taylor

Officials: Evans, Brown
Attendance: 10,521

KANSAS	MIN	FG	3FG	FT	REB	A	ST	BL	PF	TP
Dave Robisch	-	10-18	-	7-9	10	3	-	-	3	27
Roger Brown	-	6-10	-	3-5	9	1	-	-	1	15
Bud Stallworth	-	6-13	-	1-3	3	0	-	-	5	13
Bob Kivisto	-	2-4	-	5-8	2	3	-	-	0	9
Aubrey Nash	-	2-4	-	2-3	3	1	-	-	4	6
Pierre Russell	-	0-3	-	3-5	5	2	-	-	5	3
Randy Canfield	-	0-0	-	0-0	1	0	-	-	2	0
Mark Mathews	-	0-0	-	0-1	0	0	-	-	0	0
TOTALS	-	26-52	-	21-34	33	10	-	-	20	73
Percentages		50.0		61.8						

Coach: Ted Owens

73-71

30	1H	38
43	2H	33

ELITE 8

DRAKE	MIN	FG	3FG	FT	REB	A	ST	BL	PF	TP
Leon Huff	-	8-14	-	4-5	4	0	-	-	5	20
Jeff Halliburton	-	8-20	-	1-4	7	5	-	-	3	17
Tom Bush	-	6-9	-	4-6	15	0	-	-	5	16
Bobby Jones	-	5-14	-	0-0	5	2	-	-	3	10
Al Sakys	-	2-4	-	0-1	5	2	-	-	5	4
Jim Nordrum	-	1-1	-	0-0	1	0	-	-	2	2
Tony Johnson	-	0-1	-	1-2	0	1	-	-	0	1
Dave Wicklund	-	0-1	-	1-1	2	1	-	-	0	1
TOTALS	-	30-64	-	11-19	39	11	-	-	23	71
Percentages		46.9		57.9						

Coach: Maury John

Officials: Honzo, Woolridge
Attendance: 10,550

UCLA	MIN	FG	3FG	FT	REB	A	ST	BL	PF	TP
Sidney Wicks	-	5-13	-	8-12	15	0	-	-	4	18
Curtis Rowe	-	3-6	-	6-12	12	1	-	-	2	12
Henry Bibby	-	4-18	-	3-3	6	1	-	-	4	11
Terry Schofield	-	3-9	-	0-0	3	1	-	-	1	6
Steve Patterson	-	2-8	-	1-1	5	2	-	-	2	5
Rick Betchley	-	1-1	-	2-2	0	1	-	-	0	4
Larry Farmer	-	0-3	-	1-2	4	1	-	-	2	1
Kenny Booker	-	0-4	-	0-0	2	0	-	-	0	0
John Ecker	-	0-0	-	0-0	0	0	-	-	1	0
TOTALS	-	18-62	-	21-32	47	7	-	-	16	57
Percentages		29.0		65.6						

Coach: John Wooden

57-55

27	1H	31
30	2H	24

ELITE 8

LONG BEACH STATE	MIN	FG	3FG	FT	REB	A	ST	BL	PF	TP
Ed Ratleff	-	8-14	-	2-4	4	2	-	-	5	18
George Trapp	-	5-13	-	5-6	16	5	-	-	3	15
Chuck Terry	-	4-4	-	3-4	6	7	-	-	3	11
Bob Lynn	-	3-10	-	1-3	5	0	-	-	4	7
Dwight Taylor	-	0-2	-	2-4	2	0	-	-	2	2
Bernard Williams	-	1-7	-	0-0	4	1	-	-	3	2
Eric McWilliams	-	0-1	-	0-0	2	2	-	-	2	0
TOTALS	-	21-51	-	13-21	39	17	-	-	22	55
Percentages		41.2		61.9						

Coach: Jerry Tarkanian

Attendance: 14,003

92-89 — FINAL 4

39	1H	36
35	2H	38
11	OT1	11
7	OT2	4

VILLANOVA	MIN	FG	3FG	FT	REB	A	ST	BL	PF	TP
Hank Siemiontkowski	36	11-20	-	9-10	15	3	-	-	5	31
Howard Porter	50	10-20	-	2-3	16	1	-	-	4	22
Tom Ingelsby	50	5-10	-	4-7	4	3	-	-	1	14
Clarence Smith	50	5-14	-	3-6	11	3	-	-	1	13
Chris Ford	50	3-6	-	2-2	1	7	-	-	4	8
Joe McDowell	14	2-3	-	0-3	3	1	-	-	1	4
TOTALS	250	36-73	-	20-31	50	18	-	-	16	92
Percentages		49.3		64.5						

Coach: Jack Kraft

WESTERN KENTUCKY	MIN	FG	3FG	FT	REB	A	ST	BL	PF	TP
Jerry Dunn	50	11-33	-	3-6	8	6	-	-	5	25
Jim McDaniels	44	10-24	-	2-4	17	2	-	-	5	22
Jim Rose	50	8-21	-	2-3	8	1	-	-	2	18
Clarence Glover	50	5-15	-	2-4	20	0	-	-	4	12
Rex Bailey	47	5-11	-	2-3	8	7	-	-	1	12
Chuck Witt	5	0-1	-	0-0	0	0	-	-	3	0
Gary Sundmacker	4	0-0	-	0-0	0	1	-	-	1	0
TOTALS	250	39-105	-	11-20	61	17	-	-	21	89
Percentages		37.1		55.0						

Coach: John Oldham

Officials: Bain, Brown
Attendance: 31,428

68-60 — FINAL 4

32	1H	25
36	2H	35

UCLA	MIN	FG	3FG	FT	REB	A	ST	BL	PF	TP
Sidney Wicks	38	5-9	-	11-13	8	3	-	-	2	21
Henry Bibby	37	6-9	-	6-6	4	1	-	-	3	18
Curtis Rowe	38	7-10	-	2-4	15	1	-	-	2	16
Steve Patterson	37	3-11	-	0-0	6	2	-	-	2	6
Kenny Booker	20	1-2	-	1-2	5	6	-	-	3	3
Terry Schofield	17	1-3	-	0-1	0	0	-	-	3	2
John Ecker	2	0-1	-	2-2	1	0	-	-	0	2
Rick Betchley	4	0-0	-	0-1	0	0	-	-	0	0
Larry Farmer	3	0-2	-	0-1	2	0	-	-	1	0
Jon Chapman	2	0-0	-	0-0	1	0	-	-	2	0
Andy Hill	2	0-0	-	0-0	0	0	-	-	0	0
TOTALS	200	23-47	-	22-30	42	13	-	-	18	68
Percentages		48.9		73.3						

Coach: John Wooden

KANSAS	MIN	FG	3FG	FT	REB	A	ST	BL	PF	TP
Dave Robisch	38	7-19	-	3-6	6	4	-	-	3	17
Bud Stallworth	35	5-10	-	2-4	5	3	-	-	5	12
Pierre Russell	34	5-12	-	2-2	4	1	-	-	4	12
Roger Brown	33	3-8	-	1-3	9	2	-	-	4	7
Aubrey Nash	32	3-9	-	1-2	3	2	-	-	1	7
Bob Kivisto	19	1-1	-	1-4	1	4	-	-	2	3
Mark Williams	3	0-1	-	2-2	0	0	-	-	2	2
Randy Canfield	2	0-0	-	0-0	0	2	-	-	1	0
Greg Douglas	2	0-0	-	0-0	1	0	-	-	0	0
Mark Mathews	2	0-0	-	0-0	0	0	-	-	0	0
TOTALS	200	24-60	-	12-23	29	18	-	-	22	60
Percentages		40.0		52.2						

Coach: Ted Owens

Officials: White, Honzo
Attendance: 31,428

77-75 — 3RD PLACE

38	1H	37
39	2H	38

WESTERN KENTUCKY	MIN	FG	3FG	FT	REB	A	ST	BL	PF	TP
Jim McDaniels	33	14-30	-	8-10	19	1	-	-	4	36
Jim Rose	39	4-12	-	3-4	2	3	-	-	3	11
Jerry Dunn	29	3-13	-	4-6	10	4	-	-	3	10
Clarence Glover	26	3-8	-	4-5	13	3	-	-	5	10
Rex Bailey	40	3-11	-	1-2	5	7	-	-	2	7
Gary Sundmacker	12	1-1	-	0-1	1	0	-	-	1	2
Steve Eaton	4	0-0	-	1-2	0	0	-	-	0	1
Chuck Witt	16	0-1	-	0-1	1	0	-	-	3	0
Danny Johnson	1	0-0	-	0-0	1	0	-	-	0	0
TOTALS	200	28-76	-	21-31	52	18	-	-	21	77
Percentages		36.8		67.7						

Coach: John Oldham

KANSAS	MIN	FG	3FG	FT	REB	A	ST	BL	PF	TP
Dave Robisch	38	9-21	-	5-8	9	1	-	-	4	23
Roger Brown	30	7-16	-	2-3	16	1	-	-	3	16
Aubrey Nash	40	4-14	-	2-3	7	4	-	-	3	10
Bud Stallworth	32	3-13	-	4-8	14	2	-	-	4	10
Pierre Russell	30	4-10	-	0-1	7	5	-	-	1	8
Bob Kivisto	20	2-3	-	0-1	2	4	-	-	1	4
Randy Canfield	10	1-6	-	2-3	5	0	-	-	5	4
TOTALS	200	30-83	-	15-27	60	17	-	-	21	75
Percentages		36.1		55.6						

Coach: Ted Owens

Officials: Honzo, White
Attendance: 31,765

68-62 — NCAA FINAL 1971

45	1H	37
23	2H	25

UCLA	MIN	FG	3FG	FT	REB	A	ST	BL	PF	TP
Steve Patterson	40	13-18	-	3-5	8	4	-	-	1	29
Henry Bibby	40	6-12	-	5-5	2	3	-	-	1	17
Curtis Rowe	40	2-3	-	4-5	8	2	-	-	0	8
Sidney Wicks	40	3-7	-	1-1	9	7	-	-	2	7
Terry Schofield	26	3-9	-	0-0	1	4	-	-	4	6
Rick Betchley	9	0-0	-	1-2	1	0	-	-	1	1
Kenny Booker	5	0-0	-	0-0	0	0	-	-	0	0
TOTALS	200	27-49	-	14-18	29	20	-	-	9	68
Percentages		55.1		77.8						

Coach: John Wooden

VILLANOVA	MIN	FG	3FG	FT	REB	A	ST	BL	PF	TP
Howard Porter	40	10-21	-	5-6	8	0	-	-	1	25
Hank Siemiontkowski	37	9-16	-	1-2	6	0	-	-	3	19
Clarence Smith	40	4-11	-	1-1	2	0	-	-	4	9
Tom Ingelsby	40	3-9	-	1-1	4	7	-	-	2	7
Chris Ford	40	0-4	-	2-3	5	10	-	-	4	2
Joe McDowell	3	0-1	-	0-0	2	1	-	-	0	0
TOTALS	200	26-62	-	10-13	27	18	-	-	14	62
Percentages		41.9		76.9						

Coach: Jack Kraft

Officials: Bain, Brown
Attendance: 31,765

NATIONAL INVITATION TOURNAMENT (NIT)

First round: North Carolina d. Massachusetts 90-49, Duke d. Dayton 68-60, Providence d. Louisville 64-58, Tennessee d. St. John's 84-83 (2OT), Georgia Tech d. La Salle 70-67, Michigan d. Syracuse 86-76, St. Bonaventure d. Purdue 94-79, Hawaii d. Oklahoma 87-86 (2OT)
Quarterfinals: North Carolina d. Providence 86-79, Duke d. Tennessee 78-64, Georgia Tech d. Michigan 78-70, St. Bonaventure d. Hawaii 73-64
Semifinals: North Carolina d. Duke 73-69, Georgia Tech d. St. Bonaventure 76-71 (2OT)
Third place: St. Bonaventure d. Duke 92-88 (OT)
Championship: North Carolina d. Georgia Tech 84-66
MVP: Bill Chamberlain, North Carolina

1971-72: Present Perfect

UCLA didn't need any help winning its sixth straight national title and eighth in nine seasons. Nevertheless, the perfect 30–0 Bruins, led by 6'11" sophomore sensation Bill Walton, got to cut down the championship nets in the homey confines of the Los Angeles Memorial Sports Arena. UCLA danced to the Final by crushing Weber State (by 32 points), Long Beach State (16) and Louisville (19), which was coached by former John Wooden assistant Denny Crum. Florida State went up against the Bruins after edging North Carolina in the other semifinal, making coach Dean Smith 0–4 in Final Fours. Walton had 24 points and 20 rebounds in UCLA's 81-76 title win to earn MOP honors. He was named the Naismith National Player of the Year (21.1 ppg, 15.5 rpg) in his first varsity season.

Kentucky legend Adolph Rupp coached his last game on March 18, 1972, a 73-54 Elite Eight loss to Florida State. In 41 seasons at the Wildcats helm, Rupp compiled an 876–190 record (.822) and won four national championships.

Major Conference Standings

ACC

	Conference			Overall		
	W	L	Pct	W	L	Pct
North Carolina⊕	9	3	.750	26	5	.839
Maryland□	8	4	.667	27	5	.844
Virginia□	8	4	.667	21	7	.750
NC State	6	6	.500	16	10	.615
Duke	6	6	.500	14	12	.538
Wake Forest	3	9	.250	8	18	.308
Clemson	2	10	.167	10	16	.385

Tournament: **North Carolina d. Maryland 73-64**
Tournament MVP: **Bob McAdoo**, North Carolina

Big Eight

	Conference			Overall		
	W	L	Pct	W	L	Pct
Kansas State⊕	12	2	.857	19	9	.679
Missouri□	10	4	.714	21	6	.778
Oklahoma	9	5	.643	14	12	.538
Nebraska	7	7	.500	14	12	.538
Kansas	7	7	.500	11	15	.423
Iowa State	5	9	.357	12	14	.462
Colorado	4	10	.286	7	19	.269
Oklahoma State	2	12	.143	4	22	.154

Big Sky

	Conference			Overall		
	W	L	Pct	W	L	Pct
Weber State⊕	10	4	.714	18	11	.621
Gonzaga	8	6	.571	14	12	.538
Idaho State	8	6	.571	14	12	.538
Northern Arizona	7	7	.500	13	10	.565
Boise State	7	7	.500	14	12	.538
Montana	7	7	.500	14	12	.538
Montana State	6	8	.429	10	16	.385
Idaho	2	12	.143	5	20	.200

Big Ten

	Conference			Overall		
	W	L	Pct	W	L	Pct
Minnesota⊕⊗	11	3	.786	18	7	.720
Ohio State	10	4	.714	18	6	.750
Indiana□	9	5	.643	17	8	.680
Michigan	9	5	.643	14	10	.583
Wisconsin	6	8	.429	13	11	.542
Michigan State	6	8	.429	13	11	.542
Purdue	6	8	.429	12	12	.500
Illinois	5	9	.357	14	10	.583
Iowa	5	9	.357	11	13	.458
Northwestern	3	11	.214	5	18	.217

Ivy

	Conference			Overall		
	W	L	Pct	W	L	Pct
Penn⊕	13	1	.929	25	3	.893
Princeton□	12	2	.857	20	7	.741
Harvard	8	6	.571	15	11	.577
Dartmouth	8	6	.571	14	12	.538
Brown	6	8	.429	10	16	.385
Yale	5	9	.357	7	17	.292
Columbia	3	11	.214	4	20	.167
Cornell	1	13	.071	5	19	.208

Mid-American

	Conference			Overall		
	W	L	Pct	W	L	Pct
Ohio⊕	7	3	.700	15	11	.577
Toledo	7	3	.700	18	7	.720
Kent State	6	4	.600	7	17	.292
Western Michigan	5	5	.500	10	14	.417
Miami (OH)	4	6	.400	12	12	.500
Bowling Green	1	9	.100	4	20	.167

MEAC

	Conference			Overall		
	W	L	Pct	W	L	Pct
NC A&T	9	3	.750	20	6	.769
Howard	8	4	.667	18	9	.667
UMES	7	5	.583	20	7	.741
Morgan State	7	5	.583	16	10	.615
South Carolina St.	6	6	.500	15	11	.577
NC Central	3	9	.250	4	20	.167
Delaware State	2	10	.167	7	15	.031

Tournament: **NC A&T d. Howard 71-62**
Tournament MOP: **Robert Lewis**, Howard

Middle Atlantic

	Conference			Overall		
	W	L	Pct	W	L	Pct
Eastern						
Temple⊕	6	0	1.000	23	8	.742
Saint Joseph's□	5	1	.833	19	9	.679
American	3	3	.500	16	8	.667
Drexel	2	4	.333	11	14	.440
Hofstra	2	4	.333	11	14	.440
La Salle	2	4	.333	6	19	.240
West Chester	1	5	.167	9	16	.360
Western						
Rider	8	2	.800	15	11	.577
Lafayette□	7	3	.700	21	6	.778
Delaware	7	3	.700	18	7	.720
Lehigh	3	7	.300	10	14	.417
Bucknell	3	7	.300	5	18	.217
Gettysburg	2	8	.200	11	12	.478

Missouri Valley

	Conference			Overall		
	W	L	Pct	W	L	Pct
Louisville⊕	12	2	.857	26	5	.839
Memphis□	12	2	.857	21	7	.750
Saint Louis	9	5	.643	18	8	.692
Bradley	8	6	.571	17	9	.654
Wichita State	6	8	.429	16	10	.615
Tulsa	5	9	.357	15	11	.577
North Texas	2	12	.143	8	18	.308
Drake	2	12	.143	7	19	.269
New Mexico State	-	-	-	19	6	.760
West Texas A&M	-	-	-	14	11	.560

Ohio Valley

	Conference			Overall		
	W	L	Pct	W	L	Pct
Eastern Kentucky⊕	9	5	.643	15	11	.577
Morehead State	9	5	.643	16	11	.593
Western Kentucky	9	5	.643	15	11	.577
Tennessee Tech	7	7	.500	14	11	.560
Murray State	6	8	.429	15	11	.577
East Tennessee St.	6	8	.429	11	14	.440
Middle Tennessee St.	5	9	.357	15	11	.577
Austin Peay	5	9	.357	10	14	.417

PCAA

	Conference			Overall		
	W	L	Pct	W	L	Pct
Long Beach State⊕⊗	10	2	.833	25	4	.862
Pacific	8	4	.667	17	9	.654
San Diego State	7	5	.583	18	10	.643
UC Santa Barbara	5	7	.417	17	9	.654
Cal State LA	5	7	.417	14	12	.538
San Jose State	5	7	.417	11	15	.423
Fresno State	2	10	.167	9	17	.346

Pac-8

	Conference			Overall		
	W	L	Pct	W	L	Pct
UCLA⊕	14	0	1.000	30	0	1.000
Washington	10	4	.714	20	6	.769
Oregon State	9	5	.643	18	10	.643
Southern California	9	5	.643	16	10	.615
California	6	8	.429	13	16	.448
Stanford	5	9	.357	10	15	.400
Washington State	3	11	.214	11	15	.423
Oregon	0	14	.000	6	20	.231

SEC

	Conference			Overall		
	W	L	Pct	W	L	Pct
Tennessee	14	4	.778	19	6	.760
Kentucky⊕	14	4	.778	21	7	.750
Alabama	13	5	.722	18	8	.692
Vanderbilt	10	8	.556	16	10	.615
Georgia	9	9	.500	14	12	.538
Mississippi	8	10	.444	13	12	.520
Mississippi State	6	12	.333	13	13	.500
Auburn	6	12	.333	10	16	.385
LSU	6	12	.333	10	16	.385
Florida	4	14	.222	10	15	.400

Southern

	Conference			Overall		
	W	L	Pct	W	L	Pct
Davidson□	8	2	.800	19	9	.679
Furman	8	3	.727	17	11	.607
William and Mary	6	4	.600	10	17	.370
East Carolina⊕	7	5	.583	14	15	.483
The Citadel	5	6	.455	12	13	.480
Richmond	3	9	.250	6	19	.240
VMI	2	10	.167	6	19	.240
Appalachian State	-	-	-	8	18	.308

Tournament: **East Carolina d. Furman 77-75 (OT)**
Tournament MOP: **Roy Simpson**, Furman

Southland

	Conference			Overall		
	W	L	Pct	W	L	Pct
Louisiana Tech	8	0	1.000	23	3	.885
UL-Lafayette○⊗	8	0	1.000	25	4	.862
Lamar	7	1	.875	13	13	.500
Texas-Arlington	5	3	.625	14	12	.538
Arkansas State	5	3	.625	12	14	.462
Abilene Christian	3	5	.375	17	8	.680
Trinity (TX)	0	8	.000	7	17	.292

Southwest

	Conference			Overall		
	W	L	Pct	W	L	Pct
Texas⊕	10	4	.714	19	9	.679
SMU	10	4	.714	16	11	.593
TCU	9	5	.643	15	9	.625
Texas A&M	9	5	.643	16	10	.615
Texas Tech	8	6	.571	14	12	.538
Arkansas	5	9	.357	8	18	.308
Baylor	4	10	.286	14	12	.538
Rice	1	13	.071	6	20	.231

WCAC

	Conference			Overall		
	W	L	Pct	W	L	Pct
San Francisco⊕	13	1	.929	20	8	.714
Santa Clara	11	3	.786	17	9	.654
Seattle	10	4	.714	17	9	.654
UNLV	8	6	.571	14	12	.538
Loyola Marymount	6	8	.429	11	15	.423
Pepperdine	5	9	.357	10	15	.400
Saint Mary's (CA)	3	11	.214	9	17	.346
Nevada	0	14	.000	2	24	.077

WAC

	Conference			Overall		
	W	L	Pct	W	L	Pct
BYU⊕	12	2	.857	21	5	.808
UTEP□	9	5	.643	20	7	.741
Arizona State	9	5	.643	18	8	.692
Colorado State	7	7	.500	15	9	.625
New Mexico	7	7	.500	15	11	.577
Utah	5	9	.357	13	12	.520
Arizona	4	10	.286	6	20	.231
Wyoming	3	11	.214	12	14	.462

Conference Standings Continue →

⊕ Automatic NCAA Tournament bid ○ At-large NCAA Tournament bid □ NIT appearance ⊗ Team record doesn't reflect games forfeited or vacated. For adjusted record, see p. 521.

ANNUAL REVIEW

YANKEE

	Conference W	L	Pct	Overall W	L	Pct
Rhode Island	8	2	.800	15	11	.577
Maine	6	4	.600	15	10	.600
Massachusetts	6	4	.600	14	12	.538
New Hampshire	5	5	.500	14	9	.609
Connecticut	5	5	.500	8	17	.320
Vermont	0	10	.000	5	19	.208

INDEPENDENTS

	Overall W	L	Pct
Oral Roberts□	26	2	.929
Hawaii○	24	3	.889
Marquette○	25	4	.862
Marshall○	23	4	.852
Northern Illinois	21	4	.840
South Carolina○	24	5	.828
Florida State○	27	6	.818
Duquesne	20	5	.800
Syracuse□	22	6	.786
Providence○	21	6	.778
Detroit	18	6	.750
Houston○	20	7	.741
Jacksonville□	20	8	.714
Villanova○	20	8	.714
Texas-Pan American	17	7	.708
Niagara□	21	9	.700
Penn State	17	8	.680

INDEPENDENTS (CONT.)

	Overall W	L	Pct
Fordham□	18	9	.667
St. Bonaventure	16	8	.667
Cincinnati	17	9	.654
Colgate	15	8	.652
St. John's□	19	11	.633
Fairleigh Dickinson	15	9	.625
Illinois State	16	10	.615
Virginia Tech	16	10	.615
Canisius	15	11	.577
Creighton	15	11	.577
Holy Cross	15	11	.577
Oklahoma City	16	12	.571
Loyola (LA)	14	11	.560
Rutgers	14	11	.560
West Virginia	13	11	.542
Hardin-Simmons	14	12	.538
DePaul	12	11	.522
Centenary	13	12	.520
Long Island	13	12	.520
Boston College	13	13	.500
Dayton	13	13	.500
Pittsburgh	12	12	.500
Air Force	12	13	.480
Fairfield	12	13	.480
Saint Francis (PA)	12	13	.480
Saint Peter's	12	13	.480

INDEPENDENTS (CONT.)

	Overall W	L	Pct
Indiana State	12	14	.462
St. Francis (NY)	12	14	.462
Utah State	12	14	.462
Xavier	12	14	.462
Army	11	13	.458
Manhattan	11	13	.458
George Washington	11	14	.440
Navy	10	13	.435
Denver	11	15	.423
Portland	10	16	.385
Seton Hall	10	16	.385
Southern Illinois	10	16	.385
Ball State	9	15	.375
Loyola-Chicago	8	14	.364
Tulane	8	18	.308
Boston U.	7	16	.304
South Alabama	7	17	.292
Iona	6	17	.261
Butler	6	20	.231
Georgia Tech	6	20	.231
Notre Dame	6	20	.231
Stetson	6	20	.231
Georgetown	3	23	.115
Southern Miss	0	24	.000

INDIVIDUAL LEADERS—SEASON

Scoring

	CL	POS	G	FG	FT	PTS	PPG
1 **Dwight Lamar**, UL-Lafayette	JR	G	29	429	196	1,054	**36.3**
2 **Richard Fuqua**, Oral Roberts	JR	G	28	423	160	1,006	**35.9**
3 **Doug Collins**, Illinois State	JR	G	26	352	143	847	**32.6**
4 **Wil Robinson**, West Virginia	SR	G	24	265	176	706	**29.4**
5 **Bird Averitt**, Pepperdine	SO	G	24	263	167	693	**28.9**
6 **John Williamson**, New Mexico State	SO	G	25	276	126	678	**27.1**
7 **Greg Kohls**, Syracuse	SR	G	28	263	222	748	**26.7**
8 **Tony Miller**, Florida	JR	G	19	195	117	507	**26.7**
9 **Les Taylor**, Murray State	JR	F	21	200	138	538	**25.6**
10 **Ted Martiniuk**, Saint Peter's	SR	G	24	233	145	611	**25.5**

Field Goal Pct

	CL	POS	G	FG	FGA	PCT
1 **Kent Martens**, Abilene Christian	SR	F/C	21	136	204	**66.7**
2 **Bob Fullerton**, Xavier	SR	F	26	149	229	**65.1**
3 **Mike Stewart**, Santa Clara	JR	C	26	202	312	**64.7**
4 **Bill Walton**, UCLA	SO	C	30	238	372	**64.0**
5 **Bill Schaeffer**, St. John's	JR	F	28	186	294	**63.3**

Minimum: 135 made

Free Throw Pct

	CL	POS	G	FT	FTA	PCT
1 **Greg Starrick**, Southern Illinois	SR	G	26	148	160	**92.5**
2 **Andy Denny**, South Alabama	SR	G	24	117	128	**91.4**
3 **John Garrett**, Southern Illinois	SR	G	26	130	146	**89.0**
4 **Larry Bullington**, Ball State	SO	G	24	142	161	**88.2**
5 **Bob Sherwin**, Army	JR	G	24	110	125	**88.0**

Minimum: 100 made

Rebounds Per Game

	CL	POS	G	REB	RPG
1 **Kermit Washington**, American	JR	C	23	455	**19.8**
2 **John Gianelli**, Pacific	SR	F	26	466	**17.9**
3 **Steve Davidson**, West Texas A&M	SR	F/C	24	420	**17.5**
4 **Mel Davis**, St. John's	JR	F	27	460	**17.0**
5 **Jim Bradley**, Northern Illinois	SO	F/C	25	398	**15.9**

INDIVIDUAL LEADERS-GAME

Points

	CL	POS	OPP	DATE	PTS
1 **Ernie Fleming**, Jacksonville	SR	F	Saint Peter's	J29	**59**
2 **Doug Collins**, Illinois State	JR	G	Ball State	J30	**55**
3 **Tony Miller**, Florida	JR	G	Chicago State	F29	**54**
4 **Richard Fuqua**, Oral Roberts	JR	G	Moorhead State	J15	**51**
Richard Fuqua, Oral Roberts	JR	G	Union (TN)	F24	**51**
Dwight Lamar, UL-Lafayette	JR	G	Lamar	F17	**51**
Dwight Lamar, UL-Lafayette	JR	G	Louisiana Tech	F14	**51**
Barry Parkhill, Virginia	JR	G	Baldwin-Wallace	D11	**51**

TEAM LEADERS-SEASON

Win-Loss Pct

	W	L	PCT
1 UCLA	30	0	**1.000**
2 Oral Roberts	26	2	**.929**
3 Penn	25	3	**.893**
4 Hawaii	24	3	**.889**
5 Marquette	25	4	**.862**
Long Beach State	25	4	**.862**
UL-Lafayette	25	4	**.862**

Scoring Offense

	G	W-L	PTS	PPG
1 Oral Roberts	28	26-2	2,943	**105.1**
2 UL-Lafayette	29	25-4	2,840	**97.9**
3 Northern Illinois	25	21-4	2,380	**95.2**
4 UCLA	30	30-0	2,838	**94.6**
5 Furman	28	17-11	2,592	**92.6**

Scoring Margin

	G	W-L	PPG	OPP PPG	MAR
1 UCLA	30	30-0	94.6	64.3	**30.3**
2 North Carolina	31	26-5	89.1	71.4	**17.7**
3 Marshall	27	23-4	92.4	76.4	**16.0**
4 Florida State	33	27-6	86.9	71.4	**15.5**
5 Long Beach State	29	25-4	84.9	69.8	**15.1**

Field Goal Pct

	G	W-L	FG	FGA	PCT
1 North Carolina	31	26-5	1,031	1,954	**52.8**
2 Abilene Christian	25	17-8	792	1,566	**50.6**
3 South Carolina	29	24-5	894	1,773	**50.4**
4 UCLA	30	30-0	1,140	2,262	**50.4**
5 UL-Lafayette	29	25-4	1,153	2,295	**50.2**

Rebounds Per Game

	G	W-L	REB	RPG
1 Oral Roberts	28	26-2	1,686	**60.2**
2 West Texas A&M	25	14-11	1,444	**57.8**
3 Pacific	26	17-9	1,495	**57.5**
4 Hawaii	27	24-3	1,462	**56.2**
5 Houston	27	20-7	1,515	**56.1**

Scoring Defense

	G	W-L	OPP PTS	OPP PPG
1 Minnesota	25	18-7	1,451	**58.0**
2 Fairleigh Dickinson	24	15-9	1,410	**58.8**
3 UTEP	27	20-7	1,636	**60.6**
4 Marquette	29	25-4	1,836	**63.3**
5 Penn	28	25-3	1,780	**63.6**

CONSENSUS ALL-AMERICAS

First Team

PLAYER	CL	POS	HT	SCHOOL	RPG	PPG
Henry Bibby	SR	G	6-1	UCLA	3.5	15.7
Jim Chones	JR	C	6-11	Marquette	11.9	20.6
Dwight Lamar	JR	G	6-1	UL-Lafayette	2.7	36.3
Bob McAdoo	JR	C	6-8	North Carolina	10.1	19.5
Ed Ratleff	JR	G/F	6-6	Long Beach State	7.6	21.4
Tom Riker	SR	C	6-10	South Carolina	10.4	19.6
Bill Walton	SO	C	6-11	UCLA	15.5	21.1

Second Team

PLAYER	CL	POS	HT	SCHOOL	RPG	PPG
Richard Fuqua	JR	G	6-4	Oral Roberts	5.0	35.9
Barry Parkhill	JR	G	6-4	Virginia	4.5	21.6
Jim Price	SR	G	6-3	Louisville	3.9	21.0
Bud Stallworth	SR	F	6-5	Kansas	7.7	25.3
Henry Wilmore	JR	F	6-3	Michigan	8.6	23.9

Selectors: AP, NABC, UPI, USBWA

AWARD WINNERS

Player of the Year

PLAYER	CL	POS	HT	SCHOOL	AWARDS
Bill Walton	SO	C	6-11	UCLA	Naismith, AP, UPI, USBWA, Rupp
Scott Martin	SR	G	6-0	Oklahoma	Frances Pomeroy Naismith*

* For the most outstanding senior player who is 6 feet or under

Coach of the Year

COACH	SCHOOL	REC	AWARDS
John Wooden	UCLA	30-0	AP, UPI, USBWA, NABC, Sporting News

Poll Progression

Preseason Poll

AP	UPI	SCHOOL
1	1	**UCLA**
2	4	**North Carolina**
3	3	**USC**
4	2	**Marquette**
5	5	**Ohio State**
6	7	**Maryland**
7	6	**Houston**
8	9	**Long Beach State**
9	8	**Louisville**
10	10	**Kentucky**
11	11	**Jacksonville**
12	13	**South Carolina**
13	18	**Michigan**
14	16	**Kansas**
15	—	**Penn**
16	—	**New Mexico**
17	15	**St. John's**
18	17	**Villanova**
19	14	**BYU**
20	—	**Oklahoma**
—	12	**New Mexico State**
—	19	**Harvard**
—	20	**Pacific**

Week of Dec 7

AP	UPI	SCHOOL	AP↓↑
1	1	**UCLA** (2-0)	
2	3	**Marquette** (2-0)	↑2
3	2	**North Carolina** (2-0)	↓1
4	4	**Ohio State** (2-0)	↑1
5	5	**Maryland** (2-0)	↑1
6	7	**Long Beach State** (2-0)	↑2
7	6	**Kentucky** (2-0)	↑3
8	11	**Jacksonville** (2-0)	↑3
9	9	**Michigan** (2-0)	↑4
10	15	**Penn** (2-0)	↑5
11	8	**South Carolina** (1-0)	↑1
12	10	**Houston** (2-1)	↓5
13	12	**USC** (1-1)	↓10
14	13	**St. John's** (1-0)	↑3
15	14	**BYU** (2-0)	↑4
16	—	**Louisville** (1-1)	↓7
17	17	**Arizona State** (2-0)	⤴
18	19	**Villanova** (2-1)	
18	—	**Florida State** (2-0)	⤴
20	20	**NC State** (2-0)	⤴
—	16	**Minnesota** (2-0)	
—	18	**Kansas** (1-1)	⤵

Week of Dec 14

AP	UPI	SCHOOL	AP↓↑
1	1	**UCLA** (4-0)	
2	2	**Marquette** (4-0)	
3	3	**South Carolina** (4-0)	↑8
4	5	**North Carolina** (3-1)	↓1
5	9	**Penn** (4-0)	↑5
6	4	**BYU** (4-0)	↑9
7	11	**Kentucky** (3-1)	
8	6	**St. John's** (3-1)	↑6
9	13	**Florida State** (5-0)	↑9
10	7	**Ohio State** (3-1)	↓6
11	8	**USC** (3-1)	↑3
12	10	**Indiana** (4-0)	⤴
13	16	**Long Beach State** (3-0)	↓7
14	—	**Jacksonville** (4-1)	↓6
15	15	**Maryland** (2-1)	↓10
16	12	**UL-Lafayette** (4-1)	⤴
17	17	**Louisville** (3-1)	↓1
18	18	**Princeton** (3-1)	⤴
19	—	**Virginia** (4-0)	⤴
20	—	**Houston** (3-2)	↓8
—	14	**Arizona State** (4-1)	⤵
—	19	**NC State** (3-1)	⤵
—	20	**Saint Louis** (3-1)	

Week of Dec 21

AP	UPI	SCHOOL	AP↓↑
1	1	**UCLA** (4-0)	
2	2	**Marquette** (5-0)	
3	3	**South Carolina** (4-0)	
4	4	**North Carolina** (5-1)	
5	5	**USC** (5-1)	↑5
6	6	**Ohio State** (4-1)	↑4
7	11	**BYU** (6-1)	↓1
8	8	**Indiana** (5-1) (A)	↑4
9	7	**Long Beach State** (5-1)	↑4
10	9	**St. John's** (5-1)	↓2
11	14	**Kentucky** (5-2)	↓4
12	10	**UL-Lafayette** (4-1)	↑4
13	20	**Penn** (4-1) (B)	↓8
14	12	**Florida State** (5-1)	↓5
15	13	**Maryland** (4-1)	
16	20	**Jacksonville** (5-1)	↓2
17	15	**Ohio** (3-1)	⤴
18	—	**Virginia** (5-0)	↑1
19	16	**Louisville** (3-1)	↓2
20	—	**Marshall** (6-0)	⤴
—	17	**Arizona State** (5-2)	
—	19	**Minnesota** (3-1)	

Week of Dec 28

AP	UPI	SCHOOL	AP↓↑
1	1	**UCLA** (6-0)	
2	2	**Marquette** (6-0)	
3	3	**South Carolina** (5-0)	
4	4	**North Carolina** (5-1)	
5	5	**USC** (6-1)	
6	6	**Ohio State** (6-1)	
7	7	**Indiana** (6-1)	↑1
8	9	**BYU** (7-1)	↓1
9	8	**St. John's** (7-1)	↑1
10	10	**Long Beach State** (7-1)	↓1
11	—	**Virginia** (7-0)	↑7
12	15	**Kentucky** (5-2)	↓1
13	11	**UL-Lafayette** (4-1)	↓1
14	19	**Penn** (5-1)	↓1
15	13	**Louisville** (5-1)	↑4
16	14	**Maryland** (6-1)	↓1
17	—	**Marshall** (7-0)	↑3
18	12	**Hawaii** (6-0)	⤴
19	—	**West Virginia** (5-0)	⤴
20	—	**Tennessee** (3-1)	⤴
—	16	**Jacksonville** (5-1)	⤵
—	17	**Florida State** (5-2)	⤵
—	18	**Villanova** (6-1)	
—	20	**Arizona State** (6-2)	

Week of Jan 4

AP	UPI	SCHOOL	AP↓↑
1	1	**UCLA** (8-0)	
2	2	**Marquette** (8-0)	
3	3	**North Carolina** (8-1)	↑1
4	4	**South Carolina** (7-1)	↓1
5	5	**Indiana** (8-1)	↑2
6	7	**Penn** (7-1)	↑8
7	6	**Louisville** (8-1)	↑8
8	8	**Long Beach State** (9-1)	↑2
9	18	**Virginia** (9-0)	↑2
10	9	**Ohio State** (7-2)	↓4
11	11	**USC** (7-2)	↓6
12	10	**Maryland** (8-1)	↑4
13	—	**Marshall** (9-1)	↑4
14	15	**Villanova** (9-1)	⤴
15	17	**UL-Lafayette** (5-1)	↓2
16	14	**Hawaii** (9-0)	↑2
17	13	**St. John's** (8-2)	↓8
18	20	**BYU** (8-2)	↓10
19	15	**Kentucky** (7-2)	↓7
20	12	**Florida State** (8-2)	⤴
—	19	**Missouri** (10-1)	

Week of Jan 11

AP	UPI	SCHOOL	AP↓↑
1	1	**UCLA** (10-0)	
2	2	**Marquette** (10-0)	
3	3	**North Carolina** (9-1)	
4	4	**South Carolina** (7-2)	
5	6	**Louisville** (9-1)	↑2
6	5	**Penn** (9-1)	
7	7	**Long Beach State** (12-1)	↑1
8	9	**Virginia** (11-0)	↑1
9	8	**Ohio State** (9-2)	↑1
10	10	**USC** (9-2)	↑1
11	13	**Villanova** (10-1)	↑3
12	12	**Florida State** (11-2)	↑8
13	16	**UL-Lafayette** (8-1)	↑2
14	15	**BYU** (10-2)	↑4
15	18	**Kentucky** (8-2)	↑4
16	14	**Illinois** (9-1)	⤴
17	20	**Indiana** (8-3)	↓12
18	11	**Missouri** (11-1)	⤴
19	—	**Hawaii** (10-1)	↓3
20	—	**Marshall** (10-2)	↓7
—	17	**Duquesne** (8-0)	
—	19	**UTEP** (11-2)	
—	20	**Maryland** (9-2)	⤵

Week of Jan 18

AP	UPI	SCHOOL	AP↓↑
1	1	**UCLA** (12-0)	
2	2	**Marquette** (12-0)	
3	3	**North Carolina** (11-1)	
4	6	**Long Beach State** (14-1)	↑3
5	4	**South Carolina** (8-2)	↓1
6	5	**Louisville** (11-1)	↓1
7	6	**Ohio State** (10-2)	↑2
8	8	**USC** (11-2)	↑2
9	11	**Virginia** (12-1)	↓1
10	9	**Penn** (9-2)	↓4
11	10	**Florida State** (13-2)	↑1
12	12	**UL-Lafayette** (11-1)	↑1
13	14	**BYU** (11-2)	↑1
14	13	**Princeton** (14-2)	⤴
15	16	**Villanova** (11-2)	↓4
16	—	**Marshall** (12-2)	↑4
17	18	**Minnesota** (8-3)	⤴
18	17	**Hawaii** (13-1)	↑1
19	18	**Tennessee** (8-2)	⤴
20	—	**Northern Illinois** (10-1)	⤴
—	15	**Maryland** (10-2)	
—	18	**Missouri** (12-2)	⤵

Week of Jan 25

AP	UPI	SCHOOL	AP↓↑
1	1	**UCLA** (14-0)	
2	2	**Marquette** (14-0)	
3	4	**Long Beach State** (15-1)	↑1
4	3	**Louisville** (12-1)	↑2
5	5	**North Carolina** (12-2)	↓2
6	6	**Ohio State** (11-2)	↑1
7	7	**USC** (11-2)	↑1
8	11	**Virginia** (12-1)	↑1
9	9	**Penn** (10-2)	↑1
10	10	**Florida State** (15-2)	↑1
11	8	**South Carolina** (10-3)	↓6
12	12	**UL-Lafayette** (12-1)	
13	13	**BYU** (12-2)	
14	18	**Marshall** (14-2)	↑2
15	19	**Hawaii** (15-1)	↑3
16	14	**Minnesota** (10-3)	↑1
17	17	**Princeton** (14-3)	↓3
18	16	**Maryland** (11-2)	⤴
19	—	**Northern Illinois** (10-1)	↑1
20	15	**Missouri** (13-2)	⤴
—	19	**Fordham** (10-4)	

Week of Feb 1

AP	UPI	SCHOOL	AP↓↑
1	1	**UCLA** (16-0)	
2	2	**Marquette** (16-0)	
3	3	**Louisville** (15-1)	↑1
4	4	**North Carolina** (13-2)	↑1
5	5	**Long Beach State** (16-1)	↓2
6	7	**Penn** (12-2)	↑3
7	9	**Virginia** (13-1)	↑1
8	6	**South Carolina** (12-3)	↑3
9	8	**Ohio State** (12-3) (C)	↓3
10	10	**BYU** (14-2)	↑3
11	16	**Marshall** (15-2)	↑3
12	11	**Florida State** (16-3)	↓2
13	13	**UL-Lafayette** (13-2)	↓1
14	15	**Hawaii** (17-1)	↑1
15	12	**Missouri** (14-2)	↑5
16	14	**Providence** (13-2)	⤴
17	17	**Jacksonville** (12-2)	⤴
18	—	**USC** (11-5)	↓11
19	20	**Minnesota** (11-4)	↓3
20	—	**Michigan** (10-6)	⤴
—	18	**UTEP** (15-3)	
—	19	**Washington** (13-3)	

Week of Feb 8

AP	UPI	SCHOOL	AP↓↑
1	1	**UCLA** (17-0)	
2	2	**Marquette** (17-0)	
3	3	**North Carolina** (16-2)	↑1
4	4	**Louisville** (16-2)	↓1
5	5	**Penn** (14-2)	↑1
6	9	**Virginia** (15-1)	↑1
7	7	**Ohio State** (14-3)	↑2
8	8	**Long Beach State** (18-2)	↓3
9	6	**South Carolina** (16-3)	↓1
10	10	**BYU** (16-2)	
11	16	**Marshall** (17-2)	
12	13	**Providence** (14-2)	↑4
13	11	**UL-Lafayette** (14-2)	
14	11	**Florida State** (17-4)	↓2
15	—	**Memphis** (14-4)	⤴
16	—	**Jacksonville** (14-2)	↑1
17	15	**Missouri** (15-3)	↓2
18	17	**Hawaii** (18-2)	↓4
19	—	**Minnesota** (12-4)	
20	—	**Duquesne** (14-2)	⤴
—	14	**Kentucky** (13-4)	
—	17	**Maryland** (14-3)	
—	17	**Villanova** (13-5)	
—	17	**Washington** (14-3)	

Week of Feb 15

AP	UPI	SCHOOL	AP↓↑
1	1	**UCLA** (19-0)	
2	2	**Marquette** (19-0)	
3	3	**North Carolina** (17-2)	
4	6	**Louisville** (18-2)	
5	5	**Penn** (16-2)	
6	7	**Virginia** (17-1)	
7	4	**South Carolina** (16-3)	↑2
8	9	**Ohio State** (15-4)	↓1
9	8	**Long Beach State** (19-3)	↓1
10	16	**Marshall** (19-2)	↑1
11	10	**BYU** (17-3)	↓1
12	13	**UL-Lafayette** (17-2)	↑1
13	15	**Providence** (14-2)	↓1
14	11	**Florida State** (19-4)	
15	12	**Missouri** (17-3)	↑2
16	17	**Hawaii** (20-2)	↑2
17	18	**Kentucky** (15-4)	⤴
18	—	**Memphis** (15-5)	↓3
19	14	**Maryland** (16-3)	⤴
20	—	**Tennessee** (13-4)	⤴
—	19	**Houston** (14-5)	
—	19	**Saint Joseph's** (15-4)	

ANNUAL REVIEW

Poll Progression Continues →

Week of Feb 22

AP	UPI	School	AP↓↑
1	1	**UCLA** (20-0)	
2	2	**Marquette** (22-0)	
3	5	**Louisville** (19-2)	↑1
4	4	**Penn** (18-2)	↑1
5	3	**North Carolina** (18-3)	↓2
6	6	**Long Beach State** (21-3)	↑3
7	7	**BYU** (18-3)	↑4
8	16	**Marshall** (21-2)	↑2
9	7	**South Carolina** (17-4)	↓2
10	12	**UL-Lafayette** (20-2)	↑2
11	13	**Florida State** (21-4)	↑3
12	11	**Maryland** (17-3)	↑7
13	10	**Virginia** (18-3)	↓7
14	9	**Missouri** (19-3)	↑1
15	14	**Ohio State** (15-5)	↓7
16	17	**Houston** (17-5)	⤴
17	18	**Hawaii** (22-2)	↓1
18	15	**Kentucky** (17-4)	↓1
19	—	**Memphis** (17-5)	↓1
20	—	**Oral Roberts** (20-1)	⤴
—	19	**Providence** (16-4)	⤵
—	19	**Toledo** (16-4)	

Week of Feb 29

AP	UPI	School	AP↓↑
1	1	**UCLA** (23-0)	
2	3	**Louisville** (20-2)	↑1
3	2	**North Carolina** (20-3)	↑2
4	4	**Penn** (20-2)	
5	5	**Marquette** (22-1)	Ⓓ ↓3
6	8	**Long Beach State** (23-3)	
7	7	**BYU** (20-3)	
8	6	**South Carolina** (19-4)	↑1
9	10	**Marshall** (22-2)	↓1
10	11	**Florida State** (23-4)	↑1
11	12	**UL-Lafayette** (22-3)	↓1
12	9	**Virginia** (20-4)	↑1
13	14	**Houston** (19-5)	↑3
14	15	**Ohio State** (16-5)	↑1
15	—	**Hawaii** (24-2)	↑2
16	15	**Michigan** (13-7)	⤴
17	—	**Oral Roberts** (22-1)	↑3
18	13	**Maryland** (18-4)	↓6
19	19	**Missouri** (19-4)	↓5
20	17	**Memphis** (19-5)	↓1
—	18	**Detroit** (17-5)	
—	20	**Duquesne** (18-4)	

Week of Mar 7

AP	UPI	School	AP↓↑
1	1	**UCLA** (25-0)	
2	3	**Penn** (23-2)	↑2
3	2	**North Carolina** (21-4)	
4	6	**Louisville** (20-3)	↓2
5	5	**Long Beach State** (23-3)	↑1
6	4	**South Carolina** (22-4)	↑2
7	7	**Marquette** (24-2)	↓2
8	8	**BYU** (20-4)	↓1
9	11	**UL-Lafayette** (23-3)	↑2
10	10	**Marshall** (23-3)	↓1
11	9	**Memphis** (21-5)	↑9
12	13	**Hawaii** (24-2)	↑3
13	14	**Maryland** (21-4)	↑5
14	—	**Florida State** (23-5)	↓4
15	18	**Virginia** (20-5)	↓3
16	16	**Minnesota** (16-6)	⤴
17	—	**Oral Roberts** (24-1)	
18	12	**Missouri** (21-4)	↑1
19	15	**Houston** (20-6)	↓6
20	—	**Indiana** (15-7)	⤴
—	17	**UTEP** (20-5)	
—	19	**Providence** (19-5)	
—	20	**Temple** (23-7)	

Final Poll

AP	UPI	School	AP↓↑
1	1	**UCLA** (26-0)	
2	2	**North Carolina** (23-4)	↑1
3	3	**Penn** (23-2)	↓1
4	4	**Louisville** (24-3)	
5	6	**Long Beach State** (23-3)	
6	5	**South Carolina** (22-4)	
7	7	**Marquette** (24-2)	
8	8	**UL-Lafayette** (24-3)	↑1
9	9	**BYU** (21-5)	↓1
10	10	**Florida State** (24-5)	↑4
11	12	**Minnesota** (17-6)	↑5
12	18	**Marshall** (23-4)	↓2
13	13	**Memphis** (21-6)	↓2
14	11	**Maryland** (23-5)	↓1
15	15	**Villanova** (19-6)	⤴
16	—	**Oral Roberts** (25-1)	↑1
17	—	**Indiana** (17-7)	↑3
18	14	**Kentucky** (20-6)	Ⓔ ⤴
19	—	**Ohio State** (18-6)	⤴
20	—	**Virginia** (21-6)	↓5
—	16	**Kansas State** (18-8)	
—	17	**UTEP** (20-6)	
—	19	**Missouri** (21-5)	⤵
—	19	**Weber State** (17-9)	

Ⓐ Indiana routs Notre Dame, 94-29, on the newly christened Branch McCracken Memorial Floor, named for the former IU coach.

Ⓑ Temple halts Penn's 48-game regular-season winning streak, 57-52, handing new coach Chuck Daly his first loss as a Quaker.

Ⓒ With Ohio State leading Minnesota 50-44 and :36 left in the game, Buckeyes center Luke Witte is knocked to the floor. Gopher Corky Taylor helps him up, then knees Witte in the groin, setting off a terrible melee. Future baseball Hall of Famer Dave Winfield, a Gophers forward, lands five punches to OSU reserve Mark Wagar's head, while Witte, who is stomped unconscious, requires 29 stitches to his face. Buckeyes coach Fred Taylor calls it "the sorriest thing I ever saw in intercollegiate athletics."

Ⓓ In Marquette's second game after star center Jim Chones left the team to sign with the ABA's New York Nets for $1.5 million, the Warriors are manhandled by Detroit. Although Chones' departure may have cost his team a shot at the NCAA title, coach Al McGuire defends the decision to pursue financial security because Chones is the oldest of six children of a working mother and a recently deceased father.

Ⓔ In Adolph Rupp's final regular-season game, Kentucky tops Tennessee, 67-66, to claim a share of the SEC title and a spot in the NCAA Tournament. Having reached the age of mandatory retirement for Kentucky state employees (70), Rupp's request for an exemption will be denied in September, when he turns 71.

1972 NCAA Tournament

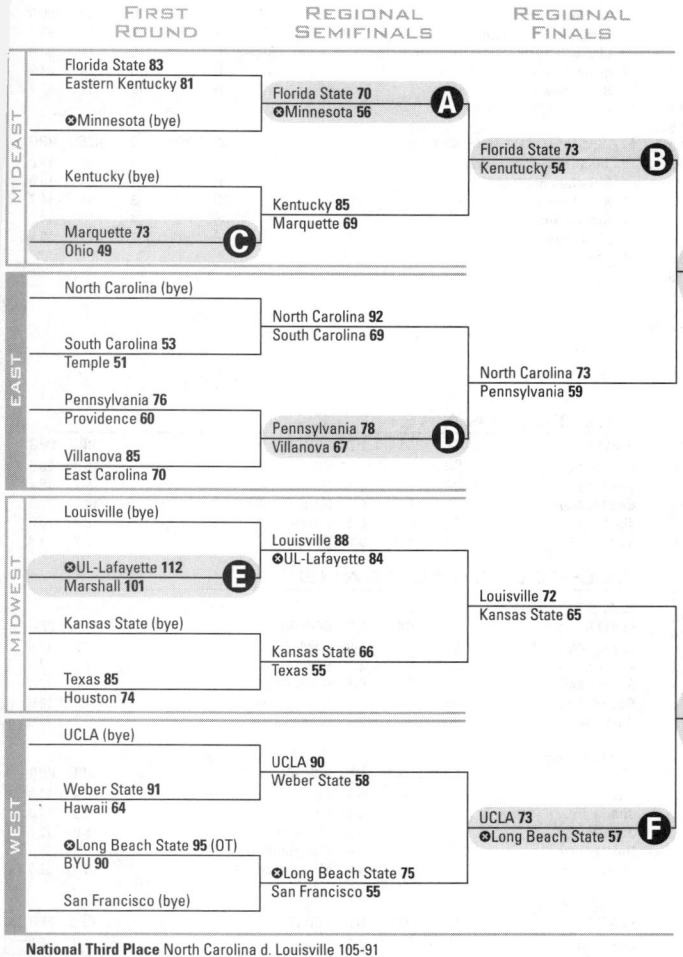

First Round / Regional Semifinals / Regional Finals

Mideast

First Round
- Florida State **83**, Eastern Kentucky **81**
- ⊗Minnesota (bye)
- Kentucky (bye)
- Marquette **73**, Ohio **49** (C)

Regional Semifinals
- Florida State **70**, ⊗Minnesota **56** (A)
- Kentucky **85**, Marquette **69**

Regional Finals
- Florida State **73**, Kenutucky **54** (B)

East

First Round
- North Carolina (bye)
- South Carolina **53**, Temple **51**
- Pennsylvania **76**, Providence **60**
- Villanova **85**, East Carolina **70**

Regional Semifinals
- North Carolina **92**, South Carolina **69**
- Pennsylvania **78**, Villanova **67** (D)

Regional Finals
- North Carolina **73**, Pennsylvania **59**

Midwest

First Round
- Louisville (bye)
- ⊗UL-Lafayette **112**, Marshall **101** (E)
- Kansas State (bye)
- Texas **85**, Houston **74**

Regional Semifinals
- Louisville **88**, ⊗UL-Lafayette **84**
- Kansas State **66**, Texas **55**

Regional Finals
- Louisville **72**, Kansas State **65**

West

First Round
- UCLA (bye)
- Weber State **91**, Hawaii **64**
- ⊗Long Beach State **95** (OT), BYU **90**
- San Francisco (bye)

Regional Semifinals
- UCLA **90**, Weber State **58**
- ⊗Long Beach State **75**, San Francisco **55**

Regional Finals
- UCLA **73**, ⊗Long Beach State **57** (F)

National Semifinals

- Florida State **79**, North Carolina **75**
- Louisville **77**, UCLA **96**

National Final

UCLA 81
Florida State 76

Los Angeles

National Third Place North Carolina d. Louisville 105-91
East Regional Third Place South Carolina d. Villanova 90-78
Mideast Regional Third Place ⊗Minnesota d. Marquette 77-72
Midwest Regional Third Place ⊗UL-Lafayette d. Texas 100-70
West Regional Third Place San Francisco d. Weber State 74-64

⊗Team participation later vacated

A Forward Dave Winfield, a future baseball Hall of Famer, scores eight points in Minnesota's loss. The Gophers are booed in Dayton because of an ugly brawl they were involved in during a regular-season game against Ohio State.

B Refusing to acknowledge rumors that he is being forced to retire, coach Adolph Rupp makes his last Tournament appearance after reaching UK's mandatory retirement age of 70.

C After routing Ohio, Marquette is disqualified when Bob Lackey refuses to sign an affidavit denying reports that he has hired an agent. Within 24 hours, Lackey signs the affidavit, clearing the way for Marquette to play Kentucky.

Ron King sinks all 10 of his free throws to lead Florida State to the Final. It's quite a turnaround for coach Hugh Durham's Seminoles, who had been put on probation twice in three years for recruiting violations.

Sophomore center Bill Walton scores 24 points and grabs 20 rebounds as UCLA ends its third unbeaten season at 30–0. Before the championship game, Bill Wall, the president of the National Association of Basketball Coaches, calls Florida State's appearance in the Final "a disgrace" because of its recent NCAA rules transgressions.

Denny Crum reaches the Final Four in his first year as a head coach, but has to witness 33 points and 21 rebounds from Bill Walton. Crum recruited Walton for UCLA when he was John Wooden's assistant.

D Coach Chuck Daly guides Penn to the regional final after three of his players score 20 points or more. Daly will later lead the Detroit Pistons to an NBA title and the Dream Team to the 1992 Olympic gold medal.

E Marshall attempts a Tournament record 112 shots and hits 42, good for 37.5%. Mike D'Antoni, future coach of the NBA Suns and Knicks, takes 22 of those shots for the Thundering Herd and scores 26 points.

F Consensus All-America and UCLA captain Henry Bibby scores 23 points and dishes four assists. During Bibby's three-year career, the Bruins go 87–3. Bibby later becomes coach at crosstown rival USC.

Tournament Leaders

INDIVIDUAL LEADERS

Scoring	CL	POS	G	PTS	PPG
1 **Dwight Lamar**, UL-Lafayette	JR	G	3	100	33.3
2 **Jim Price**, Louisville	SR	G	4	103	25.8
3 **Bob Davis**, Weber State	SR	F	3	69	23.0
Tom Riker, South Carolina	SR	C	3	69	23.0
5 **Larry Robinson**, Texas	SO	F	2	45	22.5
6 **Clyde Turner**, Minnesota	JR	F	2	44	22.0
7 **Mike Quick**, San Francisco	JR	G	2	43	21.5
8 **Roy Ebron**, UL-Lafayette	SO	C	3	63	21.0
9 **Bob McAdoo**, North Carolina	JR	C	4	82	20.5
10 **Dennis Wuycik**, North Carolina	SR	F	4	81	20.3

Minimum: 2 games

Field Goal Pct	CL	POS	G	FG	FGA	PCT
1 **Lamont King**, Long Beach State	JR	F	3	11	14	78.6
2 **George Frazier**, Marquette	JR	G/F	2	10	13	76.9
3 **Wilbert Loftin**, UL-Lafayette	SR	F	3	16	23	69.6
4 **Bill Walton**, UCLA	SO	C	4	28	41	68.3
5 **Corky Calhoun**, Penn	SR	F	3	19	28	67.9

Minimum: 10 made

Free Throw Pct	CL	POS	G	FT	FTA	PCT
1 **Jim Andrews**, Kentucky	JR	C	2	10	10	100.0
2 **Larry McNeill**, Marquette	SO	F	3	11	12	91.7
3 **Chuck Terry**, Long Beach State	SR	F	3	10	11	90.9
4 **Kevin Joyce**, South Carolina	JR	G	3	16	18	88.9
5 **Brady Small**, Weber State	JR	G	3	12	14	85.7

Minimum: 10 made

Rebounds Per Game	CL	POS	G	REB	RPG
1 **Jim Brewer**, Minnesota	JR	C	2	36	18.0
2 **Bill Walton**, UCLA	SO	C	4	64	16.0
3 **Roy Ebron**, UL-Lafayette	SO	C	3	44	14.7
4 **Bob McAdoo**, North Carolina	JR	C	4	56	14.0
5 **Jim Andrews**, Kentucky	JR	C	2	27	13.5

Minimum: 2 games

TEAM LEADERS

Scoring	G	PTS	PPG
1 **UL-Lafayette**	3	296	98.7
2 **North Carolina**	4	345	86.3
3 **UCLA**	4	340	85.0
4 **Louisville**	4	328	82.0
5 **Villanova**	3	230	76.7
6 **Florida State**	5	381	76.2
7 **Long Beach State**	3	227	75.7
8 **Marquette**	3	214	71.3
9 **Penn**	3	213	71.0
10 **South Carolina**	3	212	70.7

Minimum: 2 games

FG Pct	G	FG	FGA	PCT
1 **Penn**	3	85	167	50.9
2 **North Carolina**	4	121	242	50.0
3 **UCLA**	4	136	281	48.4
4 **Villanova**	3	93	195	47.7
5 **Kentucky**	2	50	105	47.6

FT Pct	G	FT	FTA	PCT
1 **Kentucky**	2	39	47	83.0
2 **Minnesota**	2	29	37	78.4
3 **Marquette**	3	38	50	76.0
4 **North Carolina**	4	103	138	74.6
5 **Penn**	3	43	59	72.9

Minimum: 2 games

Rebounds	G	REB	RPG
1 **UL-Lafayette**	3	165	55.0
2 **UCLA**	4	190	47.5
3 **North Carolina**	4	177	44.3
4 **Minnesota**	2	88	44.0
5 **Weber State**	3	125	41.7

Minimum: 2 games

ALL-TOURNAMENT TEAM

PLAYER	CL	POS	HT	SCHOOL	RPG	PPG
Bill Walton*	SO	C	6-11	UCLA	16.0	20.0
Ron King	JR	F	6-4	Florida State	5.2	18.4
Bob McAdoo	JR	C	6-9	North Carolina	14.0	20.5
Jim Price	SR	G	6-2	Louisville	2.8	25.8
Keith Wilkes	SO	F	6-6	UCLA	8.8	14.8

ALL-REGIONAL TEAMS

EAST

PLAYER	CL	POS	HT	SCHOOL	RPG	PPG
Dennis Wuycik*	SR	F	6-6	North Carolina	4.5	17.0
Kevin Joyce	JR	G	6-3	South Carolina	7.0	17.3
George Karl	JR	G	6-1	North Carolina	2.0	17.0
Bob McAdoo	JR	C	6-9	North Carolina	11.0	14.0
Hank Siemiontkowski	SR	F	6-7	Villanova	9.7	20.0

MIDEAST

PLAYER	CL	POS	HT	SCHOOL	RPG	PPG
Ron King*	JR	F	6-4	Florida State	5.0	14.3
Jim Andrews	JR	C	6-11	Kentucky	13.5	17.0
Jim Brewer	JR	C	6-9	Minnesota	18.0	12.0
Bob Lackey	SR	F	6-6	Marquette	8.3	18.0
Clyde Turner	JR	F	6-8	Minnesota	8.5	22.0

MIDWEST

PLAYER	CL	POS	HT	SCHOOL	RPG	PPG
Jim Price*	SR	G	6-2	Louisville	1.0	25.0
Danny Beard	SO	G/F	6-3	Kansas State	2.0	14.0
Dwight Lamar	JR	G	6-1	UL-Lafayette	2.3	33.3
Larry Robinson	SO	F	6-6	Texas	8.5	22.5
Ron Thomas	SR	F	6-5	Louisville	13.5	18.5

WEST

PLAYER	CL	POS	HT	SCHOOL	RPG	PPG
Bill Walton*	SO	C	6-11	UCLA	11.5	11.5
Henry Bibby	SR	G	6-1	UCLA	3.5	19.5
Bob Davis	SR	F	6-7	Weber State	10.0	23.0
Mike Quick	JR	G	6-2	San Francisco	1.0	21.5
Ed Ratleff	JR	G/F	6-6	Long Beach State	4.3	18.0

* Most outstanding player

1972 NCAA TOURNAMENT BOX SCORES

70-56 | 35 1H 29 | 35 2H 27 | SWEET 16

FLORIDA STATE	MIN	FG	3FG	FT	REB	A	ST	BL	PF	TP
Rowland Garrett	36	11-19	-	1-1	11	0	-	-	3	23
Reggie Royals	32	4-9	-	3-6	11	2	-	-	4	11
Ron King	27	5-11	-	1-3	5	2	-	-	1	11
Ron Harris	28	5-7	-	0-1	2	1	-	-	0	10
Otis Cole	13	3-5	-	4-4	1	2	-	-	1	10
Lawrence McCray	24	1-2	-	0-1	8	0	-	-	1	2
Otto Petty	23	0-8	-	2-3	1	6	-	-	1	2
Greg Samuel	17	0-1	-	1-1	0	4	-	-	1	1
TOTALS	**200**	**29-62**	**-**	**12-20**	**39**	**17**	**-**	**-**	**12**	**70**
Percentages		46.8		60.0						

Coach: Hugh Durham

MINNESOTA	MIN	FG	3FG	FT	REB	A	ST	BL	PF	TP
Clyde Turner	40	8-17	-	3-4	12	2	-	-	3	19
Jim Brewer	40	5-11	-	0-0	14	1	-	-	1	10
Dave Winfield	40	2-8	-	4-5	8	0	-	-	3	8
Keith Young	27	3-12	-	1-1	5	2	-	-	5	7
Bob Nix	40	1-12	-	4-5	1	2	-	-	2	6
Bob Murphy	13	3-6	-	0-0	3	1	-	-	2	6
TOTALS	**200**	**22-66**	**-**	**12-15**	**43**	**8**	**-**	**-**	**16**	**56**
Percentages		33.3		80.0						

Coach: Bill Musselman

Officials: Vidal, Filiberti
Attendance: 13,458

85-69 | 33 1H 34 | 52 2H 35 | SWEET 16

KENTUCKY	MIN	FG	3FG	FT	REB	A	ST	BL	PF	TP
Ronnie Lyons	-	6-16	-	7-8	1	-	-	-	2	19
Jim Andrews	-	5-11	-	7-7	16	-	-	-	3	17
Larry Stamper	-	7-10	-	3-5	11	-	-	-	2	17
Stan Key	-	4-5	-	6-6	5	-	-	-	0	14
Tom Parker	-	3-5	-	6-8	9	-	-	-	3	12
Rick Drewitz	-	3-4	-	0-0	2	-	-	-	2	6
Bob McCowan	-	0-0	-	0-0	0	-	-	-	1	0
TOTALS	**-**	**28-51**	**-**	**29-34**	**44**	**-**	**-**	**-**	**13**	**85**
Percentages		54.9		85.3						

Coach: Adolph Rupp

MARQUETTE	MIN	FG	3FG	FT	REB	A	ST	BL	PF	TP
Bob Lackey	-	8-14	-	5-7	6	-	-	-	4	21
Marcus Washington	-	6-24	-	2-4	4	-	-	-	5	14
Larry McNeill	-	3-10	-	3-4	8	-	-	-	5	9
George Frazier	-	4-5	-	0-0	6	-	-	-	3	8
Allie McGuire	-	3-15	-	2-2	1	-	-	-	0	8
Mike Mills	-	3-5	-	1-1	7	-	-	-	1	7
Kurt Spychalla	-	1-3	-	0-0	3	-	-	-	5	2
Guy Lam	-	0-2	-	0-0	0	-	-	-	0	0
Mark Ostrans	-	0-0	-	0-0	0	-	-	-	1	0
TOTALS	**-**	**28-78**	**-**	**13-18**	**35**	**-**	**-**	**-**	**24**	**69**
Percentages		35.9		72.2						

Coach: Al McGuire

Officials: Brown, Evans
Attendance: 13,458

92-69 | 51 1H 32 | 41 2H 37 | SWEET 16

NORTH CAROLINA	MIN	FG	3FG	FT	REB	A	ST	BL	PF	TP
George Karl	23	8-12	-	2-3	3	3	-	-	4	18
Dennis Wuycik	27	4-11	-	8-10	5	3	-	-	3	16
Steve Previs	29	5-8	-	3-4	5	4	-	-	4	13
Bob McAdoo	32	4-14	-	3-6	13	3	-	-	3	11
Bill Chamberlain	25	3-6	-	4-5	4	0	-	-	1	10
Kim Huband	19	2-5	-	4-4	4	0	-	-	3	8
Bill L. Chambers	5	2-3	-	3-4	1	1	-	-	0	7
Bobby Jones	22	1-3	-	3-4	9	2	-	-	2	5
Ray Hite	6	2-2	-	0-0	1	0	-	-	0	4
Don Johnston	7	0-1	-	0-0	2	2	-	-	0	0
Craig Corson	5	0-0	-	0-0	0	1	-	-	2	0
TOTALS	**200**	**31-65**	**-**	**30-40**	**47**	**19**	**-**	**-**	**22**	**92**
Percentages		47.7	-	75.0						

Coach: Dean Smith

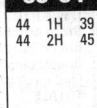

SOUTH CAROLINA	MIN	FG	3FG	FT	REB	A	ST	BL	PF	TP
Kevin Joyce	32	6-18	-	9-9	7	1	-	-	5	21
Tom Riker	38	4-13	-	2-4	10	1	-	-	4	10
Danny Traylor	24	3-6	-	3-4	2	0	-	-	4	9
Brian Winters	20	4-11	-	1-1	3	0	-	-	5	9
Rick Aydlett	25	2-4	-	2-2	4	0	-	-	4	6
Bob Carver	24	2-6	-	2-2	2	2	-	-	3	6
Casey Manning	21	0-3	-	3-3	2	0	-	-	0	3
Rick Mousa	11	1-4	-	1-4	4	1	-	-	1	3
Billy Grimes	2	1-1	-	0-1	1	0	-	-	0	2
Jimmy Powell	3	0-2	-	0-0	1	0	-	-	0	0
TOTALS	**200**	**23-68**	**-**	**23-30**	**36**	**5**	**-**	**-**	**26**	**69**
Percentages		33.8	-	76.7						

Coach: Frank McGuire

Officials: Bain, Lawson
Attendance: 10,430

78-67 | 38 1H 31 | 40 2H 36 | SWEET 16

PENN	MIN	FG	3FG	FT	REB	A	ST	BL	PF	TP
Phillip Hankinson	40	10-19	-	2-2	6	2	-	-	2	22
Corky Calhoun	31	8-11	-	5-5	7	2	-	-	4	21
Bob Morse	40	8-18	-	4-4	9	2	-	-	0	20
Al Cotler	39	3-7	-	3-4	1	6	-	-	3	9
Craig Littlepage	29	2-4	-	2-3	4	2	-	-	4	6
Ron Billingslea	11	0-1	-	0-0	1	0	-	-	2	0
John Jablonski	9	0-2	-	0-2	0	0	-	-	2	0
Zoltan Varga	1	0-0	-	0-0	0	0	-	-	0	0
TOTALS	**200**	**31-62**	**-**	**16-20**	**28**	**14**	**-**	**-**	**17**	**78**
Percentages		50.0		80.0						

Coach: Chuck Daly

VILLANOVA	MIN	FG	3FG	FT	REB	A	ST	BL	PF	TP
Hank Siemiontkowski	40	6-11	-	10-12	11	1	-	-	1	22
Tom Ingelsby	39	8-19	-	5-5	6	2	-	-	2	21
Chris Ford	40	6-11	-	2-3	4	3	-	-	3	14
Ed Hastings	30	3-3	-	0-0	2	1	-	-	4	6
Larry Moody	32	2-4	-	0-1	3	0	-	-	4	4
Bob Gohl	10	0-0	-	0-0	0	2	-	-	1	0
Joe McDowell	9	0-1	-	0-0	0	0	-	-	1	0
TOTALS	**200**	**25-49**	**-**	**17-21**	**26**	**9**	**-**	**-**	**16**	**67**
Percentages		51.0		81.0						

Coach: Jack Kraft

Officials: Scott, Smith
Attendance: 10,430

88-84 | 44 1H 39 | 44 2H 45 | SWEET 16

LOUISVILLE	MIN	FG	3FG	FT	REB	A	ST	BL	PF	TP
Jim Price	-	10-15	-	5-6	2	-	-	-	2	25
Ron Thomas	-	8-12	-	3-10	13	-	-	-	4	19
Al Vilcheck	-	5-6	-	3-6	10	-	-	-	3	13
Henry Bacon	-	5-9	-	1-2	6	-	-	-	0	11
Mike Lawhon	-	2-6	-	6-6	2	-	-	-	3	10
Ken Bradley	-	2-6	-	2-2	5	-	-	-	1	6
Larry Carter	-	2-6	-	0-1	1	-	-	-	2	4
TOTALS	**-**	**34-60**	**-**	**20-33**	**39**	**-**	**-**	**-**	**15**	**88**
Percentages		56.7		60.6						

Coach: Denny Crum

UL LAFAYETTE	MIN	FG	3FG	FT	REB	A	ST	BL	PF	TP
Dwight Lamar	-	14-42	-	1-3	0	-	-	-	2	29
Jerry Bisbano	-	6-13	-	3-4	5	-	-	-	4	15
Wilbert Loftin	-	5-7	-	2-2	10	-	-	-	4	12
Roy Ebron	-	3-10	-	5-5	12	-	-	-	4	11
Payton Townsend	-	4-6	-	2-3	7	-	-	-	3	10
Fred Saunders	-	2-10	-	0-1	11	-	-	-	4	4
Mike Haney	-	1-5	-	1-2	6	-	-	-	2	3
Steve Greene	-	0-1	-	0-0	1	-	-	-	1	0
TOTALS	**-**	**35-94**	**-**	**14-20**	**52**	**-**	**-**	**-**	**24**	**84**
Percentages		37.2		70.0						

Coach: Beryl Shipley

Officials: Hernjack, Saar
Attendance: 10,000

66-55 | 36 1H 25 | 30 2H 30 | SWEET 16

KANSAS STATE	MIN	FG	3FG	FT	REB	A	ST	BL	PF	TP
Danny Beard	-	8-18	-	4-7	2	-	-	-	1	20
David Hall	-	4-6	-	5-6	12	-	-	-	3	13
Ernie Kusnyer	-	5-9	-	2-5	6	-	-	-	3	12
Lon Kruger	-	4-9	-	3-4	3	-	-	-	1	11
Robert Zender	-	2-6	-	2-2	9	-	-	-	2	6
Steve Mitchell	-	1-2	-	0-0	2	-	-	-	2	2
Larry Williams	-	1-4	-	0-0	4	-	-	-	2	2
TOTALS	**-**	**25-54**	**-**	**16-24**	**38**	**-**	**-**	**-**	**14**	**66**
Percentages		46.3		66.7						

Coach: Jack Hartman

TEXAS	MIN	FG	3FG	FT	REB	A	ST	BL	PF	TP
Larry Robinson	-	10-14	-	2-3	3	-	-	-	3	22
Joe Lenox	-	6-12	-	2-3	2	-	-	-	4	14
B.G. Brosterhous	-	4-8	-	2-5	4	-	-	-	4	10
Harry Larrabee	-	2-10	-	1-1	8	-	-	-	5	5
Jack Louis	-	2-5	-	0-1	5	-	-	-	1	4
Jimmy Blacklock	-	0-0	-	0-0	0	-	-	-	0	0
Eric Groscurth	-	0-5	-	0-1	5	-	-	-	2	0
TOTALS	**-**	**24-54**	**-**	**7-14**	**27**	**-**	**-**	**-**	**19**	**55**
Percentages		44.4		50.0						

Coach: Leon Black

Officials: Stout, Grossman
Attendance: 10,000

SWEET 16 — UCLA 90, Weber State 58

	1H	2H
UCLA	42	48
Weber State	25	33

UCLA	MIN	FG	3FG	FT	REB	A	ST	BL	PF	TP
Henry Bibby	30	7-18	-	2-2	3	1	-	-	2	16
Larry Farmer	27	7-15	-	1-1	7	1	-	-	1	15
Swen Nater	20	5-9	-	2-4	8	0	-	-	2	12
Keith Wilkes	25	4-12	-	2-2	13	2	-	-	4	10
Andy Hill	6	3-4	-	4-4	1	1	-	-	2	10
Tommy Curtis	21	3-7	-	1-1	3	6	-	-	2	7
Greg Lee	17	3-8	-	0-0	4	6	-	-	1	6
Bill Walton	20	1-1	-	2-5	12	0	-	-	4	4
Larry Hollyfield	13	2-9	-	0-0	5	2	-	-	2	4
Gary Franklin	5	2-2	-	0-0	2	0	-	-	0	4
Jon Chapman	7	1-1	-	0-1	2	0	-	-	1	2
Vince Carson	9	0-3	-	0-1	5	2	-	-	2	0
TOTALS	**200**	**38-89**	**-**	**14-21**	**65**	**21**	**-**	**-**	**23**	**90**
Percentages		42.7		66.7						

Coach: John Wooden

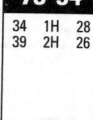

WEBER STATE	MIN	FG	3FG	FT	REB	A	ST	BL	PF	TP
Bob Davis	28	4-14	-	8-13	6	2	-	-	4	16
Riley Wimberly	22	7-15	-	0-0	5	0	-	-	0	14
Jon Knoble	32	3-8	-	3-8	9	2	-	-	4	9
Richard Cooper	31	2-10	-	4-6	12	0	-	-	4	8
Wes Van Dyke	37	2-11	-	0-1	1	1	-	-	3	4
Brady Small	34	1-12	-	2-3	2	3	-	-	0	4
Ken Gubler	5	1-2	-	0-0	1	0	-	-	2	2
Greg Soter	5	0-0	-	1-2	0	0	-	-	0	1
Rick Camac	4	0-0	-	0-0	0	0	-	-	0	0
Dave Muirbrook	2	0-0	-	0-0	0	0	-	-	0	0
Kelly McGarry	0	0-0	-	0-0	0	1	-	-	0	0
Ralph Williams	0	0-1	-	0-0	0	0	-	-	0	0
TOTALS	**200**	**20-73**	**-**	**18-33**	**36**	**9**	**-**	**-**	**17**	**58**
Percentages		27.4		54.5						

Coach: Gene Visscher

Officials: Copeland, Fou
Attendance: 15,247

SWEET 16 — Long Beach State 75, San Francisco 55

	1H	2H
Long Beach State	33	42
San Francisco	22	33

LONG BEACH STATE	MIN	FG	3FG	FT	REB	A	ST	BL	PF	TP
Ed Ratleff	-	7-17	-	2-3	5	6	-	-	0	16
Chuck Terry	-	6-14	-	4-4	4	2	-	-	1	16
Eric McWilliams	-	4-10	-	3-5	12	0	-	-	4	11
Bob Lynn	-	4-4	-	0-0	5	0	-	-	0	8
Glenn McDonald	-	3-10	-	2-3	5	2	-	-	2	8
Leonard Gray	-	3-7	-	0-0	4	5	-	-	3	6
Lamont King	-	2-4	-	2-4	1	1	-	-	3	6
Nate Stephens	-	2-4	-	0-1	3	1	-	-	1	4
Roy Miller	-	0-1	-	0-0	0	1	-	-	0	0
Tom Motley	-	0-0	-	0-0	0	1	-	-	1	0
TOTALS	**-**	**31-71**	**-**	**13-20**	**39**	**19**	**-**	**-**	**15**	**75**
Percentages		43.7		65.0						

Coach: Jerry Tarkanian

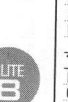

SAN FRANCISCO	MIN	FG	3FG	FT	REB	A	ST	BL	PF	TP
Mike Quick	-	7-17	-	5-6	0	3	-	-	2	19
Kevin Restani	-	4-16	-	1-5	17	1	-	-	4	9
Phil Smith	-	3-10	-	2-2	9	1	-	-	2	8
John Burks	-	3-10	-	1-1	9	0	-	-	3	7
John Boro	-	3-9	-	0-0	3	3	-	-	2	6
Byron Jones	-	1-6	-	2-4	11	0	-	-	3	4
Ron Centerwall	-	1-1	-	0-0	1	0	-	-	0	2
John Hancock	-	0-3	-	0-0	0	0	-	-	0	0
Anthony Lewis	-	0-1	-	0-0	2	0	-	-	1	0
TOTALS	**-**	**22-73**	**-**	**11-18**	**52**	**8**	**-**	**-**	**17**	**55**
Percentages		30.1		61.1						

Coach: Bob Gaillard

Officials: Wedge, Wortman
Attendance: 15,247

ELITE 8 — Florida State 73, Kentucky 54

	1H	2H
Florida State	34	39
Kentucky	28	26

FLORIDA STATE	MIN	FG	3FG	FT	REB	A	ST	BL	PF	TP
Ron King	33	9-19	-	4-4	8	0	-	-	0	22
Otto Petty	32	2-5	-	9-9	6	8	-	-	2	13
Reggie Royals	40	4-13	-	4-5	12	1	-	-	3	12
Lawrence McCray	31	6-13	-	0-2	5	0	-	-	3	12
Ron Harris	28	3-7	-	0-0	5	2	-	-	3	6
Rowland Garrett	21	2-4	-	1-1	3	2	-	-	2	5
Greg Samuel	8	1-2	-	1-1	1	2	-	-	0	3
Otis Cole	7	0-1	-	0-0	0	0	-	-	0	0
TOTALS	**200**	**27-64**	**-**	**19-22**	**40**	**15**	**-**	**-**	**13**	**73**
Percentages		42.2		86.4						

Coach: Hugh Durham

KENTUCKY	MIN	FG	3FG	FT	REB	A	ST	BL	PF	TP
Jim Andrews	40	7-14	-	3-3	11	1	-	-	1	17
Tom Parker	35	5-13	-	0-1	6	1	-	-	3	10
Ronnie Lyons	33	5-13	-	0-0	2	3	-	-	3	10
Larry Stamper	40	2-6	-	5-7	9	1	-	-	2	9
Bob McCowan	30	2-4	-	1-1	2	7	-	-	4	5
Stan Key	17	1-4	-	0-0	1	2	-	-	3	2
Rick Drewitz	5	0-0	-	1-1	0	1	-	-	0	1
TOTALS	**200**	**22-54**	**-**	**10-13**	**31**	**16**	**-**	**-**	**16**	**54**
Percentages		40.7		76.9						

Coach: Adolph Rupp

Officials: Brown, Filiberti
Attendance: 13,458

ELITE 8 — North Carolina 73, Penn 59

	1H	2H
North Carolina	37	36
Penn	35	24

NORTH CAROLINA	MIN	FG	3FG	FT	REB	A	ST	BL	PF	TP
Dennis Wuycik	30	7-12	-	4-5	4	2	-	-	4	18
Bob McAdoo	38	5-10	-	7-10	9	0	-	-	0	17
George Karl	19	5-9	-	6-7	1	1	-	-	4	16
Bill Chamberlain	26	2-6	-	3-3	2	0	-	-	1	7
Kim Huband	19	2-3	-	3-3	2	1	-	-	4	7
Bobby Jones	20	2-4	-	0-1	6	5	-	-	3	4
Steve Previs	34	1-3	-	0-0	5	4	-	-	1	2
Bill L. Chambers	4	1-1	-	0-0	2	0	-	-	0	2
Ray Hite	4	0-0	-	0-0	0	0	-	-	1	0
Don Johnston	4	0-0	-	0-0	1	0	-	-	0	0
Craig Corson	2	0-0	-	0-0	1	0	-	-	0	0
TOTALS	**200**	**25-48**	**-**	**23-29**	**33**	**13**	**-**	**-**	**18**	**73**
Percentages		52.1		79.3						

Coach: Dean Smith

PENN	MIN	FG	3FG	FT	REB	A	ST	BL	PF	TP
Bob Morse	34	5-14	-	4-6	6	0	-	-	4	14
Phillip Hankinson	39	5-19	-	2-2	9	2	-	-	5	12
Ron Billingslea	25	5-7	-	2-3	3	1	-	-	4	12
Al Cotler	33	2-7	-	6-6	1	3	-	-	4	10
Corky Calhoun	39	3-8	-	1-2	7	3	-	-	2	7
Craig Littlepage	19	1-1	-	2-4	4	0	-	-	4	4
Zoltan Varga	9	0-0	-	0-0	1	1	-	-	0	0
John Jablonski	2	0-0	-	0-0	0	0	-	-	0	0
TOTALS	**200**	**21-56**	**-**	**17-23**	**31**	**10**	**-**	**-**	**23**	**59**
Percentages		37.5		73.9						

Coach: Chuck Daly

Officials: Bain, Scott
Attendance: 10,078

ELITE 8 — Louisville 72, Kansas State 65

	1H	2H
Louisville	42	30
Kansas State	26	39

LOUISVILLE	MIN	FG	3FG	FT	REB	A	ST	BL	PF	TP
Jim Price	-	11-16	-	3-4	0	-	-	-	1	25
Ron Thomas	-	6-10	-	6-10	14	-	-	-	4	18
Mike Lawhon	-	3-8	-	4-5	7	-	-	-	1	10
Henry Bacon	-	4-10	-	0-3	5	-	-	-	3	8
Al Vilcheck	-	4-9	-	0-0	7	-	-	-	5	8
Bill Bunton	-	1-2	-	1-1	6	-	-	-	1	3
Ken Bradley	-	0-2	-	0-0	0	-	-	-	0	0
Larry Carter	-	0-1	-	0-0	0	-	-	-	1	0
TOTALS	**-**	**29-58**	**-**	**14-23**	**39**	**-**	**-**	**-**	**16**	**72**
Percentages		50.0		60.9						

Coach: Denny Crum

KANSAS STATE	MIN	FG	3FG	FT	REB	A	ST	BL	PF	TP
Lon Kruger	-	3-8	-	8-9	2	-	-	-	4	14
Ernie Kusnyer	-	4-6	-	5-5	6	-	-	-	4	13
Larry Williams	-	6-8	-	0-1	3	-	-	-	1	12
Danny Beard	-	4-9	-	0-1	2	-	-	-	4	8
David Hall	-	4-9	-	0-2	10	-	-	-	3	8
Steve Mitchell	-	3-7	-	0-0	5	-	-	-	1	6
Robert Zender	-	2-6	-	0-1	4	-	-	-	1	4
Robert Chipman	-	0-1	-	0-2	0	-	-	-	1	0
Lindbergh White	-	0-2	-	0-0	0	-	-	-	0	0
TOTALS	**-**	**26-56**	**-**	**13-21**	**32**	**-**	**-**	**-**	**19**	**65**
Percentages		46.4		61.9						

Coach: Jack Hartman

Officials: Hernjack, Grossman
Attendance: 10,000

ELITE 8 — UCLA 73, Long Beach State 57

	1H	2H
UCLA	34	39
Long Beach State	23	34

UCLA	MIN	FG	3FG	FT	REB	A	ST	BL	PF	TP
Henry Bibby	38	10-17	-	3-4	4	4	-	-	2	23
Bill Walton	37	7-10	-	5-7	11	1	-	-	3	19
Keith Wilkes	34	4-10	-	6-7	6	2	-	-	3	14
Greg Lee	32	2-6	-	2-3	3	4	-	-	0	6
Larry Farmer	36	2-7	-	1-3	3	2	-	-	3	5
Swen Nater	3	2-2	-	1-2	1	0	-	-	0	5
Andy Hill	2	0-0	-	1-3	0	1	-	-	0	1
Tommy Curtis	6	0-0	-	0-0	0	1	-	-	1	0
Larry Hollyfield	6	0-1	-	0-0	0	0	-	-	2	0
Vince Carson	3	0-0	-	0-0	1	0	-	-	1	0
Jon Chapman	2	0-0	-	0-0	0	0	-	-	0	0
Gary Franklin	1	0-0	-	0-0	0	0	-	-	0	0
TOTALS	**200**	**27-53**	**-**	**19-29**	**29**	**15**	**-**	**-**	**15**	**73**
Percentages		50.9		65.5						

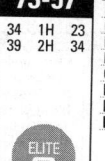

Coach: John Wooden

LONG BEACH STATE	MIN	FG	3FG	FT	REB	A	ST	BL	PF	TP
Ed Ratleff	38	7-19	-	3-6	3	3	-	-	3	17
Glenn McDonald	31	3-3	-	2-2	5	2	-	-	0	8
Eric McWilliams	25	2-4	-	3-3	5	1	-	-	4	7
Leonard Gray	18	2-5	-	3-4	3	0	-	-	4	7
Chuck Terry	40	2-6	-	2-2	4	3	-	-	4	6
Bob Lynn	23	2-6	-	2-2	8	0	-	-	2	6
Lamont King	11	2-2	-	0-0	0	0	-	-	2	4
Nate Stephens	14	1-5	-	0-0	3	0	-	-	1	2
TOTALS	**200**	**21-50**	**-**	**15-19**	**31**	**9**	**-**	**-**	**20**	**57**
Percentages		42.0		78.9						

Coach: Jerry Tarkanian

Officials: Copeland, Wortman
Attendance: 15,152

79-75 | 45 1H 32 | 34 2H 43 | FINAL 4

FLORIDA STATE	MIN	FG	3FG	FT	REB	A	ST	BL	PF	TP
Ron King	38	6-17	-	10-10	5	2	-	-	1	22
Reggie Royals	32	6-8	-	6-7	10	4	-	-	5	18
Rowland Garrett	34	4-8	-	3-7	5	1	-	-	4	11
Otto Petty	27	3-5	-	4-7	1	6	-	-	5	10
Lawrence McCray	26	3-6	-	3-6	9	1	-	-	3	9
Greg Samuel	13	2-4	-	1-4	1	0	-	-	0	5
Ron Harris	26	1-6	-	2-2	4	2	-	-	2	4
Otis Cole	3	0-0	-	0-0	0	0	-	-	0	0
Larry Gay	1	0-1	-	0-0	0	0	-	-	0	0
TOTALS	**200**	**25-55**	**-**	**29-43**	**35**	**16**	**-**	**-**	**20**	**79**
Percentages		45.5		67.4						

Coach: Hugh Durham

NORTH CAROLINA	MIN	FG	3FG	FT	REB	A	ST	BL	PF	TP
Bob McAdoo	28	10-19	-	4-5	15	1	-	-	5	24
Dennis Wuycik	34	7-16	-	6-6	6	0	-	-	4	20
George Karl	30	5-14	-	1-3	6	5	-	-	3	11
Bobby Joneps	31	4-8	-	1-1	9	2	-	-	3	9
Bill Chamberlain	23	2-5	-	2-3	10	3	-	-	4	6
Steve Previs	32	1-5	-	3-6	3	8	-	-	4	5
Kim Huband	11	0-1	-	0-0	2	0	-	-	2	0
Don Johnston	6	0-1	-	0-0	0	0	-	-	1	0
Bill L. Chambers	3	0-1	-	0-1	0	0	-	-	1	0
Craig Corson	1	0-0	-	0-0	0	0	-	-	0	0
Ray Hite	1	0-0	-	0-0	0	1	-	-	0	0
TOTALS	**200**	**29-70**	**-**	**17-25**	**51**	**20**	**-**	**-**	**27**	**75**
Percentages		41.4		68.0						

Coach: Dean Smith

Officials: Scott, Brown
Attendance: 15,189

96-77 | 39 1H 31 | 57 2H 46 | FINAL 4

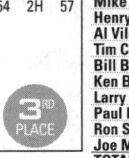

UCLA	MIN	FG	3FG	FT	REB	A	ST	BL	PF	TP
Bill Walton	36	11-13	-	11-12	21	1	-	-	2	33
Larry Farmer	27	6-12	-	3-5	4	1	-	-	2	15
Keith Wilkes	31	5-11	-	2-2	6	2	-	-	0	12
Greg Lee	30	3-6	-	4-6	4	8	-	-	1	10
Tommy Curtis	22	4-5	-	0-0	2	3	-	-	2	8
Larry Hollyfield	14	3-6	-	0-0	4	1	-	-	1	6
Andy Hill	5	1-1	-	4-4	0	0	-	-	1	6
Henry Bibby	21	1-5	-	0-0	3	2	-	-	5	2
Vince Carson	4	1-1	-	0-0	0	0	-	-	1	2
Swen Nater	4	0-0	-	2-4	1	0	-	-	1	2
Jon Chapman	3	0-0	-	0-1	1	1	-	-	0	0
Gary Franklin	3	0-1	-	0-0	2	0	-	-	0	0
TOTALS	**200**	**35-61**	**-**	**26-34**	**48**	**19**	**-**	**-**	**16**	**96**
Percentages		57.4		76.5						

Coach: John Wooden

LOUISVILLE	MIN	FG	3FG	FT	REB	A	ST	BL	PF	TP
Jim Price	38	11-23	-	8-9	5	2	-	-	3	30
Henry Bacon	32	5-11	-	5-7	4	4	-	-	0	15
Larry Carter	20	4-8	-	0-0	2	2	-	-	0	8
Al Vilcheck	25	3-6	-	0-0	1	0	-	-	5	6
Ron Thomas	21	2-4	-	0-0	3	1	-	-	5	4
Paul Pry	2	2-3	-	0-0	1	0	-	-	1	4
Bill Bunton	23	1-5	-	1-1	4	0	-	-	1	3
Ron Stallings	7	1-2	-	0-1	1	0	-	-	2	2
Ken Bradley	5	1-3	-	0-0	2	2	-	-	1	2
Tim Cooper	3	0-1	-	2-2	1	0	-	-	1	2
Mike Lawhon	22	0-7	-	1-2	3	0	-	-	3	1
Joe Meiman	2	0-1	-	0-0	1	0	-	-	0	0
TOTALS	**200**	**30-74**	**-**	**17-22**	**28**	**11**	**-**	**-**	**22**	**77**
Percentages		40.5		77.3						

Coach: Denny Crum

Officials: Hernjack, Copeland
Attendance: 15,189

105-91 | 51 1H 34 | 54 2H 57 | 3RD PLACE

NORTH CAROLINA	MIN	FG	3FG	FT	REB	A	ST	BL	PF	TP
Bob McAdoo	37	12-20	-	6-6	19	2	-	-	1	30
Dennis Wuycik	34	8-12	-	11-16	8	2	-	-	2	27
George Karl	28	6-8	-	4-5	2	3	-	-	5	16
Bobby Jones	21	4-8	-	3-4	4	5	-	-	5	11
Bill Chamberlain	18	4-6	-	1-1	4	5	-	-	5	9
Steve Previs	33	2-5	-	3-5	4	7	-	-	4	7
Bill L. Chambers	3	0-0	-	4-4	0	0	-	-	0	4
Ray Hite	7	0-0	-	1-3	1	0	-	-	1	1
Kim Huband	12	0-0	-	0-0	2	1	-	-	1	0
Don Johnston	4	0-0	-	0-0	0	0	-	-	0	0
Craig Corson	2	0-0	-	0-0	2	0	-	-	0	0
Darrell Elston	1	0-0	-	0-0	0	0	-	-	0	0
TOTALS	**200**	**36-59**	**-**	**33-44**	**46**	**25**	**-**	**-**	**24**	**105**
Percentages		61.0		75.0						

Coach: Dean Smith

LOUISVILLE	MIN	FG	3FG	FT	REB	A	ST	BL	PF	TP
Jim Price	36	9-17	-	5-7	4	4	-	-	5	23
Ron Thomas	32	5-11	-	4-6	10	0	-	-	4	14
Mike Lawhon	27	4-10	-	5-6	2	2	-	-	3	13
Henry Bacon	31	3-8	-	6-8	4	4	-	-	3	12
Al Vilcheck	19	3-5	-	2-3	5	1	-	-	3	8
Tim Cooper	11	2-5	-	4-5	0	2	-	-	4	8
Bill Bunton	18	2-4	-	1-2	5	0	-	-	2	5
Ken Bradley	6	1-4	-	0-0	4	3	-	-	2	2
Larry Carter	6	1-5	-	0-0	0	0	-	-	0	2
Paul Pry	4	1-2	-	0-0	1	0	-	-	0	2
Ron Stallings	4	1-5	-	0-0	2	0	-	-	2	2
Joe Meiman	6	0-2	-	0-0	1	1	-	-	3	0
TOTALS	**200**	**32-78**	**-**	**27-37**	**38**	**17**	**-**	**-**	**31**	**91**
Percentages		41.0		73.0						

Coach: Denny Crum

Officials: Hernjack, Copeland
Attendance: 15,063

81-76 | 50 1H 39 | 31 2H 37 | NCAA FINAL 1972

UCLA	MIN	FG	3FG	FT	REB	A	ST	BL	PF	TP
Bill Walton	34	9-17	-	6-11	20	2	-	-	4	24
Keith Wilkes	38	11-16	-	1-2	10	3	-	-	4	23
Henry Bibby	40	8-17	-	2-3	3	1	-	-	2	18
Tommy Curtis	24	4-14	-	0-1	4	6	-	-	1	8
Larry Farmer	33	2-6	-	0-0	6	0	-	-	2	4
Larry Hollyfield	9	1-6	-	0-0	2	3	-	-	2	2
Swen Nater	6	1-2	-	0-1	1	0	-	-	0	2
Greg Lee	16	0-0	-	0-0	2	4	-	-	0	0
TOTALS	**200**	**36-78**	**-**	**9-18**	**48**	**19**	**-**	**-**	**15**	**81**
Percentages		46.2		50.0						

Coach: John Wooden

FLORIDA STATE	MIN	FG	3FG	FT	REB	A	ST	BL	PF	TP
Ron King	31	12-20	-	3-3	6	1	-	-	1	27
Ron Harris	26	7-13	-	2-3	6	1	-	-	1	16
Reggie Royals	33	5-7	-	5-6	10	2	-	-	5	15
Lawrence McCray	23	3-6	-	2-5	6	3	-	-	4	8
Greg Samuel	31	3-10	-	0-0	1	7	-	-	1	6
Rowland Garrett	37	1-9	-	1-1	5	0	-	-	1	3
Otto Petty	9	0-0	-	1-1	0	2	-	-	1	1
Otis Cole	10	0-2	-	0-0	2	1	-	-	1	0
TOTALS	**200**	**31-67**	**-**	**14-19**	**36**	**17**	**-**	**-**	**15**	**76**
Percentages		46.3		73.7						

Coach: Hugh Durham

Officials: Brown, Scott
Attendance: 15,063

National Invitation Tournament (NIT)

First round: Lafayette d. Virginia 72-71, Jacksonville d. Fordham 94-75, Syracuse d. Davidson 81-77, Maryland d. Saint Joseph's 67-55, Oral Roberts d. Memphis 94-74, St. John's d. Missouri 82-81 (OT), Princeton d. Indiana 68-60, Niagara d. UTEP 76-57
Quarterfinals: Jacksonville d. Lafayette 87-76, Maryland d. Syracuse 71-65, St. John's d. Oral Roberts 94-78, Niagara d. Princeton 65-60
Semifinals: Maryland d. Jacksonville 91-77, Niagara d. St. John's 69-67
Third place: Jacksonville d. St. John's 83-80
Championship: Maryland d. Niagara 100-69
MVP: Tom McMillen, Maryland

1972-73: Sheer Wizardry

It was becoming as regular as the seasons. John Wooden, the Wizard of Westwood, coached UCLA to yet another NCAA championship *and* a second straight 30–0 record with an 87-66 dismantling of Memphis State (known today as Memphis) at the St. Louis Arena. This was the first season the NCAA allowed freshmen to play on varsity squads and the school that benefited most was Indiana. Bob Knight reached his first Final Four as a coach with a team led by freshman point guard Quinn Buckner. But the biggest impact player was still Bill Walton, who, for the second straight season, was selected as national Player of the Year, averaging 20.4 ppg, 16.9 rpg and 5.6 apg. In the national semifinals, UCLA dumped Knight's Hoosiers 70-59, with Walton getting 14 points, 17 boards and 9 assists. Walton's performance in the Final was perhaps the greatest ever: He connected on 21 of his 22 field goal attempts for a championship-game record 44 points and received his second straight Tournament MOP award.

The nation's No. 2-ranked team, 27–0 NC State, was banned from the Tournament because of NCAA violations, so a showdown between the two best teams of this season would have to wait until the next.

Major Conference Standings

ACC	Conference W	L	Pct	Overall W	L	Pct
NC State	12	0	1.000	27	0	1.000
North Carolina□	8	4	.667	25	8	.758
Maryland⊕	7	5	.583	23	7	.767
Virginia	4	8	.333	13	12	.520
Clemson	4	8	.333	12	14	.462
Duke	4	8	.333	12	14	.462
Wake Forest	3	9	.250	12	15	.444

Tournament: **NC State d. Maryland 76-74**
Tournament MVP: **Tom Burleson,** NC State

Big Eight	Conference W	L	Pct	Overall W	L	Pct
Kansas State⊕	12	2	.857	23	5	.821
Colorado	9	5	.643	13	13	.500
Missouri□	9	5	.643	21	6	.778
Oklahoma	8	6	.571	18	8	.692
Iowa State	7	7	.500	16	10	.615
Nebraska	4	10	.286	9	17	.346
Kansas	4	10	.286	8	18	.308
Oklahoma State	3	11	.214	7	19	.269

Big Sky	Conference W	L	Pct	Overall W	L	Pct
Weber State⊕	13	1	.929	20	7	.741
Idaho State	10	4	.714	18	8	.692
Montana State	9	5	.643	17	9	.654
Montana	7	7	.500	13	13	.500
Gonzaga	6	8	.429	14	12	.538
Boise State	5	9	.357	11	15	.423
Idaho	3	11	.214	7	19	.269
Northern Arizona	3	11	.214	6	20	.231

Big Ten	Conference W	L	Pct	Overall W	L	Pct
Indiana⊕	11	3	.786	22	6	.786
Minnesota□	10	4	.714	21	5	.808
Purdue	8	6	.571	15	9	.625
Illinois	8	6	.571	14	10	.583
Ohio State	8	6	.571	14	10	.583
Iowa	6	8	.429	13	11	.542
Michigan	6	8	.429	13	11	.542
Michigan State	6	8	.429	13	11	.542
Wisconsin	5	9	.357	11	13	.458
Northwestern	2	12	.143	5	19	.208

Ivy	Conference W	L	Pct	Overall W	L	Pct
Penn⊕	12	2	.857	21	7	.750
Princeton	11	3	.786	16	9	.640
Brown	10	4	.714	14	12	.538
Harvard	7	7	.500	14	12	.538
Yale	6	8	.429	9	16	.360
Columbia	5	9	.357	7	18	.280
Dartmouth	4	10	.286	6	20	.231
Cornell	1	13	.071	4	22	.154

Mid-American	Conference W	L	Pct	Overall W	L	Pct
Miami (OH)⊕	9	2	.818	18	9	.667
Toledo	7	5	.583	15	11	.577
Bowling Green	7	5	.583	13	13	.500
Ohio	6	5	.545	16	10	.615
Kent State	5	7	.417	10	16	.385
Central Michigan	4	6	.400	13	13	.500
Western Michigan	2	10	.167	8	18	.308

MEAC	Conference W	L	Pct	Overall W	L	Pct
UMES	10	2	.833	26	5	.839
Howard	9	3	.750	22	6	.786
Morgan State	8	4	.667	20	8	.714
NC A&T	7	5	.583	16	11	.593
South Carolina St.	3	9	.250	17	14	.548
Delaware State	3	9	.250	10	13	.435
NC Central	2	10	.167	5	18	.217

Tournament: **NC A&T d. Howard 86-81**
Tournament MOP: **William Harris,** NC A&T

Middle Atlantic	Conference W	L	Pct	Overall W	L	Pct
Eastern Division						
Saint Joseph's⊕	6	0	1.000	22	6	.786
Temple	5	1	.833	17	10	.630
American□	4	2	.667	21	5	.808
La Salle	3	3	.500	15	10	.600
Drexel	2	4	.333	14	7	.667
Hofstra	1	5	.167	8	16	.333
West Chester	0	6	.000	5	21	.192
Western Division						
Lafayette	7	3	.700	16	10	.615
Delaware	6	4	.600	14	11	.560
Gettysburg	6	4	.600	14	11	.560
Bucknell	6	4	.600	11	14	.440
Lehigh	3	7	.300	8	17	.320
Rider	2	8	.200	12	14	.462

Missouri Valley	Conference W	L	Pct	Overall W	L	Pct
Memphis⊕	12	2	.857	24	6	.800
Louisville□	11	3	.786	23	7	.767
Saint Louis	10	4	.714	19	7	.731
Tulsa	10	4	.714	18	8	.692
New Mexico State	6	8	.429	12	14	.462
Wichita State	6	8	.429	10	16	.385
Drake	5	9	.357	14	12	.538
Bradley	4	10	.286	12	14	.462
North Texas	4	10	.286	9	16	.360
West Texas A&M	2	12	.143	9	17	.346

Ohio Valley	Conference W	L	Pct	Overall W	L	Pct
Austin Peay⊕⊗	11	3	.786	22	7	.759
Murray State	9	5	.643	17	8	.680
Morehead State	9	5	.643	14	11	.560
Tennessee Tech	7	7	.500	14	11	.560
Eastern Kentucky	7	7	.500	12	13	.480
Western Kentucky	6	8	.429	10	16	.385
Middle Tennessee St.	5	9	.357	12	13	.480
East Tennessee St.	2	12	.143	9	17	.346

PCAA	Conference W	L	Pct	Overall W	L	Pct
Long Beach State⊕⊗	10	2	.833	26	3	.897
UC Santa Barbara	8	4	.667	17	9	.654
San Diego State	7	5	.583	15	11	.577
Pacific	6	6	.500	14	12	.538
San Jose State	6	6	.500	11	14	.440
Cal State LA	4	8	.333	11	14	.440
Fresno State	1	11	.083	10	16	.385

Pac-8	Conference W	L	Pct	Overall W	L	Pct
UCLA⊕	14	0	1.000	30	0	1.000
Southern California□	9	5	.643	18	10	.643
Oregon	8	6	.571	16	10	.615
Stanford	7	7	.500	14	11	.560
Washington	6	8	.429	16	11	.593
Oregon State	6	8	.429	15	11	.577
California	4	10	.286	11	15	.423
Washington State	2	12	.143	6	20	.231

SEC	††††Conference W	L	Pct	Overall W	L	Pct
Kentucky⊕	14	4	.778	20	8	.714
Vanderbilt	13	5	.722	20	6	.769
Alabama□	13	5	.722	22	8	.733
Tennessee	13	5	.722	15	9	.625
LSU	9	9	.500	14	10	.583
Mississippi	8	10	.444	14	12	.538
Florida	7	11	.389	11	15	.423
Georgia	5	13	.278	10	16	.385
Mississippi State	4	14	.222	11	15	.423
Auburn	4	14	.222	6	20	.231

Southern	Conference W	L	Pct	Overall W	L	Pct
Davidson	9	1	.900	18	9	.667
Furman⊕	11	2	.846	20	9	.690
East Carolina	7	7	.500	13	13	.500
The Citadel	6	7	.462	11	15	.423
William and Mary	5	6	.455	10	17	.370
Richmond	5	9	.357	8	16	.333
Appalachian State	3	8	.273	6	20	.231
VMI	3	9	.250	7	19	.269

Tournament: **Furman d. Davidson 99-81**
Tournament MOP: **Clyde Mayes,** Furman

Southland	Conference W	L	Pct	Overall W	L	Pct
UL-Lafayette○⊗	12	0	.000	24	5	.828
McNeese State⊗	10	2	.833	19	7	.731
Louisiana Tech	10	2	.833	18	8	.692
Texas-Arlington⊗	8	4	.667	13	13	.500
Lamar⊗	6	6	.500	11	13	.458
Abilene Christian	4	8	.333	8	18	.308
Arkansas State⊗	2	10	.167	7	17	.292

Southwest	Conference W	L	Pct	Overall W	L	Pct
Texas Tech⊕	12	2	.857	19	8	.704
Texas A&M	9	5	.643	17	9	.654
Arkansas	9	5	.643	16	10	.615
Baylor	8	6	.571	14	11	.560
Texas	7	7	.500	13	12	.520
SMU	7	7	.500	10	15	.400
Rice	2	12	.143	7	19	.269
TCU	2	12	.143	4	21	.160

WCAC	Conference W	L	Pct	Overall W	L	Pct
San Francisco⊕	12	2	.857	23	5	.821
Santa Clara	11	3	.786	19	7	.731
Pepperdine	7	7	.500	14	11	.560
Loyola Marymount	7	7	.500	10	16	.385
Seattle	6	8	.429	13	15	.464
UNLV	6	8	.429	13	15	.464
Nevada	5	9	.357	10	16	.385
Saint Mary's (CA)	2	12	.143	7	19	.269

WAC	Conference W	L	Pct	Overall W	L	Pct
Arizona State⊕	10	4	.714	19	9	.679
New Mexico□	9	5	.643	21	6	.778
BYU	9	5	.643	19	7	.731
Arizona	9	5	.643	16	10	.615
UTEP	6	8	.429	16	10	.615
Colorado State	5	9	.357	13	15	.464
Wyoming	4	10	.286	9	17	.346
Utah	4	10	.286	8	19	.296

⊕ Automatic NCAA Tournament bid ○ At-large NCAA Tournament bid □ NIT appearance ⊗ Team record doesn't reflect games forfeited or vacated. For adjusted record, see p. 521.

YANKEE

	Conference W	L	PCT	Overall W	L	PCT
Massachusetts□	10	2	.833	20	7	.741
Connecticut	9	3	.750	15	10	.600
Boston U.	7	4	.636	15	10	.600
Maine	6	6	.500	13	10	.565
Rhode Island	5	6	.455	7	18	.280
New Hampshire	2	10	.167	11	15	.423
Vermont	2	10	.167	8	16	.333

INDEPENDENTS

	Overall W	L	PCT
Providence○	27	4	.871
Marquette○	25	4	.862
Houston○	23	4	.852
Syracuse○	24	5	.828
Virginia Tech□	22	5	.815
Jacksonville○	21	6	.778
Oklahoma City○	21	6	.778
Oral Roberts□	21	6	.778
South Carolina○	22	7	.759
Marshall□	20	7	.741
Northeastern	19	7	.731
St. John's○	19	7	.731
Centenary	19	8	.704
Florida State	18	8	.692
Northern Illinois	17	8	.680
Fairfield□	18	9	.667
Duquesne	16	8	.667
Cincinnati	17	9	.654

INDEPENDENTS (CONT.)

	Overall W	L	PCT
Denver	17	9	.654
George Washington	17	9	.654
Penn State	15	8	.652
Detroit	16	9	.640
Hardin-Simmons	16	9	.640
Indiana State	16	10	.615
Manhattan□	16	10	.615
Utah State	16	10	.615
Notre Dame□	18	12	.600
Air Force	14	10	.583
Creighton	15	11	.577
Hawaii	15	11	.577
Rutgers□	15	11	.577
Stetson	15	11	.577
DePaul	14	11	.560
South Alabama	14	11	.560
Trinity (TX)	14	11	.560
Canisius	13	11	.542
Butler	14	12	.538
Charlotte	14	12	.538
Corpus Christi	13	12	.520
Illinois State	13	12	.520
Long Island	13	12	.520
Navy	13	12	.520
Dayton	13	13	.500
Fairleigh Dickinson	13	13	.500
St. Bonaventure	13	13	.500
Portland State	12	12	.500

INDEPENDENTS (CONT.)

	Overall W	L	PCT
Georgetown	12	14	.462
Pittsburgh	12	14	.462
Tulane	12	14	.462
Army	11	13	.458
Boston College	11	14	.440
Colgate	11	14	.440
Villanova	11	14	.440
Fordham	12	16	.429
Southern Illinois	11	15	.423
West Virginia	10	15	.400
Cleveland State	9	14	.391
Ball State	9	15	.375
Niagara	9	16	.360
Loyola-Chicago	8	15	.348
Holy Cross	9	17	.346
Southern Miss	8	16	.333
St. Francis (NY)	8	16	.333
Portland	9	19	.321
Seton Hall	8	17	.320
Saint Peter's	8	18	.308
Georgia Tech	7	18	.280
Iona	6	16	.273
Samford	5	20	.200
Saint Francis (PA)	5	21	.192
Texas-Pan American	4	22	.154
Xavier	3	23	.115

INDIVIDUAL LEADERS—SEASON

Scoring

	CL	POS	G	FG	FT	PTS	PPG
1 **Bird Averitt**, Pepperdine	JR	G	25	352	144	848	**33.9**
2 **Raymond Lewis**, Cal. State LA	SO	G	24	325	139	789	**32.9**
3 **Willie Biles**, Tulsa	JR	G	26	323	142	788	**30.3**
4 **Aron Stewart**, Richmond	JR	F	19	242	90	574	**30.2**
5 **James "Fly" Williams**, Austin Peay	FR	G	29	360	134	854	**29.4**
6 **Dwight Lamar**, UL-Lafayette	SR	G	28	339	130	808	**28.9**
7 **Ozie Edwards**, Oklahoma City	SR	F	27	332	103	767	**28.4**
8 **Martin Terry**, Arkansas	SR	G	26	264	207	735	**28.3**
9 **John Williamson**, New Mexico State	JR	G	18	202	86	490	**27.2**
10 **Doug Collins**, Illinois State	SR	G	25	269	112	650	**26.0**

Field Goal Pct

	CL	POS	G	FG	FGA	PCT
1 **Elton Hayes**, Lamar	SR	C	24	146	222	**65.8**
2 **Bill Walton**, UCLA	JR	C	30	277	426	**65.0**
3 **Mike Stewart**, Santa Clara	SR	C	26	186	291	**63.9**
4 **Bill Schaeffer**, St. John's	SR	F	26	265	420	**63.1**
5 **Ernie Losch**, Tulane	SR	C	25	151	240	**62.9**

Minimum: 140 made

Free Throw Pct

	CL	POS	G	FT	FTA	PCT
1 **Donald Smith**, Dayton	JR	G	26	111	122	**91.0**
2 **Mark Jellison**, Northeastern	SR	G	26	122	136	**89.7**
3 **Eddie Palubinskas**, LSU	JR	G	24	137	153	**89.5**
4 **John Johnson**, Denver	JR	G	26	108	121	**89.3**
5 **Jimmy Lee**, Syracuse	SO	G	29	93	105	**88.6**

Minimum: 80 made

Rebounds Per Game

	CL	POS	G	REB	RPG
1 **Kermit Washington**, American	SR	C	25	511	**20.4**
2 **Marvin Barnes**, Providence	JR	C	30	571	**19.0**
3 **Pete Padgett**, Nevada	FR	C	26	462	**17.8**
4 **Jim Bradley**, Northern Illinois	JR	F/C	24	426	**17.8**
5 **Bill Walton**, UCLA	JR	C	30	506	**16.9**

INDIVIDUAL LEADERS—GAME

Points

	CL	POS	OPP	DATE	PTS
1 **Bird Averitt**, Pepperdine	JR	G	Nevada	J6	**57**
Doug Collins, Illinois State	SR	G	New Orleans	J3	**57**
3 **Bird Averitt**, Pepperdine	JR	G	Nevada	F17	**56**
4 **Raymond Lewis**, Cal State LA	SO	G	Long Beach State	F23	**53**
5 **Allan Bristow**, Virginia Tech	SR	F	George Washington	F21	**52**
Greg Williams, Seattle	SR	F	UNLV	M2	**52**

Rebounds

	CL	POS	OPP	DATE	REB
1 **David Vaughn**, Oral Roberts	SO	C	Brandeis	J8	**34**
2 **Kermit Washington**, American	SR	C	Towson	F17	**33**
3 **Jim Bradley**, Northern Illinois	JR	F/C	Wisconsin-Milwaukee	F19	**31**
Kermit Washington, American	SR	C	La Salle	F21	**31**
5 **Marvin Barnes**, Providence	JR	C	Assumption	F22	**30**
Bill Campion, Manhattan	SO	C	Hofstra	F10	**30**
Pete Padgett, Nevada	FR	C	Loyola Marymount	J4	**30**

TEAM LEADERS—SEASON

Win-Loss Pct

	W	L	PCT
1 **UCLA**	30	0	**1.000**
NC State	27	0	**1.000**
3 **Long Beach State** ⊗	26	3	**.897**
4 **Providence**	27	4	**.871**
5 **Marquette**	25	4	**.862**

Scoring Offense

	G	W-L	PTS	PPG
1 **Oral Roberts**	27	21-6	2,626	**97.3**
2 **UL-Lafayette**	29	24-5	2,800	**96.6**
3 **Austin Peay**	29	22-7	2,700	**93.1**
4 **NC State**	27	27-0	2,509	**92.9**
5 **Houston**	27	23-4	2,472	**91.6**

Scoring Margin

	G	W-L	PPG	OPP PPG	MAR
1 **NC State**	27	27-0	92.9	71.1	**21.8**
2 **UCLA**	30	30-0	81.3	60.1	**21.2**
3 **Long Beach State**	29	26-3	90.1	72.3	**17.8**
4 **Saint Joseph's**	28	22-6	77.8	63.0	**14.8**
5 **Houston**	27	23-4	91.6	77.1	**14.5**

Field Goal Pct

	G	W-L	FG	FGA	PCT
1 **North Carolina**	33	25-8	1,150	2,181	**52.7**
2 **Maryland**	30	23-7	1,089	2,094	**52.0**
3 **NC State**	27	27-0	1,054	2,028	**52.0**
4 **UCLA**	30	30-0	1,054	2,032	**51.9**
5 **St. John's**	26	19-7	932	1,804	**51.7**

Rebound Margin

	G	W-L	REB	OPP REB	MAR
1 **Manhattan**	26	16-10	56.5	38.0	**18.5**
2 **American**	26	21-5	56.7	40.3	**16.4**
3 **Oral Roberts**	27	21-6	65.6	50.3	**15.3**
4 **UCLA**	30	30-0	49.0	33.9	**15.1**
5 **Houston**	27	23-4	54.7	40.8	**13.9**

Scoring Defense

	G	W-L	OPP PTS	OPP PPG
1 **UTEP**	26	16-10	1,460	**56.2**
2 **Penn**	28	21-7	1,606	**57.4**
3 **Fairleigh Dickinson**	26	13-13	1,523	**58.6**
4 **Air Force**	24	14-10	1,420	**59.2**
5 **UCLA**	30	30-0	1,802	**60.1**

CONSENSUS ALL-AMERICAS

First Team

PLAYER	CL	POS	HT	SCHOOL	RPG	PPG
Doug Collins	SR	G	6-6	Illinois State	5.0	26.0
Ernie DiGregorio	SR	G	6-0	Providence	3.2	24.5
Dwight Lamar	SR	G	6-1	UL-Lafayette	3.4	28.9
Ed Ratleff	SR	G/F	6-6	Long Beach State	8.7	22.8
David Thompson	SO	F	6-4	NC State	8.1	24.7
Bill Walton	JR	C	6-11	UCLA	16.9	20.4
Keith Wilkes	JR	F	6-6	UCLA	6.6	14.8

Second Team

PLAYER	CL	POS	HT	SCHOOL	RPG	PPG
Jim Brewer	SR	F	6-9	Minnesota	11.6	14.1
Tom Burleson	JR	C	7-2	NC State	12.0	17.9
Larry Finch	SR	G	6-2	Memphis	1.3	24.0
Kevin Joyce	SR	G	6-3	South Carolina	4.8	20.4
Tom McMillen	JR	C	6-11	Maryland	9.8	21.2
Kermit Washington	SR	C	6-8	American	20.4	20.8

Selectors: AP, NABC, UPI, USBWA

AWARD WINNERS

Player of the Year

PLAYER	CL	POS	HT	SCHOOL	AWARDS
Bill Walton	JR	C	6-11	UCLA	Naismith, AP, UPI, USBWA, Rupp, Sullivan†
Bobby Sherwin	SR	G	5-11	Army	Frances Pomeroy Naismith*

† Top amateur athlete in U.S.

* For the most outstanding senior player who is 6 feet or under

Coach of the Year

COACH	SCHOOL	REC	AWARDS
John Wooden	UCLA	30-0	AP, UPI, USBWA, Sporting News
Gene Bartow	Memphis	24-6	NABC

ANNUAL REVIEW

POLL PROGRESSION

PRESEASON POLL

AP	UPI	SCHOOL
1	1	UCLA
2	2	Florida State
3	3	Maryland
4	4	Minnesota
5	5	Marquette
6	8	Long Beach State
7	13	UL-Lafayette
8	10	NC State
9	9	Penn
10	6	Ohio State
11	14	Memphis
12	15	BYU
13	7	Kentucky
14	—	Tennessee
15	11	Houston
16	—	South Carolina
17	15	Kansas State
18	19	Oral Roberts
19	—	Michigan
20	17	USC
20	—	Louisville
—	12	North Carolina
—	18	Providence
—	20	UTEP

WEEK OF DEC 5

AP	UPI	SCHOOL	AP↓↑
1	1	UCLA (3-0)	
2	2	Florida State (1-0)	
3	3	Maryland (2-0)	
4	4	Minnesota (2-0)	
5	5	Marquette (1-0)	
6	7	NC State (2-0)	↑2
7	6	Long Beach State (1-0)	↓1
8	9	Kentucky (1-0)	↑5
9	10	Penn (1-0)	
10	8	UL-Lafayette (1-0)	↓3
11	13	Memphis (1-0)	
12	15	Oral Roberts (0-0)	↑6
13	12	North Carolina (2-0)	⤴
14	19	Tennessee (1-0)	
15	17	Ohio State (1-1)	↓5
16	11	Kansas State (2-0)	↑1
17	15	USC (1-0)	↑3
18	13	Michigan (1-0)	↑1
19	18	Providence (0-0)	⤴
20	—	Houston (3-1)	↓5
—	19	Jacksonville (1-0)	

WEEK OF DEC 12

AP	UPI	SCHOOL	AP↓↑
1	1	UCLA (3-0)	
2	2	Florida State (3-0)	
3	4	Maryland (3-0)	
4	3	Marquette (3-0)	↑1
5	5	Minnesota (3-0)	↓1
6	6	NC State (4-0)	
7	7	Long Beach State (3-0)	
8	8	UL-Lafayette (4-0)	↑2
9	11	Penn (3-0)	
10	17	Oral Roberts (2-0)	↑2
11	9	North Carolina (4-0)	↑2
12	10	Missouri (5-0)	⤴
13	19	Vanderbilt (5-0)	⤴
14	14	Providence (1-0)	↑5
15	12	Indiana (3-0)	⤴
16	15	Houston (5-1)	↑4
17	—	BYU (3-1)	⤴
18	—	Michigan (3-1)	
19	—	Memphis (7-2)	↓8
20	—	Kansas State (3-1)	↓4
—	13	South Carolina (2-1)	
—	16	Oklahoma (6-0)	
—	18	San Francisco (4-0)	
—	20	Iowa (3-0)	

WEEK OF DEC 19

AP	UPI	SCHOOL	AP↓↑
1	1	UCLA (4-0)	
2	3	Maryland (4-0)	↑1
3	2	Marquette (4-0)	↑1
4	4	NC State (6-0)	↑2
5	5	Minnesota (4-0)	
6	6	Long Beach State (4-0)	↑1
7	9	Florida State (4-1)	↓5
8	8	UL-Lafayette (6-0)	
9	10	Indiana (5-0)	↑6
10	7	Missouri (7-0)	↑2
11	11	Penn (4-0)	↓2
12	12	Vanderbilt (7-0)	↑1
13	14	North Carolina (6-1)	↓2
14	18	Houston (7-1)	↑2
15	—	BYU (5-1)	↑2
16	—	Oral Roberts (4-1)	↓6
17	15	Kansas State (6-1)	↑3
18	13	Providence (3-1)	↓4
19	—	Oklahoma (6-0)	⤴
20	—	Santa Clara (4-2)	⤴
—	16	New Mexico (6-0)	
—	17	Furman (4-0)	
—	19	San Francisco (5-1)	
—	20	Marshall (6-1)	

WEEK OF DEC 26

AP	UPI	SCHOOL	AP↓↑
1	1	UCLA (6-0)	
2	4	Maryland (5-0)	
3	2	Marquette (5-0)	
4	3	NC State (8-0)	
5	5	Minnesota (6-0)	
6	6	Long Beach State (8-0)	
7	7	Missouri (8-0)	↑3
8	8	Penn (5-0)	↑3
9	9	UL-Lafayette (6-0)	↓1
10	10	Vanderbilt (8-0)	↑2
11	12	North Carolina (7-1)	↑2
12	17	Florida State (5-2)	↓5
13	—	Houston (7-1)	↑1
14	14	BYU (6-1)	↑1
15	14	Indiana (5-1)	↓6
16	11	Kansas State (7-1)	↑1
17	12	Providence (5-1)	↑1
18	—	Alabama (3-1)	⤴
19	—	Oklahoma (6-0)	
20	—	San Francisco (7-1)	⤴
—	14	Washington (8-1)	
—	17	Michigan (6-1)	
—	19	South Carolina (6-2)	
—	20	Louisville (6-1)	

WEEK OF JAN 2

AP	UPI	SCHOOL	AP↓↑
1	1	UCLA (8-0)	
2	4	Maryland (7-0)	
3	2	Marquette (8-0)	
4	5	NC State (8-0)	
5	6	Long Beach State (11-0)	↑1
6	3	Minnesota (9-0)	↓1
7	7	Missouri (10-0)	
8	8	UL-Lafayette (6-0)	↑1
9	9	North Carolina (10-1)	↑2
10	—	Houston (8-2)	↑3
11	11	Vanderbilt (8-1)	↓1
12	14	San Francisco (8-1)	↑8
13	13	Providence (5-1)	↑4
14	—	Alabama (5-1)	↑4
15	18	BYU (8-2)	↓1
16	10	New Mexico (9-0)	⤴
17	20	Penn (5-2)	↓9
18	16	Kansas State (9-2)	↓2
19	19	Florida State (7-3)	↓7
20	—	Indiana (6-2)	↓5
—	12	St. John's (8-2)	
—	15	Louisville (8-2)	
—	17	South Carolina (7-3)	

WEEK OF JAN 9

AP	UPI	SCHOOL	AP↓↑
1	1	UCLA (10-0)	
2	2	Maryland (9-0)	
3	4	NC State (9-0)	↑1
4	3	Marquette (10-0)	↓1
5	5	Missouri (11-0)	↑2
6	8	Long Beach State (11-1)	↓1
7	6	North Carolina (12-1)	↑2
8	7	Minnesota (9-1)	↓2
9	9	Vanderbilt (10-1)	↑2
10	15	Houston (10-2)	
11	10	Providence (7-1)	↑2
12	11	San Francisco (10-1)	
13	13	UL-Lafayette (7-1)	↓5
14	17	Alabama (7-1)	
15	—	Jacksonville (10-2)	⤴
16	16	Indiana (8-2)	↑4
17	14	Kansas State (9-2)	↑1
18	12	St. John's (8-2)	⤴
18	—	Florida State (8-3)	↑1
20	18	Louisville (10-2)	⤴
—	19	Penn (7-2)	⤵
—	20	South Carolina (9-3)	

WEEK OF JAN 16

AP	UPI	SCHOOL	AP↓↑
1	1	UCLA (12-0)	
2	2	NC State (12-0)	↑1
3	3	Maryland (10-1)	↓1
4	4	North Carolina (13-1)	↑3
5	6	Long Beach State (13-1)	↑1
6	5	Minnesota (10-1)	↑2
7	7	Marquette (11-1)	↓3
8	8	Missouri (12-1)	↓3
9	9	Providence (10-1)	↑2
10	13	San Francisco (12-1)	↑2
11	16	Alabama (8-1)	↑3
12	12	Houston (11-2)	↓2
13	15	UL-Lafayette (10-1)	
14	10	Kansas State (11-2)	↑3
15	—	Jacksonville (11-2)	
16	11	Indiana (10-2)	
17	14	St. John's (9-2)	↑1
18	19	Vanderbilt (10-3)	↓9
19	18	Florida State (10-3)	↓1
20	19	Louisville (11-2)	
—	17	Michigan (10-3)	

WEEK OF JAN 23

AP	UPI	SCHOOL	AP↓↑
1	1	UCLA (14-0)	
2	2	NC State (12-0)	
3	3	North Carolina (15-1)	↑1
4	4	Maryland (12-1)	↓1
5	5	Long Beach State (15-1)	
6	6	Indiana (11-2)	↑10
7	11	Missouri (13-2)	↑1
8	7	Minnesota (11-2)	↓2
9	11	Alabama (10-1)	↑2
10	8	Marquette (12-2)	↓3
11	9	Houston (12-2)	↑1
12	10	UL-Lafayette (12-1)	↑1
13	17	Jacksonville (13-2)	↑2
14	13	Providence (10-2)	↓5
15	14	St. John's (11-2)	↑2
16	19	San Francisco (12-2)	↓6
17	—	Memphis (12-3)	⤴
18	15	Kansas State (11-3)	↓4
19	18	New Mexico (15-2)	⤴
20	—	Purdue (10-3)	⤴
—	16	Vanderbilt (12-3)	⤵
—	19	Oregon State (10-5)	

WEEK OF JAN 30

AP	UPI	SCHOOL	AP↓↑
1	1	UCLA (16-0) (A)	
2	2	NC State (14-0)	
3	3	Maryland (14-1)	↑1
4	4	Long Beach State (16-1)	↑1
5	5	Indiana (13-2)	↑1
6	7	Alabama (13-1)	↑3
7	10	Missouri (14-2)	
8	8	North Carolina (15-3)	↓5
9	6	Minnesota (12-2)	↓1
10	9	Marquette (14-2)	
11	11	Houston (13-2)	
12	12	Providence (12-2)	↑2
13	15	UL-Lafayette (13-1)	↓1
14	14	St. John's (13-2)	↑1
15	—	Jacksonville (14-3)	↓2
16	19	San Francisco (14-2)	
17	16	Memphis (14-3)	
18	13	Kansas State (13-3)	
19	—	Oral Roberts (15-2)	⤴
20	—	USC (13-4)	⤴
—	17	Oregon State (11-5)	
—	18	BYU (14-4)	
—	19	South Carolina (12-5)	

WEEK OF FEB 6

AP	UPI	SCHOOL	AP↓↑
1	1	UCLA (17-0)	
2	2	NC State (16-0)	
3	3	Long Beach State (17-1)	↑1
4	4	Indiana (14-2)	↑1
5	5	Minnesota (14-2)	↑4
6	6	North Carolina (16-3)	↑2
7	10	Marquette (16-2)	↑3
8	9	Missouri (15-2)	↓1
9	8	Maryland (14-3)	↓6
10	7	Alabama (14-2)	↓4
11	11	Houston (15-2)	
12	15	Providence (14-2) (B)	
13	14	UL-Lafayette (16-1)	
14	13	St. John's (15-2)	
15	16	Memphis (16-3)	↑2
16	—	Jacksonville (16-3)	↓1
17	17	San Francisco (16-2)	↓1
18	12	Kansas State (14-3)	
19	—	Oral Roberts (16-3)	
20	18	New Mexico (16-3)	⤴
—	18	Oregon State (12-5)	
—	20	BYU (15-4)	

WEEK OF FEB 13

AP	UPI	SCHOOL	AP↓↑
1	1	UCLA (18-0)	
2	2	NC State (19-0)	
3	3	Long Beach State (19-1)	
4	4	Minnesota (15-2)	↑1
5	5	Marquette (18-2)	↑2
6	6	North Carolina (18-4)	
7	8	Houston (17-2)	↑4
8	11	Providence (16-2)	↑4
9	13	St. John's (17-2)	↑5
10	7	Maryland (16-3)	↓1
11	10	Indiana (14-4)	↓7
12	12	Missouri (16-3)	↓4
13	19	Jacksonville (18-3)	↑3
14	17	UL-Lafayette (18-2)	↓1
15	9	Kansas State (16-3)	↑3
16	15	Memphis (17-4)	↓1
17	—	Alabama (14-4)	↓7
18	18	New Mexico (18-3)	↑2
19	—	Virginia Tech (14-3)	⤴
20	16	BYU (17-4)	⤴
—	14	USC (14-5)	
—	20	Oregon State (14-5)	

EEK OF FEB 20

AP	UPI	SCHOOL	AP↓↑
1	1	**UCLA** (21-0)	
2	2	**NC State** (21-0)	
3	3	**Long Beach State** (20-1)	
4	4	**Minnesota** (16-2)	
5	5	**Marquette** (20-2)	
6	6	**North Carolina** (20-4)	
7	8	**Providence** (18-2)	↑1
8	9	**Maryland** (17-4)	↑2
9	10	**Houston** (18-3)	↓2
10	14	**Indiana** (15-5)	↑1
11	13	**St. John's** (18-3)	↓2
12	15	**UL-Lafayette** (19-2)	↑2
13	7	**Kansas State** (18-3)	↑2
14	11	**Memphis** (19-4)	↑2
15	12	**New Mexico** (21-3)	↑3
16	—	**Missouri** (17-4)	↓4
17	—	**Purdue** (14-5)	⤴
18	16	**Alabama** (16-4)	↓1
19	—	**Virginia Tech** (15-4)	
20	—	**Jacksonville** (19-4)	↓7
—	17	**San Francisco** (19-3)	
—	17	**Louisville** (18-6)	
—	19	**Oral Roberts** (20-4)	
—	19	**South Carolina** (17-5)	

WEEK OF FEB 27

AP	UPI	SCHOOL	AP↓↑
1	1	**UCLA** (23-0)	
2	2	**NC State** (23-0)	
3	3	**Minnesota** (18-2)	↑1
4	5	**Long Beach State** (22-2)	↓1
5	4	**Marquette** (22-2)	
6	6	**Providence** (21-2)	↑1
7	7	**North Carolina** (21-5)	↓1
8	9	**Houston** (20-3)	↑1
9	11	**Maryland** (19-4)	↓1
10	10	**Memphis** (21-4)	↑4
11	12	**UL-Lafayette** (22-2)	↑1
12	13	**Indiana** (17-5)	↓2
13	15	**Missouri** (18-4)	↑3
14	—	**Syracuse** (20-4)	⤴
15	14	**New Mexico** (23-4)	
16	8	**Kansas State** (19-4)	↓3
17	—	**St. John's** (18-5)	↓6
18	19	**Jacksonville** (20-5)	↑2
19	19	**South Carolina** (18-5)	⤴
20	—	**Purdue** (15-6)	↓3
—	15	**Weber State** (19-6)	
—	17	**San Francisco** (20-4)	
—	17	**Tennessee** (14-6)	
—	19	**Saint Joseph's** (20-5)	

WEEK OF MAR 6

AP	UPI	SCHOOL	AP↓↑
1	1	**UCLA** (25-0)	
2	2	**NC State** (25-0)	
3	4	**Minnesota** (20-2)	
4	3	**Long Beach State** (24-2)	
5	6	**Providence** (22-2)	↑1
6	5	**Marquette** (22-3)	↓1
7	9	**Houston** (22-3)	↑1
8	7	**North Carolina** (22-6)	↓1
9	10	**Indiana** (18-5)	↑3
10	13	**Maryland** (20-5)	↓1
11	8	**Kansas State** (21-4)	↑5
12	15	**Missouri** (20-4)	↑1
13	14	**Syracuse** (22-4)	↑1
14	12	**UL-Lafayette** (22-3)	↓3
15	11	**Memphis** (21-5)	↓5
16	—	**Jacksonville** (21-5)	↑2
17	17	**St. John's** (19-6)	
18	20	**Saint Joseph's** (22-5)	⤴
19	—	**Kentucky** (18-7)	⤴
19	—	**San Francisco** (21-4)	⤴
—	16	**Arizona State** (15-7)	
—	18	**New Mexico** (25-5)	⤵
—	19	**Weber State** (19-7)	

FINAL POLL

AP	UPI	SCHOOL	AP↓↑
1	1	**UCLA** (26-0) Ⓒ	
2	2	**NC State** (27-0) Ⓓ	
3	3	**Long Beach State** (24-2)	↑1
4	5	**Providence** (23-2)	↑1
5	4	**Marquette** (23-3)	↑1
6	6	**Indiana** (19-5)	↑3
7	7	**UL-Lafayette** (23-3)	↑7
8	10	**Maryland** (22-6)	↑2
9	7	**Kansas State** (22-4)	↑2
10	9	**Minnesota** (20-4)	↓7
11	12	**North Carolina** (22-7)	↓3
12	11	**Memphis** (21-5)	↑3
13	18	**Houston** (22-3)	↓6
14	14	**Syracuse** (22-4)	↓1
15	17	**Missouri** (21-5)	↓3
16	13	**Arizona State** (18-7)	⤴
17	15	**Kentucky** (19-7)	↑2
18	20	**Penn** (20-5)	⤴
19	—	**Austin Peay** (22-5) Ⓔ	⤴
20	—	**San Francisco** (22-4)	↓1
—	16	**South Carolina** (20-6)	
—	19	**Weber State** (20-7)	

Ⓐ Notre Dame fans boo UCLA players and hurl objects during introductions, prompting coach John Wooden to wag a finger at his counterpart, Digger Phelps. The Bruins then beat the Irish, 82-63, for their 61st consecutive victory, surpassing San Francisco's mark of 60 straight from 1955 to '57. UCLA will keep the streak going for another year.

Ⓑ On Jan. 31, Providence's Marvin "Bad News" Barnes is charged with assault with a deadly weapon stemming from an October 1972 incident in which he struck teammate Larry Ketvirtis with a tire iron, fracturing his cheekbone, in retaliation for an inadvertent Ketvirtis elbow during practice that had dislodged some of Barnes' teeth. Barnes continues playing and, despite the distraction, Providence wins two road games in the days that follow, and another 15 straight to reach the Final Four.

Ⓒ UCLA becomes the second squad to go wire to wire as the No. 1-ranked team in back-to-back seasons. (Ohio State held down the top spot throughout 1960-61 and '61-62.)

Ⓓ NC State tops Maryland, 76-74, in the ACC championship game. The team, however, is on NCAA probation for having allowed visiting recruit David Thompson to participate in a pickup game with assistant coach Eddie Biedenbach, and is ineligible for postseason play.

Ⓔ In the first season the NCAA allows freshmen on varsity teams, Austin Peay's James "Fly" Williams averages 29.4 ppg—a mark for freshmen that will stand until LSU's Chris Jackson breaks it in 1988-89.

1973 NCAA Tournament (A)

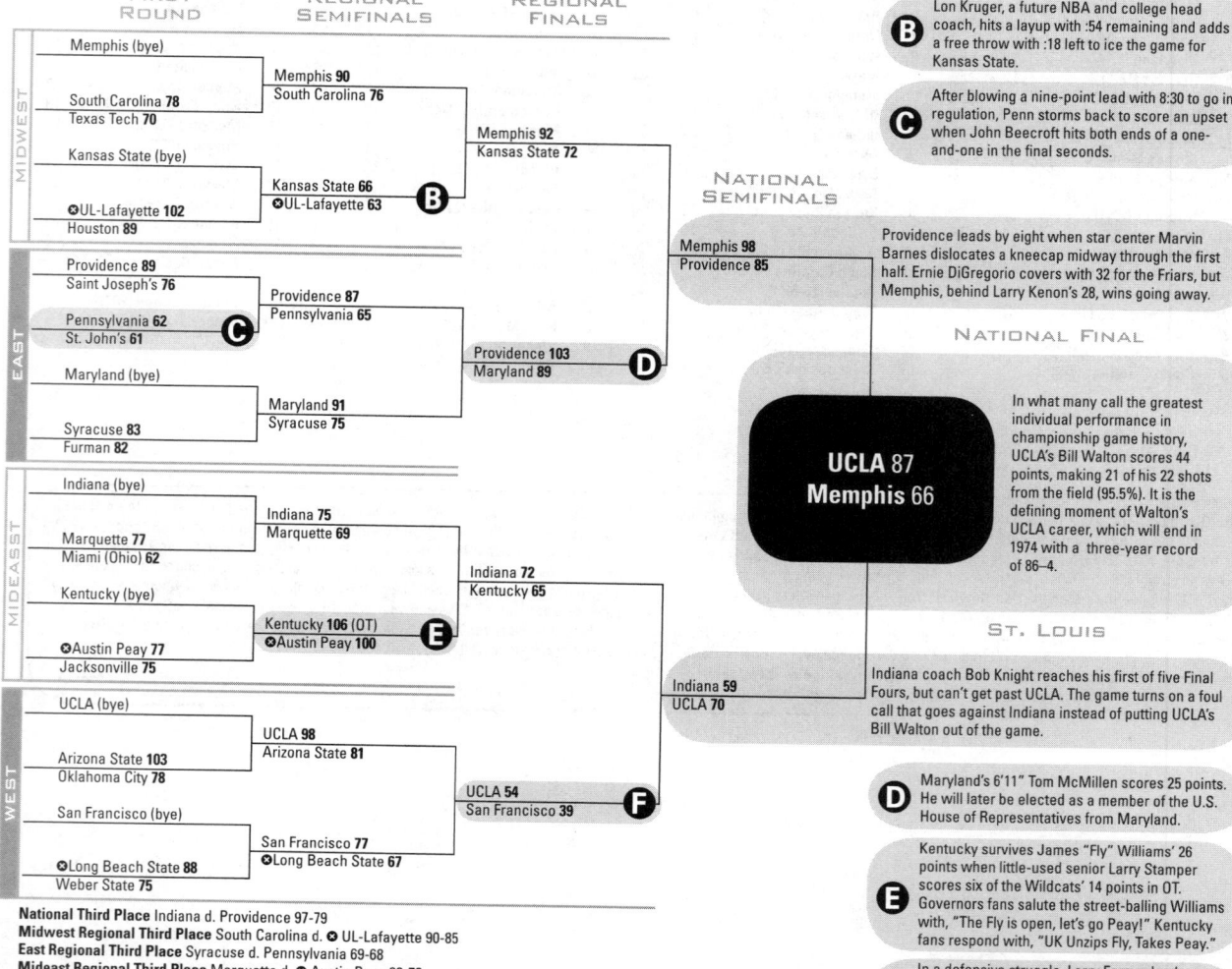

First Round / Regional Semifinals / Regional Finals / National Semifinals / National Final

MIDWEST

First Round:
- Memphis (bye)
- South Carolina **78**, Texas Tech **70**
- Kansas State (bye)
- ⊗UL-Lafayette **102**, Houston **89**

Regional Semifinals:
- Memphis **90**, South Carolina **76**
- Kansas State **66**, ⊗UL-Lafayette **63** (B)

Regional Final:
- Memphis **92**, Kansas State **72**

EAST

First Round:
- Providence **89**, Saint Joseph's **76**
- Pennsylvania **62**, St. John's **61** (C)
- Maryland (bye)
- Syracuse **83**, Furman **82**

Regional Semifinals:
- Providence **87**, Pennsylvania **65**
- Maryland **91**, Syracuse **75**

Regional Final:
- Providence **103**, Maryland **89** (D)

MIDEAST

First Round:
- Indiana (bye)
- Marquette **77**, Miami (Ohio) **62**
- Kentucky (bye)
- ⊗Austin Peay **77**, Jacksonville **75**

Regional Semifinals:
- Indiana **75**, Marquette **69**
- Kentucky **106** (OT), ⊗Austin Peay **100** (E)

Regional Final:
- Indiana **72**, Kentucky **65**

WEST

First Round:
- UCLA (bye)
- Arizona State **103**, Oklahoma City **78**
- San Francisco (bye)
- ⊗Long Beach State **88**, Weber State **75**

Regional Semifinals:
- UCLA **98**, Arizona State **81**
- San Francisco **77**, ⊗Long Beach State **67**

Regional Final:
- UCLA **54**, San Francisco **39** (F)

National Semifinals
- Memphis **98**, Providence **85**
- Indiana **59**, UCLA **70**

National Final — St. Louis

UCLA 87
Memphis 66

National Third Place Indiana d. Providence 97-79
Midwest Regional Third Place South Carolina d. ⊗ UL-Lafayette 90-85
East Regional Third Place Syracuse d. Pennsylvania 69-68
Mideast Regional Third Place Marquette d. ⊗ Austin Peay 88-73
West Regional Third Place ⊗ Long Beach State d. Arizona State 84-80

⊗ Team participation later vacated

A The old Thursday-Saturday format for the semifinals and championship game is changed to Saturday-Monday. For the first time, the Final is played in prime time, called on NBC by Curt Gowdy.

B Lon Kruger, a future NBA and college head coach, hits a layup with :54 remaining and adds a free throw with :18 left to ice the game for Kansas State.

C After blowing a nine-point lead with 8:30 to go in regulation, Penn storms back to score an upset when John Beecroft hits both ends of a one-and-one in the final seconds.

Providence leads by eight when star center Marvin Barnes dislocates a kneecap midway through the first half. Ernie DiGregorio covers with 32 for the Friars, but Memphis, behind Larry Kenon's 28, wins going away.

In what many call the greatest individual performance in championship game history, UCLA's Bill Walton scores 44 points, making 21 of his 22 shots from the field (95.5%). It is the defining moment of Walton's UCLA career, which will end in 1974 with a three-year record of 86–4.

Indiana coach Bob Knight reaches his first of five Final Fours, but can't get past UCLA. The game turns on a foul call that goes against Indiana instead of putting UCLA's Bill Walton out of the game.

D Maryland's 6'11" Tom McMillen scores 25 points. He will later be elected as a member of the U.S. House of Representatives from Maryland.

E Kentucky survives James "Fly" Williams' 26 points when little-used senior Larry Stamper scores six of the Wildcats' 14 points in OT. Governors fans salute the street-balling Williams with, "The Fly is open, let's go Peay!" Kentucky fans respond with, "UK Unzips Fly, Takes Peay."

F In a defensive struggle, Larry Farmer leads the Bruins with 13 points. The Dons limit Bill Walton to nine, but can't keep him off the glass as he gathers 14 boards. It will be the last time (through 2009) that two teams combine to score fewer than 95 points in a regional final.

Tournament Leaders

Individual Leaders

Scoring

	CL	POS	G	PTS	PPG
1 **Larry Finch**, Memphis	SR	G	4	107	26.8
2 **Jim Andrews**, Kentucky	SR	C	2	53	26.5
3 **Ernie DiGregorio**, Providence	SR	G	5	128	25.6
4 **Dwight Lamar**, UL-Lafayette	SR	G	3	75	25.0
5 **Steve Downing**, Indiana	SR	C	4	99	24.8
6 **James "Fly" Williams**, Austin Peay	FR	G	3	74	24.7
7 **Larry Kenon**, Memphis	JR	F	4	96	24.0
8 **Bill Walton**, UCLA	JR	C	4	95	23.8
9 **Tom McMillen**, Maryland	JR	C	2	43	21.5
10 **John Lucas**, Maryland	FR	G	2	41	20.5

Minimum: 2 games

Field Goal Pct

	CL	POS	G	FG	FGA	PCT
1 **Bill Walton**, UCLA	JR	C	4	45	59	76.3
2 **Tom McMillen**, Maryland	JR	C	2	18	26	69.2
3 **Jim Andrews**, Kentucky	SR	C	2	26	39	66.7
4 **Bob Dooms**, Syracuse	JR	C	3	14	23	60.9
George Frazier, Marquette	SR	G/F	3	14	23	60.9

Minimum: 10 made

Free Throw Pct

	CL	POS	G	FT	FTA	PCT
1 **Ronald Haigler**, Penn	SO	F	3	10	10	100.0
2 **Ed Ratleff**, Long Beach State	SR	G/F	3	15	16	93.8
3 **Kevin Stacom**, Providence	JR	G	5	20	22	90.9
4 **Larry Finch**, Memphis	SR	G	4	39	44	88.6
5 **Bill Laurie**, Memphis	SR	G	4	12	14	85.7

Minimum: 10 made

Rebounds Per Game

	CL	POS	G	REB	RPG
1 **Bill Walton**, UCLA	JR	C	4	58	14.5
2 **Larry Kenon**, Memphis	JR	F	4	57	14.3
3 **Ronnie Robinson**, Memphis	SR	F	4	56	14.0
4 **Howard Jackson**, Austin Peay	JR	F	3	39	13.0
5 **Rudy Hackett**, Syracuse	SO	F	3	38	12.7
Danny Traylor, South Carolina	SR	F/C	3	38	12.7

Minimum: 2 games

Team Leaders

Scoring

	G	PTS	PPG
1 **Maryland**	2	180	90.0
2 **Providence**	5	443	88.6
3 **Arizona State**	3	264	88.0
4 **Memphis**	4	346	86.5
5 **Kentucky**	2	171	85.5
6 **UL-Lafayette**	3	250	83.3
Austin Peay	3	250	83.3
8 **South Carolina**	3	244	81.3
9 **Long Beach State**	3	239	79.7
10 **Marquette**	3	234	78.0

Minimum: 2 games

FG Pct

	G	FG	FGA	PCT
1 **UCLA**	4	139	251	55.4
2 **Maryland**	2	79	151	52.3
3 **Providence**	5	188	368	51.1
4 **Memphis**	4	138	276	50.0
Kentucky	2	81	162	50.0

FT Pct

	G	FT	FTA	PCT
1 **Penn**	3	29	35	82.9
2 **Providence**	5	67	83	80.7
3 **Maryland**	2	22	28	78.6
4 **Marquette**	3	36	46	78.3
5 **South Carolina**	3	44	59	74.6

Minimum: 2 games

Rebounds

	G	REB	RPG
1 **UL-Lafayette**	3	139	46.3
2 **Kentucky**	2	92	46.0
3 **Arizona State**	3	132	44.0
4 **Long Beach State**	3	126	42.0
5 **Austin Peay**	3	125	41.7

Minimum: 2 games

All-Tournament Team

PLAYER	CL	POS	HT	SCHOOL	RPG	PPG
Bill Walton*	JR	C	6-11	UCLA	14.5	23.8
Ernie DiGregorio	SR	G	6-0	Providence	3.4	25.6
Steve Downing	SR	C	6-8	Indiana	10.5	24.8
Larry Finch	SR	G	6-2	Memphis	2.5	26.8
Larry Kenon	JR	F	6-9	Memphis	14.3	24.0

All-Regional Teams

East

PLAYER	CL	POS	HT	SCHOOL	RPG	PPG
Ernie DiGregorio*	SR	G	6-0	Providence	2.7	26.3
Marvin Barnes	JR	C	6-8	Providence	15.0	20.0
Dennis Duval	JR	G	6-2	Syracuse	4.0	20.0
Tom McMillen	JR	C	6-11	Maryland	6.0	21.5
Kevin Stacom	JR	G	6-5	Providence	3.3	17.3

Mideast

PLAYER	CL	POS	HT	SCHOOL	RPG	PPG
Steve Downing*	SR	C	6-8	Indiana	11.5	26.0
Jim Andrews	SR	C	6-11	Kentucky	12.0	26.5
Quinn Buckner	FR	G	6-2	Indiana	9.0	10.0
Howard Jackson	JR	F	6-7	Austin Peay	13.0	17.7
Larry McNeill	JR	F	6-9	Marquette	10.7	16.7

Midwest

PLAYER	CL	POS	HT	SCHOOL	RPG	PPG
Larry Finch*	SR	G	6-2	Memphis	1.5	28.5
Alex English	FR	F	6-8	South Carolina	11.0	18.7
Larry Kenon	JR	F	6-9	Memphis	13.5	24.0
Dwight Lamar	SR	G	6-1	UL-Lafayette	5.0	25.0
Ronnie Robinson	SR	F	6-9	Memphis	16.5	12.5

West

PLAYER	CL	POS	HT	SCHOOL	RPG	PPG
Bill Walton*	JR	C	6-11	UCLA	14.0	18.5
Mike Contreras	SR	G	6-2	Arizona State	4.0	20.0
Tommy Curtis	JR	G	5-11	UCLA	1.0	9.5
Mike Quick	SR	G	6-3	San Francisco	4.0	16.5
Phil Smith	JR	G	6-4	San Francisco	4.5	18.5

* Most outstanding player

1973 NCAA TOURNAMENT BOX SCORES

90-76 (SWEET 16)

	1H	2H
Memphis	39	51
South Carolina	24	52

MEMPHIS	MIN	FG	3FG	FT	REB	A	ST	BL	PF	TP
Larry Kenon	-	16-30	-	2-6	20	4	1	4	4	34
Larry Finch	-	8-17	-	9-10	1	4	0	0	4	25
Ronnie Robinson	-	5-16	-	1-4	17	3	2	0	2	11
Billy Buford	-	5-7	-	0-0	10	4	3	1	3	10
Bill Laurie	-	0-1	-	6-7	1	4	2	0	4	6
Bill Cook	-	2-5	-	0-0	0	1	0	0	1	4
Doug McKinney	-	0-0	-	0-0	0	0	0	0	1	0
Wes Westfall	-	0-1	-	0-0	0	0	0	0	0	0
TOTALS	-	36-77	-	18-27	49	20	8	5	19	90
Percentages		46.8		66.7						

Coach: Gene Bartow

SOUTH CAROLINA	MIN	FG	3FG	FT	REB	A	ST	BL	PF	TP
Alex English	38	9-15	-	1-1	8	0	1	0	5	19
Kevin Joyce	39	8-21	-	2-2	2	6	2	1	2	18
Brian Winters	36	5-11	-	4-4	8	4	0	1	5	14
Mike Dunleavy	36	4-10	-	4-4	0	1	3	1	3	12
Danny Traylor	37	5-12	-	0-4	6	1	0	3	3	10
Bob Mathias	1	1-1	-	0-0	1	0	0	1	0	2
Tommy Cox	1	0-0	-	1-2	1	0	0	0	0	1
Casey Manning	7	0-0	-	0-0	0	0	1	0	4	0
Mark Greiner	4	0-0	-	0-0	1	0	0	0	0	0
Jimmy Walsh	1	0-0	-	0-0	0	0	0	0	0	0
TOTALS	200	32-70	-	12-17	27	12	7	7	22	76
Percentages		45.7		70.6						

Coach: Frank McGuire

Officials: Grossman, Hernjack
Attendance: 10,060

66-63 (SWEET 16)

	1H	2H
Kansas State	38	28
UL-Lafayette	26	37

KANSAS STATE	MIN	FG	3FG	FT	REB	A	ST	BL	PF	TP
Lon Kruger	38	6-11	-	4-6	2	4	-	-	2	16
Ernie Kusnyer	36	7-15	-	1-3	7	3	-	-	4	15
Robert Chipman	40	4-6	-	3-5	2	6	-	-	1	11
Gene McVey	23	4-5	-	1-4	3	1	-	-	2	9
Steve Mitchell	17	4-7	-	0-0	5	1	-	-	5	8
Larry Williams	24	2-8	-	0-0	7	0	-	-	2	4
Jerry Thurston	16	1-3	-	1-2	3	3	-	-	2	3
Danny Beard	6	0-1	-	0-0	1	0	-	-	0	0
TOTALS	200	28-56	-	10-20	30	18	-	-	18	66
Percentages		50.0		50.0						

Coach: Jack Hartman

UL-LAFAYETTE	MIN	FG	3FG	FT	REB	A	ST	BL	PF	TP
Dwight Lamar	39	8-21	-	2-2	4	3	-	-	2	18
Roy Ebron	37	5-15	-	6-7	12	2	-	-	4	16
Larry Fogle	29	4-14	-	2-3	7	0	-	-	3	10
Fred Saunders	28	4-8	-	0-0	7	2	-	-	4	8
Robert Wilson	24	3-7	-	1-2	6	0	-	-	2	7
Jerry Bisbano	38	2-7	-	0-0	2	1	-	-	5	4
Andre Brown	3	0-0	-	0-0	1	0	-	-	1	0
Percy Wells	2	0-0	-	0-0	0	1	-	-	0	0
TOTALS	200	26-72	-	11-14	39	9	-	-	21	63
Percentages		36.1		78.6						

Coach: Beryl Shipley

Officials: Howell, Moreau
Attendance: 10,060

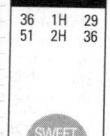

87-65 (SWEET 16)

	1H	2H
Providence	36	51
Penn	29	36

PROVIDENCE	MIN	FG	3FG	FT	REB	A	ST	BL	PF	TP
Marvin Barnes	-	10-10	-	0-0	13	0	-	-	3	20
Ernie DiGregorio	-	9-21	-	0-0	3	10	-	-	2	18
Nehru King	-	7-11	-	4-4	6	1	-	-	2	18
Kevin Stacom	-	7-9	-	2-2	5	5	-	-	0	16
Charles Crawford	-	6-6	-	0-0	3	0	-	-	1	12
Francis Costello	-	1-3	-	0-0	4	4	-	-	4	2
Richard Dunphy	-	0-0	-	1-2	1	0	-	-	0	1
Al Baker	-	0-1	-	0-0	3	0	-	-	0	0
Gary Bello	-	0-0	-	0-0	0	0	-	-	0	0
Dave Modest	-	0-0	-	0-0	0	0	-	-	0	0
TOTALS	-	40-61	-	7-8	38	20	-	-	12	87
Percentages		65.6		87.5						

Coach: Dave Gavitt

PENN	MIN	FG	3FG	FT	REB	A	ST	BL	PF	TP
Phillip Hankinson	-	9-29	-	1-3	9	2	-	-	1	19
Ronald Haigler	-	7-15	-	4-4	12	0	-	-	4	18
Bob Bigelow	-	5-19	-	0-0	6	6	-	-	3	10
Zoltan Varga	-	5-9	-	0-0	2	2	-	-	1	10
John Beecroft	-	1-6	-	0-0	1	4	-	-	0	2
Keith Hansen	-	1-1	-	0-0	0	0	-	-	1	2
Larry Lewis	-	1-6	-	0-0	5	0	-	-	1	2
Craig Littlepage	-	1-1	-	0-0	0	0	-	-	3	2
Stephen Batory	-	0-1	-	0-0	0	0	-	-	0	0
Bill Finger	-	0-1	-	0-0	0	1	-	-	0	0
Bruce Frank	-	0-1	-	0-0	0	0	-	-	0	0
John Jablonski	-	0-0	-	0-0	0	0	-	-	0	0
TOTALS	-	30-89	-	5-7	35	15	-	-	14	65
Percentages		33.7		71.4						

Coach: Chuck Daly

Officials: Wilcoxen, Lawson
Attendance: 11,003

91-75 (SWEET 16)

	1H	2H
Maryland	35	56
Syracuse	34	41

MARYLAND	MIN	FG	3FG	FT	REB	A	ST	BL	PF	TP
Jim O'Brien	-	8-14	-	6-7	6	-	-	-	2	22
John Lucas	-	9-17	-	3-4	5	-	-	-	2	21
Tom McMillen	-	8-10	-	2-2	6	-	-	-	2	18
Bob Bodell	-	5-11	-	2-2	1	-	-	-	1	12
Len Elmore	-	5-10	-	0-0	14	-	-	-	2	10
Darrell Brown	-	3-4	-	0-1	4	-	-	-	2	6
Maurice Howard	-	1-1	-	0-0	0	-	-	-	0	2
Owen Brown	-	0-0	-	0-0	1	-	-	-	1	0
Billy Hahn	-	0-0	-	0-0	0	-	-	-	0	0
Rich Porac	-	0-1	-	0-0	0	-	-	-	0	0
Tom Roy	-	0-0	-	0-0	1	-	-	-	1	0
Howard White	-	0-0	-	0-0	1	-	-	-	1	0
TOTALS	-	39-68	-	13-16	39	-	-	-	14	91
Percentages		57.4		81.2						

Coach: Lefty Driesell

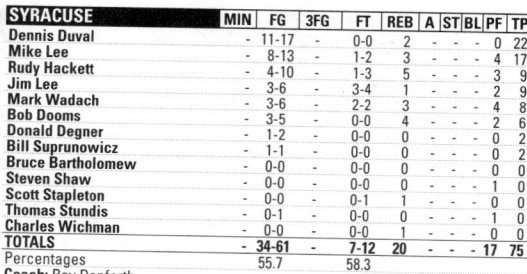

SYRACUSE	MIN	FG	3FG	FT	REB	A	ST	BL	PF	TP
Dennis Duval	-	11-17	-	0-0	2	-	-	-	0	22
Mike Lee	-	8-13	-	1-2	3	-	-	-	4	17
Rudy Hackett	-	4-10	-	1-3	5	-	-	-	3	9
Jim Lee	-	3-6	-	3-4	1	-	-	-	2	9
Mark Wadach	-	3-6	-	2-2	3	-	-	-	4	8
Bob Dooms	-	3-5	-	0-0	4	-	-	-	2	6
Donald Degner	-	1-2	-	0-0	0	-	-	-	0	2
Bill Suprunowicz	-	1-1	-	0-0	0	-	-	-	0	2
Bruce Bartholomew	-	0-0	-	0-0	0	-	-	-	0	0
Steven Shaw	-	0-0	-	0-0	0	-	-	-	1	0
Scott Stapleton	-	0-0	-	0-1	1	-	-	-	0	0
Thomas Stundis	-	0-1	-	0-0	0	-	-	-	1	0
Charles Wichman	-	0-0	-	0-0	1	-	-	-	0	0
TOTALS	-	34-61	-	7-12	20	-	-	-	17	75
Percentages		55.7		58.3						

Coach: Roy Danforth

Officials: Shosid, Bain
Attendance: 11,003

75-69 (SWEET 16)

	1H	2H
Indiana	35	40
Marquette	38	31

INDIANA	MIN	FG	3FG	FT	REB	A	ST	BL	PF	TP
Steve Downing	40	12-17	-	5-11	10	0	2	0	2	29
Steve Green	40	8-15	-	0-1	6	7	1	0	3	16
John Ritter	32	5-9	-	4-4	6	2	0	0	2	14
Jim Crews	24	3-4	-	0-0	1	2	0	0	1	6
John Laskowski	24	1-2	-	4-4	1	1	0	1	1	6
Quinn Buckner	40	2-6	-	0-2	7	4	5	1	3	4
TOTALS	200	31-53	-	13-22	31	16	8	2	12	75
Percentages		58.5		59.1						

Coach: Bob Knight

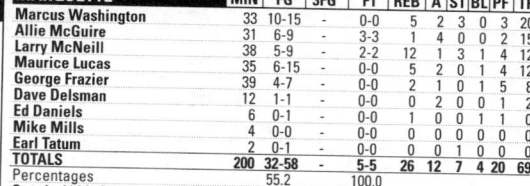

MARQUETTE	MIN	FG	3FG	FT	REB	A	ST	BL	PF	TP
Marcus Washington	33	10-15	-	0-0	5	2	3	0	3	20
Allie McGuire	31	6-9	-	3-3	1	4	0	0	2	15
Larry McNeill	38	5-9	-	2-2	12	1	3	1	4	12
Maurice Lucas	35	6-15	-	0-0	5	2	0	1	4	12
George Frazier	39	4-7	-	0-0	2	1	0	1	5	8
Dave Delsman	12	1-1	-	0-0	0	2	0	0	1	2
Ed Daniels	6	0-1	-	0-0	1	0	0	1	1	0
Mike Mills	4	0-0	-	0-0	0	0	0	0	0	0
Earl Tatum	2	0-1	-	0-0	0	0	1	0	0	0
TOTALS	200	32-58	-	5-5	26	12	7	4	20	69
Percentages		55.2		100.0						

Coach: Al McGuire

Officials: Brown, Evans
Technicals: Indiana (coach Knight)
Attendance: 15,581

106-100 (SWEET 16)

	1H	2H	OT1
Kentucky	43	49	14
Austin Peay	47	45	8

KENTUCKY	MIN	FG	3FG	FT	REB	A	ST	BL	PF	TP
Jim Andrews	-	15-19	-	0-0	14	2	-	-	1	30
Kevin Grevey	-	10-24	-	1-2	13	6	-	-	4	21
Ronnie Lyons	-	6-16	-	0-0	4	3	-	-	0	12
Mike Flynn	-	3-8	-	4-6	6	6	-	-	5	10
Larry Stamper	-	5-9	-	0-0	7	2	-	-	0	10
Jimmy Dan Conner	-	4-7	-	1-1	2	3	-	-	4	9
Bob Guyette	-	4-9	-	0-0	8	1	-	-	1	8
Steve Lochmueller	-	2-2	-	0-0	1	0	-	-	1	4
Ray Edelman	-	1-3	-	0-0	0	0	-	-	0	2
Rick Drewitz	-	0-0	-	0-0	0	0	-	-	0	0
Jerry Hale	-	0-0	-	0-0	1	0	-	-	0	0
TOTALS	-	50-97	-	6-9	56	23	-	-	16	106
Percentages		51.5		66.7						

Coach: Joe B. Hall

AUSTIN PEAY	MIN	FG	3FG	FT	REB	A	ST	BL	PF	TP
James "Fly" Williams	35	13-31	-	0-0	6	1	-	-	4	26
Howard Jackson	41	10-19	-	3-7	18	3	-	-	2	23
Ed Childress	42	10-19	-	2-2	5	2	-	-	3	22
Percy Howard	29	7-10	-	0-0	9	0	-	-	4	14
Danny Odums	42	5-10	-	1-1	2	5	-	-	2	11
Jerry Wanstrath	21	0-3	-	2-2	4	1	-	-	0	2
Kemp Hampton	3	1-3	-	0-0	2	1	-	-	0	2
Richard Jimmerson	6	0-2	-	0-0	0	0	-	-	0	0
Robert Turner	6	0-2	-	0-0	1	0	-	-	0	0
TOTALS	225	46-99	-	8-12	47	13	-	-	15	100
Percentages		46.5		66.7						

Coach: Lake Kelly

Officials: Soriano, Ditty
Attendance: 15,581

98-81

	1H	2H
UCLA	51	47
Arizona State	37	44

SWEET 16

UCLA	MIN	FG	3FG	FT	REB	A	ST	BL	PF	TP
Bill Walton	-	13-18	-	2-2	14	6	-	-	3	28
Larry Hollyfield	-	9-16	-	2-2	5	6	-	-	3	20
Keith Wilkes	-	6-14	-	0-0	10	1	-	-	2	12
Larry Farmer	-	5-10	-	0-0	4	0	-	-	2	10
Tommy Curtis	-	2-3	-	3-3	1	5	-	-	2	7
Dave Meyers	-	2-3	-	2-3	5	4	-	-	1	6
Swen Nater	-	2-5	-	0-2	2	0	-	-	2	4
Pete Trgovich	-	2-5	-	0-0	2	1	-	-	0	4
Greg Lee	-	1-2	-	1-1	0	4	-	-	0	3
Casey Corliss	-	0-0	-	2-2	0	0	-	-	1	2
Gary Franklin	-	1-2	-	0-0	2	1	-	-	0	2
Vince Carson	-	0-0	-	0-2	1	1	-	-	0	0
Ralph Drollinger	-	0-0	-	0-0	0	0	-	-	1	0
Bob Webb	-	0-2	-	0-0	0	0	-	-	2	0
TOTALS	**-**	**43-80**	**-**	**12-17**	**46**	**29**	**-**	**-**	**19**	**98**
Percentages		53.8		70.6						

Coach: John Wooden

ARIZONA STATE	MIN	FG	3FG	FT	REB	A	ST	BL	PF	TP
Jim Owens	-	8-20	-	6-8	4	1	-	-	2	22
Mike Contreras	-	9-20	-	0-0	4	1	-	-	3	18
Gary Jackson	-	3-8	-	4-6	4	1	-	-	3	10
Ron Kennedy	-	2-7	-	5-6	8	5	-	-	5	9
James Brown	-	2-6	-	2-3	6	0	-	-	2	6
Mark Wasley	-	3-8	-	0-0	10	1	-	-	1	6
Rudy White	-	3-6	-	0-0	2	0	-	-	0	6
Ken Gray	-	2-4	-	0-1	2	2	-	-	0	4
Mike Moon	-	0-2	-	0-0	1	0	-	-	0	0
Jack Schrader	-	0-1	-	0-0	3	1	-	-	1	0
TOTALS	**-**	**32-82**	**-**	**17-24**	**44**	**12**	**-**	**-**	**17**	**81**
Percentages		39.0		70.8						

Coach: Ned Wulk

Officials: Copeland, Fouty
Attendance: 12,671

77-67

	1H	2H
San Francisco	37	40
Long Beach State	31	36

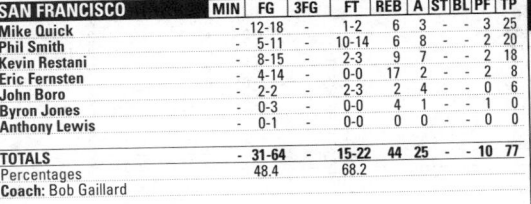

SWEET 16

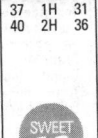

SAN FRANCISCO	MIN	FG	3FG	FT	REB	A	ST	BL	PF	TP
Mike Quick	-	12-18	-	1-2	6	3	-	-	3	25
Phil Smith	-	5-11	-	10-14	6	8	-	-	2	20
Kevin Restani	-	8-15	-	2-3	9	7	-	-	2	18
Eric Fernsten	-	4-14	-	0-0	17	2	-	-	2	8
John Boro	-	2-2	-	2-3	2	4	-	-	0	6
Byron Jones	-	0-3	-	0-0	4	1	-	-	1	0
Anthony Lewis	-	0-1	-	0-0	0	0	-	-	0	0
TOTALS	**-**	**31-64**	**-**	**15-22**	**44**	**25**	**-**	**-**	**10**	**77**
Percentages		48.4		68.2						

Coach: Bob Gaillard

LONG BEACH STATE	MIN	FG	3FG	FT	REB	A	ST	BL	PF	TP
Nate Stephens	-	9-20	-	0-1	16	1	-	-	1	18
Ed Ratleff	-	4-18	-	4-4	7	7	-	-	3	12
Roscoe Pondexter	-	5-14	-	1-2	6	1	-	-	3	11
Leonard Gray	-	4-6	-	2-2	8	5	-	-	2	10
Rick Aberegg	-	4-10	-	0-0	1	9	-	-	5	8
Ernie Douse	-	2-5	-	0-0	4	0	-	-	2	4
Glenn McDonald	-	2-9	-	0-0	2	0	-	-	1	4
Lamont King	-	0-0	-	0-0	0	0	-	-	2	0
TOTALS	**-**	**30-82**	**-**	**7-9**	**44**	**23**	**-**	**-**	**19**	**67**
Percentages		36.6		77.8						

Coach: Jerry Tarkanian

Officials: White, Wortman
Technicals: USF (Coach Gaillard); LBS (Aberegg)
Attendance: 12,632

92-72

	1H	2H
Memphis	49	43
Kansas State	34	38

ELITE 8

MEMPHIS	MIN	FG	3FG	FT	REB	A	ST	BL	PF	TP
Larry Finch	39	10-16	-	12-12	2	3	1	0	2	32
Ronnie Robinson	38	7-10	-	0-0	16	2	1	1	3	14
Larry Kenon	27	7-12	-	0-0	7	1	1	1	4	14
Wes Westfall	18	5-6	-	0-0	6	0	0	0	5	10
Bill Laurie	39	2-4	-	4-4	3	11	1	0	2	8
Bill Cook	18	3-6	-	2-2	3	3	0	0	0	8
Billy Buford	14	2-5	-	0-0	3	1	1	0	4	4
Jim Liss	1	1-1	-	0-0	0	0	0	0	0	2
Clarence Jones	3	0-0	-	0-0	0	0	0	0	1	0
Ken Andrews	1	0-0	-	0-0	0	0	0	0	1	0
Doug McKinney	1	0-1	-	0-0	0	1	1	0	0	0
Jerry Tetzlaff	1	0-1	-	0-2	2	0	0	0	0	0
TOTALS	**200**	**37-62**	**-**	**18-20**	**42**	**22**	**6**	**2**	**22**	**92**
Percentages		59.7		90.0						

Coach: Gene Bartow

KANSAS STATE	MIN	FG	3FG	FT	REB	A	ST	BL	PF	TP
Ernie Kusnyer	33	8-19	-	5-10	5	2	1	1	4	21
Lon Kruger	40	6-12	-	3-3	5	4	3	0	3	15
Steve Mitchell	24	6-14	-	0-1	6	0	1	0	3	12
Gene McVey	16	4-7	-	4-4	4	1	0	0	1	12
Larry Williams	23	2-8	-	0-0	5	0	1	1	2	4
Jerry Thurston	17	2-3	-	0-2	1	1	2	0	2	4
Robert Chipman	25	1-4	-	1-2	2	2	2	1	1	3
Danny Beard	15	0-3	-	1-2	1	2	2	0	1	1
Doug Snider	7	0-3	-	0-0	0	0	2	0	2	0
TOTALS	**200**	**29-73**	**-**	**14-24**	**29**	**12**	**14**	**3**	**19**	**72**
Percentages		39.7		58.3						

Coach: Jack Hartman

Officials: Howell, Moreau
Attendance: 10,060

103-89

	1H	2H
Providence	50	53
Maryland	51	38

ELITE 8

PROVIDENCE	MIN	FG	3FG	FT	REB	A	ST	BL	PF	TP
Ernie DiGregorio	27	14-21	-	2-2	3	5	-	-	5	30
Kevin Stacom	40	10-17	-	4-5	2	1	-	-	3	24
Marvin Barnes	40	8-18	-	3-5	15	0	-	-	2	19
Nehru King	25	7-9	-	1-3	7	2	-	-	1	15
Francis Costello	28	2-5	-	4-4	6	2	-	-	4	8
Charles Crawford	40	2-4	-	3-3	5	0	-	-	2	7
TOTALS	**200**	**43-74**	**-**	**17-22**	**38**	**10**	**-**	**-**	**17**	**103**
Percentages		58.1		77.3						

Coach: Dave Gavitt

MARYLAND	MIN	FG	3FG	FT	REB	A	ST	BL	PF	TP
Tom McMillen	-	10-16	-	5-5	6	0	-	-	4	25
John Lucas	-	9-20	-	2-2	6	4	-	-	5	20
Len Elmore	-	7-11	-	0-1	10	0	-	-	5	14
Jim O'Brien	-	3-9	-	2-2	3	2	-	-	1	8
Tom Roy	-	4-5	-	0-2	5	0	-	-	3	8
Bob Bodell	-	2-8	-	0-0	7	3	-	-	3	4
Owen Brown	-	2-4	-	0-0	1	0	-	-	0	4
Maurice Howard	-	2-6	-	0-0	0	1	-	-	1	4
Darrell Brown	-	1-3	-	0-0	1	3	-	-	0	2
Howard White	-	0-1	-	0-0	0	0	-	-	0	0
TOTALS	**-**	**40-83**	**-**	**9-12**	**39**	**13**	**-**	**-**	**22**	**89**
Percentages		48.2		75.0						

Coach: Lefty Driesell

Officials: Shosid, Bain
Attendance: 10,400

72-65

	1H	2H
Indiana	45	27
Kentucky	32	33

ELITE 8

INDIANA	MIN	FG	3FG	FT	REB	A	ST	BL	PF	TP
Steve Downing	40	10-22	-	3-4	13	0	3	0	3	23
Quinn Buckner	39	8-21	-	0-1	11	5	3	0	3	16
Steve Green	32	5-13	-	4-4	6	2	3	2	3	14
John Laskowski	24	4-5	-	2-4	6	3	1	0	1	10
John Ritter	38	4-5	-	1-1	2	1	0	0	2	9
Jim Crews	25	0-2	-	0-0	1	2	0	0	0	0
Tom Abernethy	2	0-0	-	0-0	1	0	0	0	0	0
TOTALS	**200**	**31-68**	**-**	**10-14**	**40**	**13**	**10**	**2**	**12**	**72**
Percentages		45.6		71.4						

Coach: Bob Knight

KENTUCKY	MIN	FG	3FG	FT	REB	A	ST	BL	PF	TP
Jim Andrews	37	11-20	-	1-2	10	3	1	6	3	23
Kevin Grevey	36	7-14	-	0-0	8	3	0	0	4	14
Mike Flynn	36	4-10	-	0-0	2	2	0	0	4	8
Ronnie Lyons	23	3-7	-	2-2	2	3	1	0	0	8
Bob Guyette	16	3-4	-	0-0	3	0	1	2	1	6
Steve Lochmueller	3	2-3	-	0-0	1	0	0	0	3	4
Jimmy Dan Conner	37	1-6	-	0-0	10	6	0	0	2	2
Jerry Hale	5	0-1	-	0-0	0	0	0	0	0	0
Larry Stamper	5	0-0	-	0-0	0	0	0	0	0	0
Ray Edelman	2	0-0	-	0-0	0	1	0	0	0	0
TOTALS	**200**	**31-65**	**-**	**3-4**	**36**	**18**	**3**	**8**	**17**	**65**
Percentages		47.7		75.0						

Coach: Joe B. Hall

Officials: Ditty, Brown
Attendance: 16,000

54-39

	1H	2H
UCLA	23	31
San Francisco	22	17

ELITE 8

UCLA	MIN	FG	3FG	FT	REB	A	ST	BL	PF	TP
Larry Farmer	-	5-10	-	3-3	4	1	-	-	0	13
Tommy Curtis	-	6-9	-	0-1	1	4	-	-	1	12
Keith Wilkes	-	6-13	-	0-0	1	1	-	-	0	12
Bill Walton	-	4-7	-	1-2	14	2	-	-	0	9
Gary Franklin	-	1-2	-	0-0	2	0	-	-	0	2
Greg Lee	-	1-4	-	0-0	1	0	-	-	0	2
Dave Meyers	-	1-3	-	0-0	3	1	-	-	3	2
Pete Trgovich	-	1-2	-	0-0	0	0	-	-	0	2
Vince Carson	-	0-0	-	0-0	1	0	-	-	1	0
Larry Hollyfield	-	0-3	-	0-0	1	0	-	-	0	0
Swen Nater	-	0-2	-	0-0	1	0	-	-	0	0
Bob Webb	-	0-1	-	0-0	0	0	-	-	1	0
TOTALS	**-**	**25-56**	**-**	**4-6**	**29**	**9**	**-**	**-**	**6**	**54**
Percentages		44.6		66.7						

Coach: John Wooden

SAN FRANCISCO	MIN	FG	3FG	FT	REB	A	ST	BL	PF	TP
Phil Smith	40	8-13	-	1-1	3	1	-	-	0	17
Mike Quick	40	4-9	-	0-0	2	1	-	-	1	8
Kevin Restani	40	4-11	-	0-0	9	2	-	-	0	8
Eric Fernsten	40	2-5	-	0-0	8	0	-	-	3	4
John Boro	40	0-3	-	2-2	0	1	-	-	3	2
TOTALS	**200**	**18-41**	**-**	**3-3**	**22**	**5**	**-**	**-**	**7**	**39**
Percentages		43.9		100.0						

Coach: Bob Gaillard

Officials: White, Copeland
Attendance: 12,075

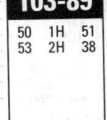

98-85

	1H	2H
Memphis	40	58
Providence	49	36

FINAL 4

MEMPHIS	MIN	FG	3FG	FT	REB	A	ST	BL	PF	TP
Larry Kenon	40	14-27	-	0-4	22	4	0	3	1	28
Ronnie Robinson	40	11-17	-	2-3	16	1	2	0	2	24
Larry Finch	34	7-16	-	7-9	6	5	1	0	4	21
Bill Cook	21	3-6	-	2-3	1	5	0	0	2	8
Wes Westfall	13	2-3	-	3-4	2	2	0	1	0	7
Billy Buford	25	3-7	-	0-0	3	4	0	1	2	6
Bill Laurie	25	1-3	-	2-3	1	3	2	0	4	4
Clarence Jones	2	0-1	-	0-0	0	0	0	0	0	0
TOTALS	**200**	**41-80**	**-**	**16-26**	**51**	**24**	**5**	**5**	**15**	**98**
Percentages		51.2		61.5						

Coach: Gene Bartow

PROVIDENCE	MIN	FG	3FG	FT	REB	A	ST	BL	PF	TP
Ernie DiGregorio	39	15-36	-	2-2	2	7	1	0	4	32
Kevin Stacom	37	6-15	-	3-3	5	3	1	1	5	15
Marvin Barnes	11	5-7	-	2-3	3	1	0	0	4	12
Francis Costello	38	5-5	-	1-1	8	3	0	0	5	11
Charles Crawford	38	5-12	-	0-0	15	1	1	0	3	10
Nehru King	30	2-6	-	0-0	1	0	1	0	1	4
Richard Dunphy	3	0-1	-	1-2	1	0	0	0	0	1
Al Baker	3	0-0	-	0-0	1	0	0	0	0	0
Gary Bello	1	0-0	-	0-0	0	0	0	0	0	0
TOTALS	**200**	**38-82**	**-**	**9-11**	**36**	**15**	**4**	**1**	**22**	**85**
Percentages		46.3		81.8						

Coach: Dave Gavitt

Officials: Ditty, White
Technicals: Memphis (Robinson)
Attendance: 19,029

70-59

	1H	2H
UCLA	40	30
Indiana	22	37

FINAL 4

UCLA	MIN	FG	3FG	FT	REB	A	ST	BL	PF	TP
Tommy Curtis	-	9-15	-	4-7	2	4	-	-	2	22
Bill Walton	-	7-12	-	0-0	17	9	-	-	4	14
Keith Wilkes	-	5-10	-	3-4	6	1	-	-	3	13
Larry Hollyfield	-	5-6	-	0-0	2	2	-	-	1	10
Larry Farmer	-	3-6	-	1-2	3	0	-	-	4	7
Dave Meyers	-	2-3	-	0-0	5	0	-	-	1	4
Greg Lee	-	0-1	-	0-0	0	1	-	-	0	0
Swen Nater	-	0-0	-	0-0	0	0	-	-	1	0
TOTALS	**-**	**31-53**	**-**	**8-13**	**35**	**17**	**-**	**-**	**16**	**70**
Percentages		58.5		61.5						

Coach: John Wooden

INDIANA	MIN	FG	3FG	FT	REB	A	ST	BL	PF	TP
Steve Downing	-	12-20	-	2-4	5	2	-	-	5	26
John Ritter	-	6-10	-	1-1	2	6	-	-	3	13
Jim Crews	-	4-10	-	0-0	2	2	-	-	3	8
Quinn Buckner	-	3-10	-	0-1	5	4	-	-	2	6
Doug Allen	-	1-1	-	0-0	0	0	-	-	0	2
Steve Green	-	1-7	-	0-0	5	2	-	-	2	2
John Laskowski	-	1-8	-	0-0	4	1	-	-	0	2
Tom Abernethy	-	0-1	-	0-0	1	0	-	-	1	0
Steven Ahlfeld	-	0-0	-	0-0	0	1	-	-	0	0
Jerry Memering	-	0-0	-	0-0	0	0	-	-	0	0
Craig Morris	-	0-0	-	0-0	0	0	-	-	0	0
Donald Noort	-	0-0	-	0-0	1	0	-	-	0	0
Trent Smock	-	0-0	-	0-0	0	0	-	-	0	0
Franklin Wilson	-	0-0	-	0-0	0	0	-	-	0	0
TOTALS	**-**	**28-67**	**-**	**3-6**	**25**	**18**	**-**	**-**	**16**	**59**
Percentages		41.8		50.0						

Coach: Bob Knight

Officials: Shosid, Howell
Technicals: UCLA (Meyers), Indiana (coach Knight)
Attendance: 19,029

97-79

	1H	2H
Indiana	51	46
Providence	42	37

3RD PLACE

INDIANA	MIN	FG	3FG	FT	REB	A	ST	BL	PF	TP
Steve Downing	39	10-17	-	1-1	14	2	-	-	3	21
John Ritter	27	8-15	-	5-8	7	2	-	-	5	21
Steve Green	33	8-13	-	0-1	7	7	-	-	4	16
Quinn Buckner	34	5-9	-	5-5	8	8	-	-	3	15
John Laskowski	17	4-7	-	0-0	5	0	-	-	3	8
Jim Crews	32	3-10	-	0-1	4	3	-	-	3	6
Steven Ahlfeld	7	1-2	-	4-4	1	1	-	-	2	6
Tom Abernethy	5	1-1	-	0-0	1	0	-	-	1	2
Franklin Wilson	1	1-1	-	0-1	1	0	-	-	0	2
Doug Allen	1	0-1	-	0-0	0	0	-	-	0	0
Jerry Memering	1	0-0	-	0-0	1	0	-	-	0	0
Craig Morris	1	0-0	-	0-0	0	0	-	-	0	0
Donald Noort	1	0-0	-	0-0	0	0	-	-	0	0
Trent Smock	1	0-0	-	0-0	0	1	-	-	0	0
TOTALS	**200**	**41-76**	**-**	**15-21**	**49**	**24**	**-**	**-**	**24**	**97**
Percentages		53.9		71.4						

Coach: Bob Knight

PROVIDENCE	MIN	FG	3FG	FT	REB	A	ST	BL	PF	TP
Kevin Stacom	40	10-21	-	9-10	7	2	-	-	3	29
Francis Costello	35	8-15	-	3-4	4	0	-	-	3	19
Ernie DiGregorio	38	7-22	-	3-4	7	7	-	-	4	17
Nehru King	28	2-10	-	0-0	5	0	-	-	3	4
Charles Crawford	20	1-4	-	2-3	5	0	-	-	4	4
Richard Dunphy	5	0-1	-	4-4	1	0	-	-	3	4
Al Baker	28	0-2	-	2-2	7	0	-	-	0	2
Mark McAndrew	3	0-1	-	0-0	1	0	-	-	0	0
Gary Bello	2	0-1	-	0-0	0	0	-	-	0	0
Dave Modest	1	0-1	-	0-0	0	0	-	-	0	0
TOTALS	**200**	**28-78**	**-**	**23-27**	**37**	**9**	**-**	**-**	**20**	**79**
Percentages		35.9		85.2						

Coach: Dave Gavitt

Officials: Ditty, White
Attendance: 19,301

87-66

	1H	2H
UCLA	39	48
Memphis	39	27

NCAA FINAL 1973

UCLA	MIN	FG	3FG	FT	REB	A	ST	BL	PF	TP
Bill Walton	33	21-22	-	2-5	13	2	0	1	4	44
Keith Wilkes	39	8-14	-	0-0	7	1	1	0	2	16
Larry Hollyfield	30	4-7	-	0-0	3	9	1	1	4	8
Greg Lee	34	1-1	-	3-3	3	14	0	0	2	5
Tommy Curtis	11	1-4	-	2-2	3	0	0	2	1	4
Dave Meyers	10	2-7	-	0-0	3	0	0	0	1	4
Larry Farmer	33	1-4	-	0-0	2	0	0	1	2	2
Swen Nater	7	1-1	-	0-0	3	0	0	0	2	2
Gary Franklin	1	1-2	-	0-1	1	0	0	0	0	2
Vince Carson	1	0-0	-	0-0	0	0	0	0	0	0
Bob Webb	1	0-0	-	0-0	0	0	0	0	0	0
TOTALS	**200**	**40-62**	**-**	**7-11**	**38**	**26**	**2**	**5**	**18**	**87**
Percentages		64.5		63.6						

Coach: John Wooden

MEMPHIS	MIN	FG	3FG	FT	REB	A	ST	BL	PF	TP
Larry Finch	38	9-21	-	11-13	1	2	-	0	2	29
Larry Kenon	34	8-16	-	4-4	8	3	-	1	3	20
Billy Buford	38	3-7	-	1-2	3	1	-	0	1	7
Ronnie Robinson	33	3-6	-	0-1	7	1	-	0	4	6
Bill Cook	18	1-4	-	2-2	0	2	-	0	1	4
Bill Laurie	21	0-1	-	0-0	0	2	-	0	0	0
Wes Westfall	10	0-1	-	0-0	0	0	-	0	5	0
Clarence Jones	4	0-0	-	0-0	0	0	-	0	0	0
Ken Andrews	1	0-0	-	0-0	0	0	-	0	0	0
Jim Liss	1	0-1	-	0-0	0	0	-	0	0	0
Doug McKinney	1	0-0	-	0-0	0	0	-	0	0	0
Jerry Tetzlaff	1	0-0	-	0-2	0	0	-	0	1	0
TOTALS	**200**	**24-57**	**-**	**18-24**	**19**	**11**	**-**	**1**	**17**	**66**
Percentages		42.1		75.0						

Coach: Gene Bartow

Officials: Howell, Shosid
Technicals: UCLA (Hollyfield), Memphis (Kenon)
Attendance: 19,301

National Invitation Tournament (NIT)

First round: Notre Dame d. Southern California 69-65, Louisville d. Texas-Pan American 97-84, North Carolina d. Oral Roberts 82-65, Massachusetts d. Missouri 78-71, Fairfield d. Marshall 80-76, Virginia Tech d. New Mexico 65-63, Minnesota d. Rutgers 68-59, Alabama d. Manhattan 87-86
Quarterfinals: North Carolina d. Massachusetts 73-63, Notre Dame d. Louisville 79-71, Virginia Tech d. Fairfield 77-76, Alabama d. Minnesota 69-65
Semifinals: Virginia Tech d. Alabama 74-73. Notre Dame d. North Carolina 78-71
Third place: North Carolina d. Alabama 88-69
Championship: Virginia Tech d. Notre Dame 92-91 (OT)
MVP: John Shumate, Notre Dame

1973-74: THE UNTHINKABLE

On Jan. 19, 1974, the team that had last beaten UCLA—a stunning 88 games ago—did it again. The 71-70 Notre Dame victory proved the Bruins mortal, and they lost twice more before reaching their eighth straight Final Four and a national semifinal match against No. 1-ranked NC State (30–1). The Wolfpack's lone regular-season loss had come in December against—guess who?—UCLA, 84-66, in St. Louis. At Greensboro Coliseum in March, however, coach Norm Sloan's crew prevailed in a thrilling 80-77 double-overtime win. The Pack's David Thompson—who had suffered a head injury during the East Regional final against Pittsburgh that required 15 stitches to close—scored 28 points and pulled down 10 rebounds, while his 7'4" teammate, Tom Burleson, had 20 points and 14 rebounds and helped "hold" Bill Walton to 29 points and 18 boards.

In the Final, the Wolfpack beat Marquette, 76-64, and Thompson, who scored 21, was named the Tournament's Most Outstanding Player. Despite averaging career lows in points (19.3) and rebounds (14.7), Walton took home his third straight Naismith National Player of the Year trophy.

MAJOR CONFERENCE STANDINGS

ACC

	Conference			Overall		
	W	L	Pct	W	L	Pct
NC State ⊕	12	0	1.000	30	1	.968
Maryland	9	3	.750	23	5	.821
North Carolina □	9	3	.750	22	6	.786
Virginia .	4	8	.333	11	16	.407
Clemson	3	9	.250	14	12	.538
Wake Forest	3	9	.250	13	13	.500
Duke	2	10	.167	10	16	.385

Tournament: **NC State d. Maryland 103-100 (OT)**
Tournament MVP: **Tom Burleson**, NC State

BIG EIGHT

	Conference			Overall		
	W	L	Pct	W	L	Pct
Kansas ⊕	13	1	.929	23	7	.767
Kansas State	11	3	.786	19	8	.704
Oklahoma	9	5	.643	18	8	.692
Nebraska	7	7	.500	14	12	.538
Iowa State	6	8	.429	15	11	.577
Colorado	4	10	.286	9	17	.346
Missouri	3	11	.214	12	14	.462
Oklahoma State	3	11	.214	9	17	.346

BIG SKY

	Conference			Overall		
	W	L	Pct	W	L	Pct
Idaho State ⊕	11	3	.786	21	8	.724
Montana	11	3	.786	19	8	.704
Weber State	8	6	.571	14	12	.538
Gonzaga	7	7	.500	13	13	.500
Boise State	6	8	.429	12	14	.462
Idaho	5	9	.357	12	14	.462
Montana State	5	9	.357	11	15	.423
Northern Arizona	3	11	.214	6	20	.231

BIG TEN

	Conference			Overall		
	W	L	Pct	W	L	Pct
Indiana	12	2	.857	23	5	.821
Michigan ⊕	12	2	.857	22	5	.815
Purdue □	10	4	.714	21	9	.700
Wisconsin	8	6	.571	16	8	.667
Michigan State	8	6	.571	13	11	.542
Minnesota	6	8	.429	12	12	.500
Iowa	5	9	.357	8	16	.333
Ohio State	4	10	.286	9	15	.375
Northwestern	3	11	.214	9	15	.375
Illinois	2	12	.143	5	18	.217

IVY

	Conference			Overall		
	W	L	Pct	W	L	Pct
Penn ⊕	13	1	.929	21	6	.778
Brown	11	3	.786	17	9	.654
Princeton	11	3	.786	16	10	.615
Harvard	9	5	.643	11	13	.458
Yale	5	9	.357	8	16	.333
Columbia	4	10	.286	5	20	.200
Dartmouth	2	12	.143	4	22	.154
Cornell	1	13	.071	3	23	.115

MID-AMERICAN

	Conference			Overall		
	W	L	Pct	W	L	Pct
Ohio ⊕	9	3	.750	16	11	.593
Toledo	8	4	.667	19	9	.679
Bowling Green	7	5	.583	15	11	.577
Central Michigan	6	6	.500	14	12	.538
Miami (OH)	6	6	.500	13	13	.500
Western Michigan	5	7	.417	13	13	.500
Kent State	1	11	.083	9	17	.346

MEAC

	Conference			Overall		
	W	L	Pct	W	L	Pct
UMES □	11	1	.917	27	2	.931
Morgan State	11	1	.917	28	5	.848
NC A&T	7	5	.583	16	10	.615
Delaware State	5	7	.417	18	11	.621
Howard	4	8	.333	11	18	.379
South Carolina St.	2	10	.167	13	15	.464
NC Central	2	10	.167	5	16	.238

Tournament: **UMES d. Morgan State 77-62**
Tournament MOP: **Talvin Skinner**, UMES

MIDDLE ATLANTIC

	Conference			Overall		
	W	L	Pct	W	L	Pct
EASTERN						
Saint Joseph's ⊕	5	1	.833	19	11	.633
La Salle	5	1	.833	18	10	.643
Temple	4	2	.667	16	9	.640
American	4	2	.667	16	10	.615
Drexel	2	4	.333	15	9	.625
Hofstra	1	5	.167	8	16	.333
West Chester	0	6	.000	11	15	.423
WESTERN						
Rider	8	2	.800	13	13	.500
Lafayette	7	3	.700	17	9	.654
Delaware	7	3	.700	15	11	.577
Gettysburg	4	6	.400	15	10	.600
Bucknell	2	8	.200	8	16	.333
Lehigh	2	8	.200	3	21	.125

MISSOURI VALLEY

	Conference			Overall		
	W	L	Pct	W	L	Pct
Louisville ⊕	11	1	.917	21	7	.750
Bradley	9	3	.750	20	8	.714
Tulsa	7	6	.538	18	8	.692
New Mexico State	7	6	.538	14	11	.560
Wichita State	6	7	.462	11	15	.423
West Texas A&M	5	8	.385	11	15	.423
North Texas	4	8	.333	13	13	.500
Saint Louis	4	8	.333	9	16	.360
Drake	3	9	.250	13	13	.500

OHIO VALLEY

	Conference			Overall		
	W	L	Pct	W	L	Pct
Austin Peay ⊕	10	4	.714	17	10	.630
Morehead State	10	4	.714	17	9	.654
Middle Tennessee St.	9	5	.643	18	8	.692
Western Kentucky	8	6	.571	15	10	.600
Murray State	6	8	.429	12	13	.480
Eastern Kentucky	6	8	.429	8	15	.348
Tennessee Tech	4	10	.286	7	18	.280
East Tennessee St.	3	11	.214	8	18	.308

PCAA

	Conference			Overall		
	W	L	Pct	W	L	Pct
Long Beach State	12	0	1.000	24	2	.923
Cal State LA ⊕	8	4	.667	17	10	.630
UC Santa Barbara	7	5	.583	16	10	.615
Fresno State	5	7	.417	16	9	.640
Pacific	4	8	.333	14	12	.538
San Diego State	4	8	.333	7	19	.269
San Jose State	2	10	.167	11	15	.423

PAC-8

	Conference			Overall		
	W	L	Pct	W	L	Pct
UCLA ⊕	12	2	.857	26	4	.867
Southern California	11	3	.786	24	5	.828
Oregon	9	5	.643	15	11	.577
Washington	7	7	.500	16	10	.615
Oregon State	6	8	.429	13	13	.500
Stanford	5	9	.357	11	14	.440
California	3	11	.214	9	17	.346
Washington State	3	11	.214	8	21	.276

SEC

	Conference			Overall		
	W	L	Pct	W	L	Pct
Alabama	15	3	.833	22	4	.846
Vanderbilt ⊕	15	3	.833	23	5	.821
Tennessee	12	6	.667	17	9	.654
Mississippi	9	9	.500	15	10	.600
Florida	9	9	.500	15	11	.577
Kentucky	9	9	.500	13	13	.500
Mississippi State	8	10	.444	16	10	.615
LSU	6	12	.333	12	14	.462
Auburn	5	13	.278	10	16	.385
Georgia	2	16	.111	6	20	.231

SOUTHERN

	Conference			Overall		
	W	L	Pct	W	L	Pct
Furman ⊕	11	1	.917	22	9	.710
Richmond	10	4	.714	16	12	.571
Davidson	7	3	.700	18	9	.667
East Carolina	8	6	.571	13	12	.520
William and Mary	5	6	.455	9	18	.333
The Citadel	4	9	.308	10	14	.417
VMI	3	9	.250	6	18	.250
Appalachian State	1	11	.083	5	20	.200

Tournament: **Furman d. Richmond 62-60**
Tournament MOP: **Aron Stewart**, Richmond

SOUTHLAND

	Conference			Overall		
	W	L	Pct	W	L	Pct
Arkansas State	4	0	1.000	17	8	.680
Texas-Arlington	2	2	.500	7	18	.280
Lamar	0	4	.000	6	19	.240
McNeese State	-	-	-	20	5	.800
Louisiana Tech	-	-	-	8	13	.381
UL-Lafayette	-	-	-	-	-	-

Note: UL-Lafayette did not field a team due to NCAA sanctions; McNeese State and Louisiana Tech were not eligible for conference play because of recruiting irregularities

SOUTHWEST

	Conference			Overall		
	W	L	Pct	W	L	Pct
Texas ⊕	11	3	.786	12	15	.444
Texas Tech	10	4	.714	17	9	.654
SMU	10	4	.714	15	12	.556
Texas A&M	7	7	.500	15	11	.577
Arkansas	6	8	.429	10	16	.385
Baylor	5	9	.357	12	13	.480
Rice	5	9	.357	11	17	.393
TCU	2	12	.143	8	17	.320

Conference Standings Continue →

⊕ Automatic NCAA Tournament bid ○ At-large NCAA Tournament bid □ NIT appearance ✪ Team record doesn't reflect games forfeited or vacated. For adjusted record, see p. 521.

WCAC

	Conference			Overall		
	W	L	Pct	W	L	Pct
San Francisco⊕	12	2	.857	19	9	.679
Seattle	11	3	.786	15	11	.577
UNLV	10	4	.714	20	6	.769
Loyola Marymount	6	8	.429	13	14	.481
Saint Mary's (CA)	5	9	.357	15	13	.536
Nevada	4	10	.286	11	15	.423
Santa Clara	4	10	.286	9	18	.333
Pepperdine	4	10	.286	8	18	.308

WAC

	Conference			Overall		
	W	L	Pct	W	L	Pct
New Mexico⊕	10	4	.714	22	7	.759
Utah□	9	5	.643	22	8	.733
Arizona	9	5	.643	19	7	.731
Arizona State	9	5	.643	18	9	.667
UTEP	8	6	.571	18	7	.720
BYU	6	8	.429	11	15	.423
Colorado State	5	9	.357	12	14	.462
Wyoming	0	14	.000	4	22	0.153

YANKEE

	Conference			Overall		
	W	L	Pct	W	L	Pct
Massachusetts□	11	1	.917	21	5	.808
Connecticut□	9	3	.750	19	8	.704
New Hampshire	8	4	.667	16	9	.640
Rhode Island	6	5	.545	11	14	.440
Vermont	3	9	.250	9	17	.346
Boston U.	2	9	.182	9	16	.360
Maine	2	10	.167	14	10	.583

INDEPENDENTS

	Overall		
	W	L	Pct
Notre Dame○	26	3	.897
Providence○	28	4	.875
Pittsburgh○	25	4	.862
Charlotte	22	4	.846
Centenary	21	4	.840
Marquette○	26	5	.839
South Carolina○	22	5	.815
Oral Roberts○	23	6	.793
South Alabama	22	6	.786
Creighton○	23	7	.767
St. John's□	20	7	.741
Ga. Southern	19	7	.731
Southern Illinois	19	7	.731
Syracuse○	19	7	.731
VCU	17	7	.708
Cincinnati□	19	8	.704
Boston College□	21	9	.700
Florida State	18	8	.692
Rutgers□	18	8	.692
Dayton○	20	9	.690
Hawaii□	19	9	.679
Jacksonville□	20	10	.667
Manhattan□	18	9	.667
Mercer	16	8	.667
Detroit	17	9	.654
Fairfield□	17	9	.654
Houston	17	9	.654
Illinois State	17	9	.654
Marshall	17	9	.654
St. Bonaventure	17	9	.654
Stetson	17	9	.654
DePaul	16	9	.640
Memphis□	19	11	.633
UL-Monroe	16	10	.615
Utah State	16	10	.615
Colgate	15	10	.600
Portland State	16	11	.593
Seton Hall□	16	11	.593
Texas-Pan American	13	9	.591
George Washington	15	11	.577
Portland	15	11	.577

INDEPENDENTS (CONT.)

	Overall		
	W	L	Pct
Saint Francis (PA)	15	11	.577
Ball State	14	12	.538
Butler	14	12	.538
Canisius	14	12	.538
Milwaukee	14	12	.538
Penn State	14	12	.538
Northeastern	12	11	.522
Long Island	13	12	.520
Duquesne	12	12	.500
Georgetown	13	13	.500
Oklahoma City	13	13	.500
Virginia Tech	13	13	.500
Indiana State	12	14	.462
Loyola-Chicago	12	14	.462
Niagara	12	14	.462
Tulane	12	14	.462
Air Force	11	13	.458
Iona	11	13	.458
St. Francis (NY)	11	13	.458
Fairleigh Dickinson	11	14	.440
Hardin-Simmons	11	14	.440
South Florida	11	14	.440
Denver	11	15	.423
Southern Miss	11	15	.423
Navy	9	13	.409
West Virginia	10	15	.400
Fordham	8	17	.320
Northern Illinois	8	17	.320
Eastern Michigan	8	18	.308
Holy Cross	8	18	.308
Saint Peter's	8	18	.308
Xavier	8	18	.308
Villanova	7	19	.269
Army	6	18	.250
Houston Baptist	6	19	.240
Cleveland State	6	20	.231
Samford	6	20	.231
Buffalo	5	20	.200
Georgia Tech	5	21	.192
Georgia State	1	25	.038

INDIVIDUAL LEADERS—SEASON

Scoring

	CL	POS	G	FG	FT	PTS	PPG
1 **Larry Fogle**, Canisius	SO	F	25	326	183	835	**33.4**
2 **Bruce King**, Texas-Pan American	SR	F	22	257	167	681	**31.0**
3 **James "Fly" Williams**, Austin Peay	SO	G	25	272	143	687	**27.5**
4 **Aron Stewart**, Richmond	SR	F	25	269	125	663	**26.5**
5 **David Thompson**, NC State	JR	F	31	325	155	805	**26.0**
6 **Larry Bullington**, Ball State	SR	G	26	255	154	664	**25.5**
7 **Frank Oleynick**, Seattle	SO	G	26	249	155	653	**25.1**
8 **James Outlaw**, North Carolina A&T	SR	G	26	265	117	647	**24.9**
9 **Willie Biles**, Tulsa	SR	G	26	257	127	641	**24.7**
10 **John Shumate**, Notre Dame	SO	F/C	29	281	141	703	**24.2**

Field Goal Pct

	CL	POS	G	FG	FGA	PCT
1 **Al Fleming**, Arizona	SO	F	26	136	204	**66.7**
2 **Bill Walton**, UCLA	SR	C	27	232	349	**66.5**
3 **Fred Cox**, Mississippi	SR	C	25	152	242	**62.8**
4 **John Shumate**, Notre Dame	SO	F/C	29	281	448	**62.7**
5 **Al Skinner**, Massachusetts	SR	F	26	196	316	**62.0**

Minimum: 5 made per game

Free Throw Pct

	CL	POS	G	FT	FTA	PCT
1 **Rickey Medlock**, Arkansas	JR	G	26	87	95	**91.6**
2 **John Snow**, Tennessee	SR	G	26	81	91	**89.0**
3 **Tom Ferrell**, Marshall	SR	G	26	128	145	**88.3**
4 **Terry Compton**, Vanderbilt	SR	G	28	89	102	**87.3**
5 **Lon Kruger**, Kansas State	SR	G	27	122	140	**87.1**

Minimum: 3 made per game

Rebounds Per Game

	CL	POS	G	REB	RPG
1 **Marvin Barnes**, Providence	SR	C	32	597	**18.7**
2 **Carlos McCullough**, Texas-Pan American	SR	C	22	358	**16.3**
3 **Brad Robinson**, Kent State	SR	F	26	423	**16.3**
4 **Bill Campion**, Manhattan	JR	C	27	419	**15.5**
5 **Pete Padgett**, Nevada	SO	C	26	395	**15.2**

INDIVIDUAL LEADERS—GAME

Points

	CL	POS	OPP	DATE	PTS
1 **Robert Hawkins**, Illinois State	JR	G/F	Northern Illinois	F20	**58**
2 **Stan Davis**, Appalachian State	SR	G	Carson-Newman	J24	**56**
3 **Larry Fogle**, Canisius	SO	F	Saint Peter's	F9	**55**
Bruce King, Texas-Pan American	SR	F	Baptist	J22	**55**
5 **Marvin Barnes**, Providence	SR	C	Austin Peay	D15	**52**

Rebounds

	CL	POS	OPP	DATE	REB
1 **Clyde Burwell**, Geo. Washington	JR	C	St. Mary's (MD)	D10	**33**
2 **Bob Warner**, Maine	SO	C	Trinity (CT)	J15	**28**
Eddie Woods, Oral Roberts	SR	C	Lamar	J21	**28**
4 **Marvin Barnes**, Providence	SR	C	Brown	F12	**27**
Rich Kelley, Stanford	JR	C	Kentucky	D22	**27**
C. McCullough, Tex.-Pan American	SR	C	Samford	J5	**27**
Joe C. Meriweather, So. Illinois	JR	C	Indiana State	F18	**27**
Henry Ray, McNeese State	JR	G	Texas-Arlington	F19	**27**
Bill Walton, UCLA	SR	C	Maryland	D1	**27**

TEAM LEADERS—SEASON

Win-Loss Pct

	W	L	PCT
1 **NC State**	30	1	**.968**
2 **UMES**	27	2	**.931**
3 **Long Beach State**	24	2	**.923**
4 **Notre Dame**	26	3	**.897**
5 **Providence**	28	4	**.875**

Scoring Offense

	G	W-L	PTS	PPG
1 **UMES**	29	27-2	2,831	**97.6**
2 **Oral Roberts**	29	23-6	2,744	**94.6**
3 **VCU**	24	17-7	2,266	**94.4**
4 **NC State**	31	30-1	2,833	**91.4**
5 **Utah**	30	22-8	2,726	**90.9**

Scoring Margin

	G	W-L	PPG	OPP PPG	MAR
1 **Charlotte**	26	22-4	90.2	69.4	**20.8**
2 **UCLA**	30	26-4	82.3	62.7	**19.6**
3 **Long Beach State**	26	24-2	80.2	61.1	**19.1**
4 **Notre Dame**	29	26-3	89.9	73.0	**16.9**
5 **Maryland**	28	23-5	85.7	69.0	**16.7**

Field Goal Pct

	G	W-L	FG	FGA	PCT
1 **Notre Dame**	29	26-3	1,056	1,992	**53.0**
2 **Long Beach State**	26	24-2	887	1,680	**52.8**
3 **North Carolina**	28	22-6	1,015	1,952	**52.0**
4 **Massachusetts**	26	21-5	878	1,709	**51.4**
5 **Charlotte**	26	22-4	996	1,948	**51.1**

Free Throw Pct

	G	W-L	FT	FTA	PCT
1 **Vanderbilt**	28	23-5	477	595	**80.2**
2 **Princeton**	26	16-10	332	423	**78.5**
3 **Davidson**	27	18-9	488	623	**78.3**
4 **Seattle**	26	15-11	366	479	**76.4**
5 **Denver**	26	11-15	311	410	**75.9**

Rebound Margin

	G	W-L	REB	OPP REB	MAR
1 **Massachusetts**	26	21-5	43.7	30.7	**13.0**
VCU	24	17-7	55.1	42.1	**13.0**
3 **Arkansas State**	25	17-8	50.3	39.2	**11.1**
4 **Iona**	24	11-13	51.0	40.0	**11.0**
5 **Maryland**	28	23-5	47.0	36.1	**10.9**

Scoring Defense

	G	W-L	OPP PTS	OPP PPG
1 **UTEP**	25	18-7	1,413	**56.5**
2 **Temple**	25	16-9	1,417	**56.7**
3 **Princeton**	26	16-10	1,520	**58.5**
4 **Marquette**	31	26-5	1,857	**59.9**
5 **Saint Joseph's**	30	19-11	1,807	**60.2**

CONSENSUS ALL-AMERICAS

First Team

PLAYER	CL	POS	HT	SCHOOL	RPG	PPG
Marvin Barnes	SR	C	6-8	Providence	18.7	22.1
John Shumate	SO	F/C	6-9	Notre Dame	11.0	24.2
David Thompson	JR	F	6-4	NC State	7.9	26.0
Bill Walton	SR	C	6-11	UCLA	14.7	19.3
Keith Wilkes	SR	F	6-6	UCLA	6.6	16.7

Second Team

PLAYER	CL	POS	HT	SCHOOL	RPG	PPG
Len Elmore	SR	C	6-9	Maryland	14.7	14.6
Larry Fogle	SO	F	6-5	Canisius	14.0	33.4
Bobby Jones	SR	F	6-9	North Carolina	9.8	16.1
Billy Knight	SR	G/F	6-6	Pittsburgh	13.4	21.8
Campy Russell	JR	F	6-8	Michigan	11.1	23.7

Selectors: AP, NABC, UPI, USBWA

AWARD WINNERS

Player of the Year

PLAYER	CL	POS	HT	SCHOOL	AWARDS
Bill Walton	SR	C	6-11	UCLA	Naismith, UPI, USBWA, Rupp
David Thompson	JR	F	6-4	NC State	AP
Mike Robinson	SR	G	5-11	Michigan State	Frances Pomeroy Naismith*

* For the most outstanding senior player who is 6 feet or under

Coach of the Year

COACH	SCHOOL	REC	AWARDS
Norm Sloan	NC State	30-1	AP, USBWA
Digger Phelps	Notre Dame	26-3	UPI, Sporting News
Al McGuire	Marquette	26-5	NABC

Poll Progression

Preseason Poll

AP	School
1	UCLA
2	NC State
3	Indiana
4	Maryland
5	North Carolina
6	Providence
7	Marquette
8	Notre Dame
9	Louisville
10	Kentucky
11	San Francisco
12	Long Beach State
13	Kansas
14	Houston
15	Arizona
16	Penn
17	Jacksonville
18	Alabama
19	UNLV
20	Memphis

Week of Dec 4

AP	School	
1	UCLA (2-0)	
2	NC State (0-0)	
3	Indiana (1-0)	
4	Maryland (0-1)	
5	North Carolina (1-0)	
6	Providence (1-0)	
7	Marquette (1-0)	
8	Notre Dame (1-0)	
9	Louisville (0-1)	
10	Kentucky (1-0)	
11	San Francisco (1-1)	
12	Long Beach State (1-0)	
13	Kansas State (1-0)	⤴
14	Houston (0-1)	
15	Arizona (1-1)	
16	Penn (1-0)	
17	Jacksonville (1-1)	
18	Alabama (1-0)	
19	UNLV (0-1)	Ⓐ
20	Memphis (2-0)	

Week of Dec 11

AP	UPI	School	AP↓↑
1	1	UCLA (3-0)	
2	2	NC State (2-0)	
3	3	Indiana (3-0)	
4	5	Maryland (1-1)	
5	4	North Carolina (2-0)	
6	7	Notre Dame (4-0)	↑2
7	6	Marquette (4-0)	
8	8	Providence (1-0)	↓2
9	10	Louisville (3-1)	
10	9	Memphis (4-0)	↑10
11	17	Penn (3-0)	↑5
12	12	Long Beach State (2-1)	
13	11	Alabama (2-0)	↑5
14	17	Arizona (3-1)	↑1
15	14	Kansas State (3-1)	↓2
16	13	South Carolina (3-0)	⤴
17	—	San Francisco (1-2)	↓6
18	—	Syracuse (3-0)	⤴
19	—	Jacksonville (3-1)	↓2
20	19	USC (2-1)	⤴
—	15	Cincinnati (3-0)	
—	16	New Mexico (4-0)	
—	19	Vanderbilt (4-0)	

Week of Dec 18

AP	UPI	School	AP↓↑
1	1	UCLA (4-0)	
2	5	Maryland (2-1)	↑2
3	3	Notre Dame (5-0)	↑3
4	2	North Carolina (5-0)	↑1
5	6	NC State (2-1)	↓3
6	4	Marquette (5-0)	↑1
7	7	Indiana (4-1)	↓4
8	9	Louisville (4-1)	↑1
9	8	Providence (3-1)	↓1
10	11	Alabama (3-0)	↑3
11	13	Long Beach State (5-1)	↑1
12	19	Memphis (6-1)	↓2
13	11	Kansas State (5-1)	↑2
14	19	Arizona (5-1)	
15	14	South Carolina (4-0)	↑1
16	10	USC (4-1)	↑4
17	17	Vanderbilt (6-0)	⤴
18	—	Syracuse (4-0)	
19	—	Jacksonville (4-1)	
20	15	Cincinnati (5-0)	⤴
—	15	New Mexico (7-0)	
—	18	Oklahoma (4-1)	

Week of Dec 25

AP	UPI	School	AP↓↑
1	1	UCLA (6-0)	
2	4	Maryland (4-1)	
3	2	Notre Dame (6-0)	
4	3	North Carolina (6-0)	
5	5	NC State (3-1)	
6	6	Marquette (7-0)	
7	7	Indiana (5-1)	
8	9	Louisville (6-1)	
9	8	Providence (6-1)	
10	12	Long Beach State (7-1)	↑1
11	11	Vanderbilt (7-0)	↑6
12	15	Arizona (5-1)	↑2
13	17	Alabama (4-1)	↓3
14	10	USC (6-1)	↑2
15	17	Syracuse (5-0)	↑3
16	19	Memphis (7-2)	↓4
17	13	New Mexico (8-0)	⤴
18	—	Kansas State (5-2)	↓5
19	16	UNLV (7-1)	⤴
20	—	Austin Peay (5-1)	⤴
—	14	Oklahoma (5-1)	
—	20	South Carolina (4-1)	⤵

Week of Jan 2

AP	UPI	School	AP↓↑
1	1	UCLA (8-0)	
2	2	Notre Dame (7-0)	↑1
3	3	Maryland (5-1)	↓1
4	4	North Carolina (7-0)	
5	5	NC State (6-1)	
6	6	Marquette (9-0)	
7	10	Alabama (6-1)	↑6
8	8	Indiana (7-2)	↓1
9	11	Long Beach State (9-1)	↑1
10	12	Vanderbilt (8-0)	↑1
11	7	USC (9-1)	↑3
12	9	New Mexico (10-0)	↑5
13	14	Louisville (7-2)	↓5
14	13	Providence (8-2)	↓5
15	18	Arizona (8-2)	↓3
16	18	UNLV (9-1)	↑4
17	16	Wisconsin (7-1)	⤴
18	—	Memphis (8-3)	↓2
19	—	Syracuse (7-1)	↓4
20	—	Austin Peay (5-1)	
—	15	Missouri (6-2)	
—	17	South Carolina (5-2)	
—	18	Purdue (7-3)	

Week of Jan 8

AP	UPI	School	AP↓↑
1	1	UCLA (9-0)	
2	2	Notre Dame (7-0)	
3	3	Maryland (7-1)	
4	4	NC State (7-1)	↑1
5	5	North Carolina (7-1)	↓1
6	8	Vanderbilt (9-0)	↑4
7	6	Marquette (10-1)	↓1
8	7	New Mexico (12-0)	↑4
9	9	Long Beach State (10-1)	
10	11	Providence (9-2)	↑4
11	9	Louisville (8-2)	↑2
12	12	Alabama (6-2)	↓5
13	12	Indiana (7-3)	↓5
14	15	Wisconsin (8-1)	↑4
15	14	South Carolina (7-2)	⤴
16	18	UNLV (9-1)	↓1
17	16	USC (9-2)	↓6
18	—	Michigan (9-2)	⤴
19	19	Memphis (10-3)	↓1
20	—	Hawaii (11-0)	⤴
—	17	Missouri (8-3)	
—	20	Dayton (8-2)	

Week of Jan 15

AP	UPI	School	AP↓↑
1	1	UCLA (11-0)	
2	2	Notre Dame (8-0)	
3	3	NC State (9-1)	↑1
4	4	Maryland (8-2)	↓1
5	5	North Carolina (9-1)	
6	6	Marquette (12-1)	↑1
7	7	Providence (11-2)	↑3
8	8	Vanderbilt (10-1)	↓2
9	10	Long Beach State (12-1)	
10	11	Alabama (9-2)	↑2
11	13	South Carolina (9-2)	↑4
12	9	Indiana (9-3)	↑1
13	14	USC (12-2)	↑4
14	18	Michigan (10-2)	↑4
15	12	New Mexico (12-2)	↓7
16	15	Louisville (9-3)	↓5
17	—	Pittsburgh (12-1)	⤴
18	16	Missouri (10-3)	⤴
19	18	Wisconsin (9-2)	↓6
20	—	Cincinnati (10-3)	⤴
—	17	Arizona State (10-4)	
—	20	Syracuse (8-3)	

Week of Jan 22

AP	UPI	School	AP↓↑
1	1	Notre Dame (10-0) Ⓑ	↑1
2	2	UCLA (13-1) Ⓑ	↓1
3	3	NC State (11-1)	
4	5	North Carolina (12-1)	↑1
5	4	Maryland (10-2)	↓1
6	6	Marquette (14-1)	
7	8	Vanderbilt (12-1)	↑1
8	7	Providence (13-2)	↓1
9	10	Alabama (10-2)	↑1
10	9	Long Beach State (12-1)	↓1
11	13	Indiana (11-3)	↑1
12	11	USC (12-2)	↑1
13	14	South Carolina (10-3)	↓2
14	15	Louisville (10-3)	↑2
15	20	Michigan (11-2)	↓1
16	12	Pittsburgh (13-1)	↑1
17	16	Wisconsin (10-2)	↑2
18	—	Centenary (12-0)	⤴
19	—	New Mexico (12-3)	↓4
20	18	Arizona State (11-4)	⤴
—	17	Kansas (11-3)	
—	19	UTEP (12-2)	

Week of Jan 29

AP	UPI	School	AP↓↑
1	1	UCLA (15-1) Ⓒ	↑1
2	2	NC State (13-1)	↑1
3	3	Notre Dame (12-1) Ⓒ	↓2
4	4	North Carolina (14-2)	
5	5	Marquette (16-1)	↑1
6	6	Maryland (11-3)	↓1
7	7	Vanderbilt (14-1)	
8	9	Alabama (13-2)	↑1
9	8	Providence (15-2)	↓1
10	12	Long Beach State (14-2)	
11	11	USC (14-2)	↑1
12	13	Indiana (12-3)	↓1
13	10	Pittsburgh (14-1)	↑3
14	15	South Carolina (12-3)	↓1
15	13	Louisville (11-3)	↓1
16	17	Wisconsin (11-2)	↑1
17	—	New Mexico (14-3)	↑2
18	16	Kansas (12-3)	⤴
19	—	Oral Roberts (16-2)	⤴
20	—	Michigan (12-3)	↓5
—	18	UTEP (14-3)	
—	19	Purdue (12-5)	
—	19	Syracuse (12-3)	

Week of Feb 5

AP	UPI	School	AP↓↑
1	1	UCLA (16-1)	
2	2	NC State (15-1)	
3	3	Notre Dame (15-1)	
4	4	North Carolina (15-2)	
5	6	Vanderbilt (16-1)	↑2
6	5	Marquette (17-2)	↓1
7	7	Maryland (13-4)	↓1
8	8	Alabama (15-2)	
9	14	Long Beach State (16-2)	↑1
10	9	Pittsburgh (17-1)	↑3
11	12	Providence (16-3)	↓2
12	11	Indiana (13-3)	
13	17	South Carolina (13-3)	↑1
14	10	USC (14-3)	↓3
15	13	Louisville (14-3)	
16	—	Michigan (14-3)	↑4
17	16	Kansas (13-4)	↑1
18	15	UTEP (15-3)	⤴
19	—	Oral Roberts (16-3)	
20	—	UMES (19-0) Ⓓ	⤴
—	18	Creighton (16-4)	
—	18	Penn (15-4)	
—	18	Syracuse (13-4)	

Week of Feb 12

AP	UPI	School	AP↓↑
1	1	UCLA (18-1)	
2	2	NC State (17-1)	
3	3	Notre Dame (18-1)	
4	4	North Carolina (17-2)	
5	5	Vanderbilt (18-1)	
6	6	Maryland (15-4)	↑1
7	8	Pittsburgh (19-1)	↑3
8	11	Alabama (16-3)	
9	7	Marquette (18-3)	↓3
10	10	Long Beach State (18-2)	↓1
11	12	Providence (18-3)	
12	9	Indiana (14-3)	
13	13	USC (16-3)	↑1
14	16	South Carolina (16-3)	↓1
15	15	Michigan (15-3)	↑1
16	14	Kansas (15-4)	↑1
17	18	Creighton (18-4)	⤴
18	17	Louisville (14-4)	↓3
19	19	Utah (16-5)	⤴
20	—	Arizona (16-5)	⤴
—	20	Purdue (14-6)	

Week of Feb 19

AP	UPI	SCHOOL	AP↓↑
1	1	**NC State** (20-1)	↑1
2	2	**Notre Dame** (20-1)	↑1
3	3	**UCLA** (18-3)	Ⓑ ↓2
4	5	**Vanderbilt** (20-1)	↑1
5	6	**Maryland** (17-4)	↑1
6	4	**North Carolina** (18-3)	↓2
7	8	**Pittsburgh** (21-1)	
8	11	**Alabama** (18-3)	
9	7	**Marquette** (19-3)	
10	10	**Indiana** (16-3)	↑2
11	12	**Providence** (21-3)	
12	9	**USC** (18-3)	Ⓔ ↑1
13	13	**Long Beach State** (20-2)	↓3
14	16	**South Carolina** (16-4)	
15	16	**Creighton** (19-4)	↑2
16	14	**Kansas** (16-5)	
17	18	**Utah** (17-5)	↑2
18	15	**Kansas State** (17-5)	⤴
19	—	**Michigan** (16-4)	↓4
20	20	**Louisville** (15-5)	↓2
—	19	**New Mexico** (17-5)	

Week of Feb 26

AP	UPI	SCHOOL	AP↓↑
1	1	**NC State** (22-1)	
2	2	**Notre Dame** (22-1)	
3	3	**UCLA** (20-3)	
4	4	**North Carolina** (20-3)	↑2
5	5	**Maryland** (19-4)	
6	8	**Vanderbilt** (21-2)	↓2
7	10	**Alabama** (20-3)	↑1
8	7	**Marquette** (21-3)	↑1
9	6	**Indiana** (18-3)	↑1
10	9	**USC** (20-3)	↑2
11	11	**Pittsburgh** (22-2)	↓4
12	13	**Providence** (23-3)	↓1
13	11	**Long Beach State** (21-2)	
14	16	**South Carolina** (19-4)	
15	14	**Kansas** (17-5)	↑1
16	16	**Creighton** (21-5)	↓1
17	—	**Michigan** (17-4)	↑2
18	—	**Arizona** (19-6)	⤴
19	18	**New Mexico** (19-6)	⤴
20	20	**Louisville** (17-5)	
—	15	**Kansas State** (18-5)	⤵
—	19	**UTEP** (18-6)	

Week of Mar 5

AP	UPI	SCHOOL	AP↓↑
1	1	**NC State** (24-1)	
2	2	**Notre Dame** (24-1)	
3	3	**UCLA** (22-3)	
4	5	**Maryland** (21-4)	↑1
5	6	**Vanderbilt** (23-2)	↑1
6	4	**North Carolina** (21-4)	Ⓕ ↓2
7	7	**USC** (22-3)	↑3
8	8	**Providence** (25-3)	↑4
9	12	**Long Beach State** (23-2)	↑4
10	11	**South Carolina** (21-4)	↑4
11	9	**Marquette** (22-4)	↓3
12	16	**Alabama** (21-4)	↓5
13	10	**Indiana** (19-4)	↓4
14	17	**Pittsburgh** (23-3)	↓3
15	13	**Kansas** (19-5)	
16	19	**Michigan** (19-4)	↑1
17	14	**New Mexico** (20-6)	↑2
18	15	**Louisville** (19-5)	↑2
19	18	**Creighton** (21-5)	↓3
20	—	**Oral Roberts** (21-4)	⤴
—	20	**Syracuse** (19-6)	

Week of Mar 12

AP	UPI	SCHOOL	AP↓↑
1	1	**NC State** (26-1)	
2	2	**UCLA** (23-3)	↑1
3	3	**Notre Dame** (25-2)	↓1
4	4	**Maryland** (23-5)	
5	6	**Providence** (27-3)	↑3
6	7	**Vanderbilt** (23-3)	↓1
7	5	**Marquette** (23-4)	↑4
8	8	**North Carolina** (22-5)	↓2
9	11	**Long Beach State** (23-2)	
10	9	**Indiana** (20-4)	↑3
11	19	**Alabama** (22-4)	↑1
12	12	**Michigan** (20-4)	↑4
13	14	**Pittsburgh** (24-3)	↑1
14	10	**Kansas** (21-5)	↑1
15	13	**USC** (22-4)	↓8
16	15	**Louisville** (21-5)	↑2
17	18	**New Mexico** (21-6)	
18	16	**South Carolina** (22-5)	↓8
19	17	**Creighton** (22-6)	
20	19	**Dayton** (20-7)	⤴

Week of Mar 19

AP	SCHOOL	AP↓↑
1	**NC State** (28-1)	
2	**UCLA** (25-3)	
3	**Marquette** (25-4)	↑4
4	**Maryland** (23-5)	
5	**Notre Dame** (26-3)	↓2
6	**Kansas** (23-5)	↑8
7	**Michigan** (22-5)	↑5
8	**Providence** (28-4)	↓3
9	**Long Beach State** (23-2)	
10	**North Carolina** (22-6)	↓2
11	**Indiana** (21-5)	↓1
11	**Vanderbilt** (23-5)	↓5
13	**Alabama** (22-4)	↓2
14	**USC** (23-4)	↑1
15	**Pittsburgh** (25-4)	↓2
16	**Dayton** (20-9)	↑4
17	**South Carolina** (22-5)	↑1
18	**Oral Roberts** (23-5)	⤴
18	**Purdue** (18-9)	⤴
20	**New Mexico** (22-7)	↓3

FINAL POLL

AP	SCHOOL	AP↓↑
1	**NC State** (30-1)	
2	**UCLA** (26-4)	
3	**Marquette** (26-5)	
4	**Maryland** (23-5)	
5	**Notre Dame** (26-3)	
6	**Michigan** (22-5)	↑1
7	**Kansas** (23-7)	↓1
8	**Providence** (28-4)	
9	**Indiana** (23-5)	↑2
10	**Long Beach State** (23-2)	↓1
11	**Purdue** (21-9)	↑7
12	**North Carolina** (22-6)	↓2
13	**Vanderbilt** (23-5)	↓2
14	**Alabama** (22-4)	↓1
15	**Utah** (22-8)	⤴
16	**Pittsburgh** (25-4)	↓1
17	**USC** (24-5)	↓3
18	**Oral Roberts** (23-5)	
19	**South Carolina** (22-5)	↓2
20	**Dayton** (20-9)	↓4

Ⓐ Jerry Tarkanian, who never lost a home game in five years coaching Long Beach State, drops his UNLV home debut to Texas Tech, 82-76.

Ⓑ Notre Dame scores the final 12 points, ending with a jumper by Dwight Clay that gives the Irish a 71-70 victory over UCLA. The Bruins' run of 88 consecutive victories is over, a streak bookended by losses to Notre Dame in South Bend. Bill Walton, who missed the previous three games with a back injury, hits 12 of 14 from the floor but misses a potential game-winning shot in the final seconds.

Ⓒ At Pauley Pavilion, UCLA exacts revenge on Notre Dame, 94-75, to reclaim the top spot in the rankings.

Ⓓ Undefeated Division I newcomer Maryland-Eastern Shore makes its first and only poll appearance before losing to Morgan State. UMES will finish 27–2, the highest winning percentage (.931) for a team in its first D1 season.

Ⓔ UCLA drops back-to-back games at Oregon and Oregon State, both of which lose the same weekend to Pac-8 rival Southern California, which is now tied with the Bruins for first place in the conference.

Ⓕ The Tar Heels score eight in the final :17, including a 35-footer by Walter Davis that ties up the March 2 game against Duke. Fans at Carmichael Auditorium pour onto the court, mob Davis and delay the start of overtime. UNC goes on to win, 96–92.

1974 NCAA Tournament

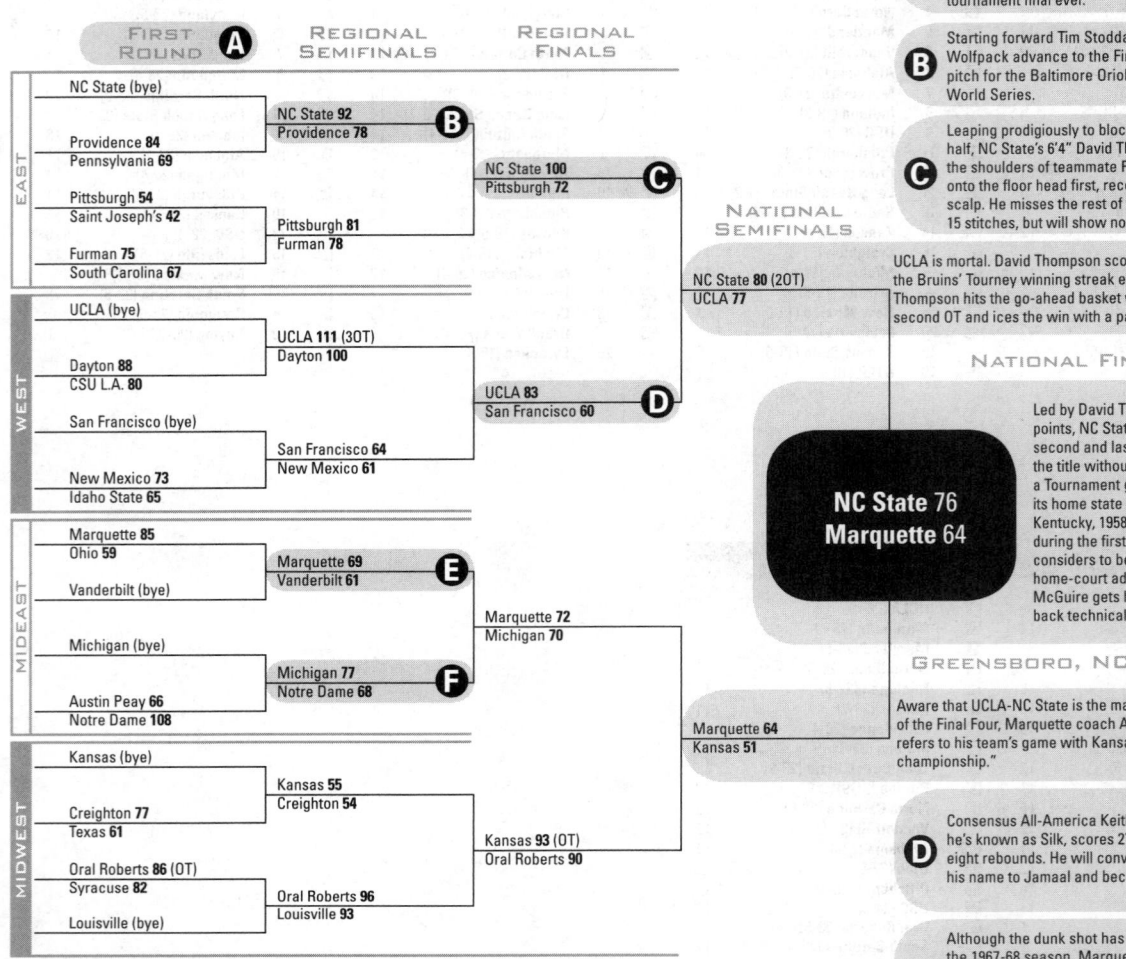

First Round (A)

East
- NC State (bye)
- Providence **84**, Pennsylvania **69**
- Pittsburgh **54**, Saint Joseph's **42**
- Furman **75**, South Carolina **67**

West
- UCLA (bye)
- Dayton **88**, CSU L.A. **80**
- San Francisco (bye)
- New Mexico **73**, Idaho State **65**

Mideast
- Marquette **85**, Ohio **59**
- Vanderbilt (bye)
- Michigan (bye)
- Austin Peay **66**, Notre Dame **108**

Midwest
- Kansas (bye)
- Creighton **77**, Texas **61**
- Oral Roberts **86** (OT), Syracuse **82**
- Louisville (bye)

Regional Semifinals

- NC State **92**, Providence **78** (B)
- Pittsburgh **81**, Furman **78**
- UCLA **111** (3OT), Dayton **100**
- San Francisco **64**, New Mexico **61**
- Marquette **69**, Vanderbilt **61** (E)
- Michigan **77**, Notre Dame **68** (F)
- Kansas **55**, Creighton **54**
- Oral Roberts **96**, Louisville **93**

Regional Finals

- NC State **100**, Pittsburgh **72** (C)
- UCLA **83**, San Francisco **60** (D)
- Marquette **72**, Michigan **70**
- Kansas **93** (OT), Oral Roberts **90**

National Semifinals

- NC State **80** (2OT), UCLA **77**
- Marquette **64**, Kansas **51**

National Final

NC State 76
Marquette 64

Greensboro, NC

National Third Place UCLA d. Kansas 78-61
East Regional Third Place Providence d. Furman 95-83
West Regional Third Place New Mexico d. Dayton 66-61
Mideast Regional Third Place Notre Dame d. Vanderbilt 118-88
Midwest Regional Third Place Creighton d. Louisville 80-71

A A great Maryland team built around Len Elmore, John Lucas and Tom McMillen misses the Big Dance after losing to NC State, 103-100, in overtime in what is considered the greatest ACC tournament final ever.

B Starting forward Tim Stoddard helps the Wolfpack advance to the Final Four. He will pitch for the Baltimore Orioles in the 1979 World Series.

C Leaping prodigiously to block a shot in the first half, NC State's 6'4" David Thompson flips over the shoulders of teammate Phil Spence and falls onto the floor head first, receiving a cut on his scalp. He misses the rest of the game and gets 15 stitches, but will show no further effects.

UCLA is mortal. David Thompson scores 28 points as the Bruins' Tourney winning streak ends at 38 games. Thompson hits the go-ahead basket with :53 left in the second OT and ices the win with a pair of free throws.

Led by David Thompson's 21 points, NC State becomes the second and last team to win the title without ever playing a Tournament game outside its home state (the other was Kentucky, 1958). Overwrought during the first half by what he considers to be the Wolfpack's home-court advantage, Al McGuire gets hit with back-to-back technicals.

Aware that UCLA-NC State is the marquee matchup of the Final Four, Marquette coach Al McGuire refers to his team's game with Kansas as "a Class B championship."

D Consensus All-America Keith Wilkes, so smooth he's known as Silk, scores 27 points and grabs eight rebounds. He will convert to Islam, change his name to Jamaal and become an NBA star.

E Although the dunk shot has been illegal since the 1967-68 season, Marquette's Bo Ellis gets away with one that increases a late lead to eight points. Protests by Vanderbilt are ultimately ignored.

F Three years after a near-fatal infection and blood clot that forced him to miss the 1971-72 season, Notre Dame co-captain John Shumate scores 34 to lead the Irish.

TOURNAMENT LEADERS

INDIVIDUAL LEADERS

SCORING

	CL	POS	G	PTS	PPG
1 **John Shumate**, Notre Dame	SO	F/C	3	86	28.7
2 **Campy Russell**, Michigan	JR	F	2	57	28.5
3 **Sam McCants**, Oral Roberts	JR	G	3	79	26.3
4 **Mike Sylvester**, Dayton	SR	F	3	76	25.3
5 **David Thompson**, NC State	JR	F	4	97	24.3
6 **Don Smith**, Dayton	SR	G	3	70	23.3
7 **Billy Knight**, Pittsburgh	SR	G/F	3	64	21.3
8 **Bruce Grimm**, Furman	FR	G	3	63	21.0
9 **Gene Harmon**, Creighton	SR	F	3	60	20.0
10 **Bill Walton**, UCLA	SR	C	4	79	19.8

MINIMUM: 2 GAMES

FIELD GOAL PCT

	CL	POS	G	FG	FGA	PCT
1 **Danny Brown**, Louisville	FR	G	2	12	16	75.0
2 **John Shumate**, Notre Dame	SO	F/C	3	35	50	70.0
3 **Bill Hagins**, New Mexico	JR	C	3	11	16	68.8
Howard Smith, San Francisco	SO	F	2	11	16	68.8
5 **Kevin Restani**, San Francisco	SR	F	2	17	25	68.0

MINIMUM: 10 MADE

FREE THROW PCT

	CL	POS	G	FT	FTA	PCT
1 **Wesley Cox**, Louisville	FR	C	2	14	14	100.0
Gene Harmon, Creighton	SR	F	3	10	10	100.0
3 **Monte Towe**, NC State	JR	G	4	22	24	91.7
4 **John Shumate**, Notre Dame	SO	F/C	3	16	18	88.9
5 **Maurice Lucas**, Marquette	JR	C	5	16	19	84.2

MINIMUM: 10 MADE

REBOUNDS PER GAME

	CL	POS	G	REB	RPG
1 **Marvin Barnes**, Providence	SR	C	3	51	17.0
2 **Campy Russell**, Michigan	JR	F	2	32	16.0
3 **Tom Burleson**, NC State	SR	C	4	61	15.3
4 **Bill Walton**, UCLA	SR	C	4	54	13.5
5 **Clyde Mayes**, Furman	JR	F	3	37	12.3

MINIMUM: 2 GAMES

TEAM LEADERS

SCORING

	G	PTS	PPG
1 **Notre Dame**	3	294	98.0
2 **Oral Roberts**	3	272	90.7
3 **UCLA**	4	349	87.3
4 **NC State**	4	348	87.0
5 **Providence**	3	257	85.7
6 **Dayton**	3	249	83.0
7 **Louisville**	2	164	82.0
8 **Furman**	3	236	78.7
9 **Vanderbilt**	2	149	74.5
10 **Michigan**	2	147	73.5

MINIMUM: 2 GAMES

FG PCT

	G	FG	FGA	PCT
1 **Notre Dame**	3	128	240	53.3
2 **Creighton**	3	92	173	53.2
3 **UCLA**	4	154	301	51.2
4 **Dayton**	3	101	200	50.5
5 **Louisville**	2	65	131	49.6

FT PCT

	G	FT	FTA	PCT
1 **San Francisco**	2	14	16	87.5
2 **Vanderbilt**	2	35	42	83.3
3 **Dayton**	3	47	59	79.7
4 **Notre Dame**	3	38	48	79.2
5 **Furman**	3	40	52	76.9

MINIMUM: 2 GAMES

REBOUNDS

	G	REB	RPG
1 **Oral Roberts**	3	139	46.3
2 **Notre Dame**	3	133	44.3
Providence	3	133	44.3
4 **NC State**	4	176	44.0
5 **UCLA**	4	168	42.0

MINIMUM: 2 GAMES

ALL-TOURNAMENT TEAM

PLAYER	CL	POS	HT	SCHOOL	RPG	PPG
David Thompson*	JR	F	6-4	NC State	7.3	24.3
Tom Burleson	SR	C	7-4	NC State	15.3	19.0
Maurice Lucas	JR	C	6-9	Marquette	12.0	16.0
Monte Towe	JR	G	5-7	NC State	3.3	15.5
Bill Walton	SR	C	6-11	UCLA	13.5	19.8

ALL-REGIONAL TEAMS

EAST

PLAYER	CL	POS	HT	SCHOOL	RPG	PPG
Tom Burleson*	SR	C	7-4	NC State	18.0	21.0
David Thompson*	JR	F	6-4	NC State	6.0	24.0
Bruce Grimm	FR	G	6-1	Furman	3.3	21.0
Billy Knight	SR	G/F	6-6	Pittsburgh	8.0	21.3
Monte Towe	JR	G	5-7	NC State	4.0	17.0

MIDEAST

PLAYER	CL	POS	HT	SCHOOL	RPG	PPG
Campy Russell*	JR	F	6-8	Michigan	16.0	28.5
Wayman Britt	SO	G	6-2	Michigan	8.0	15.0
Bo Ellis	FR	F	6-9	Marquette	9.3	15.7
Jeff Fosnes	SO	F	6-6	Vanderbilt	7.0	17.0
John Shumate	SO	F/C	6-9	Notre Dame	11.3	28.7

MIDWEST

PLAYER	CL	POS	HT	SCHOOL	RPG	PPG
Sam McCants*	JR	G	6-5	Oral Roberts	8.7	26.3
Gene Harmon	SR	F	6-7	Creighton	6.7	20.0
Danny Knight	JR	C	6-10	Kansas	4.5	10.5
Roger Morningstar	JR	F	6-6	Kansas	5.5	17.0
Allen Murphy	JR	G/F	6-5	Louisville	5.0	19.5

WEST

PLAYER	CL	POS	HT	SCHOOL	RPG	PPG
Bill Walton*	SR	C	6-11	UCLA	14.0	22.0
Dave Meyers	JR	F	6-7½	UCLA	8.0	20.0
Don Smith	SR	G	6-0	Dayton	3.7	23.3
Mike Sylvester	SR	F	6-5	Dayton	10.0	25.3
Keith Wilkes	SR	F	6-6	UCLA	7.5	20.5

* MOST OUTSTANDING PLAYER

1974 NCAA TOURNAMENT BOX SCORES

NC STATE	MIN	FG	3FG	FT	REB	A	ST	BL	PF	TP
David Thompson	40	16-29	-	8-10	10	1	4	1	2	40
Tom Burleson	31	7-19	-	2-5	24	0	0	2	3	16
Monte Towe	35	5-14	-	5-6	4	2	2	0	3	15
Morris Rivers	36	3-16	-	5-6	3	2	4	0	3	11
Steve Nuce	9	1-2	-	4-4	4	1	0	0	2	6
Tim Stoddard	29	1-6	-	0-0	3	7	1	0	4	2
Phil Spence	11	1-2	-	0-0	2	2	0	0	2	2
Mark Moeller	9	0-0	-	0-0	2	0	1	0	0	0
TOTALS	**200**	**34-88**	**-**	**24-31**	**52**	**15**	**12**	**3**	**19**	**92**
Percentages		38.6		77.4						

Coach: Norm Sloan

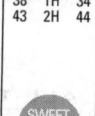

92-78

44	1H	39
48	2H	39

SWEET 16

PROVIDENCE	MIN	FG	3FG	FT	REB	A	ST	BL	PF	TP
Kevin Stacom	33	8-17	-	2-2	4	2	1	0	5	18
Bob Cooper	26	7-13	-	3-4	10	3	1	2	2	17
Marvin Barnes	39	5-14	-	4-7	13	2	0	5	5	14
Gary Bello	36	4-10	-	1-2	3	3	2	0	1	9
Joseph Hassett	18	4-11	-	0-0	1	0	1	0	2	8
Rick Santos	20	3-5	-	0-0	3	0	1	0	5	6
Mark McAndrew	13	2-2	-	0-0	0	0	0	0	2	4
Al Baker	14	1-3	-	0-1	3	0	0	0	4	2
Richard Dunphy	1	0-0	-	0-0	0	0	0	0	0	0
TOTALS	**200**	**34-75**	**-**	**10-16**	**37**	**10**	**6**	**7**	**26**	**78**
Percentages		45.3		62.5						

Coach: Dave Gavitt

Officials: Richards, Goddard
Attendance: 12,400

PITTSBURGH	MIN	FG	3FG	FT	REB	A	ST	BL	PF	TP
Bill Knight	40	12-20	-	10-11	7	2	1	0	4	34
Lewis Hill	25	6-13	-	0-2	1	0	1	0	2	12
Kirk Bruce	22	6-9	-	0-0	6	0	0	0	2	12
Mickey Martin	33	5-14	-	0-0	4	0	0	0	4	10
Tom Richards	25	3-5	-	0-0	1	2	0	0	3	6
Keith Starr	21	1-4	-	1-3	4	3	1	0	3	3
Ken Wagoner	12	1-1	-	0-0	2	1	0	0	1	2
Willie Kelly	8	1-2	-	0-0	2	0	0	2	2	2
James Bolla	14	0-1	-	0-0	0	0	0	0	0	0
TOTALS	**200**	**35-69**	**-**	**11-16**	**27**	**8**	**3**	**2**	**21**	**81**
Percentages		50.7		68.8						

Coach: Charles "Buzz" Ridl

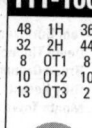

81-78

38	1H	34
43	2H	44

SWEET 16

FURMAN	MIN	FG	3FG	FT	REB	A	ST	BL	PF	TP
Bruce Grimm	38	9-18	-	9-11	6	3	1	0	4	27
Fessor Leonard	33	7-13	-	3-3	5	1	0	0	5	17
Clyde Mayes	40	6-11	-	0-1	8	3	1	1	2	12
Ed Kelley	31	3-7	-	3-4	0	3	2	0	4	9
Craig Lynch	28	3-6	-	0-0	4	2	0	1	2	6
Baron Hill	10	1-2	-	2-2	1	0	0	0	1	4
Bud Bierly	17	1-3	-	1-1	4	0	2	0	4	3
Gary Clark	2	0-0	-	0-0	0	0	0	0	0	0
Mike Hall	1	0-0	-	0-0	0	0	0	0	0	0
TOTALS	**200**	**30-60**	**-**	**18-22**	**28**	**12**	**6**	**2**	**22**	**78**
Percentages		50.0		81.8						

Coach: Joe Williams

Officials: Bain, Galvan
Attendance: 12,400

UCLA	MIN	FG	3FG	FT	REB	A	ST	BL	PF	TP
Dave Meyers	-	13-25	-	2-4	14	-	-	-	5	28
Bill Walton	-	13-23	-	1-3	19	-	-	-	2	27
Marques Johnson	-	5-8	-	4-5	5	-	-	-	2	14
Keith Wilkes	-	7-15	-	0-1	7	-	-	-	5	14
Greg Lee	-	6-10	-	0-0	3	-	-	-	3	12
Andre McCarter	-	4-8	-	2-3	1	-	-	-	2	10
Pete Trgovich	-	2-6	-	0-0	0	-	-	-	2	4
Gary Franklin	-	1-1	-	0-1	0	-	-	-	1	2
Tommy Curtis	-	0-0	-	0-0	0	-	-	-	1	0
Richard Washington	-	0-1	-	0-1	1	-	-	-	0	0
TOTALS	**-**	**51-97**	**-**	**9-18**	**50**	**-**	**-**	**-**	**23**	**111**
Percentages		52.6		50.0						

Coach: John Wooden

111-100

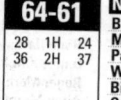

48	1H	36
32	2H	44
8	OT1	8
10	OT2	10
13	OT3	2

SWEET 16

DAYTON	MIN	FG	3FG	FT	REB	A	ST	BL	PF	TP
Mike Sylvester	-	12-21	-	12-13	13	-	-	-	4	36
Donald Smith	-	12-23	-	2-2	4	-	-	-	2	26
Johnny Davis	-	7-13	-	3-7	4	-	-	-	4	17
Joe Fisher	-	6-6	-	3-3	5	-	-	-	4	15
Allen Elijah	-	1-4	-	0-0	4	-	-	-	4	2
Jim Testerman	-	1-3	-	0-0	3	-	-	-	4	2
John VonLehman	-	1-4	-	0-0	0	-	-	-	1	2
TOTALS	**-**	**40-74**	**-**	**20-25**	**33**	**-**	**-**	**-**	**23**	**100**
Percentages		54.1		80.0						

Coach: Don Donoher

Officials: Copeland, Stout
Attendance: 13,314

SAN FRANCISCO	MIN	FG	3FG	FT	REB	A	ST	BL	PF	TP
Howard Smith	-	8-12	-	2-2	3	-	-	-	0	18
Kevin Restani	-	7-12	-	0-0	4	-	-	-	2	14
Jeff Randell	-	3-9	-	2-2	6	-	-	-	3	8
Eric Fernsten	-	3-5	-	1-1	3	-	-	-	3	7
Phil Smith	-	3-13	-	1-2	1	-	-	-	2	7
John Boro	-	1-1	-	2-2	3	-	-	-	2	4
Russ Coleman	-	2-3	-	0-0	1	-	-	-	5	4
Brad Quanstrom	-	1-1	-	0-0	1	-	-	-	1	2
TOTALS	**-**	**28-56**	**-**	**8-9**	**22**	**-**	**-**	**-**	**18**	**64**
Percentages		50.0		88.9						

Coach: Bob Gaillard

64-61

28	1H	24
36	2H	37

SWEET 16

NEW MEXICO	MIN	FG	3FG	FT	REB	A	ST	BL	PF	TP
Bernard Hardin	-	7-14	-	2-3	7	-	-	-	3	16
Mark Saiers	-	6-7	-	0-0	5	-	-	-	3	12
Pat King	-	3-3	-	4-4	1	-	-	-	2	10
Wendell Taylor	-	4-8	-	2-2	2	-	-	-	0	10
Bill Hagins	-	4-6	-	1-2	4	-	-	-	0	9
Gabe Nava	-	2-8	-	0-0	2	-	-	-	3	4
Bruce Battle	-	0-1	-	0-0	1	-	-	-	0	0
Mike Patterson	-	0-0	-	0-0	1	-	-	-	1	0
Rich Pokorski	-	0-1	-	0-0	0	-	-	-	0	0
Bob Toppert	-	0-1	-	0-0	0	-	-	-	0	0
TOTALS	**-**	**26-49**	**-**	**9-11**	**23**	**-**	**-**	**-**	**12**	**61**
Percentages		53.1		81.8						

Coach: Norm Ellenberger

Officials: Wortman, Weiler
Attendance: 13,314

MARQUETTE	MIN	FG	3FG	FT	REB	A	ST	BL	PF	TP
Bo Ellis	35	7-10	-	2-2	9	1	1	1	2	16
Maurice Lucas	39	5-18	-	5-6	11	3	0	1	1	15
Lloyd Walton	39	5-5	-	4-4	2	4	0	0	3	14
Earl Tatum	23	7-10	-	0-0	5	1	1	2	5	14
Ed Daniels	12	2-3	-	2-2	0	0	1	0	2	6
Marcus Washington	23	2-6	-	0-0	3	0	0	0	2	4
Rick Campbell	20	0-0	-	0-0	3	1	0	0	2	0
Dave Delsman	5	0-2	-	0-0	1	1	0	0	1	0
John Bryant	1	0-0	-	0-0	0	0	0	0	0	0
Jerry Homan	1	0-0	-	0-0	0	0	0	0	0	0
Greg Johnson	1	0-0	-	0-0	0	0	0	0	0	0
Paul Vollmer	1	0-0	-	0-0	0	0	0	0	0	0
TOTALS	**200**	**28-54**	**-**	**13-14**	**34**	**11**	**3**	**4**	**18**	**69**
Percentages		51.9		92.9						

Coach: Al McGuire

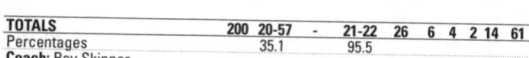

69-61

40	1H	30
29	2H	31

SWEET 16

VANDERBILT	MIN	FG	3FG	FT	REB	A	ST	BL	PF	TP
Jeff Fosnes	39	6-15	-	2-2	4	0	2	1	2	14
Joe Ford	40	5-8	-	3-4	1	3	0	0	2	13
Terry Compton	34	4-13	-	4-4	5	0	1	0	2	12
Butch Feher	37	3-12	-	4-4	4	0	1	0	2	10
Jan van Breda Kolff	40	2-5	-	4-4	10	3	0	1	3	8
Lee Fowler	7	0-2	-	4-4	0	0	0	0	3	4
Bill Ligon	3	0-2	-	0-0	2	0	0	0	0	0
TOTALS	**200**	**20-57**	**-**	**21-22**	**26**	**6**	**4**	**2**	**14**	**61**
Percentages		35.1		95.5						

Coach: Roy Skinner

MICHIGAN	MIN	FG	3FG	FT	REB	A	ST	BL	PF	TP
Campy Russell	40	16-32	-	4-7	18	1	0	0	1	36
Wayman Britt	39	9-16	-	0-2	7	4	1	2	5	18
C.J. Kupec	36	5-16	-	2-2	8	4	0	0	5	12
Joe Johnson	40	1-5	-	3-4	2	2	3	0	1	5
Steve Grote	30	2-7	-	0-0	4	1	1	0	5	4
Lionel Worrell	10	0-1	-	1-2	2	0	0	0	1	1
Charles Rogers	4	0-0	-	1-2	2	0	0	0	1	1
John Whitten	1	0-0	-	0-0	0	0	0	0	0	0
TOTALS	**200**	**33-77**	**-**	**11-19**	**43**	**12**	**5**	**2**	**19**	**77**
Percentages		42.9		57.9						

Coach: Johnny Orr

77-68

34	1H	29
43	2H	39

SWEET 16

NOTRE DAME	MIN	FG	3FG	FT	REB	A	ST	BL	PF	TP
John Shumate	40	14-22	-	6-8	17	2	2	0	3	34
Gary Novak	33	5-15	-	1-2	12	1	0	1	3	11
Gary Brokaw	40	4-16	-	2-4	3	3	3	0	3	10
Dwight Clay	39	3-10	-	0-0	2	8	0	0	4	6
Bill Paterno	13	2-5	-	1-2	4	1	0	0	3	5
Adrian Dantley	27	1-7	-	0-0	6	0	0	1	3	2
Ray Martin	8	0-0	-	0-0	0	0	0	0	2	0
TOTALS	**200**	**29-75**	**-**	**10-16**	**44**	**15**	**5**	**2**	**21**	**68**
Percentages		38.7		62.5						

Coach: Digger Phelps

55-54 (Sweet 16)

30	1H	33
25	2H	21

KANSAS	MIN	FG	3FG	FT	REB	A	ST	BL	PF	TP
Roger Morningstar	-	9-19	-	0-0	5	1	-	-	3	18
Norman Cook	-	4-7	-	3-4	7	3	-	-	1	11
Richard Suttle	-	5-13	-	0-0	6	0	-	-	2	10
Tom Kivisto	-	2-8	-	2-2	3	10	-	-	3	6
Dale Greenlee	-	2-8	-	0-1	4	3	-	-	1	4
Tommie Smith	-	2-3	-	0-0	1	0	-	-	1	4
Danny Knight	-	1-4	-	0-0	1	2	-	-	0	2
TOTALS	-	25-62	-	5-7	27	19	-	-	11	55
Percentages		40.3		71.4						

Coach: Ted Owens

CREIGHTON	MIN	FG	3FG	FT	REB	A	ST	BL	PF	TP
Gene Harmon	-	7-13	-	2-2	6	4	-	-	0	16
Doug Brookins	-	5-14	-	0-0	15	2	-	-	0	10
Ralph Bobik	-	2-7	-	4-5	1	0	-	-	2	8
Ted Weubben	-	3-7	-	0-1	3	1	-	-	5	6
Tom Anderson	-	2-2	-	0-0	1	1	-	-	0	4
Charles Butler	-	2-2	-	0-0	2	0	-	-	1	4
Mike Heck	-	2-3	-	0-0	1	0	-	-	2	4
Richie Smith	-	1-1	-	0-0	0	1	-	-	0	2
TOTALS	-	24-49	-	6-8	29	9	-	-	10	54
Percentages		49.0		75.0						

Coach: Eddie Sutton

Officials: Crowley, Folsom
Attendance: 10,575

96-93 (Sweet 16)

51	1H	51
45	2H	42

ORAL ROBERTS	MIN	FG	3FG	FT	REB	A	ST	BL	PF	TP
Sam McCants	-	11-33	-	8-10	8	10	-	-	0	30
Al Boswell	-	10-26	-	3-5	9	3	-	-	4	23
Greg McDougald	-	7-16	-	0-0	9	1	-	-	4	14
Anthony Roberts	-	6-12	-	2-2	14	0	-	-	1	14
Eddie Woods	-	6-9	-	1-2	6	0	-	-	5	13
Willis Collins	-	1-2	-	0-0	1	0	-	-	1	2
Duane Fox	-	0-1	-	0-0	1	0	-	-	4	0
TOTALS	-	41-99	-	14-19	48	14	-	-	19	96
Percentages		41.4		73.7						

Coach: Ken Trickey

LOUISVILLE	MIN	FG	3FG	FT	REB	A	ST	BL	PF	TP
Allen Murphy	-	12-21	-	2-2	10	2	-	-	4	26
Wesley Cox	-	5-13	-	12-12	9	3	-	-	1	22
Danny Brown	-	7-10	-	0-0	3	3	-	-	2	14
Bill Butler	-	5-7	-	1-2	7	2	-	-	2	11
Ike Whitfield	-	4-6	-	1-4	2	0	-	-	2	9
Terry Howard	-	3-7	-	1-2	1	0	-	-	2	7
Junior Bridgeman	-	1-5	-	2-4	3	0	-	-	5	4
Stanley Bunton	-	0-0	-	0-0	0	0	-	-	0	0
Bill Harmon	-	0-0	-	0-0	0	0	-	-	0	0
TOTALS	-	37-69	-	19-26	35	10	-	-	18	93
Percentages		53.6		73.1						

Coach: Denny Crum

100-72 (Elite 8)

47	1H	41
53	2H	31

NC STATE	MIN	FG	3FG	FT	REB	A	ST	BL	PF	TP
Tom Burleson	31	9-19	-	8-8	12	0	1	3	4	26
Monte Towe	36	6-17	-	7-7	4	6	3	0	2	19
Morris Rivers	37	8-12	-	1-4	8	3	1	0	2	17
Phil Spence	31	4-10	-	2-3	14	4	1	0	3	10
David Thompson	10	3-4	-	2-3	2	0	0	0	0	8
Tim Stoddard	22	3-9	-	1-2	6	1	1	0	3	7
Greg Hawkins	12	1-4	-	5-6	1	1	0	0	2	7
Steve Nuce	12	1-4	-	2-2	2	1	0	0	2	4
Bill Lake	1	0-0	-	2-2	0	0	0	0	0	2
Mark Moeller	4	0-0	-	0-0	0	0	0	0	0	0
Mike Buurma	1	0-0	-	0-0	0	0	0	0	0	0
Bruce Dayhuff	1	0-0	-	0-0	0	0	0	0	0	0
Dwight Johnson	1	0-0	-	0-0	0	0	0	0	0	0
Craig Kuszmaul	1	0-0	-	0-0	0	0	0	0	0	0
TOTALS	200	35-79	-	30-37	49	16	7	3	18	100
Percentages		44.3		81.1						

Coach: Norm Sloan

PITTSBURGH	MIN	FG	3FG	FT	REB	A	ST	BL	PF	TP
Bill Knight	39	9-19	-	1-2	10	4	0	1	2	19
Mickey Martin	36	6-13	-	0-0	2	0	0	0	3	12
Tom Richards	26	3-7	-	4-4	2	1	0	0	3	10
Lewis Hill	24	5-12	-	0-1	3	0	0	0	3	10
Keith Starr	17	2-7	-	0-0	2	0	0	0	1	4
James Bolla	6	2-3	-	0-0	0	0	0	0	2	4
Marvin Abrams	3	2-3	-	0-0	1	0	1	0	2	4
Kirk Bruce	21	0-5	-	3-4	1	1	0	0	3	3
Willie Kelly	10	1-3	-	1-2	2	0	0	0	4	3
Sam Fleming	5	1-1	-	1-3	1	0	0	0	1	3
Ken Wagoner	8	0-0	-	0-0	0	1	0	0	5	0
Bob Shrewsbury	3	0-2	-	0-0	0	1	1	0	1	0
Mark Disco	1	0-0	-	0-0	2	0	0	0	1	0
Greg McBride	1	0-1	-	0-0	0	0	0	0	0	0
TOTALS	200	31-76	-	10-16	26	8	2	1	31	72
Percentages		40.8		62.5						

Coach: Charles "Buzz" Ridl

Officials: Bain, Galvan
Technicals: NC State (Stoddard), Pittsburgh (Bruce)
Attendance: 12,400

83-60 (Elite 8)

35	1H	23
48	2H	37

UCLA	MIN	FG	3FG	FT	REB	A	ST	BL	PF	TP
Keith Wilkes	34	13-28	-	1-1	8	3	-	-	0	27
Bill Walton	36	7-12	-	3-5	9	4	-	-	3	17
Dave Meyers	25	6-11	-	0-0	2	1	-	-	3	12
Greg Lee	35	3-6	-	2-2	4	5	-	-	0	8
Tommy Curtis	24	3-7	-	0-0	2	0	-	-	0	6
Marques Johnson	14	2-3	-	1-2	5	0	-	-	1	5
Richard Washington	3	2-2	-	0-0	1	0	-	-	1	4
Andre McCarter	14	1-2	-	0-1	2	2	-	-	2	2
Gary Franklin	4	1-1	-	0-0	0	0	-	-	0	2
Ralph Drollinger	4	0-2	-	0-0	2	1	-	-	0	0
Pete Trgovich	4	0-0	-	0-0	1	1	-	-	0	0
Bob Webb	3	0-0	-	0-0	1	0	-	-	0	0
TOTALS	200	38-74	-	7-11	37	17	-	-	10	83
Percentages		51.4		63.6						

Coach: John Wooden

SAN FRANCISCO	MIN	FG	3FG	FT	REB	A	ST	BL	PF	TP
Kevin Restani	37	10-13	-	0-0	7	0	-	-	1	20
Phil Smith	37	9-20	-	0-0	4	3	-	-	3	18
Howard Smith	25	3-4	-	3-3	3	0	-	-	5	9
Brad Quanstrom	7	3-4	-	0-0	2	1	-	-	0	6
Eric Fernsten	28	1-3	-	1-2	5	0	-	-	5	3
Jeff Randell	29	0-6	-	2-2	7	0	-	-	3	2
Marlon Redmond	4	1-3	-	0-0	0	0	-	-	0	2
Russ Coleman	17	0-2	-	0-0	1	2	-	-	1	0
John Boro	12	0-3	-	0-0	1	3	-	-	1	0
Tony Styles	4	0-2	-	0-0	1	0	-	-	0	0
TOTALS	200	27-60	-	6-7	31	9	-	-	19	60
Percentages		45.0		85.7						

Coach: Bob Gaillard

Officials: Weiler, Copeland
Attendance: 13,314

72-70 (Elite 8)

37	1H	39
35	2H	31

MARQUETTE	MIN	FG	3FG	FT	REB	A	ST	BL	PF	TP
Marcus Washington	27	7-16	-	3-5	2	0	2	0	3	17
Bo Ellis	38	6-10	-	3-4	10	1	0	2	2	15
Lloyd Walton	37	6-10	-	1-2	2	2	2	0	4	13
Earl Tatum	31	4-8	-	0-2	5	1	2	2	2	8
Maurice Lucas	29	4-10	-	0-0	7	0	0	0	5	8
Jerry Homan	18	1-4	-	2-2	7	0	0	0	2	4
Dave Delsman	7	0-0	-	4-4	1	0	0	0	1	4
Rick Campbell	9	1-1	-	1-1	0	1	0	0	2	3
Ed Daniels	4	0-0	-	0-0	0	0	1	0	0	0
TOTALS	200	29-59	-	14-20	34	5	7	4	21	72
Percentages		49.2		70.0						

Coach: Al McGuire

MICHIGAN	MIN	FG	3FG	FT	REB	A	ST	BL	PF	TP
Campy Russell	40	7-18	-	7-9	14	0	0	1	3	21
Steve Grote	32	5-13	-	5-6	3	1	1	0	5	15
Wayman Britt	40	5-15	-	2-2	9	6	1	0	4	12
C.J. Kupec	40	3-10	-	6-8	7	1	0	1	3	12
Joe Johnson	40	4-8	-	0-0	1	6	1	0	1	8
Lionel Worrell	8	0-0	-	2-2	2	1	0	0	2	2
TOTALS	200	24-64	-	22-27	36	15	3	2	18	70
Percentages		37.5		81.5						

Coach: Johnny Orr

Technicals: Marquette (coach McGuire, 2)

93-90 (Elite 8)

45	1H	44
36	2H	37
12	OT1	9

KANSAS	MIN	FG	3FG	FT	REB	A	ST	BL	PF	TP
Danny Knight	-	9-16	-	1-2	8	1	0	1	4	19
Dale Greenlee	-	8-14	-	2-2	2	8	0	0	3	18
Roger Morningstar	-	6-8	-	4-5	6	1	0	0	4	16
Tom Kivisto	-	5-12	-	3-4	1	10	1	0	3	13
Richard Suttle	-	5-10	-	2-2	6	2	0	1	4	12
Norman Cook	-	5-7	-	0-1	7	3	0	1	2	10
Tommie Smith	-	2-6	-	1-2	5	3	0	0	1	5
TOTALS	-	40-73	-	13-18	35	28	1	3	21	93
Percentages		54.8		72.2						

Coach: Ted Owens

ORAL ROBERTS	MIN	FG	3FG	FT	REB	A	ST	BL	PF	TP
Sam McCants	-	8-24	-	8-11	10	7	-	-	2	24
Al Boswell	-	7-23	-	4-4	3	6	-	-	4	18
Greg McDougald	-	5-11	-	3-4	6	1	-	-	4	13
Anthony Roberts	-	6-9	-	0-0	6	2	-	-	0	12
Eddie Woods	-	4-7	-	3-5	6	0	-	-	5	11
Duane Fox	-	4-8	-	0-0	5	1	-	-	4	8
Willis Collins	-	2-6	-	0-0	7	0	-	-	3	4
TOTALS	-	36-88	-	18-24	43	17	-	-	22	90
Percentages		40.9		75.0						

Coach: Ken Trickey

Officials: Howell, Nichols
Technicals: Kansas (bench)
Attendance: 10,575

80-77

	1H	2H	OT1	OT2
NC State	35	30	2	13
UCLA	35	30	2	10

FINAL 4

NC STATE	MIN	FG	3FG	FT	REB	A	ST	BL	PF	TP
David Thompson	45	12-25	-	4-6	10	2	1	2	3	28
Tom Burleson	42	9-20	-	2-6	14	0	2	2	4	20
Monte Towe	50	4-10	-	4-4	2	3	2	0	4	12
Tim Stoddard	41	4-11	-	1-2	9	5	3	0	5	9
Morris Rivers	50	3-8	-	1-2	2	4	0	0	3	7
Phil Spence	19	2-3	-	0-0	5	1	0	0	0	4
Greg Hawkins	3	0-0	-	0-0	0	0	0	0	0	0
TOTALS	**250**	**34-77**	**-**	**12-20**	**42**	**15**	**8**	**4**	**19**	**80**
Percentages		44.2		60.0						

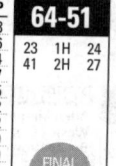

Coach: Norm Sloan

UCLA	MIN	FG	3FG	FT	REB	A	ST	BL	PF	TP
Bill Walton	50	13-21	-	3-3	18	4	0	-	2	29
Keith Wilkes	49	5-17	-	5-5	7	0	0	-	5	15
Dave Meyers	42	6-9	-	0-1	8	1	1	-	4	12
Tommy Curtis	45	4-8	-	3-4	5	2	1	-	5	11
Greg Lee	50	4-11	-	0-0	4	10	2	-	2	8
Andre McCarter	5	1-2	-	0-0	0	0	0	-	0	2
Marques Johnson	9	0-3	-	0-0	0	0	0	-	0	0
TOTALS	**250**	**33-71**	**-**	**11-13**	**42**	**17**	**4**	**-**	**18**	**77**
Percentages		46.5		84.6						

Coach: John Wooden

Officials: Weil. Galvan
Attendance: 15,829

64-51

	1H	2H
Marquette	23	41
Kansas	24	27

FINAL 4

MARQUETTE	MIN	FG	3FG	FT	REB	A	ST	BL	PF	TP
Maurice Lucas	36	7-11	-	4-4	14	2	1	4	2	18
Marcus Washington	32	5-12	-	6-11	3	1	2	0	4	16
Earl Tatum	33	5-11	-	4-6	3	0	1	0	3	14
Lloyd Walton	22	2-7	-	3-4	1	7	2	0	4	7
Bo Ellis	39	2-9	-	1-2	10	0	2	1	3	5
Dave Delsman	9	0-1	-	2-2	0	1	0	0	1	2
Jerry Homan	7	1-2	-	0-0	0	0	0	0	2	2
Ed Daniels	14	0-2	-	0-0	0	3	1	0	1	0
Rick Campbell	6	0-1	-	0-0	1	1	0	0	0	0
Barry Brennan	0	0-0	-	0-0	0	0	0	0	0	0
John Bryant	0	0-0	-	0-0	0	0	0	0	0	0
Greg Johnson	0	0-0	-	0-0	0	0	0	0	0	0
Paul Vollmer	0	0-0	-	0-0	0	0	0	0	0	0
TOTALS	**198**	**22-56**	**-**	**20-29**	**32**	**15**	**9**	**5**	**20**	**64**
Percentages		39.3		69.0						

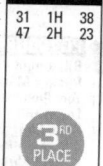

Coach: Al McGuire

KANSAS	MIN	FG	3FG	FT	REB	A	ST	BL	PF	TP
Richard Suttle	28	8-13	-	3-4	9	1	0	4	2	19
Roger Morningstar	40	5-13	-	0-0	5	2	0	0	4	10
Tom Kivisto	40	2-7	-	2-5	2	9	1	0	4	6
Dale Greenlee	34	3-7	-	0-0	3	0	0	0	4	6
Tommie Smith	13	3-4	-	0-0	4	1	1	0	3	6
Norman Cook	35	1-3	-	2-4	5	1	1	0	5	4
Danny Knight	10	0-5	-	0-0	5	1	0	0	3	0
TOTALS	**200**	**22-52**	**-**	**7-13**	**33**	**15**	**3**	**4**	**25**	**51**
Percentages		42.3		53.8						

Coach: Ted Owens

Officials: Brown Howell
Attendance: 15,829

78-61

	1H	2H
UCLA	31	47
Kansas	38	23

3RD PLACE

UCLA	MIN	FG	3FG	FT	REB	A	ST	BL	PF	TP
Pete Trgovich	30	6-9	-	2-2	2	2	0	1	1	14
Keith Wilkes	20	6-10	-	0-0	5	1	3	0	0	12
Bob Webb	11	4-7	-	2-2	0	0	0	0	1	10
Richard Washington	18	4-6	-	0-1	5	1	0	1	1	8
Dave Meyers	14	3-5	-	2-2	1	1	0	0	3	8
Ralph Drollinger	21	1-6	-	5-8	6	2	0	1	4	7
Bill Walton	20	3-3	-	0-3	8	4	0	2	1	6
Andre McCarter	24	1-4	-	2-2	4	6	1	0	1	4
Marques Johnson	10	2-3	-	0-2	2	1	0	0	0	4
Gary Franklin	13	1-2	-	0-0	3	1	0	0	1	2
Wilbert Olinde	5	1-1	-	0-0	2	0	0	0	0	2
Jim Spillane	6	0-1	-	1-2	1	1	1	0	2	1
Tommy Curtis	4	0-0	-	0-0	0	0	0	0	0	0
Greg Lee	4	0-2	-	0-0	0	0	0	0	2	0
TOTALS	**200**	**32-59**	**-**	**14-24**	**39**	**20**	**5**	**5**	**17**	**78**
Percentages		54.2		58.3						

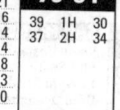

Coach: John Wooden

KANSAS	MIN	FG	3FG	FT	REB	A	ST	BL	PF	TP
Dale Greenlee	23	7-12	-	3-3	3	2	1	-	2	17
Danny Knight	26	5-10	-	2-2	5	1	0	-	2	12
Norman Cook	34	3-11	-	3-4	8	1	1	-	4	9
Tom Kivisto	38	2-5	-	4-5	3	5	2	-	3	8
Tommie Smith	19	3-7	-	0-0	4	0	0	-	4	6
Richard Suttle	22	2-11	-	0-0	7	0	0	-	5	4
Roger Morningstar	33	1-7	-	1-2	6	2	1	-	4	3
David Taynor	2	1-4	-	0-0	0	0	0	-	0	2
Donnie Von Moore	3	0-2	-	0-0	2	0	0	-	0	0
TOTALS	**200**	**24-69**	**-**	**13-16**	**38**	**11**	**5**	**-**	**24**	**61**
Percentages		34.8		81.2						

Coach: Ted Owens

Officials: Weiler, Galvan
Technicals: UCLA (Drollinger)
Attendance: 15,742

76-64

	1H	2H
NC State	39	37
Marquette	30	34

NCAA FINAL 1974

NC STATE	MIN	FG	3FG	FT	REB	A	ST	BL	PF	TP
David Thompson	40	7-12	-	7-8	7	2	3	1	3	21
Monte Towe	38	5-10	-	6-7	3	2	1	0	1	16
Morris Rivers	40	4-9	-	6-9	2	5	3	0	2	14
Tom Burleson	36	6-9	-	2-6	11	0	1	7	4	14
Tim Stoddard	26	3-4	-	2-2	7	2	3	0	5	8
Phil Spence	18	1-2	-	1-2	3	3	1	0	2	3
Mark Moeller	2	0-0	-	0-0	0	0	0	0	0	0
TOTALS	**200**	**26-46**	**-**	**24-34**	**33**	**14**	**12**	**8**	**17**	**76**
Percentages		56.5		70.6						

Coach: Norm Sloan

MARQUETTE	MIN	FG	3FG	FT	REB	A	ST	BL	PF	TP
Maurice Lucas	40	7-13	-	7-9	13	0	0	1	4	21
Bo Ellis	39	6-16	-	0-0	11	1	3	0	5	12
Marcus Washington	35	3-13	-	5-8	4	0	5	0	3	11
Lloyd Walton	25	4-10	-	0-0	2	2	0	0	2	8
Earl Tatum	20	2-7	-	0-0	3	1	0	1	4	4
Rick Campbell	12	2-3	-	0-0	1	0	1	0	3	4
Ed Daniels	17	1-3	-	1-2	0	2	0	0	3	3
Jerry Homan	6	0-4	-	1-2	6	1	0	1	2	1
Dave Delsman	5	0-0	-	0-0	0	0	0	0	2	0
Barry Brennan	1	0-0	-	0-0	0	0	0	0	1	0
TOTALS	**200**	**25-69**	**-**	**14-21**	**40**	**7**	**9**	**3**	**29**	**64**
Percentages		36.2		66.7						

Coach: Al McGuire

Officials: Howell, Brown
Technicals: Marquette (coach McGuire, 2)
Attendance: 15,742

National Invitation Tournament (NIT)

First Round: UMES d. Manhattan 84-81, Jacksonville d. Massachusetts 73-69, Hawaii d. Fairfield 66-65, Purdue d. North Carolina 82-71, Memphis d. Seton Hall 73-72, Utah d. Rutgers 102-89, Connecticut d. St. John's 82-70, Boston College d. Cincinnati 63-62

Quarterfinals: Jacksonville d. UMES 85-83, Purdue d. Hawaii 85-72, Utah d. Memphis 92-78, Boston College d. Connecticut 76-75

Semifinals: Purdue d. Jacksonville 78-63, Utah d. Boston College 117-93,

Third place: Boston College d. Jacksonville 87-77

Championship: Purdue d. Utah 87-81

MVP: Mike Sojourner, Utah

1974-75: Wooden's Finale

UCLA reclaimed the national title in 1975—the Bruins' 10th championship in 12 years. In their national semifinal, UCLA (28–3) needed overtime against Louisville, coached by former John Wooden assistant Denny Crum. Holding a one-point lead with :20 left, Cardinals reserve Terry Howard missed the front end of a one-and-one, setting up a 12-footer by Richard Washington that gave UCLA a 75-74 win. (Louisville's 37-33 halftime lead was the only intermission deficit the Bruins faced in 20 Final Four games during their 10 championship runs.) After the game, the 64-year-old Wooden announced that he would retire after the Final against Kentucky. The Bruins responded by sending the Wizard of Westwood out in style. In the title game, UCLA downed Joe B. Hall's Wildcats, 92-85, at the San Diego Sports Arena (despite 34 points from UK's Kevin Grevey) using a tight rotation of six players—four of whom scored in double figures, led by Richard Washington's 28 and Dave Meyers' 24. In 27 seasons at UCLA, Wooden went 620–147 overall and 21–3 in Final Four games. UCLA won all but two of its 151 games at Pauley Pavilion during his reign. NC State's David Thompson was named the Naismith National Player of the Year.

Major Conference Standings

ACC

	Conference			Overall		
	W	L	Pct	W	L	Pct
Maryland○	10	2	.833	24	5	.828
NC State	8	4	.667	22	6	.786
North Carolina⊕	8	4	.667	23	8	.742
Clemson□	8	4	.667	17	11	.607
Virginia	4	8	.333	12	13	.480
Duke	2	10	.167	13	13	.500
Wake Forest	2	10	.167	13	13	.500

Tournament: **North Carolina d. NC State 70-66**
Tournament MVP: **Phil Ford**, North Carolina

BIG EIGHT

	Conference			Overall		
	W	L	Pct	W	L	Pct
Kansas⊕	11	3	.786	19	8	.704
Kansas State○	10	4	.714	20	9	.690
Missouri	9	5	.643	18	9	.667
Nebraska	7	7	.500	14	12	.538
Oklahoma	6	8	.429	13	13	.500
Oklahoma State	5	9	.357	10	16	.385
Iowa State	4	10	.286	10	16	.385
Colorado	4	10	.286	7	19	.269

BIG SKY

	Conference			Overall		
	W	L	Pct	W	L	Pct
Montana⊕	13	1	.929	19	8	.704
Idaho State	9	5	.643	16	10	.615
Boise State	7	7	.500	13	13	.500
Gonzaga	7	7	.500	13	13	.500
Weber State	6	8	.429	11	15	.423
Montana State	5	9	.357	11	15	.423
Northern Arizona	5	9	.357	9	17	.346
Idaho	4	10	.286	10	16	.385

BIG TEN

	Conference			Overall		
	W	L	Pct	W	L	Pct
Indiana⊕	18	0	1.000	31	1	.969
Michigan○	12	6	.667	19	8	.704
Minnesota	11	7	.611	18	8	.692
Purdue	11	7	.611	17	11	.607
Michigan State	10	8	.556	17	9	.654
Ohio State	8	10	.444	14	14	.500
Iowa	7	11	.389	10	16	.385
Wisconsin	5	13	.278	8	18	.308
Illinois	4	14	.222	8	18	.308
Northwestern	4	14	.222	6	20	.231

EAST COAST

	Conference			Overall		
	W	L	Pct	W	L	Pct
Eastern Section						
La Salle⊕	5	1	.833	22	7	.759
American	5	1	.833	16	10	.615
Temple	4	2	.667	7	19	.269
Hofstra	3	3	.500	11	13	.458
Saint Joseph's	3	3	.500	8	17	.320
West Chester	1	5	.167	8	17	.320
Drexel	0	6	.000	12	11	.522
Western Section						
Lafayette□	7	1	.875	22	6	.786
Rider	5	3	.625	16	11	.593
Bucknell	4	4	.500	14	12	.538
Delaware	4	4	.500	12	13	.480
Lehigh	0	8	.000	1	23	.042

Tournament: **La Salle d. Lafayette 92-85**

IVY

	Conference			Overall		
	W	L	Pct	W	L	Pct
Penn⊕	13	1	.929	23	5	.821
Princeton□	12	2	.857	22	8	.733
Brown	9	5	.643	14	12	.538
Harvard	9	5	.643	12	13	.480
Dartmouth	5	9	.357	8	18	.308
Cornell	4	10	.286	7	18	.280
Columbia	2	12	.143	4	22	.154
Yale	2	12	.143	3	20	.130

MID-AMERICAN

	Conference			Overall		
	W	L	Pct	W	L	Pct
Central Michigan⊕	10	4	.714	22	6	.786
Toledo	9	5	.643	17	9	.654
Bowling Green	9	5	.643	18	10	.643
Miami (OH)	8	5	.615	19	7	.731
Western Michigan	8	6	.571	16	10	.615
Eastern Michigan	4	9	.308	12	14	.462
Ohio	4	10	.286	12	14	.462
Kent State	3	11	.214	6	20	.231

MEAC

	Conference			Overall		
	W	L	Pct	W	L	Pct
NC A&T	10	2	.833	18	7	.720
Morgan State	8	4	.667	19	10	.655
Delaware State	7	5	.583	15	9	.625
South Carolina St.	7	5	.583	14	11	.560
Howard	6	6	.500	13	13	.500
NC Central	4	8	.333	10	16	.385
UMES	0	12	.000	2	24	.077

Tournament: **NC A&T d. Morgan State 83-77**
Tournament MOP: **Marvin Webster**, Morgan State

MISSOURI VALLEY

	Conference			Overall		
	W	L	Pct	W	L	Pct
Louisville⊕	12	2	.857	28	3	.903
New Mexico State○	11	3	.786	20	7	.741
Drake	9	5	.643	19	10	.655
Bradley	7	7	.500	15	11	.577
Wichita State	6	8	.429	11	15	.423
Tulsa	5	9	.357	15	14	.517
West Texas A&M	3	11	.214	9	17	.346
North Texas	3	11	.214	6	20	.231
Southern Illinois□	-	-	-	18	9	.667

OHIO VALLEY

	Conference			Overall		
	W	L	Pct	W	L	Pct
Middle Tenn. St.⊕	12	2	.857	23	5	.821
Western Kentucky	11	3	.786	16	8	.667
Austin Peay	10	4	.714	17	10	.630
Tennessee Tech	7	7	.500	13	12	.520
Morehead State	5	9	.357	13	13	.500
East Tennessee St.	5	9	.357	9	14	.391
Murray State	3	11	.214	10	15	.400
Eastern Kentucky	3	11	.214	7	18	.280

Tournament: **Middle Tenn. St. d. Austin Peay 89-75**
Tournament MVP: **Steve Peeler**, Middle Tenn. State

PCAA

	Conference			Overall		
	W	L	Pct	W	L	Pct
Long Beach State+	8	2	.800	19	7	.731
San Diego State⊕	6	4	.600	14	13	.519
Fresno State	5	5	.500	16	10	.615
San Jose State	4	6	.400	16	13	.552
Cal State Fullerton	4	6	.400	13	11	.542
Pacific	3	7	.300	12	14	.462

+ Ineligible for postseason play

PAC-8

	Conference			Overall		
	W	L	Pct	W	L	Pct
UCLA⊕	12	2	.857	28	3	.903
Oregon State○	10	4	.714	19	12	.613
Southern California	8	6	.571	18	8	.692
California	7	7	.500	17	9	.654
Oregon□	6	8	.429	21	9	.700
Washington	6	8	.429	16	10	.615
Stanford	6	8	.429	12	14	.462
Washington State	1	13	.071	10	16	.385

SEC

	Conference			Overall		
	W	L	Pct	W	L	Pct
Kentucky⊕	15	3	.833	26	5	.839
Alabama○	15	3	.833	22	5	.815
Auburn	12	6	.667	18	8	.692
Tennessee	12	6	.667	18	8	.692
Vanderbilt	10	8	.556	15	11	.577
Florida	8	10	.444	12	16	.429
LSU	6	12	.333	10	16	.385
Mississippi State	5	13	.278	9	17	.346
Mississippi	4	14	.222	8	18	.308
Georgia	3	15	.167	8	17	.320

SOUTHERN

	Conference			Overall		
	W	L	Pct	W	L	Pct
Furman⊕	12	0	1.000	22	7	.759
East Carolina	11	3	.786	19	9	.679
William and Mary	6	5	.545	16	12	.571
VMI	6	6	.500	13	13	.500
Richmond	7	7	.500	10	16	.385
Davidson	4	6	.400	7	19	.269
The Citadel	2	11	.154	5	15	.250
Appalachian State	1	11	.083	3	23	.115

Tournament: **Furman d. William and Mary 66-55**
Tournament MOP: **Clyde Mayes**, Furman

SOUTHLAND

	Conference			Overall		
	W	L	Pct	W	L	Pct
McNeese State	6	2	.750	16	8	.667
Louisiana Tech	5	3	.625	12	13	.480
Lamar	4	4	.500	7	16	.304
Arkansas State	3	5	.375	13	12	.520
Texas-Arlington	2	6	.250	6	20	.231
UL-Lafayette	-	-	-	-	-	-

SOUTHWEST

	Conference			Overall		
	W	L	Pct	W	L	Pct
Texas A&M⊕	12	2	.857	20	7	.741
Texas Tech	11	3	.786	18	8	.692
Arkansas	11	3	.786	17	9	.654
Texas	6	8	.429	10	15	.400
Baylor	6	8	.429	10	16	.385
TCU	4	10	.286	9	16	.360
SMU	4	10	.286	8	18	.308
Rice	2	12	.143	5	21	.192

Conference Standings Continue →

⊕ Automatic NCAA Tournament bid ○ At-large NCAA Tournament bid □ NIT appearance ⊗ Team record doesn't reflect games forfeited or vacated. For adjusted record, see p. 521.

WCAC

	Conference W	Conference L	Conference Pct	Overall W	Overall L	Overall Pct
UNLV⊛	13	1	.929	24	5	.828
San Francisco	9	5	.643	19	7	.731
Pepperdine	8	6	.571	17	8	.680
Loyola Marymount	7	7	.500	14	12	.538
Saint Mary's (CA)	7	7	.500	14	12	.538
Seattle	6	8	.429	8	18	.308
Santa Clara	4	10	.286	10	16	.385
Nevada	2	12	.143	10	16	.385

WAC

	Conference W	Conference L	Conference Pct	Overall W	Overall L	Overall Pct
Arizona State⊛	12	2	.857	25	4	.862
UTEP○	10	4	.714	20	6	.769
Arizona	9	5	.643	22	7	.759
Utah	7	7	.500	17	9	.654
Colorado State	6	8	.429	14	12	.538
BYU	5	9	.357	12	14	.462
New Mexico	4	10	.286	13	13	.500
Wyoming	3	11	.214	10	16	.385

YANKEE

	Conference W	Conference L	Conference Pct	Overall W	Overall L	Overall Pct
Massachusetts□	10	2	.833	18	8	.692
Connecticut□	9	3	.750	18	10	.643
Vermont	8	4	.667	16	10	.615
Boston U.	7	4	.636	12	13	.480
Rhode Island	3	7	.300	5	20	.200
New Hampshire	2	10	.167	6	18	.250
Maine	1	10	.091	11	14	.440

INDEPENDENTS

	Overall W	Overall L	Overall Pct
Texas-Pan American	22	2	.917
Charlotte	23	3	.885
Centenary	25	4	.862
Marquette○	23	4	.852
Stetson	22	4	.846
Cincinnati○	23	6	.793
Utah State○	21	6	.778
Rutgers⊛$	22	7	.759
Creighton○	20	7	.741
Memphis□	20	7	.741
South Alabama	19	7	.731
Syracuse⊛$	23	9	.719
Holy Cross□	20	8	.714
Oral Roberts□	20	8	.714
Boston College⊛$	21	9	.700
Florida State	18	8	.692
Portland State	18	8	.692
UC Santa Barbara	18	8	.692
VCU	17	8	.680
South Carolina□	19	9	.679
St. John's□	21	10	.677
Notre Dame○	19	10	.655
Detroit	17	9	.654
Providence□	20	11	.645
Georgetown⊛$	18	10	.643
George Washington	17	10	.630
Pittsburgh□	18	11	.621
Houston	16	10	.615
Illinois State	16	10	.615
Tulane	16	10	.615
Virginia Tech	16	10	.615
Canisius	15	10	.600
DePaul	15	10	.600
South Florida	15	10	.600
UL-Monroe	15	10	.600
Seton Hall	16	11	.593
Jacksonville	15	11	.577
Duquesne	14	11	.560
Hawaii	14	11	.560
Saint Peter's□	15	12	.556
Cleveland State	13	11	.542
Manhattan□	14	12	.538
Air Force	13	12	.520

INDEPENDENTS (CONT.)

	Overall W	Overall L	Overall Pct
Long Island	13	12	.520
St. Bonaventure	14	13	.519
West Virginia	14	13	.519
Cal State LA	13	13	.500
Marshall	13	13	.500
Navy	12	12	.500
Northeastern	12	12	.500
Fairfield	13	14	.481
Niagara	13	14	.481
Fordham	12	13	.480
Penn State	11	12	.478
Indiana State	12	14	.462
Oklahoma City	12	14	.462
Saint Louis	12	14	.462
Fairleigh Dickinson	11	13	.458
Portland	13	16	.448
Saint Francis (PA)	11	14	.440
Georgia Tech	11	15	.423
Southern Miss	11	15	.423
Xavier	11	15	.423
Ball State	10	15	.400
Loyola-Chicago	10	15	.400
Butler	10	16	.385
Dayton	10	16	.385
Denver	10	16	.385
Northern Illinois	8	15	.348
Houston Baptist	9	17	.346
Mercer	9	17	.346
Samford	9	17	.346
Villanova	9	18	.333
Colgate	8	16	.333
Buffalo	8	17	.320
Georgia Southern	8	18	.308
Georgia State	8	18	.308
Milwaukee	8	18	.308
St. Francis (NY)	7	19	.269
Hardin-Simmons	5	20	.200
Charleston Southern	4	16	.200
Iona	4	19	.174
Army	3	22	.120

$ Defeated regional opponents to earn an automatic NCAA bid

INDIVIDUAL LEADERS—SEASON

SCORING	CL	POS	G	FG	FT	PTS	PPG
1 **Bob McCurdy**, Richmond	SR	F	26	321	213	855	**32.9**
2 **Adrian Dantley**, Notre Dame	SO	F	29	315	253	883	**30.4**
3 **David Thompson**, NC State	SR	F	28	347	144	838	**29.9**
4 **Luther Burden**, Utah	JR	G	26	295	157	747	**28.7**
5 **Hercle Ivy**, Iowa State	JR	G	26	315	107	737	**28.3**
6 **Mike Coleman**, Southern Miss	SR	F	20	233	98	564	**28.2**
7 **Frank Oleynick**, Seattle	JR	G	26	287	135	709	**27.3**
8 **Don Scaife**, Arkansas State	SR	G	25	289	100	678	**27.1**
9 **Marshall Rogers**, Texas-Pan American	JR	G	22	248	92	588	**26.7**
10 **Alvan Adams**, Oklahoma	JR	C	26	279	133	691	**26.6**

FIELD GOAL PCT	CL	POS	G	FG	FGA	PCT
1 **Bernard King**, Tennessee	FR	F	25	273	439	**62.2**
2 **Bob Fleischer**, Duke	SR	F	26	178	287	**62.0**
3 **Joe C. Meriweather**, Southern Illinois	SR	C	27	229	370	**61.9**
4 **Dan Roundfield**, Central Michigan	SR	F	28	216	353	**61.2**
5 **Mike Glenn**, Southern Illinois	SO	G	27	196	321	**61.1**

MINIMUM: 5 MADE PER GAME

FREE THROW PCT	CL	POS	G	FT	FTA	PCT
1 **Frank Oleynick**, Seattle	JR	G	26	135	152	**88.8**
2 **Norm Caldwell**, Florida	SO	G	28	102	115	**88.7**
3 **Doug Brookins**, Creighton	SR	C	27	98	111	**88.3**
4 **Eddie Johnson**, Auburn	SO	G	24	102	116	**87.9**
5 **Dan Kraft**, Air Force	SR	G	25	83	95	**87.4**

MINIMUM: 3 MADE PER GAME

REBOUNDS PER GAME	CL	POS	G	REB	RPG
1 **John Irving**, Hofstra	SO	F	21	323	**15.4**
2 **Bob Warner**, Maine	JR	C	25	352	**14.1**
3 **Cedric Roane**, UMES	SR	F	26	356	**13.7**
4 **Clyde Mayes**, Furman	SR	F	29	394	**13.6**
5 **Bill Robinzine**, DePaul	SR	F	25	338	**13.5**

INDIVIDUAL LEADERS—GAME

POINTS	CL	POS	OPP	DATE	PTS
1 **David Thompson**, NC State	SR	F	Buffalo State	D5	**57**
2 **Bob McCurdy**, Richmond	SR	F	Appalachian State	F26	**53**
3 **Rick Whitlow**, Illinois State	SR	G	Southern Illinois	J4	**51**
4 **Adrian Dantley**, Notre Dame	SO	F	Air Force	F10	**49**
5 **Anthony Roberts**, Oral Roberts	SO	F	Illinois State	J6	**48**

REBOUNDS	CL	POS	OPP	DATE	PTS
1 **Mike Coleman**, Southern Miss	SR	F	Wisconsin-Milwaukee	F13	**26**
Tommie Lipsey, Cal State LA	JR	F	Azusa Pacific	F6	**26**
Sam Pellom, Buffalo	FR	C	Rochester	F25	**26**
4 **Alvan Adams**, Oklahoma	JR	C	Iowa State	M5	**25**
Leon Douglas, Alabama	JR	C	Kentucky	M6	**25**
Marion Hillard, Memphis	JR	C	Florida State	D9	**25**
Clyde Mayes, Furman	SR	F	NC State	F8	**25**
Ruben Rodriguez, Long Island	SR	C	CW Post	F11	**25**
George Walls, Denver	SR	C	Phillips	F20	**25**

TEAM LEADERS—SEASON

WIN-LOSS PCT	W	L	PCT
1 **Indiana**	31	1	**.969**
2 **Texas-Pan American**	22	2	**.917**
3 **Louisville**	28	3	**.903**
UCLA	28	3	**.903**
5 **Charlotte**	23	3	**.885**

SCORING OFFENSE	G	W-L	PTS	PPG
1 **South Alabama**	26	19-7	2,412	**92.8**
2 **NC State**	28	22-6	2,596	**92.7**
3 **Houston**	26	16-10	2,407	**92.6**
4 **Kentucky**	31	26-5	2,858	**92.2**
5 **Illinois State**	26	16-10	2,375	**91.3**

SCORING MARGIN	G	W-L	PPG	OPP PPG	MAR
1 **Charlotte**	26	23-3	88.9	65.2	**23.7**
2 **Indiana**	32	31-1	88.0	65.9	**22.1**
3 **Maryland**	29	24-5	89.9	74.6	**15.3**
4 **NC State**	28	22-6	92.7	77.9	**14.8**
5 **Texas-Pan American**	24	22-2	87.0	73.2	**13.8**

FIELD GOAL PCT	G	W-L	FG	FGA	PCT
1 **Maryland**	29	24-5	1,049	1,918	**54.7**
2 **North Carolina**	31	23-8	1,037	1,933	**53.6**
3 **Arkansas**	26	17-9	807	1,524	**53.0**
4 **Tennessee**	26	18-8	927	1,756	**52.8**
5 **Duke**	26	13-13	864	1,672	**51.7**

FREE THROW PCT	G	W-L	FT	FTA	PCT
1 **Vanderbilt**	26	15-11	530	692	**76.6**
2 **Florida**	28	12-16	456	596	**76.5**
3 **Seattle**	26	8-18	303	399	**75.9**
4 **Maryland**	29	24-5	509	672	**75.7**
5 **Drake**	29	19-10	402	533	**75.4**

REBOUND MARGIN	G	W-L	REB	OPP REB	MAR
1 **Stetson**	26	22-4	47.1	34.7	**12.4**
2 **South Alabama**	26	19-7	52.6	42.2	**10.4**
3 **Texas-Pan American**	24	22-2	45.6	35.7	**9.9**
4 **Maryland**	29	24-5	43.5	34.4	**9.1**
5 **Minnesota**	26	18-8	39.6	30.8	**8.8**

SCORING DEFENSE	G	W-L	OPP PTS	OPP PPG
1 **UTEP**	26	20-6	1,491	**57.3**
2 **New Mexico State**	27	20-7	1,601	**59.3**
3 **Minnesota**	26	18-8	1,577	**60.7**
4 **Princeton**	30	22-8	1,835	**61.2**
5 **Marquette**	27	23-4	1,679	**62.2**

CONSENSUS ALL-AMERICAS

FIRST TEAM

PLAYER	CL	POS	HT	SCHOOL	RPG	PPG
Adrian Dantley	SO	F	6-5	Notre Dame	10.2	30.4
John Lucas	JR	G	6-4	Maryland	4.2	19.5
Scott May	JR	F	6-7	Indiana	6.6	16.3
Dave Meyers	SR	F	6-8	UCLA	7.9	18.3
David Thompson	SR	F	6-4	NC State	8.2	29.9

SECOND TEAM

PLAYER	CL	POS	HT	SCHOOL	RPG	PPG
Luther Burden	JR	G	6-2	Utah	5.0	28.7
Leon Douglas	JR	C	6-10	Alabama	13.1	20.7
Kevin Grevey	SR	F	6-5	Kentucky	6.4	23.5
Ron Lee	JR	G	6-4	Oregon	5.6	18.4
Gus Williams	SR	G	6-2	Southern California	4.6	21.2

SELECTORS: AP, NABC, UPI, USBWA

AWARD WINNERS

PLAYER OF THE YEAR

PLAYER	CL	POS	HT	SCHOOL	AWARDS
David Thompson	SR	F	6-4	NC State	Naismith, AP, UPI, USBWA, NABC, Rupp
Monte Towe	SR	G	5-7	NC State	Frances Pomeroy Naismith*

* FOR THE MOST OUTSTANDING SENIOR PLAYER WHO IS 6 FEET OR UNDER

COACH OF THE YEAR

COACH	SCHOOL	REC	AWARDS
Bob Knight	Indiana	31-1	AP, UPI, USBWA, NABC, Sporting News

Poll Progression

Preseason Poll

AP	School
1	NC State
2	UCLA
3	Indiana
4	Maryland
5	Marquette
6	Kansas
7	South Carolina
8	Louisville
9	Alabama
10	USC
11	North Carolina
12	Notre Dame
13	Purdue
14	Providence
15	Memphis
16	Kentucky
17	Michigan
18	Minnesota
19	Arizona
20	Penn

Week of Dec 3

AP	School	AP↓↑
1	NC State (1-0)	
2	UCLA (2-0)	
3	Indiana (1-0)	
4	Maryland (1-0)	
5	South Carolina (2-0)	↑2
6	Louisville (0-0)	↑2
7	Kansas (1-0)	↓1
8	Marquette (0-0)	↓3
9	North Carolina (1-0)	↑2
10	USC (1-0)	
11	Alabama (0-0)	↓2
12	Purdue (1-0)	↑1
13	Notre Dame (1-0)	↓1
14	Penn (2-0)	↑6
15	Kentucky (1-0)	↑1
16	Memphis (1-0)	↓1
17	Providence (0-0)	↓3
18	Arizona (1-0)	↑1
19	Michigan (1-0)	↓2
20	Houston (0-0)	⤴

Week of Dec 10

AP	UPI	School	AP↓↑
1	1	NC State (4-0) (A)	
2	2	UCLA (4-0)	
3	3	Indiana (3-0)	
4	4	Louisville (2-0)	↑2
5	10	Maryland (3-0)	↓1
6	6	USC (3-0)	↑4
7	7	Marquette (2-0)	↑1
8	5	North Carolina (3-0)	↑1
9	9	Kansas (3-1)	↓2
10	8	Alabama (2-0)	↑1
11	11	Notre Dame (3-0)	↑2
12	13	Penn (3-0)	↑2
13	12	South Carolina (2-1)	↓8
14	18	Memphis (2-0)	↑2
15	16	Purdue (2-1)	↓3
16	19	Michigan (2-0)	↑3
17	15	Arizona (3-0)	↑1
18	19	Oregon (3-0)	⤴
19	—	Oklahoma (2-1)	⤴
20	—	Providence (2-0)	↓3
—	14	Arizona State (3-0)	
—	16	Oregon State (4-0)	

Week of Dec 17

AP	UPI	School	AP↓↑
1	1	NC State (5-0)	
2	2	Indiana (5-0)	↑1
3	3	UCLA (4-0)	↓1
4	4	Louisville (3-0)	
5	6	Maryland (5-0)	
6	7	Marquette (3-0)	↑1
7	5	USC (4-0)	↓1
8	8	Alabama (3-0)	↑2
9	17	Penn (5-0)	↑3
10	9	North Carolina (3-1)	↓2
11	17	Memphis (4-0)	↑3
12	11	Notre Dame (4-1)	↓1
13	13	Arizona (6-0)	↑4
14	14	South Carolina (2-1)	↓1
15	12	Purdue (5-1)	
16	—	Providence (4-0)	↑4
17	19	Oklahoma (4-1)	↑2
18	—	Kansas (4-3)	↓9
19	16	Oregon (4-0)	↓1
20	20	Kentucky (3-1)	⤴
—	10	Arizona State (7-0)	
—	13	Washington (6-0)	

Week of Dec 24

AP	UPI	School	AP↓↑
1	1	NC State (6-0)	
2	2	Indiana (7-0)	
3	3	UCLA (6-0)	
4	4	Louisville (4-0)	
5	7	Maryland (6-0)	
6	5	USC (7-0)	↑1
7	6	Alabama (4-0)	↑1
8	8	North Carolina (4-1)	↑2
9	11	Penn (6-0)	
10	12	Arizona (7-0)	↑3
11	10	South Carolina (4-1)	↑3
12	16	Providence (5-0)	↑4
13	19	Notre Dame (4-2)	↓1
14	18	Marquette (3-2)	↓8
15	13	Purdue (5-1)	
16	—	Memphis (6-1)	↓5
17	15	Kentucky (5-1)	↑3
18	17	Oklahoma (5-1)	↓1
19	14	Oregon (4-0)	
20	20	Rutgers (7-1)	⤴
—	9	Arizona State (8-0)	

Week of Dec 31

AP	UPI	School	AP↓↑
1	1	NC State (8-0)	
2	2	Indiana (10-0)	
3	3	UCLA (8-0)	
4	4	Louisville (7-0)	
5	5	USC (8-0)	↑1
6	6	Alabama (5-0)	↑1
7	7	Maryland (7-1)	↓2
8	8	North Carolina (5-1)	
9	9	Kentucky (7-1)	↑8
10	13	Providence (7-1)	↑2
11	10	Oregon (7-0)	↑8
12	16	Penn (7-1)	↓3
13	14	Marquette (5-2)	↑1
14	18	Arizona (8-1)	↓4
15	12	South Carolina (5-2)	↓4
16	11	Arizona State (9-1)	⤴
17	15	Michigan (7-1)	⤴
18	—	Purdue (5-3)	↓3
19	20	Memphis (8-2)	↓3
19	—	Notre Dame (4-3) (B)	↓6
—	17	Kansas (6-4)	
—	19	Bradley (6-1)	

Week of Jan 7

AP	UPI	School	AP↓↑
1	1	Indiana (12-0)	↑1
2	2	UCLA (10-0)	↑1
3	4	Louisville (8-0)	↑1
4	3	NC State (9-1) (C)	↓3
5	6	Maryland (9-1)	↑2
6	5	USC (10-1)	↓1
7	9	Kentucky (8-1)	↑2
8	8	Alabama (7-1)	↓2
9	7	Oregon (9-0)	↑2
10	13	Arizona (10-1)	↑4
11	11	Michigan (9-1)	↑6
12	10	Arizona State (11-1)	↑4
13	14	Marquette (6-2)	
14	15	La Salle (10-1)	⤴
15	12	North Carolina (5-3)	↓7
16	16	South Carolina (6-3)	↓1
17	—	Minnesota (9-1)	⤴
18	—	Tennessee (7-1)	⤴
19	16	Providence (7-3)	↓9
19	16	Wake Forest (7-3)	⤴
—	16	Washington (9-2)	
—	20	New Mexico State (9-2)	
—	20	Rutgers (10-2)	

Week of Jan 14

AP	UPI	School	AP↓↑
1	1	Indiana (14-0)	
2	2	UCLA (12-0)	
3	4	Louisville (11-0)	
4	3	NC State (10-1)	
5	6	Maryland (11-1)	
6	5	USC (12-1)	
7	7	Alabama (9-1)	↑1
8	9	Oregon (10-1)	↑1
9	8	Arizona State (13-1)	↑3
10	10	Kentucky (9-2)	↓3
11	11	La Salle (12-1)	↑3
12	12	Marquette (9-2)	↑1
13	13	Arizona (12-2)	↓3
14	14	North Carolina (7-3)	↑1
15	—	Providence (9-3)	↑4
16	—	Minnesota (10-2)	↑1
17	17	Rutgers (10-2)	⤴
18	16	Tennessee (8-2)	
19	—	Michigan (9-3)	↓8
20	15	South Carolina (8-3)	↓4
—	17	Bradley (8-3)	
—	19	New Mexico State (9-3)	
—	19	Penn (9-3)	

Week of Jan 21

AP	UPI	School	AP↓↑
1	1	Indiana (16-0)	
2	3	Louisville (12-0) (D)	↑1
3	4	Maryland (13-1)	↑2
4	2	UCLA (13-1)	↓2
5	5	NC State (11-2)	↓1
6	6	Alabama (11-1)	↑1
7	7	USC (13-2)	↓1
8	9	Oregon (12-1)	
9	11	La Salle (14-1)	↑2
10	8	Arizona State (15-1)	↓1
11	10	Kentucky (11-2)	↓1
12	12	Marquette (11-2)	
13	13	Arizona (14-2)	
14	14	North Carolina (8-4)	
15	18	Stanford (8-6)	⤴
16	—	Providence (10-3)	↓1
17	—	Minnesota (11-3)	↓1
18	19	Kansas (9-4)	⤴
19	—	Rutgers (10-3)	↓2
20	—	Auburn (8-3)	⤴
20	—	Purdue (10-4)	⤴
—	15	South Carolina (9-4)	⤴
—	16	UNLV (12-3)	
—	17	Creighton (12-4)	
—	19	Utah (11-3)	

Week of Jan 28

AP	UPI	School	AP↓↑
1	1	Indiana (18-0)	
2	2	NC State (12-2)	↑3
3	3	Louisville (13-1)	↓1
4	4	UCLA (14-2)	
5	7	Kentucky (13-2)	↑6
6	5	USC (13-2)	↑1
7	10	La Salle (16-1)	↑2
8	8	Maryland (13-3)	↓5
9	6	Alabama (13-2)	↓3
10	11	North Carolina (10-4)	↑4
11	12	Oregon (12-2)	↓3
12	9	Arizona State (16-2)	↓2
13	17	Marquette (11-3)	↓1
14	—	Auburn (10-3)	↑6
15	13	Arizona (15-3)	↓2
16	20	Notre Dame (9-6) (E)	⤴
17	17	Stanford (9-6)	↓2
18	—	Tennessee (11-3)	⤴
19	14	South Carolina (11-4)	⤴
20	—	Kansas (10-5)	↓2
—	14	Creighton (13-4)	
—	16	UNLV (13-3)	
—	17	Oregon State (12-6)	

Week of Feb 4

AP	UPI	School	AP↓↑
1	1	Indiana (20-0)	
2	2	UCLA (15-2)	↑2
3	3	Louisville (15-1)	
4	4	Maryland (14-3)	↑4
5	5	Kentucky (15-2)	
6	6	NC State (13-3)	↓4
7	7	Alabama (15-2)	↑2
8	8	USC (13-3)	↓2
9	10	Oregon (15-2)	↑2
10	9	Arizona State (17-2)	↑2
11	12	Marquette (13-3)	↑2
12	11	North Carolina (11-5)	↓2
13	18	La Salle (16-3)	↓6
14	16	Notre Dame (11-6)	↑2
15	18	Tennessee (12-3)	↑3
16	15	Clemson (11-7)	⤴
17	13	Arizona (15-4)	↓2
18	18	Creighton (15-4)	⤴
19	—	Rutgers (14-4)	⤴
20	—	Penn (14-4)	⤴
—	14	Oregon State (12-7)	
—	16	UNLV (15-3)	

Week of Feb 11

AP	UPI	School	AP↓↑
1	1	Indiana (22-0)	
2	2	UCLA (17-2)	
3	3	Maryland (17-3)	↑1
4	5	Kentucky (17-2)	↑1
5	4	NC State (16-3)	↑1
6	7	Louisville (16-2)	↓3
7	6	Alabama (17-2)	
8	8	Arizona State (17-2)	↑2
9	12	Marquette (15-3)	↑2
10	9	USC (14-4)	↓2
11	10	North Carolina (15-5)	↑1
12	13	La Salle (18-3)	↑1
13	—	Oregon (15-4)	↓4
14	—	Penn (16-4)	↑6
15	—	Texas-Pan American (19-1)	⤴
16	—	Notre Dame (12-7)	↓2
17	11	Oregon State (13-8)	⤴
18	—	Clemson (11-8)	↓2
19	14	Arizona (15-4)	↓2
20	16	Creighton (15-4)	↓2
—	15	UNLV (17-3)	
—	17	New Mexico State (16-5)	
—	18	South Carolina (13-6)	
—	19	Utah State (16-4)	
—	20	UTEP (14-4)	

WEEK OF FEB 18

AP	UPI	SCHOOL	AP↓↑
1	1	**Indiana** (24-0)	
2	2	**UCLA** (19-2)	
3	3	**Maryland** (18-3)	
4	4	**NC State** (18-3)	↑1
5	5	**Alabama** (19-2)	↑2
6	6	**Louisville** (17-2)	
7	8	**Kentucky** (19-3)	↓3
8	7	**Arizona State** (19-2)	
9	9	**Marquette** (17-3)	
10	10	**USC** (15-5)	
11	18	**Notre Dame** (15-7)	↑5
12	—	**Penn** (18-4)	↑2
13	12	**North Carolina** (15-6)	↓2
14	—	**Creighton** (18-4)	↑6
15	13	**Arizona** (17-4)	↑4
16	—	**Clemson** (13-8)	↑2
17	16	**La Salle** (19-4)	↓5
18	—	**Centenary** (22-3)	↥
19	—	**Texas-Pan American** (20-2)	↓4
20	11	**Oregon State** (14-9)	↓3
—	14	**UTEP** (16-4)	
—	15	**Utah State** (17-4)	
—	17	**UNLV** (18-4)	
—	18	**Kansas** (15-6)	
—	20	**South Carolina** (15-6)	

WEEK OF FEB 25

AP	UPI	SCHOOL	AP↓↑
1	1	**Indiana** (26-0)	
2	2	**Maryland** (19-3)	↑1
3	4	**Louisville** (20-2)	↑3
4	5	**Kentucky** (20-3)	↑3
5	3	**UCLA** (20-3)	↓3
6	9	**Marquette** (20-3)	↑3
7	6	**NC State** (19-4)	↓3
8	7	**Alabama** (20-3)	↓3
9	7	**Arizona State** (20-3)	↓1
10	14	**Penn** (20-4)	↑2
11	15	**Clemson** (15-8)	↑5
12	12	**USC** (16-6)	↓2
13	—	**Creighton** (19-4)	↑1
14	13	**North Carolina** (16-7)	↓1
15	11	**UTEP** (18-4) F	↥
16	—	**Notre Dame** (16-8)	↓5
17	10	**Oregon State** (16-9)	↑3
18	—	**Texas-Pan American** (21-2)	↑1
19	18	**Arizona** (18-5)	↓4
20	18	**Washington** (16-7)	↥
—	16	**Utah State** (19-5)	
—	16	**UNLV** (20-4)	
—	18	**New Mexico State** (19-5)	

WEEK OF MAR 4

AP	UPI	SCHOOL	AP↓↑
1	1	**Indiana** (28-0)	
2	2	**Maryland** (22-3)	
3	4	**Louisville** (22-2)	
4	3	**UCLA** (22-3)	↑1
5	7	**Marquette** (21-3)	↑1
6	6	**Kentucky** (21-4)	↓2
7	5	**Alabama** (22-3)	↑1
8	9	**NC State** (20-5)	↓1
9	8	**Arizona State** (22-3)	
10	12	**Penn** (23-4)	
11	11	**USC** (18-6)	↑1
12	13	**North Carolina** (19-7)	↑2
13	18	**Creighton** (19-4)	
14	14	**Clemson** (16-9)	↓3
15	10	**Oregon State** (17-9)	↑2
16	—	**Notre Dame** (18-8)	
17	—	**Texas-Pan American** (22-2)	↑1
18	16	**UTEP** (19-5)	↓3
19	20	**Arizona** (20-5)	
20	—	**Rutgers** (20-6)	↥
—	15	**Utah State** (19-5)	
—	16	**UNLV** (20-4)	
—	19	**Cincinnati** (20-5)	

WEEK OF MAR 11

AP	UPI	SCHOOL	AP↓↑
1	1	**Indiana** (29-0)	
2	2	**UCLA** (23-3) G	↑2
3	3	**Louisville** (24-2)	
4	5	**Maryland** (22-4)	↓2
5	6	**Marquette** (22-3)	
6	4	**Kentucky** (22-4)	
7	10	**North Carolina** (21-7)	↑5
8	7	**Arizona State** (23-3)	↑1
9	9	**NC State** (22-6)	↓1
10	8	**Alabama** (22-4)	↓3
11	11	**Penn** (23-4)	↓1
12	15	**Notre Dame** (18-8)	↑4
13	12	**USC** (18-7)	↓2
14	19	**Clemson** (17-10)	
15	—	**Oregon State** (17-10)	
16	—	**Rutgers** (22-6)	↑4
17	20	**UTEP** (20-5)	↑1
17	—	**Centenary** (23-4)	↥
17	—	**Cincinnati** (21-5)	↥
20	—	**Texas-Pan American** (22-2)	↓3
—	13	**Utah State** (21-5)	
—	14	**UNLV** (21-4)	
—	16	**Creighton** (20-6)	↧
—	17	**Arizona** (20-6)	↧
—	18	**New Mexico State** (20-6)	

WEEK OF MAR 18

AP	SCHOOL	AP↓↑
1	**Indiana** (30-0)	
2	**UCLA** (24-3)	
3	**Louisville** (25-2)	
4	**Maryland** (23-4)	
5	**Kentucky** (23-4)	↑1
6	**North Carolina** (22-7)	↑1
7	**Arizona State** (24-3)	↑1
8	**NC State** (22-6)	↑1
9	**Notre Dame** (19-8)	↑3
10	**Marquette** (23-4)	↓5
11	**Alabama** (22-5)	↓1
12	**Cincinnati** (22-5)	↑5
13	**Oregon State** (18-10)	↑2
14	**Drake** (19-10)	↥
15	**Penn** (23-5)	↓4
16	**UNLV** (23-4)	↥
17	**Kansas State** (19-8)	↥
18	**USC** (18-8)	↓5
19	**Centenary** (25-4)	↓2
20	**Syracuse** (21-7)	↥

WEEK OF MAR 25

AP	SCHOOL	AP↓↑
1	**UCLA** (26-3)	↑1
2	**Kentucky** (25-4)	↑3
3	**Indiana** (31-1)	↓2
4	**Louisville** (27-2)	↓1
5	**Maryland** (24-5)	↓1
6	**Syracuse** (23-7)	↑14
7	**Arizona State** (25-4)	
8	**NC State** (22-6)	
9	**North Carolina** (23-8)	↓3
10	**Marquette** (23-4)	
11	**Alabama** (22-5)	
12	**Cincinnati** (23-6)	
13	**Princeton** (22-8)	↥
14	**Notre Dame** (19-10)	↓5
15	**Kansas State** (20-9)	↑2
16	**Drake** (20-10)	↓2
17	**Penn** (23-5)	↓2
18	**Centenary** (25-4)	↑1
19	**Michigan** (19-8)	↥
20	**UNLV** (24-5)	↓4

FINAL POLL

AP	SCHOOL	AP↓↑
1	**UCLA** (28-3)	
2	**Kentucky** (26-5)	
3	**Indiana** (31-1)	
4	**Louisville** (28-3)	
5	**Maryland** (24-5)	
6	**Syracuse** (23-9)	
7	**NC State** (22-6)	↑1
8	**Arizona State** (25-4)	↓1
9	**North Carolina** (23-8)	
10	**Alabama** (22-5)	↑1
11	**Marquette** (23-4)	↓1
12	**Princeton** (22-8)	↑1
13	**Cincinnati** (23-6)	↓1
14	**Notre Dame** (19-10)	
15	**Kansas State** (20-9)	
16	**Drake** (20-10)	
17	**UNLV** (26-5)	↑3
18	**Oregon State** (18-12)	↥
19	**Michigan** (19-8)	
20	**Providence** (17-10)	↥

A David Thompson scores a school-record 57 points in a 144-88 victory over Buffalo. Later in the week, Virginia roughs up Thompson during a 101-72 Wolfpack win, leading NC State coach Norm Sloan to sputter, "I thought we were playing the Russians."

B After a 4–0 start, Notre Dame drops games to Indiana and UCLA. The Irish will also lose to No. 17 Kentucky on Dec. 28.

C Wake Forest upsets its first No. 1 team, toppling NC State, 83-78. The loss ends the Wolfpack's string of 36 victories.

D With a 55-53 victory over Drake, Louisville wins its 11th consecutive overtime game dating back to 1968—an NCAA record.

E Notre Dame rejoins the Top 20 despite six losses (five against ranked opponents). Adrian Dantley scores 32 in ND's 84-78 victory over UCLA on Jan. 25 in South Bend, avenging an early-season defeat at Pauley Pavillion.

F Led by defensive aces Gary Brewster and Charlie Draper, UTEP beats No. 8 Arizona State and No. 15 Arizona on consecutive days to jump onto the AP poll.

G In John Wooden's final regular-season game against USC, UCLA's Pete Trgovich steals the ball from Gus Williams and sinks two free throws with :23 remaining, securing a 72-68 win and another Pac-8 title (Wooden's seventh) for the Bruins. Wooden will finish his 29-year coaching career with a 664–162 record.

1975 NCAA Tournament

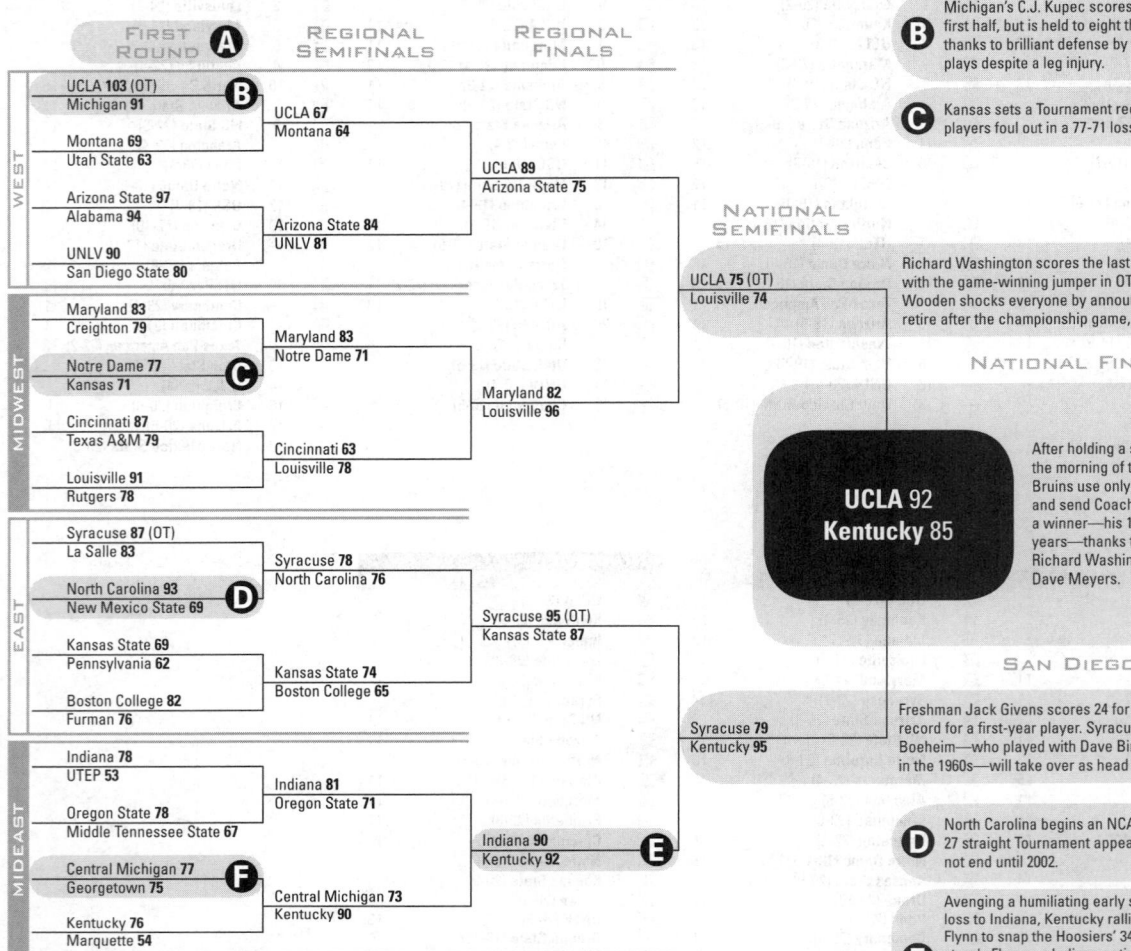

First Round (A)

West
- UCLA 103 (OT), Michigan 91 (B)
- Montana 69, Utah State 63
- Arizona State 97, Alabama 94
- UNLV 90, San Diego State 80

Midwest
- Maryland 83, Creighton 79
- Notre Dame 77, Kansas 71 (C)
- Cincinnati 87, Texas A&M 79
- Louisville 91, Rutgers 78

East
- Syracuse 87 (OT), La Salle 83
- North Carolina 93, New Mexico State 69 (D)
- Kansas State 69, Pennsylvania 62
- Boston College 82, Furman 76

Mideast
- Indiana 78, UTEP 53
- Oregon State 78, Middle Tennessee State 67
- Central Michigan 77, Georgetown 75 (F)
- Kentucky 76, Marquette 54

Regional Semifinals

- UCLA 67, Montana 64
- Arizona State 84, UNLV 81
- Maryland 83, Notre Dame 71
- Cincinnati 63, Louisville 78
- Syracuse 78, North Carolina 76
- Kansas State 74, Boston College 65
- Indiana 81, Oregon State 71
- Central Michigan 73, Kentucky 90

Regional Finals

- UCLA 89, Arizona State 75
- Maryland 82, Louisville 96
- Syracuse 95 (OT), Kansas State 87
- Indiana 90, Kentucky 92 (E)

National Semifinals

- UCLA 75 (OT), Louisville 74
- Syracuse 79, Kentucky 95

National Third Place Louisville d. Syracuse 96-88 (OT)
West Regional Third Place UNLV d. Montana 75-67
Midwest Regional Third Place Cincinnati d. Notre Dame 95-87 (OT)
East Regional Third Place North Carolina d. Boston College 110-90
Mideast Regional Third Place Central Michigan d. Oregon State 88-87

A The Tournament expands to 32 teams and, for the first time, teams other than conference champions can be chosen for at-large bids.

B Michigan's C.J. Kupec scores 20 points in the first half, but is held to eight the rest of the way thanks to brilliant defense by Dave Meyers, who plays despite a leg injury.

C Kansas sets a Tournament record when six players foul out in a 77-71 loss to the Irish.

Richard Washington scores the last of his 26 points with the game-winning jumper in OT. Afterwards, John Wooden shocks everyone by announcing that he'll retire after the championship game, at age 64.

National Final

UCLA 92
Kentucky 85

After holding a secret practice the morning of the game, the Bruins use only six players and send Coach Wooden out a winner—his 10th title in 12 years—thanks to 28 points from Richard Washington and 24 from Dave Meyers.

San Diego

Freshman Jack Givens scores 24 for Kentucky, then a record for a first-year player. Syracuse assistant Jim Boeheim—who played with Dave Bing for Syracuse in the 1960s—will take over as head coach in 1976.

D North Carolina begins an NCAA-record string of 27 straight Tournament appearances that does not end until 2002.

E Avenging a humiliating early season 24-point loss to Indiana, Kentucky rallies behind Mike Flynn to snap the Hoosiers' 34-game winning streak. Flynn, an Indiana native, scores 22. IU All-America Scott May starts despite a broken arm but is ineffective; teammate Kent Benson gets 33 points and 23 rebounds.

F Georgetown's Jonathan Smith heaves a 30-foot desperation shot at the buzzer and collides with CMU's Leonard Drake. Somehow, Smith is called for a charge and Drake makes both ends of a one-and-one, eliminating the Hoyas and their furious coach, John Thompson.

TOURNAMENT LEADERS

INDIVIDUAL LEADERS

SCORING

	CL	POS	G	PTS	PPG
1 **Adrian Dantley**, Notre Dame	SO	F	3	92	30.7
2 **Chuckie Williams**, Kansas State	JR	G	3	87	29.0
3 **Jimmy Lee**, Syracuse	SR	G	5	119	23.8
4 **John Lucas**, Maryland	JR	G	3	70	23.3
5 **Mitch Kupchak**, North Carolina	JR	F/C	3	66	22.0
6 **Richard Washington**, UCLA	SO	F/C	5	108	21.6
7 **Eric Hays**, Montana	SR	F	3	64	21.3
Dan Roundfield, Central Michigan	SR	F	3	64	21.3
9 **Rudy Hackett**, Syracuse	SR	F	5	106	21.2
10 **Kent Benson**, Indiana	SO	C	3	63	21.0

MINIMUM: 2 GAMES

FIELD GOAL PCT

	CL	POS	G	FG	FGA	PCT
1 **Tom LaGarde**, North Carolina	SO	C	3	11	15	73.3
Jim Bostic, New Mexico State	SR	F	1	11	15	73.3
3 **Mitch Kupchak**, North Carolina	JR	F/C	3	29	40	72.5
4 **Phil Sellers**, Rutgers	JR	F	1	12	17	70.6
5 **Ralph Drollinger**, UCLA	JR	C	5	14	20	70.0
Gary Jackson, Arizona State	JR	F	3	14	20	70.0

MINIMUM: 10 MADE

FREE THROW PCT

	CL	POS	G	FT	FTA	PCT
1 **Ed Stahl**, North Carolina	SR	C	3	12	12	100.0
2 **Phil Ford**, North Carolina	FR	G	3	17	18	94.4
3 **Mike Evans**, Kansas State	FR	G	3	14	15	93.3
4 **Steve Sheppard**, Maryland	SO	F	3	11	12	91.7
5 **Bill Collins**, Boston College	JR	C	3	10	11	90.9

MINIMUM: 10 MADE

REBOUNDS PER GAME

	CL	POS	G	REB	RPG
1 **Mike Franklin**, Cincinnati	SR	C	3	49	16.3
2 **Kent Benson**, Indiana	SO	C	3	42	14.0
3 **Jack Schrader**, Arizona State	SR	F	3	38	12.7
4 **Richard Washington**, UCLA	SO	F/C	5	60	12.0
5 **Lewis Brown**, UNLV	SO	C	3	34	11.3
Ken McKenzie, Montana	SR	C	3	34	11.3

MINIMUM: 2 GAMES

TEAM LEADERS

SCORING

	G	PTS	PPG
1 **North Carolina**	3	279	93.0
2 **Kentucky**	5	438	87.6
3 **Louisville**	5	435	87.0
4 **Syracuse**	5	427	85.4
5 **Arizona State**	3	256	85.3
6 **UCLA**	5	426	85.2
7 **Indiana**	3	249	83.0
8 **Maryland**	3	248	82.7
9 **UNLV**	3	246	82.0
10 **Cincinnati**	3	245	81.7

MINIMUM: 2 GAMES

FG PCT

	G	FG	FGA	PCT
1 **North Carolina**	3	113	187	60.4
2 **Maryland**	3	97	182	53.3
3 **Louisville**	5	173	331	52.3
4 **Indiana**	3	100	199	50.2
5 **Oregon State**	3	106	211	50.2

FT PCT

	G	FT	FTA	PCT
1 **Boston College**	3	47	58	81.0
2 **North Carolina**	3	53	67	79.1
3 **Maryland**	3	54	69	78.3
4 **Kansas State**	3	38	50	76.0
5 **Cincinnati**	3	49	68	72.1

MINIMUM: 2 GAMES

REBOUNDS

	G	REB	RPG
1 **Louisville**	5	224	44.8
2 **UCLA**	5	223	44.6
3 **Kentucky**	5	221	44.2
4 **Notre Dame**	3	122	40.7
5 **Central Michigan**	3	121	40.3
Cincinnati	3	121	40.3
Kansas State	3	121	40.3

MINIMUM: 2 GAMES

ALL-TOURNAMENT TEAM

PLAYER	CL	POS	HT	SCHOOL	RPG	PPG
Richard Washington*	SO	F/C	6-10	UCLA	12.0	21.6
Kevin Grevey	SR	F	6-5	Kentucky	3.6	20.2
Jimmy Lee	SR	G	6-2	Syracuse	3.8	23.8
Dave Meyers	SR	F	6-8	UCLA	9.6	17.8
Allen Murphy	SR	G/F	6-5	Louisville	4.0	20.4

ALL-REGIONAL TEAMS

EAST

PLAYER	CL	POS	HT	SCHOOL	RPG	PPG
Chuckie Williams*	JR	G	6-3	Kansas State	4.3	29.0
Rudy Hackett	SR	F	6-9	Syracuse	9.7	21.3
Brad Hoffman	SR	G	5-11	North Carolina	1.7	17.3
Mitch Kupchak	JR	F/C	6-10	North Carolina	9.7	22.0
Jimmy Lee	SR	G	6-2	Syracuse	3.7	23.0

MIDEAST

PLAYER	CL	POS	HT	SCHOOL	RPG	PPG
Kent Benson*	SO	C	6-10	Indiana	14.0	21.0
Jimmy Dan Conner	SR	F/G	6-4	Kentucky	3.3	12.7
Mike Flynn	SR	G	6-3	Kentucky	5.7	13.7
Steve Green	SR	F	6-7	Indiana	2.0	18.8
Dan Roundfield	SR	F	6-8	Central Michigan	9.3	21.3

MIDWEST

PLAYER	CL	POS	HT	SCHOOL	RPG	PPG
Phillip Bond*	SO	G	6-2	Louisville	3.7	11.0
Junior Bridgeman	SR	G/F	6-5	Louisville	7.3	23.0
Adrian Dantley	SO	F	6-5	Notre Dame	9.0	30.7
John Lucas	JR	G	6-4	Maryland	3.0	23.3
Robert Miller	FR	C	6-11	Cincinnati	7.7	16.7

WEST

PLAYER	CL	POS	HT	SCHOOL	RPG	PPG
Marques Johnson*	SO	F	6-7	UCLA	10.3	21.3
Eric Hays	SR	F	6-3	Montana	6.3	21.3
Lionel Hollins	SR	G	6-3	Arizona State	2.0	15.0
Robert Smith	SO	G	5-10	UNLV	1.7	10.7
Richard Washington	SO	F/C	6-10	UCLA	13.3	18.0

* MOST OUTSTANDING PLAYER

1975 NCAA TOURNAMENT BOX SCORES

67-64

UCLA	MIN	FG	3FG	FT	REB	A	ST	BL	PF	TP
Richard Washington	38	7-17	-	2-2	11	3	0	0	3	16
Pete Trgovich	37	6-11	-	4-6	3	3	1	1	3	16
Dave Meyers	36	6-14	-	0-0	5	3	0	0	1	12
Ralph Drollinger	24	3-5	-	2-4	9	0	0	1	3	8
Marques Johnson	22	3-7	-	1-2	6	2	0	1	1	7
Andre McCarter	34	3-8	-	0-2	1	1	2	0	1	6
Raymond Townsend	2	1-1	-	0-0	1	0	0	0	0	2
Jim Spillane	4	0-1	-	0-0	0	1	0	0	2	0
Casey Corliss	2	0-1	-	0-0	0	0	0	0	1	0
Gavin Smith	1	0-0	-	0-0	0	0	0	0	0	0
TOTALS	**200**	**29-65**	**-**	**9-16**	**36**	**13**	**3**	**3**	**15**	**67**
Percentages		44.6		56.2						

Coach: John Wooden

34	1H	33
33	2H	31

SWEET 16

MONTANA	MIN	FG	3FG	FT	REB	A	ST	BL	PF	TP
Eric Hays	36	13-16	-	6-7	7	6	3	0	2	32
Ken McKenzie	38	9-22	-	2-6	10	2	0	1	3	20
Larry Smedley	34	5-12	-	0-0	5	0	0	0	2	10
Michael Richardson	35	1-5	-	0-0	4	2	4	0	4	2
Tom Peck	31	0-1	-	0-0	4	4	0	0	1	0
Ben Demers	14	0-2	-	0-0	0	0	0	0	1	0
Tim Stambaugh	8	0-2	-	0-0	2	0	0	0	0	0
T.M. Blaine	4	0-1	-	0-0	0	1	0	0	0	0
TOTALS	**200**	**28-61**	**-**	**8-13**	**32**	**15**	**7**	**1**	**13**	**64**
Percentages		45.9		61.5						

Coach: Jud Heathcote

Officials: Wortman, Fout
Attendance: 9,797

84-81

ARIZONA STATE	MIN	FG	3FG	FT	REB	A	ST	BL	PF	TP
Scott Lloyd	33	8-13	-	1-1	3	3	0	-	4	17
Gary Jackson	22	8-11	-	1-2	6	2	1	-	0	17
Jack Schrader	40	5-9	-	3-4	15	5	0	-	4	13
Lionel Hollins	31	6-16	-	0-3	3	6	1	-	3	12
Rudy White	21	6-11	-	0-0	6	1	2	-	4	12
Mike Moon	29	3-10	-	0-0	6	6	1	-	2	6
James Holliman	16	2-5	-	2-3	3	0	0	-	1	6
Ken Wright	8	0-2	-	1-2	0	0	0	-	2	1
TOTALS	**200**	**38-77**	**-**	**8-15**	**42**	**23**	**5**	**-**	**20**	**84**
Percentages		49.4		53.3						

Coach: Ned Wulk

42	1H	50
42	2H	31

SWEET 16

UNLV	MIN	FG	3FG	FT	REB	A	ST	BL	PF	TP
Ricky Sobers	40	6-18	-	8-10	3	4	2	0	5	20
Eddie Owens	30	8-15	-	0-0	6	3	0	0	3	16
Robert Smith	40	5-11	-	3-3	1	5	3	0	1	13
Glen Gondrezick	19	5-8	-	2-2	3	3	1	1	5	12
Jackie Robinson	26	4-9	-	0-0	7	1	0	1	0	8
Lewis Brown	25	3-5	-	0-1	9	1	0	0	2	6
Boyd Batts	19	2-6	-	2-2	4	1	0	0	3	6
Mike Milke	1	0-0	-	0-0	0	0	0	0	0	0
TOTALS	**200**	**33-72**	**-**	**15-18**	**33**	**18**	**6**	**2**	**19**	**81**
Percentages		45.8		83.3						

Coach: Jerry Tarkanian

Officials: Pace
Weiler
Attendance: 9,797

83-71

MARYLAND	MIN	FG	3FG	FT	REB	A	ST	BL	PF	TP
John Lucas	40	8-12	-	8-8	0	3	0	0	3	24
Owen Brown	39	7-13	-	4-5	9	1	0	0	4	18
Brad Davis	39	4-12	-	8-10	4	9	0	1	0	16
Maurice Howard	27	5-9	-	0-0	4	2	1	0	4	10
Steve Sheppard	20	4-8	-	1-1	4	1	0	0	3	9
Tom Roy	31	3-4	-	0-0	6	2	0	0	4	6
John Boyle	1	0-0	-	0-0	0	0	0	0	1	0
Billy Hahn	1	0-0	-	0-0	1	0	0	0	0	0
John Newsome	1	0-0	-	0-1	0	0	0	0	0	0
Chris Patton	1	0-0	-	0-0	1	0	0	0	0	0
TOTALS	**200**	**31-58**	**-**	**21-25**	**29**	**18**	**1**	**1**	**19**	**83**
Percentages		53.4		84.0						

Coach: Lefty Driesell

38	1H	36
45	2H	35

SWEET 16

NOTRE DAME	MIN	FG	3FG	FT	REB	A	ST	BL	PF	TP
Adrian Dantley	39	10-18	-	5-8	11	2	-	0	5	25
Bill Paterno	37	7-16	-	3-4	7	1	-	0	2	17
Dave Batton	25	6-8	-	0-2	1	2	-	0	2	12
Toby Knight	33	5-10	-	1-2	12	1	-	1	3	11
Jeff Carpenter	24	1-3	-	2-2	3	4	-	0	4	4
Ray Martin	16	1-3	-	0-0	2	1	-	0	4	2
Don Williams	17	0-7	-	0-1	3	2	-	0	2	0
Dwight Clay	8	0-1	-	0-0	1	0	-	0	1	0
Dave Kuzmicz	1	0-1	-	0-0	0	0	-	0	0	0
TOTALS	**200**	**30-67**	**-**	**11-19**	**40**	**13**	**-**	**1**	**23**	**71**
Percentages		44.8		57.9						

Coach: Digger Phelps

Officials: Howell, Diehl
Technicals: Maryland (Roy
Notre Dame (bench)
Attendance: 6,800

78-63

LOUISVILLE	MIN	FG	3FG	FT	REB	A	ST	BL	PF	TP
Junior Bridgeman	36	8-15	-	4-5	8	4	0	1	2	20
Ricky Gallon	17	7-11	-	2-5	6	0	0	1	1	16
Allen Murphy	25	4-9	-	5-7	6	1	2	0	4	13
Philip Bond	31	2-4	-	6-7	7	6	0	0	2	10
Ike Whitfield	17	4-4	-	0-0	4	1	1	0	0	8
Danny Brown	6	2-2	-	0-0	0	0	0	0	0	4
Wesley Cox	19	1-5	-	1-2	2	1	0	0	0	3
Bill Bunton	26	1-1	-	0-0	8	0	0	1	2	2
Terry Howard	8	0-1	-	2-2	1	1	0	0	0	2
Rick Wilson	13	0-1	-	0-0	1	2	0	0	1	0
Stanley Bunton	1	0-1	-	0-0	0	0	0	0	0	0
Bill Harmon	1	0-0	-	0-0	0	0	0	0	0	0
TOTALS	**200**	**29-54**	**-**	**20-28**	**43**	**16**	**3**	**3**	**12**	**78**
Percentages		53.7		71.4						

Coach: Denny Crum

42	1H	25
36	2H	38

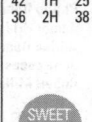

SWEET 16

CINCINNATI	MIN	FG	3FG	FT	REB	A	ST	BL	PF	TP
Mike Jones	35	9-18	-	0-1	6	0	0	0	2	18
Steve Collier	29	4-14	-	4-6	0	4	1	0	4	12
Robert Miller	26	5-8	-	1-2	7	0	0	1	3	11
Hal Ward	27	3-7	-	0-0	0	2	0	0	4	6
Garry Kamstra	24	3-7	-	0-0	1	5	0	0	3	6
Mike Franklin	27	2-5	-	0-0	13	0	0	1	5	4
Brian Williams	25	2-11	-	0-0	2	2	1	1	1	4
Mike Artis	6	1-4	-	0-0	1	1	1	0	0	2
Bob Sherlock	1	0-0	-	0-0	0	1	0	0	1	0
TOTALS	**200**	**29-74**	**-**	**5-9**	**30**	**15**	**3**	**3**	**23**	**63**
Percentages		39.2		55.6						

Coach: Gale Catlett

Officials: Hernjack, Nichols
Attendance: 6,800

78-76

SYRACUSE	MIN	FG	3FG	FT	REB	A	ST	BL	PF	TP
Jim Lee	40	12-18	-	0-0	0	0	1	0	3	24
Jim Williams	39	9-11	-	1-2	0	4	2	0	4	19
Kevin King	23	4-7	-	4-6	2	0	1	1	5	12
Christopher Sease	37	4-8	-	2-4	6	1	0	1	2	10
Rudy Hackett	31	3-7	-	0-0	1	2	0	0	4	6
Earnie Seibert	26	3-9	-	0-0	9	2	0	0	2	6
Bob Parker	2	0-0	-	1-2	0	0	0	0	0	1
Ross Kindel	2	0-0	-	0-0	0	0	0	0	0	0
TOTALS	**200**	**35-60**	**-**	**8-14**	**18**	**9**	**4**	**2**	**20**	**78**
Percentages		58.3		57.1						

Coach: Roy Danforth

41	1H	42
37	2H	34

SWEET 16

NORTH CAROLINA	MIN	FG	3FG	FT	REB	A	ST	BL	PF	TP
Phil Ford	37	7-10	-	10-10	1	5	1	0	4	24
Brad Hoffman	36	10-12	-	0-0	1	2	1	0	1	20
Mitch Kupchak	37	6-11	-	0-0	8	2	0	3	3	12
Tom LaGarde	31	5-6	-	2-2	7	0	0	0	1	12
Walter Davis	27	2-4	-	0-0	2	1	0	1	5	4
Ed Stahl	7	2-4	-	0-0	1	0	0	0	1	4
John Kuester	9	0-1	-	0-0	0	1	0	0	1	0
Mickey Bell	8	0-0	-	0-1	1	0	0	0	0	0
Bruce Buckley	3	0-0	-	0-2	0	0	0	0	0	0
Bill B. Chambers	2	0-1	-	0-0	0	0	0	0	1	0
Dave Hanners	2	0-0	-	0-0	0	0	0	0	1	0
Tom Zaliagiris	1	0-0	-	0-0	0	0	0	0	0	0
TOTALS	**200**	**32-49**	**-**	**12-15**	**21**	**11**	**2**	**4**	**18**	**76**
Percentages		65.3		80.0						

Coach: Dean Smith

Officials: Dreith
Overby
Attendance: 10,981

74-65

KANSAS STATE	MIN	FG	3FG	FT	REB	A	ST	BL	PF	TP
Chuckie Williams	-	15-25	-	2-2	3	1	2	0	3	32
Carl Gerlach	-	9-10	-	2-4	13	1	0	2	3	20
Mike Evans	-	3-6	-	1-2	5	2	2	1	1	7
Dan Droge	-	3-9	-	0-0	7	3	0	0	3	6
Doug Snider	-	3-3	-	0-0	4	6	0	1	3	6
Bobby Noland	-	1-1	-	1-1	0	1	0	0	1	3
TOTALS	**-**	**34-54**	**-**	**6-9**	**32**	**14**	**4**	**4**	**14**	**74**
Percentages		63.0		66.7						

Coach: Jack Hartman

39	1H	36
35	2H	29

SWEET 16

BOSTON COLLEGE	MIN	FG	3FG	FT	REB	A	ST	BL	PF	TP
Bill Collins	40	8-16	-	2-2	8	0	1	2	2	18
Will Morrison	40	7-20	-	3-4	9	0	0	1	3	17
Bob Carrington	34	5-15	-	4-5	4	3	2	0	5	14
Jeff Bailey	30	5-14	-	0-0	3	1	0	1	1	10
Mel Weldon	40	2-10	-	2-2	2	2	2	0	4	6
Mike Shirey	15	0-0	-	0-0	1	1	1	0	0	0
Jeff Jurgens	1	0-0	-	0-0	0	0	0	0	0	0
TOTALS	**200**	**27-75**	**-**	**11-13**	**27**	**7**	**6**	**4**	**15**	**65**
Percentages		36.0		84.6						

Coach: Bob Zuffelato

Officials: Galvan, Lawso
Attendance: 10,981

81-71 (SWEET 16)

	1H	2H
Indiana	48	33
Oregon State	27	44

INDIANA	MIN	FG	3FG	FT	REB	A	ST	BL	PF	TP
Steve Green	36	14-19	-	6-6	2	2	0	-	2	34
Kent Benson	38	11-18	-	1-2	9	3	2	-	3	23
Bob Wilkerson	36	4-8	-	2-2	5	10	0	-	4	10
Quinn Buckner	21	3-7	-	0-0	2	1	2	-	4	6
John Laskowski	38	2-4	-	0-1	6	6	0	-	0	4
Wayne Radford	17	1-1	-	0-0	5	1	0	-	1	2
Jim Crews	1	0-0	-	2-2	1	0	0	-	0	2
Scott May	3	0-2	-	0-0	0	0	0	-	1	0
Tom Abernethy	2	0-0	-	0-0	1	0	0	-	1	0
Steven Ahlfeld	2	0-0	-	0-0	0	0	0	-	0	0
Mark Haymore	2	0-0	-	0-0	0	0	0	-	1	0
Donald Noort	2	0-0	-	0-0	0	0	0	-	0	0
John Kamstra	1	0-0	-	0-1	0	0	0	-	0	0
James Wisman	1	0-0	-	0-0	0	0	0	-	0	0
TOTALS	200	35-59	-	11-14	31	23	4	-	17	81
Percentages		59.3		78.6						

Coach: Bob Knight

OREGON STATE	MIN	FG	3FG	FT	REB	A	ST	BL	PF	TP
Don Smith	38	6-11	-	2-3	2	1	0	0	4	14
Paul Miller	32	4-10	-	1-2	9	5	1	0	4	9
George Tucker	24	4-12	-	0-0	4	1	0	0	0	8
Ricky Lee	16	4-7	-	0-1	3	0	0	1	0	8
Roosevelt Daniel	10	3-4	-	2-2	1	0	0	0	1	8
Lonnie Shelton	11	3-5	-	1-1	6	0	0	0	5	7
Charlie Neal	38	3-6	-	0-2	2	4	1	0	3	6
Doug Oxsen	22	2-4	-	0-0	4	3	0	0	0	4
Carl Runyon	7	2-5	-	0-0	1	1	0	0	0	4
Tim Hennessey	2	1-1	-	1-3	1	0	0	0	2	3
TOTALS	200	32-65	-	7-14	33	15	2	1	19	71
Percentages		49.2		50.0						

Coach: Ralph Miller

Officials: Korte, Sherwood
Attendance: 13,458

90-73 (SWEET 16)

	1H	2H
Kentucky	44	46
Central Michigan	37	36

KENTUCKY	MIN	FG	3FG	FT	REB	A	ST	BL	PF	TP
Kevin Grevey	34	6-17	-	5-6	4	2	-	-	3	17
Mike Phillips	22	7-12	-	1-3	7	1	-	-	3	15
Jack Givens	22	6-12	-	0-0	6	1	-	-	2	12
Mike Flynn	26	5-8	-	1-2	11	4	-	-	3	11
Rick Robey	14	5-9	-	1-2	7	0	-	-	4	11
Jimmy Dan Conner	28	4-10	-	0-0	2	4	-	-	4	8
Larry Johnson	23	2-5	-	2-3	2	4	-	-	3	6
Bob Guyette	21	3-6	-	0-0	7	3	-	-	1	6
Jerry Hale	2	1-2	-	0-0	0	0	-	-	0	2
G.J. Smith	1	1-1	-	0-0	0	0	-	-	0	2
Dan Hall	4	0-1	-	0-0	0	0	-	-	1	0
Merionc Haskins	1	0-0	-	0-0	0	0	-	-	0	0
James Lee	1	0-0	-	0-0	1	0	-	-	2	0
Reggie Warford	1	0-0	-	0-0	0	0	-	-	0	0
TOTALS	200	40-83	-	10-16	47	19	-	-	26	90
Percentages		48.2		62.5						

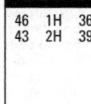

Coach: Joe B. Hall

CENTRAL MICHIGAN	MIN	FG	3FG	FT	REB	A	ST	BL	PF	TP
Dan Roundfield	-	6-18	-	8-13	11	2	-	-	3	20
James McElroy	-	8-20	-	1-3	5	4	-	-	4	17
Russ Davis	-	4-6	-	2-2	5	0	-	-	5	10
Jim Helmink	-	4-13	-	2-2	6	3	-	-	3	10
Leonard Drake	-	3-9	-	3-5	12	1	-	-	1	9
Darryl Alexander	-	2-4	-	1-2	3	0	-	-	1	5
Dennis Parks	-	1-1	-	0-0	0	1	-	-	0	2
Al Cicotte	-	0-0	-	0-0	0	0	-	-	0	0
Kurt Kaeding	-	0-2	-	0-1	2	0	-	-	0	0
Jerry McClain	-	0-3	-	0-0	2	0	-	-	0	0
TOTALS	-	28-76	-	17-28	46	11	-	-	17	73
Percentages		36.8		60.7						

Coach: Dick Parfitt

Officials: Filiberti, Soriano
Attendance: 13,458

89-75 (ELITE 8)

	1H	2H
UCLA	46	43
Arizona State	36	39

UCLA	MIN	FG	3FG	FT	REB	A	ST	BL	PF	TP
Marques Johnson	37	14-20	-	7-8	12	3	2	1	1	35
Richard Washington	34	8-13	-	0-0	12	2	1	3	5	16
Dave Meyers	38	4-15	-	3-4	13	3	3	3	3	11
Andre McCarter	40	2-5	-	5-8	5	5	0	1	1	9
Ralph Drollinger	9	3-4	-	3-3	3	0	0	0	5	9
Pete Trgovich	40	4-14	-	0-1	4	5	2	0	3	8
Wilbert Olinde	2	0-0	-	1-2	1	0	0	0	1	1
TOTALS	200	35-71	-	19-26	50	18	8	8	19	89
Percentages		49.3		73.1						

Coach: John Wooden

ARIZONA STATE	MIN	FG	3FG	FT	REB	A	ST	BL	PF	TP
Scott Lloyd	38	8-13	-	4-8	9	0	0	0	4	20
Lionel Hollins	38	8-22	-	0-1	0	6	0	1	4	16
Rudy White	34	6-13	-	3-4	5	3	1	1	5	15
Jack Schrader	27	4-12	-	1-2	12	1	2	2	4	9
Mike Moon	18	2-5	-	0-0	0	1	0	0	1	4
Gary Jackson	12	2-4	-	0-0	2	0	0	0	2	4
Ken Wright	8	2-4	-	0-1	3	0	0	0	0	4
James Holliman	23	1-5	-	1-2	7	1	0	0	3	3
Greg White	2	0-0	-	0-0	0	0	0	0	0	0
TOTALS	200	33-78	-	9-18	38	12	3	4	23	75
Percentages		42.3		50.0						

Coach: Ned Wulk

Officials: Wortman, Fouty
Attendance: 8,534

96-82 (ELITE 8)

	1H	2H
Louisville	42	54
Maryland	37	45

LOUISVILLE	MIN	FG	3FG	FT	REB	A	ST	BL	PF	TP
Philip Bond	39	9-17	-	5-6	4	7	1	0	2	23
Allen Murphy	24	10-18	-	0-0	4	1	0	0	5	20
Wesley Cox	34	6-9	-	3-4	9	2	0	1	2	15
Bill Bunton	34	6-8	-	1-3	12	2	1	1	4	13
Junior Bridgeman	29	3-11	-	7-10	3	4	4	0	4	13
Ike Whitfield	11	2-4	-	0-0	0	0	1	0	1	4
Danny Brown	7	2-4	-	0-0	0	0	0	0	1	4
Ricky Gallon	15	1-2	-	0-1	6	1	0	1	0	2
Terry Howard	1	0-0	-	2-2	0	0	0	0	0	2
Rick Wilson	4	0-0	-	0-0	0	0	0	0	1	0
Stanley Bunton	1	0-0	-	0-0	0	0	0	0	0	0
Bill Harmon	1	0-0	-	0-0	0	0	0	0	0	0
TOTALS	200	39-73	-	18-26	38	17	7	3	20	96
Percentages		53.4		69.2						

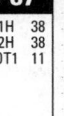

Coach: Denny Crum

MARYLAND	MIN	FG	3FG	FT	REB	A	ST	BL	PF	TP
John Lucas	40	11-19	-	5-6	6	1	1	0	4	27
Owen Brown	40	8-22	-	3-4	7	0	0	0	4	19
Tom Roy	39	5-9	-	6-6	20	0	2	3	3	16
Steve Sheppard	26	2-6	-	6-6	5	2	0	2	3	10
Brad Davis	33	3-7	-	2-2	2	7	3	0	5	8
Maurice Howard	19	1-6	-	0-1	0	0	1	0	5	2
Chris Patton	2	0-0	-	0-0	0	0	0	0	2	0
Billy Hahn	1	0-0	-	0-0	0	0	0	0	0	0
TOTALS	200	30-69	-	22-25	40	10	7	3	25	82
Percentages		43.5		88.0						

Coach: Lefty Driesell

Officials: Howell, Nichols
Technicals: Maryland (bench)
Attendance: 5,200

95-87 (ELITE 8)

	1H	2H	OT1
Syracuse	36	40	19
Kansas State	38	38	11

SYRACUSE	MIN	FG	3FG	FT	REB	A	ST	BL	PF	TP
Rudy Hackett	45	10-21	-	8-16	16	8	0	3	3	28
Jim Lee	37	10-17	-	5-7	3	4	2	0	5	25
Christopher Sease	40	5-12	-	2-2	10	0	1	1	4	12
Jim Williams	35	4-8	-	2-2	3	2	3	1	5	10
Kevin King	19	4-7	-	2-2	4	2	1	2	1	10
Ross Kindel	19	3-5	-	2-2	4	2	2	0	3	8
Earnie Seibert	26	1-4	-	0-0	3	2	0	0	3	2
Steven Shaw	3	0-0	-	0-1	1	0	0	0	0	0
Larry Arrington	1	0-0	-	0-0	0	0	0	0	0	0
TOTALS	225	37-74	-	21-32	44	20	9	7	24	95
Percentages		50.0		65.6						

Coach: Roy Danforth

KANSAS STATE	MIN	FG	3FG	FT	REB	A	ST	BL	PF	TP
Chuckie Williams	45	14-27	-	7-9	7	4	2	0	2	35
Mike Evans	43	6-21	-	8-8	7	5	2	1	5	20
Dan Droge	45	5-15	-	1-2	18	1	2	0	4	11
Doug Snider	24	5-10	-	1-3	6	0	1	0	4	11
Darryl Winston	12	4-6	-	0-0	0	1	1	0	2	8
Bobby Noland	26	0-1	-	2-2	5	1	2	0	5	2
Carl Gerlach	28	0-4	-	0-0	4	0	0	0	5	0
Jim Molinari	2	0-0	-	0-0	0	1	0	0	1	0
TOTALS	225	34-84	-	19-24	47	13	10	1	28	87
Percentages		40.5		79.2						

Coach: Jack Hartman

Officials: Galvan, Lawson
Attendance: 9,295

92-90 (ELITE 8)

	1H	2H
Kentucky	44	48
Indiana	44	46

KENTUCKY	MIN	FG	3FG	FT	REB	A	ST	BL	PF	TP
Mike Flynn	38	9-13	-	4-5	3	2	1	0	4	22
Kevin Grevey	34	6-19	-	5-6	3	5	1	0	4	17
Jimmy Dan Conner	31	8-20	-	1-3	5	5	2	1	0	17
Rick Robey	17	3-6	-	4-4	4	1	1	0	5	10
Mike Phillips	13	4-4	-	2-2	4	0	1	0	5	10
Jack Givens	29	4-7	-	0-0	6	2	1	0	0	8
Larry Johnson	11	3-5	-	0-1	1	1	0	0	0	6
Bob Guyette	22	0-1	-	2-4	7	1	3	0	4	2
Dan Hall	3	0-0	-	0-0	1	0	0	0	0	0
Merionc Haskins	2	0-0	-	0-0	0	0	0	0	0	0
TOTALS	200	37-75	-	18-25	34	17	10	1	22	92
Percentages		49.3		72.0						

Coach: Joe B. Hall

INDIANA	MIN	FG	3FG	FT	REB	A	ST	BL	PF	TP
Kent Benson	40	13-18	-	7-9	23	5	0	0	3	33
Steve Green	35	10-17	-	1-1	4	1	0	2	4	21
Bob Wilkerson	40	6-15	-	2-2	11	6	1	0	3	14
John Laskowski	33	4-13	-	4-6	3	3	1	0	3	12
Quinn Buckner	37	3-11	-	2-2	7	4	1	1	5	8
Scott May	7	1-4	-	0-0	0	0	0	0	2	2
Wayne Radford	4	0-0	-	0-0	0	0	0	0	1	0
Tom Abernethy	3	0-1	-	0-0	0	0	0	0	0	0
Steven Ahlfeld	1	0-0	-	0-0	0	0	0	0	0	0
TOTALS	200	37-79	-	16-20	48	19	3	3	21	90
Percentages		46.8		80.0						

Coach: Bob Knight

Officials: Soriano, Korte
Technicals: Indiana (bench, Green)
Attendance: 13,458

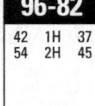

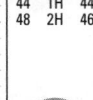

75-74 (FINAL 4)

	1H	2H	OT1
UCLA	33	32	10
Louisville	37	28	9

UCLA	MIN	FG	3FG	FT	REB	A	ST	BL	PF	TP
Richard Washington	43	11-19	-	4-6	8	2	1	0	4	26
Dave Meyers	44	6-16	-	4-6	7	2	0	0	3	16
Pete Trgovich	35	6-12	-	0-0	2	3	3	1	5	12
Marques Johnson	36	5-10	-	0-0	11	1	1	0	2	10
Andre McCarter	45	3-12	-	0-0	2	4	0	0	2	6
Ralph Drollinger	14	1-2	-	1-2	4	1	0	1	5	3
Jim Spillane	6	1-2	-	0-0	1	0	0	0	1	2
Wilbert Olinde	2	0-0	-	0-0	0	0	0	0	0	0
TOTALS	**225**	**33-73**	**-**	**9-14**	**35**	**13**	**5**	**2**	**22**	**75**
Percentages		45.2		64.3						

Coach: John Wooden

LOUISVILLE	MIN	FG	3FG	FT	REB	A	ST	BL	PF	TP
Allen Murphy	40	14-28	-	5-7	2	1	1	0	2	33
Wesley Cox	38	5-8	-	4-11	16	4	2	1	2	14
Junior Bridgeman	42	4-15	-	4-4	15	5	0	1	4	12
Bill Bunton	35	3-4	-	1-2	7	3	0	1	2	7
Philip Bond	39	2-6	-	2-2	3	8	0	0	1	6
Danny Brown	6	1-1	-	0-0	1	0	0	0	0	2
Ricky Gallon	11	0-3	-	0-0	2	0	0	0	2	0
Ike Whitfield	10	0-0	-	0-0	1	0	0	0	1	0
Terry Howard	2	0-0	-	0-1	0	0	0	0	0	0
Rick Wilson	2	0-0	-	0-0	0	0	0	0	0	0
TOTALS	**225**	**29-65**	**-**	**16-27**	**47**	**21**	**3**	**3**	**14**	**74**
Percentages		44.6		59.3						

Coach: Denny Crum

Officials: Wortman, Nichols
Attendance: 15,151

95-79 (FINAL 4)

	1H	2H
Kentucky	44	51
Syracuse	32	47

KENTUCKY	MIN	FG	3FG	FT	REB	A	ST	BL	PF	TP
Jack Givens	28	10-20	-	4-8	11	2	0	1	2	24
Kevin Grevey	29	5-13	-	4-5	3	3	1	0	5	14
Jimmy Dan Conner	35	5-9	-	2-4	5	3	2	1	4	12
Mike Flynn	30	4-9	-	3-5	3	7	2	0	4	11
Mike Phillips	14	5-6	-	0-2	4	0	4	0	4	10
Rick Robey	25	3-8	-	3-7	11	2	0	0	4	9
Bob Guyette	12	2-3	-	3-4	6	0	1	0	3	7
Larry Johnson	13	2-4	-	0-0	1	3	2	0	3	4
Merionc Haskins	5	0-0	-	2-2	1	1	0	0	0	2
James Lee	5	1-4	-	0-1	2	0	0	0	1	2
Jerry Hale	1	0-1	-	0-0	3	0	0	0	0	0
Dan Hall	1	0-0	-	0-0	1	0	0	0	1	0
G.J. Smith	1	0-1	-	0-0	0	0	0	0	0	0
Reggie Warford	1	0-0	-	0-0	0	0	0	0	0	0
TOTALS	**200**	**37-78**	**-**	**21-38**	**51**	**21**	**12**	**2**	**31**	**95**
Percentages		47.4		55.3						

Coach: Joe B. Hall

SYRACUSE	MIN	FG	3FG	FT	REB	A	ST	BL	PF	TP
Jim Lee	39	10-17	-	3-3	3	3	1	1	4	23
Christopher Sease	31	7-11	-	4-4	10	1	0	1	4	18
Rudy Hackett	26	4-6	-	6-9	5	3	0	2	5	14
Bob Parker	11	2-3	-	4-7	2	0	0	0	3	8
Kevin King	29	2-8	-	1-3	5	5	1	1	1	5
Jim Williams	24	2-9	-	0-1	2	3	0	0	5	4
Earnie Seibert	15	2-3	-	0-2	6	1	0	1	5	4
Ross Kindel	16	1-3	-	1-2	1	2	1	0	1	3
Steven Shaw	6	0-0	-	0-0	2	2	1	0	2	0
Martin Byrnes	1	0-0	-	0-1	1	0	0	0	0	0
Lawrence Kelley	1	0-1	-	0-0	0	0	0	0	0	0
Mark Meadors	1	0-0	-	0-0	1	0	0	0	0	0
TOTALS	**200**	**30-61**	**-**	**19-32**	**38**	**20**	**4**	**6**	**30**	**79**
Percentages		49.2		59.4						

Coach: Roy Danforth

Officials: Soriano, Galvan
Technicals: Syracuse (Hackett)
Attendance: 15,151

96-88 (3RD PLACE)

	1H	2H	OT1
Louisville	42	36	18
Syracuse	26	52	10

LOUISVILLE	MIN	FG	3FG	FT	REB	A	ST	BL	PF	TP
Bill Bunton	40	10-16	-	4-5	6	3	1	1	4	24
Junior Bridgeman	37	7-14	-	7-8	11	9	2	0	2	21
Allen Murphy	35	9-18	-	2-2	8	2	2	0	5	20
Philip Bond	40	5-7	-	2-3	4	8	0	0	1	12
Ricky Gallon	21	5-7	-	1-2	7	0	0	0	0	11
Wesley Cox	18	1-3	-	2-4	12	4	1	1	3	4
Danny Brown	10	2-5	-	0-1	1	1	1	0	2	4
Bill Harmon	11	0-2	-	0-1	2	1	0	0	1	0
Ike Whitfield	5	0-0	-	0-0	2	1	0	0	0	0
Rick Wilson	5	0-0	-	0-0	0	2	1	0	0	0
Terry Howard	3	0-0	-	0-0	0	1	0	0	0	0
TOTALS	**225**	**39-72**	**-**	**18-26**	**53**	**32**	**8**	**2**	**18**	**96**
Percentages		54.2		69.2						

Coach: Denny Crum

SYRACUSE	MIN	FG	3FG	FT	REB	A	ST	BL	PF	TP
Rudy Hackett	42	12-22	-	4-4	13	3	2	2	5	28
Jim Lee	45	12-29	-	3-3	5	1	0	0	1	27
Jim Williams	32	4-7	-	2-3	1	5	7	0	5	10
Kevin King	25	3-12	-	4-5	5	7	2	2	5	10
Christopher Sease	36	3-8	-	0-0	3	5	2	0	5	6
Bob Parker	15	3-5	-	0-0	3	1	0	0	3	6
Earnie Seibert	11	0-1	-	1-2	3	2	0	0	1	1
Ross Kindel	13	0-2	-	0-0	0	3	0	0	1	0
Martin Byrnes	4	0-0	-	0-0	0	0	2	0	0	0
Mark Meadors	1	0-0	-	0-0	1	0	0	0	0	0
Steven Shaw	1	0-0	-	0-0	0	0	1	0	0	0
TOTALS	**225**	**37-86**	**-**	**14-17**	**34**	**27**	**16**	**4**	**26**	**88**
Percentages		43.0		82.4						

Coach: Roy Danforth

Officials: Galvan, Soriano
Attendance: 15,151

92-85 (NCAA FINAL 1975)

	1H	2H
UCLA	43	49
Kentucky	40	45

UCLA	MIN	FG	3FG	FT	REB	A	ST	BL	PF	TP
Richard Washington	40	12-23	-	4-5	12	3	0	0	4	28
Dave Meyers	40	9-18	-	6-7	11	1	0	3	4	24
Pete Trgovich	40	7-16	-	2-4	5	4	0	0	4	16
Ralph Drollinger	16	4-6	-	2-5	13	0	0	1	4	10
Andre McCarter	40	3-6	-	2-3	2	14	2	0	1	8
Marques Johnson	24	3-9	-	0-1	7	1	1	3	2	6
TOTALS	**200**	**38-78**	**-**	**16-25**	**50**	**23**	**3**	**7**	**19**	**92**
Percentages		48.7		64.0						

Coach: John Wooden

KENTUCKY	MIN	FG	3FG	FT	REB	A	ST	BL	PF	TP
Kevin Grevey	36	13-30	-	8-10	5	1	1	0	4	34
Bob Guyette	24	7-11	-	2-2	7	3	1	0	3	16
Mike Flynn	25	3-9	-	4-5	3	2	1	0	4	10
Jimmy Dan Conner	38	4-12	-	1-2	5	6	2	0	1	9
Jack Givens	25	3-10	-	2-3	6	1	0	0	3	8
Mike Phillips	16	1-7	-	2-3	6	0	0	1	4	4
Rick Robey	14	1-3	-	0-0	9	1	1	0	5	2
Dan Hall	3	1-1	-	0-0	1	0	0	0	0	2
Larry Johnson	17	0-3	-	0-0	3	1	0	0	3	0
James Lee	2	0-0	-	0-0	0	1	0	0	1	0
TOTALS	**200**	**33-86**	**-**	**19-25**	**45**	**16**	**6**	**1**	**28**	**85**
Percentages		38.4		76.0						

Coach: Joe B. Hall

Officials: Nichols, Wortman
Technicals: UCLA (Meyers)
Attendance: 15,151

National Invitation Tournament (NIT)

First round: Manhattan d. Massachusetts 68-51, Providence d. Clemson 91-84, Pittsburgh d. Southern Illinois 70-65, St. John's d. Lafayette 94-76, South Carolina d. Connecticut 71-61, Princeton d. Holy Cross 84-63, Oral Roberts d. Memphis 97-95, Oregon d. Saint Peter's 85-79
Quarterfinals: Providence d. Pittsburgh 101-80, St. John's d. Manhattan 57-56, Oregon d. Oral Roberts 68-59, Princeton d. South Carolina 86-67
Semifinals: Providence d. St. John's 85-72, Princeton d. Oregon 58-57
Third place: Oregon d. St. John's 80-76 (OT)
Championship: Princeton d. Providence 80-69
MVP: Ron Lee, Oregon

1975-76: Coming Up Big Ten

As the post-John Wooden era began, teams other than UCLA finally had a chance to shine. And shine Indiana did. The Hoosiers went 32–0—the last Division I team (through 2008-09) to complete a perfect season. In its NCAA national semifinal, Indiana coach Bob Knight used a six-man rotation similar to the one Wooden employed in the 1975 championship game. Ironically, the Hoosiers used it in their 65-51 elimination of the Bruins, who were guided to the Final Four by first-year coach Gene Bartow. Five Hoosiers played 33 minutes or more, and the sixth played just 11. The Final was an all-Big Ten affair, though it was hardly a contest, as Indiana prevailed over Michigan, 86-68.

Scott May and Kent Benson paced the Hoosiers throughout the Tournament, and in the title game the duo combined for 51 points and 17 rebounds. Benson was named Tourney MOP, while May took home the Naismith Player of the Year award. Maryland's John Lucas was selected by Houston as the No. 1 overall pick in the NBA draft.

Major Conference Standings

ACC	Conference			Overall		
	W	L	Pct	W	L	Pct
North Carolina○	11	1	.917	25	4	.862
Maryland	7	5	.583	22	6	.786
NC State□	7	5	.583	21	9	.700
Clemson	5	7	.417	18	10	.643
Wake Forest	5	7	.417	17	10	.630
Virginia⊕	4	8	.333	18	12	.600
Duke	3	9	.250	13	14	.481

Tournament: **Virginia d. North Carolina 67-62**
Tournament MVP: **Wally Walker**, Virginia

BIG EIGHT	Conference			Overall		
	W	L	Pct	W	L	Pct
Missouri⊕	12	2	.857	26	5	.839
Kansas State□	11	3	.786	20	8	.714
Nebraska	10	4	.714	19	8	.704
Kansas	6	8	.429	13	13	.500
Oklahoma	6	8	.429	9	17	.346
Oklahoma State	4	10	.286	10	16	.385
Colorado	4	10	.286	7	19	.269
Iowa State	3	11	.214	3	24	.111

BIG SKY	Conference			Overall		
	W	L	Pct	W	L	Pct
Weber State	9	5	.643	21	11	.656
Boise State⊕	9	5	.643	18	11	.621
Idaho State	9	5	.643	16	11	.593
Northern Arizona	8	6	.571	15	12	.556
Montana	7	7	.500	13	12	.520
Montana State	6	8	.429	9	16	.360
Gonzaga	5	9	.357	13	13	.500
Idaho	3	11	.214	7	19	.269

Tournament: **Boise State d. Weber State 77-70 (2OT)**
Tournament MVP: **Jimmie Watts**, Weber State

BIG TEN	Conference			Overall		
	W	L	Pct	W	L	Pct
Indiana⊕	18	0	1.000	32	0	1.000
Michigan○	14	4	.778	25	7	.781
Purdue	11	7	.611	16	11	.593
Michigan State	10	8	.556	14	13	.519
Iowa	9	9	.500	19	10	.655
Minnesota	8	10	.444	16	10	.615
Illinois	7	11	.389	14	13	.519
Northwestern	7	11	.389	12	15	.444
Wisconsin	4	14	.222	10	16	.385
Ohio State	2	16	.111	6	20	.231

EAST COAST	Conference			Overall		
	W	L	Pct	W	L	Pct
Eastern Section						
Saint Joseph's	4	1	.800	10	16	.385
Drexel	3	2	.600	17	6	.739
Hofstra⊕	3	2	.600	18	12	.600
Temple	3	2	.600	9	18	.333
La Salle	1	4	.200	11	15	.423
American	1	4	.200	9	16	.360
Western Section						
Lafayette	9	1	.900	19	7	.731
Rider	6	4	.600	14	13	.519
Bucknell	5	5	.500	13	13	.500
Delaware	4	6	.400	10	15	.400
West Chester	4	6	.400	8	17	.320
Lehigh	2	8	.200	9	15	.375

Tournament: **Hofstra d. Temple 79-72**

IVY	Conference			Overall		
	W	L	Pct	W	L	Pct
Princeton⊕	14	0	1.000	22	5	.815
Penn	11	3	.786	17	9	.654
Dartmouth	7	7	.500	16	10	.615
Columbia	6	8	.429	8	17	.320
Brown	6	8	.429	7	19	.269
Yale	5	9	.357	7	21	.250
Cornell	4	10	.286	8	18	.308
Harvard	3	11	.214	8	18	.308

METRO	Conference			Overall		
	W	L	Pct	W	L	Pct
Cincinnati⊕	-	-	-	25	6	.806
Louisville□	-	-	-	20	8	.714
Memphis○	-	-	-	21	9	.700
Tulane	-	-	-	18	9	.667
Georgia Tech	-	-	-	13	14	.481
Saint Louis	-	-	-	13	14	.481

Tournament: **Cincinnati d. Memphis 103-95**
Tournament MVP: **Dexter Reed**, Memphis

MID-AMERICAN	Conference			Overall		
	W	L	Pct	W	L	Pct
Western Michigan⊕	15	1	.938	25	3	.893
Miami (OH)	14	2	.875	18	8	.692
Toledo	13	3	.813	18	7	.720
Central Michigan	8	8	.500	12	14	.462
Bowling Green	8	8	.500	12	15	.444
Kent State	7	9	.438	12	14	.462
Ohio	7	9	.438	11	15	.423
Ball State	5	11	.313	11	14	.440
Northern Illinois	2	14	.125	5	21	.192
Eastern Michigan	1	15	.063	7	20	.259

MEAC	Conference			Overall		
	W	L	Pct	W	L	Pct
NC A&T□	11	1	.917	20	6	.769
Morgan State	11	1	.917	22	6	.786
South Carolina St.	8	4	.667	17	8	.680
Howard	5	7	.417	9	19	.321
Delaware State	4	8	.333	6	17	.261
NC Central	2	10	.167	8	20	.286
UMES	1	11	.083	2	21	.087

Tournament: **NC A&T d. Morgan State 83-77**
Tournament MOP: **James Sparrow**, NC A&T

MISSOURI VALLEY	Conference			Overall		
	W	L	Pct	W	L	Pct
Wichita State⊕	10	2	.833	18	10	.643
Southern Illinois	9	3	.750	16	10	.615
West Texas A&M	8	4	.667	19	7	.731
New Mexico State	4	8	.333	15	12	.556
Bradley	4	8	.333	13	13	.500
Tulsa	4	8	.333	9	18	.333
Drake	3	9	.250	8	19	.296

OHIO VALLEY	Conference			Overall		
	W	L	Pct	W	L	Pct
Western Kentucky⊕	11	3	.786	20	9	.690
Austin Peay	10	4	.714	20	7	.741
Tennessee Tech	7	7	.500	14	10	.583
Morehead State	7	7	.500	13	14	.481
Middle Tennessee St.	6	8	.429	16	12	.571
Eastern Kentucky	6	8	.429	10	15	.400
Murray State	5	9	.357	9	17	.346
East Tennessee St.	4	10	.286	6	20	.231

Tournament: **Western Kentucky d. Morehead St. 65-60**
Tournament MVP: **Johnny Britt**, Western Kentucky

PCAA	Conference			Overall		
	W	L	Pct	W	L	Pct
Cal State Fullerton	6	4	.600	15	10	.600
Long Beach State	6	4	.600	14	12	.538
San Jose State	5	5	.500	17	10	.630
San Diego State⊕	5	5	.500	16	13	.552
Pacific	4	6	.400	14	14	.500
Fresno State	4	6	.400	12	14	.462

Tournament: **San Diego State d. Pacific 76-64**
Tournament MVP: **Will Connelly**, San Diego State

PAC-8	Conference			Overall		
	W	L	Pct	W	L	Pct
UCLA⊕⊗	12	2	.857	27	5	.844
Oregon State⊗	10	4	.714	18	9	.667
Oregon□⊗	10	4	.714	19	11	.633
Washington○⊗	9	5	.643	22	6	.786
Washington State⊗	8	6	.571	18	8	.692
California⊗	4	10	.286	12	14	.462
Stanford⊗	3	11	.214	9	18	.333
Southern California⊗	0	14	.000	11	16	.407

SEC	Conference			Overall		
	W	L	Pct	W	L	Pct
Alabama⊕	15	3	.833	23	5	.821
Tennessee○	14	4	.778	21	6	.778
Vanderbilt	12	6	.667	16	11	.593
Kentucky□	11	7	.611	20	10	.667
Auburn	11	7	.611	16	10	.615
Florida	7	11	.389	12	14	.462
Georgia	7	11	.389	12	15	.444
Mississippi State	6	12	.333	13	13	.500
LSU	5	13	.278	12	14	.462
Mississippi	2	16	.111	6	21	.222

SOUTHERN	Conference			Overall		
	W	L	Pct	W	L	Pct
VMI⊕	9	3	.750	22	10	.688
William and Mary	8	3	.727	15	13	.536
Richmond	7	7	.500	14	14	.500
East Carolina	7	7	.500	11	15	.423
Appalachian State	6	6	.500	13	14	.481
The Citadel	6	7	.462	10	17	.370
Furman	5	7	.417	9	18	.333
Davidson	1	9	.100	5	21	.192

Tournament: **VMI d. Richmond 41-33**
Tournament MOP: **Ron Carter**, VMI

SOUTHLAND	Conference			Overall		
	W	L	Pct	W	L	Pct
Louisiana Tech	9	1	.900	15	11	.577
McNeese State	7	3	.700	16	11	.593
Lamar	6	4	.600	10	14	.417
UL-Lafayette	4	6	.400	7	19	.269
Arkansas State	3	7	.300	10	15	.400
Texas-Arlington	1	9	.100	6	21	.222

SOUTHWEST	Conference			Overall		
	W	L	Pct	W	L	Pct
Texas A&M	14	2	.875	21	6	.778
Texas Tech⊕	13	3	.813	25	6	.806
SMU	10	6	.625	16	12	.571
Arkansas	9	7	.563	19	9	.679
Baylor	8	8	.500	12	15	.444
Houston	7	9	.438	17	11	.607
TCU	6	10	.375	11	16	.407
Texas	4	12	.250	9	17	.346
Rice	1	15	.063	3	24	.111

Tournament: **Texas Tech d. Texas A&M 74-72**
Tournament MVP: **Rick Bullock**, Texas Tech

Conference Standings Continue →

⊕ Automatic NCAA Tournament bid ○ At-large NCAA Tournament bid □ NIT appearance ⊗ Team record doesn't reflect games forfeited or vacated. For adjusted record, see p. 521.

WCAC

	Conference W	L	Pct	Overall W	L	Pct
Pepperdine⊕	10	2	.833	22	6	.786
San Francisco□	9	3	.750	22	8	.733
Nevada	7	5	.583	12	14	.462
Seattle⊗	6	6	.500	11	16	.407
Santa Clara	4	8	.333	10	16	.385
Loyola Marymount	4	8	.333	7	19	.269
Saint Mary's (CA)	2	10	.167	3	23	.115

WAC

	Conference W	L	Pct	Overall W	L	Pct
Arizona⊕	11	3	.786	24	9	.727
UTEP	9	5	.643	19	7	.731
Utah	9	5	.643	19	8	.704
New Mexico	8	6	.571	16	11	.593
BYU	6	8	.429	12	14	.462
Colorado State	6	8	.429	10	16	.385
Arizona State⊗	5	9	.357	16	11	.593
Wyoming	2	12	.143	10	17	.370

YANKEE

	Conference W	L	Pct	Overall W	L	Pct
Massachusetts	11	1	.917	21	6	.778
Connecticut⊕	7	5	.583	19	10	.655
Rhode Island	7	5	.583	14	12	.538
Vermont	6	6	.500	15	10	.600
Maine	5	7	.417	14	11	.560
New Hampshire	3	9	.250	8	18	.308
Boston U.	3	9	.250	7	19	.269

INDEPENDENTS

	Overall W	L	Pct
Rutgers⊕$	31	2	.939
UNLV○	29	2	.935
Marquette○	27	2	.931
North Texas	22	4	.846
Centenary	22	5	.815
Charlotte□	24	6	.800
Texas-Pan American	20	5	.800
Notre Dame○	23	6	.793
St. John's○	23	6	.793
Florida State⊗	21	6	.778
Oral Roberts	20	6	.769
Georgetown⊕$	21	7	.750
Virginia Tech○	21	7	.750
George Washington	20	7	.741
Illinois State	20	7	.741
Creighton	19	7	.731
UL-Monroe	18	7	.720
Detroit	19	8	.704
South Florida	19	8	.704
New Orleans	18	8	.692
DePaul○	20	9	.690
Syracuse⊕$	20	9	.690
Holy Cross□	22	10	.688
Seton Hall	18	9	.667
South Alabama	18	9	.667
South Carolina	18	9	.667
Providence□	21	11	.656
Stetson	17	9	.654
UC Santa Barbara	17	9	.654
Air Force	16	9	.640
VCU	16	9	.640
Saint Peter's□	19	11	.633
Portland State⊗	17	10	.630
St. Bonaventure	17	10	.630
Mercer	15	10	.600
Villanova	16	11	.593
Niagara□	17	12	.586
Long Island	15	12	.556
Colgate	13	11	.542
Xavier	14	12	.538

INDEPENDENTS (cont.)

	Overall W	L	Pct
West Virginia	15	13	.536
Georgia State	12	11	.522
Indiana State	13	12	.520
Dayton	14	13	.519
Hardin-Simmons	14	13	.519
Manhattan	14	14	.500
Saint Francis (PA)	14	14	.500
Jacksonville	13	13	.500
St. Francis (NY)	13	13	.500
Marshall	13	14	.481
Duquesne	12	13	.480
Northeastern	12	13	.480
Fairfield	12	14	.462
Utah State⊗	12	14	.462
Butler	12	15	.444
Denver	12	15	.444
Pittsburgh	12	15	.444
Army	11	14	.440
Iona	11	15	.423
Wisconsin-Milwaukee	11	15	.423
Southern Miss	11	15	.423
Navy	10	14	.417
Fairleigh Dickinson	9	13	.409
Georgia Southern	11	16	.407
Hawaii	11	16	.407
Penn State	10	15	.400
Buffalo	10	16	.385
Loyola-Chicago	10	16	.385
Canisius	10	17	.370
Boston College	9	17	.346
Oklahoma City	9	18	.333
Portland⊗	9	18	.333
Fordham	7	19	.269
Cleveland State	6	19	.240
Houston Baptist	5	21	.192
Charleston Southern	3	23	.115
Samford	3	23	.115

$ Defeated regional opponents to earn an automatic NCAA bid

$ Defeated regional opponents to earn an automatic NCAA bid

INDIVIDUAL LEADERS—SEASON

SCORING	CL	POS	G	FG	FT	PTS	PPG
1 **Marshall Rogers**, Texas-Pan American	SR	G	25	361	197	919	**36.8**
2 **Freeman Williams**, Portland State	SO	G	27	356	122	834	**30.9**
3 **Terry Furlow**, Michigan State	SR	G/F	27	308	177	793	**29.4**
4 **Adrian Dantley**, Notre Dame	JR	F	29	300	229	829	**28.6**
5 **Kenny Carr**, NC State	JR	F	30	322	154	798	**26.6**
6 **Lee Dixon**, Hardin-Simmons	SR	G/F	27	302	103	707	**26.2**
7 **Todd Tripucka**, Lafayette	SR	F	26	256	167	679	**26.1**
8 **Otis Birdsong**, Houston	JR	G	28	302	126	730	**26.1**
9 **Ernie Grunfeld**, Tennessee	JR	G/F	27	255	173	683	**25.3**
10 **Willie Smith**, Missouri	SR	G	31	300	183	783	**25.3**

FIELD GOAL PCT	CL	POS	G	FG	FGA	PCT
1 **Sidney Moncrief**, Arkansas	FR	G	28	149	224	**66.5**
2 **Bob Brown**, East Tennessee State	JR	C	26	181	274	**66.1**
3 **Duke Thorpe**, Virginia Tech	JR	F	28	165	251	**65.7**
4 **Roger Shute**, Texas-Arlington	SR	F/C	27	136	209	**65.1**
5 **Corky Abrams**, Southern Illinois	JR	F	25	145	224	**64.7**

MINIMUM: 5 MADE PER GAME

FREE THROW PCT	CL	POS	G	FT	FTA	PCT
1 **Tad Dufelmeier**, Loyola-Chicago	JR	G	25	71	80	**88.8**
2 **Buzzy O'Connell**, Stetson	JR	G	26	68	77	**88.3**
3 **Leonard Drake**, Central Michigan	JR	G	26	101	115	**87.8**
4 **Terry Furlow**, Michigan State	SR	G/F	27	177	202	**87.6**
5 **Ken Rood**, Hofstra	JR	G	30	77	88	**87.5**

MINIMUM: 2.5 MADE PER GAME

REBOUNDS PER GAME	CL	POS	G	REB	RPG
1 **Sam Pellom**, Buffalo	SO	C	26	420	**16.2**
2 **Dwayne Barnette**, Samford	SR	F/C	23	354	**15.4**
3 **John Irving**, Hofstra	JR	F	29	423	**14.6**
4 **John Thomas**, Connecticut	SR	C	29	402	**13.9**
5 **John Rudd**, McNeese State	SR	F	24	328	**13.7**
6 **DeCarsta Webster**, Indiana State	SO	C	25	339	**13.6**
7 **Ira Terrell**, SMU	SR	F	28	374	**13.4**
8 **Bob Stephens**, Drexel	FR	F	23	307	**13.3**
9 **Bernard King**, Tennessee	SO	F	25	325	**13.0**
Dave Kyle, Cleveland State	JR	C	25	325	**13.0**

INDIVIDUAL LEADERS—GAME

POINTS	CL	POS	OPP	DATE	PTS
1 **Marshall Rogers**, Tex.-Pan American	SR	G	Texas Lutheran	F16	**58**
2 **Terry Furlow**, Michigan State	SR	G/F	Iowa	J5	**50**
3 **Terry Furlow**, Michigan State	SR	G/F	Northwestern	J8	**48**
Marshall Rogers, Tex.-Pan American	SR	G	Texas-Arlington	J17	**48**
5 **Mike McConathy**, Louisiana Tech	JR	G	Lamar	F23	**47**

REBOUNDS	CL	POS	OPP	DATE	PTS
1 **Sam Pellom**, Buffalo	SO	C	VCU	F18	**31**
2 **John Irving**, Hofstra	JR	F	Long Island	D20	**28**
Mike Phillips, Kentucky	SO	C	Tennessee	J10	**28**
4 **Kerry Davis**, Cal State Fullerton	JR	C	Central Michigan	D15	**27**
Greg Kelser, Michigan State	FR	F	Wisconsin	J3	**27**
John Irving, Hofstra	JR	F	Long Island	M2	**27**

TEAM LEADERS—SEASON

WIN-LOSS PCT	W	L	PCT
1 **Indiana**	32	0	**1.000**
2 **Rutgers**	31	2	**.939**
3 **UNLV**	29	2	**.935**
4 **Marquette**	27	2	**.931**
5 **Western Michigan**	25	3	**.893**

SCORING OFFENSE	G	W-L	PTS	PPG
1 **UNLV**	31	29-2	3,426	**110.5**
2 **North Texas**	26	22-4	2,497	**96.0**
3 **Texas-Pan American**	25	20-5	2,391	**95.6**
4 **Rutgers**	33	31-2	3,079	**93.3**
5 **Notre Dame**	29	23-6	2,579	**88.9**

SCORING MARGIN	G	W-L	PPG	OPP PPG	MAR
1 **UNLV**	31	29-2	110.5	89.0	**21.5**
2 **Indiana**	32	32-0	82.1	64.8	**17.3**
3 **Rutgers**	33	31-2	93.3	76.9	**16.4**
4 **Charlotte**	30	24-6	84.5	69.0	**15.5**
5 **Texas-Pan American**	25	20-5	95.6	80.7	**14.9**

FIELD GOAL PCT	G	W-L	FG	FGA	PCT
1 **Maryland**	28	22-6	996	1,854	**53.7**
2 **Arkansas**	28	19-9	910	1,715	**53.1**
3 **Oregon State**	27	18-9	839	1,594	**52.6**
4 **North Carolina**	29	25-4	966	1,838	**52.6**
5 **Duke**	27	13-14	968	1,853	**52.2**

FREE THROW PCT	G	W-L	FT	FTA	PCT
1 **Morehead State**	27	13-14	452	577	**78.3**
2 **Bradley**	26	13-13	443	572	**77.4**
3 **Central Michigan**	26	12-14	328	425	**77.2**
4 **Ohio**	26	11-15	412	534	**77.2**
5 **Michigan State**	27	14-13	443	576	**76.9**

REBOUND MARGIN	G	W-L	REB	OPP REB	MAR
1 **Notre Dame**	29	23-6	46.3	34.1	**12.2**
2 **Buffalo**	26	10-16	51.5	39.7	**11.8**
3 **Virginia Tech**	28	21-7	45.6	35.3	**10.3**
4 **Connecticut**	29	19-10	43.0	32.8	**10.2**
Charlotte	30	24-6	44.4	34.2	**10.2**

SCORING DEFENSE	G	W-L	OPP PTS	OPP PPG
1 **Princeton**	27	22-5	1,427	**52.9**
2 **UTEP**	26	19-7	1,480	**56.9**
3 **Colgate**	24	13-11	1,390	**57.9**
4 **Drexel**	23	17-6	1,364	**59.3**
5 **Marquette**	29	27-2	1,742	**60.1**

CONSENSUS ALL-AMERICAS

FIRST TEAM

PLAYER	CL	POS	HT	SCHOOL	RPG	PPG
Kent Benson	JR	C	6-11	Indiana	8.8	17.3
Adrian Dantley	JR	F	6-5	Notre Dame	10.1	28.6
John Lucas	SR	G	6-4	Maryland	3.9	19.9
Scott May	SR	F	6-7	Indiana	7.7	23.5
Richard Washington	JR	F/C	6-10	UCLA	8.6	20.1

SECOND TEAM

PLAYER	CL	POS	HT	SCHOOL	RPG	PPG
Phil Ford	SO	G	6-2	North Carolina	1.9	18.6
Bernard King	SO	F	6-7	Tennessee	13.0	25.2
Mitch Kupchak	SR	F/C	6-10	North Carolina	11.3	17.6
Phil Sellers	SR	F	6-5	Rutgers	10.2	19.2
Earl Tatum	SR	F/G	6-6	Marquette	7.0	18.3

SELECTORS: AP, NABC, UPI, USBWA

AWARD WINNERS

PLAYER OF THE YEAR

PLAYER	CL	POS	HT	SCHOOL	AWARDS
Scott May	SR	F	6-7	Indiana	Naismith, AP, UPI, NABC, Rupp
Adrian Dantley	JR	F	6-5	Notre Dame	USBWA
Frank Alagia	SR	G	5-9	St. John's	Frances Pomeroy Naismith*

* FOR THE MOST OUTSTANDING SENIOR PLAYER WHO IS 6 FEET OR UNDER

COACH OF THE YEAR

COACH	SCHOOL	REC	AWARDS
Bob Knight	Indiana	32-0	AP, USBWA
Tom Young	Rutgers	31-2	UPI, Sporting News
Johnny Orr	Michigan	25-7	NABC

Poll Progression

Preseason Poll

AP	SCHOOL
1	Indiana
2	UCLA
3	Maryland
4	Marquette
5	North Carolina
6	Kentucky
7	Notre Dame
8	Louisville
9	Tennessee
10	Cincinnati
11	Arizona
12	Alabama
13	NC State
14	Kansas State
15	San Francisco
16	Michigan
17	Providence
18	Arizona State
19	Memphis
19	Charlotte
20	Syracuse

Week of Dec 2

AP	SCHOOL	AP↓↑
1	**Indiana** (1-0)	
2	**Maryland** (1-0)	↑1
3	**Marquette** (0-0)	↑1
4	**North Carolina** (1-0)	↑1
5	**UCLA** (0-1)	↓3
6	**Louisville** (1-0)	↑2
7	**Kentucky** (0-0)	↓1
8	**Tennessee** (1-0)	↑1
9	**Notre Dame** (1-0)	↓2
10	**Cincinnati** (1-0)	
11	**Arizona** (1-0)	
12	**San Francisco** (1-0)	↑3
13	**NC State** (1-0)	
14	**Alabama** (0-0)	↓2
15	**Providence** (3-0)	↑2
16	**Michigan** (0-0)	
17	**Auburn** (0-0)	⤴
18	**Kansas State** (0-1)	↓4
19	**Arizona State** (0-0)	↓1
20	**Washington** (2-0)	⤴

Week of Dec 9

AP	UPI	SCHOOL	AP↓↑
1	1	**Indiana** (1-0)	
2	3	**Maryland** (3-0)	
3	2	**Marquette** (2-0)	
4	4	**North Carolina** (3-0)	
5	5	**UCLA** (2-1)	
6	7	**Louisville** (2-0)	
7	6	**Tennessee** (3-0)	↑1
8	8	**Notre Dame** (3-0)	↑1
9	11	**Cincinnati** (4-0)	↑1
10	9	**Arizona** (4-0)	↑1
11	10	**Alabama** (3-0)	↑3
12	14	**San Francisco** (3-0)	
13	18	**NC State** (3-0)	
14	16	**Kentucky** (0-1)	↓7
15	13	**Washington** (4-0)	↑5
16	11	**UNLV** (4-0)	⤴
17	—	**Auburn** (2-0)	
18	19	**Michigan** (1-1)	↓2
19	—	**Arizona State** (3-0)	
20	—	**Missouri** (4-0)	⤴
—	15	**USC** (4-0)	
—	17	**Rutgers** (3-0)	
—	20	**Kansas State** (2-2)	⤵

Week of Dec 16

AP	UPI	SCHOOL	AP↓↑
1	1	**Indiana** (3-0)	
2	3	**Maryland** (5-0)	
3	2	**Marquette** (3-0)	
4	4	**North Carolina** (4-0)	
5	6	**Notre Dame** (5-1)	↑
6	5	**UCLA** (2-1)	↓
7	9	**Cincinnati** (6-0)	↑
8	7	**Alabama** (4-0)	↑
9	13	**NC State** (4-0)	↑
10	15	**Louisville** (3-1)	↓
11	10	**Tennessee** (4-1)	↓
12	11	**Washington** (5-0)	↑
13	8	**UNLV** (6-0)	↑
14	16	**San Francisco** (5-1)	↓
15	14	**Rutgers** (6-0)	
16	12	**Michigan** (3-1)	↑
17	—	**Auburn** (3-0)	
18	17	**St. John's** (6-0)	
19	18	**Arizona State** (5-0)	
20	—	**Kentucky** (2-2)	↓
—	19	**Arizona** (5-2)	↓
—	20	**Wichita State** (3-0)	

Week of Dec 23

AP	UPI	SCHOOL	AP↓↑
1	1	**Indiana** (6-0)	
2	2	**Maryland** (6-0)	
3	3	**North Carolina** (5-0)	↑1
4	4	**UCLA** (3-1)	↑2
5	6	**Notre Dame** (5-1)	
6	9	**Cincinnati** (7-0) Ⓐ	↑1
7	5	**Marquette** (5-1)	↓4
8	7	**Alabama** (6-0)	
9	12	**NC State** (5-0)	
10	14	**Tennessee** (6-1)	↑1
11	10	**Louisville** (5-1)	↓1
12	8	**UNLV** (8-0)	↑1
13	13	**Washington** (7-0)	↓1
14	16	**San Francisco** (7-1)	
15	15	**Rutgers** (7-0)	
16	11	**Michigan** (5-1)	
17	17	**St. John's** (7-0)	↑1
18	18	**Kentucky** (4-3)	↑2
19	—	**Centenary** (7-1)	⤴
19	—	**Minnesota** (5-0)	⤴
—	19	**Arizona State** (6-1)	⤵
—	19	**Kansas State** (6-2)	
—	19	**USC** (7-1)	

Week of Dec 30

AP	UPI	SCHOOL	AP↓↑
1	1	**Indiana** (8-0)	
2	2	**Maryland** (7-0)	
3	3	**North Carolina** (6-0)	
4	4	**UCLA** (6-1)	
5	6	**Notre Dame** (5-1)	
6	5	**Marquette** (5-1)	↑1
7	14	**Cincinnati** (8-1)	↓1
8	7	**Alabama** (6-0)	
9	8	**NC State** (7-0)	
10	9	**UNLV** (11-0)	↑2
11	9	**Louisville** (7-1)	
12	13	**Tennessee** (7-1)	↓2
13	12	**Washington** (8-0)	
14	16	**Rutgers** (7-0)	↑1
15	11	**St. John's** (9-0)	↑2
16	19	**Minnesota** (8-0)	↑3
17	15	**Michigan** (5-1)	↓1
18	—	**Centenary** (8-1)	↑1
19	17	**San Francisco** (9-2)	↓5
20	—	**La Salle** (7-0)	⤴
—	18	**Iowa** (9-0)	
—	19	**Duquesne** (5-1)	

Week of Jan 6

AP	UPI	SCHOOL	AP↓↑
1	1	**Indiana** (10-0)	
2	2	**Maryland** (10-0)	
3	3	**UCLA** (10-1)	↑1
4	4	**Marquette** (8-1)	↑2
5	6	**UNLV** (13-0)	↑5
6	8	**North Carolina** (7-1)	↓3
7	7	**Wake Forest** (10-0)	⤴
8	5	**Washington** (11-0)	↑5
9	12	**Tennessee** (8-1)	↑3
10	9	**Alabama** (8-1)	↓2
11	16	**NC State** (8-1)	↓2
12	11	**Rutgers** (10-0)	↑2
13	14	**Notre Dame** (5-3)	↓8
14	10	**St. John's** (10-1)	↑1
15	—	**Cincinnati** (9-2)	↓8
16	17	**Louisville** (7-2)	↓5
17	—	**Minnesota** (8-1)	↓1
18	15	**USC** (11-1)	⤴
19	13	**Michigan** (7-2)	↓2
20	—	**San Francisco** (10-3)	↓1
—	17	**Missouri** (10-2)	
—	19	**Kentucky** (5-4)	
—	20	**Iowa** (10-1)	

Week of Jan 13

AP	UPI	SCHOOL	AP↓↑
1	1	**Indiana** (12-0)	
2	4	**Maryland** (11-1)	
3	2	**Marquette** (9-1)	↑
4	6	**UNLV** (16-0)	↑
5	5	**Wake Forest** (11-1)	↑
6	3	**Washington** (13-0)	↑
7	7	**North Carolina** (10-1)	↓
8	8	**UCLA** (11-2)	↓
9	10	**Tennessee** (9-1)	
10	11	**Rutgers** (11-0)	↑
11	9	**Alabama** (10-1)	↓
12	12	**St. John's** (11-1)	↑
13	14	**NC State** (10-1)	↓
14	—	**Cincinnati** (11-2)	↑
15	16	**Notre Dame** (6-3)	↓
16	13	**Michigan** (9-3)	↑
17	20	**Oregon State** (9-4)	
18	—	**Centenary** (14-2)	
19	19	**West Texas A&M** (10-1)	
20	15	**Missouri** (11-2)	
—	17	**Arizona State** (8-1)	
—	17	**DePaul** (9-2)	

Week of Jan 20

AP	UPI	SCHOOL	AP↓↑
1	1	**Indiana** (14-0)	
2	3	**Maryland** (13-1)	
3	2	**Marquette** (11-1)	
4	5	**UNLV** (18-0)	
5	4	**North Carolina** (12-1)	↑2
6	7	**UCLA** (13-2)	↑2
7	8	**Rutgers** (13-0)	↑3
8	6	**Washington** (14-1)	↓2
9	10	**St. John's** (13-1)	↑3
10	12	**Tennessee** (10-2)	↓1
11	13	**NC State** (11-2)	↑2
12	9	**Alabama** (11-2)	↓1
13	11	**Oregon State** (11-4)	↑4
14	17	**Wake Forest** (11-3)	↓9
15	16	**Notre Dame** (9-3)	
16	20	**Cincinnati** (13-2)	↓2
17	14	**Michigan** (11-3)	↓1
18	15	**Missouri** (14-2)	↑2
19	18	**West Texas A&M** (12-1)	
20	—	**Virginia Tech** (12-2)	⤴
—	19	**Utah** (11-4)	

Week of Jan 27

AP	UPI	SCHOOL	AP↓↑
1	1	**Indiana** (16-0)	
2	2	**Marquette** (14-1)	↑1
3	3	**UNLV** (20-0)	↑1
4	4	**North Carolina** (12-2)	↑1
5	6	**Rutgers** (15-0)	↑2
6	5	**Washington** (16-1)	↑2
7	7	**Maryland** (13-2)	↓5
8	12	**NC State** (13-2)	↑3
9	9	**Tennessee** (12-2)	↑1
10	11	**Notre Dame** (11-3)	↑5
11	8	**Alabama** (13-2)	↑1
12	10	**UCLA** (14-3)	↓6
13	14	**Missouri** (15-2)	↑5
14	16	**St. John's** (14-2)	↓5
15	13	**Michigan** (12-3)	↑2
16	15	**Oregon State** (12-5)	↓3
17	19	**Princeton** (11-3)	⤴
18	—	**Cincinnati** (13-3)	↓2
19	—	**Centenary** (16-3)	⤴
20	18	**West Texas A&M** (13-2)	↓1
—	17	**Utah** (12-4)	
—	20	**Wake Forest** (11-5)	⤵

Week of Feb 3

AP	UPI	SCHOOL	AP↓↑
1	1	**Indiana** (18-0)	
2	2	**Marquette** (16-1)	
3	4	**UNLV** (23-0)	
4	3	**North Carolina** (15-2)	
5	6	**Maryland** (15-3)	↑2
6	5	**Washington** (17-1)	
7	7	**Rutgers** (16-0)	↓2
8	8	**Tennessee** (14-2)	↑1
9	9	**UCLA** (15-3)	↑3
10	10	**NC State** (14-3)	↓2
11	12	**Notre Dame** (12-4)	↓1
12	13	**St. John's** (15-2)	↑2
13	10	**Missouri** (17-2)	
14	15	**Alabama** (13-3)	↓3
15	19	**Princeton** (12-3)	↑2
16	14	**Michigan** (13-4)	↓1
16	20	**Cincinnati** (15-3)	↑2
17	—	**Western Michigan** (16-0)	⤴
18	—	**Centenary** (18-3)	↑1
19	—	**Virginia Tech** (15-3)	⤴
20	—	**North Texas** (16-2) Ⓑ	⤴
—	14	**Michigan** (13-4)	
—	16	**Utah** (14-4)	
—	17	**Louisville** (13-4)	
—	18	**Oregon State** (12-6)	⤵

Week of Feb 10

AP	UPI	SCHOOL	AP↓↑
1	1	**Indiana** (19-0) Ⓒ	
2	2	**Marquette** (18-1)	
3	3	**North Carolina** (18-2)	↑
4	4	**Maryland** (17-3)	↑
5	5	**Rutgers** (19-0)	↑
6	6	**UCLA** (17-3)	↑
7	8	**UNLV** (23-1) Ⓓ	↓
8	7	**Tennessee** (16-2)	
9	9	**Washington** (18-2)	↓
10	10	**Notre Dame** (14-4)	↑
11	12	**Alabama** (15-3)	↑
12	15	**NC State** (16-4)	↓
13	19	**Cincinnati** (17-3)	↑
14	13	**Missouri** (18-3)	↓
15	17	**Western Michigan** (18-0)	↑
16	11	**Michigan** (14-5)	
17	18	**St. John's** (17-3)	↓
18	—	**Virginia Tech** (18-3)	↑
19	—	**Centenary** (20-3) Ⓔ	↓
20	—	**North Texas** (16-2)	
—	14	**Utah** (16-4)	
—	15	**Louisville** (16-4)	
—	19	**West Texas State** (15-3)	

Week of Feb 17

AP	UPI	SCHOOL	AP↓↑
	1	**Indiana** (21-0)	
	2	**Marquette** (19-1)	
	3	**North Carolina** (20-2)	
	5	**Rutgers** (21-0)	↑1
	4	**UCLA** (19-3)	↑1
	6	**UNLV** (24-1)	↑1
	7	**Maryland** (18-4)	↓3
	10	**Notre Dame** (17-4)	↑2
	9	**Tennessee** (17-3)	↓1
	13	**Alabama** (17-3)	↑1
	8	**Washington** (19-3)	↓2
	15	**NC State** (18-4)	
	17	**Cincinnati** (18-3)	
	12	**Missouri** (20-3)	
	11	**Michigan** (16-5)	↑1
	16	**St. John's** (18-3)	↑1
	—	**Western Michigan** (20-1)	↓2
	—	**Virginia Tech** (19-4)	
	14	**Louisville** (17-4)	⤴
	—	**Centenary** (20-4)	↓1
—	17	**San Francisco** (21-4)	
—	19	**Utah** (17-5)	
—	20	**Texas A&M** (17-5)	

Week of Feb 24

AP	UPI	SCHOOL	AP↓↑
1	1	**Indiana** (23-0)	
2	2	**Marquette** (22-1)	
3	4	**Rutgers** (23-0)	↑1
4	3	**North Carolina** (22-2)	↓1
5	5	**UNLV** (26-1)	↑1
6	6	**Notre Dame** (20-4)	↑2
7	10	**Alabama** (19-3)	↑3
8	9	**Washington** (21-3)	↑3
9	7	**UCLA** (20-4)	↓4
10	8	**Maryland** (19-5)	↓3
11	12	**Tennessee** (18-4)	↓2
12	13	**Missouri** (22-3)	↑2
13	11	**Michigan** (18-5)	↑2
14	14	**St. John's** (20-3)	↑2
15	18	**NC State** (19-5)	↓3
16	—	**Western Michigan** (20-1)	↑1
17	—	**Oregon** (17-9)	⤴
18	19	**Cincinnati** (19-4)	↓5
19	—	**Centenary** (22-4)	↑1
20	16	**Texas A&M** (20-5)	⤴
—	15	**Louisville** (18-5)	⤵
—	17	**Florida State** (18-5)	
—	20	**Arizona** (19-8)	

Week of Mar 2

AP	UPI	SCHOOL	AP↓↑
1	1	**Indiana** (25-0)	
2	2	**Marquette** (23-1)	
3	4	**Rutgers** (25-0)	
4	3	**North Carolina** (24-2)	
5	5	**UNLV** (26-1)	
6	7	**Alabama** (20-3)	↑1
7	6	**UCLA** (22-4)	↑2
8	10	**Notre Dame** (21-5)	↓2
9	8	**Maryland** (21-5)	↑1
10	11	**Washington** (22-4)	↓2
11	9	**Michigan** (20-5)	↑2
12	13	**Tennessee** (19-5)	↓1
13	18	**Cincinnati** (21-4)	↑5
14	19	**Western Michigan** (22-1)	↑2
15	14	**Missouri** (22-4)	↓3
16	16	**St. John's** (21-4)	↓2
17	20	**NC State** (19-7)	↓2
18	12	**Florida State** (20-5)	⤴
19	—	**Texas A&M** (21-5)	↑1
20	—	**Centenary** (23-5)	↓1
—	15	**Arizona** (21-8)	
—	17	**Louisville** (19-6)	

Week of Mar 9

AP	UPI	SCHOOL	AP↓↑
1	1	**Indiana** (26-0)	
2	2	**Marquette** (25-1)	
3	3	**Rutgers** (28-0) (F)	
4	4	**UNLV** (28-1)	↑1
5	6	**North Carolina** (25-3)	↓1
6	5	**UCLA** (23-4)	↑1
7	8	**Notre Dame** (22-5)	↑1
8	7	**Alabama** (21-4)	↓2
9	14	**Tennessee** (21-5)	↑3
10	11	**Missouri** (24-4)	↑5
11	10	**Washington** (22-5)	↓1
12	13	**Maryland** (22-6)	↓3
13	15	**Virginia** (18-11) (G)	⤴
14	9	**Michigan** (21-6)	↓3
15	16	**Cincinnati** (23-5)	↓2
16	19	**Western Michigan** (24-2)	↓2
17	18	**St. John's** (23-5)	↓1
18	12	**Arizona** (22-8)	⤴
19	—	**Texas Tech** (24-5)	⤴
20	—	**Centenary** (23-5)	
—	16	**Florida State** (20-6)	⤵
—	19	**Princeton** (22-4)	

AP	SCHOOL	AP↓↑
	Indiana (28-0)	
	Marquette (26-1)	
	UNLV (29-1)	↑1
	Rutgers (29-0)	↓1
	UCLA (24-4)	↑1
	Alabama (22-4)	↑2
	Notre Dame (23-5)	
	North Carolina (25-4)	↓3
	Michigan (22-6)	↑5
	Western Michigan (25-2)	↑6
	Maryland (22-6)	↑1
	Cincinnati (24-6)	↑3
	Tennessee (21-6)	↓4
	Missouri (25-4)	↓4
	Arizona (23-8)	↑3
	Texas Tech (25-5)	↑3
	DePaul (20-8)	⤴
	Virginia (18-12)	↓5
	Centenary (23-5)	↑1
	Pepperdine (22-5)	⤴

(A) Cincinnati shoots 59% from the floor in the first half and breaks a 25-year-old NCAA record by hitting 55 field goals in a 120-49 rout of Saint Joseph's of Indiana. It's the Bearcats' highest point total since 1960.

(B) Led by sophomore forwards Fred Mitchell and Melvin Davis, North Texas debuts in the polls with a 16–2 record and goes on to finish 22–4, just a year after going 6–20.

(C) Indiana needs a Kent Benson tip-in at the buzzer to force overtime against Michigan. The Hoosiers take their first lead of the game with 1:26 left in the extra period and hold on for a 72-67 win.

(D) UNLV, which was unranked in the preseason poll but has reeled off 23 straight wins, loses to Pepperdine, 93-91. The Runnin' Rebels will finish the regular season a sparkling 29–1.

(E) Center Robert Parish gets 25 points and 19 rebounds in a 113-94 Centenary romp over Hardin-Simmons. The Gentlemen shoot 60% from the field.

(F) Rutgers captain Phil Sellers hits three crunch-time drives as the undefeated Scarlet Knights beat St. John's in the final of the ECAC Metro Division playoff. Rutgers won't lose a game until the Final Four.

(G) In the Miracle in Landover, an unheralded Virginia squad led by "Wonderful" Wally Walker upsets three ranked teams—NC State, Maryland and North Carolina—on successive nights to win the school's first (and still only) ACC tournament title.

1976 NCAA Tournament

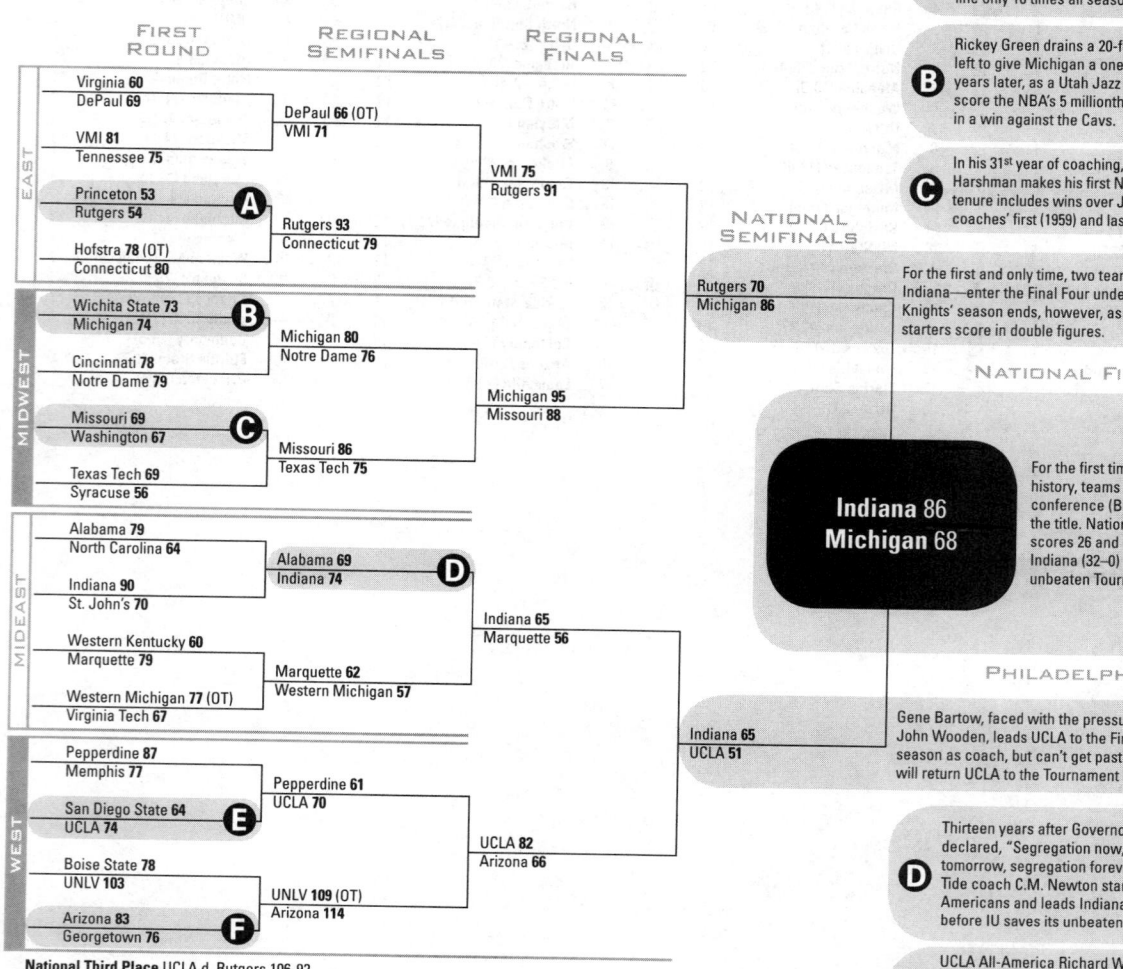

East

First Round
- Virginia **60**, DePaul **69**
- VMI **81**, Tennessee **75**
- Princeton **53**, Rutgers **54** (A)
- Hofstra **78** (OT), Connecticut **80**

Regional Semifinals
- DePaul **66** (OT), VMI **71**
- Rutgers **93**, Connecticut **79**

Regional Finals
- VMI **75**, Rutgers **91**

Midwest

First Round
- Wichita State **73**, Michigan **74** (B)
- Cincinnati **78**, Notre Dame **79**
- Missouri **69**, Washington **67** (C)
- Texas Tech **69**, Syracuse **56**

Regional Semifinals
- Michigan **80**, Notre Dame **76**
- Missouri **86**, Texas Tech **75**

Regional Finals
- Michigan **95**, Missouri **88**

Mideast

First Round
- Alabama **79**, North Carolina **64**
- Indiana **90**, St. John's **70**
- Western Kentucky **60**, Marquette **79**
- Western Michigan **77** (OT), Virginia Tech **67**

Regional Semifinals
- Alabama **69**, Indiana **74** (D)
- Marquette **62**, Western Michigan **57**

Regional Finals
- Indiana **65**, Marquette **56**

West

First Round
- Pepperdine **87**, Memphis **77**
- San Diego State **64**, UCLA **74** (E)
- Boise State **78**, UNLV **103**
- Arizona **83**, Georgetown **76** (F)

Regional Semifinals
- Pepperdine **61**, UCLA **70**
- UNLV **109** (OT), Arizona **114**

Regional Finals
- UCLA **82**, Arizona **66**

National Semifinals
- Rutgers **70**, Michigan **86**
- Indiana **65**, UCLA **51**

National Final

Philadelphia

Indiana 86
Michigan 68

For the first time in Tournament history, teams from the same conference (Big Ten) meet for the title. National POY Scott May scores 26 and Kent Benson 25 as Indiana (32–0) becomes the seventh unbeaten Tournament champion.

National Third Place UCLA d. Rutgers 106-92

For the first and only time, two teams—Rutgers and Indiana—enter the Final Four undefeated. The Scarlet Knights' season ends, however, as all five Michigan starters score in double figures.

Gene Bartow, faced with the pressure of replacing John Wooden, leads UCLA to the Final Four in his first season as coach, but can't get past Indiana. Bartow will return UCLA to the Tournament in 1977.

A Rutgers' Tom Young calls two timeouts to ice Princeton's Peter Molloy, who ends up missing a free throw with :04 left. Molloy had gone to the line only 16 times all season, making nine.

B Rickey Green drains a 20-foot jumper with :06 left to give Michigan a one-point win. Thirteen years later, as a Utah Jazz reserve, Green will score the NBA's 5 millionth point, hitting a three in a win against the Cavs.

C In his 31st year of coaching, Washington's Marv Harshman makes his first NCAA appearance. His tenure includes wins over John Wooden in the coaches' first (1959) and last (1975) meetings.

D Thirteen years after Governor George Wallace declared, "Segregation now, segregation tomorrow, segregation forever!" Crimson Tide coach C.M. Newton starts five African-Americans and leads Indiana late in the game, before IU saves its unbeaten season.

E UCLA All-America Richard Washington scores 25 points. UNLV fans, anticipating a future matchup with the Bruins, complain about the choice of Los Angeles as the West Regional site, holding signs that read "Unfair Court Los Angeles Advantage."

F For the first time in a Tournament game, both teams are coached by African-Americans: Fred Snowden of Arizona and John Thompson Jr. of Georgetown.

Tournament Leaders

INDIVIDUAL LEADERS

Scoring	CL	POS	G	PTS	PPG
1 **Willie Smith**, Missouri	SR	G	3	94	31.3
2 **Adrian Dantley**, Notre Dame	JR	F	2	58	29.0
3 **Ron Norwood**, DePaul	JR	G/F	2	51	25.5
4 **Will Bynum**, VMI	JR	F	3	76	25.3
5 **Marcos Leite**, Pepperdine	JR	C	2	50	25.0
6 **Leon Douglas**, Alabama	SR	C	2	47	23.5
7 **Scott May**, Indiana	SR	F	5	113	22.6
8 **Eddie Owens**, UNLV	JR	F	2	45	22.5
9 **Jeff Tyson**, Western Michigan	SR	F	2	43	21.5
10 **Rick Bullock**, Texas Tech	SR	C	2	42	21.0

Minimum: 2 games

Field Goal Pct	CL	POS	G	FG	FGA	PCT
1 **Glen Williams**, St. John's	JR	G	1	10	15	66.7
2 **Jackie Robinson**, UNLV	JR	F	2	10	16	62.5
3 **Stephen Hefele**, Rutgers	SO	G	5	11	18	61.1
4 **Ron Carter**, VMI	SO	G	3	22	37	59.5
5 **Adrian Dantley**, Notre Dame	JR	F	2	22	37	59.5

Minimum: 10 made

Free Throw Pct	CL	POS	G	FT	FTA	PCT
1 **Al Weston**, Connecticut	SR	G	2	14	14	100.0
Robert Smith, UNLV	JR	G	2	11	11	100.0
3 **Bob Wilkerson**, Indiana	SR	G	5	11	12	91.7
4 **Jim Rappis**, Arizona	SR	G	3	10	11	90.9
5 **Tom Cutter**, Western Michigan	JR	C	2	14	16	87.5
Adrian Dantley, Notre Dame	JR	F	2	14	16	87.5

Minimum: 10 made

Rebounds Per Game	CL	POS	G	REB	RPG
1 **John Thomas**, Connecticut	SR	C	2	30	15.0
2 **Tom Cutter**, Western Michigan	JR	C	2	28	14.0
3 **Al Fleming**, Arizona	SR	F	3	39	13.0
Mike Russell, Texas Tech	SO	C	2	26	13.0
5 **Phil Hubbard**, Michigan	FR	F	5	61	12.2

Minimum: 2 games

TEAM LEADERS

Scoring	G	PTS	PPG
1 **UNLV**	2	212	106.0
2 **Arizona**	3	263	87.7
3 **Missouri**	3	243	81.0
4 **Michigan**	5	403	80.6
5 **Rutgers**	5	400	80.0
6 **Connecticut**	2	159	79.5
7 **Notre Dame**	2	155	77.5
8 **UCLA**	5	383	76.6
9 **Indiana**	5	380	76.0
10 **VMI**	3	227	75.7

Minimum: 2 games

FG Pct	G	FG	FGA	PCT
1 **Arizona**	3	102	197	51.8
2 **Indiana**	5	151	298	50.7
3 **VMI**	3	88	176	50.0
4 **Notre Dame**	2	67	135	49.6
5 **UCLA**	5	164	332	49.4

FT Pct	G	FT	FTA	PCT
1 **Notre Dame**	2	21	26	80.8
2 **Michigan**	5	81	107	75.7
3 **Marquette**	3	17	23	73.9
4 **Indiana**	5	78	106	73.6
5 **Connecticut**	2	35	48	72.9

Minimum: 2 games

Rebounds	G	REB	RPG
1 **UNLV**	2	94	47.0
2 **Arizona**	3	135	45.0
3 **Connecticut**	2	84	42.0
4 **Western Michigan**	2	81	40.5
5 **Missouri**	3	119	39.7

Minimum: 2 games

ALL-TOURNAMENT TEAM

PLAYER	CL	POS	HT	SCHOOL	RPG	PPG
Kent Benson*	JR	C	6-11	Indiana	9.0	18.8
Tom Abernethy	SR	F	6-7	Indiana	5.4	10.4
Rickey Green	JR	G	6-2	Michigan	5.0	17.4
Marques Johnson	JR	F	6-7	UCLA	10.0	18.6
Scott May	SR	F	6-7	Indiana	7.6	22.6

ALL-REGIONAL TEAMS

EAST

PLAYER	CL	POS	HT	SCHOOL	RPG	PPG
Eddie Jordan*	JR	G	6-1	Rutgers	4.7	19.0
Will Bynum	JR	F	6-5	VMI	5.7	25.3
Ron Carter	SO	G	6-5	VMI	11.0	18.3
Mike Dabney	SR	G	6-4	Rutgers	4.0	18.0
Tony Hanson	JR	F	6-5	Connecticut	9.0	17.5
Al Weston	SR	G	5-10	Connecticut	2.5	21.0

MIDEAST

PLAYER	CL	POS	HT	SCHOOL	RPG	PPG
Kent Benson*	JR	C	6-10	Indiana	9.0	17.7
Scott May*	SR	F	6-7	Indiana	8.7	24.3
Tom Cutter	JR	C	6-8	Western Michigan	14.0	19.0
Anthony Murray	SO	G	6-2	Alabama	4.0	14.0
Earl Tatum	SR	F/G	6-6	Marquette	6.7	16.7

MIDWEST

PLAYER	CL	POS	HT	SCHOOL	RPG	PPG
Willie Smith*	SR	G	6-2	Missouri	6.3	31.3
Rick Bullock	SR	C	6-9	Texas Tech	9.5	21.0
Adrian Dantley	JR	F	6-5	Notre Dame	6.5	29.0
Rickey Green	JR	G	6-1	Michigan	4.3	17.7
Phil Hubbard	FR	F	6-7	Michigan	12.3	15.3

WEST

PLAYER	CL	POS	HT	SCHOOL	RPG	PPG
Richard Washington*	JR	F/C	6-10	UCLA	8.0	21.0
Al Fleming	SR	F	6-8	Arizona	13.0	10.7
Herman Harris	JR	G	6-5	Arizona	4.3	20.7
Marques Johnson	JR	F	6-7	UCLA	8.7	17.0
Jim Rappis	SR	G	6-2	Arizona	2.0	16.0

* Most outstanding player

1976 NCAA TOURNAMENT BOX SCORES

VMI 71-66 DePaul (SWEET 16)

31	1H	33
31	2H	29
9	OT1	4

VMI	MIN	FG	3FG	FT	REB	A	ST	BL	PF	TP
Will Bynum	43	7-12	-	8-10	6	1	0	0	4	22
Ron Carter	45	8-14	-	5-10	12	1	4	2	4	21
Dave Montgomery	32	4-12	-	4-7	14	0	2	1	3	12
John Krovic	45	4-12	-	0-2	5	2	1	0	2	8
Curt Reppart	37	1-3	-	3-10	3	0	0	0	4	5
George Borojevich	15	1-3	-	1-3	1	0	0	0	4	3
Kelly Lombard	8	0-0	-	0-0	0	1	0	0	1	0
TOTALS	225	25-56	-	21-42	41	5	7	3	22	71
Percentages		44.6		50.0						

Coach: Bill Blair

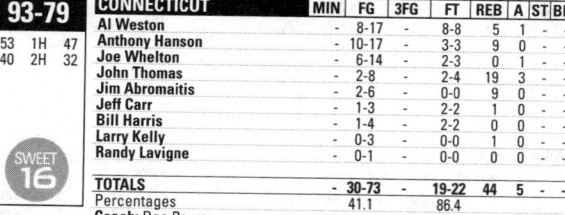

DEPAUL	MIN	FG	3FG	FT	REB	A	ST	BL	PF	TP
Ron Norwood	39	9-20	-	5-7	3	2	1	0	5	23
Dave Corzine	30	6-15	-	2-4	15	1	0	4	5	14
Curtis Watkins	33	4-12	-	2-4	8	0	0	0	5	10
Randy Ramsey	43	4-8	-	0-0	1	2	2	1	2	8
Joe Ponsetto	36	2-3	-	1-6	3	4	1	0	4	5
Gary Garland	10	1-3	-	0-0	4	0	0	0	5	2
Emmett McGovern	10	1-6	-	0-0	3	0	0	0	2	2
Randy Hook	5	1-1	-	0-1	0	0	1	0	2	2
Andy Pancratz	13	0-5	-	0-0	4	0	0	0	5	0
Gary Wydra	5	0-0	-	0-0	0	0	0	0	0	0
Greg Coehlo	1	0-1	-	0-0	0	0	0	0	0	0
TOTALS	225	28-74	-	10-22	41	9	5	5	35	66
Percentages		37.8		45.5						

Coach: Ray Meyer

Officials: Sonano, Sylvester
Technicals: DePaul (Corzi
Attendance: 10,362

Rutgers 93-79 Connecticut (SWEET 16)

53	1H	47
40	2H	32

RUTGERS	MIN	FG	3FG	FT	REB	A	ST	BL	PF	TP
Abdel Anderson	-	6-16	-	7-9	11	0	-	-	2	19
Mike Dabney	-	8-16	-	2-4	6	0	-	-	2	18
Eddie Jordan	-	6-10	-	6-6	5	5	-	-	1	18
Hollis Copeland	-	8-11	-	0-0	4	0	-	-	5	16
Stephen Hefele	-	7-9	-	0-0	7	2	-	-	2	14
Phil Sellers	-	4-13	-	0-2	5	3	-	-	3	8
James Bailey	-	0-4	-	0-2	4	1	-	-	4	0
Mark Conlin	-	0-0	-	0-0	1	0	-	-	3	0
Jeff Kleinbaum	-	0-2	-	0-0	2	0	-	-	0	0
Stan Nance	-	0-1	-	0-0	0	0	-	-	0	0
TOTALS	-	39-82	-	15-23	45	11	-	-	22	93
Percentages		47.6		65.2						

Coach: Tom Young

CONNECTICUT	MIN	FG	3FG	FT	REB	A	ST	BL	PF	TP
Al Weston	-	8-17	-	8-8	5	1	-	-	2	24
Anthony Hanson	-	10-17	-	3-3	9	0	-	-	4	23
Joe Whelton	-	6-14	-	2-3	0	1	-	-	3	14
John Thomas	-	2-8	-	2-4	19	3	-	-	4	6
Jim Abromaitis	-	2-6	-	0-0	9	0	-	-	3	4
Jeff Carr	-	1-3	-	2-2	1	0	-	-	1	4
Bill Harris	-	1-4	-	2-2	0	0	-	-	1	4
Larry Kelly	-	0-3	-	0-0	1	0	-	-	1	0
Randy Lavigne	-	0-1	-	0-0	0	0	-	-	0	0
TOTALS	-	30-73	-	19-22	44	5	-	-	19	79
Percentages		41.1		86.4						

Coach: Dee Rowe

Officials: Bain, White
Attendance: 10,362

Michigan 80-76 Notre Dame (SWEET 16)

40	1H	41
40	2H	35

MICHIGAN	MIN	FG	3FG	FT	REB	A	ST	BL	PF	TP
Rickey Green	39	8-16	-	4-4	4	3	1	0	1	20
John Robinson	38	5-13	-	5-6	8	1	1	1	2	15
Steve Grote	29	4-10	-	6-6	4	3	2	0	5	14
Wayman Britt	25	6-9	-	0-0	3	1	1	0	5	12
Phil Hubbard	36	5-13	-	1-2	10	0	1	0	4	11
Tom Staton	15	3-6	-	0-1	2	0	1	0	3	6
Dave Baxter	12	1-5	-	0-0	1	1	0	0	0	2
Tom Bergen	4	0-0	-	0-0	0	0	0	0	0	0
Alan Hardy	2	0-1	-	0-0	1	1	0	0	0	0
TOTALS	200	32-73	-	16-19	33	10	7	1	20	80
Percentages		43.8		84.2						

Coach: Johnny Orr

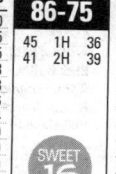

NOTRE DAME	MIN	FG	3FG	FT	REB	A	ST	BL	PF	TP
Adrian Dantley	39	12-19	-	7-8	5	1	1	0	1	31
Don Williams	34	6-13	-	3-4	2	3	0	0	3	15
Bill Paterno	20	5-9	-	0-0	4	1	1	0	2	10
Dave Batton	34	2-8	-	2-2	13	4	0	2	2	6
Bruce Flowers	24	3-6	-	0-0	9	3	1	0	5	6
Bernard Rencher	2	1-1	-	2-3	0	0	0	0	0	4
Ray Martin	26	1-2	-	0-1	2	4	1	0	5	2
Toby Knight	20	1-4	-	0-0	5	1	0	3	4	2
Jeff Carpenter	1	0-0	-	0-0	0	0	0	0	1	0
TOTALS	200	31-62	-	14-18	40	17	4	5	23	76
Percentages		50.0		77.8						

Coach: Digger Phelps

Officials: Morgan, Wortman
Attendance: 11,753

Missouri 86-75 Texas Tech (SWEET 16)

45	1H	36
41	2H	39

MISSOURI	MIN	FG	3FG	FT	REB	A	ST	BL	PF	TP
Willie Smith	39	13-21	-	4-6	10	7	0	0	2	30
Jim Kennedy	36	7-14	-	1-3	6	1	0	0	3	15
Kim Anderson	32	7-12	-	1-2	11	1	1	3	4	15
James Clabon	31	4-10	-	0-0	5	2	0	3	4	8
Stan Ray	18	4-7	-	0-0	6	0	0	0	3	8
Jeff Currie	24	2-4	-	2-3	3	1	0	1	1	6
Scott Sims	16	0-1	-	4-4	3	2	0	0	2	4
Danny Van Rheen	2	0-0	-	0-0	1	0	0	0	0	0
Brad Droy	1	0-0	-	0-0	0	0	0	0	0	0
Dave Stallman	1	0-0	-	0-0	0	0	0	0	1	0
TOTALS	200	37-69	-	12-18	45	14	1	7	20	86
Percentages		53.6		66.7						

Coach: Norm Stewart

TEXAS TECH	MIN	FG	3FG	FT	REB	A	ST	BL	PF	TP
Rick Bullock	31	8-20	-	7-12	14	1	0	1	5	23
Mike Russell	39	6-15	-	2-4	14	1	3	1	1	14
Geoff Huston	24	4-10	-	2-2	1	3	1	0	2	10
Mike Edwards	18	4-8	-	2-5	4	0	1	0	4	10
Grant Dukes	12	4-8	-	0-0	3	0	0	0	1	8
Grady Newton	29	3-6	-	0-0	4	2	1	0	3	6
Steve Dunn	22	2-9	-	0-2	2	3	0	0	1	4
Keith Kitchens	16	0-7	-	0-0	0	0	0	0	1	0
Rudy Liggins	7	0-3	-	0-0	0	0	0	0	2	0
Stanley Lee	1	0-0	-	0-0	0	0	0	0	0	0
Bob Rudolph	1	0-1	-	0-0	0	0	0	0	0	0
TOTALS	200	31-87	-	13-25	42	10	6	2	20	75
Percentages		35.6		52.0						

Coach: Gerald Myers

Officials: Nichols, Folsom
Technicals: Missouri (bench)
Attendance: 11,753

Indiana 74-69 Alabama (SWEET 16)

37	1H	29
37	2H	40

INDIANA	MIN	FG	3FG	FT	REB	A	ST	BL	PF	TP
Scott May	40	9-22	-	7-9	16	0	0	0	2	25
Kent Benson	33	7-11	-	1-2	5	3	0	1	4	15
Bob Wilkerson	40	6-12	-	2-2	12	4	0	0	1	14
Quinn Buckner	31	5-8	-	2-5	2	4	1	0	4	12
Tom Abernethy	40	2-6	-	4-5	6	3	0	0	1	8
Wayne Radford	9	0-1	-	0-0	1	0	1	0	1	0
Richard Valavicius	6	0-0	-	0-1	0	0	0	0	0	0
James Wisman	1	0-0	-	0-0	0	0	0	0	0	0
TOTALS	200	29-60	-	16-24	42	14	2	1	13	74
Percentages		48.3		66.7						

Coach: Bob Knight

ALABAMA	MIN	FG	3FG	FT	REB	A	ST	BL	PF	TP
T.R. Dunn	37	7-14	-	2-2	5	1	2	1	5	16
Anthony Murray	38	7-11	-	1-2	7	4	2	0	1	15
Leon Douglas	39	5-16	-	2-6	7	3	0	2	4	12
Keith McCord	25	5-9	-	1-2	3	0	0	0	2	11
Rickey Brown	25	3-7	-	1-2	5	0	0	0	4	7
Reginald King	25	2-6	-	0-0	6	0	0	1	5	4
Greg McElveen	7	1-4	-	0-0	1	1	0	0	1	2
Tommy Bonds	4	1-2	-	0-0	0	0	0	0	1	2
TOTALS	200	31-69	-	7-14	34	9	4	4	23	69
Percentages		44.9		50.0						

Coach: C.M. Newton

Officials: Turner, Brown
Attendance: 14,150

Marquette 62-57 Western Michigan (SWEET 16)

28	1H	25
34	2H	32

MARQUETTE	MIN	FG	3FG	FT	REB	A	ST	BL	PF	TP
Butch Lee	36	8-14	-	0-0	0	4	1	1	2	16
Lloyd Walton	34	6-12	-	0-0	1	5	2	0	4	12
Earl Tatum	35	5-12	-	0-0	8	2	0	1	4	10
Jerome Whitehead	35	5-10	-	0-0	7	0	0	1	1	10
Bo Ellis	38	3-7	-	2-2	7	0	1	4	4	8
Gary Rosenberger	8	1-4	-	2-2	0	0	0	0	0	4
Bernard Toone	7	1-1	-	0-0	0	0	0	0	0	2
Ulice Payne	4	0-1	-	0-0	1	0	0	0	0	0
Bill Neary	3	0-0	-	0-0	2	0	0	0	0	0
TOTALS	200	29-61	-	4-4	26	11	4	7	15	62
Percentages		47.5		100.0						

Coach: Al McGuire

WESTERN MICHIGAN	MIN	FG	3FG	FT	REB	A	ST	BL	PF	TP
Tom Cutter	40	8-12	-	5-5	17	1	0	1	1	21
Jeff Tyson	38	8-16	-	2-4	5	3	0	2	5	18
Jimmie Harvey	28	4-13	-	2-4	2	1	0	0	0	10
Marty Murray	24	2-9	-	0-0	2	1	0	0	2	4
Paul Griffin	31	1-2	-	0-0	9	6	2	0	3	2
Jim Kurzen	30	1-2	-	0-0	0	2	0	0	2	2
Dale Debruin	9	0-0	-	0-1	3	1	0	0	0	0
TOTALS	200	24-54	-	9-14	38	15	2	3	13	57
Percentages		44.4		64.3						

Coach: Eldon Miller

Officials: Herrold, Ditty
Attendance: 14,150

UCLA	MIN	FG	3FG	FT	REB	A	ST	BL	PF	TP
Marques Johnson	39	6-14	-	6-6	10	2	-	-	3	18
Richard Washington	37	7-18	-	2-5	6	4	-	-	2	16
David Greenwood	24	5-9	-	0-0	7	0	-	-	5	10
Raymond Townsend	37	4-6	-	0-0	4	3	-	-	2	8
Ralph Drollinger	14	4-7	-	0-0	6	2	-	-	5	8
Gavin Smith	4	3-4	-	0-2	0	0	-	-	0	6
Andre McCarter	39	2-4	-	0-0	2	7	-	-	1	4
Jim Spillane	4	0-0	-	0-0	0	0	-	-	0	0
Brett Vroman	2	0-0	-	0-0	1	0	-	-	1	0
TOTALS	200	31-62	-	8-13	36	18	-	-	19	70
Percentages		50.0		61.5						

Coach: Gene Bartow

70-61
40 1H 35
30 2H 26
SWEET 16

PEPPERDINE	MIN	FG	3FG	FT	REB	A	ST	BL	PF	TP
Marcos Leite	40	4-14	-	8-10	8	1	-	-	3	16
Dennis Johnson	39	7-14	-	2-5	6	0	-	-	2	16
Flintie Williams	38	4-10	-	2-2	0	2	-	-	3	10
Ollie Matson	34	4-9	-	2-3	5	3	-	-	5	10
Dick Skophammer	39	4-11	-	0-0	9	2	-	-	4	8
Ray Ellis	4	0-0	-	1-2	2	0	-	-	0	1
Howie Dallmar	3	0-0	-	0-0	2	0	-	-	1	0
Brian Goorjian	3	0-0	-	0-0	0	0	-	-	0	0
TOTALS	200	23-58	-	15-22	32	8	-	-	18	61
Percentages		39.7		68.2						

Coach: Gary Colson

Officials: Galvan, Fouty
Attendance: 12,683

ARIZONA	MIN	FG	3FG	FT	REB	A	ST	BL	PF	TP
Herman Harris	45	13-22	-	5-10	9	9	-	-	4	31
James Rappis	32	10-14	-	4-4	1	12	-	-	5	24
Robert Elliott	30	7-11	-	6-9	12	0	-	-	4	20
Philip Taylor	36	7-15	-	4-9	15	1	-	-	3	18
Al Fleming	23	3-7	-	0-2	11	1	-	-	5	6
Jerome Gladney	8	2-2	-	2-3	3	0	-	-	0	6
Leonard Gordy	30	2-5	-	1-3	6	2	-	-	5	5
Gilbert Myles	12	0-0	-	3-4	0	0	-	-	2	3
Gary Harrison	6	0-0	-	1-2	0	0	-	-	0	1
Sylvester Maxey	2	0-0	-	0-0	0	0	-	-	1	0
Timothy Marshall	1	0-0	-	0-0	0	0	-	-	0	0
TOTALS	225	44-76	-	26-46	57	25	-	-	29	114
Percentages		57.9		56.5						

Coach: Fred Snowden

114-109
51 1H 47
52 2H 56
11 OT1 6
SWEET 16

UNLV	MIN	FG	3FG	FT	REB	A	ST	BL	PF	TP
Sam Smith	28	9-20	-	8-10	5	0	-	-	5	26
Lewis Brown	36	10-19	-	4-5	16	0	-	-	4	24
Eddie Owens	27	9-18	-	3-3	1	1	-	-	5	21
Robert Smith	39	4-10	-	10-10	1	4	-	-	4	18
Boyd Batts	34	4-12	-	0-2	9	1	-	-	3	8
Glen Gondrezick	30	4-9	-	0-1	5	2	-	-	5	8
Jackie Robinson	17	1-3	-	0-1	4	0	-	-	5	2
Reggie Theus	13	1-5	-	0-1	4	3	-	-	2	2
Mike Milke	1	0-0	-	0-0	0	0	-	-	1	0
TOTALS	225	42-96	-	25-33	45	11	-	-	34	109
Percentages		43.8		75.8						

Coach: Jerry Tarkanian

Officials: Dreith, Menz
Attendance: 12,683

RUTGERS	MIN	FG	3FG	FT	REB	A	ST	BL	PF	TP
Mike Dabney	38	9-17	-	5-6	2	3	1	-	2	23
Eddie Jordan	37	7-11	-	9-10	4	5	6	-	3	23
Phil Sellers	33	6-9	-	4-5	12	1	0	-	4	16
Abdel Anderson	26	3-5	-	2-6	9	1	0	-	4	8
Hollis Copeland	24	4-8	-	0-0	5	0	0	-	4	8
James Bailey	16	3-6	-	0-0	5	0	1	-	4	6
Stephen Hefele	18	2-4	-	0-3	1	1	1	-	2	4
Mike Palko	1	1-1	-	0-0	0	0	0	-	0	2
Jeff Kleinbaum	2	0-0	-	1-2	0	0	0	-	0	1
Mark Conlin	3	0-0	-	0-0	1	0	0	-	0	0
Stan Nance	1	0-0	-	0-0	0	0	0	-	0	0
Bruce Scherer	1	0-0	-	0-0	1	0	0	-	0	0
TOTALS	200	35-61	-	21-32	40	11	9	-	23	91
Percentages		57.4		65.6						

Coach: Tom Young

91-75
48 1H 34
43 2H 41
ELITE 8

VMI	MIN	FG	3FG	FT	REB	A	ST	BL	PF	TP
Will Bynum	35	12-20	-	10-12	7	2	2	-	5	34
Ron Carter	34	6-12	-	3-4	7	2	4	-	4	15
John Krovic	35	5-19	-	0-0	4	2	1	-	1	10
George Borojevich	22	2-6	-	1-2	6	0	0	-	2	5
Dave Montgomery	22	2-3	-	1-2	4	0	1	-	5	5
Curt Reppart	27	2-4	-	0-1	2	2	3	-	5	4
Dave Slomski	1	1-2	-	0-0	2	0	0	-	0	2
Kelly Lombard	9	0-0	-	0-1	0	0	0	-	5	0
Saul Smith	9	0-2	-	0-0	3	0	0	-	3	0
Pat Kelley	4	0-2	-	0-0	0	0	0	-	0	0
Harlan Niehaus	1	0-0	-	0-0	0	0	0	-	0	0
Dan Stephans	1	0-0	-	0-0	0	0	0	-	0	0
TOTALS	200	30-70	-	15-22	35	8	11	-	30	75
Percentages		42.9		68.2						

Coach: Bill Blair

Officials: Bain, White
Attendance: 9,193

MICHIGAN	MIN	FG	3FG	FT	REB	A	ST	BL	PF	TP
Rickey Green	40	9-25	-	5-7	2	7	-	-	4	23
John Robinson	39	6-12	-	9-10	16	4	-	-	2	21
Phil Hubbard	39	8-10	-	4-7	18	1	-	-	3	20
Dave Baxter	31	6-12	-	6-8	5	4	-	-	2	18
Wayman Britt	35	3-10	-	1-2	3	2	-	-	3	7
Steve Grote	9	2-4	-	0-0	1	1	-	-	5	4
Tom Staton	4	1-2	-	0-0	2	1	-	-	0	2
Alan Hardy	2	0-0	-	0-0	0	0	-	-	2	0
Tom Bergen	1	0-0	-	0-0	0	0	-	-	0	0
TOTALS	200	35-75	-	25-34	47	20	-	-	21	95
Percentages		46.7		73.5						

Coach: Johnny Orr

95-88
50 1H 37
45 2H 51
ELITE 8

MISSOURI	MIN	FG	3FG	FT	REB	A	ST	BL	PF	TP
Willie Smith	39	18-35	-	7-11	7	3	-	-	4	43
Jim Kennedy	29	8-10	-	0-1	8	1	-	-	5	16
Stan Ray	35	6-12	-	1-2	15	1	-	-	3	13
Jeff Currie	34	3-8	-	1-3	2	2	-	-	5	7
Kim Anderson	23	2-6	-	0-3	7	2	-	-	5	4
Mark Anderson	19	1-4	-	1-2	0	1	-	-	4	3
Scott Sims	6	1-2	-	0-0	2	0	-	-	2	2
James Clabon	13	0-2	-	0-0	2	1	-	-	1	0
Dave Stallman	1	0-0	-	0-0	0	0	-	-	0	0
Danny Van Rheen	1	0-0	-	0-0	0	0	-	-	0	0
TOTALS	200	39-79	-	10-22	43	11	-	-	29	88
Percentages		49.4		45.5						

Coach: Norm Stewart

Officials: Nichols, Wortman
Attendance: 8,378

INDIANA	MIN	FG	3FG	FT	REB	A	ST	BL	PF	TP
Kent Benson	40	8-12	-	2-2	9	0	-	1	2	18
Scott May	27	7-10	-	1-2	3	2	-	0	3	15
Tom Abernethy	40	4-7	-	4-5	5	1	-	0	2	12
Quinn Buckner	40	4-9	-	1-2	8	5	-	0	2	9
Bob Wilkerson	23	2-3	-	2-2	3	7	-	0	1	6
Jim Crews	17	1-2	-	0-0	1	3	-	0	1	2
Wayne Radford	7	1-4	-	0-0	0	0	-	0	0	2
Richard Valavicius	6	0-0	-	1-2	2	0	-	0	0	1
TOTALS	200	27-47	-	11-15	31	18	-	1	11	65
Percentages		57.4		73.3						

Coach: Bob Knight

65-56
36 1H 35
29 2H 21
ELITE 8

MARQUETTE	MIN	FG	3FG	FT	REB	A	ST	BL	PF	TP
Earl Tatum	36	10-15	-	2-2	6	2	0	1	5	22
Bo Ellis	36	4-6	-	1-2	7	3	0	0	3	9
Butch Lee	31	4-18	-	0-0	2	0	0	0	1	8
Jerome Whitehead	35	3-10	-	1-2	9	0	0	1	4	7
Bernard Toone	8	2-5	-	2-2	4	0	1	0	0	6
Lloyd Walton	40	1-9	-	0-0	2	2	0	1	3	2
Gary Rosenberger	8	1-2	-	0-1	1	1	0	0	2	2
Bill Neary	6	0-1	-	0-0	2	0	0	0	0	0
TOTALS	200	25-66	-	6-9	33	8	1	3	18	56
Percentages		37.9		66.7						

Coach: Al McGuire

Officials: Ditty, Brown
Technicals: Marquette (coach McGuire, 2)
Attendance: 14,150

UCLA	MIN	FG	3FG	FT	REB	A	ST	BL	PF	TP
Richard Washington	37	11-24	-	0-0	10	4	-	-	2	22
Raymond Townsend	37	7-12	-	2-4	3	4	-	-	1	16
Marques Johnson	37	7-14	-	0-0	7	4	-	-	4	14
David Greenwood	26	4-8	-	2-2	4	1	-	-	2	10
Andre McCarter	37	4-7	-	1-2	3	5	-	-	0	9
Brad Holland	2	2-2	-	0-0	0	0	-	-	0	4
Ralph Drollinger	12	1-5	-	1-3	6	0	-	-	3	3
Jim Spillane	4	1-1	-	0-0	0	0	-	-	1	2
Gavin Smith	2	1-1	-	0-0	1	0	-	-	0	2
Roy Hamilton	2	0-0	-	0-0	0	0	-	-	0	0
Wilbert Olinde	2	0-0	-	0-0	0	0	-	-	0	0
Brett Vroman	2	0-0	-	0-1	1	0	-	-	0	0
TOTALS	200	38-74	-	6-12	35	18	-	-	13	82
Percentages		51.4		50.0						

Coach: Gene Bartow

82-66
38 1H 35
44 2H 31
ELITE 8

ARIZONA	MIN	FG	3FG	FT	REB	A	ST	BL	PF	TP
Herman Harris	37	9-19	-	0-0	1	4	-	-	3	18
Al Fleming	37	6-17	-	2-3	16	5	-	-	4	14
Philip Taylor	37	7-12	-	0-0	7	1	-	-	3	14
Robert Elliott	36	4-9	-	2-3	6	2	-	-	2	10
James Rappis	34	1-8	-	2-2	2	2	-	-	3	4
Jerome Gladney	4	1-2	-	0-0	1	1	-	-	1	2
Sylvester Maxey	3	0-1	-	2-2	0	1	-	-	0	2
Larry Demic	1	1-1	-	0-0	1	0	-	-	0	2
Leonard Gordy	3	0-0	-	0-0	0	0	-	-	0	0
Gilbert Myles	3	0-0	-	0-0	1	0	-	-	0	0
Brian Jung	2	0-0	-	0-0	0	0	-	-	0	0
Robert Aleksa	1	0-0	-	0-0	0	0	-	-	0	0
Gary Harrison	1	0-0	-	0-0	0	0	-	-	0	0
Timothy Marshall	1	0-0	-	0-0	0	1	-	-	1	0
TOTALS	200	29-69	-	8-10	35	17	-	-	18	66
Percentages		42.0		80.0						

Coach: Fred Snowden

Officials: Galvan, Fouty
Attendance: 12,459

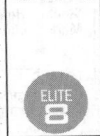

86-70 — FINAL 4

	1H	2H
Michigan	46	40
Rutgers	29	41

MICHIGAN	MIN	FG	3FG	FT	REB	A	ST	BL	PF	TP
John Robinson	38	8-13	-	4-5	16	3	-	-	2	20
Phil Hubbard	38	8-13	-	0-3	13	1	-	-	4	16
Rickey Green	30	7-16	-	2-2	6	5	-	-	4	16
Steve Grote	31	4-13	-	6-6	4	1	-	-	4	14
Wayman Britt	34	5-9	-	1-1	5	5	-	-	4	11
Dave Baxter	19	2-5	-	1-2	3	2	-	-	0	5
Tom Staton	4	1-1	-	2-2	0	2	-	-	1	4
Tom Bergen	1	0-0	-	0-0	0	0	-	-	0	0
Alan Hardy	1	0-0	-	0-0	0	0	-	-	0	0
Bobby Jones	1	0-0	-	0-0	0	0	-	-	0	0
Len Lillard	1	0-0	-	0-0	0	0	-	-	0	0
Lloyd Schinnerer	1	0-0	-	0-0	0	0	-	-	0	0
Joel Thompson	1	0-0	-	0-0	0	0	-	-	1	0
TOTALS	**200**	**35-70**	**-**	**16-21**	**47**	**19**	**-**	**-**	**20**	**86**
Percentages		50.0		76.2						

Coach: Johnny Orr

RUTGERS	MIN	FG	3FG	FT	REB	A	ST	BL	PF	TP
Eddie Jordan	25	6-20	-	4-4	4	6	-	-	4	16
Hollis Copeland	36	7-12	-	1-1	5	2	-	-	3	15
Phil Sellers	32	5-13	-	1-3	8	1	-	-	4	11
Mike Dabney	37	5-18	-	0-1	5	2	-	-	4	10
James Bailey	23	1-3	-	4-6	6	1	-	-	0	6
Abdel Anderson	19	3-8	-	0-1	6	0	-	-	3	6
Mark Conlin	16	2-2	-	0-0	1	2	-	-	2	4
Stephen Hefele	12	1-1	-	0-0	1	1	-	-	2	2
TOTALS	**200**	**30-77**	**-**	**10-16**	**36**	**15**	**-**	**-**	**22**	**70**
Percentages		39.0		62.5						

Coach: Tom Young

Officials: Wortman, Fo…
Attendance: 17,540

65-51 — FINAL 4

	1H	2H
Indiana	34	31
UCLA	26	25

INDIANA	MIN	FG	3FG	FT	REB	A	ST	BL	PF	TP
Kent Benson	38	6-15	-	4-6	9	0	0	0	4	16
Scott May	40	5-16	-	4-6	4	5	2	0	2	14
Tom Abernethy	33	7-8	-	0-1	6	2	1	0	3	14
Quinn Buckner	40	6-14	-	0-1	3	2	1	0	3	12
Bob Wilkerson	38	1-5	-	3-4	19	7	2	1	3	5
Jim Crews	11	1-1	-	2-3	3	3	1	0	0	4
TOTALS	**200**	**26-59**	**-**	**13-21**	**44**	**19**	**7**	**1**	**15**	**65**
Percentages		44.1		61.9						

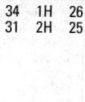

Coach: Bob Knight

UCLA	MIN	FG	3FG	FT	REB	A	ST	BL	PF	TP
Richard Washington	38	6-15	-	3-4	8	3	0	0	3	15
Marques Johnson	36	6-10	-	0-1	6	0	1	0	2	12
Gavin Smith	9	3-4	-	0-0	0	0	1	0	3	6
David Greenwood	26	2-5	-	1-2	10	0	0	2	2	5
Raymond Townsend	36	2-10	-	0-0	3	2	2	0	1	4
Andre McCarter	27	2-9	-	0-0	4	3	0	0	5	4
Ralph Drollinger	8	0-3	-	2-2	1	0	0	0	3	2
Chris Lippert	1	0-0	-	2-2	0	0	0	0	0	2
Roy Hamilton	4	0-1	-	1-2	0	0	0	0	0	1
Jim Spillane	7	0-2	-	0-0	1	2	0	0	0	0
Brad Holland	4	0-2	-	0-0	0	0	1	0	0	0
Brett Vroman	3	0-0	-	0-0	1	0	0	0	2	0
Wilbert Olinde	1	0-0	-	0-0	0	0	0	0	0	0
TOTALS	**200**	**21-61**	**-**	**9-13**	**34**	**10**	**5**	**2**	**21**	**51**
Percentages		34.4		69.2						

Coach: Gene Bartow

Officials: Brown, Bain
Attendance: 17,540

106-92 — 3RD PLACE

	1H	2H
UCLA	57	49
Rutgers	49	43

UCLA	MIN	FG	3FG	FT	REB	A	ST	BL	PF	TP
Marques Johnson	40	11-21	-	8-12	18	6	4	2	1	30
Andre McCarter	40	11-19	-	4-4	5	11	2	0	1	26
Ralph Drollinger	29	6-8	-	0-0	16	3	0	4	5	12
Richard Washington	22	5-8	-	1-2	0	2	0	0	4	11
Raymond Townsend	22	3-7	-	2-2	2	2	3	0	3	8
Gavin Smith	15	3-9	-	2-2	4	0	1	0	2	8
David Greenwood	19	2-4	-	1-2	8	0	0	0	5	5
Jim Spillane	7	2-3	-	0-0	0	0	0	0	1	4
Wilbert Olinde	4	1-1	-	0-0	1	1	0	0	0	2
Brett Vroman	2	0-0	-	0-0	1	0	0	0	1	0
TOTALS	**200**	**44-80**	**-**	**18-24**	**55**	**25**	**10**	**6**	**23**	**106**
Percentages		55.0		75.0						

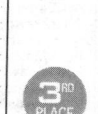

Coach: Gene Bartow

RUTGERS	MIN	FG	3FG	FT	REB	A	ST	BL	PF	TP
Phil Sellers	32	8-21	-	7-10	12	3	0	0	3	23
Mike Dabney	31	9-18	-	3-5	5	4	6	0	3	21
Hollis Copeland	38	9-19	-	0-2	13	4	2	0	3	18
Abdel Anderson	27	4-13	-	5-6	4	2	1	0	2	13
Eddie Jordan	39	4-16	-	0-2	4	7	3	0	3	8
James Bailey	23	3-10	-	1-1	5	1	0	2	2	7
Stephen Hefele	9	1-3	-	0-1	5	0	0	0	4	2
Mark Conlin	1	0-0	-	0-0	0	0	1	0	0	0
TOTALS	**200**	**38-100**	**-**	**16-27**	**48**	**21**	**13**	**2**	**20**	**92**
Percentages		38.0		59.3						

Coach: Tom Young

Officials: Fouty, Bain
Technicals: Rutgers (Dabney)
Attendance: 17,540

86-68 — NCAA FINAL 1976

	1H	2H
Indiana	29	57
Michigan	35	33

INDIANA	MIN	FG	3FG	FT	REB	A	ST	BL	PF	TP
Scott May	39	10-17	-	6-6	8	2	2	0	4	26
Kent Benson	39	11-20	-	3-5	9	2	1	1	3	25
Quinn Buckner	39	5-10	-	6-9	8	4	5	1	4	16
Tom Abernethy	35	4-8	-	3-3	4	1	1	0	2	11
James Wisman	21	0-1	-	2-3	1	6	0	0	4	2
Jim Crews	12	0-1	-	2-2	1	4	0	0	1	2
Richard Valavicius	4	1-1	-	0-0	0	0	1	0	0	2
Mark Haymore	1	1-1	-	0-0	1	0	0	0	0	2
Wayne Radford	7	0-1	-	0-0	1	0	0	0	0	0
Bob Wilkerson	2	0-1	-	0-0	0	0	0	0	1	0
Bob Bender	1	0-0	-	0-0	0	0	0	0	0	0
TOTALS	**200**	**32-61**	**-**	**22-28**	**33**	**19**	**10**	**2**	**19**	**86**
Percentages		52.5		78.6						

Coach: Bob Knight

MICHIGAN	MIN	FG	3FG	FT	REB	A	ST	BL	PF	TP
Rickey Green	39	7-16	-	4-5	6	2	1	0	3	18
Steve Grote	35	4-9	-	4-6	1	3	3	0	4	12
Wayman Britt	31	5-6	-	1-1	3	2	1	0	5	11
Phil Hubbard	31	4-8	-	2-2	11	0	0	1	5	10
John Robinson	38	4-8	-	0-1	6	5	1	0	2	8
Tom Staton	9	2-5	-	3-4	2	0	2	0	3	7
Alan Hardy	4	1-2	-	0-0	2	0	0	2	0	2
Dave Baxter	6	0-2	-	0-0	0	0	1	0	2	0
Tom Bergen	5	0-1	-	0-0	0	0	0	0	1	0
Joel Thompson	2	0-0	-	0-0	0	0	0	0	0	0
TOTALS	**200**	**27-57**	**-**	**14-19**	**31**	**12**	**9**	**3**	**25**	**68**
Percentages		47.4		73.7						

Coach: Johnny Orr

Officials: Wortman, Brown
Attendance: 17,540

National Invitation Tournament (NIT)

First round: Charlotte d. San Francisco 79-74, Holy Cross d. Saint Peter's 84-78, Kentucky d. Niagara 67-61, Providence d. North Carolina A&T 84-68
Quarterfinals: Charlotte d. Oregon 79-72, NC State d. Holy Cross 78-68, Kentucky d. Kansas State 81-78, Providence d. Louisville 73-67
Semifinals: Charlotte d. NC State 80-79, Kentucky d. Providence 79-78
Third place: NC State d. Providence 74-69
Championship: Kentucky d. Charlotte 71-67
MVP: Cedric Maxwell, Charlotte

1976-77: So Long, Al

Marquette coach Al McGuire pulled a John Wooden, leading his team to the NCAA title and retiring a champion after the season. Not that the Warriors (today's Golden Eagles) didn't get some help: Three top-ranked teams—UCLA, Michigan and Kentucky—were upset in the NCAA regionals, and UNLV and Charlotte each made the Final Four for the first time. (Charlotte, led by Cedric Maxwell, was making its first Tournament appearance.) Marquette squeaked by Maxwell and the 49ers, 51-49, on a buzzer-beater by Jerome Whitehead. In the Final, the Warriors knocked off North Carolina, 67-59, at the Omni in Atlanta, to deny Dean Smith his first shot at winning a national championship game. Butch Lee scored 19 points and was named the Tournament's Most Outstanding Player.

Marquette's seven losses were the most by an NCAA champion, surpassing Kentucky's six in 1958. (In 1988, Kansas won with 11 losses.) UCLA's Marques Johnson was the Naismith Player of the Year, averaging 21.4 ppg and 11.1 rpg. Indiana's Kent Benson was chosen by Milwaukee as the No. 1 overall pick in the NBA draft. Perhaps most important, the NCAA decided before the season to decriminalize the dunk shot, banned in warmups and games since the 1967-68 season.

Major Conference Standings

ACC

	Conference			Overall		
	W	L	Pct	W	L	Pct
North Carolina⊛	9	3	.750	28	5	.848
Clemson	8	4	.667	22	6	.786
Wake Forest○	8	4	.667	22	8	.733
Maryland	7	5	.583	19	8	.704
NC State	6	6	.500	17	11	.607
Duke	2	10	.167	14	13	.519
Virginia	2	10	.167	12	17	.414

Tournament: **North Carolina d. Virginia 75-69**
Tournament MVP: **John Kuester**, North Carolina

Big Eight

	Conference			Overall		
	W	L	Pct	W	L	Pct
Kansas State⊛⊗	11	3	.786	23	8	.742
Missouri	9	5	.643	21	8	.724
Oklahoma	9	5	.643	18	10	.643
Kansas	8	6	.571	18	10	.643
Nebraska⊗	7	7	.500	15	14	.517
Colorado	5	9	.357	11	16	.407
Oklahoma State	4	10	.286	10	17	.370
Iowa State	3	11	.214	8	19	.296

Tournament: **Kansas State d. Missouri 72-67 (OT)**
Tournament MVP: **Mike Evans**, Kansas State

Big Sky

	Conference			Overall		
	W	L	Pct	W	L	Pct
Idaho State⊛	13	1	.929	25	5	.833
Weber State	11	3	.786	20	8	.714
Montana⊗	8	6	.571	17	9	.654
Gonzaga	7	7	.500	11	16	.407
Montana State	6	8	.429	11	15	.423
Northern Arizona	5	9	.357	11	15	.423
Boise State	5	9	.357	10	16	.385
Idaho	3	11	.214	5	21	.192

Tournament: **Idaho State d. Weber State 61-55**
Tournament MVP: **Ed Thompson**, Idaho State

Big Ten

	Conference			Overall		
	W	L	Pct	W	L	Pct
Michigan⊛	16	2	.889	26	4	.867
Minnesota⊗	15	3	.833	24	3	.889
Purdue○⊗	14	4	.778	19	9	.679
Iowa⊗	12	6	.667	18	9	.667
Indiana⊗	11	7	.611	14	13	.519
Michigan State⊗	9	9	.500	10	17	.370
Illinois⊗	8	10	.444	14	16	.467
Wisconsin⊗	7	11	.389	9	18	.333
Northwestern⊗	7	11	.389	7	20	.304
Ohio State⊗	4	14	.222	9	18	.333

East Coast

	Conference			Overall		
	W	L	Pct	W	L	Pct
East Section						
Hofstra⊛	4	1	.800	23	7	.767
Temple	4	1	.800	17	11	.607
La Salle	3	2	.600	17	12	.586
American	2	3	.400	13	13	.500
Saint Joseph's	2	3	.400	13	13	.500
Drexel	0	5	.000	11	13	.458
West Section						
Lafayette	9	1	.900	21	6	.778
Delaware	7	3	.700	12	13	.480
Lehigh	6	4	.600	12	15	.444
Bucknell	5	5	.500	10	15	.400
West Chester	2	8	.200	11	14	.440
Rider	1	9	.100	8	18	.308

Tournament: **Hofstra d. La Salle 92-81**

East. Collegiate

	Conference			Overall		
	W	L	Pct	W	L	Pct
Eastern						
Rutgers□	7	1	.875	18	10	.643
Villanova□	6	1	.857	23	10	.697
George Washington	5	3	.625	14	12	.538
Massachusetts□	3	4	.429	20	11	.645
Western						
West Virginia	5	5	.500	18	11	.621
Penn State	5	5	.500	11	15	.423
Duquesne⊛	3	7	.300	15	15	.500
Pittsburgh	1	9	.100	6	21	.222

Tournament: **Duquesne d. Villanova 57-54**
Tournament MVP: **Norm Nixon**, Duquesne

Ivy

	Conference			Overall		
	W	L	Pct	W	L	Pct
Princeton⊛	13	1	.929	21	5	.808
Penn	12	2	.857	18	8	.692
Columbia	8	6	.571	16	10	.615
Harvard	6	8	.429	9	16	.360
Cornell⊗	5	9	.357	8	18	.308
Brown	5	9	.357	6	20	.231
Yale	4	10	.286	6	20	.231
Dartmouth	3	11	.214	4	22	.154

Note: Columbia and Princeton also played in NJ-NY 7

Metro 7

	Conference			Overall		
	W	L	Pct	W	L	Pct
Louisville○	6	1	.857	21	7	.750
Cincinnati⊛	4	2	.667	25	5	.833
Georgia Tech	3	3	.500	18	10	.643
Tulane	3	3	.500	10	17	.370
Memphis□	2	4	.333	20	9	.690
Florida State	2	4	.333	16	11	.593
Saint Louis	1	5	.167	7	19	.269

Tournament: **Cincinnati d. Georgia Tech 74-61**
Tournament MVP: **Gary Yoder**, Cincinnati

Mid-American

	Conference			Overall		
	W	L	Pct	W	L	Pct
Miami (OH)	13	3	.813	20	6	.769
Central Michigan⊛	13	3	.813	18	10	.643
Toledo	12	4	.750	21	6	.778
Northern Illinois	10	6	.625	13	14	.481
Western Michigan	8	8	.500	14	13	.519
Ball State	7	9	.438	11	14	.440
Bowling Green	5	11	.313	9	18	.333
Ohio	4	12	.250	9	17	.346
Eastern Michigan	4	12	.250	9	18	.333
Kent State	4	12	.250	8	19	.296

MEAC

	Conference			Overall		
	W	L	Pct	W	L	Pct
SC State	10	2	.833	15	11	.577
Howard	8	4	.667	18	10	.643
NC Central	8	4	.667	13	15	.464
Morgan State	7	5	.583	18	11	.621
UMES	6	6	.500	7	19	.269
NC A&T	3	9	.250	3	24	.111
Delaware State	0	12	.000	2	25	.074

Tournament: **Morgan State d. Howard 82-77**
Tournament MOP: **Eric Evans**, Morgan State

Missouri Valley

	Conference			Overall		
	W	L	Pct	W	L	Pct
Southern Illinois⊛	8	4	.667	22	7	.759
New Mexico State	8	4	.667	17	10	.630
Wichita State	7	5	.583	18	10	.643
West Texas A&M	7	5	.583	18	12	.600
Drake	5	7	.417	10	17	.370
Bradley	4	8	.333	9	18	.333
Tulsa	3	9	.250	6	21	.222
Indiana State□	-	-	-	25	3	.893
Creighton□	-	-	-	21	7	.750

Tournament: **Southern Illinois d. West Texas A&M 82-69**

NJ-NY 7

	Conference			Overall		
	W	L	Pct	W	L	Pct
Seton Hall□	3	1	.750	18	11	.621
Columbia	3	1	.750	16	10	.615
St. John's○	3	2	.600	22	9	.710
Manhattan	3	2	.600	13	14	.481
Rutgers	3	3	.500	18	10	.643
Princeton	1	2	.333	21	5	.808
Fordham	0	5	.000	5	21	.192

Ohio Valley

	Conference			Overall		
	W	L	Pct	W	L	Pct
Austin Peay	13	1	.929	24	4	.857
Middle Tenn. State⊛	9	5	.643	20	9	.690
Murray State	9	5	.643	17	10	.630
Morehead State	9	5	.643	15	10	.600
East Tennessee State	6	8	.429	12	14	.462
Western Kentucky	6	8	.429	10	16	.385
Eastern Kentucky	3	11	.214	8	16	.333
Tennessee Tech	1	13	.071	7	19	.269

Tournament: **Middle Tenn. State d. Austin Peay 77-65**
Tournament MVP: **Bob Martin**, Middle Tennessee State

Conference Standings Continue →

⊛ Automatic NCAA Tournament bid ○ At-large NCAA Tournament bid □ NIT appearance ⊗ Team record doesn't reflect games forfeited or vacated. For adjusted record, see p. 521.

PCAA

	Conference W	Conference L	Conference Pct	Overall W	Overall L	Overall Pct
Long Beach State⊕	9	3	.750	21	8	.724
San Diego State	9	3	.750	13	15	.464
San Jose State	8	4	.667	17	12	.586
Cal State Fullerton	7	5	.583	16	10	.615
Pacific	5	7	.417	11	14	.440
UC Santa Barbara	3	9	.250	8	18	.308
Fresno State	1	11	.083	7	20	.259

Tournament: **Long Beach State d. San Jose State 76-63**
Tournament MVP: **Michael Wiley**, Long Beach State

PAC-8

	Conference W	Conference L	Conference Pct	Overall W	Overall L	Overall Pct
UCLA⊕	11	3	.786	24	5	.828
Oregon□	9	5	.643	19	10	.655
Washington State	8	6	.571	19	8	.704
Washington	8	6	.571	17	10	.630
Oregon State	8	6	.571	16	13	.552
California	7	7	.500	12	15	.444
Stanford	3	11	.214	11	16	.407
Southern California	2	12	.143	6	20	.231

SEC

	Conference W	Conference L	Conference Pct	Overall W	Overall L	Overall Pct
Kentucky○	16	2	.889	26	4	.867
Tennessee⊕	16	2	.889	22	6	.786
Alabama□	14	4	.778	25	6	.806
Florida	10	8	.556	17	9	.654
LSU	8	10	.444	15	12	.556
Mississippi State	6	12	.333	14	13	.519
Auburn	6	12	.333	13	13	.500
Vanderbilt	6	12	.333	10	16	.385
Mississippi	5	13	.278	11	16	.407
Georgia	3	15	.167	9	18	.333

SOUTHERN

	Conference W	Conference L	Conference Pct	Overall W	Overall L	Overall Pct
VMI⊕	8	2	.800	26	4	.867
Furman	8	2	.800	18	10	.643
Appalachian State	8	4	.667	17	12	.586
William and Mary	7	4	.636	16	14	.533
East Carolina	3	9	.250	10	18	.357
Davidson	2	8	.200	5	22	.185
The Citadel	2	9	.182	8	19	.296
Chattanooga	-	-	-	27	5	.844
Western Carolina	-	-	-	8	16	.333
Marshall	-	-	-	8	19	.296

Tournament: **VMI d. Appalachian State 69-67 (OT)**
Tournament MOP: **Dave Montgomery**, VMI

SOUTHLAND

	Conference W	Conference L	Conference Pct	Overall W	Overall L	Overall Pct
UL-Lafayette	8	2	.800	21	8	.724
McNeese State	7	3	.700	20	7	.741
Lamar	6	4	.600	12	17	.414
Arkansas State	4	6	.400	14	13	.519
Louisiana Tech	4	6	.400	13	13	.500
Texas-Arlington	1	9	.100	3	24	.111

SOUTHWEST

	Conference W	Conference L	Conference Pct	Overall W	Overall L	Overall Pct
Arkansas⊕	16	0	1.000	26	2	.929
Houston□	13	3	.813	29	8	.784
Texas Tech	12	4	.750	20	9	.690
Texas A&M	8	8	.500	14	14	.500
Texas	8	8	.500	13	13	.500
SMU	7	9	.438	8	19	.296
Baylor	5	11	.313	11	17	.393
Rice	3	13	.188	9	18	.333
TCU	0	16	.000	3	23	.115

Tournament: **Arkansas d. Houston 80-74**
Tournament MVP: **Ron Brewer**, Arkansas

SUN BELT

	Conference W	Conference L	Conference Pct	Overall W	Overall L	Overall Pct
Charlotte○	5	1	.833	28	5	.848
New Orleans	4	2	.667	18	10	.643
South Alabama	3	3	.500	17	10	.630
Georgia State	2	4	.333	10	18	.357
Jacksonville	2	4	.333	10	19	.345
South Florida	2	4	.333	9	18	.333

Tournament: **Charlotte d. New Orleans 71-70**
Tournament MVP: **Cedric Maxwell**, Charlotte

WCAC

	Conference W	Conference L	Conference Pct	Overall W	Overall L	Overall Pct
San Francisco⊕	14	0	1.000	29	2	.935
Santa Clara	9	5	.643	17	10	.630
Nevada	7	7	.500	15	12	.556
Seattle	7	7	.500	14	14	.500
Portland	6	8	.429	11	15	.423
Pepperdine	5	9	.357	13	13	.500
Loyola Marymount	4	10	.286	11	15	.423
Saint Mary's (CA)	4	10	.286	11	16	.407

WAC

	Conference W	Conference L	Conference Pct	Overall W	Overall L	Overall Pct
Utah⊕	11	3	.786	22	7	.759
Arizona○	10	4	.714	21	6	.778
New Mexico	8	6	.571	19	11	.633
Wyoming	8	6	.571	17	10	.630
Arizona State	6	8	.429	15	13	.536
Colorado State	6	8	.429	13	12	.520
BYU	4	10	.286	12	15	.444
UTEP	3	11	.214	11	15	.423

INDEPENDENTS

	Overall W	Overall L	Overall Pct
UNLV○	29	3	.906
Syracuse⊕$	26	4	.867
Detroit○⊗	25	4	.862
Old Dominion□	25	4	.862
Providence○	24	5	.828
Holy Cross⊕$	23	6	.793
St. Bonaventure□	23	6	.793
Marquette○⊗	25	7	.781
North Texas	21	6	.778
Illinois State□	22	7	.759
Notre Dame○	22	7	.759
Oral Roberts□	21	7	.750
Army	20	8	.714

INDEPENDENTS (CONT.)

	Overall W	Overall L	Overall Pct
Wisconsin-Milwaukee	19	8	.704
Georgetown□	19	9	.679
Virginia Tech□	19	10	.655
James Madison	17	9	.654
Northwestern State (LA)	17	9	.654
Texas-Pan American	17	9	.654
Connecticut	17	10	.630
Portland State	17	10	.630
UNC Wilmington	16	10	.615
Iona	15	10	.600
Dayton	16	11	.593
Fairfield	16	11	.593
Georgia Southern	16	11	.593
Richmond	15	11	.577
Saint Francis (PA)	15	11	.577
DePaul	15	12	.556
UL-Monroe	15	12	.556
Stetson	15	12	.556
Utah State	15	12	.556
Colgate	13	11	.542
Navy	13	11	.542
Oklahoma City	14	12	.538
South Carolina	14	12	.538
Valparaiso	13	12	.520
Catholic	13	13	.500
Fairleigh Dickinson	13	13	.500
Loyola-Chicago	13	13	.500
Maine	13	13	.500
Niagara	13	13	.500
Rhode Island	13	13	.500
Saint Peter's	13	13	.500
VCU	13	13	.500
Butler	13	14	.481
New Hampshire	12	14	.462
Northeastern	12	14	.462
St. Francis (NY)	12	14	.462
Denver	12	15	.444
Air Force	11	16	.407
Southern Miss	11	16	.407
Siena	9	15	.375
Cleveland State	10	17	.370
Xavier	10	17	.370
Centenary	11	19	.367
Long Island	9	16	.360
Hawaii	9	18	.333
Vermont⊗	8	17	.320
Boston College	8	18	.308
Charleston Southern	8	19	.296
Boston U.	7	19	.269
Robert Morris	7	19	.269
Samford	7	19	.269
Mercer	6	19	.240
Hardin-Simmons	6	21	.222
Houston Baptist	6	23	.207
Buffalo	5	21	.192
Wagner	3	21	.125
Canisius	3	22	.120

$ Defeated regional opponents to earn an automatic NCAA bid

$ Defeated regional opponents to earn an automatic NCAA bid

INDIVIDUAL LEADERS—SEASON

Scoring

Scoring	CL	POS	G	FG	FT	PTS	PPG
1 **Freeman Williams**, Portland State	JR	G	26	417	176	1,010	**38.8**
2 **Anthony Roberts**, Oral Roberts	SR	F	28	402	147	951	**34.0**
3 **Larry Bird**, Indiana State	SO	F	28	375	168	918	**32.8**
4 **Otis Birdsong**, Houston	SR	G	36	452	186	1,090	**30.3**
5 **Rich Laurel**, Hofstra	SR	G	30	355	198	908	**30.3**
6 **Calvin Natt**, UL-Monroe	SO	F	27	307	168	782	**29.0**
7 **Mike McConathy**, Louisiana Tech	SR	G	26	258	200	716	**27.5**
8 **Roger Phegley**, Bradley	JR	G/F	27	272	195	739	**27.4**
9 **Billy Reynolds**, Northwestern State (LA)	SR	G	26	270	146	686	**26.4**
10 **Tony Hanson**, Connecticut	SR	F	27	253	196	702	**26.0**

Field Goal Pct

Field Goal Pct	CL	POS	G	FG	FGA	PCT
1 **Joe Senser**, West Chester	SO	F	25	130	186	**69.9**
2 **Dave Montgomery**, VMI	JR	C	30	161	247	**65.2**
3 **Sidney Moncrief**, Arkansas	SO	G	28	157	242	**64.9**
4 **Cedric Maxwell**, Charlotte	SR	C	31	244	381	**64.0**
5 **Frank Sowinski**, Princeton	JR	F	26	163	258	**63.2**

Minimum: 5 made per game

Free Throw Pct

Free Throw Pct	CL	POS	G	FT	FTA	PCT
1 **Robert Smith**, UNLV	SR	G	32	98	106	**92.5**
2 **Kevin Kelly**, Vermont	JR	G	25	71	77	**92.2**
3 **Phil Thieneman**, Virginia Tech	SR	G	29	98	107	**91.6**
4 **Buck O'Brien**, Seattle	SR	G	26	89	99	**89.9**
5 **Chris Fagan**, Colgate	SR	G	24	110	123	**89.4**

Minimum: 2.5 made per game

Rebounds Per Game

Rebounds Per Game	CL	POS	G	REB	RPG
1 **Glenn Mosley**, Seton Hall	SR	F	29	473	**16.3**
2 **John Irving**, Hofstra	SR	F	27	440	**16.3**
3 **Robert Elmore**, Wichita State	SR	C	28	441	**15.8**
4 **Bob Stephens**, Drexel	SO	F	23	340	**14.8**
5 **Mark Landsberger**, Arizona State	JR	F/C	25	359	**14.4**
6 **Bernard King**, Tennessee	JR	F	26	371	**14.3**
7 **Larry Bird**, Indiana State	SO	F	28	373	**13.3**
8 **Bruce King**, Iowa	SR	C	25	332	**13.3**
9 **Edgar Jones**, Nevada	SO	F/C	27	355	**13.1**
10 **Phil Hubbard**, Michigan	SO	F	30	389	**13.0**

TEAM LEADERS—SEASON

Win-Loss Pct

Win-Loss Pct	W	L	PCT
1 **San Francisco**	29	2	**.935**
2 **Arkansas**	26	2	**.929**
3 **UNLV**	29	3	**.906**
4 **Indiana State**	25	3	**.893**
5 **Minnesota**⊗	24	3	**.889**

Scoring Offense

Scoring Offense	G	W-L	PTS	PPG
1 **UNLV**	32	29-3	3,426	**107.1**
2 **Houston**	37	29-8	3,482	**94.1**
3 **San Francisco**	31	29-2	2,904	**93.7**
4 **North Texas**	27	21-6	2,468	**91.4**
5 **Detroit**	29	25-4	2,629	**90.7**

Scoring Margin

Scoring Margin	G	W-L	PPG	OPP PPG	MAR
1 **UNLV**	32	29-3	107.1	87.7	**19.4**
2 **Clemson**	28	22-6	86.6	68.9	**17.7**
3 **Old Dominion**	29	25-4	88.3	70.9	**17.4**
4 **Detroit**	29	25-4	90.7	73.9	**16.8**
5 **Syracuse**	30	26-4	86.9	70.2	**16.7**

Field Goal Pct

Field Goal Pct	G	W-L	FG	FGA	PCT
1 **Arkansas**	28	26-2	849	1,558	**54.5**
2 **UNC Wilmington**	26	16-10	816	1,500	**54.4**
3 **West Texas A&M**	30	17-13	885	1,634	**54.2**
4 **Utah**	29	22-7	936	1,733	**54.0**
5 **North Carolina**	33	28-5	1,054	1,961	**53.7**

Free Throw Pct

Free Throw Pct	G	W-L	FT	FTA	PCT
1 **Utah**	29	22-7	499	638	**78.2**
2 **Marquette**	32	25-7	446	573	**77.8**
3 **Princeton**	26	21-5	391	507	**77.1**
4 **UNLV**	32	29-3	610	793	**76.9**
5 **Georgia Tech**	28	18-10	434	565	**76.8**

Rebound Margin

Rebound Margin	G	W-L	REB	OPP REB	MAR
1 **Notre Dame**	29	22-7	42.4	31.6	**10.8**
2 **Indiana State**	28	25-3	44.0	33.9	**10.1**
3 **San Francisco**	31	29-2	47.0	37.1	**9.9**
4 **Arizona**	27	21-6	46.7	37.0	**9.7**
5 **Navy**	24	13-11	41.0	32.3	**8.7**

Scoring Defense

Scoring Defense	G	W-L	OPP PTS	OPP PPG
1 **Princeton**	26	21-5	1,343	**51.7**
2 **Marquette**	32	25-7	1,900	**59.4**
3 **Toledo**	27	21-6	1,604	**59.4**
4 **Arkansas**	28	26-2	1,701	**60.8**
5 **Oregon**	29	19-10	1,766	**60.9**

Field Goal Pct Defense

Field Goal Pct Defense	G	W-L	OPP FG	OPP FGA	OPP PCT
1 **Minnesota**	27	24-3	766	1,886	**40.6**
2 **Princeton**	26	21-5	548	1,336	**41.0**
3 **Oral Roberts**	28	21-7	796	1,922	**41.4**
4 **Kansas**	28	18-10	727	1,726	**42.1**
5 **Syracuse**	30	26-4	830	1,970	**42.1**

CONSENSUS ALL-AMERICAS

First Team

PLAYER	CL	POS	HT	SCHOOL	RPG	PPG
Kent Benson	SR	C	6-11	Indiana	10.5	19.8
Otis Birdsong	SR	G	6-4	Houston	4.4	30.3
Phil Ford	JR	G	6-3	North Carolina	1.9	18.7
Rickey Green	SR	G	6-2	Michigan	2.9	19.5
Marques Johnson	SR	F	6-7	UCLA	11.1	21.4
Bernard King	JR	F	6-7	Tennessee	14.3	25.8

Second Team

PLAYER	CL	POS	HT	SCHOOL	RPG	PPG
Greg Ballard	SR	F	6-7	Oregon	9.8	21.7
Bill Cartwright	SO	C	6-11	San Francisco	8.5	19.4
Rod Griffin	JR	F	6-7	Wake Forest	8.6	20.5
Ernie Grunfeld	SR	G/F	6-6	Tennessee	6.3	22.8
Phil Hubbard	SO	F	6-7	Michigan	13.0	19.6
Butch Lee	JR	G	6-0	Marquette	3.8	19.6
Mychal Thompson	JR	C	6-10	Minnesota	8.9	22.0

Selectors: AP, NABC, UPI, USBWA

AWARD WINNERS

Player of the Year

PLAYER	CL	POS	HT	SCHOOL	AWARDS
Marques Johnson	SR	F	6-7	UCLA	Naismith, AP, UPI, USBWA, Wooden, NABC, Rupp
Jeff Jonas	SR	G	5-11	Utah	Frances Pomeroy Naismith*

* For the most outstanding senior player who is 6 feet or under

Coach of the Year

COACH	SCHOOL	REC	AWARDS
Bob Gaillard	San Francisco	29-2	AP, UPI
Eddie Sutton	Arkansas	26-2	USBWA
Dean Smith	North Carolina	28-5	NABC
Lee Rose	Charlotte	28-5	Sporting News

Poll Progression

Preseason Poll Ⓐ

AP	UPI	School
1	2	Michigan
2	1	Marquette
3	3	North Carolina
4	4	UCLA
5	5	Indiana
6	6	Kentucky
7	7	UNLV
8	11	Maryland
9	8	Louisville
10	9	Arizona
11	12	San Francisco
12	10	Cincinnati
13	—	Alabama
14	—	Notre Dame
15	14	NC State
16	13	Tennessee
17	18	Rutgers
18	—	DePaul
19	—	Charlotte
20	15	Missouri
—	16	Wichita State
—	17	Georgetown
—	19	Pennsylvania
—	20	Purdue

Week of Nov 30

AP	UPI	School	AP↓↑
1	—	Michigan (1-0)	
2	—	Marquette (0-0)	
3	—	UCLA (2-0)	↑1
4	—	Indiana (1-0)	↑1
5	—	Kentucky (1-0) Ⓑ	↑1
6	—	UNLV (1-0)	↑1
7	—	Louisville (0-0)	↑2
8	—	Notre Dame (1-0)	↑6
9	—	North Carolina (1-1)	↓6
10	—	San Francisco (3-0)	↑1
11	—	Arizona (1-0)	↓1
12	—	Cincinnati (0-0)	
13	—	Alabama (1-0)	
14	—	Wake Forest (2-0)	⤴
15	—	Tennessee (1-0)	↑1
16	—	Maryland (0-1)	↓8
17	—	Southern Illinois (1-0)	⤴
18	—	DePaul (0-1)	
19	—	Rutgers (0-0)	↓2
20	—	Charlotte (1-0)	↓1

Week of Dec 7

AP	UPI	School	AP↓↑
1	1	Michigan (2-0)	
2	2	Marquette (1-0)	
3	3	UCLA (3-0)	
4	5	Kentucky (2-0)	↑1
5	4	UNLV (3-0)	↑1
6	8	San Francisco (4-0)	↑4
7	11	Notre Dame (3-0)	↑1
8	10	Cincinnati (3-0)	↑4
9	7	Arizona (4-0)	↑2
10	6	Alabama (4-0)	↑3
11	14	Wake Forest (4-0)	↑3
12	9	North Carolina (2-1)	↓3
13	12	Indiana (1-1)	↓9
14	16	Louisville (1-1)	↓7
15	13	Tennessee (2-0)	
16	20	Clemson (4-0)	⤴
17	15	Maryland (3-1)	↓1
18	18	Southern Illinois (3-0)	↓1
19	—	DePaul (2-1)	↓1
20	—	Syracuse (3-1)	⤴
—	17	Washington (3-0)	
—	19	Oregon (2-1)	

Week of Dec 14

AP	UPI	School	AP↓↑
1	1	Michigan (3-0)	
2	2	Marquette (4-0)	
3	3	Kentucky (4-0)	↑1
4	4	Notre Dame (5-0)	↑3
5	5	San Francisco (7-0)	↑1
6	9	Cincinnati (5-0)	↑2
7	7	Alabama (4-0)	↑3
8	8	Arizona (7-0)	↑1
9	10	UCLA (3-1)	↓6
10	12	Wake Forest (5-0)	↑1
11	6	North Carolina (4-1)	↑1
12	11	UNLV (4-1)	↓7
13	14	Clemson (4-0)	↑3
14	13	Maryland (3-1)	↑3
15	15	Syracuse (6-1)	↑5
16	19	Indiana (1-2)	↓3
17	—	Louisville (3-2)	↓3
18	16	Southern Illinois (5-1)	
19	—	Arkansas (5-0)	⤴
20	—	St. John's (5-0)	⤴
—	17	Purdue (4-2)	
—	18	Minnesota (4-0)	
—	20	Oregon (3-1)	

Week of Dec 21

AP	UPI	School	AP↓↑
1	1	Michigan (4-0)	
2	2	Notre Dame (6-0)	↑2
3	3	San Francisco (10-0)	↑2
4	6	Cincinnati (7-0)	↑2
5	4	Alabama (6-0)	↑2
6	5	Marquette (4-1)	↓4
7	7	Kentucky (6-1)	↓4
8	8	UCLA (5-1)	↑1
9	12	Wake Forest (6-0)	↑1
10	9	North Carolina (4-1)	↑1
11	10	Clemson (7-0)	↑2
12	11	UNLV (6-1)	
13	13	Louisville (4-2)	↑4
14	14	Arizona (7-1)	↓6
15	—	Maryland (6-1)	↓1
16	15	Utah (5-3)	⤴
17	17	Syracuse (7-1)	↓2
18	—	Arkansas (6-0)	↑1
19	—	Tennessee (5-2)	⤴
20	16	Minnesota (6-0)	⤴
—	18	Oregon (5-1)	
—	19	Missouri (6-2)	
—	20	Georgetown (4-0)	

Week of Dec 28

AP	UPI	School	AP↓↑
1	1	Michigan (5-0)	
2	2	Notre Dame (7-0)	
3	3	San Francisco (12-0)	
4	4	Alabama (6-0)	↑1
5	5	Cincinnati (7-0)	↓1
6	7	Kentucky (6-1)	↑1
7	10	Wake Forest (7-0)	↑2
8	8	UCLA (7-1)	
9	6	North Carolina (5-1)	↑1
10	11	Clemson (7-0)	↑1
11	9	UNLV (8-1)	↑1
12	14	Marquette (4-2)	↓6
13	13	Arizona (8-1)	↑1
14	15	Louisville (5-2)	↓1
15	12	Minnesota (8-0)	↑5
16	16	Maryland (7-1)	↓1
17	17	Arkansas (8-0)	↑1
18	18	Syracuse (7-1)	↓1
19	—	Utah (6-3)	↓3
20	—	Auburn (5-0)	⤴
—	19	Iowa (7-0)	
—	20	Oregon (5-1)	

Week of Jan 4

AP	UPI	School	AP↓↑
1	1	San Francisco (15-0)	↑2
2	4	Cincinnati (9-0)	↑3
3	2	Kentucky (7-1)	↑3
4	5	Alabama (9-0)	
5	3	Michigan (6-1)	↓4
6	7	North Carolina (6-1)	↑3
7	6	UCLA (9-1)	↑1
8	8	Notre Dame (7-1)	↓6
9	9	UNLV (10-1)	↑2
10	13	Wake Forest (9-1)	↓3
11	10	Arizona (10-1)	↑2
12	11	Marquette (7-2)	
13	12	Minnesota (9-0)	↑2
14	16	Louisville (7-2)	
15	18	Maryland (9-1)	↑1
16	15	Clemson (9-1)	↓6
17	14	Providence (8-2)	⤴
18	—	Arkansas (8-1)	↓1
19	—	Syracuse (8-2)	↓1
20	—	Memphis (10-1)	⤴
—	17	Missouri (9-2)	
—	18	Purdue (6-3)	
—	20	Utah (9-3)	⤵

Week of Jan 11

AP	UPI	School	AP↓↑
1	1	San Francisco (17-0)	
2	3	Kentucky (9-1)	↑1
3	2	Cincinnati (10-0)	↓1
4	4	Alabama (12-0)	
5	5	North Carolina (8-1)	↑1
6	6	Michigan (9-1)	↓1
7	8	Wake Forest (11-1)	↑3
8	7	UNLV (10-1)	↑1
9	11	Minnesota (10-0)	↑4
10	10	Arizona (11-1)	↑1
11	9	Marquette (9-2)	↑1
12	12	UCLA (11-2)	↓5
13	14	Louisville (9-2)	↑1
14	—	Maryland (11-2)	↑1
15	18	Providence (11-2)	↑2
16	16	Arkansas (10-1)	↑2
17	—	Clemson (10-2)	↓1
18	—	Memphis (13-1)	↑2
19	—	Notre Dame (7-3)	↓11
20	15	Oregon (11-2)	⤴
—	13	Purdue (8-3)	
—	17	Tennessee (8-2)	
—	19	Holy Cross (10-1)	
—	19	St. John's (9-2)	

Week of Jan 18

AP	UPI	School	AP↓↑
1	1	San Francisco (19-0)	
2	3	Cincinnati (11-0)	↑1
3	4	Alabama (14-0)	↑1
4	2	North Carolina (10-1)	↑1
5	5	Michigan (10-1)	↑1
6	7	Kentucky (10-2)	↓4
7	6	UNLV (11-1)	↑1
8	8	Marquette (10-2)	↑3
9	9	Wake Forest (12-2)	↓2
10	10	UCLA (13-2)	↑2
11	13	Minnesota (11-1)	↓2
12	16	Louisville (10-2)	↑1
13	18	Maryland (12-2)	↑1
14	11	Tennessee (11-2)	⤴
15	17	Providence (13-2)	
16	14	Arizona (12-2)	↓6
17	15	Arkansas (12-1)	↓1
18	19	Memphis (14-1)	
19	12	Purdue (10-3)	⤴
20	—	Syracuse (13-2)	⤴
—	20	Utah (12-3)	

Week of Jan 25

AP	UPI	School	AP↓↑
1	1	San Francisco (19-0)	
2	2	Michigan (13-1)	↑3
3	4	Alabama (14-1)	
4	3	North Carolina (11-2)	
5	5	UNLV (13-1)	↑2
6	7	Kentucky (12-2)	
7	6	Tennessee (13-2)	↑7
8	9	UCLA (13-2)	↑2
9	8	Marquette (13-2)	↓1
10	11	Wake Forest (14-2)	↓1
11	10	Louisville (12-2)	↑1
12	12	Cincinnati (12-2)	↓10
13	14	Minnesota (12-1)	↓2
14	15	Providence (15-2)	↑1
15	16	Arkansas (14-1)	↑2
16	13	Arizona (14-2)	
17	—	Syracuse (14-2)	↑3
18	17	Purdue (11-4)	↑1
19	—	Clemson (13-3)	⤴
20	—	Memphis (16-2)	↓2
—	18	Oregon (12-4)	
—	19	Indiana State (16-1)	
—	20	Missouri (14-3)	

Week of Feb 1

AP	UPI	School	AP↓↑
1	1	San Francisco (21-0)	
2	2	UCLA (15-2)	↑6
3	6	Kentucky (14-2)	↑3
4	3	UNLV (13-1)	↑1
5	8	Wake Forest (16-2)	↑5
6	4	Marquette (14-2)	↑3
7	5	Michigan (15-2)	↓5
8	9	Alabama (15-2)	↓5
9	7	Louisville (15-2)	↑2
10	16	Minnesota (15-1)	↑3
11	10	Tennessee (14-2)	↓4
12	11	Cincinnati (14-2)	
13	12	North Carolina (11-4)	↓9
14	13	Arkansas (17-1)	↑1
15	17	Providence (17-2)	↓1
16	18	Clemson (15-3)	↑3
17	—	Syracuse (16-2)	
18	14	Purdue (13-4)	
19	15	Arizona (15-3)	↓3
20	—	Detroit (16-1)	⤴
—	19	Missouri (16-3)	
—	20	Utah (15-4)	

Week of Feb 8

AP	UPI	School	AP↓↑
1	1	San Francisco (23-0)	
2	2	UCLA (18-2)	
3	5	Kentucky (16-2)	
4	6	Wake Forest (18-2)	↑1
5	4	Michigan (17-2)	↑2
6	3	Louisville (16-2)	↑3
7	9	Alabama (17-2)	↑1
8	14	Minnesota (16-1)	↑2
9	7	Marquette (14-2)	↓3
10	8	UNLV (15-2)	↓6
11	10	Tennessee (16-3)	
12	11	Cincinnati (15-3)	
13	12	Arkansas (19-1)	↑1
14	12	North Carolina (13-4)	↓1
15	20	Clemson (17-3)	↑1
16	16	Providence (18-2)	↓1
17	19	Syracuse (18-2)	
18	14	Arizona (16-3)	↑1
19	—	Detroit (18-1)	↑1
20	—	VMI (18-1)	⤴
—	17	Utah (16-4)	
—	18	Missouri (17-4)	

[WE]EK OF FEB 15

UPI	SCHOOL	AP↓↑
1	**San Francisco** (25-0)	
2	**Kentucky** (18-2)	↑1
3	**UCLA** (19-3)	↓1
8	**Alabama** (19-2)	↑3
4	**Michigan** (18-3)	
7	**UNLV** (20-2)	↑4
9	**Wake Forest** (19-3)	↓3
5	**Louisville** (18-3)	↓2
6	**Marquette** (16-3)	
12	**Cincinnati** (18-3)	↑2
10	**Arkansas** (22-1)	↑2
15	**Minnesota** (18-2)	↓4
11	**North Carolina** (17-4)	↑1
13	**Tennessee** (17-4)	↓3
19	**Detroit** (20-1)	↑4
16	**Providence** (20-3)	
14	**Arizona** (18-3)	↑1
20	**Clemson** (18-4)	↓3
—	**VMI** (21-1)	↑1
18	**Syracuse** (19-3)	↓3
17	**Notre Dame** (15-5)	

WEEK OF FEB 22

AP	UPI	SCHOOL	AP↓↑
1	1	**San Francisco** (27-0)	
2	2	**Kentucky** (20-2)	
3	3	**Michigan** (20-3)	↑2
4	4	**UNLV** (22-2)	↑2
5	6	**UCLA** (20-4)	↓2
6	7	**Arkansas** (24-1)	↑5
7	5	**Tennessee** (19-4)	↑7
8	11	**Alabama** (19-3)	↓4
9	8	**North Carolina** (18-4)	↑4
10	10	**Louisville** (19-4) Ⓒ	↓2
11	9	**Wake Forest** (20-4)	↓4
12	12	**Providence** (22-3)	↑4
13	16	**Minnesota** (20-3)	↓1
14	17	**Cincinnati** (19-4)	↓4
15	13	**Syracuse** (21-3)	↑5
16	18	**Detroit** (22-2)	↓1
17	—	**Oregon** (17-7)	↥
18	—	**Marquette** (16-6)	↓9
19	—	**Clemson** (19-5)	↓1
20	14	**Utah** (19-5)	↥
—	15	**Creighton** (21-3)	
—	19	**Houston** (22-6)	
—	19	**Oral Roberts** (20-5) Ⓓ	

WEEK OF MAR 1

AP	UPI	SCHOOL	AP↓↑
1	1	**San Francisco** (29-0)	
2	2	**Kentucky** (22-2)	
3	3	**Michigan** (21-3)	
4	4	**UCLA** (22-4)	↑1
5	6	**UNLV** (23-2)	↓1
6	5	**North Carolina** (22-4)	↑3
7	7	**Arkansas** (25-1)	↓1
8	8	**Providence** (24-3)	↑4
9	13	**Minnesota** (22-3)	↑4
10	9	**Louisville** (21-5)	
11	10	**Tennessee** (20-5)	↓4
12	12	**Alabama** (20-4)	↓4
13	11	**Syracuse** (23-3)	↑2
14	20	**Cincinnati** (22-4)	
15	17	**Detroit** (24-2)	↑1
16	14	**Wake Forest** (20-6)	↓5
17	15	**Arizona** (21-4)	↥
18	—	**Clemson** (21-5)	↑1
19	—	**Marquette** (18-6) Ⓔ	↓1
20	—	**Utah** (20-6)	
—	16	**Indiana State** (23-2)	
—	18	**Houston** (24-6)	
—	19	**Oral Roberts** (21-5)	

WEEK OF MAR 8

AP	UPI	SCHOOL	AP↓↑
1	1	**Michigan** (24-3)	↑2
2	4	**UCLA** (23-4)	↑2
3	2	**San Francisco** (29-1)	↓2
4	3	**North Carolina** (25-4)	↑2
5	6	**UNLV** (25-2)	
6	5	**Kentucky** (23-3)	↓4
7	8	**Tennessee** (21-5)	↑4
8	7	**Arkansas** (26-1)	↓1
9	17	**Minnesota** (24-3)	
10	9	**Syracuse** (25-3)	↑3
11	12	**Cincinnati** (25-4)	↑3
12	18	**Alabama** (22-4)	
13	15	**Providence** (24-4)	↓5
14	13	**Louisville** (21-6)	↓4
15	—	**Notre Dame** (20-6)	↥
16	14	**Marquette** (20-7)	↑3
17	19	**Detroit** (24-3)	↓2
18	—	**Charlotte** (23-3) Ⓕ	↥
19	10	**Utah** (21-6)	↑1
20	—	**Arizona** (21-5)	↓3
—	11	**Kansas State** (22-7)	
—	16	**Indiana State** (25-2)	
—	20	**Purdue** (19-8)	

[FI]NAL POLL

UPI	SCHOOL	AP↓↑
—	**Michigan** (25-3)	
—	**UCLA** (24-4)	
—	**Kentucky** (25-3)	↑3
—	**UNLV** (26-2)	↑1
—	**North Carolina** (25-4)	↓1
—	**Syracuse** (26-3)	↑4
—	**Marquette** (21-7)	↑9
—	**San Francisco** (29-2)	↓5
—	**Wake Forest** (23-6)	↥
—	**Notre Dame** (21-6)	↑5
—	**Alabama** (25-4)	↑1
—	**Detroit** (25-3)	↑5
—	**Minnesota** (22-3)	↓4
—	**Utah** (22-6)	↑5
—	**Tennessee** (22-6)	↓8
—	**Kansas State** (23-7)	↥
—	**Charlotte** (24-3)	↑1
—	**Arkansas** (26-2)	↓10
—	**Louisville** (21-7)	↓5
—	**VMI** (26-3)	↥

Ⓐ The NCAA reinstates the dunk, which was made illegal in 1967-68.
Ⓑ Adolph Rupp, who won 876 games and four NCAA titles in his 41-year coaching career, watches approvingly from midcourt on Nov. 28 as Kentucky, in its first game at 23,500-seat Rupp Arena, defeats Wisconsin, 72-64.
Ⓒ Louisville forward Larry Williams breaks a foot in a 91-67 win at Tulsa. The Cardinals limp into the postseason, dropping two of their last four regular-season games and losing to Georgia Tech in the Metro tournament.
Ⓓ Anthony Roberts of Oral Roberts torches North Carolina A&T for a school-record 66 points. Eighteen days later, he will score 65 against Oregon. Roberts will finish second to Portland State's Freeman Williams with 34.0 ppg.
Ⓔ With Al McGuire set to retire after the season, Marquette goes into a tailspin that leaves the Warriors on the bubble for the NCAA Tournament. "I thought it was Tap City," McGuire later says, but the Warriors rally to win four of their last five.
Ⓕ Charlotte emerges behind stars Cedric "Cornbread" Maxwell and Lew Massey. The 49ers will make a Cinderella run to the Final Four, where they'll lose on a disputed last-second basket by Marquette's Jerome Whitehead.

1977 NCAA Tournament

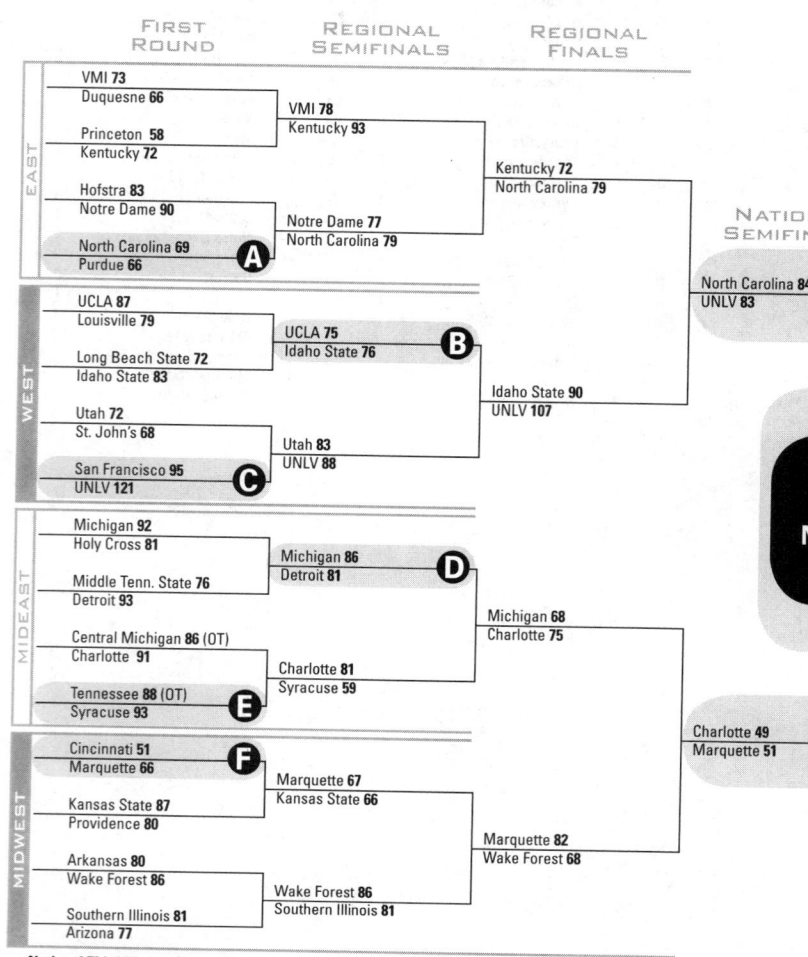

East

First Round
- VMI **73**, Duquesne **66**
- Princeton **58**, Kentucky **72**
- Hofstra **83**, Notre Dame **90**
- North Carolina **69**, Purdue **66** (A)

Regional Semifinals
- VMI **78**, Kentucky **93**
- Notre Dame **77**, North Carolina **79**

Regional Finals
- Kentucky **72**, North Carolina **79**

West

First Round
- UCLA **87**, Louisville **79**
- Long Beach State **72**, Idaho State **83**
- Utah **72**, St. John's **68**
- San Francisco **95**, UNLV **121** (C)

Regional Semifinals
- UCLA **75**, Idaho State **76** (B)
- Utah **83**, UNLV **88**

Regional Finals
- Idaho State **90**, UNLV **107**

Mideast

First Round
- Michigan **92**, Holy Cross **81**
- Middle Tenn. State **76**, Detroit **93**
- Central Michigan **86** (OT), Charlotte **91**
- Tennessee **88** (OT), Syracuse **93** (E)

Regional Semifinals
- Michigan **86**, Detroit **81** (D)
- Charlotte **81**, Syracuse **59**

Regional Finals
- Michigan **68**, Charlotte **75**

Midwest

First Round
- Cincinnati **51**, Marquette **66** (F)
- Kansas State **87**, Providence **80**
- Arkansas **80**, Wake Forest **86**
- Southern Illinois **81**, Arizona **77**

Regional Semifinals
- Marquette **67**, Kansas State **66**
- Wake Forest **86**, Southern Illinois **81**

Regional Finals
- Marquette **82**, Wake Forest **68**

National Semifinals

North Carolina **84**
UNLV **83**

UNLV coach Jerry Tarkanian reaches his first Final Four, but his Rebels go down as Mike O'Koren scores 31 and Phil Ford, who hurt his right elbow against Notre Dame and re-injured it in practice, hits 12.

Charlotte **49**
Marquette **51**

Charlotte's dreams of a title matchup with UNC end when a long pass from Marquette's Butch Lee evades UNCC's Cedric Maxwell's hands and reaches Jerome Whitehead, who hits the game-winner.

National Final

Marquette 67
North Carolina 59

Al McGuire's Warriors make 23 of 25 free throws, leading to an upset of the heavily favored Tar Heels and denying Dean Smith his first national title. Rather than join the celebration, McGuire sits on the bench by himself, his face buried in his hands, crying. He retires shortly thereafter.

Atlanta

National Third Place UNLV d. Charlotte 106-94

A UNC freshman Mike O'Koren misses the front end of a one-and-one in the final minute and is on the brink of tears. He regains his composure and forces a turnover with :13 seconds left, feeding Phil Ford for an insurance basket.

B UCLA makes a stunning early exit, despite 21 points and 13 rebounds from Marques Johnson, who plays through the pain of an impacted wisdom tooth. Gene Bartow, 52–9 in his two UCLA seasons, has had enough. He leaves to become coach at UAB.

C Six UNLV players will be chosen in the 1977 NBA draft, a record for the most from one school. The top three (all second-rounders) are Glen Gondrezick, Eddie Owens and Larry Moffett.

D Michigan's Phil Hubbard grabs 26 rebounds to lead the Wolverines. Before the game, Detroit coach Dick Vitale, perhaps prepping for his post-coaching broadcast career, says he feels like Chuck Wepner going up against Muhammad Ali.

E Bernard King gets 23 points and 12 rebounds, but the Vols are ousted in King's only Tournament game. Tennessee made the NCAA field in 1976, but King was out with a dislocated left thumb.

F Marquette's halftime talk gets heated when coach Al McGuire harshly criticizes a shot taken by reserve Bernard Toone, who proceeds to slam a folding chair on the floor and storm out of the locker room. Assistant coach Rick Majerus eventually coaxes Toone back.

TOURNAMENT LEADERS

INDIVIDUAL LEADERS

SCORING

	CL	POS	G	PTS	PPG
1 **Mike Glenn**, Southern Illinois	SR	G	2	65	32.5
2 **Cedric Maxwell**, Charlotte	SR	C	5	123	24.6
3 **Steve Hayes**, Idaho State	SR	C	3	72	24.0
4 **Ron Carter**, VMI	JR	G	2	46	23.0
Terry Tyler, Detroit	JR	F	2	46	23.0
6 **John Long**, Detroit	JR	F	2	45	22.5
7 **Eddie Owens**, UNLV	SR	F	5	110	22.0
Rickey Green, Michigan	SR	G	3	66	22.0
Curtis Redding, Kansas State	FR	F	2	44	22.0
10 **Rod Griffin**, Wake Forest	SO	F	3	64	21.3

MINIMUM: 2 GAMES

FIELD GOAL PCT

	CL	POS	G	FG	FGA	PCT
1 **Bruce Flowers**, Notre Dame	JR	F	2	11	14	78.6
2 **Corky Abrams**, Southern Illinois	SR	F	2	10	13	76.9
3 **Rick Robey**, Kentucky	JR	F/C	3	16	22	72.7
4 **Truman Claytor**, Kentucky	SO	G	3	21	29	72.4
5 **Terry Tyler**, Detroit	JR	F	2	20	28	71.4

MINIMUM: 10 MADE

FREE THROW PCT

	CL	POS	G	FT	FTA	PCT
1 **Winford Boynes**, San Francisco	SO	G	1	10	10	100.0
2 **Phil Ford**, North Carolina	JR	G	5	20	21	95.2
3 **Butch Lee**, Marquette	JR	G	5	14	15	93.3
4 **Greg Griffin**, Idaho State	SR	F	3	13	14	92.9
5 **Robert Smith**, UNLV	SR	G	5	11	12	91.7
Leroy McDonald, Wake Forest	JR	F	3	11	12	91.7
Rick Robey, Kentucky	JR	F/C	3	11	12	91.7

MINIMUM: 10 MADE

REBOUNDS PER GAME

	CL	POS	G	REB	RPG
1 **Phil Hubbard**, Michigan	SO	F	3	45	15.0
2 **Marques Johnson**, UCLA	SR	F	2	27	13.5
3 **Jeff Cook**, Idaho State	SO	C	3	40	13.3
4 **Toby Knight**, Notre Dame	SR	F/C	2	26	13.0
5 **Cedric Maxwell**, Charlotte	SR	C	5	64	12.8

MINIMUM: 2 GAMES

TEAM LEADERS

SCORING

	G	PTS	PPG
1 **UNLV**	5	505	101.0
2 **Detroit**	2	174	87.0
3 **Notre Dame**	2	167	83.5
4 **Idaho State**	3	249	83.0
5 **Michigan**	3	246	82.0
6 **Southern Illinois**	2	162	81.0
UCLA	2	162	81.0
8 **Wake Forest**	3	240	80.0
9 **Kentucky**	3	237	79.0
10 **Charlotte**	5	390	78.0

MINIMUM: 2 GAMES

FG PCT

	G	FG	FGA	PCT
1 **Notre Dame**	2	65	111	58.6
2 **Southern Illinois**	2	72	128	56.3
3 **Kentucky**	3	96	176	54.5
4 **Detroit**	2	79	145	54.5
5 **Kansas State**	2	65	124	52.4

FT PCT

	G	FT	FTA	PCT
1 **Marquette**	5	79	95	83.2
2 **Wake Forest**	3	66	80	82.5
3 **Kansas State**	2	23	28	82.1
4 **Kentucky**	3	45	55	81.8
5 **Charlotte**	5	96	119	80.7

MINIMUM: 2 GAMES

REBOUNDS

	G	REB	RPG
1 **Idaho State**	3	140	46.7
2 **UCLA**	2	77	38.5
3 **Kansas State**	2	75	37.5
4 **UNLV**	5	186	37.2
5 **VMI**	2	71	35.5

MINIMUM: 2 GAMES

ALL-TOURNAMENT TEAM

PLAYER	CL	POS	HT	SCHOOL	RPG	PPG
Butch Lee*	JR	G	6-0	Marquette	3.4	17.6
Walter Davis	SR	F	6-5	North Carolina	6.8	17.0
Bo Ellis	SR	F	6-9	Marquette	5.8	14.8
Cedric Maxwell	SR	C	6-8	Charlotte	12.8	24.6
Mike O'Koren	FR	F	6-7	North Carolina	7.2	17.2
Jerome Whitehead	JR	C	6-10	Marquette	8.8	9.6

ALL-REGIONAL TEAMS

EAST

PLAYER	CL	POS	HT	SCHOOL	RPG	PPG
John Kuester*	SR	G	6-3	North Carolina	2.0	11.7
Ron Carter	JR	G	6-5	VMI	8.0	23.0
Walter Davis	SR	F	6-5	North Carolina	7.0	14.5
Jack Givens	JR	F	6-4	Kentucky	6.0	19.7
Toby Knight	SR	F/C	6-9	Notre Dame	13.0	20.5

MIDEAST

PLAYER	CL	POS	HT	SCHOOL	RPG	PPG
Cedric Maxwell*	SR	C	6-8	Charlotte	12.0	25.3
Rickey Green	SR	G	6-2	Michigan	3.7	22.0
Phil Hubbard	SO	F	6-7	Michigan	15.0	17.3
John Long	JR	F	6-5	Detroit	5.0	22.5
Lew Massey	JR	F	6-6	Charlotte	7.0	15.7

MIDWEST

PLAYER	CL	POS	HT	SCHOOL	RPG	PPG
Butch Lee*	JR	G	6-0	Marquette	3.7	19.3
Skip Brown	SR	G	6-1	Wake Forest	2.7	19.3
Bo Ellis	SR	F	6-9	Marquette	5.0	18.7
Mike Glenn	SR	G	6-2	Southern Illinois	2.5	32.5
Jerry Schellenberg	SR	G	6-6	Wake Forest	4.7	19.3

WEST

PLAYER	CL	POS	HT	SCHOOL	RPG	PPG
Eddie Owens*	SR	F	6-7	UNLV	5.0	20.7
Robert Smith*	SR	G	5-11	UNLV	2.0	15.0
Steve Hayes	SR	C	7-0	Idaho State	12.0	24.0
Marques Johnson	SR	F	6-7	UCLA	13.5	19.0
Jeff Jonas	SR	G	5-11	Utah	4.0	11.5
Ed Thompson	SR	G	6-3	Idaho State	3.0	14.3

* MOST OUTSTANDING PLAYER

1977 NCAA TOURNAMENT BOX SCORES

KENTUCKY	MIN	FG	3FG	FT	REB	A	ST	BL	PF	TP
Truman Claytor	36	13-15	-	3-4	4	6	4	0	3	29
Jack Givens	36	9-16	-	8-9	9	3	0	1	1	26
James Lee	30	4-8	-	4-4	5	0	2	0	3	12
Mike Phillips	21	5-8	-	0-0	4	0	0	1	3	10
Rick Robey	18	4-7	-	0-1	7	0	0	0	2	8
Jay Shidler	17	2-3	-	0-0	1	1	0	0	1	4
Merionc Haskins	11	2-2	-	0-0	0	0	0	0	0	4
Larry Johnson	22	0-4	-	0-0	2	6	0	0	3	0
Dwane Casey	5	0-0	-	0-0	2	2	0	0	0	0
LaVon Williams	4	0-2	-	0-0	1	0	1	0	1	0
TOTALS	**200**	**39-65**	**-**	**15-18**	**35**	**18**	**7**	**2**	**17**	**93**
Percentages		60.0		83.3						

Coach: Joe B. Hall

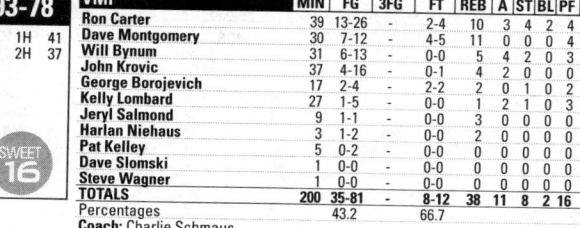

93-78

44	1H	41
49	2H	37

SWEET 16

VMI	MIN	FG	3FG	FT	REB	A	ST	BL	PF	TP
Ron Carter	39	13-26	-	2-4	10	3	4	2	4	28
Dave Montgomery	30	7-12	-	4-5	11	0	0	0	4	18
Will Bynum	31	6-13	-	0-0	5	4	2	0	3	12
John Krovic	37	4-16	-	0-1	4	2	0	0	0	8
George Borojevich	17	2-4	-	2-2	2	0	1	0	2	6
Kelly Lombard	27	1-5	-	0-0	1	2	1	0	3	2
Jeryl Salmond	9	1-1	-	0-0	3	0	0	0	0	2
Harlan Niehaus	3	1-2	-	0-0	2	0	0	0	0	2
Pat Kelley	5	0-2	-	0-0	0	0	0	0	0	0
Dave Slomski	1	0-0	-	0-0	0	0	0	0	0	0
Steve Wagner	1	0-0	-	0-0	0	0	0	0	0	0
TOTALS	**200**	**35-81**	**-**	**8-12**	**38**	**11**	**8**	**2**	**16**	**78**
Percentages		43.2		66.7						

Coach: Charlie Schmaus

Officials: Ba Galvan
Attendance: 14,500

NORTH CAROLINA	MIN	FG	3FG	FT	REB	A	ST	BL	PF	TP
Phil Ford	39	10-22	-	9-9	2	5	2	0	3	29
Mike O'Koren	34	6-10	-	4-6	5	4	0	0	5	16
John Kuester	34	5-11	-	4-4	1	7	1	0	1	14
Walter Davis	29	4-12	-	0-0	8	2	2	1	2	8
Tom Zaliagiris	14	3-6	-	0-0	0	0	1	0	2	6
Rich Yonaker	24	1-6	-	0-0	4	2	0	0	2	2
Steve Krafcisin	11	1-1	-	0-0	1	1	0	0	1	2
Bruce Buckley	9	1-1	-	0-0	1	0	0	0	2	2
Dudley Bradley	3	0-1	-	0-0	0	0	2	0	3	0
David Colescott	2	0-0	-	0-0	0	1	0	0	0	0
Jeff Wolf	1	0-0	-	0-0	0	0	0	0	0	0
TOTALS	**200**	**31-70**	**-**	**17-19**	**22**	**22**	**8**	**1**	**21**	**79**
Percentages		44.3		89.5						

Coach: Dean Smith

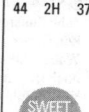

79-77

30	1H	40
49	2H	37

SWEET 16

NOTRE DAME	MIN	FG	3FG	FT	REB	A	ST	BL	PF	TP
Toby Knight	35	10-13	-	2-3	14	2	1	-	2	22
Rich Branning	40	5-7	-	8-9	2	1	2	-	2	18
Don Williams	39	6-14	-	5-5	1	1	2	-	4	17
Bruce Flowers	27	5-5	-	1-3	5	2	1	-	5	11
Dave Batton	23	3-5	-	0-0	4	2	0	-	3	6
Bill Paterno	32	1-1	-	1-2	3	0	0	-	2	3
Bill Hanzlik	3	0-0	-	0-0	1	0	0	-	1	0
Jeff Carpenter	1	0-0	-	0-0	0	0	0	-	0	0
TOTALS	**200**	**30-45**	**-**	**17-22**	**30**	**8**	**6**	**-**	**19**	**77**
Percentages		66.7		77.3						

Coach: Digger Phelps

Officials: Sanders, Turne
Technicals: North Carolina (O'Koren)
Attendance: 14,500

IDAHO STATE	MIN	FG	3FG	FT	REB	A	ST	BL	PF	TP
Steve Hayes	38	11-20	-	5-7	12	0	0	0	3	27
Ed Thompson	40	4-10	-	6-8	4	5	1	0	3	14
Greg Griffin	33	4-14	-	4-4	8	2	0	0	4	12
Jeff Cook	32	4-10	-	0-0	14	2	1	1	4	8
Brand Robinson	10	4-7	-	0-0	5	2	0	0	0	8
Ernie Wheeler	29	0-2	-	4-4	1	5	1	0	2	4
Scott Goold	11	1-4	-	0-0	1	2	0	0	2	2
Paul Wilson	7	0-2	-	1-2	1	0	0	1	1	1
TOTALS	**200**	**28-69**	**-**	**20-25**	**46**	**18**	**3**	**2**	**19**	**76**
Percentages		40.6		80.0						

Coach: Jim Killingsworth

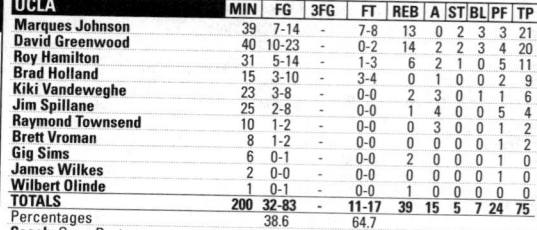

76-75

32	1H	38
44	2H	37

SWEET 16

UCLA	MIN	FG	3FG	FT	REB	A	ST	BL	PF	TP
Marques Johnson	39	7-14	-	7-8	13	0	2	3	3	21
David Greenwood	40	10-23	-	0-2	14	2	2	3	4	20
Roy Hamilton	31	5-14	-	1-3	6	2	1	0	5	11
Brad Holland	15	3-10	-	3-4	0	1	0	0	2	9
Kiki Vandeweghe	23	3-8	-	0-0	2	3	0	1	1	6
Jim Spillane	25	2-8	-	0-0	1	4	0	0	5	4
Raymond Townsend	10	1-2	-	0-0	0	3	0	0	1	2
Brett Vroman	8	1-2	-	0-0	0	0	0	0	1	2
Gig Sims	6	0-1	-	0-0	2	0	0	0	1	0
James Wilkes	2	0-0	-	0-0	0	0	0	0	1	0
Wilbert Olinde	1	0-1	-	0-0	1	0	0	0	0	0
TOTALS	**200**	**32-83**	**-**	**11-17**	**39**	**15**	**5**	**7**	**24**	**75**
Percentages		38.6		64.7						

Coach: Gene Bartow

Officials: Nichols, Wirtz
Attendance: 19,298

UNLV	MIN	FG	3FG	FT	REB	A	ST	BL	PF	TP
Robert Smith	-	8-14	-	5-5	3	6	-	-	3	21
Eddie Owens	-	8-20	-	0-0	5	2	-	-	3	16
Reggie Theus	-	3-8	-	8-9	3	5	-	-	2	14
Glen Gondrezick	-	6-12	-	1-2	5	1	-	-	5	13
Tony Smith	-	5-10	-	0-1	3	1	-	-	3	10
Sam Smith	-	4-10	-	0-2	2	2	-	-	3	8
Lewis Brown	-	2-6	-	0-0	2	0	-	-	1	4
Larry Moffett	-	1-7	-	0-0	17	0	-	-	4	2
TOTALS	**-**	**37-87**	**-**	**14-19**	**40**	**17**	**-**	**-**	**24**	**88**
Percentages		42.5		73.7						

Coach: Jerry Tarkanian

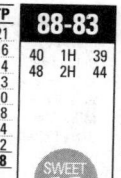

88-83

40	1H	39
48	2H	44

SWEET 16

UTAH	MIN	FG	3FG	FT	REB	A	ST	BL	PF	TP
Jay Judkins	-	10-18	-	3-4	7	3	-	-	2	23
Earl Williams	-	6-11	-	6-6	8	3	-	-	2	18
Buster Matheney	-	6-10	-	2-5	13	0	-	-	5	14
Jeff Jonas	-	3-11	-	6-9	3	15	-	-	4	12
Greg Deane	-	4-7	-	2-2	0	0	-	-	5	10
Mike Dunn	-	1-1	-	0-1	2	1	-	-	1	2
Coby Leavitt	-	0-0	-	2-2	2	0	-	-	2	2
Donnie Rice	-	1-2	-	0-0	0	0	-	-	0	2
TOTALS	**-**	**31-60**	**-**	**21-29**	**35**	**22**	**-**	**-**	**21**	**83**
Percentages		51.7		72.4						

Coach: Jerry Pimm

Officials: Fouty, Palesse
Attendance: 21,639

MICHIGAN	MIN	FG	3FG	FT	REB	A	ST	BL	PF	TP
John Robinson	33	12-18	-	1-2	7	0	0	0	2	25
Phil Hubbard	40	8-19	-	6-7	26	2	2	1	3	22
Steve Grote	29	7-14	-	2-3	3	5	0	0	2	16
Rickey Green	40	4-13	-	3-5	5	7	2	0	1	11
Tom Staton	33	4-8	-	0-1	3	4	5	1	4	8
Alan Hardy	8	1-3	-	0-0	2	0	0	0	0	2
Joel Thompson	6	1-1	-	0-0	1	1	0	0	0	2
Dave Baxter	11	0-2	-	0-0	0	0	0	0	1	0
TOTALS	**200**	**37-78**	**-**	**12-18**	**47**	**19**	**9**	**2**	**13**	**86**
Percentages		47.4		66.7						

Coach: Johnny Orr

86-81

48	1H	44
38	2H	37

SWEET 16

DETROIT	MIN	FG	3FG	FT	REB	A	ST	BL	PF	TP
John Long	39	12-24	-	1-1	7	0	1	2	3	25
Terry Tyler	39	8-12	-	1-1	9	1	1	0	2	17
Dennis Boyd	38	8-16	-	0-0	1	7	5	0	2	16
Terry Duerod	34	5-12	-	1-2	0	7	2	0	3	11
Ron Bostick	26	3-9	-	0-0	10	0	0	1	4	6
Jeff Whitlow	15	1-3	-	0-0	2	0	0	0	4	2
Turono Anderson	6	1-3	-	0-0	0	1	0	0	0	2
Wilbert McCormick	2	1-2	-	0-0	1	0	0	0	0	2
Wilbur Ross	1	0-0	-	0-0	0	0	0	0	0	0
TOTALS	**200**	**39-81**	**-**	**3-4**	**30**	**16**	**9**	**3**	**18**	**81**
Percentages		48.1		75.0						

Coach: Dick Vitale

Officials: Brown, Birk
Attendance: 22,286

CHARLOTTE	MIN	FG	3FG	FT	REB	A	ST	BL	PF	TP
Cedric Maxwell	38	4-6	-	11-11	5	3	2	3	1	19
Chad Kinch	31	6-8	-	4-6	1	5	0	0	0	16
Lew Massey	28	7-12	-	0-0	6	1	2	0	3	14
Kevin King	34	6-9	-	1-2	7	2	1	1	0	13
Melvin Watkins	33	6-8	-	1-2	1	7	0	1	2	13
Jeff Gruber	10	1-4	-	2-2	0	1	1	0	1	4
Phil Scott	13	0-3	-	2-2	4	0	1	1	4	2
Lee Whitfield	6	0-0	-	0-1	1	1	1	0	0	0
Mike Hester	4	0-2	-	0-0	1	0	0	0	1	0
Ken Angel	2	0-1	-	0-0	0	0	0	0	0	0
Todd Crowley	1	0-0	-	0-0	0	0	0	0	0	0
TOTALS	**200**	**30-53**	**-**	**21-26**	**26**	**20**	**8**	**6**	**12**	**81**
Percentages		56.6		80.8						

Coach: Lee Rose

81-59

38	1H	22
43	2H	37

SWEET 16

SYRACUSE	MIN	FG	3FG	FT	REB	A	ST	BL	PF	TP
Martin Byrnes	33	7-7	-	2-3	3	4	1	0	4	16
Dale Shackleford	25	8-14	-	0-0	6	2	1	0	5	16
Roosevelt Bouie	29	6-8	-	0-0	5	0	3	2	2	12
William Drew	18	4-13	-	0-0	3	3	1	0	3	8
Jim Williams	25	2-8	-	0-0	1	3	0	0	3	4
Louis Orr	29	1-5	-	0-0	1	1	2	0	3	2
Ross Kindel	16	0-3	-	1-2	0	1	0	0	1	1
Lawrence Kelley	21	0-7	-	0-0	2	1	1	0	0	0
Hal Cohen	2	0-0	-	0-0	0	0	0	0	0	0
Kevin James	2	0-0	-	0-0	0	0	0	0	0	0
TOTALS	**200**	**28-65**	**-**	**3-5**	**21**	**15**	**9**	**2**	**21**	**59**
Percentages		43.1		60.0						

Coach: Jim Boeheim

Officials: Jacob, Burke
Attendance: 22,286

Marquette 67, Kansas State 66 (Sweet 16)

	1H	2H
Marquette	28	39
Kansas State	36	30

MARQUETTE	MIN	FG	3FG	FT	REB	A	ST	BL	PF	TP
Butch Lee	40	12-23	-	2-2	4	2	2	0	1	26
Bo Ellis	40	5-14	-	9-11	3	1	0	1	2	19
Jim Boylan	22	4-4	-	0-0	2	0	2	0	1	8
Bernard Toone	19	2-4	-	4-5	5	0	1	0	4	8
Jim Dudley	13	2-3	-	0-0	3	1	0	0	3	4
Jerome Whitehead	23	1-9	-	0-0	6	1	0	0	2	2
Bill Neary	25	0-2	-	0-0	3	0	1	0	2	0
Gary Rosenberger	18	0-4	-	0-0	1	0	1	0	0	0
TOTALS	**200**	**26-63**	**-**	**15-18**	**27**	**5**	**7**	**1**	**15**	**67**
Percentages		41.3		83.3						

Coach: Al McGuire

KANSAS STATE	MIN	FG	3FG	FT	REB	A	ST	BL	PF	TP
Larry Dassie	36	7-12	-	4-4	6	0	0	2	4	18
Mike Evans	40	8-14	-	0-0	0	3	1	0	4	16
Darryl Winston	40	5-6	-	2-4	11	2	2	0	2	12
Curtis Redding	36	4-16	-	4-4	14	4	0	1	5	12
Scott Langton	40	3-5	-	2-2	5	3	0	0	3	8
Dan Droge	6	0-1	-	0-0	0	0	0	0	1	0
Tyrone Ladson	2	0-0	-	0-0	0	0	1	0	0	0
TOTALS	**200**	**27-54**	**-**	**12-14**	**36**	**12**	**4**	**3**	**19**	**66**
Percentages		50.0		85.7						

Coach: Jack Hartman

Officials: Wortman, Buckiewicz
Technicals: Marquette (coach McGuire)
Attendance: 10,185

Wake Forest 86, Southern Illinois 81 (Sweet 16)

	1H	2H
Wake Forest	34	52
Southern Illinois	35	46

WAKE FOREST	MIN	FG	3FG	FT	REB	A	ST	BL	PF	TP
Skip Brown	40	7-15	-	11-12	2	8	3	0	1	25
Rod Griffin	39	8-9	-	6-8	5	0	0	0	3	22
Jerry Schellenberg	37	9-16	-	4-4	6	2	1	1	1	22
Leroy McDonald	28	2-3	-	5-6	4	0	2	2	2	9
Frank Johnson	40	4-10	-	0-0	0	4	3	0	3	8
Larry Harrison	9	0-1	-	0-0	3	2	0	0	3	0
John Hendler	4	0-1	-	0-0	1	0	0	0	1	0
Don Mulnix	3	0-0	-	0-0	0	0	0	0	1	0
TOTALS	**200**	**30-55**	**-**	**26-30**	**21**	**16**	**9**	**3**	**15**	**86**
Percentages		54.5		86.7						

Coach: Carl Tacy

SOUTHERN ILLINOIS	MIN	FG	3FG	FT	REB	A	ST	BL	PF	TP
Mike Glenn	40	15-23	-	0-0	4	3	1	0	3	30
Richard Ford	36	7-10	-	3-4	6	3	0	1	5	17
Gary Wilson	32	6-13	-	0-3	7	2	0	0	4	12
Corky Abrams	34	3-4	-	2-2	3	0	0	0	4	8
Wayne Abrams	23	2-5	-	3-4	6	5	1	0	2	7
Barry Smith	8	2-2	-	0-1	3	0	0	0	1	4
Alfred Grant	10	1-7	-	1-1	5	1	0	0	1	3
Tom Harris	7	0-0	-	0-0	0	2	0	0	2	0
Mel Hughlett	7	0-0	-	0-0	1	0	0	0	0	0
Al Williams	3	0-0	-	0-0	0	0	0	0	0	0
TOTALS	**200**	**36-64**	**-**	**9-15**	**35**	**16**	**2**	**1**	**22**	**81**
Percentages		56.2		60.0						

Coach: Paul Lambert

Officials: Reed, Copeland
Attendance: 10,185

North Carolina 79, Kentucky 72 (Elite 8)

	1H	2H
North Carolina	53	26
Kentucky	41	31

NORTH CAROLINA	MIN	FG	3FG	FT	REB	A	ST	BL	PF	TP
Walter Davis	37	7-11	-	7-9	6	2	-	-	2	21
John Kuester	32	3-5	-	13-14	3	2	-	-	1	19
Mike O'Koren	36	6-10	-	2-2	7	1	-	-	2	14
Rich Yonaker	24	4-7	-	0-0	5	0	-	-	5	8
Steve Krafcisin	14	0-0	-	8-8	3	1	-	-	2	8
Tom Zaliagiris	27	1-1	-	3-3	0	0	-	-	2	5
Phil Ford	15	1-3	-	0-0	0	5	-	-	4	2
Dudley Bradley	3	1-1	-	0-0	1	0	-	-	0	2
David Colescott	5	0-0	-	0-0	0	1	-	-	1	0
Bruce Buckley	4	0-0	-	0-0	0	0	-	-	2	0
Jeff Wolf	2	0-0	-	0-0	0	0	-	-	1	0
John Virgil	1	0-0	-	0-0	0	0	-	-	0	0
TOTALS	**200**	**23-38**	**-**	**33-36**	**25**	**12**	**-**	**-**	**22**	**79**
Percentages		60.5		91.7						

Coach: Dean Smith

KENTUCKY	MIN	FG	3FG	FT	REB	A	ST	BL	PF	TP
Jack Givens	38	10-18	-	6-6	4	3	-	-	1	26
Rick Robey	23	5-6	-	5-5	3	0	-	-	5	15
Mike Phillips	20	6-7	-	0-0	3	1	-	-	3	12
Larry Johnson	38	3-11	-	3-4	6	5	-	-	5	9
James Lee	23	2-9	-	2-2	6	2	-	-	4	6
Truman Claytor	27	2-6	-	0-0	2	1	-	-	5	4
Merionc Haskins	16	0-0	-	0-1	0	0	-	-	1	0
Jay Shidler	13	0-4	-	0-0	0	1	-	-	2	0
Dwane Casey	2	0-0	-	0-0	0	0	-	-	0	0
TOTALS	**200**	**28-61**	**-**	**16-18**	**24**	**13**	**-**	**-**	**26**	**72**
Percentages		45.9		88.9						

Coach: Joe B. Hall

Officials: Bain, Galvan
Attendance: 14,500

UNLV 107, Idaho State 90 (Elite 8)

	1H	2H
UNLV	51	56
Idaho State	52	38

UNLV	MIN	FG	3FG	FT	REB	A	ST	BL	PF	TP
Eddie Owens	28	10-19	-	4-5	3	0	1	0	3	24
Tony Smith	20	7-10	-	4-4	2	4	1	0	1	18
Reggie Theus	29	6-12	-	4-5	3	6	1	0	3	16
Sam Smith	27	6-16	-	4-4	2	2	1	0	3	16
Robert Smith	24	4-8	-	2-2	2	2	2	0	4	10
Larry Moffett	29	4-8	-	0-1	16	1	0	3	5	8
Lewis Brown	13	4-8	-	0-0	4	0	0	0	3	8
Glen Gondrezick	26	3-8	-	1-2	9	3	1	1	4	7
Mike Milke	1	0-0	-	0-0	0	0	1	0	1	0
Matt Porter	1	0-0	-	0-0	0	0	0	0	0	0
John Rodriguez	1	0-0	-	0-0	0	0	0	0	0	0
Gary Wagner	1	0-1	-	0-0	0	0	0	0	0	0
TOTALS	**200**	**44-90**	**-**	**19-23**	**41**	**18**	**8**	**4**	**27**	**107**
Percentages		48.9		82.6						

Coach: Jerry Tarkanian

IDAHO STATE	MIN	FG	3FG	FT	REB	A	ST	BL	PF	TP
Ed Thompson	38	8-16	-	11-15	3	4	2	1	3	27
Greg Griffin	28	5-13	-	7-7	7	1	0	0	4	17
Steve Hayes	33	7-10	-	2-3	13	1	0	1	2	16
Jeff Cook	33	5-10	-	0-0	10	2	1	1	1	10
Brand Robinson	10	2-6	-	2-2	1	0	0	0	4	6
Ernie Wheeler	20	2-5	-	1-2	2	2	0	0	1	5
Paul Wilson	7	1-2	-	1-2	0	0	1	0	3	3
Scott Goold	18	1-4	-	0-0	1	1	0	0	3	2
Brian Bemis	5	0-0	-	2-2	0	0	0	0	1	2
Mark McQuaid	5	1-1	-	0-0	3	0	0	0	0	2
Stan Klos	2	0-1	-	0-0	0	1	0	0	0	0
Kelly Gardner	1	0-0	-	0-0	0	0	0	0	1	0
TOTALS	**200**	**32-68**	**-**	**26-33**	**40**	**12**	**4**	**3**	**23**	**90**
Percentages		47.1		78.8						

Coach: Jim Killingsworth

Officials: Fouty, Palesse
Attendance: 19,298

Charlotte 75, Michigan 68 (Elite 8)

	1H	2H
Charlotte	40	35
Michigan	27	41

CHARLOTTE	MIN	FG	3FG	FT	REB	A	ST	BL	PF	TP
Cedric Maxwell	39	10-16	-	5-8	13	1	3	4	4	25
Lew Massey	35	6-13	-	7-9	11	3	0	0	4	19
Chad Kinch	34	3-10	-	5-5	3	6	0	0	2	11
Melvin Watkins	34	2-7	-	2-2	6	3	5	0	2	6
Kevin King	33	2-3	-	2-3	3	4	3	2	2	6
Jeff Gruber	13	3-3	-	0-0	0	0	0	0	2	6
Phil Scott	11	1-1	-	0-1	1	0	0	2	1	2
Mike Hester	1	0-0	-	0-0	0	0	0	0	0	0
TOTALS	**200**	**27-53**	**-**	**21-28**	**37**	**17**	**11**	**8**	**17**	**75**
Percentages		50.9		75.0						

Coach: Lee Rose

MICHIGAN	MIN	FG	3FG	FT	REB	A	ST	BL	PF	TP
Rickey Green	40	9-19	-	2-6	2	6	5	0	1	20
Phil Hubbard	39	5-14	-	4-4	7	0	2	2	4	14
John Robinson	26	5-9	-	1-2	4	1	0	0	4	11
Steve Grote	29	3-8	-	1-2	3	4	2	0	5	7
Alan Hardy	14	3-8	-	0-0	4	0	0	1	4	6
Joel Thompson	8	3-5	-	0-0	1	0	0	0	2	6
Dave Baxter	12	2-7	-	0-0	0	0	1	0	3	4
Tom Staton	31	0-4	-	0-0	3	4	2	0	5	0
Tom Bergen	1	0-0	-	0-0	0	0	0	0	0	0
TOTALS	**200**	**30-74**	**-**	**8-14**	**24**	**15**	**12**	**3**	**28**	**68**
Percentages		40.5		57.1						

Coach: Johnny Orr

Officials: Brown, Burke
Attendance: 22,301

Marquette 82, Wake Forest 68 (Elite 8)

	1H	2H
Marquette	31	51
Wake Forest	35	33

MARQUETTE	MIN	FG	3FG	FT	REB	A	ST	BL	PF	TP
Bo Ellis	40	8-14	-	4-6	7	1	1	1	3	20
Butch Lee	40	8-15	-	3-4	2	1	2	0	2	19
Bernard Toone	24	6-11	-	6-6	2	0	0	0	2	18
Gary Rosenberger	12	2-4	-	5-6	2	0	1	0	1	9
Bill Neary	39	3-5	-	1-2	6	1	0	0	4	7
Jim Boylan	29	3-5	-	1-2	5	2	2	1	2	7
Jerome Whitehead	13	1-5	-	0-0	5	0	0	1	4	2
Jim Dudley	3	0-1	-	0-0	0	0	0	0	0	0
TOTALS	**200**	**31-60**	**-**	**20-26**	**29**	**5**	**6**	**3**	**18**	**82**
Percentages		51.7		76.9						

Coach: Al McGuire

WAKE FOREST	MIN	FG	3FG	FT	REB	A	ST	BL	PF	TP
Jerry Schellenberg	40	7-12	-	5-8	5	3	2	0	2	19
Rod Griffin	37	6-10	-	4-4	4	0	0	0	4	16
Larry Harrison	21	4-5	-	3-4	4	1	0	2	4	11
Skip Brown	40	5-12	-	0-1	5	6	3	0	4	10
Frank Johnson	33	3-13	-	0-0	4	0	0	0	4	6
Leroy McDonald	21	0-0	-	4-4	5	1	0	1	3	4
Don Mulnix	5	1-2	-	0-0	1	0	0	0	1	2
John Hendler	3	0-0	-	0-0	0	0	0	0	1	0
TOTALS	**200**	**26-54**	**-**	**16-21**	**28**	**11**	**5**	**3**	**23**	**68**
Percentages		48.1		76.2						

Coach: Carl Tacy

Officials: Copeland, Wortman
Attendance: 8,935

84-83 — FINAL 4

NORTH CAROLINA	MIN	FG	3FG	FT	REB	A	ST	BL	PF	TP
Mike O'Koren	26	14-19	-	3-5	8	1	-	-	1	31
Walter Davis	35	7-7	-	5-6	5	1	-	-	3	19
Phil Ford	37	4-10	-	4-5	6	9	-	-	2	12
Rich Yonaker	26	5-7	-	1-4	9	2	-	-	0	11
John Kuester	34	2-5	-	5-7	6	3	-	-	0	9
Bruce Buckley	14	1-5	-	0-0	2	0	-	-	3	2
Jeff Wolf	11	0-1	-	0-0	1	0	-	-	0	0
Dudley Bradley	6	0-1	-	0-0	1	0	-	-	0	0
Steve Krafcisin	4	0-0	-	0-1	2	0	-	-	1	0
Tom Zaliagiris	4	0-1	-	0-0	0	0	-	-	0	0
David Colescott	3	0-0	-	0-0	0	0	-	-	1	0
TOTALS	200	33-56	-	18-28	40	16	-	-	11	84
Percentages		58.9		64.3						

Coach: Dean Smith

43	1H	49
41	2H	34

UNLV	MIN	FG	3FG	FT	REB	A	ST	BL	PF	TP
Sam Smith	37	10-18	-	0-0	2	0	-	-	1	20
Eddie Owens	30	7-15	-	0-0	2	0	-	-	4	14
Larry Moffett	31	6-9	-	1-2	9	1	-	-	5	13
Tony Smith	12	6-8	-	0-2	1	1	-	-	3	12
Robert Smith	30	4-11	-	0-1	1	3	-	-	1	8
Glen Gondrezick	27	4-8	-	0-0	5	2	-	-	4	8
Reggie Theus	26	4-11	-	0-0	5	4	-	-	4	8
Lewis Brown	7	0-0	-	0-0	1	0	-	-	0	0
TOTALS	200	41-80	-	1-5	26	11	-	-	22	83
Percentages		51.2		20.0						

Coach: Jerry Tarkanian

Officials: Brc Copeland
Attendance: 16,086

51-49 — FINAL 4

MARQUETTE	MIN	FG	3FG	FT	REB	A	ST	BL	PF	TP
Jerome Whitehead	40	10-16	-	1-2	16	0	-	-	1	21
Butch Lee	40	5-18	-	1-1	3	2	-	-	3	11
Jim Boylan	37	4-9	-	0-0	3	6	-	-	2	8
Bernard Toone	20	2-6	-	2-2	1	0	-	-	3	6
Bo Ellis	40	2-8	-	0-0	5	0	-	-	4	4
Gary Rosenberger	5	0-0	-	1-2	1	0	-	-	0	1
Bill Neary	18	0-1	-	0-0	2	0	-	-	3	0
TOTALS	200	23-58	-	5-7	31	8	-	-	16	51
Percentages		39.7		71.4						

Coach: Al McGuire

25	1H	22
26	2H	27

CHARLOTTE	MIN	FG	3FG	FT	REB	A	ST	BL	PF	TP
Cedric Maxwell	40	5-6	-	7-9	12	2	-	-	2	17
Lew Massey	38	7-13	-	0-0	8	0	-	-	1	14
Melvin Watkins	23	2-4	-	2-3	0	1	-	-	5	6
Chad Kinch	38	1-7	-	2-2	4	2	-	-	2	4
Kevin King	38	2-7	-	0-0	5	4	-	-	2	4
Jeff Gruber	18	2-6	-	0-0	0	0	-	-	0	4
Phil Scott	5	0-0	-	0-0	0	0	-	-	0	0
TOTALS	200	19-43	-	11-14	29	9	-	-	12	49
Percentages		44.2		78.6						

Coach: Lee Rose

Officials: Fout Galvan
Attendance: 16,086

106-94 — 3RD PLACE

UNLV	MIN	FG	3FG	FT	REB	A	ST	BL	PF	TP
Eddie Owens	35	14-28	-	6-8	8	2	-	-	2	34
Reggie Theus	30	11-18	-	2-5	5	8	-	-	4	24
Larry Moffett	26	6-9	-	0-0	6	0	-	-	4	12
Robert Smith	30	4-7	-	2-2	1	3	-	-	1	10
Sam Smith	24	5-10	-	0-0	5	2	-	-	2	10
Glen Gondrezick	27	3-8	-	1-2	7	2	-	-	4	7
Lewis Brown	11	3-9	-	1-1	5	0	-	-	5	7
Tony Smith	17	1-6	-	0-0	0	3	-	-	0	2
TOTALS	200	47-95	-	12-18	37	20	-	-	22	106
Percentages		49.5		66.7						

Coach: Jerry Tarkanian

50	1H	55
56	2H	39

CHARLOTTE	MIN	FG	3FG	FT	REB	A	ST	BL	PF	TP
Cedric Maxwell	39	9-15	-	12-13	16	3	-	-	2	30
Chad Kinch	35	11-20	-	8-8	12	3	-	-	5	30
Lew Massey	31	11-19	-	0-0	7	2	-	-	3	22
Phil Scott	7	2-4	-	0-0	6	1	-	-	3	4
Melvin Watkins	29	1-5	-	0-0	4	5	-	-	2	2
Jeff Gruber	17	1-1	-	0-0	0	0	-	-	1	2
Kevin King	17	1-4	-	0-2	0	1	-	-	1	2
Ken Angel	0	0-1	-	2-3	2	1	-	-	1	2
Todd Crowley	16	0-0	-	0-0	0	0	-	-	0	0
Lee Whitfield	8	0-0	-	0-0	0	1	-	-	0	0
Mike Hester	0	0-1	-	0-0	3	0	-	-	0	0
Jerry Winston	0	0-2	-	0-0	0	0	-	-	0	0
TOTALS	199	36-72	-	22-26	50	17	-	-	18	94
Percentages		50.0		84.6						

Coach: Lee Rose

Officials: Brown, Fouty
Attendance: 16,086

67-59 — NCAA FINAL 1977

MARQUETTE	MIN	FG	3FG	FT	REB	A	ST	BL	PF	TP
Butch Lee	40	6-14	-	7-7	3	2	3	0	1	19
Bo Ellis	39	5-9	-	4-5	9	3	1	1	4	14
Jim Boylan	33	5-7	-	4-4	4	0	1	0	3	14
Jerome Whitehead	39	2-8	-	4-4	11	2	0	2	2	8
Bernard Toone	29	3-6	-	0-1	0	0	0	0	1	6
Gary Rosenberger	8	1-1	-	4-4	1	1	0	0	1	6
Bill Neary	12	0-2	-	0-0	0	0	0	0	1	0
TOTALS	200	22-47	-	23-25	28	8	5	3	13	67
Percentages		46.8		92.0						

Coach: Al McGuire

39	1H	27
28	2H	32

NORTH CAROLINA	MIN	FG	3FG	FT	REB	A	ST	BL	PF	TP
Walter Davis	33	6-13	-	8-10	8	3	2	0	4	20
Mike O'Koren	31	6-10	-	2-4	11	1	1	1	5	14
Phil Ford	38	3-10	-	0-0	2	5	0	0	3	6
Rich Yonaker	25	3-5	-	0-0	4	1	1	0	0	6
John Kuester	31	2-6	-	1-2	0	6	1	0	5	5
Tom Zaliagiris	10	2-3	-	0-0	0	0	1	0	3	4
Steve Krafcisin	10	1-1	-	0-0	0	0	0	0	0	2
Dudley Bradley	5	1-1	-	0-0	0	0	0	0	2	2
Bruce Buckley	10	0-1	-	0-0	0	0	0	0	1	0
Jeff Wolf	3	0-1	-	0-0	1	0	0	0	0	0
David Colescott	1	0-0	-	0-0	0	0	0	0	0	0
Woody Coley	1	0-0	-	0-0	0	0	0	0	0	0
Ged Doughton	1	0-0	-	0-0	0	0	0	0	0	0
John Virgil	1	0-0	-	0-0	0	0	0	0	1	0
TOTALS	200	24-51	-	11-16	26	16	6	1	24	59
Percentages		47.1		68.8						

Coach: Dean Smith

Officials: Copeland, Galvan
Technicals: Marquette (Toone)
Attendance: 16,086

ANNUAL REVIEW

National Invitation Tournament (NIT)

First round: Alabama d. Memphis, 86-63, Virginia Tech d. Georgetown 83-79, Illinois State d. Creighton 65-58, Houston d. Indiana State 83-82, Villanova d. Old Dominion 71-68 (OT), Massachusetts d. Seton Hall 86-85, Oregon d. Oral Roberts 90-89, St. Bonaventure d. Rutgers 79-77
Quarterfinals: Alabama d. Virginia Tech 79-72, Houston d. Illinois State 91-90, Villanova d. Massachusetts 81-71, St. Bonaventure d. Oregon 76-73
Semifinals: Houston d. Alabama 82-76, St. Bonaventure d. Villanova 86-82
Third place: Villanova d. Alabama 102-89
Championship: St. Bonaventure d. Houston 94-91
MVP: Greg Sanders, St. Bonaventure

1977-78: Joe B. Champ

Kentucky hadn't won a national title since Adolph Rupp's fourth in 1958. When Rupp died on Dec. 10, 1977, the pressure on current coach Joe B. Hall and his Wildcats intensified, and continued to do so with every Tournament win. In the title game at the St. Louis Checkerdome against Duke, senior forward Jack "Goose" Givens delivered a Final performance that ranks among the best ever, scoring 41 points to give Kentucky (30–2) a 94-88 win. For Duke, it was quite a turnaround: The Blue Devils had finished last in the ACC the previous four seasons. Givens was named Most Outstanding Player. After averaging 17.7 ppg as a senior, Marquette's Butch Lee was named the Naismith POY. Minnesota's Mychal Thompson went to Portland as the No. 1 pick in the NBA draft, but the canniest selection was by the Celtics, who obtained the future rights to Indiana State's Larry Bird with the No. 6 pick.

The biggest—and most tragic—story of the year was the Dec. 13, 1977, crash of a plane transporting the Evansville Purple Aces to their game against Middle Tennessee State. All 15 players and coaches and 14 others on board were killed.

Major Conference Standings

ACC

	Conference W	L	PCT	Overall W	L	PCT
North Carolina○	9	3	.750	23	8	.742
Duke⊕	8	4	.667	27	7	.794
NC State□	7	5	.583	21	10	.677
Virginia□	6	6	.500	20	8	.714
Wake Forest	6	6	.500	19	10	.655
Clemson	3	9	.250	15	12	.556
Maryland	3	9	.250	15	13	.536

Tournament: **Duke d. Wake Forest 85-77**
Tournament MVP: **Jim Spanarkel**, Duke

Big Eight

	Conference W	L	PCT	Overall W	L	PCT
Kansas○	13	1	.929	24	5	.828
Nebraska□	9	5	.643	22	8	.733
Iowa State	9	5	.643	14	13	.519
Kansas State	7	7	.500	18	11	.621
Oklahoma	7	7	.500	14	13	.519
Missouri⊕	4	10	.286	14	16	.467
Oklahoma State	4	10	.286	10	16	.385
Colorado	3	11	.214	9	18	.333

Tournament: **Missouri d. Kansas State 71-68 (2 OT)**
Tournament MVP: **Stan Ray**, Missouri

Big Sky

	Conference W	L	PCT	Overall W	L	PCT
Montana	12	2	.857	20	9	.690
Idaho State	11	3	.786	16	10	.615
Weber State⊕	9	5	.643	19	10	.655
Boise State	8	6	.571	13	14	.481
Gonzaga	7	7	.500	14	15	.483
Northern Arizona	4	10	.286	10	15	.400
Montana State	4	10	.286	10	16	.385
Idaho	1	13	.071	4	22	.154

Tournament: **Weber State d. Montana 62-55 (OT)**
Tournament MVP: **Bruce Collins**, Weber State

Big Ten

	Conference W	L	PCT	Overall W	L	PCT
Michigan State⊕	15	3	.833	25	5	.833
Indiana○	12	6	.667	21	8	.724
Minnesota	12	6	.667	17	10	.630
Michigan	11	7	.611	16	11	.593
Purdue	11	7	.611	16	11	.593
Ohio State	9	9	.500	15	12	.556
Illinois	7	11	.389	13	14	.481
Iowa	5	13	.278	12	15	.444
Northwestern	4	14	.222	8	19	.296
Wisconsin	4	14	.222	8	19	.296

East Coast

	Conference W	L	PCT	Overall W	L	PCT
East Section						
La Salle⊕	5	0	1.000	18	12	.600
Temple□	4	1	.800	24	5	.828
American	2	3	.400	16	12	.571
Drexel	2	3	.400	13	13	.500
Saint Joseph's	2	3	.400	13	15	.464
Hofstra	0	5	.000	8	19	.296
West Section						
Lafayette	10	0	1.000	23	8	.742
Delaware	5	5	.500	16	11	.593
Bucknell	5	5	.500	13	15	.464
Lehigh	5	5	.500	8	18	.308
Rider	4	6	.400	11	16	.407
West Chester	1	9	.100	6	19	.240

Tournament: **La Salle d. Temple 73-72**
Tournament MVP: **Michael Brooks**, La Salle

Eastern 8

	Conference W	L	PCT	Overall W	L	PCT
Eastern Division						
Rutgers	7	3	.700	24	7	.774
Villanova⊕	7	3	.700	23	9	.719
Pittsburgh	5	5	.500	16	11	.593
Massachusetts	5	5	.500	15	12	.556
Western Division						
Duquesne	5	5	.500	11	17	.393
George Washington	4	6	.400	15	11	.577
Penn State	4	6	.400	8	19	.296
West Virginia	3	7	.300	12	16	.429

Tournament: **Villanova d. West Virginia 63-59**
Tournament MVP: **Alex Bradley**, Villanova

Ivy

	Conference W	L	PCT	Overall W	L	PCT
Penn⊕	12	2	.857	20	8	.714
Columbia	11	3	.786	15	11	.577
Princeton	11	3	.786	17	9	.654
Harvard	7	7	.500	11	15	.423
Dartmouth	5	9	.357	10	16	.385
Cornell	5	9	.357	9	17	.346
Yale	3	11	.214	8	16	.333
Brown	2	12	.143	4	22	.154

Note: Columbia and Princeton also played in NJ-NY 7

Metro 7

	Conference W	L	PCT	Overall W	L	PCT
Florida State○	11	1	.917	23	6	.793
Louisville⊕	9	3	.750	23	7	.767
Memphis	7	5	.583	19	9	.679
Cincinnati	6	6	.500	17	10	.630
Georgia Tech	6	6	.500	15	12	.556
Saint Louis	2	10	.167	7	20	.259
Tulane	1	11	.083	5	22	.185

Tournament: **Louisville d. Florida State 94-93**
Tournament MVP: **Rick Wilson**, Louisville

Mid-American

	Conference W	L	PCT	Overall W	L	PCT
Miami (OH)⊕	12	4	.750	19	9	.679
Toledo	11	5	.688	21	6	.778
Central Michigan	11	5	.688	16	10	.615
Bowling Green	10	6	.625	12	15	.444
Northern Illinois	9	7	.563	11	16	.407
Eastern Michigan	7	9	.438	11	16	.407
Ohio	6	10	.375	13	14	.481
Ball State	6	10	.375	10	15	.400
Western Michigan	4	12	.250	7	20	.259
Kent State	4	12	.250	6	21	.222

MEAC

	Conference W	L	PCT	Overall W	L	PCT
NC A&T	11	1	.917	20	8	.714
Morgan State	9	3	.750	15	12	.556
Howard	8	4	.667	15	9	.625
SC State	5	7	.417	16	12	.571
Delaware State	5	7	.417	10	15	.400
UMES	2	10	.167	7	19	.269
NC Central	2	10	.167	6	20	.231

Tournament: **NC A&T d. Morgan State 66-63**
Tournament MOP: **James Sparrow**, NC A&T

Missouri Valley

	Conference W	L	PCT	Overall W	L	PCT
Creighton⊕	12	4	.750	19	9	.679
Indiana State□	11	5	.688	23	9	.719
Southern Illinois	11	5	.688	17	10	.630
New Mexico State	9	7	.563	15	14	.517
Bradley	8	8	.500	14	14	.500
Wichita State	8	8	.500	13	14	.481
Tulsa	7	9	.438	9	18	.333
West Texas A&M	4	12	.250	8	19	.296
Drake	2	14	.125	6	22	.214

Tournament: **Creighton d. Indiana State 54-52**

NJ-NY 7

	Conference W	L	PCT	Overall W	L	PCT
Rutgers□	5	1	.833	24	7	.774
St. John's⊕	5	1	.833	21	7	.750
Princeton	3	2	.600	17	9	.654
Manhattan	3	2	.600	12	14	.462
Columbia	3	3	.500	15	11	.577
Seton Hall	1	5	.167	16	11	.593
Fordham	0	6	.000	8	18	.308

Ohio Valley

	Conference W	L	PCT	Overall W	L	PCT
Middle Tenn. State	10	4	.714	18	8	.692
East Tenn. State	10	4	.714	18	9	.667
Western Kentucky⊕	9	5	.643	16	14	.533
Eastern Kentucky	8	6	.571	15	11	.577
Austin Peay	8	6	.571	15	12	.556
Tennessee Tech	7	7	.500	11	15	.423
Murray State	4	10	.286	8	17	.320
Morehead State	0	14	.000	4	19	.174

Tournament: **Western Kentucky d. Austin Peay 77-69**
Tournament MVP: **Otis Howard**, Austin Peay

PCAA

	Conference W	L	PCT	Overall W	L	PCT
Fresno State	11	3	.786	21	6	.778
San Diego State	11	3	.786	19	9	.679
Cal State Fullerton⊕	9	5	.643	23	9	.719
Pacific	9	5	.643	17	10	.630
Long Beach State	7	7	.500	16	13	.552
San Jose State	4	10	.286	8	19	.296
UC Santa Barbara	3	11	.214	8	19	.296
UC Irvine	2	12	.143	8	17	.320

Tournament: **Cal State Fullerton d. Long Beach St. 64-53**
Tournament MVP: **Greg Bunch**, Cal State Fullerton

Pac-8

	Conference W	L	PCT	Overall W	L	PCT
UCLA⊕	14	0	1.000	25	3	.893
Oregon State	9	5	.643	16	11	.593
Washington State	7	7	.500	16	11	.593
Southern California	7	7	.500	14	13	.519
Oregon	6	8	.429	16	11	.593
Washington	6	8	.429	14	13	.519
California	4	10	.286	11	16	.407
Stanford	3	11	.214	13	14	.481

SEC

	Conference W	L	PCT	Overall W	L	PCT
Kentucky⊕	16	2	.889	30	2	.938
Mississippi State	13	5	.722	18	9	.667
LSU	12	6	.667	18	9	.667
Alabama	11	7	.611	17	10	.630
Florida	8	10	.444	15	12	.556
Auburn	8	10	.444	13	14	.481
Tennessee	6	12	.333	11	16	.407
Vanderbilt	6	12	.333	10	17	.370
Georgia	5	13	.278	11	16	.407
Mississippi	5	13	.278	10	17	.370

Conference Standings Continue →

⊕ Automatic NCAA Tournament bid ○ At-large NCAA Tournament bid □ NIT appearance ⊗ Team record doesn't reflect games forfeited or vacated. For adjusted record, see p. 521.

SOUTHERN

	Conference W	L	PCT	Overall W	L	PCT
Appalachian State	9	3	.750	15	13	.536
VMI	7	3	.700	21	7	.750
Marshall	8	5	.615	14	15	.483
Furman⊕	7	5	.583	19	11	.633
Chattanooga	7	5	.583	16	11	.593
Western Carolina	4	8	.333	7	19	.269
Davidson	3	7	.300	9	18	.333
The Citadel	2	11	.154	8	19	.296

Tournament: **Furman d. Marshall 69-53**
Tournament MOP: **Jonathan Moore**, Furman

SOUTHLAND

	Conference W	L	PCT	Overall W	L	PCT
McNeese State	8	2	.800	20	8	.714
Lamar	8	2	.800	18	9	.667
UL-Lafayette	7	3	.700	19	8	.704
Texas-Arlington	3	7	.300	10	17	.370
Arkansas State	2	8	.200	9	18	.333
Louisiana Tech	2	8	.200	6	21	.222

SOUTHWEST

	Conference W	L	PCT	Overall W	L	PCT
Texas□	14	2	.875	26	5	.839
Arkansas○	14	2	.875	32	4	.889
Houston⊕	11	5	.688	25	8	.758
Texas Tech	10	6	.625	19	10	.655
Baylor	8	8	.500	14	13	.519
SMU	6	10	.375	10	18	.357
Texas A&M	5	11	.313	12	15	.444
Rice	2	14	.125	4	22	.154
TCU	2	14	.125	4	22	.154

Tournament: **Houston d. Texas 92-90**
Tournament MVP: **Mike Schultz,** Houston

SWAC

	Conference W	L	PCT	Overall W	L	PCT
Southern U.	9	3	.750	23	5	.821
Jackson State	9	3	.750	21	5	.808
Alcorn State	8	4	.667	22	7	.759
Texas Southern	7	5	.583	16	10	.615
Prairie View A&M	3	9	.250	14	13	.519
Miss. Valley State	3	9	.250	15	20	.429
Grambling	3	9	.250	10	14	.417

SUN BELT

	Conference W	L	PCT	Overall W	L	PCT
Charlotte	9	1	.900	20	7	.741
New Orleans	8	2	.800	21	6	.778
Jacksonville	6	4	.600	14	14	.500
South Alabama	3	7	.300	18	10	.643
South Florida	2	8	.200	13	14	.481
Georgia State	2	8	.200	5	21	.192

Tournament: **New Orleans d. South Alabama 22-20**
Tournament MVP: **Nate Mills**, New Orleans

WCAC

	Conference W	L	PCT	Overall W	L	PCT
San Francisco⊕	12	2	.857	23	6	.793
Nevada	10	4	.714	19	8	.704
Portland	9	5	.643	19	8	.704
Santa Clara	8	6	.571	21	8	.724
Seattle	6	8	.429	11	16	.407
Saint Mary's (CA)	5	9	.357	13	14	.481
Loyola Marymount	4	10	.286	11	15	.423
Pepperdine	2	12	.143	7	19	.269

WAC

	Conference W	L	PCT	Overall W	L	PCT
New Mexico⊕	13	1	.929	24	4	.857
Utah○	12	2	.857	23	6	.793
Colorado State	8	6	.571	18	9	.667
Arizona	6	8	.429	15	11	.577
Arizona State	6	8	.429	13	14	.481
BYU	6	8	.429	12	18	.400
Wyoming	3	11	.214	12	15	.444
UTEP	2	12	.143	10	16	.385

INDEPENDENTS

	Overall W	L	PCT
DePaul○	27	3	.900
Detroit□	25	4	.862
Illinois State□	24	4	.857
Marquette○	24	4	.857
Texas-Pan American	22	4	.846
VCU□	24	5	.828
Fairfield□	22	5	.815
North Texas	22	6	.786
Syracuse○	22	6	.786
Rhode Island⊕$	24	7	.774
Providence○	24	8	.750
Utah State□	21	7	.750
Georgetown□	23	8	.742
Notre Dame○	23	8	.742
Holy Cross	20	7	.741
UL-Monroe	20	7	.741
UNC Wilmington	19	7	.731
St. Bonaventure⊕$	21	8	.724
UNLV	20	8	.714
Virginia Tech	19	8	.704
James Madison	18	8	.692
Maine	17	8	.680
Army□	19	9	.679
Dayton□	19	10	.655
St. Francis (NY)	16	9	.640
Iona	17	10	.630
William and Mary	16	10	.615
Air Force	15	10	.600
Loyola-Chicago	16	11	.593
Mercer	16	11	.593
Oklahoma City	16	11	.593
Boston College	15	11	.577

INDEPENDENTS (CONT.)

	Overall W	L	PCT
Butler	15	11	.577
Saint Francis (PA)	15	11	.577
South Carolina□	16	12	.571
Siena	13	10	.565
Navy	14	11	.560
Wisconsin-Milwaukee	15	12	.556
Niagara	14	12	.538
Northeastern	14	12	.538
Southern Miss	13	12	.520
Portland State	14	13	.519
Stetson	14	13	.519
Oral Roberts	13	14	.481
Xavier	13	14	.481
Cleveland State	12	13	.480
Tennessee State	11	12	.478
Catholic	12	14	.462
Georgia Southern	12	15	.444
Northwestern State (LA)	12	15	.444
Connecticut	11	15	.423
Old Dominion	11	15	.423
Vermont	11	15	.423
Boston U.	10	15	.400
Hardin-Simmons	10	16	.385
Campbell	9	15	.375
Centenary	10	17	.370
Denver	10	17	.370
Colgate	9	17	.346
East Carolina	9	17	.346
Long Island	8	18	.308
Saint Peter's	8	18	.308
Charleston Southern	8	19	.296
Samford	8	19	.296
Canisius	7	19	.269
Houston Baptist	7	19	.269
New Hampshire	7	19	.269
Wagner	7	19	.269
Fairleigh Dickinson	6	18	.250
Evansville	1	3	.250
Valparaiso	6	19	.240
Robert Morris	4	19	.174
Richmond	4	22	.154
Hawaii	1	26	.037

$ Defeated regional opponents to earn an automatic NCAA bid

$ Defeated regional opponents to earn an automatic NCAA bid

INDIVIDUAL LEADERS—SEASON

SCORING	CL	POS	G	FG	FT	PTS	PPG
1 **Freeman Williams**, Portland State	SR	G	27	410	149	969	**35.9**
2 **Larry Bird**, Indiana State	JR	F	32	403	153	959	**30.0**
3 **Purvis Short**, Jackson State	SR	F	22	285	80	650	**29.5**
4 **Oliver Mack**, East Carolina	JR	G	25	292	115	699	**28.0**
5 **Roger Phegley**, Bradley	SR	G/F	24	237	189	663	**27.6**
6 **Frankie Sanders**, Southern U.	JR	G/F	27	316	108	740	**27.4**
7 **Ron Carter**, VMI	SR	G	28	274	188	736	**26.3**
8 **John Gerdy**, Davidson	JR	F	26	292	86	670	**25.8**
9 **Michael Brooks**, La Salle	SO	F	28	288	120	696	**24.9**
10 **Dave Caligaris**, Northeastern	SR	G/F	26	283	105	640	**24.6**

FIELD GOAL PCT	CL	POS	G	FG	FGA	PCT
1 **Joe Senser**, West Chester	JR	F	25	135	197	**68.5**
2 **Mike O'Koren**, North Carolina	SO	F	27	173	269	**64.3**
3 **Pat Cummings**, Cincinnati	JR	C	27	212	330	**64.2**
4 **Mel Daniels**, Stetson	SR	C	32	167	263	**63.5**
5 **Mark Young**, Fairfield	JR	C	27	180	284	**63.4**

MINIMUM: 5 MADE PER GAME

FREE THROW PCT	CL	POS	G	FT	FTA	PCT
1 **Carlos Gibson**, Marshall	JR	G	28	84	89	**94.4**
2 **Mark Tucker**, Oklahoma State	JR	G	26	114	125	**91.2**
3 **Anthony Williams**, Jacksonville	SR	G	28	70	77	**90.9**
4 **Brian Appel**, Hofstra	SO	G	24	67	74	**90.5**
5 **Ronnie Perry**, Holy Cross	SO	G	27	181	201	**90.0**

MINIMUM: 2.5 MADE PER GAME

REBOUNDS PER GAME	CL	POS	G	REB	RPG
1 **Ken Williams**, North Texas	SR	C	28	411	**14.7**
2 **Henry Taylor**, Texas-Pan American	SR	C	26	368	**14.2**
3 **Dean Uthoff**, Iowa State	SO	C	27	378	**14.0**
4 **Reggie King**, Alabama	JR	F	27	359	**13.3**
5 **Calvin Natt**, UL-Monroe	JR	F	27	356	**13.2**
6 **Tony Searcy**, Appalachian State	SR	F	28	359	**12.8**
7 **Michael Brooks**, La Salle	SO	F	28	358	**12.8**
8 **Jeff Ruland**, Iona	FR	C	26	332	**12.8**
9 **Wayne Cooper**, New Orleans	SR	F/C	27	343	**12.7**
Larry Knight, Loyola-Chicago	JR	F	27	343	**12.7**

TEAM LEADERS—SEASON

WIN-LOSS PCT	W	L	PCT
1 **Kentucky**	30	2	**.938**
2 **DePaul**	27	3	**.900**
3 **UCLA**	25	3	**.893**
4 **Arkansas**	32	4	**.889**
5 **Detroit**	25	4	**.862**

SCORING OFFENSE	G	W-L	PTS	PPG
1 **New Mexico**	28	24-4	2,731	**97.5**
2 **Texas-Pan American**	26	22-4	2,487	**95.7**
3 **Southern U.**	28	23-5	2,653	**94.8**
4 **Detroit**	29	25-4	2,730	**94.1**
5 **Houston**	33	25-8	3,015	**91.4**

SCORING MARGIN	G	W-L	PPG	OPP PPG	MAR
1 **UCLA**	28	25-3	85.3	67.4	**17.9**
2 **Detroit**	29	25-4	94.1	77.2	**16.9**
3 **Syracuse**	28	22-6	87.8	71.6	**16.2**
4 **Kansas**	29	24-5	81.6	66.4	**15.2**
5 **Texas-Pan American**	26	22-4	95.7	80.7	**15.0**

FIELD GOAL PCT	G	W-L	FG	FGA	PCT
1 **Arkansas**	36	32-4	1,060	1,943	**54.6**
2 **Southern U.**	28	23-5	1,107	2,031	**54.5**
3 **Kentucky**	32	30-2	1,040	1,922	**54.1**
4 **UNC Wilmington**	26	19-7	809	1,499	**54.0**
5 **San Francisco**	29	23-6	1,020	1,907	**53.5**

FREE THROW PCT	G	W-L	FT	FTA	PCT
1 **Duke**	34	27-7	665	841	**79.1**
2 **Furman**	30	19-11	557	721	**77.3**
3 **St. Bonaventure**	29	21-8	454	590	**76.9**
4 **Bradley**	28	14-14	470	615	**76.4**
5 **Morehead State**	23	4-19	363	475	**76.4**

REBOUND MARGIN	G	W-L	REB	OPP REB	MAR
1 **Alcorn State**	29	22-7	52.3	36.0	**16.3**
2 **Southern U.**	28	23-5	43.1	31.4	**11.7**
3 **South Carolina State**	28	16-12	49.1	38.4	**10.7**
4 **South Alabama**	28	18-10	40.0	31.1	**8.9**
5 **LSU**	27	18-9	46.2	37.5	**8.7**

SCORING DEFENSE	G	W-L	OPP PTS	OPP PPG
1 **Fresno State**	27	21-6	1,417	**52.5**
2 **Princeton**	26	17-9	1,431	**55.0**
3 **Marquette**	28	24-4	1,722	**61.5**
4 **Arkansas**	36	32-4	2,218	**61.6**
5 **Middle Tennessee State**	26	18-8	1,623	**62.4**

FIELD GOAL PCT DEFENSE	G	W-L	OPP FG	OPP FGA	OPP PCT
1 **Delaware State**	25	10-15	733	1,802	**40.7**
2 **Kansas**	29	24-5	705	1,729	**40.8**
3 **Utah State**	28	21-7	803	1,915	**41.9**
4 **Air Force**	25	15-10	637	1,516	**42.0**
5 **Indiana**	29	21-8	723	1,720	**42.0**

CONSENSUS ALL-AMERICAS

FIRST TEAM

PLAYER	CL	POS	HT	SCHOOL	RPG	PPG
Larry Bird	JR	F	6-9	Indiana State	11.5	30.0
Phil Ford	SR	G	6-2	North Carolina	2.1	20.8
David Greenwood	JR	F	6-9	UCLA	11.4	17.5
Butch Lee	SR	G	6-0	Marquette	3.6	17.7
Mychal Thompson	SR	C	6-10	Minnesota	10.9	22.0

SECOND TEAM

PLAYER	CL	POS	HT	SCHOOL	RPG	PPG
Ron Brewer	SR	G	6-4	Arkansas	3.1	18.0
Jack Givens	SR	F	6-4	Kentucky	6.8	18.1
Rod Griffin	SR	F	6-7	Wake Forest	10.0	21.5
Rick Robey	SR	F/C	6-10	Kentucky	8.2	14.4
Freeman Williams	SR	G	6-4	Portland State	4.9	35.9

SELECTORS: AP, NABC, UPI, USBWA

AWARD WINNERS

PLAYER OF THE YEAR

PLAYER	CL	POS	HT	SCHOOL	AWARDS
Butch Lee	SR	G	6-2	Marquette	Naismith, AP, UPI, Rupp
Phil Ford	SR	G	6-2	North Carolina	USBWA, Wooden, NABC
Mike Scheib	SR	G	5-8	Susquehanna	Frances Pomeroy Naismith*

* FOR THE MOST OUTSTANDING SENIOR PLAYER WHO IS 6 FEET OR UNDER.

COACH OF THE YEAR

COACH	SCHOOL	REC	AWARDS
Eddie Sutton	Arkansas	32-4	AP, UPI
Ray Meyer	DePaul	27-3	USBWA
Abe Lemons	Texas	26-5	NABC (shared)
Bill Foster	Duke	27-7	NABC (shared), Sporting News

Poll Progression

Preseason Poll

AP	UPI	School
1	1	**North Carolina**
2	1	**Kentucky**
3	3	**Marquette**
4	4	**Notre Dame**
5	5	**San Francisco**
6	6	**UCLA**
7	9	**Arkansas**
8	—	**UNLV**
9	8	**Cincinnati**
10	10	**Louisville**
11	11	**Syracuse**
12	7	**Purdue**
13	12	**Michigan**
14	13	**Maryland**
15	19	**Alabama**
16	—	**Minnesota**
17	14	**Wake Forest**
18	20	**Holy Cross**
19	—	**Detroit**
20	14	**St. John's**
—	14	**Indiana State**
—	14	**Utah**
—	18	**Kansas State**

Week of Nov 27

AP	School	AP↓↑
1	**Kentucky** (1-0)	↑1
2	**North Carolina** (1-0)	↓1
3	**Notre Dame** (1-0)	↑1
4	**Marquette** (0-0)	↓1
5	**San Francisco** (1-0)	
6	**UCLA** (2-0)	
7	**Arkansas** (1-0)	
8	**Cincinnati** (1-0)	↑1
9	**Louisville** (0-0)	↑1
10	**UNLV** (1-0)	↓2
11	**Purdue** (1-0)	↑1
12	**Syracuse** (1-0)	↓1
13	**Michigan** (1-0)	
14	**Maryland** (2-0)	
15	**Alabama** (0-0)	
16	**St. John's** (2-0)	↑4
17	**Holy Cross** (0-0)	↑1
18	**Wake Forest** (1-0)	↓1
19	**Detroit** (0-0)	
20	**Utah** (1-0)	⤴

Week of Dec 6

AP	UPI	School	AP↓↑
1	1	**Kentucky** (1-0)	
2	2	**North Carolina** (4-0)	
3	3	**Notre Dame** (3-0)	
4	4	**Marquette** (2-0)	
5	5	**UCLA** (4-0)	↑1
6	6	**Arkansas** (4-0)	↑1
7	7	**Cincinnati** (3-0)	↑1
8	9	**San Francisco** (2-1)	↓3
9	11	**Michigan** (3-0)	↑4
10	—	**UNLV** (3-0)	
11	8	**Indiana State** (3-0) Ⓐ	⤴
12	12	**Maryland** (4-0)	↑2
13	15	**St. John's** (4-0)	↑3
14	13	**Utah** (2-0)	↑6
15	18	**Holy Cross** (2-0)	↑2
16	18	**Louisville** (1-1)	↓7
17	—	**Detroit** (2-0)	↑2
18	10	**Syracuse** (4-1)	↓6
19	15	**Kansas** (3-0)	⤴
20	17	**Providence** (3-0)	⤴
—	14	**Purdue** (2-1)	⤵
—	20	**New Mexico** (3-0)	

Week of Dec 13

AP	UPI	School	AP↓↑
1	1	**Kentucky** (3-0)	
2	2	**Notre Dame** (6-0)	↑
3	3	**Marquette** (4-0)	↑
4	5	**Arkansas** (6-0)	↑2
5	4	**North Carolina** (5-1)	↓3
6	8	**Cincinnati** (4-0)	↑1
7	7	**Indiana State** (5-0)	↑4
8	6	**UCLA** (4-1)	↓3
9	—	**UNLV** (5-0)	↑1
10	9	**Louisville** (3-1)	↑6
11	11	**San Francisco** (3-1)	↓3
12	10	**Syracuse** (6-1)	↑6
13	12	**Holy Cross** (5-0)	↑2
14	13	**Providence** (5-0)	↑6
15	14	**Michigan** (4-1)	↓6
16	—	**Detroit** (4-0)	↑1
17	16	**Purdue** (4-1)	⤴
18	18	**Maryland** (5-1)	↓6
19	—	**Kansas State** (5-0)	⤴
20	17	**Kansas** (5-1)	↓1
—	15	**Utah** (3-1)	⤵
—	19	**St. John's** (5-1)	⤵
—	20	**Virginia** (5-0)	

Week of Dec 20

AP	UPI	School	AP↓↑
1	1	**Kentucky** (7-0)	
2	2	**Marquette** (5-0)	↑1
3	3	**North Carolina** (6-1)	↑2
4	5	**Arkansas** (6-0)	
5	4	**Notre Dame** (6-1)	↓3
6	7	**Indiana State** (7-0)	↑1
7	6	**UCLA** (6-1)	↑1
8	10	**Louisville** (4-1)	↑2
9	—	**UNLV** (9-0)	
10	8	**Syracuse** (8-1)	↑2
11	9	**San Francisco** (6-1)	
12	12	**Cincinnati** (5-1)	↓6
13	11	**Holy Cross** (5-0)	
14	13	**Providence** (5-0)	
15	—	**Detroit** (6-0)	↑1
16	14	**Kansas** (6-1)	↑4
17	15	**Utah** (5-1)	⤴
18	20	**Alabama** (4-1)	⤴
19	19	**Virginia** (5-0)	⤴
20	18	**Maryland** (6-1)	↓2
—	16	**Indiana** (6-1)	
—	17	**Purdue** (6-2)	⤵

Week of Dec 27

AP	UPI	School	AP↓↑
1	1	**Kentucky** (7-0)	
2	2	**North Carolina** (7-1)	↑1
3	4	**Arkansas** (8-0)	↑1
4	3	**Notre Dame** (7-1)	↑1
5	5	**Marquette** (5-1)	↓3
6	8	**Indiana State** (7-0)	
7	6	**Louisville** (6-1)	↑1
8	7	**UCLA** (8-1)	↓1
9	—	**UNLV** (11-0)	
10	10	**Syracuse** (8-1)	
11	11	**Cincinnati** (6-1)	↑1
12	9	**Holy Cross** (6-0)	↑1
13	13	**Providence** (6-0)	↑1
14	14	**Maryland** (7-1)	↑6
15	11	**Indiana** (6-1)	⤴
16	17	**Virginia** (5-0)	↑3
17	18	**Kansas** (7-2)	↓1
18	15	**Florida State** (8-0)	⤴
19	19	**San Francisco** (6-3)	↓8
20	—	**Detroit** (6-1)	↓5
—	16	**Utah State** (5-1)	
—	19	**Nebraska** (9-0)	

Week of Jan 3

AP	UPI	School	AP↓↑
1	1	**Kentucky** (8-0)	
2	2	**North Carolina** (10-1)	
3	3	**Arkansas** (10-0)	
4	4	**Marquette** (7-1)	↑1
5	6	**Notre Dame** (7-2)	↓1
6	7	**Indiana State** (8-0)	
7	5	**UCLA** (9-1)	↑1
8	8	**Syracuse** (10-1)	↑2
9	—	**UNLV** (13-0)	
10	9	**Louisville** (7-2)	↓3
11	10	**Indiana** (8-1)	↑4
12	13	**Cincinnati** (7-1)	↓1
13	14	**Virginia** (7-0)	↑3
14	11	**Kansas** (9-2)	↑3
15	12	**Maryland** (9-1)	↓1
16	18	**Holy Cross** (7-1)	↓4
17	18	**Providence** (7-1)	↓4
18	16	**Michigan State** (8-1)	⤴
19	20	**San Francisco** (8-3)	
20	15	**Georgetown** (8-2)	⤴
—	16	**Utah State** (8-1)	

Week of Jan 10

AP	UPI	School	AP↓↑
1	1	**Kentucky** (11-0)	
2	2	**North Carolina** (12-1) Ⓑ	
3	3	**Arkansas** (13-0)	
4	4	**Marquette** (10-1)	
5	6	**Notre Dame** (7-2)	
6	7	**Indiana State** (10-0)	
7	5	**UCLA** (11-1)	
8	9	**Syracuse** (11-1)	
9	8	**Louisville** (9-2)	↑1
10	10	**Kansas** (11-2)	↑4
11	—	**UNLV** (14-1)	↓2
12	11	**Michigan State** (10-1)	↑6
13	14	**Holy Cross** (9-1)	↑3
14	15	**Providence** (11-1)	↑3
15	—	**Virginia** (8-1)	↓2
16	18	**NC State** (10-1)	⤴
17	12	**Georgetown** (10-2)	↑3
18	13	**Indiana** (8-2)	↓7
19	19	**Cincinnati** (8-3)	↓7
20	—	**DePaul** (11-1)	⤴
—	15	**New Mexico** (9-2)	
—	15	**Nebraska** (12-1)	
—	20	**Texas** (10-2)	

Week of Jan 17

AP	UPI	School	AP↓↑
1	1	**Kentucky** (12-0)	
2	2	**Marquette** (12-1)	↑2
3	3	**UCLA** (13-1)	↑4
4	5	**Indiana State** (12-0)	↑2
5	4	**North Carolina** (13-2)	↓3
6	6	**Arkansas** (14-1)	↓3
7	10	**Notre Dame** (8-3)	↓2
8	8	**Kansas** (13-2)	↑2
9	7	**Louisville** (10-2)	
10	9	**Michigan State** (12-1)	↑2
11	11	**Syracuse** (12-2)	↓3
12	19	**Providence** (13-1)	↑2
13	14	**Virginia** (10-1)	↑2
14	16	**Holy Cross** (11-1)	↓1
15	17	**Texas** (12-2)	⤴
16	—	**UNLV** (15-2)	↓5
17	18	**Duke** (12-3)	⤴
18	20	**DePaul** (13-1)	↑2
19	15	**Georgetown** (12-2)	↓2
20	13	**New Mexico** (10-2)	⤴
—	12	**San Francisco** (12-4)	

Week of Jan 24

AP	UPI	School	AP↓↑
1	1	**Kentucky** (14-0)	
2	2	**Marquette** (14-1)	
3	3	**North Carolina** (15-2)	↑2
4	4	**Arkansas** (16-1)	↑2
5	8	**Notre Dame** (11-3)	↑2
6	5	**UCLA** (13-2)	↓3
7	7	**Michigan State** (14-1)	↑3
8	6	**Kansas** (15-2)	
9	10	**Providence** (15-1)	↑3
10	11	**Syracuse** (13-2)	↑1
11	20	**Duke** (14-3)	↑6
12	9	**Louisville** (11-3)	↓3
13	13	**Indiana State** (13-2)	↓9
14	12	**New Mexico** (13-2)	↑6
15	17	**Texas** (13-2)	
16	14	**Georgetown** (13-2)	↑3
17	16	**Florida State** (14-2)	⤴
18	—	**Virginia** (12-2)	↓5
19	19	**DePaul** (14-2)	↓1
20	—	**Illinois State** (16-2)	⤴
—	15	**San Francisco** (12-4)	
—	18	**Colorado State** (12-3)	

Week of Jan 31

AP	UPI	School	AP↓↑
1	1	**Kentucky** (14-1) Ⓒ	
2	4	**Arkansas** (19-1)	↑2
3	2	**Marquette** (15-2)	↓1
4	7	**Notre Dame** (14-3)	↑1
5	6	**UCLA** (14-2)	↑1
6	3	**North Carolina** (16-3)	↓3
7	5	**Michigan State** (15-1)	
8	9	**Kansas** (16-3)	
9	10	**Louisville** (12-3)	↑3
10	8	**New Mexico** (15-2)	↑4
11	15	**Virginia** (14-2)	↑7
12	17	**Texas** (16-2)	↑3
13	13	**DePaul** (16-2)	↑6
14	11	**Georgetown** (15-2)	↑2
15	12	**Florida State** (15-2)	↑2
16	16	**Providence** (16-2)	↓7
17	18	**Duke** (15-4)	↓6
18	19	**Syracuse** (14-3)	↓8
19	—	**Illinois State** (18-2)	↑1
20	14	**San Francisco** (15-4)	⤴
—	20	**Nebraska** (16-3)	

Week of Feb 7

AP	UPI	School	AP↓↑
1	1	**Kentucky** (16-1)	
2	3	**Arkansas** (21-1)	
3	2	**Marquette** (17-2)	
4	5	**Notre Dame** (16-3)	
5	4	**UCLA** (16-2)	
6	8	**New Mexico** (17-2)	↑4
7	7	**North Carolina** (18-4)	↓1
8	6	**Kansas** (18-3)	
9	9	**Louisville** (14-3)	
10	10	**Michigan State** (16-3)	↓3
11	11	**DePaul** (18-2)	↑2
12	12	**Texas** (18-3)	
13	19	**Virginia** (15-3)	↓2
14	16	**Wake Forest** (15-3)	⤴
15	—	**Illinois State** (18-2)	↑4
16	14	**Florida State** (16-3)	↓1
17	16	**Detroit** (18-1)	⤴
18	—	**Syracuse** (15-4)	
19	18	**Nebraska** (18-3)	⤴
20	—	**Providence** (17-4)	↓4
—	13	**Purdue** (13-6)	
—	15	**Georgetown** (15-4)	⤵
—	20	**San Francisco** (17-4)	⤵

[WE]EK OF FEB 14

UPI	SCHOOL	AP↓↑
3	**Arkansas** (23-1)	↑1
1	**Marquette** (19-2)	↑1
2	**Kentucky** (17-2)	Ⓓ ↓2
4	**UCLA** (18-2)	↑1
5	**New Mexico** (19-2)	↑1
6	**Kansas** (20-3)	↑2
9	**Notre Dame** (16-4)	↓3
10	**DePaul** (20-2)	↑3
11	**Louisville** (16-3)	
7	**Michigan State** (18-3)	
8	**North Carolina** (20-5)	↓4
14	**Texas** (19-3)	
13	**Providence** (18-4)	↑7
12	**Florida State** (18-3)	↑2
19	**Illinois State** (20-2)	
19	**Syracuse** (16-4)	↑2
16	**Virginia** (17-4)	↓4
15	**Georgetown** (17-4)	⤴
—	**Detroit** (18-2)	↓2
16	**Duke** (17-5)	⤴
18	**St. John's** (16-4)	

WEEK OF FEB 21

AP	UPI	SCHOOL	AP↓↑
1	1	**Marquette** (21-2)	↑1
2	2	**Kentucky** (20-2)	↑1
3	3	**UCLA** (20-2)	↑1
4	4	**Arkansas** (25-2)	Ⓔ ↓3
5	5	**New Mexico** (21-2)	
6	6	**Kansas** (22-3)	
7	7	**DePaul** (22-2)	↑1
8	8	**North Carolina** (22-5)	↑3
9	12	**Notre Dame** (17-5)	↓2
10	9	**Michigan State** (19-4)	
11	11	**Providence** (22-4)	↑2
12	10	**Florida State** (19-4)	↑2
13	14	**Duke** (19-5)	↑7
14	12	**Texas** (21-4)	↓2
15	17	**Illinois State** (21-2)	
16	—	**Detroit** (21-2)	↑3
17	14	**Syracuse** (18-4)	↓1
18	16	**Georgetown** (19-4)	
19	—	**Minnesota** (16-7)	⤴
20	19	**Louisville** (16-6)	↓11
—	17	**Utah** (19-5)	
—	19	**Indiana** (16-7)	
—	19	**NC State** (17-6)	

WEEK OF FEB 28

AP	UPI	SCHOOL	AP↓↑
1	1	**Kentucky** (22-2)	↑1
2	2	**UCLA** (22-2)	↑1
3	3	**Marquette** (22-3)	↓2
4	4	**Arkansas** (27-2)	
5	5	**Kansas** (23-3)	↑1
6	7	**DePaul** (23-2)	↑1
7	10	**Notre Dame** (19-5)	↑2
8	6	**New Mexico** (22-3)	↓3
9	8	**Michigan State** (21-4)	↑1
10	9	**North Carolina** (23-6)	↓2
11	11	**Florida State** (21-4)	↑1
12	12	**Texas** (22-4)	↑2
13	—	**Illinois State** (23-2)	↑2
14	14	**Syracuse** (21-4)	↑3
15	17	**Duke** (20-6)	↓2
16	—	**Detroit** (23-2)	
17	14	**Georgetown** (21-5)	↑1
18	16	**Providence** (22-6)	↓7
19	13	**Utah** (21-5)	⤴
20	—	**Louisville** (18-6)	
—	18	**Georgia Tech** (14-11)	
—	19	**Indiana** (18-7)	
—	19	**St. John's** (18-6)	

WEEK OF MAR 6

AP	UPI	SCHOOL	AP↓↑
1	1	**Kentucky** (24-2)	
2	2	**UCLA** (24-2)	
3	3	**Marquette** (24-3)	
4	7	**DePaul** (25-2)	↑2
5	4	**New Mexico** (24-3)	↑3
6	5	**Michigan State** (23-4)	↑3
7	6	**Arkansas** (28-3)	↓3
8	9	**Duke** (23-6)	Ⓕ ↑7
9	8	**Kansas** (24-4)	↓4
10	11	**Notre Dame** (19-6)	↓3
11	10	**North Carolina** (23-7)	↓1
12	14	**Louisville** (22-6)	↑8
13	12	**Florida State** (23-5)	↓2
14	16	**Houston** (25-7)	⤴
15	18	**Utah** (22-5)	↑4
16	19	**Texas** (22-5)	↓4
17	—	**Illinois State** (24-3)	↓4
18	—	**Syracuse** (22-5)	↓4
19	—	**Detroit** (24-3)	↓3
20	13	**San Francisco** (22-5)	⤴
—	15	**Indiana** (20-7)	
—	17	**Utah State** (21-6)	
—	20	**Georgetown** (21-6)	⌈

[FI]NAL POLL

SCHOOL	AP↓↑
Kentucky (26-2)	
UCLA (26-2)	
DePaul (26-2)	↑1
Michigan State (24-4)	↑2
Arkansas (29-3)	↑2
Notre Dame (21-6)	↑4
Duke (24-6)	↑1
Marquette (24-4)	↓5
Louisville (23-6)	↑3
Kansas (24-5)	↓1
San Francisco (23-5)	↑9
New Mexico (24-4)	↓7
Indiana (21-7)	⤴
Utah (23-5)	↑1
Florida State (23-6)	↓2
North Carolina (23-8)	↓5
Texas (23-5)	↓1
Detroit (25-3)	↑1
Miami (OH) (18-9)	⤴
Penn (20-7)	⤴

[…] Indiana State, where John Wooden coached before going to UCLA, makes its debut in the AP poll mainly because of junior forward Larry Bird. A skinny kid from French Lick, Bird originally enrolled at Indiana in 1974 but left after a month because he was intimidated by the large campus. He will finish the season second in scoring with 30.0 ppg.

[…] North Carolina converts 16 of 17 second-half shots against Virginia, setting an NCAA record for the highest shooting percentage in one half (94.1%).

[…] Alabama upsets Kentucky, 78-62, on Jan. 23, the first win in school history over a No. 1 team. The victory is especially meaningful to Crimson Tide coach C.M. Newton, who played on Kentucky's 1951 NCAA championship team.

Ⓓ LSU beats Kentucky, 95-94, in overtime on Feb. 11 in Baton Rouge—the first time the Tigers have defeated a No. 1 team. The victory avenges a 20-point loss in Lexington on Jan. 14, after which Tigers coach Dale Brown accused the Wildcats of "brutalizing the game of basketball."

Ⓔ After rising to the top spot for the first time in school history, Arkansas (which is led by the Triplets—Sidney Moncrief, Marvin Delph and Ron Brewer) loses four days later at Houston, 84-75.

Ⓕ A young Duke squad that doesn't have a senior in the starting lineup climbs into the Top 10. The Blue Devils hope to return to the Final Four for the first time since making three appearances between 1964 and '66.

1978 NCAA Tournament

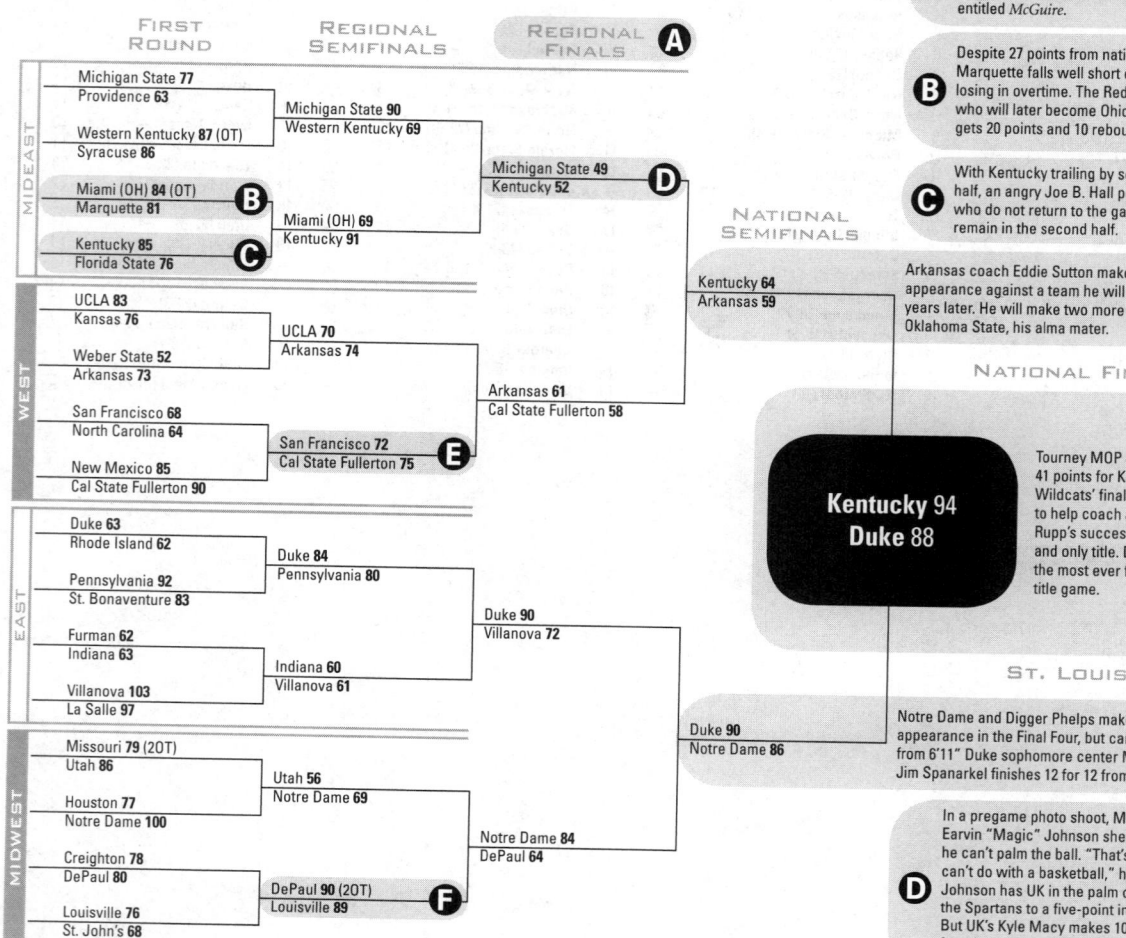

First Round

Mideast
- Michigan State **77**, Providence **63**
- Western Kentucky **87** (OT), Syracuse **86**
- Miami (OH) **84** (OT), Marquette **81** (B)
- Kentucky **85**, Florida State **76** (C)

West
- UCLA **83**, Kansas **76**
- Weber State **52**, Arkansas **73**
- San Francisco **68**, North Carolina **64**
- New Mexico **85**, Cal State Fullerton **90**

East
- Duke **63**, Rhode Island **62**
- Pennsylvania **92**, St. Bonaventure **83**
- Furman **62**, Indiana **63**
- Villanova **103**, La Salle **97**

Midwest
- Missouri **79** (2OT), Utah **86**
- Houston **77**, Notre Dame **100**
- Creighton **78**, DePaul **80**
- Louisville **76**, St. John's **68**

Regional Semifinals

- Michigan State **90**, Western Kentucky **69**
- Miami (OH) **69**, Kentucky **91**
- UCLA **70**, Arkansas **74**
- San Francisco **72**, Cal State Fullerton **75** (E)
- Duke **84**, Pennsylvania **80**
- Indiana **60**, Villanova **61**
- Utah **56**, Notre Dame **69**
- DePaul **90** (2OT), Louisville **89** (F)

Regional Finals (A)

- Michigan State **49**, Kentucky **52** (D)
- Arkansas **61**, Cal State Fullerton **58**
- Duke **90**, Villanova **72**
- Notre Dame **84**, DePaul **64**

National Semifinals

- Kentucky **64**, Arkansas **59**
- Duke **90**, Notre Dame **86**

National Final

Kentucky 94
Duke 88

St. Louis

National Third Place Arkansas d. Notre Dame 71-69

Arkansas coach Eddie Sutton makes his first Final Four appearance against a team he will be coaching seven years later. He will make two more appearances with Oklahoma State, his alma mater.

Tourney MOP Jack Givens scores 41 points for Kentucky, including the Wildcats' final 16 in the first half, to help coach Joe B. Hall—Adolph Rupp's successor—win his first and only title. Duke's 88 points are the most ever for a losing team in a title game.

Notre Dame and Digger Phelps make their only appearance in the Final Four, but can't overcome 29 points from 6'11" Duke sophomore center Mike Gminski. Duke's Jim Spanarkel finishes 12 for 12 from the line.

A A year after he led Marquette to its first and only national title, Al McGuire joins Billy Packer and Dick Enberg courtside for NBC's telecasts. In 2005, Enberg will write a one-man theatrical play entitled *McGuire*.

B Despite 27 points from national POY Butch Lee, Marquette falls well short of defending its title, losing in overtime. The Redskins' Randy Ayers, who will later become Ohio State head coach, gets 20 points and 10 rebounds.

C With Kentucky trailing by seven points at the half, an angry Joe B. Hall pulls three starters, who do not return to the game until 12 minutes remain in the second half.

D In a pregame photo shoot, MSU freshman Earvin "Magic" Johnson sheepishly reveals he can't palm the ball. "That's the only thing I can't do with a basketball," he says. For a half, Johnson has UK in the palm of his hand, leading the Spartans to a five-point intermission lead. But UK's Kyle Macy makes 10 consecutive free throws late in the second half to postpone MSU's Final Four trip by a year.

E After upsetting No. 4-ranked New Mexico, Fullerton overcomes a 12-point halftime deficit against the Dons, finally pulling ahead on a late Keith Anderson basket. The Titans seal the win after USF gets a technical for calling a timeout it doesn't have.

F DePaul's Dave Corzine scores 46 points, including the game-winner with :20 left, and passes George Mikan as the school's all-time scoring leader.

Tournament Leaders

Individual Leaders

Scoring

	CL	POS	G	PTS	PPG
1 **Dave Corzine**, DePaul	SR	F	3	82	27.3
2 **Bill Cartwright**, San Francisco	JR	C	2	50	25.0
Mike Woodson, Indiana	SO	G/F	2	50	25.0
4 **Keven McDonald**, Penn	SR	G	2	47	23.5
5 **Keith Herron**, Villanova	JR	F	3	67	22.3
6 **Darrell Griffith**, Louisville	SO	G	2	44	22.0
Buster Matheney, Utah	SR	F	2	44	22.0
8 **Mike Gminski**, Duke	SO	C	5	109	21.8
9 **Greg Kelser**, Michigan State	JR	F	3	65	21.7
10 **Roy Hamilton**, UCLA	JR	G	2	42	21.0

Minimum: 2 games

Field Goal Pct

	CL	POS	G	FG	FGA	PCT
1 **Michael Brooks**, La Salle	SO	F	1	14	17	82.3
2 **Bill Cartwright**, San Francisco	JR	C	2	18	23	78.3
3 **Greg Kelser**, Michigan State	JR	F	3	29	40	72.5
4 **Rick Robey**, Kentucky	SR	F/C	5	22	31	71.0
5 **Hal Cohen**, Syracuse	SO	G	1	11	16	68.8

Minimum: 10 made

Free Throw Pct

	CL	POS	G	FT	FTA	PCT
1 **Gary Garland**, DePaul	JR	G	3	12	13	92.3
2 **John Harrell**, Duke	JR	G	5	10	11	90.9
3 **Mike Gminski**, Duke	SO	C	5	19	21	90.5
4 **Marvin Delph**, Arkansas	SR	G	5	15	17	88.2
5 **Mike Phillips**, Kentucky	SR	C	5	13	15	86.7

Minimum: 10 made

Rebounds Per Game

	CL	POS	G	REB	RPG
1 **Greg Kelser**, Michigan State	JR	F	3	37	12.3
2 **Darrell Allums**, UCLA	SO	F	2	21	10.5
Danny Vranes, Utah	FR	F	2	21	10.5
Larry Williams, Louisville	JR	F	2	21	10.5
5 **Gene Banks**, Duke	FR	F	5	50	10.0
Bill Cartwright, San Francisco	JR	C	2	20	10.0

Minimum: 2 games

Team Leaders

Scoring

	G	PTS	PPG
1 **Penn**	2	172	86.0
2 **Duke**	5	415	83.0
3 **Louisville**	2	165	82.5
4 **Notre Dame**	5	408	81.6
5 **Villanova**	3	236	78.7
6 **DePaul**	3	234	78.0
Western Kentucky	2	156	78.0
8 **Kentucky**	5	386	77.2
9 **Miami (OH)**	2	153	76.5
UCLA	2	153	76.5

Minimum: 2 games

FG Pct

	G	FG	FGA	PCT
1 **Michigan State**	3	92	156	59.0
2 **Kentucky**	5	152	277	54.9
3 **Indiana**	2	52	95	54.7
4 **Arkansas**	5	134	251	53.4
5 **Duke**	5	154	295	52.2

FT Pct

	G	FT	FTA	PCT
1 **Miami (OH)**	2	29	35	82.9
2 **Duke**	5	107	131	81.7
3 **DePaul**	3	42	53	79.3
4 **Kentucky**	5	82	105	78.1
5 **Louisville**	2	37	48	77.1

Minimum: 2 games

Rebounds

	G	REB	RPG
1 **Duke**	5	182	36.4
2 **Western Kentucky**	2	72	36.0
UCLA	2	72	36.0
4 **San Francisco**	2	71	35.5
5 **Penn**	2	70	35.0

Minimum: 2 games

All-Tournament Team

PLAYER	CL	POS	HT	SCHOOL	RPG	PPG
Jack Givens*	SR	F	6-4	Kentucky	7.4	20.2
Ron Brewer	SR	G	6-4	Arkansas	4.4	19.0
Mike Gminski	SO	C	6-11	Duke	9.4	21.8
Rick Robey	SR	F/C	6-10	Kentucky	6.8	12.0
Jim Spanarkel	JR	G	6-5	Duke	4.4	20.4

All-Regional Teams

East

PLAYER	CL	POS	HT	SCHOOL	RPG	PPG
Jim Spanarkel*	JR	G	6-5	Duke	5.3	20.3
Gene Banks	FR	F	6-7	Duke	10.0	17.3
Mike Gminski	SO	C	6-11	Duke	10.0	20.0
Keith Herron	SR	F	6-6	Villanova	3.7	22.3
Bobby Willis	JR	G	6-2	Penn	4.5	12.0

Mideast

PLAYER	CL	POS	HT	SCHOOL	RPG	PPG
Kyle Macy*	SO	G	6-3	Kentucky	2.0	11.3
Jack Givens	SR	F	6-4	Kentucky	6.7	12.3
Earvin "Magic" Johnson	FR	G	6-9	Michigan State	6.7	11.0
Greg Kelser	JR	F	6-7	Michigan State	12.3	21.7
Mike Phillips	SR	C	6-10	Kentucky	6.0	16.0

Midwest

PLAYER	CL	POS	HT	SCHOOL	RPG	PPG
Kelly Tripucka*	FR	F	6-7	Notre Dame	6.3	17.3
Rich Branning	SO	G	6-3	Notre Dame	1.3	13.3
Dave Corzine	SR	F	6-11	DePaul	9.0	27.3
Gary Garland	JR	G	6-4	DePaul	3.3	16.0
Rick Wilson	SR	G/F	6-4	Louisville	4.0	17.5

West

PLAYER	CL	POS	HT	SCHOOL	RPG	PPG
Ron Brewer*	SR	G	6-4	Arkansas	3.7	19.7
Keith Anderson	JR	G	6-2	Cal State Fullerton	4.7	19.3
Greg Bunch	SR	F	6-6	Cal State Fullerton	9.0	17.0
Marvin Delph	SR	G	6-4	Arkansas	7.7	19.0
Sidney Moncrief	JR	G	6-4	Arkansas	6.7	16.0

* Most outstanding player

1978 NCAA TOURNAMENT BOX SCORES

90-69

SWEET 16

	1H	2H
Michigan State	39	51
Western Kentucky	29	40

MICHIGAN STATE	MIN	FG	3FG	FT	REB	A	ST	BL	PF	TP
Robert Chapman	39	10-12	-	3-6	3	2	0	0	3	23
Greg Kelser	31	11-18	-	1-2	13	1	0	1	5	23
Earvin "Magic" Johnson	39	3-17	-	7-11	9	14	1	0	2	13
Ron Charles	21	4-4	-	5-6	8	0	0	2	3	13
Jay Vincent	27	6-8	-	0-0	6	1	0	0	4	12
Mike Brkovich	3	1-1	-	0-0	1	1	0	0	1	2
Alfred Brown	1	1-1	-	0-0	1	1	0	1	0	2
Donald Flowers	1	1-1	-	0-0	0	1	0	0	0	2
Terry Donnelly	35	0-1	-	0-0	1	4	0	0	0	0
Sten Feldreich	2	0-0	-	0-0	1	0	0	0	3	0
Dan Riewald	1	0-0	-	0-0	0	0	0	0	0	0
TOTALS	**200**	**37-63**	**-**	**16-25**	**43**	**25**	**1**	**4**	**21**	**90**
Percentages		58.7		64.0						

Coach: Jud Heathcote

WESTERN KENTUCKY	MIN	FG	3FG	FT	REB	A	ST	BL	PF	TP
Greg Jackson	-	8-12	-	5-10	6	0	1	2	1	21
Aaron Bryant	-	5-7	-	2-2	7	0	0	1	5	12
James Johnson	-	5-8	-	2-5	7	0	0	2	5	12
Darryl Turner	-	6-19	-	0-0	4	4	0	0	5	12
Mike Reese	-	3-6	-	0-3	3	2	1	0	2	6
Mike Prince	-	2-7	-	0-0	1	3	1	0	0	4
John Rahn	-	1-4	-	0-0	3	0	0	0	1	2
Steve Ashby	-	0-1	-	0-0	0	5	0	0	1	0
Greg Burbach	-	0-1	-	0-0	0	3	0	0	2	0
Don Thomas	-	0-0	-	0-0	0	0	0	0	0	0
TOTALS	**-**	**30-65**	**-**	**9-20**	**31**	**17**	**3**	**5**	**22**	**69**
Percentages		46.2		45.0						

Coach: Jim Richards

Officials: MacArthur, Clymer
Attendance: 13,458

91-69

SWEET 16

	1H	2H
Kentucky	46	45
Miami (OH)	30	39

KENTUCKY	MIN	FG	3FG	FT	REB	A	ST	BL	PF	TP
Mike Phillips	21	11-13	-	2-3	4	1	0	0	2	24
Rick Robey	29	6-8	-	2-2	7	5	1	0	1	14
Truman Claytor	30	6-7	-	1-1	1	3	0	0	3	13
Jack Givens	31	6-13	-	0-1	9	5	0	0	4	12
James Lee	20	4-9	-	4-5	8	3	1	0	1	12
Fred Cowan	8	3-5	-	0-0	1	0	0	1	3	6
Kyle Macy	33	1-3	-	0-0	0	2	1	0	1	2
Chuck Aleksinas	5	1-4	-	0-0	3	0	0	0	1	2
LaVon Williams	5	1-1	-	0-0	0	1	0	0	1	2
Dwane Casey	1	1-1	-	0-0	0	0	0	0	0	2
Scott Courts	1	1-1	-	0-0	1	0	0	0	1	2
Jay Shidler	15	0-1	-	0-0	0	4	0	0	2	0
Tim Stephens	1	0-0	-	0-0	2	1	0	0	1	0
TOTALS	**200**	**41-66**	**-**	**9-12**	**36**	**25**	**3**	**1**	**21**	**91**
Percentages		62.1		75.0						

Coach: Joe B. Hall

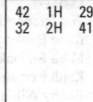

MIAMI (OH)	MIN	FG	3FG	FT	REB	A	ST	BL	PF	TP
Randy Ayers	39	9-11	-	0-0	8	3	0	2	5	18
Rick Goins	31	6-10	-	0-0	2	1	0	0	1	12
Archie Aldridge	34	4-10	-	3-4	3	2	0	1	2	11
John Shoemaker	38	2-8	-	6-6	0	4	1	0	1	10
Bill Lake	12	2-4	-	2-2	0	1	0	0	2	6
Tom Dunn	25	2-3	-	0-0	1	3	0	0	1	4
Terry Brady	8	1-4	-	0-0	4	0	0	0	1	2
Jim Harkins	4	0-0	-	2-3	1	0	0	0	1	2
Todd Jones	3	1-1	-	0-0	0	0	1	0	2	2
Rick Lantz	2	1-3	-	0-0	2	0	0	0	0	2
Brian Bays	2	0-0	-	0-1	0	0	0	0	0	0
Rich Babcock	1	0-2	-	0-0	0	0	0	0	1	0
Phil Griesinger	1	0-1	-	0-0	0	0	0	0	0	0
TOTALS	**200**	**28-57**	**-**	**13-16**	**21**	**14**	**2**	**3**	**17**	**69**
Percentages		49.1		81.2						

Coach: Darrell Hedric

Officials: Jacob, Bishop
Attendance: 13,458

74-70

SWEET 16

	1H	2H
Arkansas	42	32
UCLA	29	41

ARKANSAS	MIN	FG	3FG	FT	REB	A	ST	BL	PF	TP
Marvin Delph	40	11-14	-	1-1	10	0	1	0	2	23
Sidney Moncrief	39	7-13	-	7-13	11	1	0	1	3	21
Ron Brewer	40	5-14	-	8-10	5	5	0	0	0	18
Steve Schall	20	4-7	-	0-0	2	1	2	1	4	8
Jim Counce	39	0-1	-	2-2	3	3	2	0	0	2
Alan Zahn	21	1-1	-	0-0	2	1	0	0	3	2
U.S. Reed	1	0-0	-	0-2	0	0	0	0	0	0
TOTALS	**200**	**28-50**	**-**	**18-28**	**33**	**11**	**5**	**2**	**12**	**74**
Percentages		56.0		64.3						

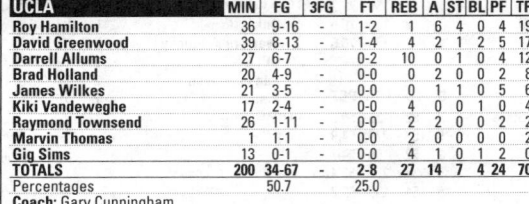

Coach: Eddie Sutton

UCLA	MIN	FG	3FG	FT	REB	A	ST	BL	PF	TP
Roy Hamilton	36	9-16	-	1-2	1	6	4	0	4	19
David Greenwood	39	8-13	-	1-4	4	2	1	2	5	17
Darrell Allums	27	6-7	-	0-2	10	0	1	0	4	12
Brad Holland	20	4-9	-	0-0	0	2	0	0	2	8
James Wilkes	21	3-5	-	0-0	0	1	1	0	5	6
Kiki Vandeweghe	17	2-4	-	0-0	4	0	0	1	0	4
Raymond Townsend	26	1-11	-	0-0	2	2	0	0	2	2
Marvin Thomas	1	1-1	-	0-0	2	0	0	0	0	2
Gig Sims	13	0-1	-	0-0	4	1	0	1	2	0
TOTALS	**200**	**34-67**	**-**	**2-8**	**27**	**14**	**7**	**4**	**24**	**70**
Percentages		50.7		25.0						

Coach: Gary Cunningham

Officials: Nichols, Fouty
Attendance: 17,750

75-72

SWEET 16

	1H	2H
Cal State Fullerton	32	43
San Francisco	44	28

CAL STATE FULLERTON	MIN	FG	3FG	FT	REB	A	ST	BL	PF	TP
Greg Bunch	37	11-15	-	2-2	12	1	-	-	2	24
Kevin Heenan	36	7-13	-	1-1	5	2	-	-	1	15
Keith Anderson	37	6-15	-	0-2	4	8	-	-	3	12
Mike Linden	40	3-9	-	1-2	2	5	-	-	3	7
Mike Niles	13	3-6	-	1-3	3	0	-	-	5	7
Steve Shaw	15	3-7	-	0-0	3	0	-	-	0	6
Greg Palm	22	2-4	-	0-0	4	1	-	-	4	4
TOTALS	**200**	**35-69**	**-**	**5-10**	**33**	**17**	**-**	**-**	**18**	**75**
Percentages		50.7		50.0						

Coach: Bobby Dye

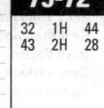

SAN FRANCISCO	MIN	FG	3FG	FT	REB	A	ST	BL	PF	TP
Bill Cartwright	35	9-11	-	9-15	9	1	-	-	2	27
Winford Boynes	37	8-14	-	1-2	2	3	-	-	3	17
Doug Jemison	34	5-12	-	3-4	11	0	-	-	3	13
James Hardy	14	3-4	-	1-2	4	0	-	-	0	7
John Cox	34	2-9	-	0-0	4	4	-	-	0	4
Sam Williams	17	2-6	-	0-0	2	0	-	-	4	4
Rod Williams	29	0-3	-	0-0	3	3	-	-	4	0
TOTALS	**200**	**29-59**	**-**	**14-23**	**35**	**11**	**-**	**-**	**16**	**72**
Percentages		49.2		60.9						

Coach: Bob Gaillard

Officials: Weiler, Bain
Technicals: San Francisco (team)
Attendance: 17,750

84-80

SWEET 16

	1H	2H
Duke	44	40
Penn	40	40

DUKE	MIN	FG	3FG	FT	REB	A	ST	BL	PF	TP
Eugene Banks	-	8-17	-	5-6	10	2	4	0	4	21
Jim Spanarkel	-	6-14	-	9-9	6	3	2	1	1	21
Mike Gminski	-	6-14	-	2-3	10	0	1	7	1	14
Bob Bender	-	3-5	-	2-5	4	5	1	0	1	8
Kenny Dennard	-	4-4	-	0-1	5	2	1	0	4	8
John Harrell	-	2-4	-	2-3	2	3	0	0	4	6
Scott Goetsch	-	1-2	-	0-0	4	0	0	1	1	2
Harold Morrison	-	0-1	-	2-2	0	0	0	0	0	2
Jim Suddath	-	1-1	-	0-0	1	0	0	0	1	2
Steve Gray	-	0-0	-	0-0	0	0	0	0	0	0
TOTALS	**-**	**31-62**	**-**	**22-29**	**42**	**15**	**9**	**9**	**17**	**84**
Percentages		50.0		75.9						

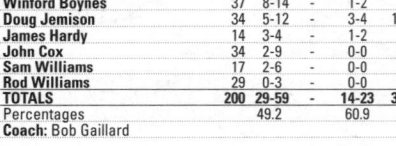

Coach: Bill E. Foster

PENN	MIN	FG	3FG	FT	REB	A	ST	BL	PF	TP
Tony Price	-	6-16	-	5-6	7	6	2	-	4	17
Bobby Willis	-	7-14	-	2-3	3	7	3	-	3	16
Tim Smith	-	6-10	-	1-2	3	0	2	-	3	13
Tom Crowley	-	5-7	-	2-4	3	1	1	-	3	12
Keven McDonald	-	5-9	-	0-1	5	1	0	-	4	10
Stan Greene	-	2-7	-	2-2	1	2	1	-	5	6
Matthew White	-	3-6	-	0-2	11	0	0	-	4	6
James Salters	-	0-0	-	0-0	0	1	0	-	3	0
TOTALS	**-**	**34-69**	**-**	**12-20**	**33**	**18**	**9**	**-**	**29**	**80**
Percentages		49.3		60.0						

Coach: Bob Weinhauer

Officials: Herrold, Savidge
Technicals: Duke (Gminski)
Attendance: 10,689

61-60

SWEET 16

	1H	2H
Villanova	35	26
Indiana	43	17

VILLANOVA	MIN	FG	3FG	FT	REB	A	ST	BL	PF	TP
Keith Herron	37	11-16	-	1-2	5	2	1	-	2	23
Reggie Robinson	35	5-13	-	2-2	7	1	1	-	3	12
Rory Sparrow	35	5-9	-	2-4	2	6	2	-	4	12
Alex Bradley	33	1-11	-	4-4	12	0	1	-	3	6
Robert Rigsby	28	2-2	-	0-1	3	3	1	-	4	4
Steve Lincoln	22	2-3	-	0-0	1	2	1	-	1	4
Jay Underman	8	0-0	-	0-0	0	1	0	-	2	0
Marty Caron	2	0-0	-	0-0	0	0	0	-	1	0
TOTALS	**200**	**26-54**	**-**	**9-13**	**30**	**15**	**7**	**-**	**20**	**61**
Percentages		48.1		69.2						

Coach: Rollie Massimino

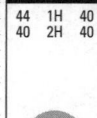

INDIANA	MIN	FG	3FG	FT	REB	A	ST	BL	PF	TP
Mike Woodson	40	11-19	-	2-2	4	0	1	0	3	24
Wayne Radford	39	8-19	-	6-8	6	1	0	0	3	22
Ray Tolbert	18	4-8	-	0-2	4	1	0	1	5	8
James Wisman	37	1-3	-	4-4	1	10	3	0	0	6
Tom Baker	25	0-0	-	0-0	1	3	0	0	3	0
Butch Carter	19	0-0	-	0-0	1	3	0	0	1	0
Steve Risley	14	0-0	-	0-1	2	0	1	0	1	0
Jim Roberson	8	0-0	-	0-0	1	0	0	1	1	0
TOTALS	**200**	**24-49**	**-**	**12-17**	**20**	**18**	**5**	**2**	**17**	**60**
Percentages		49.0		70.6						

Coach: Bob Knight

Officials: Kelley, Winters
Attendance: 10,689

69-56 — SWEET 16

	1H	2H
Notre Dame	28	41
Utah	26	30

NOTRE DAME	MIN	FG	3FG	FT	REB	A	ST	BL	PF	TP
Kelly Tripucka	29	8-11	-	4-5	4	3	2	0	3	20
Dave Batton	37	6-12	-	3-5	6	3	3	1	2	15
Rich Branning	39	3-7	-	5-7	0	5	2	0	3	11
Don Williams	38	5-14	-	0-1	2	3	2	0	2	10
Bill Hanzlik	11	2-3	-	3-3	2	1	0	0	4	7
Bill Laimbeer	18	1-3	-	2-5	5	0	0	0	2	4
Tracy Jackson	10	1-1	-	0-0	2	0	0	0	0	2
Bruce Flowers	15	0-1	-	0-1	3	2	2	0	5	0
Stan Wilcox	3	0-0	-	0-0	0	0	1	0	0	0
Jeff Carpenter	0	0-0	-	0-0	0	0	0	0	0	0
Randy Haefner	0	0-0	-	0-0	0	0	0	0	0	0
Tim Healy	0	0-0	-	0-0	0	0	0	0	0	0
Gilbert Salinas	0	0-0	-	0-0	1	0	0	0	0	0
Orlando Woolridge	0	0-0	-	0-0	0	0	0	0	0	0
TOTALS	200	26-52	-	17-27	25	17	12	1	21	69
Percentages		50.0		63.0						

Coach: Digger Phelps

UTAH	MIN	FG	3FG	FT	REB	A	ST	BL	PF	TP
Jay Judkins	40	7-17	-	2-2	4	0	1	0	3	16
Danny Vranes	40	6-10	-	2-3	11	1	1	0	4	14
Buster Matheney	24	4-9	-	0-0	4	0	1	2	5	8
Greg Deane	16	1-3	-	6-7	3	1	2	0	2	8
Earl Williams	24	2-2	-	0-0	1	3	1	0	1	4
Tom Chambers	16	2-5	-	0-1	3	0	0	0	3	4
Michael Grey	32	1-4	-	0-0	1	3	0	0	5	2
Scott Martin	8	0-1	-	0-0	0	2	0	0	2	0
Karl Bankowski	0	0-2	-	0-0	0	0	0	0	1	0
Jay Judkins	0	0-0	-	0-0	0	0	0	0	0	0
Coby Leavitt	0	0-0	-	0-0	0	0	0	0	0	0
TOTALS	200	23-53	-	10-13	27	10	6	2	26	56
Percentages		43.4		76.9						

Coach: Jerry Pimm

Officials: Galvan, Diehl
Attendance: 10,300

90-89 — SWEET 16

	1H	2H	OT1	OT2
DePaul	36	38	8	8
Louisville	35	39	8	7

DEPAUL	MIN	FG	3FG	FT	REB	A	ST	BL	PF	TP
Dave Corzine	50	18-28	-	10-10	9	1	0	3	3	46
Curtis Watkins	47	6-10	-	4-5	8	2	0	1	2	16
Gary Garland	47	3-11	-	4-4	2	4	2	1	1	10
Joe Ponsetto	44	4-4	-	0-0	4	7	1	1	3	8
Randy Ramsey	45	1-3	-	4-5	4	4	0	0	4	6
William Dise	8	2-3	-	0-0	1	1	0	0	2	4
Clyde Bradshaw	9	0-2	-	0-1	1	0	0	0	1	0
Gary Wydra	0	0-0	-	0-0	0	0	0	0	0	0
TOTALS	250	34-61	-	22-25	29	19	3	6	16	90
Percentages		55.7		88.0						

Coach: Ray Meyer

LOUISVILLE	MIN	FG	3FG	FT	REB	A	ST	BL	PF	TP
Bobby Turner	48	9-18	-	5-5	8	2	1	0	2	23
Rick Wilson	42	9-20	-	2-3	6	1	1	0	3	20
Darrell Griffith	48	9-15	-	1-3	3	5	3	1	5	19
Larry Williams	44	6-12	-	1-2	9	1	3	0	4	13
Ricky Gallon	44	5-12	-	2-4	3	0	2	2	4	12
Tony Branch	8	1-2	-	0-0	0	3	1	0	1	2
Dave Smith	12	0-0	-	0-0	2	0	0	1	1	0
Roger Burkman	4	0-0	-	0-0	1	1	1	0	3	0
TOTALS	250	39-79	-	11-17	32	13	12	4	23	89
Percentages		49.4		64.7						

Coach: Denny Crum

Officials: Howell, Wortman
Attendance: 10,300

52-49 — ELITE 8

	1H	2H
Kentucky	22	30
Michigan State	27	22

KENTUCKY	MIN	FG	3FG	FT	REB	A	ST	BL	PF	TP
Kyle Macy	40	4-10	-	10-11	1	3	1	0	2	18
Jack Givens	34	6-12	-	2-3	7	0	0	1	3	14
Mike Phillips	30	3-5	-	4-4	8	1	2	0	1	10
Rick Robey	30	3-4	-	0-0	4	1	0	0	1	6
James Lee	20	1-1	-	0-0	1	2	0	0	4	2
Jay Shidler	10	1-2	-	0-0	1	0	0	0	2	2
Truman Claytor	30	0-5	-	0-0	0	3	0	0	2	0
LaVon Williams	6	0-0	-	0-0	1	0	0	0	1	0
TOTALS	200	18-39	-	16-18	23	10	3	1	16	52
Percentages		46.2		88.9						

Coach: Joe B. Hall

MICHIGAN STATE	MIN	FG	3FG	FT	REB	A	ST	BL	PF	TP
Greg Kelser	40	9-12	-	1-3	13	1	3	2	3	19
Robert Chapman	32	5-9	-	0-0	1	1	1	0	5	10
Jay Vincent	38	4-7	-	0-0	1	2	0	0	1	8
Earvin "Magic" Johnson	39	2-10	-	2-2	4	5	2	0	4	6
Ron Charles	16	2-3	-	0-0	0	0	0	0	0	4
Terry Donnelly	34	0-0	-	2-2	0	5	0	1	5	2
Mike Brkovich	1	0-0	-	0-0	0	0	0	0	0	0
TOTALS	200	22-41	-	5-7	19	14	6	3	18	49
Percentages		53.7		71.4						

Coach: Jud Heathcote

Officials: Clymer, Bishop
Attendance: 13,458

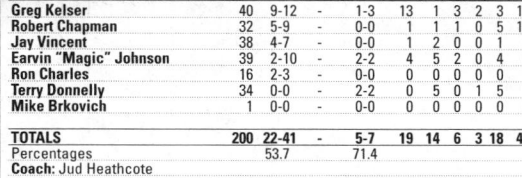

61-58 — ELITE 8

	1H	2H
Arkansas	39	22
Cal State Fullerton	24	34

ARKANSAS	MIN	FG	3FG	FT	REB	A	ST	BL	PF	TP
Ron Brewer	39	11-19	-	0-0	3	2	-	-	4	22
Marvin Delph	40	7-13	-	0-0	5	2	-	-	2	14
Sidney Moncrief	39	4-7	-	3-4	4	1	-	-	4	11
Steve Schall	40	5-6	-	0-0	9	2	-	-	2	10
Jim Counce	40	2-2	-	0-2	1	7	-	-	4	4
U.S. Reed	2	0-0	-	0-0	1	0	-	-	0	0
TOTALS	200	29-47	-	3-6	23	14	-	-	16	61
Percentages		61.7		50.0						

Coach: Eddie Sutton

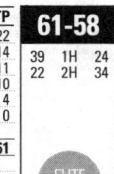

CAL STATE FULLERTON	MIN	FG	3FG	FT	REB	A	ST	BL	PF	TP
Keith Anderson	37	11-22	-	1-1	9	4	-	-	1	23
Kevin Heenan	40	5-14	-	1-2	0	1	-	-	2	11
Mike Niles	26	4-6	-	3-4	3	0	-	-	4	11
Greg Bunch	40	3-9	-	3-4	10	1	-	-	3	9
Mike Linden	38	1-7	-	0-0	3	4	-	-	1	2
Steve Shaw	16	1-4	-	0-0	3	1	-	-	1	2
Greg Palm	3	0-0	-	0-0	0	0	-	-	1	0
TOTALS	200	25-62	-	8-11	28	11	-	-	13	58
Percentages		40.3		72.7						

Coach: Bobby Dye

Officials: Weiler, Bain
Attendance: 18,144

90-72 — ELITE 8

	1H	2H
Duke	46	44
Villanova	32	40

DUKE	MIN	FG	3FG	FT	REB	A	ST	BL	PF	TP
Jim Spanarkel	35	9-11	-	4-6	5	6	2	0	3	22
Mike Gminski	35	10-17	-	1-1	10	2	2	1	3	21
Eugene Banks	34	6-10	-	5-6	10	9	1	0	4	17
Kenny Dennard	29	8-12	-	0-0	4	2	1	1	4	16
John Harrell	26	3-4	-	2-2	1	2	0	0	1	8
Jim Suddath	12	2-3	-	0-0	0	2	0	0	2	4
Steve Gray	3	1-1	-	0-0	0	0	0	0	0	2
Bob Bender	15	0-1	-	0-0	2	2	1	0	2	0
Scott Goetsch	6	0-1	-	0-0	1	0	0	0	1	0
Harold Morrison	3	0-0	-	0-0	1	0	0	0	1	0
Bruce Bell	1	0-0	-	0-0	1	1	0	0	0	0
Rob Hardy	1	0-0	-	0-0	1	0	0	0	0	0
TOTALS	200	39-60	-	12-15	36	26	7	2	21	90
Percentages		65.0		80.0						

Coach: Bill E. Foster

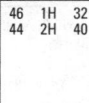

VILLANOVA	MIN	FG	3FG	FT	REB	A	ST	BL	PF	TP
Keith Herron	35	8-19	-	4-7	2	1	0	0	4	20
Reggie Robinson	29	8-17	-	0-0	4	0	1	3	0	16
Robert Rigsby	34	3-8	-	8-10	13	4	2	0	3	14
Alex Bradley	32	3-7	-	4-6	5	0	0	0	2	10
Steve Lincoln	18	2-3	-	0-0	1	2	0	0	2	4
Jay Underman	6	2-3	-	0-0	1	1	0	0	1	4
Rory Sparrow	33	1-4	-	0-0	2	8	2	0	4	2
Larry Sock	1	1-2	-	0-0	0	0	0	0	0	2
Marty Caron	4	0-0	-	0-0	0	0	0	0	1	0
Tom Sienkiewicz	4	0-3	-	0-0	0	0	0	0	1	0
Bruce Anders	2	0-0	-	0-0	0	0	0	0	0	0
Ron Cowan	2	0-1	-	0-0	0	0	1	1	1	0
TOTALS	200	28-67	-	16-23	28	16	6	3	19	72
Percentages		41.8		69.6						

Coach: Rollie Massimino

Officials: Kelley, Winters
Technicals: Villanova (coach Massimino)
Attendance: 10,804

84-64 — ELITE 8

	1H	2H
Notre Dame	37	47
DePaul	33	31

NOTRE DAME	MIN	FG	3FG	FT	REB	A	ST	BL	PF	TP
Kelly Tripucka	34	9-22	-	0-0	11	0	2	0	2	18
Rich Branning	37	6-12	-	3-3	4	7	0	0	0	15
Don Williams	27	5-12	-	4-4	3	1	0	0	2	14
Bill Laimbeer	28	4-8	-	4-7	10	0	0	2	4	12
Dave Batton	30	1-5	-	5-6	6	5	0	0	1	7
Bruce Flowers	12	2-2	-	3-3	1	1	0	0	4	7
Tracy Jackson	17	2-4	-	1-1	4	2	2	1	1	5
Bill Hanzlik	10	2-3	-	0-0	3	1	2	0	2	4
Jeff Carpenter	0	1-1	-	0-0	0	0	0	0	0	2
Stan Wilcox	5	0-1	-	0-0	1	0	0	0	0	0
Randy Haefner	0	0-0	-	0-0	0	0	0	0	0	0
Gilbert Salinas	0	0-0	-	0-0	0	0	0	0	0	0
Orlando Woolridge	0	0-0	-	0-0	0	0	0	0	0	0
TOTALS	200	32-70	-	20-24	43	17	6	3	16	84
Percentages		45.7		83.3						

Coach: Digger Phelps

DEPAUL	MIN	FG	3FG	FT	REB	A	ST	BL	PF	TP
Gary Garland	39	8-16	-	2-2	6	2	2	0	5	18
Dave Corzine	39	6-11	-	5-7	7	1	0	2	2	17
Curtis Watkins	36	4-8	-	0-0	6	1	0	0	4	8
Joe Ponsetto	30	4-12	-	0-0	6	3	0	0	5	8
Clyde Bradshaw	15	3-8	-	0-0	0	1	0	0	2	6
William Dise	10	2-6	-	1-2	3	0	1	1	2	5
Randy Ramsey	29	1-5	-	0-0	4	2	0	0	1	2
Randy Hook	1	0-0	-	0-0	0	0	0	0	0	0
Gary Wydra	1	0-0	-	0-0	0	0	0	0	0	0
TOTALS	200	28-66	-	8-11	32	10	3	3	21	64
Percentages		42.4		72.7						

Coach: Ray Meyer

Officials: Howell, Wortman
Attendance: 10,110

ANNUAL REVIEW

FINAL 4: Kentucky 64, Arkansas 59 (1H: 32-30; 2H: 32-29)

KENTUCKY	MIN	FG	3FG	FT	REB	A	ST	BL	PF	TP
Jack Givens	38	10-16	-	3-4	9	0	1	-	2	23
James Lee	27	4-8	-	5-5	8	0	0	-	4	13
Rick Robey	34	3-6	-	2-2	8	0	2	-	2	8
Kyle Macy	33	2-8	-	3-4	3	3	0	-	4	7
Jay Shidler	25	3-5	-	0-0	2	4	0	-	4	6
Mike Phillips	17	1-6	-	3-4	2	1	0	-	4	5
Truman Claytor	17	1-2	-	0-1	0	2	0	-	4	2
LaVon Williams	3	0-0	-	0-0	0	0	0	-	1	0
Dwane Casey	2	0-0	-	0-0	0	0	0	-	0	0
Fred Cowan	2	0-0	-	0-0	0	0	0	-	1	0
Tim Stephens	2	0-0	-	0-0	0	0	0	-	0	0
TOTALS	**200**	**24-51**	**-**	**16-20**	**32**	**10**	**3**	**-**	**26**	**64**
Percentages		47.1		80.0						

Coach: Joe B. Hall

ARKANSAS	MIN	FG	3FG	FT	REB	A	ST	BL	PF	TP
Ron Brewer	39	5-12	-	6-8	5	1	3	0	2	16
Marvin Delph	40	5-13	-	5-6	8	0	0	2	3	15
Sidney Moncrief	40	5-11	-	3-7	5	0	1	2	3	13
Jim Counce	32	2-2	-	2-3	2	2	0	2	4	6
Steve Schall	21	3-5	-	0-0	3	0	1	0	5	6
Alan Zahn	17	1-1	-	1-2	2	1	1	0	3	3
U.S. Reed	11	0-0	-	0-0	0	0	1	1	2	0
TOTALS	**200**	**21-44**	**-**	**17-26**	**25**	**4**	**7**	**7**	**22**	**59**
Percentages		47.7		65.4						

Coach: Eddie Sutton

Officials: Howell, Bain
Technicals: Kentucky (coa[ch] Hall)
Attendance: 18,721

FINAL 4: Duke 90, Notre Dame 86 (1H: 43-29; 2H: 47-57)

DUKE	MIN	FG	3FG	FT	REB	A	ST	BL	PF	TP
Mike Gminski	36	13-17	-	3-4	5	2	0	1	2	29
Eugene Banks	39	8-15	-	6-7	12	3	0	0	1	22
Jim Spanarkel	37	4-11	-	12-12	4	5	2	0	1	20
Kenny Dennard	34	2-3	-	3-5	7	0	2	0	5	7
John Harrell	26	0-2	-	6-6	2	3	1	0	2	6
Bob Bender	19	0-1	-	2-3	2	5	0	0	2	2
Scott Goetsch	5	1-1	-	0-0	0	1	0	0	0	2
Jim Suddath	4	1-3	-	0-0	0	0	0	0	2	2
TOTALS	**200**	**29-53**	**-**	**32-37**	**32**	**19**	**5**	**1**	**15**	**90**
Percentages		54.7		86.5						

Coach: Bill E. Foster

NOTRE DAME	MIN	FG	3FG	FT	REB	A	ST	BL	PF	TP
Don Williams	34	8-15	-	0-1	2	2	1	0	2	16
Kelly Tripucka	32	5-17	-	2-2	9	1	3	0	3	12
Tracy Jackson	16	5-6	-	1-2	0	1	0	0	4	11
Dave Batton	21	3-6	-	4-4	2	0	0	0	1	10
Bruce Flowers	17	5-8	-	0-0	6	2	1	0	3	10
Rich Branning	37	4-10	-	0-0	1	5	1	0	3	8
Bill Hanzlik	17	3-8	-	2-2	6	2	2	0	5	8
Bill Laimbeer	20	1-5	-	5-6	10	2	0	1	5	7
Stan Wilcox	6	2-2	-	0-0	0	0	1	0	0	4
TOTALS	**200**	**36-77**	**-**	**14-17**	**36**	**15**	**9**	**1**	**26**	**86**
Percentages		46.8		82.4						

Coach: Digger Phelps

Officials: Kelley, Clymer
Technicals: Notre Dame (Hanzlik)
Attendance: 18,721

3RD PLACE: Arkansas 71, Notre Dame 69 (1H: 40-36; 2H: 31-33)

ARKANSAS	MIN	FG	3FG	FT	REB	A	ST	BL	PF	TP
Marvin Delph	30	7-10	-	7-8	5	0	0	0	4	21
Ron Brewer	40	7-16	-	6-6	6	3	0	0	3	20
Sidney Moncrief	38	3-6	-	4-6	4	3	1	1	4	10
Alan Zahn	28	4-6	-	2-3	2	1	1	0	2	10
Steve Schall	40	3-9	-	0-0	11	3	1	2	3	6
Chris Bennett	9	1-2	-	0-0	0	0	1	0	1	2
Jim Counce	8	1-3	-	0-0	0	1	0	0	1	2
U.S. Reed	7	0-0	-	0-0	1	0	0	0	1	0
TOTALS	**200**	**26-52**	**-**	**19-23**	**29**	**11**	**4**	**3**	**19**	**71**
Percentages		50.0		82.6						

Coach: Eddie Sutton

NOTRE DAME	MIN	FG	3FG	FT	REB	A	ST	BL	PF	TP
Dave Batton	30	6-12	-	3-3	7	0	0	1	3	15
Bruce Flowers	18	4-9	-	4-6	5	4	0	0	4	12
Tracy Jackson	21	5-8	-	1-2	2	0	3	0	2	11
Kelly Tripucka	28	3-6	-	4-6	5	1	0	0	2	10
Bill Hanzlik	14	4-5	-	0-0	2	5	3	0	4	8
Don Williams	28	2-8	-	1-2	3	1	2	0	0	5
Rich Branning	34	1-8	-	1-2	1	4	0	0	3	3
Bill Laimbeer	13	1-1	-	0-0	3	0	0	0	2	2
Stan Wilcox	11	1-2	-	0-0	1	0	0	0	1	2
Orlando Woolridge	3	0-0	-	1-2	1	0	0	0	1	1
TOTALS	**200**	**27-59**	**-**	**15-23**	**30**	**15**	**8**	**1**	**22**	**69**
Percentages		45.8		65.2						

Coach: Digger Phelps

Officials: Howell, Kelley
Technicals: Arkansas (bench)
Attendance: 18,721

NCAA FINAL 1978: Kentucky 94, Duke 88 (1H: 45-38; 2H: 49-50)

KENTUCKY	MIN	FG	3FG	FT	REB	A	ST	BL	PF	TP
Jack Givens	37	18-27	-	5-8	8	3	-	0	4	41
Rick Robey	32	8-11	-	4-6	11	0	-	1	2	20
Kyle Macy	38	3-3	-	3-4	0	8	-	0	1	9
Truman Claytor	24	3-5	-	2-4	0	3	-	0	2	8
James Lee	20	4-8	-	0-0	4	2	-	0	4	8
Mike Phillips	11	1-4	-	2-2	2	1	-	0	5	4
Jay Shidler	15	1-5	-	0-1	1	3	-	0	3	2
LaVon Williams	11	1-3	-	0-0	4	0	-	0	2	2
Fred Cowan	8	0-2	-	0-0	2	0	-	0	1	0
Chuck Aleksinas	1	0-0	-	0-0	0	0	-	0	1	0
Scott Courts	1	0-0	-	0-0	0	0	-	0	0	0
Chris Gettelfinger	1	0-0	-	0-0	0	0	-	0	0	0
Tim Stephens	1	0-0	-	0-0	0	0	-	0	0	0
Dwane Casey	0	0-0	-	0-0	0	0	-	0	0	0
TOTALS	**200**	**39-68**	**-**	**16-25**	**32**	**20**	**-**	**1**	**25**	**94**
Percentages		57.4		64.0						

Coach: Joe B. Hall

DUKE	MIN	FG	3FG	FT	REB	A	ST	BL	PF	TP
Eugene Banks	37	6-12	-	10-12	8	2	0	0	2	22
Jim Spanarkel	40	8-16	-	5-6	2	3	2	0	4	21
Mike Gminski	37	6-16	-	8-8	12	2	1	1	3	20
Kenny Dennard	31	5-7	-	0-0	9	2	1	0	5	10
Bob Bender	16	1-2	-	5-5	1	4	1	0	3	7
John Harrell	24	2-2	-	0-0	0	1	1	0	3	4
Jim Suddath	9	1-3	-	2-3	2	0	0	0	1	4
Scott Goetsch	6	0-1	-	0-0	1	0	0	0	1	0
TOTALS	**200**	**29-59**	**-**	**30-34**	**35**	**14**	**6**	**1**	**22**	**88**
Percentages		49.2		88.2						

Coach: Bill E. Foster

Officials: Bain, Clymer
Technicals: Duke (bench)
Attendance: 18,721

National Invitation Tournament (NIT)

First round: Georgetown d. Virginia 70-68 (OT), Nebraska d. Utah State 67-66, Texas d. Temple 72-58, Rutgers d. Army 72-70, Indiana State d. Illinois State 73-71, NC State d. South Carolina 82-70, Detroit d. VCU 94-86, Dayton d. Fairfield 108-93
Quarterfinals: Georgetown d. Dayton 71-62, Texas d. Nebraska 67-48, Rutgers d. Indiana State 57-56, NC State d. Detroit 84-77
Semifinals: Texas d. Rutgers 96-76, NC State d. Georgetown 86-85
Third place: Rutgers d. Georgetown 85-72
Championship: Texas d. NC State 101-93
MVP: Ron Baxter, Texas and Jim Krivacs, Texas

1978-79: Bird vs. Magic

The season, the Tournament and college basketball itself could be summed up in three words: Bird versus Magic. March Madness hit an all-time peak in anticipation of the 1979 Final. Indiana State senior Larry Bird faced off against Michigan State sophomore Earvin "Magic" Johnson in the highest-rated college basketball telecast in history. But the game did not match the hype. Magic had 24 points, seven rebounds and five assists to Bird's 19 points and 13 rebounds in a 75-64 win for the 26–6 Spartans at the Special Events Center in Salt Lake City. It was the Sycamores' only loss of the season. With 53 points, 17 rebounds and 15 assists in the Final Four, Johnson earned the Tournament's Most Outstanding Player award and was chosen by the Los Angeles Lakers as the No. 1 overall pick in the NBA draft. Bird was named Naismith Player of the Year after averaging 28.6 ppg and 14.9 rpg.

For the first time, teams were assigned seeds for the 1979 Tournament, with Indiana State, North Carolina, UCLA and Notre Dame receiving the inaugural No. 1s. The Tournament field expanded from 32 teams to 40.

Major Conference Standings

ACC

	Conference			Overall		
	W	L	Pct	W	L	Pct
North Carolina ⊕	9	3	.750	23	6	.793
Duke ○	9	3	.750	22	8	.733
Virginia □	7	5	.583	19	10	.655
Maryland □	6	6	.500	19	11	.633
Clemson □	5	7	.417	19	10	.655
NC State	3	9	.250	18	12	.600
Wake Forest	3	9	.250	12	15	.444

Tournament: **North Carolina d. Duke 71-63**
Tournament MVP: **Dudley Bradley**, North Carolina

Big Eight

	Conference			Overall		
	W	L	Pct	W	L	Pct
Oklahoma ⊕	10	4	.714	21	10	.677
Kansas	8	6	.571	18	11	.621
Kansas State	8	6	.571	16	12	.571
Missouri	8	6	.571	13	15	.464
Nebraska	7	7	.500	14	13	.519
Iowa State	6	8	.429	11	16	.407
Oklahoma State	5	9	.357	12	15	.444
Colorado	4	10	.286	14	13	.519

Tournament: **Oklahoma d. Kansas 80-65**
Tournament MVP: **Al Beal**, Oklahoma

Big Sky

	Conference			Overall		
	W	L	Pct	W	L	Pct
Weber State ⊕	10	4	.714	25	9	.735
Idaho State	8	6	.571	14	13	.519
Northern Arizona	8	6	.571	13	14	.481
Gonzaga	7	7	.500	16	10	.615
Montana	7	7	.500	14	13	.519
Montana State	6	8	.429	15	11	.577
Boise State	6	8	.429	11	15	.423
Idaho	4	10	.286	11	15	.423

Tournament: **Weber State d. Northern Arizona 92-70**
Tournament MVP: **Bruce Collins**, Weber State

Big Ten

	Conference			Overall		
	W	L	Pct	W	L	Pct
Michigan State ⊕	13	5	.722	26	6	.813
Purdue □	13	5	.722	27	8	.771
Iowa ○	13	5	.722	20	8	.714
Ohio State □	12	6	.667	19	12	.613
Indiana □	10	8	.556	22	12	.647
Michigan	8	10	.444	15	12	.556
Illinois	7	11	.389	19	11	.633
Wisconsin	6	12	.333	12	15	.444
Minnesota	6	12	.333	11	16	.407
Northwestern	2	16	.111	6	21	.222

East Coast

	Conference			Overall		
	W	L	Pct	W	L	Pct
East Section						
Temple ⊕	13	0	1.000	25	4	.862
Saint Joseph's □	11	3	.786	19	11	.633
La Salle	10	3	.769	15	13	.536
Drexel	7	6	.538	18	9	.667
American	7	5	.583	14	13	.519
Hofstra	3	9	.250	8	19	.296
West Section						
Bucknell	12	6	.667	18	9	.667
Lafayette	9	9	.500	16	12	.571
Rider	7	9	.438	11	15	.423
West Chester	5	13	.278	8	18	.308
Lehigh	4	13	.235	8	18	.308
Delaware	3	15	.167	5	22	.185

Tournament: **Temple d. Saint Joseph's 61-60**

Eastern 8

	Conference			Overall		
	W	L	Pct	W	L	Pct
Villanova	9	1	.900	13	13	.500
Rutgers ⊕	7	3	.700	22	9	.710
West Virginia	7	3	.700	16	12	.571
Pittsburgh	6	4	.600	18	11	.621
George Washington	5	5	.500	13	14	.481
Penn State	4	6	.400	12	18	.400
Duquesne	2	8	.200	13	13	.500
Massachusetts	0	10	.000	5	22	.185

Tournament: **Rutgers d. Pittsburgh 61-57**
Tournament MVP: **James Bailey**, Rutgers

Ivy

	Conference			Overall		
	W	L	Pct	W	L	Pct
Penn ⊕	13	1	.929	25	7	.781
Columbia	10	4	.714	17	9	.654
Princeton	7	7	.500	14	12	.538
Dartmouth	6	8	.429	14	12	.538
Brown	6	8	.429	8	18	.308
Harvard	6	8	.429	8	21	.276
Yale	5	9	.357	11	15	.423
Cornell	3	11	.214	8	18	.308

Note: Columbia and Princeton also played in NJ-NY 7

Metro

	Conference			Overall		
	W	L	Pct	W	L	Pct
Louisville ○	9	1	.900	24	8	.750
Florida State	7	3	.700	19	10	.655
Memphis	5	5	.500	13	15	.464
Virginia Tech ⊕	4	6	.400	22	9	.710
Cincinnati	4	6	.400	13	14	.481
Saint Louis	3	7	.300	10	17	.370
Tulane	2	8	.200	8	19	.296

Tournament: **Virginia Tech d. Florida State 68-60**
Tournament MVP: **Dale Solomon**, Virginia Tech

Mid-American

	Conference			Overall		
	W	L	Pct	W	L	Pct
Toledo ⊕	13	3	.813	22	8	.733
Central Michigan □	13	3	.813	19	9	.679
Ohio	10	6	.625	16	11	.593
Ball State	9	7	.563	16	11	.593
Northern Illinois	8	8	.500	14	13	.519
Kent State	7	9	.438	13	14	.481
Bowling Green	6	10	.375	14	13	.519
Miami (OH)	6	10	.375	9	18	.333
Eastern Michigan	5	11	.313	9	18	.333
Western Michigan	3	13	.188	7	23	.233

MEAC

	Conference			Overall		
	W	L	Pct	W	L	Pct
NC A&T	11	1	.917	20	7	.741
Delaware State	7	5	.583	18	10	.643
Morgan State	6	6	.500	18	12	.600
Howard	6	6	.500	16	12	.571
UMES	5	7	.417	7	16	.304
NC Central	4	8	.333	5	21	.192
SC State	3	9	.250	8	19	.296

Tournament: **NC A&T d. Howard 48-46**
Tournament MOP: **Larry Spriggs**, Howard

Missouri Valley

	Conference			Overall		
	W	L	Pct	W	L	Pct
Indiana State ⊕	16	0	1.000	33	1	.971
New Mexico State ○	11	5	.688	22	10	.688
Drake	8	8	.500	15	12	.556
Southern Illinois	8	8	.500	15	13	.536
Creighton	8	8	.500	14	13	.519
Wichita State	8	8	.500	14	14	.500
Tulsa	7	9	.438	13	14	.481
Bradley	3	13	.188	9	17	.346
West Texas A&M	3	13	.188	8	19	.296

Tournament: **Indiana State d. New Mexico State 69-59**

NJ-NY 7

	Conference			Overall		
	W	L	Pct	W	L	Pct
Rutgers	6	0	1.000	22	9	.710
Seton Hall	5	1	.833	16	11	.593
St. John's ○	3	3	.500	21	11	.656
Columbia	3	3	.500	17	9	.654
Princeton	2	4	.333	14	12	.538
Fordham	1	5	.167	7	22	.241
Manhattan	1	6	.143	6	20	.231

Ohio Valley

	Conference			Overall		
	W	L	Pct	W	L	Pct
Eastern Kentucky ⊕	9	3	.750	21	8	.724
Western Kentucky	7	5	.583	17	11	.607
Middle Tenn. State	7	5	.583	16	11	.593
Morehead State	7	5	.583	14	13	.519
Tennessee Tech	7	5	.583	11	15	.423
Austin Peay	3	9	.250	8	18	.308
Murray State	2	10	.167	4	22	.154

Tournament: **Eastern Kentucky d. Western Kentucky 78-77**
Tournament MVP: **Greg Jackson**, Western Kentucky

PCAA

	Conference			Overall		
	W	L	Pct	W	L	Pct
Pacific ⊕	11	3	.786	18	12	.600
Utah State ○	9	5	.643	19	11	.633
Fresno State	9	5	.643	16	12	.571
Cal State Fullerton	7	7	.500	16	11	.593
Long Beach State	7	7	.500	16	12	.571
UC Santa Barbara	6	8	.429	12	15	.444
San Jose State	4	10	.286	7	20	.259
UC Irvine	3	11	.214	9	17	.346

Tournament: **Pacific d. Utah State 82-73**
Tournament MVP: **Ron Cornelius**, Pacific

Pac-10

	Conference			Overall		
	W	L	Pct	W	L	Pct
UCLA ⊕	15	3	.833	25	5	.833
Southern California ○	14	4	.778	20	9	.690
Oregon State □	11	7	.611	18	10	.643
Washington State	10	8	.556	18	9	.667
Arizona	10	8	.556	16	11	.593
Arizona State	7	11	.389	16	14	.533
Oregon	7	11	.389	12	15	.444
Stanford	6	12	.333	12	15	.444
Washington	6	12	.333	11	16	.407
California	4	14	.222	6	21	.222

Southeastern

	Conference			Overall		
	W	L	Pct	W	L	Pct
LSU ○	14	4	.778	23	6	.793
Tennessee ⊕	12	6	.667	21	12	.636
Mississippi State □	11	7	.611	19	9	.679
Alabama □	11	7	.611	22	11	.667
Vanderbilt	11	7	.611	18	9	.667
Kentucky □	10	8	.556	19	12	.613
Georgia	7	11	.389	14	14	.500
Mississippi	6	12	.333	11	16	.407
Auburn	5	13	.278	13	16	.448
Florida	3	15	.167	8	19	.296

Tournament: **Tennessee d. Kentucky 75-69 (OT)**
Tournament MVP: **Kyle Macy**, Kentucky

Conference Standings Continue →

⊕ Automatic NCAA Tournament bid ○ At-large NCAA Tournament bid □ NIT appearance ⊗ Team record doesn't reflect games forfeited or vacated. For adjusted record, see p. 521.

SOUTHERN

	Conference W	L	PCT	Overall W	L	PCT
Appalachian State⊛	11	3	.786	23	6	.793
Furman	9	3	.750	20	9	.690
The Citadel	10	4	.714	20	7	.741
Western Carolina	5	7	.417	14	14	.500
Marshall	5	8	.385	11	16	.407
Davidson	3	7	.300	8	19	.296
Chattanooga	3	8	.273	14	13	.519
VMI	2	8	.200	12	15	.444

Tournament: **Appalachian State d. Furman 86-83**
Tournament MOP: **Darryl Robinson**, Appalachian State

SOUTHLAND

	Conference W	L	PCT	Overall W	L	PCT
Lamar⊛	9	1	.900	23	9	.719
Louisiana Tech	6	4	.600	17	8	.680
UL-Lafayette	6	4	.600	16	11	.593
Arkansas State	5	5	.500	15	12	.556
McNeese State	3	7	.300	10	17	.370
Texas-Arlington	1	9	.100	11	16	.407

SOUTHWEST

	Conference W	L	PCT	Overall W	L	PCT
Arkansas⊛	13	3	.813	25	5	.833
Texas○	13	3	.813	21	8	.724
Texas A&M□	11	5	.688	24	9	.727
Texas Tech□	9	7	.563	19	11	.633
Baylor	9	7	.563	16	12	.571
Houston	6	10	.375	16	15	.516
SMU	6	10	.375	11	16	.407
Rice	4	12	.250	7	20	.259
TCU	1	15	.063	6	21	.222

Tournament: **Arkansas d. Texas 39-38**
Tournament MVP: **Sidney Moncrief**, Arkansas

SWAC

	Conference W	L	PCT	Overall W	L	PCT
Alcorn State□	12	0	1.000	28	1	.966
Grambling	6	6	.500	16	11	.593
Southern U.	6	6	.500	16	12	.571
Texas Southern	6	6	.500	13	14	.481
Miss. Valley State	5	7	.417	15	16	.484
Jackson State	4	8	.333	13	14	.481
Prairie View A&M	3	9	.250	17	14	.548

SUN BELT

	Conference W	L	PCT	Overall W	L	PCT
South Alabama○	10	0	1.000	20	7	.741
Charlotte	6	4	.600	16	11	.593
South Florida	6	4	.600	14	14	.500
Jacksonville⊛	5	5	.500	19	11	.633
New Orleans	3	7	.300	11	16	.407
Georgia State	0	10	.000	7	20	.259

Tournament: **Jacksonville d. South Florida 68-54**
Tournament MVP: **James Ray**, Jacksonville

TAAC

	Conference W	L	PCT	Overall W	L	PCT
UL-Monroe□	-	-	-	23	6	.793
Mercer	-	-	-	21	6	.778
Oklahoma City	-	-	-	18	11	.621
Texas-Pan American	-	-	-	13	13	.500
Houston Baptist	-	-	-	11	16	.407
Samford	-	-	-	10	15	.400
Centenary	-	-	-	9	20	.310
Hardin-Simmons	-	-	-	7	20	.259

Note: Conference did not play a formal schedule
Tournament: **UL-Monroe d. Mercer 90-69**
Tournament MVP: **Calvin Natt**, UL-Monroe

WCAC

	Conference W	L	PCT	Overall W	L	PCT
San Francisco⊛	12	2	.857	22	7	.759
Pepperdine○	10	4	.714	22	10	.688
Nevada□	9	5	.643	21	7	.750
Seattle	8	6	.571	16	11	.593
Santa Clara	6	8	.429	13	14	.481
Portland	5	9	.357	18	10	.643
Saint Mary's (CA)	5	9	.357	13	15	.464
Loyola Marymount	1	13	.071	5	21	.192

WAC

	Conference W	L	PCT	Overall W	L	PCT
BYU⊛	10	2	.833	20	8	.714
Utah○	9	3	.750	20	10	.667
New Mexico□	8	4	.667	19	10	.655
Wyoming	5	7	.417	15	12	.556
San Diego State	4	8	.333	15	12	.556
UTEP	3	9	.250	11	15	.423
Colorado State	3	9	.250	11	16	.407

INDEPENDENTS

	Overall W	L	PCT
Syracuse○	26	4	.867
Georgetown⊛$	24	5	.828
DePaul○	26	6	.813
Notre Dame○	24	6	.800
VCU	20	5	.800
Iona⊛$	23	6	.793
Detroit○	22	6	.786
Tennessee State	20	6	.769
Old Dominion□	23	7	.767
Marquette○	22	7	.759
Wagner□	21	7	.750
Connecticut⊛$	21	8	.724
UNLV	21	8	.724
UNC Wilmington	19	8	.704
Boston College	21	9	.700
James Madison	18	8	.692
Rhode Island□	20	9	.690
George Mason	17	8	.680

INDEPENDENTS (CONT.)

	Overall W	L	PCT
St. Bonaventure□	19	9	.679
Illinois State	20	10	.667
Dayton□	19	10	.655
Boston U.	17	9	.654
Fairfield	17	9	.654
Georgia Tech	17	9	.654
Oral Roberts	17	10	.630
Holy Cross□	17	11	.607
Cleveland State	15	10	.600
East Tennessee State	16	11	.593
Maine	14	10	.583
Army	14	11	.560
Denver	15	12	.556
South Carolina	15	12	.556
Stetson	15	12	.556
Siena	14	12	.538
St. Francis (NY)	14	12	.538
Navy	13	12	.520
Xavier	14	13	.519
Northeastern	13	13	.500
Saint Francis (PA)	13	13	.500
Robert Morris	13	14	.481
Southern Miss	13	14	.481
Air Force	12	13	.480
Long Island	12	13	.480
Canisius	12	14	.462
Colgate	12	14	.462
Evansville	13	16	.448
East Carolina	12	15	.444
Loyola-Chicago	12	15	.444
Butler	11	16	.407
North Texas	11	16	.407
Saint Peter's	10	15	.400
Campbell	10	16	.385
New Hampshire	10	16	.385
Providence	10	16	.385
Richmond	10	16	.385
Hawaii	10	17	.370
Vermont	9	17	.346
William and Mary	9	17	.346
Ga. Southern	9	18	.333
Fairleigh Dickinson	8	18	.308
Wisconsin-Milwaukee	8	18	.308
Northwestern State (LA)	7	19	.269
Arkansas-Little Rock	6	20	.231
Catholic	6	20	.231
Niagara	6	20	.231
Portland State	6	21	.222
Baltimore	4	21	.160
Valparaiso	4	21	.160
Charleston Southern	2	25	.074

$ Defeated regional opponents to earn an automatic NCAA bid

$ Defeated regional opponents to earn an automatic NCAA bid

INDIVIDUAL LEADERS—SEASON

Scoring

	CL	POS	G	FG	FT	PTS	PPG
1 **Lawrence Butler**, Idaho State	SR	G	27	310	192	812	**30.1**
2 **Larry Bird**, Indiana State	SR	F	34	376	221	973	**28.6**
3 **Nick Galis**, Seton Hall	SR	G	27	293	157	749	**27.7**
4 **James Tillman**, Eastern Kentucky	JR	F	29	309	162	780	**26.9**
5 **Paul Dawkins**, Northern Illinois	SR	F	26	291	113	695	**26.7**
6 **John Gerdy**, Davidson	SR	F	27	289	143	721	**26.7**
7 **Ernie Hill**, Oklahoma City	JR	G	29	287	197	771	**26.6**
8 **John Stroud**, Mississippi	JR	F	27	277	155	709	**26.3**
9 **Jon Manning**, North Texas	SR	C	27	305	89	699	**25.9**
10 **Steve Stielper**, James Madison	JR	F	26	253	162	662	**25.5**

Field Goal Pct

	CL	POS	G	FG	FGA	PCT
1 **Murray Brown**, Florida State	JR	C	29	237	343	**69.1**
2 **Jeff Ruland**, Iona	SO	C	29	233	347	**67.1**
3 **Steve Johnson**, Oregon State	SO	F/C	27	197	298	**66.1**
4 **Jonathan Green**, Tennessee State	SO	F	24	120	183	**65.6**
5 **Wiley Peck**, Mississippi State	SR	F	28	154	239	**64.4**

Minimum: 5 made per game

Free Throw Pct

	CL	POS	G	FT	FTA	PCT
1 **Darrell Mauldin**, Campbell	JR	G	26	70	76	**92.1**
2 **Kurt Kanaskie**, La Salle	JR	F	21	55	60	**91.7**
3 **Jim Krivacs**, Texas	SR	G	29	101	111	**91.0**
4 **Tom Orner**, Butler	SR	G	27	70	77	**90.9**
5 **Ronnie Perry**, Holy Cross	JR	G	28	178	196	**90.8**

Minimum: 2.5 made per game

Rebounds Per Game

	CL	POS	G	REB	RPG
1 **Monti Davis**, Tennessee State	JR	F	26	421	**16.2**
2 **Bill Cartwright**, San Francisco	SR	C	29	455	**15.7**
3 **Lionel Garrett**, Southern U.	SR	F	28	433	**15.5**
4 **Larry Bird**, Indiana State	SR	F	34	505	**14.9**
5 **Larry Knight**, Loyola-Chicago	SR	F	27	386	**14.3**
6 **Larry Smith**, Alcorn State	JR	F/C	29	398	**13.7**
7 **Michael Brooks**, La Salle	JR	F	26	347	**13.3**
8 **Bob Stephens**, Drexel	SR	F	27	360	**13.3**
9 **David Lawrence**, McNeese State	JR	F	27	343	**12.7**
10 **Lorenza Watson**, VCU	SR	C	25	313	**12.5**

INDIVIDUAL LEADERS—GAME

Points

	CL	POS	OPP	DATE	PTS
1 **Matt Teahan**, Denver	SR	C	Nebraska Wesleyan	F26	**61**
2 **Steve Stielper**, James Madison	JR	F	Robert Morris	J27	**51**
3 **Vinnie Johnson**, Baylor	SR	G	TCU	F20	**50**
4 **Larry Bird**, Indiana State	SR	F	Wichita State	F25	**49**
5 **Larry Bird**, Indiana State	SR	F	Butler	D16	**48**
Nick Galis, Seton Hall	SR	G	Santa Clara	D22	**48**
B.B. Flenory, Duquesne	JR	G	Ohio	D30	**48**
Mike Woodson, Indiana	JR	G/F	Illinois	M3	**48**

Rebounds

	CL	POS	OPP	DATE	REB
1 **Monti Davis**, Tennessee State	JR	F	Alabama State	F8	**30**
2 **Lionel Garrett**, Southern U.	SR	F	Bishop	F16	**29**
3 **James Donaldson**, Washington State	SR	C	Seattle Pacific	N24	**25**
Lloyd Terry, New Orleans	JR	F	Georgia State	F10	**25**
5 **Wiley Peck**, Mississippi State	SR	F	Memphis	D7	**24**
Wiley Peck, Mississippi State	SR	F	Alabama	J27	**24**
David Lawrence, McNeese State	JR	F	Lamar	F14	**24**
James Connolly, La Salle	SR	F	Hofstra	F21	**24**

TEAM LEADERS—SEASON

Win-Loss Pct

	W	L	PCT
1 Indiana State	33	1	.971
2 Alcorn State	28	1	.966
3 Syracuse	26	4	.867
4 Temple	25	4	.862
5 Arkansas	25	5	.833
UCLA	25	5	.833

Scoring Offense

	G	W-L	PTS	PPG
1 UNLV	29	21-8	2,700	93.1
2 Alcorn State	29	28-1	2,678	92.3
3 Wichita State	28	14-14	2,485	88.8
4 Syracuse	30	26-4	2,660	88.7
5 New Mexico	29	19-10	2,567	88.5

Scoring Margin

	G	W-L	PPG	OPP PPG	MAR
1 Syracuse	30	26-4	88.7	71.5	17.2
2 Notre Dame	30	24-6	79.7	64.1	15.6
3 Indiana State	34	33-1	86.8	72.8	14.0
4 Alcorn State	29	28-1	92.3	78.9	13.4
5 Michigan State	32	26-6	75.7	62.6	13.1

Field Goal Pct

	G	W-L	FG	FGA	PCT
1 UCLA	30	25-5	1,053	1,897	55.5
2 Fairfield	26	17-9	792	1,468	54.0
3 Arkansas	30	25-5	849	1,587	53.5
4 Citadel	27	20-7	864	1,616	53.5
5 Syracuse	30	26-4	1,052	1,970	53.4

Free Throw Pct

	G	W-L	FT	FTA	PCT
1 Saint Francis (PA)	26	13-13	350	446	78.5
2 Kentucky	31	19-12	666	858	77.6
3 Fairfield	26	17-9	513	666	77.0
4 Villanova	26	13-13	394	514	76.7
5 DePaul	32	26-6	517	676	76.5

Rebound Margin

	G	W-L	RPG	OPP RPG	MAR
1 Alcorn State	29	28-1	50.1	36.3	13.8
2 Tennessee State	26	20-6	49.7	37.9	11.8
3 Pittsburgh	29	18-11	41.3	30.6	10.7
4 Syracuse	30	26-4	48.2	38.1	10.1
5 Arkansas	30	25-5	44.1	34.8	9.3

Scoring Defense

	G	W-L	OPP PTS	OPP PPG
1 Princeton	26	14-12	1,452	55.8
2 Dartmouth	26	14-12	1,488	57.2
3 Fresno State	28	16-12	1,632	58.3
4 Montana	27	14-13	1,628	60.3
5 Indiana	34	22-12	2,080	61.2

Field Goal Pct Defense

	G	W-L	OPP FG	OPP FGA	OPP PCT
1 Illinois	30	19-11	738	1,828	40.4
2 Tennessee State	26	20-6	717	1,707	42.0
3 Wyoming	27	15-12	667	1,582	42.2
4 Indiana	34	22-12	847	2,008	42.2
5 Princeton	26	14-12	548	1,287	42.6

CONSENSUS ALL-AMERICAS

FIRST TEAM

PLAYER	CL	POS	HT	SCHOOL	RPG	PPG
Larry Bird	SR	F	6-9	Indiana State	14.9	28.6
Mike Gminski	JR	C	6-11	Duke	9.2	18.8
David Greenwood	SR	F	6-9	UCLA	10.3	19.9
Earvin "Magic" Johnson	SO	G	6-9	Michigan State	7.3	17.1
Sidney Moncrief	SR	G	6-4	Arkansas	9.6	22.0

SECOND TEAM

PLAYER	CL	POS	HT	SCHOOL	RPG	PPG
Bill Cartwright	SR	C	6-11	San Francisco	15.7	24.5
Calvin Natt	SR	F	6-6	UL-Monroe	10.9	24.4
Mike O'Koren	JR	F	6-7	North Carolina	7.2	14.8
Jim Paxson	SR	G/F	6-6	Dayton	4.2	23.2
Jim Spanarkel	SR	G	6-5	Duke	3.0	15.9
Kelly Tripucka	SO	F	6-7	Notre Dame	4.3	14.3
Sylvester "Sly" Williams	JR	F	6-7	Rhode Island	8.4	23.9

SELECTORS: AP, NABC, UPI, USBWA

AWARD WINNERS

PLAYER OF THE YEAR

PLAYER	CL	POS	HT	SCHOOL	AWARDS
Larry Bird	SR	F	6-9	Indiana State	Naismith, AP, UPI, USBWA, Wooden, NABC, Rupp
Alton Byrd	SR	G	5-7	Columbia	Frances Pomeroy Naismith*

* FOR THE MOST OUTSTANDING SENIOR PLAYER WHO IS 6 FEET OR UNDER.

COACH OF THE YEAR

COACH	SCHOOL	REC	AWARDS
Bill Hodges	Indiana State	33-1	AP, UPI, Sporting News
Dean Smith	North Carolina	23-6	USBWA
Ray Meyer	DePaul	26-6	NABC

Bob Gibbons' Top High School Senior Recruits

PLAYER	POS	HT	HIGH SCHOOL	A-A TEAMS	COLLEGE	CAREER NOTES
1 Ralph Sampson	C	7-4	Harrisonburg (VA) HS	McD, P	Virginia	3-time National POY; No. 1 overall pick, '82 NBA draft (Rockets); 15.4 ppg (9 seasons); 4-time All-Star
2 Clark Kellogg	F	6-8	St. Joseph's HS, Cleveland	McD, P	Ohio State	Big Ten MVP; No. 8 pick, '82 NBA draft (Pacers); 18.9 ppg (five seasons)
3 Sam Bowie	C	7-1	Lebanon (PA) HS	McD, P	Kentucky	2-time All-America; No. 2 pick, '84 NBA draft (Blazers); 10.9 ppg, 7.5 rpg (9 seasons)
4 James Worthy	F	6-9	Ashbrook HS, Gastonia, NC	McD, P	North Carolina	NCAA title, Tournament MOP, '82; No. 1 overall pick, '82 NBA draft (Lakers); 3 NBA titles; Basketball HOF
5 Derrick Hord	G/F	6-7	Tennessee HS, Bristol, TN	McD, P	Kentucky	1st Team All-SEC, '81-'82 (16.3 ppg); No. 67 pick, '83 NBA draft (Cavs); no NBA games played
6 Isiah Thomas	PG	6-1	St. Joseph's HS, Westchester, IL	McD, P	Indiana	NCAA title, Tournament MOP, '81; No. 2 pick, '81 NBA draft (Pistons); 2 NBA titles; NBA coach; Basketball HOF
7 Antoine Carr	F	6-9	Wichita Heights HS, Wichita, KS	McD, P	Wichita State	17.0 ppg (four seasons); All-America, '83; 47 pts in final college game; No. 8 pick, '83 NBA draft (Pistons); 9.3 ppg (16 seasons)
8 Ricky Ross	2G	6-5	Wichita (KS) HS	McD, P	Kansas/Tulsa	Transferred to Tulsa after 1 year; 17.3 ppg as a senior; No. 53 pick, '84 NBA draft (Bullets); no NBA games played
9 Darren Daye	SF	6-7	John F. Kennedy HS, Granada Hills, CA	McD, P	UCLA	10.1 ppg (4 seasons); No. 57 pick, '83 NBA draft (Bullets); 6.8 ppg (5 seasons)
10 Steve Stipanovich	C	6-11	DeSmet HS, St. Louis	McD, P	Missouri	All-America, '83; No. 2 pick, '83 NBA draft (Pacers); 13.2 ppg, 7.8 rpg (five seasons)
11 Dominique Wilkins	SF	6-7	Washington (NC) HS	McD, P	Georgia	SEC POY, '81; No. 3 pick, '83 NBA draft (Jazz); 24.8 ppg (15 seasons); 9-time All-Star; Basketball HOF
12 Teddy Grubbs	SF	6-8	Martin Luther King HS, Chicago	McD, P	DePaul	4-year starter; 7.9 ppg (4 seasons); undrafted
13 Sidney Green	PF	6-9	Thomas Jefferson HS, Brooklyn, NY	McD, P	UNLV	17.9 ppg (4 seasons); No. 5 pick, '83 NBA draft (Bulls); 7.5 ppg (10 seasons)
14 Ray McCoy	PG	6-1	Bloom HS, Chicago Heights, IL	McD, P	San Francisco/ DePaul	Transferred to DePaul after 1 year; undrafted
15 Quintin Dailey	2G	6-4	Cardinal Gibbons, Baltimore	McD, P	San Francisco	20.5 ppg (3 seasons); No. 7 pick, '82 NBA draft (Bulls) 14.1 ppg (10 seasons)
16 Tim Andree	C	6-10	Brother Rice HS, Birmingham, MI	McD, P	Notre Dame	4.0 ppg, 2.7 rpg (4 seasons); No. 98 pick, '83 NBA draft (Bulls); no NBA games played
17 Jimmy Braddock	PG	6-1	Baylor Prep, Chattanooga, TN	McD	North Carolina	NCAA title, '82; No. 107, in '83 NBA draft (Nuggets); no NBA games played
18 John Paxson	PG	6-2	Bishop Alter HS, Kettering, OH	McD, P	Notre Dame	2-time All-America; At ND, 12.2 ppg,3.7 apg (four seasons); No. 19 pick, '83 draft (Spurs); 3 NBA titles
19 Horace Owens	2G	6-4	Dobbins Tech, Philadelphia	McD	Rhode Island	Left URI 5th-leading scorer (1,765 pts); No. 44 pick, '83 NBA draft (Nets); no NBA games played
20 Dirk Minniefield	2G	6-3	Lafayette HS, Lexington, KY	McD, P	Kentucky	8.7 PPG (4 seasons); No. 33 pick, '83 NBA draft (Mavs); 5.3 ppg (3 seasons)

Other Standouts

PLAYER	POS	HT	HIGH SCHOOL	A-A TEAMS	COLLEGE	CAREER NOTES
32 Terry Cummings	PF	6-9	Carver HS, Chicago		DePaul	16.4 ppg (3 seasons); No. 2 pick, '82 NBA draft (Clippers); 16.4 ppg, 7.3 rpg (18 seasons); 2-time All-Star
39 Byron Scott	2G	6-5	Morningside HS, Inglewood, CA	McD, P	Arizona State	17.5 ppg (4 seasons); No. 4 pick, '83 NBA draft (Clippers); 3 NBA titles; NBA coach
42 Dale Ellis	SF	6-7	Marietta (GA) HS	P	Tennessee	17.5 ppg (4 seasons); No. 9 pick, '83 NBA draft (Mavs); 15.7 ppg (17 seasons); 27.5 ppg, '88-89

Abbreviations: McD=McDonald's; P=Parade

Poll Progression

Preseason Poll

AP	UPI	School
1	1	Duke
2	2	UCLA
3	3	Notre Dame
4	5	Louisville
5	5	Kansas
6	7	Texas
7	4	Michigan State
8	8	Michigan
9	13	Syracuse
10	11	Indiana
11	14	Kentucky
12	9	NC State
13	10	USC
14	17	LSU
15	18	Rutgers
16	12	North Carolina
17	16	San Francisco
18	20	Marquette
19	15	Alabama
20	—	UNLV
—	19	Minnesota

Week of Nov 28

AP	School	AP↓↑
1	Duke (1-0)	
2	UCLA (3-0)	
3	Notre Dame (0-0)	
4	Kansas (0-0)	↑1
5	Louisville (3-1)	↓1
6	NC State (3-0)	↑6
7	Michigan State (0-0)	
8	Michigan (0-0)	
9	Syracuse (1-0)	
10	Kentucky (0-0)	↑1
11	LSU (1-0)	↑3
12	USC (0-0)	↑1
13	Texas (0-1)	↓7
14	North Carolina (0-0)	↑2
15	San Francisco (1-0)	↑2
16	Rutgers (0-0)	↓1
17	Marquette (0-0)	↑1
18	UNLV (1-0)	↑2
19	Maryland (1-0)	⤴
20	Indiana (1-2)	↓10

Week of Dec 5

AP	School	AP↓↑
1	Duke (4-0)	
2	UCLA (3-0)	
3	Notre Dame (2-0)	
4	Michigan State (1-0)	↑3
5	Kansas (3-0)	↓1
6	Michigan (2-0)	↑2
7	Louisville (3-1)	↓2
8	NC State (4-1)	↓2
9	Syracuse (4-0)	
10	Kentucky (2-0)	
11	USC (2-0)	↑1
12	LSU (4-0)	↓1
13	Texas (3-1)	
14	North Carolina (3-1)	
15	UNLV (3-0)	↑3
16	Marquette (2-0)	↑1
17	San Francisco (3-1)	↓2
18	Rutgers (2-1)	↓2
19	Maryland (2-2)	
20	Georgetown (3-0)	⤴

Week of Dec 12

AP	UPI	School	AP↓↑
1	1	Duke (5-0)	
2	2	Notre Dame (4-0)	↑1
3	3	Michigan State (2-0)	↑1
4	4	Louisville (5-1)	↑3
5	5	UCLA (3-1)	↓3
6	6	Kentucky (3-0) Ⓐ	↑4
7	7	NC State (6-1)	↑1
8	8	Kansas (4-1)	↓3
9	9	Michigan (3-1)	↓3
10	11	Syracuse (5-0)	↓1
11	10	LSU (5-0)	↑1
12	13	USC (3-0)	↓1
13	12	North Carolina (4-1)	↑1
14	14	Marquette (4-0)	↑2
15	—	UNLV (3-0)	
16	15	Georgetown (5-0)	↑4
17	17	Texas (4-2)	↓4
18	19	Illinois (6-0)	⤴
19	—	San Francisco (5-2)	↓2
20	16	Indiana State (6-0)	⤴
—	18	Long Beach State (4-0)	
—	20	Arkansas (2-0)	

Week of Dec 19

AP	UPI	School	AP↓↑
1	1	Duke (6-0)	
2	2	Notre Dame (4-0)	
3	3	UCLA (4-1)	↑2
4	5	NC State (7-1)	↑3
5	4	Michigan State (3-1)	↓2
6	6	North Carolina (5-1)	↑7
7	8	Kansas (5-1)	↑1
8	9	Syracuse (6-0)	↑2
9	7	Michigan (4-1)	
10	10	LSU (6-0)	↑1
11	12	Kentucky (3-1)	↓5
12	11	Louisville (6-2)	↓8
13	13	Marquette (5-0)	↑1
14	14	Georgetown (6-0)	↑2
15	16	Illinois (7-0)	↑3
16	15	Indiana State (8-0)	↑4
17	18	Texas A&M (8-1)	⤴
18	—	UNLV (5-1)	↓3
19	19	Texas (5-2)	↓2
20	—	USC (6-2)	↓8
—	17	Long Beach State (6-0)	
—	20	Arkansas (4-0)	

Week of Dec 26

AP	UPI	School	AP↓↑
1	1	Duke (6-0)	
2	2	Notre Dame (4-0)	
3	3	UCLA (6-1)	
4	4	Michigan State (4-1)	↑1
5	6	North Carolina (6-1)	↑1
6	5	Illinois (9-0)	↑9
7	8	LSU (7-0)	↑3
8	7	Michigan (4-1)	↑1
9	—	NC State (7-2)	↓5
10	9	Louisville (7-2)	↑2
11	11	Indiana State (8-0)	↑5
12	10	Texas A&M (9-2)	↑5
13	15	Kentucky (4-2)	↓2
14	—	UNLV (8-1)	↑4
15	12	Georgetown (7-1)	↓1
16	17	Marquette (6-1)	↓3
17	13	Long Beach State (7-0)	⤴
18	14	Kansas (5-3)	↓11
19	18	Syracuse (6-2)	↓11
20	—	Arkansas (6-0)	⤴
—	16	Washington State (7-0)	
—	19	Maryland (7-2)	
—	20	Texas (5-2)	↱

Week of Jan 3

AP	UPI	School	AP↓↑
1	1	Michigan State (7-1) Ⓑ	↑3
2	2	Notre Dame (5-1)	
3	4	North Carolina (8-1)	↑2
4	3	Illinois (12-0)	↑2
5	7	Duke (6-2)	↓4
6	5	UCLA (7-2)	↓3
7	6	LSU (8-0)	
8	10	NC State (8-2)	↑1
9	8	Kentucky (5-2)	↑4
10	14	Texas A&M (11-2)	↑2
11	9	Indiana State (9-0)	
12	18	Georgetown (9-1)	↑3
13	12	Michigan (6-2)	↓5
14	15	Arkansas (7-0)	↑6
15	11	Long Beach State (8-0)	↑2
16	16	Louisville (8-3)	↓6
17	19	Marquette (8-1)	↓1
18	13	Mississippi State (8-0)	⤴
19	17	Kansas (8-3)	↓1
20	20	Maryland (11-2)	⤴

Week of Jan 9

AP	UPI	School	AP↓↑
1	1	Michigan State (9-1)	
2	2	Notre Dame (6-1)	
3	4	North Carolina (10-1)	
4	3	Illinois (14-0)	
5	5	LSU (10-0)	↑2
6	6	UCLA (9-2)	
7	7	Duke (9-2)	↓2
8	8	NC State (11-2)	
9	9	Indiana State (11-0)	↑2
10	10	Arkansas (9-0)	↑4
11	12	Texas A&M (11-2)	↓1
12	13	Louisville (10-3) Ⓒ	↑4
13	11	Marquette (10-1)	↑4
14	16	Georgetown (10-2)	↓2
15	14	Kansas (8-3)	↑4
16	20	Michigan (7-3)	↓3
17	—	Kentucky (9-4)	↓8
18	15	Temple (11-0)	⤴
19	17	Long Beach State (8-2)	↓4
20	18	Syracuse (9-2)	⤴
—	19	USC (6-3)	

Week of Jan 16

AP	UPI	School	AP↓↑
1	1	Notre Dame (8-1)	↑1
2	3	North Carolina (12-2)	↑1
3	4	UCLA (11-2)	↑3
4	2	Illinois (15-1)	
5	5	Indiana State (14-0)	↑4
6	6	Michigan State (9-3)	↓5
7	7	Louisville (12-3)	↑5
8	9	Duke (10-3)	↓1
9	8	LSU (12-2)	↓4
10	14	Georgetown (12-2)	↑4
11	13	Arkansas (10-2)	↓1
12	15	Syracuse (12-2)	↑8
13	10	Marquette (11-2)	
14	18	NC State (11-4)	↓6
15	17	Texas A&M (13-3)	↓4
16	11	Ohio State (9-1)	⤴
17	12	Temple (12-1)	↑1
18	16	Alabama (10-4)	⤴
19	—	Maryland (11-4)	⤴
20	19	Kansas (9-4)	↓5
—	20	USC (9-4)	

Week of Jan 23

AP	UPI	School	AP↓↑
1	1	Notre Dame (11-1)	
2	2	North Carolina (14-2)	
3	3	Indiana State (14-0)	↑2
4	4	Michigan State (11-3)	↑2
5	5	Louisville (15-3)	↑2
6	7	UCLA (12-3)	↓3
7	6	Duke (12-3)	↑1
8	8	Illinois (16-2)	↓4
9	10	LSU (13-2)	
10	9	Ohio State (11-4)	↑6
11	12	Georgetown (14-2)	↓1
12	13	Syracuse (14-2)	
13	11	Marquette (13-2)	
14	14	Texas A&M (15-3)	↑1
15	18	Arkansas (11-3)	↓4
16	15	Temple (12-1)	↑1
17	16	Texas (11-4)	⤴
18	20	Alabama (11-4)	
19	17	Vanderbilt (12-2)	⤴
20	19	NC State (11-6)	↓6

Week of Jan 30

AP	UPI	School	AP↓↑
1	1	Notre Dame (12-2)	
2	2	Indiana State (18-0)	↑1
3	4	Duke (14-3)	↑4
4	6	North Carolina (15-3)	↓2
5	3	UCLA (14-3)	↑1
6	5	Louisville (17-3)	↓1
7	7	Ohio State (13-4)	↑3
8	8	Syracuse (18-2)	↑4
9	10	Georgetown (16-2)	↑2
10	12	LSU (15-3)	↓1
11	11	Texas (15-4)	↑6
12	9	Marquette (14-3)	↑1
13	15	Alabama (13-4)	↑5
14	17	Illinois (16-4)	↓6
15	13	Michigan State (11-5)	↓11
16	14	Texas A&M (17-4)	↓2
17	—	Maryland (14-5)	⤴
18	18	Temple (15-3)	↓2
19	—	Arkansas (13-4)	↓4
20	16	Vanderbilt (14-3)	↓1
—	19	Weber State (19-4)	
—	20	Purdue (15-5)	

Week of Feb 6

AP	UPI	School	AP↓↑
1	1	Notre Dame (15-2)	
2	2	Indiana State (20-0)	
3	4	Duke (16-3)	
4	3	UCLA (16-3)	↑1
5	5	Louisville (19-3)	↑1
6	6	North Carolina (16-4)	↓2
7	10	Syracuse (18-2)	↑1
8	7	LSU (19-3)	↑2
9	8	Marquette (16-3)	↑3
10	9	Michigan State (14-5)	↑5
11	11	Texas A&M (20-4)	↑5
12	15	Texas (16-5)	↓1
13	12	Ohio State (13-6)	↓6
14	14	Arkansas (15-4)	↑5
15	13	Iowa (15-4)	⤴
16	—	Alabama (13-5)	↓3
17	16	Vanderbilt (15-4)	↑3
18	19	Georgetown (16-4)	↓9
19	17	Temple (17-3)	↓1
20	—	Illinois (17-5)	↓6
—	18	Purdue (17-5)	
—	19	USC (13-6)	

Week of Feb 13

AP	UPI	School	AP↓↑
1	2	**Indiana State** (23-0)	↑1
2	1	**UCLA** (18-3)	↑2
3	3	**Notre Dame** (17-3)	↓2
4	4	**North Carolina** (18-4)	↑2
5	6	**Duke** (17-4)	↓2
6	5	**LSU** (20-3)	↑2
7	7	**Syracuse** (20-2)	
8	8	**Michigan State** (16-5)	↑2
9	9	**Louisville** (21-4)	↓4
10	10	**Marquette** (17-4)	↓1
11	11	**Arkansas** (18-4)	↑3
12	12	**Texas** (18-5)	
13	13	**Purdue** (19-5)	⤴
14	15	**Iowa** (16-5)	↑1
15	14	**Temple** (19-3)	↑4
16	16	**Georgetown** (18-4)	↑2
17	18	**Ohio State** (16-7)	↓4
18	20	**Detroit** (18-4)	⤴
19	17	**Vanderbilt** (16-5)	↓2
20	—	**Alabama** (15-7)	↓4
—	18	**Texas A&M** (20-6)	⤵

Week of Feb 20

AP	UPI	School	AP↓↑
1	1	**UCLA** (20-3)	↑1
2	2	**Indiana State** (24-0)	↓1
3	3	**Notre Dame** (19-3)	
4	4	**North Carolina** (20-4)	
5	5	**LSU** (21-3)	↑1
6	7	**Duke** (19-5)	↓1
7	8	**Michigan State** (18-5)	↑1
8	6	**Syracuse** (21-2)	↓1
9	9	**Marquette** (19-4)	↑1
10	12	**Arkansas** (20-4)	↑1
11	10	**Texas** (20-5)	↑1
12	11	**Iowa** (18-5)	↑2
13	14	**Louisville** (22-6)	↓4
14	13	**Ohio State** (16-7)	↑3
15	15	**Temple** (20-3)	
16	18	**Detroit** (20-4)	↑2
17	16	**Georgetown** (20-4)	↓1
18	17	**Purdue** (20-6)	↓5
19	19	**Vanderbilt** (18-6)	
20	20	**DePaul** (18-4)	⤴

Week of Feb 27

AP	UPI	School	AP↓↑
1	1	**Indiana State** (24-0)	↑1
2	2	**Notre Dame** (22-3)	↑1
3	3	**UCLA** (21-4)	↓2
4	4	**Michigan State** (20-5)	↑3
5	6	**Duke** (20-6) Ⓓ	↑1
6	5	**Syracuse** (24-2)	↑2
7	7	**North Carolina** (21-5)	↓3
8	8	**LSU** (22-4)	↓3
9	9	**Arkansas** (21-4)	↑1
10	12	**Marquette** (19-5)	↓1
11	10	**Iowa** (19-6)	↑1
12	13	**Temple** (22-3)	↑3
13	16	**Louisville** (23-6)	
14	14	**Texas** (20-6)	↓3
15	11	**DePaul** (20-4)	↑5
16	15	**Georgetown** (22-4)	↑1
17	17	**Ohio State** (17-8)	↓3
18	20	**Detroit** (21-5)	↓2
19	18	**Purdue** (21-7)	↓1
20	19	**San Francisco** (21-6)	⤴

Week of Mar 6

AP	UPI	School	AP↓↑
1	1	**Indiana State** (29-0)	
2	2	**UCLA** (23-4)	↑1
3	3	**North Carolina** (23-5)	↑4
4	4	**Michigan State** (21-6)	
5	5	**Notre Dame** (22-5)	↓3
6	7	**Duke** (22-7)	↓1
7	6	**Arkansas** (23-4)	↑2
8	8	**DePaul** (22-4)	↑7
9	9	**LSU** (22-5)	↓1
10	10	**Syracuse** (25-3)	↓4
11	12	**Georgetown** (24-4)	↑5
12	13	**Marquette** (21-6)	↓2
13	16	**Temple** (25-3)	↓1
14	11	**Iowa** (20-7)	↓3
15	15	**Texas** (21-7)	↓1
16	14	**Purdue** (23-7)	↑3
17	20	**Detroit** (22-5)	↑1
18	19	**Louisville** (23-7)	↓5
19	17	**San Francisco** (21-6)	↑1
20	18	**Tennessee** (20-11)	⤴

Final Poll

AP	School	AP↓↑
1	**Indiana State** (30-0)	
2	**UCLA** (24-4)	
3	**Michigan State** (22-6)	↑1
4	**Notre Dame** (23-5)	↑1
5	**Arkansas** (24-4)	↑2
6	**DePaul** (23-5)	↑2
7	**LSU** (23-5)	↑2
8	**Syracuse** (26-3)	↑2
9	**North Carolina** (23-6)	↓6
10	**Marquette** (22-6)	↑2
11	**Duke** (22-8)	↓5
12	**San Francisco** (22-6)	↑7
13	**Louisville** (24-7)	↑5
14	**Pennsylvania** (23-5) Ⓔ	⤴
15	**Purdue** (24-7)	↑1
16	**Oklahoma** (21-9)	⤴
17	**St. John's** (20-10)	⤴
18	**Rutgers** (22-8)	⤴
19	**Toledo** (22-7)	⤴
20	**Iowa** (20-8)	↓6

Ⓐ Trailing Kansas by six with :31 left in overtime, Kentucky squeezes out a 67-66 win in Lexington. After junior guard Kyle Macy swishes a 15-footer to tie the game, Jayhawks guard Darnell Valentine calls a timeout—but Kansas has none left. Macy hits the technical free throw for the victory.

Ⓑ Michigan State reaches No. 1 for the first time in school history. The Spartans stay on top for two weeks, but drop two in a row before righting themselves to win 13 of their last 14. Their 6'9" sophomore star, Earvin "Magic" Johnson, will average 17.1 points, 8.8 assists and 7.3 rebounds a game for the season.

Ⓒ After holding UL-Lafayette's Andrew Toney to 12 points in a 73-60 victory on Jan. 6, Louisville's 6'4" Darrell Griffith reveals he has been undergoing "concentration sessions" with university psychologist and pep band member Dr. Stanley Frager.

Ⓓ At halftime of their Feb. 24 game, Duke leads North Carolina 7-0. Duke is the first team to hold an opponent scoreless in a half since 1938. The Tar Heels break the shutout 48 seconds into the second half, but the Blue Devils win, 47-40.

Ⓔ With Tournament wins over Iona and North Carolina, Penn debuts in the national polls. Tony Price (27 points vs. Iona, 26 vs. UNC) will lead the Quakers to their only Final Four appearance.

1979 NCAA Tournament

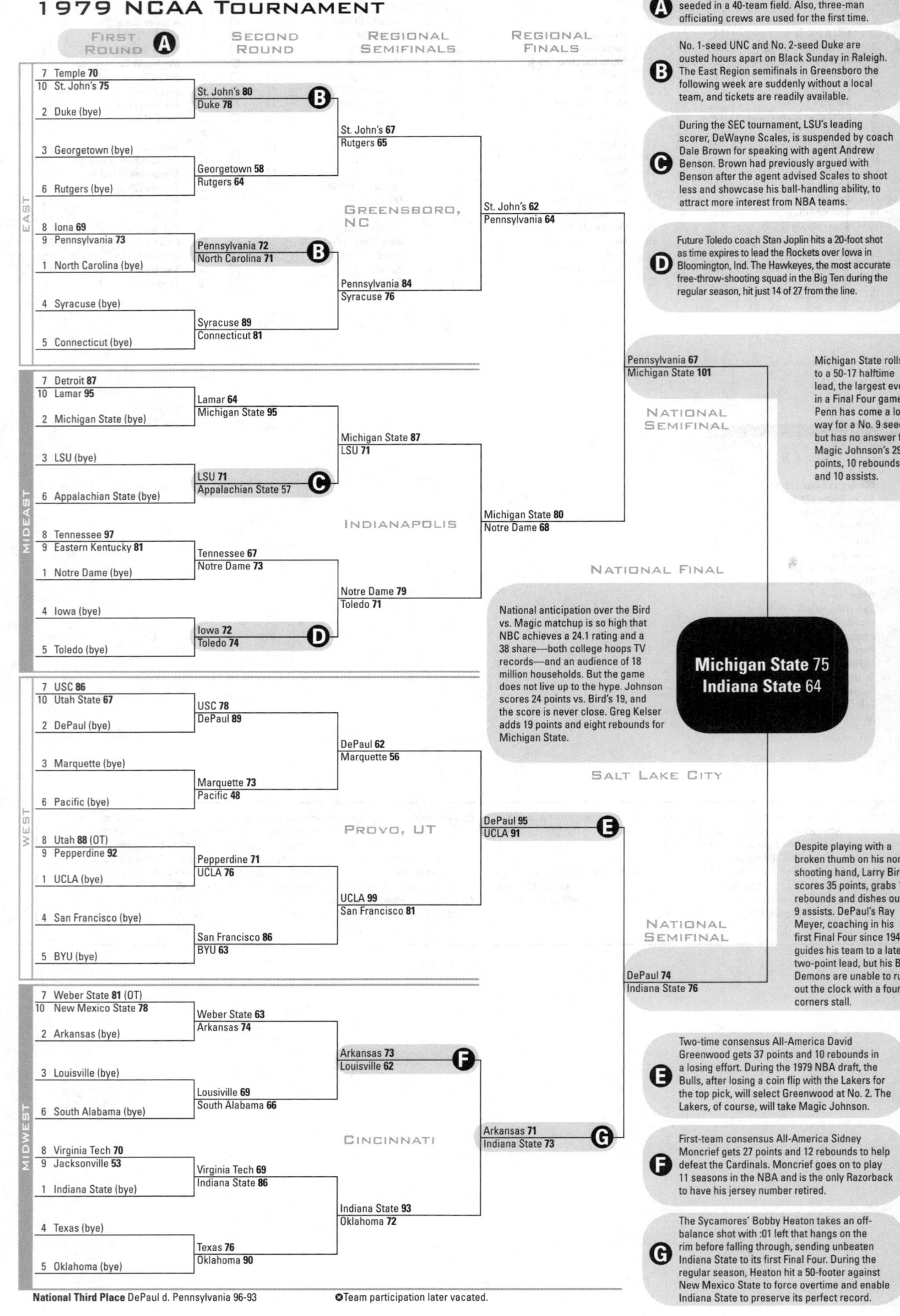

First Round (A) | Second Round | Regional Semifinals | Regional Finals

East — Greensboro, NC

First Round
- 7 Temple 70
- 10 St. John's 75
- 2 Duke (bye)
- 3 Georgetown (bye)
- 6 Rutgers (bye)
- 8 Iona 69
- 9 Pennsylvania 73
- 1 North Carolina (bye)
- 4 Syracuse (bye)
- 5 Connecticut (bye)

Second Round
- St. John's 80 / Duke 78 (B)
- Georgetown 58 / Rutgers 64
- Pennsylvania 72 / North Carolina 71 (B)
- Syracuse 89 / Connecticut 81

Regional Semifinals
- St. John's 67 / Rutgers 65
- Pennsylvania 84 / Syracuse 76

Regional Final
- St. John's 62 / Pennsylvania 64

Mideast — Indianapolis

First Round
- 7 Detroit 87
- 10 Lamar 95
- 2 Michigan State (bye)
- 3 LSU (bye)
- 6 Appalachian State (bye)
- 8 Tennessee 97
- 9 Eastern Kentucky 81
- 1 Notre Dame (bye)
- 4 Iowa (bye)
- 5 Toledo (bye)

Second Round
- Lamar 64 / Michigan State 95
- LSU 71 / Appalachian State 57 (C)
- Tennessee 67 / Notre Dame 73
- Iowa 72 / Toledo 74 (D)

Regional Semifinals
- Michigan State 87 / LSU 71
- Notre Dame 79 / Toledo 71

Regional Final
- Michigan State 80 / Notre Dame 68

West — Provo, UT

First Round
- 7 USC 86
- 10 Utah State 67
- 2 DePaul (bye)
- 3 Marquette (bye)
- 6 Pacific (bye)
- 8 Utah 88 (OT)
- 9 Pepperdine 92
- 1 UCLA (bye)
- 4 San Francisco (bye)
- 5 BYU (bye)

Second Round
- USC 78 / DePaul 89
- Marquette 73 / Pacific 48
- Pepperdine 71 / UCLA 76
- San Francisco 86 / BYU 63

Regional Semifinals
- DePaul 62 / Marquette 56
- UCLA 99 / San Francisco 81

Regional Final
- DePaul 95 / UCLA 91 (E)

Midwest — Cincinnati

First Round
- 7 Weber State 81 (OT)
- 10 New Mexico State 78
- 2 Arkansas (bye)
- 3 Louisville (bye)
- 6 South Alabama (bye)
- 8 Virginia Tech 70
- 9 Jacksonville 53
- 1 Indiana State (bye)
- 4 Texas (bye)
- 5 Oklahoma (bye)

Second Round
- Weber State 63 / Arkansas 74
- Lousiville 69 / South Alabama 66
- Virginia Tech 69 / Indiana State 86
- Texas 76 / Oklahoma 90

Regional Semifinals
- Arkansas 73 / Louisville 62 (F)
- Indiana State 93 / Oklahoma 72

Regional Final
- Arkansas 71 / Indiana State 73 (G)

National Semifinal

- Pennsylvania 67 / Michigan State 101
- DePaul 74 / Indiana State 76

National Final — Salt Lake City

Michigan State 75
Indiana State 64

National Third Place DePaul d. Pennsylvania 96-93

⊗Team participation later vacated.

A For the first time, all Tournament teams are seeded in a 40-team field. Also, three-man officiating crews are used for the first time.

B No. 1-seed UNC and No. 2-seed Duke are ousted hours apart on Black Sunday in Raleigh. The East Region semifinals in Greensboro the following week are suddenly without a local team, and tickets are readily available.

C During the SEC tournament, LSU's leading scorer, DeWayne Scales, is suspended by coach Dale Brown for speaking with agent Andrew Benson. Brown had previously argued with Benson after the agent advised Scales to shoot less and showcase his ball-handling ability, to attract more interest from NBA teams.

D Future Toledo coach Stan Joplin hits a 20-foot shot as time expires to lead the Rockets over Iowa in Bloomington, Ind. The Hawkeyes, the most accurate free-throw-shooting squad in the Big Ten during the regular season, hit just 14 of 27 from the line.

Michigan State rolls to a 50-17 halftime lead, the largest ever in a Final Four game. Penn has come a long way for a No. 9 seed, but has no answer for Magic Johnson's 29 points, 10 rebounds and 10 assists.

National anticipation over the Bird vs. Magic matchup is so high that NBC achieves a 24.1 rating and a 38 share—both college hoops TV records—and an audience of 18 million households. But the game does not live up to the hype. Johnson scores 24 points vs. Bird's 19, and the score is never close. Greg Kelser adds 19 points and eight rebounds for Michigan State.

Despite playing with a broken thumb on his non-shooting hand, Larry Bird scores 35 points, grabs 16 rebounds and dishes out 9 assists. DePaul's Ray Meyer, coaching in his first Final Four since 1943, guides his team to a late two-point lead, but his Blue Demons are unable to run out the clock with a four-corners stall.

E Two-time consensus All-America David Greenwood gets 37 points and 10 rebounds in a losing effort. During the 1979 NBA draft, the Bulls, after losing a coin flip with the Lakers for the top pick, will select Greenwood at No. 2. The Lakers, of course, will take Magic Johnson.

F First-team consensus All-America Sidney Moncrief gets 27 points and 12 rebounds to help defeat the Cardinals. Moncrief goes on to play 11 seasons in the NBA and is the only Razorback to have his jersey number retired.

G The Sycamores' Bobby Heaton takes an off-balance shot with :01 left that hangs on the rim before falling through, sending unbeaten Indiana State to its first Final Four. During the regular season, Heaton hit a 50-footer against New Mexico State to force overtime and enable Indiana State to preserve its perfect record.

TOURNAMENT LEADERS

INDIVIDUAL LEADERS

SCORING

	CL	POS	G	PTS	PPG
1 **Bill Cartwright**, San Francisco	SR	C	2	58	29.0
2 **Larry Bird**, Indiana State	SR	F	5	136	27.2
3 **Ricardo Brown**, Pepperdine	JR	G	2	53	26.5
4 **Greg Kelser**, Michigan State	SR	F	5	127	25.4
5 **David Greenwood**, UCLA	SR	F	3	74	24.7
6 **Raymond Whitley**, Oklahoma	SO	G	2	49	24.5
7 **Tony Price**, Penn	SR	F	6	142	23.7
8 **Mark Aguirre**, DePaul	SO	F	5	117	23.4
9 **Sidney Moncrief**, Arkansas	SR	G	3	70	23.3
10 **Roy Hamilton**, UCLA	SR	G	3	66	22.0

MINIMUM: 2 GAMES

FIELD GOAL PCT

	CL	POS	G	FG	FGA	PCT
1 **Steve Schall**, Arkansas	SR	C	3	17	19	89.5
2 **Raymond Whitley**, Oklahoma	SO	G	2	19	24	79.2
3 **Alex Gilbert**, Indiana State	JR	F	5	26	34	76.5
4 **David Johnson**, Weber State	JR	F	2	20	27	74.1
5 **Steve Smith**, Southern California	SR	G	2	16	22	72.7

MINIMUM: 12 MADE

FREE THROW PCT

	CL	POS	G	FT	FTA	PCT
1 **Sidney Moncrief**, Arkansas	SR	G	3	26	27	96.3
2 **Kelly Tripucka**, Notre Dame	SO	F	3	17	18	94.4
3 **Brad Holland**, UCLA	SR	G	3	13	14	92.9
Michael McKay, Connecticut	FR	F	1	13	14	92.9
5 **Scott Hastings**, Arkansas	SO	F	3	12	13	92.3

MINIMUM: 12 MADE

REBOUNDS PER GAME

	CL	POS	G	REB	RPG
1 **Lionel Green**, LSU	SR	C	2	31	15.5
2 **Larry Bird**, Indiana State	SR	F	5	67	13.4
3 **Dick Miller**, Toledo	JR	F	2	24	12.0
4 **Clarence Kea**, Lamar	JR	F	2	23	11.5
5 **Greg Kelser**, Michigan State	SR	F	5	53	10.6

MINIMUM: 2 GAMES

TEAM LEADERS

SCORING

	G	PTS	PPG
1 **UCLA**	3	266	88.7
2 **Michigan State**	5	438	87.6
3 **San Francisco**	2	167	83.5
4 **DePaul**	5	416	83.2
5 **Syracuse**	2	165	82.5
6 **Tennessee**	2	164	82.0
Southern California	2	164	82.0
8 **Pepperdine**	2	163	81.5
9 **Oklahoma**	2	162	81.0
10 **Lamar**	2	159	79.5

MINIMUM: 2 GAMES

FG PCT

	G	FG	FGA	PCT
1 **San Francisco**	2	72	122	59.0
2 **Arkansas**	3	83	143	58.0
3 **Michigan State**	5	167	295	56.6
4 **Southern California**	2	69	122	56.6
Syracuse	2	69	122	56.6

FT PCT

	G	FT	FTA	PCT
1 **Louisville**	2	37	42	88.1
2 **Marquette**	2	27	32	84.4
3 **Arkansas**	3	52	64	81.3
4 **DePaul**	5	94	121	77.7
5 **St. John's**	4	44	58	75.9

MINIMUM: 2 GAMES

REBOUNDS

	G	REB	RPG
1 **Lamar**	2	94	47.0
2 **Tennessee**	2	85	42.5
3 **LSU**	2	78	39.0
4 **Michigan State**	5	184	36.8
5 **Pepperdine**	2	70	35.0

MINIMUM: 2 GAMES

ALL-TOURNAMENT TEAM

PLAYER	CL	POS	HT	SCHOOL	RPG	PPG
Earvin "Magic" Johnson*	SO	G	6-9	Michigan State	8.8	21.8
Mark Aguirre	SO	F	6-7	DePaul	6.6	23.4
Larry Bird	SR	F	6-9	Indiana State	13.4	27.2
Gary Garland	SR	G	6-4	DePaul	6.6	19.4
Greg Kelser	SR	F	6-7	Michigan State	10.6	25.4

ALL-REGIONAL TEAMS

EAST

PLAYER	CL	POS	HT	SCHOOL	RPG	PPG
Reggie Carter	JR	G	6-3	St. John's	3.3	16.8
Wayne McKoy	SO	C	6-8	St. John's	7.3	16.3
Ron Plair	SO	F	6-4	St. John's	6.8	10.5
Tony Price	SR	F	6-7	Penn	8.0	23.3
Tim Smith	SR	G	6-5	Penn	6.8	15.0

MIDEAST

PLAYER	CL	POS	HT	SCHOOL	RPG	PPG
Greg Kelser*	SR	F	6-7	Michigan State	12.0	26.7
Bill Hanzlik	JR	G/F	6-7	Notre Dame	3.3	16.3
Earvin "Magic" Johnson	SO	G	6-9	Michigan State	9.0	18.7
Jim Swaney	JR	F	6-7½	Toledo	4.0	19.0
Kelly Tripucka	SO	F	6-7	Notre Dame	3.7	17.7

MIDWEST

PLAYER	CL	POS	HT	SCHOOL	RPG	PPG
Larry Bird*	SR	F	6-9	Indiana State	12.7	27.3
Sidney Moncrief	SR	G	6-4	Arkansas	8.3	23.3
Carl Nicks	JR	G	6-1	Indiana State	2.0	18.3
Steve Schall	SR	C	6-10	Arkansas	6.3	12.7
Raymond Whitley	SO	G	6-3	Oklahoma	1.0	24.5

WEST

PLAYER	CL	POS	HT	SCHOOL	RPG	PPG
Gary Garland*	SR	G	6-4	DePaul	5.7	18.7
Bill Cartwright	SR	C	6-11	San Francisco	8.5	29.0
David Greenwood	SR	F	6-9	UCLA	8.3	24.7
Roy Hamilton	SR	G	6-2	UCLA	2.7	22.0
Curtis Watkins	SR	F	6-6	DePaul	8.0	23.3

* MOST OUTSTANDING PLAYER

1979 NCAA TOURNAMENT BOX SCORES

Sweet 16: St. John's 67, Rutgers 65

	1H	2H
St. John's	34	33
Rutgers	38	27

ST. JOHN'S	MIN	FG	3FG	FT	REB	A	ST	BL	PF	TP
Reggie Carter	38	9-16	-	4-5	5	0	0	0	2	22
Gordon Thomas	28	7-10	-	0-1	2	3	3	0	2	14
Wayne Mckoy	27	5-12	-	0-0	7	1	1	0	4	10
Bernard Rencher	26	3-9	-	1-1	0	4	2	0	3	7
Rudy Wright	21	2-4	-	2-2	4	0	1	0	0	6
Frank Gilroy	27	2-5	-	0-0	8	0	2	2	4	4
Ron Plair	25	2-7	-	0-0	3	0	0	0	5	4
Rick Bollinger	8	0-1	-	0-0	1	1	0	0	1	0
TOTALS	200	30-64	-	7-9	30	9	9	2	21	67
Percentages		46.9		77.8						

Coach: Lou Carnesecca

RUTGERS	MIN	FG	3FG	FT	REB	A	ST	BL	PF	TP
James Bailey	38	9-15	-	1-1	6	0	1	4	2	19
Kelvin Troy	38	6-10	-	3-5	10	2	1	1	2	15
Abdel Anderson	38	5-10	-	2-5	7	1	2	0	1	12
Daryl Strickland	32	4-10	-	3-5	3	3	0	0	4	11
Tom Brown	38	2-4	-	2-2	1	6	0	0	3	6
Jon McDaniel	4	0-0	-	2-2	0	0	0	0	0	2
Darius Griffin	10	0-0	-	0-0	1	1	1	0	2	0
William Clarke	2	0-0	-	0-1	0	1	0	0	0	0
TOTALS	200	26-49	-	13-21	28	14	5	5	14	65
Percentages		53.1		61.9						

Coach: Tom Young

Officials: Ga Muncy, Jim Bain, Don Sh
Technicals: None
Attendance: 9102

Sweet 16: Penn 84, Syracuse 76

	1H	2H
Penn	50	34
Syracuse	37	39

PENN	MIN	FG	3FG	FT	REB	A	ST	BL	PF	TP
Tony Price	35	7-10	-	6-7	7	6	2	1	4	20
Tim Smith	35	9-17	-	0-0	8	3	2	0	2	18
James Salters	34	5-9	-	4-4	1	2	2	0	3	14
Matthew White	24	5-10	-	1-3	8	3	1	0	4	11
Kenneth Hall	17	0-2	-	11-12	1	1	0	0	1	11
Bobby Willis	30	4-13	-	0-0	1	5	2	0	1	8
Thomas Leifsen	13	1-1	-	0-0	2	0	0	0	1	2
Vincent Ross	12	0-1	-	0-0	3	0	2	0	3	0
TOTALS	200	31-63	-	22-26	31	20	11	1	19	84
Percentages		49.2		84.6						

Coach: Bob Weinhauer

SYRACUSE	MIN	FG	3FG	FT	REB	A	ST	BL	PF	TP
Dale Shackleford	38	7-10	-	2-2	4	7	0	0	4	16
Roosevelt Bouie	38	5-8	-	3-6	14	0	2	6	1	13
Marty Headd	32	5-14	-	3-5	3	2	3	0	2	13
Louis Orr	30	5-10	-	3-8	6	0	1	0	4	13
Eddie Moss	24	5-9	-	1-2	3	4	0	1	5	11
Mark Cubit	15	3-6	-	0-0	0	3	3	0	5	6
Rick Harmon	7	1-1	-	0-0	0	0	0	0	2	2
Danny Schayes	3	1-1	-	0-0	0	0	0	0	0	2
Hal Cohen	13	0-1	-	0-0	1	3	1	0	1	0
TOTALS	200	32-60	-	12-23	31	19	10	7	24	76
Percentages		53.3		52.2						

Coach: Jim Boeheim

Officials: Paul Galvan, Ed Maracich, Reggie Copelar
Technicals: None
Attendance: 9102

Sweet 16: Michigan State 87, LSU 71

	1H	2H
Michigan State	36	51
LSU	19	52

MICHIGAN STATE	MIN	FG	3FG	FT	REB	A	ST	BL	PF	TP
Earvin "Magic" Johnson	-	5-16	-	14-15	5	12	3	0	2	24
Ron Charles	-	6-10	-	6-10	14	1	1	0	1	18
Greg Kelser	-	6-15	-	3-5	9	1	3	2	5	15
Mike Brkovich	-	4-7	-	3-4	3	3	1	0	0	11
Robert Gonzalez	-	4-7	-	1-2	1	0	2	0	1	9
Terry Donnelly	-	2-5	-	0-0	1	2	0	0	2	4
Don Brkovich	-	1-1	-	0-0	1	1	0	0	0	2
Rick Kaye	-	1-1	-	0-0	1	0	0	0	1	2
Mike Longaker	-	1-3	-	0-0	0	0	0	0	1	2
Gerald Gilkie	-	0-1	-	0-0	0	0	0	0	0	0
Gregory Lloyd	-	0-0	-	0-0	0	1	0	0	2	0
TOTALS	-	30-66	-	27-36	35	21	10	2	15	87
Percentages		45.5		75.0						

Coach: Jud Heathcote

LSU	MIN	FG	3FG	FT	REB	A	ST	BL	PF	TP
Jordy Hultberg	-	11-20	-	3-4	3	3	0	1	4	25
Lionel Green	-	5-8	-	2-2	15	0	1	3	4	12
Al Green	-	4-9	-	3-4	3	1	2	0	3	11
Rick Mattick	-	3-3	-	1-1	4	0	0	1	3	7
Gus Rudolph	-	3-3	-	0-0	4	0	1	1	2	6
Brian Bergeron	-	2-6	-	0-0	1	0	0	0	0	4
Ethan Martin	-	2-6	-	0-0	2	7	1	0	1	4
Greg Cook	-	1-2	-	0-0	6	1	1	1	5	2
Ernest Brown	-	0-4	-	0-2	0	1	1	0	5	0
Andy Campbell	-	0-0	-	0-0	0	0	0	0	1	0
Willie Sims	-	0-3	-	0-0	0	0	0	0	0	0
TOTALS	-	31-64	-	9-13	37	14	7	7	28	71
Percentages		48.4		69.2						

Coach: Dale Brown

Officials: Bob Herrold, Pete Pavia, Frank Buckiewicz
Technicals: LSU (bench, 2)
Attendance: 17,423

Sweet 16: Notre Dame 79, Toledo 71

	1H	2H
Notre Dame	43	36
Toledo	33	38

NOTRE DAME	MIN	FG	3FG	FT	REB	A	ST	BL	PF	TP
Kelly Tripucka	33	8-12	-	8-8	4	1	-	-	4	24
Bill Hanzlik	29	4-6	-	6-8	4	2	-	-	4	14
Orlando Woolridge	25	5-11	-	1-2	6	0	-	-	2	11
Rich Branning	31	4-9	-	2-3	2	3	-	-	2	10
Bill Laimbeer	29	3-5	-	2-2	5	1	-	-	3	8
Bruce Flowers	11	1-1	-	4-4	3	2	-	-	2	6
Tracy Jackson	22	2-6	-	0-2	6	1	-	-	0	4
Mike Mitchell	16	1-1	-	0-0	1	4	-	-	0	2
Stan Wilcox	4	0-1	-	0-0	0	1	-	-	0	0
TOTALS	200	28-52	-	23-29	31	15	-	-	17	79
Percentages		53.8		79.3						

Coach: Digger Phelps

TOLEDO	MIN	FG	3FG	FT	REB	A	ST	BL	PF	TP
Jim Swaney	35	10-14	-	6-6	4	1	-	-	3	26
Dick Miller	39	8-15	-	2-4	10	5	-	-	4	18
Jay Lehman	32	4-8	-	0-0	2	5	-	-	4	8
Tim Selgo	22	4-6	-	0-0	2	1	-	-	1	8
Harvey Knuckles	23	3-10	-	1-2	3	1	-	-	5	7
Kevin Appel	12	2-3	-	0-0	3	1	-	-	0	4
Stan Joplin	30	0-5	-	0-2	3	4	-	-	1	0
Ken Montague	6	0-0	-	0-0	0	0	-	-	0	0
Dennis Mathis	1	0-0	-	0-0	0	0	-	-	2	0
TOTALS	200	31-61	-	9-14	27	18	-	-	20	71
Percentages		50.8		64.3						

Coach: Bob Nichols

Officials: Booker Turner, Jim Burch, Bob Sitov
Technicals: None
Attendance: 17,423

Sweet 16: DePaul 62, Marquette 56

	1H	2H
DePaul	31	31
Marquette	28	28

DEPAUL	MIN	FG	3FG	FT	REB	A	ST	BL	PF	TP
Mark Aguirre	40	7-17	-	5-5	4	4	1	0	1	19
Curtis Watkins	40	6-12	-	7-8	7	1	1	1	2	19
Gary Garland	40	7-14	-	1-2	8	3	3	0	2	15
Clyde Bradshaw	40	2-7	-	3-4	3	6	3	0	4	7
James Mitchem	30	1-5	-	0-0	3	1	0	1	3	2
Wiliam Madey	10	0-0	-	0-1	0	2	0	0	0	0
TOTALS	200	23-55	-	16-20	25	17	8	2	12	62
Percentages		41.8		80.0						

Coach: Ray Meyer

MARQUETTE	MIN	FG	3FG	FT	REB	A	ST	BL	PF	TP
Bernard Toone	40	11-21	-	4-4	7	0	0	0	2	26
Robert Byrd	40	4-5	-	1-1	11	1	1	0	2	9
Sam Worthen	40	4-10	-	0-0	5	5	0	1	5	8
Michael Wilson	37	2-6	-	2-2	1	1	1	4	5	6
Odell Ball	28	2-5	-	1-2	3	0	0	0	5	5
Oliver Lee	10	1-3	-	0-0	3	0	0	0	1	2
Tony Davis	2	0-0	-	0-0	0	0	0	0	0	0
Artie Green	2	0-3	-	0-0	0	1	0	0	1	0
Dean Marquardt	1	0-0	-	0-0	0	0	0	0	0	0
TOTALS	200	24-53	-	8-9	30	8	2	5	21	56
Percentages		45.3		88.9						

Coach: Hank Raymonds

Officials: Paul Housman, Mickey Crowley, Lenny Wirtz
Technicals: None
Attendance: 15,139

Sweet 16: UCLA 99, San Francisco 81

	1H	2H
UCLA	41	58
San Francisco	43	38

UCLA	MIN	FG	3FG	FT	REB	A	ST	BL	PF	TP
Roy Hamilton	39	15-20	-	6-9	4	7	0	0	2	36
Brad Holland	39	11-18	-	0-0	2	6	1	0	1	22
David Greenwood	38	6-11	-	7-8	5	3	1	1	3	19
Kiki Vandeweghe	39	5-12	-	1-1	13	1	1	0	2	11
James Wilkes	25	4-5	-	0-1	3	2	0	0	1	8
Tyren Naulls	1	1-1	-	1-2	1	0	0	0	0	3
Darrell Allums	11	0-1	-	0-0	3	1	0	0	4	0
Gig Sims	5	0-1	-	0-0	0	0	0	2	4	0
Rennie Kelly	1	0-0	-	0-0	0	0	0	0	0	0
Mike Sanders	1	0-0	-	0-0	0	1	0	0	0	0
Marvin Thomas	1	0-1	-	0-0	0	1	0	0	0	0
TOTALS	200	42-70	-	15-21	31	21	4	3	17	99
Percentages		60.0		71.4						

Coach: Gary Cunningham

SAN FRANCISCO	MIN	FG	3FG	FT	REB	A	ST	BL	PF	TP
Bill Cartwright	35	12-19	-	10-12	9	1	0	1	4	34
Billy Reid	34	5-10	-	3-4	2	4	1	0	4	13
Guy Williams	37	5-12	-	2-6	2	3	1	0	4	12
Wallace Bryant	20	5-9	-	0-0	4	1	0	0	1	10
Bart Bowers	28	2-4	-	0-0	5	1	0	0	2	4
Doug Jemison	26	2-5	-	0-0	8	0	0	0	5	4
Ken McAllister	7	1-3	-	0-0	1	0	0	0	0	2
Erik Gilberg	2	1-1	-	0-0	0	1	0	0	1	2
Marvin Deloatch	6	0-2	-	0-0	0	0	0	0	0	0
David Cornelious	5	0-0	-	0-0	0	3	0	0	1	0
TOTALS	200	33-65	-	15-22	31	14	2	1	22	81
Percentages		50.8		68.2						

Coach: Dan Belluomini

Officials: Jody Silvester, Roy Clymer, Ron Spitler
Technicals: None
Attendance: 15,139

ARKANSAS	MIN	FG	3FG	FT	REB	A	ST	BL	PF	TP
Sidney Moncrief	40	7-12	-	13-14	12	1	-	-	4	27
U.S. Reed	34	8-17	-	2-5	3	2	-	-	0	18
Scott Hastings	40	3-9	-	4-5	8	2	-	-	3	10
Steve Schall	25	2-3	-	4-4	7	0	-	-	5	8
Alan Zahn	40	3-5	-	0-0	3	4	-	-	4	6
James Crockett	7	2-3	-	0-0	1	0	-	-	2	4
Tony Brown	14	0-1	-	0-1	1	1	-	-	1	0
TOTALS	**200**	**25-50**	**-**	**23-29**	**35**	**10**	**-**	**-**	**19**	**73**
Percentages		50.0		79.3						

Coach: Eddie Sutton

73-62

38 1H 26
35 2H 36

SWEET 16

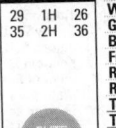

LOUISVILLE	MIN	FG	3FG	FT	REB	A	ST	BL	PF	TP
Scooter McCray	40	5-12	-	4-4	7	2	-	-	4	14
Darrell Griffith	30	5-14	-	2-2	2	1	-	-	5	12
Bobby Turner	30	3-9	-	6-6	7	0	-	-	1	12
Larry Williams	40	5-10	-	1-2	6	5	-	-	3	11
Tony Branch	24	3-5	-	4-5	3	1	-	-	5	10
Derek Smith	23	0-4	-	3-4	2	0	-	-	4	3
Roger Burkman	9	0-0	-	0-0	0	1	-	-	5	0
Jerry Eaves	4	0-0	-	0-0	0	0	-	-	1	0
TOTALS	**200**	**21-54**	**-**	**20-23**	**27**	**10**	**-**	**-**	**28**	**62**
Percentages		38.9		87.0						

Coach: Denny Crum

Officials: Art White, Richie Weiler, Hank Nichols
Technicals: None
Attendance: 17,252

INDIANA STATE	MIN	FG	3FG	FT	REB	A	ST	BL	PF	TP
Larry Bird	-	11-19	-	7-8	15	5	1	0	0	29
Carl Nicks	-	8-16	-	4-9	3	5	1	0	2	20
Alex Gilbert	-	6-7	-	0-3	9	0	0	1	2	12
Bobby Heaton	-	3-3	-	3-3	2	0	1	0	2	9
Leroy Staley	-	3-6	-	3-4	7	0	0	0	3	9
Brad Miley	-	3-3	-	0-0	3	1	0	0	1	6
Rich Nemcek	-	1-1	-	2-3	2	0	0	0	0	4
Steve Reed	-	0-3	-	4-4	2	2	0	0	5	4
Tom Crowder	-	0-0	-	0-0	1	0	0	0	1	0
Eric Curry	-	0-1	-	0-0	1	0	0	0	0	0
Rod McNelly	-	0-1	-	0-0	2	0	0	0	0	0
Scott Turner	-	0-0	-	0-0	0	0	0	0	0	0
TOTALS	**-**	**35-60**	**-**	**23-34**	**47**	**13**	**3**	**1**	**16**	**93**
Percentages		58.3		67.6						

Coach: Bill Hodges

93-72

45 1H 37
48 2H 35

SWEET 16

OKLAHOMA	MIN	FG	3FG	FT	REB	A	ST	BL	PF	TP
Raymond Whitley	36	9-12	-	6-9	1	0	0	0	4	24
John McCullough	36	6-10	-	2-2	7	3	3	0	5	14
Aaron Curry	33	5-15	-	1-2	4	2	4	1	3	11
Al Beal	22	5-7	-	0-0	4	0	0	0	5	10
Terry Stotts	37	2-11	-	1-2	2	2	1	0	4	5
Cary Carrabine	19	2-7	-	0-2	0	1	0	0	0	4
Lester Pace	13	2-6	-	0-0	1	0	0	0	4	4
Ingram Purvis	2	0-1	-	0-0	0	0	0	0	0	0
Donny Calvert	1	0-1	-	0-0	0	0	0	0	1	0
Kyle Dodd	1	0-0	-	0-0	0	0	0	0	1	0
TOTALS	**200**	**31-70**	**-**	**10-17**	**19**	**8**	**8**	**1**	**27**	**72**
Percentages		44.3		58.8						

Coach: Dave Bliss

Officials: Charles Range, Phil Robinson, Rich Ballesteros
Technicals: Oklahoma (Beal)
Attendance: 17,252

PENN	MIN	FG	3FG	FT	REB	A	ST	BL	PF	TP
Tony Price	29	7-11	-	7-12	4	0	1	-	4	21
Tim Smith	39	7-14	-	2-2	3	0	1	-	4	16
Bobby Willis	35	3-8	-	4-4	3	5	4	-	3	10
James Salters	31	2-6	-	3-4	0	5	2	-	2	7
Kenneth Hall	15	2-3	-	1-1	1	0	0	-	0	5
Matthew White	24	0-3	-	3-4	9	0	0	-	5	3
Vincent Ross	16	1-1	-	0-0	5	0	2	-	2	2
Thomas Leifsen	11	0-0	-	0-0	0	0	0	-	1	0
TOTALS	**200**	**22-46**	**-**	**20-27**	**25**	**10**	**10**	**-**	**21**	**64**
Percentages		47.8		74.1						

Coach: Bob Weinhauer

64-62

29 1H 26
35 2H 36

ELITE 8

ST. JOHN'S	MIN	FG	3FG	FT	REB	A	ST	BL	PF	TP
Ron Plair	37	9-9	-	3-3	6	1	2	1	3	21
Wayne Mckoy	28	7-14	-	1-4	7	1	0	0	3	15
Gordon Thomas	26	3-9	-	4-4	3	6	0	0	0	10
Bernard Rencher	25	3-8	-	0-0	3	5	1	1	5	6
Frank Gilroy	34	0-4	-	4-4	6	2	0	1	5	4
Reggie Carter	28	2-9	-	0-1	3	1	0	0	5	4
Rudy Wright	12	1-1	-	0-0	3	0	1	0	0	2
Tom Calabrese	10	0-1	-	0-0	0	1	0	0	1	0
TOTALS	**200**	**25-55**	**-**	**12-16**	**31**	**17**	**4**	**3**	**22**	**62**
Percentages		45.5		75.0						

Coach: Lou Carnesecca

Officials: Reggie Copeland, Gary Muncy, Don Shea
Technicals: None
Attendance: 7216

MICHIGAN STATE	MIN	FG	3FG	FT	REB	A	ST	BL	PF	TP
Greg Kelser	39	15-25	-	4-8	13	1	1	2	4	34
Earvin "Magic" Johnson	40	6-10	-	7-8	5	13	2	0	2	19
Mike Brkovich	38	5-10	-	3-4	3	1	0	0	1	13
Ron Charles	32	2-4	-	2-2	4	0	0	0	4	6
Terry Donnelly	36	1-1	-	2-2	2	0	1	1	3	4
Robert Gonzalez	11	1-2	-	0-0	3	0	0	0	2	2
Jay Vincent	3	1-2	-	0-0	0	0	0	0	0	2
Mike Longaker	1	0-0	-	0-0	0	0	0	0	0	0
TOTALS	**200**	**31-54**	**-**	**18-24**	**30**	**15**	**4**	**3**	**16**	**80**
Percentages		57.4		75.0						

Coach: Jud Heathcote

80-68

34 1H 23
46 2H 45

ELITE 8

NOTRE DAME	MIN	FG	3FG	FT	REB	A	ST	BL	PF	TP
Tracy Jackson	31	9-13	-	1-4	6	1	0	0	4	19
Bill Hanzlik	30	7-12	-	5-5	6	4	1	0	5	19
Kelly Tripucka	34	4-11	-	0-0	4	1	2	1	4	8
Rich Branning	33	4-14	-	0-0	3	4	1	0	4	8
Bill Laimbeer	20	3-5	-	1-2	4	1	1	2	3	7
Stan Wilcox	14	2-4	-	0-0	1	2	0	0	0	4
Orlando Woolridge	18	1-6	-	1-2	3	0	0	0	1	3
Bruce Flowers	16	0-1	-	0-0	6	1	2	1	3	0
Mike Mitchell	4	0-0	-	0-0	0	0	0	0	0	0
TOTALS	**200**	**30-66**	**-**	**8-13**	**32**	**14**	**7**	**4**	**24**	**68**
Percentages		45.5		61.5						

Coach: Digger Phelps

Officials: Bob Herrold, Booker Turner, Frank Buckiewicz
Technicals: None
Attendance: 17,423

DEPAUL	MIN	FG	3FG	FT	REB	A	ST	BL	PF	TP
Gary Garland	40	10-20	-	4-4	8	8	2	0	3	24
Curtis Watkins	38	9-10	-	6-6	8	3	1	1	4	24
Mark Aguirre	40	9-16	-	2-3	3	2	1	0	3	20
James Mitchem	40	6-10	-	2-5	9	1	0	1	2	14
Clyde Bradshaw	40	3-8	-	7-11	5	7	1	0	4	13
Wiliam Madey	1	0-0	-	0-0	0	0	0	0	0	0
Chris Nikitas	1	0-0	-	0-0	0	1	0	0	0	0
TOTALS	**200**	**37-64**	**-**	**21-29**	**33**	**22**	**5**	**2**	**16**	**95**
Percentages		57.8		72.4						

Coach: Ray Meyer

95-91

51 1H 34
44 2H 57

ELITE 8

UCLA	MIN	FG	3FG	FT	REB	A	ST	BL	PF	TP
David Greenwood	-	17-24	-	3-4	10	2	0	2	4	37
Brad Holland	-	6-15	-	7-8	2	2	1	0	4	19
Kiki Vandeweghe	-	7-17	-	3-3	9	1	2	1	2	17
Roy Hamilton	-	8-12	-	0-2	2	10	2	0	4	16
James Wilkes	-	1-3	-	0-0	2	1	1	0	5	2
Darrell Allums	-	0-0	-	0-0	1	1	0	1	4	0
Tyren Naulls	-	0-0	-	0-0	0	0	0	0	1	0
Mike Sanders	-	0-0	-	0-0	0	0	0	0	1	0
Gig Sims	-	0-0	-	0-0	2	0	0	1	0	0
Marvin Thomas	-	0-2	-	0-0	1	0	0	0	2	0
TOTALS	**-**	**39-73**	**-**	**13-17**	**29**	**17**	**6**	**5**	**27**	**91**
Percentages		53.4		76.5						

Coach: Gary Cunningham

Officials: Jody Silvester, Roy Clymer, Lenny Wirtz
Technicals: None
Attendance: 13,126

INDIANA STATE	MIN	FG	3FG	FT	REB	A	ST	BL	PF	TP
Larry Bird	40	12-22	-	7-8	10	3	-	-	3	31
Carl Nicks	33	5-11	-	3-4	0	3	-	-	4	13
Alex Gilbert	22	6-9	-	0-0	2	0	-	-	3	12
Bobby Heaton	16	4-5	-	0-0	1	0	-	-	0	8
Brad Miley	35	3-3	-	0-0	4	3	-	-	2	6
Leroy Staley	22	1-4	-	1-3	3	0	-	-	1	3
Steve Reed	32	0-1	-	0-0	0	5	-	-	3	0
TOTALS	**200**	**31-55**	**-**	**11-15**	**20**	**14**	**-**	**-**	**16**	**73**
Percentages		56.4		73.3						

Coach: Bill Hodges

73-71

37 1H 39
36 2H 32

ELITE 8

ARKANSAS	MIN	FG	3FG	FT	REB	A	ST	BL	PF	TP
Sidney Moncrief	-	10-16	-	4-4	8	2	-	-	2	24
Steve Schall	-	6-7	-	0-2	4	2	-	-	4	12
U.S. Reed	-	4-8	-	3-3	4	2	-	-	5	11
Scott Hastings	-	3-7	-	4-4	3	3	-	-	2	10
Alan Zahn	-	5-7	-	0-0	3	3	-	-	3	10
Mike Young	-	2-2	-	0-0	1	1	-	-	1	4
Tony Brown	-	0-0	-	0-0	0	1	-	-	0	0
TOTALS	**-**	**30-47**	**-**	**11-13**	**23**	**14**	**-**	**-**	**17**	**71**
Percentages		63.8		84.6						

Coach: Eddie Sutton

Officials: Richie Weiler, Hank Nichols, Phil Robinson
Technicals: None
Attendance: 17,166

101-67 — 1H: Michigan State 50, Penn 17; 2H: Michigan State 51, Penn 50 — FINAL 4

MICHIGAN STATE	MIN	FG	3FG	FT	REB	A	ST	BL	PF	TP
Earvin "Magic" Johnson	35	9-10	-	11-12	10	10	3	0	2	29
Greg Kelser	34	12-19	-	4-6	9	3	1	4	2	28
Mike Brkovich	24	6-10	-	0-0	1	3	1	0	4	12
Terry Donnelly	23	3-5	-	0-0	3	3	0	0	0	6
Gregory Lloyd	7	0-2	-	6-7	0	1	2	0	1	6
Rick Kaye	7	2-2	-	1-3	2	1	0	0	1	5
Ron Charles	19	2-2	-	0-0	6	0	0	2	4	4
Mike Longaker	9	2-2	-	0-0	2	1	2	0	0	4
Jay Vincent	9	0-1	-	3-4	1	0	0	0	2	3
Robert Gonzalez	22	1-5	-	0-0	3	1	1	0	2	2
Don Brkovich	3	1-1	-	0-1	1	0	0	0	1	2
Jaimie Huffman	5	0-0	-	0-1	2	1	0	0	2	0
Gerald Gilkie	3	0-1	-	0-0	1	0	0	0	1	0
TOTALS	**200**	**38-60**	**-**	**25-34**	**41**	**24**	**10**	**6**	**22**	**101**
Percentages		63.3		73.5						

Coach: Jud Heathcote

PENN	MIN	FG	3FG	FT	REB	A	ST	BL	PF	TP
Tony Price	-	7-18	-	4-4	7	0	1	0	5	18
Matthew White	-	5-12	-	3-4	11	1	1	0	4	13
Bobby Willis	-	4-13	-	1-3	6	6	3	1	2	9
Theodore Flick	-	0-6	-	6-6	2	1	1	0	3	6
Kenneth Hall	-	3-8	-	0-1	2	1	2	0	1	6
David Jackson	-	1-2	-	4-4	1	0	0	0	0	6
Vincent Ross	-	2-6	-	0-0	6	0	0	1	3	4
Angelo Reynolds	-	1-3	-	0-0	0	0	0	0	3	2
James Salters	-	1-5	-	0-0	1	3	0	0	2	2
Thomas Leifsen	-	0-1	-	1-2	4	0	0	0	1	1
Thomas Condon	-	0-0	-	0-0	2	0	0	0	2	0
Edward Kuhl	-	0-2	-	0-0	0	0	0	0	0	0
Tim Smith	-	0-6	-	0-0	0	0	0	0	5	0
TOTALS	**-**	**24-82**	**-**	**19-24**	**42**	**12**	**8**	**2**	**31**	**67**
Percentages		29.3		79.2						

Coach: Bob Weinhauer

Officials: Richie Weiler, Frank Buckiewicz, Jody Silvester
Technicals: None
Attendance: 15,410

76-74 — 1H: Indiana State 45, DePaul 42; 2H: Indiana State 31, DePaul 32 — FINAL 4

INDIANA STATE	MIN	FG	3FG	FT	REB	A	ST	BL	PF	TP
Larry Bird	-	16-19	-	3-4	16	9	1	0	3	35
Alex Gilbert	-	6-7	-	0-1	5	0	0	2	2	12
Carl Nicks	-	4-13	-	2-2	1	5	1	0	3	10
Bobby Heaton	-	3-6	-	0-0	3	0	0	0	2	6
Steve Reed	-	3-5	-	0-0	2	2	0	0	0	6
Brad Miley	-	2-2	-	0-0	3	3	2	0	1	4
Leroy Staley	-	1-4	-	1-2	2	0	0	0	3	3
TOTALS	**-**	**35-56**	**-**	**6-9**	**32**	**19**	**4**	**2**	**14**	**76**
Percentages		62.5		66.7						

Coach: Bill Hodges

DEPAUL	MIN	FG	3FG	FT	REB	A	ST	BL	PF	TP
Mark Aguirre	40	9-18	-	1-2	5	2	2	0	3	19
Gary Garland	40	9-18	-	1-3	4	8	4	0	2	19
Curtis Watkins	40	8-11	-	0-0	2	2	1	0	4	16
James Mitchem	40	6-11	-	0-0	5	0	1	1	4	12
Clyde Bradshaw	40	4-8	-	0-0	3	4	3	0	1	8
TOTALS	**200**	**36-66**	**-**	**2-5**	**19**	**16**	**11**	**1**	**14**	**74**
Percentages		54.5		40.0						

Coach: Ray Meyer

Officials: Hank Nichols, Gary Muncy, Lenny Wirtz
Technicals: None
Attendance: 15,410

96-93 — 1H: DePaul 54, Penn 43; 2H: DePaul 31, Penn 42; OT1: DePaul 11, Penn 8 — 3RD PLACE

DEPAUL	MIN	FG	3FG	FT	REB	A	ST	BL	PF	TP
Mark Aguirre	45	10-23	-	14-15	14	2	1	0	3	34
Gary Garland	36	9-18	-	4-4	12	5	3	0	5	22
Curtis Watkins	31	7-9	-	4-5	11	2	1	3	5	18
James Mitchem	45	3-11	-	5-6	5	2	1	2	4	11
Clyde Bradshaw	43	2-6	-	4-5	2	7	3	0	3	8
Chris Nikitas	11	0-0	-	2-2	1	1	0	0	0	2
Wiliam Madey	12	0-1	-	1-2	3	0	0	1	1	1
Dennis McGuire	2	0-0	-	0-0	0	0	0	0	1	0
TOTALS	**225**	**31-68**	**-**	**34-39**	**48**	**19**	**9**	**6**	**22**	**96**
Percentages		45.6		87.2						

Coach: Ray Meyer

PENN	MIN	FG	3FG	FT	REB	A	ST	BL	PF	TP
Tony Price	43	14-27	-	3-4	14	2	3	3	5	31
Tim Smith	27	8-16	-	0-3	3	2	1	1	5	16
Bobby Willis	36	5-13	-	4-5	5	9	1	0	3	14
James Salters	37	4-11	-	0-0	1	2	2	0	3	8
Kenneth Hall	27	3-7	-	1-1	1	4	3	0	1	7
Vincent Ross	19	2-3	-	3-6	10	0	1	0	5	7
Matthew White	17	2-7	-	0-0	7	1	0	0	5	4
Thomas Leifsen	4	2-3	-	0-0	2	0	0	0	0	4
Theodore Flick	11	1-6	-	0-0	3	0	0	0	3	2
Thomas Condon	3	0-1	-	0-0	1	0	0	0	1	0
David Jackson	1	0-0	-	0-0	0	0	0	0	0	0
TOTALS	**225**	**41-94**	**-**	**11-19**	**47**	**20**	**11**	**4**	**31**	**93**
Percentages		43.6		57.9						

Coach: Bob Weinhauer

Officials: Richie Weiler, Frank Buckiewicz, Jody Silvester
Technicals: None
Attendance: 15,410

75-64 — 1H: Michigan State 37, Indiana State 28; 2H: Michigan State 38, Indiana State 36 — NCAA FINAL 1979

MICHIGAN STATE	MIN	FG	3FG	FT	REB	A	ST	BL	PF	TP
Earvin "Magic" Johnson	35	8-15	-	8-10	7	5	1	0	3	24
Greg Kelser	32	7-13	-	5-6	8	9	2	2	4	19
Terry Donnelly	39	5-5	-	5-6	4	0	1	0	2	15
Ron Charles	31	3-3	-	1-2	7	0	1	0	5	7
Mike Brkovich	39	1-2	-	3-7	4	1	0	0	1	5
Jay Vincent	19	2-5	-	1-2	2	0	1	0	4	5
Robert Gonzalez	3	0-0	-	0-0	0	0	0	0	0	0
Mike Longaker	2	0-0	-	0-0	0	0	0	0	0	0
TOTALS	**200**	**26-43**	**-**	**23-33**	**32**	**15**	**6**	**2**	**19**	**75**
Percentages		60.5		69.7						

Coach: Jud Heathcote

INDIANA STATE	MIN	FG	3FG	FT	REB	A	ST	BL	PF	TP
Larry Bird	-	7-21	-	5-8	13	2	5	1	3	19
Carl Nicks	-	7-14	-	3-6	2	4	1	0	5	17
Bobby Heaton	-	4-14	-	2-2	6	2	0	0	2	10
Steve Reed	-	4-9	-	0-0	0	9	0	0	4	8
Alex Gilbert	-	2-3	-	0-4	4	0	0	1	4	4
Leroy Staley	-	2-2	-	0-1	3	0	0	0	2	4
Rich Nemcek	-	1-1	-	0-0	0	1	0	0	3	2
Brad Miley	-	0-0	-	0-1	3	0	0	0	1	0
TOTALS	**-**	**27-64**	**-**	**10-22**	**31**	**18**	**6**	**2**	**24**	**64**
Percentages		42.2		45.5						

Coach: Bill Hodges

Officials: Hank Nichols, Gary Muncy, Lenny Wirtz
Technicals: Indiana State (Bird)
Attendance: 15,410

National Invitation Tournament (NIT)

First round: Clemson d. Kentucky 68-67 (OT), Virginia d. UL-Monroe 79-78, Old Dominion d. Wagner 83-81, Maryland d. Rhode Island 67-65 (3OT), Nevada d. Oregon State 62-61, Ohio State d. Saint Joseph's 80-66, Alabama d. St. Bonaventure 98-89, Indiana d. Texas Tech 78-59, Texas A&M d. New Mexico 79-68, Dayton d. Holy Cross 105-81, Purdue d. Central Michigan 97-80, Alcorn State d. Mississippi State 80-78
Second round: Texas A&M d. Nevada 67-64, Purdue d. Dayton 84-70, Old Dominion d. Clemson 61-59, Ohio State d. Maryland 79-72, Alabama d. Virginia 90-88, Indiana d. Alcorn State 73-69
Third round: Indiana, Ohio State drew byes; Alabama d. Texas A&M 72-68, Purdue d. Old Dominion 67-59
Semifinals: Indiana d. Ohio State 64-55, Purdue d. Alabama 87-68
Third place: Alabama d. Ohio State 96-86
Championship: Indiana d. Purdue 53-52
MVP: Butch Carter, Indiana and Ray Tolbert, Indiana

1979-80: Doctors of Dunk

They were entertaining to say the least. Denny Crum's Louisville Cardinals sprinted to a 33–3 record and won the NCAA title behind the play of aerial artist Darrell "Dr. Dunkenstein" Griffith. In their NCAA championship matchup with UCLA—coached by Larry Brown, the second of John Wooden's successors to lead the Bruins to the Final Four—Griffith scored 23 points and was pivotal in a 14-4 run that sealed the 59-54 win at Indianapolis' Market Square Arena. Griffith scored 34 in the national semifinals, shot a combined 23 of 27 from the field in the Final Four and was named Tournament MOP. After two Tournaments with seedings, only one of eight No. 1s—Indiana State in 1979—had managed to make it to the Final Four. Louisville was seeded No. 2 and UCLA, whose participation in the Tournament was later vacated for using ineligible players, was a No. 8.

The Big East Conference played its inaugural season, with three members (Georgetown, St. John's and Syracuse) making the NCAA Tournament. The Naismith POY award went to DePaul's Mark Aguirre. Purdue 7-footer Joe Barry Carroll was selected by Golden State as the No. 1 overall pick in the NBA draft.

Major Conference Standings

ACC

	Conference			Overall		
	W	L	Pct	W	L	Pct
Maryland ○	11	3	.786	24	7	.774
North Carolina ○	9	5	.643	21	8	.724
NC State ○	9	5	.643	20	8	.714
Clemson ○	8	6	.571	23	9	.719
Duke ⊕	7	7	.500	24	9	.727
Virginia □	7	7	.500	24	10	.706
Wake Forest	4	10	.286	13	14	.481
Georgia Tech	1	13	.071	8	18	.308

Tournament: **Duke d. Maryland 73-72**
Tournament MVP: **Albert King**, Maryland

Big East

	Conference			Overall		
	W	L	Pct	W	L	Pct
Syracuse ○	5	1	.833	26	4	.867
Georgetown ○	5	1	.833	26	6	.813
St. John's ○	5	1	.833	24	5	.828
Connecticut □	3	3	.500	20	9	.690
Boston College □	2	4	.333	19	10	.655
Seton Hall	1	5	.167	14	13	.519
Providence	0	6	.000	11	16	.407

Tournament: **Georgetown d. Syracuse 87-81**
Tournament MVP: **Craig Shelton**, Georgetown

Big Eight

	Conference			Overall		
	W	L	Pct	W	L	Pct
Missouri ○	11	3	.786	25	6	.806
Kansas State ⊕	8	6	.571	22	9	.710
Nebraska □	8	6	.571	18	13	.581
Colorado	7	7	.500	17	10	.630
Kansas	7	7	.500	15	14	.517
Oklahoma	6	8	.429	15	12	.556
Iowa State	5	9	.357	11	16	.407
Oklahoma State	4	10	.286	10	17	.370

Tournament: **Kansas State d. Kansas 79-58**
Tournament MVP: **Rolando Blackman**, Kansas State

Big Sky

	Conference			Overall		
	W	L	Pct	W	L	Pct
Weber State ⊕	13	1	.929	26	3	.897
Idaho	9	5	.643	17	10	.630
Montana	8	6	.571	17	11	.607
Montana State	7	7	.500	14	12	.538
Northern Arizona	5	9	.357	14	12	.538
Idaho State	5	9	.357	9	17	.346
Nevada	5	9	.357	10	19	.345
Boise State	4	10	.286	10	16	.385

Tournament: **Weber State d. Montana 50-42**
Tournament MVP: **Bruce Collins**, Weber State

Big Ten

	Conference			Overall		
	W	L	Pct	W	L	Pct
Indiana ⊕	13	5	.722	21	8	.724
Ohio State ○	12	6	.667	21	8	.724
Purdue ○	11	7	.611	23	10	.697
Iowa ○	10	8	.556	23	10	.697
Minnesota □	10	8	.556	21	11	.656
Illinois □	8	10	.444	22	13	.629
Michigan □	8	10	.444	17	13	.567
Wisconsin	7	11	.389	15	14	.517
Michigan State	6	12	.333	12	15	.444
Northwestern	5	13	.278	10	17	.370

East Coast

	Conference			Overall		
	W	L	Pct	W	L	Pct
East Section						
Saint Joseph's □	10	1	.909	21	9	.700
Temple	8	3	.727	14	12	.538
La Salle ⊕	7	4	.636	22	9	.710
Hofstra	6	5	.545	14	14	.500
American	5	6	.455	13	14	.481
Drexel	4	7	.364	12	15	.444
West Section						
Bucknell	13	3	.813	20	7	.741
Lafayette □	13	3	.813	21	8	.724
Delaware	7	9	.438	9	19	.321
Rider	5	11	.313	10	18	.357
Lehigh	2	14	.125	5	20	.200
West Chester	1	15	.063	3	23	.115

Tournament: **La Salle d. Saint Joseph's 59-49**

ECAC Metro

	Conference			Overall		
	W	L	Pct	W	L	Pct
Iona ⊕ ⊗	-	-	-	29	5	.853
St. Peter's □	-	-	-	22	9	.710
Long Island	-	-	-	14	12	.538
Wagner	-	-	-	14	13	.519
Siena	-	-	-	14	14	.500
Fairleigh Dickinson	-	-	-	13	14	.481
St. Francis (NY)	-	-	-	11	15	.423
Fairfield	-	-	-	11	16	.407
Fordham	-	-	-	11	17	.393
Army	-	-	-	9	17	.346
Manhattan	-	-	-	4	22	.154

Tournament: **Iona d. St. Peter's 64-46**
Note: Conference did not play a formal schedule

ECAC North

	Conference			Overall		
	W	L	Pct	W	L	Pct
Northeastern	19	7	.731	19	8	.704
Boston U. □	19	7	.731	21	9	.700
Holy Cross ⊕	16	10	.615	19	11	.633
Rhode Island	14	12	.538	15	13	.536
Maine	14	12	.538	15	13	.536
Canisius	13	13	.500	13	14	.481
Vermont	12	14	.462	12	15	.444
Niagara	11	15	.423	11	16	.407
Colgate	8	17	.320	8	17	.320
New Hampshire	4	22	.154	4	22	.154

Tournament: **Holy Cross d. Boston U. 81-75**
Tournament MVP: **Ronnie Perry**, Holy Cross

ECAC South

	Conference			Overall		
	W	L	Pct	W	L	Pct
Old Dominion ⊕	-	-	-	25	5	.833
James Madison	-	-	-	18	8	.692
Navy	-	-	-	14	13	.519
Richmond	-	-	-	13	14	.481
Baltimore	-	-	-	12	15	.444
William and Mary	-	-	-	12	15	.444
Saint Francis (PA)	-	-	-	12	16	.429
Towson	-	-	-	9	17	.346
Catholic	-	-	-	8	19	.296
Robert Morris	-	-	-	7	19	.269
George Mason	-	-	-	5	21	.192

Note: Conference did not play a formal schedule
Tournament: **Old Dominion d. Navy 62-51 (OT)**

EAA

	Conference			Overall		
	W	L	Pct	W	L	Pct
Villanova ⊕	7	3	.700	23	8	.742
Duquesne □	7	3	.700	18	10	.643
Rutgers	7	3	.700	14	14	.500
St. Bonaventure	5	5	.500	16	11	.593
Pittsburgh □	5	5	.500	17	12	.586
George Washington	5	5	.500	15	11	.577
West Virginia	4	6	.400	15	14	.517
Massachusetts	0	10	.000	2	24	.077

Tournament: **Villanova d. West Virginia 74-62**
Tournament MVP: **Lowes Moore**, West Virginia

Ivy

	Conference			Overall		
	W	L	Pct	W	L	Pct
Penn ⊕	11	3	.786	17	12	.586
Princeton	11	3	.786	15	15	.500
Brown	9	5	.643	12	14	.462
Yale	8	6	.571	16	10	.615
Harvard	6	8	.429	11	15	.423
Columbia	5	9	.357	10	16	.385
Dartmouth	3	11	.214	6	20	.231
Cornell	3	11	.214	5	19	.208

Playoff: **Penn d. Princeton 50-49**

Metro

	Conference			Overall		
	W	L	Pct	W	L	Pct
Louisville ⊕	12	0	1.000	33	3	.917
Virginia Tech ○	8	4	.667	21	8	.724
Florida State ○	7	5	.583	22	9	.710
Memphis	5	7	.417	13	14	.481
Saint Louis	4	8	.333	12	15	.444
Cincinnati	3	9	.250	13	15	.464
Tulane	3	9	.250	10	17	.370

Tournament: **Louisville d. Florida State 81-72**
Tournament MVP: **Darrell Griffith**, Louisville

Mid-American

	Conference			Overall		
	W	L	Pct	W	L	Pct
Toledo ⊕	14	2	.875	23	6	.793
Bowling Green □	11	5	.688	20	10	.667
Northern Illinois	9	7	.563	16	13	.552
Kent State	7	9	.438	16	11	.593
Ball State	7	9	.438	14	15	.483
Western Michigan	7	9	.438	12	14	.462
Eastern Michigan	7	9	.438	11	16	.407
Miami (OH)	7	9	.438	9	18	.333
Central Michigan	6	10	.375	12	13	.480
Ohio	5	11	.313	8	18	.308

Tournament: **Toledo d. Bowling Green 85-70**
Tournament MVP: **Jim Swaney**, Toledo

MEAC

	Conference			Overall		
	W	L	Pct	W	L	Pct
Howard	-	-	-	21	7	.750
UMES	-	-	-	16	9	.640
Delaware State	-	-	-	15	12	.556
South Carolina State	-	-	-	12	17	.414
Morgan State	-	-	-	7	16	.304
NC Central	-	-	-	8	18	.308
NC A&T	-	-	-	8	19	.296
Florida A&M	-	-	-	7	22	.241

Note: Conference was transitioning to Division I; conference records not recognized by NCAA
Tournament: **Howard d. South Carolina St. 75-69**
Tournament MOP: **Larry Spriggs**, Howard

Conference Standings Continue →

⊕ Automatic NCAA Tournament bid ○ At-large NCAA Tournament bid □ NIT appearance ⊗ Team record doesn't reflect games forfeited or vacated. For adjusted record, see p. 521.

MIDWESTERN CITY

	Conference W	L	PCT	Overall W	L	PCT
Loyola-Chicago□	5	0	1.000	19	10	.655
Oral Roberts	4	1	.800	18	10	.643
Oklahoma City	3	2	.600	13	15	.464
Butler	2	3	.400	12	15	.444
Evansville	1	4	.200	18	10	.643
Xavier	0	5	.000	8	18	.308

Tournament: **Oral Roberts d. Loyola-Chicago 103-93**
Tournament MVP: **Calvin Garrett**, Oral Roberts

MISSOURI VALLEY

	Conference W	L	PCT	Overall W	L	PCT
Bradley⊛	13	3	.813	23	10	.697
West Texas A&M□	9	7	.563	19	11	.633
Wichita State□	9	7	.563	17	12	.586
Creighton	9	7	.563	16	12	.571
New Mexico State	8	8	.500	17	10	.630
Indiana State	8	8	.500	16	11	.593
Drake	6	10	.375	15	12	.556
Southern Illinois	5	11	.313	9	17	.346
Tulsa	5	11	.313	8	19	.296

Tournament: **Bradley d. West Texas A&M 62-59**

OHIO VALLEY

	Conference W	L	PCT	Overall W	L	PCT
Murray State□	10	2	.833	23	8	.742
Western Kentucky⊛	10	2	.833	21	8	.724
Eastern Kentucky	7	5	.583	15	12	.556
Morehead State	7	5	.583	15	12	.556
Middle Tenn. State	5	7	.417	13	13	.500
Austin Peay	2	10	.167	8	18	.308
Tennessee Tech	1	11	.083	5	21	.192

Tournament: **Western Kentucky d. Murray State 54-51**
Tournament MVP: **Craig McCormick**, Western Kentucky

PCAA

	Conference W	L	PCT	Overall W	L	PCT
Utah State○	11	2	.846	18	9	.667
Long Beach State□	11	3	.786	22	12	.647
Fresno State	8	4	.667	17	7	.708
San Jose State⊛	7	6	.538	17	12	.586
Pacific	7	7	.500	15	16	.484
UC Santa Barbara	5	9	.357	11	16	.407
Cal State Fullerton	4	10	.286	10	17	.370
UC Irvine	1	13	.071	9	18	.333

Tournament: **San Jose State d. Long Beach State 57-55**
Tournament MVP: **Wally Rank**, San Jose State

PAC-10

	Conference W	L	PCT	Overall W	L	PCT
Oregon State⊛⊗	16	2	.889	26	4	.867
Arizona State○	15	3	.833	22	7	.759
Washington State○	14	4	.778	22	6	.786
UCLA○⊗	12	6	.667	22	10	.686
Washington□	9	9	.500	18	10	.643
Arizona	6	12	.333	12	15	.444
Southern California	5	13	.278	12	15	.444
Oregon	5	13	.278	10	17	.370
Stanford	5	13	.278	7	19	.269
California	3	15	.167	8	19	.296

SEC

	Conference W	L	PCT	Overall W	L	PCT
Kentucky○	15	3	.833	29	6	.829
LSU⊛	14	4	.778	26	6	.813
Tennessee○	12	6	.667	18	11	.621
Alabama□	12	6	.667	18	12	.600
Mississippi□	9	9	.500	17	13	.567
Georgia	7	11	.389	14	13	.519
Vanderbilt	7	11	.389	13	13	.500
Mississippi State	7	11	.389	13	14	.481
Auburn	5	13	.278	10	18	.357
Florida	2	16	.111	7	21	.250

Tournament: **LSU d. Kentucky 80-78**
Tournament MVP: **DeWayne Scales**, LSU

SOUTHERN

	Conference W	L	PCT	Overall W	L	PCT
Furman⊛	14	1	.933	23	7	.767
Marshall	10	6	.625	17	12	.586
Western Carolina	9	7	.563	17	10	.630
East Tennessee St.	8	7	.533	15	13	.536
Chattanooga	7	9	.438	13	14	.481
The Citadel	6	10	.375	14	13	.519
Appalachian State	6	10	.375	12	16	.429
VMI	6	10	.375	11	16	.407
Davidson	4	11	.267	8	18	.308

Tournament: **Furman d. Marshall 80-62**
Tournament MOP: **Jonathan Moore**, Furman

SOUTHLAND

	Conference W	L	PCT	Overall W	L	PCT
Lamar⊛	8	2	.800	22	11	.667
UL-Lafayette□	5	5	.500	21	9	.700
Arkansas State	5	5	.500	15	12	.556
McNeese State	5	5	.500	15	12	.556
Louisiana Tech	4	6	.400	17	10	.630
Texas-Arlington	3	7	.300	14	13	.519

SOUTHWEST

	Conference W	L	PCT	Overall W	L	PCT
Texas A&M⊛	14	2	.875	26	8	.765
Arkansas○	13	3	.813	21	8	.724
Texas□	10	6	.625	19	11	.633
Texas Tech	8	8	.500	16	13	.552
Houston	8	8	.500	14	14	.500
SMU	7	9	.438	16	12	.571
Baylor	6	10	.375	11	16	.407
Rice	4	12	.250	7	19	.269
TCU	2	14	.125	7	19	.269

Tournament: **Texas A&M d. Arkansas 52-50**
Tournament MVP: **David Britton**, Texas A&M

SWAC

	Conference W	L	PCT	Overall W	L	PCT
Alcorn State○	12	0	1.000	28	2	.933
Grambling□	8	4	.667	22	8	.733
Jackson State	7	5	.583	15	14	.517
Southern U.	6	6	.500	14	15	.483
Texas Southern	5	7	.417	9	17	.346
Prairie View A&M	2	10	.167	10	18	.357
Miss. Valley State	2	10	.167	3	24	.111

Tournament: **Alcorn State d. Grambling 83-61**
Tournament MVP: **Larry Smith**, Alcorn State

SUN BELT

	Conference W	L	PCT	Overall W	L	PCT
South Alabama○	12	2	.857	23	6	.793
Jacksonville□	10	4	.714	20	9	.690
UAB□	10	4	.714	18	12	.600
Charlotte	9	5	.643	15	12	.556
VCU⊛	8	6	.571	18	12	.600
Georgia State	4	10	.286	6	21	.222
New Orleans	2	12	.143	5	21	.192
South Florida	1	13	.071	6	21	.222

Tournament: **VCU d. UAB 105-88**
Tournament MVP: **Edmund Sherod**, VCU

TAAC

	Conference W	L	PCT	Overall W	L	PCT
UL-Monroe	6	0	1.000	18	10	.643
Texas-Pan American	4	2	.667	19	9	.679
Mercer	3	3	.500	16	12	.571
Centenary	3	3	.500	15	14	.517
Samford	3	3	.500	8	19	.296
Houston Baptist	2	4	.333	14	13	.519
Hardin-Simmons	0	6	.000	5	21	.192
Arkansas-Little Rock*	-	-	-	16	10	.615
Northwestern St. (LA)*	-	-	-	5	20	.200
Georgia Southern*	-	-	-	5	22	.185

* Not eligible for conference play
Tournament: **Centenary d. UL-Monroe 79-77**
Tournament MVP: **George Lett**, Centenary

WCAC

	Conference W	L	PCT	Overall W	L	PCT
San Francisco	11	5	.688	22	7	.759
Loyola Marymount⊛⊗	10	6	.625	14	14	.500
Saint Mary's (CA)⊗	9	7	.563	13	14	.481
Gonzaga⊗	8	8	.500	14	13	.519
Santa Clara⊗	8	8	.500	15	12	.556
Pepperdine□	9	7	.563	17	11	.607
Portland	9	7	.563	17	11	.607
Seattle⊗	8	8	.500	12	15	.444
San Diego⊗	1	15	.062	5	20	.200

WAC

	Conference W	L	PCT	Overall W	L	PCT
BYU⊛	13	1	.929	24	5	.828
UTEP□	10	4	.714	20	8	.714
Utah	10	4	.714	18	10	.643
Wyoming	8	6	.571	18	10	.643
Colorado State	5	9	.357	10	17	.370
Hawaii	4	10	.286	13	14	.481
New Mexico	3	11	.214	7	21	.250
San Diego State	3	11	.214	6	21	.222
Air Force	-	-	-	8	17	.320

INDEPENDENTS

	Overall W	L	PCT
DePaul○	26	2	.929
Notre Dame○	22	6	.786
Tennessee State	19	7	.731
UNLV□	23	9	.719
Cleveland State	18	8	.692
Illinois State□	20	9	.690
Marquette○	18	9	.667
UNC Wilmington	19	10	.655
Penn State□	18	10	.643
Southern Miss	17	10	.630
South Carolina	16	11	.593
Campbell	15	12	.556
East Carolina	15	12	.556
Stetson	15	12	.556
Detroit	14	13	.519
Dayton	13	14	.481
North Texas	13	14	.481
Wisconsin-Milwaukee	9	17	.346
Valparaiso	8	18	.308
Portland State	5	21	.192
Charleston Southern	2	23	.080

INDIVIDUAL LEADERS—SEASON

Scoring

		CL	POS	G	FG	FT	PTS	PPG
1	**Tony Murphy**, Southern U.	SR	G	29	377	178	932	**32.1**
2	**Lewis Lloyd**, Drake	JR	F	27	324	167	815	**30.2**
3	**Harry Kelly**, Texas Southern	FR	F	26	313	127	753	**29.0**
4	**Kenny Page**, New Mexico	SO	G	28	314	156	784	**28.0**
5	**James Tillman**, Eastern Kentucky	SR	F	27	288	158	734	**27.2**
6	**Earl Belcher**, St. Bonaventure	JR	G	24	241	164	646	**26.9**
7	**Russell Bowers**, American	JR	F	27	288	150	726	**26.9**
8	**Carl Nicks**, Indiana State	SR	G	27	267	189	723	**26.8**
9	**Mark Aguirre**, DePaul	SO	F	28	281	187	749	**26.8**
10	**Andrew Toney**, UL-Lafayette	SR	G	24	239	149	627	**26.1**

Field Goal Pct

		CL	POS	G	FG	FGA	PCT
1	**Steve Johnson**, Oregon State	JR	F/C	30	211	297	**71.0**
2	**Ron Charles**, Michigan State	SR	F	27	169	250	**67.6**
3	**Cherokee Rhone**, Centenary	SO	C	28	193	290	**66.6**
4	**Roosevelt Bouie**, Syracuse	SR	C	30	189	289	**65.4**
5	**Murray Brown**, Florida State	SR	F	31	230	356	**64.6**

Minimum: 5 made per game

Free Throw Pct

		CL	POS	G	FT	FTA	PCT
1	**Brian Magid**, George Washington	SR	G	26	79	85	**92.9**
2	**Randy Nesbit**, The Citadel	SR	G	27	74	80	**92.5**
3	**Kyle Macy**, Kentucky	SR	G	35	104	114	**91.2**
4	**Greg Manning**, Maryland	JR	G	30	79	87	**90.8**
5	**Eddie White**, Gonzaga	SR	G	26	116	130	**89.2**

Minimum: 2.5 made per game

Rebounds Per Game

		CL	POS	G	REB	RPG
1	**Larry Smith**, Alcorn State	SR	F/C	26	392	**15.1**
2	**Lewis Lloyd**, Drake	JR	F	27	406	**15.0**
3	**Rickey Brown**, Mississippi State	SR	F/C	27	389	**14.4**
4	**Monti Davis**, Tennessee State	SR	F	26	347	**13.3**
5	**Gary Hooker**, Murray State	SR	F	29	356	**12.3**
6	**Trent Grooms**, Kent State	SR	F	26	319	**12.3**
7	**Joe Schoen**, Saint Francis (PA)	JR	F	25	303	**12.1**
8	**Kenneth Green**, Texas-Pan American	JR	F	28	337	**12.0**
9	**Jeff Ruland**, Iona	JR	C	34	407	**12.0**
10	**Antonio Martin**, Oral Roberts	SR	F	28	334	**11.9**

INDIVIDUAL LEADERS—GAME

Points

	CL	POS	OPP	DATE	PTS
1 **Michael Brooks**, La Salle	SR	F	BYU	D15	**51**
2 **Tony Murphy**, Southern U.	SR	G	Mississippi Valley St.	J21	**50**
Mike Olliver, Lamar	JR	G	Portland State	J12	**50**
4 **Jim McCloskey**, Loyola Marymount	JR	F	Saint Mary's (CA)	J4	**49**
5 **Harry Kelly**, Texas Southern	FR	F	Paul Quinn	D10	**48**

Rebounds

	CL	POS	OPP	DATE	REB
1 **Guy Charles**, Northwestern St. (LA)	SR	F	Nicholls State	F27	**25**
2 **Monti Davis**, Tennessee State	SR	F	NC Central	D1	**24**
Sidney Green, UNLV	FR	F/C	Nevada	D7	**24**
4 **Rickey Brown**, Mississippi State	SR	F/C	Vanderbilt	D6	**23**
Monti Davis, Tennessee State	SR	F	Towson	F23	**23**
Bryant Johnson, Miss. Valley State	SR	F	Jackson State	F23	**23**
John Lombardo, St. Francis (NY)	SR	F/C	Canisius	D8	**23**
Larry Smith, Alcorn State	SR	F/C	Mississippi Valley St.	J7	**23**
Alan Taylor, BYU	SR	F	San Diego State	M1	**23**

TEAM LEADERS—SEASON

Win-Loss Pct

	W	L	PCT
1 **Alcorn State**	28	2	**.933**
2 **DePaul**	26	2	**.929**
3 **Louisville**	33	3	**.917**
4 **Weber State**	26	3	**.897**
5 **Oregon State** ⊗	26	4	**.867**
Syracuse	26	4	**.867**

Scoring Offense

	G	W-L	PTS	PPG
1 **Alcorn State**	30	28-2	2,729	**91.0**
2 **Drake**	27	15-12	2,398	**88.8**
3 **Oral Roberts**	28	18-10	2,447	**87.4**
4 **Utah State**	27	18-9	2,329	**86.3**
5 **Syracuse**	30	26-4	2,575	**85.8**

Scoring Margin

	G	W-L	PPG	OPP PPG	MAR
1 **Alcorn State**	30	28-2	91.0	73.6	**17.4**
2 **Syracuse**	30	26-4	85.8	70.4	**15.4**
3 **South Alabama**	29	23-6	76.4	64.5	**11.9**
Weber State	29	26-3	75.2	63.3	**11.9**
5 **Georgetown**	32	26-6	80.1	68.8	**11.3**

Field Goal Pct

	G	W-L	FG	FGA	PCT
1 **Missouri**	31	25-6	936	1,635	**57.2**
2 **Maryland**	31	24-7	985	1,789	**55.1**
3 **Oregon State**	30	26-4	943	1,732	**54.4**
4 **Syracuse**	30	26-4	1025	1,902	**53.9**
5 **Toledo**	29	23-6	923	1,724	**53.5**

Free Throw Pct

	G	W-L	FT	FTA	PCT
1 **Oral Roberts**	28	18-10	481	610	**78.9**
2 **Southern U.**	29	14-15	417	537	**77.7**
3 **St. Bonaventure**	27	16-11	467	610	**76.6**
4 **Utah State**	27	18-9	605	794	**76.2**
5 **Kentucky**	35	29-6	609	802	**75.9**

Rebound Margin

	G	W-L	RPG	OPP RPG	MAR
1 **Alcorn State**	30	28-2	49.2	33.8	**15.4**
2 **Tennessee State**	26	19-7	46.5	34.3	**12.2**
3 **Wyoming**	28	18-10	41.0	30.8	**10.2**
4 **Northeastern**	27	19-8	39.2	31.2	**8.0**
5 **South Alabama**	29	23-6	39.3	31.7	**7.6**

Scoring Defense

	G	W-L	OPP PTS	OPP PPG
1 **Saint Peter's**	31	22-9	1,563	**50.4**
2 **Princeton**	30	15-15	1,654	**55.1**
3 **Penn State**	28	18-10	1,600	**57.1**
4 **Wyoming**	28	18-10	1,644	**58.7**
5 **Fresno State**	24	17-7	1,412	**58.8**

Field Goal Pct Defense

	G	W-L	OPP FG	OPP FGA	OPP PCT
1 **Penn State**	28	18-10	543	1,309	**41.5**
2 **Saint Peter's**	31	22-9	590	1,396	**42.3**
3 **UNC Wilmington**	29	19-10	719	1,685	**42.7**
4 **Wichita State**	29	17-12	776	1,818	**42.7**
5 **Old Dominion**	30	25-5	775	1,814	**42.7**

CONSENSUS ALL-AMERICAS

First Team

PLAYER	CL	POS	HT	SCHOOL	RPG	PPG
Mark Aguirre	SO	F	6-7	DePaul	7.7	26.8
Michael Brooks	SR	F	6-7	La Salle	11.5	24.1
Joe Barry Carroll	SR	C	7-1	Purdue	9.2	22.3
Darrell Griffith	SR	G	6-4	Louisville	4.8	22.9
Kyle Macy	SR	G	6-3	Kentucky	2.4	15.4

Second Team

PLAYER	CL	POS	HT	SCHOOL	RPG	PPG
Mike Gminski	SR	C	6-11	Duke	10.9	21.3
Albert King	JR	F	6-6	Maryland	6.7	21.7
Mike O'Koren	SR	F	6-8	North Carolina	7.4	14.7
Kelvin Ransey	SR	G	6-1	Ohio State	4.1	16.2
Sam Worthen	SR	G	6-5	Marquette	4.4	16.9

Selectors: AP, NABC, UPI, USBWA

AWARD WINNERS

Player of the Year

PLAYER	CL	POS	HT	SCHOOL	AWARDS
Mark Aguirre	SO	F	6-7	DePaul	Naismith, AP, UPI, USBWA, Rupp
Darrell Griffith	SR	G	6-4	Louisville	Wooden
Michael Brooks	SR	F	6-7	La Salle	NABC
Jim Sweeney	SR	G	6-0	Boston College	Frances Pomeroy Naismith*

* For the most outstanding senior player who is 6 feet or under

Coach of the Year

COACH	SCHOOL	REC	AWARDS
Ray Meyer	DePaul	26-2	AP, UPI, USBWA
Lute Olson	Iowa	23-10	NABC, Sporting News

Bob Gibbons' Top High School Senior Recruits

PLAYER	POS	HT	HIGH SCHOOL	A-A TEAMS	COLLEGE	CAREER NOTES
1 **Sam Perkins**	C	6-9	Shaker HS, Latham, NY	McD, P	North Carolina	NCAA title, '82; No. 4 pick, '84 NBA draft (Mavs); All-Rookie team, '85; 11.9 ppg (17 seasons)
2 **Russell Cross**	C	6-11	Hugh Manley HS, Chicago	McD, P	Purdue	16.4 ppg, 6.7 rpg (3 seasons); No. 6 pick, '83 NBA draft (Warriors); 3.7 ppg (1 season)
3 **Derek Harper**	PG	6-3	North Shore HS, West Palm Beach, FL	McD, P	Illinois	2nd team All-America, '83; No. 11 pick, '83 NBA draft (Mavs); 13.3 ppg (16 seasons)
4 **Clyde Drexler**	G/F	6-7	Ross Sterling HS, Houston		Houston	Final Four, '82 and '83; No. 14 pick, '83 NBA draft (Blazers); 10-time All-Star; Olympic gold medal, '92; Basketball HOF, '04
5 **Earl Jones**	C	6-11	Spingarn HS, Washington, DC	McD, P	District of Columbia	23.9 ppg (4 seasons); No. 23 pick, '84 NBA draft (Lakers); played in 14 NBA games
6 **Mel Turpin**	C	6-11	Fork Union (VA) Military Academy		Kentucky	12.3 ppg, 5.9 rpg (4 seasons); No. 6 pick, '84 NBA draft (Bullets); 8.5 ppg (5 seasons)
7 **Vern Fleming**	2G	6-6	Mater Christi HS, Astoria, NY	P	Georgia	19.8 ppg, '84; Olympic gold medal, '84; No. 18 pick, '84 NBA draft (Pacers); 11.3 ppg (12 seasons)
8 **Glenn "Doc" Rivers**	PG	6-3	Proviso East HS, Maywood, IL	McD, P	Marquette	13.9 ppg (3 seasons); 2nd-round pick, '83 NBA draft (Hawks); 10.9 ppg (12 seasons); All-Star, '88; NBA title as coach, '08
9 **Tim McCormick**	C	6-10	Clarkston (MI) HS	McD, P	Michigan	NIT MVP, '84; No. 12 pick, '84 NBA draft (Cavs); 8.3 ppg (8 seasons)
10 **Kenny Fields**	PF	6-8	Verbum Dei HS, Los Angeles	P	UCLA	15.0 ppg, 6.1 rpg (4 seasons); No. 21 pick, '84 NBA draft (Bucks); 6.2 ppg (4 seasons)
11 **Gary Springer**	PF	6-7	Benjamin Franklin HS, New York	McD, P	Iona	3-time first team All-MAAC; Iona's 3rd leading scorer all-time; 6th-round pick, '84 NBA draft (76ers)
12 **Lancaster Gordon**	2G	6-3	Jim Hill HS, Jackson, MS		Louisville	12.0 ppg (4 seasons); No. 8 pick, '84 NBA draft (Clippers); 5.6 ppg (4 seasons)
13 **Charles Sitton**	PF	6-8	McMinnville (OH) HS	McD, P	Oregon State	13.3 ppg (4 seasons); 2nd-round pick, '84 draft (Mavs); 2.1 ppg (1 season)
14 **James Banks**	SF	6-6	Hoke Smith HS, Atlanta	McD, P	Georgia	Final Four, '83; 1,430 points, 654 rebounds at UGA; 3rd-round pick, '84 NBA draft (76ers)
15 **Ralph Jackson**	PG	6-3	Inglewood (CA) HS	McD, P	UCLA	8.4 ppg, 4.7 apg (3 seasons); 4th-round pick, '84 NBA draft (Pacers); 1 NBA game
16 **Barry Spencer**	SF	6-7	Catholic Central HS, Detroit	McD, P	Notre Dame	4 years with Fighting Irish as starting forward; undrafted
17 **Leonard Mitchell**	F	6-7	St. Martinsville (LA) HS	P	LSU	First team All-SEC, '82; At LSU, 12.8 ppg, 7.8 rpg (4 seasons); 3rd-round pick, '84 NBA draft (Cavs)
18 **Jim Master**	2G	6-4	Paul Harding HS, Fort Wayne, IN	McD, P	Kentucky	3rd team All-SEC, '82; Led SEC in FG% (89.6), '82; 6th-round pick, '84 draft (Hawks)
19 **John Stockton**	PG	6-1	Gonzaga Prep, Spokane, WA		Gonzaga	20.9 ppg, 7.2 apg in '84; No. 16 pick, '84 NBA draft (Jazz); NBA's all-time leader in assists, steals; 2 Olympic gold medals, '92, '96
20 **Joe Kleine**	C	6-11	Slater (MO) HS	P	Notre Dame/ Arkansas	No. 6 pick, '85 NBA draft (Kings); 4.8 ppg (15 seasons); Olympic gold medal, '84

Other Standouts

PLAYER	POS	HT	HIGH SCHOOL	A-A TEAMS	COLLEGE	CAREER NOTES
27 **Terence Stansbury**	2G	6-5	Newark (DE) HS		Temple	Temple's 2nd-leading scorer all-time; No. 15 pick, '84 NBA draft (Mavs); 6.3 ppg (3 seasons)
29 **Otis Thorpe**	C	6-9	Lake Worth (FL) HS		Providence	14.4 ppg, 8.0 rpg (4 seasons); No. 9 pick, '84 NBA draft (Kings); 14.0 ppg, 8.2 rpg (17 seasons); NBA title, '94
39 **Alvin Robertson**	2G	6-3	Barberton (OH) HS		Crowder JC/ Arkansas	12.5 ppg (4 seasons); No. 7 pick, '84 NBA draft (Spurs); 14.0 ppg (9 seasons); NBA's Most Improved Player, Defensive POY, '86; 4-time All-Star

Abbreviations: McD=McDonald's; P=Parade

Poll Progression

Preseason Poll

AP	UPI	SCHOOL
1	1	Indiana
2	5	Kentucky
3	6	Duke
4	2	Ohio State
5	3	Notre Dame
6	4	North Carolina
7	8	LSU
8	7	UCLA
9	9	DePaul
10	14	Louisville
11	11	Purdue
12	12	Syracuse
13	9	Virginia
14	13	Texas A&M
15	17	BYU
16	15	St. John's
17	16	Oregon State
18	19	Marquette
19	—	Georgetown
20	—	Kansas
—	18	Iowa
—	20	UNLV

Week of Dec 4

AP	UPI	SCHOOL	AP↓↑
1	1	**Indiana** (1-0)	
2	2	**Duke** (3-0)	↑1
3	3	**Ohio State** (1-0)	↑1
4	4	**Notre Dame** (1-0)	↑1
5	6	**Kentucky** (3-1)	↓3
6	5	**LSU** (1-0)	↑1
7	8	**UCLA** (2-0)	↑1
8	7	**North Carolina** (1-1)	↓2
9	11	**St. John's** (2-0)	↑7
10	10	**DePaul** (0-0)	↓1
11	12	**Syracuse** (1-0)	↑1
12	9	**Purdue** (1-0)	↓1
13	13	**Virginia** (2-0)	
14	15	**Louisville** (1-0)	↓4
15	14	**Oregon State** (2-0)	↑2
16	16	**Marquette** (1-0)	↑2
17	16	**Georgetown** (1-0)	↑2
18	18	**BYU** (1-1)	↓3
19	18	**Kansas** (1-0)	↑1
20	—	**Iowa** (1-0)	⤴
—	20	**Arkansas** (1-0)	

Week of Dec 11

AP	UPI	SCHOOL	AP↓↑
1	1	**Indiana** (3-0)	
2	2	**Duke** (5-0)	
3	3	**Ohio State** (3-0)	
4	4	**Notre Dame** (4-0)	
5	5	**Kentucky** (5-1)	
6	7	**LSU** (3-0)	
7	6	**UCLA** (3-0)	
8	8	**North Carolina** (3-1)	
9	9	**Purdue** (4-0)	↑3
10	11	**Syracuse** (4-0)	↑1
11	10	**DePaul** (2-0)	↓1
12	13	**Louisville** (3-0) Ⓐ	↑2
13	17	**Virginia** (4-0)	
14	12	**Oregon State** (5-0) Ⓑ	↑1
15	15	**St. John's** (3-1)	↓6
16	16	**Georgetown** (2-0)	↑1
17	14	**Iowa** (4-0)	↑3
18	18	**BYU** (3-1)	
19	—	**Missouri** (6-0)	⤴
20	19	**Arkansas** (4-0)	⤴
—	20	**Southern California** (4-0)	

Week of Dec 18

AP	UPI	SCHOOL	AP↓↑
1	1	**Duke** (6-0)	
2	2	**Ohio State** (5-0)	
3	3	**Kentucky** (7-1)	
4	5	**Notre Dame** (6-0)	
5	4	**Indiana** (4-1)	↓
6	7	**DePaul** (4-0)	↑
7	6	**LSU** (4-0)	↓
8	9	**North Carolina** (4-1)	
9	7	**Purdue** (5-0)	
10	10	**Syracuse** (5-0)	
11	11	**Louisville** (5-0)	↑
12	14	**Virginia** (5-0)	↑
13	13	**Iowa** (6-0)	↑
14	12	**UCLA** (3-2)	↓
15	15	**St. John's** (5-1)	
16	16	**Missouri** (8-0)	↑
17	17	**Georgetown** (4-1)	↓1
18	18	**BYU** (6-1)	
19	20	**Oregon State** (6-1)	↓5
20	19	**Arkansas** (5-0)	

Week of Dec 26

AP	UPI	SCHOOL	AP↓↑
1	1	**Duke** (8-0)	
2	2	**Kentucky** (10-1)	↑1
3	3	**Notre Dame** (7-0)	↑1
4	5	**DePaul** (7-0)	↑2
5	6	**LSU** (6-0)	↑2
6	4	**North Carolina** (5-1)	↑2
7	7	**Ohio State** (6-1)	↓5
8	9	**Purdue** (6-1)	↑1
9	11	**Syracuse** (6-0)	↑1
10	8	**Indiana** (5-2)	↓5
11	10	**Iowa** (8-0)	↑2
12	12	**Louisville** (6-1)	↓1
13	14	**Missouri** (10-0)	↑3
14	18	**Virginia** (7-1)	↓2
15	16	**St. John's** (6-1)	
16	15	**UCLA** (5-2)	↓2
17	13	**Georgetown** (7-1)	
18	17	**Oregon State** (8-1)	↑1
19	19	**Arkansas** (6-1)	↑1
20	20	**BYU** (7-2)	↓2

Week of Jan 2

AP	UPI	SCHOOL	AP↓↑
1	1	**Duke** (10-0)	
2	2	**Kentucky** (11-1)	
3	3	**DePaul** (8-0)	↑1
4	6	**LSU** (8-0)	↑1
5	5	**Ohio State** (7-1)	↑2
6	4	**North Carolina** (5-1)	
7	8	**Notre Dame** (7-1)	↓4
8	7	**Purdue** (7-1)	
9	10	**Syracuse** (8-0)	
10	9	**Iowa** (9-0)	↑1
11	11	**Indiana** (7-2)	↓1
12	14	**Missouri** (10-0)	↑1
13	17	**Virginia** (9-1)	↑1
14	12	**Oregon State** (11-1)	↑4
15	15	**Louisville** (8-2)	↓3
16	16	**UCLA** (7-2)	
17	13	**St. John's** (8-1)	↓2
18	20	**Georgetown** (8-2)	↓1
19	—	**BYU** (9-3)	↑1
20	19	**Illinois** (10-2)	⤴
—	18	**Weber State** (11-1)	

Week of Jan 8

AP	UPI	SCHOOL	AP↓↑
1	1	**Duke** (12-0)	
2	2	**DePaul** (11-0)	↑1
3	3	**Ohio State** (9-1)	↑2
4	4	**Kentucky** (12-2)	↓2
5	5	**Syracuse** (11-0)	↑4
6	6	**LSU** (9-2)	↓2
7	8	**Notre Dame** (7-1)	
8	10	**Virginia** (12-1)	↑5
9	7	**Oregon State** (13-1)	↑5
10	9	**Purdue** (8-2)	↓2
11	12	**Louisville** (10-2)	↑4
12	11	**Iowa** (10-1)	↓2
13	14	**Missouri** (11-1)	↓1
14	13	**St. John's** (9-1)	↑3
15	15	**North Carolina** (6-3)	↓9
16	19	**UCLA** (8-3) Ⓒ	
17	—	**BYU** (11-3)	↑2
18	16	**Clemson** (10-1)	⤴
19	17	**Indiana** (7-4)	↓8
20	—	**Georgetown** (9-3)	↓2
—	18	**Tennessee** (9-1)	
—	20	**Weber State** (12-1)	

Week of Jan 15

AP	UPI	SCHOOL	AP↓↑
1	1	**DePaul** (12-0)	↑1
2	2	**Ohio State** (11-1)	↑1
3	3	**Syracuse** (14-0)	↑2
4	4	**Oregon State** (15-1)	↑5
5	5	**Duke** (12-2)	↓4
6	9	**Kentucky** (13-3)	↓2
7	6	**Louisville** (12-2)	↑4
8	7	**Notre Dame** (9-2)	↓1
9	10	**North Carolina** (8-3)	↑6
10	8	**St. John's** (11-1)	↑4
11	11	**Purdue** (10-3)	↓1
12	15	**Virginia** (12-2)	↓4
13	12	**Iowa** (11-2)	↓1
14	17	**LSU** (9-3)	↓8
15	13	**Missouri** (12-2)	↓2
16	16	**NC State** (11-1)	⤴
17	14	**Clemson** (11-2)	↑1
18	20	**BYU** (12-3)	↓1
19	—	**Indiana** (9-4)	
20	18	**Tennessee** (11-3)	⤴
—	19	**Weber State** (15-1)	

Week of Jan 22

AP	UPI	SCHOOL	AP↓↑
1	1	**DePaul** (15-0)	
2	2	**Oregon State** (17-1)	↑2
3	3	**Duke** (15-2)	↑2
4	4	**Ohio State** (12-2)	↓2
5	9	**Kentucky** (15-3)	↑1
6	5	**Syracuse** (15-1)	↓3
7	6	**Louisville** (13-2)	
8	8	**Notre Dame** (11-2)	
9	7	**St. John's** (14-1)	↑1
10	10	**Missouri** (14-2)	↑5
11	11	**LSU** (11-4)	↑3
12	13	**Clemson** (12-3)	↑5
13	12	**North Carolina** (10-4)	↓4
14	15	**Purdue** (11-4)	↓3
15	14	**Maryland** (13-2)	⤴
16	16	**Indiana** (11-4)	↑3
17	19	**Virginia** (13-2)	↓5
18	16	**Weber State** (17-1)	⤴
19	18	**Tennessee** (12-4)	↑1
20	—	**BYU** (13-4)	↓2
—	20	**Arizona State** (12-4)	

Week of Jan 29

AP	UPI	SCHOOL	AP↓↑
1	1	**DePaul** (17-0)	
2	2	**Oregon State** (18-1)	
3	6	**Kentucky** (17-3)	↑2
4	3	**Syracuse** (17-1)	↑2
5	7	**Duke** (16-3)	↓2
6	4	**Ohio State** (14-3)	↓2
7	5	**Louisville** (16-2)	
8	9	**Notre Dame** (13-2)	
9	8	**St. John's** (17-1)	
10	10	**LSU** (13-4)	↑1
11	11	**North Carolina** (12-4)	↑2
12	13	**Maryland** (14-3)	↑3
13	14	**Virginia** (16-4)	↑4
14	12	**Missouri** (15-3)	↓4
15	15	**Weber State** (18-1)	↑3
16	17	**Clemson** (13-4)	↓4
17	20	**Purdue** (12-5)	↓3
18	16	**Indiana** (12-5)	↓2
19	18	**BYU** (15-4)	↑1
20	19	**Kansas State** (15-3)	⤴

Week of Feb 5

AP	UPI	SCHOOL	AP↓↑
1	1	**DePaul** (19-0)	
2	2	**Syracuse** (20-1)	↑2
3	3	**Louisville** (19-2)	↑4
4	4	**Oregon State** (20-2)	↓2
5	6	**Kentucky** (19-4)	↓2
6	7	**LSU** (16-4)	↑4
7	5	**Maryland** (16-3)	↑5
8	8	**St. John's** (19-2)	↑1
9	9	**Notre Dame** (15-3)	↓1
10	12	**Duke** (17-4)	↓5
11	11	**North Carolina** (16-4)	
12	10	**Purdue** (14-5)	↑5
13	13	**Ohio State** (14-5)	↓7
14	14	**BYU** (17-4)	↑5
15	15	**Missouri** (16-4)	↓1
16	—	**Clemson** (15-5)	
17	17	**Weber State** (19-2)	↓2
18	—	**Virginia** (16-6)	↓5
19	16	**Arizona State** (16-4)	⤴
20	18	**Indiana** (13-6)	↓2
—	19	**Kansas State** (16-4)	↱
—	20	**Texas A&M** (17-5)	

Week of Feb 12

AP	UPI	SCHOOL	AP↓↑
1	1	**DePaul** (20-0)	
2	2	**Syracuse** (21-1)	
3	3	**Louisville** (21-2)	
4	4	**Oregon State** (22-2)	
5	5	**Kentucky** (21-4)	
6	6	**LSU** (18-4)	
7	8	**St. John's** (21-2)	↑1
8	7	**Maryland** (17-4)	↓1
9	9	**Ohio State** (16-5)	↑4
10	16	**Clemson** (17-5)	↑6
11	11	**North Carolina** (16-5)	
12	13	**Notre Dame** (16-4)	↓3
13	14	**BYU** (18-4)	↑1
14	10	**Missouri** (18-4)	↑1
15	12	**Purdue** (15-6)	↓3
16	19	**Duke** (17-6)	↓6
17	15	**Weber State** (21-2)	
18	18	**Arizona State** (17-5)	↑1
19	17	**Kansas State** (18-4)	⤴
20	—	**Iowa** (16-5)	⤴
—	20	**NC State** (16-5)	

…ek of Feb 19

	UPI	SCHOOL	AP↓↑
[illegible]	1	**DePaul** (23-0)	
[illegible]	3	**Louisville** (25-2)	↑1
[illegible]	4	**Kentucky** (24-4)	↑2
[illegible]	2	**Syracuse** (22-2)	↓2
[illegible]	6	**LSU** (20-4)	↑1
[illegible]	5	**Oregon State** (23-3)	↓2
[illegible]	11	**St. John's** (21-3)	
[illegible]	8	**North Carolina** (19-5)	↑3
[illegible]	7	**Maryland** (19-5)	↓1
[illegible]	10	**Notre Dame** (19-4)	↑2
[illegible]	11	**Ohio State** (17-6)	↓2
12	18	**Clemson** (18-6)	↓2
13	9	**Missouri** (20-4)	↑1
14	14	**BYU** (20-4)	↓1
15	15	**Purdue** (16-7)	
16	16	**Weber State** (23-2)	↑1
17	—	**Duke** (18-7)	↓1
18	17	**Arizona State** (19-5)	
19	13	**Indiana** (16-7) Ⓓ	↥
20	19	**Washington State** (19-4)	↥
—	20	**NC State** (18-6)	

Week of Feb 26

AP	UPI	SCHOOL	AP↓↑
1	1	**DePaul** (25-0)	
2	3	**Kentucky** (26-4)	↑1
3	2	**Syracuse** (24-2)	↑1
4	4	**Louisville** (26-3) Ⓔ	↓2
5	6	**LSU** (21-5)	
6	5	**Oregon State** (24-3)	
7	7	**Maryland** (21-5)	↑2
8	8	**St. John's** (23-3)	↓1
9	11	**Ohio State** (19-6)	↑2
10	9	**North Carolina** (20-6)	↓2
11	9	**Missouri** (22-4)	↑2
12	13	**BYU** (22-4)	↑2
13	12	**Indiana** (18-7)	↑6
14	15	**Notre Dame** (20-5)	↓4
15	14	**Arizona State** (20-5)	↑3
16	16	**Weber State** (24-2)	
17	19	**Clemson** (19-7)	↓5
18	—	**Purdue** (17-8)	↓3
19	17	**NC State** (20-6)	↥
20	20	**Georgetown** (21-5)	↥
—	18	**Texas A&M** (22-7)	
—	20	**Iona** (25-4)	

FINAL POLL

AP	UPI	SCHOOL	AP↓↑
1	1	**DePaul** (26-1) Ⓕ	
2	4	**Louisville** (28-3)	↑2
3	2	**LSU** (24-5)	↑2
4	3	**Kentucky** (28-5)	↓2
5	5	**Oregon State** (26-3)	↑1
6	6	**Syracuse** (25-3)	↓3
7	7	**Indiana** (20-7)	↑6
8	8	**Maryland** (23-6)	↓1
9	11	**Notre Dame** (22-5)	↑5
10	9	**Ohio State** (20-7)	↓1
11	10	**Georgetown** (24-5)	↑9
12	12	**BYU** (24-4)	
13	13	**St. John's** (24-4)	↓5
14	16	**Duke** (22-8)	↥
15	15	**North Carolina** (21-7)	↓5
16	14	**Missouri** (23-5)	↓5
17	17	**Weber State** (26-2)	↓1
18	19	**Arizona State** (21-6)	↓3
19	—	**Iona** (28-4)	↥
20	—	**Purdue** (18-9)	↓2
—	18	**Texas A&M** (24-7)	
—	20	**Kansas State** (21-8)	

Ⓐ Louisville's Darrell Griffith scores 32 points in a 77-75 win over Tennessee in Knoxville, but 6'8" sophomore center Scooter McCray injures a knee and is out for the season. He's replaced in the starting lineup by his little brother, 6'6" freshman Rodney.

Ⓑ Oregon State's Steve Johnson hits all 13 of his field goal attempts in a 104-80 victory over Hawaii-Hilo.

Ⓒ Coach Larry Brown and sharpshooter Kiki Vandeweghe have the Bruins back in the Top 20. After three straight losses—to Southern California, Arizona State and Notre Dame—they will drop out of the polls for good. In the NCAA Tournament, however, they get on a roll that takes them to the Final Four.

Ⓓ Indiana's Mike Woodson returns from back surgery and hits his first three shots in a victory over Iowa. IU will win its last six Big Ten games, capping the run with a 76-73 overtime thriller against Ohio State (and future broadcaster Clark Kellogg).

Ⓔ Louisville's 18-game winning steak ends at Madison Square Garden in New York City when 6'11" Jeff Ruland leads coach Jim Valvano's Iona to a 77-60 victory. It will be the third and final loss of the season for the Cardinals.

Ⓕ DePaul loses in double overtime, 76-74, to Notre Dame. The Blue Demons' Mark Aguirre will be named an All-America and consensus player of the year.

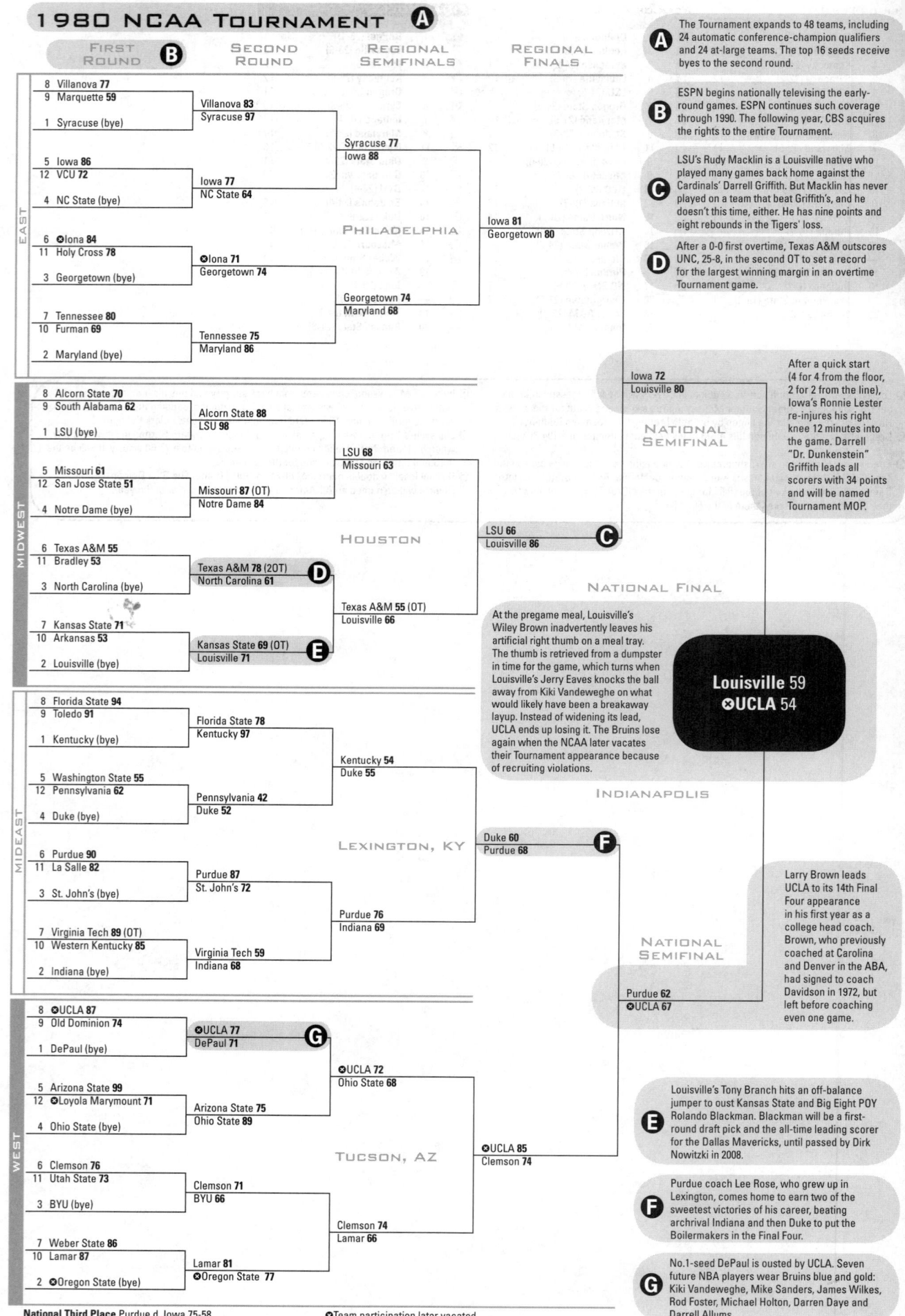

1980 NCAA TOURNAMENT (A)

First Round (B) · Second Round · Regional Semifinals · Regional Finals

EAST — Philadelphia

First Round
- 8 Villanova **77**, 9 Marquette **59**; 1 Syracuse (bye)
- 5 Iowa **86**, 12 VCU **72**; 4 NC State (bye)
- 6 ⊗Iona **84**, 11 Holy Cross **78**; 3 Georgetown (bye)
- 7 Tennessee **80**, 10 Furman **69**; 2 Maryland (bye)

Second Round
- Villanova **83**, Syracuse **97**
- Iowa **77**, NC State **64**
- ⊗Iona **71**, Georgetown **74**
- Tennessee **75**, Maryland **86**

Regional Semifinals
- Syracuse **77**, Iowa **88**
- Georgetown **74**, Maryland **68**

Regional Final
- Iowa **81**, Georgetown **80**

MIDWEST — Houston

First Round
- 8 Alcorn State **70**, 9 South Alabama **62**; 1 LSU (bye)
- 5 Missouri **61**, 12 San Jose State **51**; 4 Notre Dame (bye)
- 6 Texas A&M **55**, 11 Bradley **53**; 3 North Carolina (bye)
- 7 Kansas State **71**, 10 Arkansas **53**; 2 Louisville (bye)

Second Round
- Alcorn State **88**, LSU **98**
- Missouri **87** (OT), Notre Dame **84**
- Texas A&M **78** (2OT), North Carolina **61** (D)
- Kansas State **69** (OT), Louisville **71** (E)

Regional Semifinals
- LSU **68**, Missouri **63**
- Texas A&M **55** (OT), Louisville **66**

Regional Final
- LSU **66**, Louisville **86** (C)

MIDEAST — Lexington, KY

First Round
- 8 Florida State **94**, 9 Toledo **91**; 1 Kentucky (bye)
- 5 Washington State **55**, 12 Pennsylvania **62**; 4 Duke (bye)
- 6 Purdue **90**, 11 La Salle **82**; 3 St. John's (bye)
- 7 Virginia Tech **89** (OT), 10 Western Kentucky **85**; 2 Indiana (bye)

Second Round
- Florida State **78**, Kentucky **97**
- Pennsylvania **42**, Duke **52**
- Purdue **87**, St. John's **72**
- Virginia Tech **59**, Indiana **68**

Regional Semifinals
- Kentucky **54**, Duke **55**
- Purdue **76**, Indiana **69**

Regional Final
- Duke **60**, Purdue **68** (F)

WEST — Tucson, AZ

First Round
- 8 ⊗UCLA **87**, 9 Old Dominion **74**; 1 DePaul (bye)
- 5 Arizona State **99**, 12 ⊗Loyola Marymount **71**; 4 Ohio State (bye)
- 6 Clemson **76**, 11 Utah State **73**; 3 BYU (bye)
- 7 Weber State **86**, 10 Lamar **87**; 2 ⊗Oregon State (bye)

Second Round
- ⊗UCLA **77**, DePaul **71** (G)
- Arizona State **75**, Ohio State **89**
- Clemson **71**, BYU **66**
- Lamar **81**, ⊗Oregon State **77**

Regional Semifinals
- ⊗UCLA **72**, Ohio State **68**
- Clemson **74**, Lamar **66**

Regional Final
- ⊗UCLA **85**, Clemson **74**

National Semifinals — Indianapolis

- Iowa **72**, Louisville **80**
- Purdue **62**, ⊗UCLA **67**

National Final

Louisville 59
⊗UCLA 54

At the pregame meal, Louisville's Wiley Brown inadvertently leaves his artificial right thumb on a meal tray. The thumb is retrieved from a dumpster in time for the game, which turns when Louisville's Jerry Eaves knocks the ball away from Kiki Vandeweghe on what would likely have been a breakaway layup. Instead of widening its lead, UCLA ends up losing it. The Bruins lose again when the NCAA later vacates their Tournament appearance because of recruiting violations.

After a quick start (4 for 4 from the floor, 2 for 2 from the line), Iowa's Ronnie Lester re-injures his right knee 12 minutes into the game. Darrell "Dr. Dunkenstein" Griffith leads all scorers with 34 points and will be named Tournament MOP.

Larry Brown leads UCLA to its 14th Final Four appearance in his first year as a college head coach. Brown, who previously coached at Carolina and Denver in the ABA, had signed to coach Davidson in 1972, but left before coaching even one game.

National Third Place Purdue d. Iowa 75-58

⊗Team participation later vacated

A The Tournament expands to 48 teams, including 24 automatic conference-champion qualifiers and 24 at-large teams. The top 16 seeds receive byes to the second round.

B ESPN begins nationally televising the early-round games. ESPN continues such coverage through 1990. The following year, CBS acquires the rights to the entire Tournament.

C LSU's Rudy Macklin is a Louisville native who played many games back home against the Cardinals' Darrell Griffith. But Macklin has never played on a team that beat Griffith's, and he doesn't this time, either. He has nine points and eight rebounds in the Tigers' loss.

D After a 0-0 first overtime, Texas A&M outscores UNC, 25-8, in the second OT to set a record for the largest winning margin in an overtime Tournament game.

E Louisville's Tony Branch hits an off-balance jumper to oust Kansas State and Big Eight POY Rolando Blackman. Blackman will be a first-round draft pick and the all-time leading scorer for the Dallas Mavericks, until passed by Dirk Nowitzki in 2008.

F Purdue coach Lee Rose, who grew up in Lexington, comes home to earn two of the sweetest victories of his career, beating archrival Indiana and then Duke to put the Boilermakers in the Final Four.

G No.1-seed DePaul is ousted by UCLA. Seven future NBA players wear Bruins blue and gold: Kiki Vandeweghe, Mike Sanders, James Wilkes, Rod Foster, Michael Holton, Darren Daye and Darrell Allums.

Tournament Leaders

INDIVIDUAL LEADERS

Scoring	CL	POS	G	PTS	PPG
1 **Kelvin Ransey**, Ohio State	SR	G	2	54	27.0
2 **Joe Barry Carroll**, Purdue	SR	C	6	158	26.3
3 **Mike Olliver**, Lamar	JR	G	3	75	25.0
4 **Reggie Johnson**, Tennessee	SR	F	2	49	24.5
5 **Murray Brown**, Florida State	SR	F	2	48	24.0
6 **Greg Manning**, Maryland	JR	G	2	47	23.5
Isiah Thomas, Indiana	FR	G	2	47	23.5
8 **Eric "Sleepy" Floyd**, Georgetown	SO	G	3	70	23.3
9 **Darrell Griffith**, Louisville	SR	G	5	116	23.2
10 **Eric Santifer**, Syracuse	FR	G	2	43	21.5

Minimum: 2 games

Field Goal Pct	CL	POS	G	FG	FGA	PCT
1 **Mark Dressler**, Missouri	SO	F	3	27	35	77.1
2 **Murray Brown**, Florida State	SR	F	2	21	28	75.0
Eric Santifer, Syracuse	FR	G	2	18	24	75.0
4 **Buck Williams**, Maryland	SO	F/C	2	16	23	69.6
5 **Greg Manning**, Maryland	JR	G	2	20	29	69.0

Minimum: 12 made

Note: Field goal statistics for Iona-Holy Cross game were not available

Free Throw Pct	CL	POS	G	FT	FTA	PCT
1 **Cliff Pruitt**, UCLA	SO	F	6	14	15	93.3
2 **John Pinone**, Villanova	FR	C	2	13	14	92.9
3 **Glenn Vickers**, Iona	SR	G	2	19	21	90.5
4 **Fred Cowan**, Kentucky	JR	C	2	16	18	88.9
5 **Rod Foster**, UCLA	FR	G	6	15	17	88.2

Minimum: 12 made

Rebounds Per Game	CL	POS	G	REB	RPG
1 **Louis Orr**, Syracuse	SR	F	2	24	12.0
Buck Williams, Maryland	SO	F/C	2	24	12.0
3 **Larry Smith**, Alcorn State	SR	F/C	2	22	11.0
4 **Alton Lister**, Arizona State	JR	C	2	21	10.5
5 **Rudy Macklin**, LSU	JR	F	3	31	10.3

Minimum: 2 games

TEAM LEADERS

Scoring	G	PTS	PPG
1 **Arizona State**	2	174	87.0
Syracuse	2	174	87.0
3 **Florida State**	2	172	86.0
4 **Villanova**	2	160	80.0
5 **Alcorn State**	2	158	79.0
6 **Ohio State**	2	157	78.5
7 **Lamar**	3	234	78.0
8 **Tennessee**	2	155	77.5
Iona	2	155	77.5
10 **LSU**	3	232	77.3

Minimum: 2 games

FG Pct	G	FG	FGA	PCT
1 **Maryland**	2	67	115	58.3
2 **Missouri**	3	84	149	56.4
3 **Florida State**	2	68	122	55.7
4 **Villanova**	2	57	104	54.8
5 **Georgetown**	3	95	174	54.6

FT Pct	G	FT	FTA	PCT
1 **Kentucky**	2	39	45	86.7
2 **Villanova**	2	46	54	85.2
3 **Syracuse**	2	46	55	83.6
4 **UCLA**	6	136	166	81.9
5 **Iowa**	6	122	159	76.7

Minimum: 2 games

Rebounds	G	REB	RPG
1 **Arizona State**	2	95	47.5
2 **Kentucky**	2	83	41.5
3 **Tennessee**	2	76	38.0
Ohio State	2	76	38.0
5 **Texas A&M**	3	109	36.3

Minimum: 2 games

ALL-TOURNAMENT TEAM

PLAYER	CL	POS	HT	SCHOOL	RPG	PPG
Darrell Griffith*	SR	G	6-4	Louisville	5.4	23.2
Joe Barry Carroll	SR	C	7-1	Purdue	9.8	26.3
Rod Foster†	FR	G	6-1	UCLA	1.5	14.2
Rodney McCray	FR	F/C	6-7	Louisville	8.6	9.0
Kiki Vandeweghe†	SR	F	6-8	UCLA	7.3	19.8

ALL-REGIONAL TEAMS

EAST

PLAYER	CL	POS	HT	SCHOOL	RPG	PPG
Eric "Sleepy" Floyd*	SO	G	6-3	Georgetown	3.3	23.3
Vince Brookins	JR	F	6-5	Iowa	4.3	15.5
John Duren	SR	G	6-3	Georgetown	3.0	8.7
Louis Orr	SR	F	6-8	Syracuse	12.0	18.0
Craig Shelton	SR	F	6-7	Georgetown	4.3	16.7

MIDEAST

PLAYER	CL	POS	HT	SCHOOL	RPG	PPG
Joe Barry Carroll*	SR	C	7-1	Purdue	9.8	26.5
Fred Cowan	JR	C	6-8	Kentucky	6.5	20.0
Mike Gminski	SR	C	6-11	Duke	6.7	17.7
Drake Morris	JR	F	6-6	Purdue	4.0	17.5
Isiah Thomas	FR	G	6-1	Indiana	2.0	23.5

MIDWEST

PLAYER	CL	POS	HT	SCHOOL	RPG	PPG
Darrell Griffith*	SR	G	6-4	Louisville	6.7	19.7
David Britton	SR	G	6-4	Texas A&M	4.3	16.3
Wiley Brown	SO	F	6-8	Louisville	5.7	13.3
Mark Dressler	SO	F	6-7	Missouri	7.7	21.0
DeWayne Scales	JR	F	6-8	LSU	6.0	12.3

WEST

PLAYER	CL	POS	HT	SCHOOL	RPG	PPG
Mike Sanders*	SO	F/C	6-6	UCLA	12.0	16.8
Rod Foster	FR	G	6-1	UCLA	1.3	15.0
Larry Nance	JR	F	6-10	Clemson	9.3	14.5
Kelvin Ransey	SR	G	6-1	Ohio State	4.0	27.0
Kiki Vandeweghe	SR	F	6-8	UCLA	8.0	20.3

* Most outstanding player
† Honor later vacated

1980 NCAA TOURNAMENT BOX SCORES

Iowa 88-77 Syracuse

	1H	2H
Iowa	40	48
Syracuse	33	44

IOWA	MIN	FG	3FG	FT	REB	A	ST	BL	PF	TP
Vincent Brookins	-	5-10	-	11-12	5	-	-	-	4	21
Kevin Boyle	-	8-12	-	2-2	5	-	-	-	3	18
Steve Krafcisin	-	6-9	-	2-2	3	-	-	-	5	14
Kenny Arnold	-	2-7	-	8-13	5	-	-	-	1	12
Steve Waite	-	4-5	-	2-3	5	-	-	-	2	10
Ronnie Lester	-	3-10	-	3-5	3	-	-	-	1	9
Bob Hansen	-	1-2	-	2-2	1	-	-	-	4	4
TOTALS	-	29-55	-	30-39	27	-	-	-	20	88
Percentages		52.7		76.9						

Coach: Lute Olson

SYRACUSE	MIN	FG	3FG	FT	REB	A	ST	BL	PF	TP
Louis Orr	-	10-17	-	5-5	16	-	-	-	2	25
Roosevelt Bouie	-	7-8	-	4-5	3	-	-	-	5	18
Eric Santifer	-	5-9	-	4-4	3	-	-	-	4	14
Danny Schayes	-	2-7	-	6-9	2	-	-	-	3	10
Eddie Moss	-	4-7	-	0-0	1	-	-	-	5	8
Tony Bruin	-	1-5	-	0-0	3	-	-	-	3	2
Hal Cohen	-	0-2	-	0-0	1	-	-	-	4	0
Marty Headd	-	0-7	-	0-0	3	-	-	-	2	0
TOTALS	-	29-62	-	19-23	32	-	-	-	28	77
Percentages		46.8		82.6						

Coach: Jim Boeheim

Officials: Pa Galvan, Dale Kelley, Booke Turner
Technicals: Syracuse (co Boeheim)
Attendance: 17,569

Georgetown 74-68 Maryland

	1H	2H
Georgetown	38	36
Maryland	39	29

GEORGETOWN	MIN	FG	3FG	FT	REB	A	ST	BL	PF	TP
Eric "Sleepy" Floyd	35	8-17	-	2-2	4	3	6	1	2	18
John Duren	37	7-15	-	0-0	4	7	2	0	3	14
Eric Smith	29	3-6	-	7-11	1	2	3	0	1	13
Craig Shelton	25	3-5	-	1-2	2	0	1	0	4	7
Al Dutch	11	3-5	-	1-2	4	0	0	0	0	7
Mike Frazier	13	3-4	-	0-0	5	0	0	0	3	6
Ed Spriggs	22	2-3	-	1-3	5	0	0	0	0	5
Mike Hancock	15	2-4	-	0-0	2	1	1	0	1	4
Terry Fenlon	8	0-1	-	0-0	0	1	0	0	1	0
Jeff Bullis	5	0-0	-	0-0	0	0	0	0	0	0
TOTALS	200	31-60	-	12-20	27	14	13	1	15	74
Percentages		51.7		60.0						

Coach: John Thompson Jr.

MARYLAND	MIN	FG	3FG	FT	REB	A	ST	BL	PF	TP
Greg Manning	40	9-14	-	1-1	1	2	1	0	3	19
Charles Williams	39	8-10	-	2-4	15	0	2	2	4	18
Albert King	39	6-18	-	3-3	6	5	4	0	5	15
Ernest Graham	38	3-8	-	0-1	9	4	1	0	3	6
Greg Morley	27	3-4	-	0-0	1	6	3	0	3	6
Reggie Jackson	14	2-4	-	0-0	1	2	1	0	2	4
Taylor Baldwin	3	0-0	-	0-0	0	0	0	0	0	0
TOTALS	200	31-58	-	6-9	33	19	12	2	20	68
Percentages		53.4		66.7						

Coach: Lefty Driesell

Officials: Bob Wortman, Jim Bain, Tony Rhodes
Technicals: None
Attendance: 17,569

LSU 68-63 Missouri

	1H	2H
LSU	39	29
Missouri	40	23

LSU	MIN	FG	3FG	FT	REB	A	ST	BL	PF	TP
DeWayne Scales	35	7-17	-	3-6	7	0	-	-	4	17
Rudy Macklin	30	6-13	-	4-5	4	1	-	-	3	16
Howard Carter	25	4-10	-	2-2	0	2	-	-	1	10
Ethan Martin	38	3-9	-	3-3	0	6	-	-	2	9
Willie Sims	20	3-5	-	2-3	2	1	-	-	2	8
Greg Cook	36	1-3	-	2-2	10	5	-	-	3	4
Jordy Hultberg	8	2-3	-	0-0	0	0	-	-	0	4
Tyrone Black	5	0-0	-	0-0	0	0	-	-	1	0
Gus Rudolph	3	0-0	-	0-0	0	0	-	-	1	0
TOTALS	200	26-60	-	16-21	23	15	-	-	17	68
Percentages		43.3		76.2						

Coach: Dale Brown

MISSOURI	MIN	FG	3FG	FT	REB	A	ST	BL	PF	TP
Mark Dressler	39	9-11	-	2-4	7	2	-	-	4	20
Larry Drew	39	7-10	-	2-3	2	4	-	-	2	16
Ricky Frazier	29	6-11	-	0-0	8	1	-	-	3	12
Steve Stipanovich	28	4-9	-	2-2	5	3	-	-	4	10
Tom Dore	19	0-3	-	3-4	6	2	-	-	4	3
Jon Sundvold	40	1-5	-	0-0	4	6	-	-	4	2
Mike Foster	5	0-0	-	0-0	0	0	-	-	1	0
Carl Amos	1	0-0	-	0-0	0	0	-	-	0	0
TOTALS	200	27-49	-	9-13	32	18	-	-	22	63
Percentages		55.1		69.2						

Coach: Norm Stewart

Officials: Charles Range, Richie Weiler, Elbert Fielden
Technicals: None
Attendance: 15,400

Louisville 66-55 Texas A&M

	1H	2H	OT1
Louisville	35	18	13
Texas A&M	33	20	2

LOUISVILLE	MIN	FG	3FG	FT	REB	A	ST	BL	PF	TP
Darrell Griffith	43	9-24	-	6-8	6	2	1	0	2	24
Wiley Brown	36	5-10	-	5-6	6	1	2	0	0	15
Jerry Eaves	26	4-7	-	0-0	3	3	1	0	2	8
Derek Smith	38	2-6	-	2-2	10	5	1	1	4	6
Rodney McCray	35	0-4	-	4-8	8	3	1	1	2	4
Poncho Wright	20	2-5	-	0-0	0	1	0	0	2	4
Tony Branch	4	0-0	-	3-4	0	1	1	0	0	3
Roger Burkman	23	1-2	-	0-1	3	0	1	0	4	2
TOTALS	225	23-58	-	20-29	36	16	8	2	16	66
Percentages		39.7		69.0						

Coach: Denny Crum

TEXAS A&M	MIN	FG	3FG	FT	REB	A	ST	BL	PF	TP
David Britton	44	7-15	-	2-2	3	7	1	2	4	16
Vernon Smith	40	6-13	-	0-0	8	0	0	1	4	12
Rynn Wright	43	4-8	-	3-4	8	2	2	1	5	11
Rudy Woods	24	4-7	-	0-0	9	0	0	3	4	8
Claude Riley	15	2-7	-	0-0	2	1	0	0	3	4
David Goff	43	0-3	-	2-2	2	6	1	0	2	2
Steve Sylestine	11	1-3	-	0-0	0	0	1	0	1	2
Tyrone Ladson	5	0-0	-	0-0	0	0	0	0	1	0
TOTALS	225	24-56	-	7-8	32	16	5	7	24	55
Percentages		42.9		87.5						

Coach: Shelby Metcalf

Officials: Gary Muncy, Tom Fincken, George Solomon
Technicals: None
Attendance: 15,400

Duke 55-54 Kentucky

	1H	2H
Duke	37	18
Kentucky	23	31

DUKE	MIN	FG	3FG	FT	REB	A	ST	BL	PF	TP
Mike Gminski	38	8-18	-	1-3	7	0	-	-	3	17
Vince Taylor	37	7-9	-	1-3	1	2	-	-	3	15
Eugene Banks	38	3-6	-	5-9	6	5	-	-	2	11
Kenny Dennard	35	3-5	-	0-1	5	2	-	-	5	6
Bob Bender	36	0-1	-	4-7	1	4	-	-	2	4
Mike Tissaw	2	1-1	-	0-1	0	0	-	-	1	2
Tom Emma	5	0-0	-	0-0	0	0	-	-	1	0
Allen Williams	4	0-0	-	0-0	0	0	-	-	0	0
Jim Suddath	3	0-0	-	0-0	0	0	-	-	0	0
Chip Engelland	2	0-0	-	0-0	0	0	-	-	0	0
TOTALS	200	22-40	-	11-24	20	13	-	-	17	55
Percentages		55.0		45.8						

Coach: Bill E. Foster

KENTUCKY	MIN	FG	3FG	FT	REB	A	ST	BL	PF	TP
Fred Cowan	27	7-11	-	12-14	6	1	-	-	1	26
LaVon Williams	37	2-6	-	2-2	9	1	-	-	3	6
Kyle Macy	35	3-9	-	0-0	0	3	-	-	2	6
Dirk Minniefield	35	2-4	-	2-2	6	1	-	-	4	6
Derrick Hord	20	2-5	-	0-0	2	3	-	-	3	4
Charles Hurt	14	1-3	-	0-0	1	0	-	-	3	2
Jay Shidler	10	1-3	-	0-0	1	1	-	-	1	2
Sam Bowie	9	1-4	-	0-0	3	0	-	-	5	2
Chuck Verderber	9	0-2	-	0-0	2	0	-	-	1	0
Tom Heitz	4	0-0	-	0-0	1	0	-	-	0	0
TOTALS	200	19-47	-	16-18	31	10	-	-	23	54
Percentages		40.4		88.9						

Coach: Joe B. Hall

Officials: Bob Herrold, Rich Ballesteros, Bob Dibler
Technicals: None
Attendance: 23,320

Purdue 76-69 Indiana

	1H	2H
Purdue	37	39
Indiana	26	43

PURDUE	MIN	FG	3FG	FT	REB	A	ST	BL	PF	TP
Drake Morris	38	7-14	-	6-8	3	1	2	0	4	20
Keith Edmonson	36	5-9	-	10-12	4	2	1	0	3	20
Joe Barry Carroll	27	5-11	-	1-4	8	0	1	1	3	11
Michael Scearce	15	1-2	-	9-11	1	1	0	0	0	11
Arnette Hallman	33	2-4	-	5-7	9	2	0	0	5	9
Brian Walker	35	2-5	-	1-2	1	5	3	0	3	5
Steven Walker	6	0-0	-	0-0	0	0	0	0	1	0
Kevin Stallings	4	0-0	-	0-0	0	0	1	0	0	0
Roosevelt Barnes	3	0-0	-	0-0	0	0	1	0	0	0
Ted Benson	2	0-1	-	0-0	0	0	0	0	1	0
Jon Kitchel	1	0-0	-	0-0	0	0	0	0	0	0
TOTALS	200	22-46	-	32-44	26	11	9	1	20	76
Percentages		47.8		72.7						

Coach: Lee Rose

INDIANA	MIN	FG	3FG	FT	REB	A	ST	BL	PF	TP
Isiah Thomas	40	13-20	-	4-4	2	5	1	0	4	30
Mike Woodson	35	5-12	-	4-5	6	1	0	0	5	14
Ray Tolbert	37	3-7	-	0-2	11	0	0	2	5	6
Butch Carter	28	2-6	-	1-2	5	6	2	0	4	5
Phil Isenbarger	12	2-4	-	0-0	2	0	0	0	3	4
James Thomas	4	0-2	-	4-4	2	0	2	0	1	4
Ted Kitchel	11	1-2	-	0-0	1	0	0	0	1	2
Tony Brown	7	1-1	-	0-0	0	1	1	0	0	2
Glen Grunwald	7	1-2	-	0-0	1	0	0	0	2	2
Landon Turner	15	0-2	-	0-0	3	1	0	0	5	0
Charles Franz	2	0-0	-	0-0	0	0	0	0	2	0
Steve Risley	2	0-0	-	0-0	0	0	0	0	1	0
TOTALS	200	28-58	-	13-17	33	14	6	2	33	69
Percentages		48.3		76.5						

Coach: Bob Knight

Officials: Dan Wooldridge, Blaine Sylvester, Lou Moser
Technicals: Indiana (coach Knight)
Attendance: 21,700

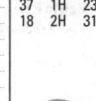

72-68 — SWEET 16

		1H	2H
UCLA		35	37
OHIO STATE		31	37

UCLA	MIN	FG	3FG	FT	REB	A	ST	BL	PF	TP
Mike Sanders	37	7-11	-	5-6	8	1	1	-	4	19
Rod Foster	35	6-11	-	7-8	4	2	2	-	3	19
Kiki Vandeweghe	35	3-13	-	6-6	5	2	0	-	2	12
Darren Daye	22	4-6	-	2-4	4	0	3	-	1	10
James Wilkes	31	1-6	-	6-8	9	2	4	-	2	8
Cliff Pruitt	8	1-1	-	2-2	0	0	0	-	0	4
Michael Holton	25	0-2	-	0-1	2	0	1	-	0	0
Darrell Allums	7	0-2	-	0-0	1	0	0	-	2	0
TOTALS	**200**	**22-52**	**-**	**28-35**	**33**	**7**	**11**	**-**	**14**	**72**
Percentages		42.3		80.0						
Coach: Larry Brown										

OHIO STATE	MIN	FG	3FG	FT	REB	A	ST	BL	PF	TP
Kelvin Ransey	39	13-23	-	3-3	4	2	0	0	5	29
Clark Kellogg	33	6-10	-	0-0	8	2	1	2	5	12
Herbert Williams	40	5-12	-	0-2	10	0	0	3	2	10
Carter Scott	28	2-3	-	2-2	3	5	3	0	5	6
J.R. Ellinghausen	10	2-2	-	0-0	0	0	0	0	1	4
James Smith	19	1-3	-	0-1	4	2	0	0	2	2
Anthony Hall	11	1-1	-	0-0	2	1	2	0	4	2
Todd Penn	7	1-2	-	0-0	0	1	1	0	2	2
Larry Huggins	6	0-0	-	1-2	0	0	0	0	0	1
John Miller	7	0-1	-	0-0	0	0	0	0	1	0
TOTALS	**200**	**31-57**	**-**	**6-10**	**31**	**13**	**7**	**5**	**27**	**68**
Percentages		54.4		60.0						
Coach: Eldon Miller										

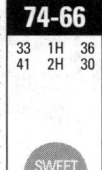

Officials: Hank Nichols, Don Shea, Larry Lembo
Technicals: None
Attendance: 7,670

74-66 — SWEET 16

		1H	2H
CLEMSON		33	41
LAMAR		36	30

CLEMSON	MIN	FG	3FG	FT	REB	A	ST	BL	PF	TP
Larry Nance	35	6-14	-	4-5	11	2	0	2	2	16
John Campbell	31	7-12	-	1-3	12	3	0	0	3	15
Billy Williams	37	3-12	-	6-8	3	5	1	1	3	12
Fred Gilliam	19	5-9	-	0-0	4	1	0	0	1	10
Bobby Conrad	29	2-3	-	4-5	3	2	1	0	2	8
Mitchell Wiggins	18	3-4	-	0-2	2	0	0	0	2	6
Chris Dodds	14	2-5	-	0-0	1	1	0	0	0	4
Horace Wyatt	13	1-4	-	1-2	5	2	1	0	2	3
Bob Fuzy	1	0-0	-	0-0	0	0	0	0	0	0
Marvin Key	1	0-0	-	0-0	0	0	0	0	0	0
Rick McKinstry	1	0-0	-	0-0	0	0	0	0	0	0
Bill Ross	1	0-0	-	0-0	0	0	0	0	0	0
TOTALS	**200**	**29-63**	**-**	**16-25**	**41**	**16**	**3**	**3**	**15**	**74**
Percentages		46.0		64.0						
Coach: Bill C. Foster										

LAMAR	MIN	FG	3FG	FT	REB	A	ST	BL	PF	TP
Mike Olliver	40	9-20	-	2-2	1	1	-	-	4	20
B.B. Davis	28	6-21	-	4-6	7	2	-	-	5	16
Clarence Kea	30	3-8	-	6-8	12	0	-	-	5	12
Cestrakiah Lewis	39	4-8	-	0-0	6	1	-	-	3	8
Robert Williams	23	2-5	-	2-2	6	0	-	-	4	6
Alvin Brooks	40	2-4	-	0-0	5	8	-	-	2	4
TOTALS	**200**	**26-66**	**-**	**14-18**	**37**	**12**	**-**	**-**	**23**	**66**
Percentages		39.4		77.8						
Coach: Billy Tubbs										

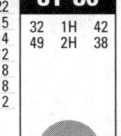

Officials: Blaine Sylvester, Robert Adams, David Pollock
Technicals: None
Attendance: 7,670

81-80 — ELITE 8

		1H	2H
IOWA		32	49
GEORGETOWN		42	38

IOWA	MIN	FG	3FG	FT	REB	A	ST	BL	PF	TP
Vincent Brookins	39	10-17	-	2-2	4	0	1	1	1	22
Steve Waite	22	4-4	-	7-7	4	2	0	0	3	15
Kevin Boyle	34	7-11	-	0-0	3	4	1	0	4	14
Kenny Arnold	32	5-8	-	2-2	2	3	1	0	1	12
Ronnie Lester	39	2-7	-	4-4	2	9	1	0	3	8
Bob Hansen	13	2-2	-	4-4	1	1	0	0	1	8
Steve Krafcisin	21	1-2	-	0-1	3	1	0	1	2	2
TOTALS	**200**	**31-51**	**-**	**19-20**	**19**	**20**	**4**	**2**	**15**	**81**
Percentages		60.8		95.0						
Coach: Lute Olson										

GEORGETOWN	MIN	FG	3FG	FT	REB	A	ST	BL	PF	TP
Eric "Sleepy" Floyd	36	11-14	-	9-10	3	2	1	0	0	31
Craig Shelton	32	7-10	-	2-3	5	0	0	1	5	16
John Duren	38	5-9	-	0-0	3	8	1	0	2	10
Mike Frazier	15	4-5	-	1-1	3	0	1	0	4	9
Eric Smith	28	2-5	-	0-0	0	2	0	0	1	4
Mike Hancock	12	2-3	-	0-0	1	0	0	0	1	4
Ed Spriggs	15	0-2	-	2-2	2	0	0	1	2	2
Al Dutch	12	1-4	-	0-0	3	0	0	0	3	2
Jeff Bullis	6	1-2	-	0-0	1	0	0	0	0	2
Terry Fenlon	6	0-1	-	0-0	0	1	0	0	1	0
TOTALS	**200**	**33-55**	**-**	**14-16**	**21**	**13**	**3**	**2**	**19**	**80**
Percentages		60.0		87.5						
Coach: John Thompson Jr.										

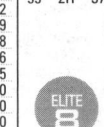

Officials: Dale Kelley, Booker Turner, Tony Rhodes
Technicals: None
Attendance: 15,981

86-66 — ELITE 8

		1H	2H
LOUISVILLE		31	55
LSU		29	37

LOUISVILLE	MIN	FG	3FG	FT	REB	A	ST	BL	PF	TP
Darrell Griffith	18	7-12	-	3-4	8	7	-	-	4	17
Wiley Brown	31	8-10	-	0-1	5	1	-	-	2	16
Derek Smith	33	4-9	-	5-9	10	3	-	-	4	13
Rodney McCray	38	4-8	-	4-6	10	2	-	-	1	12
Jerry Eaves	31	3-3	-	3-5	2	2	-	-	1	9
Roger Burkman	26	2-2	-	4-5	0	7	-	-	3	8
Poncho Wright	13	1-5	-	4-4	4	0	-	-	1	6
Tony Branch	6	1-3	-	3-4	0	0	-	-	1	5
Steve Clark	1	0-0	-	0-1	1	0	-	-	0	0
Daryl Cleveland	1	0-0	-	0-0	0	0	-	-	0	0
Greg Deuser	1	0-0	-	0-0	0	0	-	-	0	0
Marty Pulliam	1	0-0	-	0-0	0	0	-	-	0	0
TOTALS	**200**	**30-52**	**-**	**26-39**	**40**	**22**	**-**	**-**	**17**	**86**
Percentages		57.7		66.7						
Coach: Denny Crum										

LSU	MIN	FG	3FG	FT	REB	A	ST	BL	PF	TP
Jordy Hultberg	20	8-10	-	1-3	1	1	-	-	2	17
Howard Carter	29	5-14	-	2-3	7	0	-	-	5	12
DeWayne Scales	27	5-11	-	2-2	6	0	-	-	5	12
Willie Sims	22	4-8	-	2-2	1	1	-	-	5	10
Rudy Macklin	34	4-7	-	1-2	8	1	-	-	4	9
Greg Cook	25	2-4	-	0-1	7	5	-	-	5	4
Ethan Martin	31	1-11	-	0-0	2	8	-	-	4	2
Joe Costello	6	0-1	-	0-0	0	0	-	-	0	0
Mark Alcorn	1	0-0	-	0-0	0	0	-	-	0	0
Brian Bergeron	1	0-1	-	0-0	0	0	-	-	0	0
Tyrone Black	1	0-0	-	0-0	0	0	-	-	0	0
Andy Campbell	1	0-0	-	0-0	0	0	-	-	0	0
Duane DeArmond	1	0-0	-	0-0	0	0	-	-	0	0
Gus Rudolph	1	0-1	-	0-0	1	0	-	-	1	0
TOTALS	**200**	**29-68**	**-**	**8-13**	**33**	**16**	**-**	**-**	**31**	**66**
Percentages		42.6		61.5						
Coach: Dale Brown										

Officials: Charles Range, Richie Weiler, George Solomon
Technicals: Louisville (Wright)
Attendance: 15,400

68-60 — ELITE 8

		1H	2H
PURDUE		28	40
DUKE		30	30

PURDUE	MIN	FG	3FG	FT	REB	A	ST	BL	PF	TP
Joe Barry Carroll	35	10-16	-	6-6	6	0	1	1	4	26
Keith Edmonson	37	4-11	-	4-6	5	1	0	1	3	12
Drake Morris	30	1-7	-	8-9	5	3	1	0	4	10
Arnette Hallman	37	4-7	-	1-2	4	0	0	1	1	9
Brian Walker	36	2-4	-	1-4	5	6	3	0	3	5
Michael Scearce	12	1-4	-	0-0	2	0	2	0	0	2
Ted Benson	5	0-1	-	2-2	2	0	0	0	0	2
Kevin Stallings	4	1-2	-	0-0	1	1	0	0	1	2
Steven Walker	3	0-0	-	0-0	0	0	0	0	1	0
Roosevelt Barnes	1	0-0	-	0-0	0	0	0	0	0	0
TOTALS	**200**	**23-52**	**-**	**22-29**	**30**	**11**	**7**	**3**	**17**	**68**
Percentages		44.2		75.9						
Coach: Lee Rose										

DUKE	MIN	FG	3FG	FT	REB	A	ST	BL	PF	TP
Mike Gminski	33	6-16	-	5-6	9	0	0	2	3	17
Eugene Banks	35	5-9	-	4-4	4	2	2	0	5	14
Kenny Dennard	22	5-7	-	1-2	4	0	0	0	5	11
Bob Bender	34	3-7	-	4-4	2	3	3	0	4	10
Jim Suddath	10	2-2	-	0-0	0	2	0	0	1	4
Vince Taylor	33	1-7	-	0-0	4	2	0	0	4	2
Chip Engelland	10	1-4	-	0-0	1	1	0	0	1	2
Tom Emma	11	0-0	-	0-1	0	0	0	0	1	0
Mike Tissaw	7	0-0	-	0-0	1	0	0	0	1	0
Allen Williams	5	0-0	-	0-0	0	0	0	0	0	0
TOTALS	**200**	**23-52**	**-**	**14-17**	**25**	**10**	**5**	**2**	**25**	**60**
Percentages		44.2		82.4						
Coach: Bill E. Foster										

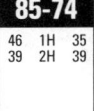

Officials: Bob Herrold, Rich Ballesteros, Dan Wooldridge
Technicals: None
Attendance: 22,800

85-74 — ELITE 8

		1H	2H
UCLA		46	39
CLEMSON		35	39

UCLA	MIN	FG	3FG	FT	REB	A	ST	BL	PF	TP
Kiki Vandeweghe	38	7-10	-	8-11	9	4	0	0	3	22
Mike Sanders	35	7-12	-	8-8	10	4	1	0	4	22
Rod Foster	35	6-13	-	0-0	1	3	1	0	4	12
Darren Daye	18	2-4	-	3-4	3	0	1	0	2	7
Michael Holton	28	2-3	-	2-4	2	2	0	2	2	6
Cliff Pruitt	18	3-5	-	0-1	3	4	0	1	1	6
Darrell Allums	6	2-2	-	2-3	3	0	0	0	2	6
James Wilkes	21	0-4	-	2-2	4	0	2	0	4	2
Randy Arrillaga	1	1-2	-	0-0	0	0	0	0	0	2
TOTALS	**200**	**30-55**	**-**	**25-33**	**35**	**17**	**5**	**3**	**22**	**85**
Percentages		54.5		75.8						
Coach: Larry Brown										

CLEMSON	MIN	FG	3FG	FT	REB	A	ST	BL	PF	TP
Billy Williams	32	9-19	-	0-0	3	2	1	-	3	18
Larry Nance	31	5-12	-	3-4	6	0	2	-	4	13
Fred Gilliam	28	5-11	-	3-4	9	5	0	-	3	13
Bobby Conrad	28	2-6	-	5-7	1	7	2	-	5	9
Chris Dodds	24	3-6	-	2-2	2	4	0	-	1	8
John Campbell	16	2-3	-	1-2	3	1	0	-	2	5
Horace Wyatt	22	2-3	-	0-0	5	0	0	-	5	4
Mitchell Wiggins	18	2-7	-	0-2	3	0	0	-	3	4
Bill Ross	1	0-0	-	0-0	0	0	0	-	0	0
TOTALS	**200**	**30-67**	**-**	**14-21**	**32**	**19**	**5**	**-**	**26**	**74**
Percentages		44.8		66.7						
Coach: Bill C. Foster										

Officials: Larry Lembo, Hank Nichols, Blaine Sylvester
Technicals: None
Attendance: 6,355

80-72 (FINAL 4)

	1H	2H
Louisville	34	46
Iowa	29	43

LOUISVILLE	MIN	FG	3FG	FT	REB	A	ST	BL	PF	TP
Darrell Griffith	36	14-21	-	6-8	5	6	3	2	1	34
Rodney McCray	37	5-7	-	4-4	9	3	2	2	2	14
Derek Smith	37	3-7	-	7-8	8	2	0	0	2	13
Jerry Eaves	22	2-4	-	4-5	4	1	0	0	1	8
Roger Burkman	22	2-3	-	3-4	2	0	1	0	3	7
Wiley Brown	29	1-3	-	0-2	5	2	0	0	4	2
Poncho Wright	15	1-2	-	0-0	3	1	0	0	1	2
Tony Branch	2	0-0	-	0-0	0	0	0	0	0	0
Daryl Cleveland	0	0-0	-	0-0	0	0	0	0	0	0
Greg Deuser	0	0-0	-	0-0	0	0	0	0	0	0
Marty Pulliam	0	0-0	-	0-0	0	0	0	0	0	0
TOTALS	**200**	**28-47**	**-**	**24-31**	**36**	**15**	**6**	**4**	**14**	**80**
Percentages		59.6		77.4						

Coach: Denny Crum

IOWA	MIN	FG	3FG	FT	REB	A	ST	BL	PF	TP
Kenny Arnold	39	9-17	-	2-2	3	5	1	0	1	20
Vincent Brookins	33	6-18	-	2-2	6	2	1	0	5	14
Steve Krafcisin	32	4-5	-	4-4	3	0	0	1	5	12
Ronnie Lester	12	4-4	-	2-2	1	1	0	0	2	10
Steve Waite	29	4-6	-	1-1	2	0	2	0	5	9
Bob Hansen	17	2-8	-	3-4	4	4	1	0	2	7
Kevin Boyle	38	0-8	-	0-0	7	5	2	0	2	0
Mark Gannon	0	0-0	-	0-0	0	0	0	0	0	0
Mike Henry	0	0-0	-	0-0	0	0	0	0	1	0
TOTALS	**200**	**29-66**	**-**	**14-15**	**26**	**17**	**7**	**1**	**23**	**72**
Percentages		43.9		93.3						

Coach: Lute Olson

Officials: H Nichols, Bo Turner, Larry Lembo
Technicals: None
Attendance: 16,637

67-62 (FINAL 4)

	1H	2H
UCLA	33	34
Purdue	25	37

UCLA	MIN	FG	3FG	FT	REB	A	ST	BL	PF	TP
Kiki Vandeweghe	40	9-12	-	6-6	5	2	0	0	1	24
Mike Sanders	38	3-7	-	6-6	6	1	4	1	2	12
Rod Foster	23	4-7	-	1-2	3	1	0	0	5	9
Cliff Pruitt	16	3-7	-	2-2	1	0	0	0	1	8
Darren Daye	24	1-5	-	4-5	3	3	0	0	2	6
Michael Holton	33	1-3	-	2-2	1	2	0	0	1	4
James Wilkes	8	2-2	-	0-0	1	0	0	0	5	4
Darrell Allums	16	0-0	-	0-2	4	2	0	0	3	0
Gig Sims	2	0-3	-	0-0	3	0	0	1	1	0
TOTALS	**200**	**23-46**	**-**	**21-25**	**27**	**11**	**4**	**2**	**21**	**67**
Percentages		50.0		84.0						

Coach: Larry Brown

PURDUE	MIN	FG	3FG	FT	REB	A	ST	BL	PF	TP
Keith Edmonson	37	9-16	-	5-6	3	1	1	0	3	23
Joe Barry Carroll	40	8-14	-	1-4	8	1	0	2	3	17
Drake Morris	30	5-14	-	2-2	6	2	0	0	2	12
Brian Walker	37	1-3	-	4-5	1	5	2	0	4	6
Arnette Hallman	33	1-7	-	0-0	7	1	0	0	4	2
Roosevelt Barnes	5	1-1	-	0-0	0	0	0	0	1	2
Steven Walker	12	0-1	-	0-0	1	2	0	0	4	0
Michael Scearce	5	0-2	-	0-0	3	0	0	1	0	0
Kevin Stallings	1	0-0	-	0-0	0	0	0	0	0	0
TOTALS	**200**	**25-58**	**-**	**12-17**	**29**	**12**	**3**	**3**	**21**	**62**
Percentages		43.1		70.6						

Coach: Lee Rose

Officials: Rich Weiler, Rober Rhodes, Bob Herrold
Technicals: None
Attendance: 16,637

75-58 (3RD PLACE)

	1H	2H
Purdue	32	43
Iowa	27	31

PURDUE	MIN	FG	3FG	FT	REB	A	ST	BL	PF	TP
Joe Barry Carroll	37	14-17	-	7-11	12	2	0	4	3	35
Keith Edmonson	35	6-11	-	5-8	4	3	1	2	2	17
Arnette Hallman	34	4-9	-	0-3	3	2	2	0	3	8
Drake Morris	22	3-3	-	1-1	1	3	1	0	3	7
Steven Walker	25	1-3	-	2-3	4	4	1	0	2	4
Kevin Stallings	12	1-3	-	2-2	1	3	1	0	1	4
Brian Walker	19	0-1	-	0-0	5	4	2	0	3	0
Roosevelt Barnes	8	0-2	-	0-0	1	0	0	0	0	0
Ted Benson	3	0-0	-	0-0	0	0	0	0	1	0
John Anthrop	2	0-0	-	0-0	0	1	0	0	1	0
Michael Scearce	2	0-0	-	0-0	0	0	0	0	1	0
Jon Kitchel	1	0-0	-	0-0	1	0	0	0	0	0
TOTALS	**200**	**29-49**	**-**	**17-28**	**32**	**22**	**8**	**6**	**20**	**75**
Percentages		59.2		60.7						

Coach: Lee Rose

IOWA	MIN	FG	3FG	FT	REB	A	ST	BL	PF	TP
Kenny Arnold	39	8-14	-	3-5	2	3	1	0	2	19
Bob Hansen	30	4-13	-	2-2	4	3	1	0	4	10
Kevin Boyle	36	3-8	-	3-4	7	2	1	0	4	9
Steve Waite	27	3-5	-	2-5	7	1	1	1	4	8
Steve Krafcisin	24	2-8	-	2-2	6	1	1	0	5	6
Vincent Brookins	20	2-6	-	0-1	6	2	0	1	5	4
Mark Gannon	15	1-8	-	0-0	3	0	0	0	0	2
Mike Henry	4	0-1	-	0-0	1	0	0	1	1	0
Mikev Heller	3	0-2	-	0-0	1	0	0	0	1	0
Mike Arens	1	0-0	-	0-0	0	0	0	0	0	0
Tom Grogan	1	0-0	-	0-0	0	0	0	0	0	0
Jon Darsee	0	0-0	-	0-0	0	0	0	0	0	0
TOTALS	**200**	**23-65**	**-**	**12-19**	**37**	**12**	**5**	**3**	**26**	**58**
Percentages		35.4		63.2						

Coach: Lute Olson

Officials: Booker Turner, Robert Rhodes, Bob Herrold
Technicals: Purdue (Edmonson)
Attendance: 16,637

59-54 (NCAA FINAL 1980)

	1H	2H
Louisville	26	33
UCLA	28	26

LOUISVILLE	MIN	FG	3FG	FT	REB	A	ST	BL	PF	TP
Darrell Griffith	38	9-16	-	5-8	2	3	1	1	3	23
Derek Smith	36	3-9	-	3-4	5	1	2	0	2	9
Wiley Brown	34	4-12	-	0-2	7	3	1	1	3	8
Jerry Eaves	30	4-7	-	0-2	3	3	1	0	3	8
Rodney McCray	36	2-4	-	3-4	11	2	0	3	4	7
Poncho Wright	12	2-4	-	0-0	4	0	2	0	1	4
Roger Burkman	11	0-1	-	0-0	1	1	1	0	4	0
Tony Branch	3	0-0	-	0-0	0	0	0	0	0	0
TOTALS	**200**	**24-53**	**-**	**11-20**	**33**	**13**	**8**	**5**	**20**	**59**
Percentages		45.3		55.0						

Coach: Denny Crum

UCLA	MIN	FG	3FG	FT	REB	A	ST	BL	PF	TP
Rod Foster	38	6-15	-	4-4	1	5	6	0	3	16
Kiki Vandeweghe	37	4-9	-	6-6	7	0	1	0	3	14
Mike Sanders	34	4-10	-	2-4	6	0	1	0	4	10
Cliff Pruitt	16	2-8	-	2-2	6	1	1	2	2	6
Michael Holton	29	1-3	-	2-2	2	3	1	0	2	4
James Wilkes	24	1-4	-	0-0	6	0	0	1	3	2
Darren Daye	13	1-3	-	0-0	1	2	0	0	1	2
Tony Anderson	5	0-0	-	0-0	0	0	0	0	0	0
Darrell Allums	4	0-0	-	0-0	2	0	0	0	0	0
TOTALS	**200**	**19-52**	**-**	**16-18**	**31**	**11**	**10**	**3**	**18**	**54**
Percentages		36.5		88.9						

Coach: Larry Brown

Officials: Hank Nichols, Richie Weiler, Larry Lembo
Technicals: None
Attendance: 16,637

National Invitation Tournament (NIT)

First round: Saint Peter's d. Connecticut 71-56, Illinois State d. West Texas A&M 80-63, Texas d. Saint Joseph's 70-61, Minnesota d. Bowling Green 64-50, Murray State d. Jacksonville 53-49, Virginia d. Lafayette 67-56, Illinois d. Loyola-Chicago 105-87, Alabama d. Penn State 53-49, Boston College d. Boston U. 95-74, UTEP d. Wichita State 58-56, Duquesne d. Pittsburgh 65-63, UL-Lafayette d. UAB 74-72, Michigan d. Nebraska 76-69, Mississippi d. Grambling 76-74, UNLV d. Washington 93-73, Long Beach State d. Pepperdine 104-87

Second round: Saint Peter's d. Duquesne 34-33, Virginia d. Boston College 57-55, UL-Lafayette d. Texas 77-76, Minnesota d. Mississippi 58-56, Murray State d. Alabama 70-62, Illinois d. Illinois State 75-65, Michigan d. UTEP 74-65, UNLV d. Long Beach State 90-81

Third round: UNLV d. Saint Peter's 67-62, Minnesota d. UL-Lafayette 94-73, Illinois d. Murray State 65-63, Virginia d. Michigan 79-68

Semifinals: Virginia d. UNLV 90-71, Minnesota d. Illinois 65-63

Third place: Illinois d. UNLV 84-74

Championship: Virginia d. Minnesota 58-55

MVP: Ralph Sampson, Virginia

1980-81: Fantastic Finishes

Before the Tournament, the NCAA announced that CBS had won the rights to broadcast future episodes of March Madness. You couldn't really blame the people at NBC, the lame-duck network, for being disappointed.

Dramatic endings ruled the 1981 Tournament (Arkansas' U.S. Reed, Kansas State's Rolando Blackman and BYU's Danny Ainge all hit memorable buzzer beaters). The day of the NCAA Final itself began badly for the country, with President Ronald Reagan being shot outside a Washington, D.C., hotel. The NCAA considered cancelling the Final but, with Reagan out of danger, the show went on in Philadelphia.

Unfortunately, Dean Smith's hopes for his first championship did not survive. Led by 23 points from sophomore Isiah Thomas, Indiana took out North Carolina, 63-50, for the Hoosiers' fourth title and coach Bob Knight's second. After starting the season 7–5, the 26–9 Hoosiers dominated the Tournament, winning their five games by an average margin of 22.6 points.

DePaul (27–1) was the nation's top-ranked team heading into the Tournament, but coach Ray Meyer's squad was one-and-done for the second straight season, this time beaten by Saint Joseph's, 49-48. Ralph Sampson and Virginia beat LSU, 78-74, in the last national third-place game.

Major Conference Standings

ACC

	Conference			Overall		
	W	L	PCT	W	L	PCT
Virginia○	13	1	.929	29	4	.879
North Carolina⊕	10	4	.714	29	8	.784
Wake Forest○	9	5	.643	22	7	.759
Maryland○	8	6	.571	21	10	.677
Clemson□	6	8	.429	20	11	.645
Duke□	6	8	.429	17	13	.567
NC State	4	10	.286	14	13	.519
Georgia Tech	0	14	.000	4	23	.148

Tournament: **North Carolina d. Maryland 61-60**
Tournament MVP: **Sam Perkins**, North Carolina

BIG EAST

	Conference			Overall		
	W	L	PCT	W	L	PCT
Boston College○	10	4	.714	23	7	.767
Georgetown⊕	9	5	.643	20	12	.625
Connecticut□	8	6	.571	20	9	.690
Villanova○	8	6	.571	20	11	.645
St. John's□	8	6	.571	17	11	.607
Syracuse□	6	8	.429	22	12	.647
Seton Hall	4	10	.286	11	16	.407
Providence	3	11	.214	10	18	.357

Tournament: **Syracuse d. Villanova 83-80 (3OT)**
Tournament MVP: **Leo Rautins**, Syracuse

BIG EIGHT

	Conference			Overall		
	W	L	PCT	W	L	PCT
Missouri○	10	4	.714	22	10	.688
Kansas⊕	9	5	.643	24	8	.750
Kansas State○	9	5	.643	24	9	.727
Nebraska	9	5	.643	15	12	.556
Oklahoma State	8	6	.571	18	9	.667
Colorado	5	9	.357	16	12	.571
Oklahoma	4	10	.286	9	18	.333
Iowa State	2	12	.143	9	18	.333

Tournament: **Kansas d. Kansas State 80-68**
Tournament MVP: **Darnell Valentine**, Kansas

BIG SKY

	Conference			Overall		
	W	L	PCT	W	L	PCT
Idaho⊕	12	2	.857	25	4	.862
Montana	11	3	.786	19	9	.679
Montana State	11	3	.786	16	11	.593
Idaho State	6	8	.429	12	14	.462
Nevada	5	9	.357	11	15	.423
Weber State	5	9	.357	8	19	.296
Boise State	4	10	.286	7	19	.269
Northern Arizona	2	12	.143	8	17	.320

Tournament: **Idaho d. Montana 70-64**
Tournament MVP: **Ken Owens**, Idaho

BIG TEN

	Conference			Overall		
	W	L	PCT	W	L	PCT
Indiana⊕	14	4	.778	26	9	.743
Iowa○	13	5	.722	21	7	.750
Illinois○	12	6	.667	21	8	.724
Purdue□	10	8	.556	21	11	.656
Minnesota□	9	9	.500	19	11	.633
Ohio State	9	9	.500	14	13	.519
Michigan□	8	10	.444	19	11	.633
Michigan State	7	11	.389	13	14	.481
Wisconsin	5	13	.278	11	16	.407
Northwestern	3	15	.167	9	18	.333

EAST COAST

	Conference			Overall		
	W	L	PCT	W	L	PCT
East Section						
American□	11	0	1.000	24	6	.800
Saint Joseph's⊕	9	2	.818	25	8	.758
Temple□	9	2	.818	20	8	.714
La Salle	8	3	.727	14	13	.519
Drexel	6	5	.545	14	13	.519
Hofstra	5	6	.455	12	15	.444
West Section						
Lafayette	8	8	.500	15	13	.536
Rider	8	8	.500	14	14	.500
Lehigh	6	10	.375	14	12	.538
Bucknell	6	10	.375	12	16	.429
Delaware	3	13	.188	6	19	.240
West Chester	2	14	.125	7	20	.259

Tournament: **Saint Joseph's d. American 63-60**

ECAC METRO

	Conference			Overall		
	W	L	PCT	W	L	PCT
Fordham□	-	-	-	19	9	.679
Saint Peter's	-	-	-	17	9	.654
Siena	-	-	-	17	10	.630
Long Island⊕	-	-	-	18	11	.621
Wagner	-	-	-	16	11	.593
Iona	-	-	-	15	14	.517
Fairleigh Dickinson	-	-	-	12	14	.462
Fairfield	-	-	-	13	13	.500
St. Francis (NY)	-	-	-	10	16	.385
Army	-	-	-	7	19	.269
Manhattan	-	-	-	6	20	.231

Tournament: **Long Island d. Iona 77-72**
Note: Conference did not play a formal schedule

ECAC NORTH

	Conference			Overall		
	W	L	PCT	W	L	PCT
Northeastern⊕	21	5	.808	24	6	.800
Holy Cross□	18	8	.692	20	10	.667
Vermont	15	11	.577	16	12	.571
Boston U.	13	13	.500	13	14	.481
Maine	13	13	.500	14	14	.500
Canisius	11	15	.423	11	15	.423
Niagara	11	15	.423	11	15	.423
Colgate	11	17	.393	11	18	.379
New Hampshire	7	19	.269	7	19	.269

Tournament: **Northeastern d. Holy Cross 81-79 (OT)**
Tournament MVP: **Perry Moss**, Northeastern

ECAC SOUTH

	Conference			Overall		
	W	L	PCT	W	L	PCT
James Madison⊕	-	-	-	21	9	.700
Old Dominion□	-	-	-	18	10	.643
Saint Francis (PA)	-	-	-	17	10	.630
William and Mary	-	-	-	16	12	.571
Richmond	-	-	-	15	14	.517
Towson	-	-	-	13	14	.481
George Mason	-	-	-	10	16	.385
Navy	-	-	-	9	16	.360
Robert Morris	-	-	-	9	18	.333
Baltimore	-	-	-	5	21	.192
Catholic	-	-	-	4	20	.167

Tournament: **James Madison d. Richmond 69-60**
Note: Conference did not play a formal schedule

EAA

	Conference			Overall		
	W	L	PCT	W	L	PCT
Rhode Island□	10	3	.769	21	8	.724
Duquesne□	10	3	.769	20	10	.667
West Virginia□	9	4	.692	23	10	.697
Pittsburgh⊕	8	5	.615	19	12	.613
Rutgers	7	6	.538	16	14	.533
St. Bonaventure	6	7	.462	14	13	.519
George Washington	4	9	.308	8	19	.296
Massachusetts	0	13	.000	3	24	.111

Tournament: **Pittsburgh d. Duquesne 64-60**
Tournament MVP: **Lenny McMillan**, Pittsburgh

IVY

	Conference			Overall		
	W	L	PCT	W	L	PCT
Princeton⊕	13	1	.929	18	10	.643
Penn□	13	1	.929	20	8	.714
Harvard	9	5	.643	16	10	.615
Brown	5	9	.357	9	17	.346
Columbia	5	9	.357	9	17	.346
Cornell	4	10	.286	7	19	.269
Yale	4	10	.286	7	19	.269
Dartmouth	3	11	.214	10	16	.385

Playoff: **Princeton d. Penn 54-40**

METRO

	Conference			Overall		
	W	L	PCT	W	L	PCT
Louisville⊕	11	1	.917	21	9	.700
Florida State	7	5	.583	17	11	.607
Cincinnati	6	6	.500	16	13	.552
Virginia Tech	6	6	.500	15	13	.536
Memphis	5	7	.417	13	14	.481
Tulane	4	8	.333	12	15	.444
Saint Louis	3	9	.250	9	18	.333

Tournament: **Louisville d. Cincinnati 42-31**
Tournament MVP: **Rodney McCray**, Louisville

Conference Standings Continue →

⊕ Automatic NCAA Tournament bid ○ At-large NCAA Tournament bid □ NIT appearance ✪ Team record doesn't reflect games forfeited or vacated. For adjusted record, see p. 521.

MID-AMERICAN

	Conference			Overall		
	W	L	PCT	W	L	PCT
Ball State⊕	10	6	.625	20	10	.667
Toledo□	10	6	.625	21	10	.677
Northern Illinois	10	6	.625	17	12	.586
Bowling Green	10	6	.625	15	12	.556
Western Michigan	10	6	.625	15	13	.536
Eastern Michigan	8	8	.500	13	14	.481
Miami (OH)	6	10	.375	11	15	.423
Ohio	6	10	.375	7	20	.259
Central Michigan	5	11	.313	12	14	.462
Kent State	5	11	.313	7	19	.269

Tournament: **Ball State d. Northern Illinois 79-66**
Tournament MVP: **Ray McCallum**, Ball State

MEAC

	Conference			Overall		
	W	L	PCT	W	L	PCT
NC A&T□	7	3	.700	21	8	.724
Florida A&M	6	4	.600	17	11	.607
Howard⊕	6	4	.600	17	12	.586
Bethune-Cookman	4	6	.400	13	15	.464
South Carolina State	4	6	.400	11	15	.423
Delaware State	3	7	.300	8	18	.308

Tournament: **Howard d. NC A&T 66-63**
Tournament MOP: **Larry Spriggs**, Howard

MIDWESTERN CITY

	Conference			Overall		
	W	L	PCT	W	L	PCT
Xavier	8	3	.727	12	16	.429
Oklahoma City○	7	4	.636	14	15	.483
Loyola-Chicago	7	4	.636	13	15	.464
Evansville	6	5	.545	19	9	.679
Oral Roberts	6	5	.545	11	16	.407
Detroit	1	5	.167	9	18	.333
Butler	1	10	.091	5	22	.185

Tournament: **Oklahoma City d. Xavier 82-76**
Tournament MVP: **Anthony Hicks**, Xavier

MISSOURI VALLEY

	Conference			Overall		
	W	L	PCT	W	L	PCT
Wichita State○	12	4	.750	26	7	.788
Tulsa□	11	5	.688	26	7	.788
Creighton⊕	11	5	.688	21	9	.700
Bradley	10	6	.625	18	9	.667
Drake□	10	6	.625	18	11	.621
West Texas A&M	7	9	.438	16	11	.593
New Mexico State	7	9	.438	10	17	.370
Indiana State	4	12	.250	9	18	.333
Southern Illinois	0	16	.000	7	20	.259

Tournament: **Creighton d. Wichita State 70-64**

OHIO VALLEY

	Conference			Overall		
	W	L	PCT	W	L	PCT
Western Kentucky⊕	12	2	.857	21	8	.724
Murray State	10	4	.714	17	10	.630
Middle Tenn. State	9	5	.643	18	9	.667
Austin Peay	7	7	.500	14	13	.519
Eastern Kentucky	7	7	.500	10	16	.385
Akron	5	9	.357	8	18	.308
Morehead State	4	10	.286	11	15	.423
Tennessee Tech	2	12	.143	6	20	.231

Tournament: **Western Kentucky d. Murray State 71-67**
Tournament MVP: **Lamont Sleets**, Murray State

PCAA

	Conference			Overall		
	W	L	PCT	W	L	PCT
Fresno State⊕	12	2	.857	25	4	.862
San Jose State□	10	4	.714	21	9	.700
UC Irvine	9	5	.643	17	10	.630
Long Beach State	9	5	.643	15	13	.536
Utah State	5	9	.357	12	16	.429
UC Santa Barbara	5	9	.357	11	16	.407
Pacific	4	10	.286	14	13	.519
Cal State Fullerton	2	12	.143	4	23	.148

Tournament: **Fresno State d. San Jose St. 52-48**
Tournament MVP: **Sid Williams**, San Jose St.

PAC-10

	Conference			Overall		
	W	L	PCT	W	L	PCT
Oregon State⊕⊗	17	1	.944	26	2	.926
Arizona State○	16	2	.889	24	4	.857
UCLA○	13	5	.722	20	7	.741
Southern California	9	9	.500	14	13	.519
Washington	8	10	.444	14	13	.519
Arizona	8	10	.444	13	14	.481
Oregon	6	12	.333	13	14	.481
California	5	13	.278	13	14	.481
Stanford	5	13	.278	9	18	.333
Washington State	3	15	.167	10	17	.370

SEC

	Conference			Overall		
	W	L	PCT	W	L	PCT
LSU○	17	1	.944	31	5	.861
Kentucky○	15	3	.833	22	6	.786
Tennessee○	12	6	.667	21	8	.724
Alabama□	10	8	.556	18	11	.621
Georgia□	9	9	.500	19	12	.613
Mississippi⊕	8	10	.444	16	14	.533
Vanderbilt	7	11	.389	15	14	.517
Florida	5	13	.278	12	16	.429
Auburn	4	14	.222	11	16	.407
Mississippi State	3	15	.167	8	19	.296

Tournament: **Mississippi d. Georgia 66-62**
Tournament MVP: **Dominique Wilkins**, Georgia

SOUTHERN

	Conference			Overall		
	W	L	PCT	W	L	PCT
Chattanooga⊕	11	5	.688	21	9	.700
Appalachian State	11	5	.688	20	9	.690
Davidson	11	5	.688	13	14	.481
Western Carolina	9	7	.563	18	10	.643
East Tenn. State	9	7	.563	13	14	.481
Marshall	8	8	.500	18	10	.643
Furman	8	8	.500	11	16	.407
VMI	3	13	.188	4	23	.148
The Citadel	2	14	.125	9	17	.346

Tournament: **Chattanooga d. Appalachian State 59-55**
Tournament MOP: **Nick Morken**, Chattanooga

SOUTHLAND

	Conference			Overall		
	W	L	PCT	W	L	PCT
Lamar⊕	8	2	.800	25	5	.833
Texas-Arlington□	7	3	.700	20	8	.714
Louisiana Tech	7	3	.700	20	10	.667
UL-Lafayette	6	4	.600	15	13	.536
Arkansas State	2	8	.200	12	15	.444
McNeese State	0	10	.000	11	21	.344

Tournament: **Lamar d. Louisiana Tech 83-69**
Tournament MVP: **Mike Olliver**, Lamar

SOUTHWEST

	Conference			Overall		
	W	L	PCT	W	L	PCT
Arkansas○	13	3	.813	24	8	.750
Houston⊕	10	6	.625	21	9	.700
Baylor	10	6	.625	15	12	.556
Texas A&M	8	8	.500	15	12	.556
Texas Tech	8	8	.500	15	13	.536
Texas	7	9	.438	15	15	.500
Rice	7	9	.438	12	15	.444
TCU	6	10	.375	11	18	.379
SMU	3	13	.188	7	20	.259

Tournament: **Houston d. Texas 84-59**
Tournament MVP: **Rob Williams**, Houston

SWAC

	Conference			Overall		
	W	L	PCT	W	L	PCT
Southern U.⊕	8	4	.667	17	11	.607
Alcorn State	8	4	.667	17	12	.586
Grambling	7	5	.583	18	11	.621
Jackson State	7	5	.583	16	13	.552
Texas Southern	7	5	.583	13	13	.500
Miss. Valley State	4	8	.333	11	16	.407
Prairie View A&M	1	11	.083	2	23	.080

Tournament: **Southern d. Jackson State 69-63**
Tournament MVP: **Alvin Jackson**, Southern

SUN BELT

	Conference			Overall		
	W	L	PCT	W	L	PCT
VCU⊕	9	3	.750	24	5	.828
South Alabama□	9	3	.750	25	6	.806
UAB○	9	3	.750	23	9	.719
South Florida□	7	5	.583	18	11	.621
Jacksonville	4	8	.333	8	19	.296
Charlotte	3	9	.250	10	17	.370
Georgia State	1	11	.083	4	23	.148

Tournament: **VCU d. UAB 62-61 (OT)**
Tournament MVP: **Kenny Stancell**, VCU

TAAC

	Conference			Overall		
	W	L	PCT	W	L	PCT
Houston Baptist	9	3	.750	18	10	.643
Mercer⊕	7	4	.636	18	12	.600
Centenary	7	5	.583	16	12	.571
UL-Monroe	8	4	.667	15	13	.536
Arkansas-Little Rock	5	6	.455	13	13	.500
Northwestern St. (LA)	5	7	.417	11	17	.393
Samford	5	6	.455	10	17	.370
Hardin-Simmons	4	8	.333	9	18	.333
Georgia Southern	2	9	.182	5	22	.185

Tournament: **Mercer d. Houston Baptist 72-67**
Tournament MVP: **Tony Gattis**, Mercer

WCAC

	Conference			Overall		
	W	L	PCT	W	L	PCT
San Francisco⊕	11	3	.786	24	7	.774
Pepperdine	11	3	.786	16	12	.571
Gonzaga	9	5	.643	19	8	.704
Portland	7	7	.500	17	10	.630
Santa Clara	7	7	.500	14	13	.519
Loyola Marymount	5	9	.357	9	19	.321
San Diego	3	11	.214	10	16	.385
Saint Mary's (CA)	3	11	.214	9	18	.333

WAC

	Conference			Overall		
	W	L	PCT	W	L	PCT
Utah○	13	3	.813	25	5	.833
Wyoming⊕	13	3	.813	24	6	.800
BYU○	12	4	.750	25	7	.781
UTEP□	9	7	.563	18	12	.600
San Diego State	8	8	.500	15	12	.556
Hawaii	7	9	.438	14	13	.519
New Mexico	6	10	.375	11	15	.423
Air Force	3	13	.188	9	18	.333
Colorado State	1	15	.063	3	24	.111

INDEPENDENTS

	Overall		
	W	L	PCT
DePaul○	27	2	.931
Notre Dame○	23	6	.793
Southern Miss□	20	7	.741
Cleveland State	18	9	.667
Stetson	18	9	.667
Tennessee State	17	9	.654
Marquette□	20	11	.645
Illinois State	17	10	.630
Penn State	17	10	.630
South Carolina	17	10	.630
Dayton□	18	11	.621
Texas-Pan American□	18	11	.621
UNLV	16	12	.571
North Texas	15	12	.556
Southeastern Louisiana	14	13	.519
UNC Wilmington	13	13	.500
New Orleans	13	14	.481
East Carolina	12	14	.462
Valparaiso	12	15	.444
Campbell	11	16	.407
Charleston Southern	8	19	.296
Northern Iowa	8	19	.296
Portland State	7	20	.259
Nicholls State	6	22	.214

INDIVIDUAL LEADERS—SEASON

Scoring	CL	POS	G	FG	FT	PTS	PPG
1 **Zam Fredrick**, South Carolina	SR	G	27	300	181	781	**28.9**
2 **Mike Ferrara**, Colgate	SR	G	27	298	176	772	**28.6**
3 **Kevin Magee**, UC Irvine	JR	F/C	27	280	183	743	**27.5**
4 **Lewis Lloyd**, Drake	SR	F	29	298	166	762	**26.3**
5 **Rob Williams**, Houston	SO	G	30	298	153	749	**25.0**
6 **Rubin Jackson**, Oklahoma City	JR	F	29	293	133	719	**24.8**
7 **Franklin Edwards**, Cleveland State	SR	G	27	265	134	664	**24.6**
8 **Earl Belcher**, St. Bonaventure	SR	G	26	244	149	637	**24.5**
9 **Danny Ainge**, BYU	SR	G	32	309	164	782	**24.4**
10 **Mike McGee**, Michigan	SR	G/F	30	309	114	732	**24.4**

Field Goal Pct	CL	POS	G	FG	FGA	PCT
1 **Steve Johnson**, Oregon State	SR	F/C	28	235	315	**74.6**
2 **Kevin Magee**, UC Irvine	JR	F/C	27	280	417	**67.1**
3 **Orlando Woolridge**, Notre Dame	SR	F	28	156	240	**65.0**
4 **Buck Williams**, Maryland	JR	F/C	31	183	283	**64.7**
5 **Thomas Best**, Lafayette	SO	F	28	164	255	**64.3**

Minimum: 5 made per game

Free Throw Pct	CL	POS	G	FT	FTA	PCT
1 **Dave Hildahl**, Portland State	SR	G	21	76	82	**92.7**
2 **Jack Moore**, Nebraska	JR	G	27	118	128	**92.2**
3 **Steve Bontrager**, Oral Roberts	SR	G	27	73	81	**90.1**
4 **Jim Stack**, Northwestern	JR	G	26	81	90	**90.0**
5 **John Leonard**, Manhattan	JR	G	26	123	138	**89.1**

Minimum: 2.5 made per game

Rebounds Per Game	CL	POS	G	REB	RPG
1 **Darryl Watson**, Mississippi Valley State	SR	F	27	379	**14.0**
2 **Wayne Sappleton**, Loyola-Chicago	JR	F	28	374	**13.4**
3 **Michael Cage**, San Diego State	FR	F	27	355	**13.1**
4 **Kevin Magee**, UC Irvine	JR	F/C	27	337	**12.5**
5 **LaSalle Thompson**, Texas	SO	F/C	30	370	**12.3**
6 **Clark Kellogg**, Ohio State	SO	F	27	324	**12.0**
7 **Bruce Atkins**, Duquesne	JR	F	30	352	**11.7**
8 **Buck Williams**, Maryland	JR	F/C	31	363	**11.7**
9 **Carl Henry**, Oklahoma City	SO	G/F	29	338	**11.7**
10 **Ralph Sampson**, Virginia	SO	C	33	378	**11.5**

INDIVIDUAL LEADERS—GAME

Points	CL	POS	OPP	DATE	PTS
1 **Mike Ferrara**, Colgate	SR	G	Siena	F26	**50**
2 **Franklin Edwards**, Cleveland State	SR	G	Xavier	F25	**49**
3 **Mark Aguirre**, DePaul	JR	F	Maine	J6	**47**
4 **Russell Bowers**, American	SR	F	Harvard	D6	**45**
5 **Kenny Page**, New Mexico	JR	G	BYU	J15	**44**

Rebounds	CL	POS	OPP	DATE	REB
1 **Michael Cage**, San Diego State	FR	F	La Salle	D29	**26**
Wayne Sappleton, Loyola-Chicago	JR	F	Oral Roberts	F21	**26**
3 **Albert Culton**, Texas-Arlington	JR	F	Northeastern	J9	**24**
4 **Jonathan Green**, Tennessee State	SR	F	Austin Peay	D1	**23**
Sidney Green, UNLV	SO	F/C	Texas State	D23	**23**
Danny Schayes, Syracuse	SR	C	Georgetown	F9	**23**
Darryl Watson, Miss. Valley State	SR	F	Prairie View A&M	D9	**23**
Darryl Watson, Miss. Valley State	SR	F	Texas Southern	J31	**23**
Mark West, Old Dominion	SO	C	Texas Wesleyan	D3	**23**

TEAM LEADERS—SEASON

Win-Loss Pct	W	L	PCT
1 **DePaul**	27	2	**.931**
2 **Oregon State** ⊗	26	2	**.929**
3 **Virginia**	29	4	**.879**
4 **Fresno State**	25	4	**.862**
Idaho	25	4	**.862**

Scoring Offense	G	W-L	PTS	PPG
1 **UC Irvine**	27	17-10	2,332	**86.4**
2 **West Texas A&M**	27	16-11	2,309	**85.5**
3 **Oklahoma City**	29	14-15	2,421	**83.5**
4 **San Francisco**	31	24-7	2,579	**83.2**
5 **Long Island**	29	18-11	2,390	**82.4**

Scoring Margin	G	W-L	PPG	OPP PPG	MAR
1 **Wyoming**	30	24-6	73.6	57.5	**16.1**
2 **Oregon State**	28	26-2	76.6	60.9	**15.7**
3 **Fresno State**	29	25-4	66.1	50.7	**15.4**
4 **Wichita State**	33	26-7	80.9	66.5	**14.4**
5 **DePaul**	29	27-2	78.9	66.1	**12.8**

Field Goal Pct	G	W-L	FG	FGA	PCT
1 **Oregon State**	28	26-2	862	1,528	**56.4**
2 **Notre Dame**	29	23-6	824	1,492	**55.2**
3 **Idaho**	29	25-4	816	1,484	**55.0**
4 **UC Irvine**	27	17-10	934	1,703	**54.8**
5 **Pepperdine**	28	16-12	918	1,709	**53.7**

Free Throw Pct	G	W-L	FT	FTA	PCT
1 **Connecticut**	29	20-9	487	623	**78.2**
2 **Idaho State**	26	12-14	405	522	**77.6**
3 **Davidson**	27	13-14	477	626	**76.2**
4 **St. John's**	28	17-11	463	612	**75.7**
5 **Tennessee**	29	21-8	424	561	**75.6**

Rebound Margin	G	W-L	RPG	OPP RPG	MAR
1 **Northeastern**	30	24-6	44.9	32.0	**12.9**
2 **Wyoming**	30	24-6	42.0	30.3	**11.7**
3 **Wichita State**	33	26-7	44.1	34.0	**10.1**
4 **Mississippi Valley State**	27	11-16	47.1	39.0	**8.1**
5 **San Francisco**	31	24-7	40.1	32.6	**7.5**

Scoring Defense	G	W-L	OPP PTS	OPP PPG
1 **Fresno State**	29	25-4	1,470	**50.7**
2 **Princeton**	28	18-10	1,438	**51.4**
3 **Saint Peter's**	26	17-9	1,338	**51.5**
4 **Air Force**	27	9-18	1,518	**56.2**
5 **San Jose State**	30	21-9	1,699	**56.6**

Field Goal Pct Defense	G	W-L	OPP FG	OPP FGA	OPP PCT
1 **Wyoming**	30	24-6	637	1,589	**40.1**
2 **Penn State**	27	17-10	547	1,338	**40.9**
3 **South Florida**	29	18-11	701	1,682	**41.7**
4 **Saint Peter's**	26	17-9	521	1,248	**41.7**
5 **Air Force**	27	9-18	561	1,343	**41.8**

CONSENSUS ALL-AMERICAS

FIRST TEAM

PLAYER	CL	POS	HT	SCHOOL	RPG	PPG
Mark Aguirre	JR	F	6-7	DePaul	8.6	23.0
Danny Ainge	SR	G	6-5	BYU	4.8	24.4
Steve Johnson	SR	F/C	6-11	Oregon State	7.7	21.0
Ralph Sampson	SO	C	7-4	Virginia	11.5	17.7
Isiah Thomas	SO	G	6-1	Indiana	3.1	16.0

SECOND TEAM

PLAYER	CL	POS	HT	SCHOOL	RPG	PPG
Sam Bowie	SO	C	7-1	Kentucky	9.1	17.4
Jeff Lamp	SR	G	6-6	Virginia	4.2	18.2
Rudy Macklin	SR	F	6-7	LSU	9.8	15.9
Kelly Tripucka	SR	F	6-7	Notre Dame	5.8	18.2
Danny Vranes	SR	F	6-7	Utah	7.7	17.5
Al Wood	SR	G/F	6-6	North Carolina	6.3	18.1

SELECTORS: AP, NABC, UPI, USBWA

AWARD WINNERS

PLAYER OF THE YEAR

PLAYER	CL	POS	HT	SCHOOL	AWARDS
Ralph Sampson	SO	C	7-4	Virginia	Naismith, AP, UPI, USBWA, Rupp
Danny Ainge	SR	G	6-5	BYU	Wooden, NABC
Terry Adolph	SR	G	6-0	West Texas A&M	Frances Pomeroy Naismith*

* FOR THE MOST OUTSTANDING SENIOR PLAYER WHO IS 6 FEET OR UNDER

COACH OF THE YEAR

COACH	SCHOOL	REC	AWARDS
Ralph Miller	Oregon State	26-2	AP, UPI, USBWA, NABC (shared)
Jack Hartman	Kansas State	24-9	NABC (shared)
Dale Brown	LSU	31-5	Sporting News, CBS/Chevrolet

BOB GIBBONS' TOP HIGH SCHOOL SENIOR RECRUITS

PLAYER	POS	HT	HIGH SCHOOL	A-A TEAMS	COLLEGE	CAREER NOTES
1 Michael Jordan	2G	6-5	E.A. Laney HS, Wilmington, NC	McD, P	North Carolina	ACC FOY, '81; NCAA title, '82; No. 3 pick, '84 NBA draft (Bulls); 5-time NBA MVP; 6-time Finals MVP; All-time ppg leader (30.1)
2 Aubrey Sherrod	2G	6-4	Wichita Heights HS, Wichita, KS	McD, P	Wichita State	McDonald's game MVP; at WSU, 14.9 ppg (4 seasons); 2nd-round pick, '85 NBA draft (Bulls); no NBA games played
3 Patrick Ewing	C	7-0	Rindge & Latin HS, Cambridge, MA	McD, P	Georgetown	NCAA title, Tournament MOP, '82; No. 1 overall pick, '85 NBA draft (Knicks); 24,815 pts (17 seasons); 11-time All-Star
4 Manuel Forrest	F	6-7	Moore HS, Louisville, KY	McD, P	Louisville	8.4 ppg, 4.1 rpg (4 seasons); 12.8 ppg as Sr.; undrafted
5 Stuart Gray	C	7-0	John F. Kennedy HS, Granada Hills, CA	McD, P	UCLA	7.5 ppg, 6.5 rpg (3 seasons); 2nd-round pick, '84 NBA draft (Pacers); 2.3 ppg (7 seasons)
6 Greg Dreiling	C	7-1	Kaupun-Mt. Carmel HS, Wichita, KS	McD, P	Wichita State/ Kansas	10.8 ppg, 5.8 rpg (4 seasons); 2nd-round pick, '86 draft (Pacers); 2.1 ppg (10 seasons)
7 Anthony Jones	SF	6-6	Dunbar HS, Washington, DC	McD, P	Georgetown/UNLV	Transferred after 2 years; at UNLV, 18.0 ppg as Sr.; No. 21 pick, '86 NBA draft (Bullets); 3.6 ppg (3 seasons)
8 Bobby Lee Hurt	C	6-9	S.R. Butler HS, Huntsville, AL	McD, P	Alabama	13.5 ppg, 8.0 rpg, 63.1 FG% (4 seasons); 6th-round pick, '86 NBA draft (Warriors); played overseas
9 John Flowers	C	6-10	Southside HS, Fort Wayne, IN	McD, P	Indiana/UNLV	At UNLV, 6.6 ppg, 4.4. rpg (2 seasons); 6th-round pick, '86 NBA draft (Kings); no NBA games played
10 Mark Acres	PF	6-9	Palos Verdes (CA) HS	McD, P	Oral Roberts	18.5 ppg (4 seasons); 2nd-round pick, '85 NBA draft (Mavs); 4.1 rpg (6 seasons)
11 Walter Downing	PF	6-8	Providence HS, New Lenox, IL	McD, P	DePaul/Marquette	Transferred after 2 years; in college, 208 blocks (4 seasons); 6th-round pick, '86 NBA draft (Lakers); no NBA games played
12 Adrian Branch	SF	6-8	DeMatha Catholic HS, Hyattsville, MD	McD, P	Maryland	16.4 ppg (4 seasons); 2-time All-America; 2nd-round pick, '85 NBA draft (Bulls); 6.4 ppg (4 seasons); NBA title
13 Mike Payne	PF	6-10	Quincy (IL) Senior HS II	McD, P	Iowa	857 rebounds (4 seasons); 3rd-round pick, '85 NBA draft (Rockets); no NBA games played; played overseas
14 Sam Vincent	PG	6-3	Eastern HS, Lansing, MI	McD, P	Michigan State	All-America, '85; At MSU, 16.8 ppg (4 seasons); No. 20 pick, '85 NBA draft (Celtics); 7.8 ppg (7 seasons); NBA head coach
15 Milt Wagner	2G	6-5	Camden (NJ) HS	McD, P	Louisville	Titles in HS, NCAA, NBA; 2nd-round pick, '86 NBA draft (Mavs); 4.1 ppg (2 seasons); played overseas
16 Eric Turner	PG	6-2	Central HS, Flint, MI	P	Michigan	14.4 ppg, 5.0 apg (3 seasons); All-America,'83; 2nd-round pick, '84 NBA draft (Pistons); no NBA games played
17 Dwayne Polee	2G	6-5	Manual Arts HS, Los Angeles	McD, P	UNLV/Pepperdine	Transferred after 1 year; in college, 12.9 ppg (4 seasons); 3rd-round pick, '86 NBA draft (Clippers); 1 NBA game
18 Dan Palombizio	PF	6-8	Rogers HS, Michigan City, IN		Purdue/Ball State	Transferred after 2 years; at Ball State, 26.3 ppg, 11.0 rpg as Jr.; 7th-round pick, '86 NBA draft (76ers); no NBA games played
19 Joe Ward	SF	6-5	Griffin (GA) HS	P	Clemson/Georgia	11.2 ppg (4 seasons); 1st team All-SEC, '86; 2nd-round pick, '86 NBA draft (Suns); played overseas
20 Buzz Peterson	PG	6-4	Asheville (NC) HS	McD, P	North Carolina	NCAA title, '82; UNC team captain, '82-'85; college head coach (4 teams, 12 seasons)

OTHER STANDOUTS

PLAYER	POS	HT	HIGH SCHOOL	A-A TEAMS	COLLEGE	CAREER NOTES
23 Chris Mullin	SF	6-6	Xaverian HS, Brooklyn, NY	McD	St. John's	National POY, '85; No. 7 pick, '85 NBA draft (Warriors); 17,911 pts (16 seasons); 5-time All-Star; 2 Olympic gold medals, '84, '92
65 A.C. Green	F	6-8	Benson Polytechnic HS, Portland, OR		Oregon State	14.7 ppg, 7.7 rpg (4 seasons); 3rd team All-America, '85; No. 23 pick, '85 NBA draft (Lakers); 3 NBA titles; NBA record for consecutive games
144 Charles Barkley	PF	6-6	Leeds (AL) HS		Auburn	13.6 ppg, 9.3 rpg (3 seasons); No. 5 pick, '84 NBA draft (76ers); 11-time All-Star; NBA MVP, '93; 2 Olympic gold medals, '92, '96

Abbreviations: McD=McDonald's; P=Parade

Poll Progression

Preseason Poll

AP	UPI	School	
1	1	Kentucky	
2	2	DePaul	(A)
3	3	Louisville	
4	5	Maryland	
5	4	Indiana	
6	8	UCLA	
7	6	Oregon State	
8	7	Virginia	
9	9	Ohio State	
10	12	Notre Dame	
11	10	Missouri	
12	13	LSU	
13	11	North Carolina	
14	15	Iowa	
15	14	Texas A&M	
16	16	Georgetown	
17	19	St. John's	
18	17	BYU	
19	20	Syracuse	
20	—	Arkansas	
—	18	Kansas State	
—	20	Arizona State	

Week of Dec 2

AP	School	AP↓↑
1	DePaul (2-0)	↑1
2	Kentucky (1-0)	↓1
3	UCLA (2-0)	↑3
4	Maryland (1-0) (B)	
5	Indiana (2-0)	
6	Oregon State (1-0)	↑1
7	Virginia (3-0)	↑1
8	Louisville (0-1)	↓5
9	Ohio State (1-0)	
10	North Carolina (3-0)	↑3
11	Arkansas (2-1)	↑9
12	Iowa (2-0)	↑2
13	Notre Dame (0-1)	↓3
14	Texas A&M (1-0)	↑1
15	LSU (2-1)	↓3
16	St. John's (2-0)	↑1
17	Missouri (2-1)	↓6
18	Syracuse (1-0)	↑1
19	BYU (1-1)	↓1
19	Georgetown (1-2)	↓3

Week of Dec 9

AP	UPI	School	AP↓↑
1	2	DePaul (3-0)	
2	1	Kentucky (3-0)	
3	3	UCLA (3-0)	
4	4	Maryland (4-0)	
5	5	Oregon State (3-0)	↑1
6	7	Virginia (4-0)	↑1
7	6	Indiana (2-1)	↓2
8	9	Ohio State (2-1)	↑1
9	13	Notre Dame (3-1)	↑4
10	8	North Carolina (5-1)	
11	11	LSU (3-1)	↑4
12	12	Texas A&M (2-0)	↑2
13	10	Wake Forest (4-0)	⤴
14	14	Missouri (4-1)	↑3
15	20	Arizona State (3-0)	⤴
16	15	Iowa (3-1)	↓4
17	—	Arkansas (3-2)	↓6
18	16	Michigan (3-0)	⤴
19	17	BYU (2-1)	
20	—	Syracuse (2-1)	↓2
—	18	Georgetown (3-2)	⤵
—	18	Minnesota (3-0)	

Week of Dec 16

AP	UPI	School	AP↓↑
1	2	DePaul (5-0)	
2	1	Kentucky (4-0)	
3	3	UCLA (5-0)	
4	4	Oregon State (5-0)	↑1
5	5	Virginia (5-0)	↑1
6	11	Notre Dame (4-1)	↑3
7	10	Ohio State (2-1)	↑1
8	6	North Carolina (6-1)	↑2
9	9	Maryland (5-1) (C)	↓5
10	12	LSU (4-1)	↑1
11	7	Indiana (5-2)	↓4
12	8	Wake Forest (6-0)	↑1
13	14	Texas A&M (5-0)	↓1
14	13	Arizona State (5-0)	↑1
15	17	Michigan (6-0)	↑3
16	15	Iowa (5-1)	
17	16	Illinois (4-0)	⤴
18	19	BYU (4-1)	↑1
19	—	Arkansas (4-2)	↓2
20	18	Louisville (1-3) (C)	⤴
—	20	Missouri (5-2)	⤵

Week of Dec 23

AP	UPI	School	AP↓↑
1	2	DePaul (8-0)	
2	1	Kentucky (6-0)	
3	3	UCLA (6-0)	
4	4	Oregon State (5-0)	
5	5	Virginia (5-0)	
6	7	North Carolina (7-1)	↑2
7	8	Wake Forest (8-0)	↑5
8	11	Notre Dame (4-1)	↓2
9	9	Maryland (6-1)	
10	12	LSU (6-1)	
11	6	Arizona State (6-0)	↑3
12	10	Texas A&M (7-0)	↑1
13	13	Michigan (7-0)	↑2
14	14	Iowa (6-1)	↑2
15	16	Indiana (5-3)	↓4
16	17	South Alabama (8-0)	⤴
17	20	Arkansas (6-2)	↑2
18	—	Illinois (5-1)	↓1
19	15	Utah (7-0)	⤴
20	18	BYU (6-2)	↓2
—	19	Tennessee (6-1)	

Week of Dec 30

AP	UPI	School	AP↓↑
1	1	DePaul (10-0)	
2	2	Oregon State (8-0)	↑2
3	4	Virginia (6-0)	↑2
4	5	Notre Dame (6-1) (D)	↑4
5	3	Kentucky (6-1) (D)	↓3
6	6	North Carolina (9-1)	
7	7	UCLA (6-1)	↓4
8	8	Wake Forest (8-0)	↓1
9	9	Maryland (8-1)	
10	11	LSU (8-1)	
11	12	Texas A&M (7-1)	↑1
12	13	Michigan (7-0)	↑1
13	10	Arizona State (8-1)	↓2
14	15	Iowa (6-1)	
15	14	Indiana (7-4)	
16	16	Illinois (7-1)	↑2
17	17	South Alabama (8-1)	↓1
18	18	Tennessee (8-1)	⤴
19	19	BYU (8-2)	↑1
20	20	Utah (9-1)	↓1

Week of Jan 6

AP	UPI	School	AP↓↑
1	1	DePaul (12-0)	
2	2	Oregon State (9-0)	
3	4	Virginia (8-0)	
4	3	Kentucky (8-1)	↑1
5	5	Notre Dame (7-1)	↓1
6	7	Wake Forest (10-0)	↑2
7	6	UCLA (7-1)	
8	8	Maryland (10-1)	↑1
9	10	LSU (10-1)	↑1
10	9	Michigan (9-0)	↑2
11	11	Iowa (8-1)	↑3
12	16	Illinois (8-1)	↑4
13	12	Tennessee (9-1)	↑5
14	17	Arizona State (8-2)	↓1
15	15	South Alabama (10-1)	↑2
16	13	North Carolina (9-3)	↓10
17	18	BYU (10-2)	↑2
18	19	Utah (11-1)	↑2
19	14	Minnesota (9-1)	⤴
20	20	Clemson (11-1)	⤴

Week of Jan 13

AP	UPI	School	AP↓↑
1	1	Oregon State (12-0) (E)	↑1
2	2	Virginia (11-0) (F)	↑1
3	4	Kentucky (10-1)	↑1
4	3	DePaul (13-1)	↓3
5	5	Wake Forest (12-0)	↑1
6	6	LSU (12-1)	↑3
7	10	Notre Dame (8-2)	↓2
8	9	UCLA (8-2)	↓1
9	8	Michigan (10-1)	↑1
10	7	Maryland (11-2)	↓2
11	12	Tennessee (10-2)	↑2
12	14	Arizona State (11-2)	↑2
13	11	South Alabama (13-1)	↑2
14	16	Iowa (9-2)	↓3
15	13	BYU (12-2)	↑2
16	15	Utah (13-1)	↑2
17	17	North Carolina (10-4)	↓1
18	—	Illinois (9-2)	↓6
19	—	Clemson (12-2)	↑1
20	20	Minnesota (9-2)	↓1
—	18	Connecticut (10-0)	
—	19	Indiana (9-5)	

Week of Jan 20

AP	UPI	School	AP↓↑
1	1	Oregon State (13-0)	
2	2	Virginia (13-0)	
3	3	DePaul (15-1)	↑1
4	4	Wake Forest (14-0)	↑2
5	5	LSU (14-1)	↑1
6	6	Kentucky (11-2)	↓3
7	9	Arizona State (13-2)	↑5
8	12	Tennessee (12-2)	↑3
9	8	Iowa (11-2)	↑5
10	7	Maryland (12-3)	
11	10	South Alabama (15-1)	↑2
12	14	UCLA (9-3)	↓4
13	13	Notre Dame (9-3)	↓6
14	11	Utah (15-1)	↑2
15	15	Illinois (11-2)	↑3
16	16	Michigan (11-2)	↓7
17	18	North Carolina (12-4)	
18	—	BYU (13-3)	↓3
19	—	Clemson (13-3)	
20	17	Connecticut (12-1)	⤴
—	19	Indiana (10-6)	
—	20	Kansas (12-2)	

Week of Jan 27

AP	UPI	School	AP↓↑
1	1	Oregon State (15-0)	
1	2	Virginia (16-0)	↑1
3	3	DePaul (16-1)	
4	4	LSU (17-1)	↑1
5	7	Arizona State (14-2)	↑2
6	6	Wake Forest (15-1)	↓3
7	5	Kentucky (13-3)	↓1
8	9	Notre Dame (12-3)	↑5
9	8	Utah (17-1)	↑5
10	10	UCLA (11-3)	↑2
11	15	Tennessee (13-3)	↓3
12	11	North Carolina (14-4)	↑5
13	12	Iowa (12-3)	↓4
14	13	Maryland (13-4)	↓4
15	16	BYU (15-3)	↑3
16	14	South Alabama (16-2)	↓5
17	20	Michigan (12-3)	↓1
18	18	Kansas (14-2)	⤴
19	—	Minnesota (11-4)	⤴
20	19	Connecticut (13-2)	
—	17	Indiana (11-7)	

Week of Feb 3

AP	UPI	School	AP↓↑
1	2	Virginia (18-0)	
2	1	Oregon State (17-0)	↓1
3	3	DePaul (18-1)	
4	4	LSU (19-1)	
5	5	Arizona State (15-2)	
6	6	Kentucky (15-3)	↑1
7	7	Utah (18-1)	↑2
8	8	Wake Forest (17-2)	↓2
9	9	Notre Dame (14-3)	↓1
10	12	Tennessee (15-3)	↑1
11	10	North Carolina (16-4)	↑1
12	14	UCLA (12-4)	↓2
13	11	Maryland (15-4)	↑1
14	15	Michigan (14-3)	↑3
15	16	Iowa (13-4)	↓2
16	19	BYU (15-4)	↓1
17	13	Indiana (13-7)	⤴
18	—	Illinois (13-4)	⤴
19	20	Wichita State (16-2)	⤴
20	17	South Alabama (17-3)	↓4
—	18	Connecticut (15-3)	⤵

Week of Feb 10

AP	UPI	School	AP↓↑
1	2	Virginia (20-0)	
2	1	Oregon State (19-0)	
3	3	DePaul (21-1)	
4	4	LSU (21-1)	
5	5	Arizona State (18-2)	
6	6	Utah (20-1)	↑1
7	7	Wake Forest (19-2)	↑1
8	10	UCLA (14-4)	↑4
9	8	Tennessee (16-4)	↑1
10	9	North Carolina (18-5)	↑1
11	11	Kentucky (16-4)	↓5
12	14	Notre Dame (16-4)	↓3
13	12	Michigan (16-3)	↑1
14	13	Iowa (15-4)	↑1
15	17	BYU (17-4)	↑1
16	19	Wichita State (18-2)	↑3
17	—	Illinois (14-5)	↑1
18	18	South Alabama (19-3)	↑2
19	16	Maryland (15-6)	↓6
20	15	Indiana (14-8)	↓3
—	20	Idaho (19-3)	

Poll Progression Continues →

Week of Feb 17

AP	UPI	SCHOOL	AP↓↑
1	2	**Virginia** (22-0)	
2	1	**Oregon State** (21-0)	
3	3	**DePaul** (22-1)	
4	4	**LSU** (23-1)	
5	5	**Wake Forest** (21-2)	↑2
6	6	**UCLA** (16-4)	↑2
7	8	**Arizona State** (19-3)	↓2
8	9	**Tennessee** (18-4)	↑1
9	7	**Utah** (21-2)	↓3
10	10	**Kentucky** (18-4)	↑1
11	11	**Notre Dame** (18-4)	↑1
12	12	**Iowa** (17-4)	↑2
13	13	**North Carolina** (19-6)	↓3
14	15	**Wichita State** (19-2)	↑2
15	18	**Illinois** (16-5)	↑2
16	14	**Indiana** (16-8)	↑4
17	19	**BYU** (18-5)	↓2
18	—	**Michigan** (16-5)	↓5
19	—	**Lamar** (20-2)	⤴
20	—	**Maryland** (16-7)	↓1
—	16	**Idaho** (20-3)	
—	17	**Arkansas** (18-6)	
—	19	**Kansas State** (17-5)	

Week of Feb 24

AP	UPI	SCHOOL	AP↓↑
1	1	**Oregon State** (23-0)	↑1
2	4	**LSU** (26-1)	↑2
3	3	**Virginia** (23-1)	↓2
4	2	**DePaul** (24-1)	↓1
5	5	**Arizona State** (20-3)	↑2
6	6	**Notre Dame** (20-4)	↑5
7	7	**Utah** (23-2)	↑2
8	8	**Iowa** (19-4)	↑4
9	9	**Kentucky** (20-4)	↑1
10	12	**Tennessee** (19-5)	↓2
11	10	**North Carolina** (21-6)	↑2
12	11	**Wake Forest** (21-4)	↓7
13	13	**UCLA** (17-5)	↓7
14	14	**Illinois** (18-5)	↑1
15	19	**BYU** (20-5)	↑2
16	15	**Indiana** (17-9)	
17	20	**Maryland** (17-7)	↑3
18	16	**Arkansas** (20-6)	⤴
19	18	**Wichita State** (20-4)	↓5
20	—	**Louisville** (17-8)	⤴
—	17	**Idaho** (22-3)	

Week of Mar 3

AP	UPI	SCHOOL	AP↓↑
1	1	**Oregon State** (25-0)	
2	2	**DePaul** (25-1)	↑2
3	3	**LSU** (27-2)	↓1
4	4	**Virginia** (24-2)	↓1
5	5	**Arizona State** (22-3)	
6	7	**Notre Dame** (22-4)	
7	8	**Kentucky** (22-4)	↑2
8	6	**Iowa** (21-4)	
9	9	**Utah** (24-3)	↓2
10	12	**Tennessee** (20-6)	
11	10	**Wake Forest** (22-5)	↑1
12	11	**North Carolina** (22-7)	↓1
13	14	**UCLA** (18-6)	
14	13	**Indiana** (19-9)	↑2
15	15	**Arkansas** (22-6)	↑3
16	17	**Illinois** (19-6)	↓2
17	18	**Louisville** (19-8)	↑3
18	19	**BYU** (21-6)	↓3
19	16	**Wyoming** (21-6)	⤴
20	—	**Maryland** (18-8)	↓3
—	20	**Missouri** (21-8)	

Final Poll

AP	UPI	SCHOOL	AP↓↑
1	1	**DePaul** (27-1)	
2	2	**Oregon State** (26-1)	
3	5	**Arizona State** (24-3) Ⓖ	
4	4	**LSU** (28-3)	
5	3	**Virginia** (25-3)	
6	6	**North Carolina** (25-7)	
7	9	**Notre Dame** (22-5)	
8	8	**Kentucky** (22-5)	
9	7	**Indiana** (21-9)	
10	11	**UCLA** (20-6)	
11	14	**Wake Forest** (22-6)	
12	13	**Louisville** (21-8)	
13	12	**Iowa** (21-6)	↓[illegible]
14	10	**Utah** (24-4)	↓[illegible]
15	15	**Tennessee** (20-7)	↓[illegible]
16	17	**BYU** (22-6)	↑[illegible]
17	16	**Wyoming** (23-5)	↑[illegible]
18	20	**Maryland** (20-9)	↑[illegible]
19	18	**Illinois** (20-7)	↓[illegible]
20	—	**Arkansas** (22-7)	↓[illegible]
—	19	**Kansas** (19-7)	

Ⓐ Heading into the final season of the Mark Aguirre era, coach Ray Meyer says, "We'll have a real good year but it will be tough to duplicate last year. As long as we make the NCAA Tournament, I'll be happy."

Ⓑ Maryland's 86-64 win over Navy on Nov. 28 is coach Lefty Driesell's 400th career victory.

Ⓒ After opening with three straight losses, Louisville hands Maryland its first defeat of the season, 78-67, in Freedom Hall. The Cardinals, however, will lose four of their next five before turning themselves around for what will be a 21-win season.

Ⓓ Notre Dame beats Kentucky, 67-61, ending a six-game losing streak in Louisville's Freedom Hall. Irish coach Digger Phelps walks up to a local sports columnist, jabs a finger at him and shouts, "This one was for you ... *you!*"

Ⓔ Oregon State tops the polls for the first time in school history. Coach Ralph Miller takes a glass-half-empty approach: "You've got to keep on winning or you go down in the polls."

Ⓕ After unbeaten Virginia moves to No. 2 behind 7'4" sophomore Ralph Sampson, Jeff Lamp, the team's senior captain, says, "Who cares where we're ranked? I was hoping we could stay at No. 3."

Ⓖ Arizona State upsets Oregon State, its first win ever over a No. 1 team.

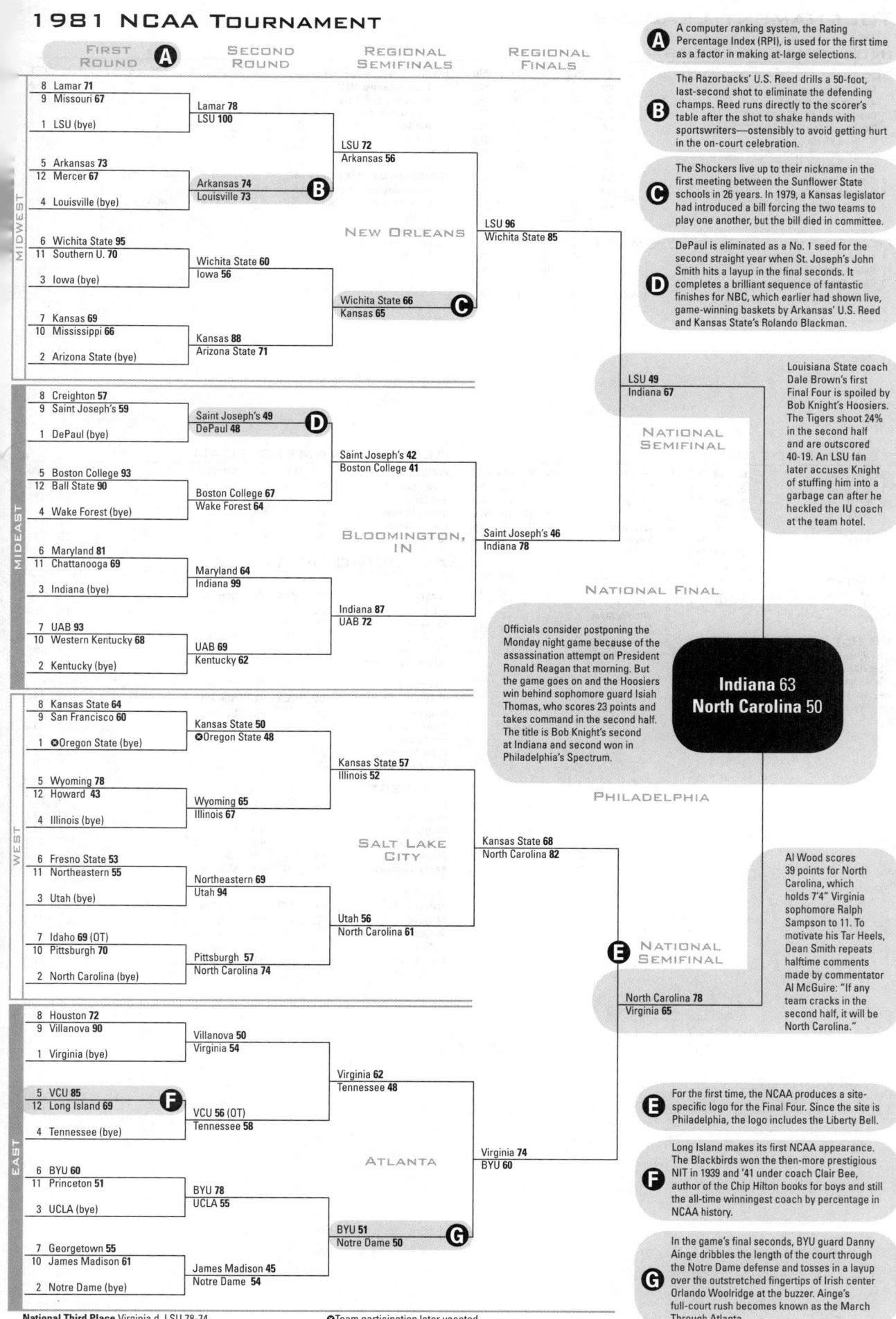

1981 NCAA Tournament

First Round (A) | Second Round | Regional Semifinals | Regional Finals

Midwest — New Orleans

First Round
- 8 Lamar **71**, 9 Missouri **67**
- 1 LSU (bye)
- 5 Arkansas **73**, 12 Mercer **67**
- 4 Louisville (bye)
- 6 Wichita State **95**, 11 Southern U. **70**
- 3 Iowa (bye)
- 7 Kansas **69**, 10 Mississippi **66**
- 2 Arizona State (bye)

Second Round
- Lamar **78**, LSU **100**
- Arkansas **74**, Louisville **73** (B)
- Wichita State **60**, Iowa **56**
- Kansas **88**, Arizona State **71**

Regional Semifinals
- LSU **72**, Arkansas **56**
- Wichita State **66**, Kansas **65** (C)

Regional Final
- LSU **96**, Wichita State **85**

Mideast — Bloomington, IN

First Round
- 8 Creighton **57**, 9 Saint Joseph's **59**
- 1 DePaul (bye)
- 5 Boston College **93**, 12 Ball State **90**
- 4 Wake Forest (bye)
- 6 Maryland **81**, 11 Chattanooga **69**
- 3 Indiana (bye)
- 7 UAB **93**, 10 Western Kentucky **68**
- 2 Kentucky (bye)

Second Round
- Saint Joseph's **49**, DePaul **48** (D)
- Boston College **67**, Wake Forest **64**
- Maryland **64**, Indiana **99**
- UAB **69**, Kentucky **62**

Regional Semifinals
- Saint Joseph's **42**, Boston College **41**
- Indiana **87**, UAB **72**

Regional Final
- Saint Joseph's **46**, Indiana **78**

West — Salt Lake City

First Round
- 8 Kansas State **64**, 9 San Francisco **60**
- 1 ⊗Oregon State (bye)
- 5 Wyoming **78**, 12 Howard **43**
- 4 Illinois (bye)
- 6 Fresno State **53**, 11 Northeastern **55**
- 3 Utah (bye)
- 7 Idaho **69** (OT), 10 Pittsburgh **70**
- 2 North Carolina (bye)

Second Round
- Kansas State **50**, ⊗Oregon State **48**
- Wyoming **65**, Illinois **67**
- Northeastern **69**, Utah **94**
- Pittsburgh **57**, North Carolina **74**

Regional Semifinals
- Kansas State **57**, Illinois **52**
- Utah **56**, North Carolina **61**

Regional Final
- Kansas State **68**, North Carolina **82**

East — Atlanta

First Round
- 8 Houston **72**, 9 Villanova **90**
- 1 Virginia (bye)
- 5 VCU **85**, 12 Long Island **69** (F)
- 4 Tennessee (bye)
- 6 BYU **60**, 11 Princeton **51**
- 3 UCLA (bye)
- 7 Georgetown **55**, 10 James Madison **61**
- 2 Notre Dame (bye)

Second Round
- Villanova **50**, Virginia **54**
- VCU **56** (OT), Tennessee **58**
- BYU **78**, UCLA **55**
- James Madison **45**, Notre Dame **54**

Regional Semifinals
- Virginia **62**, Tennessee **48**
- BYU **51**, Notre Dame **50** (G)

Regional Final
- Virginia **74**, BYU **60**

National Semifinal
- LSU **49**, Indiana **67**

Louisiana State coach Dale Brown's first Final Four is spoiled by Bob Knight's Hoosiers. The Tigers shoot 24% in the second half and are outscored 40-19. An LSU fan later accuses Knight of stuffing him into a garbage can after he heckled the IU coach at the team hotel.

National Semifinal (E)
- North Carolina **78**, Virginia **65**

Al Wood scores 39 points for North Carolina, which holds 7'4" Virginia sophomore Ralph Sampson to 11. To motivate his Tar Heels, Dean Smith repeats halftime comments made by commentator Al McGuire: "If any team cracks in the second half, it will be North Carolina."

National Final — Philadelphia

Indiana 63
North Carolina 50

Officials consider postponing the Monday night game because of the assassination attempt on President Ronald Reagan that morning. But the game goes on and the Hoosiers win behind sophomore guard Isiah Thomas, who scores 23 points and takes command in the second half. The title is Bob Knight's second at Indiana and second won in Philadelphia's Spectrum.

National Third Place Virginia d. LSU 78-74

⊗Team participation later vacated

A A computer ranking system, the Rating Percentage Index (RPI), is used for the first time as a factor in making at-large selections.

B The Razorbacks' U.S. Reed drills a 50-foot, last-second shot to eliminate the defending champs. Reed runs directly to the scorer's table after the shot to shake hands with sportswriters—ostensibly to avoid getting hurt in the on-court celebration.

C The Shockers live up to their nickname in the first meeting between the Sunflower State schools in 26 years. In 1979, a Kansas legislator had introduced a bill forcing the two teams to play one another, but the bill died in committee.

D DePaul is eliminated as a No. 1 seed for the second straight year when St. Joseph's John Smith hits a layup in the final seconds. It completes a brilliant sequence of fantastic finishes for NBC, which earlier had shown live, game-winning baskets by Arkansas' U.S. Reed and Kansas State's Rolando Blackman.

E For the first time, the NCAA produces a site-specific logo for the Final Four. Since the site is Philadelphia, the logo includes the Liberty Bell.

F Long Island makes its first NCAA appearance. The Blackbirds won the then-more prestigious NIT in 1939 and '41 under coach Clair Bee, author of the Chip Hilton books for boys and still the all-time winningest coach by percentage in NCAA history.

G In the game's final seconds, BYU guard Danny Ainge dribbles the length of the court through the Notre Dame defense and tosses in a layup over the outstretched fingertips of Irish center Orlando Woolridge at the buzzer. Ainge's full-court rush becomes known as the March Through Atlanta.

Tournament Leaders

INDIVIDUAL LEADERS

Scoring

	CL	POS	G	PTS	PPG
1 **Mike Olliver**, Lamar	SR	G	2	54	27.0
2 **Albert King**, Maryland	SR	F	2	47	23.5
3 **Charles Bradley**, Wyoming	SR	G	2	45	22.5
4 **Pete Harris**, Northeastern	SR	G	2	44	22.0
5 **Al Wood**, North Carolina	SR	G/F	5	109	21.8
6 **John Bagley**, Boston College	SO	G	3	65	21.7
7 **Cliff Levingston**, Wichita State	SO	C	4	86	21.5
8 **Danny Ainge**, BYU	SR	G	4	83	20.8
9 **Danny Vranes**, Utah	SR	F	2	40	20.0
10 **Tony Guy**, Kansas	JR	G	3	59	19.7

Minimum: 2 games

Field Goal Pct

	CL	POS	G	FG	FGA	PCT
1 **Ray McCallum**, Ball State	SO	G	1	13	19	68.4
2 **Byron Scott**, Arizona State	SO	G	1	15	22	68.2
3 **Randy Reed**, Kansas State	JR	F	4	22	33	66.7
4 **Fred Roberts**, BYU	JR	F	4	23	35	65.7
5 **Greg Cook**, LSU	SR	C	5	28	43	65.1

Minimum: 12 made

Free Throw Pct

	CL	POS	G	FT	FTA	PCT
1 **Oliver Robinson**, UAB	JR	G/F	3	17	17	100.0
Al Gooden, Ball State	SR	F	1	13	13	100.0
3 **Jeff Lamp**, Virginia	SR	G	5	25	26	96.2
4 **Jeff Jones**, Virginia	JR	G	5	13	14	92.9
Ed Nealy, Kansas State	JR	F	4	13	14	92.9

Minimum: 12 made

Rebounds Per Game

	CL	POS	G	REB	RPG
1 **Cliff Levingston**, Wichita State	SO	C	4	53	13.3
2 **Buck Williams**, Maryland	JR	F/C	2	26	13.0
3 **Danny Vranes**, Utah	SR	F	2	25	12.5
4 **Tracy Jackson**, Notre Dame	SR	G	2	23	11.5
5 **Tom Chambers**, Utah	SR	F	2	20	10.0

Minimum: 2 games

TEAM LEADERS

Scoring

		G	PTS	PPG
1	**Indiana**	5	394	78.8
2	**LSU**	5	391	78.2
3	**UAB**	3	234	78.0
4	**Wichita State**	4	306	76.5
5	**Utah**	2	150	75.0
6	**Lamar**	2	149	74.5
7	**Kansas**	3	222	74.0
8	**Maryland**	2	145	72.5
9	**Wyoming**	2	143	71.5
10	**VCU**	2	141	70.5

Minimum: 2 games

FG Pct

		G	FG	FGA	PCT
1	**Villanova**	2	56	99	56.6
2	**VCU**	2	52	93	55.9
3	**Lamar**	2	62	114	54.4
4	**Indiana**	5	153	284	53.9
5	**Wyoming**	2	56	104	53.8

FT Pct

		G	FT	FTA	PCT
1	**Illinois**	2	17	20	85.0
2	**Virginia**	5	95	115	82.6
3	**UAB**	3	84	105	80.0
4	**Wyoming**	2	31	40	77.5
5	**Indiana**	5	88	116	75.9

Minimum: 2 games

Rebounds

		G	REB	RPG
1	**Utah**	2	81	40.5
2	**LSU**	5	182	36.4
3	**Wichita State**	4	145	36.3
4	**Maryland**	2	67	33.5
5	**North Carolina**	5	165	33.0

Minimum: 2 games

ALL-TOURNAMENT TEAM

PLAYER	CL	POS	HT	SCHOOL	RPG	PPG
Isiah Thomas*	SO	G	6-1	Indiana	2.6	18.2
Jeff Lamp	SR	G	6-6	Virginia	5.8	17.8
James Thomas	SO	G	6-6	Indiana	4.4	4.6
Landon Turner	JR	F/C	6-10	Indiana	5.4	13.2
Al Wood	SR	G/F	6-6	North Carolina	9.6	21.8

ALL-REGIONAL TEAMS

EAST

PLAYER	CL	POS	HT	SCHOOL	RPG	PPG
Jeff Lamp*	SR	G	6-6	Virginia	4.7	15.3
Danny Ainge	SR	G	6-5	BYU	2.3	20.8
Lee Raker	SR	F	6-6	Virginia	2.0	10.3
Ralph Sampson	SO	C	7-4	Virginia	9.7	16.0
Orlando Woolridge	SR	F	6-9	Notre Dame	4.0	11.0

MIDEAST

PLAYER	CL	POS	HT	SCHOOL	RPG	PPG
Isiah Thomas*	SO	G	6-1	Indiana	3.0	18.0
Glenn Marcus	SR	G	5-10	UAB	2.0	16.3
Ray Tolbert	SR	F/C	6-9	Indiana	7.3	19.0
Bryan Warrick	JR	G	6-5	Saint Joseph's	2.3	12.3
Randy Wittman	JR	G/F	6-6	Indiana	2.0	12.7

MIDWEST

PLAYER	CL	POS	HT	SCHOOL	RPG	PPG
Rudy Macklin*	SR	F	6-7	LSU	11.7	22.3
Greg Cook	SR	C	6-9	LSU	7.0	13.3
Cliff Levingston	SO	C	6-8	Wichita State	13.3	21.5
Ethan Martin	SR	G	6-0	LSU	1.0	11.0
Randy Smithson	SR	G	6-1	Wichita State	2.8	13.3

WEST

PLAYER	CL	POS	HT	SCHOOL	RPG	PPG
Al Wood*	SR	G/F	6-6	North Carolina	10.7	17.3
Rolando Blackman	SR	G	6-6	Kansas State	4.8	13.8
Ed Nealy	JR	F	6-7	Kansas State	8.8	10.8
Sam Perkins	FR	F/C	6-9	North Carolina	9.0	16.7
James Worthy	SO	F	6-9	North Carolina	7.0	17.0

* Most outstanding player

1981 NCAA TOURNAMENT BOX SCORES

LSU 72-56 Arkansas (Sweet 16)

LSU	MIN	FG	3FG	FT	REB	A	ST	BL	PF	TP
Ethan Martin	30	5-8	-	6-6	3	8	2	0	5	16
Rudy Macklin	37	6-13	-	3-8	9	1	0	0	1	15
Greg Cook	22	4-7	-	4-4	7	0	1	0	5	12
Leonard Mitchell	40	4-8	-	2-3	7	2	4	2	4	10
Willie Sims	19	4-4	-	1-1	5	2	0	0	0	9
Howard Carter	40	4-13	-	0-1	3	2	0	0	2	8
Johnny Jones	11	1-3	-	0-1	3	1	1	0	0	2
John Tudor	1	0-1	-	0-0	0	1	0	0	0	0
TOTALS	200	28-57	-	16-24	37	17	8	2	17	72
Percentages		49.1		66.7						

Coach: Dale Brown

	1H	2H
LSU	34	38
Arkansas	18	38

ARKANSAS	MIN	FG	3FG	FT	REB	A	ST	BL	PF	TP
Scott Hastings	27	6-12	-	2-2	7	0	0	0	5	14
Darrell Walker	31	6-14	-	0-1	4	4	4	0	4	12
U.S. Reed	40	4-10	-	2-4	5	1	2	2	0	10
Keith Peterson	27	4-11	-	1-2	2	1	1	0	2	9
Tony Brown	34	4-7	-	0-0	4	2	2	1	4	8
Brad Friess	19	1-2	-	0-0	0	0	1	0	2	2
Carey Kelly	6	0-1	-	1-2	1	0	1	0	1	1
Mike Young	7	0-1	-	0-0	0	0	0	0	2	0
Greg Skulman	6	0-1	-	0-0	1	0	0	0	0	0
Ricky Norton	3	0-0	-	0-0	0	3	0	0	1	0
TOTALS	200	25-59	-	6-11	24	11	11	3	21	56
Percentages		42.4		54.5						

Coach: Eddie Sutton

Officials: Hank Nichols, George Solomon, Willie McJunkin **Technicals:** LSU (Cook, Sims), Arkansas (Walker) **Attendance:** 34,036

Wichita State 66-65 Kansas (Sweet 16)

WICHITA STATE	MIN	FG	3FG	FT	REB	A	ST	BL	PF	TP
Cliff Levingston	38	6-16	-	6-8	14	1	0	1	2	18
Randy Smithson	40	7-14	-	2-3	4	7	0	0	3	16
Antoine Carr	37	6-10	-	4-6	9	0	1	2	4	16
Mike Jones	21	4-7	-	0-0	1	3	1	0	1	8
Tony Martin	25	1-5	-	0-0	2	0	0	1	1	2
Jay Jackson	23	1-7	-	0-0	6	1	0	0	3	2
Karl Papke	13	1-2	-	0-0	1	4	0	0	3	2
James Gibbs	2	1-1	-	0-0	0	0	0	0	0	2
Mark Denny	1	0-0	-	0-0	0	1	0	0	0	0
TOTALS	200	27-62	-	12-17	37	17	2	4	17	66
Percentages		43.5		70.6						

Coach: Gene Smithson

	1H	2H
Wichita State	33	33
Kansas	32	33

KANSAS	MIN	FG	3FG	FT	REB	A	ST	BL	PF	TP
Darnell Valentine	36	8-13	-	5-9	2	6	4	0	2	21
John Crawford	34	5-9	-	1-3	5	1	0	1	4	11
David Magley	35	4-10	-	2-2	7	4	1	1	1	10
Tony Guy	36	4-12	-	1-2	2	0	2	0	1	9
Art Housey	35	3-7	-	0-0	6	2	1	1	4	6
Victor Mitchell	12	2-5	-	0-0	1	1	0	0	2	4
Booty Neal	12	2-5	-	0-0	1	1	1	0	1	4
TOTALS	200	28-61	-	9-16	24	15	9	3	15	65
Percentages		45.9		56.2						

Coach: Ted Owens

Officials: Bob Herrold, Burrell Crowell, Tom Fraim **Technicals:** Kansas (Mitchell, Crawford) **Attendance:** 21,192

Saint Joseph's 42-41 Boston College (Sweet 16)

SAINT JOSEPH'S	MIN	FG	3FG	FT	REB	A	ST	BL	PF	TP
Bryan Warrick	40	7-11	-	6-10	2	1	1	0	2	20
Tony Costner	32	4-7	-	0-0	4	0	1	1	4	8
Jeff Clark	40	2-6	-	1-1	2	1	1	0	1	5
John Smith	39	2-4	-	0-1	6	2	0	0	2	4
Lonnie McFarlan	25	2-9	-	0-0	6	2	2	0	3	4
Boo Williams	24	0-7	-	1-3	8	0	1	1	4	1
TOTALS	200	17-44	-	8-15	28	6	6	2	16	42
Percentages		38.6		53.3						

Coach: Jim Lynam

	1H	2H
Saint Joseph's	18	24
Boston College	22	19

BOSTON COLLEGE	MIN	FG	3FG	FT	REB	A	ST	BL	PF	TP
John Bagley	32	4-14	-	3-4	2	1	0	0	4	11
Jay Murphy	22	4-9	-	2-2	7	0	0	0	0	10
Martin Clark	31	4-8	-	1-1	3	0	1	0	3	9
Burnett Adams	18	1-6	-	3-5	5	1	0	1	3	5
Dwan Chandler	30	2-4	-	0-0	2	2	0	0	1	4
Chris Foy	22	0-0	-	2-4	3	1	1	0	3	2
Tim O'Shea	19	0-0	-	0-0	0	0	1	0	0	0
Rich Shrigley	17	0-1	-	0-0	5	1	0	0	0	0
Joe Beaulieu	9	0-1	-	0-0	1	0	1	0	0	0
TOTALS	200	15-43	-	11-16	28	6	4	1	14	41
Percentages		34.9		68.8						

Coach: Tom Davis

Officials: Paul Galvan, Byron Johnson, Mickey Crowley **Technicals:** None **Attendance:** 12,000

Indiana 87-72 UAB (Sweet 16)

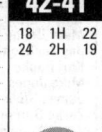

INDIANA	MIN	FG	3FG	FT	REB	A	ST	BL	PF	TP
Isiah Thomas	39	7-12	-	13-15	4	8	3	0	4	27
Randy Wittman	40	7-11	-	6-7	4	3	1	0	1	20
Ray Tolbert	39	8-12	-	1-1	9	2	0	1	3	17
Ted Kitchel	17	3-8	-	3-4	1	0	0	0	3	9
James Thomas	27	3-4	-	1-2	6	3	0	0	2	7
Steve Bouchie	16	2-7	-	1-2	3	2	1	0	2	5
Tony Brown	1	1-1	-	0-0	0	0	0	0	0	2
Landon Turner	11	0-3	-	0-2	1	0	0	1	3	0
Steve Risley	7	0-1	-	0-0	2	0	0	0	2	0
Charles Franz	1	0-0	-	0-0	0	0	0	0	0	0
Glen Grunwald	1	0-0	-	0-0	1	0	0	0	0	0
Phil Isenbarger	1	0-0	-	0-0	1	1	0	0	0	0
TOTALS	200	31-59	-	25-33	32	19	5	2	20	87
Percentages		52.5		75.8						

Coach: Bob Knight

	1H	2H
Indiana	42	45
UAB	37	35

UAB	MIN	FG	3FG	FT	REB	A	ST	BL	PF	TP
Oliver Robinson	-	6-15	-	5-5	2	1	0	0	4	17
Chris Giles	-	6-11	-	1-3	3	1	1	0	3	13
Glenn Marcus	-	6-10	-	1-1	1	4	1	0	5	13
Donnie Speer	-	3-8	-	2-2	7	0	0	1	3	8
Norman Anchrum	-	2-5	-	3-4	3	0	0	2	5	7
Leon Morris	-	1-4	-	4-4	2	1	0	0	0	6
Luellen Foster	-	2-3	-	1-1	1	0	1	0	5	5
Craig Lane	-	1-5	-	0-2	3	0	0	0	4	2
Jonath Nicholas	-	0-0	-	1-2	1	0	0	0	0	1
Tim Almquist	-	0-0	-	0-0	1	0	0	0	0	0
Murry Bartow	-	0-0	-	0-0	0	0	0	0	0	0
Bill McCammon	-	0-1	-	0-0	0	0	0	0	0	0
Tim Richards	-	0-0	-	0-0	0	0	0	0	0	0
Scott Simcik	-	0-1	-	0-0	0	0	0	0	0	0
TOTALS	-	27-63	-	18-24	24	7	3	3	29	72
Percentages		42.9		75.0						

Coach: Gene Bartow

Officials: Dale Kelley, James Howell, Bob Dibler **Technicals:** None **Attendance:** 17,091

Kansas State 57-52 Illinois (Sweet 16)

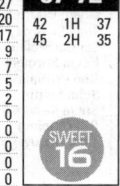

KANSAS STATE	MIN	FG	3FG	FT	REB	A	ST	BL	PF	TP
Rolando Blackman	-	4-9	-	4-6	3	1	1	-	0	12
Ed Nealy	-	4-9	-	4-4	14	0	3	-	0	12
Tyrone Adams	-	5-6	-	1-2	2	4	0	-	3	11
Tim Jankovich	-	2-5	-	4-7	2	5	1	-	2	8
Randy Reed	-	3-3	-	1-2	2	0	0	-	1	7
Eduardo Galvao	-	1-6	-	3-4	0	0	0	-	1	5
Fred Barton	-	1-1	-	0-0	1	1	1	-	1	2
Les Craft	-	0-0	-	0-0	1	0	1	-	1	0
TOTALS	-	20-39	-	17-25	25	11	7	-	9	57
Percentages		51.3		68.0						

Coach: Jack Hartman

	1H	2H
Kansas State	30	27
Illinois	27	25

ILLINOIS	MIN	FG	3FG	FT	REB	A	ST	BL	PF	TP
Eddie Johnson	40	7-15	-	1-1	9	0	0	1	4	15
Perry Range	40	5-9	-	0-0	4	2	0	0	3	10
Mark Smith	32	5-10	-	0-0	6	5	0	0	5	10
James Griffin	14	4-7	-	0-0	1	0	0	0	5	8
Craig Tucker	17	2-10	-	1-2	1	0	0	0	2	5
Derek Holcomb	23	2-4	-	0-0	7	0	1	0	3	4
Derek Harper	33	0-7	-	0-0	6	7	0	2	0	0
Quinn Richardson	1	0-0	-	0-0	0	0	0	0	0	0
TOTALS	200	25-62	-	2-3	34	14	1	3	22	52
Percentages		40.3		66.7						

Coach: Lou Henson

Officials: Booker Turner, Ken Lauderdale, Lou Moser **Technicals:** None

North Carolina 61-56 Utah (Sweet 16)

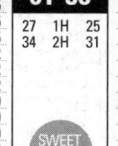

NORTH CAROLINA	MIN	FG	3FG	FT	REB	A	ST	BL	PF	TP
Al Wood	36	7-12	-	1-3	6	0	2	1	1	15
James Worthy	35	4-6	-	7-10	10	6	0	2	2	15
Sam Perkins	33	7-14	-	1-2	11	0	0	4	4	15
Matt Doherty	25	3-5	-	6-8	2	2	0	0	2	12
Jimmy Black	35	1-3	-	0-1	2	8	1	0	4	2
Mike Pepper	22	1-2	-	0-0	1	0	0	0	3	2
Pete Budko	9	0-1	-	0-0	0	0	0	0	1	0
Jim Braddock	3	0-0	-	0-0	0	0	0	0	0	0
Chris Brust	1	0-0	-	0-0	1	0	0	0	0	0
Eric Kenny	1	0-0	-	0-0	0	0	0	0	0	0
TOTALS	200	23-43	-	15-24	33	16	3	7	17	61
Percentages		53.5		62.5						

Coach: Dean Smith

	1H	2H
North Carolina	27	34
Utah	25	31

UTAH	MIN	FG	3FG	FT	REB	A	ST	BL	PF	TP
Scott Martin	40	6-13	-	3-3	1	8	3	0	4	15
Danny Vranes	40	5-14	-	3-4	14	1	1	1	1	13
Tom Chambers	24	4-9	-	3-4	8	1	1	1	4	11
Pace Mannion	38	5-8	-	0-0	5	2	0	0	2	10
Chris Winans	11	1-1	-	1-2	0	1	0	0	1	3
Karl Bankowski	23	1-9	-	0-0	2	2	1	0	5	2
Craig Hammer	18	1-4	-	0-0	1	2	0	0	1	2
Peter Williams	5	0-0	-	0-0	0	0	0	0	3	0
Angelo Robinson	1	0-0	-	0-0	0	0	0	0	0	0
TOTALS	200	23-58	-	10-13	31	17	6	2	21	56
Percentages		39.7		76.9						

Coach: Jerry Pimm

Officials: Tom Fincken, Bob Wortman, David Pollock **Technicals:** North Carolina (Worthy)

VIRGINIA	MIN	FG	3FG	FT	REB	A	ST	BL	PF	TP
Jeff Lamp	36	8-11	-	2-2	5	2	0	0	0	18
Jeff Jones	33	3-6	-	4-5	3	5	4	0	2	10
Lee Raker	17	4-5	-	2-2	3	0	1	0	1	10
Ralph Sampson	34	4-13	-	1-2	5	1	1	4	1	9
Othell Wilson	34	2-3	-	5-6	2	2	2	0	1	9
Terry Gates	32	2-2	-	0-0	4	1	1	0	1	4
Ricky Stokes	4	1-3	-	0-0	0	0	0	0	2	2
Lewis Lattimore	4	0-0	-	0-0	1	0	0	0	2	0
Craig Robinson	4	0-0	-	0-0	1	0	0	0	0	0
Louis Collins	1	0-0	-	0-0	1	0	0	0	0	0
Jeff Klein	1	0-0	-	0-0	0	0	0	0	0	0
TOTALS	**200**	**24-43**	**-**	**14-17**	**25**	**11**	**9**	**4**	**10**	**62**
Percentages		55.8		82.4						

Coach: Terry Holland

62-48

27	1H	26
35	2H	22

SWEET 16

TENNESSEE	MIN	FG	3FG	FT	REB	A	ST	BL	PF	TP
Dale Ellis	39	6-12	-	1-2	9	1	0	0	4	13
Gary Carter	39	4-9	-	1-2	4	2	0	0	4	9
Howard Wood	39	4-9	-	0-0	4	2	3	0	1	8
Michael Brooks	27	3-8	-	0-0	1	6	2	0	2	6
Steve Ray	33	2-4	-	0-0	0	1	0	0	1	4
Ed Littleton	13	2-3	-	0-0	0	2	0	0	3	4
Tyrone Beaman	7	2-2	-	0-0	0	2	0	0	3	4
Willie Burton	1	0-1	-	0-0	0	0	0	1	0	0
Dan Federmann	1	0-0	-	0-0	0	0	0	0	0	0
Anthony Love	1	0-0	-	0-0	0	1	0	0	0	0
TOTALS	**200**	**23-48**	**-**	**2-4**	**18**	**17**	**5**	**1**	**18**	**48**
Percentages		47.9		50.0						

Coach: Don DeVoe

Officials: Jan Burroughs, Richie Weiler Edgar Cartott
Technicals: None
Attendance: 15,461

BYU	MIN	FG	3FG	FT	REB	A	ST	BL	PF	TP
Danny Ainge	40	4-10	-	4-4	1	3	3	0	2	12
Fred Roberts	28	5-6	-	1-3	5	0	0	0	5	11
Steve Craig	31	5-13	-	0-0	3	1	2	0	5	10
Greg Ballif	18	3-6	-	4-5	0	1	1	0	1	10
Timo Saarelainen	14	2-3	-	0-0	2	1	0	0	2	4
Steve Trumbo	40	1-8	-	0-2	9	2	0	1	1	2
Greg Kite	22	1-2	-	0-0	5	0	0	0	4	2
Gary Furniss	7	0-0	-	0-0	1	0	0	0	0	0
TOTALS	**200**	**21-48**	**-**	**9-14**	**26**	**8**	**6**	**1**	**20**	**51**
Percentages		43.8		64.3						

Coach: Frank Arnold

51-50

18	1H	28
33	2H	22

SWEET 16

NOTRE DAME	MIN	FG	3FG	FT	REB	A	ST	BL	PF	TP
Orlando Woolridge	40	8-10	-	1-2	6	2	0	0	1	17
Kelly Tripucka	37	7-12	-	0-2	2	3	1	0	3	14
Tracy Jackson	36	3-7	-	5-5	11	4	1	2	3	11
John Paxson	40	1-5	-	2-3	4	6	0	0	3	4
Tim Andree	33	1-3	-	0-1	2	1	1	0	4	2
Joe Kleine	6	1-1	-	0-0	0	0	0	0	0	2
Tom Sluby	5	0-0	-	0-0	0	0	0	0	2	0
Bill Varner	3	0-0	-	0-1	0	0	0	0	0	0
TOTALS	**200**	**21-38**	**-**	**8-14**	**25**	**16**	**3**	**2**	**16**	**50**
Percentages		55.3		57.1						

Coach: Digger Phelps

Officials: Lenny Wirtz, Ec Maracich, Mar Reischling
Technicals: None
Attendance: 15,461

LSU	MIN	FG	3FG	FT	REB	A	ST	BL	PF	TP
Rudy Macklin	28	9-11	-	3-3	10	1	0	1	2	21
Greg Cook	32	9-10	-	1-3	7	1	0	0	3	19
Leonard Mitchell	33	7-12	-	3-5	6	0	2	0	4	17
Ethan Martin	35	5-8	-	3-3	0	10	4	0	3	13
Howard Carter	26	5-10	-	1-2	0	5	2	0	3	11
Willie Sims	18	2-5	-	3-4	1	2	0	0	2	7
Brian Bergeron	8	0-0	-	4-4	0	1	0	0	0	4
Tyrone Black	4	1-3	-	0-0	1	0	0	0	0	2
Matt England	1	1-1	-	0-0	0	0	0	0	0	2
Johnny Jones	8	0-1	-	0-0	0	0	0	0	0	0
John Tudor	4	0-0	-	0-0	1	0	0	0	0	0
Andy Campbell	1	0-0	-	0-0	0	0	0	0	0	0
Joe Costello	1	0-0	-	0-0	1	0	0	0	0	0
Brian Kistler	1	0-0	-	0-0	0	0	0	0	0	0
TOTALS	**200**	**39-61**	**-**	**18-24**	**27**	**20**	**8**	**1**	**17**	**96**
Percentages		63.9		75.0						

Coach: Dale Brown

96-85

48	1H	33
48	2H	52

ELITE 8

WICHITA STATE	MIN	FG	3FG	FT	REB	A	ST	BL	PF	TP
Antoine Carr	30	9-13	-	4-5	5	1	0	2	5	22
Cliff Levingston	40	8-12	-	3-4	10	3	3	0	4	19
Randy Smithson	32	8-11	-	2-3	1	5	0	0	3	18
Tony Martin	35	5-14	-	0-0	3	10	1	0	4	10
Mark Denny	11	5-10	-	0-0	4	1	0	0	2	10
Jay Jackson	21	2-6	-	0-1	6	4	0	0	2	4
Karl Papke	6	1-3	-	0-1	1	0	1	0	2	2
Mike Jones	15	0-5	-	0-1	0	0	0	0	0	0
James Gibbs	8	0-1	-	0-0	0	0	0	0	1	0
Zarko Durisic	1	0-0	-	0-0	0	0	0	0	0	0
Zoran Radovic	1	0-0	-	0-0	0	0	0	0	0	0
TOTALS	**200**	**38-75**	**-**	**9-15**	**30**	**24**	**5**	**2**	**23**	**85**
Percentages		50.7		60.0						

Coach: Gene Smithson

Officials: Hank Nichols, George Solomon, Willie McJunkin
Technicals: LSU (Mitchell)
Attendance: 32,747

INDIANA	MIN	FG	3FG	FT	REB	A	ST	BL	PF	TP
Ray Tolbert	37	6-8	-	2-4	5	2	0	-	1	14
Landon Turner	29	7-8	-	0-0	5	2	0	-	5	14
James Thomas	24	6-7	-	0-0	3	1	0	-	0	12
Isiah Thomas	36	3-8	-	2-3	1	12	3	-	2	8
Randy Wittman	13	4-4	-	0-0	0	1	0	-	0	8
Phil Isenbarger	3	3-4	-	0-0	0	2	0	-	3	6
Glen Grunwald	8	1-1	-	2-2	1	1	0	-	1	4
Ted Kitchel	20	1-4	-	1-2	3	3	1	-	4	3
Steve Risley	17	1-2	-	0-1	2	2	1	-	0	2
Steve Bouchie	3	1-2	-	0-0	1	1	0	-	0	2
Charles Franz	3	1-1	-	0-0	0	0	0	-	1	2
Mike Lafave	3	1-1	-	0-0	5	0	0	-	0	2
Tony Brown	4	0-1	-	1-2	1	2	0	-	2	1
TOTALS	**200**	**35-51**	**-**	**8-14**	**27**	**29**	**5**	**-**	**19**	**78**
Percentages		68.6		57.1						

Coach: Bob Knight

78-46

32	1H	16
46	2H	30

ELITE 8

SAINT JOSEPH'S	MIN	FG	3FG	FT	REB	A	ST	BL	PF	TP
Jeff Clark	31	3-4	-	5-6	4	0	0	-	4	11
Bryan Warrick	38	3-10	-	3-3	0	3	1	-	1	9
Tony Costner	34	3-8	-	1-2	4	0	1	-	5	7
Lonnie McFarlan	20	1-7	-	4-6	2	2	0	-	0	6
Kevin Springman	3	1-3	-	3-4	0	0	0	-	0	5
Boo Williams	34	2-4	-	0-0	4	0	0	-	3	4
John Smith	32	1-6	-	0-0	2	3	1	-	3	2
Steve Kearney	3	0-0	-	2-3	1	0	0	-	1	2
Bill Mitchell	3	0-0	-	0-1	0	0	0	-	0	0
Tony Dicaro	2	0-0	-	0-0	0	1	0	-	0	0
TOTALS	**200**	**14-42**	**-**	**18-25**	**17**	**9**	**3**	**-**	**17**	**46**
Percentages		33.3		72.0						

Coach: Jim Lynam

Officials: Dale Kelley, James Howell, Bob Dibler
Technicals: None
Attendance: 17,112

NORTH CAROLINA	MIN	FG	3FG	FT	REB	A	ST	BL	PF	TP
Al Wood	37	10-17	-	1-1	17	3	0	1	3	21
Sam Perkins	33	7-14	-	2-2	11	4	1	1	3	16
Matt Doherty	28	6-7	-	4-6	5	3	2	0	2	16
James Worthy	33	6-16	-	3-4	4	5	2	0	3	15
Jimmy Black	34	1-3	-	6-6	1	3	0	0	2	8
Mike Pepper	14	2-2	-	0-0	0	1	1	0	2	4
Jim Braddock	6	1-1	-	0-0	0	1	0	0	0	2
Pete Budko	10	0-0	-	0-0	0	0	0	0	1	0
Chris Brust	2	0-0	-	0-0	0	0	0	0	0	0
Jeb Barlow	1	0-0	-	0-0	0	0	0	0	0	0
Cecil Exum	1	0-0	-	0-0	0	0	0	0	0	0
Eric Kenny	1	0-1	-	0-0	1	0	0	0	0	0
TOTALS	**200**	**33-61**	**-**	**16-19**	**39**	**20**	**6**	**2**	**16**	**82**
Percentages		54.1		84.2						

Coach: Dean Smith

82-68

42	1H	29
40	2H	39

ELITE 8

KANSAS STATE	MIN	FG	3FG	FT	REB	A	ST	BL	PF	TP
Rolando Blackman	38	10-17	-	1-1	10	2	0	0	1	21
Randy Reed	28	6-12	-	7-7	5	0	0	1	4	19
Ed Nealy	28	6-10	-	0-0	7	3	3	0	4	12
Tim Jankovich	36	1-6	-	2-4	0	7	0	0	3	4
Tyrone Adams	27	2-9	-	0-1	7	3	0	0	2	4
Eduardo Galvao	25	2-8	-	0-0	1	2	1	0	4	4
Fred Barton	8	2-4	-	0-0	0	0	0	0	0	4
Les Craft	8	0-2	-	0-0	0	0	0	0	0	0
Steve Reid	2	0-1	-	0-0	0	0	0	0	1	0
TOTALS	**200**	**29-69**	**-**	**10-13**	**30**	**17**	**4**	**1**	**19**	**68**
Percentages		42.0		76.9						

Coach: Jack Hartman

Officials: Booker Turner, Ken Lauderdale, Lou Moser
Technicals: North Carolina (coach Smith, Perkins, Worthy)
Attendance: 15,429

VIRGINIA	MIN	FG	3FG	FT	REB	A	ST	BL	PF	TP
Ralph Sampson	36	9-16	-	4-7	12	1	0	4	2	22
Jeff Lamp	38	7-15	-	4-5	7	2	0	0	3	18
Lee Raker	22	4-9	-	4-4	2	1	1	0	2	12
Jeff Jones	31	2-4	-	6-6	0	4	2	0	3	10
Othell Wilson	30	3-7	-	4-4	5	5	3	1	4	10
Terry Gates	33	1-2	-	0-1	2	0	0	0	3	2
Lewis Lattimore	4	0-0	-	0-1	0	0	0	0	1	0
Ricky Stokes	4	0-1	-	0-0	0	0	1	0	0	0
Louis Collins	1	0-1	-	0-0	0	0	0	0	1	0
Jeff Klein	1	0-0	-	0-0	1	0	0	0	0	0
TOTALS	**200**	**26-55**	**-**	**22-28**	**29**	**13**	**7**	**5**	**19**	**74**
Percentages		47.3		78.6						

Coach: Terry Holland

74-60

28	1H	31
46	2H	29

ELITE 8

BYU	MIN	FG	3FG	FT	REB	A	ST	BL	PF	TP
Danny Ainge	38	4-13	-	5-5	3	5	0	0	4	13
Fred Roberts	36	6-8	-	0-1	7	5	1	1	5	12
Steve Craig	27	4-8	-	4-4	1	3	1	0	5	12
Steve Trumbo	34	4-8	-	3-4	8	2	0	0	2	11
Greg Ballif	14	2-4	-	2-2	3	0	0	0	3	6
Greg Kite	37	2-6	-	0-1	5	0	0	1	4	4
Gary Furniss	4	1-1	-	0-0	2	0	0	0	0	2
Timo Saarelainen	8	0-2	-	0-0	0	0	0	0	1	0
Craig Christensen	1	0-1	-	0-0	0	0	0	0	0	0
Richie Webb	1	0-0	-	0-0	1	0	0	0	0	0
TOTALS	**200**	**23-51**	**-**	**14-17**	**30**	**15**	**2**	**2**	**24**	**60**
Percentages		45.1		82.4						

Coach: Frank Arnold

Officials: James Burroughs, Richie Weiler, Edgar Cartotto
Technicals: BYU (Ainge)
Attendance: 15,461

INDIANA	MIN	FG	3FG	FT	REB	A	ST	BL	PF	TP
Landon Turner	38	7-19	-	6-7	8	0	0	0	1	20
Isiah Thomas	26	6-8	-	2-3	2	4	0	0	4	14
Ted Kitchel	23	3-8	-	4-4	6	0	0	0	3	10
Randy Wittman	37	3-10	-	2-2	2	2	0	0	0	8
Ray Tolbert	36	3-7	-	1-2	6	5	1	0	3	7
Glen Grunwald	3	1-2	-	1-2	2	0	0	0	1	3
James Thomas	17	0-4	-	2-2	9	2	1	2	1	2
Charles Franz	2	0-0	-	2-2	0	0	0	0	1	2
Steve Risley	10	0-2	-	1-2	2	1	0	0	0	1
Steve Bouchie	2	0-1	-	0-0	2	0	0	0	0	0
Tony Brown	2	0-1	-	0-1	0	0	0	0	0	0
Phil Isenbarger	2	0-1	-	0-0	0	0	0	0	0	0
Mike Lafave	2	0-0	-	0-0	2	0	0	0	1	0
TOTALS	**200**	**23-63**	**-**	**21-27**	**41**	**14**	**2**	**2**	**15**	**67**
Percentages		36.5		77.8						
Coach: Bob Knight										

67-49

27	1H	30
40	2H	19

FINAL 4

LSU	MIN	FG	3FG	FT	REB	A	ST	BL	PF	TP
Howard Carter	32	5-10	-	0-0	6	1	1	1	3	10
Leonard Mitchell	37	3-10	-	3-4	10	0	1	0	3	9
Ethan Martin	31	2-8	-	3-3	3	8	0	0	4	7
Greg Cook	34	3-5	-	0-0	5	0	0	0	5	6
John Tudor	3	1-3	-	4-4	2	0	0	0	3	6
Willie Sims	14	2-8	-	1-2	1	0	2	0	0	5
Rudy Macklin	35	2-12	-	0-0	8	0	0	1	1	4
Tyrone Black	1	1-1	-	0-0	1	0	0	0	0	2
Johnny Jones	9	0-2	-	0-1	2	1	0	0	3	0
Brian Bergeron	3	0-0	-	0-0	0	1	0	0	0	0
Joe Costello	1	0-0	-	0-0	0	0	0	0	0	0
TOTALS	**200**	**19-59**	**-**	**11-14**	**38**	**11**	**4**	**2**	**22**	**49**
Percentages		32.2		78.6						
Coach: Dale Brown										

Officials: Ken Lauderdale, Lou Moser, Booker Turner
Technicals: LSU (coach Brown)
Attendance: 18,276

NORTH CAROLINA	MIN	FG	3FG	FT	REB	A	ST	BL	PF	TP
Al Wood	36	14-19	-	11-13	10	1	0	0	3	39
Sam Perkins	40	4-7	-	3-5	9	1	1	1	4	11
Jimmy Black	32	4-6	-	2-3	1	4	2	0	4	10
James Worthy	40	2-8	-	4-7	3	1	1	2	2	8
Matt Doherty	32	0-1	-	8-9	4	3	1	0	1	8
Eric Kenny	1	1-1	-	0-0	1	0	0	0	0	2
Mike Pepper	11	0-4	-	0-0	1	0	0	0	2	0
Jim Braddock	8	0-1	-	0-0	0	1	0	0	0	0
TOTALS	**200**	**25-47**	**-**	**28-37**	**29**	**11**	**5**	**3**	**16**	**78**
Percentages		53.2		75.7						
Coach: Dean Smith										

78-65

27	1H	27
51	2H	38

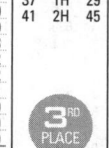

FINAL 4

VIRGINIA	MIN	FG	3FG	FT	REB	A	ST	BL	PF	TP
Jeff Lamp	39	7-18	-	4-4	7	4	3	0	5	18
Lee Raker	26	5-9	-	3-3	5	1	1	0	5	13
Jeff Jones	36	5-13	-	1-1	3	5	1	0	3	11
Ralph Sampson	36	3-10	-	5-7	9	1	1	3	3	11
Othell Wilson	23	4-7	-	0-0	2	3	1	0	4	8
Terry Gates	23	1-1	-	0-0	4	0	0	0	4	2
Lewis Lattimore	2	1-1	-	0-0	1	0	0	0	0	2
Ricky Stokes	15	0-2	-	0-0	1	0	0	0	3	0
TOTALS	**200**	**26-61**	**-**	**13-15**	**32**	**14**	**7**	**3**	**27**	**65**
Percentages		42.6		86.7						
Coach: Terry Holland										

Officials: Dale Kelley, James Howell, Bob Dibler
Technicals: None
Attendance: 18,276

VIRGINIA	MIN	FG	3FG	FT	REB	A	ST	BL	PF	TP
Jeff Lamp	38	7-13	-	11-11	8	1	0	-	3	25
Lee Raker	29	7-14	-	7-8	5	3	0	-	2	21
Ralph Sampson	17	3-8	-	4-4	11	2	0	-	5	10
Othell Wilson	32	1-6	-	7-8	1	2	1	-	1	9
Terry Gates	24	2-5	-	4-5	5	0	0	-	5	8
Jeff Jones	26	1-2	-	0-0	2	2	2	-	0	2
Lewis Lattimore	18	1-4	-	0-0	6	1	0	-	3	2
Craig Robinson	4	0-2	-	1-2	1	0	0	-	0	1
Jeff Klein	6	0-1	-	0-0	0	1	1	-	3	0
Ricky Stokes	4	0-3	-	0-0	0	1	0	-	0	0
Louis Collins	2	0-0	-	0-0	0	0	0	-	0	0
TOTALS	**200**	**22-58**	**-**	**34-38**	**39**	**13**	**4**	**-**	**22**	**78**
Percentages		37.9		89.5						
Coach: Terry Holland										

78-74

37	1H	29
41	2H	45

3RD PLACE

LSU	MIN	FG	3FG	FT	REB	A	ST	BL	PF	TP
Greg Cook	40	8-14	-	5-8	8	0	0	-	2	21
Leonard Mitchell	36	7-12	-	2-5	12	1	2	-	5	16
Howard Carter	24	7-14	-	0-0	6	1	1	-	5	14
Willie Sims	21	5-10	-	3-4	3	2	2	-	3	13
Ethan Martin	37	3-8	-	0-1	1	7	4	-	5	6
Johnny Jones	14	2-6	-	0-0	2	2	0	-	3	4
Rudy Macklin	16	0-3	-	0-0	5	0	0	-	5	0
John Tudor	9	0-1	-	0-0	1	0	0	-	2	0
Brian Bergeron	2	0-0	-	0-0	0	0	0	-	0	0
Tyrone Black	1	0-1	-	0-0	2	0	0	-	0	0
TOTALS	**200**	**32-69**	**-**	**10-18**	**40**	**13**	**9**	**-**	**30**	**74**
Percentages		46.4		55.6						
Coach: Dale Brown										

Officials: Dale Kelley, James Howell, Bob Dibler
Technicals: None
Attendance: 18,276

INDIANA	MIN	FG	3FG	FT	REB	A	ST	BL	PF	TP
Isiah Thomas	40	8-17	-	7-8	2	5	4	0	4	23
Randy Wittman	40	7-13	-	2-2	4	0	0	0	2	16
Landon Turner	34	5-8	-	2-2	6	1	1	0	5	12
Ray Tolbert	40	1-4	-	3-6	11	0	2	1	0	5
Steve Risley	13	1-1	-	3-4	4	0	0	0	1	5
James Thomas	29	1-4	-	0-0	4	8	1	0	2	2
Ted Kitchel	4	0-1	-	0-0	0	0	0	0	3	0
TOTALS	**200**	**23-48**	**-**	**17-22**	**31**	**14**	**8**	**1**	**17**	**63**
Percentages		47.9		77.3						
Coach: Bob Knight										

63-50

27	1H	26
36	2H	24

NCAA FINAL 1981

NORTH CAROLINA	MIN	FG	3FG	FT	REB	A	ST	BL	PF	TP
Al Wood	38	6-13	-	6-9	6	2	0	0	4	18
Sam Perkins	39	5-8	-	1-2	8	1	2	1	3	11
James Worthy	31	3-11	-	1-2	6	2	1	1	5	7
Jimmy Black	36	3-4	-	0-0	2	6	4	0	5	6
Mike Pepper	23	2-5	-	2-2	1	0	2	0	1	6
Matt Doherty	24	1-2	-	0-1	4	0	0	0	4	2
Jim Braddock	4	0-2	-	0-0	0	1	0	0	1	0
Chris Brust	3	0-0	-	0-0	0	0	0	0	0	0
Pete Budko	1	0-1	-	0-0	1	0	0	0	0	0
Eric Kenny	1	0-1	-	0-0	1	0	0	0	0	0
TOTALS	**200**	**20-47**	**-**	**10-16**	**29**	**12**	**9**	**2**	**23**	**50**
Percentages		42.6		62.5						
Coach: Dean Smith										

Officials: Ken Lauderdale, Lou Moser, Booker Turner
Technicals: Indiana (Turner)
Attendance: 18,276

National Invitation Tournament (NIT)

First round: Dayton d. Fordham 66-65 (2OT), Georgia d. Old Dominion 74-60, UTEP d. San Jose St. 57-53, South Alabama d. Texas-Arlington 74-71, Toledo d. Texas-Pan American 91-83, Minnesota d. Drake 90-77, Connecticut d. South Florida 65-55, Purdue d. Rhode Island 84-58, Michigan d. Duquesne 74-58, Duke d. North Carolina A&T 79-69, Temple d. Clemson 90-82, Alabama d. St. John's 73-69 (OT), Holy Cross d. Southern Miss 56-54, Syracuse d. Marquette 88-81, Tulsa d. Texas-Pan American 81-71, West Virginia d. Penn 67-64
Second round: Michigan d. Toledo 80-68, South Alabama d. Georgia 73-72, Tulsa d. UTEP 76-72, Minnesota d. Connecticut 84-66, Duke d. Alabama 75-70, West Virginia d. Temple 77-76 (OT), Syracuse d. Holy Cross 77-57, Purdue d. Dayton 50-46
Third round: Syracuse d. Michigan 91-76, West Virginia d. Minnesota 80-69, Tulsa d. South Alabama 69-68, Purdue d. Duke 81-69
Semifinals: Tulsa d. West Virginia 89-87, Syracuse d. Purdue 70-63
Third place: Purdue d. West Virginia 75-72 (OT)
Championship: Tulsa d. Syracuse 86-84 (OT)
MVP: Greg Stewart, Tulsa

1981-82: Dean Does It

After six frustrating trips to the Final Four, it took a freshman to get Dean Smith his first championship. But Michael Jordan was no ordinary frosh. He teamed with two other North Carolina greats, Sam Perkins and James Worthy, to lead the Tar Heels (32–2) to the Final at the Superdome in New Orleans, where they faced Georgetown and Patrick Ewing. Jordan hit a jumper with :15 left to give UNC a 63-62 lead. Then the Hoyas' Fred Brown made an errant pass that went straight into the hands of Worthy. Worthy had 28 points on 13-of-17 shooting, earning Tournament MOP honors. Smith joined Pete Newell as the only coaches to lead basketball teams to an NCAA title, an NIT championship and an Olympic gold medal.

The 1982 Final Four was the first to be broadcast by CBS. The possession arrow was introduced during the regular season, eliminating in-game jump balls. On Dec. 21, 1981, Cincinnati beat Bradley, 75-73, in seven overtimes, still the longest game in NCAA history. Bradley went on to win the NIT. Virginia's Ralph Sampson picked up his second Naismith Player of the Year award. The Los Angeles Lakers selected Worthy as the first pick in the NBA draft.

Major Conference Standings

ACC

	Conference			Overall		
	W	L	PCT	W	L	PCT
North Carolina⊕	12	2	.857	32	2	.941
Virginia○	12	2	.857	30	4	.882
Wake Forest○	9	5	.643	21	9	.700
NC State○	7	7	.500	22	10	.688
Maryland□	5	9	.357	16	13	.552
Clemson□	4	10	.286	14	14	.500
Duke	4	10	.286	10	17	.370
Georgia Tech	3	11	.214	10	16	.385

Tournament: **North Carolina d. Virginia 47-45**
Tournament: MVP: **James Worthy**, North Carolina

Big East

	Conference			Overall		
	W	L	PCT	W	L	PCT
Villanova○	11	3	.786	24	8	.750
Georgetown⊕	10	4	.714	30	7	.811
St. John's○	9	5	.643	21	9	.700
Boston College○	8	6	.571	22	10	.688
Connecticut□	7	7	.500	17	11	.607
Syracuse□	7	7	.500	16	13	.552
Seton Hall	2	12	.143	11	16	.407
Providence	2	12	.143	10	17	.370

Tournament: **Georgetown d. Villanova 72-54**
Tournament MVP: **Eric "Sleepy" Floyd**, Georgetown

Big Eight

	Conference			Overall		
	W	L	PCT	W	L	PCT
Missouri⊕	12	2	.857	27	4	.871
Kansas State○	10	4	.714	23	8	.742
Oklahoma□	8	6	.571	22	11	.667
Nebraska	7	7	.500	16	12	.571
Oklahoma State	7	7	.500	15	12	.556
Iowa State	5	9	.357	10	17	.370
Kansas	4	10	.286	13	14	.481
Colorado	3	11	.214	11	16	.407

Tournament: **Missouri d. Oklahoma 68-63**
Tournament MVP: **Ricky Frazier**, Missouri

Big Sky

	Conference			Overall		
	W	L	PCT	W	L	PCT
Idaho⊕	13	1	.929	27	3	.900
Montana	10	4	.714	17	10	.630
Nevada	9	5	.643	19	9	.679
Weber State	6	8	.429	15	13	.536
Boise State	6	8	.429	12	14	.462
Idaho State	5	9	.357	14	12	.538
Montana State	5	9	.357	11	18	.379
Northern Arizona	2	12	.143	6	20	.231

Tournament: **Idaho d. Nevada 85-80**
Tournament MVP: **Ken Owens**, Idaho

Big Ten

	Conference			Overall		
	W	L	PCT	W	L	PCT
Minnesota⊕	14	4	.778	23	6	.793
Iowa○	12	6	.667	21	8	.724
Ohio State○	12	6	.667	21	10	.677
Indiana○	12	6	.667	19	10	.655
Purdue□	11	7	.611	18	14	.563
Illinois□	10	8	.556	18	11	.621
Michigan State	7	11	.389	11	17	.393
Michigan	7	11	.389	7	20	.259
Northwestern	5	13	.278	8	19	.296
Wisconsin⊗	3	15	.167	6	21	.222

East Coast

	Conference			Overall		
	W	L	PCT	W	L	PCT
East Section						
Temple□	11	0	1.000	19	8	.704
Saint Joseph's⊕	10	1	.909	25	5	.833
American□	8	3	.727	21	9	.700
Drexel	7	4	.636	19	11	.633
La Salle	7	4	.636	16	13	.552
Hofstra	4	7	.364	12	16	.429
West Section						
West Chester	8	8	.500	13	14	.481
Lafayette	7	9	.438	12	15	.444
Rider	7	9	.438	11	16	.407
Delaware	6	10	.375	9	17	.346
Lehigh	3	13	.188	9	17	.346
Bucknell	3	13	.188	7	20	.259

Tournament: **Saint Joseph's d. Drexel 75-65**

ECAC Metro

	Conference			Overall		
	W	L	PCT	W	L	PCT
North Division						
Fairleigh Dickinson	12	3	.800	16	11	.593
Long Island□	11	4	.733	20	10	.667
Siena	8	7	.533	15	13	.536
St. Francis (NY)	8	7	.533	10	17	.370
Marist	6	9	.400	12	14	.462
Wagner	1	14	.067	4	22	.154
South Division						
Robert Morris⊕	9	5	.643	17	13	.567
Baltimore	8	6	.571	15	13	.536
Loyola (MD)	7	7	.500	11	16	.407
Towson	7	7	.500	10	17	.370
Saint Francis (PA)	3	11	.214	6	20	.231

Tournament: **Robert Morris d. Long Island 85-84**
Tournament MVP: **Tom Parks**, Robert Morris

ECAC North

	Conference			Overall		
	W	L	PCT	W	L	PCT
Northeastern⊕	8	1	.889	23	7	.767
Canisius	7	2	.778	19	8	.704
Niagara	7	2	.778	19	10	.655
Boston U.	6	2	.750	19	9	.679
Holy Cross	4	4	.500	16	11	.593
Maine	3	7	.300	7	19	.269
Vermont	2	8	.200	10	16	.385
Colgate	2	8	.200	8	17	.320
New Hampshire	2	9	.182	9	18	.333

Tournament: **Northeastern d. Niagara 62-59**
Tournament MVP: **Perry Moss**, Northeastern

ECAC South

	Conference			Overall		
	W	L	PCT	W	L	PCT
James Madison○	10	1	.909	24	6	.800
Richmond□	6	4	.600	18	11	.621
Old Dominion⊕	5	4	.556	18	12	.600
William and Mary	6	5	.545	16	12	.556
Towson	5	7	.417	10	17	.370
Navy	2	4	.333	12	14	.462
Saint Francis (PA)	2	5	.286	6	20	.231
George Mason	2	6	.250	13	14	.481
East Carolina	2	8	.200	10	17	.370

Tournament: **Old Dominion d. James Madison 58-57**

EAA

	Conference			Overall		
	W	L	PCT	W	L	PCT
West Virginia○	13	1	.929	27	4	.871
Rutgers□	9	5	.643	20	10	.667
Pittsburgh⊕	8	6	.571	20	10	.667
St. Bonaventure	7	7	.500	14	14	.500
George Washington	7	7	.500	13	14	.481
Duquesne	5	9	.357	11	16	.407
Rhode Island	4	10	.286	10	17	.370
Massachusetts	3	11	.214	7	20	.259

Tournament: **Pittsburgh d. West Virginia 79-72**
Tournament MVP: **Clyde Vaughan**, Pittsburgh

Ivy

	Conference			Overall		
	W	L	PCT	W	L	PCT
Penn⊕	12	2	.857	17	10	.630
Columbia	9	5	.643	16	10	.615
Princeton	9	5	.643	13	13	.500
Yale	7	7	.500	13	13	.500
Cornell	7	7	.500	10	16	.385
Harvard	6	8	.429	11	15	.423
Brown	5	9	.357	5	21	.192
Dartmouth	1	13	.071	7	19	.269

Metro

	Conference			Overall		
	W	L	PCT	W	L	PCT
Memphis⊕⊗	10	2	.833	24	5	.828
Louisville○	8	4	.667	23	10	.697
Tulane□	8	4	.667	19	9	.679
Virginia Tech□	7	5	.583	20	11	.645
Cincinnati	4	8	.333	15	12	.556
Florida State	4	8	.333	11	17	.393
Saint Louis	1	11	.083	6	21	.222

Tournament: **Memphis d. Louisville 73-62**
Tournament MVP: **Keith Lee**, Memphis

Metro Atlantic

	Conference			Overall		
	W	L	PCT	W	L	PCT
Saint Peter's□	9	1	.900	20	9	.690
Fordham□	8	2	.800	18	11	.621
Iona□	7	3	.700	24	9	.727
Manhattan	3	7	.300	11	16	.407
Fairfield	3	7	.300	11	18	.379
Army	0	10	.000	5	22	.185

Tournament: **Iona d. Saint Peter's 66-61 (OT)**
Tournament MVP: **Rory Grimes**, Iona

Mid-American

	Conference			Overall		
	W	L	PCT	W	L	PCT
Ball State	12	4	.750	17	11	.607
Bowling Green	10	6	.625	18	11	.621
Northern Illinois⊕	9	7	.563	16	14	.533
Eastern Michigan	8	8	.500	15	12	.556
Western Michigan	8	8	.500	15	14	.517
Ohio	8	8	.500	13	14	.481
Miami (OH)	8	8	.500	11	16	.407
Toledo	7	9	.438	15	11	.577
Kent State	6	10	.375	10	16	.385
Central Michigan	4	12	.250	10	16	.385

Tournament: **Northern Illinois d. Ball State 79-75**
Tournament MVP: **Allen Rayhorn**, Northern Illinois

MEAC

	Conference			Overall		
	W	L	PCT	W	L	PCT
NC A&T⊕	10	2	.833	19	9	.679
Howard	9	3	.750	17	11	.607
South Carolina State	7	5	.583	10	15	.400
Florida A&M	5	7	.417	10	17	.370
Delaware State	4	8	.333	13	13	.500
Bethune-Cookman	4	8	.333	10	18	.357
UMES	3	9	.250	6	20	.231

Tournament: **NC A&T d. Howard 79-67**
Tournament MOP: **Eric Boyd**, NC A&T

⊕ Automatic NCAA Tournament bid ○ At-large NCAA Tournament bid □ NIT appearance ⊗ Team record doesn't reflect games forfeited or vacated. For adjusted record, see p. 521.

MIDWESTERN CITY

	CONFERENCE W	L	PCT	OVERALL W	L	PCT
Evansville⊕	10	2	.833	23	6	.793
Oral Roberts□	8	4	.667	18	12	.600
Loyola-Chicago	8	4	.667	17	12	.586
Oklahoma City	6	6	.500	14	14	.500
Detroit	6	6	.500	10	17	.370
Butler	3	9	.250	7	20	.259
Xavier	1	11	.083	8	20	.286

Tournament: **Evansville d. Loyola-Chicago 81-72**
Tournament MVP: **Brad Leaf**, Evansville

MISSOURI VALLEY

	CONFERENCE W	L	PCT	OVERALL W	L	PCT
Bradley□	13	3	.813	26	10	.722
Tulsa⊕	12	4	.750	24	6	.800
Wichita State	12	4	.750	23	6	.793
New Mexico State	10	6	.625	17	11	.607
Illinois State	9	7	.563	17	12	.586
Drake	7	9	.438	12	15	.444
Southern Illinois	7	9	.438	11	16	.407
Creighton	4	12	.250	7	20	.259
West Texas A&M	3	13	.188	11	15	.423
Indiana State	2	14	.125	9	18	.333

Tournament: **Tulsa d. Illinois State 90-77**

OHIO VALLEY

	CONFERENCE W	L	PCT	OVERALL W	L	PCT
Murray State□	13	3	.813	20	8	.714
Western Kentucky□	13	3	.813	19	10	.655
Middle Tenn. State⊕	12	4	.750	22	8	.733
Morehead State	11	5	.688	17	10	.630
Tennessee Tech	8	8	.500	12	14	.462
Youngstown State	5	11	.313	8	18	.308
Austin Peay	4	12	.250	6	20	.231
Akron	3	13	.188	7	19	.269
Eastern Kentucky	3	13	.188	5	21	.192

Tournament: **Middle Tenn. St. d. Western Kentucky 54-52**
Tournament MVP: **Craig McCormick**, Western Kentucky

PCAA

	CONFERENCE W	L	PCT	OVERALL W	L	PCT
Fresno State⊕	13	1	.929	27	3	.900
UC Irvine□	10	4	.714	23	7	.767
Cal State Fullerton	9	5	.643	18	14	.563
San Jose State	7	7	.500	13	13	.500
Long Beach State	7	7	.500	12	16	.429
UC Santa Barbara	5	9	.357	10	16	.385
Pacific	3	11	.214	7	20	.259
Utah State	2	12	.143	4	23	.148
UNLV□	-	-	-	20	10	.667

Tournament: **Fresno State d. Cal State Fullerton 69-57**
Tournament MVP: **Donald Mason**, Fresno State

PAC-10

	CONFERENCE W	L	PCT	OVERALL W	L	PCT
Oregon State⊕⊗	16	2	.889	25	5	.833
UCLA	14	4	.778	21	6	.778
Southern California○	13	5	.722	19	9	.679
Washington□	11	7	.611	19	10	.655
Washington State	10	8	.556	16	14	.533
California	8	10	.444	14	13	.519
Arizona State	8	10	.444	13	14	.481
Arizona	4	14	.222	9	18	.333
Oregon	4	14	.222	9	18	.333
Stanford	2	16	.111	7	20	.259

SEC

	CONFERENCE W	L	PCT	OVERALL W	L	PCT
Kentucky○	13	5	.722	22	8	.733
Tennessee○	13	5	.722	20	10	.667
Alabama⊕	12	6	.667	24	7	.774
Mississippi□	11	7	.611	18	12	.600
LSU□	11	7	.611	14	14	.500
Georgia□	10	8	.556	19	12	.613
Vanderbilt	7	11	.389	15	13	.536
Auburn	7	11	.389	14	14	.500
Mississippi State	4	14	.222	8	19	.296
Florida	2	16	.111	5	22	.185

Tournament: **Alabama d. Kentucky 48-46**
Tournament MVP: **Dirk Minniefield**, Kentucky

SOUTHERN

	CONFERENCE W	L	PCT	OVERALL W	L	PCT
Chattanooga⊕	15	1	.938	27	4	.871
Western Carolina	11	5	.688	19	8	.704
Davidson	9	7	.563	14	15	.483
Marshall	8	8	.500	16	11	.593
East Tennessee St.	8	8	.500	13	15	.464
The Citadel	7	9	.438	14	14	.500
Furman	7	9	.438	11	16	.407
Appalachian State	6	10	.375	11	15	.423
VMI	1	15	.063	1	25	.038

Tournament: **Chattanooga d. Davidson 69-58**
Tournament MOP: **Russ Schoene**, Chattanooga

SOUTHLAND

	CONFERENCE W	L	PCT	OVERALL W	L	PCT
UL-Lafayette⊕	8	2	.800	24	8	.750
Lamar□	7	3	.700	22	7	.759
Texas-Arlington	6	4	.600	16	12	.571
McNeese State	4	6	.400	14	15	.483
Arkansas State	3	7	.300	15	11	.577
Louisiana Tech	2	8	.200	11	16	.407
North Texas	-	-	-	15	12	.556

Tournament: **UL-Lafayette d. Texas-Arlington 81-75**
Tournament MVP: **Alford Turner**, UL-Lafayette

SOUTHWEST

	CONFERENCE W	L	PCT	OVERALL W	L	PCT
Arkansas⊕	12	4	.750	23	6	.793
Houston○	11	5	.688	25	8	.758
Texas A&M□	10	6	.625	20	11	.645
Baylor	9	7	.563	17	11	.607
TCU	9	7	.563	16	13	.552
Texas Tech	8	8	.500	17	11	.607
Texas	6	10	.375	16	11	.593
Rice	6	10	.375	15	15	.500
SMU	1	15	.063	6	21	.222

Tournament: **Arkansas d. Houston 84-69**
Tournament MVP: **Alvin Robertson**, Arkansas

SWAC

	CONFERENCE W	L	PCT	OVERALL W	L	PCT
Alcorn State⊕	10	2	.833	22	8	.733
Jackson State	10	2	.833	19	9	.679
Texas Southern	8	4	.667	21	8	.724
Grambling	8	4	.667	12	17	.414
Mississippi Valley St.	4	8	.333	6	20	.231
Southern U.	3	9	.250	7	18	.280
Prairie View A&M	1	11	.083	2	23	.080

Tournament: **Alcorn State d. Jackson State 87-77**
Tournament MVP: **Albert Irving**, Alcorn State

SUN BELT

	CONFERENCE W	L	PCT	OVERALL W	L	PCT
UAB⊕	9	1	.900	25	6	.806
VCU	7	3	.700	17	11	.607
Jacksonville	5	5	.500	14	13	.519
South Florida	4	6	.400	17	11	.607
Charlotte	3	7	.300	15	12	.556
South Alabama	2	8	.200	12	16	.429

Tournament: **UAB d. VCU 94-83**
Tournament MVP: **Oliver Robinson**, UAB

TAAC

	CONFERENCE W	L	PCT	OVERALL W	L	PCT
Arkansas-Little Rock	12	4	.750	19	8	.704
Northwestern State (LA)	10	6	.625	19	9	.679
UL-Monroe⊕	9	7	.563	19	11	.633
Centenary	9	7	.563	17	12	.586
Mercer	8	8	.500	16	11	.593
Georgia Southern	8	8	.500	14	13	.519
Houston Baptist	8	8	.500	13	14	.481
Samford	6	10	.375	11	15	.423
Hardin-Simmons	2	14	.125	6	20	.231

Tournament: **UL-Monroe d. Centenary 98-85**
Tournament MVP: **Donald Wilson**, UL-Monroe

WCAC

	CONFERENCE W	L	PCT	OVERALL W	L	PCT
Pepperdine ⊕	14	0	1.000	22	7	.759
San Francisco○	11	3	.786	25	6	.806
Portland	9	5	.643	17	10	.630
Santa Clara	7	7	.500	16	11	.593
Gonzaga	7	7	.500	15	12	.556
San Diego	4	10	.286	11	15	.423
Saint Mary's (CA)	3	11	.214	11	16	.407
Loyola Marymount	1	13	.071	3	24	.111

WAC

	CONFERENCE W	L	PCT	OVERALL W	L	PCT
Wyoming⊕	14	2	.875	23	7	.767
UTEP	11	5	.688	20	8	.714
San Diego State□	11	5	.688	20	9	.690
Hawaii	9	7	.563	17	10	.630
BYU□	9	7	.563	17	13	.567
New Mexico	7	9	.438	14	14	.500
Utah	6	10	.375	11	17	.393
Air Force	3	13	.188	8	19	.296
Colorado State	2	14	.125	8	19	.296

INDEPENDENTS

	OVERALL W	L	PCT
DePaul○	26	2	.929
Marquette○	23	9	.719
Dayton□	21	9	.700
New Orleans	18	8	.692
Cleveland State	17	10	.630
Southeastern Louisiana	16	11	.593
Southern Miss	15	11	.577
Penn State	15	12	.556
Tennessee State	13	12	.520
Eastern Illinois	14	13	.519
Illinois-Chicago	14	13	.519
Western Illinois	14	13	.519
Wisconsin-Green Bay	14	13	.519
Charleston Southern	13	13	.500
South Carolina	14	15	.483
UNC Wilmington	13	14	.481
Northern Iowa	12	15	.444
Stetson	12	15	.444
Campbell	11	16	.407
East Carolina	10	17	.370
Notre Dame	10	17	.370
U.S. International	9	18	.333
Valparaiso	9	18	.333
Texas-San Antonio	8	19	.296
Nicholls State	6	20	.231
Texas-Pan American	5	20	.200
Utica	4	22	.154
Georgia State	4	23	.148

INDIVIDUAL LEADERS—SEASON

Scoring	CL	POS	G	FG	FT	PTS	PPG
1 **Harry Kelly**, Texas Southern	JR	F	29	336	190	862	**29.7**
2 **Ricky Pierce**, Rice	SR	G/F	30	314	177	805	**26.8**
3 **Dan Callandrillo**, Seton Hall	SR	G	27	250	198	698	**25.9**
4 **Kevin Magee**, UC Irvine	SR	F/C	29	272	188	732	**25.2**
5 **Quintin Dailey**, San Francisco	JR	G	30	286	183	755	**25.2**
6 **Willie Jackson**, Centenary	SO	F	29	273	147	693	**23.9**
7 **Mitchell Wiggins**, Florida State	JR	G	22	223	77	523	**23.8**
8 **Perry Moss**, Northeastern	SR	G	30	279	152	710	**23.7**
9 **Melvin McLaughlin**, Central Michigan	JR	G	25	255	71	581	**23.2**
10 **Joe Jakubick**, Akron	SO	G	26	235	124	594	**22.8**

Field Goal Pct	CL	POS	G	FG	FGA	PCT
1 **Mark McNamara**, California	SR	F/C	27	231	329	**70.2**
2 **Dale Ellis**, Tennessee	JR	F	30	257	393	**65.4**
3 **Orlando Phillips**, Pepperdine	JR	F	29	181	280	**64.6**
4 **Albert Culton**, Texas-Arlington	SR	F	28	200	311	**64.3**
5 **Kevin Magee**, UC Irvine	SR	F/C	29	272	424	**64.2**

Minimum: 5 made per game

Free Throw Pct	CL	POS	G	FT	FTA	PCT
1 **Rod Foster**, UCLA	JR	G	27	95	100	**95.0**
2 **Jack Moore**, Nebraska	SR	G	27	123	131	**93.9**
3 **Joe Dykstra**, Western Illinois	JR	F	26	147	161	**91.3**
4 **Byron Williams**, Idaho State	SR	F	26	70	78	**89.7**
5 **Jim Master**, Kentucky	SO	G	30	95	106	**89.6**

Minimum: 2.5 made per game

Rebounds Per Game	CL	POS	G	REB	RPG
1 **LaSalle Thompson**, Texas	JR	F/C	27	365	**13.5**
2 **Wayne Sappleton**, Loyola-Chicago	SR	F	29	376	**13.0**
3 **Darren Tillis**, Cleveland State	SR	F/C	27	346	**12.8**
4 **Mark McNamara**, California	SR	F/C	27	341	**12.6**
5 **Riley Clarida**, Long Island	SR	F	30	369	**12.3**
6 **Audie Norris**, Jackson State	SR	C	28	341	**12.2**
7 **Kevin Magee**, UC Irvine	SR	F/C	29	353	**12.2**
8 **Clinton Cobb**, Texas-Pan American	SR	F	25	302	**12.1**
9 **Terry Cummings**, DePaul	JR	F	28	334	**11.9**
10 **Don Robinson**, U.S. International	SR	C	26	308	**11.8**

INDIVIDUAL LEADERS—GAME

Points	CL	POS	OPP	DATE	PTS
1 **Harry Kelly**, Texas Southern	JR	F	Texas College	F16	**51**
2 **Steve Barker**, Samford	SR	G/F	Illinois-Chicago	N30	**47**
3 **Kevin Magee**, UC Irvine	SR	F/C	Loyola Marymount	D15	**46**
4 **Daryl Powell**, Marist	JR	F	Wagner	J21	**43**
5 **Quintin Dailey**, San Francisco	JR	G	Pepperdine	F27	**42**

Rebounds	CL	POS	OPP	DATE	REB
1 **Kevin Magee**, UC Irvine	SR	F/C	Long Beach State	J30	**25**
2 **Terry White**, UTEP	SR	F/C	Texas Southern	D12	**24**
Don Robinson, U.S. International	SR	C	Hawaii Pacific	J30	**24**
Doug Hashley, Montana State	JR	F	Nevada	F26	**24**
5 **Steve Trumbo**, BYU	SR	F	Air Force	J21	**23**

TEAM LEADERS—SEASON

Win-Loss Pct	W	L	PCT
1 **North Carolina**	32	2	**.941**
2 **DePaul**	26	2	**.929**
3 **Fresno State**	27	3	**.900**
Idaho	27	3	**.900**
5 **Virginia**	30	4	**.882**

Scoring Offense	G	W-L	PTS	PPG
1 **Long Island**	30	20-10	2,605	**86.8**
2 **Texas Southern**	29	21-8	2,429	**83.8**
3 **North Texas**	27	15-12	2,258	**83.6**
4 **San Francisco**	31	25-6	2,527	**81.5**
5 **Houston**	33	25-8	2,685	**81.4**

Scoring Margin	G	W-L	PPG	OPP PPG	MAR
1 **Oregon State**	30	25-5	69.6	55.0	**14.6**
2 **Georgetown**	37	30-7	67.6	53.5	**14.1**
3 **Idaho**	30	27-3	71.3	57.5	**13.8**
4 **Virginia**	34	30-4	70.7	57.2	**13.5**
5 **Chattanooga**	31	27-4	72.6	59.9	**12.7**

Field Goal Pct	G	W-L	FG	FGA	PCT
1 **UC Irvine**	30	23-7	920	1,639	**56.1**
2 **Mississippi**	30	18-12	696	1,281	**54.3**
3 **Pepperdine**	29	22-7	929	1,714	**54.2**
4 **Tennessee**	30	20-10	792	1,462	**54.2**
5 **Missouri**	31	27-4	815	1,511	**53.9**

Free Throw Pct	G	W-L	FT	FTA	PCT
1 **Western Illinois**	27	14-13	447	569	**78.6**
2 **Northwestern State (LA)**	28	19-9	489	624	**78.4**
3 **Western Carolina**	27	19-8	481	623	**77.2**
4 **Idaho State**	26	14-12	393	522	**75.3**
5 **Ohio State**	31	21-10	415	552	**75.2**

Rebound Margin	G	W-L	RPG	OPP RPG	MAR
1 **Northeastern**	30	23-7	41.2	30.8	**10.4**
2 **Wyoming**	30	23-7	36.4	26.7	**9.7**
3 **BYU**	30	17-13	37.3	29.3	**8.0**
4 **Alabama**	31	24-7	37.3	29.5	**7.8**
5 **Pepperdine**	29	22-7	37.7	30.0	**7.7**

Scoring Defense	G	W-L	OPP PTS	OPP PPG
1 **Fresno State**	30	27-3	1,412	**47.1**
2 **NC State**	32	22-10	1,570	**49.1**
3 **Princeton**	26	13-13	1,277	**49.1**
4 **Wyoming**	30	23-7	1,545	**51.5**
5 **James Madison**	30	24-6	1,559	**52.0**

Field Goal Pct Defense	G	W-L	OPP FG	OPP FGA	OPP PCT
1 **Wyoming**	30	23-7	584	1,470	**39.7**
2 **Georgetown**	37	30-7	757	1,808	**41.9**
3 **Idaho**	30	27-3	696	1,662	**41.9**
4 **NC State**	32	22-10	621	1,481	**41.9**
5 **Missouri**	31	27-4	742	1,766	**42.0**

CONSENSUS ALL-AMERICAS

FIRST TEAM

PLAYER	CL	POS	HT	SCHOOL	RPG	PPG
Terry Cummings	JR	F	6-9	DePaul	11.9	22.3
Quintin Dailey	JR	G	6-4	San Francisco	5.2	25.2
Eric "Sleepy" Floyd	SR	G	6-3	Georgetown	3.4	16.7
Ralph Sampson	JR	C	7-4	Virginia	11.4	15.8
James Worthy	JR	F	6-9	North Carolina	6.3	15.6

SECOND TEAM

PLAYER	CL	POS	HT	SCHOOL	RPG	PPG
Dale Ellis	JR	F	6-7	Tennessee	6.3	21.2
Kevin Magee	SR	F/C	6-8	UC Irvine	12.2	25.2
John Paxson	JR	G	6-2	Notre Dame	2.0	16.4
Sam Perkins	SO	F/C	6-9	North Carolina	7.8	14.3
Paul Pressey	SR	F	6-5	Tulsa	6.4	13.2

SELECTORS: AP, NABC, UPI, USBWA

AWARD WINNERS

PLAYER OF THE YEAR

PLAYER	CL	POS	HT	SCHOOL	AWARDS
Ralph Sampson	JR	C	7-4	Virginia	Naismith, AP, UPI, USBWA, Wooden, NABC, Rupp
Jack Moore	SR	G	5-9	Nebraska	Frances Pomeroy Naismith*

* FOR THE MOST OUTSTANDING SENIOR PLAYER WHO IS 6 FEET OR UNDER

COACH OF THE YEAR

COACH	SCHOOL	REC	AWARDS
Ralph Miller	Oregon State	25-5	AP, Sporting News
Norm Stewart	Missouri	27-4	UPI
John Thompson Jr.	Georgetown	30-7	USBWA
Don Monson	Idaho	27-3	NABC
Gene Keady	Purdue	18-14	CBS/Chevrolet

BOB GIBBONS' TOP HIGH SCHOOL SENIOR RECRUITS

PLAYER	POS	HT	HIGH SCHOOL	A-A TEAMS	COLLEGE	CAREER NOTES
1 **Billy Thompson**	F	6-7	Camden (NJ) HS	McD, P	Louisville	NCAA title, '86; No. 19 pick, '86 NBA draft (Hawks); 8.6 ppg, 5.4 rpg (5 seasons)
2 **Wayman Tisdale**	C	6-9	Booker T. Washington HS, Tulsa, OK	McD, P	Oklahoma	3-time All-America; Olympic gold medal, '84; No. 2 pick, '85 NBA draft (Pacers); 15.3 ppg (12 seasons)
3 **Efrem Winters**	C	6-10	Martin Luther King HS, Chicago	McD, P	Illinois	Illinois' 2nd-leading rebounder (893); 4th-round pick, '86 NBA draft (Hawks)
4 **Kenny Walker**	F	6-8	Crawford County HS, Roberta, GA	McD, P	Kentucky	2-time All-America; No. 5 pick, '86 NBA draft (Knicks); 7.0 ppg (7 seasons); NBA Slam Dunk Champ, '89
5 **Alphonso "Buck" Johnson**	SF	6-6	Birmingham (AL) Hayes HS	McD, P	Alabama	15.3 ppg, 7.6 rpg (4 seasons); No. 20 pick, '86 NBA draft (Rockets); 9.1 ppg (7 seasons); played overseas
6 **Willie Cutts**	PG	6-2	Bryant (AR) HS	McD, P	Arkansas/Ark. St.	Transferred to Arkansas State after 1 year; undrafted
7 **Brad Daugherty**	C/F	6-11	Charles D. Owen HS, Swannanoa, NC	McD, P	North Carolina	First team All-America, '86; No. 1 overall pick, '86 NBA draft (Cavs); 19.0 ppg (8 seasons); 5-time All-Star
8 **Len Bias**	F	6-8	Northwestern HS, Hyattsville, MD	P	Maryland	Consensus All-America, '86; No. 2 pick, '86 NBA draft (Celtics)
9 **Dell Curry**	2G	6-5	Fort Defiance (VA) HS	McD, P	Virginia Tech	Virginia Tech's 2nd-leading scorer (2,389 pts); No. 15 pick, '86 NBA draft (Jazz); 11.7 ppg (16 seasons); NBA Sixth Man Award, '94
10 **Curtis Hunter**	2G	6-4	Southern HS, Durham, NC	McD, P	North Carolina	4 years at UNC; 7th-round pick, '87 NBA draft (Nuggets); played overseas
11 **Johnny Dawkins**	PG	6-2	Mackin HS, Washington, DC	McD, P	Duke	Duke's 2nd-leading scorer (2,556 pts); Naismith Award winner, '86; No. 10 pick, '86 NBA draft (Spurs); 11.1 ppg (9 seasons)
12 **Ron Kellogg**	SF	6-5	Omaha (NE) Northwest HS	P	Kansas	11.6 ppg (4 seasons); 2-time All-Big Eight; 2nd-round pick, '86 NBA draft (Hawks)
13 **Ernest Myers**	2G	6-3	St. Nicholas Tolentine HS, Bronx, NY	McD, P	NC State	9.3 ppg (4 seasons); 11.3 ppg as Fr. on '83 NCAA title team; undrafted
14 **David Wingate**	2G	6-5	Dunbar HS, Baltimore	P	Georgetown	12.8 ppg (4 seasons); NCAA title, '84; 2nd-round pick, '86 NBA draft (76ers); 5.6 ppg (15 seasons)
15 **Montel Hatcher**	PG	6-1	Santa Monica (CA) HS	McD	UCLA	9.4 ppg (4 seasons); 7th-round pick, '87 NBA draft (Pacers)
16 **Baskerville Holmes**	SF	6-7	Westside HS, Memphis, TN		Memphis	8.4 ppg (4 seasons); 3rd-round pick, '86 NBA draft (Bucks)
17 **Kerry Trotter**	SF	6-6	Creighton Prep School, Omaha, NE	McD, P	Marquette	1,221 pts (4 seasons); 12 ppg as Jr.; undrafted; played overseas
18 **Tim Kempton**	C/F	6-9	St. Dominic HS, Oyster Bay, NY	McD, P	Notre Dame	25.9 mins. per game (4 seasons); 6th-round pick, '86 NBA draft (Clippers); 4.5 ppg (8 seasons)
19 **George Almones**	2G	6-4	Kathleen HS, Lakeland, FL		UL-Lafayette	1,436 points, 402 assists, 145 steals (3 seasons); 6th-round pick, '85 NBA draft (Nets)
20 **Harold Pressley**	SF	6-6	Saint Bernard HS, Uncasville, CT	McD, P	Villanova	Big East Defensive POY, first-team All-Big East, '86; No. 17 pick, '86 NBA draft (Kings); 9.0 ppg, (4 seasons)

OTHER STANDOUTS

PLAYER	POS	HT	HIGH SCHOOL	A-A TEAMS	COLLEGE	CAREER NOTES
36 **Chuck Person**	F	6-7	Brantley (AL) HS		Auburn	18.3 ppg, 7.5 rpg (4 seasons); No. 4 pick, '86 NBA draft (Pacers); 14.7 ppg (13 seasons); NBA ROY, '87
38 **Mark Price**	PG	6-0	Enid (OK) HS		Georgia Tech	17.4 ppg, 4.0 apg (4 seasons); 2nd-round pick, '86 NBA draft (Mavs); 15.2 ppg, 6.7 apg (12 seasons); 4-time All-Star; NBA all-time FT% leader
72 **Walter Berry**	F	6-8	Ben Franklin HS, New York		San Jacinto JC/ St. John's	National POY, '86; No. 14 pick, '86 NBA draft (Blazers); 14.1 ppg (3 seasons); played overseas

Abbreviations: McD=McDonald's; P=Parade

Poll Progression

Preseason Poll

AP	UPI	School	
1	1	North Carolina	(A)
2	2	UCLA	
3	3	Kentucky	
4	4	Louisville	
5	5	Georgetown	
6	7	Wichita State	
7	6	Virginia	
8	9	DePaul	
9	8	Iowa	
10	10	Minnesota	
11	12	Tulsa	
12	11	Indiana	
13	14	Wake Forest	
14	17	UAB	
15	15	Missouri	
16	13	Georgia	
17	18	LSU	
18	19	Arkansas	
19	—	Notre Dame	
20	—	Alabama	
—	16	San Francisco	
—	20	UNLV	

Week of Dec 1

AP	School	AP↓↑
1	North Carolina (1-0)	
2	Kentucky (1-0)	↑1
3	Louisville (0-0)	↑1
4	Wichita State (1-0)	↑2
5	Virginia (3-0)	↑2
6	Iowa (1-0)	↑3
7	DePaul (0-0)	↑1
8	UCLA (1-1) (B)	↓6
9	Tulsa (1-0)	↑2
10	Minnesota (0-0)	
11	UAB (2-0)	↑3
12	Indiana (1-0)	
13	Arkansas (1-0)	↑5
14	San Francisco (1-0)	⤴
15	BYU (2-1)	⤴
16	Missouri (0-0)	↓1
17	Alabama (1-0)	↑3
18	UNLV (2-0)	⤴
19	Notre Dame (1-0)	
20	Georgetown (1-2)	↓15

Week of Dec 8

AP	UPI	School	AP↓↑
1	1	North Carolina (3-0)	
2	2	Kentucky (2-0) (C)	
3	3	Louisville (2-0)	
4	6	Wichita State (3-0)	
5	4	Virginia (5-0)	
6	5	Iowa (3-0)	
7	7	DePaul (2-0)	
8	9	Minnesota (3-0)	↑2
9	12	UAB (3-0)	↑2
10	8	Indiana (2-0) (C)	↑2
11	10	Arkansas (3-0)	↑2
12	14	San Francisco (3-0)	↑2
13	11	Missouri (3-0)	↑3
14	16	Tulsa (2-1)	↓5
15	13	UNLV (4-0)	↑3
16	19	Alabama (4-0)	↑1
17	20	UCLA (2-2)	↓9
18	17	UL-Lafayette (5-0)	⤴
19	15	Oregon State (2-0)	⤴
20	—	Georgetown (3-2)	
—	18	Villanova (3-0)	

Week of Dec 15

AP	UPI	School	AP
1	1	North Carolina (4-0)	
2	2	Kentucky (4-0)	
3	3	Louisville (4-0)	
4	4	Wichita State (5-0)	
5	6	Virginia (6-0)	
6	5	Iowa (5-0)	
7	7	DePaul (4-0)	
8	9	Minnesota (4-0)	
9	8	Arkansas (5-0)	↑2
10	12	San Francisco (5-0)	↑2
11	10	Missouri (5-0)	↑2
12	14	Tulsa (5-1)	↑2
13	11	Indiana (4-1)	↓3
14	15	Alabama (5-0)	↑2
15	13	UL-Lafayette (8-0)	↑3
16	19	UAB (3-1)	↓7
17	—	UCLA (3-2)	
18	16	Villanova (5-0)	⤴
19	17	Georgetown (5-2)	↑1
20	—	Oregon State (3-1)	↓1
—	18	Georgia (3-1)	
—	20	UC Irvine (6-0)	

Week of Dec 22

AP	UPI	School	AP↓↑
1	1	North Carolina (5-0)	
2	2	Kentucky (6-0)	
3	4	Wichita State (6-0)	↑1
4	3	Virginia (8-0)	↑1
5	5	Minnesota (5-1)	↑3
6	6	Arkansas (6-0)	↑3
7	8	San Francisco (7-0)	↑3
8	9	Louisville (5-1)	↓5
9	10	Missouri (6-0)	↑2
10	11	Iowa (6-1)	↓4
11	7	Indiana (6-1)	↑2
12	14	Alabama (7-0)	↑2
13	12	DePaul (5-1)	↓6
14	16	Tulsa (6-1)	↓2
15	—	UCLA (4-2)	↑2
16	15	Oregon State (5-1)	↑4
17	13	Georgetown (7-2)	↑2
18	17	Houston (7-1)	⤴
19	—	UAB (5-2)	↓3
20	20	Villanova (6-1)	↓2
—	18	NC State (7-0)	
—	19	Kansas (5-2)	

Week of Dec 29

AP	UPI	School	AP↓↑
1	1	North Carolina (6-0)	
2	4	Wichita State (7-0)	↑1
3	2	Virginia (8-0)	↑1
4	3	Kentucky (6-1)	↓2
5	6	Arkansas (7-0)	↑1
6	8	San Francisco (10-0)	↑1
7	7	Missouri (7-0)	↑2
8	5	DePaul (7-1)	↑5
9	11	Minnesota (5-1)	↓4
10	9	Iowa (6-1)	
11	10	Indiana (6-1)	
12	14	Alabama (7-0)	
13	16	Tulsa (7-1)	↑1
14	13	Louisville (6-2)	↓6
15	12	Oregon State (6-1)	↑1
16	—	UCLA (5-2)	↓1
17	15	Georgetown (8-2)	
18	17	Houston (7-1)	
19	19	Villanova (7-1)	↑1
20	18	NC State (7-0)	⤴
—	20	Wake Forest (6-1)	

Week of Jan 5

AP	UPI	School	AP↓↑
1	1	North Carolina (9-0)	
2	2	Virginia (11-0)	↑1
3	3	Kentucky (8-1)	↑1
4	5	Missouri (9-0)	↑3
5	4	DePaul (11-1)	↑3
6	6	Minnesota (8-1)	↑3
7	7	Iowa (8-1)	↑3
8	10	San Francisco (11-1)	↓2
9	12	Wichita State (10-2)	↓7
10	14	Tulsa (9-1)	↑3
11	11	Arkansas (8-1)	↓6
12	8	Louisville (8-2)	↑2
13	9	Georgetown (11-2)	↑4
14	16	Houston (10-1)	↑4
15	15	NC State (11-1)	↑5
16	17	Alabama (9-1)	↓4
17	19	Oregon State (9-2)	↓2
18	13	Idaho (11-0)	⤴
19	—	UCLA (6-4)	↓3
20	18	St. John's (9-1)	⤴
—	20	Indiana (6-3)	⤵

Week of Jan 12

AP	UPI	School	AP↓↑
1	1	North Carolina (12-0) (D)	
2	3	Missouri (11-0)	↑2
3	2	Virginia (12-1)	↓1
4	4	DePaul (12-1)	↑1
5	5	Iowa (10-1)	↑2
6	6	Kentucky (9-2)	↓3
7	8	San Francisco (13-1)	↑1
8	7	Georgetown (13-2)	↑5
9	10	Arkansas (10-1)	↑2
10	12	Houston (11-1)	↑4
11	9	Minnesota (9-2)	↓5
12	15	NC State (13-1)	↑3
13	16	Alabama (11-1)	↑3
14	11	Idaho (13-0)	↑4
15	14	Oregon State (10-2)	↑2
16	17	Wichita State (11-3)	↓7
17	13	Louisville (10-3)	↓5
18	19	Tulsa (10-2)	↓8
19	18	Texas (10-0)	⤴
20	—	Virginia Tech (10-1)	⤴
—	20	Kansas State (10-2)	

Week of Jan 19

AP	UPI	School	AP↓↑
1	1	North Carolina (14-0)	
2	2	Missouri (14-0)	
3	3	Virginia (16-1)	
4	4	DePaul (15-1)	
5	6	Minnesota (11-2)	↑6
6	6	Iowa (11-2)	↓1
7	5	Texas (13-0)	↑12
8	8	Idaho (15-0)	↑6
9	9	Kentucky (10-3)	↓3
10	12	Tulsa (13-2)	↑8
11	13	San Francisco (15-2)	↓4
12	10	Oregon State (12-2)	↑3
13	11	Georgetown (14-3)	↓5
14	15	NC State (14-2)	↓2
15	14	Arkansas (11-2)	↓6
16	17	Alabama (12-2)	↓3
17	17	Louisville (11-4)	
18	16	Kansas State (12-2)	⤴
19	—	Houston (11-3)	↓9
20	—	Tennessee (11-3)	⤴
—	19	Villanova (12-2)	
—	20	Fresno State (13-1)	

Week of Jan 26

AP	UPI	School	AP↓↑
1	1	Missouri (16-0) (E)	↑1
2	2	North Carolina (14-1)	↓1
3	3	Virginia (18-1)	
4	4	DePaul (16-1)	
5	5	Texas (14-0)	↑2
6	6	Iowa (13-2)	
7	8	Kentucky (12-3)	↑2
8	7	Oregon State (14-2)	↑4
9	12	San Francisco (17-2)	↑2
10	9	Minnesota (12-3)	↓5
11	10	Idaho (16-1)	↓3
12	11	Arkansas (13-2)	↑3
13	14	Alabama (14-2)	↑3
14	13	Kansas State (14-2)	↑4
15	15	Tennessee (13-3)	↑5
16	16	Tulsa (13-3)	↓6
17	17	NC State (15-3)	↓3
18	20	Wake Forest (13-3)	⤴
19	18	Fresno State (15-1)	⤴
20	19	Villanova (13-3)	⤴

Week of Feb 2

AP	UPI	School	AP↓↑
1	1	Missouri (18-0)	
2	2	North Carolina (16-1)	
3	4	Virginia (20-1)	
4	3	DePaul (18-1)	
5	5	Iowa (15-2)	↑1
6	6	Minnesota (14-3)	↑4
7	8	San Francisco (19-2)	↑2
8	10	Alabama (16-2)	↑5
9	9	Kentucky (14-4)	↓2
10	7	Oregon State (15-3)	↓2
11	12	Tulsa (15-3)	↑5
12	11	Texas (14-3)	↓7
13	16	Wake Forest (14-4)	↑5
14	14	Arkansas (15-3)	↓2
15	15	Idaho (17-2)	↓4
16	17	Tennessee (14-4)	↓1
17	13	Fresno State (17-1)	↑2
18	19	West Virginia (17-1)	⤴
19	18	Kansas State (14-4)	↓5
19	—	Memphis (14-3)	⤴
—	20	Georgetown (16-5)	

Week of Feb 9

AP	UPI	School	AP↓↑
1	1	Virginia (22-1)	↑2
2	2	North Carolina (18-2)	
3	3	DePaul (20-1)	↑1
4	4	Missouri (19-1)	↓3
5	5	Iowa (17-2)	
6	6	Oregon State (16-3)	↑4
7	7	Tulsa (16-3)	↑4
8	10	Arkansas (16-3)	↑6
9	8	Minnesota (15-4)	↓3
10	11	Alabama (17-3)	↓2
11	13	West Virginia (19-1)	↑7
12	9	Kentucky (15-5)	↓3
13	12	Idaho (19-2)	↑2
14	18	Memphis (16-3)	↑5
15	14	Kansas State (16-4)	↑4
16	19	Wake Forest (15-5)	↓3
17	15	San Francisco (19-4)	↓10
18	16	Fresno State (18-2)	↓1
19	—	Washington (17-3)	⤴
20	17	Georgetown (18-5)	⤴
—	20	Wyoming (17-5)	

…ek of Feb 16

AP	UPI	SCHOOL	AP↓↑
	1	**Virginia** (25-1)	
	2	**North Carolina** (20-2)	
	3	**DePaul** (23-1)	
	4	**Missouri** (21-1)	
	5	**Oregon State** (18-3)	↑1
	7	**Tulsa** (18-4)	↑1
	6	**Iowa** (18-3)	↓2
	8	**Minnesota** (17-4)	↑1
	10	**West Virginia** (21-1)	↑2
	9	**Kentucky** (17-5)	↑2
	11	**Idaho** (21-2)	↑2
	13	**Memphis** (18-3)	↑2
	12	**Georgetown** (20-5)	↑7
	18	**Wake Forest** (17-5)	↑2
	14	**Fresno State** (20-2)	↑3
	19	**San Francisco** (21-4)	↑1
7	17	**Arkansas** (18-5)	↓9
8	16	**Kansas State** (17-5)	↓3
9	15	**Alabama** (17-5)	↓9
0	—	**Indiana** (14-7)	⤴
—	20	**Tennessee** (16-6)	

Week of Feb 23

AP	UPI	SCHOOL	AP↓↑
1	1	**Virginia** (26-1)	
2	2	**North Carolina** (22-2)	
3	3	**DePaul** (24-1)	
4	4	**Oregon State** (20-3)	↑1
5	5	**Missouri** (23-2)	↓1
6	6	**West Virginia** (23-1)	↑3
7	9	**Kentucky** (19-5)	↑3
8	10	**Tulsa** (19-4)	↓2
9	8	**Idaho** (23-2)	↑2
10	13	**Memphis** (19-3)	↑2
11	7	**Iowa** (19-4)	↓4
12	11	**Georgetown** (21-6)	↑1
13	14	**Minnesota** (18-5)	↓5
14	12	**Fresno State** (22-2)	↑1
15	15	**Arkansas** (19-5)	↑2
16	17	**San Francisco** (23-4)	
17	16	**Alabama** (19-5)	↑2
18	20	**Wake Forest** (18-6)	↓4
19	18	**Tennessee** (18-6)	⤴
20	—	**UCLA** (18-5)	⤴
—	19	**Kansas State** (18-6)	⤵

Week of Mar 2

AP	UPI	SCHOOL	AP↓↑
1	1	**North Carolina** (24-2)	↑1
2	2	**DePaul** (26-1)	↑1
3	3	**Virginia** (27-2)	Ⓕ ↓2
4	4	**Oregon State** (22-3)	
5	5	**Missouri** (23-3)	
6	6	**Idaho** (24-2)	↑3
7	7	**Minnesota** (20-5)	↑6
8	8	**Georgetown** (23-6)	↑4
9	13	**West Virginia** (24-2)	↓3
10	14	**Tulsa** (21-5)	↓2
11	10	**Iowa** (20-5)	
12	9	**Fresno State** (24-2)	↑2
13	11	**Memphis** (21-4)	↓3
14	15	**Arkansas** (21-5)	↑1
15	12	**Kentucky** (20-6)	↓8
16	18	**Wake Forest** (19-7)	↑2
17	16	**Kansas State** (20-6)	⤴
18	—	**Alabama** (20-6)	↓1
19	—	**UCLA** (19-6)	↑1
20	—	**UAB** (23-5)	⤴
—	17	**Wyoming** (20-6)	
—	18	**Louisville** (18-8)	
—	20	**Pepperdine** (20-6)	
—	20	**Tennessee** (18-8)	⤵

Final Poll

AP	UPI	SCHOOL	AP↓↑
1	1	**North Carolina** (27-2)	
2	2	**DePaul** (26-1)	
3	3	**Virginia** (29-3)	
4	4	**Oregon State** (23-4)	
5	5	**Missouri** (26-3)	
6	7	**Georgetown** (26-6)	↑2
7	6	**Minnesota** (22-5)	
8	8	**Idaho** (26-2)	↓2
9	9	**Memphis** (23-4)	↑4
10	11	**Tulsa** (24-5)	
11	10	**Fresno State** (26-2)	Ⓖ ↑1
12	13	**Arkansas** (23-5)	↑2
13	12	**Alabama** (23-6)	↑5
14	17	**West Virginia** (26-3)	↓5
15	14	**Kentucky** (22-7)	
16	16	**Iowa** (20-7)	↓5
17	—	**UAB** (23-5)	↑3
18	19	**Wake Forest** (20-8)	↓2
19	—	**UCLA** (21-6)	
20	20	**Louisville** (20-9)	⤴
—	15	**Wyoming** (22-6)	
—	18	**Kansas State** (21-7)	⤵

Ⓐ *Sports Illustrated* wants to shoot coach Dean Smith and his starting five for its cover, but because of his rule about freshmen not receiving media attention, Smith keeps Michael Jordan out of the picture.

Ⓑ After being put on probation for recruiting violations, UCLA blows a 12-point halftime lead in a 57-54 loss to Rutgers. The Bruins will be left out of the NCAA Tournament for the first time in 20 years.

Ⓒ Kentucky and Indiana are in the Top 10, but an album recorded by Wildcats coach Joe B. Hall, Hoosiers coach Bob Knight and TV analyst Al McGuire fails to make the country charts.

Ⓓ North Carolina's 65-60 victory over Virginia on Jan. 9 marks the second time in two weeks that the Tar Heels have won a battle between No. 1 and No. 2. The first was an 82-69 thrashing of Kentucky on Dec. 26.

Ⓔ After beating Kansas and Oklahoma, Missouri becomes the first Big Eight team to be ranked No. 1 since Kansas State in the 1959 end-of-season polls.

Ⓕ Maryland knocks off Virginia 47-46 in overtime. The Terrapins' total is the smallest ever in an OT victory over a No. 1 team.

Ⓖ Coach Boyd Grant's Fresno State team allows opponents only 47.1 ppg for the season, the stingiest defense since Oklahoma State allowed 45.5 in 1951-52.

1982 NCAA Tournament

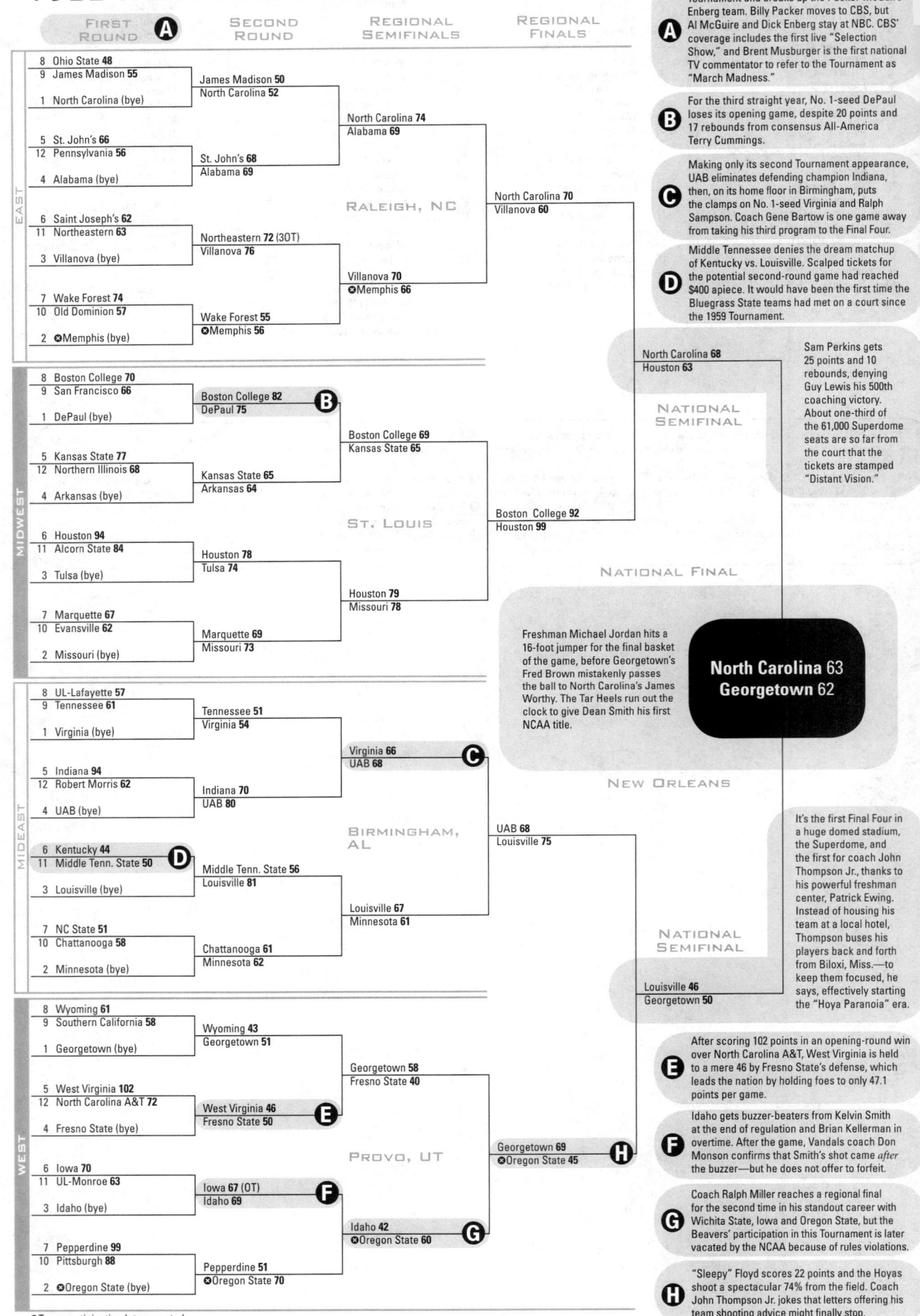

First Round (A) — Second Round — Regional Semifinals — Regional Finals

East — Raleigh, NC

First Round
- 8 Ohio State **48** / 9 James Madison **55**
- 1 North Carolina (bye)
- 5 St. John's **66** / 12 Pennsylvania **56**
- 4 Alabama (bye)
- 6 Saint Joseph's **62** / 11 Northeastern **63**
- 3 Villanova (bye)
- 7 Wake Forest **74** / 10 Old Dominion **57**
- 2 ⊗Memphis (bye)

Second Round
- James Madison **50** / North Carolina **52**
- St. John's **68** / Alabama **69**
- Northeastern **72** (3OT) / Villanova **76**
- Wake Forest **55** / ⊗Memphis **56**

Regional Semifinals
- North Carolina **74** / Alabama **69**
- Villanova **70** / ⊗Memphis **66**

Regional Final
- North Carolina **70** / Villanova **60**

Midwest — St. Louis

First Round
- 8 Boston College **70** / 9 San Francisco **66**
- 1 DePaul (bye)
- 5 Kansas State **77** / 12 Northern Illinois **68**
- 4 Arkansas (bye)
- 6 Houston **94** / 11 Alcorn State **84**
- 3 Tulsa (bye)
- 7 Marquette **67** / 10 Evansville **62**
- 2 Missouri (bye)

Second Round
- Boston College **82** / DePaul **75** (B)
- Kansas State **65** / Arkansas **64**
- Houston **78** / Tulsa **74**
- Marquette **69** / Missouri **73**

Regional Semifinals
- Boston College **69** / Kansas State **65**
- Houston **79** / Missouri **78**

Regional Final
- Boston College **92** / Houston **99**

Mideast — Birmingham, AL

First Round
- 8 UL-Lafayette **57** / 9 Tennessee **61**
- 1 Virginia (bye)
- 5 Indiana **94** / 12 Robert Morris **62**
- 4 UAB (bye)
- 6 Kentucky **44** / 11 Middle Tenn. State **50** (D)
- 3 Louisville (bye)
- 7 NC State **51** / 10 Chattanooga **58**
- 2 Minnesota (bye)

Second Round
- Tennessee **51** / Virginia **54**
- Indiana **70** / UAB **80**
- Middle Tenn. State **56** / Louisville **81**
- Chattanooga **61** / Minnesota **62**

Regional Semifinals
- Virginia **66** / UAB **68** (C)
- Louisville **67** / Minnesota **61**

Regional Final
- UAB **68** / Louisville **75**

West — Provo, UT

First Round
- 8 Wyoming **61** / 9 Southern California **58**
- 1 Georgetown (bye)
- 5 West Virginia **102** / 12 North Carolina A&T **72**
- 4 Fresno State (bye)
- 6 Iowa **70** / 11 UL-Monroe **63**
- 3 Idaho (bye)
- 7 Pepperdine **99** / 10 Pittsburgh **88**
- 2 ⊗Oregon State (bye)

Second Round
- Wyoming **43** / Georgetown **51**
- West Virginia **46** / Fresno State **50** (E)
- Iowa **67** (OT) / Idaho **69** (F)
- Pepperdine **51** / ⊗Oregon State **70**

Regional Semifinals
- Georgetown **58** / Fresno State **40**
- Idaho **42** / ⊗Oregon State **60** (G)

Regional Final
- Georgetown **69** / ⊗Oregon State **45** (H)

New Orleans

National Semifinal
- North Carolina **68** / Houston **63**

Sam Perkins gets 25 points and 10 rebounds, denying Guy Lewis his 500th coaching victory. About one-third of the 61,000 Superdome seats are so far from the court that the tickets are stamped "Distant Vision."

National Semifinal
- Louisville **46** / Georgetown **50**

It's the first Final Four in a huge domed stadium, the Superdome, and the first for coach John Thompson Jr., thanks to his powerful freshman center, Patrick Ewing. Instead of housing his team at a local hotel, Thompson buses his players back and forth from Biloxi, Miss.—to keep them focused, he says, effectively starting the "Hoya Paranoia" era.

National Final

North Carolina 63
Georgetown 62

Freshman Michael Jordan hits a 16-foot jumper for the final basket of the game, before Georgetown's Fred Brown mistakenly passes the ball to North Carolina's James Worthy. The Tar Heels run out the clock to give Dean Smith his first NCAA title.

⊗Team participation later vacated

A CBS takes over the broadcast rights to the Tournament and breaks up the Packer-McGuire-Enberg team. Billy Packer moves to CBS, but Al McGuire and Dick Enberg stay at NBC. CBS' coverage includes the first live "Selection Show," and Brent Musburger is the first national TV commentator to refer to the Tournament as "March Madness."

B For the third straight year, No. 1-seed DePaul loses its opening game, despite 20 points and 17 rebounds from consensus All-America Terry Cummings.

C Making only its second Tournament appearance, UAB eliminates defending champion Indiana, then, on its home floor in Birmingham, puts the clamps on No. 1-seed Virginia and Ralph Sampson. Coach Gene Bartow is one game away from taking his third program to the Final Four.

D Middle Tennessee denies the dream matchup of Kentucky vs. Louisville. Scalped tickets for the potential second-round game had reached $400 apiece. It would have been the first time the Bluegrass State teams had met on a court since the 1959 Tournament.

E After scoring 102 points in an opening-round win over North Carolina A&T, West Virginia is held to a mere 46 by Fresno State's defense, which leads the nation by holding foes to only 47.1 points per game.

F Idaho gets buzzer-beaters from Kelvin Smith at the end of regulation and Brian Kellerman in overtime. After the game, Vandals coach Don Monson confirms that Smith's shot came *after* the buzzer—but he does not offer to forfeit.

G Coach Ralph Miller reaches a regional final for the second time in his standout career with Wichita State, Iowa and Oregon State, but the Beavers' participation in this Tournament is later vacated by the NCAA because of rules violations.

H "Sleepy" Floyd scores 22 points and the Hoyas shoot a spectacular 74% from the field. Coach John Thompson Jr. jokes that letters offering his team shooting advice might finally stop.

Tournament Leaders

Individual Leaders

Scoring	CL	POS	G	PTS	PPG
1 **Perry Moss**, Northeastern	SR	G	2	55	27.5
2 **Ricky Frazier**, Missouri	SR	F	2	49	24.5
3 **Oliver Robinson**, UAB	SR	G/F	3	66	22.0
4 **Orlando Phillips**, Pepperdine	JR	F	2	43	21.5
5 **Trent Tucker**, Minnesota	SR	G	2	42	21.0
6 **Michael Brooks**, Tennessee	SO	G	2	40	20.0
7 **Randy Breuer**, Minnesota	JR	C	2	39	19.5
Dale Ellis, Tennessee	JR	F	2	39	19.5
Billy Goodwin, St. John's	JR	G	2	39	19.5
10 **Ralph Sampson**, Virginia	JR	C	2	38	19.0

Minimum: 2 games

Field Goal Pct	CL	POS	G	FG	FGA	PCT
1 **Jeff Jones**, Virginia	SR	G	2	13	15	86.7
2 **Keith Lee**, Memphis	FR	C	2	14	19	73.7
3 **Orlando Phillips**, Pepperdine	JR	F	2	19	26	73.1
4 **Jimmy Black**, North Carolina	SR	G	5	16	22	72.7
5 **Charles Jones**, Louisville	SO	F	4	16	23	69.6

Minimum: 12 FG made

Free Throw Pct	CL	POS	G	FT	FTA	PCT
1 **Les Craft**, Kansas State	JR	F	3	12	12	100.0
2 **Oliver Robinson**, UAB	SR	G/F	3	12	13	92.3
3 **Ken Owens**, Idaho	SR	G	2	15	17	88.2
4 **Lester Conner**, Oregon State	SR	G/F	3	13	15	86.7
5 **Luellen Foster**, UAB	SR	G	3	12	14	85.7
Eddie Phillips, Alabama	SR	F	2	12	14	85.7

Minimum: 12 made

Rebounds Per Game	CL	POS	G	REB	RPG
1 **Ralph Sampson**, Virginia	JR	C	2	30	15.0
2 **Randy Breuer**, Minnesota	JR	C	2	21	10.5
Michael Payne, Iowa	FR	F	2	21	10.5
Steve Stipanovich, Missouri	JR	C	2	21	10.5
5 **Ed Pinckney**, Villanova	FR	C	3	30	10.0

Minimum: 2 games

Team Leaders

Scoring	G	PTS	PPG
1 **Houston**	5	413	82.6
2 **Indiana**	2	164	82.0
3 **Boston College**	4	313	78.3
4 **Missouri**	2	151	75.5
5 **Pepperdine**	2	150	75.0
6 **West Virginia**	2	148	74.0
7 **UAB**	3	216	72.0
8 **Alabama**	2	138	69.0
Kansas State	3	207	69.0
10 **Villanova**	3	206	68.7

Minimum: 2 games

FG Pct	G	FG	FGA	PCT
1 **Wake Forest**	2	50	84	59.5
2 **West Virginia**	2	54	94	57.5
3 **Georgetown**	5	115	203	56.6
4 **Pepperdine**	2	58	104	55.8
5 **North Carolina**	5	120	216	55.6

FT Pct	G	FT	FTA	PCT
1 **UAB**	3	56	70	80.0
2 **Idaho**	2	39	50	78.0
3 **Wyoming**	2	34	45	75.6
4 **Alabama**	2	40	53	75.5
5 **Pepperdine**	2	34	46	73.9

Minimum: 2 games

Rebounds	G	REB	RPG
1 **Indiana**	2	84	42.0
2 **Virginia**	2	72	36.0
3 **Houston**	5	166	33.2
4 **Boston College**	4	130	32.5
Northeastern	2	65	32.5
St. John's	2	65	32.5

Minimum: 2 games

All-Tournament Team

PLAYER	CL	POS	HT	SCHOOL	RPG	PPG
James Worthy*	JR	F	6-9	North Carolina	5.0	17.4
Patrick Ewing	FR	C	7-0	Georgetown	7.6	13.2
Eric "Sleepy" Floyd	SR	G	6-3	Georgetown	3.2	16.0
Michael Jordan	FR	G	6-6	North Carolina	3.8	13.2
Sam Perkins	SO	F/C	6-9	North Carolina	7.8	16.0

All-Regional Teams

East

PLAYER	CL	POS	HT	SCHOOL	RPG	PPG
James Worthy*	JR	F	6-9	North Carolina	5.7	15.0
Jimmy Black	SR	G	6-2	North Carolina	1.7	11.3
Sam Perkins	SO	F/C	6-9	North Carolina	7.3	15.0
Ed Pinckney	FR	C	6-9	Villanova	10.0	15.3
John Pinone	JR	C	6-8	Villanova	8.7	15.0

Mideast

PLAYER	CL	POS	HT	SCHOOL	RPG	PPG
Oliver Robinson*	SR	G/F	6-4	UAB	4.0	22.0
Lancaster Gordon	SO	G	6-3	Louisville	2.3	13.0
Charles Jones	SO	F	6-8	Louisville	4.0	12.0
Ralph Sampson	JR	C	7-4	Virginia	15.0	19.0
Derek Smith	SR	G	6-6	Louisville	5.7	16.0

Midwest

PLAYER	CL	POS	HT	SCHOOL	RPG	PPG
Robert Williams*	JR	G	6-2	Houston	3.0	17.8
John Bagley	JR	G	6-0	Boston College	3.8	18.0
Ricky Frazier	SR	F	6-6	Missouri	7.5	24.5
John Garris	JR	F	6-8	Boston College	6.8	12.5
Larry Micheaux	JR	F	6-9	Houston	8.0	12.0

West

PLAYER	CL	POS	HT	SCHOOL	RPG	PPG
Eric "Sleepy" Floyd*	SR	G	6-3	Georgetown	2.7	16.3
Lester Conner	SR	G/F	6-4	Oregon State	6.0	17.7
Patrick Ewing	FR	C	7-0	Georgetown	5.7	11.7
Rod Higgins	SR	F	6-7	Fresno State	3.5	15.0
Charlie Sitton	SO	F	6-8	Oregon State	4.0	14.0

* Most outstanding player

1982 NCAA TOURNAMENT BOX SCORES

NORTH CAROLINA	MIN	FG	3FG	FT	REB	A	ST	BL	PF	TP
Matt Doherty	35	5-9	-	6-6	2	3	0	-	2	16
James Worthy	35	4-11	-	8-8	8	3	0	-	3	16
Sam Perkins	39	5-8	-	5-7	5	1	1	-	2	15
Jimmy Black	39	6-7	-	2-4	2	6	0	-	1	14
Michael Jordan	33	3-6	-	5-5	3	3	1	-	4	11
Buzz Peterson	7	1-1	-	0-1	1	0	1	-	1	2
Chris Brust	5	0-1	-	0-0	1	0	0	-	1	0
Jeb Barlow	3	0-0	-	0-0	1	0	0	-	0	0
Jim Braddock	2	0-0	-	0-0	0	1	0	-	0	0
Cecil Exum	1	0-0	-	0-0	0	0	0	-	0	0
Warren Martin	1	0-0	-	0-0	0	0	0	-	0	0
TOTALS	**200**	**24-43**	**-**	**26-31**	**23**	**17**	**3**	**-**	**14**	**74**
Percentages		55.8		83.9						

Coach: Dean Smith

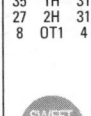

74-69

41	1H	36
33	2H	33

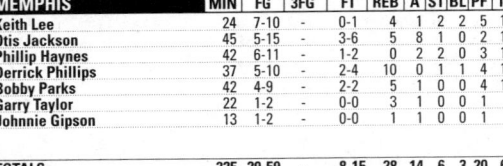

SWEET 16

ALABAMA	MIN	FG	3FG	FT	REB	A	ST	BL	PF	TP
Eddie Phillips	20	7-9	-	2-4	2	0	0	0	5	16
Bobby Lee Hurt	30	6-8	-	0-0	8	0	0	1	5	12
Ennis Whatley	40	4-13	-	2-2	2	4	2	0	3	10
Eric Richardson	36	5-7	-	0-0	0	6	0	0	3	10
Mike Davis	34	3-6	-	1-2	1	1	0	0	3	7
Phillip Lockett	19	1-3	-	4-6	3	0	0	0	5	6
Cliff Windham	9	2-4	-	2-2	2	0	0	0	2	6
Terry Williams	12	1-3	-	0-0	1	0	0	1	1	2
TOTALS	**200**	**29-53**	**-**	**11-16**	**19**	**11**	**2**	**2**	**27**	**69**
Percentages		54.7		68.8						

Coach: Wimp Sanderson

Officials: Jim Bain, Mike Tanco, Rich Ballesteros **Technicals:** None **Attendance:** 12,400

VILLANOVA	MIN	FG	3FG	FT	REB	A	ST	BL	PF	TP
John Pinone	-	8-17	-	3-6	12	3	2	0	3	19
Aaron Howard	-	8-10	-	0-1	2	0	1	0	4	16
Ed Pinckney	-	4-8	-	8-12	10	1	2	6	2	16
Stewart Granger	-	4-9	-	2-2	2	6	2	0	4	10
Mike Mulquin	-	1-2	-	5-5	1	0	0	0	0	7
Dwayne McClain	-	1-5	-	0-0	1	8	1	0	4	2
Frank Dobbs	-	0-0	-	0-0	0	1	0	0	0	0
Gary McLain	-	0-0	-	0-0	0	1	0	0	0	0
John Sices	-	0-0	-	0-0	0	0	0	0	1	0
TOTALS	**-**	**26-51**	**-**	**18-26**	**28**	**20**	**8**	**6**	**18**	**70**
Percentages		51.0		69.2						

Coach: Rollie Massimino

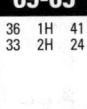

70-66

35	1H	31
27	2H	31
8	OT1	4

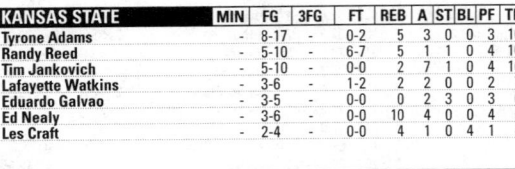

SWEET 16

MEMPHIS	MIN	FG	3FG	FT	REB	A	ST	BL	PF	TP
Keith Lee	24	7-10	-	0-1	4	1	2	2	5	14
Otis Jackson	45	5-15	-	3-6	5	8	1	0	2	13
Phillip Haynes	42	6-11	-	1-2	0	2	2	0	3	13
Derrick Phillips	37	5-10	-	2-4	10	0	1	1	4	12
Bobby Parks	42	4-9	-	2-2	5	1	0	0	4	10
Garry Taylor	22	1-2	-	0-0	3	1	0	0	1	2
Johnnie Gipson	13	1-2	-	0-0	1	1	0	0	1	2
TOTALS	**225**	**29-59**	**-**	**8-15**	**28**	**14**	**6**	**3**	**20**	**66**
Percentages		49.2		53.3						

Coach: Dana Kirk

Officials: Joe Forte, Tom Rucker, Bob Wortman **Technicals:** None **Attendance:** 12,400

BOSTON COLLEGE	MIN	FG	3FG	FT	REB	A	ST	BL	PF	TP
Michael Adams	29	7-8	-	6-8	3	3	1	0	0	20
John Garris	29	7-14	-	4-5	7	1	0	4	3	18
Jay Murphy	24	2-6	-	7-8	7	2	1	1	3	11
John Bagley	38	4-12	-	2-2	4	2	2	0	2	10
Martin Clark	23	2-5	-	3-3	6	2	0	0	2	7
Dwan Chandler	25	1-3	-	0-0	0	0	2	0	2	2
Burnett Adams	1	0-0	-	1-2	0	0	0	0	1	1
Rich Shrigley	23	0-1	-	0-0	2	4	0	0	4	0
Mark Schmidt	8	0-0	-	0-0	1	0	1	0	0	0
TOTALS	**200**	**23-49**	**-**	**23-28**	**30**	**14**	**7**	**5**	**17**	**69**
Percentages		46.9		82.1						

Coach: Tom Davis

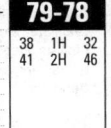

69-65

36	1H	41
33	2H	24

SWEET 16

KANSAS STATE	MIN	FG	3FG	FT	REB	A	ST	BL	PF	TP
Tyrone Adams	-	8-17	-	0-2	5	3	0	0	3	16
Randy Reed	-	5-10	-	6-7	5	1	1	0	4	16
Tim Jankovich	-	5-10	-	0-0	2	7	1	0	4	10
Lafayette Watkins	-	3-6	-	1-2	2	2	0	0	2	7
Eduardo Galvao	-	3-5	-	0-0	0	2	3	0	3	6
Ed Nealy	-	3-6	-	0-0	10	4	0	0	4	6
Les Craft	-	2-4	-	0-0	4	1	0	4	1	4
TOTALS	**-**	**29-58**	**-**	**7-11**	**28**	**20**	**5**	**4**	**21**	**65**
Percentages		50.0		63.6						

Coach: Jack Hartman

Officials: Denny Bishop, Paul Housman, Charles Range **Technicals:** None **Attendance:** 18,050

HOUSTON	MIN	FG	3FG	FT	REB	A	ST	BL	PF	TP
Lynden Rose	33	7-11	-	2-2	2	5	0	0	2	16
Michael Young	34	6-11	-	3-5	3	2	1	1	5	15
Clyde Drexler	37	5-9	-	4-6	10	3	2	1	4	14
Hakeem Olajuwon	25	5-9	-	3-7	11	0	3	3	4	13
Larry Micheaux	28	5-6	-	1-2	9	0	0	1	4	11
Robert Williams	32	4-15	-	2-3	2	0	1	0	3	10
Eric Davis	11	0-0	-	0-0	1	0	1	0	1	0
TOTALS	**200**	**32-61**	**-**	**15-25**	**38**	**10**	**8**	**6**	**23**	**79**
Percentages		52.5		60.0						

Coach: Guy V. Lewis

79-78

38	1H	32
41	2H	46

SWEET 16

MISSOURI	MIN	FG	3FG	FT	REB	A	ST	BL	PF	TP
Ricky Frazier	39	11-20	-	7-11	8	1	3	0	3	29
Steve Stipanovich	40	7-14	-	3-6	12	2	1	1	4	17
Jon Sundvold	39	6-12	-	2-2	3	2	0	1	1	14
Marvin McCrary	21	2-5	-	0-0	4	4	0	0	3	4
Greg Cavener	15	2-5	-	0-4	3	5	1	0	2	4
Mark Dressler	9	1-1	-	2-2	2	0	0	0	3	4
Prince Bridges	27	0-2	-	3-4	1	2	1	0	4	3
Michael Walker	8	1-2	-	0-0	0	1	0	0	0	2
Ron Jones	2	0-0	-	1-2	0	0	0	0	0	1
TOTALS	**200**	**30-61**	**-**	**18-31**	**33**	**17**	**6**	**2**	**20**	**78**
Percentages		49.2		58.1						

Coach: Norm Stewart

Officials: Dick Paparo, Don Shea, Bob Herrold **Technicals:** None **Attendance:** 18,050

UAB	MIN	FG	3FG	FT	REB	A	ST	BL	PF	TP
Oliver Robinson	40	8-17	-	7-7	5	9	1	0	2	23
Luellen Foster	37	4-7	-	4-5	3	4	2	0	1	12
Jonath Nicholas	27	4-6	-	3-4	5	0	2	1	3	11
Donnie Speer	16	4-7	-	2-2	2	0	1	1	4	10
Chris Giles	40	2-7	-	1-2	6	2	1	0	3	5
Norman Anchrum	27	2-10	-	1-3	3	0	1	2	3	5
Craig Lane	7	0-0	-	2-2	1	1	0	0	1	2
Raymond Gause	6	0-1	-	0-0	0	0	0	0	1	0
TOTALS	**200**	**24-55**	**-**	**20-25**	**25**	**16**	**8**	**4**	**18**	**68**
Percentages		43.6		80.0						

Coach: Gene Bartow

68-66

33	1H	37
35	2H	29

SWEET 16

VIRGINIA	MIN	FG	3FG	FT	REB	A	ST	BL	PF	TP
Ralph Sampson	37	8-18	-	3-6	21	2	0	2	4	19
Jeff Jones	33	9-9	-	0-0	1	4	0	0	3	18
Jim Miller	26	3-10	-	4-4	5	1	0	0	4	10
Tim Mullen	30	3-7	-	1-1	3	1	0	0	5	7
Craig Robinson	21	2-5	-	2-2	4	0	0	0	3	6
Kenton Edelin	23	2-4	-	0-3	7	2	2	0	3	4
Ricky Stokes	26	1-3	-	0-1	3	2	2	0	2	2
Othell Wilson	4	0-1	-	0-0	0	0	0	0	0	0
TOTALS	**200**	**28-57**	**-**	**10-17**	**44**	**12**	**4**	**2**	**24**	**66**
Percentages		49.1		58.8						

Coach: Terry Holland

Officials: Booker Turner, Charles Vacca, Jody Silvester **Technicals:** Virginia (coach Holland, bench) **Attendance:** 16,754

LOUISVILLE	MIN	FG	3FG	FT	REB	A	ST	BL	PF	TP
Lancaster Gordon	39	10-14	-	3-4	4	0	1	0	3	23
Derek Smith	22	5-5	-	7-10	6	4	3	0	4	17
Rodney McCray	35	3-5	-	2-2	6	2	1	1	3	8
Jerry Eaves	39	2-7	-	2-2	2	1	1	0	1	6
Charles Jones	30	3-3	-	0-1	3	1	5	1	1	6
Wiley Brown	14	1-3	-	0-0	3	1	0	0	1	2
Scooter McCray	9	0-2	-	2-2	0	5	1	1	0	2
Milt Wagner	2	1-1	-	0-0	0	0	0	0	0	2
Poncho Wright	10	0-3	-	1-3	2	1	0	0	3	1
TOTALS	**200**	**25-43**	**-**	**17-24**	**26**	**15**	**12**	**3**	**16**	**67**
Percentages		58.1		70.8						

Coach: Denny Crum

67-61

32	1H	31
35	2H	30

SWEET 16

MINNESOTA	MIN	FG	3FG	FT	REB	A	ST	BL	PF	TP
Randy Breuer	40	9-15	-	4-6	12	1	0	3	2	22
Trent Tucker	39	10-19	-	2-2	2	3	3	0	4	22
Gary Holmes	28	3-4	-	1-2	4	1	0	0	2	7
Darryl Mitchell	36	3-8	-	0-0	0	2	4	0	4	6
John Wiley	30	1-4	-	0-0	5	7	2	0	4	2
Zebedee Howell	6	0-0	-	2-2	1	0	0	0	0	2
Jim Petersen	12	0-3	-	0-0	0	2	0	3	3	0
Tommy Davis	9	0-3	-	0-0	3	1	0	0	1	0
TOTALS	**200**	**26-56**	**-**	**9-12**	**27**	**17**	**9**	**6**	**20**	**61**
Percentages		46.4		75.0						

Coach: Jim Dutcher

Officials: Larry Lembo, Jim McDaniel, Jack Hannon **Technicals:** None **Attendance:** 16,754

GEORGETOWN	MIN	FG	3FG	FT	REB	A	ST	BL	PF	TP
Eric "Sleepy" Floyd	35	7-9	-	2-2	4	1	0	0	3	16
Patrick Ewing	31	7-8	-	1-1	6	0	1	2	3	15
Eric Smith	36	3-7	-	4-4	5	4	1	0	1	10
Fred Brown	18	1-1	-	7-9	3	2	1	0	4	9
Ed Spriggs	27	0-2	-	2-2	2	0	0	0	1	2
Gene Smith	15	1-2	-	0-0	0	3	1	0	0	2
Bill Martin	14	1-2	-	0-0	2	0	0	0	0	2
Anthony Jones	10	1-1	-	0-0	0	0	0	0	0	2
Mike Hancock	14	0-1	-	0-0	1	0	0	0	1	0
TOTALS	200	21-33	-	16-18	23	10	4	2	13	58
Percentages		63.6		88.9						

Coach: John Thompson Jr.

58-40
25 1H 20
33 2H 20
SWEET 16

FRESNO STATE	MIN	FG	3FG	FT	REB	A	ST	BL	PF	TP
Rod Higgins	39	6-11	-	0-0	3	1	1	0	4	12
Desi Barmore	26	4-8	-	0-0	2	0	0	1	3	8
Bernard Thompson	27	1-3	-	5-5	2	1	1	0	5	7
Bobby Davis	26	2-5	-	3-4	3	3	1	0	1	7
Donald Mason	30	1-7	-	0-0	1	1	3	0	2	2
Tyrone Bradley	26	1-2	-	0-0	0	0	1	0	3	2
John Weatherspoon	1	1-2	-	0-0	0	0	0	0	0	2
Omel Nieves	15	0-0	-	0-0	1	1	0	0	1	0
Mitch Arnold	9	0-0	-	0-0	0	2	0	0	0	0
Dan Sezzi	1	0-1	-	0-0	0	0	0	0	0	0
TOTALS	200	16-39	-	8-9	12	9	7	1	19	40
Percentages		41.0		88.9						

Coach: Boyd Grant

Officials: Hank Nichols, John Dabrow, Bob Dibler
Technicals: None
Attendance: 15,237

OREGON STATE	MIN	FG	3FG	FT	REB	A	ST	BL	PF	TP
Lester Conner	39	10-14	-	4-4	10	5	1	0	3	24
Charlie Sitton	39	7-9	-	2-3	7	2	1	0	2	16
A.C. Green	18	4-6	-	0-1	4	0	0	0	3	8
Danny Evans	36	2-9	-	2-2	2	1	0	0	4	6
Rob Holbrook	25	1-3	-	2-2	5	3	0	0	3	4
William Brew	39	1-5	-	0-1	2	2	1	1	2	2
Jamie Stangel	1	0-0	-	0-0	1	0	0	0	0	0
Alan Tait	1	0-0	-	0-0	0	0	0	0	0	0
Jeff Wilson	1	0-0	-	0-0	1	0	0	0	0	0
Greg Wiltjer	1	0-0	-	0-0	1	0	0	0	1	0
TOTALS	200	25-46	-	10-13	33	13	3	1	18	60
Percentages		54.3		76.9						

Coach: Ralph Miller

60-42
31 1H 25
29 2H 17
SWEET 16

IDAHO	MIN	FG	3FG	FT	REB	A	ST	BL	PF	TP
Gordie Herbert	39	4-9	-	4-5	5	4	1	-	3	12
Phil Hopson	39	5-9	-	0-0	5	2	0	-	3	10
Brian Kellerman	39	4-7	-	2-2	1	2	1	-	2	10
Ken Owens	39	2-6	-	3-5	2	2	2	-	4	7
Pete Prigge	4	1-2	-	0-0	0	0	0	-	1	2
Kelvin Smith	34	0-3	-	1-2	3	0	0	-	5	1
Kevin Haatvedt	1	0-0	-	0-0	0	0	0	-	0	0
Matt Haskins	1	0-0	-	0-0	0	0	0	-	0	0
Mike Maben	1	0-1	-	0-0	0	0	0	-	0	0
Antwine Murchison	1	0-0	-	0-1	0	0	0	-	0	0
Ben Ross	1	0-0	-	0-0	0	0	0	-	0	0
Freeman Watkins	1	0-1	-	0-0	0	0	0	-	1	0
TOTALS	200	16-38	-	10-15	16	10	4	-	19	42
Percentages		42.1		66.7						

Coach: Don Monson

Officials: Dale Kelley, Jerry Yarborough, George Solomon
Technicals: Idaho (coach Monson)
Attendance: 15,237

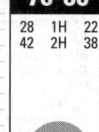

NORTH CAROLINA	MIN	FG	3FG	FT	REB	A	ST	BL	PF	TP
Michael Jordan	30	5-9	-	5-7	1	2	2	0	2	15
James Worthy	37	6-10	-	2-3	5	4	0	2	2	14
Sam Perkins	38	4-8	-	5-5	7	2	1	3	4	13
Matt Doherty	37	4-8	-	5-5	1	3	0	0	2	13
Jimmy Black	38	4-5	-	3-4	3	10	2	0	2	11
Buzz Peterson	8	1-2	-	0-0	1	0	0	0	0	2
Jeb Barlow	2	1-1	-	0-0	0	0	0	0	0	2
Chris Brust	4	0-0	-	0-0	0	0	0	0	0	0
Jim Braddock	2	0-0	-	0-0	0	0	0	0	0	0
Cecil Exum	2	0-1	-	0-0	0	0	0	0	0	0
Warren Martin	1	0-0	-	0-0	0	0	0	0	0	0
Lynwood Robinson	1	0-0	-	0-0	0	0	0	0	0	0
TOTALS	200	25-44	-	20-24	18	21	5	5	12	70
Percentages		56.8		83.3						

Coach: Dean Smith

70-60
28 1H 22
42 2H 38
ELITE 8

VILLANOVA	MIN	FG	3FG	FT	REB	A	ST	BL	PF	TP
Ed Pinckney	39	8-13	-	2-4	10	0	2	0	3	18
John Pinone	37	6-11	-	2-3	6	4	1	0	5	14
Aaron Howard	18	3-5	-	0-0	0	0	0	0	5	6
Stewart Granger	35	2-8	-	0-0	1	6	0	0	4	4
Dwayne McClain	21	2-7	-	0-0	2	0	0	1	3	4
Frank Dobbs	18	1-5	-	2-2	1	1	0	0	0	4
Gary McLain	6	2-2	-	0-0	0	0	0	0	0	4
Mike Mulquin	21	1-2	-	0-0	3	1	0	0	2	2
John Sices	2	1-1	-	0-0	0	0	0	0	0	2
Martin Lutchaunig	1	1-1	-	0-0	0	0	0	0	0	2
Jeff Sherry	2	0-0	-	0-0	0	0	0	0	0	0
TOTALS	200	27-55	-	6-9	23	12	3	1	22	60
Percentages		49.1		66.7						

Coach: Rollie Massimino

Officials: Joe Forte, Tom Rucker, Bob Wortman
Technicals: None
Attendance: 12,400

HOUSTON	MIN	FG	3FG	FT	REB	A	ST	BL	PF	TP
Robert Williams	39	9-17	-	7-10	5	2	0	0	3	25
Larry Micheaux	35	7-11	-	4-7	7	0	2	3	2	18
Clyde Drexler	35	6-9	-	3-6	9	1	2	0	5	15
Lynden Rose	34	6-10	-	3-5	1	7	3	1	5	15
Reid Gettys	8	0-0	-	10-10	2	0	0	0	0	10
Michael Young	31	3-12	-	0-0	7	1	1	0	4	6
Hakeem Olajuwon	11	2-3	-	2-2	3	0	2	2	4	6
Eric Davis	7	0-0	-	4-4	3	1	0	0	0	4
TOTALS	200	33-62	-	33-44	37	12	10	6	23	99
Percentages		53.2		75.0						

Coach: Guy V. Lewis

99-92
46 1H 43
53 2H 49
ELITE 8

BOSTON COLLEGE	MIN	FG	3FG	FT	REB	A	ST	BL	PF	TP
John Bagley	35	11-18	-	4-6	4	5	0	0	4	26
Jay Murphy	27	9-18	-	5-7	11	1	0	0	1	23
John Garris	25	6-11	-	7-9	5	1	0	2	5	19
Rich Shrigley	30	5-6	-	0-3	3	3	1	0	4	10
Michael Adams	30	4-10	-	0-0	2	1	1	0	5	8
Martin Clark	25	1-3	-	0-0	6	3	0	0	5	2
Burnett Adams	4	1-2	-	0-0	2	0	1	0	3	2
Mark Schmidt	1	1-2	-	0-0	1	0	0	0	1	2
Dwan Chandler	23	0-1	-	0-0	2	0	2	0	5	0
TOTALS	200	38-71	-	16-25	36	14	5	2	33	92
Percentages		53.5		64.0						

Coach: Tom Davis

Officials: Denny Bishop, Paul Housman, Charles Range
Technicals: None
Attendance: 15,627

LOUISVILLE	MIN	FG	3FG	FT	REB	A	ST	BL	PF	TP
Charles Jones	27	5-7	-	9-13	4	2	0	0	2	19
Derek Smith	29	5-12	-	4-4	6	1	0	2	4	14
Jerry Eaves	33	6-9	-	1-1	3	2	0	0	3	13
Lancaster Gordon	28	4-7	-	3-4	2	5	2	0	3	11
Rodney McCray	26	3-4	-	0-3	11	3	0	0	2	6
Scooter McCray	20	3-3	-	0-0	3	1	2	0	2	6
Milt Wagner	19	2-2	-	0-0	1	4	2	0	1	4
Poncho Wright	9	1-2	-	0-0	1	0	0	0	0	2
Wiley Brown	9	0-2	-	0-0	1	2	0	1	1	0
TOTALS	200	29-48	-	17-25	32	20	6	3	18	75
Percentages		60.4		68.0						

Coach: Denny Crum

75-68
40 1H 32
35 2H 36
ELITE 8

UAB	MIN	FG	3FG	FT	REB	A	ST	BL	PF	TP
Oliver Robinson	39	9-21	-	2-2	6	0	1	0	4	20
Luellen Foster	39	5-9	-	3-4	3	3	2	0	4	13
Chris Giles	33	6-11	-	0-0	8	2	0	0	5	12
Norman Anchrum	30	3-7	-	3-4	6	0	0	1	5	9
Jonath Nicholas	25	3-7	-	2-2	1	4	2	0	3	8
Craig Lane	13	1-3	-	2-2	1	0	1	0	1	4
Marvin Johnson	2	1-1	-	0-0	1	0	0	0	0	2
Donnie Speer	14	0-3	-	0-2	0	0	0	0	2	0
Raymond Gause	5	0-0	-	0-0	1	0	0	0	1	0
TOTALS	200	28-62	-	12-16	27	9	6	1	25	68
Percentages		45.2		75.0						

Coach: Gene Bartow

Officials: Booker Turner, Charles Vacca, Jody Silvester
Technicals: None
Attendance: 16,754

GEORGETOWN	MIN	FG	3FG	FT	REB	A	ST	BL	PF	TP
Eric "Sleepy" Floyd	-	9-12	-	4-5	3	2	1	0	1	22
Patrick Ewing	-	6-9	-	1-2	3	0	1	1	5	13
Fred Brown	-	4-4	-	1-1	7	2	1	0	4	9
Ed Spriggs	-	4-5	-	0-1	5	0	0	1	2	8
Anthony Jones	-	3-4	-	1-2	0	2	0	0	1	7
Mike Hancock	-	1-2	-	2-2	6	0	0	0	0	4
Eric Smith	-	1-2	-	2-4	1	3	1	0	1	4
Kurt Kaull	-	1-1	-	0-0	0	0	0	0	0	2
Ron Blaylock	-	0-0	-	0-0	0	0	0	0	0	0
David Blue	-	0-0	-	0-0	0	1	0	0	0	0
Bill Martin	-	0-0	-	0-0	0	0	0	0	0	0
Gene Smith	-	0-0	-	0-0	0	1	0	0	0	0
TOTALS	-	29-39	-	11-17	25	11	4	2	14	69
Percentages		74.4		64.7						

Coach: John Thompson Jr.

69-45
42 1H 25
27 2H 20
ELITE 8

OREGON STATE	MIN	FG	3FG	FT	REB	A	ST	BL	PF	TP
Lester Conner	40	6-10	-	1-2	1	5	2	0	3	13
Charlie Sitton	29	6-9	-	0-0	2	1	0	1	5	12
A.C. Green	33	3-4	-	4-8	5	0	0	0	2	10
Danny Evans	22	4-13	-	0-0	2	1	0	0	4	8
Rob Holbrook	27	1-7	-	0-0	1	2	0	0	4	2
William Brew	38	0-6	-	0-0	2	3	0	0	2	0
Jamie Stangel	6	0-1	-	0-0	0	0	0	0	0	0
Greg Wiltjer	4	0-2	-	0-0	2	0	0	0	0	0
Alan Tait	1	0-0	-	0-0	0	0	0	0	0	0
TOTALS	200	20-52	-	5-10	15	12	2	1	20	45
Percentages		38.5		50.0						

Coach: Ralph Miller

Officials: Hank Nichols, Bob Dibler, John Dabrow
Technicals: None
Attendance: 11,986

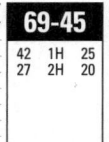

68-63

North Carolina	31 1H 37 2H
Houston	29 1H 34 2H

FINAL 4

NORTH CAROLINA	MIN	FG	3FG	FT	REB	A	ST	BL	PF	TP
Sam Perkins	39	9-11	-	7-7	10	1	1	0	1	25
Michael Jordan	39	7-14	-	4-4	5	2	0	0	4	18
James Worthy	39	7-10	-	0-0	4	3	2	2	3	14
Jimmy Black	38	1-2	-	4-6	3	4	1	0	4	6
Matt Doherty	37	2-7	-	1-2	1	5	1	0	1	5
Jim Braddock	3	0-0	-	0-0	0	0	0	0	0	0
Buzz Peterson	3	0-0	-	0-0	1	0	0	0	0	0
Chris Brust	1	0-0	-	0-0	0	0	0	0	1	0
Warren Martin	1	0-0	-	0-0	0	0	0	0	0	0
TOTALS	**200**	**26-44**	**-**	**16-19**	**24**	**15**	**5**	**2**	**14**	**68**
Percentages		59.1		84.2						
Coach: Dean Smith										

HOUSTON	MIN	FG	3FG	FT	REB	A	ST	BL	PF	TP
Lynden Rose	36	10-15	-	0-2	2	3	2	0	2	20
Larry Micheaux	37	8-14	-	2-3	6	0	1	2	2	18
Clyde Drexler	40	6-12	-	5-6	9	3	2	0	3	17
Robert Williams	35	0-8	-	2-2	1	2	1	0	1	2
Hakeem Olajuwon	20	1-3	-	0-0	6	0	1	2	4	2
Michael Young	15	1-7	-	0-1	3	1	0	0	0	2
Eric Davis	4	1-2	-	0-0	0	0	1	0	3	2
Robert Williams	12	0-1	-	0-0	1	0	2	0	2	0
Benny Anders	1	0-2	-	0-0	0	0	0	0	2	0
TOTALS	**200**	**27-64**	**-**	**9-14**	**28**	**9**	**10**	**4**	**19**	**63**
Percentages		42.2		64.3						
Coach: Guy V. Lewis										

Officials: Bob Dibler, Hank Nichols, John Dabrow
Technicals: None
Attendance: 61,612

50-46

Georgetown	24 1H 26 2H
Louisville	22 1H 24 2H

FINAL 4

GEORGETOWN	MIN	FG	3FG	FT	REB	A	ST	BL	PF	TP
Eric Smith	36	6-10	-	2-4	2	1	0	1	2	14
Eric "Sleepy" Floyd	31	3-11	-	7-8	5	3	1	0	4	13
Patrick Ewing	37	3-8	-	2-2	10	1	2	1	2	8
Ed Spriggs	20	2-2	-	1-3	7	0	2	1	2	5
Fred Brown	36	1-3	-	2-3	3	2	2	1	4	4
Anthony Jones	13	2-4	-	0-0	3	0	2	0	1	4
Mike Hancock	15	1-3	-	0-0	2	0	0	0	0	2
Bill Martin	8	0-0	-	0-0	1	0	0	0	0	0
Gene Smith	4	0-0	-	0-0	0	0	0	0	1	0
TOTALS	**200**	**18-41**	**-**	**14-20**	**33**	**7**	**9**	**4**	**16**	**50**
Percentages		43.9		70.0						
Coach: John Thompson Jr.										

LOUISVILLE	MIN	FG	3FG	FT	REB	A	ST	BL	PF	TP
Derek Smith	26	4-8	-	2-4	6	1	0	2	4	10
Jerry Eaves	34	4-9	-	0-0	4	1	2	0	1	8
Rodney McCray	30	2-5	-	4-4	5	2	1	2	5	8
Charles Jones	21	4-7	-	0-2	6	0	2	0	0	8
Wiley Brown	13	2-5	-	0-0	1	0	1	0	1	4
Poncho Wright	12	1-3	-	2-2	0	0	0	0	1	4
Lancaster Gordon	29	1-6	-	0-0	1	3	2	0	2	2
Milt Wagner	20	1-4	-	0-0	2	1	0	0	3	2
Scooter McCray	15	0-1	-	0-0	0	1	0	2	1	0
TOTALS	**200**	**19-48**	**-**	**8-12**	**25**	**9**	**8**	**6**	**18**	**46**
Percentages		39.6		66.7						
Coach: Denny Crum										

Officials: Tom Rucker, Bob Wortman, Joe Forte
Technicals: None
Attendance: 61,612

63-62

North Carolina	31 1H 32 2H
Georgetown	32 1H 30 2H

NCAA FINAL 1982

NORTH CAROLINA	MIN	FG	3FG	FT	REB	A	ST	BL	PF	TP
James Worthy	38	13-17	-	2-7	4	0	3	0	3	28
Michael Jordan	34	7-13	-	2-2	9	2	2	0	2	16
Sam Perkins	38	3-7	-	4-6	7	1	0	1	2	10
Matt Doherty	39	1-3	-	2-3	3	1	0	0	0	4
Jimmy Black	38	1-4	-	2-2	3	7	1	0	2	4
Chris Brust	4	0-0	-	1-2	1	1	0	0	1	1
Buzz Peterson	7	0-3	-	0-0	1	1	1	0	0	0
Jim Braddock	2	0-0	-	0-0	0	1	0	0	1	0
TOTALS	**200**	**25-47**	**-**	**13-22**	**28**	**14**	**7**	**1**	**11**	**63**
Percentages		53.2		59.1						
Coach: Dean Smith										

GEORGETOWN	MIN	FG	3FG	FT	REB	A	ST	BL	PF	TP
Patrick Ewing	37	10-15	-	3-3	11	1	3	2	4	23
Eric "Sleepy" Floyd	39	9-17	-	0-0	3	5	4	0	2	18
Eric Smith	35	6-8	-	2-2	3	5	0	0	5	14
Fred Brown	29	1-2	-	2-2	2	5	2	0	4	4
Anthony Jones	10	1-3	-	0-0	0	0	0	0	0	2
Ed Spriggs	30	0-2	-	1-2	1	0	2	0	2	1
Mike Hancock	8	0-2	-	0-0	0	0	0	0	1	0
Gene Smith	7	0-0	-	0-0	0	0	0	0	1	0
Bill Martin	5	0-2	-	0-0	0	0	0	0	1	0
TOTALS	**200**	**27-51**	**-**	**8-9**	**20**	**16**	**11**	**2**	**20**	**62**
Percentages		52.9		88.9						
Coach: John Thompson Jr.										

Officials: Bob Dibler, Hank Nichols, John Dabrow
Technicals: None
Attendance: 61,612

National Invitation Tournament (NIT)

First round: Oklahoma d. Oral Roberts 81-73, Purdue d. Western Kentucky 72-65, Illinois d. Long Island 126-78, Washington d. BYU 66-63, Texas A&M d. Lamar 60-58, Dayton d. Connecticut 76-75 (OT), UNLV d. Murray State 87-61, Georgia d. Temple 73-60, Rutgers d. Iona 55-51, Bradley d. Texas-Pan American 76-65, Tulane d. LSU 83-72, UC Irvine d. San Diego State 70-69, Syracuse d. Saint Peter's 84-75, Virginia Tech d. Fordham 69-58, Maryland d. Richmond 60-50, Mississippi d. Clemson 53-49
Second round: Tulane d. UNLV 56-51, Oklahoma d. UC Irvine 80-77, Bradley d. Syracuse 95-81, Georgia d. Maryland 83-69, Dayton d. Illinois 61-58, Texas A&M d. Washington 69-65, Virginia Tech d. Mississippi 61-59, Purdue d. Rutgers 98-65
Third round: Oklahoma d. Dayton 91-82, Bradley d. Tulane 77-61, Georgia d. Virginia Tech 90-73, Purdue d. Texas A&M 86-68
Semifinals: Bradley d. Oklahoma 84-68, Purdue d. Georgia 61-60
Championship: Bradley d. Purdue 67-58
MVP: Mitchell Anderson, Bradley

1982-83: SPECIAL V

David vs. Goliath had nothing on the 1983 Tournament Final. Under the guidance of Jim Valvano, NC State (26–10) shocked Guy Lewis' Houston Cougars, 54-52, at the Pit in Albuquerque, N.M. During a span of nine games in the ACC and NCAA tournaments, the Wolfpack trailed with a minute or less to play *seven* times and won all nine, inspring the nickname the Cardiac Pack. On their way to the championship game, NC State survived two overtimes against Pepperdine and had one-point wins over UNLV and Virginia. The Phi Slama Jama Cougars, led by Hakeem Olajuwon and Clyde Drexler, were riding a 26-game winning streak and cruised into the Final by beating Louisville, 94-81.

With time expiring and the score tied at 52, NC State guard Dereck Whittenburg launched a desperation 35-footer that missed badly. Lorenzo Charles retrieved the ball and dunked it with :02 left. Valvano's team was the first NCAA champ to have lost 10 or more games during the season.

Olajuwon was named Tournament MOP, the first from a losing team since 1971. Virginia's Ralph Sampson (1981-83) joined Bill Walton (1972-74) as the only three-time Naismith Player of the Year winners. Sampson was chosen as the first pick in the 1983 NBA draft, by the Houston Rockets.

MAJOR CONFERENCE STANDINGS

AMCU-8	Conference			Overall		
	W	L	PCT	W	L	PCT
Western Illinois	9	3	.750	20	11	.645
Eastern Illinois	8	4	.667	13	18	.419
SW Missouri State	6	3	.667	13	15	.464
Illinois-Chicago	7	4	.636	16	12	.571
Northern Iowa	6	5	.545	13	18	.419
Valparaiso	4	9	.308	13	15	.464
Cleveland State	1	4	.200	8	20	.286
Wisconsin-Green Bay	2	11	.154	9	19	.321

ATLANTIC 10	Conference			Overall		
	W	L	PCT	W	L	PCT
EAST						
Rutgers○	11	3	.786	23	8	.742
Saint Joseph's	8	6	.571	15	13	.536
Temple	5	9	.357	14	15	.483
Massachusetts	4	10	.286	9	20	.310
Rhode Island	3	11	.214	9	19	.321
WEST						
West Virginia⊕	10	4	.714	23	8	.742
St. Bonaventure□	10	4	.714	20	10	.667
Penn State	9	5	.643	17	11	.607
Duquesne	6	8	.429	12	16	.429
George Washington	4	10	.286	14	15	.483

Tournament: **West Virginia d. Temple 86-78**
Tournament MVP: **Terence Stansbury**, Temple

ACC	Conference			Overall		
	W	L	PCT	W	L	PCT
North Carolina○	12	2	.857	28	8	.778
Virginia○	12	2	.857	29	5	.853
NC State⊕	8	6	.571	26	10	.722
Maryland○	8	6	.571	20	10	.667
Wake Forest□	7	7	.500	20	12	.625
Georgia Tech	4	10	.286	13	15	.464
Duke	3	11	.214	11	17	.393
Clemson	2	12	.143	11	20	.355

Tournament: **NC State d. Virginia 81-78**
Tournament MVP: **Sidney Lowe**, NC State

BIG EAST	Conference			Overall		
	W	L	PCT	W	L	PCT
St. John's⊕	12	4	.750	28	5	.848
Boston College○	12	4	.750	25	7	.781
Villanova○	12	4	.750	24	8	.750
Georgetown○	11	5	.688	22	10	.688
Syracuse○	9	7	.563	21	10	.677
Pittsburgh	6	10	.375	13	15	.464
Connecticut	5	11	.313	12	16	.429
Providence	4	12	.250	12	19	.387
Seton Hall	1	15	.063	6	23	.207

Tournament: **St. John's d. Boston College 85-77**
Tournament MVP: **Chris Mullin**, St. John's

BIG EIGHT	Conference			Overall		
	W	L	PCT	W	L	PCT
Missouri○	12	2	.857	26	8	.765
Oklahoma○	10	4	.714	24	9	.727
Oklahoma State⊕	9	5	.643	24	7	.774
Nebraska□	9	5	.643	22	10	.688
Iowa State	5	9	.357	13	15	.464
Kansas	4	10	.286	13	16	.448
Kansas State	4	10	.286	12	16	.429
Colorado	3	11	.214	13	15	.464

Tournament: **Oklahoma State d. Missouri 93-92 (2OT)**
Tournament MVP: **Leroy Combs**, Oklahoma State

BIG SKY	Conference			Overall		
	W	L	PCT	W	L	PCT
Weber State⊕	10	4	.714	23	8	.742
Nevada	10	4	.714	18	11	.621
Montana	9	5	.643	22	7	.759
Idaho□	9	5	.643	20	9	.690
Idaho State	7	7	.500	10	17	.370
Boise State	5	9	.357	10	17	.370
Northern Arizona	3	11	.214	10	16	.385
Montana State	3	11	.214	10	17	.370

Tournament: **Weber State d. Nevada 87-78**
Tournament MVP: **Ken Green**, Nevada

BIG TEN	Conference			Overall		
	W	L	PCT	W	L	PCT
Indiana⊕	13	5	.722	24	6	.800
Iowa○	11	7	.611	21	10	.710
Purdue○	11	7	.611	21	9	.700
Ohio State○	11	7	.611	20	10	.667
Illinois○	11	7	.611	21	11	.656
Minnesota□	9	9	.500	18	11	.621
Michigan State□	9	9	.500	17	13	.567
Northwestern□	8	10	.444	17	13	.567
Michigan	7	11	.389	15	13	.536
Wisconsin⊗	3	15	.167	8	20	.286

EAST COAST	Conference			Overall		
	W	L	PCT	W	L	PCT
EAST						
La Salle⊕	7	2	.778	18	14	.563
American	7	2	.778	20	10	.667
Hofstra	7	2	.778	18	9	.667
Drexel	5	4	.556	14	15	.483
Towson	2	7	.222	7	21	.250
WEST						
Rider	10	3	.769	20	9	.690
Bucknell	8	5	.615	17	11	.607
Delaware	4	9	.308	11	14	.440
Lafayette	3	10	.231	7	21	.250
Lehigh	2	11	.154	10	16	.385

Tournament: **La Salle d. American 75-73**

ECAC METRO	Conference			Overall		
	W	L	PCT	W	L	PCT
NORTH						
Long Island	11	3	.786	20	9	.690
Fairleigh Dickinson	9	5	.643	17	12	.586
Marist	7	7	.500	14	15	.483
St. Francis (NY)	7	7	.500	10	18	.357
Siena	6	8	.429	12	16	.429
Wagner	2	12	.143	10	18	.357
SOUTH						
Robert Morris⊕	12	2	.857	23	8	.742
Saint Francis (PA)	7	7	.500	12	17	.414
Baltimore	4	10	.286	10	18	.357
Loyola (MD)	3	11	.214	4	24	.143

Tournament: **Robert Morris d. Long Island 79-67**
Tournament MVP: **Chipper Harris**, Robert Morris

ECAC NORTH	Conference			Overall		
	W	L	PCT	W	L	PCT
Boston U.⊕	8	2	.800	21	10	.677
New Hampshire	8	2	.800	16	12	.571
Holy Cross	5	3	.625	17	13	.567
Maine	6	4	.600	12	14	.462
Niagara	5	4	.556	11	18	.379
Northeastern	4	6	.400	13	15	.464
Canisius	3	6	.333	11	17	.393
Vermont	3	7	.300	10	19	.345
Colgate	0	8	.000	3	24	.111

Tournament: **Boston U. d. Holy Cross 63-62**
Tournament MVP: **Mike Alexander**, Boston U.

ECAC SOUTH	Conference			Overall		
	W	L	PCT	W	L	PCT
William and Mary□	9	0	1.000	20	9	.690
James Madison⊕	6	3	.667	20	11	.645
Navy	3	3	.500	18	11	.621
George Mason	3	6	.333	15	12	.556
East Carolina	3	7	.300	16	13	.552
Richmond	2	7	.222	12	16	.429

Tournament: **James Madison d. William & Mary 41-38**
Tournament MVP: **Derek Steele**, James Madison

IVY	Conference			Overall		
	W	L	PCT	W	L	PCT
Princeton⊕	12	2	.857	20	9	.690
Penn	11	3	.786	17	9	.654
Yale	7	7	.500	12	14	.462
Columbia	7	7	.500	10	16	.385
Cornell	6	8	.429	10	16	.385
Brown	6	8	.429	9	17	.346
Harvard	4	10	.286	12	14	.462
Dartmouth	3	11	.214	7	19	.269

METRO	Conference			Overall		
	W	L	PCT	W	L	PCT
Louisville⊕	12	0	1.000	32	4	.889
Virginia Tech□	7	5	.583	23	11	.676
Tulane□	7	5	.583	19	12	.613
Memphis○⊗	6	6	.500	23	8	.742
Florida State	5	7	.417	14	14	.500
Southern Miss	3	9	.250	14	14	.500
Cincinnati	1	11	.083	11	17	.393

Tournament: **Louisville d. Tulane 66-51**
Tournament MVP: **Rodney McCray**, Louisville

Conference Standings Continue →

⊕ Automatic NCAA Tournament bid ○ At-large NCAA Tournament bid □ NIT appearance ⊗ Team record doesn't reflect games forfeited or vacated. For adjusted record, see p. 521.

METRO ATLANTIC

	Conference			Overall		
	W	L	Pct	W	L	Pct
Iona□	8	2	.800	22	9	.710
Saint Peter's	7	3	.700	22	5	.815
Fordham□	7	3	.700	19	11	.633
Manhattan	4	6	.400	15	13	.536
Fairfield	2	8	.200	13	15	.464
Army	2	8	.200	11	18	.379

Tournament: **Fordham d. Iona 54-53**
Tournament MVP: **Mark Murphy**, Fordham

MID-AMERICAN

	Conference			Overall		
	W	L	Pct	W	L	Pct
Bowling Green□	15	3	.833	21	9	.700
Ohio⊕	12	6	.667	23	9	.719
Ball State	10	8	.556	17	12	.586
Toledo	10	8	.556	17	12	.586
Miami (OH)	10	8	.556	13	15	.464
Kent State	9	9	.500	15	13	.536
Eastern Michigan	8	10	.444	12	16	.429
Northern Illinois	8	10	.444	11	16	.407
Central Michigan	5	13	.278	10	17	.370
Western Michigan	3	15	.167	5	23	.179

Tournament: **Ohio d. Bowling Green 59-56**
Tournament MVP: **John Devereaux**, Ohio

MEAC

	Conference			Overall		
	W	L	Pct	W	L	Pct
Howard	11	1	.917	19	9	.679
NC A&T⊕	9	3	.750	23	8	.742
South Carolina State	5	7	.417	13	15	.464
Maryland Eastern Shore	5	7	.417	10	19	.345
Delaware State	5	7	.417	8	19	.296
Florida A&M	4	8	.333	7	21	.250
Bethune-Cookman	3	9	.250	5	21	.192

Tournament: **NC A&T d. Howard 71-64**
Tournament MOP: **Joe Binion**, NC A&T

MIDWESTERN CITY

	Conference			Overall		
	W	L	Pct	W	L	Pct
Loyola-Chicago	12	2	.857	19	10	.655
Xavier⊕	10	4	.714	22	8	.733
Oral Roberts	10	4	.714	14	14	.500
Butler	9	5	.643	15	13	.536
Evansville	6	8	.429	13	16	.448
Detroit	6	8	.429	12	17	.414
Saint Louis	2	12	.143	5	23	.179
Oklahoma City	1	13	.071	4	22	.154

Tournament: **Xavier d. Loyola-Chicago 82-76**
Tournament MVP: **Alfredrick Hughes**, Loyola-Chicago

MISSOURI VALLEY

	Conference			Overall		
	W	L	Pct	W	L	Pct
Wichita State	17	1	.944	25	3	.893
Illinois State⊕	13	5	.722	24	7	.774
New Mexico State	11	7	.611	18	11	.621
Tulsa□	11	7	.611	19	12	.613
Bradley	10	8	.556	16	13	.552
Drake	9	9	.500	13	15	.464
Indiana State	5	13	.278	9	19	.321
Southern Illinois	5	13	.278	9	19	.321
West Texas	5	13	.278	8	20	.286
Creighton	4	14	.222	8	19	.296

Tournament: **Illinois State d. Tulsa 84-64**

OHIO VALLEY

	Conference			Overall		
	W	L	Pct	W	L	Pct
Murray State□	11	3	.786	21	8	.724
Morehead State⊕	10	4	.714	19	11	.633
Tennessee Tech	9	5	.643	16	12	.571
Akron	7	7	.500	14	15	.483
Eastern Kentucky	7	7	.500	10	17	.370
Youngstown State	5	9	.357	15	12	.556
Austin Peay	4	10	.286	11	16	.407
Middle Tennessee St.	3	11	.214	7	20	.259

Tournament: **Morehead State d. Akron 81-65**
Tournament MVP: **Guy Minnifield**, Morehead State

PCAA

	Conference			Overall		
	W	L	Pct	W	L	Pct
UNLV⊕	15	1	.938	28	3	.903
Cal State Fullerton□	12	4	.750	21	8	.724
Utah State○	10	6	.625	20	9	.690
Fresno State□	9	7	.563	25	10	.714
UC Irvine	8	8	.500	16	12	.571
San Jose State	7	9	.438	14	15	.483
Long Beach State	6	10	.375	13	16	.448
Pacific	4	12	.250	7	21	.250
UC Santa Barbara	1	15	.063	7	20	.259

Tournament: **UNLV d. Fresno State 66-63**
Tournament MVP: **Sidney Green**, UNLV

PAC-10

	Conference			Overall		
	W	L	Pct	W	L	Pct
UCLA⊕	15	3	.833	23	6	.793
Washington State○	14	4	.778	23	7	.767
Oregon State□	12	6	.667	20	11	.645
Arizona State□	12	6	.667	19	14	.576
Southern California	11	7	.611	17	11	.607
Washington	7	11	.389	16	15	.516
California	7	11	.389	14	14	.500
Stanford	6	12	.333	14	14	.500
Oregon	5	13	.278	9	18	.333
Arizona	1	17	.056	4	24	.143

SEC

	Conference			Overall		
	W	L	Pct	W	L	Pct
Kentucky○	13	5	.722	23	8	.742
LSU□	10	8	.556	19	13	.594
Mississippi□	10	8	.556	18	13	.581
Georgia⊕	9	9	.500	24	10	.706
Tennessee○	9	9	.500	20	12	.625
Mississippi State	9	9	.500	17	12	.586
Vanderbilt□	9	9	.500	19	14	.576
Alabama○	8	10	.444	20	12	.625
Auburn	8	10	.444	15	13	.536
Florida	5	13	.278	13	18	.419

Tournament: **Georgia d. Alabama 86-71**
Tournament MVP: **Vern Fleming**, Georgia

SOUTHERN

	Conference			Overall		
	W	L	Pct	W	L	Pct
Chattanooga⊕	15	1	.938	26	4	.867
Marshall	13	3	.813	20	8	.714
East Tennessee St.□	12	4	.750	22	9	.710
Western Carolina	9	7	.563	17	12	.586
Davidson	8	8	.500	13	15	.464
The Citadel	7	9	.438	12	16	.429
Furman	4	12	.250	9	20	.310
Appalachian State	3	13	.188	6	21	.222
VMI	1	15	.063	2	25	.074

Tournament: **Chattanooga d. East Tennessee State 70-62**
Tournament MOP: **Willie White**, Chattanooga

SOUTHLAND

	Conference			Overall		
	W	L	Pct	W	L	Pct
Lamar⊕	9	3	.750	23	8	.742
Louisiana Tech	8	4	.667	19	9	.679
McNeese State	6	6	.500	16	13	.552
UL-Monroe	6	6	.500	14	14	.500
Arkansas State	5	7	.417	17	12	.586
North Texas	5	7	.417	15	15	.500
Texas-Arlington	3	9	.250	9	19	.321

Tournament: **Lamar d. North Texas 75-54**
Tournament MVPs: **Kenneth Lyons**, North Texas and **Lamont Robinson**, Lamar

SOUTHWEST

	Conference			Overall		
	W	L	Pct	W	L	Pct
Houston⊕	16	0	1.000	31	3	.912
Arkansas○	14	2	.875	26	4	.867
Texas A&M	10	6	.625	17	14	.548
TCU□	9	7	.563	23	11	.676
SMU	9	7	.563	19	11	.633
Texas Tech	7	9	.438	12	19	.387
Baylor	4	12	.250	12	16	.429
Rice	2	14	.125	8	20	.286
Texas	1	15	.063	6	22	.214

Tournament: **Houston d. TCU 62-59**
Tournament MVP: **Michael Young**, Houston

SWAC

	Conference			Overall		
	W	L	Pct	W	L	Pct
Alabama State□	12	2	.857	22	6	.786
Texas Southern	12	2	.857	22	7	.759
Alcorn State⊕	10	4	.714	22	10	.688
Southern U.	7	7	.500	16	14	.533
Miss. Valley State	6	8	.429	11	17	.393
Jackson State	4	10	.286	6	24	.200
Grambling	3	11	.214	6	22	.214
Prairie View A&M	2	12	.143	4	22	.154

Tournament: **Alcorn State d. Texas Southern 81-69**

SUN BELT

	Conference			Overall		
	W	L	Pct	W	L	Pct
VCU○	12	2	.857	24	7	.774
Old Dominion□	12	2	.857	19	10	.655
UAB⊕	9	5	.643	19	14	.576
South Florida□	8	6	.571	22	10	.688
South Alabama	6	8	.429	16	12	.571
Charlotte	5	9	.357	8	20	.286
Western Kentucky	4	10	.286	12	16	.429
Jacksonville	0	14	.000	7	22	.241

Tournament: **UAB d. South Florida 64-47**
Tournament MVP: **Cliff Pruitt**, UAB

TAAC

	Conference			Overall		
	W	L	Pct	W	L	Pct
Ark.-Little Rock	12	2	.857	23	6	.793
Houston Baptist	10	4	.714	20	9	.690
Ga. Southern⊕	8	6	.571	18	12	.600
Centenary	8	6	.571	16	13	.552
Mercer	6	8	.429	13	15	.464
Samford	6	8	.429	13	15	.464
Northwestern St. (LA)	5	9	.357	9	19	.321
Hardin-Simmons	1	13	.071	3	25	.107
Nicholls State	-	-	-	16	12	.571

Tournament: **Ga. Southern d. Ark.-Little Rock 68-67**
Tournament MVP: **Jimmy Lampley**, Ark.-Little Rock

WCAC

	Conference			Overall		
	W	L	Pct	W	L	Pct
Pepperdine⊕	10	2	.833	20	9	.690
Santa Clara	9	3	.750	21	7	.750
Saint Mary's (CA)	7	5	.583	14	12	.538
Gonzaga	5	7	.417	13	14	.481
San Diego	5	7	.417	11	15	.423
Portland	4	8	.333	10	18	.357
Loyola Marymount	2	10	.167	9	18	.333

WAC

	Conference			Overall		
	W	L	Pct	W	L	Pct
UTEP□	11	5	.688	19	10	.655
Utah⊕	11	5	.688	18	14	.563
BYU	11	5	.688	15	14	.517
Hawaii	9	7	.563	17	11	.607
San Diego State	8	8	.500	18	10	.643
Wyoming	8	8	.500	16	13	.552
New Mexico	6	10	.375	14	15	.483
Colorado State	6	10	.375	11	17	.393
Air Force	2	14	.125	11	16	.407

INDEPENDENTS

	Overall		
	W	L	Pct
New Orleans□	23	7	.767
UL-Lafayette○	22	7	.759
South Carolina□	22	9	.710
Stetson	19	9	.679
Southeastern Louisiana	18	9	.667
Marquette○	19	10	.655
Notre Dame□	19	10	.655
Dayton	18	10	.643
DePaul□	21	12	.636
Charleston Southern	13	14	.481
Utica	11	15	.423
Tennessee State	11	16	.407
UNC Wilmington	11	16	.407
Brooklyn	11	17	.393
Campbell	11	17	.393
UTSA	10	17	.370
Georgia State	9	19	.321
Texas-Pan American	7	21	.250
U.S. International	3	25	.107

INDIVIDUAL LEADERS—SEASON

SCORING	CL	POS	G	FG	FT	PTS	PPG
1 **Harry Kelly**, Texas Southern	SR	F	29	333	169	835	**28.8**
2 **Jeff Malone**, Mississippi State	SR	G	29	323	131	777	**26.8**
3 **Carlos Yates**, George Mason	SO	G/F	27	257	209	723	**26.8**
4 **Charlie Bradley**, South Florida	SO	F	32	333	189	855	**26.7***
5 **Joe Jakubick**, Akron	JR	G	29	296	182	774	**26.7***
6 **Greg Goorjian**, Loyola Marymount	SR	G	23	245	111	601	**26.1**
7 **Alfredrick Hughes**, Loyola-Chicago	SO	G/F	29	318	108	744	**25.7**
8 **Wayman Tisdale**, Oklahoma	FR	F/C	33	338	134	810	**24.5**
9 **Kenneth Lyons**, North Texas	SR	F	30	282	164	728	**24.3**
10 **Willie Jackson**, Centenary	JR	F	29	271	155	697	**24.0**

* Official ppg differs from average reported by school; conference used three-point line not recognized by NCAA

FIELD GOAL PCT	CL	POS	G	FG	FGA	PCT
1 **Troy Mikell**, East Tenn. State	SR	F/C	29	197	292	**67.5**
2 **Orlando Phillips**, Pepperdine	SR	F	29	223	338	**66.0**
3 **Eugene McDowell**, Florida	SO	C	31	203	314	**64.6**
4 **Charles Barkley**, Auburn	SO	F	28	161	250	**64.4**
5 **Tommy Best**, Saint Peter's	JR	F	27	138	215	**64.2**

MINIMUM: 5 MADE PER GAME

FREE THROW PCT	CL	POS	G	FT	FTA	PCT
1 **Rob Gonzalez**, Colorado	SR	G	28	75	82	**91.5**
2 **Charles Fisher**, James Madison	SR	G	31	95	104	**91.3**
3 **Mike Waitkus**, Brown	FR	G	26	97	108	**89.8**
4 **Phil Cox**, Vanderbilt	SO	G	33	113	126	**89.7**
5 **William Hobdy**, Grambling	SR	G	27	78	87	**89.7**

MINIMUM: 2.5 MADE PER GAME

REBOUNDS PER GAME	CL	POS	G	REB	RPG
1 **Xavier McDaniel**, Wichita State	SO	F	28	403	**14.4**
2 **Franklin Giles**, South Carolina State	JR	F/C	28	360	**12.9**
3 **Michael Cage**, San Diego State	JR	F	28	354	**12.6**
4 **Mark Halsel**, Northeastern	JR	F	28	350	**12.5**
5 **Jeff Cross**, Maine	JR	F	26	310	**11.9**
6 **Sidney Green**, UNLV	SR	F	31	368	**11.9**
7 **Harry Kelly**, Texas Southern	SR	F	29	340	**11.7**
8 **Ralph Sampson**, Virginia	SR	C	33	386	**11.7**
9 **Hakeem Olajuwon**, Houston	SO	C	34	388	**11.4**
10 **Sam Mosley**, Nevada	SR	F	29	325	**11.2**

INDIVIDUAL LEADERS—GAME

POINTS	CL	POS	OPP	DATE	PTS
1 **Harry Kelly**, Texas Southern	SR	F	Jarvis Christian	F23	**60**
2 **Wayman Tisdale**, Oklahoma	FR	F/C	Abilene Christian	D6	**51**
3 **Kenneth Lyons**, North Texas	SR	F	Louisiana Tech	M10	**47**
4 **Wayman Tisdale**, Oklahoma	FR	F/C	Iowa State	F5	**46**
Melvin McLaughlin, Central Michigan	SR	G	Bowling Green	M2	**46**
Antoine Carr, Wichita State	SR	F/C	Southern Illinois	M5	**46**

REBOUNDS	CL	POS	OPP	DATE	REB
1 **Carey Scurry**, Long Island	SO	F	Marist	F8	**26**
2 **Franklin Giles**, South Carolina St.	JR	F/C	Delaware State	J8	**24**
3 **Michael Zeno**, Long Beach State	SR	F	Loyola Marymount	J3	**22**
Hakeem Olajuwon, Houston	SO	C	SMU	J8	**22**
Xavier McDaniel, Wichita State	SO	F	Tulsa	J13	**22**
Ed Pinckney, Villanova	SO	C	Georgetown	J31	**22**
Hakeem Olajuwon, Houston	SO	C	Louisville	A2	**22**

TEAM LEADERS—SEASON

WIN-LOSS PCT	W	L	PCT
1 **Houston**	31	3	**.912**
2 **UNLV**	28	3	**.903**
3 **Wichita State**	25	3	**.893**
4 **Louisville**	32	4	**.889**
5 **Arkansas**	26	4	**.867**
Chattanooga	26	4	**.867**

SCORING OFFENSE	G	W-L	PTS	PPG
1 **Boston College**	32	25-7	2,697	**84.3**
2 **Syracuse**	31	21-10	2,612	**84.3**
3 **South Carolina State**	28	13-15	2,353	**84.0**
4 **Alabama State**	28	22-6	2,352	**84.0**
5 **Houston**	34	31-3	2,800	**82.4**

SCORING MARGIN	G	W-L	PPG	OPP PPG	MAR
1 **Houston**	34	31-3	82.4	64.9	**17.5**
2 **Virginia**	34	29-5	81.9	65.0	**16.9**
3 **Oklahoma**	33	24-9	82.3	70.7	**11.6**
4 **North Carolina**	36	28-8	77.0	65.7	**11.3**
St. John's	33	28-5	75.2	63.9	**11.3**

FIELD GOAL PCT	G	W-L	FG	FGA	PCT
1 **Kentucky**	31	23-8	869	1,564	**55.6**
2 **Stanford**	28	14-14	752	1,373	**54.8**
3 **New Orleans**	30	23-7	937	1,714	**54.7**
4 **Pepperdine**	29	20-9	900	1,653	**54.4**
5 **Houston Baptist**	29	20-9	712	1,319	**54.0**

FREE THROW PCT	G	W-L	FT	FTA	PCT
1 **Western Illinois**	31	20-11	526	679	**77.5**
2 **Dayton**	28	18-10	453	586	**77.3**
3 **UC Santa Barbara**	27	7-20	413	535	**77.2**
4 **William and Mary**	29	20-9	470	609	**77.2**
5 **St. John's**	33	28-5	649	843	**77.0**

REBOUND MARGIN	G	W-L	RPG	OPP RPG	MAR
1 **Wichita State**	28	25-3	42.4	33.6	**8.8**
2 **Virginia**	34	29-5	40.6	32.3	**8.3**
3 **Houston**	34	31-3	41.6	33.4	**8.2**
4 **Wyoming**	29	16-13	34.7	27.1	**7.6**
5 **Alcorn State**	32	22-10	39.8	32.9	**6.9**

SCORING DEFENSE	G	W-L	OPP PTS	OPP PPG
1 **Princeton**	29	20-9	1,507	**52.0**
2 **Fresno State**	35	25-10	1,880	**53.7**
3 **James Madison**	31	20-11	1,670	**53.9**
4 **Notre Dame**	29	19-10	1,619	**55.8**
5 **Arkansas State**	29	17-12	1,651	**56.9**

FIELD GOAL PCT DEFENSE	G	W-L	OPP FG	OPP FGA	OPP PCT
1 **Wyoming**	29	16-13	599	1,441	**41.6**
2 **Virginia**	34	29-5	863	2,071	**41.7**
3 **Idaho**	29	20-9	661	1,582	**41.8**
4 **Montana**	29	21-8	663	1,574	**42.1**
5 **Memphis**	31	23-8	831	1,965	**42.3**

CONSENSUS ALL-AMERICAS

FIRST TEAM

PLAYER	CL	POS	HT	SCHOOL	RPG	PPG
Dale Ellis	SR	F	6-7	Tennessee	6.5	22.6
Patrick Ewing	SO	C	7-0	Georgetown	10.2	17.7
Michael Jordan	SO	G	6-6	North Carolina	5.5	20.0
Keith Lee	SO	C	6-9	Memphis	10.8	18.7
Sam Perkins	JR	F/C	6-9	North Carolina	9.4	16.9
Ralph Sampson	SR	C	7-4	Virginia	11.7	19.1
Wayman Tisdale	FR	F/C	6-9	Oklahoma	10.3	24.5

SECOND TEAM

PLAYER	CL	POS	HT	SCHOOL	RPG	PPG
Clyde Drexler	JR	F	6-7	Houston	8.8	15.9
Sidney Green	SR	F	6-9	UNLV	11.9	22.1
John Paxson	SR	G	6-2	Notre Dame	2.2	17.7
Steve Stipanovich	SR	C	6-11	Missouri	8.8	18.4
Jon Sundvold	SR	G	6-0	Missouri	2.4	17.1
Darrell Walker	SR	G	6-4	Arkansas	5.7	18.2
Randy Wittman	SR	G/F	6-6	Indiana	4.5	19.0

SELECTORS: AP, NABC, UPI, USBWA

AWARD WINNERS

PLAYER OF THE YEAR

PLAYER	CL	POS	HT	SCHOOL	AWARDS
Ralph Sampson	SR	C	7-4	Virginia	Naismith, AP, UPI, USBWA, Wooden, NABC, Rupp
Ray McCallum	SR	G	5-10	Ball State	Frances Pomeroy Naismith*

* FOR THE MOST OUTSTANDING SENIOR PLAYER WHO IS 6 FEET OR UNDER

COACH OF THE YEAR

COACH	SCHOOL	REC	AWARDS
Guy V. Lewis	Houston	31-3	AP
Jerry Tarkanian	UNLV	28-3	UPI
Lou Carnesecca	St. John's	28-5	USBWA, NABC, CBS/Chevrolet
Denny Crum	Louisville	32-4	Sporting News

BOB GIBBONS' TOP HIGH SCHOOL SENIOR RECRUITS

PLAYER	POS	HT	HIGH SCHOOL	A-A TEAMS	COLLEGE	CAREER NOTES
1 Dwayne Washington	PG	6-2	Boys & Girls HS, Brooklyn, NY	McD, P, USA	Syracuse	3-time first-team All-America; at SU, 15.6 ppg (3 seasons); No. 13 pick, '86 NBA draft (Nets); 8.6 ppg (3 seasons); nicknamed "Pearl"
2 James Blackmon	2G	6-3	Marion (IN) HS	McD, P, USA	Kentucky	6.8 ppg (4 seasons); 3-year starter; Final Four, '84; 5th-round pick, '87 NBA draft (Nets); no NBA games played
3 Winston Bennett	PF	6-7	Male HS, Louisville, KY	McD, P	Kentucky	10.5 ppg, 6.0 rpg (4 seasons); 3rd-round pick, '88 NBA draft (Cavs); 4.8 ppg (3 seasons)
4 Reggie Williams	SF	6-7	Dunbar HS, Baltimore	McD, P, USA	Georgetown	NCAA title, '84; No. 4 pick, '87 NBA draft (Clippers); 12.5 ppg (10 seasons)
5 Dallas Comegys	C	6-9	Roman Catholic HS, Philadelphia	McD, P	DePaul	17.5 ppg as Sr.; No. 21 pick, '87 NBA draft (Hawks) 6.0 ppg (2 seasons); played overseas
6 Bruce Dalrymple	2G	6-3	St. Johnsbury (VT) Academy	McD, P	Georgia Tech	ACC ROY, '84; at GT, 12.6 ppg, 5.9 rpg (4 seasons); 2nd-round pick, '87 NBA draft (Suns); no NBA games played
7 David Popson	PF	6-10	Bishop O'Reilly HS, Kingston, PA	McD, P, USA	North Carolina	10.0 ppg as Sr.; 4th-round pick, '87 NBA draft (Pistons); 1.9 ppg (3 seasons)
8 Tom Sheehey	PF	6-8	McQuaid Jesuit HS, Rochester, NY	McD, P	Virginia	9.8 ppg (4 seasons); 4th-round pick, '87 NBA draft (Celtics); no NBA games played; played overseas
9 Kenny Smith	PG	6-3	Archbishop Molloy HS, Jamaica, NY	McD, P	North Carolina	2nd in assists (768); No. 6 pick, '87 NBA draft (Kings); 12.8 ppg (10 seasons); 2 NBA titles
10 Tom Curry	C	6-9	Redemptorist HS, Baton Rouge, LA	McD, P	Marshall	13.1 ppg, 5.3 rpg (4 seasons); undrafted
11 Joe Wolf	C	6-10	Kohler (WI) HS	McD, P	North Carolina	9.6 ppg, 5.5 rpg (4 seasons); No. 13 pick, '87 NBA draft (Clippers); 4.2 ppg (11 seasons)
12 Ricky Winslow	PF	6-8	Jack Yates HS, Houston	McD, P	Houston	Final Four, '84; at UH, 12.5 ppg, 7.8 rpg (4 seasons); 2nd-round pick, '87 NBA draft (Bulls); played in 7 NBA games
13 Frank Ford	2G	6-4	Osceola HS, Kissimmee, FL	McD, P	Auburn	Started 127 straight games (4 seasons); 6th-round pick, '87 NBA draft (Lakers); no NBA games played
14 Mike Smith	BF	6-9	Los Altos HS, Hacienda Heights, CA	McD, P	BYU	19.0 ppg, 7.6 rpg (4 seasons); No. 13 pick, '89 NBA draft (Celtics); 5.0 ppg (3 seasons); played overseas
15 Steve Alford	PG	6-2	New Castle (IN) Chrysler HS		Indiana	2-time All-America; Olympic gold medal, '84; 2nd-round pick, '87 NBA draft (Mavs); 4.4 ppg (4 seasons); college head coach (3 teams, 12 seasons)
16 Gerald White	PG	6-2	Richmond Academy, Augusta, GA		Auburn	7.2 ppg, 5.1 apg (4 seasons); 7th-round pick, '87 NBA draft (Mavs); no NBA games played
17 Terry Long	PF	6-8	Richmond (VA) HS	P	Maryland	Most Improved Player, '84; undrafted
18 Curtis Aiken	PG	5-11	Bennett HS, Buffalo, NY	P	Pittsburgh	10.0 ppg, 3.2 apg (4 seasons); captain of team, '87-88; undrafted
19 Rico Washington	F	6-6	Franklin HS, Philadelphia	P	Weber State	21.0 ppg, 10.6 rpg (2 seasons); first-team All-Big Sky; undrafted
20 Nikita Wilson	PF	6-8	Leesville (LA) HS	P	LSU	12.6 ppg, 6.4 rpg (4 seasons); 2nd-round pick, '87 NBA draft (Blazers); 15 games played

OTHER STANDOUTS

PLAYER	POS	HT	HIGH SCHOOL	A-A TEAMS	COLLEGE	CAREER NOTES
24 Tyrone Bogues	PG	5-3	Dunbar HS, Baltimore		Wake Forest	8.3 ppg, 6.6 apg (4 seasons); No. 12 pick, '87 NBA draft (Bullets); 7.7 apg (14 seasons); shortest NBA player ever (5-3)
48 Reggie Miller	SF	6-6	Riverside (CA) Polytechnic HS		UCLA	17.2 ppg (4 seasons); No. 11 pick, '87 NBA draft (Pacers); Olympic gold medal, '96; 5-time NBA All-Star; NBA all-time leader in 3pt FGs
52 Mark Jackson	PG	6-4	Bishop Loughlin HS, Brooklyn, NY		St. John's	10.1 ppg, 5.6 apg (4 seasons); No. 18 pick, '87 NBA draft (Knicks); 9.6 ppg, 8.0 apg (17 seasons); 2nd in assists in NBA history
132 Dan Majerle	F	6-7	Traverse City (MI) HS		Central Michigan	21.8 ppg, 8.9 rpg (4 seasons); No. 14 pick, '88 NBA draft (Suns); 35.8 3pt FG% (14 seasons); 3-time all-star

Abbreviations: McD=McDonald's; P=Parade; USA=USA Today

Poll Progression

Preseason Poll

AP	UPI	School
1	1	Virginia
2	3	Georgetown
3	2	North Carolina
4	4	Kentucky
5	7	Villanova
6	9	Memphis
7	6	UCLA
8	5	Louisville
9	7	Indiana
10	10	Oregon State
11	12	Iowa
12	13	Alabama
13	15	Tennessee
14	11	Houston
15	14	Missouri
16	—	NC State
17	20	Arkansas
18	16	Marquette
19	19	St. John's
20	18	Oklahoma
20	—	UNLV
—	17	DePaul

Week of Nov 30

AP	School	AP↓↑
1	Virginia (2-0)	
2	Georgetown (2-0)	
3	Kentucky (1-0)	↑1
4	Villanova (1-0)	↑1
5	Memphis (2-0)	↑1
6	UCLA (1-0)	↑1
7	Louisville (3-0)	↑1
8	Indiana (2-0)	↑1
9	Missouri (1-0)	↑6
10	Iowa (2-0)	↑1
11	Houston (2-0)	↑3
12	St. John's (3-0)	↑7
13	Alabama (1-0)	↓1
14	Tennessee (1-0)	↓1
15	North Carolina (0-2)	↓12
16	Arkansas (1-0)	↑1
17	Marquette (0-0)	↑1
18	NC State (1-0)	↓2
19	UNLV (1-0)	↑1
19	Oregon State (0-1)	↓9

Week of Dec 7

AP	UPI	School	AP↓↑
1	1	Virginia (4-0)	
2	2	Kentucky (3-0)	↑1
3	3	Georgetown (5-0)	↓1
4	5	Memphis (4-0)	↑1
5	4	UCLA (3-0)	↑1
6	7	Indiana (3-0)	↑2
7	6	Iowa (4-0)	↑3
8	8	Missouri (2-0)	↑1
9	10	Houston (4-0)	↑2
10	9	Villanova (1-1)	↓6
11	11	Alabama (2-0)	↑2
12	13	St. John's (5-0)	
13	12	Louisville (4-1)	↓6
14	14	Tennessee (2-0)	
15	16	Arkansas (3-0)	↑1
16	19	Marquette (2-0)	↑1
17	17	North Carolina (2-2) (A)	↓2
18	18	NC State (2-0)	
19	—	UNLV (3-0)	↑1
20	15	Purdue (4-0)	⤴
—	20	DePaul (3-1)	

Week of Dec 14

AP	UPI	School	AP↓↑
1	1	Virginia (6-0)	
2	2	Kentucky (5-0)	
3	4	Memphis (6-0)	↑1
4	3	UCLA (4-0)	↑1
5	5	Indiana (6-0)	↑1
6	7	Georgetown (6-1)	↓2
7	6	Iowa (6-0)	
8	8	Missouri (6-0)	
9	10	St. John's (7-0)	↑3
10	9	Alabama (4-0)	↑1
11	12	Tennessee (4-0)	↑3
12	11	Louisville (5-1)	↑1
13	13	Arkansas (4-0)	↑2
14	14	Houston (5-1)	↓5
15	17	NC State (4-0)	↑3
16	15	Syracuse (6-0)	⤴
17	16	North Carolina (3-2)	
18	19	UNLV (5-0)	
19	18	Villanova (2-2)	↓9
20	—	West Virginia (5-0)	⤴
—	20	Minnesota (5-0)	

Week of Dec 21

AP	UPI	School	AP↓↑
1	1	Virginia (8-0)	
2	2	Kentucky (7-0)	
3	3	UCLA (5-0)	↑1
4	4	Memphis (7-0)	↓1
5	5	Indiana (7-0)	
6	6	Missouri (6-0)	↑2
7	8	St. John's (9-0)	↑2
8	7	Alabama (5-0)	↑2
9	10	Tennessee (6-0)	↑2
10	9	Iowa (6-1)	↓3
11	12	Georgetown (6-2)	↓6
12	14	Arkansas (5-0)	↑1
13	13	Syracuse (8-0)	↑3
14	11	Louisville (7-1)	↓2
15	15	NC State (4-0)	
16	20	West Virginia (8-0)	↑4
17	18	UNLV (5-0)	↑1
18	16	Villanova (3-2)	↑1
19	17	Houston (6-2)	↓5
20	—	Tulsa (5-1)	⤴
—	19	San Diego State (6-0)	

Week of Dec 28

AP	UPI	School	AP↓↑
1	1	Indiana (8-0)	↑4
2	2	Memphis (8-0)	↑2
3	4	Kentucky (7-1)	↓1
4	3	Virginia (8-1) (B)	↓3
5	5	UCLA (6-1)	↓2
6	6	Alabama (6-0)	↑2
7	7	St. John's (9-0)	
8	8	Tennessee (7-0)	↑1
9	10	Iowa (6-1)	↑1
10	13	Georgetown (7-2)	↑1
11	14	Arkansas (6-0)	↑1
12	12	Missouri (8-1)	↓6
13	9	Louisville (8-1)	↑1
14	11	Syracuse (9-0)	↓1
15	15	UNLV (7-0)	↑2
16	17	Villanova (4-2)	↑2
17	18	NC State (4-1)	↓2
18	16	Houston (7-2)	↑1
19	20	Tulsa (5-1)	↑1
20	—	West Virginia (8-1)	↓4
—	19	UL-Lafayette (8-0)	

Week of Jan 4

AP	UPI	School	AP↓↑
1	1	Indiana (10-0)	
2	2	Memphis (9-0)	
3	3	Kentucky (8-1)	
4	4	Virginia (10-1)	
5	5	Alabama (8-0)	↑1
6	6	UCLA (7-1)	↓1
7	7	St. John's (10-0)	
8	8	Iowa (8-1)	↑1
9	9	Syracuse (10-0)	↑5
10	12	Arkansas (7-0)	↑1
11	13	UNLV (10-0)	↑4
12	11	Tennessee (8-1)	↓4
13	10	Louisville (8-2)	
14	14	Villanova (6-2)	↑2
15	15	Missouri (9-2)	↓3
16	18	NC State (5-1)	↑1
17	17	Georgetown (8-3)	↓7
18	16	North Carolina (8-3)	⤴
19	19	Houston (8-2)	↓1
20	—	Purdue (9-1)	⤴
—	20	Minnesota (7-1)	

Week of Jan 11

AP	UPI	School	AP↓↑
1	1	Memphis (11-1)	↑1
2	2	Virginia (11-1)	↑2
3	3	St. John's (13-0)	↑4
4	4	Indiana (10-1)	↓3
5	5	UCLA (9-1)	↑1
6	6	Kentucky (11-2)	↓3
7	7	Arkansas (11-0)	↑3
8	9	UNLV (12-0)	↑3
9	8	Louisville (11-2)	↑4
10	10	Alabama (9-2)	↓5
11	11	North Carolina (10-3)	↑7
12	12	Iowa (9-2)	↓4
13	14	Syracuse (11-2)	↓4
14	15	Missouri (10-2)	↑1
15	17	Villanova (8-2)	↓1
16	13	Houston (11-2)	↑3
17	16	Minnesota (10-1)	⤴
18	18	Tennessee (10-2)	↓6
19	19	NC State (7-2)	↓3
20	—	Ohio State (9-2)	⤴
—	20	Illinois State (10-1)	

Week of Jan 18

AP	UPI	School	AP↓↑
1	1	UCLA (11-1) (C)	↑4
2	2	Indiana (12-1)	↑2
3	3	North Carolina (12-3)	↑8
4	5	Arkansas (13-0)	↑3
5	9	UNLV (14-0)	↑3
6	3	Memphis (12-1)	↓5
7	6	Virginia (12-2)	↓5
8	7	St. John's (14-1)	↓5
9	8	Louisville (13-2)	
10	10	Iowa (10-2)	↑2
11	13	Kentucky (11-3)	↓5
12	11	Missouri (12-2)	↑2
13	14	Villanova (10-2)	↑2
14	12	Houston (13-2)	↑2
15	15	Syracuse (12-2)	↓2
16	18	Minnesota (10-3)	↑1
17	—	Virginia Tech (14-1)	⤴
18	19	Oklahoma State (12-1)	⤴
19	16	Georgetown (11-4)	⤴
20	—	Auburn (10-3)	⤴
—	17	Illinois State (12-1)	
—	20	NC State (8-3)	⤵
—	20	Tennessee (10-3)	⤵

Week of Jan 25

AP	UPI	School	AP↓↑
1	1	UCLA (13-1)	
2	2	Indiana (14-1)	
3	3	North Carolina (15-3)	
4	8	UNLV (16-0)	↑1
5	5	Memphis (14-1)	↑1
6	4	Virginia (15-2)	↑1
7	6	St. John's (17-1)	↑1
8	7	Louisville (15-2)	↑1
9	9	Houston (15-2)	↑5
10	10	Kentucky (13-3)	↑1
11	12	Villanova (12-3)	↑2
12	11	Arkansas (15-1)	↓8
13	13	Missouri (14-3)	↓1
14	16	Iowa (12-3)	↓4
15	15	Georgetown (13-4)	↑4
16	17	Minnesota (12-3)	
17	14	Illinois State (14-1)	⤴
18	18	Syracuse (13-3)	↓3
19	20	Wake Forest (13-2)	⤴
20	—	Oklahoma State (13-2)	↓2
—	18	Washington State (13-2)	

Week of Feb 1

AP	UPI	School	AP↓↑
1	1	North Carolina (17-3)	↑2
2	3	UNLV (18-0)	↑2
3	2	Virginia (17-2)	↑3
4	5	Memphis (16-1)	↑1
5	4	St. John's (18-1)	↑2
6	6	Indiana (15-2)	↓4
7	7	UCLA (14-2)	↓6
8	8	Houston (16-2)	↑1
9	9	Arkansas (17-1)	↑3
10	10	Missouri (16-3)	↑3
11	11	Villanova (13-3)	
12	12	Louisville (16-3)	↓4
13	13	Iowa (13-4)	↑1
14	16	Georgetown (15-4)	↑1
15	15	Kentucky (13-4)	↓5
16	14	Illinois State (15-1)	↑1
17	18	Minnesota (13-3)	↓1
18	17	Washington State (15-2)	⤴
19	—	Georgia (14-3)	⤴
20	—	Syracuse (13-4)	↓2
—	19	Oklahoma (16-4)	
—	20	Auburn (12-5)	

Week of Feb 8

AP	UPI	School	AP↓↑
1	1	North Carolina (20-3)	
2	3	UNLV (20-0)	
3	2	Virginia (19-2)	
4	4	Indiana (16-2)	↑2
5	5	UCLA (16-2)	↑2
6	6	Houston (18-2)	↑2
7	7	St. John's (19-2)	↓2
8	9	Arkansas (19-1)	↑1
9	10	Memphis (18-2)	↓5
10	8	Missouri (18-3)	
11	11	Louisville (19-3)	↑1
12	14	Villanova (14-4)	↓1
13	12	Kentucky (14-5)	↑2
14	13	Georgetown (16-5)	
15	16	Syracuse (15-5)	↑5
16	—	Wichita State (17-3)	⤴
17	16	Illinois State (17-2)	↓1
18	18	Purdue (15-4)	⤴
19	15	Minnesota (14-4)	↓2
20	—	Iowa (13-6)	↓7
—	19	Georgia (15-4)	⤵
—	20	Tennessee (14-5)	

Poll Progression Continues →

Week of Feb 15

AP	UPI	School	AP↓↑
1	2	**UNLV** (22-0)	↑1
2	1	**Indiana** (19-2)	↑2
3	3	**North Carolina** (21-4)	↓2
4	4	**Houston** (20-2)	↑2
5	5	**Virginia** (19-3)	↓2
6	6	**St. John's** (20-2)	↑1
7	7	**Arkansas** (20-1)	↑1
8	9	**Villanova** (17-4)	↑4
9	8	**Louisville** (21-3)	↑2
10	11	**UCLA** (17-3)	↓5
11	12	**Kentucky** (16-5)	↑2
12	10	**Missouri** (19-4)	↓2
13	13	**Memphis** (18-4)	↓4
14	14	**Georgetown** (16-6)	
15	—	**Wichita State** (18-3)	↑1
16	15	**Iowa** (15-6)	↑4
17	17	**Syracuse** (16-5)	↓2
18	18	**Boston College** (17-4)	⤴
19	—	**Oklahoma** (18-6)	⤴
20	—	**Ohio State** (15-6)	⤴
—	16	**Tennessee** (15-7)	
—	19	**Chattanooga** (17-3)	
—	20	**Oklahoma State** (17-4)	

Week of Feb 22

AP	UPI	School	AP↓↑
1	1	**UNLV** (24-0)	
2	2	**Houston** (22-2)	↑2
3	3	**Virginia** (21-3)	↑2
4	4	**Indiana** (20-3)	↓2
5	6	**Louisville** (22-3)	↑4
6	5	**Arkansas** (22-1)	↑1
7	7	**Villanova** (19-4)	↑1
8	9	**UCLA** (19-3)	↑2
9	8	**St. John's** (22-3)	↓3
10	10	**Kentucky** (18-5)	↑1
11	11	**North Carolina** (21-6)	↓8
12	—	**Wichita State** (21-3)	↑3
13	14	**Syracuse** (18-5)	↑4
14	13	**Memphis** (19-4)	↓1
15	12	**Missouri** (20-6)	↓3
16	15	**Ohio State** (17-6)	↑5
17	17	**Iowa** (16-7)	↓1
18	18	**Georgetown** (17-7)	↓4
19	16	**Boston College** (18-5)	↓1
20	20	**Tennessee** (16-7)	⤴
—	19	**Chattanooga** (19-3)	

Week of Mar 1

AP	UPI	School	AP↓↑
1	1	**Houston** (23-2) Ⓓ	↑1
2	2	**Virginia** (23-3)	↑1
3	3	**Louisville** (24-3)	↑2
4	5	**Villanova** (21-4)	↑3
5	4	**Arkansas** (24-1)	↑1
6	7	**UCLA** (21-3)	↑2
7	6	**Kentucky** (20-5)	↑3
8	10	**North Carolina** (23-6)	↑3
9	11	**UNLV** (24-2) Ⓓ	↓8
10	8	**St. John's** (23-4)	↓1
11	12	**Indiana** (20-5)	↓7
12	—	**Wichita State** (23-3)	
13	9	**Missouri** (22-6)	↑2
14	14	**Ohio State** (18-7)	↑1
15	13	**Boston College** (20-5)	↑4
16	16	**Georgetown** (19-7)	↑2
17	18	**Memphis** (19-5)	↓3
18	—	**Syracuse** (18-6)	↓5
19	17	**Chattanooga** (21-3)	⤴
20	—	**Purdue** (18-6)	⤴
—	15	**Washington State** (20-5)	
—	19	**Oklahoma** (20-7)	
—	20	**Iowa** (17-8)	⤵

Week of Mar 8

AP	UPI	School	AP↓↑
1	1	**Houston** (25-2)	
2	2	**Virginia** (25-3) Ⓔ	
3	3	**Louisville** (27-3)	
4	4	**UCLA** (22-4)	↑2
5	6	**North Carolina** (25-6)	↑3
6	5	**Arkansas** (25-2)	↓1
7	7	**Indiana** (22-5)	↑4
8	8	**St. John's** (24-4)	↑2
9	11	**UNLV** (25-2)	
10	10	**Kentucky** (21-6)	↓3
11	—	**Wichita State** (25-3)	↑1
12	9	**Missouri** (24-6)	↑1
13	12	**Villanova** (21-6)	↓9
14	13	**Boston College** (22-5)	↑1
15	14	**Georgetown** (21-8)	↑1
16	17	**Ohio State** (19-8)	↓2
17	18	**Memphis** (21-6)	
18	15	**Chattanooga** (23-3)	↑1
19	19	**Oklahoma** (23-7)	⤴
20	—	**Syracuse** (19-8)	↓2
—	16	**Washington State** (21-5)	
—	20	**Illinois State** (21-6)	

Final Poll

AP	UPI	School	AP↓↑
1	1	**Houston** (27-2)	
2	2	**Louisville** (29-3)	↑1
3	3	**St. John's** (27-4)	↑5
4	4	**Virginia** (27-4)	↓2
5	5	**Indiana** (23-5)	↑2
6	6	**UNLV** (28-2)	↑3
7	7	**UCLA** (23-5)	↓3
8	8	**North Carolina** (26-7)	↓3
9	9	**Arkansas** (25-3)	↓3
10	12	**Missouri** (26-7)	↑2
11	13	**Boston College** (24-6)	↑3
12	10	**Kentucky** (21-7)	↓2
13	11	**Villanova** (22-7)	
14	—	**Wichita State** (25-3)	↓3
15	16	**Chattanooga** (26-3)	↑3
16	14	**NC State** (20-10) Ⓕ	⤴
17	17	**Memphis** (22-7)	
18	15	**Georgia** (21-9)	⤴
19	19	**Oklahoma State** (24-6)	⤴
20	20	**Georgetown** (21-9)	↓5
—	18	**Illinois State** (24-6)	

Ⓐ Defending champion North Carolina loses its first two games for the first time since 1919 and struggles in its third outing, a 70-68 triple-overtime win over Tulane.

Ⓑ Ho, ho, ho! On Christmas Eve, Chaminade, a little-known school in Hawaii, shocks Virginia, 77-72, in Honolulu. It's the only time the top-ranked team has been beaten by a non-D1 opponent.

Ⓒ When Memphis State, Virginia and St. John's all lose, UCLA climbs to the No. 1 spot for the first time since 1979.

Ⓓ After UNLV loses two straight to unranked Cal State Fullerton and West Virginia and plunges to No. 9—the second biggest one-week drop for a No. 1 team in the history of the AP poll. Houston's fraternity of dunkers, Phi Slama Jama, takes over the top spot.

Ⓔ For Ralph Sampson's final home game, all personnel in Virginia's University Hall wear tuxedoes. The big fella misses four foul shots with the game on the line, but then hits a soft eight-foot hook with :03 remaining to pull out a 83-81 victory over Maryland.

Ⓕ NC State beats Virginia, 81-78, in the ACC tournament final to creep back into the polls. Jim Valvano's Wolfpack, built around guards Dereck Whittenburg and Sidney Lowe, are the season's only Top 20 team with double-digit losses.

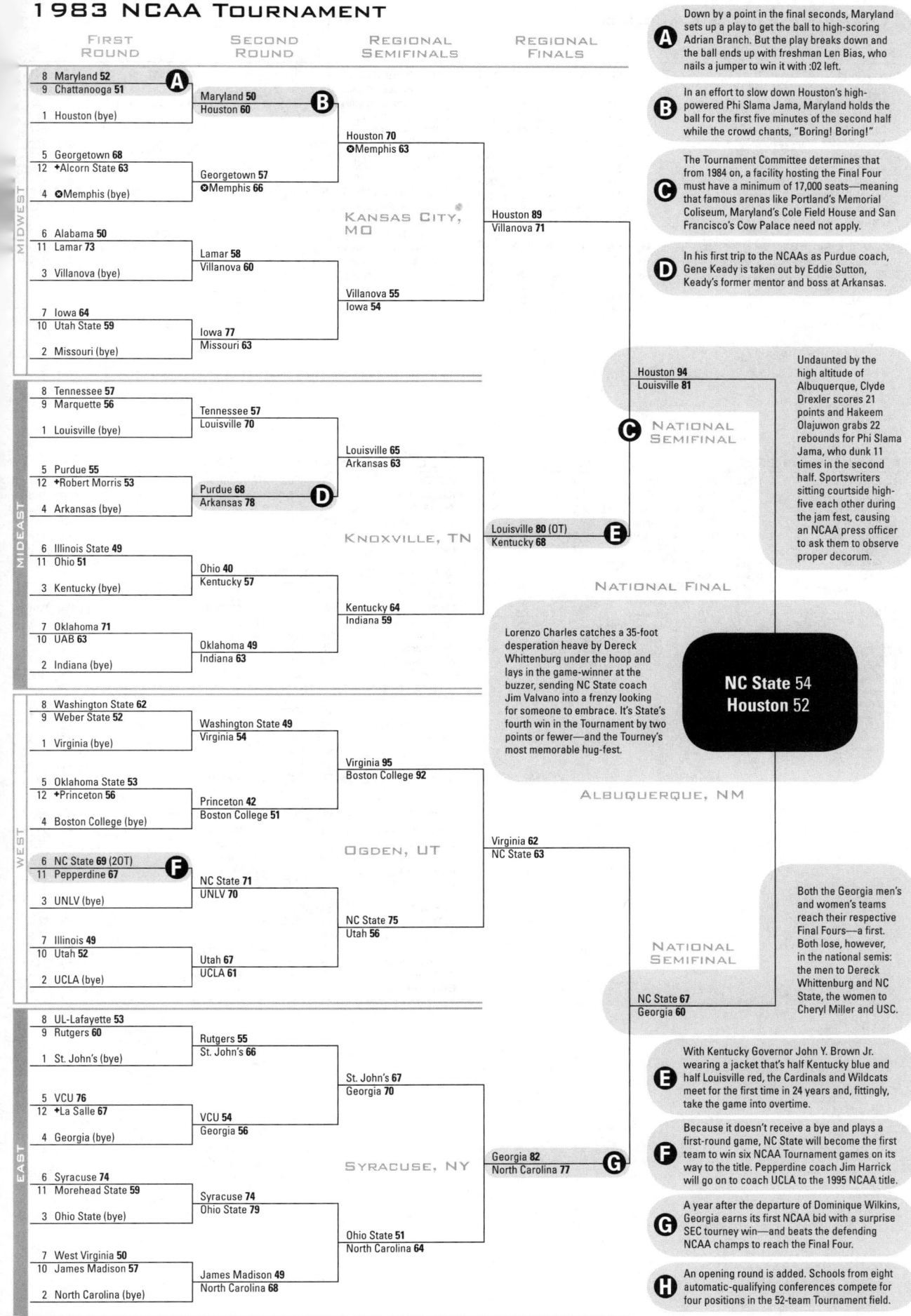

1983 NCAA Tournament

First Round | Second Round | Regional Semifinals | Regional Finals

Midwest (Kansas City, MO)

First Round
- 8 Maryland **52**, 9 Chattanooga **51** (A)
- 1 Houston (bye)
- 5 Georgetown **68**, 12 +Alcorn State **63**
- 4 ✪Memphis (bye)
- 6 Alabama **50**, 11 Lamar **73**
- 3 Villanova (bye)
- 7 Iowa **64**, 10 Utah State **59**
- 2 Missouri (bye)

Second Round
- Maryland **50**, Houston **60** (B)
- Georgetown **57**, ✪Memphis **66**
- Lamar **58**, Villanova **60**
- Iowa **77**, Missouri **63**

Regional Semifinals
- Houston **70**, ✪Memphis **63**
- Villanova **55**, Iowa **54**

Regional Final
- Houston **89**, Villanova **71**

Mideast (Knoxville, TN)

First Round
- 8 Tennessee **57**, 9 Marquette **56**
- 1 Louisville (bye)
- 5 Purdue **55**, 12 +Robert Morris **53**
- 4 Arkansas (bye)
- 6 Illinois State **49**, 11 Ohio **51**
- 3 Kentucky (bye)
- 7 Oklahoma **71**, 10 UAB **63**
- 2 Indiana (bye)

Second Round
- Tennessee **57**, Louisville **70**
- Purdue **68**, Arkansas **78** (D)
- Ohio **40**, Kentucky **57**
- Oklahoma **49**, Indiana **63**

Regional Semifinals
- Louisville **65**, Arkansas **63**
- Kentucky **64**, Indiana **59**

Regional Final
- Louisville **80** (OT), Kentucky **68** (E)

West (Ogden, UT)

First Round
- 8 Washington State **62**, 9 Weber State **52**
- 1 Virginia (bye)
- 5 Oklahoma State **53**, 12 +Princeton **56**
- 4 Boston College (bye)
- 6 NC State **69** (2OT), 11 Pepperdine **67** (F)
- 3 UNLV (bye)
- 7 Illinois **49**, 10 Utah **52**
- 2 UCLA (bye)

Second Round
- Washington State **49**, Virginia **54**
- Princeton **42**, Boston College **51**
- NC State **71**, UNLV **70**
- Utah **67**, UCLA **61**

Regional Semifinals
- Virginia **95**, Boston College **92**
- NC State **75**, Utah **56**

Regional Final
- Virginia **62**, NC State **63**

East (Syracuse, NY)

First Round
- 8 UL-Lafayette **53**, 9 Rutgers **60**
- 1 St. John's (bye)
- 5 VCU **76**, 12 +La Salle **67**
- 4 Georgia (bye)
- 6 Syracuse **74**, 11 Morehead State **59**
- 3 Ohio State (bye)
- 7 West Virginia **50**, 10 James Madison **57**
- 2 North Carolina (bye)

Second Round
- Rutgers **55**, St. John's **66**
- VCU **54**, Georgia **56**
- Syracuse **74**, Ohio State **79**
- James Madison **49**, North Carolina **68**

Regional Semifinals
- St. John's **67**, Georgia **70**
- Ohio State **51**, North Carolina **64**

Regional Final
- Georgia **82**, North Carolina **77** (G)

National Semifinal (Albuquerque, NM)

Houston **94**, Louisville **81** (C)

Undaunted by the high altitude of Albuquerque, Clyde Drexler scores 21 points and Hakeem Olajuwon grabs 22 rebounds for Phi Slama Jama, who dunk 11 times in the second half. Sportswriters sitting courtside high-five each other during the jam fest, causing an NCAA press officer to ask them to observe proper decorum.

National Semifinal

NC State **67**, Georgia **60**

Both the Georgia men's and women's teams reach their respective Final Fours—a first. Both lose, however, in the national semis: the men to Dereck Whittenburg and NC State, the women to Cheryl Miller and USC.

National Final

NC State 54
Houston 52

Lorenzo Charles catches a 35-foot desperation heave by Dereck Whittenburg under the hoop and lays in the game-winner at the buzzer, sending NC State coach Jim Valvano into a frenzy looking for someone to embrace. It's State's fourth win in the Tournament by two points or fewer—and the Tourney's most memorable hug-fest.

A Down by a point in the final seconds, Maryland sets up a play to get the ball to high-scoring Adrian Branch. But the play breaks down and the ball ends up with freshman Len Bias, who nails a jumper to win it with :02 left.

B In an effort to slow down Houston's high-powered Phi Slama Jama, Maryland holds the ball for the first five minutes of the second half while the crowd chants, "Boring! Boring!"

C The Tournament Committee determines that from 1984 on, a facility hosting the Final Four must have a minimum of 17,000 seats—meaning that famous arenas like Portland's Memorial Coliseum, Maryland's Cole Field House and San Francisco's Cow Palace need not apply.

D In his first trip to the NCAAs as Purdue coach, Gene Keady is taken out by Eddie Sutton, Keady's former mentor and boss at Arkansas.

E With Kentucky Governor John Y. Brown Jr. wearing a jacket that's half Kentucky blue and half Louisville red, the Cardinals and Wildcats meet for the first time in 24 years and, fittingly, take the game into overtime.

F Because it doesn't receive a bye and plays a first-round game, NC State will become the first team to win six NCAA Tournament games on its way to the title. Pepperdine coach Jim Harrick will go on to coach UCLA to the 1995 NCAA title.

G A year after the departure of Dominique Wilkins, Georgia earns its first NCAA bid with a surprise SEC tourney win—and beats the defending NCAA champs to reach the Final Four.

H An opening round is added. Schools from eight automatic-qualifying conferences compete for four positions in the 52-team Tournament field.

H **+Opening round** Alcorn State d. Xavier 81-75; Robert Morris d. Georgia Southern 64-54; Princeton d. North Carolina A&T 53-41; La Salle d. Boston U. 70-58

✪ Team participation later vacated

Tournament Leaders

INDIVIDUAL LEADERS

Scoring	CL	POS	G	PTS	PPG
1 **Steve Black**, La Salle	SO	G	2	46	23.0
2 **Patrick Ewing**, Georgetown	SO	C	2	43	21.5
Chris Mullin, St. John's	SO	G/F	2	43	21.5
Eric Santifer, Syracuse	SR	G	2	43	21.5
5 **Adrian Branch**, Maryland	SO	G/F	2	42	21.0
Michael Phelps, Alcorn State	SO	G	2	42	21.0
7 **Keith Lee**, Memphis	SO	C	2	41	20.5
8 **Greg Stokes**, Iowa	SO	C	3	61	20.3
9 **Dereck Whittenburg**, NC State	SR	G	6	120	20.0
Bob Hansen, Iowa	SR	G	3	60	20.0

Minimum: 2 games

Field Goal Pct	CL	POS	G	FG	FGA	PCT
1 **Len Bias**, Maryland	FR	F	2	12	16	75.0
2 **Ralph Sampson**, Virginia	SR	C	3	23	31	74.2
3 **Joe Kleine**, Arkansas	SO	C	2	14	20	70.0
4 **Chris Mullin**, St. John's	SO	G/F	2	16	24	66.7
5 **Hakeem Olajuwon**, Houston	SO	C	5	42	64	65.6

Minimum: 12 made

Free Throw Pct	CL	POS	G	FT	FTA	PCT
1 **John Pinone**, Villanova	SR	C	3	15	15	100.0
2 **Rick Carlisle**, Virginia	JR	G	3	12	13	92.3
3 **Bob Hansen**, Iowa	SR	G	3	18	20	90.0
4 **Calvin Duncan**, VCU	SO	G	2	15	17	88.2
5 **Matt Doherty**, North Carolina	JR	F	3	14	16	87.5
John Garris, Boston College	SR	F	2	14	16	87.5

Minimum: 12 made

Rebounds Per Game	CL	POS	G	REB	RPG
1 **Hakeem Olajuwon**, Houston	SO	C	5	65	13.0
2 **Keith Lee**, Memphis	SO	C	2	23	11.5
3 **Ralph Sampson**, Virginia	SR	C	3	34	11.3
4 **Ed Pinckney**, Villanova	SO	C	3	33	11.0
Jay Murphy, Boston College	JR	F	2	22	11.0

Minimum: 2 games

TEAM LEADERS

Scoring	G	PTS	PPG
1 **Louisville**	4	296	74.0
Syracuse	2	148	74.0
3 **Houston**	5	365	73.0
4 **Alcorn State**	2	144	72.0
5 **Boston College**	2	143	71.5
6 **Arkansas**	2	141	70.5
7 **Virginia**	3	211	70.3
8 **North Carolina**	3	209	69.7
9 **La Salle**	2	137	68.5
10 **Georgia**	4	268	67.0

Minimum: 2 games

FG Pct	G	FG	FGA	PCT
1 **Purdue**	2	51	84	60.7
2 **Kentucky**	3	77	136	56.6
3 **Rutgers**	2	46	82	56.1
4 **Arkansas**	2	54	99	54.5
5 **Louisville**	4	123	228	53.9

FT Pct	G	FT	FTA	PCT
1 **North Carolina**	3	55	70	78.6
2 **Washington State**	2	29	37	78.4
3 **Georgetown**	2	37	48	77.1
4 **Rutgers**	2	23	30	76.7
5 **VCU**	2	32	42	76.2

Minimum: 2 games

Rebounds	G	REB	RPG
1 **La Salle**	2	83	41.5
2 **Houston**	5	185	37.0
3 **Boston College**	2	72	36.0
4 **Washington State**	2	67	33.5
5 **Virginia**	3	100	33.3

Minimum: 2 games

ALL-TOURNAMENT TEAM

PLAYER	CL	POS	HT	SCHOOL	RPG	PPG
Hakeem Olajuwon*	SO	C	7-0	Houston	13.0	18.8
Thurl Bailey	SR	F	6-11	NC State	7.0	16.8
Sidney Lowe	SR	G	6-0	NC State	3.5	6.7
Milt Wagner	SO	G	6-5	Louisville	1.5	16.8
Dereck Whittenburg	SR	G	6-1	NC State	2.3	20.0

ALL-REGIONAL TEAMS

EAST

PLAYER	CL	POS	HT	SCHOOL	RPG	PPG
James Banks*	JR	F	6-6	Georgia	4.7	14.7
Terry Fair	SR	F	6-5	Georgia	7.0	15.7
Vern Fleming	JR	G	6-5	Georgia	5.7	14.3
Michael Jordan	SO	G	6-6	North Carolina	5.3	19.7
Chris Mullin	SO	G/F	6-6	St. John's	3.5	21.5

MIDEAST

PLAYER	CL	POS	HT	SCHOOL	RPG	PPG
Lancaster Gordon*	JR	G	6-3	Louisville	2.0	20.3
Jim Master	JR	G	6-5	Kentucky	2.3	13.3
Scooter McCray	SR	F	6-9	Louisville	5.3	11.3
Mel Turpin	JR	C	6-11	Kentucky	7.7	16.0
Darrell Walker	SR	G	6-4	Arkansas	7.0	19.0

MIDWEST

PLAYER	CL	POS	HT	SCHOOL	RPG	PPG
Hakeem Olajuwon*	SO	C	7-0	Houston	8.3	17.7
Larry Micheaux	SR	F	6-9	Houston	8.3	15.7
John Pinone	SR	C	6-8	Villanova	6.0	17.0
Greg Stokes	SO	C	6-10	Iowa	8.7	20.3
Michael Young	JR	G/F	6-7	Houston	6.0	17.7

WEST

PLAYER	CL	POS	HT	SCHOOL	RPG	PPG
Dereck Whittenburg*	SR	G	6-1	NC State	2.3	21.5
Thurl Bailey	SR	F	6-11	NC State	6.8	16.5
Lorenzo Charles	SO	F	6-7	NC State	9.5	14.5
John Garris	SR	F	6-8	Boston College	9.0	16.0
Ralph Sampson	SR	C	7-4	Virginia	11.3	19.0

* Most outstanding player

1983 NCAA TOURNAMENT BOX SCORES

Houston 70-63 Memphis (Sweet 16)

	1H	2H
Houston	34	36
Memphis	34	29

HOUSTON	MIN	FG	3FG	FT	REB	A	ST	BL	PF	TP
Hakeem Olajuwon	33	10-14	-	1-2	6	0	1	2	3	21
Michael Young	35	6-12	-	5-7	5	0	0	0	1	17
Larry Micheaux	34	2-6	-	6-7	7	0	1	2	4	10
Clyde Drexler	32	4-8	-	0-0	7	4	6	1	5	8
Alvin Franklin	23	0-4	-	4-4	0	3	0	0	0	4
Benny Anders	6	2-3	-	0-0	0	0	0	0	1	4
Reid Gettys	20	1-3	-	0-0	0	4	1	0	2	2
Derek Giles	8	1-1	-	0-0	0	0	2	0	0	2
Bryan Williams	5	1-1	-	0-0	1	0	0	2	1	2
David Rose	4	0-1	-	0-0	1	1	0	0	0	0
TOTALS	200	27-53	-	16-20	27	12	11	7	17	70
Percentages		50.9		80.0						

Coach: Guy V. Lewis

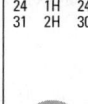

MEMPHIS	MIN	FG	3FG	FT	REB	A	ST	BL	PF	TP
Bobby Parks	40	7-12	-	3-4	5	2	2	0	5	17
Keith Lee	38	6-15	-	1-2	8	0	0	2	3	13
Derrick Phillips	38	5-5	-	3-4	5	1	0	0	1	13
Phillip Haynes	40	4-10	-	2-4	3	1	1	0	3	10
Andre Turner	40	5-13	-	0-0	2	8	4	0	2	10
Baskerville Holmes	4	0-1	-	0-0	0	0	0	0	0	0
TOTALS	200	27-56	-	9-14	23	12	7	2	14	63
Percentages		48.2		64.3						

Coach: Dana Kirk

Officials: Richie Weiler, Larry Lembo, Booker Turner
Technicals: None
Attendance: 17,036

Villanova 55-54 Iowa (Sweet 16)

	1H	2H
Villanova	24	31
Iowa	24	30

VILLANOVA	MIN	FG	3FG	FT	REB	A	ST	BL	PF	TP
John Pinone	-	6-12	-	6-6	9	1	1	1	4	18
Stewart Granger	-	5-9	-	1-4	1	4	1	0	1	11
Dwayne McClain	-	5-9	-	0-0	1	1	1	0	3	10
Ed Pinckney	-	2-6	-	4-4	11	3	2	1	4	8
Mike Mulquin	-	2-2	-	0-0	1	1	0	0	4	4
Gary McLain	-	0-1	-	2-2	0	0	0	0	2	2
Harold Pressley	-	1-5	-	0-0	3	3	1	1	0	2
Frank Dobbs	-	0-0	-	0-0	0	0	0	0	0	0
TOTALS	-	21-44	-	13-16	26	13	6	3	18	55
Percentages		47.7		81.2						

Coach: Rollie Massimino

IOWA	MIN	FG	3FG	FT	REB	A	ST	BL	PF	TP
Greg Stokes	39	10-15	-	2-4	11	1	2	1	3	22
Bob Hansen	40	9-15	-	3-4	8	3	0	0	2	21
Mark Gannon	30	2-5	-	0-0	1	0	2	0	3	4
Michael Payne	23	1-6	-	1-2	2	1	0	0	5	3
Steve Carfino	39	1-7	-	0-0	5	5	4	0	3	2
Andre Banks	23	1-4	-	0-1	2	0	1	1	0	2
Craig Anderson	6	0-1	-	0-0	0	0	0	0	0	0
TOTALS	200	24-53	-	6-11	29	10	9	2	16	54
Percentages		45.3		54.5						

Coach: Lute Olson

Officials: John Dabrow, Tom Harrington, Jim Clark
Technicals: None
Attendance: 17,036

Louisville 65-63 Arkansas (Sweet 16)

	1H	2H
Louisville	27	38
Arkansas	37	26

LOUISVILLE	MIN	FG	3FG	FT	REB	A	ST	BL	PF	TP
Lancaster Gordon	34	9-12	-	1-2	4	0	4	0	1	19
Scooter McCray	36	7-12	-	3-5	4	1	0	2	3	17
Milt Wagner	35	5-12	-	0-0	1	6	1	1	3	10
Charles Jones	29	3-4	-	0-1	2	3	3	0	4	6
Billy Thompson	22	3-6	-	0-0	4	1	1	1	3	6
Rodney McCray	33	2-5	-	1-2	5	2	1	0	4	5
Jeff Hall	11	1-3	-	0-0	0	0	0	0	1	2
TOTALS	200	30-54	-	5-10	20	13	10	4	19	65
Percentages		55.6		50.0						

Coach: Denny Crum

ARKANSAS	MIN	FG	3FG	FT	REB	A	ST	BL	PF	TP
Joe Kleine	38	8-13	-	5-6	7	0	0	0	4	21
Darrell Walker	38	5-11	-	5-7	8	2	0	0	3	15
Leroy Sutton	35	5-5	-	2-2	1	0	0	1	3	12
Charles Balentine	29	3-6	-	1-3	3	0	1	0	1	7
Alvin Robertson	35	2-8	-	0-3	3	7	5	0	4	4
Carey Kelly	14	2-3	-	0-0	7	1	0	1	1	4
Ricky Norton	9	0-1	-	0-0	0	0	0	0	0	0
John Snively	2	0-2	-	0-0	0	0	0	0	0	0
TOTALS	200	25-49	-	13-21	29	10	6	2	16	63
Percentages		51.0		61.9						

Coach: Eddie Sutton

Technicals: None
Attendance: 12,489

Kentucky 64-59 Indiana (Sweet 16)

	1H	2H
Kentucky	32	32
Indiana	29	30

KENTUCKY	MIN	FG	3FG	FT	REB	A	ST	BL	PF	TP
Mel Turpin	36	8-13	-	0-0	5	1	0	1	2	16
Kenny Walker	22	6-6	-	1-2	3	0	0	1	1	13
Jim Master	31	4-7	-	4-4	3	1	1	0	1	12
Dirk Minniefield	32	5-7	-	1-3	5	5	1	0	4	11
Bret Bearup	14	4-5	-	0-0	1	0	0	2	2	8
Charles Hurt	36	0-2	-	2-4	2	2	0	0	2	2
Dickey Beal	15	0-2	-	2-2	0	2	1	0	1	2
Derrick Hord	11	0-1	-	0-0	1	0	0	0	0	0
Roger Harden	2	0-0	-	0-0	0	0	0	0	0	0
Troy McKinley	1	0-0	-	0-0	0	0	0	0	0	0
TOTALS	200	27-43	-	10-15	20	11	3	4	13	64
Percentages		62.8		66.7						

Coach: Joe B. Hall

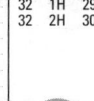

INDIANA	MIN	FG	3FG	FT	REB	A	ST	BL	PF	TP
Randy Wittman	40	8-16	-	2-2	5	1	1	-	1	18
Uwe Blab	34	6-12	-	5-9	3	0	1	-	4	17
Tony Brown	40	3-6	-	2-2	4	6	0	-	3	8
Steve Bouchie	39	4-10	-	0-0	4	2	1	-	4	8
James Thomas	36	2-4	-	0-0	7	3	1	-	3	4
Mike Giomi	5	2-2	-	0-0	0	0	0	-	0	4
Winston Morgan	6	0-0	-	0-0	0	1	0	-	2	0
TOTALS	200	25-50	-	9-13	23	13	4	-	17	59
Percentages		50.0		69.2						

Coach: Bob Knight

Officials: Hank Nichols, Joe Forte, Paul Housman
Technicals: None
Attendance: 12,489

Virginia 95-92 Boston College (Sweet 16)

	1H	2H
Virginia	45	50
Boston College	44	48

VIRGINIA	MIN	FG	3FG	FT	REB	A	ST	BL	PF	TP
Rick Carlisle	32	7-13	-	8-8	5	1	0	0	3	22
Ralph Sampson	19	9-13	-	1-3	11	1	1	4	5	19
Othell Wilson	36	8-18	-	2-5	3	9	0	1	2	18
Ricky Stokes	26	4-4	-	4-5	1	5	0	0	4	12
Craig Robinson	36	2-7	-	5-9	15	1	0	1	3	9
Jim Miller	28	4-12	-	0-0	2	1	0	0	5	8
Kenton Edelin	18	2-3	-	1-4	11	0	0	0	5	5
Tim Mullen	4	0-2	-	2-2	1	1	0	0	0	2
Dan Merrifield	1	0-0	-	0-0	0	0	0	0	0	0
TOTALS	200	36-72	-	23-36	49	19	1	6	27	95
Percentages		50.0		63.9						

Coach: Terry Holland

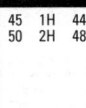

BOSTON COLLEGE	MIN	FG	3FG	FT	REB	A	ST	BL	PF	TP
John Garris	36	8-15	-	9-10	12	1	0	4	2	25
Jay Murphy	31	9-15	-	5-8	12	0	0	1	2	23
Michael Adams	34	7-22	-	4-5	5	8	1	0	2	18
Dominic Pressley	27	4-8	-	3-6	5	3	1	1	4	11
Terrence Talley	13	3-6	-	0-0	3	0	0	0	4	6
Martin Clark	26	1-4	-	2-3	3	3	0	0	4	4
Roger McCready	4	1-2	-	1-2	0	0	0	0	1	3
Stu Primus	19	1-5	-	0-0	3	0	0	0	5	2
Burnett Adams	8	0-1	-	0-0	1	0	0	0	5	0
Tim O'Shea	2	0-0	-	0-0	1	0	0	0	0	0
TOTALS	200	34-78	-	24-34	45	15	2	6	29	92
Percentages		43.6		70.6						

Coach: Gary Williams

Officials: Mike Tanco, Jim Bain, Don Rutledge
Technicals: None
Attendance: 12,084

NC State 75-56 Utah (Sweet 16)

	1H	2H
NC State	30	45
Utah	26	30

NC STATE	MIN	FG	3FG	FT	REB	A	ST	BL	PF	TP
Dereck Whittenburg	38	10-13	-	7-7	2	3	0	0	3	27
Lorenzo Charles	35	7-9	-	4-4	3	0	0	0	1	18
Thurl Bailey	37	4-10	-	2-2	9	1	0	4	0	10
Terry Gannon	18	4-5	-	2-2	1	2	1	0	1	10
Sidney Lowe	39	2-2	-	0-0	4	5	2	1	1	4
George McClain	10	1-1	-	0-0	1	1	0	0	0	2
Ernie Myers	2	0-1	-	2-2	0	0	0	0	0	2
Cozell McQueen	13	0-0	-	1-2	2	0	0	0	1	1
Mike Warren	1	0-0	-	1-2	0	0	0	0	0	1
Alvin Battle	4	0-0	-	0-0	0	0	0	0	0	0
Walt Densmore	1	0-0	-	0-1	1	0	0	0	0	0
Quinton Leonard	1	0-0	-	0-0	0	0	0	0	0	0
Harold Thompson	1	0-0	-	0-0	0	0	0	0	1	0
TOTALS	200	28-41	-	19-22	23	12	3	5	8	75
Percentages		68.3		86.4						

Coach: Jim Valvano

UTAH	MIN	FG	3FG	FT	REB	A	ST	BL	PF	TP
Peter Williams	38	7-15	-	1-1	6	1	1	0	2	15
Pace Mannion	38	6-10	-	1-4	4	4	2	0	4	13
Angelo Robinson	31	4-12	-	0-0	1	1	0	0	2	8
Chris Winans	31	3-4	-	0-0	8	4	1	0	3	6
Manny Hendrix	29	2-6	-	0-0	0	1	0	1	1	4
George Furgis	17	1-3	-	0-0	1	0	1	0	2	2
David Cecil	8	1-1	-	0-0	0	0	0	0	1	2
Mike Bozner	2	1-2	-	0-0	3	1	0	0	1	2
Clyde Rivers	2	1-3	-	0-0	0	0	0	0	1	2
John White	2	1-2	-	0-0	2	0	0	0	0	2
Mark Hill	1	0-0	-	0-0	1	0	0	0	0	0
Scott Hill	1	0-2	-	0-0	0	1	0	0	1	0
TOTALS	200	27-60	-	2-5	26	13	5	1	18	56
Percentages		45.0		40.0						

Coach: Jerry Pimm

Technicals: None
Attendance: 12,084

70-67 — SWEET 16

	1H	2H
Georgia	27	43
St. John's	29	38

GEORGIA	MIN	FG	3FG	FT	REB	A	ST	BL	PF	TP
Terry Fair	40	11-21	-	5-8	9	3	5	3	2	27
Lamar Heard	33	3-5	-	5-6	5	2	1	0	4	11
James Banks	40	4-8	-	2-3	3	2	0	1	3	10
Vern Fleming	35	5-11	-	0-0	4	2	0	0	5	10
Gerald Crosby	26	3-9	-	2-2	1	0	2	0	4	8
Donald Hartry	18	1-3	-	2-2	0	2	1	0	1	4
Richard Corhen	7	0-2	-	0-1	3	1	0	0	0	0
Troy Hitchcock	1	0-0	-	0-0	0	0	1	0	0	0
TOTALS	200	27-59	-	16-22	25	12	10	4	19	70
Percentages		45.8		72.7						

Coach: Hugh Durham

ST. JOHN'S	MIN	FG	3FG	FT	REB	A	ST	BL	PF	TP
Chris Mullin	40	6-11	-	7-8	3	4	0	0	2	19
David Russell	40	4-8	-	6-7	12	1	1	0	3	14
Billy Goodwin	33	6-12	-	0-2	6	4	0	0	4	12
Kevin Williams	20	4-7	-	4-4	2	1	0	0	5	12
Bill Wennington	33	5-8	-	0-0	10	2	0	3	3	10
Bob Kelly	20	0-2	-	0-0	1	3	1	0	3	0
Trevor Jackson	7	0-0	-	0-0	1	0	1	1	1	0
Ron Stewart	7	0-2	-	0-0	1	1	0	0	2	0
TOTALS	200	25-50	-	17-21	36	16	3	4	23	67
Percentages		50.0		81.0						

Coach: Lou Carnesecca

Technicals: None
Attendance: 23,286

64-51 — SWEET 16

	1H	2H
North Carolina	29	35
Ohio State	30	21

NORTH CAROLINA	MIN	FG	3FG	FT	REB	A	ST	BL	PF	TP
Michael Jordan	36	5-15	-	7-9	7	0	0	1	3	17
Sam Perkins	23	5-12	-	5-6	6	0	2	0	4	15
Jim Braddock	38	2-3	-	6-6	2	3	0	0	1	10
Matt Doherty	39	2-5	-	4-4	2	3	0	0	1	8
Brad Daugherty	28	4-6	-	0-0	6	1	0	0	4	8
Warren Martin	17	2-3	-	0-0	1	1	0	1	0	4
Curtis Hunter	10	1-1	-	0-0	1	2	0	0	2	2
John Brownlee	5	0-0	-	0-0	0	0	1	0	0	0
Steve Hale	2	0-0	-	0-0	0	1	0	0	1	0
Cecil Exum	1	0-0	-	0-0	0	0	0	0	1	0
Timo Makkonen	1	0-0	-	0-0	0	0	0	0	0	0
TOTALS	200	21-45	-	22-25	25	11	3	2	17	64
Percentages		46.7		88.0						

Coach: Dean Smith

OHIO STATE	MIN	FG	3FG	FT	REB	A	ST	BL	PF	TP
Joe Concheck	27	5-9	-	4-5	5	1	0	0	3	14
Tony Campbell	38	6-12	-	1-2	6	0	0	0	2	13
Troy Taylor	33	3-9	-	4-5	2	4	3	0	4	10
Granville Waiters	35	2-5	-	1-3	5	0	1	2	4	5
Larry Huggins	26	2-5	-	0-0	3	0	0	0	1	4
Ronnie Stokes	19	1-2	-	0-0	0	4	0	0	4	2
Keith Wesson	8	1-1	-	0-0	2	0	0	0	2	2
Clinton Smith	1	0-0	-	1-2	0	0	0	0	1	1
David Jones	8	0-2	-	0-0	2	0	1	0	2	0
Alan Kortokrax	2	0-0	-	0-0	0	0	0	0	0	0
Henry Grace	1	0-0	-	0-0	0	0	0	0	0	0
Mitch Haas	1	0-0	-	0-0	0	0	1	0	0	0
Derrick Polk	1	0-0	-	0-0	0	0	0	0	0	0
TOTALS	200	20-45	-	11-17	25	9	6	2	23	51
Percentages		44.4		64.7						

Coach: Eldon Miller

Officials: Jody Silvester, Ron Spitler, Woody Mayfield
Technicals: None
Attendance: 23,286

89-71 — ELITE 8

	1H	2H
Houston	37	52
Villanova	27	44

HOUSTON	MIN	FG	3FG	FT	REB	A	ST	BL	PF	TP
Larry Micheaux	35	11-17	-	8-10	12	2	1	4	2	30
Michael Young	37	9-16	-	2-2	6	3	1	0	2	20
Hakeem Olajuwon	31	10-11	-	0-1	13	1	2	8	4	20
Clyde Drexler	36	6-12	-	0-1	5	3	1	0	5	12
Alvin Franklin	24	2-5	-	0-0	2	2	0	0	1	4
David Rose	1	1-1	-	1-2	0	0	0	0	0	3
Reid Gettys	21	0-1	-	0-2	4	3	0	0	3	0
Benny Anders	5	0-3	-	0-0	0	0	0	0	2	0
Dan Bunce	2	0-0	-	0-0	0	0	0	0	0	0
Eric Dickens	2	0-1	-	0-0	0	0	0	0	0	0
Gary Orsak	2	0-0	-	0-1	0	0	0	0	0	0
Bryan Williams	2	0-0	-	0-0	1	0	0	1	2	0
Derek Giles	1	0-0	-	0-0	0	0	0	0	0	0
Renaldo Thomas	1	0-0	-	0-0	0	0	0	0	0	0
TOTALS	200	39-67	-	11-19	43	14	5	13	21	89
Percentages		58.2		57.9						

Coach: Guy V. Lewis

VILLANOVA	MIN	FG	3FG	FT	REB	A	ST	BL	PF	TP
Ed Pinckney	36	6-11	-	6-9	12	5	2	1	4	18
John Pinone	34	7-17	-	4-4	9	1	1	0	4	18
Dwayne McClain	29	8-14	-	1-1	7	0	1	0	2	17
Stewart Granger	33	3-15	-	2-2	1	3	1	0	4	8
Mike Mulquin	11	1-3	-	1-1	1	0	0	0	4	3
Wyatt Maker	5	1-1	-	0-1	2	0	0	0	1	2
Chuck Everson	2	1-1	-	0-0	1	0	0	0	0	2
Dwight Wilbur	2	1-4	-	0-0	2	1	0	0	1	2
Harold Pressley	26	0-9	-	1-2	3	1	0	0	1	1
Gary McLain	15	0-3	-	0-0	2	3	0	0	2	0
Frank Dobbs	3	0-0	-	0-0	0	0	0	0	1	0
Martin Lutchaunig	2	0-4	-	0-0	1	0	0	0	0	0
Roland Massimino	2	0-0	-	0-0	0	0	0	0	0	0
TOTALS	200	28-82	-	15-20	41	14	5	1	24	71
Percentages		34.1		75.0						

Coach: Rollie Massimino

Officials: Richie Weiler, Larry Lembo, Booker Turner
Technicals: None
Attendance: 17,036

80-68 — ELITE 8

	1H	2H	OT1
Louisville	30	32	18
Kentucky	37	25	6

LOUISVILLE	MIN	FG	3FG	FT	REB	A	ST	BL	PF	TP
Lancaster Gordon	42	11-21	-	2-3	1	2	4	0	1	24
Milt Wagner	39	7-10	-	4-4	2	4	2	0	2	18
Rodney McCray	42	7-7	-	1-2	8	2	1	2	3	15
Charles Jones	38	4-9	-	4-6	7	2	0	2	1	12
Scooter McCray	40	3-6	-	1-1	7	4	3	1	3	7
Billy Thompson	13	2-4	-	0-1	2	1	0	0	1	4
Jeff Hall	9	0-0	-	0-0	0	0	1	0	1	0
Robbie Valentine	1	0-0	-	0-0	0	0	0	0	0	0
Chris West	1	0-0	-	0-0	0	0	0	0	0	0
TOTALS	225	34-57	-	12-17	27	15	11	5	12	80
Percentages		59.6		70.6						

Coach: Denny Crum

KENTUCKY	MIN	FG	3FG	FT	REB	A	ST	BL	PF	TP
Jim Master	40	9-13	-	0-0	2	2	0	0	4	18
Mel Turpin	36	8-13	-	2-2	9	1	3	1	4	18
Dirk Minniefield	37	6-13	-	0-0	3	5	3	0	4	12
Derrick Hord	30	4-9	-	1-2	2	0	0	0	1	9
Charles Hurt	31	3-5	-	1-2	6	1	0	0	3	7
Kenny Walker	26	1-3	-	0-0	1	0	0	0	1	2
Bret Bearup	9	1-1	-	0-2	3	0	0	0	0	2
Dickey Beal	15	0-0	-	0-0	0	4	0	0	3	0
Roger Harden	1	0-0	-	0-0	0	0	0	0	0	0
TOTALS	225	32-57	-	4-8	26	13	6	1	20	68
Percentages		56.1		50.0						

Coach: Joe B. Hall

Officials: Hank Nichols, Joe Forte, Paul Housman
Technicals: None
Attendance: 12,489

63-62 — ELITE 8

	1H	2H
NC State	28	35
Virginia	33	29

NC STATE	MIN	FG	3FG	FT	REB	A	ST	BL	PF	TP
Dereck Whittenburg	39	11-16	-	2-2	3	4	1	0	4	24
Thurl Bailey	38	7-17	-	0-0	6	0	1	0	4	14
Lorenzo Charles	35	4-5	-	3-4	10	1	0	0	2	11
Sidney Lowe	40	2-8	-	4-4	0	8	0	0	1	8
Ernie Myers	6	2-3	-	0-0	0	0	0	0	0	4
Alvin Battle	7	0-1	-	1-2	2	0	0	0	0	1
George McClain	2	0-1	-	1-2	0	0	0	0	0	1
Cozell McQueen	23	0-3	-	0-0	6	1	4	1	4	0
Terry Gannon	10	0-1	-	0-0	0	0	0	1	0	0
TOTALS	200	26-55	-	11-14	27	14	6	1	16	63
Percentages		47.3		78.6						

Coach: Jim Valvano

VIRGINIA	MIN	FG	3FG	FT	REB	A	ST	BL	PF	TP
Ralph Sampson	33	8-10	-	7-11	11	2	1	4	4	23
Rick Carlisle	37	4-7	-	0-1	4	4	0	0	1	8
Craig Robinson	34	4-9	-	0-0	5	1	0	0	4	8
Ricky Stokes	21	3-3	-	2-3	1	2	0	1	2	8
Othell Wilson	35	3-5	-	1-2	2	9	0	0	3	7
Jim Miller	15	3-5	-	0-0	0	0	0	0	0	6
Kenton Edelin	19	1-1	-	0-2	4	1	0	0	3	2
Tim Mullen	6	0-1	-	0-0	0	0	0	0	0	0
TOTALS	200	26-41	-	10-19	27	19	1	5	17	62
Percentages		63.4		52.6						

Coach: Terry Holland

Officials: Gary Muncy, Dale Kelley, Phil Robinson
Technicals: None
Attendance: 12,087

82-77 — ELITE 8

	1H	2H
Georgia	37	45
North Carolina	35	42

GEORGIA	MIN	FG	3FG	FT	REB	A	ST	BL	PF	TP
James Banks	37	7-10	-	6-6	5	3	-	0	3	20
Vern Fleming	39	6-16	-	5-8	8	5	-	0	3	17
Gerald Crosby	33	6-12	-	5-8	3	2	-	0	3	17
Terry Fair	22	5-6	-	1-2	6	1	-	0	4	11
Lamar Heard	40	4-6	-	0-0	9	2	-	0	1	8
Richard Corhen	18	3-6	-	1-4	3	1	-	2	3	7
Donald Hartry	8	1-1	-	0-0	0	1	-	0	0	2
Derrick Floyd	3	0-0	-	0-0	0	1	-	0	0	0
TOTALS	200	32-57	-	18-28	34	16	-	2	17	82
Percentages		56.1		64.3						

Coach: Hugh Durham

NORTH CAROLINA	MIN	FG	3FG	FT	REB	A	ST	BL	PF	TP
Michael Jordan	34	11-23	-	4-5	6	0	-	1	5	26
Brad Daugherty	29	6-10	-	3-3	9	0	-	1	4	15
Sam Perkins	38	5-9	-	4-4	11	2	-	3	3	14
Matt Doherty	38	3-8	-	4-4	2	4	-	0	3	10
Jim Braddock	36	5-9	-	0-1	2	7	-	0	2	10
Curtis Hunter	13	1-3	-	0-0	0	0	-	0	5	2
Steve Hale	7	0-1	-	0-0	0	0	-	0	4	0
Warren Martin	5	0-0	-	0-0	2	0	-	0	0	0
TOTALS	200	31-63	-	15-17	32	13	-	5	26	77
Percentages		49.2		88.2						

Coach: Dean Smith

Technicals: None
Attendance: 22,984

94-81 (FINAL 4)

HOUSTON	MIN	FG	3FG	FT	REB	A	ST	BL	PF	TP
Clyde Drexler	37	10-15	-	1-2	7	6	1	0	2	21
Hakeem Olajuwon	36	9-14	-	3-7	22	0	1	8	4	21
Michael Young	35	7-18	-	2-3	4	3	2	1	2	16
Alvin Franklin	29	5-8	-	3-4	1	3	5	0	0	13
Benny Anders	19	5-9	-	3-5	6	2	2	1	4	13
Larry Micheaux	23	4-7	-	0-1	3	1	0	0	5	8
Bryan Williams	1	1-1	-	0-0	0	0	0	0	0	2
Reid Gettys	13	0-0	-	0-0	1	4	0	0	2	0
David Rose	6	0-2	-	0-0	0	0	0	0	3	0
Derek Giles	1	0-0	-	0-1	0	0	0	0	0	0
TOTALS	**200**	**41-74**	**-**	**12-23**	**44**	**19**	**11**	**10**	**22**	**94**
Percentages		55.4		52.2						

Coach: Guy V. Lewis

	1H	2H
Houston	36	58
Louisville	41	40

LOUISVILLE	MIN	FG	3FG	FT	REB	A	ST	BL	PF	TP
Milt Wagner	36	12-23	-	0-0	2	4	1	1	4	24
Lancaster Gordon	36	6-15	-	5-6	6	2	1	0	3	17
Charles Jones	33	3-10	-	6-8	11	1	1	2	3	12
Scooter McCray	35	5-8	-	0-0	6	4	2	2	4	10
Rodney McCray	35	3-6	-	2-8	5	5	1	0	4	8
Billy Thompson	15	1-4	-	4-5	5	1	2	1	4	6
Jeff Hall	8	2-4	-	0-0	1	0	0	0	0	4
Robbie Valentine	1	0-0	-	0-0	0	0	0	0	0	0
Chris West	1	0-0	-	0-0	0	0	0	0	1	0
TOTALS	**200**	**32-70**	**-**	**17-27**	**36**	**17**	**8**	**6**	**23**	**81**
Percentages		45.7		63.0						

Coach: Denny Crum

Officials: Hank Nichols, Paul Housman, Joe Forte
Technicals: Houston (bench)
Attendance: 17,327

67-60 (FINAL 4)

NC STATE	MIN	FG	3FG	FT	REB	A	ST	BL	PF	TP
Dereck Whittenburg	39	8-18	-	4-4	0	6	0	0	1	20
Thurl Bailey	38	9-17	-	2-5	10	1	0	2	3	20
Sidney Lowe	37	4-6	-	2-2	5	11	1	0	3	10
Cozell McQueen	38	4-5	-	0-0	13	1	1	4	5	8
Lorenzo Charles	29	2-2	-	1-2	6	0	0	0	1	5
Terry Gannon	12	1-4	-	2-2	1	0	1	0	0	4
Alvin Battle	7	0-0	-	0-0	2	0	0	1	0	0
TOTALS	**200**	**28-52**	**-**	**11-15**	**37**	**19**	**3**	**7**	**13**	**67**
Percentages		53.8		73.3						

Coach: Jim Valvano

	1H	2H
NC State	33	34
Georgia	22	38

GEORGIA	MIN	FG	3FG	FT	REB	A	ST	BL	PF	TP
Vern Fleming	31	7-17	-	0-0	11	2	0	-	4	14
James Banks	35	5-19	-	3-5	2	0	0	-	3	13
Gerald Crosby	35	5-15	-	2-2	1	2	3	-	3	12
Lamar Heard	35	3-5	-	2-3	10	1	3	-	2	8
Richard Corhen	16	3-6	-	0-1	7	1	0	-	2	6
Terry Fair	32	2-9	-	1-2	6	0	6	-	3	5
Donald Hartry	14	1-3	-	0-0	0	1	0	-	3	2
Derrick Floyd	2	0-0	-	0-0	0	0	0	-	0	0
TOTALS	**200**	**26-74**	**-**	**8-13**	**37**	**7**	**12**	**-**	**20**	**60**
Percentages		35.1		61.5						

Coach: Hugh Durham

Officials: Larry Lembo, Richie Weiler, Booker Turner
Technicals: None
Attendance: 17,327

54-52 (NCAA FINAL 1983)

NC STATE	MIN	FG	3FG	FT	REB	A	ST	BL	PF	TP
Thurl Bailey	39	7-16	-	1-2	5	0	0	0	1	15
Dereck Whittenburg	39	6-17	-	2-2	5	1	0	0	3	14
Sidney Lowe	40	4-9	-	0-1	0	8	5	0	2	8
Terry Gannon	18	3-4	-	1-2	1	2	1	0	3	7
Cozell McQueen	34	1-5	-	2-2	12	1	1	1	4	4
Lorenzo Charles	25	2-7	-	0-0	7	0	0	1	2	4
Alvin Battle	4	0-1	-	2-2	1	1	0	0	1	2
Ernie Myers	1	0-0	-	0-0	1	0	0	0	0	0
TOTALS	**200**	**23-59**	**-**	**8-11**	**32**	**13**	**7**	**2**	**16**	**54**
Percentages		39.0		72.7						

Coach: Jim Valvano

	1H	2H
NC State	33	21
Houston	25	27

HOUSTON	MIN	FG	3FG	FT	REB	A	ST	BL	PF	TP
Hakeem Olajuwon	38	7-15	-	6-7	18	1	-	7	1	20
Benny Anders	17	4-9	-	2-5	2	1	-	0	2	10
Michael Young	30	3-10	-	0-4	8	1	-	1	0	6
Alvin Franklin	35	2-6	-	0-1	0	3	-	0	0	4
Clyde Drexler	25	1-5	-	2-2	2	0	-	0	4	4
Reid Gettys	20	2-2	-	0-0	2	2	-	0	3	4
Larry Micheaux	18	2-6	-	0-0	6	0	-	0	1	4
Bryan Williams	10	0-1	-	0-0	4	1	-	0	3	0
David Rose	7	0-1	-	0-0	1	0	-	0	2	0
TOTALS	**200**	**21-55**	**-**	**10-19**	**43**	**9**	**-**	**8**	**16**	**52**
Percentages		38.2		52.6						

Coach: Guy V. Lewis

Officials: Hank Nichols, Paul Housman, Joe Forte
Technicals: None
Attendance: 17,327

National Invitation Tournament (NIT)

First round: Vanderbilt d. East Tenn. St. 79-74, South Florida d. Fordham 81-69, New Orleans d. LSU 99-94 (OT), Oregon State d. Idaho 77-59, DePaul d. Minnesota 76-73, South Carolina d. Old Dominion 100-90, TCU d. Tulsa 64-62, Iona d. St. Bonaventure 90-76, Fresno State d. UTEP 71-64, Virginia Tech d. William and Mary 85-79, Northwestern d. Notre Dame 71-57, Wake Forest d. Murray State 87-80, Nebraska d. Tulane 72-65, Mississippi d. Alabama State 87-75, Arizona State d. Cal St. Fullerton 87-83, Michigan State d. Bowling Green 72-71
Second round: Nebraska d. Iona 85-73, Mississippi d. South Florida 65-57, Fresno State d. Michigan State 72-58, Wake Forest d. Vanderbilt 75-68, South Carolina d. Virginia Tech 75-68, TCU d. Arizona State 78-76, Oregon State d. New Orleans 88-71, DePaul d. Northwestern 65-63
Third round: Nebraska d. TCU 67-57, Wake Forest d. South Carolina 78-61, Fresno State d. Oregon State 76-67, DePaul d. Mississippi 75-67
Semifinals: Fresno State d. Wake Forest 86-62, DePaul d. Nebraska 68-58
Championship: Fresno State d. DePaul 69-60
MVP: Ron Anderson, Fresno State

1983-84: Second Chances

Both teams in the 1984 NCAA Final were looking for redemption. Houston and coach Guy V. Lewis, making their third straight Final Four appearance, were still smarting from NC State's shocking championship victory in 1983. John Thompson Jr. and Georgetown were two years removed from their own heartbreaking Final loss to North Carolina. The title game at Seattle's Kingdome featured the two best college centers—the Hoyas' Patrick Ewing and the Cougars' Hakeem Olajuwon. But the difference-makers were Georgetown forwards Reggie Williams and Michael Graham, who combined for 33 points to lead the Hoyas to a 84-75 win. Olajuwon finished with 15 points and nine rebounds. Ewing scored 10, grabbed nine boards and was named Most Outstanding Player. His 18 Final Four points tied Indiana forward Marv Huffman's 1940 record for lowest scoring total by an MOP. Georgetown's Tournament opponents averaged just 49.6 points per game. Thompson became the first African-American coach to win an NCAA Division I title.

UNC's Michael Jordan (19.6 ppg, 55.1% shooting) was Naismith POY. He was chosen third in the 1984 NBA draft by the Chicago Bulls, after Olajuwon (Houston Rockets) and Kentucky's Sam Bowie (Portland Trail Blazers).

Major Conference Standings

AMCU-8

	Conference			Overall		
	W	L	PCT	W	L	PCT
Illinois-Chicago	12	2	.857	22	7	.759
Northern Iowa	10	4	.714	18	10	.643
Missouri State	9	5	.643	18	10	.643
Eastern Illinois	7	7	.500	15	13	.536
Western Illinois	6	8	.429	17	13	.567
Wisc.-Green Bay	5	9	.357	9	19	.321
Cleveland State	4	10	.286	14	16	.467
Valparaiso	3	11	.214	9	19	.321

Tournament: **Western Illinois d. Cleveland State 73-64**
Tournament MVP: **Todd Hutcheson**, Western Illinois

ATLANTIC 10

	Conference			Overall		
	W	L	PCT	W	L	PCT
Temple ○	18	0	1.000	26	5	.839
Saint Joseph's □	13	5	.722	20	9	.690
George Washington	11	7	.611	17	12	.586
West Virginia ⊕	9	9	.500	20	12	.625
Rutgers	9	9	.500	15	13	.536
St. Bonaventure	8	10	.444	18	13	.581
Duquesne	8	10	.444	10	18	.357
Massachusetts	6	12	.333	12	17	.414
Rhode Island	5	13	.278	6	22	.214
Penn State	3	15	.167	5	22	.185

Tournament: **West Virginia d. St. Bonaventure 59-56**
Tournament MVP: **Lester Rowe**, West Virginia

ACC

	Conference			Overall		
	W	L	PCT	W	L	PCT
North Carolina ○	14	0	1.000	28	3	.903
Maryland ⊕	9	5	.643	24	8	.750
Wake Forest ○	7	7	.500	23	9	.719
Duke ○	7	7	.500	24	10	.706
Virginia ○	6	8	.429	21	12	.636
Georgia Tech □	6	8	.429	18	11	.621
NC State □	4	10	.286	19	14	.576
Clemson	3	11	.214	14	14	.500

Tournament: **Maryland d. Duke 74-62**
Tournament MVP: **Len Bias**, Maryland

BIG EAST

	Conference			Overall		
	W	L	PCT	W	L	PCT
Georgetown ⊕	14	2	.875	34	3	.919
Syracuse ○	12	4	.750	23	9	.719
Villanova ○	12	4	.750	19	12	.613
Boston College □	8	8	.500	18	12	.600
St. John's ○	8	8	.500	18	12	.600
Pittsburgh □	6	10	.375	18	13	.581
Providence	5	11	.313	15	14	.517
Connecticut	5	11	.313	13	15	.464
Seton Hall	2	14	.125	9	19	.321

Tournament: **Georgetown d. Syracuse 82-71 (OT)**
Tournament MVP: **Patrick Ewing**, Georgetown

BIG EIGHT

	Conference			Overall		
	W	L	PCT	W	L	PCT
Oklahoma ○	13	1	.929	29	5	.853
Kansas ⊕	9	5	.643	22	10	.688
Nebraska □	7	7	.500	18	12	.600
Colorado	6	8	.429	16	13	.552
Iowa State □	6	8	.429	16	13	.552
Missouri	5	9	.357	16	14	.533
Kansas State	5	9	.357	14	15	.483
Oklahoma State	5	9	.357	13	15	.464

Tournament: **Kansas d. Oklahoma 79-78**
Tournament MVP: **Wayman Tisdale**, Oklahoma

BIG SKY

	Conference			Overall		
	W	L	PCT	W	L	PCT
Weber State □	12	2	.857	23	8	.742
Montana	9	5	.643	23	7	.767
Nevada ⊕	7	7	.500	17	14	.548
Montana State	7	7	.500	14	15	.483
Boise State	6	8	.429	15	13	.536
Idaho State	6	8	.429	12	20	.375
Northern Arizona	5	9	.357	13	15	.464
Idaho	4	10	.286	9	19	.321

Tournament: **Nevada d. Montana 71-69**
Tournament MVP: **Curtis High**, Nevada

BIG TEN

	Conference			Overall		
	W	L	PCT	W	L	PCT
Illinois ⊕	15	3	.833	26	5	.839
Purdue ○	15	3	.833	22	7	.759
Indiana ○	13	5	.722	22	9	.710
Michigan □	11	7	.611	23	10	.697
Michigan State	9	9	.500	15	13	.536
Ohio State □	8	10	.444	15	14	.517
Northwestern	7	11	.389	12	16	.429
Minnesota	6	12	.333	15	13	.536
Iowa	6	12	.333	13	15	.464
Wisconsin ⊗	4	14	.222	8	20	.286

EAST COAST

	Conference			Overall		
	W	L	PCT	W	L	PCT
Bucknell	14	2	.875	24	5	.828
Rider ⊕	11	5	.688	20	11	.645
Drexel	10	6	.625	17	12	.586
Hofstra	9	7	.563	14	14	.500
Lafayette	9	7	.563	12	17	.414
Delaware	6	10	.375	11	16	.407
Towson	5	11	.313	10	19	.345
American	5	11	.313	6	22	.214
Lehigh	3	13	.188	4	23	.148

Tournament: **Rider d. Bucknell 73-71 (OT)**
Tournament MVP: **Kevin Thomas**, Rider

ECAC METRO

	Conference			Overall		
	W	L	PCT	W	L	PCT
Long Island ⊕	11	5	.688	20	11	.645
Robert Morris	11	5	.688	17	13	.567
Fairleigh Dickinson	10	6	.625	17	12	.586
Loyola (MD)	10	6	.625	16	12	.571
Siena	8	8	.500	15	13	.536
Marist	8	8	.500	14	15	.483
Saint Francis (PA)	8	8	.500	12	15	.444
Wagner	5	11	.313	8	20	.286
St. Francis (NY)	1	15	.063	2	26	.071

Tournament: **Long Island d. Robert Morris 87-81**
Tournament MVP: **Carey Scurry**, Long Island

ECAC NAC

	Conference			Overall		
	W	L	PCT	W	L	PCT
Northeastern ⊕	14	0	1.000	27	5	.844
Canisius	9	5	.643	19	11	.633
Boston U.	9	5	.643	16	13	.552
New Hampshire	8	6	.571	15	13	.536
Maine	7	7	.500	17	10	.630
Niagara	5	9	.357	10	18	.357
Vermont	3	11	.214	7	21	.250
Colgate	1	13	.071	5	22	.185

Tournament: **Northeastern d. Canisius 85-75**
Tournament MVP: **Mark Halsel**, Northeastern

ECAC SOUTH

	Conference			Overall		
	W	L	PCT	W	L	PCT
Richmond ⊕	7	3	.700	22	10	.688
Navy	6	4	.600	24	8	.750
William and Mary	6	4	.600	14	14	.500
George Mason	5	5	.500	21	7	.750
James Madison	5	5	.500	15	14	.517
East Carolina	1	9	.100	4	24	.143

Tournament: **Richmond d. Navy 74-55**
Tournament MVP: **Johnny Newman**, Richmond

IVY

	Conference			Overall		
	W	L	PCT	W	L	PCT
Princeton ⊕	10	4	.714	18	10	.643
Cornell	9	5	.643	16	10	.615
Harvard	9	5	.643	15	11	.577
Penn	7	7	.500	10	16	.385
Brown	6	8	.429	11	15	.423
Dartmouth	6	8	.429	11	15	.423
Columbia	5	9	.357	8	18	.308
Yale	4	10	.286	7	19	.269

METRO

	Conference			Overall		
	W	L	PCT	W	L	PCT
Memphis ⊕⊗	11	3	.786	26	7	.788
Louisville ○	11	3	.786	24	11	.686
Florida State □	9	5	.643	20	11	.645
Virginia Tech □	8	6	.571	22	13	.629
Tulane	7	7	.500	17	11	.607
South Carolina	5	9	.357	12	16	.429
Southern Miss	4	10	.286	13	15	.464
Cincinnati	0	14	.000	3	25	.107

Tournament: **Memphis d. Virginia Tech 78-65**
Tournament MVP: **Keith Lee**, Memphis

METRO ATLANTIC

	Conference			Overall		
	W	L	PCT	W	L	PCT
Iona ⊕	11	3	.786	23	8	.742
Saint Peter's □	11	3	.786	23	6	.793
La Salle □	11	3	.786	20	11	.645
Fordham □	7	7	.500	19	15	.559
Holy Cross	5	9	.357	12	18	.400
Fairfield	5	9	.357	10	18	.357
Army	4	10	.286	11	17	.393
Manhattan	2	12	.143	9	19	.321

Tournament: **Iona d. Fordham 72-61**
Tournament MVP: **Steve Burtt Sr.**, Iona

MID-AMERICAN

	Conference			Overall		
	W	L	PCT	W	L	PCT
Miami (OH) ⊕	16	2	.889	24	6	.800
Ohio	14	4	.778	20	8	.714
Bowling Green	11	7	.611	18	10	.643
Toledo	11	7	.611	18	11	.621
Northern Illinois	9	9	.500	12	15	.444
Kent State	8	10	.444	15	14	.517
Eastern Michigan	8	10	.444	12	17	.414
Central Michigan	6	12	.333	11	16	.407
Ball State	5	13	.278	8	19	.296
Western Michigan	2	16	.111	4	22	.154

Tournament: **Miami (OH) d. Kent State 42-40**
Tournament MVP: **Chuck Stahl**, Miami (OH)

⊕ Automatic NCAA Tournament bid ○ At-large NCAA Tournament bid □ NIT appearance ⊗ Team record doesn't reflect games forfeited or vacated. For adjusted record, see p. 521.

MEAC

	Conference			Overall		
	W	L	PCT	W	L	PCT
NC A&T⊕	9	1	.900	22	7	.759
Howard	7	3	.700	15	14	.517
South Carolina State	6	4	.600	13	16	.448
Delaware State	3	7	.300	12	16	.429
UMES	3	7	.300	7	21	.250
Bethune-Cookman	2	8	.200	6	22	.214
Florida A&M*	-	-	-	7	19	.269

*Ineligible for conference competition
Tournament: **NC A&T d. Howard 65-58**
Tournament MOP: **Eric Boyd**, NC A&T

MIDWESTERN CITY

	Conference			Overall		
	W	L	PCT	W	L	PCT
Oral Roberts⊕	11	3	.786	21	10	.677
Loyola-Chicago	10	4	.714	20	9	.690
Xavier□	9	5	.643	22	11	.667
Evansville	7	7	.500	15	14	.517
Butler	7	7	.500	13	15	.464
Saint Louis	5	9	.357	12	16	.429
Detroit	4	10	.286	8	20	.286
Oklahoma City	3	11	.214	8	19	.296

Tournament: **Oral Roberts d. Xavier 68-66**
Tournament MVP: **Sam Potter**, Oral Roberts

MISSOURI VALLEY

	Conference			Overall		
	W	L	PCT	W	L	PCT
Tulsa⊕	13	3	.813	27	4	.871
Illinois State○	13	3	.813	23	8	.742
Wichita State□	11	5	.688	18	12	.600
Creighton□	8	8	.500	17	14	.548
Bradley	7	9	.438	15	13	.536
Southern Illinois	7	9	.438	15	13	.536
Indiana State	6	10	.375	14	14	.500
Drake	4	12	.250	8	20	.286
West Texas	3	13	.188	8	19	.296

Tournament: **Tulsa d. Creighton 70-68 (OT)**

OHIO VALLEY

	Conference			Overall		
	W	L	PCT	W	L	PCT
Morehead State⊕	12	2	.857	25	6	.806
Tennessee Tech	11	3	.786	18	10	.643
Youngstown State	9	5	.643	18	11	.621
Murray State	7	7	.500	15	13	.536
Austin Peay	5	9	.357	11	16	.407
Eastern Kentucky	5	9	.357	11	16	.407
Middle Tennessee State	4	10	.286	11	16	.407
Akron	3	11	.214	8	19	.296

Tournament: **Morehead State d. Youngstown State 47-44**
Tournament MVP: **Earl Harrison**, Morehead State

PCAA

	Conference			Overall		
	W	L	PCT	W	L	PCT
UNLV⊕	16	2	.889	29	6	.829
UC Irvine	14	4	.778	19	10	.655
Fresno State○	13	5	.722	25	8	.758
Utah State□	12	6	.667	19	11	.633
New Mexico State	9	9	.500	13	15	.464
Cal State Fullerton	8	10	.444	17	13	.567
San Jose State	6	12	.333	10	18	.357
Long Beach State	6	12	.333	9	19	.321
UC Santa Barbara	5	13	.278	10	17	.370
Pacific	1	17	.056	3	27	.100

Tournament: **Fresno State d. UNLV 51-49**
Tournament MVP: **Richie Adams**, UNLV

PAC-10

	Conference			Overall		
	W	L	PCT	W	L	PCT
Washington⊕	15	3	.833	24	7	.774
Oregon State○	15	3	.833	22	7	.759
Oregon□	11	7	.611	16	13	.552
UCLA	10	8	.556	17	11	.607
Stanford	8	10	.444	19	12	.613
Arizona State	8	10	.444	13	15	.464
Arizona	8	10	.444	11	17	.393
Southern California	6	12	.333	11	20	.355
California	5	13	.278	12	16	.429
Washington State	4	14	.222	10	18	.357

SEC

	Conference			Overall		
	W	L	PCT	W	L	PCT
Kentucky⊕	14	4	.778	29	5	.853
Auburn○	12	6	.667	20	11	.645
LSU○	11	7	.611	18	11	.621
Florida□	11	7	.611	16	13	.552
Alabama○	10	8	.556	18	12	.600
Tennessee□	9	9	.500	21	14	.600
Georgia□	8	10	.444	17	13	.567
Vanderbilt	8	10	.444	14	15	.483
Mississippi State	4	14	.222	9	19	.321
Mississippi	3	15	.167	8	20	.286

Tournament: **Kentucky d. Auburn 51-49**
Tournament MVP: **Charles Barkley**, Auburn

SOUTHERN

	Conference			Overall		
	W	L	PCT	W	L	PCT
Marshall⊕	13	3	.813	25	6	.806
Chattanooga□	12	4	.750	24	7	.774
Western Carolina	9	7	.563	15	13	.536
The Citadel	8	8	.500	14	14	.500
Appalachian State	8	8	.500	13	16	.448
Furman	7	9	.438	12	17	.414
East Tennessee State	6	10	.375	9	19	.321
Davidson	5	11	.313	9	19	.321
VMI	4	12	.250	8	19	.296

Tournament: **Marshall d. Appalachian St. 111-107 (2OT)**
Tournament MOP: **LaVerne Evans**, Marshall

SOUTHLAND

	Conference			Overall		
	W	L	PCT	W	L	PCT
Lamar□	11	1	.917	26	5	.839
UL-Monroe	9	3	.750	17	12	.586
Louisiana Tech⊕	8	4	.667	26	7	.788
McNeese State	6	6	.500	16	15	.516
Arkansas State	4	8	.333	13	15	.464
North Texas	3	9	.250	9	19	.321
Texas-Arlington	1	11	.083	5	23	.179

Tournament: **Louisiana Tech d. Lamar 68-65**
Tournament MVP: **Willie Simmons**, Louisiana Tech

SOUTHWEST

	Conference			Overall		
	W	L	PCT	W	L	PCT
Houston⊕	15	1	.938	32	5	.865
Arkansas○	14	2	.875	25	7	.781
SMU○	12	4	.750	25	8	.758
Texas Tech	10	6	.625	17	12	.586
Texas A&M	7	9	.438	16	14	.533
Rice	6	10	.375	13	17	.433
TCU	4	12	.250	11	17	.393
Texas	3	13	.188	7	21	.250
Baylor	1	15	.063	5	23	.179

Tournament: **Houston d. Arkansas 57-56**
Tournament MVP: **Hakeem Olajuwon**, Houston

SWAC

	Conference			Overall		
	W	L	PCT	W	L	PCT
Alabama State	11	3	.786	22	6	.786
Alcorn State⊕	11	3	.786	21	10	.677
Southern U.	10	4	.714	16	12	.571
Grambling	7	7	.500	17	12	.586
Mississippi Valley State	6	8	.429	15	13	.536
Texas Southern	6	8	.429	12	17	.414
Jackson State	5	9	.357	10	18	.357
Prairie View A&M	0	14	.000	2	26	.071

Tournament: **Alcorn State d. Texas Southern 78-69**
Tournament MVP: **Michael Phelps**, Alcorn State

SUN BELT

	Conference			Overall		
	W	L	PCT	W	L	PCT
VCU○	11	3	.786	23	7	.767
South Alabama□	9	5	.643	22	8	.733
Old Dominion□	9	5	.643	19	12	.613
South Florida	9	5	.643	17	11	.607
UAB⊕	8	6	.571	23	11	.676
Western Kentucky	5	9	.357	12	17	.414
Jacksonville	3	11	.214	12	16	.429
Charlotte	2	12	.143	9	19	.321

Tournament: **UAB d. Old Dominion 62-60**
Tournament MVP: **McKinley Singleton**, UAB

TAAC

	Conference			Overall		
	W	L	PCT	W	L	PCT
Houston Baptist⊕	11	3	.786	24	7	.774
Samford	10	4	.714	22	8	.733
Ga. Southern	8	6	.571	16	12	.571
Arkansas-Little Rock	7	7	.500	14	15	.483
Centenary	7	7	.500	12	16	.429
Mercer	6	8	.429	14	14	.500
Hardin-Simmons	5	9	.357	9	21	.300
Northwestern St. (LA)	2	12	.143	6	22	.214
Nicholls State*	-	-	-	19	7	.731
Georgia State*	-	-	-	6	22	.214

*Ineligible for conference competition
Tournament: **Houston Baptist d. Samford 81-76**
Tournament MVP: **Craig Beard**, Samford

WCAC

	Conference			Overall		
	W	L	PCT	W	L	PCT
San Diego⊕	9	3	.750	18	10	.643
Santa Clara□	7	5	.583	22	10	.688
Saint Mary's (CA)	7	5	.583	12	16	.429
Gonzaga	6	6	.500	17	11	.607
Pepperdine	6	6	.500	15	13	.536
Loyola Marymount	5	7	.417	12	15	.444
Portland	2	10	.167	11	17	.393

WAC

	Conference			Overall		
	W	L	PCT	W	L	PCT
UTEP⊕	13	3	.813	27	4	.871
BYU○	12	4	.750	20	11	.645
New Mexico□	10	6	.625	24	11	.686
Wyoming	9	7	.563	17	13	.567
Colorado State	9	7	.563	16	14	.533
San Diego State	6	10	.375	15	13	.536
Hawaii	6	10	.375	12	16	.429
Utah	4	12	.250	11	19	.367
Air Force	3	13	.188	8	19	.296

Tournament: **UTEP d. New Mexico 44-38**
Tournament MVP: **Juden Smith**, UTEP

INDEPENDENTS

	Overall		
	W	L	PCT
DePaul○	27	3	.900
UTSA	20	8	.714
UL-Lafayette□	23	10	.697
Stetson	19	9	.679
Dayton○	21	11	.656
Notre Dame□	21	12	.636
Marquette□	17	13	.567
Charleston Southern	15	13	.536
New Orleans	14	14	.500
Texas-Pan American	13	14	.481
Tennessee State	12	15	.444
Utica	11	15	.423
Southeastern Louisiana	11	17	.393
UNC Wilmington	11	17	.393
Campbell	10	18	.357
Brooklyn	8	20	.286
Monmouth	6	21	.222
Eastern Washington	4	22	.154
U.S. International	2	26	.071

INDIVIDUAL LEADERS—SEASON

SCORING	CL	POS	G	FG	FT	PTS	PPG
1 **Joe Jakubick**, Akron	SR	G	27	304	206	814	**30.1**
2 **Lewis Jackson**, Alabama State	SR	G	28	305	202	812	**29.0**
3 **Devin Durrant**, BYU	SR	F	31	312	242	866	**27.9**
4 **Alfredrick Hughes**, Loyola-Chicago	JR	G/F	29	326	148	800	**27.6**
5 **Wayman Tisdale**, Oklahoma	SO	F/C	34	369	181	919	**27.0**
6 **Joe Dumars**, McNeese State	JR	G	31	275	267	817	**26.4**
7 **Brett Crawford**, U.S. International	JR	F	25	257	100	614	**24.6**
8 **Michael Cage**, San Diego State	SR	F	28	250	186	686	**24.5**
9 **Steve Burtt Sr.**, Iona	SR	G	31	309	131	749	**24.2**
10 **Leon Wood**, Cal State Fullerton	SR	G	30	254	211	719	**24.0**

FIELD GOAL PCT	CL	POS	G	FG	FGA	PCT
1 **Hakeem Olajuwon**, Houston	JR	C	37	249	369	**67.5**
2 **Bobby Lee Hurt**, Alabama	JR	F	30	168	253	**66.4**
3 **Patrick Ewing**, Georgetown	JR	C	37	242	368	**65.8**
4 **A.C. Green**, Oregon State	JR	F	23	134	204	**65.7**
5 **Keith Walker**, Utica	JR	F	25	125	191	**65.4**

Minimum: 5 made per game

FREE THROW PCT	CL	POS	G	FT	FTA	PCT
1 **Steve Alford**, Indiana	FR	G	31	137	150	**91.3**
2 **Joe Carrabino**, Harvard	JR	F	26	153	169	**90.5**
3 **Chris Mullin**, St. John's	JR	G/F	27	169	187	**90.4**
4 **Bob Ferry**, Harvard	JR	G	24	84	93	**90.3**
5 **Vince Cunningham**, Texas-San Antonio	JR	G	27	94	107	**87.9**

Minimum: 2.5 made per game

ASSISTS PER GAME	CL	POS	G	AST	APG
1 **Craig Lathen**, Illinois-Chicago	JR	G	29	274	**9.4**
2 **Danny Tarkanian**, UNLV	SR	G	34	289	**8.5**
3 **Reid Gettys**, Houston	JR	G	37	309	**8.4**
4 **Andre LaFleur**, Northeastern	FR	G	32	252	**7.9**
5 **Tony William**, Florida State	SR	G	28	215	**7.7**
6 **Shawn Teague**, Boston U.	JR	G	29	218	**7.5**
7 **Robbie Weingard**, Hofstra	JR	G	28	208	**7.4**
8 **Carl Smith**, Massachusetts	FR	G	29	212	**7.3**
9 **Jim Les**, Bradley	SO	G	22	158	**7.2**
10 **John Stockton**, Gonzaga	SR	G	28	201	**7.2**

REBOUNDS PER GAME	CL	POS	G	REB	RPG
1 **Hakeem Olajuwon**, Houston	JR	C	37	500	**13.5**
2 **Carey Scurry**, Long Island	JR	F	31	418	**13.5**
3 **Xavier McDaniel**, Wichita State	JR	F	30	393	**13.1**
4 **Donald Newman**, Arkansas-Little Rock	SR	F/C	27	348	**12.9**
5 **Michael Cage**, San Diego State	SR	F	28	352	**12.6**
6 **Jeff Cross**, Maine	SR	F	27	339	**12.6**
7 **Mike Brown**, George Washington	JR	F/C	29	351	**12.1**
8 **Robert Sanders**, Mississippi Valley State	SR	F	28	338	**12.1**
9 **Joe Binion**, NC A&T	SR	F	29	335	**11.6**
10 **Jon Koncak**, SMU	JR	C	33	378	**11.5**

INDIVIDUAL LEADERS—GAME

POINTS	CL	POS	OPP	DATE	PTS
1 **Wayman Tisdale**, Oklahoma	SO	F/C	UTSA	D28	**61**
2 **Napoleon Johnson**, Grambling	SR	C	Alabama State	F3	**52**
3 **Tony Costner**, Saint Joseph's	SR	F/C	Alaska-Anchorage	D30	**47**
4 **Vern Fleming**, Georgia	SR	G	Vanderbilt	F27	**44**
5 **Brett Crawford**, U.S. International	JR	F	Stanford	J2	**43**
Carey Scurry, Long Island	JR	F	Loyola (MD)	F18	**43**
7 **Alfredrick Hughes**, Loyola-Chicago	JR	G/F	DePaul	F15	**42**
Derrick Gervin, Tex.-San Antonio	JR	F	Texas State	F27	**42**
Brett Crawford, U.S. International	JR	F	Miss. Valley State	M1	**42**
Joe Jakubick, Akron	SR	G	Illinois-Chicago	M3	**42**

REBOUNDS	CL	POS	OPP	DATE	REB
1 **Donald Newman**, Ark.-Little Rock	SR	F/C	Centenary	J26	**29**
2 **Hakeem Olajuwon**, Houston	JR	C	Texas Tech	J12	**25**
3 **Carey Scurry**, Long Island	JR	F	Saint Francis (PA)	J21	**23**
Xavier McDaniel, Wichita State	JR	F	Illinois State	J26	**23**
Xavier McDaniel, Wichita State	JR	F	Texas State	F6	**23**

TEAM LEADERS—SEASON

WIN-LOSS PCT	W	L	PCT
1 **Georgetown**	34	3	**.919**
2 **North Carolina**	28	3	**.903**
3 **DePaul**	27	3	**.900**
4 **UTEP**	27	4	**.871**
Tulsa	27	4	**.871**

SCORING OFFENSE	G	W-L	PTS	PPG
1 **Tulsa**	31	27-4	2,816	**90.8**
2 **Alabama State**	28	22-6	2,485	**88.8**
3 **Oklahoma**	34	29-5	2,953	**86.9**
4 **Marshall**	31	25-6	2,589	**83.5**
5 **Oral Roberts**	31	21-10	2,569	**82.9**

SCORING MARGIN	G	W-L	PPG	OPP PPG	MAR
1 **Georgetown**	37	34-3	74.3	57.9	**16.4**
2 **North Carolina**	31	28-3	80.1	64.8	**15.3**
3 **Oklahoma**	34	29-5	86.9	72.6	**14.3**
4 **Lamar**	31	26-5	78.5	64.8	**13.7**
5 **UNLV**	35	29-6	82.1	68.7	**13.4**

FIELD GOAL PCT	G	W-L	FG	FGA	PCT
1 **Houston Baptist**	31	24-7	797	1,445	**55.2**
2 **North Carolina**	31	28-3	966	1,779	**54.3**
3 **SMU**	33	25-8	1,023	1,892	**54.1**
4 **Navy**	32	24-8	873	1,616	**54.0**
5 **Maryland**	32	24-8	941	1,745	**53.9**

FREE THROW PCT	G	W-L	FT	FTA	PCT
1 **Harvard**	26	15-11	535	651	**82.2**
2 **North Carolina**	31	28-3	551	704	**78.3**
3 **Illinois State**	31	23-8	510	659	**77.4**
4 **Fairfield**	28	10-18	508	657	**77.3**
5 **Saint Louis**	28	12-16	400	521	**76.8**

REBOUND MARGIN	G	W-L	RPG	OPP RPG	MAR
1 **Northeastern**	32	27-5	40.1	30.3	**9.8**
2 **Georgetown**	37	34-3	40.0	30.5	**9.5**
3 **Saint Joseph's**	29	20-9	39.4	30.3	**9.1**
4 **Auburn**	31	20-11	36.9	28.5	**8.4**
5 **George Washington**	29	17-12	38.3	30.8	**7.5**

SCORING DEFENSE	G	W-L	OPP PTS	OPP PPG
1 **Princeton**	28	18-10	1,403	**50.1**
2 **Fresno State**	33	25-8	1,802	**54.6**
3 **Tulane**	28	17-11	1,535	**54.8**
4 **Oregon State**	29	22-7	1,618	**55.8**
5 **Illinois**	31	26-5	1,737	**56.0**

FIELD GOAL PCT DEFENSE	G	W-L	OPP FG	OPP FGA	OPP PCT
1 **Georgetown**	37	34-3	799	2,025	**39.5**
2 **DePaul**	30	27-3	687	1,658	**41.4**
3 **Memphis**	33	26-7	796	1,904	**41.8**
4 **Kentucky**	34	29-5	796	1,894	**42.0**
5 **Southern U.**	28	16-12	746	1,768	**42.2**

CONSENSUS ALL-AMERICAS

FIRST TEAM

PLAYER	CL	POS	HT	SCHOOL	RPG	PPG
Patrick Ewing	JR	C	7-0	Georgetown	10.0	16.4
Michael Jordan	JR	G	6-6	North Carolina	5.3	19.6
Hakeem Olajuwon	JR	C	7-0	Houston	13.5	16.8
Sam Perkins	SR	F/C	6-9	North Carolina	9.6	17.6
Wayman Tisdale	SO	F/C	6-9	Oklahoma	9.7	27.0

SECOND TEAM

PLAYER	CL	POS	HT	SCHOOL	RPG	PPG
Michael Cage	SR	F	6-9	San Diego State	12.6	24.5
Devin Durrant	SR	F	6-7	BYU	5.2	27.9
Keith Lee	JR	C	6-10	Memphis	10.8	18.4
Chris Mullin	JR	G/F	6-6	St. John's	4.4	22.9
Mel Turpin	SR	C	6-11	Kentucky	6.4	15.2
Leon Wood	SR	G	6-3	Cal St. Fullerton	2.6	24.0

SELECTORS: AP, NABC, UPI, USBWA

AWARD WINNERS

PLAYER OF THE YEAR

PLAYER	CL	POS	HT	SCHOOL	AWARDS
Michael Jordan	JR	G	6-6	North Carolina	Naismith, AP, UPI, USBWA, Wooden, NABC, Rupp
Ricky Stokes	SR	G	5-10	Virginia	Frances Pomeroy Naismith*

* FOR THE MOST OUTSTANDING SENIOR PLAYER WHO IS 6 FEET OR UNDER

COACH OF THE YEAR

COACH	SCHOOL	REC	AWARDS
Ray Meyer	DePaul	27-3	AP, UPI
Gene Keady	Purdue	22-7	USBWA, CBS/Chevrolet
Marv Harshman	Washington	24-7	NABC
John Thompson Jr.	Georgetown	34-3	Sporting News

BOB GIBBONS' TOP HIGH SCHOOL SENIOR RECRUITS

PLAYER	POS	HT	HIGH SCHOOL	A-A TEAMS	COLLEGE	CAREER NOTES
1 **Danny Manning**	F	6-10	Lawrence (KS) HS	McD, P, USA	Kansas	National POY, '88; NCAA Tournament MOP, '88; No. 1 pick, '88 NBA draft (Clippers); 14.0 ppg (15 seasons); 2-time All-Star
2 **John Williams**	F	6-8	Crenshaw HS, Los Angeles	McD, P, USA	LSU	15.8 ppg, 7.6 rpg (2 seasons); No. 12 pick, '86 NBA draft (Bullets); 10.1 ppg (8 seasons)
3 **Cedric Henderson**	F	6-9	Marietta HS, Atlanta		Georgia	15.5 ppg (1 season); 2nd-round pick, '86 NBA draft (Hawks); played in 8 NBA games
4 **Delray Brooks**	2G	6-4	Rogers HS, Michigan City, IN	McD, P, USA	Indiana/Providence	Transferred after 2 years; For PC, 14.4 ppg in '87 Final Four run; undrafted
5 **Chris Washburn**	C	6-11	Laurinburg (NC) Institute	McD, P, USA	North Carolina State	16.4 ppg (2 seasons); No. 3 pick, '86 NBA draft (Warriors); Played in 72 NBA games
6 **Kevin Walls**	PG	6-2	Camden (NJ) HS	McD, P, USA	Louisville	NCAA title, '86; benched by Denny Crum in '87, quit team
7 **Gary Grant**	PG	6-3	McKinley HS, Canton, Ohio	McD, P	Michigan	2,222 points, 731 assists (4 seasons); No. 15 pick, '88 NBA draft (Sonics); 7.9 ppg, 5.5 apg (13 seasons)
8 **Troy Lewis**	2G	6-4	Anderson (IN) HS	McD, P	Purdue	2-time All-Big Ten; at Purdue, 16.4 ppg (4 seasons); undrafted
9 **Al Lorenzen**	F	6-9	Kennedy HS, Cedar Rapids, IA	McD, P	Iowa	Iowa Mr. Basketball, '84; at Iowa, 6.6 ppg (3 seasons); played overseas
10 **Derrick Lewis**	F	6-7	Archbishop Carroll HS, Washington, DC	McD, P	Maryland	Maryland's all-time blocks leader (339); 11.5 ppg, 7.5 rpg (4 seasons); 3rd-round pick in '88 NBA draft (Bulls)
11 **Duane Ferrell**	SF	6-6	Calvert Hall HS, Towson, MD	McD, P	Georgia Tech	14.3 ppg (4 seasons); undrafted; 6.4 ppg in NBA (11 seasons)
12 **Chris Sandle**	SF	6-7	Poly HS, Long Beach, CA	McD, P	Arizona State/UTEP	Transferred to UTEP after 2 years; 17.1 ppg as senior.; played overseas
13 **David Rivers**	PG	5-11	St. Anthony HS, Jersey City, NJ	McD, P	Notre Dame	2-time All-America; ND 2nd all-time assists leader; No. 25 pick, '88 NBA draft (Lakers); 3.4 ppg (3 seasons)
14 **Charles Smith**	PF	6-9	Warren Harding HS, Bridgeport, CT	McD, P	Pittsburgh	Big East POY, '88; No. 3 pick, '88 NBA draft (76ers); 14.4 ppg, 5.8 rpg (9 seasons)
15 **Ed Davender**	2G	6-2	Boys & Girls HS, Brooklyn, NY	McD, P	Kentucky	1,637 points (4 seasons); 3rd-round pick, '88 NBA draft
16 **Michael Brown**	2G	6-4	Dunbar HS, Baltimore	McD, P	Syracuse/Clemson	Transferred after 1 year; sharpshooter off bench; undrafted
17 **Roger McClendon**	2G	6-5	Centennial HS, Champaign, IL	McD, P	Cincinnati	Cincinnati's 4th all-time leading scorer (1,789 points); undrafted
18 **Craig McMillan**	2G	6-6	Cloverdale (CA) HS	McD, P	Arizona	9.2 ppg (4 seasons); Final Four, '88; undrafted
19 **Shelton Jones**	F	6-8	Amityville (NY) Memorial HS	McD	St. John's	18.6 ppg, 8.8 rpg as senior; 2nd-round pick, '88 NBA draft (Spurs); played in 51 NBA games
20 **Cedric Jenkins**	F	6-9	Terrell County HS, Dawson, GA	McD, P	Kentucky	Scored 271 points (4 seasons); undrafted

OTHER STANDOUTS

PLAYER	POS	HT	HIGH SCHOOL	A-A TEAMS	COLLEGE	CAREER NOTES
21 **Derrick Chievous**	SF	6-6	Holy Cross HS, Flushing, NY	McD, P	Missouri	19.8 ppg, 7.5 rpg (4 seasons); UM's all-time leading scorer (2,580 pts); No. 16 pick, '88 NBA draft (Rockets); 7.1 ppg (3 seasons)
51 **Vernon Maxwell**	2G	6-3	Buchholz HS, Gainesville, FL		Florida	16.6 ppg as Soph.; 2nd-round pick, '88 NBA draft (Nuggets); 12.8 ppg (13 seasons); 2 NBA titles
67 **Mark Plansky**	SF	6-7	Wakefield (MA) HS		Villanova	NCAA title, '85; at Villanova, 9.1 ppg (4 seasons); undrafted

Abbreviations: McD=McDonald's; P=Parade; USA=USA Today

Poll Progression

Preseason Poll

AP	SCHOOL
1	North Carolina
2	Kentucky
3	Houston
4	Georgetown
5	Memphis
6	Louisville
7	Iowa
8	Maryland
9	UCLA
10	Oregon State
11	LSU
12	Michigan State
13	Fresno State
14	Arkansas
15	Boston College
16	Georgia
17	Kansas
18	DePaul
19	Indiana
20	Oklahoma

Week of Nov 29

AP	SCHOOL	AP↓↑
1	**Kentucky** (1-0) Ⓐ	↑1
2	**North Carolina** (1-0)	↓1
3	**Georgetown** (2-0)	↑1
4	**Memphis** (2-0)	↑1
5	**Iowa** (1-0)	↑2
6	**Maryland** (1-0)	↑2
7	**NC State** (4-0)	⤴
8	**Houston** (1-1)	↓5
9	**UCLA** (2-0)	
10	**Oregon State** (0-0)	
11	**Michigan State** (2-0)	↑1
12	**LSU** (1-0)	↓1
13	**Georgia** (2-0)	↑3
14	**Arkansas** (2-1)	
15	**Boston College** (0-0)	
16	**DePaul** (1-0)	↑2
17	**Fresno State** (1-1)	↓4
18	**Wichita State** (1-0)	⤴
19	**St. John's** (2-0)	⤴
20	**VCU** (0-0)	⤴

Week of Dec 6

AP	UPI	SCHOOL	AP↓↑
1	2	**North Carolina** (4-0)	↑1
2	1	**Kentucky** (2-0)	↓1
3	3	**Georgetown** (4-0)	
4	4	**Memphis** (4-0)	
5	5	**Iowa** (3-0)	
6	6	**Houston** (3-1)	↑2
7	7	**UCLA** (3-0)	↑2
8	13	**NC State** (5-1)	↓1
9	9	**LSU** (4-0)	↑3
10	8	**Georgia** (3-0)	↑3
11	15	**Maryland** (2-1)	↓5
12	12	**Boston College** (3-0)	↑3
13	14	**DePaul** (3-0)	↑3
14	18	**Wichita State** (4-0)	↑4
15	16	**Arkansas** (3-1)	↓1
16	10	**St. John's** (3-0)	↑3
17	20	**Michigan State** (3-1)	↓6
18	17	**Oregon State** (1-1)	↓8
19	11	**Purdue** (5-0)	⤴
20	—	**Fresno State** (3-1)	↓3
—	19	**Ohio State** (3-0)	

Week of Dec 13

AP	UPI	SCHOOL	AP
1	2	**North Carolina** (5-0)	
2	1	**Kentucky** (3-0)	
3	3	**Houston** (5-1)	↑
4	4	**DePaul** (5-0)	↑
5	5	**Georgetown** (5-1) Ⓑ	↓
6	6	**NC State** (7-1)	↑
6	8	**Memphis** (4-1)	↓
8	9	**Boston College** (5-0)	↑
9	11	**Maryland** (4-1)	↑
10	13	**LSU** (4-1)	↓1
11	7	**Purdue** (6-0)	↑8
12	10	**Georgia** (5-1)	↓2
13	12	**St. John's** (4-0)	↑3
14	14	**Oregon State** (2-1)	↑4
15	17	**UCLA** (3-1)	↓8
16	16	**Louisville** (2-2)	⤴
17	19	**Michigan State** (3-1)	
18	20	**Iowa** (3-2)	↓13
19	—	**Wake Forest** (5-0)	⤴
20	15	**UTEP** (5-0)	⤴
—	18	**Michigan** (3-1)	

Week of Dec 20

AP	UPI	SCHOOL	AP↓↑
1	2	**North Carolina** (5-0)	
2	1	**Kentucky** (5-0) Ⓒ	
3	3	**Houston** (7-1)	
4	4	**DePaul** (7-0)	
5	5	**Georgetown** (7-1)	
6	6	**Boston College** (7-0)	↑2
7	7	**Purdue** (7-0)	↑4
8	11	**Maryland** (5-1)	↑1
9	9	**UCLA** (4-1)	↑6
10	8	**Louisville** (4-2) Ⓓ	↑6
11	13	**LSU** (4-1)	↓1
12	10	**St. John's** (6-0)	↑1
13	18	**NC State** (7-2)	↓7
14	12	**Georgia** (6-1)	↓2
15	14	**Oregon State** (4-1)	↓1
16	17	**Memphis** (5-2)	↓10
17	20	**Wake Forest** (5-0)	↑2
18	16	**UTEP** (6-0)	↑2
19	19	**Michigan State** (5-1)	↓2
20	15	**Michigan** (7-0)	⤴

Week of Dec 27

AP	UPI	SCHOOL	AP↓↑
1	2	**North Carolina** (6-0)	
2	1	**Kentucky** (7-0)	
3	3	**Houston** (10-1)	
4	4	**DePaul** (8-0)	
5	5	**Georgetown** (8-1)	
6	6	**Maryland** (6-1)	↑2
7	8	**UCLA** (6-1)	↑2
8	7	**St. John's** (7-0)	↑4
9	9	**LSU** (6-1)	↑2
10	11	**Wake Forest** (6-0)	↑7
11	13	**Georgia** (7-1)	↑3
12	18	**Boston College** (7-1)	↓6
13	17	**NC State** (8-2)	
14	14	**Louisville** (4-3)	↓4
15	14	**Michigan** (8-0)	↑5
16	10	**UTEP** (8-0)	↑2
17	11	**Memphis** (6-2)	↓1
18	19	**Purdue** (7-2)	↓11
19	—	**Oregon State** (4-2)	↓4
20	16	**Illinois** (8-1)	⤴
—	20	**Arkansas** (7-2)	

Week of Jan 3

AP	UPI	SCHOOL	AP↓↑
1	2	**North Carolina** (8-0)	
2	1	**Kentucky** (8-0)	
3	3	**DePaul** (9-0)	↑1
4	4	**Georgetown** (10-1)	↑1
5	6	**Maryland** (8-1)	↑1
6	8	**UCLA** (7-1)	↑1
7	5	**Houston** (10-2)	↓4
8	9	**Wake Forest** (9-0)	↑2
9	14	**LSU** (7-1)	
10	7	**UTEP** (11-0)	↑6
11	11	**Georgia** (7-1)	
12	12	**NC State** (10-2)	↑1
13	10	**St. John's** (8-1)	↓5
14	13	**Illinois** (9-1)	↑6
15	16	**Oregon State** (7-2)	↑4
16	15	**Fresno State** (10-2)	⤴
17	—	**Boston College** (8-2)	↓5
18	18	**UNLV** (9-1)	⤴
19	19	**Memphis** (8-3)	↓2
20	—	**Virginia** (9-0)	⤴
—	17	**Iowa** (7-2)	
—	20	**Louisville** (5-4)	⤵

Week of Jan 10

AP	UPI	SCHOOL	AP↓↑
1	2	**North Carolina** (10-0)	
2	1	**Kentucky** (10-0)	
3	3	**DePaul** (11-0)	
4	4	**Georgetown** (12-1)	
5	6	**Maryland** (10-1)	
6	7	**UCLA** (9-1)	
7	5	**Houston** (12-2)	
8	8	**UTEP** (13-0)	↑2
9	10	**Illinois** (11-1)	↑5
10	9	**St. John's** (10-1)	↑3
11	17	**LSU** (8-2)	↓2
12	13	**Wake Forest** (10-1)	↓4
13	11	**Fresno State** (11-2)	↑3
14	12	**UNLV** (10-1)	↑4
15	18	**Georgia** (8-2)	↓4
16	14	**Oregon State** (8-2)	↓1
17	15	**Oklahoma** (12-1)	⤴
18	20	**Boston College** (10-2)	↓1
19	—	**Memphis** (10-3)	
20	16	**Tulsa** (13-0)	⤴
—	19	**Arkansas** (11-2)	

Week of Jan 17

AP	UPI	SCHOOL	AP↓↑
1	1	**North Carolina** (12-0)	
2	2	**DePaul** (13-0)	↑1
3	3	**Kentucky** (12-1)	↓1
4	5	**Houston** (16-2)	↑3
5	4	**UTEP** (14-0)	↑3
6	6	**Georgetown** (13-2)	↓2
7	7	**Maryland** (11-2)	↓2
8	8	**UNLV** (14-1)	↑6
9	11	**UCLA** (10-2)	↓3
10	9	**Illinois** (12-2)	↓1
11	10	**Oregon State** (9-2)	↑5
12	13	**Wake Forest** (11-2)	
13	12	**Tulsa** (15-0)	↑7
14	16	**St. John's** (11-3)	↓4
15	18	**LSU** (10-3)	↓4
16	20	**Boston College** (11-3)	↑2
17	15	**Fresno State** (12-2)	↓4
18	—	**Memphis** (11-3)	↑1
19	14	**Purdue** (11-3)	⤴
20	17	**Oklahoma** (13-2)	↓3
—	19	**Arkansas** (13-2)	

Week of Jan 24

AP	UPI	SCHOOL	AP↓↑
1	1	**North Carolina** (14-0)	
2	2	**DePaul** (14-0)	
3	3	**Kentucky** (14-2)	
4	4	**Georgetown** (15-2)	↑2
5	5	**Maryland** (13-2)	↑2
6	9	**UNLV** (16-1)	↑2
7	6	**Houston** (16-3)	↓3
8	8	**UTEP** (16-1)	↓3
9	7	**Illinois** (13-2)	↑1
10	14	**LSU** (11-3)	↑5
11	12	**Oklahoma** (15-2)	↑9
12	13	**Tulsa** (16-1)	↑1
13	15	**Memphis** (12-3)	↑5
14	10	**Louisville** (11-4)	⤴
15	16	**UCLA** (11-3)	↓6
16	11	**Arkansas** (15-2)	⤴
17	17	**Wake Forest** (12-3)	↓5
18	18	**Georgia** (12-3)	⤴
19	—	**Virginia** (12-2)	⤴
20	—	**Syracuse** (12-3)	⤴
—	19	**Washington** (13-3)	
—	20	**Oregon State** (9-4)	⤵

Week of Jan 31

AP	UPI	SCHOOL	AP↓↑
1	1	**North Carolina** (17-0)	
2	2	**DePaul** (16-0)	
3	3	**Kentucky** (15-2)	
4	4	**Georgetown** (17-2)	
5	6	**UNLV** (18-1)	↑1
6	5	**Houston** (17-3)	↑1
7	8	**UTEP** (18-1)	↑1
8	7	**Illinois** (15-2)	↑1
9	11	**Memphis** (14-3)	↑4
10	9	**Maryland** (13-3)	↓5
11	10	**Tulsa** (17-1)	↑1
12	13	**Oklahoma** (16-3)	↓1
13	12	**Syracuse** (14-3)	↑7
14	16	**LSU** (12-5)	↓4
15	15	**Wake Forest** (13-4)	↑2
16	14	**Purdue** (13-4)	⤴
17	19	**Louisville** (12-5)	↓3
18	—	**Georgia Tech** (14-3)	⤴
19	17	**Auburn** (12-5)	⤴
20	—	**UCLA** (12-4)	↓5
—	18	**Arkansas** (15-4)	⤵
—	20	**Oregon State** (12-4)	

Week of Feb 7

AP	UPI	SCHOOL	AP↓↑
1	1	**North Carolina** (20-0)	
2	2	**DePaul** (17-0)	
3	3	**Georgetown** (19-2)	↑1
4	5	**UNLV** (20-1)	↑1
5	4	**Houston** (19-3)	↑1
6	8	**Kentucky** (16-3)	↓3
7	6	**UTEP** (20-1)	
8	6	**Illinois** (17-2)	
9	9	**Memphis** (16-3)	
10	10	**Oklahoma** (18-3)	↑2
11	11	**Purdue** (15-4)	↑5
12	12	**Tulsa** (18-2)	↓1
13	13	**Maryland** (14-4)	↓3
14	17	**Wake Forest** (15-4)	↑1
15	15	**Louisville** (15-5)	↑2
16	14	**Auburn** (14-5)	↑3
17	16	**Washington** (15-4)	⤴
18	—	**Georgia Tech** (15-5)	
19	18	**Syracuse** (14-5)	↓6
20	—	**LSU** (13-5)	↓6
—	19	**Arkansas** (16-4)	
—	20	**Temple** (16-2)	

Week of Feb 14

AP	UPI	SCHOOL	AP↓↑
[illegible]	1	**North Carolina** (21-1) (E)	
[illegible]	2	**Georgetown** (21-2)	↑1
[illegible]	3	**DePaul** (18-1)	↓1
[illegible]	4	**Houston** (21-3)	↑1
[illegible]	5	**UNLV** (22-1)	↓1
[illegible]	6	**Kentucky** (18-3)	
[illegible]	7	**Illinois** (19-2)	↑1
[illegible]	9	**Memphis** (17-3)	↑1
[illegible]	10	**Oklahoma** (20-3)	↑1
[illegible]	8	**UTEP** (21-2)	↓3
[illegible]	11	**Purdue** (17-4)	
2	12	**Tulsa** (20-2)	
3	15	**Wake Forest** (17-4)	↑1
4	13	**Arkansas** (19-4) (E)	⤴
5	14	**Washington** (17-4)	↑2
6	—	**Syracuse** (15-5)	↑3
7	20	**Indiana** (16-5)	⤴
7	—	**LSU** (15-5)	↑3
9	—	**Duke** (19-5)	⤴
20	17	**Temple** (18-2)	⤴
—	16	**Auburn** (14-6)	⤵
—	17	**Illinois State** (17-4)	
—	17	**Maryland** (14-6)	⤵

Week of Feb 21

AP	UPI	SCHOOL	AP↓↑
1	1	**North Carolina** (23-1)	
2	2	**Georgetown** (23-2)	
3	3	**Houston** (23-3)	↑1
4	4	**Kentucky** (20-3)	↑2
5	5	**DePaul** (19-2)	↓2
6	6	**Illinois** (20-3)	↑1
7	7	**UNLV** (23-2)	↓2
8	8	**Oklahoma** (22-3)	↑1
9	9	**UTEP** (22-2)	↑1
10	10	**Tulsa** (22-2)	↑2
11	11	**Arkansas** (21-4)	↑3
12	13	**Memphis** (19-4)	↓4
13	12	**Purdue** (18-5)	↓2
14	19	**Duke** (21-5)	↑5
15	—	**Wake Forest** (18-5)	↓2
16	16	**Syracuse** (17-5)	
17	17	**Temple** (20-2)	↑3
18	14	**Washington** (18-5)	↓3
19	18	**Auburn** (16-6)	⤴
20	15	**Oregon State** (18-5)	⤴
—	20	**Illinois State** (19-4)	

Week of Feb 28

AP	UPI	SCHOOL	AP↓↑
1	1	**North Carolina** (24-1)	
2	2	**Houston** (25-3)	↑1
3	3	**Kentucky** (21-3)	↑1
4	4	**Georgetown** (24-3)	↓2
5	5	**DePaul** (21-2)	
6	7	**Oklahoma** (24-3)	↑2
7	6	**UNLV** (25-2)	
8	8	**UTEP** (24-2)	↑1
9	11	**Tulsa** (23-2)	↑1
10	10	**Illinois** (20-4)	↓4
11	9	**Purdue** (19-5)	↑2
12	12	**Arkansas** (22-5)	↓1
13	13	**Washington** (20-5)	↑5
14	14	**Memphis** (20-5)	↓2
15	18	**Duke** (22-6)	↓1
16	17	**Syracuse** (18-6)	
17	16	**Wake Forest** (19-6)	↓2
18	15	**Temple** (21-3)	↓1
19	19	**Maryland** (18-7)	⤴
20	20	**Oregon State** (19-6)	

Week of Mar 6

AP	UPI	SCHOOL	AP↓↑
1	1	**North Carolina** (26-1)	
2	2	**Georgetown** (26-3)	↑2
3	3	**Kentucky** (23-4)	
4	4	**DePaul** (24-2)	↑1
5	5	**Houston** (26-4)	↓3
6	6	**Oklahoma** (27-3)	
7	7	**Illinois** (22-4)	↑3
8	8	**Arkansas** (24-5)	↑4
9	9	**UTEP** (25-3)	↓1
10	10	**UNLV** (25-4)	↓3
11	11	**Purdue** (20-6)	
12	13	**Tulsa** (24-3)	↓3
13	12	**Washington** (21-6)	
14	14	**Maryland** (20-7)	↑5
15	15	**Temple** (24-3)	↑3
16	—	**Duke** (22-8)	↓1
17	20	**Memphis** (21-6)	↓3
18	18	**Louisville** (21-9)	⤴
19	—	**Wake Forest** (20-7)	↓2
20	17	**Oregon State** (20-6)	
—	16	**Illinois State** (21-6)	
—	19	**Weber State** (21-6)	

FINAL POLL

AP	UPI	SCHOOL	AP↓↑
1	1	**North Carolina** (27-2)	
2	2	**Georgetown** (29-3)	
3	3	**Kentucky** (26-4)	
4	4	**DePaul** (26-2) (F)	
5	5	**Houston** (28-4)	
6	6	**Illinois** (24-4)	↑1
7	8	**Oklahoma** (29-4)	↓1
8	7	**Arkansas** (24-6)	
9	9	**UTEP** (27-3)	
10	11	**Purdue** (22-6)	↑1
11	10	**Maryland** (23-7)	↑3
12	12	**Tulsa** (27-3)	
13	13	**UNLV** (27-5)	↓3
14	14	**Duke** (24-9)	↑2
15	15	**Washington** (22-6)	↓2
16	16	**Memphis** (24-6)	↑1
17	20	**Oregon State** (22-6)	↑3
18	16	**Syracuse** (22-8)	⤴
19	—	**Wake Forest** (21-8)	
20	—	**Temple** (25-4)	↓5
—	18	**Indiana** (20-8)	
—	19	**Auburn** (20-10)	

(A) Avenging an 80-68 loss in the 1983 Mideast Regional final, Kentucky crushes Louisville in Rupp Arena, 65-44. 7'1" Wildcat Sam Bowie, returning from a two-year layoff because of leg injuries, has 7 points, 10 rebounds, 5 blocks, 5 assists and 3 steals.

(B) After opening a cupcake schedule with wins over Hawaii-Hilo (twice), Morgan State, St. Francis (Pa.), and Saint Leo, Georgetown finally plays a ranked team—No. 13 DePaul—and loses 63-61.

(C) With Cincinnati's own fans in Riverfront Coliseum chanting "Bor-ing! Bor-ing!" the unranked Bearcats play stall-ball against Kentucky and still lose, 24-11. Cincinnati's points tie for the fourth-lowest total scored by one team since 1938.

(D) Before a Dec. 17 game between NC State and Louisville, CBS commentator Tom Brookshier says of the Cards, "They have a collective IQ of about 40, but they can play basketball." The network quickly apologizes. "I said a very stupid thing," Brookshier admits. Louisville beats NC State, 83-79.

(E) Arkansas' Charles Balantine hits a baseline jumper with :04 remaining to beat North Carolina, 65-64, in Pine Bluff, Ark., ending a 21-game Tar Heels winning streak. Despite the loss, UNC remains No. 1.

(F) Ray Meyer, who will turn over the coaching reins at DePaul to his son, Joey, after the season, is named Coach of the Year. Meyer's record in his 42 seasons at DePaul is 724–354.

1984 NCAA Tournament

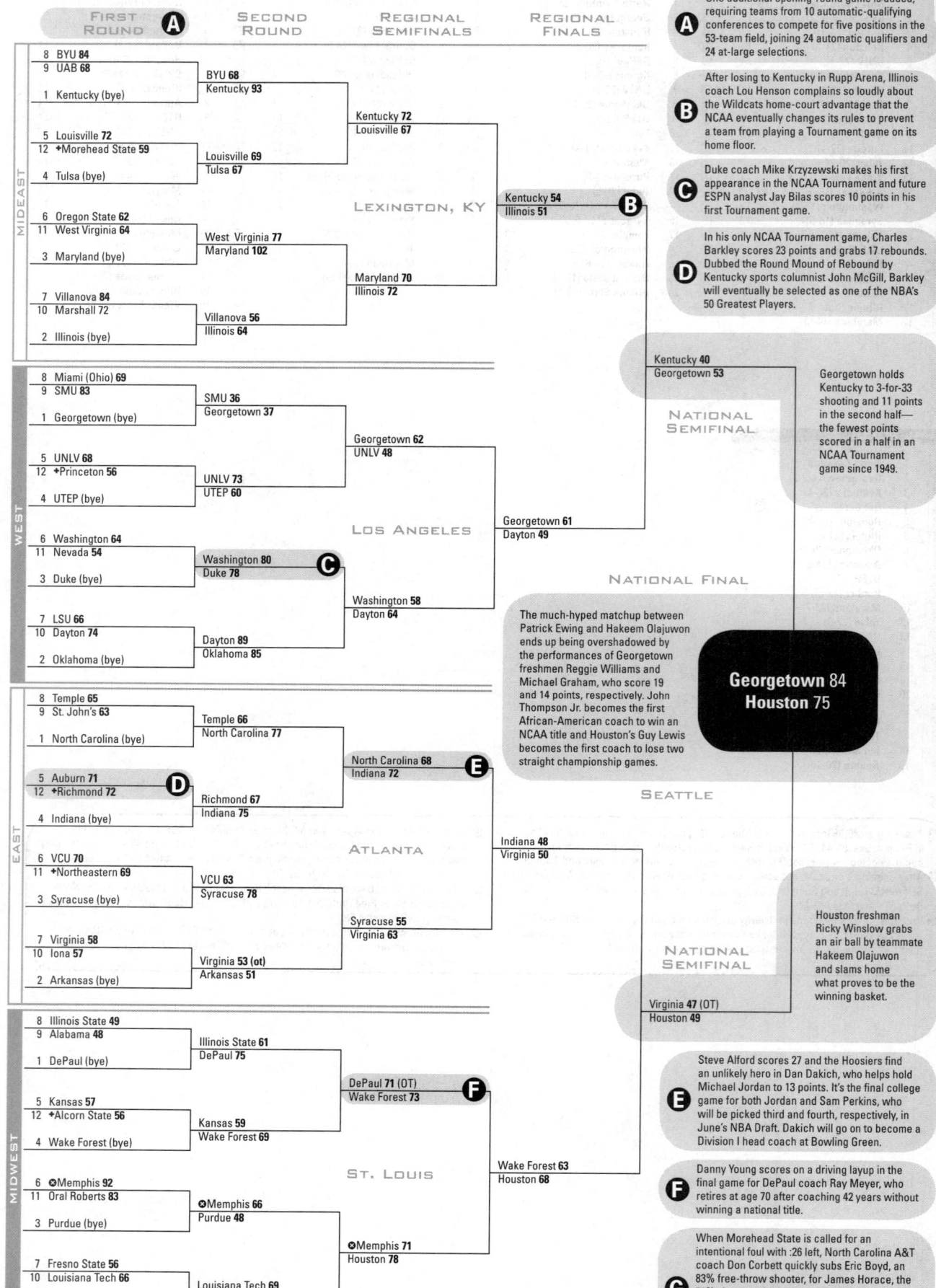

First Round (A) | Second Round | Regional Semifinals | Regional Finals

Mideast — Lexington, KY

First Round
- 8 BYU **84**, 9 UAB **68**
- 1 Kentucky (bye)
- 5 Louisville **72**, 12 +Morehead State **59**
- 4 Tulsa (bye)
- 6 Oregon State **62**, 11 West Virginia **64**
- 3 Maryland (bye)
- 7 Villanova **84**, 10 Marshall 72
- 2 Illinois (bye)

Second Round
- BYU **68**, Kentucky **93**
- Louisville **69**, Tulsa **67**
- West Virginia **77**, Maryland **102**
- Villanova **56**, Illinois **64**

Regional Semifinals
- Kentucky **72**, Louisville **67**
- Maryland **70**, Illinois **72**

Regional Final
- Kentucky **54**, Illinois **51** (B)

West — Los Angeles

First Round
- 8 Miami (Ohio) **69**, 9 SMU **83**
- 1 Georgetown (bye)
- 5 UNLV **68**, 12 +Princeton **56**
- 4 UTEP (bye)
- 6 Washington **64**, 11 Nevada **54**
- 3 Duke (bye)
- 7 LSU **66**, 10 Dayton **74**
- 2 Oklahoma (bye)

Second Round
- SMU **36**, Georgetown **37**
- UNLV **73**, UTEP **60**
- Washington **80**, Duke **78** (C)
- Dayton **89**, Oklahoma **85**

Regional Semifinals
- Georgetown **62**, UNLV **48**
- Washington **58**, Dayton **64**

Regional Final
- Georgetown **61**, Dayton **49**

East — Atlanta

First Round
- 8 Temple **65**, 9 St. John's **63**
- 1 North Carolina (bye)
- 5 Auburn **71**, 12 +Richmond **72** (D)
- 4 Indiana (bye)
- 6 VCU **70**, 11 +Northeastern **69**
- 3 Syracuse (bye)
- 7 Virginia **58**, 10 Iona **57**
- 2 Arkansas (bye)

Second Round
- Temple **66**, North Carolina **77**
- Richmond **67**, Indiana **75**
- VCU **63**, Syracuse **78**
- Virginia **53 (ot)**, Arkansas **51**

Regional Semifinals
- North Carolina **68**, Indiana **72** (E)
- Syracuse **55**, Virginia **63**

Regional Final
- Indiana **48**, Virginia **50**

Midwest — St. Louis

First Round
- 8 Illinois State **49**, 9 Alabama **48**
- 1 DePaul (bye)
- 5 Kansas **57**, 12 +Alcorn State **56**
- 4 Wake Forest (bye)
- 6 ⊗Memphis **92**, 11 Oral Roberts **83**
- 3 Purdue (bye)
- 7 Fresno State **56**, 10 Louisiana Tech **66**
- 2 Houston (bye)

Second Round
- Illinois State **61**, DePaul **75**
- Kansas **59**, Wake Forest **69**
- ⊗Memphis **66**, Purdue **48**
- Louisiana Tech **69**, Houston **77**

Regional Semifinals
- DePaul **71** (OT), Wake Forest **73** (F)
- ⊗Memphis **71**, Houston **78**

Regional Final
- Wake Forest **63**, Houston **68**

National Semifinal

- Kentucky **40**, Georgetown **53**

Georgetown holds Kentucky to 3-for-33 shooting and 11 points in the second half—the fewest points scored in a half in an NCAA Tournament game since 1949.

National Semifinal

- Virginia **47** (OT), Houston **49**

Houston freshman Ricky Winslow grabs an air ball by teammate Hakeem Olajuwon and slams home what proves to be the winning basket.

National Final — Seattle

Georgetown 84
Houston 75

The much-hyped matchup between Patrick Ewing and Hakeem Olajuwon ends up being overshadowed by the performances of Georgetown freshmen Reggie Williams and Michael Graham, who score 19 and 14 points, respectively. John Thompson Jr. becomes the first African-American coach to win an NCAA title and Houston's Guy Lewis becomes the first coach to lose two straight championship games.

(G) **+Opening round** Morehead State d. North Carolina A&T 70-69; Princeton d. San Diego 65-56; Richmond d. Rider 89-65; Northeastern d. Long Island 90-87; Alcorn State d. Houston Baptist 79-60

⊗Team participation later vacated

A One additional opening-round game is added, requiring teams from 10 automatic-qualifying conferences to compete for five positions in the 53-team field, joining 24 automatic qualifiers and 24 at-large selections.

B After losing to Kentucky in Rupp Arena, Illinois coach Lou Henson complains so loudly about the Wildcats home-court advantage that the NCAA eventually changes its rules to prevent a team from playing a Tournament game on its home floor.

C Duke coach Mike Krzyzewski makes his first appearance in the NCAA Tournament and future ESPN analyst Jay Bilas scores 10 points in his first Tournament game.

D In his only NCAA Tournament game, Charles Barkley scores 23 points and grabs 17 rebounds. Dubbed the Round Mound of Rebound by Kentucky sports columnist John McGill, Barkley will eventually be selected as one of the NBA's 50 Greatest Players.

E Steve Alford scores 27 and the Hoosiers find an unlikely hero in Dan Dakich, who helps hold Michael Jordan to 13 points. It's the final college game for both Jordan and Sam Perkins, who will be picked third and fourth, respectively, in June's NBA Draft. Dakich will go on to become a Division I head coach at Bowling Green.

F Danny Young scores on a driving layup in the final game for DePaul coach Ray Meyer, who retires at age 70 after coaching 42 years without winning a national title.

G When Morehead State is called for an intentional foul with :26 left, North Carolina A&T coach Don Corbett quickly subs Eric Boyd, an 83% free-throw shooter, for James Horace, the 51% shooter who had been fouled. Morehead protests, whereupon officials ask ESPN announcers Tom Hammond and Larry Conley to determine from a replay who should be shooting. The announcers confirm Horace.

Tournament Leaders

Individual Leaders

Scoring

	CL	POS	G	PTS	PPG
1 **Kevin Mullin**, Princeton	SR	F	2	56	28.0
2 **Roosevelt Chapman**, Dayton	SR	F	4	105	26.3
3 **Reggie Lewis**, Northeastern	FR	F	2	52	26.0
4 **Devin Durrant**, BYU	SR	F	2	51	25.5
5 **Johnny Newman**, Richmond	SO	F	3	71	23.7
Detlef Schrempf, Washington	JR	F	3	71	23.7
7 **Keith Lee**, Memphis	JR	C	3	70	23.3
8 **Ed Pinckney**, Villanova	JR	C	2	46	23.0
9 **Jon Koncak**, SMU	JR	C	2	45	22.5
10 **Kelvin Johnson**, Richmond	JR	G	3	65	21.7

Minimum: 2 games

Field Goal Pct

	CL	POS	G	FG	FGA	PCT
1 **Kenton Edelin**, Virginia	SR	F	5	12	14	85.7
2 **Reggie Lewis**, Northeastern	FR	F	2	23	30	76.7
3 **Michael Brown**, VCU	SO	F	2	13	17	76.5
4 **Kelvin Johnson**, Richmond	JR	G	3	29	38	76.3
5 **Andre Turner**, Memphis	SO	G	3	13	18	72.2

Minimum: 12 made

Free Throw Pct

	CL	POS	G	FT	FTA	PCT
1 **Wayman Tisdale**, Oklahoma	SO	F/C	1	12	12	100.0
2 **Steve Alford**, Indiana	FR	G	3	21	22	95.5
3 **Kenny Walker**, Kentucky	SO	F	4	13	14	92.9
4 **Damon Goodwin**, Dayton	SO	G/F	4	12	13	92.3
5 **Kevin Mullin**, Princeton	SR	F	2	18	20	90.0

Minimum: 12 made

Rebounds Per Game

	CL	POS	G	REB	RPG
1 **Keith Lee**, Memphis	JR	C	3	37	12.3
2 **Ed Pinckney**, Villanova	JR	C	2	24	12.0
3 **Brett Applegate**, BYU	SR	F	2	23	11.5
Sam Perkins, North Carolina	SR	F/C	2	23	11.5
5 **Hakeem Olajuwon**, Houston	JR	C	5	57	11.4

Minimum: 2 games

Team Leaders

Scoring

	G	PTS	PPG
1 **Maryland**	2	172	86.0
2 **Northeastern**	2	159	79.5
3 **Memphis**	3	229	76.3
4 **BYU**	2	152	76.0
Richmond	3	228	76.0
6 **DePaul**	2	146	73.0
7 **North Carolina**	2	145	72.5
8 **West Virginia**	2	141	70.5
9 **Villanova**	2	140	70.0
10 **Houston**	5	347	69.4

Minimum: 2 games

FG Pct

	G	FG	FGA	PCT
1 **Northeastern**	2	64	98	65.3
2 **Maryland**	2	66	116	56.9
3 **Indiana**	3	74	135	54.8
4 **Richmond**	3	93	170	54.7
5 **Princeton**	2	41	75	54.7

FT Pct

	G	FT	FTA	PCT
1 **Princeton**	2	39	46	84.8
2 **Syracuse**	2	39	48	81.3
3 **West Virginia**	2	23	29	79.3
4 **BYU**	2	42	53	79.3
5 **Maryland**	2	40	51	78.4

Minimum: 2 games

Rebounds

	G	REB	RPG
1 **Memphis**	3	120	40.0
2 **North Carolina**	2	76	38.0
3 **DePaul**	2	73	36.5
4 **BYU**	2	72	36.0
5 **Syracuse**	2	68	34.0

Minimum: 2 games

All-Tournament Team

PLAYER	CL	POS	HT	SCHOOL	RPG	PPG
Patrick Ewing*	JR	C	7-0	Georgetown	9.4	11.8
Alvin Franklin	SO	G	6-2	Houston	2.8	16.2
Michael Graham	FR	F	6-9	Georgetown	5.8	7.2
Hakeem Olajuwon	JR	C	7-0	Houston	11.4	19.4
Michael Young	SR	G/F	6-7	Houston	7.0	15.8

All-Regional Teams

East

PLAYER	CL	POS	HT	SCHOOL	RPG	PPG
Jim Miller*	JR	F/C	6-8	Virginia	2.0	10.3
Steve Alford	FR	G	6-2	Indiana	3.3	18.3
Uwe Blab	JR	C	7-2	Indiana	6.0	14.0
Sam Perkins	SR	F/C	6-9	North Carolina	11.5	19.0
Olden Polynice	FR	C	6-10	Virginia	6.3	10.8

Mideast

PLAYER	CL	POS	HT	SCHOOL	RPG	PPG
Dickey Beal*	SR	G	5-9	Kentucky	2.3	10.7
Sam Bowie	SR	C	7-1	Kentucky	10.7	11.7
Bruce Douglas	SO	G	6-3	Illinois	5.3	10.3
Lancaster Gordon	SR	G	6-3	Louisville	4.3	19.7
Mel Turpin	SR	C	6-11	Kentucky	5.3	14.0

Midwest

PLAYER	CL	POS	HT	SCHOOL	RPG	PPG
Hakeem Olajuwon*	JR	C	7-0	Houston	12.3	23.3
William Bedford	FR	C	6-11	Memphis	6.7	15.7
Kenny Green	SO	F	6-6	Wake Forest	11.3	21.0
Delaney Rudd	JR	G	6-2	Wake Forest	1.3	10.0
Michael Young	SR	G/F	6-7	Houston	7.7	14.7

West

PLAYER	CL	POS	HT	SCHOOL	RPG	PPG
Patrick Ewing*	JR	C	7-0	Georgetown	9.7	13.7
Roosevelt Chapman	SR	F	6-4	Dayton	7.5	26.3
Michael Jackson	SO	G	6-2	Georgetown	2.0	12.3
Detlef Schrempf	JR	F	6-9	Washington	8.7	23.7
Ed Young	SO	C	6-7	Dayton	4.8	6.3

* Most outstanding player

1984 NCAA TOURNAMENT BOX SCORES

Sweet 16: Kentucky 72-67 Louisville

KENTUCKY	MIN	FG	3FG	FT	REB	A	ST	BL	PF	TP
Dickey Beal	39	6-9	-	3-4	2	9	6	0	3	15
Jim Master	30	6-10	-	3-4	4	0	0	0	3	15
Mel Turpin	32	6-10	-	2-2	5	2	0	2	3	14
Winston Bennett	15	4-9	-	2-4	5	0	0	0	3	10
Sam Bowie	38	3-9	-	2-2	12	2	1	3	3	8
Kenny Walker	35	2-7	-	4-4	6	3	2	1	3	8
James Blackmon	10	1-1	-	0-0	1	0	0	0	0	2
Roger Harden	1	0-0	-	0-0	0	0	0	0	1	0
TOTALS	200	28-55	-	16-20	35	16	9	6	19	72
Percentages		50.9	-	80.0						

Coach: Joe B. Hall

72-67

	1H	2H
Kentucky	32	40
Louisville	36	31

LOUISVILLE	MIN	FG	3FG	FT	REB	A	ST	BL	PF	TP
Lancaster Gordon	34	10-18	-	5-6	3	2	1	0	2	25
Milt Wagner	36	10-17	-	2-2	2	5	1	0	2	22
Charles Jones	37	2-9	-	4-4	9	0	3	0	1	8
Manuel Forrest	35	3-4	-	0-1	4	2	2	1	5	6
Billy Thompson	26	2-8	-	0-3	5	1	0	0	4	4
Jeff Hall	11	1-4	-	0-0	0	0	1	0	3	2
Mark McSwain	15	0-1	-	0-0	0	1	0	0	1	0
Barry Sumpter	5	0-0	-	0-0	0	0	0	0	2	0
James Jeter	1	0-0	-	0-0	0	0	0	0	0	0
TOTALS	200	28-61	-	11-16	23	11	8	1	20	67
Percentages		45.9	-	68.8						

Coach: Denny Crum

Officials: Ha Nichols, Jim Clark, Dick Paparo **Technicals:** None **Attendance:** 23,525

Sweet 16: Illinois 72-70 Maryland

ILLINOIS	MIN	FG	3FG	FT	REB	A	ST	BL	PF	TP
George Montgomery	33	5-5	-	5-8	7	1	0	-	4	15
Doug Altenberger	39	4-9	-	4-7	2	2	2	-	5	12
Quinn Richardson	37	4-4	-	4-4	1	6	1	-	2	12
Bruce Douglas	38	4-10	-	3-5	6	8	1	-	3	11
Efrem Winters	33	5-12	-	1-2	6	2	0	-	2	11
Scott Meents	12	3-4	-	1-2	2	1	1	-	5	7
Tom Schafer	7	2-2	-	0-1	0	0	0	-	0	4
Tony Wysinger	1	0-0	-	0-1	1	0	0	-	0	0
TOTALS	200	27-46	-	18-30	25	20	5	-	21	72
Percentages		58.7	-	60.0						

Coach: Lou Henson

72-70

	1H	2H
Illinois	30	42
Maryland	32	38

MARYLAND	MIN	FG	3FG	FT	REB	A	ST	BL	PF	TP
Adrian Branch	37	6-11	-	7-9	3	3	2	0	4	19
Len Bias	38	8-17	-	0-0	8	2	0	2	2	16
Ben Coleman	37	5-13	-	2-3	9	0	0	1	4	12
Herman Veal	34	5-7	-	0-1	9	0	0	0	4	10
Keith Gatlin	32	3-7	-	1-1	3	10	0	0	4	7
Jeff Adkins	12	1-3	-	0-1	1	3	0	0	3	2
Terry Long	4	1-1	-	0-0	0	0	0	0	0	2
Jeff Baxter	3	1-2	-	0-0	0	0	0	0	1	2
Mark Fothergill	3	0-1	-	0-0	1	0	0	0	2	0
TOTALS	200	30-62	-	10-15	34	18	2	3	24	70
Percentages		48.4	-	66.7						

Coach: Lefty Driesell

Officials: Jody Silvester, John Dabrow, Gene Monje **Technicals:** None **Attendance:** 23,525

Sweet 16: Georgetown 62-48 UNLV

GEORGETOWN	MIN	FG	3FG	FT	REB	A	ST	BL	PF	TP
Patrick Ewing	33	5-10	-	6-7	15	1	0	6	2	16
Michael Jackson	32	2-8	-	12-12	2	4	1	0	2	16
Horace Broadnax	24	3-5	-	3-5	4	2	0	0	0	9
Reggie Williams	20	2-4	-	3-4	2	3	0	0	2	7
Bill Martin	30	3-6	-	0-2	6	0	1	0	2	6
David Wingate	22	3-6	-	0-0	3	0	1	0	2	6
Fred Brown	6	1-2	-	0-1	3	1	1	0	1	2
Gene Smith	17	0-2	-	0-3	3	1	0	0	2	0
Michael Graham	13	0-0	-	0-1	5	0	1	0	2	0
Ralph Dalton	3	0-0	-	0-0	0	0	0	0	0	0
TOTALS	200	19-43	-	24-35	43	12	5	6	15	62
Percentages		44.2	-	68.6						

Coach: John Thompson Jr.

62-48

	1H	2H
Georgetown	22	40
UNLV	21	27

UNLV	MIN	FG	3FG	FT	REB	A	ST	BL	PF	TP
John Flowers	31	3-9	-	4-6	2	1	2	0	3	10
Danny Tarkanian	34	3-9	-	2-3	2	3	1	0	5	8
Eric Booker	24	3-7	-	2-4	3	0	2	0	1	8
Freddie Banks	18	4-11	-	0-0	2	0	1	0	4	8
Richie Adams	31	2-8	-	2-4	7	0	3	2	5	6
Frank James	28	2-8	-	0-2	2	1	0	0	4	4
Jeff Collins	17	1-4	-	0-0	3	0	0	0	4	2
Ed Catchings	15	0-2	-	2-2	6	0	0	0	0	2
Paul Brozovich	2	0-0	-	0-0	1	0	0	0	0	0
TOTALS	200	18-58	-	12-21	28	5	9	2	26	48
Percentages		31.0	-	57.1						

Coach: Jerry Tarkanian

Officials: Paul Galvan, Paul Housman, Don Rutledge **Technicals:** UNLV (Booker) **Attendance:** 12,542

Sweet 16: Dayton 64-58 Washington

DAYTON	MIN	FG	3FG	FT	REB	A	ST	BL	PF	TP
Roosevelt Chapman	39	7-12	-	8-13	9	3	4	2	3	22
Sedric Toney	30	6-8	-	2-3	2	2	1	0	3	14
Damon Goodwin	39	2-8	-	4-5	5	0	0	0	0	8
Larry Schellenberg	33	2-4	-	4-6	7	3	1	1	1	8
Ed Young	37	3-8	-	0-2	7	0	0	0	2	6
Dan Christie	15	0-0	-	6-6	3	0	0	0	3	6
Jeff Zern	2	0-1	-	0-0	0	0	0	0	0	0
Rory Dahlinghaus	1	0-0	-	0-0	0	0	0	0	0	0
Anthony Grant	1	0-0	-	0-0	0	0	0	0	0	0
Ted Harris	1	0-0	-	0-0	0	0	0	0	0	0
Jim Shields	1	0-0	-	0-0	0	0	0	0	0	0
Jeff Tressler	1	0-0	-	0-0	0	0	0	0	0	0
TOTALS	200	20-41	-	24-35	33	8	6	3	12	64
Percentages		48.8	-	68.6						

Coach: Don Donoher

64-58

	1H	2H
Dayton	21	43
Washington	22	36

WASHINGTON	MIN	FG	3FG	FT	REB	A	ST	BL	PF	TP
Detlef Schrempf	40	8-19	-	2-4	11	1	0	0	5	18
Paul Fortier	33	4-8	-	0-0	7	2	4	1	4	8
Chris Welp	28	3-8	-	1-2	8	1	1	0	4	7
Alvin Vaughn	22	3-11	-	1-2	1	2	2	0	4	7
Shag Williams	21	3-6	-	0-2	5	1	0	1	1	6
Reggie Rogers	12	3-4	-	0-3	4	0	0	1	1	6
Clay Damon	13	1-6	-	0-0	1	0	0	0	1	2
Gary Gardner	6	1-3	-	0-0	0	0	0	0	4	2
Tim Kuyper	6	1-1	-	0-0	0	0	0	0	0	2
David Koehler	18	0-1	-	0-0	0	4	2	0	2	0
Pete Shimer	1	0-0	-	0-0	0	0	0	0	1	0
TOTALS	200	27-67	-	4-13	37	11	9	3	27	58
Percentages		40.3	-	30.8						

Coach: Marv Harshman

Officials: Jim Bain, Dale Kelley, John Moreau **Technicals:** None **Attendance:** 12,542

Sweet 16: Indiana 72-68 North Carolina

INDIANA	MIN	FG	3FG	FT	REB	A	ST	BL	PF	TP
Steve Alford	40	9-13	-	9-10	6	3	2	0	2	27
Uwe Blab	36	5-7	-	6-8	3	0	1	1	3	16
Stew Robinson	34	5-8	-	4-7	4	3	3	0	2	14
Mike Giomi	27	2-4	-	3-4	6	2	0	0	4	7
Daniel Dakich	33	2-3	-	0-0	3	3	0	0	5	4
Marty Simmons	18	1-1	-	2-5	2	2	0	0	2	4
Todd Meier	7	0-1	-	0-0	2	0	0	0	1	0
Charles Franz	4	0-0	-	0-1	0	0	0	0	0	0
Courtney Witte	1	0-0	-	0-0	0	0	0	0	0	0
TOTALS	200	24-37	-	24-35	26	13	6	1	19	72
Percentages		64.9	-	68.6						

Coach: Bob Knight

72-68

	1H	2H
Indiana	32	40
North Carolina	28	40

NORTH CAROLINA	MIN	FG	3FG	FT	REB	A	ST	BL	PF	TP
Sam Perkins	35	8-17	-	10-12	9	2	0	0	3	26
Michael Jordan	26	6-14	-	1-2	1	1	1	0	5	13
Kenny Smith	32	3-8	-	2-2	0	5	0	0	2	8
Matt Doherty	37	3-8	-	1-2	7	4	1	1	5	7
Joe Wolf	16	2-4	-	1-2	10	1	0	0	3	5
Steve Hale	23	2-4	-	0-1	3	2	2	0	5	4
Brad Daugherty	23	1-3	-	1-2	4	0	1	1	2	3
Buzz Peterson	4	1-4	-	0-0	0	0	0	0	1	2
Dave Popson	3	0-0	-	0-0	0	0	0	0	0	0
Cecil Exum	1	0-0	-	0-0	0	0	0	0	1	0
TOTALS	200	26-62	-	16-23	34	15	5	2	27	68
Percentages		41.9	-	69.6						

Coach: Dean Smith

Officials: Booker Turner, Ron Spitler, Mike Tanco **Technicals:** None **Attendance:** 16,723

Sweet 16: Virginia 63-55 Syracuse

VIRGINIA	MIN	FG	3FG	FT	REB	A	ST	BL	PF	TP
Othell Wilson	37	4-8	-	9-11	6	3	3	0	5	17
Olden Polynice	31	4-8	-	4-7	5	0	0	1	2	12
Kenton Edelin	34	4-4	-	2-4	14	1	2	0	2	10
Rick Carlisle	33	3-7	-	2-5	5	7	0	0	1	8
Ricky Stokes	21	4-7	-	0-3	2	3	2	0	3	8
Jim Miller	25	2-9	-	1-2	2	0	0	0	5	5
Tom Sheehey	11	1-2	-	0-0	1	1	1	0	1	2
Dan Merrifield	5	0-0	-	1-3	1	1	0	0	0	1
Kenny Johnson	1	0-0	-	0-0	0	0	0	0	0	0
Tim Mullen	1	0-0	-	0-1	0	0	0	0	0	0
Anthony Solomon	1	0-0	-	0-0	0	0	0	0	0	0
TOTALS	200	22-45	-	19-36	36	16	8	1	19	63
Percentages		48.9	-	52.8						

Coach: Terry Holland

63-55

	1H	2H
Virginia	26	37
Syracuse	16	39

SYRACUSE	MIN	FG	3FG	FT	REB	A	ST	BL	PF	TP
Rafael Addison	38	7-18	-	4-5	4	0	1	1	5	18
Sean Kerins	35	5-14	-	0-0	12	3	2	0	3	10
Dwayne Washington	32	3-10	-	2-2	0	3	1	0	5	8
Gene Waldron	31	4-8	-	0-0	1	6	1	0	5	8
Wendell Alexis	24	2-6	-	2-2	8	3	3	1	5	6
Greg Monroe	16	1-4	-	0-1	2	5	0	0	2	2
Sonny Spera	2	1-1	-	0-0	1	0	0	0	1	2
Howard Triche	2	0-0	-	1-2	2	0	0	0	3	1
Andre Hawkins	19	0-0	-	0-0	3	0	0	0	5	0
George Papadakos	1	0-0	-	0-0	2	0	0	0	0	0
TOTALS	200	23-61	-	9-12	35	20	8	2	34	55
Percentages		37.7	-	75.0						

Coach: Jim Boeheim

Officials: Bob Dibler, Charles Vacca, Sonny Holmes **Technicals:** None **Attendance:** 16,723

73-71 (SWEET 16)

	1H	2H	OT1	Final
Wake Forest	35	32	6	73
DePaul	39	28	4	71

WAKE FOREST	MIN	FG	3FG	FT	REB	A	ST	BL	PF	TP
Kenny Green	38	11-19	-	3-4	13	0	2	0	4	25
Anthony Teachey	45	4-11	-	9-14	6	3	4	2	3	17
Delaney Rudd	42	4-7	-	4-5	2	1	0	0	2	12
Danny Young	41	4-8	-	0-0	5	9	2	0	2	8
Mark Cline	32	3-9	-	2-4	9	1	0	0	0	8
Lee Garber	15	1-4	-	1-1	1	2	0	1	2	3
Muggsy Bogues	6	0-1	-	0-0	0	0	1	0	1	0
John Toms	5	0-3	-	0-0	2	0	0	0	0	0
Chuck Kepley	1	0-0	-	0-0	0	0	0	0	1	0
TOTALS	225	27-62	-	19-28	38	16	9	3	15	73
Percentages		43.5	-	67.9						

Coach: Carl Tacy

DEPAUL	MIN	FG	3FG	FT	REB	A	ST	BL	PF	TP
Dallas Comegys	37	8-15	-	1-2	13	0	0	1	4	17
Jerry McMillan	37	7-11	-	0-0	5	0	2	0	3	14
Tyrone Corbin	44	5-11	-	3-3	5	4	2	0	4	13
Kenny Patterson	42	3-12	-	2-4	3	9	4	0	3	8
Marty Embry	31	3-5	-	2-4	9	4	0	3	4	8
Kevin Holmes	16	4-5	-	0-0	2	1	1	0	4	8
Tony Jackson	18	1-7	-	1-2	3	0	2	0	1	3
TOTALS	225	31-66	-	9-15	40	18	11	4	23	71
Percentages		47.0	-	60.0						

Coach: Ray Meyer

Officials: James Howell, Norm Borucki, Larry Lembo
Technicals: None
Attendance: 20,143

78-71 (SWEET 16)

	1H	2H	Final
Houston	41	37	78
Memphis	40	31	71

HOUSTON	MIN	FG	3FG	FT	REB	A	ST	BL	PF	TP
Hakeem Olajuwon	40	9-17	-	7-15	13	3	1	4	4	25
Alvin Franklin	38	7-13	-	10-12	2	2	1	0	2	24
Michael Young	38	5-22	-	3-5	9	2	1	0	1	13
Ricky Winslow	36	5-7	-	2-4	12	1	2	0	2	12
Reid Gettys	39	2-5	-	0-0	3	9	1	0	3	4
Benny Anders	5	0-2	-	0-0	0	0	0	0	1	0
Greg Anderson	4	0-0	-	0-0	1	0	0	0	0	0
TOTALS	200	28-66	-	22-36	40	17	6	4	11	78
Percentages		42.4	-	61.1						

Coach: Guy V. Lewis

MEMPHIS	MIN	FG	3FG	FT	REB	A	ST	BL	PF	TP
William Bedford	31	10-12	-	1-2	4	0	0	3	5	21
Phillip Haynes	40	7-14	-	1-1	5	1	0	0	0	15
Keith Lee	39	6-13	-	3-6	10	3	1	6	5	15
Andre Turner	38	5-8	-	0-0	3	7	2	0	4	10
Baskerville Holmes	22	4-8	-	0-0	4	4	0	0	5	8
Derrick Phillips	11	1-3	-	0-0	1	0	0	0	0	2
Willie Becton	8	0-2	-	0-0	2	0	0	0	2	0
Ricky McCoy	7	0-1	-	0-0	2	0	0	1	1	0
Jon Albright	3	0-0	-	0-0	0	0	0	0	2	0
Larry Bush	1	0-0	-	0-0	1	0	0	0	1	0
TOTALS	200	33-61	-	5-9	32	15	3	10	25	71
Percentages		54.1	-	55.6						

Coach: Dana Kirk

Officials: Joe Forte, Tom Rucker, Tim Higgins
Technicals: None
Attendance: 20,143

54-51 (ELITE 8)

	1H	2H	Final
Kentucky	24	30	54
Illinois	22	29	51

KENTUCKY	MIN	FG	3FG	FT	REB	A	ST	BL	PF	TP
Mel Turpin	39	6-12	-	1-2	6	2	0	0	2	13
Sam Bowie	37	3-6	-	5-7	14	1	1	1	2	11
Dickey Beal	39	3-6	-	3-4	3	6	2	0	2	9
Winston Bennett	15	3-4	-	2-2	0	0	0	0	4	8
Jim Master	34	3-6	-	0-0	1	1	0	0	3	6
Kenny Walker	26	3-4	-	0-0	2	3	0	0	0	6
Bret Bearup	3	0-0	-	1-2	0	0	0	0	0	1
James Blackmon	7	0-0	-	0-0	0	0	0	0	1	0
TOTALS	200	21-38	-	12-17	26	13	3	1	14	54
Percentages		55.3	-	70.6						

Coach: Joe B. Hall

ILLINOIS	MIN	FG	3FG	FT	REB	A	ST	BL	PF	TP
Quinn Richardson	35	8-11	-	0-0	3	3	0	0	3	16
Doug Altenberger	40	5-11	-	3-4	3	3	0	0	2	13
Bruce Douglas	40	3-9	-	1-2	5	11	3	0	3	7
Efrem Winters	37	3-9	-	1-3	4	0	0	0	1	7
George Montgomery	28	2-4	-	0-0	2	0	0	0	3	4
Scott Meents	19	2-6	-	0-0	3	0	0	2	3	4
Tony Wysinger	1	0-0	-	0-0	0	0	0	0	0	0
TOTALS	200	23-50	-	5-9	20	17	3	2	15	51
Percentages		46.0	-	55.6						

Coach: Lou Henson

Officials: Hank Nichols, Jim Clark, Dick Paparo
Technicals: None
Attendance: 23,525

61-49 (ELITE 8)

	1H	2H	Final
Georgetown	30	31	61
Dayton	24	25	49

GEORGETOWN	MIN	FG	3FG	FT	REB	A	ST	BL	PF	TP
Patrick Ewing	35	6-10	-	3-3	7	3	2	3	1	15
Michael Jackson	38	6-17	-	2-3	0	4	2	0	3	14
Reggie Williams	17	3-3	-	2-2	2	0	1	0	2	8
Michael Graham	13	4-7	-	0-0	5	0	0	0	1	8
David Wingate	24	2-6	-	2-2	4	0	2	0	0	6
Bill Martin	22	2-4	-	2-4	10	0	0	0	3	6
Ralph Dalton	10	1-2	-	0-0	3	0	0	0	1	2
Fred Brown	9	1-1	-	0-0	0	0	0	0	1	2
Gene Smith	26	0-0	-	0-1	2	1	0	0	1	0
Horace Broadnax	6	0-2	-	0-0	0	1	0	0	1	0
TOTALS	200	25-52	-	11-15	33	9	7	3	14	61
Percentages		48.1	-	73.3						

Coach: John Thompson Jr.

DAYTON	MIN	FG	3FG	FT	REB	A	ST	BL	PF	TP
Ed Young	40	6-9	-	2-2	5	0	1	1	4	14
Roosevelt Chapman	40	5-10	-	3-4	5	2	2	2	2	13
Sedric Toney	34	3-13	-	0-0	4	0	1	0	2	6
Dan Christie	17	2-7	-	2-2	1	0	0	0	4	6
Damon Goodwin	35	2-7	-	0-0	2	1	0	0	3	4
Larry Schellenberg	29	2-2	-	0-0	3	3	1	0	1	4
Ted Harris	5	1-3	-	0-0	0	0	0	0	2	2
TOTALS	200	21-51	-	7-8	20	6	5	3	18	49
Percentages		41.2	-	87.5						

Coach: Don Donoher

Officials: Paul Galvan, Paul Housman, Don Rutledge
Technicals: None
Attendance: 12,564

50-48 (ELITE 8)

	1H	2H	Final
Virginia	23	27	50
Indiana	26	22	48

VIRGINIA	MIN	FG	3FG	FT	REB	A	ST	BL	PF	TP
Jim Miller	29	8-11	-	3-3	3	1	1	-	1	19
Olden Polynice	38	4-7	-	4-6	6	0	1	-	2	12
Rick Carlisle	32	2-5	-	4-5	3	4	0	-	0	8
Kenton Edelin	38	1-2	-	3-4	7	1	2	-	2	5
Othell Wilson	34	2-9	-	0-0	1	3	0	-	5	4
Ricky Stokes	25	1-5	-	0-0	2	1	1	-	2	2
Tom Sheehey	4	0-0	-	0-0	1	1	0	-	0	0
TOTALS	200	18-39	-	14-18	23	11	5	-	12	50
Percentages		46.2	-	77.8						

Coach: Terry Holland

INDIANA	MIN	FG	3FG	FT	REB	A	ST	BL	PF	TP
Uwe Blab	39	5-14	-	2-2	8	1	1	1	4	12
Mike Giomi	39	5-9	-	2-2	7	0	1	0	4	12
Stew Robinson	32	4-8	-	0-0	1	6	1	0	2	8
Steve Alford	38	2-7	-	2-2	1	2	1	0	2	6
Dan Dakich	23	2-3	-	0-0	1	3	0	0	4	4
Todd Meier	9	2-2	-	0-0	0	0	0	0	1	4
Marty Simmons	16	1-2	-	0-0	1	4	0	0	1	2
Charles Franz	3	0-0	-	0-0	0	0	0	0	0	0
Darryl Thomas	1	0-0	-	0-0	0	0	0	0	0	0
TOTALS	200	21-45	-	6-6	19	16	4	1	18	48
Percentages		46.7	-	100.0						

Coach: Bob Knight

Officials: Booker Turner, Ron Spitler, Mike Tanco
Technicals: None
Attendance: 16,723

68-63 (ELITE 8)

	1H	2H	Final
Houston	34	34	68
Wake Forest	31	32	63

HOUSTON	MIN	FG	3FG	FT	REB	A	ST	BL	PF	TP
Hakeem Olajuwon	40	14-16	-	1-5	12	2	2	3	3	29
Michael Young	40	7-18	-	1-6	8	1	2	1	0	15
Ricky Winslow	36	4-9	-	2-2	6	0	2	0	3	10
Alvin Franklin	35	2-5	-	5-6	2	3	1	0	0	9
Reid Gettys	37	1-4	-	0-0	3	10	0	0	2	2
Benny Anders	4	1-3	-	0-0	0	1	0	0	1	2
Derek Giles	1	0-1	-	1-2	2	0	0	0	1	1
Eric Dickens	4	0-0	-	0-0	0	1	0	0	1	0
Renaldo Thomas	3	0-0	-	0-0	0	0	0	0	0	0
TOTALS	200	29-56	-	10-21	33	18	7	4	11	68
Percentages		51.8	-	47.6						

Coach: Guy V. Lewis

WAKE FOREST	MIN	FG	3FG	FT	REB	A	ST	BL	PF	TP
Kenny Green	40	8-14	-	2-2	16	2	0	0	2	18
Anthony Teachey	40	5-8	-	3-3	7	2	3	2	4	13
Delaney Rudd	40	6-13	-	0-0	1	5	0	0	4	12
Mark Cline	26	5-10	-	0-0	3	1	0	0	2	10
Danny Young	38	4-8	-	0-0	1	7	1	1	3	8
Lee Garber	12	0-4	-	2-3	1	1	0	0	2	2
Muggsy Bogues	2	0-0	-	0-0	0	0	0	0	1	0
John Toms	2	0-0	-	0-0	0	0	0	0	2	0
TOTALS	200	28-57	-	7-8	29	18	4	3	20	63
Percentages		49.1	-	87.5						

Coach: Carl Tacy

Officials: Larry Lembo, Charles Howell, Norm Borucki
Technicals: None
Attendance: 18,652

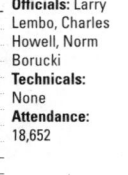

ANNUAL REVIEW

53-40 (22 1H 29; 31 2H 11) — FINAL 4

GEORGETOWN	MIN	FG	3FG	FT	REB	A	ST	BL	PF	TP
Michael Jackson	33	4-9	-	4-6	10	3	0	0	2	12
David Wingate	25	5-8	-	1-2	3	2	1	0	0	11
Michael Graham	33	4-6	-	0-2	6	1	0	3	3	8
Patrick Ewing	29	4-6	-	0-0	9	1	0	0	3	8
Gene Smith	17	2-4	-	1-2	2	1	0	0	2	5
Horace Broadnax	12	2-4	-	1-2	1	0	0	0	0	5
Reggie Williams	18	1-7	-	0-0	3	2	0	0	3	2
Bill Martin	5	1-4	-	0-0	1	0	0	0	1	2
Ralph Dalton	17	0-1	-	0-0	4	0	0	0	1	0
Fred Brown	11	0-1	-	0-1	2	1	0	0	4	0
TOTALS	**200**	**23-50**	**-**	**7-15**	**41**	**11**	**1**	**3**	**19**	**53**
Percentages		46.0	-	46.7						
Coach: John Thompson Jr.										

KENTUCKY	MIN	FG	3FG	FT	REB	A	ST	BL	PF	TP
Sam Bowie	34	3-10	-	4-4	11	1	0	2	3	10
Dickey Beal	35	2-8	-	2-2	1	4	2	0	4	6
Jim Master	23	2-7	-	2-2	1	0	0	0	1	6
Mel Turpin	27	2-11	-	1-2	5	1	1	1	2	5
James Blackmon	22	2-5	-	1-2	1	2	3	0	3	5
Kenny Walker	29	1-3	-	2-2	3	1	1	0	3	4
Winston Bennett	24	1-8	-	0-0	7	0	0	0	5	2
Bret Bearup	4	0-0	-	2-2	0	0	0	0	0	2
Roger Harden	2	0-1	-	0-0	2	0	0	0	1	0
TOTALS	**200**	**13-53**	**-**	**14-16**	**31**	**9**	**7**	**3**	**22**	**40**
Percentages		24.5	-	87.5						
Coach: Joe B. Hall										

Officials: Ro Spitler, Mike Tanco, Booke Turner
Technicals: None
Attendance: 38,471

49-47 (25 1H 23; 18 2H 20; 6 OT1 4) — FINAL 4

HOUSTON	MIN	FG	3FG	FT	REB	A	ST	BL	PF	TP
Michael Young	45	8-16	-	1-4	7	1	0	0	1	17
Hakeem Olajuwon	45	4-5	-	4-6	11	1	2	5	3	12
Ricky Winslow	44	4-7	-	0-0	7	0	2	1	2	8
Alvin Franklin	45	2-7	-	2-2	4	7	1	0	1	6
Reid Gettys	45	3-7	-	0-0	3	6	0	0	3	6
Marvin Alexander	0	0-0	-	0-0	0	0	0	0	0	0
Eric Dickens	0	0-0	-	0-0	0	0	0	0	0	0
TOTALS	**225**	**21-42**	**-**	**7-12**	**32**	**15**	**5**	**6**	**10**	**49**
Percentages		50.0	-	58.3						
Coach: Guy V. Lewis										

VIRGINIA	MIN	FG	3FG	FT	REB	A	ST	BL	PF	TP
Othell Wilson	45	5-12	-	2-2	3	5	2	1	2	12
Jim Miller	37	6-15	-	0-0	4	1	0	0	2	12
Olden Polynice	43	4-7	-	1-1	7	0	1	0	1	9
Rick Carlisle	29	3-14	-	2-2	6	0	0	0	2	8
Kenton Edelin	39	1-2	-	0-0	3	2	0	1	3	2
Ricky Stokes	24	1-1	-	0-2	2	3	2	0	4	2
Tom Sheehey	8	1-3	-	0-0	1	1	0	0	0	2
TOTALS	**225**	**21-54**	**-**	**5-7**	**26**	**12**	**5**	**2**	**14**	**47**
Percentages		38.9	-	71.4						
Coach: Terry Holland										

Officials: Jim Clark, Hank Nichols, Dick Paparo
Technicals: None
Attendance: 38,471

84-75 (40 1H 30; 44 2H 45) — NCAA FINAL 1984

GEORGETOWN	MIN	FG	3FG	FT	REB	A	ST	BL	PF	TP
Reggie Williams	26	9-18	-	1-2	7	3	-	0	2	19
David Wingate	32	5-10	-	6-9	1	3	-	0	4	16
Michael Graham	24	7-9	-	0-2	5	0	-	1	4	14
Michael Jackson	35	3-4	-	5-5	0	6	-	0	4	11
Patrick Ewing	30	4-8	-	2-2	9	3	-	4	4	10
Bill Martin	16	3-6	-	0-0	2	0	-	0	0	6
Fred Brown	15	1-2	-	2-2	4	4	-	0	4	4
Horace Broadnax	8	2-3	-	0-0	0	0	-	0	2	4
Ralph Dalton	13	0-0	-	0-0	2	0	-	1	1	0
Victor Morris	1	0-0	-	0-0	0	0	-	0	0	0
TOTALS	**200**	**34-60**	**-**	**16-22**	**30**	**19**	**-**	**6**	**25**	**84**
Percentages		56.7	-	72.7						
Coach: John Thompson Jr.										

HOUSTON	MIN	FG	3FG	FT	REB	A	ST	BL	PF	TP
Alvin Franklin	38	8-15	-	5-6	2	9	0	0	3	21
Michael Young	37	8-21	-	2-3	5	1	2	1	3	18
Hakeem Olajuwon	32	6-9	-	3-7	9	0	0	2	4	15
Reid Gettys	29	3-3	-	0-0	1	7	0	0	2	6
Eric Dickens	6	2-3	-	1-2	0	0	0	0	5	5
Benny Anders	10	2-2	-	0-2	0	0	1	0	0	4
Ricky Winslow	33	0-1	-	2-2	6	3	0	1	4	2
Greg Anderson	6	1-1	-	0-0	2	0	0	0	0	2
Gary Orsak	1	1-1	-	0-0	0	0	0	0	0	2
Derek Giles	2	0-0	-	0-0	0	0	0	0	0	0
Renaldo Thomas	2	0-0	-	0-0	0	0	0	0	0	0
Marvin Alexander	1	0-0	-	0-0	1	0	0	0	0	0
Stacey Belcher	1	0-0	-	0-0	0	0	0	0	0	0
Braxton Clark	1	0-0	-	0-0	0	0	0	0	0	0
Jamie Weaver	1	0-0	-	0-0	0	0	0	0	0	0
TOTALS	**200**	**31-56**	**-**	**13-22**	**26**	**20**	**3**	**4**	**21**	**75**
Percentages		55.4	-	59.1						
Coach: Guy V. Lewis										

Officials: Ron Spitler, Mike Tanco, Booker Turner
Technicals: Houston (grabbing the rim)
Attendance: 38,471

National Invitation Tournament (NIT)

First round: Notre Dame d. Old Dominion 67-62, Chattanooga d. Georgia 74-69 (OT), Lamar d. New Mexico 64-61, UL-Lafayette d. Utah State 94-92, South Alabama d. Florida 88-87, Tennessee d. Saint Peter's 54-40, Nebraska d. Creighton 56-54, Xavier d. Ohio State 60-57, Florida State d. NC State 74-71, Marquette d. Iowa State 73-53, Virginia Tech d. Georgia Tech 77-74, Michigan d. Wichita State 94-70, Santa Clara d. Oregon 66-53, Weber State d. Fordham 75-63, Boston College d. Saint Joseph's 75-63, Pittsburgh d. La Salle 95-91

Second round: Pittsburgh d. Florida State 66-63, Virginia Tech d. South Alabama 68-66, Santa Clara d. Lamar 76-74, Michigan d. Marquette 83-70, Xavier d. Nebraska 58-57, Tennessee d. Chattanooga 68-66, UL-Lafayette d. Weber State 74-72 (2OT), Notre Dame d. Boston College 66-52

Third round: UL-Lafayette d. Santa Clara 97-76, Michigan d. Xavier 63-62, Notre Dame d. Pittsburgh 72-64, Virginia Tech d. Tennessee 72-68

Semifinals: Michigan d. Virginia Tech 78-75, Notre Dame d. UL-Lafayette 65-59

Third place: Virginia Tech d. UL-Lafayette 71-70

Championship: Michigan d. Notre Dame 83-63

MVP: Tim McCormick, Michigan

1984-85: Super Nova

The Tournament field expanded to 64 teams. By the time that number was down to two, many fans believed they had watched one of the greatest Tournaments ever. And that was before No. 8-seed Villanova stunned Big East foe and No. 1-ranked Georgetown for the championship at Lexington's Rupp Arena.

The Hoyas were the first team in nine years to make it back to the Final Four as defending national champion. Led by center Patrick Ewing, their three losses during the season came by a combined five points. Rollie Massimino's Wildcats (25–10, 9–7 in the Big East) played a nearly perfect game in the Final, shooting a title-game record 78.6% from the field to win, 66-64, and become the lowest seed ever to win the Tourney. Ed Pinckney was named Most Outstanding Player.

A third Big East team, St. John's, also reached the national semifinals—the only time one conference has produced three-quarters of the Final Four. Ewing was named Naismith POY after averaging 14.6 ppg along with 9.2 rpg and nearly four blocks per game. He was selected as the first pick of the 1985 NBA draft by the New York Knicks.

Major Conference Standings

AMCU-8

	Conference			Overall		
	W	L	Pct	W	L	Pct
Cleveland State	11	3	.786	21	8	.724
Western Illinois	10	4	.714	14	14	.500
Eastern Illinois	9	5	.643	20	10	.667
Missouri State	8	6	.571	17	13	.567
Illinois-Chicago	7	7	.500	14	14	.500
Northern Iowa	6	8	.429	12	16	.429
Valparaiso	4	10	.286	8	20	.286
Wisc.-Green Bay	1	13	.071	4	24	.143

Tournament: **Eastern Illinois d. Missouri State 75-64**

ATLANTIC 10

	Conference			Overall		
	W	L	Pct	W	L	Pct
West Virginia□	16	2	.889	20	9	.690
Temple⊕	15	3	.833	25	6	.806
Saint Joseph's□	13	5	.722	19	12	.613
Rutgers	9	9	.500	16	14	.533
George Washington	9	9	.500	14	14	.500
Massachusetts	9	9	.500	13	15	.464
St. Bonaventure	7	11	.389	14	15	.483
Duquesne	6	12	.333	12	18	.400
Penn State	4	14	.222	8	19	.296
Rhode Island	2	16	.111	8	20	.286

Tournament: **Temple d. Rutgers 59-51**
Tournament MVP: **Granger Hall**, Temple

ACC

	Conference			Overall		
	W	L	Pct	W	L	Pct
Georgia Tech⊕	9	5	.643	27	8	.771
North Carolina○	9	5	.643	27	9	.750
NC State○	9	5	.643	23	10	.697
Duke○	8	6	.571	23	8	.742
Maryland○	8	6	.571	25	12	.676
Clemson□	5	9	.357	16	13	.552
Wake Forest□	5	9	.357	15	14	.517
Virginia□	3	11	.214	17	16	.515

Tournament: **Georgia Tech d. North Carolina 57-54**
Tournament MVP: **Mark Price**, Georgia Tech

BIG EAST

	Conference			Overall		
	W	L	Pct	W	L	Pct
St. John's○	15	1	.938	31	4	.886
Georgetown⊕	14	2	.875	35	3	.921
Villanova○	9	7	.563	25	10	.714
Syracuse○	9	7	.563	22	9	.710
Pittsburgh○	8	8	.500	17	12	.586
Boston College○	7	9	.438	20	11	.645
Connecticut	6	10	.375	13	15	.464
Providence	3	13	.188	11	20	.355
Seton Hall	1	15	.063	10	18	.357

Tournament: **Georgetown d. St. John's 92-80**
Tournament MVP: **Patrick Ewing**, Georgetown

BIG EIGHT

	Conference			Overall		
	W	L	Pct	W	L	Pct
Oklahoma⊕	13	1	.929	31	6	.838
Kansas○	11	3	.786	26	8	.765
Iowa State○	7	7	.500	21	13	.618
Missouri□	7	7	.500	18	14	.563
Nebraska□	5	9	.357	16	14	.533
Kansas State	5	9	.357	14	14	.500
Colorado	5	9	.357	11	17	.393
Oklahoma State	3	11	.214	12	16	.429

Tournament: **Oklahoma d. Iowa State 73-71**
Tournament MVP: **Wayman Tisdale**, Oklahoma

BIG SKY

	Conference			Overall		
	W	L	Pct	W	L	Pct
Nevada⊕	11	3	.786	21	10	.677
Montana□	10	4	.714	22	8	.733
Weber State	9	5	.643	20	9	.690
Northern Arizona	8	6	.571	17	12	.586
Montana State	7	7	.500	11	17	.393
Boise State	5	9	.357	16	13	.552
Idaho State	5	9	.357	15	18	.455
Idaho	1	13	.071	8	22	.267

Tournament: **Nevada d. Idaho State 79-63**
Tournament MVP: **Dwayne Randall**, Nevada

BIG TEN

	Conference			Overall		
	W	L	Pct	W	L	Pct
Michigan⊕	16	2	.889	26	4	.867
Illinois○	12	6	.667	26	9	.743
Purdue○	11	7	.611	20	9	.690
Ohio State○	11	7	.611	20	10	.667
Iowa○	10	8	.556	21	11	.656
Michigan State○	10	8	.556	19	10	.655
Indiana□	7	11	.389	19	14	.576
Minnesota	6	12	.333	13	15	.464
Wisconsin	5	13	.278	14	14	.500
Northwestern	2	16	.111	6	22	.214

EAST COAST

	Conference			Overall		
	W	L	Pct	W	L	Pct
Bucknell	10	4	.714	19	10	.655
Lafayette	8	6	.571	15	13	.536
Drexel	8	6	.571	10	18	.357
Rider	7	7	.500	14	15	.483
Delaware	7	7	.500	12	16	.429
Lehigh⊕	6	8	.429	12	19	.387
Hofstra	5	9	.357	14	15	.483
Towson	5	9	.357	7	21	.250

Tournament: **Lehigh d. Bucknell 76-74 (OT)**
Tournament MVP: **Mike Polaha**, Lehigh

ECAC METRO

	Conference			Overall		
	W	L	Pct	W	L	Pct
Marist	11	3	.786	17	12	.586
Fairleigh Dickinson⊕	10	4	.714	21	10	.677
Long Island	9	5	.643	15	13	.536
Loyola (MD)	8	6	.571	16	14	.533
Saint Francis (PA)	6	8	.429	9	19	.321
Wagner	5	9	.357	11	17	.393
Robert Morris	4	10	.286	9	19	.321
St. Francis (NY)	3	11	.214	7	21	.250

Tournament: **Fairleigh Dickinson d. Loyola (MD) 63-59**
Tournament MVP: **Larry Hampton**, Fairleigh Dickinson

ECAC NAC

	Conference			Overall		
	W	L	Pct	W	L	Pct
Northeastern⊕	13	3	.813	22	9	.710
Canisius□	13	3	.813	20	10	.667
Siena	12	4	.750	22	7	.759
Niagara	11	5	.688	16	12	.571
Boston U.	9	7	.563	15	15	.500
Maine	5	11	.313	11	17	.393
Vermont	5	11	.313	9	19	.321
New Hampshire	4	12	.250	7	22	.241
Colgate	0	16	.000	5	21	.192
Hartford	-	-	-	7	21	.250

Tournament: **Northeastern d. Boston U. 68-67**
Tournament MVP: **Reggie Lewis**, Northeastern

ECAC SOUTH

	Conference			Overall		
	W	L	Pct	W	L	Pct
Navy⊕	11	3	.786	26	6	.813
Richmond□	11	3	.786	21	11	.656
George Mason	10	4	.714	18	11	.621
William and Mary	9	5	.643	16	12	.571
James Madison	7	7	.500	14	14	.500
UNC Wilmington	4	10	.286	12	16	.429
American	3	11	.214	9	19	.321
East Carolina	1	13	.071	7	21	.250

Tournament: **Navy d. Richmond 85-76**
Tournament MVP: **Vernon Butler**, Navy

GULF STAR

	Conference			Overall		
	W	L	Pct	W	L	Pct
Southeastern Louisiana	9	1	.900	18	9	.667
Nicholls State	6	4	.600	17	10	.630
Sam Houston State	5	4	.556	16	12	.571
Stephen F. Austin	4	5	.444	16	10	.615
Texas State	2	8	.200	6	20	.231
Northwestern St. (LA)	2	8	.200	3	25	.107

IVY

	Conference			Overall		
	W	L	Pct	W	L	Pct
Penn⊕	10	4	.714	13	14	.481
Columbia	9	5	.643	13	13	.500
Cornell	8	6	.571	14	12	.538
Harvard	7	7	.500	15	9	.625
Yale	7	7	.500	14	12	.538
Princeton	7	7	.500	11	15	.423
Brown	5	9	.357	9	18	.333
Dartmouth	3	11	.214	5	21	.192

METRO

	Conference			Overall		
	W	L	Pct	W	L	Pct
Memphis⊕✪	13	1	.929	31	4	.886
Virginia Tech○	10	4	.714	20	9	.690
Cincinnati□	8	6	.571	17	14	.548
South Carolina	6	8	.429	15	13	.536
Tulane	6	8	.429	15	13	.536
Louisville□	6	8	.429	19	18	.514
Florida State	4	10	.286	14	16	.467
Southern Miss	3	11	.214	7	21	.250

Tournament: **Memphis d. Florida State 90-86 (OT)**
Tournament MVP: **Dean Shaffer**, Florida State

METRO ATLANTIC

	Conference			Overall		
	W	L	Pct	W	L	Pct
Iona⊕	11	3	.786	26	5	.839
Fordham□	9	5	.643	19	12	.613
La Salle	8	6	.571	15	13	.536
Holy Cross	8	6	.571	9	19	.321
Army	7	7	.500	16	13	.552
Saint Peter's	5	9	.357	15	14	.517
Manhattan	4	10	.286	8	20	.286
Fairfield	4	10	.286	11	17	.393

Tournament: **Iona d. Fordham 57-54**
Tournament MVP: **Tony Hargraves**, Iona

MID-AMERICAN

	Conference			Overall		
	W	L	Pct	W	L	Pct
Ohio⊕	14	4	.778	22	8	.733
Miami (OH)○	13	5	.722	20	11	.645
Toledo	11	7	.611	16	12	.571
Kent State□	11	7	.611	17	13	.567
Eastern Michigan	9	9	.500	15	13	.536
Ball State	8	10	.444	13	16	.448
Western Michigan	7	11	.389	12	16	.429
Northern Illinois	7	11	.389	11	16	.407
Bowling Green	6	12	.333	12	15	.444
Central Michigan	4	14	.222	9	18	.333

Tournament: **Ohio d. Miami (OH) 74-64**
Tournament MVP: **Ron Harper**, Miami (OH)

Conference Standings Continue →

⊕ Automatic NCAA Tournament bid ○ At-large NCAA Tournament bid □ NIT appearance ✪ Team record doesn't reflect games forfeited or vacated. For adjusted record, see p. 521.

MEAC

	Conference W	L	Pct	Overall W	L	Pct
NC A&T⊕	10	2	.833	19	10	.655
Howard	9	3	.750	16	12	.571
Delaware State	7	4	.636	12	17	.414
South Carolina St.	7	4	.636	11	16	.407
Bethune-Cookman	4	6	.400	8	19	.296
UMES	2	10	.167	3	25	.107
Morgan State	1	11	.083	3	25	.107

Tournament: **NC A&T d. Howard 71-69**
Tournament MOP: **Eric Boyd**, NC A&T

MIDWESTERN CITY

	Conference W	L	Pct	Overall W	L	Pct
Loyola-Chicago⊕	13	1	.929	27	6	.818
Butler□	9	5	.643	19	10	.655
Oral Roberts	8	6	.571	15	15	.500
Detroit	8	6	.571	16	12	.571
Xavier	7	7	.500	16	13	.552
Saint Louis	6	8	.429	13	15	.464
Evansville	4	10	.286	13	16	.448
Oklahoma City	1	13	.071	6	20	.231

Tournament: **Loyola-Chicago d. Oral Roberts 89-83**
Tournament MVP: **Alfredrick Hughes**, Loyola-Chicago

MISSOURI VALLEY

	Conference W	L	Pct	Overall W	L	Pct
Tulsa○	12	4	.750	23	8	.742
Illinois State○	11	5	.688	22	8	.733
Wichita State⊕	11	5	.688	18	13	.581
Creighton	9	7	.563	20	12	.625
Bradley□	9	7	.563	17	13	.567
Southern Illinois	6	10	.375	14	14	.500
Indiana State	6	10	.375	14	15	.483
Drake	4	12	.250	12	15	.444
West Texas	4	12	.250	11	17	.393

Tournament: **Wichita State d. Tulsa 84-82**

OHIO VALLEY

	Conference W	L	Pct	Overall W	L	Pct
Tennessee Tech□	11	3	.786	19	9	.679
Youngstown State	9	5	.643	19	11	.633
Eastern Kentucky	9	5	.643	16	13	.552
Murray State	8	6	.571	19	9	.679
Middle Tenn. State⊕	7	7	.500	17	14	.548
Akron	6	8	.429	12	14	.462
Austin Peay	4	10	.286	8	19	.296
Morehead State	2	12	.143	7	20	.259

Tournament: **Middle Tenn. St. d. Youngstown State 66-63**
Tournament MVP: **John Keshock**, Youngstown State

PCAA

	Conference W	L	Pct	Overall W	L	Pct
UNLV⊕	17	1	.944	28	4	.875
Fresno State□	15	3	.833	23	9	.719
Cal State Fullerton	11	7	.611	17	13	.567
Utah State	10	8	.556	17	11	.607
San Jose State	10	8	.556	16	13	.552
UC Irvine	8	10	.444	13	17	.433
UC Santa Barbara	8	10	.444	12	16	.429
Pacific	5	13	.278	9	19	.321
New Mexico State	4	14	.222	7	20	.259
Long Beach St.	2	16	.111	4	23	.148

Tournament: **UNLV d. Cal State Fullerton 79-61**
Tournament MVP: **Richie Adams**, UNLV

PAC-10

	Conference W	L	Pct	Overall W	L	Pct
Washington⊕	13	5	.722	22	10	.688
Southern California○	13	5	.722	19	10	.655
Oregon State○	12	6	.667	22	9	.710
Arizona○	12	6	.667	21	10	.677
UCLA□	12	6	.667	21	12	.636
Oregon	8	10	.444	15	16	.484
Arizona State	7	11	.389	12	16	.429
California	5	13	.278	13	15	.464
Washington State	5	13	.278	13	15	.464
Stanford	3	15	.167	11	17	.393

SEC

	Conference W	L	Pct	Overall W	L	Pct
LSU○	13	5	.722	19	10	.655
Georgia○⊗	12	6	.667	22	9	.710
Alabama○	11	7	.611	23	10	.697
Kentucky○	11	7	.611	18	13	.581
Florida□	9	9	.500	18	12	.600
Mississippi State	9	9	.500	13	15	.464
Auburn⊕	8	10	.444	22	12	.647
Tennessee□	8	10	.444	22	15	.595
Mississippi	5	13	.278	11	17	.393
Vanderbilt	4	14	.222	11	17	.393

Tournament: **Auburn d. Alabama 53-49 (OT)**
Tournament MVP: **Chuck Person**, Auburn

SOUTHERN

	Conference W	L	Pct	Overall W	L	Pct
Chattanooga□	14	2	.875	24	8	.750
Marshall⊕	12	4	.750	21	13	.618
The Citadel	11	5	.688	18	11	.621
Western Carolina	8	8	.500	14	14	.500
VMI	7	9	.438	16	14	.533
Appalachian State	7	9	.438	14	14	.500
Davidson	6	10	.375	10	20	.333
Furman	4	12	.250	7	21	.250
East Tennessee State	3	13	.188	9	18	.333

Tournament: **Marshall d. VMI 70-65**
Tournament MOP: **Gay Elmore**, VMI

SOUTHLAND

	Conference W	L	Pct	Overall W	L	Pct
Louisiana Tech⊕	11	1	.917	29	3	.906
McNeese State	9	3	.750	18	10	.643
Lamar□	8	4	.667	20	12	.625
Arkansas State	6	6	.500	14	14	.500
UL-Monroe	4	8	.333	17	12	.586
Texas-Arlington	3	9	.250	12	16	.429
North Texas	1	11	.083	5	23	.179

Tournament: **Louisiana Tech d. Lamar 70-69**
Tournament MVP: **Jerry Everett**, Lamar

SOUTHWEST

	Conference W	L	Pct	Overall W	L	Pct
Texas Tech⊕	12	4	.750	23	8	.742
SMU○	10	6	.625	23	10	.697
Texas A&M□	10	6	.625	19	11	.633
Arkansas○	10	6	.625	22	13	.629
TCU	8	8	.500	16	12	.571
Houston□	8	8	.500	16	14	.533
Texas	7	9	.438	15	13	.536
Baylor	4	12	.250	11	17	.393
Rice	3	13	.188	11	16	.407

Tournament: **Texas Tech d. Arkansas 67-64**
Tournament MVP: **Joe Kleine**, Arkansas

SWAC

	Conference W	L	Pct	Overall W	L	Pct
Alcorn State□	13	1	.929	23	7	.767
Southern U.⊕	9	5	.643	19	11	.633
Miss. Valley State	7	7	.500	18	11	.621
Alabama State	7	7	.500	14	17	.452
Texas Southern	6	8	.429	11	17	.393
Jackson State	6	8	.429	10	16	.385
Grambling	4	10	.286	8	19	.296
Prairie View A&M	4	10	.286	5	22	.185

Tournament: **Southern d. Alcorn State 85-70**
Tournament MVP: **Byron Gabriel**, Southern

SUN BELT

	Conference W	L	Pct	Overall W	L	Pct
VCU⊕	12	2	.857	26	6	.813
UAB○	11	3	.786	25	9	.735
Old Dominion○	9	5	.643	19	12	.613
South Florida□	6	8	.429	18	12	.600
South Alabama	6	8	.429	15	13	.536
Jacksonville	6	8	.429	15	14	.517
Western Kentucky	5	9	.357	14	14	.500
Charlotte	1	13	.071	5	23	.179

Tournament: **VCU d. Old Dominion 87-82**
Tournament MVP: **Mike Schlegel**, VCU

TAAC

	Conference W	L	Pct	Overall W	L	Pct
Ga. Southern	11	3	.786	24	5	.828
Mercer⊕	10	4	.714	22	9	.710
Houston Baptist	10	4	.714	21	8	.724
Arkansas-Little Rock	9	5	.643	17	13	.567
Samford	7	7	.500	18	12	.600
Hardin-Simmons	7	7	.500	11	17	.393
Centenary	2	12	.143	7	21	.250
Georgia State	0	14	.000	2	26	.071

Tournament: **Mercer d. Ark.-Little Rock 105-96**
Tournament MVP: **Sam Mitchell**, Mercer

WCAC

	Conference W	L	Pct	Overall W	L	Pct
Pepperdine⊕	11	1	.917	23	9	.719
Santa Clara□	9	3	.750	20	9	.690
Saint Mary's (CA)	7	5	.583	15	12	.556
San Diego	5	7	.417	16	11	.593
Gonzaga	4	8	.333	15	13	.536
Portland	3	9	.250	14	14	.500
Loyola Marymount	3	9	.250	11	16	.407

WAC

	Conference W	L	Pct	Overall W	L	Pct
UTEP○	12	4	.750	22	10	.688
San Diego State⊕	11	5	.688	23	8	.742
Colorado State	9	7	.563	18	12	.600
New Mexico□	9	7	.563	19	13	.594
BYU	9	7	.563	15	14	.517
Utah	8	8	.500	15	16	.484
Wyoming	7	9	.438	15	14	.517
Hawaii	5	11	.313	10	18	.357
Air Force	2	14	.125	8	20	.286

Tournament: **San Diego St. d. UTEP 87-81**
Tournament MVP: **Luster Goodwin**, UTEP

INDEPENDENTS

	Overall W	L	Pct
Notre Dame○	21	9	.700
Dayton○	19	10	.655
DePaul○	19	10	.655
Marquette□	20	11	.645
UTSA	18	10	.643
Chicago State	16	11	.593
Radford	16	12	.571
Utica	15	12	.556
UL-Lafayette□	17	14	.548
Brooklyn	15	13	.536
Charleston Southern	13	15	.464
Eastern Washington	12	15	.444
Monmouth	12	15	.444
Stetson	12	16	.429
Texas-Pan American	12	16	.429
New Orleans	11	19	.367
Florida A&M	10	18	.357
UCF	10	18	.357
Tennessee State	9	19	.321
Augusta	8	20	.286
Campbell	5	22	.185
U.S. International	1	27	.036

INDIVIDUAL LEADERS—SEASON

SCORING	CL	POS	G	FG	FT	PTS	PPG
1 **Xavier McDaniel**, Wichita State	SR	F	31	351	142	844	**27.2**
2 **Alfredrick Hughes**, Loyola-Chicago	SR	G/F	33	366	136	868	**26.3**
3 **Dan Palombizio**, Ball State	JR	F	29	279	204	762	**26.3**
4 **Joe Dumars**, McNeese State	SR	G	27	248	201	697	**25.8**
5 **Terry Catledge**, South Alabama	SR	F	28	285	148	718	**25.6**
6 **Derrick Gervin**, UTSA	JR	F	28	272	174	718	**25.6**
7 **Wayman Tisdale**, Oklahoma	JR	F/C	37	370	192	932	**25.2**
8 **Keith Smith**, Loyola Marymount	JR	G	27	283	112	678	**25.1**
9 **Sam Mitchell**, Mercer	SR	F	31	294	186	774	**25.0**
10 **Ron Harper**, Miami (OH)	JR	G/F	31	312	148	772	**24.9**

FIELD GOAL PCT	CL	POS	G	FG	FGA	PCT
1 **Keith Walker**, Utica	SR	F	27	154	216	**71.3**
2 **Vernon Moore**, Creighton	SR	G	32	265	393	**67.4**
3 **Dave Hoppen**, Nebraska	JR	C	30	270	418	**64.6**
4 **David Robinson**, Navy	SO	C	32	302	469	**64.4**
5 **John Staves**, Southern U.	JR	F	29	164	257	**63.8**

MINIMUM: 5 MADE PER GAME

FREE THROW PCT	CL	POS	G	FT	FTA	PCT
1 **Craig Collins**, Penn State	SR	G	27	94	98	**95.9**
2 **Steve Alford**, Indiana	SO	G	32	116	126	**92.1**
3 **Steve Eggink**, Marist	SR	G	28	81	88	**92.0**
4 **Dennis Nutt**, TCU	SR	G	28	77	84	**91.7**
5 **Bruce Timko**, Youngstown State	JR	G	30	78	86	**90.7**

MINIMUM: 2.5 MADE PER GAME

ASSISTS PER GAME	CL	POS	G	AST	APG
1 **Robbie Weingard**, Hofstra	SR	G	24	228	**9.5**
2 **Carl Golston**, Loyola-Chicago	JR	G	33	305	**9.2**
3 **Jim Les**, Bradley	JR	G	30	263	**8.8**
4 **Taurence Chisholm**, Delaware	FR	G	28	224	**8.0**
5 **Brian Carr**, Nebraska	SO	G	30	237	**7.9**
6 **Glen James**, Brooklyn	SR	G	28	211	**7.5**
7 **Carlton Clarington**, Tennessee Tech	SR	G	28	210	**7.5**
8 **Butch Moore**, SMU	JR	G	33	247	**7.5**
9 **Shawn Teague**, Boston U.	SR	G	30	217	**7.2**
10 **Aaron McCarthy**, Weber State	SR	G	29	209	**7.2**

REBOUNDS PER GAME	CL	POS	G	REB	RPG
1 **Xavier McDaniel**, Wichita State	SR	F	31	460	**14.8**
2 **Benoit Benjamin**, Creighton	JR	C	32	451	**14.1**
3 **Carey Scurry**, Long Island	SR	F	28	394	**14.1**
4 **Karl Towns**, Monmouth	SR	F/C	26	319	**12.3**
5 **Robert Sanders**, Mississippi Valley State	SR	F	29	344	**11.9**
6 **Alex Stivrins**, Colorado	SR	F	27	317	**11.7**
7 **David Robinson**, Navy	SO	C	32	370	**11.6**
8 **Terry Catledge**, South Alabama	SR	F	28	322	**11.5**
9 **Tony Neal**, Cal State Fullerton	SR	F	29	326	**11.2**
10 **Joe Williams**, Alabama State	SR	F	26	288	**11.1**

INDIVIDUAL LEADERS—GAME

POINTS	CL	POS	OPP	DATE	PTS
1 **Wayman Tisdale**, Oklahoma	JR	F/C	Southwestern (TX)	D10	**55**
2 **Derrick Gervin**, UTSA	JR	F	Baylor	J2	**51**
3 **Barry Stevens**, Iowa State	SR	G	Morgan State	J3	**47**
Alfredrick Hughes, Loyola-Chicago	SR	G/F	Detroit	F9	**47**
5 **Jim McCaffrey**, Holy Cross	JR	G	Iona	J31	**46**

ASSISTS	CL	POS	OPP	DATE	AST
1 **Brian Carr**, Nebraska	SO	G	Evansville	J3	**18**
2 **James Smith**, Rider	JR	F	Texas-Arlington	D21	**17**
Reid Gettys, Houston	JR	G	Rice	F17	**17**
4 **Bryan Williams**, UC Irvine	SR	G	Pepperdine	D20	**16**
Robbie Weingard, Hofstra	SR	G	Charlotte	D21	**16**
Brian Ellerbe, Rutgers	SR	G	NC State	D27	**16**
Reggie Watson, Georgia Southern	JR	G	Centenary	J26	**16**
Glenn Daniels, Long Island	SR	G	Robert Morris	F21	**16**
Glen James, Brooklyn	SR	G	UMES	F25	**16**
Elston Harris, Mercer	JR	G	Georgia State	J12	**16**

REBOUNDS	CL	POS	OPP	DATE	REB
1 **Terry Catledge**, South Alabama	SR	F	Charlotte	J20	**26**
2 **Karl Towns**, Monmouth	SR	F/C	Morgan State	J12	**23**
Vernon Butler, Navy	JR	F	Delaware	J21	**23**
Dennis Williams, South Carolina St.	SR	F/C	Bethune-Cookman	M7	**23**
5 **Wayman Tisdale**, Oklahoma	JR	F/C	Arkansas-Little Rock	N26	**22**
Dan Palombizio, Ball State	JR	F	Northern Illinois	J16	**22**
Benoit Benjamin, Creighton	JR	C	Briar Cliff	D4	**22**
Robert Sanders, Miss. Valley State	SR	F	Alabama State	J28	**22**
Xavier McDaniel, Wichita State	SR	F	Bradley	F23	**22**

TEAM LEADERS—SEASON

WIN-LOSS PCT	W	L	PCT
1 **Georgetown**	35	3	**.921**
2 **Louisiana Tech**	29	3	**.906**
3 **Memphis** ⊗	31	4	**.886**
St. John's	31	4	**.886**
5 **UNLV**	28	4	**.875**

SCORING OFFENSE	G	W-L	PTS	PPG
1 **Oklahoma**	37	31-6	3328	**89.9**
2 **Alcorn State**	30	23-7	2555	**85.2**
3 **Southern U.**	30	19-11	2515	**83.8**
4 **Loyola-Chicago**	33	27-6	2757	**83.5**
5 **Utah State**	28	17-11	2292	**81.9**

SCORING MARGIN	G	W-L	PPG	OPP PPG	MAR
1 **Georgetown**	38	35-3	74.3	57.3	**17.0**
2 **Oklahoma**	37	31-6	89.9	75.6	**14.3**
3 **Navy**	32	26-6	78.4	65.3	**13.1**
4 **Louisiana Tech**	32	29-3	77.9	65.1	**12.8**
5 **Illinois**	35	26-9	68.9	57.2	**11.7**

FIELD GOAL PCT	G	W-L	FG	FGA	PCT
1 **Navy**	32	26-6	946	1,726	**54.8**
2 **St. John's**	35	31-4	978	1,806	**54.2**
3 **North Carolina**	36	27-9	1,039	1,925	**54.0**
4 **Iona**	31	26-5	898	1,669	**53.8**
5 **Michigan State**	29	19-10	837	1,559	**53.7**
Kansas	34	26-8	1,019	1,898	**53.7**

FREE THROW PCT	G	W-L	FT	FTA	PCT
1 **Harvard**	24	15-9	450	555	**81.1**
2 **Davidson**	30	10-20	539	692	**77.9**
3 **Weber State**	29	20-9	495	641	**77.2**
4 **The Citadel**	29	18-11	529	688	**76.9**
5 **UTSA**	28	18-10	454	591	**76.8**

REBOUND MARGIN	G	W-L	RPG	OPP RPG	MAR
1 **Georgetown**	38	35-3	39.6	30.5	**9.1**
2 **Michigan**	30	26-4	36.7	28.8	**7.9**
Eastern Kentucky	29	16-13	40.8	32.9	**7.9**
4 **Iowa**	32	21-11	41.4	33.8	**7.6**
5 **Washington**	32	22-10	34.3	26.9	**7.4**

SCORING DEFENSE	G	W-L	OPP PTS	OPP PPG
1 **Fresno State**	32	23-9	1696	**53.0**
2 **Princeton**	26	11-15	1429	**55.0**
3 **Colgate**	26	5-21	1451	**55.8**
4 **Temple**	31	25-6	1736	**56.0**
5 **Illinois**	35	26-9	2001	**57.2**

FIELD GOAL PCT DEFENSE	G	W-L	OPP FG	OPP FGA	OPP PCT
1 **Georgetown**	38	35-3	833	2,064	**40.4**
2 **Illinois**	35	26-9	832	1,989	**41.8**
3 **West Virginia**	29	20-9	693	1,652	**41.9**
4 **Iowa**	32	21-11	767	1,826	**42.0**
5 **Memphis**	35	31-4	911	2,152	**42.3**

CONSENSUS ALL-AMERICAS

FIRST TEAM

PLAYER	CL	POS	HT	SCHOOL	RPG	PPG
Johnny Dawkins	JR	G	6-2	Duke	4.5	18.8
Patrick Ewing	SR	C	7-0	Georgetown	9.2	14.6
Keith Lee†	SR	C	6-10	Memphis	9.2	19.7
Xavier McDaniel	SR	F	6-7	Wichita State	14.8	27.2
Chris Mullin	SR	G/F	6-6	St. John's	4.8	19.8
Wayman Tisdale	JR	F/C	6-9	Oklahoma	10.2	25.2

SECOND TEAM

PLAYER	CL	POS	HT	SCHOOL	RPG	PPG
Len Bias	JR	F	6-8	Maryland	6.8	18.9
Jon Koncak	SR	C	7-0	SMU	10.7	17.2
Mark Price	JR	G	6-0	Georgia Tech	2.0	16.7
Kenny Walker	JR	F	6-8	Kentucky	10.2	22.9
Dwayne Washington	SO	G	6-2	Syracuse	2.9	15.2

SELECTORS: AP, NBC, UPI, USBWA

† HONOR LATER VACATED

AWARD WINNERS

PLAYER OF THE YEAR

PLAYER	CL	POS	HT	SCHOOL	AWARDS
Patrick Ewing	SR	C	7-0	Georgetown	Naismith, AP, NABC
Chris Mullin	SR	G/F	6-6	St. John's	UPI, USBWA, Wooden, Rupp
Bubba Jennings	SR	G	5-11	Texas Tech	Frances Pomeroy Naismith*

* FOR THE MOST OUTSTANDING SENIOR PLAYER WHO IS 6 FEET OR UNDER.

COACH OF THE YEAR

COACH	SCHOOL	REC	AWARDS
Bill Frieder	Michigan	26-4	AP
Lou Carnesecca	St. John's	31-4	UPI, USBWA, Sporting News
John Thompson	Georgetown	35-3	NABC
Dale Brown	LSU	19-10	CBS/Chevrolet

BOB GIBBONS' TOP HIGH SCHOOL SENIOR RECRUITS

PLAYER	POS	HT	HIGH SCHOOL	A-A TEAMS	COLLEGE	CAREER NOTES
1 Jeff Lebo	PG	6-3	Carlisle (Pa.) HS	McD, P, USA	North Carolina	116-25 record (4 seasons); undrafted; played in 4 NBA games; college head coach (3 teams, 10 seasons)
2 J. "Pooh" Richardson	PG	6-1	Ben Franklin Boys HS, Philadelphia	McD, P	UCLA	12.0 ppg, 6.8 apg (4 seasons); No. 10 pick, '89 NBA draft (Wolves); 11.1 ppg, 6.5 apg (10 seasons)
3 Rick Calloway	SF	6-6	Withrow HS, Cincinnati	McD, P	Indiana/Kansas	NCAA title, '87; transferred after 1 year; picked in CBA draft; played in NBA (Kings); 3.2 ppg (1 season)
4 Rod Strickland	PG	6-2	Oak Hill Academy, Mouth of Wilson, VA	P	DePaul	First team All-America, '87; No. 19 pick, '88 NBA draft (Knicks); 7,987 assists (17 seasons)
5 Tony Kimbro	SF	6-7	Seneca HS, Louisville, KY	McD, P, USA	Louisville	Kentucky Mr. Basketball, '85; NCAA title, '86; 6 points in NCAA title game; undrafted
6 Tom Hammonds	F	6-8	Crestview HS, Crestview, FL	McD, P	Georgia Tech	5th-leading scorer all-time (2,081 pts); No. 9 pick, '89 NBA draft (Bullets); 5.3 ppg, 3.3 rpg (12 seasons)
7 Walker Lambiotte	SF	6-6	Central HS, Woodstock, VA	McD, P	NC State/ Northwestern	McDonald's game MVP, '85; at Northwestern, 17.4 ppg (2 seasons); undrafted
8 Kevin Madden	G/F	6-5	Robert E. Lee HS, Stauton, VA	McD, P, USA	North Carolina	2nd team All-ACC, '89; knee injury; undrafted; played overseas
9 Ed Horton	PF	6-8	Lanphier HS, Springfield, IL	McD, P	Iowa	First team All-Big Ten; 2nd-round pick, '89 NBA draft (Bullets); 4.5 ppg (1 season)
10 Danny Ferry	F/C	6-10	DeMatha HS, Hyattsville, MD	McD, USA	Duke	Naismith Award, '89; No. 2 pick, '89 NBA draft (Clippers); 7.0 ppg (13 seasons); NBA team executive
11 Tito Horford	C	7-0	Marian Christian HS, Houston	McD, P, USA	Miami (FL)	14.3 ppg, 9.3 rpg (3 seasons); No. 39 pick, '88 NBA draft (Bucks); 1.5 ppg (3 seasons); son Al in NBA
12 Jerome Lane	SF	6-6	St. Vincent/St. Mary HS, Akron, OH	McD, P	Pittsburgh	Led NCAA in rpg, '86-87 (13.5); glass shatterer; No. 23 pick, '88 NBA draft (Nuggets); 5.8 rpg (5 seasons)
13 Glen Rice	SF	6-7	Northwestern HS, Flint, MI	P	Michigan	NCAA title, '89; No. 4 pick, '89 NBA draft (Heat); 18.3 ppg (15 seasons); 3-time All-Star (MVP, '97); 1 NBA title
14 Terry Dozier	F	6-9	Dunbar HS, Baltimore	McD, P	South Carolina	At USC, 4-year starter; undrafted; played overseas; played in 9 NBA games
15 Irving Thomas	F	6-8	Carol City (FL) HS	McD, P	Kentucky/ Florida State	Transferred after 2 years; undrafted; played 1 year in NBA (Lakers)
16 Steve Bucknall	F/G	6-6	Governor Dummer Academy, Byfield, MA	McD, P	North Carolina	2nd team All-ACC, '89; undrafted; played overseas
17 Roy Marble	G/F	6-6	Beecher HS, Flint, MI	McD, P	Iowa	Left Iowa as all-time leading scorer (2,116 pts); No. 23 pick, '89 NBA draft (Hawks); 1.9 ppg (2 seasons)
18 Michael Jones	SF	6-7	Oak Hill Academy, Mouth of Wilson, VA	P	Auburn	All-SEC as freshman; at Auburn, 13.1 ppg (3 seasons); 3rd-round pick, '88 NBA draft (Bucks); no NBA games played
19 Pervis Ellison	C/F	6-10	Savannah (Ga.) HS	McD	Louisville	NCAA title, Tournament MOP, '86; No. 1 overall pick, '89 NBA draft (Kings); 9.5 ppg (11 seasons)
20 Mark Stevenson	G/F	6-5	Roman Catholic HS, Philadelphia	McD, P	Notre Dame/ Duquesne	Transferred after 3 years; at Duquesne, 27.2 ppg (1 season); 2nd-round pick in '90 CBA draft

OTHER STANDOUTS

PLAYER	POS	HT	HIGH SCHOOL	A-A TEAMS	COLLEGE	CAREER NOTES
26 Bo Kimble	G/F	6-5	Dobbins Technical HS, Philadelphia		USC/ Loyola Marymount	Transferred after 1 year; at Loyola, 35.3 ppg as Sr.; No. 8 pick, '90 NBA draft (Clippers); 5.5 ppg (3 seasons)
33 Sean Elliott	SF	6-7	Cholla HS, Tucson, AZ	McD	Arizona	Wooden Award, '89; No. 3 pick, '89 NBA draft (Spurs); 14.2 ppg (12 seasons); 1-time All-Star
44 Hank Gathers	PF	6-6	Dobbins Technical HS, Philadelphia		USC/ Loyola Marymount	Transferred after 1 year; Led NCAA in ppg, rpg, '88-'89; fatal collapse in WCC tournament game, '90

Abbreviations: McD=McDonald's; P=Parade; USA=USA Today

Poll Progression

Preseason Poll

AP	School
1	Georgetown
2	Illinois
3	DePaul
4	Indiana
5	Oklahoma
6	Duke
7	St. John's
8	Memphis
9	Washington
10	SMU
11	UNLV
12	Syracuse
13	NC State
14	LSU
15	Virginia Tech
16	Arkansas
17	Louisville
18	Kentucky
19	Kansas
20	Georgia Tech

Week of Nov 27

AP	UPI	School	AP↓↑
1	1	Georgetown (1-0)	
2	2	DePaul (1-0)	↑1
3	3	St. John's (0-0)	↑4
4	6	Duke (0-0)	↑2
5	7	Memphis (0-0)	↑3
6	4	Louisville (1-0)	↑11
7	5	Illinois (3-1)	↓5
8	9	Washington (0-0)	↑1
9	8	SMU (1-0)	↑1
10	10	Oklahoma (1-1)	↓5
11	12	NC State (1-0)	↑2
12	13	Indiana (0-1)	↓8
13	11	UAB (3-0)	⤴
14	—	Syracuse (0-0)	↓2
15	20	Virginia Tech (1-0)	
16	14	LSU (0-0)	↓2
17	18	Arkansas (1-0)	↓1
18	—	Georgia Tech (1-0)	↑2
19	19	North Carolina (1-0)	⤴
20	15	Kansas (2-1)	↓1
20	16	UNLV (0-1)	↓9
—	17	Kentucky (0-0)	Γ

Week of Dec 4

AP	UPI	School	AP↓↑
1	1	Georgetown (3-0)	
2	2	DePaul (2-0)	
3	3	St. John's (2-0)	
4	4	Duke (3-0)	
5	6	Memphis (2-0)	
6	7	Louisville (2-0) (A)	
7	5	Illinois (5-1)	
8	9	SMU (1-0)	↑1
9	8	Washington (2-0)	↓1
10	10	NC State (2-0)	↑1
11	12	Indiana (1-1)	↑1
12	13	Syracuse (1-0)	↑2
13	11	LSU (2-0)	↑3
14	19	Virginia Tech (2-0)	↑1
15	14	Georgia Tech (3-0)	↑3
16	18	North Carolina (2-0)	↑3
17	16	Oklahoma (2-2)	↓7
18	15	UAB (4-1)	↓5
19	17	Kansas (3-1)	↑1
20	20	UNLV (1-1)	

Week of Dec 11

AP	UPI	School	AP↓↑
1	1	Georgetown (5-0)	
2	2	DePaul (5-0)	
3	3	Duke (5-0)	↑1
4	4	St. John's (4-0)	↓1
5	5	Memphis (4-0)	
6	6	Illinois (9-1)	↑1
7	7	SMU (4-0)	↑1
8	9	Washington (4-0)	↑1
9	8	NC State (5-0)	↑1
10	10	Syracuse (4-0)	↑2
11	11	Virginia Tech (4-0)	↑3
12	14	Georgia Tech (3-0)	↑3
13	12	North Carolina (4-0)	↑3
14	17	Louisville (3-1)	↓8
15	12	Oklahoma (5-2) (B)	↑2
16	16	Indiana (2-2)	↓5
17	18	UAB (5-1)	↑1
18	15	Kansas (6-1)	↑1
19	19	LSU (4-1)	↓6
20	—	Michigan (5-0)	⤴
—	20	Arkansas (3-1)	
—	20	Louisiana Tech (5-0)	

Week of Dec 18

AP	UPI	School	AP↓↑
1	1	Georgetown (7-0)	
2	2	Duke (5-0)	↑1
3	4	Memphis (5-0)	↑2
4	3	Illinois (10-1)	↑2
5	5	DePaul (6-1)	↓3
6	6	SMU (6-0)	↑1
7	7	Washington (4-0) (C)	↑1
8	8	St. John's (5-1)	↓4
9	10	Syracuse (5-0)	↑1
10	9	North Carolina (5-0)	↑3
11	11	Oklahoma (6-2)	↑4
12	15	Louisville (4-1)	↑2
13	13	Georgia Tech (4-1)	↓1
14	17	NC State (5-1)	↓5
15	12	Kansas (7-1)	↑3
16	14	Indiana (5-2)	
17	—	Virginia Tech (6-1)	↓6
18	20	Michigan (6-0)	↑2
19	19	LSU (4-1)	
20	—	Louisiana Tech (8-0)	⤴
—	16	Arkansas (5-1)	
—	18	Maryland (7-1)	

Week of Dec 25

AP	UPI	School	AP↓↑
1	1	Georgetown (9-0)	
2	2	Duke (7-0)	
3	4	Memphis (8-0)	
4	3	SMU (9-0)	↑2
5	8	St. John's (6-1)	↑3
6	6	Syracuse (6-0)	↑3
7	5	North Carolina (7-0)	↑3
8	7	Illinois (11-2)	↓4
9	9	DePaul (7-2)	↓4
10	13	Georgia Tech (6-1)	↑3
11	12	Washington (5-1)	↓4
12	11	Kansas (8-1)	↑3
13	14	Michigan (8-0)	↑5
14	—	NC State (6-1)	
15	10	Indiana (6-2)	↑1
16	18	Virginia Tech (7-1)	↑1
17	17	Oklahoma (6-3)	↓6
18	19	LSU (6-1)	↑1
19	16	Louisiana Tech (9-0)	↑1
20	—	Louisville (6-2)	↓8
—	15	Arkansas (8-1)	
—	20	Maryland (8-1)	

Week of Jan 1 (D)

AP	UPI	School	AP↓↑
1	1	Georgetown (11-0)	
2	2	Duke (9-0)	
3	3	Memphis (8-0)	
4	4	St. John's (8-1)	↑1
5	5	Syracuse (8-0)	↑1
6	6	Illinois (11-2)	↑2
7	8	SMU (9-1)	↓3
8	7	Georgia Tech (9-1)	↑2
9	9	North Carolina (8-1)	↓2
10	10	DePaul (8-2)	↓1
11	11	Kansas (8-2) (D)	↑1
12	12	Indiana (8-2)	↑3
13	14	Oklahoma (9-3)	↑4
14	15	LSU (8-1)	↑4
15	13	Washington (7-2)	↓4
16	17	Michigan (8-1)	↓3
17	—	NC State (7-2)	↓3
18	18	Louisiana Tech (10-1)	↑1
19	16	Maryland (10-2)	⤴
20	19	VCU (8-1)	⤴
—	20	Ohio State (8-1)	

Week of Jan 8

AP	UPI	School	AP↓↑
1	1	Georgetown (13-0)	
2	2	Duke (10-0)	
3	4	St. John's (10-1)	↑1
4	3	SMU (11-1)	↑3
5	6	North Carolina (10-1)	↑4
6	5	Memphis (9-1)	↓3
7	8	Syracuse (8-1)	↓2
8	7	Oklahoma (10-3)	↑5
9	10	Georgia Tech (10-2)	↓1
10	9	Kansas (10-2)	↑1
11	11	Indiana (9-3)	↑1
12	17	Boston College (10-1)	⤴
13	15	DePaul (9-3)	↓3
14	13	Louisiana Tech (11-1)	↑4
15	16	Illinois (11-4)	↓9
16	20	Villanova (9-1) (E)	⤴
17	14	Michigan State (11-1)	⤴
18	—	VCU (9-1)	↑2
19	—	Iowa (13-2)	⤴
20	12	Oregon State (11-1)	⤴
—	18	LSU (9-2)	Γ
—	19	Washington (9-3)	Γ

Week of Jan 15

AP	UPI	School	AP↓↑
1	1	Georgetown (15-0)	
2	2	Duke (12-0)	
3	3	SMU (14-1)	↑1
4	4	St. John's (11-1)	↓1
5	5	Memphis (11-1)	↑1
6	7	North Carolina (12-2)	↓1
7	6	Syracuse (10-1)	
8	9	Indiana (11-3)	↑3
9	8	Kansas (12-2)	↑1
10	14	DePaul (10-3)	↑3
11	13	Illinois (13-4)	↑4
12	12	Louisiana Tech (13-1)	↑2
13	10	Oklahoma (11-3)	↓5
14	11	Oregon State (13-1)	↑6
15	17	Boston College (11-2)	↓3
16	19	VCU (10-1)	↑2
17	15	Georgia Tech (10-3)	↓8
18	16	Villanova (9-3)	↓2
19	18	Michigan State (12-2)	↓2
20	20	Tulsa (11-2)	⤴

Week of Jan 22

AP	UPI	School	AP↓↑
1	1	Georgetown (17-0)	
2	2	SMU (15-1)	↑1
3	3	St. John's (13-1)	↑1
4	4	Memphis (13-1)	↑1
5	5	Duke (13-2)	↓3
6	6	Illinois (15-4)	↑5
7	10	DePaul (13-3)	↑3
8	9	North Carolina (14-3)	↓2
9	7	Oklahoma (13-4)	↑4
10	8	Oregon State (14-1)	↑4
11	12	Syracuse (11-2)	↓4
12	11	Louisiana Tech (15-1)	
13	13	Indiana (11-4)	↓5
14	15	Villanova (12-3)	↑4
15	14	Kansas (13-3)	↓6
16	17	Georgia Tech (13-3)	↑1
17	16	Tulsa (14-2)	↑3
18	—	Michigan (12-3)	⤴
19	—	VCU (12-2)	↓3
20	19	UNLV (13-2)	⤴
—	18	Washington (12-5)	
—	19	UAB (13-4)	

Week of Jan 29

AP	UPI	School	AP↓↑
1	1	St. John's (15-1)	↑2
2	2	Georgetown (18-1) (F)	↓1
3	3	Memphis (15-1)	↑1
4	4	SMU (16-2)	↓2
5	7	Illinois (17-4)	↑1
6	5	Duke (14-3)	↓1
7	6	Oklahoma (15-4)	↑2
8	9	Georgia Tech (15-3)	↑8
9	8	Syracuse (12-3)	↑2
10	11	Michigan (14-3)	↑8
11	14	North Carolina (14-4)	↓3
12	10	Tulsa (16-2)	↑5
13	15	DePaul (13-4)	↓6
14	12	Oregon State (14-2)	↓4
15	16	Louisiana Tech (16-2)	↓3
16	13	UNLV (15-2)	↑4
17	17	Maryland (16-5)	⤴
18	18	Villanova (13-4)	↓4
19	20	Kansas (15-4)	↓4
20	19	UAB (18-4)	⤴

Week of Feb 5

AP	UPI	School	AP↓↑
1	1	St. John's (18-1)	
2	2	Georgetown (19-2)	
3	3	Memphis (17-1)	
4	4	SMU (18-2)	
5	5	Duke (16-3)	↑1
6	8	Syracuse (15-3)	↑3
7	9	Oklahoma (17-4)	
8	10	Michigan (16-3)	↑2
9	6	Illinois (18-5)	↓4
10	7	Georgia Tech (16-4)	↓2
11	12	UNLV (17-2)	↑5
12	13	Iowa (18-4)	⤴
13	14	Kansas (18-4)	↑6
14	16	Louisiana Tech (18-2)	↑1
15	15	North Carolina (16-5)	↓4
16	11	Oregon State (16-4)	↓2
17	17	Tulsa (17-3)	↓5
18	—	DePaul (14-5)	↓5
19	18	Villanova (14-5)	↓1
20	19	Maryland (18-6)	↓3
—	20	UAB (19-5)	Γ

Poll Progression Continues →

Week of Feb 12

AP	UPI	SCHOOL	AP↓↑
1	1	**St. John's** (19-1)	
2	2	**Georgetown** (21-2)	
3	7	**Michigan** (18-3)	↑5
4	5	**Oklahoma** (19-4)	↑3
5	3	**Memphis** (17-2)	↓2
6	5	**Georgia Tech** (18-4)	↑4
7	4	**Duke** (17-4)	↓2
8	8	**Syracuse** (16-4)	↓2
9	9	**SMU** (18-4)	↓5
10	10	**Kansas** (20-4)	↑3
11	11	**Iowa** (19-4)	↑1
12	13	**Louisiana Tech** (20-2)	↑2
13	12	**North Carolina** (18-5)	↑2
14	16	**UNLV** (18-3)	↓3
15	14	**Tulsa** (18-4)	↑2
16	18	**Villanova** (15-6)	↑3
17	15	**Illinois** (18-7)	↓8
18	17	**Oregon State** (17-4)	↓2
19	—	**UAB** (21-5)	⅃
20	19	**Maryland** (19-7)	
—	20	**DePaul** (15-6)	Γ

Week of Feb 19

AP	UPI	SCHOOL	AP↓↑
1	1	**St. John's** (22-1)	
2	2	**Georgetown** (23-2)	
3	6	**Michigan** (20-3)	
4	4	**Memphis** (20-2)	↑1
5	3	**Oklahoma** (21-4)	↓1
6	5	**Duke** (18-4)	↑1
7	7	**Syracuse** (19-4)	↑1
8	9	**Georgia Tech** (18-5)	↓2
9	8	**SMU** (20-5)	
10	10	**Louisiana Tech** (22-2)	↑2
11	11	**UNLV** (20-3)	↑3
12	12	**Tulsa** (19-4)	↑3
13	15	**North Carolina** (19-6)	
14	16	**Iowa** (19-6)	↓3
15	13	**Kansas** (20-6)	↓5
16	14	**Illinois** (20-7)	↑1
17	18	**VCU** (20-4)	⅃
18	—	**Georgia** (17-6)	⅃
19	17	**Oregon State** (18-5)	↓1
20	—	**Boston College** (18-6)	⅃
—	19	**Maryland** (19-9)	Γ
—	20	**UAB** (21-6)	Γ
—	20	**Southern California** (16-6)	

Week of Feb 26

AP	UPI	SCHOOL	AP↓↑
1	1	**St. John's** (24-1)	
2	2	**Georgetown** (25-2)	
3	3	**Michigan** (21-3)	
4	4	**Memphis** (22-2)	
5	5	**Duke** (20-5)	↑1
6	6	**Oklahoma** (22-5)	↓1
7	7	**Louisiana Tech** (24-2)	↑3
8	11	**North Carolina** (21-6)	↑5
9	10	**UNLV** (23-3)	↑2
10	13	**Georgia Tech** (19-6)	↓2
11	8	**Kansas** (22-6)	↑4
12	12	**Syracuse** (19-6)	↓5
13	9	**SMU** (21-6)	↓4
14	15	**Georgia** (19-6)	↑4
15	14	**Tulsa** (20-5)	↓3
16	19	**NC State** (18-7)	⅃
17	18	**VCU** (21-5)	
18	16	**Illinois** (21-8)	↓2
19	17	**Arizona** (20-7)	⅃
20	—	**Loyola-Chicago** (20-5)	⅃
—	20	**LSU** (17-8)	

Week of Mar 5

AP	UPI	SCHOOL	A
1	1	**Georgetown** (27-2)	
2	2	**St. John's** (25-2)	
3	3	**Michigan** (23-3)	
4	5	**Oklahoma** (25-5)	
5	4	**Memphis** (24-3)	↓
6	7	**North Carolina** (22-7)	↑
7	9	**Duke** (21-6)	↓
8	6	**Louisiana Tech** (25-2)	↓
9	11	**Georgia Tech** (21-7)	↑
10	8	**Kansas** (24-6)	↑
11	10	**UNLV** (24-3)	↓
12	15	**VCU** (25-5)	↑
13	12	**Syracuse** (20-7)	↓
14	14	**Illinois** (22-8)	↑
15	13	**Tulsa** (21-6)	
16	18	**Loyola-Chicago** (22-5)	↑
17	20	**Georgia** (20-7)	↓3
18	17	**NC State** (19-8)	↓2
19	19	**LSU** (19-8)	⅃
20	16	**SMU** (21-8)	↓7

Final Poll Ⓖ

AP	UPI	SCHOOL	AP↓↑
1	1	**Georgetown** (30-2)	
2	2	**Michigan** (25-3)	↑1
3	3	**St. John's** (27-3)	↓1
4	5	**Oklahoma** (28-5)	
5	4	**Memphis** (27-3)	
6	6	**Georgia Tech** (24-7)	↑3
7	7	**North Carolina** (24-8)	↓1
8	8	**Louisiana Tech** (27-2)	
9	9	**UNLV** (27-3)	↑2
10	12	**Duke** (22-7)	↓3
11	11	**VCU** (25-5)	↑1
12	10	**Illinois** (24-8)	↑2
13	13	**Kansas** (25-7)	↓3
14	17	**Loyola-Chicago** (25-5)	↑2
15	15	**Syracuse** (21-8)	↓2
16	18	**NC State** (20-9)	↑2
17	16	**Texas Tech** (23-7)	⅃
18	14	**Tulsa** (23-7)	↓3
19	—	**Georgia** (21-8)	↓2
20	19	**LSU** (19-9)	↓1
—	20	**Michigan State** (19-9)	

Ⓐ In the newly-renovated Freedom Hall, Louisville beats Virginia Commonwealth, 67-55, but star guard Milt Wagner goes down with an ankle injury and is lost for the season.
Ⓑ Oklahoma junior Wayman Tisdale, a star on the gold-medal 1984 U.S. Olympic team, lights up Texas State on Dec. 10 for 55 points.
Ⓒ Washington gets off to a promising start for coach Marv Harshman. After the season, Harshman will retire with 654 victories in 40 seasons at Pacific Lutheran, Washington State and Washington.
Ⓓ Kentucky's Kenny "Sky" Walker outscores Kansas' Danny Manning, 36-30, in the Wildcats' 92-89 win on Dec. 31 in Freedom Hall. The Wildcats will go 18–12, and after the season Joe B. Hall will announce his retirement.
Ⓔ Villanova makes its first appearance in the polls, joining fellow Big East teams Georgetown, St. John's, Syracuse and Boston College.
Ⓕ After being ranked No. 1 since the preseason, Georgetown loses back-to-back games—66-65 at home to St. John's on Jan. 26 and 65-63 at Syracuse the next week.
Ⓖ The consensus All-America team includes four players who will finish their careers with at least 2,000 points and 1,000 rebounds: Wayman Tisdale (Oklahoma), Patrick Ewing (Georgetown), Keith Lee (Memphis State) and Xavier McDaniel (Wichita State).

1985 NCAA Tournament

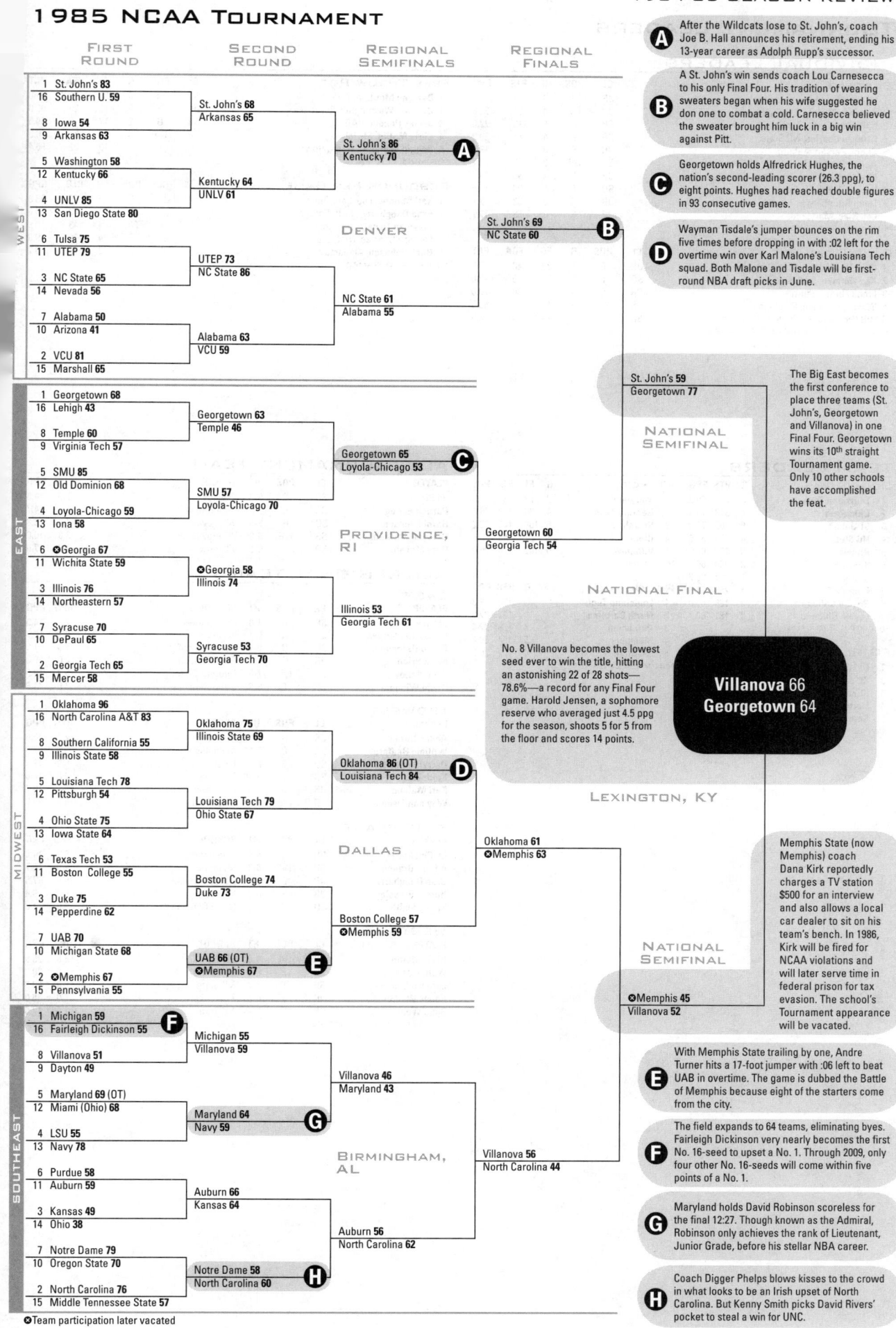

West (Denver)

First Round
- 1 St. John's **83**, 16 Southern U. **59**
- 8 Iowa **54**, 9 Arkansas **63**
- 5 Washington **58**, 12 Kentucky **66**
- 4 UNLV **85**, 13 San Diego State **80**
- 6 Tulsa **75**, 11 UTEP **79**
- 3 NC State **65**, 14 Nevada **56**
- 7 Alabama **50**, 10 Arizona **41**
- 2 VCU **81**, 15 Marshall **65**

Second Round
- St. John's **68**, Arkansas **65**
- Kentucky **64**, UNLV **61**
- UTEP **73**, NC State **86**
- Alabama **63**, VCU **59**

Regional Semifinals
- St. John's **86**, Kentucky **70** (A)
- NC State **61**, Alabama **55**

Regional Finals
- St. John's **69**, NC State **60** (B)

East (Providence, RI)

First Round
- 1 Georgetown **68**, 16 Lehigh **43**
- 8 Temple **60**, 9 Virginia Tech **57**
- 5 SMU **85**, 12 Old Dominion **68**
- 4 Loyola-Chicago **59**, 13 Iona **58**
- 6 ⊗Georgia **67**, 11 Wichita State **59**
- 3 Illinois **76**, 14 Northeastern **57**
- 7 Syracuse **70**, 10 DePaul **65**
- 2 Georgia Tech **65**, 15 Mercer **58**

Second Round
- Georgetown **63**, Temple **46**
- SMU **57**, Loyola-Chicago **70**
- ⊗Georgia **58**, Illinois **74**
- Syracuse **53**, Georgia Tech **70**

Regional Semifinals
- Georgetown **65**, Loyola-Chicago **53** (C)
- Illinois **53**, Georgia Tech **61**

Regional Finals
- Georgetown **60**, Georgia Tech **54**

Midwest (Dallas)

First Round
- 1 Oklahoma **96**, 16 North Carolina A&T **83**
- 8 Southern California **55**, 9 Illinois State **58**
- 5 Louisiana Tech **78**, 12 Pittsburgh **54**
- 4 Ohio State **75**, 13 Iowa State **64**
- 6 Texas Tech **53**, 11 Boston College **55**
- 3 Duke **75**, 14 Pepperdine **62**
- 7 UAB **70**, 10 Michigan State **68**
- 2 ⊗Memphis **67**, 15 Pennsylvania **55**

Second Round
- Oklahoma **75**, Illinois State **69**
- Louisiana Tech **79**, Ohio State **67**
- Boston College **74**, Duke **73**
- UAB **66** (OT), ⊗Memphis **67** (E)

Regional Semifinals
- Oklahoma **86** (OT), Louisiana Tech **84** (D)
- Boston College **57**, ⊗Memphis **59**

Regional Finals
- Oklahoma **61**, ⊗Memphis **63**

Southeast (Birmingham, AL)

First Round
- 1 Michigan **59**, 16 Fairleigh Dickinson **55** (F)
- 8 Villanova **51**, 9 Dayton **49**
- 5 Maryland **69** (OT), 12 Miami (Ohio) **68**
- 4 LSU **55**, 13 Navy **78**
- 6 Purdue **58**, 11 Auburn **59**
- 3 Kansas **49**, 14 Ohio **38**
- 7 Notre Dame **79**, 10 Oregon State **70**
- 2 North Carolina **76**, 15 Middle Tennessee State **57**

Second Round
- Michigan **55**, Villanova **59**
- Maryland **64**, Navy **59** (G)
- Auburn **66**, Kansas **64**
- Notre Dame **58**, North Carolina **60** (H)

Regional Semifinals
- Villanova **46**, Maryland **43**
- Auburn **56**, North Carolina **62**

Regional Finals
- Villanova **56**, North Carolina **44**

National Semifinal
- St. John's **59**, Georgetown **77**
- ⊗Memphis **45**, Villanova **52**

National Final (Lexington, KY)

Villanova 66
Georgetown 64

No. 8 Villanova becomes the lowest seed ever to win the title, hitting an astonishing 22 of 28 shots—78.6%—a record for any Final Four game. Harold Jensen, a sophomore reserve who averaged just 4.5 ppg for the season, shoots 5 for 5 from the floor and scores 14 points.

The Big East becomes the first conference to place three teams (St. John's, Georgetown and Villanova) in one Final Four. Georgetown wins its 10th straight Tournament game. Only 10 other schools have accomplished the feat.

Memphis State (now Memphis) coach Dana Kirk reportedly charges a TV station $500 for an interview and also allows a local car dealer to sit on his team's bench. In 1986, Kirk will be fired for NCAA violations and will later serve time in federal prison for tax evasion. The school's Tournament appearance will be vacated.

⊗Team participation later vacated

A After the Wildcats lose to St. John's, coach Joe B. Hall announces his retirement, ending his 13-year career as Adolph Rupp's successor.

B A St. John's win sends coach Lou Carnesecca to his only Final Four. His tradition of wearing sweaters began when his wife suggested he don one to combat a cold. Carnesecca believed the sweater brought him luck in a big win against Pitt.

C Georgetown holds Alfredrick Hughes, the nation's second-leading scorer (26.3 ppg), to eight points. Hughes had reached double figures in 93 consecutive games.

D Wayman Tisdale's jumper bounces on the rim five times before dropping in with :02 left for the overtime win over Karl Malone's Louisiana Tech squad. Both Malone and Tisdale will be first-round NBA draft picks in June.

E With Memphis State trailing by one, Andre Turner hits a 17-foot jumper with :06 left to beat UAB in overtime. The game is dubbed the Battle of Memphis because eight of the starters come from the city.

F The field expands to 64 teams, eliminating byes. Fairleigh Dickinson very nearly becomes the first No. 16-seed to upset a No. 1. Through 2009, only four other No. 16-seeds will come within five points of a No. 1.

G Maryland holds David Robinson scoreless for the final 12:27. Though known as the Admiral, Robinson only achieves the rank of Lieutenant, Junior Grade, before his stellar NBA career.

H Coach Digger Phelps blows kisses to the crowd in what looks to be an Irish upset of North Carolina. But Kenny Smith picks David Rivers' pocket to steal a win for UNC.

Tournament Leaders

INDIVIDUAL LEADERS

Scoring

		CL	POS	G	PTS	PPG
1	**Kenny Walker**, Kentucky	JR	F	3	75	25.0
2	**Wayman Tisdale**, Oklahoma	JR	F/C	4	91	22.8
3	**Chris Mullin**, St. John's	SR	G/F	5	110	22.0
4	**Lorenzo Charles**, NC State	SR	F	4	81	20.3
5	**Chuck Person**, Auburn	JR	F	3	57	19.0
6	**Adrian Branch**, Maryland	SR	G/F	3	56	18.7
	Karl Malone, Louisiana Tech	JR	F	3	56	18.7
8	**Walter Berry**, St. John's	SO	F	5	93	18.6
9	**Doug Altenberger**, Illinois	JR	G	3	53	17.7
	Len Bias, Maryland	JR	F	3	53	17.7

Minimum: 3 games

Field Goal Pct

		CL	POS	G	FG	FGA	PCT
1	**Brad Daugherty**, North Carolina	JR	C	4	29	40	72.5
2	**Ken Norman**, Illinois	SO	F	3	18	25	72.0
3	**Frank Ford**, Auburn	SR	G	3	21	30	70.0
4	**Wayman Tisdale**, Oklahoma	JR	F/C	4	41	59	69.5
5	**Bill Wennington**, St. John's	SR	C	5	24	35	68.6

Minimum: 15 made and 3 games

Free Throw Pct

		CL	POS	G	FT	FTA	PCT
1	**Dwayne McClain**, Villanova	SR	F/G	6	24	25	96.0
2	**Dwayne Washington**, Syracuse	JR	G	2	18	20	90.0
3	**James Ponder**, UAB	SR	G	2	17	19	89.5
4	**Chris Mullin**, St. John's	SR	G/F	5	32	37	86.5
5	**Reggie Williams**, Georgetown	SO	F	6	19	22	86.4

Minimum: 15 made

Rebounds Per Game

		CL	POS	G	REB	RPG
1	**Karl Malone**, Louisiana Tech	JR	F	3	40	13.3
2	**Brad Daugherty**, North Carolina	JR	C	4	43	10.8
	Wayman Tisdale, Oklahoma	JR	F/C	4	43	10.8
4	**Lorenzo Charles**, NC State	SR	F	4	39	9.8
5	**Buck Johnson**, Alabama	JR	F	3	29	9.7

Minimum: 3 games

TEAM LEADERS

Scoring

		G	PTS	PPG
1	**Louisiana Tech**	3	241	80.3
2	**Oklahoma**	4	318	79.5
3	**St. John's**	5	365	73.0
4	**NC State**	4	272	68.0
5	**Illinois**	3	203	67.7
6	**Kentucky**	3	200	66.7
7	**Georgetown**	6	397	66.2
8	**Georgia Tech**	4	250	62.5
9	**Boston College**	3	186	62.0
10	**Loyola Chicago**	3	182	60.7

Minimum: 3 games

FG Pct

		G	FG	FGA	PCT
1	**Oklahoma**	4	137	250	54.8
2	**St. John's**	5	128	237	54.0
3	**Illinois**	3	83	154	53.9
4	**North Carolina**	4	99	193	51.3
5	**Georgetown**	6	152	305	49.8

Minimum: 3 games

FT Pct

		G	FT	FTA	PCT
1	**Maryland**	3	28	34	82.3
2	**Georgia Tech**	4	86	112	76.8
3	**St. John's**	5	109	143	76.2
4	**Illinois**	3	37	49	75.5
5	**Villanova**	6	102	136	75.0

Minimum: 3 games

Rebounds

		G	REB	RPG
1	**Louisiana Tech**	3	130	43.3
2	**North Carolina**	4	131	32.8
3	**Oklahoma**	4	128	32.0
4	**Memphis**	5	154	30.8
5	**NC State**	4	122	30.5

Minimum: 3 games

ALL-TOURNAMENT TEAM

PLAYER	CL	POS	HT	SCHOOL	RPG	PPG
Ed Pinckney*	SR	C	6-9	Villanova	8.0	14.5
Patrick Ewing	SR	C	7-0	Georgetown	6.5	14.7
Harold Jensen	SO	G	6-5	Villanova	1.7	6.8
Dwayne McClain	SR	F/G	6-6	Villanova	3.8	15.0
Gary McLain	SR	G	6-5	Villanova	1.7	7.0

ALL-REGIONAL TEAMS

EAST

PLAYER	CL	POS	HT	SCHOOL	RPG	PPG
Patrick Ewing*	SR	C	7-0	Georgetown	7.3	14.5
Doug Altenberger	JR	G	6-4	Illinois	3.3	17.7
Bruce Dalrymple	SO	G	6-4	Georgia Tech	7.3	11.0
Mark Price	JR	G	6-0	Georgia Tech	2.0	16.3
John Salley	JR	F/C	7-0	Georgia Tech	6.3	12.5
David Wingate	JR	F	6-5	Georgetown	3.5	11.8

MIDWEST

PLAYER	CL	POS	HT	SCHOOL	RPG	PPG
Andre Turner*	JR	G	5-11	Memphis	2.0	15.8
William Bedford	SO	C	6-11	Memphis	6.5	13.0
Darryl Kennedy	SO	F	6-5	Oklahoma	8.5	17.5
Keith Lee	SR	C	6-10	Memphis	7.0	16.8
Karl Malone	JR	F	6-9	Louisiana Tech	13.3	18.7
Wayman Tisdale	JR	F/C	6-9	Oklahoma	10.8	22.8

SOUTHEAST

PLAYER	CL	POS	HT	SCHOOL	RPG	PPG
Ed Pinckney*	SR	C	6-9	Villanova	8.3	14.8
Adrian Branch	SR	G/F	6-8	Maryland	4.0	18.7
Brad Daugherty	JR	C	6-11	North Carolina	10.8	17.5
Harold Pressley	JR	F	6-7	Villanova	6.3	9.8
Kenny Smith	SO	G	6-3	North Carolina	3.0	11.0

WEST

PLAYER	CL	POS	HT	SCHOOL	RPG	PPG
Chris Mullin*	SR	G/F	6-6	St. John's	4.8	25.5
Walter Berry	SO	F	6-8	St. John's	9.0	20.3
Lorenzo Charles	SR	F	6-7	NC State	9.8	20.3
Kenny Walker	JR	F	6-8	Kentucky	8.0	25.0
Spud Webb	SR	G	5-7	NC State	1.8	17.0

* Most outstanding player

1985 NCAA TOURNAMENT BOX SCORES

86-70 — SWEET 16

39	1H	38
47	2H	32

ST. JOHN'S	MIN	FG	3FG	FT	REB	A	ST	BL	PF	TP
Chris Mullin	40	11-23	-	8-10	5	7	2	0	0	30
Walter Berry	36	7-13	-	8-11	12	2	0	3	4	22
Mark Jackson	19	3-4	-	6-8	2	4	2	0	2	12
Willie Glass	38	4-5	-	2-2	9	3	0	0	1	10
Bill Wennington	24	4-7	-	2-2	3	2	0	0	4	10
Ron Stewart	16	1-1	-	0-0	2	0	0	0	1	2
Mike Moses	21	0-3	-	0-0	0	1	0	0	2	0
Shelton Jones	6	0-0	-	0-0	0	0	0	0	0	0
TOTALS	200	30-56	-	26-33	33	19	4	3	14	86
Percentages		53.6	-	78.8						

Coach: Lou Carnesecca

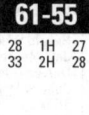

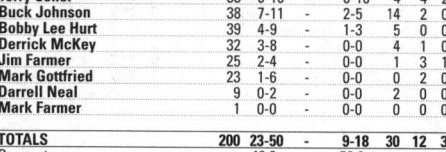

KENTUCKY	MIN	FG	3FG	FT	REB	A	ST	BL	PF	TP
Kenny Walker	36	10-14	-	3-3	8	4	1	1	5	23
Roger Harden	28	6-10	-	1-1	2	7	0	0	3	13
Ed Davender	25	5-10	-	1-2	3	3	1	0	2	11
Troy McKinley	16	4-6	-	0-0	2	1	1	0	1	8
Winston Bennett	24	2-2	-	2-2	3	0	0	0	5	6
Richard Madison	29	2-9	-	1-3	4	1	0	0	1	5
Bret Bearup	19	1-3	-	0-0	3	2	0	0	5	2
Cedric Jenkins	3	1-1	-	0-0	1	0	0	0	0	2
James Blackmon	13	0-4	-	0-0	1	1	1	1	1	0
Robert Lock	3	0-0	-	0-0	0	0	0	0	1	0
Paul Andrews	2	0-0	-	0-0	0	0	0	0	0	0
Leroy Byrd	1	0-0	-	0-0	0	0	0	0	0	0
Todd Ziegler	1	0-0	-	0-0	0	0	0	0	0	0
TOTALS	200	31-59	-	8-11	27	19	4	2	24	70
Percentages		52.5	-	72.7						

Coach: Joe B. Hall

Officials: John Clougherty, Bob Dibler, Willie McJunkin **Technicals:** St. John's (Mullin) **Attendance:** 17,022

61-55 — SWEET 16

28	1H	27
33	2H	28

NC STATE	MIN	FG	3FG	FT	REB	A	ST	BL	PF	TP
Spud Webb	38	5-12	-	4-6	4	5	1	0	4	14
Lorenzo Charles	35	5-11	-	4-6	6	3	0	0	0	14
Bennie Bolton	30	4-8	-	3-4	1	1	1	1	2	11
Russell Pierre	29	2-4	-	4-5	6	0	1	0	2	8
Terry Gannon	14	4-4	-	0-0	0	2	0	0	1	8
Cozell McQueen	25	2-5	-	0-0	4	0	1	0	5	4
Nate McMillan	22	0-2	-	2-6	5	4	1	0	3	2
Ernie Myers	6	0-1	-	0-0	0	0	0	0	2	0
John Thompson	1	0-0	-	0-0	0	0	0	0	0	0
TOTALS	200	22-47	-	17-27	26	15	5	1	19	61
Percentages		46.8	-	63.0						

Coach: Jim Valvano

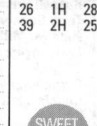

ALABAMA	MIN	FG	3FG	FT	REB	A	ST	BL	PF	TP
Terry Coner	33	6-10	-	6-10	4	4	2	0	4	18
Buck Johnson	38	7-11	-	2-5	14	2	0	1	5	16
Bobby Lee Hurt	39	4-9	-	1-3	5	0	0	1	2	9
Derrick McKey	32	3-8	-	0-0	4	1	0	1	5	6
Jim Farmer	25	2-4	-	0-0	1	3	1	0	3	4
Mark Gottfried	23	1-6	-	0-0	0	2	0	0	2	2
Darrell Neal	9	0-2	-	0-0	2	0	0	0	0	0
Mark Farmer	1	0-0	-	0-0	0	0	0	0	0	0
TOTALS	200	23-50	-	9-18	30	12	3	3	21	55
Percentages		46.0	-	50.0						

Coach: Wimp Sanderson

Officials: Dick Paparo, Jody Silvester, Bob Garibaldi **Technicals:** None **Attendance:** 17,022

65-53 — SWEET 16

26	1H	28
39	2H	25

GEORGETOWN	MIN	FG	3FG	FT	REB	A	ST	BL	PF	TP
Patrick Ewing	36	9-15	-	3-4	14	2	1	5	1	21
David Wingate	34	7-14	-	0-1	3	1	1	0	0	14
Bill Martin	37	4-7	-	0-3	3	1	0	0	2	8
Michael Jackson	35	3-8	-	2-3	7	12	0	0	2	8
Reggie Williams	24	2-7	-	4-4	5	1	0	3	3	8
Ralph Dalton	9	1-1	-	1-2	4	0	0	0	0	3
Horace Broadnax	11	0-2	-	2-2	1	0	0	0	1	2
Perry McDonald	12	0-0	-	1-2	2	0	1	0	0	1
Ralph Highsmith	1	0-0	-	0-0	0	0	0	0	0	0
Tyrone Lockhart	1	0-0	-	0-0	0	0	0	0	0	0
TOTALS	200	26-54	-	13-21	39	17	3	8	9	65
Percentages		48.1	-	61.9						

Coach: John Thompson Jr.

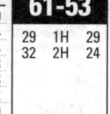

LOYOLA-CHICAGO	MIN	FG	3FG	FT	REB	A	ST	BL	PF	TP
Andre Moore	39	8-13	-	3-3	8	1	0	1	3	19
Andre Battle	39	5-13	-	0-0	3	0	3	0	4	10
Alfredrick Hughes	29	4-13	-	0-1	5	0	1	0	3	8
Carl Golston	39	3-12	-	0-0	3	7	4	1	2	6
Greg Williams	27	2-4	-	0-0	3	3	1	1	5	4
Ivan Young	17	1-5	-	0-0	3	0	0	0	0	2
Mike Cenar	7	1-2	-	0-0	0	0	0	0	2	2
Bobby Clark	1	1-2	-	0-0	2	0	0	0	0	2
Nate Brooks	1	0-0	-	0-0	0	0	0	0	1	0
Dave Klusendorf	1	0-1	-	0-0	0	0	0	0	0	0
TOTALS	200	25-65	-	3-4	27	11	9	3	20	53
Percentages		38.5	-	75.0						

Coach: Gene Sullivan

Officials: Joe Forte, Dale Kelley, Paul Housman **Technicals:** None **Attendance:** 11,913

61-53 — SWEET 16

29	1H	29
32	2H	24

GEORGIA TECH	MIN	FG	3FG	FT	REB	A	ST	BL	PF	TP
Mark Price	38	9-12	-	2-3	2	2	3	0	0	20
John Salley	36	5-12	-	4-5	4	3	0	1	3	14
Yvon Joseph	35	4-6	-	6-8	3	1	2	0	4	14
Bruce Dalrymple	36	3-4	-	2-4	4	3	2	0	2	8
Duane Ferrell	16	1-3	-	1-2	1	2	1	0	0	3
Scott Petway	28	0-2	-	2-2	2	2	3	0	2	2
Antoine Ford	7	0-0	-	0-0	1	0	0	0	1	0
Jack Mansell	2	0-0	-	0-0	0	0	0	0	0	0
John Martinson	2	0-0	-	0-0	0	0	0	0	0	0
TOTALS	200	22-39	-	17-24	17	13	11	1	12	61
Percentages		56.4	-	70.8						

Coach: Bobby Cremins

ILLINOIS	MIN	FG	3FG	FT	REB	A	ST	BL	PF	TP
Doug Altenberger	38	11-17	-	2-3	3	1	2	0	5	24
Anthony Welch	37	5-10	-	0-0	5	2	2	0	0	10
Ken Norman	38	3-3	-	3-3	7	7	3	1	3	9
Efrem Winters	36	2-5	-	0-2	4	1	1	0	3	4
Bruce Douglas	33	1-6	-	2-2	2	1	0	0	2	4
Scott Meents	6	1-2	-	0-0	0	1	0	0	4	2
Tony Wysinger	12	0-4	-	0-0	1	2	0	0	3	0
TOTALS	200	23-47	-	7-10	22	15	8	1	20	53
Percentages		48.9	-	70.0						

Coach: Lou Henson

Officials: Sonny Holmes, Don Rutledge, Mac Chauvin **Technicals:** None **Attendance:** 11,913

86-84 — SWEET 16

32	1H	28
42	2H	46
12	OT1	10

OKLAHOMA	MIN	FG	3FG	FT	REB	A	ST	BL	PF	TP
Wayman Tisdale	40	10-17	-	3-7	11	1	1	3	4	23
Darryl Kennedy	43	8-11	-	5-7	11	3	0	1	5	21
Anthony Bowie	45	8-11	-	0-1	10	7	2	0	1	16
Tim McCalister	45	5-18	-	0-0	3	3	0	0	3	10
David Johnson	31	4-5	-	2-3	4	3	1	0	5	10
Linwood Davis	19	2-5	-	2-2	1	1	0	0	2	6
Shawn Clark	1	0-0	-	0-0	0	0	0	0	0	0
Chuck Watson	1	0-0	-	0-0	0	0	0	0	0	0
TOTALS	225	37-67	-	12-20	40	18	4	4	20	86
Percentages		55.2	-	60.0						

Coach: Billy Tubbs

LOUISIANA TECH	MIN	FG	3FG	FT	REB	A	ST	BL	PF	TP
Karl Malone	45	9-19	-	2-4	16	3	0	0	4	20
Alan Davis	40	9-15	-	0-0	6	8	4	0	3	18
Willie Bland	29	7-11	-	4-6	6	1	5	0	2	18
Robert Godbolt	37	4-15	-	2-3	5	2	0	0	3	10
Willie Simmons	24	3-11	-	4-4	2	1	0	1	4	10
Wayne Smith	42	2-11	-	2-2	5	8	2	0	1	6
Adam Frank	8	0-2	-	2-2	1	3	0	0	0	2
TOTALS	225	34-84	-	16-21	41	26	11	1	17	84
Percentages		40.5	-	76.2						

Coach: Andy Russo

Technicals: None **Attendance:** 17,007

59-57 — SWEET 16

31	1H	31
28	2H	26

MEMPHIS	MIN	FG	3FG	FT	REB	A	ST	BL	PF	TP
William Bedford	-	10-13	-	3-4	8	0	-	-	3	23
Andre Turner	-	6-12	-	0-0	2	7	-	-	1	12
Willie Becton	-	4-10	-	0-0	5	0	-	-	2	8
Keith Lee	-	3-12	-	2-3	8	4	-	-	4	8
Baskerville Holmes	-	2-7	-	0-0	3	1	-	-	2	4
Vincent Askew	-	1-3	-	0-0	4	9	-	-	0	2
Dwight Boyd	-	1-1	-	0-1	0	0	-	-	0	2
TOTALS	-	27-58	-	5-8	30	21	-	-	12	59
Percentages		46.6	-	62.5						

Coach: Dana Kirk

BOSTON COLLEGE	MIN	FG	3FG	FT	REB	A	ST	BL	PF	TP
Stu Primus	-	7-13	-	0-0	3	1	-	-	2	14
Michael Adams	-	6-14	-	0-0	2	4	-	-	2	12
Terrence Talley	-	5-8	-	1-2	4	1	-	-	4	11
Trevor Gordon	-	3-3	-	3-5	6	0	-	-	4	9
Roger McCready	-	2-7	-	5-6	3	0	-	-	1	9
Dominic Pressley	-	1-2	-	0-0	1	1	-	-	0	2
Skip Barry	-	0-5	-	0-0	4	1	-	-	0	0
Troy Bowers	-	0-2	-	0-0	2	0	-	-	3	0
Mark Schmidt	-	0-1	-	0-0	0	1	-	-	0	0
Tyrone Scott	-	0-0	-	0-0	0	0	-	-	0	0
TOTALS	-	24-55	-	9-13	25	9	-	-	16	57
Percentages		43.6	-	69.2						

Coach: Gary Williams

Technicals: None **Attendance:** 17,007

ANNUAL REVIEW

Villanova 46, Maryland 43 (Sweet 16)

VILLANOVA	MIN	FG	3FG	FT	REB	A	ST	BL	PF	TP
Ed Pinckney	36	5-7	-	6-7	13	1	0	1	4	16
Dwayne McClain	40	5-9	-	2-2	4	2	0	0	3	12
Harold Pressley	35	3-12	-	1-4	10	1	0	1	2	7
Dwight Wilbur	25	1-5	-	2-2	4	3	0	0	0	4
Mark Plansky	13	2-3	-	0-0	4	2	0	0	0	4
Gary McLain	36	1-5	-	1-2	2	1	1	0	0	3
Harold Jensen	11	0-5	-	0-1	0	1	0	0	1	0
Chuck Everson	4	0-0	-	0-0	0	0	0	0	0	0
TOTALS	**200**	**17-46**	**-**	**12-18**	**37**	**11**	**1**	**2**	**10**	**46**
Percentages		37.0	-	66.7						

Coach: Rollie Massimino

46-43

	1H	
19	1H	20
27	2H	23

SWEET 16

MARYLAND	MIN	FG	3FG	FT	REB	A	ST	BL	PF	TP
Adrian Branch	39	9-19	-	3-5	5	2	1	0	3	21
Len Bias	40	4-13	-	0-0	5	1	0	0	4	8
Keith Gatlin	30	2-7	-	0-0	4	2	1	0	1	4
Jeff Adkins	29	2-7	-	0-0	4	4	1	0	2	4
Jeff Baxter	10	2-2	-	0-0	0	0	0	0	2	4
Terry Long	16	0-1	-	2-2	4	0	2	1	1	2
Derrick Lewis	24	0-2	-	0-0	5	0	0	2	4	0
Thomas Jones	12	0-2	-	0-0	2	1	0	0	3	0
TOTALS	**200**	**19-53**	**-**	**5-7**	**29**	**10**	**5**	**3**	**20**	**43**
Percentages		35.8	-	71.4						

Coach: Lefty Driesell

Officials: Tanco, Bob Showalter, R Wulkow
Technicals: None
Attendance: 16,843

North Carolina 62, Auburn 56 (Sweet 16)

NORTH CAROLINA	MIN	FG	3FG	FT	REB	A	ST	BL	PF	TP
Kenny Smith	38	9-12	-	4-5	3	6	2	0	1	22
Warren Martin	26	4-8	-	4-5	5	1	0	1	3	12
Brad Daugherty	39	5-8	-	0-2	8	3	0	2	2	10
Joe Wolf	35	4-6	-	2-2	7	3	0	0	3	10
Dave Popson	14	2-4	-	0-0	4	0	0	0	1	4
Ranzino Smith	14	1-5	-	2-2	2	1	0	0	0	4
Buzz Peterson	29	0-5	-	0-0	2	2	0	0	2	0
Curtis Hunter	5	0-1	-	0-2	1	0	0	0	0	0
TOTALS	**200**	**25-49**	**-**	**12-18**	**32**	**16**	**2**	**3**	**12**	**62**
Percentages		51.0	-	66.7						

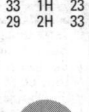

Coach: Dean Smith

62-56

	1H	
33	1H	23
29	2H	33

SWEET 16

AUBURN	MIN	FG	3FG	FT	REB	A	ST	BL	PF	TP
Frank Ford	37	8-14	-	1-2	4	3	0	0	2	17
Chuck Person	39	8-25	-	0-0	12	3	2	1	4	16
Carey Holland	22	2-2	-	4-8	1	0	0	1	2	8
Chris Morris	38	3-10	-	1-2	9	0	2	0	2	7
Gerald White	37	2-5	-	0-0	1	2	0	0	4	4
Jeff Moore	17	2-3	-	0-0	2	1	0	0	3	4
Darren Guest	5	0-0	-	0-0	1	0	0	0	0	0
Johnny Lynn	5	0-0	-	0-0	0	0	0	0	1	0
TOTALS	**200**	**25-59**	**-**	**6-12**	**30**	**9**	**4**	**2**	**18**	**56**
Percentages		42.4	-	50.0						

Coach: Sonny Smith

Officials: Tim Higgins, James Burr, J.C. Leimbach
Technicals: None
Attendance: 16,843

St. John's 69, NC State 60 (Elite 8)

ST. JOHN'S	MIN	FG	3FG	FT	REB	A	ST	BL	PF	TP
Chris Mullin	40	9-19	-	7-7	5	1	3	1	4	25
Walter Berry	40	8-12	-	3-4	5	0	1	1	2	19
Bill Wennington	36	3-5	-	8-9	10	0	1	0	2	14
Ron Stewart	19	1-3	-	5-7	3	1	0	0	0	7
Mike Moses	22	1-4	-	2-3	2	5	1	0	2	4
Willie Glass	24	0-5	-	0-0	3	2	1	0	4	0
Mark Jackson	19	0-1	-	0-1	3	5	1	1	4	0
TOTALS	**200**	**22-49**	**-**	**25-31**	**31**	**14**	**8**	**3**	**18**	**69**
Percentages		44.9	-	80.6						

Coach: Lou Carnesecca

69-60

	1H	
30	1H	29
39	2H	31

ELITE 8

NC STATE	MIN	FG	3FG	FT	REB	A	ST	BL	PF	TP
Lorenzo Charles	39	4-9	-	7-9	11	1	0	1	2	15
Spud Webb	39	5-14	-	4-5	1	9	0	0	3	14
Bennie Bolton	27	4-10	-	1-1	0	0	1	0	3	9
Cozell McQueen	40	2-4	-	4-6	11	1	0	0	4	8
Russell Pierre	25	3-6	-	0-0	3	0	1	1	5	6
Terry Gannon	18	3-7	-	0-0	1	0	0	0	4	6
Nate McMillan	11	0-3	-	2-2	3	1	0	1	5	2
Ernie Myers	1	0-0	-	0-0	0	0	0	0	1	0
TOTALS	**200**	**21-53**	**-**	**18-23**	**30**	**12**	**2**	**3**	**27**	**60**
Percentages		39.6	-	78.3						

Coach: Jim Valvano

Officials: John Clougherty, Bob Dibler, Willie McJunkin
Technicals: None
Attendance: 17,022

Georgetown 60, Georgia Tech 54 (Elite 8)

GEORGETOWN	MIN	FG	3FG	FT	REB	A	ST	BL	PF	TP
Patrick Ewing	25	5-9	-	4-9	4	1	1	0	4	14
Reggie Williams	33	4-6	-	4-4	5	2	1	0	3	12
Bill Martin	32	5-10	-	2-3	2	0	4	0	4	12
Horace Broadnax	18	3-4	-	3-4	3	1	0	0	0	9
David Wingate	34	3-8	-	1-2	1	1	0	0	3	7
Ralph Dalton	25	1-2	-	4-4	6	0	0	1	4	6
Michael Jackson	28	0-6	-	0-0	1	5	2	0	4	0
Grady Mateen	3	0-0	-	0-0	1	0	0	0	0	0
Perry McDonald	2	0-1	-	0-0	2	0	0	0	0	0
TOTALS	**200**	**21-46**	**-**	**18-26**	**25**	**10**	**8**	**1**	**22**	**60**
Percentages		45.7	-	69.2						

Coach: John Thompson Jr.

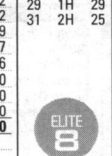

60-54

	1H	
29	1H	29
31	2H	25

ELITE 8

GEORGIA TECH	MIN	FG	3FG	FT	REB	A	ST	BL	PF	TP
John Salley	29	5-8	-	5-5	5	2	0	-	5	15
Mark Price	40	3-16	-	7-8	1	1	0	-	1	13
Bruce Dalrymple	38	3-5	-	7-7	4	0	0	-	4	13
Antoine Ford	12	2-2	-	2-2	1	1	0	-	2	6
Yvon Joseph	38	1-4	-	1-2	4	2	0	-	4	3
Scott Petway	24	1-2	-	0-0	0	4	1	-	3	2
Duane Ferrell	18	1-3	-	0-0	4	0	0	-	3	2
Jack Mansell	1	0-0	-	0-0	0	0	0	-	0	0
TOTALS	**200**	**16-40**	**-**	**22-24**	**19**	**10**	**1**	**-**	**22**	**54**
Percentages		40.0	-	91.7						

Coach: Bobby Cremins

Officials: Sonny Holmes, Don Rutledge, Mac Chauvin
Technicals: None
Attendance: 11,913

Memphis 63, Oklahoma 61 (Elite 8)

MEMPHIS	MIN	FG	3FG	FT	REB	A	ST	BL	PF	TP
Keith Lee	27	9-22	-	5-5	11	0	1	1	4	23
Andre Turner	40	5-9	-	2-5	3	12	2	0	3	12
William Bedford	24	4-5	-	4-4	4	2	0	2	4	12
Willie Becton	19	3-4	-	1-2	2	2	2	0	2	7
Baskerville Holmes	21	2-4	-	0-0	4	0	2	0	1	4
Dewayne Bailey	21	1-2	-	0-0	5	0	2	1	1	2
Dwight Boyd	11	1-2	-	0-0	0	2	0	1	0	2
Vincent Askew	37	0-1	-	1-2	1	1	1	0	1	1
TOTALS	**200**	**25-49**	**-**	**13-18**	**30**	**19**	**10**	**5**	**16**	**63**
Percentages		51.0	-	72.2						

Coach: Dana Kirk

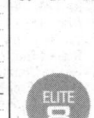

63-61

	1H	
33	1H	33
30	2H	28

ELITE 8

OKLAHOMA	MIN	FG	3FG	FT	REB	A	ST	BL	PF	TP
Darryl Kennedy	38	7-15	-	2-2	5	3	2	0	3	16
Tim McCalister	39	6-12	-	2-2	0	5	3	1	5	14
Wayman Tisdale	40	5-10	-	1-1	12	4	0	0	3	11
Anthony Bowie	40	5-12	-	0-2	2	5	1	0	2	10
David Johnson	36	3-6	-	4-6	7	2	2	0	3	10
Linwood Davis	4	0-0	-	0-0	0	1	0	0	3	0
Shawn Clark	3	0-1	-	0-0	0	0	1	0	0	0
TOTALS	**200**	**26-56**	**-**	**9-13**	**26**	**20**	**9**	**1**	**19**	**61**
Percentages		46.4	-	69.2						

Coach: Billy Tubbs

Officials: Charles Vacca, Don Shea, Hank Armstrong
Technicals: None
Attendance: 17,007

Villanova 56, North Carolina 44 (Elite 8)

VILLANOVA	MIN	FG	3FG	FT	REB	A	ST	BL	PF	TP
Harold Pressley	38	7-13	-	1-2	3	1	2	0	1	15
Gary McLain	39	3-5	-	5-6	2	2	1	0	2	11
Dwayne McClain	36	4-11	-	3-3	5	2	3	0	3	11
Harold Jensen	31	5-7	-	0-0	3	3	3	0	1	10
Ed Pinckney	38	3-6	-	3-6	7	3	3	2	3	9
Dwight Wilbur	9	0-3	-	0-0	2	1	1	0	0	0
Mark Plansky	7	0-1	-	0-0	1	1	0	0	0	0
Chuck Everson	2	0-1	-	0-0	0	0	0	0	1	0
TOTALS	**200**	**22-47**	**-**	**12-17**	**23**	**13**	**13**	**2**	**11**	**56**
Percentages		46.8	-	70.6						

Coach: Rollie Massimino

56-44

	1H	
17	1H	22
39	2H	22

ELITE 8

NORTH CAROLINA	MIN	FG	3FG	FT	REB	A	ST	BL	PF	TP
Brad Daugherty	38	7-9	-	3-6	12	0	0	0	3	17
Ranzino Smith	20	3-10	-	0-0	4	0	1	0	2	6
Curtis Hunter	16	3-4	-	0-0	2	0	1	0	2	6
Dave Popson	14	2-3	-	1-1	2	0	0	0	0	5
Kenny Smith	40	2-7	-	0-0	3	5	1	0	3	4
Joe Wolf	34	2-6	-	0-0	4	5	0	0	3	4
Warren Martin	16	1-2	-	0-0	1	1	0	2	2	2
Buzz Peterson	20	0-3	-	0-0	0	0	0	0	1	0
Cliff Morris	2	0-0	-	0-0	0	0	0	0	0	0
TOTALS	**200**	**20-44**	**-**	**4-7**	**28**	**11**	**3**	**2**	**16**	**44**
Percentages		45.5	-	57.1						

Coach: Dean Smith

Officials: Tim Higgins, James Burr, J.C. Leimbach
Technicals: None
Attendance: 16,863

GEORGETOWN	MIN	FG	3FG	FT	REB	A	ST	BL	PF	TP
Reggie Williams	33	8-15	-	4-4	4	2	1	0	1	20
Patrick Ewing	32	7-12	-	2-4	5	2	0	1	4	16
David Wingate	36	3-8	-	6-8	6	2	1	0	2	12
Bill Martin	29	4-8	-	4-4	7	0	0	0	4	12
Horace Broadnax	20	3-4	-	3-4	3	1	2	0	0	9
Michael Jackson	24	2-5	-	0-0	0	11	1	0	4	4
Ralph Dalton	17	2-2	-	0-0	1	0	0	0	3	4
Grady Mateen	3	0-1	-	0-0	0	0	0	0	0	0
Perry McDonald	3	0-1	-	0-0	1	0	1	0	0	0
Kevin Floyd	1	0-0	-	0-0	1	0	0	0	0	0
Ralph Highsmith	1	0-1	-	0-0	1	0	0	0	0	0
Tyrone Lockhart	1	0-0	-	0-0	0	0	0	0	0	0
TOTALS	**200**	**29-57**	**-**	**19-24**	**29**	**18**	**6**	**1**	**18**	**77**
Percentages		50.9	-	79.2						

Coach: John Thompson Jr.

77-59

32	1H	28
45	2H	31

FINAL 4

ST. JOHN'S	MIN	FG	3FG	FT	REB	A	ST	BL	PF	TP
Willie Glass	25	4-4	-	5-7	2	0	1	0	4	13
Bill Wennington	38	4-7	-	4-5	5	0	0	3	2	12
Walter Berry	37	4-8	-	4-5	6	3	1	2	4	12
Chris Mullin	39	4-8	-	0-0	5	1	0	0	2	8
Mark Jackson	22	3-4	-	0-2	2	5	1	0	1	6
Mike Moses	17	3-7	-	0-0	1	2	1	0	3	6
Shelton Jones	12	1-4	-	0-0	2	1	0	0	1	2
Ron Stewart	6	0-0	-	0-0	0	0	0	1	2	0
Steve Shurina	2	0-0	-	0-0	0	0	0	0	0	0
Terry Bross	1	0-0	-	0-0	0	0	0	0	1	0
Rob Cornegy	1	0-0	-	0-0	1	0	0	0	0	0
TOTALS	**200**	**23-42**	**-**	**13-19**	**24**	**12**	**4**	**6**	**20**	**59**
Percentages		54.8	-	68.4						

Coach: Lou Carnesecca

Officials: Charles Vacca, Don Rutledge, James Burr
Technicals: None
Attendance: 23,124

VILLANOVA	MIN	FG	3FG	FT	REB	A	ST	BL	PF	TP
Dwayne McClain	-	6-9	-	7-7	4	2	1	0	4	19
Ed Pinckney	-	3-7	-	6-9	9	1	0	3	3	12
Gary McLain	-	2-5	-	5-5	2	2	1	1	1	9
Harold Jensen	-	3-6	-	0-0	4	1	1	0	0	6
Mark Plansky	-	1-1	-	1-3	0	2	0	0	1	3
Harold Pressley	-	1-8	-	1-2	6	1	1	0	3	3
Chuck Everson	-	0-0	-	0-0	0	0	0	0	0	0
Dwight Wilbur	-	0-2	-	0-0	1	0	1	0	1	0
TOTALS	**-**	**16-38**	**-**	**20-26**	**26**	**9**	**5**	**4**	**13**	**52**
Percentages		42.1	-	76.9						

Coach: Rollie Massimino

52-45

23	1H	23
29	2H	22

FINAL 4

MEMPHIS	MIN	FG	3FG	FT	REB	A	ST	BL	PF	TP
Andre Turner	40	5-13	-	1-2	4	3	2	0	3	11
Keith Lee	23	3-9	-	4-4	7	1	0	1	5	10
William Bedford	32	4-9	-	0-0	7	0	1	1	4	8
Baskerville Holmes	31	4-8	-	0-0	2	0	0	0	5	8
Willie Becton	22	1-4	-	2-2	5	1	1	0	1	4
Vincent Askew	40	1-3	-	0-1	7	7	0	0	2	2
Dewayne Bailey	8	1-1	-	0-0	0	0	0	0	2	2
Dwight Boyd	3	0-2	-	0-0	0	0	0	0	0	0
John Wilfong	1	0-1	-	0-0	1	0	0	0	1	0
TOTALS	**200**	**19-50**	**-**	**7-9**	**33**	**12**	**4**	**2**	**23**	**45**
Percentages		38.0	-	77.8						

Coach: Dana Kirk

Officials: John Clougherty, Bob Dibler, Willie McJunkin
Technicals: Memphis (Bedford)
Attendance: 23,124

VILLANOVA	MIN	FG	3FG	FT	REB	A	ST	BL	PF	TP
Dwayne McClain	40	5-7	-	7-8	1	3	2	0	3	17
Ed Pinckney	37	5-7	-	6-7	6	5	2	0	3	16
Harold Jensen	34	5-5	-	4-5	1	2	1	0	2	14
Harold Pressley	40	4-6	-	3-4	4	1	3	1	1	11
Gary McLain	40	3-3	-	2-2	2	2	0	0	2	8
Dwight Wilbur	5	0-0	-	0-0	0	1	0	0	0	0
Chuck Everson	3	0-0	-	0-0	0	0	0	0	0	0
Mark Plansky	1	0-0	-	0-1	0	0	0	0	1	0
TOTALS	**200**	**22-28**	**-**	**22-27**	**14**	**14**	**8**	**1**	**12**	**66**
Percentages		78.6	-	81.5						

Coach: Rollie Massimino

66-64

29	1H	28
37	2H	36

NCAA FINAL 1985

GEORGETOWN	MIN	FG	3FG	FT	REB	A	ST	BL	PF	TP
David Wingate	39	8-14	-	0-0	2	2	1	0	4	16
Patrick Ewing	39	7-13	-	0-0	5	2	2	1	4	14
Bill Martin	37	4-6	-	2-2	5	1	0	0	2	10
Reggie Williams	29	5-9	-	0-2	4	2	1	0	3	10
Michael Jackson	37	4-7	-	0-0	0	9	1	0	4	8
Horace Broadnax	13	1-2	-	2-2	1	2	1	0	4	4
Ralph Dalton	4	0-1	-	2-2	0	0	0	0	1	2
Perry McDonald	2	0-1	-	0-0	0	0	0	0	0	0
TOTALS	**200**	**29-53**	**-**	**6-8**	**17**	**18**	**6**	**1**	**22**	**64**
Percentages		54.7	-	75.0						

Coach: John Thompson Jr.

Officials: John Clougherty, Bob Dibler, Willie McJunkin
Technicals: None
Attendance: 23,124

National Invitation Tournament (NIT)

First round: New Mexico d. Texas A&M 80-67, Nebraska d. Canisius 79-66, Marquette d. Bradley 77-64, Cincinnati d. Kent State 77-61, Louisville d. Alcorn State 77-75, Tennessee d. Tennessee Tech 65-62, UL-Lafayette d. Florida 65-64, Virginia d. West Virginia 56-55, Fresno State d. Santa Clara 79-76, South Florida d. Wake Forest 77-66, Saint Joseph's d. Missouri 68-67, UCLA d. Montana 78-47, Chattanooga d. Clemson 67-65, Lamar d. Houston 78-71, Indiana d. Butler 79-57, Richmond d. Fordham 59-57
Second round: UCLA d. Nebraska 82-63, Marquette d. Cincinnati 56-54, Fresno State d. New Mexico 66-55, Virginia d. Saint Joseph's 68-61, Indiana d. Richmond 75-53, Louisville d. South Florida 68-61, Tennessee d. UL-Lafayette 73-72, Chattanooga d. Lamar 85-84 (OT)
Third round: Tennessee d. Virginia 61-54, UCLA d. Fresno State 53-43, Indiana d. Marquette 94-82 (OT), Louisville d. Chattanooga 71-66
Semifinals: UCLA d. Louisville 75-66, Indiana d. Tennessee 74-67
Third place: Tennessee d. Louisville 100-84.
Championship: UCLA d. Indiana 65-62
MVP: Reggie Miller, UCLA

1985-86: Cardinals Rule

Nervous? Never. Louisville's big man, Pervis Ellison, took coach Denny Crum to his second national title in six years. The Cardinals downed Duke, 72-69, at Reunion Arena in Dallas. Never Nervous Pervis had 25 points and 11 rebounds against the Blue Devils, becoming the first freshman to be named MOP since Arnie Ferrin of Utah in 1944.

The 1986 Tournament was full of upsets. In the first round, two No. 14 seeds (Cleveland State and Arkansas-Little Rock) took out No. 3s (Indiana and Notre Dame). LSU became the lowest seed (No. 11) ever to reach the Final Four (a feat and seeding matched by George Mason in 2006). No. 7-seed Navy, led by David Robinson, reached the Elite Eight.

The NCAA adopted a 45-second shot clock for 1985-86 (reduced to 35 seconds for 1993-94), but it wasn't used during the Tourney. Duke's Johnny Dawkins (20.2 ppg, 3.2 apg) was named Naismith POY. Len Bias was chosen second in the NBA draft by the Boston Celtics (after Cleveland chose UNC's Brad Daugherty) but never got to play in the NBA; he died less than 48 hours after his selection due to cardiac arrest attributed to cocaine use.

Major Conference Standings

AMCU-8

	Conference W	L	Pct	Overall W	L	Pct
Cleveland State ○	13	1	.929	29	4	.879
Missouri State □	10	4	.714	24	8	.750
Eastern Illinois	8	6	.571	19	13	.594
Western Illinois	7	7	.500	13	15	.464
Illinois-Chicago	7	7	.500	13	16	.448
Valparaiso	5	9	.357	9	19	.321
Northern Iowa	3	11	.214	8	19	.296
Wisconsin-Green Bay	3	11	.214	5	23	.179

Tournament: **Cleveland State d. Eastern Illinois 70-66**
Tournament MVP: **Kevin Duckworth**, Eastern Illinois

Atlantic 10

	Conference W	L	Pct	Overall W	L	Pct
Saint Joseph's ⊕	16	2	.889	26	6	.813
Temple ○	15	3	.833	25	6	.806
West Virginia ○	15	3	.833	22	11	.667
St. Bonaventure	10	8	.556	15	13	.536
Duquesne	9	9	.500	15	14	.517
George Washington	7	11	.389	12	16	.429
Massachusetts	6	12	.333	9	19	.321
Penn State	5	13	.278	12	17	.414
Rhode Island	5	13	.278	9	19	.321
Rutgers	2	16	.111	8	21	.276

Tournament: **Saint Joseph's d. West Virginia 72-64**
Tournament MVP: **Greg Mullee**, Saint Joseph's

ACC

	Conference W	L	Pct	Overall W	L	Pct
Duke ⊕	12	2	.857	37	3	.925
Georgia Tech ○	11	3	.786	27	7	.794
North Carolina ○	10	4	.714	28	6	.824
Virginia ○	7	7	.500	19	11	.633
NC State ○	7	7	.500	21	13	.618
Maryland ○	6	8	.429	19	14	.576
Clemson □	3	11	.214	19	15	.559
Wake Forest	0	14	.000	8	21	.276

Tournament: **Duke d. Georgia Tech 68-67**
Tournament MVP: **Johnny Dawkins**, Duke

Big East

	Conference W	L	Pct	Overall W	L	Pct
St. John's ⊕	14	2	.875	31	5	.861
Syracuse ○	14	2	.875	26	6	.813
Georgetown ○	11	5	.688	24	8	.750
Villanova ○	10	6	.625	23	14	.622
Providence □	7	9	.438	17	14	.548
Pittsburgh □	6	10	.375	15	14	.517
Boston College	4	12	.250	13	15	.464
Seton Hall	3	13	.188	14	18	.438
Connecticut	3	13	.188	12	16	.429

Tournament: **St. John's d. Syracuse 70-69**
Tournament MVP: **Dwayne Washington**, Syracuse

Big Eight

	Conference W	L	Pct	Overall W	L	Pct
Kansas ⊕	13	1	.929	35	4	.897
Iowa State ○	9	5	.643	22	11	.667
Oklahoma ○	8	6	.571	26	9	.743
Nebraska ○	8	6	.571	19	11	.633
Missouri ○	8	6	.571	21	14	.600
Oklahoma State	6	8	.429	15	13	.536
Kansas State	4	10	.286	16	14	.533
Colorado	0	14	.000	8	20	.286

Tournament: **Kansas d. Iowa State 73-71**
Tournament MVP: **Danny Manning**, Kansas

Big Sky

	Conference W	L	Pct	Overall W	L	Pct
Montana □	9	5	.643	21	11	.656
Northern Arizona □	9	5	.643	19	10	.655
Idaho State	8	6	.571	15	12	.556
Weber State	7	7	.500	18	11	.621
Nevada	7	7	.500	13	15	.464
Montana State ⊕	6	8	.429	14	17	.452
Boise State	6	8	.429	12	16	.429
Idaho	4	10	.286	11	18	.379

Tournament: **Montana State d. Montana 82-77**
Tournament MVP: **Tony Hampton**, Montana State

Big South

	Conference W	L	Pct	Overall W	L	Pct
Charleston Southern	5	1	.833	21	9	.700
Winthrop	5	3	.625	20	9	.690
Augusta	4	4	.500	13	17	.433
Radford	3	4	.429	11	17	.393
UNC Asheville	4	2	.667	20	9	.690
Campbell	3	5	.375	8	19	.296
Armstrong State	3	4	.429	15	12	.556
Coastal Carolina	1	7	.125	10	17	.370

Tournament: **Charleston So. d. Augusta 68-60**
Tournament MVP: **Ben Hinson**, Charleston So.

Big Ten

	Conference W	L	Pct	Overall W	L	Pct
Michigan ⊕	14	4	.778	28	5	.848
Indiana ○	13	5	.722	21	8	.724
Michigan State ○	12	6	.667	23	8	.742
Illinois ○	11	7	.611	22	10	.688
Purdue ○	11	7	.611	22	10	.688
Iowa ○	10	8	.556	20	12	.625
Ohio State □	8	10	.444	19	14	.576
Minnesota	5	13	.278	15	16	.484
Wisconsin	4	14	.222	12	16	.429
Northwestern	2	16	.111	7	20	.259

Colonial Athletic

	Conference W	L	Pct	Overall W	L	Pct
Navy ⊕	13	1	.929	30	5	.857
Richmond ○	12	2	.857	23	7	.767
George Mason □	10	4	.714	20	12	.625
UNC Wilmington	6	8	.429	16	13	.552
East Carolina	6	8	.429	12	16	.429
American	3	11	.214	10	18	.357
William and Mary	3	11	.214	8	20	.286
James Madison	3	11	.214	5	23	.179

Tournament: **Navy d. George Mason 72-61**
Tournament MVP: **David Robinson**, Navy

East Coast

	Conference W	L	Pct	Overall W	L	Pct
Drexel ⊕	11	3	.786	19	12	.613
Hofstra	9	5	.643	17	13	.567
Bucknell	8	6	.571	17	12	.586
Lafayette	8	6	.571	14	15	.483
Lehigh	6	8	.429	13	15	.464
Rider	5	9	.357	9	19	.321
Towson	5	9	.357	8	20	.286
Delaware	4	10	.286	11	16	.407

Tournament: **Drexel d. Hofstra 80-76**
Tournament MVP: **Michael Anderson**, Drexel

ECAC Metro

	Conference W	L	Pct	Overall W	L	Pct
Fairleigh Dickinson	13	3	.813	22	8	.733
Marist ⊕	11	5	.688	19	12	.613
Loyola (MD)	10	6	.625	16	12	.571
Wagner	10	6	.625	16	13	.552
Saint Francis (PA)	8	8	.500	10	18	.357
Robert Morris	6	10	.375	10	18	.357
Monmouth	6	10	.375	9	19	.321
Long Island	4	12	.250	9	19	.321
St. Francis (NY)	4	12	.250	9	19	.321

Tournament: **Marist d. Fairleigh Dickinson 57-56**
Tournament MVP: **Rik Smits**, Marist

ECAC NAC

	Conference W	L	Pct	Overall W	L	Pct
Northeastern ⊕	16	2	.889	26	5	.839
Canisius	14	4	.778	21	8	.724
Boston U. □	13	5	.722	21	10	.677
Siena	12	6	.667	21	8	.724
Niagara	10	8	.556	14	14	.500
Hartford	10	8	.556	12	16	.429
New Hampshire	5	13	.278	11	17	.393
Vermont	5	13	.278	9	19	.321
Maine	5	13	.278	7	20	.259
Colgate	0	18	.000	1	24	.040

Tournament: **Northeastern d. Boston U. 63-54**
Tournament MVP: **Wes Fuller**, Northeastern

Gulf Star

	Conference W	L	Pct	Overall W	L	Pct
Sam Houston State	9	1	.900	27	6	.818
Stephen F. Austin	7	3	.700	22	5	.815
Northwestern State (LA)	7	3	.700	11	16	.407
Southeastern Louisiana	3	5	.375	10	18	.357
Nicholls State	2	8	.200	8	16	.333
Texas State	1	9	.100	6	22	.214

Ivy

	Conference W	L	Pct	Overall W	L	Pct
Brown ⊕	10	4	.714	16	11	.593
Penn	9	5	.643	15	11	.577
Cornell	9	5	.643	14	12	.538
Princeton	7	7	.500	13	13	.500
Yale	7	7	.500	13	13	.500
Columbia	6	8	.429	12	14	.462
Dartmouth	6	8	.429	11	15	.423
Harvard	2	12	.143	6	20	.231

Metro

	Conference W	L	Pct	Overall W	L	Pct
Louisville ⊕	10	2	.833	32	7	.821
Memphis ○ ✪	9	3	.750	28	6	.824
Virginia Tech ○	7	5	.583	22	9	.710
Southern Miss □	6	6	.500	17	12	.586
Cincinnati	5	7	.417	12	16	.429
Florida State	3	9	.250	12	17	.414
South Carolina	2	10	.167	12	16	.429

Tournament: **Louisville d. Memphis 88-79**
Tournament MVP: **Pervis Ellison**, Louisville

Metro Atlantic

	Conference W	L	Pct	Overall W	L	Pct
Fairfield ⊕	13	1	.929	24	7	.774
Iona	9	5	.643	14	15	.483
La Salle	8	6	.571	14	14	.500
Saint Peter's	7	7	.500	16	12	.571
Fordham	7	7	.500	13	17	.433
Holy Cross	6	8	.429	12	18	.400
Army	5	9	.357	9	18	.333
Manhattan	1	13	.071	2	26	.071

Tournament: **Fairfield d. Holy Cross 67-64**
Tournament MVP: **Jim McCaffrey**, Holy Cross

⊕ Automatic NCAA Tournament bid ○ At-large NCAA Tournament bid □ NIT appearance ✪ Team record doesn't reflect games forfeited or vacated. For adjusted record, see p. 521.

MID-AMERICAN	Conference			Overall		
	W	L	Pct	W	L	Pct
Miami (OH)○	16	2	.889	24	7	.774
Ohio□	14	4	.778	22	8	.733
Ball State⊕	11	7	.611	21	10	.677
Northern Illinois	10	8	.556	15	12	.556
Toledo	8	10	.444	12	17	.414
Western Michigan	7	11	.389	12	16	.429
Kent State	7	11	.389	11	16	.407
Central Michigan	7	11	.389	11	17	.393
Eastern Michigan	5	13	.278	9	18	.333
Bowling Green	5	13	.278	7	20	.259

Tournament: **Ball State d. Miami (OH) 87-79**
Tournament MVP: **Dan Palombizio**, Ball State

MEAC	Conference			Overall		
	W	L	Pct	W	L	Pct
NC A&T⊕	12	2	.857	22	8	.733
Howard	11	3	.786	19	10	.655
Delaware State	7	7	.500	11	17	.393
Coppin State	7	7	.500	10	17	.370
Morgan State	7	7	.500	7	20	.259
South Carolina State	5	9	.357	10	18	.357
UMES	5	9	.357	5	23	.179
Bethune-Cookman	4	10	.286	7	22	.241

Tournament: **NC A&T d. Howard 53-52**
Tournament MOP: **Thomas Griffis**, NC A&T

MCC	Conference			Overall		
	W	L	Pct	W	L	Pct
Xavier⊕	10	2	.833	25	5	.833
Saint Louis	8	4	.667	18	12	.600
Detroit	7	5	.583	14	15	.483
Loyola-Chicago	7	5	.583	13	16	.448
Oral Roberts	5	7	.417	10	18	.357
Evansville	3	9	.250	8	19	.296
Butler	2	10	.167	9	19	.321

Tournament: **Xavier d. Saint Louis 74-66**
Tournament MVP: **Byron Larkin**, Xavier

MISSOURI VALLEY	Conference			Overall		
	W	L	Pct	W	L	Pct
Bradley○	16	0	1.000	32	3	.914
Tulsa⊕	10	6	.625	23	9	.719
Drake□	10	6	.625	19	11	.633
Illinois State	9	7	.563	15	14	.517
Wichita State	7	9	.438	14	14	.500
Creighton	7	9	.438	12	16	.429
Indiana State	5	11	.313	11	17	.393
West Texas	4	12	.250	11	17	.393
Southern Illinois	4	12	.250	8	20	.286

Tournament: **Tulsa d. Bradley 74-58**
Tournament MOP: **Brian Rahilly**, Tulsa

OHIO VALLEY	Conference			Overall		
	W	L	Pct	W	L	Pct
Akron⊕	10	4	.714	22	8	.733
Middle Tenn. State□	10	4	.714	23	11	.676
Murray State	8	6	.571	17	12	.586
Austin Peay	8	6	.571	14	14	.500
Youngstown State	8	6	.571	12	16	.429
Tennessee Tech	6	8	.429	14	15	.483
Eastern Kentucky	5	9	.357	10	18	.357
Morehead State	1	13	.071	8	19	.296

Tournament: **Akron d. Middle Tenn. St. 68-63**
Tournament MVP: **Eric McLaughlin**, Akron

PCAA	Conference			Overall		
	W	L	Pct	W	L	Pct
UNLV⊕	16	2	.889	33	5	.868
UC Irvine□	12	6	.667	17	13	.567
New Mexico State	10	8	.556	18	12	.600
San Jose State	9	9	.500	16	12	.571
Pacific	9	9	.500	17	14	.548
Cal State Fullerton	8	10	.444	16	16	.500
Fresno State	8	10	.444	15	15	.500
Utah State	8	10	.444	12	16	.429
UC Santa Barbara	7	11	.389	12	15	.444
Long Beach State	3	15	.167	7	22	.241

Tournament: **UNLV d. New Mexico State 75-55**
Tournament MVP: **Anthony Jones**, UNLV

PAC-10	Conference			Overall		
	W	L	Pct	W	L	Pct
Arizona⊕	14	4	.778	23	9	.719
Washington○	13	5	.722	19	12	.613
California□	11	7	.611	19	10	.655
UCLA□	9	9	.500	15	14	.517
Arizona State	8	10	.444	14	14	.500
Washington State	8	10	.444	15	16	.484
Stanford	8	10	.444	14	16	.467
Oregon State	8	10	.444	12	15	.444
Oregon	6	12	.333	11	17	.393
Southern California	5	13	.278	11	17	.393

SEC	Conference			Overall		
	W	L	Pct	W	L	Pct
Kentucky⊕	17	1	.944	32	4	.889
Alabama○	13	5	.722	24	9	.727
Auburn○	13	5	.722	22	11	.667
Florida□	10	8	.556	19	14	.576
LSU○	9	9	.500	26	12	.684
Georgia□	9	9	.500	17	13	.567
Vanderbilt	7	11	.389	13	15	.464
Tennessee	5	13	.278	12	16	.429
Mississippi	4	14	.222	12	17	.414
Mississippi State	3	15	.167	8	22	.267

Tournament: **Kentucky d. Alabama 83-72**
Tournament MVP: **John Williams**, LSU

SOUTHERN	Conference			Overall		
	W	L	Pct	W	L	Pct
Chattanooga□	12	4	.750	21	10	.677
Davidson⊕	10	6	.625	20	11	.645
Marshall	10	6	.625	19	11	.633
Appalachian State	9	7	.563	17	12	.586
Western Carolina	8	8	.500	14	14	.500
East Tenn. State	8	8	.500	13	16	.448
VMI	5	11	.313	11	17	.393
Furman	5	11	.313	10	17	.370
The Citadel	5	11	.313	10	18	.357

Tournament: **Davidson d. Chattanooga 42-40**
Tournament MOP: **Gerry Born**, Davidson

SOUTHLAND	Conference			Overall		
	W	L	Pct	W	L	Pct
UL-Monroe⊕	9	3	.750	20	10	.667
McNeese State□	8	4	.667	21	11	.656
Arkansas State	7	5	.583	18	11	.621
Lamar□	6	6	.500	18	12	.600
Louisiana Tech□	6	6	.500	20	14	.588
North Texas	4	8	.333	10	18	.357
Texas-Arlington	2	10	.167	12	18	.400

Tournament: **UL-Monroe d. McNeese State 59-57**
Tournament MVP: **Arthur Hayes**, UL-Monroe

SOUTHWEST	Conference			Overall		
	W	L	Pct	W	L	Pct
TCU□	12	4	.750	22	9	.710
Texas A&M□	12	4	.750	20	12	.625
Texas□	12	4	.750	19	12	.613
SMU□	10	6	.625	18	11	.621
Texas Tech⊕	9	7	.563	17	14	.548
Houston	8	8	.500	14	14	.500
Arkansas	4	12	.250	12	16	.429
Rice	2	14	.125	9	19	.321
Baylor	3	13	.188	11	16	.407

Tournament: **Texas Tech d. Texas A&M 67-63**
Tournament MVP: **Tony Benford**, Texas Tech

SWAC	Conference			Overall		
	W	L	Pct	W	L	Pct
Southern U.	11	3	.786	19	8	.704
Alcorn State	11	3	.786	16	13	.552
Miss. Valley State⊕	10	4	.714	20	11	.645
Jackson State	9	5	.643	14	15	.483
Texas Southern	6	8	.429	9	18	.333
Grambling	4	10	.286	14	12	.538
Alabama State	4	10	.286	11	17	.393
Prairie View A&M	1	13	.071	5	25	.167

Tournament: **Miss. Valley St. d. Prairie View A&M 75-58**
Tournament MVP: **George Ivory**, Miss. Valley State

SUN BELT	Conference			Overall		
	W	L	Pct	W	L	Pct
Old Dominion○	11	3	.786	23	8	.742
Western Kentucky○	10	4	.714	23	8	.742
UAB○	9	5	.643	25	11	.694
Jacksonville⊕	9	5	.643	21	10	.677
VCU	6	8	.429	12	16	.429
South Alabama	5	9	.357	16	16	.500
South Florida	5	9	.357	14	14	.500
Charlotte	1	13	.071	8	20	.286

Tournament: **Jacksonville d. UAB 70-69**
Tournament MVP: **Otis Smith**, Jacksonville

TAAC	Conference			Overall		
	W	L	Pct	W	L	Pct
Ark.-Little Rock⊕	12	2	.857	23	11	.676
Samford	8	6	.571	16	13	.552
Hardin-Simmons	7	7	.500	15	13	.536
Houston Baptist	7	7	.500	14	14	.500
Georgia Southern	6	8	.429	15	13	.536
Mercer	6	8	.429	15	14	.517
Centenary	6	8	.429	13	17	.433
Georgia State	4	10	.286	10	18	.357
Stetson	-	-	-	10	18	.357

Tournament: **Ark.-Little Rock d. Centenary 85-63**
Tournament MVP: **Michael Clarke**, Ark.-Little Rock

WCAC	Conference			Overall		
	W	L	Pct	W	L	Pct
Pepperdine⊕	13	1	.929	25	5	.833
Loyola Marymount□	10	4	.714	19	11	.633
San Diego	9	5	.643	19	9	.679
Gonzaga	8	6	.571	15	13	.536
Santa Clara	7	7	.500	12	16	.429
Portland	4	10	.286	13	15	.464
Saint Mary's (CA)	3	11	.214	10	17	.370
San Francisco	2	12	.143	7	21	.250

WAC	Conference			Overall		
	W	L	Pct	W	L	Pct
UTEP⊕	12	4	.750	27	6	.818
Wyoming□	12	4	.750	24	12	.667
Utah○	12	4	.750	20	10	.667
BYU□	11	5	.688	18	14	.563
New Mexico□	8	8	.500	17	14	.548
San Diego State	7	9	.438	10	19	.345
Colorado State	6	10	.375	11	18	.379
Air Force	3	13	.188	10	19	.345
Hawaii	1	15	.063	4	24	.143

Tournament: **UTEP d. Wyoming 65-64**
Tournament MVP: **Eric Leckner**, Wyoming

INDEPENDENTS	Overall		
	W	L	Pct
Notre Dame○	23	6	.793
Chicago State	22	6	.786
Eastern Washington	20	8	.714
Texas-Pan American	20	8	.714
Marquette□	19	11	.633
DePaul○⊗	18	13	.581
New Orleans	16	12	.571
Dayton□	17	13	.567
UL-Lafayette	15	13	.536
Miami (FL)	14	14	.500
Tennessee State	14	14	.500
Utica	13	14	.481
Florida A&M	12	16	.429
Brooklyn	9	22	.290
U.S. International	8	20	.286
UTSA	7	24	.226
UCF	6	22	.214

INDIVIDUAL LEADERS—SEASON

SCORING	CL	POS	G	FG	FT	PTS	PPG
1 **Terrance Bailey**, Wagner	JR	G	29	321	212	854	**29.4**
2 **Scott Skiles**, Michigan State	SR	G	31	331	188	850	**27.4**
3 **Joe Yezbak**, U.S. International	JR	G	28	299	157	755	**27.0**
4 **Reggie Miller**, UCLA	JR	G	29	274	202	750	**25.9**
5 **Ron Harper**, Miami (OH)	SR	G/F	31	312	133	757	**24.4**
6 **Dell Curry**, Virginia Tech	SR	G	30	305	112	722	**24.1**
7 **Reggie Lewis**, Northeastern	JR	F	30	265	184	714	**23.8**
8 **Len Bias**, Maryland	SR	F	32	267	209	743	**23.2**
9 **Frank Ross**, American	JR	G	28	270	105	645	**23.0**
10 **Walter Berry**, St. John's	JR	F	36	327	174	828	**23.0**

FIELD GOAL PCT	CL	POS	G	FG	FGA	PCT
1 **Brad Daugherty**, North Carolina	SR	C	34	284	438	**64.8**
2 **Ken Norman**, Illinois	JR	F	32	216	337	**64.1**
3 **Kenny Gattison**, Old Dominion	SR	F/C	31	218	342	**63.7**
4 **Derrick McKey**, Alabama	SO	F/C	33	178	280	**63.6**
5 **Albert Thomas**, Centenary	SR	F	30	182	288	**63.2**

MINIMUM: 5 MADE PER GAME

FREE THROW PCT	CL	POS	G	FT	FTA	PCT
1 **Jim Barton**, Dartmouth	FR	G	26	65	69	**94.2**
2 **Damon Goodwin**, Dayton	SR	F	30	95	102	**93.1**
3 **Rick Suder**, Duquesne	SR	G	29	135	147	**91.8**
4 **Scott Coval**, William and Mary	SR	G	28	111	121	**91.7**
5 **Mike Androlewicz**, Lehigh	SR	G	28	84	93	**90.3**

MINIMUM: 2.5 MADE PER GAME

ASSISTS PER GAME	CL	POS	G	AST	APG
1 **Mark Jackson**, St. John's	JR	G	36	328	**9.1**
2 **Taurence Chisholm**, Delaware	SO	G	27	230	**8.5**
3 **Tyrone Bogues**, Wake Forest	JR	G	29	245	**8.4**
4 **Ralph Lee**, Xavier	SR	G	30	251	**8.4**
5 **Derric Thomas**, Monmouth	SO	G	25	205	**8.2**
6 **Frank Smith**, Old Dominion	SO	G	31	253	**8.2**
7 **Girard Harmon**, McNeese State	SR	G	30	243	**8.1**
8 **Drafton Davis**, Marist	SO	G	31	248	**8.0**
9 **Jim Paguaga**, Saint Francis (PA)	SR	G	28	223	**8.0**
10 **Dwight Moody**, Northwestern St. (LA)	SR	G	25	198	**7.9**

REBOUNDS PER GAME	CL	POS	G	REB	RPG
1 **David Robinson**, Navy	JR	C	35	455	**13.0**
2 **Greg Anderson**, Houston	JR	F/C	28	360	**12.9**
3 **Brad Sellers**, Ohio State	SR	F/C	33	416	**12.6**
4 **Ron Harper**, Miami (OH)	SR	G/F	31	362	**11.7**
5 **Larry Krystkowiak**, Montana	SR	F	32	364	**11.4**
6 **Walter Berry**, St. John's	JR	F	36	399	**11.1**
7 **Don Hill**, Bethune-Cookman	SR	F/C	29	317	**10.9**
8 **Kevin Carter**, Loyola (MD)	SR	F/C	28	304	**10.9**
9 **David Boone**, Marquette	JR	C	30	319	**10.6**
10 **Horace Grant**, Clemson	JR	F	34	357	**10.5**

BLOCKED SHOTS PER GAME	CL	POS	G	BLK	BPG
1 **David Robinson**, Navy	JR	C	35	207	**5.9**
2 **Tim Perry**, Temple	SO	F	31	123	**4.0**
3 **Rodney Blake**, Saint Joseph's	SO	C	32	121	**3.8**
4 **Lester Fonville**, Jackson State	JR	C	29	93	**3.2**
5 **Curtis Kitchen**, South Florida	SR	F	28	89	**3.2**

STEALS PER GAME	CL	POS	G	STL	SPG
1 **Darron Brittman**, Chicago State	SR	G	28	139	**5.0**
2 **Jim Paguaga**, St. Francis (NY)	SR	G	28	120	**4.3**
3 **Leroy Allen**, Hofstra	JR	G	28	100	**3.6**
4 **Ron Harper**, Miami (Ohio)	SR	G/F	31	101	**3.3**
5 **Harold Starks**, Providence	SR	G	26	84	**3.2**

INDIVIDUAL LEADERS—GAME

POINTS	CL	POS	OPP	DATE	PTS
1 **Anthony Watson**, San Diego State	SR	F	U.S. International	F20	**54**
2 **Terrance Bailey**, Wagner	JR	G	Brooklyn	J29	**49**
3 **Skip Henderson**, Marshall	SO	G	Charleston	J8	**46**
Terrance Bailey, Wagner	JR	G	Marist	F1	**46**
5 **Scott Skiles**, Michigan State	SR	G	Minnesota	J18	**45**
Byron Larkin, Xavier	SO	G	Loyola-Chicago	M2	**45**

ASSISTS	CL	POS	OPP	DATE	AST
1 **Grayson Marshall**, Clemson	SO	G	UMES	N25	**20**
James Johnson, Middle Tenn. State	SR	G	Freed-Hardeman	J2	**20**
3 **Frank Nardi**, Green Bay	SR	G	Northern Iowa	F24	**19**
4 **Derric Thomas**, Monmouth	SO	G	Long Island	J7	**17**
Kevin McAdoo, Detroit	SR	G	Oral Roberts	F1	**17**
Tyrone Bogues, Wake Forest	JR	G	North Carolina	F8	**17**

REBOUNDS	CL	POS	OPP	DATE	REB
1 **David Robinson**, Navy	JR	C	Fairfield	F12	**25**
Don Hill, Bethune-Cookman	SR	F/C	Morgan State	F3	**25**
3 **James Colson**, Austin Peay	JR	F/C	Samford	D30	**23**
Ron Harper, Miami (OH)	SR	G/F	Central Michigan	F26	**23**
5 **Don Hill**, Bethune-Cookman	SR	F/C	Florida A&M	N22	**22**
Darryl Martin, South Carolina	SR	F	UMES	N27	**22**
Armon Gilliam, UNLV	JR	F	Utah State	J2	**22**
Rodney Holden, Marshall	JR	F	The Citadel	J18	**22**

BLOCKED SHOTS	CL	POS	OPP	DATE	BLK
1 **David Robinson**, Navy	JR	C	UNC Wilmington	J4	**14**
2 **David Robinson**, Navy	JR	C	James Madison	J9	**12**
3 **Harold Pressley**, Villanova	SR	F	Providence	J11	**10**
David Robinson, Navy	JR	C	William and Mary	J25	**10**
David Robinson, Navy	JR	C	East Carolina	F3	**10**
Curtis Kitchen, South Florida	SR	F	Charlotte	F10	**10**
Rodney Blake, Saint Joseph's	SO	C	Penn State	F27	**10**

STEALS	CL	POS	OPP	DATE	STL
1 **Darron Brittman**, Chicago State	SR	G	McKendree	J24	**11**
Darron Brittman, Chicago State	SR	G	St. Xavier	F8	**11**
3 **Tom Gormley**, Loyola (MD)	JR	G	Towson	D21	**10**
4 **Tracy Dildy**, San Diego State	FR	G	Air Force	J2	**9**
Andre Turner, Memphis	SR	G	Virginia Tech	J27	**9**

TEAM LEADERS—SEASON

WIN-LOSS PCT	W	L	PCT
1 **Duke**	37	3	**.925**
2 **Bradley**	32	3	**.914**
3 **Kansas**	35	4	**.897**
4 **Kentucky**	32	4	**.889**
5 **Cleveland State**	29	4	**.879**

SCORING OFFENSE	G	W-L	PTS	PPG
1 **U.S. International**	28	8-20	2,542	**90.8**
2 **Cleveland State**	33	29-4	2,934	**88.9**
3 **Oklahoma**	35	26-9	3,077	**87.9**
4 **North Carolina**	34	28-6	2,945	**86.6**
5 **Syracuse**	32	26-6	2,674	**83.6**

SCORING MARGIN	G	W-L	PPG	OPP PPG	MAR
1 **Cleveland State**	33	29-4	88.9	69.6	**19.3**
2 **North Carolina**	34	28-6	86.6	69.0	**17.6**
3 **Syracuse**	32	26-6	83.6	68.3	**15.3**
4 **Memphis**	34	28-6	82.4	67.4	**15.0**
5 **Notre Dame**	29	23-6	78.9	64.8	**14.1**

FIELD GOAL PCT	G	W-L	FG	FGA	PCT
1 **Michigan State**	31	23-8	1,043	1,860	**56.1**
2 **North Carolina**	34	28-6	1,197	2,140	**55.9**
3 **Kansas**	39	35-4	1,260	2,266	**55.6**
4 **Georgia Tech**	34	27-7	1,008	1,846	**54.6**
5 **Illinois**	32	22-10	990	1,828	**54.2**

FREE THROW PCT	G	W-L	FT	FTA	PCT
1 **Michigan State**	31	23-8	490	613	**79.9**
2 **Weber State**	29	18-11	484	619	**78.2**
3 **Notre Dame**	29	23-6	567	731	**77.6**
4 **Davidson**	31	20-11	520	674	**77.2**
5 **UC Irvine**	30	17-13	597	779	**76.6**

REBOUND MARGIN	G	W-L	RPG	OPP RPG	MAR
1 **Notre Dame**	29	23-6	36.4	27.8	**8.6**
2 **Michigan**	33	28-5	37.4	29.2	**8.2**
3 **Syracuse**	32	26-6	41.0	32.9	**8.1**
Arkansas-Little Rock	34	23-11	44.6	36.5	**8.1**
5 **Cleveland State**	33	29-4	38.4	31.0	**7.4**

SCORING DEFENSE	G	W-L	OPP PTS	OPP PPG
1 **Princeton**	26	13-13	1,429	**55.0**
2 **Saint Peter's**	28	16-12	1,539	**55.0**
3 **Fresno State**	30	15-15	1,708	**56.9**
4 **NC A&T**	30	22-8	1,732	**57.7**
5 **Tulsa**	32	23-9	1,854	**57.9**

FIELD GOAL PCT DEFENSE	G	W-L	FG	FGA	PCT
1 **Saint Peter's**	28	16-12	574	1,395	**41.1**
2 **South Florida**	28	14-14	621	1,499	**41.4**
3 **TCU**	31	22-9	711	1,713	**41.5**
4 **Georgetown**	32	24-8	789	1,885	**41.9**
5 **Navy**	35	30-5	932	2,215	**42.1**

CONSENSUS ALL-AMERICAS

FIRST TEAM

PLAYER	CL	POS	HT	SCHOOL	RPG	PPG
Steve Alford	JR	G	6-2	Indiana	2.7	22.5
Walter Berry	JR	F	6-8	St. John's	11.1	23.0
Len Bias	SR	F	6-8	Maryland	7.0	23.2
Johnny Dawkins	SR	G	6-2	Duke	3.6	20.2
Kenny Walker	SR	F	6-8	Kentucky	7.7	20.0

SECOND TEAM

PLAYER	CL	POS	HT	SCHOOL	RPG	PPG
Dell Curry	SR	G	6-5	Virginia Tech	6.8	24.1
Brad Daugherty	SR	C	6-11	North Carolina	9.0	20.2
Ron Harper	SR	G/F	6-6	Miami (OH)	11.7	24.4
Danny Manning	SO	F	6-11	Kansas	6.3	16.7
David Robinson	JR	C	7-1	Navy	13.0	22.7
Scott Skiles	SR	G	6-1	Michigan State	4.4	27.4

SELECTORS: AP, NABC, UPI, USBWA

AWARD WINNERS

PLAYER OF THE YEAR

PLAYER	CL	POS	HT	SCHOOL	AWARDS
Johnny Dawkins	SR	G	6-2	Duke	Naismith
Walter Berry	JR	F	6-8	St. John's	AP, UPI, USBWA, Wooden, NABC, Rupp
Jim Les	SR	G	5-11	Bradley	Frances Pomeroy Naismith*

* FOR THE MOST OUTSTANDING SENIOR PLAYER WHO IS 6 FEET OR UNDER.

COACH OF THE YEAR

COACH	SCHOOL	REC	AWARDS
Eddie Sutton	Kentucky	32-4	AP, NABC
Mike Krzyzewski	Duke	37-3	UPI, CBS/Chevrolet
Dick Versace	Bradley	32-3	USBWA
Denny Crum	Louisville	32-7	Sporting News

BOB GIBBONS' TOP HIGH SCHOOL SENIOR RECRUITS

PLAYER	POS	HT	HIGH SCHOOL	A-A TEAMS	COLLEGE	CAREER NOTES
1 J.R. Reid	F/C	6-10	Kempsville HS, Virginia Beach, FL	McD, P, USA	North Carolina	16.2 ppg, 7.0 rpg (2 seasons); No. 5 pick, '89 NBA draft (Hornets); 13.3 ppg (11 seasons)
2 Rex Chapman	2G	6-4	Apollo HS, Owensboro, KY	McD, P, USA	Kentucky	2-time All-SEC; No. 8 pick, '88 NBA draft (Hornets); 14.6 ppg (12 seasons)
3 Terry Mills	F	6-10	Romulus (Mich.) HS	McD, P, USA	Michigan	NCAA title, '89; No. 16 pick, '90 NBA draft (Bucks); 10.8 ppg (11 seasons)
4 Derrick Coleman	C	6-10	Detroit Northern HS	McD	Syracuse	Big East POY, '90; left SU as 2nd-leading scorer (2,143 pts); No. 1 overall pick, '90 NBA draft (Nets); 16.5 ppg (15 seasons); NBA ROY, '91
5 Rumeal Robinson	PG	6-2	Rindge and Latin HS, Cambridge, MA	McD, P, USA	Michigan	NCAA title, '89; No. 10 pick, '90 NBA draft (Hawks); 7.6 ppg (6 seasons)
6 Anthony Pendleton	G	6-4	Flint (Mich.) Northwestern HS	McD, P	Iowa/USC	Transferred to USC; USC-record 9 3pt FGs vs. Long Beach State; undrafted
7 Dwayne Bryant	PG	6-3	De La Salle HS, New Orleans	McD, P	Georgetown	Left Georgetown as 5th all-time in assists (527), 3rd in 3pt FG% (39.9); undrafted
8 Stacey Augmon	SF	6-7	John Muir HS, Pasadena, CA		UNLV	NCAA title, '90; at UNLV, 2,011 pts, 1,005 reb (4 seasons); No. 9 pick, '91 NBA draft (Hawks); 8.0 ppg (15 seasons)
9 Mark Randall	F	6-8	Cherry Creek HS, Englewood, CO	McD, P	Kansas	12.3 ppg (4 seasons); No. 26 pick, '91 NBA draft (Bulls); 2.6 ppg (4 seasons)
10 Brian Oliver	2G	6-4	Wills HS, Smyrna, GA	McD, P	Georgia Tech	Final Four, '90; 21.3 ppg as Sr.; No. 32 pick, '90 NBA draft (76ers); 3.3 ppg (4 seasons)
11 Sylvester Gray	F	6-6	Bolton HS, Arlington, TN	P	Memphis	12.6 ppg, 7.6 rpg (2 seasons); No. 35 pick, '88 NBA draft (Heat); 8.0 ppg, 5.2 rpg (1 season)
12 Larry Rembert	F	6-8	Keith HS, Orrville, AL	McD, P	UAB	9.1 ppg, 4.7 rpg (4 seasons); undrafted
13 Keith Robinson	F	6-8	Grover Cleveland HS, Buffalo, NY	McD, P	Notre Dame	1,073 points, 713 rebounds (4 seasons); undrafted
14 Scott Williams	C	6-10	Glen A. Wilson HS, Hacienda Heights, CA	McD, P, USA	North Carolina	10.9 ppg, 6.2 rpg (4 seasons); undrafted; 3 NBA titles; 5.1 ppg (15 seasons)
15 Ron Huery	G/F	6-6	Whitehaven HS, Memphis	McD, P	Arkansas	1,550 points (4 seasons); undrafted
16 Dwayne Schintzius	C	7-1	Brandon (FL) HS	McD, P	Florida	14.8 ppg, 7.5 rpg (4 seasons); No. 24 pick, '90 NBA draft (Spurs); 2.7 ppg (8 seasons)
17 Nick Anderson	SF	6-5	Simeon Vocational School, Chicago	McD, P	Illinois	17.0 ppg, 7.3 rpg (2 seasons); No. 11 pick, '89 NBA draft (Magic); 14.4 ppg (13 seasons)
18 Steve Thompson	2G	6-2	Crenshaw HS, Los Angeles	McD, P	Syracuse	Left Syracuse 7th all-time scorer (1,956); undrafted
19 Anthony Allen	F	6-7	Lincoln HS, Port Arthur, TX		Georgetown	2.3 ppg (4 seasons); lettered 4 years; undrafted
20 Alaa Abdelnaby	F	6-9	Bloomfield (NJ) HS	McD, P	Duke	8.5 ppg, 3.7 rpg (4 seasons); 3rd team All-ACC, '90; No. 25 pick, '90 NBA draft (Blazers); 5.7 ppg (5 seasons)

OTHER STANDOUTS

PLAYER	POS	HT	HIGH SCHOOL	A-A TEAMS	COLLEGE	CAREER NOTES
25 Felton Spencer	C	7-0	Eastern HS, Louisville, KY	P	Louisville	Left Louisville all-time FG% leader (62.8); No. 6 pick, '90 NBA draft (Wolves); 5.2 ppg (12 seasons)
46 Lionel Simmons	F	6-6	South Philadelphia (PA) HS		La Salle	Consensus POY, '90; left 3rd all-time in NCAA points scored (3,217); No. 7 pick, '90 NBA draft (Kings); 12.8 ppg (7 seasons)
127 Gary Payton	PG	6-1	Skyline HS, Oakland, CA		Oregon State	18.1 ppg, 7.8 rpg (4 seasons); All-America, '90; No. 2 pick, '90 NBA draft (Sonics); 9-time All-Star; 16.3 ppg, 6.7 apg (17 seasons)

Abbreviations: McD=McDonald's; P=Parade; USA=USA Today

Poll Progression

Preseason Poll

AP	UPI	SCHOOL
1	2	Georgia Tech
2	3	North Carolina
3	1	Michigan
4	6	Syracuse
5	4	Kansas
6	5	Duke
7	7	Illinois
8	8	Georgetown
9	10	Louisville
10	11	Auburn
11	12	Kentucky
12	13	Notre Dame
13	—	Oklahoma
14	9	LSU
15	—	Memphis
16	16	UAB
17	14	NC State
18	18	UNLV
19	—	Maryland
19	—	Navy
—	14	Iowa
—	17	Washington
—	19	DePaul
—	20	UCLA

Week of Nov 26

AP	SCHOOL	AP↓↑
1	**North Carolina** (1-0)	↑1
2	**Georgia Tech** (0-0)	↓1
3	**Michigan** (2-0)	
4	**Syracuse** (1-0)	
5	**Kansas** (2-0)	
6	**Duke** (2-0)	
7	**Illinois** (0-0)	
8	**Georgetown** (1-0)	
9	**Louisville** (2-0)	
10	**Kentucky** (1-0)	↑1
11	**Notre Dame** (1-0)	↑1
12	**LSU** (1-0)	↑2
13	**Oklahoma** (1-0)	
14	**Memphis** (0-0)	↑1
15	**NC State** (0-0)	↑2
16	**UNLV** (1-0)	↑2
17	**Maryland** (1-0)	↑2
18	**St. John's** (2-0)	⤴
19	**Auburn** (0-1)	↓9
20	**UAB** (1-1)	↓4

Week of Dec 3

AP	UPI	SCHOOL	AP↓↑
1	1	**North Carolina** (5-0)	
2	2	**Michigan** (4-0)	↑1
3	3	**Duke** (6-0)	↑3
4	5	**Syracuse** (3-0)	
5	4	**Georgia Tech** (2-1)	↓3
6	7	**Georgetown** (2-0)	↑2
7	6	**Kansas** (3-1)	↓2
8	10	**Oklahoma** (5-0)	↑5
9	8	**Kentucky** (3-0)	↑1
10	13	**Notre Dame** (2-0)	↑1
11	11	**LSU** (5-0)	↑1
12	12	**Illinois** (2-1)	↓5
13	16	**Memphis** (2-0)	↑1
14	9	**UNLV** (4-1)	↑2
15	14	**St. John's** (3-1)	↑3
16	15	**Louisville** (2-2) (A)	↓7
17	17	**UAB** (2-1)	↑3
18	19	**Iowa** (4-0)	⤴
19	18	**Auburn** (1-1)	
19	20	**Indiana** (1-0)	⤴

Week of Dec 10

AP	UPI	SCHOOL	AP↓↑
1	1	**North Carolina** (6-0)	
2	2	**Michigan** (6-0)	
3	3	**Duke** (8-0)	
4	5	**Syracuse** (5-0)	
5	6	**Georgia Tech** (4-1)	
5	7	**Georgetown** (4-0)	↑
7	4	**Kansas** (6-1)	
8	9	**Oklahoma** (6-0)	
9	8	**Kentucky** (5-0)	
10	11	**Illinois** (5-1)	↑
11	12	**LSU** (6-0)	
12	15	**Memphis** (5-0)	↑
13	10	**UNLV** (5-1)	↑
14	13	**St. John's** (6-1)	↑
15	14	**Louisville** (3-2)	↑
16	18	**UAB** (5-1)	↑
17	16	**Notre Dame** (3-1)	↓
18	16	**Indiana** (2-1)	↑1
18	20	**DePaul** (3-0)	⤴
20	19	**Ohio State** (5-0)	⤴

Week of Dec 17

AP	UPI	SCHOOL	AP↓↑
1	1	**North Carolina** (7-0)	
2	2	**Michigan** (9-0)	
3	3	**Duke** (8-0)	
4	5	**Syracuse** (6-0)	
5	6	**Georgetown** (6-0)	
6	4	**Kansas** (8-1)	↑1
7	7	**Georgia Tech** (4-1)	↓2
8	8	**Oklahoma** (8-0)	
9	11	**LSU** (8-0)	↑2
10	11	**Memphis** (7-0)	↑2
11	9	**St. John's** (8-1)	↑3
12	10	**UNLV** (5-1)	↑1
13	14	**Kentucky** (5-1)	↓4
14	15	**UAB** (8-1)	↑2
15	13	**Illinois** (5-2)	↓5
16	17	**Louisville** (5-2)	↓1
17	16	**Indiana** (4-1)	↑1
18	18	**DePaul** (4-0)	
19	19	**Notre Dame** (4-1)	↓2
20	—	**Virginia Tech** (7-1)	⤴
—	20	**Pepperdine** (6-1)	

Week of Dec 24

AP	UPI	SCHOOL	AP↓↑
1	1	**North Carolina** (10-0)	
2	2	**Michigan** (10-0)	
3	3	**Duke** (9-0)	
4	5	**Syracuse** (7-0)	
5	7	**Georgetown** (8-0)	
6	4	**Kansas** (9-1)	
7	6	**Georgia Tech** (7-1)	
8	9	**Oklahoma** (9-0)	
9	8	**LSU** (11-0)	
10	13	**Memphis** (8-0)	
11	11	**St. John's** (9-1)	
12	12	**UNLV** (7-1)	
13	10	**Kentucky** (7-1)	
14	—	**UAB** (11-1)	
15	14	**Louisville** (6-2)	↑1
16	15	**Illinois** (7-2)	↓1
17	16	**Indiana** (6-2)	
18	17	**Notre Dame** (5-1)	↑1
19	—	**Virginia Tech** (8-1)	↑1
20	18	**DePaul** (6-2)	↓2
—	19	**UTEP** (8-1)	
—	20	**Washington** (6-2)	

Week of Dec 31

AP	UPI	SCHOOL	AP↓↑
1	1	**North Carolina** (12-0)	
2	2	**Michigan** (12-0)	
3	3	**Duke** (11-0)	
4	5	**Syracuse** (8-0)	
5	4	**Kansas** (12-1)	↑1
6	6	**Georgia Tech** (10-1)	↑1
7	7	**Oklahoma** (11-0)	↑1
8	9	**LSU** (12-0)	↑1
9	12	**Memphis** (11-0)	↑1
10	8	**St. John's** (12-1)	↑1
11	11	**Georgetown** (9-1)	↓6
12	10	**Kentucky** (9-1) (B)	↑1
13	13	**UNLV** (10-2)	↓1
14	14	**Illinois** (9-2)	↑2
15	15	**Indiana** (8-2)	↑2
16	17	**UAB** (12-2)	↓2
17	19	**Notre Dame** (6-1)	↑1
18	18	**Louisville** (6-3) (B)	↓3
19	16	**UTEP** (11-1)	⤴
20	—	**Virginia Tech** (8-2)	↓1
—	20	**NC State** (7-3)	

Week of Jan 7

AP	UPI	SCHOOL	AP↓↑
1	1	**North Carolina** (14-0)	
2	2	**Michigan** (14-0)	
3	3	**Duke** (12-0)	
4	4	**Syracuse** (10-0)	
5	5	**Georgia Tech** (10-1)	↑1
6	6	**Memphis** (12-0)	↑3
7	8	**Oklahoma** (13-0)	
8	7	**LSU** (14-0)	
9	9	**Kansas** (12-2)	↓4
10	10	**St. John's** (14-1)	
11	11	**Kentucky** (10-1)	↑1
12	12	**UNLV** (13-2)	↑1
13	15	**Georgetown** (10-2)	↓2
14	13	**UAB** (13-2)	↑2
15	14	**UTEP** (13-1)	↑4
16	16	**Notre Dame** (7-1)	↑1
17	17	**Louisville** (7-3)	↑1
18	19	**Illinois** (10-3)	↓4
19	—	**Virginia Tech** (10-2)	↑1
20	18	**Purdue** (13-2)	⤴
—	19	**Bradley** (12-1)	

Week of Jan 14

AP	UPI	SCHOOL	AP↓↑
1	1	**North Carolina** (16-0)	
2	2	**Michigan** (16-0)	
3	3	**Duke** (15-0)	
4	4	**Syracuse** (13-0)	
5	5	**Georgia Tech** (14-1)	
6	6	**Memphis** (15-0)	
7	7	**Oklahoma** (15-0)	
8	8	**Kansas** (14-2)	↑1
9	9	**St. John's** (15-2)	↑1
10	10	**UNLV** (15-2)	↑2
11	11	**Kentucky** (12-2)	
12	12	**UAB** (16-2)	↑2
13	13	**Notre Dame** (9-2)	↑3
14	14	**LSU** (15-2)	↓6
15	16	**Georgetown** (11-3)	↓2
16	20	**Virginia Tech** (12-2)	↑3
17	15	**UTEP** (14-2)	↓2
18	18	**Louisville** (9-4)	↓1
19	17	**Purdue** (14-3)	↑1
20	19	**Bradley** (16-1)	⤴

Week of Jan 21

AP	UPI	SCHOOL	AP↓↑
1	1	**North Carolina** (19-0)	
2	2	**Duke** (16-1)	↑1
3	5	**Memphis** (17-0)	↑3
4	3	**Georgia Tech** (15-1)	↑1
5	6	**Oklahoma** (17-0)	↑2
6	4	**Michigan** (17-1)	↓4
7	7	**Kansas** (16-2)	↑1
8	8	**St. John's** (17-2)	↑1
9	11	**Syracuse** (13-2)	↓5
10	10	**UNLV** (17-2)	
11	9	**Kentucky** (14-2)	
12	12	**Georgetown** (13-3)	↑3
13	14	**Louisville** (11-4)	↑5
14	13	**LSU** (16-2)	
15	16	**Purdue** (16-3)	↑4
16	15	**Notre Dame** (10-2)	↓3
17	17	**Bradley** (18-1)	↑3
18	19	**UAB** (16-4)	↓6
19	18	**UTEP** (15-3)	↓2
20	—	**Virginia Tech** (14-3)	↓4
—	20	**Pepperdine** (14-3)	

Week of Jan 28

AP	UPI	SCHOOL	AP↓↑
1	1	**North Carolina** (21-0)	
2	2	**Memphis** (20-0)	↑1
3	3	**Georgia Tech** (16-2)	↑1
4	5	**Kansas** (19-2)	↑3
5	4	**Duke** (18-2)	↓3
6	6	**Oklahoma** (18-1)	↓1
7	7	**St. John's** (19-2)	↑1
8	9	**Kentucky** (16-2)	↑3
9	8	**Michigan** (17-2)	↓3
10	11	**UNLV** (19-2)	
11	10	**Syracuse** (15-2)	↓2
12	12	**Georgetown** (16-3)	
13	13	**Bradley** (20-1)	↑4
14	18	**Notre Dame** (12-3)	↑2
15	16	**Indiana** (13-4)	⤴
16	19	**Virginia Tech** (16-4)	↑4
17	17	**LSU** (16-3)	↓3
18	15	**Louisville** (11-6)	↓5
19	14	**UTEP** (17-3)	
20	—	**Richmond** (16-2)	⤴
—	20	**Pepperdine** (16-3)	
—	20	**Purdue** (16-5)	↱

Week of Feb 4

AP	UPI	SCHOOL	AP↓↑
1	1	**North Carolina** (22-1)	
2	2	**Georgia Tech** (17-2)	↑1
3	4	**Memphis** (20-1)	↓1
4	2	**Duke** (20-2)	↑1
5	6	**Oklahoma** (20-1)	↑1
6	5	**Kansas** (20-3)	↓2
7	8	**Michigan** (19-2)	↑2
8	7	**Syracuse** (17-2)	↑3
9	9	**UNLV** (21-2)	↑1
10	10	**St. John's** (20-3)	↓3
11	11	**Georgetown** (17-3)	↑1
12	12	**Kentucky** (18-3)	↓4
13	13	**Bradley** (22-1)	
14	17	**Notre Dame** (14-3)	
15	15	**Virginia Tech** (18-4)	↑1
16	16	**Louisville** (13-6)	↑2
17	14	**UTEP** (18-3)	↑2
18	18	**Indiana** (14-5)	↓3
19	—	**Western Kentucky** (17-3)	⤴
20	—	**Alabama** (15-4)	⤴
—	19	**NC State** (14-6)	
—	20	**Virginia** (14-5)	

[WE]EK OF FEB 11

AP	UPI	SCHOOL	AP↓↑
	1	**North Carolina** (24-1)	
	2	**Duke** (22-2)	↑2
	3	**Kansas** (22-3)	↑3
	6	**Memphis** (22-2)	↓1
	5	**Georgia Tech** (18-4)	↓3
	4	**UNLV** (24-2)	↑3
	7	**St. John's** (23-3)	↑3
	10	**Oklahoma** (21-2)	↓3
	11	**Georgetown** (19-4)	↑2
	9	**Michigan** (20-3)	↓3
	8	**Kentucky** (20-3)	↑1
	13	**Syracuse** (18-3)	↓4
	12	**Bradley** (24-1)	
	14	**Notre Dame** (16-4)	
	14	**UTEP** (21-3)	↑2
	16	**Indiana** (16-5)	↑2
	18	**NC State** (17-6)	⤴
	17	**Alabama** (17-4)	↑2
19	19	**Louisville** (16-7)	↓3
20	—	**Virginia Tech** (18-6)	↓5
—	19	**Pepperdine** (19-4)	

WEEK OF FEB 18

AP	UPI	SCHOOL	AP↓↑
1	1	**North Carolina** (25-1)	
2	2	**Duke** (25-2)	
3	3	**Kansas** (24-3)	
4	4	**Memphis** (23-2)	
5	5	**Georgia Tech** (19-4)	
6	6	**St. John's** (24-3)	↑1
7	8	**Michigan** (22-3)	↑3
8	7	**Kentucky** (22-3)	↑3
9	10	**Syracuse** (20-3)	↑3
10	9	**Oklahoma** (23-3)	↓2
11	11	**UNLV** (24-3)	↓5
12	12	**Bradley** (26-1)	↑1
13	13	**Georgetown** (19-5)	↓4
14	15	**Notre Dame** (17-5)	
15	14	**Indiana** (17-5)	↑1
16	16	**Louisville** (18-7)	↑3
17	—	**Navy** (20-4) Ⓒ	⤴
18	—	**Virginia Tech** (19-6)	↑2
19	—	**Michigan State** (17-6)	⤴
20	17	**NC State** (17-8)	↓3
—	18	**Alabama** (17-6)	⤵
—	19	**UTEP** (21-5)	⤵
—	20	**Pepperdine** (20-4)	

WEEK OF FEB 25

AP	UPI	SCHOOL	AP↓↑
1	1	**Duke** (27-2) Ⓓ	↑1
2	2	**Kansas** (27-3)	↑1
3	3	**North Carolina** (25-3) Ⓓ	↓2
4	3	**Georgia Tech** (21-4)	↑1
5	5	**Kentucky** (24-3)	↑3
6	6	**Syracuse** (22-3)	↑3
7	8	**Memphis** (24-3)	↓3
8	10	**St. John's** (25-4)	↓2
9	7	**UNLV** (27-3)	↑2
10	11	**Michigan** (23-4)	↓3
11	9	**Bradley** (28-1)	↑1
12	12	**Notre Dame** (19-5)	↑2
13	14	**Louisville** (22-7)	↑3
14	13	**Oklahoma** (23-6)	↓4
15	15	**Georgetown** (20-6)	↓2
16	16	**Indiana** (18-6)	↓1
17	17	**Michigan State** (18-6)	↑2
18	18	**NC State** (18-9)	↑2
19	—	**Navy** (23-4)	↓2
20	—	**Purdue** (21-7)	⤴
—	19	**Alabama** (19-6)	
—	20	**Pepperdine** (22-4)	

WEEK OF MAR 4

AP	UPI	SCHOOL	AP↓↑
1	1	**Duke** (29-2)	
2	2	**Kansas** (28-3)	
3	4	**Kentucky** (26-3)	↑2
4	3	**North Carolina** (26-4)	↓1
5	5	**St. John's** (27-4)	↑3
6	6	**Georgia Tech** (23-5)	↓2
7	7	**Michigan** (25-4)	↑3
8	8	**Syracuse** (23-4)	↓2
9	9	**Bradley** (29-1)	↑2
10	10	**Memphis** (25-4)	↓3
11	12	**Louisville** (24-7)	↑2
12	13	**Notre Dame** (21-5)	
13	11	**UNLV** (28-4)	↓4
14	15	**Georgetown** (22-6)	↑1
15	16	**Oklahoma** (24-6)	↓1
16	14	**Indiana** (20-6)	
17	18	**Michigan State** (20-6)	
18	—	**Navy** (25-4)	↑1
19	19	**Illinois** (20-8)	⤴
20	—	**NC State** (18-11)	↓2
—	17	**UTEP** (24-5)	
—	20	**Pepperdine** (24-4)	

FINAL POLL

AP	UPI	SCHOOL	AP↓↑
1	1	**Duke** (32-2)	
2	2	**Kansas** (31-3)	
3	4	**Kentucky** (29-3) Ⓔ	
4	3	**St. John's** (30-4)	↑1
5	5	**Michigan** (27-4)	↑2
6	6	**Georgia Tech** (25-6)	
7	7	**Louisville** (26-7)	↑4
8	8	**North Carolina** (26-5)	↓4
9	9	**Syracuse** (25-5)	↓1
10	11	**Notre Dame** (23-5)	↑2
11	10	**UNLV** (31-4)	↑2
12	12	**Memphis** (27-5)	↓2
13	15	**Georgetown** (23-7)	↑1
14	13	**Bradley** (31-2)	↓5
15	17	**Oklahoma** (26-8)	
16	14	**Indiana** (21-7)	
17	—	**Navy** (27-4)	↑1
18	18	**Michigan State** (21-7)	↓1
19	20	**Illinois** (21-9)	
20	16	**UTEP** (27-5)	⤴
—	19	**Alabama** (22-8)	

Ⓐ Louisville joins Duke, Kansas and St. John's in the semis of the preseason NIT. After back-to-back losses to Kansas and St. John's, Louisville coach Denny Crum says, "Those teams are as good as any in the country. That would have been a great Final Four." Crum will prove prophetic: Louisville, Duke and Kansas will make the 1986 Final Four—along with LSU (St. John's will lose in the second round).

Ⓑ Kentucky beats Louisville, 69-64, on Dec. 28, giving first-year coach Eddie Sutton victories over Denny Crum at the helm of three different schools (Kentucky, Arkansas and Creighton).

Ⓒ Navy makes its first regular-season appearance in the AP poll. The Midshipmen are led by 7'1" junior David Robinson, who sets an NCAA record on Jan. 4 against UNC Wilmington with 14 blocked shots. Over the course of the season Robinson will block 207 shots, also an NCAA record.

Ⓓ After losses to Maryland and NC State, North Carolina cedes the top spot to Duke and its fifth-year head coach, Mike Krzyzewski. The Blue Devils will finish 37–3, the first team to play 40 games in a season since 1948.

Ⓔ Kentucky beats LSU and Alabama—each for the third time—to win the SEC tournament. The Wildcats look poised to make a run at the national title. Senior Kenny "Sky" Walker joins Len Bias of Maryland, Walter Berry of St. John's, Johnny Dawkins of Duke and Steve Alford of Indiana on the consensus All-America team.

1986 NCAA Tournament

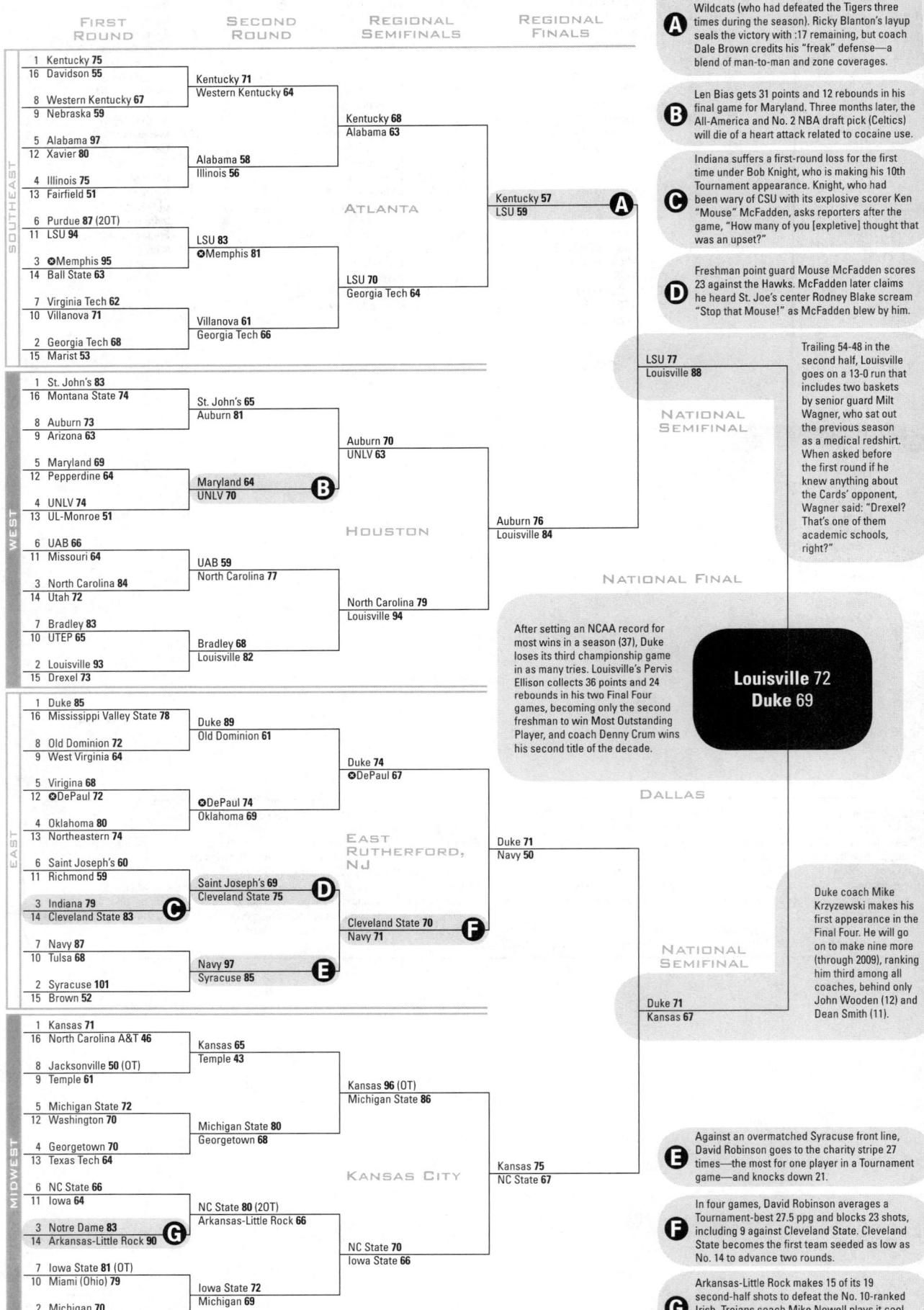

Southeast (Atlanta)

First Round
- 1 Kentucky **75**, 16 Davidson **55**
- 8 Western Kentucky **67**, 9 Nebraska **59**
- 5 Alabama **97**, 12 Xavier **80**
- 4 Illinois **75**, 13 Fairfield **51**
- 6 Purdue **87** (2OT), 11 LSU **94**
- 3 ⊗Memphis **95**, 14 Ball State **63**
- 7 Virginia Tech **62**, 10 Villanova **71**
- 2 Georgia Tech **68**, 15 Marist **53**

Second Round
- Kentucky **71**, Western Kentucky **64**
- Alabama **58**, Illinois **56**
- LSU **83**, ⊗Memphis **81**
- Villanova **61**, Georgia Tech **66**

Regional Semifinals
- Kentucky **68**, Alabama **63**
- LSU **70**, Georgia Tech **64**

Regional Final
- Kentucky **57**, LSU **59** (A)

West (Houston)

First Round
- 1 St. John's **83**, 16 Montana State **74**
- 8 Auburn **73**, 9 Arizona **63**
- 5 Maryland **69**, 12 Pepperdine **64**
- 4 UNLV **74**, 13 UL-Monroe **51**
- 6 UAB **66**, 11 Missouri **64**
- 3 North Carolina **84**, 14 Utah **72**
- 7 Bradley **83**, 10 UTEP **65**
- 2 Louisville **93**, 15 Drexel **73**

Second Round
- St. John's **65**, Auburn **81**
- Maryland **64**, UNLV **70** (B)
- UAB **59**, North Carolina **77**
- Bradley **68**, Louisville **82**

Regional Semifinals
- Auburn **70**, UNLV **63**
- North Carolina **79**, Louisville **94**

Regional Final
- Auburn **76**, Louisville **84**

East (East Rutherford, NJ)

First Round
- 1 Duke **85**, 16 Mississippi Valley State **78**
- 8 Old Dominion **72**, 9 West Virginia **64**
- 5 Virigina **68**, 12 ⊗DePaul **72**
- 4 Oklahoma **80**, 13 Northeastern **74**
- 6 Saint Joseph's **60**, 11 Richmond **59**
- 3 Indiana **79**, 14 Cleveland State **83** (C)
- 7 Navy **87**, 10 Tulsa **68**
- 2 Syracuse **101**, 15 Brown **52**

Second Round
- Duke **89**, Old Dominion **61**
- ⊗DePaul **74**, Oklahoma **69**
- Saint Joseph's **69**, Cleveland State **75** (D)
- Navy **97**, Syracuse **85** (E)

Regional Semifinals
- Duke **74**, ⊗DePaul **67**
- Cleveland State **70**, Navy **71** (F)

Regional Final
- Duke **71**, Navy **50**

Midwest (Kansas City)

First Round
- 1 Kansas **71**, 16 North Carolina A&T **46**
- 8 Jacksonville **50** (OT), 9 Temple **61**
- 5 Michigan State **72**, 12 Washington **70**
- 4 Georgetown **70**, 13 Texas Tech **64**
- 6 NC State **66**, 11 Iowa **64**
- 3 Notre Dame **83**, 14 Arkansas-Little Rock **90** (G)
- 7 Iowa State **81** (OT), 10 Miami (Ohio) **79**
- 2 Michigan **70**, 15 Akron **64**

Second Round
- Kansas **65**, Temple **43**
- Michigan State **80**, Georgetown **68**
- NC State **80** (2OT), Arkansas-Little Rock **66**
- Iowa State **72**, Michigan **69**

Regional Semifinals
- Kansas **96** (OT), Michigan State **86**
- NC State **70**, Iowa State **66**

Regional Final
- Kansas **75**, NC State **67**

National Semifinals (Dallas)
- LSU **77**, Louisville **88**
- Duke **71**, Kansas **67**

National Final
Louisville 72
Duke 69

After setting an NCAA record for most wins in a season (37), Duke loses its third championship game in as many tries. Louisville's Pervis Ellison collects 36 points and 24 rebounds in his two Final Four games, becoming only the second freshman to win Most Outstanding Player, and coach Denny Crum wins his second title of the decade.

Trailing 54-48 in the second half, Louisville goes on a 13-0 run that includes two baskets by senior guard Milt Wagner, who sat out the previous season as a medical redshirt. When asked before the first round if he knew anything about the Cards' opponent, Wagner said: "Drexel? That's one of them academic schools, right?"

Duke coach Mike Krzyzewski makes his first appearance in the Final Four. He will go on to make nine more (through 2009), ranking him third among all coaches, behind only John Wooden (12) and Dean Smith (11).

A No. 11 LSU becomes the first double-digit seed to reach the Final Four after beating the Wildcats (who had defeated the Tigers three times during the season). Ricky Blanton's layup seals the victory with :17 remaining, but coach Dale Brown credits his "freak" defense—a blend of man-to-man and zone coverages.

B Len Bias gets 31 points and 12 rebounds in his final game for Maryland. Three months later, the All-America and No. 2 NBA draft pick (Celtics) will die of a heart attack related to cocaine use.

C Indiana suffers a first-round loss for the first time under Bob Knight, who is making his 10th Tournament appearance. Knight, who had been wary of CSU with its explosive scorer Ken "Mouse" McFadden, asks reporters after the game, "How many of you [expletive] thought that was an upset?"

D Freshman point guard Mouse McFadden scores 23 against the Hawks. McFadden later claims he heard St. Joe's center Rodney Blake scream "Stop that Mouse!" as McFadden blew by him.

E Against an overmatched Syracuse front line, David Robinson goes to the charity stripe 27 times—the most for one player in a Tournament game—and knocks down 21.

F In four games, David Robinson averages a Tournament-best 27.5 ppg and blocks 23 shots, including 9 against Cleveland State. Cleveland State becomes the first team seeded as low as No. 14 to advance two rounds.

G Arkansas-Little Rock makes 15 of its 19 second-half shots to defeat the No. 10-ranked Irish. Trojans coach Mike Newell plays it cool. "Everyone thought that was an upset," he says after the game. "We're happy, but not elated."

⊗Team participation later vacated

TOURNAMENT LEADERS

INDIVIDUAL LEADERS

SCORING

	CL	POS	G	PTS	PPG
1 **David Robinson**, Navy	JR	C	4	110	27.5
2 **Johnny Dawkins**, Duke	SR	G	6	153	25.5
3 **Scott Skiles**, Michigan State	SR	G	3	75	25.0
4 **Chuck Person**, Auburn	SR	F	4	95	23.8
5 **Kenny Walker**, Kentucky	SR	F	4	94	23.5
6 **Don Redden**, LSU	SR	G/F	5	108	21.6
7 **Mark Price**, Georgia Tech	SR	G	3	60	20.0
8 **Brad Daugherty**, North Carolina	SR	C	3	59	19.7
Anthony Jones, UNLV	SR	G	3	59	19.7
10 **Chris Washburn**, NC State	SO	C	4	77	19.3

MINIMUM: 3 GAMES

FIELD GOAL PCT

	CL	POS	G	FG	FGA	PCT
1 **Ricky Blanton**, LSU	SO	F	5	19	27	70.4
2 **Kenny Walker**, Kentucky	SR	F	4	35	50	70.0
3 **Billy Thompson**, Louisville	SR	F	6	45	65	69.2
4 **Brad Daugherty**, North Carolina	SR	C	3	24	36	66.7
5 **Ronald Kellogg**, Kansas	SR	G	5	30	46	65.2

MINIMUM: 15 MADE AND 3 GAMES

FREE THROW PCT

	CL	POS	G	FT	FTA	PCT
1 **Milt Wagner**, Louisville	SR	G	6	33	36	91.7
2 **Len Bias**, Maryland	SR	F	2	21	23	91.3
3 **Derrick Taylor**, LSU	SR	G	5	17	19	89.5
4 **Scott Skiles**, Michigan State	SR	G	3	25	28	89.3
5 **Mark Alarie**, Duke	SR	F	6	27	32	84.4

MINIMUM: 15 MADE

REBOUNDS PER GAME

	CL	POS	G	REB	RPG
1 **David Robinson**, Navy	JR	C	4	47	11.8
2 **Brad Daugherty**, North Carolina	SR	C	3	33	11.0
3 **Armon Gilliam**, UNLV	JR	F	3	30	10.0
4 **Pervis Ellison**, Louisville	FR	F/C	6	57	9.5
Chuck Person, Auburn	SR	F	4	38	9.5

MINIMUM: 3 GAMES

TEAM LEADERS

SCORING

		G	PTS	PPG
1	**Louisville**	6	513	85.5
2	**North Carolina**	3	240	80.0
3	**Michigan State**	3	238	79.3
4	**LSU**	5	383	76.6
5	**Duke**	6	459	76.5
6	**Navy**	4	305	76.3
7	**Cleveland State**	3	228	76.0
8	**Auburn**	4	300	75.0
9	**Kansas**	5	374	74.8
10	**Iowa State**	3	219	73.0

MINIMUM: 3 GAMES

FG PCT

		G	FG	FGA	PCT
1	**Michigan State**	3	90	161	55.9
2	**Louisville**	6	203	366	55.5
3	**DePaul**	3	88	160	55.0
4	**Alabama**	3	92	171	53.8
5	**Georgia Tech**	3	79	148	53.4

MINIMUM: 3 GAMES

FT PCT

		G	FT	FTA	PCT
1	**Michigan State**	3	58	74	78.4
2	**Louisville**	6	107	138	77.5
3	**Auburn**	4	48	62	77.4
4	**Alabama**	3	34	45	75.6
5	**Kansas**	5	74	98	75.5

MINIMUM: 3 GAMES

REBOUNDS

		G	REB	RPG
1	**North Carolina**	3	119	39.7
2	**Louisville**	6	219	36.5
3	**Cleveland State**	3	107	35.7
	Georgia Tech	3	107	35.7
5	**Duke**	6	207	34.5

MINIMUM: 3 GAMES

ALL-TOURNAMENT TEAM

PLAYER	CL	POS	HT	SCHOOL	RPG	PPG
Pervis Ellison*	FR	F/C	6-9	Louisville	9.5	15.5
Mark Alarie	SR	F	6-8	Duke	8.8	15.8
Tommy Amaker	JR	G	6-0	Duke	2.5	6.7
Johnny Dawkins	SR	G	6-2	Duke	5.2	25.5
Billy Thompson	SR	F	6-7	Louisville	7.8	18.3

ALL-REGIONAL TEAMS

EAST

PLAYER	CL	POS	HT	SCHOOL	RPG	PPG
Johnny Dawkins*	SR	G	6-2	Duke	6.0	26.3
Mark Alarie	SR	F	6-8	Duke	9.8	17.8
Ken McFadden	FR	G	6-1	Cleveland State	2.3	16.0
David Robinson	JR	C	7-1	Navy	11.8	27.5
Kylor Whitaker	SR	G/F	6-6	Navy	2.0	14.0

MIDWEST

PLAYER	CL	POS	HT	SCHOOL	RPG	PPG
Danny Manning*	SO	F	6-11	Kansas	4.8	17.0
Charles Shackleford	FR	F/C	6-10	NC State	8.0	16.8
Scott Skiles	SR	G	6-1	Michigan State	1.3	25.0
Calvin Thompson	SR	G	6-6	Kansas	4.5	15.8
Chris Washburn	SO	C	6-11	NC State	6.8	19.3

SOUTHEAST

PLAYER	CL	POS	HT	SCHOOL	RPG	PPG
Don Redden*	SR	G/F	6-6	LSU	6.3	21.5
Winston Bennett	JR	F	6-7	Kentucky	9.0	12.3
Ricky Blanton	SO	F	6-6	LSU	8.5	9.3
Mark Price	SR	G	6-0	Georgia Tech	3.7	20.0
Kenny Walker	SR	F	6-8	Kentucky	8.0	23.5

WEST

PLAYER	CL	POS	HT	SCHOOL	RPG	PPG
Chuck Person*	SR	F	6-8	Auburn	9.5	23.8
Herbert Crook	SO	F	6-7	Louisville	7.0	14.0
Brad Daugherty	SR	C	6-11	North Carolina	11.0	19.7
Pervis Ellison	FR	F/C	6-9	Louisville	8.3	14.3
Billy Thompson	SR	F	6-7	Louisville	8.3	18.8

* MOST OUTSTANDING PLAYER

1986 NCAA TOURNAMENT BOX SCORES

68-63 (Sweet 16)

KENTUCKY	MIN	FG	3FG	FT	REB	A	ST	BL	PF	TP
Kenny Walker	40	9-19	-	4-4	7	1	2	3	4	22
Winston Bennett	39	6-11	-	2-4	12	1	0	0	3	14
Ed Davender	24	4-8	-	5-6	3	2	2	0	3	13
James Blackmon	35	5-7	-	1-4	3	0	0	0	1	11
Cedric Jenkins	23	2-3	-	2-2	4	1	0	0	5	6
Roger Harden	37	1-4	-	0-1	1	9	1	0	1	2
Richard Madison	2	0-0	-	0-0	0	0	0	0	1	0
TOTALS	**200**	**27-52**	**-**	**14-21**	**30**	**14**	**5**	**3**	**18**	**68**
Percentages		51.9		66.7						

Coach: Eddie Sutton

	1H	2H
Kentucky	32	36
Alabama	28	35

ALABAMA	MIN	FG	3FG	FT	REB	A	ST	BL	PF	TP
Terry Coner	38	7-12	-	6-7	4	4	2	0	3	20
Buck Johnson	40	6-14	-	4-4	9	0	2	0	4	16
Derrick McKey	40	4-8	-	4-4	12	1	0	1	3	12
Jim Farmer	36	3-9	-	1-2	4	0	1	0	3	7
James Jackson	16	1-4	-	1-2	1	0	0	1	2	3
Michael Ansley	11	1-3	-	1-2	1	0	1	1	2	3
Mark Gottfried	18	1-3	-	0-0	2	0	0	0	0	2
Craig Dudley	1	0-1	-	0-0	0	0	0	0	2	0
TOTALS	**200**	**23-54**	**-**	**17-21**	**33**	**5**	**6**	**3**	**19**	**63**
Percentages		42.6		81.0						

Coach: Wimp Sanderson

Officials: Booker Turn… Jim Clark, To… Fraim
Technicals: None
Attendance: 16,723

70-64 (Sweet 16)

LSU	MIN	FG	3FG	FT	REB	A	ST	BL	PF	TP
Don Redden	39	10-16	-	7-10	6	1	1	-	2	27
Derrick Taylor	40	9-18	-	5-6	3	2	5	-	1	23
Anthony Wilson	34	4-14	-	0-0	10	0	2	-	3	8
John Williams	30	2-15	-	1-2	7	3	0	-	2	5
Ricky Blanton	34	2-3	-	0-0	4	2	2	-	0	4
Oliver Brown	16	1-1	-	1-1	2	3	0	-	3	3
Jose Vargas	6	0-1	-	0-0	0	0	0	-	0	0
Bernard Woodside	1	0-0	-	0-0	0	0	0	-	0	0
TOTALS	**200**	**28-68**	**-**	**14-19**	**32**	**11**	**10**	**-**	**11**	**70**
Percentages		41.2		73.7						

Coach: Dale Brown

	1H	2H
LSU	36	34
Georgia Tech	30	34

GEORGIA TECH	MIN	FG	3FG	FT	REB	A	ST	BL	PF	TP
Mark Price	38	8-16	-	4-4	5	4	0	1	4	20
Tom Hammonds	33	7-9	-	2-2	8	0	0	0	1	16
John Salley	38	5-6	-	1-3	10	2	0	1	4	11
Duane Ferrell	38	3-6	-	0-0	4	4	1	1	3	6
Bruce Dalrymple	31	3-7	-	0-2	3	4	0	0	5	6
Chris Neal	13	2-4	-	0-0	2	4	2	0	1	4
Antoine Ford	6	0-0	-	1-2	1	0	0	0	0	1
Jack Mansell	1	0-0	-	0-0	0	0	0	0	0	0
John Martinson	1	0-0	-	0-0	0	0	0	0	0	0
Willie Reese	1	0-0	-	0-0	0	0	0	0	0	0
TOTALS	**200**	**28-48**	**-**	**8-13**	**33**	**18**	**3**	**3**	**18**	**64**
Percentages		58.3		61.5						

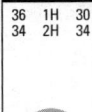

Coach: Bobby Cremins

Officials: Han… Nichols, Tom O'Neill, John Clougherty
Technicals: None
Attendance: 16,723

70-63 (Sweet 16)

AUBURN	MIN	FG	3FG	FT	REB	A	ST	BL	PF	TP
Chuck Person	37	12-22	-	1-2	11	0	2	0	1	25
Gerald White	33	3-4	-	6-7	1	10	1	0	2	12
Jeff Moore	32	5-10	-	1-2	9	4	1	0	2	11
Frank Ford	39	3-8	-	3-4	6	1	5	0	0	9
Chris Morris	39	3-8	-	3-3	8	0	1	1	4	9
Mike Jones	12	2-5	-	0-0	1	2	0	1	2	4
Terrance Howard	8	0-1	-	0-0	0	0	0	0	1	0
TOTALS	**200**	**28-58**	**-**	**14-18**	**36**	**17**	**10**	**2**	**12**	**70**
Percentages		48.3		77.8						

Coach: Sonny Smith

	1H	2H
Auburn	25	45
UNLV	34	29

UNLV	MIN	FG	3FG	FT	REB	A	ST	BL	PF	TP
Armon Gilliam	37	9-13	-	3-4	3	0	0	-	1	21
Freddie Banks	35	9-21	-	2-2	1	6	1	-	2	20
Anthony Jones	39	8-19	-	0-3	4	4	1	-	1	16
Eldridge Hudson	24	2-5	-	0-0	9	2	2	-	4	4
John Flowers	20	1-1	-	0-0	0	0	0	-	2	2
Mark Wade	36	0-0	-	0-1	3	12	2	-	5	0
Gary Graham	9	0-2	-	0-0	2	1	0	-	4	0
TOTALS	**200**	**29-61**	**-**	**5-10**	**22**	**25**	**6**	**-**	**19**	**63**
Percentages		47.5		50.0						

Coach: Jerry Tarkanian

Officials: Lenny Wirtz, Tim Higgins, Charles Vacca
Technicals: None
Attendance: 10,936

94-79 (Sweet 16)

LOUISVILLE	MIN	FG	3FG	FT	REB	A	ST	BL	PF	TP
Billy Thompson	33	10-16	-	4-5	9	5	1	2	4	24
Herbert Crook	34	5-9	-	10-10	9	2	1	0	4	20
Pervis Ellison	37	6-12	-	3-4	6	3	2	3	3	15
Milt Wagner	36	5-12	-	4-4	1	5	1	0	2	14
Jeff Hall	37	5-11	-	2-2	3	5	1	0	1	12
Mark McSwain	9	1-3	-	2-4	1	1	0	0	1	4
Kevin Walls	5	1-1	-	2-2	0	0	0	0	0	4
Tony Kimbro	6	0-1	-	1-2	1	0	0	0	2	1
Mike Abram	1	0-0	-	0-0	1	1	0	0	0	0
Kenny Payne	1	0-0	-	0-0	0	0	0	0	0	0
Robbie Valentine	1	0-0	-	0-0	0	0	0	0	0	0
TOTALS	**200**	**33-65**	**-**	**28-33**	**31**	**22**	**6**	**5**	**17**	**94**
Percentages		50.8		84.8						

Coach: Denny Crum

	1H	2H
Louisville	43	51
North Carolina	43	36

NORTH CAROLINA	MIN	FG	3FG	FT	REB	A	ST	BL	PF	TP
Joe Wolf	34	9-15	-	2-3	4	2	0	0	4	20
Brad Daugherty	39	8-14	-	3-7	15	6	0	1	4	19
Jeff Lebo	35	8-13	-	2-4	4	4	1	0	2	18
Kenny Smith	37	4-12	-	4-4	4	8	1	0	5	12
Steve Hale	31	2-10	-	0-0	6	5	0	0	5	4
Curtis Hunter	7	2-2	-	0-0	1	0	0	0	2	4
Warren Martin	6	1-1	-	0-0	3	0	0	0	3	2
Dave Popson	7	0-0	-	0-0	1	0	0	0	0	0
Steve Bucknall	1	0-0	-	0-0	0	0	0	0	0	0
James Daye	1	0-0	-	0-0	0	0	0	0	0	0
Kevin Madden	1	0-0	-	0-0	0	0	0	0	0	0
Ranzino Smith	1	0-2	-	0-0	0	0	0	0	1	0
TOTALS	**200**	**34-69**	**-**	**11-18**	**38**	**25**	**2**	**1**	**26**	**79**
Percentages		49.3		61.1						

Coach: Dean Smith

Officials: Don Rutledge, Sonny Holmes, Tom Harrington
Technicals: None
Attendance: 10,936

74-67 (Sweet 16)

DUKE	MIN	FG	3FG	FT	REB	A	ST	BL	PF	TP
Johnny Dawkins	39	11-20	-	3-4	10	1	2	1	0	25
Mark Alarie	37	6-17	-	9-9	8	1	2	0	2	21
David Henderson	33	5-14	-	1-6	4	1	2	0	3	11
Jay Bilas	19	2-3	-	2-2	4	0	1	1	4	6
Tommy Amaker	33	0-5	-	4-6	2	6	1	0	2	4
Danny Ferry	23	2-6	-	0-1	4	2	0	0	1	4
Quin Snyder	4	1-1	-	0-1	1	1	1	0	2	2
Billy King	10	0-0	-	1-4	2	1	0	0	1	1
Kevin Strickland	1	0-0	-	0-0	0	0	0	0	0	0
Weldon Williams	1	0-0	-	0-0	0	0	0	0	0	0
TOTALS	**200**	**27-66**	**-**	**20-33**	**35**	**13**	**9**	**2**	**15**	**74**
Percentages		40.9		60.6						

Coach: Mike Krzyzewski

	1H	2H
Duke	37	37
DePaul	32	35

DEPAUL	MIN	FG	3FG	FT	REB	A	ST	BL	PF	TP
Rod Strickland	37	7-11	-	1-4	3	3	2	1	3	15
Marty Embry	36	5-7	-	2-2	6	1	2	0	4	12
Dallas Comegys	28	4-6	-	2-4	3	2	0	2	3	10
Kevin Holmes	20	5-8	-	0-1	3	0	2	2	5	10
Terence Greene	20	4-7	-	0-0	2	1	0	0	4	8
Tony Jackson	31	2-6	-	2-2	4	2	0	0	5	6
Lemone Lampley	25	3-5	-	0-0	1	1	0	2	2	6
Andy Laux	3	0-1	-	0-0	0	0	0	0	1	0
TOTALS	**200**	**30-51**	**-**	**7-13**	**22**	**10**	**6**	**7**	**28**	**67**
Percentages		58.8		53.8						

Coach: Joey Meyer

Officials: Dick Paparo, Jim Bain, Tom Fincken
Technicals: None
Attendance: 19,454

71-70 (Sweet 16)

NAVY	MIN	FG	3FG	FT	REB	A	ST	BL	PF	TP
Kylor Whitaker	40	10-15	-	3-3	1	10	1	0	2	23
David Robinson	34	7-11	-	8-10	14	1	1	9	3	22
Vernon Butler	40	7-15	-	2-3	3	2	1	0	3	16
Doug Wojcik	40	1-5	-	2-3	5	7	1	0	0	4
Cliff Rees	11	2-2	-	0-0	0	1	0	0	1	4
Nathan Bailey	20	1-5	-	0-2	2	0	0	0	0	2
Carl Liebert	9	0-0	-	0-0	1	0	0	0	2	0
Derrick Turner	6	0-1	-	0-0	3	0	0	0	2	0
TOTALS	**200**	**28-54**	**-**	**15-21**	**29**	**21**	**4**	**9**	**13**	**71**
Percentages		51.9		71.4						

Coach: Paul Evans

	1H	2H
Navy	39	32
Cleveland State	30	40

CLEVELAND STATE	MIN	FG	3FG	FT	REB	A	ST	BL	PF	TP
Ken McFadden	35	8-15	-	0-1	4	0	1	0	1	16
Clinton Smith	31	8-15	-	0-0	7	0	4	1	2	16
Eric Mudd	29	5-13	-	1-2	11	0	0	0	4	11
Clinton Ransey	31	3-11	-	2-2	5	1	1	0	5	8
Paul Stewart	12	3-5	-	1-4	3	0	0	0	2	7
Eddie Bryant	24	3-5	-	0-0	1	3	0	1	2	6
Shawn Hood	15	1-2	-	1-1	1	1	1	0	0	3
Ray Salters	6	1-4	-	0-0	4	2	0	0	2	2
Bob Crawford	11	0-3	-	1-2	1	0	0	2	2	1
Steve Corbin	6	0-2	-	0-0	2	0	1	0	2	0
TOTALS	**200**	**32-75**	**-**	**6-12**	**39**	**7**	**8**	**4**	**22**	**70**
Percentages		42.7		50.0						

Coach: Kevin Mackey

Officials: Joe Forte, Paul Housman, Rick Wulkow
Technicals: None
Attendance: 19,454

96-86 (SWEET 16)

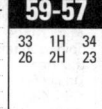

46	1H	37
34	2H	43
16	OT1	6

KANSAS	MIN	FG	3FG	FT	REB	A	ST	BL	PF	TP
Calvin Thompson	43	10-19	-	6-9	4	4	0	1	2	26
Danny Manning	25	7-12	-	3-3	3	0	1	1	5	17
Archie Marshall	31	7-12	-	2-2	13	1	0	0	2	16
Ronald Kellogg	24	7-12	-	0-0	5	2	0	0	5	14
Cedric Hunter	43	4-9	-	3-4	4	10	3	0	3	11
Greg Dreiling	32	3-10	-	4-7	7	1	0	1	0	10
Chris Piper	20	1-2	-	0-0	2	1	1	0	2	2
Mark Turgeon	7	0-1	-	0-0	0	1	1	0	2	0
TOTALS	225	39-77	-	18-25	38	20	6	3	21	96
Percentages		50.6		72.0						

Coach: Larry Brown

MICHIGAN STATE	MIN	FG	3FG	FT	REB	A	ST	BL	PF	TP
Scott Skiles	38	6-14	-	8-10	2	7	1	-	3	20
Vernon Carr	42	7-13	-	3-6	4	3	0	-	3	17
Larry Polec	39	6-7	-	4-5	11	2	2	-	5	16
Barry Fordham	45	7-9	-	1-3	5	0	0	-	3	15
Darryl Johnson	37	4-11	-	2-2	4	9	1	-	4	10
Carlton Valentine	6	2-4	-	0-0	1	0	0	-	0	4
Ralph Walker	11	0-1	-	2-2	3	0	0	-	1	2
Mark Brown	7	1-2	-	0-1	1	0	0	-	1	2
TOTALS	225	33-61	-	20-29	31	21	4	-	20	86
Percentages		54.1		69.0						

Coach: Jud Heathcote

Officials: Bob Dibler, Hank Armstrong, Peter Davis
Technicals: Kansas (coach Brown)
Attendance: 16,800

70-66 (SWEET 16)

40	1H	29
30	2H	37

NC STATE	MIN	FG	3FG	FT	REB	A	ST	BL	PF	TP
Charles Shackleford	40	9-15	-	4-6	7	0	1	0	3	22
Chris Washburn	40	10-16	-	0-0	6	1	0	2	2	20
Ernie Myers	37	7-11	-	2-3	1	2	1	0	2	16
Bennie Bolton	28	3-7	-	1-2	8	2	0	0	5	7
Nate McMillan	40	1-4	-	3-7	4	9	3	1	2	5
Vinnie Del Negro	9	0-1	-	0-1	1	0	0	0	2	0
Chucky Brown	6	0-0	-	0-0	0	1	0	0	1	0
TOTALS	200	30-54	-	10-19	27	15	5	3	17	70
Percentages		55.6		52.6						

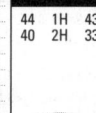

Coach: Jim Valvano

IOWA STATE	MIN	FG	3FG	FT	REB	A	ST	BL	PF	TP
Jeff Grayer	40	6-16	-	9-10	8	2	0	0	2	21
Sam Hill	33	8-13	-	5-6	9	0	2	1	3	21
Jeff Hornacek	38	3-9	-	0-0	4	8	3	0	2	6
Gary Thompkins	31	3-6	-	0-0	3	4	0	0	4	6
Ron Virgil	29	3-9	-	0-0	3	5	1	0	4	6
Elmer Robinson	16	2-6	-	0-0	8	0	0	0	4	4
Tom Schafer	6	1-2	-	0-0	1	0	0	0	0	2
David Moss	7	0-3	-	0-0	3	0	0	0	0	0
TOTALS	200	26-64	-	14-16	39	19	6	1	19	66
Percentages		40.6		87.5						

Coach: Johnny Orr

Officials: Paul Galvan, Willie McJunkin, Jody Silvester
Technicals: None
Attendance: 16,800

59-57 (ELITE 8)

33	1H	34
26	2H	23

LSU	MIN	FG	3FG	FT	REB	A	ST	BL	PF	TP
John Williams	39	7-15	-	2-4	4	1	-	-	2	16
Don Redden	34	6-13	-	3-4	8	3	-	-	3	15
Anthony Wilson	35	6-9	-	0-0	2	0	-	-	2	12
Ricky Blanton	28	5-5	-	2-2	8	3	-	-	4	12
Derrick Taylor	34	0-9	-	4-4	1	3	-	-	3	4
Oliver Brown	18	0-2	-	0-0	3	1	-	-	2	0
Neboisha Bukumirovich	6	0-0	-	0-0	0	0	-	-	0	0
Bernard Woodside	5	0-0	-	0-0	0	1	-	-	0	0
Jose Vargas	1	0-0	-	0-0	0	0	-	-	1	0
TOTALS	200	24-53	-	11-14	26	12	-	-	17	59
Percentages		45.3		78.6						

Coach: Dale Brown

KENTUCKY	MIN	FG	3FG	FT	REB	A	ST	BL	PF	TP
Kenny Walker	38	8-11	-	4-6	7	3	-	-	2	20
Roger Harden	38	6-8	-	0-0	5	5	-	-	1	12
James Blackmon	31	5-12	-	0-1	2	0	-	-	2	10
Winston Bennett	36	3-13	-	2-4	12	1	-	-	4	8
Ed Davender	35	1-6	-	3-4	4	2	-	-	4	5
Cedric Jenkins	19	1-2	-	0-1	3	1	-	-	3	2
Robert Lock	3	0-0	-	0-0	0	0	-	-	1	0
TOTALS	200	24-52	-	9-16	33	12	-	-	17	57
Percentages		46.2		56.2						

Coach: Eddie Sutton

Officials: Hank Nichols, John Clougherty, Tom Fraim
Technicals: None
Attendance: 16,453

84-76 (ELITE 8)

44	1H	43
40	2H	33

LOUISVILLE	MIN	FG	3FG	FT	REB	A	ST	BL	PF	TP
Herbert Crook	39	8-12	-	4-5	11	3	1	0	3	20
Milt Wagner	40	4-9	-	8-8	2	9	0	0	2	16
Pervis Ellison	35	7-14	-	1-3	10	0	3	2	2	15
Jeff Hall	36	7-12	-	0-0	0	2	0	0	1	14
Billy Thompson	26	5-10	-	3-4	7	4	1	0	4	13
Mark McSwain	15	2-3	-	0-0	4	2	0	0	2	4
Kevin Walls	4	1-2	-	0-0	0	0	0	0	1	2
Tony Kimbro	5	0-1	-	0-0	1	0	0	0	0	0
TOTALS	200	34-63	-	16-20	35	20	5	2	15	84
Percentages		54.0		80.0						

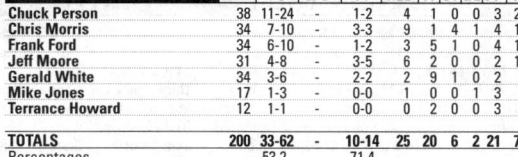

Coach: Denny Crum

AUBURN	MIN	FG	3FG	FT	REB	A	ST	BL	PF	TP
Chuck Person	38	11-24	-	1-2	4	1	0	0	3	23
Chris Morris	34	7-10	-	3-3	9	1	4	1	4	17
Frank Ford	34	6-10	-	1-2	3	5	1	0	4	13
Jeff Moore	31	4-8	-	3-5	6	2	0	0	2	11
Gerald White	34	3-6	-	2-2	2	9	1	0	2	8
Mike Jones	17	1-3	-	0-0	1	0	0	1	3	2
Terrance Howard	12	1-1	-	0-0	0	2	0	0	3	2
TOTALS	200	33-62	-	10-14	25	20	6	2	21	76
Percentages		53.2		71.4						

Coach: Sonny Smith

Officials: Don Rutledge, Lenny Wirtz, Charles Vacca
Technicals: None
Attendance: 9,650

71-50 (ELITE 8)

34	1H	22
37	2H	28

DUKE	MIN	FG	3FG	FT	REB	A	ST	BL	PF	TP
Johnny Dawkins	39	13-25	-	2-2	7	3	1	0	1	28
Mark Alarie	31	8-20	-	2-2	8	0	4	0	2	18
David Henderson	26	4-10	-	0-0	4	2	1	0	3	8
Billy King	12	2-2	-	1-2	3	0	0	1	4	5
Tommy Amaker	37	1-6	-	2-2	5	5	0	0	3	4
Jay Bilas	26	1-4	-	2-4	10	0	0	0	2	4
Danny Ferry	21	1-2	-	0-0	5	1	1	0	4	2
Kevin Strickland	2	1-2	-	0-0	0	0	0	0	0	2
Martin Nessley	3	0-0	-	0-1	2	0	0	0	0	0
Weldon Williams	2	0-0	-	0-0	1	0	0	1	1	0
John Smith	1	0-0	-	0-0	0	1	0	0	0	0
TOTALS	200	31-71	-	9-13	45	12	7	2	20	71
Percentages		43.7		69.2						

Coach: Mike Krzyzewski

NAVY	MIN	FG	3FG	FT	REB	A	ST	BL	PF	TP
David Robinson	39	10-17	-	3-4	10	0	3	2	3	23
Kylor Whitaker	29	5-12	-	0-0	3	7	0	0	2	10
Vernon Butler	32	1-5	-	6-8	6	1	0	0	3	8
Derrick Turner	20	1-1	-	1-3	1	0	0	1	2	3
Doug Wojcik	29	1-3	-	0-1	0	5	1	0	3	2
Carl Liebert	9	1-2	-	0-0	0	0	1	0	3	2
Bobby Jones	1	0-1	-	2-2	0	0	0	0	1	2
Nathan Bailey	13	0-0	-	0-1	2	1	1	0	1	0
Cliff Rees	10	0-5	-	0-0	0	0	0	0	1	0
Neal Fenton	9	0-0	-	0-0	1	1	0	0	0	0
Craig Prather	3	0-0	-	0-0	1	0	0	0	0	0
Brian Gregory	2	0-1	-	0-0	0	0	0	0	0	0
Tony Wells	2	0-1	-	0-0	1	0	0	0	1	0
Rich Brennan	1	0-0	-	0-0	0	0	0	0	0	0
Carey Manhertz	1	0-0	-	0-0	1	0	0	0	0	0
TOTALS	200	19-48	-	12-19	26	15	6	3	20	50
Percentages		39.6		63.2						

Coach: Paul Evans

Officials: Joe Forte, Dick Paparo, Tom Fincken
Technicals: None
Attendance: 19,454

75-67 (ELITE 8)

35	1H	33
40	2H	34

KANSAS	MIN	FG	3FG	FT	REB	A	ST	BL	PF	TP
Danny Manning	32	11-17	-	0-0	6	1	2	1	4	22
Greg Dreiling	33	7-11	-	5-6	12	2	0	0	4	19
Ronald Kellogg	35	5-9	-	2-4	3	2	0	0	2	12
Calvin Thompson	38	3-7	-	3-4	4	1	1	0	2	9
Cedric Hunter	40	2-4	-	1-3	0	9	2	0	4	5
Archie Marshall	12	2-4	-	0-0	1	1	0	0	3	4
Chris Piper	9	0-0	-	2-2	0	0	0	0	1	2
Mark Turgeon	1	0-0	-	2-2	0	0	0	0	0	2
TOTALS	200	30-52	-	15-21	26	16	5	1	20	75
Percentages		57.7		71.4						

Coach: Larry Brown

NC STATE	MIN	FG	3FG	FT	REB	A	ST	BL	PF	TP
Charles Shackleford	40	8-13	-	4-5	6	1	0	0	4	20
Chris Washburn	40	5-11	-	7-10	5	2	1	0	2	17
Bennie Bolton	39	6-12	-	0-0	3	2	0	0	3	12
Nate McMillan	40	4-6	-	3-4	5	7	2	2	4	11
Ernie Myers	33	2-7	-	2-4	3	4	0	0	5	6
Chucky Brown	1	0-0	-	1-2	0	0	0	0	0	1
Vinnie Del Negro	7	0-1	-	0-0	1	0	0	0	1	0
TOTALS	200	25-50	-	17-25	23	16	3	2	19	67
Percentages		50.0		68.0						

Coach: Jim Valvano

Officials: Jody Silvester, Paul Galvan, Pete Pavia
Technicals: None
Attendance: 16,800

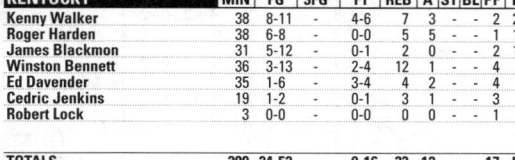

88-77

LOUISVILLE	MIN	FG	3FG	FT	REB	A	ST	BL	PF	TP
Billy Thompson	36	10-11	-	2-5	10	4	1	1	4	22
Milt Wagner	36	8-16	-	6-6	4	11	1	0	1	22
Herbert Crook	32	8-13	-	0-1	9	3	0	0	3	16
Jeff Hall	32	6-11	-	2-2	1	2	0	0	1	14
Pervis Ellison	34	5-11	-	1-2	13	1	0	1	3	11
Mark McSwain	14	1-2	-	1-1	4	0	0	1	2	3
Tony Kimbro	8	0-2	-	0-0	0	1	1	0	1	0
Kevin Walls	8	0-2	-	0-0	0	4	0	0	0	0
TOTALS	**200**	**38-68**	**-**	**12-17**	**41**	**26**	**3**	**3**	**15**	**88**
Percentages		55.9		70.6						
Coach: Denny Crum										

	1H	2H
Louisville	36	52
LSU	44	33

FINAL 4

LSU	MIN	FG	3FG	FT	REB	A	ST	BL	PF	TP
Don Redden	28	10-20	-	2-3	6	1	0	0	3	22
Derrick Taylor	39	7-17	-	2-2	1	4	3	0	2	16
Anthony Wilson	39	7-15	-	1-1	3	0	1	0	3	15
John Williams	35	7-17	-	0-1	9	6	0	0	4	14
Ricky Blanton	38	3-5	-	3-6	12	2	1	1	4	9
Oliver Brown	13	0-1	-	1-2	3	0	0	0	0	1
Jose Vargas	6	0-0	-	0-0	0	0	0	0	0	0
Bernard Woodside	2	0-0	-	0-0	0	0	0	0	0	0
TOTALS	**200**	**34-75**	**-**	**9-15**	**34**	**13**	**5**	**1**	**16**	**77**
Percentages		45.3		60.0						
Coach: Dale Brown										

Officials: Jo Forte, Dick Paparo, Len Wirtz
Technicals: None
Attendance: 16,493

71-67

DUKE	MIN	FG	3FG	FT	REB	A	ST	BL	PF	TP
Johnny Dawkins	38	11-17	-	2-4	3	0	0	0	3	24
David Henderson	33	3-12	-	7-8	4	3	2	0	1	13
Mark Alarie	35	4-13	-	4-6	8	1	4	1	3	12
Danny Ferry	15	4-5	-	0-1	3	0	0	0	1	8
Tommy Amaker	37	2-5	-	3-4	2	6	3	0	1	7
Jay Bilas	29	1-2	-	5-7	5	1	1	0	2	7
Billy King	9	0-0	-	0-0	3	1	0	0	3	0
Kevin Strickland	4	0-1	-	0-0	0	0	0	0	0	0
TOTALS	**200**	**25-55**	**-**	**21-30**	**28**	**12**	**10**	**1**	**14**	**71**
Percentages		45.5		70.0						
Coach: Mike Krzyzewski										

	1H	2H
Duke	36	35
Kansas	33	34

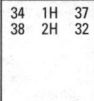

FINAL 4

KANSAS	MIN	FG	3FG	FT	REB	A	ST	BL	PF	TP
Ronald Kellogg	33	11-15	-	0-0	3	3	2	0	4	22
Calvin Thompson	39	5-12	-	3-3	5	3	1	0	1	13
Archie Marshall	19	6-10	-	1-1	2	0	0	0	3	13
Greg Dreiling	30	1-7	-	4-4	6	2	0	3	5	6
Cedric Hunter	22	2-5	-	1-4	8	3	0	0	5	5
Danny Manning	23	2-9	-	0-0	5	1	1	1	5	4
Mark Turgeon	19	1-1	-	0-0	0	5	0	0	3	2
Chris Piper	13	1-1	-	0-0	1	0	0	0	0	2
Altonio Campbell	1	0-0	-	0-0	0	1	0	0	0	0
Rodney Hull	1	0-0	-	0-0	0	0	0	0	0	0
TOTALS	**200**	**29-60**	**-**	**9-12**	**30**	**18**	**4**	**4**	**26**	**67**
Percentages		48.3		75.0						
Coach: Larry Brown										

Officials: Pau Galvan, John Clougherty, To Fincken
Technicals: Duke (Bilas)
Attendance: 16,493

72-69

LOUISVILLE	MIN	FG	3FG	FT	REB	A	ST	BL	PF	TP
Pervis Ellison	35	10-14	-	5-6	11	1	1	2	4	25
Billy Thompson	31	6-8	-	1-3	4	2	0	2	4	13
Herbert Crook	32	5-9	-	0-3	12	5	0	0	2	10
Milt Wagner	30	2-6	-	5-5	3	2	1	1	4	9
Tony Kimbro	14	2-4	-	2-2	2	2	0	2	1	6
Mark McSwain	17	2-4	-	1-2	3	2	1	0	1	5
Jeff Hall	33	2-4	-	0-0	2	2	2	0	2	4
Kevin Walls	8	0-1	-	0-0	1	0	0	0	2	0
TOTALS	**200**	**29-50**	**-**	**14-21**	**38**	**16**	**5**	**7**	**20**	**72**
Percentages		58.0		66.7						
Coach: Denny Crum										

	1H	2H
Louisville	34	38
Duke	37	32

NCAA FINAL 1986

DUKE	MIN	FG	3FG	FT	REB	A	ST	BL	PF	TP
Johnny Dawkins	40	10-19	-	4-4	4	0	2	-	1	24
David Henderson	28	5-15	-	4-4	4	4	3	-	5	14
Mark Alarie	33	4-11	-	4-4	6	0	1	-	5	12
Tommy Amaker	38	3-10	-	5-6	2	7	7	-	3	11
Jay Bilas	26	2-3	-	0-0	3	0	0	-	4	4
Danny Ferry	20	1-2	-	2-2	4	0	0	-	2	4
Billy King	13	0-1	-	0-1	0	1	0	-	2	0
Weldon Williams	2	0-1	-	0-0	0	0	0	-	0	0
TOTALS	**200**	**25-62**	**-**	**19-21**	**23**	**12**	**13**	**-**	**22**	**69**
Percentages		40.3		90.5						
Coach: Mike Krzyzewski										

Officials: Hank Nichols, Don Rutledge, Pete Pavia
Technicals: None
Attendance: 16,493

National Invitation Tournament (NIT)

First round: TCU d. Montana 76-69, McNeese State d. Dayton 86-75, Southwest Missouri St. d. Pittsburgh 59-52, Providence d. Boston U. 72-69, George Mason d. Lamar 65-63, Wyoming d. Texas A&M 79-70, Texas d. New Mexico 69-66, Florida d. Southern Miss 81-71, Georgia d. Chattanooga 95-81, Louisiana Tech d. Northern Arizona 67-61, Loyola Marymount d. California 80-75, UC Irvine d. UCLA 80-74, BYU d. SMU 67-63, Marquette d. Drake 79-59, Clemson d. Middle Tenn. St. 99-81, Ohio State d. Ohio 65-62

Second round: Florida d. TCU 77-75, Clemson d. Georgia 77-65, Providence d. George Mason 90-71, SW Missouri St. d. Marquette 83-69, Ohio State d. Texas 71-65, Louisiana Tech d. McNeese State 77-61, Wyoming d. Loyola Marymount 99-90, BYU d. Irvine 93-80

Third round: Louisiana Tech d. Providence 64-63, Florida d. SW Missouri St. 54-53, Wyoming d. Clemson 62-57, Ohio State d. BYU 79-68

Semifinals: Ohio State d. Louisiana Tech 79-66, Wyoming d. Florida 67-58

Third place: Louisiana Tech d. Florida 67-62

Championship: Ohio State d. Wyoming 73-63

MVP: Brad Sellers, Ohio State

1986-87: Smart Bombs

One Smart guy made Indiana's Bob Knight look like a genius. Keith Smart, playing at the Louisiana Superdome before what was then a title-game record crowd of 64,959, hit a baseline jumper with :04 left to lift the Hoosiers over Syracuse for IU's fifth national title. The team's fifth-leading scorer during the season, Smart hit 12 of the Hoosiers' last 15 points and was named MOP—the only junior college transfer ever to receive the award.

The three-point field goal was introduced in 1986-87, with the line set at 19 feet, nine inches from the center of the basket. (It was moved back a foot in 2006-07.) The Hoosiers—who led Division I in three-point accuracy, making 130 of 256 (50.8%)—won a 97-93 national semifinal shoot-out over UNLV. The Runnin' Rebels attempted 35 three-pointers and made a Final Four record 13. Indiana tried just four treys and hit two.

No. 14-seed Austin Peay sprang the biggest upset of the Tournament by beating No. 3-seed Illinois, 68-67. Navy's David "The Admiral" Robinson averaged 28.2 points, 11.8 rebounds and 4.5 blocks per game, was named Naismith POY and was the No. 1 pick in the NBA draft (San Antonio Spurs).

Major Conference Standings

AMCU-8	Conference			Overall		
	W	L	PCT	W	L	PCT
Missouri State○	13	1	.929	28	6	.824
Cleveland State□	10	4	.714	25	8	.758
Illinois-Chicago	9	5	.643	17	15	.531
Wisconsin-Green Bay	8	6	.571	15	14	.517
Northern Iowa	7	7	.500	13	15	.464
Valparaiso	4	10	.286	12	16	.429
Eastern Illinois	3	11	.214	9	19	.321
Western Illinois	2	12	.143	12	16	.429

Tournament: **Missouri State d. Cleveland State 90-87**
Tournament MVP: **Winston Garland**, Missouri State

ATLANTIC 10	Conference			Overall		
	W	L	PCT	W	L	PCT
Temple⊛	17	1	.944	32	4	.889
West Virginia○	15	3	.833	23	8	.742
Rhode Island□	12	6	.667	20	10	.667
Penn State	9	9	.500	15	12	.556
Saint Joseph's	9	9	.500	16	13	.552
Duquesne	7	11	.389	12	17	.414
Massachusetts	7	11	.389	11	16	.407
George Washington	6	12	.333	10	19	.345
Rutgers	5	13	.278	8	20	.286
St. Bonaventure	3	15	.167	5	23	.179

Tournament: **Temple d. West Virginia 70-57**
Tournament MVP: **Nate Blackwell**, Temple

ACC	Conference			Overall		
	W	L	PCT	W	L	PCT
North Carolina○	14	0	1.000	32	4	.889
Clemson○	10	4	.714	25	6	.806
Duke○	9	5	.643	24	9	.727
Virginia○	8	6	.571	21	10	.677
Georgia Tech○	7	7	.500	16	13	.552
NC State⊛⊗	6	8	.429	20	15	.571
Wake Forest	2	12	.143	14	15	.483
Maryland	0	14	.000	9	17	.346

Tournament: **NC State d. North Carolina 68-67**
Tournament MVP: **Vinny Del Negro**, NC State

BIG EAST	Conference			Overall		
	W	L	PCT	W	L	PCT
Georgetown⊛	12	4	.750	29	5	.853
Syracuse○	12	4	.750	31	7	.816
Pittsburgh○	12	4	.750	25	8	.758
Providence○	10	6	.625	25	9	.735
St. John's○	10	6	.625	21	9	.700
Villanova□	6	10	.375	15	16	.484
Seton Hall□	4	12	.250	15	14	.517
Boston College	3	13	.188	11	18	.379
Connecticut	3	13	.188	9	19	.321

Tournament: **Georgetown d. Syracuse 69-59**
Tournament MVP: **Reggie Williams**, Georgetown

BIG EIGHT	Conference			Overall		
	W	L	PCT	W	L	PCT
Missouri⊛	11	3	.786	24	10	.706
Oklahoma○	9	5	.643	24	10	.706
Kansas○	9	5	.643	25	11	.694
Kansas State○	8	6	.571	20	11	.645
Nebraska□	7	7	.500	21	12	.636
Iowa State	5	9	.357	13	15	.464
Oklahoma State	4	10	.286	8	20	.286
Colorado	3	11	.214	9	19	.321

Tournament: **Missouri d. Kansas 67-65**
Tournament MVP: **Danny Manning**, Kansas

BIG SKY	Conference			Overall		
	W	L	PCT	W	L	PCT
Montana State□	12	2	.857	21	8	.724
Boise State□	10	4	.714	22	8	.733
Montana	8	6	.571	18	11	.621
Nevada	7	7	.500	15	15	.500
Idaho	5	9	.357	16	14	.533
Idaho State⊛	5	9	.357	15	16	.484
Northern Arizona	5	9	.357	11	17	.393
Weber State	4	10	.286	7	22	.241

Tournament: **Idaho State d. Nevada 92-81**
Tournament MVP: **Jim Rhode**, Idaho State

BIG SOUTH	Conference			Overall		
	W	L	PCT	W	L	PCT
Charleston Southern	12	2	.857	21	9	.700
Campbell	10	4	.714	17	13	.567
UNC Asheville	5	3	.625	15	11	.577
Radford	7	7	.500	15	14	.517
Coastal Carolina	4	4	.500	12	16	.429
Winthrop	7	7	.500	8	20	.286
Armstrong State	2	6	.250	6	22	.214
Augusta	3	11	.214	8	19	.296

Tournament: **Charleston So. d. Campbell 64-63**
Tournament MVP: **Ben Hinson**, Charleston So.

BIG TEN	Conference			Overall		
	W	L	PCT	W	L	PCT
Indiana⊛	15	3	.833	30	4	.882
Purdue○	15	3	.833	25	5	.833
Iowa○	14	4	.778	30	5	.857
Illinois○	13	5	.722	23	8	.742
Michigan○	10	8	.556	20	12	.625
Ohio State○	9	9	.500	20	13	.606
Michigan State	6	12	.333	11	17	.393
Wisconsin	4	14	.222	14	17	.452
Minnesota	2	16	.111	9	19	.321
Northwestern	2	16	.111	7	21	.250

COLONIAL ATHLETIC	Conference			Overall		
	W	L	PCT	W	L	PCT
Navy⊛	13	1	.929	26	6	.813
UNC Wilmington	9	5	.643	18	12	.600
James Madison□	8	6	.571	20	10	.667
Richmond	8	6	.571	15	14	.517
George Mason	7	7	.500	15	13	.536
American	5	9	.357	13	14	.481
East Carolina	4	10	.286	12	16	.429
William and Mary	2	12	.143	5	22	.185

Tournament: **Navy d. UNC Wilmington 53-50**
Tournament MVP: **David Robinson**, Navy

EAST COAST	Conference			Overall		
	W	L	PCT	W	L	PCT
Bucknell⊛	11	3	.786	22	9	.710
Lafayette	10	4	.714	16	13	.552
Lehigh	8	6	.571	15	14	.517
Rider	8	6	.571	12	16	.429
Drexel	7	7	.500	14	14	.500
Towson	5	9	.357	14	16	.467
Hofstra	4	10	.286	10	18	.357
Delaware	3	11	.214	12	16	.429

Tournament: **Bucknell d. Towson 86-74**
Tournament MVP: **Chris Seneca**, Bucknell

ECAC METRO	Conference			Overall		
	W	L	PCT	W	L	PCT
Marist⊛	15	1	.938	20	10	.667
Fairleigh Dickinson	11	5	.688	19	10	.655
Loyola (MD)	10	6	.625	15	14	.517
Wagner	8	8	.500	16	13	.552
Robert Morris	7	9	.438	13	14	.481
Saint Francis (PA)	7	9	.438	11	16	.407
Long Island	5	11	.313	13	14	.481
St. Francis (NY)	5	11	.313	11	16	.407
Monmouth	4	12	.250	8	19	.296

Tournament: **Marist d. Fairleigh Dickinson 64-55**
Tournament MVP: **Drafton Davis**, Marist

ECAC NAC	Conference			Overall		
	W	L	PCT	W	L	PCT
Northeastern⊛	17	1	.944	27	7	.794
Niagara□	14	4	.778	21	10	.677
Boston U.	12	6	.667	18	12	.600
Siena	12	6	.667	17	12	.586
Canisius	12	6	.667	16	12	.571
Hartford	8	10	.444	14	14	.500
Maine	6	12	.333	10	18	.357
Vermont	3	15	.167	5	23	.179
Colgate	3	15	.167	4	23	.148
New Hampshire	3	15	.167	4	24	.143

Tournament: **Northeastern d. Boston U. 71-68**
Tournament MVP: **Reggie Lewis**, Northeastern

GULF STAR	Conference			Overall		
	W	L	PCT	W	L	PCT
Stephen F. Austin□	10	0	1.000	22	8	.733
Sam Houston State	6	4	.600	16	12	.571
Texas State	5	5	.500	13	15	.464
Northwestern St. (LA)	4	6	.400	15	13	.536
Southeastern La.	4	6	.400	10	21	.323
Nicholls State	1	9	.100	9	18	.333

IVY	Conference			Overall		
	W	L	PCT	W	L	PCT
Penn⊛	10	4	.714	13	14	.481
Princeton	9	5	.643	16	9	.640
Cornell	9	5	.643	15	11	.577
Dartmouth	7	7	.500	15	11	.577
Yale	7	7	.500	14	12	.538
Columbia	6	8	.429	12	14	.462
Harvard	4	10	.286	9	17	.346
Brown	4	10	.286	9	18	.333

METRO	Conference			Overall		
	W	L	PCT	W	L	PCT
Louisville	9	3	.750	18	14	.563
Memphis	8	4	.667	26	8	.765
Southern Miss.□	6	6	.500	23	11	.676
Florida State□	6	6	.500	19	11	.633
South Carolina	5	7	.417	15	14	.517
Virginia Tech	5	7	.417	10	18	.357
Cincinnati	3	9	.250	12	16	.429

Tournament: **Memphis d. Louisville 75-52**
Tournament MVP: **Marvin Alexander**, Memphis

METRO ATLANTIC	Conference			Overall		
	W	L	PCT	W	L	PCT
Saint Peter's□	11	3	.786	21	8	.724
La Salle□	10	4	.714	20	13	.606
Iona	8	6	.571	16	14	.533
Army	8	6	.571	14	15	.483
Fordham	6	8	.429	14	16	.467
Holy Cross	6	8	.429	9	19	.321
Fairfield⊛	5	9	.357	15	16	.484
Manhattan	2	12	.143	6	21	.222

Tournament: **Fairfield d. Iona 73-70 (OT)**
Tournament MVP: **Kevin Houston**, Army

Conference Standings Continue →

⊛ Automatic NCAA Tournament bid ○ At-large NCAA Tournament bid □ NIT appearance ⊗ Team record doesn't reflect games forfeited or vacated. For adjusted record, see p. 521.

MID-AMERICAN

	Conference			Overall		
	W	L	Pct	W	L	Pct
Central Michigan⊕	14	2	.875	22	8	.733
Kent State	11	5	.688	19	10	.655
Bowling Green	10	6	.625	15	14	.517
Eastern Michigan	8	8	.500	14	15	.483
Ohio	7	9	.438	14	14	.500
Miami (OH)	7	9	.438	13	15	.464
Western Michigan	7	9	.438	12	16	.429
Toledo	4	12	.250	11	17	.393
Ball State	4	12	.250	9	18	.333

Tournament: **Central Michigan d. Kent State 64-63**
Tournament MVP: **Dan Majerle**, Central Michigan

MEAC

	Conference			Overall		
	W	L	Pct	W	L	Pct
Howard	13	1	.929	25	5	.833
NC A&T⊕	12	2	.857	24	6	.800
South Carolina State	9	5	.643	14	15	.483
Coppin State	7	6	.538	8	19	.296
Bethune-Cookman	6	8	.429	10	19	.345
Morgan State	5	9	.357	8	20	.286
Delaware State	3	11	.214	4	24	.143
UMES	0	13	.000	2	24	.077
Florida A&M	-	-	-	12	16	.429

Tournament: **NC A&T d. Howard 79-58**
Tournament MOP: **Thomas Griffis**, NC A&T

MCC

	Conference			Overall		
	W	L	Pct	W	L	Pct
Evansville	8	4	.667	16	12	.571
Loyola-Chicago	8	4	.667	16	13	.552
Saint Louis□	7	5	.583	25	10	.714
Xavier⊕	7	5	.583	19	13	.594
Butler	5	7	.417	12	16	.429
Oral Roberts	5	7	.417	11	17	.393
Detroit	2	10	.167	7	21	.250

Tournament: **Xavier d. Saint Louis 81-69**
Tournament MVP: **Byron Larkin**, Xavier

MISSOURI VALLEY

	Conference			Overall		
	W	L	Pct	W	L	Pct
Tulsa○	11	3	.786	22	8	.733
Bradley	10	4	.714	17	12	.586
Wichita State⊕	9	5	.643	22	11	.667
Illinois State□	7	7	.500	19	13	.594
Drake	6	8	.429	17	14	.548
Southern Illinois	5	9	.357	12	17	.414
Creighton	4	10	.286	9	19	.321
Indiana State	4	10	.286	9	20	.310

Tournament: **Wichita State d. Tulsa 79-74**

OHIO VALLEY

	Conference			Overall		
	W	L	Pct	W	L	Pct
Middle Tenn. State○	11	3	.786	22	7	.759
Akron□	9	5	.643	21	9	.700
Eastern Kentucky	9	5	.643	19	11	.633
Austin Peay⊕	8	6	.571	20	12	.625
Morehead State	8	6	.571	14	14	.500
Murray State	6	8	.429	13	15	.464
Youngstown State	4	10	.286	11	17	.393
Tennessee Tech	1	13	.071	7	20	.259
Tennessee State	-	-	-	15	12	.556

Tournament: **Austin Peay d. Eastern Kentucky 71-68**
Tournament MVP: **Darryl Bedford**, Austin Peay

PCAA

	Conference			Overall		
	W	L	Pct	W	L	Pct
UNLV⊕	18	0	1.000	37	2	.949
UC Santa Barbara	10	8	.556	16	13	.552
San Jose State	10	8	.556	16	14	.533
Cal St. Fullerton□	9	9	.500	17	13	.567
New Mexico State	9	9	.500	15	15	.500
UC Irvine	9	9	.500	14	14	.500
Utah State	8	10	.444	15	16	.484
Long Beach State	7	11	.389	12	19	.387
Pacific	6	12	.333	10	17	.370
Fresno State	4	14	.222	9	20	.310

Tournament: **UNLV d. San Jose St. 94-69**
Tournament MVP: **Freddie Banks**, UNLV

PAC-10

	Conference			Overall		
	W	L	Pct	W	L	Pct
UCLA⊕	14	4	.778	25	7	.781
Arizona○	13	5	.722	18	12	.600
California□	10	8	.556	20	15	.571
Washington□	10	8	.556	20	15	.571
Oregon State□	10	8	.556	19	11	.633
Stanford	9	9	.500	15	13	.536
Oregon	8	10	.444	16	14	.533
Arizona State	6	12	.333	11	17	.393
Washington State	6	12	.333	10	18	.357
Southern California	4	14	.222	9	19	.321

Tournament: **UCLA d. Washington 76-64**
Tournament MOP: **Reggie Miller**, UCLA

SEC

	Conference			Overall		
	W	L	Pct	W	L	Pct
Alabama⊕✪	16	2	.889	28	5	.867
Florida○✪	12	6	.667	23	11	.676
Kentucky○	10	8	.556	18	11	.621
Georgia○	10	8	.556	18	12	.600
Auburn○	9	9	.500	18	13	.581
LSU○	8	10	.444	24	15	.615
Mississippi□	8	10	.444	15	14	.517
Vanderbilt□	7	11	.389	18	16	.529
Tennessee	7	11	.389	14	15	.483
Mississippi State	3	15	.167	7	21	.250

Tournament: **Alabama d. LSU 69-62**
Tournament MVP: **Derrick McKey**, Alabama

SOUTHERN

	Conference			Overall		
	W	L	Pct	W	L	Pct
Marshall⊕✪	15	1	.938	25	6	.806
Chattanooga□	14	2	.875	21	8	.724
Davidson	12	4	.750	20	10	.667
Furman	10	6	.625	17	12	.586
The Citadel	6	10	.375	13	15	.464
VMI	5	11	.313	11	17	.393
Western Carolina	4	12	.250	10	19	.345
Appalachian State	3	13	.188	7	21	.250
East Tenn. State	3	13	.188	7	21	.250

Tournament: **Marshall d. Davidson 66-64 (OT)**
Tournament MOP: **Derek Rucker**, Davidson

SOUTHLAND

	Conference			Overall		
	W	L	Pct	W	L	Pct
Louisiana Tech⊕	9	1	.900	22	8	.733
Arkansas State□	5	5	.500	21	13	.618
McNeese State	5	5	.500	14	14	.500
Lamar	4	6	.400	14	15	.483
North Texas	4	6	.400	11	17	.393
UL-Monroe	3	7	.300	13	15	.464

Tournament: **Louisiana Tech d. Arkansas State 58-51**
Tournament MVP: **Robert Godbolt**, Louisiana Tech

SOUTHWEST

	Conference			Overall		
	W	L	Pct	W	L	Pct
TCU○	14	2	.875	24	7	.774
Baylor□	10	6	.625	18	13	.581
Houston○	9	7	.563	18	12	.600
Texas Tech	9	7	.563	15	14	.517
Arkansas□	8	8	.500	19	14	.576
SMU	7	9	.438	16	13	.552
Texas	7	9	.438	14	17	.452
Texas A&M⊕	6	10	.375	17	14	.548
Rice	2	14	.125	8	19	.296

Tournament: **Texas A&M d. Baylor 71-46**
Tournament MVP: **Winston Crite**, Texas A&M

SWAC

	Conference			Overall		
	W	L	Pct	W	L	Pct
Grambling	11	3	.786	16	14	.533
Southern U.⊕	9	5	.643	19	12	.613
Miss. Valley State	9	5	.643	13	15	.464
Jackson State	8	6	.571	15	14	.517
Alabama State	7	7	.500	14	14	.500
Texas Southern	7	7	.500	11	18	.379
Alcorn State	3	11	.214	5	23	.179
Prairie View A&M	2	12	.143	6	22	.214

Tournament: **Southern U. d. Grambling 105-55**
Tournament MVP: **Avery Johnson**, Southern U.

SUN BELT

	Conference			Overall		
	W	L	Pct	W	L	Pct
Western Kentucky○	12	2	.857	29	9	.763
Jacksonville□	11	3	.786	19	11	.633
UAB⊕	10	4	.714	21	11	.656
VCU	7	7	.500	17	14	.548
Charlotte	6	8	.429	18	14	.563
South Alabama	6	8	.429	14	14	.500
South Florida	3	11	.214	8	20	.286
Old Dominion	1	13	.071	6	22	.214

Tournament: **UAB d. Western Kentucky 72-60**
Tournament MVP: **Tracy Foster**, UAB

TAAC

	Conference			Overall		
	W	L	Pct	W	L	Pct
Ark.-Little Rock□	16	2	.889	26	11	.703
Houston Baptist	13	5	.722	18	11	.621
Stetson	13	5	.722	18	13	.581
Georgia Southern⊕	12	6	.667	20	11	.645
Hardin-Simmons	9	9	.500	13	15	.464
UTSA	7	11	.389	13	15	.464
Mercer	7	11	.389	12	16	.429
Georgia State	7	11	.389	11	17	.393
Centenary	5	13	.278	10	17	.370
Samford	1	17	.056	4	22	.154

Tournament: **Georgia Southern d. Stetson 49-46**
Tournament MVP: **Jeff Sanders**, Georgia Southern

WCAC

	Conference			Overall		
	W	L	Pct	W	L	Pct
San Diego○	13	1	.929	24	6	.800
Gonzaga	9	5	.643	18	10	.643
Saint Mary's (CA)	7	7	.500	17	13	.567
San Francisco	6	8	.429	16	12	.571
Santa Clara⊕	6	8	.429	18	14	.563
Portland	6	8	.429	14	14	.500
Pepperdine	5	9	.357	12	18	.400
Loyola Marymount	4	10	.286	12	16	.429

Tournament: **Santa Clara d. Pepperdine 77-65**
Tournament MVP: **Jens Gordon**, Santa Clara

WAC

	Conference			Overall		
	W	L	Pct	W	L	Pct
UTEP○	13	3	.813	25	7	.781
BYU○	12	4	.750	21	11	.656
New Mexico□	11	5	.688	25	10	.714
Wyoming⊕	11	5	.688	24	10	.706
Utah□	9	7	.563	17	13	.567
Colorado State	7	9	.438	13	16	.448
Air Force	5	11	.313	12	15	.444
Hawaii	2	14	.125	7	21	.250
San Diego State	2	14	.125	5	25	.167

Tournament: **Wyoming d. New Mexico 64-62**
Tournament MVP: **Eric Leckner**, Wyoming

INDEPENDENTS

	Overall		
	W	L	Pct
DePaul○✪	28	3	.903
New Orleans○	26	4	.867
Notre Dame○	24	8	.750
Texas-Pan American	16	12	.571
Marquette□	16	13	.552
Miami (FL)	15	16	.484
Dayton	13	15	.464
UCF	12	15	.444
UMBC	12	16	.429
Chicago State	11	17	.393
UL-Lafayette	11	17	.393
U.S. International	11	17	.393
Utica	10	16	.385
Brooklyn	10	18	.357
Northern Illinois	9	19	.321
Central Connecticut State	8	21	.276
Eastern Washington	5	23	.179

INDIVIDUAL LEADERS—SEASON

SCORING	CL	POS	G	FG	3FG	FT	PTS	PPG
1 **Kevin Houston**, Army	SR	G	29	311	63	268	953	**32.9**
2 **Dennis Hopson**, Ohio State	SR	F	33	338	67	215	958	**29.0**
3 **David Robinson**, Navy	SR	C	32	350	1	202	903	**28.2**
4 **Terrance Bailey**, Wagner	SR	G	28	284	42	178	788	**28.1**
5 **Hersey Hawkins**, Bradley	JR	G	29	294	31	169	788	**27.2**
6 **Darrin Fitzgerald**, Butler	SR	G	28	250	158	76	734	**26.2**
7 **Gay Elmore**, VMI	SR	F	28	266	23	158	713	**25.5**
8 **Frank Ross**, American	SR	G	27	235	86	127	683	**25.3**
9 **Daren Queenan**, Lehigh	JR	G/F	29	260	9	191	720	**24.8**
10 **Byron Larkin**, Xavier	JR	G	32	278	32	204	792	**24.8**

FIELD GOAL PCT	CL	POS	G	FG	FGA	PCT
1 **Alan Williams**, Princeton	SR	G	25	163	232	**70.3**
2 **Tyrone Howard**, Eastern Kentucky	JR	F/C	30	156	230	**67.8**
3 **Horace Grant**, Clemson	SR	F	31	256	390	**65.6**
4 **Robert Godbolt**, Louisiana Tech	SR	F	30	191	295	**64.7**
5 **Claude Williams**, NC A&T	JR	F	29	174	273	**63.7**

MINIMUM: 5 MADE PER GAME

THREE-PT FG PER GAME	CL	POS	G	3FG	3PG
1 **Darrin Fitzgerald**, Butler	SR	G	28	158	**5.6**
2 **Scott Brooks**, UC Irvine	SR	G	28	111	**4.0**
3 **Freddie Banks**, UNLV	SR	G	39	152	**3.9**
4 **George Ivory**, Miss. Valley State	SR	G	28	109	**3.9**
5 **Tony Ross**, San Diego State	FR	G	28	104	**3.7**

THREE-PT FG PCT	CL	POS	G	3FG	3FGA	PCT
1 **Reginald Jones**, Prairie View A&M	JR	G	28	64	112	**57.1**
2 **Eric Rhodes**, Stephen F. Austin	JR	G	30	58	106	**54.7**
3 **Anthony Davis**, George Mason	JR	G	27	45	84	**53.6**
4 **Scott Dimak**, Stephen F. Austin	SO	G	30	46	86	**53.5**
5 **Steve Alford**, Indiana	SR	G	34	107	202	**53.0**

MINIMUM: 1.5 MADE PER GAME

FREE THROW PCT	CL	POS	G	FT	FTA	PCT
1 **Kevin Houston**, Army	SR	G	29	268	294	**91.2**
2 **Darryl Johnson**, Michigan State	SR	G	27	111	122	**91.0**
3 **Scott Haffner**, Evansville	SO	G	27	80	88	**90.9**
4 **Nate Blackwell**, Temple	SR	G	36	123	136	**90.4**
5 **Michael Smith**, BYU	SO	G	32	103	114	**90.4**

MINIMUM: 2.5 MADE PER GAME

ASSISTS PER GAME	CL	POS	G	AST	APG
1 **Avery Johnson**, Southern U.	JR	G	31	333	**10.7**
2 **Mark Wade**, UNLV	SR	G	38	406	**10.7**
3 **Tony Fairley**, Charleston Southern	SR	G	28	270	**9.6**
4 **Tyrone Bogues**, Wake Forest	SR	G	29	276	**9.5**
5 **Andre Van Drost**, Wagner	SR	G	28	260	**9.3**
6 **Duane Washington**, Middle Tenn. State	SR	G	29	255	**8.8**
7 **Anthony Manuel**, Bradley	SO	G	27	237	**8.8**
8 **Frank Smith**, Old Dominion	JR	G	28	229	**8.2**
9 **Drafton Davis**, Marist	JR	G	28	227	**8.1**
10 **Taurence Chisholm**, Delaware	JR	G	28	220	**7.9**

REBOUNDS PER GAME	CL	POS	G	REB	RPG
1 **Jerome Lane**, Pittsburgh	SO	F	33	444	**13.5**
2 **Chris Dudley**, Yale	SR	C	24	320	**13.3**
3 **Andre Moore**, Loyola-Illinois	SR	F	29	360	**12.4**
4 **David Robinson**, Navy	SR	C	32	378	**11.8**
5 **Brian Rowsom**, UNC Wilmington	SR	F	30	345	**11.5**
6 **Largest Agbejemisin**, Wagner	SR	C	29	333	**11.5**
7 **Bob McCann**, Morehead State	SR	F	28	317	**11.3**
8 **Melvin Stewart**, Texas Southern	SR	F/C	29	316	**10.9**
9 **Gerry Besselink**, Connecticut	SR	C	28	300	**10.7**
10 **Greg Anderson**, Houston	SR	F/C	30	318	**10.6**

BLOCKED SHOTS PER GAME	CL	POS	G	BLK	BPG
1 **David Robinson**, Navy	SR	C	32	144	**4.5**
2 **Derrick Lewis**, Maryland	JR	F	26	114	**4.4**
3 **Lester Fonville**, Jackson State	SR	C	29	112	**3.9**
4 **Rodney Blake**, Saint Joseph's	JR	C	24	87	**3.6**
5 **Dallas Comegys**, DePaul	SR	C	31	108	**3.5**

STEALS PER GAME	CL	POS	G	STL	SPG
1 **Tony Fairley**, Charleston Southern	SR	G	28	114	**4.1**
2 **Doug Usitalo**, Boise State	JR	G	30	105	**3.5**
3 **Joe Jeter**, Delaware State	SR	G	28	96	**3.4**
Roderick Ford, Texas-Arlington	JR	G	28	96	**3.4**
5 **Duane Washington**, Middle Tenn. State	SR	G	29	93	**3.2**

INDIVIDUAL LEADERS—GAME

POINTS	CL	POS	OPP	DATE	PTS
1 **Tilman Bevely**, Youngstown State	JR	G	Tennessee Tech	J26	**55**
2 **Darrin Fitzgerald**, Butler	SR	G	Detroit	F9	**54**
3 **Kevin Houston**, Army	SR	G	Fordham	F28	**53**
4 **Tony White**, Tennessee	SR	G	Auburn	F14	**51**
5 **David Robinson**, Navy	SR	C	Michigan	M12	**50**

THREE-PT FG MADE	CL	POS	OPP	DATE	3FG
1 **Gary Bossert**, Niagara	SR	G	Siena	J7	**12**
Darrin Fitzgerald, Butler	SR	G	Detroit	F9	**12**
3 **Darrin Fitzgerald**, Butler	SR	G	Loyola-Illinois	J10	**10**
Freddie Banks, UNLV	SR	G	Indiana	M28	**10**
5 Nine tied with nine					

ASSISTS	CL	POS	OPP	DATE	AST
1 **Tony Fairley**, Charleston Southern	SR	G	Armstrong Atlantic	F17	**22**
2 **Mark Wade**, UNLV	SR	G	Navy	D28	**21**
Kelvin Scarborough, New Mexico	SR	G	Hawaii	F4	**21**
4 **Avery Johnson**, Southern U.	JR	G	Texas Southern	M25	**20**
5 **Avery Johnson**, Southern U.	JR	G	Texas A&I	D16	**19**
Avery Johnson, Southern U.	JR	G	Jackson State	F6	**19**
Andre Van Drost, Wagner	SR	G	Long Island	F6	**19**

REBOUNDS	CL	POS	OPP	DATE	REB
1 **Lennell Moore**, Texas-San Antonio	JR	F	Centenary	J5	**25**
2 **Greg Anderson**, Houston	SR	F/C	Rice	F7	**24**
3 **Bruce Lefkowitz**, Penn	SR	C	Saint Francis (PA)	J13	**23**
Harry Willis, Weber State	SR	F/C	Montana State	J17	**23**
Derrick Lewis, Maryland	JR	F	James Madison	J28	**23**

BLOCKED SHOTS	CL	POS	OPP	DATE	BLK
1 **Derrick Lewis**, Maryland	JR	F	James Madison	J28	**12**
2 **Charles Smith**, Ball State	SR	F/C	Central Michigan	J7	**11**
3 **David Robinson**, Navy	SR	C	Kentucky	J25	**10**
Dallas Comegys, DePaul	SR	C	Dayton	F7	**10**
5 **Roy Brow**, Virginia Tech	JR	C	James Madison	D6	**9**
Charles Smith, Ball State	SR	F/C	Valparaiso	D12	**9**
Rik Smits, Marist	JR	C	Wagner	J5	**9**
Reuben Holmes, Alabama State	SR	F	South Carolina State	J6	**9**
Joe Arlauckas, Niagara	SR	F	Kent State	F25	**9**
Pervis Ellison, Louisville	SO	C	UCLA	F28	**9**

STEALS	CL	POS	OPP	DATE	STL
1 **Mike Boswell**, Colgate	SR	G	Niagara	J10	**10**
Tony Fairley, Charleston Southern	SR	G	UNC Ashville	J29	**10**
3 **Darryl Prue**, West Virginia	SO	F	George Mason	N29	**9**
Darryl McDonald, Texas A&M	JR	G	Lehigh	D29	**9**
Ronnie Murphy, Jacksonville	SR	F	South Florida	J11	**9**
Bruce Hodges, Sam Houston State	SR	G	Northwestern St. (LA)	J24	**9**
Andre LaFleur, Northeastern	SR	G	Maine	J24	**9**

TEAM LEADERS—SEASON

WIN-LOSS PCT	W	L	PCT
1 **UNLV**	37	2	**.949**
2 **DePaul** ⊗	28	3	**.903**
3 **North Carolina**	32	4	**.889**
Temple	32	4	**.889**
5 **Indiana**	30	4	**.882**

SCORING OFFENSE	G	W-L	PTS	PPG
1 **UNLV**	39	37-2	3,612	**92.6**
2 **North Carolina**	36	32-4	3,285	**91.2**
3 **Oklahoma**	34	24-10	3,028	**89.1**
4 **Michigan**	32	20-12	2,821	**88.2**
5 **Southern U.**	31	19-12	2,706	**87.3**

SCORING MARGIN	G	W-L	PPG	OPP PPG	MAR
1 **UNLV**	39	37-2	92.6	75.5	**17.1**
2 **North Carolina**	36	32-4	91.2	74.9	**16.3**
3 **Clemson**	31	25-6	86.1	71.5	**14.6**
4 **DePaul**	31	28-3	76.2	62.5	**13.7**
5 **Georgetown**	34	29-5	77.8	64.2	**13.6**

FIELD GOAL PCT	G	W-L	FG	FGA	PCT
1 **Princeton**	25	16-9	601	1,111	**54.1**
2 **North Carolina**	36	32-4	1,238	2,304	**53.7**
3 **Marshall**	31	25-6	946	1,777	**53.2**
4 **Clemson**	31	25-6	990	1,873	**52.9**
5 **Lafayette**	29	16-13	813	1,544	**52.7**

THREE-PT FG PER GAME	G	W-L	G	3FG	3PG
1 **Providence**	34	25-9	34	280	**8.2**
2 **UNLV**	39	37-2	39	309	**7.9**
3 **Eastern Kentucky**	30	19-11	30	216	**7.2**
4 **Butler**	28	12-16	28	198	**7.1**
5 **UC Irvine**	28	14-14	28	187	**6.7**

FREE THROW PCT	G	W-L	FT	FTA	PCT
1 **Alabama**	33	28-5	521	662	**78.7**
2 **Army**	29	14-15	491	626	**78.4**
3 **Michigan State**	28	11-17	408	529	**77.1**
4 **Northern Iowa**	28	13-15	390	507	**76.9**
5 **UC Irvine**	28	14-14	532	693	**76.8**

REBOUND MARGIN	G	W-L	RPG	OPP RPG	MAR
1 **Iowa**	35	30-5	43.1	31.5	**11.6**
2 **Pittsburgh**	33	25-8	41.5	31.8	**9.7**
3 **Western Kentucky**	38	29-9	39.6	31.5	**8.1**
4 **Georgetown**	34	29-5	40.4	32.4	**8.0**
5 **Auburn**	31	18-13	39.6	32.0	**7.6**

Scoring Defense

	G	W-L	OPP PTS	OPP PPG
1 Missouri State	34	28-6	1,958	**57.6**
2 Saint Mary's (CA)	30	17-13	1,766	**58.9**
3 Green Bay	29	15-14	1,714	**59.1**
4 Notre Dame	32	24-8	1,902	**59.4**
5 San Diego	30	24-6	1,810	**60.3**

Field Goal Pct Defense

	G	W-L	OPP FG	OPP FGA	OPP PCT
1 San Diego	30	24-6	660	1,645	**40.1**
2 Houston Baptist	29	18-11	740	1,835	**40.3**
3 Jackson State	29	15-14	703	1,721	**40.8**
4 Navy	32	26-6	814	1,961	**41.5**
5 DePaul	31	28-3	769	1,850	**41.6**

CONSENSUS ALL-AMERICAS

FIRST TEAM

PLAYER	CL	POS	HT	SCHOOL	RPG	PPG
Steve Alford	SR	G	6-2	Indiana	2.6	22.0
Danny Manning	JR	F	6-11	Kansas	9.5	23.9
David Robinson	SR	C	7-1	Navy	11.8	28.2
Kenny Smith	SR	G	6-3	North Carolina	2.2	16.9
Reggie Williams	SR	F	6-7	Georgetown	8.6	23.6

SECOND TEAM

PLAYER	CL	POS	HT	SCHOOL	RPG	PPG
Armon Gilliam	SR	F	6-9	UNLV	9.3	23.2
Horace Grant	SR	F	6-10	Clemson	9.6	21.0
Dennis Hopson	SR	F	6-5	Ohio State	8.2	29.0
Mark Jackson	SR	G	6-4	St. John's	3.7	18.9
Ken Norman	SR	F	6-8	Illinois	9.8	20.7

Selectors: AP, NABC, UPI, USBWA

AWARD WINNERS

PLAYER OF THE YEAR

PLAYER	CL	POS	HT	SCHOOL	AWARDS
David Robinson	SR	C	7-1	Navy	Naismith, AP, UPI, USBWA, Wooden, NABC, Rupp
Tyrone Bogues	SR	G	5-3	Wake Forest	Frances Pomeroy Naismith*

(For the most outstanding senior player who is 6 feet or under.)

DEFENSIVE PLAYER OF THE YEAR

PLAYER	CL	POS	HT	SCHOOL
Tommy Amaker	SR	G	6-0	Duke

COACH OF THE YEAR

COACH	SCHOOL	REC	AWARDS
Bob Knight	Indiana	30-4	Naismith
Tom Davis	Iowa	30-5	AP
John Thompson Jr.	Georgetown	29-5	UPI
John Chaney	Temple	32-4	USBWA
Rick Pitino	Providence	25-9	NABC, Sporting News
Joey Meyer	DePaul	28-3	CBS/Chevrolet

Bob Gibbons' Top High School Senior Recruits

PLAYER	POS	HT	HIGH SCHOOL	A-A TEAMS	COLLEGE	CAREER NOTES
1 Larry Johnson	F	6-7	Skyline HS, Dallas	McD, P	Odessa JC/UNLV	NCAA title, '90; No. 1 overall pick, '91 NBA draft (Hornets); NBA ROY, '92; 16.2 ppg, 7.5 rpg (10 seasons); 2-time All-Star
2 Marcus Liberty	F	6-8	Martin Luther King HS, Chicago	McD, P, USA	Illinois	12.6 ppg, 5.3 rpg (3 seasons); 2nd-round pick, '90 NBA draft (Nuggets); 7.3 ppg (4 seasons)
3 Sean Higgins	SF	6-8	Fairfax HS, Los Angeles	McD, P	Michigan	NCAA title, '89; 2nd-round pick, '90 NBA draft (Spurs); 6.3 ppg (6 seasons)
4 Eric Manuel	SF	6-6	Southwest HS, Macon, GA	McD, P, USA	Kentucky/ Oklahoma City	1 year at Kentucky; banned by NCAA for academic fraud; led Oklahoma City to '91 and '92 NAIA titles; played overseas
5 Dennis Scott	G/F	6-7	Flint Hill Prep, Falls Church, VA	McD, P, USA	Georgia Tech	ACC POY, '90; Final Four, '90; No. 4 pick, '90 NBA draft (Magic); 12.9 ppg (10 seasons); led NBA in 3pt FGs, '95-'96
6 Brian Shorter	PF	6-7	Oak Hill Academy, Mouth of Wilson, VA	McD, P	Pittsburgh	24 pts in '87 McDonald's game; Big East ROY, '88; at Pitt, 17.8 ppg, 8.4 (4 seasons); undrafted
7 Anthony Tucker	PF	6-8	McKinley HS, Washington, D.C.	McD, P	Georgetown/ Wake Forest	Transferred after 1 year; at Wake, 10.9 ppg (3 seasons); undrafted; 3.9 ppg (1 season)
8 King Rice	PG	6-0	Binghamton (NY) HS	McD, P	North Carolina	Final Four, '91; left UNC 3rd all-time in assists (629); undrafted
9 Brian Williams	C	6-10	Santa Monica (CA) Catholic HS	McD, P	Maryland/Arizona	Transferred after 1 year; No. 10 pick, '91 NBA draft (Magic); 11.0 ppg (8 seasons) as Bison Dele
10 LaBradford Smith	2G	6-4	Bay City (TX) HS	McD, P, USA	Louisville	13.6 ppg (4 seasons); No. 19 pick, '91 NBA draft (Bullets); 6.7 ppg (3 seasons)
11 Mark Macon	2G	6-5	Buena Vista HS, Saginaw, MI	McD, P	Temple	Left as A-10's all-time scorer (2,609); No. 8 pick, '91 NBA draft (Nuggets); 6.7 ppg (6 seasons)
12 LeRon Ellis	C/F	6-10	Mater Dei HS, Santa Ana, CA	P	Kentucky/Syracuse	Transferred after 2 years; No. 22 pick, '91 NBA draft (Clippers); 3.0 ppg (3 seasons)
13 Jerome Harmon	2G	6-4	Lew Wallace HS, Gary, IN	McD, P	Louisville	1 year at Louisville (14.7 ppg); undrafted; played in NBA (76ers), 4.6 ppg (1 season)
14 Perry Carter	PF	6-8	Maine Central Institute, Pittsfield, ME	McD, P	Ohio State	1,613 pts, 989 rebs (4 seasons); 2nd-round pick in CBA draft; played overseas
15 Jay Edwards	2G	6-4	Marion (IN) HS	McD, P	Indiana	Indiana Co-Mr. Basketball, '87; 2nd team All-America, '89; 2nd-round pick, '89 NBA draft (Clippers); 1.8 ppg (1 season)
16 Rodney Monroe	G	6-2	St. Maria Goretti HS, Hagerstown, MD	McD, P, USA	NC State	ACC POY, '91; 2nd-round pick, '91 NBA draft (Hawks); played in 38 NBA games
17 Greg Koubek	SF	6-6	Shenendehowa Central HS, Clifton Park, NY	McD, P	Duke	NCAA title, '91; 4 Final Fours; at Duke, 4.9 ppg, 2.5 rpg (4 seasons); undrafted
18 Lyndon Jones	PG	6-2	Marion (IN) HS	P	Indiana	Indiana Co-Mr. Basketball, '87; at Indiana, 688 pts, 306 assists (4 seasons); played in CBA, WBL
19 Treg Lee	F	6-8	St. Joseph HS, Cleveland	McD, P	Ohio State	7.0 ppg (4 seasons); undrafted; played overseas
20 John Crotty	G	6-2	Christian Brothers Academy, Lincroft, NJ	McD, P	Virginia	12.8 ppg, 5.3 apg (4 seasons); undrafted; played with 6 NBA teams; 4.0 ppg (11 seasons)

Other Standouts

PLAYER	POS	HT	HIGH SCHOOL	A-A TEAMS	COLLEGE	CAREER NOTES
41 Anderson Hunt	G	6-2	Southwestern HS, Detroit		UNLV	NCAA title and Tournament MOP, '90; undrafted; played overseas
42 Delino DeShields	PG	6-1	Seaford (DE) HS		Villanova	DNP at Villanova; No. 12 pick in '87 MLB draft; .268 bat avg (13 seasons)
54 Steve Smith	G/F	6-6	Pershing HS, Detroit		Michigan State	18.5 ppg, 6.1 rpg (4 seasons); No. 5 pick, '91 NBA draft (Heat); 14.3 ppg (14 seasons); Olympic gold medal, '00

Abbreviations: McD=McDonald's; P=Parade; USA=USA Today

Poll Progression

Preseason Poll

AP	School	
1	North Carolina	
2	Louisville	Ⓐ
3	Indiana	
4	Purdue	
5	UNLV	
6	Georgia Tech	
7	Oklahoma	
8	Kansas	
9	Navy	
10	Iowa	
11	Kentucky	
12	Auburn	
13	Alabama	
14	Illinois	
15	Syracuse	
16	Pittsburgh	
17	NC State	
18	Georgetown	
19	Arizona	
20	Cleveland State	

Week of Dec 2

AP	UPI	School	AP↓↑
1	1	North Carolina (2-0)	
2	2	UNLV (4-0)	↑3
3	3	Indiana (1-0)	
4	4	Purdue (1-0)	
5	6	Iowa (3-0)	↑5
6	5	Kansas (1-0)	↑2
7	8	Auburn (1-0)	↑5
8	7	Alabama (1-0)	↑5
9	14	Illinois (2-0)	↑5
10	14	Navy (2-1)	↓1
11	9	Oklahoma (1-1)	↓4
12	11	Pittsburgh (1-0)	↑4
13	16	Kentucky (1-0)	↓2
14	10	Western Kentucky (3-1)	⤴
15	—	Georgia Tech (1-1)	↓9
16	12	Georgetown (2-0)	↑2
17	13	Syracuse (1-0)	↓2
18	19	NC State (3-1)	↓1
19	—	Northeastern (2-1)	⤴
20	—	Arizona (0-1)	↓1
—	17	UCLA (2-0)	
—	18	Louisville (0-3)	⤵
—	20	Temple (3-1)	

Week of Dec 9

AP	UPI	School	AP↓↑
1	1	UNLV (5-0)	↑1
2	2	Indiana (3-0) Ⓑ	↑1
3	4	Purdue (3-0)	↑1
4	3	Iowa (6-0)	↑1
5	5	North Carolina (4-1)	↓4
6	6	Illinois (4-0)	↑3
7	8	Auburn (2-0)	
8	10	Western Kentucky (6-1)	↑6
9	13	Oklahoma (3-1)	↑2
10	14	Navy (3-1)	
11	7	UCLA (3-0)	⤴
12	12	Syracuse (4-0)	↑5
13	11	Georgetown (4-0)	↑3
14	9	Kansas (3-1)	↓8
15	18	NC State (5-1)	↑3
16	—	Georgia Tech (3-1)	↓1
17	17	Pittsburgh (2-1)	↓5
18	16	Alabama (2-1)	↓10
19	19	Kentucky (2-1)	↓6
20	15	Arkansas (4-0)	⤴
—	19	Wyoming (3-0)	

Week of Dec 16

AP	UPI	School	AP↓↑
1	1	UNLV (6-0)	
2	2	Purdue (5-0)	↑1
3	4	Iowa (8-0)	↑1
4	3	North Carolina (5-1)	↑1
5	5	Illinois (7-0)	↑1
6	7	Auburn (4-0)	↑1
7	9	Oklahoma (5-1)	↑2
8	6	Indiana (4-1)	↓6
9	10	Syracuse (7-0)	↑3
10	8	Georgetown (5-0)	↑3
11	12	Navy (4-1)	↓1
12	15	NC State (6-1)	↑3
13	11	Kansas (4-1)	↑1
14	13	Pittsburgh (4-1)	↑3
15	14	St. John's (6-0)	⤴
16	—	Georgia Tech (3-2)	
17	16	UCLA (3-1)	↓6
18	20	Kentucky (3-1)	↑1
19	17	DePaul (5-0)	⤴
20	19	Temple (7-1)	⤴
—	17	Arkansas (5-1)	⤵

Week of Dec 23

AP	UPI	School	AP↓↑
1	1	UNLV (9-0)	
2	2	Purdue (6-0)	
3	3	Iowa (9-0)	
4	4	North Carolina (6-1)	
5	5	Auburn (6-0)	↑1
6	8	Oklahoma (6-1)	↑1
7	7	Syracuse (8-0)	↑2
8	6	Indiana (6-1)	
9	10	Illinois (7-1)	↓4
10	9	Georgetown (7-0)	
11	13	NC State (7-1)	↑1
12	12	Navy (4-1)	↓1
13	11	Kansas (5-1)	
14	14	Pittsburgh (5-1)	
15	16	St. John's (7-0)	
16	17	Temple (8-1)	↑4
17	15	DePaul (7-0)	↑2
18	18	Kentucky (5-1)	
19	—	Georgia Tech (5-2)	↓3
20	19	Florida (8-1)	⤴
—	20	Duke (5-1)	
—	20	Cal St. Fullerton (6-1)	

Week of Dec 30

AP	UPI	School	AP↓↑
1	1	UNLV (10-0)	
2	2	Purdue (7-0)	
3	4	Iowa (11-0)	
4	3	North Carolina (8-1)	
5	6	Auburn (7-0)	
6	5	Indiana (9-1)	↑2
7	7	Syracuse (10-0)	
8	8	Georgetown (8-0)	↑2
9	10	Navy (5-1)	↑3
10	11	St. John's (8-0)	↑5
11	9	Kentucky (6-1) Ⓒ	↑7
12	14	Kansas (6-2)	↑1
13	12	Oklahoma (7-2)	↓7
14	15	Temple (8-1)	↑2
15	16	DePaul (8-0)	↑2
16	13	Illinois (8-2)	↓7
17	17	Pittsburgh (6-2)	↓3
18	—	Georgia Tech (6-2)	↑1
19	—	NC State (7-2)	↓8
20	18	Duke (6-1)	⤴
—	19	Cal St. Fullerton (7-1)	
—	20	TCU (9-3)	

Week of Jan 6

AP	UPI	School	AP↓↑
1	1	UNLV (12-0)	
2	3	Iowa (13-0)	↑1
3	2	North Carolina (11-1)	↑1
4	4	Indiana (10-1)	↑2
5	6	Syracuse (12-0)	↑2
6	5	Purdue (9-1)	↓4
7	9	DePaul (10-0)	↑8
8	7	Temple (11-1)	↑6
9	8	Kentucky (7-2)	↑2
10	12	St. John's (9-1)	
11	10	Oklahoma (9-2)	↑2
12	13	Illinois (9-2)	↑4
13	11	Auburn (7-2)	↓8
14	15	Pittsburgh (9-2)	↑3
15	14	Navy (6-2)	↓6
16	17	Georgetown (9-1)	↓8
17	16	Duke (9-1)	↑3
18	20	NC State (9-2)	↑1
19	18	Kansas (7-2)	↓7
20	—	Clemson (11-0)	⤴
—	19	TCU (10-3)	

Week of Jan 13

AP	UPI	School	AP↓↑
1	1	UNLV (14-0)	
2	3	Iowa (15-0)	
3	2	North Carolina (13-1)	
4	4	Indiana (12-1)	
5	6	Syracuse (14-0)	
6	5	Purdue (12-1)	
7	7	DePaul (12-0)	
8	10	Illinois (12-2)	↑4
9	8	Georgetown (12-1)	↑7
10	9	Auburn (9-2)	↑3
11	11	Temple (14-2)	↓3
12	14	Clemson (14-0)	↑8
13	12	St. John's (10-2)	↓3
14	13	Duke (11-2)	↑3
15	15	Alabama (10-2)	⤴
16	16	Oklahoma (10-3)	↓5
17	17	NC State (10-3)	↑1
18	18	Pittsburgh (11-3)	↓4
19	20	Navy (9-3)	↓4
20	—	Kansas (9-4)	↓1
—	19	TCU (12-3)	

Week of Jan 20

AP	UPI	School	AP↓↑
1	2	Iowa (16-0) Ⓓ	↑1
2	1	North Carolina (15-1)	↑1
3	4	Indiana (14-1)	↑1
4	3	UNLV (15-1)	↓3
5	5	Purdue (14-1)	↑1
6	6	DePaul (14-0)	↑1
7	7	Syracuse (15-1)	↓2
8	8	Temple (16-2)	↑3
9	10	Illinois (13-3)	↓1
10	12	Clemson (16-0)	↑2
11	9	Oklahoma (12-3)	↑5
12	13	Duke (13-2)	↑2
13	11	Alabama (13-2)	↑2
14	14	St. John's (12-2)	↓1
15	16	Georgetown (12-2)	↓6
16	17	Pittsburgh (13-3)	↑2
17	15	Auburn (10-3)	↓7
18	19	Navy (11-3) Ⓔ	↑1
19	18	TCU (13-3)	⤴
20	—	NC State (11-4)	↓3
—	20	Kansas (10-5)	⤵

Week of Jan 27

AP	UPI	School	AP↓↑
1	1	North Carolina (17-1)	↑1
2	3	Iowa (18-1)	↓1
3	2	UNLV (19-1)	↑1
4	4	Indiana (15-2)	↓1
5	5	Purdue (15-2)	↑1
6	6	Syracuse (17-2)	↑1
7	7	Temple (18-2)	↑1
8	8	DePaul (16-1)	↓2
9	10	Alabama (15-2)	↑4
10	9	Oklahoma (14-3)	↑1
11	13	Georgetown (14-2)	↑4
12	12	Illinois (14-4)	↓3
13	11	Duke (14-3)	↓1
14	14	Clemson (17-1)	↓4
15	18	St. John's (13-3)	↓1
16	15	TCU (16-3)	↑3
17	19	Pittsburgh (14-4)	↓1
18	17	Auburn (11-4)	↓1
19	16	Florida (15-4)	⤴
20	20	Kansas (13-5)	⤴

Week of Feb 3

AP	UPI	School	AP↓↑
1	1	UNLV (21-1)	↑2
2	2	Indiana (17-2)	↑2
3	3	North Carolina (18-2) Ⓕ	↓2
4	4	Iowa (19-2)	↓2
5	7	DePaul (18-1)	↑3
6	5	Temple (20-2)	↑1
7	6	Purdue (16-3)	↓3
8	8	Oklahoma (17-3)	↑2
9	9	Alabama (16-3)	
10	10	Georgetown (15-3)	↑1
11	11	Syracuse (17-3)	↓5
12	13	Clemson (19-2)	↑2
13	16	Pittsburgh (17-4)	↑4
14	14	Illinois (15-5)	↓2
15	12	TCU (18-3)	↑1
16	15	Duke (16-4)	↓3
17	18	Providence (16-3) Ⓖ	⤴
18	17	Kansas (15-5)	↑2
19	—	St. John's (14-4)	↓4
20	19	Auburn (12-6)	↓2
—	19	Florida (16-5)	⤵

Week of Feb 10

AP	UPI	School	AP↓↑
1	1	UNLV (23-1)	
2	2	Indiana (19-2)	
3	3	North Carolina (20-2)	
4	4	Iowa (21-2)	
5	5	DePaul (20-1)	
6	7	Temple (23-2)	
7	6	Purdue (18-3)	
8	8	Oklahoma (19-3)	
9	9	Syracuse (19-3)	↑2
10	13	Pittsburgh (19-4)	↑3
11	12	Illinois (18-5)	↑3
12	11	Clemson (21-2)	
13	10	Georgetown (16-4)	↓3
14	14	Alabama (17-4)	↓5
15	16	Duke (19-4)	↑1
16	18	St. John's (18-4)	↑3
17	17	Kansas (18-5)	↑1
18	15	TCU (19-4)	↓3
19	19	Florida (18-5)	⤴
20	—	Providence (16-5)	↓3
—	20	UTEP (18-5)	

ANNUAL REVIEW

Poll Progression Continues →

Week of Feb 17

AP	UPI	SCHOOL	AP↓↑
1	1	**UNLV** (26-1)	
2	2	**Indiana** (20-2)	
3	3	**North Carolina** (23-2)	
4	5	**DePaul** (22-1)	↑1
5	7	**Temple** (25-2)	↑1
6	6	**Purdue** (20-3)	↑1
7	4	**Iowa** (22-3)	↓3
8	8	**Pittsburgh** (21-4)	↑2
9	9	**Syracuse** (20-4)	
10	10	**Clemson** (23-2)	↑2
11	12	**Georgetown** (19-4)	↑2
12	11	**Alabama** (19-4)	↑2
13	16	**Oklahoma** (19-5)	↓5
14	13	**Illinois** (19-6)	↓3
15	14	**Kansas** (19-6)	↑2
16	15	**TCU** (20-4)	↑2
17	18	**Duke** (20-5)	↓2
18	17	**Florida** (20-6)	↑1
19	—	**Providence** (17-5)	↑1
20	—	**St. John's** (17-5)	↓4
—	19	**UTEP** (20-5)	
—	20	**New Orleans** (20-3)	
—	20	**Wyoming** (18-6)	

Week of Feb 24

AP	UPI	SCHOOL	AP↓↑
1	1	**UNLV** (28-1)	
2	3	**North Carolina** (25-2)	↑1
3	2	**Indiana** (23-2)	↓1
4	5	**DePaul** (25-1)	
5	4	**Temple** (28-2)	
6	6	**Purdue** (20-3)	
7	8	**Iowa** (23-4)	
8	7	**Georgetown** (21-4)	↑3
9	9	**Pittsburgh** (22-5)	↓1
10	10	**Alabama** (21-4)	↑2
11	11	**Syracuse** (22-5)	↓2
12	14	**Oklahoma** (21-5)	↑1
13	12	**Clemson** (24-3)	↓3
14	13	**Illinois** (19-6)	
15	15	**TCU** (22-4)	↑1
16	16	**Kansas** (21-7)	↓1
17	19	**Duke** (21-6)	
18	17	**Florida** (21-7)	
19	—	**New Orleans** (22-3)	↑
20	—	**Providence** (18-6)	↓1
—	18	**UTEP** (21-5)	
—	20	**UCLA** (19-6)	

Week of Mar 3

AP	UPI	SCHOOL	AP↓↑
1	1	**UNLV** (30-1)	
2	2	**North Carolina** (27-2)	
3	3	**Purdue** (23-3)	↑3
4	4	**Indiana** (23-4)	↓1
5	5	**DePaul** (25-2)	↓1
6	6	**Iowa** (25-4)	↑1
7	7	**Georgetown** (23-4)	↑1
8	8	**Temple** (29-3) Ⓗ	↓3
9	9	**Alabama** (23-4)	↑1
10	11	**Syracuse** (24-5)	↑1
11	10	**Pittsburgh** (23-6)	↓2
12	12	**Illinois** (21-7)	↑2
13	14	**Clemson** (25-4)	
14	15	**Duke** (22-7)	↑3
15	13	**TCU** (23-5)	
16	19	**New Orleans** (25-3)	↑3
17	17	**Oklahoma** (21-8)	↓5
18	16	**UCLA** (21-6)	↑
19	—	**Missouri** (21-9)	↑
20	18	**Notre Dame** (19-7)	↑
—	19	**Kansas** (21-8)	↓

FINAL POLL

AP	UPI	SCHOOL	AP↓↑
1	1	**UNLV** (33-1)	
2	3	**North Carolina** (29-3)	
3	2	**Indiana** (24-4)	
4	4	**Georgetown** (26-4)	
5	5	**DePaul** (26-2)	
6	7	**Iowa** (27-4)	
7	6	**Purdue** (24-4)	
8	8	**Temple** (31-3)	
9	9	**Alabama** (26-4)	
10	10	**Syracuse** (26-6)	
11	11	**Illinois** (23-7)	
12	12	**Pittsburgh** (24-7)	
13	15	**Clemson** (25-5)	
14	14	**Missouri** (24-9)	↑
15	13	**UCLA** (24-6)	↑
16	19	**New Orleans** (25-3)	
17	—	**Duke** (22-8)	↓
18	18	**Notre Dame** (22-7)	↑
19	16	**TCU** (23-6)	↓
20	—	**Kansas** (23-10)	↑
—	17	**Wyoming** (22-9)	
—	19	**Oklahoma** (22-9)	↓
—	19	**UTEP** (24-6)	

Ⓐ At the Great Alaska Shootout, Northeastern's Reggie Lewis scores 32 in an 88-84 OT victory over Louisville. After losses to Washington and Texas the next two nights, the Cardinals disappear from the AP poll—the biggest one-week drop in history.

Ⓑ *A Season on the Brink,* John Feinstein's inside account of Indiana's 1985-86 season, is released. Despite negative reviews from Bob Knight, the book becomes a bestseller.

Ⓒ Kentucky freshman sharpshooter Rex Chapman drills five of eight three-pointers for 26 points in an 85-51 victory over Louisville.

Ⓓ Iowa, one of four Big Ten schools in the Top 10, reaches No. 1 for the first time in its history, but immediately loses to Ohio State, led by 36 points from Dennis Hopson.

Ⓔ The Midshipmen spend a week in the rankings courtesy of David Robinson—who, in an 80-69 loss to Kentucky on Jan. 25, collects 45 points, 14 rebounds, 10 blocks and 8 dunks.

Ⓕ On Feb. 1, Notre Dame upsets North Carolina, 60-58, in South Bend—the fifth time in 13 years that the Irish have beaten a top-ranked team at home.

Ⓖ Rick Pitino's preseason decision to take advantage of the new three-point shot pays off for Providence. The Friars are led by point guard Billy Donovan, who has cut down his weight and beefed up his scoring.

Ⓗ A 64-61 loss to West Virginia snaps Temple's 34-game home court winning streak.

1987 NCAA Tournament (A)

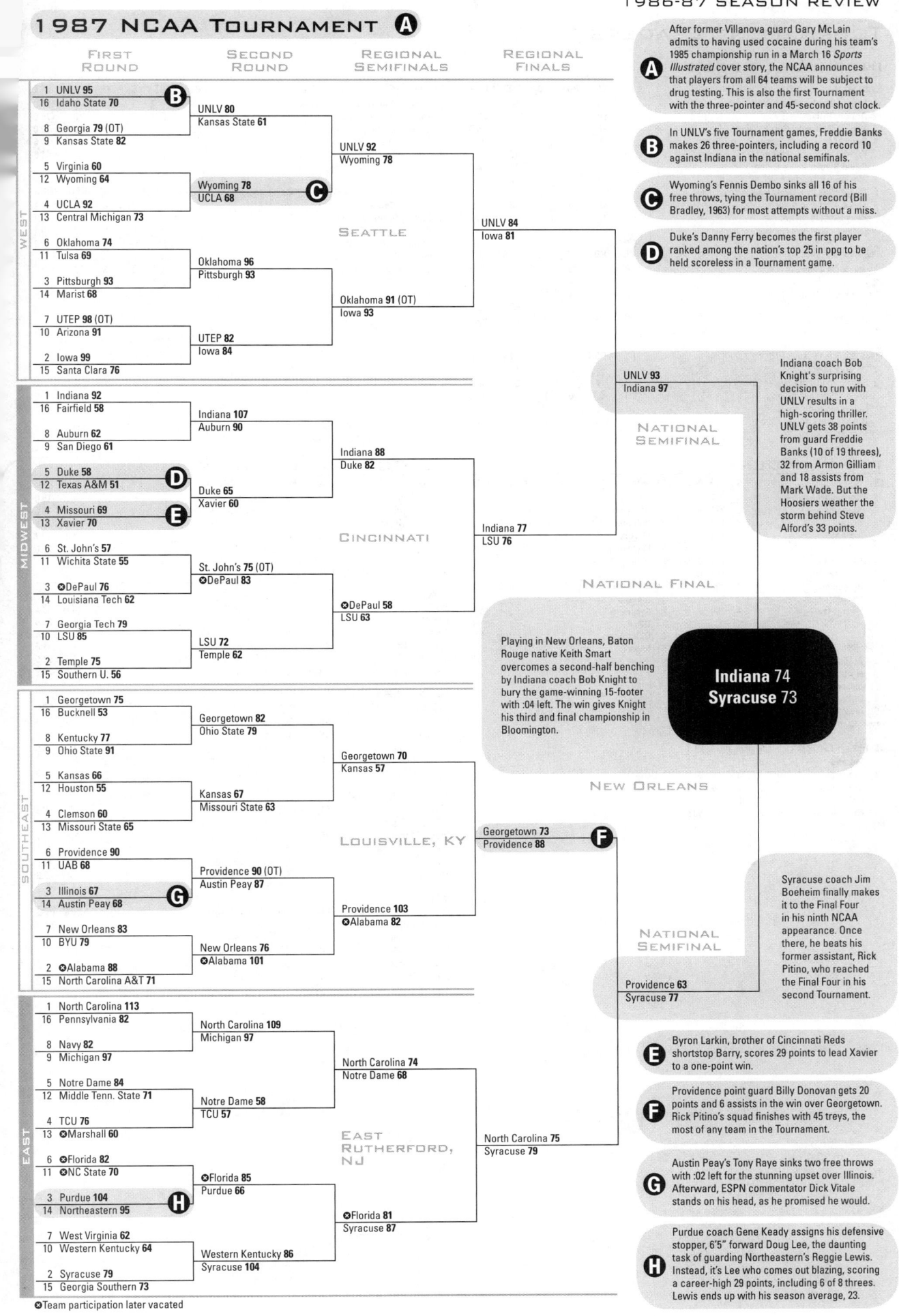

West — Seattle

First Round
- 1 UNLV **95** / 16 Idaho State **70** (B)
- 8 Georgia **79** (OT) / 9 Kansas State **82**
- 5 Virginia **60** / 12 Wyoming **64**
- 4 UCLA **92** / 13 Central Michigan **73**
- 6 Oklahoma **74** / 11 Tulsa **69**
- 3 Pittsburgh **93** / 14 Marist **68**
- 7 UTEP **98** (OT) / 10 Arizona **91**
- 2 Iowa **99** / 15 Santa Clara **76**

Second Round
- UNLV **80** / Kansas State **61**
- Wyoming **78** / UCLA **68** (C)
- Oklahoma **96** / Pittsburgh **93**
- UTEP **82** / Iowa **84**

Regional Semifinals
- UNLV **92** / Wyoming **78**
- Oklahoma **91** (OT) / Iowa **93**

Regional Finals
- UNLV **84** / Iowa **81**

Midwest — Cincinnati

First Round
- 1 Indiana **92** / 16 Fairfield **58**
- 8 Auburn **62** / 9 San Diego **61**
- 5 Duke **58** / 12 Texas A&M **51** (D)
- 4 Missouri **69** / 13 Xavier **70** (E)
- 6 St. John's **57** / 11 Wichita State **55**
- 3 ⊗DePaul **76** / 14 Louisiana Tech **62**
- 7 Georgia Tech **79** / 10 LSU **85**
- 2 Temple **75** / 15 Southern U. **56**

Second Round
- Indiana **107** / Auburn **90**
- Duke **65** / Xavier **60**
- St. John's **75** (OT) / ⊗DePaul **83**
- LSU **72** / Temple **62**

Regional Semifinals
- Indiana **88** / Duke **82**
- ⊗DePaul **58** / LSU **63**

Regional Finals
- Indiana **77** / LSU **76**

Southeast — Louisville, KY

First Round
- 1 Georgetown **75** / 16 Bucknell **53**
- 8 Kentucky **77** / 9 Ohio State **91**
- 5 Kansas **66** / 12 Houston **55**
- 4 Clemson **60** / 13 Missouri State **65**
- 6 Providence **90** / 11 UAB **68**
- 3 Illinois **67** / 14 Austin Peay **68** (G)
- 7 New Orleans **83** / 10 BYU **79**
- 2 ⊗Alabama **88** / 15 North Carolina A&T **71**

Second Round
- Georgetown **82** / Ohio State **79**
- Kansas **67** / Missouri State **63**
- Providence **90** (OT) / Austin Peay **87**
- New Orleans **76** / ⊗Alabama **101**

Regional Semifinals
- Georgetown **70** / Kansas **57**
- Providence **103** / ⊗Alabama **82**

Regional Finals
- Georgetown **73** / Providence **88** (F)

East — East Rutherford, NJ

First Round
- 1 North Carolina **113** / 16 Pennsylvania **82**
- 8 Navy **82** / 9 Michigan **97**
- 5 Notre Dame **84** / 12 Middle Tenn. State **71**
- 4 TCU **76** / 13 ⊗Marshall **60**
- 6 ⊗Florida **82** / 11 ⊗NC State **70**
- 3 Purdue **104** / 14 Northeastern **95** (H)
- 7 West Virginia **62** / 10 Western Kentucky **64**
- 2 Syracuse **79** / 15 Georgia Southern **73**

Second Round
- North Carolina **109** / Michigan **97**
- Notre Dame **58** / TCU **57**
- ⊗Florida **85** / Purdue **66**
- Western Kentucky **86** / Syracuse **104**

Regional Semifinals
- North Carolina **74** / Notre Dame **68**
- ⊗Florida **81** / Syracuse **87**

Regional Finals
- North Carolina **75** / Syracuse **79**

National Semifinal

- UNLV **93** / Indiana **97**

Indiana coach Bob Knight's surprising decision to run with UNLV results in a high-scoring thriller. UNLV gets 38 points from guard Freddie Banks (10 of 19 threes), 32 from Armon Gilliam and 18 assists from Mark Wade. But the Hoosiers weather the storm behind Steve Alford's 33 points.

National Semifinal

- Providence **63** / Syracuse **77**

Syracuse coach Jim Boeheim finally makes it to the Final Four in his ninth NCAA appearance. Once there, he beats his former assistant, Rick Pitino, who reached the Final Four in his second Tournament.

National Final — New Orleans

Indiana 74
Syracuse 73

Playing in New Orleans, Baton Rouge native Keith Smart overcomes a second-half benching by Indiana coach Bob Knight to bury the game-winning 15-footer with :04 left. The win gives Knight his third and final championship in Bloomington.

⊗Team participation later vacated

A After former Villanova guard Gary McLain admits to having used cocaine during his team's 1985 championship run in a March 16 *Sports Illustrated* cover story, the NCAA announces that players from all 64 teams will be subject to drug testing. This is also the first Tournament with the three-pointer and 45-second shot clock.

B In UNLV's five Tournament games, Freddie Banks makes 26 three-pointers, including a record 10 against Indiana in the national semifinals.

C Wyoming's Fennis Dembo sinks all 16 of his free throws, tying the Tournament record (Bill Bradley, 1963) for most attempts without a miss.

D Duke's Danny Ferry becomes the first player ranked among the nation's top 25 in ppg to be held scoreless in a Tournament game.

E Byron Larkin, brother of Cincinnati Reds shortstop Barry, scores 29 points to lead Xavier to a one-point win.

F Providence point guard Billy Donovan gets 20 points and 6 assists in the win over Georgetown. Rick Pitino's squad finishes with 45 treys, the most of any team in the Tournament.

G Austin Peay's Tony Raye sinks two free throws with :02 left for the stunning upset over Illinois. Afterward, ESPN commentator Dick Vitale stands on his head, as he promised he would.

H Purdue coach Gene Keady assigns his defensive stopper, 6'5" forward Doug Lee, the daunting task of guarding Northeastern's Reggie Lewis. Instead, it's Lee who comes out blazing, scoring a career-high 29 points, including 6 of 8 threes. Lewis ends up with his season average, 23.

Tournament Leaders

INDIVIDUAL LEADERS

Scoring	CL	POS	G	PTS	PPG
1 **Fennis Dembo**, Wyoming	JR	F	3	84	28.0
2 **Armon Gilliam**, UNLV	SR	F	5	133	26.6
3 **Reggie Williams**, Georgetown	SR	F	4	104	26.0
4 **Danny Manning**, Kansas	JR	F	3	77	25.7
Vernon Maxwell, Florida	JR	G	3	77	25.7
6 **David Rivers**, Notre Dame	JR	G	3	74	24.7
7 **Jim Farmer**, Alabama	JR	G	3	72	24.0
8 **Tim McCalister**, Oklahoma	SR	G	3	70	23.3
9 **Steve Alford**, Indiana	SR	G	6	138	23.0
Rony Seikaly, Syracuse	JR	C	6	138	23.0

Minimum: 3 games

Field Goal Pct	CL	POS	G	FG	FGA	PCT
1 **Jarvis Basnight**, UNLV	JR	F	5	18	23	78.3
2 **Kevin Gamble**, Iowa	SR	G	4	32	41	78.0
3 **Joe Wolf**, North Carolina	SR	F	4	23	33	69.7
4 **Derrick McKey**, Alabama	JR	F/C	3	21	32	65.6
5 **Darryl Wright**, Providence	SO	G	5	17	26	65.4

Minimum: 15 made and 3 games

Free Throw Pct	CL	POS	G	FT	FTA	PCT
1 **Derrick McKey**, Alabama	JR	F/C	3	19	19	100.0
2 **Reggie Williams**, Georgetown	SR	F	4	27	30	90.0
3 **Rick Calloway**, Indiana	SO	G/F	6	15	17	88.2
B.J. Armstrong, Iowa	SO	G	4	15	17	88.2
David Rivers, Notre Dame	JR	G	3	15	17	88.2

Minimum: 15 made

Three-Point FG Pct	CL	POS	G	3FG	3FGA	PCT
1 **Ranzino Smith**, North Carolina	SR	F	4	6	6	100.0
2 **Tommy Amaker**, Duke	SR	G	3	6	8	75.0
3 **Darryl Wright**, Providence	SO	G	5	7	10	70.0
4 **Billy Donovan**, Providence	SR	G	5	14	22	63.6
5 **Steve Alford**, Indiana	SR	G	6	21	34	61.8

Minimum: 6 made and 3 games

Rebounds Per Game	CL	POS	G	REB	RPG
1 **Derrick Coleman**, Syracuse	FR	C	6	73	12.2
2 **Harvey Grant**, Oklahoma	JR	F	3	32	10.7
3 **Armon Gilliam**, UNLV	SR	F	5	52	10.4
4 **Dean Garrett**, Indiana	JR	C	6	55	9.2
5 **Fennis Dembo**, Wyoming	JR	F	3	27	9.0
Eric Leckner, Wyoming	JR	C	3	27	9.0

Minimum: 3 games

TEAM LEADERS

Scoring	G	PTS	PPG
1 **North Carolina**	4	371	92.8
2 **Alabama**	3	271	90.3
3 **Iowa**	4	357	89.3
4 **Indiana**	6	535	89.2
5 **UNLV**	5	444	88.8
6 **Oklahoma**	3	261	87.0
7 **Providence**	5	434	86.8
8 **Syracuse**	6	499	83.2
9 **Florida**	3	248	82.7
10 **Georgetown**	4	300	75.0

Minimum: 3 games

FG Pct	G	FG	FGA	PCT
1 **Alabama**	3	99	169	58.6
2 **North Carolina**	4	137	246	55.7
3 **Indiana**	6	195	352	55.4
4 **DePaul**	3	83	151	55.0
5 **Iowa**	4	130	237	54.9

Minimum: 3 games

3-Pt FG Pct	G	3FG	3FGA	PCT
1 **Indiana**	6	21	40	52.5
2 **Alabama**	3	23	45	51.1
3 **Oklahoma**	3	18	36	50.0
Duke	3	16	32	50.0
Notre Dame	3	11	22	50.0

Minimum: 3 games

FT Pct	G	FT	FTA	PCT
1 **Notre Dame**	3	47	55	85.5
2 **Alabama**	3	50	59	84.8
3 **Indiana**	6	124	156	79.5
4 **Florida**	3	47	63	74.6
5 **Wyoming**	3	52	70	74.3

Minimum: 3 games

Rebounds	G	REB	RPG
1 **Indiana**	6	223	37.2
2 **Syracuse**	6	221	36.8
3 **UNLV**	5	178	35.6
4 **Oklahoma**	3	106	35.3
5 **Iowa**	4	138	34.5

Minimum: 3 games

ALL-TOURNAMENT TEAM

PLAYER	CL	POS	HT	SCHOOL	RPG	PPG
Keith Smart*	JR	G	6-1	Indiana	4.5	15.0
Steve Alford	SR	G	6-2	Indiana	2.3	23.0
Derrick Coleman	FR	C	6-9	Syracuse	12.2	10.5
Sherman Douglas	SO	G	6-0	Syracuse	4.0	16.7
Armon Gilliam	SR	F	6-9	UNLV	10.4	26.6

ALL-REGIONAL TEAMS

East

PLAYER	CL	POS	HT	SCHOOL	RPG	PPG
Rony Seikaly*	JR	C	6-10	Syracuse	9.3	26.0
Derrick Coleman	FR	C	6-9	Syracuse	10.5	10.8
Sherman Douglas	SO	G	6-0	Syracuse	2.8	17.0
J.R. Reid	FR	F/C	6-9	North Carolina	7.0	21.0
David Rivers	JR	G	6-0	Notre Dame	2.7	24.7

Midwest

PLAYER	CL	POS	HT	SCHOOL	RPG	PPG
Nikita Wilson*	SR	F/C	6-7	LSU	7.0	19.5
Steve Alford	SR	G	6-2	Indiana	1.8	20.5
Tommy Amaker	SR	G	6-0	Duke	2.7	18.0
Rick Calloway	SO	G/F	6-6	Indiana	8.5	16.8
Anthony Wilson	SR	G	6-4	LSU	4.5	18.3

Southeast

PLAYER	CL	POS	HT	SCHOOL	RPG	PPG
Billy Donovan*	SR	G	6-0	Providence	3.5	26.5
Danny Manning	JR	F	6-11	Kansas	7.7	25.7
Reggie Williams	SR	F	6-7	Georgetown	8.3	26.0
Darryl Wright	SO	G	6-5	Providence	2.0	11.8
Steve Wright	JR	C	6-9	Providence	4.0	9.8

West

PLAYER	CL	POS	HT	SCHOOL	RPG	PPG
Armon Gilliam*	SR	F	6-9	UNLV	10.5	25.3
B.J. Armstrong	SO	G	6-2	Iowa	2.0	13.0
Fennis Dembo	JR	F	6-5	Wyoming	9.0	28.0
Kevin Gamble	SR	G	6-5	Iowa	2.8	19.0
Tim McCalister	SR	G	6-3	Oklahoma	4.3	23.3

* Most outstanding player

1987 NCAA TOURNAMENT BOX SCORES

UNLV 92-78 Wyoming

	1H	2H
UNLV	38	54
Wyoming	39	39

UNLV	MIN	FG	3FG	FT	REB	A	ST	BL	PF	TP
Armon Gilliam	39	17-24	0-0	4-7	13	4	1	1	3	38
Freddie Banks	34	5-16	2-10	2-2	3	2	1	0	1	14
Gary Graham	26	2-8	1-5	8-8	0	1	1	0	4	13
Jarvis Basnight	26	4-7	0-0	0-1	5	0	0	0	3	8
Eldridge Hudson	14	3-5	0-0	0-1	2	0	1	0	1	6
David Willard	6	2-2	0-0	2-2	3	0	0	0	5	6
Gerald Paddio	15	2-9	1-7	0-0	4	2	1	1	2	5
Mark Wade	37	1-2	0-1	0-1	4	9	5	0	2	2
Richard Robinson	3	0-0	0-0	0-0	1	0	0	0	0	0
TOTALS	200	36-73	4-23	16-22	35	18	10	2	21	92
Percentages		49.3	17.4	72.7						

Coach: Jerry Tarkanian

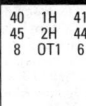

WYOMING	MIN	FG	3FG	FT	REB	A	ST	BL	PF	TP
Fennis Dembo	39	10-15	2-4	5-9	9	4	2	0	4	27
Eric Leckner	34	7-17	0-0	4-6	7	0	1	0	4	18
Turk Boyd	34	5-6	0-1	4-4	2	2	1	0	3	14
Willie Jones	29	3-6	1-1	3-4	6	5	2	2	3	10
Sean Dent	35	3-6	0-0	0-0	1	6	1	1	5	6
Tim Hunt	1	1-1	1-1	0-0	0	1	0	0	0	3
Reggie Fox	11	0-3	0-2	0-1	2	1	1	1	3	0
Jonathan Sommers	11	0-1	0-0	0-0	2	1	0	0	0	0
David Lodgins	5	0-1	0-0	0-0	2	0	0	0	2	0
Quinn Worth	1	0-0	0-0	0-0	0	0	0	0	0	0
TOTALS	200	29-56	4-9	16-24	31	20	8	4	24	78
Percentages		51.8	44.4	66.7						

Coach: Jim Brandenburg

Officials: Sam Lickliter, John Moreau, Jody Silvester
Technicals: UNLV (Hudson, Banks)
Attendance: 23,035

Iowa 93-91 Oklahoma

	1H	2H	OT1
Iowa	40	45	8
Oklahoma	41	44	6

IOWA	MIN	FG	3FG	FT	REB	A	ST	BL	PF	TP
Kevin Gamble	31	11-13	2-2	2-6	3	4	2	1	1	26
B.J. Armstrong	38	4-8	2-4	6-6	3	10	1	0	1	16
Roy Marble	43	4-13	0-0	3-5	7	2	0	0	2	11
Gerry Wright	26	4-9	0-0	2-2	5	1	0	1	5	10
Al Lorenzen	10	3-5	0-0	4-4	5	0	0	0	3	10
Brad Lohaus	33	4-8	1-2	0-0	5	3	1	1	2	9
Ed Horton	19	2-5	0-0	2-2	4	1	2	0	4	6
Jeff Moe	18	2-8	0-3	1-2	3	0	0	0	1	5
Michael Reaves	6	0-0	0-0	0-0	1	0	0	0	0	0
Bill Jones	1	0-0	0-0	0-0	0	0	0	0	1	0
TOTALS	225	34-69	5-11	20-27	36	21	6	3	20	93
Percentages		49.3	45.5	74.1						

Coach: Tom Davis

OKLAHOMA	MIN	FG	3FG	FT	REB	A	ST	BL	PF	TP
Tim McCalister	45	9-18	7-11	1-5	6	3	4	0	2	26
David Johnson	36	8-12	0-0	4-8	12	0	1	0	3	20
Darryl Kennedy	40	8-16	0-0	0-1	3	4	1	0	4	16
Harvey Grant	36	6-12	0-0	3-3	7	1	0	3	4	15
Ricky Grace	26	2-4	0-2	2-2	0	8	7	0	4	6
Dave Sieger	25	2-6	0-1	2-4	3	5	0	0	1	6
Stacey King	13	1-4	0-0	0-1	2	0	1	2	2	2
Chuck Watson	4	0-0	0-0	0-0	0	0	0	0	1	0
TOTALS	225	36-72	7-14	12-24	33	21	14	5	21	91
Percentages		50.0	50.0	50.0						

Coach: Billy Tubbs

Officials: Gerry Donaghy, Luis Grillo, Don Rutledge
Technicals: None
Attendance: 23,035

Indiana 88-82 Duke

	1H	2H
Indiana	49	39
Duke	39	43

INDIANA	MIN	FG	3FG	FT	REB	A	ST	BL	PF	TP
Rick Calloway	39	8-13	0-0	5-6	8	2	0	0	2	21
Keith Smart	30	8-11	0-0	5-6	7	3	1	0	3	21
Steve Alford	38	6-16	1-3	5-7	2	5	0	0	2	18
Darryl Thomas	22	6-10	0-0	3-3	3	0	2	1	4	15
Dean Garrett	39	4-7	0-0	3-5	9	0	0	3	2	11
Steve Eyl	14	0-0	0-0	2-4	5	3	1	0	1	2
Joe Hillman	12	0-0	0-0	0-0	2	3	0	0	1	0
Todd Meier	4	0-0	0-0	0-0	0	0	0	0	1	0
David Minor	1	0-0	0-0	0-0	0	0	0	0	0	0
Kreigh Smith	1	0-0	0-0	0-0	0	0	0	0	0	0
TOTALS	200	32-57	1-3	23-31	36	16	4	4	16	88
Percentages		56.1	33.3	74.2						

Coach: Bob Knight

DUKE	MIN	FG	3FG	FT	REB	A	ST	BL	PF	TP
Tommy Amaker	40	8-17	3-3	4-4	2	3	1	0	1	23
Danny Ferry	37	7-13	4-4	2-3	7	4	0	0	3	20
Kevin Strickland	32	5-15	1-4	0-0	6	1	1	1	5	11
John Smith	18	4-6	0-0	3-4	0	1	0	0	5	11
Robert Brickey	20	3-8	0-0	1-2	5	0	1	1	3	7
Billy King	28	3-5	0-0	0-0	4	1	2	0	3	6
Alaa Abdelnaby	7	2-3	0-0	0-0	0	0	0	0	1	4
Quin Snyder	15	0-0	0-0	0-0	0	2	0	1	3	0
Martin Nessley	3	0-0	0-0	0-0	1	0	0	0	1	0
TOTALS	200	32-67	8-11	10-13	25	12	5	3	25	82
Percentages		47.8	72.7	76.9						

Coach: Mike Krzyzewski

Officials: Don Shea, Gene Monje, James Howell
Technicals: None
Attendance: 16,902

LSU 63-58 DePaul

	1H	2H
LSU	38	25
DePaul	34	24

LSU	MIN	FG	3FG	FT	REB	A	ST	BL	PF	TP
Nikita Wilson	40	12-19	0-0	0-0	6	0	0	-	2	24
Anthony Wilson	40	7-20	3-9	0-0	5	3	0	-	1	17
Bernard Woodside	33	5-8	0-0	1-1	7	4	1	-	3	11
Jose Vargas	16	4-6	0-0	1-4	1	1	0	-	3	9
Oliver Brown	31	1-5	0-0	0-2	9	4	3	-	3	2
Darryl Joe	32	0-6	0-4	0-0	2	8	5	-	4	0
Fess Irvin	8	0-0	0-0	0-0	1	1	0	-	0	0
TOTALS	200	29-64	3-13	2-7	31	21	9	-	16	63
Percentages		45.3	23.1	28.6						

Coach: Dale Brown

DEPAUL	MIN	FG	3FG	FT	REB	A	ST	BL	PF	TP
Dallas Comegys	37	7-13	0-0	0-0	8	1	1	3	3	14
Kevin Edwards	37	4-7	1-3	3-4	1	1	0	0	2	12
Terence Greene	28	4-11	1-2	1-2	5	1	0	0	2	10
Rod Strickland	36	4-9	1-2	0-2	2	4	1	0	1	9
Stanley Brundy	26	3-3	0-0	0-0	5	1	3	0	4	6
Kevin Golden	17	2-4	0-0	2-2	1	0	0	0	2	6
Andy Laux	19	0-0	0-0	1-2	2	0	0	0	2	1
TOTALS	200	24-47	3-7	7-12	24	8	5	3	16	58
Percentages		51.1	42.9	58.3						

Coach: Joey Meyer

Officials: James Burr, Paul Housman, Tom Fraim
Technicals: None
Attendance: 16,902

Georgetown 70-57 Kansas

	1H	2H
Georgetown	34	36
Kansas	29	28

GEORGETOWN	MIN	FG	3FG	FT	REB	A	ST	BL	PF	TP
Reggie Williams	39	8-21	2-7	16-18	9	1	4	1	2	34
Charles Smith	17	5-9	1-2	2-2	2	0	1	1	2	13
Perry McDonald	34	2-3	0-0	6-11	7	0	0	1	0	10
Mark Tillmon	23	3-5	0-0	1-1	3	0	1	0	3	7
Anthony Allen	20	1-1	0-0	1-2	5	0	0	1	2	3
Ralph Highsmith	14	1-2	0-0	0-1	4	0	0	0	4	2
Bobby Winston	25	0-1	0-0	1-2	2	4	0	0	1	1
Dwayne Bryant	16	0-1	0-0	0-0	2	1	0	0	0	0
Jaren Jackson	6	0-0	0-0	0-0	1	0	1	0	1	0
Johnathan Edwards	3	0-0	0-0	0-0	1	0	0	0	1	0
Ben Gillery	2	0-0	0-0	0-0	1	0	0	0	0	0
Sam Jefferson	1	0-0	0-0	0-0	0	0	0	0	0	0
TOTALS	200	20-43	3-9	27-37	37	6	7	4	16	70
Percentages		46.5	33.3	73.0						

Coach: John Thompson Jr.

KANSAS	MIN	FG	3FG	FT	REB	A	ST	BL	PF	TP
Danny Manning	40	9-16	0-0	5-9	12	0	0	0	4	23
Cedric Hunter	34	4-12	0-0	1-2	4	1	1	0	1	9
Chris Piper	34	3-7	0-0	0-0	3	2	1	2	5	6
Mark Turgeon	27	2-5	2-4	0-0	2	4	0	0	2	6
Keith Harris	19	2-3	0-0	1-2	3	2	2	0	2	5
Kevin Pritchard	20	2-4	0-1	0-0	1	2	0	0	4	4
Jeff Gueldner	5	1-2	1-2	0-0	0	1	0	0	2	3
Scooter Barry	2	0-0	0-0	1-3	2	1	0	0	1	1
Mark Pellock	11	0-1	0-0	0-0	1	1	1	0	2	0
Milt Newton	8	0-4	0-0	0-0	0	0	0	0	2	0
TOTALS	200	23-54	3-7	8-16	28	14	5	2	25	57
Percentages		42.6	42.9	50.0						

Coach: Larry Brown

Officials: Joe Forte, Paul Galvan, Booker Turner
Technicals: Kansas (bench)

Providence 103-82 Alabama

	1H	2H
Providence	49	54
Alabama	41	41

PROVIDENCE	MIN	FG	3FG	FT	REB	A	ST	BL	PF	TP
Billy Donovan	30	6-7	5-6	9-10	3	10	1	0	5	26
Delray Brooks	36	7-11	5-6	4-5	7	4	2	0	2	23
Steve Wright	24	7-9	0-0	1-1	5	0	0	1	3	15
Darryl Wright	12	5-6	1-2	2-4	2	0	0	0	1	13
Ernie Lewis	28	3-6	3-6	0-0	3	3	0	0	5	9
Dave Kipfer	25	3-5	0-0	3-5	1	1	0	0	5	9
Marty Conlon	14	1-1	0-0	4-4	4	2	0	0	1	6
Carlton Screen	14	1-2	0-0	0-1	0	4	0	0	1	2
Jacek Duda	16	0-1	0-0	0-0	3	0	0	0	1	0
Dave Snedeker	1	0-0	0-0	0-0	1	0	0	0	0	0
TOTALS	200	33-48	14-20	23-30	29	24	3	1	24	103
Percentages		68.8	70.0	76.7						

Coach: Rick Pitino

ALABAMA	MIN	FG	3FG	FT	REB	A	ST	BL	PF	TP
Jim Farmer	36	7-19	2-9	8-8	1	3	2	0	4	24
Michael Ansley	31	6-9	0-0	2-2	6	0	0	0	2	14
Mark Gottfried	27	5-10	4-9	0-2	3	4	0	0	5	14
Terry Coner	33	5-7	0-0	2-3	2	4	0	0	3	12
Derrick McKey	37	3-6	0-1	5-5	4	2	1	1	5	11
James Jackson	22	1-5	1-2	4-4	2	0	1	0	4	7
Keith Askins	14	0-3	0-2	0-0	3	0	2	0	3	0
TOTALS	200	27-59	7-23	21-24	21	13	6	1	26	82
Percentages		45.8	30.4	87.5						

Coach: Wimp Sanderson

Officials: Bob Dibler, Dick Paparo, Dave Libbey
Technicals: None

NORTH CAROLINA	MIN	FG	3FG	FT	REB	A	ST	BL	PF	TP
J.R. Reid	35	15-18	0-0	1-3	5	0	3	1	1	31
Joe Wolf	33	6-7	1-1	0-1	7	3	1	0	1	13
Dave Popson	23	5-7	0-0	1-1	1	1	1	0	4	11
Jeff Lebo	38	2-5	0-2	3-4	2	0	0	1	1	7
Kenny Smith	34	2-8	0-4	0-0	0	12	0	0	3	4
Scott Williams	15	2-3	0-0	0-0	2	0	0	1	2	4
Steve Bucknall	14	2-3	0-0	0-0	1	1	0	0	3	4
Ranzino Smith	8	0-1	0-0	0-0	0	0	0	0	0	0
TOTALS	**200**	**34-52**	**1-7**	**5-9**	**18**	**17**	**5**	**3**	**15**	**74**
Percentages		65.4	14.3	55.6						

Coach: Dean Smith

74-68

36	1H	26
38	2H	42

SWEET 16

NOTRE DAME	MIN	FG	3FG	FT	REB	A	ST	BL	PF	TP
David Rivers	40	8-16	3-6	4-4	0	2	1	0	3	23
Donald Royal	36	7-12	0-0	5-7	10	1	0	0	4	19
Mark Stevenson	34	7-14	0-0	0-0	4	0	2	0	1	14
Gary Voce	36	3-5	0-0	2-2	6	1	1	1	3	8
Scott Hicks	38	2-9	0-1	0-0	5	3	1	0	2	4
Sean Connor	9	0-0	0-0	0-0	0	2	0	0	1	0
Jamere Jackson	3	0-0	0-0	0-0	0	0	0	0	0	0
Scott Paddock	3	0-0	0-0	0-0	1	0	0	0	0	0
Michael Smith	1	0-0	0-0	0-0	0	0	0	0	0	0
TOTALS	**200**	**27-56**	**3-7**	**11-13**	**26**	**9**	**5**	**1**	**14**	**68**
Percentages		48.2	42.9	84.6						

Coach: Digger Phelps

Officials: John Clougherty, Ly Shortnacy, Ror Spitler
Technicals: None
Attendance: 19,552

SYRACUSE	MIN	FG	3FG	FT	REB	A	ST	BL	PF	TP
Rony Seikaly	38	14-20	0-0	5-6	9	0	0	2	3	33
Howard Triche	39	8-12	0-0	1-1	4	5	0	0	2	17
Derrick Coleman	38	4-9	0-0	7-8	9	2	1	1	2	15
Greg Monroe	38	5-8	0-2	2-2	3	2	1	0	0	12
Sherman Douglas	36	4-12	0-2	2-3	4	10	0	0	3	10
Stephen Thompson	7	0-0	0-0	0-0	0	0	0	0	0	0
Derek Brower	4	0-0	0-0	0-0	1	1	0	0	1	0
TOTALS	**200**	**35-61**	**0-4**	**17-20**	**30**	**20**	**2**	**3**	**11**	**87**
Percentages		57.4	0.0	85.0						

Coach: Jim Boeheim

87-81

40	1H	33
47	2H	48

SWEET 16

FLORIDA	MIN	FG	3FG	FT	REB	A	ST	BL	PF	TP
Vernon Maxwell	35	11-23	3-6	0-0	4	0	1	0	1	25
Andrew Moten	35	7-18	1-7	3-4	2	2	4	0	3	18
Pat Lawrence	25	5-9	4-6	0-0	4	3	1	0	3	14
Kenny McClary	22	2-6	0-0	3-4	6	1	0	2	4	7
Dwayne Schintzius	29	3-10	0-0	0-0	11	3	1	3	5	6
Clifford Lett	9	2-2	1-1	1-2	1	0	0	0	2	6
Joe Lawrence	14	1-2	1-2	0-0	0	0	0	0	0	3
Chris Capers	6	1-1	0-0	0-0	1	0	1	0	0	2
Melvin Jones	15	0-3	0-0	0-0	2	2	1	0	1	0
Ronnie Montgomery	10	0-0	0-0	0-0	0	2	0	1	0	0
TOTALS	**200**	**32-74**	**10-22**	**7-10**	**31**	**13**	**9**	**6**	**19**	**81**
Percentages		43.2	45.5	70.0						

Coach: Norm Sloan

Officials: Jim Bain, Nolan Fine, Rusty Herring
Technicals: None
Attendance: 19,552

UNLV	MIN	FG	3FG	FT	REB	A	ST	BL	PF	TP
Armon Gilliam	38	11-16	0-0	5-6	10	0	2	2	4	27
Gerald Paddio	29	7-16	4-11	2-2	4	2	0	0	3	20
Freddie Banks	37	5-20	4-13	3-5	3	5	0	0	1	17
Gary Graham	14	3-10	2-5	2-2	1	2	0	0	4	10
Jarvis Basnight	25	3-3	0-0	1-2	2	0	1	0	4	7
Mark Wade	35	1-2	1-1	0-0	4	12	2	0	4	3
Eldridge Hudson	15	0-1	0-0	0-0	6	1	0	0	3	0
Richard Robinson	4	0-0	0-0	0-0	0	0	1	1	0	0
David Willard	2	0-0	0-0	0-0	1	0	0	0	2	0
Lawrence West	1	0-0	0-0	0-0	0	0	0	0	1	0
TOTALS	**200**	**30-68**	**11-30**	**13-17**	**31**	**22**	**6**	**3**	**26**	**84**
Percentages		44.1	36.7	76.5						

Coach: Jerry Tarkanian

84-81

42	1H	58
42	2H	23

ELITE 8

IOWA	MIN	FG	3FG	FT	REB	A	ST	BL	PF	TP
B.J. Armstrong	32	6-12	0-1	6-7	2	2	1	-	1	18
Kevin Gamble	27	7-11	1-2	3-3	3	2	1	-	4	18
Brad Lohaus	29	4-6	0-1	4-5	7	1	1	-	2	12
Roy Marble	35	3-11	0-1	3-7	6	5	1	-	3	9
Gerry Wright	26	3-5	0-0	2-4	3	4	2	-	3	8
Ed Horton	14	4-5	0-0	0-1	4	1	0	-	2	8
Jeff Moe	16	1-2	1-1	1-2	1	0	0	-	3	4
Michael Reaves	8	2-2	0-0	0-0	1	1	1	-	1	4
Al Lorenzen	11	0-0	0-0	0-0	1	2	0	-	3	0
Bill Jones	2	0-0	0-0	0-0	0	0	0	-	0	0
TOTALS	**200**	**30-54**	**2-6**	**19-29**	**28**	**18**	**7**	**-**	**22**	**81**
Percentages		55.6	33.3	65.5						

Coach: Tom Davis

Officials: Luis Grillo, Don Rutledge, Jody Silvester
Technicals: None
Attendance: 22,914

INDIANA	MIN	FG	3FG	FT	REB	A	ST	BL	PF	TP
Steve Alford	40	4-9	2-4	10-10	0	7	0	0	1	20
Dean Garrett	38	8-10	0-0	1-3	15	1	0	3	3	17
Darryl Thomas	39	5-11	0-0	6-6	7	0	1	0	3	16
Rick Calloway	37	5-10	0-0	1-2	5	5	1	0	4	11
Keith Smart	39	4-10	0-1	2-2	2	1	1	0	2	10
Joe Hillman	1	1-1	0-0	1-1	0	0	0	0	0	3
Steve Eyl	5	0-1	0-0	0-0	3	0	1	0	0	0
Kreigh Smith	1	0-1	0-1	0-0	1	0	0	0	0	0
TOTALS	**200**	**27-53**	**2-6**	**21-24**	**33**	**14**	**4**	**3**	**13**	**77**
Percentages		50.9	33.3	87.5						

Coach: Bob Knight

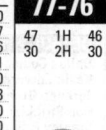

77-76

47	1H	46
30	2H	30

ELITE 8

LSU	MIN	FG	3FG	FT	REB	A	ST	BL	PF	TP
Nikita Wilson	40	9-16	0-0	2-2	6	0	0	0	3	20
Anthony Wilson	40	6-15	2-9	1-2	4	1	0	0	2	15
Fess Irvin	22	6-7	2-3	0-1	0	3	0	0	1	14
Bernard Woodside	26	6-10	1-1	0-1	7	1	1	0	5	13
Oliver Brown	34	3-6	0-0	0-2	7	8	3	0	2	6
Joe Darryl	21	1-7	1-4	1-2	2	2	1	0	3	4
Jose Vargas	17	2-4	0-0	0-0	1	2	1	1	3	4
TOTALS	**200**	**33-65**	**6-17**	**4-10**	**27**	**17**	**6**	**1**	**19**	**76**
Percentages		50.8	35.3	40.0						

Coach: Dale Brown

Officials: James Burr, Paul Housman, Tom Fraim
Technicals: Indiana (bench)
Attendance: 16,817

PROVIDENCE	MIN	FG	3FG	FT	REB	A	ST	BL	PF	TP
Billy Donovan	37	2-5	0-1	16-18	4	6	1	0	3	20
Darryl Wright	22	6-6	4-4	4-5	2	0	0	1	3	20
Steve Wright	27	5-11	0-0	2-2	3	0	1	7	3	12
Dave Kipfer	25	4-7	0-0	3-3	5	1	1	0	3	11
Carlton Screen	16	2-3	0-0	5-7	4	2	1	0	0	9
Ernie Lewis	17	3-7	1-3	0-0	4	2	0	0	5	7
Marty Conlon	15	3-5	0-0	1-1	3	1	0	0	1	7
Abdul Shamsid-deen	6	0-0	0-0	2-2	1	0	0	2	0	2
Delray Brooks	27	0-2	0-1	0-0	3	2	2	0	3	0
Jacek Duda	7	0-0	0-0	0-0	2	0	0	0	1	0
Bryan Benham	1	0-0	0-0	0-0	0	0	0	0	0	0
TOTALS	**200**	**25-46**	**5-9**	**33-38**	**31**	**14**	**6**	**10**	**22**	**88**
Percentages		54.3	55.6	86.8						

Coach: Rick Pitino

88-73

54	1H	37
34	2H	36

ELITE 8

GEORGETOWN	MIN	FG	3FG	FT	REB	A	ST	BL	PF	TP
Reggie Williams	29	9-23	2-8	5-6	9	1	1	0	4	25
Mark Tillmon	26	4-13	1-4	1-2	2	0	1	0	3	10
Charles Smith	27	4-14	1-6	0-0	5	1	0	1	5	9
Perry McDonald	28	3-11	0-0	2-5	10	0	0	0	2	8
Dwayne Bryant	20	2-6	0-2	4-4	3	2	1	0	3	8
Anthony Allen	23	1-2	0-0	5-6	4	0	1	3	3	7
Ralph Highsmith	9	1-1	0-0	0-0	5	0	0	0	1	2
Jaren Jackson	8	1-4	0-1	0-0	0	1	0	0	0	2
Johnathan Edwards	7	1-2	0-0	0-0	2	0	0	0	2	2
Bobby Winston	20	0-0	0-0	0-2	1	4	2	0	3	0
Ben Gillery	1	0-0	0-0	0-0	0	0	0	0	1	0
Sam Jefferson	1	0-0	0-0	0-0	0	0	0	0	0	0
Tom Lang	1	0-0	0-0	0-0	0	0	0	0	0	0
TOTALS	**200**	**26-76**	**4-21**	**17-25**	**41**	**9**	**6**	**4**	**27**	**73**
Percentages		34.2	19.0	68.0						

Coach: John Thompson Jr.

Officials: Joe Forte, Paul Galvan, Dick Paparo
Technicals: Georgetown (Smith), Providence (Donovan)
Attendance: 16,944

SYRACUSE	MIN	FG	3FG	FT	REB	A	ST	BL	PF	TP
Rony Seikaly	37	11-15	0-0	4-7	11	0	1	2	2	26
Sherman Douglas	38	6-13	0-1	2-5	3	9	2	0	3	14
Greg Monroe	29	3-8	2-5	4-4	1	2	0	0	4	12
Howard Triche	37	5-9	0-0	0-1	6	3	2	0	2	10
Derrick Coleman	38	2-10	0-0	4-6	14	3	2	3	2	8
Stephen Thompson	13	3-3	0-0	1-5	2	0	0	0	1	7
Derek Brower	6	1-2	0-0	0-1	1	0	0	0	2	2
Herman Harried	2	0-0	0-0	0-0	0	0	0	0	0	0
TOTALS	**200**	**31-60**	**2-6**	**15-29**	**38**	**17**	**7**	**5**	**16**	**79**
Percentages		51.7	33.3	51.7						

Coach: Jim Boeheim

79-75

41	1H	30
38	2H	45

ELITE 8

NORTH CAROLINA	MIN	FG	3FG	FT	REB	A	ST	BL	PF	TP
Kenny Smith	38	10-19	4-11	1-1	2	7	2	0	3	25
J.R. Reid	38	7-14	0-0	1-2	6	1	0	3	4	15
Joe Wolf	37	5-7	1-1	1-2	10	4	0	0	4	12
Ranzino Smith	17	4-5	3-3	0-0	1	2	1	0	0	11
Dave Popson	20	5-9	0-0	0-0	4	0	1	0	4	10
Jeff Lebo	28	0-5	0-5	2-2	3	4	0	0	3	2
Scott Williams	12	0-4	0-0	0-1	0	0	0	0	2	0
Steve Bucknall	10	0-1	0-0	0-0	0	0	0	0	3	0
TOTALS	**200**	**31-64**	**8-20**	**5-8**	**26**	**18**	**4**	**3**	**23**	**75**
Percentages		48.4	40.0	62.5						

Coach: Dean Smith

Officials: John Clougherty, Nolan Fine, Rusty Herring
Technicals: None
Attendance: 19,552

97-93 — FINAL 4

	1H	2H
Indiana	53	44
UNLV	47	46

INDIANA	MIN	FG	3FG	FT	REB	A	ST	BL	PF	TP
Steve Alford	37	10-19	2-4	11-13	4	2	0	0	4	33
Dean Garrett	40	7-10	0-0	4-5	11	1	0	2	2	18
Keith Smart	23	5-7	0-0	4-5	2	1	0	0	5	14
Rick Calloway	40	6-10	0-0	0-0	6	6	1	0	3	12
Steve Eyl	20	3-3	0-0	1-2	5	2	0	0	4	7
Joe Hillman	17	3-4	0-0	1-3	3	3	0	0	2	7
Darryl Thomas	18	3-5	0-0	0-0	4	1	0	0	3	6
Todd Meier	3	0-0	0-0	0-0	3	0	0	0	0	0
Kreigh Smith	2	0-2	0-0	0-0	1	0	0	0	0	0
TOTALS	**200**	**37-60**	**2-4**	**21-28**	**39**	**16**	**1**	**2**	**23**	**97**
Percentages		61.7	50.0	75.0						

Coach: Bob Knight

UNLV	MIN	FG	3FG	FT	REB	A	ST	BL	PF	TP
Freddie Banks	35	12-23	10-19	4-6	8	1	0	0	4	38
Armon Gilliam	39	14-26	0-0	4-6	10	1	0	3	3	32
Jarvis Basnight	22	3-4	0-0	0-1	2	1	0	0	5	6
Gerald Paddio	22	2-13	2-8	0-0	6	1	0	0	1	6
Eldridge Hudson	13	3-4	0-0	0-0	5	1	1	0	2	6
Mark Wade	35	1-6	1-6	1-2	4	18	4	0	4	4
Gary Graham	25	0-5	0-2	1-4	2	0	0	0	4	1
Richard Robinson	5	0-0	0-0	0-0	1	0	0	0	1	0
David Willard	4	0-1	0-0	0-0	0	0	0	0	2	0
TOTALS	**200**	**35-82**	**13-35**	**10-19**	**38**	**23**	**5**	**3**	**26**	**93**
Percentages		42.7	37.1	52.6						

Coach: Jerry Tarkanian

Officials: John Clougherty, Rusty Herring, Dick Paparo
Technicals: None
Attendance: 64,959

77-63 — FINAL 4

	1H	2H
Syracuse	36	41
Providence	26	37

SYRACUSE	MIN	FG	3FG	FT	REB	A	ST	BL	PF	TP
Greg Monroe	32	4-9	3-7	6-10	4	3	1	0	2	17
Rony Seikaly	31	4-11	0-0	8-11	6	2	0	2	3	16
Howard Triche	37	4-10	0-0	4-5	11	1	0	0	3	12
Sherman Douglas	35	5-11	0-1	2-6	11	6	2	0	3	12
Derrick Coleman	34	4-6	0-0	4-7	12	0	2	2	3	12
Stephen Thompson	15	3-5	0-0	1-3	5	0	0	0	1	7
Herman Harried	2	0-0	0-0	1-2	0	0	0	0	0	1
Derek Brower	14	0-1	0-0	0-0	4	1	2	0	2	0
TOTALS	**200**	**24-53**	**3-8**	**26-44**	**53**	**13**	**7**	**4**	**17**	**77**
Percentages		45.3	37.5	59.1						

Coach: Jim Boeheim

PROVIDENCE	MIN	FG	3FG	FT	REB	A	ST	BL	PF	TP
Carlton Screen	22	5-6	1-1	7-10	2	0	1	0	2	18
Delray Brooks	24	4-9	1-5	0-0	3	2	0	0	4	9
Billy Donovan	36	3-12	1-3	1-1	1	7	2	0	3	8
Dave Kipfer	29	4-10	0-0	0-1	5	0	2	0	4	8
Ernie Lewis	32	2-12	1-8	2-2	5	1	4	0	3	7
Jacek Duda	24	2-7	0-0	0-1	7	0	1	0	4	4
Darryl Wright	8	1-4	1-2	0-0	0	1	0	0	2	3
Marty Conlon	10	1-1	0-0	0-0	3	1	0	1	4	2
Steve Wright	9	1-3	0-0	0-0	4	0	1	1	5	2
Abdul Shamsid-deen	4	1-2	0-0	0-0	2	0	0	1	1	2
Dave Snedeker	2	0-0	0-0	0-0	0	0	0	0	1	0
TOTALS	**200**	**24-66**	**5-19**	**10-15**	**32**	**12**	**11**	**3**	**33**	**63**
Percentages		36.4	26.3	66.7						

Coach: Rick Pitino

Officials: Paul Galvan, Luis Grillo, Don Rutledge
Technicals: Syracuse (Coleman)
Attendance: 64,959

74-73 — NCAA FINAL 1987

	1H	2H
Indiana	34	40
Syracuse	33	40

INDIANA	MIN	FG	3FG	FT	REB	A	ST	BL	PF	TP
Steve Alford	40	8-15	7-10	0-0	3	5	2	0	2	23
Keith Smart	35	9-15	0-1	3-4	5	6	2	0	2	21
Darryl Thomas	40	8-18	0-0	4-7	7	1	0	0	1	20
Dean Garrett	33	5-10	0-0	0-0	10	0	0	3	4	10
Joe Hillman	20	0-1	0-0	0-0	2	6	3	0	2	0
Rick Calloway	14	0-3	0-0	0-0	2	1	0	0	3	0
Steve Eyl	13	0-0	0-0	0-0	1	1	0	0	2	0
Todd Meier	4	0-0	0-0	0-1	1	0	0	0	0	0
Kreigh Smith	1	0-0	0-0	0-0	0	0	0	0	1	0
TOTALS	**200**	**30-62**	**7-11**	**7-12**	**31**	**20**	**7**	**3**	**17**	**74**
Percentages		48.4	63.6	58.3						

Coach: Bob Knight

SYRACUSE	MIN	FG	3FG	FT	REB	A	ST	BL	PF	TP
Sherman Douglas	39	8-15	2-2	2-2	2	7	1	0	3	20
Rony Seikaly	34	7-13	0-0	4-6	10	1	1	3	3	18
Greg Monroe	32	5-11	2-8	0-1	2	3	2	0	1	12
Derrick Coleman	37	3-7	0-0	2-4	19	1	1	3	2	8
Howard Triche	32	3-9	0-0	2-4	1	1	0	0	4	8
Derek Brower	9	3-3	0-0	1-3	1	0	0	0	3	7
Stephen Thompson	17	0-2	0-0	0-0	3	1	0	1	0	0
TOTALS	**200**	**29-60**	**4-10**	**11-20**	**38**	**14**	**5**	**7**	**16**	**73**
Percentages		48.3	40.0	55.0						

Coach: Jim Boeheim

Officials: Joe Forte, Nolan Fine, Jody Silvester
Technicals: None
Attendance: 64,959

National Invitation Tournament (NIT)

First round: Nebraska d. Marquette 78-76, Boise State d. Utah 62-61, Washington d. Montana State 98-90, La Salle d. Villanova 86-84, Florida State d. Rhode Island 107-92, Cleveland State d. Chattanooga 92-73, Arkansas-Little Rock d. Baylor 42-41, Illinois State d. Akron 79-72, Vanderbilt d. Jacksonville 74-72, Stephen F. Austin d. James Madison 70-63, Niagara d. Seton Hall 74-65, Arkansas d. Arkansas State 67-64 (OT), Saint Louis d. Saint Peter's 76-60, Southern Miss d. Mississippi 93-75, Oregon State d. New Mexico 85-82, California d. Cal St. Fullerton 72-68

Second round: Illinois State d. Cleveland State 79-77, Arkansas-Little Rock d. Stephen F. Austin 54-48, Vanderbilt d. Florida State 109-92, Washington d. Boise State 73-68, La Salle d. Niagara 89-81, Nebraska d. Arkansas 78-71, Southern Miss d. Saint Louis 83-78, California d. Oregon State 65-62

Third round: La Salle d. Illinois State 70-50, Arkansas-Little Rock d. California 80-73, Southern Miss d. Vanderbilt 95-88, Nebraska d. Washington 81-76

Semifinals: La Salle d. Arkansas-Little Rock 92-73, Southern Miss d. Nebraska 82-75

Third place: Nebraska d. Arkansas-Little Rock 76-67

Championship: Southern Miss d. La Salle 84-80

MVP: Randolph Keys, Southern Miss

1987-88: Miracle Man

For Oklahoma, 1987-88 was about near misses. For Kansas it was about miracles. Oklahoma became the first school to reach the national championship game in both football and basketball in the same school year, but lost out on both titles. Kansas, under head coach Larry Brown, had a rocky regular season in which it went almost a month without a win over a D1 program. But the Jayhawks, led by forward Danny Manning, still managed to make the NCAA Tournament as a No. 6-seed. Then Danny and the Miracles rolled all the way to the Final Four in Kansas City, where they beat Duke and held off Big Eight rival Oklahoma for the title, 83-79.

Manning was selected the Tournament's Most Outstanding Player for setting a record with six blocked shots against Duke and scorching the Sooners for 31 points and 18 rebounds. Named the Naismith Player of the Year after averaging 24.8 ppg and 9.0 rpg, he was the top pick in the NBA draft, by the Los Angeles Clippers.

Major Conference Standings

AM. SOUTH	Conference W	L	PCT	Overall W	L	PCT
Louisiana Tech□	7	3	.700	22	9	.710
New Orleans□	7	3	.700	21	11	.656
Lamar	5	5	.500	20	11	.645
Arkansas State□	4	6	.400	21	14	.600
Tex.-Pan American	4	6	.400	14	14	.500
UL-Lafayette	3	7	.300	12	16	.429

Tournament: **Louisiana Tech d. New Orleans 66-56**

AMCU-8	Conference W	L	PCT	Overall W	L	PCT
Missouri State⊕	12	2	.857	22	7	.759
Cleveland State□	11	3	.786	22	8	.733
Wisconsin-Green Bay	9	5	.643	18	9	.667
Eastern Illinois	7	7	.500	17	11	.607
Western Illinois	6	8	.429	15	12	.556
Northern Iowa	4	10	.286	10	18	.357
Illinois-Chicago	4	10	.286	8	20	.286
Valparaiso	3	11	.214	12	16	.429

ATLANTIC 10	Conference W	L	PCT	Overall W	L	PCT
Temple⊕	18	0	1.000	32	2	.941
Rhode Island○	14	4	.778	28	7	.800
West Virginia□	12	6	.667	18	14	.563
Saint Joseph's	9	9	.500	15	14	.517
Penn State	9	9	.500	13	14	.481
St. Bonaventure	7	11	.389	13	15	.464
George Washington	7	11	.389	13	15	.464
Duquesne	6	12	.333	11	21	.344
Massachusetts	5	13	.278	10	17	.370
Rutgers	3	15	.167	7	22	.241

Tournament: **Temple d. Rhode Island 68-63**
Tournament MVP: **Tom Garrick**, Rhode Island

ACC	Conference W	L	PCT	Overall W	L	PCT
North Carolina○	11	3	.786	27	7	.794
NC State○⊗	10	4	.714	24	7	.774
Duke⊕	9	5	.643	28	7	.800
Georgia Tech○	8	6	.571	22	10	.688
Maryland○⊗	6	8	.429	18	13	.581
Virginia	5	9	.357	13	18	.419
Clemson□	4	10	.286	14	15	.483
Wake Forest	3	11	.214	10	18	.357

Tournament: **Duke d. North Carolina 65-61**
Tournament MVP: **Danny Ferry**, Duke

BIG EAST	Conference W	L	PCT	Overall W	L	PCT
Pittsburgh○	12	4	.750	24	7	.774
Syracuse⊕	11	5	.688	26	9	.743
Georgetown○	9	7	.563	20	10	.667
Villanova○	9	7	.563	24	13	.649
Seton Hall○	8	8	.500	22	13	.629
St. John's○	8	8	.500	17	12	.586
Boston College□	6	10	.375	18	15	.545
Providence	5	11	.313	11	17	.393
Connecticut□	4	12	.250	20	14	.588

Tournament: **Syracuse d. Villanova 85-68**
Tournament MVP: **Sherman Douglas**, Syracuse

BIG EIGHT	Conference W	L	PCT	Overall W	L	PCT
Oklahoma⊕	12	2	.857	35	4	.897
Kansas State○	11	3	.786	25	9	.735
Kansas○	9	5	.643	27	11	.711
Missouri○	7	7	.500	19	11	.633
Iowa State○	6	8	.429	20	12	.625
Oklahoma State	4	10	.286	14	16	.467
Nebraska	4	10	.286	13	18	.419
Colorado	3	11	.214	7	21	.250

Tournament: **Oklahoma d. Kansas State 88-83**
Tournament MVP: **Stacey King**, Oklahoma

BIG SKY	Conference W	L	PCT	Overall W	L	PCT
Boise State⊕	13	3	.813	24	6	.800
Idaho	11	5	.688	19	11	.633
Montana State	10	6	.625	19	11	.633
Idaho State	8	8	.500	15	13	.536
Nevada	8	8	.500	15	13	.536
Montana	7	9	.438	18	11	.621
Northern Arizona	7	9	.438	10	18	.357
Weber State	6	10	.375	9	21	.300
Eastern Washington	2	14	.125	6	21	.222

Tournament: **Boise State d. Montana State 63-61**
Tournament MVP: **Chris Childs**, Boise State

BIG SOUTH	Conference W	L	PCT	Overall W	L	PCT
Coastal Carolina	9	3	.750	17	11	.607
Charleston Southern	8	4	.667	17	12	.586
Radford	8	4	.667	16	14	.533
Winthrop	5	7	.417	17	13	.567
UNC Asheville	5	7	.417	13	15	.464
Augusta	4	8	.333	8	18	.308
Campbell	3	9	.250	11	16	.407

Tournament: **Winthrop d. Radford 71-56**
Tournament MVP: **Shaun Weiss**, Winthrop

BIG TEN	Conference W	L	PCT	Overall W	L	PCT
Purdue⊕	16	2	.889	29	4	.879
Michigan○	13	5	.722	26	8	.765
Iowa○	12	6	.667	24	10	.706
Illinois○	12	6	.667	23	10	.697
Indiana○	11	7	.611	19	10	.655
Ohio State□	9	9	.500	20	13	.606
Wisconsin	6	12	.333	12	16	.429
Michigan State	5	13	.278	10	18	.357
Minnesota	4	14	.222	10	18	.357
Northwestern	2	16	.111	7	21	.250

COLONIAL ATHLETIC	Conference W	L	PCT	Overall W	L	PCT
Richmond⊕	11	3	.786	26	7	.788
George Mason	9	5	.643	20	10	.667
American	9	5	.643	14	14	.500
UNC Wilmington	8	6	.571	15	14	.517
Navy	6	8	.429	12	16	.429
James Madison	5	9	.357	10	18	.357
William and Mary	5	9	.357	10	19	.345
East Carolina	3	11	.214	8	20	.286

Tournament: **Richmond d. George Mason 81-78**

EAST COAST	Conference W	L	PCT	Overall W	L	PCT
Lafayette	11	3	.786	19	10	.655
Delaware	9	5	.643	19	9	.679
Drexel	9	5	.643	18	10	.643
Lehigh⊕	8	6	.571	21	10	.677
Bucknell	7	7	.500	16	12	.571
Rider	6	8	.429	10	19	.345
Towson	4	10	.286	14	16	.467
Hofstra	2	12	.143	6	21	.222

Tournament: **Lehigh d. Towson 84-78**
Tournament MVP: **Mike Polaha**, Lehigh

ECAC METRO	Conference W	L	PCT	Overall W	L	PCT
Fairleigh Dickinson⊕	13	3	.813	23	7	.767
Marist	13	3	.813	18	9	.667
Monmouth	11	5	.688	16	13	.552
Robert Morris	9	7	.563	14	14	.500
Long Island	8	8	.500	14	14	.500
Loyola (MD)	6	10	.375	8	22	.267
St. Francis (NY)	5	11	.313	11	18	.379
Saint Francis (PA)	4	12	.250	7	20	.259
Wagner	3	13	.188	9	18	.333

Tournament: **Fairleigh Dickinson d. Monmouth 90-75**
Tournament MVP: **Jaime Latney**, Fairleigh Dickinson

ECAC NAC	Conference W	L	PCT	Overall W	L	PCT
Siena□	16	2	.889	23	6	.793
Boston U.⊕	14	4	.778	23	8	.742
Niagara	12	6	.667	15	15	.500
Hartford	12	6	.667	15	16	.484
Northeastern	11	7	.611	15	13	.536
Maine	10	8	.556	13	15	.464
Canisius	7	11	.389	7	20	.259
Colgate	3	15	.167	4	23	.148
New Hampshire	3	15	.167	4	25	.138
Vermont	2	16	.111	3	24	.111

Tournament: **Boston U. d. Niagara 79-68**
Tournament MVP: **Jeff Timberlake**, Boston U.

IVY	Conference W	L	PCT	Overall W	L	PCT
Cornell⊕	11	3	.786	17	10	.630
Dartmouth	10	4	.714	18	8	.692
Princeton	9	5	.643	17	9	.654
Yale	8	6	.571	12	14	.462
Penn	8	6	.571	10	16	.385
Harvard	6	8	.429	11	15	.423
Brown	2	12	.143	6	20	.231
Columbia	2	12	.143	6	20	.231

METRO	Conference W	L	PCT	Overall W	L	PCT
Louisville⊕	9	3	.750	24	11	.686
Florida State○	7	5	.583	19	11	.633
South Carolina	6	6	.500	19	10	.655
Virginia Tech	6	6	.500	19	10	.655
Memphis○	6	6	.500	20	12	.625
Southern Miss□	5	7	.417	19	11	.633
Cincinnati	3	9	.250	11	17	.393

Tournament: **Louisville d. Memphis 81-73**
Tournament MVP: **Herbert Crook**, Louisville

MEAC	Conference W	L	PCT	Overall W	L	PCT
La Salle⊕	14	0	1.000	24	10	.706
Saint Peter's	11	3	.786	20	9	.690
Fordham□	9	5	.643	18	15	.545
Holy Cross	8	6	.571	14	15	.483
Iona	5	9	.357	11	16	.407
Army	4	10	.286	9	19	.321
Fairfield	4	10	.286	8	20	.286
Manhattan	1	13	.071	7	23	.233

Tournament: **La Salle d. Fordham 79-70**
Tournament MVP: **Rich Tarr**, La Salle

MID-AMERICAN	Conference W	L	PCT	Overall W	L	PCT
Eastern Michigan⊕	14	2	.875	22	8	.733
Central Michigan	10	6	.625	19	13	.594
Ohio	9	7	.563	16	14	.533
Ball State	8	8	.500	14	14	.500
Bowling Green	7	9	.438	12	16	.429
Western Michigan	7	9	.438	12	17	.414
Kent State	6	10	.375	10	18	.357
Miami (OH)	6	10	.375	9	18	.333
Toledo	5	11	.313	15	12	.556

Tournament: **Eastern Michigan d. Ohio 94-80**
Tournament MVP: **Grant Long**, Eastern Michigan

⊕ Automatic NCAA Tournament bid ○ At-large NCAA Tournament bid □ NIT appearance ⊗ Team record doesn't reflect games forfeited or vacated. For adjusted record, see p. 521.

MID-EASTERN

	Conference			Overall		
	W	L	PCT	W	L	PCT
NC A&T⊕	16	0	1.000	26	3	.897
Florida A&M	11	5	.688	22	8	.733
South Carolina State	10	6	.625	16	13	.552
Howard	9	7	.563	16	13	.552
Coppin State	8	7	.533	13	14	.481
Morgan State	7	8	.467	13	17	.433
UMES	5	11	.313	7	20	.259
Bethune-Cookman	4	12	.250	6	21	.222
Delaware State	1	15	.063	3	25	.107

Tournament: **NC A&T d. Florida A&M 101-86**
Tournament MOP: **Claude Williams**, NC A&T

MCC

	Conference			Overall		
	W	L	PCT	W	L	PCT
Xavier⊕	9	1	.900	26	4	.867
Evansville□	6	4	.600	21	8	.724
Butler	5	5	.500	14	14	.500
Saint Louis	5	5	.500	14	14	.500
Loyola-Chicago	3	7	.300	13	16	.448
Detroit	2	8	.200	7	23	.233

Tournament: **Xavier d. Detroit 122-96**
Tournament MVP: **Byron Larkin**, Xavier

MISSOURI VALLEY

	Conference			Overall		
	W	L	PCT	W	L	PCT
Bradley⊕	12	2	.857	26	5	.839
Wichita State○	11	3	.786	20	10	.667
Illinois State□	9	5	.643	18	13	.581
Creighton	6	8	.429	16	16	.500
Southern Illinois	6	8	.429	12	16	.429
Drake	5	9	.357	14	14	.500
Tulsa	4	10	.286	8	20	.286
Indiana State	2	12	.143	7	21	.250

Tournament: **Bradley d. Illinois State 83-59**
Tournament MOP: **Hersey Hawkins**, Bradley

OHIO VALLEY

	Conference			Overall		
	W	L	PCT	W	L	PCT
Murray State⊕	13	1	.929	22	9	.710
Middle Tenn. State□	11	3	.786	23	11	.676
Eastern Kentucky	10	4	.714	18	11	.621
Austin Peay	10	4	.714	17	13	.567
Tennessee Tech	5	9	.357	12	16	.429
Tennessee State	4	10	.286	11	17	.393
Youngstown State	2	12	.143	7	21	.250
Morehead State	1	13	.071	5	22	.185

Tournament: **Murray State d. Austin Peay 73-70**
Tournament MVP: **Jeff Martin**, Murray State

PCAA

	Conference			Overall		
	W	L	PCT	W	L	PCT
UNLV○	15	3	.833	28	6	.824
UC Santa Barbara○	13	5	.722	22	8	.733
Utah State⊕	13	5	.722	21	10	.677
Long Beach State□	11	7	.611	17	12	.586
UC Irvine	9	9	.500	16	14	.533
New Mexico State	8	10	.444	16	16	.500
San Jose State	8	10	.444	14	15	.483
Cal St. Fullerton	7	11	.389	12	17	.414
Fresno State	6	12	.333	9	19	.321
Pacific	0	18	.000	5	24	.172

Tournament: **Utah State d. UC Irvine 86-79**
Tournament MVP: **Wayne Engelstad**, UC Irvine

PAC-10

	Conference			Overall		
	W	L	PCT	W	L	PCT
Arizona⊕	17	1	.944	35	3	.921
Oregon State○	12	6	.667	20	11	.645
UCLA	12	6	.667	16	14	.533
Stanford□	11	7	.611	21	12	.636
Oregon□	10	8	.556	16	14	.533
Washington State	7	11	.389	13	16	.448
Arizona State	6	12	.333	13	16	.448
Washington	5	13	.278	10	19	.345
California	5	13	.278	9	20	.310
Southern California	5	13	.278	7	21	.250

Tournament: **Arizona d. Oregon State 93-67**
Tournament MOP: **Sean Elliott**, Arizona

SEC

	Conference			Overall		
	W	L	PCT	W	L	PCT
Kentucky⊕⊗	13	5	.722	27	6	.818
Florida○⊗	11	7	.611	23	12	.657
Auburn○	11	7	.611	19	11	.633
Vanderbilt○	10	8	.556	20	11	.645
LSU○	10	8	.556	16	14	.533
Tennessee□	9	9	.500	16	13	.552
Georgia□	8	10	.444	20	16	.556
Mississippi State	6	12	.333	14	15	.483
Alabama	6	12	.333	14	17	.452
Mississippi	6	12	.333	13	16	.448

Tournament: **Kentucky d. Georgia 62-57**
Tournament MVP: **Rex Chapman**, Kentucky

SOUTHERN

	Conference			Overall		
	W	L	PCT	W	L	PCT
Marshall□	14	2	.875	24	8	.750
Furman	11	5	.688	18	10	.643
Davidson	9	7	.563	15	13	.536
East Tenn. State	9	7	.563	14	15	.483
Chattanooga⊕	8	8	.500	20	13	.606
Appalachian State	8	8	.500	16	13	.552
VMI	6	10	.375	13	17	.433
The Citadel	5	11	.313	8	20	.286
Western Carolina	2	14	.125	8	19	.296

Tournament: **Chattanooga d. VMI 75-61**
Tournament MOP: **Benny Green**, Chattanooga

SOUTHLAND

	Conference			Overall		
	W	L	PCT	W	L	PCT
North Texas⊕	12	2	.857	17	13	.567
UL-Monroe□	10	4	.714	21	9	.700
Sam Houston State	9	5	.643	14	14	.500
Northwestern St. (LA)	7	7	.500	16	12	.571
Texas State	6	8	.429	9	22	.290
Stephen F. Austin	4	10	.286	10	18	.357
McNeese State	4	10	.286	7	22	.241
Texas-Arlington	4	10	.286	7	22	.241

Tournament: **North Texas d. UL-Monroe 87-70**
Tournament MVP: **Tony Worrell**, North Texas

SOUTHWEST

	Conference			Overall		
	W	L	PCT	W	L	PCT
SMU⊕	12	4	.750	28	7	.800
Arkansas○	11	5	.688	21	9	.700
Baylor○	11	5	.688	23	11	.676
Houston□	10	6	.625	18	13	.581
Texas	10	6	.625	16	13	.552
Texas A&M	8	8	.500	16	15	.516
Texas Tech	4	12	.250	9	19	.321
TCU	3	13	.188	9	19	.321
Rice	3	13	.188	6	21	.222

Tournament: **SMU d. Baylor 75-64**
Tournament MVP: **Micheal Williams**, Baylor

SWAC

	Conference			Overall		
	W	L	PCT	W	L	PCT
Southern U.⊕	12	2	.857	24	7	.774
Texas Southern	11	3	.786	21	8	.724
Grambling	9	5	.643	13	17	.433
Jackson State	7	7	.500	13	15	.464
Alabama State	5	9	.357	8	20	.286
Miss. Valley State	5	9	.357	8	20	.286
Alcorn State	5	9	.357	8	21	.276
Prairie View A&M	2	12	.143	5	22	.185

Tournament: **Southern U. d. Grambling 78-62**
Tournament MVP: **Avery Johnson**, Southern U.

SUN BELT

	Conference			Overall		
	W	L	PCT	W	L	PCT
Charlotte⊕	11	3	.786	22	9	.710
VCU□	10	4	.714	23	12	.657
Old Dominion□	9	5	.643	18	12	.600
South Alabama	8	6	.571	15	14	.517
UAB	7	7	.500	16	15	.516
Western Kentucky	6	8	.429	15	13	.536
South Florida	3	11	.214	6	22	.214
Jacksonville	2	12	.143	8	21	.276

Tournament: **Charlotte d. VCU 81-79**
Tournament MVP: **Byron Dinkins**, UNC Charlotte

TAAC

	Conference			Overall		
	W	L	PCT	W	L	PCT
Arkansas-Little Rock□	15	3	.833	24	7	.774
Georgia Southern□	15	3	.833	24	7	.774
UTSA⊕	13	5	.722	22	9	.710
Hardin-Simmons	10	8	.556	18	12	.600
Mercer	8	10	.444	15	14	.517
Centenary	8	10	.444	13	15	.464
Stetson	8	10	.444	13	15	.464
Georgia State	5	13	.278	9	19	.321
Houston Baptist	4	14	.222	9	18	.333
Samford	4	14	.222	7	20	.259

Tournament: **UTSA d. Georgia Southern 76-69 (OT)**
Tournament MVP: **Frank Hampton**, UTSA

WCAC

	Conference			Overall		
	W	L	PCT	W	L	PCT
Loyola Marymount⊕	14	0	1.000	28	4	.875
Saint Mary's (CA)	9	5	.643	19	9	.679
Santa Clara□	9	5	.643	20	11	.645
Pepperdine□	8	6	.571	17	13	.567
Gonzaga	7	7	.500	16	12	.571
San Francisco	5	9	.357	13	15	.464
San Diego	3	11	.214	11	17	.393
Portland	1	13	.071	6	22	.214

Tournament: **Loyola Marymount d. Santa Clara 104-96**
Tournament MVP: **Hank Gathers**, Loyola Marymount

WAC

	Conference			Overall		
	W	L	PCT	W	L	PCT
BYU○	13	3	.813	26	6	.813
Wyoming⊕	11	5	.688	26	6	.813
Utah□	11	5	.688	19	11	.633
UTEP○	10	6	.625	23	10	.697
Colorado State□	8	8	.500	22	13	.629
New Mexico□	8	8	.500	22	14	.611
San Diego State	5	11	.313	12	17	.414
Air Force	4	12	.250	11	17	.393
Hawaii	2	14	.125	4	25	.138

Tournament: **Wyoming d. UTEP 79-75**
Tournament MVP: **Eric Leckner**, Wyoming

INDEPENDENTS

	Overall		
	W	L	PCT
Akron	21	7	.750
DePaul○⊗	22	8	.733
Notre Dame○	20	9	.690
Wright State	16	11	.593
Miami (FL)	17	14	.548
UMBC	13	15	.464
Dayton	13	18	.419
Brooklyn	11	17	.393
Central Connecticut State	10	18	.357
Marquette	10	18	.357
Nicholls State	10	18	.357
U.S. International	10	18	.357
Florida International	9	19	.321
UCF	9	19	.321
Chicago State	8	20	.286
Northern Illinois	8	20	.286
Oral Roberts	8	21	.276
Southeastern Louisiana	7	21	.250

INDIVIDUAL LEADERS—SEASON

SCORING	CL	POS	G	FG	3FG	FT	PTS	PPG
1 **Hersey Hawkins**, Bradley	SR	G	31	377	87	284	1,125	**36.3**
2 **Daren Queenan**, Lehigh	SR	G/F	31	324	20	214	882	**28.5**
3 **Anthony Mason**, Tennessee State	SR	F	28	276	40	191	783	**28.0**
4 **Gerald Hayward**, Loyola-Chicago	JR	F	29	298	39	121	756	**26.1**
5 **Jeff Martin**, Murray State	JR	F	31	304	17	181	806	**26.0**
6 **Marty Simmons**, Evansville	SR	F	29	269	59	153	750	**25.9**
7 **Steve Middleton**, Southern Illinois	SR	F	28	265	58	123	711	**25.4**
8 **Jeff Grayer**, Iowa State	SR	F	32	312	20	167	811	**25.3**
9 **Byron Larkin**, Xavier	SR	G	30	296	19	147	758	**25.3**
10 **Skip Henderson**, Marshall	SR	G	32	291	80	142	804	**25.1**

FIELD GOAL PCT	CL	POS	G	FG	FGA	PCT
1 **Arnell Jones**, Boise State	SR	F	30	187	283	**66.1**
2 **Stanley Brundy**, DePaul	JR	F	30	194	295	**65.8**
3 **Tony Holifield**, Illinois State	SR	F/C	30	177	273	**64.8**
4 **Jarvis Basnight**, UNLV	SR	F	33	184	284	**64.8**
5 **Eric Leckner**, Wyoming	SR	C	32	181	281	**64.4**

MINIMUM: 5 MADE PER GAME

THREE-PT FG PER GAME	CL	POS	G	3FG	3PG
1 **Timothy Pollard**, Mississippi Valley State	JR	G	28	132	**4.7**
2 **Jeff McGill**, Eastern Kentucky	SR	G	27	104	**3.9**
3 **Wally Lancaster**, Virginia Tech	JR	G	29	106	**3.7**
4 **Dave Mooney**, Coastal Carolina	SR	G	28	102	**3.6**
5 **Gerald Paddio**, UNLV	SR	G/F	34	118	**3.5**

THREE-PT FG PCT	CL	POS	G	3FG	3FGA	PCT
1 **Glenn Tropf**, Holy Cross	JR	G	29	52	82	**63.4**
2 **Steve Kerr**, Arizona	SR	G	38	114	199	**57.3**
3 **Mike Joseph**, Bucknell	SO	G	28	65	116	**56.0**
4 **Reginald Jones**, Prairie View A&M	SR	G	27	85	155	**54.8**
5 **Dave Orlandini**, Princeton	SR	G	26	60	110	**54.5**

MINIMUM: 1.5 MADE PER GAME

FREE THROW PCT	CL	POS	G	FT	FTA	PCT
1 **Steve Henson**, Kansas State	SO	G	34	111	120	**92.5**
2 **Archie Tullos**, Detroit	SR	G	30	139	153	**90.8**
3 **Jay Edwards**, Indiana	FR	G	23	69	76	**90.8**
4 **Jim Barton**, Dartmouth	JR	G	26	115	127	**90.6**
5 **LaBradford Smith**, Louisville	FR	G	35	143	158	**90.5**

MINIMUM: 2.5 MADE PER GAME

ASSISTS PER GAME	CL	POS	G	AST	APG
1 **Avery Johnson**, Southern U.	SR	G	30	399	**13.3**
2 **Anthony Manuel**, Bradley	JR	G	31	373	**12.0**
3 **Craig Neal**, Georgia Tech	SR	G	32	303	**9.5**
4 **Corey Gaines**, Loyola Marymount	SR	G	31	271	**8.7**
5 **Howard Evans**, Temple	SR	G	34	294	**8.6**
6 **Sherman Douglas**, Syracuse	JR	G	35	288	**8.2**
7 **Frank Smith**, Old Dominion	SR	G	30	244	**8.1**
8 **Glenn Williams**, Holy Cross	JR	G	29	234	**8.1**
9 **Drafton Davis**, Marist	SR	G	27	207	**7.7**
10 **Marc Brown**, Siena	FR	G	29	222	**7.7**

REBOUNDS PER GAME	CL	POS	G	REB	RPG
1 **Kenny Miller**, Loyola-Chicago	FR	C	29	395	**13.6**
2 **Rodney Mack**, South Carolina State	JR	F/C	29	387	**13.3**
3 **Jerome Lane**, Pittsburgh	JR	F	31	378	**12.2**
4 **Kenny Sanders**, George Mason	JR	F	29	339	**11.7**
5 **Randy White**, Louisiana Tech	JR	F	31	359	**11.6**
6 **Tyrone Canino**, Central Connecticut State	SR	F	28	321	**11.5**
7 **Oliver Johnson**, Charleston Southern	SR	F/C	29	331	**11.4**
8 **Lionel Simmons**, La Salle	SO	F	34	386	**11.4**
9 **Fred West**, Texas Southern	SO	C	29	322	**11.1**
10 **Derrick Coleman**, Syracuse	SO	C	35	384	**11.0**

BLOCKED SHOTS PER GAME	CL	POS	G	BLK	BPG
1 **Rodney Blake**, Saint Joseph's	SR	C	29	116	**4.0**
2 **Rik Smits**, Marist	SR	C	27	105	**3.9**
3 **Mike Brown**, Canisius	SR	F/C	27	100	**3.7**
4 **Tim Perry**, Temple	SR	F	33	118	**3.6**
5 **Roy Brow**, Virginia Tech	SR	C	28	100	**3.6**

STEALS PER GAME	CL	POS	G	STL	SPG
1 **Aldwin Ware**, Florida A&M	SR	G	29	142	**4.9**
2 **Marty Johnson**, Towson	SR	G	30	124	**4.1**
3 **Mookie Blaylock**, Oklahoma	JR	G	39	150	**3.8**
4 **Haywoode Workman**, Oral Roberts	JR	G	29	103	**3.6**
5 **Avery Johnson**, Southern U.	SR	G	30	106	**3.5**

INDIVIDUAL LEADERS—GAME

POINTS	CL	POS	OPP	DATE	PTS
1 **Hersey Hawkins**, Bradley	SR	G	Detroit	F22	**63**
2 **Skip Henderson**, Marshall	SR	G	The Citadel	M4	**55**
3 **Lafester Rhodes**, Iowa State	SR	C	Iowa	D19	**54**
4 **Tommie Johnson**, Central Michigan	SR	G	Wright State	D22	**53**
5 **Hersey Hawkins**, Bradley	SR	G	UC Irvine	D19	**51**
Bimbo Coles, Virginia Tech	SO	G	Southern Miss	F6	**51**

THREE-PT FG MADE	CL	POS	OPP	DATE	3FG
1 **Tommie Johnson**, Central Michigan	SR	G	Wright State	D22	**10**
Earl Watkins, UL-Lafayette	JR	G	Houston	J13	**10**
3 **Anthony Pendleton**, USC	FR	G	Long Beach State	D9	**9**
Ron Simpson, Rider	SR	F	St. Francis (NY)	D5	**9**
Brian Leahy, Saint Joseph's	SR	G	Duquesne	J17	**9**
Skip Henderson, Marshall	SR	G	The Citadel	M4	**9**
Marty Simmons, Evansville	SR	F	Saint Louis	M6	**9**
Greg Boyd, Weber State	SR	G	Nevada	M9	**9**

ASSISTS	CL	POS	OPP	DATE	AST
1 **Avery Johnson**, Southern U.	SR	G	Texas Southern	J25	**22**
2 **Anthony Manuel**, Bradley	JR	G	UC Irvine	D19	**21**
Avery Johnson, Southern U.	SR	G	Alabama State	J16	**21**
4 **Avery Johnson**, Southern U.	SR	G	Miss. Valley State	F8	**20**
Howard Evans, Temple	SR	G	Villanova	F10	**20**

REBOUNDS	CL	POS	OPP	DATE	REB
1 **Levy Middlebrooks**, Pepperdine	SR	F/C	Loyola Marymount	F20	**25**
Kenny Miller, Loyola Illinois	FR	C	Oral Roberts	D2	**25**
Rodney Mack, South Carolina State	JR	F/C	UMES	M1	**25**
4 **Jeff Grayer**, Iowa State	SR	F	U.S. International	J16	**24**
Darrell Coleman, South Florida	SR	F	Miami (FL)	M1	**24**

BLOCKED SHOTS	CL	POS	OPP	DATE	BLK
1 **Rodney Blake**, Saint Joseph's	SR	C	Cleveland State	D2	**12**
Walter Palmer, Dartmouth	SO	C	Harvard	J9	**12**
3 **Roy Brow**, Virginia Tech	SR	C	Charleston Southern	D12	**9**
Byron Hopkins, Navy	SO	C	William and Mary	J13	**9**
Tom Greis, Villanova	SO	C	Georgetown	F1	**9**
Rodney Blake, Saint Joseph's	SR	C	Penn	F23	**9**
Tim Perry, Temple	SR	F	Duquesne	F25	**9**

STEALS	CL	POS	OPP	DATE	STL
1 **Mookie Blaylock**, Oklahoma	JR	G	Centenary	D12	**13**
2 **Marty Johnson**, Towson	SR	G	Bucknell	F17	**11**
Aldwin Ware, Florida A&M	SR	G	Tuskegee	F24	**11**
4 **Avery Johnson**, Southern U.	SR	G	Tuskegee	D17	**9**
Haywoode Workman, Oral Roberts	JR	G	Oklahoma	D29	**9**
Darryl McDonald, Texas A&M	SR	G	SMU	D30	**9**
Anthony Manuel, Bradley	JR	G	Wichita State	J9	**9**
Cliff Robinson, Connecticut	JR	F/C	Georgetown	F6	**9**
Tyrone Canino, Central Conn. State	SR	F	Vermont	F6	**9**
Gary Massey, Villanova	JR	F	Providence	F20	**9**
Drafton Davis, Marist	SR	G	Robert Morris	M1	**9**

TEAM LEADERS—SEASON

WIN-LOSS PCT	W	L	PCT
1 **Temple**	32	2	**.941**
2 **Arizona**	35	3	**.921**
3 **Oklahoma**	35	4	**.897**
4 **NC A&T**	26	3	**.897**
5 **Purdue**	29	4	**.879**

SCORING OFFENSE	G	W-L	PTS	PPG
1 **Loyola Marymount**	32	28-4	3,528	**110.3**
2 **Oklahoma**	39	35-4	4,012	**102.9**
3 **Southern U.**	31	24-7	2,965	**95.6**
4 **Xavier**	30	26-4	2,840	**94.7**
5 **Iowa**	34	24-10	3,181	**93.6**

SCORING MARGIN	G	W-L	PPG	OPP PPG	MAR
1 **Oklahoma**	39	35-4	102.9	81.0	**21.9**
2 **Arizona**	38	35-3	85.1	64.2	**20.9**
3 **UNLV**	34	28-6	84.3	68.2	**16.1**
4 **Temple**	34	32-2	76.8	61.2	**15.6**
5 **Xavier**	30	26-4	94.7	79.5	**15.2**

FIELD GOAL PCT	G	W-L	FG	FGA	PCT
1 **Michigan**	34	26-8	1,198	2,196	**54.6**
2 **Arizona**	38	35-3	1,147	2,106	**54.5**
3 **North Carolina**	34	27-7	1,013	1,892	**53.5**
4 **Purdue**	33	29-4	1,018	1,912	**53.2**
5 **BYU**	32	26-6	976	1,839	**53.1**

THREE-PT FG PER GAME	G	W-L	3FG	3PG
1 **Princeton**	26	17-9	211	**8.1**
2 **Loyola Marymount**	32	28-4	251	**7.8**
3 **Oklahoma**	39	35-4	299	**7.7**
4 **George Mason**	30	20-10	219	**7.3**
5 **Bradley**	31	26-5	224	**7.2**

FREE THROW PCT	G	W-L	FT	FTA	PCT
1 **Butler**	28	14-14	413	517	**79.9**
2 **Princeton**	26	17-9	315	405	**77.8**
3 **Bucknell**	28	16-12	477	617	**77.3**
4 **UNC Asheville**	28	13-15	419	543	**77.2**
5 **Auburn**	30	19-11	406	527	**77.0**

REBOUND MARGIN	G	W-L	RPG	OPP RPG	MAR
1 **Notre Dame**	29	20-9	36.0	26.2	**9.8**
2 **South Carolina State**	29	16-13	42.9	33.5	**9.4**
3 **Arkansas-Little Rock**	31	24-7	41.3	32.5	**8.8**
4 **Georgetown**	30	20-10	39.2	31.3	**7.9**
5 **Missouri**	30	19-11	41.9	34.3	**7.6**

SCORING DEFENSE	G	W-L	PTS	PPG
1 **Georgia Southern**	31	24-7	1,725	**55.6**
2 **Boise State**	30	24-6	1,680	**56.0**
3 **Princeton**	26	17-9	1,467	**56.4**
4 **Colorado State**	35	22-13	2,007	**57.3**
5 **Saint Mary's (CA)**	28	19-9	1,640	**58.6**

FIELD GOAL PCT DEFENSE	G	W-L	OPP FG	OPP FGA	OPP PCT
1 Temple	34	32-2	777	1,981	**39.2**
2 Marist	27	18-9	617	1,537	**40.1**
3 Kansas	38	27-11	912	2,215	**41.2**
4 UNLV	34	28-6	841	2,012	**41.8**
5 Georgia Southern	31	24-7	640	1,529	**41.9**

CONSENSUS ALL-AMERICAS

FIRST TEAM

PLAYER	CL	POS	HT	SCHOOL	RPG	PPG
Sean Elliott	JR	G/F	6-8	Arizona	5.8	19.6
Gary Grant	SR	G	6-3	Michigan	3.4	21.1
Hersey Hawkins	SR	G	6-3	Bradley	7.8	36.3
Danny Manning	SR	F	6-11	Kansas	9.0	24.8
J.R. Reid	SO	F/C	6-9	North Carolina	8.9	18.0

SECOND TEAM

PLAYER	CL	POS	HT	SCHOOL	RPG	PPG
Danny Ferry	JR	F	6-10	Duke	7.6	19.1
Jerome Lane	JR	F	6-6	Pittsburgh	12.2	13.9
Mark Macon	FR	G	6-5	Temple	5.6	20.6
Mitch Richmond	SR	G	6-5	Kansas State	6.3	22.6
Rony Seikaly	SR	C	6-10	Syracuse	9.6	16.3
Michael Smith	JR	F	6-10	BYU	7.8	21.2

SELECTORS: AP, NABC, UPI, USBWA

AWARD WINNERS

PLAYER OF THE YEAR

PLAYER	CL	POS	HT	SCHOOL	AWARDS
Danny Manning	SR	F	6-11	Kansas	Naismith, Wooden, NABC
Hersey Hawkins	SR	G	6-3	Bradley	AP, UPI, USBWA, Rupp
Jerry Johnson	SR	G	6-0	Fla. Southern	Frances Pomeroy Naismith*

* FOR THE MOST OUTSTANDING SENIOR PLAYER WHO IS 6 FEET OR UNDER.

DEFENSIVE PLAYER OF THE YEAR

PLAYER	CL	POS	HT	SCHOOL
Billy King	SR	F	6-6	Duke

COACH OF THE YEAR

COACH	SCHOOL	REC	AWARDS
Larry Brown	Kansas	27-11	Naismith
John Chaney	Temple	32-2	AP, UPI, USBWA, NABC, CBS/Chevrolet

BOB GIBBONS' TOP HIGH SCHOOL SENIOR RECRUITS

PLAYER	POS	HT	HIGH SCHOOL	A-A TEAMS	COLLEGE	CAREER NOTES
1 **Alonzo Mourning**	C	6-10	Indian River HS, Chesapeake, VA	McD, P, USA	Georgetown	16.7 ppg, 8.6 rpg (4 seasons); No. 2 pick, '92 NBA draft (Hornets); 7-time All-Star; 2-time Defensive POY
2 **Billy Owens**	F	6-8	Carlisle (Pa.) HS	McD, P, USA	Syracuse	1,840 points (3 seasons); No. 3 pick, '91 NBA draft (Kings); 11.7 ppg (10 seasons)
3 **Shawn Kemp**	PF	6-11	Concord HS, Elkhart, IN	McD, P	Kentucky/TVCC	DNP in college; No. 17 pick, '89 NBA draft (Sonics); 6-time All-Star; 14.6 ppg, 8.4 rpg (14 seasons)
4 **Stanley Roberts**	C	7-0	Lower Richland HS, Hopkins, SC	McD, P	LSU	14.1 ppg, 9.8 rpg; No. 23 pick, '91 NBA draft (Magic); 8.5 ppg (8 years)
5 **Kenneth Williams**	PF	6-9	Northeastern HS, Elizabeth City, NC	McD, P, USA	North Carolina	Recruited by UNC but DNP; 2nd-round pick, '90 NBA draft (Pacers); 4.8 ppg (4 seasons)
6 **Anthony Peeler**	2G	6-5	Paseo HS, Kansas City, MO	McD, P	Missouri	Left Missouri 3rd-leading scorer; Big Eight POY, '92; No. 15 pick, '92 NBA draft (Lakers); 9.7 ppg (13 seasons)
7 **Malik Sealy**	F	6-7	St. Nicholas of Tolentine HS, Bronx, NY	McD, P	St. John's	18.9 ppg (4 seasons); No. 14 pick, '92 NBA draft (Pacers); 10.1 ppg (8 seasons)
8 **Chris Mills**	SF	6-6	Fairfax HS, Los Angeles	McD, P, USA	Kentucky/Arizona	Transferred after 1 year; Pac-10 POY, '93; No. 22 pick, '93 NBA draft (Cavs); 11.2 ppg (10 seasons)
9 **Matt Steigenga**	F	6-7	South Christian HS, Grand Rapids, MI	McD, P	Michigan State	1,296 points (4 seasons); 2nd-round pick, '92 NBA draft (Bulls); played in 2 NBA games
10 **Darrick Martin**	PG	5-11	St. Anthony HS, Long Beach, CA	McD, P	UCLA	Left UCLA 3rd in assists (636); undrafted; 6.9 ppg in NBA (13 seasons)
11 **LaPhonso Ellis**	C/F	6-8	Lincoln Senior HS, East St. Louis, IL	McD, P	Notre Dame	Left Notre Dame 2nd in blocks (200); No. 5 pick, '92 NBA draft (Nuggets); All-Rookie team, '93; 11.9 ppg (10 seasons)
12 **Lee Mayberry**	PG	6-2	Will Rogers HS, Tulsa, OK	McD, P	Arkansas	Left Arkansas 3rd-leading scorer; No. 23 pick, '92 NBA draft (Bucks); 5.1 ppg (7 seasons)
13 **Eric Anderson**	PF	6-9	St. Francis DeSales HS, Chicago	McD, P	Indiana	4-year starter; Final Four, '92; undrafted
14 **Jerrod Mustaf**	C/F	6-10	DeMatha Catholic HS, Hyattsville, MD	McD, P	Maryland	18.5 ppg, 7.7 rpg as Soph.; No. 17 pick, '90 NBA draft (Knicks); 4.0 ppg (4 seasons)
15 **Chris Jackson**	PG	6-1	Gulfport (MS) HS	P, USA	LSU	2-time All-America; at LSU, 29.0 ppg (2 seasons); No. 3 pick, '90 NBA draft (Nuggets); 14.6 ppg (9 seasons) as Mahmoud Abdul-Rauf
16 **Evric Gray**	PF	6-7	Bloomington (CA) HS		UNLV	Left UNLV 10th in blocks; undrafted; played in 5 NBA games; played overseas
17 **Mike Peplowski**	C	6-10	De La Salle HS, Warren, MI	P	Michigan State	10.2 ppg, 7.8 rpg (4 seasons); 2nd-round pick, '93 NBA draft (Kings); 2.9 ppg (3 seasons)
18 **Donald Hodge**	C/F	6-10	Calvin Coolidge HS, Washington, D.C.	McD, P	Temple	13.3 ppg, 7.5 rpg (2 seasons); 2nd-round pick, '91 NBA draft (Mavs); 4.7 ppg, 3.2 rpg (5 seasons)
19 **Don MacLean**	PF	6-9	Simi Valley (CA) HS	McD, P	UCLA	Left UCLA all-time leading scorer (2,608 pts); No. 19 pick, '92 NBA draft (Pistons); 10.9 ppg (9 seasons)
20 **Mark Baker**	PG	6-1	Dunbar HS, Dayton, OH	P	Ohio State	Left OSU 3rd in assists; undrafted; played in 1 NBA game, played overseas

OTHER STANDOUTS

PLAYER	POS	HT	HIGH SCHOOL	A-A TEAMS	COLLEGE	CAREER NOTES
25 **Christian Laettner**	C	6-11	Nichols School, Buffalo, NY	McD, P	Duke	2 NCAA titles; 4 Final Fours; National POY, '92; No. 3 pick, '92 NBA draft (Wolves); 12.8 ppg (13 seasons); Olympic gold medal, '92
37 **Robert Horry**	PF	6-9	Andalusia (AL) HS	P	Alabama	First-team All-SEC, '92; No. 11 pick, '92 NBA draft (Rockets); 7.0 ppg (16 seasons); 7 NBA titles
63 **Sam Cassell**	PG	6-3	Dunbar HS, Baltimore		San Jacinto JC/ Florida State	At FSU, 18.3 ppg (2 seasons); No. 24 pick, '93 NBA draft (Rockets); 15.7 ppg, 6.0 apg (15 seasons); 1-time All-Star; 2 NBA titles

Abbreviations: McD=McDonald's; P=Parade; USA=USA Today

ANNUAL REVIEW

Poll Progression

Preseason Poll

AP	School
1	Syracuse
2	Purdue
3	North Carolina
4	Pittsburgh
5	Kentucky
6	Indiana
7	Kansas
8	Missouri
9	Michigan
10	Wyoming
11	Iowa
12	Temple
13	Louisville
14	Florida
15	Duke
16	Georgetown
17	Arizona
18	Georgia Tech
19	Oklahoma
20	DePaul

Week of Dec 1

AP	UPI	School	AP↓↑
1	1	**North Carolina** (3-0)	↑2
2	5	**Kentucky** (1-0)	↑3
3	2	**Syracuse** (2-1)	↓2
4	4	**Pittsburgh** (1-0)	
5	3	**Indiana** (1-0)	↑1
6	10	**Iowa** (3-0)	↑5
7	6	**Florida** (4-0)	↑7
8	8	**Missouri** (0-0)	
9	7	**Arizona** (2-0)	↑8
10	11	**Wyoming** (1-0)	
11	14	**Purdue** (1-1)	↓9
12	15	**Temple** (0-0)	
13	9	**Duke** (1-0)	↑2
14	16	**Louisville** (0-0)	↓1
15	13	**Michigan** (2-1)	↓6
16	19	**Kansas** (1-2)	↓9
17	12	**Georgetown** (2-0)	↓1
18	17	**Oklahoma** (1-0)	↑1
19	18	**UNLV** (0-0)	⤴
20	—	**Memphis** (1-0)	⤴
—	20	**NC State** (0-0)	

Week of Dec 8

AP	UPI	School	AP↓↑
1	1	**Kentucky** (3-0)	↑1
2	5	**Pittsburgh** (2-0)	↑2
3	3	**Iowa** (6-0)	↑3
4	2	**Arizona** (5-0)	↑5
5	4	**North Carolina** (4-1) (A)	↓4
6	6	**Indiana** (2-1)	↓1
7	8	**Wyoming** (3-0)	↑3
8	7	**Syracuse** (4-2)	↓5
9	10	**Missouri** (2-0)	↓1
10	9	**Duke** (3-0)	↑3
11	13	**Temple** (1-0)	↑1
12	12	**Florida** (4-1)	↓5
13	14	**Purdue** (4-1)	↓2
14	11	**Georgetown** (3-0)	↑3
15	15	**Michigan** (4-1)	
16	16	**Oklahoma** (3-0)	↑2
17	17	**UNLV** (3-0)	↑2
18	19	**Kansas** (4-2)	↓2
19	18	**Notre Dame** (1-1)	⤴
20	—	**Memphis** (2-0)	
—	20	**Auburn** (2-0)	

Week of Dec 15

AP	UPI	School	AP↓↑
1	1	**Kentucky** (4-0)	
2	2	**Arizona** (7-0)	
3	3	**Pittsburgh** (4-0)	
4	4	**North Carolina** (5-1)	
5	5	**Indiana** (5-1)	
6	6	**Wyoming** (4-0)	
7	8	**Iowa** (6-1)	
8	10	**Temple** (4-0)	
9	9	**Syracuse** (6-2)	
10	7	**Duke** (4-0)	
11	11	**Florida** (5-1)	↑
12	13	**Purdue** (6-1)	↑
13	12	**Michigan** (7-1)	↑
14	14	**Oklahoma** (6-0)	↑
15	15	**UNLV** (5-0)	↑
16	17	**Missouri** (3-1)	↓
17	18	**Kansas** (6-2)	↑
18	16	**Georgetown** (4-1)	↓
19	20	**Memphis** (3-1)	↑
20	—	**Iowa State** (7-1)	⤴
—	19	**Illinois** (7-1)	

Week of Dec 22

AP	UPI	School	AP↓↑
1	2	**Arizona** (9-0)	↑1
2	1	**Kentucky** (6-0)	↓1
3	3	**Pittsburgh** (4-0)	
4	4	**North Carolina** (7-1)	
5	5	**Wyoming** (6-0)	↑1
6	8	**Temple** (5-0)	↑2
7	7	**Syracuse** (7-2)	↑2
8	9	**Florida** (6-1)	↑3
9	6	**Duke** (4-0)	↑1
10	10	**Purdue** (7-1)	↑2
11	11	**Michigan** (8-1)	↑2
12	13	**Oklahoma** (7-0)	↑2
13	12	**Indiana** (6-2)	↓8
14	17	**Iowa** (6-2) (B)	↓7
15	14	**UNLV** (5-0)	
16	16	**Iowa State** (8-1) (B)	↑4
17	19	**Missouri** (4-1)	↓1
18	18	**Kansas** (7-2)	↓1
19	15	**Georgetown** (6-1)	↓1
20	—	**Memphis** (3-1)	↓1
—	20	**Georgia Tech** (6-1)	

Week of Dec 29

AP	UPI	School	AP↓↑
1	1	**Arizona** (10-0)	
2	2	**Kentucky** (6-0)	
3	4	**Pittsburgh** (6-0)	
4	3	**North Carolina** (7-1)	
5	5	**Wyoming** (8-0)	
6	8	**Temple** (5-0)	
7	7	**Syracuse** (8-2)	
8	9	**Florida** (7-1)	
9	6	**Duke** (5-0)	
10	10	**Oklahoma** (10-0)	↑2
11	11	**Purdue** (8-1)	↓1
12	12	**Michigan** (9-1)	↓1
13	13	**Indiana** (7-2)	
14	15	**Iowa** (7-2)	
15	14	**UNLV** (7-0)	
16	17	**Iowa State** (9-1)	
17	17	**Kansas** (7-2)	↑1
18	16	**Georgetown** (7-1)	↑1
19	—	**Memphis** (4-2)	↑1
20	—	**Louisville** (3-2)	⤴
—	19	**Illinois** (8-2)	
—	20	**Missouri** (4-2)	↱

Week of Jan 5

AP	UPI	School	AP↓↑
1	1	**Kentucky** (9-0)	↑1
2	2	**Pittsburgh** (9-0)	↑1
3	4	**Arizona** (12-1)	↓2
4	3	**North Carolina** (9-1)	
5	5	**Wyoming** (11-0)	
6	6	**Temple** (7-0)	
7	7	**Syracuse** (10-2)	
8	8	**Oklahoma** (12-0)	↑2
9	9	**Duke** (6-1)	
10	10	**Purdue** (10-1)	↑1
11	11	**Michigan** (11-1)	↑1
12	13	**Indiana** (8-2)	↑1
13	12	**UNLV** (10-0)	↑2
14	14	**Georgetown** (9-1)	↑4
15	15	**Florida** (8-3)	↓7
16	16	**Iowa** (8-3)	↓2
17	19	**Iowa State** (11-2)	↓1
18	17	**Kansas** (8-3)	↓1
19	18	**Illinois** (9-2)	⤴
20	19	**St. John's** (8-1)	⤴

Week of Jan 12

AP	UPI	School	AP↓↑
1	1	**Arizona** (14-1)	↑2
2	2	**North Carolina** (11-1)	↑2
3	3	**Oklahoma** (14-0)	↑5
4	4	**Temple** (10-0)	↑2
5	5	**Kentucky** (10-1)	↓4
6	7	**Pittsburgh** (10-1)	↓4
7	6	**Duke** (9-1)	↑2
8	8	**Purdue** (13-1)	↑2
9	9	**Syracuse** (12-2)	↓2
10	10	**Michigan** (13-1)	↑1
11	11	**Georgetown** (11-1)	↑3
12	12	**Wyoming** (11-2)	↓7
13	13	**UNLV** (12-1)	
14	17	**Iowa State** (13-2)	↑3
15	15	**Indiana** (8-3)	↓3
16	16	**Kansas** (11-3)	↑2
17	18	**Iowa** (9-4)	↓1
18	19	**New Mexico** (14-3)	⤴
19	—	**Auburn** (9-2)	⤴
20	—	**Illinois** (11-3)	↓1
—	14	**BYU** (11-0)	
—	20	**Florida** (10-4)	↱

Week of Jan 19

AP	UPI	School	AP↓↑
1	1	**Arizona** (16-1)	
2	2	**North Carolina** (13-1)	
3	5	**Temple** (12-0)	↑1
4	3	**Kentucky** (12-1)	↑1
5	4	**Purdue** (15-1)	↑3
6	6	**Pittsburgh** (13-1)	
7	8	**Michigan** (14-1)	↑3
8	7	**UNLV** (14-1)	↑5
9	9	**Duke** (10-2)	↓2
10	12	**Iowa State** (15-2)	↑4
11	11	**Oklahoma** (14-2) (C)	↓8
12	9	**BYU** (12-0)	⤴
13	14	**Illinois** (13-3)	↑7
14	13	**Syracuse** (12-4)	↓5
15	15	**Georgetown** (11-3)	↓4
16	18	**Kansas** (12-4)	
17	16	**Wyoming** (12-3)	↓5
18	16	**UTEP** (15-2)	⤴
19	19	**Iowa** (11-5)	↓2
20	20	**NC State** (10-2)	⤴
—	20	**Florida** (12-4)	

Week of Jan 26

AP	UPI	School	AP↓↑
1	1	**Arizona** (18-1)	
2	2	**Purdue** (17-1)	↑3
3	3	**North Carolina** (14-2)	↓1
4	5	**UNLV** (17-1)	↑4
5	4	**Duke** (12-2)	↑4
6	6	**Temple** (14-1)	↓3
7	7	**BYU** (14-0)	↑5
8	8	**Michigan** (14-2)	↓1
9	9	**Kentucky** (13-2)	↓5
10	10	**Oklahoma** (16-2)	↑1
11	11	**Pittsburgh** (13-2)	↓5
12	17	**Iowa State** (16-3)	↓2
13	14	**Illinois** (14-4)	
14	12	**Florida** (14-4)	⤴
15	15	**Georgetown** (12-4)	
16	18	**Iowa** (12-5)	↑3
17	13	**Syracuse** (13-5)	↓3
18	16	**UTEP** (16-3)	
19	19	**Villanova** (14-4)	⤴
20	20	**Southern Miss** (14-2)	⤴
—	20	**Missouri** (11-4)	

Week of Feb 2

AP	UPI	School	AP↓↑
1	1	**Arizona** (20-1)	
2	3	**UNLV** (19-1)	↑2
3	5	**Duke** (13-2)	↑2
4	2	**BYU** (15-0)	↑3
5	4	**Temple** (16-1)	↑1
6	6	**Purdue** (17-2)	↓4
7	8	**Oklahoma** (18-2)	↑3
8	7	**North Carolina** (15-3)	↓5
9	9	**Pittsburgh** (15-2)	↑2
10	10	**Kentucky** (14-3)	↓1
11	11	**Michigan** (17-3)	↓3
12	12	**Syracuse** (15-5)	↑5
13	14	**Iowa** (15-5)	↑3
14	13	**Georgetown** (14-4)	↑1
15	15	**Vanderbilt** (13-4)	⤴
16	—	**Iowa State** (15-5)	↓4
17	17	**Illinois** (14-6)	↓4
18	16	**Bradley** (13-2)	⤴
19	20	**Florida** (15-5)	↓5
20	18	**St. John's** (14-3)	⤴
—	19	**UTEP** (17-4)	↱

Week of Feb 9

AP	UPI	School	AP↓↑
1	1	**Temple** (18-1)	↑4
2	2	**Purdue** (19-2)	↑4
3	3	**Arizona** (21-2)	↓2
4	4	**Oklahoma** (20-2)	↑3
5	8	**Pittsburgh** (16-2)	↑4
6	5	**North Carolina** (16-3)	↑2
7	7	**UNLV** (20-2) (D)	↓5
8	6	**BYU** (17-1)	↓4
9	9	**Duke** (16-3)	↓5
10	10	**Kentucky** (16-3)	
11	11	**Syracuse** (17-5)	↑1
12	12	**Michigan** (18-4)	↓1
13	15	**Iowa** (16-6)	
14	14	**Kansas State** (14-4)	⤴
15	20	**Bradley** (14-3)	↑3
16	—	**NC State** (14-4)	⤴
17	18	**Vanderbilt** (14-5)	↓2
18	16	**Wyoming** (17-4)	⤴
19	17	**Indiana** (13-6)	⤴
20	—	**Villanova** (16-6)	⤴
—	19	**Florida** (16-6)	↱
—	20	**Georgetown** (14-6)	↱

ANNUAL REVIEW

[We]ek of Feb 16

UPI	School	AP↓↑
1	**Temple** (20-1)	
3	**Purdue** (20-2)	
2	**Arizona** (23-2)	
4	**Oklahoma** (22-2)	
5	**North Carolina** (18-3)	↑1
6	**Duke** (18-3)	↑2
7	**BYU** (20-1)	↑1
8	**Pittsburgh** (17-3)	↓3
9	**Kentucky** (18-3)	↑1
10	**Michigan** (20-4)	↑2
11	**UNLV** (21-3)	↓4
12	**Syracuse** (18-6)	↓1
13	**Iowa** (17-6)	
14	**NC State** (16-5)	↑2
17	**Missouri** (16-5)	⤴
16	**Vanderbilt** (16-5)	↑1
18	**Bradley** (16-4)	↓2
15	**Georgetown** (16-6)	⤴
18	**Wyoming** (18-5)	↓1
20	**Loyola Marymount** (20-3)	⤴

Week of Feb 23

AP	UPI	School	AP↓↑
1	1	**Temple** (22-1)	
2	2	**Purdue** (22-2)	
3	3	**Arizona** (25-2)	
4	4	**Oklahoma** (24-2)	
5	5	**Duke** (20-3)	↑1
6	6	**Pittsburgh** (19-3)	↑2
7	10	**Michigan** (21-4)	↑3
8	8	**UNLV** (23-3)	↑3
9	9	**North Carolina** (20-4)	↓4
10	11	**Syracuse** (20-6)	↑2
11	7	**BYU** (21-2)	↓4
12	12	**Kentucky** (18-5)	↓3
13	13	**Iowa** (18-7)	
14	14	**Bradley** (19-4)	↑3
15	17	**Missouri** (17-6)	
16	20	**Wyoming** (20-5)	↑3
17	19	**Vanderbilt** (17-6)	↓1
18	—	**Southern Miss** (16-6)	⤴
19	15	**Loyola Marymount** (22-3)	↑1
20	16	**Georgia Tech** (19-6)	⤴
—	18	**NC State** (18-6)	⤵

Week of Mar 1

AP	UPI	School	AP↓↑
1	1	**Temple** (25-1)	
2	4	**Purdue** (24-2)	
3	2	**Arizona** (26-2)	
4	3	**Oklahoma** (26-2)	
5	6	**UNLV** (25-3)	↑3
6	5	**North Carolina** (21-4)	↑3
7	7	**Pittsburgh** (20-4)	↓1
8	10	**Kentucky** (20-5)	↑4
9	8	**Duke** (20-5)	↓4
10	9	**Michigan** (22-5)	↓3
11	11	**Iowa** (20-7)	↑2
12	13	**Syracuse** (21-7)	↓2
13	14	**Georgia Tech** (21-6)	↑7
14	17	**Bradley** (22-4) Ⓔ	
15	15	**BYU** (23-3)	↓4
16	12	**NC State** (20-6)	⤴
17	19	**Wyoming** (22-5)	↓1
18	16	**Loyola Marymount** (24-3)	↑1
19	18	**Vanderbilt** (18-7)	↓2
20	20	**Xavier** (22-3)	⤴
—	21	**Indiana** (16-8)	
—	22	**Louisville** (18-9)	
—	23	**Kansas** (18-10)	
—	24	**Florida** (19-9)	
—	25	**Georgetown** (17-8)	

Week of Mar 8

AP	UPI	School	AP↓↑
1	1	**Temple** (27-1)	
2	2	**Purdue** (26-2)	
3	3	**Arizona** (26-2)	
4	4	**Oklahoma** (27-3)	
5	5	**Pittsburgh** (22-5)	↑2
6	6	**Kentucky** (22-5)	↑2
7	8	**UNLV** (26-4)	↓2
8	7	**Duke** (21-6)	↑1
9	9	**North Carolina** (22-5)	↓3
10	10	**Michigan** (23-6)	
11	11	**NC State** (23-6)	↑5
12	12	**Bradley** (25-4)	↑2
13	13	**Syracuse** (22-8)	↓1
14	17	**Wyoming** (23-5)	↑3
15	15	**Iowa** (21-8)	↓4
16	16	**Loyola Marymount** (26-3)	↑2
17	14	**BYU** (24-4)	↓2
18	18	**Georgia Tech** (21-8)	↓5
19	19	**Illinois** (20-9)	⤴
20	—	**Xavier** (24-3)	
—	20	**UTEP** (21-8)	

Final Poll

AP	UPI	School	AP↓↑
1	1	**Temple** (29-1)	
2	2	**Arizona** (31-2)	↑1
3	4	**Purdue** (27-3)	↓1
4	3	**Oklahoma** (30-3)	
5	6	**Duke** (24-6)	↑3
6	5	**Kentucky** (25-5) Ⓕ	
7	7	**North Carolina** (24-6)	↑2
8	8	**Pittsburgh** (23-6)	↓3
9	9	**Syracuse** (25-8)	↑4
10	10	**Michigan** (24-7)	
11	12	**Bradley** (26-4)	↑1
12	15	**UNLV** (27-5)	↓5
13	13	**Wyoming** (26-5)	↑1
14	11	**NC State** (24-7)	↓3
15	14	**Loyola Marymount** (27-3)	↑1
16	17	**Illinois** (22-9)	↑3
17	16	**Iowa** (22-9)	↓2
18	19	**Xavier** (26-3)	↑2
19	21	**BYU** (25-5)	↓2
20	20	**Kansas State** (22-8) Ⓖ	⤴
—	18	**DePaul** (21-7)	
—	22	**Indiana** (19-9)	
—	23	**Georgia Tech** (21-9)	⤵
—	24	**SMU** (27-8)	
—	25	**UTEP** (23-9)	

Ⓐ Despite letting North Carolina score seven points in the last :09, coach C.M. Newton's Vanderbilt squad holds on for a 78-76 win. Will Perdue leads the Commodores with 23 points.

Ⓑ Iowa State center Lafester Rhodes shocks Iowa with a school-record 54 points—20 more than he scored the entire previous season—including the game-winning bucket with :23 remaining in overtime.

Ⓒ Oklahoma loses back-to-back games to LSU and Kansas State. The Sooners' 62 points (against K-State's 69) is their lowest output of the season. They will finish with an NCAA record 4,012 points.

Ⓓ UC Santa Barbara upsets UNLV for the second time in the season. Brian Shaw leads the Gauchos with 17 points and 11 rebounds.

Ⓔ Bradley's Hersey Hawkins scores 63 in a 122-107 win over Detroit. Hawkins will lead the nation with 36.3 ppg, the highest average since Portland State's Freeman Williams had 38.8 in 1976-77.

Ⓕ Kentucky finishes its 60th consecutive season with a non-losing record, an NCAA record.

Ⓖ Kansas State beats Kansas, 69-58, in the Big Eight tournament semis. In Danny Manning's senior season, Kansas limps into the NCAA Tournament with 11 losses and little hope.

1988 NCAA Tournament

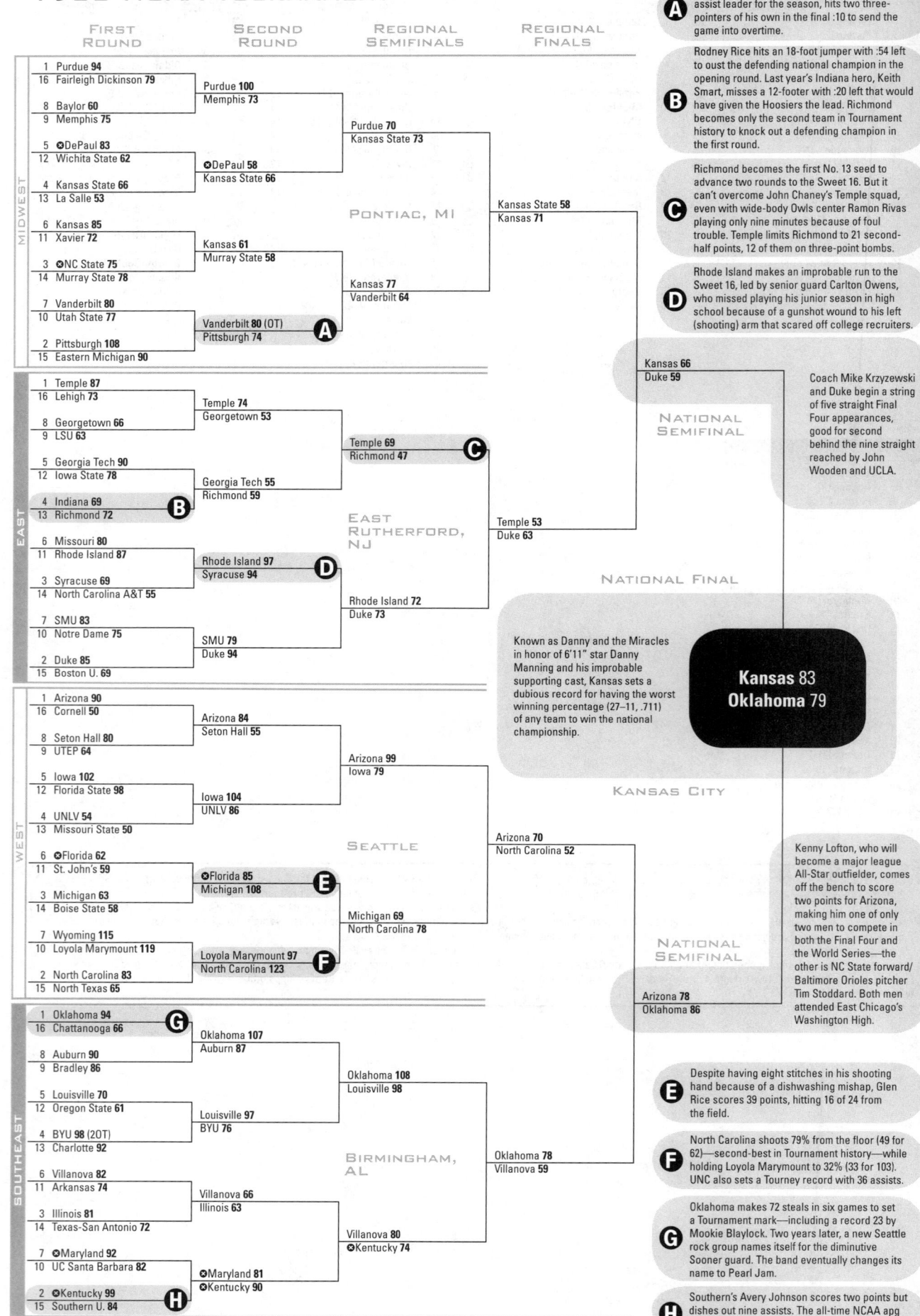

Midwest

First Round
- 1 Purdue **94**, 16 Fairleigh Dickinson **79**
- 8 Baylor **60**, 9 Memphis **75**
- 5 ⊗DePaul **83**, 12 Wichita State **62**
- 4 Kansas State **66**, 13 La Salle **53**
- 6 Kansas **85**, 11 Xavier **72**
- 3 ⊗NC State **75**, 14 Murray State **78**
- 7 Vanderbilt **80**, 10 Utah State **77**
- 2 Pittsburgh **108**, 15 Eastern Michigan **90**

Second Round
- Purdue **100**, Memphis **73**
- ⊗DePaul **58**, Kansas State **66**
- Kansas **61**, Murray State **58**
- Vanderbilt **80** (OT), Pittsburgh **74** (A)

Regional Semifinals (Pontiac, MI)
- Purdue **70**, Kansas State **73**
- Kansas **77**, Vanderbilt **64**

Regional Finals
- Kansas State **58**, Kansas **71**

East

First Round
- 1 Temple **87**, 16 Lehigh **73**
- 8 Georgetown **66**, 9 LSU **63**
- 5 Georgia Tech **90**, 12 Iowa State **78**
- 4 Indiana **69**, 13 Richmond **72** (B)
- 6 Missouri **80**, 11 Rhode Island **87**
- 3 Syracuse **69**, 14 North Carolina A&T **55**
- 7 SMU **83**, 10 Notre Dame **75**
- 2 Duke **85**, 15 Boston U. **69**

Second Round
- Temple **74**, Georgetown **53**
- Georgia Tech **55**, Richmond **59**
- Rhode Island **97**, Syracuse **94** (D)
- SMU **79**, Duke **94**

Regional Semifinals (East Rutherford, NJ)
- Temple **69**, Richmond **47** (C)
- Rhode Island **72**, Duke **73**

Regional Finals
- Temple **53**, Duke **63**

West

First Round
- 1 Arizona **90**, 16 Cornell **50**
- 8 Seton Hall **80**, 9 UTEP **64**
- 5 Iowa **102**, 12 Florida State **98**
- 4 UNLV **54**, 13 Missouri State **50**
- 6 ⊗Florida **62**, 11 St. John's **59**
- 3 Michigan **63**, 14 Boise State **58**
- 7 Wyoming **115**, 10 Loyola Marymount **119**
- 2 North Carolina **83**, 15 North Texas **65**

Second Round
- Arizona **84**, Seton Hall **55**
- Iowa **104**, UNLV **86**
- ⊗Florida **85**, Michigan **108** (E)
- Loyola Marymount **97**, North Carolina **123** (F)

Regional Semifinals (Seattle)
- Arizona **99**, Iowa **79**
- Michigan **69**, North Carolina **78**

Regional Finals
- Arizona **70**, North Carolina **52**

Southeast

First Round
- 1 Oklahoma **94**, 16 Chattanooga **66** (G)
- 8 Auburn **90**, 9 Bradley **86**
- 5 Louisville **70**, 12 Oregon State **61**
- 4 BYU **98** (2OT), 13 Charlotte **92**
- 6 Villanova **82**, 11 Arkansas **74**
- 3 Illinois **81**, 14 Texas-San Antonio **72**
- 7 ⊗Maryland **92**, 10 UC Santa Barbara **82**
- 2 ⊗Kentucky **99**, 15 Southern U. **84** (H)

Second Round
- Oklahoma **107**, Auburn **87**
- Louisville **97**, BYU **76**
- Villanova **66**, Illinois **63**
- ⊗Maryland **81**, ⊗Kentucky **90**

Regional Semifinals (Birmingham, AL)
- Oklahoma **108**, Louisville **98**
- Villanova **80**, ⊗Kentucky **74**

Regional Finals
- Oklahoma **78**, Villanova **59**

National Semifinal

- Kansas **66**, Duke **59**
- Arizona **78**, Oklahoma **86**

National Final (Kansas City)

Kansas 83
Oklahoma 79

Known as Danny and the Miracles in honor of 6′11″ star Danny Manning and his improbable supporting cast, Kansas sets a dubious record for having the worst winning percentage (27–11, .711) of any team to win the national championship.

Coach Mike Krzyzewski and Duke begin a string of five straight Final Four appearances, good for second behind the nine straight reached by John Wooden and UCLA.

Kenny Lofton, who will become a major league All-Star outfielder, comes off the bench to score two points for Arizona, making him one of only two men to compete in both the Final Four and the World Series—the other is NC State forward/Baltimore Orioles pitcher Tim Stoddard. Both men attended East Chicago's Washington High.

A Vanderbilt's Barry Goheen, the Commodores' assist leader for the season, hits two three-pointers of his own in the final :10 to send the game into overtime.

B Rodney Rice hits an 18-foot jumper with :54 left to oust the defending national champion in the opening round. Last year's Indiana hero, Keith Smart, misses a 12-footer with :20 left that would have given the Hoosiers the lead. Richmond becomes only the second team in Tournament history to knock out a defending champion in the first round.

C Richmond becomes the first No. 13 seed to advance two rounds to the Sweet 16. But it can't overcome John Chaney's Temple squad, even with wide-body Owls center Ramon Rivas playing only nine minutes because of foul trouble. Temple limits Richmond to 21 second-half points, 12 of them on three-point bombs.

D Rhode Island makes an improbable run to the Sweet 16, led by senior guard Carlton Owens, who missed playing his junior season in high school because of a gunshot wound to his left (shooting) arm that scared off college recruiters.

E Despite having eight stitches in his shooting hand because of a dishwashing mishap, Glen Rice scores 39 points, hitting 16 of 24 from the field.

F North Carolina shoots 79% from the floor (49 for 62)—second-best in Tournament history—while holding Loyola Marymount to 32% (33 for 103). UNC also sets a Tourney record with 36 assists.

G Oklahoma makes 72 steals in six games to set a Tournament mark—including a record 23 by Mookie Blaylock. Two years later, a new Seattle rock group names itself for the diminutive Sooner guard. The band eventually changes its name to Pearl Jam.

H Southern's Avery Johnson scores two points but dishes out nine assists. The all-time NCAA apg leader (12) will play and coach in the NBA.

⊗Team participation later vacated

TOURNAMENT LEADERS

INDIVIDUAL LEADERS

SCORING

	CL	POS	G	PTS	PPG
1 **Danny Manning**, Kansas	SR	F	6	163	27.2
2 **Stacey King**, Oklahoma	JR	C	6	152	25.3
Rex Chapman, Kentucky	SO	G	3	76	25.3
4 **B.J. Armstrong**, Iowa	JR	G	3	71	23.7
Tom Garrick, Rhode Island	SR	G	3	71	23.7
6 **Pervis Ellison**, Louisville	JR	F/C	3	70	23.3
7 **Sean Elliott**, Arizona	JR	G/F	5	116	23.2
8 **Mitch Richmond**, Kansas State	SR	G	4	87	21.8
9 **Glen Rice**, Michigan	JR	F	3	65	21.7
10 **Carlton Owens**, Rhode Island	SR	G	3	62	20.7

MINIMUM: 3 GAMES

FIELD GOAL PCT

	CL	POS	G	FG	FGA	PCT
1 **Winston Bennett**, Kentucky	SR	F	3	18	23	78.3
2 **Tom Greis**, Villanova	SO	C	4	19	25	76.0
3 **Tim Perry**, Temple	SR	C	4	26	36	72.2
4 **Loy Vaught**, Michigan	SO	F	3	16	23	69.6
5 **Pervis Ellison**, Louisville	JR	F/C	3	30	45	66.7

MINIMUM: 15 MADE AND 3 GAMES

FREE THROW PCT

	CL	POS	G	FT	FTA	PCT
1 **Mike Vreeswyk**, Temple	JR	F	4	18	18	100.0
LaBradford Smith, Louisville	FR	G	3	15	15	100.0
3 **Ed Davender**, Kentucky	SR	G	3	19	20	95.0
4 **Kenny Wilson**, Villanova	JR	G	4	18	19	94.7
5 **Jeff Martin**, Murray State	JR	F	2	16	17	94.1
Chris Morris, Auburn	SR	F	2	16	17	94.1

MINIMUM: 15 MADE

THREE-POINT FG PCT

	CL	POS	G	3FG	3FGA	PCT
1 **Glen Rice**, Michigan	JR	F	3	7	11	63.6
2 **William Scott**, Kansas State	SR	G	4	21	34	61.8
3 **Kenny Payne**, Louisville	JR	F	3	9	16	56.3
4 **Kevin Pritchard**, Kansas	SO	G	6	7	13	53.8
Carlton Owens, Rhode Island	SR	G	3	7	13	53.8

MINIMUM: 6 MADE AND 3 GAMES

ASSISTS PER GAME

	CL	POS	G	AST	APG
1 **Rumeal Robinson**, Michigan	FR	G	3	21	7.0
2 **Ricky Grace**, Oklahoma	SR	G	6	41	6.8
3 **Gary Grant**, Michigan	SR	G	3	20	6.7
Everette Stephens, Purdue	SR	G	3	20	6.7
Keith Williams, Louisville	SO	G	3	20	6.7

MINIMUM: 3 GAMES

REBOUNDS PER GAME

	CL	POS	G	REB	RPG
1 **Pervis Ellison**, Louisville	JR	F/C	3	33	11.0
2 **J.R. Reid**, North Carolina	SO	F/C	4	41	10.3
3 **Danny Manning**, Kansas	SR	F	6	56	9.3
Steve Kratzer, Richmond	SR	F	3	28	9.3
5 **Tim Perry**, Temple	SR	C	4	37	9.3

MINIMUM: 3 GAMES

TEAM LEADERS

SCORING

	G	PTS	PPG
1 **Iowa**	3	285	95.0
2 **Oklahoma**	6	552	92.0
3 **Louisville**	3	265	88.3
4 **Purdue**	3	264	88.0
5 **Kentucky**	3	263	87.7
6 **Rhode Island**	3	256	85.3
7 **Arizona**	5	421	84.2
8 **North Carolina**	4	336	84.0
9 **Michigan**	3	240	80.0
10 **Duke**	5	374	74.8

MINIMUM: 3 GAMES

FG PCT

	G	FG	FGA	PCT
1 **Michigan**	3	96	161	59.6
2 **Kentucky**	3	97	172	56.4
3 **North Carolina**	4	125	227	55.1
4 **Iowa**	3	99	182	54.4
5 **Louisville**	3	105	195	53.8

MINIMUM: 3 GAMES

3-PT FG PCT

	G	3FG	3FGA	PCT
1 **Michigan**	3	12	23	52.2
2 **Kansas State**	4	33	65	50.8
3 **Kentucky**	3	16	32	50.0
Rhode Island	3	10	20	50.0
5 **Purdue**	3	18	39	46.2

MINIMUM: 3 GAMES

FT PCT

	G	FT	FTA	PCT
1 **Temple**	4	76	90	84.4
2 **Villanova**	4	70	87	80.5
3 **Arizona**	5	88	110	80.0
4 **Vanderbilt**	3	33	43	76.7
5 **Kentucky**	3	53	70	75.7

MINIMUM: 3 GAMES

AST/TO RATIO

	G	AST	TO	RAT
1 **Michigan**	3	61	24	2.54
2 **Kentucky**	3	43	21	2.05
3 **Oklahoma**	6	136	77	1.77
4 **Purdue**	3	72	42	1.71
Rhode Island	3	48	28	1.71

MINIMUM: 3 GAMES

REBOUNDS

	G	REB	RPG
1 **Purdue**	3	119	39.7
2 **North Carolina**	4	146	36.5
3 **Kansas**	6	213	35.5
4 **Duke**	5	175	35.0
5 **Louisville**	3	104	34.7

MINIMUM: 3 GAMES

ALL-TOURNAMENT TEAM

PLAYER	CL	POS	HT	SCHOOL	RPG	APG	PPG
Danny Manning*	SR	F	6-11	Kansas	9.3	1.7	27.2
Sean Elliott	JR	G/F	6-8	Arizona	5.8	3.6	23.2
Stacey King	JR	C	6-10	Oklahoma	8.7	0.8	25.3
Milt Newton	JR	F	6-4½	Kansas	7.0	2.8	14.8
Dave Sieger	SR	F	6-5	Oklahoma	3.5	6.2	11.8

ALL-REGIONAL TEAMS

EAST

PLAYER	CL	POS	HT	SCHOOL	RPG	APG	PPG
Danny Ferry*	JR	F	6-10	Duke	8.5	3.5	17.5
Billy King	SR	F	6-6	Duke	4.5	3.8	6.8
Carlton Owens	SR	G	6-0	Rhode Island	2.0	5.0	20.7
Tim Perry	SR	C	6-9	Temple	9.3	0.3	15.8
Kevin Strickland	SR	G	6-5	Duke	4.3	1.8	20.8

MIDWEST

PLAYER	CL	POS	HT	SCHOOL	RPG	APG	PPG
Danny Manning*	SR	F	6-11	Kansas	7.0	1.5	26.8
Milt Newton	JR	F	6-4½	Kansas	7.8	3.3	13.5
Kevin Pritchard	SO	G	6-3	Kansas	3.0	4.3	10.8
Mitch Richmond	SR	G	6-5	Kansas State	7.5	5.0	21.8
William Scott	SR	G	6-2	Kansas State	2.5	2.0	18.8

SOUTHEAST

PLAYER	CL	POS	HT	SCHOOL	RPG	APG	PPG
Stacey King*	JR	C	6-10	Oklahoma	9.8	1.3	28.5
Rex Chapman	SO	G	6-5	Kentucky	2.7	3.7	25.3
Harvey Grant	SR	F	6-8	Oklahoma	6.0	1.0	19.8
Doug West	JR	F	6-6	Villanova	3.8	1.0	16.8
Kenny Wilson	JR	G	5-9	Villanova	2.5	4.8	14.0

WEST

PLAYER	CL	POS	HT	SCHOOL	RPG	APG	PPG
Sean Elliott*	JR	G/F	6-8	Arizona	4.5	4.3	21.3
Steve Kerr	SR	G	6-1	Arizona	3.5	4.3	12.3
J.R. Reid	SO	F/C	6-9	North Carolina	10.3	2.3	19.0
Rumeal Robinson	FR	G	6-2	Michigan	3.0	7.0	15.3
Tom Tolbert	SR	C	6-7	Arizona	5.3	0.5	15.3

* MOST OUTSTANDING PLAYER

1988 NCAA TOURNAMENT BOX SCORES

73-70 (Sweet 16)

34	1H	43
39	2H	27

KANSAS STATE	MIN	FG	3FG	FT	REB	A	ST	BL	PF	TP
Mitch Richmond	40	10-20	2-4	5-8	11	3	0	0	2	27
William Scott	33	6-11	5-5	0-0	3	0	0	0	3	17
Fred McCoy	13	4-8	0-0	0-1	6	0	0	0	2	8
Steve Henson	39	1-3	1-1	2-2	1	12	2	0	4	5
Ron Meyer	27	2-8	0-0	1-2	2	3	0	2	3	5
Charles Bledsoe	17	2-6	0-0	1-3	4	0	2	1	3	5
Mark Dobbins	23	2-4	0-0	0-0	3	0	0	0	1	4
Buster Glover	8	1-1	0-0	0-0	0	0	0	0	2	2
TOTALS	**200**	**28-61**	**8-10**	**9-16**	**30**	**18**	**4**	**3**	**20**	**73**
Percentages		45.9	80.0	56.2						

Coach: Lon Kruger

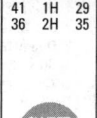

PURDUE	MIN	FG	3FG	FT	REB	A	ST	BL	PF	TP
Everette Stephens	35	7-11	5-7	1-1	5	9	0	2	2	20
Troy Lewis	38	5-11	4-8	5-6	5	2	1	0	2	19
Melvin McCants	33	5-12	0-0	3-4	2	0	0	2	3	13
Todd Mitchell	30	6-15	0-1	1-4	9	0	1	1	4	13
Tony Jones	30	1-3	0-0	0-0	4	6	2	0	4	2
Ryan Berning	3	1-1	0-0	0-0	0	0	0	0	0	2
Steve Scheffler	10	0-0	0-0	1-2	1	0	0	0	2	1
Kip Jones	21	0-0	0-0	0-0	6	1	0	0	1	0
TOTALS	**200**	**25-53**	**9-16**	**11-17**	**32**	**18**	**4**	**5**	**18**	**70**
Percentages		47.2	56.2	64.7						

Coach: Gene Keady

Officials: Do Shea, Bob Garibaldi, Fr Scagliotta **Technicals:** None **Attendance:** 31,309

77-64 (Sweet 16)

41	1H	29
36	2H	35

KANSAS	MIN	FG	3FG	FT	REB	A	ST	BL	PF	TP
Danny Manning	29	16-29	2-3	4-7	5	1	1	1	2	38
Kevin Pritchard	33	5-6	1-1	0-2	1	5	1	1	3	11
Chris Piper	33	3-5	0-0	2-2	10	2	1	0	2	8
Scooter Barry	26	2-4	0-1	4-6	3	3	0	0	0	8
Milt Newton	23	2-7	0-0	0-0	7	1	0	1	2	4
Marvin Mattox	7	0-0	0-0	4-4	0	1	0	0	2	4
Jeff Gueldner	22	1-2	0-0	0-0	2	7	1	0	2	2
Mike Maddox	1	1-1	0-0	0-0	0	0	1	0	0	2
Keith Harris	22	0-3	0-0	0-0	6	1	1	0	0	0
Clint Normore	3	0-0	0-0	0-0	1	0	0	0	0	0
Lincoln Minor	1	0-0	0-0	0-0	0	0	0	0	1	0
TOTALS	**200**	**30-57**	**3-5**	**14-21**	**35**	**21**	**6**	**3**	**14**	**77**
Percentages		52.6	60.0	66.7						

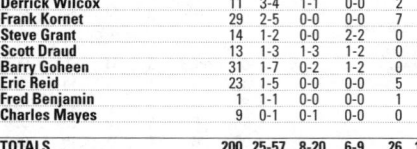

Coach: Larry Brown

VANDERBILT	MIN	FG	3FG	FT	REB	A	ST	BL	PF	TP
Barry Booker	33	8-16	6-13	0-0	3	3	0	1	1	22
Will Perdue	36	7-13	0-0	2-3	8	1	0	2	5	16
Derrick Wilcox	11	3-4	1-1	0-0	2	0	2	0	2	7
Frank Kornet	29	2-5	0-0	0-0	7	4	2	0	2	4
Steve Grant	14	1-2	0-0	2-2	0	0	0	0	1	4
Scott Draud	13	1-3	1-3	1-2	0	2	1	0	4	4
Barry Goheen	31	1-7	0-2	1-2	0	4	1	0	3	3
Eric Reid	23	1-5	0-0	0-0	5	1	0	0	0	2
Fred Benjamin	1	1-1	0-0	0-0	1	0	0	0	0	2
Charles Mayes	9	0-1	0-1	0-0	0	2	0	0	0	0
TOTALS	**200**	**25-57**	**8-20**	**6-9**	**26**	**17**	**6**	**3**	**18**	**64**
Percentages		43.9	40.0	66.7						

Coach: C.M. Newton

Officials: Jam Burr, Tom O'Neill, Terry Tackett **Technicals:** Vanderbilt (bench) **Attendance:** 31,309

69-47 (Sweet 16)

32	1H	26
37	2H	21

TEMPLE	MIN	FG	3FG	FT	REB	A	ST	BL	PF	TP
Mark Macon	40	11-23	0-6	2-4	2	3	2	0	1	24
Mike Vreeswyk	40	6-13	5-9	2-2	4	2	1	0	2	19
Howard Evans	40	4-6	3-5	0-0	1	11	0	0	1	11
Tim Perry	40	5-7	0-0	1-3	13	1	1	4	1	11
Derrick Brantley	14	1-3	0-0	0-0	4	0	2	0	1	2
Ramon Rivas	9	1-1	0-0	0-0	1	0	0	0	4	2
Duane Causwell	16	0-1	0-0	0-0	2	0	0	0	3	0
Shawn Johnson	1	0-0	0-0	0-0	0	0	0	0	0	0
TOTALS	**200**	**28-54**	**8-20**	**5-9**	**27**	**17**	**6**	**4**	**13**	**69**
Percentages		51.9	40.0	55.6						

Coach: John Chaney

RICHMOND	MIN	FG	3FG	FT	REB	A	ST	BL	PF	TP
Ken Atkinson	38	5-9	5-7	0-1	3	2	0	-	0	15
Peter Woolfolk	38	6-13	0-0	0-1	10	0	0	-	1	12
Rodney Rice	38	4-14	3-12	0-0	4	1	0	-	4	11
Steve Kratzer	33	1-3	0-0	2-6	4	0	1	-	3	4
Mike Winiecki	9	1-1	0-0	1-2	1	1	0	-	3	3
Scott Stapleton	30	1-4	0-0	0-0	5	6	0	-	0	2
Benji Taylor	8	0-3	0-3	0-0	0	1	0	-	0	0
Eric English	5	0-0	0-0	0-0	0	2	0	-	0	0
Steve Floyd	1	0-1	0-1	0-0	0	0	0	-	0	0
TOTALS	**200**	**18-48**	**8-23**	**3-10**	**27**	**13**	**1**	**-**	**11**	**47**
Percentages		37.5	34.8	30.0						

Coach: Dick Tarrant

Officials: Ed Hightower, Mac Chauvin, Tom Rucker **Technicals:** None **Attendance:** 19,591

73-72 (Sweet 16)

38	1H	37
35	2H	35

DUKE	MIN	FG	3FG	FT	REB	A	ST	BL	PF	TP
Danny Ferry	34	8-15	0-0	1-2	12	4	1	1	3	17
Robert Brickey	21	4-6	0-0	7-9	7	4	2	1	0	15
Kevin Strickland	30	5-10	1-4	3-5	3	4	0	1	1	14
John Smith	14	6-8	0-0	0-2	4	0	0	0	1	12
Quin Snyder	33	2-4	0-0	0-1	5	6	2	3	3	4
Greg Koubek	8	2-5	0-1	0-0	1	1	0	0	0	4
Billy King	34	1-7	0-0	1-2	5	4	1	0	2	3
Phil Henderson	19	1-7	0-2	0-1	2	1	2	0	0	2
Alaa Abdelnaby	7	0-2	0-0	2-2	1	2	0	0	0	2
TOTALS	**200**	**29-64**	**1-7**	**14-24**	**40**	**26**	**8**	**6**	**10**	**73**
Percentages		45.3	14.3	58.3						

Coach: Mike Krzyzewski

RHODE ISLAND	MIN	FG	3FG	FT	REB	A	ST	BL	PF	TP
Carlton Owens	39	5-13	1-2	8-8	3	4	1	0	4	19
Tom Garrick	39	7-19	0-0	0-0	2	4	0	0	2	14
John Evans	38	4-9	0-0	6-8	7	3	6	0	1	14
Mergin Sina	38	6-8	0-0	2-3	8	4	0	0	1	14
Kenny Green	29	3-9	0-0	5-8	8	3	2	2	0	11
Bonzie Colson	15	0-0	0-0	0-0	1	2	1	4	0	0
Steve Lane	1	0-0	0-0	0-0	1	0	0	0	0	0
Josh Oppenheimer	1	0-1	0-1	0-0	0	0	0	0	0	0
TOTALS	**200**	**25-59**	**1-3**	**21-27**	**30**	**20**	**10**	**6**	**8**	**72**
Percentages		42.4	33.3	77.8						

Coach: Tom Penders

Officials: Sonny Holmes, Don Rutledge, Jim Burch **Technicals:** None **Attendance:** 19,591

99-79 (Sweet 16)

38	1H	34
61	2H	45

ARIZONA	MIN	FG	3FG	FT	REB	A	ST	BL	PF	TP
Sean Elliott	39	11-18	1-5	2-2	3	8	2	0	3	25
Anthony Cook	31	8-12	0-0	3-3	6	0	0	1	2	19
Steve Kerr	39	5-11	5-10	2-3	4	8	1	0	2	17
Tom Tolbert	36	7-13	0-0	3-4	9	1	3	0	2	17
Craig McMillan	22	2-6	2-5	2-2	2	4	1	0	3	8
Kenny Lofton	11	2-3	1-2	1-2	0	1	3	0	1	6
Harvey Mason	8	2-3	2-2	0-1	1	0	0	0	0	6
Joe Turner	7	0-0	0-0	1-2	1	0	0	0	3	1
Jud Buechler	5	0-0	0-0	0-0	1	0	2	0	0	0
Craig Bergman	1	0-0	0-0	0-0	0	0	0	0	0	0
Matt Muehlebach	1	0-0	0-0	0-0	0	0	0	0	0	0
TOTALS	**200**	**37-66**	**11-24**	**14-19**	**27**	**22**	**12**	**1**	**16**	**99**
Percentages		56.1	45.8	73.7						

Coach: Lute Olson

IOWA	MIN	FG	3FG	FT	REB	A	ST	BL	PF	TP
B.J. Armstrong	34	11-21	3-7	2-3	1	7	3	-	1	27
Roy Marble	36	6-15	0-1	2-3	5	2	1	-	3	14
Bill Jones	31	4-6	0-1	4-6	6	3	1	-	3	12
Jeff Moe	26	4-9	3-8	0-0	1	1	1	-	3	11
Kent Hill	23	4-5	0-0	1-2	7	0	0	-	5	9
Ed Horton	22	2-5	0-0	0-0	3	0	1	-	5	4
Michael Reaves	20	1-6	0-3	0-0	3	1	1	-	1	2
Michael Morgan	4	0-0	0-0	0-0	0	0	0	-	1	0
Les Jepsen	2	0-0	0-0	0-0	0	0	0	-	0	0
Mark Jewell	2	0-0	0-0	0-0	2	0	0	-	1	0
Kelly Westen	0	0-0	0-0	0-0	0	0	0	-	0	0
TOTALS	**200**	**32-67**	**6-20**	**9-14**	**28**	**14**	**8**	**-**	**23**	**79**
Percentages		47.8	30.0	64.3						

Coach: Tom Davis

Officials: Nolan Fine, Luis Grillo, Jack Hannon **Technicals:** None **Attendance:** 23,229

78-69 (Sweet 16)

31	1H	30
47	2H	39

NORTH CAROLINA	MIN	FG	3FG	FT	REB	A	ST	BL	PF	TP
Scott Williams	28	5-9	0-0	9-13	7	1	0	2	3	19
J.R. Reid	32	7-14	0-0	4-7	8	1	1	0	3	18
Jeff Lebo	33	2-5	1-3	4-4	2	2	1	0	1	9
Ranzino Smith	20	3-6	2-5	0-1	0	3	1	0	0	8
Steve Bucknall	31	2-6	1-2	2-2	2	1	1	0	2	7
Rick Fox	12	3-5	1-3	0-0	1	3	0	0	2	7
Kevin Madden	18	2-4	0-1	2-2	6	3	1	0	1	6
King Rice	15	1-2	0-1	0-1	1	2	1	0	1	2
Pete Chilcutt	11	1-1	0-0	0-0	0	1	0	0	1	2
TOTALS	**200**	**26-52**	**5-15**	**21-30**	**27**	**17**	**6**	**2**	**14**	**78**
Percentages		50.0	33.3	70.0						

Coach: Dean Smith

MICHIGAN	MIN	FG	3FG	FT	REB	A	ST	BL	PF	TP
Rumeal Robinson	39	10-14	1-3	8-11	5	6	2	0	3	29
Glen Rice	39	7-16	4-8	0-0	7	3	0	2	2	18
Terry Mills	30	6-12	0-0	0-0	4	1	0	2	3	12
Gary Grant	29	3-10	1-5	0-0	3	4	1	0	5	7
Loy Vaught	26	1-3	0-0	0-0	5	0	0	0	3	2
Mark Hughes	17	0-0	0-0	1-2	2	1	0	0	5	1
Mike Griffin	19	0-0	0-0	0-0	3	0	0	0	3	0
J.P. Oosterbaan	1	0-0	0-0	0-0	1	0	0	0	0	0
TOTALS	**200**	**27-55**	**6-16**	**9-13**	**30**	**15**	**3**	**4**	**24**	**69**
Percentages		49.1	37.5	69.2						

Coach: Bill Frieder

Officials: John Clougherty, Dan Chrisman, Jim Stupin **Technicals:** None **Attendance:** 23,229

108-98 — SWEET 16

55	1H	51
53	2H	47

OKLAHOMA	MIN	FG	3FG	FT	REB	A	ST	BL	PF	TP
Harvey Grant	38	14-21	0-0	6-10	7	1	4	0	3	34
Stacey King	36	9-20	0-0	6-13	12	1	1	2	4	24
Mookie Blaylock	40	7-13	3-5	1-3	6	7	2	0	2	18
Ricky Grace	40	3-11	3-8	6-8	3	8	3	0	2	15
Dave Sieger	35	4-7	3-5	0-0	2	7	3	0	3	11
Andre Wiley	6	1-1	0-0	1-2	2	1	0	0	1	3
Terrence Mullins	5	1-1	1-1	0-0	0	0	0	0	1	3
TOTALS	**200**	**39-74**	**10-19**	**20-36**	**32**	**25**	**13**	**2**	**16**	**108**
Percentages		52.7	52.6	55.6						

Coach: Billy Tubbs

LOUISVILLE	MIN	FG	3FG	FT	REB	A	ST	BL	PF	TP
Pervis Ellison	38	11-16	0-1	1-1	14	2	0	4	3	23
Kenny Payne	31	6-12	4-8	2-2	5	2	1	0	2	18
Herbert Crook	27	7-10	0-0	2-2	2	2	3	0	3	16
Felton Spencer	24	6-9	0-0	3-5	7	1	0	0	4	15
Keith Williams	32	4-10	0-0	2-3	2	2	2	0	4	10
LaBradford Smith	22	3-8	1-2	3-3	0	5	1	0	5	10
Mike Abram	22	2-3	0-0	0-0	2	2	1	0	4	4
Craig Hawley	4	1-1	0-0	0-0	0	0	0	0	0	2
TOTALS	**200**	**40-69**	**5-11**	**13-16**	**32**	**16**	**8**	**4**	**25**	**98**
Percentages		58.0	45.5	81.2						

Coach: Denny Crum

Officials: Mickey Crowley, David Jones, Eric Harmon
Technicals: None
Attendance: 16,816

80-74 — SWEET 16

43	1H	32
37	2H	42

VILLANOVA	MIN	FG	3FG	FT	REB	A	ST	BL	PF	TP
Doug West	38	9-16	2-5	0-0	3	1	0	-	2	20
Mark Plansky	40	5-12	2-5	4-4	8	3	0	-	2	16
Kenny Wilson	40	4-10	1-3	6-6	2	6	0	-	0	15
Rodney Taylor	29	3-5	0-0	5-5	8	1	0	-	3	11
Tom Greis	22	5-5	0-0	0-0	3	3	0	-	5	10
Gary Massey	30	3-3	0-0	2-2	2	0	3	-	2	8
Pat Enright	1	0-0	0-0	0-0	0	0	0	-	0	0
TOTALS	**200**	**29-51**	**5-13**	**17-17**	**26**	**14**	**3**	**-**	**14**	**80**
Percentages		56.9	38.5	100.0						

Coach: Rollie Massimino

KENTUCKY	MIN	FG	3FG	FT	REB	A	ST	BL	PF	TP
Rex Chapman	39	11-19	5-9	3-3	1	5	2	-	3	30
Winston Bennett	22	6-9	0-0	4-4	7	0	0	-	4	16
Robert Lock	22	5-6	0-0	1-4	3	0	1	-	4	11
Eric Manuel	38	3-10	3-5	0-0	8	6	1	-	0	9
Ed Davender	40	2-12	0-2	2-2	2	3	0	-	3	6
LeRon Ellis	28	0-2	0-0	2-4	7	1	0	-	2	2
Richard Madison	11	0-1	0-0	0-0	1	0	0	-	1	0
TOTALS	**200**	**27-59**	**8-16**	**12-17**	**29**	**15**	**4**	**-**	**17**	**74**
Percentages		45.8	50.0	70.6						

Coach: Eddie Sutton

Officials: Paul Housman, Bob Dibler, Tom Harrington
Technicals: None
Attendance: 16,816

71-58 — ELITE 8

27	1H	29
44	2H	29

KANSAS	MIN	FG	3FG	FT	REB	A	ST	BL	PF	TP
Danny Manning	39	10-18	0-1	0-1	6	1	0	1	3	20
Milt Newton	29	7-10	2-3	2-2	9	7	1	0	3	18
Scooter Barry	25	5-6	1-1	4-4	5	3	1	0	1	15
Kevin Pritchard	38	2-7	1-4	3-4	3	7	2	0	3	8
Chris Piper	36	3-6	0-1	0-2	4	1	0	0	2	6
Keith Harris	15	2-3	0-0	0-0	1	0	2	0	0	4
Jeff Gueldner	11	0-3	0-1	0-0	0	2	0	0	1	0
Lincoln Minor	4	0-1	0-0	0-0	0	1	0	0	0	0
Mike Maddox	1	0-0	0-0	0-0	0	0	0	0	0	0
Marvin Mattox	1	0-0	0-0	0-1	0	0	0	0	0	0
Clint Normore	1	0-0	0-0	0-0	0	0	0	0	0	0
TOTALS	**200**	**29-54**	**4-11**	**9-14**	**28**	**22**	**6**	**1**	**13**	**71**
Percentages		53.7	36.4	64.3						

Coach: Larry Brown

KANSAS STATE	MIN	FG	3FG	FT	REB	A	ST	BL	PF	TP
William Scott	30	6-15	4-10	2-2	0	1	2	1	0	18
Mitch Richmond	37	4-14	1-5	2-4	4	5	0	0	3	11
Charles Bledsoe	33	5-6	0-0	0-4	9	1	0	1	4	10
Fred McCoy	18	3-5	0-0	3-4	5	0	0	0	2	9
Steve Henson	40	2-8	2-6	0-0	3	5	1	1	4	6
Ron Meyer	26	1-3	0-0	0-0	2	2	1	0	0	2
Buster Glover	9	1-3	0-1	0-0	1	1	0	0	0	2
Carlos Diggins	3	0-0	0-0	0-0	0	0	0	0	1	0
Mark Dobbins	3	0-0	0-0	0-0	1	0	0	0	0	0
Todd Stanfield	1	0-0	0-0	0-0	1	0	0	0	0	0
TOTALS	**200**	**22-54**	**7-22**	**7-14**	**26**	**15**	**4**	**3**	**14**	**58**
Percentages		40.7	31.8	50.0						

Coach: Lon Kruger

Officials: Booker Turner, Dick Paparo, Wally Tanner
Technicals: None
Attendance: 31,632

63-53 — ELITE 8

25	1H	28
38	2H	25

DUKE	MIN	FG	3FG	FT	REB	A	ST	BL	PF	TP
Kevin Strickland	36	9-17	3-8	0-1	5	0	2	4	0	21
Danny Ferry	38	7-11	0-3	6-8	5	4	0	1	2	20
Quin Snyder	36	1-5	1-4	6-7	8	3	1	2	3	9
Billy King	37	2-3	0-0	0-0	3	4	0	2	3	4
Robert Brickey	30	0-8	0-0	3-5	5	0	1	2	2	3
Alaa Abdelnaby	12	1-2	0-0	0-2	3	0	1	0	3	2
Phil Henderson	7	1-2	0-1	0-0	1	0	0	0	0	2
Greg Koubek	4	1-4	0-1	0-0	0	0	0	0	0	2
TOTALS	**200**	**22-52**	**4-17**	**15-23**	**30**	**11**	**5**	**11**	**13**	**63**
Percentages		42.3	23.5	65.2						

Coach: Mike Krzyzewski

TEMPLE	MIN	FG	3FG	FT	REB	A	ST	BL	PF	TP
Mark Macon	40	6-29	1-8	0-0	7	2	0	0	2	13
Tim Perry	34	6-9	0-0	1-1	7	0	1	6	4	13
Howard Evans	40	2-8	1-3	7-8	6	3	1	0	4	12
Mike Vreeswyk	39	2-12	1-6	1-1	7	0	0	0	3	6
Ramon Rivas	32	0-2	0-0	4-4	6	0	0	0	4	4
Jerome Dowdell	2	1-1	1-1	0-0	0	0	0	0	0	3
Derrick Brantley	4	1-1	0-0	0-0	1	0	0	0	2	2
Duane Causwell	9	0-1	0-0	0-0	2	0	0	0	3	0
TOTALS	**200**	**18-63**	**4-18**	**13-14**	**36**	**5**	**2**	**6**	**22**	**53**
Percentages		28.6	22.2	92.9						

Coach: John Chaney

Officials: Larry Lembo, Jim Bain, Art McDonald
Technicals: Duke (bench)
Attendance: 19,633

70-52 — ELITE 8

26	1H	28
44	2H	24

ARIZONA	MIN	FG	3FG	FT	REB	A	ST	BL	PF	TP
Sean Elliott	38	6-11	1-3	11-14	5	3	0	0	3	24
Tom Tolbert	34	8-14	0-0	5-6	6	0	0	0	3	21
Steve Kerr	39	3-4	3-4	5-6	3	3	1	0	2	14
Craig McMillan	30	4-6	1-3	0-0	3	1	2	0	1	9
Anthony Cook	29	0-2	0-0	2-2	4	0	0	0	4	2
Joe Turner	13	0-0	0-0	0-0	2	0	0	1	2	0
Kenny Lofton	8	0-0	0-0	0-0	0	1	1	0	0	0
Jud Buechler	4	0-0	0-0	0-0	1	1	0	0	0	0
Harvey Mason	4	0-2	0-1	0-0	0	1	0	0	1	0
Matt Muehlebach	1	0-0	0-0	0-0	0	0	0	0	0	0
TOTALS	**200**	**21-39**	**5-11**	**23-28**	**24**	**10**	**4**	**1**	**16**	**70**
Percentages		53.8	45.5	82.1						

Coach: Lute Olson

NORTH CAROLINA	MIN	FG	3FG	FT	REB	A	ST	BL	PF	TP
Scott Williams	30	5-7	0-1	3-4	6	0	0	1	4	13
J.R. Reid	31	4-10	0-0	2-2	9	2	1	0	4	10
Jeff Lebo	34	3-9	3-8	0-0	0	4	0	0	3	9
Ranzino Smith	23	3-12	3-10	0-0	3	0	2	0	1	9
Rick Fox	18	3-4	0-0	1-2	1	0	1	0	2	7
Steve Bucknall	21	1-1	0-0	0-0	0	2	0	0	4	2
Kevin Madden	17	1-9	0-0	0-0	2	1	0	0	2	2
Pete Chilcutt	11	0-1	0-0	0-0	1	3	0	0	0	0
King Rice	10	0-1	0-0	0-0	2	0	0	0	2	0
Jeff Denny	1	0-0	0-0	0-0	0	0	0	0	0	0
Doug Elstun	1	0-0	0-0	0-0	0	0	0	0	0	0
Rodney Hyatt	1	0-2	0-0	0-0	1	0	0	0	0	0
Joe Jenkins	1	0-0	0-0	0-0	0	0	0	0	0	0
David May	1	0-0	0-0	0-0	0	0	0	0	0	0
TOTALS	**200**	**20-56**	**6-19**	**6-8**	**25**	**12**	**4**	**1**	**22**	**52**
Percentages		35.7	31.6	75.0						

Coach: Dean Smith

Officials: Rich Ballesteros, Tim Higgins, Jody Silvester
Technicals: None
Attendance: 22,470

78-59 — ELITE 8

31	1H	38
47	2H	21

OKLAHOMA	MIN	FG	3FG	FT	REB	A	ST	BL	PF	TP
Stacey King	36	12-20	0-0	4-7	11	0	0	0	1	28
Mookie Blaylock	39	5-12	2-5	2-2	5	3	4	0	3	14
Harvey Grant	39	4-10	0-0	4-5	9	2	0	0	2	12
Ricky Grace	36	2-5	1-4	4-6	4	5	2	0	4	9
Dave Sieger	33	3-9	2-8	0-0	2	6	4	0	4	8
Andre Wiley	1	2-3	0-1	0-0	1	0	0	0	0	4
Jason Skurcenski	1	0-1	0-0	2-2	1	0	0	0	1	2
Tyrone Jones	1	0-0	0-0	1-2	0	0	0	0	0	1
Terrence Mullins	8	0-2	0-0	0-0	1	1	0	0	0	0
Tony Martin	4	0-0	0-0	0-2	0	0	0	0	2	0
Mike Bell	1	0-0	0-0	0-0	0	0	0	1	0	0
Art Pollard	1	0-0	0-0	0-0	0	1	0	0	0	0
TOTALS	**200**	**28-62**	**5-18**	**17-26**	**34**	**18**	**10**	**1**	**17**	**78**
Percentages		45.2	27.8	65.4						

Coach: Billy Tubbs

VILLANOVA	MIN	FG	3FG	FT	REB	A	ST	BL	PF	TP
Doug West	31	7-11	1-2	3-4	4	1	0	0	4	18
Kenny Wilson	38	5-14	1-5	4-5	1	4	3	0	4	15
Tom Greis	26	4-5	0-0	0-0	7	0	0	1	3	8
Mark Plansky	38	3-11	0-4	0-0	5	5	0	0	1	6
Gary Massey	24	3-4	0-0	0-1	2	1	1	0	1	6
Pat Enright	2	1-2	0-2	2-2	1	0	0	0	2	4
Rodney Taylor	30	1-5	0-0	0-0	11	0	0	0	1	2
Barry Bekkedam	3	0-0	0-0	0-0	0	0	0	0	2	0
Greg Downs	2	0-0	0-0	0-0	0	0	0	0	0	0
Chris Masotti	2	0-0	0-0	0-0	0	0	0	0	0	0
Tim Muller	2	0-2	0-1	0-0	0	0	0	0	0	0
Rob Tribuiani	2	0-0	0-0	0-0	0	0	0	0	0	0
TOTALS	**200**	**24-54**	**2-14**	**9-12**	**31**	**11**	**4**	**1**	**18**	**59**
Percentages		44.4	14.3	75.0						

Coach: Rollie Massimino

Officials: Joe Forte, David Dodge, Sam Lickliter
Technicals: Villanova (bench)
Attendance: 11,218

66-59

	1H	2H
Kansas	38	28
Duke	27	32

FINAL 4

KANSAS	MIN	FG	3FG	FT	REB	A	ST	BL	PF	TP
Danny Manning	39	12-21	0-0	1-2	10	2	4	6	3	25
Milt Newton	32	8-14	2-3	2-3	7	3	1	1	3	20
Chris Piper	29	3-4	0-0	4-4	6	3	1	1	2	10
Kevin Pritchard	36	2-6	0-1	2-2	7	5	2	1	2	6
Scooter Barry	27	1-2	0-0	3-4	1	1	0	0	4	5
Keith Harris	15	0-4	0-0	0-0	3	0	0	0	0	0
Clint Normore	11	0-0	0-0	0-0	1	1	1	0	0	0
Jeff Gueldner	9	0-1	0-0	0-0	1	1	0	0	2	0
Mike Maddox	1	0-0	0-0	0-0	0	0	0	0	0	0
Lincoln Minor	1	0-0	0-0	0-0	0	0	0	0	0	0
Marvin Mattox	0	0-0	0-0	0-0	0	0	0	0	0	0
TOTALS	**200**	**26-52**	**2-4**	**12-15**	**36**	**16**	**9**	**9**	**16**	**66**
Percentages		50.0	50.0	80.0						

Coach: Larry Brown

DUKE	MIN	FG	3FG	FT	REB	A	ST	BL	PF	TP
Danny Ferry	36	7-22	1-5	4-4	12	4	3	0	4	19
Kevin Strickland	35	5-13	0-3	0-0	6	1	1	2	2	10
Quin Snyder	28	4-10	0-3	1-2	3	5	2	0	4	9
Greg Koubek	16	3-5	2-3	0-0	4	0	0	0	2	8
Robert Brickey	27	2-9	0-0	2-5	6	0	1	1	1	6
Alaa Abdelnaby	12	1-2	0-0	2-4	0	0	0	1	2	4
Billy King	26	1-4	0-0	1-2	1	2	0	1	4	3
Phil Henderson	16	0-2	0-0	0-0	3	1	0	0	0	0
John Smith	4	0-0	0-0	0-0	0	0	1	0	0	0
Joe Cook	0	0-0	0-0	0-0	0	0	0	0	0	0
TOTALS	**200**	**23-67**	**3-14**	**10-17**	**35**	**13**	**8**	**5**	**19**	**59**
Percentages		34.3	21.4	58.8						

Coach: Mike Krzyzewski

Officials: Booker Turr Larry Lembc James Burr **Technicals:** None **Attendance:** 16,392

86-78

	1H	2H
Oklahoma	39	47
Arizona	27	51

FINAL 4

OKLAHOMA	MIN	FG	3FG	FT	REB	A	ST	BL	PF	TP
Harvey Grant	36	7-14	0-0	7-10	10	0	2	0	0	21
Stacey King	28	9-16	0-0	3-6	6	0	1	1	4	21
Ricky Grace	40	3-10	2-7	5-7	0	8	2	0	3	13
Andre Wiley	17	4-8	0-0	3-3	4	0	0	1	2	11
Dave Sieger	32	3-8	1-6	3-6	6	3	1	0	3	10
Mookie Blaylock	40	3-7	0-0	1-2	7	6	2	0	1	7
Terrence Mullins	7	1-1	1-1	0-0	1	1	0	0	0	3
TOTALS	**200**	**30-64**	**4-14**	**22-34**	**34**	**18**	**8**	**2**	**13**	**86**
Percentages		46.9	28.6	64.7						

Coach: Billy Tubbs

ARIZONA	MIN	FG	3FG	FT	REB	A	ST	BL	PF	TP
Sean Elliott	38	13-23	2-4	3-3	11	1	0	0	4	31
Anthony Cook	37	6-13	0-0	4-6	11	0	0	1	3	16
Tom Tolbert	32	5-11	0-0	1-2	13	3	0	1	4	11
Craig McMillan	25	3-6	2-4	0-0	0	3	0	0	5	8
Steve Kerr	40	2-13	2-12	0-0	2	5	1	0	2	6
Jud Buechler	6	2-2	0-0	0-0	0	0	0	0	0	4
Kenny Lofton	11	1-4	0-3	0-0	2	0	1	0	4	2
Joe Turner	7	0-0	0-0	0-0	2	0	0	0	1	0
Harvey Mason	4	0-0	0-0	0-0	0	0	0	0	1	0
TOTALS	**200**	**32-72**	**6-23**	**8-11**	**41**	**12**	**2**	**2**	**24**	**78**
Percentages		44.4	26.1	72.7						

Coach: Lute Olson

Officials: Pau Housman, Joe Forte, Luis Gri **Technicals:** None **Attendance:** 16,392

83-79

	1H	2H
Kansas	50	33
Oklahoma	50	29

NCAA FINAL 1988

KANSAS	MIN	FG	3FG	FT	REB	A	ST	BL	PF	TP
Danny Manning	36	13-24	0-1	5-7	18	2	5	2	3	31
Milt Newton	32	6-6	2-2	1-2	4	1	0	2	1	15
Kevin Pritchard	31	6-7	1-1	0-0	1	4	1	0	1	13
Chris Piper	37	4-6	0-0	0-0	7	2	3	0	3	8
Clint Normore	16	3-3	1-1	0-1	1	4	0	0	3	7
Lincoln Minor	11	1-4	0-0	2-2	1	1	1	0	1	4
Jeff Gueldner	15	1-2	0-1	0-0	2	1	1	0	0	2
Keith Harris	12	1-1	0-0	0-0	1	0	0	0	2	2
Scooter Barry	9	0-2	0-0	1-2	0	2	0	0	1	1
Mike Maddox	1	0-0	0-0	0-0	0	0	0	0	1	0
TOTALS	**200**	**35-55**	**4-6**	**9-14**	**35**	**17**	**11**	**4**	**16**	**83**
Percentages		63.6	66.7	64.3						

Coach: Larry Brown

OKLAHOMA	MIN	FG	3FG	FT	REB	A	ST	BL	PF	TP
Dave Sieger	40	7-15	7-13	1-2	5	7	3	0	2	22
Stacey King	39	7-14	0-0	3-3	7	0	1	2	3	17
Mookie Blaylock	40	6-13	2-4	0-1	5	4	7	0	4	14
Harvey Grant	40	6-14	0-0	2-3	5	1	1	1	4	14
Ricky Grace	34	4-14	1-7	3-4	7	7	1	0	4	12
Terrence Mullins	7	0-0	0-0	0-0	1	0	0	0	1	0
TOTALS	**200**	**30-70**	**10-24**	**9-13**	**30**	**19**	**13**	**3**	**18**	**79**
Percentages		42.9	41.7	69.2						

Coach: Billy Tubbs

Officials: John Clougherty, Tim Higgins, Ed Hightower **Technicals:** None **Attendance:** 16,392

National Invitation Tournament (NIT)

First round: Ohio State d. Old Dominion 86-73, Georgia d. Ga. Southern 53-48, Connecticut d. West Virginia 62-57 (OT), Evansville d. Utah 66-55, Louisiana Tech d. Arkansas-Little Rock 66-56, Boston College d. Siena 73-65, Houston d. Fordham 69-61, New Mexico d. Pepperdine 86-75, Oregon d. Santa Clara 81-65, Cleveland State d. Illinois State 89-83 (OT), Middle Tenn. St. d. Tennessee 85-80, VCU d. Marshall 81-80, Arkansas State d. UL-Monroe 70-54, Southern Miss d. Clemson 74-69, Colorado State d. New Orleans 63-54, Stanford d. Long Beach St. 80-77
Second round: Connecticut d. Louisiana Tech 65-59, VCU d. Southern Miss 93-89, Ohio State d. Cleveland State 86-80, Middle Tenn. St. d. Georgia 69-54, Boston College d. Evansville 86-81, Colorado State d. Houston 71-61, Arkansas State d. Stanford 60-59, New Mexico d. Oregon 78-59
Third round: Connecticut d. VCU 69-60, Ohio State d. New Mexico 68-65, Colorado State d. Arkansas State 69-49, Boston College d. Middle Tenn. St. 78-69
Semifinals: Ohio State d. Colorado State 64-62, Connecticut d. Boston College 73-67
Third place: Colorado State d. Boston College 58-57.
Championship: Connecticut d. Ohio State 72-67
MVP: Phil Gamble, Connecticut

1988-89: AMAZIN' BLUE

It was public, it was ugly and it may well have won the Maize and Blue its first national title. At the end of the regular season, Michigan coach Bill Frieder announced that he would move to Arizona State after the NCAA Tournament. Feisty Michigan athletic director Bo Schembechler promptly sacked Frieder and replaced him for the NCAAs with his top assistant, Steve Fisher.

The extra-motivated Wolverines proceeded to reach the Final Four at Seattle's Kingdome. After an 83-81 semifinal win over Illinois, Michigan (30–7) got 31 points from MOP Glen Rice and two free throws by Rumeal Robinson with :03 left in OT to beat Seton Hall, 80-79. The Wolverines' total Final Four victory margin of three points is the smallest for any champion. Rice set Tournament records with his 27 three-pointers and 184 points.

Kentucky's streak of 60 consecutive non-losing seasons (an NCAA record) was snapped; the Wildcats went 13–19 in coach Eddie Sutton's final campaign in Lexington. Naismith Player of the Year honors went to Duke's Danny Ferry (22.6 ppg, 7.4 rpg, 4.7 apg). Louisville's Pervis Ellison was the No. 1 pick in the NBA draft, by the Sacramento Kings.

MAJOR CONFERENCE STANDINGS

AM. SOUTH

	Conference			Overall		
	W	L	PCT	W	L	PCT
New Orleans□	7	3	.700	19	11	.633
Louisiana Tech○	6	4	.600	23	9	.719
Arkansas State□	6	4	.600	20	10	.667
UL-Lafayette	4	6	.400	17	12	.586
Texas-Pan American	4	6	.400	15	13	.536
Lamar	3	7	.300	12	16	.429

Tournament: **Louisiana Tech d. New Orleans 84-62**

AMCU-8

	Conference			Overall		
	W	L	PCT	W	L	PCT
Missouri State⊕	10	2	.833	21	10	.677
Northern Iowa	8	4	.667	19	9	.679
Eastern Illinois	7	5	.583	16	16	.500
Wisconsin-Green Bay	6	6	.500	14	14	.500
Valparaiso	4	8	.333	10	19	.345
Western Illinois	4	8	.333	9	19	.321
Illinois-Chicago	3	9	.250	13	17	.433
Cleveland State	—	—	—	16	12	.571

Tournament: **Missouri State d. Illinois-Chicago 73-67**
Tournament MVP: **Hubert Henderson**, Missouri State

ATLANTIC 10

	Conference			Overall		
	W	L	PCT	W	L	PCT
West Virginia○	17	1	.944	26	5	.839
Temple□	15	3	.833	18	12	.600
Rutgers⊕	13	5	.722	18	13	.581
Penn State□	12	6	.667	20	12	.625
Rhode Island	9	9	.500	13	15	.464
St. Bonaventure	7	11	.389	13	15	.464
Duquesne	7	11	.389	13	16	.448
Massachusetts	5	13	.278	10	18	.357
Saint Joseph's	4	14	.222	8	21	.276
George Washington	1	17	.056	1	27	.036

Tournament: **Rutgers d. Penn State 70-66**
Tournament MVP: **Tom Savage**, Rutgers

ACC

	Conference			Overall		
	W	L	PCT	W	L	PCT
NC State○	10	4	.714	22	9	.710
North Carolina⊕	9	5	.643	29	8	.784
Duke○	9	5	.643	28	8	.778
Virginia○	9	5	.643	22	11	.667
Georgia Tech○	8	6	.571	20	12	.625
Clemson○	7	7	.500	19	11	.633
Wake Forest	3	11	.214	13	15	.464
Maryland	1	13	.071	9	20	.310

Tournament: **North Carolina d. Duke 77-74**
Tournament MVP: **J.R. Reid**, North Carolina

BIG EAST

	Conference			Overall		
	W	L	PCT	W	L	PCT
Georgetown⊕	13	3	.813	29	5	.853
Seton Hall○	11	5	.688	31	7	.816
Syracuse○	10	6	.625	30	8	.789
Pittsburgh○	9	7	.563	17	13	.567
Providence○	7	9	.438	18	11	.621
Villanova□	7	9	.438	18	16	.529
St. John's□	6	10	.375	20	13	.606
Connecticut□	6	10	.375	18	13	.581
Boston College	3	13	.188	12	17	.414

Tournament: **Georgetown d. Syracuse 88-79**
Tournament MVP: **Charles Smith**, Georgetown

BIG EIGHT

	Conference			Overall		
	W	L	PCT	W	L	PCT
Oklahoma○	12	2	.857	30	6	.833
Missouri⊕	10	4	.714	29	8	.784
Kansas State○	8	6	.571	19	11	.633
Iowa State○	7	7	.500	17	12	.586
Oklahoma State□	7	7	.500	17	13	.567
Kansas	6	8	.429	19	12	.613
Nebraska□	4	10	.286	17	16	.515
Colorado	2	12	.143	7	21	.250

Tournament: **Missouri d. Oklahoma 98-86**
Tournament MVP: **Doug Smith**, Missouri

BIG SKY

	Conference			Overall		
	W	L	PCT	W	L	PCT
Boise State□	13	3	.813	23	7	.767
Idaho⊕	13	3	.813	25	6	.806
Montana	11	5	.688	20	11	.645
Nevada	10	6	.625	16	12	.571
Weber State	9	7	.563	17	11	.607
Montana State	6	10	.375	14	15	.483
Eastern Washington	5	11	.313	8	22	.267
Idaho State	4	12	.250	9	18	.333
Northern Arizona	1	15	.063	2	25	.074

Tournament: **Idaho d. Boise State 59-52**
Tournament MVP: **Riley Smith**, Idaho

BIG SOUTH

	Conference			Overall		
	W	L	PCT	W	L	PCT
Coastal Carolina	9	3	.750	14	14	.500
Campbell	8	4	.667	18	12	.600
UNC Asheville	6	6	.500	16	14	.533
Charleston Southern	6	6	.500	12	16	.429
Winthrop	5	7	.417	16	13	.552
Radford	5	7	.417	15	13	.536
Augusta	3	9	.250	5	23	.179

Tournament: **UNC Asheville d. Campbell 93-78**
Tournament MVP: **Milton Moore**, UNC Asheville

BIG TEN

	Conference			Overall		
	W	L	PCT	W	L	PCT
Indiana⊕	15	3	.833	27	8	.771
Illinois○	14	4	.778	31	5	.861
Michigan○	12	6	.667	30	7	.811
Iowa○	10	8	.556	23	10	.697
Minnesota○	9	9	.500	19	12	.613
Wisconsin□	8	10	.444	18	12	.600
Purdue	8	10	.444	15	16	.484
Ohio State□	6	12	.333	19	15	.559
Michigan State□	6	12	.333	18	15	.545
Northwestern	2	16	.111	9	19	.321

BIG WEST

	Conference			Overall		
	W	L	PCT	W	L	PCT
UNLV⊕	16	2	.889	29	8	.784
New Mexico State□	12	6	.667	21	11	.656
UC Santa Barbara□	11	7	.611	21	9	.700
Cal State Fullerton	10	8	.556	16	13	.552
Long Beach State	10	8	.556	13	15	.464
Utah State	10	8	.556	12	16	.429
Fresno State	9	9	.500	15	14	.517
UC Irvine	8	10	.444	12	17	.414
Pacific	3	15	.167	7	21	.250
San Jose State	1	17	.056	5	23	.179

Tournament: **UNLV d. New Mexico State 68-62**
Tournament MVP: **Stacey Augmon**, UNLV

COLONIAL ATHLETIC

	Conference			Overall		
	W	L	PCT	W	L	PCT
Richmond□	13	1	.929	21	10	.677
George Mason⊕	10	4	.714	20	11	.645
American	9	5	.643	17	11	.607
UNC Wilmington	9	5	.643	16	14	.533
James Madison	6	8	.429	16	14	.533
East Carolina	6	8	.429	15	14	.517
William and Mary	2	12	.143	5	23	.179
Navy	1	13	.071	6	22	.214

Tournament: **Geo. Mason d. UNC Wilmington 78-72 (OT)**
Tournament MVP: **Kenny Sanders**, George Mason

EAST COAST

	Conference			Overall		
	W	L	PCT	W	L	PCT
Bucknell⊕	11	3	.786	23	8	.742
Towson	10	4	.714	19	10	.655
Lafayette	8	6	.571	20	10	.667
Hofstra	7	7	.500	14	15	.483
Drexel	7	7	.500	12	16	.429
Delaware	6	8	.429	14	14	.500
Lehigh	5	9	.357	10	18	.357
Rider	2	12	.143	5	23	.179

Tournament: **Bucknell d. Lafayette 71-65**
Tournament MVP: **Mike Butts**, Bucknell

ECAC NAC

	Conference			Overall		
	W	L	PCT	W	L	PCT
Siena⊕	16	1	.941	25	5	.833
Boston U.	14	4	.778	21	9	.700
Northeastern	12	5	.706	17	11	.607
Canisius	11	7	.611	13	15	.464
Hartford	10	7	.588	15	13	.536
Maine	7	11	.389	9	19	.321
Niagara	6	12	.333	9	19	.321
Colgate	5	13	.278	6	22	.214
Vermont	4	14	.222	6	21	.222
New Hampshire	3	14	.176	4	22	.154

Tournament: **Siena d. Boston U. 68-67**
Tournament MVP: **Marc Brown**, Siena

IVY

	Conference			Overall		
	W	L	PCT	W	L	PCT
Princeton⊕	11	3	.786	19	8	.704
Dartmouth	10	4	.714	17	9	.654
Penn	9	5	.643	13	13	.500
Harvard	7	7	.500	11	15	.423
Cornell	7	7	.500	10	16	.385
Yale	6	8	.429	11	17	.393
Columbia	4	10	.286	8	18	.308
Brown	2	12	.143	7	19	.269

METRO

	Conference			Overall		
	W	L	PCT	W	L	PCT
Florida State○	9	3	.750	22	8	.733
Louisville⊕	8	4	.667	24	9	.727
Memphis○	8	4	.667	21	11	.656
South Carolina○	8	4	.667	19	11	.633
Cincinnati	5	7	.417	15	12	.556
Virginia Tech	2	10	.167	11	17	.393
Southern Miss	2	10	.167	10	17	.370

Tournament: **Louisville d. Florida State 87-80**
Tournament MVP: **Pervis Ellison**, Louisville

Conference Standings Continue →

⊕ Automatic NCAA Tournament bid ○ At-large NCAA Tournament bid □ NIT appearance ⊗ Team record doesn't reflect games forfeited or vacated. For adjusted record, see p. 521.

METRO ATLANTIC

	Conference			Overall		
	W	L	Pct	W	L	Pct
La Salle⊕	13	1	.929	26	6	.813
Saint Peter's□	11	3	.786	22	9	.710
Iona	8	6	.571	15	16	.484
Fordham	8	6	.571	14	15	.483
Army	6	8	.429	12	16	.429
Holy Cross	5	9	.357	13	15	.464
Manhattan	3	11	.214	7	21	.250
Fairfield	2	12	.143	7	21	.250

Tournament: **La Salle d. Saint Peter's 71-58**
Tournament MVP: **Lionel Simmons**, La Salle

MID-AMERICAN

	Conference			Overall		
	W	L	Pct	W	L	Pct
Ball State⊕	14	2	.875	29	3	.906
Kent State□⊗	12	4	.750	20	11	.645
Toledo⊗	11	5	.688	16	15	.516
Eastern Michigan⊗	8	8	.500	16	13	.552
Miami (OH)⊗	8	8	.500	13	15	.464
Bowling Green⊗	7	9	.438	12	16	.429
Central Mich.⊗	7	9	.438	12	16	.429
Western Michigan	6	10	.375	12	16	.429
Ohio⊗	6	10	.375	12	17	.414

Tournament: **Ball State d. Kent State 67-65**
Tournament MVP: **Billy Butts**, Ball State

MEAC

	Conference			Overall		
	W	L	Pct	W	L	Pct
South Carolina State⊕	14	2	.875	25	8	.758
Florida A&M	12	4	.750	20	10	.667
Coppin State	11	5	.688	18	11	.621
Morgan State	9	7	.563	15	13	.536
Bethune-Cookman	8	8	.500	12	16	.429
Delaware State	6	10	.375	11	17	.393
NC A&T	6	10	.375	9	18	.333
Howard	5	11	.313	9	19	.321
UMES	1	15	.063	1	26	.037

Tournament: **South Carolina St. d. Florida A&M 83-79**
Tournament MOP: **Travis Williams**, South Carolina St.

MCC

	Conference			Overall		
	W	L	Pct	W	L	Pct
Evansville○	10	2	.833	25	6	.806
Saint Louis□	8	4	.667	27	10	.730
Xavier⊕	7	5	.583	21	12	.636
Dayton	6	6	.500	12	17	.414
Loyola-Chicago	4	8	.333	11	17	.393
Detroit	4	8	.333	7	21	.250
Butler	3	9	.250	11	17	.393

Tournament: **Xavier d. Evansville 85-78**
Tournament MVP: **Tyrone Hill**, Xavier

MISSOURI VALLEY

	Conference			Overall		
	W	L	Pct	W	L	Pct
Creighton⊕	11	3	.786	20	11	.645
Wichita State□	10	4	.714	19	11	.633
Tulsa	10	4	.714	18	13	.581
Bradley	7	7	.500	13	14	.481
Southern Illinois□	6	8	.429	20	14	.588
Illinois State	6	8	.429	13	17	.433
Drake	6	8	.429	12	17	.414
Indiana State	0	14	.000	4	24	.143

Tournament: **Creighton d. Southern Illinois 79-77**
Tournament MVP: **Chad Gallagher**, Creighton

NORTHEAST

	Conference			Overall		
	W	L	Pct	W	L	Pct
Robert Morris⊕	12	4	.750	21	9	.700
Fairleigh Dickinson	11	5	.688	17	12	.586
Monmouth	9	7	.563	15	13	.536
Marist	9	7	.563	13	15	.464
Loyola (MD)	7	9	.438	10	18	.357
Long Island	7	9	.438	9	19	.321
Saint Francis (PA)	6	10	.375	13	16	.448
Wagner	6	10	.375	10	17	.370
St. Francis (NY)	5	11	.313	14	16	.467

Tournament: **Robert Morris d. Fairleigh Dickinson 67-66**
Tournament MVP: **Vaughn Luton**, Robert Morris

OHIO VALLEY

	Conference			Overall		
	W	L	Pct	W	L	Pct
Middle Tenn. State⊕	10	2	.833	23	8	.742
Murray State□	10	2	.833	19	11	.633
Austin Peay	8	4	.667	18	12	.600
Morehead State	5	7	.417	15	16	.484
Eastern Kentucky	4	8	.333	7	22	.241
Tennessee Tech	3	9	.250	10	20	.333
Tennessee State	2	10	.167	4	24	.143

Tournament: **Middle Tenn. State d. Austin Peay 82-79**
Tournament MVP: **Keith Rawls**, Austin Peay

PAC-10

	Conference			Overall		
	W	L	Pct	W	L	Pct
Arizona⊕	17	1	.944	29	4	.879
Stanford○	15	3	.833	26	7	.788
Oregon State○	13	5	.722	22	8	.733
UCLA○	13	5	.722	21	10	.677
California□	10	8	.556	20	13	.606
Washington	8	10	.444	12	16	.429
Arizona State	5	13	.278	12	16	.429
Washington State	4	14	.222	10	19	.345
Oregon	3	15	.167	8	21	.276
Southern California	2	16	.111	10	22	.313

Tournament: **Arizona d. Stanford 73-51**
Tournament MVP: **Sean Elliott**, Arizona

SEC

	Conference			Overall		
	W	L	Pct	W	L	Pct
Florida○	13	5	.722	21	13	.618
Alabama⊕	12	6	.667	23	8	.742
Vanderbilt○	12	6	.667	19	14	.576
Tennessee○	11	7	.611	19	11	.633
LSU○	11	7	.611	20	12	.625
Mississippi□	8	10	.444	15	15	.500
Kentucky	8	10	.444	13	19	.406
Mississippi State	7	11	.389	13	15	.464
Georgia	6	12	.333	15	16	.484
Auburn	2	16	.111	9	19	.321

Tournament: **Alabama d. Florida 72-60**
Tournament MVP: **Livingston Chatman**, Florida

SOUTHERN

	Conference			Overall		
	W	L	Pct	W	L	Pct
Chattanooga	10	4	.714	18	12	.600
Furman	9	5	.643	17	12	.586
Appalachian State	8	6	.571	20	8	.714
East Tenn. State⊕	7	7	.500	20	11	.645
The Citadel	7	7	.500	16	12	.571
Marshall	6	8	.429	15	15	.500
VMI	5	9	.357	11	17	.393
Western Carolina	4	10	.286	12	16	.429

Tournament: **East Tenn. State d. Marshall 96-73**
Tournament MOP: **John Taft**, Marshall

SOUTHLAND

	Conference			Overall		
	W	L	Pct	W	L	Pct
North Texas	10	4	.714	14	15	.483
UL-Monroe	9	5	.643	17	12	.586
McNeese State⊕	9	5	.643	16	14	.533
Sam Houston State	8	6	.571	12	16	.429
Northwestern St. (LA)	7	7	.500	13	16	.448
Texas State	6	8	.429	13	17	.433
Texas-Arlington	4	10	.286	7	21	.250
Stephen F. Austin	3	11	.214	10	18	.357

Tournament: **McNeese State d. North Texas 85-68**
Tournament MVP: **Michael Cutright**, McNeese State

SOUTHWEST

	Conference			Overall		
	W	L	Pct	W	L	Pct
Arkansas⊕	13	3	.813	25	7	.781
Texas○	12	4	.750	25	9	.735
TCU	9	7	.563	17	13	.567
Houston	8	8	.500	17	14	.548
Texas A&M	8	8	.500	16	14	.533
Texas Tech	8	8	.500	13	15	.464
SMU	7	9	.438	13	16	.448
Rice	6	10	.375	12	16	.429
Baylor	1	15	.063	5	22	.185

Tournament: **Arkansas d. Texas 100-76**
Tournament MVP: **Lenzie Howell**, Arkansas

SWAC

	Conference			Overall		
	W	L	Pct	W	L	Pct
Southern U.⊕	10	4	.714	20	11	.645
Texas Southern	10	4	.714	17	13	.567
Grambling	10	4	.714	15	14	.517
Jackson State	7	7	.500	15	13	.536
Alabama State	7	7	.500	13	16	.448
Prairie View A&M	5	9	.357	11	16	.407
Alcorn State	4	10	.286	5	23	.179
Miss. Valley State	3	11	.214	8	20	.286

Tournament: **Southern U. d. Texas Southern 86-81 (OT)**
Tournament MVP: **Charles Price**, Texas Southern

SUN BELT

	Conference			Overall		
	W	L	Pct	W	L	Pct
South Alabama⊕	11	3	.786	23	9	.719
Charlotte□	10	4	.714	17	12	.586
VCU	9	5	.643	13	15	.464
UAB□	8	6	.571	22	12	.647
Old Dominion	7	7	.500	15	13	.536
Jacksonville	5	9	.357	14	16	.467
Western Kentucky	4	10	.286	14	15	.483
South Florida	2	12	.143	7	21	.250

Tournament: **South Alabama d. Jacksonville 105-99**
Tournament MVP: **Jeff Hodge**, South Alabama

TAAC

	Conference			Overall		
	W	L	Pct	W	L	Pct
Georgia Southern□	16	2	.889	23	6	.793
Arkansas-Little Rock⊕	14	4	.778	23	8	.742
Stetson	10	8	.556	17	12	.586
Centenary	9	9	.500	16	14	.533
Georgia State	9	9	.500	14	14	.500
Mercer	9	9	.500	14	14	.500
UTSA	8	10	.444	15	13	.536
Houston Baptist	6	12	.333	9	20	.310
Samford	5	13	.278	8	19	.296
Hardin-Simmons	4	14	.222	8	19	.296

Tournament: **Arkansas-Little Rock d. Centenary 100-72**
Tournament MVP: **Jeff Cummings**, Arkansas-Little Rock

WEST COAST

	Conference			Overall		
	W	L	Pct	W	L	Pct
Saint Mary's (CA)○	12	2	.857	25	5	.833
Loyola Marymount⊕	10	4	.714	20	11	.645
Pepperdine□	10	4	.714	20	13	.606
San Francisco	8	6	.571	16	12	.571
Santa Clara□	7	7	.500	20	11	.645
Gonzaga	5	9	.357	14	14	.500
San Diego	2	12	.143	8	20	.286
Portland	2	12	.143	2	26	.071

Tournament: **Loyola Marymount d. Santa Clara 75-70 (OT)**
Tournament MVP: **Hank Gathers**, Loyola Marymount

WAC

	Conference			Overall		
	W	L	Pct	W	L	Pct
Colorado State○	12	4	.750	23	10	.697
UTEP⊕	11	5	.688	26	7	.788
New Mexico□	11	5	.688	22	11	.667
Hawaii□	9	7	.563	17	13	.567
BYU	7	9	.438	14	15	.483
Air Force	6	10	.375	14	14	.500
Utah	6	10	.375	16	17	.485
Wyoming	6	10	.375	14	17	.452
San Diego State	4	12	.250	12	17	.414

Tournament: **UTEP d. Colorado State 73-60**
Tournament MVP: **Tim Hardaway**, UTEP

INDEPENDENTS

	Overall		
	W	L	Pct
Akron□	21	8	.724
Notre Dame○	21	9	.700
DePaul○⊗	21	12	.636
Miami (FL)	19	12	.613
UMBC	17	11	.607
Wright State	17	11	.607
Marquette	13	15	.464
Mount St. Mary's	12	15	.444
Chicago State	12	16	.429
Nicholls State	12	16	.429
Northern Illinois	11	17	.393
U.S. International	11	17	.393
Liberty	10	17	.370
Central Connecticut State	10	18	.357
Florida International	10	18	.357
Southern Utah	10	18	.357
Oral Roberts	8	20	.286
UCF	7	20	.259
Davidson⊗	7	24	.226
Youngstown State	5	23	.179
Brooklyn	4	23	.148
Southeastern Louisiana	3	24	.111

INDIVIDUAL LEADERS—SEASON

SCORING	CL	POS	G	FG	3FG	FT	PTS	PPG
1 **Hank Gathers**, Loyola Marymount	JR	F	31	419	0	177	1,015	**32.7**
2 **Chris Jackson**, LSU	FR	G	32	359	84	163	965	**30.2**
3 **Lionel Simmons**, La Salle	JR	F	32	349	21	189	908	**28.4**
4 **Gerald Glass**, Mississippi	JR	F	30	326	41	148	841	**28.0**
5 **Blue Edwards**, East Carolina	JR	G	29	297	25	154	773	**26.7**
6 **Raymond Dudley**, Air Force	JR	G	28	262	105	117	746	**26.6**
7 **Bimbo Coles**, Virginia Tech	JR	G	27	249	62	157	717	**26.6**
8 **Michael Smith**, BYU	SR	G	29	286	33	160	765	**26.4**
9 **Stacey King**, Oklahoma	SR	C	33	324	0	211	859	**26.0**
10 **John Taft**, Marshall	SO	G	27	245	52	159	701	**26.0**

FIELD GOAL PCT	CL	POS	G	FG	FGA	PCT
1 **Dwayne Davis**, Florida	SO	F	33	179	248	**72.2**
2 **Cameron Burns**, Mississippi State	SO	F	28	167	249	**67.1**
3 **Dale Davis**, Clemson	SO	F/C	29	146	218	**67.0**
4 **Rodney Mack**, South Carolina State	SR	F/C	33	204	306	**66.7**
5 **Brian Parker**, Cleveland State	JR	F	28	168	253	**66.4**

MINIMUM: 5 MADE PER GAME

THREE-PT FG PER GAME	CL	POS	G	3FG	3PG
1 **Timothy Pollard**, Miss. Valley State	SR	G	28	124	**4.4**
2 **Sydney Grider**, UL-Lafayette	JR	G	29	122	**4.2**
3 **Jeff Fryer**, Loyola Marymount	JR	G	31	126	**4.1**
4 **Dana Barros**, Boston College	SR	G	29	112	**3.9**
5 **George McCloud**, Florida State	SR	G/F	30	115	**3.8**

THREE-PT FG PCT	CL	POS	G	3FG	3FGA	PCT
1 **Dave Calloway**, Monmouth	SO	G	28	48	82	**58.5**
2 **Joel Tribelhorn**, Colorado State	SR	G	33	76	135	**56.3**
3 **Mike Joseph**, Bucknell	JR	G	31	62	115	**53.9**
4 **John Bays**, Towson	SR	G	29	71	132	**53.8**
5 **Mark Anglavar**, Marquette	SO	G	28	53	99	**53.5**

MINIMUM: 1.5 MADE PER GAME

FREE THROW PCT	CL	POS	G	FT	FTA	PCT
1 **Michael Smith**, BYU	SR	G	29	160	173	**92.5**
2 **Steve Henson**, Kansas State	JR	G	30	92	100	**92.0**
3 **Larry Simmons**, UMBC	JR	G	28	83	92	**90.2**
4 **Kai Nurnberger**, Southern Illinois	SR	G	33	129	143	**90.2**
5 **Scott Haffner**, Evansville	SR	G	31	136	151	**90.1**

MINIMUM: 2.5 MADE PER GAME

ASSISTS PER GAME	CL	POS	G	AST	APG
1 **Glenn Williams**, Holy Cross	SR	G	28	278	**9.9**
2 **Chris Corchiani**, NC State	SO	G	31	266	**8.6**
3 **Sherman Douglas**, Syracuse	SR	G	38	326	**8.6**
4 **Gary Payton**, Oregon State	JR	G	30	244	**8.1**
5 **Anthony Manuel**, Bradley	SR	G	27	216	**8.0**
6 **Jeff Timberlake**, Boston U.	SR	G	30	238	**7.9**
7 **Doug Overton**, La Salle	SO	G	32	244	**7.6**
8 **Jerome "Pooh" Richardson**, UCLA	SR	G	31	236	**7.6**
9 **Carlos Sample**, Southern U.	SO	G	31	234	**7.5**
10 **Darrell McGee**, New Mexico	JR	G	33	243	**7.4**

REBOUNDS PER GAME	CL	POS	G	REB	RPG
1 **Hank Gathers**, Loyola Marymount	JR	F	31	426	**13.7**
2 **Tyrone Hill**, Xavier	JR	F	33	403	**12.2**
3 **Ron Draper**, American	JR	F	28	336	**12.0**
4 **Daryl Battles**, Southern U.	SR	F/C	31	360	**11.6**
5 **Lionel Simmons**, La Salle	JR	F	32	365	**11.4**
6 **Derrick Coleman**, Syracuse	JR	C	37	422	**11.4**
7 **Fred Burton**, Long Island	SR	F	28	309	**11.0**
8 **Rodney Mack**, South Carolina State	SR	F/C	33	361	**10.9**
9 **Kenny Sanders**, George Mason	SR	F	30	326	**10.9**
10 **Rico Washington**, Weber State	SR	C	28	303	**10.8**

BLOCKED SHOTS PER GAME	CL	POS	G	BLK	BPG
1 **Alonzo Mourning**, Georgetown	FR	F/C	34	169	**5.0**
2 **Duane Causwell**, Temple	SO	C	30	124	**4.1**
3 **Alan Ogg**, UAB	JR	C	34	129	**3.8**
4 **Derrick Coleman**, Syracuse	JR	C	37	127	**3.4**
5 **Mike Butts**, Bucknell	SR	F	31	100	**3.2**

STEALS PER GAME	CL	POS	G	STL	SPG
1 **Kenny Robertson**, Cleveland State	JR	G	28	111	**4.0**
2 **Mookie Blaylock**, Oklahoma	SR	G	35	131	**3.7**
3 **Darrion Applewhite**, Texas Southern	JR	G	30	105	**3.5**
4 **Carlton Screen**, Providence	JR	G	29	101	**3.5**
5 **Kurk Lee**, Towson	JR	G	29	98	**3.4**

INDIVIDUAL LEADERS—GAME

POINTS	CL	POS	OPP	DATE	PTS
1 **Scott Haffner**, Evansville	SR	G	Dayton	F18	**65**
2 **Danny Ferry**, Duke	SR	F	Miami (FL)	D10	**58**
3 **Chris Jackson**, LSU	FR	G	Mississippi	M4	**55**
4 **Chris Jackson**, LSU	FR	G	Florida	D10	**53**
5 **Michael Cutright**, McNeese State	SR	G	Stephen F. Austin	M2	**51**

THREE-PT FG MADE	CL	POS	OPP	DATE	3FG
1 **Dennis Scott**, Georgia Tech	SO	G	Houston	D28	**11**
Scott Haffner, Evansville	SR	G	Dayton	F18	**11**
3 **Scott Murphy**, Mount St. Mary's	SO	G	Wright State	J31	**10**
David Donerlson, Western Carolina	JR	G	Elon	F20	**10**
George McCloud, Florida State	SR	G/F	La Salle	F23	**10**

ASSISTS	CL	POS	OPP	DATE	AST
1 **Sherman Douglas**, Syracuse	SR	G	Providence	J28	**22**
2 **Ronn McMahon**, Eastern Washington	JR	G	UC Irvine	D13	**18**
Doug Overton, La Salle	SO	G	Holy Cross	F13	**18**
4 **Jeff Lebo**, North Carolina	SR	G	Chattanooga	N18	**17**
5 Eight tied with 16					

REBOUNDS	CL	POS	OPP	DATE	REB
1 **Hank Gathers**, Loyola Marymount	JR	F	U.S. International	J31	**29**
2 **Hank Gathers**, Loyola Marymount	JR	F	Nevada	D30	**26**
3 **Joey Fatta**, Baylor	SO	F	North Texas	D17	**24**
Adrian Caldwell, Lamar	SR	C	Texas-Pan American	F4	**24**
5 **Warren Bradley**, Cleveland State	SO	F	Clarion	N25	**23**
Stacey King, Oklahoma	SR	C	Loyola Marymount	D17	**23**
Ron Draper, American	JR	F	Harvard	D17	**23**
Hank Gathers, Loyola Marymount	JR	F	U.S. International	J7	**23**
Stanley Brundy, DePaul	SR	F	Loyola Marymount	J14	**23**
Elbert Boyd, Morehead State	SR	F/C	Austin Peay	J16	**23**
Tyrone Hill, Xavier	JR	F	Loyola-Chicago	F9	**23**

BLOCKED SHOTS	CL	POS	OPP	DATE	BLK
1 **Alan Ogg**, UAB	JR	C	Florida A&M	D16	**12**
Dikembe Mutombo, Georgetown	SO	C	St. John's	J23	**12**
3 **Alonzo Mourning**, Georgetown	FR	F/C	St. Leo	D7	**11**
4 **Duane Causwell**, Temple	SO	C	Penn State	D26	**10**
Kevin Cooper, Iona	JR	F/C	Northern Illinois	J74	**10**
Torsten Stein, Fairleigh Dickinson	SR	C	Rider	J9	**10**
Alonzo Mourning, Georgetown	FR	F/C	Boston College	J14	**10**
Duane Causwell, Temple	SO	C	Penn State	J19	**10**

STEALS	CL	POS	OPP	DATE	STL
1 **Mookie Blaylock**, Oklahoma	SR	G	Loyola Marymount	D17	**13**
2 **Kenny Robertson**, Cleveland State	JR	G	Wagner	D3	**12**
3 **Mark Macon**, Temple	SO	G	Notre Dame	J29	**11**
4 **Tim Keyes**, Sam Houston State	SR	G	Texas	D1	**10**
Lorenzo Neely, Eastern Michigan	SR	G	Cleveland State	D14	**10**
Kenny Robertson, Cleveland State	JR	G	Northern Iowa	F18	**10**

TEAM LEADERS—SEASON

WIN-LOSS PCT	W	L	PCT
1 **Ball State**	29	3	**.906**
2 **Arizona**	29	4	**.879**
3 **Illinois**	31	5	**.861**
4 **Georgetown**	29	5	**.853**
5 **West Virginia**	26	5	**.839**

SCORING OFFENSE	G	W-L	PTS	PPG
1 **Loyola Marymount**	31	20-11	3,486	**112.5**
2 **Oklahoma**	36	30-6	3,680	**102.2**
3 **Southern U.**	31	20-11	3,015	**97.3**
4 **Texas**	34	25-9	3,206	**94.3**
5 **LSU**	32	20-12	2,966	**92.7**

SCORING MARGIN	G	W-L	PPG	OPP PPG	MAR
1 **Saint Mary's (CA)**	30	25-5	76.1	57.6	**18.5**
2 **Arizona**	33	29-4	84.5	66.9	**17.6**
3 **Michigan**	37	30-7	91.7	74.8	**16.9**
4 **Duke**	36	28-8	86.5	69.8	**16.7**
5 **Siena**	30	25-5	85.0	69.8	**15.2**

FIELD GOAL PCT	G	W-L	FG	FGA	PCT
1 **Michigan**	37	30-7	1,325	2,341	**56.6**
2 **New Mexico**	33	22-11	992	1,819	**54.5**
3 **Syracuse**	38	30-8	1,334	2,456	**54.3**
4 **Duke**	36	28-8	1,163	2,166	**53.7**
5 **Saint Mary's (CA)**	30	25-5	859	1,606	**53.5**

THREE-PT FG PER GAME	G	W-L	3FG	3PG
1 **Loyola Marymount**	31	20-11	287	**9.3**
2 **Valparaiso**	29	10-19	257	**8.9**
3 **Oral Roberts**	28	8-20	216	**7.7**
4 **Mount St. Mary's**	27	12-15	202	**7.5**
5 **UAB**	34	22-12	247	**7.3**

FREE THROW PCT	G	W-L	FT	FTA	PCT
1 **BYU**	29	14-15	527	647	**81.5**
2 **Gonzaga**	28	14-14	485	614	**79.0**
3 **Bucknell**	31	23-8	590	749	**78.8**
4 **Kent State**	31	20-11	592	755	**78.4**
5 **LSU**	32	20-12	557	723	**77.0**

REBOUND MARGIN	G	W-L	RPG	OPP RPG	MAR
1 **Iowa**	33	23-10	41.4	31.8	**9.6**
2 **Notre Dame**	30	21-9	37.7	28.8	**8.9**
3 **Missouri**	37	29-8	42.1	34.2	**7.9**
4 **Michigan**	37	30-7	37.7	30.3	**7.4**
5 **Stanford**	33	26-7	34.8	27.7	**7.1**

SCORING DEFENSE	G	W-L	OPP PTS	OPP PPG
1 **Princeton**	27	19-8	1,430	**53.0**
2 **Saint Mary's (CA)**	30	25-5	1,728	**57.6**
3 **Boise State**	30	23-7	1,767	**58.9**
4 **Colorado State**	33	23-10	2,012	**61.0**
5 **Idaho**	31	25-6	1,894	**61.1**

Field Goal Pct Defense	G	W-L	OPP FG	OPP FGA	OPP PCT
1 Georgetown	34	29-5	795	1,993	**39.9**
2 West Virginia	31	26-5	738	1,840	**40.1**
3 Saint Mary's (CA)	30	25-5	651	1,606	**40.5**
4 Ball State	32	29-3	688	1,687	**40.8**
5 Seton Hall	38	31-7	934	2,265	**41.2**

CONSENSUS ALL-AMERICAS

FIRST TEAM

PLAYER	CL	POS	HT	SCHOOL	RPG	PPG
Sean Elliott	SR	G/F	6-8	Arizona	7.2	22.3
Pervis Ellison	SR	F/C	6-9	Louisville	8.7	17.6
Danny Ferry	SR	F	6-10	Duke	7.4	22.6
Chris Jackson	FR	G	6-1	LSU	2.5	30.2
Stacey King	SR	C	6-11	Oklahoma	10.1	26.0

SECOND TEAM

PLAYER	CL	POS	HT	SCHOOL	RPG	PPG
Mookie Blaylock	SR	G	6-1	Oklahoma	4.7	20.0
Sherman Douglas	SR	G	6-0	Syracuse	2.4	18.2
Jay Edwards	SO	G	6-4	Indiana	4.3	20.0
Todd Lichti	SR	G	6-4	Stanford	5.0	20.1
Glen Rice	SR	F	6-7	Michigan	6.3	25.6
Lionel Simmons	JR	F	6-6	La Salle	11.4	28.4

Selectors: AP, NABC, UPI, USBWA

AWARD WINNERS

PLAYER OF THE YEAR

PLAYER	CL	POS	HT	SCHOOL	AWARDS
Danny Ferry	SR	F	6-10	Duke	Naismith, UPI, USBWA
Sean Elliott	SR	G/F	6-8	Arizona	AP, Wooden, NABC, Rupp
Tim Hardaway	SR	G	6-0	UTEP	Frances Pomeroy Naismith*

* For the most outstanding senior player who is 6 feet or under.

DEFENSIVE PLAYER OF THE YEAR

PLAYER	CL	POS	HT	SCHOOL
Stacey Augmon	SO	G/F	6-8	UNLV

COACH OF THE YEAR

COACH	SCHOOL	REC	AWARDS
Mike Krzyzewski	Duke	28-8	Naismith
Bob Knight	Indiana	27-8	AP, UPI, USBWA
P.J. Carlesimo	Seton Hall	31-7	NABC, Sporting News
Lute Olson	Arizona	29-4	CBS/Chevrolet

Bob Gibbons' Top High School Senior Recruits

PLAYER	POS	HT	HIGH SCHOOL	A-A TEAMS	COLLEGE	CAREER NOTES
1 **Shaquille O'Neal**	C	7-0	Robert G. Cole HS, San Antonio	McD, P	LSU	LSU's all-time leader in blocks; National POY, '91; No. 1 overall pick, '92 NBA draft (Magic); NBA MVP, '00; 3-time Finals MVP
2 **Kenny Anderson**	PG	6-1	Archbishop Molloy HS, Jamaica, NY	McD, P, USA	Georgia Tech	Final Four, '90; No. 2 pick, '91 NBA draft (Nets); 12.6 ppg, 6.1 apg (14 seasons)
3 **Doug Edwards**	PF	6-9	Miami Senior HS	McD, P, USA	Florida State	At FSU, 17.2 ppg (4 seasons); No. 15 pick, '93 NBA draft (Hawks); 2.4 ppg (3 seasons)
4 **Deon Thomas**	PF	6-9	Simeon Vocational HS, Chicago	McD, P	Illinois	UI's all-time scoring leader (2,129 pts); No. 28 pick, '94 NBA draft (Mavs); played overseas
5 **Bobby Hurley**	PG	6-0	St. Anthony HS, Jersey City, NJ	McD, P, USA	Duke	2 NCAA titles; Tournament MOP, '92; left Duke as NCAA career assists leader; No. 7 pick, '93 NBA draft (Kings); 3.8 ppg (5 seasons)
6 **Allan Houston**	2G	6-6	Ballard HS, Louisville, KY	McD, P, USA	Tennessee	Left UT as all-time scoring leader; No. 11 pick, '93 NBA draft (Pistons); 2-time NBA All-Star; 17.3 ppg (12 seasons)
7 **Lawrence Funderburke**	PF	6-8	Wehrle HS, Columbus, OH		Indiana/Ohio State	Transferred after 1 year; in college, 14.5 ppg (4 seasons); No. 51 pick, '94 NBA draft (Kings); 6.4 ppg (7 seasons)
8 **Jimmy Jackson**	GF	6-6	Macomber-Whitney HS, Toledo, OH	McD, P, USA	Ohio State	Left OSU 6th all-time leading scorer; first-team All-America, '92; No. 4 pick, '92 NBA draft (Mavs); 14.3 ppg (14 seasons)
9 **George Lynch**	F	6-7	Flint Hill Prep, Falls Church, VA	McD	North Carolina	NCAA title, '93; left UNC 2nd all-time in rebounds; No. 12 pick, '93 NBA draft (Lakers); 6.6 ppg (12 seasons)
10 **Travis Ford**	PG	5-10	North Hopkins HS, Madisonville, KY	P	Missouri/Kentucky	Transferred after 1 year; first-team All-SEC, '93; undrafted
11 **James Robinson**	G	6-2	William B. Murrah HS, Jackson, MS	McD, P	Alabama	Left Alabama 6th all-time leading scorer; No. 21 pick, '93 NBA draft (Blazers); 7.7 ppg (8 seasons)
12 **Pat Graham**	G/F	6-5	Floyd Central HS, New Albany, IN	McD	Indiana	Indiana Mr. Basketball, '89; NCAA Final Four, '92; undrafted
13 **Tracy Murray**	SF	6-8	Glendora HS, Glendora, CA	McD	UCLA	At UCLA, 18.3 ppg (3 seasons); No. 18 pick, '92 NBA draft (Spurs); 9.0 ppg (12 seasons)
14 **Jeff Webster**	F	6-7	Carl Albert HS, Midwest City, OK	McD, P	Oklahoma	At Oklahoma, 17.8 ppg (4 seasons); No. 40 pick, '94 NBA draft (Spurs); played in 11 NBA games
15 **Billy McCaffrey**	2G	6-4	Central Catholic HS, Allentown, PA	McD, P	Duke/Vanderbilt	At Duke, NCAA title, '91; two-time All-America at Vanderbilt; undrafted
16 **Zan Mason**	F	6-7	Westchester HS, Los Angeles	P	UCLA/Loyola Marymount	Transferred after 2 years; at Loyola, 13.6 ppg, 6.8 rpg, 1.1 spg (2 seasons); undrafted
17 **Jerry Walker**	PF	6-6	St. Anthony HS, Jersey City, NJ		Seton Hall	Big East Defensive POY, '93; at SHU, 11.1 ppg (4 seasons); undrafted; played overseas
18 **Mitchell Butler**	G/F	6-5	Oakwood HS, North Hollywood, CA	McD, P	UCLA	Left UCLA 7th all-time in steals; undrafted; played on 3 NBA teams; 5.2 ppg (8 seasons)
19 **Arron Bain**	SF	6-7	Flint Hill Prep, Falls Church, VA	McD, P	Villanova	9 points in '89 McDonald's game; at Villanova, 4-year starter
20 **Edward Stokes**	C/F	7-0	St. Bernard HS, Playa del Rey, CA		Arizona	At Arizona, 8.1 ppg, 5.3 rpg (4 seasons); No. 35 pick, '93 NBA draft (Heat); played in 4 NBA games

Other Standouts

PLAYER	POS	HT	HIGH SCHOOL	A-A TEAMS	COLLEGE	CAREER NOTES
29 **Harold Miner**	2G	6-4	Inglewood (CA) HS		Southern California	First-team All-America, '92; No. 12 pick, '92 NBA draft (Heat); 9.0 ppg (4 seasons); 2-time Slam Dunk champ
58 **Calbert Cheaney**	SF	6-6	William Henry Harrison HS, Evansville, IN		Indiana	National POY, '93; No. 6 pick, '93 NBA draft (Bullets); 9.5 ppg (13 seasons)
60 **Greg Graham**	2G	6-3	Warren Central HS, Indianapolis	McD	Indiana	At Indiana, 12.0 ppg (4 seasons); No. 17 pick, '93 NBA draft (Hornets); 4.5 ppg (5 seasons)

Abbreviations: McD=McDonald's; P=Parade; USA=USA Today

Poll Progression

Preseason Poll

AP	UPI	School
1	1	Duke
2	4	Georgetown
3	2	Michigan
4	10	Louisville
5	6	Oklahoma
6	3	North Carolina
7	9	Iowa
8	8	Syracuse
9	5	Illinois
10	7	UNLV
11	11	Arizona
12	12	Villanova
13	16	Georgia Tech
14	13	Missouri
15	14	Florida
16	18	Florida State
17	—	Ohio State
18	20	NC State
19	15	Temple
20	19	Stanford
—	17	Indiana
—	20	Purdue

Week of Nov 22

AP	School	AP↓↑
1	Duke (1-0) (A)	
2	Georgetown (0-0)	
3	Michigan (0-0)	
4	Oklahoma (0-0)	↑1
5	North Carolina (2-0)	↑1
6	Syracuse (0-0)	↑2
7	Iowa (0-0)	
8	UNLV (0-0)	↑2
9	Illinois (0-0)	
10	Arizona (0-0)	↑1
11	Villanova (0-0)	↑1
12	Louisville (0-1)	↓8
13	Missouri (2-0)	↑1
14	Georgia Tech (0-0)	↓1
15	Florida (0-0)	
16	Ohio State (0-0)	↑1
17	Florida State (0-0)	↓1
18	NC State (0-0)	
19	Temple (0-0)	
20	Indiana (2-0)	⤴

Week of Nov 29

AP	UPI	School	AP↓↑
1	1	Duke (2-0)	
2	2	Michigan (3-0)	↑1
3	4	Georgetown (2-0)	↓1
4	3	Syracuse (4-0)	↑2
5	5	Oklahoma (2-1)	↓1
6	7	Iowa (1-0)	↑1
7	6	Illinois (1-0)	↑2
8	11	Missouri (3-1)	↑5
9	8	UNLV (2-1)	↓1
10	10	North Carolina (3-1)	↓5
11	9	Arizona (0-0)	↓1
12	12	Georgia Tech (1-0)	↑2
13	16	Louisville (0-1)	↓1
14	14	Florida State (1-0)	↑3
15	15	Ohio State (2-1)	↑1
16	—	NC State (1-0)	↑2
17	13	Temple (0-0)	↑2
18	17	Villanova (1-1)	↓7
19	18	Florida (2-1)	↓4
20	—	Tennessee (1-0)	⤴
—	19	Stanford (1-1)	
—	20	Seton Hall (3-0)	

Week of Dec 6

AP	UPI	School	AP↓↑
1	1	Duke (4-0)	
2	2	Michigan (5-0)	
3	3	Syracuse (7-0)	↑1
4	4	Georgetown (2-0)	↓1
5	6	Iowa (4-0)	↑1
6	7	Oklahoma (2-1)	↓1
7	9	Illinois (3-0)	
8	5	North Carolina (6-1)	↑2
9	8	UNLV (2-1)	
10	10	Arizona (2-1)	↑1
11	11	Missouri (5-2)	↓3
12	12	Georgia Tech (3-0)	
13	13	Florida State (3-0)	↑1
14	15	Ohio State (3-1)	↑1
15	14	Louisville (1-2)	↓2
16	16	Tennessee (3-0)	↑4
17	17	Villanova (3-1)	↑1
18	—	Connecticut (2-0)	⤴
19	—	NC State (2-1)	↓3
20	19	Seton Hall (5-0)	⤴
—	18	UCLA (3-0)	
—	20	Oregon State (2-0)	

Week of Dec 13

AP	UPI	School	AP↓↑
1	1	Duke (6-0)	
2	2	Michigan (8-0)	
3	3	Syracuse (8-0)	
4	5	Iowa (6-0)	↑1
5	4	Georgetown (4-0)	↓1
6	6	Illinois (6-0)	↑1
7	7	Oklahoma (5-1)	↓1
8	8	North Carolina (8-1)	
9	9	Arizona (3-1)	↑1
10	10	Missouri (7-2)	↑1
11	11	Georgia Tech (4-0)	↑1
12	12	Florida State (4-0)	↑1
13	13	UNLV (2-2)	↓4
14	14	Ohio State (4-1)	
15	16	Louisville (4-2)	
16	17	Tennessee (4-0)	
17	15	Seton Hall (7-0)	↑3
18	20	NC State (2-1)	↑1
19	18	Notre Dame (4-0)	⤴
20	19	UCLA (4-0)	⤴

Week of Dec 20

AP	UPI	School	AP↓↑
1	1	Duke (6-0)	
2	2	Michigan (9-0)	
3	3	Syracuse (10-0)	
4	4	Iowa (8-0)	
5	5	Illinois (7-0)	↑1
6	6	Georgetown (6-0)	↓1
7	8	Oklahoma (6-1) (B)	
8	7	North Carolina (9-1)	
9	9	Arizona (4-1)	
10	10	Missouri (9-2)	
11	11	Florida State (6-0)	↑1
12	12	Ohio State (6-1)	↑2
13	14	UNLV (3-2)	
14	15	Louisville (5-2)	↑1
15	13	Seton Hall (9-0)	↑2
16	16	Georgia Tech (4-1)	↓5
17	20	NC State (2-1)	↑1
18	17	South Carolina (5-0)	⤴
19	18	Tennessee (4-1)	↓3
20	—	Kansas (7-1)	⤴
—	19	Georgia (5-2)	

Week of Dec 27

AP	UPI	School	AP↓↑
1	1	Duke (7-0)	
2	2	Michigan (11-0)	
3	3	Syracuse (11-0)	
4	4	Illinois (9-0)	↑1
5	6	Georgetown (7-0)	↑1
6	7	Oklahoma (8-1)	↑1
7	5	North Carolina (10-1)	↑1
8	8	Arizona (6-1)	↑1
9	9	Iowa (10-1)	↓5
10	12	Florida State (7-0)	↑1
11	11	Missouri (10-3)	↓1
12	10	UNLV (5-2)	↑1
13	13	Seton Hall (10-0)	↑2
14	14	Louisville (6-2)	
15	15	Ohio State (7-2)	↓3
16	19	South Carolina (6-0)	↑2
17	17	Georgia Tech (5-1)	↓1
18	18	NC State (4-1)	↓1
19	20	Tennessee (6-1)	
20	—	Kansas (8-1)	
—	16	Georgia (7-2)	

Week of Jan 3

AP	UPI	School	AP↓↑
1	1	Duke (8-0)	
2	2	Syracuse (13-0)	↑1
3	3	Illinois (12-0)	↑1
4	6	Oklahoma (10-1)	↑2
5	5	Georgetown (9-0)	
6	4	North Carolina (11-1)	↑1
7	7	Michigan (12-1) (C)	↓5
8	7	Arizona (8-1)	
9	9	Iowa (11-1)	
10	10	Seton Hall (12-0)	↑3
11	13	Missouri (12-3)	
12	12	UNLV (7-2)	
13	11	Louisville (7-2)	↑1
14	14	Ohio State (9-2)	↑1
15	15	Florida State (8-1)	↓5
16	17	Tennessee (8-1)	↑3
17	18	NC State (6-1)	↑2
18	—	Kansas (10-1)	↑2
19	16	Georgia Tech (7-2)	↓2
20	20	Georgia (9-2)	⤴
—	19	UTEP (11-1)	

Week of Jan 10

AP	UPI	School	AP↓↑
1	1	Duke (11-0)	
2	2	Illinois (13-0)	↑1
3	3	Oklahoma (12-1)	↑1
4	4	Syracuse (14-1)	↓2
5	6	Iowa (13-1)	↑4
6	5	Michigan (13-1)	↑1
7	7	Georgetown (10-1)	↓2
8	8	North Carolina (13-2)	↓2
9	9	Louisville (9-2)	↑4
10	12	Missouri (13-3)	↑1
11	11	UNLV (9-2)	↑1
12	10	Arizona (9-2)	↓4
13	13	Seton Hall (13-1)	↓3
14	14	Florida State (10-1)	↑1
15	17	NC State (9-1)	↑1
16	—	Kansas (12-1)	↑2
17	18	Tennessee (10-1)	↓1
18	15	Ohio State (10-3)	↓4
19	16	Georgia Tech (10-2)	
20	18	Providence (12-0)	⤴
—	20	UTEP (13-1)	

Week of Jan 17

AP	UPI	School	AP↓↑
1	1	Duke (13-0)	
2	2	Illinois (15-0)	
3	4	Georgetown (12-1)	↑4
4	3	Louisville (12-2)	↑5
5	6	Oklahoma (13-2)	↓2
6	5	Michigan (14-2)	
7	8	Iowa (13-2)	↓2
8	8	Missouri (13-3)	↑2
9	7	Arizona (11-2)	↑3
10	10	UNLV (11-2)	↑1
11	11	Syracuse (14-3)	↓7
12	13	Seton Hall (15-1)	↑1
13	12	North Carolina (14-3)	↓5
14	14	Florida State (12-1)	
15	15	NC State (11-1)	
16	16	Ohio State (12-3)	↑2
17	—	Kansas (14-2)	↓1
18	20	Tennessee (11-2)	↓1
19	17	Indiana (13-4)	⤴
20	18	Stanford (12-3)	⤴
—	19	Providence (13-1)	↱
—	20	Georgia Tech (10-4)	↱

Week of Jan 24

AP	UPI	School	AP↓↑
1	1	Illinois (17-0)	↑1
2	2	Georgetown (14-1)	↑1
3	3	Louisville (13-2)	↑1
4	4	Oklahoma (15-2)	↑1
5	8	Missouri (16-3)	↑3
6	5	Arizona (13-2)	↑3
7	6	North Carolina (16-3)	↑6
8	7	Duke (13-2)	↓7
9	9	Seton Hall (17-1)	↑3
10	10	Michigan (15-3)	↓4
11	11	Florida State (14-1)	↑3
12	12	Iowa (14-3)	↓5
13	16	UNLV (13-3)	↓3
14	13	Syracuse (15-4)	↓3
15	15	NC State (12-2)	
16	14	Indiana (15-4)	↑3
17	17	Ohio State (12-4)	↓1
18	—	Kansas (15-3)	↓1
19	18	Stanford (14-4)	↑1
20	—	Providence (14-2)	⤴
—	19	Georgia Tech (12-5)	
—	20	Saint Mary's (CA) (16-1)	

Week of Jan 31 (D)

AP	UPI	School	AP↓↑
1	1	Oklahoma (17-2)	↑3
2	2	Illinois (18-1)	↓1
3	3	North Carolina (18-3)	↑4
4	3	Arizona (15-2)	↑2
5	6	Missouri (18-3)	
6	5	Georgetown (15-2) (E)	↓4
7	7	Louisville (14-3)	↓4
8	9	Florida State (16-1)	↑3
9	13	Iowa (15-3)	↑3
10	8	Seton Hall (18-2)	↓1
11	11	Michigan (16-4)	↓1
12	10	Duke (14-3)	↓4
13	12	NC State (14-2)	↑2
14	14	Syracuse (17-4)	
15	15	Ohio State (15-4)	↑2
16	17	UNLV (14-4)	↓3
17	16	Indiana (16-5)	↓1
18	—	West Virginia (15-2)	⤴
19	20	LSU (14-5) (E)	⤴
20	18	Stanford (15-5)	↓1
—	19	Saint Mary's (CA) (17-2)	

Poll Progression Continues →

Week of Feb 7

AP	UPI	SCHOOL	AP ↓↑
1	1	**Arizona** (17-2)	↑3
2	2	**Georgetown** (17-2)	↑4
3	3	**Missouri** (20-3)	↑2
4	4	**Louisville** (16-3)	↑3
5	5	**Oklahoma** (18-3)	↓4
6	6	**North Carolina** (18-4)	↓3
7	7	**Illinois** (18-3)	↓5
8	11	**Iowa** (17-4)	↑1
9	10	**Syracuse** (19-4)	↑5
10	9	**Michigan** (17-4)	↑1
11	8	**Seton Hall** (19-3)	↓1
12	13	**Florida State** (17-2)	↓4
13	12	**Indiana** (18-5)	↑4
14	14	**Duke** (15-4)	↓2
15	15	**West Virginia** (17-2)	↑3
16	16	**Ohio State** (15-5)	↓1
17	17	**NC State** (14-4)	↓4
18	18	**Stanford** (17-5)	↑2
19	19	**UNLV** (14-5)	↓3
20	20	**Georgia Tech** (14-6)	⤴
—	20	**Saint Mary's (CA)** (18-3)	

Week of Feb 14

AP	UPI	SCHOOL	AP ↓↑
1	1	**Oklahoma** (21-3)	F ↑4
2	2	**Arizona** (18-3)	↓1
3	3	**Missouri** (21-4)	
4	4	**Georgetown** (18-3)	↓2
5	6	**Illinois** (20-3)	↑2
6	5	**Syracuse** (21-4)	↑3
7	9	**Florida State** (19-2)	↑5
8	7	**North Carolina** (19-5)	↓2
9	8	**Indiana** (20-5)	↑4
10	10	**Louisville** (17-5)	↓6
11	12	**Duke** (17-4)	↑3
12	11	**Seton Hall** (20-4)	↓1
13	13	**Michigan** (18-5)	↓3
14	14	**West Virginia** (19-2)	↑1
15	15	**Iowa** (17-6)	↓7
16	19	**Ohio State** (17-6)	
17	16	**Stanford** (19-5)	↑1
18	17	**UNLV** (16-6)	↑1
19	18	**NC State** (15-5)	↓2
20	—	**LSU** (17-6)	⤴
—	20	**UTEP** (19-4)	
—	20	**UCLA** (14-5)	

Week of Feb 21

AP	UPI	SCHOOL	AP ↓↑
1	1	**Oklahoma** (23-3)	
2	2	**Arizona** (20-3)	
3	3	**Georgetown** (20-3)	↑1
4	6	**Indiana** (21-5)	↑5
5	4	**North Carolina** (22-5)	↑3
6	5	**Syracuse** (22-5)	
7	7	**Missouri** (22-5)	↓4
8	9	**Louisville** (18-5)	↑2
9	8	**Duke** (19-4)	↑2
10	10	**Illinois** (21-4)	↓5
11	11	**West Virginia** (22-2)	↑3
12	12	**Florida State** (19-4)	↓5
13	13	**Michigan** (19-6)	
14	16	**Iowa** (19-6)	↑1
15	14	**Seton Hall** (21-5)	↓3
16	17	**Stanford** (20-5)	↑1
17	15	**NC State** (17-5)	↑2
18	18	**UNLV** (18-6)	
19	—	**Saint Mary's (CA)** (22-3)	⤴
20	20	**Ball State** (21-2)	⤴
—	19	**Ark.-Little Rock** (18-5)	

Week of Feb 28

AP	UPI	SCHOOL	AP ↓↑
1	1	**Arizona** (22-3)	
2	2	**Georgetown** (22-3)	
3	3	**Indiana** (23-5)	
4	4	**Oklahoma** (24-4)	
5	5	**North Carolina** (24-5)	
6	6	**Syracuse** (23-5)	
7	7	**Missouri** (23-6)	
8	9	**Illinois** (23-4)	
9	8	**Duke** (21-5)	
10	10	**Michigan** (21-6)	
11	11	**Iowa** (21-6)	
12	12	**Seton Hall** (23-5)	↑
13	13	**Stanford** (23-5)	↑
14	14	**Louisville** (19-7)	↓
15	15	**West Virginia** (23-3)	↓
16	16	**Florida State** (19-6)	↓
17	—	**Saint Mary's (CA)** (24-3)	↑
18	16	**UNLV** (20-7)	
19	18	**Ball State** (23-2)	↑
20	18	**NC State** (18-7)	↓

Week of Mar 7

AP	UPI	SCHOOL	AP ↓↑
1	1	**Arizona** (24-3)	
2	2	**Oklahoma** (26-4)	↑2
3	3	**Georgetown** (23-4)	↓1
4	5	**Illinois** (25-4)	↑4
5	4	**Syracuse** (25-6)	↑1
6	6	**Indiana** (24-6)	↓3
7	7	**Duke** (22-6)	↑2
8	9	**Michigan** (23-6)	↑2
9	8	**North Carolina** (24-7)	↓4
10	10	**Missouri** (24-7)	↓3
11	11	**Seton Hall** (25-5)	↑1
12	12	**Stanford** (24-5)	↑1
13	14	**West Virginia** (25-3)	↑2
14	16	**Florida State** (21-6)	↑2
15	17	**Iowa** (21-8)	↓4
16	15	**Louisville** (20-8)	↓2
17	13	**NC State** (20-7)	↑3
18	19	**UNLV** (23-7)	
19	18	**Ball State** (25-2)	
20	—	**Saint Mary's (CA)** (25-4)	↓3
—	20	**Arkansas** (20-6)	

FINAL POLL

AP	UPI	SCHOOL	AP ↓↑
1	1	**Arizona** (27-3)	
2	2	**Georgetown** (26-4)	↑1
3	3	**Illinois** (27-4)	↑1
4	5	**Oklahoma** (28-5)	↓2
5	4	**North Carolina** (27-7)	↑4
6	8	**Missouri** (27-7)	↑4
7	9	**Syracuse** (27-7)	↓2
8	6	**Indiana** (25-7)	↓2
9	7	**Duke** (24-7)	↓2
10	10	**Michigan** (24-7)	G ↓2
11	11	**Seton Hall** (26-6)	
12	13	**Louisville** (22-8)	↑4
13	12	**Stanford** (26-6)	↓1
14	15	**Iowa** (22-9)	↑1
15	14	**UNLV** (26-7)	↑3
16	16	**Florida State** (22-7)	↓2
17	19	**West Virginia** (25-4)	↓4
18	—	**Ball State** (28-2)	↑1
19	18	**NC State** (20-8)	↓2
20	20	**Alabama** (23-7)	⤴
—	17	**Arkansas** (23-6)	

A Duke opens the season with an 80-55 pounding of Kentucky. The Wildcats are reeling from an NCAA investigation that began in the spring after an Emery Air Freight envelope, sent from the Kentucky basketball office to the father of prized recruit Chris Mills, popped open and $1,000 in cash spilled out.

B Oklahoma's Mookie Blaylock has 13 steals against Loyola Marymount on Dec. 17, tying the NCAA record he set on Dec. 12, 1987, against Centenary.

C Division II Alaska-Anchorage shocks Michigan, 70-66, in the opening round of the Utah Classic.

D Loyola Marymount and U.S. International combine for 331 points on Jan. 31, an NCAA record, in the Lions' 181-150 victory. The teams average a field goal every 11 seconds. Hank Gathers leads the winners with 41 points and 29 rebounds.

E LSU rides 26 points by freshman guard Chris Jackson to upset Georgetown, 82-80, before 54,321 fans in the Superdome—at the time, the largest crowd to watch a regular-season basketball game.

F There's a different team at No. 1 in the AP poll for the fifth straight week, a first in its 40-year history.

G Michigan coach Bill Frieder announces he's heading to Arizona State after the Tournament. But he gets an unexpected vacation when Michigan AD Bo Schembechler fires him and replaces him with assistant Steve Fisher, who coaches the team to its only NCAA championship.

1989 NCAA Tournament

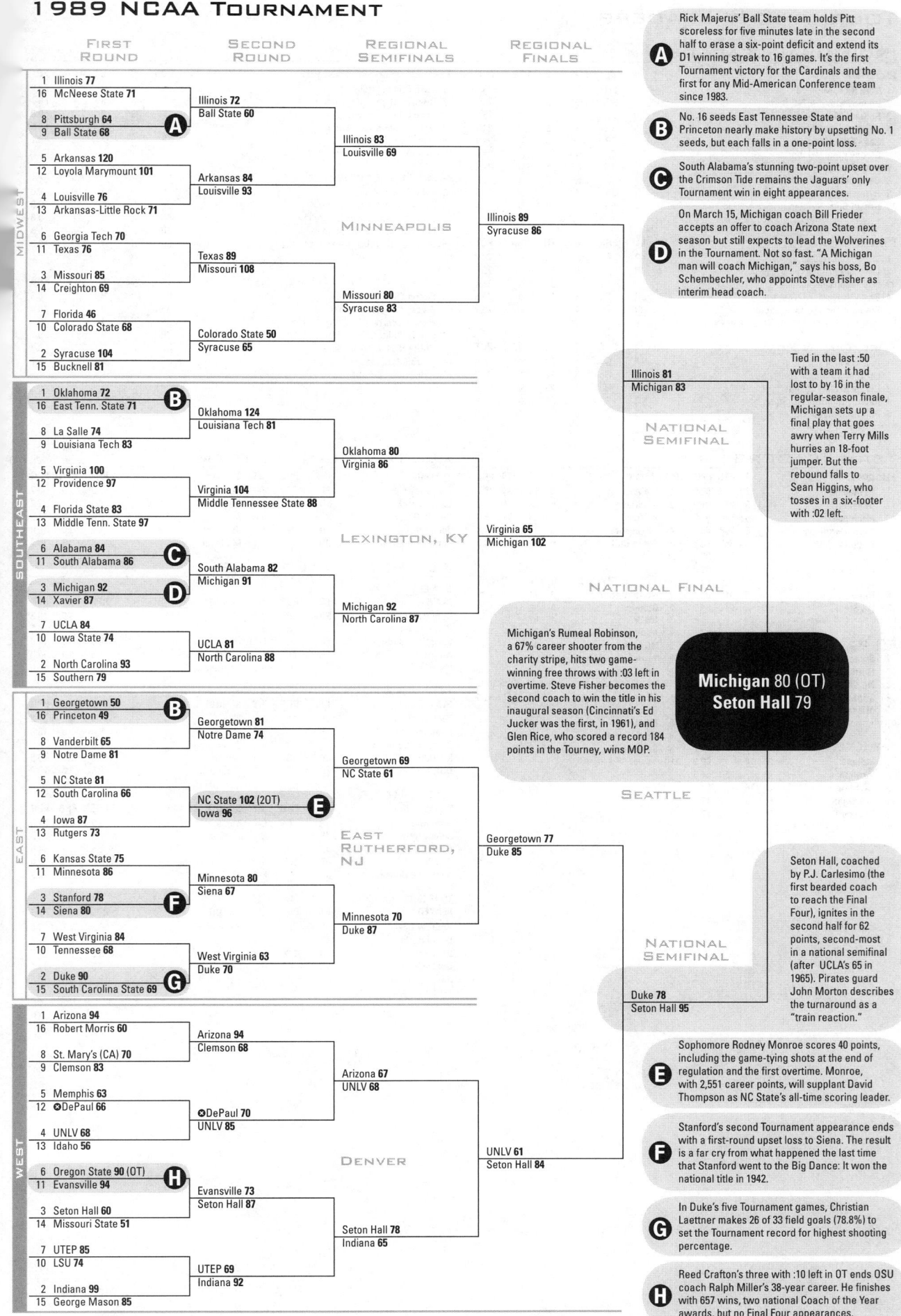

Midwest

First Round
- 1 Illinois **77**, 16 McNeese State **71**
- 8 Pittsburgh **64**, 9 Ball State **68** (A)
- 5 Arkansas **120**, 12 Loyola Marymount **101**
- 4 Louisville **76**, 13 Arkansas-Little Rock **71**
- 6 Georgia Tech **70**, 11 Texas **76**
- 3 Missouri **85**, 14 Creighton **69**
- 7 Florida **46**, 10 Colorado State **68**
- 2 Syracuse **104**, 15 Bucknell **81**

Second Round
- Illinois **72**, Ball State **60**
- Arkansas **84**, Louisville **93**
- Texas **89**, Missouri **108**
- Colorado State **50**, Syracuse **65**

Regional Semifinals (Minneapolis)
- Illinois **83**, Louisville **69**
- Missouri **80**, Syracuse **83**

Regional Finals
- Illinois **89**, Syracuse **86**

Southeast

First Round
- 1 Oklahoma **72**, 16 East Tenn. State **71** (B)
- 8 La Salle **74**, 9 Louisiana Tech **83**
- 5 Virginia **100**, 12 Providence **97**
- 4 Florida State **83**, 13 Middle Tenn. State **97**
- 6 Alabama **84**, 11 South Alabama **86** (C)
- 3 Michigan **92**, 14 Xavier **87** (D)
- 7 UCLA **84**, 10 Iowa State **74**
- 2 North Carolina **93**, 15 Southern **79**

Second Round
- Oklahoma **124**, Louisiana Tech **81**
- Virginia **104**, Middle Tennessee State **88**
- South Alabama **82**, Michigan **91**
- UCLA **81**, North Carolina **88**

Regional Semifinals (Lexington, KY)
- Oklahoma **80**, Virginia **86**
- Michigan **92**, North Carolina **87**

Regional Finals
- Virginia **65**, Michigan **102**

East

First Round
- 1 Georgetown **50**, 16 Princeton **49** (B)
- 8 Vanderbilt **65**, 9 Notre Dame **81**
- 5 NC State **81**, 12 South Carolina **66**
- 4 Iowa **87**, 13 Rutgers **73**
- 6 Kansas State **75**, 11 Minnesota **86**
- 3 Stanford **78**, 14 Siena **80** (F)
- 7 West Virginia **84**, 10 Tennessee **68**
- 2 Duke **90**, 15 South Carolina State **69** (G)

Second Round
- Georgetown **81**, Notre Dame **74**
- NC State **102** (2OT), Iowa **96** (E)
- Minnesota **80**, Siena **67**
- West Virginia **63**, Duke **70**

Regional Semifinals (East Rutherford, NJ)
- Georgetown **69**, NC State **61**
- Minnesota **70**, Duke **87**

Regional Finals
- Georgetown **77**, Duke **85**

West

First Round
- 1 Arizona **94**, 16 Robert Morris **60**
- 8 St. Mary's (CA) **70**, 9 Clemson **83**
- 5 Memphis **63**, 12 ⊗DePaul **66**
- 4 UNLV **68**, 13 Idaho **56**
- 6 Oregon State **90** (OT), 11 Evansville **94** (H)
- 3 Seton Hall **60**, 14 Missouri State **51**
- 7 UTEP **85**, 10 LSU **74**
- 2 Indiana **99**, 15 George Mason **85**

Second Round
- Arizona **94**, Clemson **68**
- ⊗DePaul **70**, UNLV **85**
- Evansville **73**, Seton Hall **87**
- UTEP **69**, Indiana **92**

Regional Semifinals (Denver)
- Arizona **67**, UNLV **68**
- Seton Hall **78**, Indiana **65**

Regional Finals
- UNLV **61**, Seton Hall **84**

⊗Team participation later vacated

National Semifinals (Seattle)

- Illinois **81**, Michigan **83**
- Duke **78**, Seton Hall **95**

National Final

Michigan 80 (OT)
Seton Hall 79

Michigan's Rumeal Robinson, a 67% career shooter from the charity stripe, hits two game-winning free throws with :03 left in overtime. Steve Fisher becomes the second coach to win the title in his inaugural season (Cincinnati's Ed Jucker was the first, in 1961), and Glen Rice, who scored a record 184 points in the Tourney, wins MOP.

Tied in the last :50 with a team it had lost to by 16 in the regular-season finale, Michigan sets up a final play that goes awry when Terry Mills hurries an 18-foot jumper. But the rebound falls to Sean Higgins, who tosses in a six-footer with :02 left.

Seton Hall, coached by P.J. Carlesimo (the first bearded coach to reach the Final Four), ignites in the second half for 62 points, second-most in a national semifinal (after UCLA's 65 in 1965). Pirates guard John Morton describes the turnaround as a "train reaction."

A Rick Majerus' Ball State team holds Pitt scoreless for five minutes late in the second half to erase a six-point deficit and extend its D1 winning streak to 16 games. It's the first Tournament victory for the Cardinals and the first for any Mid-American Conference team since 1983.

B No. 16 seeds East Tennessee State and Princeton nearly make history by upsetting No. 1 seeds, but each falls in a one-point loss.

C South Alabama's stunning two-point upset over the Crimson Tide remains the Jaguars' only Tournament win in eight appearances.

D On March 15, Michigan coach Bill Frieder accepts an offer to coach Arizona State next season but still expects to lead the Wolverines in the Tournament. Not so fast. "A Michigan man will coach Michigan," says his boss, Bo Schembechler, who appoints Steve Fisher as interim head coach.

E Sophomore Rodney Monroe scores 40 points, including the game-tying shots at the end of regulation and the first overtime. Monroe, with 2,551 career points, will supplant David Thompson as NC State's all-time scoring leader.

F Stanford's second Tournament appearance ends with a first-round upset loss to Siena. The result is a far cry from what happened the last time that Stanford went to the Big Dance: It won the national title in 1942.

G In Duke's five Tournament games, Christian Laettner makes 26 of 33 field goals (78.8%) to set the Tournament record for highest shooting percentage.

H Reed Crafton's three with :10 left in OT ends OSU coach Ralph Miller's 38-year career. He finishes with 657 wins, two national Coach of the Year awards, but no Final Four appearances.

Tournament Leaders

INDIVIDUAL LEADERS

Scoring	CL	POS	G	PTS	PPG
1 **Glen Rice**, Michigan	SR	F	6	184	30.7
2 **Rodney Monroe**, NC State	SO	G	3	88	29.3
3 **Richard Morgan**, Virginia	SR	G	4	106	26.5
4 **Willie Burton**, Minnesota	SR	F	3	74	24.7
Sean Elliott, Arizona	SR	G/F	3	74	24.7
6 **Stacey King**, Oklahoma	SR	C	3	71	23.7
7 **Danny Ferry**, Duke	SR	F	5	111	22.2
8 **Doug Smith**, Missouri	SO	F	3	66	22.0
9 **Byron Irvin**, Missouri	SR	G	3	64	21.3
10 **Bryant Stith**, Virginia	FR	G	4	82	20.5

Minimum: 3 games

Field Goal Pct	CL	POS	G	FG	FGA	PCT
1 **Christian Laettner**, Duke	FR	C	5	26	33	78.8
2 **Larry Smith**, Illinois	JR	G	5	15	20	75.0
3 **Eric Anderson**, Indiana	FR	F	3	20	28	71.4
4 **Brian Howard**, NC State	JR	F	3	17	24	70.8
5 **Stephen Thompson**, Syracuse	JR	F	4	29	41	70.7

Minimum: 15 made and 3 games

Free Throw Pct	CL	POS	G	FT	FTA	PCT
1 **Richard Morgan**, Virginia	SR	G	4	23	23	100.0
2 **LaBradford Smith**, Louisville	SO	G	3	22	24	91.7
3 **Bryant Stith**, Virginia	FR	G	4	29	33	87.9
4 **Rodney Monroe**, NC State	SO	G	3	21	24	87.5
5 **Phil Henderson**, Duke	JR	G	5	20	23	87.0

Minimum: 15 made

Three-Point FG Pct	CL	POS	G	3FG	3FGA	PCT
1 **John Crotty**, Virginia	JR	G	4	8	10	80.0
2 **Dwayne Bryant**, Georgetown	JR	G	4	6	9	66.7
3 **Sean Elliott**, Arizona	SR	G/F	3	6	10	60.0
4 **Tyrone Jones**, Oklahoma	SR	F	3	7	12	58.3
5 **Glen Rice**, Michigan	SR	F	6	27	49	55.1

Minimum: 6 made and 3 games

Assists Per Game	CL	POS	G	AST	APG
1 **John Crotty**, Virginia	JR	G	4	39	9.8
2 **Rumeal Robinson**, Michigan	JR	G	6	56	9.3
Steve Bucknall, North Carolina	SR	G	3	28	9.3
4 **Chris Corchiani**, NC State	SO	G	3	25	8.3
5 **Sherman Douglas**, Syracuse	SR	G	4	32	8.0

Minimum: 3 games

Rebounds Per Game	CL	POS	G	REB	RPG
1 **Pervis Ellison**, Louisville	SR	F/C	3	31	10.3
Stacey King, Oklahoma	SR	C	3	31	10.3
3 **Moses Scurry**, UNLV	JR	F	4	41	10.3
4 **Daryll Walker**, Seton Hall	SR	F	6	58	9.7
Willie Burton, Minnesota	SR	F	3	29	9.7
Derrick Coleman, Syracuse	JR	C	3	29	9.7

Minimum: 3 games

TEAM LEADERS

Scoring	G	PTS	PPG
1 **Oklahoma**	3	276	92.0
2 **Missouri**	3	273	91.0
3 **Michigan**	6	540	90.0
4 **North Carolina**	3	268	89.3
5 **Virginia**	4	355	88.8
6 **Indiana**	3	256	85.3
7 **Arizona**	3	255	85.0
8 **Syracuse**	4	338	84.5
9 **Duke**	5	410	82.0
10 **NC State**	3	244	81.3

Minimum: 3 games

FG Pct	G	FG	FGA	PCT
1 **Syracuse**	4	129	235	54.9
2 **North Carolina**	3	105	193	54.4
3 **NC State**	3	85	159	53.5
4 **Michigan**	6	217	409	53.1
5 **Missouri**	3	108	210	51.4

Minimum: 3 games

3-Pt FG Pct	G	3FG	3FGA	PCT
1 **Indiana**	3	14	23	60.9
2 **Virginia**	4	27	50	54.0
3 **NC State**	3	16	31	51.6
4 **Michigan**	6	43	90	47.8
5 **Missouri**	3	11	26	42.3

Minimum: 3 games

FT Pct	G	FT	FTA	PCT
1 **Indiana**	3	74	94	78.7
2 **Michigan**	6	63	84	75.0
Arizona	3	48	64	75.0
4 **Minnesota**	3	44	59	74.6
5 **Seton Hall**	6	111	150	74.0

Minimum: 3 games

Ast/TO Ratio	G	AST	TO	RAT
1 **North Carolina**	3	71	41	1.73
2 **Illinois**	5	92	58	1.59
3 **UNLV**	4	57	39	1.46
4 **Michigan**	6	125	88	1.42
5 **NC State**	3	49	35	1.40

Minimum: 3 games

Rebounds	G	REB	RPG
1 **Missouri**	3	117	39.0
Oklahoma	3	117	39.0
3 **Michigan**	6	219	36.5
4 **North Carolina**	3	109	36.3
5 **Seton Hall**	6	216	36.0

Minimum: 3 games

ALL-TOURNAMENT TEAM

PLAYER	CL	POS	HT	SCHOOL	RPG	APG	PPG
Glen Rice*	SR	F	6-7	Michigan	6.5	2.0	30.7
Danny Ferry	SR	F	6-10	Duke	7.6	3.4	22.2
Gerald Greene	SR	G	6-0	Seton Hall	3.3	4.3	11.8
John Morton	SR	G	6-1	Seton Hall	2.5	2.0	19.0
Rumeal Robinson	JR	G	6-2	Michigan	2.8	9.3	16.7

ALL-REGIONAL TEAMS

EAST

PLAYER	CL	POS	HT	SCHOOL	RPG	APG	PPG
Danny Ferry*	SR	F	6-10	Duke	7.0	3.8	19.3
Phil Henderson	JR	G	6-4	Duke	3.3	2.5	18.5
Christian Laettner	FR	C	6-11	Duke	6.3	1.5	15.0
Alonzo Mourning	FR	F/C	6-10	Georgetown	8.5	0.0	15.3
Charles Smith	SR	G	6-1	Georgetown	3.3	3.5	15.0

MIDWEST

PLAYER	CL	POS	HT	SCHOOL	RPG	APG	PPG
Nick Anderson*	JR	F	6-6	Illinois	1.0	2.5	21.3
Kenny Battle	SR	F	6-6	Illinois	5.0	2.3	13.8
Sherman Douglas	SR	G	6-0	Syracuse	2.0	8.0	18.0
Kendall Gill	JR	G	6-5	Illinois	4.0	5.0	15.5
Billy Owens	FR	F	6-8	Syracuse	8.8	2.0	20.0

SOUTHEAST

PLAYER	CL	POS	HT	SCHOOL	RPG	APG	PPG
Glen Rice*	SR	F	6-7	Michigan	5.8	2.8	31.3
John Crotty	JR	G	6-1	Virginia	3.3	9.8	19.3
Sean Higgins	JR	G	6-2	Michigan	2.5	1.3	14.5
J.R. Reid	JR	F/C	6-9	North Carolina	8.0	1.0	22.0
Rumeal Robinson	JR	G	6-2	Michigan	3.3	8.3	16.3

WEST

PLAYER	CL	POS	HT	SCHOOL	RPG	APG	PPG
Andrew Gaze*	JR	F	6-7	Seton Hall	3.8	2.8	14.8
David Butler	JR	C	6-10	UNLV	5.5	0.8	17.5
Sean Elliott	SR	G/F	6-8	Arizona	9.0	2.0	24.7
Gerald Greene	SR	G	6-0	Seton Hall	2.5	3.3	10.3
Daryll Walker	SR	F	6-8	Seton Hall	10.3	0.5	10.8

* Most outstanding player

1989 NCAA TOURNAMENT BOX SCORES

83-69 (SWEET 16)

	1H	2H
Illinois	40	43
Louisville	37	32

ILLINOIS	MIN	FG	3FG	FT	REB	A	ST	BL	PF	TP
Nick Anderson	35	12-22	0-0	0-1	5	3	3	1	1	24
Kendall Gill	38	7-17	0-3	2-2	3	5	2	0	2	16
Marcus Liberty	33	7-14	0-0	0-0	8	1	3	0	3	14
Stephen Bardo	36	3-9	1-2	2-5	8	6	2	0	2	9
Larry Smith	17	4-6	0-0	0-3	2	4	1	0	1	8
Kenny Battle	15	2-4	0-0	0-0	4	3	0	0	1	4
Lowell Hamilton	13	2-5	0-0	0-0	3	0	0	1	2	4
Ervin Small	13	2-4	0-0	0-0	2	0	0	0	4	4
TOTALS	**200**	**39-81**	**1-5**	**4-11**	**35**	**22**	**11**	**2**	**16**	**83**
Percentages		48.1	20.0	36.4						

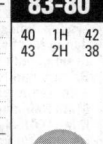

Coach: Lou Henson

LOUISVILLE	MIN	FG	3FG	FT	REB	A	ST	BL	PF	TP
Kenny Payne	33	9-15	1-3	0-0	3	1	0	0	1	19
Everick Sullivan	24	7-14	1-3	0-0	2	1	0	2	2	15
LaBradford Smith	34	2-8	2-3	8-8	1	4	1	0	3	14
Pervis Ellison	35	4-5	0-0	4-6	9	4	2	7	3	12
Tony Kimbro	25	2-7	1-4	0-0	7	0	0	4	2	5
Keith Williams	27	2-6	0-1	0-0	1	3	1	0	2	4
Felton Spencer	15	0-2	0-0	0-0	2	0	0	0	3	0
Cornelius Holden	7	0-1	0-0	0-0	1	0	0	0	0	0
TOTALS	**200**	**26-58**	**5-14**	**12-14**	**26**	**13**	**4**	**13**	**16**	**69**
Percentages		44.8	35.7	85.7						

Coach: Denny Crum

Officials: Dick Paparo, Tim Higgins, Donnee Gray
Technicals: None
Attendance: 33,560

83-80 (SWEET 16)

	1H	2H
Syracuse	40	43
Missouri	42	38

SYRACUSE	MIN	FG	3FG	FT	REB	A	ST	BL	PF	TP
Sherman Douglas	40	8-12	1-2	10-13	3	7	0	0	2	27
Billy Owens	40	10-14	1-2	4-7	8	2	1	0	3	25
Derrick Coleman	29	6-15	0-0	2-4	12	1	0	2	5	14
Stephen Thompson	37	4-7	0-0	3-5	2	1	3	1	2	11
Dave Johnson	26	1-2	0-0	2-4	1	1	0	0	1	4
Matthew Roe	14	1-2	0-0	0-0	1	0	0	0	3	2
Herman Harried	12	0-0	0-0	0-0	0	0	1	0	1	0
Richard Manning	2	0-0	0-0	0-0	0	0	0	0	1	0
TOTALS	**200**	**30-52**	**2-4**	**21-33**	**27**	**12**	**5**	**3**	**18**	**83**
Percentages		57.7	50.0	63.6						

Coach: Jim Boeheim

MISSOURI	MIN	FG	3FG	FT	REB	A	ST	BL	PF	TP
Byron Irvin	38	8-25	2-7	3-3	10	5	1	0	4	21
Doug Smith	29	7-14	0-1	2-2	13	2	0	0	3	16
Lee Coward	37	6-10	0-2	1-4	1	6	0	0	3	13
Gary Leonard	26	5-7	0-0	2-4	7	0	1	1	4	12
Greg Church	20	4-11	0-0	3-3	2	1	1	0	4	11
Mike Sandbothe	26	1-2	0-0	1-4	6	0	0	1	2	3
Anthony Peeler	15	1-5	0-1	0-0	4	2	2	0	1	2
Nathan Buntin	9	1-1	0-0	0-0	2	1	0	0	3	2
TOTALS	**200**	**33-75**	**2-11**	**12-20**	**45**	**17**	**5**	**2**	**24**	**80**
Percentages		44.0	18.2	60.0						

Coach: Norm Stewart

Officials: Rich Ballesteros, Sam Lickliter, Paul Housman
Technicals: None
Attendance: 33,560

86-80 (SWEET 16)

	1H	2H
Virginia	42	44
Oklahoma	37	43

VIRGINIA	MIN	FG	3FG	FT	REB	A	ST	BL	PF	TP
Bryant Stith	35	9-16	0-0	10-11	7	1	2	0	2	28
Richard Morgan	38	7-16	5-8	6-6	4	1	2	1	2	25
John Crotty	39	4-9	0-0	6-9	3	8	1	0	0	14
Brent Dabbs	35	4-11	0-0	2-4	14	2	0	0	2	10
Matt Blundin	28	3-4	0-0	3-6	6	2	2	0	2	9
Jeff Daniel	17	0-0	0-0	0-0	1	1	1	1	0	0
Kenny Turner	5	0-0	0-0	0-0	1	0	1	0	2	0
Dirk Katstra	3	0-0	0-0	0-0	0	0	0	0	0	0
Anthony Oliver	0	0-0	0-0	0-0	0	0	0	0	0	0
TOTALS	**200**	**27-56**	**5-8**	**27-36**	**36**	**15**	**9**	**2**	**10**	**86**
Percentages		48.2	62.5	75.0						

Coach: Terry Holland

OKLAHOMA	MIN	FG	3FG	FT	REB	A	ST	BL	PF	TP
Stacey King	35	9-15	0-0	4-5	6	1	1	0	4	22
Terrence Mullins	37	6-12	4-8	0-0	4	4	1	0	4	16
William Davis	19	5-6	0-0	2-2	3	1	0	1	3	12
Skeeter Henry	27	4-8	1-3	2-2	3	1	2	0	5	11
Tyrone Jones	19	3-5	2-4	0-0	3	1	0	0	2	8
Mookie Blaylock	33	2-12	1-6	0-0	2	5	4	0	2	5
Tony Martin	18	2-4	0-0	0-0	3	2	0	0	4	4
Mike Bell	5	1-2	0-0	0-0	1	0	0	0	0	2
Damon Patterson	7	0-0	0-0	0-0	0	0	0	0	2	0
TOTALS	**200**	**32-64**	**8-21**	**8-9**	**25**	**15**	**8**	**1**	**26**	**80**
Percentages		50.0	38.1	88.9						

Coach: Billy Tubbs

Officials: Gene Monje, Bob Dibler, Herman Ramsey
Technicals: None
Attendance: 22,314

92-87 (SWEET 16)

	1H	2H
Michigan	50	42
North Carolina	47	40

MICHIGAN	MIN	FG	3FG	FT	REB	A	ST	BL	PF	TP
Glen Rice	37	13-19	8-12	0-0	6	2	1	0	1	34
Rumeal Robinson	37	7-15	3-6	0-2	5	13	1	0	3	17
Terry Mills	33	8-11	0-0	0-2	6	1	1	1	3	16
Sean Higgins	21	5-11	2-5	2-2	2	3	1	0	0	14
Mark Hughes	20	1-2	0-0	3-4	6	0	0	1	4	5
Loy Vaught	23	1-3	0-0	2-2	6	0	1	2	5	4
Demetrius Calip	21	1-4	0-1	0-0	1	0	1	0	1	2
Mike Griffin	8	0-1	0-0	0-0	1	1	0	0	1	0
TOTALS	**200**	**36-66**	**13-24**	**7-12**	**33**	**20**	**6**	**4**	**18**	**92**
Percentages		54.5	54.2	58.3						

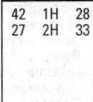

Coach: Steve Fisher

NORTH CAROLINA	MIN	FG	3FG	FT	REB	A	ST	BL	PF	TP
J.R. Reid	29	12-18	0-0	2-7	6	0	0	0	4	26
Jeff Lebo	32	6-10	5-9	2-2	1	7	0	0	3	19
Steve Bucknall	36	2-7	2-4	4-4	7	10	3	0	1	10
Kevin Madden	25	5-12	0-2	0-0	1	0	2	1	1	10
Scott Williams	28	4-9	0-0	0-0	5	0	2	0	1	8
Rick Fox	27	4-5	0-0	0-0	2	3	2	0	2	8
King Rice	14	1-3	0-1	2-2	1	4	2	0	0	4
Pete Chilcutt	9	1-2	0-0	0-0	4	0	0	0	2	2
TOTALS	**200**	**35-66**	**7-16**	**10-15**	**27**	**24**	**11**	**1**	**14**	**87**
Percentages		53.0	43.8	66.7						

Coach: Dean Smith

Officials: Don Rutledge, Tom Scott, Wally Tanner
Technicals: None
Attendance: 22,314

69-61 (SWEET 16)

	1H	2H
Georgetown	42	27
NC State	28	33

GEORGETOWN	MIN	FG	3FG	FT	REB	A	ST	BL	PF	TP
Dwayne Bryant	36	7-9	5-6	2-2	2	2	0	0	2	21
Jaren Jackson	33	7-14	3-7	0-0	2	1	1	1	2	17
Alonzo Mourning	36	5-10	0-1	2-2	12	0	1	5	4	12
John Turner	25	1-5	0-0	5-6	4	0	0	0	3	7
Bobby Winston	17	2-3	0-0	2-3	2	1	0	0	2	6
Mark Tillmon	11	1-4	0-1	1-2	2	0	0	0	5	3
Johnathan Edwards	1	1-1	0-0	0-0	0	0	0	0	0	2
Charles Smith	32	0-2	0-0	1-3	5	5	1	0	1	1
Dikembe Mutombo	4	0-0	0-0	0-0	0	0	0	0	0	0
Ronnie Thompson	4	0-2	0-1	0-0	1	0	0	0	0	0
Sam Jefferson	1	0-0	0-0	0-0	0	0	0	0	1	0
TOTALS	**200**	**24-50**	**8-16**	**13-18**	**30**	**9**	**3**	**6**	**20**	**69**
Percentages		48.0	50.0	72.2						

Coach: John Thompson Jr.

NC STATE	MIN	FG	3FG	FT	REB	A	ST	BL	PF	TP
Rodney Monroe	38	6-16	3-7	11-13	4	3	1	0	2	26
Brian Howard	33	6-9	1-1	0-0	4	1	0	1	4	13
Avie Lester	35	3-5	0-0	1-2	5	1	0	1	4	7
Chris Corchiani	39	1-5	1-2	3-4	3	4	0	0	5	6
Chucky Brown	39	2-11	0-1	1-2	12	2	0	0	1	5
Kelsey Weems	13	2-4	0-0	0-0	0	0	1	0	1	4
Mickey Hinnant	2	0-1	0-0	0-0	0	0	0	0	0	0
Brian D'Amico	1	0-0	0-0	0-0	0	0	0	0	1	0
TOTALS	**200**	**20-51**	**5-11**	**16-21**	**28**	**11**	**2**	**2**	**18**	**61**
Percentages		39.2	45.5	76.2						

Coach: Jim Valvano

Officials: Tom Lopes, Jim Bain, Rick Hartzell
Technicals: None
Attendance: 19,508

87-70 (SWEET 16)

	1H	2H
Duke	45	42
Minnesota	30	40

DUKE	MIN	FG	3FG	FT	REB	A	ST	BL	PF	TP
Phil Henderson	34	7-12	2-3	5-6	6	3	-	-	1	21
Robert Brickey	22	9-10	0-0	3-7	7	0	-	-	4	21
Danny Ferry	36	7-14	1-2	3-6	5	4	-	-	3	18
Christian Laettner	25	2-4	0-0	6-7	11	1	-	-	4	10
Quin Snyder	33	2-4	1-3	1-4	2	8	-	-	2	6
John Smith	18	1-2	0-0	3-4	4	2	-	-	0	5
Brian Davis	4	0-0	0-0	3-6	2	0	-	-	1	3
Crawford Palmer	1	1-1	0-0	0-0	1	0	-	-	0	2
Alaa Abdelnaby	16	0-2	0-0	1-2	3	1	-	-	1	1
Greg Koubek	9	0-2	0-0	0-0	1	2	-	-	0	0
Clay Buckley	1	0-0	0-0	0-0	0	0	-	-	0	0
George Burgin	1	0-0	0-0	0-0	0	0	-	-	0	0
TOTALS	**200**	**29-51**	**4-8**	**25-42**	**42**	**21**	**-**	**-**	**16**	**87**
Percentages		56.9	50.0	59.5						

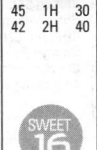

Coach: Mike Krzyzewski

MINNESOTA	MIN	FG	3FG	FT	REB	A	ST	BL	PF	TP
Willie Burton	32	12-24	2-7	0-0	5	0	-	-	4	26
Kevin Lynch	34	5-15	1-5	3-4	5	1	-	-	3	14
Walter Bond	22	2-4	0-0	2-2	6	1	-	-	2	6
Ray Gaffney	14	3-5	0-1	0-0	1	2	-	-	3	6
Jim Shikenjanski	26	2-5	0-0	0-0	2	1	-	-	4	4
Richard Coffey	11	2-3	0-0	0-0	5	0	-	-	5	4
Robert Martin	10	1-2	0-0	2-2	0	0	-	-	2	4
Melvin Newbern	27	1-8	0-0	0-0	4	7	-	-	2	2
Rob Metcalf	15	1-3	0-1	0-2	2	1	-	-	2	2
Connell Lewis	8	1-5	0-2	0-0	2	1	-	-	2	2
Mario Green	1	0-0	0-0	0-0	0	0	-	-	1	0
TOTALS	**200**	**30-74**	**3-16**	**7-10**	**32**	**14**	**-**	**-**	**30**	**70**
Percentages		40.5	18.8	70.0						

Coach: Clem Haskins

Officials: John Clougherty, Dan Chrisman, Tom O'Neill
Technicals: None
Attendance: 19,508

68-67 — SWEET 16

	1H	2H
UNLV	37	31
Arizona	36	31

UNLV	MIN	FG	3FG	FT	REB	A	ST	BL	PF	TP
Anderson Hunt	33	8-12	5-8	0-0	4	3	0	1	3	21
David Butler	32	8-17	0-0	0-2	2	1	0	2	4	16
Stacey Augmon	32	5-13	1-4	4-6	6	4	2	2	2	15
Clint Rossum	16	3-4	2-3	0-0	1	2	0	0	0	8
George Ackles	25	2-3	0-0	0-1	6	0	1	3	2	4
Greg Anthony	31	1-7	0-4	0-0	1	11	1	1	3	2
Moses Scurry	23	1-3	0-0	0-0	5	0	0	0	3	2
Barry Young	8	0-1	0-0	0-0	0	0	0	0	1	0
TOTALS	200	28-60	8-19	4-9	25	21	4	9	18	68
Percentages		46.7	42.1	44.4						

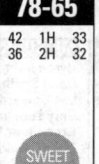

Coach: Jerry Tarkanian

ARIZONA	MIN	FG	3FG	FT	REB	A	ST	BL	PF	TP
Sean Elliott	39	8-16	1-3	5-7	14	1	2	0	1	22
Anthony Cook	33	6-9	0-0	0-0	6	1	2	4	2	12
Jud Buechler	30	4-6	0-0	2-3	7	2	0	0	4	10
Matt Muehlebach	37	3-6	2-5	0-0	2	1	0	0	1	8
Kenneth Lofton	28	3-12	2-4	0-0	2	6	0	0	1	8
Sean Rooks	14	1-3	0-0	2-3	3	0	0	1	1	4
Matt Othick	17	1-4	1-4	0-0	1	2	0	0	0	3
Wayne Womack	2	0-0	0-0	0-0	0	0	0	0	0	0
TOTALS	200	26-56	6-16	9-13	35	13	4	5	10	67
Percentages		46.4	37.5	69.2						

Coach: Lute Olson

Officials: Ed Hightower, T Rucker, Fran Scagliotta
Technicals: None
Attendance: 16,813

78-65 — SWEET 16

	1H	2H
Seton Hall	42	36
Indiana	33	32

SETON HALL	MIN	FG	3FG	FT	REB	A	ST	BL	PF	TP
John Morton	21	4-12	1-2	8-9	4	1	4	0	4	17
Andrew Gaze	38	6-12	4-7	0-0	3	2	0	0	2	16
Gerald Greene	29	3-6	2-4	7-8	3	4	1	0	3	15
Ramon Ramos	22	5-12	0-0	2-3	5	2	1	2	4	12
Daryll Walker	29	4-9	0-0	1-2	10	2	2	1	3	9
Frantz Volcy	16	1-4	0-0	2-4	5	1	0	1	3	4
Nick Katsikis	4	1-1	1-1	0-0	1	0	0	0	0	3
Michael Cooper	16	1-3	0-0	0-0	1	2	0	1	3	2
Anthony Avent	12	0-2	0-0	0-0	3	0	0	1	3	0
Pookey Wigington	12	0-0	0-0	0-1	2	0	1	0	1	0
Trevor Crowley	1	0-0	0-0	0-0	0	0	0	0	0	0
TOTALS	200	25-61	8-14	20-27	37	14	9	6	26	78
Percentages		41.0	57.1	74.1						

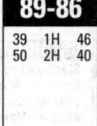

Coach: P.J. Carlesimo

INDIANA	MIN	FG	3FG	FT	REB	A	ST	BL	PF	TP
Jay Edwards	23	4-11	1-5	9-10	3	2	0	0	5	18
Eric Anderson	36	4-5	0-0	5-6	6	0	1	2	4	13
Joe Hillman	35	4-13	1-2	3-4	1	3	1	0	2	12
Todd Jadlow	22	1-5	0-0	4-6	5	0	0	0	3	6
Lyndon Jones	29	1-7	0-0	2-2	4	3	0	1	5	4
Jamal Meeks	14	2-2	0-0	0-0	1	1	0	0	0	4
Kreigh Smith	14	0-0	0-0	3-4	2	1	0	0	1	3
Brian Sloan	11	1-1	0-0	1-2	1	1	0	0	2	3
John White	7	1-1	0-0	0-2	0	0	0	0	1	2
Mark Robinson	7	0-1	0-0	0-1	2	0	1	0	1	0
Mike D'Aloisio	1	0-0	0-0	0-0	1	0	0	0	0	0
Magnus Pelkowski	1	0-0	0-0	0-0	0	0	0	0	0	0
TOTALS	200	18-46	2-7	27-37	26	11	3	3	24	65
Percentages		39.1	28.6	73.0						

Coach: Bob Knight

Officials: Jody Silvester, Dave Libbey, David Bair
Technicals: None
Attendance: 16,813

89-86 — ELITE 8

	1H	2H
Illinois	39	50
Syracuse	46	40

ILLINOIS	MIN	FG	3FG	FT	REB	A	ST	BL	PF	TP
Kenny Battle	34	12-17	0-0	4-6	3	1	1	-	3	28
Nick Anderson	40	10-18	0-0	4-7	16	2	1	-	2	24
Kendall Gill	38	8-13	2-4	0-0	8	5	3	-	1	18
Larry Smith	16	3-3	0-0	2-2	0	5	0	-	4	8
Lowell Hamilton	18	2-4	0-0	3-10	2	1	1	-	1	7
Stephen Bardo	26	1-2	0-0	0-0	3	4	0	-	5	2
Marcus Liberty	11	1-4	0-0	0-1	3	0	0	-	2	2
Ervin Small	17	0-0	0-0	0-0	1	2	1	-	3	0
TOTALS	200	37-61	2-4	13-26	36	20	7	-	21	89
Percentages		60.7	50.0	50.0						

Coach: Lou Henson

SYRACUSE	MIN	FG	3FG	FT	REB	A	ST	BL	PF	TP
Billy Owens	35	9-18	0-1	4-4	8	2	0	0	2	22
Derrick Coleman	40	5-11	0-0	7-10	10	2	1	1	4	17
Stephen Thompson	40	8-11	0-0	1-2	6	0	0	0	4	17
Sherman Douglas	39	5-10	1-2	4-4	2	8	1	0	5	15
Matthew Roe	21	4-9	4-8	1-2	0	0	0	0	2	13
Dave Johnson	19	1-3	0-1	0-2	2	2	2	0	4	2
Herman Harried	6	0-0	0-0	0-0	0	0	1	0	0	0
TOTALS	200	32-62	5-12	17-24	28	14	5	1	21	86
Percentages		51.6	41.7	70.8						

Coach: Jim Boeheim

Officials: Larry Lembo, Jim Rife, John Moreau
Technicals: None
Attendance: 33,496

102-65 — ELITE 8

	1H	2H
Michigan	44	58
Virginia	25	40

MICHIGAN	MIN	FG	3FG	FT	REB	A	ST	BL	PF	TP
Glen Rice	32	13-16	4-5	2-2	6	2	2	-	3	32
Sean Higgins	20	11-15	7-10	2-3	3	0	0	-	2	31
Rumeal Robinson	23	5-9	0-1	3-3	3	7	1	-	2	13
Terry Mills	27	4-9	0-0	0-0	5	2	1	-	2	8
Loy Vaught	21	4-6	0-0	0-1	9	2	0	-	3	8
Demetrius Calip	22	2-3	0-0	2-2	5	5	0	-	2	6
Mark Hughes	20	1-4	0-0	0-0	7	2	0	-	4	2
J.P. Oosterbaan	6	1-3	0-1	0-1	3	0	0	-	1	2
Mike Griffin	22	0-1	0-0	0-0	0	3	1	-	4	0
Rob Pelinka	5	0-4	0-3	0-0	0	0	0	-	0	0
Marc Koenig	2	0-0	0-0	0-0	0	0	2	-	0	0
TOTALS	200	41-70	11-20	9-12	41	23	7	-	23	102
Percentages		58.6	55.0	75.0						

Coach: Steve Fisher

VIRGINIA	MIN	FG	3FG	FT	REB	A	ST	BL	PF	TP
Richard Morgan	26	5-18	3-9	2-2	1	0	1	0	1	15
John Crotty	36	5-13	2-3	2-4	3	7	0	0	1	14
Brent Dabbs	37	5-10	0-0	2-4	12	0	1	0	2	12
Bryant Stith	33	3-6	1-1	2-4	3	1	1	0	3	9
Dirk Katstra	13	3-9	1-6	0-0	2	1	2	1	2	7
Mark Cooke	3	1-3	1-3	0-0	1	0	0	0	0	3
Matt Blundin	21	1-1	0-0	0-0	4	2	0	0	1	2
Kenny Turner	6	1-1	0-0	0-1	1	0	0	0	0	2
Anthony Oliver	4	0-0	0-0	1-2	2	0	0	0	2	1
Jeff Daniel	13	0-1	0-0	0-2	3	1	0	0	4	0
Curtis Williams	8	0-1	0-0	0-3	0	0	0	0	0	0
TOTALS	200	24-63	8-22	9-22	32	12	5	1	16	65
Percentages		38.1	36.4	40.9						

Coach: Terry Holland

Officials: Mickey Crowley, James Burr, Frank Bosone
Technicals: None
Attendance: 22,755

85-77 — ELITE 8

	1H	2H
Duke	38	47
Georgetown	40	37

DUKE	MIN	FG	3FG	FT	REB	A	ST	BL	PF	TP
Christian Laettner	32	9-10	0-0	6-7	9	4	1	1	3	24
Phil Henderson	36	9-15	1-1	4-4	3	2	0	1	2	23
Danny Ferry	39	8-17	0-2	5-6	7	3	0	1	3	21
Robert Brickey	32	2-6	0-0	6-8	8	0	0	0	4	10
Quin Snyder	34	1-6	0-3	2-4	3	7	0	1	5	4
John Smith	14	0-1	0-0	3-4	3	0	0	1	2	3
Alaa Abdelnaby	9	0-2	0-0	0-0	2	0	1	0	3	0
Greg Koubek	4	0-0	0-0	0-0	0	0	0	0	0	0
TOTALS	200	29-57	1-6	26-33	35	16	2	5	22	85
Percentages		50.9	16.7	78.8						

Coach: Mike Krzyzewski

GEORGETOWN	MIN	FG	3FG	FT	REB	A	ST	BL	PF	TP
Charles Smith	38	9-19	0-2	3-5	5	1	0	0	3	21
Mark Tillmon	28	6-12	2-6	2-5	4	2	2	0	3	16
Alonzo Mourning	26	5-8	0-0	1-2	5	0	0	4	2	11
Bobby Winston	23	4-8	0-0	1-3	1	1	1	0	2	9
Sam Jefferson	23	2-5	0-0	4-4	7	1	0	0	5	8
John Turner	17	2-3	0-0	0-2	1	1	0	0	1	4
Jaren Jackson	22	1-10	0-2	0-0	5	1	2	0	2	2
Dwayne Bryant	16	0-4	0-1	2-2	2	3	1	0	3	2
Dikembe Mutombo	5	1-1	0-0	0-0	0	0	0	1	2	2
Johnathan Edwards	2	1-1	0-0	0-0	1	0	0	0	1	2
TOTALS	200	31-71	2-11	13-23	31	10	6	5	24	77
Percentages		43.7	18.2	56.5						

Coach: John Thompson Jr.

Officials: Ted Hillary, David Jones, Tom Harrington
Technicals: None
Attendance: 19,514

84-61 — ELITE 8

	1H	2H
Seton Hall	34	50
UNLV	30	31

SETON HALL	MIN	FG	3FG	FT	REB	A	ST	BL	PF	TP
Andrew Gaze	33	6-9	3-6	4-6	5	1	3	2	2	19
Daryll Walker	37	5-9	0-0	2-4	15	0	1	1	2	12
Anthony Avent	9	3-5	0-0	5-6	3	0	0	0	2	11
Michael Cooper	16	5-7	0-0	0-0	5	2	0	0	1	10
Gerald Greene	30	3-4	0-0	3-5	4	3	1	0	2	9
Frantz Volcy	17	4-8	0-0	1-2	6	1	0	3	1	9
John Morton	31	2-11	0-3	2-5	1	2	0	0	2	6
Pookey Wigington	9	0-0	0-0	3-4	2	1	0	0	2	3
Nick Katsikis	1	1-1	1-1	0-0	1	0	0	0	0	3
Jose Rebimbas	1	1-1	0-0	0-0	0	0	0	0	1	2
Ramon Ramos	14	0-2	0-0	0-0	4	2	0	1	2	0
Trevor Crowley	1	0-1	0-1	0-0	0	0	0	0	0	0
Rene Monteserin	1	0-0	0-0	0-0	0	0	0	0	0	0
TOTALS	200	30-58	4-11	20-32	46	12	5	7	17	84
Percentages		51.7	36.4	62.5						

Coach: P.J. Carlesimo

UNLV	MIN	FG	3FG	FT	REB	A	ST	BL	PF	TP
Greg Anthony	31	5-15	5-10	1-2	1	4	2	0	5	16
David Butler	32	6-15	0-0	3-5	9	0	1	1	4	15
Stacey Augmon	33	4-12	0-0	0-2	3	2	2	1	1	8
Anderson Hunt	27	1-12	0-5	5-6	2	1	1	0	4	7
Moses Scurry	18	2-5	0-0	2-3	14	1	1	0	2	6
Barry Young	13	1-6	1-3	0-0	1	0	0	0	1	3
Clint Rossum	22	1-4	0-3	0-0	0	1	0	0	1	2
George Ackles	16	1-3	0-0	0-1	4	0	0	2	1	2
Stacey Cvijanovich	2	1-1	0-0	0-0	0	0	0	0	1	2
James Jones	6	0-0	0-0	0-0	0	2	0	0	2	0
TOTALS	200	22-73	6-21	11-19	34	11	7	4	22	61
Percentages		30.1	28.6	57.9						

Coach: Jerry Tarkanian

Officials: Lenny Wirtz, David Dodge, Larry Rose
Technicals: None
Attendance: 16,813

MICHIGAN	MIN	FG	3FG	FT	REB	A	ST	BL	PF	TP
Glen Rice	37	12-24	2-4	2-2	5	1	3	0	1	28
Rumeal Robinson	40	6-13	0-1	2-5	1	12	1	0	4	14
Sean Higgins	24	5-12	1-3	3-3	3	1	0	2	2	14
Loy Vaught	29	5-13	0-0	0-0	16	0	0	0	2	10
Mark Hughes	19	4-5	0-0	1-1	6	1	0	0	3	9
Terry Mills	31	4-8	0-0	0-0	9	5	0	1	4	8
Mike Griffin	17	0-1	0-0	0-0	1	3	2	0	2	0
Demetrius Calip	3	0-1	0-0	0-0	0	0	0	0	2	0
TOTALS	**200**	**36-77**	**3-8**	**8-11**	**41**	**23**	**6**	**3**	**20**	**83**
Percentages		46.8	37.5	72.7						
Coach: Steve Fisher										

83-81

39 1H 38
44 2H 43

FINAL 4

ILLINOIS	MIN	FG	3FG	FT	REB	A	ST	BL	PF	TP
Kenny Battle	-	10-17	1-1	8-10	7	1	0	1	2	29
Nick Anderson	-	6-14	0-1	5-6	7	2	2	0	1	17
Kendall Gill	-	5-9	0-2	1-1	4	2	3	0	1	11
Lowell Hamilton	-	5-14	0-0	1-2	9	0	1	0	5	11
Stephen Bardo	-	1-7	1-3	4-4	6	8	0	1	3	7
Larry Smith	-	3-5	0-1	0-0	2	1	0	0	2	6
Marcus Liberty	-	0-1	0-0	0-0	0	0	0	0	0	0
Ervin Small	-	0-0	0-0	0-0	0	0	0	0	2	0
TOTALS	**-**	**30-67**	**2-8**	**19-23**	**35**	**14**	**6**	**2**	**16**	**81**
Percentages		44.8	25.0	82.6						
Coach: Lou Henson										

Officials: Ted Hillary, David Jones, Tom Harrington
Technicals: None
Attendance: 39,187

SETON HALL	MIN	FG	3FG	FT	REB	A	ST	BL	PF	TP
Andrew Gaze	38	7-14	4-9	2-2	4	3	2	2	2	20
Daryll Walker	29	6-9	0-0	7-7	6	0	3	1	4	19
Gerald Greene	39	5-9	1-1	6-6	5	8	1	0	1	17
John Morton	19	4-8	0-1	5-6	2	2	0	0	4	13
Ramon Ramos	30	3-8	0-0	3-3	12	1	2	0	3	9
Michael Cooper	14	3-4	0-0	0-0	4	0	0	0	3	6
Anthony Avent	10	3-4	0-0	0-0	1	0	0	2	1	6
Nick Katsikis	7	1-1	1-1	0-1	1	1	0	0	1	3
Frantz Volcy	10	1-2	0-0	0-1	1	1	0	2	4	2
Khyiem Long	1	0-1	0-0	0-0	0	0	0	0	0	0
Rene Monteserin	1	0-0	0-0	0-0	0	0	0	0	0	0
Jose Rebimbas	1	0-1	0-0	0-0	0	0	0	0	0	0
Pookey Wigington	1	0-0	0-0	0-1	0	0	0	0	0	0
Trevor Crowley	0	0-1	0-0	0-0	0	0	0	0	0	0
TOTALS	**200**	**33-62**	**6-12**	**23-27**	**36**	**16**	**8**	**7**	**23**	**95**
Percentages		53.2	50.0	85.2						
Coach: P.J. Carlesimo										

95-78

33 1H 38
62 2H 40

FINAL 4

DUKE	MIN	FG	3FG	FT	REB	A	ST	BL	PF	TP
Danny Ferry	39	13-29	1-5	7-11	10	2	0	0	2	34
Phil Henderson	37	4-16	0-1	5-6	5	5	2	1	3	13
Christian Laettner	21	4-5	0-0	5-7	7	1	1	0	5	13
Quin Snyder	31	3-10	2-5	0-0	5	4	0	0	5	8
John Smith	23	1-4	1-3	3-4	6	0	1	1	2	6
Robert Brickey	11	0-3	0-0	2-2	3	2	0	0	0	2
Brian Davis	9	1-2	0-0	0-2	0	0	0	0	1	2
Greg Koubek	18	0-3	0-2	0-0	2	1	0	0	2	0
Alaa Abdelnaby	6	0-0	0-0	0-0	0	0	0	1	4	0
Clay Buckley	3	0-0	0-0	0-0	0	0	0	0	1	0
George Burgin	1	0-0	0-0	0-0	0	0	0	1	0	0
Crawford Palmer	1	0-0	0-0	0-0	0	0	0	1	0	0
TOTALS	**200**	**26-72**	**4-16**	**22-32**	**38**	**15**	**4**	**5**	**25**	**78**
Percentages		36.1	25.0	68.8						
Coach: Mike Krzyzewski										

Officials: Larry Lembo, Don Rutledge, Ed Hightower
Technicals: None
Attendance: 39,187

MICHIGAN	MIN	FG	3FG	FT	REB	A	ST	BL	PF	TP
Glen Rice	42	12-25	5-12	2-2	11	0	0	0	2	31
Rumeal Robinson	43	6-13	0-0	9-10	3	11	0	0	2	21
Sean Higgins	27	3-10	1-4	3-4	9	2	0	1	3	10
Terry Mills	34	4-8	0-0	0-0	6	2	2	3	2	8
Loy Vaught	26	4-8	0-0	0-0	7	0	1	0	2	8
Mark Hughes	25	1-1	0-0	0-0	2	0	0	0	2	2
Mike Griffin	17	0-0	0-0	0-0	4	3	0	0	4	0
Demetrius Calip	11	0-2	0-0	0-0	0	1	0	0	3	0
TOTALS	**225**	**30-67**	**6-16**	**14-16**	**42**	**19**	**3**	**4**	**20**	**80**
Percentages		44.8	37.5	87.5						
Coach: Steve Fisher										

80-79

37 1H 32
34 2H 39
9 OT1 8

NCAA FINAL 1989

SETON HALL	MIN	FG	3FG	FT	REB	A	ST	BL	PF	TP
John Morton	37	11-26	4-12	9-10	4	3	0	0	3	35
Gerald Greene	43	5-13	2-5	1-3	5	5	2	0	3	13
Daryll Walker	39	5-9	0-1	3-4	11	1	0	0	2	13
Ramon Ramos	33	4-9	0-0	1-1	5	1	1	1	2	9
Andrew Gaze	39	1-5	1-5	2-2	3	3	1	0	3	5
Anthony Avent	11	1-2	0-0	0-0	3	1	0	0	0	2
Pookey Wigington	2	1-1	0-0	0-0	0	0	0	0	1	2
Michael Cooper	14	0-0	0-0	0-0	2	0	0	1	1	0
Frantz Volcy	7	0-0	0-0	0-2	1	0	0	0	2	0
TOTALS	**225**	**28-65**	**7-23**	**16-22**	**34**	**14**	**4**	**2**	**17**	**79**
Percentages		43.1	30.4	72.7						
Coach: P.J. Carlesimo										

Officials: Mickey Crowley, Tom Rucker, John Clougherty
Technicals: None
Attendance: 39,187

National Invitation Tournament (NIT)

First round: Villanova d. Saint Peter's 76-56, UAB d. Ga. Southern 83-74, Richmond d. Temple 70-56, St. John's d. Mississippi 70-67, Wisconsin d. New Orleans 63-61, Penn State d. Murray State 89-73, Ohio State d. Akron 81-70, Saint Louis d. Southern Illinois 87-54, Connecticut d. Charlotte 67-62, California d. Hawaii 73-57, New Mexico d. Santa Clara 91-76, Michigan State d. Kent State 83-69, Wichita State d. UC Santa Barbara 70-62, Pepperdine d. New Mexico St. 84-69, Nebraska d. Arkansas State 81-79, Oklahoma State d. Boise State 69-55

Second round: Saint Louis d. Wisconsin 73-68, Villanova d. Penn State 76-67, Connecticut d. California 73-72, Ohio State d. Nebraska 85-74, UAB d. Richmond 64-61, Michigan State d. Wichita State 79-67, St. John's d. Oklahoma State 76-64, New Mexico d. Pepperdine 86-69

Third round: UAB d. Connecticut 85-79, Michigan State d. Villanova 70-63, Saint Louis d. New Mexico 66-65, St. John's d. Ohio State 83-80 (OT)

Semifinals: Saint Louis d. Michigan State 74-64, St. John's d. UAB 76-65.

Third place: UAB d. Michigan State 78-76 (OT)

Championship: St. John's d. Saint Louis 73-65

MVP: Jayson Williams, St. John's

1989-90: Runnin' Wild

UNLV won the NCAA Tournament; Loyola Marymount won the hearts of the nation. In the middle of their West Coast Conference tournament semifinal, Lions' senior star Hank Gathers collapsed on the floor and died later that night of a heart ailment. The tournament was suspended and regular-season champ Loyola Marymount earned the conference's automatic bid to the NCAAs.

In the Tournament's first round, the No. 11-seed Lions upset New Mexico State, 111-92, behind Bo Kimble's 45 points. Then they took out defending champ Michigan, 149-115—the highest scoring game in Tournament history. A two-point win over Alabama set up a meeting with No. 1-seed UNLV, in which the Rebels overwhelmed the Lions, 131-101, to reach the Final Four. At Denver's McNichols Arena, Jerry Tarkanian's Runnin' Rebels beat Georgia Tech, 90-81, then thumped Duke, 103-73, the largest margin of victory in a Final. UNLV's Anderson Hunt was selected as the Tournament MOP.

La Salle's Lionel "L-Train" Simmons was named the Naismith Player of the Year (26.5 ppg, 11.1 rpg). Simmons is the only player in NCAA history to score more than 3,000 points and grab more than 1,100 rebounds. Syracuse's Derrick Coleman was the No. 1 pick in the NBA draft, selected by the New Jersey Nets.

Major Conference Standings

AM. SOUTH	Conference W	L	PCT	Overall W	L	PCT
Louisiana Tech□	8	2	.800	20	8	.714
New Orleans□	8	2	.800	21	11	.656
Texas-Pan American	7	3	.700	21	9	.700
UL-Lafayette	4	6	.400	20	9	.690
Arkansas State	2	8	.200	15	13	.536
Lamar	1	9	.100	7	21	.250

Tournament: **New Orleans d. Tex.-Pan American 48-44**

ACC	Conference W	L	PCT	Overall W	L	PCT
Clemson○⊗	10	4	.714	26	9	.743
Duke○	9	5	.643	29	9	.763
Georgia Tech⊕	8	6	.571	28	7	.800
North Carolina○	8	6	.571	21	13	.618
Virginia○	6	8	.429	20	12	.625
NC State	6	8	.429	18	12	.600
Maryland□	6	8	.429	19	14	.576
Wake Forest	3	11	.214	12	16	.429

Tournament: **Georgia Tech d. Virginia 70-61**
Tournament MVP: **Brian Oliver**, Georgia Tech

ATLANTIC 10	Conference W	L	PCT	Overall W	L	PCT
Temple⊕	15	3	.833	20	11	.645
Penn State□	13	5	.722	25	9	.735
West Virginia	11	7	.611	16	12	.571
Rhode Island	11	7	.611	15	13	.536
Rutgers□	11	7	.611	18	17	.514
Massachusetts□	10	8	.556	17	14	.548
George Washington	6	12	.333	14	17	.452
Saint Joseph's	5	13	.278	7	21	.250
Duquesne	5	13	.278	7	22	.241
St. Bonaventure	3	15	.167	8	20	.286

Tournament: **Temple d. Massachusetts 53-51**
Tournament MOP: **Mark Macon**, Temple

BIG EAST	Conference W	L	PCT	Overall W	L	PCT
Connecticut⊕	12	4	.750	31	6	.838
Syracuse○	12	4	.750	26	7	.788
Georgetown○	11	5	.688	24	7	.774
St. John's○	10	6	.625	24	10	.706
Providence○	8	8	.500	17	12	.586
Villanova○	8	8	.500	18	15	.545
Seton Hall	5	11	.313	12	16	.429
Pittsburgh	5	11	.313	12	17	.414
Boston College	1	15	.063	8	20	.286

Tournament: **Connecticut d. Syracuse 78-75**
Tournament MVP: **Chris Smith**, Connecticut

BIG EIGHT	Conference W	L	PCT	Overall W	L	PCT
Missouri○	12	2	.857	26	6	.813
Kansas○	11	3	.786	30	5	.857
Oklahoma⊕	11	3	.786	27	5	.844
Kansas State○	7	7	.500	17	15	.531
Oklahoma State□	6	8	.429	17	14	.548
Iowa State	4	10	.286	10	18	.357
Nebraska	3	11	.214	10	18	.357
Colorado	2	12	.143	12	18	.400

Tournament: **Oklahoma d. Colorado 92-80**
Tournament MVP: **Shaun Vandiver**, Colorado

BIG SKY	Conference W	L	PCT	Overall W	L	PCT
Idaho⊕	13	3	.813	25	6	.806
Eastern Washington	11	5	.688	18	11	.621
Montana	10	6	.625	19	10	.655
Nevada	9	7	.563	15	13	.536
Montana State	8	8	.500	17	12	.586
Weber State	8	8	.500	14	15	.483
Boise State	7	9	.438	12	15	.444
Northern Arizona	3	13	.188	8	20	.286
Idaho State	3	13	.188	6	21	.222

Tournament: **Idaho d. Eastern Washington 65-62**
Tournament: **MVP Riley Smith**, Idaho

BIG SOUTH	Conference W	L	PCT	Overall W	L	PCT
Coastal Carolina	11	1	.917	23	6	.793
UNC Asheville	7	5	.583	18	12	.600
Campbell	7	5	.583	15	13	.536
Winthrop	6	6	.500	19	10	.655
Charleston Southern	4	8	.333	9	19	.321
Augusta	4	8	.333	8	20	.286
Radford	3	9	.250	7	22	.241

Tournament: **Coastal Carolina d. UNC Asheville 76-73**
Tournament MVP: **Milton Moore**, UNC Asheville

BIG TEN	Conference W	L	PCT	Overall W	L	PCT
Michigan State⊕	15	3	.833	28	6	.824
Purdue○	13	5	.722	22	8	.733
Michigan○	12	6	.667	23	8	.742
Illinois○	11	7	.611	21	8	.724
Minnesota○	11	7	.611	23	9	.719
Ohio State○	10	8	.556	17	13	.567
Indiana○	8	10	.444	18	11	.621
Wisconsin	4	14	.222	14	17	.452
Iowa	4	14	.222	12	16	.429
Northwestern	2	16	.111	9	19	.321

BIG WEST	Conference W	L	PCT	Overall W	L	PCT
UNLV⊕	16	2	.889	35	5	.875
New Mexico State○	16	2	.889	26	5	.839
UC Santa Barbara○	13	5	.722	21	9	.700
Long Beach State□	12	6	.667	23	9	.719
Utah State	8	10	.444	14	16	.467
Pacific	7	11	.389	15	14	.517
Cal State Fullerton	6	12	.333	13	16	.448
San Jose State	5	13	.278	8	20	.286
Fresno State	4	14	.222	10	19	.345
UC Irvine	3	15	.167	5	23	.179

Tournament: **UNLV d. Long Beach State 92-74**
Tournament MVP: **Larry Johnson**, UNLV

COLONIAL ATHLETIC	Conference W	L	PCT	Overall W	L	PCT
James Madison□	11	3	.786	20	11	.645
Richmond⊕	10	4	.714	22	10	.688
American	10	4	.714	20	9	.690
George Mason	10	4	.714	20	12	.625
East Carolina	6	8	.429	13	18	.419
Navy	4	10	.286	5	23	.179
UNC Wilmington	3	11	.214	8	20	.286
William and Mary	2	12	.143	6	22	.214

Tournament: **Richmond d. James Madison 77-72**
Tournament MVP: **Ken Atkinson**, Richmond

EAST COAST	Conference W	L	PCT	Overall W	L	PCT
Lehigh	8	6	.571	18	12	.600
Towson⊕	8	6	.571	18	13	.581
Hofstra	8	6	.571	13	15	.464
Delaware	7	7	.500	16	13	.552
Lafayette	7	7	.500	15	13	.536
Drexel	7	7	.500	13	15	.464
Bucknell	6	8	.429	15	14	.517
Rider	5	9	.357	10	18	.357

Tournament: **Towson d. Lehigh 73-60**
Tournament MVP: **Kurk Lee**, Towson

IVY	Conference W	L	PCT	Overall W	L	PCT
Princeton⊕	11	3	.786	20	7	.741
Yale	10	4	.714	19	7	.731
Dartmouth	7	7	.500	12	14	.462
Harvard	7	7	.500	12	14	.462
Penn	7	7	.500	12	14	.462
Brown	7	7	.500	10	16	.385
Cornell	5	9	.357	12	17	.414
Columbia	2	12	.143	4	22	.154

METRO	Conference W	L	PCT	Overall W	L	PCT
Louisville⊕	12	2	.857	27	8	.771
Southern Miss○	9	5	.643	20	12	.625
Cincinnati□	9	5	.643	20	14	.588
Memphis□	8	6	.571	18	12	.600
Florida State	6	8	.429	16	15	.516
South Carolina	6	8	.429	14	14	.500
Virginia Tech	5	9	.357	13	18	.419
Tulane	1	13	.071	4	24	.143

Tournament: **Louisville d. Southern Miss 83-80**
Tournament MOP: **LaBradford Smith**, Louisville

METRO ATLANTIC	Conference W	L	PCT	Overall W	L	PCT
North						
Holy Cross□	14	2	.875	24	6	.800
Siena	11	5	.688	16	13	.552
Fordham□	10	6	.625	20	13	.606
Canisius	5	11	.313	11	18	.379
Army	5	11	.313	10	19	.345
Niagara	5	11	.313	6	22	.214
South						
La Salle⊕	16	0	1.000	30	2	.938
Iona	8	8	.500	13	15	.464
Saint Peter's	7	9	.438	14	14	.500
Manhattan	7	9	.438	11	17	.393
Fairfield	6	10	.375	10	19	.345
Loyola (MD)	2	14	.125	4	24	.143

Tournament: **La Salle d. Fordham 71-61**
Tournament MVP: **Lionel Simmons**, La Salle

MID-AMERICAN	Conference W	L	PCT	Overall W	L	PCT
Ball State⊕	13	3	.813	26	7	.788
Kent State□	12	4	.750	21	8	.724
Bowling Green□	9	7	.563	18	11	.621
Miami (OH)	9	7	.563	14	15	.483
Eastern Michigan	8	8	.500	19	13	.594
Toledo	7	9	.438	12	16	.429
Central Michigan	6	10	.375	13	17	.433
Ohio	5	11	.313	12	16	.429
Western Michigan	3	13	.188	9	18	.333

Tournament: **Ball State d. Central Michigan 78-56**
Tournament MVP: **Billy Butts**, Ball State

⊕ Automatic NCAA Tournament bid ○ At-large NCAA Tournament bid □ NIT appearance ⊗ Team record doesn't reflect games forfeited or vacated. For adjusted record, see p. 521.

MID-CONTINENT

	Conference			Overall		
	W	L	Pct	W	L	Pct
Missouri State○	11	1	.917	22	7	.759
Wisconsin-Green Bay□	9	3	.750	24	8	.750
Northern Iowa⊕	6	6	.500	23	9	.719
Illinois-Chicago	6	6	.500	16	12	.571
Western Illinois	6	6	.500	16	13	.552
Eastern Illinois	3	9	.250	10	18	.357
Valparaiso	1	11	.083	4	24	.143
Cleveland State	-	-	-	15	13	.536

Tournament: **Northern Iowa d. Wisc.-Green Bay 53-45**
Tournament MVP: **Jason Reese**, Northern Iowa

MEAC

	Conference			Overall		
	W	L	Pct	W	L	Pct
Coppin State⊕	15	1	.938	26	7	.788
Florida A&M	13	3	.813	18	11	.621
Delaware State	9	7	.563	14	14	.500
South Carolina State	8	8	.500	13	16	.448
Bethune-Cookman	8	8	.500	10	18	.357
NC A&T	6	10	.375	12	17	.414
Howard	5	11	.313	8	20	.286
UMES	4	12	.250	10	17	.370
Morgan State	4	12	.250	8	20	.286

Tournament: **Coppin State d. NC A&T 54-50**
Tournament MOP: **Reggie Isaacs**, Coppin State

MCC

	Conference			Overall		
	W	L	Pct	W	L	Pct
Xavier○	12	2	.857	28	5	.848
Dayton⊕	10	4	.714	22	10	.688
Saint Louis□	9	5	.643	21	12	.636
Marquette□	9	5	.643	15	14	.517
Evansville	8	6	.571	17	15	.531
Detroit	3	11	.214	10	18	.357
Loyola-Chicago	3	11	.214	7	22	.241
Butler	2	12	.143	6	22	.214

Tournament: **Dayton d. Xavier 98-89**
Tournament MVP: **Negele Knight**, Dayton

MISSOURI VALLEY

	Conference			Overall		
	W	L	Pct	W	L	Pct
Southern Illinois□	10	4	.714	26	8	.765
Creighton□	9	5	.643	21	12	.636
Illinois State⊕	9	5	.643	18	13	.581
Tulsa□	9	5	.643	17	13	.567
Bradley	6	8	.429	11	20	.355
Wichita State	6	8	.429	10	19	.345
Drake	5	9	.357	13	18	.419
Indiana State	2	12	.143	8	20	.286

Tournament: **Illinois State d. Southern Illinois 81-78**
Tournament MOP: **Rickey Jackson**, Illinois State

NAC

	Conference			Overall		
	W	L	Pct	W	L	Pct
Boston U.⊕	9	3	.750	18	12	.600
Northeastern	9	3	.750	16	12	.571
Hartford	8	4	.667	17	11	.607
Maine	6	6	.500	11	17	.393
Vermont	4	8	.333	13	17	.433
Colgate	3	9	.250	8	21	.276
New Hampshire	3	9	.250	5	23	.179

Tournament: **Boston U. d. Vermont 75-57**
Tournament MVP: **Bill Brigham**, Boston U.

NORTHEAST

	Conference			Overall		
	W	L	Pct	W	L	Pct
Robert Morris⊕	12	4	.750	22	8	.733
Monmouth	11	5	.688	17	12	.586
Marist	10	6	.625	17	11	.607
Saint Francis (PA)	10	6	.625	17	11	.607
Mount St. Mary's	10	6	.625	16	12	.571
Fairleigh Dickinson	8	8	.500	16	13	.552
Wagner	6	10	.375	11	17	.393
St. Francis (NY)	4	12	.250	9	18	.333
Long Island	1	15	.063	3	23	.115

Tournament: **Robert Morris d. Monmouth 71-66**
Tournament MVP: **Alex Blackwell**, Monmouth

OHIO VALLEY

	Conference			Overall		
	W	L	Pct	W	L	Pct
Murray State⊕	10	2	.833	21	9	.700
Tennessee Tech	9	3	.750	19	9	.679
Morehead State	7	5	.583	16	13	.552
Eastern Kentucky	7	5	.583	13	17	.433
Middle Tenn. State	6	6	.500	12	15	.444
Austin Peay	2	10	.167	10	19	.345
Tennessee State	2	10	.167	7	20	.259

Tournament: **Murray State d. Eastern Kentucky 64-57**
Tournament MVP: **Popeye Jones**, Murray State

PAC-10

	Conference			Overall		
	W	L	Pct	W	L	Pct
Oregon State○	15	3	.833	22	7	.759
Arizona○	15	3	.833	25	7	.781
California○	12	6	.667	22	10	.688
UCLA⊕	11	7	.611	22	11	.667
Oregon□	10	8	.556	15	14	.517
Stanford□	9	9	.500	18	12	.600
Arizona State□	6	12	.333	15	16	.484
Southern California	6	12	.333	12	16	.429
Washington	5	13	.278	11	17	.393
Washington State	1	17	.056	7	22	.241

Tournament: **Arizona d. UCLA 94-78**
Tournament MVP: **Jud Buechler**, Arizona

SEC

	Conference			Overall		
	W	L	Pct	W	L	Pct
Georgia○	13	5	.722	20	9	.690
Alabama⊕	12	6	.667	26	9	.743
LSU○	12	6	.667	23	9	.719
Tennessee□	10	8	.556	16	14	.533
Kentucky	10	8	.556	14	14	.500
Mississippi	8	10	.444	13	17	.433
Auburn	8	10	.444	13	18	.419
Vanderbilt□	7	11	.389	21	14	.600
Mississippi State□	7	11	.389	16	14	.533
Florida	3	15	.167	7	21	.250

Tournament: **Alabama d. Mississippi 70-51**
Tournament MVP: **Melvin Cheatum**, Alabama

SOUTHERN

	Conference			Overall		
	W	L	Pct	W	L	Pct
East Tennessee State⊕	12	2	.857	27	7	.794
Marshall	9	5	.643	15	13	.536
Appalachian State	8	6	.571	19	11	.633
Chattanooga	7	7	.500	14	14	.500
VMI	7	7	.500	14	15	.483
Furman	5	9	.357	15	16	.484
The Citadel	5	9	.357	12	16	.429
Western Carolina	3	11	.214	10	18	.357

Tournament: **East Tenn. St. d. Appalachian State 96-75**
Tournament MOP: **Keith Jennings**, East Tenn. St.

SOUTHLAND

	Conference			Overall		
	W	L	Pct	W	L	Pct
UL-Monroe⊕	13	1	.929	22	8	.733
McNeese State	11	3	.786	14	13	.519
Texas State	9	5	.643	13	15	.464
Sam Houston State	8	6	.571	10	18	.357
Texas-Arlington	6	8	.429	13	16	.448
Northwestern St. (LA)	5	9	.357	10	19	.345
North Texas	3	11	.214	5	25	.167
Stephen F. Austin	1	13	.071	2	25	.074

Tournament: **UL-Monroe d. North Texas 84-68**
Tournament MVP: **Anthony Jones**, UL-Monroe

SOUTHWEST

	Conference			Overall		
	W	L	Pct	W	L	Pct
Arkansas⊕	14	2	.875	30	5	.857
Houston○	13	3	.813	25	8	.758
Texas○	12	4	.750	24	9	.727
TCU	9	7	.563	16	13	.552
Baylor□	7	9	.438	16	14	.533
Texas A&M	7	9	.438	14	17	.452
Rice	5	11	.313	11	17	.393
SMU	5	11	.313	10	18	.357
Texas Tech	0	16	.000	5	22	.185

Tournament: **Arkansas d. Houston 96-84**
Tournament MVP: **Todd Day**, Arkansas

SWAC

	Conference			Overall		
	W	L	Pct	W	L	Pct
Southern U.□	12	2	.857	25	6	.806
Texas Southern⊕	10	4	.714	19	12	.613
Alabama State	7	7	.500	15	13	.536
Miss. Valley State	7	7	.500	11	18	.379
Alcorn State	6	8	.429	7	22	.241
Prairie View A&M	5	9	.357	9	18	.333
Grambling	5	9	.357	9	19	.321
Jackson State	4	10	.286	9	19	.321

Tournament: **Texas Southern d. Southern U. 94-89**
Tournament MVP: **Charles Price**, Texas Southern

SUN BELT

	Conference			Overall		
	W	L	Pct	W	L	Pct
UAB○	12	2	.857	22	9	.710
South Florida⊕	9	5	.643	20	11	.645
Old Dominion	7	7	.500	14	14	.500
Western Kentucky	7	7	.500	13	17	.433
Charlotte	6	8	.429	16	14	.533
Jacksonville	5	9	.357	13	16	.448
South Alabama	5	9	.357	11	17	.393
VCU	5	9	.357	11	17	.393

Tournament: **South Florida d. Charlotte 81-74**
Tournament MOP: **Radenko Dobras**, South Florida

TAAC

	Conference			Overall		
	W	L	Pct	W	L	Pct
Centenary	14	2	.875	22	8	.733
UTSA	13	3	.813	22	7	.759
Ark.-Little Rock⊕	12	4	.750	20	10	.667
Ga. Southern	11	5	.688	17	11	.607
Stetson	8	8	.500	15	17	.469
Hardin-Simmons	5	11	.313	9	19	.321
Samford	4	12	.250	6	22	.214
Georgia State	3	13	.188	5	23	.179
Mercer	2	14	.125	7	20	.259

Tournament: **Ark.-Little Rock d. Centenary 105-95**
Tournament MOP: **Derrick Owens**, Ark.-Little Rock

WEST COAST

	Conference			Overall		
	W	L	Pct	W	L	Pct
Loyola Marymount⊕	13	1	.929	26	6	.813
Pepperdine	10	4	.714	17	11	.607
San Diego	9	5	.643	16	12	.571
Portland	7	7	.500	11	17	.393
Santa Clara	6	8	.429	9	19	.321
San Francisco	4	10	.286	8	20	.286
Saint Mary's (CA)	4	10	.286	7	20	.259
Gonzaga	3	11	.214	8	20	.286

Note: Conference tournament canceled due to death of Loyola Marymount's Hank Gathers

WAC

	Conference			Overall		
	W	L	Pct	W	L	Pct
Colorado State○	11	5	.688	21	9	.700
BYU○	11	5	.688	21	9	.700
Hawaii□	10	6	.625	25	10	.714
UTEP⊕	10	6	.625	21	11	.656
New Mexico□	9	7	.563	20	14	.588
Wyoming	7	9	.438	15	14	.517
Utah	7	9	.438	16	14	.533
San Diego State	4	12	.250	13	18	.419
Air Force	3	13	.188	12	20	.375

Tournament: **UTEP d. Hawaii 75-58**
Tournament MVP: **Greg Foster**, UTEP

INDEPENDENTS

	Overall		
	W	L	Pct
Wright State	21	7	.750
Northern Illinois	17	11	.607
DePaul□	20	15	.571
Akron	16	12	.571
Notre Dame○	16	13	.552
Miami (FL)	13	15	.464
Southern Utah	13	15	.464
UMKC	13	15	.464
U.S. International	12	16	.429
UMBC	12	16	.429
Liberty	11	17	.393
Youngstown State	8	20	.286
Brooklyn	7	21	.250
Florida International	7	21	.250
Central Florida	7	21	.250
Central Connecticut State	6	22	.214
Chicago State	6	22	.214
Nicholls State	4	23	.148
Davidson	4	24	.143

INDIVIDUAL LEADERS—SEASON

SCORING	CL	POS	G	FG	3FG	FT	PTS	PPG
1 **Bo Kimble**, Loyola Marymount	SR	F	32	404	92	231	1,131	**35.3**
2 **Kevin Bradshaw**, U.S. International	JR	G	28	291	72	221	875	**31.3**
3 **Dave Jamerson**, Ohio	SR	G	28	297	131	149	874	**31.2**
4 **Alphonso Ford**, Miss. Valley State	FR	G	27	289	104	126	808	**29.9**
5 **Steve Rogers**, Alabama State	SO	F	28	286	46	213	831	**29.7**
6 **Hank Gathers**, Loyola Marymount	SR	F	26	314	0	126	754	**29.0**
7 **Darryl Brooks**, Tennessee State	JR	F	24	258	95	79	690	**28.8**
8 **Chris Jackson**, LSU	SO	G	32	305	88	191	889	**27.8**
9 **Dennis Scott**, Georgia Tech	JR	G	35	336	137	161	970	**27.7**
10 **Mark Stevenson**, Duquesne	SR	F	29	297	34	160	788	**27.2**

FIELD GOAL PCT	CL	POS	G	FG	FGA	PCT
1 **Lee Campbell**, Missouri State	SR	F	29	192	275	**69.8**
2 **Stephen Scheffler**, Purdue	SR	C/F	30	173	248	**69.8**
3 **Felton Spencer**, Louisville	SR	C	35	188	276	**68.1**
4 **Brian Parker**, Cleveland State	SR	C	26	155	236	**65.7**
5 **Brian Hill**, Evansville	SR	F	32	180	278	**64.7**

MINIMUM: 5 MADE PER GAME

THREE-PT FG PER GAME	CL	POS	G	3FG	3PG
1 **Dave Jamerson**, Ohio	SR	G	28	131	**4.7**
2 **Sydney Grider**, UL-Lafayette	SR	G	29	131	**4.5**
3 **Mark Alberts**, Akron	SO	G	28	122	**4.4**
4 **Jeff Fryer**, Loyola Marymount	SR	G	28	121	**4.3**
5 **Darryl Brooks**, Tennessee State	JR	F	24	95	**4.0**

THREE-PT FG PCT	CL	POS	G	3FG	3FGA	PCT
1 **Matt Lapin**, Princeton	SR	F	27	71	133	**53.4**
2 **Mike Iuzzolino**, Saint Francis (PA)	JR	G	27	79	153	**51.6**
3 **Dan Oberbrunner**, Wisconsin-Green Bay	SR	G	31	47	93	**50.5**
4 **Lee Mayberry**, Arkansas	SO	G	35	65	129	**50.4**
5 **Dwight Pernell**, Holy Cross	SR	G	30	81	161	**50.3**

MINIMUM: 1.5 MADE PER GAME

FREE THROW PCT	CL	POS	G	FT	FTA	PCT
1 **Rob Robbins**, New Mexico	JR	F	34	101	108	**93.5**
2 **Mike Joseph**, Bucknell	SR	G	29	144	155	**92.9**
3 **Chris Jackson**, LSU	SO	G	32	191	210	**91.0**
4 **Andy Kennedy**, UAB	JR	C	31	111	123	**90.2**
5 **Steve Henson**, Kansas State	SR	G	32	101	112	**90.2**

MINIMUM: 2.5 MADE PER GAME

ASSISTS PER GAME	CL	POS	G	AST	APG
1 **Todd Lehmann**, Drexel	SR	G	28	260	**9.3**
2 **Aaron Mitchell**, UL-Lafayette	JR	G	29	264	**9.1**
3 **Keith Jennings**, East Tennesee State	JR	G	34	297	**8.7**
4 **Otis Livingston**, Idaho	JR	G	31	262	**8.5**
5 **Kenny Anderson**, Georgia Tech	FR	G	35	285	**8.1**
6 **Gary Payton**, Oregon State	SR	G	29	235	**8.1**
7 **Tony Edmond**, TCU	SR	G	29	234	**8.1**
8 **Chris Corchiani**, NC State	JR	G	30	238	**7.9**
9 **Darelle Porter**, Pittsburgh	JR	G	29	229	**7.9**
10 **Lamar Holt**, Prairie View A&M	SR	G	27	213	**7.9**

REBOUNDS PER GAME	CL	POS	G	REB	RPG
1 **Anthony Bonner**, Saint Louis	SR	F	33	456	**13.8**
2 **Eric McArthur**, UC Santa Barbara	SR	F	29	377	**13.0**
3 **Tyrone Hill**, Xavier	SR	F	32	402	**12.6**
4 **Lee Campbell**, Missouri State	SR	F	29	363	**12.5**
5 **Cedric Ceballos**, Cal State Fullerton	SR	F	29	362	**12.5**
6 **Hakim Shahid**, South Florida	SR	C	31	383	**12.4**
7 **Ron Draper**, American	SR	F	29	354	**12.2**
8 **Derrick Coleman**, Syracuse	SR	C	33	398	**12.1**
9 **Shaquille O'Neal**, LSU	FR	C	32	385	**12.0**
10 **Clarence Weatherspoon**, Southern Miss	SO	F	32	371	**11.6**

BLOCKED SHOTS PER GAME	CL	POS	G	BLK	BPG
1 **Kenny Green**, Rhode Island	SR	F	26	124	**4.8**
2 **Dikembe Mutombo**, Georgetown	JR	C	31	128	**4.1**
3 **Kevin Roberson**, Vermont	SO	C	30	114	**3.8**
4 **Lorenzo Williams**, Stetson	JR	C	32	121	**3.8**
5 **Omar Roland**, Marshall	SR	C	28	101	**3.6**

STEALS PER GAME	CL	POS	G	STL	SPG
1 **Ronn McMahon**, Eastern Washington	SR	G	29	130	**4.5**
2 **Robert Dowdell**, Coastal Carolina	JR	G	29	109	**3.8**
3 **Nadav Henefeld**, Connecticut	FR	F	37	138	**3.7**
4 **Larry Robinson**, Centenary	SR	G	30	104	**3.5**
5 **Gary Payton**, Oregon State	SR	G	29	100	**3.4**

INDIVIDUAL LEADERS—GAME

POINTS	CL	POS	OPP	DATE	PTS
1 **Dave Jamerson**, Ohio	SR	G	Charleston (WV)	D21	**60**
2 **Gary Payton**, Oregon State	SR	G	Southern California	F22	**58**
3 **Kevin Bradshaw**, U.S. International	JR	G	Loyola Marymount	D7	**54**
Bo Kimble, Loyola Marymount	SR	F	Saint Joseph's	J4	**54**
5 **Bo Kimble**, Loyola Marymount	SR	F	Oregon State	D19	**53**

THREE-PT FG MADE	CL	POS	OPP	DATE	3FG
1 **Dave Jamerson**, Ohio	SR	G	Charleston (WV)	D21	**14**
2 **Bobby Phills**, Southern U.	JR	G	Alcorn State	F3	**11**
Dave Jamerson, Ohio	SR	G	Kent State	F24	**11**
Jeff Fryer, Loyola Marymount	SR	G	Michigan	M18	**11**
5 **Chris Jackson**, LSU	SO	G	Tennessee	F10	**10**
Mark Alberts, Akron	SO	G	Southern Utah	M1	**10**
Carl Brown, Arkansas-Little Rock	SR	G	UTSA	M7	**10**

ASSISTS	CL	POS	OPP	DATE	AST
1 **Todd Lehmann**, Drexel	SR	G	Liberty	F5	**19**
2 **Kenny Anderson**, Georgia Tech	FR	G	Pittsburgh	D28	**18**
3 **Kenny Anderson**, Georgia Tech	FR	G	North Carolina	F1	**17**
4 **Chris Corchiani**, NC State	JR	G	Florida State	D2	**16**
Steve Berger, West Virginia	SR	G	Pittsburgh	D19	**16**
Larry Yarbray, Coppin State	FR	G	South Carolina State	J4	**16**
Carlton Screen, Providence	SR	G	Syracuse	J20	**16**
Derrick Daniels, Houston	SO	G	Rice	F7	**16**
Otis Livingston, Idaho	JR	G	Montana State	F8	**16**

REBOUNDS	CL	POS	OPP	DATE	REB
1 **Eric McArthur**, UC Santa Barbara	SR	F	New Mexico State	J11	**28**
2 **Hank Gathers**, Loyola Marymount	SR	F	U.S. International	D7	**27**
3 **Hakim Shahid**, South Florida	SR	C	Jacksonville	F22	**25**
4 **Derek Strong**, Xavier	SR	C	Loyola Marymount	J2	**24**
LaPhonso Ellis, Notre Dame	SO	F	Creighton	J3	**24**
Shaquille O'Neal, LSU	FR	C	Loyola Marymount	F3	**24**
Todd Mattson, Army	SR	C	Holy Cross	M3	**24**

BLOCKED SHOTS	CL	POS	OPP	DATE	BLK
1 **Shaquille O'Neal**, LSU	FR	C	Loyola Marymount	F3	**12**
2 **Barry Brown**, James Madison	JR	F/C	American	J24	**11**
3 **Luc Longley**, New Mexico	JR	F/C	Hardin-Simmons	N24	**10**
Dikembe Mutombo, Georgetown	JR	C	North Carolina	D7	**10**
Daron Jenkins, Southern Miss	JR	C	Auburn	D29	**10**
Shaquille O'Neal, LSU	FR	C	Texas	J2	**10**
Derek Stewart, Augusta	FR	F	Radford	J10	**10**
Oliver Miller, Arkansas	SO	C	Texas	F4	**10**
Damon Lopez, Fordham	JR	C	Army	F13	**10**

STEALS	CL	POS	OPP	DATE	STL
1 **Elliot Perry**, Memphis	JR	G	Tennessee	N25	**9**
Eric Murdock, Providence	JR	G	Monmouth	N30	**9**
Ronn McMahon, Eastern Washington	SR	G	Portland	D15	**9**
Bojan Popovic, South Carolina	SO	G	Tennessee	D17	**9**
Omar Roland, Marshall	SR	C	Chattanooga	J13	**9**
Larry Robinson, Centenary	SR	G	Stetson	J18	**9**
Robert Dowdell, Coastal Carolina	JR	G	Winthrop	F21	**9**

TEAM LEADERS—SEASON

WIN-LOSS PCT	W	L	PCT
1 **La Salle**	30	2	**.938**
2 **UNLV**	35	5	**.875**
3 **Arkansas**	30	5	**.857**
Kansas	30	5	**.857**
5 **Xavier**	28	5	**.848**

SCORING OFFENSE	G	W-L	PTS	PPG
1 **Loyola Marymount**	32	26-6	3,918	**122.4**
2 **Oklahoma**	32	27-5	3,243	**101.3**
3 **Southern U.**	31	25-6	3,078	**99.3**
4 **U.S. Int'l**	28	12-16	2,738	**97.8**
5 **Centenary**	30	22-8	2,877	**95.9**

SCORING MARGIN	G	W-L	PPG	OPP PPG	MAR
1 **Oklahoma**	32	27-5	101.3	80.4	**20.9**
2 **Kansas**	35	30-5	92.1	72.3	**19.8**
3 **Georgetown**	31	24-7	81.5	64.8	**16.7**
4 **Arkansas**	35	30-5	95.6	79.8	**15.8**
5 **Southern U.**	31	25-6	99.3	84.1	**15.2**

FIELD GOAL PCT	G	W-L	FG	FGA	PCT
1 **Kansas**	35	30-5	1,204	2,258	**53.3**
2 **Louisville**	35	27-8	1,097	2,078	**52.8**
3 **Princeton**	27	20-7	592	1,133	**52.3**
4 **Purdue**	30	22-8	778	1,491	**52.2**
5 **Loyola Marymount**	32	26-6	1,456	2,808	**51.9**

THREE-PT FG PER GAME	G	W-L	3FG	3PG
1 **Kentucky**	28	14-14	281	**10.0**
2 **Loyola Marymount**	32	26-6	298	**9.3**
3 **UL-Lafayette**	29	20-9	251	**8.7**
4 **East Tennessee State**	34	27-7	285	**8.4**
5 **Dayton**	32	22-10	261	**8.2**

FREE THROW PCT	G	W-L	FT	FTA	PCT
1 **Lafayette**	28	15-13	461	588	**78.4**
2 **Vanderbilt**	35	21-14	742	956	**77.6**
3 **Wisconsin-Green Bay**	32	24-8	411	532	**77.3**
4 **Murray State**	30	21-9	540	703	**76.8**
5 **Bucknell**	29	15-14	502	657	**76.4**

REBOUND MARGIN	G	W-L	RPG	OPP RPG	MAR
1 **Georgetown**	31	24-7	44.8	34.0	**10.8**
2 **Xavier**	33	28-5	40.4	30.0	**10.4**
3 **Ball State**	33	26-7	39.5	30.9	**8.6**
4 **Michigan State**	34	28-6	38.1	29.8	**8.3**
Notre Dame	29	16-13	37.9	29.6	**8.3**

SCORING DEFENSE	G	W-L	OPP PTS	OPP PPG
1 Princeton	27	20-7	1,378	**51.0**
2 Ball State	33	26-7	1,935	**58.6**
3 Colorado State	30	21-9	1,778	**59.3**
4 Wisconsin-Green Bay	32	24-8	1,913	**59.8**
5 Northern Illinois	28	17-11	1,710	**61.1**

FIELD GOAL PCT DEFENSE	G	W-L	OPP FG	OPP FGA	OPP PCT
1 Georgetown	31	24-7	713	1,929	**37.0**
2 Arizona	32	25-7	780	1,990	**39.2**
3 Ball State	33	26-7	715	1,789	**40.0**
4 Alabama	35	26-9	784	1,952	**40.2**
5 South Carolina	28	14-14	660	1,630	**40.5**

CONSENSUS ALL-AMERICAS

FIRST TEAM

PLAYER	CL	POS	HT	SCHOOL	RPG	PPG
Derrick Coleman	SR	C	6-10	Syracuse	12.1	17.9
Chris Jackson	SO	G	6-1	LSU	2.5	27.8
Larry Johnson	JR	F	6-7	UNLV	11.4	22.7
Gary Payton	SR	G	6-3	Oregon State	4.7	25.7
Lionel Simmons	SR	F	6-6	La Salle	11.1	26.5

SECOND TEAM

PLAYER	CL	POS	HT	SCHOOL	RPG	PPG
Hank Gathers	SR	F	6-7	Loyola Marymount	7.7	29.0
Kendall Gill	SR	G	6-5	Illinois	4.9	20.0
Bo Kimble	SR	F	6-5	Loyola Marymount	7.7	35.3
Alonzo Mourning	SO	F/C	6-10	Georgetown	8.5	16.5
Rumeal Robinson	SR	G	6-2	Michigan	4.2	19.2
Dennis Scott	JR	G	6-8	Georgia Tech	6.6	27.7
Doug Smith	JR	F	6-10	Missouri	9.2	19.8

SELECTORS: AP, NABC, UPI, USBWA

AWARD WINNERS

PLAYER OF THE YEAR

PLAYER	CL	POS	HT	SCHOOL	AWARDS
Lionel Simmons	SR	F	6-6	La Salle	Naismith, AP, UPI, USBWA, Wooden, NABC, Rupp
Greg Harvey	SR	G	6-0	St. John's	Frances Pomeroy Naismith*

* FOR THE MOST OUTSTANDING SENIOR PLAYER WHO IS 6 FEET OR UNDER.

DEFENSIVE PLAYER OF THE YEAR

PLAYER	CL	POS	HT	SCHOOL
Stacey Augmon	JR	G/F	6-8	UNLV

COACH OF THE YEAR

COACH	SCHOOL	REC	AWARDS
Bobby Cremins	Georgia Tech	28-7	Naismith
Jim Calhoun	Connecticut	31-6	AP, UPI, Sporting News, CBS/Chevrolet
Roy Williams	Kansas	30-5	USBWA
Jud Heathcoate	Michigan State	28-6	NABC

BOB GIBBONS' TOP HIGH SCHOOL SENIOR RECRUITS

PLAYER	POS	HT	HIGH SCHOOL	A-A TEAMS	COLLEGE	CAREER NOTES
1 Eric Montross	C	7-0	Lawrence North HS, Indianapolis	McD, P, USA	North Carolina	NCAA title, '93; No. 9 pick, '94 NBA draft (Celtics); 4.5 ppg, 4.6 rpg (8 seasons)
2 Anthony Cade	PF	6-9	Oak Hill Academy, Mouth of Wilson, VA	McD, P	Seminole JC	17.5 ppg in JC; declared for '92 NBA draft as Soph.; undrafted
3 Ed O'Bannon	F	6-8	Artesia HS, Lakewood, CA	McD, P, USA	UCLA	Wooden Award, NCAA title, '95; No. 9 pick, '95 NBA draft (Nets); 5.0 ppg (2 seasons)
4 Shawn Bradley	C	7-5	Emery County HS, Castle Dale, UT	McD, P, USA	BYU	14.8 ppg, 7.7 rpg (1 season); No. 2 pick, '93 NBA draft (76ers); 8.1 ppg, 6.3 rpg (13 seasons)
5 Clifford Rozier	PF	6-10	Southeast HS, Bradenton, FL	McD, P	North Carolina/ Louisville	Transferred after 1 year; 18.1 ppg, 11.1 rpg as Sr.; No. 16 pick, '94 draft (Warriors); 4.8 ppg (3 seasons)
6 Grant Hill	G/F	6-8	South Lakes HS, Reston, VA	McD, P	Duke	ACC POY, '94; 2 NCAA titles; No. 3 pick, '94 NBA draft (Pistons); Olympic gold medal, '96; 7-time NBA All-Star
7 Jamie Brandon	2G	6-4	Martin Luther King HS, Chicago	McD, P, USA	Illinois/LSU	At LSU, 1,055 points (3 seasons); declared for NBA draft as a junior; undrafted
8 Jamal Mashburn	PF	6-8	Cardinal Hayes HS, Bronx, NY	P	Kentucky	18.8 ppg (3 seasons); No. 4 pick, '93 NBA draft (Mavs); 19.1 ppg (11 seasons); NBA All-Star, '03
9 Dwayne Morton	SF	6-7	Central HS, Louisville, KY	McD, P	Louisville	15.0 ppg (4 seasons); 2nd-round pick, '94 NBA draft (Warriors); 4.1 ppg (1 season)
10 Luther Wright	C	7-2	Elizabeth HS, Elizabeth, NJ	McD, P	Seton Hall	7.1 ppg, 5.3 rpg (2 seasons); No. 18 pick, '93 NBA draft (Jazz); played in 15 NBA games
11 Rodney Rogers	PF	6-7	Hillside HS, Durham, NC	McD, P	Wake Forest	ACC POY, '93; No. 9 pick, '93 NBA draft (Nuggets); 10.9 ppg, 4.5 rpg (12 seasons); NBA Sixth Man Award, '00
12 Brian Reese	G/F	6-6	St. Nicholas of Tolentine HS, Bronx, NY	McD, P	North Carolina	NCAA title, '93; at UNC, 1,113 points (4 seasons); undrafted; played overseas
13 Damon Bailey	G	6-3	Bedford (IN) North Lawrence HS	McD, P, USA	Indiana	Indiana's 6th-leading scorer (1,741 points); 2nd-round pick, '94 NBA draft (Pacers); played in CBA
14 Michael Smith	PF	6-8	Dunbar HS, Washington, DC	McD, P	Providence	PC's 4th-leading rebounder; 11.8 ppg (4 seasons); 2nd-round pick, '94 NBA draft (Kings); 5.6 ppg (7 seasons)
15 Anfernee Hardaway	G/F	6-7	Treadwell HS, Memphis, TN	P	Memphis	20.0 ppg, 7.7 rpg, 5.9 apg (2 seasons); No. 3 pick, '93 NBA draft (Warriors); 15.2 ppg (14 seasons); 4-time NBA All-Star
16 Kendrick Warren	SF	6-7	Thomas Jefferson HS, Richmond, VA	McD, P	VCU	4-time first team All-CAA; VCU's all-time leading scorer (1,858 pts); played in CBA, overseas
17 Darrin Hancock	G/F	6-6	Griffin HS, Griffin, CA	McD, P	Garden City (KS) JC/Kansas	Transferred after 2 years; 2nd-round pick, '94 NBA draft (Hornets); 3.5 ppg (3 seasons)
18 Robert Phelps	2G	6-5	Nazareth HS, Brooklyn, NY		Providence	9th all-time N.Y. State HS scoring; at Providence, 782 points; undrafted
19 Khalid Reeves	2G	6-3	Christ the King HS, Middle Village, NY	McD, P	Arizona	Top-10 in 6 stat categories; No. 12 pick, '94 NBA draft (Heat); 7.8 ppg (6 seasons)
20 Antonio Lang	G/F	6-7	LeFlore HS, Mobile, AL	P	Duke	2 NCAA titles; 2nd-round pick, '94 NBA draft (Suns); 2.3 ppg (3 seasons)

OTHER STANDOUTS

PLAYER	POS	HT	HIGH SCHOOL	A-A TEAMS	COLLEGE	CAREER NOTES
34 Wesley Person	G	6-4	Brantley (AL) HS		Auburn	19.1 ppg, 6.5 rpg (4 seasons); No. 23 pick, '94 NBA draft (Suns); 11.2 ppg (11 seasons)
64 Eddie Jones	SF	6-6	Blanche Ely HS, Pompano Beach, FL		Temple	A-10 POY, '94; at Temple, 16.0 ppg, 6.3 rpg (4 seasons); No. 10 pick, '94 NBA draft (Lakers); 3-time NBA All-Star
65 Lawrence Moten	SF	6-4	Archbishop Carroll HS, Washington, DC		Syracuse	Left Syracuse as Big East all-time leading scorer (2,334 points); 2nd-round pick, '95 NBA draft (Grizzlies); 6.3 ppg (3 seasons)

Abbreviations: McD=McDonald's; P=Parade; USA=USA Today

Poll Progression

Preseason Poll

AP	UPI	SCHOOL
1	1	**UNLV**
2	3	**LSU**
3	2	**Syracuse**
4	5	**Michigan**
5	4	**Georgetown**
6	6	**Arizona**
7	7	**North Carolina**
8	8	**Illinois**
9	10	**Arkansas**
10	9	**Duke**
11	10	**Missouri**
12	14	**Louisville**
13	13	**UCLA**
14	12	**Indiana**
15	17	**Temple**
16	16	**Oklahoma**
17	19	**Notre Dame**
18	18	**Pittsburgh**
19	—	**NC State**
20	—	**Minnesota**
21	20	**Oklahoma State**
22	15	**Georgia Tech**
23	—	**Florida**
24	—	**Memphis**
25	—	**St. John's**

Week of Nov 27

AP	UPI	SCHOOL	AP↓↑
1	1	**Syracuse** (0-0)	↑2
2	3	**Arizona** (1-0)	↑4
3	4	**Georgetown** (2-0)	↑2
4	2	**Kansas** (4-0) Ⓐ	⤴
5	6	**Missouri** (3-0)	↑6
6	5	**UNLV** (3-1) Ⓐ	↓5
7	11	**Duke** (1-0)	↑3
8	8	**Illinois** (0-0)	
9	7	**LSU** (1-1)	↓7
10	12	**Michigan** (0-1)	↓6
11	9	**Arkansas** (2-0)	↓2
12	10	**North Carolina** (2-1)	↓5
13	15	**Louisville** (2-1)	↓1
14	14	**Indiana** (1-0)	
15	13	**UCLA** (1-0)	↓2
16	17	**Temple** (0-0)	↓1
17	16	**Oklahoma** (0-0)	↓1
18	—	**Pittsburgh** (0-0)	
19	—	**Notre Dame** (0-0)	↓2
20	—	**St. John's** (3-1)	↑5
21	19	**Georgia Tech** (1-0)	↑1
22	—	**Memphis** (2-0)	↑2
23	18	**Oklahoma State** (0-0)	↓2
24	20	**Florida** (0-0)	↓1
25	—	**NC State** (1-1)	↓6

Week of Dec 5

AP	UPI	SCHOOL	AP↓↑
1	1	**Syracuse** (4-0)	
2	2	**Kansas** (6-0)	↑2
3	3	**Georgetown** (3-0)	
4	4	**Missouri** (4-0)	↑1
5	5	**UNLV** (3-1)	↑1
6	6	**Duke** (3-0)	↑1
7	7	**Illinois** (2-0)	↑1
8	10	**Michigan** (3-1)	↑2
9	8	**LSU** (2-1)	
10	9	**Arkansas** (3-0)	↑1
11	11	**Louisville** (3-1)	↑2
12	12	**Oklahoma** (2-0) Ⓑ	↑5
13	14	**UCLA** (3-0)	↑2
14	13	**Indiana** (3-0)	
15	—	**St. John's** (4-1)	↑5
16	—	**Memphis** (3-0)	↑6
17	15	**North Carolina** (4-2)	↓5
18	18	**Georgia Tech** (2-0)	↑3
19	18	**NC State** (4-1)	↑6
20	17	**Arizona** (1-2) Ⓒ	↓18
21	16	**Alabama** (4-0)	⤴
22	—	**Pittsburgh** (2-1)	↓4
23	—	**Temple** (2-1)	↓7
24	20	**Oregon State** (3-0) Ⓒ	⤴
25	—	**Florida** (1-0)	↓1

Week of Dec 12

AP	UPI	SCHOOL	AP↓↑
1	1	**Syracuse** (6-0)	
2	2	**Kansas** (9-0) Ⓓ	
3	3	**Georgetown** (5-0)	
4	4	**Missouri** (7-0)	
5	5	**Illinois** (5-0)	
6	7	**Michigan** (5-1)	
7	6	**Arkansas** (5-0)	↑
8	8	**Oklahoma** (4-0)	↑
9	9	**LSU** (4-1)	
10	11	**Louisville** (6-1)	↑
11	10	**Indiana** (6-0)	↑
12	13	**Duke** (3-2)	↓
13	14	**UCLA** (4-0)	
14	12	**UNLV** (3-2)	↓
15	16	**Georgia Tech** (3-0)	↑
16	15	**NC State** (6-1)	↑
17	—	**Memphis** (4-1)	↓
18	—	**St. John's** (5-2)	↓3
19	19	**Alabama** (5-1)	↑2
20	—	**Arizona** (2-2)	
21	17	**Iowa** (6-0)	⤴
22	20	**Oklahoma State** (4-1)	⤴
23	—	**Oregon State** (4-1)	↑1
24	—	**Florida** (2-1)	↑1
25	18	**Michigan State** (6-0)	⤴

Week of Dec 19

AP	UPI	SCHOOL	AP↓↑
1	1	**Syracuse** (7-0)	
2	2	**Kansas** (10-0)	
3	3	**Georgetown** (7-0)	
4	4	**Missouri** (9-0)	
5	5	**Illinois** (6-0)	
6	6	**Michigan** (7-1)	
7	7	**Oklahoma** (4-0)	↑1
8	8	**LSU** (4-1)	↑1
9	10	**Louisville** (7-1)	↑1
10	11	**Arkansas** (5-1)	↓3
11	9	**Indiana** (7-0)	
12	14	**Duke** (3-2)	
13	12	**UNLV** (4-2)	↑1
14	13	**Georgia Tech** (5-0)	↑1
15	—	**NC State** (6-1)	↑1
16	15	**Iowa** (6-0)	↑5
17	20	**Memphis** (4-1)	
18	16	**UCLA** (4-1)	↓5
19	19	**St. John's** (8-2)	↓1
20	18	**Alabama** (6-1)	↓1
21	17	**Oregon State** (5-1)	↑2
22	—	**Arizona** (2-2)	↓2
23	—	**La Salle** (4-0)	⤴
24	—	**Oklahoma State** (6-2)	↓2
25	—	**Michigan State** (7-1)	
—	20	**Arkansas-Little Rock** (3-0)	
—	20	**North Carolina** (5-4)	

Week of Dec 26

AP	UPI	SCHOOL	AP↓↑
1	1	**Syracuse** (8-0)	
2	2	**Kansas** (11-0)	
3	3	**Georgetown** (8-0)	
4	4	**Illinois** (8-0)	↑1
5	6	**Michigan** (8-1)	↑1
6	5	**Oklahoma** (5-0)	↑1
7	6	**Missouri** (9-1)	↓3
8	11	**Louisville** (8-1)	↑1
9	12	**LSU** (6-1)	↓1
10	8	**Indiana** (8-0)	↑1
11	10	**Arkansas** (7-1)	↓1
12	9	**UNLV** (5-2)	↑1
13	14	**Duke** (5-2)	↓1
14	13	**Georgia Tech** (6-0)	
15	—	**Memphis** (6-1)	↑2
16	15	**UCLA** (6-1)	↑2
17	—	**St. John's** (9-2)	↑2
18	20	**Iowa** (7-1)	↓2
19	—	**NC State** (7-2)	↓4
20	16	**La Salle** (6-0)	↑3
21	16	**Arizona** (3-2)	↑1
22	—	**Alabama** (7-2)	↓2
23	—	**Oregon State** (6-2)	↓2
24	19	**North Carolina** (6-4)	⤴
25	—	**Minnesota** (7-1)	⤴
—	18	**Virginia** (8-1)	

Week of Jan 2

AP	UPI	SCHOOL	AP↓↑
1	1	**Syracuse** (9-0)	
2	2	**Kansas** (13-0)	
3	3	**Georgetown** (9-0)	
4	4	**Illinois** (10-0)	
5	5	**Michigan** (10-1)	
6	5	**Oklahoma** (8-0)	
7	7	**Missouri** (10-1)	
8	10	**Louisville** (9-1)	
9	8	**Indiana** (10-0)	↑1
10	9	**UNLV** (7-2)	↑2
11	11	**LSU** (6-1)	↓2
12	12	**Georgia Tech** (8-0)	↑2
13	13	**Duke** (8-2)	
14	14	**Arkansas** (8-2)	↓3
15	15	**UCLA** (8-1)	↑1
16	—	**St. John's** (9-2)	↑1
17	19	**La Salle** (7-0)	↑3
18	—	**NC State** (7-2)	↑1
19	19	**Arizona** (5-2)	↑2
20	17	**Iowa** (8-1)	↓2
21	—	**Memphis** (7-3)	↓6
22	18	**Alabama** (9-2)	
23	—	**Oregon State** (9-2)	
24	—	**Minnesota** (8-1)	↑1
25	—	**Loyola Marymount** (7-2)	⤴
—	16	**Colorado State** (10-2)	

Week of Jan 9

AP	UPI	SCHOOL	AP↓↑
1	1	**Kansas** (15-0)	↑1
2	2	**Georgetown** (11-0)	↑1
3	4	**Michigan** (10-1)	↑2
4	3	**Oklahoma** (10-0)	↑2
5	5	**Missouri** (13-1)	↑2
6	6	**Syracuse** (10-1)	↓5
7	8	**UNLV** (9-2)	↑3
8	7	**Illinois** (11-1)	↓4
9	9	**Georgia Tech** (10-0)	↑3
10	11	**Duke** (10-2)	↑3
11	10	**Louisville** (10-2)	↓3
12	14	**Arkansas** (10-2)	↑2
13	12	**Indiana** (10-1)	↓4
14	13	**LSU** (8-2)	↓3
15	16	**St. John's** (13-2)	↑1
16	15	**Minnesota** (10-1)	↑8
17	—	**NC State** (11-2)	↑1
18	17	**Arizona** (8-2)	↑1
19	19	**UCLA** (9-2)	↓4
20	—	**Memphis** (9-3)	↑1
21	—	**La Salle** (8-1)	↓4
22	—	**Oregon State** (11-2)	↑1
23	18	**Loyola Marymount** (9-3)	↑2
24	20	**Alabama** (10-3)	↓2
25	—	**Xavier** (9-1)	⤴

Week of Jan 16

AP	UPI	SCHOOL	AP↓↑
1	1	**Kansas** (18-0)	
2	2	**Georgetown** (13-0)	
3	3	**Oklahoma** (12-0)	↑1
4	4	**Missouri** (15-1)	↑1
5	5	**Syracuse** (12-1)	↑1
6	7	**Michigan** (11-2)	↓3
7	6	**Illinois** (12-1)	↑1
8	8	**Duke** (12-2)	↑2
9	9	**UNLV** (10-3)	↓2
10	10	**Louisville** (12-2)	↑1
11	11	**Georgia Tech** (11-1)	↓2
12	13	**Arkansas** (12-2)	
13	12	**LSU** (10-2)	↑1
14	14	**Indiana** (12-2)	↓1
15	17	**St. John's** (14-3)	
16	15	**UCLA** (11-2)	↑3
17	19	**La Salle** (10-1)	↑4
18	—	**Oregon State** (12-2)	↑4
19	—	**NC State** (12-3)	↓2
20	18	**Xavier** (11-1)	↑5
21	—	**Loyola Marymount** (11-3)	↑2
22	—	**Minnesota** (10-3)	↓6
23	—	**Arizona** (9-3)	↓5
24	16	**Purdue** (11-2)	⤴
25	—	**Alabama** (12-3)	↓1
—	19	**Michigan State** (14-2)	

Week of Jan 23

AP	UPI	SCHOOL	AP↓↑
1	1	**Missouri** (17-1)	↑3
2	2	**Kansas** (19-1)	↓1
3	3	**Georgetown** (14-1)	↓1
4	4	**Louisville** (14-2)	↑6
5	5	**UNLV** (12-3)	↑4
6	9	**Arkansas** (14-2)	↑6
7	8	**Michigan** (13-3)	↓1
8	7	**Duke** (13-3)	
9	6	**Oklahoma** (12-2)	↓6
10	12	**Illinois** (13-3)	↓3
11	10	**Syracuse** (12-3)	↓6
12	15	**Indiana** (13-2)	↑2
13	11	**Georgia Tech** (12-2)	↓2
13	13	**Purdue** (13-2)	↑11
15	17	**St. John's** (16-3)	
16	13	**LSU** (12-3)	↓3
17	16	**Oregon State** (14-2)	↑1
18	18	**La Salle** (12-1)	↓1
19	—	**Arizona** (11-3)	↑4
20	19	**Connecticut** (15-3)	⤴
21	—	**Minnesota** (12-3)	↑1
22	—	**Loyola Marymount** (13-3)	↓1
23	—	**UCLA** (12-3)	↓7
24	20	**Alabama** (13-4)	↑1
25	—	**Xavier** (13-2)	↓5

Week of Jan 30

AP	UPI	SCHOOL	AP↓↑
1	1	**Missouri** (19-1)	
2	2	**Kansas** (20-1)	
3	3	**Arkansas** (17-2)	↑3
4	4	**Michigan** (15-3)	↑3
5	5	**Duke** (16-3)	↑3
6	6	**Georgetown** (15-2)	↓3
7	7	**Syracuse** (14-3)	↑4
8	9	**Purdue** (15-2)	↑5
9	8	**Oklahoma** (14-2)	
10	12	**Louisville** (14-3)	↓6
11	11	**Illinois** (15-3)	↓1
12	10	**UNLV** (14-4)	↓7
13	14	**Connecticut** (17-3)	↑7
14	13	**LSU** (14-4)	↑2
15	15	**La Salle** (15-1)	↑3
16	17	**UCLA** (14-3)	↑7
17	15	**Georgia Tech** (12-4)	↓4
18	19	**St. John's** (17-4)	↓3
19	20	**Minnesota** (14-4)	↑2
20	—	**Loyola Marymount** (15-3)	↑2
21	—	**Oregon State** (15-3)	↓4
22	—	**Indiana** (13-4)	↓10
23	—	**Xavier** (15-2)	↑2
24	—	**Arizona** (12-4)	↓5
25	18	**North Carolina** (15-6)	⤴

Week of Feb 6

AP	UPI	SCHOOL	AP↓↑
1	1	**Missouri** (21-1)	
2	2	**Kansas** (22-1)	
3	3	**Arkansas** (19-2)	
4	4	**Duke** (18-3)	↑1
5	5	**Georgetown** (17-2)	↑1
6	6	**Syracuse** (16-3)	↑1
7	8	**Michigan** (16-4)	↓3
8	11	**Connecticut** (19-3)	↑5
9	7	**UNLV** (16-4)	↑3
10	9	**Purdue** (16-3)	↓2
11	12	**LSU** (16-4)	↑3
12	13	**Illinois** (16-4)	↓1
13	10	**Oklahoma** (15-3)	↓4
14	16	**La Salle** (16-1)	↑1
15	14	**Louisville** (16-4)	↓5
16	15	**Georgia Tech** (14-4)	↑1
17	18	**Minnesota** (15-4)	↑2
18	17	**Oregon State** (17-3)	↑3
19	20	**UCLA** (15-4)	↓3
20	—	**Loyola Marymount** (17-4)	
21	—	**Xavier** (17-2)	↑2
22	—	**Arizona** (14-4)	↑2
23	—	**Michigan State** (17-5)	⤴
24	—	**St. John's** (17-6)	↓6
25	—	**Indiana** (14-5)	↓3
—	19	**New Mexico State** (18-2)	

Week of Feb 13

UPI	School	AP↓↑
1	**Kansas** (24-1)	↑1
4	**Missouri** (22-2)	↓1
2	**Georgetown** (19-2)	↑2
3	**Syracuse** (18-3)	↑2
6	**Michigan** (18-4)	↑2
5	**Duke** (19-4)	↓2
7	**UNLV** (19-4)	↑2
8	**Arkansas** (20-3)	↓5
9	**LSU** (19-4) Ⓔ	↑2
13	**Connecticut** (20-4)	↓2
10	**Oklahoma** (17-3)	↑2
12	**Purdue** (17-4)	↓2
11	**Georgia Tech** (16-4)	↑3
14	**La Salle** (19-1)	
17	**Illinois** (17-5)	↓3
16	**Oregon State** (18-3)	↑2
15	**Minnesota** (16-5)	
—	**Louisville** (18-5)	↓3
20	**Loyola Marymount** (19-4)	↑1
—	**Arizona** (16-4)	↑2
—	**Michigan State** (19-5)	↑2
19	**Xavier** (19-2)	↓1
—	**UCLA** (16-5)	↓4
—	**St. John's** (19-6)	
18	**New Mexico State** (20-2)	⤴

Week of Feb 20

AP	UPI	School	AP↓↑
1	1	**Missouri** (24-2)	↑1
2	2	**Kansas** (25-2)	↓1
3	4	**Duke** (22-4)	↑3
4	5	**UNLV** (22-4)	↑3
5	3	**Georgetown** (20-3)	↓2
6	8	**Connecticut** (22-4)	↑4
7	10	**Michigan** (19-5)	↓2
8	6	**Georgia Tech** (19-4)	↑5
9	7	**Purdue** (18-4)	↑3
10	11	**Oklahoma** (19-4)	↑1
11	9	**Syracuse** (18-5)	↓7
12	13	**LSU** (20-5)	↓3
13	12	**Arkansas** (21-4)	↓5
14	14	**La Salle** (22-1)	
15	16	**Michigan State** (21-5)	↑6
16	15	**Louisville** (20-5)	↑2
17	18	**Oregon State** (19-4)	↓1
18	17	**Minnesota** (17-6)	↓1
19	19	**Xavier** (21-2)	↑3
19	—	**Illinois** (18-6)	↓4
21	—	**Arizona** (17-5)	↓1
22	—	**Loyola Marymount** (20-5)	↓3
23	—	**Clemson** (20-5)	⤴
24	19	**New Mexico State** (21-3)	↑1
25	—	**Indiana** (16-6)	⤴

Week of Feb 27

AP	UPI	School	AP↓↑
1	1	**Kansas** (27-2)	↑1
2	3	**UNLV** (24-4)	↑2
3	2	**Missouri** (25-3)	↓2
4	6	**Connecticut** (24-4)	↑2
5	4	**Duke** (23-5)	↓2
5	7	**Oklahoma** (21-4)	↑5
7	5	**Georgetown** (21-4)	↓2
8	8	**Michigan** (20-5)	↓1
9	10	**Purdue** (20-5)	
10	9	**Syracuse** (20-5)	↑1
11	11	**Georgia Tech** (20-5)	↓3
12	12	**Arkansas** (22-4)	↑1
13	14	**La Salle** (25-1)	↑1
14	13	**Michigan State** (22-5)	↑1
15	15	**LSU** (21-6)	↓3
16	15	**Oregon State** (21-4)	↑1
17	20	**Minnesota** (19-6)	↑1
18	17	**Illinois** (19-6)	↑1
19	18	**Xavier** (23-2)	
20	—	**Clemson** (22-5)	↑3
21	—	**Louisville** (20-7)	↓5
22	—	**Loyola Marymount** (22-5)	
23	—	**Arizona** (19-6)	↓2
24	19	**New Mexico State** (23-3)	
25	—	**Georgia** (19-6)	⤴

Week of Mar 6

AP	UPI	School	AP↓↑
1	1	**Oklahoma** (23-4)	↑4
2	2	**Kansas** (28-3)	↓1
3	3	**UNLV** (26-5)	↓1
4	4	**Syracuse** (22-5)	↑6
5	6	**Georgetown** (22-5)	↑2
6	5	**Missouri** (26-4)	↓3
7	8	**Michigan State** (24-5)	↑7
8	7	**Connecticut** (25-5)	↓4
9	10	**Arkansas** (23-4)	↑3
10	9	**Purdue** (21-6)	↓1
11	12	**La Salle** (28-1)	↑2
12	11	**Duke** (23-7)	↓7
13	14	**Michigan** (20-7)	↓5
14	13	**Georgia Tech** (21-6)	↓3
15	16	**Arizona** (21-6)	↑8
16	—	**LSU** (22-7)	↓1
17	15	**Clemson** (23-6)	↑3
18	18	**Louisville** (23-7)	↑3
19	20	**Minnesota** (20-7)	↓2
20	19	**Illinois** (20-7)	↓2
21	—	**Loyola Marymount** (23-5) Ⓕ	↑1
22	—	**Oregon State** (22-5)	↓6
23	17	**New Mexico State** (25-3)	↑1
24	—	**Xavier** (24-3)	↓5
25	—	**Georgia** (20-7)	

Final Poll

AP	School	AP↓↑
1	**Oklahoma** (26-4)	
2	**UNLV** (29-5)	↑1
3	**Michigan State** (26-5)	↑4
4	**Connecticut** (28-5)	↑4
5	**Kansas** (29-4)	↓3
6	**Syracuse** (24-6)	↓2
7	**Arkansas** (26-4)	↑2
8	**Georgetown** (23-6)	↓3
9	**Georgia Tech** (24-6)	↑5
10	**Purdue** (21-7)	
11	**Missouri** (26-5)	↓5
12	**La Salle** (29-1) Ⓖ	↓1
13	**Michigan** (22-7)	
14	**Arizona** (24-6)	↑1
15	**Duke** (24-8)	↓3
16	**Louisville** (26-7)	↑2
17	**Clemson** (24-8)	
18	**Illinois** (21-7)	↑2
19	**LSU** (22-8)	↓3
20	**Minnesota** (20-8)	↓1
21	**Loyola Marymount** (23-5)	
22	**Oregon State** (22-6)	
23	**Alabama** (24-8)	⤴
24	**New Mexico State** (26-4)	↓1
25	**Xavier** (26-4)	↓1

Ⓐ After upsetting UNLV, Kansas jumps to No. 4 in the AP poll, the biggest one-week leap ever for an unranked team. UNLV will fail to regain the top spot although it will win the national title this season.

Ⓑ Oklahoma rips U.S. International for 97 points in the first half, a record against a D1 opponent (final score: 173-101). The Sooners also set NCAA records for field goals made and attempted in a half (42 of 90) and field goals attempted in a game (147).

Ⓒ Oregon State hands Arizona its worst defeat of the Lute Olson era, riding Gary Payton's 25 points to an 84-61 victory.

Ⓓ New Kentucky coach Rick Pitino brings his high-octane offense to Kansas, but it fires up the Jayhawks more than the Wildcats in a 150-95 drubbing.

Ⓔ New Tennessee coach Wade Houston gets 43 points from his freshman son, Allan, but LSU holds off the Vols, 119-113, behind Chris Jackson's 49 points, 30 of which come on three-pointers.

Ⓕ Loyola Marymount star Hank Gathers collapses during the Lions' West Coast Conference tournament game against Portland and dies in the hospital two hours later from an undiagnosed heart-muscle disorder known as cardiomyopathy.

Ⓖ La Salle's Lionel Simmons completes his four-year varsity career with 3,217 points and 1,429 rebounds.

1990 NCAA TOURNAMENT

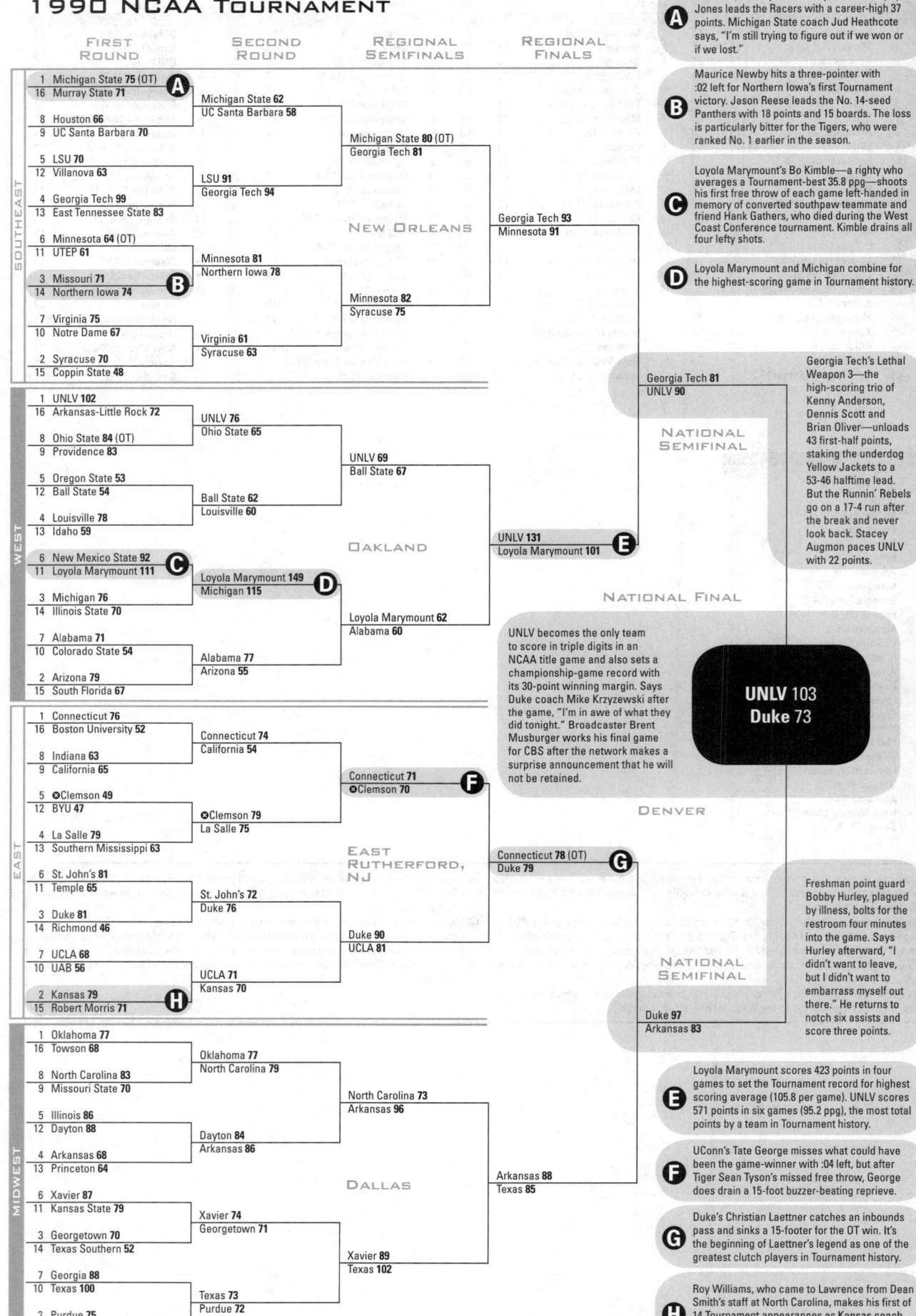

SOUTHEAST

First Round
- 1 Michigan State **75** (OT) — 16 Murray State **71** (A)
- 8 Houston **66** — 9 UC Santa Barbara **70**
- 5 LSU **70** — 12 Villanova **63**
- 4 Georgia Tech **99** — 13 East Tennessee State **83**
- 6 Minnesota **64** (OT) — 11 UTEP **61**
- 3 Missouri **71** — 14 Northern Iowa **74** (B)
- 7 Virginia **75** — 10 Notre Dame **67**
- 2 Syracuse **70** — 15 Coppin State **48**

Second Round
- Michigan State **62** — UC Santa Barbara **58**
- LSU **91** — Georgia Tech **94**
- Minnesota **81** — Northern Iowa **78**
- Virginia **61** — Syracuse **63**

Regional Semifinals (New Orleans)
- Michigan State **80** (OT) — Georgia Tech **81**
- Minnesota **82** — Syracuse **75**

Regional Finals
- Georgia Tech **93** — Minnesota **91**

WEST

First Round
- 1 UNLV **102** — 16 Arkansas-Little Rock **72**
- 8 Ohio State **84** (OT) — 9 Providence **83**
- 5 Oregon State **53** — 12 Ball State **54**
- 4 Louisville **78** — 13 Idaho **59**
- 6 New Mexico State **92** — 11 Loyola Marymount **111** (C)
- 3 Michigan **76** — 14 Illinois State **70**
- 7 Alabama **71** — 10 Colorado State **54**
- 2 Arizona **79** — 15 South Florida **67**

Second Round
- UNLV **76** — Ohio State **65**
- Ball State **62** — Louisville **60**
- Loyola Marymount **149** — Michigan **115** (D)
- Alabama **77** — Arizona **55**

Regional Semifinals (Oakland)
- UNLV **69** — Ball State **67**
- Loyola Marymount **62** — Alabama **60**

Regional Finals
- UNLV **131** — Loyola Marymount **101** (E)

EAST

First Round
- 1 Connecticut **76** — 16 Boston University **52**
- 8 Indiana **63** — 9 California **65**
- 5 ⊗Clemson **49** — 12 BYU **47**
- 4 La Salle **79** — 13 Southern Mississippi **63**
- 6 St. John's **81** — 11 Temple **65**
- 3 Duke **81** — 14 Richmond **46**
- 7 UCLA **68** — 10 UAB **56**
- 2 Kansas **79** — 15 Robert Morris **71** (H)

Second Round
- Connecticut **74** — California **54**
- ⊗Clemson **79** — La Salle **75**
- St. John's **72** — Duke **76**
- UCLA **71** — Kansas **70**

Regional Semifinals (East Rutherford, NJ)
- Connecticut **71** — ⊗Clemson **70** (F)
- Duke **90** — UCLA **81**

Regional Finals
- Connecticut **78** (OT) — Duke **79** (G)

MIDWEST

First Round
- 1 Oklahoma **77** — 16 Towson **68**
- 8 North Carolina **83** — 9 Missouri State **70**
- 5 Illinois **86** — 12 Dayton **88**
- 4 Arkansas **68** — 13 Princeton **64**
- 6 Xavier **87** — 11 Kansas State **79**
- 3 Georgetown **70** — 14 Texas Southern **52**
- 7 Georgia **88** — 10 Texas **100**
- 2 Purdue **75** — 15 UL-Monroe **63**

Second Round
- Oklahoma **77** — North Carolina **79**
- Dayton **84** — Arkansas **86**
- Xavier **74** — Georgetown **71**
- Texas **73** — Purdue **72**

Regional Semifinals (Dallas)
- North Carolina **73** — Arkansas **96**
- Xavier **89** — Texas **102**

Regional Finals
- Arkansas **88** — Texas **85**

National Semifinal (Denver)
- Georgia Tech **81** — UNLV **90**
- Duke **97** — Arkansas **83**

National Final
UNLV 103
Duke 73

UNLV becomes the only team to score in triple digits in an NCAA title game and also sets a championship-game record with its 30-point winning margin. Says Duke coach Mike Krzyzewski after the game, "I'm in awe of what they did tonight." Broadcaster Brent Musburger works his final game for CBS after the network makes a surprise announcement that he will not be retained.

Georgia Tech's Lethal Weapon 3—the high-scoring trio of Kenny Anderson, Dennis Scott and Brian Oliver—unloads 43 first-half points, staking the underdog Yellow Jackets to a 53-46 halftime lead. But the Runnin' Rebels go on a 17-4 run after the break and never look back. Stacey Augmon paces UNLV with 22 points.

Freshman point guard Bobby Hurley, plagued by illness, bolts for the restroom four minutes into the game. Says Hurley afterward, "I didn't want to leave, but I didn't want to embarrass myself out there." He returns to notch six assists and score three points.

A In the only No. 1 vs. No. 16 matchup to go to overtime, Murray State falls just short. Popeye Jones leads the Racers with a career-high 37 points. Michigan State coach Jud Heathcote says, "I'm still trying to figure out if we won or if we lost."

B Maurice Newby hits a three-pointer with :02 left for Northern Iowa's first Tournament victory. Jason Reese leads the No. 14-seed Panthers with 18 points and 15 boards. The loss is particularly bitter for the Tigers, who were ranked No. 1 earlier in the season.

C Loyola Marymount's Bo Kimble—a righty who averages a Tournament-best 35.8 ppg—shoots his first free throw of each game left-handed in memory of converted southpaw teammate and friend Hank Gathers, who died during the West Coast Conference tournament. Kimble drains all four lefty shots.

D Loyola Marymount and Michigan combine for the highest-scoring game in Tournament history.

E Loyola Marymount scores 423 points in four games to set the Tournament record for highest scoring average (105.8 per game). UNLV scores 571 points in six games (95.2 ppg), the most total points by a team in Tournament history.

F UConn's Tate George misses what could have been the game-winner with :04 left, but after Tiger Sean Tyson's missed free throw, George does drain a 15-foot buzzer-beating reprieve.

G Duke's Christian Laettner catches an inbounds pass and sinks a 15-footer for the OT win. It's the beginning of Laettner's legend as one of the greatest clutch players in Tournament history.

H Roy Williams, who came to Lawrence from Dean Smith's staff at North Carolina, makes his first of 14 Tournament appearances as Kansas coach. He will take the Jayhawks to four Final Fours and two title games without winning a title.

⊗Team participation later vacated

Tournament Leaders

Individual Leaders

Scoring	CL	POS	G	PTS	PPG
1 **Bo Kimble**, Loyola Marymount	SR	F	4	143	35.8
2 **Dennis Scott**, Georgia Tech	JR	G	5	153	30.6
3 **Travis Mays**, Texas	SR	G	4	112	28.0
4 **Steve Smith**, Michigan State	JR	G	3	75	25.0
5 **Kenny Anderson**, Georgia Tech	FR	G	5	124	24.8
6 **Jeff Fryer**, Loyola Marymount	SR	G	4	98	24.5
7 **Willie Burton**, Minnesota	SR	F	4	97	24.3
8 **Phil Henderson**, Duke	SR	G	6	130	21.7
9 **Tyrone Hill**, Xavier	SR	F	3	64	21.3
10 **Lance Blanks**, Texas	SR	G	4	85	21.3

Minimum: 3 games

Field Goal Pct	CL	POS	G	FG	FGA	PCT
1 **Johnny McNeil**, Georgia Tech	SR	C	5	15	21	71.4
2 **Alaa Abdelnaby**, Duke	SR	C	6	42	64	65.6
3 **Stephen Thompson**, Syracuse	SR	G	3	23	37	62.2
4 **Oliver Miller**, Arkansas	SO	C	5	18	29	62.1
5 **Stacey Augmon**, UNLV	JR	G/F	6	45	74	60.8

Minimum: 15 made and 3 games

Free Throw Pct	CL	POS	G	FT	FTA	PCT
1 **Steve Scheffler**, Purdue	SR	C	2	15	16	93.8
2 **Bo Kimble**, Loyola Marymount	SR	F	4	26	29	89.7
3 **Travis Mays**, Texas	SR	G	4	43	48	89.6
4 **Phil Henderson**, Duke	SR	G	6	17	19	89.5
Chris Smith, Connecticut	SO	G	4	17	19	89.5

Minimum: 15 made

Three-Point FG Pct	CL	POS	G	3FG	3FGA	PCT
1 **Kevin Lynch**, Minnesota	JR	G	4	9	16	56.3
2 **Greg Anthony**, UNLV	JR	G	6	9	17	52.9
3 **Rick Fox**, North Carolina	JR	F	3	8	16	50.0
Robert Horry, Alabama	SO	F	3	8	16	50.0
5 **Chris Smith**, Connecticut	SO	G	4	14	30	46.7
Per Stumer, Loyola Marymount	JR	F	4	7	15	46.7

Minimum: 6 made and 3 games

Assists Per Game	CL	POS	G	AST	APG
1 **James Sanders**, Alabama	SR	G	3	27	9.0
2 **Darrick Martin**, UCLA	SO	G	3	22	7.3
3 **Bobby Hurley**, Duke	FR	G	6	39	6.5
4 **King Rice**, North Carolina	JR	G	3	19	6.3
5 **Greg Anthony**, UNLV	JR	G	6	37	6.2

Minimum: 3 games

Rebounds Per Game	CL	POS	G	REB	RPG
1 **Dale Davis**, Clemson	JR	F	3	44	14.7
2 **Larry Johnson**, UNLV	JR	F	6	75	12.5
3 **Tyrone Hill**, Xavier	SR	F	3	37	12.3
Derek Strong, Xavier	SR	C	3	37	12.3
5 **Derrick Coleman**, Syracuse	SR	C	3	33	11.0

Minimum: 3 games

Blocked Shots Per Game	CL	POS	G	BLK	BPG
1 **Elden Campbell**, Clemson	SR	F	3	8	2.7
2 **Guillermo Myers**, Texas	JR	F	4	10	2.5
3 **Oliver Miller**, Arkansas	SO	C	5	10	2.0
4 **Larry Johnson**, UNLV	JR	F	6	11	1.8
5 **Alaa Abdelnaby**, Duke	SR	C	6	10	1.7
Stacey Augmon, UNLV	JR	G/F	6	10	1.7
Robert Horry, Alabama	SO	F	3	5	1.7
George Lynch, North Carolina	FR	F	3	5	1.7

Minimum: 3 games

Steals Per Game	CL	POS	G	STL	SPG
1 **Lee Mayberry**, Arkansas	SO	G	5	18	3.6
2 **Bo Kimble**, Loyola Marymount	SR	F	4	12	3.0
Trevor Wilson, UCLA	SR	F	3	9	3.0
4 **Lance Blanks**, Texas	SR	G	4	10	2.5
Jeff Fryer, Loyola Marymount	SR	G	4	10	2.5
Melvin Newbern, Minnesota	SR	G	4	10	2.5

Minimum: 3 games

Team Leaders

Scoring	G	PTS	PPG
1 **Loyola Marymount**	4	423	105.8
2 **UNLV**	6	571	95.2
3 **Texas**	4	360	90.0
4 **Georgia Tech**	5	448	89.6
5 **Arkansas**	5	421	84.2
6 **Xavier**	3	250	83.3
7 **Duke**	6	496	82.7
8 **Minnesota**	4	318	79.5
9 **North Carolina**	3	235	78.3
10 **Connecticut**	4	299	74.8

Minimum: 3 games

FG Pct	G	FG	FGA	PCT
1 **UNLV**	6	217	410	52.9
2 **Alabama**	3	83	159	52.2
3 **North Carolina**	3	91	180	50.6
4 **Michigan State**	3	86	176	48.9
Xavier	3	86	176	48.9

Minimum: 3 games

3-Pt FG Pct	G	3FG	3FGA	PCT
1 **Alabama**	3	15	35	42.9
2 **North Carolina**	3	14	33	42.4
3 **Loyola Marymount**	4	56	137	40.9
4 **Minnesota**	4	22	54	40.7
5 **Georgia Tech**	5	39	98	39.8

Minimum: 3 games

FT Pct	G	FT	FTA	PCT
1 **Loyola Marymount**	4	69	84	82.1
2 **Xavier**	3	74	92	80.4
3 **Connecticut**	4	58	78	74.4
4 **Duke**	6	136	183	74.3
5 **Ball State**	3	40	55	72.7

Minimum: 3 games

Ast/TO Ratio	G	AST	TO	RAT
1 **UCLA**	3	50	34	1.47
2 **UNLV**	6	140	99	1.41
3 **Minnesota**	4	62	48	1.29
4 **Syracuse**	3	49	38	1.29
5 **Loyola Marymount**	4	85	69	1.23

Minimum: 3 games

Rebounds	G	REB	RPG
1 **Clemson**	3	134	44.7
2 **UNLV**	6	251	41.8
3 **Ball State**	3	125	41.7
4 **Michigan State**	3	118	39.3
5 **Loyola Marymount**	4	157	39.3

Minimum: 3 games

Blocks	G	BLK	BPG
1 **UNLV**	6	33	5.5
2 **Alabama**	3	15	5.0
Clemson	3	15	5.0
4 **North Carolina**	3	13	4.3
5 **Arkansas**	5	18	3.6

Minimum: 3 games

Steals	G	STL	SPG
1 **Loyola Marymount**	4	51	12.8
2 **Connecticut**	4	48	12.0
3 **Arkansas**	5	57	11.4
4 **UCLA**	3	32	10.7
5 **UNLV**	6	54	9.0

Minimum: 3 games

All-Tournament Team

PLAYER	CL	POS	HT	SCHOOL	RPG	APG	PPG
Anderson Hunt*	SO	G	6-2	UNLV	2.2	5.0	17.2
Stacey Augmon	JR	G/F	6-8	UNLV	8.0	4.3	18.2
Phil Henderson	SR	G	6-4	Duke	4.2	2.2	21.7
Larry Johnson	JR	F	6-7	UNLV	12.5	2.2	18.8
Dennis Scott	JR	G	6-8	Georgia Tech	6.4	1.4	30.6

All-Regional Teams

East

PLAYER	CL	POS	HT	SCHOOL	RPG	APG	PPG
Christian Laettner*	SO	C	6-11	Duke	8.3	1.5	15.0
Alaa Abdelnaby	SR	C	6-10	Duke	10.0	0.8	20.0
Tate George	SR	G	6-5	Connecticut	2.3	4.0	10.0
Phil Henderson	SR	G	6-4	Duke	3.8	2.5	20.3
Chris Smith	SO	G	6-2	Connecticut	3.5	3.8	19.3

Midwest

PLAYER	CL	POS	HT	SCHOOL	RPG	APG	PPG
Lenzie Howell*	SR	G/F	6-4	Arkansas	6.3	1.8	19.8
Lance Blanks	SR	G	6-4	Texas	3.8	2.8	21.3
Lee Mayberry	SO	G	6-1	Arkansas	4.3	4.8	14.5
Travis Mays	SR	G	6-2	Texas	3.5	2.5	28.0
Oliver Miller	SO	C	6-9	Arkansas	7.0	2.0	11.3

Southeast

PLAYER	CL	POS	HT	SCHOOL	RPG	APG	PPG
Kenny Anderson*	FR	G	6-2	Georgia Tech	6.8	5.0	27.0
Willie Burton	SR	F	6-7	Minnesota	6.5	1.8	24.3
Melvin Newbern	SR	G	6-4	Minnesota	4.0	5.3	15.0
Dennis Scott	JR	G	6-8	Georgia Tech	7.0	1.8	31.0
Steve Smith	JR	G	6-7	Michigan State	7.3	4.7	25.0

West

PLAYER	CL	POS	HT	SCHOOL	RPG	APG	PPG
Stacey Augmon*	JR	G/F	6-8	UNLV	8.8	4.0	18.8
Anderson Hunt	SO	G	6-2	UNLV	2.3	5.3	13.5
Larry Johnson	JR	F	6-7	UNLV	14.8	2.0	19.0
Bo Kimble	SR	F	6-5	Loyola Marymount	10.5	2.3	35.8
Chandler Thompson	SO	G	6-3	Ball State	9.3	1.3	20.0

* Most outstanding player

1990 NCAA TOURNAMENT BOX SCORES

81-80 (Sweet 16)

GEORGIA TECH	MIN	FG	3FG	FT	REB	A	ST	BL	PF	TP
Kenny Anderson	45	13-23	3-8	2-3	4	3	3	0	0	31
Dennis Scott	45	7-22	2-10	2-2	9	1	1	0	3	18
Johnny McNeil	37	4-6	0-0	4-4	6	0	0	0	5	12
Brian Oliver	43	4-10	0-4	3-4	1	1	1	0	4	11
Malcolm Mackey	25	3-6	0-0	0-2	7	0	0	2	3	6
Karl Brown	29	1-2	1-1	0-0	1	1	2	0	3	3
Darryl Barnes	1	0-0	0-0	0-0	0	0	0	0	0	0
TOTALS	225	32-69	6-23	11-15	28	6	7	2	18	81
Percentages		46.4	26.1	73.3						

Coach: Bobby Cremins

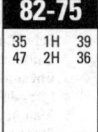

	1H	2H	OT1
Georgia Tech	39	36	6
Michigan State	35	40	5

MICHIGAN STATE	MIN	FG	3FG	FT	REB	A	ST	BL	PF	TP
Steve Smith	44	13-22	3-5	3-4	5	6	2	0	0	32
Parish Hickman	25	6-9	0-0	1-1	10	0	0	2	2	13
Dwayne Stephens	35	3-6	0-0	4-4	5	2	0	0	0	10
Mike Peplowski	19	4-5	0-0	1-1	4	1	0	0	1	9
Ken Redfield	36	3-6	0-1	1-2	5	2	1	1	4	7
Mark Montgomery	29	2-5	1-1	0-0	1	2	1	1	5	5
Matt Steigenga	25	2-9	0-0	0-0	4	3	1	0	4	4
Kirk Manns	12	0-3	0-1	0-0	1	0	0	0	1	0
TOTALS	225	33-65	4-8	10-12	35	16	5	4	17	80
Percentages		50.8	50.0	83.3						

Coach: Jud Heathcote

Officials: Jo Clougherty, Tanco, Charle Range **Technicals:** None **Attendance:** 18,172

82-75 (Sweet 16)

MINNESOTA	MIN	FG	3FG	FT	REB	A	ST	BL	PF	TP
Melvin Newbern	33	9-15	0-1	2-3	3	4	4	0	2	20
Kevin Lynch	35	7-10	2-2	2-3	2	3	1	0	1	18
Richard Coffey	32	5-8	0-0	2-2	12	3	0	1	4	12
Willie Burton	29	4-8	1-2	3-6	4	1	1	0	4	12
Robert Martin	16	4-5	0-0	2-2	3	0	0	0	2	10
Jim Shikenjanski	19	3-5	0-0	0-0	0	0	1	0	2	6
Walter Bond	24	1-4	0-1	2-3	4	1	1	2	3	4
Connell Lewis	9	0-0	0-0	0-0	0	1	0	0	0	0
Mario Green	3	0-1	0-0	0-0	1	0	0	0	1	0
TOTALS	200	33-56	3-6	13-19	29	13	8	3	19	82
Percentages		58.9	50.0	68.4						

Coach: Clem Haskins

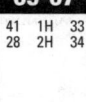

	1H	2H
Minnesota	35	47
Syracuse	39	36

SYRACUSE	MIN	FG	3FG	FT	REB	A	ST	BL	PF	TP
Billy Owens	40	8-16	2-3	0-2	9	1	1	0	5	18
Stephen Thompson	39	8-10	0-1	0-0	7	6	0	0	1	16
Derrick Coleman	40	5-13	2-4	3-8	11	4	2	1	4	15
Anthony Scott	25	3-16	2-11	2-2	4	0	0	0	3	10
LeRon Ellis	29	2-6	0-0	3-6	7	0	1	1	2	7
Michael Edwards	9	3-6	1-4	0-0	0	2	1	0	0	7
Dave Johnson	18	1-2	0-0	0-2	2	3	0	0	3	2
TOTALS	200	30-69	7-23	8-20	40	16	5	2	18	75
Percentages		43.5	30.4	40.0						

Coach: Jim Boeheim

Officials: Paul Housman, Larr Rose, Scott Thornley **Technicals:** Syracuse (Coleman) **Attendance:** 18,172

69-67 (Sweet 16)

UNLV	MIN	FG	3FG	FT	REB	A	ST	BL	PF	TP
Stacey Augmon	35	8-14	1-3	3-5	9	4	2	3	3	20
Larry Johnson	33	8-18	1-2	3-3	13	2	0	1	3	20
David Butler	35	5-10	0-0	3-4	7	3	1	0	2	13
Greg Anthony	35	2-5	2-5	1-4	3	9	1	2	1	7
Anderson Hunt	23	1-2	1-1	0-0	1	2	0	0	4	3
Travis Bice	14	1-5	1-5	0-0	0	0	0	0	0	3
Barry Young	7	1-3	1-3	0-0	0	0	0	0	2	3
Moses Scurry	11	0-1	0-0	0-0	0	0	1	0	2	0
Stacey Cvijanovich	5	0-1	0-0	0-0	1	0	1	0	1	0
James Jones	2	0-0	0-0	0-0	0	0	0	0	0	0
TOTALS	200	26-59	7-19	10-16	34	20	6	6	18	69
Percentages		44.1	36.8	62.5						

Coach: Jerry Tarkanian

	1H	2H
UNLV	41	28
Ball State	33	34

BALL STATE	MIN	FG	3FG	FT	REB	A	ST	BL	PF	TP
Chandler Thompson	26	9-19	2-3	1-5	9	2	0	-	3	21
Paris McCurdy	30	6-15	1-1	4-4	11	1	4	-	4	17
Curtis Kidd	33	4-9	0-0	3-4	12	1	0	-	3	11
Shawn Parrish	15	3-7	0-0	1-1	4	1	0	-	2	7
Billy Butts	28	2-9	2-7	0-0	1	2	0	-	1	6
Greg Miller	10	1-4	1-4	2-3	3	0	0	-	0	5
Scott Nichols	28	0-1	0-0	0-0	1	10	0	-	5	0
Emanuel Cross	20	0-4	0-2	0-0	3	1	0	-	0	0
Roman Muller	5	0-2	0-0	0-0	3	0	1	-	0	0
Mike Spicer	5	0-1	0-0	0-0	0	0	0	-	1	0
TOTALS	200	25-71	6-17	11-17	47	18	5	-	19	67
Percentages		35.2	35.3	64.7						

Coach: Dick Hunsaker

Officials: Pete Pavia, Gene Monje, Dick Paparo **Technicals:** None **Attendance:** 14,262

62-60 (Sweet 16)

LOYOLA MARYMOUNT	MIN	FG	3FG	FT	REB	A	ST	BL	PF	TP
Bo Kimble	38	9-25	1-5	0-0	6	0	4	0	3	19
Terrell Lowery	27	6-15	2-8	2-5	3	1	1	0	2	16
Jeff Fryer	36	4-13	3-10	2-2	7	2	4	0	3	13
Per Stumer	35	3-8	1-4	0-0	12	2	1	0	3	7
Tom Peabody	25	3-6	0-1	1-2	5	1	2	0	4	7
Tony Walker	18	0-5	0-0	0-0	0	1	1	0	1	0
Chris Knight	16	0-2	0-0	0-0	3	1	0	1	0	0
Christian Scott	5	0-0	0-0	0-0	0	0	0	0	1	0
TOTALS	200	25-74	7-28	5-9	36	8	13	1	17	62
Percentages		33.8	25.0	55.6						

Coach: Paul Westhead

	1H	2H
Loyola Marymount	22	40
Alabama	21	39

ALABAMA	MIN	FG	3FG	FT	REB	A	ST	BL	PF	TP
Melvin Cheatum	36	10-18	0-0	1-2	9	1	1	2	0	21
Robert Horry	36	8-16	0-3	5-7	5	3	2	3	2	21
James Sanders	40	3-7	0-3	2-3	5	5	0	0	2	8
David Benoit	20	2-5	0-0	0-0	5	0	0	1	1	4
Gary Waites	39	1-1	1-1	0-0	2	3	0	1	1	3
Keith Askins	28	1-4	0-0	1-2	9	1	0	2	5	3
Marcus Webb	1	0-0	0-0	0-0	0	0	0	0	0	0
TOTALS	200	25-51	1-7	9-14	35	13	3	9	11	60
Percentages		49.0	14.3	64.3						

Coach: Wimp Sanderson

Officials: Lenny Wirtz, John Corio, Ted Hillary **Technicals:** Loyola Marymount (Kimble) **Attendance:** 12,972

71-70 (Sweet 16)

CONNECTICUT	MIN	FG	3FG	FT	REB	A	ST	BL	PF	TP
Chris Smith	33	8-14	4-6	3-3	3	5	1	0	2	23
Tate George	30	5-12	0-1	2-2	1	4	1	1	2	12
Scott Burrell	32	2-9	0-0	5-6	15	1	2	0	3	9
John Gwynn	17	4-13	0-2	1-2	1	0	0	0	1	9
Lyman Depriest	17	4-6	0-0	0-0	2	2	1	0	2	8
Rod Sellers	19	2-3	0-0	0-1	3	0	0	0	1	4
Nadav Henefeld	22	1-3	0-1	0-0	3	3	0	0	4	2
Toraino Walker	14	1-2	0-0	0-0	2	0	1	0	4	2
Dan Cyrulik	6	1-1	0-0	0-1	0	0	1	0	2	2
Murray Williams	9	0-1	0-0	0-0	0	1	0	0	2	0
Oliver Macklin	1	0-0	0-0	0-0	0	0	0	0	0	0
TOTALS	200	28-64	4-10	11-15	30	16	7	1	23	71
Percentages		43.8	40.0	73.3						

Coach: Jim Calhoun

	1H	2H
Connecticut	38	33
Clemson	29	41

CLEMSON	MIN	FG	3FG	FT	REB	A	ST	BL	PF	TP
Dale Davis	37	6-10	0-0	3-5	17	0	0	1	2	15
Elden Campbell	33	5-11	0-0	5-7	8	1	1	3	3	15
Sean Tyson	22	5-8	0-0	1-3	4	2	2	0	0	11
Marion Cash	33	2-9	1-1	3-5	3	4	2	0	3	8
Kirkland Howling	24	2-8	1-6	2-3	1	1	0	0	2	7
Derrick Forrest	27	2-4	0-2	2-2	1	2	2	0	1	6
David Young	9	1-2	1-2	0-0	1	0	2	0	1	3
Shawn Lastinger	4	1-2	1-1	0-0	1	1	0	0	1	3
Wayne Buckingham	8	1-2	0-0	0-0	2	0	0	0	2	2
Ricky Jones	2	0-0	0-0	0-0	0	0	0	0	1	0
Colby Brown	1	0-0	0-0	0-0	0	0	0	0	0	0
TOTALS	200	25-56	4-12	16-25	38	11	9	4	16	70
Percentages		44.6	33.3	64.0						

Coach: Cliff Ellis

Officials: Jim Bain, Jim Stupin, David Bair **Technicals:** Clemson (Davis) **Attendance:** 19,502

90-81 (Sweet 16)

DUKE	MIN	FG	3FG	FT	REB	A	ST	BL	PF	TP
Phil Henderson	38	10-22	6-11	2-2	5	2	1	0	3	28
Christian Laettner	32	8-12	0-0	8-8	14	0	0	0	4	24
Alaa Abdelnaby	20	5-7	0-0	4-5	7	1	0	2	4	14
Bobby Hurley	36	3-6	1-4	5-6	4	9	2	0	3	12
Robert Brickey	33	3-8	0-0	1-3	3	3	2	1	3	7
Billy McCaffrey	12	0-4	0-0	3-4	1	2	0	0	0	3
Brian Davis	12	1-1	0-0	0-0	0	1	0	0	3	2
Thomas Hill	11	0-3	0-1	0-0	1	0	1	0	2	0
Greg Koubek	4	0-1	0-0	0-0	1	0	0	0	3	0
Crawford Palmer	2	0-0	0-0	0-0	0	1	0	0	0	0
TOTALS	200	30-64	7-16	23-28	36	19	6	3	25	90
Percentages		46.9	43.8	82.1						

Coach: Mike Krzyzewski

	1H	2H
Duke	47	43
UCLA	38	43

UCLA	MIN	FG	3FG	FT	REB	A	ST	BL	PF	TP
Don MacLean	36	9-17	0-0	3-5	15	0	2	-	3	21
Gerald Madkins	30	5-6	2-3	5-8	2	6	1	-	4	17
Trevor Wilson	39	5-18	0-1	6-10	6	3	2	-	5	16
Tracy Murray	35	6-12	3-5	0-2	9	0	0	-	3	15
Mitchell Butler	16	1-4	0-1	4-4	5	1	0	-	4	6
Darrick Martin	34	1-9	0-4	2-2	3	8	1	-	2	4
Kevin Walker	7	1-2	0-0	0-1	1	0	0	-	1	2
Keith Owens	2	0-0	0-0	0-0	0	0	0	-	1	0
Zan Mason	1	0-1	0-0	0-0	0	0	0	-	1	0
TOTALS	200	28-69	5-14	20-32	41	18	6	-	24	81
Percentages		40.6	35.7	62.5						

Coach: Jim Harrick

Officials: Jody Silvester, John Koskinen, Sonny Holmes **Technicals:** None **Attendance:** 19,502

96-73

	1H	2H
Arkansas	39	57
North Carolina	34	39

SWEET 16

ARKANSAS	MIN	FG	3FG	FT	REB	A	ST	BL	PF	TP
Lenzie Howell	36	12-18	1-1	0-0	8	0	2	0	3	25
Lee Mayberry	35	7-14	4-7	1-2	6	7	3	0	3	19
Oliver Miller	25	7-7	0-0	5-5	4	1	0	1	4	19
Todd Day	20	6-13	3-6	3-4	4	3	2	0	3	18
Arlyn Bowers	30	1-5	0-2	2-2	0	3	2	0	1	4
Ron Huery	20	2-8	0-0	0-0	6	3	1	0	3	4
Mario Credit	15	0-0	0-0	2-2	3	0	0	0	4	2
Darrell Hawkins	10	1-2	0-0	0-0	2	3	0	0	0	2
Warren Linn	1	1-1	0-0	0-0	0	0	0	0	0	2
Cannon Whitby	3	0-2	0-1	1-2	0	0	0	0	0	1
Ernie Murry	4	0-2	0-1	0-0	0	0	0	0	0	0
Larry Marks	1	0-0	0-0	0-0	0	0	0	0	0	0
TOTALS	**200**	**37-72**	**8-18**	**14-17**	**33**	**20**	**10**	**1**	**21**	**96**
Percentages		51.4	44.4	82.4						

Coach: Nolan Richardson

NORTH CAROLINA	MIN	FG	3FG	FT	REB	A	ST	BL	PF	TP
Scott Williams	28	6-15	0-1	8-8	8	0	2	2	4	20
Pete Chilcutt	35	5-10	1-3	0-0	11	3	0	0	1	11
Hubert Davis	27	4-12	2-4	1-2	3	0	0	0	2	11
King Rice	30	3-5	1-2	3-6	4	5	1	0	4	10
George Lynch	15	3-4	0-0	4-7	3	1	0	0	2	10
Rick Fox	33	4-10	1-5	0-0	8	3	0	0	4	9
Kenny Harris	7	1-1	0-0	0-0	0	0	1	0	0	2
Henrik Rodl	16	0-2	0-0	0-2	1	0	1	0	0	0
Jeff Denny	6	0-3	0-2	0-0	1	0	0	0	0	0
Matt Wenstrom	2	0-0	0-0	0-0	0	0	0	0	0	0
John Greene	1	0-0	0-0	0-0	0	0	0	0	0	0
TOTALS	**200**	**26-62**	**5-17**	**16-25**	**39**	**12**	**5**	**2**	**17**	**73**
Percentages		41.9	29.4	64.0						

Coach: Dean Smith

Officials: Rich Ballesteros, Don Rutledge, Ted Valentine
Technicals: North Carolina (coach Smith)
Attendance: 16,413

102-89

	1H	2H
Texas	41	61
Xavier	53	36

SWEET 16

TEXAS	MIN	FG	3FG	FT	REB	A	ST	BL	PF	TP
Travis Mays	39	9-21	3-9	11-12	2	2	3	0	1	32
Lance Blanks	38	9-21	0-7	10-11	5	3	2	0	5	28
Joey Wright	31	9-12	2-2	6-8	4	3	1	0	4	26
Locksley Collie	33	3-8	0-0	3-6	16	0	1	0	1	9
Hank Dudek	9	2-3	0-0	0-0	2	0	1	0	3	4
Guillermo Myers	28	1-2	0-0	1-2	7	0	1	1	4	3
Courtney Jeans	10	0-0	0-0	0-0	0	0	1	0	1	0
George Muller	5	0-0	0-0	0-0	0	0	0	0	1	0
Benford Williams	5	0-1	0-0	0-0	0	0	0	0	3	0
Gerrald Houston	1	0-0	0-0	0-0	0	0	0	0	0	0
Winn Shepard	1	0-0	0-0	0-0	0	0	0	0	0	0
TOTALS	**200**	**33-68**	**5-18**	**31-39**	**36**	**8**	**10**	**1**	**23**	**102**
Percentages		48.5	27.8	79.5						

Coach: Tom Penders

XAVIER	MIN	FG	3FG	FT	REB	A	ST	BL	PF	TP
Derek Strong	34	11-17	0-0	5-5	14	4	2	0	5	27
Tyrone Hill	34	8-14	0-1	6-9	15	5	0	2	4	22
Jamal Walker	33	6-14	0-2	2-2	3	3	1	0	3	14
Maurice Brantley	26	5-6	0-0	2-3	2	0	0	0	4	12
Jamie Gladden	36	2-7	0-0	0-2	0	1	1	0	4	4
Aaron Williams	9	1-1	0-0	2-3	1	0	0	0	1	4
Michael Davenport	16	1-7	0-5	0-0	1	1	0	0	4	2
Colin Parker	7	1-2	0-1	0-0	0	0	0	0	2	2
Jerry Butler	1	1-1	0-0	0-0	0	0	0	0	1	2
Robert Koester	1	0-0	0-0	0-0	0	0	0	0	0	0
David Minor	1	0-0	0-0	0-0	0	0	0	0	0	0
Mark Poynter	1	0-0	0-0	0-0	0	0	0	0	0	0
Dwayne Wilson	1	0-0	0-0	0-0	0	0	0	0	0	0
TOTALS	**200**	**36-69**	**0-9**	**17-24**	**36**	**14**	**4**	**2**	**28**	**89**
Percentages		52.2	0.0	70.8						

Coach: Pete Gillen

Officials: Larry Lembo, Bob Donato, Tom Harrington
Technicals: None
Attendance: 16,413

93-91

	1H	2H
Georgia Tech	47	46
Minnesota	49	42

ELITE 8

GEORGIA TECH	MIN	FG	3FG	FT	REB	A	ST	BL	PF	TP
Dennis Scott	40	12-22	7-12	9-10	4	0	3	0	3	40
Kenny Anderson	39	10-15	1-2	9-11	8	3	0	0	1	30
Brian Oliver	38	5-15	0-1	9-12	5	1	1	0	2	19
Karl Brown	30	1-3	0-1	0-0	2	2	1	0	3	2
Johnny McNeil	26	1-1	0-0	0-0	3	0	0	0	4	2
Malcolm Mackey	24	0-0	0-0	0-2	6	0	0	3	2	0
Darryl Barnes	2	0-0	0-0	0-0	1	0	0	0	0	0
James Munlyn	1	0-0	0-0	0-0	0	0	0	0	0	0
TOTALS	**200**	**29-56**	**8-16**	**27-35**	**29**	**6**	**5**	**3**	**15**	**93**
Percentages		51.8	50.0	77.1						

Coach: Bobby Cremins

MINNESOTA	MIN	FG	3FG	FT	REB	A	ST	BL	PF	TP
Willie Burton	33	15-23	5-10	0-0	7	3	1	1	3	35
Jim Shikenjanski	31	9-14	0-0	1-1	5	0	1	0	2	19
Melvin Newbern	32	8-17	1-2	0-2	5	6	3	1	4	17
Kevin Lynch	29	3-8	2-3	4-8	3	3	2	0	4	12
Richard Coffey	32	2-4	0-0	0-0	9	0	0	0	4	4
Walter Bond	28	1-6	0-2	0-0	2	3	0	0	3	2
Connell Lewis	10	1-3	0-1	0-0	3	2	0	0	2	2
Robert Martin	3	0-0	0-0	0-0	0	0	0	0	0	0
Mario Green	1	0-0	0-0	0-0	0	0	0	0	1	0
Rob Metcalf	1	0-0	0-0	0-0	0	0	0	0	0	0
TOTALS	**200**	**39-75**	**8-18**	**5-11**	**34**	**17**	**7**	**2**	**23**	**91**
Percentages		52.0	44.4	45.5						

Coach: Clem Haskins

Officials: Gerry Donaghy, Samuel Croft, Dave Libbey
Technicals: Minnesota (Burton)
Attendance: 17,782

131-101

	1H	2H
UNLV	67	64
Loyola Marymount	47	54

ELITE 8

UNLV	MIN	FG	3FG	FT	REB	A	ST	BL	PF	TP
Stacey Augmon	30	13-20	0-0	7-7	11	6	2	1	2	33
Anderson Hunt	34	11-23	4-12	4-6	4	13	6	1	1	30
Greg Anthony	30	8-10	3-4	2-3	1	8	3	0	3	21
Larry Johnson	31	10-14	0-0	0-1	18	5	0	2	2	20
David Butler	25	4-7	0-0	1-5	8	2	0	0	5	9
Moses Scurry	14	3-4	0-0	2-2	4	0	0	1	0	8
James Jones	9	2-3	0-0	3-4	3	0	0	1	1	7
Stacey Cvijanovich	10	0-0	0-0	2-2	2	0	0	0	1	2
Travis Bice	6	0-4	0-2	1-2	1	1	0	0	1	1
Barry Young	9	0-0	0-0	0-0	2	0	2	0	1	0
Chris Jeter	1	0-1	0-0	0-0	1	0	0	2	0	0
Dave Rice	1	0-0	0-0	0-0	1	0	0	0	0	0
TOTALS	**200**	**51-86**	**7-18**	**22-32**	**56**	**35**	**13**	**8**	**17**	**131**
Percentages		59.3	38.9	68.8						

Coach: Jerry Tarkanian

LOYOLA MARYMOUNT	MIN	FG	3FG	FT	REB	A	ST	BL	PF	TP
Bo Kimble	37	14-32	8-11	6-6	11	3	3	0	4	42
Jeff Fryer	36	7-24	4-16	3-3	6	2	1	0	2	21
Terrell Lowery	23	6-16	4-9	2-2	0	6	3	0	3	18
Chris Knight	19	4-8	0-0	0-0	2	2	2	2	3	8
Per Stumer	28	2-4	0-2	0-0	5	2	0	0	4	4
Tony Walker	22	1-1	0-0	2-3	2	3	3	0	3	4
Marcellus Lee	1	1-2	1-1	0-0	0	0	0	0	1	3
John O'Connell	6	0-0	0-0	1-2	2	0	0	0	2	1
Tom Peabody	22	0-2	0-2	0-1	2	4	2	0	3	0
Christian Scott	3	0-2	0-0	0-0	1	1	0	0	2	0
Jeff Roscoe	1	0-0	0-0	0-0	1	0	0	0	0	0
Marcus Slater	1	0-2	0-0	0-0	1	0	0	0	0	0
Greg Walker	1	0-1	0-0	0-0	1	0	0	0	0	0
TOTALS	**200**	**35-94**	**17-41**	**14-17**	**34**	**23**	**14**	**2**	**27**	**101**
Percentages		37.2	41.5	82.4						

Coach: Paul Westhead

Officials: James Burr, Rusty Herring, Tom Rucker
Technicals: (Kimble, coach Westhead)
Attendance: 14,298

79-78

	1H	2H	OT1
Duke	37	35	7
Connecticut	30	42	6

ELITE 8

DUKE	MIN	FG	3FG	FT	REB	A	ST	BL	PF	TP
Alaa Abdelnaby	37	9-16	0-0	9-12	14	0	1	2	2	27
Christian Laettner	38	7-8	0-0	9-11	5	2	2	1	3	23
Phil Henderson	42	7-20	4-10	3-3	3	1	0	0	2	21
Bobby Hurley	43	0-9	0-2	3-4	2	8	4	0	3	3
Brian Davis	23	1-2	0-0	0-0	3	1	1	0	4	2
Robert Brickey	14	1-4	0-0	0-0	1	1	1	0	2	2
Billy McCaffrey	5	0-2	0-0	1-2	1	1	0	0	0	1
Thomas Hill	17	0-2	0-0	0-0	3	1	0	0	0	0
Greg Koubek	6	0-1	0-1	0-0	2	0	0	0	0	0
TOTALS	**225**	**25-64**	**4-13**	**25-32**	**34**	**15**	**9**	**3**	**16**	**79**
Percentages		39.1	30.8	78.1						

Coach: Mike Krzyzewski

CONNECTICUT	MIN	FG	3FG	FT	REB	A	ST	BL	PF	TP
Nadav Henefeld	44	5-10	1-4	4-4	6	4	1	1	3	15
John Gwynn	28	6-15	0-4	3-3	4	0	0	0	3	15
Scott Burrell	22	6-10	0-0	0-0	5	1	1	0	5	12
Chris Smith	42	4-16	1-4	2-2	4	5	2	0	1	11
Tate George	27	4-8	1-2	0-0	2	4	0	0	4	9
Toraino Walker	21	4-5	0-0	1-1	5	1	1	1	3	9
Dan Cyrulik	5	2-2	0-0	0-0	1	0	0	0	0	4
Lyman Depriest	11	1-1	0-0	0-0	3	0	1	0	4	2
Rod Sellers	24	0-1	0-0	1-2	5	0	0	4	3	1
Murray Williams	1	0-0	0-0	0-0	0	0	0	0	0	0
TOTALS	**225**	**32-68**	**3-14**	**11-12**	**35**	**15**	**6**	**6**	**26**	**78**
Percentages		47.1	21.4	91.7						

Coach: Jim Calhoun

Officials: Ed Hightower, Gordon Birk, David Hall
Technicals: None
Attendance: 19,546

88-85

	1H	2H
Arkansas	43	45
Texas	36	49

ELITE 8

ARKANSAS	MIN	FG	3FG	FT	REB	A	ST	BL	PF	TP
Lenzie Howell	25	7-13	0-2	7-10	9	2	2	0	4	21
Lee Mayberry	39	8-15	1-2	1-2	5	7	4	0	2	18
Mario Credit	22	5-8	0-0	4-5	5	0	2	1	5	14
Todd Day	34	5-17	0-4	2-5	6	1	4	1	4	12
Oliver Miller	22	2-3	0-0	5-11	9	2	1	2	4	9
Ron Huery	15	2-3	0-0	2-2	2	1	2	0	0	6
Darrell Hawkins	12	3-3	0-0	0-0	1	0	0	0	3	6
Arlyn Bowers	23	0-5	0-2	2-3	3	0	0	0	4	2
Ernie Murry	5	0-2	0-1	0-0	0	0	0	0	0	0
Larry Marks	3	0-0	0-0	0-0	0	0	0	0	0	0
TOTALS	**200**	**32-69**	**1-11**	**23-38**	**40**	**13**	**15**	**4**	**26**	**88**
Percentages		46.4	9.1	60.5						

Coach: Nolan Richardson

TEXAS	MIN	FG	3FG	FT	REB	A	ST	BL	PF	TP
Travis Mays	39	6-15	4-8	4-4	2	5	0	1	5	20
Joey Wright	38	5-15	2-3	8-10	6	0	1	0	4	20
Lance Blanks	40	4-12	3-6	6-6	6	4	2	0	1	17
Locksley Collie	28	4-6	0-0	8-11	9	0	0	0	2	16
Guillermo Myers	20	3-5	0-0	0-2	4	0	1	1	5	6
Benford Williams	20	1-2	0-0	0-1	6	2	0	0	2	2
Hank Dudek	7	1-1	0-0	0-0	2	0	0	0	5	2
Winn Shepard	1	1-1	0-0	0-0	1	0	0	0	0	2
George Muller	5	0-1	0-0	0-0	0	0	0	0	3	0
Gerrald Houston	1	0-0	0-0	0-0	0	0	0	0	0	0
Courtney Jeans	1	0-2	0-0	0-0	0	0	0	0	1	0
TOTALS	**200**	**25-60**	**9-17**	**26-34**	**36**	**11**	**4**	**2**	**28**	**85**
Percentages		41.7	52.9	76.5						

Coach: Tom Penders

Officials: Tim Higgins, Mickey Crowley, Frank Bosone
Technicals: None
Attendance: 16,413

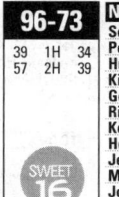

90-81

	1H	2H
UNLV	46	44
Georgia Tech	53	28

UNLV	MIN	FG	3FG	FT	REB	A	ST	BL	PF	TP
Stacey Augmon	37	9-16	1-1	3-3	9	3	2	0	3	22
Anderson Hunt	38	7-15	5-9	1-2	2	7	1	1	1	20
Larry Johnson	26	5-11	1-1	4-4	5	3	0	1	5	15
Greg Anthony	39	4-9	3-4	3-7	1	5	1	0	2	14
David Butler	31	6-10	0-0	1-3	10	1	2	0	4	13
Moses Scurry	21	3-4	0-0	0-0	11	0	0	0	4	6
Barry Young	3	0-0	0-0	0-0	0	0	0	0	0	0
Travis Bice	2	0-0	0-0	0-0	0	1	0	0	0	0
James Jones	2	0-0	0-0	0-0	0	0	0	0	0	0
Stacey Cvijanovich	1	0-0	0-0	0-0	0	0	0	0	1	0
TOTALS	**200**	**34-65**	**10-15**	**12-19**	**38**	**20**	**6**	**2**	**20**	**90**
Percentages		52.3	66.7	63.2						

Coach: Jerry Tarkanian

GEORGIA TECH	MIN	FG	3FG	FT	REB	A	ST	BL	PF	TP
Dennis Scott	39	8-17	7-14	6-9	4	0	2	0	3	29
Brian Oliver	37	9-18	0-3	6-9	3	4	0	0	3	24
Kenny Anderson	34	7-14	1-4	1-2	8	8	1	0	4	16
Karl Brown	29	2-3	0-0	0-0	2	3	0	0	5	4
Johnny McNeil	29	2-4	0-0	0-1	9	0	1	1	2	4
Malcolm Mackey	26	2-3	0-0	0-0	5	0	0	0	3	4
Darryl Barnes	6	0-0	0-0	0-0	0	0	0	0	0	0
TOTALS	**200**	**30-59**	**8-21**	**13-21**	**31**	**15**	**4**	**1**	**20**	**81**
Percentages		50.8	38.1	61.9						

Coach: Bobby Cremins

Officials: Ji Bain, Dick Paparo, Jim Stupin
Technicals: None
Attendance: 17,675

97-83

	1H	2H
Duke	46	51
Arkansas	43	40

DUKE	MIN	FG	3FG	FT	REB	A	ST	BL	PF	TP
Phil Henderson	37	10-21	3-7	5-5	8	3	1	1	2	28
Alaa Abdelnaby	27	8-12	0-0	4-5	5	0	3	1	3	20
Christian Laettner	32	5-7	0-0	9-12	14	1	2	1	4	19
Robert Brickey	24	8-10	0-0	1-3	11	3	1	0	3	17
Brian Davis	23	1-4	0-0	3-4	4	2	0	0	3	5
Bobby Hurley	36	0-2	0-1	3-6	1	6	1	0	0	3
Billy McCaffrey	5	0-1	0-0	3-4	0	1	1	0	1	3
Greg Koubek	10	1-4	0-1	0-0	0	0	0	0	2	2
Thomas Hill	4	0-0	0-0	0-0	1	0	0	0	1	0
Clay Buckley	1	0-0	0-0	0-0	0	0	0	0	0	0
Joe Cook	1	0-0	0-0	0-0	0	0	0	0	0	0
TOTALS	**200**	**33-61**	**3-9**	**28-39**	**44**	**16**	**9**	**3**	**19**	**97**
Percentages		54.1	33.3	71.8						

Coach: Mike Krzyzewski

ARKANSAS	MIN	FG	3FG	FT	REB	A	ST	BL	PF	TP
Todd Day	30	8-17	4-8	7-7	7	1	0	0	4	27
Lenzie Howell	30	5-9	1-2	7-8	6	0	1	0	3	18
Lee Mayberry	33	6-18	0-4	0-0	2	6	3	0	1	12
Darrell Hawkins	15	2-4	0-0	2-2	2	0	0	1	1	6
Mario Credit	19	2-3	0-0	1-4	3	0	1	0	5	5
Ron Huery	16	2-5	0-1	1-3	3	3	1	0	1	5
Ernie Murry	11	2-5	1-3	0-0	1	1	0	0	3	5
Oliver Miller	20	1-3	0-0	1-2	6	1	1	3	5	3
Arlyn Bowers	20	1-6	0-1	0-0	2	2	0	0	0	2
Larry Marks	3	0-0	0-0	0-0	1	0	0	0	2	0
Cannon Whitby	2	0-2	0-2	0-0	0	0	0	0	0	0
Warren Linn	1	0-1	0-0	0-0	0	0	0	0	0	0
TOTALS	**200**	**29-73**	**6-21**	**19-26**	**33**	**14**	**7**	**4**	**25**	**83**
Percentages		39.7	28.6	73.1						

Coach: Nolan Richardson

Officials: Ger Donaghy, Jam Burr, Frank Bosone
Technicals: None
Attendance: 17,675

103-73

	1H	2H
UNLV	47	56
Duke	35	38

UNLV	MIN	FG	3FG	FT	REB	A	ST	BL	PF	TP
Anderson Hunt	31	12-16	4-7	1-2	2	2	0	0	0	29
Larry Johnson	30	8-12	2-2	4-4	11	2	4	1	3	22
Greg Anthony	30	5-11	0-1	3-4	1	6	5	0	3	13
Stacey Augmon	26	6-7	0-0	0-1	4	7	2	2	5	12
James Jones	8	4-5	0-0	0-0	2	0	0	0	2	8
Moses Scurry	12	2-5	0-0	1-2	6	0	1	0	2	5
Barry Young	12	2-2	1-1	0-0	0	0	0	0	1	5
Stacey Cvijanovich	10	1-2	1-1	2-2	1	2	2	0	2	5
David Butler	27	1-4	0-0	2-2	3	3	1	0	3	4
Travis Bice	9	0-1	0-1	0-0	0	2	1	0	2	0
Chris Jeter	3	0-0	0-0	0-0	0	0	0	0	0	0
Dave Rice	2	0-2	0-1	0-0	1	0	0	0	0	0
TOTALS	**200**	**41-67**	**8-14**	**13-17**	**31**	**24**	**16**	**3**	**23**	**103**
Percentages		61.2	57.1	76.5						

Coach: Jerry Tarkanian

DUKE	MIN	FG	3FG	FT	REB	A	ST	BL	PF	TP
Phil Henderson	32	9-20	1-8	2-2	2	0	1	0	2	21
Christian Laettner	29	5-12	0-0	5-6	9	5	1	0	4	15
Alaa Abdelnaby	24	5-7	0-0	4-6	7	0	0	2	3	14
Brian Davis	21	2-5	0-0	2-3	1	0	1	1	1	6
Robert Brickey	24	2-4	0-0	0-2	3	2	0	0	2	4
Billy McCaffrey	9	1-3	0-0	2-2	2	0	0	0	1	4
Crawford Palmer	2	0-0	0-0	3-4	3	0	0	0	0	3
Bobby Hurley	32	0-3	0-2	2-2	0	3	1	0	3	2
Greg Koubek	14	1-4	0-1	0-0	2	0	0	0	0	2
Joe Cook	2	1-1	0-0	0-0	0	0	0	0	0	2
Thomas Hill	8	0-2	0-0	0-0	3	1	1	0	0	0
Clay Buckley	3	0-0	0-0	0-0	1	0	0	0	0	0
TOTALS	**200**	**26-61**	**1-11**	**20-27**	**33**	**11**	**5**	**3**	**16**	**73**
Percentages		42.6	9.1	74.1						

Coach: Mike Krzyzewski

Officials: Ed Hightower, Tim Higgins, Rich Ballesteros
Technicals: None
Attendance: 17,765

National Invitation Tournament (NIT)

First round: Penn State d. Marquette 57-54, New Orleans d. James Madison 78-74, Tennessee d. Memphis 73-71, Fordham d. Southern 106-80, Maryland d. Massachusetts 91-81, Mississippi State d. Baylor 84-75, Wisconsin-Green Bay d. Southern Illinois 73-60, Vanderbilt d. Louisiana Tech 98-90 (OT), Oklahoma State d. Tulsa 83-74, Hawaii d. Stanford 69-57, Rutgers d. Holy Cross 87-78, Cincinnati d. Bowling Green 75-60, Saint Louis d. Kent State 85-74, DePaul d. Creighton 89-72, New Mexico d. Oregon 89-78, Long Beach St. d. Arizona State 86-71

Second round: Vanderbilt d. Tennessee 89-85, Rutgers d. Fordham 81-74, Penn State d. Maryland 80-78, New Orleans d. Mississippi State 65-60, DePaul d. Cincinnati 61-59, Saint Louis d. Wisconsin-Green Bay 58-54, New Mexico d. Oklahoma State 90-88, Hawaii d. Long Beach St. 84-79

Third round: Penn State d. Rutgers 58-55, Vanderbilt d. New Orleans 88-85, Saint Louis d. DePaul 54-47, New Mexico d. Hawaii 80-58

Semifinals: Vanderbilt d. Penn State 75-62, Saint Louis d. New Mexico 80-73

Third place: Penn State d. New Mexico 83-81 (OT)

Championship: Vanderbilt 74, Saint Louis 72

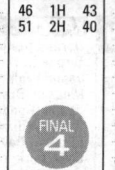

MVP: Scott Draud, Vanderbilt

1990-91: Bedeviled

At 30–0, UNLV was the first team to enter the Tournament unbeaten since Indiana State in 1979. Jerry Tarkanian's Runnin' Rebels averaged 97.7 ppg, blew out opponents by an average margin of more than 25 points and shot 53.5% from the field. They cruised into the Final Four to face Duke, the team they demolished in the 1990 Final. At the end of a game that featured 17 ties and 25 lead changes, Christian Laettner sank two free throws for a 79-77 upset. Duke (32–7) then beat Kansas, 72-65, at the Hoosier Dome in Indianapolis. It was the Blue Devils' first national title in five championship games. Coach Mike Krzyzewski joined UCLA's John Wooden as the only coaches to lead a school to four consecutive Final Fours.

Richmond became the first No. 15 seed to topple a No. 2 by beating Syracuse, 73-69, in the first round. UNLV's Larry Johnson was named the Naismith POY after averaging 22.7 ppg and 10.9 rpg. Three Rebels were selected in the first 12 picks of the NBA draft—Johnson was No. 1 (Charlotte Hornets), Stacey Augmon No. 9 (Atlanta Hawks) and Greg Anthony No. 12 (New York Knicks).

Major Conference Standings

AM. SOUTH	Conference			Overall		
	W	L	PCT	W	L	PCT
New Orleans○	9	3	.750	23	8	.742
Arkansas State□	9	3	.750	23	9	.719
Louisiana Tech⊕	8	4	.667	21	10	.677
UL-Lafayette	6	6	.500	21	10	.677
Lamar	4	8	.333	15	13	.536
Central Florida	3	9	.250	10	17	.370
Texas-Pan American	3	9	.250	7	21	.250

Tournament: **Louisiana Tech d. New Orleans 56-51**

ACC	Conference			Overall		
	W	L	PCT	W	L	PCT
Duke○	11	3	.786	32	7	.821
North Carolina⊕	10	4	.714	29	6	.829
NC State○	8	6	.571	20	11	.645
Wake Forest○	8	6	.571	19	11	.633
Virginia○	6	8	.429	21	12	.636
Georgia Tech○	6	8	.429	17	13	.567
Maryland	5	9	.357	16	12	.571
Clemson	2	12	.143	11	17	.393

Tournament: **North Carolina d. Duke 96-74**
Tournament MVP: **Rick Fox**, North Carolina

ATLANTIC 10	Conference			Overall		
	W	L	PCT	W	L	PCT
Rutgers○	14	4	.778	19	10	.655
Temple○	13	5	.722	24	10	.706
Penn State⊕	10	8	.556	21	11	.656
George Washington□	10	8	.556	19	12	.613
Massachusetts□	10	8	.556	20	13	.606
West Virginia□	10	8	.556	17	14	.548
Duquesne	10	8	.556	13	15	.464
Saint Joseph's	7	11	.389	13	17	.433
Rhode Island	6	12	.333	11	17	.393
St. Bonaventure	0	18	.000	5	23	.179

Tournament: **Penn State d. George Washington 81-75**
Tournament MOP: **Freddie Barnes**, Penn State

BIG EAST	Conference			Overall		
	W	L	PCT	W	L	PCT
Syracuse○	12	4	.750	26	6	.813
St. John's○	10	6	.625	23	9	.719
Seton Hall⊕	9	7	.563	25	9	.735
Connecticut○	9	7	.563	20	11	.645
Pittsburgh○	9	7	.563	21	12	.636
Georgetown○	8	8	.500	19	13	.594
Providence□	7	9	.438	19	13	.594
Villanova○	7	9	.438	17	15	.531
Boston College	1	15	.063	11	19	.367

Tournament: **Seton Hall d. Georgetown 74-62**
Tournament MVP: **Oliver Taylor**, Seton Hall

BIG EIGHT	Conference			Overall		
	W	L	PCT	W	L	PCT
Kansas○	10	4	.714	27	8	.771
Oklahoma State○	10	4	.714	24	8	.750
Nebraska○	9	5	.643	26	8	.765
Missouri	8	6	.571	20	10	.667
Iowa State	6	8	.429	12	19	.387
Colorado□	5	9	.357	19	14	.576
Oklahoma□	5	9	.357	20	15	.571
Kansas State	3	11	.214	13	15	.464

Tournament: **Missouri d. Nebraska 90-82**
Tournament MVP: **Doug Smith**, Missouri

BIG SKY	Conference			Overall		
	W	L	PCT	W	L	PCT
Montana⊕	13	3	.813	22	9	.710
Nevada	12	4	.750	17	14	.548
Idaho	11	5	.688	19	11	.633
Boise State□	10	6	.625	18	11	.621
Weber State	7	9	.438	12	16	.429
Idaho State	7	9	.438	11	18	.379
Montana State	6	10	.375	12	16	.429
Eastern Washington	5	11	.313	11	16	.407
Northern Arizona	1	15	.063	4	23	.148

Tournament: **Montana d. Idaho 76-68**
Tournament MVP: **Kevin Kearney**, Montana

BIG SOUTH	Conference			Overall		
	W	L	PCT	W	L	PCT
Coastal Carolina⊕	13	1	.929	24	8	.750
Radford	12	2	.857	22	7	.759
Augusta	9	5	.643	14	16	.467
Davidson	6	8	.429	10	19	.345
Winthrop	5	9	.357	8	20	.286
Charleston Southern	4	10	.286	9	19	.321
UNC Asheville	4	10	.286	8	20	.286
Campbell	3	11	.214	9	19	.321

Tournament: **Coastal Carolina d. Augusta 89-54**
Tournament MVP: **Tony Dunkin**, Coastal Carolina

BIG TEN	Conference			Overall		
	W	L	PCT	W	L	PCT
Ohio State⊕	15	3	.833	27	4	.871
Indiana○	15	3	.833	29	5	.853
Illinois	11	7	.611	21	10	.677
Michigan State○	11	7	.611	19	11	.633
Iowa○	9	9	.500	21	11	.656
Purdue○	9	9	.500	17	12	.586
Wisconsin□	8	10	.444	15	15	.500
Michigan□	7	11	.389	14	15	.483
Minnesota	5	13	.278	12	16	.429
Northwestern	0	18	.000	5	23	.179

BIG WEST	Conference			Overall		
	W	L	PCT	W	L	PCT
UNLV⊕	18	0	1.000	34	1	.971
New Mexico State○	15	3	.833	23	6	.793
Pacific	9	9	.500	14	15	.483
UC Santa Barbara	8	10	.444	14	15	.483
Utah State	8	10	.444	11	17	.393
Cal State Fullerton	7	11	.389	14	14	.500
Fresno State	7	11	.389	14	16	.467
Long Beach State	7	11	.389	11	17	.393
UC Irvine	6	12	.333	11	19	.367
San Jose State	5	13	.278	7	20	.259

Tournament: **UNLV d. Fresno State 98-74**
Tournament MVP: **Larry Johnson**, UNLV

COLONIAL ATHLETIC	Conference			Overall		
	W	L	PCT	W	L	PCT
James Madison□	12	2	.857	19	10	.655
Richmond⊕	10	4	.714	22	10	.688
American	8	6	.571	15	14	.517
George Mason	8	6	.571	14	16	.467
William and Mary	6	8	.429	13	15	.464
UNC Wilmington	6	8	.429	11	17	.393
East Carolina	4	10	.286	12	16	.429
Navy	2	12	.143	8	21	.276

Tournament: **Richmond d. George Mason 81-78**
Tournament MVP: **Jim Shields**, Richmond

EAST COAST	Conference			Overall		
	W	L	PCT	W	L	PCT
Towson⊕	10	2	.833	19	11	.633
Delaware	8	4	.667	16	13	.552
Hofstra	7	5	.583	14	14	.500
Drexel	7	5	.583	12	16	.429
Rider	4	8	.333	14	16	.467
UMBC	4	8	.333	7	22	.241
Cent. Connecticut St.	2	10	.167	4	24	.143

Tournament: **Towson d. Rider 69-63**
Tournament MVP: **Darrick Suber**, Rider

IVY	Conference			Overall		
	W	L	PCT	W	L	PCT
Princeton⊕	14	0	1.000	24	3	.889
Yale	9	5	.643	15	11	.577
Cornell	6	8	.429	13	13	.500
Brown	6	8	.429	11	15	.423
Harvard	6	8	.429	9	17	.346
Penn	6	8	.429	9	17	.346
Columbia	5	9	.357	7	19	.269
Dartmouth	4	10	.286	9	17	.346

METRO	Conference			Overall		
	W	L	PCT	W	L	PCT
Southern Miss○	10	4	.714	21	8	.724
Cincinnati□	8	6	.571	18	12	.600
Florida State⊕	9	5	.643	21	11	.656
Tulane	7	7	.500	15	13	.536
Memphis□	7	7	.500	17	15	.531
South Carolina□	5	9	.357	20	13	.606
Virginia Tech	6	8	.429	13	16	.448
Louisville	4	10	.286	14	16	.467

Tournament: **Florida State d. Louisville 76-69**
Tournament MOP: **LaBradford Smith**, Louisville

MAAC	Conference			Overall		
	W	L	PCT	W	L	PCT
Siena□	12	4	.750	25	10	.714
La Salle□	12	4	.750	19	10	.655
Saint Peter's⊕	11	5	.688	24	7	.774
Iona	11	5	.688	17	13	.567
Manhattan	8	8	.500	13	15	.464
Niagara	6	10	.375	8	20	.286
Loyola (MD)	5	11	.313	12	16	.429
Fairfield	4	12	.250	8	20	.286
Canisius	3	13	.188	10	19	.345

Tournament: **Saint Peter's d. Iona 64-58**
Tournament MVP: **Marvin Andrews**, Saint Peter's

MID-AMERICAN	Conference			Overall		
	W	L	PCT	W	L	PCT
Eastern Michigan⊕	13	3	.813	26	7	.788
Ball State□	10	6	.625	21	10	.677
Miami (OH)	10	6	.625	16	12	.571
Ohio	9	7	.563	16	12	.571
Bowling Green□	9	7	.563	17	13	.567
Central Michigan	8	8	.500	14	14	.500
Toledo	7	9	.438	17	16	.515
Kent State	4	12	.250	10	18	.357
Western Michigan	2	14	.125	5	22	.185

Tournament: **Eastern Michigan d. Toledo 67-66**
Tournament MVP: **Marcus Kennedy**, Eastern Michigan

ANNUAL REVIEW

Conference Standings Continue →

⊕ Automatic NCAA Tournament bid ○ At-large NCAA Tournament bid □ NIT appearance ✪ Team record doesn't reflect games forfeited or vacated. For adjusted record, see p. 521.

MID-CONTINENT

	Conference			Overall		
	W	L	PCT	W	L	PCT
Northern Illinois○	14	2	.875	25	6	.806
Wisc.-Green Bay⊕	13	3	.813	24	7	.774
Eastern Illinois	10	6	.625	17	12	.586
Cleveland State	8	8	.500	12	16	.429
Northern Iowa	8	8	.500	13	19	.406
Akron	6	10	.375	15	13	.536
Western Illinois	6	10	.375	13	15	.464
Illinois-Chicago	5	11	.313	15	15	.500
Valparaiso	2	14	.125	5	22	.185

Tournament: **Wisc.-Green Bay d. Northern Illinois 56-39**
Tournament MVP: **Tony Bennett**, Wisc.-Green Bay

MEAC

	Conference			Overall		
	W	L	PCT	W	L	PCT
Coppin State□	14	2	.875	19	11	.633
Delaware State	10	6	.625	19	11	.633
NC A&T	10	6	.625	17	10	.630
South Carolina State	10	6	.625	13	15	.464
Florida A&M	9	7	.563	17	14	.548
Howard	7	9	.438	8	20	.286
Morgan State	6	10	.375	7	22	.241
UMES	3	13	.188	5	23	.179
Bethune-Cookman	3	13	.188	5	24	.172

Tournament: **Florida A&M d. Delaware State 84-80 (OT)**
Tournament MOP: **Kenneth Davis**, Florida A&M

MCC

	Conference			Overall		
	W	L	PCT	W	L	PCT
Xavier⊕	11	3	.786	22	10	.688
Butler□	10	4	.714	18	11	.621
Saint Louis	8	6	.571	19	14	.576
Dayton	8	6	.571	14	15	.483
Evansville	7	7	.500	14	14	.500
Marquette	7	7	.500	11	18	.379
Loyola-Chicago	3	11	.214	10	19	.345
Detroit	2	12	.143	9	19	.321

Tournament: **Xavier d. Saint Louis 81-68**
Tournament MVP: **Jamie Gladden**, Xavier

MISSOURI VALLEY

	Conference			Overall		
	W	L	PCT	W	L	PCT
Creighton⊕	12	4	.750	24	8	.750
Missouri State□	11	5	.688	22	12	.647
Tulsa□	10	6	.625	18	12	.600
Southern Illinois□	9	7	.563	18	14	.563
Indiana State	9	7	.563	14	14	.500
Wichita State	7	9	.438	14	17	.452
Bradley	6	10	.375	8	20	.286
Drake	4	12	.250	8	21	.276
Illinois State	4	12	.250	5	23	.179

Tournament: **Creighton d. Missouri State 68-52**
Tournament MOP: **Bob Harstad**, Creighton

NAC

	Conference			Overall		
	W	L	PCT	W	L	PCT
Northeastern⊕	8	2	.800	22	11	.667
Maine	7	3	.700	13	16	.448
Vermont	5	5	.500	15	13	.536
Hartford	5	5	.500	13	16	.448
Boston U.	5	5	.500	11	18	.379
New Hampshire	0	10	.000	3	25	.107

Tournament: **Northeastern d. Maine 57-46**
Tournament MVP: **Ron Lacey**, Northeastern

NORTHEAST

	Conference			Overall		
	W	L	PCT	W	L	PCT
Saint Francis (PA)⊕	13	3	.813	24	8	.750
Fairleigh Dickinson□	13	3	.813	22	9	.710
Robert Morris	12	4	.750	17	11	.607
Monmouth	10	6	.625	19	10	.655
St. Francis (NY)	8	8	.500	15	14	.517
Mount St. Mary's	6	10	.375	8	19	.296
Long Island	4	12	.250	10	18	.357
Marist	4	12	.250	6	22	.214
Wagner	2	14	.125	4	26	.133

Tournament: **St. Francis (PA) d. Fairleigh Dickinson 97-82**
Tournament MVP: **Mike Iuzzolino**, Saint Francis (PA)

OHIO VALLEY

	Conference			Overall		
	W	L	PCT	W	L	PCT
Murray State⊕	10	2	.833	24	9	.727
Eastern Kentucky	9	3	.750	19	10	.655
Middle Tennessee St.	6	6	.500	21	9	.700
Austin Peay	6	6	.500	15	14	.517
Tennessee Tech	6	6	.500	12	16	.429
Morehead State	4	8	.333	16	13	.552
Tennessee State	1	11	.083	5	23	.179

Tournament: **Murray State d. Middle Tennessee St. 79-67**
Tournament MVP: **Popeye Jones**, Murray State

PAC-10

	Conference			Overall		
	W	L	PCT	W	L	PCT
Arizona⊕	14	4	.778	28	7	.800
UCLA○	11	7	.611	23	9	.719
Arizona State○	10	8	.556	20	10	.667
Southern California○	10	8	.556	19	10	.655
Stanford□	8	10	.444	20	13	.606
Washington State	8	10	.444	16	12	.571
Oregon State	8	10	.444	14	14	.500
California	8	10	.444	13	15	.464
Oregon	8	10	.444	13	15	.464
Washington	5	13	.278	14	14	.500

PATRIOT

	Conference			Overall		
	W	L	PCT	W	L	PCT
Fordham□	11	1	.917	25	8	.758
Lehigh	10	2	.833	19	10	.655
Holy Cross	8	4	.667	18	12	.600
Bucknell	7	5	.583	18	13	.581
Army	3	9	.250	6	22	.214
Colgate	2	10	.167	5	23	.179
Lafayette	1	11	.083	7	21	.250

Tournament: **Fordham d. Holy Cross 84-81 (OT)**
Tournament MVP: **Damon Lopez**, Fordham

SEC

	Conference			Overall		
	W	L	PCT	W	L	PCT
Kentucky*	14	4	.778	22	6	.786
Mississippi State○	13	5	.722	20	9	.690
LSU○	13	5	.722	20	10	.667
Alabama⊕	12	6	.667	23	10	.697
Vanderbilt○	11	7	.611	17	13	.567
Georgia○	9	9	.500	17	13	.567
Florida	7	11	.389	11	17	.393
Auburn	5	13	.278	13	16	.448
Tennessee	3	15	.167	12	22	.353
Mississippi	3	15	.167	9	19	.321

* Ineligible for conference title
Tournament: **Alabama d. Tennessee 88-69**
Tournament MVP: **Allan Houston**, Tennessee

SOUTHERN

	Conference			Overall		
	W	L	PCT	W	L	PCT
East Tennessee St.⊕	11	3	.786	28	5	.848
Furman□	11	3	.786	20	9	.690
Chattanooga	11	3	.786	19	10	.655
Appalachian State	7	7	.500	16	14	.533
Marshall	7	7	.500	14	14	.500
VMI	5	9	.357	10	18	.357
Western Carolina	3	11	.214	11	17	.393
The Citadel	1	13	.071	6	22	.214

Tournament: **East Tenn. St. d. Appalachian St. 101-82**
Tournament MOP: **Keith Jennings**, East Tenn. St.

SOUTHLAND

	Conference			Overall		
	W	L	PCT	W	L	PCT
UL-Monroe⊕	13	1	.929	25	8	.758
Texas-Arlington	11	3	.786	20	9	.690
North Texas	11	3	.786	17	13	.567
Stephen F. Austin	6	8	.429	11	17	.393
Sam Houston State	5	9	.357	7	20	.259
Texas State	4	10	.286	10	17	.370
McNeese State	4	10	.286	8	19	.296
Northwestern St. (LA)	2	12	.143	6	22	.214

Tournament: **UL-Monroe d. Texas-Arlington 87-60**
Tournament MVP: **Anthony Jones**, UL-Monroe

SOUTHWEST

	Conference			Overall		
	W	L	PCT	W	L	PCT
Arkansas⊕	15	1	.938	34	4	.895
Texas○	13	3	.813	23	9	.719
Houston□	10	6	.625	18	11	.621
TCU	9	7	.563	18	10	.643
Rice□	9	7	.563	16	14	.533
SMU	6	10	.375	12	17	.414
Baylor	4	12	.250	12	15	.444
Texas Tech	4	12	.250	8	23	.258
Texas A&M	2	14	.125	8	21	.276

Tournament: **Arkansas d. Texas 120-89**
Tournament MVP: **Oliver Miller**, Arkansas

SWAC

	Conference			Overall		
	W	L	PCT	W	L	PCT
Jackson State	10	2	.833	17	13	.567
Southern U.	8	4	.667	19	9	.679
Alabama State	7	5	.583	18	11	.621
Texas Southern	7	5	.583	13	17	.433
Mississippi Valley St.	4	8	.333	9	19	.321
Alcorn State	3	9	.250	8	21	.276
Grambling	3	9	.250	6	22	.214
Prairie View A&M	0	0	.000	4	21	.160

Tournament: **Jackson State d. Texas Southern 70-66**
Tournament MVP: **Lindsey Hunter**, Jackson State

SUN BELT

	Conference			Overall		
	W	L	PCT	W	L	PCT
South Alabama⊕	11	3	.786	22	9	.710
UAB□	9	5	.643	18	13	.581
South Florida□	8	6	.571	19	11	.633
Western Kentucky	8	6	.571	14	14	.500
VCU	7	7	.500	14	17	.452
Charlotte	6	8	.429	14	14	.500
Old Dominion	5	9	.357	14	18	.438
Jacksonville	2	12	.143	6	22	.214

Tournament: **South Alabama d. Old Dominion 86-81**
Tournament MOP: **Chris Gatling**, Old Dominion

TAAC

	Conference			Overall		
	W	L	PCT	W	L	PCT
UTSA	12	2	.857	21	8	.724
Centenary	10	4	.714	17	12	.586
Ga. Southern	9	5	.643	14	13	.519
Stetson	9	5	.643	15	16	.484
Georgia State⊕	7	7	.500	16	15	.516
Arkansas-Little Rock	6	8	.429	10	20	.333
Samford	2	12	.143	6	22	.214
Mercer	1	13	.071	2	25	.074

Tournament: **Georgia State d. Arkansas-Little Rock 80-60**
Tournament MOP: **Chris Collier**, Georgia State

WEST COAST

	Conference			Overall		
	W	L	PCT	W	L	PCT
Pepperdine⊕	13	1	.929	22	9	.710
Loyola Marymount	9	5	.643	16	15	.516
San Diego	8	6	.571	17	12	.586
Santa Clara	7	7	.500	16	13	.552
Saint Mary's (CA)	7	7	.500	13	17	.433
Gonzaga	5	9	.357	14	14	.500
San Francisco	4	10	.286	12	17	.414
Portland	3	11	.214	5	23	.179

Tournament: **Pepperdine d. Saint Mary's 71-68 (OT)**
Tournament MVP: **Geoff Lear**, Pepperdine

WAC

	Conference			Overall		
	W	L	PCT	W	L	PCT
Utah○	15	1	.938	30	4	.882
BYU⊕	11	5	.688	21	13	.618
New Mexico○	10	6	.625	20	10	.667
Wyoming□	8	8	.500	20	12	.625
Hawaii	7	9	.438	16	13	.552
UTEP	7	9	.438	16	13	.552
Colorado State	6	10	.375	15	14	.517
San Diego State	6	10	.375	13	16	.448
Air Force	3	13	.188	9	20	.310

Tournament: **BYU d. Utah 51-49 (OT)**
Tournament MVP: **Shawn Bradley**, BYU

INDEPENDENTS

	Overall		
	W	L	PCT
DePaul○	20	9	.690
Wright State	19	9	.679
Wisconsin-Milwaukee	18	10	.643
Southern Utah	16	12	.571
UMKC	15	14	.517
Youngstown State	12	16	.429
Brooklyn	11	16	.407
Notre Dame	12	20	.375
Miami (FL)	9	19	.321
Southeastern Louisiana	9	19	.321
Cal State Northridge	8	20	.286
Florida International	6	22	.214
Liberty	5	23	.179
Chicago State	4	24	.143
Nicholls State	3	25	.107
Northeastern Illinois	2	25	.074
U.S. International	2	26	.071

INDIVIDUAL LEADERS—SEASON

SCORING	CL	POS	G	FG	3FG	FT	PTS	PPG
1 **Kevin Bradshaw**, U.S. International	SR	G	28	358	60	278	1,054	**37.6**
2 **Alphonso Ford**, Miss. Valley St.	SO	G	28	325	86	179	915	**32.7**
3 **Von McDade**, Wisconsin-Milwaukee	SR	G	28	274	96	186	830	**29.6**
4 **Steve Rogers**, Alabama State	JR	F	29	273	56	250	852	**29.4**
5 **Terrell Lowery**, Loyola Marymount	JR	G	31	298	103	185	884	**28.5**
6 **Bobby Phills**, Southern U.	SR	G	28	260	123	152	795	**28.4**
7 **Shaquille O'Neal**, LSU	SO	C	28	312	0	150	774	**27.6**
8 **John Taft**, Marshall	SR	G	28	256	82	170	764	**27.3**
9 **Rodney Monroe**, NC State	SR	G	31	285	104	162	836	**27.0**
10 **Terrell Brandon**, Oregon	JR	G	28	273	40	159	745	**26.6**

FIELD GOAL PCT	CL	POS	G	FG	FGA	PCT
1 **Oliver Miller**, Arkansas	JR	C	38	254	361	**70.4**
2 **Warren Kidd**, Middle Tennessee State	SO	C	30	173	247	**70.0**
3 **Pete Freeman**, Akron	SR	C	28	175	250	**70.0**
4 **Lester James**, St. Francis (NY)	JR	C	29	149	215	**69.3**
5 **Marcus Kennedy**, Eastern Michigan	SR	F	33	240	352	**68.2**

MINIMUM: 5 MADE PER GAME

THREE-PT FG PER GAME	CL	POS	G	3FG	3PG
1 **Bobby Phills**, Southern U.	SR	G	28	123	**4.4**
2 **Ronnie Schmitz**, UMKC	SO	G	29	116	**4.0**
3 **Jeff Herdman**, UC Irvine	SR	F	30	112	**3.7**
4 **Doug Day**, Radford	SO	G	29	106	**3.7**
5 **Sean Jackson**, Princeton	JR	G	27	95	**3.5**

THREE-PT FG PCT	CL	POS	G	3FG	3FGA	PCT
1 **Keith Jennings**, East Tennessee State	SR	G	33	84	142	**59.2**
2 **Tony Bennett**, Wisconsin-Green Bay	JR	G	31	80	150	**53.3**
3 **Mike Iuzzolino**, Saint Francis (PA)	SR	G	32	103	195	**52.8**
4 **Ross Richardson**, Loyola Marymount	FR	G	25	61	116	**52.6**
5 **David Mitchell**, Samford	SO	F	26	41	78	**52.6**

MINIMUM: 1.5 MADE PER GAME

FREE THROW PCT	CL	POS	G	FT	FTA	PCT
1 **Darin Archbold**, Butler	JR	G	29	187	205	**91.2**
2 **William Lewis**, Monmouth	JR	G	28	91	101	**90.1**
3 **Darwyn Alexander**, Oklahoma State	JR	G	32	96	107	**89.7**
4 **Keith Jennings**, East Tennessee State	SR	G	33	136	152	**89.5**
5 **Rodney Monroe**, NC State	SR	G	31	162	183	**88.5**

MINIMUM: 2.5 MADE PER GAME

ASSISTS PER GAME	CL	POS	G	AST	APG
1 **Chris Corchiani**, NC State	SR	G	31	299	**9.6**
2 **Danny Tirado**, Jacksonville	JR	G	28	259	**9.3**
3 **Terrell Lowery**, Loyola Marymount	JR	G	31	283	**9.1**
4 **Keith Jennings**, East Tennessee State	SR	G	33	301	**9.1**
5 **Greg Anthony**, UNLV	SR	G	35	310	**8.9**
6 **Van Usher**, Tennessee Tech	JR	G	28	233	**8.3**
7 **Orlando Smart**, San Francisco	FR	G	29	237	**8.2**
8 **Ray Johnson**, Sam Houston State	JR	G	24	193	**8.0**
9 **Glover Cody**, Texas-Arlington	JR	G	29	229	**7.9**
10 **Arnold Bernard**, Missouri State	SR	G	34	257	**7.6**

REBOUNDS PER GAME	CL	POS	G	REB	RPG
1 **Shaquille O'Neal**, LSU	SO	C	28	411	**14.7**
2 **Popeye Jones**, Murray State	JR	C	33	469	**14.2**
3 **Larry Stewart**, Coppin State	SR	F	30	403	**13.4**
4 **Tim Burroughs**, Jacksonville	JR	F	27	350	**13.0**
5 **Warren Kidd**, Middle Tennessee State	SO	C	30	370	**12.3**
6 **Clarence Weatherspoon**, Southern Miss	JR	F	29	355	**12.2**
7 **Ervin Johnson**, New Orleans	SO	C	30	367	**12.2**
8 **Tom Davis**, Delaware State	SR	F	30	366	**12.2**
9 **Dikembe Mutombo**, Georgetown	SR	C	32	389	**12.2**
10 **Dale Davis**, Clemson	SR	F/C	28	340	**12.1**

BLOCKED SHOTS PER GAME	CL	POS	G	BLK	BPG
1 **Shawn Bradley**, BYU	FR	C	34	177	**5.2**
2 **Cedric Lewis**, Maryland	SR	F/C	28	143	**5.1**
3 **Shaquille O'Neal**, LSU	SO	C	28	140	**5.0**
4 **Dikembe Mutombo**, Georgetown	SR	C	32	151	**4.7**
5 **Kevin Roberson**, Vermont	JR	C	28	104	**3.7**

STEALS PER GAME	CL	POS	G	STL	SPG
1 **Van Usher**, Tennessee Tech	JR	G	28	104	**3.7**
2 **Scott Burrell**, Connecticut	SO	F	31	112	**3.6**
3 **Eric Murdock**, Providence	SR	G	32	111	**3.5**
4 **Von McDade**, Wisconsin-Milwaukee	SR	G	28	97	**3.5**
5 **Lynn Smith**, St. Francis (NY)	JR	G	29	100	**3.4**

INDIVIDUAL LEADERS—GAME

POINTS	CL	POS	OPP	DATE	PTS
1 **Kevin Bradshaw**, U.S. International	SR	G	Loyola Marymount	J5	**72**
2 **Kevin Bradshaw**, U.S. International	SR	G	Florida Int'l	J14	**59**
3 **Brent Price**, Oklahoma	JR	G	Loyola Marymount	D15	**56**
4 **Shaquille O'Neal**, LSU	SO	C	Arkansas State	D18	**53**
Kevin Bradshaw, U.S. International	SR	G	Cal State LA	J24	**53**
Kevin Bradshaw, U.S. International	SR	G	Cal State Northridge	J28	**53**

THREE-PT FG MADE	CL	POS	OPP	DATE	3FG
1 **Doug Day**, Radford	SO	G	Central Connecticut State	D12	**11**
Brent Price, Oklahoma	JR	G	Loyola Marymount	D15	**11**
Bobby Phills, Southern U.	SR	G	Manhattan	D28	**11**
Terry Brown, Kansas	SR	G	NC State	J5	**11**
5 **Kyle Kerlegan**, Cal State Northridge	SR	G	Colorado	N23	**10**
Ronnie Schmitz, UMKC	SO	G	Denver	D17	**10**
Scott Murphy, Mount St. Mary's	SR	G	Wagner	F7	**10**

ASSISTS	CL	POS	OPP	DATE	AST
1 **Chris Corchiani**, NC State	SR	G	Maryland	F27	**20**
2 **Greg Anthony**, UNLV	SR	G	Pacific	D29	**19**
Keith Jennings, East Tennessee St.	SR	G	Appalachian State	F2	**19**
4 **Terrell Lowery**, Loyola Marymount	JR	G	Saint Joseph's	D29	**18**
5 **Van Usher**, Tennessee Tech	JR	G	Western Kentucky	D28	**17**
Tyrone Buckmon, Idaho State	JR	G	Northern Arizona	J17	**17**
Danny Tirado, Jacksonville	JR	G	South Alabama	F7	**17**

REBOUNDS	CL	POS	OPP	DATE	REB
1 **Dikembe Mutombo**, Georgetown	SR	C	Connecticut	M8	**27**
2 **Popeye Jones**, Murray State	JR	C	Morehead State	F11	**23**
3 **Rob Renfroe**, Mercer	JR	C	UNC Asheville	D3	**22**
Ervin Johnson, New Orleans	SO	C	Lamar	J17	**22**
DeLon Turner, Florida A&M	SO	F	Morgan State	F7	**22**
Darrell Harris, Grambling	JR	F	Prairie View A&M	F9	**22**
Billy Owens, Syracuse	JR	F	Villanova	M8	**22**

BLOCKED SHOTS	CL	POS	OPP	DATE	BLK
1 **Shawn Bradley**, BYU	FR	C	Eastern Kentucky	D7	**14**
2 **Cedric Lewis**, Maryland	SR	F/C	South Florida	J19	**12**
3 **Dikembe Mutombo**, Georgetown	SR	C	Hawaii-Loa	N23	**11**
4 **Byron Tucker**, George Mason	JR	F	Miami (FL)	N23	**10**
Kevin Roberson, Vermont	JR	C	Hartford	J8	**10**
Damon Lopez, Fordham	SR	C	Lehigh	J16	**10**
Shaquille O'Neal, LSU	SO	C	Florida	J26	**10**
Derek Stewart, Augusta	SO	F	Davidson	J26	**10**

STEALS	CL	POS	OPP	DATE	STL
1 **Carl Thomas**, Eastern Michigan	SR	G	Chicago State	F20	**11**
2 **Delvon Anderson**, Montana	JR	G/F	Simon Fraser	N15	**10**
Shawn Griggs, LSU	SO	G	Tennessee	F23	**10**
4 13 tied with nine					

TEAM LEADERS—SEASON

WIN-LOSS PCT	W	L	PCT
1 **UNLV**	34	1	**.971**
2 **Arkansas**	34	4	**.895**
3 **Princeton**	24	3	**.889**
4 **Utah**	30	4	**.882**
5 **Ohio State**	27	4	**.871**

SCORING OFFENSE	G	W-L	PTS	PPG
1 **Southern U.**	28	19-9	2,924	**104.4**
2 **Loyola Marymount**	31	16-15	3,211	**103.6**
3 **Arkansas**	38	34-4	3,783	**99.6**
4 **UNLV**	35	34-1	3,420	**97.7**
5 **Oklahoma**	35	20-15	3,363	**96.1**

SCORING MARGIN	G	W-L	PPG	OPP PPG	MAR
1 **UNLV**	35	34-1	97.7	71.0	**26.7**
2 **Arkansas**	38	34-4	99.6	80.4	**19.2**
3 **East Tennessee State**	33	28-5	94.0	76.8	**17.2**
4 **Ohio State**	31	27-4	84.6	68.5	**16.1**
5 **North Carolina**	35	29-6	87.6	71.6	**16.0**

FIELD GOAL PCT	G	W-L	FG	FGA	PCT
1 **UNLV**	35	34-1	1,305	2,441	**53.5**
2 **Indiana**	34	29-5	1,043	1,955	**53.4**
3 **New Mexico**	30	20-10	868	1,644	**52.8**
4 **Brooklyn**	27	11-16	656	1,262	**52.0**
5 **Kansas**	35	27-8	1,086	2,097	**51.8**

THREE-PT FG PER GAME	G	W-L	3FG	3PG
1 **Texas-Arlington**	29	20-9	265	**9.1**
2 **East Tennessee State**	33	28-5	301	**9.1**
3 **Dayton**	29	14-15	256	**8.8**
4 **UC Irvine**	30	11-19	263	**8.8**
5 **Kentucky**	28	22-6	242	**8.6**

FREE THROW PCT	G	W-L	FT	FTA	PCT
1 **Butler**	29	18-11	725	922	**78.6**
2 **Monmouth**	29	19-10	422	547	**77.1**
3 **Air Force**	29	9-20	483	627	**77.0**
4 **Northwestern**	28	5-23	470	612	**76.8**
5 **Wyoming**	32	20-12	654	853	**76.7**

REBOUND MARGIN	G	W-L	RPG	OPP RPG	MAR
1 **New Orleans**	31	23-8	41.7	32.4	**9.3**
2 **Murray State**	33	24-9	43.4	34.6	**8.8**
3 **Stanford**	33	20-13	37.9	29.4	**8.5**
4 **UNLV**	35	34-1	42.5	34.8	**7.7**
5 **Northern Illinois**	31	25-6	35.5	28.0	**7.5**

SCORING DEFENSE	G	W-L	OPP PTS	OPP PPG
1 **Princeton**	27	24-3	1,320	**48.9**
2 **Northern Illinois**	31	25-6	1,781	**57.5**
3 **Yale**	26	15-11	1,508	**58.0**
4 **Wisconsin-Green Bay**	31	24-7	1,893	**61.1**
5 **Georgetown**	32	19-13	1,964	**61.4**

FIELD GOAL PCT DEFENSE	G	W-L	OPP FG	OPP FGA	OPP PCT
1 **Georgetown**	32	19-13	680	1,847	**36.8**
2 **Northern Illinois**	31	25-6	616	1,587	**38.8**
3 **Connecticut**	31	20-11	682	1,753	**38.9**
4 **New Orleans**	31	23-8	725	1,837	**39.5**
5 **Middle Tennessee State**	30	21-9	793	2,007	**39.5**

TEAM LEADERS—GAME

POINTS	OPP	DATE	SCORE
1 Loyola Marymount	U.S. International	J5	**186-140**
2 Oklahoma	Loyola Marymount	D15	**172-112**
3 Loyola Marymount	Chaminade	N25	**162-129**
Oklahoma	Angelo State	D1	**162-99**
5 Southern U.	Texas College	D6	**159-65**

FIELD GOAL PCT	OPP	DATE	FG	FGA	PCT
1 Princeton	Brown	F15	27	37	**73.0**
2 Duquesne	St. Bonaventure	F23	34	47	**72.3**
3 Xavier	Butler	F23	39	54	**72.2**
4 Monmouth	Long Island	J19	33	46	**71.7**
5 Missouri State	UL-Monroe	N23	25	35	**71.4**
Fairleigh Dickinson	Central Connecticut St.	D22	25	35	**71.4**

THREE-PT FG MADE	OPP	DATE	3FG
1 UNLV	Nevada	D8	**21**
2 Navy	Mount St. Mary's	N26	**20**
3 Loyola Marymount	Chaminade	N25	**19**
New Mexico St.	Morgan State	D29	**19**
5 Washington State	Seattle	D29	**18**
La Salle	Loyola Marymount	D31	**18**

CONSENSUS ALL-AMERICAS

FIRST TEAM

PLAYER	CL	POS	HT	SCHOOL	RPG	PPG
Kenny Anderson	SO	G	6-2	Georgia Tech	5.7	25.9
Jim Jackson	SO	G/F	6-6	Ohio State	5.5	18.9
Larry Johnson	SR	F	6-7	UNLV	10.9	22.7
Shaquille O'Neal	SO	C	7-1	LSU	14.7	27.6
Billy Owens	JR	F	6-9	Syracuse	11.6	23.3

SECOND TEAM

PLAYER	CL	POS	HT	SCHOOL	RPG	PPG
Stacey Augmon	SR	G/F	6-8	UNLV	7.3	16.5
Keith Jennings	SR	G	5-7	East Tennessee State	3.9	20.1
Christian Laettner	JR	C	6-11	Duke	8.7	19.8
Eric Murdock	SR	G	6-2	Providence	4.1	25.6
Steve Smith	SR	G	6-6	Michigan State	6.1	25.1

SELECTORS: AP, NABC, UPI, USBWA

AWARD WINNERS

PLAYER OF THE YEAR

PLAYER	CL	POS	HT	SCHOOL	AWARDS
Larry Johnson	SR	F	6-7	UNLV	Naismith, USBWA, Wooden, NABC
Shaquille O'Neal	SO	C	7-1	LSU	AP, UPI, Rupp
Keith Jennings	SR	G	5-7	East Tenn. St.	Frances Pomeroy Naismith*

* FOR THE MOST OUTSTANDING SENIOR PLAYER WHO IS 6 FEET OR UNDER.

DEFENSIVE PLAYER OF THE YEAR

PLAYER	CL	POS	HT	SCHOOL
Stacey Augmon	SR	G/F	6-8	UNLV

COACH OF THE YEAR

COACH	SCHOOL	REC	AWARDS
Randy Ayers	Ohio State	27-4	Naismith, AP, USBWA, CBS/Chevrolet
Rick Majerus	Utah	30-4	UPI
Mike Krzyzewski	Duke	32-7	NABC
Rick Pitino	Kentucky	22-6	Sporting News

BOB GIBBONS' TOP HIGH SCHOOL SENIOR RECRUITS

PLAYER	POS	HT	HIGH SCHOOL	A-A TEAMS	COLLEGE	CAREER NOTES
1 Glenn Robinson	PF	6-8	Roosevelt HS, Gary, IN	McD, P, USA	Purdue	Consensus National POY, 30.3 ppg, 10.1 rpg, '94; No. 1 overall pick, '94 NBA draft (Bucks); 20.7 ppg (11 seasons); 2-time All-Star
2 Chris Webber	C/F	6-9	Detroit Country Day School, Beverly Hills, MI	McD, P, USA	Michigan	First-team All-America, '93; No. 1 overall pick. '93 NBA draft (Magic); 20.7 ppg (15 seasons); 5-time All-Star
3 James Forrest	F	6-8	Atlanta Southside HS	McD, P	Georgia Tech	17.4 ppg, 7.4 rpg (4 seasons); undrafted; played overseas
4 Juwan Howard	C/F	6-9	Chicago Vocational HS	McD, P, USA	Michigan	15.3 ppg, 7.5 rpg (3 seasons); No. 5 pick, '94 NBA draft (Bullets); 15.3 ppg (14 seasons); All-Star, '96
5 Cherokee Parks	C	6-11	Marina HS, Huntington Beach, CA	McD, P	Duke	NCAA title, '92; at Duke, 12.5 ppg, 6.7 rpg (4 seasons); No. 12 pick, '95 NBA draft (Mavs); 4.4 ppg (9 seasons)
6 David Vaughn	C/F	6-10	White's Creek (TN) HS	McD, P, USA	Memphis	903 rebounds (4 seasons); No. 25 pick, '95 NBA draft (Magic); 2.9 ppg (4 seasons)
7 Ben Davis	C/F	6-8	Oak Hill Academy, Mouth of Wilson, VA	McD, P	Kansas/Arizona	First-team All-Pac-10, '96; 2nd-round pick, '96 NBA draft (Suns); 1.4 ppg (4 seasons)
8 Alan Henderson	F	6-9	Brebeuf Prep HS, Indianapolis	McD, P, USA	Indiana	Indiana's all-time leading rebounder (1,091); No. 16 pick, '95 NBA draft (Hawks); 7.8 ppg (12 seasons)
9 Donyell Marshall	F	6-8	Reading (PA) HS	McD, P	Connecticut	1,648 points (3 seasons); first-team All-America, '94; No. 4 pick, '94 NBA draft (Wolves); 11.4 ppg, 6.8 rpg (14 seasons)
10 Jimmy King	2G	6-4	Plano (Texas) East HS	McD, P	Michigan	11.5 ppg (4 seasons); 2nd-round pick, '95 NBA draft (Raptors); 4.5 ppg (2 seasons); played in CBA, overseas
11 Howard Nathan	PG	5-11	Peoria (IL) Manual HS	McD, P	DePaul/UL-Monroe	Illinois Mr. Basketball, '91; undrafted; played in 5 NBA games
12 Jalen Rose	SF	6-7	Detroit Southwestern HS	McD, P	Michigan	17.5 ppg, 4.7 rpg (3 seasons); No. 13 pick, '94 NBA draft (Nuggets); 14.3 ppg (13 seasons); NBA Most Improved Player, '00
13 Cory Alexander	PG	6-1	Oak Hill Academy, Mouth of Wilson, VA	McD, P	Virginia	15.1 ppg (3 seasons); 2nd-round pick, '95 NBA draft (Spurs); 5.5 ppg, 2.7 apg (7 seasons)
14 Donald Williams	2G	6-3	Garner (NC) HS	McD, P	North Carolina	NCAA title, Tournament MOP, '93; undrafted; played overseas
15 Travis Best	PG	5-11	Springfield (MA) Central HS	McD, P	Georgia Tech	2,057 pts (4 seasons); No. 23 pick, '95 NBA draft (Pacers); 7.6 ppg (10 seasons)
16 Junior Burrough	PF	6-8	Oak Hill Academy, Mouth of Wilson, VA		Virginia	15.3 ppg, 7.2 rpg (4 seasons); 2nd-round pick, '95 NBA draft (Celtics); 3.1 ppg (1 season)
17 Loren Meyer	C	6-10	Ruthven-Ayearshire HS, Ruthven, IA	P	Iowa State	1,280 points, 677 rebounds (5 seasons); No. 24 pick, '95 NBA draft (Mavs); 4.6 ppg (3 seasons)
18 Sharone Wright	C	6-10	Southwest Macon (GA) HS	McD, P	Clemson	14.2 ppg (3 seasons); No. 6 pick, '94 NBA draft (76ers); 9.7 ppg, 5.0 rpg (4 seasons)
19 Calvin Rayford	PG	5-7	Washington HS, Milwaukee	McD, P	Kansas	10.3 ppg (4 seasons); Final Four, '93; undrafted
20 Rick Brunson	2G	6-3	Salem (MA) HS	McD	Temple	1,493 points, 470 assists (4 seasons); undrafted; played on 8 NBA teams; 3.2 ppg (9 seasons)

OTHER STANDOUTS

PLAYER	POS	HT	HIGH SCHOOL	A-A TEAMS	COLLEGE	CAREER NOTES
44 Greg Ostertag	C	7-1	Duncanville (Texas) HS		Kansas	2 Final Fours; at Kansas, 7.9 ppg, 6.1 rpg (4 seasons); No. 28 pick, '95 NBA draft (Jazz); 4.6 ppg, 5.5 rpg (11 seasons)
64 Damon Stoudamire	PG	5-10	Woodrow Wilson HS, Portland		Arizona	2-time All-America; No. 7 pick, '95 draft (Raptors); 13.4 ppg (13 seasons); NBA ROY, '96
110 Tyus Edney	PG	5-10	Long Beach (CA) HS		UCLA	NCAA title, '95; at UCLA, 12.1 ppg, 5.2 apg (4 seasons); 2nd-round pick, '95 NBA draft (Kings); 7.6 ppg (4 seasons)

Abbreviations: McD=McDonald's; P=Parade; USA=USA Today

POLL PROGRESSION

PRESEASON POLL

AP	UPI	SCHOOL
1	1	**UNLV**
2	3	**Arkansas**
3	2	**Arizona**
4	5	**Michigan State**
5	4	**North Carolina**
6	6	**Duke**
7	9	**Alabama**
8	8	**Indiana**
9	7	**Georgetown**
10	11	**Ohio State**
11	10	**UCLA**
12	15	**Pittsburgh**
13	16	**Syracuse**
14	13	**LSU**
15	12	**Oklahoma**
16	17	**Georgia Tech**
17	13	**Connecticut**
18	19	**Virginia**
19	24	**Temple**
20	—	**Missouri**
21	23	**Georgia**
22	21	**Texas**
23	22	**Louisville**
24	18	**Southern Miss**
25	—	**St. John's**
—	20	**Kansas**
—	25	**Notre Dame**

WEEK OF NOV 27

AP	UPI	SCHOOL	AP↓↑
1	2	**UNLV** (0-0)	
2	1	**Arizona** (5-0)	↑1
3	3	**Arkansas** (3-1)	↓1
4	4	**North Carolina** (1-0)	↑1
5	5	**Michigan State** (1-0)	↓1
6	8	**Alabama** (1-0)	↑1
7	7	**Syracuse** (3-0)	↑6
8	9	**Duke** (3-1)	↓2
9	6	**Georgetown** (2-0)	
10	11	**Indiana** (2-1)	↓2
11	12	**Ohio State** (1-0)	↓1
12	10	**UCLA** (3-0)	↓1
13	14	**Pittsburgh** (2-0)	↓1
14	14	**Georgia Tech** (1-0)	↑2
15	13	**Connecticut** (1-0)	↑2
16	18	**Virginia** (2-1)	↑2
17	16	**Georgia** (2-0)	↑4
18	16	**Oklahoma** (2-1)	↓3
19	19	**Southern Miss** (0-0)	↑5
20	23	**LSU** (1-1)	↓6
21	22	**St. John's** (2-0)	↑4
22	19	**Texas** (0-0)	
23	19	**Missouri** (0-0)	↓3
24	—	**Villanova** (2-0)	⤴
25	21	**Louisville** (0-0)	↓2
—	24	**New Mexico State** (1-0)	
—	25	**Houston** (1-0)	

WEEK OF DEC 4

AP	UPI	SCHOOL	AP↓↑
1	1	**UNLV** (1-0)	
2	2	**Arizona** (6-0)	
3	3	**Arkansas** (5-1)	
4	4	**Syracuse** (4-0)	↑3
5	5	**Duke** (5-1)	↑3
6	6	**Georgetown** (3-0)	↑3
7	7	**Indiana** (4-1)	↑3
8	7	**UCLA** (4-0)	↑4
9	9	**Ohio State** (3-0)	↑2
10	10	**North Carolina** (3-1)	↓6
11	13	**Pittsburgh** (4-0)	↑2
12	15	**Alabama** (2-1)	↓6
13	12	**Georgia** (4-0)	↑4
14	11	**Connecticut** (3-0)	↑1
15	16	**Southern Miss** (1-0)	↑4
16	13	**Oklahoma** (4-1)	↑2
17	18	**St. John's** (3-0)	↑4
18	17	**LSU** (2-1)	↑2
19	19	**Michigan State** (1-2)	↓14
20	20	**Georgia Tech** (2-1)	↓6
21	22	**South Carolina** (4-1)	⤴
21	—	**Virginia** (3-2)	↓5
23	24	**Texas** (1-1)	↓1
24	—	**Temple** (1-1)	⤴
25	—	**Kentucky** (3-0)	⤴
—	21	**New Mexico State** (4-0)	
—	22	**Kansas** (2-1)	
—	25	**East Tennesee State** (3-1)	

WEEK OF DEC 11

AP	UPI	SCHOOL	AP↓↑
1	1	**UNLV** (2-0)	
2	2	**Arkansas** (7-1)	↑1
3	3	**Syracuse** (7-0)	↑1
4	5	**Arizona** (7-1)	↓2
5	4	**Georgetown** (5-0)	↑1
6	6	**UCLA** (6-0)	↑2
7	9	**Indiana** (7-1)	
8	7	**Ohio State** (4-0)	↑1
9	10	**North Carolina** (4-1)	↑1
10	8	**Duke** (6-2)	↓5
11	12	**Georgia** (5-0)	↑2
12	11	**LSU** (4-1)	↑6
13	14	**Oklahoma** (6-1)	↑3
14	15	**St. John's** (6-0)	↑3
15	13	**Pittsburgh** (6-1)	↓4
16	16	**Connecticut** (3-1)	↓2
17	17	**South Carolina** (5-1)	↑4
18	18	**Kentucky** (4-0)	↑7
19	22	**Virginia** (5-2)	↑2
20	21	**Alabama** (2-2)	↓8
21	20	**Michigan State** (2-2)	↓2
22	23	**Southern Miss** (2-1)	↓7
23	19	**Georgia Tech** (3-2)	↓3
24	—	**East Tenn. St.** (6-1)	⤴
25	24	**Texas** (3-2)	↓2
—	25	**Villanova** (5-1)	

WEEK OF DEC 18

AP	UPI	SCHOOL	AP↓↑
1	1	**UNLV** (3-0)	
2	2	**Arkansas** (8-1)	
3	3	**Syracuse** (9-0)	
4	4	**Arizona** (7-1)	
5	5	**UCLA** (7-0)	↑1
6	6	**Indiana** (8-1)	↑1
7	7	**Ohio State** (6-0)	↑1
8	8	**North Carolina** (6-1)	↑1
9	9	**Duke** (6-2)	↑1
10	11	**LSU** (4-1)	↑2
11	12	**Oklahoma** (8-1)	↑2
12	10	**Georgetown** (6-1)	↓7
13	14	**St. John's** (8-0)	↑1
14	16	**Pittsburgh** (7-1)	↑1
15	15	**Connecticut** (5-1) Ⓐ	↑1
16	17	**South Carolina** (7-1)	↑1
17	13	**Georgia** (6-1)	↓6
18	—	**Kentucky** (5-1)	
19	—	**Virginia** (5-2)	
20	18	**Southern Miss** (3-1)	↑2
21	19	**East Tennesee State** (7-1)	↑3
22	21	**Nebraska** (9-1)	⤴
23	—	**Texas** (3-2)	↑2
24	24	**Michigan State** (3-3)	↓3
25	22	**Princeton** (7-0)	⤴
—	20	**New Mexico State** (6-1)	
—	23	**Temple** (3-2)	
—	25	**DePaul** (6-2)	

WEEK OF DEC 25

AP	UPI	SCHOOL	AP↓↑
1	1	**UNLV** (5-0)	
2	2	**Arkansas** (9-1)	
3	4	**Syracuse** (11-0)	
4	3	**Arizona** (8-1)	
5	5	**Indiana** (10-1)	↑1
6	6	**Ohio State** (8-0)	↑1
7	7	**North Carolina** (7-1)	↑1
8	8	**Duke** (8-2) Ⓑ	↑1
9	10	**St. John's** (9-0)	↑4
10	9	**UCLA** (8-1)	↓5
11	11	**Pittsburgh** (9-1)	↑3
12	12	**South Carolina** (8-1)	↑4
13	15	**Connecticut** (6-1)	↑2
14	14	**Oklahoma** (8-2) Ⓑ	↓3
15	13	**LSU** (6-2)	↓5
16	16	**Georgetown** (6-2)	↓4
17	17	**Georgia** (7-2)	
18	—	**Kentucky** (6-2)	
19	24	**Virginia** (6-2)	
20	19	**East Tennessee St.** (8-1)	↑1
21	22	**Southern Miss** (3-1)	↓1
22	19	**Nebraska** (10-1)	
23	21	**Iowa** (9-1)	⤴
24	22	**New Mexico State** (7-1)	⤴
25	18	**Michigan State** (5-3)	↓1
—	24	**Alabama** (6-3)	

WEEK OF JAN 1

AP	UPI	SCHOOL	AP↓↑
1	1	**UNLV** (6-0)	
2	2	**Arkansas** (10-1)	
3	4	**Syracuse** (12-0)	
4	3	**Arizona** (10-1)	
5	5	**Indiana** (12-1)	
6	6	**Ohio State** (10-0)	
7	7	**North Carolina** (9-1)	
8	8	**Duke** (9-2)	
9	10	**St. John's** (9-0)	
10	9	**UCLA** (10-1)	
11	14	**Pittsburgh** (11-2)	
12	13	**Connecticut** (8-1)	↑1
13	11	**Oklahoma** (10-2)	↑1
14	12	**LSU** (7-2)	↑1
15	16	**Georgetown** (7-2)	↑1
16	—	**Kentucky** (8-2)	↑2
17	17	**East Tennessee St.** (9-1)	↑3
18	22	**Virginia** (7-2)	↑1
19	15	**Nebraska** (12-1)	↑3
20	23	**South Carolina** (9-2)	↓8
21	18	**Southern Miss** (5-1)	
22	19	**Iowa** (11-1)	↑1
23	20	**New Mexico State** (8-1)	↑1
24	25	**Georgia Tech** (7-3)	⤴
25	21	**Michigan State** (7-3)	
—	24	**Georgia** (7-3)	⤵

WEEK OF JAN 8 Ⓒ

AP	UPI	SCHOOL	AP↓↑
1	1	**UNLV** (8-0)	
2	2	**Arkansas** (13-1)	
3	3	**Indiana** (14-1)	↑2
4	4	**Ohio State** (12-0)	↑2
5	5	**North Carolina** (11-1)	↑2
6	6	**Arizona** (11-2)	↓2
7	7	**UCLA** (12-1)	↑3
8	8	**Syracuse** (13-1)	↓5
9	9	**Connecticut** (10-1)	↑3
10	10	**St. John's** (10-1)	↓1
11	—	**Kentucky** (10-2) Ⓓ	↑5
12	12	**Oklahoma** (11-2)	↑1
13	15	**Virginia** (9-2)	↑5
14	11	**Duke** (10-3)	↓6
15	13	**Georgetown** (9-2)	
16	17	**East Tennessee St.** (10-1)	↑1
17	16	**Pittsburgh** (12-3)	↓6
18	14	**Nebraska** (14-1)	↑1
19	23	**Southern Miss** (6-1)	↑2
20	19	**LSU** (8-3)	↓6
21	21	**South Carolina** (10-2)	↓1
22	20	**Iowa** (12-2)	
23	18	**New Mexico State** (9-1)	
24	22	**Georgia Tech** (9-3)	
25	—	**UTEP** (10-2)	⤴
—	24	**Michigan State** (8-4)	⤵
—	25	**Georgia** (8-4)	

WEEK OF JAN 15

AP	UPI	SCHOOL	AP↓↑
1	1	**UNLV** (11-0)	
2	2	**Arkansas** (15-1)	
3	4	**Indiana** (14-1)	
4	3	**Ohio State** (14-0)	
5	5	**North Carolina** (13-1)	
6	6	**Arizona** (13-2)	
7	7	**UCLA** (13-2)	
8	8	**Syracuse** (14-2)	
9	—	**Kentucky** (12-2)	↑2
10	10	**St. John's** (11-2)	
11	11	**Oklahoma** (13-2)	↑1
12	9	**Duke** (12-3)	↑2
13	12	**Connecticut** (12-2)	↓4
14	15	**Virginia** (10-3)	↓1
15	16	**East Tennessee St.** (12-2)	↑1
16	14	**Pittsburgh** (14-3)	↑1
17	13	**Nebraska** (16-1)	↑1
18	20	**Southern Miss** (8-1)	↑1
19	18	**Georgetown** (10-3)	↓4
20	17	**LSU** (10-3)	
21	19	**New Mexico State** (11-1)	↑2
22	22	**South Carolina** (13-3)	↓1
23	22	**Utah** (15-1)	⤴
24	—	**Iowa** (13-3)	↓2
25	21	**Seton Hall** (10-3)	⤴
—	24	**New Orleans** (13-2)	
—	25	**Wyoming** (13-2)	

WEEK OF JAN 22

AP	UPI	SCHOOL	AP↓↑
1	1	**UNLV** (13-0)	
2	2	**Arkansas** (17-1)	
3	3	**Indiana** (16-1)	
4	4	**Ohio State** (15-0)	
5	5	**Arizona** (15-2)	↑1
6	7	**Syracuse** (16-2)	↑2
7	8	**North Carolina** (13-2)	↓2
8	—	**Kentucky** (14-2)	↑1
9	6	**Duke** (15-3)	↑3
10	9	**St. John's** (13-2)	
11	10	**UCLA** (14-3)	↓4
12	13	**East Tenn. St.** (14-1)	↑3
13	11	**Oklahoma** (14-3)	↓2
14	12	**Nebraska** (16-2)	↑3
15	15	**Southern Miss** (10-1)	↑3
16	14	**LSU** (12-3)	↑4
17	16	**Pittsburgh** (14-4)	↓1
18	21	**Virginia** (11-4)	↓4
19	19	**Connecticut** (12-4)	↓6
20	17	**Utah** (17-1)	↑3
21	20	**Georgetown** (11-4)	↓2
22	18	**Michigan State** (12-4)	⤴
23	22	**New Mexico State** (12-2)	↓2
24	23	**New Orleans** (15-2)	⤴
25	—	**South Carolina** (13-4)	↓3
—	24	**Kansas** (11-4)	
—	25	**Georgia Tech** (10-5)	

WEEK OF JAN 29

AP	UPI	SCHOOL	AP↓↑
1	1	**UNLV** (15-0)	
2	2	**Arkansas** (20-1)	
3	3	**Ohio State** (17-0)	↑1
4	4	**Indiana** (18-2)	↓1
5	5	**St. John's** (15-2)	↑5
6	6	**Arizona** (16-3)	↓1
7	7	**Duke** (16-4)	↑2
8	8	**Syracuse** (17-3)	↓2
9	9	**North Carolina** (14-3)	↓2
10	10	**Kentucky** (15-3)	↓2
11	11	**Nebraska** (17-2)	↑3
12	13	**UCLA** (15-4)	↓1
13	15	**Utah** (19-1)	↑7
14	14	**LSU** (13-4)	↑2
15	18	**Virginia** (14-4)	↑3
16	12	**East Tennessee St.** (15-2)	↓4
17	16	**Southern Miss** (12-2)	↓2
18	20	**Georgetown** (12-5)	↑3
19	17	**Pittsburgh** (15-5)	↓2
20	19	**New Mexico St.** (15-2)	↑3
21	21	**Oklahoma** (14-5)	↓8
22	22	**New Orleans** (17-2)	↑2
23	25	**Georgia Tech** (12-5)	⤴
24	—	**Kansas** (13-4)	⤴
25	24	**Seton Hall** (13-4)	⤴
—	23	**Connecticut** (12-6)	⤵

WEEK OF FEB 5

AP	UPI	SCHOOL	AP↓↑
1	1	**UNLV** (18-0) Ⓔ	
2	2	**Arkansas** (22-1) Ⓔ	
3	3	**Ohio State** (18-1)	
4	4	**Indiana** (20-2)	
5	5	**Arizona** (18-3)	↑1
6	6	**Duke** (18-4)	↑1
7	8	**Syracuse** (19-3)	↑1
8	7	**St. John's** (16-3)	↓3
9	9	**North Carolina** (15-3)	
10	—	**Kentucky** (17-3)	
11	13	**Virginia** (16-4)	↑4
12	12	**Southern Miss** (14-2)	↑5
13	10	**East Tennessee St.** (18-2)	↑3
14	11	**UCLA** (16-5)	↓2
15	14	**Nebraska** (18-3)	↓4
16	16	**New Mexico State** (16-2)	↑4
17	15	**Utah** (20-2)	↓4
18	17	**Kansas** (15-4)	↑6
19	22	**LSU** (13-6)	↓5
20	19	**Georgetown** (13-6)	↓2
21	18	**New Orleans** (19-3)	↑1
22	20	**Oklahoma State** (15-4)	⤴
23	22	**Oklahoma** (15-6)	↓2
24	—	**Pittsburgh** (15-7)	↓5
25	—	**Michigan State** (13-6)	⤴
—	21	**Alabama** (13-6)	
—	24	**Texas** (14-5)	
—	25	**Mississippi State** (14-5)	

Poll Progression Continues →

Week of Feb 12

AP	UPI	School	AP↓↑
1	1	**UNLV** (20-0)	
2	2	**Ohio State** (19-1)	↑1
3	3	**Arkansas** (22-2)	↓1
4	4	**Indiana** (22-2)	
5	5	**Duke** (21-4)	↑1
6	6	**Arizona** (19-4)	↓1
7	7	**Syracuse** (20-3)	
8	8	**North Carolina** (17-4)	↑1
9	10	**Southern Miss** (17-2)	↑3
10	9	**East Tennessee St.** (21-2)	↑3
11	11	**Kansas** (17-4)	↑7
12	15	**New Mexico State** (17-2)	↑4
13	12	**St. John's** (16-5)	↓5
14	13	**Utah** (22-2)	↑3
15	14	**UCLA** (17-6)	↓1
16	—	**Kentucky** (17-5)	↓6
17	16	**Nebraska** (19-4)	↓2
18	17	**Georgetown** (15-6)	↑2
19	18	**Virginia** (17-7)	↓8
20	25	**LSU** (15-7)	↓1
21	19	**Oklahoma State** (16-5)	↑1
22	—	**Pittsburgh** (17-7)	↑2
23	—	**Mississippi State** (15-6)	⤴
24	21	**Texas** (16-5)	⤴
25	—	**Princeton** (16-2)	⤴
—	20	**Alabama** (15-6)	
—	22	**Michigan State** (13-6)	⤵
—	23	**Wake Forest** (16-7)	
—	24	**New Orleans** (19-5)	⤵

Week of Feb 19

AP	UPI	School	AP↓↑
1	1	**UNLV** (22-0)	
2	2	**Ohio State** (22-1)	
3	3	**Arkansas** (25-2)	
4	4	**Indiana** (22-3)	
5	5	**Syracuse** (22-3)	↑2
6	6	**North Carolina** (19-4)	↑2
7	7	**Duke** (22-5)	↓2
8	9	**Kansas** (19-4)	↑3
9	8	**Arizona** (20-5)	↓3
10	10	**Utah** (24-2)	↑4
11	11	**Southern Miss** (19-3)	↓2
12	—	**Kentucky** (19-5)	↑4
13	12	**East Tennessee St.** (23-3)	↓3
14	13	**Nebraska** (21-4)	↑3
15	14	**New Mexico State** (19-3)	↓3
16	15	**Oklahoma State** (18-5)	↑5
17	17	**UCLA** (18-7)	↓2
18	16	**St. John's** (17-6)	↓5
19	18	**LSU** (17-7)	↑1
20	19	**Virginia** (19-7)	↓1
21	21	**Mississippi State** (17-6)	↑2
22	—	**Pittsburgh** (18-8)	
23	20	**Princeton** (18-2)	↑2
24	24	**Seton Hall** (16-7)	⤴
25	22	**Georgetown** (15-8)	↓7
—	23	**Texas** (17-6)	⤵
—	23	**Alabama** (16-7)	
—	25	**NC State** (15-7)	

Week of Feb 26

AP	UPI	School	AP↓↑
1	1	**UNLV** (25-0)	
2	2	**Ohio State** (24-1)	
3	3	**Arkansas** (27-2)	
4	4	**North Carolina** (20-4)	↑2
5	7	**Indiana** (23-4)	↓1
6	6	**Syracuse** (24-4)	↓1
7	5	**Arizona** (22-5)	↑2
8	8	**Duke** (23-6)	↓1
9	10	**Utah** (25-2)	↑1
10	9	**Kansas** (20-5)	↓2
11	11	**New Mexico State** (21-3)	↑4
12	12	**Oklahoma State** (20-5)	↑4
13	—	**Kentucky** (20-6)	↓1
14	16	**Southern Miss** (20-4)	↓3
15	13	**Nebraska** (23-5)	↓1
16	15	**UCLA** (20-7)	↑1
17	14	**St. John's** (19-6)	↑1
18	17	**LSU** (19-7)	↑1
19	18	**East Tennessee St.** (24-4)	↓6
20	22	**Seton Hall** (18-7)	↑4
21	19	**Princeton** (20-2)	↑2
22	—	**Pittsburgh** (19-9)	
23	—	**Mississippi State** (18-7)	↓2
24	20	**Alabama** (17-8)	⤴
25	—	**Virginia** (19-9)	↓5
—	21	**Georgia Tech** (16-7)	
—	23	**Texas** (18-6)	
—	24	**NC State** (16-8)	
—	25	**Georgetown** (16-9)	⤵

Week of Mar 5

AP	UPI	School
1	1	**UNLV** (27-0)
2	2	**Ohio State** (25-1)
3	3	**Indiana** (25-4)
4	4	**Syracuse** (26-4)
5	6	**Arkansas** (28-3)
6	5	**Duke** (25-6)
7	8	**North Carolina** (22-5)
8	9	**Utah** (26-2)
9	7	**Arizona** (24-6)
10	—	**Kentucky** (22-6)
11	11	**New Mexico State** (23-4)
12	10	**Kansas** (21-6)
13	13	**Nebraska** (24-6)
14	14	**Oklahoma State** (21-6)
15	12	**East Tennessee St.** (28-4)
16	18	**LSU** (20-8)
17	15	**UCLA** (21-8)
18	16	**Mississippi State** (20-7)
19	22	**Princeton** (23-2)
20	17	**St. John's** (20-7)
21	23	**Seton Hall** (19-8)
22	19	**Southern Miss** (21-6)
23	25	**Texas** (20-7)
24	21	**Alabama** (18-9)
25	20	**DePaul** (18-8)
—	24	**Louisiana Tech** (21-9)

Final Poll

AP	UPI	School	AP↓↑
1	1	**UNLV** (30-0) Ⓕ	
2	2	**Arkansas** (31-3)	↑3
3	3	**Indiana** (27-4)	
4	4	**North Carolina** (25-5)	↑3
5	5	**Ohio State** (25-3) Ⓖ	↓3
6	6	**Duke** (26-7)	
7	8	**Syracuse** (26-5)	↓3
8	7	**Arizona** (26-6)	↑1
9	9	**Kentucky** (22-6)	↑1
10	10	**Utah** (28-3)	↓2
11	9	**Nebraska** (26-7)	↑2
12	12	**Kansas** (22-7)	
13	11	**Seton Hall** (22-8)	↑8
14	13	**Oklahoma State** (22-7)	
15	17	**New Mexico State** (23-5)	↓4
16	14	**UCLA** (23-8)	↑1
17	15	**East Tennessee St.** (28-4)	↓2
18	20	**Princeton** (24-2)	↑1
19	16	**Alabama** (21-9)	↑5
20	19	**St. John's** (20-8)	
21	18	**Mississippi State** (20-8)	↓3
22	21	**LSU** (20-9)	↓6
23	25	**Texas** (22-8)	
24	—	**DePaul** (20-8)	↑1
25	—	**Southern Miss** (21-7)	↓3
—	22	**Michigan State** (18-10)	
—	23	**Georgetown** (18-12)	
—	24	**NC State** (19-10)	

Ⓐ On Dec. 12 in Hartford, UConn sets the NCAA record for the biggest run to start a game against a Division I foe, jumping out to a 32-0 lead over New Hampshire en route to an 85-32 drubbing.

Ⓑ Duke ends Oklahoma's 51-game home court winning streak, 90-85. It's the Sooners' first nonconference loss since 1982.

Ⓒ Kevin Bradshaw of U.S. International sets a record for points against a Division I opponent with 72 against Loyola Marymount, but LMU sets a team scoring record and wins, 186-140. The combined point total falls five short of the mark set by the same two teams on Jan. 31, 1989. Bradshaw will go on to win the D1 scoring title with 37.6 ppg.

Ⓓ Jamal Mashburn scores 31 points, a Wildcats record for a freshman, as Kentucky rips Georgia, 96-84. UK is in its second year of NCAA probation and is ineligible for postseason play, but Rick Pitino will coach them to the best record in the SEC (14–4).

Ⓔ UNLV outguns Arkansas, 112-105, and the teams set a record for most total points scored in a No. 1 vs. No. 2 matchup. Stacey Augmon leads the Rebels with 32.

Ⓕ UNLV's 34–0 regular-season record is the best in NCAA history.

Ⓖ Iowa upsets Ohio State, 80-69, denying the Buckeyes an outright Big Ten championship. Indiana backs into a share of the title.

Pre-Tournament Ratings Percentage Index (RPI)

Rank	School	W-L	Sched. Strg.	SS Rank	RPI
1	**UNLV**	30-0	.5603	45	.6354
2	**Arkansas**	30-3	.5934	16	.6311
3	**North Carolina**	25-5	.5888	22	.6309
4	**Indiana**	27-4	.5620	44	.6216
5	**Nebraska**	26-7	.6045	9	.6215
6	**Arizona**	26-6	.5796	25	.6163
7	**Syracuse**	25-5	.5648	40	.6146
8	**Duke**	26-7	.5755	27	.6135
9	**Ohio State**	25-3	.5350	82	.6104
10	**Kentucky**	22-6	.5737	28	.6054
11	**Seton Hall**	21-8	.5910	19	.6052
12	**Kansas**	21-7	.5674	37	.5980
13	**Utah**	25-3	.5279	97	.5956
14	**UCLA**	22-8	.5684	34	.5930
15	**Michigan State**	18-10	.6049	8	.5914
16	**St. John's**	20-8	.5669	38	.5911
17	**Virginia**	21-11	.5970	12	.5909
18	**Oklahoma State**	22-7	.5462	59	.5898
19	**Pittsburgh**	18-11	.6170	5	.5864
20	**NC State**	19-10	.5926	17	.5853
21	**Georgetown**	14-12	.6528	1	.5844
22	**Illinois**	20-10	.5847	23	.5837
23	**Missouri**	19-10	.5649	39	.5836
24	**Georgia Tech**	16-12	.6109	7	.5799
25	**Alabama**	21-9	.5584	48	.5790
26	**Louisiana Tech**	21-9	.6042	10	.5773
27	**LSU**	19-9	.5621	43	.5766
28	**Southern Miss**	20-7	.5426	68	.5764
29	**Villanova**	16-14	.6160	6	.5756
30	**Texas**	22-8	.5391	73	.5743
31	**Wake Forest**	18-10	.5681	35	.5743
32	**Arizona State**	19-9	.5535	53	.5737
33	**Florida State**	20-10	.5647	41	.5730
34	**Purdue**	17-11	.5900	20	.5726
35	**BYU**	20-12	.5935	15	.5713
36	**Rutgers**	18-9	.5688	33	.5691
37	**Creighton**	23-7	.5252	102	.5687
38	**Wisconsin-Green Bay**	22-6	.5311	90	.5687
39	**Mississippi State**	20-8	.5227	107	.5670
40	**New Mexico State**	22-5	.4978	146	.5667
41	**Princeton**	23-2	.4882	163	.5665
42	**Saint Peter's**	24-6	.5094	126	.5657
43	**Temple**	21-9	.5317	89	.5656
44	**Oklahoma**	14-14	.6194	3	.5646
45	**Connecticut**	17-10	.5435	63	.5627
46	**Vanderbilt**	17-12	.5713	31	.5620
47	**East Tennessee State**	25-4	.4838	174	.5618
48	**Northern Illinois**	24-5	.4934	154	.5616
49	**Colorado**	15-13	.5890	21	.5604
50	**Iowa**	18-10	.5286	95	.5587

Source: Collegiate Basketball News

1991 NCAA Tournament

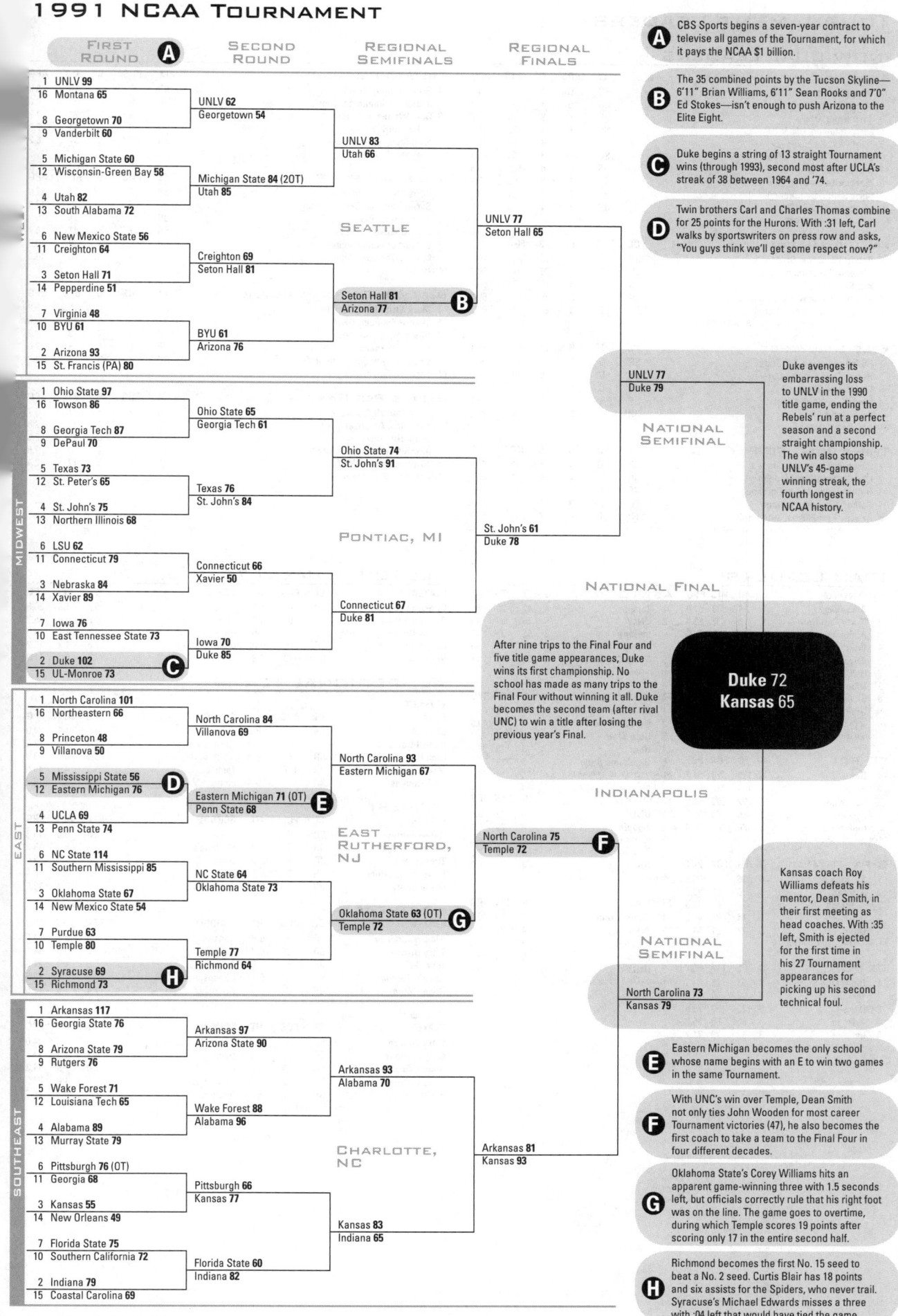

First Round (A) | Second Round | Regional Semifinals | Regional Finals

Seattle

First Round
- 1 UNLV **99**, 16 Montana **65**
- 8 Georgetown **70**, 9 Vanderbilt **60**
- 5 Michigan State **60**, 12 Wisconsin-Green Bay **58**
- 4 Utah **82**, 13 South Alabama **72**
- 6 New Mexico State **56**, 11 Creighton **64**
- 3 Seton Hall **71**, 14 Pepperdine **51**
- 7 Virginia **48**, 10 BYU **61**
- 2 Arizona **93**, 15 St. Francis (PA) **80**

Second Round
- UNLV **62**, Georgetown **54**
- Michigan State **84** (2OT), Utah **85**
- Creighton **69**, Seton Hall **81**
- BYU **61**, Arizona **76**

Regional Semifinals
- UNLV **83**, Utah **66**
- Seton Hall **81**, Arizona **77** (B)

Regional Final
- UNLV **77**, Seton Hall **65**

Midwest — Pontiac, MI

First Round
- 1 Ohio State **97**, 16 Towson **86**
- 8 Georgia Tech **87**, 9 DePaul **70**
- 5 Texas **73**, 12 St. Peter's **65**
- 4 St. John's **75**, 13 Northern Illinois **68**
- 6 LSU **62**, 11 Connecticut **79**
- 3 Nebraska **84**, 14 Xavier **89**
- 7 Iowa **76**, 10 East Tennessee State **73**
- 2 Duke **102**, 15 UL-Monroe **73** (C)

Second Round
- Ohio State **65**, Georgia Tech **61**
- Texas **76**, St. John's **84**
- Connecticut **66**, Xavier **50**
- Iowa **70**, Duke **85**

Regional Semifinals
- Ohio State **74**, St. John's **91**
- Connecticut **67**, Duke **81**

Regional Final
- St. John's **61**, Duke **78**

East — East Rutherford, NJ

First Round
- 1 North Carolina **101**, 16 Northeastern **66**
- 8 Princeton **48**, 9 Villanova **50**
- 5 Mississippi State **56**, 12 Eastern Michigan **76** (D)
- 4 UCLA **69**, 13 Penn State **74**
- 6 NC State **114**, 11 Southern Mississippi **85**
- 3 Oklahoma State **67**, 14 New Mexico State **54**
- 7 Purdue **63**, 10 Temple **80**
- 2 Syracuse **69**, 15 Richmond **73** (H)

Second Round
- North Carolina **84**, Villanova **69**
- Eastern Michigan **71** (OT), Penn State **68** (E)
- NC State **64**, Oklahoma State **73**
- Temple **77**, Richmond **64**

Regional Semifinals
- North Carolina **93**, Eastern Michigan **67**
- Oklahoma State **63** (OT), Temple **72** (G)

Regional Final
- North Carolina **75**, Temple **72** (F)

Southeast — Charlotte, NC

First Round
- 1 Arkansas **117**, 16 Georgia State **76**
- 8 Arizona State **79**, 9 Rutgers **76**
- 5 Wake Forest **71**, 12 Louisiana Tech **65**
- 4 Alabama **89**, 13 Murray State **79**
- 6 Pittsburgh **76** (OT), 11 Georgia **68**
- 3 Kansas **55**, 14 New Orleans **49**
- 7 Florida State **75**, 10 Southern California **72**
- 2 Indiana **79**, 15 Coastal Carolina **69**

Second Round
- Arkansas **97**, Arizona State **90**
- Wake Forest **88**, Alabama **96**
- Pittsburgh **66**, Kansas **77**
- Florida State **60**, Indiana **82**

Regional Semifinals
- Arkansas **93**, Alabama **70**
- Kansas **83**, Indiana **65**

Regional Final
- Arkansas **81**, Kansas **93**

Indianapolis

National Semifinal
- UNLV **77**, Duke **79**

Duke avenges its embarrassing loss to UNLV in the 1990 title game, ending the Rebels' run at a perfect season and a second straight championship. The win also stops UNLV's 45-game winning streak, the fourth longest in NCAA history.

National Semifinal
- North Carolina **73**, Kansas **79**

Kansas coach Roy Williams defeats his mentor, Dean Smith, in their first meeting as head coaches. With :35 left, Smith is ejected for the first time in his 27 Tournament appearances for picking up his second technical foul.

National Final

Duke 72
Kansas 65

After nine trips to the Final Four and five title game appearances, Duke wins its first championship. No school has made as many trips to the Final Four without winning it all. Duke becomes the second team (after rival UNC) to win a title after losing the previous year's Final.

A CBS Sports begins a seven-year contract to televise all games of the Tournament, for which it pays the NCAA $1 billion.

B The 35 combined points by the Tucson Skyline—6'11" Brian Williams, 6'11" Sean Rooks and 7'0" Ed Stokes—isn't enough to push Arizona to the Elite Eight.

C Duke begins a string of 13 straight Tournament wins (through 1993), second most after UCLA's streak of 38 between 1964 and '74.

D Twin brothers Carl and Charles Thomas combine for 25 points for the Hurons. With :31 left, Carl walks by sportswriters on press row and asks, "You guys think we'll get some respect now?"

E Eastern Michigan becomes the only school whose name begins with an E to win two games in the same Tournament.

F With UNC's win over Temple, Dean Smith not only ties John Wooden for most career Tournament victories (47), he also becomes the first coach to take a team to the Final Four in four different decades.

G Oklahoma State's Corey Williams hits an apparent game-winning three with 1.5 seconds left, but officials correctly rule that his right foot was on the line. The game goes to overtime, during which Temple scores 19 points after scoring only 17 in the entire second half.

H Richmond becomes the first No. 15 seed to beat a No. 2 seed. Curtis Blair has 18 points and six assists for the Spiders, who never trail. Syracuse's Michael Edwards misses a three with :04 left that would have tied the game.

⊗Team participation later vacated

Tournament Leaders

Individual Leaders

Scoring

	CL	POS	G	PTS	PPG
1 **Terry Dehere**, Seton Hall	SO	G	4	97	24.3
2 **Mark Macon**, Temple	SR	G	4	96	24.0
3 **Josh Grant**, Utah	JR	F	3	68	22.7
4 **Larry Johnson**, UNLV	SR	F	5	109	21.8
5 **Todd Day**, Arkansas	JR	F	4	86	21.5
6 **Calbert Cheaney**, Indiana	SO	G/F	3	64	21.3
7 **Christian Laettner**, Duke	JR	C	6	125	20.8
8 **Marcus Kennedy**, Eastern Michigan	SR	F	3	62	20.7
9 **Chris Smith**, Connecticut	JR	G	3	61	20.3
10 **Malik Sealy**, St. John's	JR	F	4	79	19.8

Minimum: 3 games

Field Goal Pct

	CL	POS	G	FG	FGA	PCT
1 **Robert Werdann**, St. John's	JR	C	4	20	26	76.9
2 **Oliver Miller**, Arkansas	JR	C	4	29	41	70.7
3 **Bill Singleton**, St. John's	SR	F	4	18	27	66.7
4 **Marcus Kennedy**, Eastern Michigan	SR	F	3	25	40	62.5
5 **George Lynch**, North Carolina	SO	F	5	28	45	62.2

Minimum: 15 made and 3 games

Free Throw Pct

	CL	POS	G	FT	FTA	PCT
1 **Rodney Monroe**, NC State	SR	G	2	17	17	100.0
2 **Hubert Davis**, North Carolina	JR	G	5	19	20	95.0
3 **Christian Laettner**, Duke	JR	C	6	49	54	90.7
4 **King Rice**, North Carolina	SR	G	5	15	17	88.2
Josh Grant, Utah	JR	F	3	15	17	88.2

Minimum: 15 made

Three-Point FG Pct

	CL	POS	G	3FG	3FGA	PCT
1 **Jason Buchanan**, St. John's	JR	G	4	8	13	61.5
2 **Chucky Sproling**, St. John's	JR	G	4	6	10	60.0
3 **Hubert Davis**, North Carolina	JR	G	5	13	23	56.5
4 **Calbert Cheaney**, Indiana	SO	G/F	3	6	11	54.5
5 **Arturas Karnisovas**, Seton Hall	FR	F	4	7	13	53.8

Minimum: 6 made and 3 games

Assists Per Game

	CL	POS	G	AST	APG
1 **Greg Anthony**, UNLV	SR	G	5	40	8.0
Jason Buchanan, St. John's	JR	G	4	32	8.0
3 **Gary Waites**, Alabama	JR	G	3	23	7.7
4 **Bobby Hurley**, Duke	SO	G	6	43	7.2
5 **King Rice**, North Carolina	SR	G	5	31	6.2

Minimum: 3 games

Rebounds Per Game

	CL	POS	G	REB	RPG
1 **Perry Carter**, Ohio State	SR	C	3	36	12.0
Byron Houston, Oklahoma State	JR	F	3	36	12.0
3 **Josh Grant**, Utah	JR	F	3	31	10.3
4 **Larry Johnson**, UNLV	SR	F	5	51	10.2
5 **Calbert Cheaney**, Indiana	SO	G	3	30	10.0
Melvin Cheatum, Alabama	JR	F	3	30	10.0

Minimum: 3 games

Blocked Shots Per Game

	CL	POS	G	BLK	BPG
1 **Mark Strickland**, Temple	JR	F	4	15	3.8
2 **Elmore Spencer**, UNLV	JR	C	5	15	3.0
3 **Oliver Miller**, Arkansas	JR	C	4	9	2.3
4 **Robert Werdann**, St. John's	JR	C	4	8	2.0
Scott Burrell, Connecticut	SO	F	3	6	2.0

Minimum: 3 games

Steals Per Game

	CL	POS	G	STL	SPG
1 **Scott Burrell**, Connecticut	SO	F	3	11	3.7
2 **Todd Day**, Arkansas	JR	F	4	11	2.8
3 **Grant Hill**, Duke	FR	G/F	6	15	2.5
Jason Buchanan, St. John's	JR	G	4	10	2.5
5 **Larry Johnson**, UNLV	SR	F	5	12	2.4

Minimum: 3 games

Team Leaders

Scoring

		G	PTS	PPG
1	**Arkansas**	4	388	97.0
2	**North Carolina**	5	432	86.4
3	**Alabama**	3	255	85.0
4	**Duke**	6	497	82.8
5	**Arizona**	3	246	82.0
6	**UNLV**	5	398	79.6
7	**Ohio State**	3	236	78.7
8	**St. John's**	4	311	77.8
9	**Utah**	3	233	77.7
10	**Indiana**	3	226	75.3

Minimum: 3 games

FG Pct

		G	FG	FGA	PCT
1	**Duke**	6	175	320	54.7
2	**St. John's**	4	114	212	53.8
3	**Alabama**	3	102	200	51.0
4	**Arizona**	3	85	168	50.6
5	**Indiana**	3	80	160	50.0

Minimum: 3 games

3-Pt FG Pct

		G	3FG	3FGA	PCT
1	**St. John's**	4	16	27	59.3
2	**Arizona**	3	16	35	45.7
3	**Alabama**	3	20	44	45.5
4	**Indiana**	3	14	31	45.2
5	**Duke**	6	27	61	44.3

Minimum: 3 games

FT Pct

		G	FT	FTA	PCT
1	**Oklahoma State**	3	53	65	81.5
2	**Temple**	4	65	86	75.6
3	**Duke**	6	120	159	75.5
4	**Arizona**	3	60	80	75.0
5	**Indiana**	3	52	73	71.2

Minimum: 3 games

Ast/TO Ratio

		G	AST	TO	RAT
1	**Temple**	4	42	28	1.50
2	**UNLV**	5	76	53	1.43
	Indiana	3	53	37	1.43
	Arizona	3	50	35	1.43
5	**North Carolina**	5	99	70	1.41

Minimum: 3 games

Rebounds

		G	REB	RPG
1	**Arkansas**	4	178	44.5
2	**North Carolina**	5	204	40.8
3	**Ohio State**	3	122	40.7
4	**Utah**	3	116	38.7
5	**Oklahoma State**	3	115	38.3

Minimum: 3 games

Blocks

		G	BLK	BPG
1	**UNLV**	5	32	6.4
2	**Temple**	4	23	5.8
3	**North Carolina**	5	28	5.6
4	**Arizona**	3	16	5.3
	Arkansas	4	21	5.3

Minimum: 3 games

Steals

		G	STL	SPG
1	**Connecticut**	3	30	10.0
2	**Arkansas**	4	37	9.3
	Seton Hall	4	37	9.3
4	**Duke**	6	55	9.2
5	**UNLV**	5	45	9.0

Minimum: 3 games

All-Tournament Team

PLAYER	CL	POS	HT	SCHOOL	RPG	APG	PPG
Christian Laettner*	JR	C	6-11	Duke	5.7	1.8	20.8
Anderson Hunt	JR	G	6-2	UNLV	2.6	0.8	15.2
Bobby Hurley	SO	G	6-0	Duke	2.7	7.2	10.8
Billy McCaffrey	SO	G	6-3	Duke	1.8	1.2	10.2
Mark Randall	SR	F/C	6-8	Kansas	7.3	3.5	11.3

All-Regional Teams

East

PLAYER	CL	POS	HT	SCHOOL	RPG	APG	PPG
Mark Macon*	SR	G	6-5	Temple	4.5	1.8	24.0
Hubert Davis	JR	G	6-4	North Carolina	2.8	3.0	17.8
Rick Fox	SR	F	6-8	North Carolina	5.3	4.0	13.8
Mik Kilgore	JR	G/F	6-7	Temple	5.3	4.0	19.5
Carl Thomas	SR	F	6-4	Eastern Michigan	5.0	2.7	16.7

Midwest

PLAYER	CL	POS	HT	SCHOOL	RPG	APG	PPG
Bobby Hurley*	SO	G	6-0	Duke	3.3	6.8	10.3
Jason Buchanan	JR	G	6-2	St. John's	3.3	8.0	15.8
Thomas Hill	SO	F	6-8	Duke	2.8	1.8	13.0
Christian Laettner	JR	C	6-11	Duke	4.3	2.3	19.8
Malik Sealy	JR	F	6-7	St. John's	7.8	2.3	19.8

Southeast

PLAYER	CL	POS	HT	SCHOOL	RPG	APG	PPG
Alonzo Jamison*	JR	F	6-6	Kansas	7.5	3.3	14.5
Terry Brown	SR	G	6-2	Kansas	3.5	0.8	14.5
Todd Day	JR	F	6-6	Arkansas	5.8	1.3	21.5
Adonis Jordan	SO	G	5-11	Kansas	3.8	2.8	12.5
Oliver Miller	JR	C	6-9	Arkansas	7.8	1.5	17.5

West

PLAYER	CL	POS	HT	SCHOOL	RPG	APG	PPG
Larry Johnson*	SR	F	6-7	UNLV	9.5	2.3	24.0
Greg Anthony	SR	G	6-2	UNLV	3.3	8.5	11.8
Stacey Augmon	SR	G/F	6-8	UNLV	6.0	2.5	14.3
Terry Dehere	SO	G	6-4	Seton Hall	4.0	1.0	24.3
Brian Williams	JR	F	6-11	Arizona	9.0	0.3	16.3

* Most outstanding player

1991 NCAA TOURNAMENT BOX SCORES

UNLV 83-66 Utah (SWEET 16)

	1H	2H
UNLV	41	42
Utah	35	31

UNLV	MIN	FG	3FG	FT	REB	A	ST	BL	PF	TP
Larry Johnson	33	10-13	0-1	3-4	13	1	4	1	2	23
Stacey Augmon	31	6-9	2-3	1-1	3	3	3	0	4	15
Elmore Spencer	26	6-14	0-0	3-9	5	0	0	2	1	15
Anderson Hunt	33	4-9	3-7	1-2	2	0	0	0	1	12
George Ackles	21	6-8	0-0	0-0	3	0	0	2	1	12
Greg Anthony	34	2-6	0-0	2-4	3	10	1	0	2	6
Evric Gray	11	0-2	0-1	0-0	1	1	1	0	1	0
Travis Bice	6	0-0	0-0	0-0	0	0	0	0	0	0
H Waldman	5	0-0	0-0	0-0	2	0	0	0	1	0
TOTALS	200	34-61	5-12	10-20	32	15	9	5	13	83
Percentages		55.7	41.7	50.0						

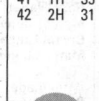

Coach: Jerry Tarkanian

UTAH	MIN	FG	3FG	FT	REB	A	ST	BL	PF	TP
Josh Grant	32	7-12	1-3	2-2	10	3	1	1	3	17
Jimmy Soto	25	4-5	3-3	1-1	3	1	0	0	3	12
Walter Watts	22	4-6	0-0	3-3	5	0	0	1	2	11
Byron Wilson	23	3-11	1-3	2-3	3	2	0	0	2	9
Tyrone Tate	27	2-4	0-0	3-3	1	7	0	0	1	7
Craig Rydalch	16	1-6	0-3	1-1	0	0	0	0	1	3
Phil Dixon	15	1-7	1-4	0-0	1	1	1	0	1	3
Paul Afeaki	16	1-2	0-0	0-0	3	0	0	1	2	2
M'Kay McGrath	14	1-1	0-0	0-0	3	0	0	0	4	2
Larry Cain	2	0-1	0-0	0-0	2	0	1	0	1	0
Barry Howard	2	0-0	0-0	0-0	1	0	0	0	0	0
Ralph McKinney	2	0-1	0-0	0-0	0	0	0	0	0	0
Sean Mooney	2	0-1	0-0	0-0	1	0	0	0	0	0
Anthony Williams	2	0-2	0-0	0-0	0	0	0	0	0	0
TOTALS	200	24-59	6-16	12-13	33	14	3	3	20	66
Percentages		40.7	37.5	92.3						

Coach: Rick Majerus

Officials: Larry Lembo, Eric Harmon, Phil Bova
Technicals: None
Attendance: 22,628

Seton Hall 81-77 Arizona (SWEET 16)

	1H	2H
Seton Hall	37	44
Arizona	37	40

SETON HALL	MIN	FG	3FG	FT	REB	A	ST	BL	PF	TP
Terry Dehere	39	8-14	2-8	10-11	6	1	1	0	1	28
Anthony Avent	31	6-13	0-0	3-6	4	1	0	1	3	15
Gordon Winchester	31	5-8	0-0	1-2	6	0	2	0	3	11
Arturas Karnisovas	19	4-8	3-4	0-0	4	0	0	0	4	11
Oliver Taylor	16	1-5	0-1	4-4	1	2	0	0	1	6
Jerry Walker	31	2-4	0-0	1-2	4	0	3	0	4	5
Bryan Caver	25	2-4	0-0	1-2	3	6	2	1	2	5
Assaf Barnea	7	0-0	0-0	0-0	0	1	0	0	1	0
Chris Davis	1	0-0	0-0	0-0	0	0	0	0	0	0
TOTALS	200	28-56	5-13	20-27	28	11	8	2	19	81
Percentages		50.0	38.5	74.1						

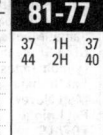

Coach: P.J. Carlesimo

ARIZONA	MIN	FG	3FG	FT	REB	A	ST	BL	PF	TP
Brian Williams	33	8-14	0-0	5-5	10	0	0	1	1	21
Chris Mills	31	9-12	2-3	0-0	5	2	1	0	2	20
Sean Rooks	27	5-13	0-0	2-2	5	2	1	1	1	12
Matt Othick	31	4-9	2-6	1-2	0	3	0	0	3	11
Matt Muehlebach	32	1-3	1-1	1-2	0	5	1	0	5	4
Khalid Reeves	17	1-5	1-3	1-2	2	1	0	0	4	4
Wayne Womack	12	1-1	0-0	1-3	4	1	0	1	0	3
Ed Stokes	17	1-4	0-0	0-0	4	1	3	1	4	2
TOTALS	200	30-61	6-13	11-16	30	15	6	4	20	77
Percentages		49.2	46.2	68.8						

Coach: Lute Olson

Officials: Gerry Donaghy, Ted Hillary, Andre Pattillo
Technicals: None
Attendance: 22,628

St. John's 91-74 Ohio State (SWEET 16)

	1H	2H
St. John's	43	48
Ohio State	24	50

ST. JOHN'S	MIN	FG	3FG	FT	REB	A	ST	BL	PF	TP
Malik Sealy	32	10-17	0-0	2-2	5	2	1	0	4	22
Robert Werdann	33	8-9	0-0	5-7	6	1	1	4	3	21
Chucky Sproling	40	6-10	2-4	1-2	4	3	4	0	3	15
Jason Buchanan	38	4-7	1-1	5-6	4	9	6	0	1	14
Bill Singleton	35	4-7	0-0	6-7	8	5	1	0	2	14
David Cain	9	1-2	0-0	1-2	0	2	1	0	0	3
Shawnelle Scott	10	1-1	0-0	0-0	0	0	0	0	0	2
Sean Muto	3	0-1	0-0	0-0	0	0	0	0	0	0
TOTALS	200	34-54	3-5	20-26	27	22	14	4	13	91
Percentages		63.0	60.0	76.9						

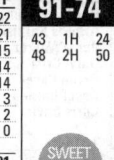

Coach: Lou Carnesecca

OHIO STATE	MIN	FG	3FG	FT	REB	A	ST	BL	PF	TP
Jim Jackson	32	7-15	0-2	5-8	4	5	1	2	1	19
Jamaal Brown	32	6-8	1-1	1-2	3	5	3	0	0	14
Mark Baker	32	5-10	0-1	3-4	0	4	1	1	3	13
Perry Carter	20	4-7	0-0	1-3	7	0	1	1	4	9
Jamie Skelton	9	4-5	1-1	0-0	2	1	2	0	1	9
Treg Lee	24	3-8	0-0	0-0	4	0	1	0	3	6
Chris Jent	27	1-6	1-5	0-0	4	2	0	0	4	3
Alex Davis	10	0-2	0-1	1-2	1	1	0	0	1	1
Bill Robinson	14	0-1	0-0	0-0	2	0	0	1	2	0
TOTALS	200	30-62	3-11	11-19	27	18	9	5	19	74
Percentages		48.4	27.3	57.9						

Coach: Randy Ayers

Officials: James Burr, Ron Zetcher, Gary Marcum
Technicals: None
Attendance: 30,461

Duke 81-67 Connecticut (SWEET 16)

	1H	2H
Duke	44	37
Connecticut	27	40

DUKE	MIN	FG	3FG	FT	REB	A	ST	BL	PF	TP
Christian Laettner	29	7-13	0-1	5-7	4	1	0	3	2	19
Greg Koubek	30	6-10	3-5	3-4	5	2	0	0	2	18
Thomas Hill	22	4-5	2-2	3-3	1	1	2	1	4	13
Bobby Hurley	38	3-7	2-4	4-5	2	7	1	0	0	12
Billy McCaffrey	26	3-5	0-0	1-2	4	2	0	0	0	7
Brian Davis	23	0-1	0-0	5-6	5	1	1	0	3	5
Grant Hill	16	0-2	0-0	3-4	5	2	1	1	4	3
Crawford Palmer	9	1-1	0-0	0-0	1	0	0	0	1	2
Marty Clark	2	1-1	0-0	0-0	1	0	0	0	1	2
Antonio Lang	4	0-0	0-0	0-0	0	0	0	0	2	0
Clay Buckley	1	0-0	0-0	0-2	0	0	0	0	0	0
TOTALS	200	25-45	7-12	24-33	28	16	5	5	19	81
Percentages		55.6	58.3	72.7						

Coach: Mike Krzyzewski

CONNECTICUT	MIN	FG	3FG	FT	REB	A	ST	BL	PF	TP
Chris Smith	40	5-18	3-9	3-4	1	3	1	0	2	16
John Gwynn	28	6-13	4-6	0-0	3	4	1	0	3	16
Scott Burrell	32	4-10	1-3	2-5	3	2	3	0	5	11
Dan Cyrulik	15	3-5	0-1	1-3	5	1	0	0	2	7
Rod Sellers	27	2-5	0-0	2-2	7	2	1	1	5	6
Toraino Walker	10	2-3	0-0	1-2	2	0	0	0	4	5
Steve Pikiell	15	1-3	1-1	0-0	3	2	0	0	3	3
Marc Suhr	2	1-2	0-0	0-0	2	0	0	0	0	2
Oliver Macklin	1	0-0	0-0	1-2	1	0	0	0	0	1
Lyman Depriest	30	0-1	0-0	0-0	0	0	1	0	2	0
TOTALS	200	24-60	9-20	10-18	27	14	7	1	26	67
Percentages		40.0	45.0	55.6						

Coach: Jim Calhoun

Officials: Jim Bain, Tom O'Neill, David Hall
Technicals: Connecticut (Sellers)
Attendance: 30,461

North Carolina 93-67 Eastern Michigan (SWEET 16)

	1H	2H
North Carolina	47	46
Eastern Michigan	42	25

NORTH CAROLINA	MIN	FG	3FG	FT	REB	A	ST	BL	PF	TP
Hubert Davis	29	5-6	5-5	3-3	4	1	1	0	1	18
Pete Chilcutt	24	8-9	0-0	2-2	5	2	2	0	0	18
Eric Montross	18	5-7	0-0	7-8	6	0	0	3	3	17
King Rice	25	4-6	1-2	3-3	3	6	1	0	2	12
George Lynch	30	5-11	0-0	0-1	7	0	0	1	3	10
Rick Fox	24	3-10	0-2	0-0	6	0	3	2	4	6
Derrick Phelps	13	2-2	0-0	0-0	0	4	1	0	1	4
Brian Reese	12	1-4	0-0	1-2	0	0	0	0	0	3
Henrik Rodl	9	1-2	0-0	0-0	0	1	1	0	0	2
Kevin Salvadori	2	1-3	0-0	0-0	2	0	0	1	0	2
Matt Wenstrom	2	0-2	0-0	1-2	3	0	0	0	0	1
Clifford Rozier	4	0-2	0-0	0-0	0	1	0	1	0	0
Pat Sullivan	4	0-0	0-0	0-2	1	1	0	0	0	0
Scott Cherry	2	0-1	0-0	0-0	1	0	0	0	0	0
Kenny Harris	2	0-1	0-0	0-0	0	0	0	0	0	0
TOTALS	200	35-66	6-9	17-23	38	16	9	8	14	93
Percentages		53.0	66.7	73.9						

Coach: Dean Smith

EASTERN MICHIGAN	MIN	FG	3FG	FT	REB	A	ST	BL	PF	TP
Carl Thomas	33	10-16	5-10	2-2	5	2	1	2	3	27
Marcus Kennedy	37	8-14	0-0	3-6	6	1	1	3	4	19
Kory Hallas	31	4-9	0-0	1-2	2	2	1	0	3	9
Charles Thomas	37	3-11	2-9	0-0	5	6	3	1	2	8
Mike Boykin	7	1-2	0-0	0-0	3	0	0	0	0	2
Joe Frasor	1	1-1	0-0	0-0	1	0	0	0	0	2
Lorenzo Neely	33	0-4	0-0	0-0	4	5	1	0	0	0
Roger Lewis	10	0-1	0-1	0-0	0	1	0	0	3	0
Kahlil Felder	7	0-0	0-0	0-0	0	1	0	0	0	0
Fenorris Pearson	2	0-1	0-0	0-0	0	0	0	0	0	0
Von Nickleberry	1	0-2	0-0	0-0	0	0	0	0	1	0
Pete Pangas	1	0-0	0-0	0-0	0	0	0	0	0	0
TOTALS	200	27-61	7-20	6-10	26	18	7	6	16	67
Percentages		44.3	35.0	60.0						

Coach: Ben Braun

Officials: Bob Dibler, David Bair, Harrell Allen
Technicals: None
Attendance: 19,544

Temple 72-63 Oklahoma State (SWEET 16)

	1H	2H	OT1
Temple	36	17	19
Oklahoma State	30	23	10

TEMPLE	MIN	FG	3FG	FT	REB	A	ST	BL	PF	TP
Mark Macon	44	11-21	1-2	3-3	3	0	3	0	5	26
Mik Kilgore	45	6-12	0-3	5-6	5	4	0	0	1	17
Donald Hodge	41	3-5	0-0	6-8	5	2	0	0	2	12
Vic Carstarphen	40	2-7	1-4	2-2	2	3	3	1	2	7
Mark Strickland	45	3-5	0-0	0-2	6	0	1	8	4	6
Michael Harden	6	0-1	0-0	2-4	0	0	1	0	0	2
James Spears	4	1-1	0-0	0-0	2	0	0	0	0	2
TOTALS	225	26-52	2-9	18-25	23	9	8	9	14	72
Percentages		50.0	22.2	72.0						

Coach: John Chaney

OKLAHOMA STATE	MIN	FG	3FG	FT	REB	A	ST	BL	PF	TP
Corey Williams	33	7-12	3-6	0-0	2	3	0	0	2	17
Byron Houston	44	6-18	1-2	1-2	7	2	1	1	4	14
John Potter	26	4-6	2-3	2-2	4	1	0	0	5	12
Sean Sutton	35	2-11	2-9	0-0	4	5	1	0	0	6
Mattias Sahlstrom	17	3-3	0-0	0-1	4	1	0	0	3	6
Cornell Hatcher	18	1-4	0-0	1-2	4	1	0	0	1	3
Dennis Burbank	1	1-1	1-1	0-0	0	0	0	0	0	3
Johnny Pittman	28	1-5	0-0	0-0	9	0	1	2	4	2
Darwyn Alexander	20	0-1	0-1	0-0	1	2	0	0	0	0
Milton Brown	1	0-0	0-0	0-0	0	0	0	0	0	0
Earl Jones	1	0-0	0-0	0-0	0	0	0	0	0	0
Mike Philpott	1	0-0	0-0	0-0	0	0	0	0	0	0
TOTALS	225	25-61	9-22	4-7	35	15	3	3	19	63
Percentages		41.0	40.9	57.1						

Coach: Eddie Sutton

Officials: Jody Silvester, Ted Valentine, Bob Garibaldi
Technicals: None
Attendance: 19,544

93-70

	1H	2H
Arkansas	40	53
Alabama	37	33

SWEET 16

ARKANSAS	MIN	FG	3FG	FT	REB	A	ST	BL	PF	TP
Todd Day	36	14-24	2-5	1-1	7	1	2	0	1	31
Lee Mayberry	32	6-12	3-7	1-2	3	4	4	0	1	16
Oliver Miller	19	7-9	0-0	1-2	7	0	1	2	2	15
Ron Huery	24	4-8	1-1	0-0	2	2	2	0	1	9
Arlyn Bowers	26	1-8	1-4	4-4	0	6	1	0	3	7
Clyde Fletcher	13	3-5	0-0	0-0	6	0	0	0	0	6
Roosevelt Wallace	13	2-9	1-1	0-0	8	1	0	0	1	5
Isaiah Morris	21	2-7	0-0	0-0	7	0	0	0	1	4
Ernie Murry	16	0-3	0-2	0-0	4	3	0	0	0	0
TOTALS	**200**	**39-85**	**8-20**	**7-9**	**44**	**17**	**10**	**2**	**10**	**93**
Percentages		45.9	40.0	77.8						

Coach: Nolan Richardson

ALABAMA	MIN	FG	3FG	FT	REB	A	ST	BL	PF	TP
James Robinson	34	7-15	3-5	4-6	2	0	0	1	1	21
Robert Horry	37	7-15	1-3	3-4	11	1	1	3	2	18
Melvin Cheatum	38	6-11	0-0	1-2	12	0	3	0	1	13
Latrell Sprewell	34	5-11	0-0	0-0	4	4	0	2	3	10
Marcus Webb	9	2-4	0-0	0-1	2	0	0	0	3	4
Gary Waites	35	1-4	0-1	0-0	3	4	1	0	2	2
Marcus Jones	7	1-1	0-0	0-0	0	2	0	0	2	2
Bryant Lancaster	5	0-1	0-1	0-0	1	1	0	0	0	0
Marcus Campbell	1	0-0	0-0	0-0	1	1	0	0	0	0
TOTALS	**200**	**29-62**	**4-10**	**8-13**	**36**	**13**	**5**	**6**	**14**	**70**
Percentages		46.8	40.0	61.5						

Coach: Wimp Sanderson

Officials: Dic Paparo, Art McDonald, La Rose
Technicals: Arkansas (bench)
Attendance: 23,287

83-65

	1H	2H
Kansas	49	34
Indiana	27	38

SWEET 16

KANSAS	MIN	FG	3FG	FT	REB	A	ST	BL	PF	TP
Terry Brown	25	7-16	4-9	5-6	6	1	1	0	1	23
Sean Tunstall	25	4-9	2-4	5-6	3	1	1	1	0	15
Alonzo Jamison	26	7-10	0-0	0-0	10	3	1	0	2	14
Adonis Jordan	35	3-10	2-5	3-4	2	1	2	0	3	11
Mark Randall	29	4-9	0-0	0-3	6	6	2	0	4	8
Richard Scott	15	4-9	0-0	0-2	3	0	0	0	2	8
Mike Maddox	24	2-4	0-1	0-1	2	5	0	0	3	4
Steve Woodberry	11	0-0	0-0	0-0	2	1	0	0	1	0
Patrick Richey	5	0-1	0-1	0-0	0	0	0	0	1	0
Kirk Wagner	5	0-0	0-0	0-0	1	0	0	0	0	0
TOTALS	**200**	**31-68**	**8-20**	**13-22**	**35**	**18**	**7**	**1**	**17**	**83**
Percentages		45.6	40.0	59.1						

Coach: Roy Williams

INDIANA	MIN	FG	3FG	FT	REB	A	ST	BL	PF	TP
Calbert Cheaney	36	8-14	3-6	4-5	6	1	1	1	4	23
Damon Bailey	31	8-14	2-5	2-4	5	2	1	3	5	20
Chris Reynolds	26	3-3	0-0	5-5	5	1	2	0	2	11
Eric Anderson	36	3-8	0-0	0-0	4	0	0	1	4	6
Jamal Meeks	33	1-2	0-0	0-0	1	4	0	0	1	2
Greg Graham	10	1-4	0-1	0-1	1	1	0	0	1	2
Lyndon Jones	8	0-1	0-0	1-2	2	0	0	0	1	1
Pat Graham	7	0-2	0-0	0-0	1	1	0	0	0	0
Matt Nover	7	0-4	0-0	0-0	3	0	0	1	0	0
Pat Knight	6	0-1	0-0	0-0	1	1	0	0	1	0
TOTALS	**200**	**24-53**	**5-12**	**12-17**	**29**	**11**	**4**	**6**	**19**	**65**
Percentages		45.3	41.7	70.6						

Coach: Bob Knight

Officials: John Clougherty, Ma Chauvin, Frank Scagliotta
Technicals: None
Attendance: 23,287

77-65

	1H	2H
UNLV	39	38
Seton Hall	36	29

ELITE 8

UNLV	MIN	FG	3FG	FT	REB	A	ST	BL	PF	TP
Larry Johnson	37	13-19	2-3	2-4	6	0	3	0	3	30
Anderson Hunt	37	5-16	3-11	0-1	3	1	1	0	1	13
Stacey Augmon	36	6-10	1-1	0-1	5	4	4	2	3	13
Greg Anthony	35	3-8	0-1	0-0	5	11	5	0	3	6
George Ackles	30	3-6	0-0	0-0	5	0	1	3	3	6
Evric Gray	7	1-2	0-0	2-2	4	0	0	0	2	4
Elmore Spencer	10	0-1	0-0	3-4	1	1	0	1	0	3
H Waldman	2	0-0	0-0	2-2	0	0	0	0	0	2
Travis Bice	4	0-1	0-0	0-0	1	0	0	0	0	0
Melvin Love	1	0-0	0-0	0-0	0	0	0	0	0	0
Dave Rice	1	0-0	0-0	0-0	0	0	0	0	0	0
TOTALS	**200**	**31-63**	**6-16**	**9-14**	**30**	**17**	**14**	**6**	**15**	**77**
Percentages		49.2	37.5	64.3						

Coach: Jerry Tarkanian

SETON HALL	MIN	FG	3FG	FT	REB	A	ST	BL	PF	TP
Terry Dehere	36	5-15	2-5	3-3	3	1	2	2	1	15
Anthony Avent	35	5-10	0-0	3-4	8	2	0	2	3	13
Oliver Taylor	26	3-11	1-4	2-2	4	2	0	0	3	9
Gordon Winchester	30	3-6	0-0	2-3	8	2	0	0	2	8
Arturas Karnisovas	26	2-6	2-3	2-2	4	1	0	0	4	8
Jerry Walker	25	3-4	0-0	1-2	4	1	2	0	3	7
Daryl Crist	2	1-1	1-1	0-0	0	0	0	0	1	3
Bryan Caver	16	1-5	0-1	0-0	2	1	0	0	1	2
Assaf Barnea	2	0-0	0-0	0-0	0	0	0	0	0	0
Chris Davis	2	0-0	0-0	0-0	0	0	0	0	0	0
TOTALS	**200**	**23-58**	**6-14**	**13-16**	**33**	**10**	**4**	**4**	**18**	**65**
Percentages		39.7	42.9	81.2						

Coach: P.J. Carlesimo

Officials: Lenny Wirtz, Ed Hightower, Rusty Herring
Technicals: None
Attendance: 23,666

78-61

	1H	2H
Duke	40	38
St. John's	27	34

ELITE 8

DUKE	MIN	FG	3FG	FT	REB	A	ST	BL	PF	TP
Bobby Hurley	36	6-10	4-7	4-6	7	4	4	0	2	20
Christian Laettner	29	5-6	0-1	9-9	5	3	4	0	0	19
Grant Hill	23	3-6	0-0	6-8	2	1	2	0	0	12
Greg Koubek	22	3-6	1-3	0-0	2	1	1	0	2	7
Billy McCaffrey	23	3-9	0-0	0-0	2	1	1	1	0	6
Thomas Hill	26	1-4	0-2	2-2	2	3	2	3	3	4
Brian Davis	20	1-4	0-0	2-3	3	1	0	0	2	4
Crawford Palmer	9	2-2	0-0	0-0	1	0	1	0	0	4
Marty Clark	3	1-1	0-0	0-0	0	0	0	0	0	2
Antonio Lang	7	0-0	0-0	0-0	0	1	1	0	0	0
Chistian Ast	1	0-0	0-0	0-0	0	0	0	0	1	0
Clay Buckley	1	0-0	0-0	0-0	0	0	1	0	0	0
TOTALS	**200**	**25-48**	**5-13**	**23-28**	**24**	**15**	**17**	**4**	**10**	**78**
Percentages		52.1	38.5	82.1						

Coach: Mike Krzyzewski

ST. JOHN'S	MIN	FG	3FG	FT	REB	A	ST	BL	PF	TP
Malik Sealy	29	8-19	1-2	2-4	6	1	2	1	2	19
Jason Buchanan	27	6-11	3-3	0-0	0	7	0	0	5	15
Bill Singleton	32	4-6	0-1	0-0	5	0	3	0	3	8
Chucky Sproling	37	2-9	2-3	0-0	3	3	0	0	2	6
Robert Werdann	12	2-2	0-0	0-0	7	0	0	0	1	4
Carl Beckett	5	1-2	1-1	0-0	1	0	1	0	0	3
Sean Muto	16	0-2	0-0	2-2	3	0	0	0	4	2
David Cain	15	1-3	0-0	0-0	0	3	0	0	1	2
Sergio Luyk	6	1-2	0-0	0-0	3	1	2	0	0	2
Shawnelle Scott	17	0-1	0-0	0-0	2	0	1	0	4	0
Terence Mullin	4	0-0	0-0	0-0	0	0	0	0	0	0
TOTALS	**200**	**25-57**	**7-10**	**4-6**	**30**	**15**	**9**	**1**	**22**	**61**
Percentages		43.9	70.0	66.7						

Coach: Lou Carnesecca

Officials: Dave Libbey, Tim Higgins, Rich Ballesteros
Technicals: None
Attendance: 25,634

75-72

	1H	2H
North Carolina	35	40
Temple	30	42

ELITE 8

NORTH CAROLINA	MIN	FG	3FG	FT	REB	A	ST	BL	PF	TP
Rick Fox	32	8-16	2-7	1-1	7	5	0	1	3	19
Hubert Davis	30	7-13	2-6	3-3	3	2	0	0	1	19
King Rice	32	2-4	2-2	6-6	2	7	1	0	0	12
George Lynch	30	5-9	0-0	0-0	8	0	0	1	3	10
Pete Chilcutt	32	3-10	0-1	1-2	9	0	1	2	1	7
Henrik Rodl	7	2-3	1-1	0-0	0	0	0	0	1	5
Brian Reese	10	1-1	0-0	0-0	2	0	0	0	0	2
Eric Montross	15	0-3	0-0	1-2	2	0	0	2	3	1
Derrick Phelps	8	0-1	0-0	0-0	2	0	0	0	0	0
Pat Sullivan	3	0-0	0-0	0-0	0	0	0	0	0	0
Clifford Rozier	1	0-1	0-0	0-0	0	1	0	0	0	0
TOTALS	**200**	**28-61**	**7-17**	**12-14**	**35**	**15**	**2**	**6**	**12**	**75**
Percentages		45.9	41.2	85.7						

Coach: Dean Smith

TEMPLE	MIN	FG	3FG	FT	REB	A	ST	BL	PF	TP
Mark Macon	38	12-23	4-9	3-3	9	1	2	0	3	31
Mik Kilgore	40	7-15	3-6	1-5	5	4	0	3	4	18
Vic Carstarphen	38	3-11	2-9	0-0	3	5	1	0	5	8
Mark Strickland	37	3-7	0-0	2-2	6	1	0	3	2	8
Donald Hodge	39	3-7	0-0	1-2	6	0	0	1	1	7
Michael Harden	5	0-0	0-0	0-0	1	1	0	0	1	0
James Spears	3	0-2	0-0	0-0	1	0	0	0	0	0
TOTALS	**200**	**28-65**	**9-24**	**7-12**	**31**	**12**	**3**	**7**	**16**	**72**
Percentages		43.1	37.5	58.3						

Coach: John Chaney

Officials: Tom Harrington, Charles Range, Joe Mingle
Technicals: None
Attendance: 19,601

93-81

	1H	2H
Kansas	35	58
Arkansas	47	34

ELITE 8

KANSAS	MIN	FG	3FG	FT	REB	A	ST	BL	PF	TP
Alonzo Jamison	28	11-14	1-1	3-5	9	2	1	0	3	26
Adonis Jordan	34	3-9	0-3	8-10	6	3	1	0	3	14
Terry Brown	26	5-12	1-5	0-0	3	1	2	0	4	11
Sean Tunstall	18	3-7	1-3	4-4	3	1	0	0	0	11
Mark Randall	27	4-5	0-0	2-4	2	3	1	0	4	10
Mike Maddox	22	3-4	0-0	2-2	4	1	0	0	2	8
Steve Woodberry	16	1-4	0-0	4-4	4	1	1	1	0	6
Kirk Wagner	5	1-1	0-0	2-2	0	0	0	0	0	4
Richard Scott	16	1-5	0-0	1-2	3	0	0	0	2	3
Patrick Richey	5	0-1	0-0	0-0	1	0	0	0	0	0
David Johanning	3	0-0	0-0	0-0	0	0	0	0	0	0
TOTALS	**200**	**32-62**	**3-12**	**26-33**	**35**	**12**	**6**	**1**	**18**	**93**
Percentages		51.6	25.0	78.8						

Coach: Roy Williams

ARKANSAS	MIN	FG	3FG	FT	REB	A	ST	BL	PF	TP
Todd Day	34	8-19	4-8	6-7	4	1	2	3	4	26
Oliver Miller	34	7-11	0-0	2-3	9	1	0	2	3	16
Ernie Murry	25	6-13	2-5	0-2	4	2	1	1	5	14
Isaiah Morris	15	5-6	0-0	1-1	5	0	1	0	3	11
Lee Mayberry	38	3-9	0-4	1-2	6	4	0	0	3	7
Arlyn Bowers	20	1-4	1-1	0-0	0	3	0	0	3	3
Ron Huery	18	1-7	0-0	0-0	1	4	0	0	2	2
Roosevelt Wallace	11	1-3	0-1	0-0	2	1	0	0	2	2
Clyde Fletcher	5	0-1	0-0	0-0	0	0	0	0	0	0
TOTALS	**200**	**32-73**	**7-19**	**10-15**	**31**	**16**	**4**	**6**	**25**	**81**
Percentages		43.8	36.8	66.7						

Coach: Nolan Richardson

Officials: Mickey Crowley, Pete Pavia, Samuel Croft
Technicals: None
Attendance: 22,717

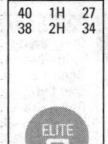

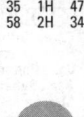

79-77

41	1H	43
38	2H	34

DUKE	MIN	FG	3FG	FT	REB	A	ST	BL	PF	TP
Christian Laettner	40	9-14	1-1	9-11	7	2	1	1	2	28
Brian Davis	21	6-12	0-0	3-4	4	1	1	0	1	15
Bobby Hurley	40	4-7	3-4	1-1	2	7	2	0	3	12
Grant Hill	33	5-8	0-0	1-1	5	5	1	0	2	11
Thomas Hill	22	2-6	0-0	2-2	2	1	1	1	2	6
Billy McCaffrey	14	2-3	0-0	1-2	0	2	0	0	1	5
Greg Koubek	22	1-6	0-3	0-0	1	3	0	1	1	2
Crawford Palmer	6	0-0	0-0	0-0	0	0	0	0	1	0
Antonio Lang	2	0-0	0-0	0-0	0	0	0	1	0	0
TOTALS	**200**	**29-56**	**4-8**	**17-21**	**21**	**21**	**6**	**4**	**13**	**79**
Percentages		51.8	50.0	81.0						
Coach: Mike Krzyzewski										

UNLV	MIN	FG	3FG	FT	REB	A	ST	BL	PF	TP
Anderson Hunt	39	11-20	4-11	3-5	4	2	1	0	0	29
Greg Anthony	35	8-18	2-2	1-1	5	6	3	0	5	19
Larry Johnson	39	5-10	0-2	3-4	13	2	1	2	3	13
George Ackles	25	3-6	0-0	1-2	5	0	0	1	4	7
Stacey Augmon	39	3-10	0-0	0-1	8	2	2	1	2	6
Evric Gray	14	1-2	0-0	0-0	1	0	0	0	2	2
Elmore Spencer	9	0-2	0-0	1-2	3	1	0	0	2	1
TOTALS	**200**	**31-68**	**6-15**	**9-15**	**39**	**13**	**7**	**4**	**18**	**77**
Percentages		45.6	40.0	60.0						
Coach: Jerry Tarkanian										

Officials: John Clougherty, Tom O'Neill, Ted Valentine
Technicals: UNLV (Johnson)
Attendance: 47,100

79-73

43	1H	34
36	2H	39

KANSAS	MIN	FG	3FG	FT	REB	A	ST	BL	PF	TP
Adonis Jordan	36	4-11	2-6	6-13	4	7	2	0	2	16
Mark Randall	34	6-11	0-0	4-6	11	4	0	0	1	16
Richard Scott	16	6-9	0-0	2-3	6	0	0	0	3	14
Mike Maddox	27	4-10	0-0	2-2	4	2	1	0	3	10
Alonzo Jamison	25	4-8	0-0	1-3	11	2	0	1	4	9
Sean Tunstall	20	1-5	1-2	2-5	2	1	1	0	2	5
Patrick Richey	10	1-1	0-0	2-2	1	0	0	0	2	4
Terry Brown	24	1-10	1-6	0-0	4	1	1	0	2	3
Steve Woodberry	6	0-0	0-0	2-2	1	0	0	0	1	2
David Johanning	1	0-0	0-0	0-0	1	0	0	0	0	0
Kirk Wagner	1	0-1	0-0	0-0	1	0	0	0	0	0
TOTALS	**200**	**27-66**	**4-14**	**21-36**	**46**	**17**	**5**	**1**	**20**	**79**
Percentages		40.9	28.6	58.3						
Coach: Roy Williams										

NORTH CAROLINA	MIN	FG	3FG	FT	REB	A	ST	BL	PF	TP
Hubert Davis	31	9-16	2-4	5-5	5	1	1	0	0	25
George Lynch	30	5-8	0-0	3-6	5	2	2	0	5	13
Rick Fox	29	5-22	0-7	3-3	9	7	0	0	5	13
Eric Montross	19	3-4	0-0	0-1	3	1	1	1	4	6
King Rice	30	1-6	0-3	3-4	0	3	0	0	2	5
Brian Reese	11	2-5	1-1	0-3	2	0	1	0	0	5
Pete Chilcutt	27	2-8	0-1	0-0	11	1	2	2	3	4
Derrick Phelps	10	1-1	0-0	0-1	1	1	1	0	4	2
Henrik Rodl	8	0-1	0-0	0-0	2	0	1	1	1	0
Clifford Rozier	3	0-0	0-0	0-0	0	0	0	0	0	0
Kenny Harris	1	0-2	0-2	0-0	0	0	1	0	0	0
Pat Sullivan	1	0-0	0-0	0-0	0	0	1	0	3	0
TOTALS	**200**	**28-73**	**3-18**	**14-23**	**38**	**16**	**11**	**4**	**27**	**73**
Percentages		38.4	16.7	60.9						
Coach: Dean Smith										

Officials: Gerry Donaghy, Ed Hightower, Pete Pavia
Technicals: UNC (Coach Smith, 2)
Attendance: 47,100

72-65

42	1H	34
30	2H	31

DUKE	MIN	FG	3FG	FT	REB	A	ST	BL	PF	TP
Christian Laettner	32	3-8	0-0	12-12	10	0	1	0	3	18
Billy McCaffrey	26	6-8	2-3	2-2	1	0	0	0	1	16
Bobby Hurley	40	3-5	2-4	4-4	1	9	2	0	1	12
Grant Hill	28	4-6	0-0	2-8	8	3	2	2	1	10
Brian Davis	24	4-5	0-0	0-2	0	1	0	0	4	8
Greg Koubek	17	2-4	1-2	0-0	4	0	1	0	1	5
Thomas Hill	23	1-5	1-1	0-0	4	1	0	0	2	3
Crawford Palmer	9	0-0	0-0	0-0	0	0	0	0	0	0
Antonio Lang	1	0-0	0-0	0-0	0	0	0	0	0	0
TOTALS	**200**	**23-41**	**6-10**	**20-28**	**28**	**14**	**6**	**2**	**13**	**72**
Percentages		56.1	60.0	71.4						
Coach: Mike Krzyzewski										

KANSAS	MIN	FG	3FG	FT	REB	A	ST	BL	PF	TP
Mark Randall	33	7-9	1-1	3-6	10	2	1	0	4	18
Terry Brown	31	6-15	4-11	0-0	4	1	3	0	1	16
Adonis Jordan	34	4-6	2-2	1-2	0	3	1	0	0	11
Richard Scott	15	3-9	0-0	0-0	2	0	0	1	1	6
Mike Maddox	19	2-4	0-0	0-0	3	4	0	1	3	4
Alonzo Jamison	29	1-10	0-2	0-0	4	5	4	0	4	2
Steve Woodberry	18	1-4	0-0	0-0	4	0	1	0	4	2
Sean Tunstall	11	1-5	0-1	0-0	1	0	0	0	3	2
David Johanning	3	1-1	0-0	0-0	2	1	0	0	1	2
Kirk Wagner	3	1-1	0-0	0-0	1	0	0	0	0	2
Patrick Richey	4	0-1	0-1	0-0	1	0	0	0	0	0
TOTALS	**200**	**27-65**	**7-18**	**4-8**	**32**	**16**	**10**	**2**	**21**	**65**
Percentages		41.5	38.9	50.0						
Coach: Roy Williams										

Officials: Mickey Crowley, Charles Range, James Burr
Technicals: None
Attendance: 47,100

National Invitation Tournament (NIT)

First round: Providence d. James Madison 98-93 (2OT), Cincinnati d. Ball State 82-55, Wisconsin d. Bowling Green 87-79 (OT), Southern Illinois d. Boise State 75-74, Colorado d. Michigan 71-64, Stanford d. Houston 93-86, Siena d. Fairleigh Dickinson 90-85, Memphis d. UAB 82-76, Oklahoma d. Tulsa 111-86, Missouri State d. Coppin State 57-47, Arkansas State d. Rice 78-71, Fordham d. South Florida 76-66, West Virginia d. Furman 86-67, South Carolina d. George Washington 69-63, Massachusetts d. La Salle 93-90, Wyoming d. Butler 63-61
Second round: Providence d. West Virginia 85-79, Oklahoma d. Cincinnati 89-81 (OT), Colorado d. Wyoming 83-75, Southern Illinois d. Missouri State 72-69, Arkansas State d. Memphis 58-57, Stanford d. Wisconsin 80-72, Massachusetts d. Fordham 78-74, Siena d. South Carolina 63-58
Third round: Oklahoma d. Providence 83-74, Massachusetts d. Siena 82-80 (OT), Colorado d. Arkansas State 81-75, Stanford d. Southern Illinois 78-68
Semifinals: Stanford d. Massachusetts 73-71, Oklahoma d. Colorado 88-78
Third place: Colorado d. Massachusetts 98-91
Championship: Stanford d. Oklahoma 78-72
MVP: Adam Keefe, Stanford

ANNUAL REVIEW

1991-92: Special K

Duke's fifth straight Final Four appearance nearly didn't happen. The record shows that Duke beat Michigan for its second straight national championship, but only because the Blue Devils escaped death in their Elite Eight game with Kentucky, when Christian Laettner caught a perfect inbounds pass from Grant Hill at the top of the key as time expired in overtime and nailed a jumper. *Sports Illustrated* called Duke's 104-103 win over Kentucky the greatest college basketball game of all time.

The Blue Devils (32–2) then squeaked by Indiana in a battle of Coach K's—Mike Krzyzewski vs. his mentor, Bob Knight—to reach the title game. Against Michigan's Fab Five freshmen, Duke turned a one-point halftime deficit into a 20-point, 71-51 win. The MOP was Duke point guard Bobby Hurley, who in 1993 set the record for career Tournament assists (145). Laettner became the top all-time Tournament scorer with 407 points and was named Naismith POY. Michigan's national semifinal Tournament appearance was later vacated by the NCAA for rules violations. Two dominant big men were chosen one-two in the NBA draft: LSU's Shaquille O'Neal (Orlando Magic) and Georgetown's Alonzo Mourning (Charlotte Hornets).

Major Conference Standings

ACC	Conference			Overall		
	W	L	PCT	W	L	PCT
Duke⊕	14	2	.875	34	2	.944
Florida State○	11	5	.688	22	10	.688
North Carolina○	9	7	.563	23	10	.697
Georgia Tech○	8	8	.500	23	12	.657
Virginia□	8	8	.500	20	13	.606
Wake Forest○	7	9	.438	17	12	.586
NC State	6	10	.375	12	18	.400
Maryland	5	11	.313	14	15	.483
Clemson	4	12	.250	14	14	.500

Tournament: **Duke d. North Carolina 94-74**
Tournament MVP: **Christian Laettner**, Duke

ATLANTIC 10	Conference			Overall		
	W	L	PCT	W	L	PCT
Massachusetts⊕	13	3	.813	30	5	.857
Temple○	11	5	.688	17	13	.567
West Virginia○	10	6	.625	20	12	.625
Rhode Island□	9	7	.563	22	10	.688
George Washington	8	8	.500	16	12	.571
Rutgers□	6	10	.375	16	15	.516
Duquesne	6	10	.375	13	15	.464
Saint Joseph's	6	10	.375	13	15	.464
St. Bonaventure	3	13	.188	9	19	.321

Tournament: **Massachusetts d. West Virginia 97-91**
Tournament MOP: **Harper Williams**, Massachusetts

BIG EAST	Conference			Overall		
	W	L	PCT	W	L	PCT
Seton Hall○	12	6	.667	23	9	.719
Georgetown○	12	6	.667	22	10	.688
St. John's○	12	6	.667	19	11	.633
Villanova□	11	7	.611	14	15	.483
Syracuse⊕	10	8	.556	22	10	.688
Connecticut○	10	8	.556	20	10	.667
Pittsburgh□	9	9	.500	18	16	.529
Boston College□	7	11	.389	17	14	.548
Providence	6	12	.333	14	17	.452
Miami (FL)	1	17	.056	8	24	.250

Tournament: **Syracuse d. Georgetown 56-54**
Tournament MVP: **Alonzo Mourning**, Georgetown

BIG EIGHT	Conference			Overall		
	W	L	PCT	W	L	PCT
Kansas⊕	11	3	.786	27	5	.844
Oklahoma State○	8	6	.571	28	8	.778
Missouri○	8	6	.571	21	9	.700
Oklahoma○	8	6	.571	21	9	.700
Nebraska○	7	7	.500	19	10	.655
Iowa State○	5	9	.357	21	13	.618
Kansas State□	5	9	.357	16	14	.533
Colorado	4	10	.286	13	15	.464

Tournament: **Kansas d. Oklahoma State 66-57**
Tournament MVP: **Byron Houston**, Oklahoma State

BIG SKY	Conference			Overall		
	W	L	PCT	W	L	PCT
Montana⊕	14	2	.875	27	4	.871
Nevada	13	3	.813	19	10	.655
Idaho	10	6	.625	18	14	.563
Weber State	10	6	.625	16	13	.552
Boise State	7	9	.438	16	13	.552
Montana State	6	10	.375	14	14	.500
Idaho State	6	10	.375	9	21	.300
Northern Arizona	3	13	.188	7	20	.259
Eastern Washington	3	13	.188	6	21	.222

Tournament: **Montana d. Nevada 73-68**
Tournament MVP: **Delvon Anderson**, Montana

BIG SOUTH	Conference			Overall		
	W	L	PCT	W	L	PCT
Radford	12	2	.857	20	9	.690
Liberty	10	4	.714	22	7	.759
Campbell⊕	7	7	.500	19	12	.613
Charleston Southern	7	7	.500	16	14	.533
Davidson	6	8	.429	11	17	.393
Coastal Carolina	6	8	.429	12	19	.387
UNC Asheville	6	8	.429	9	19	.321
Winthrop	2	12	.143	6	22	.214

Tournament: **Campbell d. Charleston Southern 67-53**
Tournament MVP: **Mark Mocnik**, Campbell

BIG TEN	Conference			Overall		
	W	L	PCT	W	L	PCT
Ohio State⊕	15	3	.833	26	6	.813
Indiana○	14	4	.778	27	7	.794
Michigan○⊗	11	7	.611	25	9	.735
Michigan State○	11	7	.611	22	8	.733
Iowa○	10	8	.556	19	11	.633
Purdue□	8	10	.444	18	15	.545
Minnesota□	8	10	.444	16	16	.500
Illinois	7	11	.389	13	15	.464
Wisconsin	4	14	.222	13	18	.419
Northwestern	2	16	.111	9	19	.321

BIG WEST	Conference			Overall		
	W	L	PCT	W	L	PCT
UNLV	18	0	1.000	26	2	.929
UC Santa Barbara□	13	5	.722	20	9	.690
New Mexico State⊕⊗	12	6	.667	25	8	.758
Long Beach State□	11	7	.611	18	12	.600
Utah State	10	8	.556	16	12	.571
Pacific	8	10	.444	14	16	.467
Cal State Fullerton	8	10	.444	12	16	.429
Fresno State	6	12	.333	15	16	.484
UC Irvine	3	15	.167	7	22	.241
San Jose State	1	17	.056	2	24	.077

Tournament: **New Mexico State d. Pacific 74-73**
Tournament MVP: **Sam Crawford**, New Mexico State

COLONIAL ATHLETIC	Conference			Overall		
	W	L	PCT	W	L	PCT
Richmond□	12	2	.857	22	8	.733
James Madison□	12	2	.857	21	11	.656
Old Dominion⊕	8	6	.571	15	15	.500
American	8	6	.571	11	18	.379
UNC Wilmington	6	8	.429	13	15	.464
East Carolina	4	10	.286	10	18	.357
William & Mary	3	11	.214	10	19	.345
George Mason	3	11	.214	7	21	.250

Tournament: **Old Dominion d. James Madison 78-73**
Tournament MVP: **Ricardo Leonard**, Old Dominion

EAST COAST	Conference			Overall		
	W	L	PCT	W	L	PCT
Hofstra	10	2	.833	20	9	.690
Towson	9	3	.750	17	13	.567
Rider	9	3	.750	16	13	.552
UMBC	8	4	.667	10	19	.345
Central Connecticut St.	3	9	.250	7	21	.250
Brooklyn	3	9	.250	5	23	.179
Buffalo	0	12	.000	2	26	.071

Tournament: **Towson d. Hofstra 69-61**
Tournament MVP: **Terrance Alexander**, Towson

GMWC	Conference			Overall		
	W	L	PCT	W	L	PCT
Cincinnati○	8	2	.800	29	5	.853
DePaul○	8	2	.800	20	9	.690
Memphis○	5	5	.500	23	11	.676
Marquette	5	5	.500	16	13	.552
UAB□	4	6	.400	20	9	.690
Saint Louis	0	10	.000	5	23	.179

Tournament: **Cincinnati d. Memphis 75-63**

IVY	Conference			Overall		
	W	L	PCT	W	L	PCT
Princeton⊕	12	2	.857	22	6	.786
Penn	9	5	.643	16	10	.615
Columbia	8	6	.571	10	16	.385
Yale	7	7	.500	17	9	.654
Brown	5	9	.357	11	15	.423
Dartmouth	5	9	.357	10	16	.385
Cornell	5	9	.357	7	19	.269
Harvard	5	9	.357	6	20	.231

METRO	Conference			Overall		
	W	L	PCT	W	L	PCT
Tulane○	8	4	.667	22	9	.710
Charlotte○	7	5	.583	23	9	.719
South Florida○	7	5	.583	19	10	.655
Louisville○	7	5	.583	19	11	.633
VCU	5	7	.417	14	15	.483
Southern Miss	5	7	.417	13	16	.448
Virginia Tech	3	9	.250	10	18	.357

Tournament: **Charlotte d. Tulane 64-63**
Tournament MOP: **Henry Williams**, Charlotte

MAAC	Conference			Overall		
	W	L	PCT	W	L	PCT
Manhattan□	13	3	.813	25	9	.735
La Salle⊕	12	4	.750	20	11	.645
Siena	11	5	.688	19	10	.655
Loyola (MD)	10	6	.625	14	14	.500
Niagara	8	8	.500	14	14	.500
Iona	8	8	.500	14	15	.483
Fairfield	4	12	.250	8	20	.286
Saint Peter's	3	13	.188	8	21	.276
Canisius	3	13	.188	8	22	.267

Tournament: **La Salle d. Manhattan 79-78**
Tournament MVP: **Randy Woods**, La Salle

MID-AMERICAN	Conference			Overall		
	W	L	PCT	W	L	PCT
Miami (OH)⊕	13	3	.813	23	8	.742
Ball State□	11	5	.688	24	9	.727
Western Michigan□	11	5	.688	21	9	.700
Ohio	10	6	.625	18	10	.643
Bowling Green	8	8	.500	14	15	.483
Central Michigan	6	10	.375	12	16	.429
Kent State	6	10	.375	9	19	.321
Eastern Michigan	4	12	.250	9	22	.290
Toledo	3	13	.188	7	20	.259

Tournament: **Miami (OH) d. Ball State 58-57**
Tournament MVP: **Bill Gillis**, Ball State

⊕ Automatic NCAA Tournament bid ○ At-large NCAA Tournament bid □ NIT appearance ⊗ Team record doesn't reflect games forfeited or vacated. For adjusted record, see p. 521.

MID-CONTINENT

	Conference			Overall		
	W	L	Pct	W	L	Pct
Wisc.-Green Bay□	14	2	.875	25	5	.833
Akron	10	6	.625	16	12	.571
Illinois-Chicago	10	6	.625	16	14	.533
Eastern Illinois⊕	9	7	.563	17	14	.548
Wright State	9	7	.563	15	13	.536
Cleveland State	7	9	.438	16	13	.552
Northern Illinois	7	9	.438	11	17	.393
Western Illinois	4	12	.250	10	18	.357
Valparaiso	2	14	.125	5	22	.185

Tournament: **Eastern Illinois d. Illinois-Chicago 83-68**
Tournament MVP: **Steve Rowe**, Eastern Illinois

MEAC

	Conference			Overall		
	W	L	Pct	W	L	Pct
NC A&T	12	4	.750	18	9	.667
Howard⊕	12	4	.750	17	14	.548
Florida A&M	11	5	.688	16	14	.533
Coppin State	9	7	.563	15	13	.536
South Carolina State	9	7	.563	14	15	.483
Delaware State	9	7	.563	12	16	.429
Morgan State	5	11	.313	6	23	.207
Bethune-Cookman	3	13	.188	4	25	.138
UMES	2	14	.125	3	25	.107

Tournament: **Howard d. Florida A&M 67-65**
Tournament MOP: **Howard Holley**, Howard

MCC

	Conference			Overall		
	W	L	Pct	W	L	Pct
Evansville⊕	8	2	.800	24	6	.800
Butler□	7	3	.700	21	10	.677
Xavier	7	3	.700	15	12	.556
Dayton	5	5	.500	15	15	.500
Loyola-Chicago	2	8	.200	13	16	.448
Detroit	1	9	.100	12	17	.414

Tournament: **Evansville d. Butler 95-76**
Tournament MVP: **Parrish Casebier**, Evansville

MISSOURI VALLEY

	Conference			Overall		
	W	L	Pct	W	L	Pct
Southern Illinois□	14	4	.778	22	8	.733
Illinois State	14	4	.778	18	11	.621
Missouri State⊕	13	5	.722	23	8	.742
Tulsa	12	6	.667	17	13	.567
Indiana State	12	6	.667	13	15	.464
Creighton	7	11	.389	9	19	.321
UNI	6	12	.333	10	18	.357
Wichita State	6	12	.333	8	20	.286
Bradley	3	15	.167	7	23	.233
Drake	3	15	.167	6	21	.222

Tournament: **Missouri St. d. Tulsa 71-68**
Tournament MOP: **Jackie Crawford**, Missouri State

NAC

	Conference			Overall		
	W	L	Pct	W	L	Pct
Delaware⊕	14	0	1.000	27	4	.871
Drexel	9	5	.643	16	14	.533
Maine	8	6	.571	17	15	.531
Vermont	7	7	.500	16	13	.552
Boston U.	5	9	.357	10	18	.357
Northeastern	5	9	.357	9	19	.321
New Hampshire	5	9	.357	7	21	.250
Hartford	3	11	.214	6	21	.222

Tournament: **Delaware d. Drexel 92-68**
Tournament MVP: **Alex Coles**, Delaware

NORTHEAST

	Conference			Overall		
	W	L	Pct	W	L	Pct
Robert Morris⊕	12	4	.750	19	12	.613
Monmouth	11	5	.688	20	9	.690
Fairleigh Dickinson	11	5	.688	14	14	.500
Wagner	9	7	.563	16	12	.571
St. Francis (NY)	8	8	.500	15	14	.517
Long Island	7	9	.438	11	18	.379
Marist	6	10	.375	10	20	.333
Saint Francis (PA)	5	11	.313	13	16	.448
Mount St. Mary's	3	13	.188	6	22	.214

Tournament: **Robert Morris d. Marist 85-81**
Tournament MVP: **Myron Walker**, Robert Morris

OHIO VALLEY

	Conference			Overall		
	W	L	Pct	W	L	Pct
Murray State⊕	11	3	.786	17	13	.567
Middle Tennessee State	9	5	.643	16	11	.593
Eastern Kentucky	9	5	.643	19	14	.576
Tennessee Tech	8	6	.571	14	15	.483
Morehead State	6	8	.429	14	15	.483
Austin Peay	6	8	.429	11	17	.393
SE Missouri State	5	9	.357	12	16	.429
Tennessee State	2	12	.143	4	24	.143

Tournament: **Murray State d. Eastern Kentucky 81-60**
Tournament MVP: **Popeye Jones**, Murray State

PAC-10

	Conference			Overall		
	W	L	Pct	W	L	Pct
UCLA⊕	16	2	.889	28	5	.848
Southern California○	15	3	.833	24	6	.800
Arizona○	13	5	.722	24	7	.774
Stanford○	10	8	.556	18	11	.621
Washington State□	9	9	.500	22	11	.667
Arizona State□	9	9	.500	19	14	.576
Oregon State	7	11	.389	15	16	.484
Washington	5	13	.278	12	17	.414
California	4	14	.222	10	18	.357
Oregon	2	16	.111	6	21	.222

PATRIOT

	Conference			Overall		
	W	L	Pct	W	L	Pct
Bucknell	11	3	.786	21	9	.700
Fordham⊕	11	3	.786	18	13	.581
Holy Cross	10	4	.714	18	11	.621
Lehigh	8	6	.571	14	15	.483
Colgate	7	7	.500	14	14	.500
Lafayette	6	8	.429	8	20	.286
Army	2	12	.143	4	24	.143
Navy	1	13	.071	6	22	.214

Tournament: **Fordham d. Bucknell 70-65**
Tournament MVP: **Fred Herzog**, Fordham

SEC

	Conference			Overall		
	W	L	Pct	W	L	Pct
EASTERN						
Kentucky⊕	12	4	.750	29	7	.806
Florida□	9	7	.563	19	14	.576
Tennessee□	8	8	.500	19	15	.559
Georgia	7	9	.438	15	14	.517
Vanderbilt□	6	10	.375	15	15	.500
South Carolina	3	13	.188	11	17	.393
WESTERN						
Arkansas○	13	3	.813	26	8	.765
LSU○	12	4	.750	21	10	.677
Alabama○	10	6	.625	26	9	.743
Mississippi State	7	9	.438	15	13	.536
Auburn	5	11	.313	12	15	.444
Mississippi	4	12	.250	11	17	.393

Tournament: **Kentucky d. Alabama 80-54**
Tournament MVP: **Jamal Mashburn**, Kentucky

SOUTHERN

	Conference			Overall		
	W	L	Pct	W	L	Pct
East Tennessee St.⊕	12	2	.857	24	7	.774
Chattanooga	12	2	.857	23	7	.767
Furman	9	5	.643	17	11	.607
Appalachian State	9	5	.643	15	14	.517
Western Carolina	5	9	.357	11	17	.393
The Citadel	3	11	.214	10	18	.357
VMI	3	11	.214	10	18	.357
Marshall	3	11	.214	7	22	.241

Tournament: **East Tennessee St. d. Chattanooga 74-62**
Tournament MOP: **Greg Dennis**, East Tennessee St.

SOUTHLAND

	Conference			Overall		
	W	L	Pct	W	L	Pct
UTSA	15	3	.833	21	8	.724
UL-Monroe⊕	12	6	.667	19	10	.655
Nicholls State	12	6	.667	15	13	.536
North Texas	12	6	.667	15	14	.517
Texas-Arlington	11	7	.611	16	13	.552
Stephen F. Austin	10	8	.556	15	13	.536
Northwestern St. (LA)	9	9	.500	15	13	.536
Texas State	4	14	.222	7	20	.259
McNeese State	4	14	.222	7	22	.241
Sam Houston State	1	17	.056	2	25	.074

Tournament: **UL-Monroe d. UTSA 81-77**
Tournament MVP: **Ryan Stuart**, UL-Monroe

SOUTHWEST

	Conference			Overall		
	W	L	Pct	W	L	Pct
Houston⊕	11	3	.786	25	6	.806
Texas○	11	3	.786	23	12	.657
TCU□	9	5	.643	23	11	.676
Rice	8	6	.571	20	11	.645
Texas Tech	6	8	.429	15	14	.517
Baylor	5	9	.357	13	15	.464
SMU	4	10	.286	10	18	.357
Texas A&M	2	12	.143	6	22	.214

Tournament: **Houston d. Texas 91-72**
Tournament MVP: **Dexter Cambridge**, Texas

SWAC

	Conference			Overall		
	W	L	Pct	W	L	Pct
Miss. Valley State⊕	11	3	.786	16	14	.533
Texas Southern	11	3	.786	15	14	.517
Southern U.	9	5	.643	18	12	.600
Alcorn State	8	6	.571	15	14	.517
Alabama State	8	6	.571	14	14	.500
Jackson State	7	7	.500	12	16	.429
Grambling	2	12	.143	4	24	.143
Prairie View A&M	0	14	.000	0	28	.000

Tournament: **Miss. Valley State d. Southern U. 85-77**
Tournament MVP: **Alphonso Ford**, Miss. Valley State

SUN BELT

	Conference			Overall		
	W	L	Pct	W	L	Pct
Louisiana Tech□	12	4	.750	22	9	.710
UL-Lafayette⊕	12	4	.750	21	11	.656
Arkansas State	11	5	.688	17	11	.607
Western Kentucky□	10	6	.625	21	11	.656
New Orleans⊗	9	7	.563	18	14	.563
South Alabama	9	7	.563	14	14	.500
Arkansas-Little Rock⊗	8	8	.500	17	13	.567
Lamar	7	9	.438	12	19	.387
Jacksonville	6	10	.375	12	17	.414
Central Florida	3	13	.188	10	18	.357
Tex.-Pan American⊗	1	15	.063	3	26	.103

Tournament: **UL-Lafayette d. Louisiana Tech 75-71**
Tournament MOP: **Todd Hill**, UL-Lafayette

TAAC

	Conference			Overall		
	W	L	Pct	W	L	Pct
Georgia Southern⊕	13	1	.929	25	6	.806
Georgia State	8	6	.571	16	14	.533
Florida International	7	7	.500	11	17	.393
Samford	7	7	.500	11	18	.379
Stetson	6	8	.429	11	17	.393
Mercer	6	8	.429	11	18	.379
Centenary	5	9	.357	10	18	.357
Southeastern Louisiana	4	10	.286	6	22	.214

Tournament: **Ga. Southern d. Georgia State 95-82**
Tournament MVP: **Charlton Young**, Ga. Southern

WEST COAST

	Conference			Overall		
	W	L	Pct	W	L	Pct
Pepperdine⊕	14	0	1.000	24	7	.774
Santa Clara	9	5	.643	14	15	.483
Gonzaga	8	6	.571	20	10	.667
Loyola Marymount	8	6	.571	15	13	.536
San Diego	6	8	.429	14	14	.500
San Francisco	4	10	.286	13	16	.448
Saint Mary's (CA)	4	10	.286	13	17	.433
Portland	3	11	.214	10	18	.357

Tournament: **Pepperdine d. Gonzaga 73-70**
Tournament MVP: **Doug Christie**, Pepperdine

WAC

	Conference			Overall		
	W	L	Pct	W	L	Pct
UTEP○	12	4	.750	27	7	.794
BYU⊕	12	4	.750	25	7	.781
New Mexico□	11	5	.688	20	13	.606
Utah□	9	7	.563	24	11	.686
Hawaii	9	7	.563	16	12	.571
Wyoming	8	8	.500	16	13	.552
Colorado State	8	8	.500	14	17	.452
Air Force	3	13	.188	9	20	.310
San Diego State	0	16	.000	2	26	.071

Tournament: **BYU d. UTEP 73-71**
Tournament MVP: **Eddie Rivera**, UTEP

INDEPENDENTS

	Overall		
	W	L	Pct
Penn State□	21	8	.724
Southern Utah	20	8	.714
UMKC	20	8	.714
Wisconsin-Milwaukee	20	8	.714
Charleston	19	8	.704
Notre Dame□	18	15	.545
Cal State Northridge	11	17	.393
Northeastern Illinois	8	20	.286
Chicago State	7	21	.250
UNC Greensboro	7	21	.250
Youngstown State	6	22	.214
Cal State Sacramento	4	24	.143

INDIVIDUAL LEADERS—SEASON

Scoring	CL	POS	G	FG	3FG	FT	PTS	PPG
1 **Brett Roberts**, Morehead State	SR	F	29	278	66	193	815	**28.1**
2 **Vin Baker**, Hartford	JR	F	27	281	41	142	745	**27.6**
3 **Alphonso Ford**, Mississippi Valley St.	JR	G	26	255	67	137	714	**27.5**
4 **Randy Woods**, La Salle	SR	G	31	272	121	182	847	**27.3**
5 **Steve Rogers**, Alabama State	SR	F	28	233	83	215	764	**27.3**
6 **Walt Williams**, Maryland	SR	G/F	29	256	89	175	776	**26.8**
7 **Harold Miner**, Southern California	JR	G	30	250	57	232	789	**26.3**
8 **Terrell Lowery**, Loyola Marymount	SR	G	26	216	84	159	675	**26.0**
9 **Reggie Cunningham**, Bethune-Cookman	SR	G/F	29	281	47	135	744	**25.7**
10 **Parrish Casebier**, Evansville	SO	G	25	210	27	187	634	**25.4**

Field Goal Pct	CL	POS	G	FG	FGA	PCT
1 **Bo Outlaw**, Houston	JR	F/C	31	156	228	**68.4**
2 **Warren Kidd**, Middle Tennessee State	JR	C	27	156	235	**66.4**
3 **Matt Fish**, UNC Wilmington	SR	C	28	206	319	**64.6**
4 **Johnny McDowell**, Texas-Arlington	JR	F/C	29	184	287	**64.1**
5 **Elmore Spencer**, UNLV	SR	C	28	174	273	**63.7**

Minimum: 5 made per game

Three-Pt FG Per Game	CL	POS	G	3FG	3PG
1 **Doug Day**, Radford	JR	G	29	117	**4.0**
2 **Mark Alberts**, Akron	JR	G	28	110	**3.9**
3 **Randy Woods**, La Salle	SR	G	31	121	**3.9**
4 **Peter McKelvey**, Portland	JR	G	28	106	**3.8**
5 **Jack Hurd**, La Salle	SR	G	31	113	**3.6**

Three-Pt FG Pct	CL	POS	G	3FG	3FGA	PCT
1 **Sean Wightman**, Western Michigan	JR	F	30	48	76	**63.2**
2 **Christian Laettner**, Duke	SR	C	35	54	97	**55.7**
3 **Lance Barker**, Valparaiso	FR	G	26	61	117	**52.1**
4 **Ronnie Battle**, Auburn	JR	G	27	71	139	**51.1**
5 **Tony Bennett**, Wisconsin-Green Bay	SR	G	30	95	186	**51.1**

Minimum: 1.5 made per game

Free Throw Pct	CL	POS	G	FT	FTA	PCT
1 **Don MacLean**, UCLA	SR	F	32	197	214	**92.1**
2 **Keith Adkins**, UNC Wilmington	JR	G	27	78	85	**91.8**
Scott Shreffler, Evansville	JR	G	24	78	85	**91.8**
4 **Matt Hildebrand**, Liberty	SO	G	29	114	125	**91.2**
5 **Jeff Lauritzen**, Indiana State	SR	G	28	82	91	**90.1**

Minimum: 2.5 made per game

Assists Per Game	CL	POS	G	AST	APG
1 **Van Usher**, Tennessee Tech	SR	G	29	254	**8.8**
2 **Sam Crawford**, New Mexico State	JR	G	33	282	**8.5**
3 **Orlando Smart**, San Francisco	SO	G	29	241	**8.3**
4 **Kevin Soares**, Nevada	SR	G	29	227	**7.8**
5 **Chuck Evans**, Mississippi State	JR	G	28	219	**7.8**
6 **Tony Walker**, Loyola Marymount	SR	G	28	218	**7.8**
7 **Dallas Dale**, Southern Miss	SR	G	29	222	**7.7**
8 **Bobby Hurley**, Duke	JR	G	31	237	**7.6**
9 **Tony Miller**, Marquette	FR	G	29	221	**7.6**
10 **Cedric Yelding**, South Alabama	JR	G	26	184	**7.1**

Rebounds Per Game	CL	POS	G	REB	RPG
1 **Popeye Jones**, Murray State	SR	C	30	431	**14.4**
2 **Shaquille O'Neal**, LSU	JR	C	30	421	**14.0**
3 **Tim Burroughs**, Jacksonville	SR	F	28	370	**13.2**
4 **Adam Keefe**, Stanford	SR	F	29	355	**12.2**
5 **Leonard White**, Southern U.	JR	F	30	367	**12.2**
6 **Jerome Sims**, Youngstown State	JR	F	28	327	**11.7**
7 **LaPhonso Ellis**, Notre Dame	SR	F	33	385	**11.7**
8 **Marcus Stokes**, UL-Lafayette	SR	F	32	370	**11.6**
9 **Darryl Johnson**, San Francisco	SR	F	27	309	**11.4**
10 **Drew Henderson**, Fairfield	JR	C	28	318	**11.4**

Blocked Shots Per Game	CL	POS	G	BLK	BPG
1 **Shaquille O'Neal**, LSU	JR	C	30	157	**5.2**
2 **Alonzo Mourning**, Georgetown	SR	F/C	32	160	**5.0**
3 **Kevin Roberson**, Vermont	SR	C	28	139	**5.0**
4 **Acie Earl**, Iowa	JR	C	30	121	**4.0**
5 **Vin Baker**, Hartford	JR	F	27	100	**3.7**

Steals Per Game	CL	POS	G	STL	SPG
1 **Victor Snipes**, Northeastern Illinois	SO	G	25	86	**3.4**
2 **Reggie Burcy**, Chicago State	SR	G	26	85	**3.3**
3 **David Corbitt**, Central Connecticut State	SO	G	28	88	**3.1**
4 **Marc Mitchell**, Wisconsin-Milwaukee	JR	G	25	78	**3.1**
5 **Kevin Soares**, Nevada	SR	G	29	90	**3.1**

INDIVIDUAL LEADERS—GAME

Points	CL	POS	OPP	DATE	PTS
1 **Brett Roberts**, Morehead State	SR	F	Middle Tennessee State	F10	**53**
2 **Jonathan Stone**, Colgate	SR	F	Brooklyn	M2	**52**
3 **Brett Roberts**, Morehead State	SR	F	UNC Greensboro	N27	**47**
4 **R. Cunningham**, Bethune-Cookman	SR	G/F	Stetson	N25	**46**
5 **Izett Buchanan**, Marist	SO	G	Mount St. Mary's	F13	**45**

Three-Pt FG Made	CL	POS	OPP	DATE	3FG
1 **Marc Rybczyk**, Central Conn. State	JR	G	Long Island	N26	**11**
Mark Alberts, Akron	JR	G	Wright State	F8	**11**
Mike Alcorn, Youngstown State	SO	G	Pittsburgh-Bradford	F24	**11**
4 **Doug Day**, Radford	JR	G	Morgan State	N30	**10**
Mark Alberts, Akron	JR	G	Lamar	D7	**10**
Dave Olson, Eastern Illinois	SR	F	Wright State	F20	**10**

Assists	CL	POS	OPP	DATE	AST
1 **Clarence Armstrong**, Drexel	SR	G	Boston U.	J25	**17**
Cedric Yelding, South Alabama	JR	G	UL-Lafayette	J26	**17**
3 **Russell Peyton**, Bucknell	JR	G	UMBC	N26	**16**
Tim Brooks, Chattanooga	JR	G	Western Carolina	F1	**16**
David Corbitt, Central Conn. State	SO	G	Buffalo	M2	**16**

Rebounds	CL	POS	OPP	DATE	REB
1 **Reginald Slater**, Wyoming	SR	F	Troy	D14	**27**
2 **Tim Burroughs**, Jacksonville	SR	F	Florida	D2	**23**
Gary Alexander, South Florida	SR	F	Northeastern Illinois	D27	**23**
4 **Fred Lewis**, South Florida	SR	F	Stetson	N22	**22**
Alonzo Mourning, Georgetown	SR	F/C	Delaware State	D9	**22**
Tim Burroughs, Jacksonville	SR	F	Iona	D28	**22**
Adam Keefe, Stanford	SR	F	Oregon	J11	**22**
Michael Smith, Providence	SO	F	Connecticut	J22	**22**
Jesse Ratliff, North Texas	JR	F	Nicholls State	J25	**22**
Darryl Johnson, San Francisco	SR	F	Pepperdine	F1	**22**
Darryl Johnson, San Francisco	SR	F	Portland	F6	**22**
Jerome Sims, Youngstown State	JR	F	Radford	F8	**22**
Thomas Gipson, North Texas	SR	C	Texas State	F10	**22**
Walt Williams, Maryland	SR	G/F	Clemson	F22	**22**

Blocked Shots	CL	POS	OPP	DATE	BLK
1 **Kevin Roberson**, Vermont	SR	C	New Hampshire	J9	**13**
2 **Kevin Roberson**, Vermont	SR	C	Cornell	J7	**11**
Shaquille O'Neal, LSU	JR	C	South Carolina	F19	**11**
Shaquille O'Neal, LSU	JR	C	Auburn	F22	**11**
5 **Shaquille O'Neal**, LSU	JR	C	Brigham Young	M19	**10**

Steals	CL	POS	OPP	DATE	STL
1 **David Edwards**, Texas A&M	SO	G	Prairie View A&M	N25	**9**
Pat Nash, North Texas	SR	G	South Alabama	D17	**9**
Willie Banks, New Mexico	SR	G	Tennessee State	D21	**9**
Damon Patterson, Oklahoma	SR	F	Morgan State	D21	**9**
Shawn Harlan, Northeastern Illinois	FR	F	Nicholls State	D21	**9**
Chuck Lightening, Towson	SR	F	George Mason	J8	**9**
Trent Smith, Centenary	FR	G/F	East Texas Baptist	J13	**9**
Andre Cradle, Long Island	SO	F	Monmouth	J18	**9**
Curtis Faust, South Carolina State	SR	G	Florida A&M	J25	**9**
Derrick Phelps, North Carolina	SO	G	Georgia Tech	F2	**9**

TEAM LEADERS—SEASON

Win-Loss Pct	W	L	PCT
1 **Duke**	34	2	**.944**
2 **UNLV**	26	2	**.929**
3 **Delaware**	27	4	**.871**
Montana	27	4	**.871**
5 **Massachusetts**	30	5	**.857**

Scoring Offense	G	W-L	PTS	PPG
1 **Northwestern State (LA)**	28	15-13	2,660	**95.0**
2 **Oklahoma**	30	21-9	2,838	**94.6**
3 **Southern U.**	30	18-12	2,809	**93.6**
4 **Georgia Southern**	31	25-6	2,836	**91.5**
5 **Loyola Marymount**	28	15-13	2,552	**91.1**

Scoring Margin	G	W-L	PPG	OPP PPG	MAR
1 **Indiana**	34	27-7	83.4	65.8	**17.6**
2 **Kansas**	32	27-5	84.5	68.1	**16.4**
3 **Arizona**	31	24-7	84.8	68.8	**16.0**
4 **Cincinnati**	34	29-5	79.0	63.1	**15.9**
5 **Duke**	36	34-2	88.0	72.6	**15.4**

Field Goal Pct	G	W-L	FG	FGA	PCT
1 **Duke**	36	34-2	1,108	2,069	**53.6**
2 **Liberty**	29	22-7	790	1,519	**52.0**
3 **UNLV**	28	26-2	817	1,583	**51.6**
4 **Kansas**	32	27-5	975	1,892	**51.5**
5 **Wisc.-Green Bay**	30	25-5	759	1,481	**51.2**

Three-Pt FG Per Game	G	W-L	3FG	3PG
1 **La Salle**	31	20-11	294	**9.5**
2 **Northwestern State (LA)**	28	15-13	259	**9.3**
3 **NC State**	30	12-18	265	**8.8**
4 **Kentucky**	36	29-7	317	**8.8**
5 **Texas-Arlington**	29	16-13	255	**8.8**

Free Throw Pct	G	W-L	FT	FTA	PCT
1 **Northwestern**	28	9-19	497	651	**76.3**
2 **Bucknell**	30	21-9	550	722	**76.2**
3 **Monmouth**	29	20-9	414	544	**76.1**
4 **Washington State**	33	22-11	554	729	**76.0**
5 **Drexel**	30	16-14	524	692	**75.7**

Rebound Margin	G	W-L	RPG	OPP RPG	MAR
1 **Delaware**	31	27-4	42.1	33.8	**8.3**
2 **Montana**	31	27-4	40.6	32.4	**8.2**
3 **Wake Forest**	29	17-12	36.8	29.1	**7.7**
4 **Providence**	31	14-17	42.8	35.3	**7.5**
5 **Michigan**	34	25-9	40.4	33.0	**7.4**

Scoring Defense	G	W-L	OPP PTS	OPP PPG
1 **Princeton**	28	22-6	1,349	**48.2**
2 **Wisconsin-Green Bay**	30	25-5	1,659	**55.3**
3 **Missouri State**	31	23-8	1,761	**56.8**
4 **Monmouth**	29	20-9	1,701	**58.7**
5 **Ball State**	33	24-9	1,959	**59.4**

FIELD GOAL PCT DEFENSE	G	W-L	OPP FG	OPP FGA	OPP PCT
1 UNLV	28	26-2	628	1,723	**36.4**
2 Princeton	28	22-6	445	1,169	**38.1**
3 Montana	31	27-4	685	1,736	**39.5**
4 Connecticut	30	20-10	734	1,843	**39.8**
5 Charleston	27	19-8	592	1,486	**39.8**

TEAM LEADERS—GAME

POINTS	OPP	DATE	SCORE
1 LSU	Northern Arizona	D28	**159-86**
2 Oklahoma	Morgan State	D21	**144-81**
3 Stetson	St. Leo	N30	**143-125**
4 Auburn	Troy	D11	**141-116**
5 Loyola Marymount	Morgan State	N22	**140-110**
Northwestern State (LA)	LeTourneau	J20	**140-51**

FIELD GOAL PCT	OPP	DATE	FG	FGA	PCT
1 Oklahoma State	Tulane	M22	28	35	**80.0**
2 Evansville	Butler	M14	31	43	**72.1**
Bradley	Chicago State	N26	31	43	**72.1**
4 Texas State	Concordia Lutheran	N30	33	46	**71.7**
5 Florida State	UNC Asheville	J2	43	60	**71.7**

THREE-PT FG MADE	OPP	DATE	3FG
1 Temple	George Washington	M3	**19**
2 La Salle	Oregon	D28	**18**
Stetson	Iona	D30	**18**
Centenary	East Texas Baptist	J13	**18**
NC State	Florida State	F10	**18**

CONSENSUS ALL-AMERICAS

FIRST TEAM

PLAYER	CL	POS	HT	SCHOOL	RPG	PPG
Jim Jackson	JR	G/F	6-6	Ohio State	6.8	22.4
Christian Laettner	SR	C	6-11	Duke	7.9	21.5
Harold Miner	JR	G	6-5	Southern California	7.0	26.3
Alonzo Mourning	SR	F/C	6-10	Georgetown	10.7	21.3
Shaquille O'Neal	JR	C	7-1	LSU	14.0	24.1

SECOND TEAM

PLAYER	CL	POS	HT	SCHOOL	RPG	PPG
Byron Houston	SR	F	6-7	Oklahoma State	8.6	20.2
Don MacLean	SR	F	6-10	UCLA	7.8	20.7
Anthony Peeler	SR	G	6-4	Missouri	5.5	23.4
Malik Sealy	SR	F	6-7	St. John's	6.8	22.6
Walt Williams	SR	G/F	6-8	Maryland	5.6	26.8

SELECTORS: AP, NABC, UPI, USBWA

AWARD WINNERS

PLAYER OF THE YEAR

PLAYER	CL	POS	HT	SCHOOL	AWARDS
Christian Laettner	SR	C	6-11	Duke	Naismith, AP, USBWA, Wooden, NABC, Rupp
Jim Jackson	JR	G/F	6-6	Ohio State	UPI
Tony Bennett	SR	G	6-0	Wisc.-Green Bay	Frances Pomeroy Naismith*

* FOR THE MOST OUTSTANDING SENIOR PLAYER WHO IS 6 FEET OR UNDER

DEFENSIVE PLAYER OF THE YEAR

PLAYER	CL	POS	HT	SCHOOL
Alonzo Mourning	SR	F/C	6-10	Georgetown

COACH OF THE YEAR

COACH	SCHOOL	REC	AWARDS
Mike Krzyzewski	Duke	34-2	Naismith, Sporting News
Roy Williams	Kansas	27-5	AP
Perry Clark	Tulane	22-9	UPI, USBWA
George Raveling	USC	24-6	NABC, CBS/Chevrolet

BOB GIBBONS' TOP HIGH SCHOOL SENIOR RECRUITS

PLAYER	POS	HT	HIGH SCHOOL	A-A TEAMS	COLLEGE	CAREER NOTES
1 **Othella Harrington**	C	6-10	Murrah HS, Jackson, MI	McD, P, USA	Georgetown	1,839 pts, 983 reb (4 seasons); 2nd-round pick, '96 NBA draft (Rockets); 7.4 ppg (13 seasons)
2 **Corliss Williamson**	PF	6-7	Russellville (AR) Senior HS	McD, P, USA	Arkansas	NCAA title, '94; at UA, 1,728 pts (3 seasons); No. 13 pick in '95 NBA draft (Kings); NBA Sixth Man award, '02
3 **Jason Kidd**	G	6-4	St. Joseph Notre Dame HS, Alameda, CA	McD, P, USA	California	First-team All-America, '94; 16.7 ppg, 8.4 apg, '94; No. 2 pick, '94 NBA draft (Mavs); 9-time All-Star
4 **Carlos Strong**	PF	6-8	Cedar Shoals HS, Athens, GA	McD, P	Georgia	12.0 ppg, 6.3 rpg (4 seasons); 3rd team All-SEC, '95; undrafted
5 **Donta Bright**	SF	6-6	Dunbar HS, Baltimore	McD, P, USA	Massachusetts	First-team All-America, '96; At UMass, 1,229 pts (4 seasons); undrafted; played overseas
6 **Rodrick Rhodes**	SF	6-7	St. Anthony's HS, Jersey City, NJ	McD, P, USA	Kentucky/USC	Transferred after 3 years; in college, 1,559 pts; No. 24 pick in '97 NBA draft (Rockets); 5.3 ppg (3 seasons)
7 **Chris Davis**	F	6-6	Oak Hill Academy, Mouth of Wilson, VA	McD	Auburn	11.6 ppg, 6.1 rpg (1 season); undrafted
8 **Walter McCarty**	F/C	6-9	Harrison HS, Evansville, IN	P	Kentucky	NCAA title, '96; at UK, 9.2 ppg, 5.1 rpg (3 seasons); No. 19 pick, '96 NBA draft (Knicks); 5.2 ppg (11 seasons)
9 **John Wallace**	PF	6-8	Greece-Athena HS, Rochester, NY	McD, P	Syracuse	Left as SU's 3rd leading scorer (2,119 pts); No. 18 pick, '96 NBA draft (Knicks); 7.6 ppg (7 seasons)
10 **Michael Evans**	PG	6-2	Booker T. Washington HS, Norfolk, VA	P	Okaloosa-Walton JC	20.6 ppg, 6.6 apg (1 season); undrafted
11 **Greg Simpson**	G	6-1	Lima (OH) Senior HS	McD, P	Ohio State/ West Virginia	2-time Ohio Mr. Basketball; Big Ten FOY, '93; transferred after 2 years; at WVa., 13.2 ppg; undrafted
12 **Richard Keene**	2G	6-5	Collinsville (IL) HS	P	Illinois	9.4 ppg (4 seasons); left Illinois all-time leader in 3pt FGs; undrafted; played in CBA
13 **Tony Delk**	2G	6-1	Haywood HS, Brownsville, TN	McD, P	Kentucky	SEC POY, '96; NCAA title, '96; No. 16 pick, '96 NBA draft (Hornets); 9.1 ppg (10 seasons)
14 **Kenyon Murray**	G/F	6-6	Battle Creek (MI) Central HS	McD, P	Iowa	Left Iowa as all-time steals leader (200); undrafted; played in CBA, USBL, overseas
15 **Steve Edwards**	2G	6-6	Miami Senior HS	McD, P	Miami (FL)	Big East All-Rookie team, '93; left as Big East leader in 3pt FGs; 12.7 ppg (4 seasons); undrafted
16 **Andre Woolridge**	PG	6-1	Benson HS, Omaha, NE		Nebraska/Iowa	Transferred after 1 year; led Big Ten with 20.2 ppg, 6.0 apg as Sr.; 3rd team AP All-America, '97; undrafted
17 **Michael Lloyd**	G	6-1	Dunbar HS, Baltimore	McD	San Jacinto CC/ Syracuse	1,871 points; at SU, 12.5 ppg, 5.2 apg (1 season); undrafted
18 **Charles Macon**	F	6-7	Michigan City (IN) HS	McD, P	Ohio State/ Central Michigan	Indiana Mr. Basketball, '92; DNP at OSU; at Central Michigan, 18.2 ppg, 7.2 rpg as Sr.
19 **Duane Spencer**	F	6-9	W.L. Cohen HS, New Orleans	McD, P	Georgetown/LSU	Transferred after 2 years; at LSU, 15.1 ppg, 7.7 rpg as Sr.; undrafted
20 **Chris Collins**	G	6-3	Glenbrook North HS, Northbrook, IL	McD	Duke	9.1 ppg, 2.4 apg (4 seasons); 2nd team All-ACC as Sr. (16.3 ppg); undrafted

OTHER STANDOUTS

PLAYER	POS	HT	HIGH SCHOOL	A-A TEAMS	COLLEGE	CAREER NOTES
41 **DeJuan Wheat**	PG	6-2	Ballard HS, Louisville, KY	P	Louisville	Left L'ville as 2nd-leading scorer (2,183 pts); 16.1 ppg (3 seasons); 2nd-round pick, '97 NBA draft (Lakers); 3.3 ppg (2 seasons)
54 **Kerry Kittles**	G/F	6-5	St. Augustine HS, New Orleans		Villanova	Left as Nova's all-time leading scorer (2,243 pts); first-team AP All-America, '96; No. 8 pick, '96 NBA draft (Nets); 14.1 ppg (8 seasons)
100 **Travis Knight**	PF	6-11	Alta HS, Sandy, UT		Connecticut	6.1 ppg, 6.0 rpg (4 seasons); No. 29 pick in '96 NBA draft (Bulls); 3.4 ppg (7 seasons)

Abbreviations: McD=McDonald's; P=Parade; USA=USA Today

Poll Progression

Preseason Poll

AP	UPI	School
1	1	**Duke**
2	2	**Indiana**
3	3	**Arkansas**
4	8	**Kentucky**
5	7	**Arizona**
6	6	**LSU**
7	5	**Ohio State**
8	4	**North Carolina**
9	9	**Seton Hall**
10	10	**St. John's**
11	11	**UCLA**
12	13	**Kansas**
13	12	**Oklahoma State**
14	17	**Utah**
15	15	**Connecticut**
16	14	**Georgetown**
17	16	**Alabama**
18	23	**DePaul**
19	21	**Oklahoma**
20	19	**Michigan**
21	20	**Iowa**
22	18	**Wake Forest**
23	24	**Georgia Tech**
24	22	**Arizona State**
25	—	**Louisville**
—	25	**Texas**

Week of Nov 25

AP	UPI	School	AP↓↑
1	1	**Duke** (0-0)	
2	3	**Arkansas** (0-0)	↑1
3	4	**Arizona** (0-0)	↑2
4	2	**UCLA** (1-0)	↑7
5	6	**Ohio State** (0-0)	↑2
6	5	**North Carolina** (1-0)	↑2
7	7	**Seton Hall** (1-0)	↑2
8	11	**St. John's** (1-0)	↑2
9	12	**LSU** (1-0)	↓3
10	9	**Indiana** (0-1)	↓8
11	8	**Oklahoma State** (2-0)	↑2
12	10	**Kansas** (1-0)	
13	15	**Kentucky** (1-1)	↓9
14	17	**Utah** (1-0)	
15	13	**Connecticut** (1-0)	
16	14	**Alabama** (1-0)	↑1
17	16	**Georgetown** (0-0)	↓1
18	18	**Georgia Tech** (2-0)	↑5
19	20	**Oklahoma** (1-0)	
20	24	**DePaul** (0-0)	↓2
21	25	**Iowa** (1-0)	
22	19	**Wake Forest** (1-0)	
23	22	**Michigan** (0-0)	↓3
24	21	**Pittsburgh** (2-0)	⤴
25	—	**Arizona State** (0-0)	↓1
—	23	**Texas** (2-0)	

Week of Dec 2

AP	UPI	School	AP↓↑
1	1	**Duke** (2-0)	
2	2	**UCLA** (2-0)	↑2
3	3	**Arizona** (1-0)	
4	3	**Ohio State** (2-0)	↑1
5	5	**North Carolina** (4-0)	↑1
6	7	**Seton Hall** (2-0)	↑1
7	8	**St. John's** (3-0)	↑1
8	6	**Oklahoma State** (5-0)	↑3
9	10	**Indiana** (1-1)	↑1
10	9	**Kansas** (3-0)	↑2
11	11	**Arkansas** (2-1)	↓9
12	12	**Connecticut** (2-0)	↑3
13	19	**Utah** (3-0)	↑1
14	17	**Kentucky** (1-1)	↓1
15	15	**Alabama** (4-0)	↑1
16	13	**LSU** (2-1)	↓7
17	16	**Georgia Tech** (3-1)	↑1
18	14	**Georgetown** (2-0)	↓1
19	22	**Oklahoma** (3-0)	
20	21	**DePaul** (1-0)	
21	23	**Iowa** (2-0)	
22	20	**Michigan State** (3-0)	⤴
23	18	**Wake Forest** (3-0)	↓1
24	—	**UNLV** (2-0)	⤴
25	25	**Michigan** (0-0)	↓2
—	24	**Pittsburgh** (3-1)	↱

Week of Dec 9

AP	UPI	School	AP↓↑
1	1	**Duke** (4-0)	
2	4	**Arizona** (3-0)	↑
3	2	**UCLA** (3-0)	↓
4	3	**Ohio State** (4-0)	
5	5	**North Carolina** (6-0)	
6	6	**Oklahoma State** (7-0)	↑
7	7	**Kansas** (4-0)	↑
8	8	**Connecticut** (4-0)	↑
9	9	**Kentucky** (3-1)	↑
10	11	**Utah** (6-0)	↑
11	10	**St. John's** (3-1)	↓4
12	14	**Seton Hall** (3-1)	↓6
13	12	**Indiana** (2-2)	↓4
13	13	**Georgia Tech** (5-1)	↑4
13	15	**Michigan State** (5-0)	↑9
16	17	**Iowa** (4-0)	↑5
17	18	**Oklahoma** (4-0)	↑2
18	22	**Michigan** (2-0)	↑7
19	16	**Arkansas** (4-2)	↓8
20	19	**Alabama** (5-1)	↓5
21	24	**Missouri** (4-0)	⤴
22	21	**Wake Forest** (4-1)	↑1
23	20	**Georgetown** (2-1)	↓5
24	—	**Charlotte** (4-1)	⤴
25	23	**LSU** (2-2)	↓9
—	25	**Virginia** (3-1)	

Week of Dec 16

AP	UPI	School	AP↓↑
1	1	**Duke** (5-0)	Ⓐ
2	4	**Arizona** (4-0)	
3	2	**UCLA** (4-0)	
4	3	**Ohio State** (5-0)	
5	5	**Oklahoma State** (9-0)	↑1
6	7	**Kansas** (5-0)	↑1
7	8	**Connecticut** (5-0)	↑1
8	9	**Kentucky** (6-1)	↑1
9	6	**North Carolina** (6-1)	↓4
10	11	**St. John's** (4-1)	↑1
11	12	**Seton Hall** (5-1)	↑1
12	14	**Michigan State** (6-0)	↑1
13	13	**Georgia Tech** (6-1)	
14	10	**Indiana** (5-2)	↓1
15	15	**Michigan** (4-1)	Ⓐ ↑3
16	16	**Oklahoma** (5-0)	↑1
17	20	**Missouri** (6-0)	↑4
18	18	**Utah** (8-1)	↓8
19	19	**Arkansas** (5-2)	
20	17	**Alabama** (6-1)	
21	22	**Wake Forest** (4-1)	↑1
22	23	**Iowa** (6-1)	↓6
23	21	**Georgetown** (4-1)	
24	—	**Charlotte** (7-1)	
25	24	**Louisville** (4-0)	⤴
—	25	**LSU** (2-2)	↱

Week of Dec 23

AP	UPI	School	AP↓↑
1	1	**Duke** (5-0)	
2	2	**UCLA** (5-0)	↑1
3	3	**Oklahoma State** (10-0)	↑2
4	4	**Kansas** (6-0)	↑2
5	5	**Connecticut** (5-0)	↑2
6	6	**Arizona** (5-1)	↓4
7	9	**Ohio State** (6-1)	↓3
8	7	**North Carolina** (7-1)	↑1
9	8	**Michigan State** (8-0)	↑3
10	10	**Indiana** (6-2)	↑4
11	12	**Michigan** (6-1)	↑4
12	13	**Seton Hall** (5-1)	↓1
13	11	**Georgia Tech** (7-2)	
14	17	**Oklahoma** (6-0)	↑2
15	14	**Arkansas** (7-2)	↑4
16	15	**Missouri** (7-0)	↑1
17	16	**Kentucky** (6-2)	↓9
18	18	**St. John's** (4-2)	↓8
19	20	**Utah** (9-1)	↓1
20	19	**Alabama** (8-1)	
21	22	**Louisville** (6-0)	↑4
22	21	**Wake Forest** (6-1)	↓1
23	23	**Iowa** (6-1)	↓1
24	24	**Georgetown** (6-1)	↓1
25	—	**Charlotte** (7-1)	↓1
—	25	**USC** (7-1)	

Week of Dec 30

AP	UPI	School	AP↓↑
1	1	**Duke** (5-0)	
2	2	**UCLA** (7-0)	
3	3	**Oklahoma State** (10-0)	
4	4	**Kansas** (8-0)	
5	5	**Connecticut** (6-0)	
6	8	**Arizona** (6-1)	
7	7	**Ohio State** (7-1)	
8	6	**North Carolina** (7-1)	
9	9	**Michigan State** (10-0)	
10	10	**Indiana** (8-2)	
11	11	**Michigan** (7-1)	
12	12	**Seton Hall** (7-1)	
13	14	**Missouri** (9-0)	↑3
14	13	**Oklahoma** (8-0)	
15	15	**Georgia Tech** (8-2)	↓2
16	17	**Arkansas** (9-2)	↓1
17	16	**Kentucky** (8-2)	
18	19	**St. John's** (6-2)	
19	18	**Alabama** (10-1)	↑1
20	20	**Wake Forest** (6-1)	↑2
21	24	**Charlotte** (7-1)	↑4
22	21	**Georgetown** (7-1)	↑2
23	—	**Syracuse** (7-0)	⤴
24	25	**Louisville** (6-1)	↓3
25	23	**USC** (8-1)	⤴
—	22	**Utah** (9-2)	↱

Week of Jan 6

AP	UPI	School	AP↓↑
1	1	**Duke** (7-0)	
2	2	**UCLA** (8-0)	
3	3	**Oklahoma State** (12-0)	
4	4	**Kansas** (10-0)	
5	5	**Connecticut** (10-0)	
6	6	**Arizona** (9-1)	
7	8	**Ohio State** (8-1)	
8	7	**North Carolina** (9-1)	
9	10	**Michigan State** (10-0)	
10	9	**Indiana** (9-2)	
11	12	**Michigan** (8-1)	
12	14	**Missouri** (11-0)	↑1
13	13	**Arkansas** (12-2)	↑3
14	15	**Georgia Tech** (11-2)	↑1
15	11	**Kentucky** (10-2)	↑2
16	16	**Alabama** (12-1)	↑3
17	18	**St. John's** (8-2)	↑1
18	17	**Seton Hall** (8-2)	↓6
19	19	**Wake Forest** (7-1)	↑1
20	21	**Syracuse** (10-0)	↑3
21	20	**Oklahoma** (10-1)	↓7
22	24	**Charlotte** (8-1)	↓1
23	22	**USC** (8-1)	↑2
24	23	**Tulane** (9-0)	⤴
25	25	**Massachusetts** (11-2)	⤴

Week of Jan 13

AP	UPI	School	AP↓↑
1	1	**Duke** (10-0)	
2	2	**UCLA** (10-0)	Ⓑ
3	3	**Oklahoma State** (14-0)	
4	4	**Ohio State** (10-1)	↑3
5	5	**Indiana** (11-2)	↑5
6	7	**Kansas** (11-1)	↓2
7	6	**Arizona** (10-2)	Ⓑ ↓1
8	8	**Connecticut** (11-1)	↓3
9	9	**Alabama** (14-1)	↑7
10	11	**Kentucky** (12-2)	↑5
11	10	**Michigan State** (11-1)	↓2
12	12	**Arkansas** (13-3)	↑1
13	13	**Missouri** (11-1)	↓1
14	13	**North Carolina** (10-2)	↓6
15	15	**Michigan** (9-2)	↓4
16	16	**Georgia Tech** (12-3)	↓2
17	18	**St. John's** (9-3)	
18	20	**Charlotte** (11-1)	↑4
19	19	**Tulane** (11-0)	↑5
20	17	**Syracuse** (11-1)	
21	21	**Seton Hall** (9-3)	↓3
22	23	**Georgetown** (9-2)	⤴
23	22	**Oklahoma** (10-2)	↓2
24	—	**Iowa State** (13-3)	⤴
25	25	**Louisville** (8-3)	⤴
—	24	**Wake Forest** (8-3)	↱

Week of Jan 20

AP	UPI	School	AP↓↑
1	1	**Duke** (12-0)	
2	2	**UCLA** (12-0)	
3	3	**Oklahoma State** (16-0)	
4	4	**Indiana** (13-2)	↑1
5	7	**Kansas** (13-1)	↑1
6	5	**Ohio State** (11-2)	↓2
7	6	**Connecticut** (13-1)	↑1
8	8	**Kentucky** (14-2)	Ⓒ ↑2
9	10	**Arkansas** (15-3)	↑3
10	11	**North Carolina** (13-2)	↑4
11	9	**Arizona** (11-3)	↓4
12	12	**Missouri** (12-2)	↑1
13	14	**Syracuse** (13-1)	↑7
14	13	**Michigan State** (12-2)	↓3
15	15	**Alabama** (14-3)	↓6
16	16	**Michigan** (10-3)	↓1
17	17	**Oklahoma** (11-2)	↑6
18	18	**Georgia Tech** (13-4)	↓2
19	22	**Charlotte** (11-2)	↓1
20	21	**Louisville** (10-3)	↑5
21	19	**Tulane** (13-1)	↓2
22	20	**St. John's** (10-4)	↓5
23	24	**UTEP** (14-1)	⤴
24	25	**Stanford** (11-1)	⤴
25	—	**UNLV** (14-2)	⤴
—	23	**Wake Forest** (9-4)	

Week of Jan 27

AP	UPI	School	AP↓↑
1	1	**Duke** (14-0)	
2	2	**UCLA** (14-0)	
3	3	**Oklahoma State** (18-0)	
4	4	**Indiana** (14-2)	
5	5	**Kansas** (14-1)	
6	6	**Connecticut** (15-1)	↑1
7	7	**Arkansas** (17-3)	↑2
8	10	**Missouri** (14-2)	↑4
9	9	**Arizona** (13-3)	↑2
10	8	**Ohio State** (12-3)	↓4
11	11	**North Carolina** (14-3)	↓1
12	12	**Syracuse** (14-2)	↑1
13	13	**Michigan State** (13-2)	↑1
14	14	**Kentucky** (14-4)	↓6
15	17	**Michigan** (11-4)	↑1
16	15	**Tulane** (15-1)	↑5
17	21	**Charlotte** (13-2)	↑2
18	18	**Oklahoma** (12-3)	↓1
19	20	**UTEP** (16-1)	↑4
20	16	**Georgia Tech** (14-5)	↓2
21	—	**UNLV** (18-2)	↑4
22	19	**Alabama** (15-4)	↓7
23	—	**Florida State** (14-5)	⤴
24	22	**Louisville** (11-4)	↓4
25	25	**USC** (13-3)	⤴
—	23	**Seton Hall** (11-5)	
—	23	**LSU** (11-4)	

Week of Feb 3

AP	UPI	School	AP↓↑
1	1	**Duke** (17-0)	
2	2	**Oklahoma State** (20-0)	↑1
3	3	**Kansas** (16-1)	↑2
4	4	**UCLA** (15-1)	↓2
5	5	**Arkansas** (17-3)	↑2
6	9	**Indiana** (15-3)	↓2
7	6	**Arizona** (15-3)	↑2
8	7	**Ohio State** (14-3)	↑2
9	8	**North Carolina** (15-3)	↑2
10	10	**Connecticut** (16-2)	↓4
11	11	**Michigan State** (14-3)	↑2
12	14	**Missouri** (14-3)	↓4
13	12	**Syracuse** (15-3)	↓1
14	13	**Tulane** (16-1)	↑2
15	16	**Michigan** (12-5)	
16	18	**USC** (14-3)	↑9
17	—	**UNLV** (19-2)	↑4
18	15	**Alabama** (17-4)	↑4
19	17	**Kentucky** (15-5)	↓5
20	21	**Charlotte** (15-3)	↓3
21	19	**Oklahoma** (14-4)	↓3
22	20	**LSU** (12-4)	⤴
23	23	**Florida State** (14-5)	
24	22	**Georgia Tech** (15-6)	↓4
25	25	**UTEP** (16-3)	↓6
—	24	**St. John's** (11-7)	

[Wee]k of Feb 10

AP	UPI	School		AP ↓↑
	1	**Duke** (18-1)	(D)	
	2	**Oklahoma State** (21-1)		
	3	**UCLA** (17-1)		↑1
	5	**Kansas** (17-2)		↓1
	6	**Indiana** (17-3)		↑2
	8	**North Carolina** (17-3)	(D)	↑3
	7	**Arizona** (17-3)		
	4	**Ohio State** (16-3)		
	11	**Missouri** (16-3)		↑3
	10	**Syracuse** (16-3)		↑3
	9	**Arkansas** (17-5)		↓6
	12	**Michigan State** (15-4)		↓1
	16	**USC** (16-3)		↑3
	13	**Tulane** (18-2)		
	—	**UNLV** (22-2)		↑2
	15	**Alabama** (19-4)		↑2
	17	**Michigan** (14-5)		↓2
	14	**Connecticut** (16-4)		↓8
	18	**Kentucky** (16-5)		
	19	**LSU** (14-5)		↑2
	21	**UTEP** (18-3)		↑4
	20	**Charlotte** (16-4)		↓2
	21	**Florida State** (15-6)		
	25	**Cincinnati** (17-3)		⤴
	—	**Seton Hall** (13-6)		⤴
—	23	**Oklahoma** (14-6)		⤵
—	24	**Georgia Tech** (16-7)		⤵

Week of Feb 17

AP	UPI	School	AP ↓↑
1	1	**Duke** (20-1)	
2	2	**UCLA** (19-1)	↑1
3	3	**Kansas** (19-2)	↑1
4	6	**North Carolina** (18-3)	↑2
5	5	**Arizona** (19-3)	↑2
6	4	**Ohio State** (17-3)	↑2
7	7	**Indiana** (18-4)	↓3
8	8	**Oklahoma State** (21-3)	↓6
9	10	**Missouri** (17-3)	
10	9	**Arkansas** (19-5)	↑1
11	11	**Michigan State** (17-4)	↑1
12	—	**UNLV** (22-2)	↑3
13	12	**Kentucky** (18-5)	↑6
14	13	**Alabama** (19-5)	↑2
15	17	**USC** (17-4)	↓2
16	16	**Florida State** (18-6)	↑7
17	14	**Syracuse** (16-5)	↓7
18	15	**Tulane** (19-3)	↓4
19	20	**Cincinnati** (19-3)	↑5
20	19	**Michigan** (15-6)	↓3
21	18	**Connecticut** (16-5)	↓3
22	21	**Seton Hall** (15-6)	↑3
23	—	**Iowa State** (18-8)	⤴
24	23	**St. John's** (14-7)	⤴
25	—	**Georgetown** (17-6)	⤴
—	22	**UTEP** (18-5)	⤵
—	24	**LSU** (14-7)	⤵
—	24	**Oklahoma** (15-6)	

Week of Feb 24

AP	UPI	School	AP ↓↑
1	1	**Duke** (21-2)	
2	3	**Indiana** (20-4)	↑5
3	2	**Kansas** (20-3)	
4	4	**UCLA** (21-2)	↓2
5	6	**Arizona** (20-4)	
6	7	**Missouri** (19-4)	↑3
7	—	**UNLV** (24-2)	↑5
8	5	**Ohio State** (17-5)	↓2
9	8	**Arkansas** (20-6)	↑1
10	10	**North Carolina** (18-5)	↓6
11	12	**Kentucky** (20-5)	↑2
12	11	**Michigan State** (18-5)	↓1
13	13	**USC** (19-4)	↑2
14	9	**Oklahoma State** (21-5)	↓6
15	15	**Tulane** (19-3)	↑3
16	14	**Alabama** (20-6)	↓2
17	16	**Michigan** (17-6)	↑3
18	17	**Georgetown** (17-6)	↑7
19	18	**Cincinnati** (20-4)	
20	22	**St. John's** (16-7)	↑4
21	24	**DePaul** (18-6)	⤴
22	19	**Syracuse** (16-7)	↓5
22	21	**Florida State** (18-8)	↓6
24	20	**Connecticut** (17-6)	↓3
25	—	**Nebraska** (17-6)	⤴
—	23	**Oklahoma** (17-6)	
—	25	**Seton Hall** (16-7)	⤵
—	25	**UTEP** (19-5)	

Week of Mar 2

AP	UPI	School	AP ↓↑
1	1	**Duke** (23-2)	
2	2	**Indiana** (21-4)	
3	3	**Kansas** (21-3)	
4	4	**Arizona** (22-4)	↑1
5	5	**Ohio State** (19-5)	↑3
6	—	**UNLV** (25-2)	↑1
7	6	**Arkansas** (22-6)	↑2
8	10	**USC** (20-4)	↑5
9	7	**UCLA** (21-4)	↓5
10	9	**Kentucky** (22-5)	↑1
11	8	**Missouri** (20-5)	↓5
12	11	**Oklahoma State** (22-5)	↑2
13	12	**Michigan State** (18-6)	↓1
14	15	**Cincinnati** (22-4)	↑5
15	19	**DePaul** (19-6)	↑6
16	13	**North Carolina** (18-7)	↓6
17	14	**Georgetown** (18-7)	↑1
18	18	**Michigan** (17-7)	↓1
19	16	**Florida State** (19-8)	↑3
20	17	**Alabama** (21-7)	↓4
21	20	**Tulane** (19-5)	↓6
22	22	**Seton Hall** (18-7)	⤴
23	23	**LSU** (18-7)	⤴
24	21	**Syracuse** (18-7)	↓2
25	—	**Massachusetts** (24-4)	⤴
—	24	**Oklahoma** (18-7)	
—	25	**St. John's** (17-8)	⤵

[W]eek of Mar 9

AP	UPI	School		AP ↓↑
1	1	**Duke** (25-2)		
2	3	**Arizona** (24-4)		↑2
3	2	**Kansas** (23-4)		
4	4	**Indiana** (22-5)		↓2
5	5	**Ohio State** (21-5)		
6	6	**Arkansas** (24-6)	(E)	↑1
7	—	**UNLV** (26-2)		↓1
8	7	**UCLA** (23-4)		↑1
9	11	**Kentucky** (23-6)		↑1
10	8	**USC** (21-5)		↓2
11	10	**Oklahoma State** (24-6)		↑1
12	12	**Cincinnati** (23-4)		↑2
13	9	**Missouri** (20-7)		↓2
14	15	**Michigan** (18-8)		↑4
15	18	**Seton Hall** (20-7)		↑7
16	16	**Michigan State** (19-7)		↓3
17	14	**Alabama** (23-7)		↑3
18	13	**Florida State** (19-8)		↑1
19	20	**DePaul** (20-7)		↓4
20	16	**North Carolina** (19-8)		↓4
21	19	**Georgetown** (19-8)		↓4
22	25	**Massachusetts** (26-4)		↑3
23	23	**LSU** (19-8)	(E)	
24	22	**Oklahoma** (20-7)		⤴
25	21	**St. John's** (19-8)		⤴
—	24	**Tulane** (20-7)		⤵

Final Poll

AP	UPI	School		AP ↓↑
1	1	**Duke** (28-2)		
2	2	**Kansas** (26-4)		↑1
3	3	**Ohio State** (23-5)		↑2
4	5	**UCLA** (25-4)		↑4
5	4	**Indiana** (23-6)	(F)	↓1
6	9	**Kentucky** (26-6)		↑3
7	—	**UNLV** (26-2)		
8	6	**USC** (23-6)		↑2
9	8	**Arkansas** (25-7)		↓3
10	7	**Arizona** (24-6)		↓8
11	10	**Oklahoma State** (26-7)		
12	11	**Cincinnati** (25-4)	(G)	
13	12	**Alabama** (25-8)		↑4
14	15	**Michigan State** (21-7)		↑2
15	16	**Michigan** (20-8)		↓1
16	13	**Missouri** (20-8)		↓3
17	21	**Massachusetts** (28-4)		↑5
18	14	**North Carolina** (21-9)		↑2
19	19	**Seton Hall** (21-8)		↓4
20	17	**Florida State** (20-9)		↓2
21	20	**Syracuse** (21-9)		⤴
22	18	**Georgetown** (21-9)		↓1
23	24	**Oklahoma** (21-8)		↑1
24	22	**DePaul** (20-8)		↓5
25	—	**LSU** (20-9)		↓2
—	23	**St. John's** (19-10)		⤵
—	25	**Tulane** (20-7)		

(A) Michigan's Fab Five— freshmen Chris Webber, Jalen Rose, Juwan Howard, Ray Jackson and Jimmy King—take defending NCAA champion Duke into OT before losing 88-85.

(B) Arizona's 71-game home court winning steak ends when Darrick Martin hits a running 12-footer with 0.3 seconds remaining to give UCLA an 89-87 victory.

(C) Off probation and in the hunt for the NCAA title, Kentucky gets 21 points and 15 rebounds from sophomore Jamal Mashburn in an 84-71 win over Vanderbilt. Mashburn is surrounded by four seniors—Richie Farmer, John Pelphrey, Deron Feldhaus and Sean Woods—all survivors of the Eddie Sutton scandal.

(D) Eric Montross, North Carolina's 7-foot center, gets battered by Duke, but the Tar Heels prevail, 75-73, on Feb. 9. It's not the first time blood has been shed in the rivalry, and it won't be the last.

(E) Down by 15 at halftime, coach Nolan Richardson's Razorbacks roar back for a 106-92 OT victory over LSU, thanks to Lee Mayberry's nine three-pointers and a defense that holds Shaquille O'Neal scoreless for the final 16:30.

(F) Indiana ends its regular season with a 61-59 road loss to the same Purdue team it whipped in Bloomington on Jan. 28, 106-65.

(G) Cincinnati rides a 16-game winning streak into the NCAA Tournament; it will advance to the Final Four for the first time since 1963.

Pre-Tournament Ratings Percentage Index (RPI)

Rank	School	W-L	Sched. Strg.	SS Rank	RPI
1	**Kansas**	24-4	.6270	3	.6539
2	**Duke**	28-2	.5800	30	.6446
3	**UCLA**	24-4	.5730	39	.6256
4	**Indiana**	23-6	.6008	18	.6251
5	**Oklahoma State**	23-7	.6084	11	.6243
6	**Ohio State**	23-5	.6019	17	.6234
7	**Kentucky**	26-6	.5882	25	.6169
8	**Massachusetts**	27-4	.5591	53	.6168
9	**Cincinnati**	25-4	.5759	37	.6146
10	**Oklahoma**	18-8	.6272	2	.6113
11	**Arizona**	24-6	.5680	44	.6077
12	**Missouri**	19-8	.5929	21	.6073
13	**Michigan State**	21-7	.5895	23	.6071
14	**North Carolina**	21-9	.5885	24	.6004
15	**UNLV**	25-2	.5011	135	.6001
16	**Memphis State**	20-10	.6127	7	.5983
17	**Arkansas**	22-7	.5686	43	.5981
18	**Georgia Tech**	21-11	.6169	6	.5980
19	**USC**	22-5	.5300	87	.5970
20	**Louisville**	18-10	.6035	14	.5918
21	**Florida State**	20-9	.5854	29	.5917
22	**Michigan**	20-8	.5633	49	.5900
23	**Nebraska**	19-9	.5784	32	.5896
24	**St. John's**	19-10	.6023	16	.5884
25	**LSU**	20-9	.5881	26	.5876
26	**Seton Hall**	20-8	.5678	45	.5864
27	**DePaul**	20-8	.5530	59	.5853
28	**Pepperdine**	23-5	.5535	58	.5848
29	**Charlotte**	21-8	.5650	47	.5842
30	**Alabama**	25-8	.5306	86	.5817
31	**Temple**	17-12	.6056	13	.5816
32	**Notre Dame**	14-14	.6517	1	.5800
33	**BYU**	25-6	.5357	77	.5800
34	**Houston**	24-5	.5001	137	.5778
35	**New Mexico State**	22-7	.5467	65	.5771
36	**Evansville**	24-5	.5083	123	.5768
37	**UTEP**	21-6	.5382	75	.5768
38	**Syracuse**	21-9	.5393	72	.5741
39	**Butler**	21-9	.5721	41	.5739
40	**Stanford**	18-10	.5629	50	.5736
41	**Kansas State**	13-13	.6255	4	.5728
42	**Texas**	22-11	.5611	51	.5707
43	**Iowa State**	17-12	.5731	38	.5704
44	**West Virginia**	20-11	.5540	56	.5690
45	**South Florida**	19-8	.5288	90	.5669
46	**Miami (OH)**	21-7	.5292	88	.5661
47	**Connecticut**	19-9	.5398	71	.5660
48	**Virginia**	15-13	.5864	28	.5650
49	**Purdue**	16-14	.5975	19	.5637
50	**Wake Forest**	17-11	.5562	55	.5627

Source: Collegiate Basketball News

1992 NCAA Tournament

Midwest

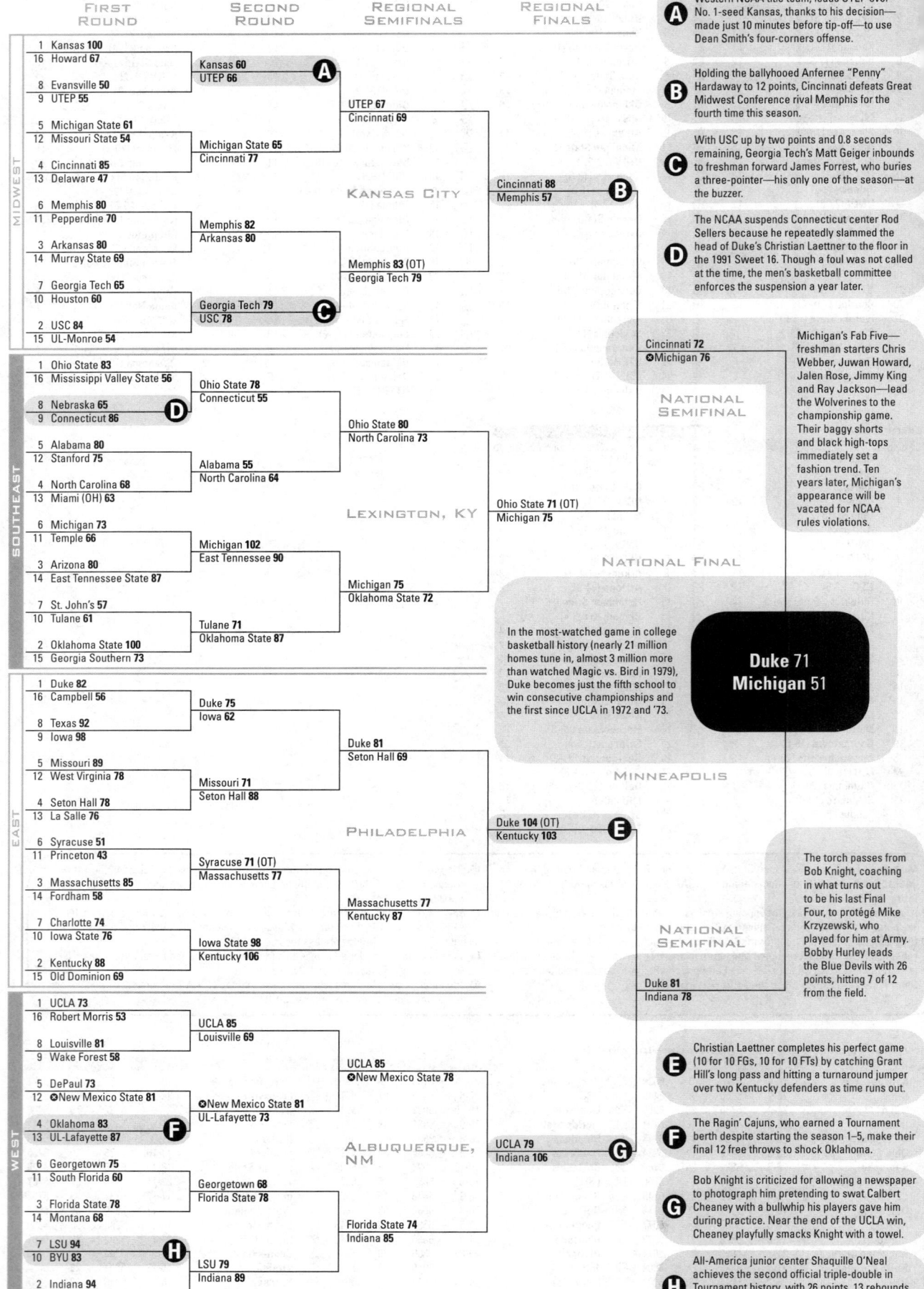

First Round
- 1 Kansas 100 / 16 Howard 67
- 8 Evansville 50 / 9 UTEP 55
- 5 Michigan State 61 / 12 Missouri State 54
- 4 Cincinnati 85 / 13 Delaware 47
- 6 Memphis 80 / 11 Pepperdine 70
- 3 Arkansas 80 / 14 Murray State 69
- 7 Georgia Tech 65 / 10 Houston 60
- 2 USC 84 / 15 UL-Monroe 54

Second Round
- Kansas 60 / UTEP 66 (A)
- Michigan State 65 / Cincinnati 77
- Memphis 82 / Arkansas 80
- Georgia Tech 79 / USC 78 (C)

Regional Semifinals (Kansas City)
- UTEP 67 / Cincinnati 69
- Memphis 83 (OT) / Georgia Tech 79

Regional Finals
- Cincinnati 88 / Memphis 57 (B)

Southeast

First Round
- 1 Ohio State 83 / 16 Mississippi Valley State 56
- 8 Nebraska 65 / 9 Connecticut 86 (D)
- 5 Alabama 80 / 12 Stanford 75
- 4 North Carolina 68 / 13 Miami (OH) 63
- 6 Michigan 73 / 11 Temple 66
- 3 Arizona 80 / 14 East Tennessee State 87
- 7 St. John's 57 / 10 Tulane 61
- 2 Oklahoma State 100 / 15 Georgia Southern 73

Second Round
- Ohio State 78 / Connecticut 55
- Alabama 55 / North Carolina 64
- Michigan 102 / East Tennessee 90
- Tulane 71 / Oklahoma State 87

Regional Semifinals (Lexington, KY)
- Ohio State 80 / North Carolina 73
- Michigan 75 / Oklahoma State 72

Regional Finals
- Ohio State 71 (OT) / Michigan 75

East

First Round
- 1 Duke 82 / 16 Campbell 56
- 8 Texas 92 / 9 Iowa 98
- 5 Missouri 89 / 12 West Virginia 78
- 4 Seton Hall 78 / 13 La Salle 76
- 6 Syracuse 51 / 11 Princeton 43
- 3 Massachusetts 85 / 14 Fordham 58
- 7 Charlotte 74 / 10 Iowa State 76
- 2 Kentucky 88 / 15 Old Dominion 69

Second Round
- Duke 75 / Iowa 62
- Missouri 71 / Seton Hall 88
- Syracuse 71 (OT) / Massachusetts 77
- Iowa State 98 / Kentucky 106

Regional Semifinals (Philadelphia)
- Duke 81 / Seton Hall 69
- Massachusetts 77 / Kentucky 87

Regional Finals
- Duke 104 (OT) / Kentucky 103 (E)

West

First Round
- 1 UCLA 73 / 16 Robert Morris 53
- 8 Louisville 81 / 9 Wake Forest 58
- 5 DePaul 73 / 12 ⊗New Mexico State 81
- 4 Oklahoma 83 / 13 UL-Lafayette 87 (F)
- 6 Georgetown 75 / 11 South Florida 60
- 3 Florida State 78 / 14 Montana 68
- 7 LSU 94 / 10 BYU 83 (H)
- 2 Indiana 94 / 15 Eastern Illinois 55

Second Round
- UCLA 85 / Louisville 69
- ⊗New Mexico State 81 / UL-Lafayette 73
- Georgetown 68 / Florida State 78
- LSU 79 / Indiana 89

Regional Semifinals (Albuquerque, NM)
- UCLA 85 / ⊗New Mexico State 78
- Florida State 74 / Indiana 85

Regional Finals
- UCLA 79 / Indiana 106 (G)

National Semifinal
- Cincinnati 72 / ⊗Michigan 76
- Duke 81 / Indiana 78

National Final (Minneapolis)

Duke 71
Michigan 51

In the most-watched game in college basketball history (nearly 21 million homes tune in, almost 3 million more than watched Magic vs. Bird in 1979), Duke becomes just the fifth school to win consecutive championships and the first since UCLA in 1972 and '73.

Michigan's Fab Five—freshman starters Chris Webber, Juwan Howard, Jalen Rose, Jimmy King and Ray Jackson—lead the Wolverines to the championship game. Their baggy shorts and black high-tops immediately set a fashion trend. Ten years later, Michigan's appearance will be vacated for NCAA rules violations.

The torch passes from Bob Knight, coaching in what turns out to be his last Final Four, to protégé Mike Krzyzewski, who played for him at Army. Bobby Hurley leads the Blue Devils with 26 points, hitting 7 of 12 from the field.

A Don Haskins, who coached the 1966 Texas Western NCAA title team, leads UTEP over No. 1-seed Kansas, thanks to his decision—made just 10 minutes before tip-off—to use Dean Smith's four-corners offense.

B Holding the ballyhooed Anfernee "Penny" Hardaway to 12 points, Cincinnati defeats Great Midwest Conference rival Memphis for the fourth time this season.

C With USC up by two points and 0.8 seconds remaining, Georgia Tech's Matt Geiger inbounds to freshman forward James Forrest, who buries a three-pointer—his only one of the season—at the buzzer.

D The NCAA suspends Connecticut center Rod Sellers because he repeatedly slammed the head of Duke's Christian Laettner to the floor in the 1991 Sweet 16. Though a foul was not called at the time, the men's basketball committee enforces the suspension a year later.

E Christian Laettner completes his perfect game (10 for 10 FGs, 10 for 10 FTs) by catching Grant Hill's long pass and hitting a turnaround jumper over two Kentucky defenders as time runs out.

F The Ragin' Cajuns, who earned a Tournament berth despite starting the season 1–5, make their final 12 free throws to shock Oklahoma.

G Bob Knight is criticized for allowing a newspaper to photograph him pretending to swat Calbert Cheaney with a bullwhip his players gave him during practice. Near the end of the UCLA win, Cheaney playfully smacks Knight with a towel.

H All-America junior center Shaquille O'Neal achieves the second official triple-double in Tournament history, with 26 points, 13 rebounds and a record 11 blocks. The Orlando Magic will make him the No. 1 pick in the 1992 NBA draft.

⊗ Team participation later vacated

TOURNAMENT LEADERS

INDIVIDUAL LEADERS

SCORING

	CL	POS	G	PTS	PPG
1 **Jamal Mashburn**, Kentucky	SO	F	4	96	24.0
2 **Jon Barry**, Georgia Tech	SR	G	3	66	22.0
3 **Terry Dehere**, Seton Hall	JR	G	3	65	21.7
4 **Tracy Murray**, UCLA	JR	F	4	82	20.5
5 **Sam Cassell**, Florida State	JR	G	3	61	20.3
6 **Byron Houston**, Oklahoma State	SR	F	3	60	20.0
Corey Williams, Oklahoma State	SR	G	3	60	20.0
8 **Sean Sutton**, Oklahoma State	SR	G	3	58	19.3
9 **Christian Laettner**, Duke	SR	C	6	115	19.2
10 **John Pelphrey**, Kentucky	SR	F	4	76	19.0

MINIMUM: 3 GAMES

FIELD GOAL PCT

	CL	POS	G	FG	FGA	PCT
1 **Eric Montross**, North Carolina	SO	C	3	24	33	72.7
2 **Sean Sutton**, Oklahoma State	SR	G	3	18	25	72.0
3 **Gordon Winchester**, Seton Hall	SR	F	3	15	22	68.2
4 **John Pelphrey**, Kentucky	SR	F	4	26	41	63.4
5 **Will Herndon**, Massachusetts	SR	F	3	15	24	62.5

MINIMUM: 15 MADE AND 3 GAMES

FREE THROW PCT

	CL	POS	G	FT	FTA	PCT
1 **John Pelphrey**, Kentucky	SR	F	4	15	15	100.0
Harold Miner, Southern California	SR	G	2	15	15	100.0
3 **Ron Bayless**, Iowa State	JR	G	2	19	20	95.0
4 **Don MacLean**, UCLA	SR	F	4	35	38	92.1
5 **Chris Hickman**, New Mexico State	SR	F	3	20	22	90.9

MINIMUM: 15 MADE

THREE-POINT FG PCT

	CL	POS	G	3FG	3FGA	PCT
1 **Corey Williams**, Oklahoma State	SR	G	3	7	9	77.8
2 **Jimmy King**, Michigan	FR	G	6	10	15	66.7
John Leahy, Seton Hall	FR	F	3	8	12	66.7
4 **Sean Sutton**, Oklahoma State	SR	G	3	7	11	63.6
5 **Eric Anderson**, Indiana	SR	F	5	6	10	60.0

MINIMUM: 6 MADE AND 3 GAMES

ASSISTS PER GAME

	CL	POS	G	AST	APG
1 **Sam Crawford**, New Mexico State	JR	G	3	28	9.3
2 **Jamal Meeks**, Indiana	SR	G	5	42	8.4
3 **Bobby Hurley**, Duke	JR	G	6	47	7.8
4 **Sean Woods**, Kentucky	SR	G	4	30	7.5
5 **Anton Brown**, Massachusetts	SR	G	3	21	7.0

MINIMUM: 3 GAMES

REBOUNDS PER GAME

	CL	POS	G	REB	RPG
1 **Doug Edwards**, Florida State	JR	F	3	32	10.7
2 **Eric Montross**, North Carolina	SO	C	3	31	10.3
3 **Chris Webber**, Michigan	FR	F/C	6	58	9.7
4 **Jamal Mashburn**, Kentucky	SO	F	4	38	9.5
5 **Harper Williams**, Massachusetts	JR	F	3	27	9.0

MINIMUM: 3 GAMES

BLOCKED SHOTS PER GAME

	CL	POS	G	BLK	BPG
1 **David Van Dyke**, UTEP	SR	F	3	12	4.0
2 **Chris Webber**, Michigan	FR	F/C	6	17	2.8
3 **David Vaughn**, Memphis	FR	F	4	10	2.5
4 **Alan Henderson**, Indiana	FR	F/C	5	11	2.2
5 **Matt Geiger**, Georgia Tech	SR	C	3	6	2.0

MINIMUM: 3 GAMES

STEALS PER GAME

	CL	POS	G	STL	SPG
1 **John Pelphrey**, Kentucky	SR	F	4	13	3.3
2 **Sam Crawford**, New Mexico State	JR	G	3	9	3.0
3 **Jamal Mashburn**, Kentucky	SO	F	4	10	2.5
4 **William Benjamin**, New Mexico State	SR	G	3	7	2.3
Cornell Hatcher, Oklahoma State	SR	G	3	7	2.3
George Lynch, North Carolina	JR	F	3	7	2.3
Prince Stewart, UTEP	SR	G	3	7	2.3

MINIMUM: 3 GAMES

TEAM LEADERS

SCORING

	G	PTS	PPG
1 **Kentucky**	4	384	96.0
2 **Indiana**	5	452	90.4
3 **Oklahoma State**	3	259	86.3
4 **Duke**	6	494	82.3
5 **UCLA**	4	322	80.5
6 **New Mexico State**	3	240	80.0
7 **Massachusetts**	3	239	79.7
8 **Seton Hall**	3	235	78.3
9 **Cincinnati**	5	391	78.2
10 **Ohio State**	4	312	78.0

MINIMUM: 3 GAMES

FG PCT

	G	FG	FGA	PCT
1 **Oklahoma State**	3	88	152	57.9
2 **Indiana**	5	156	284	54.9
3 **Kentucky**	4	137	254	53.9
4 **Georgia Tech**	3	85	166	51.2
5 **Seton Hall**	3	82	163	50.3

MINIMUM: 3 GAMES

3-PT FG PCT

	G	3FG	3FGA	PCT
1 **Oklahoma State**	3	19	38	50.0
2 **Indiana**	5	32	69	46.4
3 **UCLA**	4	23	54	42.6
4 **Duke**	6	30	71	42.3
5 **Michigan**	6	24	59	40.7

MINIMUM: 3 GAMES

FT PCT

	G	FT	FTA	PCT
1 **Georgia Tech**	3	36	44	81.8
2 **Indiana**	5	108	133	81.2
3 **Seton Hall**	3	52	67	77.6
4 **UCLA**	4	93	121	76.9
5 **North Carolina**	3	54	71	76.1

MINIMUM: 3 GAMES

AST/TO RATIO

	G	AST	TO	RAT
1 **Kentucky**	4	91	51	1.78
2 **Indiana**	5	97	62	1.56
3 **Massachusetts**	3	59	39	1.51
4 **UCLA**	4	66	54	1.22
5 **New Mexico State**	3	49	43	1.14

MINIMUM: 3 GAMES

REBOUNDS

	G	REB	RPG
1 **Ohio State**	4	159	39.8
2 **North Carolina**	3	118	39.3
3 **Michigan**	6	234	39.0
4 **Indiana**	5	192	38.4
5 **Massachusetts**	3	113	37.7

MINIMUM: 3 GAMES

BLOCKS

	G	BLK	BPG
1 **UTEP**	3	19	6.3
2 **Seton Hall**	3	17	5.7
3 **Duke**	6	31	5.2
4 **Memphis**	4	20	5.0
North Carolina	3	15	5.0

MINIMUM: 3 GAMES

STEALS

	G	STL	SPG
1 **Kentucky**	4	44	11.0
2 **New Mexico State**	3	29	9.7
3 **Massachusetts**	3	27	9.0
4 **Duke**	6	52	8.7
5 **Ohio State**	4	33	8.3

MINIMUM: 3 GAMES

ALL-TOURNAMENT TEAM

PLAYER	CL	POS	HT	SCHOOL	RPG	APG	PPG
Bobby Hurley*	JR	G	6-0	Duke	2.3	7.8	13.8
Grant Hill	SO	G/F	6-7	Duke	6.5	4.2	12.0
Christian Laettner	SR	C	6-11	Duke	7.8	1.7	19.2
Jalen Rose†	FR	G	6-8	Michigan	5.8	5.0	17.8
Chris Webber†	FR	F/C	6-9	Michigan	9.7	2.3	16.3

ALL-REGIONAL TEAMS

EAST

PLAYER	CL	POS	HT	SCHOOL	RPG	APG	PPG
Christian Laettner*	SR	C	6-11	Duke	7.5	2.3	22.0
Bobby Hurley	JR	G	6-0	Duke	2.8	9.0	12.0
Jamal Mashburn	SO	F	6-8	Kentucky	9.5	1.3	24.0
Gordon Winchester	SR	F	6-7	Seton Hall	6.7	2.0	11.3
Sean Woods	SR	G	6-2	Kentucky	2.8	7.5	16.8

MIDWEST

PLAYER	CL	POS	HT	SCHOOL	RPG	APG	PPG
Herb Jones*	SR	G/F	6-4	Cincinnati	7.8	1.8	18.8
Jon Barry	SR	G	6-5	Georgia Tech	5.3	6.3	22.0
Anthony Buford	SR	G	6-3	Cincinnati	2.3	3.8	15.5
Anfernee Hardaway	SO	G/F	6-7	Memphis	5.5	5.5	17.8
Nick Van Exel	JR	G	6-1	Cincinnati	4.3	4.0	14.5

SOUTHEAST

PLAYER	CL	POS	HT	SCHOOL	RPG	APG	PPG
Jalen Rose*	FR	G	6-8	Michigan	5.3	5.8	20.8
Lawrence Funderburke	SO	C	6-9	Ohio State	6.8	1.0	15.8
Jim Jackson	JR	G/F	6-6	Ohio State	6.8	3.8	18.5
Eric Montross	SO	C	7-0	North Carolina	10.3	0.0	18.3
Chris Webber	FR	F/C	6-9	Michigan	9.0	2.8	17.0

WEST

PLAYER	CL	POS	HT	SCHOOL	RPG	APG	PPG
Eric Anderson*	SR	F	6-9	Indiana	4.5	1.3	16.5
Damon Bailey	SO	G	6-3	Indiana	2.8	2.8	14.8
Calbert Cheaney	JR	G/F	6-7	Indiana	5.5	1.8	20.3
Alan Henderson	FR	F/C	6-9	Indiana	8.0	0.5	14.0
Tracy Murray	JR	F	6-8	UCLA	7.3	1.8	20.5

* MOST OUTSTANDING PLAYER

† HONOR LATER VACATED

1992 NCAA TOURNAMENT BOX SCORES

Cincinnati 69, UTEP 67 (Sweet 16)

	1H	2H
Cincinnati	42	27
UTEP	35	32

CINCINNATI	MIN	FG	3FG	FT	REB	A	ST	BL	PF	TP
Herb Jones	37	8-17	0-2	8-9	6	1	0	-	2	24
Anthony Buford	38	4-8	3-4	1-3	3	4	3	-	3	12
Nick Van Exel	29	4-6	2-3	2-3	1	2	1	-	0	12
Erik Martin	23	4-7	0-0	2-3	4	1	0	-	3	10
Jeff Scott	23	2-5	0-0	1-2	5	0	0	-	5	5
Corie Blount	11	2-3	0-0	0-0	3	0	0	-	4	4
Terry Nelson	13	1-3	0-0	0-0	3	0	0	-	3	2
Tarrance Gibson	13	0-3	0-3	0-0	1	1	1	-	2	0
Allen Jackson	13	0-0	0-0	0-0	0	0	1	-	1	0
TOTALS	**200**	**25-52**	**5-12**	**14-20**	**26**	**9**	**6**	**-**	**23**	**69**
Percentages		48.1	41.7	70.0						

Coach: Bob Huggins

UTEP	MIN	FG	3FG	FT	REB	A	ST	BL	PF	TP
David Van Dyke	33	6-9	0-0	6-8	4	1	2	3	5	18
Marlon Maxey	35	3-8	0-0	8-9	8	0	1	1	4	14
Johnny Melvin	33	4-6	0-1	5-6	1	4	2	1	2	13
Eddie Rivera	39	3-5	0-1	2-2	4	4	0	0	2	8
Prince Stewart	37	3-7	1-4	0-1	2	6	3	0	3	7
Ralph Davis	11	2-5	0-0	0-0	2	0	0	2	0	4
Gym Bice	5	1-1	1-1	0-0	0	0	0	0	3	3
Roy Howard	7	0-1	0-0	0-0	3	0	0	2	2	0
TOTALS	**200**	**22-42**	**2-7**	**21-26**	**24**	**15**	**8**	**9**	**21**	**67**
Percentages		52.4	28.6	80.8						

Coach: Don Haskins

Officials: J… Silvester, Fr… Scagliotta, … Herring
Technicals: UTEP (Stew…
Attendance: 14,388

Memphis 83, Georgia Tech 79 (OT) (Sweet 16)

	1H	2H	OT1
Memphis	36	38	9
Georgia Tech	42	32	5

MEMPHIS	MIN	FG	3FG	FT	REB	A	ST	BL	PF	TP
Anfernee Hardaway	41	6-19	5-14	7-12	4	7	3	4	3	24
Anthony Douglas	37	7-13	0-0	2-2	5	0	2	0	3	16
Billy Smith	28	6-11	1-3	2-2	2	0	1	0	2	15
Tony Madlock	37	2-2	0-0	6-6	5	4	0	0	1	10
David Vaughn	34	4-12	0-0	0-1	8	1	1	4	2	8
Ernest Smith	21	4-6	0-2	0-0	2	2	2	0	1	8
Kelvin Allen	9	1-1	0-0	0-0	1	0	0	0	2	2
Tim Duncan	9	0-0	0-0	0-0	1	1	0	0	3	0
Marcus Nolan	9	0-2	0-2	0-0	0	2	3	0	1	0
TOTALS	**225**	**30-66**	**6-21**	**17-23**	**28**	**17**	**12**	**8**	**18**	**83**
Percentages		45.5	28.6	73.9						

Coach: Larry Finch

GEORGIA TECH	MIN	FG	3FG	FT	REB	A	ST	BL	PF	TP
Jon Barry	43	10-21	2-9	7-8	7	6	2	0	3	29
James Forrest	39	8-13	0-0	0-0	11	1	4	1	2	16
Malcolm Mackey	45	4-10	0-0	5-6	10	0	0	0	3	13
Travis Best	44	5-14	1-5	2-3	0	4	2	0	4	13
Matt Geiger	21	2-4	0-0	1-2	3	0	0	3	5	5
Bryan Hill	9	1-3	0-0	1-1	3	2	1	1	1	3
Ivano Newbill	18	0-0	0-0	0-0	2	2	0	0	0	0
Fred Vinson	6	0-0	0-0	0-0	0	0	0	0	1	0
TOTALS	**225**	**30-65**	**3-14**	**16-20**	**36**	**15**	**9**	**5**	**19**	**79**
Percentages		46.2	21.4	80.0						

Coach: Bobby Cremins

Officials: Jam… Burr, Bob Garibaldi, Sta… Reynolds
Technicals: Memphis (Hardaway)
Attendance: 14,388

Ohio State 80, North Carolina 73 (Sweet 16)

	1H	2H
Ohio State	32	48
North Carolina	37	36

OHIO STATE	MIN	FG	3FG	FT	REB	A	ST	BL	PF	TP
Lawrence Funderburke	36	9-14	0-0	3-4	7	1	2	1	2	21
Jim Jackson	37	8-17	1-5	1-2	7	5	2	1	3	18
Chris Jent	31	5-16	3-7	2-2	6	0	0	0	1	15
Jamie Skelton	19	6-10	2-5	0-0	3	0	1	0	1	14
Mark Baker	33	3-10	0-0	0-1	1	8	1	0	1	6
Jamaal Brown	20	1-5	1-3	3-4	4	1	1	0	3	6
Rickey Dudley	11	0-0	0-0	0-0	1	0	0	0	1	0
Alex Davis	7	0-2	0-2	0-0	3	2	1	0	1	0
Bill Robinson	6	0-1	0-0	0-0	1	0	0	0	1	0
TOTALS	**200**	**32-75**	**7-22**	**9-13**	**33**	**17**	**8**	**2**	**14**	**80**
Percentages		42.7	31.8	69.2						

Coach: Randy Ayers

NORTH CAROLINA	MIN	FG	3FG	FT	REB	A	ST	BL	PF	TP
Hubert Davis	39	9-20	1-5	2-2	2	0	0	0	1	21
Eric Montross	33	8-11	0-0	5-6	12	0	0	2	3	21
George Lynch	34	3-6	0-0	3-4	10	3	1	0	4	9
Brian Reese	24	2-6	0-0	4-4	3	1	0	0	4	8
Derrick Phelps	38	2-9	0-2	2-2	4	5	1	0	3	6
Henrik Rodl	18	2-4	0-1	0-0	3	2	1	0	2	4
Kevin Salvadori	8	0-0	0-0	2-2	4	0	0	3	0	2
Pat Sullivan	5	1-1	0-0	0-0	1	1	0	0	0	2
Donald Williams	1	0-0	0-0	0-0	0	0	0	0	0	0
Matt Wenstrom	0	0-0	0-0	0-0	0	0	0	0	0	0
TOTALS	**200**	**27-57**	**1-8**	**18-20**	**39**	**12**	**3**	**5**	**17**	**73**
Percentages		47.4	12.5	90.0						

Coach: Dean Smith

Officials: Don Rutledge, Bob Dibler, Scott Thornley
Technicals: None
Attendance: 23,124

Michigan 75, Oklahoma State 72 (Sweet 16)

	1H	2H
Michigan	33	42
Oklahoma State	35	37

MICHIGAN	MIN	FG	3FG	FT	REB	A	ST	BL	PF	TP
Jalen Rose	40	8-14	2-5	7-10	11	1	1	0	1	25
Jimmy King	38	4-11	3-5	4-6	5	1	1	1	0	15
Eric Riley	26	6-9	0-0	3-8	10	1	0	1	2	15
Juwan Howard	27	4-11	0-0	5-7	5	4	2	2	4	13
Chris Webber	18	2-6	0-2	0-0	4	2	1	3	5	4
Ray Jackson	25	1-2	0-0	1-1	2	0	2	0	5	3
Freddie Hunter	9	0-1	0-0	0-0	0	0	0	0	2	0
Rob Pelinka	9	0-0	0-0	0-0	0	0	0	0	2	0
Michael Talley	4	0-1	0-0	0-0	0	1	0	0	0	0
James Voskuil	4	0-0	0-0	0-0	0	0	0	0	1	0
TOTALS	**200**	**25-55**	**5-12**	**20-32**	**37**	**10**	**7**	**7**	**22**	**75**
Percentages		45.5	41.7	62.5						

Coach: Steve Fisher

OKLAHOMA STATE	MIN	FG	3FG	FT	REB	A	ST	BL	PF	TP
Corey Williams	37	7-12	4-5	7-7	1	1	2	0	5	25
Sean Sutton	35	6-10	3-5	3-3	3	8	1	0	4	18
Darwyn Alexander	32	4-6	2-4	3-4	3	1	1	0	5	13
Bryant Reeves	24	4-7	0-0	1-2	5	0	1	1	3	9
Byron Houston	38	2-14	0-4	0-1	6	1	1	1	3	4
Randy Davis	13	0-3	0-0	3-4	6	0	0	1	5	3
Cornell Hatcher	18	0-0	0-0	0-0	1	1	0	0	3	0
Milton Brown	3	0-0	0-0	0-1	0	0	0	0	0	0
Terry Collins	0	0-0	0-0	0-0	0	0	0	0	0	0
TOTALS	**200**	**23-52**	**9-18**	**17-22**	**25**	**12**	**6**	**3**	**28**	**72**
Percentages		44.2	50.0	77.3						

Coach: Eddie Sutton

Officials: Larry Lembo, Bob Donato, Larry Rose
Technicals: None
Attendance: 23,124

Duke 81, Seton Hall 69 (Sweet 16)

	1H	2H
Duke	38	43
Seton Hall	32	37

DUKE	MIN	FG	3FG	FT	REB	A	ST	BL	PF	TP
Christian Laettner	36	6-13	2-4	2-2	6	1	1	0	3	16
Antonio Lang	20	4-4	0-0	8-10	7	0	1	0	2	16
Brian Davis	37	4-11	0-2	7-10	4	2	2	0	2	15
Grant Hill	30	5-8	0-0	3-3	4	2	0	1	3	13
Thomas Hill	30	4-8	1-2	4-4	5	1	4	1	2	13
Bobby Hurley	39	2-7	0-1	0-2	1	7	1	0	2	4
Cherokee Parks	3	1-1	0-0	0-0	1	0	0	0	0	2
Chistian Ast	1	1-1	0-0	0-0	0	0	0	0	0	2
Kenny Blakeney	1	0-0	0-0	0-0	0	0	0	0	0	0
Ron Burt	1	0-0	0-0	0-0	0	0	0	0	0	0
Marty Clark	1	0-0	0-0	0-0	0	1	0	0	0	0
Erik Meek	1	0-0	0-0	0-0	1	0	0	0	0	0
TOTALS	**200**	**27-53**	**3-9**	**24-31**	**29**	**14**	**9**	**2**	**14**	**81**
Percentages		50.9	33.3	77.4						

Coach: Mike Krzyzewski

SETON HALL	MIN	FG	3FG	FT	REB	A	ST	BL	PF	TP
Terry Dehere	34	8-16	0-2	5-5	2	6	1	0	4	21
Gordon Winchester	34	10-12	0-0	0-1	8	1	3	1	2	20
Jerry Walker	33	5-12	0-0	0-2	6	4	2	2	2	10
Bryan Caver	25	2-6	0-1	2-3	3	3	0	0	0	6
Arturas Karnishovas	17	2-4	0-0	1-3	4	0	0	1	5	5
Luther Wright	15	2-5	0-0	0-0	4	0	1	3	2	4
John Leahy	21	1-3	1-3	0-0	1	0	1	0	3	3
Danny Hurley	18	0-4	0-1	0-0	0	1	1	0	2	0
Daryl Crist	1	0-1	0-0	0-0	0	0	0	0	0	0
Jim Dickinson	1	0-0	0-0	0-0	0	0	0	0	0	0
Darrell Mims	1	0-0	0-0	0-0	0	0	0	0	0	0
TOTALS	**200**	**30-63**	**1-7**	**8-14**	**28**	**15**	**9**	**7**	**20**	**69**
Percentages		47.6	14.3	57.1						

Coach: P.J. Carlesimo

Officials: Ed Hightower, Ted Hillary, Ron Zetcher
Technicals: None
Attendance: 17,878

Kentucky 87, Massachusetts 77 (Sweet 16)

	1H	2H
Kentucky	50	37
Massachusetts	42	35

KENTUCKY	MIN	FG	3FG	FT	REB	A	ST	BL	PF	TP
Jamal Mashburn	37	11-15	1-2	7-9	6	0	2	1	3	30
John Pelphrey	30	7-13	1-4	3-3	4	4	4	1	4	18
Sean Woods	28	4-6	0-1	4-4	2	4	0	0	2	12
Deron Feldhaus	30	5-10	1-4	0-0	3	1	1	0	1	11
Richie Farmer	20	2-4	0-2	3-4	3	2	0	0	1	7
Dale Brown	20	2-7	0-2	1-3	4	2	0	0	2	5
Junior Braddy	5	1-1	0-0	0-0	0	1	0	0	0	2
Andre Riddick	2	1-2	0-0	0-0	1	0	0	0	1	2
Gimel Martinez	13	0-0	0-0	0-0	4	3	0	1	4	0
Travis Ford	12	0-0	0-0	0-0	2	2	0	0	0	0
Aminu Timberlake	3	0-1	0-0	0-0	1	0	0	1	2	0
TOTALS	**200**	**33-59**	**3-15**	**18-23**	**30**	**19**	**7**	**4**	**20**	**87**
Percentages		55.9	20.0	78.3						

Coach: Rick Pitino

MASSACHUSETTS	MIN	FG	3FG	FT	REB	A	ST	BL	PF	TP
Jim McCoy	34	7-15	1-1	6-7	2	0	4	0	1	21
Will Herndon	37	6-8	0-0	3-4	2	3	1	2	4	15
Anton Brown	36	5-8	2-2	2-2	1	5	1	0	2	14
Tony Barbee	33	4-10	2-5	0-1	6	1	0	0	2	10
Lou Roe	28	2-6	0-0	5-6	7	2	2	0	2	9
Harper Williams	18	3-7	0-0	2-2	4	3	0	1	5	8
Jerome Malloy	8	0-1	0-1	0-0	0	0	0	0	2	0
Derek Kellogg	4	0-0	0-0	0-0	0	0	0	0	0	0
Kennard Robinson	2	0-0	0-0	0-0	0	0	0	0	0	0
TOTALS	**200**	**27-55**	**5-9**	**18-22**	**22**	**14**	**8**	**3**	**18**	**77**
Percentages		49.1	55.6	81.8						

Coach: John Calipari

Officials: Lenny Wirtz, Jim Stupin, Tom Rucker
Technicals: None
Attendance: 17,878

85-78 (SWEET 16)

	1H	2H
UCLA	47	38
New Mexico State	31	47

UCLA	MIN	FG	3FG	FT	REB	A	ST	BL	PF	TP
Tracy Murray	33	7-11	3-5	4-4	5	3	3	-	3	21
Don MacLean	37	7-15	0-1	5-5	6	5	4	-	0	19
Gerald Madkins	35	4-7	2-3	5-6	5	4	1	-	5	15
Darrick Martin	24	3-5	2-2	5-6	0	1	2	-	3	13
Ed O'Bannon	18	3-6	0-0	1-1	8	1	0	-	1	7
Shon Tarver	14	2-3	0-0	1-3	2	2	1	-	0	5
Mitchell Butler	11	2-3	0-0	0-0	2	0	0	-	5	4
Tyus Edney	25	0-1	0-1	1-2	3	1	0	-	3	1
Rodney Zimmerman	3	0-0	0-0	0-0	0	0	0	-	1	0
TOTALS	200	28-51	7-12	22-27	31	17	11	-	21	85
Percentages		54.9	58.3	81.5						

Coach: Jim Harrick

NEW MEXICO STATE	MIN	FG	3FG	FT	REB	A	ST	BL	PF	TP
Sam Crawford	32	4-11	1-5	7-7	3	7	3	-	4	16
Cliff Reed	30	7-10	0-0	0-2	8	1	1	-	2	14
Eric Traylor	31	6-12	0-1	1-4	4	1	0	-	4	13
William Benjamin	35	5-9	1-4	0-0	1	6	1	-	4	11
Chris Hickman	25	1-2	0-0	7-8	4	1	0	-	4	9
Marc Thompson	14	3-6	1-1	1-2	2	0	1	-	2	8
Ron Coleman	4	2-2	0-0	0-0	1	0	0	-	0	4
Malcolm Leak	21	1-7	1-2	0-0	4	1	0	-	0	3
Brian Sitter	6	0-0	0-0	0-0	0	0	0	-	0	0
John Bartleson	1	0-0	0-0	0-0	0	0	0	-	0	0
Ron Putzi	1	0-0	0-0	0-0	0	0	0	-	0	0
TOTALS	200	29-59	4-13	16-23	27	17	6	-	20	78
Percentages		49.2	30.8	69.6						

Coach: Neil McCarthy

Officials: Dick Paparo, Bob Barnett, Tom O'Neill
Technicals: UCLA (Madkins)
Attendance: 15,914

85-74 (SWEET 16)

	1H	2H
Indiana	40	45
Florida State	38	36

INDIANA	MIN	FG	3FG	FT	REB	A	ST	BL	PF	TP
Eric Anderson	31	8-12	2-3	6-7	4	1	1	-	3	24
Greg Graham	36	6-14	2-7	5-8	7	2	2	-	1	19
Calbert Cheaney	34	6-11	1-3	4-4	11	4	1	-	2	17
Damon Bailey	35	3-8	0-3	4-7	4	2	0	-	1	10
Alan Henderson	13	3-6	0-0	2-2	3	0	0	-	4	8
Jamal Meeks	27	1-2	1-2	0-0	2	9	0	-	3	3
Chris Reynolds	14	0-1	0-0	2-4	1	1	0	-	0	2
Matt Nover	10	0-0	0-0	2-2	1	0	0	-	0	2
TOTALS	200	27-54	6-18	25-34	33	19	4	-	14	85
Percentages		50.0	33.3	73.5						

Coach: Bob Knight

FLORIDA STATE	MIN	FG	3FG	FT	REB	A	ST	BL	PF	TP
Doug Edwards	40	7-16	2-3	4-5	9	2	1	2	4	20
Sam Cassell	32	8-14	3-6	0-0	4	4	0	0	5	19
Chuck Graham	26	5-12	1-4	3-3	5	0	1	0	4	14
Bob Sura	36	3-9	1-6	2-2	1	5	2	0	4	9
Byron Wells	9	2-3	1-2	0-0	1	0	0	0	1	5
Charlie Ward	26	1-4	0-2	1-2	0	3	0	0	4	3
Rodney Dobard	20	1-2	0-0	0-2	4	0	0	0	3	2
Andre Reid	11	1-2	0-0	0-3	6	0	0	0	3	2
TOTALS	200	28-62	8-23	10-17	30	14	4	2	28	74
Percentages		45.2	34.8	58.8						

Coach: Pat Kennedy

Officials: Tom Harrington, Frank Bosone, Lynn Shortnacy
Technicals: None
Attendance: 15,914

88-57 (ELITE 8)

	1H	2H
Cincinnati	46	42
Memphis	36	21

CINCINNATI	MIN	FG	3FG	FT	REB	A	ST	BL	PF	TP
Herb Jones	36	9-13	1-3	4-4	13	2	0	0	1	23
Nick Van Exel	34	8-11	4-5	2-4	5	3	1	1	1	22
Anthony Buford	31	4-7	1-3	6-6	2	4	0	0	2	15
Corie Blount	26	5-8	0-0	3-5	4	3	1	0	3	13
Erik Martin	14	3-4	0-0	2-3	5	0	1	0	4	8
Terry Nelson	27	2-4	0-0	2-2	4	1	0	0	4	6
B.J Ward	3	0-0	0-0	1-2	1	0	0	0	0	1
Allen Jackson	10	0-2	0-1	0-0	0	0	0	0	0	0
Jeff Scott	9	0-1	0-0	0-0	0	0	0	1	3	0
Tarrance Gibson	8	0-1	0-1	0-0	0	0	0	0	1	0
Mike Reicheneker	2	0-1	0-1	0-0	1	0	0	0	0	0
TOTALS	200	31-52	6-14	20-26	35	13	3	2	15	88
Percentages		59.6	42.9	76.9						

Coach: Bob Huggins

MEMPHIS	MIN	FG	3FG	FT	REB	A	ST	BL	PF	TP
Anfernee Hardaway	27	4-9	3-7	1-2	4	3	1	0	5	12
Billy Smith	29	5-17	1-7	0-0	1	1	0	0	1	11
David Vaughn	25	3-7	0-0	3-6	2	0	1	1	3	9
Ernest Smith	28	1-6	1-4	5-6	2	0	1	0	4	8
Tim Duncan	16	3-5	0-1	0-0	3	0	0	0	2	6
Tony Madlock	25	2-5	0-1	1-3	2	4	2	0	4	5
Anthony Douglas	28	2-4	0-0	0-2	4	1	0	0	0	4
Kelvin Allen	9	0-0	0-0	2-2	4	0	0	0	2	2
Marcus Nolan	4	0-1	0-1	0-0	0	0	0	0	1	0
Todd Mundt	3	0-0	0-0	0-0	1	0	0	0	0	0
Chris Haynes	2	0-0	0-0	0-0	0	0	0	0	0	0
Leon Mitchell	2	0-1	0-0	0-0	0	0	0	0	0	0
Danyell Scott	1	0-0	0-0	0-0	1	0	0	0	0	0
Russell Young	1	0-1	0-1	0-0	0	0	0	0	1	0
TOTALS	200	20-56	5-22	12-21	24	9	5	1	23	57
Percentages		35.7	22.7	57.1						

Coach: Larry Finch

Officials: Ted Valentine, Gene Monje, John Koskinen
Technicals: None
Attendance: 14,850

75-71 (ELITE 8)

	1H	2H	OT1
Michigan	37	26	12
Ohio State	31	32	8

MICHIGAN	MIN	FG	3FG	FT	REB	A	ST	BL	PF	TP
Chris Webber	43	9-12	0-1	5-7	11	2	1	5	1	23
Jalen Rose	45	6-14	1-3	7-8	6	4	3	0	1	20
Jimmy King	43	7-10	1-1	0-0	2	3	1	1	1	15
Juwan Howard	39	4-9	0-0	2-2	4	1	0	1	1	10
Ray Jackson	26	2-3	1-1	0-0	0	3	1	1	4	5
Eric Riley	8	1-3	0-0	0-0	1	0	0	0	3	2
Rob Pelinka	10	0-2	0-1	0-0	0	0	0	0	0	0
James Voskuil	10	0-1	0-1	0-0	1	0	0	0	1	0
Freddie Hunter	1	0-0	0-0	0-0	0	0	0	0	0	0
TOTALS	225	29-54	3-8	14-17	25	13	6	8	12	75
Percentages		53.7	37.5	82.4						

Coach: Steve Fisher

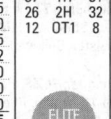

OHIO STATE	MIN	FG	3FG	FT	REB	A	ST	BL	PF	TP
Jim Jackson	42	9-21	1-6	1-4	4	2	3	0	4	20
Jamaal Brown	35	6-10	2-4	2-2	3	0	2	0	1	16
Lawrence Funderburke	36	5-10	0-0	2-3	8	2	2	0	3	12
Mark Baker	39	4-10	0-1	0-0	5	5	0	0	0	8
Chris Jent	32	2-12	2-7	0-0	1	2	1	0	4	6
Bill Robinson	19	2-4	0-0	0-0	8	0	0	0	3	4
Alex Davis	6	0-0	0-0	3-3	0	0	1	0	0	3
Jamie Skelton	6	1-1	0-0	0-0	2	1	0	1	0	2
Rickey Dudley	10	0-0	0-0	0-0	0	0	1	0	2	0
TOTALS	225	29-68	5-18	8-12	31	12	10	1	17	71
Percentages		42.6	27.8	66.7						

Coach: Randy Ayers

Officials: Gerry Donaghy, Dave Libbey, Art McDonald
Technicals: Ohio State (Jent), Michigan (Howard)
Attendance: 23,047

104-103 (ELITE 8)

	1H	2H	OT1
Duke	50	43	11
Kentucky	45	48	10

DUKE	MIN	FG	3FG	FT	REB	A	ST	BL	PF	TP
Christian Laettner	43	10-10	1-1	10-10	7	3	2	0	4	31
Bobby Hurley	45	6-12	5-10	5-6	3	10	0	0	3	22
Thomas Hill	34	6-10	2-3	5-5	3	2	3	0	3	19
Brian Davis	38	3-6	0-2	7-10	5	1	2	0	5	13
Grant Hill	37	5-10	0-0	1-2	10	7	0	1	2	11
Antonio Lang	21	2-2	0-0	0-1	3	0	0	0	4	4
Cherokee Parks	6	2-2	0-0	0-0	0	0	1	1	2	4
Marty Clark	1	0-0	0-0	0-0	0	0	0	1	0	0
TOTALS	225	34-52	8-16	28-34	31	23	8	3	23	104
Percentages		65.4	50.0	82.4						

Coach: Mike Krzyzewski

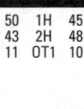

KENTUCKY	MIN	FG	3FG	FT	REB	A	ST	BL	PF	TP
Jamal Mashburn	43	11-16	3-4	3-3	10	3	2	-	5	28
Sean Woods	38	9-15	1-1	2-2	2	9	3	-	4	21
Dale Brown	30	6-11	3-5	3-5	3	0	2	-	4	18
John Pelphrey	25	5-7	3-4	3-3	1	5	2	-	4	16
Richie Farmer	15	2-3	1-2	4-6	1	1	0	-	2	9
Deron Feldhaus	37	2-6	0-2	1-2	1	5	2	-	1	5
Gimel Martinez	23	2-4	1-2	0-0	0	1	1	-	5	5
Aminu Timberlake	5	0-0	0-0	1-2	0	0	0	-	2	1
Travis Ford	7	0-2	0-1	0-0	1	0	0	-	0	0
Junior Braddy	1	0-1	0-1	0-0	0	0	0	-	0	0
Andre Riddick	1	0-0	0-0	0-0	0	0	0	-	1	0
TOTALS	225	37-65	12-22	17-23	19	24	12	-	28	103
Percentages		56.9	54.5	73.9						

Coach: Rick Pitino

Officials: Tim Higgins, Charles Range, Tom Clark
Technicals: None
Attendance: 17,878

106-79 (ELITE 8)

	1H	2H
Indiana	44	62
UCLA	29	50

INDIANA	MIN	FG	3FG	FT	REB	A	ST	BL	PF	TP
Calbert Cheaney	29	9-15	0-2	5-6	2	0	1	0	2	23
Damon Bailey	21	8-11	4-5	2-2	4	4	1	0	1	22
Eric Anderson	28	7-10	1-2	2-2	4	0	1	2	3	17
Matt Nover	23	5-7	0-0	6-6	5	0	0	0	3	16
Alan Henderson	26	4-9	0-1	2-3	12	1	0	4	4	10
Chris Reynolds	18	1-1	0-0	6-6	3	5	0	0	1	8
Jamal Meeks	28	0-1	0-1	5-6	3	9	0	0	2	5
Greg Graham	23	0-4	0-0	3-4	4	4	0	0	3	3
Todd Lindeman	2	0-1	0-0	2-4	1	0	0	0	0	2
Todd Leary	2	0-0	0-0	0-0	1	0	0	0	1	0
TOTALS	200	34-59	5-11	33-39	39	23	3	6	20	106
Percentages		57.6	45.5	84.6						

Coach: Bob Knight

UCLA	MIN	FG	3FG	FT	REB	A	ST	BL	PF	TP
Gerald Madkins	33	6-10	3-6	3-3	2	2	0	-	5	18
Tracy Murray	29	6-16	0-3	3-5	8	0	2	-	4	15
Shon Tarver	20	5-9	3-3	0-0	2	2	0	-	4	13
Don MacLean	32	4-13	0-1	4-5	3	1	0	-	2	12
Tyus Edney	30	5-15	0-6	2-3	4	4	1	-	0	12
Ed O'Bannon	21	2-4	1-2	2-4	2	1	1	-	2	7
Darrick Martin	12	0-4	0-0	2-2	1	0	0	-	3	2
Mitchell Butler	18	0-0	0-0	0-0	4	2	0	-	5	0
Rodney Zimmerman	3	0-0	0-0	0-0	1	0	0	-	0	0
George Zidek	2	0-0	0-0	0-0	1	0	0	-	1	0
Steve Elkind	0	0-1	0-0	0-0	1	0	0	-	0	0
TOTALS	200	28-72	7-21	16-22	29	12	4	-	26	79
Percentages		38.9	33.3	72.7						

Coach: Jim Harrick

Officials: John Clougherty, David Hall, Andre Pattillo
Technicals: UCLA (MacLean), Indiana (Meeks)
Attendance: 16,160

76-72

38	1H	41
38	2H	31

MICHIGAN	MIN	FG	3FG	FT	REB	A	ST	BL	PF	TP
Jimmy King	37	5-9	3-4	4-4	5	0	0	0	2	17
Chris Webber	36	8-12	0-0	0-2	11	2	3	1	1	16
Jalen Rose	37	4-13	0-2	5-6	9	3	0	0	2	13
Juwan Howard	33	3-9	0-0	6-7	8	4	1	0	4	12
James Voskuil	14	2-4	1-2	4-5	4	0	1	0	1	9
Michael Talley	13	1-3	0-0	2-3	0	2	1	0	4	4
Ray Jackson	20	1-2	0-0	1-2	5	1	0	0	1	3
Eric Riley	10	1-1	0-0	0-0	3	0	0	0	2	2
TOTALS	200	25-53	4-8	22-29	45	12	6	1	17	76
Percentages		47.2	50.0	75.9						

Coach: Steve Fisher

CINCINNATI	MIN	FG	3FG	FT	REB	A	ST	BL	PF	TP
Nick Van Exel	36	7-15	2-7	5-10	5	5	4	1	4	21
Anthony Buford	35	6-17	2-7	4-4	1	1	3	0	4	18
Herb Jones	34	5-13	2-6	2-2	5	0	1	0	1	14
Erik Martin	30	4-10	0-1	2-3	10	0	1	0	3	10
Terry Nelson	19	2-2	0-0	0-0	0	0	1	0	2	4
Tarrance Gibson	7	2-3	0-1	0-0	2	0	1	0	1	4
Corie Blount	27	0-3	0-0	1-2	4	2	0	2	4	1
Allen Jackson	6	0-1	0-0	0-0	0	0	0	1	0	0
Jeff Scott	6	0-0	0-0	0-0	0	0	0	0	3	0
TOTALS	200	26-64	6-22	14-21	27	8	11	4	22	72
Percentages		40.6	27.3	66.7						

Coach: Bob Huggins

Officials: Ed Hightower, James Burr, Rutledge
Technicals: None
Attendance: 50,379

81-78

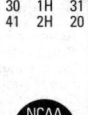

37	1H	42
44	2H	36

DUKE	MIN	FG	3FG	FT	REB	A	ST	BL	PF	TP
Bobby Hurley	37	7-12	6-9	6-8	0	4	2	0	2	26
Grant Hill	29	6-9	0-0	2-4	6	6	0	3	5	14
Thomas Hill	32	3-10	1-1	4-5	2	0	2	0	2	11
Christian Laettner	39	2-8	0-1	4-7	10	1	0	1	3	8
Cherokee Parks	9	3-5	0-0	2-3	1	0	0	0	1	8
Brian Davis	25	1-3	0-0	3-7	5	0	1	1	2	5
Marty Clark	2	0-0	0-0	5-6	1	0	0	0	0	5
Antonio Lang	27	1-5	0-0	2-2	3	0	0	1	3	4
TOTALS	200	23-52	7-11	28-42	28	11	5	6	18	81
Percentages		44.2	63.6	66.7						

Coach: Mike Krzyzewski

INDIANA	MIN	FG	3FG	FT	REB	A	ST	BL	PF	TP
Greg Graham	28	6-9	1-3	5-5	7	0	0	0	5	18
Alan Henderson	32	6-9	1-1	2-2	5	1	1	3	5	15
Calbert Cheaney	28	4-13	1-3	2-4	7	1	0	0	5	11
Damon Bailey	22	4-8	1-1	0-0	3	0	0	0	5	9
Matt Nover	20	3-4	1-1	2-2	3	0	0	0	3	9
Todd Leary	1	3-3	3-3	0-0	0	0	0	0	2	9
Jamal Meeks	18	1-2	0-1	1-2	3	8	1	0	2	3
Eric Anderson	26	1-6	0-2	0-1	4	1	1	0	2	2
Chris Reynolds	25	1-4	0-0	0-0	4	4	3	0	4	2
TOTALS	200	29-58	8-15	12-16	36	15	6	3	33	78
Percentages		50.0	53.3	75.0						

Coach: Bob Knight

Officials: Tim Higgins, Ted Valentine, John Clougherty
Technicals: Indiana (bench)
Attendance: 50,379

71-51

30	1H	31
41	2H	20

NCAA FINAL 1992

DUKE	MIN	FG	3FG	FT	REB	A	ST	BL	PF	TP
Christian Laettner	36	6-13	2-4	5-6	7	0	1	1	1	19
Grant Hill	37	8-14	0-0	2-2	10	5	3	2	2	18
Thomas Hill	35	5-10	1-2	5-8	7	0	2	0	2	16
Bobby Hurley	37	3-12	1-3	2-2	3	7	1	0	4	9
Antonio Lang	32	2-3	0-0	1-2	4	0	1	0	1	5
Cherokee Parks	13	1-3	0-0	2-2	3	0	0	1	3	4
Brian Davis	10	0-2	0-0	0-0	0	0	1	0	0	0
Chistian Ast	0	0-0	0-0	0-0	1	0	0	0	0	0
Kenny Blakeney	0	0-0	0-0	0-0	0	0	0	0	0	0
Ron Burt	0	0-0	0-0	0-0	0	0	0	0	0	0
Marty Clark	0	0-0	0-0	0-0	0	0	0	0	0	0
TOTALS	200	25-57	4-9	17-22	35	12	9	4	13	71
Percentages		43.9	44.4	77.3						

Coach: Mike Krzyzewski

MICHIGAN	MIN	FG	3FG	FT	REB	A	ST	BL	PF	TP
Chris Webber	30	6-12	0-2	2-5	11	1	2	0	4	14
Jalen Rose	37	5-12	0-3	1-2	5	4	2	0	4	11
Juwan Howard	29	4-9	0-1	1-3	3	0	0	0	3	9
Jimmy King	40	3-10	1-2	0-0	2	1	2	1	1	7
Eric Riley	19	2-6	0-0	0-0	4	1	0	0	2	4
James Voskuil	15	1-2	0-1	2-2	3	3	1	0	2	4
Rob Pelinka	10	1-2	0-0	0-0	2	1	0	0	0	2
Ray Jackson	16	0-1	0-0	0-0	1	2	1	2	1	0
Freddie Hunter	2	0-0	0-0	0-0	0	0	0	0	0	0
Jason Bossard	1	0-1	0-1	0-0	0	0	0	0	0	0
Michael Talley	1	0-2	0-1	0-0	1	0	0	0	0	0
Chip Armer	0	0-0	0-0	0-0	0	0	0	0	0	0
Chris Seter	0	0-1	0-0	0-0	1	0	0	0	0	0
TOTALS	200	22-58	1-11	6-12	33	13	8	3	17	51
Percentages		37.9	9.1	50.0						

Coach: Steve Fisher

Officials: Gerry Donaghy, Tom Harrington, Dave Libbey
Technicals: None
Attendance: 50,379

National Invitation Tournament (NIT)

First round: Kansas State d. Western Kentucky 85-74, Virginia d. Villanova 83-80, Pittsburgh d. Penn State 67-65, Washington State d. Minnesota 72-70, Tennessee d. UAB 71-68, Notre Dame d. Western Michigan 63-56, Manhattan d. Wisc.-Green Bay 67-65, Purdue d. Butler 82-56, Utah d. Ball State 72-57, New Mexico d. Louisiana Tech 90-84, Rhode Island d. Vanderbilt 68-63, Arizona State d. UC Santa Barbara 71-65, Boston College d. Southern Illinois 78-69, TCU d. Long Beach St. 73-61, Florida d. Richmond 66-52, Rutgers d. James Madison 73-69

Second round: Virginia d. Tennessee 77-52, Notre Dame d. Kansas State 64-48, Florida d. Pittsburgh 77-74, Purdue d. TCU 67-51, New Mexico d. Washington State 79-71, Manhattan d. Rutgers 62-61, Rhode Island d. Boston College 81-80 (2OT), Utah d. Arizona State 80-58

Third round: Notre Dame d. Manhattan 74-58, Florida d. Purdue 74-67, Virginia d. New Mexico 76-71, Utah d. Rhode Island 84-72

Semifinals: Virginia d. Florida 62-56, Notre Dame d. Utah 58-55

Third place: Utah d. Florida 81-78

Championship: Virginia d. Notre Dame 81-76

MVP: Bryant Stith, Virginia

1992-93: FAB FLAMEOUT

The most indelible memory of the 1993 Tournament isn't a last-second shot or a spectacular team performance—it's of a man in baggy shorts calling for a timeout. In the Final at the New Orleans Superdome, Michigan trailed North Carolina by two points with :11 left. Under extreme defensive pressure, Chris Webber—the lead member of Michigan's Fab Five (along with Juwan Howard, Jalen Rose, Ray Jackson and Jimmy King)—signaled for a timeout the Wolverines didn't have. Michigan was whistled for a technical, UNC (34–4) made the shots, got the ball and won Dean Smith his second national title, 77-71. The Tar Heels' Donald Williams scored 25 points, set a Final Four record for three-point shooting percentage (71.4%) and was named Tournament MOP.

For the first time, three No. 1 seeds (UNC, Michigan and Kentucky) reached the Final Four. The Naismith POY was Indiana's Calbert Cheaney (22.4 ppg, 6.4 rpg). Webber was the No. 1 pick in the NBA draft (by the Orlando Magic, who traded him to the Golden State Warriors for Penny Hardaway and future draft picks). In 2002, it was revealed that a booster had given $616,000 to Webber and three other Wolverines; as a result, 115 of Michigan's regular-season and Tournament victories over six seasons were either vacated or turned into forfeit losses, essentially wiping out the Fab Five's accomplishments. If Webber hadn't called the illegal timeout and the Wolverines had hit a three-pointer at the buzzer instead, the forfeit of an NCAA championship would likely be considered the sport's darkest moment.

MAJOR CONFERENCE STANDINGS

ACC	Conference			Overall		
	W	L	PCT	W	L	PCT
North Carolina○	14	2	.875	34	4	.895
Florida State○	12	4	.750	25	10	.714
Duke○	10	6	.625	24	8	.750
Wake Forest○	10	6	.625	21	9	.700
Virginia○	9	7	.563	21	10	.677
Georgia Tech⊕	8	8	.500	19	11	.633
Clemson□	5	11	.313	17	13	.567
Maryland	2	14	.125	12	16	.429
NC State	2	14	.125	8	19	.296

Tournament: **Georgia Tech d. North Carolina 77-75**
Tournament MVP: **James Forrest**, Georgia Tech

ATLANTIC 10	Conference			Overall		
	W	L	PCT	W	L	PCT
Massachusetts⊕	11	3	.786	24	7	.774
George Washington○	8	6	.571	21	9	.700
Rhode Island○	8	6	.571	19	11	.633
Saint Joseph's□	8	6	.571	18	11	.621
Temple○	8	6	.571	20	13	.606
West Virginia□	7	7	.500	17	12	.586
Rutgers	6	8	.429	13	15	.464
St. Bonaventure	0	14	.000	10	17	.370

Tournament: **Massachusetts d Temple 69-61**
Tournament MOP: **Harper Williams**, Massachusetts

BIG EAST	Conference			Overall		
	W	L	PCT	W	L	PCT
Seton Hall⊕	14	4	.778	28	7	.800
St. John's○	12	6	.667	19	11	.633
Syracuse	10	8	.556	20	9	.690
Pittsburgh	9	9	.500	17	11	.607
Providence□	9	9	.500	20	13	.606
Boston College□	9	9	.500	18	13	.581
Connecticut□	9	9	.500	15	13	.536
Georgetown□	8	10	.444	20	13	.606
Miami (FL)	7	11	.389	10	17	.370
Villanova	3	15	.167	8	19	.296

Tournament: **Seton Hall d. Syracuse 103-70**
Tournament MVP: **Terry Dehere**, Seton Hall

BIG EIGHT	Conference			Overall		
	W	L	PCT	W	L	PCT
Kansas○	11	3	.786	29	7	.806
Oklahoma State○	8	6	.571	20	9	.690
Iowa State○	8	6	.571	20	11	.645
Nebraska○	8	6	.571	20	11	.645
Kansas State○	7	7	.500	19	11	.633
Oklahoma□	7	7	.500	20	12	.625
Missouri⊕	5	9	.357	19	14	.576
Colorado	2	12	.143	10	17	.370

Tournament: **Missouri d. Kansas State 68-56**
Tournament MVP: **Chris Heller**, Missouri

BIG SKY	Conference			Overall		
	W	L	PCT	W	L	PCT
Idaho	11	3	.786	24	8	.750
Boise State⊕	10	4	.714	21	8	.724
Weber State	10	4	.714	20	8	.714
Montana	8	6	.571	17	11	.607
Idaho State	5	9	.357	10	18	.357
Montana State	5	9	.357	9	18	.333
Northern Arizona	4	10	.286	10	16	.385
Eastern Washington	3	11	.214	6	20	.231

Tournament: **Boise State d. Idaho 80-68**
Tournament MVP: **Tanoka Beard**, Boise State

BIG SOUTH	Conference			Overall		
	W	L	PCT	W	L	PCT
Towson	14	2	.875	18	9	.667
Coastal Carolina⊕	12	4	.750	22	10	.688
Campbell	10	6	.625	12	15	.444
Liberty	9	7	.563	16	14	.533
Radford ⊗	8	8	.500	14	16	.467
UMBC	7	9	.438	12	16	.429
Winthrop	5	11	.313	14	16	.467
Charleston Southern	5	11	.313	9	18	.333
UNC Asheville	2	14	.125	4	23	.148

Tournament: **Coastal Carolina d. Winthrop 78-65**
Tournament MVP: **Tony Dunkin**, Coastal Carolina

BIG TEN	Conference			Overall		
	W	L	PCT	W	L	PCT
Indiana⊕	17	1	.944	31	4	.886
Michigan○⊗	15	3	.883	31	5	.838
Iowa○	11	7	.611	23	9	.719
Illinois○	11	7	.611	19	13	.594
Minnesota□	9	9	.500	22	10	.688
Purdue○	9	9	.500	18	10	.643
Ohio State□	8	10	.444	15	13	.536
Michigan State□	7	11	.389	15	13	.536
Wisconsin□	7	11	.389	14	14	.500
Northwestern	3	15	.167	8	19	.296
Penn State	2	16	.111	7	20	.259

BIG WEST	Conference			Overall		
	W	L	PCT	W	L	PCT
New Mexico State○⊗	15	3	.833	26	8	.765
UNLV□	13	5	.722	21	8	.724
Pacific	12	6	.667	16	11	.593
Long Beach State⊕	11	7	.611	22	10	.688
UC Santa Barbara□	10	8	.556	18	11	.621
Cal State Fullerton	10	8	.556	15	12	.556
Utah State	7	11	.389	10	17	.370
Nevada	4	14	.222	9	17	.346
San Jose State	4	14	.222	7	19	.269
UC Irvine	4	14	.222	6	21	.222

Tournament: **Long Beach St. d. New Mexico St. 70-62**
Tournament MVP: **Lucious Harris**, Long Beach St.

COLONIAL ATHLETIC	Conference			Overall		
	W	L	PCT	W	L	PCT
Old Dominion□	11	3	.786	21	8	.724
James Madison□	11	3	.786	21	9	.700
Richmond	10	4	.714	15	12	.556
UNC Wilmington	6	8	.429	17	11	.607
William and Mary	6	8	.429	14	13	.519
American	6	8	.429	11	17	.393
East Carolina⊕	4	10	.286	13	17	.433
George Mason	2	12	.143	7	21	.250

Tournament: **East Carolina d. James Madison 54-49**
Tournament MVP: **Lester Lyons**, East Carolina

GMWC	Conference			Overall		
	W	L	PCT	W	L	PCT
Cincinnati○	8	2	.800	27	5	.844
Memphis○	7	3	.700	20	12	.625
Marquette○	6	4	.600	20	8	.714
UAB□	5	5	.500	21	14	.600
DePaul	3	7	.300	16	15	.516
Saint Louis	1	9	.100	12	17	.414

Tournament: **Cincinnati d. Memphis 77-72**

IVY	Conference			Overall		
	W	L	PCT	W	L	PCT
Penn⊕	14	0	1.000	22	5	.815
Columbia	10	4	.714	16	10	.615
Cornell	9	5	.643	16	10	.615
Princeton	7	7	.500	15	11	.577
Yale	6	8	.429	10	16	.385
Dartmouth	5	9	.357	11	15	.423
Harvard	3	11	.214	6	20	.231
Brown	2	12	.143	7	19	.269

METRO	Conference			Overall		
	W	L	PCT	W	L	PCT
Louisville⊕	11	1	.917	22	9	.710
Tulane○	9	3	.750	22	9	.710
VCU□	7	5	.583	20	10	.667
Charlotte	6	6	.500	15	13	.536
Southern Miss	6	6	.500	10	17	.370
South Florida	2	10	.167	8	19	.296
Virginia Tech	1	11	.083	10	18	.357

Tournament: **Louisville d. VCU 90-78**
Tournament MOP: **Dwayne Morton**, Louisville

MAAC	Conference			Overall		
	W	L	PCT	W	L	PCT
Manhattan⊕	12	2	.857	23	7	.767
Niagara□	11	3	.786	23	7	.767
Iona	9	5	.643	16	11	.593
Siena	8	6	.571	16	13	.552
Fairfield	7	7	.500	14	13	.519
Canisius	5	9	.357	10	18	.357
Saint Peter's	3	11	.214	9	18	.333
Loyola (MD)	1	13	.071	2	25	.074

Tournament: **Manhattan d. Niagara 68-67**
Tournament MVP: **Keith Bullock**, Manhattan

MID-AMERICAN	Conference			Overall		
	W	L	PCT	W	L	PCT
Ball State⊕	14	4	.778	26	8	.765
Miami (OH)□	14	4	.778	22	9	.710
Western Michigan	12	6	.667	17	12	.586
Ohio	11	7	.611	14	13	.519
Toledo	9	9	.500	12	16	.429
Eastern Michigan	8	10	.444	13	17	.433
Bowling Green	8	10	.444	11	16	.407
Kent State	7	11	.389	10	17	.370
Central Michigan	4	14	.222	8	18	.308
Akron	3	15	.167	8	18	.308

Tournament: **Ball State d. Western Michigan 79-64**
Tournament MVP: **Steve Payne**, Ball State

MID-CONTINENT	Conference			Overall		
	W	L	PCT	W	L	PCT
Cleveland State	15	1	.938	22	6	.786
Wright State⊕	10	6	.625	20	10	.667
Northern Illinois	10	6	.625	15	12	.556
Illinois-Chicago	9	7	.563	17	15	.531
Wisconsin-Green Bay	9	7	.563	13	14	.481
Valparaiso	7	9	.438	12	16	.429
Eastern Illinois	7	9	.438	10	17	.370
Western Illinois	4	12	.250	7	20	.259
Youngstown State	1	15	.063	3	23	.115

Tournament: **Wright State d. Illinois-Chicago 94-88**
Tournament MVP: **Bill Edwards**, Wright State

Conference Standings Continue →

⊕ Automatic NCAA Tournament bid ○ At-large NCAA Tournament bid □ NIT appearance ⊗ Team record doesn't reflect games forfeited or vacated. For adjusted record, see p. 521.

MEAC

	Conference			Overall		
	W	L	Pct	W	L	Pct
Coppin State⊕	16	0	1.000	22	8	.733
South Carolina State	9	7	.563	16	13	.552
NC A&T	9	7	.563	14	13	.519
Morgan State	9	7	.563	9	17	.346
Florida A&M	8	8	.500	10	18	.357
UMES	7	9	.438	13	14	.481
Delaware State	6	10	.375	13	16	.448
Howard	6	10	.375	10	18	.357
Bethune-Cookman	2	14	.125	3	24	.111

Tournament: **Coppin State d. Delaware State 80-53**
Tournament MOP: **Stephen Stewart**, Coppin State

MCC

	Conference			Overall		
	W	L	Pct	W	L	Pct
Xavier○	12	2	.857	24	6	.800
Evansville⊕	12	2	.857	23	7	.767
La Salle	9	5	.643	14	13	.519
Detroit	7	7	.500	15	12	.556
Duquesne	5	9	.357	13	15	.464
Butler	5	9	.357	11	17	.393
Loyola-Chicago	3	11	.214	7	20	.259
Dayton	3	11	.214	4	26	.133

Tournament: **Evansville d. Xavier 80-69**
Tournament MVP: **Parrish Casebier**, Evansville

MISSOURI VALLEY

	Conference			Overall		
	W	L	Pct	W	L	Pct
Illinois State	13	5	.722	19	10	.655
Southern Illinois⊕	12	6	.667	23	10	.697
Missouri State□	11	7	.611	20	11	.645
Tulsa	10	8	.556	15	14	.517
Drake	9	9	.500	14	14	.500
Northern Iowa	8	10	.444	12	15	.444
Bradley	7	11	.389	11	16	.407
Indiana State	7	11	.389	11	17	.393
Wichita State	7	11	.389	10	17	.370
Creighton	6	12	.333	8	18	.308

Tournament: **Southern Illinois d. Illinois State 70-59**
Tournament MOP: **Ashraf Amaya**, Southern Illinois

NAC

	Conference			Overall		
	W	L	Pct	W	L	Pct
Drexel	12	2	.857	22	7	.759
Northeastern	12	2	.857	20	8	.714
Delaware⊕	10	4	.714	22	8	.733
Hartford	7	7	.500	14	14	.500
Maine	4	10	.286	10	17	.370
Vermont	4	10	.286	10	17	.370
New Hampshire	4	10	.286	6	21	.222
Boston U.	3	11	.214	6	21	.222

Tournament: **Delaware d. Drexel 67-64**
Tournament MVP: **Kevin Blackhurst**, Delaware

NORTHEAST

	Conference			Overall		
	W	L	Pct	W	L	Pct
Rider⊕	14	4	.778	19	11	.633
Wagner	12	6	.667	18	12	.600
Marist	10	8	.556	14	16	.467
Mount St. Mary's	10	8	.556	13	15	.464
Fairleigh Dickinson	8	10	.444	11	17	.393
St. Francis (NY)	8	10	.444	9	18	.333
Long Island	7	11	.389	11	17	.393
Monmouth	7	11	.389	11	17	.393
Robert Morris	7	11	.389	9	18	.333
Saint Francis (PA)	7	11	.389	9	18	.333

Tournament: **Rider d. Wagner 65-64**
Tournament MVP: **Darrick Suber**, Rider

OHIO VALLEY

	Conference			Overall		
	W	L	Pct	W	L	Pct
Tennessee State⊕	13	3	.813	19	10	.655
Murray State	11	5	.688	18	12	.600
Eastern Kentucky	11	5	.688	15	12	.556
SE Missouri State	9	7	.563	16	11	.593
Tennessee Tech	9	7	.563	15	13	.536
Morehead State	6	10	.375	6	21	.222
Middle Tennessee St.	5	11	.313	10	16	.385
Tennessee-Martin	4	12	.250	7	19	.269
Austin Peay	4	12	.250	7	20	.259

Tournament: **Tennessee State d. Murray State 82-68**
Tournament MVP: **Monty Wilson**, Tennessee State

PAC-10

	Conference			Overall		
	W	L	Pct	W	L	Pct
Arizona⊕	17	1	.944	24	4	.857
California○	12	6	.667	21	9	.700
UCLA○	11	7	.611	22	11	.667
Arizona State□	11	7	.611	18	10	.643
Southern California□	9	9	.500	18	12	.600
Washington State	9	9	.500	15	12	.556
Oregon State	9	9	.500	13	14	.481
Washington	7	11	.389	13	14	.481
Oregon	3	15	.167	10	20	.333
Stanford	2	16	.111	7	23	.233

PATRIOT

	Conference			Overall		
	W	L	Pct	W	L	Pct
Bucknell	13	1	.929	23	6	.793
Holy Cross⊕	12	2	.857	23	7	.767
Colgate	9	5	.643	18	10	.643
Fordham	9	5	.643	15	16	.484
Navy	5	9	.357	8	19	.296
Lafayette	4	10	.286	7	20	.259
Army	2	12	.143	4	22	.154
Lehigh	2	12	.143	4	23	.148

Tournament: **Holy Cross d. Bucknell 98-73**
Tournament MVP: **Rob Feaster**, Holy Cross

SEC

	Conference			Overall		
	W	L	Pct	W	L	Pct
Eastern						
Vanderbilt○	14	2	.875	28	6	.824
Kentucky⊕	13	3	.813	30	4	.882
Florida□	9	7	.563	16	12	.571
Georgia□	8	8	.500	15	14	.517
South Carolina	5	11	.313	9	18	.333
Tennessee	4	12	.250	13	17	.433
Western						
Arkansas○	10	6	.625	22	9	.710
LSU○	9	7	.563	22	11	.667
Auburn□	8	8	.500	15	12	.556
Alabama□	7	9	.438	16	13	.552
Mississippi State	5	11	.313	13	16	.448
Mississippi	4	12	.250	10	18	.357

Tournament: **Kentucky d. LSU 82-65**
Tournament MVP: **Travis Ford**, Kentucky

SOUTHERN

	Conference			Overall		
	W	L	Pct	W	L	Pct
Chattanooga⊕	16	2	.889	26	7	.788
Georgia Southern	12	6	.667	19	9	.679
East Tennessee State	12	6	.667	19	10	.655
Marshall	11	7	.611	16	11	.593
Davidson	10	8	.556	14	14	.500
Appalachian State	8	10	.444	13	15	.464
Furman	8	10	.444	11	17	.393
The Citadel	8	10	.444	10	17	.370
VMI	3	15	.167	5	22	.185
Western Carolina	2	16	.111	6	21	.222

Tournament: **Chattanooga d. East Tennessee St. 86-75**
Tournament MOP: **Tim Brooks**, Chattanooga

SOUTHLAND

	Conference			Overall		
	W	L	Pct	W	L	Pct
UL-Monroe⊕	17	1	.944	26	5	.839
Nicholls State	11	7	.611	14	12	.538
Texas-Arlington	10	8	.556	16	12	.571
UTSA	10	8	.556	15	14	.517
Texas State	9	9	.500	14	13	.519
McNeese State	9	9	.500	12	15	.444
Stephen F. Austin	8	10	.444	12	14	.462
Northwestern State (LA)	7	11	.389	13	13	.500
North Texas	5	13	.278	5	21	.192
Sam Houston State	4	14	.222	6	19	.240

Tournament: **UL-Monroe d. UTSA 80-66**
Tournament MVP: **Ryan Stuart**, UL-Monroe

SOUTHWEST

	Conference			Overall		
	W	L	Pct	W	L	Pct
SMU○	12	2	.857	20	8	.714
Rice□	11	3	.786	18	10	.643
Houston□	9	5	.643	21	9	.700
Baylor	7	7	.500	16	11	.593
Texas Tech⊕	6	8	.429	18	12	.600
Texas A&M	5	9	.357	10	17	.370
Texas	4	10	.286	11	17	.393
TCU	2	12	.143	6	22	.214

Tournament: **Texas Tech d. Houston 88-74**
Tournament MVP: **Lance Hughes**, Texas Tech

SWAC

	Conference			Overall		
	W	L	Pct	W	L	Pct
Jackson State□	13	1	.929	25	9	.735
Southern U.⊕	9	5	.643	21	10	.677
Alabama State	9	5	.643	14	13	.519
Texas Southern	8	6	.571	12	15	.444
Mississippi Valley State	7	7	.500	13	15	.464
Grambling	5	9	.357	13	14	.481
Alcorn State	5	9	.357	7	20	.259
Prairie View A&M	0	14	.000	1	26	.037

Tournament: **Southern U. d. Jackson State 101-80**
Tournament MVP: **Leonard White**, Southern U.

SUN BELT

	Conference			Overall		
	W	L	Pct	W	L	Pct
New Orleans○	18	0	1.000	26	4	.867
Western Kentucky⊕	14	4	.778	26	6	.813
Arkansas State	11	7	.611	16	12	.571
UL-Lafayette	11	7	.611	17	13	.567
Arkansas-Little Rock	10	8	.556	15	12	.556
Lamar	9	9	.500	15	12	.556
South Alabama	9	9	.500	15	13	.536
Louisiana Tech	3	15	.167	7	21	.250
Jacksonville	3	15	.167	5	22	.185
Texas-Pan American	2	16	.111	2	20	.091

Tournament: **Western Kentucky d. New Orleans 72-63**
Tournament MOP: **Darnell Mee**, Western Kentucky

TAAC

	Conference			Overall		
	W	L	Pct	W	L	Pct
Florida International	9	3	.750	20	10	.667
Samford	7	5	.583	17	10	.630
Mercer	7	5	.583	13	14	.481
Stetson	6	6	.500	13	14	.481
Georgia State	5	7	.417	13	14	.481
Southeastern Louisiana	4	8	.333	12	15	.444
Centenary	4	8	.333	9	18	.333

WEST COAST

	Conference			Overall		
	W	L	Pct	W	L	Pct
Pepperdine□	11	3	.786	23	8	.742
Gonzaga	10	4	.714	19	9	.679
Santa Clara⊕	9	5	.643	19	12	.613
San Francisco	8	6	.571	19	12	.613
San Diego	7	7	.500	13	14	.481
Saint Mary's (CA)	6	8	.429	11	16	.407
Portland	3	11	.214	9	18	.333
Loyola Marymount	2	12	.143	7	20	.259

Tournament: **Santa Clara d. Pepperdine 73-63**
Tournament MVP: **Steve Nash**, Santa Clara

WAC

	Conference			Overall		
	W	L	Pct	W	L	Pct
Utah○	15	3	.833	24	7	.774
BYU○	15	3	.833	25	9	.735
New Mexico⊕	13	5	.722	24	7	.774
UTEP□	10	8	.556	21	13	.618
Colorado State	9	9	.500	17	12	.586
Fresno State	8	10	.444	13	15	.464
Wyoming	7	11	.389	13	15	.464
Hawaii	7	11	.389	12	16	.429
Air Force	3	15	.167	9	19	.321
San Diego State	3	15	.167	8	21	.276

Tournament: **New Mexico d. UTEP 76-65**
Tournament MVP: **Ike Williams**, New Mexico

INDEPENDENTS

	Overall		
	W	L	Pct
Wisconsin-Milwaukee	23	4	.852
Charleston	19	8	.704
UMKC	15	12	.556
Southern Utah	14	13	.519
Northeastern Illinois	11	16	.407
Cal State Northridge	10	17	.370
Central Florida	10	17	.370
UNC Greensboro	10	17	.370
Hofstra	9	18	.333
Notre Dame	9	18	.333
Central Connecticut State	8	19	.296
Buffalo	5	22	.185
Chicago State	4	23	.148
Cal State Sacramento	3	24	.111

INDIVIDUAL LEADERS—SEASON

SCORING	CL	POS	G	FG	3FG	FT	PTS	PPG
1 **Greg Guy**, Texas-Pan American	JR	G	19	189	67	111	556	**29.3**
2 **J.R. Rider**, UNLV	SR	G	28	282	55	195	814	**29.1**
3 **John Best**, Tennessee Tech	SR	F	28	296	4	203	799	**28.5**
4 **Vin Baker**, Hartford	SR	F	28	305	32	150	792	**28.3**
5 **Lindsey Hunter**, Jackson State	SR	G	34	320	112	155	907	**26.7**
6 **Alphonso Ford**, Mississippi Valley St.	SR	G	28	252	76	148	728	**26.0**
7 **Bill Edwards**, Wright State	SR	F	30	288	43	138	757	**25.2**
8 **Billy Ross**, Appalachian State	SR	G	28	232	93	126	683	**24.4**
9 **Glenn Robinson**, Purdue	SO	F	28	246	32	152	676	**24.1**
10 **Kenny Sykes**, Grambling	SO	G	27	242	37	123	644	**23.9**

FIELD GOAL PCT	CL	POS	G	FG	FGA	PCT
1 **Bo Outlaw**, Houston	SR	F/C	30	196	298	**65.8**
2 **Brian Grant**, Xavier	JR	C	30	223	341	**65.4**
3 **Harry Hart**, Iona	SR	C	26	151	231	**65.4**
4 **Cherokee Parks**, Duke	SO	F/C	32	161	247	**65.2**
5 **Gary Trent**, Ohio	FR	F	27	194	298	**65.1**

MINIMUM: 5 MADE PER GAME

THREE-PT FG PER GAME	CL	POS	G	3FG	3PG
1 **Bernard Haslett**, Southern Miss	JR	G	26	109	**4.2**
2 **Stevin Smith**, Arizona State	JR	G	27	113	**4.2**
3 **Mark Alberts**, Akron	SR	G	26	107	**4.1**
4 **Keith Veney**, Lamar	FR	G	27	106	**3.9**
5 **Doug Day**, Radford	SR	G	31	116	**3.7**

THREE-PT FG PCT	CL	POS	G	3FG	3FGA	PCT
1 **Jeff Anderson**, Kent State	JR	G	26	44	82	**53.7**
2 **Roosevelt Moore**, Sam Houston	JR	G	25	73	137	**53.3**
3 **Dwayne Morton**, Louisville	JR	G/F	31	51	96	**53.1**
4 **Travis Ford**, Kentucky	JR	G	34	101	191	**52.9**
5 **Greg Graham**, Indiana	JR	G	35	57	111	**51.4**

MINIMUM: 1.5 MADE PER GAME

FREE THROW PCT	CL	POS	G	FT	FTA	PCT
1 **Josh Grant**, Utah	SR	F	31	104	113	**92.0**
2 **Roger Breslin**, Holy Cross	SR	G	30	100	111	**90.1**
3 **Jeremy Lake**, Montana	SO	G	28	71	79	**89.9**
4 **Casey Schmidt**, Valparaiso	JR	G	27	70	78	**89.7**
5 **Scott Hartzell**, UNC Greensboro	FR	G	27	72	81	**88.9**

MINIMUM: 2.5 MADE PER GAME

ASSISTS PER GAME	CL	POS	G	AST	APG
1 **Sam Crawford**, New Mexico State	SR	G	34	310	**9.1**
2 **Dedan Thomas**, UNLV	JR	G	29	248	**8.6**
3 **Mark Woods**, Wright State	SR	G	30	253	**8.4**
4 **Bobby Hurley**, Duke	SR	G	32	262	**8.2**
5 **Chuck Evans**, Mississippi State	SR	G	29	235	**8.1**
6 **Jason Kidd**, California	FR	G	29	222	**7.7**
7 **Tony Miller**, Marquette	SO	G	28	213	**7.6**
8 **Nelson Haggerty**, Baylor	SO	G	26	189	**7.3**
9 **Atiim Browne**, Lamar	JR	G	27	195	**7.2**
10 **Marcell Capers**, Arizona State	JR	G	28	200	**7.1**

REBOUNDS PER GAME	CL	POS	G	REB	RPG
1 **Warren Kidd**, Middle Tennessee State	SR	C	26	386	**14.8**
2 **Jervaughn Scales**, Southern U.	JR	F	31	393	**12.7**
3 **Reggie Jackson**, Nicholls State	SO	F	26	325	**12.5**
4 **Spencer Dunkley**, Delaware	SR	C	30	367	**12.2**
5 **Dan Callahan**, Northeastern	JR	F/C	28	340	**12.1**
6 **Ervin Johnson**, New Orleans	SR	C	29	346	**11.9**
7 **Carlos Rogers**, Tennessee State	JR	C	29	339	**11.7**
8 **Malik Rose**, Drexel	FR	F	29	330	**11.4**
9 **Michael Smith**, Providence	JR	F	33	375	**11.4**
10 **Darren Brown**, Colgate	SR	F	28	317	**11.3**

BLOCKED SHOTS PER GAME	CL	POS	G	BLK	BPG
1 **Theo Ratliff**, Wyoming	SO	C	28	124	**4.4**
2 **Sharone Wright**, Clemson	SO	C	30	124	**4.1**
3 **Bo Outlaw**, Houston	SR	F/C	30	114	**3.8**
4 **Carlos Rogers**, Tennessee State	JR	C	29	93	**3.2**
5 **Theron Wilson**, Eastern Michigan	SO	F	30	96	**3.2**
Spencer Dunkley, Delaware	SR	C	30	96	**3.2**

STEALS PER GAME	CL	POS	G	STL	SPG
1 **Jason Kidd**, California	FR	G	29	110	**3.8**
2 **Jay Goodman**, Utah State	SR	G	27	102	**3.8**
3 **Mark Woods**, Wright State	SR	G	30	109	**3.6**
4 **Mike Bright**, Bucknell	SR	G	29	94	**3.2**
5 **Darnell Mee**, Western Kentucky	SR	G	32	100	**3.1**

INDIVIDUAL LEADERS—GAME

POINTS	CL	POS	OPP	DATE	PTS
1 **Alphonso Ford**, Miss. Valley State	SR	G	Alabama State	J23	**49**
Alphonso Ford, Miss. Valley State	SR	G	Southern U.	F8	**49**
3 **Lindsey Hunter**, Jackson State	SR	G	Kansas	D27	**48**
4 **Will Flemons**, Texas Tech	SR	F	Oral Roberts	F15	**47**
5 **Reggie Kemp**, Youngstown State	SR	G	Wright State	F6	**46**
Devin Boyd, Towson	SR	G	UMBC	F27	**46**

THREE-PT FG MADE	CL	POS	OPP	DATE	3FG
1 **Doug Day**, Radford	SR	G	Morgan State	D9	**11**
Lindsey Hunter, Jackson State	SR	G	Kansas	D27	**11**
Keith Veney, Lamar	FR	G	Prairie View A&M	F3	**11**
Keith Veney, Lamar	FR	G	Arkansas-Little Rock	F11	**11**
5 **Theon Dotson**, Texas Southern	JR	G	UTSA	D5	**10**
Stevin Smith, Arizona State	JR	G	Oregon	J30	**10**
Bernard Haslett, Southern Miss	JR	G	Memphis	F10	**10**

ASSISTS	CL	POS	OPP	DATE	AST
1 **Dana Harris**, UMBC	SR	G	Saint Mary's (MD)	D12	**20**
Sam Crawford, New Mexico State	SR	G	Sam Houston State	D21	**20**
3 **Nelson Haggerty**, Baylor	SO	G	Oral Roberts	F27	**19**
4 **B.J. Tyler**, Texas	JR	G	Oral Roberts	D1	**18**
5 **Gary Robb**, Chattanooga	JR	G	Southern U.	D29	**17**
Bryan Parker, Pepperdine	SR	G	Oral Roberts	J9	**17**
Sam Crawford, New Mexico State	SR	G	San Jose State	J14	**17**
Gerald Lewis, SMU	SR	G	Texas	M6	**17**

REBOUNDS	CL	POS	OPP	DATE	REB
1 **Ervin Johnson**, New Orleans	SR	C	Lamar	F18	**27**
2 **Malik Rose**, Drexel	FR	F	Vermont	J29	**26**
3 **Malik Rose**, Drexel	FR	F	Vermont	F11	**25**
Spencer Dunkley, Delaware	SR	C	UMBC	J6	**25**
5 **Todd Cauthorn**, William and Mary	SR	F	The Citadel	D5	**24**
Ervin Johnson, New Orleans	SR	C	Jacksonville	J2	**24**
Yinka Dare, George Washington	FR	C	St. Bonaventure	F6	**24**

BLOCKED SHOTS	CL	POS	OPP	DATE	BLK
1 **Jim McIlvaine**, Marquette	JR	C	Northeastern Illinois	D9	**13**
2 **Ervin Johnson**, New Orleans	SR	C	Texas A&M	D29	**12**
3 **Sharone Wright**, Clemson	SO	C	UNC Greensboro	D12	**10**
Sharone Wright, Clemson	SO	C	Maryland	J27	**10**
Bo Outlaw, Houston	SR	F/C	Texas A&M	F17	**10**
Theo Ratliff, Wyoming	SO	C	San Diego State	F25	**10**

STEALS	CL	POS	OPP	DATE	STL
1 **Terry Evans**, Oklahoma	SR	G	Florida A&M	J27	**12**
2 **Ron Arnold**, St. Francis (NY)	SR	F	Mount St. Mary's	F4	**11**
3 **Michael Finley**, Wisconsin	JR	F	Purdue	F13	**10**
4 **Robert Shepherd**, Arkansas	SR	G	Arizona	D6	**9**
Darius Mimms, Southern U.	SR	G	Baptist Christian	D14	**9**
Cam Johnson, Northern Iowa	JR	G	St. Bonaventure	D19	**9**
Hank Washington, Southeastern La.	SR	G	Texas-Pan American	D19	**9**
Angelo Hamilton, Oklahoma	SR	G	BYU	D21	**9**
Acie Earl, Iowa	SR	C	Texas Southern	D28	**9**
Darnell Mee, Western Kentucky	SR	G	Jacksonville	F11	**9**
Jay Goodman, Utah State	SR	G	San Jose State	F20	**9**
Darnell Mee, Western Kentucky	SR	G	Louisiana Tech	F25	**9**
Corey Taylor, Iona	SR	G	Loyola (MD)	F27	**9**

TEAM LEADERS—SEASON

WIN-LOSS PCT	W	L	PCT
1 **North Carolina**	34	4	**.895**
2 **Indiana**	31	4	**.886**
3 **Kentucky**	30	4	**.882**
4 **New Orleans**	26	4	**.867**
5 **Michigan** ✪	31	5	**.861**

SCORING OFFENSE	G	W-L	PTS	PPG
1 **Southern U.**	31	21-10	3,011	**97.1**
2 **Northwestern State (LA)**	26	13-13	2,357	**90.7**
3 **UNLV**	29	21-8	2,592	**89.4**
4 **Wright State**	30	20-10	2,674	**89.1**
5 **Oklahoma**	32	20-12	2,850	**89.1**

SCORING MARGIN	G	W-L	PPG	OPP PPG	MAR
1 **North Carolina**	38	34-4	86.1	68.3	**17.8**
2 **Kentucky**	34	30-4	87.5	69.8	**17.7**
3 **Cincinnati**	32	27-5	74.5	58.5	**16.0**
4 **Duke**	32	24-8	86.4	71.2	**15.2**
5 **Indiana**	35	31-4	86.5	71.6	**14.9**

FIELD GOAL PCT	G	W-L	FG	FGA	PCT
1 **Indiana**	35	31-4	1,076	2,062	**52.2**
2 **UL-Monroe**	31	26-5	1,015	1,946	**52.2**
3 **James Madison**	30	21-9	848	1,634	**51.9**
4 **Wright State**	30	20-10	987	1,912	**51.6**
5 **Kansas**	36	29-7	1,109	2,154	**51.5**

THREE-PT FG PER GAME	G	W-L	3FG	3PG
1 **Lamar**	27	15-12	271	**10.0**
Kentucky	34	30-4	340	**10.0**
3 **Arizona State**	28	18-10	263	**9.4**
4 **UNC Asheville**	27	4-23	235	**8.7**
5 **Southern California**	30	18-12	259	**8.6**

FREE THROW PCT	G	W-L	FT	FTA	PCT
1 **Utah**	31	24-7	476	602	**79.1**
2 **Charleston Southern**	27	9-18	408	526	**77.6**
3 **Valparaiso**	28	12-16	412	532	**77.4**
4 **Indiana State**	28	11-17	445	580	**76.7**
5 **BYU**	34	25-9	697	909	**76.7**

ASSISTS PER GAME	G	W-L	AST	APG
1 **Northwestern State (LA)**	26	13-13	570	**21.9**
2 **Georgia Tech**	30	19-11	588	**19.6**
3 **Kentucky**	34	30-4	665	**19.6**
4 **Kansas**	36	29-7	687	**19.1**
5 **Tennessee Tech**	28	15-13	532	**19.0**

REBOUND MARGIN	G	W-L	RPG	OPP RPG	MAR
1 **Massachusetts**	31	24-7	43.9	32.8	**11.1**
Iowa	32	23-9	42.8	31.7	**11.1**
3 **Idaho**	32	24-8	39.6	29.3	**10.3**
4 **Arizona**	28	24-4	43.1	34.2	**8.9**
North Carolina	38	34-4	41.1	32.2	**8.9**

Scoring Defense	G	W-L	OPP PTS	OPP PPG
1 Princeton	26	15-11	1,421	**54.7**
2 Yale	26	10-16	1,444	**55.5**
3 Miami (OH)	31	22-9	1,775	**57.3**
4 Cincinnati	32	27-5	1,871	**58.5**
5 Missouri State	31	20-11	1,813	**58.5**

Field Goal Pct Defense	G	W-L	OPP FG	OPP FGA	OPP PCT
1 Marquette	28	20-8	634	1,613	**39.3**
2 George Washington	30	21-9	708	1,794	**39.5**
3 Arizona	28	24-4	710	1,776	**40.0**
4 Utah	31	24-7	737	1,831	**40.3**
5 New Orleans	30	26-4	680	1,689	**40.3**

Blocked Shots Per Game	G	W-L	BLK	BPG
1 Wyoming	28	13-15	184	**6.6**
2 Syracuse	29	20-9	184	**6.3**
3 Jackson State	34	25-9	215	**6.3**
4 Navy	27	8-19	170	**6.3**
5 Northwestern State (LA)	26	13-13	157	**6.0**

Steals Per Game	G	W-L	STL	SPG
1 Centenary	27	9-18	380	**14.1**
2 Oklahoma	32	20-12	405	**12.7**
3 Southern U.	31	21-10	387	**12.5**
4 Arizona State	28	18-10	337	**12.0**
5 St. Francis (NY)	27	9-18	324	**12.0**

TEAM LEADERS—GAME

Points	OPP	DATE	SCORE
1 Southern U.	Baptist Christian	D14	**156-91**
2 Oklahoma	Florida A&M	J27	**146-65**
3 Lamar	Prairie View A&M	F3	**143-88**
4 Kansas	Oral Roberts	J14	**140-72**
5 Lamar	Prairie View A&M	D28	**138-77**

Field Goal Pct	OPP	DATE	FG	FGA	PCT
1 Samford	Loyola (LA)	D12	35	45	**77.8**
2 North Carolina	Old Dominion	D1	43	57	**75.4**
3 Oklahoma State	Tulsa	D12	28	38	**73.7**
4 Rider	St. Francis (NY)	J5	40	56	**71.4**
5 Louisville	Tulane	F27	35	50	**70.0**

Three-Pt FG Made	OPP	DATE	3FG
1 Lamar	Louisiana Tech	F28	**23**
2 Lamar	Prairie View A&M	F3	**20**
3 Northwestern State	UTSA	J21	**17**
Old Dominion	James Madison	F17	**17**
Morehead State	Tennessee Tech	F22	**17**

CONSENSUS ALL-AMERICAS

FIRST TEAM

PLAYER	CL	POS	HT	SCHOOL	RPG	PPG
Calbert Cheaney	SR	G/F	6-7	Indiana	6.4	22.4
Anfernee Hardaway	JR	G/F	6-7	Memphis	8.5	22.8
Bobby Hurley	SR	G	6-0	Duke	2.6	17.0
Jamal Mashburn	JR	F	6-8	Kentucky	8.4	21.0
Chris Webber†	SO	F/C	6-9	Michigan	10.1	19.2

SECOND TEAM

PLAYER	CL	POS	HT	SCHOOL	RPG	PPG
Terry Dehere	SR	G	6-3	Seton Hall	3.0	22.0
Grant Hill	JR	G/F	6-8	Duke	6.4	18.0
Billy McCaffrey	JR	G	6-3	Vanderbilt	2.6	20.6
Eric Montross	JR	C	7-0	North Carolina	7.6	15.8
J.R. Rider	SR	G	6-7	UNLV	8.9	29.1
Glenn Robinson	SO	F	6-8	Purdue	9.2	24.1
Rodney Rogers	JR	F	6-8	Wake Forest	7.9	21.2

Selectors: AP, NABC, UPI, USBWA

† Honor later vacated

AWARD WINNERS

PLAYER OF THE YEAR

PLAYER	CL	POS	HT	SCHOOL	AWARDS
Calbert Cheaney	SR	G/F	6-7	Indiana	Naismith, AP, UPI, USBWA, Wooden, NABC, Rupp
Sam Crawford	SR	G	5-8	New Mexico State	Frances Pomeroy Naismith*

* For the most outstanding senior player who is 6 feet or under.

DEFENSIVE PLAYER OF THE YEAR

PLAYER	CL	POS	HT	SCHOOL
Grant Hill	JR	G/F	6-8	Duke

COACH OF THE YEAR

COACH	SCHOOL	REC	AWARDS
Dean Smith	North Carolina	34-4	Naismith
Eddie Fogler	Vanderbilt	28-6	AP, UPI, USBWA, NABC, Sporting News, CBS/Chevrolet

Bob Gibbons' Top High School Senior Recruits

PLAYER	POS	HT	HIGH SCHOOL	A-A TEAMS	COLLEGE	CAREER NOTES
1 Jerry Stackhouse	SF	6-6	Oak Hill Academy, Mouth of Wilson, VA	McD, P, USA	North Carolina	15.9 ppg (2 seasons); first-team All-America, '95; No. 3 pick, '95 NBA draft (76ers); All-Rookie team, '96; 18.6 ppg (13 seasons); 2-time All-Star
2 Randy Livingston	PG	6-4	Isidore Newman HS, New Orleans	McD, P, USA	LSU	11.4 ppg, 7.6 apg (3 seasons); 2nd-round pick, '96 NBA draft (Rockets); 3.8 ppg (11 seasons)
3 Rasheed Wallace	F/C	6-10	Simon Gratz HS, Philadelphia	McD, P, USA	North Carolina	13.0 ppg, 7.4 rpg (2 seasons); 2nd team All-America, '95; No. 4 pick, '95 NBA draft (Bullets); NBA title, '04; 4-time All-Star
4 Jacque Vaughn	PG	6-0	John Muir HS, Pasadena, CA	McD, P, USA	Kansas	804 assists; 2nd team All-America; 27th pick, '97 draft (Jazz); 4.6 ppg (11 seasons); NBA title, '07
5 Darnell Robinson	C	6-10	Emeryville (CA) HS	McD, P	Arkansas	NCAA title, 9.2 ppg in Tournament, '94; 2nd-round pick, '96 NBA draft (Mavs); played overseas
6 Jason Osborne	SF	6-8	Male HS, Louisville, KY	McD, P	Louisville	10.6 ppg (2 seasons); undrafted; played overseas
7 Charles O'Bannon	G/F	6-6	Artesia HS, Lakewood, CA	McD, P	UCLA	NCAA title, '95; UCLA's 10th leading scorer all-time; No. 22 pick, '97 NBA draft (Pistons); 2.5 ppg (2 seasons)
8 Rashard Griffith	C	7-0	King HS, Chicago	McD, P	Wisconsin	17.2 ppg, 10.8 rpg as Soph.; 2nd-round pick, '95 NBA draft (Bucks); played overseas
9 Jerald Honeycutt	PF	6-9	Grambling (LA) HS	McD, P	Tulane	Left as TU's all-time leading scorer (2,209 pts); 2nd-round pick, '97 NBA draft (Bucks); 5.1 ppg (2 seasons); played overseas
10 Jeff McInnis	PG	6-4	Oak Hill Academy, Mouth of Wilson, VA	McD, P	North Carolina	1,128 points, 436 assists (3 seasons); 2nd-round pick, '96 NBA draft (Nuggets); 9.4 ppg (11 seasons)
11 Ronnie Henderson	SF	6-7	Murrah HS, Jackson, MS	McD, P	LSU	20.3 ppg, 4.5 rpg (3 seasons); 2nd-round pick, '96 NBA draft (Bullets); no NBA games played
12 Joey Beard	F	6-10	South Lakes HS, Reston, VA	McD, P	Duke/Boston U.	Transferred after 1 year; in college, 11.7 ppg, 8.2 rpg (4 seasons); undrafted; played overseas
13 Cedric Henderson	SF	6-7	East HS, Memphis, TN	McD, P	Memphis	Left Memphis 6th-leading scorer (1,697 pts); 2nd-round pick, '97 NBA draft (Cavs); 7.3 ppg (5 seasons)
14 Avondre Jones	F/C	6-10	Artesia HS, Lakewood, CA	McD, P	USC/Fresno State	Transferred after 2 seasons; at USC, 10.1 ppg and 72 blocks as Soph.; undrafted
15 Marcus Camby	C	6-11	Hartford (CT) Public HS	P	Massachusetts	15.1 ppg, 7.0 rpg (3 seasons); National POY, '96; No. 2 pick, '96 NBA draft (Raptors); Defensive POY, '07; 3-time blocks leader
16 Antonio McDyess	F/C	6-9	Quitman (MS) HS	P	Alabama	12.8 ppg, 9.3 rpg (2 seasons); No. 2 pick, '95 NBA draft (Clippers); All-Rookie team, '96; All-Star, '01
17 Keith Booth	SF	6-6	Dunbar HS, Baltimore	McD, P	Maryland	14.2 ppg, 7.3 rpg (4 seasons); No. 28 pick, '97 NBA draft (Bulls); 2.9 ppg (2 seasons)
18 Dontonio Wingfield	PF	6-8	Westover HS, Albany, OH	McD, P	Cincinnati	16.0 ppg, 9.0 rpg (1 season); 2nd-round pick, '94 NBA draft (Sonics); 3.7 ppg, 2.4 rpg (4 seasons)
19 Kiwane Garris	2G	6-2	Westinghouse HS, Chicago	P	Illinois	16.8 ppg, 4.3 apg (4 seasons); first-team All-Big Ten as Sr.; undrafted; played on 2 NBA teams; 2.3 ppg in NBA (2 seasons)
20 Scot Pollard	F/C	6-10	Kamiakin HS, Kennewick, WA	P	Kansas	Left KU as 4th all-time in rebounds (850); No. 19 pick, '97 NBA draft (Nuggets); 4.4 ppg, 4.6 rpg (11 seasons)

Other Standouts

PLAYER	POS	HT	HIGH SCHOOL	A-A TEAMS	COLLEGE	CAREER NOTES
23 Joe Smith	PF	6-9	Maury HS, Norfolk, VA	P	Maryland	20.2 ppg, 10.7 rpg (2 seasons); Naismith Award, '95; No. 1 overall pick, '95 NBA draft (Warriors); 11.9 ppg, 6.9 rpg (13 seasons)
27 Ray Allen	2G	6-5	Hillcrest HS, Dalzell, SC		Connecticut	2-time All-America; left UConn as 4th-leading scorer all-time; No. 5 pick, '96 NBA draft (Wolves); 8-time All-Star; NBA title, '08
105 Keith Van Horn	SF	6-8	Diamond Bar (CA) HS		Utah	Left Utah as all-time leading scorer (2,542 pts); first-team All-America, '97; No. 2 pick, '97 NBA draft (76ers); 16.0 ppg (9 seasons)

Abbreviations: McD=McDonald's; P=Parade; USA=USA Today

Poll Progression

Preseason Poll

AP	USA/CNN	SCHOOL
1	1	Michigan
2	4	Kansas
3	2	Duke
4	3	Indiana
5	5	Kentucky
6	6	Seton Hall
7	7	North Carolina
8	9	Memphis
9	8	Florida State
10	10	Arizona
11	13	Iowa
12	11	Georgetown
13	12	Louisville
14	15	Georgia Tech
15	16	Oklahoma
16	20	Connecticut
17	14	Tulane
18	—	Syracuse
19	24	Iowa State
20	21	Michigan State
21	18	Cincinnati
22	23	UNLV
23	—	Massachusetts
24	17	UCLA
25	22	Nebraska
—	18	Texas
—	25	New Mexico State

Week of Nov 23

AP	SCHOOL	AP↓↑
1	Michigan (0-0)	
2	Kansas (0-0)	
3	Duke (0-0)	
4	Indiana (2-0)	
5	Kentucky (0-0)	
6	Seton Hall (2-0)	
7	Florida State (2-0)	↑2
8	North Carolina (0-0)	↓1
9	Memphis (0-0)	↓1
10	Arizona (0-0)	
11	Iowa (0-0)	
12	Louisville (0-0)	↑1
13	Georgetown (0-0)	↓1
14	Georgia Tech (0-0)	
15	Oklahoma (0-0)	
16	Connecticut (0-0)	
17	Syracuse (0-0)	↑1
18	Michigan State (0-0)	↑2
19	Tulane (1-1)	↓2
20	Massachusetts (0-0)	↑3
21	UCLA (2-0)	↑3
22	UNLV (0-0)	
23	Cincinnati (0-0)	↓2
24	Iowa State (1-1)	↓5
25	Nebraska (0-0)	

Week of Nov 30

AP	USA/CNN	SCHOOL	AP↓↑
1	2	Michigan (0-0)	
2	1	Indiana (4-0)	↑2
3	4	Kansas (0-0)	↓1
4	3	Duke (0-0)	↓1
5	5	Kentucky (0-0)	
6	6	Seton Hall (4-1)	
7	7	North Carolina (0-0)	↑1
8	8	Memphis (0-0)	↑1
9	9	Arizona (0-0)	↑1
10	14	Iowa (0-0)	↑1
11	10	Florida State (2-2)	↓4
12	13	Louisville (0-0)	
13	15	Georgia Tech (0-0)	↑1
14	12	Georgetown (0-0)	↓1
15	16	Oklahoma (0-0)	
16	11	UCLA (3-1)	↑5
17	—	Syracuse (0-0)	
18	18	Michigan State (0-0)	
19	—	Massachusetts (0-0)	↑1
20	19	Tulane (1-1)	↓1
21	22	New Mexico State (3-0)	⤴
22	20	Cincinnati (0-0)	↑1
23	21	UNLV (0-0)	↓1
24	17	Purdue (1-0)	⤴
25	23	Connecticut (0-1)	↓9
—	24	Texas (0-0)	
—	25	Nebraska (0-0)	⤵

Week of Dec 7

AP	USA/CNN	SCHOOL	AP↓↑
1	1	Duke (2-0)	↑3
2	2	Kansas (2-0)	↑1
3	4	Kentucky (2-0)	↑2
4	3	Indiana (4-1)	↓2
5	5	North Carolina (3-0)	↑2
6	5	Michigan (1-1)	↓5
7	7	Seton Hall (4-1)	↓1
8	10	Iowa (3-0)	↑2
9	9	Louisville (1-0)	↑3
10	8	Florida State (3-2)	↑1
11	11	Georgetown (2-0)	↑3
12	14	Oklahoma (2-0)	↑4
13	13	UCLA (4-1)	↑3
14	12	Arizona (0-1)	↓5
15	—	Syracuse (3-0)	↑2
16	16	Arkansas (3-0)	⤴
17	17	Georgia Tech (1-1)	↓4
18	15	Purdue (3-0)	↑6
19	24	Cincinnati (1-0)	↑3
20	19	Tulane (3-1)	
21	—	Memphis (0-1) Ⓐ	↓13
22	20	UNLV (1-0)	↑1
23	22	Massachusetts (1-1)	↓4
24	18	Michigan State (1-1)	↓6
25	21	Nebraska (2-0)	⤴
—	23	Connecticut (1-1)	⤵
—	25	New Mexico State (4-1)	⤵

Week of Dec 14

AP	USA/CNN	SCHOOL	AP↓↑
1	1	Duke (4-0)	
2	2	Kansas (5-0)	
3	3	Kentucky (4-0)	
4	4	Indiana (7-1)	
5	5	North Carolina (5-0)	
6	6	Michigan (3-1)	
7	7	Seton Hall (6-1)	
8	8	Iowa (5-0)	
9	11	Oklahoma (5-0)	↑2
10	9	Florida State (3-2)	
11	12	Georgetown (4-0)	
12	15	Arkansas (3-0)	↑4
13	13	UCLA (5-1)	
14	—	Syracuse (3-0)	↑1
15	10	Arizona (2-1)	↓1
16	14	Purdue (4-0)	↑2
17	16	Georgia Tech (2-1)	
18	17	Tulane (5-1)	↑2
19	18	Cincinnati (3-0)	
20	19	Nebraska (5-0)	↑5
21	22	Louisville (1-2)	↓12
22	20	UNLV (2-0)	
23	21	Michigan State (3-1)	↑1
24	24	Connecticut (3-1)	⤴
25	—	California (3-0)	⤴
—	23	Massachusetts (2-2)	⤵
—	25	New Mexico State (5-2)	

Week of Dec 21

AP	USA/CNN	SCHOOL	AP↓↑
1	1	Duke (4-0)	
2	2	Kansas (6-0)	
3	3	Kentucky (5-0)	
4	4	Indiana (8-1)	
5	5	North Carolina (6-0)	
6	6	Michigan (5-1)	
7	7	Seton Hall (8-1)	
8	8	Iowa (6-0)	
9	9	Oklahoma (5-0)	
10	11	Arkansas (5-0)	↑2
11	13	Georgetown (5-0)	
12	10	UCLA (6-1)	↑1
13	—	Syracuse (7-0)	↑1
14	12	Arizona (2-1)	↑1
15	14	Purdue (5-0)	↑1
16	15	Georgia Tech (2-1)	↑1
17	16	Nebraska (6-0)	↑3
18	18	Florida State (5-3)	↓8
19	17	UNLV (3-0)	↑3
20	19	Michigan State (5-1)	↑3
21	25	California (4-0)	↑4
22	20	Connecticut (3-1)	↑2
23	23	Cincinnati (3-1)	↓4
24	20	Tulane (5-2)	↓6
25	—	Vanderbilt (8-1)	⤴
—	22	Massachusetts (2-2)	
—	24	New Mexico State (5-2)	

Week of Dec 28

AP	USA/CNN	SCHOOL	AP↓↑
1	1	Duke (7-0)	
2	2	Kansas (8-0)	
3	3	Kentucky (6-0)	
4	4	Indiana (10-1)	
5	5	North Carolina (7-0)	
6	6	Michigan (6-1)	
7	7	Seton Hall (9-1)	
8	8	Iowa (8-0)	
9	9	Arkansas (7-0)	↑1
10	11	Georgetown (5-0)	↑1
11	10	UCLA (7-1)	↑1
12	—	Syracuse (8-0)	↑1
13	12	Purdue (6-0)	↑2
14	13	Georgia Tech (5-1)	↑2
15	13	Oklahoma (7-1)	↓6
16	15	UNLV (4-0)	↑3
17	18	Michigan State (5-1)	↑3
18	16	Florida State (6-3)	
19	22	California (5-0)	↑2
20	20	Nebraska (7-1)	↓3
21	20	Cincinnati (4-1)	↑2
22	17	Arizona (2-2)	↓8
23	19	Connecticut (4-1)	↓1
24	25	Vanderbilt (8-1)	↑1
25	24	BYU (7-2)	⤴
—	23	Massachusetts (2-2)	

Week of Jan 4

AP	USA/CNN	SCHOOL	AP↓↑
1	1	Duke (8-0)	
2	2	Kentucky (9-0)	↑1
3	3	Michigan (10-1)	↑3
4	6	Kansas (9-1)	↓2
5	4	Indiana (11-2)	↓1
6	5	North Carolina (9-1)	↓1
7	7	Seton Hall (11-1)	
8	8	Iowa (10-0)	
9	9	Purdue (9-0)	↑4
10	11	Georgia Tech (7-1)	↑4
11	10	Oklahoma (10-1)	↑4
12	14	UNLV (6-0)	↑4
13	13	Arkansas (8-1)	↓4
14	15	Michigan State (8-1)	↑3
15	12	UCLA (9-2)	↓4
16	16	Cincinnati (6-1)	↑5
17	18	Georgetown (7-1)	↓7
18	20	Vanderbilt (11-1)	↑6
19	19	Connecticut (6-1)	↑4
20	17	Arizona (5-2)	↑2
21	—	Syracuse (8-2)	↓9
22	21	Massachusetts (5-2)	⤴
23	23	Florida State (8-4)	↓5
24	—	Pittsburgh (8-1)	⤴
25	—	Virginia (7-0)	⤴
—	22	Nebraska (9-3)	⤵
—	24	BYU (8-4)	⤵
—	25	New Mexico State (7-3)	

Week of Jan 11

AP	USA/CNN	SCHOOL	AP↓↑
1	1	Kentucky (11-0)	↑1
2	3	Michigan (12-1)	↑1
3	2	Duke (10-1)	↓2
4	5	Kansas (11-1)	
5	6	North Carolina (12-1)	↑1
6	4	Indiana (13-2) Ⓑ	↓1
7	7	Seton Hall (13-1)	
8	8	Georgia Tech (9-1)	↑2
9	10	Arkansas (11-1)	↑4
10	9	Oklahoma (11-2)	↑1
11	11	Cincinnati (9-1)	↑5
12	12	Arizona (7-2)	↑8
13	13	Iowa (11-2) Ⓑ	↓5
14	18	Virginia (9-0)	↑11
15	16	Connecticut (7-2)	↑4
16	14	UCLA (10-3)	↓1
17	15	Purdue (9-2)	↓8
18	17	UNLV (6-1)	↓6
19	24	Minnesota (10-1)	⤴
20	20	Georgetown (8-2)	↓3
21	22	Ohio State (9-2)	⤴
22	—	Boston College (9-2)	⤴
23	19	Michigan State (8-3)	↓9
24	—	Syracuse (9-2)	↓3
25	—	Utah (10-2)	⤴
—	21	Florida State (9-5)	⤵
—	23	Vanderbilt (11-3)	⤵
—	25	Nebraska (11-3)	

Week of Jan 18

AP	USA/CNN	SCHOOL	AP↓↑
1	1	Kansas (14-1)	↑3
2	2	Indiana (15-2) Ⓒ	↑4
3	4	North Carolina (14-1)	↑2
4	6	Kentucky (11-1)	↓3
5	5	Michigan (13-2) Ⓒ	↓3
6	3	Duke (12-2)	↓3
7	10	Virginia (11-0)	↑7
8	7	Arkansas (12-1)	↑1
9	8	Cincinnati (11-1)	↑2
10	9	Seton Hall (14-2)	↓3
11	12	Arizona (9-2)	↑1
12	11	Oklahoma (12-3)	↓2
13	14	Purdue (11-2)	↑4
14	13	Iowa (12-3)	↓1
15	17	UNLV (9-1)	↑3
16	16	Georgia Tech (9-3)	↓8
17	15	Connecticut (8-3)	↓2
18	18	Georgetown (10-2)	↑2
19	19	Vanderbilt (13-3)	⤴
20	23	Pittsburgh (11-2)	⤴
21	21	Michigan State (10-3)	↑2
22	24	Utah (12-2)	↑3
23	20	UCLA (11-4)	↓7
24	25	Ohio State (9-3)	↓3
25	—	Long Beach State (12-1)	⤴
—	22	Florida State (11-5)	

Week of Jan 25

AP	USA/CNN	SCHOOL	AP↓↑
1	1	Kansas (16-1)	
2	3	Indiana (17-2)	
3	2	North Carolina (16-1)	
4	4	Kentucky (13-1)	
5	5	Michigan (15-2)	
6	6	Cincinnati (13-1)	↑3
7	7	Duke (13-3)	↓1
8	8	Arizona (11-2)	↑3
9	10	Seton Hall (15-3)	↑1
10	9	UNLV (11-1)	↑5
11	11	Iowa (14-3)	↑3
12	13	Vanderbilt (14-3)	↑8
13	18	Pittsburgh (13-2)	↑7
14	15	Purdue (11-3)	↓1
15	14	Virginia (11-2)	↓8
16	12	Arkansas (12-3)	↓8
17	21	Utah (14-2)	↑5
18	17	Georgia Tech (10-4)	↓2
19	20	Florida State (13-5)	⤴
20	19	Oklahoma (12-5)	↓8
21	22	Georgetown (11-3)	↓3
22	16	Connecticut (9-4)	↓5
23	—	Tulane (14-3)	⤴
24	—	Marquette (14-2)	⤴
25	—	Houston (11-2)	⤴
—	23	UCLA (12-5)	⤵
—	24	Wisconsin (10-4)	
—	25	Xavier (12-2)	

Week of Feb 1

AP	USA/CNN	SCHOOL	AP↓↑
1	1	Indiana (19-2)	↑1
2	2	Kentucky (15-1)	↑2
3	3	Kansas (17-2)	↓2
4	4	Cincinnati (15-1)	↑2
5	6	Duke (15-3)	↑2
6	5	North Carolina (17-2)	↓3
7	9	Michigan (16-3)	↓2
8	7	Arizona (13-2)	
9	8	Iowa (14-3)	↑2
10	10	UNLV (13-1)	
11	11	Vanderbilt (16-3)	
12	15	Florida State (14-6)	↑7
13	20	Wake Forest (13-3)	⤴
14	14	Seton Hall (15-5)	↓5
15	17	Pittsburgh (13-3)	↓2
16	13	Oklahoma (14-5)	↑4
17	12	Arkansas (13-4)	↓1
18	24	Tulane (15-3)	↑5
19	16	Purdue (12-4)	↓5
20	21	Marquette (15-2)	↑4
21	18	Utah (15-3)	↓4
22	22	Georgia Tech (11-5)	↓4
23	25	Georgetown (12-4)	↓2
24	23	Virginia (12-4)	↓9
25	—	Michigan State (11-5)	⤴
—	19	UCLA (14-5)	

Poll Progression Continues →

Week of Feb 8

AP	USA/CNN	School	AP↓↑
1	1	**Indiana** (20-2)	
2	2	**Kentucky** (17-1)	
3	3	**Duke** (17-3)	↑2
4	4	**Michigan** (18-3)	↑3
5	7	**Arizona** (15-2) Ⓓ	↑3
6	6	**North Carolina** (18-3)	
7	5	**Kansas** (18-3)	↓4
8	8	**Cincinnati** (17-2)	↓4
9	15	**Wake Forest** (15-3)	↑4
10	12	**Florida State** (16-6)	↑2
11	13	**Vanderbilt** (17-4)	
12	10	**UNLV** (14-2)	↓2
13	9	**Iowa** (14-5)	↓4
14	11	**Arkansas** (15-4)	↑3
15	16	**Marquette** (17-2)	↑5
16	14	**Utah** (17-3)	↑5
17	17	**Pittsburgh** (14-4)	↓2
18	20	**Purdue** (13-5)	↑1
19	18	**Seton Hall** (16-6)	↓5
20	21	**Tulane** (16-4)	↓2
21	—	**Boston College** (13-5)	⤴
22	23	**Massachusetts** (15-4)	⤴
23	—	**Kansas State** (14-3)	⤴
24	19	**Virginia** (13-4)	
25	—	**New Orleans** (17-2)	⤴
—	22	**Oklahoma** (14-7)	⤵
—	24	**Georgia Tech** (12-6)	⤵
—	25	**Louisville** (13-5)	

Week of Feb 15

AP	USA/CNN	School	AP↓↑
1	1	**Indiana** (22-2)	
2	2	**Kentucky** (18-2)	
3	3	**North Carolina** (20-3)	↑3
4	6	**Arizona** (17-2)	↑1
5	5	**Michigan** (19-4)	↓1
6	4	**Kansas** (20-3)	↑1
7	8	**Duke** (19-4)	↓4
8	7	**Cincinnati** (19-2)	
9	9	**Florida State** (19-6)	↑1
10	11	**Wake Forest** (16-4)	↓1
11	10	**Vanderbilt** (19-4)	
12	13	**Utah** (19-3)	↑4
13	12	**Arkansas** (16-5)	↑1
14	17	**Purdue** (15-5)	↑4
15	14	**UNLV** (16-3) Ⓔ	↓3
16	18	**Seton Hall** (18-6)	↑3
17	15	**Pittsburgh** (15-5)	
18	19	**Tulane** (17-4)	↑2
19	20	**Massachusetts** (17-4)	↑3
20	16	**Iowa** (14-6)	↓7
21	23	**New Orleans** (17-2)	↑4
22	25	**Louisville** (14-6) Ⓔ	⤴
23	21	**Virginia** (15-5)	↑1
24	22	**Marquette** (17-4)	↓9
25	—	**St. John's** (14-6)	⤴
—	23	**Oklahoma** (16-7)	

Week of Feb 22

AP	USA/CNN	School	AP↓↑
1	1	**Indiana** (24-2)	
2	2	**Kentucky** (20-2)	
3	3	**North Carolina** (22-3)	
4	4	**Arizona** (19-2)	
5	5	**Michigan** (21-4)	
6	7	**Florida State** (21-6)	↑3
7	6	**Kansas** (21-4)	↓1
8	9	**Vanderbilt** (21-4)	↑3
9	10	**Duke** (20-5)	↓2
10	8	**Cincinnati** (20-3)	↓2
11	11	**Utah** (21-3)	↑1
12	12	**Wake Forest** (17-5)	↓2
13	13	**UNLV** (17-3)	↑2
14	15	**Seton Hall** (20-6)	↑2
15	14	**Arkansas** (17-6)	↓2
16	17	**Tulane** (20-4)	↑2
17	18	**Purdue** (15-6)	↓3
18	16	**Iowa** (16-6)	↑2
19	20	**New Orleans** (20-2)	↑2
20	19	**Marquette** (19-4)	↑4
21	23	**Massachusetts** (18-5)	↓2
22	22	**Virginia** (16-6)	↑1
23	—	**BYU** (21-5)	⤴
24	25	**Xavier** (18-3)	⤴
25	21	**Pittsburgh** (15-7)	↓8
—	24	**Oklahoma** (17-8)	

Week of Mar 1

AP	USA/CNN	School	AP↓↑
1	1	**North Carolina** (24-3)	↑
2	2	**Indiana** (25-3)	↓
3	3	**Arizona** (21-2)	↑
4	5	**Michigan** (22-4)	↑
5	4	**Kentucky** (21-3)	↓
6	6	**Duke** (22-5) Ⓕ	↑
7	8	**Vanderbilt** (23-4)	↑
8	7	**Kansas** (22-5)	↓
9	9	**Utah** (22-3)	↑2
10	12	**Seton Hall** (22-6)	↑4
11	11	**Florida State** (21-8)	↓5
12	10	**Cincinnati** (21-4)	↓2
13	13	**Arkansas** (18-6)	↑2
14	16	**Wake Forest** (18-6)	↓2
15	15	**Iowa** (19-6)	↑3
16	14	**UNLV** (19-4)	↓3
17	17	**New Orleans** (23-2)	↑2
18	18	**Xavier** (20-3)	↑6
19	22	**Oklahoma State** (18-5)	⤴
20	20	**Tulane** (20-6)	↓4
21	—	**BYU** (22-6)	↑2
22	25	**Louisville** (16-8)	⤴
23	24	**Massachusetts** (18-6)	↓2
24	23	**Purdue** (15-8)	↓7
25	—	**St. John's** (16-8)	⤴
—	19	**Marquette** (19-6)	⤵
—	21	**Virginia** (16-8)	⤵

Week of Mar 8

AP	USA/CNN	School	AP↓↑
1	1	**North Carolina** (25-3)	
2	2	**Indiana** (26-3)	
3	3	**Michigan** (23-4)	↑1
4	4	**Kentucky** (23-3)	↑1
5	6	**Vanderbilt** (25-4)	↑2
6	5	**Arizona** (22-3)	↓3
7	7	**Kansas** (23-5)	↑1
8	8	**Duke** (23-5)	↓2
9	10	**Seton Hall** (24-6)	↑1
10	11	**Florida State** (22-8)	↑1
11	9	**Cincinnati** (22-4)	↑1
12	12	**Wake Forest** (19-7)	↑2
13	15	**New Orleans** (25-2)	↑4
14	14	**Arkansas** (19-7)	↓1
15	13	**Utah** (22-5)	↓6
16	19	**Louisville** (18-8)	↑6
17	17	**Iowa** (19-8)	↓2
18	18	**Purdue** (17-8)	↑6
19	16	**UNLV** (20-6)	↓3
20	21	**Massachusetts** (20-6)	↑3
21	22	**Oklahoma State** (19-7)	↓2
22	—	**Xavier** (21-4)	↓4
23	20	**Tulane** (21-7)	↓3
24	24	**New Mexico State** (23-6)	⤴
25	—	**BYU** (23-7)	↓4
—	23	**Marquette** (20-6)	
—	25	**Virginia** (18-8)	

Week of Mar 15

AP	USA/CNN	School	AP↓↑
1	1	**Indiana** (28-3)	↑1
2	3	**Kentucky** (26-3)	↑2
3	4	**Michigan** (26-4)	
4	2	**North Carolina** (28-4)	↓3
5	5	**Arizona** (24-3)	↑1
6	6	**Seton Hall** (27-6)	↑3
7	7	**Cincinnati** (24-4)	↑4
8	9	**Vanderbilt** (26-5)	↓3
9	8	**Kansas** (25-6)	↓2
10	10	**Duke** (23-7)	↓2
11	11	**Florida State** (22-9)	↓1
12	12	**Arkansas** (20-8)	↑2
13	13	**Iowa** (22-8)	↑4
14	17	**Massachusetts** (23-6)	↑6
15	14	**Louisville** (20-8)	↑1
16	15	**Wake Forest** (19-8)	↓4
17	18	**New Orleans** (26-3)	↓4
18	20	**Georgia Tech** (19-10)	⤴
19	16	**Utah** (23-6)	↓4
20	25	**W. Kentucky** (24-5) Ⓖ	⤴
21	—	**New Mexico** (24-6)	⤴
22	21	**Purdue** (17-9)	↓4
23	23	**Oklahoma State** (19-8)	↓2
24	24	**New Mexico State** (25-7)	
25	19	**UNLV** (21-7)	↓6
—	21	**Virginia** (19-9)	

Final Poll

	USA/CNN	School
1		**North Carolina** (34-4)
2		**Michigan** (31-5)
3		**Kentucky** (30-4)
4		**Kansas** (29-7)
5		**Indiana** (31-4)
6		**Cincinnati** (29-5)
7		**Florida State** (25-10)
8		**Vanderbilt** (28-6)
9		**Duke** (24-8)
10		**Arkansas** (22-9)
11		**Seton Hall** (28-7)
12		**Arizona** (24-4)
13		**Temple** (20-13)
14		**Wake Forest** (21-9)
15		**Louisville** (22-9)
16		**Western Kentucky** (26-6)
17		**California** (21-9)
18		**Virginia** (21-10)
19		**Iowa** (23-9)
20		**Utah** (24-7)
21		**George Washington** (21-9)
22		**Massachusetts** (24-7)
23		**Xavier** (24-6)
24		**UCLA** (22-11)
25		**Minnesota** (20-10)

Ⓐ Despite 27 points and six assists from junior guard Anfernee "Penny" Hardaway, Memphis State starts the season with an 81-76 loss to Arkansas.

Ⓑ Indiana defeats Iowa, 75-67, on Jan. 6 to give coach Bob Knight his 600th career coaching victory. He accomplishes it in his 812th game, making him the ninth-fastest to reach the milestone.

Ⓒ Indiana goes to Ann Arbor on Jan. 12 and gets the first of two one-point victories over the sophomore edition of Michigan's Fab Five, who will nevertheless reach the Final Four for the second consecutive year.

Ⓓ In Tuscon, Arizona hands California its third straight defeat, 93-81. Afterward, Cal fires coach Lou Campanelli, replacing him with Todd Bozeman.

Ⓔ Louisville upsets UNLV, 90-86, on Valentine's Day in Las Vegas, ending the Rebels' 59-game home court winning streak.

Ⓕ Duke's Bobby Hurley dishes out a school-record 16 assists in a 98-75 victory over Florida State at Cameron Indoor Stadium, avenging a one-point road loss to FSU in January. Hurley will finish with 1,076 assists, an NCAA record.

Ⓖ Western Kentucky defeats New Orleans, 72-63, to win the Sun Belt tournament. The Hilltoppers will use that momentum to make a Tournament run to the Sweet 16.

Pre-Tournament Ratings Percentage Index (RPI)

Rank	School	W-L	Sched. Strg.	SS Rank	RPI
1	**Indiana**	28-3	.6106	6	.6517
2	**North Carolina**	28-4	.6069	9	.6500
3	**Michigan**	26-4	.6233	2	.6442
4	**Kentucky**	26-3	.5848	25	.6346
5	**Duke**	23-7	.6162	4	.6287
6	**Arizona**	24-3	.5926	18	.6285
7	**Kansas**	22-6	.6088	7	.6223
8	**Seton Hall**	26-6	.6022	12	.6213
9	**Cincinnati**	24-4	.5837	27	.6198
10	**Florida State**	22-9	.6072	8	.6113
11	**Georgia Tech**	19-10	.6181	3	.6033
12	**Massachusetts**	23-6	.5530	56	.6005
13	**Wake Forest**	19-8	.5893	20	.6004
14	**Louisville**	19-8	.6141	5	.6003
15	**Virginia**	19-9	.6067	10	.5997
16	**Arkansas**	20-8	.5961	16	.5970
17	**Vanderbilt**	26-5	.5190	99	.5952
18	**Temple**	17-12	.6379	1	.5940
19	**New Mexico**	23-6	.5657	40	.5906
20	**St. John's**	18-10	.5999	13	.5857
21	**New Orleans**	25-3	.5138	111	.5843
22	**Syracuse**	19-9	.5712	36	.5838
23	**Iowa**	21-8	.5459	63	.5820
24	**Purdue**	18-9	.5685	39	.5820
25	**Memphis State**	18-11	.6051	11	.5815
26	**Rhode Island**	18-10	.5851	24	.5790
27	**George Washington**	19-8	.5589	44	.5779
28	**Western Kentucky**	24-5	.5373	71	.5775
29	**Oklahoma State**	15-8	.5702	37	.5775
30	**Oklahoma**	16-11	.5848	25	.5736
31	**Iowa State**	19-10	.5575	45	.5724
32	**New Mexico State**	22-7	.5297	82	.5720
33	**UCLA**	21-10	.5494	58	.5718
34	**Xavier**	22-5	.5114	119	.5706
35	**Ohio State**	15-12	.5923	19	.5701
36	**Illinois**	18-12	.5751	34	.5695
37	**BYU**	24-8	.5124	114	.5677
38	**Kansas State**	19-10	.5492	59	.5675
39	**Pittsburgh**	17-10	.5562	52	.5665
40	**Missouri**	16-13	.5962	15	.5662
41	**Minnesota**	16-10	.5567	51	.5657
42	**Nebraska**	20-10	.5444	64	.5651
43	**California**	19-8	.5294	83	.5647
44	**Houston**	21-8	.5146	109	.5626
45	**West Virginia**	16-11	.5642	42	.5614
46	**LSU**	22-10	.5268	88	.5612
47	**SMU**	18-7	.5121	116	.5595
48	**Clemson**	16-12	.5568	50	.5591
49	**Utah**	22-6	.4803	181	.5588
50	**Old Dominion**	19-7	.5061	129	.5578

Source: Collegiate Basketball News

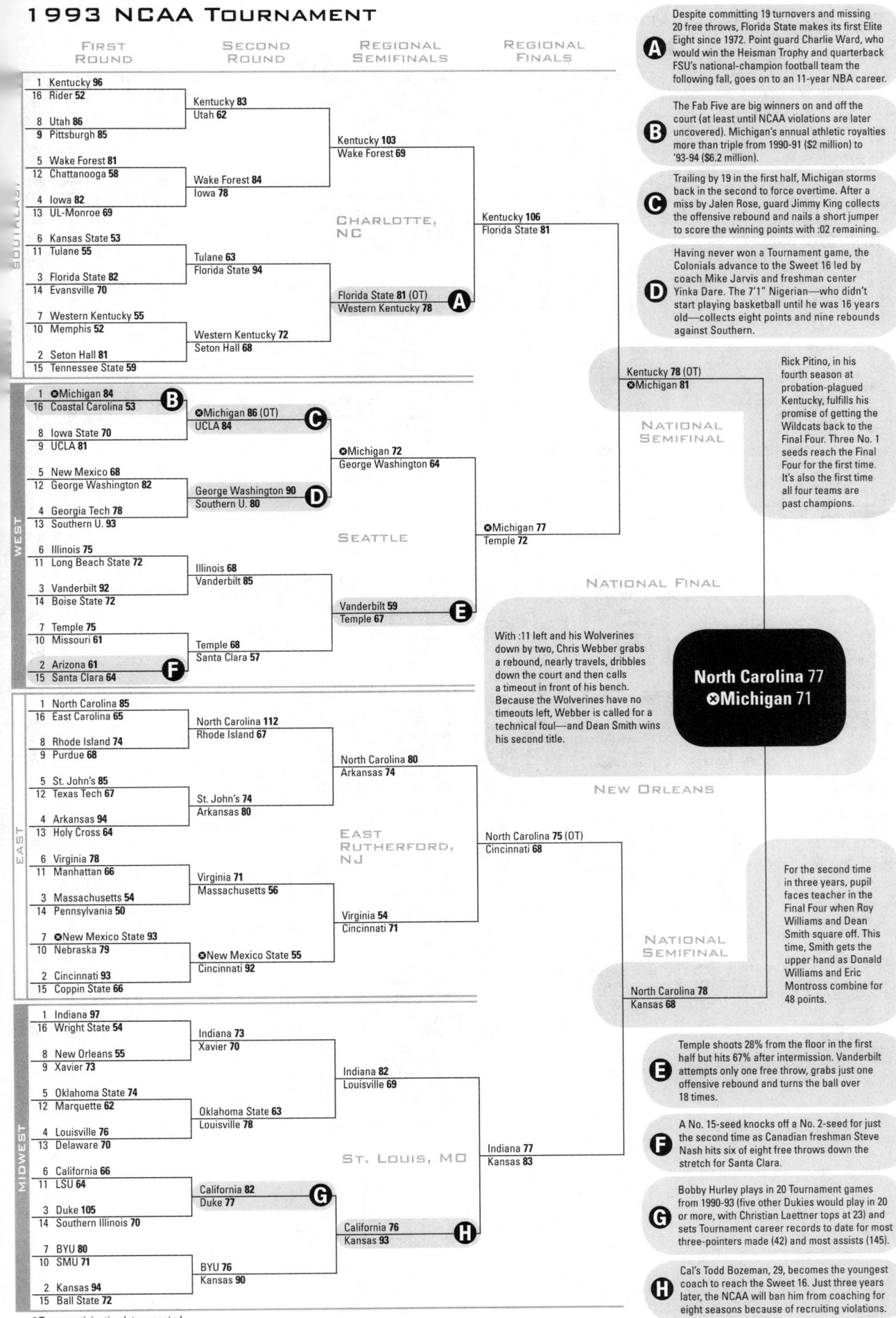

1993 NCAA Tournament

Southeast — Charlotte, NC

First Round
- 1 Kentucky **96**, 16 Rider **52**
- 8 Utah **86**, 9 Pittsburgh **85**
- 5 Wake Forest **81**, 12 Chattanooga **58**
- 4 Iowa **82**, 13 UL-Monroe **69**
- 6 Kansas State **53**, 11 Tulane **55**
- 3 Florida State **82**, 14 Evansville **70**
- 7 Western Kentucky **55**, 10 Memphis **52**
- 2 Seton Hall **81**, 15 Tennessee State **59**

Second Round
- Kentucky **83**, Utah **62**
- Wake Forest **84**, Iowa **78**
- Tulane **63**, Florida State **94**
- Western Kentucky **72**, Seton Hall **68**

Regional Semifinals
- Kentucky **103**, Wake Forest **69**
- Florida State **81** (OT), Western Kentucky **78** (A)

Regional Finals
- Kentucky **106**, Florida State **81**

West — Seattle

First Round
- 1 ⊗Michigan **84**, 16 Coastal Carolina **53** (B)
- 8 Iowa State **70**, 9 UCLA **81**
- 5 New Mexico **68**, 12 George Washington **82**
- 4 Georgia Tech **78**, 13 Southern U. **93**
- 6 Illinois **75**, 11 Long Beach State **72**
- 3 Vanderbilt **92**, 14 Boise State **72**
- 7 Temple **75**, 10 Missouri **61**
- 2 Arizona **61**, 15 Santa Clara **64** (F)

Second Round
- ⊗Michigan **86** (OT), UCLA **84** (C)
- George Washington **90**, Southern U. **80** (D)
- Illinois **68**, Vanderbilt **85**
- Temple **68**, Santa Clara **57**

Regional Semifinals
- ⊗Michigan **72**, George Washington **64**
- Vanderbilt **59**, Temple **67** (E)

Regional Finals
- ⊗Michigan **77**, Temple **72**

East — East Rutherford, NJ

First Round
- 1 North Carolina **85**, 16 East Carolina **65**
- 8 Rhode Island **74**, 9 Purdue **68**
- 5 St. John's **85**, 12 Texas Tech **67**
- 4 Arkansas **94**, 13 Holy Cross **64**
- 6 Virginia **78**, 11 Manhattan **66**
- 3 Massachusetts **54**, 14 Pennsylvania **50**
- 7 ⊗New Mexico State **93**, 10 Nebraska **79**
- 2 Cincinnati **93**, 15 Coppin State **66**

Second Round
- North Carolina **112**, Rhode Island **67**
- St. John's **74**, Arkansas **80**
- Virginia **71**, Massachusetts **56**
- ⊗New Mexico State **55**, Cincinnati **92**

Regional Semifinals
- North Carolina **80**, Arkansas **74**
- Virginia **54**, Cincinnati **71**

Regional Finals
- North Carolina **75** (OT), Cincinnati **68**

Midwest — St. Louis, MO

First Round
- 1 Indiana **97**, 16 Wright State **54**
- 8 New Orleans **55**, 9 Xavier **73**
- 5 Oklahoma State **74**, 12 Marquette **62**
- 4 Louisville **76**, 13 Delaware **70**
- 6 California **66**, 11 LSU **64**
- 3 Duke **105**, 14 Southern Illinois **70**
- 7 BYU **80**, 10 SMU **71**
- 2 Kansas **94**, 15 Ball State **72**

Second Round
- Indiana **73**, Xavier **70**
- Oklahoma State **63**, Louisville **78**
- California **82**, Duke **77** (G)
- BYU **76**, Kansas **90**

Regional Semifinals
- Indiana **82**, Louisville **69**
- California **76**, Kansas **93** (H)

Regional Finals
- Indiana **77**, Kansas **83**

National Semifinal
- Kentucky **78** (OT), ⊗Michigan **81**

Rick Pitino, in his fourth season at probation-plagued Kentucky, fulfills his promise of getting the Wildcats back to the Final Four. Three No. 1 seeds reach the Final Four for the first time. It's also the first time all four teams are past champions.

National Final — New Orleans

North Carolina 77
⊗Michigan 71

With :11 left and his Wolverines down by two, Chris Webber grabs a rebound, nearly travels, dribbles down the court and then calls a timeout in front of his bench. Because the Wolverines have no timeouts left, Webber is called for a technical foul—and Dean Smith wins his second title.

National Semifinal
- North Carolina **78**, Kansas **68**

For the second time in three years, pupil faces teacher in the Final Four when Roy Williams and Dean Smith square off. This time, Smith gets the upper hand as Donald Williams and Eric Montross combine for 48 points.

⊗Team participation later vacated

A Despite committing 19 turnovers and missing 20 free throws, Florida State makes its first Elite Eight since 1972. Point guard Charlie Ward, who would win the Heisman Trophy and quarterback FSU's national-champion football team the following fall, goes on to an 11-year NBA career.

B The Fab Five are big winners on and off the court (at least until NCAA violations are later uncovered). Michigan's annual athletic royalties more than triple from 1990-91 ($2 million) to '93-94 ($6.2 million).

C Trailing by 19 in the first half, Michigan storms back in the second to force overtime. After a miss by Jalen Rose, guard Jimmy King collects the offensive rebound and nails a short jumper to score the winning points with :02 remaining.

D Having never won a Tournament game, the Colonials advance to the Sweet 16 led by coach Mike Jarvis and freshman center Yinka Dare. The 7'1" Nigerian—who didn't start playing basketball until he was 16 years old—collects eight points and nine rebounds against Southern.

E Temple shoots 28% from the floor in the first half but hits 67% after intermission. Vanderbilt attempts only one free throw, grabs just one offensive rebound and turns the ball over 18 times.

F A No. 15-seed knocks off a No. 2-seed for just the second time as Canadian freshman Steve Nash hits six of eight free throws down the stretch for Santa Clara.

G Bobby Hurley plays in 20 Tournament games from 1990-93 (five other Dukies would play in 20 or more, with Christian Laettner tops at 23) and sets Tournament career records to date for most three-pointers made (42) and most assists (145).

H Cal's Todd Bozeman, 29, becomes the youngest coach to reach the Sweet 16. Just three years later, the NCAA will ban him from coaching for eight seasons because of recruiting violations.

Tournament Leaders

INDIVIDUAL LEADERS

Scoring

	CL	POS	G	PTS	PPG
1 **Calbert Cheaney**, Indiana	SR	G/F	4	106	26.5
2 **Lamond Murray**, California	SO	F	3	74	24.7
3 **Rodney Rogers**, Wake Forest	JR	F	3	73	24.3
4 **Billy McCaffrey**, Vanderbilt	JR	G	3	72	24.0
5 **Eddie Jones**, Temple	JR	G	4	85	21.3
6 **Rex Walters**, Kansas	SR	G	5	106	21.2
7 **Aaron McKie**, Temple	JR	G	4	82	20.5
8 **Randolph Childress**, Wake Forest	SO	G	3	60	20.0
9 **Donald Williams**, North Carolina	SO	G	6	118	19.7
10 **Jamal Mashburn**, Kentucky	JR	F	5	97	19.4

Minimum: 3 games

Field Goal Pct

	CL	POS	G	FG	FGA	PCT
1 **Corliss Williamson**, Arkansas	FR	F	3	19	25	76.0
2 **Trelonnie Owens**, Wake Forest	JR	F	3	21	30	70.0
3 **Matt Nover**, Indiana	SR	F	4	20	29	69.0
4 **Eric Montross**, North Carolina	JR	C	6	37	57	64.9
5 **Richard Scott**, Kansas	JR	F	5	20	31	64.5

Minimum: 15 made and 3 games

Free Throw Pct

	CL	POS	G	FT	FTA	PCT
1 **Greg Graham**, Indiana	SR	G	4	18	19	94.7
2 **Steve Woodberry**, Kansas	JR	G	5	16	17	94.1
3 **Rex Walters**, Kansas	SR	G	5	18	20	90.0
4 **Donald Williams**, North Carolina	SO	G	6	16	18	88.9
Erik Martin, Cincinnati	SR	F	4	16	18	88.9

Minimum: 15 made

Three-Pt FG Pct

	CL	POS	G	3FG	3FGA	PCT
1 **Sam Cassell**, Florida State	SR	G	4	12	17	70.6
2 **Ronnie McMahan**, Vanderbilt	SO	G	3	13	19	68.4
3 **Greg Minor**, Louisville	JR	G	3	9	14	64.3
4 **Kwame Evans**, George Washington	SR	G	3	8	13	61.5
5 **Rex Walters**, Kansas	SR	G	5	18	30	60.0

Minimum: 6 made and 3 games

Assists Per Game

	CL	POS	G	AST	APG
1 **Jason Kidd**, California	FR	G	3	31	10.3
2 **Nick Van Exel**, Cincinnati	SR	G	4	29	7.3
3 **Adonis Jordan**, Kansas	SR	G	5	30	6.0
4 **Charlie Ward**, Florida State	JR	G	4	22	5.5
5 **Rex Walters**, Kansas	SR	G	5	27	5.4

Minimum: 3 games

Rebounds Per Game

	CL	POS	G	REB	RPG
1 **Chris Webber**, Michigan	SO	F/C	6	68	11.3
2 **Doug Edwards**, Florida State	SR	F	4	40	10.0
3 **George Lynch**, North Carolina	SR	F	6	59	9.8
4 **Erik Martin**, Cincinnati	SR	F	4	37	9.3
5 **Lamond Murray**, California	SO	F	3	26	8.7

Minimum: 3 games

Blocked Shots Per Game

	CL	POS	G	BLK	BPG
1 **Rodney Dobard**, Florida State	SR	F	4	15	3.8
2 **Chris Webber**, Michigan	SO	F/C	6	15	2.5
3 **Eddie Jones**, Temple	JR	G	4	8	2.0
4 **Doug Edwards**, Florida State	SR	F	4	7	1.8
5 **Cypheus Bunton**, Western Kentucky	JR	F	3	5	1.7
Yinka Dare, George Washington	FR	C	3	5	1.7

Minimum: 3 games

Steals Per Game

	CL	POS	G	STL	SPG
1 **Jason Kidd**, California	FR	G	3	13	4.3
2 **Rick Brunson**, Temple	SO	G	4	14	3.5
3 **Aaron McKie**, Temple	JR	G	4	12	3.0
Nick Van Exel, Cincinnati	SR	G	4	12	3.0
5 **Charlie Ward**, Florida State	JR	G	4	11	2.8

Minimum: 3 games

TEAM LEADERS

Scoring

	G	PTS	PPG
1 **Kentucky**	5	466	93.2
2 **Kansas**	5	428	85.6
3 **Florida State**	4	338	84.5
North Carolina	6	507	84.5
5 **Arkansas**	3	248	82.7
6 **Indiana**	4	329	82.3
7 **Cincinnati**	4	324	81.0
8 **Vanderbilt**	3	236	78.7
George Washington	3	236	78.7
10 **Michigan**	6	471	78.5

Minimum: 3 games

FG Pct

	G	FG	FGA	PCT
1 **Wake Forest**	3	85	146	58.2
2 **Kentucky**	5	173	319	54.2
3 **Vanderbilt**	3	81	151	53.6
4 **Kansas**	5	152	285	53.3
5 **Indiana**	4	121	230	52.6

Minimum: 3 games

3-Pt FG Pct

	G	3FG	3FGA	PCT
1 **Kansas**	5	40	77	51.9
2 **Vanderbilt**	3	32	68	47.1
3 **Kentucky**	5	49	111	44.1
4 **North Carolina**	6	28	68	41.2
5 **Indiana**	4	23	56	41.1

Minimum: 3 games

FT Pct

	G	FT	FTA	PCT
1 **Kansas**	5	84	103	81.5
2 **Vanderbilt**	3	42	53	79.3
3 **Indiana**	4	64	87	73.6
4 **North Carolina**	6	113	155	72.9
5 **Wake Forest**	3	50	69	72.5

Minimum: 3 games

Ast/TO Ratio

	G	AST	TO	RAT
1 **Kentucky**	5	106	69	1.54
2 **Kansas**	5	102	67	1.52
3 **North Carolina**	6	106	73	1.45
4 **Arkansas**	3	54	38	1.42
5 **Indiana**	4	68	48	1.42

Minimum: 3 games

Rebounds

	G	REB	RPG
1 **Cincinnati**	4	171	42.8
2 **George Washington**	3	128	42.7
3 **Western Kentucky**	3	127	42.3
4 **Michigan**	6	242	40.3
5 **North Carolina**	6	236	39.3

Minimum: 3 games

Blocks

	G	BLK	BPG
1 **Florida State**	4	25	6.3
2 **Michigan**	6	28	4.7
Arkansas	3	14	4.7
Western Kentucky	3	14	4.7
5 **George Washington**	3	13	4.3

Minimum: 3 games

Steals

	G	STL	SPG
1 **Temple**	4	46	11.5
Cincinnati	4	46	11.5
3 **Arkansas**	3	33	11.0
4 **Kansas**	5	43	8.6
5 **North Carolina**	6	47	7.8

Minimum: 3 games

ALL-TOURNAMENT TEAM

PLAYER	CL	POS	HT	SCHOOL	RPG	APG	PPG
Donald Williams*	SO	G	6-3	North Carolina	1.7	0.7	19.7
George Lynch	SR	F	6-8	North Carolina	9.8	1.0	15.7
Jamal Mashburn	JR	F	6-8	Kentucky	6.8	4.0	19.4
Eric Montross	JR	C	7-0	North Carolina	7.0	1.0	16.8
Chris Webber†	SO	F/C	6-9	Michigan	11.3	1.7	19.2

ALL-REGIONAL TEAMS

EAST

PLAYER	CL	POS	HT	SCHOOL	RPG	APG	PPG
George Lynch*	SR	F	6-8	North Carolina	9.8	1.3	17.0
Erik Martin	SR	F	6-6	Cincinnati	9.3	2.5	17.5
Eric Montross	JR	C	7-0	North Carolina	8.3	1.3	15.5
Nick Van Exel	SR	G	6-1	Cincinnati	1.5	7.3	13.0
Donald Williams	SO	G	6-3	North Carolina	1.5	0.8	17.0

MIDWEST

PLAYER	CL	POS	HT	SCHOOL	RPG	APG	PPG
Calbert Cheaney*	SR	G/F	6-7	Indiana	8.3	1.5	26.5
Greg Graham	SR	G	6-4	Indiana	2.8	2.3	18.3
Adonis Jordan	SR	G	5-11	Kansas	3.5	6.5	13.0
Richard Scott	JR	F	6-7	Kansas	3.0	0.3	11.5
Rex Walters	SR	G	6-4	Kansas	3.3	5.5	21.8

SOUTHEAST

PLAYER	CL	POS	HT	SCHOOL	RPG	APG	PPG
Travis Ford*	JR	G	5-9	Kentucky	1.0	4.5	15.3
Mark Bell	SR	G	5-8	Western Kentucky	7.0	4.0	17.7
Rodney Dobard	SR	F	6-9	Florida State	6.5	1.5	14.5
Jamal Mashburn	JR	F	6-8	Kentucky	7.0	4.5	17.8
Jared Prickett	FR	F	6-9	Kentucky	5.3	2.8	10.3

WEST

PLAYER	CL	POS	HT	SCHOOL	RPG	APG	PPG
Chris Webber*	SO	F/C	6-9	Michigan	11.0	2.3	16.3
Juwan Howard	SO	C	6-9	Michigan	8.5	1.8	14.5
Eddie Jones	JR	G	6-6	Temple	5.5	0.8	21.3
Aaron McKie	JR	G	6-5	Temple	4.0	2.3	20.5
Jalen Rose	SO	G	6-8	Michigan	3.8	5.0	13.5

* Most outstanding player
† Honor later vacated

1993 NCAA TOURNAMENT BOX SCORES

Sweet 16 — 103-69 (1H: 60–26; 2H: 43–43)

KENTUCKY	MIN	FG	3FG	FT	REB	A	ST	BL	PF	TP
Travis Ford	33	10-11	5-6	1-2	1	4	1	-	1	26
Jamal Mashburn	30	8-13	5-5	2-4	5	5	1	-	3	23
Dale Brown	20	5-6	1-1	5-5	2	2	1	-	4	16
Rodrick Rhodes	15	3-5	2-2	0-0	1	1	1	-	2	8
Jared Prickett	24	3-3	0-0	0-2	5	5	1	-	4	6
Rodney Dent	17	3-5	0-0	0-0	1	1	0	-	1	6
Gimel Martinez	7	2-5	1-3	0-0	1	1	0	-	1	5
Tony Delk	13	1-7	1-3	0-0	5	1	2	-	1	3
Jeff Brassow	11	1-3	1-3	0-0	0	1	0	-	3	3
Junior Braddy	10	1-2	0-1	0-0	0	1	0	-	2	2
Aminu Timberlake	4	1-1	0-0	0-1	1	0	0	-	1	2
Todd Svoboda	3	1-2	0-0	0-1	2	0	0	-	0	2
Andre Riddick	13	0-0	0-0	1-2	5	1	1	-	2	1
TOTALS	200	39-63	16-24	9-17	29	23	8	-	25	103
Percentages		61.9	66.7	52.9						

Coach: Rick Pitino

WAKE FOREST	MIN	FG	3FG	FT	REB	A	ST	BL	PF	TP
Randolph Childress	30	3-8	2-5	10-11	3	2	0	0	1	18
Rodney Rogers	30	4-9	0-1	6-9	4	1	0	0	4	14
Trelonnie Owens	32	6-7	0-0	1-4	3	2	0	1	2	13
Derrick Hicks	30	2-5	0-0	4-5	3	1	1	1	4	8
Charlie Harrison	22	3-6	0-1	0-0	1	2	0	0	3	6
Travis Banks	13	1-2	0-0	1-2	2	0	1	0	0	3
David Rasmussen	4	1-1	1-1	0-0	1	0	0	0	0	3
Marc Blucas	20	0-0	0-0	2-2	3	0	0	0	1	2
Rusty LaRue	4	1-2	0-0	0-0	0	0	2	0	0	2
Stacey Castle	5	0-0	0-0	0-0	0	0	0	0	2	0
Barry Canty	4	0-1	0-1	0-0	0	0	0	0	0	0
Bobby Fitzgibbons	3	0-1	0-1	0-0	1	0	0	0	1	0
Stan King	3	0-2	0-0	0-0	1	0	0	0	2	0
TOTALS	200	21-44	3-10	24-33	22	8	4	2	20	69
Percentages		47.7	30.0	72.7						

Coach: Dave Odom

Officials: Tim Higgins, Charles Range, Jerry Petro
Technicals: None
Attendance: 22,876

Sweet 16 — 81-78 (1H: 40–40; 2H: 29–29; OT1: 12–9)

FLORIDA STATE	MIN	FG	3FG	FT	REB	A	ST	BL	PF	TP
Doug Edwards	32	8-13	0-0	3-9	9	1	0	2	5	19
Bob Sura	33	7-12	2-3	1-4	7	4	1	0	4	17
Rodney Dobard	42	7-11	0-0	2-5	13	3	0	4	0	16
Sam Cassell	43	3-14	1-5	5-7	3	3	1	1	3	12
Derrick Carroll	20	3-5	0-1	3-4	1	0	0	0	0	9
Charlie Ward	42	1-3	0-1	3-6	4	4	3	0	0	5
Byron Wells	11	1-3	0-0	1-3	4	0	0	2	3	3
Maurice Robinson	2	0-0	0-0	0-0	0	1	0	0	1	0
TOTALS	225	30-61	3-10	18-38	41	16	5	9	16	81
Percentages		49.2	30.0	47.4						

Coach:

WESTERN KENTUCKY	MIN	FG	3FG	FT	REB	A	ST	BL	PF	TP
Darnell Mee	36	7-18	2-7	5-6	5	3	2	0	5	21
Darrin Horn	33	7-14	1-3	2-3	1	3	1	1	2	17
Mark Bell	42	6-16	2-5	1-1	8	4	1	0	5	15
Chris Robinson	21	3-5	1-2	2-4	3	0	0	0	4	9
Darius Hall	26	3-6	0-0	1-2	5	0	3	0	4	7
Bryan Brown	22	3-6	0-0	0-1	4	0	0	0	4	6
Cypheus Bunton	42	1-8	0-1	1-2	7	0	2	3	3	3
Michael Fraliex	3	0-2	0-1	0-0	0	1	0	0	0	0
TOTALS	225	30-75	6-19	12-19	33	11	9	4	27	78
Percentages		40.0	31.6	63.2						

Coach: Ralph Willard

Officials: Don Rutledge, Tom O'Neill, Tom Clark
Technicals: None
Attendance: 22,876

Sweet 16 — 72-64 (1H: 35–33; 2H: 37–31)

MICHIGAN	MIN	FG	3FG	FT	REB	A	ST	BL	PF	TP
Juwan Howard	31	4-12	0-0	9-13	10	0	1	0	5	17
Jalen Rose	37	4-12	1-3	7-9	5	6	3	2	3	16
Chris Webber	36	5-9	0-1	4-8	9	0	2	2	2	14
Jimmy King	36	4-9	2-4	1-2	8	1	2	0	3	11
Ray Jackson	35	4-6	0-0	3-6	6	3	0	0	2	11
James Voskuil	6	1-1	1-1	0-0	1	0	0	0	2	3
Rob Pelinka	9	0-1	0-0	0-0	1	0	0	0	0	0
Eric Riley	9	0-0	0-0	0-0	2	0	0	0	4	0
Michael Talley	1	0-0	0-0	0-0	0	0	0	0	0	0
TOTALS	200	22-50	4-9	24-38	42	10	8	4	21	72
Percentages		44.0	44.4	63.2						

Coach: Steve Fisher

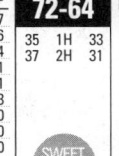

GEORGE WASHINGTON	MIN	FG	3FG	FT	REB	A	ST	BL	PF	TP
Kwame Evans	22	5-12	1-4	2-2	6	1	2	0	5	13
Sonni Holland	28	6-11	0-0	0-0	4	0	2	1	4	12
Robert Hammons	26	3-12	3-10	0-0	5	0	0	0	4	9
Dirkk Surles	22	4-10	1-5	0-0	3	1	1	0	1	9
Vaughn Jones	19	3-8	0-1	3-3	3	4	1	0	3	9
Bill Brigham	27	1-3	0-1	5-9	5	2	1	0	4	7
Alvin Pearsall	21	1-6	1-2	0-2	3	2	0	0	1	3
Omo Moses	9	1-2	0-1	0-0	0	0	0	0	5	2
Yinka Dare	19	0-5	0-0	0-0	5	0	0	1	3	0
Antoine Hart	5	0-1	0-0	0-0	1	0	0	1	0	0
Marcus Ford	1	0-0	0-0	0-0	0	0	0	0	0	0
Eric Withers	1	0-1	0-1	0-0	0	0	0	0	0	0
TOTALS	200	24-71	6-25	10-16	35	10	7	3	30	64
Percentages		33.8	24.0	62.5						

Coach: Mike Jarvis

Officials: Lenny Wirtz, Rusty Herring, Samuel Croft
Technicals: None
Attendance: 24,021

Sweet 16 — 67-59 (1H: 18–24; 2H: 49–35)

TEMPLE	MIN	FG	3FG	FT	REB	A	ST	BL	PF	TP
Eddie Jones	40	13-23	0-4	0-0	5	2	2	0	1	26
Aaron McKie	40	6-17	1-3	1-3	4	2	4	1	3	14
Derrick Battie	37	4-8	0-0	4-4	10	0	3	0	2	12
Rick Brunson	40	3-8	0-3	3-5	3	1	2	0	3	9
Jason Ivey	29	3-5	0-0	0-1	2	0	1	0	0	6
William Cunningham	14	0-1	0-0	0-0	1	0	1	0	0	0
TOTALS	200	29-62	1-10	8-13	25	5	13	1	9	67
Percentages		46.8	10.0	61.5						

Coach: John Chaney

VANDERBILT	MIN	FG	3FG	FT	REB	A	ST	BL	PF	TP
Ronnie McMahan	33	7-11	7-11	0-0	3	2	1	0	1	21
Billy McCaffrey	32	7-15	3-7	0-0	3	2	0	0	3	17
Bruce Elder	31	5-6	1-2	1-1	7	5	1	0	2	12
Chris Lawson	33	2-4	0-0	0-0	5	4	0	0	4	4
Kevin Anglin	33	1-3	1-3	0-0	1	4	0	0	1	3
Dan Hall	20	1-2	0-0	0-0	3	0	0	1	3	2
Frank Seckar	10	0-3	0-3	0-0	0	1	1	0	1	0
Bryan Milburn	8	0-0	0-0	0-0	2	0	0	1	1	0
TOTALS	200	23-44	12-26	1-1	24	18	3	2	16	59
Percentages		52.3	46.2	100.0						

Coach: Eddie Fogler

Officials: Ed Hightower, Scott Thornley, Duke Edsall
Technicals: None
Attendance: 24,021

Sweet 16 — 80-74 (1H: 45–45; 2H: 35–29)

NORTH CAROLINA	MIN	FG	3FG	FT	REB	A	ST	BL	PF	TP
George Lynch	33	9-13	0-0	5-7	10	2	1	0	4	23
Donald Williams	30	7-19	3-9	5-6	1	3	0	0	3	22
Eric Montross	37	6-8	0-0	3-6	8	1	1	2	2	15
Brian Reese	31	5-11	0-1	3-6	8	4	0	0	1	13
Derrick Phelps	35	2-5	1-1	0-1	7	7	2	0	1	5
Pat Sullivan	12	1-4	0-0	0-0	2	0	0	0	0	2
Henrik Rodl	12	0-1	0-1	0-0	1	2	1	1	1	0
Kevin Salvadori	7	0-1	0-0	0-0	2	0	0	0	1	0
Scott Cherry	3	0-0	0-0	0-0	0	0	0	0	0	0
TOTALS	200	30-62	4-12	16-26	39	19	5	3	13	80
Percentages		48.4	33.3	61.5						

Coach: Dean Smith

ARKANSAS	MIN	FG	3FG	FT	REB	A	ST	BL	PF	TP
Corliss Williamson	30	7-7	0-0	2-3	2	1	1	2	3	16
Robert Shepherd	25	5-8	3-4	0-0	3	2	2	1	0	13
Scotty Thurman	29	5-12	2-5	0-0	0	1	2	0	1	12
Clint McDaniel	23	3-12	3-8	3-4	6	1	0	1	4	12
Elmer Martin	16	2-4	0-0	3-4	5	5	0	2	2	7
Darrell Hawkins	27	2-10	1-4	0-0	4	2	0	0	2	5
Dwight Stewart	12	2-3	1-1	0-0	1	1	0	0	3	5
Roger Crawford	14	1-2	1-1	1-2	1	3	1	0	1	4
Corey Beck	18	0-2	0-0	0-0	2	5	0	0	4	0
Warren Linn	6	0-1	0-1	0-0	1	0	0	0	0	0
TOTALS	200	27-61	11-24	9-13	25	21	6	6	20	74
Percentages		44.3	45.8	69.2						

Coach: Nolan Richardson

Officials: Ted Hillary, Tom Harrington, Mike Sanzere
Technicals: None
Attendance: 19,761

Sweet 16 — 71-54 (1H: 31–24; 2H: 40–30)

CINCINNATI	MIN	FG	3FG	FT	REB	A	ST	BL	PF	TP
Nick Van Exel	39	6-21	3-11	4-5	1	11	2	0	3	19
Corie Blount	33	9-14	0-0	1-2	11	1	1	1	2	19
Erik Martin	36	5-12	0-0	5-6	12	1	1	0	3	15
Tarrance Gibson	27	3-10	1-4	0-1	6	1	2	1	3	7
LaZelle Durden	14	2-5	0-2	0-0	2	0	2	0	1	4
Curtis Bostic	13	1-3	0-0	2-4	2	0	1	0	3	4
Terry Nelson	28	1-2	0-0	1-5	7	0	2	1	2	3
Keith Gregor	8	0-0	0-0	0-0	0	0	0	0	1	0
Mike Harris	1	0-0	0-0	0-0	0	0	0	0	0	0
John Jacobs	1	0-0	0-0	0-0	0	0	0	0	0	0
TOTALS	200	27-67	4-17	13-23	41	14	11	3	18	71
Percentages		40.3	23.5	56.5						

Coach: Bob Huggins

VIRGINIA	MIN	FG	3FG	FT	REB	A	ST	BL	PF	TP
Junior Burrough	32	7-15	0-0	1-4	8	0	0	2	2	15
Jason Williford	33	5-8	0-0	2-2	6	3	3	2	3	12
Cory Alexander	39	3-14	3-7	2-3	1	4	1	0	3	11
Ted Jeffries	33	4-6	0-0	1-2	3	1	2	3	3	9
Yuri Barnes	8	1-1	0-0	2-2	1	0	1	0	3	4
Cornel Parker	34	1-5	1-3	0-0	7	3	0	1	5	3
Doug Smith	17	0-3	0-1	0-0	1	2	1	0	1	0
Shawn Wilson	3	0-0	0-0	0-0	0	0	1	0	0	0
Rahsaan Mitchell	1	0-1	0-0	0-0	0	0	0	0	0	0
TOTALS	200	21-53	4-11	8-13	27	13	9	8	20	54
Percentages		39.6	36.4	61.5						

Coach: Jeff Jones

Officials: Dave Libbey, Tom Lopes, David Hall
Technicals: Cincinnati (Van Exel)
Attendance: 19,761

INDIANA	MIN	FG	3FG	FT	REB	A	ST	BL	PF	TP
Calbert Cheaney	34	10-12	2-3	10-12	8	4	1	1	2	32
Greg Graham	35	7-11	1-4	7-7	1	3	3	1	2	22
Matt Nover	40	7-9	0-0	1-1	8	1	0	0	2	15
Damon Bailey	29	2-7	2-4	0-0	1	2	0	0	1	6
Pat Graham	19	1-3	1-2	0-1	3	3	0	0	0	3
Todd Leary	10	1-2	1-1	0-1	0	1	0	0	0	3
Chris Reynolds	3	0-0	0-0	1-2	2	0	0	0	1	1
Brian Evans	16	0-0	0-0	0-1	3	4	1	0	1	0
Alan Henderson	11	0-1	0-0	0-0	3	1	1	1	0	0
Pat Knight	3	0-0	0-0	0-0	0	0	0	0	0	0
TOTALS	**200**	**28-45**	**7-14**	**19-25**	**29**	**19**	**6**	**3**	**9**	**82**
Percentages		62.2	50.0	76.0						

Coach: Bob Knight

82-69

50	1H	43
32	2H	26

SWEET 16

LOUISVILLE	MIN	FG	3FG	FT	REB	A	ST	BL	PF	TP
Clifford Rozier	34	8-14	0-1	0-0	10	2	0	-	2	16
Greg Minor	36	5-8	5-7	0-0	6	0	0	-	4	15
James Brewer	26	4-16	2-10	3-4	0	1	0	-	4	13
Dwayne Morton	29	4-14	1-4	3-4	3	3	1	-	5	12
Troy Smith	29	3-4	0-0	2-4	6	6	2	-	2	8
Tick Rogers	6	1-2	0-1	1-1	1	1	0	-	0	3
Keith LeGree	27	1-5	0-2	0-0	3	4	1	-	3	2
Derwin Webb	11	0-0	0-0	0-0	0	0	0	-	0	0
Mike Case	1	0-0	0-0	0-0	0	0	0	-	0	0
Brian Kiser	1	0-0	0-0	0-0	0	0	0	-	0	0
Brian Hopgood	0	0-0	0-0	0-0	0	0	0	-	0	0
TOTALS	**200**	**26-63**	**8-25**	**9-13**	**29**	**17**	**4**	**-**	**20**	**69**
Percentages		41.3	32.0	69.2						

Coach: Denny Crum

Officials: Jo Clougherty, Frank Scagl Gerald Boudreaux **Technicals:** Indiana (Cheaney), Louisville (Morton) **Attendance:** 17,883

KANSAS	MIN	FG	3FG	FT	REB	A	ST	BL	PF	TP
Rex Walters	25	8-9	4-5	4-5	1	3	1	0	2	24
Adonis Jordan	31	5-9	3-4	2-2	7	6	1	0	2	15
Steve Woodberry	27	3-8	0-1	7-7	6	4	2	0	2	13
Eric Pauley	22	5-10	0-0	0-0	5	0	0	0	5	10
Darrin Hancock	18	4-7	0-0	2-3	5	1	1	0	0	10
Richard Scott	24	3-5	0-0	3-4	5	1	0	1	3	9
Patrick Richey	24	1-1	1-1	1-2	4	2	1	0	0	4
Greg Ostertag	18	2-4	0-0	0-0	5	1	0	1	0	4
Calvin Rayford	9	1-4	0-0	2-2	0	2	1	0	1	4
Greg Gurley	2	0-0	0-0	0-0	0	0	0	0	0	0
TOTALS	**200**	**32-57**	**8-11**	**21-25**	**38**	**20**	**7**	**2**	**15**	**93**
Percentages		56.1	72.7	84.0						

Coach: Roy Williams

93-76

43	1H	40
50	2H	36

SWEET 16

CALIFORNIA	MIN	FG	3FG	FT	REB	A	ST	BL	PF	TP
Lamond Murray	36	9-22	3-11	2-4	6	2	2	0	2	23
Brian Hendrick	24	7-8	0-0	1-3	7	1	0	1	4	15
Jason Kidd	37	6-12	0-3	1-2	5	10	4	0	5	13
Jerod Haase	24	4-9	2-5	0-0	0	1	1	0	3	10
K.J. Roberts	14	1-5	0-3	3-3	3	2	0	1	0	5
Monty Buckley	11	2-5	1-3	0-0	0	0	0	0	1	5
Alfred Grigsby	25	1-1	0-0	1-1	3	0	0	0	4	3
Stevie Johnson	8	1-1	0-0	0-0	2	0	0	0	1	2
Ryan Jamison	10	0-1	0-0	0-0	2	1	0	0	2	0
Brendan Graves	5	0-0	0-0	0-0	0	0	0	0	1	0
Akili Jones	5	0-1	0-1	0-0	0	1	0	0	0	0
Richard Branham	1	0-0	0-0	0-0	0	0	0	0	0	0
TOTALS	**200**	**31-65**	**6-26**	**8-13**	**28**	**18**	**7**	**2**	**23**	**76**
Percentages		47.7	23.1	61.5						

Coach: Todd Bozeman

Officials: Jam Burr, Larry Lembo, Gary Marcum **Technicals:** None **Attendance:** 17,883

KENTUCKY	MIN	FG	3FG	FT	REB	A	ST	BL	PF	TP
Jared Prickett	33	9-12	0-0	4-6	11	3	0	0	2	22
Travis Ford	31	5-9	4-7	5-6	2	6	1	0	3	19
Jamal Mashburn	36	5-13	0-4	2-3	9	7	1	0	4	12
Dale Brown	23	4-10	3-7	1-2	6	1	0	0	5	12
Gimel Martinez	13	4-6	0-0	2-2	4	1	0	0	3	10
Rodrick Rhodes	9	3-4	1-1	1-3	1	1	0	0	3	8
Junior Braddy	15	2-3	2-3	1-2	0	2	0	0	1	7
Tony Delk	11	3-5	0-0	0-1	3	0	0	0	2	6
Rodney Dent	23	2-5	0-0	1-3	5	0	0	1	4	5
Todd Svoboda	1	1-2	1-1	0-0	0	0	0	0	0	3
Andre Riddick	3	0-1	0-0	2-2	0	0	0	0	0	2
Jeff Brassow	1	0-0	0-0	0-0	1	1	0	0	0	0
Aminu Timberlake	1	0-0	0-0	0-0	1	0	0	0	0	0
TOTALS	**200**	**38-70**	**11-23**	**19-30**	**43**	**22**	**2**	**1**	**27**	**106**
Percentages		54.3	47.8	63.3						

Coach: Rick Pitino

106-81

54	1H	46
52	2H	35

ELITE 8

FLORIDA STATE	MIN	FG	3FG	FT	REB	A	ST	BL	PF	TP
Bob Sura	31	5-13	0-4	7-10	0	1	1	0	3	17
Rodney Dobard	37	7-12	0-0	2-2	2	2	0	1	3	16
Sam Cassell	35	3-11	2-3	8-10	2	0	3	0	5	16
Doug Edwards	27	4-8	2-5	5-6	7	3	1	1	5	15
Derrick Carroll	18	4-4	1-1	0-0	2	0	0	0	0	9
Charlie Ward	35	1-7	0-6	3-5	1	7	4	0	4	5
Byron Wells	4	1-3	0-0	1-2	0	1	0	0	1	3
Maurice Robinson	8	0-0	0-0	0-0	1	0	0	0	2	0
Lorenzo Hands	4	0-2	0-1	0-0	1	0	0	0	0	0
Scott Shepherd	1	0-1	0-0	0-0	1	0	0	0	1	0
TOTALS	**200**	**25-61**	**5-20**	**26-35**	**17**	**14**	**9**	**2**	**24**	**81**
Percentages		41.0	25.0	74.3						

Coach: Pat Kennedy

Officials: Gerry Donaghy, Tom Rucker, Jim Stupin **Technicals:** None **Attendance:** 22,876

MICHIGAN	MIN	FG	3FG	FT	REB	A	ST	BL	PF	TP
Jalen Rose	38	5-8	0-2	7-10	5	2	1	0	1	17
Jimmy King	39	5-14	1-4	3-4	4	2	1	1	2	14
Chris Webber	32	6-12	0-1	1-2	12	3	1	5	2	13
Juwan Howard	36	5-13	0-0	1-3	9	2	0	2	3	11
Ray Jackson	28	3-6	0-0	4-8	2	2	4	0	3	10
Eric Riley	12	4-5	0-0	1-1	4	0	0	0	3	9
Rob Pelinka	12	1-4	1-3	0-0	2	1	0	0	2	3
James Voskuil	3	0-1	0-1	0-0	0	0	0	0	0	0
TOTALS	**200**	**29-63**	**2-11**	**17-28**	**38**	**12**	**7**	**8**	**16**	**77**
Percentages		46.0	18.2	60.7						

Coach: Steve Fisher

77-72

27	1H	35
50	2H	37

ELITE 8

TEMPLE	MIN	FG	3FG	FT	REB	A	ST	BL	PF	TP
Rick Brunson	40	6-15	3-6	6-7	3	9	3	0	2	21
Aaron McKie	40	7-20	3-7	2-2	2	1	2	0	5	19
Eddie Jones	31	7-15	4-5	0-2	5	0	2	3	3	18
Derrick Battie	40	5-8	0-0	3-7	10	0	1	0	1	13
Chris Ozment	5	0-0	0-0	1-2	3	0	0	0	1	1
William Cunningham	22	0-0	0-0	0-0	3	0	0	0	5	0
Jason Ivey	13	0-1	0-0	0-0	1	0	0	0	4	0
Vic Carstarphen	5	0-0	0-0	0-0	0	0	0	0	1	0
Julian King	4	0-0	0-0	0-0	0	0	1	0	0	0
TOTALS	**200**	**25-59**	**10-18**	**12-20**	**27**	**10**	**9**	**3**	**22**	**72**
Percentages		42.4	55.6	60.0						

Coach: John Chaney

Officials: Larry Rose, Gene Monje, John Moreau **Technicals:** Temple (bench) **Attendance:** 24,196

NORTH CAROLINA	MIN	FG	3FG	FT	REB	A	ST	BL	PF	TP
George Lynch	41	7-14	0-0	7-9	14	0	6	1	2	21
Donald Williams	34	8-17	3-7	1-2	1	0	0	0	3	20
Eric Montross	35	6-8	0-0	3-6	7	0	1	1	4	15
Brian Reese	30	2-9	0-1	4-4	3	3	0	1	2	8
Pat Sullivan	13	2-4	0-0	0-0	2	2	0	0	0	4
Derrick Phelps	43	0-3	0-0	3-4	2	7	3	0	2	3
Henrik Rodl	14	1-1	0-0	0-0	0	2	0	0	1	2
Kevin Salvadori	14	1-2	0-0	0-0	5	0	1	2	1	2
Dante Calabria	1	0-0	0-0	0-0	0	0	0	0	0	0
TOTALS	**225**	**27-58**	**3-8**	**18-25**	**34**	**14**	**11**	**5**	**15**	**75**
Percentages		46.6	37.5	72.0						

Coach: Dean Smith

75-68

36	1H	37
30	2H	29
9	OT1	2

ELITE 8

CINCINNATI	MIN	FG	3FG	FT	REB	A	ST	BL	PF	TP
Nick Van Exel	44	8-24	6-13	1-2	3	5	5	1	1	23
Erik Martin	42	6-11	0-0	4-4	6	2	1	2	5	16
Tarrance Gibson	38	5-11	3-8	0-0	5	6	2	1	3	13
Corie Blount	27	3-10	0-0	2-2	9	2	1	0	4	8
Terry Nelson	38	2-3	0-1	0-0	5	2	1	1	1	4
Curtis Bostic	12	1-3	0-0	0-0	3	1	1	0	5	2
Keith Gregor	11	1-5	0-0	0-1	2	1	0	1	2	2
LaZelle Durden	10	0-2	0-2	0-0	0	0	0	0	0	0
Mike Harris	2	0-0	0-0	0-0	1	0	0	0	0	0
John Jacobs	1	0-1	0-0	0-0	0	0	0	0	0	0
TOTALS	**225**	**26-70**	**9-24**	**7-9**	**34**	**19**	**11**	**6**	**21**	**68**
Percentages		37.1	37.5	77.8						

Coach: Bob Huggins

Officials: Jody Silvester, Art McDonald, Ted Valentine **Technicals:** None **Attendance:** 19,761

KANSAS	MIN	FG	3FG	FT	REB	A	ST	BL	PF	TP
Richard Scott	26	7-10	0-0	2-4	2	0	0	0	1	16
Eric Pauley	25	6-12	0-0	1-1	4	3	1	2	2	13
Rex Walters	29	4-8	1-4	3-4	2	8	0	0	2	12
Darrin Hancock	20	3-4	0-0	6-6	4	1	1	1	2	12
Adonis Jordan	37	4-7	2-3	1-1	4	4	2	0	2	11
Steve Woodberry	26	2-3	1-2	4-4	2	4	3	0	4	9
Greg Ostertag	15	3-5	0-0	0-0	6	0	0	2	1	6
Greg Gurley	4	1-1	0-0	0-0	1	0	0	0	0	2
Calvin Rayford	3	1-1	0-0	0-0	0	2	1	0	0	2
Patrick Richey	14	0-0	0-0	0-0	2	1	0	0	1	0
Sean Pearson	1	0-1	0-1	0-0	0	0	0	0	1	0
TOTALS	**200**	**31-52**	**4-10**	**17-20**	**27**	**23**	**8**	**5**	**16**	**83**
Percentages		59.6	40.0	85.0						

Coach: Roy Williams

83-77

38	1H	34
45	2H	43

ELITE 8

INDIANA	MIN	FG	3FG	FT	REB	A	ST	BL	PF	TP
Greg Graham	33	8-14	3-4	4-5	3	2	1	-	4	23
Calbert Cheaney	40	10-19	0-2	2-2	9	1	0	-	3	22
Brian Evans	27	4-9	2-2	0-0	7	1	3	-	3	10
Matt Nover	39	3-5	0-0	3-4	7	2	1	-	2	9
Damon Bailey	27	3-7	0-1	1-2	7	4	0	-	4	7
Todd Leary	12	2-7	0-4	2-3	0	1	0	-	2	6
Pat Graham	11	0-3	0-1	0-0	0	1	0	-	1	0
Chris Reynolds	5	0-1	0-1	0-0	0	1	0	-	1	0
Alan Henderson	3	0-1	0-0	0-0	0	0	0	-	0	0
Pat Knight	3	0-0	0-0	0-0	0	0	0	-	0	0
TOTALS	**200**	**30-66**	**5-15**	**12-16**	**33**	**13**	**5**	**-**	**20**	**77**
Percentages		45.5	33.3	75.0						

Coach: Bob Knight

Officials: Dick Paparo, Bob Donato, Andre Pattillo **Technicals:** None **Attendance:** 17,883

81-78 (Final 4)

	1H	2H	OT1
Michigan	40	31	10
Kentucky	35	36	7

MICHIGAN	MIN	FG	3FG	FT	REB	A	ST	BL	PF	TP
Chris Webber	39	10-17	0-1	7-9	13	0	1	2	3	27
Jalen Rose	42	6-16	0-2	6-7	6	1	1	0	3	18
Juwan Howard	40	6-12	0-0	5-7	3	3	2	0	4	17
Ray Jackson	33	4-7	0-0	3-5	8	1	1	0	4	11
Eric Riley	12	2-4	0-0	0-0	4	1	1	1	2	4
Jimmy King	33	1-3	0-0	0-0	3	3	2	0	5	2
Rob Pelinka	23	0-1	0-1	2-2	1	0	0	0	3	2
James Voskuil	3	0-1	0-0	0-0	0	0	0	0	0	0
TOTALS	**225**	**29-61**	**0-4**	**23-30**	**38**	**9**	**8**	**3**	**24**	**81**
Percentages		47.5	0.0	76.7						

Coach: Steve Fisher

KENTUCKY	MIN	FG	3FG	FT	REB	A	ST	BL	PF	TP
Jamal Mashburn	41	10-18	1-3	5-9	6	2	2	0	5	26
Dale Brown	27	6-10	4-6	0-0	1	1	2	0	2	16
Travis Ford	45	3-10	2-6	4-4	5	6	3	0	2	12
Jared Prickett	27	1-6	0-1	7-7	7	2	0	0	5	9
Rodney Dent	27	2-6	0-0	2-2	3	1	0	1	4	6
Tony Delk	18	1-3	0-2	2-2	3	0	2	0	0	4
Andre Riddick	16	2-4	0-0	0-0	2	1	2	1	2	4
Rodrick Rhodes	14	0-1	0-1	1-2	1	0	0	0	4	1
Gimel Martinez	6	0-3	0-2	0-0	1	0	0	0	3	0
Jeff Brassow	3	0-0	0-0	0-0	0	0	0	0	0	0
Junior Braddy	1	0-0	0-0	0-0	0	0	0	0	0	0
TOTALS	**225**	**25-61**	**7-21**	**21-26**	**29**	**13**	**11**	**2**	**27**	**78**
Percentages		41.0	33.3	80.8						

Coach: Rick Pitino

Officials: Gerry Donaghy, Dick Paparo, Larry Rose
Technicals: None
Attendance: 64,151

78-68 (Final 4)

	1H	2H
North Carolina	40	38
Kansas	36	32

NORTH CAROLINA	MIN	FG	3FG	FT	REB	A	ST	BL	PF	TP
Donald Williams	29	7-11	5-7	6-6	3	0	1	0	1	25
Eric Montross	26	9-14	0-0	5-8	4	1	2	0	4	23
George Lynch	34	5-12	0-0	4-6	10	0	2	0	3	14
Brian Reese	23	3-5	0-0	1-2	4	6	0	0	0	7
Kevin Salvadori	17	3-5	0-0	0-0	3	1	0	1	0	6
Derrick Phelps	30	1-3	0-0	1-2	5	6	2	0	2	3
Henrik Rodl	20	0-0	0-0	0-0	0	2	0	0	2	0
Pat Sullivan	16	0-2	0-0	0-0	1	1	1	0	1	0
Dante Calabria	1	0-0	0-0	0-0	0	0	0	0	0	0
Scott Cherry	1	0-0	0-0	0-0	2	0	0	0	0	0
Ed Geth	1	0-0	0-0	0-0	0	0	0	0	0	0
Travis Stephenson	1	0-0	0-0	0-0	0	0	0	0	0	0
Matt Wenstrom	1	0-0	0-0	0-0	0	0	0	0	0	0
TOTALS	**200**	**28-52**	**5-7**	**17-24**	**32**	**17**	**8**	**1**	**13**	**78**
Percentages		53.8	71.4	70.8						

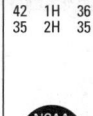

Coach: Dean Smith

KANSAS	MIN	FG	3FG	FT	REB	A	ST	BL	PF	TP
Adonis Jordan	35	7-13	5-7	0-0	1	4	1	0	1	19
Rex Walters	32	7-15	5-9	0-0	0	5	1	0	2	19
Richard Scott	23	3-5	0-0	2-2	1	1	1	0	5	8
Darrin Hancock	23	2-5	0-0	2-2	5	1	1	1	1	6
Eric Pauley	27	2-5	0-0	1-1	9	2	0	0	3	5
Steve Woodberry	20	2-5	0-2	0-0	2	2	0	0	4	4
Greg Gurley	5	1-2	1-1	0-0	0	0	0	0	0	3
Patrick Richey	17	1-4	0-0	0-0	2	0	0	2	1	2
Greg Ostertag	12	0-2	0-0	2-2	2	0	1	1	3	2
Calvin Rayford	5	0-0	0-0	0-0	0	0	0	0	0	0
Sean Pearson	1	0-1	0-1	0-0	0	0	0	0	0	0
TOTALS	**200**	**25-57**	**11-20**	**7-7**	**22**	**15**	**5**	**4**	**20**	**68**
Percentages		43.9	55.0	100.0						

Coach: Roy Williams

Officials: John Clougherty, James Burr, Ted Valentine
Technicals: None
Attendance: 64,151

77-71 (NCAA Final 1993)

	1H	2H
North Carolina	42	35
Michigan	36	35

NORTH CAROLINA	MIN	FG	3FG	FT	REB	A	ST	BL	PF	TP
Donald Williams	31	8-12	5-7	4-4	1	1	1	0	1	25
Eric Montross	31	5-11	0-0	6-9	5	0	0	1	2	16
George Lynch	28	6-12	0-0	0-0	10	1	1	2	3	12
Derrick Phelps	36	4-6	0-1	1-2	3	6	3	0	0	9
Brian Reese	27	2-7	0-1	4-4	5	3	0	0	1	8
Pat Sullivan	14	1-2	0-0	1-2	1	1	0	0	2	3
Kevin Salvadori	18	0-0	0-0	2-2	4	1	0	1	1	2
Henrik Rodl	11	1-4	0-2	0-0	0	0	2	0	0	2
Matt Wenstrom	2	0-1	0-0	0-0	0	0	0	0	0	0
Dante Calabria	1	0-0	0-0	0-0	0	0	0	0	0	0
Scott Cherry	1	0-0	0-0	0-0	0	0	0	0	0	0
TOTALS	**200**	**27-55**	**5-11**	**18-23**	**29**	**13**	**7**	**4**	**10**	**77**
Percentages		49.1	45.5	78.3						

Coach: Dean Smith

MICHIGAN	MIN	FG	3FG	FT	REB	A	ST	BL	PF	TP
Chris Webber	33	11-18	0-1	1-2	11	1	1	3	2	23
Jimmy King	34	6-13	1-5	2-2	6	4	1	0	2	15
Jalen Rose	40	5-12	2-6	0-0	1	4	0	0	3	12
Juwan Howard	34	3-8	0-0	1-1	7	3	0	0	3	7
Ray Jackson	20	2-3	0-0	2-2	1	1	1	0	5	6
Rob Pelinka	17	2-4	2-3	0-0	2	1	0	0	1	6
Eric Riley	14	1-3	0-0	0-0	3	1	1	1	1	2
Michael Talley	4	0-0	0-0	0-0	0	1	0	0	1	0
James Voskuil	4	0-1	0-0	0-0	0	1	0	0	0	0
TOTALS	**200**	**30-62**	**5-15**	**6-7**	**31**	**17**	**4**	**4**	**18**	**71**
Percentages		48.4	33.3	85.7						

Coach: Steve Fisher

Officials: Ed Hightower, Tom Harrington, Jim Stupin
Technicals: Michigan (excessive timeouts)
Attendance: 64,151

National Invitation Tournament (NIT)

First round: Old Dominion d. VCU 74-68, Boston College d. Niagara 87-83, Providence d. James Madison 73-61, Clemson d. Auburn 84-72, UAB d. Alabama 58-56, SW Missouri State d. Saint Joseph's 56-34, Georgetown d. Arizona State 78-68, Minnesota d. Florida 74-66, West Virginia d. Georgia 95-84, Miami (OH) d. Ohio State 56-53, Rice d. Wisconsin 77-73, Oklahoma d. Michigan State 88-86, Southern California d. UNLV 90-74, Jackson State d. Connecticut 90-88 (OT), UTEP d. Houston 67-61, Pepperdine d. UC Santa Barbara 53-50
Second round: UAB d. Clemson 65-64, Miami (OH) d. Old Dominion 60-58, Boston College d. Rice 101-68, Providence d. West Virginia 68-67, Minnesota d. Oklahoma 86-72, Georgetown d. UTEP 71-44, SW Missouri St. d. Jackson State 70-52, Southern California d. Pepperdine 71-59
Third round: Providence d. Boston College 75-58, Minnesota d. Southern California 76-58, UAB d. SW Missouri State 61-52, Georgetown d. Miami (OH) 66-53
Semifinals: Minnesota d. Providence 76-70, Georgetown d. UAB 45-41
Third place: UAB d. Providence 55-52
Championship: Minnesota d. Georgetown 62-61
MVP: Voshon Lenard, Minnesota

1993-94: HOG HEAVEN

Since 1978 and Kentucky's last title, the Southeastern Conference had sent each of its teams to the Tournament at least once, but all had come away empty-handed. Arkansas (31–3) changed that in its third season as a member of the SEC. The Razorbacks used an up-tempo offense and a pressure defense that coach Nolan Richardson liked to call "40 minutes of hell" to knock off Duke in the Final, 76-72, at the Charlotte Coliseum. Sophomore forward Corliss Williamson, the Tournament MOP, scored 23 points and grabbed eight rebounds. Arkansas native Bill Clinton became the first sitting U.S. president to attend the Tournament.

Before the season, the NCAA shot clock was shortened from :45 to :35 per possession. Purdue forward Glenn "Big Dog" Robinson (30.3 ppg, 10.1 rpg) was named Naismith Player of the Year and was selected by the Milwaukee Bucks with the first pick of the NBA draft.

MAJOR CONFERENCE STANDINGS

ACC	Conference			Overall		
	W	L	PCT	W	L	PCT
Duke○	12	4	.750	28	6	.824
North Carolina⊛	11	5	.688	28	7	.800
Wake Forest○	9	7	.563	21	12	.636
Maryland○	8	8	.500	18	12	.600
Virginia○	8	8	.500	18	13	.581
Georgia Tech□	7	9	.438	16	13	.552
Clemson□	6	10	.375	18	16	.529
Florida State	6	10	.375	13	14	.481
NC State	5	11	.313	11	19	.367

Tournament: **North Carolina d. Virginia 73-66**
Tournament MVP: **Jerry Stackhouse**, North Carolina

ATLANTIC 10	Conference			Overall		
	W	L	PCT	W	L	PCT
Massachusetts⊛	14	2	.875	28	7	.800
Temple○	12	4	.750	23	8	.742
George Washington○	8	8	.500	18	12	.600
West Virginia□	8	8	.500	17	12	.586
Duquesne□	8	8	.500	17	13	.567
Rhode Island	7	9	.438	11	16	.407
Rutgers	6	10	.375	11	16	.407
Saint Joseph's	5	11	.313	14	14	.500
St. Bonaventure	4	12	.250	10	17	.370

Tournament: **Massachusetts d. Temple 70-59**
Tournament MOP: **Mike Williams**, Massachusetts

BIG EAST	Conference			Overall		
	W	L	PCT	W	L	PCT
Connecticut○	16	2	.889	29	5	.853
Syracuse○	13	5	.722	23	7	.767
Boston College○	11	7	.611	23	11	.676
Providence⊛	10	8	.556	20	10	.667
Villanova□	10	8	.556	20	12	.625
Georgetown○	10	8	.556	19	12	.613
Seton Hall○	8	10	.444	17	13	.567
Pittsburgh	7	11	.389	13	14	.481
St. John's	5	13	.278	12	17	.414
Miami (FL)	0	18	.000	7	20	.259

Tournament: **Providence d. Georgetown 74-64**
Tournament MVP: **Michael Smith**, Providence

BIG EIGHT	Conference			Overall		
	W	L	PCT	W	L	PCT
Missouri○⊗	14	0	1.000	28	4	.875
Oklahoma State○	10	4	.714	24	10	.706
Kansas○	9	5	.643	27	8	.771
Nebraska⊛	7	7	.500	20	10	.667
Oklahoma□	6	8	.429	15	13	.536
Kansas State□	4	10	.286	20	14	.588
Iowa State	4	10	.286	14	13	.519
Colorado	2	12	.143	10	17	.370

Tournament: **Nebraska d. Oklahoma State 77-68**
Tournament MVP: **Eric Piatkowski**, Nebraska

BIG SKY	Conference			Overall		
	W	L	PCT	W	L	PCT
Weber State⊗	10	4	.714	20	10	.667
Idaho State⊗	10	4	.714	18	9	.667
Idaho⊗	9	5	.643	18	10	.643
Montana State⊗	8	6	.571	16	11	.593
Boise State⊛⊗	7	7	.500	17	13	.567
Montana⊗	6	8	.429	19	9	.679
Northern Arizona⊗	6	8	.429	13	13	.500
Eastern Washington⊗	0	14	.000	5	21	.192

Tournament: **Boise State d. Idaho State 85-81**
Tournament MVP: **Shambric Williams**, Boise State

BIG SOUTH	Conference			Overall		
	W	L	PCT	W	L	PCT
Towson	16	2	.889	21	9	.700
Campbell	12	4	.750	20	9	.690
Radford	13	5	.722	20	8	.714
Liberty⊛	13	5	.722	18	12	.600
UNC Greenville	11	7	.611	15	12	.556
Coastal Carolina	10	8	.556	15	11	.577
Charleston Southern	8	10	.444	9	18	.333
UMBC	5	13	.278	6	21	.222
Winthrop	3	15	.167	4	23	.148
UNC Asheville	3	15	.167	3	24	.111

Tournament: **Liberty d. Campbell 76-62**
Tournament MVP: **Peter Aluma**, Liberty

BIG TEN	Conference			Overall		
	W	L	PCT	W	L	PCT
Purdue⊛	14	4	.778	29	5	.853
Michigan○	13	5	.722	24	8	.750
Indiana○	12	6	.667	21	9	.700
Minnesota○⊗	10	8	.556	22	13	.629
Michigan State○	10	8	.556	20	12	.625
Illinois○	10	8	.556	17	11	.607
Wisconsin○	8	10	.444	18	11	.621
Penn State	6	12	.333	13	14	.481
Ohio State	6	12	.333	13	16	.448
Northwestern□	5	13	.278	15	14	.517
Iowa	5	13	.278	11	16	.407

BIG WEST	Conference			Overall		
	W	L	PCT	W	L	PCT
New Mexico State⊛⊗	12	6	.667	23	8	.742
Long Beach State	11	7	.611	17	10	.630
San Jose State	11	7	.611	15	12	.556
Utah State	11	7	.611	14	13	.519
Pacific	10	8	.556	17	14	.548
UNLV	10	8	.556	15	13	.536
UC Santa Barbara	9	9	.500	13	17	.433
Nevada	6	12	.333	11	17	.393
Cal State Fullerton	6	12	.333	8	19	.296
UC Irvine	4	14	.222	10	20	.333

Tournament: **New Mexico State d. UC Irvine 70-64**
Tournament MVPs: **James Dockery**, New Mexico State and **Chris Brown**, UC Irvine

COLONIAL ATHLETIC	Conference			Overall		
	W	L	PCT	W	L	PCT
Old Dominion□	10	4	.714	21	10	.677
James Madison⊛	10	4	.714	20	10	.667
UNC Wilmington	9	5	.643	18	10	.643
Richmond	8	6	.571	14	14	.500
East Carolina	7	7	.500	15	12	.556
George Mason	5	9	.357	10	17	.370
American	5	9	.357	8	19	.296
William and Mary	2	12	.143	4	23	.148

Tournament: **James Madison d. Old Dominion 77-76**
Tournament MVP: **Odell Hodge**, Old Dominion

EAST COAST	Conference			Overall		
	W	L	PCT	W	L	PCT
Troy	5	0	1.000	13	14	.481
Northeastern Illinois	4	1	.800	17	11	.607
Buffalo	3	2	.600	10	18	.357
Chicago State	2	3	.400	4	23	.148
Hofstra	1	4	.200	9	20	.310
Central Conn. State	0	5	.000	4	22	.154

Tournament: **Hofstra d. Northeastern Illinois 88-86 (OT)**
Tournament MVP: **Jim Shaffer**, Hofstra

GMWC	Conference			Overall		
	W	L	PCT	W	L	PCT
Marquette○	10	2	.833	24	9	.727
Saint Louis○	8	4	.667	23	6	.793
UAB○	8	4	.667	22	8	.733
Cincinnati○	7	5	.583	22	10	.688
DePaul□	4	8	.333	16	12	.571
Memphis	4	8	.333	13	16	.448
Dayton	1	11	.083	6	21	.222

Tournament: **Cincinnati d. Memphis 68-47**

IVY	Conference			Overall		
	W	L	PCT	W	L	PCT
Penn⊛	14	0	1.000	25	3	.893
Princeton	11	3	.786	18	8	.692
Yale	7	7	.500	10	16	.385
Brown	6	8	.429	12	14	.462
Dartmouth	6	8	.429	10	16	.385
Harvard	5	9	.357	9	17	.346
Columbia	4	10	.286	6	20	.231
Cornell	3	11	.214	8	18	.308

METRO	Conference			Overall		
	W	L	PCT	W	L	PCT
Louisville⊛	10	2	.833	28	6	.824
Tulane□	7	5	.583	18	11	.621
Charlotte□	7	5	.583	16	13	.552
Virginia Tech	6	6	.500	18	10	.643
VCU	5	7	.417	14	13	.519
Southern Miss□	5	7	.417	15	15	.500
South Florida	2	10	.167	10	17	.370

Tournament: **Louisville d. Southern Miss 69-61**
Tournament MOP: **Clifford Rozier**, Louisville

MAAC	Conference			Overall		
	W	L	PCT	W	L	PCT
Canisius□	12	2	.857	22	7	.759
Siena□	10	4	.714	25	8	.758
Manhattan□	10	4	.714	20	10	.667
Saint Peter's	8	6	.571	14	13	.519
Loyola (MD)⊛	6	8	.429	17	13	.567
Fairfield	4	10	.286	8	19	.296
Iona	3	11	.214	7	20	.259
Niagara	3	11	.214	6	21	.222

Tournament: **Loyola (MD) d. Manhattan 80-75**
Tournament MVP: **Tracy Bergan**, Loyola (MD)

MID-AMERICAN	Conference			Overall		
	W	L	PCT	W	L	PCT
Ohio⊛	14	4	.778	25	8	.758
Bowling Green	12	6	.667	18	10	.643
Miami (OH)□	12	6	.667	19	11	.633
Ball State	11	7	.611	16	12	.571
Eastern Michigan	10	8	.556	15	12	.556
Toledo	10	8	.556	15	12	.556
Kent State	8	10	.444	13	14	.481
Western Michigan	7	11	.389	14	14	.500
Central Michigan	4	14	.222	5	21	.192
Akron	2	16	.111	8	18	.308

Tournament: **Ohio d. Miami (OH) 89-66**
Tournament MVP: **Gary Trent**, Ohio

MID-CONTINENT	Conference			Overall		
	W	L	PCT	W	L	PCT
Wisc.-Green Bay⊛	15	3	.833	27	7	.794
Valparaiso	14	4	.778	20	8	.714
Illinois-Chicago	14	4	.778	20	9	.690
Cleveland State	9	9	.500	14	15	.483
Wright State	9	9	.500	12	18	.400
Eastern Illinois	7	11	.389	12	15	.444
Northern Illinois	7	11	.389	10	17	.370
Wisc.-Milwaukee	7	11	.389	10	17	.370
Western Illinois	5	13	.278	7	20	.259
Youngstown State	3	15	.167	5	21	.192

Tournament: **Wisc.-Green Bay d. Illinois-Chicago 61-56**
Tournament MVP: **Sherell Ford**, Illinois-Chicago

⊛ Automatic NCAA Tournament bid ○ At-large NCAA Tournament bid □ NIT appearance ⊗ Team record doesn't reflect games forfeited or vacated. For adjusted record, see p. 521.

MEAC

	Conference W	L	PCT	Overall W	L	PCT
Coppin State	16	0	1.000	22	8	.733
UMES	10	6	.625	16	12	.571
NC A&T⊕	10	6	.625	16	14	.533
South Carolina State	10	6	.625	16	13	.552
Bethune-Cookman	8	8	.500	9	18	.333
Howard	7	9	.438	10	17	.370
Delaware State	5	11	.313	8	19	.296
Morgan State	4	12	.250	8	21	.276
Florida A&M	2	14	.125	4	23	.148

Tournament: **NC A&T d. South Carolina St. 87-70**
Tournament MOP: **Phillip Allen**, NC A&T

MCC

	Conference W	L	PCT	Overall W	L	PCT
Xavier□	8	2	.800	22	8	.733
Evansville□	6	4	.600	21	11	.656
Butler	6	4	.600	16	13	.552
Detroit	5	5	.500	16	13	.552
La Salle	4	6	.400	11	16	.407
Loyola-Chicago	1	9	.100	8	19	.296

Tournament: **Detroit d. Evansville 70-65**
Tournament MVP: **Andy Elkins**, Evansville

MISSOURI VALLEY

	Conference W	L	PCT	Overall W	L	PCT
Tulsa○	15	3	.833	23	8	.742
Southern Illinois⊕	14	4	.778	23	7	.767
Bradley□	14	4	.750	23	8	.742
Illinois State	12	6	.666	16	11	.593
Northern Iowa	10	8	.556	16	13	.552
Missouri State	7	11	.389	12	15	.444
Drake	6	12	.333	11	16	.407
Wichita State	6	12	.333	9	18	.333
Creighton	3	15	.167	7	22	.241
Indiana State	3	15	.167	4	22	.154

Tournament: **Southern Illinois d. Northern Iowa 77-74**
Tournament MOP: **Cam Johnson**, Northern Iowa

NAC

	Conference W	L	PCT	Overall W	L	PCT
Drexel⊕	12	2	.857	25	5	.833
Maine	11	3	.786	20	9	.690
Hartford	9	5	.643	16	12	.571
New Hampshire	8	6	.571	15	13	.536
Delaware	7	7	.500	14	13	.519
Boston U.	4	10	.286	11	16	.407
Vermont	3	11	.214	12	15	.444
Northeastern	2	12	.143	5	22	.185

Tournament: **Drexel d. Maine 86-78**
Tournament MVP: **Malik Rose**, Drexel

NORTHEAST

	Conference W	L	PCT	Overall W	L	PCT
Rider⊕	14	4	.778	21	9	.700
Monmouth	13	5	.722	18	11	.621
Wagner	11	7	.611	16	12	.571
Robert Morris	11	7	.611	14	14	.500
Fairleigh Dickinson	10	8	.556	14	13	.519
Marist	10	8	.556	14	13	.519
Mount St. Mary's	9	9	.500	14	14	.500
Saint Francis (PA)	9	9	.500	13	15	.464
Long Island	2	16	.111	3	24	.111
St. Francis (NY)	1	17	.056	1	26	.037

Tournament: **Rider d. Monmouth 62-56**
Tournament MVP: **Charles Smith**, Rider

OHIO VALLEY

	Conference W	L	PCT	Overall W	L	PCT
Murray State□	15	1	.938	23	6	.793
Tennessee State⊕	12	4	.750	19	12	.613
Austin Peay	10	6	.625	11	16	.407
Eastern Kentucky	9	7	.563	13	14	.481
Morehead State	8	8	.500	14	14	.500
SE Missouri State	5	11	.313	10	17	.370
Tennessee Tech	5	11	.313	10	21	.323
Middle Tenn. State	5	11	.313	8	19	.296
Tennessee-Martin	3	13	.188	5	22	.185

Tournament: **Tennessee State d. Murray State 73-72**
Tournament MVP: **Carlos Rogers**, Tennessee State

PAC-10

	Conference W	L	PCT	Overall W	L	PCT
Arizona⊕	14	4	.778	29	6	.829
UCLA○	13	5	.722	21	7	.750
California○	13	5	.722	22	8	.733
Washington State○	10	8	.556	20	11	.645
Stanford□	10	8	.556	17	11	.607
Arizona State□	10	8	.556	15	13	.536
Southern California□	9	9	.500	16	12	.571
Oregon	6	12	.333	10	17	.370
Washington	3	15	.167	5	22	.185
Oregon State	2	16	.111	6	21	.222

PATRIOT

	Conference W	L	PCT	Overall W	L	PCT
Navy⊕	9	5	.643	17	13	.567
Colgate	9	5	.643	17	12	.586
Holy Cross	9	5	.643	14	14	.500
Fordham	9	5	.643	12	15	.444
Bucknell	6	8	.429	10	17	.370
Lehigh	6	8	.429	10	17	.370
Lafayette	4	10	.286	9	19	.321
Army	4	10	.286	7	20	.259

Tournament: **Navy d. Colgate 78-76**
Tournament MVP: **T.J. Hall**, Navy

SEC

	Conference W	L	PCT	Overall W	L	PCT
EASTERN						
Florida○	12	4	.750	29	8	.784
Kentucky⊕	12	4	.750	27	7	.794
Vanderbilt□	9	7	.563	20	12	.625
Georgia	7	9	.438	14	16	.467
South Carolina	4	12	.250	9	19	.321
Tennessee	2	14	.125	5	22	.185
WESTERN						
Arkansas○	14	2	.875	31	3	.912
Alabama○	12	4	.750	20	10	.667
Mississippi State□	9	7	.563	18	11	.621
Mississippi	7	9	.438	14	13	.519
LSU	5	11	.313	11	16	.407
Auburn	3	13	.188	11	17	.393

Tournament: **Kentucky d. Florida 73-60**
Tournament MVP: **Travis Ford**, Kentucky

SOUTHERN

	Conference W	L	PCT	Overall W	L	PCT
Chattanooga⊕	14	4	.778	23	7	.767
Davidson□	13	5	.722	22	8	.733
East Tenn. State	13	5	.722	16	14	.533
Appalachian State	12	6	.667	16	11	.593
Ga. Southern	9	9	.500	14	14	.500
Western Carolina	8	10	.444	12	16	.429
Marshall	7	11	.389	9	18	.333
The Citadel	6	12	.333	11	16	.407
Furman	6	12	.333	10	18	.357
VMI	2	16	.111	5	23	.179

Tournament: **Chattanooga d. Davidson 65-64**
Tournament MOP: **Chad Copeland**, Chattanooga

SOUTHLAND

	Conference W	L	PCT	Overall W	L	PCT
UL-Monroe	15	3	.833	19	9	.679
Texas State⊕	14	4	.778	25	7	.781
Nicholls State	12	6	.667	19	9	.679
North Texas	9	9	.500	14	15	.483
McNeese State	9	9	.500	11	16	.407
Texas-San Antonio	8	10	.444	12	15	.444
Sam Houston State	7	11	.389	7	20	.259
Northwestern St. (LA)	6	12	.333	11	15	.423
Stephen F. Austin	6	12	.333	9	18	.333
Texas-Arlington	4	14	.222	7	22	.241

Tournament: **Texas State d. North Texas 69-60**
Tournament MVP: **Lynwood Wade**, Texas State

SOUTHWEST

	Conference W	L	PCT	Overall W	L	PCT
Texas⊕	12	2	.857	26	8	.765
Texas A&M□	10	4	.714	19	11	.633
Texas Tech	10	4	.714	17	11	.607
Baylor	7	7	.500	16	11	.593
Rice	6	8	.429	15	14	.517
Houston	5	9	.357	8	19	.296
TCU	3	11	.214	7	20	.259
SMU	3	11	.214	6	21	.222

Tournament: **Texas d. Texas A&M 87-62**
Tournament MVP: **B.J. Tyler**, Texas

SWAC

	Conference W	L	PCT	Overall W	L	PCT
Texas Southern⊕	12	2	.857	19	11	.633
Jackson State	11	3	.786	19	10	.655
Alabama State	10	4	.714	19	10	.655
Southern U.	8	6	.571	16	11	.593
Miss. Valley State	6	8	.429	10	17	.370
Grambling	4	10	.286	9	18	.333
Alcorn State	3	11	.214	3	24	.111
Prairie View A&M	2	12	.143	5	22	.185

Tournament: **Texas Southern d. Jackson State 70-67**
Tournament MVP: **Kevin Granger**, Texas Southern

SUN BELT

	Conference W	L	PCT	Overall W	L	PCT
Western Kentucky○	14	4	.778	20	11	.645
UL-Lafayette⊕	13	5	.722	22	8	.733
New Orleans□	12	6	.667	20	10	.667
Jacksonville	11	7	.611	17	11	.607
Arkansas State	10	8	.556	15	12	.556
Texas-Pan American	9	9	.500	16	12	.571
South Alabama	9	9	.500	13	14	.481
Arkansas-Little Rock	6	12	.333	13	15	.464
Lamar	6	12	.333	10	17	.370
Louisiana Tech	0	18	.000	2	25	.074

Tournament: **UL-Lafayette d. Western Kentucky 78-72**
Tournament MOP: **Michael Allen**, UL-Lafayette

TAAC

	Conference W	L	PCT	Overall W	L	PCT
Charleston○	14	2	.875	24	4	.857
Central Florida⊕	11	5	.688	21	9	.700
Stetson	9	7	.563	14	15	.483
Georgia State	9	7	.563	13	14	.481
Centenary	8	8	.500	16	12	.571
Florida International	7	9	.438	11	16	.407
Southeastern Louisiana	7	9	.438	10	17	.370
Samford	4	12	.250	10	18	.357
Mercer	3	13	.188	5	24	.172
Florida Atlantic*	-	-	-	3	24	.111

* Ineligible for conference title
Tournament: **Central Florida d. Stetson 70-67**
Tournament MVP: **Victor Saxton**, Central Florida

WEST COAST

	Conference W	L	PCT	Overall W	L	PCT
Gonzaga□	12	2	.857	22	8	.733
Pepperdine⊕	8	6	.571	19	11	.633
San Francisco	8	6	.571	17	11	.607
San Diego	7	7	.500	18	11	.621
Santa Clara	6	8	.429	13	14	.481
Portland	6	8	.429	13	17	.433
Saint Mary's (CA)	5	9	.357	13	14	.481
Loyola Marymount	4	10	.286	6	21	.222

Tournament: **Pepperdine d. San Diego 56-53**
Tournament MVP: **Dana Jones**, Pepperdine

WAC

	Conference W	L	PCT	Overall W	L	PCT
New Mexico○	14	4	.778	23	8	.742
Fresno State□	13	5	.722	21	11	.656
BYU□	12	6	.667	22	10	.688
Hawaii⊕	11	7	.611	18	15	.545
UTEP	8	10	.444	18	12	.600
Colorado State	8	10	.444	15	13	.536
Utah	8	10	.444	14	14	.500
Wyoming	7	11	.389	14	14	.500
San Diego State	6	12	.333	12	16	.429
Air Force	3	15	.167	8	18	.308

Tournament: **Hawaii d. BYU 73-66**
Tournament MVP: **Trevor Ruffin**, Hawaii

INDEPENDENTS

	Overall W	L	PCT
Southern Utah	16	11	.593
Notre Dame	12	17	.414
Missouri-Kansas City	12	17	.414
Cal State Northridge	8	18	.308
Oral Roberts	6	21	.222
Cal State Sacramento	1	26	.037

INDIVIDUAL LEADERS—SEASON

SCORING	CL	POS	G	FG	3FG	FT	PTS	PPG
1 **Glenn Robinson**, Purdue	JR	F	34	368	79	215	1,030	**30.3**
2 **Rob Feaster**, Holy Cross	JR	F	28	261	42	221	785	**28.0**
3 **Jervaughn Scales**, Southern U.	SR	F	27	293	0	147	733	**27.1**
4 **Frankie King**, Western Carolina	JR	G	28	258	29	207	752	**26.9**
5 **Tucker Neale**, Colgate	JR	G	29	249	95	178	771	**26.6**
6 **Eddie Benton**, Vermont	SO	G	26	205	68	209	687	**26.4**
7 **Doremus Bennerman**, Siena	SR	G	33	254	102	248	858	**26.0**
8 **Tony Dumas**, **Missouri-Kansas City**	SR	G	29	229	74	221	753	**26.0**
9 **Otis Jones**, Air Force	JR	G	26	206	77	174	663	**25.5**
10 **Izett Buchanan**, Marist	SR	G	27	238	41	168	685	**25.4**

FIELD GOAL PCT	CL	POS	G	FG	FGA	PCT
1 **Mike Atkinson**, Long Beach State	JR	F	26	141	203	**69.5**
2 **Lynwood Wade**, Texas State	SR	G	32	232	356	**65.2**
3 **Anthony Miller**, Michigan State	SR	F	32	162	249	**65.1**
4 **Deon Thomas**, Illinois	SR	F	28	207	327	**63.3**
5 **Aaron Swinson**, Auburn	SR	F/C	28	234	371	**63.1**

MINIMUM: 5 MADE PER GAME

3-PT FG PER GAME	CL	POS	G	3FG	3PG
1 **Chris Brown**, UC Irvine	JR	G	26	122	**4.7**
2 **KeKe Hicks**, Coastal Carolina	JR	G	26	115	**4.4**
3 **LaZelle Durden**, Cincinnati	JR	G	25	102	**4.1**
4 **Bernard Haslett**, Southern Miss	SR	G	30	112	**3.7**
5 **Kareem Townes**, La Salle	JR	G	27	100	**3.7**

3-PT FG PCT	CL	POS	G	3FG	3FGA	PCT
1 **Brent Kell**, Evansville	SO	G	29	62	123	**50.4**
2 **Brian Santiago**, Fresno State	SR	G	32	64	128	**50.0**
3 **Brandon Born**, UT Chattanooga	JR	G/F	30	67	135	**49.6**
4 **Chris Young**, Canisius	SO	G	29	53	109	**48.6**
5 **Howard Eisley**, Boston College	SR	G	34	91	188	**48.4**

MINIMUM: 1.5 MADE PER GAME

FREE THROW PCT	CL	POS	G	FT	FTA	PCT
1 **Danny Basile**, Marist	SO	G	27	84	89	**94.4**
2 **Dandrea Evans**, Troy	SR	G	27	72	77	**93.5**
3 **Casey Schmidt**, Valparaiso	SR	G	25	75	81	**92.6**
4 **Matt Hildebrand**, Liberty	SR	G	30	149	161	**92.5**
5 **Kent Culuko**, James Madison	JR	G	30	117	127	**92.1**

MINIMUM: 2.5 MADE PER GAME

ASSISTS PER GAME	CL	POS	G	AST	APG
1 **Jason Kidd**, California	SO	G	30	272	**9.1**
2 **David Edwards**, Texas A&M	SR	G	30	265	**8.8**
3 **Tony Miller**, Marquette	JR	G	33	274	**8.3**
4 **Eathan O'Bryant**, Nevada	JR	G	28	232	**8.3**
5 **Abdul Abdullah**, Providence	SR	G	30	241	**8.0**
6 **Howard Nathan**, UL-Monroe	SO	G	23	179	**7.8**
7 **Orlando Smart**, San Francisco	SR	G	27	204	**7.6**
8 **Dan Pogue**, Campbell	SO	G	28	207	**7.4**
9 **Dedan Thomas**, UNLV	SR	G	28	205	**7.3**
10 **Nelson Haggerty**, Baylor	JR	G	22	161	**7.3**

REBOUNDS PER GAME	CL	POS	G	REB	RPG
1 **Jerome Lambert**, Baylor	JR	F	24	355	**14.8**
2 **Jervaughn Scales**, Southern U.	SR	F	27	384	**14.2**
3 **Eric Kubel**, Northwestern St. (LA)	SR	F	26	341	**13.1**
4 **Kendrick Warren**, VCU	SR	F	27	336	**12.4**
5 **Malik Rose**, Drexel	SO	F	30	371	**12.4**
6 **David Vaughn**, Memphis	SO	F	28	335	**12.0**
7 **Reggie Jackson**, Nicholls State	SR	F	26	311	**12.0**
8 **Melvin Simon**, New Orleans	SR	F	30	355	**11.8**
9 **Kebu Stewart**, UNLV	SO	F	22	256	**11.6**
10 **Carlos Rogers**, Tennessee State	SR	C	31	358	**11.5**

BLOCKED SHOTS PER GAME	CL	POS	G	BLK	BPG
1 **Grady Livingston**, Howard	JR	C	26	115	**4.4**
2 **Jim McIlvaine**, Marquette	SR	C	33	142	**4.3**
3 **Theo Ratliff**, Wyoming	JR	C	28	114	**4.1**
4 **David Vaughn**, Memphis	SO	F	28	107	**3.8**
5 **Tim Duncan**, Wake Forest	FR	F	33	124	**3.8**

STEALS PER GAME	CL	POS	G	STL	SPG
1 **Shawn Griggs**, UL-Lafayette	SR	G	30	120	**4.0**
2 **Gerald Walker**, San Francisco	SO	G	28	109	**3.9**
3 **Andre Cradle**, Long Island	SR	F	21	79	**3.8**
4 **Jason Kidd**, California	SO	G	30	94	**3.1**
5 **B.J. Tyler**, Texas	SR	G	28	87	**3.1**

INDIVIDUAL LEADERS-GAME

POINTS	CL	POS	OPP	DATE	PTS
1 **Askia Jones**, Kansas State	SR	G	Fresno State	M24	**62**
2 **Eddie Benton**, Vermont	SO	G	Drexel	J29	**54**
3 **Jervaughn Scales**, Southern U.	SR	F	Patten	N26	**52**
4 **Izett Buchanan**, Marist	SR	G	Long Island	F12	**51**
Doremus Bennerman, Siena	SR	G	Kansas State	M30	**51**

3-PT FG MADE	CL	POS	OPP	DATE	3FG
1 **Askia Jones**, Kansas State	SR	G	Fresno State	M24	**14**
2 **Al Dillard**, Arkansas	JR	G	Delaware State	D11	**12**
3 **Scott Neely**, Campbell	JR	G	Coastal Carolina	J29	**11**
Chris Brown, UC Irvine	JR	G	New Mexico State	M13	**11**
5 **Trevor Ruffin**, Hawaii	SR	G	Louisville	D30	**10**
Stevin Smith, Arizona State	SR	G	Oregon State	J27	**10**
Chris Brown, UC Irvine	JR	G	Pacific	F5	**10**

ASSISTS	CL	POS	OPP	DATE	AST
1 **Nelson Haggerty**, Baylor	JR	G	UL-Lafayette	D20	**18**
Jason Kidd, California	SO	G	Stanford	J20	**18**
3 **Danny Doyle**, Iona	SR	G	Fairfield	F19	**17**
4 **Arriel McDonald**, Minnesota	SR	G	Wisconsin	J12	**16**
Eathan O'Bryant, Nevada	JR	G	UC Irvine	J15	**16**
Kenny Harris, VCU	SR	G	Oklahoma	J20	**16**
Sean Miller, Texas-Arlington	SR	G	Northwestern St. (LA)	F19	**16**

REBOUNDS	CL	POS	OPP	DATE	REB
1 **Jervaughn Scales**, Southern U.	SR	F	Grambling State	F7	**32**
2 **Willie Fisher**, Jacksonville	JR	F	Louisiana Tech	D4	**27**
3 **Eric Kubel**, Northwestern St. (LA)	SR	F	Southeastern La.	D18	**26**
Michael Smith, Providence	SR	F	Syracuse	J25	**26**
Jerome Lambert, Baylor	JR	F	SMU	F6	**26**

BLOCKED SHOTS	CL	POS	OPP	DATE	BLK
1 **Grady Livingston**, Howard	JR	C	UMES	J13	**11**
Randy Edney, Mount St. Mary's	JR	C	Long Island	J15	**11**
Theo Ratliff, Wyoming	JR	C	BYU	F3	**11**
4 **Donyell Marshall**, Connecticut	JR	F	Hartford	J17	**10**
Pascal Fleury, UMBC	SR	C	Winthrop	J29	**10**
Cherokee Parks, Duke	JR	F/C	Clemson	M11	**10**

STEALS	CL	POS	OPP	DATE	STL
1 **Brevin Knight**, Stanford	FR	G	McNeese State	D20	**10**
Brian Bidlingmyer, Siena	JR	F	Loyola (MD)	J15	**10**
B.J. Tyler, Texas	SR	G	Houston	J29	**10**
Shawn Moore, Marshall	JR	F	East Tennessee State	J29	**10**
5 **Phil Anderson**, Delaware State	JR	G	Penn State	D29	**9**
Alex Robertson, Dayton	SR	G	Miami (OH)	D30	**9**
Andre Cradle, Long Island	SR	F	Monmouth	J29	**9**
Dana Jones, Pepperdine	SR	F	San Francisco	F18	**9**

TEAM LEADERS—SEASON

WIN-LOSS PCT	W	L	PCT
1 **Arkansas**	31	3	**.912**
2 **Penn**	25	3	**.893**
3 **Missouri**	28	4	**.875**
4 **Charleston**	24	4	**.857**
5 **Purdue**	29	5	**.853**
Connecticut	29	5	**.853**

SCORING OFFENSE	G	W-L	PTS	PPG
1 **Southern U.**	27	16-11	2,727	**101.0**
2 **Troy**	27	13-14	2,634	**97.6**
3 **Arkansas**	34	31-3	3,176	**93.4**
4 **Texas**	34	26-8	3,119	**91.7**
5 **Murray State**	29	23-6	2,611	**90.0**

SCORING MARGIN	G	W-L	PPG	OPP PPG	MAR
1 **Arkansas**	34	31-3	93.4	75.6	**17.8**
2 **Connecticut**	34	29-5	84.9	68.6	**16.3**
3 **Arizona**	35	29-6	89.3	74.4	**14.9**
4 **Southern U.**	27	16-11	101.0	87.7	**13.3**
5 **North Carolina**	35	28-7	85.6	72.4	**13.2**

FIELD GOAL PCT	G	W-L	FG	FGA	PCT
1 **Auburn**	28	11-17	854	1,689	**50.6**
2 **Michigan State**	32	20-12	944	1,875	**50.3**
3 **Radford**	28	20-8	793	1,580	**50.2**
4 **James Madison**	30	20-10	890	1,783	**49.9**
5 **North Carolina**	35	28-7	1,091	2,188	**49.9**

THREE-PT FG PER GAME	G	W-L	3FG	3PG
1 **Troy**	27	13-14	262	**9.7**
2 **New Mexico**	31	23-8	300	**9.7**
3 **Vermont**	27	12-15	240	**8.9**
4 **Arkansas**	34	31-3	301	**8.9**
Kentucky	34	27-7	301	**8.9**

FREE THROW PCT	G	W-L	FT	FTA	PCT
1 **Colgate**	29	17-12	511	665	**76.8**
2 **Wisconsin-Green Bay**	34	27-7	462	607	**76.1**
3 **Iowa State**	27	14-13	521	687	**75.8**
4 **Davidson**	30	22-8	529	704	**75.1**
5 **Vanderbilt**	32	20-12	557	742	**75.1**

ASSISTS PER GAME	G	W-L	AST	APG
1 **Arkansas**	34	31-3	687	**20.2**
2 **Oklahoma State**	34	24-10	677	**19.9**
3 **Nebraska**	30	20-10	581	**19.4**
4 **Kentucky**	34	27-7	648	**19.1**
5 **Canisius**	29	22-7	540	**18.6**

REBOUND MARGIN	G	W-L	RPG	OPP RPG	MAR
1 **Utah State**	27	14-13	38.4	29.8	**8.6**
2 **North Carolina**	35	28-7	43.7	35.3	**8.4**
Idaho	28	18-10	41.5	33.1	**8.4**
4 **UCLA**	28	21-7	43.9	36.2	**7.7**
Baylor	27	16-11	50.3	42.6	**7.7**

SCORING DEFENSE	G	W-L	OPP PTS	OPP PPG
1 **Princeton**	26	18-8	1,361	**52.3**
2 **Temple**	31	23-8	1,697	**54.7**
3 **Wisconsin-Green Bay**	34	27-7	1,872	**55.1**
4 **UAB**	30	22-8	1,806	**60.2**
5 **Marquette**	33	24-9	2,040	**61.8**

Field Goal Pct Defense

	G	W-L	OPP FG	OPP FGA	OPP PCT
1 Marquette	33	24-9	750	2,097	**35.8**
2 Temple	31	23-8	621	1,686	**36.8**
3 Wisconsin-Green Bay	34	27-7	664	1,777	**37.4**
4 Kansas	35	27-8	823	2,147	**38.3**
5 UAB	30	22-8	661	1,718	**38.5**

Blocked Shots Per Game

	G	W-L	BLK	BPG
1 Howard	27	10-17	179	**6.6**
2 Memphis	29	13-16	189	**6.5**
3 Connecticut	34	29-5	218	**6.4**
4 North Carolina	35	28-7	219	**6.3**
5 Massachusetts	35	28-7	214	**6.1**

Steals Per Game

	G	W-L	STL	SPG
1 Texas	34	26-8	453	**13.3**
2 Drake	27	11-16	337	**12.5**
3 Long Island	27	3-24	322	**11.9**
4 Troy	27	13-14	321	**11.9**
5 Saint Francis (PA)	28	13-15	327	**11.7**

TEAM LEADERS—GAME

Points

	OPP	DATE	SCORE
1 Southern U.	Patten	N26	**154-57**
2 Tennessee State	Fisk	D6	**148-57**
Southern U.	Louisiana Christian	D13	**148-90**
4 Southern U.	Paul Quinn	N29	**142-82**
5 Nicholls State	Baptist Christian	D16	**140-64**

Field Goal Pct

	OPP	DATE	FG	FGA	PCT
1 Western Michigan	Miami (OH)	J5	32	44	**72.7**
2 Monmouth	Long Island	J8	49	70	**70.0**
3 Florida Int'l	Saint Francis	D3	23	33	**69.7**
Butler	Illinois State	D9	23	33	**69.7**
5 Nicholls State	Baptist Christian	D16	58	84	**69.0**

Three-Pt FG Made

	OPP	DATE	3FG
1 Kansas State	Fresno State	M24	**23**
2 Arkansas	Montevallo	F5	**19**
3 Arkansas	Delaware State	D11	**18**
4 New Mexico	Simon Fraser	N21	**17**
Vermont	Middlebury	D8	**17**
Old Dominion	William and Mary	F2	**17**
Stetson	Southeastern La.	M3	**17**

CONSENSUS ALL-AMERICAS

FIRST TEAM

PLAYER	CL	POS	HT	SCHOOL	RPG	PPG
Grant Hill	SR	G/F	6-8	Duke	6.9	17.4
Jason Kidd	SO	G	6-4	California	6.9	16.7
Donyell Marshall	JR	F	6-9	Connecticut	8.9	25.1
Glenn Robinson	JR	F	6-8	Purdue	10.1	30.3
Clifford Rozier	JR	F/C	6-10	Louisville	11.1	18.1

SECOND TEAM

PLAYER	CL	POS	HT	SCHOOL	RPG	PPG
Melvin Booker	SR	G	6-2	Missouri	3.8	18.1
Eric Montross	SR	C	7-0	North Carolina	8.1	13.6
Lamond Murray	JR	F	6-7	California	7.9	24.3
Khalid Reeves	SR	G	6-3	Arizona	4.3	24.2
Jalen Rose	JR	G	6-8	Michigan	5.7	19.9
Corliss Williamson	SO	F	6-7	Arkansas	7.7	20.4

Selectors: AP, NABC, UPI, USBWA

AWARD WINNERS

PLAYER OF THE YEAR

PLAYER	CL	POS	HT	SCHOOL	AWARDS
Glenn Robinson	JR	F	6-8	Purdue	Naismith, AP, UPI, USBWA, Wooden, NABC, Rupp
Greg Brown	SR	G	5-7	New Mexico	Frances Pomeroy Naismith*

* For the most outstanding senior player who is 6 feet or under

DEFENSIVE PLAYER OF THE YEAR

PLAYER	CL	POS	HT	SCHOOL
Jim McIlvaine	SR	C	7-1	Marquette

COACH OF THE YEAR

COACH	SCHOOL	REC	AWARDS
Nolan Richardson	Arkansas	31-3	Naismith, NABC (shared), CBS/Chevrolet
Norm Stewart	Missouri	28-4	AP, UPI, Sporting News
Charlie Spoonhour	Saint Louis	23-6	USBWA
Gene Keady	Purdue	29-5	NABC (shared)

Bob Gibbons' Top High School Senior Recruits

PLAYER	POS	HT	HIGH SCHOOL	A-A TEAMS	COLLEGE	CAREER NOTES
1 Jerod Ward	F	6-9	Clinton (MS) HS	McD, P, USA	Michigan	9.4 ppg, 4.5 rpg; undrafted; played in CBA, overseas
2 Raef LaFrentz	C/F	6-11	MFL Mar Mac HS, Monona, IA	McD, P, USA	Kansas	2-time first-team AP All-America; 2-time Big 12 POY; No. 3 pick, '98 NBA draft (Nuggets); 10.1 ppg (10 seasons)
3 Andrae Patterson	PF	6-8	Cooper HS Abilene, TX	McD, P	Indiana	11.3 ppg, 5.7 rpg (4 seasons); 2nd-round pick, '98 NBA draft (Wolves); 3.0 ppg (2 seasons)
4 Felipe Lopez	G/F	6-5	Rice HS, New York	McD, P, USA	St. John's	16.9 ppg, 5.8 rpg (4 seasons); No. 24 pick, '98 NBA draft (Spurs); 5.8 ppg (4 seasons)
5 Samaki Walker	PF	6-9	Whitehall HS, Columbus, OH	P	Louisville	14.3 ppg, 7.3 rpg (2 seasons); No. 9 pick, '96 NBA draft (Mavs); 5.3 ppg, 4.7 rpg (10 seasons)
6 Ricky Price	G/F	6-6	Serra HS, Gardena, CA	McD, P, USA	Duke	9.2 ppg (4 seasons); 3rd team All-ACC, '96; undrafted; played overseas
7 Trajan Langdon	G	6-3	Anchorage (AK) East HS	McD, P	Duke	14.5 ppg (4 seasons); 3-time first-team All-ACC; No. 11 pick, '99 NBA draft (Cavs); 5.4 ppg (3 seasons)
8 Lorenzen Wright	C	6-10	Booker T. Washington HS, Memphis, TN	McD, P	Memphis	16.0 ppg, 10.3 rpg (2 seasons); No. 7 pick, '96 NBA draft (Clippers); 8.1 ppg, 6.5 rpg (12 seasons)
9 Curtis Staples	2G	6-2	Oak Hill Academy, Mouth of Wilson, VA	McD, P	Virginia	1,757 pts (4 seasons); left as NCAA all-time leader in 3pt FGs (413); undrafted; played in D-League
10 Adonal Foyle	C	6-10	Hamilton (NY) Central HS	McD, P	Colgate	20.4 ppg, 12.7 rpg, 5.7 bpg (3 seasons); No. 8 pick, '97 NBA draft (Warriors); 4.1 ppg, 4.8 rpg (11 seasons)
11 Maurice Taylor	PF	6-8	Henry Ford HS, Detroit	P	Michigan	12.9 ppg, 6.1 rpg (3 seasons); Big Ten FOY, '95; No. 14 pick, '97 NBA draft (Clippers); 11.0 ppg (9 seasons)
12 Danny Fortson	C	6-7	Shaler Area Senior HS, Pittsburgh	McD, P	Cincinnatti	18.8 ppg, 8.7 rpg (3 seasons); first-team AP All-America, '97; No. 10 pick, '97 NBA draft (Bucks); 8.2 ppg (10 seasons)
13 Jelani Gardner	2G	6-5	St. John Bosco HS, Bellflower, CA	McD, P, USA	California/Pepperdine	Transferred after 2 years; 2-time All-WCC; undrafted
14 Zendon Hamilton	C/F	6-10	Sewanhaka HS, Floral Park, NY	McD, P	St. John's	15.9 ppg, 8.3 rpg (4 seasons); 3-time 2nd team All-Big East; undrafted; 4.4 ppg (6 seasons)
15 Jerry Gee	PF	6-7	St. Martin de Porres HS, Waukegan, IL		Illinois	7.3 ppg (4 seasons); undrafted; played in D-League, CBA, USBL, overseas
16 Galen Robinson	PF	6-8	MacArthur HS, Houston		Houston	1,135 points (4 seasons); undrafted; played with Harlem Globetrotters, overseas
17 Maceo Baston	PF	6-9	H. Grady Spruce HS, Dallas		Michigan	10.7 ppg, 6.6 rpg (4 seasons); 2nd-round pick, '98 NBA draft (Bulls); 2.8 ppg (3 seasons); played overseas
18 Tremaine Fowlkes	SF	6-6	Crenshaw HS, Los Angeles	P	California/Fresno St.	In college, 13.4 ppg; 2nd-round pick, '98 NBA draft (Nuggets); 2.9 ppg (4 seasons)
19 Sam Jacobson	G/F	6-5	Park HS, Cottage Grove, MN		Minnesota	13.1 ppg, 4.8 rpg (4 seasons); No. 26 pick, '98 NBA draft (Lakers); 4.2 ppg (3 seasons)
20 Chris Herren	2G	6-3	Durfee HS, Fall River, MA	McD, P	Boston College/ Fresno St.	Transferred after 1 year; in college, 15.1 ppg, 5.4 (4 seasons); 2nd-round pick, '99 NBA draft; 3.2 ppg (2 seasons)

Other Standouts

PLAYER	POS	HT	HIGH SCHOOL	A-A TEAMS	COLLEGE	CAREER NOTES
25 Antoine Walker	F	6-8	Mount Carmel HS, Chicago	McD, P	Kentucky	NCAA title, '96; at UK, 11.7 ppg (2 seasons); No. 6 pick, '96 NBA draft (Celtics); 17.5 ppg (12 seasons); 3-time All-Star
56 Tony Gonzalez	PF	6-6	Huntington Beach (CA) HS		California (football)	6.4 ppg, 4.3 rpg (3 seasons); No. 13 pick, '97 NFL draft (Chiefs); 9-time All-Pro TE
72 Andre Miller	G	6-2	Verbum Dei HS, Los Angeles		Utah	WAC POY, '99; at Utah, 12.1 ppg, 5.4 apg (4 seasons); No. 8 pick, '99 NBA draft (Cavs); 14.4 ppg (9 seasons)

Abbreviations: McD=McDonald's; P=Parade; USA=USA Today

POLL PROGRESSION

PRESEASON POLL

AP	USA/CNN	SCHOOL
1	1	**North Carolina**
2	2	**Kentucky**
3	4	**Arkansas**
4	3	**Duke**
5	5	**Michigan**
6	10	**California**
7	6	**Louisville**
8	7	**Temple**
9	9	**Kansas**
10	11	**Minnesota**
11	13	**Oklahoma State**
12	7	**Indiana**
13	14	**UCLA**
14	15	**Georgia Tech**
15	12	**Georgetown**
16	18	**Virginia**
17	16	**Illinois**
18	20	**Arizona**
19	17	**Cincinnati**
20	19	**Syracuse**
21	25	**Purdue**
22	21	**Massachusetts**
23	—	**Vanderbilt**
24	—	**George Washington**
25	24	**Florida State**
—	22	**Wisconsin**
—	23	**Marquette**

WEEK OF NOV 22

AP	USA/CNN	SCHOOL	AP↓↑
1	5	**North Carolina** (2-0)	
2	1	**Kentucky** (0-0)	
3	6	**Arkansas** (0-0)	
4	4	**Duke** (0-0)	
5	3	**Michigan** (0-0)	
6	2	**Kansas** (2-0)	↑3
7	11	**Louisville** (0-0)	
8	7	**Temple** (0-0)	
9	14	**Minnesota** (2-0)	↑1
10	10	**Oklahoma State** (0-0)	↑1
11	19	**Indiana** (0-0)	↑1
12	15	**California** (1-1)	↓6
13	17	**Georgia Tech** (0-0)	↑1
14	8	**UCLA** (0-0)	↓1
15	22	**Georgetown** (0-0)	
16	18	**Virginia** (0-0)	
17	21	**Illinois** (0-0)	
18	9	**Massachusetts** (2-0)	↑4
19	12	**Arizona** (0-0)	↓1
20	16	**Syracuse** (0-0)	
21	13	**Purdue** (0-0)	
22	20	**Cincinnati** (1-1)	↓3
23	—	**George Washington** (0-0)	↑1
24	23	**Vanderbilt** (0-0)	↓1
25	—	**Wisconsin** (0-0)	⤴
—	24	**Florida State** (0-0)	⤵
—	25	**Marquette** (2-1)	

WEEK OF NOV 29

AP	USA/CNN	SCHOOL	AP↓↑
1	6	**Kentucky** (2-1)	↑1
2	1	**Arkansas** (3-0)	↑1
3	7	**Kansas** (5-1)	↑3
4	2	**North Carolina** (6-1)	↓3
5	4	**Michigan** (4-0)	
6	5	**Duke** (3-0)	↓2
7	3	**Temple** (2-0)	↑1
8	8	**Oklahoma State** (4-1)	↑2
9	9	**Massachusetts** (5-1)	↑9
10	10	**UCLA** (2-0)	↑4
11	15	**Louisville** (1-1)	↓4
12	22	**Virginia** (0-0)	↑4
13	25	**California** (2-2)	↓1
14	11	**Purdue** (3-0)	↑7
15	16	**Minnesota** (4-2)	↓6
16	18	**Illinois** (2-0)	↑1
17	17	**Georgia Tech** (3-1)	↓4
18	13	**Syracuse** (4-0)	↑2
19	14	**Arizona** (3-0)	
20	—	**Vanderbilt** (1-0)	↑4
21	12	**Indiana** (1-1)	↓10
22	23	**George Washington** (2-1)	↑1
23	19	**Cincinnati** (4-1)	↓1
24	21	**Wisconsin** (2-0)	↑1
25	—	**Georgetown** (1-1)	↓10
—	20	**Connecticut** (3-0)	
—	24	**Florida State** (2-0)	

WEEK OF DEC 6 Ⓐ

AP	USA/CNN	SCHOOL	AP↓↑
1	1	**Arkansas** (3-0)	
2	2	**North Carolina** (6-1)	
3	4	**Michigan** (4-0)	
4	5	**Duke** (3-0)	
5	3	**Temple** (2-0)	
6	6	**Kentucky** (2-1)	
7	7	**Kansas** (5-1)	
8	9	**Massachusetts** (5-1)	
9	10	**UCLA** (2-0)	
10	15	**Louisville** (1-1)	
11	11	**Purdue** (5-0)	
12	12	**Indiana** (1-1) Ⓑ	[illegible]
13	13	**Syracuse** (4-0)	[illegible]
14	14	**Arizona** (3-0)	[illegible]
15	8	**Oklahoma State** (4-1)	[illegible]
16	18	**Illinois** (2-0)	
17	16	**Minnesota** (4-2)	[illegible]
18	17	**Georgia Tech** (3-1)	[illegible]
19	21	**Wisconsin** (2-0)	[illegible]
20	19	**Cincinnati** (4-1)	[illegible]
21	20	**Connecticut** (3-0)	[illegible]
22	22	**Virginia** (2-1)	[illegible]
23	—	**Vanderbilt** (3-1)	[illegible]
24	23	**George Washington** (2-1)	[illegible]
25	25	**California** (2-2)	[illegible]
—	24	**Florida State** (2-0)	

WEEK OF DEC 13

AP	USA/CNN	SCHOOL	AP↓↑
1	1	**Arkansas** (5-0)	
2	2	**North Carolina** (7-1)	
3	3	**Duke** (5-0)	↑1
4	4	**Temple** (3-0)	↑1
5	5	**Kentucky** (3-1)	↑1
6	6	**Kansas** (8-1)	↑1
7	7	**Michigan** (5-1)	↓4
8	9	**Massachusetts** (7-1)	
9	8	**UCLA** (4-0)	
10	13	**Louisville** (3-1)	
11	11	**Purdue** (7-0)	
12	10	**Indiana** (4-1)	
13	12	**Arizona** (4-0)	↑1
14	14	**Georgia Tech** (4-1)	↑4
15	18	**Minnesota** (4-2)	↑2
16	15	**Connecticut** (5-0)	↑5
17	17	**Cincinnati** (6-1)	↑3
18	19	**Wisconsin** (4-0)	↑1
19	20	**Illinois** (4-1)	↓3
20	22	**Boston College** (6-0)	⤴
21	21	**Syracuse** (4-1)	↓8
22	16	**Oklahoma State** (5-2)	↓7
23	23	**George Washington** (4-1)	↑1
24	24	**Vanderbilt** (4-1)	↓1
25	25	**LSU** (3-0)	⤴

WEEK OF DEC 20

AP	USA/CNN	SCHOOL	AP↓↑
1	1	**Arkansas** (6-0)	
2	2	**North Carolina** (8-1)	
3	3	**Duke** (5-0)	
4	4	**Temple** (4-0)	
5	5	**Kentucky** (4-1)	
6	6	**Kansas** (9-1)	
7	9	**Michigan** (5-1)	
8	10	**Massachusetts** (7-1)	
9	7	**UCLA** (5-0)	
10	11	**Purdue** (8-0)	↑1
11	13	**Louisville** (4-1)	↓1
12	8	**Indiana** (5-1)	
13	12	**Arizona** (6-0)	
14	15	**Georgia Tech** (6-1)	
15	14	**Connecticut** (6-0)	↑1
16	16	**Minnesota** (6-2)	↓1
17	20	**Wisconsin** (5-0)	↑1
18	22	**Boston College** (6-0)	↑2
19	19	**Illinois** (5-1)	
20	21	**Cincinnati** (7-2)	↓3
21	18	**Syracuse** (6-1)	
22	17	**Oklahoma State** (6-2)	
23	23	**George Washington** (5-1)	
24	24	**Marquette** (5-2)	⤴
25	—	**Western Kentucky** (3-1)	⤴
—	25	**Vanderbilt** (4-2)	⤵

WEEK OF DEC 27

AP	USA/CNN	SCHOOL	AP↓↑
1	1	**Arkansas** (7-0)	
2	2	**North Carolina** (9-1)	
3	3	**Duke** (6-0)	
4	4	**Temple** (4-0)	
5	5	**Kentucky** (7-1)	
6	6	**Kansas** (11-1)	
7	10	**Michigan** (5-1)	
8	7	**UCLA** (6-0)	↑1
9	9	**Massachusetts** (7-1)	↓1
10	8	**Purdue** (9-0)	
11	12	**Louisville** (5-1)	
12	13	**Arizona** (8-1)	↑1
13	11	**Indiana** (5-2)	↓1
14	14	**Connecticut** (7-0)	↑1
15	15	**Georgia Tech** (7-1)	↓1
16	16	**Minnesota** (7-2)	
17	17	**Wisconsin** (6-0)	
18	18	**Cincinnati** (8-2)	↑2
19	20	**Syracuse** (7-1)	↑2
20	19	**Oklahoma State** (7-2)	↑2
21	22	**George Washington** (5-1)	↑2
22	21	**Illinois** (6-2)	↓3
23	23	**Boston College** (7-2)	↓5
24	24	**Marquette** (6-2)	
25	—	**Western Kentucky** (3-2)	
—	25	**Vanderbilt** (5-2)	

WEEK OF JAN 3

AP	USA/CNN	SCHOOL	AP↓↑
1	1	**Arkansas** (8-0)	
2	2	**North Carolina** (10-1)	
3	3	**Duke** (7-0)	
4	4	**Kentucky** (9-1)	↑1
5	5	**Kansas** (13-1)	↑1
6	6	**UCLA** (7-0)	↑2
7	7	**Temple** (6-1)	↓3
8	11	**Massachusetts** (9-1)	↑1
9	9	**Arizona** (10-1)	↑3
10	8	**Purdue** (11-0)	
11	12	**Louisville** (8-1)	
12	13	**Georgia Tech** (9-1)	↑3
13	14	**Michigan** (7-2)	↓6
14	10	**Indiana** (7-2)	↓1
15	15	**Wisconsin** (9-0)	↑2
16	16	**Connecticut** (10-1)	↓2
17	17	**Cincinnati** (10-2)	↑1
18	18	**Syracuse** (8-1)	↑1
19	19	**Minnesota** (8-3)	↓3
20	21	**Boston College** (9-2)	↑3
21	20	**Illinois** (7-2)	↑1
22	25	**Vanderbilt** (7-2)	⤴
23	24	**George Washington** (6-2)	↓2
24	—	**California** (7-2)	⤴
25	23	**Marquette** (7-3)	↓1
—	22	**Oklahoma State** (8-4)	⤵

WEEK OF JAN 10

AP	USA/CNN	SCHOOL	AP↓↑
1	1	**North Carolina** (12-1)	↑1
2	2	**Duke** (9-0)	↑1
3	4	**Kansas** (15-1)	↑2
4	3	**Arkansas** (10-1) Ⓒ	↓3
5	5	**UCLA** (9-0)	↑1
6	6	**Arizona** (12-1)	↑3
7	9	**Massachusetts** (11-1)	↑1
8	7	**Kentucky** (11-2)	↓4
9	8	**Purdue** (13-0)	↑1
10	13	**Michigan** (10-2)	↑3
11	10	**Indiana** (8-2)	↑3
12	12	**Wisconsin** (11-0)	↑3
13	11	**Temple** (7-2)	↓6
14	14	**Connecticut** (12-1)	↑2
15	15	**Louisville** (10-2)	↓4
16	16	**Syracuse** (9-1)	↑2
17	18	**Georgia Tech** (9-3)	↓5
18	19	**Minnesota** (10-3)	↑1
19	24	**California** (9-2)	↑5
20	20	**Boston College** (10-3)	
21	17	**Cincinnati** (11-3)	↓4
22	25	**UAB** (11-1)	⤴
23	—	**West Virginia** (8-1)	⤴
24	23	**Vanderbilt** (8-3)	↓2
25	—	**Missouri** (10-1)	⤴
25	—	**Xavier** (8-1)	⤴
—	21	**Oklahoma State** (10-4)	
—	22	**Illinois** (7-3)	⤵

WEEK OF JAN 17

AP	USA/CNN	SCHOOL	AP↓↑
1	1	**Kansas** (16-1)	↑2
2	1	**UCLA** (11-0)	↑3
3	4	**Arkansas** (12-1)	↑1
4	3	**North Carolina** (13-2)	↓3
5	5	**Duke** (11-1)	↓3
6	7	**Massachusetts** (13-1)	↑1
7	6	**Kentucky** (13-2)	↑1
8	8	**Indiana** (10-2)	↑3
9	9	**Arizona** (13-2)	↑3
10	12	**Connecticut** (14-1)	↑4
11	11	**Temple** (9-2)	↑2
12	10	**Purdue** (14-1)	↓3
13	14	**Louisville** (12-2)	↑2
14	15	**Wisconsin** (12-1)	↓2
15	13	**Michigan** (11-3)	↓5
16	16	**Syracuse** (10-2)	
17	17	**Georgia Tech** (10-4)	
18	20	**UAB** (13-1)	↑4
19	18	**Cincinnati** (12-3)	↑2
20	19	**Minnesota** (11-4)	↓2
21	24	**California** (10-3)	↓2
22	25	**Xavier** (11-1)	↑3
23	22	**Saint Louis** (14-0)	⤴
24	—	**West Virginia** (10-2)	↓1
25	—	**Maryland** (10-3)	⤴
—	21	**Oklahoma State** (12-4)	
—	23	**Boston College** (11-4)	⤵

WEEK OF JAN 24

AP	USA/CNN	SCHOOL	AP↓↑
1	1	**UCLA** (13-0)	↑1
2	2	**Duke** (13-1)	↑3
3	3	**Kansas** (17-2)	↓2
4	4	**North Carolina** (14-3)	
5	5	**Arkansas** (13-2)	↓2
6	9	**Connecticut** (16-1)	↑4
7	6	**Purdue** (16-1)	↑5
8	8	**Massachusetts** (15-2)	↓2
9	7	**Kentucky** (14-3)	↓2
10	13	**Temple** (11-2)	↑1
11	10	**Indiana** (11-3)	↓3
12	12	**Louisville** (14-2)	↑1
13	11	**Arizona** (14-3)	↓4
14	14	**Syracuse** (12-2)	↑2
15	15	**Michigan** (12-4)	
16	17	**Wisconsin** (12-2)	↓2
17	16	**Minnesota** (13-4)	↑3
18	21	**Maryland** (11-3)	↑7
19	24	**West Virginia** (12-2)	↑5
20	18	**UAB** (14-2)	↓2
21	19	**Georgia Tech** (11-5)	↓4
22	22	**Marquette** (11-4)	⤴
23	—	**Saint Louis** (14-1)	
24	—	**Missouri** (13-2)	⤴
25	—	**New Mexico State** (14-1)	⤴
—	20	**Cincinnati** (12-5)	⤵
—	23	**California** (10-4)	⤵
—	25	**Boston College** (13-5)	

WEEK OF JAN 31

AP	USA/CNN	SCHOOL	AP↓↑
1	1	**Duke** (15-1)	↑1
2	2	**North Carolina** (17-3)	↑2
3	4	**Kansas** (19-2)	
4	3	**UCLA** (14-1) Ⓓ	↓3
5	6	**Connecticut** (18-1)	↑1
6	5	**Arkansas** (14-2)	↓1
7	7	**Kentucky** (16-3)	↑2
8	8	**Purdue** (17-2)	↓1
9	10	**Louisville** (16-2)	↑3
10	13	**Temple** (13-2)	
11	12	**Massachusetts** (16-3)	↓3
12	9	**Arizona** (16-3)	↑1
13	14	**Michigan** (13-4)	↑2
14	11	**Indiana** (12-4)	↓3
15	15	**Syracuse** (13-3)	↓1
16	16	**Wisconsin** (13-3)	
17	17	**UAB** (16-2)	↑3
18	20	**Saint Louis** (16-1)	↑5
19	22	**California** (12-4) Ⓓ	⤴
20	25	**Missouri** (14-2)	↑4
21	21	**Maryland** (12-4)	↓3
22	18	**Minnesota** (14-6)	↓5
23	—	**New Mexico State** (16-1)	↑2
24	—	**Florida** (16-3)	⤴
25	19	**Cincinnati** (14-5)	⤴
—	23	**Marquette** (12-5)	⤵
—	24	**Boston College** (15-5)	

[We]ek of Feb 7

AP	USA/CNN	SCHOOL	AP↓↑
[illegible]	1	**North Carolina** (19-3)	↑1
[illegible]	2	**Duke** (16-2)	↓1
[illegible]	3	**Arkansas** (16-2)	↑3
[illegible]	5	**Kentucky** (18-3)	↑3
[illegible]	4	**Kansas** (20-3)	↓2
[illegible]	6	**Connecticut** (19-2)	↓1
[illegible]	9	**Louisville** (18-2)	↑2
[illegible]	8	**Temple** (16-2)	↑2
[illegible]	7	**UCLA** (15-2)	↓5
10	10	**Purdue** (18-3)	↓2
11	13	**Michigan** (15-4)	↑2
12	11	**Indiana** (14-4)	↑2
13	12	**Massachusetts** (17-4)	↓2
14	14	**Syracuse** (15-3)	↑1
15	16	**Missouri** (16-2)	↑5
16	15	**Arizona** (17-4)	↓4
17	18	**Saint Louis** (18-1)	↑1
18	19	**California** (14-4)	↑1
19	17	**UAB** (17-3)	↓2
20	21	**Florida** (18-3)	↑4
21	22	**Wisconsin** (14-4)	↓5
22	20	**Marquette** (15-5)	↥
23	23	**Minnesota** (15-7)	↓1
24	24	**Illinois** (12-5)	↥
25	—	**Xavier** (16-3)	↥
—	25	**Cincinnati** (15-6)	↧

Week of Feb 14

AP	USA/CNN	SCHOOL	AP↓↑
1	1	**Arkansas** (18-2)	Ⓔ ↑2
2	4	**North Carolina** (20-4)	↓1
3	3	**Connecticut** (21-2)	↑3
4	2	**Kansas** (21-3)	↑1
5	6	**Louisville** (20-2)	↑2
6	5	**Duke** (17-3)	↓4
7	11	**Michigan** (17-4)	↑4
8	7	**UCLA** (17-2)	↑1
9	8	**Purdue** (20-3)	↑1
10	12	**Massachusetts** (19-4)	↑3
11	10	**Kentucky** (18-5)	↓7
12	14	**Missouri** (18-2)	↑3
13	9	**Temple** (17-4)	↓5
14	13	**Syracuse** (16-4)	
15	15	**Arizona** (19-4)	↑1
16	16	**Indiana** (15-5)	↓4
17	22	**Florida** (19-4)	↑3
18	17	**Saint Louis** (19-2)	↓1
19	18	**California** (16-5)	↓1
20	19	**Minnesota** (17-7)	↑3
21	20	**UAB** (18-4)	↓2
22	21	**Marquette** (16-6)	
23	24	**Cincinnati** (16-7)	↥
24	23	**Wisconsin** (15-5)	↓3
25	—	**Georgia Tech** (13-9)	↥
—	25	**Boston College** (16-7)	

Week of Feb 21

AP	USA/CNN	SCHOOL	AP↓↑
1	1	**Arkansas** (20-2)	
2	2	**Duke** (19-3)	↑4
3	6	**Michigan** (19-4)	↑4
4	4	**North Carolina** (21-5)	↓2
5	3	**Connecticut** (22-3)	↓2
6	8	**Missouri** (20-2)	↑6
7	7	**Kentucky** (20-5)	↑4
8	9	**Temple** (19-4)	↑5
9	11	**Arizona** (21-4)	↑6
10	5	**Kansas** (21-5)	↓6
11	14	**Massachusetts** (21-5)	↓1
12	13	**Indiana** (16-5)	↑4
13	10	**Louisville** (20-4)	↓8
14	12	**Purdue** (21-4)	↓5
15	15	**UCLA** (18-3)	↓7
16	19	**Florida** (21-4)	↑1
17	18	**California** (18-5)	↑2
18	16	**Syracuse** (17-5)	↓4
19	17	**Saint Louis** (20-3)	↓1
20	20	**Minnesota** (18-8)	
21	21	**Boston College** (18-7)	↥
22	22	**Marquette** (18-7)	
23	—	**Georgia Tech** (14-9)	↑2
24	—	**Oklahoma State** (18-7)	↥
25	25	**New Mexico State** (19-3)	↥
25	—	**Penn** (19-2)	↥
—	23	**UAB** (18-6)	↧
—	24	**Cincinnati** (17-8)	↧

Week of Feb 28

AP	USA/CNN	SCHOOL	AP↓↑
1	1	**Arkansas** (22-2)	
2	2	**Duke** (21-3)	
3	5	**Michigan** (20-4)	
4	3	**Connecticut** (24-3)	↑1
5	4	**North Carolina** (23-5)	↓1
6	6	**Missouri** (22-2)	
7	8	**Kentucky** (22-5)	
8	7	**Arizona** (23-4)	↑1
9	12	**Purdue** (23-4)	↑5
10	9	**Louisville** (22-4)	↑3
11	10	**Massachusetts** (23-6)	
12	13	**Temple** (20-6)	↓4
13	11	**Kansas** (22-6)	↓3
14	15	**Syracuse** (19-5)	↑4
15	14	**UCLA** (19-4)	
16	17	**Saint Louis** (22-3)	↑3
17	16	**Indiana** (17-6)	↓5
18	20	**Minnesota** (19-9)	↑2
19	19	**Florida** (22-5)	↓3
20	18	**California** (19-6)	↓3
21	22	**Oklahoma State** (20-7)	↑3
22	21	**Marquette** (20-7)	
23	23	**Boston College** (19-8)	↓2
24	23	**UAB** (20-6)	↥
24	—	**Penn** (21-2)	↑1
—	25	**Cincinnati** (18-9)	

Week of Mar 7

AP	USA/CNN	SCHOOL	AP↓↑
1	1	**Arkansas** (24-2)	
2	2	**Connecticut** (26-3)	↑2
3	3	**Missouri** (24-2)	↑3
4	3	**North Carolina** (24-6)	Ⓕ ↑1
5	5	**Duke** (22-4)	Ⓕ ↓3
6	8	**Purdue** (25-4)	↑3
7	6	**Arizona** (25-4)	↑1
8	7	**Michigan** (20-6)	↓5
9	10	**Massachusetts** (24-6)	↑2
10	12	**Kentucky** (23-6)	↓3
11	11	**Kansas** (24-6)	↑2
12	14	**Temple** (20-6)	
13	13	**Syracuse** (21-5)	↑1
14	9	**Louisville** (24-5)	↓4
15	15	**UCLA** (20-5)	
16	17	**California** (21-6)	↑4
17	18	**Florida** (23-6)	↑2
18	16	**Indiana** (18-7)	↓1
19	21	**Marquette** (22-7)	↑3
20	19	**Minnesota** (20-10)	↓2
21	22	**Saint Louis** (22-4)	↓5
22	20	**UAB** (22-6)	↑2
23	23	**Oklahoma State** (21-8)	↓2
24	25	**Penn** (23-2)	
25	—	**Texas** (22-7)	↥
—	24	**Boston College** (20-9)	↧

Week of Mar 14

AP	USA/CNN	SCHOOL	AP↓↑
1	2	**North Carolina** (27-6)	↑3
2	1	**Arkansas** (25-3)	Ⓖ ↓1
3	4	**Purdue** (26-4)	Ⓗ ↑3
4	3	**Connecticut** (27-4)	↓2
5	5	**Missouri** (25-3)	↓2
6	6	**Duke** (23-5)	↓1
7	8	**Kentucky** (26-6)	↑3
8	7	**Massachusetts** (27-6)	↑1
9	10	**Arizona** (25-5)	↓2
10	9	**Louisville** (26-5)	↑4
11	11	**Michigan** (21-7)	↓3
12	12	**Temple** (22-7)	
13	13	**Kansas** (25-7)	↓2
14	15	**Florida** (25-7)	↑3
15	14	**Syracuse** (21-6)	↓2
16	17	**California** (22-7)	
17	16	**UCLA** (21-6)	↓2
18	18	**Indiana** (19-8)	
19	19	**Oklahoma State** (23-9)	↑4
20	24	**Texas** (25-7)	↑5
21	22	**Marquette** (22-8)	↓2
22	—	**Nebraska** (20-9)	↥
23	20	**Minnesota** (20-11)	↓3
24	21	**Saint Louis** (23-5)	↓3
25	25	**Cincinnati** (22-9)	↥
—	23	**UAB** (22-7)	↧

FINAL POLL (Post-Tournament)

USA/CNN	SCHOOL
1	**Arkansas** (31-3)
2	**Duke** (28-6)
3	**Arizona** (29-6)
4	**Florida** (29-8)
5	**Purdue** (29-5)
6	**Missouri** (28-4)
7	**Connecticut** (29-5)
8	**Michigan** (24-8)
9	**North Carolina** (28-7)
10	**Louisville** (28-6)
11	**Boston College** (23-11)
12	**Kansas** (27-8)
13	**Kentucky** (27-7)
14	**Syracuse** (23-7)
15	**Massachusetts** (28-7)
16	**Indiana** (21-9)
17	**Marquette** (24-9)
18	**Temple** (23-8)
19	**Tulsa** (23-8)
20	**Maryland** (18-12)
21	**Oklahoma State** (24-10)
22	**UCLA** (21-7)
23	**Minnesota** (21-12)
24	**Texas** (26-8)
25	**Penn** (25-3)

Ⓐ On Dec. 1, unranked Georgetown beats Southern, 108-55, and sets an NCAA record by blocking 22 shots. The Hoyas follow that with an overtime loss to Villanova that drops them to 2–2 and they stay out of the polls for the rest of the season.
Ⓑ Damon Bailey rips Kentucky for 29 points while leading Indiana to a 96-84 upset in the Hoosier Dome. He will appear on the cover of *Sports Illustrated* the following week.
Ⓒ The Razorbacks lose to Alabama, 66-64, scoring 40 points less than their season average at the time.
Ⓓ Led by Jason Kidd (18 points, 14 rebounds, 12 assists), Cal topples UCLA, 85-70. Kidd will go on to set a single-season school record of 272 assists.
Ⓔ For a record sixth consecutive week the AP poll has a new No. 1. Arkansas takes over the top spot after beating Florida, 99-87, on Feb. 12—the same day that UNC loses in Chapel Hill to Georgia Tech, 96-89.
Ⓕ North Carolina beats Duke, 87-77, at Cameron, to complete a regular-season sweep.
Ⓖ On March 21, 1994, Arkansas' No. 1 fan, President Bill Clinton, appears on the cover of *Sports Illustrated.* He vows to attend the Final Four if the Razorbacks make it.
Ⓗ In his last regular-season game, Purdue's 6'8" Glenn "Big Dog" Robinson rips Illinois for 49 points in an 87-77 victory. He will end up leading the nation with a 30.3 scoring average.

Pre-Tournament Ratings Percentage Index (RPI)

RANK	SCHOOL	W-L	Sched. Strg.	SS Rank	RPI
1	**Purdue**	26-4	.6092	6	.6607
2	**Missouri**	24-3	.5832	28	.6520
3	**North Carolina**	27-6	.5902	14	.6423
4	**Massachusetts**	27-6	.5914	13	.6385
5	**Temple**	22-7	.6184	2	.6381
6	**Arkansas**	24-3	.5593	55	.6365
7	**Louisville**	26-5	.5779	33	.6359
8	**Kentucky**	26-6	.5915	12	.6351
9	**Michigan**	21-7	.6098	5	.6339
10	**Arizona**	25-5	.5713	39	.6301
11	**Duke**	23-5	.5680	45	.6297
12	**Connecticut**	27-4	.5372	82	.6208
13	**Kansas**	24-7	.5733	37	.6207
14	**Florida**	25-7	.5637	51	.6137
15	**Indiana**	19-8	.5890	18	.6123
16	**Syracuse**	21-6	.5549	64	.6062
17	**Oklahoma State**	21-9	.5837	27	.6047
18	**Marquette**	21-8	.5743	36	.6035
19	**Nebraska**	20-9	.5865	21	.6009
20	**Cincinnati**	22-9	.5753	35	.6001
21	**Virginia**	17-12	.6292	1	.5988
22	**Wake Forest**	20-10	.5857	23	.5963
23	**California**	22-7	.5405	76	.5943
24	**Minnesota**	20-11	.5895	16	.5942
25	**Providence**	20-9	.5691	43	.5941
26	**UCLA**	21-6	.5257	92	.5930
27	**Michigan State**	19-11	.5895	17	.5928
28	**Illinois**	17-10	.5868	20	.5901
29	**UAB**	22-7	.5259	91	.5858
30	**Wisconsin**	17-10	.5793	32	.5853
31	**Saint Louis**	22-5	.4854	168	.5812
32	**Ohio**	23-7	.5285	89	.5812
33	**Oklahoma**	15-12	.6106	4	.5801
34	**Boston College**	19-10	.5580	58	.5781
35	**Charlotte**	16-12	.6038	7	.5768
36	**Southern Illinois**	22-6	.5151	107	.5761
37	**Georgetown**	16-11	.5801	30	.5757
38	**Washington State**	18-10	.5621	52	.5752
39	**Georgia Tech**	16-12	.5839	26	.5741
40	**Texas**	25-7	.4994	131	.5740
41	**Seton Hall**	17-12	.5826	29	.5733
42	**Drexel**	24-4	.4704	202	.5732
43	**Maryland**	16-11	.5725	38	.5726
44	**Western Kentucky**	19-10	.5637	50	.5725
45	**New Mexico**	21-7	.5134	109	.5720
46	**BYU**	19-9	.5434	70	.5720
47	**Villanova**	15-12	.5883	19	.5708
48	**UL-Lafayette**	21-7	.5092	116	.5701
49	**Chattanooga**	21-6	.5029	126	.5677
50	**Kansas State**	17-12	.5702	41	.5676

Source: Collegiate Basketball News

1994 NCAA Tournament

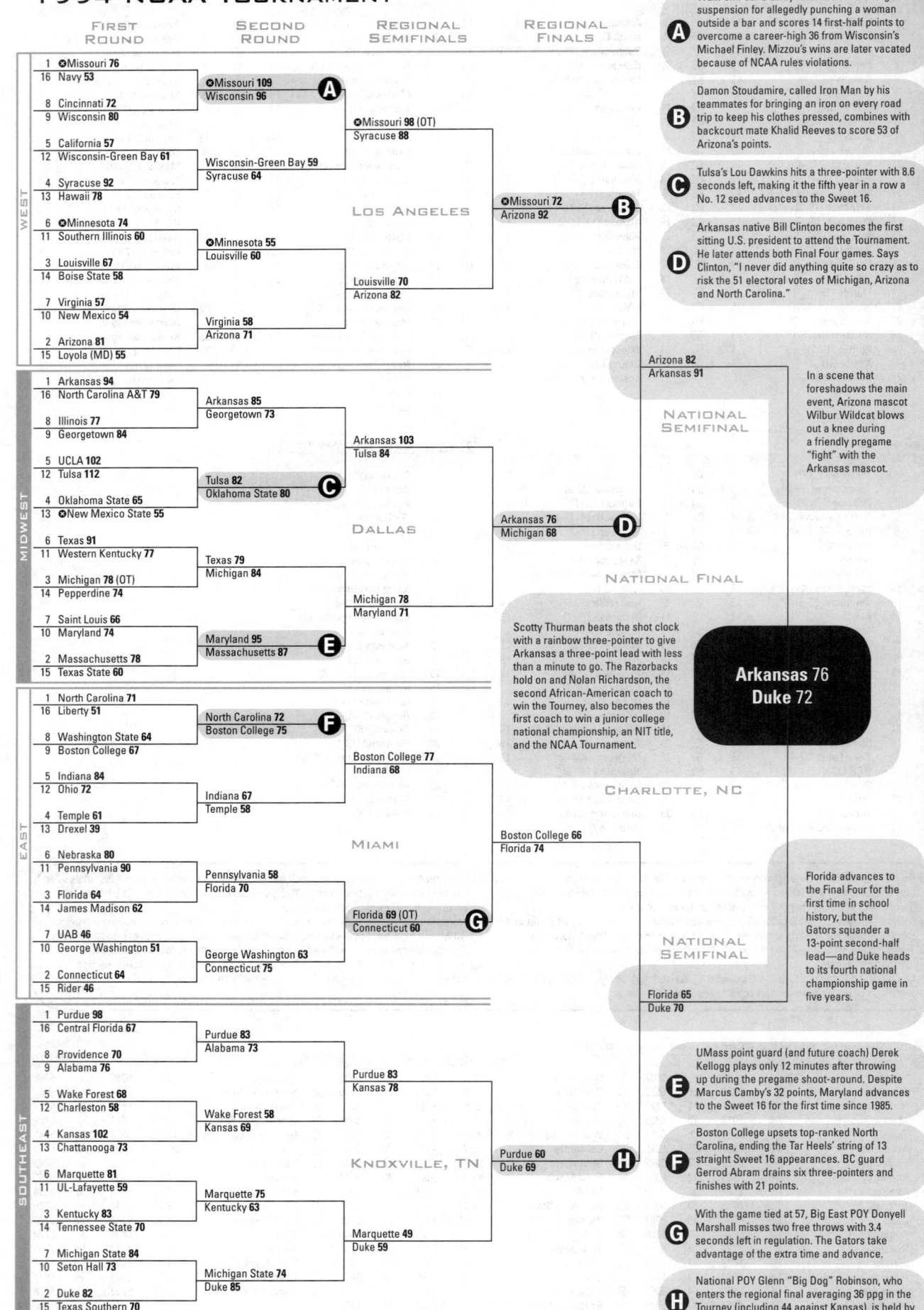

First Round · **Second Round** · **Regional Semifinals** · **Regional Finals**

West — Los Angeles

First Round

1 ⊗Missouri 76
16 Navy 53

8 Cincinnati 72
9 Wisconsin 80

5 California 57
12 Wisconsin-Green Bay 61

4 Syracuse 92
13 Hawaii 78

6 ⊗Minnesota 74
11 Southern Illinois 60

3 Louisville 67
14 Boise State 58

7 Virginia 57
10 New Mexico 54

2 Arizona 81
15 Loyola (MD) 55

Second Round

⊗Missouri 109
Wisconsin 96 (A)

Wisconsin-Green Bay 59
Syracuse 64

⊗Minnesota 55
Louisville 60

Virginia 58
Arizona 71

Regional Semifinals

⊗Missouri 98 (OT)
Syracuse 88

Louisville 70
Arizona 82

Regional Final

⊗Missouri 72
Arizona 92 (B)

Midwest — Dallas

First Round

1 Arkansas 94
16 North Carolina A&T 79

8 Illinois 77
9 Georgetown 84

5 UCLA 102
12 Tulsa 112

4 Oklahoma State 65
13 ⊗New Mexico State 55

6 Texas 91
11 Western Kentucky 77

3 Michigan 78 (OT)
14 Pepperdine 74

7 Saint Louis 66
10 Maryland 74

2 Massachusetts 78
15 Texas State 60

Second Round

Arkansas 85
Georgetown 73

Tulsa 82
Oklahoma State 80 (C)

Texas 79
Michigan 84

Maryland 95
Massachusetts 87 (E)

Regional Semifinals

Arkansas 103
Tulsa 84

Michigan 78
Maryland 71

Regional Final

Arkansas 76
Michigan 68 (D)

East — Miami

First Round

1 North Carolina 71
16 Liberty 51

8 Washington State 64
9 Boston College 67

5 Indiana 84
12 Ohio 72

4 Temple 61
13 Drexel 39

6 Nebraska 80
11 Pennsylvania 90

3 Florida 64
14 James Madison 62

7 UAB 46
10 George Washington 51

2 Connecticut 64
15 Rider 46

Second Round

North Carolina 72
Boston College 75 (F)

Indiana 67
Temple 58

Pennsylvania 58
Florida 70

George Washington 63
Connecticut 75

Regional Semifinals

Boston College 77
Indiana 68

Florida 69 (OT)
Connecticut 60 (G)

Regional Final

Boston College 66
Florida 74

Southeast — Knoxville, TN

First Round

1 Purdue 98
16 Central Florida 67

8 Providence 70
9 Alabama 76

5 Wake Forest 68
12 Charleston 58

4 Kansas 102
13 Chattanooga 73

6 Marquette 81
11 UL-Lafayette 59

3 Kentucky 83
14 Tennessee State 70

7 Michigan State 84
10 Seton Hall 73

2 Duke 82
15 Texas Southern 70

Second Round

Purdue 83
Alabama 73

Wake Forest 58
Kansas 69

Marquette 75
Kentucky 63

Michigan State 74
Duke 85

Regional Semifinals

Purdue 83
Kansas 78

Marquette 49
Duke 59

Regional Final

Purdue 60
Duke 69 (H)

National Semifinal

Arizona 82
Arkansas 91

In a scene that foreshadows the main event, Arizona mascot Wilbur Wildcat blows out a knee during a friendly pregame "fight" with the Arkansas mascot.

National Semifinal

Florida 65
Duke 70

Florida advances to the Final Four for the first time in school history, but the Gators squander a 13-point second-half lead—and Duke heads to its fourth national championship game in five years.

National Final — Charlotte, NC

Arkansas 76
Duke 72

Scotty Thurman beats the shot clock with a rainbow three-pointer to give Arkansas a three-point lead with less than a minute to go. The Razorbacks hold on and Nolan Richardson, the second African-American coach to win the Tourney, also becomes the first coach to win a junior college national championship, an NIT title, and the NCAA Tournament.

⊗Team participation later vacated

A Walk-on Paul O'Liney returns from a one-game suspension for allegedly punching a woman outside a bar and scores 14 first-half points to overcome a career-high 36 from Wisconsin's Michael Finley. Mizzou's wins are later vacated because of NCAA rules violations.

B Damon Stoudamire, called Iron Man by his teammates for bringing an iron on every road trip to keep his clothes pressed, combines with backcourt mate Khalid Reeves to score 53 of Arizona's points.

C Tulsa's Lou Dawkins hits a three-pointer with 8.6 seconds left, making it the fifth year in a row a No. 12 seed advances to the Sweet 16.

D Arkansas native Bill Clinton becomes the first sitting U.S. president to attend the Tournament. He later attends both Final Four games. Says Clinton, "I never did anything quite so crazy as to risk the 51 electoral votes of Michigan, Arizona and North Carolina."

E UMass point guard (and future coach) Derek Kellogg plays only 12 minutes after throwing up during the pregame shoot-around. Despite Marcus Camby's 32 points, Maryland advances to the Sweet 16 for the first time since 1985.

F Boston College upsets top-ranked North Carolina, ending the Tar Heels' string of 13 straight Sweet 16 appearances. BC guard Gerrod Abram drains six three-pointers and finishes with 21 points.

G With the game tied at 57, Big East POY Donyell Marshall misses two free throws with 3.4 seconds left in regulation. The Gators take advantage of the extra time and advance.

H National POY Glenn "Big Dog" Robinson, who enters the regional final averaging 36 ppg in the Tourney (including 44 against Kansas), is held by Duke to a season-low 13.

Tournament Leaders

Individual Leaders

Scoring

	CL	POS	G	PTS	PPG
1 **Gary Collier**, Tulsa	SR	F	3	94	31.3
2 **Glenn Robinson**, Purdue	JR	F	4	121	30.3
3 **Juwan Howard**, Michigan	JR	C	4	116	29.0
4 **Khalid Reeves**, Arizona	SR	G	5	137	27.4
5 **Lawrence Moten**, Syracuse	JR	G/F	3	75	25.0
6 **Melvin Booker**, Missouri	SR	G	4	90	22.5
7 **Corliss Williamson**, Arkansas	SO	F	6	130	21.7
8 **Adrian Autry**, Syracuse	SR	G	3	63	21.0
Joe Smith, Maryland	FR	F/C	3	63	21.0
10 **Alan Henderson**, Indiana	JR	F/C	3	58	19.3

Minimum: 3 games

Field Goal Pct

	CL	POS	G	FG	FGA	PCT
1 **Joseph Blair**, Arizona	SO	F	5	22	32	68.8
2 **Keith Booth**, Maryland	FR	F	3	15	22	68.2
3 **Ray Jackson**, Michigan	JR	G	4	21	32	65.6
4 **Juwan Howard**, Michigan	JR	C	4	48	74	64.9
5 **Corliss Williamson**, Arkansas	SO	F	6	55	89	61.8

Minimum: 15 made and 3 games

Free Throw Pct

	CL	POS	G	FT	FTA	PCT
1 **Dwayne Morton**, Louisville	SR	F	3	18	19	94.7
Shawn Respert, Michigan State	JR	G	2	18	19	94.7
3 **Melvin Booker**, Missouri	SR	G	4	22	24	91.7
4 **Michael Finley**, Wisconsin	JR	G/F	2	17	19	89.5
5 **Gary Collier**, Tulsa	SR	F	3	21	24	87.5

Minimum: 15 made

Three-Point FG Pct

	CL	POS	G	3FG	3FGA	PCT
1 **Steve Woodberry**, Kansas	SR	G	3	8	14	57.1
2 **Dwight Stewart**, Arkansas	JR	C	6	11	20	55.0
3 **Roney Eford**, Marquette	SO	G	3	6	11	54.5
Dwayne Morton, Louisville	SR	F	3	6	11	54.5
5 **Grant Hill**, Duke	SR	G/F	6	8	16	50.0
Todd Leary, Indiana	SR	G	3	7	14	50.0
Sean Pearson, Kansas	SO	F	3	7	14	50.0

Minimum: 6 made and 3 games

Assists Per Game

	CL	POS	G	AST	APG
1 **Duane Simpkins**, Maryland	SO	G	3	22	7.3
2 **Tony Miller**, Marquette	JR	G	3	20	6.7
Steve Woodberry, Kansas	SR	G	3	20	6.7
4 **Melvin Booker**, Missouri	SR	G	4	26	6.5
5 **Jacque Vaughn**, Kansas	FR	G	3	19	6.3

Minimum: 3 games

Rebounds Per Game

	CL	POS	G	REB	RPG
1 **Juwan Howard**, Michigan	JR	C	4	51	12.8
2 **Joe Smith**, Maryland	FR	F	3	34	11.3
3 **Glenn Robinson**, Purdue	JR	F	4	42	10.5
4 **Joseph Blair**, Arizona	SO	F	5	51	10.2
5 **Ray Owes**, Arizona	JR	F	5	50	10.0
Alan Henderson, Indiana	JR	F/C	3	30	10.0
Clifford Rozier, Louisville	SR	F	3	30	10.0

Minimum: 3 games

Blocked Shots Per Game

	CL	POS	G	BLK	BPG
1 **Cherokee Parks**, Duke	JR	F/C	6	18	3.0
Greg Ostertag, Kansas	JR	C	3	9	3.0
3 **Corliss Williamson**, Arkansas	SO	F	6	14	2.3
Alan Henderson, Indiana	JR	F/C	3	7	2.3
Clifford Rozier, Louisville	SR	F	3	7	2.3

Minimum: 3 games

Steals Per Game

	CL	POS	G	STL	SPG
1 **Tony Miller**, Marquette	JR	G	3	8	2.7
Doron Sheffer, Connecticut	SO	G	3	8	2.7
Alvin Williamson, Tulsa	JR	G	3	8	2.7
4 **Dan Cross**, Florida	JR	G	5	12	2.4
5 **Lawrence Moten**, Syracuse	JR	G/F	3	7	2.3
Jason Osborne, Louisville	FR	F	3	7	2.3
Johnny Rhodes, Maryland	SO	G	3	7	2.3
Steve Woodberry, Kansas	SR	G	3	7	2.3

Minimum: 3 games

Team Leaders

Scoring

	G	PTS	PPG
1 Missouri	4	355	88.8
2 Arkansas	5	440	88.0
3 Arizona	4	256	85.3
4 Kansas	3	249	83.0
5 Syracuse	3	244	81.3
6 Purdue	4	324	81.0
7 Maryland	3	240	80.0
8 Michigan	4	230	76.7
9 Boston College	4	285	71.3
10 Duke	5	352	70.4

Minimum: 3 games

FG Pct

	G	FG	FGA	PCT
1 Purdue	4	118	216	54.6
2 Arizona	4	120	222	54.0
3 Arkansas	5	166	332	50.0
Maryland	3	85	170	50.0
5 Syracuse	3	92	188	48.9

Minimum: 3 games

3-Pt FG Pct

	G	3FG	3FGA	PCT
1 Purdue	4	36	69	52.2
2 Marquette	3	18	41	43.9
3 Kansas	3	24	57	42.1
4 Boston College	4	33	81	40.7
5 Duke	5	27	68	39.7

Minimum: 3 games

FT Pct

	G	FT	FTA	PCT
1 Connecticut	3	58	76	76.3
2 Arizona	4	73	97	75.3
3 Syracuse	3	50	68	73.5
4 Duke	5	79	108	73.2
5 Purdue	4	50	69	72.5

Minimum: 3 games

Ast/TO Ratio

	G	AST	TO	RAT
1 Kansas	3	73	43	1.70
2 Missouri	4	72	46	1.57
3 Arkansas	5	105	75	1.40
4 Marquette	3	51	37	1.38
5 Purdue	4	66	56	1.18

Minimum: 3 games

Rebounds

	G	REB	RPG
1 Arizona	4	180	45.0
2 Kansas	3	134	44.7
3 Connecticut	3	130	43.3
4 Missouri	4	169	42.3
Michigan	4	169	42.3

Minimum: 3 games

Blocks

	G	BLK	BPG
1 Duke	5	33	6.6
2 Syracuse	3	19	6.3
3 Kansas	3	17	5.7
4 Connecticut	3	15	5.0
5 Arkansas	5	22	4.4

Minimum: 3 games

Steals

	G	STL	SPG
1 Kansas	3	30	10.0
2 Florida	5	45	9.0
3 Michigan	4	32	8.0
Maryland	3	24	8.0
5 Arkansas	5	37	7.4

Minimum: 3 games

All-Tournament Team

PLAYER	CL	POS	HT	SCHOOL	RPG	APG	PPG
Corliss Williamson*	SO	F	6-7	Arkansas	8.2	3.3	21.7
Corey Beck	JR	G	6-2	Arkansas	5.7	4.7	10.0
Grant Hill	SR	G/F	6-8	Duke	8.3	5.7	17.7
Antonio Lang	SR	F	6-8	Duke	6.2	0.8	14.5
Scotty Thurman	SO	G/F	6-6	Arkansas	3.5	3.5	16.2

All-Regional Teams

East

PLAYER	CL	POS	HT	SCHOOL	RPG	APG	PPG
Craig Brown*	SR	G	6-3	Florida	5.5	2.5	16.0
Dan Cross	JR	G	6-3	Florida	3.8	4.3	17.3
Bill Curley	SR	F	6-9	Boston College	9.8	1.0	18.5
Andrew DeClercq	JR	F/C	6-10	Florida	9.3	0.5	8.3
Howard Eisley	SR	G	6-3	Boston College	3.8	5.0	16.3

Midwest

PLAYER	CL	POS	HT	SCHOOL	RPG	APG	PPG
Juwan Howard*	JR	C	6-9	Michigan	12.8	1.0	29.0
Gary Collier	SR	F	6-4	Tulsa	5.0	2.7	31.3
Clint McDaniel	JR	G	6-4	Arkansas	4.3	0.8	9.3
Scotty Thurman	SO	G/F	6-6	Arkansas	2.0	3.8	17.0
Corliss Williamson	SO	F	6-7	Arkansas	7.0	3.0	19.5

Southeast

PLAYER	CL	POS	HT	SCHOOL	RPG	APG	PPG
Grant Hill*	SR	G/F	6-8	Duke	7.5	5.8	17.3
Jeff Capel	FR	G	6-5	Duke	3.8	4.8	11.8
Cuonzo Martin	JR	G	6-6	Purdue	4.5	1.5	18.0
Cherokee Parks	JR	F/C	6-11	Duke	9.3	0.5	15.5
Glenn Robinson	JR	F	6-8	Purdue	10.5	1.5	30.3

West

PLAYER	CL	POS	HT	SCHOOL	RPG	APG	PPG
Khalid Reeves*	SR	G	6-3	Arizona	4.5	3.3	29.3
Adrian Autry	SR	G	6-4	Syracuse	5.7	5.3	21.0
Melvin Booker	SR	G	6-2	Missouri	4.8	6.5	22.5
Lawrence Moten	JR	G/F	6-5	Syracuse	6.3	2.0	25.0
Damon Stoudamire	JR	G	5-10	Arizona	6.5	5.3	18.5

* Most outstanding player

1994 NCAA TOURNAMENT BOX SCORES

98-88 (SWEET 16)

	1H	2H	OT1
Missouri	36	43	19
Syracuse	36	43	9

MISSOURI	MIN	FG	3FG	FT	REB	A	ST	BL	PF	TP
Melvin Booker	43	7-13	2-4	8-9	4	9	3	0	4	24
Kelly Thames	30	9-15	1-1	5-7	8	1	1	0	2	24
Lamont Frazier	40	6-9	0-1	5-9	7	5	3	0	4	17
Paul O'Liney	36	4-11	1-6	5-7	1	2	2	0	1	14
Jevon Crudup	37	3-10	0-0	4-8	14	3	1	2	2	10
Mark Atkins	18	2-7	1-6	2-2	1	1	0	0	2	7
Julian Winfield	8	1-2	0-1	0-0	2	1	0	0	1	2
Marlo Finner	12	0-1	0-0	0-2	1	1	0	0	3	0
Jason Sutherland	1	0-0	0-0	0-0	0	0	0	0	1	0
TOTALS	**225**	**32-68**	**5-19**	**29-44**	**38**	**23**	**10**	**2**	**20**	**98**
Percentages		47.1	26.3	65.9						

Coach: Norm Stewart

SYRACUSE	MIN	FG	3FG	FT	REB	A	ST	BL	PF	TP
Adrian Autry	42	10-21	4-7	7-8	7	2	1	0	4	31
Lawrence Moten	42	11-22	3-9	4-4	6	1	2	0	4	29
Otis Hill	33	5-7	0-0	0-3	7	2	0	2	4	10
Lucious Jackson	35	4-10	0-4	0-2	4	3	0	1	5	8
John Wallace	40	2-8	0-0	2-2	7	4	1	0	4	6
Scott McCorkle	17	1-2	0-1	0-0	2	1	0	0	2	2
J.B. Reafsnyder	12	0-2	0-0	2-2	3	0	0	0	1	2
Lazarus Sims	4	0-1	0-0	0-0	1	1	0	0	0	0
TOTALS	**225**	**33-73**	**7-21**	**15-21**	**37**	**14**	**4**	**3**	**24**	**88**
Percentages		45.2	33.3	71.4						

Coach: Jim Boeheim

Officials: D Rutledge, T O'Neill, Bob Barnett **Technicals:** None **Attendance:** 15,157

82-70 (SWEET 16)

	1H	2H
Arizona	35	47
Louisville	26	44

ARIZONA	MIN	FG	3FG	FT	REB	A	ST	BL	PF	TP
Khalid Reeves	38	9-17	5-10	6-6	4	5	2	0	3	29
Reginald Geary	32	5-7	2-2	0-0	6	2	1	1	3	12
Damon Stoudamire	36	2-12	1-8	6-9	6	7	1	0	2	11
Joseph Blair	35	5-8	0-0	1-3	10	0	1	0	2	11
Ray Owes	34	5-10	0-0	1-2	8	1	0	1	1	11
Joseph McLean	9	1-4	1-3	0-0	0	1	0	0	1	3
Corey Williams	7	1-1	1-1	0-0	0	0	1	0	1	3
Dylan Rigdon	4	1-1	0-0	0-1	0	0	0	0	1	2
Kevin Flanagan	5	0-0	0-0	0-0	1	0	1	0	1	0
TOTALS	**200**	**29-60**	**10-24**	**14-21**	**35**	**16**	**7**	**2**	**15**	**82**
Percentages		48.3	41.7	66.7						

Coach: Lute Olson

LOUISVILLE	MIN	FG	3FG	FT	REB	A	ST	BL	PF	TP
Dwayne Morton	32	7-14	0-5	7-7	1	2	0	0	3	21
Jason Osborne	37	5-14	3-7	1-3	9	1	0	1	0	14
Greg Minor	33	6-13	1-5	0-0	12	0	0	1	5	13
DeJuan Wheat	32	2-11	2-6	2-2	0	5	1	0	3	8
Tick Rogers	21	3-8	0-2	0-0	4	0	1	0	3	6
Clifford Rozier	36	1-4	0-0	3-4	7	1	0	1	3	5
Alvin Sims	7	1-3	1-2	0-0	3	0	0	1	4	3
Brian Kiser	1	0-0	0-0	0-0	0	0	0	0	0	0
Matt Simons	1	0-0	0-0	0-0	0	0	0	0	1	0
TOTALS	**200**	**25-67**	**7-27**	**13-16**	**36**	**9**	**2**	**4**	**22**	**70**
Percentages		37.3	25.9	81.2						

Coach: Denny Crum

Officials: Ted Valentine, Bo Donato, Duke Edsall **Technicals:** None **Attendance:** 15,157

103-84 (SWEET 16)

	1H	2H
Arkansas	44	59
Tulsa	29	55

ARKANSAS	MIN	FG	3FG	FT	REB	A	ST	BL	PF	TP
Corliss Williamson	30	10-13	0-0	1-1	9	2	2	5	3	21
Scotty Thurman	29	9-13	3-5	0-0	0	5	2	1	1	21
Clint McDaniel	23	8-9	3-4	0-0	6	2	0	0	0	19
Corey Beck	31	4-7	0-1	5-7	4	7	0	0	4	13
Dwight Stewart	25	2-3	2-2	2-2	4	4	0	0	4	8
Lee Wilson	14	4-7	0-0	0-1	8	1	0	0	1	8
Darnell Robinson	18	2-4	0-1	2-4	4	2	2	1	2	6
Davor Rimac	11	1-3	1-3	2-2	0	3	0	0	2	5
Ken Biley	3	1-1	0-0	0-0	0	1	0	0	1	2
Alex Dillard	9	0-2	0-0	0-0	0	4	0	0	1	0
Elmer Martin	4	0-0	0-0	0-0	1	0	0	0	1	0
Ray Biggers	3	0-0	0-0	0-0	0	0	0	0	1	0
TOTALS	**200**	**41-62**	**9-16**	**12-17**	**36**	**31**	**6**	**7**	**21**	**103**
Percentages		66.1	56.2	70.6						

Coach: Nolan Richardson

TULSA	MIN	FG	3FG	FT	REB	A	ST	BL	PF	TP
Gary Collier	39	12-26	6-13	5-5	6	1	0	1	1	35
Shea Seals	35	4-17	2-10	9-9	11	6	2	0	3	19
Lou Dawkins	28	6-8	0-2	2-5	6	3	2	0	3	14
Alvin Williamson	38	2-10	2-8	0-0	1	5	4	0	2	6
Dewayne Bonner	7	1-1	0-0	4-4	1	1	1	0	1	6
Kwanza Johnson	22	1-5	0-0	0-0	4	3	1	0	2	2
Kevin Grawer	6	0-3	0-3	2-2	0	0	0	0	1	2
J.R. Rollo	13	0-3	0-0	0-2	1	1	0	1	2	0
Rafael Maldonado	8	0-1	0-0	0-0	0	0	2	0	1	0
Craig Hernadi	3	0-0	0-0	0-0	1	0	0	0	0	0
Jay Malham	1	0-0	0-0	0-0	0	0	0	0	0	0
TOTALS	**200**	**26-74**	**10-36**	**22-27**	**31**	**20**	**12**	**2**	**16**	**84**
Percentages		35.1	27.8	81.5						

Coach: Tubby Smith

Officials: Lenny Wirtz, Sam Lickliter, Larry Rose **Technicals:** None **Attendance:** 16,297

78-71 (SWEET 16)

	1H	2H
Michigan	39	39
Maryland	32	39

MICHIGAN	MIN	FG	3FG	FT	REB	A	ST	BL	PF	TP
Juwan Howard	36	9-16	0-0	6-9	11	2	1	1	5	24
Jalen Rose	40	5-12	1-2	5-9	5	4	0	0	1	16
Jimmy King	31	5-9	1-1	2-5	2	1	1	0	4	13
Dugan Fife	40	3-7	2-5	4-4	7	4	3	2	2	12
Ray Jackson	18	4-7	1-2	2-4	6	0	2	0	4	11
Olivier Saint-Jean	13	1-3	0-0	0-0	6	1	1	1	3	2
Makhtar N'diaye	13	0-2	0-1	0-0	2	1	0	3	4	0
Leon Derricks	8	0-2	0-0	0-0	2	2	0	0	3	0
Bobby Crawford	1	0-0	0-0	0-0	0	0	0	0	0	0
TOTALS	**200**	**27-58**	**5-11**	**19-31**	**41**	**15**	**8**	**7**	**26**	**78**
Percentages		46.6	45.5	61.3						

Coach: Steve Fisher

MARYLAND	MIN	FG	3FG	FT	REB	A	ST	BL	PF	TP
Keith Booth	29	7-11	0-0	3-11	9	0	2	1	5	17
Joe Smith	34	3-8	0-0	6-10	14	0	0	3	3	12
Duane Simpkins	36	3-13	0-4	5-5	4	5	2	0	3	11
Johnny Rhodes	32	4-14	1-5	1-3	7	6	4	0	4	10
Exree Hipp	36	4-12	1-6	0-0	6	0	2	0	4	9
Mario Lucas	13	2-6	1-3	1-2	1	0	1	0	3	6
Nick Bosnic	9	1-1	1-1	0-0	0	0	0	0	1	3
Wayne Bristol	8	0-1	0-1	3-4	1	0	0	0	2	3
Donny Judd	1	0-0	0-0	0-0	1	0	0	0	0	0
Matt Raydo	1	0-1	0-1	0-0	0	0	0	0	0	0
Kurtis Shultz	1	0-0	0-0	0-0	0	0	0	0	0	0
TOTALS	**200**	**24-67**	**4-21**	**19-35**	**43**	**11**	**11**	**4**	**25**	**71**
Percentages		35.8	19.0	54.3						

Coach: Gary Williams

Officials: Larry Lembo, William Sanchez, David Hall **Technicals:** None **Attendance:** 16,297

77-68 (SWEET 16)

	1H	2H
Boston College	40	37
Indiana	38	30

BOSTON COLLEGE	MIN	FG	3FG	FT	REB	A	ST	BL	PF	TP
Howard Eisley	37	7-12	4-6	0-0	3	4	0	0	3	18
Malcolm Huckaby	38	5-8	2-4	3-4	4	4	2	0	2	15
Gerrod Abram	33	5-10	2-3	3-4	3	2	1	0	0	15
Bill Curley	38	3-11	0-0	5-8	13	0	2	2	3	11
Mark Molinksy	12	3-4	2-3	0-0	1	2	0	0	3	8
Danya Abrams	27	2-10	0-0	2-6	2	2	2	0	2	6
Kevin Hrobowski	14	2-4	0-0	0-0	5	0	0	0	0	4
Paul Grant	1	0-0	0-0	0-0	0	0	0	0	0	0
TOTALS	**200**	**27-59**	**10-16**	**13-22**	**31**	**14**	**7**	**2**	**13**	**77**
Percentages		45.8	62.5	59.1						

Coach: Jim O'Brien

INDIANA	MIN	FG	3FG	FT	REB	A	ST	BL	PF	TP
Pat Graham	32	6-11	2-3	2-2	5	1	0	0	3	16
Brian Evans	40	5-12	2-7	2-2	6	5	2	1	3	14
Alan Henderson	39	6-11	0-0	0-0	6	0	1	2	4	12
Todd Leary	38	5-11	2-6	0-0	4	4	1	0	3	12
Damon Bailey	38	5-10	0-1	0-0	2	9	2	0	3	10
Todd Lindeman	6	2-3	0-0	0-1	1	0	0	0	0	4
Steve Hart	6	0-0	0-0	0-0	0	0	0	0	1	0
Pat Knight	1	0-1	0-0	0-0	0	0	0	0	0	0
TOTALS	**200**	**29-59**	**6-17**	**4-5**	**24**	**19**	**6**	**3**	**17**	**68**
Percentages		49.2	35.3	80.0						

Coach: Bob Knight

Officials: Charles Range, Jim Stupin, Curtis Shaw **Technicals:** None **Attendance:** 15,217

69-60 (SWEET 16)

	1H	2H	OT1
Florida	28	29	12
Connecticut	34	23	3

FLORIDA	MIN	FG	3FG	FT	REB	A	ST	BL	PF	TP
Dan Cross	43	5-14	0-2	7-11	4	4	4	0	4	17
Craig Brown	41	7-14	2-5	1-2	9	4	0	0	1	17
Dametri Hill	39	5-12	0-1	5-7	5	0	1	0	2	15
Andrew DeClercq	30	4-8	0-0	1-2	6	2	2	0	4	9
Brian Thompson	22	2-7	0-0	0-1	3	2	2	0	0	4
Martti Kuisma	15	1-5	1-4	0-0	2	0	0	0	0	3
Jason Anderson	23	0-4	0-0	2-2	5	1	1	1	4	2
Svein Dyrkolboin	6	1-2	0-0	0-0	1	1	0	0	1	2
Greg Williams	6	0-1	0-0	0-0	1	0	2	0	0	0
TOTALS	**225**	**25-67**	**3-12**	**16-25**	**36**	**14**	**12**	**1**	**16**	**69**
Percentages		37.3	25.0	64.0						

Coach: Lon Kruger

CONNECTICUT	MIN	FG	3FG	FT	REB	A	ST	BL	PF	TP
Doron Sheffer	39	7-16	2-6	2-2	5	3	4	1	2	18
Donyell Marshall	44	5-13	0-5	6-10	13	3	0	4	1	16
Donny Marshall	30	3-7	0-2	4-4	3	1	1	0	3	10
Kevin Ollie	39	1-6	0-2	4-4	4	8	1	0	1	6
Travis Knight	26	3-5	0-0	0-2	6	0	0	3	5	6
Ray Allen	20	1-5	0-2	0-0	4	0	0	0	3	2
Rudy Johnson	5	1-2	0-0	0-0	2	0	0	0	1	2
Eric Hayward	15	0-0	0-0	0-0	3	0	0	1	2	0
Brian Fair	4	0-1	0-0	0-0	0	0	0	0	0	0
Kirk King	2	0-0	0-0	0-0	0	0	0	1	2	0
Nantambu Willingham	1	0-0	0-0	0-0	1	0	0	0	0	0
TOTALS	**225**	**21-55**	**2-17**	**16-22**	**41**	**15**	**6**	**10**	**20**	**60**
Percentages		38.2	11.8	72.7						

Coach: Jim Calhoun

Officials: Tom Rucker, Ted Hillary, Mike Sanzere **Technicals:** None **Attendance:** 15,217

83-78 — SWEET 16

	1H	2H
Purdue	44	39
Kansas	42	36

PURDUE	MIN	FG	3FG	FT	REB	A	ST	BL	PF	TP
Glenn Robinson	38	15-33	6-10	8-9	7	2	3	1	3	44
Cuonzo Martin	37	9-18	8-13	3-3	5	0	1	0	0	29
Matt Waddell	35	2-8	1-3	0-1	1	7	2	0	2	5
Porter Roberts	30	0-3	0-1	3-4	7	2	0	0	2	3
Ian Stanback	20	1-2	0-0	0-0	4	1	0	0	2	2
Brandon Brantley	17	0-1	0-0	0-0	4	0	0	1	3	0
Linc Darner	11	0-0	0-0	0-0	3	1	0	0	1	0
Justin Jennings	6	0-0	0-0	0-0	3	0	0	0	1	0
Herb Dove	5	0-0	0-0	0-0	0	0	1	0	2	0
Cornelius McNairy	1	0-0	0-0	0-0	0	0	0	0	0	0
TOTALS	200	27-65	15-27	14-17	34	13	7	2	16	83
Percentages		41.5	55.6	82.4						

Coach: Gene Keady

KANSAS	MIN	FG	3FG	FT	REB	A	ST	BL	PF	TP
Sean Pearson	19	7-13	4-8	2-2	3	1	3	0	3	20
Steve Woodberry	30	6-10	3-5	1-3	3	4	2	0	1	16
Richard Scott	27	6-12	0-0	3-4	10	1	0	0	3	15
Greg Ostertag	20	4-7	0-0	0-0	5	0	0	4	2	8
Scot Pollard	20	3-4	0-0	0-0	3	0	2	1	1	6
Greg Gurley	16	2-3	1-2	0-0	3	1	1	0	0	5
Jacque Vaughn	27	1-3	0-0	2-7	0	6	1	0	3	4
Patrick Richey	17	2-7	0-1	0-0	7	2	1	0	1	4
Calvin Rayford	15	0-2	0-1	0-0	1	7	1	0	0	0
B.J. Williams	9	0-1	0-0	0-0	1	0	0	0	0	0
TOTALS	200	31-62	8-17	8-16	36	22	11	5	14	78
Percentages		50.0	47.1	50.0						

Coach: Roy Williams

Officials: Ed Hightower, Rusty Herring, Frank Scagliotta
Technicals: None
Attendance: 22,896

59-49 — SWEET 16

	1H	2H
Duke	25	34
Marquette	26	23

DUKE	MIN	FG	3FG	FT	REB	A	ST	BL	PF	TP
Grant Hill	38	10-16	1-3	1-3	9	6	1	0	2	22
Cherokee Parks	33	5-12	0-0	2-2	8	0	3	5	2	12
Jeff Capel	36	4-8	1-2	0-0	4	4	0	1	4	9
Antonio Lang	29	2-5	0-0	3-7	3	1	0	1	3	7
Chris Collins	35	2-6	1-4	0-0	0	2	1	0	0	5
Erik Meek	14	1-2	0-0	2-2	5	1	0	0	0	4
Marty Clark	10	0-3	0-1	0-0	0	0	0	0	0	0
Greg Newton	3	0-0	0-0	0-0	1	0	1	0	2	0
Joey Beard	1	0-0	0-0	0-0	0	0	0	0	0	0
Carmen Wallace	1	0-0	0-0	0-0	1	0	0	1	0	0
TOTALS	200	24-52	3-10	8-14	31	14	6	8	13	59
Percentages		46.2	30.0	57.1						

Coach: Mike Krzyzewski

MARQUETTE	MIN	FG	3FG	FT	REB	A	ST	BL	PF	TP
Roney Eford	39	3-14	2-6	4-4	11	2	0	1	3	12
Jim McIlvaine	31	4-13	0-0	3-6	5	0	1	1	1	11
Damon Key	26	3-12	1-2	1-2	8	1	0	0	3	8
Tony Miller	39	2-6	2-4	0-0	5	6	1	0	4	6
Robb Logterman	34	2-3	2-2	0-0	1	3	0	0	1	6
Amal McCaskill	21	3-5	0-0	0-0	6	1	1	1	3	6
Anthony Pieper	8	0-1	0-0	0-0	0	0	0	0	1	0
Faisal Abraham	2	0-0	0-0	0-0	0	1	0	0	0	0
TOTALS	200	17-54	7-14	8-12	36	14	3	3	16	49
Percentages		31.5	50.0	66.7						

Coach: Kevin O'Neill

Officials: Jody Silvester, Gene Monje, Samuel Kroft
Technicals: None
Attendance: 22,896

92-72 — ELITE 8

	1H	2H
Arizona	48	44
Missouri	34	38

ARIZONA	MIN	FG	3FG	FT	REB	A	ST	BL	PF	TP
Damon Stoudamire	39	8-14	4-6	7-8	10	4	0	0	2	27
Khalid Reeves	32	9-17	0-5	8-10	4	1	2	0	4	26
Reginald Geary	39	2-6	0-2	10-11	6	5	1	2	3	14
Joseph Blair	27	4-7	0-0	1-2	8	0	0	1	2	9
Ray Owes	37	0-10	0-1	5-6	10	2	1	1	2	5
Joseph McLean	6	1-1	1-1	2-2	1	0	0	0	0	5
Corey Williams	7	2-2	0-0	0-2	3	0	0	1	0	4
Jarvis Kelley	1	1-1	0-0	0-0	0	0	0	0	0	2
Kevin Flanagan	7	0-0	0-0	0-0	2	0	0	0	3	0
Dylan Rigdon	3	0-0	0-0	0-0	2	1	0	0	1	0
Andy Brown	1	0-0	0-0	0-0	0	0	0	0	0	0
Jason Richey	1	0-2	0-0	0-0	0	0	0	0	0	0
TOTALS	200	27-60	5-15	33-41	46	13	4	5	17	92
Percentages		45.0	33.3	80.5						

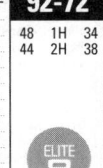

Coach: Lute Olson

MISSOURI	MIN	FG	3FG	FT	REB	A	ST	BL	PF	TP
Melvin Booker	35	5-12	1-6	3-4	5	5	0	0	4	14
Jevon Crudup	27	7-13	0-0	0-2	6	4	2	2	5	14
Paul O'Liney	27	5-18	2-10	1-2	3	1	0	0	3	13
Lamont Frazier	28	4-7	0-0	1-3	7	1	1	0	4	9
Kelly Thames	24	3-7	2-3	1-2	5	0	0	1	4	9
Marlo Finner	11	3-6	0-1	0-0	5	0	0	0	0	6
Mark Atkins	15	1-13	1-9	1-2	6	0	0	0	1	4
Chip Walther	1	1-1	1-1	0-0	0	0	0	0	0	3
Julian Winfield	11	0-1	0-0	0-0	4	0	0	0	1	0
Jason Sutherland	8	0-2	0-0	0-0	0	0	0	0	2	0
Reggie Smith	7	0-2	0-2	0-0	1	1	2	0	2	0
Derek Grimm	5	0-0	0-0	0-0	3	0	0	0	1	0
Jed Frost	1	0-1	0-1	0-0	1	1	0	0	0	0
TOTALS	200	29-83	7-33	7-15	46	13	5	3	27	72
Percentages		34.9	21.2	46.7						

Coach: Norm Stewart

Officials: Andre Pattillo, Scott Thornley, Phil Bova
Technicals: None
Attendance: 15,517

76-68 — ELITE 8

	1H	2H
Arkansas	40	36
Michigan	31	37

ARKANSAS	MIN	FG	3FG	FT	REB	A	ST	BL	PF	TP
Scotty Thurman	31	7-13	4-8	2-2	2	1	1	0	3	20
Darnell Robinson	28	6-13	0-0	2-3	4	1	0	0	2	14
Corliss Williamson	40	6-10	0-0	0-2	6	3	1	0	1	12
Clint McDaniel	31	3-7	3-6	3-4	7	0	0	0	3	12
Dwight Stewart	22	2-4	1-2	2-4	3	2	0	0	5	7
Alex Dillard	7	2-6	2-5	0-0	1	3	0	0	0	6
Corey Beck	28	1-4	0-0	2-2	2	5	2	0	2	4
Elmer Martin	3	0-0	0-0	1-2	0	0	0	0	1	1
Lee Wilson	7	0-0	0-0	0-0	2	0	0	1	1	0
Davor Rimac	2	0-0	0-0	0-0	0	0	0	0	0	0
Ray Biggers	1	0-0	0-0	0-0	0	0	0	0	0	0
TOTALS	200	27-57	10-21	12-19	27	15	4	2	17	76
Percentages		47.4	47.6	63.2						

Coach: Nolan Richardson

MICHIGAN	MIN	FG	3FG	FT	REB	A	ST	BL	PF	TP
Juwan Howard	37	11-17	0-0	8-11	13	0	1	0	3	30
Jalen Rose	39	5-19	1-7	2-5	8	1	1	0	4	13
Ray Jackson	33	6-8	0-0	0-0	5	2	1	0	4	12
Jimmy King	32	2-7	1-2	0-0	5	4	1	1	5	5
Dugan Fife	37	1-8	0-6	2-2	3	7	3	0	1	4
Olivier Saint-Jean	11	1-3	1-1	1-2	3	0	1	1	2	4
Makhtar N'diaye	8	0-2	0-1	0-0	2	0	0	0	2	0
Leon Derricks	2	0-0	0-0	0-0	0	0	0	0	0	0
Bobby Crawford	1	0-0	0-0	0-0	0	0	0	0	1	0
TOTALS	200	26-64	3-17	13-20	39	14	8	2	22	68
Percentages		40.6	17.6	65.0						

Coach: Steve Fisher

Officials: James Burr, John Hughes, Dave Libbey
Technicals: Arkansas (bench)
Attendance: 16,297

74-66 — ELITE 8

	1H	2H
Florida	35	39
Boston College	33	33

FLORIDA	MIN	FG	3FG	FT	REB	A	ST	BL	PF	TP
Craig Brown	37	7-14	5-9	2-2	5	4	2	2	3	21
Andrew DeClercq	30	8-11	0-0	0-0	13	0	2	1	3	16
Dan Cross	36	6-14	0-3	2-4	1	6	3	0	1	14
Dametri Hill	23	4-5	0-0	4-4	1	0	0	0	5	12
Jason Anderson	19	3-3	0-0	1-2	4	3	2	0	2	7
Brian Thompson	21	1-4	0-0	0-0	8	4	1	0	1	2
Greg Williams	8	0-1	0-0	2-4	0	0	1	0	2	2
Svein Dyrkolboin	11	0-0	0-0	0-0	0	0	1	1	2	0
Martti Kuisma	11	0-5	0-3	0-0	1	0	0	0	2	0
Tony Mickens	4	0-0	0-0	0-0	0	1	0	0	1	0
TOTALS	200	29-57	5-15	11-16	33	18	12	4	22	74
Percentages		50.9	33.3	68.8						

Coach: Lon Kruger

BOSTON COLLEGE	MIN	FG	3FG	FT	REB	A	ST	BL	PF	TP
Bill Curley	38	8-16	0-0	4-6	7	0	0	0	2	20
Howard Eisley	40	4-11	2-5	9-9	4	5	3	0	0	19
Danya Abrams	32	4-10	0-0	6-8	9	0	0	0	3	14
Gerrod Abram	36	3-8	2-6	1-2	3	3	1	1	5	9
Paul Grant	3	1-1	0-0	0-0	0	0	0	0	0	2
Malcolm Huckaby	39	0-5	0-4	1-2	1	5	1	0	3	1
Kevin Hrobowski	7	0-1	0-0	1-2	1	0	2	0	0	1
Mark Molinksy	5	0-0	0-0	0-0	1	0	0	0	0	0
TOTALS	200	20-52	4-15	22-29	26	13	7	1	13	66
Percentages		38.5	26.7	75.9						

Coach: Jim O'Brien

Officials: Bill Kennedy, Gerry Donaghy, Mark Reischling
Technicals: None
Attendance: 15,217

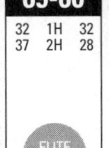

69-60 — ELITE 8

	1H	2H
Duke	32	37
Purdue	32	28

DUKE	MIN	FG	3FG	FT	REB	A	ST	BL	PF	TP
Jeff Capel	36	7-12	3-3	2-5	4	7	0	0	1	19
Antonio Lang	36	7-13	0-0	5-8	5	0	0	1	3	19
Cherokee Parks	36	5-10	0-0	5-6	10	0	1	3	0	15
Grant Hill	30	4-12	1-1	2-2	7	5	1	0	4	11
Chris Collins	38	1-6	0-5	3-5	4	2	4	0	1	5
Marty Clark	14	0-3	0-2	0-0	2	2	1	0	0	0
Erik Meek	5	0-0	0-0	0-0	3	0	0	0	1	0
Joey Beard	1	0-0	0-0	0-0	0	0	0	0	0	0
Stan Brunson	1	0-0	0-0	0-0	0	0	0	0	0	0
Tony Moore	1	0-0	0-0	0-0	0	0	0	0	0	0
Greg Newton	1	0-0	0-0	0-0	0	0	0	0	0	0
Carmen Wallace	1	0-0	0-0	0-0	0	0	0	0	0	0
TOTALS	200	24-56	4-11	17-26	35	16	7	4	10	69
Percentages		42.9	36.4	65.4						

Coach: Mike Krzyzewski

PURDUE	MIN	FG	3FG	FT	REB	A	ST	BL	PF	TP
Matt Waddell	33	6-11	2-3	2-2	2	2	0	0	3	16
Glenn Robinson	40	6-22	0-6	1-3	13	1	0	0	5	13
Cuonzo Martin	37	5-14	2-7	0-0	3	1	1	1	1	12
Ian Stanback	32	4-6	0-0	0-0	9	2	0	0	3	8
Porter Roberts	28	3-5	1-3	0-0	4	4	2	0	4	7
Herb Dove	12	1-2	0-0	0-0	4	0	0	0	3	2
Justin Jennings	3	1-2	0-0	0-0	1	0	0	0	0	2
Brandon Brantley	8	0-1	0-0	0-0	0	0	0	0	2	0
Linc Darner	7	0-0	0-0	0-0	1	2	1	0	0	0
TOTALS	200	26-63	5-19	3-5	37	12	4	1	21	60
Percentages		41.3	26.3	60.0						

Coach: Gene Keady

Officials: John Clougherty, Gerald Boudreaux, John Cahill
Technicals: Purdue (bench)
Attendance: 23,370

ANNUAL REVIEW

91-82 (Final 4)

	1H	2H
Arkansas	41	50
Arizona	41	41

ARKANSAS	MIN	FG	3FG	FT	REB	A	ST	BL	PF	TP
Corliss Williamson	37	11-18	0-0	7-9	13	5	2	1	0	29
Scotty Thurman	36	5-13	0-5	4-6	8	5	0	1	2	14
Clint McDaniel	28	4-10	2-6	2-2	5	3	1	0	3	12
Darnell Robinson	26	5-9	0-1	2-3	1	2	0	3	2	12
Corey Beck	27	2-5	1-1	4-8	4	4	0	0	4	9
Dwight Stewart	23	2-5	2-3	1-2	5	0	1	0	5	7
Alex Dillard	12	2-7	2-7	0-0	1	0	0	0	0	6
Lee Wilson	6	1-2	0-0	0-2	4	0	0	0	0	2
Davor Rimac	5	0-1	0-1	0-0	1	0	0	0	0	0
TOTALS	**200**	**32-70**	**7-24**	**20-32**	**42**	**19**	**4**	**5**	**16**	**91**
Percentages		45.7	29.2	62.5						

Coach: Nolan Richardson

ARIZONA	MIN	FG	3FG	FT	REB	A	ST	BL	PF	TP
Khalid Reeves	34	6-19	0-9	8-9	4	4	0	0	4	20
Damon Stoudamire	37	5-24	2-13	4-4	8	6	1	0	4	16
Ray Owes	35	7-15	0-1	2-2	12	0	0	0	5	16
Corey Williams	12	5-7	4-6	0-0	6	1	1	0	0	14
Joseph Blair	36	4-7	0-0	0-1	14	1	3	0	3	8
Reginald Geary	36	2-6	0-3	0-0	4	6	4	1	4	4
Kevin Flanagan	4	1-1	0-0	0-0	0	0	0	0	1	2
Joseph McLean	2	1-1	0-0	0-0	0	0	0	0	2	2
Andy Brown	1	0-0	0-0	0-0	0	0	0	0	0	0
Jarvis Kelley	1	0-0	0-0	0-0	0	0	0	0	0	0
Jason Richey	1	0-0	0-0	0-0	0	0	0	0	0	0
Dylan Rigdon	1	0-0	0-0	0-0	0	0	0	0	0	0
TOTALS	**200**	**31-80**	**6-32**	**14-16**	**48**	**18**	**9**	**1**	**23**	**82**
Percentages		38.8	18.8	87.5						

Coach: Lute Olson

Officials: T Rucker, Te Hillary, Mi Sanzere
Technicals
None
Attendance
23,674

70-65 (Final 4)

	1H	2H
Duke	32	38
Florida	39	26

DUKE	MIN	FG	3FG	FT	REB	A	ST	BL	PF	TP
Grant Hill	40	8-13	3-4	6-8	6	5	0	2	2	25
Antonio Lang	28	3-6	0-0	6-6	5	0	0	0	3	12
Cherokee Parks	40	4-11	0-0	3-4	11	2	2	3	1	11
Jeff Capel	33	3-10	2-4	1-1	3	0	0	0	3	9
Marty Clark	24	3-6	2-3	0-0	3	3	4	1	4	8
Erik Meek	10	0-1	0-0	3-4	2	0	0	0	1	3
Chris Collins	24	1-4	0-3	0-0	1	1	0	0	0	2
Greg Newton	1	0-0	0-0	0-0	0	0	0	0	2	0
TOTALS	**200**	**22-51**	**7-14**	**19-23**	**31**	**11**	**6**	**6**	**16**	**70**
Percentages		43.1	50.0	82.6						

Coach: Mike Krzyzewski

FLORIDA	MIN	FG	3FG	FT	REB	A	ST	BL	PF	TP
Dametri Hill	30	6-17	0-0	4-6	9	3	2	0	1	16
Andrew DeClercq	29	7-11	0-1	0-2	7	1	1	1	2	14
Dan Cross	39	3-14	2-5	2-4	6	8	2	0	2	10
Jason Anderson	21	4-6	0-0	1-2	4	0	0	0	4	9
Craig Brown	35	3-9	2-3	0-0	6	5	3	0	1	8
Brian Thompson	20	1-3	0-0	2-4	3	0	1	0	4	4
Martti Kuisma	12	0-2	0-0	2-2	1	0	0	0	1	2
Greg Williams	5	1-1	0-0	0-0	0	0	1	0	1	2
Svein Dyrkolboin	9	0-0	0-0	0-0	1	0	0	0	0	0
TOTALS	**200**	**25-63**	**4-9**	**11-20**	**37**	**17**	**10**	**1**	**16**	**65**
Percentages		39.7	44.4	55.0						

Coach: Lon Kruger

Officials: Jim Stupin, Dave Libbey, Ed Hightower
Technicals:
None
Attendance:
23,674

76-72 (NCAA Final 1994)

	1H	2H
Arkansas	34	42
Duke	33	39

ARKANSAS	MIN	FG	3FG	FT	REB	A	ST	BL	PF	TP
Corliss Williamson	35	10-24	0-0	3-5	8	3	2	2	3	23
Scotty Thurman	36	6-13	3-5	0-0	5	1	1	0	2	15
Corey Beck	35	5-11	0-1	5-8	10	4	1	0	3	15
Clint McDaniel	32	2-5	1-3	2-4	2	3	3	0	2	7
Dwight Stewart	29	3-11	0-5	0-0	9	4	4	0	3	6
Alex Dillard	8	1-5	1-4	1-2	1	0	0	0	1	4
Lee Wilson	5	2-2	0-0	0-0	4	0	0	0	1	4
Darnell Robinson	12	1-5	0-0	0-0	2	0	0	0	1	2
Davor Rimac	5	0-1	0-0	0-0	0	0	0	1	0	0
Ken Biley	3	0-0	0-0	0-0	0	0	0	0	1	0
TOTALS	**200**	**30-77**	**5-18**	**11-19**	**41**	**15**	**11**	**3**	**17**	**76**
Percentages		39.0	27.8	57.9						

Coach: Nolan Richardson

DUKE	MIN	FG	3FG	FT	REB	A	ST	BL	PF	TP
Antonio Lang	34	6-9	0-0	3-3	5	3	0	1	5	15
Jeff Capel	35	6-16	2-6	0-0	5	4	1	0	3	14
Cherokee Parks	30	7-10	0-0	0-1	7	0	0	2	3	14
Grant Hill	38	4-11	1-4	3-5	14	6	3	3	3	12
Chris Collins	34	4-11	4-8	0-0	0	1	1	1	1	12
Marty Clark	15	1-6	0-2	1-2	1	3	0	0	2	3
Erik Meek	14	1-2	0-0	0-0	7	0	0	0	1	2
TOTALS	**200**	**29-65**	**7-20**	**7-11**	**39**	**17**	**5**	**7**	**18**	**72**
Percentages		44.6	35.0	63.6						

Coach: Mike Krzyzewski

Officials: Jame Burr, Jody Silvester, Ted Valentine
Technicals:
None
Attendance:
23,674

National Invitation Tournament (NIT)

First round: New Orleans d. Texas A&M 79-73, Vanderbilt d. Oklahoma 77-67, Fresno State d. Southern California 79-76 (OT), Bradley d. Murray State 66-58, Northwestern d. DePaul 69-68, Xavier d. Miami (OH) 80-68, Duquesne d. Charlotte 75-73, Siena d. Georgia Tech 76-68, Tulane d. Evansville 76-63, Clemson d. Southern Miss 96-85, Old Dominion d. Manhattan 76-74, West Virginia d. Davidson 85-69, Gonzaga d. Stanford 80-76, Kansas State d. Mississippi State 78-69, BYU d. Arizona State 74-67, Villanova d. Canisius 103-79
Second round: Clemson d. West Virginia 96-79, Vanderbilt d. New Orleans 78-59, Villanova d. Duquesne 82-66, Xavier d. Northwestern 83-79 (OT), Fresno State d. BYU 68-66, Kansas State d. Gonzaga 66-64, Bradley d. Old Dominion 79-75, Siena d. Tulane 89-79
Third round: Villanova d. Xavier 76-74, Vanderbilt d. Clemson 89-74, Siena d. Bradley 75-62, Kansas State d. Fresno State 115-77
Semifinals: Vanderbilt d. Kansas State 82-76, Villanova d. Siena 66-58
Third place: Siena d. Kansas State 92-79
Championship: Villanova d. Vanderbilt 80-73
MVP: Doremus Bennerman, Siena

1994-95: They're Back

It took 20 years for UCLA to win its first championship without John Wooden. Jim Harrick's Bruins beat defending national champion Arkansas, 89-78, at the Seattle Kingdome behind Tournament MOP Ed O'Bannon's 30 points and 17 rebounds. His brother Charles added 11 points and nine boards.

Both the No. 1-seed Bruins (31–2) and No. 2-seed Razorbacks (32–7) nearly didn't make it to Seattle. In the second round, UCLA trailed Missouri, 74-73, with 4.8 seconds left when 5'10" Tyus Edney drove the length of the floor and laid the ball in off the glass at the buzzer. Arkansas barely escaped a first-round matchup against Texas Southern, 79-78, then had to go to overtime before beating both Syracuse and Memphis.

For the first time since the Tournament expanded to 16 teams in 1951, the Big Ten did not have a representative reach the Sweet 16. Maryland sophomore Joe Smith (20.8 ppg, 10.6 rpg) was the Naismith Player of the Year and became the No. 1 pick in the NBA draft (Golden State Warriors).

Major Conference Standings

AM. WEST

	Conference			Overall		
	W	L	PCT	W	L	PCT
Southern Utah	6	0	1.000	17	11	.607
Cal St. Northridge⊗	4	2	.667	8	20	.321
Cal St. Sacramento	2	4	.333	6	21	.222
Cal Poly	0	6	.000	1	26	.037

Tournament: **Southern Utah d. Cal St. Northridge 83-82**
Tournament MVP: **Sean Allen**, Southern Utah

ACC

	Conference			Overall		
	W	L	PCT	W	L	PCT
Wake Forest⊕	12	4	.750	26	6	.813
North Carolina○	12	4	.750	28	6	.824
Maryland○	12	4	.750	26	8	.765
Virginia○	12	4	.750	25	9	.735
Georgia Tech	8	8	.500	18	12	.600
Clemson□	5	11	.313	15	13	.536
Florida State	5	11	.313	12	15	.444
NC State	4	12	.250	12	15	.444
Duke	2	14	.125	13	18	.419

Tournament: **Wake Forest d. North Carolina 82-80 (OT)**
Tournament MVP: **Randolph Childress**, Wake Forest

ATLANTIC 10

	Conference			Overall		
	W	L	PCT	W	L	PCT
Massachusetts⊕	13	3	.813	29	5	.853
Temple○	10	6	.625	19	11	.633
George Washington□	10	6	.625	18	14	.563
Saint Joseph's□	9	7	.563	17	12	.586
St. Bonaventure□	9	7	.563	18	13	.581
West Virginia	7	9	.438	13	13	.500
Rutgers	7	9	.438	13	15	.464
Duquesne	5	11	.313	10	18	.357
Rhode Island	2	14	.125	7	20	.259

Tournament: **Massachusetts d. Temple 63-44**
Tournament MOP: **Lou Roe**, Massachusetts

BIG EAST

	Conference			Overall		
	W	L	PCT	W	L	PCT
Connecticut○	16	2	.889	28	5	.848
Villanova⊕	14	4	.778	25	8	.758
Syracuse○	12	6	.667	20	10	.667
Georgetown○	11	7	.611	21	10	.677
Miami (FL)□	9	9	.500	15	13	.536
Providence□	7	11	.389	17	13	.567
Seton Hall□	7	11	.389	16	14	.533
St. John's□	7	11	.389	14	14	.500
Pittsburgh	5	13	.278	10	18	.357
Boston College	2	16	.111	9	19	.321

Tournament: **Villanova d. Connecticut 94-78**
Tournament MVP: **Kerry Kittles**, Villanova

BIG EIGHT

	Conference			Overall		
	W	L	PCT	W	L	PCT
Kansas○	11	3	.786	25	6	.806
Oklahoma State⊕	10	4	.714	27	10	.730
Oklahoma○	9	5	.643	23	9	.719
Missouri○	8	6	.571	20	9	.690
Iowa State○	6	8	.429	23	11	.676
Colorado□	5	9	.357	15	13	.536
Nebraska□	4	10	.286	18	14	.563
Kansas State	3	11	.214	12	15	.444

Tournament: **Oklahoma State d. Iowa State 62-53**
Tournament MVP: **Bryant Reeves**, Oklahoma State

BIG SKY

	Conference			Overall		
	W	L	PCT	W	L	PCT
Weber State⊕	11	3	.786	21	9	.700
Montana□	11	3	.786	21	9	.700
Montana State	8	6	.571	21	8	.724
Idaho State	7	7	.500	18	10	.643
Boise State	7	7	.500	17	10	.630
Idaho	6	8	.429	12	15	.444
Northern Arizona⊗	4	10	.286	8	18	.308
Eastern Washington	2	12	.143	6	20	.231

Tournament: **Weber State d. Montana 84-62**
Tournament MVP: **Ruben Nembhard**, Weber State

BIG SOUTH

	Conference			Overall		
	W	L	PCT	W	L	PCT
UNC Greensboro	14	2	.875	23	6	.793
Charleston So.	12	4	.750	19	10	.655
UMBC	10	6	.625	13	14	.481
Radford	9	7	.563	16	12	.571
Liberty	7	9	.438	12	16	.429
UNC Asheville	7	9	.438	11	16	.407
Towson	6	10	.375	12	15	.444
Winthrop	4	12	.250	7	20	.259
Coastal Carolina	3	13	.188	6	20	.231

Tournament: **Charleston So. d. UNC Greensboro 68-67**
Tournament MVP: **Eric Burks**, Charleston So.

BIG TEN

	Conference			Overall		
	W	L	PCT	W	L	PCT
Purdue⊕	15	3	.833	25	7	.781
Michigan State○	14	4	.778	22	6	.786
Indiana○	11	7	.611	19	12	.613
Michigan○	11	7	.611	17	14	.548
Illinois○	10	8	.556	19	12	.613
Minnesota○⊗	10	8	.556	19	13	.594
Penn State□	9	9	.500	21	11	.656
Iowa□	9	9	.500	21	12	.636
Wisconsin	7	11	.389	13	14	.481
Ohio State	2	16	.111	6	22	.214
Northwestern	1	17	.056	5	22	.185

BIG WEST

	Conference			Overall		
	W	L	PCT	W	L	PCT
Utah State□	14	4	.778	21	8	.724
New Mexico State□	13	5	.722	25	10	.714
Long Beach State⊕	13	5	.722	20	10	.667
Nevada	12	6	.667	18	11	.621
Pacific⊗	9	9	.500	14	13	.519
UC Santa Barbara	8	10	.444	13	14	.481
UNLV	7	11	.389	12	16	.429
UC Irvine	6	12	.333	13	16	.448
Cal State Fullerton	5	13	.278	7	20	.259
San Jose State	3	15	.167	4	23	.148

Tournament: **Long Beach State d. Nevada 76-69 (OT)**
Tournament MVP: **Brian Green**, Nevada

COLONIAL ATHLETIC

	Conference			Overall		
	W	L	PCT	W	L	PCT
Old Dominion⊕	12	2	.857	21	12	.636
UNC Wilmington	10	4	.714	16	11	.593
James Madison	9	5	.643	16	13	.552
East Carolina	7	7	.500	18	11	.621
American	7	7	.500	9	19	.321
William and Mary	6	8	.429	8	19	.296
Richmond	3	11	.214	8	20	.286
George Mason	2	12	.143	7	20	.259

Tournament: **Old Dominion d. James Madison 80-75**
Tournament MVP: **Petey Sessoms**, Old Dominion

GMWC

	Conference			Overall		
	W	L	PCT	W	L	PCT
Memphis○	9	3	.750	24	10	.706
Saint Louis○	8	4	.667	23	8	.742
Cincinnati○⊗	7	5	.583	22	12	.647
Marquette□	7	5	.583	21	12	.636
DePaul□	6	6	.500	17	11	.607
UAB⊗	5	7	.417	14	16	.467
Dayton	0	12	.000	7	20	.259

Tournament: **Cincinnati d. Saint Louis 67-65**
Tournament MVP: **Danny Fortson**, Cincinnati

IVY

	Conference			Overall		
	W	L	PCT	W	L	PCT
Penn⊕	14	0	1.000	22	6	.786
Princeton	10	4	.714	16	10	.615
Dartmouth	10	4	.714	13	13	.500
Brown	8	6	.571	13	13	.500
Yale	5	9	.357	9	17	.346
Cornell	4	10	.286	9	17	.346
Harvard	4	10	.286	6	20	.231
Columbia⊗	1	13	.071	4	22	.154

METRO

	Conference			Overall		
	W	L	PCT	W	L	PCT
Charlotte○	8	4	.667	19	9	.679
Louisville⊕	7	5	.583	19	14	.576
Tulane○	7	5	.583	23	10	.697
Virginia Tech□	6	6	.500	25	10	.714
Southern Miss□	6	6	.500	17	13	.567
South Florida□	5	7	.417	18	12	.600
VCU	3	9	.250	16	14	.533

Tournament: **Louisville d. Southern Miss 78-64**
Tournament MOP: **DeJuan Wheat**, Louisville

MAAC

	Conference			Overall		
	W	L	PCT	W	L	PCT
Manhattan○	12	2	.857	26	5	.839
Saint Peter's⊕	10	4	.714	19	11	.633
Canisius□	10	4	.714	21	14	.600
Fairfield	6	8	.429	13	15	.464
Iona	6	8	.429	10	17	.370
Loyola (MD)	5	9	.357	9	18	.333
Siena	5	9	.357	8	19	.296
Niagara	2	12	.143	5	25	.167

Tournament: **Saint Peter's d. Manhattan 80-78 (OT)**
Tournament MVP: **Randy Holmes**, Saint Peter's

MID-AMERICAN

	Conference			Overall		
	W	L	PCT	W	L	PCT
Miami (OH)○	16	2	.889	23	7	.767
Ohio□	13	5	.722	24	10	.706
Eastern Michigan□	12	6	.667	20	10	.667
Ball State⊕	11	7	.611	19	11	.633
Bowling Green	10	8	.556	16	11	.593
Toledo	10	8	.556	16	11	.593
Western Michigan	9	9	.500	14	13	.519
Kent State	5	13	.278	8	19	.296
Akron	4	14	.222	8	18	.308
Central Michigan	0	18	.000	3	23	.115

Tournament: **Ball State d. Eastern Michigan 77-70**
Tournament MVP: **Steve Payne**, Ball State

ANNUAL REVIEW

Conference Standings Continue →

⊕ Automatic NCAA Tournament bid ○ At-large NCAA Tournament bid □ NIT appearance ⊗ Team record doesn't reflect games forfeited or vacated. For adjusted record, see p. 521.

MID-CONTINENT	Conference			Overall		
	W	L	Pct	W	L	Pct
Valparaiso	14	4	.778	20	8	.714
Western Illinois	13	5	.722	20	8	.714
Buffalo	12	6	.667	18	10	.643
Youngstown State	10	8	.556	18	10	.643
Eastern Illinois	10	8	.556	16	13	.552
Troy	10	8	.556	11	16	.407
Missouri-Kansas City	7	11	.389	7	19	.269
Central Conn. State	6	12	.333	8	18	.308
Chicago State	6	12	.333	6	20	.231
Northeastern Illinois	2	16	.111	4	22	.154

Tournament: **Valparaiso d. Western Illinois 88-85 (3OT)**
Tournament MVP: **Bryce Drew**, Valparaiso

MEAC	Conference			Overall		
	W	L	Pct	W	L	Pct
Coppin State□	15	1	.938	21	10	.677
South Carolina State	11	5	.688	15	13	.536
NC A&T⊕	10	6	.625	15	15	.500
UMES	9	7	.563	13	14	.481
Bethune-Cookman	9	7	.563	12	16	.429
Howard	8	8	.500	9	18	.333
Morgan State	5	11	.313	5	22	.185
Delaware State	3	13	.188	7	21	.250
Florida A&M	2	14	.125	5	22	.185

Tournament: **NC A&T d. Coppin State 66-64**
Tournament MOP: **Phillip Allen**, NC A&T

MCC	Conference			Overall		
	W	L	Pct	W	L	Pct
Xavier○	14	0	1.000	23	5	.821
Wisc.-Green Bay⊕	11	4	.733	22	8	.733
Illinois-Chicago	11	4	.733	18	9	.667
Detroit	9	5	.643	13	15	.464
Butler	8	7	.533	15	12	.556
La Salle	7	7	.500	13	14	.481
Northern Illinois	7	8	.467	19	10	.655
Wright State	6	8	.429	13	17	.433
Cleveland State	3	11	.214	10	17	.370
Loyola-Chicago	2	13	.133	5	22	.185
Wisc.-Milwaukee	2	13	.133	3	24	.111

Tournament: **Wisc.-Green Bay d. Wright State 73-59**
Tournament MVP: **Jeff Nordgaard**, Wisc.-Green Bay

MISSOURI VALLEY	Conference			Overall		
	W	L	Pct	W	L	Pct
Tulsa○	15	3	.833	24	8	.750
Southern Illinois⊕	13	5	.722	23	9	.719
Illinois State□	13	5	.722	20	13	.606
Bradley□	12	6	.667	20	10	.667
Evansville	11	7	.611	18	9	.667
Missouri State	9	9	.500	16	11	.593
Drake	9	9	.500	12	15	.444
Wichita State	6	12	.333	13	14	.481
Northern Iowa	4	14	.222	8	20	.286
Creighton	4	14	.222	7	19	.269
Indiana State	3	15	.167	7	19	.269

Tournament: **Southern Illinois d. Tulsa 77-62**
Tournament MOP: **Chris Carr**, Southern Illinois

NAC	Conference			Overall		
	W	L	Pct	W	L	Pct
Drexel⊕	12	4	.750	22	8	.733
New Hampshire	11	5	.688	19	9	.679
Northeastern	10	6	.625	18	11	.621
Vermont	7	9	.438	14	13	.519
Boston U.	7	9	.438	15	16	.484
Delaware	7	9	.438	12	15	.444
Hartford	7	9	.438	11	16	.407
Maine	6	10	.375	11	16	.407
Hofstra	5	11	.313	10	18	.357

Tournament: **Drexel d. Northeastern 72-52**
Tournament MVP: **Malik Rose**, Drexel

NORTHEAST	Conference			Overall		
	W	L	Pct	W	L	Pct
Rider	13	5	.722	18	11	.621
Mount St. Mary's⊕	12	6	.667	17	13	.567
Marist	12	6	.667	17	11	.607
Monmouth	11	7	.611	13	14	.481
Fairleigh Dickinson	11	7	.611	16	12	.571
Wagner	9	9	.500	10	17	.370
Long Island	8	10	.444	11	17	.393
Saint Francis (PA)	7	11	.389	12	16	.429
St. Francis (NY)	5	13	.278	9	18	.333
Robert Morris	2	16	.111	4	23	.148

Tournament: **Mount St. Mary's d. Rider 69-62**
Tournament MVP: **Silas Cheung**, Mount St. Mary's

OHIO VALLEY	Conference			Overall		
	W	L	Pct	W	L	Pct
Murray State⊕	11	5	.688	21	9	.700
Tennessee State	11	5	.688	17	10	.630
Morehead State	10	6	.625	15	12	.556
Tennessee Tech	9	7	.563	13	14	.481
Austin Peay	8	8	.500	13	16	.448
SE Missouri State	7	9	.438	13	14	.481
Eastern Kentucky	6	10	.375	9	19	.321
Middle Tenn. State	5	11	.313	12	15	.444
Tennessee-Martin	5	11	.313	7	20	.259

Tournament: **Murray State d. Austin Peay 92-84**
Tournament MVP: **Marcus Brown**, Murray State

PAC-10	Conference			Overall		
	W	L	Pct	W	L	Pct
UCLA⊕⊗	16	2	.889	31	2	.939
Arizona○⊗	13	5	.722	23	8	.742
Arizona State○⊗	12	6	.667	24	9	.727
Oregon○	11	7	.611	19	9	.679
Stanford○	10	8	.556	20	9	.690
Washington State□	10	8	.556	18	12	.600
Oregon State	6	12	.333	9	18	.333
California⊗	5	13	.278	13	14	.481
Washington⊗	5	13	.278	9	18	.333
Southern California⊗	2	16	.111	7	21	.250

PATRIOT	Conference			Overall		
	W	L	Pct	W	L	Pct
Colgate⊕	11	3	.786	17	13	.567
Bucknell	11	3	.786	13	14	.481
Navy	10	4	.714	20	9	.690
Holy Cross	9	5	.643	15	12	.556
Fordham	6	8	.429	11	17	.393
Lehigh	5	9	.357	11	16	.407
Army	4	10	.286	12	16	.429
Lafayette	0	14	.000	2	25	.074

Tournament: **Colgate d. Navy 68-63**
Tournament MVP: **Tucker Neale**, Colgate

SEC	Conference			Overall		
	W	L	Pct	W	L	Pct
Eastern						
Kentucky⊕	14	2	.875	28	5	.848
Georgia□	9	7	.563	18	10	.643
Florida○	8	8	.500	17	13	.567
Vanderbilt	6	10	.375	13	15	.464
South Carolina	5	11	.313	10	17	.370
Tennessee	4	12	.250	11	16	.407
Western						
Arkansas○	12	4	.750	32	7	.821
Mississippi State○	12	4	.750	22	8	.733
Alabama○	10	6	.625	23	10	.697
Auburn□	7	9	.438	16	13	.552
LSU	6	10	.375	12	15	.444
Mississippi	3	13	.188	8	19	.296

Tournament: **Kentucky d. Arkansas 95-93 (OT)**
Tournament MVP: **Antoine Walker**, Kentucky

SOUTHERN	Conference			Overall		
	W	L	Pct	W	L	Pct
North						
Marshall	10	4	.714	18	9	.667
East Tenn. State	9	5	.643	14	14	.500
Davidson	7	7	.500	14	13	.519
VMI	6	8	.429	10	17	.370
Appalachian State	4	10	.286	9	20	.310
South						
Chattanooga⊕	11	3	.786	19	11	.633
Western Carolina	8	6	.571	14	14	.500
The Citadel	6	8	.429	11	16	.407
Furman	6	8	.429	10	17	.370
Georgia Southern	3	11	.214	8	20	.286

Tournament: **Chattanooga d. Western Carolina 63-61**
Tournament MOP: **Frankie King**, Western Carolina

SOUTHLAND	Conference			Overall		
	W	L	Pct	W	L	Pct
Nicholls State⊕	17	1	.944	24	6	.800
Texas-San Antonio	11	7	.611	15	13	.536
UL-Monroe	11	7	.611	14	18	.438
North Texas	9	9	.500	14	13	.519
Stephen F. Austin	9	9	.500	14	14	.500
Northwestern St. (LA)	8	10	.444	13	14	.481
Texas State	7	11	.389	12	14	.462
McNeese State	7	11	.389	11	16	.407
Texas-Arlington	7	11	.389	10	17	.370
Sam Houston State	4	14	.222	7	19	.269

Tournament: **Nicholls State d. UL-Monroe 98-87**
Tournament MVP: **Reggie Jackson**, Nicholls State

SOUTHWEST	Conference			Overall		
	W	L	Pct	W	L	Pct
Texas⊕	11	3	.786	23	7	.767
Texas Tech□	11	3	.786	20	10	.667
TCU	8	6	.571	16	11	.593
Rice	8	6	.571	15	13	.536
Texas A&M	7	7	.500	14	16	.467
Houston	5	9	.357	9	19	.321
Baylor	3	11	.214	9	19	.321
SMU	3	11	.214	7	20	.259

Tournament: **Texas d. Texas Tech 107-104 (OT)**
Tournament MVP: **Terrence Rencher**, Texas

SWAC	Conference			Overall		
	W	L	Pct	W	L	Pct
Texas Southern⊕⊗	12	2	.857	22	7	.759
Miss. Valley State	10	4	.714	17	11	.607
Alabama State	8	6	.571	11	15	.423
Southern U.	7	7	.500	13	13	.500
Jackson State	7	7	.500	12	19	.387
Grambling	5	9	.357	11	17	.393
Alcorn State	4	10	.286	7	19	.269
Prairie View A&M	3	11	.214	6	21	.222

Tournament: **Texas Southern d. Miss. Valley St. 75-62**
Tournament MVP: **Kevin Adams**, Texas Southern

SUN BELT	Conference			Overall		
	W	L	Pct	W	L	Pct
Western Kentucky⊕	17	1	.944	27	4	.871
New Orleans	13	5	.722	20	11	.645
Jacksonville	12	6	.667	18	9	.667
Texas-Pan American	10	8	.556	14	14	.500
Arkansas-Little Rock	9	9	.500	17	12	.586
Louisiana Tech	9	9	.500	14	13	.519
South Alabama	7	11	.389	9	18	.333
Lamar	6	12	.333	11	16	.407
UL-Lafayette	4	14	.222	7	22	.241
Arkansas State	3	15	.167	8	20	.286

Tournament: **Western Kentucky d. Ark.-Little Rock 82-79**
Tournament MOP: **Chris Robinson**, Western Kentucky

TAAC	Conference			Overall		
	W	L	Pct	W	L	Pct
Charleston□	15	1	.938	23	6	.793
Samford	11	5	.688	16	11	.593
Stetson	11	5	.688	15	12	.556
Mercer	8	8	.500	15	14	.517
Southeastern La.	7	9	.438	12	16	.429
Central Florida	7	9	.438	11	16	.407
Centenary	7	9	.438	10	17	.370
Georgia State	6	10	.375	11	17	.393
Florida International⊕	4	12	.250	11	19	.367
Campbell	4	12	.250	8	18	.308
Florida Atlantic*	-	-	-	9	18	.333

* Ineligible for conference title
Tournament: **Florida International d. Mercer 68-57**
Tournament MVP: **James Mazyck**, Florida International

WEST COAST	Conference			Overall		
	W	L	Pct	W	L	Pct
Santa Clara○	12	2	.857	21	7	.750
Portland	10	4	.714	21	8	.724
Saint Mary's (CA)	10	4	.714	18	10	.643
Gonzaga⊕	7	7	.500	21	9	.700
San Diego	5	9	.357	11	16	.407
Loyola Marymount	4	10	.286	13	15	.464
San Francisco⊗	4	10	.286	10	19	.345
Pepperdine	4	10	.286	8	19	.296

Tournament: **Gonzaga d. Portland 80-67**
Tournament MVP: **John Rillie**, Gonzaga

WAC	Conference			Overall		
	W	L	Pct	W	L	Pct
Utah⊕	15	3	.833	28	6	.824
BYU○	13	5	.722	22	10	.688
UTEP□	13	5	.722	20	10	.667
New Mexico	9	9	.500	15	15	.500
Wyoming	9	9	.500	13	15	.464
Hawaii	8	10	.444	16	13	.552
Colorado State	7	11	.389	17	14	.548
Fresno State	7	11	.389	13	15	.464
San Diego State	5	13	.278	11	17	.393
Air Force	4	14	.222	8	20	.286

Tournament: **Utah d. Hawaii 67-54**
Tournament MVP: **Keith Van Horn**, Utah

INDEPENDENTS	Overall		
	W	L	Pct
Notre Dame	15	12	.556
Oral Roberts	10	17	.370

NDIVIDUAL LEADERS—SEASON

SCORING	CL	POS	G	FG	3FG	FT	PTS	PPG
1 **Kurt Thomas**, TCU	SR	C	27	288	3	202	781	**28.9**
2 **Frankie King**, Western Carolina	SR	G	28	249	52	193	743	**26.5**
3 **Kenny Sykes**, Grambling	SR	G	26	245	82	112	684	**26.3**
4 **Sherell Ford**, Illinois-Chicago	SR	F	27	265	47	130	707	**26.2**
5 **Tim Roberts**, Southern U.	JR	G	26	233	108	106	680	**26.2**
6 **Kareem Townes**, La Salle	SR	G	27	242	103	112	699	**25.9**
7 **Joe Griffin**, Long Island	SR	F	28	271	11	170	723	**25.8**
8 **Shawn Respert**, Michigan State	SR	G	28	229	119	139	716	**25.6**
9 **Rob Feaster**, Holy Cross	SR	F	27	225	55	169	674	**25.0**
10 **Shannon Smith**, Wisconsin-Milwaukee	JR	F	27	199	51	212	661	**24.5**

FIELD GOAL PCT	CL	POS	G	FG	FGA	PCT
1 **Shane Kline-Ruminski**, Bowling Green	SR	F	26	181	265	**68.3**
2 **George Spain**, Davidson	SR	C	27	141	210	**67.1**
3 **Rasheed Wallace**, North Carolina	SO	F/C	34	238	364	**65.4**
4 **Erick Dampier**, Mississippi State	SO	C	30	153	239	**64.0**
5 **Alexander Koul**, George Washington	FR	C	32	160	253	**63.2**

Minimum: 5 made per game

THREE-PT FG PER GAME	CL	POS	G	3FG	3PG
1 **Mitch Taylor**, Southern U.	JR	G	25	109	**4.4**
2 **Shawn Respert**, Michigan State	SR	G	28	119	**4.3**
3 **Tim Roberts**, Southern U.	JR	G	26	108	**4.2**
4 **Randy Rutherford**, Oklahoma State	SR	G	37	146	**3.9**
5 **Kareem Townes**, La Salle	SR	G	27	103	**3.8**

THREE-PT FG PCT	CL	POS	G	3FG	3FGA	PCT
1 **Brian Jackson**, Evansville	JR	G	27	53	95	**55.8**
2 **Scott Kegler**, Penn	SR	G	28	58	114	**50.9**
3 **Chris Westlake**, Wisconsin-Green Bay	SR	G	30	87	174	**50.0**
4 **Dante Calabria**, North Carolina	JR	G/F	33	66	133	**49.6**
5 **Malik Hightower**, Marshall	SR	F	27	46	95	**48.4**

Minimum: 1.5 made per game

FREE THROW PCT	CL	POS	G	FT	FTA	PCT
1 **Greg Bibb**, Tennessee Tech	JR	F	27	106	117	**90.6**
2 **Scott Hartzell**, UNC Greensboro	JR	G	29	97	108	**89.8**
3 **Marcus Brown**, Murray State	JR	G	30	189	211	**89.6**
4 **Keith Cornett**, Texas-Arlington	JR	G	27	70	79	**88.6**
5 **Arlando Johnson**, Eastern Kentucky	SR	G	28	123	139	**88.5**

Minimum: 2.5 made per game

ASSISTS PER GAME	CL	POS	G	AST	APG
1 **Nelson Haggerty**, Baylor	SR	G	28	284	**10.1**
2 **Curtis McCants**, George Mason	SO	G	27	251	**9.3**
3 **Raimonds Miglinieks**, UC Irvine	JR	G	29	245	**8.4**
4 **Eric Snow**, Michigan State	SR	G	28	217	**7.8**
5 **Jacque Vaughn**, Kansas	SO	G	31	238	**7.7**
6 **Anthony Foster**, South Alabama	SR	G	27	203	**7.5**
7 **Tony Miller**, Marquette	SR	G	33	248	**7.5**
8 **Hassan Sanders**, Southern U.	JR	G	24	179	**7.5**
9 **Ray Washington**, Nicholls State	SR	G	29	213	**7.3**
10 **Damon Stoudamire**, Arizona	SR	G	30	220	**7.3**

REBOUNDS PER GAME	CL	POS	G	REB	RPG
1 **Kurt Thomas**, TCU	SR	C	27	393	**14.6**
2 **Malik Rose**, Drexel	JR	F	30	404	**13.5**
3 **Gary Trent**, Ohio	JR	F	33	423	**12.8**
4 **Dan Callahan**, Northeastern	SR	C	29	364	**12.6**
5 **Tim Duncan**, Wake Forest	SO	F	32	401	**12.5**
6 **Adonal Foyle**, Colgate	FR	C	30	371	**12.4**
7 **Tunji Awojobi**, Boston U.	SO	F/C	31	378	**12.2**
8 **Kareem Carpenter**, Eastern Michigan	SR	F	29	343	**11.8**
9 **Marcus Mann**, Mississippi Valley State	JR	F	27	317	**11.7**
10 **Chris Ensminger**, Valparaiso	JR	C	28	315	**11.3**

BLOCKED SHOTS PER GAME	CL	POS	G	BLK	BPG
1 **Keith Closs**, Central Connecticut State	FR	C	26	139	**5.3**
2 **Theo Ratliff**, Wyoming	SR	C	28	144	**5.1**
3 **Adonal Foyle**, Colgate	FR	C	30	147	**4.9**
4 **Pascal Fleury**, UMBC	SR	C	27	124	**4.6**
5 **Lorenzo Coleman**, Tennessee Tech	SO	C	27	122	**4.5**

STEALS PER GAME	CL	POS	G	STL	SPG
1 **Roderick Anderson**, Texas	SR	G	30	101	**3.4**
2 **Greg Black**, Texas-Pan American	SR	G	28	94	**3.4**
3 **Nate Langley**, George Mason	SO	G	26	87	**3.3**
4 **Ray Washington**, Nicholls State	SR	G	29	88	**3.0**
5 **Clarence Ceasar**, LSU	SR	F	22	66	**3.0**

INDIVIDUAL LEADERS—GAME

POINTS	CL	POS	OPP	DATE	PTS
1 **Tim Roberts**, Southern U.	JR	G	Faith Baptist	D12	**56**
2 **Kareem Townes**, La Salle	SR	G	Loyola-Chicago	F4	**52**
3 **Kenny Sykes**, Grambling	SR	G	Southern U.	J8	**50**
4 **Mitch Taylor**, Southern U.	JR	G	La. Christian	D1	**48**
5 **Joe Griffin**, Long Island	SR	F	Marist	F16	**46**

THREE-PT FG MADE	CL	POS	OPP	DATE	3FG
1 **Mitch Taylor**, Southern U.	JR	G	La. Christian	D1	**12**
2 **Randy Rutherford**, Oklahoma State	SR	G	Kansas	M5	**11**
3 **KeKe Hicks**, Coastal Carolina	SR	G	Georgia Tech	N28	**10**
Keith Carmichael, Coppin State	SR	G	Kansas	D5	**10**
Byron Coast, Florida A&M	JR	G	Bethune-Cookman	F4	**10**

ASSISTS	CL	POS	OPP	DATE	AST
1 **Ray Washington**, Nicholls State	SR	G	McNeese State	J28	**20**
2 **Randy Livingston**, LSU	FR	G	George Mason	D3	**18**
Nelson Haggerty, Baylor	SR	G	TCU	F14	**18**
4 **Raimonds Miglinieks**, UC Irvine	JR	G	UNLV	F2	**17**
Tony Miller, Marquette	SR	G	Memphis	M4	**17**

REBOUNDS	CL	POS	OPP	DATE	REB
1 **Kareem Carpenter**, Eastern Mich.	SR	F	Western Michigan	F8	**27**
2 **Kareem Carpenter**, Eastern Mich.	SR	F	Central Michigan	J14	**26**
3 **Adonal Foyle**, Colgate	FR	C	Texas Southern	D3	**25**
Kurt Thomas, TCU	SR	C	Baylor	F14	**25**
5 **Tunji Awojobi**, Boston U.	SO	F/C	Vermont	J14	**23**
Tim Duncan, Wake Forest	SO	F	Winthrop	F4	**23**
Tyrone Evans, Houston	SR	G/F	Texas Tech	F15	**23**

BLOCKED SHOTS	CL	POS	OPP	DATE	BLK
1 **Keith Closs**, Central Conn. State	FR	C	Saint Francis (PA)	D21	**13**
2 **Kurt Thomas**, TCU	SR	C	Texas A&M	F25	**12**
3 **Samaki Walker**, Louisville	FR	C	Kentucky	J1	**11**
Theo Ratliff, Wyoming	SR	C	Mississippi State	D28	**11**
Theo Ratliff, Wyoming	SR	C	San Diego State	J2	**11**

STEALS	CL	POS	OPP	DATE	STL
1 **Tyus Edney**, UCLA	SR	G	George Mason	D22	**11**
2 **Brandon Born**, Chattanooga	SR	G/F	South Carolina-Aiken	N26	**10**
Mario Miller, Bethune-Cookman	JR	G	Warner Southern	D3	**10**
Tick Rogers, Louisville	JR	G	Western Carolina	D5	**10**
5 **Dave Masciale**, Long Island	JR	G	Seton Hall	D2	**9**
Dominick Young, Fresno State	SO	G	Pacific	D7	**9**
Greg Black, Texas-Pan American	SR	G	Minnesota-Duluth	J2	**9**
Darnell Woods, Boise State	SR	G	Montana	J27	**9**
Kenyon Murray, Iowa	JR	G/F	Ohio State	F18	**9**
Brevin Knight, Stanford	SO	G	Southern California	F23	**9**

TEAM LEADERS—SEASON

WIN-LOSS PCT	W	L	PCT
1 **UCLA**	31	2	**.939**
2 **Western Kentucky**	27	4	**.871**
3 **Massachusetts**	29	5	**.853**
4 **Connecticut**	28	5	**.848**
Kentucky	28	5	**.848**

SCORING OFFENSE	G	W-L	PTS	PPG
1 **TCU**	27	16-11	2,529	**93.7**
2 **Southern U.**	26	13-13	2,425	**93.3**
3 **Texas**	30	23-7	2,787	**92.9**
4 **George Mason**	27	7-20	2,499	**92.6**
5 **Troy**	27	11-16	2,468	**91.4**

SCORING MARGIN	G	W-L	PPG	OPP PPG	MAR
1 **Kentucky**	33	28-5	87.4	69.0	**18.4**
2 **Massachusetts**	34	29-5	80.9	65.7	**15.2**
3 **Penn**	28	22-6	82.2	67.5	**14.7**
4 **UCLA**	33	31-2	87.5	73.9	**13.6**
5 **Montana State**	29	21-8	84.2	70.8	**13.4**

FIELD GOAL PCT	G	W-L	FG	FGA	PCT
1 **Washington State**	30	18-12	902	1,743	**51.7**
2 **UCLA**	33	31-2	1,079	2,102	**51.3**
3 **North Carolina**	34	28-6	1,044	2,055	**50.8**
4 **Montana State**	29	21-8	930	1,832	**50.8**
5 **Bowling Green**	27	16-11	721	1,427	**50.5**

THREE-PT FG PER GAME	G	W-L	3FG	3PG
1 **Troy**	27	11-16	287	**10.6**
2 **Samford**	27	16-11	279	**10.3**
3 **Vermont**	27	14-13	268	**9.9**
4 **Baylor**	28	9-19	265	**9.5**
5 **Marshall**	27	18-9	253	**9.4**

FREE THROW PCT	G	W-L	FT	FTA	PCT
1 **BYU**	32	22-10	617	798	**77.3**
2 **Murray State**	30	21-9	553	719	**76.9**
3 **Wake Forest**	32	26-6	475	622	**76.4**
4 **Samford**	27	16-11	472	622	**75.9**
5 **Iowa State**	34	23-11	610	806	**75.7**

ASSISTS PER GAME	G	W-L	AST	APG
1 **Montana State**	29	21-8	606	**20.9**
2 **UCLA**	33	31-2	653	**19.8**
3 **Nicholls State**	30	24-6	590	**19.7**
4 **Kentucky**	33	28-5	647	**19.6**
5 **Texas Tech**	30	20-10	585	**19.5**

REBOUND MARGIN	G	W-L	RPG	OPP RPG	MAR
1 **Navy**	29	20-9	40.6	29.6	**11.0**
2 **Utah State**	29	21-8	40.9	30.4	**10.5**
3 **Texas Tech**	30	20-10	43.3	33.5	**9.8**
4 **Utah**	34	28-6	39.7	30.0	**9.7**
5 **Mississippi Valley State**	28	17-11	47.0	38.3	**8.7**

SCORING DEFENSE	G	W-L	OPP PTS	OPP PPG
1 **Princeton**	26	16-10	1,501	**57.7**
2 **Wisconsin-Green Bay**	30	22-8	1,767	**58.9**
3 **Temple**	30	19-11	1,792	**59.7**
4 **Miami (OH)**	30	23-7	1,827	**60.9**
5 **Manhattan**	31	26-5	1,929	**62.2**

Field Goal Pct Defense	G	W-L	OPP FG	OPP FGA	OPP PCT
1 Alabama	33	23-10	771	2,048	**37.6**
2 Kansas	31	25-6	768	2,032	**37.8**
3 Marquette	33	21-12	747	1,957	**38.2**
4 Mississippi State	30	22-8	698	1,821	**38.3**
5 Manhattan	31	26-5	670	1,747	**38.4**

Blocked Shots Per Game	G	W-L	BLK	BPG
1 Massachusetts	34	29-5	273	**8.0**
2 Central Conn. State	26	8-18	194	**7.5**
3 Tennessee Tech	27	13-14	181	**6.7**
4 Memphis	34	24-10	218	**6.4**
5 Wyoming	28	13-15	177	**6.3**

Steals Per Game	G	W-L	STL	SPG
1 Nicholls State	30	24-6	376	**12.5**
2 Murray State	30	21-9	351	**11.7**
3 Troy	27	11-16	315	**11.7**
4 Arkansas	39	32-7	445	**11.4**
5 Texas	30	23-7	341	**11.4**

TEAM LEADERS—GAME

Points	OPP	DATE	SCORE
1 South Alabama	Prairie View A&M	D2	**156-114**
2 George Mason	Troy	D10	**148-132**
3 George Mason	Macalester	N29	**140-99**
Southern Utah	South Alabama	D10	**140-72**
Nicholls State	Faith Baptist	D17	**140-51**
Troy	Chicago State	J23	**140-131**

Field Goal Pct	OPP	DATE	FG	FGA	PCT
1 New Mexico	Eastern N.M.	D6	44	59	**74.6**
2 Eastern Illinois	Chaminade	D20	36	49	**73.5**
3 UNC Asheville	Coastal Carolina	J9	31	44	**70.5**
Wright State	La Salle	F11	31	44	**70.5**
5 Auburn	Arkansas	J14	37	53	**69.8**

Three-Pt FG Made	OPP	DATE	3FG
1 Troy	George Mason	D10	**28**
2 Gonzaga	San Francisco	F23	**22**
3 Baylor	TCU	F14	**20**
4 Southern U.	Louisiana College	J5	**19**
5 Samford	Southeastern La.	J16	**18**
UC Santa Barbara	New Mexico State	M4	**18**

CONSENSUS ALL-AMERICAS

FIRST TEAM

PLAYER	CL	POS	HT	SCHOOL	RPG	PPG
Ed O'Bannon	SR	F	6-8	UCLA	8.3	20.
Shawn Respert	SR	G	6-3	Michigan State	4.0	25.
Joe Smith	SO	F/C	6-10	Maryland	10.6	20.
Jerry Stackhouse	SO	G/F	6-6	North Carolina	8.2	19.
Damon Stoudamire	SR	G	5-10	Arizona	4.3	22.

SECOND TEAM

PLAYER	CL	POS	HT	SCHOOL	RPG	PPG
Randolph Childress	SR	G	6-2	Wake Forest	3.6	20.1
Kerry Kittles	JR	G	6-5	Villanova	6.1	21.4
Lou Roe	SR	F	6-7	Massachusetts	8.1	16.5
Rasheed Wallace	SO	F/C	6-10	North Carolina	8.2	16.6
Corliss Williamson	JR	F	6-7	Arkansas	7.5	19.0

SELECTORS: AP, NABC, UPI, USBWA

AWARD WINNERS

PLAYER OF THE YEAR

PLAYER	CL	POS	HT	SCHOOL	AWARDS
Joe Smith	SO	F/C	6-10	Maryland	Naismith, AP, UPI, Rupp
Ed O'Bannon	SR	F	6-8	UCLA	USBWA, Wooden
Shawn Respert	SR	G	6-3	Michigan State	NABC
Tyus Edney	SR	G	5-10	UCLA	Frances Pomeroy Naismith*

* FOR THE MOST OUTSTANDING SENIOR PLAYER WHO IS 6 FEET OR UNDER.

DEFENSIVE PLAYER OF THE YEAR

PLAYER	CL	POS	HT	SCHOOL
Tim Duncan	SO	F	6-10	Wake Forest

COACH OF THE YEAR

COACH	SCHOOL	REC	AWARDS
Jim Harrick	UCLA	31-2	Naismith, NABC
Kelvin Sampson	Oklahoma	23-9	AP, USBWA
Leonard Hamilton	Miami (FL)	15-13	UPI
Jud Heathcote	Michigan State	22-6	Sporting News
Gene Keady	Purdue	25-7	CBS/Chevrolet

Bob Gibbons' Top High School Senior Recruits

PLAYER	POS	HT	HIGH SCHOOL	A-A TEAMS	COLLEGE	CAREER NOTES
1 Kevin Garnett	C	6-11	Farragut Academy, Chicago	McD, P, USA	None	Drafted straight out of HS; No. 5 pick, '95 NBA draft (Wolves); 11-time All-Star; 9-time All-NBA; NBA MVP, '04; NBA title, '08
Ron Mercer	SF	6-7	Oak Hill Academy, Mouth of Wilson, VA	McD, P, USA	Kentucky	First team All-America, '97; NCAA title, '96; No. 6 pick, '97 NBA draft (Celtics); 13.6 ppg (8 seasons)
3 Robert Traylor	C	6-8	Murray-Wright HS, Detroit	McD, P	Michigan	NIT MVP, '97; at UM, 13.3 ppg, 8.2 rpg (3 seasons); No. 6 pick, '98 NBA draft (Mavs); 4.8 ppg (7 seasons)
4 Vince Carter	G/F	6-6	Mainland HS, Daytona Beach, FL	McD, P, USA	North Carolina	12.3 ppg, 4.5 rpg (3 seasons); No. 5 pick, '98 NBA draft (Warriors); NBA ROY, '99; 8-time All-Star
5 Paul Pierce	SF	6-7	Inglewood (CA) HS	McD, P	Kansas	16.4 ppg (3 seasons); No. 10 pick, '98 draft (Celtics); 23.1 ppg (10 seasons); 6-time All-Star; NBA title, '08
6 Stephon Marbury	PG	6-1	Abraham Lincoln HS, Brooklyn, NY	McD, P, USA	Georgia Tech	18.9 ppg (1 season); No. 4 pick, '96 NBA draft (Bucks); 19.7 ppg, 7.8 apg (12 seasons); 2-time NBA All-Star
7 Jelani McCoy	C	6-10	St. Augustine HS, San Diego	McD	UCLA	UCLA's all-time leader in FG%, blocks; 2nd-round pick, '98 NBA draft (Sonics); 4.6 ppg (8 seasons)
8 Shareef Abdur-Rahim	PF	6-9	Joseph Wheeler HS, Marietta, GA	McD, P, USA	California	21.1 ppg (1 season); Pac-10 POY, '96; No. 3 pick, '96 NBA draft (Grizzlies); 18.1 ppg (12 seasons)
9 Albert White	SF	6-5	Inkster (MI) HS	McD, P	Michigan/Missouri	Transferred after 1 year; led team in points, rebounds, assists; first-team All-Big 12; undrafted; played overseas
10 Louis Bullock	2G	6-2	Laurel (MD) Baptist Academy	McD, P	Michigan	16.8 ppg (4 seasons); 2nd-round pick, '99 NBA draft (Wolves); played overseas
11 Sam Okey	PF	6-7	Cassville (WI) HS	McD, P	Wisconsin/Iowa	Transferred after 3 years; Big Ten FOY, '96; 2nd team All-Big Ten; undrafted; played in CBA
12 Kenny Thomas	C	6-9	Albuquerque (NM) HS	P	New Mexico	3-time first-team All-WAC; No. 22 pick, '99 NBA draft (Rockets); 9.7 ppg, 7.1 rpg (9 seasons)
13 Derek Hood	PF	6-7	Central HS, Kansas City, MO	McD, P	Arkansas	1,002 rebounds (4 seasons); All-SEC 2nd team, '99; undrafted; played in D-League
14 Taymon Domzalski	C/F	6-9	New Mexico Military Institute, Roswell, NM	McD, P	Duke	4.2 ppg, 3.4 rpg (4 seasons); ACC All-Freshman team, '96; undrafted
15 B.J. McKie	PG	6-1	Irmo HS, Columbia, SC	McD, P	South Carolina	3-time first-team All-SEC; left Southern California as all-time scorer (2,119 pts); undrafted; played in D-League
16 Antawn Jamison	PF	6-8	Providence HS, Charlotte, NC	McD	North Carolina	Consensus POY, '98; No. 4 pick, '98 NBA draft (Raptors); 19.6 ppg (10 seasons); 2-time All-Star; NBA Sixth Man Award, '04
17 Randell Jackson	C	6-10	Winchendon (MA) Academy	McD, P	Florida State	12.7 ppg as Sr.; undrafted; 4.1 ppg in NBA (2 seasons); played overseas
18 Ricky Moore	PG	6-2	Westside HS, Augusta, GA	P	Connecticut	NCAA title, '99 (co-captain); undrafted; played in D-League, overseas
19 Chauncey Billups	2G	6-3	George Washington HS, Denver	McD, P	Colorado	18.5 ppg (2 seasons); 2nd team All-America, '97; No. 3 pick in '97 NBA draft (Celtics); 3-time All-Star; '04 Finals MVP
20 Kris Clack	2G	6-5	Anderson HS, Austin, TX	McD	Texas	1,592 pts, 771 rebs (4 seasons); 2nd-round pick, '99 NBA draft (Celtics); played in D-League

Other Standouts

PLAYER	POS	HT	HIGH SCHOOL	A-A TEAMS	COLLEGE	CAREER NOTES
23 Courtney Alexander	G	6-5	C.E. Jordan HS, Durham, NC	P	Virginia/Fresno St.	NCAA scoring leader, '99-'00; in college, 18.8 ppg (4 years); No. 13 pick, '00 NBA draft (Mavs); 9.0 ppg (3 seasons)
128 Doug Gottlieb	PG	6-0	Tustin (CA) HS		Notre Dame/ Oklahoma St.	Transferred after 1 year; in college, 947 total assists (4 seasons); undrafted

Abbreviations: McD=McDonald's; P=Parade; USA=USA Today

Poll Progression

Preseason Poll

AP	USA/CNN	School
1	1	Arkansas
2	2	North Carolina
3	3	Massachusetts
4	4	Kentucky
5	6	Arizona
6	5	UCLA
7	14	Maryland
8	9	Duke
9	7	Indiana
10	13	Florida
11	12	Kansas
12	8	Syracuse
13	11	Cincinnati
14	10	Virginia
15	15	Georgetown
16	16	Michigan
17	17	Wisconsin
18	19	Alabama
19	18	Connecticut
20	20	Michigan State
21	22	Oklahoma State
22	21	Villanova
23	22	Georgia Tech
24	24	Wake Forest
25	—	Illinois
—	25	Memphis

Week of Nov 21

AP	School	AP↓↑
1	Arkansas (0-0)	
2	North Carolina (0-0)	
3	Massachusetts (0-0)	
4	Kentucky (0-0)	
5	Arizona (0-0)	
6	UCLA (0-0)	
7	Maryland (0-0)	
8	Duke (0-0)	
9	Kansas (0-0)	↑2
10	Florida (0-0)	
11	Indiana (0-0)	↓2
12	Cincinnati (0-0)	↑1
13	Michigan (0-0)	↑3
14	Georgetown (0-0)	↑1
15	Wisconsin (0-0)	↑2
16	Connecticut (0-0)	↑3
17	Michigan State (0-0)	↑3
18	Syracuse (0-1)	↓6
19	Oklahoma State (0-0)	↑2
20	Virginia (1-1)	↓6
21	Villanova (0-0)	↑1
22	Georgia Tech (0-0)	↑1
23	Ohio (2-0)	↗
24	Wake Forest (0-0)	
25	Alabama (1-1)	↓7

Week of Nov 28

AP	USA/CNN	School	AP↓↑
1	1	Massachusetts (1-0) (A)	↑2
2	2	North Carolina (1-0)	
3	3	Kentucky (1-0)	↑1
4	5	Arkansas (1-1) (A)	↓3
5	4	UCLA (1-0)	↑1
6	6	Duke (2-0)	↑2
7	7	Kansas (1-0)	↑2
8	12	Florida (1-0)	↑2
9	8	Arizona (2-1)	↓4
10	9	Cincinnati (1-0)	↑2
11	10	Maryland (2-1)	↓4
12	13	Arizona State (3-0)	↗
13	18	Wisconsin (1-0)	↑2
14	15	Ohio (4-0)	↑9
15	11	Minnesota (3-0)	↗
16	14	Connecticut (1-0)	
17	16	Michigan (2-1)	↓4
18	25	Michigan State (0-0)	↓1
19	17	Georgetown (0-1)	↓5
20	19	Georgia Tech (1-0)	↑2
21	—	Wake Forest (1-0)	↑3
22	20	Syracuse (0-1)	↓4
23	—	Virginia (1-1)	↓3
24	—	Villanova (2-1)	↓3
25	24	New Mexico State (3-1)	↗
—	21	Texas (0-1)	
—	22	Indiana (1-2)	↘
—	23	BYU (2-1)	

Week of Dec 5

AP	USA/CNN	School	AP↓↑
1	1	North Carolina (4-0)	↑1
2	2	UCLA (2-0) (B)	↑3
3	3	Arkansas (3-1)	↑1
4	4	Kansas (2-0)	↑3
5	5	Massachusetts (1-1)	↓4
6	9	Florida (3-0)	↑2
7	7	Kentucky (2-1)	↓4
8	8	Arizona (3-1)	↑1
9	6	Duke (3-1)	↓3
10	10	Connecticut (3-0)	↑6
11	11	Maryland (4-1)	
12	12	Minnesota (5-0)	↑3
13	13	Cincinnati (3-1)	↓3
14	14	Wisconsin (3-0)	↓1
15	17	Michigan State (2-0)	↑3
16	16	Arizona State (4-1)	↓4
17	15	Georgia Tech (4-0)	↑3
18	18	Georgetown (2-1)	↑1
19	19	Syracuse (3-1)	↑3
20	23	Virginia (3-1)	↑3
21	22	Ohio (5-2)	↓7
22	21	New Mexico State (5-1)	↑3
23	20	Michigan (3-2)	↓6
24	—	Villanova (3-1)	
25	—	Wake Forest (2-1)	↓4
—	24	BYU (3-2)	
—	25	Indiana (2-3)	

Week of Dec 12 (C)

AP	USA/CNN	School	AP↓↑
1	1	North Carolina (5-0)	
2	2	UCLA (3-0)	
3	4	Kansas (5-0)	↑1
4	3	Arkansas (6-1)	↓1
5	5	Massachusetts (3-1)	
6	7	Kentucky (4-1)	↑1
7	8	Arizona (5-1)	↑1
8	9	Florida (4-1)	↓2
9	6	Duke (5-1)	
10	10	Connecticut (4-0)	
11	11	Minnesota (6-0)	↑1
12	12	Maryland (6-2)	↓1
13	15	Arizona State (4-1)	↑3
14	13	Georgia Tech (5-0)	↑3
15	16	Georgetown (4-1)	↑3
16	14	Syracuse (4-1)	↑3
17	17	Cincinnati (4-2)	↓4
18	18	Michigan State (2-1)	↓3
19	21	Ohio (6-2)	↑2
20	23	Wisconsin (4-1)	↓6
21	—	Wake Forest (4-1)	↑4
22	25	Villanova (4-2)	↑2
23	20	Virginia (5-2)	↓3
24	19	New Mexico State (6-2)	↓2
25	22	Michigan (4-3)	↓2
—	24	Nebraska (6-1)	

Week of Dec 19

AP	USA/CNN	School	AP↓↑
1	1	North Carolina (6-0)	
2	2	UCLA (4-0)	
3	3	Arkansas (6-1)	↑1
4	4	Massachusetts (5-1)	↑1
5	6	Kentucky (5-1)	↑1
6	7	Arizona (7-1)	↑1
7	10	Kansas (5-1)	↓4
8	8	Florida (5-1)	
9	5	Duke (5-1)	
10	9	Connecticut (4-0)	
11	11	Maryland (7-2)	↑1
12	14	Georgetown (5-1)	↑3
13	13	Cincinnati (6-2)	↑4
14	16	Syracuse (5-1)	↑2
15	12	Arizona State (5-2)	↓2
16	15	Minnesota (6-2)	↓5
17	17	Michigan State (4-1)	↑1
18	19	Georgia Tech (6-1)	↓4
19	22	Wake Forest (5-1)	↑2
20	20	Wisconsin (5-1)	
21	18	New Mexico State (7-2)	↑3
22	21	Virginia (5-2)	↑1
23	—	Illinois (7-1)	↗
24	—	California (5-0)	↗
25	—	Iowa State (7-1)	↗
—	23	Indiana (5-4)	
—	24	Nebraska (7-1)	
—	25	Oklahoma State (7-2)	

Week of Dec 26

AP	USA/CNN	School	AP↓↑
1	1	North Carolina (7-0)	
2	2	UCLA (5-0)	
3	3	Arkansas (8-1)	
4	4	Massachusetts (5-1)	
5	5	Kentucky (5-1)	
6	8	Kansas (7-1)	↑1
7	7	Duke (6-1)	↑2
8	6	Connecticut (5-0)	↑2
9	11	Maryland (8-2)	↑2
10	9	Arizona (7-2)	↓4
11	10	Syracuse (7-1)	↑3
12	14	Georgetown (5-1)	
13	12	Florida (5-2)	↓5
14	17	California (6-0)	↑10
15	15	Michigan State (5-1)	↑2
16	13	Arizona State (5-1)	↓1
17	16	Georgia Tech (7-1)	↑1
18	22	Wake Forest (6-1)	↑1
19	21	Wisconsin (6-1)	↑1
20	18	Cincinnati (7-3)	↓7
21	24	Iowa State (8-1)	↑4
22	19	New Mexico State (8-2)	↓1
23	23	Nebraska (9-1)	↗
24	20	Indiana (6-4)	↗
25	—	St. John's (7-0)	↗
—	25	Minnesota (7-3)	↘

Week of Jan 2

AP	USA/CNN	School	AP↓↑
1	1	North Carolina (9-0)	
2	2	UCLA (6-0)	
3	3	Arkansas (11-1)	
4	4	Massachusetts (5-1)	
5	5	Kansas (8-1)	↑1
6	7	Connecticut (7-0)	↑2
7	11	Maryland (10-2)	↑2
8	6	Kentucky (6-2)	↓3
9	8	Arizona (9-2)	↑1
10	10	Syracuse (8-1)	↑1
11	9	Duke (9-2)	↓4
12	13	Georgetown (7-1)	
13	12	Florida (6-2)	
14	15	Michigan State (7-1)	↑1
15	14	Arizona State (9-2)	↑1
16	21	Iowa State (10-1)	↑5
17	16	California (7-1)	↓3
18	22	Wake Forest (7-1)	
19	18	Nebraska (11-1)	↑4
20	17	New Mexico State (9-2)	↑2
21	19	Indiana (8-4)	↑3
22	23	Iowa (10-2)	↗
23	—	Stanford (9-0)	↗
24	20	Georgia Tech (8-3)	↓7
25	—	Penn (6-1)	↗
—	24	Cincinnati (8-5)	↘
—	25	Virginia Tech (10-1)	

Week of Jan 9

AP	USA/CNN	School	AP↓↑
1	1	Massachusetts (8-1)	↑3
2	3	Connecticut (10-0)	↑4
3	5	Kansas (10-1)	↑2
4	2	North Carolina (10-1)	↓3
5	4	Arkansas (12-2)	↓2
6	6	UCLA (7-1) (D)	↓4
7	7	Kentucky (8-2)	↑1
8	8	Syracuse (10-1)	↑2
9	13	Maryland (11-3)	↓2
10	12	Georgetown (9-1)	↑2
11	11	Michigan State (9-1)	↑3
12	10	Arizona State (11-2)	↑3
13	9	Arizona (10-3)	↓4
14	16	Wake Forest (8-1)	↑4
15	15	Florida (7-3)	↓2
16	14	Duke (9-4) (E)	↓5
17	20	Missouri (10-1)	↗
18	25	Clemson (10-0)	↗
19	19	Iowa (11-3)	↑3
20	22	California (8-2)	↓3
21	21	Penn (8-1)	↑4
22	17	Georgia Tech (9-4)	↑2
23	24	Iowa State (11-2)	↓7
24	18	New Mexico State (10-3)	↓4
25	—	Oregon (10-1)	↗
—	23	Indiana (9-5)	↘

Week of Jan 16

AP	USA/CNN	School	AP↓↑
1	1	Massachusetts (11-1)	
2	2	Connecticut (12-0)	
3	3	North Carolina (12-1)	↑1
4	4	UCLA (9-1)	↑2
5	5	Kentucky (10-2)	↑2
6	6	Syracuse (12-1)	↑2
7	8	Kansas (11-2)	↓4
8	9	Maryland (13-3)	↑1
9	7	Arkansas (13-3)	↓4
10	10	Georgetown (11-1)	
11	11	Arizona (12-3)	↑2
12	12	Michigan State (10-2)	↓1
13	13	Arizona State (12-3)	↓1
14	15	Iowa State (13-2)	↑9
15	16	Wake Forest (9-2)	↓1
16	14	Missouri (12-2)	↑1
17	21	Oregon (11-1)	↑8
18	19	Virginia (10-3)	↗
19	17	New Mexico State (12-3)	↑5
20	22	Illinois (13-3)	↗
21	23	Stanford (11-2)	↗
22	18	Georgia Tech (9-5)	
23	—	Cincinnati (12-5)	↗
24	20	Florida (7-5)	↓9
25	—	Penn (8-2)	↓4
—	24	Clemson (10-2)	↘
—	25	Iowa (11-5)	↘

Week of Jan 23

AP	USA/CNN	School	AP↓↑
1	1	Massachusetts (13-1)	
2	2	Connecticut (14-0)	
3	3	North Carolina (14-1)	
4	4	UCLA (11-1)	
5	5	Kentucky (12-2)	
6	6	Syracuse (14-1)	
7	7	Kansas (13-2)	
8	9	Maryland (14-3)	
9	8	Arkansas (15-3)	
10	11	Michigan State (12-2)	↑2
11	12	Iowa State (15-2)	↑3
12	10	Arizona (13-4)	↓1
13	14	Arizona State (13-4)	
14	13	Georgetown (12-3)	↓4
15	17	Virginia (11-4)	↑3
16	15	Wake Forest (10-3)	↓1
17	19	Stanford (12-2)	↑4
18	22	Oregon (12-2)	↓1
19	18	Cincinnati (14-5)	↑4
20	16	Missouri (13-3)	↓4
21	21	Georgia Tech (11-6)	↑1
22	25	Villanova (11-5)	↗
23	23	Florida (9-5)	↑1
24	20	New Mexico State (13-4)	↓5
25	—	Oklahoma (14-3)	↗
—	24	Iowa (12-5)	

Week of Jan 30

AP	USA/CNN	School	AP↓↑
1	1	Massachusetts (15-1)	
2	2	North Carolina (16-1)	↑1
3	3	Kansas (15-2)	↑4
4	5	Connecticut (15-1)	↓2
5	8	Maryland (16-3)	↑3
6	4	Kentucky (13-3)	↓1
7	6	UCLA (12-2)	↓3
8	9	Arkansas (16-4)	↑1
9	10	Michigan State (14-2)	↑1
10	7	Syracuse (15-2)	↓4
11	11	Iowa State (17-2)	
12	12	Arizona (15-4)	
13	13	Georgetown (14-3)	↑1
14	15	Wake Forest (12-4)	↑2
15	17	Virginia (12-5)	
16	14	Arizona State (14-5)	↓3
17	18	Stanford (13-3)	
18	16	Missouri (14-3)	↑2
19	19	Villanova (13-5)	↑3
20	24	Alabama (14-4)	↗
21	20	Georgia Tech (13-6)	
22	21	Oregon (12-4)	↓4
23	22	Cincinnati (15-6)	↓4
24	25	Oklahoma (15-4)	↑1
25	—	Florida (10-6)	↓2
—	23	New Mexico State (14-5)	↘

Poll Progression Continues →

ANNUAL REVIEW

Week of Feb 6

AP	USA/CNN	School	AP ↓↑
1	1	**North Carolina** (18-1)	↑1
2	2	**Kansas** (17-2)	↑1
3	4	**Connecticut** (17-1)	↑1
4	5	**Massachusetts** (17-2)	↓3
5	3	**Kentucky** (15-3)	↑1
6	6	**UCLA** (14-2)	↑1
7	7	**Michigan State** (16-2)	↑2
8	10	**Maryland** (17-4)	↓3
9	8	**Arizona** (17-4)	↑3
10	9	**Syracuse** (16-3)	
11	13	**Wake Forest** (14-4)	↑3
12	11	**Arkansas** (17-5)	↓4
13	12	**Missouri** (16-3)	↑5
14	14	**Arizona State** (16-5)	↑2
15	16	**Stanford** (15-3)	↑2
16	18	**Villanova** (15-5)	↑3
17	17	**Virginia** (13-6)	↓2
18	15	**Georgia Tech** (15-6)	↑3
19	21	**Iowa State** (17-5)	↓8
20	19	**Georgetown** (14-5)	↓7
21	23	**Mississippi State** (14-4)	⤴
22	20	**Oregon** (13-5)	
23	—	**Alabama** (15-5)	↓3
24	—	**Oklahoma State** (16-6)	⤴
25	25	**Purdue** (15-5)	⤴
—	22	**New Mexico State** (16-5)	
—	24	**Minnesota** (15-6)	

Week of Feb 13

AP	USA/CNN	School	AP ↓↑
1	1	**Connecticut** (19-1)	↑2
2	2	**North Carolina** (19-2) Ⓕ	↓1
3	3	**Kansas** (18-3)	↓1
4	3	**Kentucky** (17-3)	↑1
5	5	**Massachusetts** (18-2)	↓1
6	6	**UCLA** (16-2) Ⓖ	
7	7	**Maryland** (19-4)	↑1
8	8	**Michigan State** (17-3)	↓1
9	11	**Missouri** (18-3)	↑4
10	12	**Arkansas** (19-5)	↑2
11	9	**Syracuse** (17-4)	↓1
12	10	**Arizona** (18-5)	↓3
13	13	**Arizona State** (18-5)	↑1
14	14	**Wake Forest** (15-5)	↓3
15	15	**Villanova** (17-5)	↑1
16	16	**Virginia** (16-6)	↑1
17	19	**Stanford** (15-5)	↓2
18	—	**Alabama** (17-5)	↑5
19	18	**Oregon** (14-5)	↑3
20	17	**Georgia Tech** (15-8)	↓2
21	23	**Iowa State** (18-6)	↓2
22	20	**Oklahoma State** (16-7)	↑2
23	—	**Mississippi State** (15-5)	↓2
24	25	**Minnesota** (16-6)	⤴
25	24	**Purdue** (16-6)	
—	21	**BYU** (20-5)	
—	22	**Georgetown** (14-6)	⤵

Week of Feb 20

AP	USA/CNN	School	AP ↓↑
1	1	**Kansas** (20-3)	↑2
2	3	**UCLA** (18-2)	↑4
3	2	**North Carolina** (20-3)	↓1
4	5	**Connecticut** (20-2) Ⓗ	↓3
5	6	**Massachusetts** (20-3)	
6	4	**Kentucky** (18-4)	↓2
7	7	**Maryland** (20-5)	
8	8	**Arkansas** (21-5)	↑2
9	11	**Villanova** (19-5) Ⓗ	↑6
10	12	**Wake Forest** (17-5)	↑4
11	13	**Virginia** (18-6)	↑5
12	10	**Michigan State** (18-4)	↓4
13	9	**Arizona** (19-6)	↓1
14	15	**Missouri** (18-4)	↓5
15	14	**Arizona State** (19-6)	↓2
16	19	**Mississippi State** (17-5)	↑7
17	16	**Syracuse** (17-6)	↓6
18	17	**Oklahoma State** (18-7)	↑4
19	18	**Stanford** (16-5)	↓2
20	25	**Alabama** (18-6)	↓2
21	20	**Purdue** (18-6)	↑4
22	21	**Minnesota** (17-7)	↑2
23	24	**Iowa State** (19-7)	↓2
24	22	**Georgia Tech** (16-9)	↓4
25	—	**Oklahoma** (19-6)	⤴
—	23	**Oregon** (15-6)	⤵

Week of Feb 27

AP	USA/CNN	School
1	1	**UCLA** (21-2)
2	2	**North Carolina** (21-3)
3	4	**Kansas** (21-4)
4	5	**Connecticut** (22-2)
5	3	**Kentucky** (20-4)
6	6	**Maryland** (22-5)
7	7	**Arkansas** (23-5)
8	8	**Massachusetts** (21-4)
9	11	**Wake Forest** (19-5)
10	9	**Michigan State** (20-4)
11	12	**Villanova** (21-6)
12	10	**Arizona** (21-6)
13	13	**Virginia** (19-7)
14	17	**Mississippi State** (19-5)
15	14	**Arizona State** (20-7)
16	18	**Oklahoma** (21-6)
17	16	**Purdue** (20-6)
18	20	**Oklahoma State** (19-8)
19	21	**Missouri** (18-6)
20	19	**Stanford** (17-6)
21	22	**Alabama** (19-7)
22	15	**Syracuse** (18-7)
23	22	**Georgetown** (17-7)
24	22	**Iowa State** (19-7)
25	—	**Xavier** (23-3)
—	25	**Utah** (23-5)

Week of Mar 6

AP	USA/CNN	School	AP ↓↑
1	1	**UCLA** (23-2)	
2	2	**Kansas** (22-4)	↑1
3	4	**Kentucky** (22-4)	↑2
4	3	**North Carolina** (22-4)	↓2
5	6	**Arkansas** (25-5)	↑2
6	5	**Connecticut** (23-3)	↓2
7	8	**Wake Forest** (21-5)	↑2
8	7	**Massachusetts** (24-4)	
9	9	**Michigan State** (21-4)	↑1
10	10	**Maryland** (23-6)	↓4
11	12	**Virginia** (21-7)	↑2
12	11	**Arizona** (23-6)	
13	14	**Villanova** (22-7)	↓2
14	13	**Purdue** (22-6)	↑3
15	15	**Mississippi State** (20-6)	↓1
16	18	**Oklahoma** (22-7)	
17	19	**Missouri** (19-7)	↑2
18	16	**Arizona State** (21-8)	↓3
19	17	**Oklahoma State** (20-9)	↓1
20	22	**Alabama** (20-8)	↑1
21	20	**Syracuse** (19-8)	↑1
22	21	**Utah** (24-5)	⤴
23	—	**Western Kentucky** (25-3)	⤴
24	—	**Georgetown** (18-8)	↓1
25	23	**Oregon** (18-7)	⤴
—	24	**Stanford** (17-8)	⤵
—	25	**Iowa State** (20-9)	⤵

Week of Mar 13

AP	USA/CNN	School	AP ↓↑
1	1	**UCLA** (25-2)	
2	2	**Kentucky** (25-4)	↑1
3	3	**Wake Forest** (24-5)	↑4
4	5	**North Carolina** (24-5)	
5	4	**Kansas** (23-5)	↓3
6	6	**Arkansas** (27-6)	↓1
7	7	**Massachusetts** (26-4)	↑1
8	8	**Connecticut** (25-4)	↓2
9	12	**Villanova** (25-7)	↑4
10	10	**Maryland** (24-7)	
11	9	**Michigan State** (22-5)	↓2
12	11	**Purdue** (24-6)	↑2
13	15	**Virginia** (22-8)	↓2
14	14	**Oklahoma State** (23-9)	↑5
15	13	**Arizona** (23-7)	↓3
16	16	**Arizona State** (22-8)	↑2
17	20	**Oklahoma** (23-8)	↓1
18	19	**Mississippi State** (20-7)	↓3
19	17	**Utah** (27-5)	↑3
20	21	**Alabama** (22-9)	
21	—	**Western Kentucky** (26-3)	↑2
22	—	**Georgetown** (19-9)	↑2
23	23	**Missouri** (19-8)	↓6
24	18	**Iowa State** (22-10)	⤴
25	22	**Syracuse** (19-9)	↓4
	24	**Oregon** (19-8)	⤵
	25	**Stanford** (19-8)	

Final Poll (Post-Tournament)

USA/CNN	School
1	**UCLA** (31-2)
2	**Arkansas** (32-7)
3	**North Carolina** (28-6)
4	**Oklahoma State** (27-10)
5	**Kentucky** (28-5)
6	**Connecticut** (28-5)
7	**Massachusetts** (29-5)
8	**Virginia** (25-9)
9	**Wake Forest** (26-6)
10	**Kansas** (25-6)
11	**Maryland** (26-8)
12	**Mississippi State** (22-8)
13	**Arizona State** (24-9)
14	**Memphis** (24-10)
15	**Tulsa** (24-8)
16	**Georgetown** (21-10)
17	**Syracuse** (20-10)
18	**Missouri** (20-9)
19	**Purdue** (25-7)
20	**Michigan State** (22-6)
21	**Alabama** (23-10)
22	**Utah** (28-6)
23	**Villanova** (25-8)
24	**Texas** (23-7)
25	**Arizona** (23-8)

Ⓐ NCAA champion Arkansas is routed by UMass, 104-80, in Springfield. It's the third-largest margin of defeat ever for a No. 1-ranked team.

Ⓑ As UCLA begins the 20th season since its last NCAA title, freshman J.R. Henderson sinks two free throws with 0.6 seconds remaining to beat Kentucky, 82-81, on Dec. 3 in the inaugural Wooden Classic.

Ⓒ Troy State sets NCAA records for three-pointers attempted (74) and made (28) in a 148-132 loss to George Mason.

Ⓓ UCLA stumbles at Oregon, 82-72. It will be one of only two Bruins losses during the season. The second—to California, 100-93, on Jan. 28—was later forfeited by Cal due to a pay-for-play scandal involving coach Todd Bozeman.

Ⓔ After Duke loses to Clemson on Jan. 8, coach Mike Krzyzewski—exhausted and requiring back surgery—announces that he's taking a leaving of absence for the remainder of the season.

Ⓕ To the delight of interim coach Pete Gaudet, Duke's Jeff Capel hits a 37-footer against North Carolina to force a second overtime, but the Tar Heels prevail, 102-100.

Ⓖ Before UCLA dispatches Washington, 74-66, on Feb. 9 at Hec Edmundson Pavilion in Seattle, Bruins coach Jim Harrick takes his players to tour the Kingdome, site of the Final Four.

Ⓗ Villanova knocks off UConn, 96-73, with Kerry Kittles scoring 37—a record for a Big East team against the Huskies. The two teams will meet again in the Big East tournament final, with the Wildcats also winning the rematch.

Pre-Tournament Ratings Percentage Index (RPI)

Rank	School	W-L	Sched. Strg.	SS Rank	RPI
1	**North Carolina**	24-5	.6209	3	.6608
2	**Kansas**	22-5	.6237	2	.6581
3	**Kentucky**	25-4	.6003	14	.6531
4	**Wake Forest**	24-5	.6101	9	.6514
5	**Massachusetts**	26-4	.5851	25	.6464
6	**UCLA**	25-2	.5369	80	.6380
7	**Connecticut**	25-4	.5655	41	.6369
8	**Arkansas**	26-6	.5927	22	.6367
9	**Villanova**	24-7	.6029	11	.6331
10	**Maryland**	23-7	.6020	12	.6322
11	**Michigan State**	22-5	.5663	40	.6248
12	**Oklahoma State**	21-9	.6155	7	.6241
13	**Oklahoma**	23-8	.6007	13	.6233
14	**Virginia**	22-8	.5944	21	.6191
15	**Tulsa**	22-7	.5848	26	.6114
16	**Mississippi State**	20-7	.5767	31	.6102
17	**Missouri**	19-8	.5888	23	.6098
18	**Arizona**	22-7	.5587	46	.6070
19	**Purdue**	24-6	.5379	78	.6044
20	**Oregon**	17-8	.5957	19	.6031
21	**Iowa State**	19-10	.5962	18	.6030
22	**Cincinnati**	21-11	.6059	10	.6014
23	**Indiana**	18-11	.6167	5	.5978
24	**Western Kentucky**	25-3	.4975	152	.5962
25	**Syracuse**	18-9	.5785	28	.5925
26	**Utah**	25-5	.5019	143	.5917
27	**Louisville**	19-13	.6154	8	.5917
28	**Arizona State**	22-8	.5424	67	.5908
29	**Georgetown**	19-9	.5694	35	.5888
30	**Southern Illinois**	22-8	.5525	58	.5884
31	**Temple**	19-10	.5739	32	.5880
32	**Memphis**	22-9	.5531	56	.5879
33	**Texas**	22-6	.5223	108	.5871
34	**Florida**	17-12	.5990	15	.5862
35	**Alabama**	22-9	.5405	72	.5828
36	**Virginia Tech**	20-10	.5641	43	.5821
37	**Charlotte**	19-8	.5501	60	.5812
38	**Xavier**	22-4	.4874	169	.5807
39	**Illinois**	18-11	.5768	30	.5802
40	**Saint Louis**	22-7	.5143	116	.5792
41	**Saint Joseph's**	17-11	.5859	24	.5790
42	**Tulane**	22-9	.5361	83	.5786
43	**Ohio**	22-9	.5361	83	.5764
44	**BYU**	22-9	.5387	77	.5763
45	**Michigan**	17-13	.5977	17	.5755
46	**Santa Clara**	20-6	.5054	131	.5719
47	**Stanford**	19-8	.5179	111	.5704
48	**New Mexico State**	22-9	.5272	97	.5697
49	**Charleston**	21-5	.4969	155	.5691
50	**Manhattan**	25-4	.4602	217	.5690

Source: Collegiate Basketball News

1995 NCAA Tournament

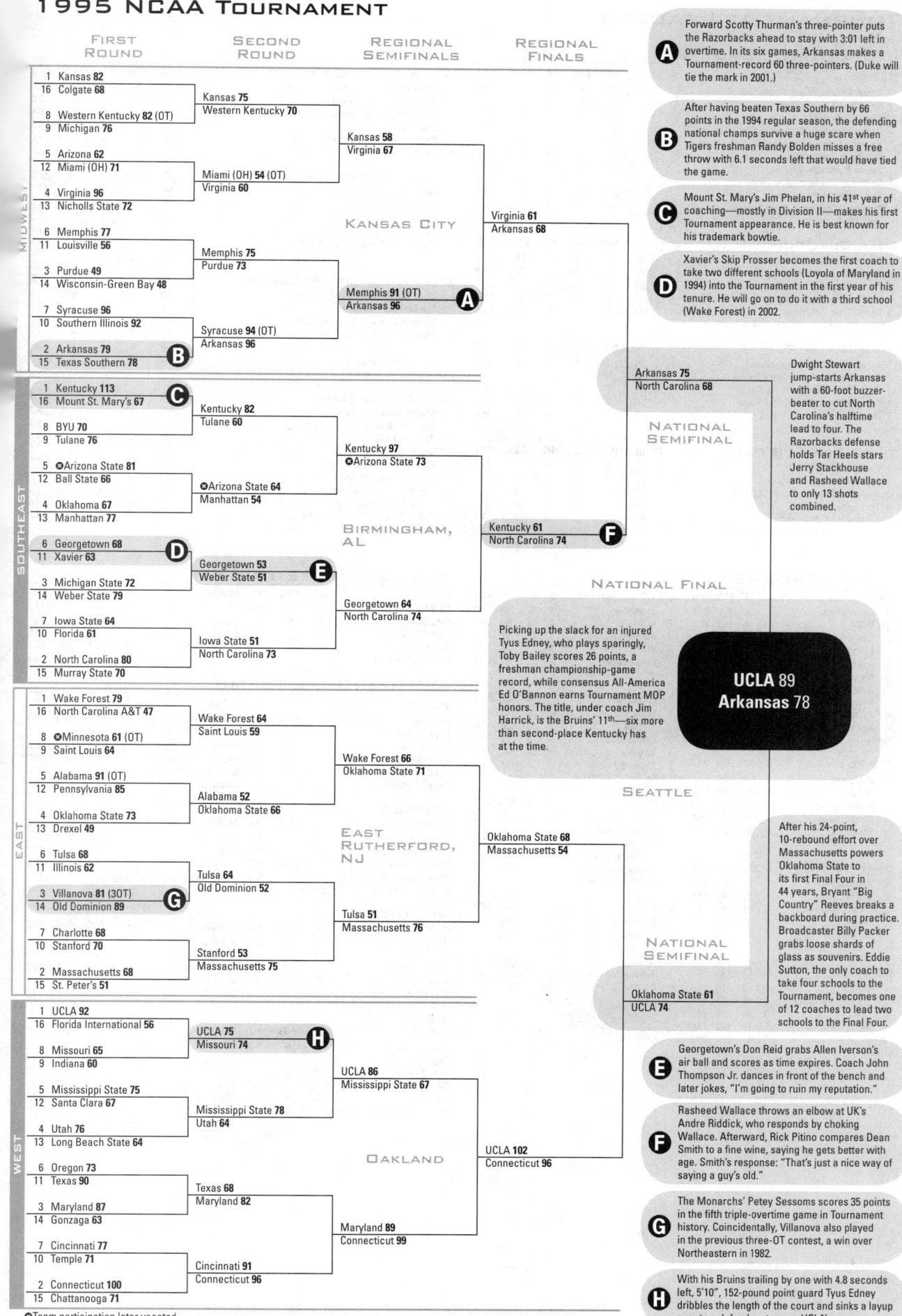

Midwest (Kansas City)

First Round
- 1 Kansas **82**, 16 Colgate **68**
- 8 Western Kentucky **82** (OT), 9 Michigan **76**
- 5 Arizona **62**, 12 Miami (OH) **71**
- 4 Virginia **96**, 13 Nicholls State **72**
- 6 Memphis **77**, 11 Louisville **56**
- 3 Purdue **49**, 14 Wisconsin-Green Bay **48**
- 7 Syracuse **96**, 10 Southern Illinois **92**
- 2 Arkansas **79**, 15 Texas Southern **78** (B)

Second Round
- Kansas **75**, Western Kentucky **70**
- Miami (OH) **54** (OT), Virginia **60**
- Memphis **75**, Purdue **73**
- Syracuse **94** (OT), Arkansas **96**

Regional Semifinals
- Kansas **58**, Virginia **67**
- Memphis **91** (OT), Arkansas **96** (A)

Regional Finals
- Virginia **61**, Arkansas **68**

Southeast (Birmingham, AL)

First Round
- 1 Kentucky **113**, 16 Mount St. Mary's **67** (C)
- 8 BYU **70**, 9 Tulane **76**
- 5 ⊗Arizona State **81**, 12 Ball State **66**
- 4 Oklahoma **67**, 13 Manhattan **77**
- 6 Georgetown **68**, 11 Xavier **63** (D)
- 3 Michigan State **72**, 14 Weber State **79**
- 7 Iowa State **64**, 10 Florida **61**
- 2 North Carolina **80**, 15 Murray State **70**

Second Round
- Kentucky **82**, Tulane **60**
- ⊗Arizona State **64**, Manhattan **54**
- Georgetown **53**, Weber State **51** (E)
- Iowa State **51**, North Carolina **73**

Regional Semifinals
- Kentucky **97**, ⊗Arizona State **73**
- Georgetown **64**, North Carolina **74**

Regional Finals
- Kentucky **61**, North Carolina **74** (F)

East (East Rutherford, NJ)

First Round
- 1 Wake Forest **79**, 16 North Carolina A&T **47**
- 8 ⊗Minnesota **61** (OT), 9 Saint Louis **64**
- 5 Alabama **91** (OT), 12 Pennsylvania **85**
- 4 Oklahoma State **73**, 13 Drexel **49**
- 6 Tulsa **68**, 11 Illinois **62**
- 3 Villanova **81** (3OT), 14 Old Dominion **89** (G)
- 7 Charlotte **68**, 10 Stanford **70**
- 2 Massachusetts **68**, 15 St. Peter's **51**

Second Round
- Wake Forest **64**, Saint Louis **59**
- Alabama **52**, Oklahoma State **66**
- Tulsa **64**, Old Dominion **52**
- Stanford **53**, Massachusetts **75**

Regional Semifinals
- Wake Forest **66**, Oklahoma State **71**
- Tulsa **51**, Massachusetts **76**

Regional Finals
- Oklahoma State **68**, Massachusetts **54**

West (Oakland)

First Round
- 1 UCLA **92**, 16 Florida International **56**
- 8 Missouri **65**, 9 Indiana **60**
- 5 Mississippi State **75**, 12 Santa Clara **67**
- 4 Utah **76**, 13 Long Beach State **64**
- 6 Oregon **73**, 11 Texas **90**
- 3 Maryland **87**, 14 Gonzaga **63**
- 7 Cincinnati **77**, 10 Temple **71**
- 2 Connecticut **100**, 15 Chattanooga **71**

Second Round
- UCLA **75**, Missouri **74** (H)
- Mississippi State **78**, Utah **64**
- Texas **68**, Maryland **82**
- Cincinnati **91**, Connecticut **96**

Regional Semifinals
- UCLA **86**, Mississippi State **67**
- Maryland **89**, Connecticut **99**

Regional Finals
- UCLA **102**, Connecticut **96**

National Semifinal
- Arkansas **75**, North Carolina **68**
- Oklahoma State **61**, UCLA **74**

National Final (Seattle)

UCLA 89
Arkansas 78

Picking up the slack for an injured Tyus Edney, who plays sparingly, Toby Bailey scores 26 points, a freshman championship-game record, while consensus All-America Ed O'Bannon earns Tournament MOP honors. The title, under coach Jim Harrick, is the Bruins' 11th—six more than second-place Kentucky has at the time.

Dwight Stewart jump-starts Arkansas with a 60-foot buzzer-beater to cut North Carolina's halftime lead to four. The Razorbacks defense holds Tar Heels stars Jerry Stackhouse and Rasheed Wallace to only 13 shots combined.

After his 24-point, 10-rebound effort over Massachusetts powers Oklahoma State to its first Final Four in 44 years, Bryant "Big Country" Reeves breaks a backboard during practice. Broadcaster Billy Packer grabs loose shards of glass as souvenirs. Eddie Sutton, the only coach to take four schools to the Tournament, becomes one of 12 coaches to lead two schools to the Final Four.

A Forward Scotty Thurman's three-pointer puts the Razorbacks ahead to stay with 3:01 left in overtime. In its six games, Arkansas makes a Tournament-record 60 three-pointers. (Duke will tie the mark in 2001.)

B After having beaten Texas Southern by 66 points in the 1994 regular season, the defending national champs survive a huge scare when Tigers freshman Randy Bolden misses a free throw with 6.1 seconds left that would have tied the game.

C Mount St. Mary's Jim Phelan, in his 41st year of coaching—mostly in Division II—makes his first Tournament appearance. He is best known for his trademark bowtie.

D Xavier's Skip Prosser becomes the first coach to take two different schools (Loyola of Maryland in 1994) into the Tournament in the first year of his tenure. He will go on to do it with a third school (Wake Forest) in 2002.

E Georgetown's Don Reid grabs Allen Iverson's air ball and scores as time expires. Coach John Thompson Jr. dances in front of the bench and later jokes, "I'm going to ruin my reputation."

F Rasheed Wallace throws an elbow at UK's Andre Riddick, who responds by choking Wallace. Afterward, Rick Pitino compares Dean Smith to a fine wine, saying he gets better with age. Smith's response: "That's just a nice way of saying a guy's old."

G The Monarchs' Petey Sessoms scores 35 points in the fifth triple-overtime game in Tournament history. Coincidentally, Villanova also played in the previous three-OT contest, a win over Northeastern in 1982.

H With his Bruins trailing by one with 4.8 seconds left, 5'10", 152-pound point guard Tyus Edney dribbles the length of the court and sinks a layup over two defenders to save UCLA's season.

⊗Team participation later vacated

ANNUAL REVIEW

Tournament Leaders

Individual Leaders

Scoring

	CL	POS	G	PTS	PPG
1 **Darryl Wilson**, Mississippi State	SR	G	3	73	24.3
2 **Ray Allen**, Connecticut	SO	G	4	96	24.0
Shea Seals, Tulsa	SO	G	3	72	24.0
4 **Donny Marshall**, Connecticut	SR	F	4	89	22.3
5 **Bryant Reeves**, Oklahoma State	SR	C	5	111	22.2
6 **Ron Riley**, Arizona State	JR	G	3	65	21.7
7 **Junior Burrough**, Virginia	SR	F	4	84	21.0
8 **Corliss Williamson**, Arkansas	JR	F	6	125	20.8
9 **Joe Smith**, Maryland	SO	F	3	62	20.7
10 **Randolph Childress**, Wake Forest	SR	G	3	58	19.3

Minimum: 3 games

Field Goal Pct

	CL	POS	G	FG	FGA	PCT
1 **Michael Wilson**, Memphis	JR	G	3	18	24	75.0
2 **Erick Dampier**, Mississippi State	SO	C	3	17	23	73.9
3 **Travis Knight**, Connecticut	JR	C	4	20	28	71.4
4 **Tim Duncan**, Wake Forest	SO	F	3	23	35	65.7
5 **Lee Wilson**, Arkansas	SO	F	6	15	23	65.2

Minimum: 15 made and 3 games

Free Throw Pct

	CL	POS	G	FT	FTA	PCT
1 **Donny Marshall**, Connecticut	SR	F	4	25	28	89.3
2 **Randolph Childress**, Wake Forest	SR	G	3	15	17	88.2
3 **Bryant Reeves**, Oklahoma State	SR	C	5	37	42	88.1
4 **Darryl Wilson**, Mississippi State	SR	G	3	22	25	88.0
5 **Doron Sheffer**, Connecticut	JR	G	4	19	22	86.4

Minimum: 15 made

Three-Point FG Pct

	CL	POS	G	3FG	3FGA	PCT
1 **Corey Beck**, Arkansas	SR	G	6	8	11	72.7
2 **Donny Marshall**, Connecticut	SR	F	4	6	10	60.0
3 **Jerry Stackhouse**, North Carolina	SO	G	5	7	12	58.3
4 **Tyus Edney**, UCLA	SR	G	6	6	12	50.0
5 **Jeremy Veal**, Arizona State	FR	G	3	9	19	47.4

Minimum: 6 made and 3 games

Assists Per Game

	CL	POS	G	AST	APG
1 **Kevin Ollie**, Connecticut	SR	G	4	32	8.0
2 **Jacque Vaughn**, Kansas	SO	G	3	21	7.0
3 **Andre Owens**, Oklahoma State	SR	G	5	33	6.6
4 **Tyus Edney**, UCLA	SR	G	6	38	6.3
5 **Rodrick Rhodes**, Kentucky	JR	F	4	24	6.0

Minimum: 3 games

Rebounds Per Game

	CL	POS	G	REB	RPG
1 **Tim Duncan**, Wake Forest	SO	F	3	43	14.3
2 **Joe Smith**, Maryland	SO	F	3	39	13.0
3 **Keith Booth**, Maryland	SO	F	3	37	12.3
4 **Junior Burrough**, Virginia	SR	F	4	49	12.3
5 **Jerome Williams**, Georgetown	JR	F	3	32	10.7

Minimum: 3 games

Blocked Shots Per Game

	CL	POS	G	BLK	BPG
1 **Erick Dampier**, Mississippi State	SO	C	3	16	5.3
2 **Tim Duncan**, Wake Forest	SO	F	3	16	5.3
3 **Marcus Camby**, Massachusetts	SO	F	4	18	4.5
Mario Bennett, Arizona State	SR	F	3	8	2.7
Greg Ostertag, Kansas	SR	C	3	8	2.7
Joe Smith, Maryland	SO	F	3	8	2.7

Minimum: 3 games

Steals Per Game

	CL	POS	G	STL	SPG
1 **Mingo Johnson**, Memphis	JR	G	3	9	3.0
2 **Edgar Padilla**, Massachusetts	SO	G	3	8	2.7
3 **Andre Owens**, Oklahoma State	SR	G	5	13	2.6
4 **Cameron Dollar**, UCLA	SO	G	6	15	2.5
Clint McDaniel, Arkansas	SR	G	6	14	2.3
Chris Garner, Memphis	SO	G	3	7	2.3
Ron Riley, Arizona State	JR	G	3	7	2.3
Alvin Williamson, Tulsa	SR	G	3	7	2.3
Darryl Wilson, Mississippi State	SR	G	3	7	2.3

Minimum: 3 games

Team Leaders

Scoring

	G	PTS	PPG
1 **Connecticut**	4	391	97.8
2 **UCLA**	5	443	88.6
3 **Kentucky**	4	353	88.3
4 **Maryland**	3	258	86.0
5 **Arkansas**	6	492	82.0
6 **Memphis**	3	243	81.0
7 **North Carolina**	5	369	73.8
8 **Mississippi State**	3	220	73.3
9 **Arizona State**	3	218	72.7
10 **Kansas**	3	215	71.7

Minimum: 3 games

FG Pct

	G	FG	FGA	PCT
1 **Maryland**	3	100	160	62.5
2 **UCLA**	5	162	309	52.4
3 **Wake Forest**	3	76	153	49.7
4 **Connecticut**	4	136	275	49.5
5 **Memphis**	3	95	200	47.5

Minimum: 3 games

3-Pt FG Pct

	G	3FG	3FGA	PCT
1 **Arizona State**	3	27	64	42.2
2 **Connecticut**	4	26	64	40.6
3 **Oklahoma State**	5	27	68	39.7
4 **Memphis**	3	18	47	38.3
5 **Arkansas**	6	60	165	36.4

Minimum: 3 games

FT Pct

	G	FT	FTA	PCT
1 **Connecticut**	4	93	118	78.8
2 **Mississippi State**	3	42	56	75.0
3 **Tulsa**	3	46	62	74.2
4 **North Carolina**	5	77	106	72.6
5 **UCLA**	5	107	150	71.3

Minimum: 3 games

Ast/TO Ratio

	G	AST	TO	RAT
1 **Kentucky**	4	100	50	2.00
2 **UCLA**	5	88	60	1.47
3 **Oklahoma State**	5	83	57	1.46
4 **Wake Forest**	3	49	34	1.44
5 **Connecticut**	4	82	57	1.44

Minimum: 3 games

Rebounds

	G	REB	RPG
1 **Maryland**	3	145	48.3
2 **Kansas**	3	135	45.0
3 **Connecticut**	4	177	44.3
4 **Virginia**	4	174	43.5
5 **Kentucky**	4	171	42.8

Minimum: 3 games

Blocks

	G	BLK	BPG
1 **Massachusetts**	4	37	9.3
2 **Wake Forest**	3	20	6.7
3 **Kansas**	3	17	5.7
4 **Mississippi State**	3	17	5.7
5 **Kentucky**	4	22	5.5

Minimum: 3 games

Steals

	G	STL	SPG
1 **Kentucky**	4	46	11.5
2 **Arkansas**	6	65	10.8
3 **Memphis**	3	29	9.7
4 **UCLA**	5	47	9.4
5 **Massachusetts**	4	35	8.8

Minimum: 3 games

All-Tournament Team

PLAYER	CL	POS	HT	SCHOOL	RPG	APG	PPG
Ed O'Bannon*	SR	F	6-8	UCLA	9.0	1.5	19.2
Toby Bailey	FR	G	6-5	UCLA	5.0	1.7	13.7
Clint McDaniel	SR	G	6-4	Arkansas	3.7	1.7	9.5
Bryant Reeves	SR	C	7-0	Oklahoma State	9.2	1.4	22.2
Corliss Williamson	JR	F	6-7	Arkansas	8.7	2.7	20.8

All-Regional Teams

East

PLAYER	CL	POS	HT	SCHOOL	RPG	APG	PPG
Bryant Reeves*	SR	C	7-0	Oklahoma State	9.3	1.8	21.5
Tim Duncan	SO	F	6-10	Wake Forest	14.3	2.0	19.3
Derek Kellogg	SR	G	6-2	Massachusetts	3.3	3.8	7.3
Scott Pierce	SR	F	6-9	Oklahoma State	4.5	0.5	6.8
Randy Rutherford	SR	G	6-3	Oklahoma State	7.3	2.0	19.0

Midwest

PLAYER	CL	POS	HT	SCHOOL	RPG	APG	PPG
Corliss Williamson*	JR	F	6-7	Arkansas	9.5	2.3	23.0
Junior Burrough	SR	F	6-8	Virginia	12.3	0.8	21.0
Harold Deane	SO	G	6-2	Virginia	3.8	3.3	17.5
Mingo Johnson	JR	G	6-2	Memphis	2.7	4.3	18.7
Scotty Thurman	JR	G/F	6-6	Arkansas	4.0	2.8	18.0

Southeast

PLAYER	CL	POS	HT	SCHOOL	RPG	APG	PPG
Jerry Stackhouse*	SO	G/F	6-6	North Carolina	8.5	4.3	17.5
Tony Delk	JR	G	6-1	Kentucky	3.0	2.0	19.0
Allen Iverson	FR	G	6-1	Georgetown	4.7	2.0	18.7
Rasheed Wallace	SO	F/C	6-10	North Carolina	6.8	0.5	11.8
Donald Williams	SR	G	6-3	North Carolina	2.8	1.8	15.8

West

PLAYER	CL	POS	HT	SCHOOL	RPG	APG	PPG
Tyus Edney*	SR	G	5-10	UCLA	2.5	8.3	13.8
Ray Allen	SO	G	6-5	Connecticut	8.0	2.5	24.0
Toby Bailey	FR	G	6-5	UCLA	5.3	1.5	13.5
Donny Marshall	SR	F	6-7	Connecticut	7.3	1.3	22.3
Ed O'Bannon	SR	F	6-8	UCLA	7.3	1.5	17.5

* Most outstanding player

1995 NCAA TOURNAMENT BOX SCORES

Virginia 67-58 Kansas

VIRGINIA	MIN	FG	3FG	FT	REB	A	ST	BL	PF	TP
Harold Deane	39	7-15	2-6	6-7	6	2	1	0	3	22
Curtis Staples	37	6-14	3-9	3-4	5	1	2	0	1	18
Junior Burrough	34	7-21	0-1	4-7	12	0	0	0	1	18
Yuri Barnes	18	1-2	0-0	3-4	5	0	1	1	4	5
Jason Williford	29	1-4	0-1	0-2	9	0	0	2	4	2
Jamal Robinson	17	1-6	0-1	0-0	2	1	0	0	3	2
Chris Alexander	17	0-1	0-0	0-0	5	1	1	1	4	0
Norman Nolan	8	0-0	0-0	0-0	0	0	0	1	1	0
Percy Ellsworth	1	0-0	0-0	0-0	0	0	0	0	0	0
TOTALS	200	23-63	5-18	16-24	44	5	5	5	21	67
Percentages		36.5	27.8	66.7						

Coach: Jeff Jones

67-58

31	1H	28
36	2H	30

KANSAS	MIN	FG	3FG	FT	REB	A	ST	BL	PF	TP
Jacque Vaughn	36	6-11	1-2	0-1	5	7	1	0	4	13
Raef LaFrentz	26	4-9	0-0	2-6	9	0	0	1	2	10
Scot Pollard	21	3-8	0-0	3-7	10	0	0	2	1	9
Greg Ostertag	18	4-8	0-0	0-2	5	1	0	2	3	8
Billy Thomas	23	1-8	0-7	5-5	3	1	0	0	3	7
Jerod Haase	34	1-6	1-5	2-2	3	2	3	0	1	5
B.J. Williams	12	2-4	0-0	0-0	2	0	0	0	5	4
Greg Gurley	12	0-3	0-3	2-2	2	0	0	0	0	2
Sean Pearson	13	0-4	0-4	0-2	1	0	1	0	1	0
C.B. McGrath	2	0-1	0-0	0-0	0	0	0	0	1	0
Joel Branstrom	1	0-0	0-0	0-0	0	0	0	0	0	0
Scott Novosell	1	0-0	0-0	0-0	0	0	0	0	0	0
Thomas Whatley	1	0-0	0-0	0-0	0	0	0	0	0	0
TOTALS	200	21-62	2-21	14-27	40	11	5	5	21	58
Percentages		33.9	9.5	51.9						

Coach: Roy Williams

Officials: John Clougherty, Ted Hillary, Jim Haney
Technicals: None
Attendance: 16,153

Arkansas 96-91 Memphis

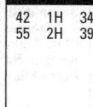

ARKANSAS	MIN	FG	3FG	FT	REB	A	ST	BL	PF	TP
Corliss Williamson	40	10-16	0-0	7-9	13	3	2	0	4	27
Alex Dillard	17	6-12	4-8	3-4	4	0	2	0	1	19
Scotty Thurman	38	5-12	4-5	3-4	2	4	0	0	2	17
Corey Beck	33	2-5	2-2	2-4	5	4	2	0	4	8
Clint McDaniel	33	2-6	1-5	2-4	4	3	4	0	4	7
Lee Wilson	11	2-5	0-0	3-6	3	0	1	0	1	7
Dwight Stewart	30	2-6	0-3	2-4	5	3	1	1	2	6
Davor Rimac	11	1-3	1-3	0-0	2	1	1	0	0	3
Elmer Martin	8	1-2	0-1	0-0	3	1	1	0	0	2
Darnell Robinson	3	0-1	0-0	0-0	0	0	0	0	2	0
Reggie Garrett	1	0-0	0-0	0-0	0	0	0	0	0	0
TOTALS	225	31-68	12-27	22-35	41	19	14	1	20	96
Percentages		45.6	44.4	62.9						

Coach: Nolan Richardson

96-91

43	1H	34
40	2H	49
13	OT1	8

MEMPHIS	MIN	FG	3FG	FT	REB	A	ST	BL	PF	TP
Mingo Johnson	33	10-18	5-9	7-10	2	5	2	0	4	32
Cedric Henderson	40	5-17	2-6	2-2	6	2	3	3	3	14
Lorenzen Wright	42	6-11	0-0	0-1	14	2	0	1	4	12
Michael Wilson	23	5-7	0-0	1-1	7	1	0	0	2	11
David Vaughn	29	2-7	0-0	3-5	9	0	0	0	2	7
Justin Wimmer	13	3-7	1-5	0-0	1	1	0	0	3	7
Chris Garner	39	2-4	1-1	0-1	5	8	3	0	5	5
Marcus Nolan	1	1-1	1-1	0-0	0	0	0	0	0	3
Rodney Newsom	4	0-3	0-1	0-0	2	0	0	0	1	0
Leon Mitchell	1	0-0	0-0	0-0	0	0	0	0	0	0
TOTALS	225	34-75	10-23	13-20	46	19	8	4	24	91
Percentages		45.3	43.5	65.0						

Coach: Larry Finch

Officials: James Burr, Larry Rose, David Hall
Technicals: Arkansas (Beck), Memphis (Johnson)
Attendance: 16,153

Kentucky 97-73 Arizona State

KENTUCKY	MIN	FG	3FG	FT	REB	A	ST	BL	PF	TP
Tony Delk	31	11-18	3-5	1-2	5	1	1	0	2	26
Rodrick Rhodes	27	6-8	1-2	3-3	5	8	1	0	0	16
Andre Riddick	20	6-8	0-0	3-6	6	0	3	1	3	15
Walter McCarty	20	3-4	0-1	4-4	5	1	1	1	2	10
Antoine Walker	16	3-13	1-1	2-2	10	2	0	1	2	9
Chris Harrison	6	2-2	2-2	0-0	0	0	0	0	0	6
Jeff Sheppard	25	2-5	0-0	0-0	1	5	3	0	3	4
Anthony Epps	18	2-3	0-1	0-0	2	7	1	1	1	4
Mark Pope	20	1-3	0-1	1-2	2	0	1	2	3	3
Jared Prickett	13	1-2	0-0	0-0	2	3	1	0	3	2
Allen Edwards	4	1-2	0-1	0-0	0	0	0	0	0	2
TOTALS	200	38-68	7-14	14-19	38	27	12	6	19	97
Percentages		55.9	50.0	73.7						

Coach: Rick Pitino

97-73

42	1H	34
55	2H	39

ARIZONA STATE	MIN	FG	3FG	FT	REB	A	ST	BL	PF	TP
Ron Riley	34	6-16	4-8	4-8	9	0	2	0	3	20
Mario Bennett	39	5-12	1-3	5-8	8	4	0	2	4	16
Jeremy Veal	27	4-9	4-6	0-0	2	0	0	0	4	12
Isaac Burton	25	4-10	4-10	0-0	7	3	1	0	2	12
Quincy Brewer	25	3-4	0-0	1-5	4	1	0	0	2	7
Marcell Capers	33	0-3	0-1	4-4	0	5	0	0	4	4
James Bacon	14	1-4	0-0	0-0	1	0	1	0	1	2
Joe Zaletel	3	0-0	0-0	0-0	0	0	0	0	0	0
TOTALS	200	23-58	13-28	14-25	31	13	4	2	20	73
Percentages		39.7	46.4	56.0						

Coach: Bill Frieder

Officials: Dick Paparo, Donnee Gray, Frank Scagliotta
Technicals: None
Attendance: 17,458

North Carolina 74-64 Georgetown

NORTH CAROLINA	MIN	FG	3FG	FT	REB	A	ST	BL	PF	TP
Rasheed Wallace	31	10-13	0-0	2-4	12	0	1	6	4	22
Donald Williams	34	6-14	4-9	4-6	2	2	0	0	2	20
Jerry Stackhouse	35	5-9	0-0	2-5	7	4	1	3	1	12
Dante Calabria	34	3-5	2-4	0-0	6	1	0	0	3	8
Jeff McInnis	32	1-8	0-5	3-4	3	4	1	0	3	5
Pierce Landry	17	1-6	1-5	0-0	5	1	0	1	3	3
Pat Sullivan	8	0-2	0-1	2-2	1	1	0	0	0	2
Serge Zwikker	8	1-2	0-0	0-0	1	0	0	1	2	2
Shammond Williams	1	0-0	0-0	0-0	0	0	0	0	0	0
TOTALS	200	27-59	7-24	13-21	37	13	3	11	18	74
Percentages		45.8	29.2	61.9						

Coach: Dean Smith

74-64

35	1H	26
39	2H	38

GEORGETOWN	MIN	FG	3FG	FT	REB	A	ST	BL	PF	TP
Allen Iverson	35	8-20	2-4	6-9	8	3	0	0	5	24
Othella Harrington	31	7-16	0-0	4-5	11	2	2	1	3	18
Jerome Williams	36	6-8	0-0	4-6	10	1	0	0	2	16
Irvin Church	14	1-5	1-3	0-0	1	0	1	0	0	3
John Jacques	28	1-9	0-3	0-0	3	1	0	0	1	2
Don Reid	21	0-2	0-0	1-2	5	0	1	2	3	1
Boubacar Aw	21	0-5	0-0	0-0	5	2	1	0	4	0
Kevin Millen	7	0-2	0-0	0-0	0	0	1	0	0	0
Eric Myles	4	0-2	0-2	0-0	0	0	0	0	0	0
Jahidi White	2	0-0	0-0	0-0	0	0	0	1	0	0
Jerry Nichols	1	0-0	0-0	0-0	0	0	0	0	0	0
TOTALS	200	23-69	3-12	15-22	43	9	6	4	18	64
Percentages		33.3	25.0	68.2						

Coach: John Thompson Jr.

Officials: Tom Harrington, Paul Janssen, Mike Sanzere
Technicals: None
Attendance: 17,458

Oklahoma State 71-66 Wake Forest

OKLAHOMA STATE	MIN	FG	3FG	FT	REB	A	ST	BL	PF	TP
Randy Rutherford	37	7-14	3-7	6-6	11	1	1	0	0	23
Bryant Reeves	40	4-15	0-0	7-8	9	2	0	2	3	15
Chianti Roberts	29	6-8	1-1	0-0	6	1	1	0	4	13
Andre Owens	36	2-3	1-1	3-5	2	3	4	1	1	8
Jason Skaer	12	2-5	2-4	1-2	1	0	0	1	0	7
Terry Collins	27	2-5	0-0	1-4	4	5	2	0	1	5
Scott Pierce	19	0-7	0-0	0-0	2	0	1	0	1	0
TOTALS	200	23-57	7-13	18-25	35	12	9	4	10	71
Percentages		40.4	53.8	72.0						

Coach: Eddie Sutton

71-66

33	1H	31
38	2H	35

WAKE FOREST	MIN	FG	3FG	FT	REB	A	ST	BL	PF	TP
Randolph Childress	40	6-16	3-11	7-8	4	6	1	0	3	22
Rusty LaRue	27	6-10	5-7	0-0	0	1	1	0	4	17
Tim Duncan	40	6-11	0-0	0-2	22	2	1	8	3	12
Travis Banks	39	4-10	0-0	0-0	8	0	1	0	2	8
Jerry Braswell	19	2-5	2-4	0-0	1	0	0	0	0	6
Ricardo Peral	25	0-3	0-3	1-2	2	2	0	1	3	1
Tony Rutland	10	0-4	0-3	0-0	0	4	0	0	1	0
TOTALS	200	24-59	10-28	8-12	37	15	4	9	16	66
Percentages		40.7	35.7	66.7						

Coach: Dave Odom

Officials: Ted Valentine, Larry Lembo, Tom Lopes
Technicals: None
Attendance: 19,689

Massachusetts 76-51 Tulsa

MASSACHUSETTS	MIN	FG	3FG	FT	REB	A	ST	BL	PF	TP
Marcus Camby	22	6-15	0-0	8-12	9	1	2	5	1	20
Derek Kellogg	33	4-7	2-4	2-2	1	4	2	1	1	12
Carmelo Travieso	28	3-9	3-8	0-0	6	2	2	1	3	9
Lou Roe	28	4-10	0-0	0-2	9	2	1	1	2	8
Donta Bright	20	4-6	0-0	0-0	3	0	1	1	4	8
Tyrone Weeks	18	2-4	0-0	2-2	7	1	0	0	1	6
Inus Norville	5	2-3	0-0	1-3	1	0	0	0	2	5
Dana Dingle	22	1-1	0-0	1-4	8	0	0	0	2	3
Edgar Padilla	10	1-2	0-0	0-0	0	2	0	0	1	2
Jeff Meyer	7	1-1	0-0	0-0	0	0	0	0	1	2
Ted Cottrell	2	0-1	0-0	1-2	0	0	0	0	0	1
Rigoberto Nunez	4	0-1	0-0	0-0	2	0	1	0	0	0
Jason Germain	1	0-0	0-0	0-0	0	0	0	0	0	0
TOTALS	200	28-60	5-12	15-27	46	12	9	9	18	76
Percentages		46.7	41.7	55.6						

Coach: John Calipari

76-51

42	1H	24
34	2H	27

TULSA	MIN	FG	3FG	FT	REB	A	ST	BL	PF	TP
Shea Seals	38	6-16	1-5	6-8	6	2	2	1	2	19
Kwanza Johnson	35	3-13	1-2	1-2	9	1	3	0	1	8
Alvin Williamson	36	2-12	0-8	2-2	1	2	1	0	1	6
J.R. Rollo	26	2-3	0-0	0-0	7	0	0	1	3	4
Ray Poindexter	18	1-3	0-0	2-4	8	1	1	3	4	4
Rafael Maldonado	15	1-4	0-0	1-2	1	0	0	0	5	3
Kevin Grawer	5	1-3	1-2	0-0	1	0	0	0	1	3
Dewayne Bonner	3	1-2	0-1	1-1	0	0	0	0	1	3
Craig Hernadi	14	0-0	0-0	1-2	0	0	0	2	0	1
Cordell Love	7	0-6	0-5	0-0	0	0	0	0	1	0
Jamie Gillin	3	0-1	0-0	0-0	1	0	0	0	1	0
TOTALS	200	17-63	3-23	14-21	34	6	8	7	19	51
Percentages		27.0	13.0	66.7						

Coach: Tubby Smith

Officials: Rusty Herring, Duke Edsall, Bill Kennedy
Technicals: None
Attendance: 19,689

86-67

40	1H	19
46	2H	48

SWEET 16

UCLA	MIN	FG	3FG	FT	REB	A	ST	BL	PF	TP
Ed O'Bannon	29	8-14	3-6	2-3	8	1	1	0	2	21
Toby Bailey	31	3-11	0-2	6-9	5	2	0	0	2	12
George Zidek	28	5-11	0-0	1-4	2	0	0	2	3	11
Tyus Edney	25	4-6	1-2	1-2	3	8	0	0	3	10
Charles O'Bannon	22	3-7	0-1	3-4	5	2	1	0	1	9
J.R. Henderson	26	2-3	0-0	4-5	2	1	3	0	2	8
Kris Johnson	7	1-2	0-0	3-6	3	1	0	0	1	5
Ike Nwankwo	5	0-1	0-0	4-4	0	1	0	0	0	4
omm'A Givens	2	2-2	0-0	0-0	2	0	0	0	1	4
Cameron Dollar	23	0-1	0-0	2-6	6	2	4	0	3	2
Kevin Dempsey	1	0-0	0-0	0-0	0	0	0	0	0	0
Bob Myers	1	0-0	0-0	0-0	0	0	0	0	0	0
TOTALS	200	28-58	4-11	26-43	36	18	9	2	18	86
Percentages		48.3	36.4	60.5						

Coach: Jim Harrick

MISSISSIPPI STATE	MIN	FG	3FG	FT	REB	A	ST	BL	PF	TP
Darryl Wilson	38	7-21	5-14	3-5	6	3	1	0	4	22
Erick Dampier	34	4-4	0-0	3-4	4	1	0	4	5	11
Marcus Bullard	19	3-9	2-6	2-2	3	2	2	0	0	10
Russell Walters	17	3-5	0-0	4-6	7	1	0	0	3	10
T.J. Honore	33	2-10	2-7	0-0	4	5	1	0	3	6
Brian Price	22	3-5	0-0	0-0	2	3	0	0	0	6
Marcus Grant	27	1-8	0-5	0-0	10	3	1	0	4	2
Whit Hughes	8	0-0	0-0	0-0	1	0	0	0	2	0
Bubba Wilson	1	0-0	0-0	0-0	0	0	0	0	0	0
Jack Young	1	0-0	0-0	0-0	0	0	0	0	0	0
TOTALS	200	23-62	9-32	12-17	37	18	5	4	21	67
Percentages		37.1	28.1	70.6						

Coach:

Officials: Silvestre, M Wood
Technicals: None
Attendance: 14,399

99-89

49	1H	41
50	2H	48

SWEET 16

CONNECTICUT	MIN	FG	3FG	FT	REB	A	ST	BL	PF	TP
Donny Marshall	35	11-22	3-3	2-4	9	2	2	0	1	27
Ray Allen	32	8-16	2-6	0-2	11	3	1	1	2	18
Travis Knight	17	6-7	0-0	3-4	4	0	1	0	5	15
Doron Sheffer	32	3-7	0-1	6-6	1	7	0	0	3	12
Eric Hayward	20	4-4	0-0	4-7	5	0	1	1	1	12
Kevin Ollie	34	2-7	0-2	5-6	4	4	1	0	0	9
Brian Fair	15	1-7	1-2	1-4	3	4	0	0	0	4
Kirk King	7	1-2	0-0	0-0	2	1	0	0	1	2
Rudy Johnson	5	0-2	0-0	0-0	2	1	0	0	2	0
Uri Cohen-Mintz	1	0-0	0-0	0-0	0	0	0	0	0	0
Marcus Thomas	1	0-0	0-0	0-0	0	0	0	0	0	0
Nantambu Willingham	1	0-0	0-0	0-0	0	0	0	0	0	0
TOTALS	200	36-74	6-14	21-33	41	22	6	2	15	99
Percentages		48.6	42.9	63.6						

Coach: Jim Calhoun

MARYLAND	MIN	FG	3FG	FT	REB	A	ST	BL	PF	TP
Johnny Rhodes	35	9-18	2-5	2-3	7	5	0	0	3	22
Joe Smith	31	10-17	0-1	2-2	14	0	0	1	3	22
Exree Hipp	30	5-11	1-1	2-4	5	4	0	0	5	13
Keith Booth	30	4-9	0-2	2-3	11	3	1	1	2	10
Duane Simpkins	36	4-11	1-5	0-0	1	5	1	0	4	9
Mario Lucas	15	3-7	0-3	1-2	2	1	1	0	1	7
Wayne Bristol	14	1-4	0-2	0-0	2	3	0	0	3	2
Matt Raydo	1	1-2	0-0	0-0	1	0	0	0	0	2
Kurtis Shultz	1	1-1	0-0	0-0	1	0	0	0	0	2
Matt Kovarik	3	0-0	0-0	0-0	1	1	0	0	3	0
Rodney Elliot	2	0-1	0-0	0-0	0	0	0	0	0	0
Sarunas Jasikevicius	1	0-1	0-0	0-0	0	0	0	0	0	0
Donny Judd	1	0-1	0-1	0-0	0	0	0	0	0	0
TOTALS	200	38-83	4-20	9-14	45	22	3	2	24	89
Percentages		45.8	20.0	64.3						

Coach: Gary Williams

Officials: Ed Hightower, David Dodge, Scott Thornle
Technicals: None
Attendance: 14,399

68-61

37	1H	25
31	2H	36

ELITE 8

ARKANSAS	MIN	FG	3FG	FT	REB	A	ST	BL	PF	TP
Corliss Williamson	35	8-13	0-0	5-6	9	3	2	0	3	21
Scotty Thurman	33	7-16	2-6	1-2	8	1	2	0	1	17
Corey Beck	30	1-5	0-2	5-6	6	3	2	0	4	7
Davor Rimac	15	2-4	2-4	0-0	0	1	0	0	1	6
Dwight Stewart	17	1-7	1-6	2-2	6	1	0	1	3	5
Lee Wilson	10	2-2	0-0	1-2	4	1	0	1	2	5
Clint McDaniel	29	1-2	0-1	2-2	1	1	2	0	3	4
Alex Dillard	12	1-5	0-2	1-1	3	2	1	0	1	3
Darnell Robinson	9	0-1	0-1	0-0	3	0	0	0	1	0
Elmer Martin	8	0-2	0-2	0-0	1	0	0	1	3	0
Reggie Garrett	2	0-1	0-0	0-0	0	0	0	0	0	0
TOTALS	200	23-58	5-24	17-21	41	13	9	3	22	68
Percentages		39.7	20.8	81.0						

Coach: Nolan Richardson

VIRGINIA	MIN	FG	3FG	FT	REB	A	ST	BL	PF	TP
Junior Burrough	39	6-14	1-1	9-11	16	1	-	0	3	22
Curtis Staples	38	6-15	4-10	0-0	4	2	-	0	4	16
Harold Deane	38	4-16	1-9	3-7	2	2	-	0	2	12
Jamal Robinson	16	3-5	0-0	0-0	3	0	-	1	3	6
Jason Williford	32	0-3	0-1	4-8	8	4	-	0	5	4
Yuri Barnes	10	0-1	0-0	1-2	0	0	-	0	2	1
Chris Alexander	23	0-2	0-0	0-0	6	0	-	0	3	0
Norman Nolan	3	0-0	0-0	0-0	0	0	-	0	0	0
Percy Ellsworth	1	0-0	0-0	0-0	0	0	-	0	0	0
TOTALS	200	19-56	6-21	17-28	39	9	-	1	22	61
Percentages		33.9	28.6	60.7						

Coach: Jeff Jones

Officials: Charles Range, John Cahill, Mark Reischling
Technicals: None
Attendance: 15,622

74-61

34	1H	31
40	2H	30

ELITE 8

NORTH CAROLINA	MIN	FG	3FG	FT	REB	A	ST	BL	PF	TP
Jerry Stackhouse	35	3-9	1-3	11-14	12	6	2	2	0	18
Donald Williams	33	7-15	2-8	2-2	4	2	0	0	0	18
Rasheed Wallace	23	5-9	0-0	2-2	3	0	0	0	4	12
Dante Calabria	31	2-3	1-1	3-4	6	2	1	1	3	8
Jeff McInnis	34	3-6	0-2	0-0	7	1	0	0	1	6
Serge Zwikker	16	2-3	0-0	1-2	4	0	1	0	0	5
Shammond Williams	6	0-0	0-0	3-4	1	0	0	0	0	3
Pierce Landry	16	1-3	0-1	0-0	1	1	1	0	1	2
Pat Sullivan	6	1-1	0-0	0-0	2	0	0	0	3	2
TOTALS	200	24-49	4-15	22-28	40	12	5	3	12	74
Percentages		49.0	26.7	78.6						

Coach: Dean Smith

KENTUCKY	MIN	FG	3FG	FT	REB	A	ST	BL	PF	TP
Tony Delk	36	7-21	5-14	0-0	4	3	4	1	2	19
Walter McCarty	24	5-9	2-4	2-2	3	2	1	1	4	14
Rodrick Rhodes	29	2-10	0-6	3-4	0	4	4	0	4	7
Andre Riddick	20	2-5	0-0	2-4	5	1	0	1	4	6
Jeff Sheppard	22	2-9	0-4	0-0	5	2	1	0	1	4
Jared Prickett	20	2-6	0-0	0-0	5	3	1	0	0	4
Anthony Epps	19	0-5	0-3	4-4	2	4	0	0	1	4
Antoine Walker	9	1-5	0-2	0-0	6	0	1	0	4	2
Mark Pope	13	0-2	0-1	1-2	3	0	1	1	2	1
Chris Harrison	7	0-3	0-2	0-0	0	0	0	0	1	0
Allen Edwards	1	0-0	0-0	0-0	0	0	0	0	0	0
TOTALS	200	21-75	7-36	12-16	33	19	13	4	23	61
Percentages		28.0	19.4	75.0						

Coach: Rick Pitino

Officials: Tim Higgins, Bob Donato, Tom Rucker
Technicals: None
Attendance: 17,721

68-54

27	1H	32
41	2H	22

ELITE 8

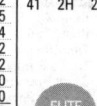

OKLAHOMA STATE	MIN	FG	3FG	FT	REB	A	ST	BL	PF	TP
Bryant Reeves	40	10-21	0-0	4-6	10	2	0	1	2	24
Randy Rutherford	38	7-14	4-10	1-2	6	2	1	2	2	19
Scott Pierce	33	6-8	0-0	0-0	8	1	1	0	3	12
Andre Owens	35	2-9	0-0	1-5	4	5	3	0	2	5
Chianti Roberts	14	2-5	0-1	0-2	5	3	0	2	5	4
Terry Collins	23	1-3	0-1	0-1	7	2	0	0	2	2
Jason Skaer	15	1-3	0-0	0-0	5	1	1	0	2	2
Kevin Miles	1	0-0	0-0	0-0	0	0	0	0	0	0
John Nelson	1	0-0	0-0	0-0	0	0	0	0	0	0
TOTALS	200	29-63	4-12	6-16	45	16	6	5	18	68
Percentages		46.0	33.3	37.5						

Coach: Eddie Sutton

MASSACHUSETTS	MIN	FG	3FG	FT	REB	A	ST	BL	PF	TP
Carmelo Travieso	34	4-10	3-8	0-0	5	1	0	0	0	11
Derek Kellogg	36	3-10	2-6	2-2	5	6	1	0	4	10
Lou Roe	32	3-11	0-0	3-4	7	2	3	1	2	9
Dana Dingle	31	3-10	0-1	3-6	5	1	2	0	4	9
Marcus Camby	23	2-10	0-0	2-3	4	1	0	4	5	6
Donta Bright	21	0-4	0-1	3-5	1	0	0	2	2	3
Tyrone Weeks	18	0-2	0-0	3-4	6	0	0	1	1	3
Rigoberto Nunez	1	1-1	1-1	0-0	0	0	0	0	0	3
Jeff Meyer	4	0-0	0-0	0-0	1	0	0	1	0	0
TOTALS	200	16-58	6-17	16-24	34	11	6	9	18	54
Percentages		27.6	35.3	66.7						

Coach: John Calipari

Officials: Andre Pattillo, Don Rutledge, Steve Welmer
Technicals: None
Attendance: 19,689

102-96

48	1H	41
54	2H	55

ELITE 8

UCLA	MIN	FG	3FG	FT	REB	A	ST	BL	PF	TP
Toby Bailey	38	10-16	0-2	6-12	9	0	1	0	2	26
Tyus Edney	40	5-11	2-3	10-10	2	10	1	0	4	22
J.R. Henderson	30	9-12	0-0	0-1	2	1	0	1	4	18
Ed O'Bannon	33	5-13	0-6	5-6	6	2	1	0	3	15
Charles O'Bannon	24	2-4	0-0	6-8	5	5	2	1	2	10
George Zidek	12	4-9	0-0	0-0	3	0	1	0	4	8
Cameron Dollar	23	1-1	0-0	1-2	6	5	3	0	3	3
TOTALS	200	36-66	2-11	28-39	33	23	9	2	22	102
Percentages		54.5	18.2	71.8						

Coach: Jim Harrick

CONNECTICUT	MIN	FG	3FG	FT	REB	A	ST	BL	PF	TP
Ray Allen	38	12-25	3-8	9-12	9	3	1	-	2	36
Doron Sheffer	35	9-20	2-8	4-4	5	4	1	-	4	24
Donny Marshall	37	3-11	1-4	8-8	9	0	0	-	4	15
Travis Knight	26	6-9	0-0	0-1	13	0	1	-	3	12
Brian Fair	13	1-3	1-2	0-0	1	2	0	-	3	3
Kevin Ollie	32	1-6	0-0	0-0	3	8	2	-	5	2
Eric Hayward	13	0-0	0-0	2-2	1	0	0	-	1	2
Kirk King	3	1-2	0-0	0-0	2	0	0	-	3	2
Rudy Johnson	2	0-0	0-0	0-0	0	0	0	-	1	0
Nantambu Willingham	1	0-0	0-0	0-0	0	0	0	-	0	0
TOTALS	200	33-76	7-22	23-27	43	17	5	-	26	96
Percentages		43.4	31.8	85.2						

Coach: Jim Calhoun

Officials: Gerry Donaghy, Tom O'Neill, Stan Reynolds
Technicals: None
Attendance: 14,399

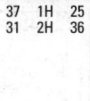

ANNUAL REVIEW

75-68

	1H	2H
Arkansas	34	41
North Carolina	38	30

ARKANSAS	MIN	FG	3FG	FT	REB	A	ST	BL	PF	TP
Corliss Williamson	29	10-17	0-0	1-1	10	1	2	1	4	21
Dwight Stewart	24	6-10	3-7	0-2	8	3	2	0	2	15
Clint McDaniel	32	3-7	3-5	4-4	5	2	1	0	3	13
Scotty Thurman	37	2-10	2-9	0-0	5	3	2	0	3	6
Davor Rimac	17	2-8	2-6	0-0	1	2	0	0	1	6
Corey Beck	30	2-9	1-1	0-0	3	10	0	0	3	5
Lee Wilson	12	1-3	0-0	2-2	4	0	2	0	1	4
Elmer Martin	5	1-1	1-1	0-0	1	1	0	0	0	3
Darnell Robinson	8	1-4	0-1	0-0	4	0	0	0	0	2
Alex Dillard	6	0-5	0-4	0-0	0	0	0	0	0	0
TOTALS	**200**	**28-74**	**12-34**	**7-9**	**41**	**22**	**9**	**1**	**17**	**75**
Percentages		37.8	35.3	77.8						

Coach: Nolan Richardson

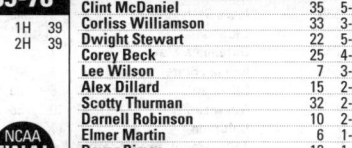

NORTH CAROLINA	MIN	FG	3FG	FT	REB	A	ST	BL	PF	TP
Donald Williams	36	7-19	5-12	0-0	6	1	1	0	1	19
Jerry Stackhouse	28	4-7	3-3	7-10	6	2	0	0	2	18
Jeff McInnis	37	3-9	2-5	5-6	7	3	0	0	4	13
Rasheed Wallace	33	4-6	0-0	2-4	10	0	0	4	4	10
Pat Sullivan	13	1-2	0-0	2-4	0	0	0	0	0	4
Dante Calabria	35	1-10	0-7	0-0	5	9	2	1	1	2
Pierce Landry	10	1-2	0-1	0-0	1	0	0	0	0	2
Serge Zwikker	6	0-1	0-0	0-0	2	0	0	0	1	0
Shammond Williams	2	0-0	0-0	0-0	1	0	0	0	0	0
TOTALS	**200**	**21-56**	**10-28**	**16-24**	**38**	**15**	**3**	**5**	**13**	**68**
Percentages		37.5	35.7	66.7						

Coach: Dean Smith

Officials: Tom Harrington, Charles Range, Gene Monje
Technicals: None
Attendance: 38,540

74-61

	1H	2H
UCLA	37	37
Oklahoma State	37	24

UCLA	MIN	FG	3FG	FT	REB	A	ST	BL	PF	TP
Tyus Edney	37	6-12	0-1	9-11	1	5	0	0	1	21
Charles O'Bannon	37	7-9	0-0	5-5	6	2	1	0	2	19
Ed O'Bannon	36	6-14	2-4	1-2	8	0	4	1	1	15
Cameron Dollar	18	1-1	0-0	7-8	3	0	2	0	0	9
George Zidek	19	2-4	0-0	2-2	2	0	0	0	4	6
J.R. Henderson	25	1-6	0-0	0-0	1	1	3	0	4	2
Toby Bailey	23	1-2	0-1	0-0	0	1	0	0	2	2
Kevin Dempsey	1	0-0	0-0	0-0	0	0	0	0	0	0
omm'A Givens	1	0-0	0-0	0-0	0	0	0	0	1	0
Kris Johnson	1	0-1	0-1	0-0	0	0	0	0	0	0
Bob Myers	1	0-0	0-0	0-0	1	0	0	0	0	0
Ike Nwankwo	1	0-0	0-0	0-0	0	0	0	0	1	0
TOTALS	**200**	**24-49**	**2-7**	**24-28**	**22**	**9**	**10**	**1**	**16**	**74**
Percentages		49.0	28.6	85.7						

Coach: Jim Harrick

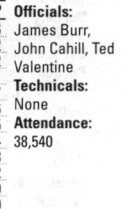

OKLAHOMA STATE	MIN	FG	3FG	FT	REB	A	ST	BL	PF	TP
Bryant Reeves	40	8-16	0-0	9-9	9	0	0	0	2	25
Randy Rutherford	40	4-13	4-11	3-4	4	1	0	0	3	15
Chianti Roberts	29	5-7	0-2	0-2	6	0	0	2	4	10
Terry Collins	22	2-6	2-3	0-0	2	5	2	0	2	6
Andre Owens	35	1-4	1-3	0-0	6	9	1	1	5	3
Scott Pierce	24	1-4	0-0	0-1	2	1	1	0	4	2
Jason Skaer	6	0-0	0-0	0-0	1	0	0	0	1	0
Chad Alexander	1	0-0	0-0	0-0	0	0	0	0	0	0
Ben Baum	1	0-0	0-0	0-0	0	0	0	0	0	0
Kevin Miles	1	0-0	0-0	0-0	1	0	0	0	0	0
John Nelson	1	0-0	0-0	0-0	0	0	0	0	0	0
TOTALS	**200**	**21-50**	**7-19**	**12-16**	**31**	**16**	**4**	**3**	**21**	**61**
Percentages		42.0	36.8	75.0						

Coach: Eddie Sutton

Officials: Dick Paparo, Tom Lopes, Andre Pattillo
Technicals: None
Attendance: 38,540

89-78

	1H	2H
UCLA	40	49
Arkansas	39	39

UCLA	MIN	FG	3FG	FT	REB	A	ST	BL	PF	TP
Ed O'Bannon	40	10-21	1-4	9-11	17	3	3	0	2	30
Toby Bailey	39	12-20	1-2	1-2	9	3	2	0	3	26
George Zidek	29	5-8	0-0	4-7	6	0	0	0	4	14
Charles O'Bannon	36	4-10	0-0	3-4	9	6	2	2	1	11
Cameron Dollar	36	1-4	0-1	4-5	3	8	4	1	4	6
J.R. Henderson	17	1-5	0-0	0-0	2	1	0	1	1	2
Tyus Edney	3	0-0	0-0	0-0	0	0	0	0	0	0
TOTALS	**200**	**33-68**	**2-7**	**21-29**	**46**	**21**	**11**	**4**	**15**	**89**
Percentages		48.5	28.6	72.4						

Coach: Jim Harrick

ARKANSAS	MIN	FG	3FG	FT	REB	A	ST	BL	PF	TP
Clint McDaniel	35	5-10	3-7	3-4	3	1	4	0	5	16
Corliss Williamson	33	3-16	0-0	6-10	4	6	4	0	1	12
Dwight Stewart	22	5-10	1-5	1-2	5	0	0	0	4	12
Corey Beck	25	4-6	2-3	1-2	3	2	3	1	3	11
Lee Wilson	7	3-4	0-0	1-2	0	0	0	1	1	7
Alex Dillard	15	2-4	2-3	0-0	2	1	0	0	1	6
Scotty Thurman	32	2-9	1-7	0-0	3	1	1	0	2	5
Darnell Robinson	10	2-3	0-1	0-0	2	0	0	2	3	4
Elmer Martin	6	1-2	1-2	0-0	3	1	1	0	2	3
Davor Rimac	12	1-1	0-0	0-0	2	3	2	0	0	2
Reggie Garrett	2	0-0	0-0	0-0	0	0	0	0	0	0
Landis Williams	1	0-0	0-0	0-0	0	0	0	0	0	0
TOTALS	**200**	**28-65**	**10-28**	**12-20**	**27**	**15**	**15**	**4**	**22**	**78**
Percentages		43.1	35.7	60.0						

Coach: Nolan Richardson

Officials: James Burr, John Cahill, Ted Valentine
Technicals: None
Attendance: 38,540

National Invitational Tournament (NIT)

First round: Penn State d. Miami 62-56, Iowa d. DePaul 96-87, Marquette d. Auburn 68-61, Coppin State d. Saint Joseph's 75-68 (OT), New Mexico St. d. Colorado 97-83, Canisius d. Seton Hall 83-71, Washington State d. Texas Tech 94-82, Nebraska d. Georgia 69-61, Ohio d. George Washington 83-71, St. Bonaventure d. Southern Miss 75-70, South Florida d. St. John's 74-67, Providence d. Charleston 72-67, Bradley d. Eastern Michigan 86-85 (2OT), Illinois State d. Utah State 93-87 (OT), Virginia Tech d. Clemson 62-54, UTEP d. Montana 90-60
Second round: Marquette d. St. Bonaventure 70-61, South Florida d. Coppin State 75-59, Washington State d. Illinois State 83-80, Canisius d. Bradley 55-53, Virginia Tech d. Providence 91-78, New Mexico St. d. UTEP 92-89, Iowa d. Ohio 66-62, Penn State d. Nebraska 65-59
Third round: Virginia Tech d. New Mexico St. 64-61, Marquette d. South Florida 67-60 (OT), Canisius d. Washington State 89-80, Penn State d. Iowa 67-64
Semifinals: Virginia Tech d. Canisius 71-59, Marquette d. Penn State 87-79
Third place: Penn State d. Canisius 66-62.
Championship: Virginia Tech d. Marquette 65-64 (OT)
MVP: Shawn Smith, Virginia Tech

1995-96: KENTUCKY REIGNS

Massachusetts—lifted from its usual also-ran status by star Marcus Camby and coach John Calipari—joined Mississippi State, Syracuse and Kentucky at the Continental Arena (now Izod Center) in East Rutherford, N.J., for the last Final Four to be played in a non-dome facility. The Wildcats beat UMass in the national semifinals, 81-74, and then turned back Syracuse, 76-67, for coach Rick Pitino's first title. Tony Delk tied a championship game record by hitting seven of 12 three-pointers (24 points in all) and was named the Tournament MOP.

In coach Pete Carril's final Tournament, No. 13-seed Princeton upset No. 4-seed—and defending champion—UCLA, 43-41, thanks to a backdoor layup by freshman Gabe Lewullis with 3.9 seconds left. It was the first time the Tigers advanced past the first round since 1983. A dubious record was set by six Tournament participants: California, Connecticut, Massachusetts, Michigan, Purdue and Texas Tech would all have their 1996 appearances vacated by the NCAA for rules violations, the most teams ever retroactively erased from a single Tournament.

Camby was the season's Naismith POY for averaging 20.5 points, 8.2 rebounds and 3.8 blocks per game. The Philadelphia 76ers selected Georgetown sophomore Allen Iverson as the No. 1 pick in the NBA draft.

MAJOR CONFERENCE STANDINGS

AM. WEST

	Conference			Overall		
	W	L	PCT	W	L	PCT
Cal Poly	5	1	.833	16	13	.552
Southern Utah	3	3	.500	15	13	.536
Cal State Northridge	2	4	.333	7	20	.259
Cal State Sacramento	2	4	.333	7	20	.259

Tournament: **Southern Utah d. Cal Poly 55-53**
Tournament MVP: **Jon Gaines**, Southern Utah

ACC

	Conference			Overall		
	W	L	PCT	W	L	PCT
Georgia Tech○	13	3	.813	24	12	.667
Wake Forest⊕	12	4	.750	26	6	.813
North Carolina○	10	6	.625	21	11	.656
Duke○	8	8	.500	18	13	.581
Maryland○	8	8	.500	17	13	.567
Clemson○	7	9	.438	18	11	.621
Virginia	6	10	.375	12	15	.444
Florida State	5	11	.313	13	14	.481
NC State	3	13	.188	15	16	.484

Tournament: **Wake Forest d. Georgia Tech 75-74**
Tournament MVP: **Tim Duncan**, Wake Forest

ATLANTIC 10

	Conference			Overall		
	W	L	PCT	W	L	PCT
EAST						
Massachusetts⊕⊗	15	1	.938	35	2	.946
Temple○	12	4	.750	20	13	.606
Saint Joseph's□	9	7	.563	19	13	.594
Rhode Island□	8	8	.500	20	14	.588
St. Bonaventure	4	12	.250	10	18	.357
Fordham	2	14	.125	4	23	.148
WEST						
Virginia Tech○	13	3	.813	23	6	.793
George Washington○	13	3	.813	21	8	.724
Xavier	8	8	.500	13	15	.464
Dayton	6	10	.375	15	14	.517
Duquesne	3	13	.188	9	18	.333
La Salle	3	13	.188	6	24	.200

Tournament: **Massachusetts d. Temple 75-61**
Tournament MOP: **Carmelo Travieso**, Massachusetts

BIG EAST

	Conference			Overall		
	W	L	PCT	W	L	PCT
BIG EAST 7						
Georgetown○	13	5	.722	29	8	.784
Syracuse○	12	6	.667	29	9	.763
Providence□	9	9	.500	18	12	.600
Miami (FL)	8	10	.444	15	13	.536
Seton Hall⊗	7	11	.389	12	16	.429
Rutgers	6	12	.333	9	18	.333
Pittsburgh	5	13	.278	10	17	.370
BIG EAST 6						
Connecticut⊕⊗	17	1	.944	32	3	.914
Villanova○	14	4	.778	26	7	.788
Boston College○	10	8	.556	19	11	.633
West Virginia	7	11	.389	12	15	.444
St. John's	5	13	.278	11	16	.407
Notre Dame	4	14	.222	9	18	.333

Tournament: **Connecticut d. Georgetown 75-74**
Tournament MVP: **Victor Page**, Georgetown

BIG EIGHT

	Conference			Overall		
	W	L	PCT	W	L	PCT
Kansas○	12	2	.857	29	5	.853
Iowa State⊕⊗	9	5	.643	24	9	.727
Oklahoma○⊗	8	6	.571	17	13	.567
Oklahoma State	7	7	.500	17	10	.630
Kansas State○	7	7	.500	17	12	.586
Missouri□	6	8	.429	18	15	.545
Nebraska□	4	10	.286	21	14	.600
Colorado	3	11	.214	9	18	.333

Tournament: **Iowa State d. Kansas 56-55**
Tournament MVP: **Dedric Willoughby**, Iowa State

BIG SKY

	Conference			Overall		
	W	L	PCT	W	L	PCT
Montana State⊕	11	3	.786	21	9	.700
Montana	10	4	.714	20	8	.714
Weber State	10	4	.714	20	10	.667
Boise State	10	4	.714	15	13	.536
Idaho State	7	7	.500	11	15	.423
Idaho	5	9	.357	12	16	.429
Northern Arizona⊗	3	11	.214	6	20	.231
Eastern Washington	0	14	.000	3	23	.115

Tournament: **Montana State d. Weber State 81-70**
Tournament MVP: **Danny Sprinkle**, Montana State

BIG SOUTH

	Conference			Overall		
	W	L	PCT	W	L	PCT
UNC Greensboro⊕	11	3	.786	20	10	.667
UNC Asheville	9	5	.643	18	10	.643
Liberty	9	5	.643	17	12	.586
Charleston Southern	9	5	.643	15	13	.536
Radford	8	6	.571	14	13	.519
Winthrop	6	8	.429	7	19	.269
UMBC	3	11	.214	5	22	.185
Coastal Carolina	1	13	.071	5	21	.192

Tournament: **UNC Greensboro d. Liberty 79-53**
Tournament MVP: **Scott Hartzell**, UNC Greensboro

BIG TEN

	Conference			Overall		
	W	L	PCT	W	L	PCT
Purdue⊕⊗	15	3	.833	26	6	.813
Penn State○	12	6	.667	21	7	.750
Indiana○⊗	12	6	.667	19	12	.613
Iowa○⊗	11	7	.611	23	9	.719
Michigan○⊗	10	8	.556	21	11	.625
Minnesota□⊗	10	8	.556	19	13	.594
Michigan State□	9	9	.500	16	16	.500
Wisconsin□⊗	8	10	.444	17	15	.531
Illinois□	7	11	.389	18	13	.581
Ohio State⊗	3	18	.143	10	17	.370
Northwestern⊗	2	16	.111	7	20	.259

BIG WEST

	Conference			Overall		
	W	L	PCT	W	L	PCT
Long Beach State	12	6	.667	17	11	.607
Pacific	11	7	.611	15	12	.556
UC Irvine	11	7	.611	15	12	.556
Utah State	10	8	.556	18	15	.545
Nevada	9	9	.500	16	13	.552
San Jose State⊕	9	9	.500	13	17	.433
New Mexico State	8	10	.444	11	15	.423
UC Santa Barbara	8	10	.444	11	15	.423
UNLV	7	11	.389	10	16	.385
Cal State Fullerton	5	13	.278	6	20	.231

Tournament: **San Jose State d. Utah State 76-75 (OT)**
Tournament MVP: **Olivier Saint-Jean**, San Jose State

COLONIAL ATHLETIC

	Conference			Overall		
	W	L	PCT	W	L	PCT
VCU⊕	14	2	.875	24	9	.727
Old Dominion	12	4	.750	18	13	.581
UNC Wilmington	9	7	.563	13	16	.448
East Carolina	8	8	.500	17	11	.607
American	8	8	.500	12	15	.444
George Mason	6	10	.375	11	16	.407
William and Mary	6	10	.375	10	16	.385
James Madison	6	10	.375	10	20	.333
Richmond	3	13	.188	8	20	.286

Tournament: **VCU d. UNC Wilmington 46-43**
Tournament MVP: **Bernard Hopkins**, VCU

C-USA

	Conference			Overall		
	W	L	PCT	W	L	PCT
RED						
Tulane□	9	5	.643	22	10	.688
UAB	6	8	.429	16	14	.533
Southern Miss	6	8	.429	12	15	.444
South Florida	2	12	.143	12	16	.429
WHITE						
Memphis○	11	3	.786	22	8	.733
Louisville○	10	4	.714	22	12	.647
Charlotte⊗	6	8	.429	14	15	.483
BLUE						
Cincinnati○	11	3	.786	28	5	.848
Marquette○	10	4	.714	23	8	.742
Saint Louis□	4	10	.286	16	14	.533
DePaul⊗	2	12	.143	11	18	.379

Tournament: **Cincinnati d. Marquette 85-84 (OT)**
Tournament MVP: **Danny Fortson**, Cincinnati

IVY

	Conference			Overall		
	W	L	PCT	W	L	PCT
Princeton⊕	12	2	.857	22	7	.759
Penn	12	2	.857	17	10	.630
Dartmouth	9	5	.643	16	10	.615
Harvard	7	7	.500	15	11	.577
Brown	5	9	.357	10	16	.385
Cornell	5	9	.357	10	16	.385
Yale	3	11	.214	8	18	.308
Columbia	3	11	.214	7	19	.269

Playoff: **Princeton d. Penn 63-56** for the title

MAAC

	Conference			Overall		
	W	L	PCT	W	L	PCT
Iona□	10	4	.714	21	8	.724
Fairfield□	10	4	.714	20	10	.667
Manhattan□	9	5	.643	17	12	.586
Loyola (MD)	8	6	.571	12	15	.444
Canisius⊕	7	7	.500	19	11	.633
Niagara	6	8	.429	13	15	.464
Saint Peter's	5	9	.357	15	12	.556
Siena	1	13	.071	5	22	.185

Tournament: **Canisius d. Fairfield 52-46**
Tournament MVP: **Micheal Meeks**, Canisius

⊕ Automatic NCAA Tournament bid ○ At-large NCAA Tournament bid □ NIT appearance ⊗ Team record doesn't reflect games forfeited or vacated. For adjusted record, see p. 521.

MID-AMERICAN

	Conference			Overall		
	W	L	PCT	W	L	PCT
Eastern Michigan⊕	14	4	.778	25	6	.806
Western Michigan⊗	13	5	.722	15	12	.556
Miami (OH)□	12	6	.667	21	8	.724
Ball State	11	7	.611	16	12	.571
Ohio	11	7	.611	16	14	.533
Toledo	9	9	.500	18	14	.563
Bowling Green	9	9	.500	14	13	.519
Kent State	8	10	.444	14	13	.519
Central Michigan	3	15	.167	6	20	.231
Akron	0	18	.000	3	23	.115

Tournament: **Eastern Michigan d. Toledo 77-63**
Tournament MVP: **Brian Tolbert**, Eastern Michigan

MID-CONTINENT

	Conference			Overall		
	W	L	PCT	W	L	PCT
Valparaiso⊕⊗	13	5	.722	21	11	.656
Western Illinois	12	6	.667	17	12	.586
Northeastern Illinois	10	8	.556	14	13	.519
Buffalo	10	8	.556	13	14	.481
UMKC	10	8	.556	12	15	.444
Central Conn. State	9	9	.500	13	15	.464
Eastern Illinois	9	9	.500	13	15	.464
Troy	8	10	.444	11	16	.407
Youngstown State	7	11	.389	12	15	.444
Chicago State	2	16	.111	2	25	.074

Tournament: **Valparaiso d. Western Illinois 75-52**
Tournament MVP: **Bryce Drew**, Valparaiso

MEAC

	Conference			Overall		
	W	L	PCT	W	L	PCT
South Carolina State⊕	14	2	.875	22	8	.733
Coppin State	14	2	.875	19	10	.655
Bethune-Cookman	8	8	.500	12	15	.444
Delaware State	8	8	.500	11	17	.393
NC A&T	7	9	.438	10	17	.370
UMES	6	10	.375	11	16	.407
Howard	6	10	.375	7	20	.259
Morgan State	6	10	.375	7	20	.259
Florida A&M	3	13	.188	8	19	.296
Hampton	--			9	17	.346

Tournament: **South Carolina St. d. Coppin State 69-56**
Tournament MOP: **Derrick Patterson**, South Carolina St.

MCC

	Conference			Overall		
	W	L	PCT	W	L	PCT
Wisc.-Green Bay○	16	0	1.000	25	4	.862
Butler	12	4	.750	19	8	.704
Northern Illinois⊕	10	6	.625	20	10	.667
Detroit	8	8	.500	18	11	.621
Wright State	8	8	.500	14	13	.519
Illinois-Chicago⊗	5	11	.313	10	18	.357
Wisc.-Milwaukee	5	11	.313	9	18	.333
Loyola-Chicago	5	11	.313	8	19	.296
Cleveland State	3	13	.188	5	21	.192

Tournament: **Northern Illinois d. Detroit 84-63**
Tournament MVP: **Chris Coleman**, Northern Illinois

MISSOURI VALLEY

	Conference			Overall		
	W	L	PCT	W	L	PCT
Bradley○	15	3	.833	22	8	.733
Illinois State□	13	5	.722	22	12	.647
Tulsa⊕	12	6	.667	22	8	.733
Missouri State	11	7	.611	16	12	.571
Creighton	9	9	.500	14	15	.483
Evansville	9	9	.500	13	14	.481
Northern Iowa	8	10	.444	14	13	.519
Drake	8	10	.444	12	15	.444
Indiana State	6	12	.333	10	16	.385
Southern Illinois	4	14	.222	11	18	.379
Wichita State	4	14	.222	8	21	.276

Tournament: **Tulsa d. Bradley 60-46**
Tournament MOP: **Shea Seals**, Tulsa

NAC

	Conference			Overall		
	W	L	PCT	W	L	PCT
Drexel⊕	17	1	.944	27	4	.871
Boston U.	13	5	.722	18	11	.621
Towson	11	7	.611	16	12	.571
Delaware	11	7	.611	15	12	.556
Maine	11	7	.611	15	13	.536
Vermont	10	8	.556	12	15	.444
Hofstra	5	13	.278	9	18	.333
New Hampshire	5	13	.278	6	21	.222
Hartford	5	13	.278	6	22	.214
Northeastern	2	16	.111	4	24	.143

Tournament: **Drexel d. Boston U. 76-67**
Tournament MVP: **Malik Rose**, Drexel

NORTHEAST

	Conference			Overall		
	W	L	PCT	W	L	PCT
Mount St. Mary's□	16	2	.889	21	8	.724
Marist□	14	4	.778	22	7	.759
Monmouth⊕	14	4	.778	20	10	.667
Rider	12	6	.667	19	11	.633
Saint Francis (PA)	11	7	.611	13	14	.481
Wagner	7	11	.389	10	17	.370
Fairleigh Dickinson	6	12	.333	7	20	.259
Long Island	5	13	.278	9	19	.321
St. Francis (NY)	3	15	.167	9	18	.333
Robert Morris	2	16	.111	5	23	.179

Tournament: **Monmouth d. Rider 60-59**
Tournament MVP: **Corey Albano**, Monmouth

OHIO VALLEY

	Conference			Overall		
	W	L	PCT	W	L	PCT
Murray State□⊗	12	4	.750	19	10	.655
Tennessee State	11	5	.688	15	13	.536
Austin Peay⊕	10	6	.625	19	11	.633
Middle Tenn. State	9	7	.563	15	12	.556
Tennessee-Martin	9	7	.563	13	14	.481
Eastern Kentucky	7	9	.438	13	14	.481
Tennessee Tech	7	9	.438	13	15	.464
SE Missouri State	5	11	.313	8	19	.296
Morehead State	2	14	.125	7	20	.259

Tournament: **Austin Peay d. Murray State 92-84**
Tournament MVP: **Bubba Wells**, Austin Peay

PAC-10

	Conference			Overall		
	W	L	PCT	W	L	PCT
UCLA⊕	16	2	.889	23	8	.742
Arizona○⊗	13	5	.722	26	7	.788
Stanford○⊗	12	6	.667	20	9	.690
California○⊗	11	7	.611	17	11	.607
Washington□	9	9	.500	16	12	.571
Oregon⊗	9	9	.500	16	13	.552
Washington State□⊗	8	10	.444	17	12	.586
Arizona State⊗	6	12	.333	11	16	.407
Southern California⊗	4	14	.222	11	19	.367
Oregon State⊗	2	16	.111	4	23	.148

PATRIOT

	Conference			Overall		
	W	L	PCT	W	L	PCT
Navy	9	3	.750	15	12	.556
Colgate⊕	9	3	.750	15	15	.500
Bucknell	8	4	.667	17	11	.607
Holy Cross⊗	8	4	.667	16	13	.552
Lafayette	4	8	.333	7	20	.259
Army	2	10	.167	7	20	.259
Lehigh	2	10	.167	4	23	.148

Tournament: **Colgate d. Holy Cross 74-65**
Tournament MVP: **Adonal Foyle**, Colgate

SEC

	Conference			Overall		
	W	L	PCT	W	L	PCT
Eastern						
Kentucky○	16	0	1.000	34	2	.944
Georgia○	9	7	.563	21	10	.677
South Carolina□	8	8	.500	19	12	.613
Vanderbilt□	7	9	.438	18	14	.563
Tennessee□	6	10	.375	14	15	.483
Florida	6	10	.375	12	16	.429
Western						
Mississippi State⊕	10	6	.625	26	8	.765
Arkansas○	9	7	.563	20	13	.606
Alabama□	9	7	.563	19	13	.594
Auburn□	6	10	.375	19	13	.594
Mississippi	6	10	.375	12	15	.444
LSU	4	12	.250	12	17	.414

Tournament: **Mississippi State d. Kentucky 84-73**
Tournament MVP: **Dontae' Jones**, Mississippi State

SOUTHERN

	Conference			Overall		
	W	L	PCT	W	L	PCT
North						
Davidson□	14	0	1.000	25	5	.833
VMI	10	4	.714	18	10	.643
Marshall	8	6	.571	17	11	.607
Appalachian State	3	11	.214	8	20	.286
East Tenn. State	3	11	.214	7	20	.259
South						
Western Carolina⊕	10	4	.714	17	13	.567
Chattanooga	9	5	.643	15	12	.556
Furman	6	8	.429	10	17	.370
The Citadel	5	9	.357	10	16	.385
Georgia Southern	2	12	.143	3	23	.115

Tournament: **Western Carolina d. Davidson 69-60**
Tournament MOP: **Anquell McCollum**, Western Carolina

SOUTHLAND

	Conference			Overall		
	W	L	PCT	W	L	PCT
UL-Monroe⊕	13	5	.722	16	14	.533
North Texas	12	6	.667	15	13	.536
UTSA	12	6	.667	14	14	.500
Stephen F. Austin	11	7	.611	17	11	.607
McNeese State	11	7	.611	15	12	.556
Sam Houston State	9	9	.500	11	16	.407
Texas-Arlington	7	11	.389	11	15	.423
Texas State	7	11	.389	11	15	.423
Nicholls State	5	13	.278	5	21	.192
Northwestern St. (LA)	3	15	.167	5	21	.192

Tournament: **UL-Monroe d. North Texas 71-60**
Tournament MVP: **Paul Marshall**, UL-Monroe

SOUTHWEST

	Conference			Overall		
	W	L	PCT	W	L	PCT
Texas Tech⊕⊗	14	0	1.000	30	2	.938
Houston	11	3	.786	17	10	.630
Texas○	10	4	.714	21	10	.677
TCU⊗	6	8	.429	15	15	.500
Rice	5	9	.357	14	14	.500
Baylor	4	10	.286	9	18	.333
Texas A&M	3	11	.214	11	16	.407
SMU	3	11	.214	8	20	.286

Tournament: **Texas Tech d. Texas 75-73**
Tournament MVP: **Reggie Freeman**, Texas

SWAC

	Conference			Overall		
	W	L	PCT	W	L	PCT
Miss. Valley State⊕	11	3	.786	22	7	.759
Jackson State	11	3	.786	16	13	.552
Southern U.	8	5	.615	17	11	.607
Texas Southern⊗	7	7	.500	11	15	.423
Alcorn State	7	7	.500	10	15	.400
Grambling	6	7	.462	12	16	.429
Alabama State	5	9	.357	9	18	.333
Prairie View A&M	0	14	.000	4	23	.148

Tournament: **Miss. Valley State d. Jackson State 83-76**
Tournament MVP: **Marcus Mann**, Miss. Valley State

SUN BELT

	Conference			Overall		
	W	L	PCT	W	L	PCT
Ark.-Little Rock□	14	4	.778	23	7	.767
New Orleans⊕	14	4	.778	21	9	.700
Jacksonville	10	8	.556	15	13	.536
Western Kentucky	10	8	.556	13	14	.481
UL-Lafayette	9	9	.500	16	12	.571
Lamar	7	11	.389	12	15	.444
South Alabama	7	11	.389	12	15	.444
Arkansas State	7	11	.389	9	18	.333
Louisiana Tech	6	12	.333	11	17	.393
Texas-Pan American	6	12	.333	9	19	.321

Tournament: **New Orleans d. Ark.-Little Rock 57-56**
Tournament MOP: **Lewis Sims**, New Orleans

TAAC

	Conference			Overall		
	W	L	PCT	W	L	PCT
East						
Charleston□	15	1	.938	25	4	.862
Campbell	11	5	.688	17	11	.607
Florida Int'l	6	10	.375	13	15	.464
Stetson	6	10	.375	10	17	.370
Central Florida⊕	6	10	.375	11	19	.367
Florida Atlantic	5	11	.313	9	18	.333
West						
Samford	11	5	.688	16	11	.593
Southeastern La.	11	5	.688	15	12	.556
Centenary	8	8	.500	11	16	.407
Mercer	7	9	.438	15	14	.517
Georgia State	6	10	.375	10	16	.385
Jacksonville State	4	12	.250	10	17	.370

Tournament: **Central Florida d. Mercer 86-77**
Tournament MVP: **Harry Kennedy**, Central Florida

WEST COAST

	Conference			Overall		
	W	L	PCT	W	L	PCT
Gonzaga□	10	4	.714	21	9	.700
Santa Clara○	10	4	.714	20	9	.690
Loyola Marymount	8	6	.571	18	11	.621
San Francisco⊗	8	6	.571	15	12	.556
Portland⊕	7	7	.500	19	11	.633
San Diego	6	8	.429	14	14	.500
Saint Mary's (CA)	5	9	.357	12	15	.444
Pepperdine	2	12	.143	10	18	.357

Tournament: **Portland d. Gonzaga 76-68**
Tournament MVP: **Kweemada King**, Portland

WAC

	Conference			Overall		
	W	L	PCT	W	L	PCT
Utah○	15	3	.833	27	7	.794
New Mexico⊕	14	4	.778	28	5	.848
Fresno State□	13	5	.722	22	11	.667
Colorado State□	11	7	.611	18	12	.600
BYU	9	9	.500	15	13	.536
San Diego State	8	10	.444	15	14	.517
Wyoming	8	10	.444	14	15	.483
Hawaii	7	11	.389	10	18	.357
UTEP	4	14	.222	13	15	.464
Air Force	1	17	.056	5	23	.179

Tournament: **New Mexico d. Utah 64-60**
Tournament MVP: **Kenny Thomas**, New Mexico

INDEPENDENTS

	Overall		
	W	L	PCT
Oral Roberts	18	9	.667
Wofford	4	22	.154

INDIVIDUAL LEADERS—SEASON

SCORING	CL	POS	G	FG	3FG	FT	PTS	PPG
1 **Kevin Granger**, Texas Southern	SR	G	24	194	30	230	648	**27.0**
2 **Marcus Brown**, Murray State	SR	G	29	254	74	185	767	**26.4**
3 **Bubba Wells**, Austin Peay	JR	F	30	312	34	131	789	**26.3**
4 **JaFonde Williams**, Hampton	SR	G	26	220	83	146	669	**25.7**
5 **Bonzi Wells**, Ball State	SO	F	28	269	31	143	712	**25.4**
6 **Anquell McCollum**, Western Carolina	SR	G	30	257	99	138	751	**25.0**
7 **Allen Iverson**, Georgetown	SO	G	37	312	87	215	926	**25.0**
8 **Eddie Benton**, Vermont	SR	G	26	187	69	193	636	**24.5**
9 **Matt Alosa**, New Hampshire	SR	G	26	199	76	150	624	**24.0**
10 **Ray Allen**, Connecticut	JR	G	35	292	115	119	818	**23.4**

FIELD GOAL PCT	CL	POS	G	FG	FGA	PCT
1 **Quadre Lollis**, Montana State	SR	F	30	212	314	**67.5**
2 **Daniel Watts**, Nevada	SR	C	29	145	221	**65.6**
3 **Lincoln Abrams**, Centenary	SR	F	27	187	286	**65.4**
4 **Alexander Koul**, George Washington	SO	C	29	163	254	**64.2**
5 **Terquin Mott**, Coppin State	JR	F/C	28	208	326	**63.8**

MINIMUM: 5 MADE PER GAME

THREE-PT FG PER GAME	CL	POS	G	3FG	3PG
1 **Dominick Young**, Fresno State	JR	G	29	120	**4.1**
2 **Darren McLinton**, James Madison	SR	G	30	122	**4.1**
3 **Keith Veney**, Marshall	JR	G	28	111	**4.0**
4 **Paul Marshall**, UL-Monroe	SR	G	30	115	**3.8**
5 **Troy Hudson**, Southern Illinois	SO	G	25	93	**3.7**

THREE-PT FG PCT	CL	POS	G	3FG	3FGA	PCT
1 **Joe Stafford**, Western Carolina	JR	F	30	58	110	**52.7**
2 **Ricky Peral**, Wake Forest	JR	F	32	51	100	**51.0**
3 **Justyn Tebbs**, Weber State	SR	G	30	50	100	**50.0**
4 **Aaron Brown**, Central Michigan	FR	F	26	51	104	**49.0**
5 **Isaac Fontaine**, Washington State	JR	G	29	66	136	**48.5**

MINIMUM: 1.5 MADE PER GAME

FREE THROW PCT	CL	POS	G	FT	FTA	PCT
1 **Mike Dillard**, Sam Houston State	JR	G	25	63	68	**92.6**
2 **Dion Cross**, Stanford	SR	G	29	81	88	**92.0**
3 **Roderick Howard**, Charlotte	JR	G	29	93	103	**90.3**
4 **Geoff Billet**, Rutgers	FR	G	26	72	80	**90.0**
5 **Steve Nash**, Santa Clara	SR	G	29	101	113	**89.4**

MINIMUM: 2.5 MADE PER GAME

ASSISTS PER GAME	CL	POS	G	AST	APG
1 **Raimonds Miglinieks**, UC Irvine	SR	G	27	230	**8.5**
2 **Curtis McCants**, George Mason	JR	G	27	223	**8.3**
3 **Dan Pogue**, Campbell	SR	G	23	183	**8.0**
4 **Pointer Williams**, McNeese State	SR	G	27	200	**7.4**
5 **Lazarus Sims**, Syracuse	SR	G	38	281	**7.4**
6 **Brevin Knight**, Stanford	JR	G	29	212	**7.3**
7 **Phillip Turner**, UC Santa Barbara	SR	G	26	190	**7.3**
8 **Reggie Geary**, Arizona	SR	G	33	231	**7.0**
9 **David Fizdale**, San Diego	SR	G	28	195	**7.0**
10 **Aaron Hutchins**, Marquette	SO	G	31	215	**6.9**

REBOUNDS PER GAME	CL	POS	G	REB	RPG
1 **Marcus Mann**, Mississippi Valley State	SR	F	29	394	**13.6**
2 **Malik Rose**, Drexel	SR	F	31	409	**13.2**
3 **Adonal Foyle**, Colgate	SO	C	29	364	**12.6**
4 **Tim Duncan**, Wake Forest	JR	F	32	395	**12.3**
5 **Scott Farley**, Mercer	SR	F	29	349	**12.0**
6 **Chris Ensminger**, Valparaiso	SR	C	32	368	**11.5**
7 **Thaddeous DeLaney**, Charleston	JR	F/C	29	330	**11.4**
8 **Alan Tomidy**, Marist	SR	C	29	329	**11.3**
9 **Quadre Lollis**, Montana State	SR	F	30	340	**11.3**
10 **Kyle Snowden**, Harvard	JR	F	26	289	**11.1**

BLOCKED SHOTS PER GAME	CL	POS	G	BLK	BPG
1 **Keith Closs**, Central Connecticut State	SO	C	28	178	**6.4**
2 **Adonal Foyle**, Colgate	SO	C	29	165	**5.7**
3 **Roy Rogers**, Alabama	SR	F	32	156	**4.9**
4 **Jerome James**, Florida A&M	SO	C	27	119	**4.4**
5 **Alan Tomidy**, Marist	SR	C	29	113	**3.9**
Peter Aluma, Liberty	JR	C	29	113	**3.9**

STEALS PER GAME	CL	POS	G	STL	SPG
1 **Pointer Williams**, McNeese State	SR	G	27	118	**4.4**
2 **Johnny Rhodes**, Maryland	SR	G	30	110	**3.7**
3 **Roderick Taylor**, Jackson State	SR	G	29	106	**3.7**
4 **Rasul Salahuddin**, Long Beach State	SR	G	28	101	**3.6**
5 **Andrell Hoard**, Northeastern Illinois	JR	G	27	97	**3.6**

INDIVIDUAL LEADERS—GAME

POINTS	CL	POS	OPP	DATE	PTS
1 **Marcus Brown**, Murray State	SR	G	Washington-St. Louis	D16	**45**
Eddie Benton, Vermont	SR	G	Hartford	F2	**45**
3 **Shanta Cotright**, Cal Poly	JR	G	George Mason	J13	**43**
JaFonde Williams, Hampton	SR	G	Maine	J29	**43**
Tunji Awojobi, Boston U.	JR	F/C	Vermont	F10	**43**
Steve Rich, Miami	SR	C	St. John's	F20	**43**

THREE-PT FG MADE	CL	POS	OPP	DATE	3FG
1 **David McMahan**, Winthrop	SR	G	Coastal Carolina	J15	**12**
2 **Troy Hudson**, Southern Illinois	SO	G	Hawaii-Hilo	D29	**11**
3 **Lance Weems**, Auburn	SR	G	Arkansas	J6	**10**
Keith Veney, Marshall	JR	G	Hampton	J6	**10**
John Gordon, Maine	SR	G	New Hampshire	J19	**10**
Mike Martinho, Buffalo	FR	G	Troy	F22	**10**

ASSISTS	CL	POS	OPP	DATE	AST
1 **Steve Nash**, Santa Clara	SR	G	Southern U.	D9	**15**
Raimonds Miglinieks, UC Irvine	SR	G	Cal State Fullerton	F10	**15**
Colby Pierce, Austin Peay	JR	G	Tennessee Tech	F12	**15**
Kyle Kessel, Texas A&M	SO	G	TCU	F26	**15**
Andre Owens, Oklahoma State	SR	G	Oklahoma	F29	**15**

REBOUNDS	CL	POS	OPP	DATE	REB
1 **Marcus Mann**, Miss. Valley State	SR	F	Jackson State	M9	**28**
2 **Larry Callis**, Wichita State	SR	F	Drake	J13	**26**
David Cully, William and Mary	SR	F/C	VMI	J17	**26**
4 **Chris Ensminger**, Valparaiso	SR	C	Northeastern Illinois	J4	**24**
5 **Scott Farley**, Mercer	SR	F	Alabama	D16	**22**
Frantz Pierre-Louis, Wagner	SO	C	Long Island	J17	**22**
Alan Tomidy, Marist	SR	C	Long Island	F8	**22**
Ernie Abercrombie, Oklahoma	SR	F	Mississippi State	F10	**22**
Greg Logan, Maine	SR	F	Vermont	F18	**22**
Tim Duncan, Wake Forest	JR	F	Georgia Tech	M10	**22**

BLOCKED SHOTS	CL	POS	OPP	DATE	BLK
1 **Roy Rogers**, Alabama	SR	F	Georgia	F10	**14**
2 **Keith Closs**, Central Conn. State	SO	C	Troy	J20	**12**
3 **Jelani McCoy**, UCLA	FR	C	Maryland	D9	**11**
Keith Closs, Central Conn. State	SO	C	Northeastern Illinois	J8	**11**
Keith Closs, Central Conn. State	SO	C	Eastern Illinois	J15	**11**
Alan Tomidy, Marist	SR	C	Long Island	F8	**11**

STEALS	CL	POS	OPP	DATE	STL
1 **Bonzi Wells**, Ball State	SO	F	Ohio	J3	**10**
Allen Iverson, Georgetown	SO	G	Miami	J13	**10**
3 **Alvin Sims**, Louisville	JR	G	VCU	N25	**9**
Jason Hamilton, Washington	SR	G	Eastern Washington	N28	**9**
Johnny Rhodes, Maryland	SR	G	North Carolina	F6	**9**

TEAM LEADERS—SEASON

WIN-LOSS PCT	W	L	PCT
1 **Massachusetts**	35	2	**.946**
2 **Kentucky**	34	2	**.944**
3 **Texas Tech**	30	2	**.938**
4 **Connecticut**	32	3	**.914**
5 **Drexel**	27	4	**.871**

SCORING OFFENSE	G	W-L	PTS	PPG
1 **Troy**	27	11-16	2,551	**94.5**
2 **Kentucky**	36	34-2	3,292	**91.4**
3 **Marshall**	28	17-11	2,560	**91.4**
4 **George Mason**	27	11-16	2,443	**90.5**
5 **Southern U.**	28	17-11	2,521	**90.0**

SCORING MARGIN	G	W-L	PPG	OPP PPG	MAR
1 **Kentucky**	36	34-2	91.4	69.4	**22.0**
2 **Connecticut**	35	32-3	82.6	64.7	**17.9**
3 **Drexel**	31	27-4	82.6	66.3	**16.3**
4 **Davidson**	30	25-5	84.3	68.2	**16.1**
5 **Kansas**	34	29-5	80.6	65.3	**15.3**

FIELD GOAL PCT	G	W-L	FG	FGA	PCT
1 **UCLA**	31	23-8	897	1,698	**52.8**
2 **Colorado State**	30	18-12	851	1,683	**50.6**
3 **Coppin State**	29	19-10	828	1,650	**50.2**
4 **Montana State**	30	21-9	898	1,800	**49.9**
5 **Weber State**	30	20-10	880	1,766	**49.8**

THREE-PT FG PER GAME	G	W-L	3FG	3PG
1 **Troy**	27	11-16	300	**11.1**
2 **Marshall**	28	17-11	284	**10.1**
3 **NC State**	31	15-16	292	**9.4**
4 **Southern Illinois**	29	11-18	268	**9.2**
5 **Samford**	27	16-11	243	**9.0**
Southern U.	28	17-11	252	**9.0**

FREE THROW PCT	G	W-L	FT	FTA	PCT
1 **Utah**	34	27-7	649	828	**78.4**
2 **Weber State**	30	20-10	519	675	**76.9**
3 **BYU**	28	15-13	587	767	**76.5**
4 **Stanford**	29	20-9	558	736	**75.8**
5 **VMI**	28	18-10	469	623	**75.3**

ASSISTS PER GAME	G	W-L	AST	APG
1 **Kentucky**	36	34-2	783	**21.8**
2 **Montana State**	30	21-9	627	**20.9**
3 **Connecticut**	35	32-3	659	**18.8**
4 **Georgia**	31	21-10	569	**18.4**
5 **Iowa**	32	23-9	576	**18.0**

REBOUND MARGIN	G	W-L	RPG	OPP RPG	MAR
1 **Mississippi Valley State**	29	22-7	48.3	36.8	**11.5**
2 **Utah State**	33	18-15	39.5	29.5	**10.0**
3 **Utah**	34	27-7	39.6	30.0	**9.6**
4 **Iowa**	32	23-9	40.5	31.4	**9.1**
5 **Connecticut**	35	32-3	43.4	34.4	**9.0**

SCORING DEFENSE	G	W-L	OPP PTS	OPP PPG
1 **Princeton**	29	22-7	1,498	**51.7**
2 **Wisconsin-Green Bay**	29	25-4	1,620	**55.9**
3 **South Alabama**	27	12-15	1,571	**58.2**
4 **Temple**	33	20-13	1,922	**58.2**
5 **UNC Wilmington**	29	13-16	1,694	**58.4**

Field Goal Pct Defense

	G	W-L	OPP FG	OPP FGA	OPP PCT
1 Temple	33	20-13	670	1741	**38.5**
2 Marquette	31	23-8	682	1772	**38.5**
3 Mississippi State	34	26-8	803	2084	**38.5**
4 Connecticut	35	32-3	840	2175	**38.6**
5 Kansas	34	29-5	777	2008	**38.7**

Blocked Shots Per Game

	G	W-L	BLK	BPG
1 Central Connecticut State	28	13-15	235	**8.4**
2 Florida A&M	27	8-19	198	**7.3**
3 Colgate	30	15-15	195	**6.5**
4 William and Mary	26	10-16	164	**6.3**
5 Massachusetts	37	35-2	232	**6.3**

Steals Per Game

	G	W-L	STL	SPG
1 McNeese State	27	15-12	330	**12.2**
2 Kentucky	36	34-2	435	**12.1**
3 Cal Poly	29	16-13	349	**12.0**
4 Northeastern Illinois	27	14-13	320	**11.9**
5 UL-Lafayette	28	16-12	327	**11.7**

TEAM LEADERS—GAME

Points

	OPP	DATE	SCORE
1 Prairie View A&M	Bay Ridge Christian	N27	**142-75**
George Mason	Troy	N28	**142-127**
3 Tulsa	Prairie View A&M	D17	**141-50**
4 George Mason	Delaware State	N25	**139-73**
5 Colorado	George Mason	D2	**132-117**

Field Goal Pct

	OPP	DATE	FG	FGA	PCT
1 UCLA	Southern California	J24	38	52	**73.1**
2 Evansville	Southern Illinois	F24	34	47	**72.3**
3 Gonzaga	Saint Mary's (CA)	J13	28	39	**71.8**
4 Weber State	Eastern Washington	J27	39	55	**70.9**
5 Tulsa	NC A&T	D2	30	43	**69.8**

Three-Pt FG Made

	OPP	DATE	3FG
1 Troy	George Mason	N28	**23**
2 Florida International	Palm Beach Atlanta	N25	**18**
Morehead State	Centre	D2	**18**
Florida A&M	Palm Beach Atlanta	D4	**18**
Southern Illinois	Hawaii-Hilo	D29	**18**
Marshall	Hampton	J6	**18**
Pacific	Nevada	F8	**18**
Long Island	St. Francis (NY)	F19	**18**

CONSENSUS ALL-AMERICAS

FIRST TEAM

PLAYER	CL	POS	HT	SCHOOL	RPG	PPG
Ray Allen	JR	G	6-5	Connecticut	6.5	23.4
Marcus Camby	JR	F/C	6-11	Massachusetts	8.2	20.5
Tony Delk	SR	G	6-1	Kentucky	4.2	17.8
Tim Duncan	JR	F	6-10	Wake Forest	12.3	19.1
Allen Iverson	SO	G	6-1	Georgetown	3.8	25.0
Kerry Kittles	SR	G	6-5	Villanova	7.1	20.4

SECOND TEAM

PLAYER	CL	POS	HT	SCHOOL	RPG	PPG
Danny Fortson	SO	C	6-7	Cincinnati	7.6	20.1
Keith Van Horn	JR	F	6-9	Utah	8.8	21.4
Jacque Vaughn	JR	G	6-1	Kansas	3.1	10.9
John Wallace	SR	F	6-8	Syracuse	8.7	22.2
Lorenzen Wright	SO	F/C	6-11	Memphis	10.4	17.4

SELECTORS: AP, NABC, UPI, USBWA

AWARD WINNERS

PLAYER OF THE YEAR

PLAYER	CL	POS	HT	SCHOOL	AWARDS
Marcus Camby	JR	F/C	6-11	Massachusetts	Naismith, AP, UPI, USBWA, Wooden, NABC, Rupp
Eddie Benton	SR	G	5-10	Vermont	Frances Naismith Pomeroy*

* FOR THE MOST OUTSTANDING SENIOR PLAYER WHO IS 6 FEET OR UNDER

DEFENSIVE PLAYER OF THE YEAR

PLAYER	CL	POS	HT	SCHOOL
Tim Duncan	JR	F	6-10	Wake Forest

COACH OF THE YEAR

COACH	SCHOOL	REC	AWARDS
John Calipari	Massachusetts	35-2	Naismith, NABC, Sporting News
Gene Keady	Purdue	26-6	AP, UPI, USBWA, CBS/Chevrolet

Bob Gibbons' Top High School Senior Recruits

PLAYER	POS	HT	HIGH SCHOOL	A-A TEAMS	COLLEGE	CAREER NOTES
1 Kobe Bryant	2G	6-6	Lower Merion HS, Ardmore, PA	McD, P, USA	None	Drafted straight out of HS; No. 13 pick '96 NBA draft (Hornets); 11-time All-Star; 2008 NBA MVP; 4-time scoring champ
2 Jermaine O'Neal	C	6-10	Eau Claire HS, Columbia, SC	McD, P, USA	None	Drafted straight out of HS; No. 17 pick '96 NBA draft (Blazers); 6-time All-Star; NBA Most Improved Player, '02
3 Corey Benjamin	G/F	6-6	Fontana (CA) HS	McD, P	Oregon State	17.5 ppg (2 seasons); No. 8 pick, '98 NBA draft (Bulls); 5.5 ppg (2 seasons)
4 Winfred Walton	PF	6-9	Pershing HS, Detroit	McD, P	Syracuse/ Fresno St.	11.1 ppg (1 season); undrafted, played in CBA
5 Tim Thomas	PF	6-9	Paterson (NJ) Catholic HS	McD, P, USA	Villanova	16.9 ppg, 6.0 rpg (1 season); No. 7 pick, '97 NBA draft (Nets); 11.6 ppg (12 seasons)
6 Jason Collier	C	7-0	Catholic Central HS, Springfield, OH	McD, P	Indiana/Georgia Tech	Transferred after 2 years; at GT, 17.1 ppg (2 seasons); No. 15 pick, '00 NBA draft (Rockets)
7 Ronnie Fields	2G	6-3	Farragut Academy, Chicago	McD, P, USA	DePaul	Declared academically ineligible at DePaul; played in CBA; 2-time All-CBA first team
8 Lester Earl	PF	6-8	Glen Oaks HS, Baton Rouge, LA	McD, P	LSU/Kansas	Transferred after 1 year; in college, 5.7 ppg, 4.5 rpg; undrafted
9 Vassil Evtimov	PF	6-9	Long Island Lutheran HS, Brookville, NY	McD, P	North Carolina	2.8 ppg (2 seasons); undrafted; played overseas
10 Mike Bibby	PG	6-1	Shadow Mountain HS, Phoenix	McD, P, USA	Arizona	NCAA title, '97; first-team All-America, Pac-10 POY '98; No. 2 pick, '98 NBA draft (Grizzlies); All-Rookie team '99
11 Loren Woods	C	7-1	Cardinal Ritter College Prep, St. Louis	McD, P	Wake Forest/Arizona	Transferred after 2 years; 15.6 ppg, 7.5 rpg as Jr.; 2nd-round pick, '01 NBA draft (Wolves); played 6 years in the NBA
12 Charles Hathaway	C	6-10	Hillwood Comprehensive HS, Nashville, TN	McD, P	Tennessee	4.9 ppg, 4.4 rpg (4-plus seasons); undrafted, played overseas
13 Nate James	SF	6-6	St. John's Catholic Prep, Frederick, MD	McD	Duke	3rd team All-ACC as senior with 12.3 ppg, 5.2 rpg; played in D-League
14 Stephen Jackson	SF	6-7	Oak Hill Academy, Mouth of Wilson, VA	McD, P	Arizona	2nd-round pick, '97 NBA draft (Suns); 15.4 ppg (9 seasons)
15 Mateen Cleaves	PG	6-1	Northern HS, Flint, MI	McD, P	Michigan State	2-time Big Ten POY; NCAA title, Final Four MOP '00; No. 14 pick, '00 NBA draft (Pistons); played 6 years in the NBA
16 Shaheen Holloway	PG	5-9	St. Patrick's HS, Elizabeth, NJ	McD, P	Seton Hall	13.7 ppg, 5.9 apg (4 seasons); 2-time 2nd team All-Big East; undrafted
17 Richard Hamilton	2G	6-6	Coatesville (PA) Area HS	McD, P	Connecticut	NCAA title, Final Four MOP '99; No. 7 pick, '99 NBA draft (Wizards); 3-time All-Star; NBA title '04
18 Ed Cota	PG	6-1	St. Thomas More Academy, Oakdale, CT	McD, P	North Carolina	3-time 2nd team All-ACC; 3rd in assists in NCAA history in D1 (1,030); undrafted, played overseas
19 Lamont Barnes	PF	6-10	University Heights Academy, Hopkinsville, KY		Temple	10.9 ppg, 6.6 rpg (4 seasons); undrafted
20 Jaraan Cornell	2G	6-3	Clay HS, South Bend, IN	P	Purdue	12.8 ppg (4 seasons); undrafted, played in CBA

Other Standouts

PLAYER	POS	HT	HIGH SCHOOL	A-A TEAMS	COLLEGE	CAREER NOTES
23 Desmond Mason	SF	6-6	Waxahachie (TX) HS		Oklahoma State	1st team All-Big 12 as senior with 18.0 ppg, 6.6 rpg; No. 17 pick, '00 NBA draft (Sonics); '01 Slam Dunk champ
62 Kenyon Martin	PF	6-8	Bryan Adams HS, Dallas		Cincinnati	Consensus POY: 18.9 ppg, 9.7 rpg, '00; No. 1 pick, '00 NBA draft; All-Rookie team '01; All-Star '04
148 Craig "Speedy" Claxton	PG	5-10	Christ the King HS, Queens, NY		Hofstra	22.8 ppg, 5.4 rpg, 6.0 apg, '00; No. 20 pick, '00 NBA draft (76ers); 9.3 ppg (7 seasons)

Abbreviations: McD=McDonald's; P=Parade; USA=USA Today

Poll Progression

Preseason Poll

AP	USA/CNN	School
1	1	**Kentucky**
2	2	**Kansas**
3	4	**Villanova**
4	3	**UCLA**
5	5	**Georgetown**
6	6	**Connecticut**
7	7	**Massachusetts**
8	10	**Iowa**
9	12	**Mississippi State**
10	11	**Utah**
11	8	**Wake Forest**
12	9	**Louisville**
13	13	**Memphis**
14	15	**Missouri**
15	19	**Maryland**
16	18	**Arkansas**
17	16	**Michigan**
18	16	**Stanford**
19	14	**Virginia**
20	21	**North Carolina**
21	20	**Cincinnati**
22	22	**Virginia Tech**
23	24	**Indiana**
24	23	**Purdue**
25	—	**California**
—	25	**Arizona**

Week of Nov 20

AP	USA/CNN	School	AP ↓↑
1	1	**Kentucky** (0-0)	
2	2	**Kansas** (0-0)	
3	3	**Villanova** (0-0)	
4	5	**UCLA** (0-0)	
5	4	**Georgetown** (2-0)	
6	6	**Connecticut** (0-0)	
7	7	**Massachusetts** (0-0)	
8	10	**Utah** (0-0)	↑2
9	12	**Mississippi State** (0-0)	
10	11	**Iowa** (0-0)	↓2
11	8	**Wake Forest** (0-0)	
12	15	**Memphis** (0-0)	↑1
13	16	**Louisville** (0-0)	↓1
14	14	**Maryland** (0-0)	↑1
15	17	**Missouri** (0-0)	↓1
16	13	**Michigan** (2-0)	↑1
17	19	**Virginia** (0-0)	↑2
18	18	**Stanford** (0-0)	
19	9	**Arizona** (2-0)	
20	22	**North Carolina** (0-0)	
21	21	**Cincinnati** (0-0)	
22	23	**Virginia Tech** (0-0)	
23	24	**Indiana** (0-0)	
24	25	**Purdue** (0-0)	
25	20	**Georgia Tech** (2-0)	⤴

Week of Nov 27

AP	USA/CNN	School	AP ↓↑
1	1	**Kentucky** (1-0)	
2	2	**Kansas** (1-0)	
3	3	**Villanova** (3-0)	
4	4	**Arizona** (4-0)	↑15
5	6	**Massachusetts** (0-0)	↑2
6	5	**Georgetown** (3-1)	↓2
7	10	**Memphis** (1-0)	↑5
8	8	**Mississippi State** (1-0)	↑1
9	9	**Connecticut** (2-1)	↓3
10	7	**Wake Forest** (1-0)	↑1
11	11	**Iowa** (2-1)	↓1
12	12	**Duke** (3-0)	⤴
13	14	**Missouri** (1-0)	↑2
14	17	**Utah** (0-1)	↓6
15	19	**Virginia** (1-0)	↑2
16	15	**Stanford** (2-0)	↑2
17	18	**North Carolina** (2-1)	↑3
18	13	**Louisville** (2-1)	↓5
19	16	**Maryland** (0-1)	↓5
20	20	**Georgia Tech** (3-1)	↑5
21	21	**Cincinnati** (0-0)	
22	23	**Virginia Tech** (0-0)	
23	22	**UCLA** (1-2)	Ⓐ ↓18
24	24	**Michigan** (2-2)	↓8
25	—	**Arkansas** (1-1)	⤴
—	25	**Tulane** (0-1)	

Week of Dec 4

AP	USA/CNN	School	AP ↓↑
1	1	**Kansas** (3-0)	
2	2	**Villanova** (5-0)	
3	3	**Massachusetts** (3-0)	
4	4	**Arizona** (5-0)	
5	5	**Kentucky** (2-1)	
6	6	**Georgetown** (5-1)	
7	9	**Memphis** (3-0)	
8	7	**Mississippi State** (3-0)	
9	11	**Connecticut** (4-1)	
10	8	**Wake Forest** (3-0)	
11	12	**Missouri** (4-0)	↑
12	10	**Iowa** (5-1)	↓
13	13	**North Carolina** (5-1)	↑
14	14	**Utah** (2-1)	
15	16	**Virginia** (2-1)	
16	15	**Georgia Tech** (5-1)	↑
17	17	**Cincinnati** (1-0)	↑
18	18	**Duke** (4-1)	↓
19	20	**Virginia Tech** (2-0)	↑
20	19	**Maryland** (2-2)	↓1
21	24	**Illinois** (3-0)	⤴
22	21	**Michigan** (5-2)	↑2
23	21	**Louisville** (3-2)	↓5
24	23	**Stanford** (3-2)	↓8
25	25	**Santa Clara** (4-1)	⤴

Week of Dec 11

AP	USA/CNN	School	AP ↓↑
1	1	**Kansas** (5-0)	
2	2	**Villanova** (7-0)	
3	3	**Massachusetts** (5-0)	
3	4	**Arizona** (7-0)	↑1
5	5	**Kentucky** (4-1)	
6	8	**Memphis** (4-0)	↑1
7	6	**Georgetown** (7-1)	↓1
8	7	**Connecticut** (6-1)	↑1
9	9	**Iowa** (7-1)	↑3
10	12	**North Carolina** (6-1)	↑3
11	11	**Wake Forest** (4-1)	↓1
12	10	**Cincinnati** (4-0)	↑5
13	14	**Utah** (5-1)	↑1
14	13	**Missouri** (5-1)	↓3
15	15	**Mississippi State** (4-1)	↓7
16	18	**Illinois** (6-0)	↑5
17	17	**Virginia Tech** (3-0)	↑2
18	16	**Michigan** (7-2)	↑4
19	20	**Georgia Tech** (5-2)	↓3
20	19	**Louisville** (5-2)	↑3
21	22	**Duke** (5-2)	↓3
22	23	**Santa Clara** (5-1)	↑3
23	21	**Virginia** (3-2)	↓8
24	25	**UCLA** (3-3)	⤴
25	—	**Syracuse** (6-0)	⤴
—	24	**Maryland** (3-3)	⤵

Week of Dec 18

AP	USA/CNN	School	AP ↓↑
1	1	**Kansas** (6-0)	
2	2	**Massachusetts** (6-0)	↑1
3	3	**Arizona** (8-0)	
4	4	**Kentucky** (5-1)	↑1
5	8	**Memphis** (5-0)	↑1
6	5	**Georgetown** (7-1)	↑1
7	7	**Villanova** (7-1)	↓5
8	6	**Connecticut** (7-1)	
9	9	**Cincinnati** (6-0)	↑3
10	10	**Iowa** (8-1)	↓1
11	11	**North Carolina** (7-1)	↓1
12	12	**Wake Forest** (4-1)	↓1
13	14	**Utah** (6-1)	
14	15	**Illinois** (7-0)	↑2
15	13	**Missouri** (6-1)	↓1
16	16	**Mississippi State** (5-1)	↓1
17	17	**Michigan** (8-2)	↑1
18	19	**Georgia** (6-1)	⤴
19	22	**Syracuse** (8-0)	↑6
20	20	**Duke** (5-2)	↑1
21	18	**Georgia Tech** (6-3)	↓2
22	24	**Virginia Tech** (3-1)	↓5
23	21	**Virginia** (3-2)	
24	—	**California** (4-0)	⤴
25	22	**Louisville** (6-3)	↓5
—	25	**Maryland** (4-3)	

Week of Dec 26

AP	USA/CNN	School	AP ↓↑
1	1	**Massachusetts** (7-0)	↑1
2	2	**Kentucky** (7-1)	↑2
3	7	**Memphis** (7-0)	↑2
4	3	**Kansas** (7-1)	↓3
5	6	**Cincinnati** (7-0)	↑4
6	4	**Georgetown** (9-1)	
7	4	**Connecticut** (8-1)	↑1
8	9	**Villanova** (8-1)	↓1
9	8	**Arizona** (8-1)	↓6
10	10	**Iowa** (10-1)	
11	11	**North Carolina** (8-1)	
12	12	**Illinois** (9-0)	↑2
13	14	**Syracuse** (9-0)	↑6
14	13	**Wake Forest** (6-1)	↓2
15	16	**Utah** (7-2)	↓2
16	16	**Georgia** (8-1)	↑2
17	15	**Mississippi State** (6-1)	↓1
18	18	**Missouri** (7-2)	↓3
19	19	**Michigan** (9-2)	↓2
20	20	**Duke** (7-2)	
21	22	**Virginia Tech** (4-1)	↑1
22	21	**Virginia** (4-2)	↑1
23	—	**UCLA** (6-3)	⤴
24	—	**Clemson** (8-0)	⤴
25	—	**Tulsa** (5-0)	⤴
—	23	**Georgia Tech** (6-5)	⤵
—	24	**Maryland** (5-3)	
—	25	**Louisville** (7-4)	⤵

Week of Jan 2

AP	USA/CNN	School	AP ↓↑
1	1	**Massachusetts** (10-0) Ⓑ	
2	2	**Kentucky** (9-1)	
3	5	**Memphis** (8-0)	
4	3	**Kansas** (7-1)	
5	4	**Cincinnati** (8-0)	
6	7	**Georgetown** (11-1)	
7	6	**Connecticut** (10-1)	
8	8	**Villanova** (10-1)	
9	9	**Arizona** (10-1)	
10	10	**Iowa** (11-1)	
11	12	**Syracuse** (11-1)	Ⓑ ↑2
12	11	**Wake Forest** (6-1)	↑2
13	15	**Illinois** (11-1)	↓1
14	14	**Georgia** (9-1)	↑2
15	16	**Utah** (8-2)	
16	13	**North Carolina** (9-2)	↓5
17	17	**Mississippi State** (8-1)	
18	18	**Virginia Tech** (6-1)	↑3
19	20	**Duke** (9-2)	↑1
20	21	**UCLA** (7-3)	↑3
21	19	**Michigan** (10-3)	↓2
22	24	**Clemson** (9-0)	↑2
23	—	**Texas** (7-2)	⤴
24	—	**Boston College** (8-2)	⤴
25	—	**New Mexico** (10-0)	⤴
—	22	**Virginia** (5-3)	⤵
—	23	**Missouri** (8-4)	⤵
—	25	**Penn State** (9-0)	

Week of Jan 8

AP	USA/CNN	School	AP ↓↑
1	1	**Massachusetts** (12-0)	
2	2	**Kentucky** (11-1) Ⓒ	
3	3	**Kansas** (10-1)	↑1
4	4	**Cincinnati** (9-0)	↑1
5	5	**Georgetown** (13-1)	↑1
6	6	**Connecticut** (12-1)	↑1
7	7	**Villanova** (12-1)	↑1
8	8	**Wake Forest** (8-1)	↑4
9	13	**Memphis** (8-2)	↓6
10	9	**North Carolina** (11-2)	↑6
11	11	**Iowa** (12-2)	↓1
12	12	**Mississippi State** (10-1)	↑5
13	10	**Utah** (9-2)	↑2
14	14	**Syracuse** (11-2)	↓3
15	15	**Virginia Tech** (7-1)	↑3
16	20	**Clemson** (10-0)	↑6
17	19	**UCLA** (9-3)	↑3
18	16	**Arizona** (10-3)	↓9
19	17	**Georgia** (10-2)	↓5
20	22	**Penn State** (11-0)	⤴
21	21	**Illinois** (11-3)	↓8
22	25	**Purdue** (11-2)	⤴
23	18	**Michigan** (11-4)	↓2
24	24	**Stanford** (8-2)	⤴
25	—	**New Mexico** (11-1)	
—	23	**Duke** (9-4)	⤵

Week of Jan 15

AP	USA/CNN	School	AP ↓↑
1	1	**Massachusetts** (14-0)	
2	2	**Kentucky** (13-1)	
3	4	**Cincinnati** (11-0)	↑1
4	3	**Kansas** (12-1)	↓1
5	5	**Connecticut** (14-1)	↑1
6	6	**Wake Forest** (10-1)	↑2
7	8	**Villanova** (13-2)	
8	7	**Georgetown** (14-2)	↓3
9	10	**Memphis** (11-2)	
10	9	**North Carolina** (12-3)	
11	13	**Virginia Tech** (9-1)	↑4
12	12	**Syracuse** (13-2)	↑2
13	15	**UCLA** (11-3)	↑4
14	14	**Penn State** (13-0)	↑6
15	11	**Utah** (11-3)	↓2
16	16	**Iowa** (13-3)	↓5
17	18	**Purdue** (13-2)	↑5
18	17	**Arizona** (11-3)	
19	20	**Clemson** (11-1)	↓3
20	19	**Michigan** (13-4)	↑3
21	21	**Mississippi State** (10-3)	↓9
22	22	**Georgia** (10-3)	↓3
23	23	**Auburn** (14-3)	⤴
24	—	**Boston College** (11-3)	⤴
25	—	**Texas Tech** (12-1)	⤴
—	24	**Stanford** (8-4)	⤵
—	25	**Illinois** (11-5)	⤵

Week of Jan 22

AP	USA/CNN	School	AP ↓↑
1	1	**Massachusetts** (16-0)	
2	2	**Kentucky** (15-1)	
3	4	**Kansas** (14-1)	↑1
4	5	**Connecticut** (16-1)	↑1
5	3	**Cincinnati** (12-1)	↓2
6	6	**Georgetown** (16-2)	↑2
7	7	**Villanova** (14-3)	
8	10	**Virginia Tech** (11-1)	↑3
9	8	**Wake Forest** (12-2)	↓3
10	9	**Utah** (14-3)	↑5
11	11	**North Carolina** (13-4)	↓1
12	15	**Memphis** (12-3)	↓3
13	12	**Arizona** (13-3)	↑5
14	14	**Penn State** (13-1)	
15	17	**UCLA** (12-4)	↓2
16	16	**Michigan** (14-4)	↑4
17	13	**Syracuse** (13-4)	↓5
18	20	**Clemson** (12-2)	↑1
19	19	**Purdue** (14-3)	↓2
20	21	**Boston College** (12-3)	↑4
21	22	**Auburn** (15-3)	↑2
22	18	**Iowa** (14-4)	↓6
23	23	**Texas Tech** (14-1)	↑3
24	—	**Marquette** (12-3)	⤴
25	—	**California** (10-4)	⤴
—	24	**Georgia** (11-4)	⤵
—	25	**Stanford** (10-4)	

Week of Jan 29

AP	USA/CNN	School	AP ↓↑
1	1	**Massachusetts** (18-0)	
2	2	**Kentucky** (17-1)	
3	3	**Kansas** (16-1)	
4	4	**Connecticut** (19-1)	
5	5	**Cincinnati** (14-1)	
6	6	**Villanova** (16-3)	↑1
7	7	**Utah** (16-3)	↑3
8	8	**North Carolina** (15-4)	↑3
9	9	**Georgetown** (17-3)	↓3
10	11	**Penn State** (15-1)	↑4
11	13	**Memphis** (14-3)	↑1
12	10	**Wake Forest** (13-3)	↓3
13	14	**Virginia Tech** (13-2)	↓5
14	12	**Arizona** (15-3)	↓1
15	20	**Texas Tech** (16-1)	↑7
16	17	**Iowa** (15-4)	↑6
17	15	**Purdue** (15-4)	↑2
18	16	**Syracuse** (14-5)	↓1
19	19	**UCLA** (13-5)	↓4
20	18	**Michigan** (14-6)	↓4
21	23	**Boston College** (12-4)	↓1
22	22	**Auburn** (15-4)	↓1
23	—	**Eastern Michigan** (15-1)	⤴
24	21	**Clemson** (12-4)	↓6
25	25	**Georgia Tech** (13-8)	⤴
—	24	**Stanford** (11-6)	

Week of Feb 5

USA/CNN	School	AP ↓↑
1	**Massachusetts** (21-0)	
2	**Kentucky** (18-1)	
3	**Kansas** (18-1)	
4	**Connecticut** (21-1)	
5	**Cincinnati** (17-1)	
6	**Villanova** (18-3)	
7	**Utah** (18-3)	
8	**Georgetown** (19-3)	↑1
9	**Wake Forest** (14-3)	↑3
10	**Penn State** (16-2)	
12	**Virginia Tech** (16-2)	↑2
11	**North Carolina** (16-5)	↓4
14	**Texas Tech** (18-1)	↑2
13	**Purdue** (17-4)	↑3
16	**Memphis** (16-4)	↓4
15	**Arizona** (16-4)	↓2
17	**UCLA** (15-5)	↑2
18	**Syracuse** (16-6)	
20	**Iowa** (15-6)	↓3
25	**Louisville** (16-6)	⤴
—	**Iowa State** (16-4)	⤴
21	**Boston College** (13-5)	↓1
19	**Michigan** (15-7)	↓3
23	**Eastern Michigan** (16-2)	↓1
24	**Stanford** (13-5)	⤴
22	**Auburn** (15-6)	⤵

Week of Feb 12

AP	USA/CNN	School	AP ↓↑
1	1	**Massachusetts** (23-0)	
2	2	**Kentucky** (20-1)	
3	3	**Connecticut** (22-1)	↑1
4	6	**Villanova** (20-3)	↑2
5	5	**Kansas** (19-2)	↓2
6	4	**Cincinnati** (18-2)	↓1
7	7	**Utah** (19-3)	
8	9	**Wake Forest** (16-3)	↑1
9	8	**Penn State** (18-2)	↑1
10	10	**Virginia Tech** (18-2)	↑1
11	11	**Purdue** (19-4)	↑3
12	12	**Texas Tech** (20-1)	↑1
13	15	**Arizona** (18-4)	↑3
14	13	**Georgetown** (19-5)	↓6
15	14	**Memphis** (17-4)	
16	16	**Syracuse** (18-6)	↑2
17	17	**North Carolina** (16-7)	↓5
18	18	**UCLA** (16-6)	↓1
19	19	**Iowa** (17-6)	
20	20	**Stanford** (15-5)	↑5
21	21	**Boston College** (15-5)	↑1
22	24	**Iowa State** (17-5)	↓1
23	22	**Eastern Michigan** (18-2)	↑1
24	23	**Louisville** (17-7)	↓4
25	—	**Mississippi State** (16-5) Ⓓ	⤴
—	25	**Michigan** (15-8)	⤵

Week of Feb 19

AP	USA/CNN	School	AP ↓↑
1	1	**Massachusetts** (25-0)	
2	2	**Kentucky** (22-1)	
3	3	**Connecticut** (24-1)	
4	5	**Villanova** (23-3)	
5	4	**Kansas** (21-2)	
6	6	**Cincinnati** (19-2)	
7	7	**Purdue** (21-4)	↑4
8	8	**Utah** (21-4)	↓1
9	9	**Texas Tech** (22-1)	↑3
10	10	**Wake Forest** (17-4)	↓2
11	11	**Georgetown** (21-5)	↑3
12	13	**Virginia Tech** (19-3)	↓2
13	14	**Arizona** (19-5)	
14	12	**Penn State** (18-4)	↓5
15	16	**Syracuse** (19-6)	↑1
16	15	**UCLA** (18-6)	↑2
17	17	**North Carolina** (18-7)	
18	19	**Iowa** (18-6)	↑1
19	18	**Memphis** (17-5)	↓4
20	20	**Boston College** (16-6)	↑1
21	25	**Louisville** (18-7)	↑3
22	24	**Iowa State** (18-6)	
23	22	**Georgia Tech** (16-10)	⤴
24	23	**Stanford** (16-6)	↓4
25	—	**Wisc.-Green Bay** (21-2)	⤴
—	21	**Eastern Michigan** (19-3)	⤵

Week of Feb 26

AP	USA/CNN	School	AP ↓↑
1	1	**Kentucky** (24-1)	↑1
2	2	**Massachusetts** (26-1)	↓1
3	3	**Kansas** (23-2)	↑2
4	4	**Connecticut** (25-2)	↓1
5	5	**Purdue** (23-4)	↑2
6	7	**Villanova** (23-4)	↓2
7	6	**Cincinnati** (21-3)	↓1
8	9	**Georgetown** (23-5)	↑3
9	8	**Texas Tech** (24-1)	
10	10	**Utah** (22-5)	↓2
11	11	**Arizona** (21-5)	↑2
12	13	**Penn State** (19-4)	↑2
13	12	**Wake Forest** (18-5)	↓3
14	15	**Memphis** (20-5)	↑5
15	14	**Syracuse** (20-7)	
16	16	**Virginia Tech** (20-4)	↓4
17	17	**UCLA** (19-7)	↓1
18	20	**Georgia Tech** (18-10)	↑5
19	19	**North Carolina** (19-8)	↓2
20	21	**Iowa** (19-7)	↓2
21	18	**Louisville** (19-8)	
22	22	**Wisc.-Green Bay** (24-2)	↑3
23	23	**Iowa State** (19-7)	↓1
24	—	**George Washington** (18-5)	⤴
25	24	**Stanford** (17-7)	↓1
—	25	**Boston College** (16-8)	⤵

Week of Mar 5

AP	USA/CNN	School	AP ↓↑
1	1	**Kentucky** (26-1)	
2	2	**Massachusetts** (28-1)	
3	3	**Connecticut** (27-2)	↑1
4	4	**Purdue** (25-4)	↑1
5	5	**Kansas** (24-3)	↓2
6	6	**Georgetown** (24-6)	↑2
7	7	**Texas Tech** (25-1)	↑2
8	9	**Cincinnati** (22-4)	↓1
9	12	**Villanova** (24-5)	↓3
10	8	**Utah** (23-5)	
11	11	**Arizona** (23-5)	
12	10	**Wake Forest** (20-5)	↑1
13	13	**Syracuse** (22-7)	↑2
14	14	**Memphis** (21-6)	
15	16	**Virginia Tech** (22-4)	↑1
16	17	**Penn State** (20-5)	↓4
17	15	**UCLA** (21-7)	
18	18	**Georgia Tech** (20-10)	
19	19	**Iowa** (21-7)	↑1
20	20	**North Carolina** (20-9)	↓1
21	25	**Marquette** (20-6)	⤴
22	21	**Louisville** (19-10)	↓1
23	22	**Iowa State** (20-8)	
24	23	**Wisc.-Green Bay** (25-3)	↓2
25	—	**Mississippi State** (19-7)	⤴
—	24	**Stanford** (17-8)	⤵

Week of Mar 12 Ⓔ

AP	USA/CNN	School	AP ↓↑
1	1	**Massachusetts** (31-1)	↑1
2	2	**Kentucky** (28-2)	↓1
3	3	**Connecticut** (30-2) Ⓕ	
4	4	**Purdue** (26-4)	
4	5	**Georgetown** (26-7) Ⓕ	↑2
4	8	**Kansas** (25-5)	↑1
7	6	**Cincinnati** (25-4)	↑1
8	7	**Texas Tech** (28-1)	↓1
9	9	**Wake Forest** (23-5)	↑3
10	12	**Villanova** (25-6)	↓1
11	11	**Arizona** (24-6)	
12	10	**Utah** (25-6)	↓2
13	15	**Georgia Tech** (22-11)	↑5
14	13	**UCLA** (23-7)	↑3
15	14	**Syracuse** (24-8)	↓2
16	17	**Memphis** (22-7)	↓2
17	16	**Iowa State** (23-8)	↑6
18	18	**Penn State** (21-6)	↓2
19	20	**Mississippi State** (22-7)	↑6
20	22	**Marquette** (22-7)	↑1
21	19	**Iowa** (22-8)	↓2
22	21	**Virginia Tech** (22-5)	↓7
23	—	**New Mexico** (27-4)	⤴
24	23	**Louisville** (20-11)	↓2
25	24	**North Carolina** (20-10)	↓5
	25	**Stanford** (19-8)	

Final Poll (Post-Tournament)

USA/CNN	School
1	**Kentucky** (34-2)
2	**Massachusetts** (35-2)
3	**Syracuse** (29-9)
4	**Mississippi State** (26-8)
5	**Kansas** (29-5)
6	**Cincinnati** (28-5)
7	**Georgetown** (29-8)
8	**Connecticut** (32-3)
9	**Wake Forest** (26-6)
10	**Texas Tech** (30-2)
11	**Arizona** (26-6)
12	**Utah** (27-7)
13	**Georgia Tech** (24-12)
14	**Louisville** (22-12)
15	**Purdue** (26-6)
16	**Georgia** (21-10)
17	**Villanova** (26-7)
18	**Arkansas** (20-13)
19	**UCLA** (23-8)
20	**Iowa State** (24-9)
21	**Virginia Tech** (23-6)
22	**Iowa** (23-9)
23	**Marquette** (23-8)
24	**North Carolina** (21-11)
25	**New Mexico** (28-5)

Ⓐ Defending champion UCLA loses to both Santa Clara and Vanderbilt in the Maui Classic.

Ⓑ In a midseason matchup of two Final Four-bound teams, UMass defeats Syracuse, 65-47. The Minutemen's 6'11" Marcus Camby, nursing an injured knee, comes off the bench to contribute 20 points, 11 rebounds, 3 blocks and 2 steals. "He was healthier than I was," gripes Syracuse coach Jim Boeheim. Camby will go on to sweep the national POY awards.

Ⓒ Kentucky rips LSU, 129-97, in Baton Rouge with a team that will send six players to the NBA: Antoine Walker, Tony Delk, Ron Mercer, Walter McCarty, Derek Anderson and Nazr Mohammed.

Ⓓ Mississippi State wins at Oklahoma, 76-71, on Feb. 10 to climb into the AP poll. The Bulldogs lose their next game to Mississippi and drop out again, but will go on to beat Kentucky in the SEC tournament final and then make the Final Four for the first time.

Ⓔ Coach Pete Carril retires with a 525–273 record in 30 seasons as a head coach, the last 29 at Princeton. His final Tigers team holds opponents to 51.7 ppg, leading the nation in scoring defense for the eighth straight season.

Ⓕ UConn's Ray Allen hits a running floater over Georgetown's Allen Iverson with :13 remaining to give the Huskies a 75-74 victory in the Big East tournament title game.

Pre-Tournament Ratings Percentage Index (RPI)

Rank	School	W-L	Sched. Strg.	SS Rank	RPI
1	**Kentucky**	28-2	.6194	6	.6840
2	**Massachusetts**	31-1	.5662	42	.6646
3	**Connecticut**	30-2	.5493	64	.6463
4	**Cincinnati**	25-4	.5826	23	.6449
5	**Villanova**	25-6	.6065	10	.6441
6	**Purdue**	25-5	.5843	20	.6398
7	**Kansas**	25-4	.5657	43	.6396
8	**Wake Forest**	23-5	.5751	30	.6370
9	**Georgia Tech**	22-11	.6518	1	.6350
10	**Texas Tech**	28-1	.5141	119	.6284
11	**Arizona**	24-6	.5735	34	.6226
12	**Georgetown**	24-7	.5798	25	.6219
13	**Iowa State**	22-8	.5999	13	.6190
14	**Penn State**	21-6	.5711	37	.6147
15	**Memphis**	22-7	.5765	28	.6146
16	**Syracuse**	24-8	.5831	22	.6144
17	**North Carolina**	20-10	.6127	8	.6140
18	**Mississippi State**	22-7	.5723	35	.6122
19	**Louisville**	19-11	.6240	3	.6070
20	**UCLA**	23-7	.5549	53	.6070
21	**Wisc.-Green Bay**	24-3	.5163	112	.6065
22	**Marquette**	22-7	.5595	49	.6059
23	**Utah**	23-6	.5516	62	.6055
24	**New Mexico**	26-4	.5145	116	.6012
25	**Bradley**	22-7	.5571	50	.5992
26	**Iowa**	22-8	.5545	56	.5982
27	**Temple**	19-12	.6199	5	.5977
28	**Indiana**	18-11	.6057	11	.5970
29	**Duke**	18-12	.6129	7	.5961
30	**Maryland**	17-12	.6112	9	.5920
31	**Santa Clara**	19-8	.5670	41	.5911
32	**Michigan**	20-11	.5838	21	.5907
33	**Eastern Michigan**	22-5	.5155	114	.5886
34	**Georgia**	19-9	.5631	45	.5880
35	**Virginia Tech**	22-5	.5063	133	.5863
36	**Arkansas**	18-12	.5915	17	.5804
37	**Stanford**	19-8	.5385	77	.5797
38	**Oklahoma**	17-12	.5943	15	.5794
39	**Tulsa**	22-7	.5192	107	.5782
40	**Clemson**	18-10	.5519	61	.5770
41	**Kansas State**	16-11	.5810	24	.5753
42	**Providence**	17-11	.5708	38	.5732
43	**Oklahoma State**	16-10	.5614	46	.5717
44	**Texas**	20-9	.5308	85	.5713
45	**Boston College**	18-10	.5463	66	.5701
46	**Minnesota**	18-12	.5712	36	.5699
47	**New Orleans**	21-8	.5249	93	.5690
48	**Arkansas-Little Rock**	21-6	.5047	136	.5679
49	**Illinois**	18-12	.5547	55	.5656
50	**George Washington**	21-7	.4886	162	.5651

Source: Collegiate Basketball News

ANNUAL REVIEW

1996 NCAA Tournament

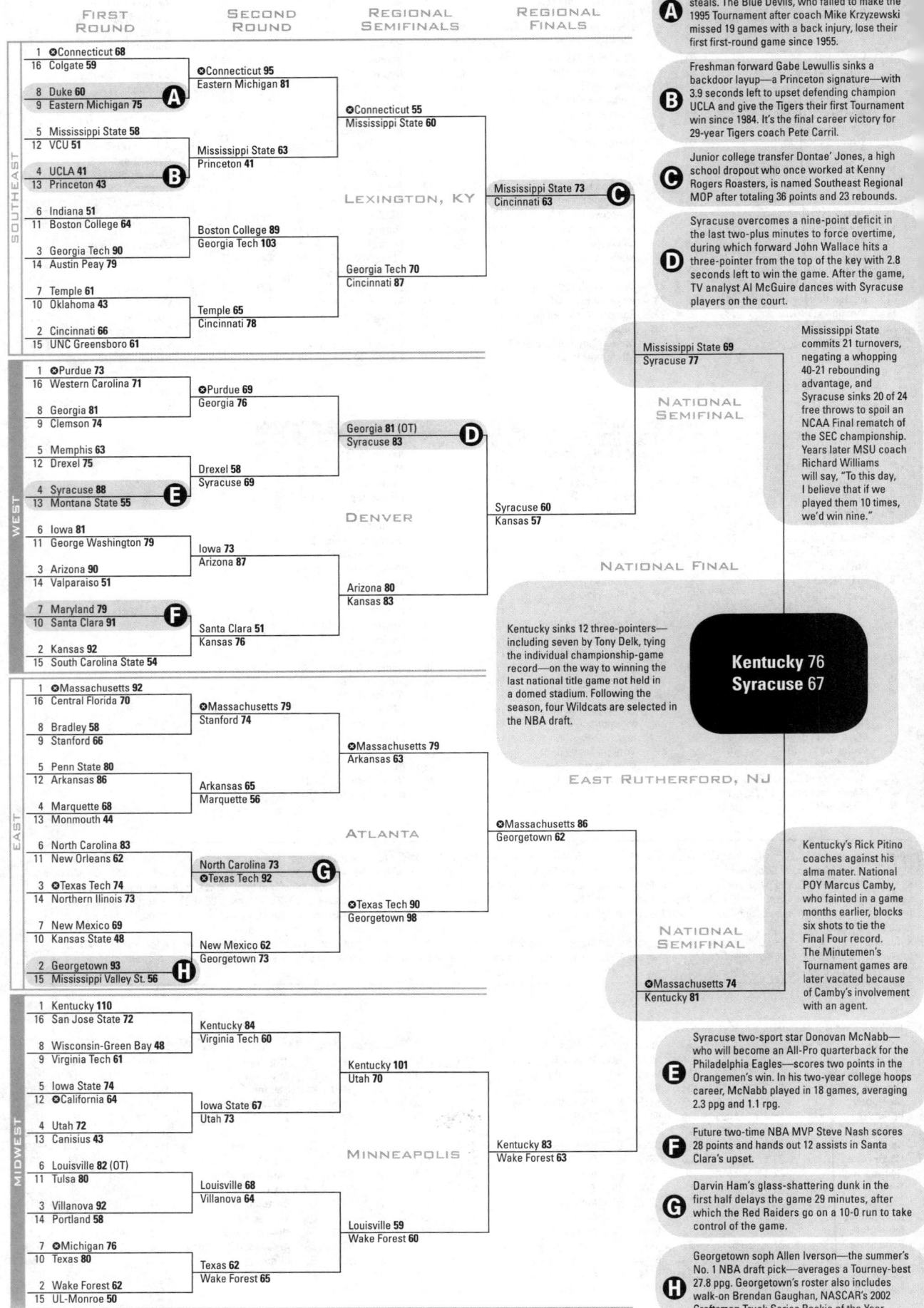

Southeast

First Round

- 1 ⊗Connecticut **68**
- 16 Colgate **59**
- 8 Duke **60** (A)
- 9 Eastern Michigan **75**
- 5 Mississippi State **58**
- 12 VCU **51**
- 4 UCLA **41** (B)
- 13 Princeton **43**
- 6 Indiana **51**
- 11 Boston College **64**
- 3 Georgia Tech **90**
- 14 Austin Peay **79**
- 7 Temple **61**
- 10 Oklahoma **43**
- 2 Cincinnati **66**
- 15 UNC Greensboro **61**

Second Round

- ⊗Connecticut **95**
- Eastern Michigan **81**
- Mississippi State **63**
- Princeton **41**
- Boston College **89**
- Georgia Tech **103**
- Temple **65**
- Cincinnati **78**

Regional Semifinals (Lexington, KY)

- ⊗Connecticut **55**
- Mississippi State **60**
- Georgia Tech **70**
- Cincinnati **87**

Regional Finals

- Mississippi State **73** (C)
- Cincinnati **63**

West

First Round

- 1 ⊗Purdue **73**
- 16 Western Carolina **71**
- 8 Georgia **81**
- 9 Clemson **74**
- 5 Memphis **63**
- 12 Drexel **75**
- 4 Syracuse **88** (E)
- 13 Montana State **55**
- 6 Iowa **81**
- 11 George Washington **79**
- 3 Arizona **90**
- 14 Valparaiso **51**
- 7 Maryland **79** (F)
- 10 Santa Clara **91**
- 2 Kansas **92**
- 15 South Carolina State **54**

Second Round

- ⊗Purdue **69**
- Georgia **76**
- Drexel **58**
- Syracuse **69**
- Iowa **73**
- Arizona **87**
- Santa Clara **51**
- Kansas **76**

Regional Semifinals (Denver)

- Georgia **81** (OT) (D)
- Syracuse **83**
- Arizona **80**
- Kansas **83**

Regional Finals

- Syracuse **60**
- Kansas **57**

East

First Round

- 1 ⊗Massachusetts **92**
- 16 Central Florida **70**
- 8 Bradley **58**
- 9 Stanford **66**
- 5 Penn State **80**
- 12 Arkansas **86**
- 4 Marquette **68**
- 13 Monmouth **44**
- 6 North Carolina **83**
- 11 New Orleans **62**
- 3 ⊗Texas Tech **74**
- 14 Northern Illinois **73**
- 7 New Mexico **69**
- 10 Kansas State **48**
- 2 Georgetown **93** (H)
- 15 Mississippi Valley St. **56**

Second Round

- ⊗Massachusetts **79**
- Stanford **74**
- Arkansas **65**
- Marquette **56**
- North Carolina **73** (G)
- ⊗Texas Tech **92**
- New Mexico **62**
- Georgetown **73**

Regional Semifinals (Atlanta)

- ⊗Massachusetts **79**
- Arkansas **63**
- ⊗Texas Tech **90**
- Georgetown **98**

Regional Finals

- ⊗Massachusetts **86**
- Georgetown **62**

Midwest

First Round

- 1 Kentucky **110**
- 16 San Jose State **72**
- 8 Wisconsin-Green Bay **48**
- 9 Virginia Tech **61**
- 5 Iowa State **74**
- 12 ⊗California **64**
- 4 Utah **72**
- 13 Canisius **43**
- 6 Louisville **82** (OT)
- 11 Tulsa **80**
- 3 Villanova **92**
- 14 Portland **58**
- 7 ⊗Michigan **76**
- 10 Texas **80**
- 2 Wake Forest **62**
- 15 UL-Monroe **50**

Second Round

- Kentucky **84**
- Virginia Tech **60**
- Iowa State **67**
- Utah **73**
- Louisville **68**
- Villanova **64**
- Texas **62**
- Wake Forest **65**

Regional Semifinals (Minneapolis)

- Kentucky **101**
- Utah **70**
- Louisville **59**
- Wake Forest **60**

Regional Finals

- Kentucky **83**
- Wake Forest **63**

National Semifinal

- Mississippi State **69**
- Syracuse **77**

Mississippi State commits 21 turnovers, negating a whopping 40-21 rebounding advantage, and Syracuse sinks 20 of 24 free throws to spoil an NCAA Final rematch of the SEC championship. Years later MSU coach Richard Williams will say, "To this day, I believe that if we played them 10 times, we'd win nine."

National Semifinal

- ⊗Massachusetts **74**
- Kentucky **81**

Kentucky's Rick Pitino coaches against his alma mater. National POY Marcus Camby, who fainted in a game months earlier, blocks six shots to tie the Final Four record. The Minutemen's Tournament games are later vacated because of Camby's involvement with an agent.

National Final

East Rutherford, NJ

Kentucky 76
Syracuse 67

Kentucky sinks 12 three-pointers—including seven by Tony Delk, tying the individual championship-game record—on the way to winning the last national title game not held in a domed stadium. Following the season, four Wildcats are selected in the NBA draft.

⊗ Team participation later vacated

A Pint-size point guard Earl Boykins, just 5'5", stuns Duke with 23 points, five assists and four steals. The Blue Devils, who failed to make the 1995 Tournament after coach Mike Krzyzewski missed 19 games with a back injury, lose their first first-round game since 1955.

B Freshman forward Gabe Lewullis sinks a backdoor layup—a Princeton signature—with 3.9 seconds left to upset defending champion UCLA and give the Tigers their first Tournament win since 1984. It's the final career victory for 29-year Tigers coach Pete Carril.

C Junior college transfer Dontae' Jones, a high school dropout who once worked at Kenny Rogers Roasters, is named Southeast Regional MOP after totaling 36 points and 23 rebounds.

D Syracuse overcomes a nine-point deficit in the last two-plus minutes to force overtime, during which forward John Wallace hits a three-pointer from the top of the key with 2.8 seconds left to win the game. After the game, TV analyst Al McGuire dances with Syracuse players on the court.

E Syracuse two-sport star Donovan McNabb—who will become an All-Pro quarterback for the Philadelphia Eagles—scores two points in the Orangemen's win. In his two-year college hoops career, McNabb played in 18 games, averaging 2.3 ppg and 1.1 rpg.

F Future two-time NBA MVP Steve Nash scores 28 points and hands out 12 assists in Santa Clara's upset.

G Darvin Ham's glass-shattering dunk in the first half delays the game 29 minutes, after which the Red Raiders go on a 10-0 run to take control of the game.

H Georgetown soph Allen Iverson—the summer's No. 1 NBA draft pick—averages a Tourney-best 27.8 ppg. Georgetown's roster also includes walk-on Brendan Gaughan, NASCAR's 2002 Craftsman Truck Series Rookie of the Year.

TOURNAMENT LEADERS

INDIVIDUAL LEADERS

SCORING

		CL	POS	G	PTS	PPG
1	**Allen Iverson**, Georgetown	SO	G	4	111	27.8
2	**Jason Sasser**, Texas Tech	SR	F	3	73	24.3
3	**Ray Allen**, Connecticut	JR	G	3	71	23.7
4	**John Wallace**, Syracuse	SR	F	6	131	21.8
5	**Stephon Marbury**, Georgia Tech	FR	G	3	61	20.3
6	**Matt Harpring**, Georgia Tech	SO	G/F	3	60	20.0
7	**DeJuan Wheat**, Louisville	JR	G	3	59	19.7
8	**Shandon Anderson**, Georgia	SR	G/F	3	58	19.3
9	**Marcus Camby**, Massachusetts	JR	F/C	5	96	19.2
10	**Tony Delk**, Kentucky	SR	G	6	113	18.8

MINIMUM: 3 GAMES

FIELD GOAL PCT

		CL	POS	G	FG	FGA	PCT
1	**Darvin Ham**, Texas Tech	JR	F	3	16	23	69.6
2	**Ricardo Peral**, Wake Forest	JR	F	4	18	26	69.2
3	**Keith LeGree**, Cincinnati	SO	G	4	15	23	65.2
4	**Otis Hill**, Syracuse	JR	C	6	38	59	64.4
5	**Edner Elisma**, Georgia Tech	JR	C	3	16	25	64.0

MINIMUM: 15 MADE AND 3 GAMES

FREE THROW PCT

		CL	POS	G	FT	FTA	PCT
1	**Steve Nash**, Santa Clara	SR	G	2	21	22	95.5
2	**Brevin Knight**, Stanford	JR	G	2	20	23	87.0
3	**Derek Anderson**, Kentucky	JR	G	6	17	20	85.0
4	**Donta Bright**, Massachusetts	SR	F	5	15	18	83.3
	Paul Pierce, Kansas	FR	F	4	15	18	83.3

MINIMUM: 15 MADE

THREE-POINT PCT

		CL	POS	G	3FG	3FGA	PCT
1	**Ricardo Peral**, Wake Forest	JR	F	4	8	11	72.7
2	**Michael Maddox**, Georgia Tech	SO	F	3	6	10	60.0
3	**John Wallace**, Syracuse	SR	F	6	7	13	53.8
4	**Rusty LaRue**, Wake Forest	SR	G/F	4	11	22	50.0
	Stephon Marbury, Georgia Tech	FR	G	3	10	20	50.0

MINIMUM: 6 MADE AND 3 GAMES

ASSISTS PER GAME

		CL	POS	G	AST	APG
1	**Drew Barry**, Georgia Tech	SR	G	3	29	9.7
	Reginald Geary, Arizona	SR	G	3	29	9.7
3	**Jacque Vaughn**, Kansas	JR	G	4	33	8.2
4	**Edgar Padilla**, Massachusetts	JR	G	5	41	8.2
5	**Lazarus Sims**, Syracuse	SR	G	6	46	7.7

MINIMUM: 3 GAMES

REBOUNDS PER GAME

		CL	POS	G	REB	RPG
1	**Tim Duncan**, Wake Forest	JR	F	4	52	13.0
2	**Danny Fortson**, Cincinnati	SO	C	4	49	12.2
3	**Derek Hood**, Arkansas	FR	F	3	30	10.0
4	**Marcus Camby**, Massachusetts	JR	F/C	5	47	9.4
5	**Dontae' Jones**, Mississippi State	SR	F	5	46	9.2

MINIMUM: 3 GAMES

BLOCKED SHOTS PER GAME

		CL	POS	G	BLK	BPG
1	**Marcus Camby**, Massachusetts	JR	F/C	5	21	4.2
2	**Tim Duncan**, Wake Forest	JR	F	4	14	3.5
3	**Scot Pollard**, Kansas	JR	C	4	12	3.0
4	**Erick Dampier**, Mississippi State	JR	C	5	12	2.4
5	**Terrell Bell**, Georgia	SR	F	3	7	2.3
	Travis Knight, Connecticut	SR	C	3	7	2.3
	Michael Maddox, Georgia Tech	SO	F	3	7	2.3

MINIMUM: 3 GAMES

STEALS PER GAME

		CL	POS	G	STL	SPG
1	**Edgar Padilla**, Massachusetts	JR	G	5	19	3.8
2	**Tick Rogers**, Louisville	SR	G	3	10	3.3
3	**Kareem Reid**, Arkansas	FR	G	3	9	3.0
4	**Antoine Walker**, Kentucky	SO	F	6	17	2.8
5	**Anthony Epps**, Kentucky	JR	G	6	16	2.7

MINIMUM: 3 GAMES

TEAM LEADERS

SCORING

		G	PTS	PPG
1	**Kentucky**	6	535	89.2
2	**Georgia Tech**	3	263	87.7
3	**Arizona**	3	257	85.7
4	**Texas Tech**	3	256	85.3
5	**Massachusetts**	5	410	82.0
6	**Georgetown**	4	326	81.5
7	**Georgia**	3	238	79.3
8	**Kansas**	4	225	75.0
9	**Syracuse**	6	444	74.0
10	**Cincinnati**	4	294	73.5

MINIMUM: 3 GAMES

FG PCT

		G	FG	FGA	PCT
1	**Utah**	3	82	155	52.9
2	**Georgia Tech**	3	98	191	51.3
3	**Arizona**	3	94	186	50.5
4	**Kentucky**	6	199	402	49.5
5	**Syracuse**	6	164	339	48.4

MINIMUM: 3 GAMES

3-PT FG PCT

		G	3FG	3FGA	PCT
1	**Kentucky**	6	44	97	45.4
2	**Wake Forest**	4	32	72	44.4
3	**Georgia Tech**	3	34	78	43.6
4	**Utah**	3	15	35	42.9
5	**Syracuse**	6	32	77	41.6

MINIMUM: 3 GAMES

FT PCT

		G	FT	FTA	PCT
1	**Utah**	3	36	42	85.7
2	**Arizona**	3	42	55	76.4
3	**Kentucky**	6	93	124	75.0
4	**Louisville**	3	50	68	73.5
5	**Wake Forest**	4	58	79	73.4

MINIMUM: 3 GAMES

AST/TO RATIO

		G	AST	TO	RAT
1	**Kentucky**	6	143	71	2.01
2	**Arizona**	3	67	42	1.60
3	**Georgia Tech**	3	64	42	1.52
4	**Georgia**	3	49	33	1.48
5	**Texas Tech**	3	53	41	1.29

MINIMUM: 3 GAMES

REBOUNDS

		G	REB	RPG
1	**Kansas**	4	187	46.8
2	**Connecticut**	3	134	44.7
3	**Arkansas**	3	132	44.0
	Georgetown	4	176	44.0
5	**Massachusetts**	5	212	42.4

MINIMUM: 3 GAMES

BLOCKS

		G	BLK	BPG
1	**Massachusetts**	5	35	7.0
2	**Connecticut**	3	20	6.7
3	**Kansas**	4	25	6.3
4	**Arizona**	3	18	6.0
5	**Kentucky**	6	33	5.5

MINIMUM: 3 GAMES

STEALS

		G	STL	SPG
1	**Kentucky**	6	71	11.8
2	**Kansas**	4	46	11.5
3	**Massachusetts**	5	57	11.4
4	**Louisville**	3	33	11.0
5	**Arkansas**	3	29	9.7

MINIMUM: 3 GAMES

ALL-TOURNAMENT TEAM

PLAYER	CL	POS	HT	SCHOOL	RPG	APG	PPG
Tony Delk*	SR	G	6-1	Kentucky	3.7	1.3	18.8
Todd Burgan	SO	G/F	6-7	Syracuse	8.5	2.0	13.2
Marcus Camby†	JR	F/C	6-11	Massachusetts	9.4	1.4	19.2
Ron Mercer	FR	G/F	6-7	Kentucky	1.5	1.3	7.8
John Wallace	SR	F	6-8	Syracuse	8.0	2.0	21.8

ALL-REGIONAL TEAMS

EAST

PLAYER	CL	POS	HT	SCHOOL	RPG	APG	PPG
Marcus Camby*	JR	F/C	6-11	Massachusetts	9.8	1.0	17.8
Donta Bright	SR	F	6-6	Massachusetts	5.5	0.8	12.8
Allen Iverson	SO	G	6-1	Georgetown	3.5	2.0	27.8
Jason Sasser	SR	F	6-7	Texas Tech	6.3	3.0	24.3
Carmelo Travieso	JR	G	6-2	Massachusetts	3.5	4.5	17.3

MIDWEST

PLAYER	CL	POS	HT	SCHOOL	RPG	APG	PPG
Tony Delk*	SR	G	6-1	Kentucky	3.3	1.5	17.3
Derek Anderson	JR	G	6-6	Kentucky	4.3	2.3	12.0
Tim Duncan	JR	F	6-10	Wake Forest	13.0	2.5	16.0
Anthony Epps	JR	G	6-2	Kentucky	3.0	5.3	8.3
Antoine Walker	SO	F	6-8	Kentucky	8.5	4.5	15.8

SOUTHEAST

PLAYER	CL	POS	HT	SCHOOL	RPG	APG	PPG
Dontae' Jones*	SR	F	6-8	Mississippi State	10.0	1.8	15.0
Darnell Burton	JR	G	6-2	Cincinnati	4.0	1.0	14.3
Erick Dampier	JR	C	6-11	Mississippi State	7.0	1.0	14.3
Danny Fortson	SO	C	6-7	Cincinnati	12.3	1.8	16.0
Darryl Wilson	SR	G	6-1	Mississippi State	2.5	1.8	17.8

WEST

PLAYER	CL	POS	HT	SCHOOL	RPG	APG	PPG
John Wallace*	SR	F	6-8	Syracuse	8.5	2.3	20.3
Shandon Anderson	SR	G/F	6-6	Georgia	7.0	2.3	19.3
Otis Hill	JR	C	6-8	Syracuse	6.8	1.0	16.3
Pertha Robinson	JR	G	6-1	Georgia	3.0	2.5	13.0
Jacque Vaughn	JR	G	6-1	Kansas	2.5	8.3	10.3

* MOST OUTSTANDING PLAYER

† HONOR LATER VACATED

1996 NCAA TOURNAMENT BOX SCORES

60-55

37	1H	25
23	2H	30

MISSISSIPPI STATE	MIN	FG	3FG	FT	REB	A	ST	BL	PF	TP
Darryl Wilson	35	9-14	7-11	2-2	2	0	0	1	3	27
Erick Dampier	40	6-15	0-0	3-4	8	2	0	4	1	15
Dontae' Jones	32	6-16	0-1	1-2	10	4	2	2	4	13
Russell Walters	35	1-2	0-0	1-2	6	1	0	0	0	3
Marcus Bullard	40	1-6	0-2	0-0	2	6	2	0	3	2
Whit Hughes	12	0-2	0-0	0-0	3	1	1	0	1	0
Bart Hyche	6	0-1	0-1	0-0	0	0	0	0	1	0
TOTALS	**200**	**23-56**	**7-15**	**7-10**	**31**	**14**	**5**	**7**	**13**	**60**
Percentages		41.1	46.7	70.0						

Coach: Richard Williams

CONNECTICUT	MIN	FG	3FG	FT	REB	A	ST	BL	PF	TP
Ray Allen	40	9-25	4-10	0-2	6	1	0	1	2	22
Doron Sheffer	36	3-14	2-7	2-2	9	5	0	1	2	10
Travis Knight	35	5-10	0-0	0-0	13	2	1	1	3	10
Kirk King	30	4-9	0-0	0-0	8	1	1	1	1	8
Rashamel Jones	17	1-5	1-2	0-0	2	0	1	0	1	3
Rudy Johnson	27	0-4	0-1	2-2	1	2	0	0	3	2
Eric Hayward	13	0-0	0-0	0-0	1	0	0	0	2	0
Dion Carson	2	0-1	0-0	0-0	0	0	0	0	0	0
TOTALS	**200**	**22-68**	**7-20**	**4-6**	**40**	**11**	**3**	**4**	**14**	**55**
Percentages		32.4	35.0	66.7						

Coach: Jim Calhoun

Officials: Dic Paparo, Jim Stupin, Mike Wood **Technicals:** None **Attendance:** 23,890

87-70

40	1H	30
47	2H	40

CINCINNATI	MIN	FG	3FG	FT	REB	A	ST	BL	PF	TP
Damon Flint	37	7-14	3-7	1-3	6	3	1	1	1	18
Danny Fortson	32	3-13	0-0	6-7	16	3	1	0	3	12
Keith Gregor	31	4-8	1-2	3-4	3	0	1	1	2	12
Art Long	24	4-12	0-0	4-4	8	1	0	0	3	12
Darnell Burton	15	5-7	2-4	0-0	4	1	1	0	3	12
Keith LeGree	37	4-4	0-0	3-6	5	6	3	1	3	11
Jackson Julson	12	2-5	0-0	2-2	2	1	1	1	1	6
Bobby Brannen	5	1-1	0-0	0-0	1	0	0	0	1	2
Melvin Levett	2	1-1	0-0	0-0	0	0	0	0	0	2
Terrance Davis	3	0-0	0-0	0-0	0	1	0	0	0	0
Ryan Fletcher	1	0-0	0-0	0-0	0	0	0	0	0	0
Rodrick Monroe	1	0-0	0-0	0-0	0	0	0	0	0	0
TOTALS	**200**	**31-65**	**6-13**	**19-26**	**45**	**16**	**8**	**4**	**17**	**87**
Percentages		47.7	46.2	73.1						

Coach: Bob Huggins

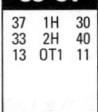

GEORGIA TECH	MIN	FG	3FG	FT	REB	A	ST	BL	PF	TP
Stephon Marbury	37	4-13	1-6	6-8	1	3	1	0	3	15
Matt Harpring	37	6-14	1-6	0-0	5	0	2	0	2	13
Michael Maddox	26	4-7	3-4	2-2	3	1	2	1	5	13
Gary Saunders	16	3-6	1-3	0-0	1	0	1	0	2	7
Drew Barry	36	2-12	2-7	0-0	4	8	3	0	2	6
Juan Gaston	12	1-4	0-2	4-4	5	0	0	0	2	6
Edner Elisma	31	2-6	0-0	0-2	12	1	2	2	3	4
John Kelly	1	1-1	1-1	0-0	0	0	0	0	1	3
Ryan Murphy	1	1-1	1-1	0-0	0	0	0	0	0	3
Bryan Brennan	1	0-1	0-0	0-0	0	0	0	0	0	0
Ashley Kelly	1	0-0	0-0	0-0	0	0	0	0	0	0
Ajani Williams	1	0-0	0-0	0-0	1	1	0	0	0	0
TOTALS	**200**	**24-65**	**10-30**	**12-16**	**32**	**14**	**11**	**3**	**20**	**70**
Percentages		36.9	33.3	75.0						

Coach: Bobby Cremins

Officials: Gene Monje, John Hughes, Ted Valentine **Technicals:** None **Attendance:** 23,890

83-81

37	1H	30
33	2H	40
13	OT1	11

SYRACUSE	MIN	FG	3FG	FT	REB	A	ST	BL	PF	TP
John Wallace	35	10-18	1-4	9-12	15	2	0	1	4	30
Otis Hill	32	8-10	0-0	3-5	11	1	0	1	5	19
Jason Cipolla	37	7-13	2-6	1-2	1	0	1	0	4	17
Lazarus Sims	45	3-7	2-5	2-2	4	10	2	1	0	10
Todd Burgan	37	2-5	0-2	3-9	11	4	3	0	4	7
J.B. Reafsnyder	14	0-3	0-0	0-0	0	1	1	0	3	0
Donovan McNabb	8	0-0	0-0	0-0	0	0	0	0	0	0
Bobby Lazor	6	0-1	0-0	0-0	0	0	0	0	0	0
Elvir Ovcina	1	0-0	0-0	0-0	0	0	1	0	0	0
Marius Janulis	0	0-1	0-0	0-0	0	0	0	0	2	0
TOTALS	**215**	**30-58**	**5-17**	**18-30**	**42**	**18**	**8**	**3**	**22**	**83**
Percentages		51.7	29.4	60.0						

Coach: Jim Boeheim

GEORGIA	MIN	FG	3FG	FT	REB	A	ST	BL	PF	TP
Shandon Anderson	40	8-19	1-3	8-9	13	1	1	1	4	25
Pertha Robinson	29	7-13	5-9	2-3	5	2	1	0	2	21
Katu Davis	37	5-14	3-8	3-4	7	6	2	0	2	16
Carlos Strong	24	1-8	0-1	2-4	1	0	1	1	5	4
Steve Jones	22	2-8	0-0	0-1	5	2	2	0	2	4
Ray Harrison	20	2-7	0-2	0-0	2	2	2	0	0	4
Terrell Bell	17	1-1	0-0	1-2	3	1	0	0	5	3
Larry Brown	10	1-3	0-0	0-2	4	0	0	1	0	2
Michael Chadwick	3	0-0	0-0	2-2	1	0	0	0	0	2
G.G. Smith	17	0-4	0-4	0-1	1	2	0	0	0	0
Jon Nordin	6	0-0	0-0	0-0	0	0	0	0	1	0
TOTALS	**225**	**27-77**	**9-27**	**18-28**	**42**	**16**	**9**	**3**	**21**	**81**
Percentages		35.1	33.3	64.3						

Coach: Tubby Smith

Officials: Tom Rucker, Mike Sanzere, Joe Shortnacy **Technicals:** None **Attendance:** 17,074

83-80

41	1H	39
42	2H	41

KANSAS	MIN	FG	3FG	FT	REB	A	ST	BL	PF	TP
Paul Pierce	27	6-11	4-6	4-4	5	0	1	0	2	20
B.J. Williams	27	8-12	0-0	2-2	9	0	1	1	4	18
Jerod Haase	29	4-13	4-11	4-4	10	8	3	0	4	16
Jacque Vaughn	37	4-10	0-3	5-7	2	11	2	0	2	13
Scot Pollard	25	2-4	0-0	3-4	4	0	0	3	2	7
Ryan Robertson	12	2-3	2-2	0-0	1	0	1	0	2	6
T.J. Pugh	7	1-4	0-1	0-0	2	0	0	0	1	2
Raef LaFrentz	23	0-4	0-0	1-2	4	1	0	1	2	1
Billy Thomas	6	0-2	0-2	0-0	1	0	2	0	3	0
Sean Pearson	4	0-1	0-1	0-0	0	1	0	0	0	0
Calvin Rayford	3	0-0	0-0	0-0	0	0	0	0	0	0
TOTALS	**200**	**27-64**	**10-26**	**19-23**	**38**	**21**	**10**	**5**	**22**	**83**
Percentages		42.2	38.5	82.6						

Coach: Roy Williams

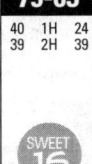

ARIZONA	MIN	FG	3FG	FT	REB	A	ST	BL	PF	TP
Miles Simon	38	6-15	2-4	7-8	4	6	2	1	3	21
Michael Dickerson	31	6-14	3-8	6-7	7	2	1	1	3	21
Corey Williams	34	7-13	2-4	0-0	5	0	0	2	2	16
Ben Davis	34	3-8	0-0	4-4	4	1	2	0	2	10
Joseph McLean	13	2-4	2-3	1-2	2	0	1	0	2	7
Jason Terry	8	1-2	0-0	1-1	0	0	0	0	2	3
Reginald Geary	35	1-4	0-3	0-0	4	8	1	1	4	2
A.J. Bramlett	4	0-0	0-0	0-0	0	0	0	1	1	0
Donnell Harris	2	0-0	0-0	0-0	0	0	0	0	0	0
Kelvin Eafon	1	0-0	0-0	0-0	0	0	0	0	0	0
TOTALS	**200**	**26-60**	**9-22**	**19-22**	**26**	**17**	**7**	**6**	**19**	**80**
Percentages		43.3	40.9	86.4						

Coach: Lute Olson

Officials: Tom O'Neill, Tim Higgins, Michael Kitts **Technicals:** None **Attendance:** 17,074

79-63

40	1H	24
39	2H	39

MASSACHUSETTS	MIN	FG	3FG	FT	REB	A	ST	BL	PF	TP
Tyrone Weeks	25	5-9	0-0	6-8	7	1	0	2	3	16
Marcus Camby	18	5-8	0-0	5-10	7	1	0	3	3	15
Carmelo Travieso	35	5-14	3-9	1-1	8	3	2	1	0	14
Dana Dingle	30	4-9	0-0	4-7	7	4	2	0	0	12
Donta Bright	33	5-14	0-1	1-1	6	0	2	0	3	11
Edgar Padilla	31	2-5	1-2	0-0	3	5	5	0	3	5
Ted Cottrell	3	0-1	0-0	2-2	2	0	0	1	0	2
Rigoberto Nunez	3	1-3	0-1	0-0	1	0	0	0	1	2
Charlton Clarke	12	0-4	0-2	1-2	1	1	1	0	0	1
Inus Norville	8	0-0	0-0	1-2	2	0	0	0	5	1
Giddel Padilla	2	0-0	0-0	0-0	0	2	0	0	0	0
TOTALS	**200**	**27-67**	**4-15**	**21-33**	**44**	**17**	**12**	**7**	**18**	**79**
Percentages		40.3	26.7	63.6						

Coach: John Calipari

ARKANSAS	MIN	FG	3FG	FT	REB	A	ST	BL	PF	TP
Pat Bradley	37	6-10	3-6	0-0	3	0	2	0	2	15
Kareem Reid	38	3-11	0-2	6-6	3	8	1	0	1	12
Lee Wilson	18	3-7	0-0	6-6	6	1	2	1	2	12
Ali Thompson	22	4-9	0-1	1-2	6	2	1	0	3	9
Darnell Robinson	17	3-6	0-1	0-0	2	0	1	0	4	6
Derek Hood	18	1-6	0-0	3-4	5	0	0	0	4	5
Landis Williams	15	1-4	0-0	0-0	3	0	0	1	3	2
Nick Davis	9	1-4	0-1	0-0	4	0	1	2	4	2
Marlon Towns	20	0-6	0-4	0-0	1	1	1	0	3	0
Antwon Hall	5	0-1	0-0	0-0	1	1	0	0	0	0
Guy Whitney	1	0-0	0-0	0-0	0	1	0	0	0	0
TOTALS	**200**	**22-64**	**3-15**	**16-18**	**34**	**14**	**9**	**4**	**26**	**63**
Percentages		34.4	20.0	88.9						

Coach: Nolan Richardson

Officials: Dave Libbey, Frank Bosone, Rick Hartzell **Technicals:** None **Attendance:** 34,614

98-90

47	1H	50
51	2H	40

GEORGETOWN	MIN	FG	3FG	FT	REB	A	ST	BL	PF	TP
Allen Iverson	38	10-29	1-5	11-18	4	5	5	0	1	32
Othella Harrington	27	10-13	0-0	3-4	6	0	0	2	5	23
Victor Page	26	4-10	0-1	9-13	4	0	1	0	2	17
Jerome Williams	35	3-5	0-0	6-6	7	3	3	0	1	12
Boubacar Aw	25	4-5	0-0	0-0	1	1	0	0	3	8
Jahidi White	7	1-1	0-0	2-3	2	0	0	0	5	4
Joseph Touomou	17	0-0	0-0	2-2	1	2	0	0	3	2
Ya-Ya Dia	13	0-2	0-0	0-0	4	0	0	0	4	0
Jerry Nichols	8	0-1	0-0	0-0	0	1	0	0	0	0
Daymond Jackson	3	0-0	0-0	0-0	0	0	0	0	0	0
Dean Berry	1	0-0	0-0	0-0	1	0	0	0	0	0
TOTALS	**200**	**32-66**	**1-6**	**33-46**	**30**	**12**	**9**	**2**	**24**	**98**
Percentages		48.5	16.7	71.7						

Coach: John Thompson Jr.

TEXAS TECH	MIN	FG	3FG	FT	REB	A	ST	BL	PF	TP
Jason Sasser	40	8-18	2-4	7-10	8	2	0	0	5	25
Cory Carr	29	4-13	3-8	5-6	5	0	0	0	4	16
Koy Smith	29	5-10	2-4	4-4	5	3	1	0	4	16
Jason Martin	30	5-9	0-1	2-4	2	2	3	0	4	12
Darvin Ham	26	4-7	0-0	1-7	7	1	0	0	5	9
Gionet Cooper	14	2-3	0-0	2-2	4	1	0	1	5	6
Tony Battie	16	1-4	0-0	2-2	4	1	0	1	5	4
Stan Bonewitz	10	1-1	0-0	0-0	0	2	0	0	0	2
Deuce Jones	3	0-0	0-0	0-0	0	0	0	0	1	0
Da'Mon Roberts	3	0-1	0-0	0-0	0	0	0	0	2	0
TOTALS	**200**	**30-66**	**7-17**	**23-35**	**35**	**12**	**4**	**2**	**35**	**90**
Percentages		45.5	41.2	65.7						

Coach: James Dickey

Officials: Ed Hightower, Bill Gracey, Zelton Steed **Technicals:** Georgetown (White) **Attendance:** 34,614

101-70 (1H: 56-34; 2H: 45-36) — SWEET 16

KENTUCKY	MIN	FG	3FG	FT	REB	A	ST	BL	PF	TP
Antoine Walker	25	9-18	0-1	1-1	8	6	1	1	1	19
Derek Anderson	18	5-9	0-1	8-8	6	1	1	0	3	18
Anthony Epps	25	5-11	3-6	1-2	4	8	3	0	0	14
Tony Delk	23	6-15	2-7	0-1	4	2	2	1	1	14
Allen Edwards	17	2-3	1-2	1-3	3	0	2	0	2	6
Jeff Sheppard	14	3-7	0-1	0-0	1	2	0	0	1	6
Wayne Turner	13	3-4	0-0	0-0	0	1	1	0	0	6
Mark Pope	20	2-4	1-1	0-1	2	0	0	1	2	5
Oliver Simmons	8	2-3	1-1	0-0	0	1	0	1	1	5
Ron Mercer	17	2-5	0-2	0-0	2	1	2	2	0	4
Walter McCarty	15	1-3	0-0	0-0	4	2	1	1	2	2
Nazr Mohammed	4	1-1	0-0	0-0	0	0	0	0	1	2
Cameron Mills	1	0-0	0-0	0-0	0	0	0	0	0	0
TOTALS	200	41-83	8-22	11-16	34	24	13	7	14	101
Percentages		49.4	36.4	68.8						

Coach: Rick Pitino

UTAH	MIN	FG	3FG	FT	REB	A	ST	BL	PF	TP
Keith Van Horn	32	8-15	1-3	6-6	8	1	1	0	1	23
Ben Caton	31	9-10	3-3	1-1	2	4	0	0	1	22
Michael Doleac	23	3-7	0-0	3-5	8	0	0	3	3	9
Brandon Jessie	29	2-10	0-2	0-0	4	1	1	0	1	4
Ben Melmeth	16	1-3	0-0	2-2	4	0	0	0	1	4
Andre Miller	35	1-3	0-0	0-1	4	9	2	1	2	2
Mark Rydalch	13	1-4	0-1	0-0	0	2	0	0	1	2
Drew Hansen	4	1-2	0-0	0-0	2	1	0	0	3	2
Paul Jonas	4	1-2	0-0	0-0	0	0	0	0	0	2
Terry Preston	5	0-1	0-1	0-0	1	0	0	0	0	0
Will Carlton	4	0-0	0-0	0-0	0	0	1	1	2	0
Doug Meacham	2	0-0	0-0	0-0	0	0	0	0	0	0
Andy Jensen	1	0-0	0-0	0-0	0	0	0	0	0	0
Kelly Leonard	1	0-0	0-0	0-0	0	0	0	0	1	0
TOTALS	200	27-57	4-10	12-15	33	18	5	5	16	70
Percentages		47.4	40.0	80.0						

Coach: Rick Majerus

Officials: Gerry Donaghy, Donnee Gray, Bob Donato
Technicals: Utah (coach Majerus)
Attendance: 30,334

60-59 (1H: 30-27; 2H: 30-32) — SWEET 16

WAKE FOREST	MIN	FG	3FG	FT	REB	A	ST	BL	PF	TP
Tim Duncan	40	9-13	1-2	8-10	13	3	0	7	4	27
Ricardo Peral	27	4-5	3-3	0-1	3	4	0	0	5	11
Rusty LaRue	39	3-8	3-6	0-0	3	3	1	0	3	9
Jerry Braswell	38	3-5	2-2	0-0	5	3	0	0	2	8
Steven Goolsby	24	1-5	1-4	0-0	2	1	1	0	1	3
Sean Allen	29	1-3	0-0	0-0	4	2	0	0	2	2
Tony Rutland	3	0-1	0-1	0-0	0	0	0	0	1	0
TOTALS	200	21-40	10-18	8-11	30	16	2	7	18	60
Percentages		52.5	55.6	72.7						

Coach: Dave Odom

LOUISVILLE	MIN	FG	3FG	FT	REB	A	ST	BL	PF	TP
Samaki Walker	25	5-14	0-0	6-10	6	0	2	-	3	16
Tick Rogers	31	6-10	1-3	0-0	3	1	4	-	2	13
B.J. Flynn	26	3-8	1-4	4-4	4	3	2	-	0	11
DeJuan Wheat	33	3-15	1-7	0-1	1	6	1	-	0	7
Alvin Sims	25	2-9	0-2	0-0	5	2	1	-	4	4
Beau Zach Smith	15	2-4	0-0	0-0	6	0	0	-	4	4
Damion Dantzler	24	1-6	0-2	0-0	4	0	0	-	3	2
Brian Kiser	2	1-3	0-1	0-0	1	1	0	-	0	2
TOTALS	181	23-69	3-19	10-15	30	13	10	-	16	59
Percentages		33.3	15.8	66.7						

Coach: Denny Crum

Officials: Scott Thornley, Jody Silvester, Kerry Sitton
Technicals: None
Attendance: 30,334

73-63 (1H: 37-29; 2H: 36-34) — ELITE 8

MISSISSIPPI STATE	MIN	FG	3FG	FT	REB	A	ST	BL	PF	TP
Dontae' Jones	34	9-17	2-6	3-3	13	0	2	2	0	23
Darryl Wilson	35	3-9	1-6	9-12	2	5	0	0	3	16
Marcus Bullard	40	3-7	1-3	4-7	4	3	1	0	2	11
Erick Dampier	31	4-10	0-0	1-4	6	2	0	0	4	9
Tyrone Washington	11	3-4	0-0	1-2	4	0	0	1	4	7
Bart Hyche	5	2-2	1-1	0-0	0	1	0	0	0	5
Russell Walters	35	0-2	0-0	1-2	10	0	0	1	1	1
Whit Hughes	9	0-0	0-0	1-3	0	0	1	0	0	1
TOTALS	200	24-51	5-16	20-33	39	11	4	4	14	73
Percentages		47.1	31.2	60.6						

Coach: Richard Williams

CINCINNATI	MIN	FG	3FG	FT	REB	A	ST	BL	PF	TP
Danny Fortson	36	6-15	0-0	12-16	13	2	1	2	5	24
Darnell Burton	35	6-20	5-16	0-0	3	2	3	0	0	17
Keith LeGree	38	5-8	1-1	0-2	5	4	1	0	5	11
Art Long	24	2-4	0-0	0-0	6	0	1	1	5	4
Jackson Julson	10	1-2	0-0	1-2	2	0	0	0	2	3
Damon Flint	35	1-12	0-7	0-0	4	1	2	0	0	2
Rodrick Monroe	9	1-2	0-0	0-0	2	0	0	0	2	2
Keith Gregor	5	0-0	0-0	0-0	0	0	0	0	0	0
Bobby Brannen	4	0-0	0-0	0-0	0	0	1	0	1	0
Terrance Davis	2	0-0	0-0	0-0	0	2	1	0	2	0
Ryan Fletcher	1	0-0	0-0	0-0	0	0	0	0	0	0
Melvin Levett	1	0-2	0-2	0-0	0	0	0	0	0	0
TOTALS	200	22-65	6-26	13-20	35	11	10	3	22	63
Percentages		33.8	23.1	65.0						

Coach: Bob Huggins

Officials: Andre Pattillo, David Dodge, Ted Hillary
Technicals: None
Attendance: 23,850

60-57 (1H: 35-26; 2H: 25-31) — ELITE 8

SYRACUSE	MIN	FG	3FG	FT	REB	A	ST	BL	PF	TP
John Wallace	40	5-16	1-1	4-6	9	1	1	1	1	15
Otis Hill	25	5-10	0-0	5-7	6	0	0	0	4	15
Jason Cipolla	32	4-9	2-4	1-2	2	2	2	0	2	11
Todd Burgan	32	3-11	0-1	2-7	8	1	2	1	4	8
J.B. Reafsnyder	16	3-5	0-0	0-0	5	0	2	0	2	6
Lazarus Sims	39	0-4	0-1	4-4	4	4	0	0	1	4
Marius Janulis	15	0-1	0-1	1-2	2	1	1	0	1	1
David Patrick	1	0-0	0-0	0-0	0	0	0	0	0	0
TOTALS	200	20-56	3-8	17-28	36	9	8	2	15	60
Percentages		35.7	37.5	60.7						

Coach: Jim Boeheim

KANSAS	MIN	FG	3FG	FT	REB	A	ST	BL	PF	TP
Jacque Vaughn	34	8-12	3-5	2-2	3	4	1	0	4	21
Paul Pierce	28	3-9	1-4	4-5	7	0	1	1	2	11
Scot Pollard	31	5-9	0-0	0-1	7	0	2	4	5	10
Raef LaFrentz	28	3-8	0-0	0-1	9	0	1	1	1	6
B.J. Williams	13	2-4	0-0	0-0	5	0	1	0	3	4
Jerod Haase	29	0-9	0-8	3-4	3	6	4	0	3	3
Ryan Robertson	12	1-3	0-2	0-0	4	2	1	0	1	2
Billy Thomas	9	0-5	0-4	0-0	0	0	0	0	1	0
T.J. Pugh	7	0-3	0-0	0-0	3	0	0	0	0	0
Calvin Rayford	5	0-0	0-0	0-0	1	0	0	0	0	0
Sean Pearson	4	0-2	0-2	0-0	0	1	0	0	0	0
TOTALS	200	22-64	4-25	9-13	42	13	11	6	23	57
Percentages		34.4	16.0	69.2						

Coach: Roy Williams

Officials: Don Rutledge, Larry Rose, Frank Scagliotta
Technicals: None
Attendance: 17,074

86-62 (1H: 38-34; 2H: 48-28) — ELITE 8

MASSACHUSETTS	MIN	FG	3FG	FT	REB	A	ST	BL	PF	TP
Marcus Camby	28	9-19	0-0	4-5	7	1	1	3	4	22
Carmelo Travieso	37	6-14	6-13	2-2	1	6	4	1	3	20
Donta Bright	30	5-14	0-0	7-9	7	2	4	2	2	17
Dana Dingle	29	2-4	0-0	6-10	4	2	1	0	3	10
Edgar Padilla	39	1-4	1-2	5-6	3	4	5	0	4	8
Tyrone Weeks	26	2-5	0-0	0-1	8	0	0	0	4	4
Ross Burns	1	1-1	0-0	0-0	0	1	0	0	0	2
Giddel Padilla	1	1-2	0-1	0-0	0	1	0	0	1	2
Charlton Clarke	2	0-0	0-0	1-2	0	0	1	0	0	1
Inus Norville	4	0-1	0-0	0-0	2	0	0	0	1	0
Ted Cottrell	1	0-0	0-0	0-0	2	0	0	0	0	0
Andrew Maclay	1	0-0	0-0	0-0	0	1	0	0	0	0
Rigoberto Nunez	1	0-1	0-0	0-0	1	0	0	0	0	0
TOTALS	200	27-65	7-16	25-35	35	18	16	6	22	86
Percentages		41.5	43.8	71.4						

Coach: John Calipari

GEORGETOWN	MIN	FG	3FG	FT	REB	A	ST	BL	PF	TP
Allen Iverson	36	6-21	4-9	7-10	2	1	2	0	4	23
Othella Harrington	30	4-9	0-0	5-8	6	2	0	0	1	13
Jerome Williams	24	4-7	0-1	1-2	8	2	2	1	3	9
Daymond Jackson	16	2-2	0-0	2-2	3	0	1	0	4	6
Joseph Touomou	24	2-4	0-1	1-1	1	2	3	0	3	5
Boubacar Aw	17	1-2	0-0	0-0	3	0	0	1	3	2
Jahidi White	16	0-1	0-0	2-4	3	0	0	1	0	2
Ya-Ya Dia	13	1-3	0-0	0-0	3	0	0	1	1	2
Victor Page	18	0-5	0-1	0-0	3	1	0	0	4	0
Jerry Nichols	3	0-2	0-2	0-1	1	0	0	0	1	0
Dean Berry	1	0-1	0-1	0-0	0	0	0	0	0	0
Godwin Owinje	1	0-0	0-0	0-0	0	0	0	0	0	0
James Reed	1	0-0	0-0	0-0	0	0	0	0	0	0
TOTALS	200	20-57	4-15	18-28	33	8	8	4	24	62
Percentages		35.1	26.7	64.3						

Coach: John Thompson Jr.

Officials: John Clougherty, Bob Garibaldi, Charles Range
Technicals: None
Attendance: 32,328

83-63 (1H: 38-19; 2H: 45-44) — ELITE 8

KENTUCKY	MIN	FG	3FG	FT	REB	A	ST	BL	PF	TP
Tony Delk	27	9-13	4-6	3-3	4	2	3	3	3	25
Derek Anderson	25	4-7	1-1	3-4	5	5	1	1	3	12
Walter McCarty	29	3-4	1-1	3-4	3	1	1	1	3	10
Antoine Walker	31	3-11	0-1	3-3	6	2	1	1	4	9
Jeff Sheppard	14	3-4	1-1	0-1	3	4	0	0	0	7
Anthony Epps	29	3-6	0-1	6-6	1	0	3	3	12	12
Allen Edwards	11	1-2	0-0	2-2	0	2	0	0	1	4
Mark Pope	17	1-4	0-0	0-0	3	0	0	0	3	2
Nazr Mohammed	1	1-1	0-0	0-0	0	0	0	0	0	2
Wayne Turner	8	0-0	0-0	0-0	0	0	0	0	2	0
Ron Mercer	6	0-1	0-0	0-0	0	0	0	0	1	0
Oliver Simmons	2	0-0	0-0	0-0	0	0	0	0	1	0
TOTALS	200	28-53	7-11	20-23	25	16	9	9	32	83
Percentages		52.8	63.6	87.0						

Coach: Rick Pitino

WAKE FOREST	MIN	FG	3FG	FT	REB	A	ST	BL	PF	TP
Tim Duncan	39	2-7	0-0	10-12	16	6	2	4	3	14
Steven Goolsby	32	4-10	4-7	2-2	7	2	0	1	4	14
Ricardo Peral	34	3-5	2-3	5-5	0	0	0	0	5	13
Jerry Braswell	39	3-12	2-6	2-3	2	2	2	0	1	10
Sean Allen	22	3-6	0-1	1-1	5	0	0	0	3	7
Rusty LaRue	30	1-4	1-4	0-0	2	0	2	0	4	3
William Stringfellow	1	1-1	0-0	0-0	0	0	0	0	0	2
Joseph Amonett	2	0-2	0-2	0-0	0	0	0	0	0	0
Armond Wilson	1	0-0	0-0	0-0	0	1	0	0	0	0
TOTALS	200	17-47	9-23	20-23	32	11	6	5	20	63
Percentages		36.2	39.1	87.0						

Coach: Dave Odom

Officials: James Burr, John Cahill, Dan Chrisman
Technicals: None
Attendance: 30,397

ANNUAL REVIEW

SYRACUSE	MIN	FG	3FG	FT	REB	A	ST	BL	PF	TP
John Wallace	40	6-14	1-1	8-10	4	2	0	2	2	21
Todd Burgan	39	6-11	2-4	5-6	7	2	3	1	1	19
Otis Hill	32	7-11	0-0	1-2	2	1	1	0	4	15
Lazarus Sims	40	3-5	1-3	4-4	5	9	2	0	2	11
Jason Cipolla	32	3-9	1-3	2-2	1	1	2	0	0	9
J.B. Reafsnyder	8	1-3	0-0	0-0	2	0	2	0	1	2
Marius Janulis	9	0-2	0-1	0-0	0	0	0	0	1	0
TOTALS	**200**	**26-55**	**5-12**	**20-24**	**21**	**15**	**10**	**3**	**11**	**77**
Percentages		47.3	41.7	83.3						
Coach: Jim Boeheim										

77-69

36	1H	36
41	2H	33

FINAL 4

MISSISSIPPI STATE	MIN	FG	3FG	FT	REB	A	ST	BL	PF	TP
Darryl Wilson	37	7-16	6-13	0-0	2	3	1	0	4	20
Dontae' Jones	37	6-16	2-8	2-2	6	2	0	1	4	16
Erick Dampier	36	4-6	0-0	4-4	14	6	1	1	1	12
Marcus Bullard	39	4-9	3-7	0-0	5	8	0	0	2	11
Russell Walters	32	5-9	0-0	0-0	6	0	0	0	5	10
Whit Hughes	10	0-0	0-0	0-0	5	1	2	0	0	0
Bart Hyche	5	0-0	0-0	0-0	1	1	0	0	1	0
Tyrone Washington	4	0-0	0-0	0-0	1	0	0	0	1	0
TOTALS	**200**	**26-56**	**11-28**	**6-6**	**40**	**21**	**4**	**2**	**18**	**69**
Percentages		46.4	39.3	100.0						
Coach: Richard Williams										

Officials: A… Pattillo, Fra… Scagliotta, … Sanzere
Technicals: None
Attendance: 19,229

KENTUCKY	MIN	FG	3FG	FT	REB	A	ST	BL	PF	TP
Tony Delk	32	7-16	1-4	5-9	2	0	1	1	2	20
Antoine Walker	32	5-10	0-0	4-5	6	4	4	1	2	14
Ron Mercer	16	4-6	1-1	0-1	0	1	2	0	1	9
Walter McCarty	23	4-8	0-1	0-0	10	4	0	1	1	8
Mark Pope	23	1-2	0-0	6-6	3	1	1	1	4	8
Anthony Epps	33	3-6	1-2	0-0	4	4	2	0	1	7
Jeff Sheppard	10	2-2	0-0	3-4	2	1	0	1	3	7
Derek Anderson	21	1-3	0-1	4-5	5	4	1	0	4	6
Wayne Turner	6	1-2	0-0	0-0	1	1	1	0	0	2
Allen Edwards	4	0-0	0-0	0-0	0	0	0	1	2	0
TOTALS	**200**	**28-55**	**3-9**	**22-30**	**33**	**20**	**12**	**6**	**20**	**81**
Percentages		50.9	33.3	73.3						
Coach: Rick Pitino										

81-74

36	1H	28
45	2H	46

FINAL 4

MASSACHUSETTS	MIN	FG	3FG	FT	REB	A	ST	BL	PF	TP
Marcus Camby	36	9-18	0-1	7-9	8	3	0	6	4	25
Donta Bright	32	7-14	0-1	1-2	9	1	2	0	5	15
Carmelo Travieso	26	3-7	2-4	2-2	4	0	1	0	4	10
Dana Dingle	31	4-6	0-0	0-0	4	0	0	0	3	8
Edgar Padilla	39	2-10	1-3	1-2	2	12	2	1	5	6
Giddel Padilla	8	2-4	0-0	0-0	1	1	1	0	2	4
Charlton Clarke	10	1-2	0-0	1-2	1	1	1	0	1	3
Inus Norville	2	1-1	0-0	0-0	0	0	0	0	0	2
Tyrone Weeks	15	0-2	0-0	1-2	2	1	1	1	0	1
Rigoberto Nunez	1	0-0	0-0	0-0	0	0	0	0	0	0
TOTALS	**200**	**29-64**	**3-9**	**13-19**	**31**	**19**	**8**	**8**	**24**	**74**
Percentages		45.3	33.3	68.4						
Coach: John Calipari										

Officials: Ed Hightower, To… Rucker, Micha… Kitts
Technicals: None
Attendance: 19,229

KENTUCKY	MIN	FG	3FG	FT	REB	A	ST	BL	PF	TP
Tony Delk	37	8-20	7-12	1-2	7	2	2	1	2	24
Ron Mercer	24	8-12	3-4	1-1	2	2	1	0	3	20
Antoine Walker	32	4-12	0-1	3-6	9	4	4	0	2	11
Derek Anderson	16	4-8	2-3	1-1	4	1	3	0	2	11
Mark Pope	27	1-6	0-2	2-2	3	2	1	0	3	4
Walter McCarty	19	2-6	0-0	0-0	3	0	0	0	4	4
Jeff Sheppard	7	1-2	0-1	0-1	2	0	0	0	3	2
Anthony Epps	35	0-6	0-3	0-0	4	7	0	0	1	0
Allen Edwards	3	0-1	0-1	0-0	0	1	0	0	0	0
TOTALS	**200**	**28-73**	**12-27**	**8-13**	**34**	**19**	**11**	**1**	**20**	**76**
Percentages		38.4	44.4	61.5						
Coach: Rick Pitino										

76-67

42	1H	33
34	2H	34

NCAA FINAL 1996

SYRACUSE	MIN	FG	3FG	FT	REB	A	ST	BL	PF	TP
John Wallace	38	11-19	2-3	5-5	10	1	0	1	5	29
Todd Burgan	39	7-10	3-5	2-5	8	1	1	0	5	19
Otis Hill	28	3-9	0-0	1-2	10	1	0	1	2	7
Lazarus Sims	39	2-5	1-4	1-2	2	7	1	0	2	6
Jason Cipolla	35	3-8	0-3	0-0	1	2	4	0	1	6
J.B. Reafsnyder	13	0-1	0-0	0-0	4	0	0	0	0	0
Marius Janulis	7	0-0	0-0	0-0	2	0	0	0	2	0
Elimu Nelson	1	0-0	0-0	0-0	0	0	0	0	0	0
TOTALS	**200**	**26-52**	**6-15**	**9-14**	**37**	**12**	**6**	**2**	**17**	**67**
Percentages		50.0	40.0	64.3						
Coach: Jim Boeheim										

Officials: John Clougherty, Scott Thornley, Dave Libbey
Technicals: None
Attendance: 19,229

National Invitation Tournament (NIT)

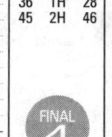

First round: Rhode Island d. Marist 82-77, Charleston d. Tennessee 55-49, South Carolina d. Davidson 100-73, Vanderbilt d. Arkansas-Little Rock 86-80, Alabama d. Illinois 72-69, Missouri d. Murray State 89-85, Fresno State d. Miami (OH) 58-57, Michigan State d. Washington 64-50, Tulane d. Auburn 87-73, Minnesota d. Saint Louis 68-52, Wisconsin d. Manhattan 55-42, Illinois State d. Mount St. Mary's 73-49, Saint Joseph's d. Iona 82-78, Nebraska d. Colorado State 91-83, Washington State d. Gonzaga 92-73, Providence d. Fairfield 91-79
Second round: South Carolina d. Vanderbilt 80-70, Alabama d. Missouri 72-49, Tulane d. Minnesota 84-65, Illinois State d. Wisconsin 77-62, Rhode Island d. Charleston 62-58 (OT), Saint Joseph's d. Providence 82-62, Fresno State d. Michigan State 80-70, Nebraska d. Washington State 82-73
Third round: Alabama d. South Carolina 68-67, Tulane d. Illinois State 83-72, Saint Joseph's d. Rhode Island 76-59, Nebraska d. Fresno State 83-71
Semifinals: Nebraska d. Tulane 90-78, Saint Joseph's d. Alabama 74-69
Championship: Nebraska d. Saint Joseph's 60-56
Third place: Tulane d. Alabama 87-76
MVP: Erick Strickland, Nebraska

1996-97: Cat Fight

In a battle of feral felines, the NCAA Final pitted Rick Pitino's defending champion Kentucky Wildcats against coach Lute Olson's surprising Arizona Wildcats. Arizona finished the regular season 19–9, just good enough for a No. 4 Tournament seed, while Kentucky had 30 wins, a No. 1 seed and looked very much like a team poised to repeat. The western Cats caught fire during the Tournament and—powered by 30 points from junior Miles Simon, the Tournament's Most Outstanding Player—beat the southeastern Cats in overtime, 84-79, at the RCA Dome in Indianapolis to win the program's first NCAA title. Arizona became the first team to beat three No. 1 seeds—Kansas, North Carolina and Kentucky (which also happen to be the three winningest programs of all time)—on its way to the championship.

Minnesota (35–5) reached the Final Four, where it lost to Kentucky, but three years later had its participation vacated for academic fraud. Wake Forest's Tim Duncan was the Naismith Player of the Year and was chosen as the No. 1 pick of the NBA draft by the San Antonio Spurs. Duncan averaged 20.8 ppg, 14.7 rpg and 3.2 apg. In May, Pitino resigned from Kentucky to become coach of the Boston Celtics.

Major Conference Standings

AM. EAST

	Conference W	L	Pct	Overall W	L	Pct
Boston U.⊕	17	1	.944	25	5	.833
Drexel□	16	2	.889	22	9	.710
Hartford	11	7	.611	17	11	.607
Hofstra	9	9	.500	12	15	.444
Delaware	8	10	.444	15	16	.484
Vermont	7	11	.389	14	13	.519
Maine	6	12	.333	11	20	.355
Northeastern	6	12	.333	7	20	.259
Towson	5	13	.278	9	19	.321
New Hampshire	5	13	.278	7	20	.259

Tournament: **Boston U. d. Drexel 68-61**
Tournament MOP: **Tunji Awojobi**, Boston U.

ACC

	Conference W	L	Pct	Overall W	L	Pct
Duke○	12	4	.750	24	9	.727
North Carolina⊕	11	5	.688	28	7	.800
Wake Forest○	11	5	.688	24	7	.774
Clemson○	9	7	.563	23	10	.697
Maryland○	9	7	.563	21	11	.656
Virginia○	7	9	.438	18	13	.581
Florida State□	6	10	.375	20	12	.625
NC State□	4	12	.250	17	15	.531
Georgia Tech	3	13	.188	9	18	.333

Tournament: **North Carolina d. NC State 64-54**
Tournament MVP: **Shammond Williams**, North Carolina

ATLANTIC 10

	Conference W	L	Pct	Overall W	L	Pct
East						
Saint Joseph's⊕	13	3	.813	26	7	.788
Rhode Island○	12	4	.750	20	10	.667
Massachusetts○	11	5	.688	19	14	.576
Temple○	10	6	.625	20	11	.645
St. Bonaventure	5	11	.313	14	14	.500
Fordham	1	15	.063	6	21	.222
West						
Xavier○	13	3	.813	23	6	.793
George Washington□	8	8	.500	15	14	.517
Virginia Tech	7	9	.438	15	16	.484
Dayton	6	10	.375	13	14	.481
La Salle	5	11	.313	10	17	.370
Duquesne	5	11	.313	9	18	.333

Tournament: **Saint Joseph's d. Rhode Island 61-56**
Tournament MOP: **Rashid Bey**, Saint Joseph's

BIG EAST

	Conference W	L	Pct	Overall W	L	Pct
Big East 7						
Georgetown○	11	7	.611	20	10	.667
Providence○	10	8	.556	24	12	.667
Pittsburgh□	10	8	.556	18	15	.545
Syracuse□	9	9	.500	19	13	.594
Miami (FL)□	9	9	.500	16	13	.552
Rutgers	5	13	.278	11	16	.407
Seton Hall	5	13	.278	10	18	.357
Big East 6						
Boston College⊕	12	6	.667	22	9	.710
Villanova○	12	6	.667	24	10	.706
West Virginia□	11	7	.611	21	10	.677
Notre Dame□	8	10	.444	16	14	.533
St. John's	8	10	.444	13	14	.481
Connecticut□	7	11	.389	18	15	.545

Tournament: **Boston College d. Villanova 70-58**
Tournament MVP: **Scoonie Penn**, Boston College

BIG SKY

	Conference W	L	Pct	Overall W	L	Pct
Northern Arizona□	14	2	.875	21	7	.750
Montana⊕	11	5	.688	21	11	.656
Montana State	10	6	.625	16	14	.533
Weber State	9	7	.563	15	13	.536
Idaho State	9	7	.563	14	13	.519
Cal State Northridge	8	8	.500	14	15	.483
Portland State	6	10	.375	9	17	.346
Eastern Washington	3	13	.188	7	19	.269
Cal State Sacramento	2	14	.125	3	23	.115

Tournament: **Montana d. Cal State Northridge 82-79**
Tournament MVP: **Trenton Cross**, Cal State Northridge

BIG SOUTH

	Conference W	L	Pct	Overall W	L	Pct
Liberty	11	3	.786	23	9	.719
UNC Asheville	11	3	.786	18	10	.643
Radford	8	6	.571	15	13	.536
Charleston Southern⊕	7	7	.500	17	13	.567
Coastal Carolina	6	8	.429	11	16	.407
UNC Greensboro	6	8	.429	10	20	.333
Winthrop	5	9	.357	12	15	.444
UMBC	2	12	.143	5	22	.185

Tournament: **Charleston Southern d. Liberty 64-54**
Tournament MVP: **Peter Aluma**, Liberty

BIG TEN

	Conference W	L	Pct	Overall W	L	Pct
Minnesota⊕✪	16	2	.889	35	5	.875
Iowa○	12	6	.667	22	10	.688
Purdue○	12	6	.667	18	12	.600
Illinois○	11	7	.611	22	10	.688
Wisconsin○	11	7	.611	18	10	.643
Michigan□✪	9	9	.500	24	11	.686
Indiana○	9	9	.500	22	11	.667
Michigan State□	9	9	.500	17	12	.586
Ohio State	5	13	.278	10	17	.370
Penn State	3	15	.167	10	17	.370
Northwestern	2	16	.111	7	22	.241

BIG 12

	Conference W	L	Pct	Overall W	L	Pct
Kansas⊕	15	1	.938	34	2	.944
Colorado○	11	5	.688	22	10	.688
Iowa State○	10	6	.625	22	9	.710
Texas Tech	10	6	.625	19	9	.679
Texas○	10	6	.625	18	12	.600
Oklahoma○	9	7	.563	19	11	.633
Nebraska□	7	9	.438	18	15	.545
Oklahoma State□	7	9	.438	17	15	.531
Baylor	6	10	.375	18	12	.600
Missouri	5	11	.313	16	17	.485
Kansas State	3	13	.188	10	17	.370
Texas A&M	3	13	.188	9	18	.333

Tournament: **Kansas d. Missouri 87-60**
Tournament MOP: **Paul Pierce**, Kansas

BIG WEST

	Conference W	L	Pct	Overall W	L	Pct
Eastern						
Utah State	12	4	.750	20	9	.690
New Mexico State✪	12	4	.750	19	9	.679
Nevada□	12	4	.750	21	10	.677
Boise State	9	7	.563	14	13	.519
Idaho	5	11	.313	13	17	.433
North Texas	5	11	.313	10	16	.385
Western						
Pacific⊕	12	4	.750	24	6	.800
Long Beach State	9	7	.563	13	14	.481
UC Santa Barbara	7	9	.438	12	15	.444
Cal State Fullerton	6	10	.375	13	14	.481
Cal Poly	6	10	.375	14	16	.467
UC Irvine	1	15	.063	1	25	.038

Tournament: **Pacific d. Nevada 63-55**
Tournament MVPs: **Corey Anders**, Pacific and **Faron Hand**, Nevada

COLONIAL ATHLETIC

	Conference W	L	Pct	Overall W	L	Pct
Old Dominion⊕	10	6	.625	22	11	.667
UNC Wilmington	10	6	.625	16	14	.533
East Carolina	9	7	.563	17	10	.630
VCU	9	7	.563	14	13	.519
James Madison	8	8	.500	16	13	.552
William and Mary	8	8	.500	12	16	.429
Richmond	7	9	.438	13	15	.464
American	7	9	.438	11	16	.407
George Mason	4	12	.250	10	17	.370

Tournament: **Old Dominion d. James Madison 62-58 (OT)**
Tournament MVP: **Odell Hodge**, Old Dominion

C-USA

	Conference W	L	Pct	Overall W	L	Pct
Red						
Tulane□	11	3	.786	20	11	.645
UAB□	7	7	.500	18	14	.563
Southern Miss	6	8	.429	12	15	.444
South Florida	2	12	.143	8	19	.296
White						
Charlotte○	10	4	.714	22	9	.710
Memphis□	10	4	.714	16	15	.516
Louisville○	9	5	.643	26	9	.743
Houston	3	11	.214	11	16	.407
Blue						
Cincinnati○	12	2	.857	26	8	.765
Marquette⊕	9	5	.643	22	9	.710
Saint Louis	4	10	.286	11	18	.379
DePaul	1	13	.071	3	23	.115

Tournament: **Marquette d. Charlotte 60-52**
Tournament MVP: **Aaron Hutchins**, Marquette

IVY

	Conference W	L	Pct	Overall W	L	Pct
Princeton⊕	14	0	1.000	24	4	.857
Dartmouth	10	4	.714	18	8	.692
Harvard	10	4	.714	17	9	.654
Penn	8	6	.571	12	14	.462
Cornell	7	7	.500	15	11	.577
Yale	3	11	.214	10	16	.385
Brown	3	11	.214	4	22	.154
Columbia	1	13	.071	6	20	.231

Conference Standings Continue →

⊕ Automatic NCAA Tournament bid ○ At-large NCAA Tournament bid □ NIT appearance ✪ Team record doesn't reflect games forfeited or vacated. For adjusted record, see p. 521.

MAAC

	Conference			Overall		
	W	L	PCT	W	L	PCT
Iona□	11	3	.786	22	8	.733
Canisius	10	4	.714	17	12	.586
Loyola (MD)	10	4	.714	13	14	.481
Saint Peter's	9	5	.643	13	15	.464
Niagara	5	9	.357	11	17	.393
Manhattan	5	9	.357	9	18	.333
Siena	4	10	.286	9	18	.333
Fairfield⊕	2	12	.143	11	19	.367

Tournament: **Fairfield d. Canisius 78-72**
Tournament MVP: **Greg Francis**, Fairfield

MID-AMERICAN

	Conference			Overall		
	W	L	PCT	W	L	PCT
Bowling Green□	13	5	.722	22	10	.688
Miami (OH)⊕	13	5	.722	21	9	.700
Ohio	12	6	.667	17	10	.630
Eastern Michigan	11	7	.611	22	10	.688
Ball State	9	9	.500	16	13	.552
Western Michigan	9	9	.500	14	14	.500
Kent State	7	11	.389	9	18	.333
Toledo	6	12	.333	13	14	.481
Akron	6	12	.333	8	18	.308
Central Michigan	4	14	.222	7	19	.269

Tournament: **Miami (OH) d. Eastern Michigan 96-76**
Tournament MVP: **Devin Davis**, Miami (OH)

MID-CONTINENT

	Conference			Overall		
	W	L	PCT	W	L	PCT
Valparaiso⊕	13	3	.813	24	7	.774
Western Illinois	11	5	.688	19	10	.655
Buffalo	11	5	.688	17	11	.607
Troy	10	6	.625	16	11	.593
Northeastern Ill.	8	8	.500	16	12	.571
UMKC	7	9	.438	10	17	.370
Youngstown State	4	12	.250	9	18	.333
Central Conn. State	4	12	.250	8	19	.296
Chicago State	4	12	.250	4	23	.148

Tournament: **Valparaiso d. Western Illinois 63-59**
Tournament MVP: **Janthony Joseph**, Western Illinois

MEAC

	Conference			Overall		
	W	L	PCT	W	L	PCT
Coppin State⊕	15	3	.833	22	9	.710
South Carolina State	12	6	.667	14	14	.500
NC A&T	11	7	.611	15	13	.536
Bethune-Cookman	9	9	.500	12	16	.429
Morgan State	8	10	.444	9	18	.333
Florida A&M	8	10	.444	8	19	.296
Hampton	7	11	.389	8	19	.296
Delaware State	7	11	.389	7	20	.259
Howard	7	11	.389	7	20	.259
UMES	6	12	.333	11	17	.393

Tournament: **Coppin State d. NC A&T 81-74 (OT)**
Tournament MOP: **Terquin Mott**, Coppin State

MCC

	Conference			Overall		
	W	L	PCT	W	L	PCT
Butler⊕	12	4	.750	23	10	.697
Detroit	11	5	.688	16	13	.552
Illinois-Chicago	11	5	.688	15	14	.517
Wisconsin-Green Bay	10	6	.625	14	14	.500
Loyola-Chicago	7	9	.438	12	15	.444
Northern Illinois	6	10	.375	12	15	.444
Cleveland State	6	10	.375	9	19	.321
Wright State	5	11	.313	7	20	.259
Wisconsin-Milwaukee	4	12	.250	8	20	.286

Tournament: **Butler d. Illinois-Chicago 69-68**
Tournament MVP: **Kelsey Wilson**, Butler

MISSOURI VALLEY

	Conference			Overall		
	W	L	PCT	W	L	PCT
Illinois State⊕	14	4	.778	24	6	.800
Missouri State□	12	6	.667	24	9	.727
Bradley□	12	6	.667	17	13	.567
Northern Iowa	11	7	.611	16	12	.571
Evansville	11	7	.611	17	14	.548
Creighton	10	8	.556	15	15	.500
Wichita State	8	10	.444	14	13	.519
Southern Illinois	6	12	.333	13	17	.433
Indiana State	6	12	.333	12	16	.429
Drake	0	18	.000	2	26	.071

Tournament: **Illinois State d. Missouri State 75-72**
Tournament MOP: **Rico Hill**, Illinois State

NORTHEAST

	Conference			Overall		
	W	L	PCT	W	L	PCT
Long Island⊕	15	3	.833	21	9	.700
Fairleigh Dickinson	13	5	.722	18	10	.643
Monmouth	12	6	.667	18	11	.621
Mount St. Mary's	10	8	.556	14	13	.519
Rider	10	8	.556	14	14	.500
Saint Francis (PA)	9	9	.500	12	15	.444
St. Francis (NY)	7	11	.389	13	15	.464
Wagner	7	11	.389	10	17	.370
Marist	4	14	.222	6	22	.214
Robert Morris	3	15	.167	4	23	.148

Tournament: **Long Island d. Monmouth 72-67**
Tournament MVP: **Charles Jones**, Long Island

OHIO VALLEY

	Conference			Overall		
	W	L	PCT	W	L	PCT
Murray State⊕	12	6	.667	20	10	.667
Austin Peay	12	6	.667	17	14	.548
Middle Tenn. State	11	7	.611	19	12	.613
Tennessee Tech	10	8	.556	15	13	.536
Eastern Illinois	9	9	.500	12	15	.444
SE Missouri State	9	9	.500	12	18	.400
Tennessee-Martin	8	10	.444	11	16	.407
Tennessee State	7	11	.389	9	18	.333
Eastern Kentucky	6	12	.333	8	18	.308
Morehead State	6	12	.333	8	19	.296

Tournament: **Murray State d. Austin Peay 88-85 (OT)**
Tournament MVP: **Chad Townsend**, Murray State

PAC-10

	Conference			Overall		
	W	L	PCT	W	L	PCT
UCLA⊕	15	3	.833	24	8	.750
Stanford○	12	6	.667	22	8	.733
California○	12	6	.667	23	9	.719
Southern California○	12	6	.667	17	11	.607
Arizona○	11	7	.611	25	9	.735
Washington□	10	8	.556	17	11	.607
Oregon□	8	10	.444	17	11	.607
Washington State	5	13	.278	13	17	.433
Oregon State	3	15	.167	7	20	.259
Arizona State	2	16	.111	10	20	.333

PATRIOT

	Conference			Overall		
	W	L	PCT	W	L	PCT
Navy⊕	10	2	.833	20	9	.690
Bucknell	9	3	.750	18	11	.621
Colgate	8	4	.667	12	16	.429
Lafayette	5	7	.417	11	17	.393
Holy Cross	5	7	.417	8	19	.296
Army	4	8	.333	10	16	.385
Lehigh	1	11	.083	1	26	.037

Tournament: **Navy d. Bucknell 76-75**
Tournament MVP: **Hassan Booker**, Navy

SEC

	Conference			Overall		
	W	L	PCT	W	L	PCT
Eastern						
South Carolina○	15	1	.938	24	8	.750
Kentucky⊕	13	3	.813	35	5	.875
Georgia○	10	6	.625	24	9	.727
Vanderbilt○	9	7	.563	19	12	.613
Florida	5	11	.313	13	17	.433
Tennessee	4	12	.250	11	16	.407
Western						
Mississippi○	11	5	.688	20	9	.690
Arkansas□	8	8	.500	18	14	.563
Alabama	6	10	.375	17	14	.548
Auburn	6	10	.375	16	15	.516
Mississippi State	6	10	.375	12	18	.400
LSU	3	13	.188	10	20	.333

Tournament: **Kentucky d. Georgia 95-68**
Tournament MVP: **Ron Mercer**, Kentucky

SOUTHERN

	Conference			Overall		
	W	L	PCT	W	L	PCT
North						
Marshall	10	4	.714	20	9	.690
Davidson	10	4	.714	18	10	.643
Appalachian State	8	6	.571	14	14	.500
VMI	7	7	.500	12	16	.429
East Tennessee State	2	12	.143	7	20	.259
South						
Chattanooga⊕	11	3	.786	24	11	.686
Western Carolina	7	7	.500	14	13	.519
The Citadel	6	8	.429	13	14	.481
Georgia Southern	5	9	.357	10	18	.357
Furman	4	10	.286	10	17	.370

Tournament: **Chattanooga d. Marshall 71-70 (OT)**
Tournament MOP: **John Brannen**, Marshall

SOUTHLAND

	Conference			Overall		
	W	L	PCT	W	L	PCT
Texas State⊕	10	6	.625	16	13	.552
McNeese State	10	6	.625	18	12	.600
UL-Monroe	10	6	.625	14	14	.500
Northwestern St. (LA)	8	8	.500	13	15	.464
Stephen F. Austin	8	8	.500	12	15	.444
Texas-Arlington	8	8	.500	12	15	.444
Nicholls State	7	9	.438	10	16	.385
Sam Houston State	7	9	.438	8	18	.308
UTSA	4	12	.250	9	17	.346

Tournament: **Texas State d. UL-Monroe 74-64**
Tournament MVP: **Dameon Sansom**, Texas State

SWAC

	Conference			Overall		
	W	L	PCT	W	L	PCT
Miss. Valley State	11	3	.786	19	10	.655
Jackson State⊕	9	5	.643	14	16	.467
Alcorn State	8	6	.571	11	17	.393
Prairie View A&M	7	7	.500	10	17	.370
Texas Southern	6	8	.429	12	16	.429
Grambling	5	9	.357	10	17	.370
Southern U.	5	9	.357	10	17	.370
Alabama State	5	9	.357	8	21	.276

Tournament: **Jackson State d. Miss. Valley State 81-74**
Tournament MVP: **Trent Pulliam**, Jackson State

SUN BELT

	Conference			Overall		
	W	L	PCT	W	L	PCT
South Alabama⊕	14	4	.778	23	7	.767
New Orleans□	14	4	.778	22	7	.759
Ark.-Little Rock	11	7	.611	18	11	.621
Lamar	10	8	.556	15	12	.556
Louisiana Tech	10	8	.556	15	14	.517
Western Kentucky	9	9	.500	12	15	.444
UL-Lafayette	9	9	.500	12	16	.429
Arkansas State	8	10	.444	15	12	.556
Jacksonville	4	14	.222	5	23	.179
Texas-Pan American	1	17	.056	3	25	.107

Tournament: **South Alabama d. Louisiana Tech 44-43**
Tournament MOP: **Rusty Yoder**, South Alabama

TAAC

	Conference			Overall		
	W	L	PCT	W	L	PCT
East						
Charleston⊕	16	0	1.000	29	3	.906
Florida International	12	4	.750	16	13	.552
Florida Atlantic	11	5	.688	16	11	.593
Campbell	8	8	.500	11	16	.407
Stetson	5	11	.313	9	18	.333
Central Florida	4	12	.250	7	19	.269
West						
Samford	11	5	.688	19	9	.679
Jacksonville State	9	7	.563	10	17	.370
Southeastern Louisiana	7	9	.438	10	18	.357
Georgia State	6	10	.375	10	17	.370
Centenary	6	10	.375	9	18	.333
Mercer	1	15	.063	3	23	.115

Tournament: **Charleston d. Florida International 83-73**
Tournament MVP: **Anthony Johnson**, Charleston

WEST COAST

	Conference			Overall		
	W	L	PCT	W	L	PCT
Saint Mary's (CA)⊕	10	4	.714	23	8	.742
Santa Clara	10	4	.714	16	11	.593
San Francisco	9	5	.643	16	13	.552
San Diego	8	6	.571	17	11	.607
Gonzaga	8	6	.571	15	12	.556
Portland	4	10	.286	9	18	.333
Pepperdine	4	10	.286	6	21	.222
Loyola Marymount	3	11	.214	7	21	.250

Tournament: **Saint Mary's (CA) d. San Francisco 66-59**
Tournament MVP: **Brad Millard**, Saint Mary's (CA)

WAC

	Conference			Overall		
	W	L	PCT	W	L	PCT
Pacific						
Hawaii□	12	4	.750	21	8	.724
Fresno State□	12	4	.750	20	12	.625
UNLV□	11	5	.688	22	10	.688
Colorado State	10	6	.625	20	9	.690
Wyoming	8	8	.500	12	16	.429
San Jose State	5	11	.313	13	14	.481
San Diego State	4	12	.250	12	15	.444
Air Force	2	14	.125	7	19	.269
Mountain						
Utah⊕	15	1	.938	29	4	.879
Tulsa○	12	4	.750	24	10	.706
New Mexico○	11	5	.688	25	8	.758
TCU□	7	9	.438	22	13	.629
SMU	7	9	.438	16	12	.571
UTEP	6	10	.375	13	13	.500
Rice	6	10	.375	12	15	.444
BYU	0	16	.000	1	25	.038

Tournament: **Utah d. TCU 89-68**
Tournament MVP: **Keith Van Horn**, Utah

INDEPENDENTS

	Overall		
	W	L	PCT
Oral Roberts□	21	7	.750
Southern Utah	9	17	.346
Wofford	7	20	.259

INDIVIDUAL LEADERS—SEASON

SCORING	CL	POS	G	FG	3FG	FT	PTS	PPG
1 **Charles Jones**, Long Island	JR	G	30	338	109	118	903	**30.1**
2 **Ed Gray**, California	SR	G	26	224	38	158	644	**24.8**
3 **Adonal Foyle**, Colgate	JR	C	28	277	1	127	682	**24.4**
4 **Raymond Tutt**, UC Santa Barbara	JR	G	27	221	55	152	649	**24.0**
5 **Antonio Daniels**, Bowling Green	SR	G	32	279	45	164	767	**24.0**
6 **Donnie Carr**, La Salle	FR	G	27	209	99	129	646	**23.9**
7 **Olivier Saint-Jean**, San Jose State	SR	F	26	225	26	143	619	**23.8**
8 **James Cotton**, Long Beach State	JR	G	27	196	63	179	634	**23.5**
9 **Roderick Blakney**, South Carolina St.	JR	G	28	216	61	162	655	**23.4**
10 **Cory Carr**, Texas Tech	JR	G	28	213	94	126	646	**23.1**

FIELD GOAL PCT	CL	POS	G	FG	FGA	PCT
1 **Todd MacCulloch**, Washington	SO	C	28	163	241	**67.6**
2 **Sean Scott**, Central Conn. St.	SR	F	24	128	191	**67.0**
3 **Rosell Ellis**, McNeese State	SR	F	30	213	319	**66.8**
4 **Ed Sears**, Ohio	SR	C	27	156	241	**64.7**
5 **Lorenzo Coleman**, Tennessee Tech	SR	C	28	198	307	**64.5**

MINIMUM: 5 MADE PER GAME

THREE-PT FG PER GAME	CL	POS	G	3FG	3PG
1 **William Fourche**, Southern U.	SR	G	27	122	**4.5**
2 **Keith Veney**, Marshall	SR	G	29	130	**4.5**
3 **Troy Hudson**, Southern Illinois	JR	G	30	134	**4.5**
4 **Dedric Willoughby**, Iowa State	SR	G	27	102	**3.8**
5 **Tom Pipkins**, Duquesne	SR	G	27	99	**3.7**
Donnie Carr, La Salle	FR	G	27	99	**3.7**

THREE-PT FG PCT	CL	POS	G	3FG	3FGA	PCT
1 **Kent McCausland**, Iowa	SO	G	29	70	134	**52.2**
2 **Bill Slack**, Central Michigan	SR	G	26	49	96	**51.0**
3 **Ross Land**, Northern Arizona	FR	G/F	28	64	126	**50.8**
4 **Marcus Carreno**, Florida Int'l	SO	G	28	52	104	**50.0**
5 **Danny Sprinkle**, Montana State	SO	G	25	61	125	**48.8**

MINIMUM: 1.5 MADE PER GAME

FREE THROW PCT	CL	POS	G	FT	FTA	PCT
1 **Aaron Zobrist**, Bradley	SR	G	30	77	85	**90.6**
2 **Keith Van Horn**, Utah	SR	F	32	151	167	**90.4**
3 **Jim Williamson**, Loyola Marymount	SR	G	28	110	122	**90.2**
4 **Marcus Wilson**, Evansville	SO	G	31	91	101	**90.1**
5 **Trajan Langdon**, Duke	SO	G	33	113	126	**89.7**

MINIMUM: 2.5 MADE PER GAME

ASSISTS PER GAME	CL	POS	G	AST	APG
1 **Kenny Mitchell**, Dartmouth	SR	G	26	203	**7.8**
2 **Brevin Knight**, Stanford	SR	G	30	234	**7.8**
3 **Kareem Gilbert**, Tennessee State	JR	G	25	191	**7.6**
4 **Jamar Smiley**, Illinois State	JR	G	30	219	**7.3**
5 **Chad Peckinpaugh**, Eastern Illinois	SO	G	27	196	**7.3**
6 **Anthony Johnson**, Charleston	SR	G	32	229	**7.2**
7 **Chad Townsend**, Murray State	JR	G	30	212	**7.1**
8 **Ed Cota**, North Carolina	FR	G	34	234	**6.9**
9 **Ali Ton**, Davidson	SO	G	28	190	**6.8**
10 **Antonio Daniels**, Bowling Green	SR	G	32	216	**6.8**

REBOUNDS PER GAME	CL	POS	G	REB	RPG
1 **Tim Duncan**, Wake Forest	SR	F	31	457	**14.7**
2 **Adonal Foyle**, Colgate	JR	C	28	368	**13.1**
3 **Lorenzo Coleman**, Tennessee Tech	SR	C	28	333	**11.9**
4 **Tony Battie**, Texas Tech	JR	F	28	329	**11.8**
5 **Muntrelle Dobbins**, Arkansas-Little Rock	SR	F	28	320	**11.4**
6 **Eric Taylor**, Saint Francis (PA)	JR	C	27	306	**11.3**
7 **Kory Billups**, Chicago State	SR	F	27	304	**11.3**
8 **Nate Huffman**, Central Michigan	SR	C	26	287	**11.0**
9 **Greg Smith**, Delaware	SR	F	31	342	**11.0**
10 **H.L. Coleman**, Wyoming	SR	F	28	303	**10.8**

BLOCKED SHOTS PER GAME	CL	POS	G	BLK	BPG
1 **Adonal Foyle**, Colgate	JR	C	28	180	**6.4**
2 **Lorenzo Coleman**, Tennessee Tech	SR	C	28	134	**4.8**
3 **Richard Lugo**, St. Francis (NY)	FR	C	28	125	**4.5**
4 **Jerome James**, Florida A&M	JR	C	27	119	**4.4**
5 **Kelvin Cato**, Iowa State	SR	C	28	118	**4.2**

STEALS PER GAME	CL	POS	G	STL	SPG
1 **Joel Hoover**, UMES	FR	G	28	90	**3.2**
2 **Philip Huyler**, Florida Atlantic	SR	G	27	86	**3.2**
3 **Kellii Taylor**, Pittsburgh	FR	G	32	101	**3.2**
4 **Moe Segar**, Saint Peter's	SR	F	28	87	**3.1**
5 **Mustafa Barksdale**, Monmouth	SR	G	27	81	**3.0**

INDIVIDUAL LEADERS-GAME

POINTS	CL	POS	OPP	DATE	PTS
1 **Keith Veney**, Marshall	SR	G	Morehead State	D14	**51**
2 **Ed Gray**, California	SR	G	Washington State	F22	**48**
3 **Charles Jones**, Long Island	JR	G	Saint Francis (PA)	J4	**46**
Bubba Wells, Austin Peay	SR	F	Morehead State	F22	**46**
5 **Jimmal Ball**, Akron	FR	G	Xavier	D21	**44**
Charles Jones, Long Island	JR	G	Mount St. Mary's	J9	**44**
Mike Jones, TCU	JR	G	Fresno State	M6	**44**

THREE-PT FG MADE	CL	POS	OPP	DATE	3FG
1 **Keith Veney**, Marshall	SR	G	Morehead State	D14	**15**
2 **Seth Chadwick**, Wofford	SR	G	Mercer	F15	**11**
3 **Shun Pearson**, Miss. Valley State	SR	G	Troy	D6	**10**
Al Coleman, Texas	SR	G	Kansas State	J12	**10**
Mark Heidersbach, Northeastern Ill.	SR	G	Troy	F12	**10**
John Knox, Jacksonville	JR	G	Arkansas-Little Rock	F17	**10**
William Fourche, Southern U.	SR	G	Prairie View A&M	F17	**10**

ASSISTS	CL	POS	OPP	DATE	AST
1 **Chad Peckinpaugh**, Eastern Illinois	SO	G	SE Missouri State	F22	**18**
2 **Sean Colson**, Charlotte	JR	G	Houston	F8	**17**
3 **Chad Townsend**, Murray State	JR	G	Eastern Illinois	F20	**16**
4 **Kareem Reid**, Arkansas	SO	G	Jackson State	N22	**15**
Chad Townsend, Murray State	JR	G	Campbellsville	D7	**15**
Colby Pierce, Austin Peay	SR	G	SE Missouri State	J4	**15**

REBOUNDS	CL	POS	OPP	DATE	REB
1 **Jim Cruse**, Indiana State	SR	F	Drake	J18	**25**
2 **Kory Billups**, Chicago State	SR	F	Western Michigan	D18	**24**
Michael Ruffin, Tulsa	SO	F	TCU	F27	**24**
4 **Tony Berg**, UMKC	SR	C	Baylor	D3	**23**
Eric Taylor, Saint Francis (PA)	JR	C	Long Island	J4	**23**
Tim Duncan, Wake Forest	SR	F	Virginia	F22	**23**
H.L. Coleman, Wyoming	SR	F	UNLV	F27	**23**

BLOCKED SHOTS	CL	POS	OPP	DATE	BLK
1 **Adonal Foyle**, Colgate	JR	C	Fairfield	N26	**12**
Adonal Foyle, Colgate	JR	C	Navy	F5	**12**
3 **Kelvin Cato**, Iowa State	SR	C	Texas-Pan American	D30	**11**
Richard Lugo, St. Francis (NY)	FR	C	Rider	F12	**11**
Jerome James, Florida A&M	JR	C	Morgan State	F17	**11**

STEALS	CL	POS	OPP	DATE	STL
1 **Phillip Huyler**, Florida Atlantic	SR	G	Campbell	J18	**11**
2 **God Shammgod**, Providence	SO	G	Brown	D21	**10**
3 **Roni Bailey**, Middle Tenn. State	SR	G	Montreat	N27	**9**
Dominick Young, Fresno State	SR	G	Northwestern	N29	**9**
Kenya Wilkins, Oregon	SR	G	Boise State	D19	**9**
Correy Childs, Tulane	SR	G	Xavier	J16	**9**
Andrell Hoard, Northeastern Illinois	SR	G	UMKC	F10	**9**

TEAM LEADERS-SEASON

WIN-LOSS PCT	W	L	PCT
1 **Kansas**	34	2	**.944**
2 **Charleston**	29	3	**.906**
3 **Minnesota**	35	5	**.886**
4 **Utah**	29	4	**.879**
5 **Kentucky**	35	5	**.875**

SCORING OFFENSE	G	W-L	PTS	PPG
1 **Long Island**	30	21-9	2,746	**91.5**
2 **Kansas**	36	34-2	3,058	**84.9**
3 **Arizona**	34	25-9	2,850	**83.8**
4 **TCU**	35	22-13	2,931	**83.7**
5 **Mississippi Valley State**	29	19-10	2,413	**83.2**
Xavier	29	23-6	2,413	**83.2**

SCORING MARGIN	G	W-L	PPG	OPP PPG	MAR
1 **Kentucky**	40	35-5	83.1	62.8	**20.3**
2 **Kansas**	36	34-2	84.9	66.1	**18.8**
3 **Cincinnati**	34	26-8	80.7	65.5	**15.2**
4 **Minnesota**	40	35-5	78.3	63.4	**14.9**
5 **Duke**	33	24-9	79.7	66.2	**13.5**

FIELD GOAL PCT	G	W-L	FG	FGA	PCT
1 **UCLA**	32	24-8	932	1,791	**52.0**
2 **Northern Arizona**	28	21-7	763	1,478	**51.6**
3 **Princeton**	28	24-4	631	1,262	**50.0**
4 **Cincinnati**	34	26-8	962	1,938	**49.6**
5 **Utah**	33	29-4	886	1,785	**49.6**

THREE-PT FG PER GAME	G	W-L	3FG	3PG
1 **Mississippi Valley State**	29	19-10	309	**10.7**
2 **Long Island**	30	21-9	301	**10.0**
3 **Cal Poly**	30	14-16	290	**9.7**
4 **Morehead State**	27	8-19	257	**9.5**
5 **Florida Int'l**	29	16-13	271	**9.3**

FREE THROW PCT	G	W-L	FT	FTA	PCT
1 **Western Kentucky**	27	12-15	342	433	**79.0**
2 **Indiana**	33	22-11	674	880	**76.6**
3 **Missouri**	33	16-17	583	769	**75.8**
4 **Harvard**	26	17-9	388	516	**75.2**
5 **Cal Poly**	30	14-16	468	625	**74.9**

ASSISTS PER GAME	G	W-L	AST	APG
1 **Kentucky**	40	35-5	776	**19.4**
2 **Morgan State**	27	9-18	518	**19.2**
3 **Montana State**	30	16-14	566	**18.9**
4 **Western Illinois**	29	19-10	539	**18.6**
5 **Xavier**	29	23-6	532	**18.3**

REBOUND MARGIN	G	W-L	RPG	OPP RPG	MAR
1 **Utah State**	29	20-9	37.4	26.6	**10.8**
2 **Kansas**	36	34-2	42.6	32.2	**10.4**
3 **Iowa**	32	22-10	38.5	28.7	**9.8**
4 **North Carolina**	35	28-7	41.6	32.2	**9.4**
5 **Cincinnati**	34	26-8	39.9	30.6	**9.3**

SCORING DEFENSE	G	W-L	OPP PTS	OPP PPG
1 **Princeton**	28	24-4	1,496	**53.4**
2 **Wisconsin-Green Bay**	28	14-14	1,515	**54.1**
3 **NC State**	32	17-15	1,749	**54.7**
4 **Wisconsin**	28	18-10	1,548	**55.3**
5 **South Alabama**	30	23-7	1,699	**56.6**

Field Goal Pct Defense

	G	W-L	OPP FG	OPP FGA	OPP PCT
1 Marquette	31	22-9	628	1,735	**36.2**
2 Wake Forest	31	24-7	667	1,832	**36.4**
3 Wisconsin-Green Bay	28	14-14	499	1,368	**36.5**
4 Wisconsin	28	18-10	502	1,329	**37.8**
5 Georgetown	30	20-10	659	1,740	**37.9**

Blocked Shots Per Game

	G	W-L	BLK	BPG
1 Colgate	28	12-16	217	**7.8**
2 Old Dominion	33	22-11	233	**7.1**
3 Georgetown	30	20-10	195	**6.5**
4 Kansas	36	34-2	222	**6.2**
5 Nebraska	33	18-15	202	**6.1**

Steals Per Game

	G	W-L	STL	SPG
1 Long Island	30	21-9	396	**13.2**
2 Kentucky	40	35-5	480	**12.0**
3 Bowling Green	32	22-10	378	**11.8**
4 Stephen F. Austin	27	12-15	313	**11.6**
5 Hartford	28	17-11	310	**11.1**

TEAM LEADERS—GAME

Points

	OPP	DATE	SCORE
1 Cal Poly	Cal Baptist	D3	**143-97**
2 Stephen F. Austin	Schreiner	N25	**138-69**
3 Arkansas	Troy	D10	**137-70**
4 Kansas	Niagara	J9	**134-73**
5 Morehead State	Asbury	N30	**130-48**
UL-Monroe	Arkansas-Monticello	D3	**130-76**
Winthrop	Johnson & Wales	D7	**130-33**

Field Goal Pct

	OPP	DATE	FG	FGA	PCT
1 Kansas	Niagara	J9	44	61	**72.1**
2 UCLA	Jackson State	D17	32	45	**71.1**
3 Louisiana Tech	Western Kentucky	F15	33	47	**70.2**
4 New Mexico	BYU	F27	36	52	**69.2**
5 Winthrop	Johnson and Wales	D7	56	81	**69.1**

Three-Pt FG Made

	OPP	DATE	3FG
1 Cal Poly	Cal Baptist	D3	**21**
Miss. Valley State	Troy	D6	**21**
Arkansas	Troy	D10	**21**
Long Island	Robert Morris	F3	**21**
5 Stephen F. Austin	Schreiner	N25	**19**
Marshall	Morehead State	D14	**19**

CONSENSUS ALL-AMERICAS

FIRST TEAM

PLAYER	CL	POS	HT	SCHOOL	RPG	PPG
Tim Duncan	SR	F	6-10	Wake Forest	14.7	20.8
Danny Fortson	JR	C	6-7	Cincinnati	9.1	21.3
Raef LaFrentz	JR	F	6-11	Kansas	9.3	18.5
Ron Mercer	SO	G/F	6-7	Kentucky	5.3	18.1
Keith Van Horn	SR	F	6-9	Utah	9.5	22.0

SECOND TEAM

PLAYER	CL	POS	HT	SCHOOL	RPG	PPG
Chauncey Billups	SO	G	6-3	Colorado	4.9	19.1
Bobby Jackson	SR	G	6-1	Minnesota	6.1	15.3
Antawn Jamison	SO	F	6-9	North Carolina	9.4	19.1
Brevin Knight	SR	G	5-10	Stanford	3.7	16.3
Jacque Vaughn	SR	G	6-1	Kansas	2.4	10.2

Selectors: AP, NABC, Sporting News, USBWA

AWARD WINNERS

PLAYER OF THE YEAR

PLAYER	CL	POS	HT	SCHOOL	AWARDS
Tim Duncan	SR	F	6-10	Wake Forest	Naismith, AP, USBWA, Wooden, NABC, Rupp
Kent McCausland	SO	G	5-11	Iowa	Frances Pomeroy Naismith*

* For the most outstanding senior player who is 6 feet or under

DEFENSIVE PLAYER OF THE YEAR

PLAYER	CL	POS	HT	SCHOOL
Tim Duncan	SR	F	6-10	Wake Forest

COACH OF THE YEAR

COACH	SCHOOL	REC	AWARDS
Roy Williams	Kansas	34-2	Naismith, Sporting News
Clem Haskins	Minnesota	35-5	AP, USBWA, NABC, CBS/Chevrolet

Bob Gibbons' Top High School Senior Recruits

PLAYER	POS	HT	HIGH SCHOOL	A-A TEAMS	COLLEGE	CAREER NOTES
1 **Tracy McGrady**	SF	6-8	Mt. Zion Christian Academy, Durham, NC	McD, P, USA	None	Drafted straight out of HS; No. 9 pick, '97 NBA draft (Raptors); 22.1 ppg (12seasons); 7-time All-Star; 2-time ppg leader
2 **Lamar Odom**	F	6-9	Christian Redemption Academy, Troy, NY, Christ The King HS, Queens, NY	McD, P, USA	Rhode Island	17.6 ppg (1 season); No. 4 pick, '99 NBA draft (Clippers); 15.1 ppg, 8.8 rpg (10 seasons)
3 **Elton Brand**	F/C	6-8	Peekskill (NY) HS	McD, P	Duke	Consensus POY, '99; at Duke, 16.2 ppg (2 seasons); No. 1 overall pick, '99 NBA draft (Bulls); co-ROY, '00; 2-time All-Star
4 **Larry Hughes**	G	6-5	Christian Brothers HS, St. Louis	McD, P	Saint Louis	C-USA FOY, '98; at SLU, 20.9 ppg (1 season); No. 8 pick, '98 NBA draft (76ers); 14.6 ppg (11 seasons)
5 **Dion Glover**	G/F	6-4	Cedar Grove HS, Decatur, GA	McD, P	Georgia Tech	18.4 ppg, 5.0 rpg (1 season); No. 20 pick, '99 NBA draft (Hawks); 8.2 ppg (6 seasons)
6 **Shane Battier**	F	6-8	Detroit Country Day School, Beverly Hills, MI	McD, P	Duke	NCAA title, '01; Naismith, Wooden Awards, '01; No. 6 pick, '01 NBA draft (Grizzlies); 10.0 ppg (8 seasons)
7 **Baron Davis**	PG	6-2	Crossroads HS, Santa Monica, CA	McD, P, USA	UCLA	13.6 ppg (2 seasons); No. 3 pick, '99 NBA draft (Hornets); 16.9 ppg, 7.3 apg (10 seasons); 2-time All-Star
8 **Kenny Gregory**	SG	6-5	Independence HS, Columbus, OH	McD, P	Kansas	2nd team All-Big 12, '01; at Kansas, 11.4 ppg (4 seasons); undrafted; played in D-League, overseas
9 **Terence Morris**	F	6-9	Thomas Johnson HS, Frederick, MD	P	Maryland	12.7 ppg (4 seasons); 2nd-round pick, '01 NBA draft (Hawks); 3.4 ppg (3 seasons)
10 **Khalid El-Amin**	PG	5-10	North HS, Minneapolis	McD, P	Connecticut	NCAA title, '99; 2nd-round pick, '00 NBA draft (Bulls); 6.3 ppg (50 games); played overseas
11 **Ricky Davis**	SF	6-7	North HS, Davenport, IA	P	Iowa	15.0 ppg, 4.8 rpg (1 season); No. 21 pick, '98 NBA draft (Hornets); 13.9 ppg (11 seasons)
12 **Chris Burgess**	F/C	6-10	Woodbridge HS, Irvine, CA	McD, P, USA	Duke/Utah	Transferred after 2 years; in college, 57.3 FG% (4 seasons); undrafted
13 **Luke Recker**	SG	6-6	DeKalb HS, Waterloo, IN	McD, P	Indiana/Iowa	Transferred after 2 years; in college, 1,880 career pts (4 seasons); undrafted
14 **Ron Artest**	SF	6-6	La Salle Academy, New York	McD, P	St. John's	13.1 ppg (2 seasons); No. 16 pick, '99 NBA draft (Bulls); 16.1 ppg (10 seasons); Defensive POY, '04
15 **Jumaine Jones**	F	6-8	Mitchell Baker HS, Camilla, GA	P	Georgia	16.6 ppg, 9.0 rpg (2 seasons); No. 27 pick, '99 NBA draft (Hawks); 7.1 ppg (8 seasons)
16 **Marcus Fizer**	PF	6-8	Arcadia (LA) HS	McD, P	Iowa State	First-team All-America, '00; No. 4 pick, '00 NBA draft (Bulls); 9.6 ppg (6 seasons); D-League MVP, '05-06
17 **Jason Collins**	C	6-11	Harvard-Westlake HS, N. Hollywood, CA	McD, P	Stanford	10.8 ppg, 6.6 rpg (4 seasons); No. 18 pick, '01 NBA draft (Rockets); 4.3 rpg (8 seasons)
18 **Ryan Humphrey**	F	6-7	Booker T. Washington HS, Tulsa, OK	McD, P	Oklahoma/Notre Dame	Transferred after 2 years; 13.3 ppg, 8.4 rpg (4 seasons); No. 19 pick, '02 NBA draft (Jazz); 2.3 ppg (3 seasons)
19 **Anthony Perry**	SG	6-3	St. Anthony's HS, Jersey City, NJ	McD, P	Georgetown	9.7 ppg, 1.6 steals (3 seasons); led team in scoring as Fr. (14.0 ppg); undrafted; played in ABA
20 **Eric Chenowith**	C	7-1	Villa Park (CA) HS	McD, P	Kansas	9.2 ppg, 6.7 rpg (4 seasons); left as 2nd in blocks; 2nd-round pick, '01 NBA draft (Knicks); no NBA games played

Other Standouts

PLAYER	POS	HT	HIGH SCHOOL	A-A TEAMS	COLLEGE	CAREER NOTES
22 **Brendan Haywood**	C	7-0	Dudley HS, Greensboro, NC	McD, P	North Carolina	2 Final Fours; 1st triple-double in UNC history; No. 20 pick, '01 NBA draft (Cavs); 5.9 rpg (8 seasons)
24 **Melvin Ely**	C	6-10	Thornton Township HS, Harvey, IL	McD, P	Fresno State	2-time WAC POY; at Fresno St., 15.7 ppg, 7.5 rpg (4 seasons); No. 12 pick, '02 NBA draft (Clippers); 5.6 ppg (7 seasons)
86 **Michael Redd**	SG	6-6	West HS, Columbus, OH		Ohio State	19.6 ppg (3 seasons); 2nd-round pick, '00 NBA draft (Bucks); 20.5 ppg (9 seasons); Olympic gold medal, '08

Abbreviations: McD=McDonald's; P=Parade; USA=USA Today

Poll Progression

Preseason Poll

AP	USA/CNN	School	
1	2	Cincinnati	
2	1	Kansas	
3	4	Kentucky	
4	3	Wake Forest	
5	6	UCLA	(A)
6	5	Utah	
7	8	Villanova	
8	7	North Carolina	
9	9	Michigan	
10	10	Duke	
11	11	Iowa State	
12	12	Syracuse	
13	18	Arkansas	
14	19	Fresno State	
15	13	Massachusetts	
16	15	Texas	
17	22	New Mexico	
18	14	Stanford	
19	16	Arizona	
20	17	Clemson	
21	21	Boston College	
22	—	Minnesota	
23	20	Iowa	
24	—	George Washington	
25	—	Marquette	
—	23	Tulane	
—	24	Indiana	
—	25	Louisville	

Week of Nov 19

AP	School	AP↓↑
1	Cincinnati (0-0)	
2	Kansas (0-0)	
3	Wake Forest (0-0)	↑1
4	Utah (0-0)	↑2
5	UCLA (0-0)	
6	Villanova (0-0)	↑1
7	North Carolina (0-0)	↑1
8	Kentucky (0-1)	↓5
9	Michigan (0-0)	
10	Duke (0-0)	
11	Iowa State (0-0)	
12	Clemson (1-0)	↑8
13	Syracuse (0-0)	↓1
14	Fresno State (0-0)	
15	Massachusetts (0-0)	
16	Arkansas (0-0)	↓3
17	Texas (0-0)	↓1
18	New Mexico (0-0)	↓1
19	Arizona (0-0)	
20	Stanford (0-0)	↓2
21	Boston College (0-0)	
22	Indiana (1-0)	⅃
23	Minnesota (0-0)	↓1
24	George Washington (0-0)	
25	Iowa (0-0)	↓2

Week of Nov 26

AP	USA/CNN	School	AP↓↑
1	1	Cincinnati (1-0)	
2	2	Kansas (1-0)	
3	3	Wake Forest (1-0)	
4	4	Utah (1-0)	
5	6	Villanova (0-0)	↑1
6	5	Duke (2-0)	↑4
7	7	Michigan (0-0)	↑2
8	8	Kentucky (0-1)	
9	15	Iowa State (0-0)	↑2
10	9	Clemson (2-0)	↑2
11	10	Arizona (1-0)	↑8
12	11	Syracuse (1-0)	↑1
13	18	UCLA (0-1)	↓8
14	12	North Carolina (0-1)	↓7
15	19	Fresno State (1-0)	↓1
16	20	Arkansas (1-0)	
17	16	Massachusetts (0-0)	↓2
18	13	Texas (1-0)	↓1
19	22	New Mexico (3-0)	↓1
20	17	Indiana (3-0)	↑2
21	14	Stanford (0-0)	↓1
22	21	Tulsa (2-0)	⅃
23	24	Boston College (1-0)	↓2
24	—	Minnesota (1-0)	↓1
25	25	George Washington (2-0)	↓1
—	23	Iowa (1-0)	Γ

Week of Dec 3

AP	USA/CNN	School	AP↓↑
1	1	Kansas (5-0)	↑1
2	2	Wake Forest (4-0)	↑1
3	3	Utah (3-0)	↑1
4	4	Cincinnati (2-1)	↓3
5	8	Villanova (3-0)	
6	5	Kentucky (3-1)	↑2
7	7	Michigan (2-0)	
8	6	Indiana (4-0)	↑12
9	15	Iowa State (2-0)	
10	10	Duke (3-1)	↓4
11	12	New Mexico (5-0)	↑8
12	9	Clemson (4-1)	↓2
13	16	Fresno State (4-0)	↑2
14	14	North Carolina (2-1)	
15	13	Arizona (2-1)	↓4
16	20	Minnesota (5-0)	↑8
17	17	UCLA (0-1)	↓4
18	11	Texas (2-0)	
19	18	Syracuse (3-1)	↓7
20	22	Boston College (2-0)	↑3
21	19	Tulsa (2-1)	↑1
22	23	Arkansas (2-1)	↓6
23	—	Xavier (3-0)	⅃
24	21	Stanford (2-1)	↓3
25	—	Virginia (3-1)	⅃
—	24	Georgetown (3-0)	
—	25	Texas Tech (3-0)	

Week of Dec 10

AP	USA/CNN	School	AP↓↑
1	1	Kansas (7-0)	
2	2	Wake Forest (6-0)	
3	3	Kentucky (5-1)	↑3
4	4	Villanova (5-0)	↑1
5	5	Michigan (5-0)	↑2
6	12	Iowa State (4-0)	↑3
7	9	Cincinnati (2-2)	↓3
8	8	Arizona (3-1) (B)	↑7
9	7	Utah (4-1)	↓6
10	6	Clemson (6-1)	↑2
11	11	North Carolina (5-1)	↑3
12	10	Indiana (6-1)	↓4
13	13	Texas (4-0)	↑5
14	14	Duke (5-2)	↓4
15	15	New Mexico (6-1)	↓4
16	16	Fresno State (5-1)	↓3
17	17	Minnesota (5-1)	↓1
18	19	Texas Tech (5-0)	⅃
19	21	Xavier (5-0)	↑4
20	20	Arkansas (3-1)	↑2
21	18	Stanford (3-1)	↑3
22	22	Louisville (4-0)	⅃
23	—	UCLA (1-2)	↓6
24	—	Alabama (7-0)	⅃
25	22	Boston College (3-1)	↓5
—	24	Georgetown (5-1)	
—	25	George Washington (5-1)	

Week of Dec 17

AP	USA/CNN	School	AP↓↑
1	1	Kansas (9-0)	
2	2	Wake Forest (7-0)	
3	3	Kentucky (7-1)	
4	4	Michigan (7-0)	↑1
5	5	Iowa State (6-0)	↑1
6	6	Arizona (5-1)	↑2
7	10	Cincinnati (2-2)	
8	8	Clemson (7-1)	↑2
9	7	Utah (5-1)	
10	12	Villanova (6-1)	↓6
11	11	Duke (7-2)	↑3
12	13	North Carolina (6-1)	↓1
13	9	Indiana (9-1)	↓1
14	14	Texas (5-1)	↓1
15	15	New Mexico (7-1)	
16	16	Minnesota (6-1)	↑1
17	19	Xavier (7-0)	↑2
18	18	Louisville (6-0)	↑4
19	21	Arkansas (4-1)	↑1
20	22	Alabama (8-0)	↑4
21	17	Fresno State (6-2)	↓5
22	20	Stanford (4-1)	↓1
23	23	Texas Tech (5-1)	↓5
24	—	UCLA (2-2)	↓1
25	25	Maryland (7-0)	⅃
—	24	Boston College (4-1)	Γ

Week of Dec 24

AP	USA/CNN	School	AP↓↑
1	1	Kansas (10-0)	
2	2	Wake Forest (8-0)	
3	3	Kentucky (8-1)	
4	4	Michigan (8-0)	
5	5	Iowa State (8-0)	
6	9	Clemson (10-1)	↑2
7	6	Cincinnati (4-2)	
8	7	Utah (6-1)	↑1
9	13	Arizona (5-2)	↓3
10	12	Villanova (7-1)	
11	10	North Carolina (9-1)	↑1
12	8	Duke (8-2)	↓1
13	11	Indiana (10-1)	
14	14	New Mexico (8-1)	↑1
15	17	Minnesota (8-1)	↑1
16	15	Louisville (8-0)	↑2
17	18	Xavier (8-0)	
18	16	Texas (6-2)	↓4
19	19	Alabama (10-0)	↑1
20	22	Texas Tech (7-1)	↑3
21	21	Maryland (8-0)	↑4
22	24	Arkansas (5-2)	↓3
23	20	Stanford (6-1)	↓1
24	—	Oregon (7-0)	⅃
25	25	Boston College (5-1)	⅃
—	23	Fresno State (6-3)	Γ

Week of Dec 31

AP	USA/CNN	School	AP↓↑
1	1	Kansas (10-0)	
2	2	Wake Forest (8-0)	
3	3	Kentucky (10-1)	
4	4	Iowa State (8-0)	↑1
5	7	Clemson (10-1)	↑1
6	6	Cincinnati (5-2)	↑1
7	8	Utah (8-1)	↑1
8	5	Michigan (9-1)	↓4
9	13	Arizona (6-2)	
10	12	Villanova (9-1)	
11	9	North Carolina (9-1)	
12	10	Indiana (13-1)	↑1
13	11	Duke (8-2)	↓1
14	15	Louisville (10-0)	↑2
15	16	Minnesota (10-1)	
16	14	New Mexico (11-1)	↓2
17	19	Xavier (9-0)	
18	17	Texas (6-2)	
19	18	Maryland (11-0)	↑2
20	22	Oregon (9-0)	↑4
21	20	Stanford (7-1)	↑2
22	24	Arkansas (6-2)	
23	21	Texas Tech (8-2)	↓3
24	—	Illinois (10-2)	⅃
25	25	Boston College (6-2)	
—	23	Alabama (10-2)	Γ

Week of Jan 7

AP	USA/CNN	School	AP↓↑
1	1	Kansas (13-0)	
2	2	Wake Forest (10-0)	
3	3	Kentucky (12-1)	
4	4	Iowa State (10-0)	
5	5	Clemson (12-1)	
6	6	Cincinnati (8-2)	
7	8	Arizona (9-2)	↑2
8	7	Villanova (11-1)	↑2
9	10	Utah (9-1)	↓2
10	9	Duke (11-2)	↑3
11	11	Minnesota (13-1)	↑4
12	13	Xavier (10-0)	↑5
13	12	North Carolina (9-2)	↓2
14	16	Louisville (11-1)	
15	15	Indiana (14-2)	↓3
16	14	Michigan (10-3)	↓8
17	20	Oregon (10-0)	↑3
18	18	New Mexico (11-2)	↓2
19	17	Maryland (12-1)	
20	21	Texas Tech (9-2)	↑3
21	22	Stanford (8-2)	
22	19	Texas (7-3)	↓4
23	23	Boston College (8-2)	↑2
24	25	Georgia (11-2)	⅃
25	24	Illinois (11-3)	↓1

Week of Jan 14

AP	USA/CNN	School	AP↓↑
1	1	Kansas (16-0)	
2	2	Wake Forest (12-0)	
3	3	Clemson (14-1)	↑2
4	6	Cincinnati (11-2)	↑2
5	4	Kentucky (14-2)	↓2
6	7	Arizona (10-2)	↑1
7	8	Minnesota (15-1)	↑4
8	5	Iowa State (11-1)	↓4
9	9	Utah (10-2)	
10	10	Louisville (13-1)	↑4
11	12	Maryland (14-1)	↑8
12	14	New Mexico (13-2)	↑6
13	13	Duke (11-4)	↓3
14	11	Xavier (11-1)	↓2
15	17	Stanford (10-2)	↑6
16	15	Villanova (12-3)	↓8
17	16	Indiana (14-3)	↓2
18	18	Michigan (11-4)	↓2
19	19	Boston College (10-2)	↑4
20	25	Mississippi (11-3)	⅃
21	24	Georgia (12-2)	↑3
22	21	North Carolina (9-4)	↓9
23	20	Texas (8-4)	↓1
24	22	Oregon (10-2)	↓7
25	23	Texas Tech (10-3)	↓5

Week of Jan 21

AP	USA/CNN	School	AP↓↑
1	1	Kansas (18-0)	
2	3	Clemson (16-1)	↑1
3	4	Kentucky (16-2) (C)	↑2
4	2	Wake Forest (13-1)	↓2
5	5	Utah (12-2)	↑4
6	8	Louisville (15-1)	↑4
7	10	Maryland (15-2)	↑4
8	6	Minnesota (16-2)	↓1
9	7	Cincinnati (12-3)	↓5
10	9	Duke (14-4)	↑3
11	11	Arizona (10-4)	↓5
12	13	Villanova (14-3)	↑4
13	16	Michigan (13-4)	↑5
14	12	Iowa State (11-3)	↓6
15	14	New Mexico (14-3)	↓3
16	15	Xavier (12-2)	↓2
17	17	Stanford (11-3)	↓2
18	22	Colorado (14-3)	⅃
19	18	North Carolina (11-4)	↑3
20	20	Texas Tech (12-3)	↑5
21	19	Indiana (15-4)	↓4
22	23	Boston College (12-3)	↓3
23	21	Texas (9-5)	
24	—	Tulsa (14-4)	⅃
25	—	Marquette (12-3)	⅃
—	24	Iowa (14-4)	
—	25	Illinois (13-4)	

Week of Jan 28

AP	USA/CNN	School	AP↓↑
1	1	Kansas (20-0)	
2	2	Wake Forest (15-1)	↑2
3	3	Kentucky (18-2)	
4	4	Utah (13-2)	↑1
5	9	Maryland (17-2)	↑2
6	5	Minnesota (18-2)	↑2
7	6	Clemson (16-3)	↓5
8	7	Cincinnati (14-3)	↑1
9	8	Louisville (16-2)	↓3
10	10	Arizona (12-4)	↑1
11	12	Iowa State (13-3)	↑3
12	11	Duke (15-5)	↓2
13	14	New Mexico (15-3)	↑2
14	13	Villanova (15-4)	↓2
15	15	Stanford (13-3)	↑2
16	16	Michigan (14-5)	↓3
17	17	Indiana (17-4)	↑4
18	20	Colorado (15-4)	
19	18	North Carolina (12-5)	
20	19	Xavier (13-3)	↓4
21	24	Tulsa (15-4)	↑3
22	22	Texas Tech (13-4)	↓2
23	21	Texas (11-5)	
24	23	Marquette (13-3)	↑1
25	—	South Carolina (13-5)	⅃
—	25	Boston College (13-4)	Γ

Poll Progression Continues →

WEEK OF FEB 4

AP	USA/CNN	SCHOOL	AP↓↑
1	1	**Kansas** (22-0)	
2	2	**Wake Forest** (18-1)	
3	3	**Kentucky** (20-2)	
4	4	**Minnesota** (19-2)	↑2
5	7	**Utah** (15-3)	↓1
6	13	**Iowa State** (15-3)	↑5
7	9	**Maryland** (17-4)	↓2
8	11	**Duke** (17-5)	↑4
9	10	**New Mexico** (16-3)	↑4
10	8	**Clemson** (17-4)	↓3
11	5	**Louisville** (18-3)	↓2
12	6	**Cincinnati** (15-4)	↓4
13	15	**Michigan** (16-5)	↑3
14	11	**Arizona** (13-5)	↓4
15	19	**Colorado** (16-4)	↑3
16	14	**Villanova** (16-5)	↓2
17	17	**Xavier** (15-3)	↑3
18	16	**Stanford** (13-4)	↓3
19	20	**South Carolina** (15-5)	↑6
20	18	**North Carolina** (13-6)	↓1
21	24	**Tulane** (16-5)	⌋
22	22	**Tulsa** (17-5)	↓1
23	21	**Texas Tech** (13-5)	↓1
24	23	**Indiana** (17-6)	↓7
25	—	**Iowa** (15-5)	⌋
—	25	**Illinois** (15-6)	

WEEK OF FEB 11

AP	USA/CNN	SCHOOL	AP↓↑
1	1	**Kansas** (23-1) (D)	
2	2	**Wake Forest** (19-2)	
3	3	**Minnesota** (20-2)	↑1
4	4	**Kentucky** (22-3)	↓1
5	5	**Utah** (17-3)	
6	7	**Duke** (19-5)	↑2
7	6	**Clemson** (19-4)	↑3
8	8	**Cincinnati** (17-4)	↑4
9	9	**Iowa State** (16-4)	↓3
10	10	**Maryland** (18-5)	↓3
11	11	**Arizona** (15-5)	↑3
12	13	**South Carolina** (17-5)	↑7
13	12	**New Mexico** (18-4)	↓4
14	14	**Michigan** (17-6)	↓1
15	16	**Colorado** (17-6)	
16	17	**North Carolina** (15-6)	↑4
17	15	**Louisville** (18-5)	↓6
18	18	**Villanova** (17-6)	↓2
19	19	**Xavier** (16-4)	↓2
20	21	**Illinois** (17-6)	⌋
21	20	**Texas Tech** (14-6)	↑2
22	22	**Stanford** (13-6)	↓4
23	23	**Tulane** (16-7)	↓2
24	25	**UCLA** (13-7)	⌋
25	—	**Charleston** (21-2)	⌋
—	24	**Tulsa** (17-6)	⌈

WEEK OF FEB 18

AP	USA/CNN	SCHOOL	AP↓↑
1	1	**Kansas** (25-1)	
2	2	**Minnesota** (22-2)	↑1
3	3	**Kentucky** (24-3)	↑1
4	4	**Wake Forest** (20-3)	↓2
5	5	**Utah** (19-3)	
6	6	**Duke** (21-5)	
7	8	**Iowa State** (18-4)	↑2
8	7	**Clemson** (20-5)	↓1
9	9	**South Carolina** (18-6)	↑3
10	10	**New Mexico** (20-4)	↑3
11	11	**Cincinnati** (19-5)	↓3
12	14	**North Carolina** (17-6)	↑4
13	12	**Arizona** (16-6)	↓2
14	13	**Maryland** (19-6)	↓4
15	15	**Louisville** (19-5)	↑2
16	17	**Xavier** (18-4)	↑3
17	19	**UCLA** (15-7)	↑7
18	16	**Michigan** (17-7)	↓4
19	18	**Villanova** (18-7)	↓1
20	22	**Stanford** (15-6)	↑2
21	20	**Colorado** (17-7)	↓6
22	24	**Charleston** (23-2)	↑3
23	21	**Illinois** (18-7)	↓3
24	25	**Indiana** (20-7)	⌋
25	—	**California** (18-6)	⌋
—	23	**Texas Tech** (15-7)	⌈

WEEK OF FEB 25

AP	USA/CNN	SCHOOL	AP↓↑
1	1	**Kansas** (27-1)	
2	2	**Minnesota** (24-2)	
3	3	**Kentucky** (26-3)	
4	4	**Utah** (20-3)	
5	5	**Wake Forest** (21-4)	
6	6	**South Carolina** (21-6)	
7	7	**Duke** (22-6)	
8	9	**North Carolina** (19-6)	
9	8	**Cincinnati** (22-5)	
10	14	**UCLA** (17-7)	
11	11	**New Mexico** (21-5)	[illegible]
12	10	**Clemson** (20-7)	[illegible]
13	12	**Iowa State** (18-6)	[illegible]
14	17	**Xavier** (20-4)	[illegible]
15	13	**Arizona** (17-7)	↓[illegible]
16	16	**Maryland** (20-7)	↓[illegible]
17	15	**Louisville** (21-6)	↓[illegible]
18	18	**Villanova** (20-7)	↑[illegible]
19	19	**Colorado** (19-7)	↑[illegible]
20	20	**Charleston** (25-2)	↑[illegible]
21	23	**Illinois** (18-8)	↑[illegible]
22	22	**Indiana** (21-8)	↑[illegible]
23	—	**Saint Joseph's** (19-6)	⌋
24	21	**Michigan** (17-9)	↓[illegible]
25	24	**Stanford** (16-7)	↓[illegible]
—	25	**California** (19-7)	⌈

WEEK OF MAR 4

AP	USA/CNN	SCHOOL	AP↓↑
1	1	**Kansas** (29-1)	
2	2	**Minnesota** (26-2)	
3	3	**Utah** (23-3)	↑1
4	4	**South Carolina** (23-6)	↑2
5	6	**North Carolina** (21-6)	↑3
6	5	**Kentucky** (27-4)	↓3
7	7	**Duke** (23-7)	
8	9	**Wake Forest** (22-5)	↓3
9	8	**UCLA** (19-7)	↑1
10	10	**Cincinnati** (24-6)	↓1
11	14	**Xavier** (22-4)	↑3
12	11	**Arizona** (19-7)	↑3
13	13	**Clemson** (21-8)	↓1
14	12	**New Mexico** (22-6)	↓3
15	21	**Illinois** (20-8)	↑6
16	15	**Iowa State** (19-7)	↓3
17	18	**Charleston** (28-2)	↑3
18	16	**Colorado** (21-8)	↑1
19	23	**Saint Joseph's** (21-6)	↑4
20	19	**Louisville** (22-7)	↓3
21	17	**Villanova** (21-8)	↓3
22	20	**Maryland** (20-9)	↓6
23	22	**Stanford** (18-7)	↑2
24	—	**Georgia** (21-7)	⌋
25	24	**Indiana** (21-9)	↓3
—	25	**Princeton** (22-3)	

WEEK OF MAR 11

AP	USA/CNN	SCHOOL	AP↓↑
1	1	**Kansas** (32-1)	
2	2	**Utah** (26-3) (E)	↑1
3	3	**Minnesota** (27-3) (F)	↓1
4	5	**North Carolina** (24-6)	↑1
5	4	**Kentucky** (30-4)	↑1
6	6	**South Carolina** (24-7)	↓2
7	7	**UCLA** (21-7)	↑2
8	8	**Duke** (23-8)	↓1
9	9	**Wake Forest** (23-6)	↓1
10	10	**Cincinnati** (25-7)	
11	11	**New Mexico** (24-7)	↑3
12	15	**Saint Joseph's** (24-6)	↑7
13	14	**Xavier** (22-5)	↓2
14	12	**Clemson** (21-9)	↓1
15	13	**Arizona** (19-9)	↓3
16	18	**Charleston** (28-2)	↑1
17	22	**Georgia** (24-8)	↑7
18	17	**Iowa State** (20-8)	↓2
19	24	**Illinois** (21-9)	↓4
20	16	**Villanova** (23-9)	↑1
21	21	**Stanford** (20-7)	↑2
22	19	**Maryland** (21-10)	
23	20	**Boston College** (21-8)	⌋
24	23	**Colorado** (21-9)	↓6
25	25	**Louisville** (23-8)	↓5

FINAL POLL (POST-TOURNAMENT)

USA/CNN	SCHOOL
1	**Arizona** (25-9)
2	**Kentucky** (35-5)
3	**Minnesota** (31-4)
4	**North Carolina** (28-7)
5	**Kansas** (34-2)
6	**Utah** (29-4)
7	**UCLA** (24-8)
8	**Clemson** (23-10)
9	**Wake Forest** (24-7)
10	**Louisville** (26-9)
11	**Duke** (24-9)
12	**Stanford** (22-8)
13	**Iowa State** (22-9)
14	**South Carolina** (24-8)
15	**Providence** (24-12)
16	**Cincinnati** (26-8)
17	**Saint Joseph's** (26-7)
18	**California** (25-9)
19	**New Mexico** (25-8)
20	**Texas** (18-12)
21	**Charleston** (29-3)
22	**Xavier** (23-6)
23	**Boston College** (22-9)
24	**Michigan** (23-11)
25	**Colorado** (22-10)

(A) The only man not named Wooden to coach UCLA to a NCAA championship, Jim Harrick, is fired on Nov. 6 over recruiting violations. The Bruins will go on to win the Pac-10 title under interim coach Steve Lavin.

(B) Arizona upsets Utah in the Wooden Classic, which will remain its season highlight until the NCAA Tournament, where the 19–9 Wildcats will knock off three No. 1-seeds on the way to winning the title.

(C) In a 77-53 home win over Auburn on Jan. 18, Kentucky's leading scorer, Derek Anderson, goes down with a knee injury. Originally thought to be only a bruise, it is diagnosed two days later as a torn ACL, sidelining him for the season.

(D) Missouri defeats Kansas, 96-94, in double OT in what is to be the Jayhawks' only loss of the regular season.

(E) Utah's Keith Van Horn hits buzzer-beaters in two straight games to send the Utes into the WAC tournament championship game, where he scores 37 to help beat TCU.

(F) Despite a last-second loss to unranked Wisconsin on March 8, Minnesota wins its first Big Ten title in 15 years. Coach Clem Haskins' Gophers will advance to the Final Four for the first time, only to have their Tournament appearance vacated later because of academic fraud.

PRE-TOURNAMENT RATINGS PERCENTAGE INDEX (RPI)

RANK	SCHOOL	W-L	Sched. Strg.	SS Rank	RPI
1	**Kansas**	31-1	.58378	22	.6742
2	**Kentucky**	29-4	.60006	11	.6572
3	**North Carolina**	24-6	.62923	1	.6569
4	**Minnesota**	26-3	.58257	23	.6522
5	**Utah**	25-3	.55821	54	.6380
6	**Wake Forest**	23-6	.58909	15	.6344
7	**Duke**	23-8	.60378	7	.6271
8	**Villanova**	22-9	.62004	2	.6229
9	**South Carolina**	23-7	.58480	19	.6202
10	**UCLA**	21-7	.58826	17	.6165
11	**Clemson**	21-9	.60257	9	.6159
12	**Saint Joseph's**	24-6	.55411	61	.6124
13	**Cincinnati**	25-7	.56606	41	.6112
14	**New Mexico**	23-7	.57012	35	.6087
15	**Tulsa**	23-9	.57100	34	.6017
16	**Indiana**	22-10	.58427	21	.6014
17	**Arizona**	19-9	.58917	14	.5994
18	**Louisville**	23-8	.55191	63	.5978
19	**Georgia**	24-8	.54329	77	.5965
20	**California**	21-8	.56033	51	.5963
21	**Maryland**	21-10	.57267	33	.5963
22	**Purdue**	17-11	.61312	4	.5945
23	**Rhode Island**	20-9	.57624	26	.5939
24	**Illinois**	21-9	.56434	44	.5934
25	**Virginia**	18-12	.60690	6	.5932
26	**Wisconsin**	18-9	.57379	31	.5919
27	**Charlotte**	21-8	.55526	58	.5917
28	**Xavier**	22-5	.50926	119	.5907
29	**Texas Tech**	19-9	.56421	45	.5893
30	**Stanford**	18-7	.55372	62	.5887
31	**Boston U.**	25-4	.49646	143	.5877
32	**Princeton**	23-3	.48028	180	.5854
33	**Vanderbilt**	18-11	.58867	16	.5847
34	**Boston College**	21-8	.53393	85	.5846
35	**Illinois State**	24-5	.49297	151	.5842
36	**Iowa State**	20-8	.53555	82	.5829
37	**Iowa**	20-9	.54596	72	.5826
38	**Temple**	19-10	.56291	47	.5818
39	**Texas**	16-11	.58428	20	.5807
40	**Michigan**	19-11	.56552	43	.5805
41	**TCU**	21-12	.57600	27	.5798
42	**SW Missouri State**	24-8	.52932	91	.5797
43	**Colorado**	21-9	.53610	81	.5785
44	**Mississippi**	19-8	.53455	83	.5785
45	**Massachusetts**	18-13	.59465	13	.5785
46	**Providence**	20-11	.55792	55	.5770
47	**Oklahoma**	19-10	.55090	66	.5752
48	**Oklahoma State**	16-14	.61978	3	.5749
49	**West Virginia**	19-9	.53167	86	.5724
50	**Hawaii**	20-7	.51532	110	.5721

Source: Collegiate Basketball News

1997 NCAA Tournament

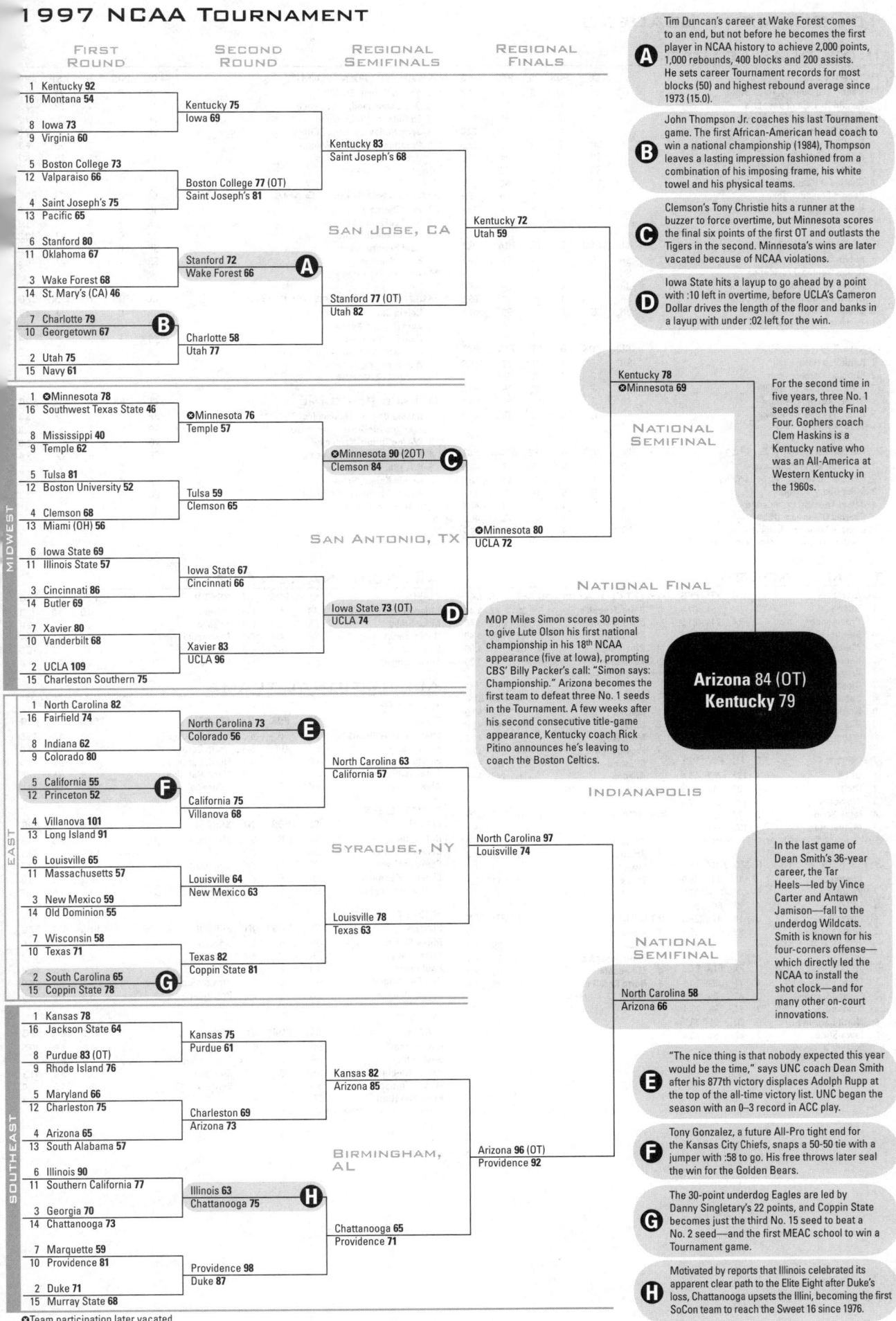

First Round · Second Round · Regional Semifinals · Regional Finals

San Jose, CA

First Round

- 1 Kentucky **92** / 16 Montana **54**
- 8 Iowa **73** / 9 Virginia **60**
- 5 Boston College **73** / 12 Valparaiso **66**
- 4 Saint Joseph's **75** / 13 Pacific **65**
- 6 Stanford **80** / 11 Oklahoma **67**
- 3 Wake Forest **68** / 14 St. Mary's (CA) **46**
- 7 Charlotte **79** / 10 Georgetown **67** (B)
- 2 Utah **75** / 15 Navy **61**

Second Round

- Kentucky **75** / Iowa **69**
- Boston College **77** (OT) / Saint Joseph's **81**
- Stanford **72** / Wake Forest **66** (A)
- Charlotte **58** / Utah **77**

Regional Semifinals

- Kentucky **83** / Saint Joseph's **68**
- Stanford **77** (OT) / Utah **82**

Regional Final

- Kentucky **72** / Utah **59**

Midwest: San Antonio, TX

First Round

- 1 ⊗Minnesota **78** / 16 Southwest Texas State **46**
- 8 Mississippi **40** / 9 Temple **62**
- 5 Tulsa **81** / 12 Boston University **52**
- 4 Clemson **68** / 13 Miami (OH) **56**
- 6 Iowa State **69** / 11 Illinois State **57**
- 3 Cincinnati **86** / 14 Butler **69**
- 7 Xavier **80** / 10 Vanderbilt **68**
- 2 UCLA **109** / 15 Charleston Southern **75**

Second Round

- ⊗Minnesota **76** / Temple **57**
- Tulsa **59** / Clemson **65**
- Iowa State **67** / Cincinnati **66**
- Xavier **83** / UCLA **96**

Regional Semifinals

- ⊗Minnesota **90** (2OT) / Clemson **84** (C)
- Iowa State **73** (OT) / UCLA **74** (D)

Regional Final

- ⊗Minnesota **80** / UCLA **72**

East: Syracuse, NY

First Round

- 1 North Carolina **82** / 16 Fairfield **74**
- 8 Indiana **62** / 9 Colorado **80**
- 5 California **55** / 12 Princeton **52** (F)
- 4 Villanova **101** / 13 Long Island **91**
- 6 Louisville **65** / 11 Massachusetts **57**
- 3 New Mexico **59** / 14 Old Dominion **55**
- 7 Wisconsin **58** / 10 Texas **71**
- 2 South Carolina **65** / 15 Coppin State **78** (G)

Second Round

- North Carolina **73** / Colorado **56** (E)
- California **75** / Villanova **68**
- Louisville **64** / New Mexico **63**
- Texas **82** / Coppin State **81**

Regional Semifinals

- North Carolina **63** / California **57**
- Louisville **78** / Texas **63**

Regional Final

- North Carolina **97** / Louisville **74**

Southeast: Birmingham, AL

First Round

- 1 Kansas **78** / 16 Jackson State **64**
- 8 Purdue **83** (OT) / 9 Rhode Island **76**
- 5 Maryland **66** / 12 Charleston **75**
- 4 Arizona **65** / 13 South Alabama **57**
- 6 Illinois **90** / 11 Southern California **77**
- 3 Georgia **70** / 14 Chattanooga **73**
- 7 Marquette **59** / 10 Providence **81**
- 2 Duke **71** / 15 Murray State **68**

Second Round

- Kansas **75** / Purdue **61**
- Charleston **69** / Arizona **73**
- Illinois **63** / Chattanooga **75** (H)
- Providence **98** / Duke **87**

Regional Semifinals

- Kansas **82** / Arizona **85**
- Chattanooga **65** / Providence **71**

Regional Final

- Arizona **96** (OT) / Providence **92**

National Semifinal

Kentucky **78** / ⊗Minnesota **69**

For the second time in five years, three No. 1 seeds reach the Final Four. Gophers coach Clem Haskins is a Kentucky native who was an All-America at Western Kentucky in the 1960s.

National Semifinal

North Carolina **58** / Arizona **66**

In the last game of Dean Smith's 36-year career, the Tar Heels—led by Vince Carter and Antawn Jamison—fall to the underdog Wildcats. Smith is known for his four-corners offense—which directly led the NCAA to install the shot clock—and for many other on-court innovations.

National Final (Indianapolis)

Arizona 84 (OT)
Kentucky 79

MOP Miles Simon scores 30 points to give Lute Olson his first national championship in his 18th NCAA appearance (five at Iowa), prompting CBS' Billy Packer's call: "Simon says: Championship." Arizona becomes the first team to defeat three No. 1 seeds in the Tournament. A few weeks after his second consecutive title-game appearance, Kentucky coach Rick Pitino announces he's leaving to coach the Boston Celtics.

A Tim Duncan's career at Wake Forest comes to an end, but not before he becomes the first player in NCAA history to achieve 2,000 points, 1,000 rebounds, 400 blocks and 200 assists. He sets career Tournament records for most blocks (50) and highest rebound average since 1973 (15.0).

B John Thompson Jr. coaches his last Tournament game. The first African-American head coach to win a national championship (1984), Thompson leaves a lasting impression fashioned from a combination of his imposing frame, his white towel and his physical teams.

C Clemson's Tony Christie hits a runner at the buzzer to force overtime, but Minnesota scores the final six points of the first OT and outlasts the Tigers in the second. Minnesota's wins are later vacated because of NCAA violations.

D Iowa State hits a layup to go ahead by a point with :10 left in overtime, before UCLA's Cameron Dollar drives the length of the floor and banks in a layup with under :02 left for the win.

E "The nice thing is that nobody expected this year would be the time," says UNC coach Dean Smith after his 877th victory displaces Adolph Rupp at the top of the all-time victory list. UNC began the season with an 0–3 record in ACC play.

F Tony Gonzalez, a future All-Pro tight end for the Kansas City Chiefs, snaps a 50-50 tie with a jumper with :58 to go. His free throws later seal the win for the Golden Bears.

G The 30-point underdog Eagles are led by Danny Singletary's 22 points, and Coppin State becomes just the third No. 15 seed to beat a No. 2 seed—and the first MEAC school to win a Tournament game.

H Motivated by reports that Illinois celebrated its apparent clear path to the Elite Eight after Duke's loss, Chattanooga upsets the Illini, becoming the first SoCon team to reach the Sweet 16 since 1976.

⊗Team participation later vacated

ANNUAL REVIEW

TOURNAMENT LEADERS

INDIVIDUAL LEADERS

SCORING

		CL	POS	G	PTS	PPG
1	**Dedric Willoughby**, Iowa State	SR	G	3	74	24.7
2	**Rashid Bey**, Saint Joseph's	JR	G	3	71	23.7
3	**Austin Croshere**, Providence	SR	F	4	91	22.8
4	**Miles Simon**, Arizona	JR	G	6	132	22.0
	Paul Pierce, Kansas	SO	F	3	66	22.0
6	**Brevin Knight**, Stanford	SR	G	3	64	21.3
7	**Keith Van Horn**, Utah	SR	F	4	83	20.8
8	**Charles O'Bannon**, UCLA	SR	F	4	80	20.0
9	**Reggie Freeman**, Texas	SR	G	3	59	19.7
10	**Bobby Jackson**, Minnesota	SR	G	5	97	19.4

MINIMUM: 3 GAMES

FIELD GOAL PCT

		CL	POS	G	FG	FGA	PCT
1	**Kelvin Cato**, Iowa State	SR	C	3	18	27	66.7
	Ruben Garces, Providence	SR	F	4	16	24	66.7
	Jelani McCoy, UCLA	JR	C	4	16	24	66.7
4	**Charles O'Bannon**, UCLA	SR	F	4	30	46	65.2
5	**Cameron Mills**, Kentucky	JR	G	6	24	39	61.5

MINIMUM: 15 MADE AND 3 GAMES

FREE THROW PCT

		CL	POS	G	FT	FTA	PCT
1	**Keith Van Horn**, Utah	SR	F	4	21	21	100.0
2	**Michael Doleac**, Utah	JR	C	4	25	26	96.2
3	**Nate Johnson**, Louisville	FR	F	5	23	25	92.0
4	**Brevin Knight**, Stanford	SR	G	3	28	31	90.3
5	**Anthony Epps**, Kentucky	SR	G	6	16	18	88.9

MINIMUM: 15 MADE

THREE-POINT FG PCT

		CL	POS	G	3FG	3FGA	PCT
1	**Cameron Mills**, Kentucky	JR	G	6	17	27	63.0
2	**Ademola Okulaja**, North Carolina	SO	F	5	6	12	50.0
3	**Mike Bibby**, Arizona	FR	G	6	18	37	48.6
4	**Jamel Thomas**, Providence	SO	G	4	9	19	47.4
5	**Charles O'Bannon**, UCLA	SR	F	4	6	13	46.2
	Charles Thomas, Minnesota	SO	G	4	6	13	46.2

MINIMUM: 6 MADE AND 3 GAMES

ASSISTS PER GAME

		CL	POS	G	AST	APG
1	**Brevin Knight**, Stanford	SR	G	3	24	8.0
2	**God Shammgod**, Providence	SO	G	4	29	7.3
3	**Ed Cota**, North Carolina	FR	G	5	36	7.2
4	**Jacy Holloway**, Iowa State	SR	G	3	21	7.0
5	**Prentice McGruder**, California	SO	G	3	20	6.7
	Jacque Vaughn, Kansas	SR	G	3	20	6.7

MINIMUM: 3 GAMES

REBOUNDS PER GAME

		CL	POS	G	REB	RPG
1	**Paul Pierce**, Kansas	SO	F	3	36	12.0
2	**Raef LaFrentz**, Kansas	JR	F	3	34	11.3
3	**A.J. Bramlett**, Arizona	SO	C	6	62	10.3
	Scot Pollard, Kansas	SR	C	3	31	10.3
	Keith Van Horn, Utah	SR	F	4	41	10.3

MINIMUM: 3 GAMES

BLOCKED SHOTS PER GAME

		CL	POS	G	BLK	BPG
1	**Kelvin Cato**, Iowa State	SR	C	3	14	4.7
2	**Scot Pollard**, Kansas	SR	C	3	12	4.0
3	**Paul Pierce**, Kansas	SO	F	3	8	2.7
4	**Jelani McCoy**, UCLA	JR	C	4	9	2.3
5	**A.J. Bramlett**, Arizona	SO	C	6	13	2.2

MINIMUM: 3 GAMES

STEALS PER GAME

		CL	POS	G	STL	SPG
1	**Rashid Bey**, Saint Joseph's	JR	G	3	10	3.3
2	**Prentice McGruder**, California	SO	G	3	9	3.0
3	**Wayne Turner**, Kentucky	SO	G	6	17	2.8
4	**Bobby Jackson**, Minnesota	SR	G	5	12	2.4
5	**Kris Clack**, Texas	SO	G	3	7	2.3
	Brevin Knight, Stanford	SR	G	3	7	2.3
	Anwar McQueen, California	SR	G	3	7	2.3

MINIMUM: 3 GAMES

TEAM LEADERS

SCORING

		G	PTS	PPG
1	**UCLA**	4	351	87.8
2	**Providence**	4	244	81.3
3	**Kentucky**	6	479	79.8
4	**Minnesota**	5	393	78.6
5	**Kansas**	3	235	78.3
6	**Arizona**	6	469	78.2
7	**Stanford**	3	229	76.3
8	**Saint Joseph's**	3	224	74.7
9	**North Carolina**	5	373	74.6
10	**Utah**	4	293	73.3

MINIMUM: 3 GAMES

FG PCT

		G	FG	FGA	PCT
1	**UCLA**	4	132	257	51.4
2	**Utah**	4	102	210	48.6
3	**Providence**	4	120	251	47.8
4	**Iowa State**	3	72	151	47.7
5	**Minnesota**	5	135	291	46.4

MINIMUM: 15 MADE AND 3 GAMES

3-PT FG PCT

		G	3FG	3FGA	PCT
1	**Chattanooga**	3	15	39	38.5
2	**Kentucky**	6	46	120	38.3
3	**UCLA**	4	23	60	38.3
4	**Iowa State**	3	18	47	38.3
5	**North Carolina**	5	29	79	36.7

MINIMUM: 3 GAMES

FT PCT

		G	FT	FTA	PCT
1	**Utah**	4	71	89	79.8
2	**Saint Joseph's**	3	66	85	77.6
3	**Stanford**	3	74	96	77.1
4	**North Carolina**	5	70	95	73.7
5	**Iowa State**	3	47	64	73.4

MINIMUM: 3 GAMES

AST/TO RATIO

		G	AST	TO	RAT
1	**Saint Joseph's**	3	39	27	1.44
	North Carolina	5	84	60	1.40
	Stanford	3	42	30	1.40
4	**Providence**	4	65	50	1.30
5	**Kentucky**	6	101	80	1.26

MINIMUM: 3 GAMES

REBOUNDS

		G	REB	RPG
1	**Kansas**	3	150	50.0
2	**UCLA**	4	167	41.8
3	**Minnesota**	5	208	41.6
4	**Providence**	4	164	41.0
	Clemson	3	123	41.0
	Arizona	6	246	41.0

MINIMUM: 3 GAMES

BLOCKS

		G	BLK	BPG
1	**Kansas**	3	29	9.7
2	**Kentucky**	6	31	5.2
3	**Arizona**	6	29	4.8
4	**Iowa State**	3	14	4.7
5	**Texas**	3	11	3.7

MINIMUM: 3 GAMES

STEALS

		G	STL	SPG
1	**Kentucky**	6	64	10.7
2	**UCLA**	4	35	8.8
3	**Saint Joseph's**	3	26	8.7
4	**Minnesota**	5	40	8.0
5	**North Carolina**	5	38	7.6

MINIMUM: 3 GAMES

ALL-TOURNAMENT TEAM

PLAYER	CL	POS	HT	SCHOOL	RPG	APG	PPG
Miles Simon*	JR	G	6-5	Arizona	4.0	3.2	22.0
Mike Bibby	FR	G	6-2	Arizona	4.8	3.3	18.0
Bobby Jackson	SR	G	6-1	Minnesota	7.4	3.0	19.4
Ron Mercer	SO	G/F	6-7	Kentucky	5.3	2.2	16.3
Scott Padgett	SO	F	6-9	Kentucky	4.2	1.5	11.0

ALL-REGIONAL TEAMS

EAST

PLAYER	CL	POS	HT	SCHOOL	RPG	APG	PPG
Shammond Williams*	JR	G	6-3	North Carolina	2.0	4.5	16.5
Vince Carter	SO	G/F	6-6	North Carolina	3.3	1.8	14.0
Ed Cota	FR	G	6-1	North Carolina	3.0	8.0	9.0
Antawn Jamison	JR	F	6-9	North Carolina	8.5	0.5	17.5
Alex Sanders	FR	F	6-7	Louisville	5.3	1.5	13.8

MIDWEST

PLAYER	CL	POS	HT	SCHOOL	RPG	APG	PPG
Bobby Jackson*	SR	G	6-1	Minnesota	7.8	2.8	18.5
Cameron Dollar	SR	G	6-1	UCLA	4.5	4.3	12.8
Sam Jacobson	JR	G/F	6-6	Minnesota	4.0	1.0	17.0
Charles O'Bannon	SR	F	6-6	UCLA	5.0	1.3	20.0
Dedric Willoughby	SR	G	6-3	Iowa State	4.3	1.0	24.7

SOUTHEAST

PLAYER	CL	POS	HT	SCHOOL	RPG	APG	PPG
Miles Simon*	JR	G	6-5	Arizona	4.0	3.3	19.5
Mike Bibby	FR	G	6-2	Arizona	3.3	3.0	17.3
Paul Pierce	SO	F	6-7	Kansas	12.0	2.3	22.0
God Shammgod	SO	G	6-0	Providence	1.3	7.3	14.0
Jamel Thomas	SO	G	6-6	Providence	6.8	2.0	15.8

WEST

PLAYER	CL	POS	HT	SCHOOL	RPG	APG	PPG
Ron Mercer*	SO	G/F	6-7	Kentucky	5.0	1.5	16.5
Rashid Bey	JR	G	5-11	Saint Joseph's	4.0	6.0	23.7
Brevin Knight	SR	G	5-10	Stanford	5.0	8.0	21.3
Wayne Turner	SO	G	6-2	Kentucky	2.5	4.0	15.0
Keith Van Horn	SR	F	6-9	Utah	10.3	1.5	20.8

* MOST OUTSTANDING PLAYER

1997 NCAA TOURNAMENT BOX SCORES

83-68 (Sweet 16)

	1H	2H
Kentucky	39	44
Saint Joseph's	27	41

KENTUCKY	MIN	FG	3FG	FT	REB	A	ST	BL	PF	TP
Ron Mercer	38	8-13	0-2	3-3	4	1	3	0	3	19
Cameron Mills	20	6-8	5-6	2-2	2	0	1	0	3	19
Wayne Turner	37	5-9	0-1	6-9	3	6	1	0	3	16
Scott Padgett	32	4-6	2-4	2-2	5	4	1	1	5	12
Anthony Epps	25	2-6	1-3	2-2	5	1	1	0	1	7
Nazr Mohammed	18	2-4	0-0	2-4	1	1	1	2	1	6
Jamaal Magloire	15	1-4	0-0	0-0	1	0	0	0	2	2
Jared Prickett	15	1-2	0-0	0-0	5	0	1	0	4	2
TOTALS	200	29-52	8-16	17-22	26	13	9	3	22	83
Percentages		55.8	50.0	77.3						

Coach: Rick Pitino

SAINT JOSEPH'S	MIN	FG	3FG	FT	REB	A	ST	BL	PF	TP
Rashid Bey	40	6-10	3-5	11-13	4	5	3	0	2	26
Dmitri Domani	37	4-5	1-1	6-7	2	2	0	0	2	15
Arthur Davis	28	4-10	1-2	4-4	2	0	2	0	3	13
Terrell Myers	19	2-9	1-4	4-6	1	0	0	0	5	9
Duval Simmonds	31	1-6	1-4	0-0	0	0	1	0	3	3
Nemanja Petrovic	16	1-2	0-0	0-0	3	0	0	0	2	2
Robert Haskins	15	0-0	0-0	0-0	3	0	0	0	0	0
Harold Rasul	14	0-0	0-0	0-0	2	0	0	0	2	0
Tim Brown	0	0-0	0-0	0-0	0	0	0	0	0	0
Bob Del Vescovo	0	0-0	0-0	0-0	0	0	0	0	0	0
John Gallagher	0	0-0	0-0	0-0	0	0	0	0	0	0
TOTALS	200	18-42	7-16	25-30	17	7	6	0	19	68
Percentages		42.9	43.8	83.3						

Coach: Phil Martelli

Officials: David Hall, Charles Range, Steve Gordon
Technicals: None
Attendance: 18,543

82-77 (Sweet 16)

	1H	2H	OT1
Utah	35	32	15
Stanford	21	46	10

UTAH	MIN	FG	3FG	FT	REB	A	ST	BL	PF	TP
Keith Van Horn	38	9-26	2-10	5-5	14	2	0	2	5	25
Andre Miller	39	7-11	0-0	5-9	7	1	1	0	4	19
Michael Doleac	31	2-7	0-1	12-12	6	1	1	0	4	16
Hanno Mottola	21	3-4	0-0	3-6	2	1	0	0	2	9
Jeff Johnsen	19	2-3	0-1	1-2	4	2	1	0	0	5
Ben Caton	34	1-5	1-3	0-1	6	2	0	0	5	3
David Jackson	8	1-1	1-1	0-2	0	1	1	0	1	3
Drew Hansen	30	1-4	0-3	0-0	4	2	1	0	5	2
Jordie McTavish	5	0-0	0-0	0-0	0	0	0	0	0	0
TOTALS	225	26-61	4-19	26-37	43	12	5	2	26	82
Percentages		42.6	21.1	70.3						

Coach: Rick Majerus

STANFORD	MIN	FG	3FG	FT	REB	A	ST	BL	PF	TP
Brevin Knight	39	7-19	1-5	12-13	6	9	1	0	4	27
Tim Young	28	5-15	0-0	2-2	15	0	1	2	5	12
Arthur Lee	40	3-9	2-6	3-4	2	0	2	0	5	11
Kris Weems	40	2-8	1-3	3-5	2	0	2	0	1	8
Peter Sauer	34	4-13	0-2	0-0	2	0	1	0	4	8
Mark Madsen	18	2-6	0-0	3-4	5	0	0	1	5	7
Pete Van Elswyk	9	0-0	0-0	2-4	0	0	0	0	4	2
David Moseley	7	0-2	0-0	2-2	1	0	0	0	0	2
Rich Jackson	10	0-0	0-0	0-0	2	0	0	0	0	0
TOTALS	225	23-72	4-16	27-34	35	9	7	3	28	77
Percentages		31.9	25.0	79.4						

Coach: Mike Montgomery

Officials: Ted Hillary, Frank Scagliotta, Tom Lopes
Technicals: Stanford (bench)
Attendance: 18,543

90-84 (Sweet 16)

	1H	2H	OT1	OT2
Minnesota	41	31	8	10
Clemson	35	37	8	4

MINNESOTA	MIN	FG	3FG	FT	REB	A	ST	BL	PF	TP
Bobby Jackson	49	11-20	2-4	12-13	9	0	2	-	4	36
Sam Jacobson	37	9-18	4-12	7-9	4	1	0	-	4	29
Courtney James	36	3-6	0-0	1-4	5	0	2	-	2	7
Charles Thomas	28	0-4	0-1	6-6	2	1	1	-	2	6
Eric Harris	22	1-1	0-0	3-4	1	3	1	-	1	5
Quincy Lewis	14	1-1	0-0	3-7	1	0	3	-	4	5
John Thomas	27	0-1	0-0	2-2	6	2	2	-	4	2
Trevor Winter	23	0-3	0-0	0-0	4	1	0	-	2	0
Miles Tarver	14	0-1	0-0	0-0	1	0	0	-	1	0
TOTALS	250	25-55	6-17	34-45	33	8	11	-	24	90
Percentages		45.5	35.3	75.6						

Coach: Clem Haskins

CLEMSON	MIN	FG	3FG	FT	REB	A	ST	BL	PF	TP
Greg Buckner	39	7-9	1-2	7-12	2	2	0	0	5	22
Terrell McIntyre	42	7-18	3-6	0-0	2	2	2	1	4	17
Mohamed Woni	26	1-1	0-0	10-10	4	1	0	0	4	12
Merl Code	42	2-14	2-10	4-5	3	2	0	0	3	10
Tom Wideman	30	5-5	0-0	0-0	10	4	1	0	2	10
Iker Iturbe	17	2-4	1-1	2-3	2	2	2	0	5	7
Harold Jamison	27	1-3	0-0	1-2	5	1	1	0	2	3
Tony Christie	13	1-1	0-0	1-2	0	0	0	0	3	3
Vincent Whitt	13	0-2	0-0	0-1	2	1	0	0	4	0
Andrius Jurkunas	1	0-1	0-1	0-0	0	0	0	0	0	0
TOTALS	250	26-58	7-20	25-35	30	15	6	1	32	84
Percentages		44.8	35.0	71.4						

Coach: Rick Barnes

Officials: Don Rutledge, Dave Libbey, Reggie Greenwood
Technicals: Minnesota (Jackson)
Attendance: 29,231

74-73 (Sweet 16)

	1H	2H	OT1
UCLA	25	39	10
Iowa State	37	27	9

UCLA	MIN	FG	3FG	FT	REB	A	ST	BL	PF	TP
Cameron Dollar	41	9-14	2-5	0-0	4	4	1	0	3	20
Charles O'Bannon	44	5-8	2-3	4-4	5	1	1	0	3	16
Toby Bailey	44	6-17	1-3	0-2	10	3	3	1	4	13
J.R. Henderson	45	4-13	0-2	4-8	12	5	2	0	4	12
Jelani McCoy	18	3-6	0-0	0-0	4	0	0	1	3	6
Kris Johnson	26	2-5	0-3	0-0	1	4	1	0	1	4
Brandon Loyd	7	1-1	1-1	0-0	0	0	0	0	1	3
TOTALS	225	30-64	6-17	8-14	36	17	8	2	19	74
Percentages		46.9	35.3	57.1						

Coach: Steve Lavin

IOWA STATE	MIN	FG	3FG	FT	REB	A	ST	BL	PF	TP
Dedric Willoughby	44	11-21	8-17	4-4	7	1	0	0	1	34
Kenny Pratt	42	6-13	0-1	2-6	6	2	2	0	4	14
Kelvin Cato	40	4-7	0-0	2-2	9	1	0	4	3	10
Jacy Holloway	45	1-5	1-3	4-4	2	6	1	0	1	7
Shawn Bankhead	41	3-7	0-0	0-0	1	5	0	0	3	6
Klay Edwards	7	1-1	0-0	0-4	2	0	1	0	0	2
Stevie Johnson	5	0-0	0-0	0-0	0	1	0	0	0	0
Tony Rampton	1	0-0	0-0	0-0	0	0	0	0	0	0
TOTALS	225	26-54	9-21	12-20	27	16	4	4	12	73
Percentages		48.1	42.9	60.0						

Coach: Tim Floyd

Officials: Jody Silvester, Michael Kitts, Raymond Perone
Technicals: None
Attendance: 29,231

63-57 (Sweet 16)

	1H	2H
North Carolina	28	35
California	26	31

NORTH CAROLINA	MIN	FG	3FG	FT	REB	A	ST	BL	PF	TP
Antawn Jamison	35	8-15	0-0	5-8	8	1	0	0	2	21
Vince Carter	29	5-10	2-4	2-2	3	0	1	0	2	14
Shammond Williams	33	4-8	4-7	0-0	2	3	1	0	0	12
Serge Zwikker	36	2-8	0-0	2-2	10	1	0	2	4	6
Ed Cota	33	1-4	1-1	2-5	2	8	2	0	1	5
Ademola Okulaja	30	2-4	1-2	0-0	6	1	1	0	3	5
Makhtar N'diaye	4	0-0	0-0	0-0	0	0	2	0	2	0
TOTALS	200	22-49	8-14	11-17	31	14	7	2	14	63
Percentages		44.9	57.1	64.7						

Coach: Dean Smith

CALIFORNIA	MIN	FG	3FG	FT	REB	A	ST	BL	PF	TP
Randy Duck	36	6-13	3-7	0-1	4	6	0	0	4	15
Sean Marks	17	4-7	3-4	0-0	2	0	0	0	1	11
Alfred Grigsby	29	3-10	0-0	4-4	7	0	1	0	3	10
Michael Stewart	23	4-8	0-0	1-3	7	0	0	2	2	9
Anwar McQueen	21	3-9	2-8	0-0	3	2	4	1	2	8
Tony Gonzalez	27	1-4	0-0	2-6	5	1	0	0	1	4
Prentice McGruder	36	0-4	0-4	0-0	6	7	2	1	2	0
Kenyon Jones	11	0-0	0-0	0-0	0	0	0	0	0	0
TOTALS	200	21-55	8-23	7-14	34	16	7	4	15	57
Percentages		38.2	34.8	50.0						

Coach: Ben Braun

Officials: James Burr, Mike Foote, Paul Janssen
Technicals: None
Attendance: 30,617

78-63 (Sweet 16)

	1H	2H
Louisville	31	47
Texas	37	26

LOUISVILLE	MIN	FG	3FG	FT	REB	A	ST	BL	PF	TP
Alvin Sims	37	9-13	1-2	6-9	8	0	3	0	2	25
Alex Sanders	35	7-11	2-2	1-2	3	1	0	0	1	17
Damion Dantzler	31	6-9	2-2	3-4	8	5	2	1	3	17
Nate Johnson	29	2-6	0-2	4-5	6	1	4	0	3	8
B.J. Flynn	29	1-5	0-2	4-8	4	5	0	0	4	6
DeJuan Wheat	21	1-8	1-5	0-0	1	5	1	0	1	3
Eric Johnson	11	1-5	0-1	0-0	1	0	0	0	2	2
Beau Zach Smith	5	0-0	0-0	0-2	2	0	0	0	2	0
Tony Williams	2	0-0	0-0	0-0	0	1	0	0	0	0
TOTALS	200	27-57	6-16	18-30	33	18	10	1	18	78
Percentages		47.4	37.5	60.0						

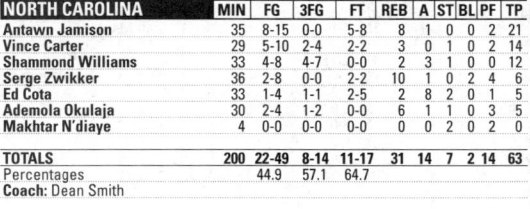

Coach: Denny Crum

TEXAS	MIN	FG	3FG	FT	REB	A	ST	BL	PF	TP
Gabe Muoneke	30	8-12	0-0	3-4	12	2	2	0	4	19
Al Coleman	24	5-11	1-5	2-2	1	0	0	0	1	13
Kris Clack	23	2-6	1-3	2-6	5	4	2	1	5	7
DeJuan Vasquez	16	3-5	1-2	0-2	1	0	2	0	3	7
Reggie Freeman	40	2-14	0-5	2-4	8	6	3	1	4	6
Sheldon Quarles	28	3-8	0-0	0-0	7	0	1	2	4	6
Brandy Perryman	21	1-5	1-4	0-0	2	1	0	0	0	3
Ira Clark	6	1-2	0-0	0-2	3	0	0	1	2	2
Dennis Jordan	12	0-2	0-0	0-0	2	1	0	0	1	0
TOTALS	200	25-65	4-19	9-20	41	14	10	5	24	63
Percentages		38.5	21.1	45.0						

Coach: Tom Penders

Officials: John Clougherty, Ed Hightower, Mike Wood
Technicals: None
Attendance: 30,617

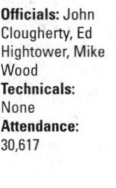

ANNUAL REVIEW

SWEET 16 — 85-82

	1H	2H	Final
Arizona	38	47	85
Kansas	36	46	82

ARIZONA	MIN	FG	3FG	FT	REB	A	ST	BL	PF	TP
Mike Bibby	35	7-11	2-4	5-6	2	5	2	0	1	21
Michael Dickerson	37	8-21	1-6	3-6	1	2	2	1	2	20
Miles Simon	27	7-12	1-2	2-2	3	1	1	0	3	17
A.J. Bramlett	30	6-14	0-0	0-1	12	0	1	0	4	12
Jason Terry	23	1-3	0-0	3-4	1	2	4	0	2	5
Eugene Edgerson	17	1-2	0-0	3-4	4	1	0	0	2	5
Bennett Davison	21	2-4	0-0	0-0	5	1	2	2	4	4
Donnell Harris	10	0-1	0-0	1-4	3	0	0	0	1	1
TOTALS	200	32-68	4-12	17-27	31	12	12	3	19	85
Percentages		47.1	33.3	63.0						

Coach: Lute Olson

KANSAS	MIN	FG	3FG	FT	REB	A	ST	BL	PF	TP
Paul Pierce	35	9-13	3-3	6-7	11	1	2	2	2	27
Raef LaFrentz	35	7-14	0-1	0-1	9	2	1	3	4	14
Ryan Robertson	18	5-10	4-7	0-0	3	2	0	2	4	14
Billy Thomas	19	5-15	3-10	0-0	3	0	0	0	1	13
Jacque Vaughn	37	3-10	0-4	2-4	3	8	0	0	4	8
Jerod Haase	14	1-3	0-0	0-0	1	2	1	0	0	2
T.J. Pugh	12	1-3	0-0	0-1	2	1	0	1	2	2
B.J. Williams	10	1-3	0-0	0-0	2	0	1	0	0	2
Scot Pollard	20	0-1	0-0	0-0	5	2	2	2	4	0
TOTALS	200	32-72	10-25	8-13	39	18	7	10	21	82
Percentages		44.4	40.0	61.5						

Coach: Roy Williams

Officials: An[illegible] Pattillo, Tim Higgins, Rick Hartzell **Technicals:** None **Attendance:** 17,647

SWEET 16 — 71-65

	1H	2H	Final
Providence	31	40	71
Chattanooga	24	41	65

PROVIDENCE	MIN	FG	3FG	FT	REB	A	ST	BL	PF	TP
Austin Croshere	32	6-11	3-6	4-7	5	2	0	3	4	19
God Shammgod	36	5-9	0-0	5-9	1	7	0	0	3	15
Jamel Thomas	33	4-9	3-4	1-2	5	2	0	1	1	12
Ruben Garces	26	5-7	0-0	2-4	8	0	2	4	4	12
Derrick Brown	33	3-13	1-5	2-4	8	0	0	0	0	9
Jason Murdock	25	2-3	0-1	0-0	6	2	1	0	2	4
Corey Wright	13	0-0	0-0	0-0	3	1	1	0	0	0
Ndongo N'diaye	2	0-1	0-0	0-0	0	0	0	0	0	0
TOTALS	200	25-53	7-16	14-26	36	14	4	8	14	71
Percentages		47.2	43.8	53.8						

Coach: Pete Gillen

CHATTANOOGA	MIN	FG	3FG	FT	REB	A	ST	BL	PF	TP
Johnny Taylor	34	10-21	0-3	2-8	9	1	1	0	4	22
Chris Mims	32	6-15	0-0	3-4	9	1	1	1	3	15
Willie Young	38	3-12	2-5	0-0	2	3	0	0	4	8
Marquis Collier	16	4-12	0-0	0-0	4	0	0	0	1	8
Isaac Conner	36	3-8	1-5	0-0	10	3	1	0	2	7
Wes Moore	28	1-2	1-1	0-0	3	3	0	0	2	3
David Phillips	15	1-4	0-1	0-0	5	1	0	0	4	2
Billy Hutchins	1	0-0	0-0	0-0	0	0	0	0	0	0
TOTALS	200	28-74	4-15	5-12	42	12	3	1	20	65
Percentages		37.8	26.7	41.7						

Coach: Mack McCarthy

Officials: Tom Harrington, Frank Bosone, Bob Garibaldi **Technicals:** Providence (Murdock), Chattanooga (Conner) **Attendance:** 17,647

ELITE 8 — 72-59

	1H	2H	Final
Kentucky	34	38	72
Utah	24	35	59

KENTUCKY	MIN	FG	3FG	FT	REB	A	ST	BL	PF	TP
Ron Mercer	38	10-17	1-2	0-0	3	2	1	0	2	21
Anthony Epps	33	2-5	2-5	9-10	3	6	1	0	0	15
Wayne Turner	35	6-12	0-1	0-3	3	4	5	0	2	12
Scott Padgett	21	4-10	1-6	2-2	5	2	0	1	2	11
Jared Prickett	28	4-8	0-1	0-2	10	4	1	0	3	8
Nazr Mohammed	18	2-6	0-0	1-2	7	0	0	1	0	5
Cameron Mills	14	0-1	0-0	0-0	1	1	0	0	3	0
Jamaal Magloire	13	0-0	0-0	0-0	1	0	0	0	2	0
TOTALS	200	28-59	4-15	12-19	33	19	8	2	14	72
Percentages		47.5	26.7	63.2						

Coach: Rick Pitino

UTAH	MIN	FG	3FG	FT	REB	A	ST	BL	PF	TP
Keith Van Horn	38	5-12	1-2	4-4	8	1	1	1	2	15
Michael Doleac	29	4-10	1-2	4-4	4	1	0	0	3	13
Andre Miller	33	4-9	1-4	2-2	3	5	1	0	1	11
Ben Caton	35	4-7	0-1	1-2	2	3	0	0	0	9
Drew Hansen	33	2-4	2-3	0-0	3	4	2	0	5	6
David Jackson	9	1-4	1-3	0-0	2	1	1	0	2	3
Hanno Mottola	13	1-4	0-0	0-0	1	2	0	0	2	2
Jeff Johnsen	7	0-0	0-0	0-0	2	0	1	0	2	0
Jordie McTavish	3	0-0	0-0	0-0	0	0	0	0	1	0
TOTALS	200	21-50	6-15	11-12	25	17	6	1	18	59
Percentages		42.0	40.0	91.7						

Coach: Rick Majerus

Officials: Ted Valentine, Tom O'Neill, Art McDonald **Technicals:** None **Attendance:** 18,543

ELITE 8 — 80-72

	1H	2H	Final
Minnesota	28	52	80
UCLA	33	39	72

MINNESOTA	MIN	FG	3FG	FT	REB	A	ST	BL	PF	TP
Quincy Lewis	17	5-9	0-1	7-7	3	2	1	2	2	17
Bobby Jackson	36	4-8	0-1	8-10	9	3	2	0	0	16
Sam Jacobson	24	7-16	0-6	0-0	2	0	0	0	4	14
Charles Thomas	21	6-11	1-3	1-2	5	2	3	0	1	14
Courtney James	31	4-6	0-0	4-6	6	4	0	0	2	12
John Thomas	20	3-6	0-0	1-1	7	0	0	0	4	7
Eric Harris	23	0-3	0-1	0-0	1	2	0	0	3	0
Trevor Winter	18	0-1	0-0	0-0	3	0	0	0	1	0
Miles Tarver	10	0-0	0-0	0-0	2	1	1	0	1	0
TOTALS	200	29-60	1-12	21-26	38	14	7	2	18	80
Percentages		48.3	8.3	80.8						

Coach: Clem Haskins

UCLA	MIN	FG	3FG	FT	REB	A	ST	BL	PF	TP
Charles O'Bannon	40	9-16	0-5	4-5	3	2	2	0	3	22
Toby Bailey	40	9-17	0-5	3-4	9	5	1	0	3	21
Kris Johnson	24	3-7	1-2	3-4	3	1	1	0	5	10
J.R. Henderson	34	4-8	0-0	1-2	4	3	3	0	4	9
Cameron Dollar	38	3-10	1-3	0-0	5	2	3	0	4	7
Brandon Loyd	8	1-1	1-1	0-0	0	0	0	0	0	3
Jelani McCoy	13	0-3	0-0	0-0	4	1	1	2	0	0
Bob Myers	3	0-0	0-0	0-0	0	0	0	0	0	0
TOTALS	200	29-62	3-16	11-15	28	14	11	2	19	72
Percentages		46.8	18.8	73.3						

Coach: Steve Lavin

Officials: Gerald Boudreaux, Rusty Herring, Ed Corbett **Technicals:** None **Attendance:** 31,930

ELITE 8 — 97-74

	1H	2H	Final
North Carolina	54	43	97
Louisville	33	41	74

NORTH CAROLINA	MIN	FG	3FG	FT	REB	A	ST	BL	PF	TP
Shammond Williams	36	6-13	4-7	6-7	2	6	2	0	2	22
Vince Carter	36	6-10	1-1	5-6	7	5	2	1	1	18
Antawn Jamison	32	6-11	0-0	3-3	6	1	1	0	3	15
Serge Zwikker	35	5-9	0-0	3-4	8	0	2	0	3	13
Ed Cota	29	4-6	0-1	5-6	3	9	3	0	2	13
Ademola Okulaja	24	5-7	1-1	0-0	5	0	2	0	2	11
Vasco Evtimov	1	1-2	0-1	0-0	0	0	0	0	1	2
Webb Tyndall	1	0-0	0-0	2-2	1	1	0	0	0	2
Makhtar N'diaye	2	0-0	0-0	1-2	1	0	0	0	1	1
Ryan Sullivan	2	0-0	0-0	0-0	0	0	0	0	0	0
Brad Frederick	1	0-1	0-1	0-0	0	0	0	0	1	0
Charlie McNairy	1	0-0	0-0	0-0	0	0	0	0	0	0
TOTALS	200	33-59	6-12	25-30	33	22	12	1	15	97
Percentages		55.9	50.0	83.3						

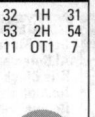

Coach: Dean Smith

LOUISVILLE	MIN	FG	3FG	FT	REB	A	ST	BL	PF	TP
Alex Sanders	34	8-15	3-5	1-2	6	2	2	0	2	20
B.J. Flynn	26	4-8	4-8	0-0	3	0	1	0	2	12
Nate Johnson	26	3-9	0-0	6-6	4	1	0	1	5	12
Alvin Sims	27	4-10	1-4	2-5	4	1	0	0	4	11
Damion Dantzler	30	4-7	0-1	2-3	9	4	1	0	4	10
DeJuan Wheat	32	2-11	2-11	0-0	2	8	1	0	1	6
Tony Williams	12	1-7	1-5	0-0	2	0	0	0	4	3
Eric Johnson	5	0-2	0-0	0-0	0	0	0	0	1	0
Beau Zach Smith	5	0-0	0-0	0-0	0	0	0	0	2	0
Matt Akridge	1	0-0	0-0	0-0	0	1	0	0	1	0
Craig Farmer	1	0-0	0-0	0-0	1	0	0	0	0	0
Jerry Johnson	1	0-0	0-0	0-0	0	0	0	0	0	0
TOTALS	200	26-69	11-34	11-16	31	17	5	1	26	74
Percentages		37.7	32.4	68.8						

Coach: Denny Crum

Officials: Curtis Shaw, John Cahill, Stan Reynolds **Technicals:** None **Attendance:** 30,230

ELITE 8 — 96-92

	1H	2H	OT1	Final
Arizona	32	53	11	96
Providence	31	54	7	92

ARIZONA	MIN	FG	3FG	FT	REB	A	ST	BL	PF	TP
Miles Simon	42	8-18	4-6	10-16	6	4	2	1	0	30
Mike Bibby	38	4-9	2-6	7-10	5	4	2	0	2	17
Bennett Davison	41	6-12	0-0	2-2	12	4	0	2	3	14
A.J. Bramlett	24	4-4	0-0	4-4	3	1	0	2	5	12
Jason Terry	27	4-8	0-3	3-4	3	5	1	0	1	11
Michael Dickerson	38	4-10	1-5	1-2	3	1	0	0	5	10
Donnell Harris	11	1-3	0-0	0-0	7	0	0	1	4	2
Eugene Edgerson	4	0-0	0-0	0-0	0	0	1	0	1	0
TOTALS	225	31-64	7-20	27-38	39	19	6	6	21	96
Percentages		48.4	35.0	71.1						

Coach: Lute Olson

PROVIDENCE	MIN	FG	3FG	FT	REB	A	ST	BL	PF	TP
God Shammgod	43	7-18	1-5	8-10	1	5	3	0	4	23
Jamel Thomas	41	9-29	3-8	2-3	11	1	3	0	4	23
Michael Brown	36	7-16	0-5	4-4	9	1	1	1	5	18
Ruben Garces	35	7-11	0-0	2-4	19	2	3	1	3	16
Austin Croshere	26	4-6	1-2	3-4	2	1	0	0	5	12
Corey Wright	26	0-4	0-3	0-0	2	6	3	0	3	0
Jason Murdock	12	0-2	0-0	0-0	2	0	0	0	3	0
Kofi Pointer	4	0-0	0-0	0-0	0	0	0	0	0	0
Ndongo N'diaye	2	0-0	0-0	0-0	0	0	1	0	0	0
TOTALS	225	34-86	5-23	19-25	46	16	14	2	27	92
Percentages		39.5	21.7	76.0						

Coach: Pete Gillen

Officials: Dick Paparo, Tom Rucker, David Day **Technicals:** Providence (Garces, Thomas, Murdock), Arizona (Harris) **Attendance:** 13,721

78-69

36	1H	31
42	2H	38

FINAL 4

KENTUCKY	MIN	FG	3FG	FT	REB	A	ST	BL	PF	TP
Ron Mercer	34	7-21	1-5	4-5	3	1	0	1	2	19
Anthony Epps	30	3-10	2-7	5-6	5	7	5	1	0	13
Cameron Mills	11	2-4	2-3	4-4	2	0	0	0	1	10
Scott Padgett	17	3-8	3-6	0-0	4	0	2	0	5	9
Wayne Turner	39	2-6	0-0	4-6	4	6	5	0	2	8
Jared Prickett	25	3-4	0-0	1-2	6	0	2	0	4	7
Nazr Mohammed	16	2-3	0-0	1-5	4	0	0	1	4	5
Allen Edwards	11	1-3	1-2	1-2	0	0	0	0	0	4
Derek Anderson	1	0-0	0-0	2-2	0	0	0	0	0	2
Jamaal Magloire	16	0-1	0-0	1-2	3	0	0	2	1	1
TOTALS	**200**	**23-60**	**9-23**	**23-34**	**31**	**14**	**14**	**5**	**19**	**78**
Percentages		38.3	39.1	67.6						
Coach: Rick Pitino										

MINNESOTA	MIN	FG	3FG	FT	REB	A	ST	BL	PF	TP
Bobby Jackson	35	8-18	2-5	5-6	6	4	2	0	3	23
Sam Jacobson	22	4-12	0-5	2-3	1	0	1	0	5	10
John Thomas	20	5-6	0-0	0-0	8	2	0	0	3	10
Courtney James	27	2-3	0-0	4-6	6	0	0	3	3	8
Eric Harris	29	2-3	1-1	0-0	5	2	0	1	1	5
Charles Thomas	14	2-7	0-1	1-2	4	1	0	0	5	5
Trevor Winter	12	2-3	0-0	0-0	2	0	0	0	1	4
Miles Tarver	22	1-2	0-0	0-2	9	1	1	0	3	2
Quincy Lewis	17	1-9	0-4	0-0	2	2	2	0	2	2
Russ Archambault	1	0-0	0-0	0-0	0	0	0	0	1	0
Aaron Stauber	1	0-1	0-0	0-0	0	0	0	0	0	0
TOTALS	**200**	**27-64**	**3-16**	**12-19**	**43**	**12**	**6**	**4**	**27**	**69**
Percentages		42.2	18.8	63.2						
Coach: Clem Haskins										

Officials: Frank Scagliotta, Dave Libbey, James Burr
Technicals: Minnesota (bench)
Attendance: 47,028

66-58

34	1H	31
32	2H	27

FINAL 4

ARIZONA	MIN	FG	3FG	FT	REB	A	ST	BL	PF	TP
Miles Simon	36	9-19	3-8	3-5	5	5	0	1	0	24
Mike Bibby	38	7-18	6-11	0-0	7	4	3	0	3	20
Donnell Harris	21	2-3	0-0	2-2	3	2	0	2	1	6
Michael Dickerson	27	1-10	1-4	2-3	6	0	0	0	2	5
Bennett Davison	10	1-2	0-0	2-4	2	0	0	1	4	4
Jason Terry	20	1-6	1-6	0-0	2	2	3	0	0	3
A.J. Bramlett	35	0-5	0-0	2-2	10	2	1	4	2	2
Eugene Edgerson	13	1-3	0-0	0-0	9	0	1	0	1	2
TOTALS	**200**	**22-66**	**11-29**	**11-16**	**44**	**15**	**8**	**8**	**13**	**66**
Percentages		33.3	37.9	68.8						
Coach: Lute Olson										

NORTH CAROLINA	MIN	FG	3FG	FT	REB	A	ST	BL	PF	TP
Vince Carter	36	8-15	1-7	4-5	6	2	4	0	4	21
Antawn Jamison	35	7-17	0-0	4-4	11	2	2	0	4	18
Serge Zwikker	32	4-12	0-0	0-0	9	0	0	1	3	8
Ed Cota	32	2-9	1-3	0-1	6	4	3	1	1	5
Shammond Williams	32	1-13	1-8	0-0	5	3	1	0	3	3
Ademola Okulaja	29	1-8	1-3	0-0	10	3	1	0	4	3
Makhtar N'diaye	4	0-0	0-0	0-0	0	0	0	0	1	0
TOTALS	**200**	**23-74**	**4-21**	**8-10**	**47**	**14**	**11**	**2**	**20**	**58**
Percentages		31.1	19.0	80.0						
Coach: Dean Smith										

Officials: John Clougherty, Andre Pattillo, Gerald Boudreaux
Technicals: None
Attendance: 47,028

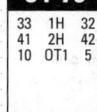

84-79

33	1H	32
41	2H	42
10	OT1	5

NCAA FINAL 1997

ARIZONA	MIN	FG	3FG	FT	REB	A	ST	BL	PF	TP
Miles Simon	40	8-18	0-2	14-17	3	1	0	0	1	30
Mike Bibby	38	5-12	3-5	6-6	9	4	3	0	1	19
Bennett Davison	29	3-9	0-0	3-3	7	0	0	0	2	9
Jason Terry	33	2-6	2-3	2-2	2	5	3	0	1	8
Donnell Harris	19	2-2	0-0	4-8	7	1	0	0	4	8
Michael Dickerson	24	1-8	1-3	2-2	4	0	0	0	0	5
A.J. Bramlett	27	1-3	0-0	1-1	6	1	1	2	5	3
Eugene Edgerson	15	0-0	0-0	2-2	5	0	0	0	2	2
TOTALS	**225**	**22-58**	**6-13**	**34-41**	**43**	**12**	**7**	**2**	**16**	**84**
Percentages		37.9	46.2	82.9						
Coach: Lute Olson										

KENTUCKY	MIN	FG	3FG	FT	REB	A	ST	BL	PF	TP
Scott Padgett	30	5-16	3-12	4-4	1	0	2	0	5	17
Ron Mercer	41	5-9	2-4	1-1	9	6	1	0	5	13
Nazr Mohammed	25	6-11	0-0	0-6	11	0	0	3	3	12
Cameron Mills	22	5-9	2-6	0-0	1	1	1	0	2	12
Anthony Epps	38	4-13	3-8	0-0	5	4	2	0	0	11
Wayne Turner	28	4-9	0-0	0-1	4	5	1	1	5	8
Jared Prickett	21	1-4	0-0	4-5	5	1	2	1	5	6
Jamaal Magloire	14	0-1	0-0	0-0	4	1	0	2	4	0
Allen Edwards	6	0-0	0-0	0-0	0	0	0	0	0	0
TOTALS	**225**	**30-72**	**10-30**	**9-17**	**40**	**18**	**9**	**7**	**29**	**79**
Percentages		41.7	33.3	52.9						
Coach: Rick Pitino										

Officials: Tim Higgins, Ted Valentine, Tom O'Neill
Technicals: None
Attendance: 47,028

National Invitation Tournament (NIT)

First round: Connecticut d. Iona 71-66, Bradley d. Drexel 66-53, Nevada d. Fresno State 97-86, Nebraska d. Washington 67-63, Florida State d. Syracuse 82-67, Michigan State d. George Washington 65-50, NC State d. Southwest Missouri St. 77-66, West Virginia d. Bowling Green 98-95, Notre Dame d. Oral Roberts 74-58, TCU d. UAB 85-62, Arkansas d. Northern Arizona 101-75, Pittsburgh d. New Orleans 82-63, Hawaii d. Oregon 71-61, UNLV d. Memphis 66-62, Michigan d. Miami 76-63, Oklahoma State d. Tulane 79-72

Second round: Arkansas d. Pittsburgh 76-71, Florida State d. Michigan State 68-63, West Virginia d. NC State 76-73, UNLV d. Hawaii 89-80, Connecticut d. Bradley 63-47, Notre Dame d. TCU 82-72, Nebraska d. Nevada 78-68, Michigan d. Oklahoma State 75-65

Third round: Florida State d. West Virginia 76-71, Arkansas d. UNLV 86-73, Michigan d. Notre Dame 67-66, Connecticut d. Nebraska 76-67

Semifinals: Florida State d. Connecticut 71-65, Michigan d. Arkansas 77-62

Championship: Michigan⊗ d. Florida State 82-73

Third place: Connecticut d. Arkansas 74-64

MVP: Robert Traylor, Michigan⊗

⊗ Team later sanctioned by NCAA

1997-98: Wildcat Strike

For the third straight Tournament, Wildcats prevailed. After Kentucky in 1996 and Arizona in '97, it was Kentucky again, this time making a champion of Rick Pitino's replacement, Tubby Smith. Kentucky came back from double-digit deficits in its last three games, climaxing with a 78-69 victory over Utah in the Final at the Alamodome in San Antonio. Jeff Sheppard (16 points and the Tournament's Most Outstanding Player), Scott Padgett, Jamaal Magloire and Nazr Mohammed all excelled for Smith. The comeback that may have better satisfied Kentucky fans was the 86-84 win after being 18 points down to Duke in the South Regional final, which helped ease the painful memory of Christian Laettner's 1992 game-winner.

Another first-year coach, Bill Guthridge (who replaced North Carolina legend Dean Smith), led the Tar Heels to a 34–4 record and a Final Four berth. UNC forward Antawn Jamison (22.2 ppg, 10.5 rpg) was named Naismith POY. Pacific's talented seven-footer, Michael Olowokandi (22.2 ppg, 11.2 rpg), was chosen as the first pick of the NBA draft by the Los Angeles Clippers.

Major Conference Standings

Am. East

	Conference			Overall		
	W	L	Pct	W	L	Pct
Delaware⊕	12	6	.667	20	10	.667
Boston U.	12	6	.667	19	11	.633
Hofstra	11	7	.611	19	12	.613
Vermont	11	7	.611	16	11	.593
Hartford	11	7	.611	15	12	.556
Drexel	10	8	.556	13	15	.464
Northeastern	9	9	.500	14	14	.500
New Hampshire	6	12	.333	10	17	.370
Towson	4	14	.222	8	20	.286
Maine	4	14	.222	7	20	.259

Tournament: **Delaware d. Boston U. 66-58**
Tournament MOP: **Darryl Presley**, Delaware

ACC

	Conference			Overall		
	W	L	Pct	W	L	Pct
Duke○	15	1	.938	32	4	.889
North Carolina⊕	13	3	.813	34	4	.895
Maryland○	10	6	.625	21	11	.656
Clemson○	7	9	.438	18	14	.563
Wake Forest□	7	9	.438	16	14	.533
Georgia Tech□	6	10	.375	19	14	.576
Florida State○	6	10	.375	18	14	.563
NC State□	5	11	.313	17	15	.531
Virginia	3	13	.188	11	19	.367

Tournament: **North Carolina d. Duke 83-68**
Tournament MVP: **Antawn Jamison**, North Carolina

Atlantic 10

	Conference			Overall		
	W	L	Pct	W	L	Pct
East						
Temple○	13	3	.813	21	9	.700
Rhode Island○	12	4	.750	25	9	.735
Massachusetts○	12	4	.750	21	11	.656
St. Bonaventure□	6	10	.375	17	15	.531
Saint Joseph's	3	13	.188	11	17	.393
Fordham	2	14	.125	6	21	.222
West						
Xavier⊕	11	5	.688	22	8	.733
George Washington○	11	5	.688	24	9	.727
Dayton□	11	5	.688	21	12	.636
Virginia Tech	5	11	.313	10	17	.370
Duquesne	5	11	.313	11	19	.367
La Salle	5	11	.313	9	18	.333

Tournament: **Xavier d. George Washington 77-63**
Tournament MOP: **James Posey**, Xavier

Big East

	Conference			Overall		
	W	L	Pct	W	L	Pct
Big East 7						
Syracuse○	12	6	.667	26	9	.743
Miami (FL)○	11	7	.611	18	10	.643
Seton Hall□	9	9	.500	15	15	.500
Providence	7	11	.389	13	16	.448
Georgetown□	6	12	.333	16	15	.516
Rutgers	6	12	.333	14	15	.483
Pittsburgh	6	12	.333	11	16	.407
Big East 6						
Connecticut⊕	15	3	.833	32	5	.865
St. John's○	13	5	.722	22	10	.688
West Virginia○	11	7	.611	24	9	.727
Villanova	8	10	.444	12	17	.414
Notre Dame	7	11	.389	13	14	.481
Boston College	6	12	.333	15	16	.484

Tournament: **Connecticut d. Syracuse 69-64**
Tournament MVP: **Khalid El-Amin**, Connecticut

Big Sky

	Conference			Overall		
	W	L	Pct	W	L	Pct
Northern Arizona⊕	13	3	.813	21	8	.724
Weber State	12	4	.750	14	13	.519
Eastern Washington	10	6	.625	16	11	.593
Portland State	10	6	.625	15	12	.556
Montana State	9	7	.563	19	11	.633
Montana	9	7	.563	16	14	.533
Cal St. Northridge	7	9	.438	12	16	.429
Idaho State	2	14	.125	6	20	.231
Cal State Sacramento	0	16	.000	1	25	.038

Tournament: **Northern Arizona d. Montana State 77-50**
Tournament MVP: **Dan McClintock**, Northern Arizona

Big South

	Conference			Overall		
	W	L	Pct	W	L	Pct
UNC Asheville	11	1	.917	19	9	.679
Radford⊕	10	2	.833	20	10	.667
UMBC	6	6	.500	14	14	.500
Liberty	5	7	.417	11	17	.393
Coastal Carolina	4	8	.333	8	19	.296
Winthrop	4	8	.333	7	20	.259
Charleston Southern	2	10	.167	5	22	.185

Tournament: **Radford d. UNC Asheville 63-61**
Tournament MVP: **Kevin Robinson**, Radford

Big Ten

	Conference			Overall		
	W	L	Pct	W	L	Pct
Michigan State○	13	3	.813	22	8	.733
Illinois○	13	3	.813	23	10	.697
Purdue○	12	4	.750	28	8	.778
Michigan⊕✪	11	5	.688	25	9	.714
Iowa□	9	7	.563	20	11	.645
Indiana○	9	7	.563	20	12	.625
Penn State□	8	8	.500	19	13	.594
Minnesota□✪	6	10	.375	20	15	.571
Wisconsin	3	13	.188	12	19	.387
Northwestern	3	13	.188	10	17	.370
Ohio State	1	15	.063	8	22	.267

Tournament: **Michigan d. Purdue 76-67**
Tournament MOP: **Robert Traylor**, Michigan

Big 12

	Conference			Overall		
	W	L	Pct	W	L	Pct
Kansas⊕	15	1	.938	35	4	.897
Oklahoma State○	11	5	.688	22	7	.759
Oklahoma○	11	5	.688	22	11	.667
Nebraska○	10	6	.625	20	12	.625
Missouri□	8	8	.500	17	15	.531
Baylor	8	8	.500	14	14	.500
Kansas State□	7	9	.438	17	12	.586
Colorado	7	9	.438	13	14	.481
Texas Tech	7	9	.438	13	14	.481
Texas	6	10	.375	14	17	.452
Iowa State	5	11	.313	12	18	.400
Texas A&M	1	15	.063	7	20	.259

Tournament: **Kansas d. Oklahoma 72-58**
Tournament MOP: **Paul Pierce**, Kansas

Big West

	Conference			Overall		
	W	L	Pct	W	L	Pct
Eastern						
Utah State⊕	13	3	.813	25	8	.758
Nevada	11	5	.688	16	12	.571
Boise State	9	7	.563	17	13	.567
Idaho	9	7	.563	15	12	.556
New Mexico State✪	8	8	.500	18	12	.600
North Texas	4	12	.250	5	21	.192
Western						
Pacific□	14	2	.875	23	10	.697
Cal Poly	7	9	.438	14	14	.500
Cal State Fullerton	6	10	.375	12	16	.429
UC Irvine	6	10	.375	9	18	.333
Long Beach State	5	11	.313	10	19	.345
UC Santa Barbara	4	12	.250	7	19	.269

Tournament: **Utah State d. Pacific 78-63**
Tournament MVP: **Marcus Saxon**, Utah State

Colonial Athletic

	Conference			Overall		
	W	L	Pct	W	L	Pct
William and Mary	13	3	.813	20	7	.741
UNC Wilmington□	13	3	.813	20	11	.645
Richmond⊕	12	4	.750	23	8	.742
Old Dominion	8	8	.500	12	16	.429
James Madison	6	10	.375	11	16	.407
George Mason	6	10	.375	9	18	.333
East Carolina	5	11	.313	10	17	.370
American	5	11	.313	9	19	.321
VCU	4	12	.250	9	19	.321

Tournament: **Richmond d. UNC Wilmington 79-64**
Tournament MVP: **Daryl Oliver**, Richmond

C-USA

	Conference			Overall		
	W	L	Pct	W	L	Pct
American						
Cincinnati⊕	14	2	.875	27	6	.818
Charlotte○	13	3	.813	20	11	.645
Saint Louis○	11	5	.688	22	11	.667
Marquette□	8	8	.500	20	11	.645
Louisville	5	11	.313	12	20	.375
DePaul	3	13	.188	7	23	.233
National						
Memphis□	12	4	.750	17	12	.586
UAB□	10	6	.625	21	12	.636
Southern Miss□	9	7	.563	22	11	.667
South Florida	7	9	.438	17	13	.567
Houston	2	14	.125	9	20	.310
Tulane	2	14	.125	7	22	.241

Tournament: **Cincinnati d. Charlotte 71-57**
Tournament MVP: **Kenyon Martin**, Cincinnati

Ivy

	Conference			Overall		
	W	L	Pct	W	L	Pct
Princeton⊕	14	0	1.000	27	2	.931
Penn	10	4	.714	17	12	.586
Yale	7	7	.500	12	14	.462
Harvard	6	8	.429	13	13	.500
Columbia	6	8	.429	11	15	.423
Cornell	6	8	.429	9	17	.346
Dartmouth	4	10	.286	7	19	.269
Brown	3	11	.214	6	20	.231

⊕ Automatic NCAA Tournament bid ○ At-large NCAA Tournament bid □ NIT appearance ✪ Team record doesn't reflect games forfeited or vacated. For adjusted record, see p. 521.

MAAC

	Conference			Overall		
	W	L	PCT	W	L	PCT
Iona⊕	15	3	.833	27	6	.818
Rider□	12	6	.667	18	10	.643
Siena	10	8	.556	17	12	.586
Niagara	10	8	.556	14	13	.519
Canisius	9	9	.500	13	14	.481
Loyola (MD)	9	9	.500	12	16	.429
Fairfield	7	11	.389	12	15	.444
Manhattan	7	11	.389	12	17	.414
Marist	7	11	.389	11	17	.393
Saint Peter's	4	14	.222	8	19	.296

Tournament: **Iona d. Siena 90-75**
Tournament MVP: **John McDonald**, Iona

MID-AMERICAN

	Conference			Overall		
	W	L	PCT	W	L	PCT
EAST						
Akron	13	5	.722	17	10	.630
Miami (OH)	9	9	.500	17	12	.586
Kent State	9	9	.500	13	17	.433
Marshall	7	11	.389	11	16	.407
Bowling Green	7	11	.389	10	16	.385
Ohio	3	15	.167	5	21	.192
WEST						
Ball State□	14	4	.778	21	8	.724
Western Michigan○	14	4	.778	21	8	.724
Eastern Michigan⊕	13	5	.722	20	10	.667
Toledo	10	8	.556	15	12	.556
Northern Illinois	6	12	.333	10	16	.385
Central Michigan	3	15	.167	5	21	.192

Tournament: **Eastern Michigan d. Miami (OH) 92-77**
Tournament MVP: **Earl Boykins**, Eastern Michigan

MID-CONTINENT

	Conference			Overall		
	W	L	PCT	W	L	PCT
Valparaiso⊕	13	3	.813	23	10	.697
Oral Roberts	12	4	.750	19	12	.613
Youngstown State	11	5	.688	20	9	.690
Western Illinois	11	5	.688	16	11	.593
Buffalo	9	7	.563	15	13	.536
UMKC	7	9	.438	9	18	.333
Southern Utah	4	12	.250	7	20	.259
Northeastern Illinois	3	13	.188	6	19	.240
Chicago State	2	14	.125	2	25	.074

Tournament: **Valparaiso d. Youngstown State 67-48**
Tournament MVP: **Bryce Drew**, Valparaiso

MEAC

	Conference			Overall		
	W	L	PCT	W	L	PCT
Coppin State	17	1	.944	21	8	.724
South Carolina St.⊕	16	2	.889	22	8	.733
Hampton	11	7	.611	14	12	.538
Morgan State	11	7	.611	12	16	.429
Florida A&M	8	10	.444	11	17	.393
Delaware State	7	11	.389	9	18	.333
UMES	7	11	.389	9	18	.333
NC A&T	7	11	.389	8	19	.296
Howard	5	13	.278	8	20	.286
Bethune-Cookman	1	17	.056	1	26	.037
Norfolk State	-	-		6	21	.222

Tournament: **South Carolina St. d. Coppin State 66-61**
Tournament MOP: **Roderick Blakney**, South Carolina St.

MCC

	Conference			Overall		
	W	L	PCT	W	L	PCT
Detroit○	12	2	.857	25	6	.806
Illinois-Chicago○	12	2	.857	22	6	.786
Butler⊕	8	6	.571	22	11	.667
Wisconsin-Green Bay	7	7	.500	17	12	.586
Loyola-Chicago	6	8	.429	15	15	.500
Cleveland State	6	8	.429	12	15	.444
Wright State	3	11	.214	10	18	.357
Wisconsin-Milwaukee	2	12	.143	3	24	.111

Tournament: **Butler d. Wisconsin-Green Bay 70-51**
Tournament MVP: **Jon Neuhouser**, Butler

MISSOURI VALLEY

	Conference			Overall		
	W	L	PCT	W	L	PCT
Illinois State⊕	16	2	.889	25	6	.806
Creighton□	12	6	.667	18	10	.643
Wichita State	11	7	.611	16	15	.516
Missouri State	11	7	.611	16	16	.500
Indiana State	10	8	.556	16	11	.593
Bradley	9	9	.500	15	14	.517
Evansville	9	9	.500	15	15	.500
Southern Illinois	8	10	.444	14	16	.467
Northern Iowa	4	14	.222	10	17	.370
Drake	0	18	.000	3	24	.111

Tournament: **Illinois State d. Missouri State 84-74**
Tournament MOP: **Dan Muller**, Illinois State

NORTHEAST

	Conference			Overall		
	W	L	PCT	W	L	PCT
Long Island□	14	2	.875	21	11	.656
Fairleigh Dickinson⊕	13	3	.813	23	7	.767
Saint Francis (PA)	10	6	.625	17	10	.630
St. Francis (NY)	10	6	.625	15	12	.556
Mount St. Mary's	8	8	.500	13	15	.464
Wagner	7	9	.438	13	16	.448
Robert Morris	4	12	.250	8	19	.296
Central Conn. State	3	13	.188	4	22	.154
Monmouth	3	13	.188	4	23	.148

Tournament: **Fairleigh Dickinson d. Long Island 105-91**
Tournament MVP: **Rahshon Turner**, Fairleigh Dickinson

OHIO VALLEY

	Conference			Overall		
	W	L	PCT	W	L	PCT
Murray State⊕	16	2	.889	29	4	.879
Eastern Illinois	13	5	.722	16	11	.593
Middle Tenn. State	12	6	.667	19	9	.679
Austin Peay	11	7	.611	17	11	.607
SE Missouri State	10	8	.556	14	13	.519
Tennessee State	8	10	.444	13	16	.448
Eastern Kentucky	8	10	.444	10	17	.370
Tennessee Tech	5	13	.278	9	21	.300
Tennessee-Martin	5	13	.278	7	20	.259
Morehead State	2	16	.111	3	23	.115

Tournament: **Murray State d. Tennessee State 92-69**
Tournament MVP: **Chad Townsend**, Murray State

PAC-10

	Conference			Overall		
	W	L	PCT	W	L	PCT
Arizona⊕	17	1	.944	30	5	.857
Stanford○	15	3	.833	30	5	.857
UCLA○	12	6	.667	24	9	.727
Washington○	11	7	.611	20	10	.667
Arizona State□	8	10	.444	18	14	.563
Oregon	8	10	.444	13	14	.481
California	8	10	.444	12	15	.444
Southern California	5	13	.278	9	19	.321
Oregon State	3	15	.167	13	17	.433
Washington State	3	15	.167	10	19	.345

PATRIOT

	Conference			Overall		
	W	L	PCT	W	L	PCT
Lafayette	10	2	.833	19	9	.679
Navy⊕	10	2	.833	19	11	.633
Bucknell	8	4	.667	13	15	.464
Colgate	5	7	.417	10	18	.357
Lehigh	4	8	.333	10	17	.370
Holy Cross	3	9	.250	7	20	.259
Army	2	10	.167	8	19	.296

Tournament: **Navy d. Lafayette 93-85**
Tournament MVP: **Skip Victor**, Navy

SEC

	Conference			Overall		
	W	L	PCT	W	L	PCT
EASTERN						
Kentucky⊕	14	2	.875	35	4	.897
South Carolina○	11	5	.688	23	8	.742
Tennessee○	9	7	.563	20	9	.690
Vanderbilt□	7	9	.438	20	13	.606
Georgia□	7	9	.438	20	15	.571
Florida□	6	10	.375	14	15	.483
WESTERN						
Mississippi○	12	4	.750	22	7	.759
Arkansas○	11	5	.688	24	9	.727
Auburn□	7	9	.438	16	14	.533
Alabama	6	10	.375	15	16	.484
Mississippi State	4	12	.250	15	15	.500
LSU	2	14	.125	9	18	.333

Tournament: **Kentucky d. South Carolina 86-56**
Tournament MVP: **Wayne Turner**, Kentucky

SOUTHERN

	Conference			Overall		
	W	L	PCT	W	L	PCT
NORTH						
Appalachian State	13	2	.867	21	8	.724
Davidson⊕	13	2	.867	20	10	.667
VMI	8	7	.533	14	13	.519
Western Carolina	6	9	.400	12	15	.444
East Tenn. State	6	9	.400	11	16	.407
UNC Greensboro	6	9	.400	9	19	.321
SOUTH						
Chattanooga	7	7	.500	13	15	.464
The Citadel	6	8	.429	15	13	.536
Wofford	6	8	.429	9	18	.333
Furman	5	9	.357	9	20	.310
Georgia Southern	4	10	.286	10	18	.357

Tournament: **Davidson d. Appalachian State 66-62**
Tournament MOP: **Ben Ebong**, Davidson

SOUTHLAND

	Conference			Overall		
	W	L	PCT	W	L	PCT
Nicholls State⊕	15	1	.938	19	10	.655
Texas State	10	6	.625	17	11	.607
UTSA	10	6	.625	16	11	.593
Northwestern St. (LA)	10	6	.625	13	14	.481
Texas-Arlington	8	8	.500	13	16	.448
UL-Monroe	8	8	.500	13	16	.448
Sam Houston State	7	9	.438	9	17	.346
Stephen F. Austin	6	10	.375	10	16	.385
McNeese State	4	12	.250	7	19	.269
Southeastern La.	2	14	.125	6	20	.231

Tournament: **Nicholls State d. Texas-Arlington 84-81**
Tournament MVP: **Donald Harris**, Texas-Arlington

SWAC

	Conference			Overall		
	W	L	PCT	W	L	PCT
Texas Southern	12	4	.750	15	16	.484
Jackson State	11	5	.688	14	13	.519
Grambling	10	6	.625	16	12	.571
Southern U.	10	6	.625	14	13	.519
Alcorn State	8	8	.500	12	15	.444
Prairie View A&M⊕	6	10	.375	13	17	.433
Alabama State	6	10	.375	11	17	.393
Miss. Valley State	6	10	.375	6	21	.222
Arkansas-Pine Bluff	3	13	.188	4	23	.148

Tournament: **Prairie View A&M d. Texas Southern 59-57**
Tournament MVP: **Tamarron Sharpe**, Prairie View A&M

SUN BELT

	Conference			Overall		
	W	L	PCT	W	L	PCT
South Alabama⊕	14	4	.778	21	7	.750
Arkansas State	14	4	.778	20	9	.690
UL-Lafayette	12	6	.667	18	13	.581
Arkansas-Little Rock	10	8	.556	15	13	.536
New Orleans	9	9	.500	15	12	.556
Louisiana Tech	9	9	.500	12	15	.444
Lamar	7	11	.389	15	14	.517
Western Kentucky	6	12	.333	10	19	.345
Jacksonville	6	12	.333	8	19	.296
Texas-Pan American	3	15	.167	3	24	.111

Tournament: **South Alabama d. UL-Lafayette 62-59**
Tournament MOP: **Toby Madison**, South Alabama

TAAC

	Conference			Overall		
	W	L	PCT	W	L	PCT
EAST						
Charleston⊕	14	2	.875	24	6	.800
Florida International	13	3	.813	21	8	.724
Central Florida	11	5	.688	17	11	.607
Stetson	8	8	.500	11	15	.423
Florida Atlantic	5	11	.313	5	22	.185
Campbell	4	12	.250	10	17	.370
WEST						
Georgia State	11	5	.688	16	12	.571
Samford	9	7	.563	14	13	.519
Centenary	8	8	.500	10	20	.333
Jacksonville State	6	10	.375	12	14	.462
Troy	5	11	.313	7	20	.259
Mercer	2	14	.125	5	21	.192

Tournament: **Charleston d. Florida International 72-63**
Tournament MVP: **Sedric Webber**, Charleston

WEST COAST

	Conference			Overall		
	W	L	PCT	W	L	PCT
Gonzaga□	10	4	.714	24	10	.706
Pepperdine	9	5	.643	17	10	.630
Santa Clara	8	6	.571	18	10	.643
San Francisco⊕	7	7	.500	19	11	.633
Portland	7	7	.500	14	13	.519
Saint Mary's (CA)	7	7	.500	12	15	.444
San Diego	5	9	.357	14	14	.500
Loyola Marymount	3	11	.214	7	20	.259

Tournament: **San Francisco d. Gonzaga 80-67**
Tournament MVP: **Hakeem Ward**, San Francisco

WAC

	Conference			Overall		
	W	L	PCT	W	L	PCT
PACIFIC						
TCU○	14	0	1.000	27	6	.818
Fresno State□	10	4	.714	21	13	.618
Tulsa	9	5	.643	19	12	.613
Hawaii□	8	6	.571	21	9	.700
SMU	6	8	.429	18	10	.643
San Diego State	5	9	.357	13	15	.464
Rice	3	11	.214	6	22	.214
San Jose State	1	13	.071	3	23	.115
MOUNTAIN						
Utah○	12	2	.857	30	4	.882
New Mexico○	11	3	.786	24	8	.750
Wyoming□	9	5	.643	19	9	.679
Colorado State□	8	6	.571	20	9	.690
UNLV⊕	7	7	.500	20	13	.606
BYU	4	10	.286	9	21	.300
UTEP	3	11	.214	12	14	.462
Air Force	2	12	.143	10	16	.385

Tournament: **UNLV d. New Mexico 56-51**
Tournament MVP: **Kenny Thomas**, New Mexico

INDIVIDUAL LEADERS—SEASON

SCORING	CL	POS	G	FG	3FG	FT	PTS	PPG
1 **Charles Jones**, Long Island	SR	G	30	326	116	101	869	**29.0**
2 **Earl Boykins**, Eastern Michigan	SR	G	29	266	85	129	746	**25.7**
3 **Lee Nailon**, TCU	JR	F	32	329	1	137	796	**24.9**
4 **Brett Eppehimer**, Lehigh	JR	G	27	195	92	185	667	**24.7**
5 **Cory Carr**, Texas Tech	SR	G	27	209	67	143	628	**23.3**
6 **Pat Garrity**, Notre Dame	SR	F	27	214	40	159	627	**23.2**
7 **Mike Powell**, Loyola (MD)	SR	G	28	197	46	207	647	**23.1**
8 **Bonzi Wells**, Ball State	SR	G	29	238	53	133	662	**22.8**
9 **Xavier Singletary**, Howard	SO	G	23	158	71	127	514	**22.3**
10 **Michael Olowokandi**, Pacific	SR	C	33	310	0	114	734	**22.2**

FIELD GOAL PCT	CL	POS	G	FG	FGA	PCT
1 **Todd MacCulloch**, Washington	JR	C	30	225	346	**65.0**
2 **Ryan Moss**, Arkansas-Little Rock	JR	F	28	167	257	**65.0**
3 **Jarrett Stephens**, Penn State	JR	F	31	165	258	**64.0**
4 **Isaac Spencer**, Murray State	SO	F	33	171	270	**63.3**
5 **Brad Miller**, Purdue	SR	F	34	191	302	**63.2**

MINIMUM: 5 MADE PER GAME

THREE-PT FG PER GAME	CL	POS	G	3FG	3PG
1 **Curtis Staples**, Virginia	SR	G	30	130	**4.3**
2 **Cedric Foster**, Miss. Valley State	SR	G	22	86	**3.9**
3 **Charles Jones**, Long Island	SR	G	30	116	**3.9**
4 **Demond Mallet**, McNeese State	SO	G	26	94	**3.6**
5 **Cory Johnson**, SE Missouri State	JR	G	27	95	**3.5**

THREE-PT FG PCT	CL	POS	G	3FG	3FGA	PCT
1 **Jim Cantamessa**, Siena	SO	F	29	66	117	**56.4**
2 **Coby Turner**, Dayton	JR	F	33	61	118	**51.7**
3 **Royce Olney**, New Mexico	SR	G	25	80	156	**51.3**
4 **Mike Beam**, Harvard	JR	G	25	41	80	**51.3**
5 **Kenyan Weaks**, Florida	SO	G	26	61	120	**50.8**

MINIMUM: 1.5 MADE PER GAME

FREE THROW PCT	CL	POS	G	FT	FTA	PCT
1 **Matt Sundblad**, Lamar	JR	G	27	96	104	**92.3**
2 **Louis Bullock**, Michigan	JR	G	34	123	135	**91.1**
3 **Shammond Williams**, North Carolina	SR	G	38	133	146	**91.1**
4 **Kevin Ault**, Missouri State	SO	G	32	99	110	**90.0**
Clifton Ellis, Texas State	JR	G	28	72	80	**90.0**

MINIMUM: 2.5 MADE PER GAME

ASSISTS PER GAME	CL	POS	G	AST	APG
1 **Ahlon Lewis**, Arizona State	SR	G	32	294	**9.2**
2 **Chico Fletcher**, Arkansas State	SO	G	29	240	**8.3**
3 **Sean Colson**, UNC Charlotte	SR	G	29	231	**8.0**
4 **Ed Cota**, North Carolina	SO	G	37	274	**7.4**
5 **Charles Jones**, Long Island	SR	G	30	221	**7.4**
6 **Anthony Carter**, Hawaii	SR	G	29	212	**7.3**
7 **Rafer Alston**, Fresno State	JR	G	33	240	**7.3**
8 **Mateen Cleaves**, Michigan State	SO	G	30	217	**7.2**
9 **Craig Claxton**, Hofstra	SO	G	31	224	**7.2**
10 **Michael Wheeler**, Wagner	JR	G	28	197	**7.0**

REBOUNDS PER GAME	CL	POS	G	REB	RPG
1 **Ryan Perryman**, Dayton	SR	F	33	412	**12.5**
2 **Eric Taylor**, Saint Francis (PA)	SR	F/C	27	321	**11.9**
3 **Raef LaFrentz**, Kansas	SR	F	30	342	**11.4**
4 **Tremaine Fowlkes**, Fresno State	JR	F	32	359	**11.2**
5 **Michael Olowokandi**, Pacific	SR	C	33	369	**11.2**
6 **T.J. Lux**, Northern Illinois	JR	C	26	289	**11.1**
7 **Thad Burton**, Wright State	SR	F/C	28	305	**10.9**
8 **Allen Ledbetter**, Maine	JR	C	27	294	**10.9**
9 **Rahshon Turner**, Fairleigh Dickinson	SR	F	29	313	**10.8**
10 **Kenyon Ross**, Miss. Valley State	SR	F	27	291	**10.8**

BLOCKED SHOTS PER GAME	CL	POS	G	BLK	BPG
1 **Jerome James**, Florida A&M	SR	C	27	125	**4.6**
2 **Calvin Booth**, Penn State	JR	C	32	140	**4.4**
3 **Alvin Jones**, Georgia Tech	FR	C	33	141	**4.3**
4 **Etan Thomas**, Syracuse	SO	C	35	138	**3.9**
5 **Brian Skinner**, Baylor	SR	F/C	28	98	**3.5**

STEALS PER GAME	CL	POS	G	STL	SPG
1 **Bonzi Wells**, Ball State	SR	G	29	103	**3.6**
2 **Pepe Sanchez**, Temple	SO	G	27	93	**3.4**
3 **Willie Coleman**, DePaul	JR	G	30	100	**3.3**
4 **J.R. Camel**, Montana	JR	G	29	90	**3.1**
5 **Jason Rowe**, Loyola (MD)	SO	G	28	86	**3.1**

INDIVIDUAL LEADERS—GAME

POINTS	CL	POS	OPP	DATE	PTS
1 **Charles Jones**, Long Island	SR	G	Medgar Evers	N26	**53**
Lee Nailon, TCU	JR	F	Miss. Valley State	D12	**53**
3 **Roderic Hall**, UTSA	SR	G	Maine	D6	**52**
4 **Mike Jones**, TCU	SR	G	Delaware State	D3	**51**
5 **Lee Nailon**, TCU	JR	F	Hawaii	F12	**46**

THREE-PT FG MADE	CL	POS	OPP	DATE	3FG
1 **Melvin Levett**, Cincinnati	JR	G	Eastern Kentucky	D20	**10**
Mike Martinho, Buffalo	JR	G	Rochester	F3	**10**
3 **Wes Moore**, Chattanooga	JR	G	Wofford	N15	**9**
Jarmica Reese, Air Force	SR	G	Doane	N22	**9**
Mark Poag, Old Dominion	JR	F	VMI	N25	**9**
Derrick Dial, Eastern Michigan	SR	G	Marshall	J5	**9**
Tyson Wheeler, Rhode Island	SR	G	Saint Joseph's	J6	**9**
Joe Sibbitt, Austin Peay	JR	G	Tennessee-Martin	J24	**9**
Davanzio Carter, Stephen F. Austin	SR	G/F	Southeastern La.	J24	**9**
Jim Peterson, Ohio	SR	G	Central Michigan	F5	**9**
Curtis Staples, Virginia	SR	G	Georgia Tech	F14	**9**
Mike Warhank, Montana	SO	G	Eastern Washington	F21	**9**
Bryce Drew, Valparaiso	SR	G	Western Illinois	F25	**9**

ASSISTS	CL	POS	OPP	DATE	AST
1 **Michael Johnson**, Oklahoma	JR	G	North Texas	D22	**18**
Sean Colson, Charlotte	SR	G	Houston	F28	**18**
3 **Jason Williams**, Florida	SO	G	Duquesne	D3	**17**
Rafer Alston, Fresno State	JR	G	North Florida	D22	**17**
5 **Ahlon Lewis**, Arizona State	SR	G	Northern Arizona	D3	**16**
Mick Wheeler, Wagner	JR	G	Fairleigh Dickinson	F21	**16**
7 **Ishua Benjamin**, NC State	SR	G	Sam Houston State	D18	**15**
Rafer Alston, Fresno State	JR	G	TCU	F5	**15**
Chico Fletcher, Arkansas State	SO	G	Jacksonville	F19	**15**
Michael Lewis, Indiana	SO	G	Iowa	F28	**15**
Earl Boykins, Eastern Michigan	SR	G	Toledo	F28	**15**

REBOUNDS	CL	POS	OPP	DATE	REB
1 **Nick Davis**, Arkansas	SR	C	Jackson State	N21	**23**
Kenyon Martin, Cincinnati	SO	C	DePaul	F21	**23**
3 **Thad Burton**, Wright State	SR	F/C	Old Dominion	N18	**22**
Eric Taylor, Saint Francis (PA)	SR	F/C	Norfolk State	N18	**22**
E. Adekunle, Saint Francis (PA)	SR	F	Long Island	F16	**22**

BLOCKED SHOTS	CL	POS	OPP	DATE	BLK
1 **Alvin Jones**, Georgia Tech	FR	C	Winthrop	N24	**11**
2 **Rashon Turner**, Fairleigh Dickinson	SR	F	Hartford	N22	**10**
Brian Skinner, Baylor	SR	F/C	Eastern Washington	N29	**10**
Calvin Booth, Penn State	JR	C	George Mason	D8	**10**
Kenyon Martin, Cincinnati	SO	C	DePaul	F21	**10**

STEALS	CL	POS	OPP	DATE	STL
1 **Ali Ton**, Davidson	JR	G	Tufts	N29	**11**
2 **Todd Burgan**, Syracuse	SR	F	Colgate	N30	**10**
Antrone Lee, Long Beach State	SO	F	UC Irvine	F19	**10**
4 **Bonzi Wells**, Ball State	SR	G	Akron	J3	**9**
Bonzi Wells, Ball State	SR	G	Kent State	J5	**9**
James Posey, Xavier	JR	F	Fordham	J10	**9**
John Linehan, Providence	FR	G	Pittsburgh	J10	**9**
Bonzi Wells, Ball State	SR	G	Eastern Michigan	F11	**9**
Reggie Crenshaw, Austin Peay	SR	F	Tennessee Tech	F14	**9**
Mateen Cleaves, Michigan State	SO	G	Minnesota	F14	**9**
Willie Coleman, DePaul	JR	G	Louisville	F28	**9**
Bennett Davison, Arizona	SR	F	Stanford	F28	**9**

TEAM LEADERS—SEASON

WIN-LOSS PCT	W	L	PCT
1 **Princeton**	27	2	**.931**
2 **Kansas**	35	4	**.897**
2 **Kentucky**	35	4	**.897**
4 **North Carolina**	34	4	**.895**
5 **Duke**	32	4	**.889**

SCORING OFFENSE	G	W-L	PTS	PPG
1 **TCU**	33	27-6	3,209	**97.2**
2 **Long Island**	32	21-11	3,102	**96.9**
3 **Arizona**	35	30-5	3,177	**90.8**
4 **Florida International**	29	21-8	2,533	**87.3**
5 **Murray State**	33	29-4	2,862	**86.7**

SCORING MARGIN	G	W-L	PPG	OPP PPG	MAR
1 **Duke**	36	32-4	85.6	64.1	**21.5**
2 **TCU**	33	27-6	97.2	77.9	**19.3**
3 **Kansas**	39	35-4	84.6	67.4	**17.2**
4 **North Carolina**	38	34-4	81.9	65.6	**16.3**
5 **Arizona**	35	30-5	90.8	74.6	**16.2**

FIELD GOAL PCT	G	W-L	FG	FGA	PCT
1 **North Carolina**	38	34-4	1,131	2,184	**51.8**
2 **Northern Arizona**	29	21-8	806	1,577	**51.1**
3 **Murray State**	33	29-4	1,037	2,070	**50.1**
4 **Princeton**	29	27-2	684	1,374	**49.8**
5 **Pacific**	33	23-10	841	1,692	**49.7**

THREE-PT FG PER GAME	G	W-L	3FG	3PG
1 **Florida**	29	14-15	285	**9.8**
2 **Long Island**	32	21-11	310	**9.7**
3 **North Texas**	26	5-21	250	**9.6**
4 **New Mexico**	32	24-8	301	**9.4**
5 **Princeton**	29	27-2	265	**9.1**

FREE THROW PCT	G	W-L	FT	FTA	PCT
1 **Siena**	29	17-12	574	715	**80.3**
2 **Montana State**	30	19-11	437	570	**76.7**
3 **Purdue**	36	28-8	657	864	**76.0**
4 **Montana**	30	16-14	472	621	**76.0**
5 **New Mexico**	32	24-8	430	568	**75.7**

Assists Per Game

		G	W-L	AST	APG
1	Montana State	30	19-11	624	**20.8**
2	Fresno State	34	21-13	685	**20.1**
3	Arizona State	32	18-14	639	**20.0**
4	TCU	33	27-6	651	**19.7**
5	Arizona	35	30-5	677	**19.3**

Rebound Margin

		G	W-L	RPG	OPP RPG	MAR
1	Utah	34	30-4	37.0	27.1	**9.9**
2	Stanford	35	30-5	41.3	31.9	**9.4**
3	Fairleigh Dickinson	30	23-7	45.7	36.5	**9.2**
4	Kansas	39	35-4	43.1	34.2	**8.9**
	Michigan State	30	22-8	39.9	31.0	**8.9**

Scoring Defense

		G	W-L	OPP PTS	OPP PPG
1	Princeton	29	27-2	1,491	**51.4**
2	South Alabama	28	21-7	1,526	**54.5**
3	Charleston	30	24-6	1,662	**55.4**
4	Utah	34	30-4	1,959	**57.6**
5	Wyoming	28	19-9	1,656	**59.1**

Field Goal Pct Defense

		G	W-L	OPP FG	OPP FGA	OPP PCT
1	Miami (FL)	28	18-10	634	1,672	**37.9**
2	Bradley	29	15-14	617	1,614	**38.2**
3	Kentucky	39	35-4	892	2,324	**38.4**
4	North Carolina	38	34-4	923	2,403	**38.4**
5	Wyoming	28	19-9	541	1,405	**38.5**

Blocked Shots Per Game

		G	W-L	BLK	BPG
1	Texas	31	14-17	203	**6.5**
2	Florida A&M	28	11-17	182	**6.5**
3	Georgia Tech	33	19-14	209	**6.3**
4	Iona	33	27-6	205	**6.2**
5	Fairleigh Dickinson	30	23-7	185	**6.2**

Steals Per Game

		G	W-L	STL	SPG
1	Long Island	32	21-11	478	**14.9**
2	West Virginia	33	24-9	407	**12.3**
3	Ball State	29	21-8	349	**12.0**
4	Xavier	30	22-8	354	**11.8**
5	North Texas	26	5-21	303	**11.7**

TEAM LEADERS—GAME

Points

		OPP	DATE	SCORE
1	Long Island	Medgar Evers	N26	**179-62**
2	TCU	Texas-Pan American	N29	**153-87**
3	TCU	Delaware State	D3	**138-75**
4	TCU	Morgan State	D6	**133-74**
5	Southeastern Louisiana	Texas College	N22	**129-97**

Field Goal Pct

		OPP	DATE	FG	FGA	PCT
1	Purdue	Long Island	N14	47	61	**77.0**
2	Air Force	Doane	N22	45	60	**75.0**
3	Nebraska	UNC Wilmington	D5	34	47	**72.3**
4	Utah	Loyola Marymount	N25	33	46	**71.7**
5	Northwestern	Troy	D2	33	47	**70.2**

Three-Pt FG Made

		OPP	DATE	3FG
1	Arkansas State	Cal Poly SLO	D19	**19**
	Monmouth	Long Island	F21	**19**
3	Oral Roberts	Jarvis Christian	N15	**18**
	Georgia	Charleston So.	N22	**18**
	New Mexico	Holy Cross	D29	**18**
	Wake Forest	North Carolina	J31	**18**
	New Mexico	UTEP	F19	**18**

CONSENSUS ALL-AMERICAS

First Team

PLAYER	CL	POS	HT	SCHOOL	RPG	PPG
Mike Bibby	SO	G	6-2	Arizona	3.0	17.2
Antawn Jamison	JR	F	6-9	North Carolina	10.5	22.2
Raef LaFrentz	SR	F	6-11	Kansas	11.4	19.8
Paul Pierce	JR	F	6-7	Kansas	6.7	20.4
Miles Simon	SR	G	6-5	Arizona	3.5	17.2

Second Team

PLAYER	CL	POS	HT	SCHOOL	RPG	PPG
Vince Carter	JR	G/F	6-6	North Carolina	5.1	15.6
Mateen Cleaves	SO	G	6-2	Michigan State	2.5	16.1
Pat Garrity	SR	F	6-9	Notre Dame	8.3	23.2
Richard Hamilton	SO	G/F	6-6	Connecticut	4.4	21.5
Ansu Sesay	SR	F	6-9	Mississippi	7.6	18.6

Selectors: AP, NABC, Sporting News, USBWA

AWARD WINNERS

Player of the Year

PLAYER	CL	POS	HT	SCHOOL	AWARDS
Antawn Jamison	JR	F	6-9	North Carolina	Naismith, AP, USBWA, Wooden, NABC, Rupp
Earl Boykins	SR	G	5-5	Eastern Michigan	Frances Pomeroy Naismith*

* For the most outstanding senior player who is 6 feet or under

Defensive Player of the Year

PLAYER	CL	POS	HT	SCHOOL
Steve Wojciechowski	SR	G	5-11	Duke

Coach of the Year

COACH	SCHOOL	REC	AWARDS
Bill Guthridge	North Carolina	34-4	Naismith, NABC, Sporting News, CBS/Chevrolet
Tom Izzo	Michigan State	22-8	AP, USBWA

Bob Gibbons' Top High School Senior Recruits

	PLAYER	POS	HT	HIGH SCHOOL	A-A TEAMS	COLLEGE	CAREER NOTES
1	**Rashard Lewis**	F	6-9	Alief-Elsik HS, Alief, TX	McD, P, USA	None	Drafted straight out of HS; 2nd-round pick, '98 NBA draft (Sonics); 16.9 ppg (11 seasons); All-Star, '05, '09
2	**Al Harrington**	F	6-8	St. Patrick HS, Elizabeth, NJ	McD, P, USA	None	Drafted stright out of HS; No. 25 pick, '98 NBA draft (Pacers); 13.0 ppg (10 seasons); career-high 20.1 ppg, '08-09
3	**Jaron Rush**	F	6-7	Pembroke Hill HS, Kansas City, MO	McD, P	UCLA	11.4 ppg, 7.3 rpg as freshman; suspended during sophomore year; entered NBA draft; undrafted
4	**Joel Przybilla**	C	7-1	Monticello (MN) HS	McD, P	Minnesota	14.2 ppg, 8.4 rpg as sophomore; No. 9 pick, '00 draft (Bucks); 4.2 ppg, 6.4 rpg (9 seasons)
5	**Quentin Richardson**	F	6-6	Whitney Young HS, Chicago	McD, P, USA	DePaul	17.9 ppg, 10.2 rpg (2 seasons); No. 18 pick, '00 NBA draft (Clippers); 11.5 ppg, 5.0 rpg (9 seasons)
6	**Dan Gadzuric**	C	6-10	Gov. Dummer Academy, Byfield, MA	McD, P	UCLA	10.5 ppg, 6.6 rpg; 2nd-round pick, '02 NBA draft (Bucks); 5.0 ppg, 4.6 rpg (7 seasons)
7	**Jason Capel**	F	6-8	St. John's Catholic Prep, Frederick, MD	McD, P	North Carolina	1,447 pts; 15.6 ppg as senior; undrafted; head coach at Oklahoma
8	**Vincent Yarbrough**	F	6-7	Cleveland (TN) HS	McD, P	Tennessee	Left Tennessee as 8th-leading scorer (1,737 pts); 2nd-round pick, '02 NBA draft (Nuggets); 6.8 ppg (1 season)
9	**Mike Miller**	F	6-8	Mitchell (SD) HS	McD, P	Florida	13.3 ppg, 6.0 rpg (2 seasons); No. 5 pick, '00 NBA draft (Magic); NBA ROY '01; NBA Sixth Man award '06
10	**Stromile Swift**	F/C	6-9	Fair Park HS, Shreveport, LA	McD, P, USA	LSU	13.4 ppg, 7.0 rpg (2 seasons); No. 2 pick, '00 NBA draft (Grizzlies); 8.6 ppg, 4.7 rpg (8 seasons)
11	**Ronald Curry**	PG	6-2	Hampton (VA) HS	McD, P	North Carolina	Led team in assists as Soph. (119); QB, UNC football team; 7th-round pick, '02 NFL draft (Raiders); WR in NFL
12	**Korleone Young**	PF	6-7	Hargrave Military Academy, Chatham, VA	McD, P, USA	None	Drafted straight out of HS; 2nd-round pick, '98 NBA draft (Pistons); played in 3 NBA games, CBA, overseas
13	**Michael Wright**	PF	6-8	Farragut Academy, Chicago		Arizona	15.1 ppg, 8.4 rpg (3 seasons); 3rd team All-America, '01; 2nd-round pick, '01 NBA draft (Knicks)
14	**Tayshaun Prince**	G/F	6-8	Dominguez HS, Compton, CA	McD, P	Kentucky	SEC POY, '01; at UK, 13.1 ppg, 5.6 rpg (4 seasons); No. 23 pick, '02 NBA draft (Pistons); 4-time NBA All-Defensive 2nd team
15	**Keyon Dooling**	PG	6-4	Dillard HS, Fort Lauderdale, FL	P	Missouri	12.1 ppg (2 seasons); No. 10 pick, '00 NBA draft (Clippers); 7.2 ppg (9 seasons)
16	**Erick Barkley**	PG	6-0	Maine Central Inst., Pittsfield, ME	McD	St. John's	14.6 ppg, 4.6 apg (2 seasons); No. 28 pick, '00 NBA draft (Blazers); played in 27 NBA games
17	**Lloyd Price**	G/F	6-4	Oak Hill Academy, Mouth of Wilson, VA		Xavier	9.2 ppg as junior; transferred after 3 years due to academic problems; also attended Fairleigh Dickinson and Kentucky-Wesleyan
18	**Adam Harrington**	G	6-5	Pioneer Valley Regional HS, Northfield, MA	P	NC State/Auburn	11.6 ppg as freshman; transfered after 1 year; 15.5 ppg as sophomore; entered draft after junior year; undrafted
19	**Corey Maggette**	F	6-6	Fenwick HS, Oak Park, IL	McD, P	Duke	10.6 ppg (1 season); No. 13 pick, '99 NBA draft (Sonics); 16.3 ppg, 5.1 rpg (10 seasons)
20	**Ray Young**	G	6-5	St. Joseph's Notre Dame HS, Alameda, CA	McD, P	UCLA	10.1 ppg as senior; undrafted; played in USBL, CBA

Other Standouts

	PLAYER	POS	HT	HIGH SCHOOL	A-A TEAMS	COLLEGE	CAREER NOTES
22	**Richard Jefferson**	F	6-7	Moon Valley HS, Phoenix	McD, P	Arizona	11.2 ppg (3 seasons); No. 13 pick, '01 NBA draft (Rockets); '02 All-Rookie 2nd team
33	**Frank Williams**	G	6-3	Manual HS, Peoria, IL	McD, P	Illinois	14.3 ppg (3 seasons); No. 25 pick, '02 draft (Nuggets); 2.9 ppg (3 seasons)
35	**Luke Walton**	PF	6-8	University, San Diego		Arizona	1 of 3 Pac-10 players with 1,000 pts, 500 rebs, 500 assists; 2nd-round pick, '03 NBA draft (Lakers); son of Hall of Famer Bill Walton

Abbreviations: McD=McDonald's; P=Parade; USA=USA Today

Poll Progression

Preseason Poll

AP	ESPN/USA	SCHOOL
1	1	**Arizona**
2	4	**Kansas**
3	2	**Duke**
4	2	**North Carolina**
5	7	**Clemson**
6	5	**UCLA**
7	8	**South Carolina**
8	9	**Kentucky**
9	6	**Purdue**
10	11	**Xavier**
11	10	**New Mexico**
12	13	**Connecticut**
13	15	**Fresno State**
14	12	**Stanford**
15	16	**Iowa**
16	14	**Utah**
17	18	**Indiana**
18	17	**Charlotte**
19	22	**Georgia**
20	21	**Oklahoma**
21	25	**Rhode Island**
22	24	**Texas**
23	—	**Mississippi**
24	—	**Temple**
25	19	**Louisville**
—	20	**Michigan**
—	23	**Maryland**

Week of Nov 18

AP	SCHOOL	AP↓↑
1	**Arizona** (0-0)	
2	**Kansas** (2-0)	
3	**Duke** (1-0)	
4	**North Carolina** (1-0)	
5	**Clemson** (1-0)	
6	**South Carolina** (1-0)	↑1
7	**UCLA** (0-0)	↓1
8	**Purdue** (2-0)	↑1
9	**Kentucky** (0-0)	↓1
10	**Xavier** (0-0)	
11	**New Mexico** (1-0)	
12	**Connecticut** (2-0)	
13	**Fresno State** (1-0)	
14	**Iowa** (2-0)	↑1
15	**Stanford** (0-0)	↓1
16	**Utah** (1-0)	
17	**Charlotte** (0-0)	↑1
18	**Temple** (2-0)	↑6
19	**Oklahoma** (1-0)	↑1
20	**Rhode Island** (1-0)	↑1
21	**Mississippi** (0-0)	↑2
22	**Louisville** (0-0)	↑3
23	**Indiana** (0-1)	↓6
24	**Illinois State** (1-0)	⤴
25	**Georgia** (1-1)	↓6

Week of Nov 25

AP	ESPN/USA	SCHOOL	AP↓↑
1	1	**Arizona** (1-0)	
2	2	**Kansas** (4-0)	
3	4	**Duke** (2-0)	
4	3	**North Carolina** (3-0)	
5	8	**South Carolina** (2-0)	↑1
6	5	**Purdue** (3-0)	↑2
7	6	**UCLA** (0-0)	
8	7	**Kentucky** (1-0)	Ⓐ ↑1
9	10	**Xavier** (2-0)	↑1
10	9	**New Mexico** (4-0)	↑1
11	11	**Connecticut** (3-0)	↑1
12	15	**Fresno State** (2-0)	↑1
13	12	**Clemson** (3-1)	↓8
14	16	**Iowa** (2-0)	
15	13	**Stanford** (1-0)	
16	14	**Utah** (3-0)	
17	18	**Mississippi** (2-0)	↑4
18	17	**Oklahoma** (3-0)	↑1
19	19	**Louisville** (0-0)	↑3
20	20	**Temple** (2-1)	↓2
21	21	**Indiana** (1-1)	↑2
22	24	**Georgia** (3-1)	↑3
23	—	**Rhode Island** (1-1)	↓3
24	—	**Maryland** (2-1)	⤴
25	23	**Charlotte** (0-1)	↓8
—	22	**Princeton** (3-0)	
—	25	**Florida State** (3-0)	
—	25	**Wake Forest** (3-0)	

Week of Dec 2 Ⓑ

AP	ESPN/USA	SCHOOL	AP↓↑
1	1	**Duke** (6-0)	[illegible]
2	3	**Kansas** (6-0)	
3	2	**North Carolina** (6-0)	[illegible]
4	4	**Arizona** (4-1)	[illegible]
5	6	**South Carolina** (3-0)	
6	5	**Purdue** (5-1)	
7	7	**Kentucky** (4-1)	↑[illegible]
8	8	**New Mexico** (5-0)	↑[illegible]
9	9	**Xavier** (3-0)	
10	12	**Iowa** (3-0)	↑[illegible]
11	10	**Utah** (5-0)	↑[illegible]
12	11	**Stanford** (4-0)	↑[illegible]
13	13	**Connecticut** (5-1)	↓2
14	14	**Mississippi** (3-0)	↑3
15	15	**UCLA** (2-1)	↓8
16	17	**Fresno State** (3-1)	↓4
17	16	**Clemson** (3-2)	↓4
18	21	**Arkansas** (4-0)	⤴
19	18	**Florida State** (4-1)	⤴
20	19	**Temple** (2-1)	
21	22	**Georgia** (5-1)	↑1
22	23	**Georgia Tech** (4-0)	⤴
23	—	**Maryland** (3-1)	↑1
24	24	**Wake Forest** (5-0)	⤴
25	20	**Princeton** (4-0)	⤴
—	25	**Louisville** (2-1)	⤵

Week of Dec 9

AP	ESPN/USA	SCHOOL	AP↓↑
1	1	**Duke** (8-0)	
2	2	**North Carolina** (9-0)	↑1
3	3	**Kansas** (8-1)	↓1
4	5	**Kentucky** (6-1)	↑3
5	8	**South Carolina** (5-0)	
6	4	**Arizona** (5-2)	↓2
7	9	**Xavier** (5-0)	↑2
8	7	**Purdue** (6-2)	↓2
9	6	**Utah** (7-0)	↑2
10	10	**Iowa** (6-0)	
11	11	**Stanford** (5-0)	↑1
12	14	**UCLA** (3-1)	↑3
13	13	**Connecticut** (7-1)	
14	12	**New Mexico** (5-1)	↓6
15	16	**Arkansas** (6-0)	↑3
16	15	**Florida State** (6-1)	↑3
17	18	**Clemson** (5-2)	
18	21	**Fresno State** (3-1)	↓2
19	22	**Maryland** (4-2)	↑4
20	17	**Temple** (4-1)	
21	19	**Mississippi** (4-1)	↓7
22	20	**Princeton** (6-0)	↑3
23	25	**Georgia** (5-2)	↓2
24	23	**Georgia Tech** (5-1)	↓2
25	24	**Wake Forest** (6-1)	↓1

Week of Dec 16

AP	ESPN/USA	SCHOOL	AP↓↑
1	1	**North Carolina** (10-0)	↑1
2	3	**Kansas** (11-1)	↑1
3	2	**Duke** (9-1)	↓2
4	4	**Kentucky** (8-1)	
5	5	**Arizona** (7-2)	↑1
6	8	**South Carolina** (5-0)	↓1
7	6	**Utah** (9-0)	↑2
8	7	**Purdue** (8-2)	
9	9	**Stanford** (5-0)	↑2
10	10	**Xavier** (6-1)	↓3
11	11	**UCLA** (4-1)	↑1
12	12	**Connecticut** (8-1)	↑1
13	14	**Arkansas** (7-0)	↑2
14	15	**New Mexico** (7-1)	
15	13	**Iowa** (7-1)	↓5
16	16	**Temple** (6-1)	↑4
17	17	**Florida State** (7-1)	↓1
18	18	**Mississippi** (5-1)	↑3
19	19	**Princeton** (7-1)	↑3
20	21	**Georgia** (7-2)	↑3
21	—	**Michigan** (6-2)	⤴
22	20	**Maryland** (5-3)	↓3
23	22	**Wake Forest** (6-1)	↑2
24	24	**TCU** (9-0)	⤴
25	23	**Syracuse** (7-0)	⤴
—	25	**Clemson** (5-3)	⤵

Week of Dec 23

AP	ESPN/USA	SCHOOL	AP↓↑
1	1	**North Carolina** (12-0)	
2	3	**Kansas** (13-1)	
3	2	**Duke** (10-1)	
4	4	**Kentucky** (9-2)	
5	5	**Arizona** (7-2)	
6	6	**Utah** (10-0)	↑1
7	7	**Purdue** (9-2)	↑1
8	8	**Stanford** (7-0)	↑1
9	9	**UCLA** (6-1)	↑2
10	10	**South Carolina** (6-1)	↓4
11	11	**Connecticut** (9-1)	↑1
12	14	**Arkansas** (8-0)	↑1
13	13	**Xavier** (6-2)	↓3
14	12	**New Mexico** (7-1)	
15	15	**Iowa** (8-1)	
16	16	**Mississippi** (7-1)	↑2
17	18	**Florida State** (8-2)	
18	17	**Princeton** (8-1)	↑1
19	19	**Syracuse** (9-0)	↑6
20	20	**Maryland** (5-3)	↑2
21	22	**Clemson** (7-3)	⤴
22	—	**Rhode Island** (5-1)	⤴
23	—	**West Virginia** (9-1)	⤴
24	21	**Temple** (6-3)	↓8
25	25	**TCU** (9-1)	↓1
—	23	**Georgia Tech** (7-2)	
—	24	**Marquette** (6-0)	

Week of Dec 30

AP	ESPN/USA	SCHOOL	AP↓↑
1	1	**North Carolina** (13-0)	
2	3	**Kansas** (15-1)	
3	2	**Duke** (10-1)	
4	4	**Utah** (11-0)	↑2
5	5	**Purdue** (11-2)	↑2
6	7	**Kentucky** (10-2)	↓2
7	8	**Stanford** (9-0)	↑1
8	6	**Arizona** (8-3)	↓3
9	9	**UCLA** (8-1)	
10	11	**Connecticut** (11-1)	↑1
11	10	**South Carolina** (7-1)	↓1
12	13	**New Mexico** (8-1)	↑2
13	12	**Xavier** (7-2)	
14	14	**Iowa** (11-1)	↑1
15	15	**Florida State** (9-2)	↑2
16	17	**Mississippi** (8-1)	
17	16	**Princeton** (10-1)	↑1
18	20	**Michigan** (10-3)	⤴
19	19	**Syracuse** (11-1)	
20	18	**Maryland** (7-3)	
21	21	**Clemson** (9-3)	
22	23	**West Virginia** (11-1)	↑1
23	24	**Arkansas** (9-2)	Ⓒ ↓11
24	—	**Rhode Island** (6-1)	↓2
25	25	**Marquette** (8-0)	⤴
—	22	**Temple** (6-3)	⤵

Week of Jan 6

AP	ESPN/USA	SCHOOL	AP↓↑
1	1	**North Carolina** (15-0)	
2	2	**Duke** (12-1)	↑1
3	3	**Utah** (12-0)	↑1
4	4	**Kansas** (17-2)	↓2
5	5	**Arizona** (10-3)	↑3
6	6	**Kentucky** (12-2)	
7	7	**Stanford** (12-0)	
8	8	**Connecticut** (13-1)	↑2
9	9	**Purdue** (12-3)	↓4
10	12	**UCLA** (9-2)	↓1
11	11	**Iowa** (13-1)	↑3
12	10	**New Mexico** (10-1)	
13	13	**Florida State** (12-2)	↑2
14	14	**Mississippi** (10-1)	↑2
15	15	**Princeton** (11-1)	↑2
16	16	**South Carolina** (8-2)	↓5
17	18	**Michigan** (12-3)	↑1
18	19	**Syracuse** (12-1)	↑1
19	17	**Xavier** (8-3)	↓6
20	20	**Marquette** (10-0)	↑5
21	23	**Hawaii** (11-1)	⤴
22	24	**Arkansas** (11-2)	↑1
23	25	**Rhode Island** (8-2)	↑1
24	22	**Clemson** (10-4)	↓3
25	21	**West Virginia** (12-2)	↓3

Week of Jan 13

AP	ESPN/USA	SCHOOL	AP↓↑
1	1	**North Carolina** (17-0)	
2	2	**Duke** (14-1)	
3	3	**Kansas** (19-2)	↑1
4	4	**Utah** (13-0)	↓1
5	5	**Arizona** (13-3)	
6	6	**Kentucky** (14-2)	Ⓓ
7	7	**Stanford** (14-0)	
8	9	**UCLA** (12-2)	↑2
9	8	**Purdue** (14-3)	
10	10	**Connecticut** (14-2)	↓2
11	11	**Mississippi** (12-1)	↑3
12	12	**Princeton** (13-1)	↑3
13	14	**Iowa** (13-2)	↓2
14	17	**South Carolina** (10-2)	↑2
15	13	**New Mexico** (11-2)	↓3
16	15	**Syracuse** (14-1)	↑3
17	16	**Florida State** (12-4)	↓4
18	19	**Xavier** (10-3)	↑1
19	18	**Michigan** (13-4)	↓2
20	23	**Rhode Island** (10-2)	↑3
21	20	**West Virginia** (14-2)	↑4
22	22	**Arkansas** (13-2)	
23	21	**Marquette** (10-2)	↓3
24	24	**Hawaii** (11-2)	↓3
25	—	**Oklahoma State** (12-1)	⤴
—	24	**Clemson** (10-5)	⤵

Week of Jan 20

AP	ESPN/USA	SCHOOL	AP↓↑
1	1	**Duke** (16-1)	↑1
2	2	**North Carolina** (18-1)	↓1
3	3	**Kansas** (21-2)	
4	4	**Utah** (15-0)	
5	6	**Stanford** (16-0)	↑2
6	5	**Arizona** (15-3)	↓1
7	7	**Kentucky** (16-2)	↓1
8	8	**Connecticut** (16-2)	↑2
9	10	**UCLA** (13-3)	↓1
10	12	**Iowa** (15-2)	↑3
11	11	**Princeton** (13-1)	↑1
12	9	**Purdue** (15-4)	↓3
13	14	**Mississippi** (12-2)	↓2
14	17	**South Carolina** (11-3)	
15	15	**Syracuse** (15-2)	
16	16	**Michigan** (14-4)	↑3
17	13	**New Mexico** (13-3)	↓2
18	19	**Arkansas** (14-3)	↑4
19	18	**Xavier** (11-4)	↓1
20	20	**Florida State** (13-5)	↓3
21	25	**Cincinnati** (13-2)	⤴
22	22	**Rhode Island** (12-3)	↓2
23	21	**West Virginia** (15-3)	↓2
24	24	**Hawaii** (12-2)	
25	23	**Clemson** (11-6)	⤴

Week of Jan 27 Ⓔ

AP	ESPN/USA	SCHOOL	AP↓↑
1	1	**Duke** (18-1)	
2	2	**North Carolina** (20-1)	
3	3	**Utah** (17-0)	↑1
4	5	**Stanford** (18-0)	↑1
5	4	**Kansas** (22-3)	↓2
6	6	**Arizona** (17-3)	
7	7	**Kentucky** (18-2)	
8	9	**UCLA** (15-3)	↑1
9	8	**Connecticut** (17-3)	↓1
10	10	**Purdue** (17-4)	↑2
11	11	**Princeton** (14-1)	
12	12	**Mississippi** (14-2)	↑1
13	14	**South Carolina** (13-3)	↑1
14	13	**New Mexico** (14-3)	↑3
15	15	**Arkansas** (16-3)	↑3
16	16	**Iowa** (15-4)	↓6
17	19	**West Virginia** (17-3)	↑6
18	20	**Cincinnati** (15-3)	↑3
19	17	**Michigan** (15-5)	↓3
20	18	**Syracuse** (15-4)	↓5
21	21	**Rhode Island** (13-4)	↑1
22	25	**Michigan State** (13-4)	⤴
23	24	**Maryland** (12-6)	⤴
24	22	**Xavier** (12-5)	↓5
25	—	**Indiana** (14-5)	⤴
—	23	**Florida State** (14-6)	⤵

[WEE]K OF FEB 3

AP	ESPN/USA	SCHOOL	AP↓↑
	1	**Duke** (20-1)	
	2	**North Carolina** (22-1)	
	3	**Kansas** (24-3)	↑2
	4	**Arizona** (19-3)	↑2
	5	**Utah** (18-1)	↓2
	6	**UCLA** (17-3)	↑2
	7	**Connecticut** (19-3)	↑2
	9	**Kentucky** (19-3)	↓1
	10	**Stanford** (18-2)	↓5
	8	**Purdue** (19-4)	
	11	**Princeton** (16-1)	
	12	**New Mexico** (16-3)	↑2
	13	**South Carolina** (16-3)	
	14	**Arkansas** (18-3)	↑1
	15	**West Virginia** (18-3)	↑2
	19	**Michigan State** (15-4)	↑6
	16	**Mississippi** (14-4)	↓5
	18	**Michigan** (16-6)	↑1
	17	**Syracuse** (17-4)	↑1
	20	**Cincinnati** (16-4)	↓2
	22	**Xavier** (14-5)	↑3
	25	**George Washington** (18-3)	⤴
	24	**Massachusetts** (16-5)	⤴
	21	**Iowa** (15-6)	↓8
	—	**Maryland** (13-7)	↓2
—	23	**Rhode Island** (14-5)	↱

WEEK OF FEB 10

AP	ESPN/USA	SCHOOL	AP↓↑
1	1	**North Carolina** (24-1)	↑1
2	2	**Duke** (21-2)	↓1
3	4	**Arizona** (21-3)	↑1
4	3	**Kansas** (26-3)	↓1
5	5	**Utah** (20-1)	
6	6	**Connecticut** (21-3)	↑1
7	8	**Kentucky** (21-3)	↑1
8	7	**Purdue** (20-4)	↑2
9	10	**UCLA** (18-4)	↓3
10	9	**Princeton** (18-1)	↑1
11	11	**New Mexico** (18-3)	↑1
12	12	**Arkansas** (20-3)	↑2
13	15	**Michigan State** (17-4)	↑3
14	13	**Stanford** (19-3)	↓5
15	14	**South Carolina** (17-4)	↓2
16	17	**West Virginia** (19-4)	↓1
17	18	**George Washington** (20-3)	↑5
18	16	**Mississippi** (15-5)	↓1
19	21	**Cincinnati** (17-5)	↑1
20	22	**Massachusetts** (17-6)	↑3
21	19	**Michigan** (17-7)	↓3
22	—	**TCU** (20-4)	⤴
23	20	**Syracuse** (17-5)	↓4
24	25	**Maryland** (14-7)	↑1
25	24	**Rhode Island** (17-5)	⤴
—	23	**Xavier** (15-6)	↱

WEEK OF FEB 17

AP	ESPN/USA	SCHOOL	AP↓↑
1	1	**North Carolina** (26-1)	
2	2	**Duke** (23-2)	
3	3	**Arizona** (22-3)	
4	4	**Kansas** (28-3)	
5	6	**Purdue** (22-4)	↑3
6	5	**Utah** (21-2)	↓1
7	7	**Connecticut** (22-4)	↓1
8	10	**Kentucky** (22-4)	↓1
9	8	**Princeton** (20-1)	↑1
10	11	**Stanford** (21-3)	↑4
11	9	**New Mexico** (19-3)	
12	12	**UCLA** (19-5)	↓3
13	13	**South Carolina** (19-4)	↑2
14	15	**Michigan State** (18-5)	↓1
15	14	**Mississippi** (17-5)	↑3
16	16	**Arkansas** (20-5)	↓4
17	18	**Cincinnati** (19-5)	↑2
18	20	**Massachusetts** (19-6)	↑2
19	22	**TCU** (22-4)	↑3
20	19	**West Virginia** (20-5)	↓4
21	17	**Syracuse** (19-5)	↑2
22	21	**Michigan** (18-7)	↓1
23	—	**Illinois** (18-8)	⤴
24	23	**George Washington** (20-5)	↓7
25	—	**Maryland** (15-8)	↓1
—	24	**Xavier** (16-6)	
—	25	**Rhode Island** (18-6)	↱

WEEK OF FEB 24

AP	ESPN/USA	SCHOOL	AP↓↑
1	1	**Duke** (25-2)	↑1
2	2	**Arizona** (24-3)	↑1
3	3	**North Carolina** (26-2)	↓2
4	4	**Kansas** (30-3)	
5	5	**Utah** (22-2)	↑1
6	6	**Connecticut** (24-4)	↑1
7	8	**Kentucky** (24-4)	↑1
8	9	**Stanford** (23-3)	↑2
9	7	**Princeton** (23-1)	
10	12	**Michigan State** (20-5)	↑4
11	10	**Purdue** (22-6)	↓6
12	14	**Arkansas** (22-5)	↑4
13	13	**Mississippi** (19-5)	↑2
14	11	**South Carolina** (20-5)	↓1
15	18	**TCU** (24-4)	↑4
16	15	**New Mexico** (21-4)	↓5
17	17	**Cincinnati** (21-5)	
18	16	**UCLA** (20-6)	↓6
19	19	**West Virginia** (22-5)	↑1
20	20	**Massachusetts** (20-7)	↓2
21	21	**Michigan** (19-8)	↑1
22	23	**Illinois** (20-8)	↑1
23	22	**Syracuse** (20-6)	↓2
24	—	**Temple** (19-6)	⤴
25	—	**Oklahoma State** (20-4)	⤴
—	24	**Xavier** (18-6)	
—	25	**Maryland** (16-9)	↱

[W]EEK OF MAR 3

AP	ESPN/USA	SCHOOL	AP↓↑
1	1	**Duke** (27-2)	
2	2	**Arizona** (25-3)	
3	3	**Kansas** (31-3)	↑1
3	4	**North Carolina** (27-3)	
5	5	**Utah** (25-2)	
6	6	**Connecticut** (26-4)	
7	7	**Kentucky** (26-4)	
8	8	**Princeton** (25-1)	↑1
9	9	**Purdue** (24-6)	↑2
10	10	**Mississippi** (21-5)	↑3
11	11	**Stanford** (24-4)	↓3
12	12	**Michigan State** (20-6)	↓2
13	14	**TCU** (26-4)	↑2
14	13	**Cincinnati** (23-5)	↑3
15	15	**South Carolina** (21-6)	↓1
16	16	**Arkansas** (22-7)	↓4
17	18	**Michigan** (21-8)	↑4
18	20	**Illinois** (21-8)	↑4
19	17	**UCLA** (21-7)	↓1
20	19	**New Mexico** (21-6)	↓4
21	24	**Maryland** (18-9)	⤴
22	21	**Syracuse** (22-7)	↑1
23	22	**West Virginia** (22-7)	↓4
24	25	**Temple** (20-7)	
25	—	**Oklahoma State** (21-5)	
—	23	**Massachusetts** (20-9)	↱

WEEK OF MAR 10

AP	ESPN/USA	SCHOOL	AP↓↑
1	1	**North Carolina** (30-3) F	↑2
2	2	**Kansas** (34-3)	↑1
3	3	**Duke** (29-3) F	↓2
4	4	**Arizona** (27-4)	↓2
5	6	**Kentucky** (29-4)	↑2
6	5	**Connecticut** (29-4)	
7	7	**Utah** (25-3)	↓2
8	8	**Princeton** (26-1)	
9	11	**Cincinnati** (26-5)	↑5
10	10	**Stanford** (26-4)	↑1
11	9	**Purdue** (26-7) G	↓2
12	12	**Michigan** (24-8) G	↑5
13	14	**Mississippi** (22-6)	↓3
14	13	**South Carolina** (22-6)	↑1
15	16	**TCU** (27-5)	↓2
16	15	**Michigan State** (20-7)	↓4
17	17	**Arkansas** (23-8)	↓1
18	18	**New Mexico** (23-7)	↑2
19	20	**UCLA** (22-8)	
20	22	**Maryland** (19-10)	↑1
21	19	**Syracuse** (24-8)	↑1
22	23	**Illinois** (22-9)	↓4
23	21	**Xavier** (22-7)	⤴
24	24	**Temple** (21-8)	
25	—	**Murray State** (29-3)	⤴
—	25	**Oklahoma** (22-10)	

FINAL POLL (POST-TOURNAMENT)

USA/CNN	SCHOOL
1	**Kentucky** (35-4)
2	**Utah** (30-4)
3	**North Carolina** (34-4)
4	**Stanford** (30-5)
5	**Duke** (32-4)
6	**Arizona** (30-5)
7	**Connecticut** (32-5)
8	**Kansas** (35-4)
9	**Purdue** (28-8)
10	**Michigan State** (22-8)
11	**Rhode Island** (25-9)
12	**UCLA** (24-9)
13	**Syracuse** (26-9)
14	**Cincinnati** (27-6)
15	**Maryland** (21-11)
16	**Princeton** (27-2)
17	**Michigan** (25-9)
18	**West Virginia** (24-9)
19	**South Carolina** (23-8)
20	**Mississippi** (22-7)
21	**New Mexico** (24-8)
22	**Arkansas** (24-9)
23	**Valparaiso** (23-10)
24	**Washington** (20-10)
25	**TCU** (27-6)

- **A** Kentucky opens its first season under Rick Pitino's replacement, Tubby Smith—the first African-American head coach in Wildcats history—with an 88-49 win over Morehead State in Rupp Arena.
- **B** Long Island blasts Medgar Evers, 179-62, on Nov. 26, the most lopsided game in NCAA history. The Blackbirds score 98 second-half points, another NCAA record.
- **C** It's a blue Christmas for Razorbacks fans. At the Puerto Rico Classic, Arkansas loses back-to-back games—on Dec. 24 to D2 American University-Puerto Rico and on the 25th to Murray State.
- **D** Kentucky beats Georgia, 90-79, on Jan. 6. In the stands, Donna Smith—wife of UK coach Tubby and mother of both Bulldogs point guard G.G. and Wildcats backup guard Saul—wears the colors of both schools.
- **E** Oklahoma State beats Texas A&M, 94-62, on Jan. 24, earning coach Eddie Sutton career victory No. 600.
- **F** North Carolina knocks off Duke, 83-68, in the ACC tournament and replaces its foe as No. 1 in the polls for the third time this season. The first was on Feb. 5, when the Heels thumped the Blue Devils, 97-73, in Chapel Hill.
- **G** Michigan beats Purdue, 76-67, in the final of the first Big Ten tournament. The Wolverines 6'8", 300-pound center Robert "Tractor" Traylor, who scores 24 points, celebrates by vaulting the press tables to bear-hug his grandmother.

PRE-TOURNAMENT RATINGS PERCENTAGE INDEX (RPI)

RANK	SCHOOL	W-L	Sched. Strg.	SS Rank	RPI
1	**North Carolina**	30-3	.6145	4	.6768
2	**Duke**	27-3	.6002	11	.6687
3	**Kentucky**	29-4	.5984	14	.6608
4	**Kansas**	33-3	.5833	29	.6586
5	**Connecticut**	29-4	.5926	21	.6544
6	**Arizona**	27-4	.5953	19	.6518
7	**Maryland**	19-10	.6679	1	.6388
8	**Purdue**	26-7	.6000	12	.6345
9	**South Carolina**	22-7	.6088	8	.6327
10	**Stanford**	25-4	.5638	44	.6325
11	**Michigan**	23-8	.6128	6	.6276
12	**Mississippi**	20-6	.5834	28	.6217
13	**UCLA**	21-8	.6004	10	.6179
14	**New Mexico**	23-7	.5866	23	.6157
15	**Michigan State**	20-7	.5865	24	.6139
16	**Cincinnati**	26-5	.5368	74	.6137
17	**Syracuse**	24-8	.5781	34	.6134
18	**TCU**	26-5	.5297	89	.6069
19	**Arkansas**	23-7	.5607	45	.6068
20	**Massachusetts**	21-10	.5964	15	.6026
21	**Princeton**	25-1	.4739	192	.6004
22	**Rhode Island**	22-8	.5595	49	.5984
23	**Xavier**	22-7	.5489	64	.5982
24	**Tennessee**	20-8	.5665	41	.5980
25	**Indiana**	19-11	.6068	9	.5974
26	**Temple**	21-8	.5526	60	.5974
27	**Illinois**	22-9	.5600	48	.5969
28	**Clemson**	18-13	.6206	3	.5963
29	**Illinois-Chicago**	22-5	.5280	92	.5961
30	**Utah**	24-3	.4763	182	.5958
31	**Charlotte**	19-10	.5989	13	.5953
32	**St. John's**	21-9	.5647	42	.5934
33	**Illinois State**	23-5	.5187	107	.5919
34	**George Washington**	24-8	.5337	79	.5895
35	**Wake Forest**	15-13	.6313	2	.5874
36	**Oklahoma State**	21-6	.5184	109	.5872
37	**Nebraska**	20-11	.5813	31	.5848
38	**Detroit**	22-5	.4995	137	.5843
39	**Florida State**	17-13	.5938	20	.5823
40	**Iona**	26-5	.4842	174	.5774
41	**Washington**	18-9	.5504	63	.5759
42	**UNLV**	19-12	.5746	36	.5732
43	**Murray State**	25-3	.4582	217	.5730
44	**Vanderbilt**	18-12	.5725	37	.5729
45	**Hawaii**	19-8	.5293	90	.5728
46	**West Virginia**	20-8	.5118	119	.5717
47	**Saint Louis**	21-10	.5345	78	.5703
48	**Utah State**	22-7	.5150	114	.5700
49	**Miami (FL)**	18-9	.5328	80	.5698
50	**Butler**	19-10	.5509	61	.5687

Source: Collegiate Basketball News

ANNUAL REVIEW

1998 NCAA Tournament

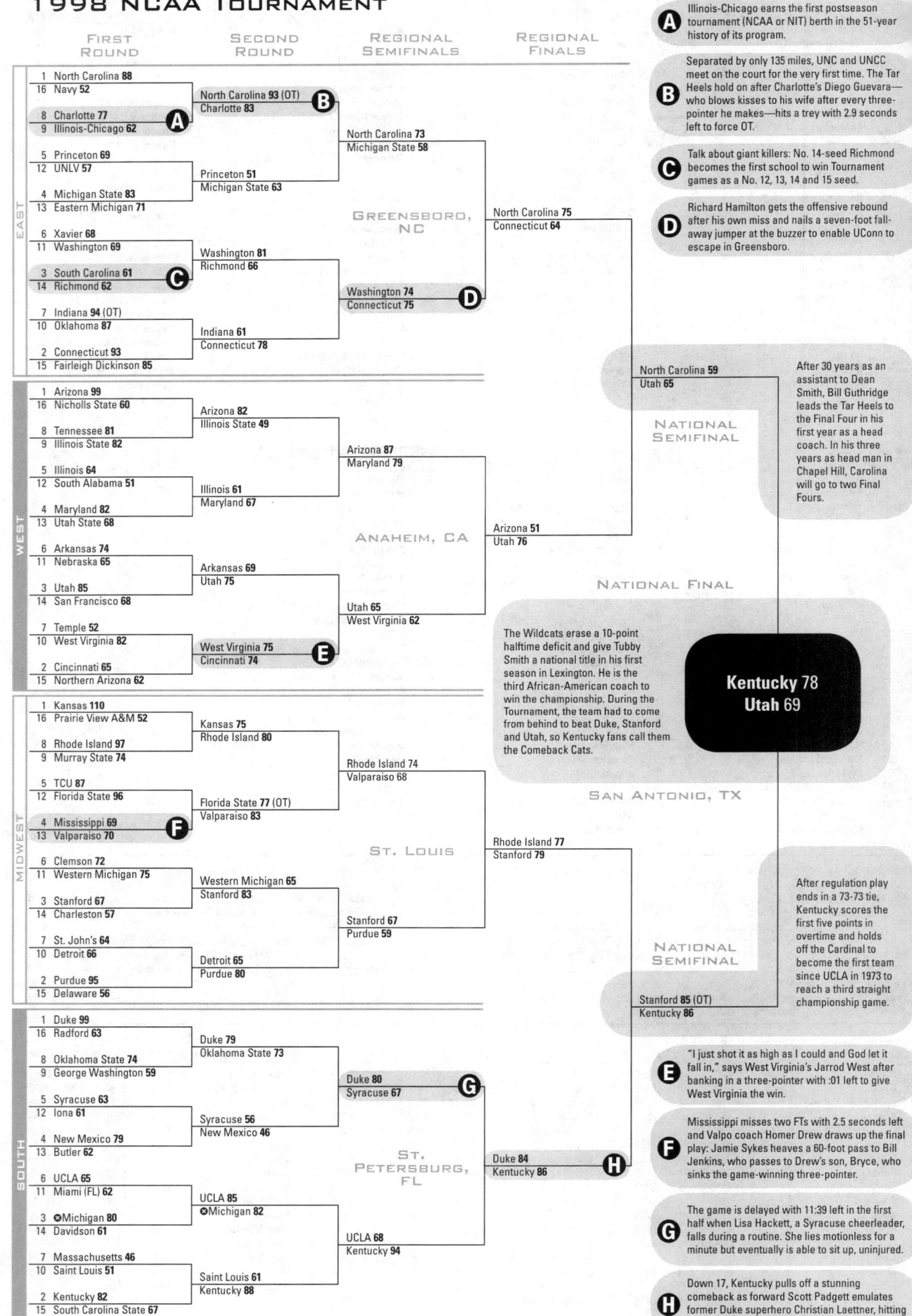

East (Greensboro, NC)

First Round
- 1 North Carolina **88** / 16 Navy **52**
- 8 Charlotte **77** / 9 Illinois-Chicago **62** (A)
- 5 Princeton **69** / 12 UNLV **57**
- 4 Michigan State **83** / 13 Eastern Michigan **71**
- 6 Xavier **68** / 11 Washington **69**
- 3 South Carolina **61** / 14 Richmond **62** (C)
- 7 Indiana **94** (OT) / 10 Oklahoma **87**
- 2 Connecticut **93** / 15 Fairleigh Dickinson **85**

Second Round
- North Carolina **93** (OT) / Charlotte **83** (B)
- Princeton **51** / Michigan State **63**
- Washington **81** / Richmond **66**
- Indiana **61** / Connecticut **78**

Regional Semifinals
- North Carolina **73** / Michigan State **58**
- Washington **74** / Connecticut **75** (D)

Regional Finals
- North Carolina **75** / Connecticut **64**

West (Anaheim, CA)

First Round
- 1 Arizona **99** / 16 Nicholls State **60**
- 8 Tennessee **81** / 9 Illinois State **82**
- 5 Illinois **64** / 12 South Alabama **51**
- 4 Maryland **82** / 13 Utah State **68**
- 6 Arkansas **74** / 11 Nebraska **65**
- 3 Utah **85** / 14 San Francisco **68**
- 7 Temple **52** / 10 West Virginia **82**
- 2 Cincinnati **65** / 15 Northern Arizona **62**

Second Round
- Arizona **82** / Illinois State **49**
- Illinois **61** / Maryland **67**
- Arkansas **69** / Utah **75**
- West Virginia **75** / Cincinnati **74** (E)

Regional Semifinals
- Arizona **87** / Maryland **79**
- Utah **65** / West Virginia **62**

Regional Finals
- Arizona **51** / Utah **76**

Midwest (St. Louis)

First Round
- 1 Kansas **110** / 16 Prairie View A&M **52**
- 8 Rhode Island **97** / 9 Murray State **74**
- 5 TCU **87** / 12 Florida State **96**
- 4 Mississippi **69** / 13 Valparaiso **70** (F)
- 6 Clemson **72** / 11 Western Michigan **75**
- 3 Stanford **67** / 14 Charleston **57**
- 7 St. John's **64** / 10 Detroit **66**
- 2 Purdue **95** / 15 Delaware **56**

Second Round
- Kansas **75** / Rhode Island **80**
- Florida State **77** (OT) / Valparaiso **83**
- Western Michigan **65** / Stanford **83**
- Detroit **65** / Purdue **80**

Regional Semifinals
- Rhode Island 74 / Valparaiso 68
- Stanford **67** / Purdue **59**

Regional Finals
- Rhode Island **77** / Stanford **79**

South (St. Petersburg, FL)

First Round
- 1 Duke **99** / 16 Radford **63**
- 8 Oklahoma State **74** / 9 George Washington **59**
- 5 Syracuse **63** / 12 Iona **61**
- 4 New Mexico **79** / 13 Butler **62**
- 6 UCLA **65** / 11 Miami (FL) **62**
- 3 ✪Michigan **80** / 14 Davidson **61**
- 7 Massachusetts **46** / 10 Saint Louis **51**
- 2 Kentucky **82** / 15 South Carolina State **67**

Second Round
- Duke **79** / Oklahoma State **73**
- Syracuse **56** / New Mexico **46**
- UCLA **85** / ✪Michigan **82**
- Saint Louis **61** / Kentucky **88**

Regional Semifinals
- Duke **80** / Syracuse **67** (G)
- UCLA **68** / Kentucky **94**

Regional Finals
- Duke **84** / Kentucky **86** (H)

✪Team participation later vacated

National Semifinal

North Carolina **59** / Utah **65**

After 30 years as an assistant to Dean Smith, Bill Guthridge leads the Tar Heels to the Final Four in his first year as a head coach. In his three years as head man in Chapel Hill, Carolina will go to two Final Fours.

National Semifinal

Stanford **85** (OT) / Kentucky **86**

After regulation play ends in a 73-73 tie, Kentucky scores the first five points in overtime and holds off the Cardinal to become the first team since UCLA in 1973 to reach a third straight championship game.

National Final (San Antonio, TX)

Kentucky 78
Utah 69

The Wildcats erase a 10-point halftime deficit and give Tubby Smith a national title in his first season in Lexington. He is the third African-American coach to win the championship. During the Tournament, the team had to come from behind to beat Duke, Stanford and Utah, so Kentucky fans call them the Comeback Cats.

A Illinois-Chicago earns the first postseason tournament (NCAA or NIT) berth in the 51-year history of its program.

B Separated by only 135 miles, UNC and UNCC meet on the court for the very first time. The Tar Heels hold on after Charlotte's Diego Guevara—who blows kisses to his wife after every three-pointer he makes—hits a trey with 2.9 seconds left to force OT.

C Talk about giant killers: No. 14-seed Richmond becomes the first school to win Tournament games as a No. 12, 13, 14 and 15 seed.

D Richard Hamilton gets the offensive rebound after his own miss and nails a seven-foot fall-away jumper at the buzzer to enable UConn to escape in Greensboro.

E "I just shot it as high as I could and God let it fall in," says West Virginia's Jarrod West after banking in a three-pointer with :01 left to give West Virginia the win.

F Mississippi misses two FTs with 2.5 seconds left and Valpo coach Homer Drew draws up the final play: Jamie Sykes heaves a 60-foot pass to Bill Jenkins, who passes to Drew's son, Bryce, who sinks the game-winning three-pointer.

G The game is delayed with 11:39 left in the first half when Lisa Hackett, a Syracuse cheerleader, falls during a routine. She lies motionless for a minute but eventually is able to sit up, uninjured.

H Down 17, Kentucky pulls off a stunning comeback as forward Scott Padgett emulates former Duke superhero Christian Laettner, hitting a three with :39 left to capture the lead for good.

Tournament Leaders

Individual Leaders

Scoring

	CL	POS	G	PTS	PPG
1 **Khalid El-Amin**, Connecticut	FR	G	4	93	23.3
2 **Richard Hamilton**, Connecticut	SO	G/F	4	90	22.5
3 **Mateen Cleaves**, Michigan State	SO	G	3	65	21.7
Todd MacCulloch, Washington	JR	C	3	65	21.7
5 **Bryce Drew**, Valparaiso	SR	G	3	62	20.7
6 **Arthur Lee**, Stanford	JR	G	5	103	20.6
7 **Michael Doleac**, Utah	SR	C	6	115	19.2
8 **Toby Bailey**, UCLA	SR	G	3	56	18.7
Todd Burgan, Syracuse	SR	G	3	56	18.7
10 **Cuttino Mobley**, Rhode Island	SR	G	4	74	18.5

Minimum: 3 games

Field Goal Pct

	CL	POS	G	FG	FGA	PCT
1 **Shane Battier**, Duke	FR	F	4	17	24	70.8
Brent Solheim, West Virginia	SR	F	3	17	24	70.8
3 **Mark Madsen**, Stanford	JR	F	5	32	49	65.3
4 **Tim Young**, Stanford	JR	C	5	28	43	65.1
5 **Heshimu Evans**, Kentucky	JR	G	6	20	32	62.5

Minimum: 15 made and 3 games

Free Throw Pct

	CL	POS	G	FT	FTA	PCT
1 **Arthur Lee**, Stanford	JR	G	5	35	35	100.0
Shammond Williams, North Carolina	SR	G	5	20	20	100.0
3 **Scott Padgett**, Kentucky	JR	F	6	21	23	91.3
4 **Zoran Viskovic**, Valparaiso	SO	C	3	15	17	88.2
5 **Khalid El-Amin**, Connecticut	FR	G	4	23	27	85.2

Minimum: 15 made

Three-Point FG Pct

	CL	POS	G	3FG	3FGA	PCT
1 **Mike Chappell**, Duke	FR	G	4	6	7	85.7
2 **Sarunas Jasikevicius**, Maryland	SR	G	3	8	13	61.5
3 **Deon Luton**, Washington	SO	G	3	9	18	50.0
4 **Toby Bailey**, UCLA	SR	G	3	6	13	46.2
Ryan Mendez, Stanford	FR	G	5	6	13	46.2

Minimum: 6 made and 3 games

Assists Per Game

	CL	POS	G	AST	APG
1 **Ed Cota**, North Carolina	SO	G	5	35	7.0
2 **Andre Miller**, Utah	JR	G	6	41	6.8
3 **Tyson Wheeler**, Rhode Island	SR	G	4	27	6.8
4 **Terrell Stokes**, Maryland	JR	G	3	17	5.7
5 **Arthur Lee**, Stanford	JR	G	5	28	5.6

Minimum: 3 games

Rebounds Per Game

	CL	POS	G	REB	RPG
1 **Antawn Jamison**, North Carolina	JR	F	5	63	12.6
2 **Mark Madsen**, Stanford	JR	F	5	61	12.2
3 **Todd MacCulloch**, Washington	JR	C	3	36	12.0
4 **Ryan Blackwell**, Syracuse	SO	F	3	29	9.7
5 **Brad Miller**, Purdue	SR	C	3	28	9.3

Minimum: 3 games

Blocked Shots Per Game

	CL	POS	G	BLK	BPG
1 **Etan Thomas**, Syracuse	SO	F	3	13	4.3
2 **Jamaal Magloire**, Kentucky	SO	F	6	18	3.0
3 **Nazr Mohammed**, Kentucky	JR	C	6	15	2.5
Antonio Reynolds-Dean, Rhode Island	JR	F	4	10	2.5
5 **Patrick Femerling**, Washington	JR	C	3	6	2.0

Minimum: 3 games

Steals Per Game

	CL	POS	G	STL	SPG
1 **Jason Hart**, Syracuse	SO	G	3	11	3.7
Damian Owens, West Virginia	SR	F	3	11	3.7
3 **Brian Cardinal**, Purdue	SO	F	3	10	3.3
4 **Brad Miller**, Purdue	SR	C	3	9	3.0
5 **Bryce Drew**, Valparaiso	SR	G	3	8	2.7
Jarrod West, West Virginia	SR	G	3	8	2.7

Minimum: 3 games

Team Leaders

Scoring

		G	PTS	PPG
1	**Kentucky**	6	514	85.7
2	**Duke**	4	342	85.5
3	**Rhode Island**	4	328	82.0
4	**Arizona**	4	319	79.8
5	**Purdue**	3	234	78.0
6	**North Carolina**	5	388	77.6
7	**Connecticut**	4	310	77.5
8	**Stanford**	5	381	76.2
9	**Maryland**	3	228	76.0
10	**Washington**	3	224	74.7

Minimum: 3 games

FG Pct

		G	FG	FGA	PCT
1	**Kentucky**	6	186	363	51.2
2	**Utah**	6	152	303	50.2
3	**Washington**	3	87	174	50.0
4	**Duke**	4	130	262	49.6
5	**Rhode Island**	4	121	245	49.4

Minimum: 3 games

3-Pt FG Pct

		G	3FG	3FGA	PCT
1	**Kentucky**	6	39	99	39.4
2	**Maryland**	3	21	54	38.9
3	**Valparaiso**	3	22	57	38.6
4	**Duke**	4	29	76	38.2
5	**Rhode Island**	4	28	77	36.4

Minimum: 3 games

FT Pct

		G	FT	FTA	PCT
1	**Stanford**	5	80	99	80.8
2	**Valparaiso**	3	47	59	79.7
3	**Purdue**	3	39	49	79.6
4	**Connecticut**	4	76	99	76.8
5	**Kentucky**	6	103	138	74.6

Minimum: 3 games

Ast/TO Ratio

		G	AST	TO	RAT
1	**Purdue**	3	68	38	1.79
2	**Maryland**	3	63	40	1.58
3	**Kentucky**	6	113	74	1.53
4	**North Carolina**	5	77	53	1.45
5	**Duke**	4	73	51	1.43

Minimum: 3 games

Rebounds

		G	REB	RPG
1	**North Carolina**	5	223	44.6
2	**Arizona**	4	178	44.5
3	**Stanford**	5	222	44.4
4	**Purdue**	3	127	42.3
5	**Maryland**	3	125	41.7

Minimum: 3 games

Blocks

		G	BLK	BPG
1	**Kentucky**	6	48	8.0
2	**Syracuse**	3	16	5.3
3	**Rhode Island**	4	21	5.3
4	**North Carolina**	5	25	5.0
5	**Arizona**	4	19	4.8

Minimum: 3 games

Steals

		G	STL	SPG
1	**Purdue**	3	32	10.7
2	**UCLA**	3	31	10.3
3	**West Virginia**	3	31	10.3
4	**Arizona**	4	40	10.0
5	**Syracuse**	3	28	9.3

Minimum: 3 games

All-Tournament Team

PLAYER	CL	POS	HT	SCHOOL	RPG	APG	PPG
Jeff Sheppard*	SR	G	6-3	Kentucky	4.8	2.3	16.5
Michael Doleac	SR	C	6-11	Utah	7.5	1.3	19.2
Arthur Lee	JR	G	6-1	Stanford	3.2	5.6	20.6
Andre Miller	JR	G	6-2	Utah	7.5	6.8	16.7
Scott Padgett	JR	F	6-9	Kentucky	5.5	2.2	13.7

All-Regional Teams

East

PLAYER	CL	POS	HT	SCHOOL	RPG	APG	PPG
Antawn Jamison*	JR	F	6-9	North Carolina	12.8	0.8	19.0
Vince Carter	JR	G/F	6-6	North Carolina	6.0	1.8	17.5
Ed Cota	SO	G	6-1	North Carolina	4.3	7.0	8.3
Khalid El-Amin	FR	G	5-10	Connecticut	3.8	4.0	23.3
Richard Hamilton	SO	G/F	6-6	Connecticut	4.8	2.3	22.5
Shammond Williams	SR	G	6-3	North Carolina	4.5	3.0	21.0

Midwest

PLAYER	CL	POS	HT	SCHOOL	RPG	APG	PPG
Arthur Lee*	JR	G	6-1	Stanford	3.3	5.8	19.3
Bryce Drew	SR	G	6-3	Valparaiso	3.7	5.0	20.7
Mark Madsen	JR	F	6-8	Stanford	11.3	1.8	16.3
Cuttino Mobley	SR	G	6-4	Rhode Island	4.3	2.5	18.5
Tyson Wheeler	SR	G	5-10	Rhode Island	4.0	6.8	17.0

South

PLAYER	CL	POS	HT	SCHOOL	RPG	APG	PPG
Wayne Turner*	JR	G	6-2	Kentucky	3.8	6.3	10.8
Trajan Langdon	JR	G	6-3	Duke	3.0	2.8	10.5
Roshown McLeod	SR	F	6-8	Duke	7.0	3.0	17.5
Scott Padgett	JR	F	6-9	Kentucky	5.5	2.5	13.8
Jeff Sheppard	SR	G	6-3	Kentucky	4.8	1.8	14.0

West

PLAYER	CL	POS	HT	SCHOOL	RPG	APG	PPG
Andre Miller*	JR	G	6-2	Utah	6.3	7.3	17.0
Mike Bibby	SO	G	6-2	Arizona	4.0	3.8	17.8
Michael Doleac	SR	C	6-11	Utah	7.5	1.5	21.0
Alex Jensen	SO	F	6-7	Utah	7.0	1.0	7.5
Hanno Mottola	SO	C	6-11	Utah	5.0	0.8	10.3

* Most outstanding player

1998 NCAA TOURNAMENT BOX SCORES

73-58

NORTH CAROLINA	MIN	FG	3FG	FT	REB	A	ST	BL	PF	TP
Antawn Jamison	34	7-15	0-0	6-11	14	0	1	1	2	20
Vince Carter	31	7-13	0-2	6-8	10	0	0	1	1	20
Shammond Williams	33	7-13	2-6	2-2	9	2	0	1	1	18
Ed Cota	33	3-7	0-0	5-6	2	8	0	0	2	11
Makhtar N'diaye	29	2-6	0-1	0-0	7	0	0	1	3	4
Ademola Okulaja	29	0-4	0-1	0-0	4	1	0	0	4	0
Brendan Haywood	4	0-0	0-0	0-0	1	0	0	0	0	0
Brad Frederick	2	0-0	0-0	0-0	0	0	0	0	0	0
Brian Bersticker	1	0-0	0-0	0-0	0	0	0	0	0	0
Michael Brooker	1	0-0	0-0	0-0	0	0	0	0	0	0
Terrence Newby	1	0-1	0-0	0-0	0	0	0	0	0	0
Max Owens	1	0-0	0-0	0-0	0	0	0	0	0	0
Scott Williams	1	0-0	0-0	0-0	0	0	0	0	0	0
TOTALS	**200**	**26-59**	**2-10**	**19-27**	**47**	**11**	**1**	**4**	**13**	**73**
Percentages		44.1	20.0	70.4						

Coach: Bill Guthridge

	1H	2H
North Carolina	38	35
Michigan State	24	34

SWEET 16

MICHIGAN STATE	MIN	FG	3FG	FT	REB	A	ST	BL	PF	TP
Mateen Cleaves	39	7-21	2-9	2-3	4	5	2	0	4	18
Charlie Bell	25	5-7	2-3	1-1	4	2	0	0	2	13
Morris Peterson	23	3-11	0-3	3-4	3	1	1	1	3	9
Jason Klein	23	2-11	2-8	0-0	2	1	0	0	2	6
Antonio Smith	29	0-4	0-0	4-4	7	0	0	0	4	4
Andre Hutson	26	2-6	0-0	0-0	3	1	0	1	4	4
DuJuan Wiley	19	2-6	0-0	0-0	3	0	0	1	2	4
David Thomas	7	0-0	0-0	0-0	1	0	0	0	0	0
A.J. Granger	6	0-2	0-2	0-0	2	0	1	0	1	0
Steve Cherry	1	0-0	0-0	0-0	0	0	0	0	0	0
Doug Davis	1	0-0	0-0	0-0	0	0	0	0	0	0
Ken Miller	1	0-0	0-0	0-0	0	0	0	0	0	0
TOTALS	**200**	**21-68**	**6-25**	**10-12**	**29**	**10**	**4**	**3**	**22**	**58**
Percentages		30.9	24.0	83.3						

Coach: Tom Izzo

Officials: Tim Higgins, Jim Haney, Reggi Greenwood **Technicals:** None **Attendance:** 23,235

75-74

CONNECTICUT	MIN	FG	3FG	FT	REB	A	ST	BL	PF	TP
Richard Hamilton	28	8-16	2-5	4-4	6	1	0	0	4	22
Khalid El-Amin	35	7-20	2-8	3-4	2	4	2	0	2	19
Kevin Freeman	35	2-3	0-0	6-6	2	0	0	0	3	10
Jake Voskuhl	25	3-4	0-0	3-3	6	0	0	2	4	9
Ricky Moore	35	1-3	0-1	2-3	1	2	2	1	2	4
Rashamel Jones	14	2-3	0-0	0-0	4	0	0	0	1	4
Monquencio Hardnett	11	1-2	0-0	2-2	2	2	1	0	2	4
Sowleymane Wane	7	1-1	0-0	1-1	2	0	0	1	3	3
Antric Klaiber	9	0-0	0-0	0-0	1	0	0	0	2	0
E.J. Harrison	1	0-0	0-0	0-0	0	0	0	0	0	0
TOTALS	**200**	**25-52**	**4-14**	**21-23**	**26**	**9**	**5**	**4**	**23**	**75**
Percentages		48.1	28.6	91.3						

Coach: Jim Calhoun

	1H	2H
Connecticut	47	28
Washington	39	35

SWEET 16

WASHINGTON	MIN	FG	3FG	FT	REB	A	ST	BL	PF	TP
Donald Watts	40	7-19	1-4	7-8	7	4	0	0	1	22
Todd MacCulloch	30	7-12	0-0	4-5	10	0	0	0	2	18
Deon Luton	37	6-14	1-5	4-4	0	1	1	0	2	17
Patrick Femerling	18	3-4	0-0	1-3	2	1	0	3	2	7
Chris Walcott	16	3-6	0-0	0-0	7	0	0	0	3	6
Jan Wooten	31	1-3	0-1	0-0	4	3	0	0	3	2
Thalo Green	16	1-2	0-0	0-0	0	3	1	0	4	2
Chris Thompson	5	0-0	0-0	0-0	0	0	0	0	0	0
Dan Dickau	4	0-1	0-0	0-0	0	0	0	0	0	0
Michael Johnson	3	0-1	0-0	0-0	0	0	0	0	0	0
TOTALS	**200**	**28-62**	**2-10**	**16-20**	**30**	**12**	**2**	**3**	**17**	**74**
Percentages		45.2	20.0	80.0						

Coach: Bob Bender

Officials: Don Rutledge, Zelto Steed, Ron Foxcroft **Technicals:** None **Attendance:** 23,235

87-79

ARIZONA	MIN	FG	3FG	FT	REB	A	ST	BL	PF	TP
Mike Bibby	39	7-12	5-6	7-9	5	4	4	1	1	26
Miles Simon	36	6-14	2-5	4-4	7	6	0	0	2	18
Bennett Davison	29	6-7	0-0	4-6	7	1	2	3	1	16
Michael Dickerson	28	5-14	0-3	2-4	5	2	1	1	3	12
A.J. Bramlett	31	4-6	0-0	3-4	5	0	1	1	4	11
Eugene Edgerson	11	0-3	0-0	2-2	2	0	0	1	0	2
Donnell Harris	9	0-1	0-0	2-2	2	0	1	1	2	2
Jason Terry	17	0-5	0-2	0-0	1	5	1	0	1	0
TOTALS	**200**	**28-62**	**7-16**	**24-31**	**34**	**18**	**10**	**8**	**14**	**87**
Percentages		45.2	43.8	77.4						

Coach: Lute Olson

	1H	2H
Arizona	42	45
Maryland	33	46

SWEET 16

MARYLAND	MIN	FG	3FG	FT	REB	A	ST	BL	PF	TP
Laron Profit	34	8-21	2-5	1-3	10	2	0	2	4	19
Rodney Elliot	27	6-16	2-5	2-3	6	1	2	2	5	16
Terrell Stokes	35	4-11	3-7	0-0	7	7	1	0	2	11
Terence Morris	15	4-8	3-6	0-0	2	1	2	2	1	11
Mike Mardesich	19	3-7	0-0	2-2	4	1	1	0	5	8
Sarunas Jasikevicius	34	1-7	1-4	4-6	3	4	0	0	1	7
Obinna Ekezie	23	1-5	0-0	1-3	3	2	0	0	5	3
Matt Kovarik	12	1-2	0-0	0-0	0	1	0	0	1	2
LaRon Cephas	1	1-1	0-0	0-0	3	0	0	0	0	2
TOTALS	**200**	**29-78**	**11-27**	**10-17**	**38**	**19**	**6**	**6**	**24**	**79**
Percentages		37.2	40.7	58.8						

Coach: Gary Williams

Officials: Gene Monje, Ted Valentine, James Burr **Technicals:** None **Attendance:** 17,838

65-62

UTAH	MIN	FG	3FG	FT	REB	A	ST	BL	PF	TP
Michael Doleac	33	6-11	0-0	13-14	9	3	1	0	2	25
Andre Miller	36	4-8	1-2	5-5	2	8	3	0	3	14
Britton Johnsen	23	2-6	0-2	3-4	4	1	1	0	2	7
Drew Hansen	34	2-5	1-4	0-2	5	1	2	1	4	5
Trace Caton	6	2-5	1-2	0-0	0	0	0	0	0	5
Hanno Mottola	20	2-4	0-1	0-0	0	1	0	0	2	4
Alex Jensen	34	1-6	0-2	1-2	6	0	0	0	3	3
David Jackson	6	1-1	0-0	0-0	1	0	1	0	0	2
Nate Althoff	4	0-0	0-0	0-0	0	0	0	0	1	0
Jordie McTavish	4	0-0	0-0	0-0	1	0	0	0	0	0
TOTALS	**200**	**20-46**	**3-13**	**22-27**	**28**	**14**	**8**	**1**	**17**	**65**
Percentages		43.5	23.1	81.5						

Coach: Rick Majerus

	1H	2H
Utah	34	31
West Virginia	28	34

SWEET 16

WEST VIRGINIA	MIN	FG	3FG	FT	REB	A	ST	BL	PF	TP
Brent Solheim	34	6-9	0-0	4-4	7	1	0	2	4	16
Damian Owens	33	5-9	0-0	2-6	9	5	6	0	4	12
Jarrod West	32	4-13	2-7	1-2	2	3	4	0	4	11
Adrian Pledger	26	4-8	0-0	1-2	5	2	2	0	2	9
Brian Lewin	21	4-5	0-0	0-0	2	0	0	1	4	8
Marcus Goree	23	1-3	0-0	2-2	2	1	1	0	0	4
Jarett Kearse	10	1-4	0-1	0-0	0	2	0	0	1	2
Greg Jones	15	0-4	0-2	0-0	0	1	0	0	1	0
Elton Scott	3	0-0	0-0	0-0	0	0	0	0	0	0
Carl Williams	3	0-2	0-0	0-0	2	0	0	0	0	0
TOTALS	**200**	**25-57**	**2-10**	**10-16**	**29**	**15**	**13**	**3**	**20**	**62**
Percentages		43.9	20.0	62.5						

Coach: Gale Catlett

Officials: Dave Libbey, Mike Wood, Charles Range **Technicals:** West Virginia (bench) **Attendance:** 17,838

74-68

RHODE ISLAND	MIN	FG	3FG	FT	REB	A	ST	BL	PF	TP
Cuttino Mobley	38	5-12	4-6	2-2	5	2	0	0	4	16
Antonio Reynolds-Dean	35	6-8	0-0	4-8	11	1	1	3	2	16
Luther Clay	32	5-9	0-0	4-5	3	1	1	1	4	14
Preston Murphy	27	2-6	1-3	7-8	3	1	0	0	2	12
Tyson Wheeler	36	4-14	1-8	1-2	5	7	1	0	1	10
Josh King	20	1-5	1-4	0-0	3	1	0	0	1	3
David Arigbabu	10	0-1	0-0	3-4	2	0	0	0	1	3
John Bennett	1	0-0	0-0	0-0	1	0	0	0	0	0
Tory Jefferson	1	0-0	0-0	0-0	0	0	0	0	0	0
TOTALS	**200**	**23-55**	**7-21**	**21-29**	**33**	**13**	**3**	**4**	**15**	**74**
Percentages		41.8	33.3	72.4						

Coach: Jim Harrick

	1H	2H
Rhode Island	44	30
Valparaiso	39	29

SWEET 16

VALPARAISO	MIN	FG	3FG	FT	REB	A	ST	BL	PF	TP
Bryce Drew	36	6-16	3-7	3-3	3	3	3	0	4	18
Zoran Viskovic	28	5-9	0-0	3-4	7	1	1	1	1	13
Jamie Sykes	34	3-9	3-3	2-2	3	3	0	0	2	11
Bob Jenkins	23	4-8	1-1	2-2	8	1	0	0	5	11
Jason Jenkins	9	2-4	1-2	0-0	2	1	0	0	0	5
Bill Jenkins	26	2-8	0-3	0-1	5	0	1	0	4	4
Antanas Vilcinskas	21	2-3	0-0	0-0	1	0	0	0	4	4
Jared Nuness	23	1-6	0-2	0-0	3	2	0	0	2	2
TOTALS	**200**	**25-63**	**8-18**	**10-12**	**32**	**11**	**5**	**1**	**22**	**68**
Percentages		39.7	44.4	83.3						

Coach: Homer Drew

Officials: John Clougherty, Rick Hartzell, Leslie Jones **Technicals:** None **Attendance:** 22,172

67-59

STANFORD	MIN	FG	3FG	FT	REB	A	ST	BL	PF	TP
Mark Madsen	26	6-8	0-0	3-5	13	1	1	0	5	15
Arthur Lee	34	3-11	1-2	6-6	4	3	0	0	0	13
Jarron Collins	23	5-9	0-1	2-3	11	2	1	0	3	12
David Moseley	16	3-10	2-5	2-2	3	0	0	0	0	10
Peter Sauer	22	4-10	1-4	0-0	4	3	0	0	0	9
Tim Young	20	3-5	0-0	0-0	4	2	0	1	4	6
Michael McDonald	6	0-1	0-0	2-2	0	1	0	0	2	2
Kris Weems	31	0-10	0-3	0-1	6	2	1	0	0	0
Ryan Mendez	11	0-2	0-1	0-0	4	0	0	0	1	0
Mark Seaton	8	0-0	0-0	0-0	1	0	0	0	1	0
Pete Van Elswyk	3	0-0	0-0	0-0	1	0	0	0	0	0
TOTALS	**200**	**24-66**	**4-16**	**15-19**	**51**	**14**	**3**	**1**	**16**	**67**
Percentages		36.4	25.0	78.9						

Coach: Mike Montgomery

	1H	2H
Stanford	37	30
Purdue	26	33

SWEET 16

PURDUE	MIN	FG	3FG	FT	REB	A	ST	BL	PF	TP
Brad Miller	29	5-11	0-1	3-4	11	2	2	1	4	13
Chad Austin	35	4-18	2-9	2-2	5	3	1	1	0	12
Brian Cardinal	28	4-11	1-6	2-4	8	3	2	0	4	11
Mike Robinson	30	3-11	1-4	2-2	6	2	1	1	3	9
Alan Eldridge	29	2-8	1-6	0-0	4	3	1	1	1	5
Jaraan Cornell	18	1-3	1-3	2-2	1	1	1	0	1	5
Gary McQuay	18	1-3	0-0	0-0	4	0	1	2	4	2
Tony Mayfield	13	1-2	0-0	0-0	0	3	0	0	3	2
TOTALS	**200**	**21-67**	**6-29**	**11-14**	**39**	**17**	**9**	**6**	**20**	**59**
Percentages		31.3	20.7	78.6						

Coach: Gene Keady

Officials: Tom Lopes, John Cahill, Bob Donato **Technicals:** None **Attendance:** 22,172

DUKE	MIN	FG	3FG	FT	REB	A	ST	BL	PF	TP
Elton Brand	29	10-14	0-0	0-2	14	0	1	1	3	20
Shane Battier	20	6-7	0-0	2-3	7	1	2	3	3	14
William Avery	23	4-6	3-5	0-0	4	6	3	0	3	11
Chris Carrawell	27	4-9	0-1	2-4	5	2	1	0	1	10
Trajan Langdon	36	2-13	1-8	2-2	3	2	0	0	0	7
Steve Wojciechowski	26	1-4	1-4	3-4	4	2	0	0	3	6
Roshown McLeod	24	2-9	0-2	2-4	5	3	1	1	4	6
Mike Chappell	8	2-3	2-2	0-0	2	0	0	0	1	6
Chris Burgess	4	0-0	0-0	0-0	0	0	0	0	0	0
Jay Heaps	1	0-0	0-0	0-0	0	0	0	0	0	0
J.D. Simpson	1	0-0	0-0	0-0	0	0	0	0	0	0
Todd Singleton	1	0-0	0-0	0-0	0	0	0	0	0	0
TOTALS	**200**	**31-65**	**7-22**	**11-19**	**44**	**16**	**8**	**5**	**18**	**80**
Percentages		47.7	31.8	57.9						

Coach: Mike Krzyzewski

80-67

40	1H	30
40	2H	37

SWEET 16

SYRACUSE	MIN	FG	3FG	FT	REB	A	ST	BL	PF	TP
Todd Burgan	37	7-16	4-7	2-3	10	0	1	0	3	20
Jason Hart	36	6-11	1-4	2-2	2	3	3	0	4	15
Ryan Blackwell	37	4-13	0-2	3-6	9	3	2	0	3	11
Etan Thomas	32	2-5	0-0	5-8	6	1	2	3	2	9
Allen Griffin	19	3-6	0-1	0-0	1	2	4	0	1	6
Marius Janulis	24	1-7	1-5	0-0	2	1	3	0	5	3
Elvir Ovcina	11	1-5	0-2	1-2	3	0	0	1	0	3
Damone Brown	1	0-0	0-0	0-0	0	0	0	0	0	0
Malik Campbell	1	0-0	0-0	0-0	0	0	0	0	0	0
Erik Frazier	1	0-0	0-0	0-0	0	0	0	0	0	0
Jason Mallin	1	0-0	0-0	0-0	0	0	0	0	0	0
TOTALS	**200**	**24-63**	**6-21**	**13-21**	**33**	**10**	**15**	**4**	**18**	**67**
Percentages		38.1	28.6	61.9						

Coach: Jim Boeheim

Officials: Scott Thornley, Andre Pattillo, David Hall
Technicals: None
Attendance: 40,589

KENTUCKY	MIN	FG	3FG	FT	REB	A	ST	BL	PF	TP
Scott Padgett	24	6-8	1-2	6-6	6	4	1	0	3	19
Jeff Sheppard	28	7-14	2-6	0-0	4	3	1	0	3	16
Nazr Mohammed	19	6-9	0-0	3-5	7	0	0	6	3	15
Heshimu Evans	21	3-4	0-0	4-4	2	1	1	1	1	10
Allen Edwards	20	5-6	0-1	0-0	2	5	0	1	3	10
Wayne Turner	26	4-7	0-0	0-0	3	4	3	0	1	8
Ryan Hogan	3	2-4	2-3	0-1	2	0	0	0	0	6
Myron Anthony	9	2-4	1-1	0-0	1	0	0	0	0	5
Jamaal Magloire	15	1-1	0-0	1-2	5	0	2	6	2	3
Michael Bradley	9	1-5	0-0	0-0	4	1	0	0	1	2
Cameron Mills	13	0-3	0-1	0-0	1	0	0	0	0	0
Saul Smith	11	0-1	0-0	0-1	1	3	1	0	1	0
Steve Masiello	2	0-2	0-0	0-0	2	0	1	0	0	0
TOTALS	**200**	**37-68**	**6-14**	**14-19**	**40**	**21**	**10**	**14**	**18**	**94**
Percentages		54.4	42.9	73.7						

Coach: Tubby Smith

94-68

40	1H	23
54	2H	45

SWEET 16

UCLA	MIN	FG	3FG	FT	REB	A	ST	BL	PF	TP
Kris Johnson	33	7-15	3-8	1-2	8	1	0	0	3	18
Toby Bailey	35	4-15	1-5	7-8	11	3	0	2	4	16
J.R. Henderson	36	5-20	0-0	0-0	9	1	1	0	2	10
Travis Reed	31	2-13	0-0	3-5	10	0	2	3	3	7
Earl Watson	34	1-8	0-4	4-4	2	2	2	1	2	6
Rico Hines	18	1-2	0-0	2-2	4	0	1	0	3	4
Kevin Daley	3	2-3	0-1	0-0	1	0	1	0	0	4
Billy Knight	2	1-2	0-1	1-1	2	0	0	0	0	3
Brandon Loyd	3	0-0	0-0	0-0	1	1	0	0	0	0
Sean Farnham	2	0-0	0-0	0-0	0	0	0	0	0	0
Matt Harbour	1	0-1	0-0	0-0	1	0	1	0	0	0
Vince McGautha	1	0-0	0-0	0-0	0	0	0	0	0	0
Todd Ramasar	1	0-0	0-0	0-0	1	1	0	0	0	0
TOTALS	**200**	**23-79**	**4-19**	**18-22**	**50**	**9**	**8**	**6**	**17**	**68**
Percentages		29.1	21.1	81.8						

Coach: Steve Lavin

Officials: Donnee Gray, Steve Welmer, Jody Silvester
Technicals: None
Attendance: 40,589

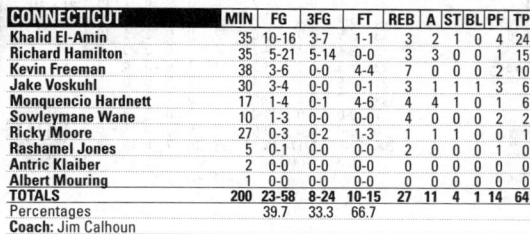

NORTH CAROLINA	MIN	FG	3FG	FT	REB	A	ST	BL	PF	TP
Antawn Jamison	35	9-19	0-1	2-4	11	1	0	0	1	20
Shammond Williams	34	6-16	1-7	6-6	2	3	1	0	0	19
Vince Carter	33	5-9	1-2	1-1	3	2	1	2	1	12
Ademola Okulaja	29	5-8	2-3	0-0	7	2	0	1	3	12
Ed Cota	37	4-8	0-1	0-0	8	9	1	0	1	8
Makhtar N'diaye	30	2-3	0-0	0-0	4	0	1	2	4	4
Brendan Haywood	2	0-0	0-0	0-0	0	0	0	0	0	0
TOTALS	**200**	**31-63**	**4-14**	**9-11**	**35**	**17**	**4**	**5**	**10**	**75**
Percentages		49.2	28.6	81.8						

Coach: Bill Guthridge

75-64

36	1H	32
39	2H	32

ELITE 8

CONNECTICUT	MIN	FG	3FG	FT	REB	A	ST	BL	PF	TP
Khalid El-Amin	35	10-16	3-7	1-1	3	2	1	0	4	24
Richard Hamilton	35	5-21	5-14	0-0	3	3	0	0	1	15
Kevin Freeman	38	3-6	0-0	4-4	7	0	0	0	2	10
Jake Voskuhl	30	3-4	0-0	0-1	3	1	1	1	3	6
Monquencio Hardnett	17	1-4	0-1	4-6	4	4	1	0	1	6
Sowleymane Wane	10	1-3	0-0	0-0	4	0	0	0	2	2
Ricky Moore	27	0-3	0-2	1-3	1	1	1	0	0	1
Rashamel Jones	5	0-1	0-0	0-0	2	0	0	0	1	0
Antric Klaiber	2	0-0	0-0	0-0	0	0	0	0	0	0
Albert Mouring	1	0-0	0-0	0-0	0	0	0	0	0	0
TOTALS	**200**	**23-58**	**8-24**	**10-15**	**27**	**11**	**4**	**1**	**14**	**64**
Percentages		39.7	33.3	66.7						

Coach: Jim Calhoun

Officials: Mark Reischling, Eddie Jackson, Dick Cartmell
Technicals: None
Attendance: 23,235

UTAH	MIN	FG	3FG	FT	REB	A	ST	BL	PF	TP
Andre Miller	36	7-15	0-1	4-8	14	13	2	1	4	18
Michael Doleac	34	6-9	0-1	4-4	11	0	0	1	3	16
Hanno Mottola	27	7-12	0-1	0-1	5	0	0	0	1	14
Alex Jensen	35	4-7	0-1	3-5	10	2	1	0	4	11
David Jackson	25	3-6	1-2	3-4	2	2	0	0	1	10
Britton Johnsen	14	1-1	0-0	2-4	0	0	0	1	2	4
Drew Hansen	24	1-4	1-3	0-0	4	1	0	0	4	3
Trace Caton	3	0-0	0-0	0-0	0	0	0	0	0	0
Jordie McTavish	2	0-1	0-1	0-0	0	1	0	0	0	0
TOTALS	**200**	**29-55**	**2-10**	**16-26**	**46**	**19**	**3**	**3**	**19**	**76**
Percentages		52.7	20.0	61.5						

Coach: Rick Majerus

76-51

29	1H	20
47	2H	31

ELITE 8

ARIZONA	MIN	FG	3FG	FT	REB	A	ST	BL	PF	TP
Jason Terry	28	5-11	4-9	2-2	5	3	1	1	3	16
A.J. Bramlett	29	4-7	0-0	2-6	6	0	2	0	5	10
Mike Bibby	35	3-15	0-7	1-2	3	1	1	0	3	7
Miles Simon	33	1-9	0-3	4-8	4	4	0	0	2	6
Bennett Davison	29	2-5	0-0	2-4	10	0	0	1	4	6
Michael Dickerson	26	2-12	0-3	2-2	2	2	0	0	3	6
Donnell Harris	9	0-0	0-0	0-0	1	0	0	0	0	0
Eugene Edgerson	8	0-1	0-0	0-0	1	0	0	0	1	0
Quynn Tebbs	2	0-0	0-0	0-0	0	0	0	0	0	0
Ortege Jenkins	1	0-0	0-0	0-0	0	0	0	0	0	0
TOTALS	**200**	**17-60**	**4-22**	**13-24**	**32**	**10**	**4**	**2**	**21**	**51**
Percentages		28.3	18.2	54.2						

Coach: Lute Olson

Officials: Gerald Boudreaux, Tony Greene, Tom Rucker
Technicals: None
Attendance: 17,851

STANFORD	MIN	FG	3FG	FT	REB	A	ST	BL	PF	TP
Arthur Lee	36	9-15	3-6	5-5	4	7	2	0	4	26
Mark Madsen	30	6-15	0-0	3-3	5	1	0	0	3	15
Tim Young	32	6-7	0-0	2-3	12	2	0	0	3	14
David Moseley	16	2-5	2-4	2-2	2	1	0	0	5	8
Kris Weems	27	2-5	1-2	1-3	2	0	1	1	2	6
Ryan Mendez	17	2-5	2-4	0-0	2	2	1	0	0	6
Peter Sauer	19	1-6	0-2	2-2	2	2	1	0	0	4
Jarron Collins	18	0-4	0-1	0-0	4	0	2	0	1	0
Michael McDonald	5	0-1	0-0	0-0	0	1	0	0	0	0
TOTALS	**200**	**28-63**	**8-19**	**15-18**	**33**	**16**	**7**	**1**	**18**	**79**
Percentages		44.4	42.1	83.3						

Coach: Mike Montgomery

79-77

38	1H	38
41	2H	39

ELITE 8

RHODE ISLAND	MIN	FG	3FG	FT	REB	A	ST	BL	PF	TP
Tyson Wheeler	34	9-14	4-7	2-5	1	5	1	0	0	24
Cuttino Mobley	35	6-10	3-4	5-6	5	3	1	0	3	20
Preston Murphy	24	2-6	0-1	6-8	2	1	3	0	4	10
Luther Clay	35	3-7	0-0	2-2	6	2	0	1	2	8
Antonio Reynolds-Dean	33	4-12	0-0	0-0	10	3	2	2	4	8
Josh King	27	3-6	1-4	0-0	1	0	1	1	2	7
David Arigbabu	12	0-1	0-0	0-0	3	1	0	1	4	0
TOTALS	**200**	**27-56**	**8-16**	**15-21**	**28**	**15**	**8**	**5**	**19**	**77**
Percentages		48.2	50.0	71.4						

Coach: Jim Harrick

Officials: Frank Scagliotta, Michael Kitts, Larry Rose
Technicals: Stanford (Moseley)
Attendance: 22,172

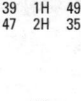

KENTUCKY	MIN	FG	3FG	FT	REB	A	ST	BL	PF	TP
Jeff Sheppard	32	5-11	1-3	7-9	11	0	0	0	4	18
Wayne Turner	36	5-14	0-1	6-8	5	8	2	0	1	16
Heshimu Evans	24	5-8	2-2	2-2	11	1	0	0	3	14
Scott Padgett	38	4-10	3-5	1-2	6	1	0	0	3	12
Allen Edwards	20	4-8	2-5	1-2	2	2	0	0	4	11
Nazr Mohammed	16	4-10	0-0	0-2	5	0	0	0	2	8
Cameron Mills	13	1-1	1-1	2-2	3	1	1	0	1	5
Jamaal Magloire	16	1-1	0-0	0-0	1	0	1	1	2	2
Saul Smith	5	0-0	0-0	0-0	1	0	0	1	0	0
TOTALS	**200**	**29-63**	**9-17**	**19-27**	**44**	**14**	**4**	**1**	**21**	**86**
Percentages		46.0	52.9	70.4						

Coach: Tubby Smith

86-84

39	1H	49
47	2H	35

ELITE 8

DUKE	MIN	FG	3FG	FT	REB	A	ST	BL	PF	TP
Roshown McLeod	30	7-20	2-7	3-7	8	3	0	0	4	19
Trajan Langdon	37	6-14	3-8	3-4	5	4	0	0	2	18
Chris Carrawell	27	5-11	0-2	2-2	5	2	0	1	1	12
Shane Battier	24	3-6	0-0	5-6	8	0	0	1	3	11
Steve Wojciechowski	32	3-5	3-5	1-3	3	4	3	0	4	10
Mike Chappell	6	2-2	2-2	0-0	0	0	0	0	0	6
Elton Brand	21	1-4	0-0	2-4	2	0	0	2	5	4
William Avery	20	2-4	0-1	0-0	4	1	1	0	1	4
Chris Burgess	3	0-1	0-0	0-0	0	0	0	1	2	0
TOTALS	**200**	**29-67**	**10-25**	**16-26**	**35**	**14**	**4**	**5**	**22**	**84**
Percentages		43.3	40.0	61.5						

Coach: Mike Krzyzewski

Officials: Tom Harrington, Mike Sanzere, Curtis Shaw
Technicals: None
Attendance: 40,589

65-59 (Final 4)

	1H	2H
Utah	35	30
North Carolina	22	37

UTAH	MIN	FG	3FG	FT	REB	A	ST	BL	PF	TP
Andre Miller	37	7-15	0-3	2-7	14	7	1	0	1	16
Michael Doleac	25	6-11	0-1	4-7	5	1	0	1	2	16
Hanno Mottola	29	2-9	1-4	4-6	1	0	0	1	3	9
Alex Jensen	34	3-4	1-1	0-0	5	3	2	0	4	7
Britton Johnsen	16	3-7	1-2	0-0	2	0	1	1	1	7
Drew Hansen	33	1-1	1-1	2-2	6	2	1	0	2	5
Jordie McTavish	3	1-2	1-2	0-0	0	1	0	0	1	3
Trace Caton	5	1-3	0-2	0-0	1	0	0	0	0	2
David Jackson	18	0-2	0-1	0-0	0	0	0	0	1	0
TOTALS	**200**	**24-54**	**5-17**	**12-22**	**34**	**14**	**5**	**3**	**15**	**65**
Percentages		44.4	29.4	54.5						

Coach: Rick Majerus

NORTH CAROLINA	MIN	FG	3FG	FT	REB	A	ST	BL	PF	TP
Vince Carter	32	10-16	1-4	0-1	5	0	0	3	3	21
Antawn Jamison	37	7-19	0-1	0-2	12	1	1	0	4	14
Ed Cota	38	4-9	0-4	0-0	7	7	1	0	2	8
Ademola Okulaja	37	3-8	1-5	0-0	9	1	3	0	3	7
Shammond Williams	34	2-12	1-9	2-2	2	5	0	0	0	7
Brendan Haywood	8	1-2	0-0	0-0	3	0	0	0	2	2
Makhtar N'diaye	14	0-3	0-0	0-2	2	0	0	2	5	0
TOTALS	**200**	**27-69**	**3-23**	**2-7**	**40**	**14**	**5**	**5**	**19**	**59**
Percentages		39.1	13.0	28.6						

Coach: Bill Guthridge

Officials: J[illegible] Clougherty, Andre Patt[illegible] Don Rutledg[illegible] **Technicals:** None **Attendance:** 40,509

86-85 (Final 4)

	1H	2H	OT1
Kentucky	32	41	13
Stanford	37	36	12

KENTUCKY	MIN	FG	3FG	FT	REB	A	ST	BL	PF	TP
Jeff Sheppard	33	9-15	4-8	5-7	6	4	2	0	3	27
Nazr Mohammed	24	7-14	0-0	4-6	5	0	1	3	4	18
Allen Edwards	26	4-10	1-2	2-3	3	1	0	0	1	11
Scott Padgett	38	2-8	0-3	6-6	6	2	3	0	3	10
Wayne Turner	35	2-8	0-0	4-9	2	4	2	1	2	8
Jamaal Magloire	19	2-3	0-0	2-2	4	1	0	2	2	6
Heshimu Evans	28	2-7	0-2	0-0	6	2	0	1	2	4
Cameron Mills	7	1-1	0-0	0-0	2	0	0	0	2	2
Saul Smith	14	0-1	0-0	0-0	2	2	0	0	2	0
Michael Bradley	1	0-0	0-0	0-0	0	0	0	0	1	0
TOTALS	**225**	**29-67**	**5-15**	**23-33**	**36**	**16**	**8**	**7**	**22**	**86**
Percentages		43.3	33.3	69.7						

Coach: Tubby Smith

STANFORD	MIN	FG	3FG	FT	REB	A	ST	BL	PF	TP
Arthur Lee	41	6-12	5-8	9-9	3	5	0	0	4	26
Kris Weems	41	6-23	3-11	2-3	1	4	0	1	1	17
Mark Madsen	34	5-6	0-0	1-1	16	0	0	2	5	11
Tim Young	28	5-11	0-0	0-0	7	2	0	1	5	10
Peter Sauer	22	3-4	2-3	0-0	7	0	0	1	2	8
Jarron Collins	20	1-3	0-0	5-7	5	0	1	0	3	7
Ryan Mendez	11	1-4	1-4	0-0	1	0	0	0	1	3
David Moseley	15	0-3	0-2	2-2	1	0	0	0	1	2
Pete Van Elswyk	3	0-1	0-0	1-2	0	0	1	0	1	1
Mark Seaton	6	0-0	0-0	0-0	2	1	0	0	0	0
Michael McDonald	4	0-1	0-0	0-0	1	1	0	0	0	0
TOTALS	**225**	**27-68**	**11-28**	**20-24**	**44**	**13**	**2**	**5**	**23**	**85**
Percentages		39.7	39.3	83.3						

Coach: Mike Montgomery

Officials: Tim Higgins, Bob Donato, Larry Rose **Technicals:** None **Attendance:** 40,509

78-69 (NCAA Final 1998)

	1H	2H
Kentucky	31	47
Utah	41	28

KENTUCKY	MIN	FG	3FG	FT	REB	A	ST	BL	PF	TP
Scott Padgett	33	6-11	1-5	4-4	5	1	0	0	4	17
Jeff Sheppard	34	7-14	0-2	2-2	4	3	2	0	1	16
Heshimu Evans	23	3-4	2-2	2-2	6	0	1	1	1	10
Nazr Mohammed	13	5-9	0-0	0-0	2	0	0	2	4	10
Cameron Mills	12	2-4	2-4	2-2	0	1	0	0	0	8
Jamaal Magloire	22	2-3	0-0	3-3	2	1	0	3	4	7
Wayne Turner	27	2-5	0-1	2-4	2	4	3	0	0	6
Allen Edwards	24	2-7	0-3	0-0	1	5	1	0	0	4
Saul Smith	7	0-0	0-0	0-0	0	0	0	0	0	0
Michael Bradley	5	0-0	0-0	0-0	1	0	0	0	1	0
TOTALS	**200**	**29-57**	**5-17**	**15-17**	**23**	**15**	**7**	**6**	**15**	**78**
Percentages		50.9	29.4	88.2						

Coach: Tubby Smith

UTAH	MIN	FG	3FG	FT	REB	A	ST	BL	PF	TP
Andre Miller	37	6-15	0-3	4-7	6	5	2	0	5	16
Michael Doleac	34	5-12	1-1	4-6	10	1	3	2	2	15
Hanno Mottola	28	4-10	1-3	6-6	8	0	0	0	4	15
Alex Jensen	35	5-6	1-1	3-3	2	2	0	0	2	14
Britton Johnsen	16	3-4	1-2	0-0	4	0	0	0	0	7
Drew Hansen	32	1-6	0-2	0-0	5	1	3	0	2	2
David Jackson	10	0-1	0-1	0-0	0	1	0	0	2	0
Trace Caton	5	0-1	0-1	0-0	0	0	0	0	0	0
Jordie McTavish	3	0-0	0-0	0-0	0	2	0	0	1	0
TOTALS	**200**	**24-55**	**4-14**	**17-22**	**35**	**12**	**8**	**2**	**18**	**69**
Percentages		43.6	28.6	77.3						

Coach: Rick Majerus

Officials: James Burr, Donnee Gray, Mike Sanzere **Technicals:** None **Attendance:** 40,509

National Invitation Tournament (NIT)

First round: Wake Forest d. UNC Wilmington 56-52, Vanderbilt d. St. Bonaventure 73-61, Georgia d. Iowa 100-93, NC State d. Kansas State 59-39, Penn State d. Rider 82-68, Dayton d. Long Island 95-92, Georgetown d. Florida 71-69, Georgia Tech d. Seton Hall 88-78, Hawaii d. Arizona State 90-73, Gonzaga d. Wyoming 69-55, Fresno St d. Pacific 73-70, Memphis d. Ball State 90-67, Marquette d. Creighton 80-68, Auburn d. Southern Miss 77-62, Minnesota d. Colorado State 77-65, UAB d. Missouri 93-86

Second round: Vanderbilt d. Wake Forest 72-68, Georgia d. NC State 61-55, Penn State d. Dayton 77-74, Georgia Tech d. Georgetown 80-79, Hawaii d. Gonzaga 78-70, Fresno St d. Memphis 83-80, Marquette d. Auburn 75-60, Minnesota d. UAB 79-66

Third round: Georgia d. Vanderbilt 79-65, Penn State d. Georgia Tech 77-70, Fresno St d. Hawaii 85-83, Minnesota d. Marquette 73-71

Semifinals: Penn State d. Georgia 66-60, Minnesota d. Fresno St 91-89

Championship: Minnesota✪ d. Penn State 79-72

Third place: Georgia d. Fresno State 95-79

MVP: Kevin Clark, Minnesota✪

✪ Team later sanctioned by NCAA

1998-99: UConn Can

The '90s were a frustrating decade for Connecticut coach Jim Calhoun—the Huskies fell shy of the Final Four three times, with Elite Eight losses in 1990, '95 and '98. But at last they broke through in 1999, becoming the first team since Texas Western in 1966 to win the national championship in its first Final Four appearance. Duke, Michigan State and Ohio State joined UConn for the final weekend at the Tropicana Dome in St. Petersburg, Fla. The Huskies' Richard "Rip" Hamilton scored 27 points in the 77-74 championship game win over Duke and was named Tournament MOP.

But the early part of the Tournament was a trip through Wally World. Miami of Ohio forward Wally Szczerbiak—who, during the season, averaged 24.2 ppg (third in Division I), 8.5 rebounds and 2.9 assists per game—scored an unreal 43 of Miami's 59 points in a first-round upset of Washington. Szczerbiak scored 90 points in three games as Miami advanced to the Sweet 16 (where it lost to Kentucky) for the first time since 1978.

Norm Stewart retired after 32 years as Missouri head coach. Stormin' Norman finished with a Division I record of 728–374, at Mizzou and Northern Iowa.

Major Conference Standings

AM. EAST

	Conference			Overall		
	W	L	PCT	W	L	PCT
Delaware⊕	15	3	.833	25	6	.806
Drexel	15	3	.833	20	9	.690
Hofstra□	14	4	.778	22	10	.688
Maine	13	5	.722	19	9	.679
Hartford	9	9	.500	11	16	.407
Vermont	7	11	.389	11	16	.407
Northeastern	6	12	.333	10	18	.357
Boston U.	5	13	.278	9	18	.333
Towson	4	14	.222	6	22	.214
New Hampshire	2	16	.111	4	23	.148

Tournament: **Delaware d. Drexel 86-67**
Tournament MOP: **John Gordon**, Delaware

ACC

	Conference			Overall		
	W	L	PCT	W	L	PCT
Duke⊕	16	0	1.000	37	2	.949
Maryland○	13	3	.813	28	6	.824
North Carolina○	10	6	.625	24	10	.706
Wake Forest□	7	9	.438	17	14	.548
NC State□	6	10	.375	19	14	.576
Georgia Tech□	6	10	.375	15	16	.484
Clemson□	5	11	.313	20	15	.571
Florida State	5	11	.313	13	17	.433
Virginia	4	12	.250	14	16	.467

Tournament: **Duke d. North Carolina 96-73**
Tournament MVP: **Elton Brand**, Duke

ATLANTIC 10

	Conference			Overall		
	W	L	PCT	W	L	PCT
EAST						
Temple○	13	3	.813	24	11	.686
Rhode Island⊕	10	6	.625	20	13	.606
Massachusetts	9	7	.563	14	16	.467
St. Bonaventure	8	8	.500	14	15	.483
Fordham	5	11	.313	12	15	.444
Saint Joseph's	5	11	.313	12	18	.400
WEST						
George Washington○	13	3	.813	20	9	.690
Xavier□	12	4	.750	25	11	.694
La Salle	8	8	.500	13	15	.464
Virginia Tech	7	9	.438	13	15	.464
Dayton	5	11	.313	11	17	.393
Duquesne	1	15	.063	5	23	.179

Tournament: **Rhode Island d. Temple 62-59**
Tournament MOP: **Lamar Odom**, Rhode Island

BIG EAST

	Conference			Overall		
	W	L	PCT	W	L	PCT
Connecticut⊕	16	2	.889	34	2	.944
Miami (FL)○	15	3	.833	23	7	.767
St. John's○	14	4	.778	28	9	.757
Villanova○	10	8	.556	21	11	.656
Syracuse○	10	8	.556	21	12	.636
Rutgers□	9	9	.500	19	13	.594
Providence□	9	9	.500	16	14	.533
Seton Hall□	8	10	.444	15	15	.500
Notre Dame	8	10	.444	14	16	.467
Georgetown□	6	12	.333	15	16	.484
Pittsburgh	5	13	.278	14	16	.467
West Virginia	4	14	.222	10	19	.345
Boston College	3	15	.167	6	21	.222

Tournament: **Connecticut d. St. John's 82-63**
Tournament MVP: **Kevin Freeman**, Connecticut

BIG SKY

	Conference			Overall		
	W	L	PCT	W	L	PCT
Weber State⊕	13	3	.813	25	8	.758
Northern Arizona	12	4	.750	21	8	.724
Portland State	9	7	.563	17	11	.607
Cal State Northridge	9	7	.563	17	12	.586
Montana State	9	7	.563	16	13	.552
Eastern Washington	7	9	.438	10	17	.370
Montana	6	10	.375	13	14	.481
Idaho State	4	12	.250	6	20	.231
Cal State Sacramento	3	13	.188	3	23	.115

Tournament: **Weber State d. Northern Arizona 82-75**
Tournament MVP: **Eddie Gill**, Weber State

BIG SOUTH

	Conference			Overall		
	W	L	PCT	W	L	PCT
Winthrop⊕	9	1	.900	21	8	.724
Radford	8	2	.800	20	8	.714
UNC Asheville	5	5	.500	11	18	.379
Charleston Southern	4	6	.400	12	16	.429
Coastal Carolina	4	6	.400	7	20	.259
Liberty	0	10	.000	4	23	.148

Tournament: **Winthrop d. Radford 86-74**
Tournament MVP: **Heson Groves**, Winthrop

BIG TEN

	Conference			Overall		
	W	L	PCT	W	L	PCT
Michigan State⊕	15	1	.938	33	5	.868
Ohio State○⊗	12	4	.750	27	9	.750
Indiana○	9	7	.563	23	11	.676
Wisconsin○	9	7	.563	22	10	.688
Iowa○	9	7	.563	20	10	.667
Minnesota○	8	8	.500	17	11	.607
Purdue○	7	9	.438	21	13	.618
Northwestern□	6	10	.375	15	14	.517
Penn State	5	11	.313	13	14	.481
Michigan⊗	5	11	.313	12	19	.387
Illinois	3	13	.188	14	18	.438

Tournament: **Michigan State d. Illinois 67-50**
Tournament MOP: **Mateen Cleaves**, Michigan State

BIG 12

	Conference			Overall		
	W	L	PCT	W	L	PCT
Texas○	13	3	.813	19	13	.594
Kansas⊕	11	5	.688	23	10	.697
Missouri○	11	5	.688	20	9	.690
Oklahoma○	11	5	.688	22	11	.667
Oklahoma State○	10	6	.625	23	11	.676
Nebraska□	10	6	.625	20	13	.606
Kansas State□	7	9	.438	20	13	.606
Colorado□	7	9	.438	18	15	.545
Iowa State	6	10	.375	15	15	.500
Texas A&M	5	11	.313	12	15	.444
Texas Tech	5	11	.313	13	17	.433
Baylor	0	16	.000	6	24	.200

Tournament: **Kansas d. Oklahoma State 53-37**
Tournament MOP: **Jeff Boschee**, Kansas

BIG WEST

	Conference			Overall		
	W	L	PCT	W	L	PCT
EASTERN						
Boise State	12	4	.750	21	8	.724
New Mexico State⊕	12	4	.750	23	10	.697
Idaho	11	5	.688	16	11	.593
Utah State	8	8	.500	15	13	.536
Nevada	4	12	.250	8	18	.308
North Texas	4	12	.250	4	22	.154
WESTERN						
UC Santa Barbara	12	4	.750	15	13	.536
Pacific	9	7	.563	14	13	.519
Long Beach State	9	7	.563	13	15	.464
Cal State Fullerton	7	9	.438	13	14	.481
Cal Poly	6	10	.375	11	16	.407
UC Irvine	2	14	.125	6	20	.231

Tournament: **New Mexico State d. Boise State 79-69**
Tournament MVP: **Billy Keys**, New Mexico St.

COLONIAL ATHLETIC

	Conference			Overall		
	W	L	PCT	W	L	PCT
George Mason⊕	13	3	.813	19	11	.633
Old Dominion□	11	5	.688	25	9	.735
Richmond	10	6	.625	15	12	.556
James Madison	9	7	.563	16	11	.593
UNC Wilmington	9	7	.563	11	17	.393
VCU	8	8	.500	15	16	.484
East Carolina	7	9	.438	13	14	.481
William and Mary	3	13	.188	8	19	.296
American	2	14	.125	7	21	.250

Tournament: **George Mason d. Old Dominion 63-58**
Tournament MVP: **George Evans**, George Mason

C-USA

	Conference			Overall		
	W	L	PCT	W	L	PCT
AMERICAN						
Cincinnati○	12	4	.750	27	6	.818
Louisville○	11	5	.688	19	11	.633
Charlotte⊕	10	6	.625	23	11	.676
DePaul□	10	6	.625	18	13	.581
Saint Louis	8	8	.500	15	16	.484
Marquette	6	10	.375	14	15	.483
NATIONAL						
UAB○	10	6	.625	20	12	.625
South Florida	6	10	.375	14	14	.500
Southern Miss	6	10	.375	14	16	.467
Memphis	6	10	.375	13	15	.464
Tulane	6	10	.375	12	15	.444
Houston	5	11	.313	10	17	.370

Tournament: **Charlotte d. Louisville 68-59**
Tournament MVP: **Galen Young**, Charlotte

IVY

	Conference			Overall		
	W	L	PCT	W	L	PCT
Penn⊕	13	1	.929	21	6	.778
Princeton□	11	3	.786	22	8	.733
Dartmouth	10	4	.714	14	12	.538
Harvard	7	7	.500	13	13	.500
Cornell	6	8	.429	11	15	.423
Columbia	5	9	.357	10	16	.385
Brown	2	12	.143	4	22	.154
Yale	2	12	.143	4	22	.154

Conference Standings Continue →

⊕ Automatic NCAA Tournament bid ○ At-large NCAA Tournament bid □ NIT appearance ⊗ Team record doesn't reflect games forfeited or vacated. For adjusted record, see p. 521.

MAAC

	Conference			Overall		
	W	L	PCT	W	L	PCT
Siena⊛	13	5	.722	25	6	.806
Niagara	13	5	.722	17	12	.586
Iona	12	6	.667	16	14	.533
Canisius	11	7	.611	15	12	.556
Saint Peter's	10	8	.556	14	15	.483
Marist	8	10	.444	16	12	.571
Fairfield	7	11	.389	12	15	.444
Rider	7	11	.389	12	16	.429
Loyola (MD)	6	12	.333	13	15	.464
Manhattan	3	15	.167	5	22	.185

Tournament: **Siena d. Saint Peter's 82-67**
Tournament MVP: **Marcus Faison**, Siena

MID-AMERICAN

	Conference			Overall		
	W	L	PCT	W	L	PCT
East						
Miami (OH)○	15	3	.833	24	8	.750
Kent State⊛	13	5	.722	23	7	.767
Akron	12	6	.667	18	9	.667
Bowling Green	12	6	.667	18	10	.643
Ohio	12	6	.667	18	10	.643
Marshall	11	7	.611	16	11	.593
Buffalo	1	17	.056	5	24	.172
West						
Toledo□	11	7	.611	19	9	.679
Ball State	10	8	.556	16	11	.593
Central Michigan	7	11	.389	10	16	.385
Western Michigan	6	12	.333	11	15	.423
Eastern Michigan	5	13	.278	5	20	.200
Northern Illinois	2	16	.111	6	20	.231

Tournament: **Kent State d. Miami (OH) 49-43**
Tournament MVP: **John Whorton**, Kent State

MID-CONTINENT

	Conference			Overall		
	W	L	PCT	W	L	PCT
Valparaiso⊛	10	4	.714	23	9	.719
Oral Roberts	10	4	.714	17	11	.607
Western Illinois	9	5	.643	16	12	.571
Youngstown State	9	5	.643	14	14	.500
Southern Utah	6	8	.429	13	17	.433
IUPUI	6	8	.429	11	16	.407
UMKC	3	11	.214	8	22	.267
Chicago State	3	11	.214	3	24	.111

Tournament: **Valparaiso d. Oral Roberts 73-69**
Tournament MVP: **Milo Stovall**, Valparaiso

MEAC

	Conference			Overall		
	W	L	PCT	W	L	PCT
South Carolina State	14	4	.778	17	12	.586
Coppin State	14	4	.778	15	14	.517
Morgan State	12	6	.667	14	14	.500
Norfolk State	11	7	.611	15	12	.556
Bethune-Cookman	10	9	.526	11	16	.407
NC A&T	9	9	.500	13	15	.464
Hampton	8	10	.444	8	19	.296
Florida A&M⊛	8	11	.421	12	19	.387
UMES	7	11	.389	10	17	.370
Delaware State	5	13	.278	8	19	.296
Howard	2	16	.111	2	25	.074

Tournament: **Florida A&M d. South Carolina State 64-61**
Tournament MOP: **Monroe Pippins**, Florida A&M

MCC

	Conference			Overall		
	W	L	PCT	W	L	PCT
Detroit⊛	12	2	.857	25	6	.806
Butler□	11	3	.786	22	10	.688
Wisconsin-Green Bay	9	5	.643	20	11	.645
Loyola-Chicago	7	7	.500	9	18	.333
Cleveland State	6	8	.429	14	14	.500
Wisconsin-Milwaukee	5	9	.357	8	19	.296
Wright State	4	10	.286	9	18	.333
Illinois-Chicago	2	12	.143	7	21	.250

Tournament: **Detroit d. Butler 72-65**
Tournament MVP: **Rashad Phillips**, Detroit

MISSOURI VALLEY

	Conference			Overall		
	W	L	PCT	W	L	PCT
Evansville○	13	5	.722	23	10	.697
Creighton⊛	11	7	.611	22	9	.710
Missouri State○	11	7	.611	22	11	.667
Bradley□	11	7	.611	17	12	.586
Indiana State	10	8	.556	15	12	.556
Southern Illinois	10	8	.556	15	12	.556
Illinois State	7	11	.389	16	15	.516
Wichita State	6	12	.333	13	17	.433
Northern Iowa	6	12	.333	9	18	.333
Drake	5	13	.278	10	17	.370

Tournament: **Creighton d. Evansville 70-61**
Tournament MOP: **Rodney Buford**, Creighton

NORTHEAST

	Conference			Overall		
	W	L	PCT	W	L	PCT
UMBC	17	3	.850	19	9	.679
St. Francis (NY)	16	4	.800	20	8	.714
Robert Morris	12	8	.600	15	12	.556
Central Conn. State	11	9	.550	19	13	.594
Mount St. Mary's⊛	10	10	.500	15	15	.500
Long Island	10	10	.500	10	17	.370
Fairleigh Dickinson	9	11	.450	12	16	.429
Saint Francis (PA)	7	13	.350	9	17	.346
Wagner	7	13	.350	9	18	.333
Quinnipiac	6	14	.300	9	18	.333
Monmouth	5	15	.250	5	21	.192

Tournament: **Mount St. Mary's d. Central Conn. St. 72-56**
Tournament MVP: **Gregory Harris**, Mount St. Mary's

OHIO VALLEY

	Conference			Overall		
	W	L	PCT	W	L	PCT
Murray State⊛	16	2	.889	27	6	.818
SE Missouri State	15	3	.833	20	9	.690
Morehead State	9	9	.500	13	15	.464
Tennessee State	9	9	.500	12	15	.444
Austin Peay	9	9	.500	11	16	.407
Middle Tenn. State	9	9	.500	12	19	.387
Eastern Illinois	8	10	.444	13	16	.448
Tennessee Tech	8	10	.444	12	15	.444
Tennessee-Martin	5	13	.278	8	18	.308
Eastern Kentucky	2	16	.111	3	23	.115

Tournament: **Murray State d. SE Missouri State 62-61**
Tournament MVP: **Aubrey Reese**, Murray State

PAC-10

	Conference			Overall		
	W	L	PCT	W	L	PCT
Stanford⊛	15	3	.833	26	7	.788
Arizona○⊗	13	5	.722	22	7	.759
UCLA○⊗	12	6	.667	22	9	.710
Washington○	10	8	.556	17	12	.586
California□	8	10	.444	22	11	.667
Oregon□	8	10	.444	19	13	.594
Southern California□	7	11	.389	15	13	.536
Oregon State	7	11	.389	13	14	.481
Arizona State	6	12	.333	14	16	.467
Washington State	4	14	.222	10	19	.345

PATRIOT

	Conference			Overall		
	W	L	PCT	W	L	PCT
Lafayette⊛	10	2	.833	22	8	.733
Navy	9	3	.750	20	7	.741
Bucknell	9	3	.750	16	13	.552
Colgate	7	5	.583	14	14	.500
Army	4	8	.333	8	19	.296
Holy Cross	3	9	.250	7	20	.259
Lehigh	0	12	.000	6	22	.214

Tournament: **Lafayette d. Bucknell 67-63**
Tournament MVP: **Brian Ehlers**, Lafayette

SEC

	Conference			Overall		
	W	L	PCT	W	L	PCT
Eastern						
Tennessee○	12	4	.750	21	9	.700
Kentucky⊛	11	5	.688	28	9	.757
Florida○	10	6	.625	22	9	.710
Georgia□	6	10	.375	15	15	.500
Vanderbilt	5	11	.313	14	15	.483
South Carolina	3	13	.188	8	21	.276
Western						
Auburn○	14	2	.875	29	4	.879
Arkansas○	9	7	.563	23	11	.676
Mississippi○	8	8	.500	20	13	.606
Mississippi State□	8	8	.500	20	13	.606
Alabama□	6	10	.375	17	15	.531
LSU	4	12	.250	12	15	.444

Tournament: **Kentucky d. Arkansas 76-63**
Tournament MVP: **Scott Padgett**, Kentucky

SOUTHERN

	Conference			Overall		
	W	L	PCT	W	L	PCT
North						
Appalachian State	13	3	.813	21	8	.724
Davidson	11	5	.688	16	11	.593
East Tenn. State	9	7	.563	17	11	.607
VMI	9	7	.563	12	15	.444
UNC Greensboro	5	11	.313	7	20	.259
Western Carolina	2	14	.125	8	21	.276
South						
Charleston⊛	16	0	1.000	28	3	.903
Chattanooga	9	7	.563	16	12	.571
Wofford	8	8	.500	11	16	.407
Georgia Southern	6	10	.375	11	17	.393
Furman	5	11	.313	12	16	.429
The Citadel	3	13	.188	9	18	.333

Tournament: **Charleston d. Appalachian State 77-67**
Tournament MOP: **Marshall Phillips**, Appalachian State

SOUTHLAND

	Conference			Overall		
	W	L	PCT	W	L	PCT
Texas State	13	5	.722	19	9	.679
UTSA⊛	12	6	.667	18	11	.621
Nicholls State	12	6	.667	14	15	.483
UL-Monroe	12	6	.667	13	14	.481
Lamar	11	7	.611	17	11	.607
McNeese State	11	7	.611	13	15	.464
Northwestern St. (LA)	8	10	.444	11	15	.423
Texas-Arlington	8	10	.444	10	16	.385
Sam Houston State	7	11	.389	10	16	.385
Southeastern Louisiana	3	15	.167	6	20	.231
Stephen F. Austin	2	16	.111	4	22	.154

Tournament: **UTSA d. Texas State 71-63**
Tournament MVP: **Steve Meyer**, UTSA

SWAC

	Conference			Overall		
	W	L	PCT	W	L	PCT
Alcorn State⊛	14	2	.875	23	7	.767
Southern U.	13	3	.813	21	7	.750
Jackson State	11	5	.688	16	12	.571
Mississippi Valley St.	10	6	.625	14	13	.519
Alabama State	8	8	.500	11	16	.407
Texas Southern	6	10	.375	8	19	.296
Grambling	5	11	.313	6	21	.222
Prairie View A&M	4	12	.250	6	21	.222
Arkansas-Pine Bluff	1	15	.063	3	24	.111

Tournament: **Alcorn State d. Southern 89-83**
Tournament MVP: **Reuben Stiff**, Alcorn State

SUN BELT

	Conference			Overall		
	W	L	PCT	W	L	PCT
Louisiana Tech	10	4	.714	19	9	.679
Arkansas State⊛	9	5	.643	18	12	.600
Florida International	7	7	.500	13	16	.448
UL-Lafayette	7	7	.500	13	16	.448
Western Kentucky	7	7	.500	13	16	.448
South Alabama	6	8	.429	11	16	.407
New Orleans	5	9	.357	14	16	.467
Arkansas-Little Rock	5	9	.357	12	15	.444

Tournament: **Arkansas St. d. Western Kentucky 65-48**
Tournament MOP: **Chico Fletcher**, Arkansas St.

TAAC

	Conference			Overall		
	W	L	PCT	W	L	PCT
Samford⊛	15	1	.938	24	6	.800
Central Florida	13	3	.813	19	10	.655
Georgia State	11	5	.688	17	13	.567
Stetson	10	6	.625	14	13	.519
Centenary	9	7	.563	14	14	.500
Jacksonville	7	9	.438	12	15	.444
Campbell	6	10	.375	9	18	.333
Troy	6	10	.375	9	18	.333
Mercer	5	11	.313	8	18	.308
Jacksonville State	3	13	.188	8	18	.308
Florida Atlantic	3	13	.188	6	20	.231

Tournament: **Samford d. Central Florida 89-67**
Tournament MVP: **Marc Salyers**, Samford

WEST COAST

	Conference			Overall		
	W	L	PCT	W	L	PCT
Gonzaga⊛	12	2	.857	28	7	.800
San Diego	9	5	.643	18	9	.667
Pepperdine□	9	5	.643	19	13	.594
Santa Clara	8	6	.571	14	15	.483
Loyola Marymount	6	8	.429	11	16	.407
Saint Mary's (CA)	5	9	.357	13	18	.419
San Francisco	4	10	.286	12	18	.400
Portland	3	11	.214	9	18	.333

Tournament: **Gonzaga d. Santa Clara 91-66**
Tournament MVP: **Matt Santangelo**, Gonzaga

WAC

	Conference			Overall		
	W	L	PCT	W	L	PCT
Pacific						
Utah⊛	14	0	1.000	28	5	.848
New Mexico○	9	5	.643	25	9	.735
Fresno State□⊗	9	5	.643	21	12	.636
UTEP	8	6	.571	16	12	.571
BYU	6	8	.429	12	16	.429
San Jose State	5	9	.357	12	16	.429
Hawaii	3	11	.214	6	20	.231
San Diego State	2	12	.143	4	22	.154
Mountain						
UNLV□	9	5	.643	16	13	.552
Tulsa○	9	5	.643	23	10	.697
Rice	8	6	.571	18	10	.643
TCU□	7	7	.500	21	11	.656
Wyoming□	7	7	.500	18	10	.643
Colorado State□	7	7	.500	19	11	.633
SMU	7	7	.500	15	15	.500
Air Force	2	12	.143	10	16	.385

Tournament: **Utah d. New Mexico 60-45**
Tournament MVP: **Alex Jenson**, Utah

INDEPENDENTS

	Overall		
	W	L	PCT
Denver	10	17	.370
Texas-Pan American	5	22	.185

INDIVIDUAL LEADERS—SEASON

SCORING	CL	POS	G	FG	3FG	FT	PTS	PPG
1 **Alvin Young**, Niagara	SR	G	29	253	65	157	728	**25.1**
2 **Ray Minlend**, St. Francis (NY)	SR	G	28	210	31	229	680	**24.3**
3 **Wally Szczerbiak**, Miami (OH)	SR	F	32	270	63	172	775	**24.2**
4 **Brian Merriweather**, Tex.-Pan American	SO	G	27	239	110	53	641	**23.7**
5 **Damian Woolfolk**, Norfolk State	JR	G	27	237	46	115	635	**23.5**
6 **Quincy Lewis**, Minnesota	SR	G/F	27	226	53	120	625	**23.1**
7 **Jason Hartman**, Portland State	SR	F	28	198	79	164	639	**22.8**
8 **Lee Nailon**, TCU	SR	F	31	266	4	171	707	**22.8**
9 **Maurice Evans**, Wichita State	SO	G/F	28	211	69	141	632	**22.6**
10 **Harold Arceneaux**, Weber State	JR	F	32	266	34	147	713	**22.3**

FIELD GOAL PCT	CL	POS	G	FG	FGA	PCT
1 **Todd MacCulloch**, Washington	SR	C	29	210	317	**66.2**
2 **Quincy Gause**, Georgia State	SR	F	23	144	221	**65.2**
3 **Ryan Moss**, Arkansas-Little Rock	SR	F	24	135	210	**64.3**
4 **Elton Brand**, Duke	SO	F	39	255	411	**62.0**
5 **Damous Anderson**, Florida State	JR	F	23	115	190	**60.5**

MINIMUM: 5 MADE PER GAME

THREE-PT FG PER GAME	CL	POS	G	3FG	3PG
1 **Brian Merriweather**, Texas-Pan American	SO	G	27	110	**4.1**
2 **Shannon Taylor**, Eastern Washington	SR	G	27	103	**3.8**
3 **Alan Barksdale**, Arkansas-Little Rock	JR	G	25	95	**3.8**
4 **Josh Heard**, Tennessee Tech	JR	G	27	98	**3.6**
5 **Fred Warrick**, Coppin State	SR	G	29	98	**3.4**

THREE-PT FG PCT	CL	POS	G	3FG	3FGA	PCT
1 **Rodney Thomas**, IUPUI	JR	G	26	59	113	**52.2**
2 **Ross Land**, Northern Arizona	JR	G/F	29	83	163	**50.9**
3 **Brian Grawer**, Missouri	SO	G	29	64	129	**49.6**
4 **Ryan Borowicz**, Wisconsin-Green Bay	SR	G	31	78	159	**49.1**
5 **Alan Puckett**, The Citadel	FR	F	27	55	113	**48.7**

MINIMUM: 1.5 MADE PER GAME

FREE THROW PCT	CL	POS	G	FT	FTA	PCT
1 **Lonnie Cooper**, Louisiana Tech	SR	G	25	70	76	**92.1**
2 **Haywood Eaddy**, Loyola Marymount	SR	G	21	79	88	**89.8**
3 **Marcus Wilson**, Evansville	SR	G	33	165	184	**89.7**
4 **Jermel President**, Charleston	SR	G	31	94	105	**89.5**
5 **Arthur Lee**, Stanford	SR	G	33	140	158	**88.6**

MINIMUM: 2.5 MADE PER GAME

ASSISTS PER GAME	CL	POS	G	AST	APG
1 **Doug Gottlieb**, Oklahoma State	JR	G	34	299	**8.8**
2 **Chico Fletcher**, Arkansas State	JR	G	30	250	**8.3**
3 **Ali Ton**, Davidson	SR	G	25	190	**7.6**
4 **Ed Cota**, North Carolina	JR	G	32	238	**7.4**
5 **Chris Herren**, Fresno State	SR	G	25	181	**7.2**
6 **Mateen Cleaves**, Michigan State	JR	G	38	274	**7.2**
7 **Prince Fowler**, TCU	SR	G	32	226	**7.1**
8 **Devan Clark**, Southern U.	SO	G	28	194	**6.9**
9 **Shawnta Rogers**, George Washington	SR	G	29	196	**6.8**
10 **Tim Hill**, Harvard	SR	G	26	172	**6.6**

REBOUNDS PER GAME	CL	POS	G	REB	RPG
1 **Ian McGinnis**, Dartmouth	SO	F	26	317	**12.2**
2 **Todd MacCulloch**, Washington	SR	C	29	345	**11.9**
3 **Jeff Foster**, SW Texas State	SR	C	28	316	**11.3**
4 **Chris Mihm**, Texas	SO	C	32	351	**11.0**
5 **K'Zell Wesson**, La Salle	SR	F/C	28	301	**10.8**
6 **William "Bud" Eley**, Southeast Missouri State	SR	C	29	310	**10.7**
7 **Quentin Richardson**, DePaul	FR	F	31	327	**10.5**
8 **Michael Ruffin**, Tulsa	SR	F	33	342	**10.4**
9 **Derek Hood**, Arkansas	SR	F	34	349	**10.3**
10 **Eric Dow**, Denver	SR	F	27	276	**10.2**

BLOCKED SHOTS PER GAME	CL	POS	G	BLK	BPG
1 **Tarvis Williams**, Hampton	SO	F	27	135	**5.0**
2 **Henry Jordan**, Mississippi Valley State	SO	C	27	108	**4.0**
3 **Etan Thomas**, Syracuse	JR	C	33	131	**4.0**
4 **Wojciech Myrda**, UL-Monroe	FR	C	27	96	**3.6**
5 **Calvin Booth**, Penn State	SR	C	27	95	**3.5**

STEALS PER GAME	CL	POS	G	STL	SPG
1 **Shawnta Rogers**, George Washington	SR	G	29	103	**3.6**
2 **Tim Winn**, St. Bonaventure	JR	G	23	81	**3.5**
3 **Jason Rowe**, Loyola (MD)	JR	G	28	95	**3.4**
4 **John Linehan**, Providence	SO	G	30	98	**3.3**
5 **Cookie Belcher**, Nebraska	JR	G	32	102	**3.2**

INDIVIDUAL LEADERS—GAME

POINTS	CL	POS	OPP	DATE	PTS
1 **Lee Nailon**, TCU	SR	F	Gonzaga	D30	**44**
Alvin Young, Niagara	SR	G	Siena	F8	**44**
3 **Wally Szczerbiak**, Miami (OH)	SR	F	Washington	M12	**43**
4 **Keion Brooks**, Wright State	SR	G	Illinois-Chicago	J4	**41**
Marquise Gainous, TCU	JR	F	UNLV	J23	**41**
Rayford Young, Texas Tech	JR	G	Kansas	F13	**41**
Donald Hand, Virginia	SO	G	NC State	F14	**41**

THREE-PT FG MADE	CL	POS	OPP	DATE	3FG
1 **Pat Bradley**, Arkansas	SR	G	North Texas	D30	**10**
2 **Marcus Wilson**, Evansville	SR	G	Tennessee-Martin	N18	**9**
Anton Reese, Georgia State	JR	G	Kansas State	N29	**9**
Matt Sundblad, Lamar	SR	G	Loyola (LA)	D2	**9**
Clay McKnight, Pacific	JR	G	Fresno State	D7	**9**
Leslie Ballard, Radford	SR	G	VCU	D8	**9**
B. Merriweather, Tex.-Pan American	SO	G	New Mexico	D8	**9**
J. Rasmussen, Fairleigh Dickinson	SR	G	Siena	D12	**9**
Chris Crosby, Washington State	JR	F	Idaho	D20	**9**
Kevin Morris, Georgia State	SR	G	VCU	D22	**9**
Leslie Ballard, Radford	SR	G	Coastal Carolina	J18	**9**
Melvin Watson, Howard	SR	G	Bethune-Cookman	J25	**9**
Fred Warrick, Coppin State	SR	G	Howard	F1	**9**
Danny Sprinkle, Montana State	SR	G	Sacramento State	F4	**9**
Kenny Price, Colorado	SR	G	Texas	M5	**9**
Johnny Hemsley, Miami (FL)	JR	G	Lafayette	M12	**9**

ASSISTS	CL	POS	OPP	DATE	AST
1 **Doug Gottlieb**, Oklahoma State	JR	G	Florida Atlantic	D1	**18**
2 **Chico Fletcher**, Arkansas State	JR	G	TCU	N23	**17**
Jermaine Johnson, Texas-Arlington	SR	G	Sam Houston State	D28	**17**
4 **Prince Fowler**, TCU	SR	G	Central Oklahoma	D12	**16**
Prince Fowler, TCU	SR	G	Wyoming	F11	**16**

REBOUNDS	CL	POS	OPP	DATE	REB
1 **Darren Phillip**, Fairfield	JR	F	Loyola (MD)	D5	**24**
2 **Lee Nailon**, TCU	SR	F	SMU	J11	**22**
Troy Mack, Wichita State	SO	F	Missouri State	J18	**22**
4 **Matt Nelson**, Northern Illinois	FR	C	Chicago State	N14	**21**
Elton Brand, Duke	SO	F	Fresno State	N28	**21**
William "Bud" Eley, SE Missouri St.	SR	C	Missouri State	D22	**21**
Reginald Poole, UL-Lafayette	SR	F	Hawaii	D27	**21**
Darien Robinson, Delaware State	SR	F	Morgan State	J18	**21**
Evan Eschmeyer, Northwestern	SR	C	Penn State	J20	**21**
Todd MacCulloch, Washington	SR	C	UCLA	J31	**21**
Shawn Marion, UNLV	JR	F	TCU	F22	**21**

BLOCKED SHOTS	CL	POS	OPP	DATE	BLK
1 **Tarvis Williams**, Hampton	SO	F	NC A&T	J9	**12**
2 **Stromile Swift**, LSU	FR	F	Alabama	F10	**11**
3 **Tarvis Williams**, Hampton	SO	F	Maine	N14	**10**
Joel Przybilla, Minnesota	FR	C	Fresno State	D4	**10**
William "Bud" Eley, SE Missouri St.	SR	C	Morehead State	J4	**10**

STEALS	CL	POS	OPP	DATE	STL
1 **Richard Duncan**, Middle Tenn. State	SR	G	Eastern Kentucky	F20	**12**
2 **Dionte Harvey**, Southern U.	SR	G	Prairie View A&M	N23	**10**
Aaron Bates, Southern U.	SR	F	Southeastern Louisiana	D5	**10**
Ivan Wagner, Texas	JR	G	Texas A&M	F3	**10**
5 **Rick Mickens**, Central Conn. State	JR	G	Brown	N20	**9**
Damon Cobb, UAB	SR	G	Tulsa	N22	**9**
Jocquinn Arch, Prairie View A&M	SR	G	Alcorn State	N25	**9**
Mark Bigelow, BYU	FR	F	Arizona	N28	**9**
Faragi Phillips, Miss. Valley State	SR	G	Arkansas-Pine Bluff	D7	**9**
Sam Sutton, Saint Francis (PA)	SO	F	Fairleigh Dickinson	J2	**9**
Rob Dye, Bradley	JR	G	Missouri State	J13	**9**
Damon Arnette, Florida Atlantic	SR	G	Centenary	J25	**9**
Alvin Young, Niagara	SR	G	Saint Peter's	J30	**9**
Kevin Braswell, Georgetown	FR	G	Notre Dame	F10	**9**
John Linehan, Providence	SO	G	Georgetown	F27	**9**
Terrance Roberson, Fresno State	JR	F	Tulsa	M4	**9**

TEAM LEADERS—SEASON

WIN-LOSS PCT	W	L	PCT
1 **Duke**	37	2	**.949**
2 **Connecticut**	34	2	**.944**
3 **Charleston**	28	3	**.903**
4 **Auburn**	29	4	**.879**
5 **Michigan State**	33	5	**.868**

SCORING OFFENSE	G	W-L	PTS	PPG
1 **Duke**	39	37-2	3,581	**91.8**
2 **TCU**	32	21-11	2,776	**86.8**
3 **Siena**	31	25-6	2,686	**86.6**
4 **Norfolk State**	27	15-12	2,330	**86.3**
5 **Cal Poly**	27	11-16	2,293	**84.9**

SCORING MARGIN	G	W-L	PPG	OPP PPG	MAR
1 **Duke**	39	37-2	91.8	67.2	**24.6**
2 **Auburn**	33	29-4	81.2	61.6	**19.6**
3 **Maryland**	34	28-6	84.5	66.4	**18.1**
4 **Connecticut**	36	34-2	77.3	61.3	**16.0**
5 **Utah**	33	28-5	71.3	55.4	**15.9**

FIELD GOAL PCT	G	W-L	FG	FGA	PCT
1 **Northern Arizona**	29	21-8	783	1,497	**52.3**
2 **Duke**	39	37-2	1,244	2,422	**51.4**
3 **Evansville**	33	23-10	879	1,739	**50.5**
4 **Maryland**	34	28-6	1,044	2,108	**49.5**
5 **TCU**	32	21-11	1,006	2,050	**49.1**

THREE-PT FG PER GAME	G	W-L	3FG	3PG
1 **Cal Poly**	27	11-16	255	**9.4**
2 **Florida**	31	22-9	289	**9.3**
3 **Samford**	30	24-6	278	**9.3**
4 **Air Force**	26	10-16	233	**9.0**
5 **Portland State**	28	17-11	250	**8.9**

Free Throw Pct	G	W-L	FT	FTA	PCT
1 Siena	31	25-6	672	854	**78.7**
2 Evansville	33	23-10	515	667	**77.2**
3 Western Michigan	26	11-15	435	568	**76.6**
4 Miami (OH)	32	24-8	436	570	**76.5**
5 Robert Morris	27	15-12	452	594	**76.1**

Assists Per Game	G	W-L	AST	APG
1 TCU	32	21-11	650	**20.3**
2 Montana State	29	16-13	583	**20.1**
3 Maryland	34	28-6	674	**19.8**
4 Wyoming	28	18-10	540	**19.3**
5 Fresno State	33	21-12	600	**18.2**

Rebound Margin	G	W-L	RPG	OPP RPG	MAR
1 Navy	27	20-7	43.6	33.7	**9.9**
2 Michigan State	38	33-5	36.3	27.1	**9.2**
Auburn	33	29-4	44.0	34.8	**9.2**
4 North Carolina	34	24-10	39.9	31.0	**8.9**
5 Duke	39	37-2	42.2	33.4	**8.8**

Scoring Defense	G	W-L	OPP PTS	OPP PPG
1 Princeton	30	22-8	1,581	**52.7**
2 Wisconsin	32	22-10	1,766	**55.2**
3 Detroit	31	25-6	1,713	**55.3**
4 Utah	33	28-5	1,827	**55.4**
5 Wisconsin-Green Bay	31	20-11	1,736	**56.0**

Field Goal Pct Defense	G	W-L	OPP FG	OPP FGA	OPP PCT
1 Kansas State	33	20-13	729	1,963	**37.1**
2 Detroit	31	25-6	590	1,583	**37.3**
3 Northwestern	29	15-14	577	1,548	**37.3**
4 Texas State	28	19-9	597	1,601	**37.3**
5 Old Dominion	34	25-9	797	2,116	**37.7**

Blocked Shots Per Game	G	W-L	BLK	BPG
1 Iona	30	16-14	220	**7.3**
2 Old Dominion	34	25-9	248	**7.3**
3 Syracuse	33	21-12	229	**6.9**
4 Mississippi Valley State	27	14-13	187	**6.9**
5 Tennessee	30	21-9	190	**6.3**

Steals Per Game	G	W-L	STL	SPG
1 Maryland	34	28-6	431	**12.7**
2 Radford	28	20-8	340	**12.1**
3 Southern U.	28	21-7	324	**11.6**
4 McNeese State	28	13-15	319	**11.4**
5 Pittsburgh	30	14-16	338	**11.3**

TEAM LEADERS—GAME

Points	OPP	DATE	SCORE
1 Prairie View A&M	Southwestern Adventist	D6	**134-75**
2 TCU	Central Oklahoma	D12	**133-108**
3 Maryland	North Texas	D23	**132-57**
4 Texas-Arlington	Sam Houston State	D28	**125-123**
5 Sam Houston State	Texas-Arlington	D28	**123-125**

Field Goal Pct	OPP	DATE	FG	FGA	PCT
1 New Orleans	Wisconsin-Green Bay	N28	26	34	**76.5**
2 Wisconsin-Green Bay	Miami (OH)	D5	30	41	**73.2**
3 Utah	San Jose State	J23	28	40	**70.0**
4 Northern Arizona	St. Bonaventure	D18	28	41	**68.3**
5 Northern Iowa	Drake	F22	30	44	**68.2**

Three-Pt FG Made	OPP	DATE	3FG
1 Cincinnati	Oakland (MI)	D5	**24**
2 Arkansas	North Texas	D30	**19**
3 Tulsa	North Texas	D8	**18**
Fresno State	San Diego State	J28	**18**
Saint Joseph's	Temple	F9	**18**

CONSENSUS ALL-AMERICAS

FIRST TEAM

PLAYER	CL	POS	HT	SCHOOL	RPG	PPG
Elton Brand	SO	F	6-8	Duke	9.8	17.7
Mateen Cleaves	JR	G	6-2	Michigan State	1.6	11.7
Richard Hamilton	JR	G/F	6-6	Connecticut	4.8	21.5
Andre Miller	SR	G	6-2	Utah	5.4	15.8
Jason Terry	SR	G	6-2	Arizona	3.3	21.9

SECOND TEAM

PLAYER	CL	POS	HT	SCHOOL	RPG	PPG
Evan Eschmeyer	SR	C	6-11	Northwestern	10.1	19.6
Steve Francis	JR	G	6-3	Maryland	4.5	17.0
Trajan Langdon	SR	G	6-3	Duke	3.4	17.3
Chris Porter	JR	F	6-7	Auburn	8.6	16.0
Wally Szczerbiak	SR	F	6-8	Miami (OH)	8.5	24.2

Selectors: AP, NABC, Sporting News, USBWA

AWARD WINNERS

PLAYER OF THE YEAR

PLAYER	CL	POS	HT	SCHOOL	AWARDS
Elton Brand	SO	F	6-8	Duke	Naismith, AP, USBWA, Wooden, NABC, Rupp
Shawnta Rogers	SR	G	5-4	George Washington	Frances Pomeroy Naismith*

* For the most outstanding senior player who is 6 feet or under

DEFENSIVE PLAYER OF THE YEAR

PLAYER	CL	POS	HT	SCHOOL
Shane Battier	SO	F	6-8	Duke

COACH OF THE YEAR

COACH	SCHOOL	REC	AWARDS
Mike Krzyzewski	Duke	37-2	Naismith, NABC
Cliff Ellis	Auburn	29-4	AP, USBWA, Sporting News, CBS/Chevrolet

Bob Gibbons' Top High School Senior Recruits

PLAYER	POS	HT	HIGH SCHOOL	A-A TEAMS	COLLEGE	CAREER NOTES
1 Damien Wilkins	F	6-6	Dr. Phillips HS, Orlando, FL	McD, P	NC State/Georgia	Transferred after 1 year; undrafted; signed by Sonics in '04, 8.0 ppg (4 seasons)
2 Jonathan Bender	F	6-11	Picayune Memorial (MS) HS	McD, P	None	Drafted straight out of HS; No. 5 pick, '99 NBA draft (Raptors); 5.6 ppg (7 seasons)
3 LaVell Blanchard	F	6-7	Ann Arbor (MI) Pioneer HS	McD, P, USA	Michigan	Led team with 15.8 ppg, 7.4 rpg; All-Big Ten as senior; undrafted
4 Donnell Harvey	PF	6-8	Randolph-Clay HS, Cuthbert, GA	McD, P, USA	Florida	10.1 ppg, 7.0 rpg (1 season); No. 22 pick, '00 NBA draft (Mavs)
5 Jason Williams	PG	6-2	St. Joseph's HS, Metuchen, NJ	McD, P, USA	Duke	19.3 ppg (3 seasons); consensus POY, '02; No. 2 pick, '02 NBA draft (Bulls); 9.5 ppg (1 season)
6 Joseph Forte	G	6-4	DeMatha Catholic HS, Hyattsville, MD	McD, P, USA	North Carolina	18.7 ppg (2 seas.); co-ACC POY, '01; No. 21 pick, '01 NBA draft (Celtics)
7 DerMarr Johnson	F	6-9	Maine Central Inst., Pittsfield, ME	McD, P, USA	Cincinnati	12.6 ppg (1 season); No. 6 pick, '00 NBA draft (Hawks); 6.2 ppg (7 seasons)
8 Nick Collison	C/F	6-9	Iowa Falls (IA) HS	McD, P	Kansas	Left KU as 2nd-leading scorer, 3rd-leading rebounder; first-team All-America, '03; No. 12 pick, '03 NBA draft (Sonics); 8.2 ppg (4 seasons)
9 Travis Watson	PF	6-7	Oak Hill Academy, Mouth of Wilson, VA	P	Virginia	13.0 ppg, 9.4 rpg (4 seasons); led ACC in rebounds, '02-'04; undrafted, played overseas
10 Jason Richardson	F	6-6	Arthur Hill HS, Saginaw, MI	McD, P	Michigan State	9.6 ppg (2 seasons); No. 5 pick, '01 NBA draft (Warriors); 2-time Slam Dunk champ; 18.8 ppg (7 seasons)
11 Casey Jacobsen	G/F	6-6	Glendora (CA) HS	McD, P	Stanford	Left SU as 3rd-leading scorer (1,723 pts); 2-time All-America; No. 22 pick, '02 NBA draft (Suns); 5.2 ppg (4 seasons)
12 Jason Parker	C/F	6-8	West Charlotte (NC) HS	P	Kentucky	All-SEC freshman team, '00-'01; dismissed from team; undrafted
13 Keith Bogans	G/F	6-4	DeMatha HS, Hyattsville, MD	McD, P	Kentucky	1,923 points (4 seasons); SEC POY, 3rd team All-America, '03; 2nd-round pick, '03 NBA draft (Bucks); 7.9 ppg (5 seasons)
14 Kenny Satterfield	G	6-2	Rice HS, New York	McD, P	Cincinnati	11.9 ppg, 5.2 apg (2 seasons); No. 53 pick, '01 NBA draft (Mavs)
15 Carlos Boozer	PF	6-9	Douglas HS, Juneau, AK	McD, P	Duke	14.9 ppg (3 seasons); NCAA title, '01; 2nd-round pick, '02 NBA draft (Cavs); 16.9 ppg, 9.9 rpg (6 seasons); 2-time All-Star
16 Brett Nelson	G	6-3	St. Albans (WV) HS	McD, P	Florida	First-team All-SEC as Soph.; left Gators 2nd in 3-pt FGs (274); undrafted
17 Tony Robertson	G	6-3	St. Andrew's HS, Barrington, RI	P	Connecticut	1,160 points (4 seasons); undrafted; played overseas
18 Jason Kapono	F	6-8	Artesia HS, Los Angeles	McD, P	UCLA	4-time first-team All-Pac 10; 2nd-round pick, '03 NBA draft (Cavs); 7.3 ppg (5 seasons); NBA title, '06
19 Marvin Stone	C/F	6-10	Grissom HS, Huntsville, AL	McD, P	Kentucky/Louisville	5.3 ppg, 4.2 rpg; at Louisville, 10.3 ppg, 7.1 rpg; undrafted
20 Mike Dunleavy	G/F	6-9	Jesuit HS, Portland, OR	McD, P	Duke	NCAA title '01, 21 pts in title game; 2nd team All-America, '02; No. 3 pick, '02 NBA draft (Cavs); 12.4 ppg (6 seasons)

Other Standouts

PLAYER	POS	HT	HIGH SCHOOL	A-A TEAMS	COLLEGE	CAREER NOTES
22 Jason Gardner	PG	5-10	North Central HS, Indianapolis	McD, P	Arizona	1,984 points; 20.4 ppg as junior; 2nd team All-America '03; undrafted
35 Joe Johnson	F	6-6	Central HS, Little Rock, AR		Arkansas	15.0 ppg (2 seasons); No. 10 pick, '01 NBA draft (Celtics); 2-time All-Star
71 Gilbert Arenas	G	6-4	Grant HS, Van Nuys, CA		Arizona	15.8 ppg (2 seasons); 2nd-round pick, '01 NBA draft (Warriors); 3-time All-Star

Abbreviations: McD=McDonald's; P=Parade; USA=USA Today

POLL PROGRESSION

PRESEASON POLL

AP	ESPN/USA	SCHOOL	AP↓↑
1	1	Duke	
2	3	Connecticut	
3	2	Stanford	
4	6	Kentucky	
5	4	Michigan State	
6	5	Maryland	
7	7	Temple	
8	8	Kansas	
9	9	Tennessee	
10	12	Utah	
11	11	North Carolina	
12	13	UCLA	
13	18	Oklahoma State	
14	14	Washington	
15	15	Cincinnati	
16	16	Purdue	
17	10	Xavier	
18	20	Arizona	
19	19	Arkansas	
20	21	New Mexico	
20	22	Syracuse	
22	17	Indiana	
23	25	Rhode Island	
24	23	Massachusetts	
25	24	TCU	

WEEK OF NOV 17

AP	SCHOOL	AP↓↑
1	Duke (1-0)	
2	Connecticut (1-0)	
3	Stanford (1-0)	
4	Kentucky (0-0)	
5	Michigan State (1-0)	
6	Maryland (1-0)	
7	Temple (2-0)	
8	Kansas (1-0)	
9	Utah (1-0)	↑1
10	North Carolina (1-0)	↑1
11	UCLA (0-0)	↑1
12	Arizona (1-0)	↑6
13	Oklahoma State (0-0)	
14	Washington (0-0)	
15	Purdue (1-0)	↑1
16	Xavier (0-0)	↑1
17	Cincinnati (0-0)	↓2
18	Tennessee (1-1)	↓9
19	Arkansas (1-0)	
20	New Mexico (1-0)	
21	Indiana (3-0)	↑1
22	Syracuse (0-0)	↓2
23	Massachusetts (0-0)	↑1
24	Clemson (1-0)	⤴
25	Rhode Island (2-1)	↓2

WEEK OF NOV 24

AP	ESPN/USA	SCHOOL	AP↓↑
1	1	Duke (3-0)	
2	3	Connecticut (2-0)	
3	2	Stanford (3-0)	
4	4	Kentucky (2-0)	
5	5	Maryland (3-0)	↑1
6	6	Temple (4-0)	↑1
7	9	Michigan State (2-1)	↓2
8	7	Kansas (3-0)	
9	8	North Carolina (3-0)	↑1
10	12	UCLA (1-0)	↑1
11	15	Arizona (1-0)	↑1
12	17	Oklahoma State (3-0)	↑1
13	10	Xavier (2-0)	↑3
14	11	Purdue (4-0)	↑1
15	14	Cincinnati (1-0)	↑2
16	16	Washington (1-0)	↓2
17	13	Indiana (4-0)	↑4
18	21	Utah (1-1)	↓9
19	18	Syracuse (2-0)	↑3
20	20	New Mexico (2-0)	
21	19	Arkansas (4-1)	↓2
22	24	Clemson (3-0)	↑2
23	23	St. John's (2-0)	⤴
24	—	Miami (Ohio) (3-0)	⤴
25	22	Tennessee (2-2)	↓7
—	25	Massachusetts (1-1)	⤵

WEEK OF DEC 1

AP	ESPN/USA	SCHOOL	AP↓↑
1	1	Connecticut (4-0)	↑1
2	2	Maryland (7-0)	↑3
3	3	North Carolina (6-0)	↑6
4	4	Duke (5-1)	↓3
5	5	Stanford (4-1)	↓2
6	7	Cincinnati (4-0)	↑9
7	6	Kansas (4-0)	↑1
8	8	Kentucky (5-1)	↓4
9	9	Michigan State (4-1)	↓2
10	10	Temple (4-1)	↓4
11	15	Oklahoma State (4-0)	↑1
12	11	Syracuse (5-0)	↑7
13	13	Arizona (3-0)	↓2
14	12	Purdue (6-1)	
15	14	Washington (4-0)	↑1
16	16	Indiana (6-1)	↑1
17	18	New Mexico (4-0)	↑3
18	19	UCLA (2-2)	↓8
19	17	Arkansas (5-1)	↑2
20	21	Pittsburgh (6-1)	⤴
21	20	Utah (3-2)	↓3
22	23	Miami (Ohio) (4-0)	↑2
23	22	Xavier (4-2)	↓10
24	24	Clemson (5-1)	↓2
25	25	St. John's (3-2)	↓2

WEEK OF DEC 8

AP	ESPN/USA	SCHOOL	AP↓↑
1	1	Connecticut (6-0)	
2	2	Maryland (9-0)	
3	3	Duke (7-1)	↑1
4	4	Cincinnati (5-0)	↑2
5	5	Kentucky (7-1)	↑3
6	7	Stanford (4-2)	↓1
7	6	North Carolina (8-1) (A)	↓4
8	10	Arizona (4-0)	↑5
9	9	Purdue (7-1)	↑5
10	8	Kansas (5-1)	↓3
11	11	Indiana (8-1)	↑5
12	15	New Mexico (5-0)	↑5
13	12	Syracuse (7-1)	↓1
14	13	Michigan State (4-3)	↓5
15	16	UCLA (4-2)	↑3
16	14	Temple (4-3)	↓6
17	19	Clemson (7-1)	↑7
18	20	St. John's (6-2)	↑7
19	21	Oklahoma State (4-2)	↓8
20	18	Pittsburgh (7-2)	
21	25	Tennessee (6-2)	⤴
22	17	Washington (4-2)	↓7
23	23	Arkansas (5-2)	↓4
24	—	Minnesota (5-0)	⤴
25	22	Utah (4-3)	↓4
—	24	Auburn (8-0)	

WEEK OF DEC 15

AP	ESPN/USA	SCHOOL	AP↓↑
1	1	Connecticut (8-0)	
2	2	Duke (9-1)	↑1
3	4	Kentucky (9-1)	↑2
4	3	Cincinnati (6-0)	
5	5	Maryland (10-1)	↓3
6	7	Stanford (5-2)	
7	6	North Carolina (10-1)	
8	8	Purdue (10-1)	↑1
9	9	Arizona (5-0)	
10	10	Indiana (10-2) (B)	↑1
11	12	New Mexico (6-0)	↑1
12	13	UCLA (5-2)	↑3
13	11	Kansas (6-2)	↓3
14	14	Michigan State (6-3)	
15	15	St. John's (8-2)	↑3
16	16	Clemson (8-1)	↑1
17	21	Minnesota (6-0)	↑7
18	17	Oklahoma State (5-2)	↑1
19	18	Auburn (9-0)	⤴
20	23	Arkansas (6-2)	↑3
21	20	Syracuse (7-3)	↓8
22	19	Pittsburgh (7-4)	↓2
23	24	Wisconsin (9-1)	⤴
24	—	Oklahoma (5-1)	⤴
25	—	Iowa (7-1)	⤴
—	21	Temple (4-4)	⤵
—	25	Tennessee (6-3)	⤵
—	25	Washington (4-3)	⤵

WEEK OF DEC 22

AP	ESPN/USA	SCHOOL	AP↓↑
1	1	Connecticut (8-0)	
2	2	Duke (10-1)	
3	4	Kentucky (10-1)	
4	3	Cincinnati (9-0)	
5	5	Maryland (11-1)	
6	7	Stanford (7-2)	
7	6	North Carolina (12-1)	
8	9	Arizona (6-0)	
9	8	Purdue (11-1)	↓1
10	10	Indiana (11-2)	
11	13	New Mexico (7-0)	
12	12	UCLA (6-2)	
13	11	Kansas (8-2)	
14	15	St. John's (9-2)	↑1
15	14	Michigan State (6-3)	↓1
16	16	Clemson (9-1)	
17	18	Minnesota (7-1)	
18	17	Auburn (11-0)	↑1
19	20	Arkansas (8-2)	↑1
20	23	Wisconsin (10-1)	↑3
21	25	Iowa (8-1)	↑4
22	21	Syracuse (7-3)	↓1
23	—	Oklahoma (6-1) (C)	↑1
24	22	Pittsburgh (7-4)	↓2
25	19	Oklahoma State (6-3)	↓7
—	24	Temple (6-4)	

WEEK OF DEC 29

AP	ESPN/USA	SCHOOL	AP↓↑
1	1	Connecticut (9-0)	
2	2	Duke (11-1)	
3	3	Cincinnati (11-0)	↑1
4	4	Maryland (13-1)	↑1
5	5	Stanford (9-2)	↑1
6	7	Arizona (6-0)	↑2
7	6	Kentucky (10-3)	↓4
8	10	Indiana (12-2)	↑2
9	9	North Carolina (12-2)	↓2
10	11	UCLA (7-2)	↑2
11	8	Purdue (12-2)	↓2
12	12	St. John's (10-2)	↑2
13	13	Michigan State (9-3)	↑2
14	16	Clemson (10-1)	↑2
15	17	New Mexico (8-1)	↓4
16	18	Minnesota (8-1)	↑1
17	15	Auburn (11-0)	↑1
18	14	Kansas (8-3)	↓5
19	20	Wisconsin (12-1)	↑1
20	19	Arkansas (9-2)	↓1
21	24	Iowa (9-1)	
22	22	Syracuse (8-3)	
23	23	Pittsburgh (8-4)	↑1
24	—	TCU (10-2)	⤴
25	21	Oklahoma State (7-3)	
—	25	Temple (6-4)	

WEEK OF JAN 5

AP	ESPN/USA	SCHOOL	AP↓↑
1	1	Connecticut (11-0)	
2	2	Duke (13-1)	
3	3	Cincinnati (12-0)	
4	4	Stanford (11-2)	↑1
5	6	Maryland (13-2)	↓1
6	5	Kentucky (12-3)	↑1
7	8	UCLA (9-2)	↑3
8	11	Arizona (8-1)	↓2
9	7	Purdue (12-2)	↑2
10	9	St. John's (11-2)	↑2
11	10	North Carolina (13-3)	↓2
12	12	Michigan State (11-3)	↑1
13	13	Indiana (14-3)	↓5
14	14	Auburn (13-0)	↑3
15	15	New Mexico (12-1)	
16	17	Minnesota (9-1)	
17	19	Iowa (11-1)	↑4
18	16	Kansas (9-3)	
19	18	Arkansas (11-2)	↑1
20	21	Syracuse (10-3)	↑2
21	20	Clemson (11-3)	↓7
22	24	TCU (12-2)	↑2
23	22	Oklahoma State (9-3)	↑2
24	23	Wisconsin (12-3)	↓5
25	—	California (9-2)	⤴
—	25	Ohio State (12-3)	

WEEK OF JAN 12

AP	ESPN/USA	SCHOOL	AP↓↑
1	1	Connecticut (13-0)	
2	2	Duke (15-1)	
3	3	Cincinnati (15-0)	
4	4	Stanford (13-2)	
5	5	Maryland (15-2)	
6	6	Kentucky (14-3)	
7	8	Arizona (11-1)	
8	9	Auburn (15-0)	
9	7	North Carolina (14-3)	
10	12	UCLA (11-3)	
11	13	St. John's (13-3)	
12	16	Iowa (12-1)	
13	11	Purdue (13-3)	
14	10	Michigan State (12-4)	
15	14	Kansas (11-3)	
16	15	New Mexico (14-2)	
17	19	Wisconsin (14-3)	
18	18	Syracuse (11-3)	
19	17	Minnesota (10-2)	
20	24	TCU (12-2)	
21	23	Ohio State (13-3)	
22	21	Oklahoma State (11-3)	
23	20	Indiana (14-5)	
24	22	Arkansas (11-4)	
25	25	Clemson (12-4)	

WEEK OF JAN 19

AP	ESPN/USA	SCHOOL	AP↓↑
1	1	Connecticut (15-0)	
2	2	Duke (17-1)	
3	3	Stanford (15-2)	↑1
4	4	Maryland (16-2)	↑1
5	5	Cincinnati (16-1)	↓2
6	6	Auburn (17-0) (D)	↑8
7	7	Kentucky (15-4)	↓1
8	9	St. John's (15-3)	↑2
9	11	Arizona (12-2)	↓1
10	8	North Carolina (15-4)	↑1
11	10	Michigan State (14-4)	↑1
12	13	New Mexico (16-2)	↑3
13	12	UCLA (12-4)	↓6
14	15	Iowa (13-2)	↑3
15	16	Wisconsin (16-3)	↑9
16	14	Purdue (14-4)	↓7
17	17	Minnesota (11-3)	↓1
18	18	Indiana (16-5)	↓5
19	19	Kansas (12-4)	↓1
20	20	Syracuse (12-4)	
21	22	TCU (14-3)	↑1
22	21	Arkansas (13-4)	↓3
23	23	Oklahoma State (12-4)	
24	—	Louisville (10-3)	⤴
25	—	Miami (FL) (11-3)	⤴
—	24	Ohio State (13-5)	
—	25	Oklahoma (13-4)	

WEEK OF JAN 26

AP	ESPN/USA	SCHOOL	AP↓↑
1	1	Connecticut (17-0)	
2	2	Duke (19-1)	
3	3	Stanford (17-2)	
4	4	Maryland (18-2)	
5	5	Cincinnati (18-1)	
6	6	Kentucky (17-4)	↑1
7	7	Auburn (18-1)	↓1
8	8	Michigan State (16-4)	↑3
9	10	St. John's (16-4)	↓1
10	9	North Carolina (17-4)	
11	11	UCLA (14-4)	↑2
12	13	Wisconsin (18-3)	↑3
13	12	Arizona (13-3)	↓4
14	14	Purdue (15-5)	↑2
15	17	Ohio State (15-5)	⤴
16	18	Iowa (13-4)	↓2
17	16	Syracuse (14-5)	↑3
18	19	New Mexico (16-4)	↓6
19	21	Minnesota (12-4)	↓2
20	15	Indiana (16-6)	↓2
21	22	Arkansas (14-5)	↑1
22	20	Kansas (13-5)	↓3
23	25	Miami (FL) (12-4)	↑2
24	24	TCU (15-4)	↓3
25	—	Florida (14-3)	⤴
—	23	Oklahoma State (13-5)	⤵

Poll Progression Continues →

ANNUAL REVIEW

Week of Feb 2

AP	ESPN/USA	School	AP↓↑
1	1	**Connecticut** (19-0)	
2	2	**Duke** (21-1)	
3	3	**Cincinnati** (20-1)	↑2
4	4	**Stanford** (18-3)	↓1
5	5	**Kentucky** (19-4)	↑1
6	7	**Auburn** (20-1)	↑1
7	6	**Maryland** (19-3)	↓3
8	8	**Michigan State** (18-4)	
9	10	**St. John's** (17-5)	
10	11	**Arizona** (15-3)	Ⓔ ↑3
11	12	**Wisconsin** (19-3)	↑1
12	9	**North Carolina** (18-5)	↓2
13	13	**UCLA** (15-5)	↓2
14	14	**Iowa** (15-4)	↑2
15	15	**Ohio State** (16-6)	
16	16	**Syracuse** (15-6)	↑1
17	18	**New Mexico** (17-4)	↑1
18	17	**Purdue** (15-6)	↓4
18	20	**Minnesota** (13-5)	↑1
20	24	**Utah** (16-4)	⤴
21	19	**Indiana** (17-7)	↓1
22	—	**Charleston** (18-2)	⤴
23	23	**Arkansas** (15-6)	↓2
24	—	**Missouri** (15-4)	⤴
25	—	**Miami (FL)** (13-5)	↓2
—	21	**Oklahoma State** (15-5)	
—	22	**Kansas** (14-6)	⤵
—	25	**Gonzaga** (18-4)	

Week of Feb 9

AP	ESPN/USA	School	AP↓↑
1	1	**Duke** (23-1)	↑1
2	2	**Connecticut** (20-1)	Ⓕ ↓1
3	3	**Auburn** (22-1)	↑3
4	5	**Cincinnati** (21-2)	↓1
5	4	**Michigan State** (20-4)	↑3
6	6	**Stanford** (19-4)	↓2
7	7	**Maryland** (20-4)	
8	9	**Kentucky** (20-4)	↓3
9	12	**UCLA** (17-5)	↑4
10	11	**Arizona** (16-4)	
11	8	**St. John's** (18-6)	↓2
12	10	**North Carolina** (19-6)	
13	13	**Ohio State** (17-6)	↑2
14	16	**Utah** (18-4)	↑6
15	14	**Wisconsin** (19-5)	↓4
16	21	**Miami (FL)** (15-5)	↑9
17	15	**Indiana** (18-7)	↑4
18	17	**Syracuse** (16-7)	Ⓕ ↓2
19	18	**Iowa** (15-6)	↓5
20	25	**Charleston** (21-2)	↑2
21	19	**Purdue** (16-7)	↓3
22	20	**Minnesota** (14-6)	↓4
23	24	**Florida** (16-5)	⤴
24	22	**Kansas** (18-6)	⤴
25	23	**New Mexico** (17-6)	↓8

Week of Feb 16

AP	ESPN/USA	School	AP↓↑
1	1	**Duke** (25-1)	
2	2	**Connecticut** (22-1)	
3	3	**Auburn** (24-1)	
4	4	**Michigan State** (22-4)	↑1
5	5	**Maryland** (22-4)	↑2
6	9	**Kentucky** (20-6)	↑2
7	8	**Stanford** (20-5)	↓1
8	10	**Arizona** (18-4)	↑2
9	6	**Cincinnati** (21-4)	↓5
10	7	**St. John's** (20-6)	↑1
11	11	**Ohio State** (19-6)	↑2
12	13	**Utah** (20-4)	↑2
13	13	**Wisconsin** (21-5)	↑2
14	12	**North Carolina** (19-7)	↓2
15	16	**Miami (FL)** (17-5)	↑1
16	15	**UCLA** (17-7)	↓7
17	18	**Purdue** (18-7)	↑4
18	21	**Charleston** (23-2)	↑2
19	17	**Indiana** (19-8)	↓2
20	20	**Iowa** (16-7)	↓1
21	19	**Syracuse** (17-8)	↓3
22	—	**Missouri** (18-5)	⤴
23	24	**Florida** (17-6)	
24	22	**New Mexico** (20-6)	↑1
25	—	**Miami (Ohio)** (19-4)	⤴
—	23	**Minnesota** (14-8)	⤵
—	25	**Texas** (15-10)	

Week of Feb 23

AP	ESPN/USA	School	A[illegible]
1	1	**Duke** (27-1)	
2	2	**Auburn** (25-1)	
3	3	**Michigan State** (25-4)	
4	4	**Connecticut** (23-2)	
5	5	**Maryland** (23-4)	
6	6	**Stanford** (22-5)	↑
7	9	**Arizona** (20-4)	↑
8	7	**St. John's** (22-6)	↑
9	8	**Cincinnati** (23-4)	
10	10	**Ohio State** (21-6)	↑
11	13	**Miami (Fla.)** (19-5)	↑
12	12	**Utah** (22-4)	
13	11	**Kentucky** (21-7)	↓[illegible]
14	14	**North Carolina** (21-7)	
15	16	**UCLA** (19-7)	↑1
16	15	**Wisconsin** (21-6)	↓3
17	18	**Charleston** (25-2)	↑1
18	19	**Iowa** (17-7)	↑2
19	24	**Florida** (18-6)	↑4
20	17	**Indiana** (20-9)	↓1
21	21	**New Mexico** (21-6)	↑3
22	23	**Texas** (17-10)	⤴
23	22	**Purdue** (18-9)	↓6
24	20	**Syracuse** (18-9)	↓3
24	—	**Temple** (18-9)	⤴
—	25	**Minnesota** (15-8)	

Week of Mar 2

AP	ESPN/USA	School	AP↓↑
1	1	**Duke** (29-1)	
2	2	**Michigan State** (26-4)	Ⓖ ↑1
3	3	**Connecticut** (25-2)	↑1
4	4	**Auburn** (26-2)	↓2
5	5	**Maryland** (25-4)	
6	6	**Stanford** (24-5)	
7	7	**Cincinnati** (25-4)	↑2
8	8	**Utah** (24-4)	↑4
9	10	**Miami (FL)** (21-5)	↑2
10	9	**St. John's** (23-7)	↓2
11	12	**Ohio State** (22-7)	Ⓖ ↓1
12	13	**UCLA** (21-7)	↑3
13	11	**Arizona** (20-6)	↓6
14	14	**Kentucky** (22-8)	↓1
15	15	**North Carolina** (22-8)	↓1
16	16	**Charleston** (28-2)	↑1
17	17	**Indiana** (22-9)	Ⓖ ↑3
18	25	**Tennessee** (20-7)	⤴
19	18	**Wisconsin** (21-8)	↓3
20	19	**Iowa** (18-8)	↓2
21	23	**Florida** (19-7)	↓2
22	—	**Arkansas** (20-9)	⤴
23	24	**Minnesota** (17-9)	Ⓖ ⤴
24	—	**Missouri** (20-7)	⤴
25	21	**New Mexico** (22-7)	↓4
—	20	**Syracuse** (19-10)	⤵
—	22	**Texas** (18-11)	⤵

Week of Mar 9

AP	ESPN/USA	School	AP↓↑
1	1	**Duke** (32-1)	
2	2	**Michigan State** (29-4)	
3	3	**Connecticut** (28-2)	
4	4	**Auburn** (27-3)	
5	5	**Maryland** (26-5)	
6	6	**Utah** (27-4)	↑2
7	7	**Stanford** (25-6)	↓1
8	11	**Kentucky** (25-8)	↑6
9	8	**St. John's** (25-8)	↑1
10	12	**Miami (FL)** (22-6)	↓1
11	9	**Cincinnati** (26-5)	↓4
12	10	**Arizona** (22-6)	↑1
13	13	**North Carolina** (24-9)	↑2
14	14	**Ohio State** (23-8)	↓3
15	15	**UCLA** (22-8)	↓3
16	16	**Charleston** (28-2)	
17	19	**Arkansas** (22-10)	↑5
18	17	**Wisconsin** (22-9)	↑1
19	18	**Indiana** (22-10)	↓2
20	—	**Tennessee** (20-8)	↓2
21	20	**Iowa** (18-9)	↓1
22	22	**Kansas** (22-9)	⤴
23	25	**Florida** (20-8)	↓2
24	—	**Charlotte** (22-10)	⤴
25	24	**New Mexico** (24-8)	
—	21	**Syracuse** (21-11)	
—	23	**Texas** (19-12)	

Final Poll (Post-Tournament)

ESPN/USA	School
1	**Connecticut** (34-2)
2	**Duke** (37-2)
3	**Michigan State** (33-5)
4	**Ohio State** (27-9)
5	**Kentucky** (28-9)
5	**St. John's** (28-9)
7	**Auburn** (29-4)
8	**Maryland** (28-6)
9	**Stanford** (26-7)
10	**Utah** (28-5)
11	**Cincinnati** (27-6)
12	**Gonzaga** (28-7)
12	**Miami (FL)** (23-7)
14	**Temple** (24-11)
15	**Iowa** (20-10)
16	**Arizona** (22-7)
17	**Florida** (22-9)
18	**North Carolina** (24-10)
19	**Oklahoma** (22-11)
20	**Miami (Ohio)** (24-8)
21	**UCLA** (22-9)
22	**Purdue** (21-13)
23	**Kansas** (23-10)
24	**SW Missouri State** (22-11)
25	**Arkansas** (23-11)

Ⓐ The College of Charleston upsets North Carolina on Dec. 5, 66-64; Danny Johnson's winning bucket comes with 0.1 seconds left on the clock.

Ⓑ Coaching his 1,000th game, Indiana's Bob Knight kicks the scorer's table while protesting a traveling call and gets hit with a technical during the Hoosiers' 70-61 loss to Kentucky.

Ⓒ American University-Puerto Rico's Ramon Gomez knocks Tim Heskett of Oklahoma unconscious with an elbow to the head with 5:02 left in the first half. Referees award the Sooners a 2-0 victory by forfeit.

Ⓓ Undefeated Auburn demolishes Florida, 88-69, on Jan. 16 and cracks the Top 10 for the first time. The Tigers will lose four days later at Kentucky, 72-62, but go on to win the SEC regular-season title and head to the NCAA Tournament with a sparkling 27–3 record.

Ⓔ Arizona's Jason Terry sets a school career record for steals (245) and then hits the game-winning shot in a 79-78 victory over Stanford on Jan. 28.

Ⓕ The top-ranked and undefeated Huskies get a wakeup call. Syracuse hands UConn its first loss, 59-42, in Hartford.

Ⓖ In the Big Ten tournament, bottom-seed Illinois defeats ranked opponents Minnesota, Indiana and Ohio State before falling to Michigan State in the final. Despite the loss, Ohio State is the nation's most improved team, having gone 8–22 in 1997-98.

Pre-Tournament Ratings Percentage Index (RPI)

Rank	School	W-L	Sched. Strg.	SS Rank	RPI
1	**Duke**	32-1	.6203	3	.6999
2	**Michigan State**	28-4	.6117	8	.6741
3	**Connecticut**	28-2	.5709	29	.6598
4	**Stanford**	23-6	.6157	5	.6549
5	**Maryland**	25-5	.5957	16	.6513
6	**Kentucky**	25-8	.6008	11	.6377
7	**North Carolina**	24-9	.6238	2	.6374
8	**Auburn**	27-3	.5484	63	.6346
9	**Cincinnati**	25-5	.5680	35	.6324
10	**St. John's**	25-8	.6053	10	.6319
11	**Miami**	22-6	.5832	21	.6306
12	**Wisconsin**	22-9	.5876	18	.6181
13	**Arizona**	22-6	.5562	54	.6155
14	**Iowa**	18-9	.6142	6	.6147
15	**Kansas**	21-9	.6004	12	.6136
16	**Indiana**	22-10	.5894	17	.6120
17	**Charlotte**	22-10	.6000	13	.6111
18	**Ohio State**	22-8	.5553	55	.6104
19	**UCLA**	22-8	.5696	32	.6097
20	**Utah**	24-4	.5213	107	.6059
21	**Louisville**	19-10	.5842	20	.5998
22	**Miami (Ohio)**	22-7	.5563	53	.5972
23	**Purdue**	19-12	.5966	15	.5943
24	**Minnesota**	17-10	.5829	22	.5936
25	**Tennessee**	20-8	.5535	57	.5936
26	**Kent State**	21-6	.5382	79	.5910
27	**Washington**	16-11	.6063	9	.5898
28	**Temple**	21-10	.5642	39	.5898
29	**Arkansas**	22-10	.5613	42	.5895
30	**Tulsa**	22-9	.5550	56	.5877
31	**Missouri**	20-8	.5441	69	.5823
32	**Charleston**	25-2	.4553	229	.5814
33	**Villanova**	20-10	.5498	62	.5811
34	**Florida**	20-8	.5344	87	.5806
35	**Creighton**	21-8	.5334	91	.5805
36	**SW Missouri State**	20-10	.5611	44	.5790
37	**Syracuse**	20-11	.5524	59	.5780
38	**George Washington**	20-8	.5334	89	.5756
39	**Siena**	25-5	.4876	156	.5738
40	**Oregon**	15-11	.5823	23	.5731
41	**TCU**	18-10	.5567	52	.5713
42	**Gonzaga**	24-6	.4847	163	.5701
43	**Nebraska**	19-12	.5600	47	.5693
44	**Texas**	19-12	.5613	41	.5684
45	**Mississippi**	16-12	.5711	28	.5675
46	**DePaul**	17-12	.5686	34	.5674
47	**UAB**	20-11	.5448	66	.5674
48	**Rutgers**	18-12	.5694	33	.5668
49	**Oklahoma**	19-10	.5411	74	.5666
50	**Evansville**	21-9	.5252	102	.5663

Source: Collegiate Basketball News

ANNUAL REVIEW

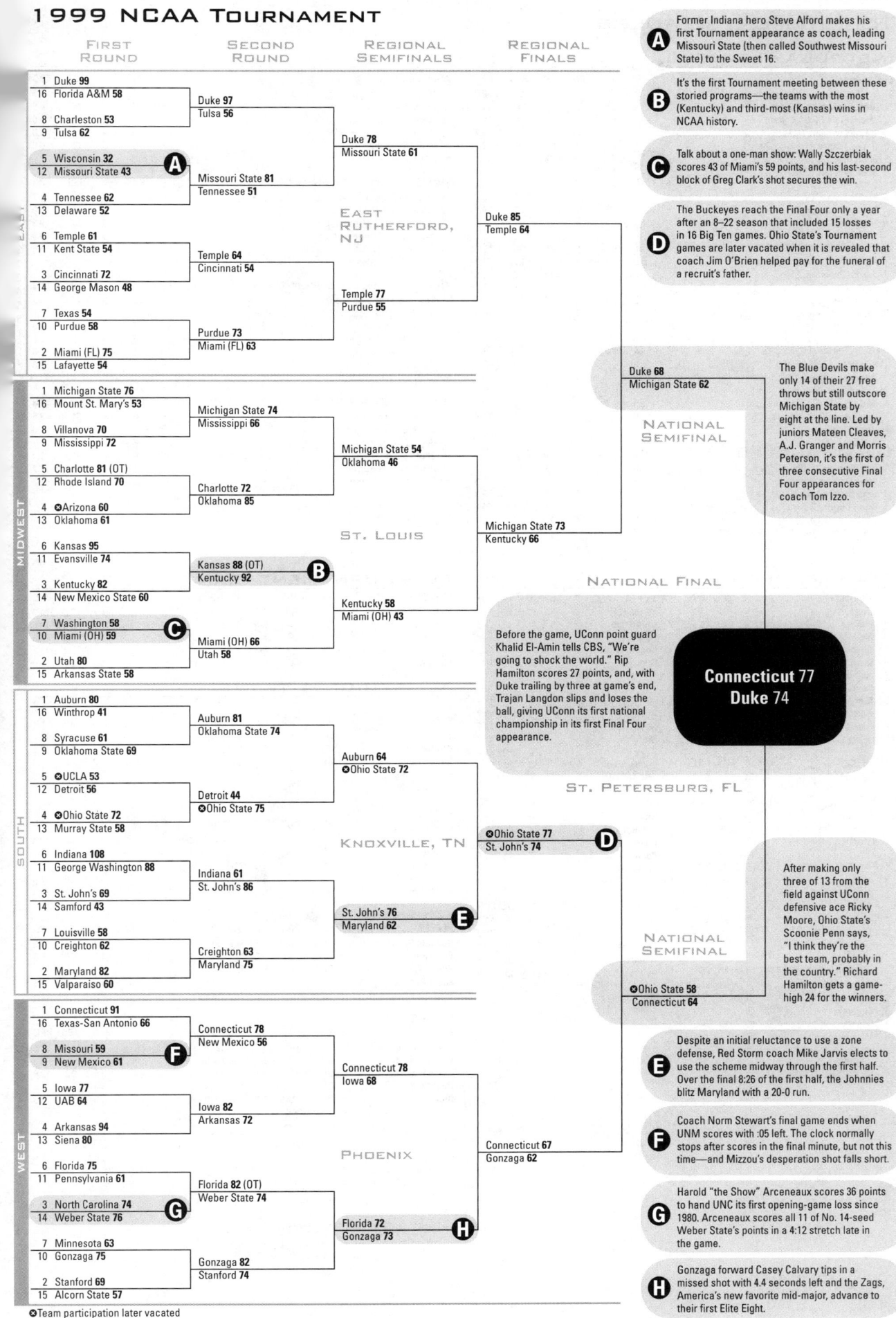

1999 NCAA Tournament

First Round | Second Round | Regional Semifinals | Regional Finals

East — East Rutherford, NJ

First Round
- 1 Duke **99** / 16 Florida A&M **58**
- 8 Charleston **53** / 9 Tulsa **62**
- 5 Wisconsin **32** / 12 Missouri State **43** (A)
- 4 Tennessee **62** / 13 Delaware **52**
- 6 Temple **61** / 11 Kent State **54**
- 3 Cincinnati **72** / 14 George Mason **48**
- 7 Texas **54** / 10 Purdue **58**
- 2 Miami (FL) **75** / 15 Lafayette **54**

Second Round
- Duke **97** / Tulsa **56**
- Missouri State **81** / Tennessee **51**
- Temple **64** / Cincinnati **54**
- Purdue **73** / Miami (FL) **63**

Regional Semifinals
- Duke **78** / Missouri State **61**
- Temple **77** / Purdue **55**

Regional Finals
- Duke **85** / Temple **64**

Midwest — St. Louis

First Round
- 1 Michigan State **76** / 16 Mount St. Mary's **53**
- 8 Villanova **70** / 9 Mississippi **72**
- 5 Charlotte **81** (OT) / 12 Rhode Island **70**
- 4 ⊗Arizona **60** / 13 Oklahoma **61**
- 6 Kansas **95** / 11 Evansville **74**
- 3 Kentucky **82** / 14 New Mexico State **60**
- 7 Washington **58** / 10 Miami (OH) **59** (C)
- 2 Utah **80** / 15 Arkansas State **58**

Second Round
- Michigan State **74** / Mississippi **66**
- Charlotte **72** / Oklahoma **85**
- Kansas **88** (OT) / Kentucky **92** (B)
- Miami (OH) **66** / Utah **58**

Regional Semifinals
- Michigan State **54** / Oklahoma **46**
- Kentucky **58** / Miami (OH) **43**

Regional Finals
- Michigan State **73** / Kentucky **66**

South — Knoxville, TN

First Round
- 1 Auburn **80** / 16 Winthrop **41**
- 8 Syracuse **61** / 9 Oklahoma State **69**
- 5 ⊗UCLA **53** / 12 Detroit **56**
- 4 ⊗Ohio State **72** / 13 Murray State **58**
- 6 Indiana **108** / 11 George Washington **88**
- 3 St. John's **69** / 14 Samford **43**
- 7 Louisville **58** / 10 Creighton **62**
- 2 Maryland **82** / 15 Valparaiso **60**

Second Round
- Auburn **81** / Oklahoma State **74**
- Detroit **44** / ⊗Ohio State **75**
- Indiana **61** / St. John's **86**
- Creighton **63** / Maryland **75**

Regional Semifinals
- Auburn **64** / ⊗Ohio State **72**
- St. John's **76** / Maryland **62** (E)

Regional Finals
- ⊗Ohio State **77** / St. John's **74** (D)

West — Phoenix

First Round
- 1 Connecticut **91** / 16 Texas-San Antonio **66**
- 8 Missouri **59** / 9 New Mexico **61** (F)
- 5 Iowa **77** / 12 UAB **64**
- 4 Arkansas **94** / 13 Siena **80**
- 6 Florida **75** / 11 Pennsylvania **61**
- 3 North Carolina **74** / 14 Weber State **76** (G)
- 7 Minnesota **63** / 10 Gonzaga **75**
- 2 Stanford **69** / 15 Alcorn State **57**

Second Round
- Connecticut **78** / New Mexico **56**
- Iowa **82** / Arkansas **72**
- Florida **82** (OT) / Weber State **74**
- Gonzaga **82** / Stanford **74**

Regional Semifinals
- Connecticut **78** / Iowa **68**
- Florida **72** / Gonzaga **73** (H)

Regional Finals
- Connecticut **67** / Gonzaga **62**

National Semifinal

Duke **68** / Michigan State **62**

The Blue Devils make only 14 of their 27 free throws but still outscore Michigan State by eight at the line. Led by juniors Mateen Cleaves, A.J. Granger and Morris Peterson, it's the first of three consecutive Final Four appearances for coach Tom Izzo.

National Semifinal

⊗Ohio State **58** / Connecticut **64**

After making only three of 13 from the field against UConn defensive ace Ricky Moore, Ohio State's Scoonie Penn says, "I think they're the best team, probably in the country." Richard Hamilton gets a game-high 24 for the winners.

National Final — St. Petersburg, FL

Connecticut 77
Duke 74

Before the game, UConn point guard Khalid El-Amin tells CBS, "We're going to shock the world." Rip Hamilton scores 27 points, and, with Duke trailing by three at game's end, Trajan Langdon slips and loses the ball, giving UConn its first national championship in its first Final Four appearance.

⊗Team participation later vacated

A Former Indiana hero Steve Alford makes his first Tournament appearance as coach, leading Missouri State (then called Southwest Missouri State) to the Sweet 16.

B It's the first Tournament meeting between these storied programs—the teams with the most (Kentucky) and third-most (Kansas) wins in NCAA history.

C Talk about a one-man show: Wally Szczerbiak scores 43 of Miami's 59 points, and his last-second block of Greg Clark's shot secures the win.

D The Buckeyes reach the Final Four only a year after an 8–22 season that included 15 losses in 16 Big Ten games. Ohio State's Tournament games are later vacated when it is revealed that coach Jim O'Brien helped pay for the funeral of a recruit's father.

E Despite an initial reluctance to use a zone defense, Red Storm coach Mike Jarvis elects to use the scheme midway through the first half. Over the final 8:26 of the first half, the Johnnies blitz Maryland with a 20-0 run.

F Coach Norm Stewart's final game ends when UNM scores with :05 left. The clock normally stops after scores in the final minute, but not this time—and Mizzou's desperation shot falls short.

G Harold "the Show" Arceneaux scores 36 points to hand UNC its first opening-game loss since 1980. Arceneaux scores all 11 of No. 14-seed Weber State's points in a 4:12 stretch late in the game.

H Gonzaga forward Casey Calvary tips in a missed shot with 4.4 seconds left and the Zags, America's new favorite mid-major, advance to their first Elite Eight.

Tournament Leaders

INDIVIDUAL LEADERS

Scoring	CL	POS	G	PTS	PPG
1 **Wally Szczerbiak**, Miami (OH)	SR	F	3	90	30.0
2 **Richard Hamilton**, Connecticut	JR	G/F	6	145	24.2
3 **Michael Redd**, Ohio State	SO	G	5	99	19.8
4 **Trajan Langdon**, Duke	SR	G	5	91	18.2
5 **Danny Moore**, Missouri State	SR	F	3	52	17.3
6 **Elton Brand**, Duke	SO	F	6	102	17.0
Scott Padgett, Kentucky	SR	F	4	68	17.0
8 **Scott Pohlman**, Auburn	SO	G	3	49	16.3
9 **Richie Frahm**, Gonzaga	JR	G	4	65	16.3
Bootsy Thornton, St. John's	JR	G	4	65	16.3

Minimum: 3 games

Field Goal Pct	CL	POS	G	FG	FGA	PCT
1 **Andre Hutson**, Michigan State	SO	F	5	22	31	71.0
2 **Jason Singleton**, Ohio State	SR	G	5	19	29	65.5
3 **Casey Calvary**, Gonzaga	SO	F	4	15	23	65.2
4 **Elton Brand**, Duke	SO	F	6	37	57	64.9
5 **Edmund Saunders**, Connecticut	SO	F	6	17	27	63.0

Minimum: 15 made and 3 games

Free Throw Pct	CL	POS	G	FT	FTA	PCT
1 **Richie Frahm**, Gonzaga	JR	G	4	17	18	94.4
Arthur Lee, Stanford	JR	G	2	17	18	94.4
3 **Pepe Sanchez**, Temple	JR	G	4	15	16	93.8
4 **Wally Szczerbiak**, Miami (OH)	SR	F	3	15	17	88.2
5 **Lavor Postell**, St. John's	JR	F	4	24	29	82.8

Minimum: 15 made

Three-Point FG Pct	CL	POS	G	3FG	3FGA	PCT
1 **A.J. Granger**, Michigan State	JR	F	5	8	11	72.7
2 **Allen Phillips**, Missouri State	FR	G	3	7	12	58.3
3 **Greg Stolt**, Florida	SR	F	3	9	16	56.3
4 **Brian Cardinal**, Purdue	JR	F	3	7	13	53.8
5 **Trajan Langdon**, Duke	SR	G	5	17	32	53.1

Minimum: 6 made and 3 games

Assists Per Game	CL	POS	G	AST	APG
1 **Mateen Cleaves**, Michigan State	JR	G	5	38	7.6
2 **Erick Barkley**, St. John's	FR	G	4	26	6.5
3 **Pepe Sanchez**, Temple	JR	G	4	24	6.0
Wayne Turner, Kentucky	SR	G	4	24	6.0
Eddie Shannon, Florida	SR	G	3	18	6.0

Minimum: 3 games

Rebounds Per Game	CL	POS	G	REB	RPG
1 **Eduardo Najera**, Oklahoma	JR	F	3	35	11.7
2 **Elton Brand**, Duke	SO	F	6	60	10.0
3 **Danny Moore**, Missouri State	SR	F	3	28	9.3
Mamadou N'diaye, Auburn	JR	C	3	28	9.3
5 **Antonio Smith**, Michigan State	SR	G	5	44	8.8

Minimum: 3 games

Blocked Shots Per Game	CL	POS	G	BLK	BPG
1 **Ken Johnson**, Ohio State	SO	C	5	21	4.2
2 **Ron Artest**, St. John's	SO	F	4	10	2.5
3 **Elton Brand**, Duke	SO	F	6	12	2.0
Jamaal Magloire, Kentucky	JR	F	4	8	2.0
Terence Morris, Maryland	SO	F	3	6	2.0
Mamadou N'diaye, Auburn	JR	C	3	6	2.0

Minimum: 3 games

Steals Per Game	CL	POS	G	STL	SPG
1 **Pepe Sanchez**, Temple	JR	G	4	14	3.5
2 **Brian Cardinal**, Purdue	JR	F	3	9	3.0
3 **Jay Heard**, Auburn	FR	G	3	8	2.7
Eddie Shannon, Florida	SR	G	3	8	2.7
Brent Wright, Florida	SO	F	3	8	2.7

Minimum: 3 games

TEAM LEADERS

Scoring	G	PTS	PPG
1 **Duke**	6	501	83.5
2 **Florida**	3	229	76.3
3 **St. John's**	4	305	76.3
4 **Connecticut**	6	455	75.8
5 **Iowa**	3	227	75.7
6 **Auburn**	3	225	75.0
7 **Kentucky**	4	298	74.5
8 **Maryland**	3	219	73.0
Gonzaga	4	292	73.0
10 **Ohio State**	5	354	70.8

Minimum: 3 games

FG Pct	G	FG	FGA	PCT
1 **Kentucky**	4	104	204	51.0
2 **Duke**	6	170	337	50.4
3 **Connecticut**	6	173	358	48.3
4 **St. John's**	4	103	224	46.0
5 **Purdue**	3	62	136	45.6

Minimum: 3 games

3-Pt FG Pct	G	3FG	3FGA	PCT
1 **Duke**	6	49	104	47.1
2 **Gonzaga**	4	37	84	44.0
3 **Iowa**	3	28	64	43.8
4 **Kentucky**	4	30	69	43.5
5 **St. John's**	4	26	63	41.3

Minimum: 3 games

FT Pct	G	FT	FTA	PCT
1 **Miami (OH)**	3	27	33	81.8
2 **Michigan State**	5	67	88	76.1
3 **Kentucky**	4	60	81	74.1
4 **Connecticut**	6	88	119	74.0
5 **Missouri State**	3	40	55	72.7

Minimum: 3 games

Ast/TO Ratio	G	AST	TO	RAT
1 **Miami (OH)**	3	34	22	1.55
2 **Ohio State**	5	70	49	1.43
3 **St. John's**	4	60	47	1.28
4 **Kentucky**	4	62	51	1.22
5 **Gonzaga**	4	59	53	1.11

Minimum: 3 games

Rebounds	G	REB	RPG
1 **Auburn**	3	128	42.7
Missouri State	3	128	42.7
3 **Maryland**	3	125	41.7
Duke	6	250	41.7
5 **Connecticut**	6	234	39.0

Minimum: 3 games

Blocks	G	BLK	BPG
1 **Ohio State**	5	29	5.8
2 **Kentucky**	4	22	5.5
3 **Duke**	6	30	5.0
4 **Connecticut**	6	26	4.3
5 **St. John's**	4	15	3.8

Minimum: 3 games

Steals	G	STL	SPG
1 **Florida**	3	37	12.3
2 **Iowa**	3	29	9.7
Maryland	3	29	9.7
4 **Temple**	4	37	9.3
5 **Auburn**	3	27	9.0

Minimum: 3 games

ALL-TOURNAMENT TEAM

PLAYER	CL	POS	HT	SCHOOL	RPG	APG	PPG
Richard Hamilton*	JR	G/F	6-6	Connecticut	4.7	2.0	24.2
Elton Brand	SO	F	6-8	Duke	10.0	0.8	17.0
Khalid El-Amin	SO	G	5-10	Connecticut	3.3	5.2	14.0
Trajan Langdon	SR	G	6-3	Duke	3.4	2.2	18.2
Ricky Moore	SR	G	6-2	Connecticut	5.3	3.2	8.0

ALL-REGIONAL TEAMS

EAST

PLAYER	CL	POS	HT	SCHOOL	RPG	APG	PPG
Trajan Langdon*	SR	G	6-3	Duke	3.3	2.3	19.7
William Avery	SO	G	6-2	Duke	5.8	3.0	14.8
Elton Brand	SO	F	6-8	Duke	8.0	1.0	17.3
Mark Karcher	SO	F	6-5	Temple	3.5	2.0	12.8
Pepe Sanchez	JR	G	6-4	Temple	6.0	6.0	14.0

MIDWEST

PLAYER	CL	POS	HT	SCHOOL	RPG	APG	PPG
Morris Peterson*	JR	G/F	6-6	Michigan State	7.4	1.0	9.8
Mateen Cleaves	JR	G	6-2	Michigan State	2.0	7.0	11.3
A.J. Granger	JR	F	6-9	Michigan State	4.3	0.5	12.0
Scott Padgett	SR	F	6-9	Kentucky	4.5	2.0	17.0
Wally Szczerbiak	SR	F	6-8	Miami (OH)	7.3	3.0	30.0

SOUTH

PLAYER	CL	POS	HT	SCHOOL	RPG	APG	PPG
Scoonie Penn*	JR	G	5-10	Ohio State	7.3	4.5	17.5
Erick Barkley	FR	G	6-1	St. John's	4.0	6.5	15.0
Ken Johnson	SO	C	6-11	Ohio State	3.5	0.0	8.0
Lavor Postell	JR	F	6-6	St. John's	8.5	2.0	15.5
Michael Redd	SO	G	6-6	Ohio State	6.0	3.3	21.0

WEST

PLAYER	CL	POS	HT	SCHOOL	RPG	APG	PPG
Richard Hamilton*	JR	G/F	6-6	Connecticut	4.0	2.0	23.5
Casey Calvary	SO	F	6-8	Gonzaga	7.5	0.8	9.5
Kevin Freeman	JR	F	6-7	Connecticut	8.5	0.3	12.0
Quentin Hall	SR	G	5-9	Gonzaga	5.3	2.0	12.3
Ricky Moore	SR	G	6-2	Connecticut	4.0	4.0	7.3

* Most outstanding player

1999 NCAA TOURNAMENT BOX SCORES

78-61 (Sweet 16)

	1H	2H
Duke	39	39
Missouri State	30	31

DUKE	MIN	FG	3FG	FT	REB	A	ST	BL	PF	TP
Trajan Langdon	33	9-14	4-6	2-2	5	2	0	0	1	24
Elton Brand	34	6-11	0-0	2-5	13	1	4	5	1	14
William Avery	30	4-10	3-8	1-3	6	2	1	0	3	12
Chris Carrawell	31	3-7	0-1	3-5	3	4	1	0	1	9
Nate James	14	2-4	1-3	2-2	5	4	0	0	4	7
Corey Maggette	15	3-7	0-2	0-2	7	0	0	0	1	6
Shane Battier	31	2-5	1-3	0-0	8	3	2	2	3	5
D. Bryant	1	0-0	0-0	1-2	0	0	0	0	0	1
Chris Burgess	8	0-0	0-0	0-0	2	0	0	1	2	0
Justin Caldbeck	1	0-0	0-0	0-0	0	0	0	0	0	0
Ryan Caldbeck	1	0-0	0-0	0-0	0	0	0	0	0	0
J.D. Simpson	1	0-0	0-0	0-0	0	0	0	0	0	0
TOTALS	**200**	**29-58**	**9-23**	**11-21**	**49**	**16**	**8**	**8**	**16**	**78**
Percentages		50.0	39.1	52.4						

Coach: Mike Krzyzewski

MISSOURI STATE	MIN	FG	3FG	FT	REB	A	ST	BL	PF	TP
Allen Phillips	22	6-12	4-5	0-0	6	1	2	0	1	16
Danny Moore	34	5-15	0-0	5-6	5	2	1	3	2	15
William Fontleroy	33	4-11	0-2	2-4	9	2	0	0	4	10
Scott Brakebill	15	3-5	0-0	2-2	5	0	1	0	2	8
Kevin Ault	32	2-7	1-5	0-0	3	3	4	0	2	5
Ryan Bettenhausen	10	1-2	0-0	0-0	1	0	1	0	1	2
Paul Murans	1	1-1	0-0	0-0	0	0	0	0	0	2
Butch Tshomba	1	1-1	0-0	0-0	4	0	0	0	0	2
Ken Stringer	27	0-2	0-0	1-2	5	2	1	1	1	1
Ron Bruton	16	0-3	0-0	0-0	7	0	0	0	1	0
Matt Rueter	7	0-1	0-0	0-0	2	1	0	0	3	0
Eric Judd	1	0-1	0-1	0-0	0	0	0	0	0	0
Brandon Miller	1	0-1	0-1	0-0	0	0	0	0	1	0
TOTALS	**200**	**23-62**	**5-14**	**10-14**	**47**	**11**	**10**	**4**	**18**	**61**
Percentages		37.1	35.7	71.4						

Coach: Steve Alford

Officials: Ted Hillary, Tom Lopes, Tom Eades
Technicals: None
Attendance: 19,233

77-55 (Sweet 16)

	1H	2H
Temple	47	30
Purdue	32	23

TEMPLE	MIN	FG	3FG	FT	REB	A	ST	BL	PF	TP
Mark Karcher	30	8-17	5-12	0-0	4	2	2	1	1	21
Pepe Sanchez	39	6-12	1-5	4-4	6	9	6	1	1	17
Kevin Lyde	25	6-6	0-0	2-2	8	1	0	0	0	14
Quincy Wadley	24	3-5	1-1	2-3	4	0	0	0	3	9
Rasheed Brokenborough	40	3-9	1-4	1-2	2	1	3	0	0	8
Lamont Barnes	16	3-4	0-0	1-3	2	0	1	0	3	7
Ron Rollerson	8	0-0	0-0	1-2	1	0	0	0	1	1
Keaton Sanders	16	0-2	0-1	0-0	2	0	1	0	1	0
Mamadou Cello Barry	1	0-0	0-0	0-0	0	0	0	0	0	0
Damien Reid	1	0-0	0-0	0-0	0	0	0	0	0	0
TOTALS	**200**	**29-55**	**8-23**	**11-16**	**29**	**13**	**13**	**2**	**10**	**77**
Percentages		52.7	34.8	68.8						

Coach: John Chaney

PURDUE	MIN	FG	3FG	FT	REB	A	ST	BL	PF	TP
Jaraan Cornell	35	5-13	4-9	0-1	3	3	0	0	2	14
Alan Eldridge	26	3-5	3-5	0-0	1	1	0	0	1	9
John Allison	7	2-2	0-0	3-4	3	1	0	1	0	7
Carson Cunningham	6	2-3	2-2	0-0	1	1	0	0	0	6
Brian Cardinal	32	2-2	1-1	0-0	4	1	2	0	4	5
Tony Mayfield	25	2-5	1-2	0-0	1	3	1	1	1	5
Mayhard Lewis	10	2-2	1-1	0-0	0	0	0	0	0	5
Mike Robinson	10	1-2	1-1	1-2	1	0	0	1	2	4
Cameron Stephens	31	0-5	0-0	0-0	3	2	0	0	1	0
Rodney Smith	10	0-3	0-1	0-0	1	0	0	0	0	0
Greg McQuay	7	0-0	0-0	0-0	0	1	0	0	2	0
Chad Kerkhof	1	0-0	0-0	0-0	0	0	0	0	0	0
TOTALS	**200**	**19-42**	**13-22**	**4-7**	**18**	**13**	**3**	**3**	**13**	**55**
Percentages		45.2	59.1	57.1						

Coach: Gene Keady

Officials: John Clougherty, Rusty Herring, Randy McCall
Technicals: Purdue (Cornell, coach Keady)
Attendance: 19,233

54-46 (Sweet 16)

	1H	2H
Michigan State	26	28
Oklahoma	25	21

MICHIGAN STATE	MIN	FG	3FG	FT	REB	A	ST	BL	PF	TP
Andre Hutson	30	3-3	0-0	6-10	5	0	0	0	1	12
Morris Peterson	23	4-8	0-1	3-4	7	0	1	0	1	11
A.J. Granger	24	4-5	2-2	0-0	7	0	1	0	4	10
Mateen Cleaves	32	3-14	0-4	3-4	2	2	0	0	4	9
Charlie Bell	26	3-3	3-3	0-0	2	1	1	1	1	9
Jason Klein	22	1-5	1-3	0-0	0	2	1	1	1	3
Antonio Smith	23	0-1	0-0	0-0	7	0	1	0	4	0
Thomas Kelley	11	0-4	0-2	0-0	1	1	1	0	0	0
Doug Davis	9	0-2	0-0	0-0	0	4	0	0	2	0
TOTALS	**200**	**18-45**	**6-15**	**12-18**	**31**	**10**	**6**	**2**	**18**	**54**
Percentages		40.0	40.0	66.7						

Coach: Tom Izzo

OKLAHOMA	MIN	FG	3FG	FT	REB	A	ST	BL	PF	TP
Michael Johnson	40	4-15	1-4	3-4	2	1	2	0	2	12
Ryan Humphrey	31	4-8	0-0	2-5	10	1	2	1	5	10
Alex Spaulding	34	3-7	0-1	1-3	4	0	0	0	4	7
Eduardo Najera	31	2-8	1-4	2-2	7	0	1	2	2	7
Victor Avila	9	2-3	0-0	0-0	1	0	0	0	0	4
Eric Martin	33	1-8	1-5	0-0	2	2	0	0	2	3
Tim Heskett	10	1-2	1-1	0-0	2	1	0	0	1	3
Renzi Stone	12	0-0	0-0	0-0	0	0	1	0	1	0
TOTALS	**200**	**17-51**	**4-15**	**8-14**	**28**	**5**	**6**	**3**	**17**	**46**
Percentages		33.3	26.7	57.1						

Coach: Kelvin Sampson

Officials: John Cahill, Ed Corbett, Michael Kitts
Technicals: None
Attendance: 42,440

58-43 (Sweet 16)

	1H	2H
Kentucky	26	32
Miami (OH)	19	24

KENTUCKY	MIN	FG	3FG	FT	REB	A	ST	BL	PF	TP
Scott Padgett	23	5-9	2-5	5-6	4	2	1	1	3	17
Heshimu Evans	28	4-7	0-1	3-3	10	4	2	0	1	11
Wayne Turner	30	3-6	0-0	1-2	3	3	2	0	2	7
Saul Smith	20	2-4	2-4	1-2	4	0	0	0	2	7
Jules Camara	17	3-3	0-0	0-0	5	0	0	0	1	6
Jamaal Magloire	21	1-4	0-0	3-4	6	0	0	0	3	5
Desmond Allison	13	1-3	1-2	0-0	2	0	0	0	2	3
Tayshaun Prince	18	1-2	0-1	0-0	3	0	0	1	0	2
Michael Bradley	18	0-1	0-0	0-0	3	1	0	0	3	0
Ryan Hogan	8	0-2	0-1	0-0	0	1	0	0	0	0
Todd Tackett	2	0-1	0-1	0-0	0	0	0	0	0	0
J.P. Blevins	1	0-0	0-0	0-0	0	0	0	0	0	0
Steve Masiello	1	0-0	0-0	0-0	0	0	0	0	0	0
TOTALS	**200**	**20-42**	**5-15**	**13-17**	**40**	**11**	**5**	**3**	**16**	**58**
Percentages		47.6	33.3	76.5						

Coach: Tubby Smith

MIAMI (OH)	MIN	FG	3FG	FT	REB	A	ST	BL	PF	TP
Wally Szczerbiak	38	8-16	4-10	3-4	2	2	2	0	4	23
Damon Frierson	38	3-10	2-3	1-2	5	2	1	0	1	9
Anthony Taylor	23	1-4	1-1	4-4	0	0	1	0	1	7
Rob Mestas	36	1-4	0-2	0-0	4	1	0	0	3	2
John Estick	25	1-2	0-0	0-1	3	0	0	1	3	2
Jason Stewart	14	0-4	0-2	0-0	2	0	1	0	1	0
Mike Ensminger	12	0-2	0-0	0-0	1	0	1	0	0	0
Jason Grunkemeyer	6	0-2	0-2	0-0	2	0	0	0	0	0
Refiloe Lethunya	5	0-0	0-0	0-0	1	1	0	0	0	0
Rich Allendorf	1	0-0	0-0	0-0	0	0	0	0	0	0
Ben Helmers	1	0-0	0-0	0-0	0	0	0	0	0	0
Jay Locklier	1	0-0	0-0	0-0	0	0	0	0	0	0
TOTALS	**200**	**14-44**	**7-20**	**8-11**	**20**	**6**	**6**	**1**	**13**	**43**
Percentages		31.8	35.0	72.7						

Coach: Charlie Coles

Officials: Mike Sanzere, Charles Range, Dick Paparo
Technicals: None
Attendance: 42,440

72-64 (Sweet 16)

	1H	2H
Ohio State	31	41
Auburn	26	38

OHIO STATE	MIN	FG	3FG	FT	REB	A	ST	BL	PF	TP
James Penn	36	9-16	4-7	4-4	3	4	3	1	4	26
Michael Redd	36	9-19	1-3	3-4	10	2	1	0	2	22
Brian Brown	33	2-9	1-4	4-6	6	4	1	1	0	9
Jason Singleton	21	3-4	0-0	1-3	2	1	1	0	4	7
Ken Johnson	25	2-4	0-0	0-2	2	0	0	1	4	4
George Reese	27	1-4	0-0	0-3	3	0	1	0	0	2
Boban Savovic	12	1-3	0-2	0-0	0	0	0	0	1	2
Jon Sanderson	6	0-2	0-0	0-1	2	0	0	0	1	0
Neshaun Coleman	4	0-1	0-1	0-0	3	0	0	0	0	0
TOTALS	**200**	**27-62**	**6-17**	**12-23**	**31**	**11**	**7**	**3**	**16**	**72**
Percentages		43.5	35.3	52.2						

Coach: Jim O'Brien

AUBURN	MIN	FG	3FG	FT	REB	A	ST	BL	PF	TP
Chris Porter	32	6-10	2-3	1-2	11	2	0	0	5	15
Doc Robinson	33	5-13	2-3	2-3	0	6	0	0	3	14
Daymeon Fishback	23	4-10	3-6	1-2	9	1	0	0	1	12
Bryant Smith	33	4-9	0-3	2-2	2	1	2	0	1	10
Scott Pohlman	24	2-8	1-5	2-2	2	3	0	0	2	7
Mamadou N'diaye	34	1-3	0-0	1-2	11	1	1	3	3	3
Mack McGadney	6	1-3	0-0	0-0	1	0	1	0	1	2
Jay Heard	9	0-3	0-2	1-2	1	0	1	0	1	1
Reggie Sharp	3	0-0	0-0	0-0	0	0	0	0	0	0
Adrian Chilliest	2	0-0	0-0	0-0	0	0	0	0	0	0
Abe Smith	1	0-0	0-0	0-0	0	0	0	0	0	0
TOTALS	**200**	**23-59**	**8-22**	**10-15**	**37**	**14**	**5**	**3**	**17**	**64**
Percentages		39.0	36.4	66.7						

Coach: Cliff Ellis

Officials: Tim Higgins, Lonnie Dixon, Dick Cartmell
Technicals: None
Attendance: 23,898

76-62 (Sweet 16)

	1H	2H
St. John's	38	38
Maryland	19	43

ST. JOHN'S	MIN	FG	3FG	FT	REB	A	ST	BL	PF	TP
Erick Barkley	37	5-11	3-5	11-14	3	9	2	0	4	24
Bootsy Thornton	34	7-13	0-3	3-4	6	1	0	0	4	17
Tyrone Grant	36	4-9	0-0	1-4	6	0	3	2	4	9
Ron Artest	39	2-5	1-2	3-5	7	4	3	6	1	8
Lavor Postell	36	2-11	0-2	4-5	6	1	1	0	2	8
Reggie Jessie	11	1-3	0-0	2-2	2	0	0	0	1	4
Donald Emanuel	3	1-1	0-0	0-0	0	0	1	0	0	2
Chudney Gray	3	0-0	0-0	2-2	1	1	0	0	0	2
Collin Charles	1	0-0	0-0	2-2	0	0	0	0	0	2
TOTALS	**200**	**22-53**	**4-12**	**28-38**	**31**	**16**	**10**	**8**	**16**	**76**
Percentages		41.5	33.3	73.7						

Coach: Mike Jarvis

MARYLAND	MIN	FG	3FG	FT	REB	A	ST	BL	PF	TP
Steve Francis	33	5-13	1-5	2-2	6	2	2	0	4	13
Terence Morris	37	3-10	1-3	2-2	4	1	3	3	5	9
Laron Profit	28	2-7	0-1	5-6	8	1	0	0	3	9
Terrell Stokes	30	1-5	1-4	3-4	1	7	0	0	3	6
Danny Miller	19	2-3	1-1	1-1	0	1	1	1	4	6
Lonny Baxter	13	2-7	0-0	2-2	8	1	0	0	4	6
Brian Watkins	11	3-3	0-0	0-0	3	0	1	0	3	6
Juan Dixon	17	2-7	1-5	0-0	3	1	1	0	0	5
Mike Mardesich	10	1-3	0-0	0-0	1	0	0	0	1	2
LaRon Cephas	1	0-1	0-0	0-0	1	0	0	0	0	0
Norman Fields	1	0-1	0-1	0-0	0	0	0	0	0	0
TOTALS	**200**	**21-60**	**5-20**	**15-17**	**35**	**14**	**8**	**4**	**27**	**62**
Percentages		35.0	25.0	88.2						

Coach: Gary Williams

Officials: Curtis Shaw, David Hall, Kerry Sitton
Technicals: None
Attendance: 23,898

ANNUAL REVIEW

Connecticut 78-68 Iowa (Sweet 16)

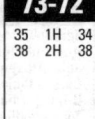

	1H	2H
Connecticut	40	38
Iowa	35	33

CONNECTICUT	MIN	FG	3FG	FT	REB	A	ST	BL	PF	TP
Richard Hamilton	38	8-17	1-4	7-8	3	4	0	1	2	24
Khalid El-Amin	26	6-10	1-2	8-10	3	5	2	0	4	21
Albert Mouring	15	4-6	3-4	0-0	3	4	0	0	1	11
Kevin Freeman	32	4-6	0-0	2-2	6	0	2	0	1	10
Ricky Moore	34	2-5	1-3	1-2	5	5	0	0	0	6
Jake Voskuhl	23	1-2	0-0	2-2	4	0	0	0	4	4
Edmund Saunders	18	1-2	0-0	0-0	2	0	0	0	3	2
E.J. Harrison	6	0-0	0-0	0-0	0	0	0	0	0	0
Sowleymane Wane	6	0-0	0-0	0-0	0	0	1	1	1	0
Rashamel Jones	2	0-0	0-0	0-0	0	0	0	0	0	0
TOTALS	200	26-48	6-13	20-24	26	18	5	2	16	78
Percentages		54.2	46.2	83.3						

Coach: Jim Calhoun

IOWA	MIN	FG	3FG	FT	REB	A	ST	BL	PF	TP
J.R. Koch	23	5-7	2-3	2-2	3	1	0	-	4	14
Jess Settles	24	3-11	1-5	4-4	6	2	0	-	4	11
Kent McCausland	28	3-7	3-7	0-0	0	1	2	-	1	9
Guy Rucker	14	4-6	0-0	0-0	6	0	0	-	1	8
Joey Range	18	3-4	0-0	1-2	0	1	2	-	2	7
Jacob Jaacks	16	2-5	0-1	3-5	5	1	0	-	2	7
Dean Oliver	31	2-10	1-4	0-3	2	2	0	-	2	5
Ryan Luehrsmann	19	2-7	1-3	0-0	1	1	1	-	4	5
Marcelo Gomes	1	1-1	0-0	0-0	1	0	0	-	0	2
Jason Bauer	21	0-0	0-0	0-0	6	2	0	-	1	0
Josiah Bilskemper	1	0-1	0-0	0-0	0	0	1	-	0	0
Duez Henderson	1	0-0	0-0	0-0	0	0	0	-	0	0
Morris Peterson	1	0-0	0-0	0-0	0	0	0	-	0	0
Jason Price	1	0-1	0-0	0-0	0	0	0	-	0	0
Jason Smith	1	0-1	0-0	0-0	1	0	0	-	0	0
TOTALS	200	25-61	8-23	10-16	31	11	6	-	21	68
Percentages		41.0	34.8	62.5						

Coach: Tom Davis

Officials: Jo Silvester, Fra Bosone, Jac Sweeney **Technicals:** None **Attendance:** 17,975

Gonzaga 73-72 Florida (Sweet 16)

	1H	2H
Gonzaga	35	38
Florida	34	38

GONZAGA	MIN	FG	3FG	FT	REB	A	ST	BL	PF	TP
Richie Frahm	30	6-10	5-8	0-0	5	4	1	0	3	17
Casey Calvary	25	5-6	0-0	2-2	5	0	0	0	3	12
Matt Santangelo	35	3-13	2-6	3-4	2	7	2	0	2	11
Axel Dench	16	2-5	1-1	3-4	2	1	0	1	4	8
Quentin Hall	33	2-5	1-3	2-6	1	4	5	0	1	7
Jeremy Eaton	22	2-6	0-0	1-2	4	1	1	1	4	5
Mike Leasure	10	2-3	1-1	0-0	1	0	0	0	0	5
Ryan Floyd	12	1-2	1-2	0-0	2	1	0	0	0	3
Mike Nilson	11	1-2	1-1	0-0	2	0	1	0	3	3
Mark Spink	6	1-3	0-0	0-0	3	0	0	0	1	2
TOTALS	200	25-55	12-22	11-18	27	18	10	2	21	73
Percentages		45.5	54.5	61.1						

Coach: Dan Monson

FLORIDA	MIN	FG	3FG	FT	REB	A	ST	BL	PF	TP
Greg Stolt	33	6-10	4-7	0-0	1	1	1	2	2	16
Brent Wright	26	4-10	0-0	7-7	7	1	1	0	4	15
Mike Miller	29	4-7	1-3	1-2	11	3	1	0	0	10
Kenyan Weaks	25	3-8	0-3	3-3	3	1	3	0	2	9
Teddy Dupay	21	3-11	0-6	1-4	1	1	3	0	2	7
Eddie Shannon	27	3-5	0-2	0-0	0	7	2	0	4	6
Udonis Haslem	15	2-4	0-0	2-4	5	0	0	0	5	6
Major Parker	17	1-2	1-2	0-0	4	1	2	1	1	3
Ladarius Halton	7	0-3	0-1	0-0	1	0	0	0	0	0
TOTALS	200	26-60	6-24	14-20	33	15	13	3	20	72
Percentages		43.3	25.0	70.0						

Coach: Billy Donovan

Officials: Tom Rucker, Rick Hartzell, Ed Hightower **Technicals:** None **Attendance:** 17,975

Duke 85-64 Temple (Elite 8)

	1H	2H
Duke	43	42
Temple	31	33

DUKE	MIN	FG	3FG	FT	REB	A	ST	BL	PF	TP
Trajan Langdon	32	6-7	5-6	6-8	1	2	0	0	2	23
Elton Brand	37	8-10	0-0	5-6	8	0	1	1	3	21
William Avery	36	4-12	3-7	2-2	4	4	0	0	2	13
Chris Carrawell	34	3-6	0-0	6-9	7	7	0	2	1	12
Corey Maggette	14	3-5	0-2	2-2	4	2	1	0	1	8
Shane Battier	32	2-3	2-2	0-0	4	2	2	1	1	6
Chris Burgess	9	1-2	0-0	0-1	1	0	0	1	2	2
Nate James	4	0-0	0-0	0-0	0	2	0	0	1	0
Taymon Domzalski	1	0-0	0-0	0-0	0	0	0	0	0	0
J.D. Simpson	1	0-0	0-0	0-0	0	0	0	0	0	0
TOTALS	200	27-45	10-17	21-28	29	19	4	5	13	85
Percentages		60.0	58.8	75.0						

Coach: Mike Krzyzewski

TEMPLE	MIN	FG	3FG	FT	REB	A	ST	BL	PF	TP
Lamont Barnes	39	7-12	0-0	5-6	6	2	1	2	1	19
Mark Karcher	38	7-25	3-15	2-3	4	3	2	0	4	19
Rasheed Brokenborough	35	4-7	2-2	2-2	1	0	1	0	2	12
Pepe Sanchez	39	5-10	0-5	0-0	5	4	1	0	2	10
Kevin Lyde	18	1-5	0-0	0-0	3	0	2	0	3	2
Ron Rollerson	3	1-1	0-0	0-0	2	0	0	0	0	2
Quincy Wadley	18	0-4	0-3	0-0	1	1	0	0	2	0
Keaton Sanders	8	0-1	0-1	0-0	1	0	1	0	4	0
Mamadou Cello Barry	1	0-1	0-0	0-0	1	0	0	0	0	0
Damien Reid	1	0-1	0-1	0-0	0	0	0	1	0	0
TOTALS	200	25-67	5-27	9-11	24	10	8	2	19	64
Percentages		37.3	18.5	81.8						

Coach: John Chaney

Officials: Gerard Boudreaux, Ted Valentine, Scott Thornley **Technicals:** Temple (coach Chaney) **Attendance:** 19,557

Michigan State 73-66 Kentucky (Elite 8)

	1H	2H
Michigan State	35	38
Kentucky	36	30

MICHIGAN STATE	MIN	FG	3FG	FT	REB	A	ST	BL	PF	TP
Morris Peterson	33	6-13	0-2	7-8	10	1	0	0	3	19
Andre Hutson	29	6-10	0-0	2-4	5	1	0	0	3	14
A.J. Granger	18	4-5	3-3	3-3	2	0	0	0	2	14
Mateen Cleaves	37	4-11	2-5	0-0	4	11	0	0	0	10
Charlie Bell	27	3-5	1-2	0-0	3	2	2	0	3	7
Antonio Smith	33	1-2	0-0	2-2	7	0	2	0	2	4
Jason Klein	18	1-6	1-5	0-0	1	0	0	0	3	3
Thomas Kelley	2	1-1	0-0	0-0	0	0	0	0	0	2
Doug Davis	3	0-0	0-0	0-0	0	2	0	0	0	0
TOTALS	200	26-53	7-17	14-17	32	17	4	0	16	73
Percentages		49.1	41.2	82.4						

Coach: Tom Izzo

KENTUCKY	MIN	FG	3FG	FT	REB	A	ST	BL	PF	TP
Tayshaun Prince	24	3-3	2-2	4-4	2	1	0	1	2	12
Heshimu Evans	20	5-10	2-2	0-0	6	1	0	0	4	12
Scott Padgett	30	3-8	2-6	3-5	3	2	0	2	4	11
Jamaal Magloire	26	3-5	0-0	3-4	1	0	1	3	3	9
Desmond Allison	23	3-8	0-2	1-1	2	2	1	1	1	7
Wayne Turner	35	2-8	0-3	1-2	2	8	1	0	1	5
Michael Bradley	12	2-4	0-0	0-0	4	0	1	0	0	4
Jules Camara	11	2-4	0-0	0-0	0	0	0	0	0	4
Ryan Hogan	6	1-2	0-0	0-0	3	1	0	0	0	2
Saul Smith	13	0-1	0-1	0-0	1	0	1	0	1	0
TOTALS	200	24-53	6-16	12-16	24	15	5	7	16	66
Percentages		45.3	37.5	75.0						

Coach: Tubby Smith

Officials: James Burr, Bob Donato, Reggie Greenwood **Technicals:** None **Attendance:** 42,519

Ohio State 77-74 St. John's (Elite 8)

	1H	2H
Ohio State	41	36
St. John's	33	41

OHIO STATE	MIN	FG	3FG	FT	REB	A	ST	BL	PF	TP
James Penn	38	7-13	3-6	5-6	8	8	2	0	2	22
Michael Redd	38	8-17	3-4	1-3	6	5	0	1	0	20
Jason Singleton	21	6-7	0-0	1-1	2	2	1	0	4	13
Ken Johnson	37	6-9	0-0	0-0	4	0	0	7	3	12
Boban Savovic	15	1-2	1-2	4-5	3	3	0	0	1	7
George Reese	19	1-3	0-0	1-2	2	1	2	1	3	3
Brian Brown	28	0-1	0-1	0-1	1	2	0	0	4	0
Neshaun Coleman	2	0-1	0-1	0-0	0	0	0	0	0	0
Jon Sanderson	2	0-0	0-0	0-0	0	0	0	0	1	0
TOTALS	200	29-53	7-14	12-18	26	21	5	9	18	77
Percentages		54.7	50.0	66.7						

Coach: Jim O'Brien

ST. JOHN'S	MIN	FG	3FG	FT	REB	A	ST	BL	PF	TP
Lavor Postell	38	8-19	4-7	4-6	9	2	0	0	2	24
Bootsy Thornton	37	7-12	1-3	3-4	3	1	0	0	1	18
Erick Barkley	37	4-15	1-3	4-7	7	7	0	0	4	13
Ron Artest	31	4-10	1-5	0-0	9	2	0	0	4	9
Tyrone Grant	19	1-5	0-0	1-2	7	1	0	0	3	3
Chudney Gray	7	1-1	0-0	1-2	0	0	0	0	4	3
Reggie Jessie	24	1-4	0-0	0-0	5	1	0	0	2	2
Donald Emanuel	6	0-0	0-0	2-2	1	0	0	0	1	2
Albert Richardson	1	0-0	0-0	0-0	0	0	0	0	0	0
TOTALS	200	26-66	7-18	15-23	41	14	0	0	21	74
Percentages		39.4	38.9	65.2						

Coach: Mike Jarvis

Officials: Dave Libbey, Gene Monje, Mark Whitehead **Technicals:** None **Attendance:** 24,248

Connecticut 67-62 Gonzaga (Elite 8)

	1H	2H
Connecticut	31	36
Gonzaga	32	30

CONNECTICUT	MIN	FG	3FG	FT	REB	A	ST	BL	PF	TP
Richard Hamilton	37	9-16	0-2	3-6	4	2	0	0	2	21
Kevin Freeman	37	4-14	0-0	5-7	15	0	2	1	3	13
Ricky Moore	38	3-6	0-0	6-6	3	3	1	0	2	12
Edmund Saunders	23	4-8	0-0	0-2	7	0	0	0	3	8
Jake Voskuhl	19	3-5	0-0	0-0	9	1	0	1	4	6
Khalid El-Amin	24	0-12	0-6	5-6	4	4	0	0	2	5
Rashamel Jones	7	1-2	0-0	0-0	2	0	0	0	0	2
Albert Mouring	8	0-1	0-1	0-0	1	0	1	0	1	0
E.J. Harrison	7	0-1	0-0	0-0	2	2	1	0	1	0
TOTALS	200	24-65	0-9	19-27	47	12	5	2	18	67
Percentages		36.9	0.0	70.4						

Coach: Jim Calhoun

GONZAGA	MIN	FG	3FG	FT	REB	A	ST	BL	PF	TP
Quentin Hall	33	6-12	2-5	4-6	8	1	1	0	5	18
Jeremy Eaton	25	4-8	0-0	3-4	4	1	2	3	3	11
Casey Calvary	33	4-7	1-1	0-1	8	1	0	2	3	9
Richie Frahm	32	2-11	1-7	2-2	2	2	1	0	0	7
Mike Leasure	8	1-3	1-2	4-4	3	0	0	0	2	7
Ryan Floyd	11	0-2	0-1	4-4	1	2	1	0	2	4
Axel Dench	10	2-3	0-1	0-0	2	0	2	0	2	4
Matt Santangelo	29	1-9	0-4	0-1	0	2	1	0	2	2
Mike Nilson	15	0-1	0-0	0-0	4	1	0	0	3	0
Mark Spink	4	0-1	0-0	0-0	1	0	0	0	1	0
TOTALS	200	20-57	5-21	17-22	33	10	8	5	23	62
Percentages		35.1	23.8	77.3						

Coach: Dan Monson

Officials: Andre Pattillo, Larry Rose, Bobby Hunt **Technicals:** None **Attendance:** 18,053

DUKE	MIN	FG	3FG	FT	REB	A	ST	BL	PF	TP
Elton Brand	29	7-10	0-0	4-5	15	1	0	1	4	18
William Avery	35	6-14	2-4	0-1	5	0	1	0	0	14
Chris Carrawell	30	3-8	1-1	6-12	4	1	0	0	0	13
Corey Maggette	17	3-7	0-1	3-6	4	0	0	0	0	9
Trajan Langdon	37	3-9	1-4	0-1	6	3	0	0	2	7
Shane Battier	33	2-5	0-3	1-2	6	1	1	2	3	5
Nate James	7	1-2	0-0	0-0	0	0	1	0	0	2
Chris Burgess	12	0-1	0-0	0-0	4	1	0	2	2	0
TOTALS	**200**	**25-56**	**4-13**	**14-27**	**44**	**7**	**3**	**5**	**11**	**68**
Percentages		44.6	30.8	51.9						
Coach: Mike Krzyzewski										

68-62

32	1H	20
36	2H	42

FINAL 4

MICHIGAN STATE	MIN	FG	3FG	FT	REB	A	ST	BL	PF	TP
Morris Peterson	30	6-17	0-2	3-4	8	1	2	0	5	15
Andre Hutson	24	6-8	0-0	1-1	5	1	0	0	2	13
Mateen Cleaves	36	5-16	2-9	0-2	3	10	1	0	3	12
Antonio Smith	34	3-7	0-0	0-0	10	0	0	0	5	6
A.J. Granger	20	2-6	1-3	0-0	4	0	0	0	2	5
Jason Klein	14	2-6	1-3	0-0	2	0	1	0	2	5
Thomas Kelley	14	2-8	0-1	0-0	4	0	1	0	2	4
Charlie Bell	23	0-2	0-0	2-4	3	1	0	0	3	2
Doug Davis	5	0-0	0-0	0-0	0	0	0	0	0	0
TOTALS	**200**	**26-70**	**4-18**	**6-11**	**39**	**13**	**5**	**0**	**24**	**62**
Percentages		37.1	22.2	54.5						
Coach: Tom Izzo										

Officials: Dave Libbey, Curtis Shaw, John Cahill
Technicals: None
Attendance: 41,340

CONNECTICUT	MIN	FG	3FG	FT	REB	A	ST	BL	PF	TP
Richard Hamilton	33	10-17	1-3	3-5	5	1	0	1	3	24
Khalid El-Amin	34	8-15	0-1	2-2	1	6	3	0	1	18
Ricky Moore	37	1-7	0-2	4-4	8	1	1	0	2	6
Kevin Freeman	29	2-4	0-0	1-1	7	0	0	0	3	5
Edmund Saunders	23	2-3	0-0	1-3	5	0	0	1	3	5
Rashamel Jones	8	2-3	0-0	0-0	0	0	1	0	1	4
Jake Voskuhl	19	1-2	0-0	0-0	5	1	1	1	5	2
Sowleymane Wane	8	0-2	0-0	0-0	4	0	0	0	2	0
Albert Mouring	5	0-2	0-0	0-0	0	0	0	0	0	0
E.J. Harrison	4	0-0	0-0	0-0	0	0	0	0	1	0
TOTALS	**200**	**26-55**	**1-6**	**11-15**	**35**	**9**	**6**	**3**	**21**	**64**
Percentages		47.3	16.7	73.3						
Coach: Jim Calhoun										

64-58

36	1H	35
28	2H	23

FINAL 4

OHIO STATE	MIN	FG	3FG	FT	REB	A	ST	BL	PF	TP
Michael Redd	37	7-18	0-2	1-2	8	3	2	0	2	15
Scoonie Penn	40	3-13	2-7	3-5	5	4	2	0	3	11
Jason Singleton	36	4-8	0-0	1-3	6	4	0	2	3	9
Boban Savovic	20	2-4	1-3	2-2	3	1	0	1	3	7
Ken Johnson	30	3-8	0-0	0-0	5	0	0	3	1	6
Brian Brown	21	2-8	0-2	1-2	2	2	1	0	1	5
George Reese	14	2-4	0-0	1-4	3	0	0	0	2	5
Neshaun Coleman	2	0-0	0-0	0-0	0	0	0	0	1	0
TOTALS	**200**	**23-63**	**3-14**	**9-18**	**32**	**14**	**5**	**6**	**16**	**58**
Percentages		36.5	21.4	50.0						
Coach: Jim O'Brien										

Officials: James Burr, Larry Rose, Mark Whitehead
Technicals: None
Attendance: 41,340

CONNECTICUT	MIN	FG	3FG	FT	REB	A	ST	BL	PF	TP
Richard Hamilton	38	10-22	2-4	5-6	7	3	2	0	1	27
Ricky Moore	37	6-10	1-1	0-1	8	2	1	0	4	13
Khalid El-Amin	22	5-12	0-2	2-4	4	4	0	0	3	12
Kevin Freeman	32	3-6	0-0	0-0	8	0	0	3	1	6
Albert Mouring	17	3-4	0-1	0-1	3	0	0	1	1	6
Edmund Saunders	11	1-3	0-0	2-4	3	0	0	0	3	4
Sowleymane Wane	8	2-2	0-0	0-0	0	0	1	0	4	4
Rashamel Jones	6	1-1	0-0	1-2	2	0	0	0	0	3
Jake Voskuhl	28	1-1	0-0	0-0	3	2	0	2	3	2
Antric Klaiber	1	0-0	0-0	0-0	0	0	0	0	0	0
TOTALS	**200**	**32-61**	**3-8**	**10-18**	**38**	**11**	**4**	**6**	**20**	**77**
Percentages		52.5	37.5	55.6						
Coach: Jim Calhoun										

77-74

37	1H	39
40	2H	35

NCAA FINAL 1999

DUKE	MIN	FG	3FG	FT	REB	A	ST	BL	PF	TP
Trajan Langdon	38	7-15	5-10	6-7	1	1	3	0	2	25
Elton Brand	38	5-8	0-0	5-8	13	0	2	2	3	15
William Avery	36	3-12	1-3	4-4	4	5	0	0	4	11
Chris Carrawell	31	3-7	0-2	3-4	4	2	1	2	4	9
Corey Maggette	8	3-7	0-1	2-2	0	0	0	0	2	8
Shane Battier	33	2-7	1-3	1-2	4	2	0	0	3	6
Chris Burgess	7	0-0	0-0	0-0	0	0	0	0	1	0
Nate James	6	0-0	0-0	0-0	1	0	0	0	0	0
TOTALS	**197**	**23-56**	**7-19**	**21-27**	**27**	**10**	**6**	**4**	**19**	**74**
Percentages		41.1	36.8	77.8						
Coach: Mike Krzyzewski										

Officials: Tim Higgins, Gerald Boudreaux, Scott Thornley
Technicals: None
Attendance: 41,340

National Invitation Tournament (NIT)

First round: Butler d. Bradley 51-50, California d. Fresno State 79-71, Clemson d. Georgia 77-57, Colorado d. Pepperdine 65-61, Colorado State d. Mississippi State 69-56, DePaul d. Northwestern 69-64, TCU d. Kansas State 72-71, Nebraska d. UNLV 68-53, NC State d. Providence 92-86, Old Dominion d. Seton Hall 75-56, Oregon d. Georgia Tech 67-64, Princeton d. Georgetown 54-47, Rutgers d. Hofstra 58-45, Xavier d. Toledo 86-84, Wake Forest d. Alabama 73-57, Wyoming d. Southern California 81-77
Second round: Butler d. Old Dominion 75-62, Xavier d. Wake Forest 87-76, Princeton d. NC State 61-58, Oregon d. Wyoming 93-72, TCU d. Nebraska 101-89, Clemson d. Rutgers 78-68, California d. DePaul 58-57, Colorado State d. Colorado 86-76
Third round: Clemson d. Butler 89-69, Oregon d. TCU 77-68, California d. Colorado State 71-62, Xavier d. Princeton 65-58
Semifinals: California d. Oregon 85-69, Clemson d. Xavier 79-76
Championship: California d. Clemson 61-60
Third place: Xavier d. Oregon 106-75
MVP: Sean Lampley, California

1999-2000: Flint Lock

It wasn't so much the Final Four as it was the Go Figure Eight. Michigan State was the lone No. 1 seed to survive until the final weekend at the RCA Dome in Indianapolis, where the Spartans were joined by No. 5-seed Florida and two No. 8's: Wisconsin and North Carolina. In the end, though, Michigan State was the one that prevailed, as coach Tom Izzo won his first national championship and the school's second in an 89-76 victory over Florida. The Spartans were led by a trio of players known as the Flintstones—Mateen Cleaves, Morris Peterson and Charlie Bell, all of whom hailed from Flint, Mich. Cleaves, who was named the the Tournament MOP, rolled his right ankle at the start of the second half, but returned to finish with 18 points.

Cincinnati forward Kenyon Martin—the Naismith Player of the Year and No. 1 pick in the NBA draft (New Jersey Nets)—broke his right leg during the Conference USA tournament. Bob Huggins' Bearcats wound up losing to Tulsa in the second round of the NCAA Tournament.

CBS signed a stunning $6 billion contract with the NCAA for the right to televise the Tournament from 2003 (when the previous contract expired) through 2014.

Major Conference Standings

AMERICA EAST	Conference			Overall		
	W	L	PCT	W	L	PCT
Hofstra⊕	16	2	.889	24	7	.774
Maine	15	3	.833	24	7	.774
Delaware□	14	4	.778	24	8	.750
Vermont	11	7	.611	16	12	.571
Drexel	9	9	.500	13	17	.433
Towson	7	11	.389	11	17	.393
Hartford	6	12	.333	10	19	.345
Northeastern	5	13	.278	7	21	.250
Boston U.	5	13	.278	7	22	.241
New Hampshire	2	16	.111	3	25	.107

Tournament: **Hofstra d. Delaware 76-69**
Tournament MVP: **Craig "Speedy" Claxton**, Hofstra

ACC	Conference			Overall		
	W	L	PCT	W	L	PCT
Duke⊕	15	1	.938	29	5	.853
Maryland○	11	5	.688	25	10	.714
Virginia□	9	7	.563	19	12	.613
North Carolina○	9	7	.563	22	14	.611
Wake Forest□	7	9	.438	22	14	.611
Florida State	6	10	.375	12	17	.414
NC State□	5	11	.313	20	14	.588
Georgia Tech	5	11	.313	13	17	.433
Clemson	4	12	.250	10	20	.333

Tournament: **Duke d. Maryland 81-68**
Tournament MVP: **Jason Williams**, Duke

ATLANTIC 10	Conference			Overall		
	W	L	PCT	W	L	PCT
East Division						
Temple⊕	14	2	.875	27	6	.818
St. Bonaventure○	11	5	.688	21	10	.677
Massachusetts□	9	7	.563	17	16	.515
Fordham	7	9	.438	14	15	.483
Saint Joseph's	7	9	.438	13	16	.448
Rhode Island	2	14	.125	5	25	.167
West Division						
Dayton○	11	5	.688	22	9	.710
Xavier□	9	7	.563	21	12	.636
George Washington	9	7	.563	15	15	.500
Virginia Tech	8	8	.500	16	15	.516
La Salle	5	11	.313	11	17	.393
Duquesne	4	12	.250	9	20	.310

Tournament: **Temple d. St. Bonaventure 65-44**
Tournament MOP: **Quincy Wadley**, Temple

BIG EAST	Conference			Overall		
	W	L	PCT	W	L	PCT
Syracuse○	13	3	.813	26	6	.813
Miami (FL)○	13	3	.813	23	11	.676
St. John's⊕	12	4	.750	25	8	.758
Connecticut○	10	6	.625	25	10	.714
Seton Hall○	10	6	.625	22	10	.688
Villanova□	8	8	.500	20	13	.606
Notre Dame□	8	8	.500	22	15	.595
Georgetown□	6	10	.375	19	15	.559
West Virginia	6	10	.375	14	14	.500
Rutgers□	6	10	.375	15	16	.484
Pittsburgh	5	11	.313	13	15	.464
Providence	4	12	.250	11	19	.367
Boston College	3	13	.188	11	19	.367

Tournament: **St. John's d. Connecticut 80-70**
Tournament MVP: **Bootsy Thornton**, St. John's

BIG SKY	Conference			Overall		
	W	L	PCT	W	L	PCT
Montana	12	4	.750	17	11	.607
Eastern Washington	12	4	.750	15	12	.556
Northern Arizona⊕	11	5	.688	20	11	.645
Cal State Northridge	10	6	.625	20	10	.667
Weber State	10	6	.625	18	10	.643
Portland State	7	9	.438	15	14	.517
Montana State	4	12	.250	12	17	.414
Sacramento State	3	13	.188	9	18	.333
Idaho State	3	13	.188	8	19	.296

Tournament: **N. Arizona d. Cal St. Northridge 85-81 (OT)**
Tournament MVP: **Ross Land**, Northern Arizona

BIG SOUTH	Conference			Overall		
	W	L	PCT	W	L	PCT
Radford	12	2	.857	18	10	.643
Winthrop⊕	11	3	.786	21	9	.700
Elon	7	7	.500	13	15	.464
UNC Asheville	7	7	.500	11	19	.367
Coastal Carolina	7	7	.500	10	18	.357
High Point	5	9	.357	11	17	.393
Liberty	4	10	.286	14	14	.500
Charleston So.	3	11	.214	8	21	.276

Tournament: **Winthrop d. UNC Asheville 75-62**
Tournament MVP: **Greg Lewis**, Winthrop

BIG TEN	Conference			Overall		
	W	L	PCT	W	L	PCT
Michigan State⊕	13	3	.813	32	7	.821
Ohio State○⊗	13	3	.813	23	7	.767
Purdue○	12	4	.750	24	10	.706
Illinois○	11	5	.688	22	10	.688
Indiana○	10	6	.625	20	9	.690
Wisconsin○	8	8	.500	22	14	.611
Michigan□	6	10	.375	15	14	.517
Iowa	6	10	.375	14	16	.467
Penn State□	5	11	.313	19	16	.543
Minnesota	4	12	.250	12	16	.429
Northwestern	0	16	.000	5	25	.167

Tournament: **Michigan State d. Illinois 76-61**
Tournament MOP: **Morris Peterson**, Michigan State

BIG 12	Conference			Overall		
	W	L	PCT	W	L	PCT
Iowa State⊕	14	2	.875	32	5	.865
Texas○	13	3	.813	24	9	.727
Oklahoma○	12	4	.750	27	7	.794
Oklahoma State○	12	4	.750	27	7	.794
Kansas○	11	5	.688	24	10	.706
Missouri○	10	6	.625	18	13	.581
Colorado□	7	9	.438	18	14	.563
Baylor	4	12	.250	14	15	.483
Nebraska	4	12	.250	11	19	.367
Texas A&M	4	12	.250	8	20	.286
Texas Tech	3	13	.188	12	16	.429
Kansas State	2	14	.125	9	19	.321

Tournament: **Iowa State d. Oklahoma 70-58**
Tournament MOP: **Marcus Fizer**, Iowa State

BIG WEST	Conference			Overall		
	W	L	PCT	W	L	PCT
Eastern Division						
Utah State⊕	16	0	1.000	28	6	.824
New Mexico State□	11	5	.688	22	10	.688
Boise State	6	10	.375	12	15	.444
Idaho	6	10	.375	12	17	.414
Nevada	6	10	.375	9	20	.310
North Texas	5	11	.313	7	20	.259
Western Division						
Long Beach State□	15	1	.938	24	6	.800
UC Santa Barbara	10	6	.625	14	14	.500
UC Irvine	7	9	.438	14	14	.500
Pacific	6	10	.375	11	18	.379
Cal Poly	5	11	.313	10	18	.357
Cal State Fullerton	3	13	.188	8	19	.296

Tournament: **Utah State d. New Mexico State 71-66**
Tournament MVPs: **Shawn Daniels**, New Mexico State and **Troy Rolle**, Utah State

COLONIAL	Conference			Overall		
	W	L	PCT	W	L	PCT
James Madison	12	4	.750	20	9	.690
George Mason	12	4	.750	19	11	.633
Richmond	11	5	.688	18	12	.600
UNC Wilmington⊕	8	8	.500	18	13	.581
VCU	7	9	.438	14	14	.500
William and Mary	6	10	.375	11	17	.393
Old Dominion	6	10	.375	11	19	.367
American	5	11	.313	11	18	.379
East Carolina	5	11	.313	10	18	.357

Tournament: **UNC Wilmington d. Richmond 57-47**
Tournament MVP: **Brett Blizzard**, UNC Wilmington

C-USA	Conference			Overall		
	W	L	PCT	W	L	PCT
American Division						
Cincinnati○	16	0	1.000	29	4	.879
Louisville○	10	6	.625	19	12	.613
DePaul○	9	7	.563	21	12	.636
Marquette□	8	8	.500	15	14	.517
Saint Louis⊕	7	9	.438	19	14	.576
Charlotte□	7	9	.438	17	16	.515
National Division						
Tulane□	8	8	.500	20	11	.645
South Florida□	8	8	.500	17	14	.548
Southern Miss	7	9	.438	17	12	.586
UAB	7	9	.438	14	14	.500
Memphis	7	9	.438	15	16	.484
Houston	2	14	.125	9	22	.290

Tournament: **Saint Louis d. DePaul 56-49**
Tournament MVP: **Justin Love**, Saint Louis

IVY	Conference			Overall		
	W	L	PCT	W	L	PCT
Penn⊕	14	0	1.000	21	8	.724
Princeton□	11	3	.786	19	11	.633
Columbia	7	7	.500	13	14	.481
Harvard	7	7	.500	12	15	.444
Dartmouth	5	9	.357	9	18	.333
Yale	5	9	.357	7	20	.259
Brown	4	10	.286	8	19	.296
Cornell	3	11	.214	10	17	.370

⊕ Automatic NCAA Tournament bid ○ At-large NCAA Tournament bid □ NIT appearance ⊗ Team record doesn't reflect games forfeited or vacated. For adjusted record, see p. 521.

MAAC

	Conference			Overall		
	W	L	Pct	W	L	Pct
Siena□	15	3	.833	24	9	.727
Iona⊕	13	5	.722	20	11	.645
Fairfield	11	7	.611	14	15	.483
Niagara	10	8	.556	17	12	.586
Marist	10	8	.556	14	14	.500
Manhattan	9	9	.500	12	15	.444
Rider	8	10	.444	16	14	.533
Canisius	8	10	.444	10	20	.333
Loyola (MD)	4	14	.222	7	21	.250
Saint Peter's	2	16	.111	5	23	.179

Tournament: **Iona d. Siena 84-80**
Tournament MVP: **Dyree Wilson**, Iona

MID-AMERICAN

	Conference			Overall		
	W	L	Pct	W	L	Pct
East Division						
Bowling Green□	14	4	.778	22	8	.733
Kent State State□	13	5	.722	23	8	.742
Marshall	11	7	.611	21	9	.700
Akron	11	7	.611	17	11	.607
Ohio	11	7	.611	20	13	.606
Miami (OH)	8	10	.444	15	15	.500
Buffalo	3	15	.167	5	23	.179
West Division						
Ball State⊕	11	7	.611	22	9	.710
Toledo	11	7	.611	18	13	.581
Eastern Michigan	9	9	.500	15	13	.536
Northern Illinois	7	11	.389	13	15	.464
Western Michigan	6	12	.333	10	18	.357
Central Michigan	2	16	.111	6	23	.207

Tournament: **Ball State d. Miami (OH) 61-58**
Tournament MVP: **Duane Clemens**, Ball State

MID-CONTINENT

	Conference			Overall		
	W	L	Pct	W	L	Pct
Oakland	11	5	.688	13	17	.433
Valparaiso⊕	10	6	.625	19	13	.594
Southern Utah	10	6	.625	16	13	.552
UMKC	10	6	.625	16	13	.552
Youngstown State	9	7	.563	12	16	.429
Oral Roberts	8	8	.500	13	17	.433
Chicago State	7	9	.438	10	18	.357
IUPUI	4	12	.250	7	21	.250
Western Illinois	3	13	.188	8	22	.267

Tournament: **Valparaiso d. Southern Utah 71-62**
Tournament MVP: **Lubos Barton**, Valparaiso

MEAC

	Conference			Overall		
	W	L	Pct	W	L	Pct
South Carolina State⊕	14	5	.737	20	14	.588
Hampton	13	5	.722	17	12	.586
Coppin State	13	5	.722	15	15	.500
Bethune-Cookman	12	6	.667	14	15	.483
Norfolk State	11	7	.611	12	16	.429
NC A&T	11	8	.579	14	15	.483
UMES	8	10	.444	12	17	.414
Florida A&M	7	11	.389	9	22	.290
Delaware State	5	13	.278	6	22	.214
Morgan State	5	13	.278	5	24	.172
Howard	1	17	.056	1	27	.036

Tournament: **South Carolina State d. Coppin State 70-53**
Tournament MOP: **Mike Wiatre**, South Carolina State

MCC

	Conference			Overall		
	W	L	Pct	W	L	Pct
Butler⊕	12	2	.857	23	8	.742
Cleveland State	9	5	.643	16	14	.533
Detroit	8	6	.571	20	12	.625
Wisconsin-Milwaukee	6	8	.429	15	14	.517
Wisconsin-Green Bay	6	8	.429	14	16	.467
Wright State	6	8	.429	11	17	.393
Illinois-Chicago	5	9	.357	11	20	.355
Loyola-Chicago	4	10	.286	14	14	.500

Tournament: **Butler d. Detroit 62-43**
Tournament MVP: **Mike Marshall**, Butler

MISSOURI VALLEY

	Conference			Overall		
	W	L	Pct	W	L	Pct
Indiana State○	14	4	.778	22	10	.688
Missouri State□	13	5	.722	23	11	.676
Southern Illinois□	12	6	.667	20	13	.606
Creighton⊕	11	7	.611	23	10	.697
Bradley	10	8	.556	14	16	.467
Evansville	9	9	.500	18	12	.600
Northern Iowa	7	11	.389	14	15	.483
Wichita State	5	13	.278	12	17	.414
Illinois State	5	13	.278	10	20	.333
Drake	4	14	.222	11	18	.379

Tournament: **Creighton d. Missouri State 57-45**
Tournament MOP: **Ryan Sears**, Creighton

MOUNTAIN WEST

	Conference			Overall		
	W	L	Pct	W	L	Pct
UNLV○	10	4	.714	23	8	.742
Utah○	10	4	.714	23	9	.719
New Mexico□	9	5	.643	18	14	.563
Wyoming	8	6	.571	19	12	.613
Colorado State	8	6	.571	18	12	.600
BYU□	7	7	.500	22	11	.667
Air Force	4	10	.286	8	20	.286
San Diego State	0	14	.000	5	23	.179

Tournament: **UNLV d. BYU 79-56**
Tournament MVP: **Mark Dickel**, UNLV

NORTHEAST

	Conference			Overall		
	W	L	Pct	W	L	Pct
Central Conn. State⊕	15	3	.833	25	6	.806
Fairleigh Dickinson	13	5	.722	17	11	.607
Robert Morris	13	5	.722	18	12	.600
Quinnipiac	12	6	.667	18	10	.643
St. Francis (NY)	12	6	.667	18	12	.600
Monmouth	9	9	.500	12	16	.429
UMBC	7	11	.389	11	18	.379
Saint Francis (PA)	7	11	.389	10	18	.357
Mount St. Mary's	7	11	.389	9	20	.310
Wagner	6	12	.333	11	16	.407
Long Island	5	13	.278	8	19	.296
Sacred Heart	2	16	.111	3	25	.107

Tournament: **Central Conn. State d. Robert Morris 63-46**
Tournament MVP: **Rick Mickens**, Central Conn. State

OHIO VALLEY

	Conference			Overall		
	W	L	Pct	W	L	Pct
SE Missouri State⊕	14	4	.778	24	7	.774
Murray State	14	4	.778	23	9	.719
Austin Peay	11	7	.611	18	10	.643
Eastern Illinois	11	7	.611	17	12	.586
Tennessee Tech	11	7	.611	16	12	.571
Middle Tenn. State	10	8	.556	15	13	.536
Tennessee-Martin	7	11	.389	10	19	.345
Tennessee State	6	12	.333	7	22	.241
Morehead State	4	14	.222	9	18	.333
Eastern Kentucky	2	16	.111	6	21	.222

Tournament: **SE Missouri State d. Murray State 67-56**
Tournament MVP: **Roderick Johnson**, SE Missouri State

PAC-10

	Conference			Overall		
	W	L	Pct	W	L	Pct
Arizona⊕	15	3	.833	27	7	.794
Stanford○	15	3	.833	27	4	.871
Oregon○	13	5	.722	22	8	.733
UCLA○	10	8	.556	21	12	.636
Arizona State□	10	8	.556	19	13	.594
Southern California	9	9	.500	16	14	.533
California□	7	11	.389	18	15	.545
Oregon State	5	13	.278	13	16	.448
Washington	5	13	.278	10	20	.333
Washington State	1	17	.056	6	22	.214

PATRIOT LEAGUE

	Conference			Overall		
	W	L	Pct	W	L	Pct
Lafayette⊕	11	1	.917	24	7	.774
Navy	11	1	.917	23	6	.793
Bucknell	8	4	.667	17	11	.607
Colgate	4	8	.333	13	16	.448
Holy Cross	3	9	.250	10	18	.357
Lehigh	3	9	.250	8	21	.276
Army	2	10	.167	5	23	.179

Tournament: **Lafayette d. Navy 87-61**
Tournament MVP: **Stefan Ciosici**, Lafayette

SEC

	Conference			Overall		
	W	L	Pct	W	L	Pct
Eastern						
Tennessee○	12	4	.750	26	7	.788
Florida○	12	4	.750	29	8	.784
Kentucky○	12	4	.750	23	10	.697
Vanderbilt□	8	8	.500	19	11	.633
South Carolina	5	11	.313	15	17	.469
Georgia	3	13	.188	10	20	.333
Western						
LSU○	12	4	.750	28	6	.824
Auburn○	9	7	.563	24	10	.706
Arkansas⊕	7	9	.438	19	15	.559
Alabama	6	10	.375	13	16	.448
Mississippi□	5	11	.313	19	14	.576
Mississippi State	5	11	.313	14	16	.467

Tournament: **Arkansas d. Auburn 75-67**
Tournament MVP: **Brandon Dean**, Arkansas

SOUTHERN

	Conference			Overall		
	W	L	Pct	W	L	Pct
North						
Appalachian State⊕	13	3	.813	23	9	.719
Davidson	10	6	.625	15	13	.536
UNC Greensboro	9	7	.563	15	13	.536
East Tenn. State	8	8	.500	14	15	.483
Western Carolina	7	9	.438	14	14	.500
VMI	1	15	.063	6	23	.207
South						
Charleston	13	3	.813	24	6	.800
Ga. Southern	10	6	.625	16	12	.571
Wofford	8	8	.500	14	16	.467
Chattanooga	6	10	.375	10	19	.345
Furman	5	10	.333	14	18	.438
The Citadel	5	10	.333	10	20	.333

Tournament: **Appalachian State d. Charleston 68-56**
Tournament MOP: **Tyson Patterson**, Appalachian State

SOUTHLAND

	Conference			Overall		
	W	L	Pct	W	L	Pct
Sam Houston State	15	3	.833	22	7	.759
UL-Monroe	13	5	.722	19	9	.679
UTSA	12	6	.667	15	13	.536
Northwestern St. (LA)	11	7	.611	17	13	.567
Texas-Arlington	11	7	.611	15	12	.556
Lamar⊕	8	10	.444	15	16	.484
Texas State	8	10	.444	12	17	.414
Nicholls State	8	10	.444	11	17	.393
Southeastern Louisiana	5	13	.278	10	17	.370
McNeese State	5	13	.278	6	21	.222
Stephen F. Austin	3	15	.167	6	21	.222

Tournament: **Lamar d. Northwestern State (LA) 62-55**
Tournament MVP: **Landon Rowe**, Lamar

SWAC

	Conference			Overall		
	W	L	Pct	W	L	Pct
Alcorn State	15	3	.833	19	10	.655
Alabama A&M	14	4	.778	18	10	.643
Southern U.	14	4	.778	18	11	.621
Jackson State⊕	10	8	.556	17	16	.515
Texas Southern	10	8	.556	15	14	.517
Alabama State	10	8	.556	13	15	.464
Miss. Valley State	6	12	.333	6	21	.222
Prairie View A&M	5	13	.278	7	20	.259
Arkansas-Pine Bluff	5	13	.278	6	21	.222
Grambling	0	18	.000	1	30	.032

Tournament: **Jackson State d. Southern U. 76-61**
Tournament MVP: **Vincent Jones**, Jackson State

SUN BELT

	Conference			Overall		
	W	L	Pct	W	L	Pct
UL-Lafayette⊕	13	3	.813	25	9	.735
South Alabama	13	3	.813	20	10	.667
Louisiana Tech	12	4	.750	21	8	.724
Florida International	9	7	.563	16	14	.533
Western Kentucky	8	8	.500	11	18	.379
Arkansas State	7	9	.438	10	18	.357
New Orleans	6	10	.375	11	18	.379
Denver	3	13	.188	6	22	.214
Arkansas-Little Rock	1	15	.063	4	24	.143

Tournament: **UL-Lafayette d. South Alabama 51-50**
Tournament MOP: **Virgil Stanescu**, South Alabama

TAAC

	Conference			Overall		
	W	L	Pct	W	L	Pct
Troy	13	5	.722	17	11	.607
Georgia State	13	5	.722	17	12	.586
Samford⊕	12	6	.667	21	11	.656
Jacksonville State	12	6	.667	17	11	.607
Central Florida	10	8	.556	14	18	.438
Campbell	10	8	.556	12	16	.429
Stetson	8	10	.444	13	15	.464
Mercer	7	11	.389	12	21	.364
Jacksonville	5	13	.278	8	19	.296
Florida Atlantic	0	18	.000	2	28	.067

Tournament: **Samford d. Central Florida 78-69**
Tournament MVP: **Marc Salyers**, Samford

WEST COAST

	Conference			Overall		
	W	L	Pct	W	L	Pct
Pepperdine○	12	2	.857	25	9	.735
Gonzaga⊕	11	3	.786	26	9	.743
San Diego	10	4	.714	20	9	.690
Santa Clara	9	5	.643	19	12	.613
San Francisco	7	7	.500	19	9	.679
Portland	4	10	.286	10	18	.357
Saint Mary's (CA)	3	11	.214	8	20	.286
Loyola Marymount	0	14	.000	2	26	.071

Tournament: **Gonzaga d. Pepperdine 69-65**
Tournament MVP: **Casey Calvary**, Gonzaga

WAC

	Conference			Overall		
	W	L	Pct	W	L	Pct
Tulsa○	12	2	.857	32	5	.865
Fresno State○⊗	11	3	.786	24	10	.706
SMU□	9	5	.643	21	9	.700
TCU	8	6	.571	18	14	.563
San Jose State	6	8	.429	15	15	.500
Hawaii	5	9	.357	17	12	.586
UTEP	4	10	.286	13	15	.464
Rice	1	13	.071	5	22	.185

Tournament: **Fresno State d. Tulsa 75-72**
Tournament MVP: **Courtney Alexander**, Fresno State

INDEPENDENTS

	Overall		
	W	L	Pct
Texas-Pan American	12	16	.429
Albany (NY)	11	17	.393
Centenary	10	18	.357
Belmont	7	21	.250
Stony Brook	6	23	.207

ANNUAL REVIEW

INDIVIDUAL LEADERS—SEASON

SCORING	CL	POS	G	FG	3FG	FT	PTS	PPG
1 **Courtney Alexander**, Fresno State	SR	G	27	252	58	107	669	**24.8**
2 **SirValiant Brown**, George Washington	FR	G	30	222	73	221	738	**24.6**
3 **Ronnie McCollum**, Centenary	JR	G	28	226	92	123	667	**23.8**
4 **Eddie House**, Arizona State	SR	G	32	263	73	137	736	**23.0**
Harold Arceneaux, Weber State	SR	F	28	213	38	180	644	**23.0**
6 **Rashad Phillips**, Detroit	SR	G	32	226	102	181	735	**23.0**
7 **Demond Stewart**, Niagara	JR	G	29	217	55	176	665	**22.9**
8 **Marcus Fizer**, Iowa State	JR	F	37	327	15	175	844	**22.8**
9 **Craig "Speedy" Claxton**, Hofstra	SR	G	31	253	51	149	706	**22.8**
10 **Troy Murphy**, Notre Dame	SO	F	37	274	30	261	839	**22.7**

FIELD GOAL PCT	CL	POS	G	FG	FGA	PCT
1 **Brendan Haywood**, North Carolina	JR	C	36	191	274	**69.7**
2 **John Whorton**, Kent State	SR	C	31	159	250	**63.6**
3 **Joel Przybilla**, Minnesota	SO	C	21	122	199	**61.3**
4 **Stromile Swift**, LSU	SO	F	34	208	342	**60.8**
5 **Patrick Chambers**, Arkansas-Pine Bluff	SR	F	27	174	287	**60.6**

MINIMUM: 5 MADE PER GAME

THREE-PT FG PER GAME	CL	POS	G	3FG	3PG
1 **Brian Merriweather**, Texas-Pan American	JR	G	28	114	**4.1**
2 **Josh Heard**, Tennessee Tech	SR	G	28	112	**4.0**
3 **Tevis Stukes**, Baylor	SR	G	29	100	**3.4**
4 **Adam Fellers**, Campbell	SO	G	28	96	**3.4**
Gordon Scott, Idaho	SR	G	28	96	**3.4**

THREE-PT FG PCT	CL	POS	G	3FG	3FGA	PCT
1 **Jonathan Whitworth**, Middle Tennessee State	JR	G	28	50	99	**50.5**
2 **Jason Thornton**, Central Florida	SO	F	32	94	190	**49.5**
3 **Aki Palmer**, Colorado State	JR	G	30	70	143	**49.0**
4 **Pete Conway**, Montana State	FR	G	29	44	90	**48.9**
5 **Stephen Brown**, Idaho State	SR	G	27	65	133	**48.9**

MINIMUM: 1.5 MADE PER GAME

FREE THROW PCT	CL	POS	G	FT	FTA	PCT
1 **Clay McKnight**, Pacific	SR	G	24	74	78	**94.9**
2 **Troy Bell**, Boston College	FR	G	27	161	180	**89.4**
3 **Lee Nosse**, Middle Tenn. State	JR	C	28	83	93	**89.2**
4 **Khalid El-Amin**, Connecticut	JR	G	35	107	120	**89.2**
Brad Buddenborg, Oakland	SO	G	28	107	120	**89.2**

MINIMUM: 2.5 MADE PER GAME

ASSISTS PER GAME	CL	POS	G	AST	APG
1 **Mark Dickel**, UNLV	SR	G	31	280	**9.0**
2 **Doug Gottlieb**, Oklahoma State	SR	G	34	293	**8.6**
3 **Chico Fletcher**, Arkansas State	SR	G	28	232	**8.3**
4 **Brandon Granville**, Southern California	SO	G	30	248	**8.3**
5 **Ed Cota**, North Carolina	SR	G	35	284	**8.1**
6 **Pepe Sanchez**, Temple	SR	G	25	201	**8.0**
7 **Casey Rogers**, Western Carolina	SO	G	28	213	**7.6**
8 **Cornelius Jackson**, Marshall	JR	G	30	218	**7.3**
9 **Elliott Prasse-Freeman**, Harvard	FR	G	27	196	**7.3**
10 **Eddie Gill**, Weber State	SR	G	28	195	**7.0**

REBOUNDS PER GAME	CL	POS	G	REB	RPG
1 **Darren Phillip**, Fairfield	SR	F	29	405	**14.0**
2 **Josh Sankes**, Holy Cross	JR	C	28	334	**11.9**
3 **Larry Abney**, Fresno State	SR	F	34	402	**11.8**
4 **Shaun Stonerook**, Ohio	SR	F	33	387	**11.7**
5 **Jarrett Stephens**, Penn State	SR	F	35	368	**10.5**
6 **Darren Fenn**, Canisius	JR	C	30	315	**10.5**
7 **Chris Mihm**, Texas	JR	C	33	346	**10.5**
8 **Darrell Neal**, Norfolk State	JR	F	27	282	**10.4**
9 **Troy Murphy**, Notre Dame	SO	F	37	380	**10.3**
10 **Matt Williams**, Montana	SR	F	28	287	**10.3**

BLOCKED SHOTS PER GAME	CL	POS	G	BLK	BPG
1 **Ken Johnson**, Ohio State	JR	C	30	161	**5.4**
2 **Wojciech Myrda**, UL-Monroe	SO	C	28	144	**5.1**
3 **Loren Woods**, Arizona	JR	C	26	102	**3.9**
4 **Joel Przybilla**, Minnesota	SO	C	21	81	**3.9**
5 **Sitapha Savane**, Navy	SR	C	29	111	**3.8**

STEALS PER GAME	CL	POS	G	STL	SPG
1 **Carl Williams**, Liberty	SR	G/F	28	107	**3.8**
2 **Rick Mickens**, Central Connecticut State	SR	G	26	93	**3.6**
3 **Pepe Sanchez**, Temple	SR	G	25	85	**3.4**
4 **Fred House**, Southern Utah	JR	G/F	29	98	**3.4**
5 **Eric Coley**, Tulsa	SR	F	37	123	**3.3**

INDIVIDUAL LEADERS—GAME

POINTS	CL	POS	OPP	DATE	PTS
1 **Eddie House**, Arizona State	SR	G	California	J8	**61**
2 **David Webber**, Central Michigan	SO	G	Ball State	F24	**51**
3 **Damon Stringer**, Cleveland State	SR	G	Wisconsin-Milwaukee	J29	**47**
4 **Eddie House**, Arizona State	SR	G	San Diego State	D18	**46**
5 **Nate Green**, Indiana State	SR	G	Eastern Illinois	D19	**45**
Detric Golden, Troy	SR	G	Jacksonville	F5	**45**

THREE-PT FG MADE	CL	POS	OPP	DATE	3FG
1 **Spencer Gloger**, Princeton	FR	F	UAB	D18	**10**
Jason Harris, Fordham	JR	G	Quinnipiac	D21	**10**
Marc Polite, Eastern Illinois	SR	F	Arkansas State	D23	**10**
Donta Wade, Providence	JR	G	Notre Dame	F23	**10**
Desmond Ferguson, Detroit	SR	G/F	Wisconsin-Milwaukee	F26	**10**
Jason Stewart, Miami (OH)	SR	F	Marshall	M6	**10**

ASSISTS	CL	POS	OPP	DATE	AST
1 **Mateen Cleaves**, Michigan State	SR	G	Michigan	M4	**20**
2 **Mark Dickel**, UNLV	SR	G	Wyoming	M10	**18**
3 **Ed Cota**, North Carolina	SR	G	UNLV	D4	**17**
4 **Doug Gottlieb**, Oklahoma State	SR	G	North Texas	N27	**16**
Marquis Sykes, Morehead State	FR	G	Tennessee State	F10	**16**
Earl Watson, UCLA	JR	G	Maryland	M18	**16**

REBOUNDS	CL	POS	OPP	DATE	REB
1 **Larry Abney**, Fresno State	SR	F	SMU	F17	**35**
2 **David Bluthenthal**, USC	SO	F	Arizona State	J20	**28**
3 **Darren Phillip**, Fairfield	SR	C	Marist	J5	**25**
4 **Larry Abney**, Fresno State	SR	F	Tulsa	J29	**24**
5 **Darrell Tucker**, San Francisco	FR	F	Fresno State	D8	**23**

BLOCKED SHOTS	CL	POS	OPP	DATE	BLK
1 **Loren Woods**, Arizona	JR	C	Oregon	F3	**14**
2 **Derrick Davenport**, TCU	JR	C	Alaska-Fairbanks	N20	**12**
3 **Wojciech Myrda**, UL-Monroe	SO	C	Nicholls State	D30	**11**
Samuel Dalembert, Seton Hall	FR	C	St. John's	J18	**11**
Ken Johnson, Ohio State	JR	C	St. John's	J22	**11**
Derrick Davenport, TCU	JR	C	Rice	M3	**11**

STEALS	CL	POS	OPP	DATE	STL
1 **Jeff Trepagnier**, Southern California	JR	G	Utah State	N24	**10**
Mike Kelley, Wisconsin	JR	G	Texas	D7	**10**
Collis Temple, LSU	FR	G	Florida	J12	**10**
4 **Eddie Gill**, Weber State	SR	G	Alabama	N19	**9**
Jason Harris, Fordham	JR	G	Holy Cross	N27	**9**
Jimmal Ball, Akron	SR	G	Eastern Michigan	J22	**9**
Pepe Sanchez, Temple	SR	G	Maryland	F13	**9**
Justin Gainey, NC State	SR	G	Virginia	M10	**9**

TEAM LEADERS—SEASON

WIN-LOSS PCT	W	L	PCT
1 **Cincinnati**	29	4	**.879**
2 **Stanford**	27	4	**.871**
3 **Iowa State**	32	5	**.865**
Tulsa	32	5	**.865**
5 **Duke**	29	5	**.853**

SCORING OFFENSE	G	W-L	PTS	PPG
1 **Duke**	34	29-5	2,992	**88.0**
2 **TCU**	32	18-14	2,813	**87.9**
3 **Siena**	33	24-9	2,862	**86.7**
4 **Florida**	37	29-8	3,102	**83.8**
5 **Wyoming**	31	19-12	2,567	**82.8**

SCORING MARGIN	G	W-L	PPG	OPP PPG	MAR
1 **Stanford**	31	27-4	78.9	59.7	**19.3**
2 **Tulsa**	37	32-5	80.4	62.9	**17.5**
3 **Duke**	34	29-5	88.0	71.3	**16.7**
4 **Cincinnati**	33	29-4	77.6	61.5	**16.1**
5 **Michigan State**	39	32-7	74.1	58.9	**15.2**

FIELD GOAL PCT	G	W-L	FG	FGA	PCT
1 **Samford**	32	21-11	825	1,649	**50.0**
2 **Long Beach State**	30	24-6	884	1,784	**49.6**
3 **Austin Peay**	28	18-10	797	1,618	**49.3**
4 **Bowling Green**	30	22-8	777	1,578	**49.2**
5 **North Carolina**	36	22-14	1,014	2,066	**49.1**

THREE-PT FG PER GAME	G	W-L	3FG	3PG
1 **Tennessee Tech**	28	16-12	279	**10.0**
2 **Samford**	32	21-11	313	**9.8**
3 **Belmont**	28	7-21	273	**9.8**
4 **Missouri**	31	18-13	291	**9.4**
5 **Texas-Arlington**	27	15-12	247	**9.1**

REBOUND MARGIN	G	W-L	RPG	OPP RPG	MAR
1 **Michigan State**	39	32-7	39.0	27.3	**11.7**
2 **Stanford**	31	27-4	42.2	32.5	**9.7**
3 **Texas Southern**	29	15-14	39.3	30.7	**8.6**
4 **Kansas**	34	24-10	44.3	36.0	**8.3**
5 **LSU**	34	28-6	40.4	32.4	**8.0**

SCORING DEFENSE	G	W-L	OPP PTS	OPP PPG
1 **Princeton**	30	19-11	1,637	**54.6**
2 **Temple**	33	27-6	1,808	**54.8**
3 **Butler**	31	23-8	1,728	**55.7**
4 **Wisconsin**	36	22-14	2,007	**55.8**
5 **UNC Wilmington**	31	18-13	1,781	**57.5**

FIELD GOAL PCT DEFENSE	G	W-L	OPP FG	OPP FGA	OPP PCT
1 **Stanford**	31	27-4	667	1,893	**35.2**
2 **Temple**	33	27-6	633	1,747	**36.2**
3 **Princeton**	30	19-11	577	1,558	**37.0**
4 **Ohio State**	30	23-7	654	1,730	**37.8**
5 **SE Missouri State**	31	24-7	670	1,765	**38.0**

TEAM LEADERS—GAME

Points

	OPP	DATE	SCORE
1 TCU	Grambling	D30	**143-110**
2 TCU	North Texas	J3	**134-91**
3 Florida	New Hampshire	N29	**131-72**
Tennessee Tech	Toccoa Falls (GA)	J11	**131-57**
5 Marshall	Western Michigan	D20	**127-126**
Long Beach State	Cal State Monterey	D22	**127-57**

Field Goal Pct

	OPP	DATE	FG	FGA	PCT
1 Long Beach State	Cal State Monterey	D22	56	70	**80.0**
2 Wright State	Cleveland State	F10	29	40	**72.5**
3 North Carolina	NC State	J8	27	38	**71.1**
4 Appalachian State	Tennessee Wesleyan	D30	44	62	**71.0**
5 Sam Houston State	Texas-Arlington	M2	41	59	**69.5**

Three-Pt FG Made

	OPP	DATE	3FG
1 Southern California	Oregon State	J29	**20**
2 Belmont	Valparaiso	J10	**19**
3 Siena	Saint Peter's	D4	**18**
Tennessee Tech	Toccoa Falls (GA)	J11	**18**
Cal Poly	Cal State Fullerton	F12	**18**
Detroit	Wisconsin-Milwaukee	F26	**18**

CONSENSUS ALL-AMERICAS

FIRST TEAM

PLAYER	CL	POS	HT	SCHOOL	RPG	PPG
Chris Carrawell	SR	F	6-6	Duke	6.1	16.9
Marcus Fizer	JR	F	6-8	Iowa State	7.7	22.8
A.J. Guyton	SR	G	6-1	Indiana	2.8	19.7
Kenyon Martin	SR	F	6-9	Cincinnati	9.7	18.9
Chris Mihm	JR	C	7-0	Texas	10.5	17.7
Troy Murphy	SO	F	6-10	Notre Dame	10.3	22.7

SECOND TEAM

PLAYER	CL	POS	HT	SCHOOL	RPG	PPG
Courtney Alexander	SR	G	6-6	Fresno State	4.7	24.8
Shane Battier	JR	F	6-8	Duke	5.6	17.4
Mateen Cleaves	SR	G	6-2	Michigan State	1.8	12.1
Scoonie Penn	SR	G	5-10	Ohio State	4.4	15.6
Morris Peterson	SR	G/F	6-6	Michigan State	6.0	16.8
Stromile Swift	SO	F	6-9	LSU	8.2	16.2

Selectors: AP, NABC, Sporting News, USBWA

AWARD WINNERS

PLAYER OF THE YEAR

PLAYER	CL	POS	HT	SCHOOL	AWARDS
Kenyon Martin	SR	F	6-9	Cincinnati	Naismith, AP, USBWA, Wooden, NABC, Rupp
Scoonie Penn	SR	G	5-10	Ohio State	Frances Pomeroy Naismith*

* For the most outstanding senior player who is 6 feet or under

DEFENSIVE PLAYERS OF THE YEAR

PLAYER	CL	POS	HT	SCHOOL
Shane Battier	JR	F	6-8	Duke
Kenyon Martin	SR	F	6-9	Cincinnati

COACH OF THE YEAR

COACH	SCHOOL	REC	AWARDS
Mike Montgomery	Stanford	27-4	Naismith
Larry Eustachy	Iowa State	32-5	AP, USBWA
Gene Keady	Purdue	24-10	NABC
Bob Huggins	Cincinnati	29-4	Sporting News (shared)
Bill Self	Tulsa	32-5	Sporting News (shared)
Mike Krzyzewski	Duke	29-5	CBS/Chevrolet

Bob Gibbons' Top High School Senior Recruits

PLAYER	POS	HT	HIGH SCHOOL	A-A TEAMS	COLLEGE	CAREER NOTES
1 Zach Randolph	F/C	6-8	Marion (IN) HS	McD, P, USA	Michigan State	Left MSU after 1 season; No. 19 pick '01 NBA draft (Blazers); 9 seasons, 16.7 ppg, 8.3 rpg
2 Darius Miles	G/F	6-9	East St. Louis (IL) Senior HS	McD, P, USA	None	Drafted straight out of HS; No. 3 pick, '00 NBA draft (Clippers); '01 All-Rookie team; 10.1 ppg (7 seasons)
3 Eddie Griffin	PF	6-8	Roman Catholic HS, Philadelphia	McD, P, USA	Seton Hall	*Sporting News* FOY, '01; No. 7 pick, '01 NBA draft (Nets); 7.2 ppg (5 seasons); died in car accident
4 Gerald Wallace	F	6-7	Childersburg (AL) HS	McD, P, USA	Alabama	All-SEC freshman team (9.8 ppg, 6.0 rpg), '01; No. 25 pick, '01 NBA draft (Kings); 12.3 ppg (8 seasons)
5 Marcus Taylor	G	6-3	Waverly HS, Lansing, MI	McD, P, USA	Michigan State	Led Big Ten in assists as sophomore; 2nd-round pick, '02 NBA draft (Wolves); played in CBA, overseas
6 Chris Duhon	PG	6-1	Salmen HS, Slidell, LA	McD, P	Duke	Duke's all-time steals leader (300); ACC ROY '01; 2nd-round pick, '04 NBA draft (Bulls); 7.8 ppg (5 seasons)
7 DeShawn Stevenson	G	6-5	Washington Union HS, Fresno, CA	McD, P	None	Drafted straight out of HS; No. 23 pick, '00 NBA draft (Jazz); 8.6 ppg (9 seasons)
8 Jared Jeffries	PF	6-10	North HS, Bloomington, IN	McD, P	Indiana	Big Ten POY, '02; 14.4 ppg, 7.2 rpg (2 years); No. 11 pick, '02 NBA draft (Wizards); 5.3 ppg (7 seasons)
9 Andre Brown	PF	6-8	Leo Catholic HS, Chicago	McD, P	DePaul	855 rebounds at DePaul; undrafted; played overseas, D-League; 75 NBA games for 3 teams
10 Mario Austin	C	6-10	Sumter County HS, York, AL	McD, P	Mississippi State	First-team All-SEC, 2nd-round pick, '03 NBA draft (Bulls); played overseas
11 Taliek Brown	PG	6-1	St. John's Prep HS, Astoria, NY	McD, P	Connecticut	Connecticut's all-time assists leader (722); NCAA title, '04; undrafted
12 Darius Rice	F	6-9	Lanier HS, Jackson, MS	McD, P	Miami (FL)	2nd team All-Big East, '02-'04; led team in points all 4 years; undrafted; played in D-League
13 Alton Ford	F/C	6-8	Charles H. Milby HS, Houston	McD, P	Houston	10.8 ppg, 5.9 rpg (1 season); 2nd-round pick, '01 NBA draft (Suns); 2.5 ppg (3 seasons)
14 Omar Cook	PG	6-1	Christ the King HS, Middle Village, NY	McD, P	St. John's	Led Big East, 8.7 apg, 15.3 ppg '01 (1 season); 2nd-round pick, '01 NBA draft (Magic); 22 NBA games
15 Abdou Diame	PF	6-8	Oak Hill Academy, Mouth of Wilson, VA	P	Auburn/ Jacksonville State	Tranferred after 2 years; 5.4 ppg at Jacksonville State; undrafted; played overseas
16 Jerome Harper	F	6-6	W.J. Keenan HS, Columbia, SC	McD, P	Indian Hill CC	Academics kept him from D1; played 2 years at CC; undrafted
17 Brian Boddicker	PF	6-9	Duncanville (TX) HS	McD, P	Texas	Texas' 2nd all-time 3-pt FG% (40.4%); 7.3 ppg, 4.2 rpg (4 seasons); undrafted; played overseas
18 Brian Morrison	G	6-2	Lake Washington HS, Kirkland, WA		North Carolina/UCLA	Tranferred after 2 seasons; 7.7 ppg at UCLA; undrafted; played in D-League
19 Andre Barrett	PG	5-9	Rice HS, New York	McD, P	Seton Hall	SHU's 2nd all-time assists leader (662); first-team All-Big East, '04; undrafted; played in 67 NBA games thru '09
20 Rolando Howell	PF	6-9	Lower Richland HS, Hopkins, SC	McD, P	South Carolina	9.5 ppg, 5.8 rpg (4 seasons); undrafted, played overseas

Other Standouts

PLAYER	POS	HT	HIGH SCHOOL	A-A TEAMS	COLLEGE	CAREER NOTES
24 Justin Reed	F	6-7	Provine HS, Jackson, MS	P	Mississippi	SEC FOY, '01; first-team All-SEC, '04; 2nd-round pick, '04 NBA draft (Celtics); 3.5 ppg (3 seasons)
51 Dwyane Wade	G	6-3	Richards HS, Oak Lawn, IL		Marquette	AP All-American, Final Four, '03; No. 5 pick, '03 NBA draft (Heat); NBA Finals MVP '06; 5-time All-Star
87 Jameer Nelson	PG	6-0	Chester (PA) HS		Saint Joseph's	National POY '04; No. 20 pick, '04 NBA draft (Nuggets); 2nd team All-Rookie '05; '09 All-Star

Abbreviations: McD=McDonald's; P=Parade; USA=USA Today

POLL PROGRESSION

PRESEASON POLL

AP	ESPN/USA	SCHOOL
1	1	Connecticut
2	3	Cincinnati
3	2	Michigan State
4	4	Auburn
5	6	Ohio State
6	5	North Carolina
7	7	Temple
8	8	Florida
9	9	Arizona
10	10	Duke
11	11	Kansas
12	14	UCLA
13	13	Stanford
14	12	Kentucky
15	15	Utah
16	18	Illinois
17	17	Syracuse
18	19	St. John's
19	16	Tennessee
20	20	DePaul
21	22	Texas
22	25	Oklahoma State
23	21	Purdue
24	—	Gonzaga
25	24	Miami (FL.)
—	23	Maryland

WEEK OF NOV 16

AP	SCHOOL	AP↓↑
1	Cincinnati (0-0)	↑1
2	Michigan State (0-0)	↑1
3	Auburn (0-0)	↑1
4	Ohio State (0-0)	↑1
5	North Carolina (0-0)	↑1
6	Temple (0-0)	↑1
7	Florida (0-0)	↑1
8	Connecticut (1-1)	↓7
9	Stanford (2-0)	↑4
10	Arizona (0-0)	↓1
11	Kansas (0-0)	
12	UCLA (0-0)	
13	Syracuse (2-0)	↑4
14	Kentucky (0-0)	
15	St. John's (0-0)	↑3
16	Utah (0-0)	↓1
17	Illinois (0-0)	↓1
18	Duke (0-2)	↓8
19	Tennessee (0-0)	
20	DePaul (0-0)	
21	Texas (0-0)	
22	Iowa (1-1)	⤴
23	Oklahoma State (0-0)	↓1
24	Purdue (0-0)	↓1
25	Gonzaga (0-0)	↓1

WEEK OF NOV 23

AP	ESPN/USA	SCHOOL	AP↓↑
1	1	Cincinnati (1-0)	
2	3	Auburn (2-0)	↑1
3	2	Michigan State (1-0)	↓1
4	6	North Carolina (0-0)	↑1
5	4	Temple (1-0)	↑1
6	5	Florida (1-0)	↑1
7	7	Connecticut (2-1)	↑1
8	9	Arizona (2-0)	↑2
9	7	Stanford (3-0)	
10	11	Kansas (1-0)	↑1
11	10	Kentucky (2-0)	↑3
12	14	Ohio State (0-1) (A)	↓8
13	12	UCLA (1-0)	↓1
14	13	Syracuse (2-0)	↓1
15	16	Illinois (1-0)	↑2
16	15	Duke (1-2)	↑2
17	18	Tennessee (0-0)	↑2
18	19	DePaul (1-0)	↑2
19	17	Utah (2-1)	↓3
20	20	Texas (1-0)	↑1
21	23	Oklahoma State (2-0)	↑2
22	21	Purdue (0-0)	↑2
23	—	Iowa (2-1)	↓1
24	22	Maryland (2-0)	⤴
25	25	Gonzaga (1-0)	
—	24	Miami (FL) (1-0)	

WEEK OF NOV 30

AP	ESPN/USA	SCHOOL	AP↓↑
1	1	Cincinnati (4-0)	
2	2	North Carolina (3-0)	
3	3	Stanford (5-0)	
4	4	Arizona (4-0)	
5	8	Connecticut (3-1)	
6	6	Kansas (4-0)	[illegible]
7	5	Auburn (2-1)	[illegible]
8	7	Michigan State (3-1)	[illegible]
9	11	Texas (4-0)	↑[illegible]
10	9	Temple (1-1)	↓[illegible]
11	10	Florida (3-1)	↓[illegible]
12	13	UCLA (2-0)	↑[illegible]
13	12	Kentucky (3-1)	↓[illegible]
14	14	Syracuse (3-0)	
15	17	Ohio State (0-1)	↓[illegible]
16	16	Illinois (2-0)	↓[illegible]
17	15	Duke (3-2)	↓1
18	18	Tennessee (3-0)	↓1
19	21	Purdue (2-1)	↑3
20	19	Utah (2-1)	↓1
21	22	Oklahoma State (4-0)	
22	20	DePaul (3-1)	↓4
23	24	Indiana (2-0)	⤴
24	23	Maryland (4-1)	
25	—	Gonzaga (2-0)	
—	25	Miami (FL) (2-0)	

WEEK OF DEC 7

AP	ESPN/USA	SCHOOL	AP↓↑
1	1	Cincinnati (5-0)	
2	2	Arizona (6-0)	↑2
3	3	Stanford (5-0)	
4	5	Michigan State (6-1) (B)	↑4
5	4	Kansas (6-0)	↑1
6	6	Connecticut (5-1)	↓1
7	7	North Carolina (5-1) (B)	↓5
8	8	Auburn (4-1)	↓1
9	10	Florida (5-1)	↑2
10	12	Texas (4-1)	↓1
11	11	UCLA (3-0)	↑1
12	9	Syracuse (6-0)	↑2
13	16	Ohio State (2-1)	↑2
14	13	Duke (5-2)	↑3
15	14	Indiana (4-0)	↑8
16	15	Tennessee (6-0)	↑2
17	17	Oklahoma State (6-0)	↑4
18	21	Wake Forest (5-0)	⤴
19	18	Temple (2-2)	↓9
20	20	DePaul (4-2)	↑2
21	19	Maryland (6-2)	↑3
22	24	Illinois (3-2)	↓6
23	22	Kentucky (3-3)	↓10
24	—	Gonzaga (4-1)	↑1
25	23	Purdue (3-2)	↓6
—	25	Utah (3-2)	⤵

WEEK OF DEC 14

AP	ESPN/USA	SCHOOL	AP↓↑
1	1	Cincinnati (7-0)	
2	2	Stanford (6-0)	↑1
3	4	Connecticut (7-1)	↑3
4	3	Arizona (7-1)	↓2
5	5	Michigan State (7-2)	↓1
6	7	Auburn (5-1)	↑2
7	9	North Carolina (7-2)	
8	6	Kansas (7-1)	↓3
9	8	Florida (6-1)	
10	10	Syracuse (7-0)	↑2
11	11	Duke (6-2)	↑3
12	13	Ohio State (3-1)	↑1
13	12	Tennessee (8-0)	↑3
14	15	Oklahoma State (7-0)	↑3
15	16	Texas (5-2)	↓5
16	14	Maryland (8-2)	↑5
17	18	Temple (3-2)	↑2
18	17	UCLA (3-1) (C)	↓7
19	20	DePaul (6-2)	↑1
20	22	Illinois (5-2)	↑2
21	19	Indiana (6-1)	↓6
22	—	Gonzaga (5-2) (C)	↑2
23	24	Oklahoma (8-0)	⤴
24	21	Purdue (6-2)	↑1
25	23	Wake Forest (5-1)	↓7
—	25	Utah (5-2)	

WEEK OF DEC 21

AP	ESPN/USA	SCHOOL	AP↓↑
1	1	Stanford (8-0)	↑1
2	3	Connecticut (7-1)	↑1
3	2	Arizona (9-1)	↑1
4	4	Cincinnati (8-1)	↓3
5	5	Michigan State (8-2)	
6	7	North Carolina (8-2)	↑1
7	6	Auburn (7-1)	↓1
8	8	Florida (7-1)	↑1
9	9	Syracuse (7-0)	↑1
10	10	Duke (7-2)	↑1
11	12	Tennessee (9-0)	↑2
12	11	Kansas (8-2)	↓4
13	13	Oklahoma State (9-0)	↑1
14	14	Texas (6-2)	↑1
15	17	Illinois (6-2)	↑5
16	20	Ohio State (5-2)	↓4
17	15	Maryland (8-2)	↓1
18	16	UCLA (4-1)	
19	19	Temple (4-2)	↓2
20	18	Indiana (7-1)	↑1
21	21	Oklahoma (9-0)	↑2
22	25	Gonzaga (7-2)	
23	22	Wake Forest (7-1)	↑2
24	23	DePaul (7-3)	↓5
25	—	NC State (7-0)	⤴
—	24	Utah (7-2)	

WEEK OF DEC 28

AP	ESPN/USA	SCHOOL	AP↓↑
1	1	Stanford (9-0)	
2	2	Connecticut (8-1)	
3	3	Cincinnati (9-1)	↑1
4	5	Auburn (10-1)	↑3
5	4	Arizona (9-2)	↓2
6	7	Florida (9-1)	↑2
7	9	Syracuse (8-0)	↑2
8	6	Michigan State (8-3)	↓3
9	8	Duke (8-2)	↑1
10	10	Kansas (9-2)	↑2
11	11	Oklahoma State (10-0)	↑2
12	12	Indiana (8-1)	↑8
13	14	North Carolina (8-4)	↓7
14	16	Maryland (9-2)	↑3
15	18	Ohio State (6-2)	↑1
16	13	Tennessee (11-1)	↓5
17	17	Temple (5-2)	↑2
18	15	Texas (6-3)	↓4
19	19	Wake Forest (8-1)	↑4
20	20	Illinois (6-3)	↓5
21	24	Utah (8-2)	⤴
22	22	Oklahoma (9-1)	↓1
23	21	UCLA (6-2)	↓5
24	23	DePaul (8-3)	
25	—	Tulsa (11-1)	⤴
—	25	Kentucky (6-4)	

WEEK OF JAN 4

AP	ESPN/USA	SCHOOL	AP↓↑
1	1	Stanford (11-0)	
2	2	Connecticut (9-1)	
3	3	Cincinnati (12-1)	
4	5	Auburn (12-1)	
5	4	Arizona (11-2)	
6	6	Florida (11-1)	
7	8	Syracuse (9-0)	
8	7	Duke (9-2)	↑1
9	9	Kansas (10-2)	↑1
10	11	Indiana (10-1)	↑2
11	10	Michigan State (9-4) (D)	↓3
12	15	Maryland (11-2)	↑2
13	18	Ohio State (8-2)	↑2
14	14	North Carolina (9-4)	↓1
15	13	Tennessee (12-1)	↑1
16	12	Oklahoma State (10-1)	↓5
17	16	Texas (8-3)	↑1
18	22	Utah (11-2)	↑3
19	17	Illinois (8-3)	↑1
20	19	Oklahoma (11-1)	↑2
21	—	LSU (12-0)	⤴
22	25	Tulsa (13-1)	↑3
23	23	DePaul (10-3)	↑1
24	20	UCLA (8-2)	↓1
25	24	Kentucky (8-4)	⤴
—	21	Temple (6-3)	⤵

WEEK OF JAN 11

AP	ESPN/USA	SCHOOL	AP↓↑
1	1	Cincinnati (14-1)	↑2
2	2	Arizona (13-2)	↑3
3	3	Stanford (12-1)	↓2
4	5	Auburn (13-1)	
5	4	Connecticut (11-2)	↓3
6	7	Duke (11-2)	↑2
7	6	Syracuse (11-0)	
8	8	Kansas (12-2)	↑1
9	10	Indiana (12-1)	↑1
10	9	Florida (12-2)	↓4
11	11	Michigan State (11-4)	
12	12	Tennessee (14-1)	↑3
13	14	North Carolina (11-4)	↑1
14	13	Oklahoma State (12-1)	↑2
15	15	Texas (9-3)	↑2
16	17	Oklahoma (13-1)	↑4
17	18	Ohio State (9-3)	↓4
18	16	Maryland (11-4)	↓6
19	22	Tulsa (14-1)	↑3
20	23	Kentucky (10-4)	↑5
21	19	DePaul (11-3)	↑2
22	21	Illinois (9-4)	↓3
23	20	Temple (8-3)	⤴
24	—	LSU (13-1)	↓3
25	—	Louisville (10-3)	⤴
—	24	Utah (11-3)	⤵
—	25	UCLA (9-3)	⤵

WEEK OF JAN 18

AP	ESPN/USA	SCHOOL	AP↓↑
1	1	Cincinnati (16-1)	
2	2	Arizona (15-2)	
3	3	Stanford (14-1)	
4	4	Auburn (15-1)	
5	6	Duke (13-2)	↑1
6	5	Syracuse (14-0)	↑1
7	8	Kansas (14-2)	↑1
8	7	Connecticut (12-3)	↓3
9	9	Florida (13-2)	↑1
10	10	Michigan State (12-4)	↑1
11	11	Indiana (13-2)	↓2
12	12	Oklahoma State (13-1)	↑2
13	15	Ohio State (11-3)	↑4
14	13	Texas (11-4)	↑1
15	17	Tulsa (16-1)	↑4
16	14	Tennessee (15-2)	↓4
17	16	Oklahoma (14-2)	↓1
18	18	Kentucky (11-5)	↑2
19	23	St. John's (12-2)	⤴
20	24	Vanderbilt (12-2)	⤴
21	21	North Carolina (11-6)	↓8
22	20	Utah (13-3)	⤴
23	22	DePaul (12-4)	↓2
24	—	Maryland (11-5)	↓6
25	19	UCLA (10-4)	⤴
—	25	Illinois (9-6)	⤵

WEEK OF JAN 25

AP	ESPN/USA	SCHOOL	AP↓↑
1	1	Cincinnati (18-1)	
2	2	Stanford (15-1)	↑1
3	3	Duke (15-2)	↑2
4	5	Syracuse (15-0)	↑2
5	4	Arizona (16-3)	↓3
6	6	Connecticut (13-3)	↑2
7	7	Auburn (16-2)	↓3
8	10	Ohio State (13-3)	↑5
9	8	Michigan State (13-5)	↑1
10	9	Florida (14-3)	↓1
11	13	Tennessee (16-2)	↑5
12	11	Kansas (15-3)	↓5
13	15	Tulsa (18-1)	↑2
14	12	Indiana (14-3)	↓3
15	16	Oklahoma State (14-2)	↓3
16	18	Kentucky (13-5)	↑2
17	14	Texas (12-5)	↓3
18	17	Oklahoma (15-3)	↓1
19	19	Utah (14-3)	↑3
20	22	Vanderbilt (12-3)	
21	25	NC State (13-3)	⤴
22	21	Maryland (13-5)	↑2
23	24	Temple (12-4)	⤴
23	—	Southern California (12-5)	⤴
25	23	St. John's (12-4)	↓6
—	20	UCLA (11-5)	⤵

Week of Feb 1

AP	ESPN/USA	SCHOOL	AP↓↑
	1	**Cincinnati** (20-1)	
	2	**Stanford** (17-1)	
	3	**Duke** (16-2)	
	4	**Syracuse** (17-0)	
	8	**Ohio State** (14-3)	↑3
	9	**Tennessee** (18-2)	↑5
	7	**Connecticut** (15-4)	↓1
	6	**Michigan State** (15-5)	↑1
	5	**Arizona** (17-4)	↓4
	10	**Auburn** (17-3)	↓3
	11	**Indiana** (15-3)	↑3
	12	**Florida** (15-4)	↓2
	14	**Oklahoma State** (16-2)	↑2
	17	**Kentucky** (15-5)	↑2
	15	**Kansas** (16-4)	↓3
	13	**Texas** (14-5)	↑1
	16	**Tulsa** (20-2)	↓4
	17	**Oklahoma** (16-3)	
	19	**Utah** (16-3)	
	24	**Iowa State** (16-3)	⤴
	20	**Temple** (14-4)	↑2
	25	**LSU** (16-3)	⤴
	—	**Oregon** (15-3)	⤴
24	23	**Vanderbilt** (13-4)	↓4
25	21	**Maryland** (14-6)	↓3
—	22	**NC State** (14-4)	⤵

Week of Feb 8

AP	ESPN/USA	SCHOOL	AP↓↑
1	1	**Cincinnati** (22-1)	
2	2	**Stanford** (19-1)	
3	3	**Duke** (18-2)	
4	4	**Syracuse** (19-0)	
5	6	**Ohio State** (16-3)	
6	5	**Michigan State** (17-6)	↑2
7	7	**Arizona** (19-4)	↑2
8	9	**Tennessee** (19-3)	↓2
9	8	**Auburn** (19-3)	↑1
10	9	**Indiana** (17-3)	↑1
11	14	**Kentucky** (17-5)	↑3
12	11	**Florida** (17-4)	
13	12	**Connecticut** (16-5)	↓6
14	13	**Oklahoma State** (18-2)	↓1
15	15	**Tulsa** (22-2)	↑2
16	17	**Oklahoma** (18-3)	↑2
17	21	**Iowa State** (19-3)	↑3
18	16	**Texas** (15-6)	↓2
19	19	**Temple** (16-4)	↑2
20	18	**Kansas** (17-5)	↓5
21	20	**Utah** (17-4)	↓2
22	23	**Vanderbilt** (15-4)	↑2
23	22	**Maryland** (16-6)	↑2
24	—	**Oregon** (16-4)	↓1
25	25	**LSU** (17-4)	↓3
—	24	**NC State** (15-5)	

Week of Feb 15

AP	ESPN/USA	SCHOOL	AP↓↑
1	1	**Cincinnati** (23-1)	
2	2	**Stanford** (21-1)	
3	3	**Duke** (19-3)	
4	4	**Arizona** (21-4)	↑3
5	6	**Tennessee** (21-3)	↑3
6	5	**Michigan State** (18-6)	
7	7	**Ohio State** (17-4)	↓2
8	9	**Oklahoma State** (20-2)	↑6
9	8	**Syracuse** (20-2) (E)	↓5
10	10	**Indiana** (18-4)	
11	12	**Florida** (18-5)	↑1
12	11	**Auburn** (19-4)	↓3
13	13	**Tulsa** (22-2)	↑2
14	17	**Iowa State** (21-3)	↑3
15	15	**Temple** (18-4)	↑4
16	23	**LSU** (19-4)	↑9
17	14	**Texas** (17-6)	↑1
18	18	**Connecticut** (17-6)	↓5
19	16	**Kentucky** (17-7)	↓8
20	19	**Oklahoma** (19-4)	↓4
21	20	**Utah** (19-4)	
22	22	**Maryland** (17-7)	↑1
23	25	**Seton Hall** (18-4)	⤴
24	21	**Kansas** (18-6)	↓4
25	—	**Purdue** (17-7)	⤴
—	24	**Vanderbilt** (16-5)	⤵

Week of Feb 22 (F)

AP	ESPN/USA	SCHOOL	AP↓↑
1	1	**Stanford** (22-1)	↑1
2	2	**Duke** (21-3)	↑1
3	3	**Cincinnati** (24-2)	↓2
4	4	**Arizona** (23-4)	
5	5	**Michigan State** (20-6)	↑1
6	6	**Ohio State** (18-5)	↑1
7	7	**Tennessee** (21-4)	↓2
8	12	**Temple** (20-4)	↑7
9	10	**Florida** (20-5)	↑2
10	9	**Oklahoma State** (21-3)	↓2
11	8	**Auburn** (21-4)	↑1
12	13	**Tulsa** (25-2)	↑1
13	11	**Syracuse** (21-3)	↓4
14	15	**Texas** (19-6)	↑3
15	17	**LSU** (21-4)	↑1
16	14	**Indiana** (18-5)	↓6
17	18	**Iowa State** (22-4)	↓3
18	16	**Kentucky** (19-7)	↑1
19	19	**Maryland** (19-7)	↑3
20	20	**Oklahoma** (20-5)	
21	25	**Purdue** (19-7)	↑4
22	21	**Connecticut** (18-7)	↓4
23	23	**Kansas** (19-7)	↑1
24	22	**Vanderbilt** (17-6)	⤴
25	24	**Utah** (19-5)	↓4

Week of Feb 29

AP	ESPN/USA	SCHOOL	AP↓↑
1	1	**Stanford** (24-1)	
2	2	**Cincinnati** (26-2)	↑1
3	3	**Arizona** (24-4)	↑1
4	4	**Duke** (22-4)	↓2
5	7	**Temple** (22-4)	↑3
6	5	**Ohio State** (20-5)	
7	6	**Michigan State** (21-7)	↓2
8	8	**Florida** (22-5)	↑1
9	9	**Syracuse** (23-3)	↑4
10	14	**Iowa State** (24-4)	↑7
11	10	**Tennessee** (22-5)	↓4
12	16	**LSU** (23-4)	↑3
13	11	**Oklahoma State** (22-4)	↓3
14	12	**Indiana** (19-6)	↑2
15	17	**Tulsa** (26-3)	↓3
16	15	**Texas** (20-7)	↓2
17	19	**Maryland** (21-7)	↑2
18	21	**St. John's** (20-6)	⤴
19	13	**Auburn** (21-6)	↓8
20	22	**Purdue** (21-7)	↑1
21	20	**Oklahoma** (22-5)	↓1
22	18	**Kentucky** (20-8)	↓4
23	23	**Kansas** (21-7)	
24	24	**Connecticut** (19-8)	↓2
25	—	**Illinois** (18-8)	⤴
—	25	**Vanderbilt** (17-8)	⤵

Week of Mar 7

AP	ESPN/USA	SCHOOL	AP↓↑
1	1	**Cincinnati** (28-2)	↑1
2	3	**Stanford** (25-2)	↓1
3	2	**Duke** (24-4)	↑1
4	5	**Ohio State** (22-5)	↑2
5	4	**Michigan State** (23-7)	↑2
6	7	**Temple** (23-5)	↓1
7	9	**Iowa State** (26-4)	↑3
8	8	**Tennessee** (24-5)	↑3
9	6	**Arizona** (24-6)	↓6
10	11	**LSU** (25-4)	↑2
11	10	**Florida** (23-6)	↓3
12	12	**Syracuse** (24-4)	↓3
13	15	**Texas** (22-7)	↑3
14	17	**Tulsa** (27-3)	↑1
15	18	**Oklahoma** (24-5)	↑6
16	16	**Kentucky** (22-8)	↑6
17	14	**Oklahoma State** (23-5)	↓4
18	13	**Indiana** (20-7)	↓4
19	20	**St. John's** (21-7)	↓1
20	19	**Maryland** (22-8)	↓3
21	22	**Connecticut** (21-8)	↑3
22	21	**Purdue** (21-8)	↓2
23	—	**Miami (FL)** (20-9)	⤴
24	24	**Kansas** (22-8)	↓1
25	—	**Illinois** (19-8)	
—	23	**Auburn** (21-8)	⤵
—	25	**Oregon** (21-7)	

Week of Mar 14

AP	ESPN/USA	SCHOOL	AP↓↑
1	1	**Duke** (27-4)	↑2
2	2	**Michigan State** (26-7)	↑3
3	3	**Stanford** (26-3)	↓1
4	4	**Arizona** (26-6)	↑5
5	5	**Temple** (26-5)	↑1
6	7	**Iowa State** (29-4)	↑1
7	6	**Cincinnati** (28-3) (G)	↓6
8	8	**Ohio State** (22-6)	↓4
9	12	**St. John's** (24-7)	↑10
10	9	**LSU** (26-5)	
11	10	**Tennessee** (24-6)	↓3
12	13	**Oklahoma** (26-6)	↑3
13	11	**Florida** (24-7)	↓2
14	15	**Oklahoma State** (24-6)	↑3
15	18	**Texas** (23-8)	↓2
16	14	**Syracuse** (24-5)	↓4
17	16	**Maryland** (24-9)	↑3
18	19	**Tulsa** (29-4)	↓4
19	20	**Kentucky** (22-9)	↓3
20	21	**Connecticut** (24-9)	↑1
21	23	**Illinois** (21-9)	↑4
22	17	**Indiana** (20-8)	↓4
23	25	**Miami (FL)** (21-10)	
24	22	**Auburn** (23-9)	⤴
25	24	**Purdue** (21-9)	↓3

FINAL POLL (Post-Tournament)

ESPN/USA	SCHOOL
1	**Michigan State** (32-7)
2	**Florida** (29-8)
3	**Iowa State** (32-5)
4	**Duke** (29-5)
5	**Stanford** (27-4)
6	**Oklahoma State** (27-7)
7	**Cincinnati** (29-4)
8	**Arizona** (27-7)
9	**Tulsa** (32-5)
10	**Temple** (27-6)
11	**North Carolina** (22-14)
12	**Syracuse** (26-6)
13	**LSU** (28-6)
14	**Tennessee** (26-7)
15	**Purdue** (24-10)
16	**Wisconsin** (22-14)
17	**Ohio State** (23-7)
18	**St. John's** (25-8)
19	**Oklahoma** (27-7)
20	**Miami (FL)** (23-11)
21	**Texas** (24-9)
22	**Kentucky** (23-10)
23	**UCLA** (21-12)
24	**Gonzaga** (26-9)
25	**Maryland** (25-10)

(A) Notre Dame's David Graves hits a 15-footer as time expires, giving the Irish an upset over Ohio State on Nov. 16 in the Preseason NIT.
(B) North Carolina gets beaten by Michigan State, 86-76. It's the first Tar Heel loss in a home opener since 1928.
(C) Gonzaga defeats UCLA, 59-43, the Bruins' lowest point output in Pauley Pavilion since it opened in 1966.
(D) After missing the first 13 games of Michigan State's season with a stress fracture in his right foot, Mateen Cleaves returns to the starting lineup in time for Big Ten play. The Spartans will win 17 of their last 20 and the regular-season conference title.
(E) Unranked Louisville stuns Syracuse, 82-69, on Feb. 10, making the Orangemen the fourth ranked team the Cardinals have defeated in a 19–12 season. The others are North Carolina on Dec. 23, Utah on Jan. 6 and DePaul on Jan. 20.
(F) Fresno State's Larry Abney hauls in 35 rebounds against SMU on Feb. 17, the most by a D1 player since Pacific's Keith Swagerty grabbed 39 against UC Santa Barbara on March 5, 1965.
(G) Cincinnati's Kenyon Martin breaks his right fibula and tears tendons in his right leg during a 68-58 loss to Saint Louis, ending his season and undermining the Bearcats' hopes of winning their first NCAA title since 1962.

Pre-Tournament Ratings Percentage Index (RPI)

RANK	SCHOOL	W-L	Sched. Strg.	SS Rank	RPI
1	**Cincinnati**	28-3	.6076	5	.6726
2	**Kentucky**	21-9	.6456	1	.6467
3	**Duke**	27-4	.5737	24	.6459
4	**Arizona**	26-6	.5934	10	.6443
5	**St. John's**	24-7	.6149	2	.6412
6	**Temple**	26-5	.5699	30	.6379
7	**Iowa State**	26-4	.5570	53	.6362
8	**Texas**	23-8	.6120	3	.6323
9	**Stanford**	25-3	.5289	99	.6257
10	**Oklahoma**	26-6	.5653	39	.6247
11	**Michigan State**	26-7	.5630	44	.6247
12	**LSU**	26-5	.5507	64	.6236
13	**Tennessee**	23-6	.5691	32	.6221
14	**Connecticut**	24-9	.5934	9	.6218
15	**Syracuse**	24-5	.5452	76	.6205
16	**Maryland**	24-9	.5987	6	.6203
17	**Florida**	24-7	.5616	46	.6141
18	**Kansas**	22-9	.5930	12	.6139
19	**Oklahoma State**	23-6	.5511	61	.6102
20	**Indiana**	20-8	.5747	23	.6094
21	**Auburn**	22-9	.5673	35	.6014
22	**Illinois**	21-9	.5692	31	.6007
23	**Ohio State**	22-6	.5277	102	.5994
24	**Tulsa**	29-4	.4994	148	.5992
25	**Fresno State**	24-9	.5712	27	.5975
26	**UCLA**	19-11	.5961	8	.5941
27	**Oregon**	21-7	.5431	79	.5933
28	**Utah State**	24-5	.5212	114	.5906
29	**Louisville**	18-11	.5828	18	.5873
30	**Wisconsin**	18-13	.5976	7	.5870
31	**Purdue**	20-9	.5467	75	.5867
32	**Saint Louis**	19-13	.5931	11	.5866
33	**Missouri**	18-12	.5820	21	.5832
34	**Gonzaga**	24-8	.5356	89	.5831
35	**DePaul**	20-11	.5672	36	.5829
36	**SW Missouri State**	22-10	.5612	48	.5822
37	**North Carolina**	18-13	.5893	13	.5813
38	**Miami (FL)**	21-10	.5509	62	.5805
39	**Kent State**	19-7	.5409	83	.5799
40	**St. Bonaventure**	21-9	.5395	84	.5783
41	**Vanderbilt**	19-10	.5535	60	.5780
42	**Dayton**	22-8	.5165	121	.5747
43	**Villanova**	19-12	.5702	29	.5741
44	**Ball State**	21-8	.5198	116	.5741
45	**Arkansas**	19-14	.5874	16	.5730
46	**Indiana State**	22-9	.5279	101	.5719
47	**BYU**	19-10	.5617	45	.5693
48	**Pepperdine**	24-8	.5100	131	.5693
49	**SMU**	20-8	.5242	109	.5692
50	**Seton Hall**	20-9	.5222	111	.5691

Source: Collegiate Basketball News

ANNUAL REVIEW

2000 NCAA Tournament

West

First Round
- 1 Arizona 71
- 16 Jackson State 47
- 8 Wisconsin 66
- 9 ⊗Fresno State 56
- 5 Texas 77
- 12 Indiana State 61
- 4 LSU 64
- 13 Southeast Missouri State 61
- 6 Purdue 62
- 11 Dayton 61
- 3 Oklahoma 74
- 14 Winthrop 50
- 7 Louisville 66
- 10 Gonzaga 77
- 2 St. John's 61
- 15 Northern Arizona 56

Second Round
- Arizona 59
- Wisconsin 66
- Texas 67
- LSU 72
- Purdue 66
- Oklahoma 62
- Gonzaga 82 (A)
- St. John's 76

Regional Semifinals (Albuquerque, NM)
- Wisconsin 61
- LSU 48
- Purdue 75
- Gonzaga 66

Regional Finals
- Wisconsin 64
- Purdue 60

Midwest

First Round
- 1 Michigan State 65
- 16 Valparaiso 38
- 8 Utah 48
- 9 Saint Louis 45
- 5 Kentucky 85 (2OT)
- 12 St. Bonaventure 80
- 4 Syracuse 79
- 13 Samford 65
- 6 UCLA 65
- 11 Ball State 57
- 3 Maryland 74
- 14 Iona 59
- 7 Auburn 72
- 10 Creighton 69
- 2 Iowa State 88
- 15 Central Connecticut State 78

Second Round
- Michigan State 73
- Utah 61
- Kentucky 50
- Syracuse 52
- UCLA 105
- Maryland 70
- Auburn 60
- Iowa State 79

Regional Semifinals (Auburn Hills, MI)
- Michigan State 75 (B)
- Syracuse 58
- UCLA 56 (C)
- Iowa State 80

Regional Finals
- Michigan State 75
- Iowa State 64

East

First Round
- 1 Duke 85
- 16 Lamar 55
- 8 Kansas 81 (OT)
- 9 DePaul 77
- 5 Florida 69 (OT)
- 12 Butler 68
- 4 Illinois 68
- 13 Pennsylvania 58
- 6 Indiana 57 (D)
- 11 Pepperdine 77
- 3 Oklahoma State 86
- 14 Hofstra 66
- 7 Oregon 71 (OT)
- 10 Seton Hall 72
- 2 Temple 73 (E)
- 15 Lafayette 47

Second Round
- Duke 69
- Kansas 64
- Florida 93
- Illinois 76
- Pepperdine 67
- Oklahoma State 75
- Seton Hall 67 (OT) (F)
- Temple 65

Regional Semifinals (Syracuse, NY)
- Duke 78
- Florida 87
- Oklahoma State 68
- Seton Hall 66

Regional Finals
- Florida 77
- Oklahoma State 65

South

First Round
- 1 Stanford 84
- 16 South Carolina State 65
- 8 North Carolina 84
- 9 Missouri 70
- 5 Connecticut 75
- 12 Utah State 67
- 4 Tennessee 63
- 13 UL-Lafayette 58
- 6 Miami (FL) 75
- 11 Arkansas 71
- 3 ⊗Ohio State 87
- 14 Appalachian State 61
- 7 Tulsa 89
- 10 UNLV 62
- 2 Cincinnati 64 (H)
- 15 UNC Wilmington 47

Second Round
- Stanford 53
- North Carolina 60
- Connecticut 61 (G)
- Tennessee 65
- Miami (FL) 75
- ⊗Ohio State 62
- Tulsa 69
- Cincinnati 61

Regional Semifinals (Austin, TX)
- North Carolina 74
- Tennessee 69
- Miami (FL) 71
- Tulsa 80

Regional Finals
- North Carolina 59
- Tulsa 55

⊗Team participation later vacated

National Semifinal
- Wisconsin 41
- Michigan State 53

Add up all the seed numbers of the Final Four teams—including two No. 8s—and you get 22, the highest ever. The 13 losses for Wisconsin and UNC are the most for any Final Four teams since Tournament seeding was introduced in 1979.

National Semifinal
- Florida 71
- North Carolina 59

Key UNC reserve Julius Peppers notches the first half of a unique career double. Four years after playing in the Final Four, Peppers, an All-Pro defensive end, will play in the Super Bowl for the losing Carolina Panthers.

National Final (Indianapolis)

Michigan State 89
Florida 76

Florida becomes the first No. 5 seed to play in the championship game, but cannot overcome 11 Michigan State three-pointers. The Spartans, playing in their first title game since 1979, overcome an ankle injury to point guard and MOP Mateen Cleaves with the help of 21 points from wing Morris Peterson.

A The Zags reach the Sweet 16 for the second straight year by dominating the Red Storm in the paint, with inside players scoring 43 of their points.

B The Spartans trail by 14 points in the second half, but come back to tie the game at 58 and then go on a 17-0 run to end the game.

C After throwing down 14 alley-oops in a romp over Maryland, UCLA's high-flying attack is grounded by the physical play of Iowa State. The Cyclones front line, led by burly power forward Marcus Fizer with his 16 points, dominates.

D Pepperdine, a tough matchup for any team because of its four left-handed starters, upsets Indiana in what turns out to be Bob Knight's final game as Hoosiers head coach.

E In the battle of eastern Pennsylvania, Temple's Pepe Sanchez dishes out 15 assists but scores zero points in the Owls' victory.

F Shaheen Holloway sprains an ankle eight minutes in, but backup Ty Shine scores a career-high 26 points, including a game-winning three in OT. It's an emotional win for Seton Hall, where two months earlier a dorm fire claimed the lives of three students.

G Slowed by a sprained ankle he suffered during the Utah State game, point guard Khalid El-Amin plays only 13 minutes and scores three points. The defending champion Huskies lose their composure and the game, turning the ball over 15 times.

H Ranked No. 1 for much of the season, Cincinnati drops to a No. 2 seed in the Tournament after Kenyon Martin breaks his leg in the Conference USA tournament.

TOURNAMENT LEADERS

INDIVIDUAL LEADERS

SCORING	CL	POS	G	PTS	PPG
1 **Marcus Fizer**, Iowa State	JR	F	4	80	20.0
2 **Joseph Forte**, North Carolina	FR	G	5	95	19.0
Johnny Hemsley, Miami (FL)	SR	G	3	57	19.0
4 **Richie Frahm**, Gonzaga	SR	G	3	55	18.3
5 **Shane Battier**, Duke	JR	F	3	53	17.7
6 **Morris Peterson**, Michigan State	SR	G/F	6	105	17.5
Jamaal Tinsley, Iowa State	JR	G	4	70	17.5
8 **Desmond Mason**, Oklahoma State	SR	F	4	68	17.0
Matt Santangelo, Gonzaga	SR	G	3	51	17.0
10 **Rimas Kaukenas**, Seton Hall	SR	G	3	49	16.3

MINIMUM: 3 GAMES

FIELD GOAL PCT	CL	POS	G	FG	FGA	PCT
1 **Casey Calvary**, Gonzaga	JR	F	3	15	21	71.4
2 **Stevie Johnson**, Iowa State	SR	F	4	15	22	68.2
Greg McQuay, Purdue	SR	C	4	15	22	68.2
4 **Udonis Haslem**, Florida	SO	F	6	33	50	66.0
5 **Andy Kowske**, Wisconsin	JR	F	5	22	35	62.9

MINIMUM: 15 MADE AND 3 GAMES

FREE THROW PCT	CL	POS	G	FT	FTA	PCT
1 **Morris Peterson**, Michigan State	SR	G/F	6	20	22	90.9
2 **C.J. Black**, Tennessee	SR	F	3	17	19	89.5
3 **Mateen Cleaves**, Michigan State	SR	G	6	17	21	81.0
4 **Shane Battier**, Duke	JR	F	3	20	25	80.0
Joseph Forte, North Carolina	FR	G	5	16	20	80.0

MINIMUM: 15 MADE

THREE-POINT FG PCT	CL	POS	G	3FG	3FGA	PCT
1 **Rimas Kaukenas**, Seton Hall	SR	G	3	8	14	57.1
2 **Michael Nurse**, Iowa State	SO	G	4	14	25	56.0
3 **Brett Nelson**, Florida	FR	G	6	14	27	51.8
4 **Desmond Mason**, Oklahoma State	SR	F	4	8	16	50.0
Jamaal Tinsley, Iowa State	JR	G	4	8	16	50.0
Earl Watson, UCLA	JR	G	3	7	14	50.0

MINIMUM: 6 MADE AND 3 GAMES

ASSISTS PER GAME	CL	POS	G	AST	APG
1 **Earl Watson**, UCLA	JR	G	3	33	11.0
2 **Doug Gottlieb**, Oklahoma State	SR	G	4	36	9.0
3 **Ed Cota**, North Carolina	SR	G	5	37	7.4
4 **Jason Hart**, Syracuse	SR	G	3	21	7.0
Vernon Jennings, Miami (FL)	SR	G/F	3	21	7.0

MINIMUM: 3 GAMES

REBOUNDS PER GAME	CL	POS	G	REB	RPG
1 **Eric Coley**, Tulsa	SR	F	4	43	10.8
2 **Brendan Haywood**, North Carolina	JR	C	5	48	9.6
3 **Marcus Fizer**, Iowa State	JR	F	4	36	9.0
Carlos Boozer, Duke	FR	F	3	27	9.0
5 **Mario Bland**, Miami (FL)	SR	F	3	26	8.7
Jerome Moiso, UCLA	SO	F/C	3	26	8.7

MINIMUM: 3 GAMES

BLOCKED SHOTS PER GAME	CL	POS	G	BLK	BPG
1 **Shane Battier**, Duke	JR	F	3	13	4.3
2 **Samuel Dalembert**, Seton Hall	FR	C	3	10	3.3
3 **Brendan Haywood**, North Carolina	JR	C	5	15	3.0
Etan Thomas, Syracuse	SR	F	3	9	3.0
5 **Stromile Swift**, LSU	SO	F	3	8	2.7

MINIMUM: 3 GAMES

STEALS PER GAME	CL	POS	G	STL	SPG
1 **Mike Kelley**, Wisconsin	JR	G	5	19	3.8
2 **Eric Coley**, Tulsa	SR	F	4	14	3.5
3 **Jason Williams**, Duke	FR	G	3	9	3.0
4 **Jamaal Tinsley**, Iowa State	JR	G	4	11	2.8
5 **Earl Watson**, UCLA	JR	G	3	8	2.7

MINIMUM: 3 GAMES

TEAM LEADERS

SCORING	G	PTS	PPG
1 **Florida**	6	473	78.8
2 **Iowa State**	4	311	77.8
3 **Duke**	3	229	76.3
4 **UCLA**	3	226	75.3
5 **Gonzaga**	3	225	75.0
6 **Miami (FL)**	3	221	73.7
7 **Oklahoma State**	4	294	73.5
8 **Tulsa**	4	293	73.3
9 **Michigan State**	6	430	71.7
10 **Seton Hall**	3	205	68.3

MINIMUM: 3 GAMES

FG PCT	G	FG	FGA	PCT
1 **Iowa State**	4	110	214	51.4
2 **Gonzaga**	3	77	159	48.4
3 **Michigan State**	6	146	307	47.6
4 **UCLA**	3	86	181	47.5
5 **Miami (FL)**	3	72	157	45.9

MINIMUM: 3 GAMES

3-PT FG PCT	G	3FG	3FGA	PCT
1 **Miami (FL)**	3	23	43	53.5
2 **UCLA**	3	25	62	40.3
3 **Iowa State**	4	27	68	39.7
4 **Oklahoma State**	4	23	58	39.7
5 **Michigan State**	6	43	110	39.1

MINIMUM: 3 GAMES

FT PCT	G	FT	FTA	PCT
1 **Tennessee**	3	60	76	79.0
2 **Michigan State**	6	95	121	78.5
3 **Iowa State**	4	64	83	77.1
Duke	3	64	83	77.1
5 **Syracuse**	3	30	39	76.9

MINIMUM: 3 GAMES

AST/TO RATIO	G	AST	TO	RAT
1 **Oklahoma State**	4	75	51	1.47
2 **Duke**	3	36	30	1.20
3 **Wisconsin**	5	65	56	1.16
4 **Michigan State**	6	76	66	1.15
5 **Gonzaga**	3	50	44	1.14

MINIMUM: 3 GAMES

REBOUNDS	G	REB	RPG
1 **Duke**	3	126	42.0
2 **North Carolina**	5	203	40.6
3 **Tulsa**	4	161	40.3
4 **Miami (FL)**	3	118	39.3
5 **Iowa State**	4	156	39.0

MINIMUM: 3 GAMES

BLOCKS	G	BLK	BPG
1 **Duke**	3	20	6.7
2 **North Carolina**	5	30	6.0
3 **UCLA**	3	17	5.7
4 **Seton Hall**	3	14	4.7
5 **Tennessee**	3	13	4.3

MINIMUM: 3 GAMES

STEALS	G	STL	SPG
1 **Tulsa**	4	41	10.3
2 **UCLA**	3	29	9.7
3 **Wisconsin**	5	42	8.4
4 **Florida**	6	43	7.2
5 **Syracuse**	3	21	7.0
Tennessee	3	21	7.0

MINIMUM: 3 GAMES

ALL-TOURNAMENT TEAM

PLAYER	CL	POS	HT	SCHOOL	RPG	APG	PPG
Mateen Cleaves*	SR	G	6-2	Michigan State	2.0	4.5	14.2
Charlie Bell	JR	G	6-3	Michigan State	6.0	2.8	7.2
A.J. Granger	SR	F	6-9	Michigan State	4.3	1.7	11.8
Udonis Haslem	SO	F	6-8	Florida	4.3	1.0	14.2
Morris Peterson	SR	G/F	6-6	Michigan State	4.3	1.2	17.5

ALL-REGIONAL TEAMS

EAST

PLAYER	CL	POS	HT	SCHOOL	RPG	APG	PPG
Mike Miller*	SO	F	6-8	Florida	9.0	1.8	14.8
Shane Battier	JR	F	6-8	Duke	7.3	2.3	17.7
Udonis Haslem	SO	F	6-8	Florida	4.8	1.5	12.0
Fredrik Jonzen	SO	F	6-10	Oklahoma State	8.5	1.3	15.8
Brett Nelson	FR	G	6-3	Florida	2.3	3.5	11.0

MIDWEST

PLAYER	CL	POS	HT	SCHOOL	RPG	APG	PPG
Morris Peterson*	SR	G/F	6-6	Michigan State	4.3	0.5	16.0
Mateen Cleaves	SR	G	6-2	Michigan State	1.5	5.5	14.0
Marcus Fizer	JR	F	6-8	Iowa State	9.0	0.8	20.0
A.J. Granger	SR	F	6-9	Michigan State	2.5	2.0	12.8
Andre Hutson	JR	F	6-8	Michigan State	7.0	1.8	12.8
Jamaal Tinsley	JR	G	6-3	Iowa State	5.5	6.5	17.5

SOUTH

PLAYER	CL	POS	HT	SCHOOL	RPG	APG	PPG
Joseph Forte*	FR	G	6-4	North Carolina	6.5	1.5	20.0
Jason Capel	SO	F	6-8	North Carolina	6.5	3.0	9.8
Eric Coley	SR	F	6-5	Tulsa	10.8	3.0	11.0
Ed Cota	SR	G	6-1	North Carolina	5.5	7.3	7.3
Brandon Kurtz	SR	C	6-10	Tulsa	7.5	1.3	9.0

WEST

PLAYER	CL	POS	HT	SCHOOL	RPG	APG	PPG
Jon Bryant*	SR	G	6-2	Wisconsin	2.3	1.3	16.8
Brian Cardinal	SR	F	6-8	Purdue	6.3	2.3	12.3
Carson Cunningham	JR	G	6-1	Purdue	2.3	3.8	11.3
Mike Kelley	JR	G	6-3	Wisconsin	2.3	5.0	5.8
Andy Kowske	JR	F	6-8	Wisconsin	9.5	0.3	11.5
Mike Robinson	SR	F	6-6	Purdue	5.3	3.3	8.0

* MOST OUTSTANDING PLAYER

2000 NCAA TOURNAMENT BOX SCORES

61-48 (Sweet 16)

	1H	2H
Wisconsin	22	39
LSU	14	34

WISCONSIN	MIN	FG	3FG	FT	REB	A	ST	BL	PF	TP
Jon Bryant	32	6-14	3-9	1-2	3	4	0	0	1	16
Andy Kowske	31	3-5	0-0	2-2	4	0	1	1	3	8
Maurice Linton	25	4-8	0-0	0-0	3	0	2	0	2	8
Mark Vershaw	30	2-8	1-2	2-2	5	3	1	0	3	7
Kirk Penney	12	2-6	1-4	0-0	0	0	0	0	0	5
Roy Boone	10	0-1	0-0	5-8	3	2	0	0	1	5
Mike Kelley	35	1-2	0-0	1-2	4	5	5	0	3	3
Duany Duany	9	1-3	1-3	0-0	1	0	0	0	0	3
Charlie Wills	9	1-6	0-1	0-0	2	0	1	0	4	2
Travon Davis	5	0-1	0-0	2-2	0	1	0	0	0	2
Julian Swartz	1	1-1	0-0	0-0	0	0	1	0	0	2
Erik Faust	1	0-0	0-0	0-0	0	0	0	0	0	0
TOTALS	200	21-55	6-19	13-18	25	15	11	1	17	61
Percentages		38.2	31.6	72.2						

Coach: Dick Bennett

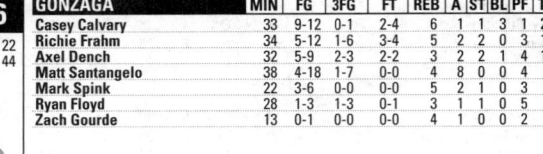

LSU	MIN	FG	3FG	FT	REB	A	ST	BL	PF	TP
Stromile Swift	37	3-5	1-1	5-7	10	2	1	0	2	12
Jabari Smith	33	5-12	1-3	1-1	7	0	0	2	3	12
Jermaine Williams	17	3-4	1-1	0-0	2	0	2	0	4	7
Brian Beshara	33	2-7	1-5	0-0	8	2	3	0	2	5
Lamont Roland	28	2-7	0-2	1-2	4	2	0	0	2	5
Torris Bright	26	1-7	0-6	2-2	2	0	1	0	4	4
Collis Temple	17	1-3	1-3	0-0	3	0	0	0	1	3
Ronald DuPree	5	0-1	0-0	0-0	0	0	0	0	0	0
Brad Bridgewater	4	0-1	0-0	0-0	0	0	0	0	0	0
TOTALS	200	17-47	5-21	9-12	36	6	7	2	18	48
Percentages		36.2	23.8	75.0						

Coach: John Brady

Officials: Jo Cahill, Larry Rose, Verne Harris
Technicals: None
Attendance: 16,004

75-66 (Sweet 16)

	1H	2H
Purdue	35	40
Gonzaga	22	44

PURDUE	MIN	FG	3FG	FT	REB	A	ST	BL	PF	TP
Jaraan Cornell	24	5-13	2-7	6-8	7	2	0	0	4	18
Carson Cunningham	30	3-6	2-5	6-8	3	3	0	0	1	14
Greg McQuay	28	5-7	0-0	1-3	7	0	1	0	3	11
Brian Cardinal	34	3-8	0-3	4-6	8	5	1	0	3	10
Mike Robinson	35	4-10	0-0	0-0	4	3	0	0	0	8
Rodney Smith	13	1-3	0-1	3-4	6	0	0	1	1	5
Mayhard Lewis	19	2-6	0-3	0-1	3	0	1	0	0	4
Chad Kerkhof	10	1-1	1-1	0-0	2	2	1	0	1	3
Kenneth Lowe	1	1-1	0-0	0-0	0	0	0	0	0	2
John Allison	5	0-1	0-0	0-0	0	0	0	0	3	0
Adam Wetzel	1	0-0	0-0	0-0	0	0	0	0	0	0
TOTALS	200	25-56	5-20	20-30	40	15	4	1	16	75
Percentages		44.6	25.0	66.7						

Coach: Gene Keady

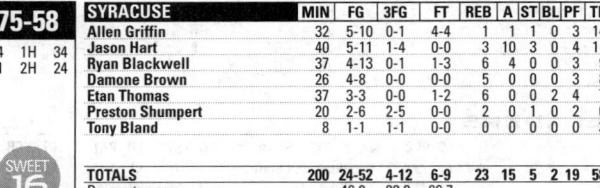

GONZAGA	MIN	FG	3FG	FT	REB	A	ST	BL	PF	TP
Casey Calvary	33	9-12	0-1	2-4	6	1	1	3	1	20
Richie Frahm	34	5-12	1-6	3-4	5	2	2	0	3	14
Axel Dench	32	5-9	2-3	2-2	3	2	2	1	4	14
Matt Santangelo	38	4-18	1-7	0-0	4	8	0	0	4	9
Mark Spink	22	3-6	0-0	0-0	5	2	1	0	3	6
Ryan Floyd	28	1-3	1-3	0-1	3	1	1	0	5	3
Zach Gourde	13	0-1	0-0	0-0	4	1	0	0	2	0
TOTALS	200	27-61	5-20	7-11	30	17	7	4	22	66
Percentages		44.3	25.0	63.6						

Coach: Mark Few

Officials: Joh Clougherty, Ed Corbett, Mike Thibodeaux
Technicals: None
Attendance: 16,004

75-58 (Sweet 16)

	1H	2H
Michigan State	24	51
Syracuse	34	24

MICHIGAN STATE	MIN	FG	3FG	FT	REB	A	ST	BL	PF	TP
Morris Peterson	34	6-10	5-9	4-4	3	2	0	1	2	21
A.J. Granger	33	7-11	2-4	3-3	4	3	0	2	1	19
Charlie Bell	29	3-7	2-4	4-4	6	4	1	0	1	12
Andre Hutson	34	5-7	0-0	1-4	5	1	1	0	2	11
Mateen Cleaves	38	4-12	2-6	0-0	1	7	1	0	1	10
Mike Chappell	15	0-1	0-0	1-2	4	0	0	0	2	1
Aloysius Anagonye	4	0-0	0-0	1-2	1	0	0	0	4	1
Jason Richardson	11	0-1	0-0	0-0	3	0	0	0	0	0
David Thomas	2	0-0	0-0	0-0	1	0	0	0	0	0
TOTALS	200	25-49	11-23	14-19	28	17	3	3	13	75
Percentages		51.0	47.8	73.7						

Coach: Tom Izzo

SYRACUSE	MIN	FG	3FG	FT	REB	A	ST	BL	PF	TP
Allen Griffin	32	5-10	0-1	4-4	1	1	1	0	3	14
Jason Hart	40	5-11	1-4	0-0	3	10	3	0	4	11
Ryan Blackwell	37	4-13	0-1	1-3	6	4	0	0	3	9
Damone Brown	26	4-8	0-0	0-0	5	0	0	0	3	8
Etan Thomas	37	3-3	0-0	1-2	6	0	0	2	4	7
Preston Shumpert	20	2-6	2-5	0-0	2	0	1	0	2	6
Tony Bland	8	1-1	1-1	0-0	0	0	0	0	0	3
TOTALS	200	24-52	4-12	6-9	23	15	5	2	19	58
Percentages		46.2	33.3	66.7						

Coach: Jim Boeheim

Officials: Scott Thornley, Bob Sitov, Rick Hartzell
Technicals: None
Attendance: 21,214

80-56 (Sweet 16)

	1H	2H
Iowa State	40	40
UCLA	28	28

IOWA STATE	MIN	FG	3FG	FT	REB	A	ST	BL	PF	TP
Michael Nurse	38	6-9	4-5	0-0	3	1	2	0	2	16
Marcus Fizer	33	7-15	0-0	2-2	9	1	0	2	3	16
Stevie Johnson	33	6-11	0-0	4-7	8	0	1	0	1	16
Jamaal Tinsley	35	5-14	1-2	3-4	9	11	4	0	1	14
Kantrail Horton	36	3-7	1-3	2-2	3	3	1	0	0	9
Brandon Hawkins	8	2-2	0-0	1-2	1	1	1	0	1	5
Martin Rancik	7	2-2	0-0	0-0	2	0	0	0	3	4
Richard Evans	4	0-0	0-0	0-0	1	1	0	1	1	0
Paul Shirley	4	0-0	0-0	0-0	4	0	0	0	2	0
Brad Davis	1	0-0	0-0	0-0	0	0	0	0	0	0
Thomas Watkins	1	0-0	0-0	0-0	0	0	0	0	0	0
TOTALS	200	31-60	6-10	12-17	40	18	9	3	14	80
Percentages		51.7	60.0	70.6						

Coach: Larry Eustachy

UCLA	MIN	FG	3FG	FT	REB	A	ST	BL	PF	TP
Jerome Moiso	31	5-12	0-0	5-5	10	0	0	3	2	15
Earl Watson	33	3-7	2-5	0-0	2	5	0	1	5	8
Jason Kapono	30	3-11	1-4	1-2	4	3	0	0	4	8
Jaron Rush	27	3-10	0-5	0-0	6	0	3	1	0	6
Dan Gadzuric	17	3-6	0-0	0-0	3	0	0	3	2	6
Ryan Bailey	8	2-5	0-1	2-2	1	0	0	0	1	6
Billy Knight	11	1-1	1-1	1-2	1	0	0	0	1	4
Rico Hines	7	1-1	0-0	0-0	2	0	1	0	0	2
Matt Barnes	19	0-6	0-1	1-2	1	0	2	0	2	1
Ray Young	10	0-2	0-0	0-0	1	0	0	0	1	0
Sean Farnham	5	0-1	0-0	0-0	0	0	1	0	0	0
Brandon Brooks	2	0-0	0-0	0-0	0	0	0	0	0	0
TOTALS	200	21-62	4-17	10-13	31	8	7	8	18	56
Percentages		33.9	23.5	76.9						

Coach: Steve Lavin

Officials: Ted Valentine, Donnee Gray, Karl Hess
Technicals: None
Attendance: 21,214

87-78 (Sweet 16)

	1H	2H
Florida	40	47
Duke	33	45

FLORIDA	MIN	FG	3FG	FT	REB	A	ST	BL	PF	TP
Brett Nelson	28	6-12	3-5	0-0	2	4	1	0	2	15
Udonis Haslem	27	5-8	0-0	3-5	8	4	2	1	2	13
Teddy Dupay	21	3-9	2-4	4-6	1	1	0	0	1	12
Mike Miller	30	2-9	0-2	6-8	9	4	1	1	4	10
Brent Wright	28	3-11	0-1	4-4	8	3	2	0	2	10
Matt Bonner	11	4-5	0-1	0-0	1	0	0	0	2	8
Justin Hamilton	13	3-3	1-1	0-0	0	0	1	0	1	7
Major Parker	12	1-2	1-1	3-4	0	0	1	0	0	6
Donnell Harvey	12	2-2	0-0	0-0	1	1	0	1	3	4
Kenyan Weaks	18	1-3	0-0	0-0	1	4	0	0	3	2
TOTALS	200	30-64	7-15	20-27	31	21	8	3	20	87
Percentages		46.9	46.7	74.1						

Coach: Billy Donovan

DUKE	MIN	FG	3FG	FT	REB	A	ST	BL	PF	TP
Shane Battier	39	6-11	1-3	7-9	9	1	1	4	1	20
Chris Carrawell	37	6-14	1-3	3-3	6	3	3	0	4	16
Jason Williams	38	6-20	1-9	0-1	4	7	3	0	5	13
Nate James	32	6-12	0-3	0-1	8	0	0	0	3	12
Carlos Boozer	21	3-5	0-0	5-8	9	1	0	1	5	11
Mike Dunleavy Jr.	21	1-4	0-1	2-3	4	0	0	0	3	4
Matt Christensen	10	1-2	0-0	0-0	0	0	0	0	1	2
Andre Buckner	1	0-0	0-0	0-0	0	0	0	0	0	0
Nick Horvath	1	0-0	0-0	0-0	0	0	0	0	0	0
TOTALS	200	29-68	3-19	17-25	40	12	7	5	22	78
Percentages		42.6	15.8	68.0						

Coach: Mike Krzyzewski

Officials: Jody Silvester, Eddie Jackson, Mark Whitehead
Technicals: None
Attendance: 30,681

68-66 (Sweet 16)

	1H	2H
Oklahoma State	35	33
Seton Hall	36	30

OKLAHOMA STATE	MIN	FG	3FG	FT	REB	A	ST	BL	PF	TP
Desmond Mason	39	5-13	2-3	4-4	6	2	1	1	2	16
Fredrik Jonzen	35	6-13	0-0	3-4	7	1	0	2	2	15
Brian Montonati	19	7-12	0-0	1-4	3	0	2	0	4	15
Glendon Alexander	18	2-7	1-4	4-6	0	1	0	0	2	9
Joe Adkins	29	1-8	0-3	5-5	5	2	0	1	1	7
Doug Gottlieb	34	1-4	0-1	0-0	7	12	0	0	2	2
Alex Webber	15	1-2	0-0	0-0	1	0	0	0	0	2
Andre Williams	11	1-2	0-0	0-0	5	1	0	0	1	2
TOTALS	200	24-61	3-11	17-23	34	19	3	4	14	68
Percentages		39.3	27.3	73.9						

Coach: Eddie Sutton

SETON HALL	MIN	FG	3FG	FT	REB	A	ST	BL	PF	TP
Rimas Kaukenas	40	5-15	3-6	4-4	3	3	1	1	4	17
Darius Lane	40	7-24	2-18	0-0	2	1	0	0	1	16
Ty Shine	40	4-16	2-10	1-2	7	3	0	0	4	11
Charles Manga	12	3-3	0-0	1-1	3	0	0	0	4	7
Samuel Dalembert	24	3-4	0-0	0-0	10	0	0	1	3	6
Greg Morton	32	2-3	0-0	0-1	7	0	0	1	1	4
Al Harris	6	1-2	0-0	2-2	4	1	1	0	0	4
Kevin Wilkins	6	0-2	0-0	1-2	1	0	0	0	1	1
TOTALS	200	25-69	7-34	9-12	37	8	2	3	18	66
Percentages		36.2	20.6	75.0						

Coach: Tommy Amaker

Officials: Ted Hillary, Mike Wood, Steve Welmer
Technicals: None
Attendance: 30,681

NORTH CAROLINA	MIN	FG	3FG	FT	REB	A	ST	BL	PF	TP
Joseph Forte	36	8-13	2-5	4-4	5	2	1	1	2	22
Ed Cota	39	4-9	0-1	3-5	7	5	1	0	4	11
Brendan Haywood	26	5-10	0-0	1-4	5	0	0	4	5	11
Kris Lang	28	5-12	0-0	0-0	3	0	1	2	3	10
Jason Capel	38	3-9	1-2	2-2	5	5	2	0	1	9
Julius Peppers	20	2-3	0-0	2-2	6	0	0	2	4	6
Max Owens	12	2-2	1-1	0-0	0	0	1	0	0	5
Terrence Newby	1	0-0	0-0	0-0	0	0	0	0	0	0
TOTALS	**200**	**29-58**	**4-9**	**12-17**	**31**	**12**	**6**	**9**	**19**	**74**
Percentages		50.0	44.4	70.6						
Coach: Bill Guthridge										

74-69

36	1H	39
38	2H	30

SWEET 16

TENNESSEE	MIN	FG	3FG	FT	REB	A	ST	BL	PF	TP
C.J. Black	21	6-7	1-1	4-4	5	0	1	1	4	17
Vincent Yarbrough	38	4-11	1-5	4-4	3	3	1	0	3	13
Ron Slay	24	4-11	0-3	4-4	7	1	2	0	1	12
Isiah Victor	21	3-8	1-1	4-6	4	1	3	2	2	11
Jon Higgins	35	3-7	2-5	0-0	4	0	0	0	1	8
Tony Harris	32	1-10	1-6	1-2	4	4	0	0	3	4
Harris Walker	17	0-3	0-0	2-2	3	1	1	1	0	2
Charles Hathaway	12	0-2	0-0	2-2	4	1	1	0	3	2
TOTALS	**200**	**21-59**	**6-21**	**21-24**	**34**	**11**	**9**	**4**	**17**	**69**
Percentages		35.6	28.6	87.5						
Coach: Jerry Green										

Officials: David Hall, Bob Donato, Michael Kitts
Technicals: None
Attendance: 16,731

TULSA	MIN	FG	3FG	FT	REB	A	ST	BL	PF	TP
Eric Coley	34	7-11	0-1	3-4	9	2	4	3	0	17
Brandon Kurtz	33	5-8	0-0	7-12	10	3	3	0	3	17
Greg Harrington	27	4-6	2-3	4-6	4	0	0	0	4	14
Marcus Hill	30	4-9	0-2	5-7	5	5	1	0	3	13
Tony Heard	31	3-9	2-7	3-4	3	2	0	0	4	11
David Shelton	19	2-6	0-1	2-4	3	0	1	0	4	6
Dante Swanson	18	1-6	0-3	0-0	1	0	1	0	0	2
Kevin Johnson	4	0-0	0-0	0-0	0	0	0	0	0	0
Deangelo McDaniel	4	0-1	0-0	0-0	2	0	0	0	1	0
TOTALS	**200**	**26-56**	**4-17**	**24-37**	**37**	**12**	**10**	**3**	**19**	**80**
Percentages		46.4	23.5	64.9						
Coach: Bill Self										

80-71

31	1H	25
49	2H	46

SWEET 16

MIAMI (FL)	MIN	FG	3FG	FT	REB	A	ST	BL	PF	TP
Vernon Jennings	37	5-8	2-3	5-6	4	7	3	0	4	17
Mario Bland	31	5-15	1-2	6-8	9	0	0	0	4	17
Johnny Hemsley	34	4-10	3-7	2-2	4	0	0	0	5	13
John Salmons	35	4-8	1-1	1-2	5	2	1	0	2	10
James Jones	10	2-2	2-2	0-0	2	1	1	1	1	6
LeRoy Hurd	17	2-3	1-2	0-1	4	0	1	0	2	5
Dwayne Wimbley	15	1-5	0-0	1-2	3	0	0	1	2	3
Elton Tyler	18	0-6	0-0	0-0	2	0	2	0	4	0
Paulo Coelho	2	0-0	0-0	0-0	1	0	0	0	1	0
Tarik El-Bassiouni	1	0-0	0-0	0-0	0	0	0	0	1	0
TOTALS	**200**	**23-57**	**10-17**	**15-21**	**34**	**10**	**8**	**2**	**26**	**71**
Percentages		40.4	58.8	71.4						
Coach: Leonard Hamilton										

Officials: Gerald Boudreaux, Duke Edsall, Mike Sanzere
Technicals: None
Attendance: 16,731

WISCONSIN	MIN	FG	3FG	FT	REB	A	ST	BL	PF	TP
Jon Bryant	35	6-12	5-9	1-2	2	1	1	0	1	18
Andy Kowske	27	6-10	0-0	2-2	8	0	0	0	4	14
Roy Boone	16	3-6	0-0	6-10	2	2	2	1	2	12
Mark Vershaw	30	2-9	0-2	3-6	7	3	1	0	1	7
Mike Kelley	36	2-3	0-0	1-4	1	5	1	0	2	5
Maurice Linton	23	2-3	1-2	0-0	1	2	0	0	3	5
Duany Duany	8	1-2	1-2	0-0	3	1	1	0	3	3
Charlie Wills	16	0-1	0-0	0-0	5	0	0	0	3	0
Travon Davis	6	0-0	0-0	0-0	1	0	0	0	2	0
Kirk Penney	3	0-1	0-1	0-0	0	0	0	0	0	0
TOTALS	**200**	**22-47**	**7-16**	**13-24**	**30**	**14**	**6**	**1**	**21**	**64**
Percentages		46.8	43.8	54.2						
Coach: Dick Bennett										

64-60

31	1H	28
33	2H	32

ELITE 8

PURDUE	MIN	FG	3FG	FT	REB	A	ST	BL	PF	TP
Carson Cunningham	31	4-12	3-8	2-2	2	2	1	0	2	13
Brian Cardinal	27	4-8	2-4	3-5	4	1	1	0	4	13
Mike Robinson	35	4-10	0-0	4-5	1	4	0	0	3	12
Greg McQuay	31	4-5	0-0	2-3	12	0	0	2	3	10
Mayhard Lewis	18	3-5	1-2	0-0	5	1	0	0	2	7
Jaraan Cornell	32	1-9	1-7	0-2	2	1	1	1	4	3
John Allison	3	1-1	0-0	0-0	0	0	0	0	0	2
Rodney Smith	15	0-3	0-2	0-0	1	1	0	0	1	0
Chad Kerkhof	7	0-0	0-0	0-0	0	0	1	0	2	0
Kenneth Lowe	1	0-0	0-0	0-0	0	0	0	0	0	0
TOTALS	**200**	**21-53**	**7-23**	**11-17**	**27**	**10**	**4**	**3**	**21**	**60**
Percentages		39.6	30.4	64.7						
Coach: Gene Keady										

Officials: Dick Paparo, Tony Greene, Tim Higgins
Technicals: None
Attendance: 16,004

MICHIGAN STATE	MIN	FG	3FG	FT	REB	A	ST	BL	PF	TP
A.J. Granger	37	5-8	2-4	6-6	0	2	0	0	2	18
Morris Peterson	36	5-13	1-3	7-7	7	0	1	1	3	18
Andre Hutson	24	6-9	0-0	5-5	11	2	0	0	4	17
Mateen Cleaves	35	4-12	1-4	1-2	1	2	2	2	4	10
Charlie Bell	26	3-11	1-6	2-2	5	2	3	0	4	9
Mike Chappell	15	1-2	0-1	0-0	0	1	0	0	0	2
Aloysius Anagonye	8	0-0	0-0	1-2	1	0	0	0	4	1
Jason Richardson	13	0-1	0-1	0-0	2	0	0	0	1	0
David Thomas	3	0-0	0-0	0-0	0	0	0	0	1	0
Adam Ballinger	1	0-0	0-0	0-0	0	0	0	0	0	0
Mat Ishbia	1	0-0	0-0	0-0	0	0	0	0	0	0
Brandon Smith	1	0-0	0-0	0-0	0	0	0	0	0	0
TOTALS	**200**	**24-56**	**5-19**	**22-24**	**27**	**9**	**6**	**3**	**23**	**75**
Percentages		42.9	26.3	91.7						
Coach: Tom Izzo										

75-64

34	1H	31
41	2H	33

ELITE 8

IOWA STATE	MIN	FG	3FG	FT	REB	A	ST	BL	PF	TP
Jamaal Tinsley	34	5-13	3-8	5-7	3	2	0	3	4	18
Michael Nurse	40	5-11	5-9	2-2	4	1	0	0	5	17
Marcus Fizer	36	6-15	1-6	2-2	4	1	0	0	4	15
Kantrail Horton	32	1-5	0-3	4-4	6	2	0	0	2	6
Paul Shirley	16	1-3	0-0	2-2	4	2	0	0	5	4
Stevie Johnson	29	1-1	0-0	0-1	5	0	0	0	0	2
Brandon Hawkins	13	1-2	0-0	0-0	7	0	1	0	2	2
TOTALS	**200**	**20-50**	**9-26**	**15-18**	**33**	**8**	**1**	**3**	**22**	**64**
Percentages		40.0	34.6	83.3						
Coach: Larry Eustachy										

Officials: Curtis Shaw, Frank Bosone, Lonnie Dixon
Technicals: Iowa State (bench, 2), Michigan State (bench)
Attendance: 21,214

FLORIDA	MIN	FG	3FG	FT	REB	A	ST	BL	PF	TP
Mike Miller	30	4-8	2-6	4-6	5	0	2	0	2	14
Donnell Harvey	22	4-6	0-0	2-2	6	1	1	1	3	10
Udonis Haslem	21	4-7	0-0	2-2	4	0	0	1	2	10
Brent Wright	28	2-5	1-2	4-6	2	3	0	2	1	9
Brett Nelson	21	3-7	1-2	2-2	3	4	2	0	1	9
Kenyan Weaks	16	3-6	0-2	3-4	3	1	2	0	1	9
Justin Hamilton	21	4-6	0-2	0-0	5	0	1	0	1	8
Teddy Dupay	23	1-4	1-3	2-2	1	0	0	1	0	5
Matt Bonner	10	1-1	1-1	0-0	1	1	0	0	0	3
Major Parker	8	0-1	0-0	0-0	0	0	0	1	2	0
TOTALS	**200**	**26-51**	**6-18**	**19-24**	**29**	**11**	**8**	**5**	**14**	**77**
Percentages		51.0	33.3	79.2						
Coach: Billy Donovan										

77-65

43	1H	31
34	2H	34

ELITE 8

OKLAHOMA STATE	MIN	FG	3FG	FT	REB	A	ST	BL	PF	TP
Fredrik Jonzen	24	6-9	0-0	2-2	7	2	0	0	2	14
Glendon Alexander	22	5-10	3-8	0-0	1	0	0	0	1	13
Joe Adkins	26	4-14	2-7	2-2	2	7	1	0	2	12
Desmond Mason	39	2-8	2-5	3-4	3	1	1	0	3	9
Brian Montonati	35	4-10	0-0	1-2	6	3	1	0	5	9
Andre Williams	13	2-4	0-0	0-0	4	0	1	2	4	4
Alex Webber	6	2-2	0-0	0-0	1	0	0	0	2	4
Doug Gottlieb	32	0-2	0-0	0-2	2	7	2	0	1	0
Zac Cazzelle	1	0-0	0-0	0-0	0	0	0	0	0	0
Jason Keep	1	0-0	0-0	0-0	0	0	0	0	0	0
Rodney Sooter	1	0-0	0-0	0-0	0	0	0	0	0	0
TOTALS	**200**	**25-59**	**7-20**	**8-12**	**26**	**20**	**6**	**2**	**20**	**65**
Percentages		42.4	35.0	66.7						
Coach: Eddie Sutton										

Officials: James Burr, Dick Cartmell, Dave Libbey
Technicals: Oklahoma State (bench)
Attendance: 30,388

NORTH CAROLINA	MIN	FG	3FG	FT	REB	A	ST	BL	PF	TP
Joseph Forte	39	10-17	1-7	7-8	8	1	1	0	2	28
Jason Capel	40	2-7	1-4	3-4	6	3	2	0	0	8
Brendan Haywood	32	4-10	0-0	0-2	8	1	1	3	3	8
Julius Peppers	30	2-4	0-0	2-2	8	2	2	0	3	6
Ed Cota	40	2-6	0-1	1-2	2	4	2	0	1	5
Kris Lang	18	2-6	0-0	0-1	3	0	0	0	1	4
Max Owens	1	0-0	0-0	0-0	0	0	0	0	1	0
TOTALS	**200**	**22-50**	**2-12**	**13-19**	**35**	**11**	**8**	**3**	**11**	**59**
Percentages		44.0	16.7	68.4						
Coach: Bill Guthridge										

59-55

30	1H	31
29	2H	24

ELITE 8

TULSA	MIN	FG	3FG	FT	REB	A	ST	BL	PF	TP
Dante Swanson	18	6-8	2-2	1-1	0	0	1	0	1	15
Marcus Hill	30	3-9	1-5	4-6	3	2	0	1	0	11
Brandon Kurtz	26	5-10	0-1	1-2	9	0	1	0	2	11
Tony Heard	33	3-8	2-6	0-0	3	2	3	0	2	8
Eric Coley	24	3-7	0-0	0-0	4	1	2	0	5	6
Greg Harrington	33	1-6	0-4	0-0	2	3	0	1	4	2
David Shelton	17	1-9	0-2	0-0	2	0	2	0	4	2
Kevin Johnson	8	0-1	0-0	0-0	1	1	0	0	1	0
Charlie Davis	6	0-0	0-0	0-0	1	0	0	1	0	0
Deangelo McDaniel	5	0-1	0-0	0-0	1	0	0	1	0	0
TOTALS	**200**	**22-59**	**5-20**	**6-9**	**26**	**9**	**9**	**4**	**19**	**55**
Percentages		37.3	25.0	66.7						
Coach: Bill Self										

Officials: Andre Pattillo, Tom O'Neill, Tom Eades
Technicals: None
Attendance: 16,731

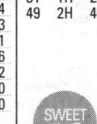

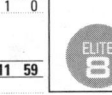

MICHIGAN STATE	MIN	FG	3FG	FT	REB	A	ST	BL	PF	TP
Morris Peterson	33	7-15	2-8	4-4	7	0	1	0	3	20
Mateen Cleaves	36	1-7	0-0	9-11	4	1	2	0	3	11
Andre Hutson	32	3-7	0-0	4-5	10	0	0	0	2	10
Mike Chappell	9	2-4	0-2	1-1	0	0	0	2	1	5
Charlie Bell	30	2-9	0-3	0-0	8	2	0	0	2	4
Aloysius Anagonye	12	1-1	0-0	0-0	2	0	0	0	2	2
A.J. Granger	32	0-3	0-1	1-2	7	1	0	0	4	1
Jason Richardson	10	0-0	0-0	0-0	0	0	0	0	1	0
Adam Ballinger	3	0-0	0-0	0-0	1	0	0	1	0	0
David Thomas	3	0-0	0-0	0-0	0	0	0	0	0	0
TOTALS	200	16-46	2-14	19-23	39	4	3	3	18	53
Percentages		34.8	14.3	82.6						

Coach: Tom Izzo

53-41

19 1H 17
34 2H 24

FINAL 4

WISCONSIN	MIN	FG	3FG	FT	REB	A	ST	BL	PF	TP
Roy Boone	25	6-9	1-1	5-6	3	0	0	0	2	18
Kirk Penney	14	2-3	2-3	0-0	2	0	0	0	0	6
Mark Vershaw	31	2-11	0-1	1-1	2	3	0	0	3	5
Travon Davis	10	1-1	1-1	1-2	2	1	0	0	2	4
Mike Kelley	30	1-2	0-1	0-0	7	3	2	0	3	2
Jon Bryant	27	1-5	0-3	0-0	1	1	0	0	3	2
Andy Kowske	20	1-2	0-0	0-2	0	0	0	4	4	2
Charlie Wills	19	1-4	0-1	0-0	1	0	0	0	2	2
Duany Duany	11	0-2	0-1	0-0	0	0	0	0	0	0
Maurice Linton	10	0-4	0-1	0-0	1	0	0	0	0	0
Erik Faust	1	0-0	0-0	0-0	0	0	0	0	0	0
Robert Smith	1	0-0	0-0	0-0	0	0	0	0	0	0
Julian Swartz	1	0-0	0-0	0-0	0	0	0	0	0	0
TOTALS	200	15-43	4-13	7-11	19	8	2	4	19	41
Percentages		34.9	30.8	63.6						

Coach: Dick Bennett

Officials: J
Clougherty,
Andre Patti
Tim Higgins
Technicals:
None
Attendance
43,116

FLORIDA	MIN	FG	3FG	FT	REB	A	ST	BL	PF	TP
Brett Nelson	22	5-10	2-6	1-2	6	4	0	0	2	13
Mike Miller	29	3-13	0-6	4-6	7	1	1	0	1	10
Udonis Haslem	20	5-7	0-0	0-0	5	0	0	0	4	10
Donnell Harvey	20	2-7	0-0	4-5	7	1	1	2	4	8
Kenyan Weaks	18	2-5	1-4	1-4	1	1	2	0	1	6
Major Parker	13	2-3	2-3	0-0	3	1	1	0	1	6
Brent Wright	20	1-3	1-1	2-4	7	2	1	0	3	5
Justin Hamilton	18	2-5	1-2	0-0	3	3	1	0	2	5
Teddy Dupay	26	1-8	0-6	2-2	2	0	1	0	2	4
Matt Bonner	14	2-3	0-0	0-0	2	0	1	0	3	4
TOTALS	200	25-64	7-28	14-23	43	13	9	2	23	71
Percentages		39.1	25.0	60.9						

Coach: Billy Donovan

71-59

37 1H 34
34 2H 25

FINAL 4

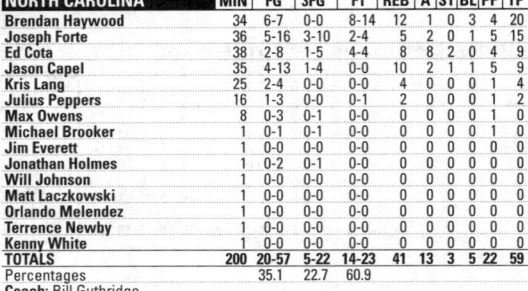

NORTH CAROLINA	MIN	FG	3FG	FT	REB	A	ST	BL	PF	TP
Brendan Haywood	34	6-7	0-0	8-14	12	1	0	3	4	20
Joseph Forte	36	5-16	3-10	2-4	5	2	0	1	5	15
Ed Cota	38	2-8	1-5	4-4	8	8	2	0	4	9
Jason Capel	35	4-13	1-4	0-0	10	2	1	1	5	9
Kris Lang	25	2-4	0-0	0-0	4	0	0	0	1	4
Julius Peppers	16	1-3	0-0	0-1	2	0	0	0	1	2
Max Owens	8	0-3	0-1	0-0	0	0	0	0	1	0
Michael Brooker	1	0-1	0-1	0-0	0	0	0	0	1	0
Jim Everett	1	0-0	0-0	0-0	0	0	0	0	0	0
Jonathan Holmes	1	0-2	0-1	0-0	0	0	0	0	0	0
Will Johnson	1	0-0	0-0	0-0	0	0	0	0	0	0
Matt Laczkowski	1	0-0	0-0	0-0	0	0	0	0	0	0
Orlando Melendez	1	0-0	0-0	0-0	0	0	0	0	0	0
Terrence Newby	1	0-0	0-0	0-0	0	0	0	0	0	0
Kenny White	1	0-0	0-0	0-0	0	0	0	0	0	0
TOTALS	200	20-57	5-22	14-23	41	13	3	5	22	59
Percentages		35.1	22.7	60.9						

Coach: Bill Guthridge

Officials:
Jody Silveste
Donnee Gray,
John Cahill
Technicals:
Florida (Parke
North Carolina
(Forte, Pepper
Attendance:
43,116

MICHIGAN STATE	MIN	FG	3FG	FT	REB	A	ST	BL	PF	TP
Morris Peterson	32	7-14	3-8	4-6	2	5	1	0	3	21
A.J. Granger	34	7-11	3-5	2-2	9	1	0	0	2	19
Mateen Cleaves	33	7-11	3-4	1-1	2	4	0	0	1	18
Charlie Bell	33	3-6	1-2	2-3	8	5	2	0	2	9
Jason Richardson	15	4-7	0-0	1-2	2	0	1	0	1	9
Andre Hutson	23	2-4	0-0	2-2	1	3	0	0	4	6
Mike Chappell	6	2-4	1-3	0-0	1	0	1	0	4	5
Adam Ballinger	6	1-1	0-0	0-0	0	0	0	0	2	2
Aloysius Anagonye	11	0-0	0-0	0-0	3	0	0	1	0	0
David Thomas	4	0-0	0-0	0-0	1	1	0	0	1	0
Steve Cherry	1	0-0	0-0	0-0	0	0	0	0	0	0
Mat Ishbia	1	0-1	0-0	0-0	0	0	0	0	0	0
Brandon Smith	1	0-0	0-0	0-0	0	0	0	0	0	0
TOTALS	200	33-59	11-22	12-16	29	19	5	1	20	89
Percentages		55.9	50.0	75.0						

Coach: Tom Izzo

89-76

43 1H 32
46 2H 44

NCAA FINAL 2000

FLORIDA	MIN	FG	3FG	FT	REB	A	ST	BL	PF	TP
Udonis Haslem	28	10-12	0-0	7-7	2	0	0	1	4	27
Brent Wright	29	5-8	0-1	3-5	10	4	1	0	4	13
Brett Nelson	26	4-10	3-6	0-0	4	3	2	0	1	11
Mike Miller	31	2-5	1-2	5-6	3	2	0	0	0	10
Donnell Harvey	16	3-11	0-0	3-4	6	0	0	1	2	9
Kenyan Weaks	22	1-3	1-1	0-0	1	1	2	0	2	3
Major Parker	12	1-3	1-3	0-0	0	2	0	0	2	3
Teddy Dupay	15	0-4	0-2	0-0	0	1	0	0	2	0
Justin Hamilton	14	0-1	0-1	0-0	0	0	0	0	1	0
Matt Bonner	7	0-3	0-2	0-0	3	0	0	0	1	0
TOTALS	200	26-60	6-18	18-22	29	13	5	2	19	76
Percentages		43.3	33.3	81.8						

Coach: Billy Donovan

Officials: James
Burr, Gerald
Boudreaux,
David Hall
Technicals:
None
Attendance:
43,116

National Invitation Tournament (NIT)

First Round: Siena d. Massachusetts 66-65, Penn State d. Princeton 55-41, Kent State d. Rutgers 73-62, Villanova d. Delaware 72-63, Notre Dame d. Michigan 75-65, Xavier d. Marquette 67-63, BYU d. Bowling Green 81-54, Southern Illinois d. Colorado 94-92, NC State d. Tulane 64-60, Arizona State d. New Mexico State 83-77, SW Missouri State d. SMU 77-64, Mississippi d. Charlotte 62-45, Wake Forest d. Vanderbilt 83-68, New Mexico d. South Florida 64-58, Georgetown d. Virginia 115-111 (3OT), California d. Long Beach State 70-66

Second Round: Penn State d. Siena 105-103, Kent State d. Villanova 81-67, Notre Dame d. Xavier 76-64, BYU d. Southern Illinois 82-57, NC State d. Arizona State 60-57, Mississippi d. SW Missouri State 70-48, Wake Forest d. New Mexico 72-65, California d. Georgetown 60-49

Third Round: Penn State d. Kent State 81-74, Notre Dame d. BYU 64-52, NC State d. Mississippi 77-54, Wake Forest d. California 76-59

Semifinals: Notre Dame d. Penn State 73-52, Wake Forest d. NC State 62-59

Championship: Wake Forest d. Notre Dame 71-61

Third place: Penn State d. NC State 74-72

MVP: Robert O'Kelley, Wake Forest

2000-01: Dance Fever

In 2001, the Big Dance got a little bigger—not to mention wilder. The NCAA added another team and one more game—an opening round "play-in" between teams seeded No. 64 and 65. Northwestern State (La.) beat Winthrop, 71-67, for the opportunity to lose to No. 1-seed Illinois, 96-54, in the first round. The extra game must have shaken the Tournament's balance, because 13 of the 32 first-round games were won by the lower-seeded team. Among the notable upsets: Hampton (No. 15) over Iowa State (2), 58-57; Indiana State (13) over Oklahoma (4), 70-68; Kent State (13) over Indiana (4), 77-73; Gonzaga (12) over Virginia (5), 86-85; Utah State (12) over Ohio State (5), 77-68.

Even with the early turmoil, the Final Four was filled with familiar names: Arizona, Michigan State, Maryland and overall No. 1-seed Duke—which ultimately beat Arizona, 82-72, for the title. Duke's Shane Battier was the Tournament MOP after his 18-point, 11-rebound Final. Battier was also Naismith Player of the Year and the sixth pick in the NBA draft (Memphis Grizzlies).

Major Conference Standings

America East

	Conference			Overall		
	W	L	PCT	W	L	PCT
Hofstra ⊕	16	2	.889	26	5	.839
Delaware	14	4	.778	20	10	.667
Drexel	12	6	.667	15	12	.556
Maine	10	8	.556	18	11	.621
Boston U.	9	9	.500	14	14	.500
Northeastern	8	10	.444	10	19	.345
Towson	7	11	.389	12	17	.414
Vermont	7	11	.389	12	17	.414
New Hampshire	6	12	.333	7	21	.250
Hartford	1	17	.056	4	24	.143

Tournament: **Hofstra d. Delaware 68-54**
Tournament MVP: **Roberto Gittens**, Hofstra

ACC

	Conference			Overall		
	W	L	PCT	W	L	PCT
Duke ⊕	13	3	.813	35	4	.897
North Carolina ○	13	3	.813	26	7	.788
Maryland ○	10	6	.625	25	11	.694
Virginia ○	9	7	.563	20	9	.690
Wake Forest ○	8	8	.500	19	11	.633
Georgia Tech ○	8	8	.500	17	13	.567
NC State	5	11	.313	13	16	.448
Florida State	4	12	.250	9	21	.300
Clemson	2	14	.125	12	19	.387

Tournament: **Duke d. North Carolina 79-53**
Tournament MVP: **Shane Battier**, Duke

Atlantic 10

	Conference			Overall		
	W	L	PCT	W	L	PCT
Saint Joseph's ○	14	2	.875	26	7	.788
Xavier ○	12	4	.750	21	8	.724
Temple ⊕	12	4	.750	24	13	.649
Massachusetts	11	5	.688	15	15	.500
Dayton □	9	7	.563	21	13	.618
St. Bonaventure □	9	7	.563	18	12	.600
George Washington	6	10	.375	14	18	.438
La Salle	5	11	.313	12	17	.414
Fordham	4	12	.250	12	17	.414
Duquesne	3	13	.188	9	21	.300
Rhode Island	3	13	.188	7	23	.233

Tournament: **Temple d. Massachusetts 76-65**
Tournament MOP: **Lynn Greer**, Temple

Big East

	Conference			Overall		
	W	L	PCT	W	L	PCT
East Division						
Boston College ⊕	13	3	.813	27	5	.844
Providence ○	11	5	.688	21	10	.677
Connecticut □	8	8	.500	20	12	.625
Villanova □	8	8	.500	18	13	.581
Miami (FL) □	8	8	.500	16	13	.552
St. John's ⊗	8	8	.500	14	15	.483
Virginia Tech	2	14	.125	8	19	.296
West Division						
Notre Dame ○	11	5	.688	20	10	.667
Georgetown ○	10	6	.625	25	8	.758
Syracuse ○	10	6	.625	25	9	.735
West Virginia □	8	8	.500	17	12	.586
Pittsburgh □	7	9	.438	19	14	.576
Seton Hall □	5	11	.313	16	15	.516
Rutgers	3	13	.188	11	16	.407

Tournament: **Boston College d. Pittsburgh 79-57**
Tournament MVP: **Troy Bell**, Boston College

Big Sky

	Conference			Overall		
	W	L	PCT	W	L	PCT
Cal State Northridge ⊕	13	3	.813	22	10	.688
Eastern Washington	11	5	.688	17	11	.607
Idaho State	10	6	.625	14	14	.500
Montana State	8	8	.500	16	14	.533
Northern Arizona	8	8	.500	15	14	.517
Weber State	8	8	.500	15	14	.517
Montana	6	10	.375	11	16	.407
Portland State	6	10	.375	9	18	.333
Sacramento State	2	14	.125	5	22	.185

Tournament: **Cal State Northridge d. Eastern Washington 73-58**
Tournament MVP: **Brian Heinle**, Cal State Northridge

Big South

	Conference			Overall		
	W	L	PCT	W	L	PCT
Radford	12	2	.857	19	10	.655
Winthrop ⊕	11	3	.786	18	13	.581
UNC Asheville	9	5	.643	15	13	.536
Charleston Southern	6	8	.429	10	19	.345
Coastal Carolina	6	8	.429	8	20	.286
Liberty	5	9	.357	13	15	.464
Elon	4	10	.286	9	20	.310
High Point	3	11	.214	8	20	.286

Tournament: **Winthrop d. Radford 67-65 OT**
Tournament MVP: **Andrey Savtchenko**, Radford

Big Ten

	Conference			Overall		
	W	L	PCT	W	L	PCT
Michigan State ○	13	3	.813	28	5	.848
Illinois ○	13	3	.813	27	8	.771
Ohio State ○ ⊗	11	5	.688	20	11	.645
Indiana ○	10	6	.625	21	13	.618
Wisconsin ○	9	7	.563	18	11	.621
Iowa ⊕	7	9	.438	23	12	.657
Penn State ○	7	9	.438	21	12	.636
Purdue □	6	10	.375	17	15	.531
Minnesota □	5	11	.313	18	14	.563
Michigan	4	12	.250	10	18	.357
Northwestern	3	13	.188	11	19	.367

Tournament: **Iowa d. Indiana 63-61**
Tournament MOP: **Reggie Evans**, Iowa

Big 12

	Conference			Overall		
	W	L	PCT	W	L	PCT
Iowa State ○	13	3	.813	25	6	.806
Kansas ○	12	4	.750	26	7	.788
Oklahoma ⊕	12	4	.750	26	7	.788
Texas ○	12	4	.750	25	9	.735
Oklahoma State ○	10	6	.625	20	10	.667
Missouri ○	9	7	.563	20	13	.606
Nebraska	7	9	.438	14	16	.467
Baylor □	6	10	.375	19	12	.613
Colorado	5	11	.313	15	15	.500
Kansas State	4	12	.250	11	18	.379
Texas A&M	3	13	.188	10	20	.333
Texas Tech	3	13	.188	9	19	.321

Tournament: **Oklahoma d. Texas 54-45**
Tournament MOP: **Nolan Johnson**, Oklahoma

Big West

	Conference			Overall		
	W	L	PCT	W	L	PCT
UC Irvine □	15	1	.938	25	5	.833
Utah State ⊕	13	3	.813	28	6	.824
Long Beach State	10	6	.625	18	13	.581
UC Santa Barbara	9	7	.563	13	15	.464
Pacific	8	8	.500	18	12	.600
Boise State	8	8	.500	17	14	.548
Cal Poly	3	13	.188	9	19	.321
Idaho	3	13	.188	6	21	.222
Cal State Fullerton	3	13	.188	5	23	.179

Tournament: **Utah State d. Pacific 50-38**
Tournament MVP: **Bernard Rock**, Utah State

Colonial Athletic

	Conference			Overall		
	W	L	PCT	W	L	PCT
Richmond □	12	4	.750	22	7	.759
UNC Wilmington □	11	5	.688	19	11	.633
George Mason ⊕	11	5	.688	18	12	.600
VCU	9	7	.563	16	14	.533
Old Dominion	7	9	.438	13	18	.419
William and Mary	7	9	.438	11	17	.393
East Carolina	6	10	.375	14	14	.500
James Madison	6	10	.375	12	17	.414
American	3	13	.188	7	20	.259

Tournament: **George Mason d. UNC Wilmington 35-33**
Tournament MVP: **Erik Herring**, George Mason

C-USA

	Conference			Overall		
	W	L	PCT	W	L	PCT
American Division						
Cincinnati ○	11	5	.688	25	10	.714
Charlotte ⊕	10	6	.625	22	11	.667
Marquette	9	7	.563	15	14	.517
Saint Louis	8	8	.500	17	14	.548
Louisville	8	8	.500	12	19	.387
DePaul	4	12	.250	12	18	.400
National Division						
Southern Miss □	11	5	.688	22	9	.710
Memphis □	10	6	.625	21	15	.583
South Florida	9	7	.563	18	13	.581
UAB	8	8	.500	17	14	.548
Houston	6	10	.375	9	20	.310
Tulane	2	14	.125	9	21	.300

Tournament: **Charlotte d. Cincinnati 80-72**
Tournament MVP: **Rodney White**, Charlotte

Ivy

	Conference			Overall		
	W	L	PCT	W	L	PCT
Princeton ⊕	11	3	.786	16	11	.593
Brown	9	5	.643	15	12	.556
Penn	9	5	.643	12	17	.414
Harvard	7	7	.500	14	12	.538
Columbia	7	7	.500	12	15	.444
Yale	7	7	.500	10	17	.370
Dartmouth	3	11	.214	8	19	.296
Cornell	3	11	.214	7	20	.259

MAAC

	Conference			Overall		
	W	L	PCT	W	L	PCT
Iona ⊕	12	6	.667	22	11	.667
Siena	12	6	.667	20	11	.645
Niagara	12	6	.667	15	13	.536
Rider	11	7	.611	16	12	.571
Marist	11	7	.611	17	13	.567
Manhattan	11	7	.611	14	15	.483
Canisius	9	9	.500	20	11	.645
Fairfield	8	10	.444	12	16	.429
Loyola (MD)	2	16	.111	6	23	.207
Saint Peter's	2	16	.111	4	24	.143

Tournament: **Iona d. Canisius 74-67**
Tournament MVP: **Nakiea Miller**, Iona

Conference Standings Continue →

⊕ Automatic NCAA Tournament bid ○ At-large NCAA Tournament bid □ NIT appearance ⊗ Team record doesn't reflect games forfeited or vacated. For adjusted record, see p. 521.

MID-AMERICAN

	Conference W	L	Pct	Overall W	L	Pct
East Division						
Kent State⊛	13	5	.722	24	10	.706
Marshall	12	6	.667	18	9	.667
Ohio	12	6	.667	19	11	.633
Bowling Green	10	8	.556	15	14	.517
Miami (OH)	10	8	.556	17	16	.515
Akron	9	9	.500	12	16	.429
Buffalo	2	16	.111	4	24	.143
West Division						
Central Michigan	14	4	.778	20	8	.714
Toledo□	12	6	.667	22	11	.667
Ball State	11	7	.611	18	12	.600
Western Michigan	7	11	.389	7	21	.250
Northern Illinois	4	14	.222	5	23	.179
Eastern Michigan	1	17	.056	3	25	.107

Tournament: **Kent State d. Miami (OH) 67-61**
Tournament MVP: **Trevor Huffman**, Kent State

MID-CONTINENT

	Conference W	L	Pct	Overall W	L	Pct
Southern Utah⊛	13	3	.813	25	6	.806
Valparaiso	13	3	.813	24	8	.750
Youngstown State	11	5	.688	19	11	.633
UMKC	9	7	.563	14	16	.467
Oakland	8	8	.500	12	16	.429
IUPUI	6	10	.375	11	18	.379
Oral Roberts	5	11	.313	10	19	.345
Western Illinois	5	11	.313	5	23	.179
Chicago State	2	14	.125	5	23	.179

Tournament: **Southern Utah d. Valparaiso 62-59**
Tournament MVP: **Fred House**, Southern Utah

MEAC

	Conference W	L	Pct	Overall W	L	Pct
Hampton⊛	14	4	.778	25	7	.781
South Carolina State	14	4	.778	19	13	.594
Delaware State	11	7	.611	13	15	.464
Norfolk State	11	7	.611	12	17	.414
Coppin State	11	8	.579	13	15	.464
UMES	10	8	.556	12	16	.429
NC A&T	8	10	.444	13	17	.433
Howard	8	10	.444	10	18	.357
Bethune-Cookman	5	13	.278	10	19	.345
Florida A&M	4	14	.222	6	22	.214
Morgan State	4	15	.211	6	23	.207

Tournament: **Hampton d. South Carolina State 70-68**
Tournament MOP: **Tarvis Williams**, Hampton

MCC

	Conference W	L	Pct	Overall W	L	Pct
Butler⊛	11	3	.786	24	8	.750
Detroit□	10	4	.714	25	12	.676
Cleveland State	9	5	.643	19	13	.594
Wright State	8	6	.571	18	11	.621
Wisconsin-Milwaukee	7	7	.500	15	13	.536
Illinois-Chicago	5	9	.357	11	17	.393
Wisconsin-Green Bay	4	10	.286	11	17	.393
Loyola-Chicago	2	12	.143	7	21	.250

Tournament: **Butler d. Detroit 53-38**
Tournament MVP: **LaVall Jordan**, Butler

MISSOURI VALLEY

	Conference W	L	Pct	Overall W	L	Pct
Creighton○	14	4	.778	24	8	.750
Illinois State□	12	6	.667	21	9	.700
Bradley□	12	6	.667	19	12	.613
Indiana State⊛	10	8	.556	22	12	.647
Southern Illinois	10	8	.556	16	14	.533
Evansville	9	9	.500	14	16	.467
Missouri State	8	10	.444	13	16	.448
Drake	8	10	.444	12	16	.429
Wichita State	4	14	.222	9	19	.321
Northern Iowa	3	15	.167	7	24	.226

Tournament: **Indiana State d. Bradley 69-63**
Tournament MOP: **Michael Menser**, Indiana State

MOUNTAIN WEST

	Conference W	L	Pct	Overall W	L	Pct
BYU⊛	10	4	.714	24	9	.727
Wyoming□	10	4	.714	20	10	.667
Utah□	10	4	.714	19	12	.613
UNLV	7	7	.500	16	13	.552
New Mexico□	6	8	.429	21	13	.618
Colorado State	6	8	.429	15	13	.536
San Diego State	4	10	.286	14	14	.500
Air Force	3	11	.214	8	21	.276

Tournament: **BYU d. New Mexico 69-65**
Tournament MVP: **Mekeli Wesley**, BYU

NORTHEAST

	Conference W	L	Pct	Overall W	L	Pct
St. Francis (NY)	16	4	.800	18	11	.621
Monmouth⊛	15	5	.750	21	10	.677
UMBC	13	7	.650	18	11	.621
Long Island	12	8	.600	12	16	.429
Wagner	11	9	.550	16	13	.552
Central Conn. State	11	9	.550	14	14	.500
Fairleigh Dickinson	10	10	.500	13	15	.464
Saint Francis (PA)	9	11	.450	9	18	.333
Mount St. Mary's	7	13	.350	7	21	.250
Robert Morris	7	13	.350	7	22	.241
Sacred Heart	6	14	.300	7	21	.250
Quinnipiac	3	17	.150	6	21	.222

Tournament: **Monmouth d. St. Francis (NY) 67-64**
Tournament MVP: **Rahsaan Johnson**, Monmouth

OHIO VALLEY

	Conference W	L	Pct	Overall W	L	Pct
Tennessee Tech	13	3	.813	20	9	.690
Eastern Illinois⊛	11	5	.688	21	10	.677
Murray State	11	5	.688	17	12	.586
Austin Peay	10	6	.625	22	10	.688
SE Missouri State	8	8	.500	18	12	.600
Tennessee State	7	9	.438	10	19	.345
Morehead State	6	10	.375	12	16	.429
Tennessee-Martin	5	11	.313	10	18	.357
Eastern Kentucky	1	15	.063	7	19	.269

Tournament: **Eastern Illinois d. Austin Peay 84-83**
Tournament MVP: **Kyle Hill**, Eastern Illinois

PAC-10

	Conference W	L	Pct	Overall W	L	Pct
Stanford⊛	16	2	.889	31	3	.912
Arizona○	15	3	.833	28	8	.778
UCLA○	14	4	.778	23	9	.719
Southern California○	11	7	.611	24	10	.706
California○	11	7	.611	20	11	.645
Oregon	5	13	.278	14	14	.500
Arizona State	5	13	.278	13	16	.448
Washington State	5	13	.278	12	16	.429
Oregon State	4	14	.222	10	20	.333
Washington	4	14	.222	10	20	.333

PATRIOT LEAGUE

	Conference W	L	Pct	Overall W	L	Pct
Holy Cross⊛	10	2	.833	22	8	.733
Navy	9	3	.750	19	12	.613
Colgate	6	6	.500	13	15	.464
Lehigh	6	6	.500	13	16	.448
Bucknell	4	8	.333	14	15	.483
Lafayette	4	8	.333	12	16	.429
Army	3	9	.250	9	19	.321

Tournament: **Holy Cross d. Navy 68-64 OT**
Tournament MVP: **Josh Sankes**, Holy Cross

SEC

	Conference W	L	Pct	Overall W	L	Pct
Eastern						
Florida○	12	4	.750	24	7	.774
Kentucky⊛	12	4	.750	24	10	.706
Georgia○	9	7	.563	16	15	.516
Tennessee○	8	8	.500	22	11	.667
South Carolina□	6	10	.375	15	15	.500
Vanderbilt	4	12	.250	15	15	.500
Western						
Mississippi○	11	5	.688	27	8	.771
Arkansas○	10	6	.625	20	11	.645
Alabama□	8	8	.500	25	11	.694
Mississippi State□	7	9	.438	18	13	.581
Auburn□	7	9	.438	18	14	.563
LSU	2	14	.125	13	16	.448

Tournament: **Kentucky d. Mississippi 77-55**
Tournament MVP: **Tayshaun Prince**, Kentucky

SOUTHERN

	Conference W	L	Pct	Overall W	L	Pct
North						
East Tenn. State	13	3	.813	18	10	.643
UNC Greensboro⊛	10	6	.625	19	12	.613
Davidson	7	9	.438	15	17	.469
Appalachian State	7	9	.438	11	20	.355
VMI	5	11	.313	9	19	.321
Western Carolina	3	13	.188	6	25	.194
South						
Charleston	12	4	.750	22	7	.759
The Citadel	9	7	.563	16	12	.571
Chattanooga	9	7	.563	17	13	.567
Georgia Southern	9	7	.563	15	15	.500
Wofford	7	9	.438	12	16	.429
Furman	5	11	.313	10	16	.385

Tournament: **UNC Greensboro d. Chattanooga 67-66**
Tournament MOP: **Toot Young**, Chattanooga

SOUTHLAND

	Conference W	L	Pct	Overall W	L	Pct
McNeese State□	17	3	.850	22	9	.710
Nicholls State	12	8	.600	14	14	.500
UTSA	12	8	.600	14	15	.483
Northwestern St. (LA)⊛	11	9	.550	19	13	.594
Sam Houston State	11	9	.550	16	13	.552
Texas-Arlington	11	9	.550	13	15	.464
Texas State	10	10	.500	13	15	.464
UL-Monroe	8	12	.400	11	17	.393
Lamar	7	13	.350	9	18	.333
Stephen F. Austin	6	14	.300	9	17	.346
Southeastern Louisiana	5	15	.250	8	21	.276

Tournament: **Northwestern State (LA) d. McNeese State 72-71**
Tournament MVP: **Michael Byars-Dawson**, Northwestern State (LA)

SWAC

	Conference W	L	Pct	Overall W	L	Pct
Alabama State⊛	15	3	.833	22	9	.710
Miss. Valley State	14	4	.778	18	9	.667
Alabama A&M	13	5	.722	17	11	.607
Alcorn State	13	5	.722	15	15	.500
Southern U.	8	10	.444	11	16	.407
Grambling	8	10	.444	8	18	.308
Jackson State	7	11	.389	7	23	.233
Texas Southern	5	13	.278	7	22	.241
Prairie View A&M	5	13	.278	6	22	.214
Ark.-Pine Bluff	2	16	.111	2	25	.074

Tournament: **Alabama State d. Alcorn State 62-52**
Tournament MVP: **Tyrone Levett**, Alabama State

SUN BELT

	Conference W	L	Pct	Overall W	L	Pct
East Division						
Western Kentucky⊛	14	2	.875	24	7	.774
Louisiana Tech	10	6	.625	17	12	.586
Arkansas State	10	6	.625	17	13	.567
Arkansas-Little Rock	9	7	.563	18	11	.621
Florida Int'l	5	11	.313	8	21	.276
Middle Tenn State	1	15	.063	5	22	.185
West Division						
South Alabama□	11	5	.688	22	11	.667
New Orleans	10	6	.625	17	12	.586
UL-Lafayette	10	6	.625	16	13	.552
New Mexico State	10	6	.625	14	14	.500
Denver	5	11	.313	10	18	.357
North Texas	1	15	.063	4	24	.143

Tournament: **Western Kentucky d. South Alabama 64-54**
Tournament MOP: **Chris Marcus**, Western Kentucky

TRANS AMERICA

	Conference W	L	Pct	Overall W	L	Pct
Georgia State⊛	16	2	.889	29	5	.853
Troy	12	6	.667	19	12	.613
Jacksonville	11	7	.611	18	10	.643
Stetson	11	7	.611	17	12	.586
Samford	11	7	.611	15	14	.517
Mercer	10	8	.556	13	15	.464
Jacksonville State	6	12	.333	9	19	.321
Campbell	5	13	.278	7	21	.250
Florida Atlantic	5	13	.278	7	24	.226
Central Florida	3	15	.167	8	23	.258

Tournament: **Georgia State d. Troy 79-55**
Tournament MVP: **Thomas Terrell**, Georgia State

WEST COAST

	Conference W	L	Pct	Overall W	L	Pct
Gonzaga⊛	13	1	.929	26	7	.788
Pepperdine□	12	2	.857	22	9	.710
Santa Clara	10	4	.714	20	12	.625
San Diego	7	7	.500	16	13	.552
San Francisco	5	9	.357	12	18	.400
Loyola Marymount	5	9	.357	9	19	.321
Portland	4	10	.286	11	17	.393
Saint Mary's (CA)	0	14	.000	2	27	.069

Tournament: **Gonzaga d. Santa Clara 80-77**
Tournament MVP: **Dan Dickau**, Gonzaga

WAC

	Conference W	L	Pct	Overall W	L	Pct
Fresno State○✪	13	3	.813	26	7	.788
UTEP□	10	6	.625	23	9	.719
Tulsa□	10	6	.625	26	11	.703
TCU	9	7	.563	20	11	.645
SMU	8	8	.500	18	12	.600
Hawaii⊛	8	8	.500	17	14	.548
San Jose State	6	10	.375	14	14	.500
Rice	5	11	.313	14	16	.467
Nevada	3	13	.188	10	18	.357

Tournament: **Hawaii d. Tulsa 78-72 (OT)**
Tournament MVP: **Carl English**, Hawaii

INDEPENDENTS

	Overall W	L	Pct
Stony Brook	17	11	.607
Belmont	13	15	.464
Texas-Pan American	12	17	.414
Centenary	8	19	.296
Albany (NY)	6	22	.214

INDIVIDUAL LEADERS—SEASON

SCORING	CL	POS	G	FG	3FG	FT	PTS	PPG
1 **Ronnie McCollum**, Centenary	SR	G	27	244	85	214	787	**29.1**
2 **Kyle Hill**, Eastern Illinois	SR	G	31	250	86	151	737	**23.8**
3 **DeWayne Jefferson**, Miss. Valley St.	SR	G	27	216	107	98	637	**23.6**
4 **Tarise Bryson**, Illinois State	SR	G	30	208	62	207	685	**22.8**
5 **Henry Domercant**, Eastern Illinois	SO	G/F	31	256	79	115	706	**22.8**
6 **Rashad Phillips**, Detroit	SR	G	35	232	136	185	785	**22.4**
7 **Brandon Wolfram**, UTEP	SR	F	32	251	6	206	714	**22.3**
8 **Rasual Butler**, La Salle	JR	F	29	231	97	82	641	**22.1**
9 **Brandon Armstrong**, Pepperdine	JR	G	31	240	76	128	684	**22.1**
10 **Marvin O'Connor**, Saint Joseph's	JR	G	32	240	99	127	706	**22.1**

FIELD GOAL PCT	CL	POS	G	FG	FGA	PCT
1 **Michael Bradley**, Villanova	JR	C	31	254	367	**69.2**
2 **Nakiea Miller**, Iona	SR	C	27	163	244	**66.8**
3 **Kimani Ffriend**, Nebraska	SR	C	28	144	231	**62.3**
4 **Andre Hutson**, Michigan State	SR	F	32	173	278	**62.2**
5 **George Evans**, George Mason	SR	F	30	233	380	**61.3**

MINIMUM: 5 MADE PER GAME

THREE-POINT FG PER GAME	CL	POS	G	3FG	3PG
1 **DeWayne Jefferson**, Miss. Valley State	SR	G	27	107	**4.0**
2 **Rashad Phillips**, Detroit	SR	G	35	136	**3.9**
3 **Brian Merriweather**, Tex.-Pan American	SR	G	29	108	**3.7**
4 **Cory Schwab**, Northern Arizona	SR	F	29	105	**3.6**
5 **Demond Mallet**, McNeese State	SR	G	31	107	**3.5**

THREE-POINT FG PCT	CL	POS	G	3FG	3FGA	PCT
1 **Amory Sanders**, SE Missouri State	SR	G	24	53	95	**55.8**
2 **David Falknor**, Akron	JR	F	22	47	87	**54.0**
3 **Cary Cochran**, Nebraska	JR	G	30	78	165	**47.3**
4 **Casey Jacobsen**, Stanford	SO	G	34	84	178	**47.2**
5 **Tim Erickson**, Idaho State	SR	G	28	82	177	**46.3**

MINIMUM: 1.5 MADE PER GAME

FREE THROW PCT	CL	POS	G	FT	FTA	PCT
1 **Gary Buchanan**, Villanova	SO	G	31	97	103	**94.2**
2 **Brent Jolly**, Tennessee Tech	SO	G	29	95	102	**93.1**
3 **Ryan Mendez**, Stanford	SR	F	34	94	101	**93.1**
4 **Rashad Phillips**, Detroit	SR	G	35	185	202	**91.6**
5 **Ronnie McCollum**, Centenary	SR	G	27	214	236	**90.7**

MINIMUM: 2.5 MADE PER GAME

ASSISTS PER GAME	CL	POS	G	AST	APG
1 **Markus Carr**, Cal State Northridge	JR	G	32	286	**8.9**
2 **Omar Cook**, St. John's	FR	G	29	252	**8.7**
3 **Sean Kennedy**, Marist	JR	G	27	219	**8.1**
4 **Tito Maddox**, Fresno State	SO	G	25	200	**8.0**
5 **Ashley Robinson**, Mississippi Valley State	JR	G	27	201	**7.4**
6 **Brandon Pardon**, Bowling Green	JR	G	29	204	**7.0**
7 **Jeremy Stanton**, Evansville	SR	G	26	181	**7.0**
8 **Kirk Hinrich**, Kansas	SO	G	33	229	**6.9**
9 **Steve Blake**, Maryland	SO	G	36	248	**6.9**
10 **Allen Griffin**, Syracuse	SR	G	34	220	**6.5**

REBOUNDS PER GAME	CL	POS	G	REB	RPG
1 **Chris Marcus**, Western Kentucky	JR	C	31	374	**12.1**
2 **Reggie Evans**, Iowa	JR	F	35	416	**11.9**
3 **J.R. VanHoose**, Marshall	JR	C	27	299	**11.1**
4 **David West**, Xavier	SO	F	29	316	**10.9**
5 **Eddie Griffin**, Seton Hall	FR	F	30	323	**10.8**
6 **Jeremy Jefferson**, Arkansas-Pine Bluff	JR	F	23	246	**10.7**
7 **Brian Carroll**, Loyola (MD)	SR	F	27	286	**10.6**
8 **Eric Mann**, VMI	SR	C	28	294	**10.5**
Joe Breakenridge, Northern Iowa	SR	F	28	294	**10.5**
10 **Alvin Jones**, Georgia Tech	SR	C	30	312	**10.4**

BLOCKED SHOTS PER GAME	CL	POS	G	BLK	BPG
1 **Tarvis Williams**, Hampton	SR	F	32	147	**4.6**
2 **Eddie Griffin**, Seton Hall	FR	F	30	133	**4.4**
3 **Wojciech Myrda**, UL-Monroe	JR	C	28	123	**4.4**
4 **Kris Hunter**, Jacksonville	SR	C	28	114	**4.1**
5 **Ken Johnson**, Ohio State	SR	C	31	125	**4.0**

STEALS PER GAME	CL	POS	G	STL	SPG
1 **Greedy Daniels**, TCU	JR	G	25	108	**4.3**
2 **Desmond Cambridge**, Alabama A&M	JR	G	28	107	**3.8**
3 **Senecca Wall**, Sam Houston State	SR	G	29	103	**3.6**
4 **John Linehan**, Providence	JR	G	26	81	**3.1**
5 **Fred House**, Southern Utah	SR	G/F	31	93	**3.0**

INDIVIDUAL LEADERS—GAME

POINTS	CL	POS	OPP	DATE	PTS
1 **Oliver Morton**, Chattanooga	SR	G	Pikeville	J24	**50**
2 **Trevor Diggs**, UNLV	SR	G	Wyoming	M3	**49**
3 **Senecca Wall**, Sam Houston State	SR	G	Texas-Arlington	M6	**45**
4 **Okechi Egbe**, Tennessee-Martin	SO	F	Bethel	N20	**44**
Ronnie McCollum, Centenary	SR	G	Northwestern State (LA)	F21	**44**

THREE-POINT FG MADE	CL	POS	OPP	DATE	3FG
1 **Cory Schwab**, Northern Arizona	SR	F	Cal Poly	D2	**11**
Ron Williamson, Howard	SO	G	Georgetown	D16	**11**
3 **Ravonte Dantzler**, South Alabama	SR	G	Alabama State	D9	**10**
Ryan Dillon, Cal State Fullerton	FR	G	Boise State	J31	**10**
5 **Shane Battier**, Duke	SR	F	Princeton	N14	**9**
Abe Jackson, Boise State	JR	F	Gonzaga	D9	**9**
Thomas Terrell, Georgia State	JR	F	Jacksonville	J8	**9**
Greg Buth, Dartmouth	SR	G	Albany (NY)	J20	**9**
E.J. Gallup, Albany (NY)	FR	G	Army	F3	**9**
Chris Miller, Texas Southern	SO	G	Prairie View A&M	F3	**9**
Dan Dickau, Gonzaga	JR	G	Santa Clara	F22	**9**
Rashad Phillips, Detroit	SR	G	Cleveland State	M4	**9**

ASSISTS	CL	POS	OPP	DATE	AST
1 **Omar Cook**, St. John's	FR	G	Stony Brook	N18	**17**
Tito Maddox, Fresno State	SO	G	TCU	J10	**17**
3 **Greedy Daniels**, TCU	JR	G	Central Oklahoma	D9	**16**
Flinder Boyd, Dartmouth	JR	G	Albany (NY)	J20	**16**
Sean Peterson, Ga. Southern	JR	G	East Tennessee State	F10	**16**

REBOUNDS	CL	POS	OPP	DATE	REB
1 **Clifton Jones**, Old Dominion	SR	F	UNC Wilmington	F26	**23**
2 **Jamahl Mosley**, Colorado	SR	F	Missouri	J10	**22**
3 **Chris Marcus**, Western Kentucky	JR	C	Tennessee State	N25	**21**
Eddie Griffin, Seton Hall	FR	F	Saint Peter's	N27	**21**
Kelly Wise, Memphis	JR	C	Tennessee	D5	**21**
Kelly Wise, Memphis	JR	C	Miami (FL)	D21	**21**
David West, Xavier	SO	F	George Washington	F3	**21**
Ron Robinson, Central Conn. State	FR	F	Mount St. Mary's	F5	**21**

BLOCKED SHOTS	CL	POS	OPP	DATE	BLK
1 **D'or Fischer**, Northwestern State (LA)	FR	C	SW Texas State	J22	**13**
Kyle Davis, Auburn	FR	C	Miami (FL)	M14	**13**
3 **Tarvis Williams**, Hampton	SR	F	Delaware State	J13	**12**
4 **Walter Harper**, Alcorn State	JR	C	Southern Miss	N21	**11**
Gerrick Morris, South Florida	FR	C	George Washington	N28	**11**
Jason Jennings, Arkansas State	JR	C	Morris Brown	D18	**11**

STEALS	CL	POS	OPP	DATE	STL
1 **Greedy Daniels**, TCU	JR	G	Arkansas-Pine Bluff	D30	**12**
2 **Morris Scott**, Florida A&M	SR	G	Alabama State	N27	**10**
3 **Fred House**, Southern Utah	SR	G/F	Idaho State	N25	**9**
Fred House, Southern Utah	SR	G/F	Western Oregon	D19	**9**
5 18 tied with eight					

TEAM LEADERS—SEASON

WIN-LOSS PCT	W	L	PCT
1 **Stanford**	31	3	**.912**
2 **Duke**	35	4	**.897**
3 **Georgia State**	29	5	**.853**
4 **Michigan State**	28	5	**.848**
5 **Boston College**	27	5	**.844**

SCORING OFFENSE	G	W-L	PTS	PPG
1 **TCU**	31	20-11	2,902	**93.6**
2 **Duke**	39	35-4	3,538	**90.7**
3 **Maryland**	36	25-11	3,067	**85.2**
4 **Virginia**	29	20-9	2,464	**85.0**
5 **McNeese State**	31	22-9	2,580	**83.2**

SCORING MARGIN	G	W-L	PPG	OPP PPG	MAR
1 **Duke**	39	35-4	90.7	70.5	**20.2**
2 **Stanford**	34	31-3	83.2	65.5	**17.7**
3 **Michigan State**	33	28-5	77.4	61.8	**15.6**
4 **Arizona**	36	28-8	81.3	66.3	**15.0**
5 **Florida**	31	24-7	80.9	67.1	**13.8**

FIELD GOAL PCT	G	W-L	FG	FGA	PCT
1 **Stanford**	34	31-3	953	1,865	**51.1**
2 **Gonzaga**	33	26-7	915	1,793	**51.0**
3 **Austin Peay**	32	22-10	935	1,845	**50.7**
4 **Kansas**	33	26-7	1,002	1,996	**50.2**
5 **Villanova**	31	18-13	845	1,708	**49.5**

THREE-POINT FG PER GAME	G	W-L	3FG	3PG
1 **Duke**	39	35-4	407	**10.4**
2 **Belmont**	28	13-15	288	**10.3**
3 **Samford**	29	15-14	284	**9.8**
4 **Miss. Valley State**	27	18-9	250	**9.3**
5 **Charlotte**	33	22-11	305	**9.2**

REBOUND MARGIN	G	W-L	RPG	OPP RPG	MAR
1 **Michigan State**	33	28-5	42.5	27.1	**15.4**
2 **Western Kentucky**	31	24-7	40.0	30.4	**9.6**
3 **Georgetown**	33	25-8	44.9	35.6	**9.3**
4 **Iowa State**	31	25-6	39.6	30.8	**8.8**
5 **Mississippi State**	31	18-13	41.2	33.3	**7.9**

Scoring Defense

	G	W-L	OPP PTS	OPP PPG
1 Wisconsin	29	18-11	1,641	**56.6**
2 Utah State	34	28-6	1,959	**57.6**
3 Princeton	27	16-11	1,569	**58.1**
4 UNC Wilmington	30	19-11	1,751	**58.4**
5 Miami (OH)	33	17-16	1,928	**58.4**

Field Goal Pct Defense

	G	W-L	OPP FG	OPP FGA	OPP PCT
1 Kansas	33	26-7	782	2,069	**37.8**
2 Holy Cross	30	22-8	628	1,642	**38.2**
3 Illinois	35	27-8	748	1,936	**38.6**
4 Georgetown	33	25-8	745	1,922	**38.8**
5 Texas	34	25-9	734	1,889	**38.9**

TEAM LEADERS—GAME

Points

	OPP	DATE	SCORE
1 TCU	Central Oklahoma	D9	**141-92**
2 TCU	Ark.-Pine Bluff	D30	**130-71**
3 Florida	Florida A&M	D10	**125-50**
4 Georgetown	Howard	D16	**123-90**
Maryland	Norfolk State	D23	**123-79**

Field Goal Pct

	OPP	DATE	FG	FGA	PCT
1 BYU	Elon	N21	34	48	**70.8**
2 Towson	Northeastern	J13	31	44	**70.5**
3 Indiana	Wisconsin	F24	33	47	**70.2**
4 Georgia	Mississippi State	F28	40	57	**70.2**
5 Wake Forest	Mount St. Mary's	N16	42	60	**70.0**
Northern Illinois	Rockford	D6	49	70	**70.0**

Three-point FG Made

	OPP	DATE	3FG
1 Samford	Troy	J13	**23**
2 Northern Arizona	Cal Poly	D2	**20**
3 Delaware	New Hampshire	D7	**18**
Lafayette	Fordham	D11	**18**
Howard	Georgetown	D16	**18**
Duke	NC A&T	D30	**18**
Wisconsin-Milwaukee	Illinois-Chicago	J11	**18**
Dartmouth	Albany (NY)	J20	**18**
Duke	Monmouth	M15	**18**

CONSENSUS ALL-AMERICAS

First Team

PLAYER	CL	POS	HT	SCHOOL	RPG	PPG
Shane Battier	SR	F	6-8	Duke	7.3	19.9
Joseph Forte	SO	G	6-4	North Carolina	6.1	20.9
Casey Jacobsen	SO	G	6-6	Stanford	4.0	18.1
Troy Murphy	JR	F	6-10	Notre Dame	9.2	21.8
Jason Williams	SO	G	6-2	Duke	3.3	21.6

Second Team

PLAYER	CL	POS	HT	SCHOOL	RPG	PPG
Troy Bell	SO	G	6-1	Boston College	4.3	20.4
Michael Bradley	JR	C	6-10	Villanova	9.8	20.8
Tayshaun Prince	JR	G/F	6-9	Kentucky	6.5	16.9
Jason Richardson	SO	G/F	6-6	Michigan State	5.9	14.7
Jamaal Tinsley	SR	G	6-3	Iowa State	3.8	14.3

SELECTORS: AP, NABC, SPORTING NEWS, USBWA

AWARD WINNERS

Player of the Year

PLAYER	CL	POS	HT	SCHOOL	AWARDS
Shane Battier	SR	F	6-8	Duke	Naismith, AP, USBWA, Wooden, Rupp
Jason Williams	SO	G	6-2	Duke	NABC
Rashad Phillips	SR	G	5-10	Detroit	Frances Pomeroy Naismith*

* FOR THE MOST OUTSTANDING SENIOR PLAYER WHO IS 6 FEET OR UNDER

Defensive Player of the Year

PLAYER	CL	POS	HT	SCHOOL
Shane Battier	SR	F	6-8	Duke

Coach of the Year

COACH	SCHOOL	REC	AWARDS
Rod Barnes	Mississippi	27-8	Naismith
Matt Doherty	North Carolina	26-7	AP
Al Skinner	Boston College	27-5	USBWA, Sporting News, CBS/Chevrolet
Tom Izzo	Michigan State	28-5	NABC

Bob Gibbons' Top High School Senior Recruits

PLAYER	POS	HT	HIGH SCHOOL	A-A TEAMS	COLLEGE	CAREER NOTES
1 Eddy Curry	C	6-11	Thornwood HS, South Holland, IL	McD, P, USA	None	Drafted straight out of HS; No. 4 pick, '01 NBA draft (Bulls); led NBA in FG% in '02 and '03; 13.4 ppg (8 seasons)
2 Kwame Brown	F/C	6-11	Glynn Academy, Brunswick, GA	McD, P, USA	None	Drafted straight out of HS; No. 1 overall pick, '01 NBA draft (Wizards); 7.0 ppg, 5.8 rpg (8 seasons)
3 Tyson Chandler	C	7-1	Dominguez HS, Compton, CA	McD, P	None	Drafted straight out of HS; No. 2 pick, '01 NBA draft (Clippers); 8.2 ppg, 9.0 rpg (8 seasons)
4 Dajuan Wagner	G	6-2	Camden (NJ) HS	McD, P, USA	Memphis	21.2 ppg (1 season); No. 6 pick, '02 NBA draft (Cavs); 9.4 ppg (4 seasons); played overseas
5 David Lee	F	6-8	Chaminade Prep, St. Louis, MO	McD, P	Florida	2nd team All-SEC in '05; 2nd-round pick, '05 NBA draft (Knicks); 10.9 ppg, 9.0 rpg (4 seasons)
6 DeSagana Diop	C	7-0	Oak Hill Academy, Mouth of Wilson, VA	McD, P	None	Drafted straight out of HS; No. 8 pick, '01 NBA draft (Cavs); 2.1 ppg, 3.9 rpg (8 seasons)
7 Ousmane Cisse	PF	6-7	St. Jude Catholic HS, Montgomery, AL	McD, P	None	Drafted straight out of HS; 2nd-round pick, '01 NBA draft (Nuggets); led Israeli League in rebounding, '05-'06
8 Kelvin Torbert	G	6-4	Northwestern HS, Flint, MI	McD, P, USA	Michigan State	1,195 pts (4 seasons); 3rd team All-Big Ten, '04; undrafted, plays overseas
9 Rick Rickert	F/C	6-10	East HS, Duluth, MN	McD, P	Minnesota	Big Ten FOY, '02; 1st team All-Big Ten, '03; 2nd-round pick, '03 NBA draft (Wolves)
10 Maurice Williams	PG	6-2	Murrah HS, Jackson, MS	McD, P	Alabama	SEC FOY, '02; 2nd-round pick, '03 NBA draft (Jazz); 13.5 ppg, 4.8 apg (6 seasons); '09 All-Star
11 David Harrison	C	6-11	Brentwood (TN) Academy	McD, P	Colorado	First-team All-Big 12, '05; No. 29 pick, '04 NBA draft (Pacers); 5.0 ppg (4 seasons)
12 Aaron Miles	PG	6-1	Jefferson HS, Portland, OR	McD, P	Kansas	Kansas' all-time assist leader (954); undrafted, played overseas
13 Jawad Williams	F	6-8	St. Edward HS, Lakewood, OH	McD, P	North Carolina	12.7 ppg (4 seasons) undrafted, played in D-League; 10 games for Cavs in '08-'09
14 Wayne Simien	F	6-8	Leavenworth (KS) HS	McD, P	Kansas	First-team All-America, '05; No. 29 pick, '05 NBA draft (Heat); 3.3 ppg (2 seasons); played in Spain
15 James White	F	6-6	Hargrave Military Academy, Chatham, VA	McD, P	Florida/Cincinnati	At Cincy, 16.3 ppg as a senior; 2nd-round pick, '06 NBA draft (Blazers)
16 Julius Hodge	G/F	6-6	St. Raymond HS, Bronx, NY	McD, P	NC State	2,040 points (4 seasons); ACC POY, '04; No. 20 pick, '05 NBA draft (Nuggets)
17 Cedric Bozeman	G/F	6-6	Mater Dei HS, Santa Ana, CA	McD, P	UCLA	Pac-10 leader in assists, '04; undrafted; played 23 games for Hawks, '07
18 T.J. Ford	PG	5-10	Willowridge HS, Sugar Land, TX	McD, P	Texas	Won Naismith, Wooden Awards, '03; No. 8 pick, '03 NBA draft (Bucks); 12.4 ppg, 6.5 apg (5 seasons)
19 John Allen	F	6-6	Coatesville (PA) HS	P	Seton Hall	All-Big East Rookie team, '02; undrafted; played in USBL, overseas
20 Pierre Pierce	G	6-4	Westmont (IL) HS	P	Iowa	1,072 points, 305 assists (3 seasons); undrafted; legal troubles; played overseas

Other Standouts

PLAYER	POS	HT	HIGH SCHOOL	A-A TEAMS	COLLEGE	CAREER NOTES
21 Josh Childress	G/F	6-6	Mayfair HS, Lakewood, CA	McD, P	Stanford	1st team All-America, '04; No. 6 pick, '04 NBA draft (Hawks); played in Euroleague
77 Ben Gordon	G	6-2	Mt. Vernon (NY) HS		Connecticut	1,795 pts (3 seasons); No. 3 pick, '04 NBA draft (Bulls); Sixth Man Award, '05; 18.5 ppg (5 seasons)
99 Emeka Okafor	C	6-9	Bellaire (TX) HS		Connecticut	First-team All-America, '04; No. 2 pick, '04 NBA draft (Bobcats); 14.0 ppg, 10.7 rpg (5 seasons)

Abbreviations: McD=McDonald's; P=Parade; USA=USA Today

Poll Progression

Preseason Poll

AP	ESPN/USA	School
1	1	Arizona
2	2	Duke
3	5	Michigan State
4	3	Stanford
5	7	Maryland
6	4	North Carolina
7	6	Kansas
8	9	Illinois
9	8	Tennessee
10	10	Seton Hall
11	11	Florida
12	12	Kentucky
13	16	Utah
14	13	Connecticut
15	15	Arkansas
16	17	Notre Dame
17	19	UCLA
18	14	Cincinnati
19	22	Wisconsin
20	18	Wake Forest
21	20	DePaul
22	21	Oklahoma
23	24	Southern California
24	25	Virginia
25	23	Iowa State

Week of Nov 14

AP	School	AP↓↑
1	Arizona (0-0)	
2	Duke (0-0)	
3	Michigan State (0-0)	
4	Kansas (2-0)	↑3
5	Stanford (0-0)	↓1
6	Maryland (0-0)	↓1
7	North Carolina (2-0)	↓1
8	Illinois (0-0)	
9	Tennessee (0-0)	
10	Seton Hall (0-0)	
11	Florida (0-0)	
12	Utah (0-0)	↑1
13	Connecticut (0-0)	↑1
14	UCLA (1-1)	↑3
15	Arkansas (0-0)	
16	Notre Dame (0-0)	↓1
17	Cincinnati (0-0)	↑1
18	Wake Forest (0-0)	↑2
19	Wisconsin (0-0)	
20	Kentucky (0-2)	↓8
21	Oklahoma (0-0)	↑1
22	DePaul (0-0)	↓1
23	Southern California (0-0)	
24	St. John's (1-1)	⤴
25	Virginia (0-0)	↓1

Week of Nov 21

AP	ESPN/USA	School	AP↓↑
1	2	Arizona (1-0)	
2	1	Duke (2-0)	
3	4	Kansas (3-0)	↑1
4	3	Michigan State (1-0)	↓1
5	5	Stanford (1-0)	
6	6	Maryland (0-0)	
7	7	North Carolina (3-0)	
8	8	Illinois (1-0)	
9	9	Tennessee (2-0)	
10	10	Seton Hall (1-0)	
11	11	Florida (1-0)	
12	12	Connecticut (1-0)	↑1
13	14	Utah (1-0)	↓1
14	15	Notre Dame (1-0)	↑2
15	17	UCLA (1-1)	↓1
16	13	Cincinnati (1-0)	↑1
17	16	Wake Forest (2-0)	↑1
18	20	Wisconsin (0-0)	↑1
19	19	Oklahoma (2-0)	↑2
20	23	Southern California (1-0)	↑3
21	22	DePaul (1-0)	↑1
22	21	Kentucky (0-2)	↓2
23	24	St. John's (2-1)	↑1
24	18	Arkansas (1-1)	↓9
25	—	Virginia (1-0)	
—	25	Temple (3-0)	

Week of Nov 28

AP	ESPN/USA	School	AP↓↑
1	1	Duke (5-0)	↑1
2	4	Kansas (5-0)	↑1
3	2	Michigan State (3-0)	↑1
4	3	Stanford (4-0)	↑1
5	5	Arizona (3-1)	↓4
6	6	North Carolina (3-0)	↑1
7	7	Tennessee (3-0)	↑2
8	9	Seton Hall (2-0)	↑2
9	8	Illinois (4-1)	↓1
10	10	Florida (1-0)	↑1
11	11	Notre Dame (3-0)	↑3
12	12	Wake Forest (4-0)	↑5
13	14	Maryland (1-2)	↓7
14	13	Oklahoma (5-0)	↑5
15	18	Southern California (3-0)	↑5
16	16	Connecticut (3-1)	↓4
17	15	Temple (4-1) (A)	⤴
18	20	Utah (3-1)	↓5
19	21	St. John's (3-1)	↑4
20	19	Syracuse (4-0)	⤴
21	22	Virginia (3-0)	↑4
22	17	Cincinnati (2-1)	↓6
23	23	Wisconsin (1-1)	↓5
24	—	Dayton (2-1)	⤴
25	24	Arkansas (3-1)	↓1
—	25	DePaul (3-1)	⤵

Week of Dec 5

AP	ESPN/USA	School	AP↓↑
1	1	Duke (7-0)	
2	2	Michigan State (5-0)	↑1
3	4	Kansas (7-0)	↓1
4	3	Stanford (6-0)	
5	5	Arizona (5-1)	
6	6	Tennessee (6-0)	↑1
7	8	Seton Hall (4-0)	↑1
8	9	Florida (3-0)	↑2
9	7	Illinois (5-2)	
10	10	Notre Dame (4-0)	↑1
11	11	Wake Forest (6-0)	↑1
12	15	Southern California (4-0)	↑3
13	14	Syracuse (7-0)	↑7
14	12	North Carolina (3-2) (B)	↓8
15	13	Connecticut (6-1)	↑1
16	19	Virginia (4-0)	↑5
17	20	Wisconsin (3-1)	↑6
18	18	Cincinnati (3-1)	↑4
19	17	Maryland (3-3)	↓6
20	16	Oklahoma (5-1)	↓6
21	21	Arkansas (5-1)	↑4
22	22	Utah (4-2)	↓4
23	—	Alabama (3-0)	⤴
24	24	St. John's (4-2)	↓5
25	—	Iowa State (5-0)	⤴
—	23	Temple (4-3)	⤵
—	25	Texas (5-1)	

Week of Dec 12

AP	ESPN/USA	School	AP↓↑
1	1	Duke (9-0)	
2	2	Michigan State (7-0)	
3	3	Stanford (6-0)	↑1
4	4	Tennessee (8-0)	↑2
5	5	Illinois (7-2)	↑4
6	7	Wake Forest (7-0)	↑5
7	6	Arizona (5-2)	↓2
8	9	Florida (5-1)	
9	10	Seton Hall (5-1)	↓2
10	8	Kansas (7-1)	↓7
11	11	Connecticut (7-1)	↑4
12	12	Syracuse (8-0)	↑1
13	13	Southern California (6-0)	↓1
14	14	Virginia (6-0)	↑2
15	15	North Carolina (5-2)	↓1
16	17	Wisconsin (5-1)	↑1
17	18	Cincinnati (3-1)	↑1
18	22	Alabama (6-0)	↑5
19	16	Oklahoma (6-1)	↑1
20	19	Maryland (5-3)	↓1
21	20	Notre Dame (4-2)	↓11
22	25	Iowa (7-0)	⤴
23	—	Mississippi (7-0)	⤴
24	23	Georgetown (7-0)	⤴
25	21	Arkansas (6-2)	↓4
—	24	Charlotte (6-1)	

Week of Dec 19

AP	ESPN/USA	School	AP↓↑
1	1	Duke (9-0)	
2	2	Michigan State (8-0)	
3	3	Stanford (6-0)	
4	4	Tennessee (9-0)	
5	5	Illinois (8-2)	
6	6	Wake Forest (8-0)	
7	7	Florida (6-1)	↑1
8	11	Seton Hall (6-1)	↑1
9	9	Kansas (9-1)	↑1
10	8	Arizona (5-3)	↓3
11	12	Connecticut (8-1)	
12	10	Syracuse (9-0)	
13	13	Southern California (7-0)	
14	14	Virginia (6-0)	
15	16	North Carolina (6-2)	
16	15	Wisconsin (7-1)	
17	18	Alabama (7-0)	↑1
18	17	Oklahoma (7-1)	↑1
19	21	Iowa (8-0)	↑3
20	19	Maryland (6-3)	
21	24	Notre Dame (5-2)	
22	20	Cincinnati (5-2)	↓5
23	22	Georgetown (9-0)	↑1
24	25	Mississippi (8-0)	↓1
25	23	Arkansas (6-2)	

Week of Dec 26

AP	ESPN/USA	School	AP↓↑
1	1	Michigan State (9-0)	↑1
2	2	Stanford (9-0)	↑1
3	3	Duke (10-1)	↓2
4	4	Wake Forest (10-0)	↑2
5	7	Florida (9-1)	↑2
6	5	Tennessee (10-1)	↓2
7	8	Kansas (10-1)	↑2
8	9	Virginia (8-0)	↑6
9	6	Illinois (9-3)	↓4
10	11	Connecticut (9-1)	↑1
11	12	Seton Hall (7-2)	↓3
12	10	Arizona (8-3)	↓2
13	14	Wisconsin (8-1)	↑3
14	16	North Carolina (7-2)	↑1
15	13	Syracuse (9-1)	↓3
16	15	Southern California (9-1)	↓3
17	17	Oklahoma (9-1)	↑1
18	19	Maryland (7-3)	↑2
19	18	Cincinnati (8-2)	↑3
20	20	Alabama (9-1)	↓3
21	21	Georgetown (10-0)	↑2
22	23	Notre Dame (7-2)	↓1
23	22	Iowa (9-1)	↓4
24	24	Mississippi (11-1)	
25	—	Iowa State (10-1)	⤴
—	25	Texas (8-2)	

Week of Jan 2

AP	ESPN/USA	School	AP↓↑
1	1	Michigan State (11-0)	
2	2	Stanford (11-0)	
3	3	Duke (11-1)	
4	4	Wake Forest (11-0) (C)	
5	6	Florida (10-1)	
6	5	Tennessee (13-1)	
7	7	Kansas (11-1)	
8	9	Virginia (10-0)	
9	8	Illinois (10-3)	
10	10	Connecticut (11-1)	
11	11	Seton Hall (9-2)	
12	12	Wisconsin (9-1)	↑1
13	14	North Carolina (9-2)	↑1
14	13	Syracuse (11-1)	↑1
15	16	Oklahoma (11-1)	↑2
16	15	Arizona (8-4)	↓4
17	17	Maryland (9-3)	↑1
18	18	Alabama (10-1)	↑2
19	20	Georgetown (11-0)	↑2
20	19	Southern California (10-2)	↓4
21	25	Notre Dame (8-2)	↑1
22	21	Mississippi (12-1)	↑2
23	—	Iowa State (11-1)	↑2
24	22	Texas (10-2)	⤴
25	24	Cincinnati (9-3)	↓6
—	23	Iowa (11-2)	⤵

Week of Jan 9 (D)

AP	ESPN/USA	School	AP↓↑
1	1	Stanford (13-0)	↑1
2	2	Duke (13-1)	↑1
3	3	Michigan State (12-1)	↓2
4	4	Tennessee (14-1)	↑2
5	5	Kansas (12-1)	↑2
6	6	Wake Forest (12-1)	↓2
7	8	Illinois (12-3)	↑2
8	7	Florida (10-2)	↓3
9	11	North Carolina (11-2)	↑4
10	9	Virginia (11-1)	↓2
11	10	Syracuse (13-1)	↑3
12	13	Georgetown (13-0)	↑7
13	12	Connecticut (12-2)	↓3
14	16	Maryland (11-3)	↑3
15	15	Seton Hall (10-3)	↓4
16	14	Alabama (12-1)	↑2
17	17	Wisconsin (10-2)	↓5
18	23	Iowa State (13-1)	↑5
19	18	Southern California (12-2)	↑1
20	21	Mississippi (13-1)	↑2
21	20	Arizona (8-5)	↓5
22	19	Oklahoma (11-2)	↓7
23	22	Texas (11-2)	↑1
24	—	Boston College (11-0)	⤴
25	25	Notre Dame (9-3)	↓4
—	24	Iowa (12-2)	

Week of Jan 16

AP	ESPN/USA	School	AP↓↑
1	1	Stanford (15-0)	
2	2	Duke (15-1)	
3	3	Michigan State (14-1)	
4	4	Tennessee (16-1)	
5	5	Kansas (13-1)	
6	6	North Carolina (13-2)	↑3
7	7	Florida (11-2)	↑1
8	9	Syracuse (15-1)	↑3
9	11	Georgetown (15-0)	↑3
10	8	Wake Forest (13-2)	↓4
11	10	Illinois (13-4)	↓4
12	14	Maryland (12-4)	↑2
13	13	Virginia (11-3)	↓3
14	16	Iowa (14-2)	⤴
15	12	Alabama (13-2)	↑1
16	15	Connecticut (13-3)	↓2
17	17	Arizona (10-5)	↑4
18	19	Seton Hall (11-4)	↓3
19	18	Wisconsin (10-4)	↓2
20	—	Missouri (12-3)	⤴
21	22	Mississippi (14-2)	↓1
22	21	Oklahoma (12-3)	
23	23	Iowa State (13-3)	↓5
24	20	Southern California (12-3)	↓5
25	25	Boston College (12-1)	↓1
—	24	Texas (12-3)	⤵

Week of Jan 23

AP	ESPN/USA	School	AP↓↑
1	1	Stanford (17-0)	
2	2	Duke (17-1)	
3	3	Michigan State (15-1)	
4	4	Kansas (15-1)	↑1
5	6	North Carolina (15-2)	↑1
6	5	Tennessee (17-2)	↓2
7	7	Illinois (15-4)	↑4
8	10	Maryland (14-4)	↑4
9	8	Wake Forest (14-3)	↑1
10	11	Georgetown (16-1)	↓1
11	8	Syracuse (15-2)	↓3
12	13	Arizona (12-5)	↑5
13	12	Virginia (13-3)	
14	14	Florida (11-4)	↓7
15	16	Wisconsin (11-4)	↑4
16	19	Seton Hall (12-5)	↑2
17	18	Iowa State (15-3)	↑6
18	15	Alabama (14-3)	↓3
19	21	Mississippi (15-3)	↑2
20	23	Texas (15-3)	⤴
21	17	Iowa (14-4)	↓7
22	—	Fresno State (16-2)	⤴
23	25	Boston College (13-2)	↑2
24	20	Connecticut (13-5)	↓9
25	22	Southern California (13-4)	↓1
—	24	Oklahoma (13-4)	⤵

Poll Progression Continues →

Week of Jan 30

AP	ESPN/USA	School	AP↓↑
1	1	**Stanford** (19-0)	
2	2	**Duke** (19-1)	
3	3	**Kansas** (17-1)	↑1
4	4	**North Carolina** (17-2)	↑1
5	5	**Michigan State** (16-2)	↓2
6	6	**Illinois** (16-4)	↑1
7	9	**Arizona** (14-5)	↑5
8	7	**Tennessee** (17-3)	↓2
9	10	**Maryland** (14-5)	↓1
10	16	**Wisconsin** (13-4)	↑5
11	11	**Virginia** (14-4)	↑2
12	8	**Syracuse** (16-3)	↓1
13	14	**Florida** (13-4)	↑1
14	13	**Georgetown** (17-2)	↓4
15	18	**Iowa State** (17-3)	↑2
16	12	**Wake Forest** (14-5)	↓7
17	15	**Alabama** (16-3)	↑1
18	17	**Iowa** (16-4)	↑3
19	22	**Fresno State** (17-2)	↑3
20	20	**Boston College** (14-2)	↑3
21	19	**Southern California** (15-4)	↑4
22	25	**Seton Hall** (12-6)	↓6
23	—	**Notre Dame** (13-5)	⤴
24	21	**Oklahoma** (15-4)	⤴
25	—	**Georgia** (13-7)	⤴
—	23	**Connecticut** (13-6)	⤵
—	24	**Texas** (15-5)	⤵

Week of Feb 6

AP	ESPN/USA	School	AP↓↑
1	1	**North Carolina** (19-2)	↑3
2	2	**Stanford** (20-1)	↓1
3	3	**Duke** (20-2)	↓1
4	4	**Michigan State** (18-2)	↑1
5	5	**Kansas** (18-2)	↓2
6	9	**Virginia** (15-4)	↑5
7	6	**Illinois** (17-5)	↓1
8	11	**Florida** (15-4)	↑5
9	7	**Syracuse** (18-3)	↑3
10	8	**Tennessee** (18-4)	↓2
11	10	**Arizona** (15-6)	↓4
12	14	**Iowa State** (19-3)	↑3
13	13	**Maryland** (15-6)	↓4
14	16	**Iowa** (17-4)	↑4
15	12	**Georgetown** (18-3)	↓1
16	18	**Wisconsin** (14-5)	↓6
17	20	**Boston College** (16-2)	↑3
18	17	**Alabama** (17-4)	↓1
19	15	**Wake Forest** (15-5)	↓3
20	23	**Notre Dame** (14-5)	↑3
21	21	**Oklahoma** (17-4)	↑3
22	19	**Southern California** (16-5)	↓1
23	22	**Fresno State** (18-3)	↓4
24	—	**Xavier** (17-3)	⤴
25	24	**Mississippi** (17-4)	⤴
—	25	**Texas** (16-6)	

Week of Feb 13

AP	ESPN/USA	School	AP↓↑
1	1	**North Carolina** (21-2)	
2	2	**Stanford** (22-1)	
3	3	**Duke** (22-2)	
4	5	**Illinois** (19-5)	↑3
5	4	**Michigan State** (19-3)	↓1
6	6	**Kansas** (19-3)	↓1
7	9	**Iowa State** (21-3)	↑5
8	8	**Arizona** (17-6)	↑3
9	11	**Boston College** (18-2)	↑8
10	7	**Syracuse** (19-4)	↓1
11	9	**Florida** (16-5) Ⓔ	↓3
12	12	**Virginia** (16-6)	↓6
13	14	**Oklahoma** (19-4)	↑8
14	21	**Notre Dame** (16-5)	↑6
15	13	**Tennessee** (18-6)	↓5
16	19	**Mississippi** (19-4)	↑9
17	18	**Maryland** (15-8)	↓4
18	16	**Georgetown** (19-4)	↓3
19	20	**Wisconsin** (15-6)	↓3
20	22	**Fresno State** (20-3)	↑3
21	17	**Alabama** (18-5)	↓3
22	25	**Kentucky** (15-7) Ⓔ	⤴
23	15	**Wake Forest** (16-7)	↓4
24	—	**UCLA** (15-6)	⤴
25	24	**Iowa** (17-6)	↓11
—	23	**Southern California** (16-6)	⤵

Week of Feb 20

AP	ESPN/USA	School
1	1	**Stanford** (23-1)
2	2	**North Carolina** (21-3)
3	4	**Illinois** (21-5)
4	3	**Duke** (23-3)
5	5	**Michigan State** (20-3) Ⓕ
6	6	**Iowa State** (22-3)
7	7	**Florida** (18-5)
8	8	**Arizona** (18-7)
9	11	**Virginia** (18-6)
10	9	**Boston College** (19-3)
11	10	**Kansas** (19-5)
12	13	**Mississippi** (21-4)
13	16	**Kentucky** (17-7)
14	14	**Alabama** (20-5)
15	23	**UCLA** (17-6)
16	15	**Oklahoma** (20-5)
17	12	**Syracuse** (19-6)
18	18	**Notre Dame** (17-6)
19	17	**Wisconsin** (16-7)
20	20	**Maryland** (16-9)
21	19	**Georgetown** (20-5)
22	21	**Tennessee** (18-8)
23	24	**Saint Joseph's** (21-4)
24	22	**Wake Forest** (17-8)
25	—	**Providence** (18-7)
—	25	**Fresno State** (20-5)

Week of Feb 27

AP	ESPN/USA	School	AP↓↑
1	1	**Stanford** (25-1)	
2	2	**Duke** (25-3)	↑2
3	3	**Michigan State** (22-3)	↑2
4	4	**North Carolina** (22-4)	↓2
5	5	**Illinois** (22-6)	↓2
6	6	**Florida** (20-5)	↑1
7	9	**Virginia** (19-6)	↑2
8	8	**Iowa State** (23-4)	↓2
9	7	**Arizona** (19-7)	↓1
10	11	**Kansas** (21-5)	↑1
11	10	**Boston College** (20-4)	↓1
12	18	**UCLA** (19-6)	↑3
13	13	**Notre Dame** (19-6)	↑5
14	12	**Mississippi** (22-5)	↓2
15	15	**Kentucky** (18-8)	↓2
16	16	**Maryland** (18-9)	↑4
17	17	**Oklahoma** (21-6)	↓1
18	22	**Saint Joseph's** (23-4)	↑5
19	13	**Syracuse** (20-7)	↓2
20	19	**Alabama** (20-7)	↓6
21	20	**Georgetown** (21-6)	
22	24	**Wisconsin** (17-8)	↓3
23	21	**Wake Forest** (19-9)	↑1
24	—	**Texas** (21-7)	⤴
25	—	**Xavier** (21-5)	⤴
—	23	**Tennessee** (19-9)	⤵
—	25	**Fresno State** (21-5)	

Week of Mar 6

AP	ESPN/USA	School	AP↓↑
1	1	**Stanford** (27-1)	
2	3	**Michigan State** (24-3)	↑1
3	2	**Duke** (26-4)	↓1
4	4	**Illinois** (23-6)	↑1
5	6	**Florida** (22-5)	↑1
6	5	**North Carolina** (23-5)	↓2
7	8	**Iowa State** (25-4)	↑1
8	7	**Arizona** (21-7)	↑1
9	10	**Kansas** (23-5)	↑1
10	9	**Boston College** (23-4)	↑1
11	13	**Maryland** (20-9)	↑5
12	12	**Virginia** (20-7)	↓5
13	17	**UCLA** (20-7)	↓1
14	11	**Mississippi** (23-6)	
15	15	**Kentucky** (19-9)	
16	16	**Oklahoma** (23-6)	↑1
17	14	**Syracuse** (22-7)	↑2
18	19	**Georgetown** (23-6)	↑3
19	18	**Notre Dame** (19-8)	↓6
20	22	**Texas** (23-7)	↑4
21	23	**Saint Joseph's** (24-5)	↓3
22	20	**Wake Forest** (19-9)	↑1
23	21	**Wisconsin** (18-9)	↓1
24	—	**Ohio State** (20-9)	⤴
25	25	**Fresno State** (24-5)	⤴
—	24	**Tennessee** (21-9)	
—	25	**Alabama** (21-8)	⤵

Week of Mar 13 Ⓖ

AP	ESPN/USA	School	AP↓↑
1	1	**Duke** (29-4)	↑2
2	2	**Stanford** (28-2)	↓1
3	3	**Michigan State** (24-4)	↓1
4	6	**Illinois** (24-7)	
5	4	**Arizona** (23-7)	↑3
6	5	**North Carolina** (25-6)	
7	7	**Boston College** (26-4)	↑3
8	8	**Florida** (23-6)	↓3
9	10	**Kentucky** (22-9)	↑6
10	9	**Iowa State** (25-5)	↓3
11	11	**Maryland** (21-10)	
12	12	**Kansas** (24-6)	↓3
13	14	**Oklahoma** (26-6)	↑3
14	13	**Mississippi** (25-7)	
15	18	**UCLA** (21-8)	↓2
16	15	**Virginia** (20-8)	↓4
17	16	**Syracuse** (24-8)	
18	17	**Texas** (25-8)	↑2
19	19	**Notre Dame** (19-9)	
20	21	**Indiana** (21-12)	⤴
21	20	**Georgetown** (23-7)	↓3
22	23	**Saint Joseph's** (25-6)	↓1
23	22	**Wake Forest** (19-10)	↓1
24	25	**Iowa** (22-11)	⤴
25	24	**Wisconsin** (18-10)	↓2

Final Poll (Post-Tournamen[t])

ESPN/USA	School
1	**Duke** (35-4)
2	**Arizona** (28-8)
3	**Michigan State** (28-5)
4	**Maryland** (25-11)
5	**Stanford** (31-3)
6	**Illinois** (27-8)
7	**Kansas** (26-7)
8	**Kentucky** (24-10)
9	**Mississippi** (27-8)
10	**North Carolina** (26-7)
11	**Boston College** (27-5)
12	**UCLA** (23-9)
13	**Florida** (24-7)
14	**Southern California** (24-10)
15	**Iowa State** (25-6)
16	**Temple** (24-13)
17	**Georgetown** (25-8)
18	**Syracuse** (25-9)
19	**Oklahoma** (26-7)
20	**Gonzaga** (26-7)
21	**Virginia** (20-9)
22	**Cincinnati** (25-10)
23	**Notre Dame** (20-10)
24	**Saint Joseph's** (26-7)
25	**Penn State** (21-12)

Ⓐ Temple's 69-61 win is new Indiana coach Mike Davis' first loss. The previous September, Bob Knight was forced to resign after violating IU president Myles Brand's zero-tolerance bad-behavior policy by grabbing a student forcefully by the arm and yelling at him. Knight went 659-242 in his 29 seasons at Indiana.

Ⓑ Brendan Haywood collects 18 points, 14 rebounds and 10 blocks against Miami on Dec. 4, becoming the first North Carolina player to achieve a triple-double.

Ⓒ Wake Forest defeats Navy, 90-58, on Dec. 29 to extend its winning streak to 16 games, the school's longest since 1926-27. The Demon Deacons will beat Virginia to run the streak to 17 before losing to North Carolina on Jan. 6.

Ⓓ Arizona State's Eddie House becomes the first player in the 2000s to score at least 60 points, posting 61 in a double-OT victory over California.

Ⓔ Kentucky's Tayshaun Prince hits a baby hook with 3.3 seconds remaining on Feb. 6 to give the Wildcats a 71-70 home win over Florida.

Ⓕ With a 66-57 victory over Indiana, Michigan State's senior class gets its 108th career victory, tying Indiana's Big Ten record, set and matched by the Hoosier classes of 1976 and '94.

Ⓖ In Denny Crum's last home game in Freedom Hall, Louisville gets drilled by UAB, 74-61, in the Conference USA tournament. The Cards finish 12–19, Crum's second losing season in four years.

Pre-Tournament Ratings Percentage Index (RPI)

Rank	School	W-L	Sched. Strg.	SS Rank	RPI
1	**Duke**	29-4	.6088	5	.6776
2	**Stanford**	26-2	.5647	50	.6617
3	**North Carolina**	25-6	.5980	14	.6475
4	**Michigan State**	24-4	.5750	39	.6463
5	**Illinois**	24-7	.5937	19	.6397
6	**Boston College**	25-4	.5641	53	.6364
7	**Arizona**	22-7	.5975	16	.6355
8	**Mississippi**	24-7	.5938	18	.6352
9	**Kentucky**	22-9	.6068	8	.6351
10	**Texas**	25-8	.6086	6	.6331
11	**UCLA**	21-8	.6061	11	.6293
12	**Kansas**	22-6	.5737	42	.6263
13	**Iowa State**	24-5	.5540	59	.6202
14	**Indiana**	21-12	.6237	3	.6183
15	**Tennessee**	22-10	.6064	10	.6177
16	**Oklahoma**	26-6	.5516	63	.6173
17	**Florida**	23-6	.5409	77	.6116
18	**Wisconsin**	18-10	.6089	4	.6115
19	**Syracuse**	24-8	.5644	52	.6071
20	**Fresno State**	25-6	.5391	79	.6037
21	**Maryland**	21-10	.5842	25	.6033
22	**Southern California**	20-9	.5826	27	.6023
23	**Georgia**	16-14	.6362	1	.6017
24	**Penn State**	19-11	.5984	13	.6016
25	**Iowa**	22-11	.5742	41	.6014
26	**Notre Dame**	19-9	.5770	37	.5982
27	**Creighton**	24-7	.5483	68	.5973
28	**Wake Forest**	19-10	.5815	29	.5958
29	**Providence**	20-9	.5665	45	.5942
30	**Butler**	21-7	.5508	65	.5934
31	**Cincinnati**	23-9	.5578	55	.5911
32	**Virginia**	20-8	.5472	69	.5897
33	**Georgia State**	25-4	.5023	139	.5892
34	**Ohio State**	20-10	.5661	47	.5892
35	**California**	20-10	.5647	51	.5877
36	**Saint Joseph's**	25-6	.5023	140	.5877
37	**Temple**	21-12	.5746	40	.5873
38	**Georgia Tech**	17-12	.5979	15	.5857
39	**BYU**	24-8	.5345	85	.5823
40	**Mississippi State**	16-12	.6077	7	.5815
41	**Xavier**	21-7	.5179	106	.5799
42	**Arkansas**	20-10	.5539	60	.5791
43	**Georgetown**	23-7	.5075	125	.5787
44	**Richmond**	21-6	.5166	109	.5787
45	**Missouri**	18-12	.5778	36	.5770
46	**Villanova**	18-12	.5808	30	.5759
47	**Hofstra**	26-4	.4712	207	.5733
48	**Charlotte**	21-10	.5381	80	.5729
49	**Oklahoma State**	19-9	.5372	81	.5712
50	**Alabama**	21-10	.5288	94	.5711

Source: Collegiate Basketball News

ANNUAL REVIEW

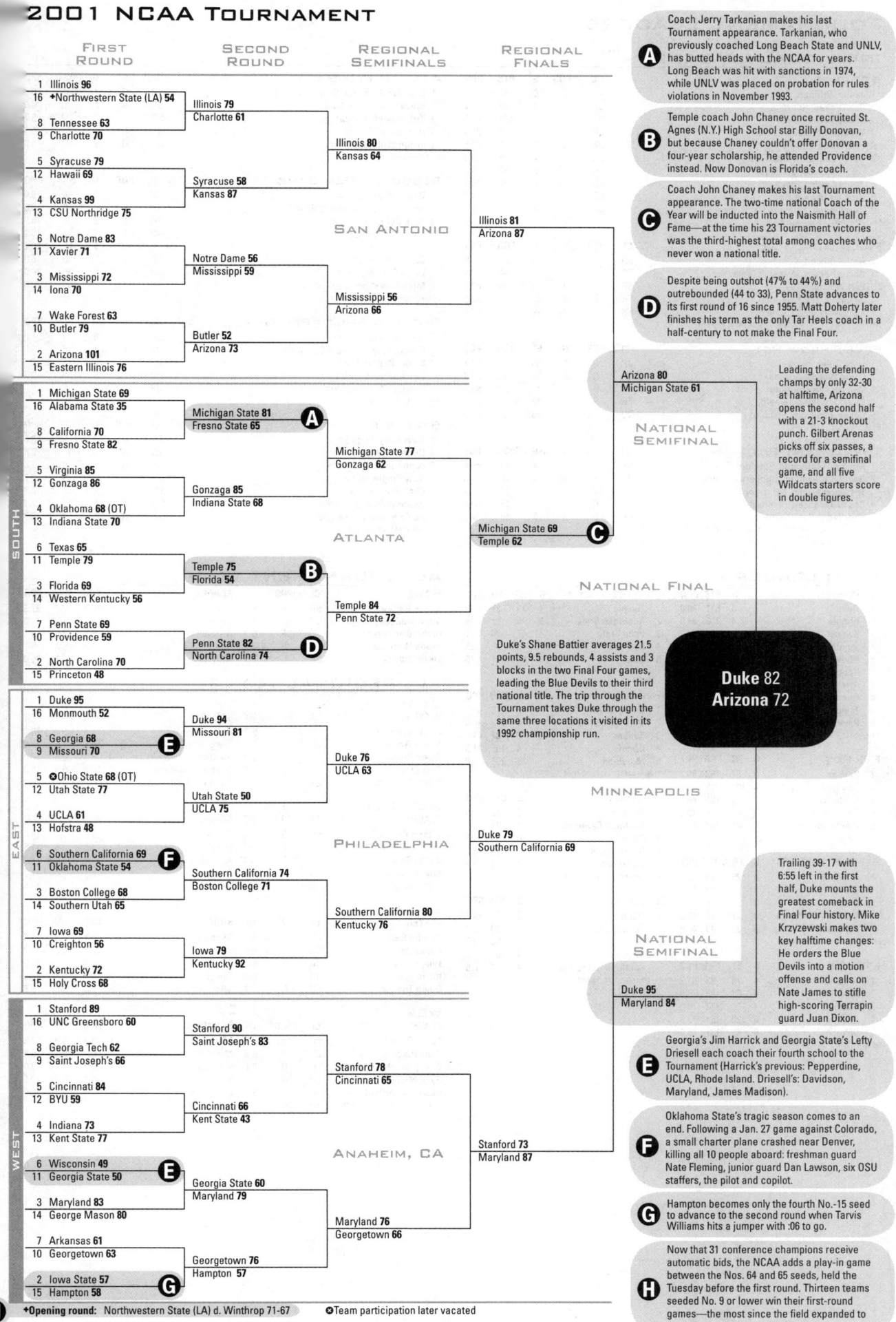

2001 NCAA Tournament

San Antonio

First Round
- 1 Illinois **96**
- 16 ✦Northwestern State (LA) **54**
- 8 Tennessee **63**
- 9 Charlotte **70**
- 5 Syracuse **79**
- 12 Hawaii **69**
- 4 Kansas **99**
- 13 CSU Northridge **75**
- 6 Notre Dame **83**
- 11 Xavier **71**
- 3 Mississippi **72**
- 14 Iona **70**
- 7 Wake Forest **63**
- 10 Butler **79**
- 2 Arizona **101**
- 15 Eastern Illinois **76**

Second Round
- Illinois **79**, Charlotte **61**
- Syracuse **58**, Kansas **87**
- Notre Dame **56**, Mississippi **59**
- Butler **52**, Arizona **73**

Regional Semifinals
- Illinois **80**, Kansas **64**
- Mississippi **56**, Arizona **66**

Regional Finals
- Illinois **81**, Arizona **87**

South — Atlanta

First Round
- 1 Michigan State **69**
- 16 Alabama State **35**
- 8 California **70**
- 9 Fresno State **82**
- 5 Virginia **85**
- 12 Gonzaga **86**
- 4 Oklahoma **68** (OT)
- 13 Indiana State **70**
- 6 Texas **65**
- 11 Temple **79**
- 3 Florida **69**
- 14 Western Kentucky **56**
- 7 Penn State **69**
- 10 Providence **59**
- 2 North Carolina **70**
- 15 Princeton **48**

Second Round
- Michigan State **81**, Fresno State **65** (A)
- Gonzaga **85**, Indiana State **68**
- Temple **75**, Florida **54** (B)
- Penn State **82**, North Carolina **74** (D)

Regional Semifinals
- Michigan State **77**, Gonzaga **62**
- Temple **84**, Penn State **72**

Regional Finals
- Michigan State **69**, Temple **62** (C)

East — Philadelphia

First Round
- 1 Duke **95**
- 16 Monmouth **52**
- 8 Georgia **68** (E)
- 9 Missouri **70**
- 5 ⊗Ohio State **68** (OT)
- 12 Utah State **77**
- 4 UCLA **61**
- 13 Hofstra **48**
- 6 Southern California **69** (F)
- 11 Oklahoma State **54**
- 3 Boston College **68**
- 14 Southern Utah **65**
- 7 Iowa **69**
- 10 Creighton **56**
- 2 Kentucky **72**
- 15 Holy Cross **68**

Second Round
- Duke **94**, Missouri **81**
- Utah State **50**, UCLA **75**
- Southern California **74**, Boston College **71**
- Iowa **79**, Kentucky **92**

Regional Semifinals
- Duke **76**, UCLA **63**
- Southern California **80**, Kentucky **76**

Regional Finals
- Duke **79**, Southern California **69**

West — Anaheim, CA

First Round
- 1 Stanford **89**
- 16 UNC Greensboro **60**
- 8 Georgia Tech **62**
- 9 Saint Joseph's **66**
- 5 Cincinnati **84**
- 12 BYU **59**
- 4 Indiana **73**
- 13 Kent State **77**
- 6 Wisconsin **49** (E)
- 11 Georgia State **50**
- 3 Maryland **83**
- 14 George Mason **80**
- 7 Arkansas **61**
- 10 Georgetown **63**
- 2 Iowa State **57** (G)
- 15 Hampton **58**

Second Round
- Stanford **90**, Saint Joseph's **83**
- Cincinnati **66**, Kent State **43**
- Georgia State **60**, Maryland **79**
- Georgetown **76**, Hampton **57**

Regional Semifinals
- Stanford **78**, Cincinnati **65**
- Maryland **76**, Georgetown **66**

Regional Finals
- Stanford **73**, Maryland **87**

Minneapolis

National Semifinal
- Arizona **80**, Michigan State **61**

Leading the defending champs by only 32-30 at halftime, Arizona opens the second half with a 21-3 knockout punch. Gilbert Arenas picks off six passes, a record for a semifinal game, and all five Wildcats starters score in double figures.

National Semifinal
- Duke **95**, Maryland **84**

Trailing 39-17 with 6:55 left in the first half, Duke mounts the greatest comeback in Final Four history. Mike Krzyzewski makes two key halftime changes: He orders the Blue Devils into a motion offense and calls on Nate James to stifle high-scoring Terrapin guard Juan Dixon.

National Final

Duke 82
Arizona 72

Duke's Shane Battier averages 21.5 points, 9.5 rebounds, 4 assists and 3 blocks in the two Final Four games, leading the Blue Devils to their third national title. The trip through the Tournament takes Duke through the same three locations it visited in its 1992 championship run.

(H) ✦**Opening round:** Northwestern State (LA) d. Winthrop 71-67

⊗Team participation later vacated

A Coach Jerry Tarkanian makes his last Tournament appearance. Tarkanian, who previously coached Long Beach State and UNLV, has butted heads with the NCAA for years. Long Beach was hit with sanctions in 1974, while UNLV was placed on probation for rules violations in November 1993.

B Temple coach John Chaney once recruited St. Agnes (N.Y.) High School star Billy Donovan, but because Chaney couldn't offer Donovan a four-year scholarship, he attended Providence instead. Now Donovan is Florida's coach.

C Coach John Chaney makes his last Tournament appearance. The two-time national Coach of the Year will be inducted into the Naismith Hall of Fame—at the time his 23 Tournament victories was the third-highest total among coaches who never won a national title.

D Despite being outshot (47% to 44%) and outrebounded (44 to 33), Penn State advances to its first round of 16 since 1955. Matt Doherty later finishes his term as the only Tar Heels coach in a half-century to not make the Final Four.

E Georgia's Jim Harrick and Georgia State's Lefty Driesell each coach their fourth school to the Tournament (Harrick's previous: Pepperdine, UCLA, Rhode Island. Driesell's: Davidson, Maryland, James Madison).

F Oklahoma State's tragic season comes to an end. Following a Jan. 27 game against Colorado, a small charter plane crashed near Denver, killing all 10 people aboard: freshman guard Nate Fleming, junior guard Dan Lawson, six OSU staffers, the pilot and copilot.

G Hampton becomes only the fourth No.-15 seed to advance to the second round when Tarvis Williams hits a jumper with :06 to go.

H Now that 31 conference champions receive automatic bids, the NCAA adds a play-in game between the Nos. 64 and 65 seeds, held the Tuesday before the first round. Thirteen teams seeded No. 9 or lower win their first-round games—the most since the field expanded to 64 teams.

Tournament Leaders

Individual Leaders

Scoring

	CL	POS	G	PTS	PPG
1 **Jason Williams**, Duke	SO	G	6	154	25.7
2 **Dan Dickau**, Gonzaga	JR	G	3	68	22.7
3 **Shane Battier**, Duke	SR	F	6	135	22.5
4 **Tayshaun Prince**, Kentucky	JR	G/F	3	64	21.3
5 **Lynn Greer**, Temple	JR	G	4	82	20.5
6 **Casey Jacobsen**, Stanford	SO	G	4	76	19.0
Casey Calvary, Gonzaga	SR	F	3	57	19.0
8 **Jason Collins**, Stanford	SO	C	4	74	18.5
9 **Nick Collison**, Kansas	SO	F	3	55	18.3
10 **Sam Clancy**, Southern California	JR	F	4	72	18.0

Minimum: 3 games

Field Goal Pct

	CL	POS	G	FG	FGA	PCT
1 **Nick Collison**, Kansas	SO	F	3	23	32	71.9
2 **Andre Hutson**, Michigan State	SR	F	5	31	44	70.5
3 **Earl Watson**, UCLA	SR	G	3	22	35	62.9
4 **Jason Parker**, Kentucky	FR	F	3	15	24	62.5
5 **Titus Ivory**, Penn State	SR	G	3	18	29	62.1

Minimum: 15 made and 3 games

Free Throw Pct

	CL	POS	G	FT	FTA	PCT
1 **Lynn Greer**, Temple	JR	G	4	33	34	97.1
2 **Loren Woods**, Arizona	SR	C	6	30	33	90.9
3 **Dan Dickau**, Gonzaga	JR	G	3	19	21	90.5
4 **David Hawkins**, Temple	FR	G	4	15	17	88.2
5 **Casey Jacobsen**, Stanford	SO	G	4	20	23	87.0

Minimum: 15 made

Three-Point Pct

	CL	POS	G	3FG	3FGA	PCT
1 **Michael McDonald**, Stanford	SR	G	4	8	13	61.5
2 **David Bluthenthal**, Southern California	JR	F	4	9	16	56.3
Tayshaun Prince, Kentucky	JR	G/F	3	9	16	56.3
4 **Casey Jacobsen**, Stanford	SO	G	4	8	15	53.3
5 **Titus Ivory**, Penn State	SR	G	3	10	19	52.6

Minimum: 6 made and 3 games

Assists Per Game

	CL	POS	G	AST	APG
1 **Brandon Granville**, Southern California	JR	G	4	26	6.5
2 **Steve Blake**, Maryland	SO	G	5	30	6.0
3 **Kirk Hinrich**, Kansas	SO	G	3	17	5.7
4 **Lynn Greer**, Temple	JR	G	4	21	5.3
5 **Jason Williams**, Duke	SO	G	6	31	5.2

Minimum: 3 games

Rebounds Per Game

	CL	POS	G	REB	RPG
1 **Dan Gadzuric**, UCLA	JR	C	3	36	12.0
2 **Sam Clancy**, Southern California	JR	F	4	43	10.8
3 **Nick Collison**, Kansas	SO	F	3	31	10.3
4 **Shane Battier**, Duke	SR	F	6	61	10.2
5 **Lonny Baxter**, Maryland	JR	F/C	5	50	10.0
Casey Calvary, Gonzaga	SR	F	3	30	10.0
Drew Gooden, Kansas	SO	F	3	30	10.0
Mike Sweetney, Georgetown	FR	F	3	30	10.0

Minimum: 3 games

Blocked Shots Per Game

	CL	POS	G	BLK	BPG
1 **Loren Woods**, Arizona	SR	C	6	24	4.0
Sam Clancy, Southern California	JR	F	4	16	4.0
3 **Shane Battier**, Duke	SR	F	6	16	2.7
Dan Gadzuric, UCLA	JR	C	3	8	2.7
Donald Little, Cincinnati	JR	C	3	8	2.7

Minimum: 3 games

Steals Per Game

	CL	POS	G	STL	SPG
1 **Titus Ivory**, Penn State	SR	G	3	9	3.0
2 **Gilbert Arenas**, Arizona	SO	G	6	17	2.8
3 **Juan Dixon**, Maryland	JR	G	5	14	2.8
4 **Billy Knight**, UCLA	JR	G	3	8	2.7
5 **Chris Duhon**, Duke	FR	G	6	14	2.3
Jason Williams, Duke	SO	G	6	14	2.3
Kevin Braswell, Georgetown	JR	G	3	7	2.3

Minimum: 3 games

Team Leaders

Scoring

	G	PTS	PPG
1 **Duke**	6	521	86.8
2 **Illinois**	4	336	84.0
3 **Kansas**	3	250	83.3
4 **Stanford**	4	330	82.5
5 **Maryland**	5	409	81.8
6 **Kentucky**	3	240	80.0
7 **Arizona**	6	479	79.8
8 **Gonzaga**	3	233	77.7
9 **Temple**	4	300	75.0
10 **Penn State**	3	223	74.3

Minimum: 3 games

FG Pct

	G	FG	FGA	PCT
1 **Kansas**	3	87	159	54.7
2 **Stanford**	4	103	208	49.5
3 **Kentucky**	3	89	181	49.2
4 **Gonzaga**	3	82	169	48.5
5 **Cincinnati**	3	81	167	48.5

Minimum: 3 games

3-Pt FG Pct

	G	3FG	3FGA	PCT
1 **Stanford**	4	28	60	46.7
2 **Kentucky**	3	28	62	45.2
3 **Gonzaga**	3	22	49	44.9
4 **Southern California**	4	22	52	42.3
5 **Kansas**	3	20	49	40.8

Minimum: 3 games

FT Pct

	G	FT	FTA	PCT
1 **Temple**	4	76	93	81.7
2 **Illinois**	4	67	85	78.8
3 **Stanford**	4	96	123	78.0
4 **Arizona**	6	120	154	77.9
5 **Duke**	6	99	131	75.6

Minimum: 3 games

Ast/TO Ratio

	G	AST	TO	RAT
1 **Temple**	4	39	25	1.56
2 **Michigan State**	5	76	55	1.38
3 **Penn State**	3	47	36	1.31
4 **Kentucky**	3	49	39	1.26
5 **Duke**	6	97	81	1.20

Minimum: 3 games

Rebounds

	G	REB	RPG
1 **Georgetown**	3	139	46.3
2 **Michigan State**	5	223	44.6
3 **Kansas**	3	132	44.0
4 **Illinois**	4	165	41.3
5 **Maryland**	5	205	41.0

Minimum: 3 games

Blocks

	G	BLK	BPG
1 **Arizona**	6	42	7.0
2 **Southern California**	4	24	6.0
3 **Duke**	6	33	5.5
4 **Georgetown**	3	16	5.3
5 **Cincinnati**	3	15	5.0

Minimum: 3 games

Steals

	G	STL	SPG
1 **UCLA**	3	32	10.7
2 **Penn State**	3	30	10.0
3 **Duke**	6	56	9.3
4 **Arizona**	6	51	8.5
Southern California	4	34	8.5

Minimum: 3 games

All-Tournament Team

PLAYER	CL	POS	HT	SCHOOL	RPG	APG	PPG
Shane Battier*	SR	F	6-8	Duke	10.2	2.3	22.5
Mike Dunleavy Jr.	SO	G/F	6-9	Duke	4.3	1.7	12.0
Richard Jefferson	JR	F	6-7	Arizona	6.3	2.0	13.5
Jason Williams	SO	G	6-2	Duke	3.3	5.2	25.7
Loren Woods	SR	C	7-1	Arizona	7.7	1.7	16.0

All-Regional Teams

East

PLAYER	CL	POS	HT	SCHOOL	RPG	APG	PPG
Jason Williams*	SO	G	6-2	Duke	3.5	5.8	28.8
Shane Battier	SR	F	6-8	Duke	10.5	1.5	23.0
David Bluthenthal	JR	F	6-7	Southern California	6.3	0.5	16.0
Sam Clancy	JR	F	6-7	Southern California	10.8	0.3	18.0
Brian Scalabrine	SR	C	6-9	Southern California	6.0	3.3	10.3

Midwest

PLAYER	CL	POS	HT	SCHOOL	RPG	APG	PPG
Gilbert Arenas*	SO	G	6-4	Arizona	5.0	1.8	16.3
Robert Archibald	JR	F	6-11	Illinois	5.5	0.5	11.5
Jason Gardner	SO	G	5-10	Arizona	3.0	3.0	11.8
Richard Jefferson	JR	F	6-7	Arizona	5.5	1.8	11.3
Loren Woods	SR	C	7-1	Arizona	6.8	1.8	15.8

South

PLAYER	CL	POS	HT	SCHOOL	RPG	APG	PPG
Charlie Bell*	SR	G	6-3	Michigan State	5.8	3.5	13.8
Casey Calvary	SR	F	6-8	Gonzaga	10.0	4.3	19.0
Lynn Greer	JR	G	6-1	Temple	2.3	5.3	20.5
Kevin Lyde	JR	C	6-9	Temple	7.5	1.8	13.8
David Thomas	SR	G	6-7	Michigan State	7.0	2.0	8.8

West

PLAYER	CL	POS	HT	SCHOOL	RPG	APG	PPG
Lonny Baxter*	JR	F/C	6-8	Maryland	10.0	0.3	17.8
Juan Dixon	JR	G	6-3	Maryland	4.5	3.0	16.5
Casey Jacobsen	SO	G	6-6	Stanford	4.3	2.5	19.0
Ryan Mendez	SR	G/F	6-7	Stanford	4.8	3.0	12.5
Kenny Satterfield	SO	G	6-2	Cincinnati	6.0	5.0	16.0

* Most outstanding player

2001 NCAA TOURNAMENT BOX SCORES

Illinois 80, Kansas 64 (Sweet 16)

	1H	2H
Illinois	41	39
Kansas	29	35

ILLINOIS	MIN	FG	3FG	FT	REB	A	ST	BL	PF	TP
Frank Williams	36	11-24	3-7	5-5	5	3	3	0	0	30
Lucas Johnson	25	3-4	2-3	7-8	5	3	0	0	3	15
Sergio McClain	32	4-8	0-3	2-2	10	1	2	0	3	10
Damir Krupalija	15	3-6	0-2	1-3	7	0	1	0	5	7
Brian Cook	19	3-5	0-1	0-0	4	2	2	0	5	6
Cory Bradford	24	1-13	1-9	1-2	0	1	2	0	1	4
Robert Archibald	15	1-1	0-0	2-4	8	0	0	1	4	4
Marcus Griffin	16	1-2	0-0	0-0	1	0	0	0	5	2
Joe Cross	1	1-1	0-0	0-0	0	0	0	0	0	2
Sean Harrington	15	0-1	0-1	0-2	0	0	1	0	0	0
Jerrance Howard	1	0-0	0-0	0-0	0	0	0	0	0	0
Brett Melton	1	0-0	0-0	0-0	1	0	0	0	0	0
TOTALS	200	28-65	6-26	18-26	41	10	11	1	26	80
Percentages		43.1	23.1	69.2						

Coach: Bill Self

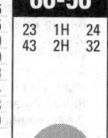

KANSAS	MIN	FG	3FG	FT	REB	A	ST	BL	PF	TP
Nick Collison	28	8-11	1-1	6-14	7	0	1	0	5	23
Kirk Hinrich	28	4-6	1-1	5-6	2	2	2	0	5	14
Drew Gooden	33	5-11	0-3	3-6	9	1	0	2	4	13
Kenny Gregory	40	3-11	1-5	4-7	6	2	3	0	1	11
Jeff Boschee	40	1-7	1-7	0-0	2	2	0	0	3	3
Eric Chenowith	22	0-0	0-0	0-2	2	2	0	0	2	0
Brett Ballard	7	0-0	0-0	0-0	1	1	1	0	3	0
Jeff Carey	1	0-0	0-0	0-0	0	0	1	0	0	0
Lewis Harrison	1	0-0	0-0	0-0	0	0	1	0	0	0
TOTALS	200	21-46	4-17	18-35	29	10	9	2	23	64
Percentages		45.7	23.5	51.4						

Coach: Roy Williams

Officials: Dave Libbey, Mike Wood, Doug Shows **Technicals:** None **Attendance:** 28,962

Arizona 66, Mississippi 56 (Sweet 16)

	1H	2H
Arizona	23	43
Mississippi	24	32

ARIZONA	MIN	FG	3FG	FT	REB	A	ST	BL	PF	TP
Loren Woods	38	4-8	0-0	8-8	11	0	0	3	2	16
Richard Jefferson	34	7-16	0-1	1-2	11	1	2	1	4	15
Jason Gardner	37	2-7	0-2	6-6	1	1	0	0	1	10
Michael Wright	28	5-9	0-0	0-0	7	0	0	0	2	10
Gilbert Arenas	30	4-12	0-4	0-1	4	1	3	0	4	8
Luke Walton	17	1-3	0-1	2-4	2	0	2	0	2	4
Eugene Edgerson	13	1-1	0-0	1-1	5	0	0	0	2	3
Lamont Frazier	3	0-1	0-0	0-0	0	0	1	0	0	0
TOTALS	200	24-57	0-8	18-22	41	3	8	4	17	66
Percentages		42.1	0.0	81.8						

Coach: Lute Olson

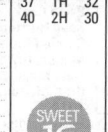

MISSISSIPPI	MIN	FG	3FG	FT	REB	A	ST	BL	PF	TP
Justin Reed	29	7-12	0-1	2-4	9	2	3	0	4	16
Rahim Lockhart	34	3-11	0-0	5-7	7	2	2	1	4	11
Jason Flanigan	28	3-7	2-2	0-0	3	0	3	0	4	8
David Sanders	27	2-3	0-0	4-5	2	0	0	0	3	8
Aaron Harper	23	3-13	1-8	0-0	4	2	0	0	3	7
Jason Holmes	19	1-4	1-4	0-0	3	3	0	0	2	3
Jason Harrison	14	1-5	1-4	0-0	0	3	0	0	4	3
Emmanuel Wade	13	0-1	0-1	0-0	1	1	0	0	0	0
John Gunn	7	0-1	0-0	0-0	1	0	0	0	1	0
Richard Kirklin	5	0-1	0-1	0-0	0	0	0	0	0	0
John Pilger	1	0-0	0-0	0-0	0	0	0	0	0	0
TOTALS	200	20-58	5-21	11-16	30	13	8	1	25	56
Percentages		34.5	23.8	68.8						

Coach: Rod Barnes

Officials: Tom Rucker, Bob Donato, Bob Staffen **Technicals:** None **Attendance:** 28,962

Michigan State 77, Gonzaga 62 (Sweet 16)

	1H	2H
Michigan State	37	40
Gonzaga	32	30

MICHIGAN STATE	MIN	FG	3FG	FT	REB	A	ST	BL	PF	TP
Charlie Bell	35	5-12	3-5	8-10	10	3	0	0	1	21
Andre Hutson	29	8-11	0-0	3-4	10	3	0	0	2	19
Jason Richardson	34	5-13	2-6	0-1	7	3	0	0	2	12
Zach Randolph	19	4-8	0-0	2-4	5	0	0	0	1	10
Marcus Taylor	23	3-9	0-4	0-0	0	5	0	0	1	6
Mike Chappell	11	2-3	1-2	0-0	6	2	0	0	2	5
Adam Ballinger	10	2-2	0-0	0-0	0	0	0	0	1	4
David Thomas	18	0-4	0-0	0-0	5	3	0	0	3	0
Aloysius Anagonye	17	0-2	0-0	0-0	3	0	0	0	4	0
Jason Andreas	4	0-1	0-0	0-0	1	0	0	0	0	0
TOTALS	200	29-65	6-20	13-19	47	19	0	0	17	77
Percentages		44.6	30.0	68.4						

Coach: Tom Izzo

GONZAGA	MIN	FG	3FG	FT	REB	A	ST	BL	PF	TP
Dan Dickau	40	6-17	5-9	2-3	4	2	0	0	4	19
Casey Calvary	38	6-15	2-2	3-5	11	3	0	2	1	17
Mark Spink	24	4-7	0-0	2-2	5	1	1	0	2	10
Blake Stepp	37	3-11	2-10	0-0	3	2	2	0	2	8
Zach Gourde	18	1-2	0-0	2-2	2	0	1	0	4	4
Anthony Reason	12	1-3	0-1	0-1	0	5	1	0	2	2
Cory Violette	8	1-2	0-0	0-0	2	0	0	0	2	2
Alex Hernandez	13	0-1	0-0	0-0	0	0	0	0	3	0
Germayne Forbes	5	0-0	0-0	0-0	0	0	0	0	0	0
Kyle Bankhead	3	0-0	0-0	0-0	0	0	0	0	0	0
Jay Sherrell	1	0-0	0-0	0-0	1	0	0	0	0	0
Jimmy Tricco	1	0-0	0-0	0-0	0	0	0	0	0	0
TOTALS	200	22-58	9-22	9-13	28	13	5	2	20	62
Percentages		37.9	40.9	69.2						

Coach: Mark Few

Officials: Tom Lopes, Larry Rose, Olandis Poole **Technicals:** None **Attendance:** 26,873

Temple 84, Penn State 72 (Sweet 16)

	1H	2H
Temple	39	45
Penn State	21	51

TEMPLE	MIN	FG	3FG	FT	REB	A	ST	BL	PF	TP
Lynn Greer	40	5-15	1-4	10-10	2	3	1	0	1	21
Greg Jefferson	21	7-9	0-0	1-1	7	0	2	0	3	15
Alex Wesby	40	5-12	3-8	1-2	6	2	0	0	4	14
Quincy Wadley	40	3-9	2-7	5-6	6	1	2	0	1	13
Kevin Lyde	30	5-11	0-0	3-5	13	3	1	4	3	13
David Hawkins	18	1-3	0-0	6-6	5	0	0	0	4	8
Ron Rollerson	9	0-0	0-0	0-0	0	0	0	0	1	0
Mamadou Cello Barry	1	0-0	0-0	0-0	1	0	0	1	0	0
Rouldra Thomas	1	0-0	0-0	0-0	0	0	0	1	0	0
TOTALS	200	26-59	6-19	26-30	40	9	6	6	17	84
Percentages		44.1	31.6	86.7						

Coach: John Chaney

PENN STATE	MIN	FG	3FG	FT	REB	A	ST	BL	PF	TP
Titus Ivory	37	6-9	4-7	4-4	7	9	1	1	4	20
Gyasi Cline-Heard	38	6-11	0-1	6-10	6	2	0	3	4	18
Joe Crispin	28	4-11	4-10	0-0	3	2	0	0	5	12
Brandon Watkins	12	4-7	3-4	1-2	0	2	0	0	4	12
Jon Crispin	33	2-10	2-8	0-0	1	0	0	0	2	6
Ndu Egekeze	7	1-1	0-0	0-1	1	0	0	0	1	2
Tyler Smith	21	0-1	0-0	1-2	2	0	1	1	0	1
Marcus Banta	8	0-2	0-0	1-2	1	0	0	0	1	1
Jamaal Tate	11	0-3	0-3	0-0	1	0	0	1	1	0
Sharif Chambliss	2	0-0	0-0	0-0	0	0	0	0	1	0
Ken Krimmel	1	0-0	0-0	0-0	0	0	0	0	0	0
B.J. Vossekuil	1	0-0	0-0	0-0	0	0	0	0	0	0
Scott Witkowsky	1	0-2	0-0	0-0	1	0	0	0	0	0
TOTALS	200	23-57	13-33	13-21	23	15	2	6	23	72
Percentages		40.4	39.4	61.9						

Coach: Jerry Dunn

Officials: Gerald Boudreaux, Karl Hess, Curtis Shaw **Technicals:** None **Attendance:** 26,873

Duke 76, UCLA 63 (Sweet 16)

	1H	2H
Duke	33	43
UCLA	26	37

DUKE	MIN	FG	3FG	FT	REB	A	ST	BL	PF	TP
Jason Williams	37	11-21	6-13	6-6	2	4	3	0	0	34
Shane Battier	39	6-14	2-7	10-11	11	1	4	1	2	24
Mike Dunleavy Jr.	30	3-11	0-6	1-2	5	3	3	0	3	7
Chris Duhon	38	0-2	0-2	4-7	5	4	4	0	2	4
Casey Sanders	16	0-1	0-0	3-4	3	0	0	1	2	3
Carlos Boozer	22	1-2	0-0	0-0	6	0	2	1	4	2
Nate James	13	1-4	0-3	0-0	3	1	1	1	2	2
Reggie Love	3	0-0	0-0	0-0	0	0	0	1	1	0
Andre Buckner	1	0-0	0-0	0-0	0	0	0	0	0	0
J.D. Simpson	1	0-0	0-0	0-0	0	0	0	0	0	0
TOTALS	200	22-55	8-31	24-30	35	13	17	5	16	76
Percentages		40.0	25.8	80.0						

Coach: Mike Krzyzewski

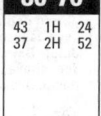

UCLA	MIN	FG	3FG	FT	REB	A	ST	BL	PF	TP
Earl Watson	39	7-12	1-2	2-2	6	5	1	1	4	17
Billy Knight	28	4-13	2-5	3-4	4	0	1	0	3	13
Jason Kapono	33	3-10	2-5	4-6	5	2	3	0	4	12
Dan Gadzuric	38	5-12	0-0	0-1	9	1	1	2	2	10
Matt Barnes	31	3-8	0-0	3-5	11	3	2	0	5	9
Ray Young	19	1-4	0-2	0-0	0	0	0	0	3	2
T.J. Cummings	6	0-0	0-0	0-0	0	0	0	0	3	0
Ryan Bailey	5	0-1	0-0	0-0	0	0	2	0	0	0
Jason Flowers	1	0-0	0-0	0-0	0	0	0	0	0	0
TOTALS	200	23-60	5-14	12-18	35	11	10	3	24	63
Percentages		38.3	35.7	66.7						

Coach: Steve Lavin

Officials: Ed Corbett, Ted Hillary, John Hughes **Technicals:** None **Attendance:** 20,270

Southern California 80, Kentucky 76 (Sweet 16)

	1H	2H
Southern California	43	37
Kentucky	24	52

SOUTHERN CALIFORNIA	MIN	FG	3FG	FT	REB	A	ST	BL	PF	TP
David Bluthenthal	35	7-13	6-9	7-8	3	1	1	0	2	27
Sam Clancy	39	6-12	0-0	5-10	7	0	2	4	3	17
Jeff Trepagnier	40	5-8	1-2	3-3	6	3	4	1	4	14
Brian Scalabrine	35	6-11	0-1	1-1	6	4	2	0	3	13
Brandon Granville	28	3-7	1-2	0-1	2	8	0	0	4	7
Jarvis Turner	5	1-1	0-0	0-2	2	0	1	0	1	2
Robert Hutchinson	12	0-0	0-0	0-0	1	2	1	0	1	0
Desmon Farmer	6	0-1	0-0	0-0	0	0	0	0	0	0
TOTALS	200	28-53	8-14	16-25	27	18	11	5	18	80
Percentages		52.8	57.1	64.0						

Coach: Henry Bibby

KENTUCKY	MIN	FG	3FG	FT	REB	A	ST	BL	PF	TP
Keith Bogans	35	10-22	3-8	0-3	4	1	0	0	4	23
Jason Parker	39	9-13	0-0	4-8	13	0	1	2	4	22
Saul Smith	32	5-8	5-7	2-2	3	4	3	0	4	17
Tayshaun Prince	36	2-8	0-4	2-2	8	5	0	1	1	6
Marvin Stone	6	2-3	0-0	0-0	2	0	0	0	1	4
Gerald Fitch	29	1-5	0-2	0-0	6	4	1	0	1	2
Erik Daniels	5	1-2	0-0	0-0	2	0	0	0	0	2
Cliff Hawkins	10	0-2	0-0	0-0	0	1	0	0	2	0
J.P. Blevins	7	0-3	0-2	0-0	1	0	0	0	0	0
Marquis Estill	7	0-3	0-0	0-1	1	0	0	0	0	0
TOTALS	200	30-69	8-23	8-16	40	15	5	3	17	76
Percentages		43.5	34.8	50.0						

Coach: Tubby Smith

Officials: Ted Valentine, Tom O'Neill, Joe Lindsay **Technicals:** None **Attendance:** 20,270

78-65 — 1H: 34–38, 2H: 44–27 — SWEET 16

STANFORD	MIN	FG	3FG	FT	REB	A	ST	BL	PF	TP
Casey Jacobsen	37	8-13	2-4	9-10	4	3	0	0	1	27
Ryan Mendez	34	6-7	2-2	2-2	6	5	0	0	2	16
Jason Collins	34	4-7	0-0	7-10	8	1	1	5	2	15
Jarron Collins	35	6-11	0-1	2-4	7	2	1	2	3	14
Teyo Johnson	9	2-2	0-0	0-0	2	2	0	0	1	4
Tony Giovacchini	5	1-1	0-0	0-0	1	0	0	0	2	2
Michael McDonald	22	0-1	0-0	0-0	3	2	1	0	4	0
Julius Barnes	21	0-1	0-1	0-1	2	0	0	0	1	0
Justin Davis	3	0-0	0-0	0-2	2	0	0	0	1	0
TOTALS	**200**	**27-43**	**4-8**	**20-29**	**35**	**15**	**3**	**7**	**17**	**78**
Percentages		62.8	50.0	69.0						

Coach: Mike Montgomery

CINCINNATI	MIN	FG	3FG	FT	REB	A	ST	BL	PF	TP
Kenny Satterfield	38	7-16	1-4	9-10	7	6	3	0	3	24
Steve Logan	34	5-16	1-6	0-0	1	1	0	0	3	11
B.J. Grove	29	3-6	0-0	2-4	2	0	1	1	3	8
Leonard Stokes	28	3-6	0-0	0-0	4	0	2	0	4	6
Immanuel McElroy	20	3-5	0-0	0-1	1	0	1	0	1	6
Donald Little	12	2-5	0-0	2-2	2	0	0	2	4	6
Jamaal Davis	27	2-6	0-0	0-0	4	0	1	0	3	4
Antwan Jones	9	0-2	0-1	0-0	0	0	1	0	2	0
Rodney Crawford	2	0-0	0-0	0-0	1	0	0	0	1	0
Field Williams	1	0-1	0-1	0-0	0	0	0	0	0	0
TOTALS	**200**	**25-63**	**2-12**	**13-17**	**22**	**7**	**9**	**3**	**24**	**65**
Percentages		39.7	16.7	76.5						

Coach: Bob Huggins

Officials: T[illegible] Greene, Lo[illegible] Dixon, Mike[illegible] Stuart **Technicals:** Cincinnati (Satterfield) **Attendance:** 18,008

76-66 — 1H: 38–36, 2H: 38–30 — SWEET 16

MARYLAND	MIN	FG	3FG	FT	REB	A	ST	BL	PF	TP
Lonny Baxter	32	9-14	0-0	8-13	14	0	2	1	1	26
Juan Dixon	34	4-8	1-4	4-6	5	1	3	2	2	13
Tahj Holden	14	3-4	0-0	4-5	5	1	0	0	2	10
Danny Miller	20	2-5	0-1	3-4	3	3	1	0	3	7
Mike Mardesich	8	2-3	0-0	1-2	3	0	0	0	3	5
Byron Mouton	22	2-7	0-1	0-0	7	1	0	0	1	4
Terence Morris	20	1-11	0-0	2-2	6	2	1	4	0	4
Drew Nicholas	14	1-3	0-0	2-2	0	3	0	0	0	4
Chris Wilcox	5	1-3	0-0	0-0	1	0	0	0	0	2
Steve Blake	31	0-4	0-3	1-2	2	5	3	0	3	1
TOTALS	**200**	**25-62**	**1-9**	**25-36**	**46**	**16**	**10**	**7**	**15**	**76**
Percentages		40.3	11.1	69.4						

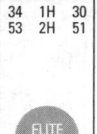

Coach: Gary Williams

GEORGETOWN	MIN	FG	3FG	FT	REB	A	ST	BL	PF	TP
Kevin Braswell	37	3-12	3-9	8-11	6	2	3	1	3	17
Demetrius Hunter	29	4-12	3-9	0-0	2	0	0	0	3	11
Mike Sweetney	27	3-7	0-0	4-6	11	3	0	1	3	10
Lee Scruggs	19	4-9	0-3	2-2	6	0	1	2	3	10
Gerald Riley	17	2-8	1-4	0-0	0	1	0	0	2	5
Wesley Wilson	14	1-3	0-0	2-2	6	0	0	1	4	4
Victor Samnick	9	1-2	0-0	2-2	2	0	0	0	1	4
Anthony Perry	19	1-6	1-5	0-0	2	0	1	0	3	3
Nathaniel Burton	9	1-2	0-0	0-0	0	0	1	1	1	2
Ruben Boumtje-Boumtje	19	0-3	0-0	0-0	3	1	0	1	5	0
Omari Faulkner	1	0-1	0-0	0-0	0	0	0	0	0	0
TOTALS	**200**	**20-65**	**8-30**	**18-23**	**38**	**7**	**6**	**7**	**28**	**66**
Percentages		30.8	26.7	78.3						

Coach: Craig Esherick

Officials: Sc[illegible] Thornley, Ma[illegible] Reischling, T[illegible] Eades **Technicals:** None **Attendance:** 18,008

87-81 — 1H: 34–30, 2H: 53–51 — ELITE 8

ARIZONA	MIN	FG	3FG	FT	REB	A	ST	BL	PF	TP
Gilbert Arenas	37	7-13	2-4	5-6	4	0	4	0	3	21
Jason Gardner	37	4-9	3-6	7-11	5	5	2	0	2	18
Loren Woods	29	3-3	0-0	12-13	5	0	1	7	2	18
Richard Jefferson	23	2-6	0-3	6-7	6	1	1	1	4	10
Luke Walton	19	1-4	1-1	6-9	3	3	0	0	3	9
Eugene Edgerson	18	1-1	0-0	3-4	4	0	1	0	3	5
Michael Wright	20	0-0	0-0	4-4	2	1	0	0	3	4
Justin Wessel	13	1-3	0-0	0-2	2	1	0	1	2	2
Lamont Frazier	4	0-1	0-0	0-0	0	0	0	0	1	0
TOTALS	**200**	**19-40**	**6-14**	**43-56**	**31**	**11**	**9**	**9**	**23**	**87**
Percentages		47.5	42.9	76.8						

Coach: Lute Olson

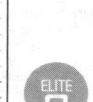

ILLINOIS	MIN	FG	3FG	FT	REB	A	ST	BL	PF	TP
Robert Archibald	24	6-7	0-0	13-15	7	0	0	0	5	25
Cory Bradford	34	8-14	6-11	0-0	1	1	2	0	1	22
Frank Williams	31	3-15	1-6	2-2	1	5	1	0	2	9
Lucas Johnson	18	2-2	2-2	2-2	2	2	1	0	5	8
Damir Krupalija	13	2-4	1-2	2-3	5	0	1	1	5	7
Brian Cook	10	2-4	0-1	0-0	2	1	0	0	5	4
Sean Harrington	15	1-5	1-4	0-0	0	0	1	0	1	3
Sergio McClain	29	1-5	0-0	0-0	6	6	1	0	5	2
Marcus Griffin	24	0-6	0-0	1-3	4	0	2	0	5	1
Nate Mast	1	0-0	0-0	0-0	0	0	0	0	2	0
Brett Melton	1	0-1	0-1	0-0	0	0	0	0	0	0
TOTALS	**200**	**25-63**	**11-27**	**20-25**	**28**	**15**	**9**	**1**	**36**	**81**
Percentages		39.7	40.7	80.0						

Coach: Bill Self

Officials: Tim Higgins, Micha[illegible] Kitts, Reggie Greenwood **Technicals:** None **Attendance:** 30,212

69-62 — 1H: 30–27, 2H: 39–35 — ELITE 8

MICHIGAN STATE	MIN	FG	3FG	FT	REB	A	ST	BL	PF	TP
David Thomas	30	8-10	1-2	2-3	7	2	2	0	1	19
Charlie Bell	36	6-14	2-7	0-0	4	3	1	0	2	14
Andre Hutson	34	2-5	0-0	7-10	10	4	0	1	3	11
Jason Richardson	31	4-11	1-3	2-3	2	2	0	0	1	11
Zach Randolph	24	3-5	0-0	2-6	14	3	0	0	2	8
Marcus Taylor	17	2-5	0-0	0-0	1	3	0	0	1	4
Aloysius Anagonye	19	1-1	0-0	0-0	1	2	0	1	5	2
Mike Chappell	7	0-3	0-3	0-0	0	0	0	0	0	0
Adam Ballinger	2	0-0	0-0	0-0	0	0	0	0	0	0
TOTALS	**200**	**26-54**	**4-15**	**13-22**	**39**	**19**	**3**	**2**	**15**	**69**
Percentages		48.1	26.7	59.1						

Coach: Tom Izzo

TEMPLE	MIN	FG	3FG	FT	REB	A	ST	BL	PF	TP
Lynn Greer	40	7-21	2-7	6-7	0	3	2	0	2	22
Kevin Lyde	40	10-15	0-0	1-3	8	1	0	1	4	21
Alex Wesby	34	3-6	2-5	1-1	6	0	0	0	5	9
Quincy Wadley	40	2-12	0-7	0-0	4	2	1	0	3	4
David Hawkins	29	1-7	0-4	2-2	2	0	1	0	3	4
Ron Rollerson	9	1-2	0-0	0-0	5	0	0	0	0	2
Greg Jefferson	7	0-0	0-0	0-0	0	0	1	0	1	0
Rouldra Thomas	1	0-0	0-0	0-0	0	0	0	0	0	0
TOTALS	**200**	**24-63**	**4-23**	**10-13**	**25**	**6**	**5**	**1**	**18**	**62**
Percentages		38.1	17.4	76.9						

Coach: John Chaney

Officials: James Burr, Andre Pattillo, Mark Whitehead **Technicals:** None **Attendance:** 25,995

79-69 — 1H: 43–38, 2H: 36–31 — ELITE 8

DUKE	MIN	FG	3FG	FT	REB	A	ST	BL	PF	TP
Jason Williams	37	10-26	3-11	5-5	7	6	2	0	3	28
Shane Battier	40	7-16	2-6	4-4	10	1	3	3	2	20
Chris Duhon	30	4-10	3-6	2-2	4	1	2	0	2	13
Mike Dunleavy Jr.	34	4-6	1-3	2-2	3	1	1	0	2	11
Nate James	19	2-2	0-0	0-0	3	1	0	0	1	4
Casey Sanders	18	1-1	0-0	0-0	1	0	0	0	3	2
Carlos Boozer	22	0-2	0-0	1-2	4	1	2	1	2	1
TOTALS	**200**	**28-63**	**9-26**	**14-15**	**32**	**11**	**10**	**4**	**15**	**79**
Percentages		44.4	34.6	93.3						

Coach: Mike Krzyzewski

SOUTHERN CALIFORNIA	MIN	FG	3FG	FT	REB	A	ST	BL	PF	TP
Sam Clancy	39	8-19	0-0	3-6	11	1	1	4	3	19
David Bluthenthal	38	6-13	2-2	3-6	13	1	2	0	2	17
Brian Scalabrine	37	4-12	3-5	2-2	2	4	0	2	4	13
Jeff Trepagnier	39	4-9	1-3	2-2	6	2	0	1	4	11
Jarvis Turner	4	3-4	0-0	0-0	1	0	1	0	3	6
Desmon Farmer	3	1-3	0-1	0-0	0	1	1	0	0	2
Brandon Granville	34	0-3	0-2	1-2	3	7	2	0	1	1
Robert Hutchinson	6	0-1	0-1	0-0	0	0	0	0	1	0
TOTALS	**200**	**26-64**	**6-14**	**11-18**	**36**	**16**	**7**	**7**	**18**	**69**
Percentages		40.6	42.9	61.1						

Coach: Henry Bibby

Officials: Mike Sanzere, Steve Olson, Ed Hightower **Technicals:** None **Attendance:** 20,270

87-73 — 1H: 42–32, 2H: 45–41 — ELITE 8

MARYLAND	MIN	FG	3FG	FT	REB	A	ST	BL	PF	TP
Lonny Baxter	29	11-18	0-0	2-3	6	1	1	1	4	24
Juan Dixon	35	7-10	2-3	1-2	3	3	3	0	1	17
Tahj Holden	20	3-6	3-4	5-8	2	0	0	1	2	14
Steve Blake	28	3-5	3-3	4-4	1	7	1	0	4	13
Terence Morris	22	5-8	1-2	0-1	10	0	0	1	4	11
Drew Nicholas	17	2-4	0-1	2-3	1	3	0	0	2	6
Danny Miller	26	1-1	0-0	0-0	1	3	2	0	1	2
Byron Mouton	14	0-3	0-0	0-0	4	1	1	1	3	0
Mike Mardesich	7	0-0	0-0	0-0	2	0	0	0	1	0
Chris Wilcox	2	0-0	0-0	0-0	1	0	0	0	1	0
TOTALS	**200**	**32-55**	**9-13**	**14-21**	**31**	**18**	**8**	**4**	**23**	**87**
Percentages		58.2	69.2	66.7						

Coach: Gary Williams

STANFORD	MIN	FG	3FG	FT	REB	A	ST	BL	PF	TP
Ryan Mendez	36	6-11	4-7	2-4	3	2	0	0	4	18
Casey Jacobsen	39	4-11	2-4	4-4	9	2	2	1	1	14
Michael McDonald	34	4-11	3-6	1-2	2	7	1	0	5	12
Jason Collins	29	3-7	0-1	6-8	5	3	0	0	4	12
Jarron Collins	24	3-6	0-0	3-3	2	0	0	2	4	9
Teyo Johnson	23	3-6	1-2	1-2	4	2	1	0	4	8
Julius Barnes	6	0-3	0-2	0-0	0	1	1	0	0	0
Tony Giovacchini	5	0-0	0-0	0-0	0	0	0	0	0	0
Justin Davis	4	0-1	0-0	0-0	1	0	0	0	0	0
TOTALS	**200**	**23-56**	**10-22**	**17-23**	**26**	**17**	**5**	**3**	**22**	**73**
Percentages		41.1	45.5	73.9						

Coach: Mike Montgomery

Officials: John Clougherty, Kerry Sitton, Art McDonald **Technicals:** None **Attendance:** 17,979

80-61 — FINAL 4

	1H	2H
Arizona	32	48
Michigan State	30	31

ARIZONA	MIN	FG	3FG	FT	REB	A	ST	BL	PF	TP
Jason Gardner	38	6-11	3-7	6-6	1	1	3	1	1	21
Richard Jefferson	34	6-13	3-5	2-4	8	2	2	2	1	17
Michael Wright	23	6-10	0-0	1-1	3	0	0	1	2	13
Gilbert Arenas	27	4-7	1-2	3-4	2	7	6	0	2	12
Loren Woods	37	5-13	0-0	1-1	8	2	0	3	2	11
Eugene Edgerson	17	3-4	0-0	0-0	6	1	0	0	1	6
Luke Walton	16	0-1	0-0	0-0	1	2	0	0	0	0
Lamont Frazier	4	0-1	0-0	0-0	0	0	0	0	1	0
Justin Wessel	3	0-0	0-0	0-0	0	0	1	0	1	0
Travis Hanour	1	0-0	0-0	0-0	0	0	0	0	0	0
TOTALS	200	30-60	7-14	13-16	29	15	12	7	11	80
Percentages		50.0	50.0	81.2						

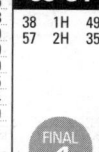

Coach: Lute Olson

MICHIGAN STATE	MIN	FG	3FG	FT	REB	A	ST	BL	PF	TP
Andre Hutson	37	9-14	0-0	2-2	5	0	0	2	2	20
Zach Randolph	24	5-8	0-0	2-4	5	0	0	0	3	12
Marcus Taylor	20	3-9	1-4	1-2	1	2	1	0	3	8
David Thomas	20	4-6	0-0	0-0	5	2	1	0	1	8
Jason Richardson	28	2-11	1-4	1-2	7	2	0	0	2	6
Charlie Bell	36	1-10	0-6	1-1	10	3	0	0	1	3
Mike Chappell	12	0-0	0-0	2-2	0	2	0	0	1	2
Adam Ballinger	9	1-1	0-0	0-1	2	0	0	1	0	2
Aloysius Anagonye	8	0-1	0-0	0-0	2	0	0	0	4	0
Brandon Smith	3	0-0	0-0	0-0	0	0	0	0	1	0
Jason Andreas	1	0-0	0-0	0-0	0	0	0	0	0	0
Mat Ishbia	1	0-1	0-0	0-0	0	0	0	0	0	0
Adam Wolfe	1	0-0	0-0	0-0	0	0	0	0	0	0
TOTALS	200	25-61	2-14	9-14	37	11	2	3	18	61
Percentages		41.0	14.3	64.3						

Coach: Tom Izzo

Officials: Tim Higgins, Tony Greene, Bob Donato
Technicals: Arizona (Jefferson)
Attendance: 45,406

95-84 — FINAL 4

	1H	2H
Duke	38	57
Maryland	49	35

DUKE	MIN	FG	3FG	FT	REB	A	ST	BL	PF	TP
Shane Battier	40	6-12	4-7	9-11	8	2	2	4	3	25
Jason Williams	33	7-19	1-9	8-12	3	4	2	0	4	23
Carlos Boozer	25	7-8	0-0	5-8	4	0	0	0	4	19
Chris Duhon	33	3-10	1-5	3-3	2	6	3	0	4	10
Nate James	30	4-10	1-4	0-0	9	1	0	0	3	9
Casey Sanders	14	2-4	0-0	1-1	5	0	0	2	2	5
Mike Dunleavy Jr.	24	2-8	0-2	0-0	3	2	1	1	3	4
Andre Buckner	1	0-0	0-0	0-0	0	0	0	0	0	0
TOTALS	200	31-71	7-27	26-35	34	15	8	7	23	95
Percentages		43.7	25.9	74.3						

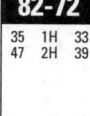

Coach: Mike Krzyzewski

MARYLAND	MIN	FG	3FG	FT	REB	A	ST	BL	PF	TP
Juan Dixon	38	6-17	4-10	3-3	8	0	1	0	2	19
Steve Blake	31	5-8	2-4	1-2	4	5	0	0	4	13
Lonny Baxter	25	2-10	0-0	6-8	10	0	0	1	5	10
Terence Morris	20	4-7	1-1	1-2	8	0	0	0	4	10
Byron Mouton	18	4-6	0-0	1-2	7	1	2	0	2	9
Drew Nicholas	12	1-5	0-0	5-6	3	1	0	0	2	7
Mike Mardesich	12	3-4	0-0	0-0	5	1	1	0	1	6
Danny Miller	21	1-4	0-3	2-2	1	2	0	0	1	4
Tahj Holden	17	2-4	0-0	0-2	4	0	0	0	4	4
Chris Wilcox	6	1-1	0-0	0-0	0	0	0	0	1	2
TOTALS	200	29-66	7-18	19-27	50	10	4	1	26	84
Percentages		43.9	38.9	70.4						

Coach: Gary Williams

Officials: Dave Libbey, Mark Reischling, Ted Hillary
Technicals: None
Attendance: 45,406

82-72 — NCAA FINAL 2001

	1H	2H
Duke	35	47
Arizona	33	39

DUKE	MIN	FG	3FG	FT	REB	A	ST	BL	PF	TP
Mike Dunleavy Jr.	32	8-17	5-9	0-1	3	0	0	0	3	21
Shane Battier	40	7-14	1-5	3-6	11	6	0	2	1	18
Jason Williams	29	5-15	2-11	4-6	3	4	3	0	4	16
Carlos Boozer	30	5-9	0-0	2-3	12	1	0	2	3	12
Chris Duhon	39	3-5	1-1	2-3	4	6	0	0	2	9
Nate James	20	2-3	0-1	2-3	3	0	1	1	3	6
Casey Sanders	10	0-1	0-0	0-0	2	1	1	0	1	0
TOTALS	200	30-64	9-27	13-22	38	18	5	5	17	82
Percentages		46.9	33.3	59.1						

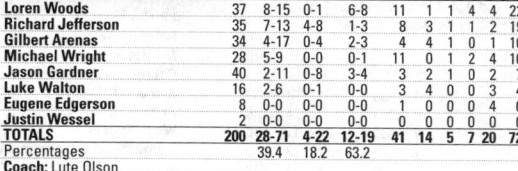

Coach: Mike Krzyzewski

ARIZONA	MIN	FG	3FG	FT	REB	A	ST	BL	PF	TP
Loren Woods	37	8-15	0-1	6-8	11	1	1	4	4	22
Richard Jefferson	35	7-13	4-8	1-3	8	3	1	1	2	19
Gilbert Arenas	34	4-17	0-4	2-3	4	4	1	0	1	10
Michael Wright	28	5-9	0-0	0-1	11	0	1	2	4	10
Jason Gardner	40	2-11	0-8	3-4	3	2	1	0	2	7
Luke Walton	16	2-6	0-1	0-0	3	4	0	0	3	4
Eugene Edgerson	8	0-0	0-0	0-0	1	0	0	0	4	0
Justin Wessel	2	0-0	0-0	0-0	0	0	0	0	0	0
TOTALS	200	28-71	4-22	12-19	41	14	5	7	20	72
Percentages		39.4	18.2	63.2						

Coach: Lute Olson

Officials: Scott Thornley, Gerald Boudreaux, Ed Corbett
Technicals: None
Attendance: 45,994

National Invitation Tournament (NIT)

First Round: Connecticut d. South Carolina 72-65, Detroit d. Bradley 68-49, Richmond d. West Virginia 79-56, Dayton d. UNC Wilmington 68-59, Alabama d. Seton Hall 85-79, Toledo d. South Alabama 76-67, Purdue d. Illinois State 90-79, Auburn d. Miami 60-58, Minnesota d. Villanova 87-78, Tulsa d. UC Irvine 75-71, Pittsburgh d. St. Bonaventure 84-75, Mississippi State d. Southern Miss 75-68, Pepperdine d. Wyoming 72-69, New Mexico d. Baylor 83-73, UTEP d. McNeese State 84-74, Memphis d. Utah 71-62
Second Round: Detroit d. Connecticut 67-61, Dayton d. Richmond 71-56, Alabama d. Toledo 79-69, Purdue d. Auburn 79-61, Tulsa d. Minnesota 73-70, Mississippi State d. Pittsburgh 66-61, New Mexico d. Pepperdine 81-75, Memphis d. UTEP 90-65
Third Round: Detroit d. Dayton 59-42, Alabama d. Purdue 85-77, Tulsa d. Mississippi State 77-75, Memphis d. New Mexico 81-63
Semifinals: Alabama d. Detroit 74-63, Tulsa d. Memphis 72-64
Championship: Tulsa d. Alabama 79-60
Third place: Memphis d. Detroit 86-71
MVP: Marcus Hill, Tulsa

2001-02: Terrapin Station

Gary Williams' nearly constant scowl turned to a sweet smile as the Maryland Terrapins (32–4) downed Indiana, 64-52, to claim the school's first national championship. The 116 combined points remains the lowest total in a title game since the 1985 introduction of the shot clock. Maryland got hot at the right time, winning 19 of its last 20 games, besting its six Tournament victims by eight points or more. Senior guard Juan Dixon was selected as MOP after scoring 18 points against the Hoosiers.

Indiana made its remarkable run to the Final as a No. 5 seed, knocking off Utah and UNC-Wilmington to meet the nation's No. 1 team, Duke, in the Sweet 16. Led by Big Ten POY Jared Jeffries and hot-shooting Jarrad Odle, the Hoosiers erased a 17-point second-half deficit to go ahead 74-73. Duke's Jason Williams missed the game-tying free throw with :04 to go. Williams was named the Naismith POY after averaging 21.3 ppg and was the second pick in the NBA draft (Chicago Bulls), after China's Yao Ming (Houston Rockets).

Major Conference Standings

America East

	Conference			Overall		
	W	L	Pct	W	L	Pct
Boston U.⊕	13	3	.813	22	10	.688
Vermont	13	3	.813	21	8	.724
Hartford	10	6	.625	14	18	.438
New Hampshire	8	8	.500	11	17	.393
Maine	7	9	.438	12	18	.400
Binghamton	6	10	.375	9	19	.321
Albany (NY)	5	11	.313	8	20	.286
Northeastern	5	11	.313	7	21	.250
Stony Brook	5	11	.313	6	22	.214

Tournament: **Boston U. d. Maine 60-44**
Tournament MVP: **Billy Collins**, Boston U.

ACC

	Conference			Overall		
	W	L	Pct	W	L	Pct
Maryland○	15	1	.938	32	4	.889
Duke⊕	13	3	.813	31	4	.886
NC State○	9	7	.563	23	11	.676
Wake Forest○	9	7	.563	21	13	.618
Virginia□	7	9	.438	17	12	.586
Georgia Tech	7	9	.438	15	16	.484
Clemson	4	12	.250	13	17	.433
Florida State	4	12	.250	12	17	.414
North Carolina	4	12	.250	8	20	.286

Tournament: **Duke d. NC State 91-61**
Tournament MVP: **Carlos Boozer**, Duke

Atlantic Sun

	Conference			Overall		
	W	L	Pct	W	L	Pct
Georgia State□	14	6	.700	20	11	.645
Troy	14	6	.700	18	10	.643
Florida Atlantic⊕	13	7	.650	19	12	.613
Jacksonville	12	8	.600	18	12	.600
Samford	12	8	.600	15	14	.517
Central Florida	12	8	.600	17	12	.586
Jacksonville State	8	12	.400	13	16	.448
Belmont	8	12	.400	11	17	.393
Stetson	7	13	.350	10	16	.385
Campbell	6	14	.300	8	19	.296
Mercer	4	16	.200	6	23	.207

Tournament: **Florida Atlantic d. Georgia State 76-75**
Tournament MVP: **Thomas Terrell**, Georgia State

Atlantic 10

	Conference			Overall		
	W	L	Pct	W	L	Pct
East Division						
Saint Joseph's□	12	4	.750	19	12	.613
Temple□	12	4	.750	19	15	.559
St. Bonaventure□	8	8	.500	17	13	.567
Massachusetts	6	10	.375	13	16	.448
Fordham	4	12	.250	8	20	.286
Rhode Island	4	12	.250	8	20	.286
West Division						
Xavier⊕	14	2	.875	26	6	.813
Richmond□	11	5	.688	22	14	.611
Dayton□	10	6	.625	21	11	.656
La Salle	6	10	.375	15	17	.469
George Washington	5	11	.313	12	16	.429
Duquesne	4	12	.250	9	19	.321

Tournament: **Xavier d. Richmond 73-60**
Tournament MOP: **David West**, Xavier

Big East

	Conference			Overall		
	W	L	Pct	W	L	Pct
East Division						
Connecticut⊕	13	3	.813	27	7	.794
Miami (FL)○	10	6	.625	24	8	.750
St. John's○✪	9	7	.563	20	12	.625
Boston College○	8	8	.500	20	12	.625
Villanova□	7	9	.438	19	13	.594
Providence	6	10	.375	15	16	.484
Virginia Tech	4	12	.250	10	18	.357
West Division						
Pittsburgh○	13	3	.813	29	6	.829
Notre Dame○	10	6	.625	22	11	.667
Syracuse□	9	7	.563	23	13	.639
Georgetown	9	7	.563	19	11	.633
Rutgers□	8	8	.500	18	13	.581
Seton Hall	5	11	.313	12	18	.400
West Virginia	1	15	.063	8	20	.286

Tournament: **Connecticut d. Pittsburgh 74-65 2OT**
Tournament MVP: **Caron Butler**, Connecticut

Big Sky

	Conference			Overall		
	W	L	Pct	W	L	Pct
Montana State□	12	2	.857	20	10	.667
Eastern Washington	10	4	.714	17	13	.567
Weber State	8	6	.571	18	11	.621
Montana⊕	7	7	.500	16	15	.516
Northern Arizona	7	7	.500	14	14	.500
Portland State	6	8	.429	12	16	.429
Idaho State	3	11	.214	10	17	.370
Sacramento State	3	11	.214	9	19	.321

Tournament: **Montana d. Eastern Washington 70-66**
Tournament MVP: **Dan Trammel**, Montana

Big South

	Conference			Overall		
	W	L	Pct	W	L	Pct
Winthrop⊕	10	4	.714	19	12	.613
UNC Asheville	10	4	.714	13	15	.464
Radford	9	5	.643	15	16	.484
Charleston Southern	8	6	.571	12	17	.414
Elon	7	7	.500	13	16	.448
High Point	5	9	.357	11	19	.367
Coastal Carolina	5	9	.357	8	20	.286
Liberty	2	12	.143	5	25	.167

Tournament: **Winthrop d. High Point 70-48**
Tournament MVP: **Greg Lewis**, Winthrop

Big Ten

	Conference			Overall		
	W	L	Pct	W	L	Pct
Ohio State⊕✪	11	5	.688	24	8	.750
Illinois○	11	5	.688	26	9	.743
Indiana○	11	5	.688	25	12	.676
Wisconsin○	11	5	.688	19	13	.594
Michigan State○	10	6	.625	19	12	.613
Minnesota□	9	7	.563	18	13	.581
Northwestern	7	9	.438	16	13	.552
Iowa□	5	11	.313	19	16	.543
Purdue	5	11	.313	13	18	.419
Michigan	5	11	.313	11	18	.379
Penn State	3	13	.188	7	21	.250

Tournament: **Ohio State d. Iowa 81-64**
Tournament MOP: **Boban Savovic**, Ohio State

Big 12

	Conference			Overall		
	W	L	Pct	W	L	Pct
Kansas○	16	0	1.000	33	4	.892
Oklahoma⊕	13	3	.813	31	5	.861
Oklahoma State○	10	6	.625	23	9	.719
Texas Tech○	10	6	.625	23	9	.719
Texas○	10	6	.625	22	12	.647
Missouri○	9	7	.563	24	12	.667
Nebraska	6	10	.375	13	15	.464
Kansas State	6	10	.375	13	16	.448
Colorado	5	11	.313	15	14	.517
Baylor	4	12	.250	14	16	.467
Iowa State	4	12	.250	12	19	.387
Texas A&M	3	13	.188	9	22	.290

Tournament: **Oklahoma d. Kansas 64-55**
Tournament MOP: **Hollis Price**, Oklahoma

Big West

	Conference			Overall		
	W	L	Pct	W	L	Pct
UC Irvine□	13	5	.722	21	11	.656
Utah State□	13	5	.722	23	8	.742
Pacific	11	7	.611	20	10	.667
UC Santa Barbara⊕	11	7	.611	20	11	.645
Cal State Northridge	11	7	.611	12	16	.429
Cal Poly	9	9	.500	15	12	.556
Long Beach State	9	9	.500	13	17	.433
Idaho	6	12	.333	9	19	.321
UC Riverside	5	13	.278	8	18	.308
Cal State Fullerton	2	16	.111	5	22	.185

Tournament: **UC Santa Barbara d. Utah State 60-56**
Tournament MVP: **Nick Jones**, UC Santa Barbara

Colonial Athletic

	Conference			Overall		
	W	L	Pct	W	L	Pct
UNC Wilmington⊕	14	4	.778	23	10	.697
George Mason□	13	5	.722	19	10	.655
VCU	11	7	.611	21	11	.656
Drexel	11	7	.611	14	14	.500
Delaware	9	9	.500	14	16	.467
Old Dominion	7	11	.389	13	16	.448
Towson	7	11	.389	11	18	.379
William and Mary	7	11	.389	10	19	.345
James Madison	6	12	.333	14	15	.483
Hofstra	5	13	.278	12	20	.375

Tournament: **UNC Wilmington d. VCU 66-51**
Tournament MVP: **Brett Blizzard**, UNC Wilmington

C-USA

	Conference			Overall		
	W	L	Pct	W	L	Pct
American Division						
Cincinnati⊕	14	2	.875	31	4	.886
Marquette○	13	3	.813	26	7	.788
Charlotte○	11	5	.688	18	12	.600
Saint Louis	9	7	.563	15	16	.484
Louisville□	8	8	.500	19	13	.594
East Carolina	5	11	.313	12	18	.400
DePaul	2	14	.125	9	19	.321
National Division						
Memphis□	12	4	.750	27	9	.750
Houston□	9	7	.563	18	15	.545
South Florida□	8	8	.500	19	13	.594
TCU	6	10	.375	16	15	.516
UAB	6	10	.375	13	17	.433
Tulane	5	11	.313	14	15	.483
Southern Miss	4	12	.250	10	17	.370

Tournament: **Cincinnati d. Marquette 77-63**
Tournament MVP: **Steve Logan**, Cincinnati

⊕ Automatic NCAA Tournament bid ○ At-large NCAA Tournament bid □ NIT appearance ✪ Team record doesn't reflect games forfeited or vacated. For adjusted record, see p. 521.

HORIZON

	Conference			Overall		
	W	L	Pct	W	L	Pct
Butler□	12	4	.750	26	6	.813
Detroit□	11	5	.688	18	13	.581
Wisconsin-Milwaukee	11	5	.688	16	13	.552
Wright State	9	7	.563	17	11	.607
Loyola-Chicago	9	7	.563	17	13	.567
Illinois-Chicago⊕	8	8	.500	20	14	.588
Cleveland State	6	10	.375	12	16	.429
Wisconsin-Green Bay	4	12	.250	9	21	.300
Youngstown State	2	14	.125	5	23	.179

Tournament: **Illinois-Chicago d. Loyola-Chicago 76-75 OT**
Tournament MVP: **Cedrick Banks**, Illinois-Chicago

IVY

	Conference			Overall		
	W	L	Pct	W	L	Pct
Penn⊕	11	3	.786	25	7	.781
Yale□	11	3	.786	21	11	.656
Princeton□	11	3	.786	16	12	.571
Brown	8	6	.571	17	10	.630
Harvard	7	7	.500	14	12	.538
Columbia	4	10	.286	11	17	.393
Dartmouth	2	12	.143	9	18	.333
Cornell	2	12	.143	5	22	.185

Note: Yale d. Princeton 76-60; **Penn d. Yale 77-58** for the title.

MAAC

	Conference			Overall		
	W	L	Pct	W	L	Pct
Marist	13	5	.722	19	9	.679
Rider	13	5	.722	17	11	.607
Manhattan□	12	6	.667	20	9	.690
Niagara	12	6	.667	18	14	.563
Iona	10	8	.556	13	17	.433
Siena⊕	9	9	.500	17	19	.472
Fairfield	9	9	.500	12	17	.414
Canisius	5	13	.278	10	20	.333
Loyola (MD)	4	14	.222	5	23	.179
Saint Peter's	3	15	.167	4	24	.143

Tournament: **Siena d. Niagara 92-77**
Tournament MVP: **Dwayne Archbold**, Siena

MID-AMERICAN

	Conference			Overall		
	W	L	Pct	W	L	Pct
East Division						
Kent State State⊕	17	1	.944	30	6	.833
Bowling Green□	12	6	.667	24	9	.727
Ohio	11	7	.611	17	11	.607
Miami (OH)	9	9	.500	13	18	.419
Marshall	8	10	.444	15	15	.500
Buffalo	7	11	.389	12	18	.400
Akron	5	13	.278	10	21	.323
West Division						
Ball State□	12	6	.667	23	12	.657
Toledo	11	7	.611	16	14	.533
Western Michigan	10	8	.556	17	13	.567
Northern Illinois	8	10	.444	12	16	.429
Central Michigan	5	13	.278	9	19	.321
Eastern Michigan	2	16	.111	6	24	.200

Tournament: **Kent State d. Bowling Green 70-59**
Tournament MVP: **Trevor Huffman**, Kent State

MID-CONTINENT

	Conference			Overall		
	W	L	Pct	W	L	Pct
Valparaiso⊕	12	2	.857	25	8	.758
Oakland	10	4	.714	17	13	.567
Oral Roberts	10	4	.714	17	14	.548
Southern Utah	8	6	.571	11	16	.407
UMKC	7	7	.500	18	11	.621
IUPUI	6	8	.429	15	15	.500
Western Illinois	3	11	.214	12	16	.429
Chicago State	0	14	.000	2	26	.071

Tournament: **Valparaiso d. IUPUI 88-55**
Tournament MVP: **Milo Stovall**, Valparaiso

MEAC

	Conference			Overall		
	W	L	Pct	W	L	Pct
Hampton⊕	17	1	.944	26	7	.788
Delaware State	12	6	.667	16	13	.552
Howard	11	7	.611	18	13	.581
South Carolina State	11	7	.611	15	16	.484
NC A&T	10	8	.556	11	17	.393
Norfolk State	9	9	.500	10	19	.345
Florida A&M	9	9	.500	9	19	.321
Bethune-Cookman	8	10	.444	12	17	.414
UMES	7	11	.389	11	18	.379
Coppin State	3	15	.167	6	25	.194
Morgan State	2	16	.111	3	25	.107

Tournament: **Hampton d. Howard 80-62**
Tournament MOP: **Tommy Adams**, Hampton

MISSOURI VALLEY

	Conference			Overall		
	W	L	Pct	W	L	Pct
Creighton⊕	14	4	.778	23	9	.719
Southern Illinois○	14	4	.778	28	8	.778
Illinois State	12	6	.667	17	14	.548
Missouri State	11	7	.611	17	15	.531
Wichita State	9	9	.500	15	15	.500
Drake	9	9	.500	14	15	.483
Northern Iowa	8	10	.444	14	15	.483
Bradley	5	13	.278	9	20	.310
Evansville	4	14	.222	7	21	.250
Indiana State	4	14	.222	6	22	.214

Tournament: **Creighton d. Southern Illinois 84-76**
Tournament MOP: **Kyle Korver**, Creighton

MOUNTAIN WEST

	Conference			Overall		
	W	L	Pct	W	L	Pct
Wyoming○	11	3	.786	22	9	.710
Utah○	10	4	.714	21	9	.700
UNLV□	9	5	.643	21	11	.656
San Diego State⊕	7	7	.500	21	12	.636
BYU□	7	7	.500	18	12	.600
New Mexico□	6	8	.429	16	14	.533
Colorado State	3	11	.214	12	18	.400
Air Force	3	11	.214	9	19	.321

Tournament: **San Diego State d. UNLV 78-75**
Tournament MVP: **Randy Holcomb**, San Diego State

NORTHEAST

	Conference			Overall		
	W	L	Pct	W	L	Pct
Central Conn. State⊕	19	1	.950	27	5	.844
UMBC	15	5	.750	20	9	.690
Wagner□	15	5	.750	19	10	.655
Monmouth	14	6	.700	18	12	.600
St. Francis (NY)	13	7	.650	18	11	.621
Robert Morris	11	9	.550	12	18	.400
Quinnipiac	10	10	.500	14	16	.467
Sacred Heart	7	13	.350	8	20	.286
Saint Francis (PA)	5	15	.250	6	21	.222
Long Island	5	15	.250	5	22	.185
Fairleigh Dickinson	4	16	.200	4	25	.138
Mount St. Mary's	2	18	.100	3	24	.111

Tournament: **Central Conn. State d. Quinnipiac 78-71**
Tournament MVP: **Damian Battles**, Central Conn. State

OHIO VALLEY

	Conference			Overall		
	W	L	Pct	W	L	Pct
Tennessee Tech□	15	1	.938	27	7	.794
Morehead State	11	5	.688	18	11	.621
Murray State⊕	10	6	.625	19	13	.594
Austin Peay	8	8	.500	14	18	.438
Tennessee-Martin	7	9	.438	15	14	.517
Eastern Illinois	7	9	.438	15	16	.484
Tennessee State	7	9	.438	11	17	.393
SE Missouri State	4	12	.250	6	22	.214
Eastern Kentucky	3	13	.188	7	20	.259

Tournament: **Murray State d. Tennessee Tech 70-69**
Tournament MVP: **Justin Burdine**, Murray State

PAC-10

	Conference			Overall		
	W	L	Pct	W	L	Pct
Oregon○	14	4	.778	26	9	.743
Arizona⊕	12	6	.667	24	10	.706
California○	12	6	.667	23	9	.719
Southern California○	12	6	.667	22	10	.688
Stanford○	12	6	.667	20	10	.667
UCLA○	11	7	.611	21	12	.636
Arizona State□	7	11	.389	14	15	.483
Washington	5	13	.278	11	18	.379
Oregon State	4	14	.222	12	17	.414
Washington State	1	17	.056	6	21	.222

Tournament: **Arizona d. Southern California 81-71**
Tournament MOP: **Luke Walton**, Arizona

PATRIOT LEAGUE

	Conference			Overall		
	W	L	Pct	W	L	Pct
American	10	4	.714	18	12	.600
Holy Cross⊕	9	5	.643	18	15	.545
Colgate	8	6	.571	17	11	.607
Lafayette	8	6	.571	15	14	.517
Bucknell	8	6	.571	13	16	.448
Army	6	8	.429	12	16	.429
Navy	5	9	.357	10	20	.333
Lehigh	2	12	.143	5	23	.179

Tournament: **Holy Cross d. American 58-54**
Tournament MVP: **Tim Szatko**, Holy Cross

SEC

	Conference			Overall		
	W	L	Pct	W	L	Pct
Eastern						
Florida○	10	6	.625	22	9	.710
Georgia○⊗	10	6	.625	22	10	.688
Kentucky○	10	6	.625	22	10	.688
Tennessee	7	9	.438	15	16	.484
South Carolina□	6	10	.375	22	15	.595
Vanderbilt□	6	10	.375	17	15	.531
Western						
Alabama○	12	4	.750	27	8	.771
Mississippi State⊕	10	6	.625	27	8	.771
Mississippi○	9	7	.563	20	11	.645
LSU□	6	10	.375	19	15	.559
Arkansas	6	10	.375	14	15	.483
Auburn	4	12	.250	12	16	.429

Tournament: **Mississippi State d. Alabama 61-58**
Tournament MVP: **Mario Austin**, Mississippi State

SOUTHERN

	Conference			Overall		
	W	L	Pct	W	L	Pct
North						
Davidson⊕	11	5	.688	21	10	.677
UNC Greensboro□	11	5	.688	20	11	.645
East Tennesee State	11	5	.688	18	10	.643
Western Carolina	6	10	.375	12	16	.429
Appalachian State	5	11	.313	10	18	.357
VMI	5	11	.313	10	18	.357
South						
Charleston	9	7	.563	21	9	.700
Ga. Southern	9	7	.563	16	12	.571
Chattanooga	9	7	.563	16	14	.533
The Citadel	8	8	.500	17	12	.586
Furman	7	9	.438	17	14	.548
Wofford	5	11	.313	11	18	.379

Tournament: **Davidson d. Furman 62-57**
Tournament MOP: **Peter Anderer**, Davidson

SOUTHLAND

	Conference			Overall		
	W	L	Pct	W	L	Pct
McNeese State⊕	17	3	.850	21	9	.700
UL-Monroe	15	5	.750	20	12	.625
UTSA	13	7	.650	19	10	.655
Lamar	11	9	.550	15	14	.517
Stephen F. Austin	10	10	.500	13	15	.464
Texas State	10	10	.500	12	16	.429
Sam Houston State	9	11	.450	14	14	.500
Texas-Arlington	9	11	.450	12	15	.444
Northwestern State (LA)	9	11	.450	13	18	.419
Southeastern Louisiana	6	14	.300	7	20	.259
Nicholls State	1	19	.050	2	25	.074

Tournament: **McNeese State d. UL-Monroe 65-43**
Tournament MVP: **Fred Gentry**, McNeese State

SWAC

	Conference			Overall		
	W	L	Pct	W	L	Pct
Alcorn State⊕	16	2	.889	21	10	.677
Alabama A&M	12	6	.667	19	10	.655
Alabama State	12	6	.667	19	13	.594
Texas Southern	10	8	.556	11	17	.393
Miss. Valley State	9	9	.500	12	17	.414
Prairie View A&M	8	10	.444	10	20	.333
Jackson State	8	10	.444	9	19	.321
Grambling	7	11	.389	9	19	.321
Southern U.	6	12	.333	7	20	.259
Arkansas-Pine Bluff	2	16	.111	2	26	.071

Tournament: **Alcorn State d. Alabama State 70-67**
Tournament MVP: **Marcus Fleming**, Alcorn State

SUN BELT

	Conference			Overall		
	W	L	Pct	W	L	Pct
East Division						
Western Kentucky⊕	13	1	.929	28	4	.875
Arkansas-Little Rock	8	6	.571	18	11	.621
Middle Tennesee State	6	8	.429	14	15	.483
Arkansas State	5	9	.357	15	16	.484
Florida International	4	10	.286	10	20	.333
West Division						
UL-Lafayette□	11	4	.733	20	11	.645
New Mexico State	11	4	.733	20	12	.625
New Orleans	9	6	.600	15	14	.517
North Texas	8	7	.533	15	14	.517
Denver	3	12	.200	8	20	.286
South Alabama	2	13	.133	7	21	.250

Tournament: **Western Kentucky d. UL-Lafayette 76-70**
Tournament MOP: **Derek Robinson**, Western Kentucky

WEST COAST

	Conference			Overall		
	W	L	Pct	W	L	Pct
Gonzaga⊕	13	1	.929	29	4	.879
Pepperdine○	13	1	.929	22	9	.710
San Francisco	8	6	.571	13	15	.464
Santa Clara	8	6	.571	13	15	.464
San Diego	7	7	.500	16	13	.552
Saint Mary's (CA)	3	11	.214	9	20	.310
Loyola Marymount	2	12	.143	9	20	.310
Portland	2	12	.143	6	24	.200

Tournament: **Gonzaga d. Pepperdine 96-90**
Tournament MVP: **Dan Dickau**, Gonzaga

WAC

	Conference			Overall		
	W	L	Pct	W	L	Pct
Hawaii⊕	15	3	.833	27	6	.818
Tulsa○	15	3	.833	27	7	.794
Louisiana Tech□	14	4	.778	22	10	.688
SMU	10	8	.556	15	14	.517
Nevada	9	9	.500	17	13	.567
Fresno State□	9	9	.500	19	15	.559
Boise State	6	12	.333	13	17	.433
Rice	5	13	.278	10	19	.345
San Jose State	4	14	.222	10	22	.313
UTEP	3	15	.167	10	22	.313

Tournament: **Hawaii d. Tulsa 73-59**
Tournament MVP: **Predrag Savovic**, Hawaii

INDEPENDENTS

	Overall		
	W	L	Pct
Texas-Pan American	20	10	.667
Centenary	14	13	.519
Morris Brown	4	25	.138

INDIVIDUAL LEADERS—SEASON

Scoring	CL	POS	G	FG	3FG	FT	PTS	PPG
1 **Jason Conley**, VMI	FR	F	28	285	79	171	820	**29.3**
2 **Henry Domercant**, Eastern Illinois	JR	G/F	31	262	104	189	817	**26.4**
3 **Mire Chatman**, Tex.-Pan American	SR	G	29	265	65	165	760	**26.2**
4 **J.R. Bremer**, St. Bonaventure	SR	G	30	231	88	188	738	**24.6**
5 **Melvin Ely**, Fresno State	SR	C	28	246	0	161	653	**23.3**
6 **Lynn Greer**, Temple	SR	G	31	226	95	172	719	**23.2**
7 **Nick Stapleton**, Austin Peay	SR	G	32	270	72	130	742	**23.2**
8 **Keith McLeod**, Bowling Green	SR	G	33	224	89	218	755	**22.9**
9 **Chris Davis**, North Texas	JR	G	29	217	46	173	653	**22.5**
10 **Ricky Minard**, Morehead State	SO	G	29	227	65	127	646	**22.3**

Field Goal Pct	CL	POS	G	FG	FGA	PCT
1 **Adam Mark**, Belmont	SO	F	26	150	212	**70.8**
2 **Carlos Boozer**, Duke	JR	C	35	230	346	**66.5**
3 **David Harrison**, Colorado	FR	C	27	139	218	**63.8**
4 **Rolan Roberts**, Southern Illinois	SR	C	36	209	346	**60.4**
5 **Jermaine Hall**, Wagner	JR	F	29	240	400	**60.0**

Minimum: 5 made per game

Three-point FG Per Game	CL	POS	G	3FG	3PG
1 **Cain Doliboa**, Wright State	SR	G	28	104	**3.7**
2 **Jobey Thomas**, Charlotte	SR	G	30	110	**3.7**
3 **Dan Dickau**, Gonzaga	SR	G	32	117	**3.7**
4 **Wes Burtner**, Belmont	SR	F	28	100	**3.6**
Jason Morgan, St. Francis (NY)	SR	G	28	100	**3.6**

Three-point FG Pct	CL	POS	G	3FG	3FGA	PCT
1 **Dante Swanson**, Tulsa	JR	G	33	73	149	**49.0**
2 **Cain Doliboa**, Wright State	SR	G	28	104	217	**47.9**
3 **Jake Sullivan**, Iowa State	SO	G	28	60	127	**47.2**
4 **Jeff Boschee**, Kansas	SR	G	37	110	237	**46.4**
5 **Ray Abellard**, Central Florida	JR	G	29	80	173	**46.2**

Minimum: 2 made per game

Free Throw Pct	CL	POS	G	FT	FTA	PCT
1 **Cary Cochran**, Nebraska	SR	G	28	71	77	**92.2**
2 **Gary Buchanan**, Villanova	JR	G	32	112	123	**91.1**
3 **Cain Doliboa**, Wright State	SR	G	28	80	88	**90.9**
4 **Salim Stoudamire**, Arizona	FR	G	34	103	114	**90.4**
5 **Jake Sullivan**, Iowa State	SO	G	28	117	130	**90.0**

Minimum: 2.5 made per game

Assists Per Game	CL	POS	G	AST	APG
1 **T.J. Ford**, Texas	FR	G	33	273	**8.3**
2 **Steve Blake**, Maryland	JR	G	36	286	**7.9**
3 **Edward Scott**, Clemson	JR	G	30	238	**7.9**
4 **Sean Kennedy**, Marist	SR	G	28	222	**7.9**
5 **Chris Thomas**, Notre Dame	FR	G	33	252	**7.6**
6 **Matt Montague**, BYU	SR	G	30	217	**7.2**
7 **Brandin Knight**, Pittsburgh	JR	G	35	251	**7.2**
8 **Mychal Covington**, Oakland	SR	G	28	198	**7.1**
9 **Reggie Kohn**, South Florida	JR	G	32	220	**6.9**
10 **Aaron Miles**, Kansas	FR	G	37	252	**6.8**

Rebounds Per Game	CL	POS	G	REB	RPG
1 **Jeremy Bishop**, Quinnipiac	JR	F	29	347	**12.0**
2 **Bruce Jenkins**, NC A&T	SR	F	28	329	**11.8**
3 **Curtis Borchardt**, Stanford	JR	C	29	332	**11.4**
4 **Drew Gooden**, Kansas	JR	F	37	423	**11.4**
5 **Corey Jackson**, Nevada	SR	F	29	323	**11.1**
6 **Reggie Evans**, Iowa	SR	F	34	378	**11.1**
7 **Trevor Gaines**, Vermont	SR	C	29	320	**11.0**
8 **Theron Smith**, Ball State	JR	F	35	381	**10.9**
9 **Ryan Humphrey**, Notre Dame	SR	F	31	337	**10.9**
10 **Stephane Pelle**, Colorado	JR	F	29	314	**10.8**

Blocked Shots Per Game	CL	POS	G	BLK	BPG
1 **Wojciech Myrda**, UL-Monroe	SR	C	32	172	**5.4**
2 **D'or Fischer**, Northwestern State (LA)	SO	C	30	133	**4.4**
3 **Emeka Okafor**, Connecticut	FR	C	34	138	**4.1**
4 **Justin Rowe**, Maine	JR	C	30	121	**4.0**
5 **Deng Gai**, Fairfield	FR	F	29	115	**4.0**

Steals Per Game	CL	POS	G	STL	SPG
1 **Desmond Cambridge**, Alabama A&M	SR	G	29	160	**5.5**
2 **John Linehan**, Providence	SR	G	31	139	**4.5**
3 **Mire Chatman**, Texas-Pan American	SR	G	29	105	**3.6**
4 **Marques Green**, St. Bonaventure	SO	G	30	102	**3.4**
5 **Marcus Hatten**, St. John's	JR	G	32	105	**3.3**

INDIVIDUAL LEADERS—GAME

Points	CL	POS	OPP	DATE	PTS
1 **Desmond Cambridge**, Alabama A&M	SR	G	Texas Southern	F25	**50**
2 **Casey Jacobsen**, Stanford	JR	G	Arizona State	J31	**49**
3 **Lynn Greer**, Temple	SR	G	Wisconsin	D3	**47**
4 **Mire Chatman**, Texas-Pan American	SR	G	Corpus Christi	F9	**46**
5 **T.J. Sorrentine**, Vermont	SO	G	Northeastern	J17	**45**
Mike Helms, Oakland	SO	G	Western Michigan	D29	**45**
Errick Greene, Maine	SR	G	Norfolk State	D11	**45**

Three-point FG Made	CL	POS	OPP	DATE	3FG
1 **Ronald Blackshear**, Marshall	SO	G	Akron	M1	**14**
2 **Clarence Gilbert**, Missouri	SR	G	Colorado	F23	**12**
3 **T.J. Sorrentine**, Vermont	SO	G	Northeastern	J17	**11**
4 **Wes Burtner**, Belmont	SR	F	Troy	F9	**10**
Ronnie Jones, Wisc.-Milwaukee	JR	G	Youngstown State	J2	**10**
Earnest Porter, Nicholls State	JR	G	Troy	D17	**10**

Assists	CL	POS	OPP	DATE	AST
1 **Brad Boyd**, UL-Lafayette	SO	F	North Texas	J24	**17**
Sean Peterson, Ga. Southern	SR	G	Western Carolina	J21	**17**
Imari Sawyer, DePaul	SO	G	Youngstown State	N25	**17**
4 **Kevin Braswell**, Georgetown	SR	G	Rutgers	M2	**16**
Steve Logan, Cincinnati	SR	G	Coppin State	D8	**16**

Rebounds	CL	POS	OPP	DATE	REB
1 **Andre Brown**, DePaul	SO	F	TCU	F6	**27**
Amien Hicks, Morris Brown	JR	F	Clark Atlanta	J14	**27**
3 **Jamal Brown**, TCU	JR	F	North Texas	D23	**26**
4 **Nicholas Egland**, Southern U.	FR	G	Arkansas-Pine Bluff	J12	**25**
5 **Ellis Myles**, Louisville	SO	F	Tennessee State	D1	**23**

Blocked Shots	CL	POS	OPP	DATE	BLK
1 **Wojciech Myrda**, UL-Monroe	SR	C	UTSA	J17	**13**
2 **D'or Fischer**, Northwestern St. (LA)	SO	C	Siena	N21	**12**
3 **Wojciech Myrda**, UL-Monroe	SR	C	Nicholls State	F16	**11**
4 **Cedric Suitt**, Pepperdine	SR	C	San Diego	J26	**10**
Wojciech Myrda, UL-Monroe	SR	C	Sam Houston State	J24	**10**
Wojciech Myrda, UL-Monroe	SR	C	Texas-Arlington	J7	**10**
Wojciech Myrda, UL-Monroe	SR	C	Stephen F. Austin	J5	**10**
Wojciech Myrda, UL-Monroe	SR	C	Holy Cross	D29	**10**
Deng Gai, Fairfield	FR	F	St. Francis (NY)	D11	**10**

Steals	CL	POS	OPP	DATE	STL
1 **Jehiel Lewis**, Navy	SR	G	Bucknell	J12	**12**
2 **Travis Demanby**, Fresno State	JR	G	Oklahoma State	F10	**11**
John Linehan, Providence	SR	G	Rutgers	J22	**11**
Drew Schifino, West Virginia	FR	G	Arkansas-Monticello	D1	**11**
Chris Thomas, Notre Dame	FR	G	New Hampshire	N16	**11**

TEAM LEADERS—SEASON

Win-Loss Pct	W	L	PCT
1 **Kansas**	33	4	**.892**
2 **Maryland**	32	4	**.889**
3 **Cincinnati**	31	4	**.886**
Duke	31	4	**.886**
5 **Western Kentucky**	28	4	**.875**

Scoring Offense	G	W-L	PTS	PPG
1 **Kansas**	37	33-4	3,365	**90.9**
2 **Duke**	35	31-4	3,112	**88.9**
3 **Oregon**	35	26-9	2,994	**85.5**
4 **TCU**	31	16-15	2,645	**85.3**
5 **Maryland**	36	32-4	3,060	**85.0**

Scoring Margin	G	W-L	PPG	OPP PPG	MAR
1 **Duke**	35	31-4	88.9	69.2	**19.7**
2 **Cincinnati**	35	31-4	78.2	60.4	**17.8**
3 **Kansas**	37	33-4	90.9	74.7	**16.2**
4 **Gonzaga**	33	29-4	81.1	66.6	**14.5**
5 **Maryland**	36	32-4	85.0	70.9	**14.1**

Field Goal Pct	G	W-L	FG	FGA	PCT
1 **Kansas**	37	33-4	1,259	2,487	**50.6**
2 **Duke**	35	31-4	1,093	2,209	**49.5**
3 **Bowling Green**	33	24-9	834	1,709	**48.8**
4 **Oregon**	35	26-9	1,014	2,082	**48.7**
5 **Ohio State**	32	24-8	825	1,702	**48.5**

Three-point FG Per Game	G	W-L	3FG	3PG
1 **St. Bonaventure**	30	17-13	314	**10.5**
2 **Dartmouth**	27	9-18	263	**9.7**
3 **Nebraska**	28	13-15	267	**9.5**
4 **Belmont**	28	11-17	264	**9.4**
5 **Troy**	28	18-10	258	**9.2**

Assists Per Game	G	W-L	AST	APG
1 **Kansas**	37	33-4	767	**20.7**
2 **Maryland**	36	32-4	714	**19.8**
3 **Notre Dame**	33	22-11	629	**19.1**
4 **Texas Tech**	32	23-9	588	**18.4**
5 **Belmont**	28	11-17	506	**18.1**

Rebound Margin	G	W-L	RPG	OPP RPG	MAR
1 **Gonzaga**	33	29-4	41.5	32.6	**8.9**
2 **Louisiana Tech**	32	22-10	40.9	32.2	**8.8**
3 **Kansas**	37	33-4	44.3	35.5	**8.7**
4 **Stanford**	30	20-10	41.8	33.3	**8.5**
5 **Dayton**	32	21-11	39.9	31.7	**8.3**

Scoring Defense	G	W-L	OPP PTS	OPP PPG
1 **Columbia**	28	11-17	1,596	**57.0**
2 **Princeton**	28	16-12	1,606	**57.4**
3 **Butler**	32	26-6	1,849	**57.8**
4 **Utah State**	31	23-8	1,800	**58.1**
5 **Northwestern**	29	16-13	1,715	**59.1**

Field Goal Pct Defense	G	W-L	OPP FG	OPP FGA	OPP PCT
1 **VCU**	32	21-11	767	2,052	**37.4**
2 **Cincinnati**	35	31-4	761	2,035	**37.4**
3 **Charleston**	30	21-9	663	1,762	**37.6**
4 **Davidson**	31	21-10	692	1,822	**38.0**
5 **Connecticut**	34	27-7	830	2,182	**38.0**

Blocked Shots Per Game

	G	W-L	BLK	BPG
1 Connecticut	34	27-7	236	**6.9**
2 Rutgers	31	18-13	215	**6.9**
3 Fairfield	29	12-17	199	**6.9**
4 UL-Monroe	32	20-12	217	**6.8**
5 Georgetown	30	19-11	191	**6.4**

Steals Per Game

	G	W-L	STL	SPG
1 Alabama A&M	29	19-10	395	**13.6**
2 Arkansas-Pine Bluff	28	2-26	311	**11.1**
3 Providence	31	15-16	342	**11.0**
4 Syracuse	36	23-13	394	**10.9**
5 Tennessee-Martin	29	15-14	310	**10.7**

TEAM LEADERS—GAME

Points

POINTS	OPP	DATE	SCORE
1 Sacred Heart	Fairleigh Dickinson	D1	**133-130**
Western Carolina	Toccoa Falls (GA)	N26	**133-58**
3 Fairleigh Dickinson	Sacred Heart	D1	**130-133**
4 Long Island	Fairleigh Dickinson	F23	**122-115**
5 UNLV	New Mexico	M7	**120-117**

Field Goal Pct

FIELD GOAL PCT	OPP	DATE	FG	FGA	PCT
1 UCLA	South Carolina	N21	35	48	**72.9**
2 Air Force	Montana State	N30	25	35	**71.4**
3 Colorado State	Denver	D15	27	38	**71.1**
4 Houston	Tennessee	D30	35	50	**70.0**
5 BYU	Fort Lewis	D12	39	56	**69.6**

Three-Point FG Made

THREE-POINT FG MADE	OPP	DATE	3FG
1 Missouri	Colorado	F23	**20**
Nicholls State	Troy	D17	**20**
3 Louisville	South Florida	F1	**19**
St. Bonaventure	Temple	J16	**19**
5 Richmond	Duquesne	M2	**18**
Nebraska	Kansas	F24	**18**
Temple	Fordham	J30	**18**
Lafayette	Howard	D30	**18**
Cincinnati	UL-Monroe	D20	**18**

CONSENSUS ALL-AMERICAS

First Team

PLAYER	CL	POS	HT	SCHOOL	RPG	PPG
Dan Dickau	SR	G	6-1	Gonzaga	3.0	21.0
Juan Dixon	SR	G	6-3	Maryland	4.6	20.4
Drew Gooden	JR	F	6-10	Kansas	11.4	19.8
Steve Logan	SR	G	6-0	Cincinnati	3.1	22.0
Jason Williams	JR	G	6-2	Duke	3.5	21.3

Second Team

PLAYER	CL	POS	HT	SCHOOL	RPG	PPG
Sam Clancy	SR	F	6-7	Southern California	9.4	19.1
Mike Dunleavy	JR	G/F	6-9	Duke	7.2	17.3
Casey Jacobsen	JR	G	6-6	Stanford	4.5	21.9
Jared Jeffries	SO	F	6-10	Indiana	7.6	15.0
David West	JR	F	6-8	Xavier	9.8	18.3

SELECTORS: AP, NABC, SPORTING NEWS, USBWA

AWARD WINNERS

Player of the Year

PLAYER	CL	POS	HT	SCHOOL	AWARDS
Jason Williams	JR	G	6-2	Duke	Naismith, AP, USBWA, Wooden, NABC (shared), Rupp
Drew Gooden	JR	F	6-10	Kansas	NABC (shared)
Steve Logan	SR	G	6-0	Cincinnati	Frances Pomeroy Naismith*

* THE MOST OUTSTANDING SENIOR PLAYER WHO IS 6 FEET OR UNDER

Defensive Player of the Year

PLAYER	CL	POS	HT	SCHOOL
John Linehan	SR	G	5-9	Providence

Coach of the Year

COACH	SCHOOL	REC	AWARDS
Ben Howland	Pittsburgh	29-6	Naismith, AP, USBWA, Sporting News
Kelvin Sampson	Oklahoma	31-5	NABC, CBS/Chevrolet

Bob Gibbons' Top High School Senior Recruits

PLAYER	POS	HT	HIGH SCHOOL	A-A TEAMS	COLLEGE	CAREER NOTES
1 Raymond Felton	PG	6-1	Latta (SC) HS	McD, P, USA	North Carolina	698 assists (4 seasons); first-team All-ACC; No. 5 pick '05 NBA draft (Bobcats); 13.6 ppg (4 seasons)
2 Carmelo Anthony	F	6-7	Oak Hill Academy, Mouth of Wilson, VA	McD, P, USA	Syracuse	NCAA Tourney MOP '03; 22.2 ppg in 1 year; No. 3 pick, '03 NBA draft (Nuggets); 2-time All-Star
3 Paul Davis	F/C	6-11	Rochester (MI) HS	McD, P	Michigan State	13.2 ppg at MSU; 2nd-round pick, '06 NBA draft (Clippers); 3 seasons
4 Amare Stoudemire	F/C	6-10	Cypress Creek HS, Orlando, FL	McD, P, USA	None	Drafted straight out of HS; No. 9 pick, '02 NBA draft (Suns); '03 ROY; '07 All-NBA team; 4-time All-Star
5 Chris Bosh	F/C	6-10	Lincoln HS, Dallas, TX	McD, P	Georgia Tech	15.6 ppg/9.0 rpg in 1 year; No. 4 pick, '03 NBA draft (Raptors); '04 All-Rookie team; 4-time All-Star
6 J.J. Redick	G	6-4	Cave Spring HS, Roanoke, VA	McD, P	Duke	2-time ACC POY; '06 National POY; No. 11 pick, '06 NBA draft (Magic); 5.5 ppg (3 seasons)
7 Rashad McCants	G	6-4	New Hampton (NH) Prep	McD, P	North Carolina	Led ACC: 20.0 ppg as Soph.; No. 14 pick, '05 NBA draft (Wolves); 10.0 ppg (3 seasons)
8 Brad Buckman	C	6-9	Westlake HS, Austin, TX	McD, P	Texas	8.5 ppg, 6.2 rpg (4 seasons); undrafted; played in D-League
9 Sean May	PF	6-8	Bloomington (IN) North HS	McD, P	North Carolina	First-team All-ACC, '05; MOP, '05 NCAA title; No. 13 pick, '05 NBA draft (Bobcats); 8.5 ppg (3 seasons)
10 Andre Iguodala	G/F	6-6	Lanphier, HS, Springfield, IL	P	Arizona	All-Pac-10, '04; No. 9 pick, '04 NBA draft (76ers); 15.6 ppg, 5.7 rpg (5 seasons)
11 Jason Fraser	F/C	6-9	Amityville (NY) HS	McD, P	Villanova	5.9 ppg (2 seasons); career derailed by injuries; undrafted; played with Harlem Globetrotters
12 Bracey Wright	G	6-3	The Colony (TX) HS	McD, P	Indiana	17.6 ppg in 3 years; 2nd-round pick, '05 NBA draft (Wolves); played 26 NBA games, D-League
13 Anthony Roberson	G	6-2	Saginaw (MI) HS	McD, P	Florida	17.5 ppg as a Sr.; entered draft as a Jr.; undrafted; played 65 NBA games
14 Hassan Adams	G/F	6-4	Westchester HS, Los Angeles, CA	McD, P, USA	Arizona	1,818 points for Arizona; 2nd-round pick, '06 NBA draft (Nets); 2.5 ppg (2 seasons)
15 Travis Garrison	PF	6-8	DeMatha HS, Hyattsville, MD	McD, P	Maryland	7.4 ppg (4 seasons); played in D-League and overseas
16 Kevin Bookout	C	6-9	Stroud (OK) HS	P	Oklahoma	1,108 pts (4 seasons); 3-time All-America in the shot put; played in D-League
17 Dee Brown	PG	6-0	Proviso East HS, Maywood, IL	McD	Illinois	2nd team All-America ('05, '06); 2nd-round pick, '06 NBA draft (Jazz); played 68 NBA games
18 Daniel Horton	G	6-3	Cedar Hill (TX) HS	McD, P	Michigan	14.7 ppg, 4.4 apg (4 seasons); signed by Miami (1 game); played in D-League
19 Shavlik Randolph	PF	6-10	Broughton HS, Raleigh, NC	McD, P	Duke	6.3 ppg (3 seasons); declared for draft early; undrafted; played 89 NBA games
20 Torin Francis	C	6-10	Tabor Academy, Marion, MA	McD, P	Notre Dame	11.5 ppg, 8.6 rpg (4 seasons); undrafted; played in Greece and Israel

Other Standouts

PLAYER	POS	HT	HIGH SCHOOL	A-A TEAMS	COLLEGE	CAREER NOTES
27 Jarrett Jack	G	6-5	Academy HS, Worchester, MA		Georgia Tech	No. 5 all-time in assists at GT (543); No. 22 pick, '05 NBA draft (Nuggets); 10.4 (4 seasons)
46 Randy Foye	G	6-3	East Side HS, Newark, NJ		Villanova	First-team All-America as senior (20.5 ppg); No. 7 pick, '06 NBA draft (Celtics); All-Rookie team, '07
55 Brandon Roy	G/F	6-6	Garfield HS, Seattle, WA		Washington	Pac-10 POY, '06; No. 6 pick, '06 NBA draft (Wolves); '07 ROY (16.8 ppg); 2-time NBA All-Star

Abbreviations: McD=McDonald's; P=Parade; USA=USA Today

Poll Progression

Preseason Poll Poll

AP	ESPN/USA	School
1	1	Duke
2	3	Maryland
3	2	Illinois
4	4	Kentucky
5	6	UCLA
6	5	Florida
7	7	Kansas
8	9	Missouri
9	8	Iowa
10	10	Saint Joseph's
11	11	Virginia
12	13	Memphis
13	15	Stanford
14	14	Georgetown
15	12	Michigan State
16	17	Temple
17	16	Boston College
18	18	Oklahoma State
19	19	North Carolina
20	24	USC
21	20	Syracuse
22	21	Indiana
23	22	Texas
24	—	Alabama
25	23	Oklahoma
—	25	Fresno Sate

Week of Nov 13

ESPN/USA	School
1	Duke (0-0)
2	Illinois (0-0)
3	Kentucky (0-0)
4	UCLA (0-0)
5	Kansas (0-0)
6	Maryland (1-1)
7	Florida (1-1)
8	Missouri (0-0)
9	Saint Joseph's (0-0)
10	Iowa (0-0)
11	Virginia (0-0)
12	Arizona (2-0)
13	Michigan State (0-0)
14	Memphis (0-0)
15	Georgetown (0-0)
16	Stanford (0-0)
17	Boston College (0-0)
18	Oklahoma State (0-0)
19	Syracuse (0-0)
20	Indiana (0-0)
20	North Carolina (0-0)
22	Texas (0-0)
23	USC (0-0)
24	Oklahoma (0-0)
25	Temple (0-2)

Week of Nov 20 (A)

AP	ESPN/USA	School
1	1	Duke (1-0)
2	2	Illinois (1-0)
3	4	UCLA (0-0)
4	3	Kansas (0-0)
5	9	Missouri (2-0)
6	5	Maryland (2-1)
7	6	Florida (2-1)
8	7	Arizona (3-0) (B)
9	8	Iowa (3-0)
10	12	Kentucky (1-1)
11	10	Virginia (2-0)
12	14	Memphis (3-0)
13	11	Michigan State (2-0)
14	13	Stanford (1-0)
15	16	Oklahoma State (2-0)
16	15	Georgetown (1-0)
17	17	Boston College (1-0)
18	18	Syracuse (3-0)
19	19	Saint Joseph's (1-1)
20	20	Indiana (1-0)
21	25	Western Kentucky (2-0)
22	22	Alabama (2-0)
23	21	Fresno State (2-0)
24	—	USC (1-1)
25	—	Temple (0-2)
—	23	Oklahoma (1-1)
—	24	Texas (0-1)

Week of Nov 27

AP	ESPN/USA	School	
1	1	Duke (4-0)	
2	2	Illinois (5-0)	
3	5	Missouri (5-0)	
4	3	Arizona (3-0)	
5	4	Maryland (3-1)	
6	6	Florida (2-1)	
7	13	Iowa (4-1)	
8	7	Kansas (2-1)	
9	8	Virginia (3-0)	↑
10	11	UCLA (2-1)	↓
11	9	Stanford (3-0)	↑
12	10	Syracuse (5-0)	↑
13	14	Kentucky (2-1)	↓
14	12	Oklahoma State (6-0)	↑
15	15	Boston College (3-0)	↑
16	25	Ball State (2-1)	
17	18	Western Kentucky (4-0)	↑
18	16	Georgetown (3-1)	↓
19	21	Saint Joseph's (2-1)	
20	19	Memphis (4-2)	↓8
21	22	Alabama (3-1)	↑1
22	17	Michigan State (2-2)	↓9
23	—	Marquette (5-0)	⤴
24	20	Fresno State (3-1)	↓1
25	23	Wake Forest (4-1)	⤴
—	24	Indiana (3-1)	⤵

Week of Dec 4

AP	ESPN/USA	School	AP↓↑
1	1	Duke (6-0)	
2	3	Missouri (7-0)	↑1
3	2	Maryland (5-1)	↑2
4	5	Kansas (4-1)	↑4
5	6	Illinois (6-1)	↓3
6	4	Florida (4-1)	
7	8	Arizona (3-1)	↓3
8	7	Virginia (4-0)	↑1
9	9	Syracuse (8-0)	↑3
10	10	Oklahoma State (8-0)	↑4
11	12	Kentucky (3-1)	↑2
12	11	Iowa (6-2)	↓5
13	13	Boston College (5-0)	↑2
14	14	Stanford (3-1)	↓3
15	20	Ball State (4-1)	↑1
16	19	Alabama (5-1)	↑5
17	21	Marquette (7-0)	↑6
18	24	Saint Joseph's (4-1)	↑1
19	15	Georgetown (5-1)	↓1
20	18	UCLA (2-2)	↓10
21	16	Fresno State (6-1)	↑3
22	23	Memphis (6-2)	↓2
23	22	Wake Forest (5-1)	↑2
24	16	Michigan State (4-2)	↓2
25	25	Western Kentucky (4-2)	↓8

Week of Dec 11

AP	ESPN/USA	School	AP↓↑
1	1	Duke (8-0)	
2	3	Missouri (9-0)	
3	2	Maryland (7-1)	
4	5	Kansas (6-1)	
5	4	Florida (6-1)	↑1
6	7	Arizona (5-1)	↑1
7	6	Virginia (5-0)	↑1
8	9	Oklahoma State (9-0)	↑2
9	10	Kentucky (5-1)	↑2
10	8	Illinois (7-2)	↓5
11	11	Boston College (7-0)	↑2
12	13	Stanford (3-1)	↑2
13	12	Syracuse (9-1)	↓4
14	16	Marquette (9-0)	↑3
15	15	Iowa (7-3)	↓3
16	18	Saint Joseph's (5-1) (C)	↑2
17	17	UCLA (4-2)	↑3
18	14	Georgetown (6-1)	↑1
19	20	Wake Forest (6-2)	↑4
20	23	Ball State (5-2)	↓5
21	24	Indiana (6-2)	⤴
22	21	Alabama (6-2)	↓6
23	19	Michigan State (5-3)	↑1
24	22	Oklahoma (5-1)	⤴
25	—	Gonzaga (7-2)	⤴
—	25	Western Kentucky (6-2)	⤵

Week of Dec 18

AP	ESPN/USA	School	AP↓↑
1	1	Duke (9-0)	
2	2	Maryland (8-1)	↑1
3	4	Kansas (8-1)	↑1
4	3	Florida (7-1)	↑1
5	5	Virginia (5-0)	↑2
6	6	Oklahoma State (9-0)	↑2
7	8	Kentucky (6-1)	↑2
8	9	Missouri (9-1)	↓6
9	7	Illinois (8-2)	↑1
10	11	Boston College (9-0)	↑1
11	10	Arizona (5-2)	↓5
12	12	Iowa (9-3)	↑3
13	13	Stanford (4-1)	↓1
14	15	Marquette (9-0)	
15	18	Saint Joseph's (6-1)	↑1
16	16	Georgetown (8-1)	↑2
17	17	Michigan State (6-3)	↑6
18	14	Syracuse (9-2)	↓5
19	19	UCLA (5-2)	↓2
20	20	Wake Forest (7-2)	↓1
21	23	Ball State (6-2)	↓1
22	21	Oklahoma (7-1)	↑2
23	22	Alabama (7-2)	↓1
24	24	Gonzaga (9-2)	↑1
25	25	Cincinnati (7-1)	⤴

Week of Dec 25

AP	ESPN/USA	School	AP↓↑
1	1	Duke (10-0)	
2	3	Kansas (9-1)	↑1
3	2	Florida (9-1)	↑1
4	4	Virginia (8-0)	↑1
5	5	Oklahoma State (12-0)	↑1
6	8	Kentucky (7-2)	↑1
7	7	Illinois (10-2)	↑2
8	6	Maryland (8-2)	↓6
9	9	Iowa (10-3)	↑3
10	10	Missouri (9-2)	↓2
11	13	Boston College (11-1)	↓1
12	14	Oklahoma (9-1)	↑10
13	12	Michigan State (9-3)	↑4
14	16	Arizona (6-3)	↓3
15	17	UCLA (7-2)	↑4
16	15	Stanford (6-2)	↓3
17	20	Cincinnati (11-1)	↑8
18	11	Syracuse (10-2)	
19	19	Marquette (10-1)	↓5
20	18	Georgetown (9-2)	↓4
21	21	Alabama (9-2)	↑2
22	22	Gonzaga (10-2)	↑2
23	24	Butler (11-0)	⤴
24	23	Miami (FL) (11-0)	⤴
25	25	Wake Forest (8-3)	↓5

Week of Jan 1

AP	ESPN/USA	School	AP↓↑
1	1	Duke (11-0)	
2	3	Kansas (10-1)	
3	2	Florida (11-1)	
4	4	Virginia (9-0)	
5	5	Oklahoma State (13-0)	
6	8	Kentucky (8-2) (D)	
7	7	Illinois (11-2)	
8	6	Maryland (10-2)	
9	9	Iowa (11-3)	
10	11	Oklahoma (10-1)	↑2
11	12	Boston College (11-1)	
12	13	Stanford (7-2)	↑4
13	16	Cincinnati (12-1)	↑4
14	15	UCLA (9-2)	↑1
15	14	Arizona (8-3)	↓1
16	10	Syracuse (11-2)	↑2
17	18	Missouri (9-3)	↓7
18	19	Alabama (10-2)	↑3
19	17	Michigan State (9-4)	↓6
20	20	Butler (13-0)	↑3
21	21	Miami (FL) (13-0)	↑3
22	22	Gonzaga (11-2)	
23	24	Wake Forest (9-3)	↑2
24	23	Georgetown (9-3)	↓4
25	25	Marquette (11-2)	↓6

Week of Jan 8

AP	ESPN/USA	School	AP↓↑
1	3	Kansas (12-1)	↑1
2	1	Duke (12-1)	↓1
3	2	Florida (12-1)	
4	4	Maryland (11-2)	↑4
5	7	Oklahoma (11-1)	↑5
6	6	Oklahoma State (13-1) (E)	↓1
7	5	Virginia (9-1)	↓3
8	9	Kentucky (9-3)	↓2
9	10	Illinois (12-3)	↓2
10	12	Cincinnati (13-1)	↑3
11	14	UCLA (11-2)	↑3
12	8	Syracuse (13-2)	↑4
13	13	Iowa (12-4)	↓4
14	11	Stanford (8-3)	↓2
15	15	Alabama (13-2)	↑4
16	16	Boston College (12-2)	↓5
17	17	Missouri (11-3)	
18	18	Gonzaga (12-2)	↑4
19	19	Wake Forest (11-3)	↑4
20	21	Arizona (9-4)	↓5
21	20	Miami (Fla.) (14-1)	
22	24	Mississippi State (14-1)	⤴
23	25	Pittsburgh (14-1)	⤴
24	23	Butler (13-1)	↓4
25	22	Michigan State (9-5)	↓6

Week of Jan 15

AP	ESPN/USA	School	AP↓↑
1	1	Duke (14-1)	↑1
2	2	Florida (14-1)	↑1
3	3	Maryland (13-2)	↑1
4	4	Kansas (13-2)	↓3
5	5	Oklahoma (13-1)	
6	6	Oklahoma State (15-1)	
7	8	Cincinnati (15-1)	↑3
8	7	Syracuse (15-2)	↑4
9	11	UCLA (12-3)	↑2
10	9	Virginia (10-2)	↓3
11	10	Illinois (13-4)	↓2
12	12	Kentucky (10-4)	↓4
13	14	Gonzaga (15-2)	↑5
14	13	Wake Forest (13-3)	↑5
15	18	Arizona (11-4)	↑5
16	17	Alabama (14-3)	↓2
17	15	Iowa (13-5)	↓4
18	24	USC (13-2)	⤴
19	16	Stanford (9-4)	↓5
20	23	Georgia (14-2)	⤴
21	19	Missouri (12-4)	↓4
22	21	Boston College (13-3)	↓6
23	22	Oregon (12-4)	⤴
24	20	Miami (FL) (15-2)	↓3
25	—	Indiana (11-5)	⤴
—	25	Butler (15-2)	⤵

Week of Jan 22

AP	ESPN/USA	School	AP↓↑
1	1	Duke (16-1)	
2	2	Kansas (15-2)	↑2
3	3	Maryland (14-3)	
4	5	Cincinnati (17-1)	↑3
5	4	Florida (15-2)	↓3
6	6	Oklahoma (14-2)	↓1
7	7	Virginia (12-2)	↑3
8	9	Kentucky (12-4)	↑4
9	8	Illinois (14-4)	↑2
10	12	Arizona (13-4)	↑5
11	11	Oklahoma State (15-3)	↓5
12	10	Syracuse (16-3)	↓4
13	13	UCLA (13-4)	↓4
14	14	Alabama (16-3)	↑2
15	17	Georgia (15-3)	↑5
16	18	Gonzaga (16-3)	↓3
17	14	Stanford (11-4)	↑2
18	20	Missouri (14-4)	↑3
19	21	Oregon (14-4)	↑4
20	23	Ohio State (14-2)	⤴
21	16	Wake Forest (13-5)	↓7
22	19	Miami (FL) (17-2)	↑2
23	22	USC (14-3)	↓5
24	—	Texas (13-4)	⤴
25	—	Connecticut (12-3)	⤴
—	24	Iowa (13-7)	⤵
—	25	Pittsburgh (16-3)	

ANNUAL REVIEW

K of Jan 29

AP	ESPN/USA	School	AP↓↑
	1	**Duke** (18-1)	
	2	**Kansas** (17-2)	
	3	**Maryland** (16-3)	
	4	**Cincinnati** (19-1)	
	6	**Florida** (15-3)	
	7	**Oklahoma** (15-3)	
	8	**Alabama** (17-3)	↑7
	5	**Virginia** (14-3)	↓1
	9	**Oklahoma State** (17-3)	↑2
	11	**Kentucky** (13-5)	↓2
	14	**Gonzaga** (18-3)	↑5
	12	**Illinois** (15-5)	↓3
	13	**UCLA** (14-5)	
	10	**Syracuse** (17-4)	↓2
	16	**Miami (Fla.)** (18-2)	↑7
	17	**Georgia** (16-4)	↓1
	22	**Connecticut** (14-3)	↑8
	15	**Stanford** (12-5)	↓1
	18	**Arizona** (13-6)	↓9
	23	**Texas Tech** (15-3)	⤴
	21	**Pittsburgh** (18-3)	⤴
22	24	**Missouri** (15-5)	↓4
23	20	**USC** (15-4)	
24	19	**Wake Forest** (14-6)	↓3
25	—	**Ohio State** (15-3)	↓5
—	25	**Indiana** (13-6)	

Week of Feb 5

AP	ESPN/USA	School	AP↓↑
1	1	**Duke** (20-1)	
2	2	**Kansas** (19-2)	
3	3	**Maryland** (18-3)	
4	4	**Oklahoma** (17-3)	↑2
5	6	**Alabama** (19-3)	↑2
6	5	**Cincinnati** (20-2)	↓2
7	9	**Kentucky** (15-5)	↑3
8	7	**Florida** (16-4)	↓3
9	10	**Gonzaga** (20-3)	↑2
10	8	**Virginia** (14-5)	↓2
11	13	**Arizona** (15-6)	↑8
12	11	**Miami (Fla.)** (19-3)	↑3
13	15	**Oregon** (17-5)	⤴
14	12	**Oklahoma State** (17-5)	↓5
15	18	**UCLA** (15-6)	↓2
16	22	**Ohio State** (17-3)	↑9
17	19	**Georgia** (17-5)	↓1
18	23	**Marquette** (19-3)	⤴
19	16	**Wake Forest** (16-6)	↑5
20	20	**Stanford** (13-6)	↓2
21	14	**Illinois** (15-7)	↓9
22	—	**Missouri** (16-6)	
23	17	**Syracuse** (17-6)	↓9
24	25	**Texas Tech** (16-4)	↓4
25	24	**USC** (16-5)	↓2
—	21	**Pittsburgh** (19-4)	⤵

Week of Feb 12

AP	ESPN/USA	School	AP↓↑
1	1	**Duke** (22-1)	
2	2	**Kansas** (21-2)	
3	3	**Maryland** (19-3)	
4	4	**Oklahoma** (19-3)	
5	5	**Cincinnati** (22-2)	↑1
6	6	**Florida** (18-4)	↑2
7	7	**Alabama** (20-4)	↓2
8	8	**Gonzaga** (22-3)	↑1
9	10	**Arizona** (17-6)	↑2
10	9	**Kentucky** (16-6)	↓3
11	12	**Marquette** (21-3)	↑7
12	14	**Stanford** (15-6)	↑8
13	11	**Miami (Fla.)** (20-4)	↓1
14	16	**Pittsburgh** (21-4)	⤴
15	13	**Virginia** (15-6)	↓5
16	15	**Oklahoma State** (18-6)	↓2
17	18	**Oregon** (17-7)	↓4
18	19	**Illinois** (17-7)	↑3
19	17	**Wake Forest** (17-7)	
20	23	**UCLA** (16-7)	↓5
21	22	**Georgia** (18-6)	↓4
22	24	**Indiana** (16-7)	⤴
23	20	**Ohio State** (17-5)	↓7
24	—	**NC State** (18-6)	⤴
25	25	**USC** (16-6)	
—	21	**Syracuse** (18-7)	⤵

Week of Feb 19

AP	ESPN/USA	School	AP↓↑
1	1	**Kansas** (23-2)	↑1
2	2	**Maryland** (21-3) Ⓕ	↑1
3	3	**Duke** (23-2) Ⓕ	↓2
4	4	**Cincinnati** (24-2)	↑1
5	6	**Alabama** (22-4)	↑2
6	5	**Oklahoma** (20-4)	↓2
7	7	**Gonzaga** (24-3)	↑1
8	8	**Florida** (19-5)	↓2
9	9	**Marquette** (22-3)	↑2
10	11	**Stanford** (17-6)	↑2
11	10	**Pittsburgh** (22-4)	↑3
12	12	**Kentucky** (17-7)	↓2
13	14	**Oklahoma State** (20-6)	↑3
14	16	**Arizona** (17-8)	↓5
15	17	**Oregon** (18-7)	↑2
16	19	**Illinois** (19-7)	↑2
17	13	**Miami (Fla.)** (21-5)	↓4
18	20	**Georgia** (19-7)	↑3
19	18	**Ohio State** (18-5)	↑4
20	21	**Wake Forest** (18-8)	↓1
21	22	**USC** (18-6)	↑5
22	15	**Virginia** (16-7)	↓7
23	23	**Indiana** (17-8)	↓1
24	—	**Western Kentucky** (23-3)	⤴
25	—	**UCLA** (17-8)	↓5
—	24	**Xavier** (19-4)	
—	25	**Syracuse** (19-7)	

Week of Feb 26

AP	ESPN/USA	School	AP↓↑
1	1	**Kansas** (25-2)	
2	2	**Maryland** (23-3)	
3	3	**Duke** (25-2)	
4	4	**Cincinnati** (26-2)	
5	5	**Oklahoma** (22-4)	↑1
6	6	**Alabama** (23-5)	↓1
7	7	**Gonzaga** (26-3)	
8	10	**Florida** (20-6)	
9	9	**Marquette** (23-4)	
10	8	**Pittsburgh** (23-4)	↑1
11	11	**Kentucky** (19-7)	↑1
12	12	**Oklahoma State** (22-6)	↑1
13	13	**Oregon** (20-7)	↑2
14	14	**Arizona** (18-8)	
15	16	**Illinois** (21-7)	↑1
16	15	**Georgia** (20-7)	↑2
17	19	**Stanford** (17-8)	↓7
18	17	**Ohio State** (19-6)	↑1
19	20	**USC** (19-7)	↑1
20	23	**Western Kentucky** (25-3)	↑4
21	25	**California** (20-5)	⤴
22	18	**Miami (FL)** (21-6)	↓5
23	—	**Connecticut** (19-6)	⤴
24	22	**Wake Forest** (18-10)	↓4
25	21	**Indiana** (18-9)	↓2
—	24	**Xavier** (20-5)	

Week of Mar 5

AP	ESPN/USA	School	AP↓↑
1	1	**Kansas** (27-2)	
2	2	**Maryland** (25-3)	
3	3	**Duke** (26-3)	
4	4	**Oklahoma** (24-4)	↑1
5	5	**Cincinnati** (27-3)	↓1
6	6	**Gonzaga** (28-3)	↑1
7	7	**Pittsburgh** (25-4)	↑3
8	8	**Alabama** (24-6)	↓2
9	9	**Oregon** (22-7)	↑4
10	15	**Illinois** (23-7)	↑5
11	12	**Florida** (21-7)	↓3
12	11	**Kentucky** (20-8)	↓1
13	10	**Marquette** (24-5)	↓4
14	13	**Oklahoma State** (23-7)	↓2
15	14	**Arizona** (19-9)	↓1
16	18	**Stanford** (19-8)	↑1
17	19	**Georgia** (21-8)	↓1
18	21	**Western Kentucky** (26-3)	↑2
19	24	**Connecticut** (21-6)	↑4
20	16	**Miami (FL)** (23-6)	↑2
21	17	**Ohio State** (20-7)	↓3
22	20	**USC** (20-8)	↓3
23	22	**Indiana** (19-10)	↑2
24	23	**Xavier** (22-5)	⤴
25	25	**California** (21-7)	↓4

Week of Mar 12 Ⓖ

AP	ESPN/USA	School	AP↓↑
1	1	**Duke** (29-3)	↑2
2	2	**Kansas** (29-3)	↓1
3	3	**Oklahoma** (27-4)	↑1
4	4	**Maryland** (26-4)	↓2
5	5	**Cincinnati** (30-3)	
6	6	**Gonzaga** (29-3)	
7	8	**Arizona** (22-9)	↑8
8	8	**Alabama** (26-7)	
9	7	**Pittsburgh** (27-5)	↓2
10	13	**Connecticut** (24-6)	↑9
11	11	**Oregon** (23-8)	↓2
12	10	**Marquette** (26-6)	↑1
13	16	**Illinois** (24-8)	↓3
14	12	**Ohio State** (23-7)	↑7
15	14	**Florida** (22-8)	↓4
16	15	**Kentucky** (20-9)	↓4
17	18	**Mississippi State** (26-7)	⤴
18	16	**USC** (22-9)	↑4
19	20	**Western Kentucky** (28-3)	↓1
20	22	**Oklahoma State** (23-8)	↓6
21	21	**Miami (FL)** (24-7)	↓1
22	19	**Xavier** (25-5)	↑2
23	—	**Georgia** (21-9)	↓6
24	23	**Stanford** (19-9)	↓8
25	24	**Hawaii** (27-5)	⤴
—	25	**NC State** (22-10)	

Final Poll (Post-Tournament)

ESPN/USA	School
1	**Maryland** (32-4)
2	**Kansas** (33-4)
3	**Indiana** (25-12)
4	**Oklahoma** (31-5)
5	**Duke** (31-4)
6	**Connecticut** (27-7)
6	**Oregon** (26-9)
8	**Cincinnati** (31-4)
9	**Pittsburgh** (29-6)
10	**Arizona** (24-10)
11	**Illinois** (26-9)
12	**Kent State** (30-6)
13	**Kentucky** (22-10)
14	**Alabama** (27-8)
15	**Missouri** (24-12)
16	**Gonzaga** (29-4)
17	**Ohio State** (24-8)
18	**Marquette** (26-7)
19	**Texas** (22-12)
20	**UCLA** (21-12)
21	**Mississippi State** (27-8)
22	**Southern Illinois** (28-8)
23	**Florida** (22-9)
24	**Xavier** (26-6)
25	**NC State** (23-11)

Ⓐ Bob Knight returns to coaching after a year off, guiding Texas Tech to a 75-55 win over William and Mary on Nov. 19 in Lubbock. The Red Raiders, who went 9–19 in 2000-01, will post a 23–9 record and receive an NCAA Tournament bid.

Ⓑ After upsetting Florida, Arizona rockets from unranked to No. 8, the second-biggest jump in the history of the AP Top 25.

Ⓒ After his Saint Joseph's team trounces Drexel, 85-64, coach Phil Martelli says that his Drexel counterpart, Bruiser Flint, "was fighting with sticks; we were fighting with bazookas." Eleven days later, Georgia State will muzzle the bazookas, beating St. Joe's for its first win ever over a ranked opponent.

Ⓓ Kentucky fans, angry that former UK coach Rick Pitino has returned to the college ranks at archrival Louisville, boo him loudly in his first return to Rupp Arena. The Wildcats oblige with an 82-62 victory.

Ⓔ During Texas' upset of Oklahoma State, Longhorns guard T.J. Ford dives for a loose ball and gets into a scuffle with Cowboys fans, including one who shoves him. Ford will end up with 273 assists, the third-best single-season total for a freshman in NCAA history.

Ⓕ Led by Juan Dixon, Maryland rocks Duke, 87-73, in Cole Fieldhouse, the seventh win over a top-ranked team in Terps history.

Ⓖ VMI's Jason Conley ends the season with 29.3 ppg, making him the first freshman to lead the nation in scoring.

Pre-Tournament Ratings Percentage Index (RPI)

Rank	School	W-L	Sched. Strg.	SS Rank	RPI
1	**Kansas**	27-3	.60700	7	.6723
2	**Cincinnati**	30-3	.58829	18	.6630
3	**Maryland**	26-4	.60022	10	.6613
4	**Duke**	29-3	.56644	39	.6601
5	**Oklahoma**	27-4	.59419	12	.6587
6	**Arizona**	22-9	.63641	1	.6458
7	**Alabama**	26-7	.59329	14	.6371
8	**Connecticut**	24-6	.58018	27	.6355
9	**Mississippi State**	26-7	.58926	17	.6325
10	**Kentucky**	19-9	.61277	5	.6238
11	**Illinois**	24-8	.58559	20	.6210
12	**Pittsburgh**	26-5	.54875	62	.6195
13	**Florida**	22-8	.57017	32	.6135
14	**Georgia**	21-9	.58446	21	.6126
15	**Texas Tech**	23-8	.57521	29	.6120
16	**Ohio State**	23-7	.56345	47	.6111
17	**Xavier**	25-5	.53750	78	.6110
18	**Indiana**	19-11	.61513	3	.6108
19	**Miami**	24-7	.56109	52	.6103
20	**Gonzaga**	28-3	.49843	153	.6061
21	**Oklahoma State**	23-8	.56689	38	.6054
22	**Texas**	20-11	.60843	6	.6049
23	**Marquette**	26-6	.52545	102	.6030
24	**Wake Forest**	20-12	.60430	9	.5996
25	**USC**	22-9	.56164	50	.5991
26	**UCLA**	19-11	.59129	15	.5962
27	**California**	22-8	.54135	70	.5954
28	**Kent State**	26-5	.51966	108	.5951
29	**Hawaii**	27-5	.51073	129	.5943
30	**Western Kentucky**	26-3	.49027	175	.5929
31	**Utah**	19-8	.56291	49	.5928
32	**NC State**	22-10	.56602	41	.5908
33	**Oregon**	22-8	.53605	81	.5899
34	**Michigan State**	18-11	.58194	25	.5894
35	**Tulsa**	25-6	.51644	118	.5876
36	**Stanford**	19-9	.54702	64	.5857
37	**Charlotte**	18-11	.58824	19	.5850
38	**Penn**	25-6	.51267	125	.5842
39	**San Diego State**	19-11	.58211	24	.5830
40	**St. John's**	20-11	.57081	31	.5827
41	**Notre Dame**	20-10	.55739	56	.5812
42	**Boston College**	20-11	.56834	36	.5801
43	**Villanova**	17-12	.59705	11	.5801
44	**Creighton**	22-8	.52845	95	.5734
45	**Pepperdine**	21-8	.51767	114	.5730
46	**Arkansas**	14-15	.62226	2	.5725
47	**Mississippi**	19-10	.54049	73	.5720
48	**South Carolina**	17-14	.58380	22	.5693
49	**UNLV**	20-10	.52790	97	.5686
50	**Virginia**	17-11	.55916	55	.5685

Source: Collegiate Basketball News

2002 NCAA Tournament

First Round | Second Round | Regional Semifinals | Regional Finals

South — Lexington, KY

First Round
- 1 Duke **84**, 16 Winthrop **37**
- 8 Notre Dame **82**, 9 Charlotte **63**
- 5 Indiana **75**, 12 Utah **56**
- 4 USC **89** (OT), 13 UNC Wilmington **93**
- 6 California **82**, 11 Pennsylvania **75**
- 3 Pittsburgh **71**, 14 Central Connecticut State **54**
- 7 Oklahoma State **61**, 10 Kent State **69**
- 2 Alabama **86**, 15 Florida Atlantic **78**

Second Round
- Duke **84**, Notre Dame **77**
- Indiana **76**, UNC Wilmington **67**
- California **50**, Pittsburgh **63**
- Kent State **71**, Alabama **58**

Regional Semifinals
- Duke **73**, Indiana **74** (A)
- Pittsburgh **73** (OT), Kent State **78** (B)

Regional Final
- Indiana **81**, Kent State **69**

West — San Jose, CA

First Round
- 1 Cincinnati **90**, 16 Boston University **52**
- 8 UCLA **80**, 9 Mississippi **58**
- 5 Miami (FL) **80**, 12 Missouri **93**
- 4 ⊗Ohio State **69**, 13 Davidson **64**
- 6 Gonzaga **66**, 11 Wyoming **73** (D)
- 3 Arizona **86**, 14 UC Santa Barbara **81**
- 7 Xavier **70**, 10 Hawaii **58** (E)
- 2 Oklahoma **71**, 15 Illinois-Chicago **63**

Second Round
- Cincinnati **101** (OT), UCLA **105**
- Missouri **83**, ⊗Ohio State **67**
- Wyoming **60**, Arizona **68**
- Xavier **65**, Oklahoma **78**

Regional Semifinals
- UCLA **73**, Missouri **82** (C)
- Arizona **67**, Oklahoma **88**

Regional Final
- Missouri **75**, Oklahoma **81**

East — Syracuse, NY

First Round
- 1 Maryland **85**, 16 +Siena **70**
- 8 Wisconsin **80**, 9 St. John's **70**⊗
- 5 Marquette **69**, 12 Tulsa **71**
- 4 Kentucky **83**, 13 Valparaiso **68**
- 6 Texas Tech **68**, 11 Southern Illinois **76** (F)
- 3 ⊗Georgia **85**, 14 Murray State **68**
- 7 NC State **69**, 10 Michigan State **58**
- 2 Connecticut **78**, 15 Hampton **67**

Second Round
- Maryland **87**, Wisconsin **57**
- Tulsa **82**, Kentucky **87**
- Southern Illinois **77**, ⊗Georgia **75**
- NC State **74**, Connecticut **77**

Regional Semifinals
- Maryland **78**, Kentucky **68**
- Southern Illinois **59**, Connecticut **71**

Regional Final
- Maryland **90**, Connecticut **82**

Midwest — Madison, WI

First Round
- 1 Kansas **70**, 16 Holy Cross **59**
- 8 Stanford **84**, 9 Western Kentucky **68**
- 5 Florida **82** (2OT), 12 Creighton **83** (G)
- 4 Illinois **93**, 13 San Diego State **64**
- 6 Texas **70**, 11 Boston College **57**
- 3 Mississippi State **70**, 14 McNeese State **58**
- 7 Wake Forest **83**, 10 Pepperdine **74**
- 2 Oregon **81**, 15 Montana **62**

Second Round
- Kansas **86**, Stanford **63**
- Creighton **60**, Illinois **72**
- Texas **68**, Mississippi State **64**
- Wake Forest **87**, Oregon **92**

Regional Semifinals
- Kansas **73**, Illinois **69**
- Texas **70**, Oregon **72**

Regional Final
- Kansas **104**, Oregon **86**

National Semifinals — Atlanta

- Indiana **73**, Oklahoma **64**
- Maryland **97**, Kansas **88**

National Final

Maryland 64
Indiana 52

Indiana holds the lead for just 11 seconds as Tournament MOP Juan Dixon scores 18 points to lead Maryland to its first title. While disgruntled Hoosiers fans tear down road signs, burn couches and throw beer bottles at police officers in Bloomington, 24 people are injured during celebrations in College Park.

Two unheralded players help IU upset Oklahoma. Defensive stopper Dane Fife smothers Sooners star Hollis Price, limiting him to six points on 1-for-11 shooting, and forward Jeff Newton comes off the bench to score 19 points in 23 minutes.

Before the season, Kansas coach Roy Williams had taped pictures of the Georgia Dome to each player's locker for motivation. But in Atlanta, forward Drew Gooden signals for a timeout that Kansas doesn't have, allowing Juan Dixon to seal the game when he converts the ensuing technical foul.

A Duke's first-team All-America point guard, Jason Williams, is fouled after hitting a three-pointer with 4.2 seconds left, but misses the ensuing freebie. With the upset, Indiana improves to 6–1 all-time against No. 1 seeds and Mike Davis is able to exhale—briefly—in his role as Bob Knight's successor.

B Antonio Gates—who will become an All-Pro tight end for the San Diego Chargers—scores 22 points to extend Kent State's national-best winning streak to 21 games.

C Behind the play of Clarence Gilbert and Kareem Rush, Missouri becomes the first No. 12 seed to advance to a regional final.

D Gonzaga's talented guards, Blake Stepp and Dan Dickau, combine to shoot a dismal 8-for-37 from the floor, enabling the Cowboys to pull off the upset.

E Xavier's Thad Matta becomes the second coach (after Skip Prosser) to take different schools to the Tournament in his first year at each school. In 2000-01, Matta led Butler to a Tourney berth.

F Texas Tech, 9–19 the previous season, improves to 23–9 and advances to the Tournament in its first season under former Indiana coach Bob Knight. It is Knight's 25th trip to the NCAAs.

G Terrell Taylor, the MVC's Sixth Man of the Year, hits a three-pointer with 0.2 seconds left in regulation to give Creighton the lead. The Bluejays bench storms the court, leaving Billy Donovan screaming futilely for a technical foul call.

H Siena becomes the first team with a losing record (16–18) to win a Tournament game since 1955.

+Opening round: Siena d. Alcorn State 81-77 (H)

⊗Team participation later vacated

Tournament Leaders

Individual Leaders

Scoring

	CL	POS	G	PTS	PPG
1 **Caron Butler**, Connecticut	SO	F	4	106	26.5
2 **Juan Dixon**, Maryland	SR	G	6	155	25.8
3 **Tayshaun Prince**, Kentucky	SR	G/F	3	71	23.7
4 **Aaron McGhee**, Oklahoma	JR	F	5	109	21.8
5 **Frank Williams**, Illinois	SR	G	3	60	20.0
6 **Luke Jackson**, Oregon	SO	G/F	4	79	19.8
7 **Jermaine Dearman**, Southern Illinois	JR	F	3	59	19.7
8 **Fred Jones**, Oregon	SR	G	4	76	19.0
9 **Antonio Gates**, Kent State	JR	F	4	75	18.8
Luke Ridnour, Oregon	SO	G	4	75	18.8

Minimum: 3 games

Field Goal Pct

	CL	POS	G	FG	FGA	PCT
1 **Emeka Okafor**, Connecticut	FR	C	4	15	21	71.4
Channing Frye, Arizona	FR	C	3	15	21	71.4
3 **Jeff Newton**, Indiana	JR	F	6	25	36	69.4
4 **Deginald Erskin**, Texas	JR	F	3	19	29	65.5
5 **Carlos Boozer**, Duke	JR	F	3	20	31	64.5

Minimum: 15 made and 3 games

Free Throw Pct

	CL	POS	G	FT	FTA	PCT
1 **Tahj Holden**, Maryland	JR	F	6	15	15	100.0
2 **Byron Mouton**, Maryland	SR	G	6	16	17	94.1
3 **Aaron Miles**, Kansas	FR	G	5	19	21	90.5
4 **Maurice Williams**, Alabama	FR	G	2	17	19	89.5
5 **AJ Moye**, Indiana	SO	G	6	16	18	88.9

Minimum: 15 made

Three-Point FG Pct

	CL	POS	G	3FG	3FGA	PCT
1 **Brian Boddicker**, Texas	SO	F	3	6	8	75.0
2 **Kirk Hinrich**, Kansas	JR	G	5	7	11	63.6
3 **Frank Williams**, Illinois	SR	G	3	12	20	60.0
4 **Dane Fife**, Indiana	SR	G	6	11	19	57.9
5 **Daniel Ewing**, Duke	FR	G	3	7	13	53.8

Minimum: 6 made and 3 games

Assists Per Game

	CL	POS	G	AST	APG
1 **Brandin Knight**, Pittsburgh	JR	G	3	22	7.3
2 **Steve Blake**, Maryland	JR	G	6	40	6.7
3 **T.J. Ford**, Texas	FR	G	3	18	6.0
4 **Aaron Miles**, Kansas	FR	G	5	29	5.8
5 **Luke Walton**, Arizona	JR	F	3	17	5.7
Frank Williams, Illinois	SR	G	3	17	5.7

Minimum: 3 games

Rebounds Per Game

	CL	POS	G	REB	RPG
1 **Drew Gooden**, Kansas	JR	F	5	61	12.2
2 **Nick Collison**, Kansas	JR	F	5	56	11.2
3 **Jermaine Dearman**, Southern Illinois	JR	F	3	28	9.3
James Thomas, Texas	SO	F/C	3	28	9.3
5 **Matt Barnes**, UCLA	SR	F	3	27	9.0
Dan Gadzuric, UCLA	SR	C	3	27	9.0

Minimum: 3 games

Blocked Shots Per Game

	CL	POS	G	BLK	BPG
1 **Channing Frye**, Arizona	FR	C	3	9	3.0
2 **Emeka Okafor**, Connecticut	FR	C	4	11	2.8
3 **Lonny Baxter**, Maryland	SR	F/C	6	13	2.2
4 **Dan Gadzuric**, UCLA	SR	C	3	6	2.0
Rolan Roberts, Southern Illinois	SR	C	3	6	2.0

Minimum: 3 games

Steals Per Game

	CL	POS	G	STL	SPG
1 **Andrew Mitchell**, Kent State	SR	G	4	15	3.8
2 **Chris Duhon**, Duke	SO	G	3	9	3.0
T.J. Ford, Texas	FR	G	3	9	3.0
4 **Luther Head**, Illinois	FR	G	3	8	2.7
Jason Williams, Duke	JR	G	3	8	2.7

Minimum: 3 games

Team Leaders

Scoring

		G	PTS	PPG
1	**UCLA**	3	258	86.0
2	**Kansas**	5	421	84.2
3	**Maryland**	6	501	83.5
4	**Missouri**	4	333	83.3
5	**Oregon**	4	331	82.8
6	**Duke**	3	241	80.3
7	**Kentucky**	3	238	79.3
8	**Illinois**	3	234	78.0
9	**Connecticut**	4	308	77.0
10	**Oklahoma**	5	382	76.4

Minimum: 3 games

FG Pct

		G	FG	FGA	PCT
1	**Indiana**	6	149	292	51.0
2	**Connecticut**	4	103	204	50.5
3	**Illinois**	3	83	166	50.0
4	**Kansas**	5	155	325	47.7
5	**Maryland**	6	170	357	47.6

Minimum: 3 games

3-Pt FG Pct

		G	3FG	3FGA	PCT
1	**Indiana**	6	47	93	50.5
2	**Illinois**	3	33	72	45.8
3	**Connecticut**	4	22	48	45.8
4	**Kentucky**	3	22	54	40.7
5	**Oregon**	4	35	87	40.2

Minimum: 3 games

FT Pct

		G	FT	FTA	PCT
1	**Maryland**	6	124	154	80.5
2	**UCLA**	3	41	51	80.4
3	**Oklahoma**	5	97	121	80.2
4	**Texas**	3	39	52	75.0
5	**Kent State**	4	62	83	74.7

Minimum: 3 games

Ast/TO Ratio

		G	AST	TO	RAT
1	**Oklahoma**	5	67	42	1.60
2	**Southern Illinois**	3	49	32	1.53
3	**Oregon**	4	70	48	1.46
4	**Kentucky**	3	49	34	1.44
5	**Illinois**	3	61	44	1.39

Minimum: 3 games

Rebounds

		G	REB	RPG
1	**Kansas**	5	232	46.4
2	**Missouri**	4	178	44.5
3	**UCLA**	3	122	40.7
4	**Oklahoma**	5	197	39.4
5	**Texas**	3	117	39.0
	Arizona	3	117	39.0

Minimum: 3 games

Blocks

		G	BLK	BPG
1	**Connecticut**	4	22	5.5
2	**Illinois**	3	15	5.0
	Duke	3	15	5.0
	Arizona	3	15	5.0
5	**Maryland**	6	28	4.7

Minimum: 3 games

Steals

		G	STL	SPG
1	**Duke**	3	32	10.7
2	**Illinois**	3	31	10.3
3	**Oregon**	4	36	9.0
4	**Texas**	3	26	8.7
	Kentucky	3	26	8.7

Minimum: 3 games

All-Tournament Team

PLAYER	CL	POS	HT	SCHOOL	RPG	APG	PPG
Juan Dixon*	SR	G	6-3	Maryland	3.8	3.2	25.8
Lonny Baxter	SR	F/C	6-8	Maryland	8.5	0.7	15.7
Dane Fife	SR	G	6-4	Indiana	2.0	2.7	7.3
Kyle Hornsby	JR	G	6-5	Indiana	2.8	2.7	9.3
Chris Wilcox	SO	F/C	6-10	Maryland	5.5	1.0	13.5

All-Regional Teams

East

PLAYER	CL	POS	HT	SCHOOL	RPG	APG	PPG
Lonny Baxter*	SR	F/C	6-8	Maryland	7.5	1.0	18.8
Caron Butler	SO	F	6-7	Connecticut	7.3	4.0	26.5
Juan Dixon	SR	G	6-3	Maryland	3.8	3.5	26.0
Rolan Roberts	SR	C	6-6	Southern Illinois	7.0	2.0	15.0
Tony Robertson	JR	G	6-3	Connecticut	2.3	0.8	13.3

Midwest

PLAYER	CL	POS	HT	SCHOOL	RPG	APG	PPG
Drew Gooden*	JR	F	6-10	Kansas	13.0	2.8	16.8
Nick Collison	JR	F	6-9	Kansas	11.5	1.3	14.5
Fred Jones	SR	G	6-4	Oregon	4.0	4.0	19.0
Keith Langford	FR	G	6-4	Kansas	4.0	1.5	11.5
Luke Ridnour	SO	G	6-2	Oregon	2.0	4.3	18.8
James Thomas	SO	F/C	6-8	Texas	9.3	0.0	10.3

South

PLAYER	CL	POS	HT	SCHOOL	RPG	APG	PPG
Tom Coverdale*	JR	G	6-2	Indiana	3.8	5.8	11.5
Dane Fife	SR	G	6-4	Indiana	1.5	2.5	7.5
Antonio Gates	JR	F	6-5	Kent State	7.3	2.0	18.8
Trevor Huffman	SR	G	6-2	Kent State	2.0	3.8	15.8
Jared Jeffries	SO	F	6-10	Indiana	8.5	1.0	17.0

West

PLAYER	CL	POS	HT	SCHOOL	RPG	APG	PPG
Hollis Price*	JR	G	6-1	Oklahoma	3.5	2.3	18.3
Ebi Ere	JR	G	6-5	Oklahoma	7.0	1.5	15.3
Rickey Paulding	SO	G	6-5	Missouri	5.3	2.3	18.3
Kareem Rush	JR	F	6-6	Missouri	6.5	3.5	17.3
Quannas White	JR	G	6-1	Oklahoma	3.3	6.3	6.5

* Most outstanding player

2002 NCAA TOURNAMENT BOX SCORES

74-73

	1H	2H
Indiana	29	45
Duke	42	31

INDIANA	MIN	FG	3FG	FT	REB	A	ST	BL	PF	TP
Jared Jeffries	38	9-21	1-3	5-7	15	1	2	1	2	24
Jarrad Odle	18	7-9	0-0	1-3	5	0	0	0	2	15
AJ Moye	17	3-5	0-1	8-10	3	0	2	0	0	14
Jeff Newton	25	3-3	0-0	2-5	10	1	0	2	2	8
Tom Coverdale	29	1-3	0-1	4-6	4	7	1	0	4	6
Dane Fife	38	1-3	1-3	0-0	3	1	2	0	4	3
Donald Perry	17	1-4	0-1	0-0	4	1	1	0	1	2
Kyle Hornsby	16	1-4	0-1	0-0	2	2	0	0	1	2
George Leach	2	0-0	0-0	0-0	0	0	0	0	1	0
TOTALS	**200**	**26-52**	**2-10**	**20-31**	**46**	**13**	**8**	**3**	**17**	**74**
Percentages		50.0	20.0	64.5						

Coach: Mike Davis

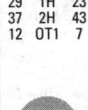

DUKE	MIN	FG	3FG	FT	REB	A	ST	BL	PF	TP
Carlos Boozer	35	7-10	0-0	5-9	9	3	2	1	3	19
Mike Dunleavy Jr.	35	5-16	3-8	4-5	6	0	3	1	4	17
Jason Williams	35	6-19	3-9	0-1	7	4	1	0	3	15
Chris Duhon	37	3-5	1-2	0-0	1	3	5	0	4	7
Dahntay Jones	27	3-8	0-1	0-2	1	1	1	1	5	6
Daniel Ewing	25	2-8	2-4	0-0	3	1	2	0	3	6
Casey Sanders	6	1-1	0-0	1-2	2	0	0	0	4	3
TOTALS	**200**	**27-67**	**9-24**	**10-19**	**29**	**12**	**14**	**3**	**26**	**73**
Percentages		40.3	37.5	52.6						

Coach: Mike Krzyzewski

Officials: B[illegible] Benedict, D[illegible] Hall, Tony Greene **Technicals:** None **Attendance:** 22,338

78-73

	1H	2H	OT1
Kent State	29	37	12
Pittsburgh	23	43	7

KENT STATE	MIN	FG	3FG	FT	REB	A	ST	BL	PF	TP
Antonio Gates	43	7-11	0-0	8-9	8	4	0	1	4	22
Trevor Huffman	42	7-13	3-6	0-2	1	3	1	0	4	17
Andrew Mitchell	44	3-16	0-6	6-6	3	3	5	0	1	12
Eric Thomas	31	4-7	2-3	2-2	4	0	0	0	1	12
John Edwards	15	2-2	0-0	2-2	1	0	0	0	3	6
Nate Gerwig	18	1-3	0-0	3-4	2	0	1	0	1	5
Demetric Shaw	25	2-6	0-2	0-0	2	0	4	0	2	4
Eric Haut	4	0-0	0-0	0-0	1	0	0	0	0	0
Bryan Bedford	3	0-0	0-0	0-0	2	0	0	0	0	0
TOTALS	**225**	**26-58**	**5-17**	**21-25**	**24**	**10**	**11**	**1**	**16**	**78**
Percentages		44.8	29.4	84.0						

Coach: Stan Heath

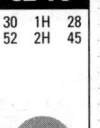

PITTSBURGH	MIN	FG	3FG	FT	REB	A	ST	BL	PF	TP
Julius Page	45	7-12	1-4	3-4	3	2	0	2	0	18
Brandin Knight	42	7-16	4-10	0-0	5	6	0	0	5	18
Jaron Brown	32	5-11	0-2	3-4	8	1	3	1	4	13
Chevon Troutman	17	3-6	0-0	3-7	8	1	1	0	2	9
Ontario Lett	30	4-9	0-0	0-0	4	2	1	0	3	8
Donatas Zavackas	40	2-7	1-6	0-0	5	1	1	0	2	5
Chad Johnson	16	1-2	0-0	0-0	2	2	0	0	4	2
Toree Morris	3	0-0	0-0	0-0	0	0	0	0	1	0
TOTALS	**225**	**29-63**	**6-22**	**9-15**	**35**	**15**	**6**	**3**	**21**	**73**
Percentages		46.0	27.3	60.0						

Coach: Ben Howland

Officials: Duk[illegible] Edsall, John Higgins, Stan Reynolds **Technicals:** None **Attendance:** 22,338

82-73

	1H	2H
Missouri	30	52
UCLA	28	45

MISSOURI	MIN	FG	3FG	FT	REB	A	ST	BL	PF	TP
Clarence Gilbert	36	7-12	4-8	5-7	0	0	3	0	2	23
Kareem Rush	33	8-14	4-8	0-2	9	4	1	0	2	20
Rickey Paulding	27	6-12	2-4	1-4	1	1	0	1	5	15
Arthur Johnson	36	5-12	0-0	4-5	14	3	1	1	3	14
Wesley Stokes	14	1-4	0-2	4-4	3	3	0	0	2	6
Travon Bryant	26	1-3	0-0	0-0	7	0	2	1	1	2
Justin Gage	17	1-2	0-1	0-0	3	3	1	0	3	2
Josh Kroenke	6	0-1	0-0	0-0	2	2	0	0	1	0
Najeeb Echols	1	0-0	0-0	0-0	0	0	0	0	0	0
Jeffrey Ferguson	1	0-0	0-0	0-0	0	0	0	0	0	0
Michael Griffin	1	0-0	0-0	0-0	0	0	0	0	0	0
Duane John	1	0-0	0-0	0-0	0	0	0	0	0	0
Ryan Kiernan	1	0-0	0-0	0-0	1	0	0	0	0	0
TOTALS	**200**	**29-60**	**10-23**	**14-22**	**40**	**16**	**8**	**3**	**19**	**82**
Percentages		48.3	43.5	63.6						

Coach: Quin Snyder

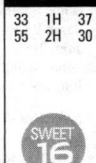

UCLA	MIN	FG	3FG	FT	REB	A	ST	BL	PF	TP
Matt Barnes	33	10-20	2-5	1-2	11	4	1	1	4	23
Billy Knight	31	6-14	0-4	4-4	5	1	3	0	4	16
Dan Gadzuric	34	4-9	0-0	3-4	8	1	0	4	2	11
Cedric Bozeman	28	4-11	0-1	0-1	3	2	0	0	1	8
Jason Kapono	31	3-8	0-1	1-3	3	4	2	0	0	7
Ryan Walcott	15	2-3	1-2	1-2	1	1	0	0	1	6
T.J. Cummings	7	1-4	0-2	0-0	4	0	1	0	3	2
Dijon Thompson	14	0-4	0-1	0-0	3	1	0	0	0	0
Andre Patterson	5	0-2	0-1	0-0	1	0	0	1	2	0
John Hoffart	1	0-0	0-0	0-0	0	0	0	0	0	0
Josiah Johnson	1	0-0	0-0	0-0	0	0	0	0	0	0
TOTALS	**200**	**30-75**	**3-17**	**10-16**	**39**	**14**	**7**	**6**	**17**	**73**
Percentages		40.0	17.6	62.5						

Coach: Steve Lavin

Officials: Karl Hess, Joe Lindsay, John Clougherty **Technicals:** None **Attendance:** 18,040

88-67

	1H	2H
Oklahoma	33	55
Arizona	37	30

OKLAHOMA	MIN	FG	3FG	FT	REB	A	ST	BL	PF	TP
Hollis Price	28	9-16	6-11	2-2	4	3	1	0	4	26
Aaron McGhee	30	6-12	1-1	8-8	8	1	1	0	3	21
Daryan Selvy	28	7-12	1-1	0-0	6	1	0	1	2	15
Ebi Ere	35	5-14	2-7	2-2	8	1	1	1	1	14
Jason Detrick	22	3-9	0-3	2-2	6	4	2	0	4	8
Jabahri Brown	18	1-2	0-0	0-0	1	0	1	0	4	2
Quannas White	25	0-4	0-2	1-2	2	6	1	0	3	1
Jozsef Szendrei	3	0-0	0-0	1-2	1	0	0	1	0	1
Blake Johnston	8	0-0	0-0	0-0	0	2	1	0	0	0
Richard Ainooson	1	0-0	0-0	0-0	0	0	0	0	0	0
Michael Cano	1	0-0	0-0	0-0	0	0	0	0	0	0
Michael Liggett	1	0-1	0-0	0-0	0	0	0	0	0	0
TOTALS	**200**	**31-70**	**10-25**	**16-18**	**36**	**18**	**8**	**3**	**21**	**88**
Percentages		44.3	40.0	88.9						

Coach: Kelvin Sampson

ARIZONA	MIN	FG	3FG	FT	REB	A	ST	BL	PF	TP
Jason Gardner	38	4-15	1-6	5-5	3	2	1	0	3	14
Will Bynum	20	3-8	1-5	3-3	3	0	0	0	3	10
Luke Walton	39	3-9	0-2	3-4	8	8	0	0	1	9
Channing Frye	22	4-4	0-0	1-3	5	0	0	2	4	9
Salim Stoudamire	31	2-8	2-6	2-2	3	0	1	0	2	8
Isaiah Fox	18	4-6	0-0	0-1	2	0	0	1	0	8
Rick Anderson	25	2-4	1-2	2-4	4	1	0	1	5	7
Andrew Zahn	1	1-3	0-1	0-0	1	0	0	0	0	2
Dennis Latimore	3	0-0	0-0	0-0	1	0	0	0	0	0
Anas Fellah	1	0-0	0-0	0-0	0	0	0	0	0	0
Jason Ranne	1	0-0	0-0	0-0	0	0	0	0	0	0
Mike Schwertley	1	0-0	0-0	0-0	0	0	0	0	0	0
TOTALS	**200**	**23-57**	**5-22**	**16-22**	**30**	**11**	**2**	**4**	**18**	**67**
Percentages		40.4	22.7	72.7						

Coach: Lute Olson

Officials: Larry Rose, Pat Driscoll, Tim Higgins **Technicals:** Arizona (Frye), Oklahoma (Brown) **Attendance:** 18,040

78-68

	1H	2H
Maryland	39	39
Kentucky	33	35

MARYLAND	MIN	FG	3FG	FT	REB	A	ST	BL	PF	TP
Juan Dixon	37	6-15	3-8	4-4	7	4	1	0	2	19
Lonny Baxter	30	6-9	0-0	4-4	5	0	0	0	3	16
Chris Wilcox	30	4-10	0-1	7-8	2	1	1	0	1	15
Byron Mouton	31	5-9	0-0	4-5	6	2	1	0	1	14
Drew Nicholas	20	3-6	2-4	0-0	3	5	1	0	2	8
Steve Blake	31	2-9	0-3	0-1	3	5	2	0	3	4
Tahj Holden	13	0-0	0-0	2-2	2	0	1	1	3	2
Ryan Randle	8	0-1	0-0	0-0	1	0	0	0	1	0
TOTALS	**200**	**26-59**	**5-16**	**21-24**	**29**	**17**	**7**	**1**	**16**	**78**
Percentages		44.1	31.2	87.5						

Coach: Gary Williams

KENTUCKY	MIN	FG	3FG	FT	REB	A	ST	BL	PF	TP
Tayshaun Prince	38	6-15	3-7	2-2	7	2	1	0	2	17
Keith Bogans	28	6-14	2-6	1-3	2	2	2	0	3	15
Marquis Estill	19	4-4	0-0	4-4	2	0	0	1	5	12
Jules Camara	27	4-11	0-1	2-4	8	1	2	2	3	10
Chuck Hayes	23	3-6	0-1	1-2	7	1	1	0	1	7
Cliff Hawkins	35	2-8	2-3	0-0	5	7	2	0	3	6
Erik Daniels	7	0-1	0-0	1-2	1	0	0	0	2	1
Gerald Fitch	13	0-2	0-1	0-0	0	0	0	1	0	0
J.P. Blevins	5	0-0	0-0	0-0	0	0	0	0	0	0
Rashaad Carruth	5	0-1	0-0	0-0	0	0	0	0	1	0
TOTALS	**200**	**25-62**	**7-19**	**11-17**	**32**	**13**	**8**	**4**	**20**	**68**
Percentages		40.3	36.8	64.7						

Coach: Tubby Smith

Officials: Steve Welmer, Paul Janssen, Ed Hightower **Technicals:** None **Attendance:** 29,633

71-59

	1H	2H
Connecticut	40	31
Southern Illinois	28	31

CONNECTICUT	MIN	FG	3FG	FT	REB	A	ST	BL	PF	TP
Caron Butler	38	6-16	1-2	6-9	4	2	1	1	2	19
Ben Gordon	23	4-7	2-3	2-4	5	5	1	0	0	12
Tony Robertson	28	4-9	1-2	1-2	3	1	0	0	2	10
Taliek Brown	33	2-5	1-2	4-6	7	4	2	0	4	9
Emeka Okafor	22	4-5	0-0	1-2	6	1	1	1	4	9
Johnnie Selvie	30	3-7	0-0	2-3	2	1	1	0	4	8
Mike Hayes	17	1-1	0-0	2-4	2	0	0	0	2	4
Justin Brown	7	0-2	0-0	0-0	1	0	0	0	1	0
Shamon Tooles	2	0-0	0-0	0-0	0	0	0	0	3	0
TOTALS	**200**	**24-52**	**5-9**	**18-30**	**30**	**14**	**6**	**2**	**22**	**71**
Percentages		46.2	55.6	60.0						

Coach: Jim Calhoun

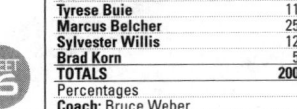

SOUTHERN ILLINOIS	MIN	FG	3FG	FT	REB	A	ST	BL	PF	TP
Rolan Roberts	34	11-16	0-0	2-4	8	2	1	1	3	24
Jermaine Dearman	27	6-12	0-0	5-11	9	1	0	0	4	17
Kent Williams	30	2-11	0-5	3-4	2	2	1	0	4	7
Darren Brooks	25	3-8	1-4	0-0	3	0	0	0	1	7
Stetson Hairston	31	0-5	0-2	2-2	3	1	1	0	3	2
Tyrese Buie	11	1-5	0-1	0-0	4	2	0	0	1	2
Marcus Belcher	25	0-3	0-2	0-0	2	3	1	0	5	0
Sylvester Willis	12	0-0	0-0	0-0	1	0	0	0	0	0
Brad Korn	5	0-0	0-0	0-0	1	0	1	0	2	0
TOTALS	**200**	**23-60**	**1-14**	**12-21**	**33**	**11**	**5**	**1**	**23**	**59**
Percentages		38.3	7.1	57.1						

Coach: Bruce Weber

Officials: Dave Libbey, Tom O'Neill, Art McDonald **Technicals:** Southern Illinois (bench) **Attendance:** 29,633

Kansas 73, Illinois 69 (Sweet 16)

	1H	2H
Kansas	40	33
Illinois	34	35

KANSAS	MIN	FG	3FG	FT	REB	A	ST	BL	PF	TP
Drew Gooden	34	5-14	0-1	5-6	13	4	0	2	0	15
Keith Langford	26	5-7	0-2	5-6	3	3	1	1	1	15
Aaron Miles	35	5-11	1-3	2-2	7	5	1	0	2	13
Nick Collison	20	5-12	0-0	1-2	9	2	1	0	5	11
Wayne Simien	24	3-5	0-0	1-1	6	0	0	0	3	7
Jeff Boschee	37	2-5	2-5	0-1	0	1	1	0	3	6
Kirk Hinrich	17	1-3	1-2	0-0	2	1	0	0	4	3
Jeff Carey	6	1-1	0-0	1-1	1	0	0	0	2	3
Brett Ballard	1	0-0	0-0	0-0	0	0	0	0	0	0
TOTALS	**200**	**27-58**	**4-13**	**15-19**	**41**	**16**	**4**	**3**	**20**	**73**
Percentages		46.6	30.8	78.9						

Coach: Roy Williams

ILLINOIS	MIN	FG	3FG	FT	REB	A	ST	BL	PF	TP
Frank Williams	37	6-18	3-7	0-0	5	4	1	0	2	15
Robert Archibald	20	4-4	0-0	7-10	10	1	0	1	5	15
Brian Cook	38	6-17	1-4	0-0	9	2	1	2	3	13
Cory Bradford	35	3-10	3-7	0-0	2	1	1	0	2	9
Sean Harrington	24	3-5	2-4	0-0	1	2	2	0	1	8
Damir Krupalija	18	1-5	1-1	1-2	4	1	2	0	3	4
Luther Head	17	1-2	0-1	1-2	1	6	2	0	2	3
Lucas Johnson	10	0-2	0-2	2-4	1	2	1	0	2	2
Nick Smith	1	0-0	0-0	0-0	0	0	0	0	0	0
TOTALS	**200**	**24-63**	**10-26**	**11-18**	**33**	**19**	**10**	**3**	**20**	**69**
Percentages		38.1	38.5	61.1						

Coach: Bill Self

Officials: Ed Corbett, Michael Kitts, Mike Wood
Technicals: None
Attendance: 16,310

Oregon 72, Texas 70 (Sweet 16)

	1H	2H
Oregon	41	31
Texas	28	42

OREGON	MIN	FG	3FG	FT	REB	A	ST	BL	PF	TP
Luke Jackson	35	10-17	2-6	3-4	6	8	0	0	0	25
Luke Ridnour	39	8-15	4-9	0-0	1	5	3	0	3	20
Robert Johnson	34	5-6	0-0	0-0	7	0	0	0	2	10
Chris Christoffersen	30	3-6	0-0	1-4	7	0	1	4	4	7
Fred Jones	24	2-6	0-2	0-0	4	5	2	0	3	4
Mark Michaelis	8	2-2	0-0	0-0	0	0	0	0	1	4
James Davis	9	1-3	0-1	0-1	0	1	1	0	0	2
Anthony Lever	13	0-2	0-0	0-0	3	1	2	1	1	0
Brian Helquist	8	0-0	0-0	0-1	2	1	0	0	2	0
TOTALS	**200**	**31-57**	**6-18**	**4-10**	**30**	**21**	**9**	**5**	**16**	**72**
Percentages		54.4	33.3	40.0						

Coach: Ernie Kent

TEXAS	MIN	FG	3FG	FT	REB	A	ST	BL	PF	TP
James Thomas	27	7-13	0-0	1-4	11	0	0	0	1	15
Brian Boddicker	24	4-6	3-4	2-2	8	0	0	0	2	13
T.J. Ford	32	3-10	0-1	2-2	1	5	7	1	2	8
Brandon Mouton	26	4-13	0-4	0-0	5	3	1	0	1	8
Royal Ivey	19	3-10	0-1	2-2	3	0	2	0	4	8
Deginald Erskin	21	3-8	0-0	0-0	5	0	0	0	0	6
Jason Klotz	15	3-4	0-0	0-0	3	1	1	0	3	6
Sydmill Harris	18	1-4	0-2	2-3	1	1	0	0	0	4
Fredie Williams	16	1-4	0-0	0-1	2	1	0	0	2	2
Terrell Ross	2	0-0	0-0	0-0	1	0	0	0	0	0
TOTALS	**200**	**29-72**	**3-12**	**9-14**	**40**	**11**	**11**	**1**	**15**	**70**
Percentages		40.3	25.0	64.3						

Coach: Rick Barnes

Officials: Mike Sanzere, Ted Valentine, Bob Donato
Technicals: None
Attendance: 16,310

Indiana 81, Kent State 69 (Elite 8)

	1H	2H
Indiana	40	41
Kent State	28	41

INDIANA	MIN	FG	3FG	FT	REB	A	ST	BL	PF	TP
Dane Fife	35	6-8	5-6	0-0	1	1	0	0	4	17
Kyle Hornsby	34	6-8	4-5	0-0	2	7	1	0	1	16
Tom Coverdale	27	4-7	3-4	3-4	0	7	0	0	2	14
Jared Jeffries	39	4-7	1-1	1-3	7	1	0	1	1	10
AJ Moye	8	2-3	1-2	4-4	1	0	0	0	1	9
Donald Perry	17	1-1	0-0	4-10	2	2	2	0	2	6
Jarrad Odle	23	2-5	1-1	0-0	3	0	0	0	3	5
Jeff Newton	15	2-2	0-0	0-0	4	0	1	0	2	4
George Leach	2	0-1	0-0	0-0	1	0	0	0	0	0
TOTALS	**200**	**27-42**	**15-19**	**12-21**	**21**	**18**	**4**	**1**	**16**	**81**
Percentages		64.3	78.9	57.1						

Coach: Mike Davis

KENT STATE	MIN	FG	3FG	FT	REB	A	ST	BL	PF	TP
Antonio Gates	40	10-18	0-1	2-4	8	2	2	0	1	22
Andrew Mitchell	37	7-17	1-4	4-4	4	2	4	1	4	19
Trevor Huffman	40	2-7	1-3	3-4	3	4	0	0	5	8
Demetric Shaw	29	2-7	0-1	4-4	8	0	0	0	4	8
John Edwards	17	2-2	0-0	2-4	1	0	0	1	2	6
Eric Thomas	22	2-9	0-4	0-0	3	1	1	0	2	4
Bryan Bedford	6	1-2	0-0	0-0	0	0	0	0	2	2
Nate Gerwig	7	0-0	0-0	0-0	0	0	0	0	1	0
Eric Haut	2	0-2	0-1	0-0	0	0	0	0	0	0
TOTALS	**200**	**26-64**	**2-14**	**15-20**	**27**	**9**	**7**	**2**	**21**	**69**
Percentages		40.6	14.3	75.0						

Coach: Stan Heath

Officials: Mark Whitehead, Scott Thornley, Tom Nunez
Technicals: None
Attendance: 22,435

Oklahoma 81, Missouri 75 (Elite 8)

	1H	2H
Oklahoma	41	40
Missouri	33	42

OKLAHOMA	MIN	FG	3FG	FT	REB	A	ST	BL	PF	TP
Hollis Price	35	6-13	4-7	2-3	4	3	0	0	4	18
Ebi Ere	28	6-11	1-1	4-4	6	3	1	0	4	17
Aaron McGhee	20	5-10	1-2	4-6	3	0	1	1	4	15
Quannas White	35	3-6	0-0	6-6	7	7	2	0	3	12
Jabahri Brown	20	3-5	0-0	1-2	2	1	1	0	4	7
Daryan Selvy	32	0-5	0-1	4-4	7	1	0	0	3	4
Jason Detrick	10	1-2	0-0	1-2	2	1	2	0	3	3
Blake Johnston	9	1-4	1-3	0-1	2	1	0	0	0	3
Jozsef Szendrei	11	0-0	0-0	2-4	2	0	0	0	1	2
TOTALS	**200**	**25-56**	**7-14**	**24-32**	**35**	**17**	**7**	**1**	**26**	**81**
Percentages		44.6	50.0	75.0						

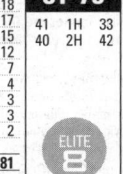

Coach: Kelvin Sampson

MISSOURI	MIN	FG	3FG	FT	REB	A	ST	BL	PF	TP
Rickey Paulding	36	7-12	3-5	5-6	5	4	1	1	3	22
Kareem Rush	27	5-10	2-6	5-6	3	2	1	1	5	17
Arthur Johnson	26	4-6	0-0	1-8	4	1	0	1	5	9
Travon Bryant	21	4-7	0-1	1-3	9	1	1	0	4	9
Clarence Gilbert	37	1-16	1-9	4-6	4	3	1	0	1	7
Justin Gage	23	2-3	0-0	2-2	5	1	1	0	3	6
Wesley Stokes	17	1-2	1-1	2-2	4	4	0	0	1	5
Najeeb Echols	10	0-1	0-0	0-1	2	0	0	0	3	0
Josh Kroenke	2	0-0	0-0	0-0	1	0	0	0	2	0
Jake Jackson	1	0-0	0-0	0-0	0	0	0	0	0	0
TOTALS	**200**	**24-57**	**7-22**	**20-34**	**37**	**16**	**5**	**3**	**27**	**75**
Percentages		42.1	31.8	58.8						

Coach: Quin Snyder

Officials: John Cahill, Terry Moore, John Hughes
Technicals: Oklahoma (bench)
Attendance: 18,040

Maryland 90, Connecticut 82 (Elite 8)

	1H	2H
Maryland	44	46
Connecticut	37	45

MARYLAND	MIN	FG	3FG	FT	REB	A	ST	BL	PF	TP
Lonny Baxter	36	7-12	0-0	15-18	9	1	1	1	2	29
Juan Dixon	39	10-18	3-5	4-4	1	3	1	0	3	27
Chris Wilcox	25	5-10	0-0	3-4	4	0	1	1	4	13
Tahj Holden	14	2-3	1-1	3-3	2	0	0	0	4	8
Steve Blake	27	1-3	1-1	2-2	4	6	1	0	3	5
Byron Mouton	34	1-4	0-1	2-2	3	1	2	0	3	4
Drew Nicholas	21	0-1	0-1	2-2	2	3	1	0	1	2
Ryan Randle	3	1-2	0-0	0-0	1	0	0	0	3	2
Calvin McCall	1	0-0	0-0	0-0	0	0	0	0	0	0
TOTALS	**200**	**27-53**	**5-9**	**31-35**	**26**	**14**	**7**	**2**	**23**	**90**
Percentages		50.9	55.6	88.6						

Coach: Gary Williams

CONNECTICUT	MIN	FG	3FG	FT	REB	A	ST	BL	PF	TP
Caron Butler	33	9-13	3-5	11-14	7	4	1	0	3	32
Tony Robertson	28	5-10	1-4	4-4	1	1	2	1	3	15
Taliek Brown	34	5-10	2-4	0-0	2	3	0	0	4	12
Ben Gordon	25	1-7	1-4	5-6	1	3	0	0	0	8
Johnnie Selvie	37	2-7	0-0	3-4	6	1	0	1	3	7
Emeka Okafor	23	2-5	0-0	2-4	6	0	0	1	4	6
Justin Brown	10	1-3	0-0	0-0	2	0	0	1	2	2
Mike Hayes	8	0-0	0-0	0-2	1	0	0	1	4	0
Scott Hazelton	1	0-0	0-0	0-0	0	0	0	0	0	0
Shamon Tooles	1	0-0	0-0	0-0	0	0	0	0	0	0
TOTALS	**200**	**25-55**	**7-17**	**25-34**	**26**	**12**	**3**	**5**	**23**	**82**
Percentages		45.5	41.2	73.5						

Coach: Jim Calhoun

Officials: Tom Rucker, Zelton Steed, Dick Cartmell
Technicals: None
Attendance: 29,252

Kansas 104, Oregon 86 (Elite 8)

	1H	2H
Kansas	48	56
Oregon	42	44

KANSAS	MIN	FG	3FG	FT	REB	A	ST	BL	PF	TP
Nick Collison	30	12-20	0-0	1-5	15	2	0	3	2	25
Keith Langford	22	6-7	0-0	8-9	8	1	3	1	2	20
Drew Gooden	31	7-13	0-0	4-6	20	2	1	0	2	18
Kirk Hinrich	31	5-10	1-2	3-3	9	2	5	1	3	14
Jeff Boschee	33	4-11	2-7	0-0	2	0	0	0	0	10
Wayne Simien	10	2-5	0-0	3-4	3	0	0	0	2	7
Aaron Miles	30	2-10	0-2	2-2	2	8	0	0	2	6
Bryant Nash	1	1-3	0-0	0-0	1	0	0	0	0	2
Chris Zerbe	1	1-1	0-0	0-0	2	0	0	0	0	2
Jeff Carey	5	0-0	0-0	0-0	1	0	0	0	0	0
Brett Ballard	3	0-1	0-1	0-0	0	0	0	0	0	0
Larry Harrison	1	0-0	0-0	0-0	0	0	0	0	0	0
Todd Kappelmann	1	0-0	0-0	0-0	0	0	0	0	0	0
Michael Lee	1	0-0	0-0	0-0	0	0	0	0	0	0
TOTALS	**200**	**40-81**	**3-12**	**21-29**	**61**	**17**	**9**	**5**	**13**	**104**
Percentages		49.4	25.0	72.4						

Coach: Roy Williams

OREGON	MIN	FG	3FG	FT	REB	A	ST	BL	PF	TP
Fred Jones	37	13-23	3-8	3-3	2	4	4	1	2	32
Anthony Lever	24	5-10	3-6	0-0	4	1	1	0	3	13
Robert Johnson	32	4-16	0-0	2-2	10	5	1	0	2	10
Luke Ridnour	33	3-13	3-9	0-0	3	7	3	0	2	9
Luke Jackson	32	3-7	0-0	1-2	7	2	0	0	4	7
Chris Christoffersen	17	3-6	0-0	1-3	3	1	1	1	3	7
Mark Michaelis	10	2-3	1-1	0-0	0	0	0	0	0	5
James Davis	7	1-5	1-4	0-0	1	1	1	0	0	3
Brian Helquist	4	0-1	0-0	0-0	0	0	0	0	1	0
Ben Lindquist	3	0-0	0-0	0-0	1	0	0	0	1	0
Jay Anderson	1	0-0	0-0	0-0	0	0	0	0	0	0
TOTALS	**200**	**34-84**	**11-28**	**7-10**	**31**	**21**	**11**	**2**	**18**	**86**
Percentages		40.5	39.3	70.0						

Coach: Ernie Kent

Officials: James Burr, Leslie Jones, Tom Lopes
Technicals: None
Attendance: 16,310

73-64

	1H	2H
Indiana	30	43
Oklahoma	34	30

FINAL 4

INDIANA	MIN	FG	3FG	FT	REB	A	ST	BL	PF	TP
Jeff Newton	23	7-10	0-0	5-8	6	2	0	4	2	19
Jarrad Odle	24	5-10	1-1	0-0	1	1	1	0	2	11
Donald Perry	11	2-3	1-1	5-6	4	1	0	0	0	10
AJ Moye	20	4-6	1-1	0-0	3	1	0	1	2	9
Jared Jeffries	27	2-5	1-1	3-4	8	4	1	1	3	8
Kyle Hornsby	26	2-4	2-4	1-2	2	1	3	0	2	7
Dane Fife	34	1-4	1-2	0-0	1	5	0	0	2	3
Tom Coverdale	29	1-5	1-3	0-1	4	4	1	0	3	3
George Leach	6	1-1	0-0	1-3	2	0	0	2	1	3
TOTALS	**200**	**25-48**	**8-13**	**15-24**	**31**	**19**	**6**	**8**	**17**	**73**
Percentages		52.1	61.5	62.5						

Coach: Mike Davis

OKLAHOMA	MIN	FG	3FG	FT	REB	A	ST	BL	PF	TP
Aaron McGhee	30	8-15	0-1	6-7	8	0	2	0	5	22
Ebi Ere	34	7-12	1-5	0-0	5	1	0	0	2	15
Jabahri Brown	19	4-5	0-0	1-2	6	0	0	0	3	9
Hollis Price	35	1-11	1-7	3-4	3	3	2	0	3	6
Jason Detrick	22	1-6	0-2	4-4	3	0	2	0	2	6
Daryan Selvy	24	2-10	0-2	0-1	8	1	2	1	4	4
Blake Johnston	4	1-1	0-0	0-0	0	0	0	0	0	2
Quannas White	24	0-5	0-1	0-0	1	1	0	0	3	0
Jozsef Szendrei	8	0-1	0-0	0-0	2	0	0	0	0	0
TOTALS	**200**	**24-66**	**2-18**	**14-18**	**36**	**6**	**8**	**1**	**22**	**64**
Percentages		36.4	11.1	77.8						

Coach: Kelvin Sampson

Officials: D
Libbey, Duk
Edsall, Mich
Kitts
Technicals:
None
Attendance:
53,378

97-88

	1H	2H
Maryland	44	53
Kansas	37	51

FINAL 4

MARYLAND	MIN	FG	3FG	FT	REB	A	ST	BL	PF	TP
Juan Dixon	37	10-18	5-11	8-11	3	2	2	0	2	33
Chris Wilcox	26	8-15	0-0	2-3	9	1	1	4	4	18
Tahj Holden	24	4-5	0-1	5-5	5	0	1	1	4	13
Byron Mouton	29	4-9	0-0	4-4	6	2	1	0	2	12
Steve Blake	32	1-7	1-4	5-9	3	11	1	0	4	8
Drew Nicholas	23	2-9	1-5	2-2	2	2	0	0	2	7
Lonny Baxter	14	2-4	0-0	0-0	7	0	1	2	5	4
Ryan Randle	15	1-3	0-0	0-1	2	0	0	2	1	2
TOTALS	**200**	**32-70**	**7-21**	**26-35**	**37**	**18**	**7**	**9**	**24**	**97**
Percentages		45.7	33.3	74.3						

Coach: Gary Williams

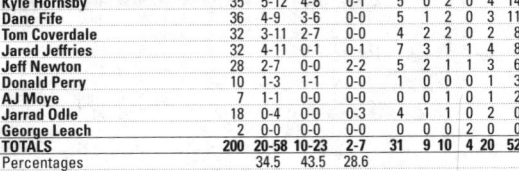

KANSAS	MIN	FG	3FG	FT	REB	A	ST	BL	PF	TP
Nick Collison	33	9-14	0-0	3-4	10	1	1	1	3	21
Jeff Boschee	38	6-16	5-13	0-0	3	2	1	0	3	17
Drew Gooden	28	5-12	2-2	3-5	9	3	1	1	4	15
Aaron Miles	28	1-7	0-4	10-12	3	10	2	0	4	12
Kirk Hinrich	29	4-8	2-3	1-2	4	4	1	0	5	11
Keith Langford	24	2-6	0-1	4-8	5	2	0	0	4	8
Wayne Simien	14	2-3	0-0	0-0	5	0	0	1	2	4
Jeff Carey	4	0-1	0-0	0-0	0	0	0	0	1	0
Brett Ballard	2	0-0	0-0	0-0	0	0	0	0	1	0
TOTALS	**200**	**29-67**	**9-23**	**21-31**	**39**	**22**	**6**	**3**	**27**	**88**
Percentages		43.3	39.1	67.7						

Coach: Roy Williams

Officials: Ed
Corbett, Ed
Hightower, Tim
Higgins
Technicals:
None
Attendance:
53,378

64-52

	1H	2H
Maryland	31	33
Indiana	25	27

NCAA FINAL 2002

MARYLAND	MIN	FG	3FG	FT	REB	A	ST	BL	PF	TP
Juan Dixon	38	6-9	2-4	4-4	5	3	5	0	1	18
Lonny Baxter	32	6-15	0-0	3-8	14	0	1	3	1	15
Chris Wilcox	24	4-8	0-0	2-4	7	0	1	1	3	10
Drew Nicholas	22	1-2	0-1	5-6	3	0	1	0	0	7
Steve Blake	33	2-6	0-3	2-2	6	3	2	0	2	6
Byron Mouton	27	1-5	0-0	2-2	4	1	2	1	2	4
Tahj Holden	20	0-2	0-1	2-2	3	4	0	1	3	2
Ryan Randle	4	1-1	0-0	0-0	0	0	0	0	1	2
TOTALS	**200**	**21-48**	**2-9**	**20-28**	**42**	**11**	**12**	**6**	**13**	**64**
Percentages		43.8	22.2	71.4						

Coach: Gary Williams

INDIANA	MIN	FG	3FG	FT	REB	A	ST	BL	PF	TP
Kyle Hornsby	35	5-12	4-8	0-1	5	0	2	0	4	14
Dane Fife	36	4-9	3-6	0-0	5	1	2	0	3	11
Tom Coverdale	32	3-11	2-7	0-0	4	2	2	0	2	8
Jared Jeffries	32	4-11	0-1	0-1	7	3	1	1	4	8
Jeff Newton	28	2-7	0-0	2-2	5	2	1	1	3	6
Donald Perry	10	1-3	1-1	0-0	1	0	0	0	1	3
AJ Moye	7	1-1	0-0	0-0	0	0	1	0	1	2
Jarrad Odle	18	0-4	0-0	0-3	4	1	1	0	2	0
George Leach	2	0-0	0-0	0-0	0	0	0	2	0	0
TOTALS	**200**	**20-58**	**10-23**	**2-7**	**31**	**9**	**10**	**4**	**20**	**52**
Percentages		34.5	43.5	28.6						

Coach: Mike Davis

Officials: Dick
Cartmell, James
Burr, Tony
Greene
Technicals:
None
Attendance:
53,406

National Invitation Tournament (NIT)

Opening Round: Richmond d. Wagner 74-67, Montana State d. Utah State 77-69, Ball State d. South Florida 98-92, Saint Joseph's d. George Mason 73-64, Louisiana Tech d. UL-Lafayette 83-63, Vanderbilt d. Houston 59-50, Dayton d. Detroit 80-69, Tennessee Tech d. Georgia State 64-62

First Round: Syracuse d. St. Bonaventure 76-66, Butler d. Bowling Green 81-69, Minnesota d. New Mexico 96-62, Richmond d. Montana State 63-48, Ball State d. Saint Joseph's 76-54, LSU d. Iowa 63-61, UNLV d. Arizona State 96-91, South Carolina d. Virginia 74-67, Temple d. Fresno State 81-75, Louisville d. Princeton 66-65, Villanova d. Manhattan 84-69, Louisiana Tech d. Vanderbilt 83-68, Tennessee Tech d. Dayton 68-59, Yale d. Rutgers 67-65, BYU d. UC Irvine 78-55, Memphis d. UNC Greensboro 82-62

Second Round: Syracuse d. Butler 66-65, Richmond d. Minnesota 67-66, Ball State d. LSU 75-65, South Carolina d. UNLV 75-65, Temple d. Louisville 65-62, Villanova d. Louisiana Tech 67-64, Tennessee Tech d. Yale 80-61, Memphis d. BYU 80-69

Third Round: Syracuse d. Richmond 62-46, South Carolina d. Ball State 82-47, Temple d. Villanova 63-57, Memphis d. Tennessee Tech 79-73

Semifinals: South Carolina d. Syracuse 66-59, Memphis d. Temple 78-77

Championship: Memphis d. South Carolina 72-62

Third place: Temple d. Syracuse 65-64

MVP: Dajuan Wagner, Memphis

2002-03: SWEET ORANGE

The coach and team that "had never" finally did: Syracuse (30–5) gave Jim Boeheim his first national title in three Final appearances and 27 seasons as head coach. The Orangemen downed Texas and Naismith POY T.J. Ford, 95-84, in one semi and Kansas blew by Dwyane Wade's Marquette, 94-61, in the other. Carmelo Anthony, the Tournament MOP, had 20 points and 10 rebounds against the Jayhawks in the Final, which the Orangemen iced, 81-78, when Hakim Warrick blocked Michael Lee's potential game-tying three with 1.5 seconds left. Even after his phenomenal freshman campaign, Anthony had to take a backseat in the NBA draft while schoolboy LeBron James (Cleveland Cavaliers) and Serbia's Darko Milicic (Detroit Pistons) were chosen before him. Anthony then became the third pick (Denver Nuggets), followed by Georgia Tech's Chris Bosh (Toronto Raptors) and Wade (Miami Heat).

MAJOR CONFERENCE STANDINGS

AMERICA EAST

	Conference			Overall		
	W	L	Pct	W	L	Pct
Boston U.□	13	3	.813	20	11	.645
Vermont⊕	11	5	.688	21	12	.636
Hartford	10	6	.625	16	13	.552
Binghamton	9	7	.563	14	13	.519
Northeastern	8	8	.500	16	15	.516
Maine	8	8	.500	14	16	.467
Stony Brook	7	9	.438	13	15	.464
Albany (NY)	3	13	.188	7	21	.250
New Hampshire	3	13	.188	5	23	.179

Tournament: **Vermont d. Boston U. 56-55**
Tournament MVP: **Matt Sheftic**, Vermont

ACC

	Conference			Overall		
	W	L	Pct	W	L	Pct
Wake Forest○	13	3	.813	25	6	.806
Duke⊕	11	5	.688	26	7	.788
Maryland○	11	5	.688	21	10	.677
NC State○	9	7	.563	18	13	.581
Georgia Tech□	7	9	.438	16	15	.516
North Carolina□	6	10	.375	19	16	.543
Virginia□	6	10	.375	16	16	.500
Clemson	5	11	.313	15	13	.536
Florida State	4	12	.250	14	15	.483

Tournament: **Duke d. NC State 84-77**
Tournament MVP: **Daniel Ewing**, Duke

ATLANTIC SUN

	Conference			Overall		
	W	L	Pct	W	L	Pct
North Division						
Belmont	12	4	.750	17	12	.586
Jacksonville State	10	6	.625	20	10	.667
Samford	9	7	.563	13	15	.464
Georgia State	8	8	.500	14	15	.483
Gardner-Webb	2	14	.125	5	24	.172
Campbell	1	15	.063	5	22	.185
South Division						
Troy⊕	14	2	.875	26	6	.813
Mercer	14	2	.875	23	6	.793
Central Florida	11	5	.688	21	11	.656
Jacksonville	8	8	.500	13	16	.448
Stetson	4	12	.250	6	20	.231
Florida Atlantic	3	13	.188	7	21	.250

Tournament: **Troy d. Central Florida 80-69**
Tournament MVP: **Ben Fletcher**, Troy

ATLANTIC 10

	Conference			Overall		
	W	L	Pct	W	L	Pct
East Division						
Saint Joseph's○	12	4	.750	23	7	.767
Rhode Island□	10	6	.625	19	12	.613
Temple□	10	6	.625	18	16	.529
Massachusetts	6	10	.375	11	18	.379
St. Bonaventure✪	7	9	.438	13	14	.481
Fordham	1	15	.063	2	26	.143
West Division						
Xavier○	15	1	.938	26	6	.813
Dayton⊕	14	2	.875	24	6	.800
Richmond□	10	6	.625	15	14	.517
La Salle	6	10	.375	12	17	.414
George Washington	5	11	.313	12	17	.414
Duquesne	4	12	.250	9	21	.300

Tournament: **Dayton d. Temple 79-72**
Tournament MOP: **Ramod Marshall**, Dayton

BIG EAST

	Conference			Overall		
	W	L	Pct	W	L	Pct
East Division						
Boston College□	10	6	.625	19	12	.613
Connecticut○	10	6	.625	23	10	.697
Providence□	8	8	.500	18	14	.563
Villanova□	8	8	.500	15	16	.484
St. John's□✪	7	9	.438	21	13	.618
Miami (FL)	4	12	.250	11	17	.393
Virginia Tech✪	4	12	.250	11	18	.379
West Division						
Syracuse○	13	3	.813	30	5	.857
Pittsburgh⊕	13	3	.813	28	5	.848
Notre Dame○	10	6	.625	24	10	.706
Seton Hall□	10	6	.625	17	13	.567
Georgetown□	6	10	.375	19	15	.559
West Virginia	5	11	.313	14	15	.483
Rutgers	4	12	.250	12	16	.429

Tournament: **Pittsburgh d. Connecticut 74-56**
Tournament MVP: **Julius Page**, Pittsburgh

BIG SKY

	Conference			Overall		
	W	L	Pct	W	L	Pct
Weber State⊕	14	0	1.000	26	6	.813
Eastern Washington□	9	5	.643	18	13	.581
Idaho State	7	7	.500	15	14	.517
Montana	7	7	.500	13	17	.433
Northern Arizona	6	8	.429	15	13	.536
Sacramento State	5	9	.357	12	17	.414
Montana State	5	9	.357	11	16	.407
Portland State	3	11	.214	5	22	.185

Tournament: **Weber State d. Eastern Washington 60-57**
Tournament MVP: **Jermaine Boyette**, Weber State

BIG SOUTH

	Conference			Overall		
	W	L	Pct	W	L	Pct
Winthrop	11	3	.786	20	10	.667
Charleston Southern	8	6	.571	14	14	.500
Liberty	8	6	.571	14	15	.483
Elon	8	6	.571	12	15	.444
UNC Asheville⊕	7	7	.500	15	17	.469
Radford	6	8	.429	10	20	.333
Coastal Carolina	5	9	.357	13	15	.464
High Point	3	11	.214	7	20	.259

Tournament: **UNC Asheville d. Radford 85-71**
Tournament MVP: **Andre Smith**, UNC Asheville

BIG TEN

	Conference			Overall		
	W	L	Pct	W	L	Pct
Wisconsin○	12	4	.750	24	8	.750
Illinois⊕	11	5	.688	25	7	.781
Purdue○	10	6	.625	19	11	.633
Michigan State○	10	6	.625	22	13	.629
Michigan✪	10	6	.625	17	13	.567
Indiana○	8	8	.500	21	13	.618
Minnesota□	8	8	.500	19	14	.576
Iowa□	7	9	.438	17	14	.548
Ohio State□	7	9	.438	17	15	.531
Northwestern	3	13	.188	12	17	.414
Penn State	2	14	.125	7	21	.250

Tournament: **Illinois d. Ohio State 72-59**
Tournament MOP: **Brian Cook**, Illinois

BIG 12

	Conference			Overall		
	W	L	Pct	W	L	Pct
Kansas○	14	2	.875	30	8	.789
Texas○	13	3	.813	26	7	.788
Oklahoma⊕	12	4	.750	27	7	.794
Oklahoma State○	10	6	.625	22	10	.688
Missouri○	9	7	.563	22	11	.667
Colorado○	9	7	.563	20	12	.625
Texas Tech□	6	10	.375	22	13	.629
Texas A&M	6	10	.375	14	14	.500
Iowa State□	5	11	.313	17	14	.548
Baylor	5	11	.313	14	14	.500
Kansas State	4	12	.250	13	17	.433
Nebraska	3	13	.188	11	19	.367

Tournament: **Oklahoma d. Missouri 49-47**
Tournament MOP: **Hollis Price**, Oklahoma

BIG WEST

	Conference			Overall		
	W	L	Pct	W	L	Pct
UC Santa Barbara□	14	4	.778	18	14	.563
UC Irvine	13	5	.722	20	9	.690
Utah State⊕	12	6	.667	24	9	.727
Cal Poly	10	8	.556	16	14	.533
Idaho	9	9	.500	13	15	.464
Cal State Northridge	8	10	.444	14	15	.483
Cal State Fullerton	8	10	.444	10	19	.345
Pacific	7	11	.389	12	16	.429
UC Riverside	5	13	.278	6	18	.250
Long Beach State	4	14	.222	5	22	.185

Tournament: **Utah State d. Cal Poly 57-54**
Tournament MVP: **Desmond Penigar**, Utah State

COLONIAL ATHLETIC

	Conference			Overall		
	W	L	Pct	W	L	Pct
UNC Wilmington⊕	15	3	.833	24	7	.774
VCU	12	6	.667	18	10	.643
Drexel□	12	6	.667	19	12	.613
George Mason	11	7	.611	16	12	.571
Delaware	9	9	.500	15	14	.517
Old Dominion	9	9	.500	12	15	.444
James Madison	8	10	.444	13	17	.433
William and Mary	7	11	.389	12	16	.429
Hofstra	6	12	.333	8	21	.276
Towson	1	17	.056	4	24	.143

Tournament: **UNC Wilmington d. Drexel 70-62**
Tournament MVP: **Brett Blizzard**, UNC Wilmington

C-USA

	Conference			Overall		
	W	L	Pct	W	L	Pct
American Division						
Marquette○	14	2	.875	27	6	.818
Louisville⊕	11	5	.688	25	7	.781
Cincinnati○	9	7	.563	17	12	.586
Saint Louis□	9	7	.563	16	14	.533
DePaul□	8	8	.500	16	13	.552
Charlotte	8	8	.500	13	16	.448
East Carolina	3	13	.188	12	15	.444
National Division						
Memphis○	13	3	.813	23	7	.767
UAB□	8	8	.500	21	13	.618
Tulane	8	8	.500	16	15	.516
South Florida	7	9	.438	15	14	.517
Houston	6	10	.375	8	20	.286
Southern Miss	5	11	.313	13	16	.448
TCU	3	13	.188	9	19	.321

Tournament: **Louisville d. UAB 83-78**
Tournament MVP: **Luke Whitehead**, Louisville

HORIZON

	Conference			Overall		
	W	L	Pct	W	L	Pct
Butler○	14	2	.875	27	6	.818
Wisc.-Milwaukee⊕	13	3	.813	24	8	.750
Illinois-Chicago□	12	4	.750	21	9	.700
Detroit	9	7	.563	18	12	.600
Loyola-Chicago	9	7	.563	15	16	.484
Wright State	4	12	.250	10	18	.357
Wisconsin-Green Bay	4	12	.250	10	20	.333
Youngstown State	4	12	.250	9	20	.310
Cleveland State	3	13	.188	8	22	.267

Tournament: **Wisconsin-Milwaukee d. Butler 69-52**
Tournament MVP: **Clay Tucker**, Wisconsin-Milwaukee

IVY

	Conference			Overall		
	W	L	Pct	W	L	Pct
Penn⊕	14	0	1.000	22	6	.786
Brown□	12	2	.857	17	12	.586
Princeton	10	4	.714	16	11	.593
Yale	8	6	.571	14	13	.519
Harvard	4	10	.286	12	15	.444
Cornell	4	10	.286	9	18	.333
Dartmouth	4	10	.286	8	19	.296
Columbia	0	14	.000	2	25	.074

⊕ Automatic NCAA Tournament bid ○ At-large NCAA Tournament bid □ NIT appearance ✪ Team record doesn't reflect games forfeited or vacated. For adjusted record, see p. 521.

MAAC

	Conference			Overall		
	W	L	PCT	W	L	PCT
Manhattan⊕	14	4	.778	23	7	.767
Fairfield□	13	5	.722	19	12	.613
Siena□	12	6	.667	21	11	.656
Niagara	12	6	.667	17	12	.586
Iona	11	7	.611	17	12	.586
Marist	8	10	.444	13	16	.448
Rider	7	11	.389	12	16	.429
Canisius	6	12	.333	10	18	.357
Saint Peter's	6	12	.333	10	19	.345
Loyola (MD)	1	17	.056	4	24	.143

Tournament: **Manhattan d. Fairfield 69-54**
Tournament MVP: **Luis Flores**, Manhattan

MID-AMERICAN

	Conference			Overall		
	W	L	PCT	W	L	PCT
East Division						
Kent State State□	12	6	.667	21	10	.677
Miami (OH)	11	7	.611	13	15	.464
Akron	9	9	.500	14	14	.500
Marshall	9	9	.500	14	15	.483
Ohio	8	10	.444	14	16	.467
Buffalo	2	16	.111	5	23	.179
West Division						
Central Michigan⊕	14	4	.778	25	7	.781
Northern Illinois	11	7	.611	17	14	.548
Western Michigan□	10	8	.556	20	11	.645
Eastern Michigan	8	10	.444	14	14	.500
Bowling Green	8	10	.444	13	16	.448
Ball State	8	10	.444	13	17	.433
Toledo	7	11	.389	13	16	.448

Tournament: **Central Michigan d. Kent State 77-67**
Tournament MVP: **Chris Kaman**, Central Michigan

MID-CONTINENT

	Conference			Overall		
	W	L	PCT	W	L	PCT
Valparaiso□	12	2	.857	20	11	.645
IUPUI⊕	10	4	.714	20	14	.588
Oakland	10	4	.714	17	11	.607
Oral Roberts	9	5	.643	18	10	.643
UMKC	7	7	.500	9	20	.310
Southern Utah	5	9	.357	11	17	.393
Western Illinois	3	11	.214	7	21	.250
Chicago State	0	14	.000	3	27	.100

Tournament: **IUPUI d. Valparaiso 66-64**
Tournament MVP: **Josh Murray**, IUPUI

MEAC

	Conference			Overall		
	W	L	PCT	W	L	PCT
South Carolina State⊕	15	3	.833	20	11	.645
Delaware State	13	5	.722	15	12	.556
Hampton	13	5	.722	19	11	.633
Coppin State	11	7	.611	11	17	.393
Florida A&M	11	7	.611	17	12	.586
Norfolk State	10	8	.556	14	15	.483
Howard	9	9	.500	13	17	.433
Morgan State	6	12	.333	7	22	.241
Bethune-Cookman	5	13	.278	8	22	.267
UMES	5	13	.278	5	23	.179
NC A&T	1	17	.056	1	26	.037

Tournament: **South Carolina State d. Hampton 72-67**
Tournament MOP: **Dustin Braddick**, South Carolina St.

MISSOURI VALLEY

	Conference			Overall		
	W	L	PCT	W	L	PCT
Southern Illinois○	16	2	.889	24	7	.774
Creighton⊕	15	3	.833	29	5	.853
Wichita State□	12	6	.667	18	12	.600
Missouri State	12	6	.667	17	12	.586
Evansville	8	10	.444	12	16	.429
Bradley	8	10	.444	12	18	.400
Northern Iowa	7	11	.389	11	17	.393
Drake	5	13	.278	10	20	.333
Illinois State	5	13	.278	8	21	.276
Indiana State	2	16	.111	7	24	.226

Tournament: **Creighton d. Southern Illinois 80-56**
Tournament MOP: **Kyle Korver**, Creighton

MOUNTAIN WEST

	Conference			Overall		
	W	L	PCT	W	L	PCT
Utah○	11	3	.786	25	8	.758
BYU○	11	3	.786	23	9	.719
UNLV□	8	6	.571	21	11	.656
Wyoming□	8	6	.571	21	11	.656
San Diego State□	6	8	.429	16	14	.533
Colorado State⊕	5	9	.357	19	14	.576
New Mexico	4	10	.286	10	18	.357
Air Force	3	11	.214	12	16	.429

Tournament: **Colorado State d. UNLV 62-61**
Tournament MVP: **Matt Nelson**, Colorado State

NORTHEAST

	Conference			Overall		
	W	L	PCT	W	L	PCT
Wagner⊕	14	4	.778	21	11	.656
Monmouth	13	5	.722	15	13	.536
Central Conn. State	12	6	.667	15	13	.536
Quinnipiac	10	8	.556	17	12	.586
Saint Francis (PA)	10	8	.556	14	14	.500
Fairleigh Dickinson	9	9	.500	15	14	.517
St. Francis (NY)	9	9	.500	14	16	.467
Robert Morris	7	11	.389	10	17	.370
Long Island	7	11	.389	9	19	.321
Mount St. Mary's	6	12	.333	11	16	.407
Sacred Heart	6	12	.333	8	21	.276
UMBC	5	13	.278	7	20	.259

Tournament: **Wagner d. St. Francis (NY) 78-61**
Tournament MVP: **Jermaine Hall**, Wagner

OHIO VALLEY

	Conference			Overall		
	W	L	PCT	W	L	PCT
Austin Peay⊕	13	3	.813	23	8	.742
Morehead State	13	3	.813	20	9	.690
Tennessee Tech	11	5	.688	20	12	.625
Murray State	9	7	.563	17	12	.586
Eastern Illinois	9	7	.563	14	15	.483
Tennessee-Martin	7	9	.438	14	14	.500
Eastern Kentucky	5	11	.313	11	17	.393
SE Missouri State	5	11	.313	11	19	.367
Tennessee State	0	16	.000	2	25	.074

Tournament: **Austin Peay d. Tennessee Tech 63-57**
Tournament MVP: **Josh Lewis**, Austin Peay

PAC-10

	Conference			Overall		
	W	L	PCT	W	L	PCT
Arizona○	17	1	.944	28	4	.875
Stanford○	14	4	.778	24	9	.727
California○	13	5	.722	22	9	.710
Arizona State○	11	7	.611	20	12	.625
Oregon⊕	10	8	.556	23	10	.697
Oregon State	6	12	.333	13	15	.464
Southern California	6	12	.333	13	17	.433
Washington	5	13	.278	10	17	.370
UCLA	6	12	.333	10	19	.345
Washington State	2	16	.111	7	20	.259

Tournament: **Oregon d. Southern California 74-66**
Tournament MOP: **Luke Ridnour**, Oregon

PATRIOT LEAGUE

	Conference			Overall		
	W	L	PCT	W	L	PCT
Holy Cross⊕	13	1	.929	26	5	.839
American	9	5	.643	16	14	.533
Colgate	9	5	.643	14	14	.500
Lehigh	8	6	.571	16	12	.571
Bucknell	7	7	.500	14	15	.483
Lafayette	6	8	.429	13	16	.448
Navy	4	10	.286	8	20	.286
Army	0	14	.000	5	22	.185

Tournament: **Holy Cross d. American 72-64**
Tournament MVP: **Patrick Whearty**, Holy Cross

SEC

	Conference			Overall		
	W	L	PCT	W	L	PCT
Eastern Division						
Kentucky⊕	16	0	1.000	32	4	.889
Florida○	12	4	.750	25	8	.758
Georgia⊗	11	5	.688	19	8	.704
Tennessee□	9	7	.563	17	12	.586
South Carolina	5	11	.313	12	16	.429
Vanderbilt	3	13	.188	11	18	.379
Western Division						
Mississippi State○	9	7	.563	21	10	.677
LSU○	8	8	.500	21	11	.656
Auburn○	8	8	.500	22	12	.647
Alabama○	7	9	.438	17	12	.586
Mississippi	4	12	.250	14	15	.483
Arkansas	4	12	.250	9	19	.321

Tournament: **Kentucky d. Mississippi State 64-57**
Tournament MVP: **Keith Bogans**, Kentucky

SOUTHERN

	Conference			Overall		
	W	L	PCT	W	L	PCT
North Division						
East Tenn. State⊕	11	5	.688	20	11	.645
Appalachian State	11	5	.688	19	10	.655
Davidson	11	5	.688	17	10	.630
Western Carolina	6	10	.375	9	19	.321
VMI	3	13	.188	10	20	.333
UNC Greensboro	3	13	.188	7	22	.241
South Division						
Charleston□	13	3	.813	25	8	.758
Chattanooga	11	5	.688	21	9	.700
Georgia Southern	8	8	.500	16	13	.552
Wofford	8	8	.500	14	15	.483
Furman	8	8	.500	14	17	.452
The Citadel	3	13	.188	8	20	.286

Tournament: **East Tenn. State d. Chattanooga 97-90**
Tournament MOP: **Tim Smith**, East Tenn. State

SOUTHLAND

	Conference			Overall		
	W	L	PCT	W	L	PCT
Sam Houston State⊕	17	3	.850	23	7	.767
Stephen F. Austin	16	4	.800	21	8	.724
Texas-Arlington	13	7	.650	16	13	.552
Texas State	11	9	.550	17	12	.586
McNeese State	10	10	.500	15	14	.517
Lamar	10	10	.500	13	14	.481
UL-Monroe	10	10	.500	12	16	.429
Southeastern Louisiana	9	11	.450	11	16	.407
UTSA	7	13	.350	10	17	.370
Northwestern State (LA)	6	14	.300	6	21	.222
Nicholls State	1	19	.050	3	25	.107

Tournament: **Sam Houston St. d. Stephen F. Austin 69-66 OT**
Tournament MVP: **Donald Cole**, Stephen F. Austin

SWAC

	Conference			Overall		
	W	L	PCT	W	L	PCT
Prairie View A&M	14	4	.778	17	12	.586
Miss. Valley State	13	5	.722	15	14	.517
Texas Southern⊕	11	7	.611	18	13	.581
Alabama State	11	7	.611	14	15	.483
Alcorn State	10	8	.556	14	19	.424
Grambling	9	9	.500	12	18	.400
Jackson State	9	9	.500	10	18	.357
Southern U.	5	13	.278	9	20	.310
Alabama A&M	4	14	.222	8	19	.296
Arkansas-Pine Bluff	4	14	.222	4	24	.143

Tournament: **Texas Southern d. Alcorn State 77-68**
Tournament MVP: **Ra'Kim Hollis**, Texas Southern

SUN BELT

	Conference			Overall		
	W	L	PCT	W	L	PCT
East Division						
Western Kentucky⊕	12	2	.857	24	9	.727
Middle Tenn. State	9	5	.643	16	14	.533
Arkansas-Little Rock	8	6	.571	18	12	.600
Arkansas State	6	8	.429	13	15	.464
Florida International⊗	1	13	.071	8	21	.276
West Division						
UL-Lafayette□	12	3	.800	20	10	.667
New Mexico State	9	6	.600	20	9	.690
Denver	7	8	.467	17	15	.531
New Orleans	7	8	.467	15	14	.517
South Alabama	7	8	.467	14	14	.500
North Texas	2	13	.133	7	21	.250

Tournament: **Western Kentucky d. Middle Tenn. St. 64-52**
Tournament MOP: **Patrick Sparks**, Western Kentucky

WEST COAST

	Conference			Overall		
	W	L	PCT	W	L	PCT
Gonzaga○	12	2	.857	24	9	.727
San Diego⊕	10	4	.714	18	12	.600
San Francisco	9	5	.643	15	14	.517
Pepperdine	7	7	.500	15	13	.536
Saint Mary's (CA)	6	8	.429	15	15	.500
Santa Clara	4	10	.286	13	15	.464
Portland	4	10	.286	11	17	.393
Loyola Marymount	4	10	.286	11	20	.355

Tournament: **San Diego d. Gonzaga 72-63**
Tournament MVP: **Jason Keep**, San Diego

WAC

	Conference			Overall		
	W	L	PCT	W	L	PCT
Fresno State	13	5	.722	20	8	.714
Tulsa⊕	12	6	.667	23	10	.697
Rice	11	7	.611	19	10	.655
SMU	11	7	.611	17	13	.567
Nevada□	11	7	.611	18	14	.563
Hawaii□	9	9	.500	19	12	.613
Louisiana Tech	9	9	.500	12	15	.444
Boise State	7	11	.389	13	16	.448
San Jose State	4	14	.222	7	21	.250
UTEP	3	15	.167	6	24	.200

Note: Fresno State was ineligible for NCAA Tournament.
Tournament: **Tulsa d. Nevada 75-64**
Tournament MVP: **Kevin Johnson**, Tulsa

INDEPENDENTS

	Overall		
	W	L	PCT
Centenary	14	14	.500
Corpus Christi	14	15	.483
Texas-Pan American	10	20	.333
IPFW	9	21	.300
Morris Brown	8	20	.286
Savannah State	3	24	.111

OTHERS

(Reclassifying & provisional teams that are not eligible for the NCAA Tournament.)

	Overall		
	W	L	PCT
Birmingham Southern	19	9	.679
Lipscomb	8	20	.286

INDIVIDUAL LEADERS—SEASON

SCORING	CL	POS	G	FG	3FG	FT	PTS	PPG
1 **Ruben Douglas**, New Mexico	SR	G	28	218	94	253	783	**28.0**
2 **Henry Domercant**, Eastern Illinois	SR	G	29	252	84	222	810	**27.9**
3 **Mike Helms**, Oakland	JR	G	28	241	74	196	752	**26.9**
4 **Michael Watson**, UMKC	JR	G	29	247	118	128	740	**25.5**
5 **Troy Bell**, Boston College	SR	G	31	224	106	227	781	**25.2**
6 **Keydren Clark**, Saint Peter's	FR	G	29	231	109	151	722	**24.9**
7 **Luis Flores**, Manhattan	JR	G	30	231	56	221	739	**24.6**
8 **Chris Williams**, Ball State	SR	G	30	226	64	220	736	**24.5**
9 **Mike Sweetney**, Georgetown	JR	F	34	264	0	248	776	**22.8**
10 **Kevin Martin**, Western Carolina	SO	G	24	161	50	174	546	**22.8**

FIELD GOAL PCT	CL	POS	G	FG	FGA	PCT
1 **Adam Mark**, Belmont	JR	F	28	199	297	**67.0**
2 **Rickey White**, Maine	SR	F	24	131	198	**66.2**
3 **Matt Nelson**, Colorado State	SO	C	31	205	319	**64.3**
4 **Armond Williams**, Illinois-Chicago	SO	F	30	168	263	**63.9**
5 **Michael Harris**, Rice	SO	F	28	172	276	**62.3**

MINIMUM: 5 MADE PER GAME

THREE-POINT FG PER GAME	CL	POS	G	3FG	3PG
1 **Terrence Woods**, Florida A&M	JR	G	28	139	**5.0**
2 **Demon Brown**, Charlotte	JR	G	29	137	**4.7**
3 **Michael Watson**, UMKC	JR	G	29	118	**4.1**
4 **Brad Boyd**, UL-Lafayette	JR	G	27	104	**3.9**
5 **Kyle Korver**, Creighton	SR	G/F	34	129	**3.8**

THREE-POINT FG PCT	CL	POS	G	3FG	3FGA	PCT
1 **Jeff Schiffner**, Penn	JR	G	28	74	150	**49.3**
2 **Kyle Korver**, Creighton	SR	F	34	129	269	**48.0**
3 **Terrence Woods**, Florida A&M	JR	G	28	139	304	**45.7**
4 **Chez Marks**, Morehead State	SR	G	29	82	180	**45.6**
5 **Tyson Dorsey**, Samford	JR	G	27	75	165	**45.5**

MINIMUM: 2.5 MADE PER GAME

FREE THROW PCT	CL	POS	G	FT	FTA	PCT
1 **Steve Drabyn**, Belmont	JR	G	29	78	82	**95.1**
2 **Matt Logie**, Lehigh	SR	G	28	91	96	**94.8**
3 **Hollis Price**, Oklahoma	SR	G	34	130	140	**92.9**
4 **Brian Dux**, Canisius	SR	G	28	115	125	**92.0**
5 **J.J. Redick**, Duke	FR	G	33	102	111	**91.9**

MINIMUM: 2.5 MADE PER GAME

ASSISTS PER GAME	CL	POS	G	AST	APG
1 **Martell Bailey**, Illinois-Chicago	JR	G	30	244	**8.1**
2 **Marques Green**, St. Bonaventure	JR	G	27	216	**8.0**
3 **T.J. Ford**, Texas	SO	G	33	254	**7.7**
4 **Elliott Prasse-Freeman**, Harvard	SR	G	27	207	**7.7**
5 **Antawn Dobie**, Long Island	SR	G	26	193	**7.4**
6 **Richard Little**, VMI	JR	G	30	216	**7.2**
7 **Steve Blake**, Maryland	SR	G	31	221	**7.1**
8 **Chris Thomas**, Notre Dame	SO	G	34	236	**6.9**
9 **Raymond Felton**, North Carolina	FR	G	35	236	**6.7**
10 **Luke Ridnour**, Oregon	JR	G	33	218	**6.6**

REBOUNDS PER GAME	CL	POS	G	REB	RPG
1 **Brandon Hunter**, Ohio	SR	F	30	378	**12.6**
2 **Amien Hicks**, Morris Brown	SR	F	24	298	**12.4**
3 **Adam Sonn**, Belmont	SR	C	29	352	**12.1**
4 **Chris Kaman**, Central Michigan	JR	C	31	373	**12.0**
5 **David West**, Xavier	SR	F	32	379	**11.8**
6 **Louis Truscott**, Houston	SR	F	28	315	**11.3**
7 **Emeka Okafor**, Connecticut	SO	C	33	370	**11.2**
8 **Kenny Adeleke**, Hofstra	SO	F	29	320	**11.0**
James Singleton, Murray State	SR	F	29	320	**11.0**
10 **James Thomas**, Texas	JR	C	33	363	**11.0**

BLOCKED SHOTS PER GAME	CL	POS	G	BLK	BPG
1 **Emeka Okafor**, Connecticut	SO	C	33	156	**4.7**
2 **Nick Billings**, Binghamton	SO	C	27	117	**4.3**
3 **Justin Rowe**, Maine	SR	C	25	105	**4.2**
4 **Deng Gai**, Fairfield	SO	F	25	96	**3.8**
5 **Robert Battle**, Drexel	SR	C	31	116	**3.7**

STEALS PER GAME	CL	POS	G	STL	SPG
1 **Alexis McMillan**, Stetson	SR	F	22	87	**4.0**
2 **Zakee Wadood**, East Tennessee State	JR	F	29	93	**3.2**
3 **Jay Heard**, Jacksonville State	SR	G	30	95	**3.2**
4 **Eric Bush**, UAB	SR	G	34	106	**3.1**
5 **Marcus Hatten**, St. John's	SR	G	34	100	**2.9**

INDIVIDUAL LEADERS—GAME

POINTS	CL	POS	OPP	DATE	PTS
1 **Michael Watson**, UMKC	JR	G	Oral Roberts	F22	**54**
2 **Antawn Dobie**, Long Island	SR	G	St. Francis (NY)	F22	**53**
3 **Ron Williamson**, Howard	SR	G	NC A&T	J21	**52**
4 **Richard Toussaint**, Bethune-Cookman	SR	G	Morgan State	M11	**49**
5 **Chris Williams**, Ball State	SR	G	Akron	J4	**48**
Keydren Clark, Saint Peter's	FR	G	Northern Arizona	N23	**48**

THREE-POINT FG MADE	CL	POS	OPP	DATE	3FG
1 **Terrence Woods**, Florida A&M	JR	G	Coppin State	M1	**12**
2 **Terrence Woods**, Florida A&M	JR	G	NC A&T	F1	**11**
Ron Williamson, Howard	SR	G	NC A&T	J21	**11**
4 **Chris Hill**, Michigan State	SO	G	Syracuse	F23	**10**
Michael Watson, UMKC	JR	G	Oral Roberts	F22	**10**
Keydren Clark, Saint Peter's	FR	G	Northern Arizona	N23	**10**

ASSISTS	CL	POS	OPP	DATE	AST
1 **Antawn Dobie**, Long Island	SR	G	St. Francis (NY)	D15	**17**
Zakee Smith, Cal State Fullerton	JR	G	Pepperdine	D4	**17**
3 **Malcolm Campbell**, Alabama State	JR	G	Mississippi Valley State	F10	**16**
Blake Stepp, Gonzaga	JR	G	Long Beach State	D20	**16**
5 **Antawn Dobie**, Long Island	SR	G	Saint Francis (NY)	F22	**15**
Mike Slattery, Delaware	SO	G	William and Mary	F1	**15**
Mike Slattery, Delaware	SO	G	UNC Greensboro	D19	**15**

REBOUNDS	CL	POS	OPP	DATE	REB
1 **Brandon Hunter**, Ohio	SR	F	Akron	J8	**26**
2 **Erroyl Bing**, East Carolina	JR	F	South Florida	J25	**24**
Brandon Hunter, Ohio	SR	F	St. Bonaventure	D31	**24**
4 **Chris Jackson**, New Mexico State	SR	C	North Texas	F1	**23**
Nick Collison, Kansas	SR	F	Texas	J27	**23**
Willie Neal, Miss. Valley State	SR	C	Arkansas-Pine Bluff	J4	**23**

BLOCKED SHOTS	CL	POS	OPP	DATE	BLK
1 **David Harrison**, Colorado	SO	C	Nebraska	M8	**11**
Jordan Cornette, Notre Dame	SO	F	Belmont	N17	**11**
3 **Nick Billings**, Binghamton	SO	C	Northeastern	F22	**10**
William McDonald, Grambling	SR	F	Prairie View A&M	F15	**10**
Nick Billings, Binghamton	SO	C	Boston U.	F9	**10**
David Harrison, Colorado	SO	C	Stetson	N24	**10**

STEALS	CL	POS	OPP	DATE	STL
1 **Marcus Hatten**, St. John's	SR	G	Syracuse	F18	**10**
Joseph Frazier, Cal St. Northridge	SO	G	Bethany (CA)	D7	**10**
Rawle Marshall, Oakland	SO	G	Texas A&M	D2	**10**
4 **Aaron Miles**, Kansas	SO	G	Iowa State	F16	**9**
5 **Matt Crenshaw**, IUPUI	JR	G	Chicago State	M1	**8**
Joseph Frazier, Cal St. Northridge	SO	G	Cal Poly	F13	**8**
Tony Dobbins, Richmond	JR	G	Massachusetts	F12	**8**
Marcus Banks, UNLV	SR	G	Colorado State	F3	**8**
Errick Craven, Southern California	SO	G	Oregon	F2	**8**
Alexis McMillan, Stetson	SR	F	Campbell	J25	**8**
Alexis McMillan, Stetson	SR	F	Jacksonville	J10	**8**
Marcus Banks, UNLV	SR	G	IPFW	J2	**8**
Terry Conerway, Texas State	JR	G	Arkansas	D21	**8**
Eric Bush, UAB	SR	G	Corpus Christi	D19	**8**
Mike Gale, Centenary	JR	G	Jarvis Christian	D17	**8**
Tim Smith, East Tenn. State	FR	G	Virginia-Wise	D14	**8**
Jeremy Bishop, Quinnipiac	SR	F	Hofstra	D1	**8**
A.J. Diggs, California	JR	G	Cleveland State	N30	**8**

TEAM LEADERS—SEASON

WIN-LOSS PCT	W	L	PCT
1 **Kentucky**	32	4	**.889**
2 **Arizona**	28	4	**.875**
3 **Syracuse**	30	5	**.857**
4 **Creighton**	29	5	**.853**
5 **Pittsburgh**	28	5	**.848**

SCORING OFFENSE	G	W-L	PTS	PPG
1 **Arizona**	32	28-4	2,725	**85.2**
2 **Appalachian State**	29	19-10	2,434	**83.9**
3 **Kansas**	38	30-8	3,141	**82.7**
4 **East Tennessee State**	31	20-11	2,543	**82.0**
5 **Louisville**	32	25-7	2,612	**81.6**

SCORING MARGIN	G	W-L	PPG	OPP PPG	MAR
1 **Kansas**	38	30-8	82.7	66.9	**15.8**
2 **Pittsburgh**	33	28-5	74.9	59.2	**15.7**
3 **Arizona**	32	28-4	85.2	70.7	**14.5**
4 **Creighton**	34	29-5	79.1	64.8	**14.3**
5 **Kentucky**	36	32-4	77.3	64.1	**13.1**

FIELD GOAL PCT	G	W-L	FG	FGA	PCT
1 **Morehead State**	29	20-9	854	1,674	**51.0**
2 **Pittsburgh**	33	28-5	893	1,766	**50.6**
3 **Colorado State**	33	19-14	876	1,733	**50.5**
4 **Central Michigan**	32	25-7	864	1,714	**50.4**
5 **Creighton**	34	29-5	974	1,956	**49.9**

THREE-POINT FG PER GAME	G	W-L	3FG	3PG
1 **Mississippi Valley State**	29	15-14	299	**10.3**
2 **St. Bonaventure**	27	13-14	271	**10.0**
3 **Davidson**	27	17-10	269	**10.0**
4 **Troy**	32	26-6	312	**9.8**
5 **UMKC**	29	9-20	272	**9.4**

ASSISTS PER GAME	G	W-L	AST	APG
1 **Maryland**	31	21-10	573	**18.5**
2 **Illinois**	32	25-7	575	**18.0**
3 **Georgia**	27	19-8	483	**17.9**
4 **Pittsburgh**	33	28-5	589	**17.8**
5 **SE Missouri State**	30	11-19	535	**17.8**

REBOUND MARGIN	G	W-L	RPG	OPP RPG	MAR
1 **Wake Forest**	31	25-6	41.7	32.0	**9.6**
2 **Kansas**	38	30-8	41.8	33.9	**7.9**
Holy Cross	31	26-5	36.5	28.6	**7.9**
4 **Vermont**	33	21-12	39.2	31.9	**7.4**
5 **Utah State**	33	24-9	35.0	28.0	**7.0**

Scoring Defense	G	W-L	OPP PTS	OPP PPG
1 **Air Force**	28	12-16	1596	**57.0**
2 **Miami (OH)**	28	13-15	1643	**58.7**
3 **Holy Cross**	31	26-5	1821	**58.7**
4 **Bucknell**	29	14-15	1706	**58.8**
5 **Pittsburgh**	33	28-5	1955	**59.2**

Field Goal Pct Defense	G	W-L	OPP FG	OPP FGA	OPP PCT
1 **Saint Joseph's**	30	23-7	609	1639	**37.2**
2 **Illinois**	32	25-7	657	1741	**37.7**
3 **Maryland**	31	21-10	704	1864	**37.8**
4 **Connecticut**	33	23-10	817	2157	**37.9**
5 **Syracuse**	35	30-5	878	2253	**39.0**

Blocked Shots Per Game	G	W-L	BLK	BPG
1 **Connecticut**	33	23-10	253	**7.7**
2 **Syracuse**	35	30-5	247	**7.1**
3 **Colorado**	32	20-12	214	**6.7**
4 **Binghamton**	27	14-13	176	**6.5**
5 **Maryland**	31	21-10	198	**6.4**

Steals Per Game	G	W-L	STL	SPG
1 **UAB**	34	21-13	394	**11.6**
2 **East Tennessee State**	31	20-11	354	**11.4**
3 **Stetson**	26	6-20	282	**10.8**
4 **Jacksonville State**	30	20-10	314	**10.5**
5 **Maryland**	31	21-10	322	**10.4**

TEAM LEADERS—GAME

Points	OPP	DATE	SCORE
1 **Drake**	Grinnell	D11	**162-110**
2 **St. Francis (NY)**	Long Island	F22	**142-140**
3 **Long Island**	St. Francis (NY)	F22	**140-142**
4 **Centenary**	Arkansas Baptist	F1	**124-75**
5 **Arkansas State**	Lyon	D7	**120-55**

Field Goal Pct	OPP	DATE	FG	FGA	PCT
1 **Southern Utah**	Montana Tech	D19	32	41	**78.0**
2 **Stephen F. Austin**	LeTourneau	N26	44	57	**77.2**
3 **Morehead State**	Asbury	N30	39	53	**73.6**
4 **Chattanooga**	Appalachian State	M6	34	47	**72.3**
5 **Delaware State**	Fairleigh Dickinson	D7	31	43	**72.1**

Three-Point FG Made	OPP	DATE	3FG
1 **Arkansas State**	Lyon	D7	20
2 **Temple**	Charlotte	D4	19
Davidson	Washington and Lee	N30	19
4 **Washington State**	Gonzaga	D7	18
Air Force	Texas-Pan American	D5	18

CONSENSUS ALL-AMERICAS

FIRST TEAM

PLAYER	CL	POS	HT	SCHOOL	RPG	PPG
T.J. Ford	SO	G	5-10	Texas	3.9	15.0
Dwyane Wade	JR	G	6-4	Marquette	6.3	21.5
Nick Collison	SR	F	6-9	Kansas	10.0	18.5
Josh Howard	SR	F	6-6	Wake Forest	8.3	19.5
David West	SR	F	6-9	Xavier	11.8	20.1

SECOND TEAM

PLAYER	CL	POS	HT	SCHOOL	RPG	PPG
Troy Bell	SR	G	6-1	Boston College	4.6	25.2
Jason Gardner	SR	G	5-10	Arizona	4.0	14.8
Hollis Price	SR	G	6-1	Oklahoma	2.7	18.0
Carmelo Anthony	FR	F	6-8	Syracuse	10.0	22.2
Kyle Korver	SR	G/F	6-7	Creighton	6.4	17.8

Selectors: AP, NABC, Sporting News, USBWA

AWARD WINNERS

PLAYER OF THE YEAR

PLAYER	CL	POS	HT	SCHOOL	AWARDS
T.J. Ford	SO	G	5-10	Texas	Naismith, Wooden
David West	SR	F	6-9	Xavier	AP, USBWA, Rupp
Nick Collison	SR	F	6-9	Kansas	NABC
Jason Gardner	SR	G	5-10	Arizona	Frances Pomeroy Naismith *

* For the most outstanding senior player who is 6 feet or under

DEFENSIVE PLAYER OF THE YEAR

PLAYER	CL	POS	HT	SCHOOL
Emeka Okafor	SO	C	6-10	Connecticut

COACH OF THE YEAR

COACH	SCHOOL	REC	AWARDS
Tubby Smith	Kentucky	32-4	Naismith, AP, USBWA, NABC, Sporting News, CBS/Chevrolet

Bob Gibbons' Top High School Senior Recruits

PLAYER	POS	HT	HIGH SCHOOL	A-A TEAMS	COLLEGE	CAREER NOTES
1 **LeBron James**	G/F	6-7	St. Vincent-St. Mary HS, Akron, OH	McD, MJ, P, USA	None	Drafted straight out of HS; No. 1 pick, '03 NBA draft (Cavs); ROY '04; 5-time All-Star; MVP '09
2 **Luol Deng**	F	6-8	Blair Academy, Blairstown, NJ	McD, P, USA	Duke	15.1 ppg, 1 season at Duke; No. 7 pick, '04 NBA draft (Suns); 15.4 ppg (5 seasons)
3 **Shannon Brown**	F	6-3	Proviso East HS, Maywood, IL	McD, MJ, P	Michigan State	Second-team All-Big Ten, '05-'06; 1,183 pts at MSU; No. 25 pick, '06 NBA draft (Cavs); 3 seasons
4 **Ndudi Ebi**	F	6-9	Westbury Christian HS, Houston	McD, MJ, P, USA	None	Drafted straight out of HS; No. 26 pick, '03 NBA draft (Wolves); 2.1 ppg (2 seasons); played in Italy with Carife Ferrara team
5 **David Padgett**	C	6-11	Reno (NV) HS	McD, P	Kansas/Louisville	Transferred after 1 year; second-team All-Big East as a junior; undrafted
6 **Travis Outlaw**	F	6-10	Starkville (MS) HS	McD, P	None	Drafted straight out of HS; No. 23 pick, '03 NBA draft (Blazers); 9.6 ppg (6 seasons)
7 **Kendrick Perkins**	C	6-10	Clifton J. Ozen HS, Beaumont, TX	McD, P	None	Drafted straight out of HS; No. 27 pick, '03 NBA draft (Grizzlies); 5.6 ppg and 5.7 rpg in 6 seasons (Celtics)
8 **Charlie Villanueva**	PF	6-9	Blair Academy, Blairstown, NJ	McD	Connecticut	NCAA title '04; No. 7 pick, '05 NBA draft; first-team All-Rookie, '05-'06; 16.2 ppg in '08-'09
9 **James Lang**	C	6-10	Central Park Christian HS, Birmingham, AL	McD	None	Drafted straight out of HS; 2nd-round pick, '03 NBA draft (Hornets); much-injured; played 11 NBA games and D-League
10 **Chris Paul**	PG	5-11	West Forsyth HS, Clemmons, NC	McD, MJ, P	Wake Forest	395 assists in 2 seasons; No. 4 pick, '05 NBA draft (Hornets); NBA ROY, '06; NBA asst leader, '07-09
11 **Mustafa Shakur**	PG	6-3	Friends Central HS, Wynnewood, PA	McD, USA	Arizona	670 assists at Arizona; undrafted; playing in Greece with Panellinios
12 **Linas Kleiza**	PF	6-8	Montrose Christian HS, Rockville, MD	P	Missouri	Led Tigers in rebounding, '04-05; No. 27, pick '05 NBA draft (Blazers); 8.3 ppg in 4 seasons (Nuggets)
13 **Leon Powe**	PF	6-8	Oakland (CA) Tech HS	McD, P	California	All Pac-10 '06; 2nd-round pick, '06 NBA draft (Celtics); NBA title, '08
14 **Brandon Bass**	PF	6-8	Capitol HS, Baton Rouge, LA	McD, P	LSU	SEC POY, '05; 2nd-round pick, '05 NBA draft (Hornets); 6.9 ppg (4 seasons)
15 **Brian Butch**	C	7-0	Appleton (WI) West HS	McD, P, USA	Wisconsin	9.0 ppg, 5.4 rpg (4 seasons); All-Big Ten honorable mention '06-'07; undrafted, played in Germany
16 **Trevor Ariza**	F	6-8	Westchester HS, Los Angeles	P	UCLA	First-team Pac-10 All-Freshman, '04; 2nd-round pick, '04 NBA draft (Knicks); (5 seasons)
17 **Kris Humphries**	PF	6-8	Hopkins HS, Minnetonka, MN	McD, MJ, P	Minnesota	Big Ten FOY, '04; No. 14 pick, '04 NBA draft (Jazz); 4.2 ppg, 3.0 rpg (5 seasons)
18 **Mike Jones**	G	6-4	Thayer Academy, Braintree, MA	McD, P	Maryland	10.5 ppg as a junior; holds UMd. single-game record for 3-pointers (9); undrafted; playing in Romania
19 **J.R. Giddens**	G/F	6-5	John Marshall HS, Oklahoma City	McD, MJ, P	Kansas/New Mexico	Transferred after 2 years; 15.8 ppg as junior (UNM), No. 30 pick, '08 NBA draft (Celtics)
20 **Von Wafer**	G/F	6-5	Heritage Christian Academy, Cleveland, TX	McD, P	Florida State	12.5 ppg as a Soph.; 2nd-round pick, '05 NBA draft (Lakers); 6.2 ppg (4 seasons)

Other Standouts

PLAYER	POS	HT	HIGH SCHOOL	A-A TEAMS	COLLEGE	CAREER NOTES
34 **Adam Morrison**	F	6-7	Mead HS, Spokane, WA		Gonzaga	USBWA Co-POY, '06; 19.7 ppg (1,867 pts), 3 seasons; No. 3 pick, '06 NBA draft (Bobcats)
114 **Acie Law IV**	G	6-3	Kimball HS, Dallas		Texas A&M	First-team All-American '06-07; Wooden Award finalist; No. 11 pick, '07 NBA draft (Hawks); 3.6 ppg, (2 seasons)

Abbreviations: McD=McDonald's; MJ=Jordan Brand; P=Parade; USA=USA Today

Poll Progression

Preseason Poll

AP	ESPN/USA	School
1	1	**Arizona**
2	2	**Kansas**
3	3	**Oklahoma**
4	5	**Texas**
5	4	**Pittsburgh**
6	6	**Duke**
7	7	**Florida**
8	8	**Alabama**
9	10	**Michigan State**
10	11	**Xavier**
11	9	**Oregon**
12	13	**Mississippi State**
13	15	**Maryland**
14	12	**UCLA**
15	14	**Connecticut**
16	16	**Georgia**
17	17	**Kentucky**
18	19	**Marquette**
19	18	**Missouri**
20	23	**Western Kentucky**
21	21	**Indiana**
22	22	**Gonzaga**
23	20	**Cincinnati**
24	24	**Minnesota**
25	—	**Tulsa**
—	25	**Illinois**

Week of Nov 19

AP	ESPN/USA	School	AP↓↑
1	1	**Arizona** (0-0)	
2	2	**Kansas** (0-0)	
3	5	**Texas** (1-0)	↑1
4	8	**Alabama** (1-0)	↑4
5	4	**Pittsburgh** (0-0)	
6	6	**Duke** (0-0)	
7	3	**Oklahoma** (0-1)	↓4
8	7	**Florida** (0-0)	↓1
9	10	**Michigan State** (0-0)	
10	9	**Oregon** (0-0)	↑1
11	11	**Xavier** (0-0)	↓1
12	13	**Mississippi State** (0-0)	
12	15	**Maryland** (0-0)	↑1
14	14	**Connecticut** (0-0)	↑1
15	12	**UCLA** (0-0)	↓1
16	19	**Marquette** (1-0)	↑2
17	17	**Kentucky** (0-0)	
18	16	**Georgia** (0-1)	↓2
19	23	**Western Kentucky** (0-0)	↑1
20	18	**Missouri** (0-0)	↓1
21	22	**Gonzaga** (0-0)	↑1
22	21	**Indiana** (0-0)	↓1
23	20	**Cincinnati** (0-0)	
24	24	**Minnesota** (0-0)	
25	—	**Tulsa** (0-0)	
—	25	**Illinois** (0-0)	

Week of Nov 26

AP	ESPN/USA	School	AP↓↑
1	1	**Arizona** (1-0)	
2	2	**Kansas** (2-0)	
3	3	**Texas** (2-0)	
4	6	**Alabama** (2-0)	
5	5	**Pittsburgh** (1-0)	
6	4	**Duke** (1-0)	
7	7	**Florida** (3-0)	↑1
8	8	**Oklahoma** (2-1)	↓1
9	10	**Michigan State** (1-0)	
10	9	**Oregon** (1-0)	
11	11	**Maryland** (1-0)	↑1
12	12	**Connecticut** (1-0)	↑2
13	13	**Marquette** (3-0)	↑3
14	14	**UCLA** (0-1)	↑1
15	16	**Kentucky** (1-0)	↑2
16	15	**Xavier** (2-1)	↓5
17	18	**Georgia** (1-1)	↑1
18	17	**Missouri** (1-0)	↑2
19	20	**Indiana** (0-0)	↑3
20	21	**Gonzaga** (1-0)	↑1
21	19	**Cincinnati** (1-0)	↑2
22	24	**Tulsa** (2-0)	↑3
23	23	**Mississippi State** (0-1)	↓11
24	22	**Minnesota** (1-0)	
25	—	**Wisconsin** (3-0)	⤴
—	25	**Illinois** (1-0)	

Week of Dec 3

AP	ESPN/USA	School	AP↓↑
1	1	**Arizona** (2-0)	
2	2	**Texas** (4-0)	↑1
3	5	**Alabama** (4-0)	↑1
4	3	**Duke** (3-0)	↑2
5	4	**Pittsburgh** (3-0)	
6	7	**Oklahoma** (3-1)	↑2
7	6	**Oregon** (3-0)	↑3
8	9	**Florida** (4-1)	↓1
9	8	**Maryland** (3-0)	↑2
10	11	**Indiana** (4-0)	↑9
11	12	**Connecticut** (3-0)	↑1
12	14	**North Carolina** (5-0)	⤴
13	10	**Marquette** (4-0)	
14	13	**Kansas** (2-2)	↓12
15	15	**Missouri** (2-0)	↑3
16	16	**Xavier** (2-1)	
17	22	**Stanford** (4-1)	⤴
18	18	**Kentucky** (2-1)	↓3
19	19	**Tulsa** (3-0)	↑3
20	17	**Minnesota** (2-0)	↑4
21	21	**Michigan State** (2-2)	↓12
22	23	**Virginia** (3-1)	⤴
23	—	**Wisconsin** (4-0)	↑2
24	24	**Mississippi State** (2-1)	↓1
25	20	**Illinois** (3-0)	⤴
—	25	**Gonzaga** (2-2)	⤵

Week of Dec 10

AP	ESPN/USA	School	AP↓↑
1	1	**Arizona** (4-0)	
2	4	**Alabama** (6-0)	↑1
3	2	**Duke** (5-0)	↑1
4	3	**Pittsburgh** (5-0)	↑1
5	5	**Oregon** (5-0)	↑2
6	8	**Oklahoma** (4-1)	
7	6	**Indiana** (6-0) (A)	↑3
8	7	**Texas** (5-1)	↓6
9	9	**Connecticut** (5-0)	↑2
10	15	**Notre Dame** (8-1) (B)	⤴
11	10	**Missouri** (4-0)	↑4
12	12	**Kentucky** (4-1)	↑6
13	11	**Xavier** (4-1)	↑3
14	17	**Florida** (6-2)	↓6
15	14	**Illinois** (5-0)	↑10
16	13	**Marquette** (5-1)	↓3
17	18	**Tulsa** (4-0)	↑2
18	16	**Maryland** (4-2) (A)	↓9
19	20	**Stanford** (4-1)	↓2
20	19	**Kansas** (3-3)	↓6
21	21	**Michigan State** (4-2)	
22	22	**North Carolina** (5-2)	↓10
23	24	**Creighton** (6-0)	⤴
24	22	**Mississippi State** (5-1)	
25	—	**Charleston** (6-0)	⤴
—	25	**Minnesota** (4-1)	⤵

Week of Dec 17

AP	ESPN/USA	School	AP↓↑
1	1	**Arizona** (5-0)	
2	4	**Alabama** (7-0)	
3	2	**Duke** (5-0)	
4	3	**Pittsburgh** (6-0)	
5	5	**Oregon** (6-0)	
6	6	**Indiana** (8-0)	↑1
7	7	**Oklahoma** (5-1)	↓1
8	8	**Connecticut** (6-0)	↑1
9	11	**Notre Dame** (9-1)	↑1
10	9	**Texas** (5-2)	↓2
11	10	**Missouri** (6-0)	
12	12	**Illinois** (7-0)	↑3
13	13	**Florida** (7-2)	↑1
14	14	**Marquette** (6-1)	↑2
15	15	**Michigan State** (5-2)	↑6
16	17	**Mississippi State** (6-1)	↑8
17	21	**Stanford** (5-1)	↑2
18	16	**Kentucky** (5-2)	↓6
19	18	**Kansas** (5-3)	↑1
20	19	**Creighton** (7-0)	↑3
21	20	**Xavier** (5-2)	↓8
22	22	**Tulsa** (5-1)	↓5
23	24	**North Carolina** (5-2)	↓1
24	23	**Maryland** (4-3)	↓6
25	—	**Minnesota** (6-1)	⤴
—	25	**NC State** (5-0)	

Week of Dec 24

AP	ESPN/USA	School	AP↓↑
1	3	**Alabama** (8-0)	↑1
2	2	**Pittsburgh** (8-0)	↑2
3	1	**Duke** (6-0)	
4	4	**Arizona** (5-1)	↓3
5	5	**Oklahoma** (6-1)	↑2
6	6	**Connecticut** (7-0)	↑2
7	7	**Illinois** (8-0)	↑5
8	8	**Notre Dame** (10-1)	↑1
9	10	**Texas** (7-2)	↑1
10	11	**Indiana** (8-1)	↓4
11	9	**Oregon** (8-1)	↓6
12	13	**Florida** (8-2)	↑1
13	12	**Marquette** (7-1)	↑1
14	14	**Kentucky** (6-2)	↑4
15	15	**Michigan State** (7-2)	
16	17	**Mississippi State** (7-1)	
17	16	**Missouri** (6-1)	↓6
18	18	**Creighton** (9-0)	↑2
19	19	**Kansas** (6-3)	
20	21	**Tulsa** (6-1)	↑2
21	20	**Xavier** (6-2)	
22	23	**North Carolina** (7-2)	↑1
23	22	**Maryland** (4-3)	↑1
24	—	**LSU** (7-1)	⤴
25	—	**Wake Forest** (6-0)	⤴
—	24	**NC State** (6-1)	
—	25	**Texas Tech** (7-1)	

Week of Dec 31

AP	ESPN/USA	School	AP↓↑
1	3	**Alabama** (9-0)	
2	2	**Pittsburgh** (9-0)	
3	1	**Duke** (7-0)	
4	4	**Arizona** (6-1)	
5	5	**Connecticut** (8-0)	↑1
6	6	**Notre Dame** (10-1)	↑2
7	8	**Texas** (7-2)	↑2
8	10	**Mississippi State** (8-1)	↑8
9	7	**Oregon** (9-1)	↑2
10	11	**Oklahoma** (6-2)	↓5
11	12	**Illinois** (8-1)	↓4
12	13	**Florida** (10-2)	
13	9	**Marquette** (8-1)	
14	14	**Michigan State** (8-2)	↑1
15	15	**Creighton** (10-0)	↑3
16	16	**Missouri** (6-1)	↑1
17	18	**Indiana** (8-2)	↓7
18	17	**Kansas** (7-3)	↑1
19	19	**Xavier** (8-2)	↑2
20	21	**Kentucky** (6-3)	↓6
21	25	**LSU** (8-1)	↑3
22	20	**Maryland** (6-3)	↑1
23	23	**Wake Forest** (7-0)	↑2
24	—	**Louisville** (7-1)	⤴
25	22	**Texas Tech** (8-1)	⤴
—	24	**NC State** (8-1)	

Week of Jan 7

AP	ESPN/USA	School	AP↓↑
1	1	**Duke** (9-0)	↑2
2	2	**Arizona** (9-1)	↑2
3	3	**Connecticut** (9-0)	↑2
4	4	**Alabama** (10-1)	↓3
5	6	**Notre Dame** (12-1)	↑1
6	5	**Pittsburgh** (10-1)	↓4
7	8	**Mississippi State** (10-1)	↑1
8	7	**Texas** (9-2)	↓1
9	9	**Oklahoma** (8-2)	↑1
10	11	**Illinois** (10-1)	↑1
11	12	**Florida** (11-2)	↑1
12	10	**Oregon** (10-2)	↓3
13	13	**Missouri** (8-1)	↑3
14	14	**Kansas** (9-3)	↑4
15	15	**Indiana** (10-2)	↑2
16	16	**Creighton** (11-1)	↓1
17	18	**Wake Forest** (9-0)	↑6
18	19	**Kentucky** (9-3)	↑2
19	25	**Louisville** (8-1)	↑5
20	24	**Georgia** (9-3)	⤴
21	17	**Maryland** (7-3)	↑1
22	22	**Xavier** (9-3)	↓2
23	21	**Texas Tech** (9-1)	↑2
24	23	**Marquette** (8-3)	↓11
25	20	**Michigan State** (8-4)	↓11

Week of Jan 14

AP	ESPN/USA	School	AP↓↑
1	1	**Duke** (11-0)	
2	2	**Arizona** (11-1)	
3	3	**Pittsburgh** (12-1)	↑3
4	4	**Texas** (10-2)	↑4
5	5	**Oklahoma** (10-2)	↑4
6	6	**Connecticut** (10-1)	↓3
6	7	**Florida** (13-2)	↑5
8	8	**Illinois** (12-1)	↑2
9	10	**Alabama** (11-2)	↓5
10	9	**Notre Dame** (13-2)	↓5
11	11	**Missouri** (10-2)	↑2
12	12	**Kansas** (11-3)	↑2
13	14	**Creighton** (13-1)	↑3
14	13	**Mississippi State** (10-3)	↓7
15	18	**Louisville** (10-1)	↑4
16	16	**Kentucky** (11-3)	↑2
17	15	**Maryland** (9-3)	↑4
18	17	**Indiana** (11-3)	↓3
19	20	**Wake Forest** (10-1)	↓2
20	22	**Georgia** (9-4)	
21	21	**Marquette** (10-3)	↑3
22	19	**Oregon** (10-4)	↓10
23	—	**LSU** (11-2)	⤴
24	24	**Oklahoma State** (12-1)	⤴
25	—	**Syracuse** (10-1) (C)	⤴
—	23	**Xavier** (10-4)	⤵
—	25	**Texas Tech** (10-2)	⤵

Week of Jan 21

AP	ESPN/USA	School	AP↓↑
1	1	**Arizona** (13-1)	↑1
2	2	**Pittsburgh** (14-1)	↑1
3	3	**Duke** (12-1)	↓2
4	4	**Texas** (12-2)	
5	5	**Florida** (15-2)	↑1
6	6	**Kansas** (13-3)	↑6
7	7	**Oklahoma** (11-3)	↓2
8	10	**Kentucky** (13-3)	↑8
9	14	**Louisville** (12-1)	↑6
10	9	**Creighton** (15-1)	↑3
11	8	**Connecticut** (11-2)	↓5
12	11	**Maryland** (10-4)	↑5
13	17	**Oklahoma State** (14-1)	↑11
14	16	**Indiana** (13-3)	↑4
15	13	**Alabama** (12-3)	↓6
16	12	**Notre Dame** (14-3)	↓6
17	18	**Wake Forest** (12-1)	↑2
18	15	**Illinois** (12-3)	↓10
19	22	**Georgia** (10-4)	↑1
20	19	**Marquette** (12-3)	↑1
21	20	**Missouri** (10-3)	↓10
22	23	**Mississippi State** (10-4)	↓8
23	21	**Oregon** (12-4)	↓1
24	—	**Auburn** (15-2)	⤴
25	—	**California** (12-2)	⤴
—	24	**Xavier** (12-4)	
—	25	**Texas Tech** (11-2)	

Week of Jan 28

AP	ESPN/USA	School	AP↓↑
1	1	**Arizona** (15-1)	
2	2	**Pittsburgh** (15-1)	
3	3	**Texas** (13-2)	↑1
4	4	**Florida** (16-2)	↑1
5	5	**Duke** (13-2)	↓2
6	6	**Oklahoma** (13-3)	↑1
7	7	**Kentucky** (15-3)	↑1
8	8	**Louisville** (15-1)	↑1
9	11	**Oklahoma State** (16-1)	↑4
10	9	**Maryland** (12-4)	↑2
11	10	**Notre Dame** (16-3)	↑5
12	13	**Kansas** (13-5)	↓6
13	14	**Illinois** (14-3)	↑5
14	12	**Connecticut** (12-3)	↓3
15	17	**Georgia** (12-4)	↑4
16	15	**Creighton** (17-2)	↓6
17	18	**Wake Forest** (13-2)	
18	16	**Marquette** (13-3)	↑2
19	20	**Indiana** (14-4)	↓5
20	24	**California** (14-2)	↑5
21	22	**Mississippi State** (12-4)	↑1
22	19	**Oregon** (14-4)	↑1
23	21	**Alabama** (12-5)	↓8
24	—	**Syracuse** (13-2)	⤴
25	25	**Missouri** (11-4)	↓4
—	23	**Xavier** (14-4)	

Poll Progression Continues →

Week of Feb 4

AP	ESPN/USA	School	AP↓↑
1	1	**Florida** (18-2)	↑3
2	2	**Arizona** (16-2)	↓1
3	3	**Texas** (14-3)	
4	4	**Pittsburgh** (15-2)	↓2
5	6	**Louisville** (16-1)	↑3
6	7	**Kentucky** (16-3)	↑1
7	5	**Oklahoma** (15-3)	↓1
8	8	**Maryland** (14-4)	↑2
9	9	**Duke** (14-3)	↓4
10	10	**Notre Dame** (18-3)	↑1
11	12	**Oklahoma State** (17-2)	↓2
12	11	**Kansas** (15-5)	
13	13	**Creighton** (19-2)	↑3
14	15	**Wake Forest** (15-2)	↑3
15	14	**Marquette** (15-3)	↑3
16	16	**Illinois** (15-4)	↓3
17	18	**Georgia** (13-5)	↓2
18	17	**Connecticut** (13-4)	↓4
19	21	**Syracuse** (14-3)	↑5
20	19	**Xavier** (15-4)	┘
21	22	**Missouri** (13-4)	↑4
22	20	**Alabama** (13-5)	↑1
23	24	**Mississippi State** (13-5)	↓2
24	25	**Purdue** (14-4)	┘
25	—	**Stanford** (16-5)	┘
—	23	**Oregon** (15-5)	┌

Week of Feb 11

AP	ESPN/USA	School	AP↓↑
1	1	**Arizona** (18-2)	↑1
2	2	**Louisville** (18-1)	↑3
3	3	**Kentucky** (18-3)	↑3
4	5	**Florida** (19-3)	↓3
5	4	**Oklahoma** (16-3)	↑2
6	6	**Texas** (15-4)	↓3
7	7	**Pittsburgh** (16-3)	↓3
8	8	**Duke** (16-3)	↑1
9	10	**Kansas** (17-5)	↑3
10	9	**Notre Dame** (19-4)	
11	11	**Marquette** (17-3)	↑4
12	12	**Creighton** (21-2)	↑1
13	14	**Oklahoma State** (18-3)	↓2
14	13	**Illinois** (16-4)	↑2
15	17	**Wake Forest** (16-3)	↓1
16	15	**Maryland** (14-5)	↓8
17	18	**Syracuse** (16-3)	↑2
18	16	**Xavier** (17-4) (D)	↑2
19	20	**Mississippi State** (15-5)	↑4
20	22	**Georgia** (13-6)	↓3
21	21	**Missouri** (14-5)	
22	23	**California** (16-4)	┘
23	19	**Connecticut** (14-5)	↓5
24	24	**Stanford** (17-6)	↑1
25	—	**Saint Joseph's** (17-3)	┘
—	25	**Purdue** (15-5)	┌

Week of Feb 18

AP	ESPN/USA	School	AP↓↑
1	1	**Arizona** (20-2)	
2	2	**Kentucky** (20-3)	↑1
3	4	**Texas** (17-4)	↑3
4	3	**Louisville** (19-2)	↓2
5	5	**Oklahoma** (17-4)	
6	6	**Kansas** (19-5)	↑3
7	7	**Florida** (20-4)	↓3
8	8	**Duke** (17-4)	
9	9	**Pittsburgh** (17-4)	↓2
10	11	**Wake Forest** (17-3)	↑5
11	12	**Marquette** (18-4)	
12	10	**Notre Dame** (19-5)	↓2
13	13	**Maryland** (15-6)	↑3
14	14	**Xavier** (18-4)	↑4
15	17	**Syracuse** (17-4)	↑2
16	16	**Oklahoma State** (19-4)	↓3
17	18	**Creighton** (22-3)	↓5
18	20	**California** (18-4)	↑4
19	19	**Mississippi State** (16-5)	
20	15	**Illinois** (16-5)	↓6
21	21	**Stanford** (19-6)	↑3
22	24	**Georgia** (14-7)	↓2
23	—	**Utah** (19-4)	┘
24	23	**Purdue** (16-6)	┘
25	—	**Dayton** (18-4)	┘
—	22	**Missouri** (15-6)	┌
—	24	**Connecticut** (15-6)	┌

Week of Feb 25

AP	ESPN/USA	School	AP↓↑
1	1	**Arizona** (21-2)	
2	2	**Kentucky** (22-3)	
3	3	**Oklahoma** (19-4)	
4	4	**Florida** (22-4)	
5	6	**Texas** (18-5)	
6	5	**Duke** (19-4)	
7	7	**Kansas** (20-6)	
8	8	**Pittsburgh** (19-4)	
9	10	**Notre Dame** (21-5)	
10	11	**Marquette** (20-4)	
11	9	**Louisville** (19-4)	
12	12	**Wake Forest** (19-4)	
13	13	**Xavier** (20-4)	
14	14	**Maryland** (17-7)	
15	15	**Syracuse** (19-4)	
16	17	**Oklahoma State** (20-5)	
17	18	**Creighton** (24-3)	
18	16	**Illinois** (18-5)	↑
19	19	**Stanford** (21-6)	↑
20	20	**Mississippi State** (17-6)	↓
21	22	**Georgia** (16-7)	↑
22	23	**Utah** (20-4)	↑
23	21	**California** (19-5)	↓
24	—	**Memphis** (18-5)	┘
25	25	**Dayton** (19-5)	
—	24	**Connecticut** (17-6)	

Week of Mar 4 (E)

AP	ESPN/USA	School	AP↓↑
1	1	**Arizona** (23-2)	
2	2	**Kentucky** (24-3)	
3	3	**Florida** (24-4)	↑1
4	4	**Texas** (20-5)	↑1
5	5	**Oklahoma** (20-5)	↓2
6	6	**Kansas** (22-6)	↑1
7	7	**Pittsburgh** (21-4)	↑1
8	8	**Marquette** (22-4)	↑2
9	10	**Wake Forest** (21-4)	↑3
10	9	**Duke** (20-5)	↓4
11	11	**Xavier** (22-4)	↑2
12	12	**Syracuse** (21-4)	↑3
13	12	**Maryland** (19-7)	↑1
14	14	**Illinois** (20-5)	↑4
15	15	**Louisville** (20-5) (F)	↓4
16	16	**Notre Dame** (21-7)	↓7
17	17	**Stanford** (22-7)	↑2
18	—	**Memphis** (20-5)	↑6
19	19	**Creighton** (25-4)	↓2
20	18	**Oklahoma State** (20-7)	↓4
21	22	**Dayton** (21-5)	↑4
22	20	**California** (20-6)	↑1
23	21	**Mississippi State** (18-7)	↓3
24	24	**Wisconsin** (21-6)	┘
25	25	**Georgia** (17-8)	↓4
—	23	**Utah** (22-5)	┌

Week of Mar 11

AP	ESPN/USA	School	AP↓↑
1	1	**Arizona** (25-2)	
2	2	**Kentucky** (26-3) (G)	
3	3	**Texas** (22-5)	↑1
4	4	**Kansas** (24-6)	↑2
5	5	**Pittsburgh** (23-4)	↑2
6	6	**Oklahoma** (21-6)	↓1
7	7	**Florida** (24-6)	↓4
8	8	**Marquette** (23-4)	
9	9	**Wake Forest** (23-4)	
10	10	**Xavier** (24-4)	↑1
11	11	**Syracuse** (23-4)	↑1
12	12	**Duke** (21-6)	↓2
13	13	**Illinois** (21-6)	↑1
14	15	**Maryland** (19-8)	↓1
15	14	**Stanford** (23-7)	↑2
16	24	**Memphis** (22-5)	↑2
17	19	**Notre Dame** (22-8)	↓1
18	18	**Wisconsin** (22-6)	↑6
19	17	**Creighton** (26-4)	
20	16	**Louisville** (21-6)	↓5
21	22	**Georgia** (19-8)	↑4
22	21	**Dayton** (21-5)	↓1
23	20	**Oklahoma State** (21-6)	↓3
24	23	**California** (20-7)	↓2
25	—	**Saint Joseph's** (22-5)	┘
—	25	**Mississippi State** (19-8)	┌

Week of Mar 18

AP	ESPN/USA	School	AP↓↑
1	1	**Kentucky** (29-3)	↑1
2	2	**Arizona** (25-3)	↓1
3	3	**Oklahoma** (24-6)	↑3
4	4	**Pittsburgh** (26-4)	↑1
5	5	**Texas** (22-6)	↓2
6	6	**Kansas** (25-7)	↓2
7	7	**Duke** (24-6)	↑5
8	9	**Wake Forest** (24-5)	↑1
9	11	**Marquette** (23-5)	↓1
10	8	**Florida** (24-7)	↓3
11	10	**Illinois** (24-6)	↑2
12	14	**Xavier** (25-5)	↓2
13	12	**Syracuse** (24-5)	↓2
14	13	**Louisville** (24-6)	↑6
15	15	**Creighton** (29-4)	↑4
16	18	**Dayton** (24-5)	↑6
17	17	**Maryland** (19-9)	↓3
18	16	**Stanford** (23-8)	↓3
19	22	**Memphis** (23-6)	↓3
20	21	**Mississippi State** (21-9)	┘
21	19	**Wisconsin** (22-7)	↓3
22	20	**Notre Dame** (22-9)	↓5
23	24	**Connecticut** (21-9)	┘
24	25	**Missouri** (21-10)	┘
25	—	**Georgia** (19-8)	↓4
—	23	**Oklahoma State** (21-9)	┌

Final Poll (Post-Tournament

ESPN/USA	School
1	**Syracuse** (30-5)
2	**Kansas** (30-8)
3	**Texas** (26-7)
4	**Kentucky** (32-4)
5	**Arizona** (28-4)
6	**Marquette** (27-6)
7	**Oklahoma** (27-7)
8	**Pittsburgh** (28-5)
9	**Duke** (26-7)
10	**Maryland** (21-10)
11	**Connecticut** (23-10)
12	**Wake Forest** (25-6)
13	**Illinois** (25-7)
13	**Wisconsin** (24-8)
15	**Notre Dame** (24-10)
16	**Florida** (25-8)
17	**Xavier** (26-6)
18	**Michigan State** (22-13)
19	**Louisville** (25-7)
20	**Stanford** (24-9)
21	**Butler** (27-6)
22	**Missouri** (22-11)
23	**Creighton** (29-5)
24	**Oklahoma State** (22-10)
25	**Dayton** (25-6)

(A) In a rematch of the 2002 NCAA Final, referees rule that a half-court shot by Maryland's Steve Blake did not beat the buzzer at the end of regulation, enabling Indiana to defeat the Terrapins in overtime, 80-74.

(B) On successive nights, Notre Dame stuns two Top-10 teams: defending champion Maryland and Texas. The Irish become the third team to jump from unranked on the AP poll to No. 10.

(C) After beating No. 13 Missouri, 76-69, on Jan. 13, Syracuse makes its first appearance in this season's polls. The Orangemen are led by Carmelo Anthony, who will set an NCAA freshman record with 22 double-doubles during the season. (His record will be broken in 2007-08 by fellow one-and-done frosh Michael Beasley of Kansas State, who gets 28.)

(D) David West scores a career-high 47 in Xavier's 85-77 win over Dayton on Feb. 8. The 6'9" West will be named Player of the Year by both the AP and the U.S. Basketball Writers Association.

(E) UCLA finishes the season 10–19, ending at 54 the Bruins' run of consecutive winning seasons (1949-2002)—an NCAA record.

(F) After rising to No. 2 in the AP poll the week of Feb. 11, Louisville loses four of its next five games, culminating with a 78-73 loss to Marquette at home.

(G) Kentucky defeats Florida, 69-67, on March 8 in Gainesville to complete a 16–0 run through the SEC. The Wildcats take a 23-game winning streak into the NCAA Tournament.

Pre-Tournament Ratings Percentage Index (RPI)

Rank	School	W-L	Sched. Strg.	SS Rank	RPI
1	**Kentucky**	29-3	.5824	25	.6693
2	**Arizona**	25-3	.5784	30	.6555
3	**Oklahoma**	24-6	.6169	3	.6530
4	**Texas**	22-6	.6149	4	.6491
5	**Georgia**	19-8	.6379	1	.6434
6	**Kansas**	23-7	.6093	8	.6399
7	**Syracuse**	24-5	.5749	35	.6321
8	**Wake Forest**	24-5	.5735	38	.6320
9	**Marquette**	23-5	.5733	39	.6313
10	**Louisville**	24-6	.5784	29	.6308
11	**Pittsburgh**	26-4	.5537	58	.6304
12	**Duke**	24-6	.5722	42	.6266
13	**Dayton**	24-5	.5614	50	.6230
14	**Notre Dame**	22-9	.6121	6	.6230
15	**Florida**	24-7	.5726	41	.6210
16	**Xavier**	25-5	.5418	71	.6193
17	**Utah**	23-7	.5809	27	.6181
18	**Stanford**	23-8	.5832	24	.6180
19	**Missouri**	21-10	.6127	5	.6173
20	**Illinois**	24-6	.5545	56	.6145
21	**BYU**	23-8	.5883	18	.6139
22	**Oklahoma State**	20-9	.5946	13	.6129
23	**Creighton**	29-4	.5172	114	.6087
24	**Mississippi State**	21-9	.5867	20	.6077
25	**Wisconsin**	22-7	.5544	57	.6034
26	**Memphis**	23-6	.5344	82	.6029
27	**Saint Joseph's**	23-6	.5301	85	.5956
28	**Connecticut**	21-9	.5638	48	.5943
29	**Purdue**	18-10	.5862	21	.5938
30	**Cincinnati**	17-11	.6103	7	.5938
31	**Michigan State**	19-12	.5959	12	.5922
32	**Arizona State**	18-11	.5941	14	.5906
33	**California**	21-8	.5398	76	.5894
34	**Southern Illinois**	24-6	.5174	113	.5875
35	**Butler**	24-5	.5048	136	.5869
36	**Alabama**	17-11	.5781	31	.5848
37	**Maryland**	19-9	.5569	55	.5841
38	**Auburn**	19-11	.5820	26	.5837
39	**LSU**	21-10	.5495	62	.5822
40	**UNLV**	21-10	.5532	59	.5818
41	**Seton Hall**	17-12	.5967	11	.5815
42	**Colorado**	20-11	.5581	54	.5802
43	**Texas Tech**	18-12	.5759	34	.5796
44	**Indiana**	20-12	.5640	47	.5795
45	**Gonzaga**	23-8	.5275	89	.5793
46	**Weber State**	25-4	.4833	188	.5775
47	**Boston College**	18-11	.5772	33	.5763
48	**Central Michigan**	23-6	.5064	134	.5762
49	**Wisconsin-Milwaukee**	23-7	.5237	104	.5754
50	**North Carolina**	17-15	.6037	10	.5750

Source: Collegiate Basketball News

2003 NCAA Tournament

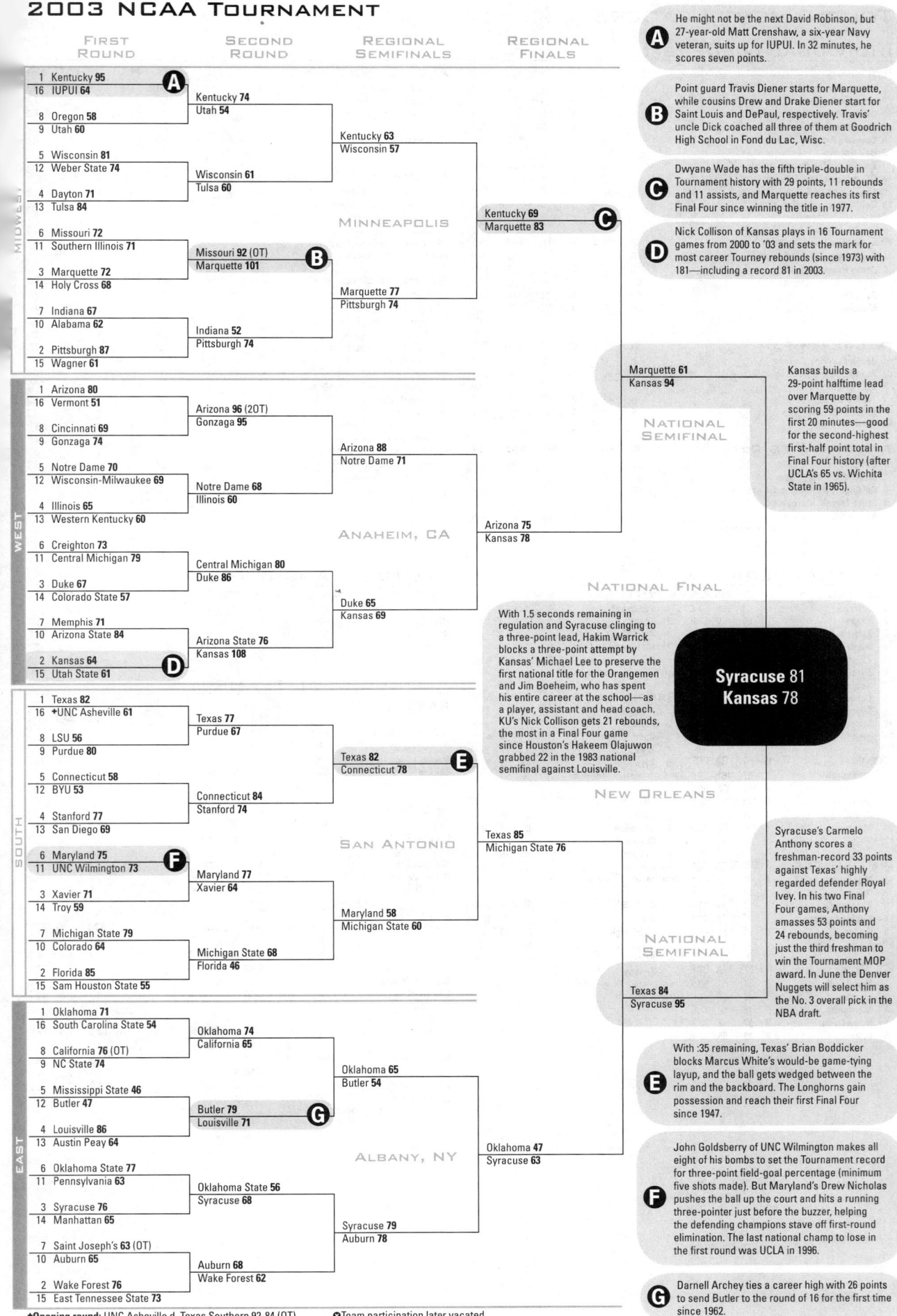

Midwest (Minneapolis)

First Round
- 1 Kentucky **95**, 16 IUPUI **64** (A)
- 8 Oregon **58**, 9 Utah **60**
- 5 Wisconsin **81**, 12 Weber State **74**
- 4 Dayton **71**, 13 Tulsa **84**
- 6 Missouri **72**, 11 Southern Illinois **71**
- 3 Marquette **72**, 14 Holy Cross **68**
- 7 Indiana **67**, 10 Alabama **62**
- 2 Pittsburgh **87**, 15 Wagner **61**

Second Round
- Kentucky **74**, Utah **54**
- Wisconsin **61**, Tulsa **60**
- Missouri **92** (OT), Marquette **101** (B)
- Indiana **52**, Pittsburgh **74**

Regional Semifinals
- Kentucky **63**, Wisconsin **57**
- Marquette **77**, Pittsburgh **74**

Regional Finals
- Kentucky **69**, Marquette **83** (C)

West (Anaheim, CA)

First Round
- 1 Arizona **80**, 16 Vermont **51**
- 8 Cincinnati **69**, 9 Gonzaga **74**
- 5 Notre Dame **70**, 12 Wisconsin-Milwaukee **69**
- 4 Illinois **65**, 13 Western Kentucky **60**
- 6 Creighton **73**, 11 Central Michigan **79**
- 3 Duke **67**, 14 Colorado State **57**
- 7 Memphis **71**, 10 Arizona State **84**
- 2 Kansas **64**, 15 Utah State **61** (D)

Second Round
- Arizona **96** (2OT), Gonzaga **95**
- Notre Dame **68**, Illinois **60**
- Central Michigan **80**, Duke **86**
- Arizona State **76**, Kansas **108**

Regional Semifinals
- Arizona **88**, Notre Dame **71**
- Duke **65**, Kansas **69**

Regional Finals
- Arizona **75**, Kansas **78**

South (San Antonio)

First Round
- 1 Texas **82**, 16 +UNC Asheville **61**
- 8 LSU **56**, 9 Purdue **80**
- 5 Connecticut **58**, 12 BYU **53**
- 4 Stanford **77**, 13 San Diego **69**
- 6 Maryland **75**, 11 UNC Wilmington **73** (F)
- 3 Xavier **71**, 14 Troy **59**
- 7 Michigan State **79**, 10 Colorado **64**
- 2 Florida **85**, 15 Sam Houston State **55**

Second Round
- Texas **77**, Purdue **67**
- Connecticut **84**, Stanford **74**
- Maryland **77**, Xavier **64**
- Michigan State **68**, Florida **46**

Regional Semifinals
- Texas **82**, Connecticut **78** (E)
- Maryland **58**, Michigan State **60**

Regional Finals
- Texas **85**, Michigan State **76**

East (Albany, NY)

First Round
- 1 Oklahoma **71**, 16 South Carolina State **54**
- 8 California **76** (OT), 9 NC State **74**
- 5 Mississippi State **46**, 12 Butler **47**
- 4 Louisville **86**, 13 Austin Peay **64**
- 6 Oklahoma State **77**, 11 Pennsylvania **63**
- 3 Syracuse **76**, 14 Manhattan **65**
- 7 Saint Joseph's **63** (OT), 10 Auburn **65**
- 2 Wake Forest **76**, 15 East Tennessee State **73**

Second Round
- Oklahoma **74**, California **65**
- Butler **79**, Louisville **71** (G)
- Oklahoma State **56**, Syracuse **68**
- Auburn **68**, Wake Forest **62**

Regional Semifinals
- Oklahoma **65**, Butler **54**
- Syracuse **79**, Auburn **78**

Regional Finals
- Oklahoma **47**, Syracuse **63**

National Semifinal (New Orleans)
- Marquette **61**, Kansas **94**
- Texas **84**, Syracuse **95**

National Final
Syracuse 81, Kansas 78

+**Opening round:** UNC Asheville d. Texas Southern 92-84 (OT)

✪Team participation later vacated

A He might not be the next David Robinson, but 27-year-old Matt Crenshaw, a six-year Navy veteran, suits up for IUPUI. In 32 minutes, he scores seven points.

B Point guard Travis Diener starts for Marquette, while cousins Drew and Drake Diener start for Saint Louis and DePaul, respectively. Travis' uncle Dick coached all three of them at Goodrich High School in Fond du Lac, Wisc.

C Dwyane Wade has the fifth triple-double in Tournament history with 29 points, 11 rebounds and 11 assists, and Marquette reaches its first Final Four since winning the title in 1977.

D Nick Collison of Kansas plays in 16 Tournament games from 2000 to '03 and sets the mark for most career Tourney rebounds (since 1973) with 181—including a record 81 in 2003.

Kansas builds a 29-point halftime lead over Marquette by scoring 59 points in the first 20 minutes—good for the second-highest first-half point total in Final Four history (after UCLA's 65 vs. Wichita State in 1965).

With 1.5 seconds remaining in regulation and Syracuse clinging to a three-point lead, Hakim Warrick blocks a three-point attempt by Kansas' Michael Lee to preserve the first national title for the Orangemen and Jim Boeheim, who has spent his entire career at the school—as a player, assistant and head coach. KU's Nick Collison gets 21 rebounds, the most in a Final Four game since Houston's Hakeem Olajuwon grabbed 22 in the 1983 national semifinal against Louisville.

Syracuse's Carmelo Anthony scores a freshman-record 33 points against Texas' highly regarded defender Royal Ivey. In his two Final Four games, Anthony amasses 53 points and 24 rebounds, becoming just the third freshman to win the Tournament MOP award. In June the Denver Nuggets will select him as the No. 3 overall pick in the NBA draft.

E With :35 remaining, Texas' Brian Boddicker blocks Marcus White's would-be game-tying layup, and the ball gets wedged between the rim and the backboard. The Longhorns gain possession and reach their first Final Four since 1947.

F John Goldsberry of UNC Wilmington makes all eight of his bombs to set the Tournament record for three-point field-goal percentage (minimum five shots made). But Maryland's Drew Nicholas pushes the ball up the court and hits a running three-pointer just before the buzzer, helping the defending champions stave off first-round elimination. The last national champ to lose in the first round was UCLA in 1996.

G Darnell Archey ties a career high with 26 points to send Butler to the round of 16 for the first time since 1962.

Tournament Leaders

INDIVIDUAL LEADERS

Scoring	CL	POS	G	PTS	PPG
1 **Dahntay Jones**, Duke	SR	F	3	74	24.7
2 **Marquis Daniels**, Auburn	SR	G	3	70	23.3
3 **Dwyane Wade**, Marquette	JR	G	5	109	21.8
4 **Chris Thomas**, Notre Dame	SO	G	3	64	21.3
5 **Carmelo Anthony**, Syracuse	FR	F	6	121	20.2
6 **Ben Gordon**, Connecticut	SO	G	3	59	19.7
Emeka Okafor, Connecticut	SO	C	3	59	19.7
8 **Drew Nicholas**, Maryland	SR	G	3	57	19.0
9 **Nick Collison**, Kansas	SR	F	6	112	18.7
10 **Keith Langford**, Kansas	SO	G	6	109	18.2

Minimum: 3 games

Field Goal Pct	CL	POS	G	FG	FGA	PCT
1 **Kevin Bookout**, Oklahoma	FR	F	4	18	25	72.0
2 **Jaron Brown**, Pittsburgh	JR	G	3	18	27	66.7
3 **Nick Collison**, Kansas	SR	F	6	48	74	64.9
4 **Josh Pace**, Syracuse	SO	G	6	23	36	63.9
5 **Marquis Estill**, Kentucky	SR	F/C	4	30	47	63.8

Minimum: 15 made and 3 games

Free Throw Pct	CL	POS	G	FT	FTA	PCT
1 **Jason Gardner**, Arizona	SR	G	4	20	21	95.2
2 **Alan Anderson**, Michigan State	SO	G	4	16	18	88.9
3 **T.J. Ford**, Texas	SO	G	5	34	39	87.2
4 **Torin Francis**, Notre Dame	FR	F	3	16	19	84.2
Dahntay Jones, Duke	SR	F	3	16	19	84.2

Minimum: 15 made

Three-Point FG Pct	CL	POS	G	3FG	3FGA	PCT
1 **Darnell Archey**, Butler	SR	G	3	11	16	68.8
2 **Mike Monserez**, Butler	JR	G	3	7	12	58.3
3 **De'Angelo Alexander**, Oklahoma	FR	G	4	8	14	57.1
4 **Steve Novak**, Marquette	FR	F	5	14	25	56.0
5 **Michael Lee**, Kansas	SO	G	6	6	11	54.5

Minimum: 6 made and 3 games

Assists Per Game	CL	POS	G	AST	APG
1 **T.J. Ford**, Texas	SO	G	5	51	10.2
2 **Luke Walton**, Arizona	SR	F	4	29	7.3
3 **Brandin Knight**, Pittsburgh	SR	G	3	21	7.0
4 **Steve Blake**, Maryland	SR	G	3	19	6.3
5 **Aaron Miles**, Kansas	SO	G	6	37	6.2

Minimum: 3 games

Rebounds Per Game	CL	POS	G	REB	RPG
1 **Nick Collison**, Kansas	SR	F	6	81	13.5
2 **Emeka Okafor**, Connecticut	SO	C	3	40	13.3
3 **Torin Francis**, Notre Dame	FR	F	3	38	12.7
4 **Channing Frye**, Arizona	SO	C	4	41	10.3
5 **Carmelo Anthony**, Syracuse	FR	F	6	59	9.8

Minimum: 3 games

Blocked Shots Per Game	CL	POS	G	BLK	BPG
1 **Emeka Okafor**, Connecticut	SO	C	3	14	4.7
2 **Kyle Davis**, Auburn	JR	C	3	12	4.0
Casey Sanders, Duke	SR	C	3	12	4.0
4 **Nick Collison**, Kansas	SR	F	6	15	2.5
Channing Frye, Arizona	SO	C	4	10	2.5

Minimum: 3 games

Steals Per Game	CL	POS	G	STL	SPG
1 **Chris Duhon**, Duke	JR	G	3	10	3.3
Devin Harris, Wisconsin	SO	G	3	10	3.3
3 **Steve Blake**, Maryland	SR	G	3	9	3.0
4 **Gerry McNamara**, Syracuse	FR	G	6	15	2.5
5 **Marquis Daniels**, Auburn	SR	G	3	7	2.3
Brandin Knight, Pittsburgh	SR	G	3	7	2.3

Minimum: 3 games

TEAM LEADERS

Scoring	G	PTS	PPG
1 **Arizona**	4	339	84.8
2 **Texas**	5	410	82.0
3 **Kansas**	6	491	81.8
4 **Marquette**	5	394	78.8
5 **Pittsburgh**	3	235	78.3
6 **Syracuse**	6	462	77.0
7 **Kentucky**	4	301	75.3
8 **Connecticut**	3	221	73.7
9 **Duke**	3	218	72.7
10 **Michigan State**	4	283	70.8

Minimum: 3 games

FG Pct	G	FG	FGA	PCT
1 **Pittsburgh**	3	87	161	54.0
2 **Kansas**	6	195	386	50.5
3 **Syracuse**	6	172	342	50.3
4 **Kentucky**	4	115	233	49.4
5 **Marquette**	5	139	296	47.0

Minimum: 3 games

3-Pt FG Pct	G	3FG	3FGA	PCT
1 **Marquette**	5	40	81	49.4
2 **Duke**	3	24	54	44.4
3 **Pittsburgh**	3	17	39	43.6
4 **Michigan State**	4	27	62	43.5
5 **Butler**	3	23	53	43.4

Minimum: 3 games

FT Pct	G	FT	FTA	PCT
1 **Maryland**	3	41	50	82.0
2 **Arizona**	4	60	77	77.9
3 **Marquette**	5	76	98	77.5
4 **Notre Dame**	3	37	48	77.1
5 **Duke**	3	42	55	76.4

Minimum: 3 games

Ast/TO Ratio	G	AST	TO	RAT
1 **Pittsburgh**	3	56	30	1.87
2 **Texas**	5	72	49	1.47
3 **Arizona**	4	75	54	1.39
4 **Marquette**	5	76	56	1.36
5 **Wisconsin**	3	37	29	1.28

Minimum: 3 games

Rebounds	G	REB	RPG
1 **Arizona**	4	174	43.5
2 **Kansas**	6	252	42.0
3 **Connecticut**	3	124	41.3
4 **Texas**	5	197	39.4
5 **Syracuse**	6	230	38.3

Minimum: 3 games

Blocks	G	BLK	BPG
1 **Duke**	3	24	8.0
2 **Syracuse**	6	36	6.0
3 **Connecticut**	3	17	5.7
4 **Auburn**	3	16	5.3
5 **Kansas**	6	29	4.8

Minimum: 3 games

Steals	G	STL	SPG
1 **Duke**	3	31	10.3
2 **Pittsburgh**	3	29	9.7
3 **Syracuse**	6	57	9.5
4 **Arizona**	4	37	9.3
5 **Kansas**	6	48	8.0

Minimum: 3 games

ALL-TOURNAMENT TEAM

PLAYER	CL	POS	HT	SCHOOL	RPG	APG	PPG
Carmelo Anthony*	FR	F	6-8	Syracuse	9.8	2.5	20.2
Nick Collison	SR	F	6-9	Kansas	13.5	3.7	18.7
Kirk Hinrich	SR	G	6-3	Kansas	3.2	3.0	16.0
Keith Langford	SO	G	6-4	Kansas	4.5	1.3	18.2
Gerry McNamara	FR	G	6-2	Syracuse	1.8	3.5	13.3

ALL-REGIONAL TEAMS

EAST

PLAYER	CL	POS	HT	SCHOOL	RPG	APG	PPG
Carmelo Anthony*	FR	F	6-8	Syracuse	8.8	1.8	17.0
Joel Cornette	SR	F/C	6-9	Butler	8.0	2.3	14.7
Marquis Daniels	SR	G	6-6	Auburn	7.0	3.0	23.3
Ebi Ere	SR	G	6-5	Oklahoma	6.0	1.3	11.0
Hakim Warrick	SO	F	6-9	Syracuse	6.0	2.3	12.3

MIDWEST

PLAYER	CL	POS	HT	SCHOOL	RPG	APG	PPG
Dwyane Wade*	JR	G	6-4	Marquette	6.8	6.5	22.5
Keith Bogans	SR	G	6-5	Kentucky	2.8	1.0	12.8
Marquis Estill	SR	F/C	6-9	Kentucky	7.3	0.8	17.3
Robert Jackson	SR	F	6-10	Marquette	8.0	1.8	13.0
Steve Novak	FR	F	6-10	Marquette	1.5	0.5	11.8

SOUTH

PLAYER	CL	POS	HT	SCHOOL	RPG	APG	PPG
T.J. Ford*	SO	G	5-10	Texas	5.3	9.5	15.3
Paul Davis	FR	C	6-11	Michigan State	5.3	0.5	11.5
Erazem Lorbek	FR	F	6-10	Michigan State	5.5	0.5	12.0
Brandon Mouton	JR	G	6-4	Texas	3.0	1.0	16.0
Emeka Okafor	SO	C	6-10	Connecticut	13.3	0.0	19.7

WEST

PLAYER	CL	POS	HT	SCHOOL	RPG	APG	PPG
Kirk Hinrich*	SR	G	6-3	Kansas	4.0	2.8	15.5
Nick Collison	SR	F	6-9	Kansas	11.3	3.5	20.3
Jason Gardner	SR	G	5-10	Arizona	3.5	5.0	17.0
Keith Langford	SO	G	6-4	Kansas	5.0	1.0	16.8
Luke Walton	SR	F	6-8	Arizona	7.3	7.3	15.5

* Most outstanding player

2003 NCAA TOURNAMENT BOX SCORES

Kentucky 63, Wisconsin 57 (Sweet 16)

		1H	2H
Kentucky		32	31
Wisconsin		28	29

KENTUCKY	MIN	FG	3FG	FT	REB	A	ST	BL	PF	TP
Marquis Estill	32	12-18	0-0	4-10	6	0	-	1	3	28
Erik Daniels	32	2-3	0-0	5-6	6	2	-	0	1	9
Gerald Fitch	31	3-7	0-1	1-2	1	1	-	0	2	7
Keith Bogans	15	2-6	1-2	0-0	2	1	-	1	0	5
Cliff Hawkins	28	1-4	0-1	2-2	1	2	-	1	3	4
Chuck Hayes	28	2-5	0-0	0-0	7	0	-	1	2	4
Jules Camara	10	2-2	0-0	0-2	3	1	-	0	3	4
Antwain Barbour	15	0-2	0-0	2-2	2	1	-	0	0	2
Kelenna Azubuike	9	0-2	0-1	0-0	0	1	-	0	3	0
TOTALS	**200**	**24-49**	**1-5**	**14-24**	**28**	**9**	**-**	**4**	**17**	**63**
Percentages		49.0	20.0	58.3						

Coach: Tubby Smith

WISCONSIN	MIN	FG	3FG	FT	REB	A	ST	BL	PF	TP
Kirk Penney	40	6-12	5-7	3-4	6	3	0	0	2	20
Devin Harris	36	6-9	1-2	2-3	3	4	3	0	4	15
Michael Wilkinson	35	4-11	1-5	4-7	3	1	2	0	5	13
Alando Tucker	36	1-4	0-1	2-2	7	0	1	0	3	4
Boo Wade	18	1-1	1-1	0-0	2	1	1	0	0	3
Freddie Owens	27	1-8	0-5	0-0	2	0	0	0	2	2
Dave Mader	5	0-0	0-0	0-0	1	0	0	1	4	0
Andreas Helmigk	3	0-0	0-0	0-0	0	0	0	0	0	0
TOTALS	**200**	**19-45**	**8-21**	**11-16**	**24**	**9**	**7**	**1**	**20**	**57**
Percentages		42.2	38.1	68.8						

Coach: Bo Ryan

Officials: Frank Scagliotta, Jim Haney, Bob Donato
Technicals: None
Attendance: 28,168

Marquette 77, Pittsburgh 74 (Sweet 16)

		1H	2H
Marquette		34	43
Pittsburgh		34	40

MARQUETTE	MIN	FG	3FG	FT	REB	A	ST	BL	PF	TP
Dwyane Wade	29	10-19	0-1	2-3	3	4	3	1	2	22
Scott Merritt	34	4-6	0-0	9-11	3	0	1	0	4	17
Robert Jackson	36	6-8	0-0	4-6	4	1	1	0	2	16
Steve Novak	16	3-6	3-5	0-0	3	1	0	0	4	9
KaRon Bradley	11	2-4	2-2	0-0	1	1	1	0	1	6
Travis Diener	36	2-8	0-2	0-2	2	8	1	1	1	4
Todd Towsend	25	1-2	1-2	0-0	5	0	0	0	2	3
Terry Sanders	8	0-1	0-0	0-0	2	1	0	1	2	0
Joe Chapman	5	0-0	0-0	0-0	1	0	0	0	0	0
TOTALS	**200**	**28-54**	**6-12**	**15-22**	**24**	**16**	**7**	**3**	**18**	**77**
Percentages		51.9	50.0	68.2						

Coach: Tom Crean

PITTSBURGH	MIN	FG	3FG	FT	REB	A	ST	BL	PF	TP
Brandin Knight	36	6-13	2-7	2-2	1	11	1	0	4	16
Chevon Troutman	34	6-7	0-0	3-3	5	2	1	0	3	15
Jaron Brown	32	5-10	0-2	4-6	6	0	0	3	2	14
Julius Page	38	5-11	1-4	1-2	0	4	1	0	2	12
Ontario Lett	21	2-7	0-0	2-2	6	0	0	1	4	6
Donatas Zavackas	17	2-2	1-1	0-0	5	0	0	0	2	5
Carl Krauser	17	2-4	0-0	0-0	2	1	2	0	1	4
Toree Morris	5	1-1	0-0	0-0	0	0	1	0	1	2
TOTALS	**200**	**29-55**	**4-14**	**12-15**	**25**	**18**	**6**	**4**	**19**	**74**
Percentages		52.7	28.6	80.0						

Coach: Ben Howland

Officials: Dick Cartmell, Ed Hightower, Eddie Jackson
Technicals: None
Attendance: 28,168

Arizona 88, Notre Dame 71 (Sweet 16)

		1H	2H
Arizona		53	35
Notre Dame		40	31

ARIZONA	MIN	FG	3FG	FT	REB	A	ST	BL	PF	TP
Jason Gardner	34	6-12	3-5	4-4	2	6	3	0	1	19
Luke Walton	32	7-14	0-0	2-2	7	8	0	1	3	16
Channing Frye	33	7-17	0-0	0-0	12	0	1	3	2	14
Hassan Adams	22	7-9	0-1	0-0	4	1	3	0	0	14
Salim Stoudamire	19	4-6	3-4	0-0	1	2	0	0	5	11
Rick Anderson	31	3-9	1-2	2-3	12	2	1	0	3	9
Andre Iguodala	19	1-5	0-1	1-2	3	0	2	1	2	3
Chris Rodgers	3	1-1	0-0	0-0	1	0	2	0	0	2
Isaiah Fox	4	0-2	0-0	0-0	1	0	0	0	1	0
Jason Ranne	2	0-1	0-1	0-0	0	0	0	0	0	0
Fil Torres	1	0-0	0-0	0-0	0	0	0	0	0	0
TOTALS	**200**	**36-76**	**7-14**	**9-11**	**43**	**19**	**12**	**5**	**17**	**88**
Percentages		47.4	50.0	81.8						

Coach: Lute Olson

NOTRE DAME	MIN	FG	3FG	FT	REB	A	ST	BL	PF	TP
Torin Francis	40	10-11	1-1	4-6	10	0	0	2	0	25
Chris Thomas	40	6-14	3-5	5-5	5	5	3	0	2	20
Danny Miller	33	4-13	2-6	1-2	7	1	0	0	3	11
Matt Carroll	28	4-14	3-7	0-1	4	2	1	0	1	11
Chris Quinn	11	1-2	1-1	0-0	0	1	1	0	1	3
Jordan Cornette	24	0-2	0-2	1-2	4	4	0	2	5	1
Torrian Jones	11	0-2	0-1	0-2	0	1	1	0	1	0
Tom Timmermans	10	0-1	0-0	0-0	2	1	0	0	3	0
Rick Cornett	2	0-0	0-0	0-0	0	0	0	0	0	0
Dan Lustig	1	0-0	0-0	0-0	0	0	0	0	0	0
TOTALS	**200**	**25-59**	**10-23**	**11-18**	**32**	**15**	**6**	**4**	**16**	**71**
Percentages		42.4	43.5	61.1						

Coach: Mike Brey

Officials: Emanuel Upton, Larry Rose, Mark Whitehead
Technicals: None
Attendance: 17,607

Kansas 69, Duke 65 (Sweet 16)

		1H	2H
Kansas		35	34
Duke		35	30

KANSAS	MIN	FG	3FG	FT	REB	A	ST	BL	PF	TP
Nick Collison	40	14-22	0-0	5-7	19	4	1	3	1	33
Keith Langford	37	5-17	0-3	3-4	8	0	0	1	2	13
Aaron Miles	33	2-8	1-4	1-2	2	7	1	0	3	6
Jeff Graves	17	3-5	0-0	0-2	7	1	1	0	4	6
Michael Lee	25	2-3	0-0	1-2	2	0	0	0	1	5
Bryant Nash	15	2-3	0-0	0-0	3	0	0	1	1	4
Kirk Hinrich	33	1-9	0-5	0-0	3	2	1	0	4	2
TOTALS	**200**	**29-67**	**1-12**	**10-17**	**44**	**14**	**4**	**5**	**16**	**69**
Percentages		43.3	8.3	58.8						

Coach: Roy Williams

DUKE	MIN	FG	3FG	FT	REB	A	ST	BL	PF	TP
Dahntay Jones	35	9-22	4-7	1-2	7	1	1	1	3	23
Daniel Ewing	35	5-12	2-4	1-2	3	2	2	0	4	13
Chris Duhon	40	5-7	2-3	0-0	6	3	0	0	2	12
J.J. Redick	37	2-16	1-11	0-0	3	4	1	0	2	5
Casey Sanders	28	1-2	0-0	3-4	7	1	1	5	3	5
Shelden Williams	13	2-4	0-0	0-0	3	0	0	1	2	4
Sean Dockery	10	1-2	1-1	0-0	1	0	1	0	0	3
Lee Melchionni	1	0-0	0-0	0-0	0	0	0	0	0	0
Michael Thompson	1	0-0	0-0	0-0	0	0	0	0	2	0
TOTALS	**200**	**25-65**	**10-26**	**5-8**	**30**	**11**	**6**	**7**	**18**	**65**
Percentages		38.5	38.5	62.5						

Coach: Mike Krzyzewski

Officials: Donnee Gray, James Burr, Tom Lopes
Technicals: None
Attendance: 17,607

Texas 82, Connecticut 78 (Sweet 16)

		1H	2H
Texas		44	38
Connecticut		38	40

TEXAS	MIN	FG	3FG	FT	REB	A	ST	BL	PF	TP
Brandon Mouton	34	10-18	4-7	3-4	5	0	1	1	2	27
T.J. Ford	35	3-15	0-4	7-7	4	9	2	0	4	13
James Thomas	29	2-9	0-0	9-13	15	0	0	1	2	13
Royal Ivey	34	2-6	0-0	6-6	6	1	0	1	3	10
Brian Boddicker	17	2-5	1-4	1-2	4	1	0	1	4	6
Jason Klotz	10	3-6	0-0	0-0	4	0	0	0	2	6
Deginald Erskin	9	1-4	0-0	3-4	4	0	0	1	0	5
Brad Buckman	16	1-3	0-0	0-0	6	1	2	0	1	2
Sydmill Harris	11	0-3	0-3	0-0	0	0	0	0	3	0
Terrell Ross	5	0-0	0-0	0-0	0	1	0	0	0	0
TOTALS	**200**	**24-69**	**5-18**	**29-36**	**48**	**13**	**5**	**5**	**21**	**82**
Percentages		34.8	27.8	80.6						

Coach: Rick Barnes

CONNECTICUT	MIN	FG	3FG	FT	REB	A	ST	BL	PF	TP
Emeka Okafor	35	8-16	0-0	5-6	17	0	0	6	4	21
Ben Gordon	26	6-15	2-6	2-4	1	0	2	0	4	16
Taliek Brown	31	4-10	0-0	1-3	3	7	2	0	2	9
Rashad Anderson	21	3-10	2-6	0-1	5	1	0	0	2	8
Denham Brown	20	4-6	0-0	0-2	3	2	2	0	3	8
Mike Hayes	20	3-6	0-0	2-3	5	1	0	0	3	8
Marcus White	22	1-4	0-0	2-4	4	1	1	1	2	4
Tony Robertson	21	1-4	0-1	2-2	1	1	0	1	1	4
Hilton Armstorng	3	0-0	0-0	0-0	1	0	0	0	0	0
Shamon Tooles	1	0-0	0-0	0-0	0	0	0	0	0	0
TOTALS	**200**	**30-71**	**4-13**	**14-25**	**40**	**13**	**7**	**8**	**21**	**78**
Percentages		42.3	30.8	56.0						

Coach: Jim Calhoun

Officials: Bill Vinovich, Mike Eades, Reggie Cofer
Technicals: Connecticut (bench)
Attendance: 33,009

Michigan State 60, Maryland 58 (Sweet 16)

		1H	2H
Michigan State		29	31
Maryland		24	34

MICHIGAN STATE	MIN	FG	3FG	FT	REB	A	ST	BL	PF	TP
Paul Davis	22	5-7	0-0	3-3	5	0	0	1	2	13
Alan Anderson	29	4-8	0-0	2-2	5	2	1	0	2	10
Maurice Ager	20	4-8	2-4	0-0	4	1	0	0	3	10
Chris Hill	28	3-14	2-7	0-0	3	5	1	0	3	8
Adam Ballinger	16	2-5	1-2	3-3	1	1	2	1	1	8
Erazem Lorbek	16	1-3	1-2	2-4	1	0	1	0	5	5
Aloysius Anagonye	22	2-4	0-0	0-0	8	0	0	0	2	4
Kelvin Torbert	33	1-6	0-1	0-0	2	0	2	1	1	2
Rashi Johnson	9	0-1	0-1	0-0	1	1	1	0	0	0
Jason Andreas	3	0-0	0-0	0-0	1	0	0	0	0	0
Tim Bograkos	2	0-0	0-0	0-0	0	0	0	0	1	0
TOTALS	**200**	**22-56**	**6-17**	**10-12**	**31**	**10**	**8**	**3**	**20**	**60**
Percentages		39.3	35.3	83.3						

Coach: Tom Izzo

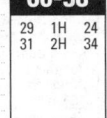

MARYLAND	MIN	FG	3FG	FT	REB	A	ST	BL	PF	TP
Drew Nicholas	35	6-14	1-7	5-5	2	0	0	-	0	18
Steve Blake	36	3-9	1-5	4-4	6	3	0	-	2	11
Tahj Holden	34	2-7	0-2	4-6	9	1	3	-	3	8
Jamar Smith	21	3-6	0-0	1-1	5	0	1	-	1	7
Ryan Randle	22	2-10	0-0	2-2	4	0	0	-	3	6
John Gilchrist	21	2-3	0-0	0-0	2	2	0	-	0	4
Calvin McCall	21	2-4	0-1	0-0	1	1	0	-	2	4
Nik Caner-Medley	6	0-0	0-0	0-0	2	1	0	-	1	0
Andre Collins	2	0-1	0-1	0-0	1	0	0	-	1	0
Travis Garrison	2	0-0	0-0	0-0	0	0	0	-	2	0
TOTALS	**200**	**20-54**	**2-16**	**16-18**	**32**	**8**	**4**	**-**	**15**	**58**
Percentages		37.0	12.5	88.9						

Coach: Gary Williams

Officials: Duke Edsall, Ed Corbett, Michael Kitts
Technicals: None
Attendance: 33,009

65-54 (Sweet 16)

32	1H	23
33	2H	31

OKLAHOMA	MIN	FG	3FG	FT	REB	A	ST	BL	PF	TP
Ebi Ere	30	11-19	2-4	1-4	8	0	0	0	3	25
Kevin Bookout	29	8-9	0-0	0-0	8	0	0	1	4	16
Hollis Price	37	5-16	2-5	0-0	1	5	2	0	0	12
Quannas White	35	0-4	0-1	4-5	6	5	3	0	3	4
Jabahri Brown	31	2-5	0-0	0-1	11	3	1	0	2	4
De'Angelo Alexander	15	0-1	0-0	2-2	1	0	0	0	0	2
Johnnie Gilbert	14	1-1	0-0	0-0	1	2	0	0	5	2
Blake Johnston	8	0-0	0-0	0-0	0	0	0	0	1	0
Jozsef Szendrei	1	0-0	0-0	0-0	1	0	0	0	0	0
TOTALS	**200**	**27-55**	**4-10**	**7-12**	**37**	**15**	**6**	**1**	**18**	**65**
Percentages		49.1	40.0	58.3						

Coach: Kelvin Sampson

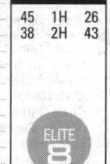

BUTLER	MIN	FG	3FG	FT	REB	A	ST	BL	PF	TP
Joel Cornette	36	9-17	0-0	3-7	8	3	1	2	4	21
Duane Lightfoot	28	4-6	0-0	0-0	1	0	2	0	3	8
Mike Monserez	39	2-3	2-2	1-2	7	5	0	0	4	7
Brandon Miller	36	2-7	0-3	3-3	0	2	0	0	3	7
Darnell Archey	37	1-5	1-3	3-3	2	0	3	0	2	6
Lewis Curry	14	1-3	1-3	2-2	2	0	0	0	0	5
Avery Sheets	6	0-1	0-1	0-0	0	0	1	0	0	0
Nick Gardner	1	0-0	0-0	0-0	0	0	0	0	2	0
Bruce Horan	1	0-1	0-1	0-0	0	0	0	0	0	0
Michael Moore	1	0-0	0-0	0-0	0	0	0	0	0	0
Rob Walls	1	0-0	0-0	0-0	0	0	0	0	0	0
TOTALS	**200**	**19-43**	**4-13**	**12-17**	**20**	**10**	**7**	**2**	**18**	**54**
Percentages		44.2	30.8	70.6						

Coach: Todd Lickliter

Officials: Jo Cahill, Mike Scyphers, Ti Higgins **Technicals:** Butler (Miller Oklahoma (White) **Attendance:** 15,093

79-78 (Sweet 16)

37	1H	27
42	2H	51

SYRACUSE	MIN	FG	3FG	FT	REB	A	ST	BL	PF	TP
Carmelo Anthony	34	7-17	2-4	2-3	8	3	2	1	2	18
Hakim Warrick	25	6-12	0-0	3-4	4	1	3	0	5	15
Josh Pace	22	7-13	0-0	0-1	2	2	1	0	1	14
Duany Duany	26	3-9	2-6	4-4	5	0	1	0	0	12
Gerry McNamara	37	2-6	1-4	4-5	2	3	0	0	2	9
Jeremy McNeil	27	3-6	0-0	0-0	7	0	0	4	3	6
Billy Edelin	17	1-2	0-0	3-4	6	4	1	0	2	5
Craig Forth	12	0-1	0-0	0-0	1	1	1	2	2	0
TOTALS	**200**	**29-66**	**5-14**	**16-21**	**35**	**14**	**9**	**7**	**17**	**79**
Percentages		43.9	35.7	76.2						

Coach: Jim Boeheim

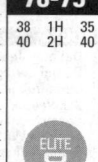

AUBURN	MIN	FG	3FG	FT	REB	A	ST	BL	PF	TP
Marquis Daniels	38	12-21	0-1	3-5	9	4	2	0	3	27
Nathan Watson	29	5-8	4-7	2-2	1	2	2	0	3	16
Lewis Monroe	35	4-7	3-5	1-2	2	1	0	0	4	12
Derrick Bird	38	3-10	3-9	2-2	4	5	0	0	2	11
Brandon Robinson	20	2-8	0-0	4-4	9	2	1	0	0	8
Kyle Davis	20	1-6	0-0	0-0	6	0	0	4	4	2
Marco Killingsworth	18	0-3	0-0	2-2	5	0	0	0	3	2
Troy Gaines	1	0-0	0-0	0-0	0	1	0	0	0	0
Rodney Tucker	1	0-0	0-0	0-0	0	0	0	1	0	0
TOTALS	**200**	**27-63**	**10-22**	**14-17**	**36**	**15**	**5**	**5**	**19**	**78**
Percentages		42.9	45.5	82.4						

Coach: Cliff Ellis

Officials: John Clougherty, Jo Higgins, Rick Hartzell **Technicals:** None **Attendance:** 15,093

83-69 (Elite 8)

45	1H	26
38	2H	43

MARQUETTE	MIN	FG	3FG	FT	REB	A	ST	BL	PF	TP
Dwyane Wade	35	11-16	2-2	5-6	11	11	1	4	3	29
Robert Jackson	35	10-16	0-0	4-6	15	2	1	1	4	24
Steve Novak	27	5-8	5-8	1-1	0	0	1	0	2	16
Travis Diener	34	2-8	1-6	1-2	2	7	3	0	1	6
Todd Towsend	17	1-2	1-2	0-0	2	0	0	0	3	3
KaRon Bradley	13	1-2	1-1	0-0	0	1	0	0	0	3
Scott Merritt	22	1-3	0-0	0-0	3	0	0	1	4	2
Terry Sanders	10	0-0	0-0	0-0	1	0	0	0	3	0
Joe Chapman	3	0-0	0-0	0-0	0	0	0	0	0	0
Chris Grimm	2	0-0	0-0	0-0	0	0	0	0	1	0
Tony Gries	1	0-0	0-0	0-0	0	0	0	0	0	0
Jared Sichting	1	0-0	0-0	0-0	1	0	0	0	1	0
TOTALS	**200**	**31-55**	**10-19**	**11-15**	**35**	**21**	**6**	**6**	**22**	**83**
Percentages		56.4	52.6	73.3						

Coach: Tom Crean

KENTUCKY	MIN	FG	3FG	FT	REB	A	ST	BL	PF	TP
Gerald Fitch	34	6-10	0-3	3-4	2	3	0	0	3	15
Keith Bogans	24	4-11	3-7	4-6	3	0	0	0	1	15
Marquis Estill	25	3-8	0-0	4-7	6	1	0	2	2	10
Erik Daniels	28	4-9	0-0	1-1	5	1	3	0	3	9
Cliff Hawkins	27	4-11	0-1	1-2	2	3	2	0	2	9
Jeff Carrier	2	1-2	1-2	2-2	1	0	0	0	0	5
Antwain Barbour	15	2-4	0-1	0-0	2	1	0	0	1	4
Jules Camara	17	1-2	0-0	0-0	2	1	1	0	1	2
Chuck Hayes	17	0-3	0-0	0-2	7	3	2	0	5	0
Kelenna Azubuike	8	0-3	0-1	0-0	2	0	0	0	1	0
Bernard Cote	1	0-0	0-0	0-0	0	0	0	0	0	0
Ravi Moss	1	0-0	0-0	0-0	0	1	1	0	0	0
Brandon Stockton	1	0-1	0-1	0-0	0	0	1	0	0	0
TOTALS	**200**	**25-64**	**4-16**	**15-24**	**32**	**14**	**10**	**2**	**19**	**69**
Percentages		39.1	25.0	62.5						

Coach: Tubby Smith

Officials: David Hall, Karl Hess, Scott Thornley **Technicals:** None **Attendance:** 28,383

78-75 (Elite 8)

38	1H	35
40	2H	40

KANSAS	MIN	FG	3FG	FT	REB	A	ST	BL	PF	TP
Kirk Hinrich	39	10-23	6-17	2-3	5	5	2	2	3	28
Keith Langford	39	5-15	0-3	3-4	3	1	1	0	2	13
Jeff Graves	32	6-6	0-0	1-3	15	1	1	0	3	13
Nick Collison	34	2-7	0-1	4-6	9	2	1	3	4	8
Michael Lee	20	3-7	2-3	0-0	1	0	2	0	1	8
Aaron Miles	27	2-7	0-2	2-2	4	7	5	0	5	6
Bryant Nash	9	1-2	0-0	0-0	0	0	1	0	2	2
TOTALS	**200**	**29-67**	**8-26**	**12-18**	**37**	**16**	**13**	**5**	**20**	**78**
Percentages		43.3	30.8	66.7						

Coach: Roy Williams

ARIZONA	MIN	FG	3FG	FT	REB	A	ST	BL	PF	TP
Jason Gardner	40	6-15	3-10	8-8	3	4	2	0	0	23
Luke Walton	38	5-14	2-2	6-9	10	6	0	0	2	18
Hassan Adams	26	3-4	1-1	4-4	4	0	3	0	4	11
Rick Anderson	18	4-8	3-5	0-0	5	0	0	0	4	11
Channing Frye	25	3-6	0-0	0-0	5	2	0	1	4	6
Salim Stoudamire	21	1-4	1-4	1-2	0	1	0	0	0	4
Andre Iguodala	30	1-4	0-0	0-0	7	3	3	1	3	2
Isaiah Fox	2	0-0	0-0	0-0	0	0	0	0	0	0
TOTALS	**200**	**23-55**	**10-22**	**19-23**	**34**	**16**	**8**	**2**	**17**	**75**
Percentages		41.8	45.5	82.6						

Coach: Lute Olson

Officials: Kerry Sitton, Ted Valentine, Tony Greene **Technicals:** None **Attendance:** 17,439

85-76 (Elite 8)

43	1H	38
42	2H	38

TEXAS	MIN	FG	3FG	FT	REB	A	ST	BL	PF	TP
T.J. Ford	37	4-12	0-0	11-13	1	10	1	0	3	19
Brandon Mouton	33	4-11	1-3	7-10	0	3	1	1	1	16
Brian Boddicker	31	6-10	3-6	0-0	6	0	0	1	4	15
Sydmill Harris	18	4-6	2-4	2-2	0	1	0	0	2	12
Brad Buckman	18	3-4	0-0	5-6	4	0	3	0	3	11
James Thomas	15	1-2	0-0	3-5	7	0	1	1	4	5
Jason Klotz	14	2-3	0-0	0-0	2	0	0	0	2	4
Royal Ivey	25	1-3	0-1	1-2	6	1	0	0	2	3
Terrell Ross	6	0-0	0-0	0-0	0	1	0	1	0	0
Deginald Erskin	3	0-0	0-0	0-0	0	0	0	0	1	0
TOTALS	**200**	**25-51**	**6-14**	**29-38**	**26**	**16**	**6**	**4**	**22**	**85**
Percentages		49.0	42.9	76.3						

Coach: Rick Barnes

MICHIGAN STATE	MIN	FG	3FG	FT	REB	A	ST	BL	PF	TP
Paul Davis	20	4-9	0-0	7-12	7	1	0	1	2	15
Erazem Lorbek	29	6-11	1-2	1-2	9	1	0	0	3	14
Chris Hill	29	3-7	3-6	1-2	2	3	1	0	4	10
Maurice Ager	24	3-7	2-3	2-2	2	0	0	0	4	10
Alan Anderson	29	3-6	0-0	3-3	4	3	0	1	5	9
Kelvin Torbert	32	3-6	2-3	0-0	3	0	0	0	4	8
Aloysius Anagonye	24	2-3	0-0	4-5	4	2	0	0	2	8
Adam Ballinger	7	1-3	0-1	0-0	2	1	0	0	1	2
Rashi Johnson	4	0-2	0-1	0-0	0	0	0	0	2	0
Tim Bograkos	1	0-0	0-0	0-0	1	0	0	0	1	0
Adam Wolfe	1	0-0	0-0	0-0	0	0	0	0	0	0
TOTALS	**200**	**25-54**	**8-16**	**18-26**	**34**	**11**	**1**	**2**	**28**	**76**
Percentages		46.3	50.0	69.2						

Coach: Tom Izzo

Officials: Bruce Hicks, Gerald Boudreaux, Mike Stuart **Technicals:** None **Attendance:** 30,169

63-47 (Elite 8)

30	1H	20
33	2H	27

SYRACUSE	MIN	FG	3FG	FT	REB	A	ST	BL	PF	TP
Carmelo Anthony	40	9-16	1-4	1-2	10	1	2	0	3	20
Hakim Warrick	35	6-9	0-0	1-3	9	4	2	1	4	13
Gerry McNamara	39	4-10	1-6	0-0	0	3	5	0	0	9
Billy Edelin	21	1-2	0-0	7-10	6	3	1	0	1	9
Duany Duany	24	3-7	0-2	2-4	5	1	2	0	0	8
Jeremy McNeil	23	1-1	0-0	0-0	2	1	0	0	2	2
Craig Forth	17	1-3	0-0	0-0	3	3	1	1	3	2
Josh Pace	1	0-0	0-0	0-0	0	0	0	0	0	0
TOTALS	**200**	**25-48**	**2-12**	**11-19**	**35**	**16**	**13**	**2**	**13**	**63**
Percentages		52.1	16.7	57.9						

Coach: Jim Boeheim

OKLAHOMA	MIN	FG	3FG	FT	REB	A	ST	BL	PF	TP
De'Angelo Alexander	24	5-9	2-5	2-4	6	0	2	1	5	14
Jabahri Brown	24	4-6	0-0	1-1	7	0	1	1	2	9
Hollis Price	36	3-17	2-11	0-0	0	2	4	0	2	8
Ebi Ere	23	2-8	0-4	3-6	5	2	1	1	0	7
Blake Johnston	16	2-6	1-4	0-0	1	3	2	1	2	5
Quannas White	26	1-8	0-4	0-0	0	2	0	0	4	2
Kevin Bookout	22	1-4	0-0	0-0	4	1	2	0	0	2
Johnnie Gilbert	23	0-0	0-0	0-0	2	0	1	0	1	0
Jozsef Szendrei	6	0-0	0-0	0-0	1	0	0	0	0	0
TOTALS	**200**	**18-58**	**5-28**	**6-11**	**26**	**10**	**13**	**4**	**16**	**47**
Percentages		31.0	17.9	54.5						

Coach: Kelvin Sampson

Officials: Bill Gracey, Dave Libbey, Terry Moore **Technicals:** None **Attendance:** 15,207

94-61

59	1H	30
35	2H	31

FINAL 4

KANSAS	MIN	FG	3FG	FT	REB	A	ST	BL	PF	TP
Keith Langford	32	11-14	0-1	1-3	5	4	1	1	1	23
Aaron Miles	29	7-12	2-4	2-3	5	4	0	1	2	18
Kirk Hinrich	25	6-13	3-7	3-4	1	3	2	0	1	18
Michael Lee	22	4-8	3-3	2-2	6	4	2	0	1	13
Nick Collison	26	6-7	0-0	0-0	15	5	0	1	2	12
Jeff Graves	27	2-4	0-0	1-4	9	1	2	2	4	5
Bryant Nash	18	1-4	0-1	1-1	4	0	1	0	3	3
Moulaye Niang	4	1-3	0-0	0-0	1	0	0	0	0	2
Jeff Hawkins	6	0-3	0-2	0-0	0	0	0	0	0	0
Stephen Vinson	5	0-2	0-1	0-0	1	1	0	0	1	0
Christian Moody	3	0-0	0-0	0-0	2	0	0	0	0	0
Brett Olson	3	0-1	0-0	0-0	2	0	0	0	0	0
TOTALS	**200**	**38-71**	**8-19**	**10-17**	**51**	**22**	**8**	**5**	**15**	**94**
Percentages		53.5	42.1	58.8						

Coach: Roy Williams

MARQUETTE	MIN	FG	3FG	FT	REB	A	ST	BL	PF	TP
Dwyane Wade	29	7-15	1-1	4-8	6	4	2	1	3	19
Robert Jackson	30	6-12	0-0	3-4	9	0	1	1	1	15
Scott Merritt	24	5-14	0-0	2-2	11	0	0	1	1	12
Travis Diener	35	1-11	1-5	2-2	1	2	2	0	2	5
KaRon Bradley	14	1-7	1-3	0-0	1	1	1	0	1	3
Steve Novak	18	1-7	0-5	0-0	3	0	0	0	2	2
Terry Sanders	11	1-1	0-0	0-0	4	0	0	0	3	2
Chris Grimm	5	1-1	0-0	0-0	1	0	0	0	0	2
Todd Towsend	22	0-3	0-1	1-2	2	0	1	0	3	1
Joe Chapman	10	0-3	0-1	0-0	0	0	0	0	1	0
Tony Gries	1	0-0	0-0	0-0	0	0	0	0	0	0
Jared Sichting	1	0-0	0-0	0-0	0	0	0	0	0	0
TOTALS	**200**	**23-74**	**3-16**	**12-18**	**38**	**7**	**7**	**3**	**17**	**61**
Percentages		31.1	18.8	66.7						

Coach: Tom Crean

Officials: Karl Hess, Michael Kitts, Tom Lopes
Technicals: None
Attendance: 54,432

95-84

48	1H	45
47	2H	39

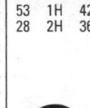

FINAL 4

SYRACUSE	MIN	FG	3FG	FT	REB	A	ST	BL	PF	TP
Carmelo Anthony	37	12-19	3-4	6-7	14	1	3	0	3	33
Gerry McNamara	37	6-12	3-8	4-4	3	4	4	0	2	19
Hakim Warrick	34	6-11	0-0	6-8	7	4	0	1	4	18
Josh Pace	20	5-6	0-0	2-2	3	2	0	1	2	12
Billy Edelin	20	2-6	0-0	1-2	3	3	1	0	0	5
Duany Duany	14	1-2	1-1	1-2	1	0	0	0	1	4
Craig Forth	21	0-0	0-0	2-4	4	0	1	0	5	2
Jeremy McNeil	17	0-0	0-0	2-2	1	0	0	0	4	2
TOTALS	**200**	**32-56**	**7-13**	**24-31**	**36**	**14**	**9**	**2**	**21**	**95**
Percentages		57.1	53.8	77.4						

Coach: Jim Boeheim

TEXAS	MIN	FG	3FG	FT	REB	A	ST	BL	PF	TP
Brandon Mouton	39	9-23	5-9	2-2	3	3	0	0	3	25
Brad Buckman	23	6-6	0-0	2-5	7	0	0	1	5	14
James Thomas	25	4-7	0-0	5-11	9	0	0	0	3	13
T.J. Ford	33	3-8	1-2	5-6	4	13	4	0	4	12
Brian Boddicker	17	3-5	3-4	3-4	5	0	0	1	4	12
Royal Ivey	30	1-8	0-1	2-2	0	4	2	0	3	4
Sydmill Harris	16	1-5	1-5	0-0	0	0	0	0	1	3
Jason Klotz	7	0-0	0-0	1-2	1	0	0	0	2	1
Deginald Erskin	6	0-1	0-0	0-0	2	0	0	0	1	0
Terrell Ross	4	0-0	0-0	0-0	0	0	0	0	0	0
TOTALS	**200**	**27-63**	**10-21**	**20-32**	**31**	**20**	**6**	**2**	**26**	**84**
Percentages		42.9	47.6	62.5						

Coach: Rick Barnes

Officials: Dave Libbey, Donnee Gray, Larry Rose
Technicals: None
Attendance: 54,432

81-78

53	1H	42
28	2H	36

NCAA FINAL 2003

SYRACUSE	MIN	FG	3FG	FT	REB	A	ST	BL	PF	TP
Carmelo Anthony	37	7-16	3-5	3-4	10	7	1	0	2	20
Gerry McNamara	34	6-13	6-10	0-0	0	1	1	0	2	18
Billy Edelin	27	4-10	0-0	4-6	2	2	3	0	1	12
Duany Duany	13	4-6	2-3	1-2	4	0	1	0	3	11
Josh Pace	21	4-9	0-0	0-0	8	2	3	0	2	8
Hakim Warrick	31	2-4	0-0	2-4	2	1	0	2	3	6
Craig Forth	24	3-4	0-0	0-1	3	0	1	3	5	6
Jeremy McNeil	13	0-1	0-0	0-0	5	0	0	2	4	0
TOTALS	**200**	**30-63**	**11-18**	**10-17**	**34**	**13**	**10**	**7**	**22**	**81**
Percentages		47.6	61.1	58.8						

Coach: Jim Boeheim

KANSAS	MIN	FG	3FG	FT	REB	A	ST	BL	PF	TP
Nick Collison	40	8-14	0-0	3-10	21	3	3	3	5	19
Keith Langford	23	7-9	0-1	5-10	2	0	1	0	5	19
Kirk Hinrich	38	6-20	3-12	1-1	2	4	1	1	1	16
Jeff Graves	37	7-13	0-0	2-7	16	3	1	0	2	16
Michael Lee	23	2-8	1-5	0-0	1	1	2	0	1	5
Aaron Miles	34	1-5	0-2	0-0	6	7	1	0	1	2
Bryant Nash	5	0-2	0-0	1-2	1	0	0	0	1	1
TOTALS	**200**	**31-71**	**4-20**	**12-30**	**49**	**18**	**9**	**4**	**16**	**78**
Percentages		43.7	20.0	40.0						

Coach: Roy Williams

Officials: Dick Cartmell, Gerald Boudreaux, Reggie Cofer
Technicals: None
Attendance: 54,524

National Invitation Tournament (NIT)

Opening Round: Iowa d. Valparaiso 62-60, Siena d. Villanova 74-59, Temple d. Drexel 68-59, Boston College d. Fairfield 90-78, Western Michigan d. Illinois-Chicago 63-62, Charleston d. Kent State 72-66, Providence d. Richmond 67-49, Iowa State d. Wichita State 76-65

First Round: Georgetown d. Tennessee 70-60, North Carolina d. DePaul 83-72, Georgia Tech d. Ohio State 72-58, Virginia d. Brown 89-73, Rhode Island d. Seton Hall 61-60, St. John's d. Boston U. 62-57, Minnesota d. Saint Louis 62-52, UAB d. UL-Lafayette 82-80, Texas Tech d. Nevada 66-54, San Diego St. d. UC Santa Barbara 67-62 (OT), Hawaii d. UNLV 85-68, Wyoming d. Eastern Washington 78-71, Temple d. Boston College 75-62, Iowa d. Iowa State 54-53, Providence d. Charleston 69-64, Siena d. Western Michigan 68-62

Second Round: Texas Tech d. San Diego State 57-48, St. John's d. Virginia 73-63, Minnesota d. Hawaii 84-70, North Carolina d. Wyoming 90-74, Georgia Tech d. Iowa 79-78, Georgetown d. Providence 67-58, Temple d. Rhode Island 61-53, UAB d. Siena 80-71

Third Round: Georgetown d. North Carolina 79-74, Texas Tech d. Georgia Tech 80-72, St. John's d. UAB 79-71, Minnesota d. Temple 63-58 (OT)

Semifinals: Georgetown d. Minnesota 88-74, St. John's d. Texas Tech 64-63

Championship: St. John's⊗ d. Georgetown 70-67

Third place: Texas Tech d. Minnesota 71-61

MVP: Marcus Hatten, St. John's⊗

⊗Team later sanctioned by NCAA.

2003-04: A Husky Double

Saint Joseph's had reached No. 1 in the polls for the first time, but lost in the Elite Eight when Oklahoma State's John Lucas III drained a game-winning three with 6.9 seconds left. In the Final Four in San Antonio, No. 3-seed Georgia Tech beat the No. 2-seed Cowboys, 67-65, and No. 2-seed Connecticut downed No. 1-seed Duke, 79-78. The cumulative three-point differential was the smallest ever for the two games of a Final Four Saturday. Behind the NBA's No. 2 and No. 3 draft picks, Emeka Okafor and Ben Gordon, the Huskies (33–6) crushed Georgia Tech, 82-73, for their school's second title. But UConn really made history when its women's team beat Tennessee the following night. Never before had a school won both the men's and women's D1 national titles in the same year.

Major Conference Standings

America East

	Conference W	L	Pct	Overall W	L	Pct
Boston U.□	17	1	.944	23	6	.793
Vermont⊕	15	3	.833	22	9	.710
Northeastern	13	5	.722	19	11	.633
Maine	12	6	.667	20	10	.667
Binghamton	10	8	.556	14	16	.467
Hartford	6	12	.333	12	17	.414
New Hampshire	5	13	.278	10	20	.333
Stony Brook	5	13	.278	10	20	.333
UMBC	4	14	.222	7	21	.250
Albany (NY)	3	15	.167	5	23	.179

Tournament: **Vermont d. Maine 72-53**
Tournament MVP: **Taylor Coppenrath**, Vermont

ACC

	Conference W	L	Pct	Overall W	L	Pct
Duke○	13	3	.813	31	6	.838
NC State○	11	5	.688	21	10	.677
Georgia Tech○	9	7	.563	28	10	.737
Wake Forest○	9	7	.563	21	10	.677
North Carolina○	8	8	.500	19	11	.633
Maryland⊕	7	9	.438	20	12	.625
Virginia□	6	10	.375	18	13	.581
Florida State□	6	10	.375	19	14	.576
Clemson	3	13	.188	10	18	.357

Tournament: **Maryland d. Duke 95-87 OT**
Tournament MVP: **John Gilchrist**, Maryland

Atlantic Sun

	Conference W	L	Pct	Overall W	L	Pct
Troy□	18	2	.900	24	7	.774
Central Florida⊕	17	3	.850	25	6	.806
Belmont□	15	5	.750	21	9	.700
Georgia State	14	6	.700	20	9	.690
Stetson	10	10	.500	12	15	.444
Mercer	9	11	.450	12	18	.400
Jacksonville	8	12	.400	13	15	.464
Florida Atlantic	6	14	.300	9	19	.321
Gardner-Webb	6	14	.300	9	20	.310
Lipscomb	4	16	.200	7	21	.250
Campbell	3	17	.150	3	24	.111

Tournament: **Central Florida d. Troy 60-55**
Tournament MVP: **Dexter Lyons**, Central Florida

Atlantic 10

	Conference W	L	Pct	Overall W	L	Pct
East Division						
Saint Joseph's○	16	0	1.000	30	2	.938
Temple□	9	7	.563	15	14	.517
Rhode Island□	7	9	.438	20	14	.588
Massachusetts	4	12	.250	10	19	.345
St. Bonaventure	3	13	.188	7	21	.250
Fordham	3	13	.188	6	22	.214
West Division						
Dayton○	12	4	.750	24	9	.727
George Washington□	11	5	.688	18	12	.600
Xavier⊕	10	6	.625	26	11	.703
Richmond○	10	6	.625	20	13	.606
Duquesne	6	10	.375	12	17	.414
La Salle	5	11	.313	10	20	.333

Tournament: **Xavier d. Dayton 58-49**
Tournament MOP: **Lionel Chalmers**, Xavier

Big East

	Conference W	L	Pct	Overall W	L	Pct
Pittsburgh○	13	3	.813	31	5	.861
Connecticut⊕	12	4	.750	33	6	.846
Syracuse○	11	5	.688	23	8	.742
Providence○	11	5	.688	20	9	.690
Boston College○	10	6	.625	24	10	.706
Seton Hall○	10	6	.625	21	10	.677
Notre Dame□	9	7	.563	19	13	.594
West Virginia□	7	9	.438	17	14	.548
Rutgers□	7	9	.438	20	13	.606
Virginia Tech	7	9	.438	15	14	.517
Villanova□	6	10	.375	18	17	.514
Miami (FL)	4	12	.250	14	16	.467
Georgetown	4	12	.250	13	15	.464
St. John's⊗	1	15	.063	6	21	.222

Tournament: **Connecticut d. Pittsburgh 61-58**
Tournament MVP: **Ben Gordon**, Connecticut

Big Sky

	Conference W	L	Pct	Overall W	L	Pct
Eastern Washington⊕	11	3	.786	17	13	.567
Northern Arizona	7	7	.500	15	14	.517
Weber State	7	7	.500	15	14	.517
Sacramento State	7	7	.500	13	15	.464
Idaho State	7	7	.500	13	18	.419
Montana State	6	8	.429	14	13	.519
Montana	6	8	.429	10	18	.357
Portland State	5	9	.357	11	16	.407

Tournament: **Eastern Wash. d. Northern Arizona 71-59**
Tournament MVP: **Brendon Merritt**, Eastern Washington

Big South

	Conference W	L	Pct	Overall W	L	Pct
Birmingham Southern	12	4	.750	20	7	.741
Liberty⊕	12	4	.750	18	15	.545
High Point	10	6	.625	19	11	.633
Winthrop	10	6	.625	16	12	.571
Coastal Carolina	8	8	.500	14	15	.483
Radford	7	9	.438	12	16	.429
UNC Asheville	6	10	.375	9	20	.310
VMI	4	12	.250	6	22	.214
Charleston Southern	3	13	.188	6	22	.214

Tournament: **Liberty d. High Point 89-44**
Tournament MVP: **Danny Gathings**, High Point

Big Ten

	Conference W	L	Pct	Overall W	L	Pct
Illinois○	13	3	.813	26	7	.788
Wisconsin⊕	12	4	.750	25	7	.781
Michigan State○	12	4	.750	18	12	.600
Iowa□	9	7	.563	16	13	.552
Michigan□	8	8	.500	23	11	.676
Northwestern	8	8	.500	14	15	.483
Purdue□	7	9	.438	17	14	.548
Indiana	7	9	.438	14	15	.483
Ohio State	6	10	.375	14	16	.467
Minnesota	3	13	.188	12	18	.400
Penn State	3	13	.188	9	19	.321

Tournament: **Wisconsin d. Illinois 70-53**
Tournament MOP: **Devin Harris**, Wisconsin

Big 12

	Conference W	L	Pct	Overall W	L	Pct
Oklahoma State⊕	14	2	.875	31	4	.886
Texas○	12	4	.750	25	8	.758
Kansas○	12	4	.750	24	9	.727
Colorado□	10	6	.625	18	11	.621
Texas Tech○	9	7	.563	23	11	.676
Missouri□	9	7	.563	16	14	.533
Oklahoma□	8	8	.500	20	11	.645
Iowa State□	7	9	.438	20	13	.606
Nebraska□	6	10	.375	18	13	.581
Kansas State	6	10	.375	14	14	.500
Baylor	3	13	.188	8	21	.276
Texas A&M	0	16	.000	7	21	.250

Tournament: **Oklahoma State d. Texas 65-49**
Tournament MOP: **Tony Allen**, Oklahoma State

Big West

	Conference W	L	Pct	Overall W	L	Pct
Utah State□	17	1	.944	25	4	.862
Pacific⊕	17	1	.944	25	8	.758
UC Santa Barbara	10	8	.556	16	12	.571
Idaho	9	9	.500	14	16	.467
Cal State Northridge	7	11	.389	14	16	.467
Cal State Fullerton	7	11	.389	11	17	.393
UC Riverside	7	11	.389	11	17	.393
Cal Poly	6	12	.333	11	16	.407
UC Irvine	6	12	.333	11	17	.393
Long Beach State	4	14	.222	6	21	.222

Tournament: **Pacific d. Cal State Northridge 75-73**
Tournament MVP: **Ian Boylan**, Cal State Northridge

Colonial Athletic

	Conference W	L	Pct	Overall W	L	Pct
VCU⊕	14	4	.778	23	8	.742
Drexel□	13	5	.722	18	11	.621
George Mason□	12	6	.667	23	10	.697
Old Dominion	11	7	.611	17	12	.586
Delaware	10	8	.556	16	12	.571
Hofstra	10	8	.556	14	15	.483
UNC Wilmington	9	9	.500	15	15	.500
Towson	4	14	.222	8	21	.276
William and Mary	4	14	.222	7	21	.250
James Madison	3	15	.167	7	21	.250

Tournament: **VCU d. George Mason 55-54**
Tournament MVP: **Domonic Jones**, VCU

C-USA

	Conference W	L	Pct	Overall W	L	Pct
DePaul○	12	4	.750	22	10	.688
Cincinnati⊕	12	4	.750	25	7	.781
Memphis○	12	4	.750	22	8	.733
Charlotte○	12	4	.750	21	9	.700
UAB○	12	4	.750	22	10	.688
Louisville○	9	7	.563	20	10	.667
Saint Louis□	9	7	.563	19	13	.594
Marquette□	8	8	.500	19	12	.613
TCU	7	9	.438	12	17	.414
Southern Miss	6	10	.375	13	15	.464
East Carolina	5	11	.313	13	14	.481
Tulane	4	12	.250	11	17	.393
Houston	3	13	.188	9	18	.333
South Florida	1	15	.063	7	20	.259

Tournament: **Cincinnati d. DePaul 55-50**
Tournament MVP: **Tony Bobbitt**, Cincinnati

Horizon

	Conference W	L	Pct	Overall W	L	Pct
Wisc.-Milwaukee□	13	3	.813	20	11	.645
Illinois-Chicago⊕	12	4	.750	24	8	.750
Wisconsin-Green Bay	11	5	.688	17	11	.607
Detroit	10	6	.625	19	11	.633
Wright State	10	6	.625	14	14	.500
Butler	8	8	.500	16	14	.533
Loyola-Chicago	4	12	.250	9	20	.310
Youngstown State	4	12	.250	8	20	.286
Cleveland State	0	16	.000	4	25	.138

Tournament: **Illinois-Chicago d. Wisc.-Milwaukee 65-62**
Tournament MVP: **Armond Williams**, Illinois-Chicago

Ivy

	Conference W	L	Pct	Overall W	L	Pct
Princeton⊕	13	1	.929	20	8	.714
Penn	10	4	.714	17	10	.630
Brown	10	4	.714	14	13	.519
Yale	7	7	.500	12	15	.444
Cornell	6	8	.429	11	16	.407
Columbia	6	8	.429	10	17	.370
Harvard	3	11	.214	4	23	.148
Dartmouth	1	13	.071	3	25	.107

⊕ Automatic NCAA Tournament bid ○ At-large NCAA Tournament bid □ NIT appearance ⊗ Team record doesn't reflect games forfeited or vacated. For adjusted record, see p. 521.

MAAC

	Conference			Overall		
	W	L	Pct	W	L	Pct
Manhattan⊕	16	2	.889	25	6	.806
Niagara□	13	5	.722	22	10	.688
Fairfield	12	6	.667	19	11	.633
Saint Peter's	12	6	.667	17	12	.586
Rider	10	8	.556	17	14	.548
Siena	9	9	.500	14	16	.467
Iona	8	10	.444	11	18	.379
Canisius	5	13	.278	10	20	.333
Marist	4	14	.222	6	22	.214
Loyola (MD)	1	17	.056	1	27	.036

Tournament: **Manhattan d. Niagara 62-61**
Tournament MVP: **Luis Flores**, Manhattan

MID-AMERICAN

	Conference			Overall		
	W	L	Pct	W	L	Pct
East Division						
Kent State State□	13	5	.722	22	9	.710
Miami (OH)	12	6	.667	18	11	.621
Buffalo	11	7	.611	17	12	.586
Marshall	8	10	.444	12	17	.414
Akron	7	11	.389	13	15	.464
Ohio	7	11	.389	10	20	.333
West Division						
Western Michigan⊕	15	3	.833	26	5	.839
Toledo□	12	6	.667	20	11	.645
Ball State	10	8	.556	14	15	.483
Bowling Green	8	10	.444	14	17	.452
Eastern Michigan	7	11	.389	13	15	.464
Northern Illinois	5	13	.278	10	20	.333
Central Michigan	2	16	.111	6	24	.200

Tournament: **Western Michigan d. Kent State 77-66**
Tournament MVP: **Mike Williams**, Western Michigan

MID-CONTINENT

	Conference			Overall		
	W	L	Pct	W	L	Pct
Valparaiso⊕	11	5	.688	18	13	.581
IUPUI	10	6	.625	21	11	.656
Oral Roberts	10	6	.625	17	11	.607
Centenary	10	6	.625	16	12	.571
UMKC	9	7	.563	15	14	.517
Chicago State	9	7	.563	12	20	.375
Oakland	6	10	.375	13	17	.433
Southern Utah	6	10	.375	10	18	.357
Western Illinois	1	15	.063	3	25	.107

Tournament: **Valparaiso d. IUPUI 75-70**
Tournament MVP: **Odell Bradley**, IUPUI

MEAC

	Conference			Overall		
	W	L	Pct	W	L	Pct
South Carolina State	14	4	.778	18	11	.621
Coppin State	14	4	.778	18	14	.563
Delaware State	11	7	.611	13	15	.464
Hampton	11	7	.611	13	17	.433
Florida A&M⊕	10	8	.556	15	17	.469
Norfolk State	10	8	.556	12	17	.414
Morgan State	9	9	.500	11	16	.407
Bethune-Cookman	7	11	.389	8	21	.276
UMES	6	12	.333	8	21	.276
Howard	4	14	.222	6	22	.214
NC A&T	3	15	.167	3	25	.107

Tournament: **Florida A&M d. Coppin State 58-51**
Tournament MOP: **Terrence Woods**, Florida A&M

MISSOURI VALLEY

	Conference			Overall		
	W	L	Pct	W	L	Pct
Southern Illinois○	17	1	.944	25	5	.833
Creighton□	12	6	.667	20	9	.690
Northern Iowa⊕	12	6	.667	21	10	.677
Wichita State□	12	6	.667	21	11	.656
Missouri State	9	9	.500	19	14	.576
Bradley	7	11	.389	15	16	.484
Drake	7	11	.389	12	16	.429
Indiana State	5	13	.278	9	19	.321
Evansville	5	13	.278	7	22	.241
Illinois State	4	14	.222	10	19	.345

Tournament: **Northern Iowa d. Missouri State 79-74**
Tournament MOP: **Ben Jacobson**, Northern Iowa

MOUNTAIN WEST

	Conference			Overall		
	W	L	Pct	W	L	Pct
Air Force○	12	2	.857	22	7	.759
BYU○	10	4	.714	21	9	.700
Utah⊕	9	5	.643	24	9	.727
UNLV□	7	7	.500	18	13	.581
New Mexico	5	9	.357	14	14	.500
San Diego State	5	9	.357	14	16	.467
Colorado State	4	10	.286	13	16	.448
Wyoming	4	10	.286	11	17	.393

Tournament: **Utah d. UNLV 73-70**
Tournament MVP: **Nick Jacobson**, Utah

NORTHEAST

	Conference			Overall		
	W	L	Pct	W	L	Pct
Monmouth⊕	12	6	.667	21	12	.636
St. Francis (NY)	12	6	.667	15	13	.536
Fairleigh Dickinson	11	7	.611	17	12	.586
Robert Morris	10	8	.556	14	15	.483
Saint Francis (PA)	10	8	.556	13	15	.464
Wagner	10	8	.556	13	16	.448
Central Conn. State	9	9	.500	14	14	.500
Sacred Heart	8	10	.444	12	15	.444
Mount St. Mary's	8	10	.444	10	19	.345
Quinnipiac	5	13	.278	9	20	.310
Long Island	4	14	.222	8	19	.296

Tournament: **Monmouth d. Central Conn. State 67-55**
Tournament MVP: **Blake Hamilton**, Monmouth

OHIO VALLEY

	Conference			Overall		
	W	L	Pct	W	L	Pct
Austin Peay□	16	0	1.000	22	10	.688
Murray State⊕	14	2	.875	28	6	.824
Morehead State	10	6	.625	16	13	.552
Eastern Kentucky	8	8	.500	14	15	.483
Jacksonville State	7	9	.438	14	14	.500
Tennessee Tech	7	9	.438	13	15	.464
Samford	7	9	.438	12	16	.429
Tennessee State	6	10	.375	7	21	.250
Tennessee-Martin	5	11	.313	10	18	.357
SE Missouri State	4	12	.250	11	16	.407
Eastern Illinois	4	12	.250	6	21	.222

Tournament: **Murray State d. Austin Peay 66-60**
Tournament MVP: **Cuthbert Victor**, Murray State

PAC-10

	Conference			Overall		
	W	L	Pct	W	L	Pct
Stanford⊕	17	1	.944	30	2	.938
Washington○	12	6	.667	19	12	.613
Arizona○	11	7	.611	20	10	.667
Oregon□	9	9	.500	18	13	.581
California	9	9	.500	13	15	.464
Southern California	8	10	.444	13	15	.464
Washington State	7	11	.389	13	16	.448
UCLA	7	11	.389	11	17	.393
Oregon State	6	12	.333	12	16	.429
Arizona State	4	14	.222	10	17	.370

Tournament: **Stanford d. Washington 77-66**
Tournament MOP: **Josh Childress**, Stanford

PATRIOT LEAGUE

	Conference			Overall		
	W	L	Pct	W	L	Pct
Lehigh⊕	10	4	.714	20	11	.645
American	10	4	.714	18	13	.581
Lafayette	9	5	.643	18	10	.643
Bucknell	9	5	.643	14	15	.483
Holy Cross	7	7	.500	13	15	.464
Colgate	6	8	.429	15	14	.517
Army	3	11	.214	6	21	.222
Navy	2	12	.143	5	23	.179

Tournament: **Lehigh d American 59-57**
Tournament MVP: **Austen Rowland**, Lehigh

SEC

	Conference			Overall		
	W	L	Pct	W	L	Pct
Eastern						
Kentucky⊕	13	3	.813	27	5	.844
Florida○	9	7	.563	20	11	.645
Vanderbilt○	8	8	.500	23	10	.697
South Carolina○	8	8	.500	23	11	.676
Georgia□	7	9	.438	16	14	.533
Tennessee□	7	9	.438	15	14	.517
Western						
Mississippi State○	14	2	.875	26	4	.867
LSU□	8	8	.500	18	11	.620
Alabama○	8	8	.500	20	13	.606
Auburn	5	11	.313	14	14	.500
Mississippi	5	11	.313	13	15	.464
Arkansas	4	12	.250	12	16	.429

Tournament: **Kentucky d. Florida 89-73**
Tournament MVP: **Gerald Fitch**, Kentucky

SOUTHERN

	Conference			Overall		
	W	L	Pct	W	L	Pct
North						
East Tennessee State⊕	15	1	.938	27	6	.818
Chattanooga	10	6	.625	19	11	.633
Elon	7	9	.438	12	18	.400
UNC Greensboro	7	9	.438	11	17	.393
Western Carolina	6	10	.375	13	15	.464
Appalachian State	4	12	.250	9	21	.300
South						
Ga. Southern	11	5	.688	21	8	.724
Charleston	11	5	.688	20	9	.690
Davidson	11	5	.688	17	12	.586
Furman	8	8	.500	17	12	.586
Wofford	4	12	.250	9	20	.310
The Citadel	2	14	.125	6	22	.214

Tournament: **East Tenn. State d. Chattanooga 78-62**
Tournament MOP: **Tim Smith**, East Tenn. State

SOUTHLAND

	Conference			Overall		
	W	L	Pct	W	L	Pct
Southeastern La.	11	5	.688	20	9	.690
Texas-Arlington	11	5	.688	17	12	.586
UTSA⊕	11	5	.688	19	14	.576
Stephen F. Austin	10	6	.625	21	9	.700
Sam Houston State	8	8	.500	13	15	.464
Texas State	8	8	.500	13	15	.464
Northwestern State (LA)	8	8	.500	11	17	.393
UL-Monroe	8	8	.500	12	19	.387
McNeese State	7	9	.438	11	16	.407
Lamar	5	11	.313	11	18	.379
Nicholls State	1	15	.063	6	21	.222

Tournament: **UTSA d. Stephen F. Austin 74-70**
Tournament MVP: **LeRoy Hurd**, UTSA

SWAC

	Conference			Overall		
	W	L	Pct	W	L	Pct
Miss. Valley State	16	2	.889	22	7	.759
Alabama State⊕	11	7	.611	16	15	.516
Texas Southern	10	8	.556	14	15	.483
Southern U.	9	9	.500	12	16	.429
Alabama A&M	9	9	.500	13	17	.433
Jackson State	9	9	.500	12	17	.414
Alcorn State	9	9	.500	11	18	.379
Grambling	9	9	.500	11	18	.379
Prairie View A&M	7	11	.389	7	20	.259
Arkansas-Pine Bluff	1	17	.056	1	26	.037

Tournament: **Alabama State d. Alabama A&M 63-58**
Tournament MVP: **Malcolm Campbell**, Alabama State

SUN BELT

	Conference			Overall		
	W	L	Pct	W	L	Pct
East Division						
Arkansas-Little Rock	9	5	.643	17	12	.586
Middle Tenn. State	8	6	.571	17	12	.586
Western Kentucky	8	6	.571	15	13	.536
Arkansas State	7	7	.500	17	11	.607
Florida International✪	1	13	.071	5	22	.185
West Division						
UL-Lafayette⊕✪	12	3	.800	20	9	.690
New Orleans	9	6	.600	17	14	.548
North Texas	8	7	.533	13	15	.464
Denver	6	9	.400	14	13	.519
South Alabama	6	9	.400	12	16	.429
New Mexico State	6	9	.400	13	14	.481

Tournament: **UL-Lafayette d. New Orleans 67-58**
Tournament MOP: **Bo McCalebb**, New Orleans

WEST COAST

	Conference			Overall		
	W	L	Pct	W	L	Pct
Gonzaga⊕	14	0	1.000	28	3	.903
Saint Mary's (CA)	9	5	.643	19	12	.613
Pepperdine	9	5	.643	15	16	.484
San Francisco	7	7	.500	17	14	.548
Santa Clara	6	8	.429	16	16	.500
Loyola Marymount	5	9	.357	15	14	.517
Portland	5	9	.357	11	17	.393
San Diego	1	13	.071	4	26	.133

Tournament: **Gonzaga d. Saint Mary's (CA) 84-71**
Tournament MVP: **Ronny Turiaf**, Gonzaga

WAC

	Conference			Overall		
	W	L	Pct	W	L	Pct
UTEP○	13	5	.722	24	8	.750
Nevada⊕	13	5	.722	25	9	.735
Rice□	12	6	.667	22	11	.667
Boise State□	12	6	.667	23	10	.697
Hawaii□	11	7	.611	21	12	.636
Fresno State	10	8	.556	14	15	.483
Louisiana Tech	8	10	.444	15	15	.500
SMU	5	13	.278	12	18	.400
Tulsa	5	13	.278	9	20	.310
San Jose State	1	17	.056	6	23	.207

Tournament: **Nevada d. UTEP 66-60**
Tournament MVP: **Kirk Snyder**, Nevada

INDEPENDENTS

	Overall		
	W	L	Pct
Corpus Christi	15	11	.577
Texas-Pan American	14	14	.500
Savannah State	4	24	.143
IPFW	3	25	.107

INDIVIDUAL LEADERS—SEASON

SCORING	CL	POS	G	FG	3FG	FT	PTS	PPG
1 **Keydren Clark**, Saint Peter's	SO	G	29	233	112	197	775	**26.7**
2 **Kevin Martin**, Western Carolina	JR	G	27	208	51	206	673	**24.9**
3 **David Hawkins**, Temple	SR	G	29	224	84	177	709	**24.4**
4 **Taylor Coppenrath**, Vermont	JR	F	24	203	14	159	579	**24.1**
5 **Luis Flores**, Manhattan	SR	G	31	234	68	208	744	**24.0**
6 **Michael Watson**, UMKC	SR	G	29	225	96	134	680	**23.4**
7 **Mike Helms**, Oakland	SR	G	30	224	79	168	695	**23.2**
8 **Odell Bradley**, IUPUI	SR	F	29	235	31	170	671	**23.1**
9 **Ike Diogu**, Arizona State	SO	F	27	179	14	243	615	**22.8**
10 **Derrick Tarver**, Akron	SR	G	27	196	47	173	612	**22.7**

FIELD GOAL PCT	CL	POS	G	FG	FGA	PCT
1 **Nigel Dixon**, Western Kentucky	SR	C	28	179	264	**67.8**
2 **Sean Finn**, Dayton	SR	C	33	175	264	**66.3**
3 **Adam Mark**, Belmont	SR	F	30	233	352	**66.2**
4 **David Harrison**, Colorado	JR	C	29	186	295	**63.1**
5 **Cuthbert Victor**, Murray State	SR	F	34	190	302	**62.9**

MINIMUM: 5 MADE PER GAME

THREE-POINT FG PER GAME	CL	POS	G	3FG	3PG
1 **Terrence Woods**, Florida A&M	SR	G	31	140	**4.5**
2 **Keydren Clark**, Saint Peter's	SO	G	29	112	**3.9**
3 **Marques Green**, St. Bonaventure	SR	G	27	98	**3.6**
4 **Ken Tutt**, Oral Roberts	FR	G	28	101	**3.6**
5 **Erik Benzel**, Denver	JR	G	27	97	**3.6**

THREE-POINT FG PCT	CL	POS	G	3FG	3FGA	PCT
1 **Brad Lechtenberg**, San Diego	SR	G	23	71	139	**51.1**
2 **James Odoms**, Mercer	JR	G	23	59	121	**48.8**
3 **Tyson Dorsey**, Samford	SR	G	28	74	152	**48.7**
4 **Antonio Burks**, Stephen F. Austin	SR	F	30	78	164	**47.6**
5 **Trey Guidry**, Illinois State	JR	G	29	86	187	**46.0**

MINIMUM: 2.5 MADE PER GAME

FREE THROW PCT	CL	POS	G	FT	FTA	PCT
1 **Blake Ahearn**, Missouri State	FR	G	33	117	120	**97.5**
2 **J.J. Redick**, Duke	SO	G	37	143	150	**95.3**
3 **Jake Sullivan**, Iowa State	SR	G	33	83	89	**93.3**
4 **Steve Drabyn**, Belmont	SR	G	30	96	105	**91.4**
Chris Hernandez, Stanford	SO	G	30	96	105	**91.4**

MINIMUM: 2.5 MADE PER GAME

ASSISTS PER GAME	CL	POS	G	AST	APG
1 **Greg Davis**, Troy	SR	G	31	256	**8.3**
2 **Martell Bailey**, Illinois-Chicago	SR	G	32	250	**7.8**
3 **Aaron Miles**, Kansas	JR	G	33	242	**7.3**
4 **Andres Rodriguez**, American	SR	G	31	225	**7.3**
5 **Raymond Felton**, North Carolina	SO	G	30	212	**7.1**
6 **Maurice Searight**, Grambling	SO	G	28	195	**7.0**
7 **Blake Stepp**, Gonzaga	SR	G	31	207	**6.7**
8 **Jerel Blassingame**, UNLV	JR	G	31	205	**6.6**
9 **Walker Russell Jr.**, Jacksonville State	SO	G	28	182	**6.5**
Mike McGrain, San Diego	JR	G	26	169	**6.5**

REBOUNDS PER GAME	CL	POS	G	REB	RPG
1 **Paul Millsap**, Louisiana Tech	FR	F	30	374	**12.5**
2 **Jaime Lloreda**, LSU	SR	F	22	256	**11.6**
3 **Emeka Okafor**, Connecticut	JR	C	36	415	**11.5**
4 **Nate Lofton**, Southeastern Louisiana	JR	C	29	315	**10.9**
5 **Nigel Wyatte**, Wagner	SR	F	28	292	**10.4**
6 **Charles Gaines**, Southern Miss	SR	F	28	290	**10.4**
7 **Nigel Dixon**, Western Kentucky	SR	C	28	287	**10.3**
8 **Cuthbert Victor**, Murray State	SR	F	34	347	**10.2**
9 **Odartey Blankson**, UNLV	JR	F	31	315	**10.2**
10 **Kris Humphries**, Minnesota	FR	F	29	293	**10.1**

BLOCKED SHOTS PER GAME	CL	POS	G	BLK	BPG
1 **Anwar Ferguson**, Houston	SR	C	27	111	**4.1**
2 **Emeka Okafor**, Connecticut	JR	C	36	147	**4.1**
3 **D'or Fischer**, West Virginia	JR	C	31	124	**4.0**
Gerrick Morris, South Florida	SR	C	27	108	**4.0**
5 **Nick Billings**, Binghamton	JR	C	30	105	**3.5**

STEALS PER GAME	CL	POS	G	STL	SPG
1 **Marques Green**, St. Bonaventure	SR	G	27	107	**4.0**
2 **Obie Trotter**, Alabama A&M	SO	G	29	88	**3.0**
3 **Chakowby Hicks**, Norfolk State	JR	G	29	86	**3.0**
4 **Zakee Wadood**, East Tennessee State	SR	F	33	92	**2.8**
5 **Jameer Nelson**, Saint Joseph's	SR	G	32	89	**2.8**

INDIVIDUAL LEADERS—GAME

POINTS	CL	POS	OPP	DATE	PTS
1 **Alex Loughton**, Old Dominion	SO	F	Charlotte	D6	**45**
2 **Derrick Tarver**, Akron	SR	G	Wright State	D30	**44**
Derrick Tarver, Akron	SR	G	Hampton	D1	**44**
Kevin Martin, Western Carolina	JR	G	Georgia	N21	**44**
5 **Taylor Coppenrath**, Vermont	JR	F	Maine	M13	**43**
Marques Green, St. Bonaventure	SR	G	Niagara	D17	**43**

THREE-POINT FG MADE	CL	POS	OPP	DATE	3FG
1 **Earnest Crumbley**, Florida Atlantic	SR	G	Campbell	F26	**11**
Kevin Bettencourt, Bucknell	SO	G	Saint Francis (PA)	D6	**11**
3 **Erik Benzel**, Denver	JR	G	Southern Utah	J2	**10**
Derrick Tarver, Akron	SR	G	Wright State	D30	**10**
Kelly Golob, Northern Arizona	SO	G	San Diego	D20	**10**
Brendan Plavich, Charlotte	JR	G	Syracuse	N26	**10**

ASSISTS	CL	POS	OPP	DATE	AST
1 **Andres Rodriguez**, American	SR	G	Navy	J14	**19**
2 **Raymond Felton**, North Carolina	SO	G	George Mason	D7	**18**
3 **Francisco Garcia**, Louisville	SO	F	Murray State	J3	**15**
Jay Straight, Wyoming	JR	G	Winthrop	D20	**15**
Maurice Searight, Grambling	SO	G	Texas College	D11	**15**
Martell Bailey, Illinois-Chicago	SR	G	Evansville	N25	**15**

REBOUNDS	CL	POS	OPP	DATE	REB
1 **Nate Lofton**, Southeastern Louisiana	JR	C	UTSA	M10	**22**
Caleb Green, Oral Roberts	FR	F	Southern Utah	F28	**22**
Emeka Okafor, Connecticut	JR	C	Notre Dame	F21	**22**
4 **Lawrence Roberts**, Mississippi State	JR	F	Alabama	M6	**21**
Sean May, North Carolina	SO	C	Duke	F5	**21**
Nigel Wyatte, Wagner	SR	F	Quinnipiac	F2	**21**
Nate Lofton, Southeastern Louisiana	JR	C	Lamar	J21	**21**
Paul Millsap, Louisiana Tech	FR	F	Nevada	J8	**21**
Adam Baumann, Youngstown State	SR	C	Oakland	D20	**21**
Cortney Scott, Oakland	JR	F	Saginaw Valley	D16	**21**
Sean May, North Carolina	SO	C	Akron	D14	**21**
Jaime Lloreda, LSU	SR	F	McNeese State	N24	**21**

BLOCKED SHOTS	CL	POS	OPP	DATE	BLK
1 **Gerrick Morris**, South Florida	SR	C	Houston	F21	**10**
Nick Billings, Binghamton	JR	C	Hartford	J31	**10**
Emeka Okafor, Connecticut	JR	C	Army	D6	**10**
Gerrick Morris, South Florida	SR	C	Wright State	N29	**10**
5 **D'or Fischer**, West Virginia	JR	C	Rhode Island	M19	**9**
Gerrick Morris, South Florida	SR	C	Southern Miss	F13	**9**
Gerrick Morris, South Florida	SR	C	TCU	F9	**9**
Greg Jenkins, Iona	SR	C	Manhattan	J25	**9**
Emeka Okafor, Connecticut	JR	C	Oklahoma	J11	**9**
Kendall Dartez, Louisville	SR	C	Holy Cross	D7	**9**

STEALS	CL	POS	OPP	DATE	STL
1 **Linas Lekavicius**, American	FR	G	Bucknell	F7	**9**
James Denson, Jacksonville State	SR	G	Morehead State	J24	**9**
Edward O'Neil, Charleston Southern	SR	G	Coastal Carolina	J13	**9**
Derrick Obasohan, Texas-Arlington	SR	F	Wichita State	D22	**9**
Ryan Price, McNeese State	SO	G	George Mason	D18	**9**
Michael Ross, Eastern Michigan	JR	G	Concordia (MI)	N25	**9**

TEAM LEADERS—SEASON

WIN-LOSS PCT	W	L	PCT
1 **Saint Joseph's**	30	2	.938
Stanford	30	2	.938
3 **Gonzaga**	28	3	.903
4 **Oklahoma State**	31	4	.886
5 **Mississippi State**	26	4	.867

SCORING OFFENSE	G	W-L	PTS	PPG
1 **Arizona**	30	20-10	2,614	**87.1**
2 **Troy**	31	24-7	2,624	**84.6**
3 **Wake Forest**	31	21-10	2,590	**83.5**
4 **North Carolina**	30	19-11	2,464	**82.1**
5 **Chattanooga**	30	19-11	2,463	**82.1**

SCORING MARGIN	G	W-L	PPG	OPP PPG	MAR
1 **Gonzaga**	31	28-3	81.8	66.2	**15.6**
2 **Saint Joseph's**	32	30-2	77.4	62.3	**15.1**
3 **Connecticut**	39	33-6	78.8	63.9	**14.9**
4 **Duke**	37	31-6	79.8	65.0	**14.8**
5 **Oklahoma State**	35	31-4	77.1	62.5	**14.6**

FIELD GOAL PCT	G	W-L	FG	FGA	PCT
1 **Oklahoma State**	35	31-4	1,002	1,953	**51.3**
2 **Gonzaga**	31	28-3	899	1,765	**50.9**
3 **Utah State**	29	25-4	711	1,397	**50.9**
4 **Murray State**	34	28-6	994	2,009	**49.5**
5 **Michigan State**	30	18-12	748	1,519	**49.2**

THREE-POINT FG PER GAME	G	W-L	3FG	3PG
1 **Troy**	31	24-7	364	**11.7**
2 **Saint Joseph's**	32	30-2	313	**9.8**
3 **Belmont**	30	21-9	293	**9.8**
4 **Samford**	28	12-16	264	**9.4**
5 **St. Francis (NY)**	28	15-13	258	**9.2**

ASSISTS PER GAME	G	W-L	AST	APG
1 **Sam Houston State**	28	13-15	530	**18.9**
2 **Murray State**	34	28-6	636	**18.7**
3 **Arizona**	30	20-10	560	**18.7**
4 **Gonzaga**	31	28-3	556	**17.9**
5 **North Carolina**	30	19-11	538	**17.9**

REBOUND MARGIN	G	W-L	RPG	OPP RPG	MAR
1 **Connecticut**	39	33-6	44.7	34.9	**9.7**
2 **Gonzaga**	31	28-3	39.7	31.5	**8.2**
3 **Mississippi State**	30	26-4	41.0	33.1	**8.0**
4 **Rhode Island**	34	20-14	40.6	33.1	**7.5**
5 **Utah**	33	24-9	34.5	27.2	**7.4**

Scoring Defense	G	W-L	OPP PTS	OPP PPG
1 Air Force	29	22-7	1,475	**50.9**
2 Pittsburgh	36	31-5	2,031	**56.4**
3 Princeton	28	20-8	1,591	**56.8**
4 Wisconsin	32	25-7	1,823	**57.0**
5 Utah	33	24-9	1,893	**57.4**

Field Goal Pct Defense	G	W-L	OPP FG	OPP FGA	OPP PCT
1 Connecticut	39	33-6	924	2,502	**36.9**
2 Louisville	30	20-10	638	1,672	**38.2**
3 Gonzaga	31	28-3	725	1,890	**38.4**
4 Stanford	32	30-2	671	1,745	**38.5**
5 Pittsburgh	36	31-5	765	1,984	**38.6**

Blocked Shots Per Game	G	W-L	BLK	BPG
1 Connecticut	39	33-6	315	**8.1**
2 Maryland	32	20-12	215	**6.7**
3 Syracuse	31	23-8	205	**6.6**
4 Duke	37	31-6	240	**6.5**
5 Jacksonville	28	13-15	169	**6.0**

Steals Per Game	G	W-L	STL	SPG
1 UAB	32	22-10	371	**11.6**
2 East Tenn. State	33	27-6	382	**11.6**
3 Drake	28	12-16	321	**11.5**
4 Troy	31	24-7	354	**11.4**
5 Ga. Southern	29	21-8	327	**11.3**

TEAM LEADERS—GAME

Points	OPP	DATE	SCORE
1 Troy	Oakwood	N24	**140-66**
2 Chattanooga	Emmanuel (GA)	N29	**125-78**
3 Central Michigan	Tri-State	D30	**124-103**
Chattanooga	Tennessee Wesleyan	N26	**124-58**
5 Lamar	Huston-Tillotson	D3	**123-76**

Field Goal Pct	OPP	DATE	FG	FGA	PCT
1 Iowa State	Georgia	M17	29	39	**74.4**
2 Michigan State	Ohio State	F7	33	45	**73.3**
3 Air Force	BYU	J24	29	40	**72.5**
4 Wyoming	Tennessee State	D17	39	54	**72.2**
5 Bucknell	Navy	J17	33	46	**71.7**

Three-point FG Made	OPP	DATE	3FG
1 Troy	Oakwood	N24	**26**
2 Troy	Lipscomb	J10	**21**
3 Saint Joseph's	Temple	J31	**20**
Ohio	Duquesne	J7	**20**
Northern Arizona	San Jose Christian	N26	**20**

CONSENSUS ALL-AMERICAS

FIRST TEAM

PLAYER	CL	POS	HT	SCHOOL	RPG	PPG
Andre Emmett	SR	G	6-5	Texas Tech	6.6	20.6
Ryan Gomes	JR	F	6-7	Providence	9.4	18.9
Jameer Nelson	SR	G	6-0	Saint Joseph's	4.7	20.6
Emeka Okafor	JR	C	6-10	Connecticut	11.5	17.6
Lawrence Roberts	JR	F	6-9	Mississippi State	10.1	16.9

SECOND TEAM

PLAYER	CL	POS	HT	SCHOOL	RPG	PPG
Josh Childress	JR	F	6-8	Stanford	7.5	15.7
Devin Harris	JR	G	6-3	Wisconsin	4.3	19.5
Julius Hodge	JR	G/F	6-6	NC State	6.4	18.2
Luke Jackson	SR	F	6-7	Oregon	7.2	21.2
Blake Stepp	SR	G	6-4	Gonzaga	4.6	14.6

Selectors: AP, NABC, Sporting News, USBWA

AWARD WINNERS

PLAYER OF THE YEAR

PLAYER	CL	POS	HT	SCHOOL	AWARDS
Jameer Nelson	SR	G	6-0	Saint Joseph's	Naismith, AP, USBWA, Wooden, NABC (shared), Rupp, Frances Pomeroy Naismith*
Emeka Okafor	JR	C	6-10	Connecticut	NABC (shared)

* For the most outstanding senior player who is 6 feet or under

DEFENSIVE PLAYER OF THE YEAR

PLAYER	CL	POS	HT	SCHOOL
Emeka Okafor	JR	C	6-10	Connecticut

COACH OF THE YEAR

COACH	SCHOOL	REC	AWARD
Phil Martelli	Saint Joseph's	30-2	Naismith, AP, USBWA, NABC (shared), CBS/Chevrolet
Mike Montgomery	Stanford	30-2	NABC (shared), Sporting News

Bob Gibbons' Top High School Senior Recruits

PLAYER	POS	HT	HIGH SCHOOL	A-A TEAMS	COLLEGE	CAREER NOTES
1 Dwight Howard	PF	6-11	Southwest Atlanta Christian Academy	McD, MJ, P, USA	None	Drafted straight out of HS; No. 1 overall pick, '04 NBA draft (Magic); NBA Defensive POY '09; 5 seasons, 17.3 ppg, 12.5 rpg
2 Shaun Livingston	PG	6-7	Peoria (IL) Central HS	McD, P, USA	None	Drafted straight out of HS; No. 4 pick, '04 NBA draft (Clippers); 7.3 ppg (4 seasons)
3 Joshua Smith	F	6-9	Oak Hill Academy, Mouth of Wilson, VA	McD, P, USA	None	Drafted straight out of HS; No. 17 pick, '04 NBA draft (Hawks), 14.0 ppg, 7.4 rpg (5 seasons)
4 Al Jefferson	PF	6-9	Prentiss (MS) HS	McD, MJ, P, USA	None	Drafted straight out of HS; No. 15 pick, '04 NBA draft (Celtics); traded to Wolves, '07; 5 seasons, 14.9 ppg, 8.5 rpg
5 Sebastian Telfair	PG	6-0	Abraham Lincoln HS, Brooklyn, NY	McD, P, USA	None	Drafted straight out of HS; No. 13 pick, '04 NBA draft (Blazers); 8.2 ppg, 4.0 apg (5 seasons)
6 Robert Swift	C	7-1	Bakersfield (CA) HS	McD, P	None	Drafted straight out of HS; No. 12 pick, '04 NBA draft (Sonics); 4.3 ppg, 3.0 rpg (4 seasons)
7 Marvin Williams	PF	6-9	Bremerton (WA) HS	McD, P	North Carolina	No. 2 pick '05 NBA draft (Hawks); 12.5 ppg (4 seasons); NCAA title, '05
8 Earl J.R. Smith	G/F	6-6	St. Benedict's Prep, Newark, NJ	McD, P	None	Drafted straight out of HS; No. 18 pick, '04 NBA draft (Hornets); 11.9 ppg (5 seasons)
9 Rudy Gay	PF	6-8	Archbishop Spalding HS, Severn, MD	McD, MJ, P	Connecticut	15.2 ppg as sophomore; No. 8 pick, '06 NBA draft (Rockets); 16.7 ppg (3 seasons)
10 Randolph Morris	C	6-11	Landmark Christian HS, Fairburn, GA	McD, P	Kentucky	12.6 ppg, 6.0 rpg, 3 seasons; undrafted; 46 NBA games with Knicks, Hawks
11 Glen Davis	F/C	6-8	University Lab School, Baton Rouge, LA	McD, P	LSU	'06 SEC POY at LSU; 2nd-round pick, '07 NBA draft (Celtics); NBA title, '08
12 Malik Hairston	G/F	6-6	Renaissance HS, Detroit	McD, MJ, P	Oregon	2nd-round pick, '08 NBA draft (Suns); 15 games with Spurs in '09
13 Mike Williams	PF	6-8	Wilcox Central HS, Camden, AL	McD, P	Texas/Cincinnati	Tranferred to Cincy in '06; injured all of '07-'08; 9.8 ppg, 5.7 rpg as Sr. in '08-'09
14 Jordan Farmar	PG	6-2	Taft HS, Woodland Hills, CA	McD, MJ, P	UCLA	Pac-10 FOY; All-Pac-10 as Soph.; No. 26 pick, '06 NBA draft (Lakers)
15 LaMarcus Aldridge	F/C	6-10	Seagoville HS, Dallas	McD, MJ, P	Texas	13.8 ppg, 8.2 rpg at UT; No. 2 pick, '06 NBA draft (Bulls); '07 All-Rookie team
16 Rajon Rondo	PG	6-2	Oak Hill Academy, Mouth of Wilson, VA	McD, MJ, P	Kentucky	9.6 ppg in 2 seasons at UK; No. 21 pick, '06 NBA draft (Suns); NBA title, '08 (Celtics)
17 DeMarcus Nelson	G	6-3	Sheldon HS, Sacramento, CA	McD, P	Duke	ACC Defensive POY ('08); undrafted; signed with Warriors, '08, Bulls, '09
18 Jawann McClellan	G	6-5	Charles H. Milby HS, Houston	McD, P	Arizona	7.7 ppg, 3.3 rpg in 4 seasons at UA; undrafted; played in D-League
19 Joe Crawford	G	6-4	Renaissance HS, Detroit	McD, MJ, P	Kentucky	4 seasons at UK; 17.9 ppg as Sr.; 2nd-round pick, '08 NBA draft (Lakers)
20 Daniel Gibson	G	6-3	Jesse Jones HS, Houston	McD, MJ, P	Texas	Big 12 FOY; 13.8 ppg, 3.5 apg, 2 seasons; 2nd-round pick, '06 NBA draft (Cavs)

Other Standouts

PLAYER	POS	HT	HIGH SCHOOL	A-A TEAMS	COLLEGE	CAREER NOTES
42 Corey Brewer	F	6-7	Portland (TN) HS	McD, MJ, P	Florida	Final Four MOP '07; No. 7 pick, '07 NBA draft (Wolves)
48 Joakim Noah	F/C	6-11	Lawrenceville (NJ) HS		Florida	Final Four MOP '06; 2nd-team AP All-America, 2007; No. 9 pick, '07 NBA draft (Bulls)
94 Taurean Green	PG	6-0	Cardinal Gibbons HS, Raleigh, NC		Florida	2nd-round pick, '07 NBA draft (Blazers); 2 seasons NBA; 1 season D-League

Abbreviations: McD=McDonald's; MJ=Jordan Brand; P=Parade; USA=USA Today

ANNUAL REVIEW

Poll Progression

Preseason Poll

AP	ESPN/USA	SCHOOL	AP↓↑
1	1	**Connecticut**	
2	2	**Duke**	
3	3	**Michigan State**	
4	4	**Arizona**	
5	6	**Missouri**	
6	5	**Kansas**	
7	7	**Syracuse**	
8	8	**Florida**	
9	10	**North Carolina**	
10	9	**Kentucky**	
11	11	**Texas**	
12	13	**Illinois**	
13	18	**Saint Joseph's**	
14	15	**Oklahoma**	
15	14	**Wisconsin**	
16	12	**Gonzaga**	
17	16	**Louisville**	
18	19	**Cincinnati**	
19	21	**Wake Forest**	
20	17	**Stanford**	
21	19	**Notre Dame**	
22	22	**Pittsburgh**	
23	23	**Marquette**	
24	—	**NC State**	
25	24	**Oklahoma State**	
—	25	**Maryland**	

Week of Nov 25

AP	ESPN/USA	SCHOOL	AP↓↑
1	1	**Connecticut** (3-0)	
2	2	**Duke** (1-0)	
3	4	**Michigan State** (1-0)	
4	3	**Arizona** (0-0)	
5	6	**Missouri** (0-0)	
6	5	**Kansas** (1-0)	
7	7	**Syracuse** (0-0)	
8	8	**Florida** (0-0)	
9	10	**North Carolina** (1-0)	
10	9	**Kentucky** (1-0)	
11	11	**Texas** (1-0)	
12	12	**Illinois** (1-0)	
13	14	**Saint Joseph's** (1-0)	
14	13	**Oklahoma** (2-0)	
15	15	**Wisconsin** (1-0)	
16	21	**Gonzaga** (1-0)	
17	16	**Louisville** (0-0)	
18	18	**Wake Forest** (2-0)	↑1
19	19	**Cincinnati** (1-0)	↓1
20	17	**Stanford** (0-0)	
21	20	**Notre Dame** (1-1)	
22	22	**Pittsburgh** (2-0)	
23	23	**Marquette** (3-0)	
24	—	**Oklahoma State** (1-0)	↑1
25	—	**NC State** (0-0)	↓1
—	24	**Maryland** (1-0)	
—	25	**Texas Tech** (3-0)	

Week of Dec 2

AP	ESPN/USA	SCHOOL	AP↓↑
1	1	**Kansas** (2-0)	↑5
2	2	**Florida** (2-0)	↑6
3	4	**Connecticut** (4-1)	↓2
4	5	**Missouri** (1-0)	↑1
5	6	**Michigan State** (3-1)	↓2
6	6	**Duke** (3-1)	↓4
7	8	**Arizona** (1-1)	↓3
8	9	**Texas** (3-0)	↑3
9	3	**Kentucky** (2-0)	↑1
10	10	**North Carolina** (3-0)	↓1
11	11	**Illinois** (3-0)	↑1
12	14	**Saint Joseph's** (3-0)	↑1
13	15	**Georgia Tech** (5-0)	⤴
14	12	**Oklahoma** (3-0)	
15	13	**Wisconsin** (3-0)	
16	18	**Syracuse** (1-1)	↓9
17	24	**Gonzaga** (3-1)	↓1
18	16	**Wake Forest** (3-0)	
19	19	**Cincinnati** (3-0)	
20	21	**Purdue** (4-0)	⤴
21	17	**Stanford** (3-0)	↓1
22	22	**Pittsburgh** (4-0)	
23	20	**Notre Dame** (2-0)	↓2
24	23	**Marquette** (4-0)	↓1
25	—	**Oklahoma State** (3-0)	↓1
—	25	**Maryland** (3-0)	

Week of Dec 9

AP	ESPN/USA	SCHOOL	AP↓↑
1	1	**Florida** (5-0)	
2	3	**Connecticut** (6-1)	
3	4	**Missouri** (3-0)	↑
4	5	**Duke** (5-1)	↑
5	7	**Kansas** (3-1)	↓
6	6	**Texas** (4-0)	↑
7	8	**North Carolina** (5-0)	↑
8	2	**Kentucky** (4-0)	↑
9	9	**Arizona** (2-1)	↓
10	10	**Georgia Tech** (7-0)	↑
11	11	**Oklahoma** (5-0)	↑
12	15	**Saint Joseph's** (5-0)	
13	13	**Stanford** (4-0)	↑8
14	14	**Illinois** (4-1)	↓3
15	12	**Wake Forest** (5-0)	↑3
16	16	**Purdue** (6-0)	↑4
17	18	**Gonzaga** (6-1)	
18	17	**Cincinnati** (4-0)	↑1
19	21	**Syracuse** (2-1)	↓3
20	23	**Pittsburgh** (6-0)	↑2
21	20	**Michigan State** (3-3)	↓16
22	21	**Marquette** (6-0)	↑2
23	19	**Wisconsin** (4-1)	↓8
24	—	**Iowa** (6-0)	⤴
25	24	**Dayton** (6-0)	⤴
—	25	**Louisville** (2-1)	

Week of Dec 16

AP	ESPN/USA	SCHOOL	AP↓↑
1	2	**Connecticut** (7-1)	↑1
2	1	**Kentucky** (5-0) Ⓐ	↑6
3	3	**Duke** (6-1)	↑1
4	4	**North Carolina** (6-0)	↑3
5	6	**Georgia Tech** (8-0)	↑5
6	7	**Kansas** (5-1)	↓1
7	5	**Arizona** (4-1)	↑2
8	8	**Oklahoma** (7-0)	↑3
9	11	**Stanford** (5-0)	↑4
10	14	**Missouri** (3-1)	↓7
11	10	**Texas** (5-1)	↓5
11	12	**Saint Joseph's** (7-0)	↑1
13	15	**Gonzaga** (7-1)	↑4
14	9	**Wake Forest** (5-0)	↑1
15	13	**Florida** (5-2) Ⓑ	↓14
16	16	**Cincinnati** (4-0)	↑2
17	17	**Purdue** (7-1)	↓1
18	20	**Pittsburgh** (7-0)	↑2
19	21	**Syracuse** (3-1)	
20	22	**Louisville** (4-1) Ⓑ	⤴
21	19	**Illinois** (6-2)	↓7
22	18	**Wisconsin** (6-1)	↑1
23	23	**Marquette** (6-1)	↓1
24	24	**Dayton** (8-0)	↑1
25	—	**Maryland** (5-2)	⤴
—	25	**Michigan State** (3-4) Ⓐ	⤵

Week of Dec 23

AP	ESPN/USA	SCHOOL	AP↓↑
1	2	**Connecticut** (8-1)	
2	1	**Kentucky** (6-0)	
3	3	**Duke** (8-1)	
4	4	**Georgia Tech** (10-0)	↑1
5	5	**Arizona** (5-1)	↑2
6	8	**Stanford** (7-0)	↑3
7	7	**Oklahoma** (8-0)	↑1
8	6	**Wake Forest** (7-0)	↑6
9	9	**North Carolina** (6-1)	↓5
10	10	**Saint Joseph's** (8-0)	↑1
11	14	**Missouri** (4-1)	↓1
12	11	**Kansas** (6-2)	↓6
13	13	**Florida** (6-2)	↑2
14	12	**Cincinnati** (6-0)	↑2
15	18	**Gonzaga** (7-2)	↓2
16	17	**Pittsburgh** (10-0)	↑2
17	21	**Syracuse** (5-1)	↑2
18	16	**Texas** (5-2)	↓7
19	15	**Wisconsin** (7-1)	↑3
20	20	**Louisville** (5-1)	
21	19	**Illinois** (6-2)	
22	22	**Purdue** (8-2)	↓5
23	23	**Dayton** (9-0)	↑1
24	25	**Maryland** (6-2)	↑1
25	—	**Vanderbilt** (8-0)	⤴
—	24	**Marquette** (6-2)	⤵

Week of Dec 31

AP	ESPN/USA	SCHOOL	AP↓↑
1	1	**Connecticut** (9-1)	
2	2	**Duke** (8-1)	↑1
3	3	**Georgia Tech** (11-0)	↑1
4	4	**Arizona** (7-1)	↑1
5	7	**Stanford** (9-0)	↑1
6	5	**Wake Forest** (7-0)	↑2
7	8	**Oklahoma** (8-0)	
8	6	**Kentucky** (7-1)	↓6
9	9	**North Carolina** (7-1)	
10	10	**Saint Joseph's** (9-0)	
11	14	**Louisville** (7-1)	↑9
12	11	**Cincinnati** (8-0)	↑2
13	13	**Kansas** (6-2)	↓1
14	12	**Florida** (8-2)	↓1
15	16	**Pittsburgh** (12-0)	↑1
16	18	**Gonzaga** (8-2)	↓1
17	20	**Syracuse** (7-1)	
18	15	**Wisconsin** (8-1)	↑1
19	17	**Texas** (5-2)	↓1
20	19	**Illinois** (7-2)	↑1
21	21	**Purdue** (9-2)	↑1
22	24	**Vanderbilt** (9-0)	↑3
23	22	**Missouri** (4-3)	↓12
24	—	**Mississippi State** (10-0)	⤴
25	23	**Marquette** (8-2)	⤴
—	25	**Florida State** (11-1)	

Week of Jan 6

AP	ESPN/USA	SCHOOL	AP↓↑
1	1	**Connecticut** (11-1)	
2	2	**Duke** (10-1)	
3	3	**Arizona** (9-1)	↑1
4	6	**Stanford** (11-0)	↑1
5	4	**Wake Forest** (9-0)	↑1
6	7	**Oklahoma** (10-0)	↑1
7	5	**Kentucky** (9-1)	↑1
8	8	**Georgia Tech** (12-1)	↓5
9	9	**Saint Joseph's** (11-0)	↑1
10	12	**Louisville** (9-1)	↑1
11	10	**Cincinnati** (9-0)	↑1
12	13	**North Carolina** (8-2)	↓3
13	14	**Kansas** (8-2)	
14	11	**Florida** (9-2)	
15	15	**Pittsburgh** (14-0)	
16	17	**Gonzaga** (10-2)	
17	19	**Syracuse** (9-1)	
18	16	**Texas** (7-2)	↑1
19	20	**Illinois** (9-2)	↑1
20	21	**Vanderbilt** (11-0)	↑2
21	18	**Wisconsin** (9-2)	↓3
22	—	**Mississippi State** (11-0)	↑2
23	22	**Marquette** (9-2)	↑2
24	25	**Purdue** (10-3)	↓3
25	—	**Providence** (8-1)	⤴
—	23	**Creighton** (9-0)	
—	24	**Oklahoma State** (9-1)	
—	25	**Texas Tech** (12-2)	

Week of Jan 13

AP	ESPN/USA	SCHOOL	AP↓↑
1	1	**Connecticut** (13-1)	
2	2	**Duke** (12-1)	
3	4	**Stanford** (13-0)	↑1
4	3	**Wake Forest** (11-0)	↑1
5	5	**Kentucky** (10-1)	↑2
6	6	**Saint Joseph's** (13-0)	↑3
7	8	**Arizona** (10-2)	↓4
8	9	**Louisville** (11-1)	↑2
9	11	**North Carolina** (10-2)	↑3
10	7	**Cincinnati** (11-0)	↑1
11	13	**Oklahoma** (10-1)	↓5
12	14	**Georgia Tech** (12-2)	↓4
13	15	**Pittsburgh** (16-0) Ⓒ	↑2
14	12	**Kansas** (9-2)	↓1
15	10	**Florida** (11-2)	↓1
16	17	**Gonzaga** (12-2)	
17	19	**Syracuse** (11-1)	
18	16	**Texas** (9-2)	
19	18	**Wisconsin** (11-2)	↑2
20	24	**Mississippi State** (13-0)	↑2
21	21	**Marquette** (11-2)	↑2
22	22	**Texas Tech** (13-2)	⤴
23	23	**Vanderbilt** (12-1)	↓3
24	20	**Creighton** (12-0)	⤴
25	25	**Illinois** (10-3)	↓6

Week of Jan 20

AP	ESPN/USA	SCHOOL	AP↓↑
1	1	**Duke** (14-1)	↑1
2	2	**Stanford** (14-0)	↑1
3	3	**Saint Joseph's** (15-0)	↑3
4	4	**Connecticut** (14-2)	↓3
5	6	**Louisville** (13-1)	↑3
6	5	**Cincinnati** (13-0)	↑4
7	11	**North Carolina** (11-3) Ⓓ	↑2
8	9	**Pittsburgh** (18-0)	↑5
9	8	**Kentucky** (11-2)	↓4
10	7	**Wake Forest** (11-2)	↓6
11	13	**Georgia Tech** (14-2)	↑1
12	10	**Kansas** (11-2)	↑2
13	16	**Syracuse** (13-1)	↑4
14	12	**Arizona** (11-3)	↓7
15	15	**Gonzaga** (14-2)	↑1
16	14	**Texas** (11-2)	↑2
17	17	**Florida** (11-3)	↓2
18	18	**Texas Tech** (14-2)	↑4
19	20	**Mississippi State** (14-1)	↑1
20	21	**Oklahoma** (10-3)	↓9
21	19	**Wisconsin** (11-3)	↓2
22	22	**Vanderbilt** (13-2)	↑1
23	23	**Purdue** (12-4)	⤴
24	25	**Oklahoma State** (12-2)	⤴
25	—	**South Carolina** (16-2)	⤴
—	24	**Creighton** (13-1)	⤵

Week of Jan 27

AP	ESPN/USA	SCHOOL	AP↓↑
1	1	**Duke** (16-1)	
2	2	**Stanford** (16-0)	
3	3	**Saint Joseph's** (17-0)	
4	4	**Louisville** (15-1)	↑1
5	5	**Kentucky** (13-2)	↑4
6	8	**Connecticut** (15-3)	↓2
7	6	**Pittsburgh** (19-1)	↑1
8	7	**Cincinnati** (14-1)	↓2
9	9	**Arizona** (13-3)	↑5
10	10	**Gonzaga** (15-2)	↑5
11	11	**Mississippi State** (16-1)	↑8
12	15	**North Carolina** (12-4)	↓5
13	14	**Texas Tech** (16-2)	↑5
14	16	**Georgia Tech** (15-3)	↓3
15	12	**Kansas** (12-3)	↓3
16	18	**Texas** (12-3)	
17	13	**Wisconsin** (13-3)	↑4
18	19	**Oklahoma State** (14-2)	↑6
19	17	**Wake Forest** (11-4)	↓9
20	22	**Syracuse** (13-3)	↓7
21	21	**Purdue** (14-4)	↑2
22	20	**Florida** (12-4)	↓5
23	24	**Providence** (13-3)	⤴
24	23	**South Carolina** (17-2)	↑1
25	25	**Oklahoma** (11-4)	↓5

Week of Feb 3

AP	ESPN/USA	SCHOOL	AP↓↑
1	1	**Duke** (18-1)	
2	2	**Stanford** (18-0)	
3	3	**Saint Joseph's** (18-0)	
4	4	**Pittsburgh** (20-1)	↑3
5	5	**Connecticut** (17-3)	↑1
6	6	**Louisville** (16-2)	↓2
7	7	**Mississippi State** (18-1)	↑4
8	8	**Gonzaga** (17-2)	↑2
9	9	**Kentucky** (14-3)	↓4
10	10	**Cincinnati** (15-2)	↓2
11	14	**Texas** (14-3)	↑5
12	12	**Arizona** (14-4)	↓3
13	13	**Oklahoma State** (15-2)	↑5
14	11	**Wisconsin** (14-3)	↑3
15	16	**Georgia Tech** (16-4)	↓1
16	15	**Wake Forest** (13-4)	↑3
17	19	**North Carolina** (13-5)	↓5
18	20	**Syracuse** (14-3)	↑2
19	18	**Texas Tech** (16-4)	↓6
20	17	**Kansas** (13-4)	↓5
21	21	**Florida** (13-5)	↑1
22	22	**Oklahoma** (13-4)	↑3
23	23	**Providence** (14-4)	
24	—	**Utah State** (17-1)	⤴
25	24	**South Carolina** (18-3)	↓1
—	25	**Vanderbilt** (14-4)	

k of Feb 10

AP	ESPN/USA	SCHOOL	AP↓↑
	1	**Duke** (20-1)	
	2	**Stanford** (20-0) Ⓔ	
	3	**Saint Joseph's** (20-0)	
	4	**Pittsburgh** (22-1)	
	5	**Connecticut** (19-3)	
	6	**Mississippi State** (19-1)	↑1
	7	**Gonzaga** (19-2)	↑1
	8	**Kentucky** (16-3)	↑1
	9	**Louisville** (17-3)	↓3
	10	**Oklahoma State** (17-2)	↑3
	11	**Texas** (16-3)	
	13	**Kansas** (15-4)	↑8
	12	**Cincinnati** (16-3)	↓3
	17	**North Carolina** (14-6)	↑3
	16	**Georgia Tech** (17-5)	
	15	**Arizona** (14-6)	↓4
	14	**Wisconsin** (15-4)	↓3
	19	**Texas Tech** (17-5)	↑1
	23	**Utah State** (19-1)	↑5
	18	**Wake Forest** (13-6)	↓4
	—	**NC State** (14-5)	⤴
	20	**Florida** (14-6)	↓1
	24	**Southern Illinois** (18-2)	⤴
24	21	**Providence** (15-5)	↓1
	22	**South Carolina** (19-4)	
—	25	**Syracuse** (14-5)	⤵

Week of Feb 17

AP	ESPN/USA	SCHOOL	AP↓↑
1	1	**Stanford** (21-0)	↑1
2	2	**Saint Joseph's** (22-0)	↑1
3	3	**Duke** (21-2)	↓2
4	5	**Mississippi State** (21-1)	↑2
5	4	**Pittsburgh** (23-2)	↓1
6	6	**Gonzaga** (21-2)	↑1
7	7	**Oklahoma State** (19-2)	↑3
8	8	**Connecticut** (19-5)	↓3
9	9	**Kentucky** (17-4)	↓1
10	11	**Louisville** (17-4)	↓1
11	12	**Texas** (17-4)	
12	10	**Wisconsin** (17-4)	↑5
13	18	**NC State** (16-5)	↑8
14	13	**Arizona** (16-6)	↑2
15	15	**Wake Forest** (15-6)	↑5
16	19	**North Carolina** (15-7)	↓2
17	14	**Cincinnati** (17-4)	↓4
18	16	**Georgia Tech** (18-6)	↓3
19	17	**Providence** (17-5)	↑5
20	21	**Southern Illinois** (20-2)	↑3
21	20	**Kansas** (15-6)	↓9
22	23	**Texas Tech** (18-6)	↓4
23	—	**Memphis** (18-4)	⤴
24	—	**LSU** (17-4)	⤴
25	22	**South Carolina** (20-5)	
—	24	**Syracuse** (16-5)	
—	25	**Utah State** (20-2)	⤵

Week of Feb 24

AP	ESPN/USA	SCHOOL	AP↓↑
1	1	**Stanford** (23-0)	
2	2	**Saint Joseph's** (24-0)	
3	3	**Pittsburgh** (24-2)	↑2
4	5	**Gonzaga** (23-2)	↑2
5	4	**Duke** (22-3)	↓2
6	6	**Oklahoma State** (21-2)	↑1
7	7	**Mississippi State** (21-2)	↓3
8	8	**Connecticut** (21-5)	
9	9	**Kentucky** (19-4)	
10	10	**Texas** (19-4)	↑1
11	11	**Wake Forest** (17-6)	↑4
12	16	**North Carolina** (16-7)	↑4
13	13	**Providence** (18-5)	↑6
14	19	**NC State** (17-6)	↓1
15	12	**Cincinnati** (18-5)	↑2
16	17	**Southern Illinois** (22-2)	↑4
17	14	**Arizona** (17-7)	↓3
18	20	**Georgia Tech** (19-7)	
19	22	**Memphis** (19-4)	↑4
20	18	**Kansas** (17-6)	↑1
21	21	**Louisville** (17-6)	↓11
22	15	**Wisconsin** (17-6)	↓10
23	24	**Illinois** (18-5)	⤴
24	23	**Utah State** (22-2)	⤴
25	25	**Texas Tech** (19-7)	↓3

Week of Mar 2

AP	ESPN/USA	SCHOOL	AP↓↑
1	1	**Stanford** (25-0)	
2	2	**Saint Joseph's** (26-0)	
3	3	**Duke** (24-3)	↑2
4	4	**Gonzaga** (25-2)	
5	5	**Mississippi State** (23-2)	↑2
6	6	**Pittsburgh** (25-3)	↓3
7	8	**Connecticut** (23-5)	↑1
8	7	**Oklahoma State** (22-3)	↓2
9	9	**Kentucky** (21-4)	
10	10	**Texas** (21-4)	
11	11	**Wake Forest** (19-6)	
12	13	**Providence** (20-5)	↑1
13	12	**Cincinnati** (20-5)	↑2
14	16	**North Carolina** (17-8)	↓2
15	15	**Southern Illinois** (24-2)	↑1
16	19	**NC State** (18-7)	↓2
17	14	**Wisconsin** (19-6)	↑5
18	20	**Illinois** (20-5)	↑5
19	22	**Georgia Tech** (20-8)	↓1
20	23	**Memphis** (20-5)	↓1
21	18	**Kansas** (18-7)	↓1
22	17	**Arizona** (18-8)	↓5
23	21	**Utah State** (24-2)	↑1
24	—	**Syracuse** (19-6)	⤴
25	24	**Louisville** (18-7)	↓4
—	25	**Michigan State** (17-9)	

Week of Mar 9

AP	ESPN/USA	SCHOOL	AP↓↑
1	1	**Saint Joseph's** (27-0)	↑1
2	2	**Stanford** (26-1)	↓1
3	3	**Gonzaga** (26-2)	↑1
4	5	**Mississippi State** (25-2)	↑1
5	4	**Duke** (25-3)	↓2
6	6	**Pittsburgh** (27-3)	
7	7	**Oklahoma State** (24-3)	↑1
8	8	**Kentucky** (23-4)	↑1
9	9	**Connecticut** (24-6)	↓2
10	10	**Wisconsin** (21-6)	↑7
11	11	**Texas** (21-6)	↓1
12	13	**Illinois** (22-5)	↑6
13	12	**Cincinnati** (21-6)	
14	18	**Georgia Tech** (22-8)	↑5
15	14	**Wake Forest** (19-9)	↓4
16	19	**North Carolina** (18-9)	↓2
17	20	**NC State** (19-8)	↓1
18	15	**Kansas** (20-7)	↑3
19	23	**Syracuse** (21-6)	↑5
20	17	**Providence** (20-7)	↓8
21	16	**Arizona** (19-8)	↑1
22	21	**Utah State** (25-2)	↑1
23	24	**Memphis** (21-6)	↓3
24	22	**Southern Illinois** (25-4)	↓9
25	25	**Air Force** (22-5)	⤴

Week of Mar 16 Ⓕ

AP	ESPN/USA	SCHOOL	AP↓↑
1	1	**Stanford** (29-1)	↑1
2	4	**Kentucky** (26-4)	↑6
3	2	**Gonzaga** (27-2)	
4	3	**Oklahoma State** (27-3)	↑3
5	5	**Saint Joseph's** (27-1)	↓4
6	6	**Duke** (27-5)	↓1
7	7	**Connecticut** (27-6)	↑2
8	9	**Mississippi State** (25-3)	↓4
9	8	**Pittsburgh** (29-4)	↓3
10	10	**Wisconsin** (24-6)	
11	12	**Cincinnati** (24-6)	↑2
12	11	**Texas** (23-7)	↓1
13	13	**Illinois** (24-6)	↓1
14	15	**Georgia Tech** (23-9)	
15	17	**NC State** (20-9)	↑2
16	14	**Kansas** (21-8)	↑2
17	16	**Wake Forest** (19-9)	↓2
18	20	**North Carolina** (18-10)	↓2
19	21	**Maryland** (19-11)	⤴
20	24	**Syracuse** (21-7)	↓1
21	19	**Providence** (20-8)	↓1
22	18	**Arizona** (20-9)	↓1
23	23	**Southern Illinois** (25-4)	↑1
24	—	**Memphis** (21-7)	↓1
25	22	**Utah State** (25-3)	↓3
25	—	**Boston College** (23-9)	⤴
—	25	**Michigan State** (18-11)	

Final Poll (Post-Tournament)

ESPN/USA	SCHOOL
1	**Connecticut** (33-6)
2	**Duke** (31-6)
3	**Georgia Tech** (28-10)
4	**Oklahoma State** (31-4)
5	**Saint Joseph's** (30-2)
6	**Stanford** (30-2)
7	**Pittsburgh** (31-5)
8	**Kentucky** (27-5)
9	**Kansas** (24-9)
10	**Texas** (25-8)
11	**Illinois** (26-7)
12	**Gonzaga** (28-3)
13	**Mississippi State** (26-4)
14	**Xavier** (26-11)
15	**Wake Forest** (21-10)
16	**Wisconsin** (25-7)
17	**Alabama** (20-13)
18	**Cincinnati** (25-7)
19	**Syracuse** (23-8)
20	**NC State** (21-10)
21	**Nevada** (25-9)
22	**North Carolina** (19-11)
23	**UAB** (22-10)
24	**Maryland** (20-12)
25	**Vanderbilt** (23-10)

Ⓐ On Dec. 13, a world-record basketball crowd of 78,129 gathers at Ford Field, home of the Detroit Lions, to watch Kentucky defeat Michigan State, 79-74.

Ⓑ After losing back-to-back games to previously unranked Maryland and Louisville, Florida suffers the biggest one-week drop for a top-ranked team in AP poll history. Louisville's win on Dec. 13 is the 400th of Rick Pitino's NCAA career.

Ⓒ Off to its best start since the 1927-28 season, Pittsburgh goes on the road for the first time in a month and survives two overtimes to beat Miami, 84-80, and remain undefeated.

Ⓓ North Carolina's 86-83 win over Connecticut on Jan. 17 gives the Tar Heels their 10th victory over a top-ranked team, tying the NCAA record set by UCLA. UNC will take sole possession of the record with a victory over Illinois in the 2005 NCAA championship game and extend it to 12 on March 4, 2006, with a 83-76 victory over Duke.

Ⓔ Stanford alum Tiger Woods is among the fans who storm the floor after Nick Robinson hits a 35-foot jumper in the final seconds on Feb. 7 to give the Cardinal a win over Arizona, 80-77, keeping its unbeaten season intact.

Ⓕ For the first time in school history, Texas Tech wins 20 games or more for the third straight season. Andre Emmett (20.6 ppg) becomes the leading scorer in the Big 12 for the second straight season, the leading career scorer in Tech history and the 13th All-America coached by Bob Knight.

Pre-Tournament Ratings Percentage Index (RPI)

RANK	SCHOOL	W-L	Sched. Strg.	SS Rank	RPI
1	**Kentucky**	26-4	.6146	7	.6762
2	**Duke**	27-5	.6282	4	.6750
3	**Saint Joseph's**	27-1	.5672	42	.6622
4	**Mississippi State**	25-3	.5624	48	.6473
5	**Connecticut**	27-6	.5976	16	.6441
6	**Oklahoma State**	26-3	.5598	53	.6431
7	**Pittsburgh**	28-4	.5610	50	.6407
8	**Texas**	23-7	.6077	10	.6374
9	**Stanford**	29-1	.5253	106	.6371
10	**Cincinnati**	24-6	.5925	21	.6352
11	**Gonzaga**	27-2	.5358	82	.6332
12	**Florida**	20-10	.6392	1	.6303
13	**Wisconsin**	24-6	.5839	28	.6299
14	**Georgia Tech**	23-9	.5974	17	.6285
15	**NC State**	20-9	.6084	9	.6252
16	**Maryland**	19-11	.6338	3	.6238
17	**Syracuse**	21-7	.5940	18	.6237
18	**Kansas**	20-8	.6087	8	.6228
19	**North Carolina**	18-10	.6228	5	.6203
20	**Wake Forest**	19-9	.5994	15	.6197
21	**Providence**	20-8	.5862	26	.6188
22	**Boston College**	23-9	.5894	23	.6155
23	**Louisville**	20-9	.6046	12	.6135
24	**Illinois**	24-6	.5503	64	.6117
25	**Alabama**	17-12	.6389	2	.6091
26	**Southern Illinois**	25-4	.5273	101	.6076
27	**Vanderbilt**	21-9	.5837	29	.6071
28	**Seton Hall**	19-9	.5931	19	.6061
29	**Nevada**	22-8	.5763	34	.6025
30	**Texas Tech**	22-10	.5804	30	.5996
31	**BYU**	19-8	.5762	35	.5986
32	**Charlotte**	21-8	.5536	62	.5982
33	**UAB**	20-9	.5841	27	.5981
34	**Memphis**	21-7	.5430	73	.5976
35	**Xavier**	23-10	.5690	40	.5966
36	**Utah**	23-8	.5481	65	.5939
37	**DePaul**	21-9	.5545	60	.5920
38	**Michigan State**	18-11	.5928	20	.5905
39	**LSU**	18-10	.5794	32	.5895
40	**Dayton**	24-8	.5299	93	.5884
41	**Arizona**	20-9	.5568	58	.5859
42	**South Carolina**	23-10	.5379	79	.5848
43	**Manhattan**	24-5	.5076	138	.5844
44	**Utah State**	24-3	.4777	197	.5817
45	**Western Michigan**	26-4	.4817	185	.5813
46	**Richmond**	20-12	.5756	37	.5791
47	**UTEP**	22-7	.5229	107	.5791
48	**Notre Dame**	17-12	.5877	24	.5790
49	**Georgia**	16-13	.6015	14	.5779
50	**Oklahoma**	19-10	.5580	56	.5777

Source: Collegiate Basketball News

ANNUAL REVIEW

2004 NCAA Tournament

St. Louis

First Round
- 1 Kentucky **96** / 16 +Florida A&M **76**
- 8 Washington **100** / 9 UAB **102**
- 5 Providence **58** / 12 Pacific **66**
- 4 Kansas **78** / 13 Illinois-Chicago **53**
- 6 Boston College **58** / 11 Utah **51**
- 3 Georgia Tech **65** / 14 Northern Iowa **60**
- 7 Michigan State **66** / 10 Nevada **72**
- 2 Gonzaga **76** / 15 Valparaiso **49**

Second Round
- Kentucky **75** / UAB **76** (A)
- Pacific **63** / Kansas **78**
- Boston College **54** / Georgia Tech **57**
- Nevada **91** / Gonzaga **72** (C)

Regional Semifinals
- UAB **74** / Kansas **100**
- Georgia Tech **72** / Nevada **67**

Regional Finals
- Kansas **71** (OT) / Georgia Tech **79** (B)

East Rutherford, NJ

First Round
- 1 Saint Joseph's **82** / 16 Liberty **63**
- 8 Texas Tech **76** / 9 Charlotte **73**
- 5 Florida **60** / 12 Manhattan **75**
- 4 Wake Forest **79** / 13 VCU **78**
- 6 Wisconsin **76** / 11 Richmond **64**
- 3 Pittsburgh **53** / 14 Central Florida **44**
- 7 Memphis **59** / 10 South Carolina **43** (F)
- 2 Oklahoma State **75** / 15 Eastern Washington **56**

Second Round
- Saint Joseph's **70** / Texas Tech **65**
- Manhattan **80** / Wake Forest **84**
- Wisconsin **55** / Pittsburgh **59**
- Memphis **53** / Oklahoma State **70**

Regional Semifinals
- Saint Joseph's **84** / Wake Forest **80** (D)
- Pittsburgh **51** / Oklahoma State **63**

Regional Finals
- Saint Joseph's **62** / Oklahoma State **64** (E)

Atlanta

First Round
- 1 Duke **96** / 16 Alabama State **61**
- 8 Seton Hall **80** / 9 Arizona **76**
- 5 Illinois **72** / 12 Murray State **53**
- 4 Cincinnati **80** / 13 East Tennessee State **77**
- 6 North Carolina **63** / 11 Air Force **52**
- 3 Texas **66** / 14 Princeton **49**
- 7 Xavier **80** / 10 Louisville **70**
- 2 Mississippi State **85** / 15 Monmouth **52**

Second Round
- Duke **90** / Seton Hall **62**
- Illinois **92** / Cincinnati **68**
- North Carolina **75** / Texas **78**
- Xavier **89** / Mississippi State **74**

Regional Semifinals
- Duke **75** / Illinois **62**
- Texas **71** / Xavier **79**

Regional Finals
- Duke **66** / Xavier **63**

Phoenix

First Round
- 1 Stanford **71** / 16 Texas-San Antonio **45**
- 8 Alabama **65** / 9 Southern Illinois **64**
- 5 Syracuse **80** / 12 BYU **75** (H)
- 4 Maryland **86** / 13 UTEP **83**
- 6 Vanderbilt **71** / 11 Western Michigan **58**
- 3 NC State **62** / 14 ✪UL-Lafayette **52**
- 7 DePaul **76** (2OT) / 10 Dayton **69**
- 2 Connecticut **70** / 15 Vermont **53**

Second Round
- Stanford **67** / Alabama **70** (G)
- Syracuse **72** / Maryland **70**
- Vanderbilt **75** / NC State **73**
- DePaul **55** / Connecticut **72**

Regional Semifinals
- Alabama **80** / Syracuse **71**
- Vanderbilt **53** / Connecticut **73**

Regional Finals
- Alabama **71** / Connecticut **87**

San Antonio

National Semifinal
- Georgia Tech **67** / Oklahoma State **65**
- Duke **78** / Connecticut **79**

National Final
- **Connecticut 82**
- **Georgia Tech 73**

Emeka Okafor, who wasn't heavily recruited until the spring of his senior year in high school, scores 24 points, rips down 15 rebounds and blocks a pair of shots, making him the easy choice as the Tournament's Most Outstanding Player. UConn coach Jim Calhoun improves his Final Four record to 4–0 .

Georgia Tech's Will Bynum and Oklahoma State's Tony Allen were high school teammates at Chicago's Crane Tech Prep. Allen will go on to play guard for the Boston Celtics, while Bynum—who hits the game-winning layup with one tick left—will play professionally in Israel and Detroit.

After Emeka Okafor picks up two quick fouls, Jim Calhoun keeps his All-America center on the bench for the final 16 minutes of the first half. But Okafor is key to the Huskies' second-half comeback, finishing with 18 points and playing lockdown D in the game's last minutes.

A After player introductions, UAB forward Sidney Ball removes his warmup top and realizes he forgot to put on his game jersey. The opening tap is delayed while Ball runs back to the locker room to dress.

B Kansas is the third school that Bill Self has coached to the Elite Eight in five seasons, joining Tulsa in 2000 and Illinois in 2001.

C With Nevada's victory over Gonzaga, a No. 10 seed advances to the Sweet 16 for the eighth straight year.

D TV analyst Billy Packer, an outspoken critic of Saint Joseph's No. 1 seed, works the game between the Hawks and Wake Forest, his alma mater. After the St. Joe's win, Packer concedes the Hawks are indeed deserving of a top seed.

E OSU's John Lucas—with his father, the former NBA player and coach of the same name, watching from the stands—nails a game-winning three with 6.9 seconds left. St. Joe's Jameer Nelson's last-second fadeaway misses.

F South Carolina remains winless in the Tournament since 1973, losing its fifth straight first-round game. In all, the Gamecocks are 4–9 in Tournament games.

G Twice in the regular season, Stanford won on wild shots at the buzzer. But luck runs out for the No. 1 seed when Dan Grunfield misses a last-ditch three-pointer.

H Gerry McNamara explodes for 43 points, including nine three-pointers. McNamara's 28 first-half points are three shy of the Syracuse school record, and his nine threes tie him for third-most made in a Tournament game.

+Opening round: Florida A&M d. Lehigh 72-57

✪Team participation later vacated

Tournament Leaders

Individual Leaders

Scoring	CL	POS	G	PTS	PPG
1 **Gerry McNamara**, Syracuse	SO	G	3	80	26.7
2 **Jameer Nelson**, Saint Joseph's	SR	G	4	98	24.5
3 **Hakim Warrick**, Syracuse	JR	F	3	67	22.3
4 **Lionel Chalmers**, Xavier	SR	G	4	87	21.8
5 **Ben Gordon**, Connecticut	JR	G	6	127	21.2
6 **Chris Paul**, Wake Forest	FR	G	3	63	21.0
7 **Kirk Snyder**, Nevada	JR	G	3	58	19.3
8 **Delonte West**, Saint Joseph's	JR	G	4	77	19.3
9 **Kennedy Winston**, Alabama	JR	F	4	75	18.8
10 **Brandon Mouton**, Texas	SR	G	3	56	18.7

Minimum: 3 games

Field Goal Pct	CL	POS	G	FG	FGA	PCT
1 **Shavlik Randolph**, Duke	SO	F	5	20	26	76.9
2 **Kevinn Pinkney**, Nevada	JR	F	3	16	23	69.6
3 **Roger Powell**, Illinois	JR	F	3	20	30	66.7
4 **Ivan McFarlin**, Oklahoma State	JR	F	5	27	42	64.3
5 **Joey Graham**, Oklahoma State	JR	F	5	27	43	62.8

Minimum: 15 made and 3 games

Free Throw Pct	CL	POS	G	FT	FTA	PCT
1 **Tony Allen**, Oklahoma State	SR	G	5	20	22	90.9
2 **Ben Gordon**, Connecticut	JR	G	6	39	43	90.7
3 **Royal Ivey**, Texas	SR	G	3	19	21	90.5
4 **Kirk Snyder**, Nevada	JR	G	3	16	18	88.9
5 **Chris Duhon**, Duke	SR	G	5	15	17	88.2

Minimum: 15 made

Three-Point FG Pct	CL	POS	G	3FG	3FGA	PCT
1 **Brandon Mouton**, Texas	SR	G	3	8	12	66.7
2 **Mario Moore**, Vanderbilt	SO	G	3	11	17	64.7
3 **Brian Boddicker**, Texas	SR	F	3	8	13	61.5
4 **Dedrick Finn**, Xavier	SO	G	4	10	18	55.6
5 **Gerry McNamara**, Syracuse	SO	G	3	15	29	51.7

Minimum: 6 made and 3 games

Assists Per Game	CL	POS	G	AST	APG
1 **Aaron Miles**, Kansas	JR	G	4	34	8.5
2 **Chris Paul**, Wake Forest	FR	G	3	21	7.0
Deron Williams, Illinois	SO	G	3	21	7.0
4 **Luther Head**, Illinois	JR	G	3	17	5.7
5 **Taliek Brown**, Connecticut	SR	G	6	33	5.5

Minimum: 3 games

Rebounds Per Game	CL	POS	G	REB	RPG
1 **Emeka Okafor**, Connecticut	JR	C	6	68	11.3
2 **Anthony Myles**, Xavier	SR	F	4	42	10.5
3 **Wayne Simien**, Kansas	JR	F	4	41	10.3
4 **Ivan McFarlin**, Oklahoma State	JR	F	5	45	9.0
5 **Shelden Williams**, Duke	SO	F	5	43	8.6

Minimum: 3 games

Blocked Shots Per Game	CL	POS	G	BLK	BPG
1 **Jermareo Davidson**, Alabama	FR	F	4	9	2.3
2 **Shelden Williams**, Duke	SO	F	5	11	2.2
3 **Emeka Okafor**, Connecticut	JR	C	6	13	2.2
4 **Brad Buckman**, Texas	SO	F	3	6	2.0
Jeremy McNeil, Syracuse	SR	C	3	6	2.0

Minimum: 3 games

Steals Per Game	CL	POS	G	STL	SPG
1 **Jameer Nelson**, Saint Joseph's	SR	G	4	11	2.8
2 **Mario Moore**, Vanderbilt	SO	G	3	8	2.7
3 **Morris Finley**, UAB	SR	G	3	7	2.3
Carldell Johnson, UAB	SO	G	3	7	2.3
5 **Jarrett Jack**, Georgia Tech	SO	G	6	13	2.2

Minimum: 3 games

Team Leaders

Scoring	G	PTS	PPG
1 **UAB**	3	252	84.0
2 **Kansas**	4	327	81.8
3 **Wake Forest**	3	243	81.0
4 **Duke**	5	402	80.4
5 **Xavier**	4	311	77.8
6 **Connecticut**	6	463	77.2
7 **Nevada**	3	230	76.7
8 **Illinois**	3	226	75.3
9 **Saint Joseph's**	4	298	74.5
10 **Syracuse**	3	223	74.3

Minimum: 3 games

FG Pct	G	FG	FGA	PCT
1 **Wake Forest**	3	84	162	51.8
2 **Oklahoma State**	5	127	250	50.8
3 **Kansas**	4	109	220	49.5
4 **Illinois**	3	88	179	49.2
5 **Connecticut**	6	160	336	47.6

Minimum: 3 games

3-Pt FG Pct	G	3FG	3FGA	PCT
1 **Texas**	3	23	44	52.3
2 **Syracuse**	3	20	42	47.6
3 **Xavier**	4	33	77	42.9
Illinois	3	24	56	42.9
5 **Vanderbilt**	3	29	68	42.6

Minimum: 3 games

FT Pct	G	FT	FTA	PCT
1 **Nevada**	3	66	82	80.5
2 **Alabama**	4	78	101	77.2
3 **Duke**	5	97	127	76.4
4 **UAB**	3	61	81	75.3
5 **Xavier**	4	82	110	74.6

Minimum: 3 games

Ast/TO Ratio	G	AST	TO	RAT
1 **Illinois**	3	62	24	2.58
2 **UAB**	3	54	36	1.50
3 **Duke**	5	80	57	1.40
4 **Saint Joseph's**	4	59	43	1.37
5 **Alabama**	4	51	38	1.34

Minimum: 3 games

Rebounds	G	REB	RPG
1 **Connecticut**	6	261	44.0
2 **Kansas**	4	164	41.0
3 **Nevada**	3	116	38.7
4 **Duke**	5	189	37.8
5 **Xavier**	4	151	37.8

Minimum: 3 games

Blocks	G	BLK	BPG
1 **Alabama**	4	21	5.3
2 **Connecticut**	6	27	4.5
3 **Duke**	5	22	4.4
4 **Kansas**	4	17	4.3
5 **Syracuse**	3	11	3.7

Minimum: 3 games

Steals	G	STL	SPG
1 **UAB**	3	30	10.0
2 **Georgia Tech**	6	55	9.2
3 **Saint Joseph's**	4	35	8.8
4 **Kansas**	4	34	8.5
5 **Duke**	5	41	8.2

Minimum: 3 games

All-Tournament Team

PLAYER	CL	POS	HT	SCHOOL	RPG	APG	PPG
Emeka Okafor*	JR	C	6-10	Connecticut	11.3	1.5	13.5
Rashad Anderson	SO	G/F	6-5	Connecticut	4.5	1.5	17.3
Will Bynum	JR	G	6-0	Georgia Tech	1.7	1.8	9.3
Ben Gordon	JR	G	6-3	Connecticut	4.3	3.2	21.2
Luke Schenscher	JR	C	7-1	Georgia Tech	7.0	0.7	10.8

All-Regional Teams

Atlanta

PLAYER	CL	POS	HT	SCHOOL	RPG	APG	PPG
Luol Deng*	FR	F	6-8	Duke	6.3	3.0	18.0
Lionel Chalmers	SR	G	6-0	Xavier	3.5	3.8	21.8
Anthony Myles	SR	F	6-9	Xavier	10.5	0.8	12.0
Romain Sato	SR	G	6-5	Xavier	7.3	2.0	18.3
Shelden Williams	SO	F	6-9	Duke	9.3	1.0	13.8

East Rutherford, NJ

PLAYER	CL	POS	HT	SCHOOL	RPG	APG	PPG
John Lucas*	JR	G	5-11	Oklahoma State	3.3	4.5	13.5
Tony Allen	SR	G	6-4	Oklahoma State	6.5	4.0	15.8
Joey Graham	JR	F	6-7	Oklahoma State	5.8	1.0	12.8
Jameer Nelson	SR	G	6-0	Saint Joseph's	4.3	5.0	24.5
Delonte West	JR	G	6-4	Saint Joseph's	5.3	5.0	19.3

Phoenix

PLAYER	CL	POS	HT	SCHOOL	RPG	APG	PPG
Ben Gordon*	JR	G	6-3	Connecticut	5.3	3.8	22.0
Rashad Anderson	SO	G/F	6-5	Connecticut	4.5	1.8	18.0
Chuck Davis	JR	F	6-8	Alabama	6.3	2.0	16.3
Emeka Okafor	JR	C	6-10	Connecticut	11.5	1.8	9.8
Kennedy Winston	JR	F	6-6	Alabama	5.5	3.3	18.8

St. Louis

PLAYER	CL	POS	HT	SCHOOL	RPG	APG	PPG
Jarrett Jack*	SO	G	6-3	Georgia Tech	5.8	4.5	12.8
Aaron Miles	JR	G	6-1	Kansas	3.3	8.5	8.0
Clarence Moore	SR	F	6-5	Georgia Tech	6.0	1.5	8.3
Wayne Simien	JR	F	6-9	Kansas	10.3	3.0	18.0
Kirk Snyder	JR	G	6-6	Nevada	5.0	4.0	19.3

* Most outstanding player

2004 NCAA TOURNAMENT BOX SCORES

100-74 — 56 1H 41 / 44 2H 33 — SWEET 16

KANSAS	MIN	FG	3FG	FT	REB	A	ST	BL	PF	TP
Wayne Simien	28	6-8	0-0	18-20	9	5	1	1	4	30
J.R. Giddens	29	8-14	2-6	0-0	4	0	1	1	3	18
Aaron Miles	35	4-7	0-0	5-6	4	10	4	0	0	13
Jeff Graves	15	4-6	0-0	5-5	8	0	0	0	3	13
Keith Langford	33	3-8	1-3	2-4	4	5	0	0	1	9
David Padgett	24	2-5	0-0	3-4	6	0	1	1	3	7
Michael Lee	15	2-4	1-1	0-1	2	1	0	0	0	5
Christian Moody	10	1-1	0-0	0-0	1	0	0	0	4	2
Jeff Hawkins	4	0-1	0-0	2-2	1	0	1	0	1	2
Omar Wilkes	1	0-1	0-0	1-2	1	0	0	0	0	1
Bryant Nash	2	0-0	0-0	0-0	0	0	1	0	0	0
Moulaye Niang	2	0-0	0-0	0-0	1	0	0	0	0	0
Nick Bahe	1	0-0	0-0	0-0	1	0	0	0	0	0
Jeremy Case	1	0-1	0-0	0-0	0	0	0	0	0	0
TOTALS	200	30-56	4-10	36-44	42	21	9	3	19	100
Percentages		53.6	40.0	81.8						

Coach: Bill Self

UAB	MIN	FG	3FG	FT	REB	A	ST	BL	PF	TP
Morris Finley	27	4-19	3-13	2-2	2	2	3	0	3	13
Tony Johnson	24	5-7	1-2	0-0	3	1	3	0	4	11
Demario Eddins	31	2-4	0-1	6-8	5	2	0	1	2	10
Gabe Kennedy	22	3-7	0-0	4-4	1	0	1	0	4	10
Marques Lewis	18	3-6	0-0	4-6	6	0	1	1	2	10
Donnell Taylor	13	1-6	1-3	4-4	2	2	3	0	1	7
Ronnell Taylor	19	2-7	1-3	0-0	5	1	0	0	3	5
Carldell Johnson	22	1-6	1-5	0-0	0	3	1	0	4	3
Derrick Broom	2	1-3	1-2	0-0	1	0	1	0	1	3
Sidney Ball	18	1-4	0-2	0-0	2	1	0	1	3	2
Brandon Tobias	3	0-0	0-0	0-0	0	0	0	1	0	0
Lee Cobb	1	0-2	0-2	0-0	1	0	0	0	0	0
TOTALS	200	23-71	8-33	20-24	28	12	13	4	27	74
Percentages		32.4	24.2	83.3						

Coach: Mike Anderson

Officials: P Adams, Bob Donato, Ton Greene **Technicals:** UAB (coach Anderson, 2) **Attendance:** 30,801

72-67 — 34 1H 39 / 38 2H 28 — SWEET 16

GEORGIA TECH	MIN	FG	3FG	FT	REB	A	ST	BL	PF	TP
Marvin Lewis	36	7-13	4-9	5-6	5	2	1	0	3	23
Will Bynum	21	3-7	2-4	1-2	3	1	1	0	2	9
Jarrett Jack	28	3-10	0-1	2-4	2	3	1	0	2	8
Isma'il Muhammad	29	3-11	0-1	1-2	8	1	1	0	4	7
Luke Schenscher	28	3-7	0-0	1-1	9	1	1	2	3	7
Anthony McHenry	25	3-5	0-0	0-0	6	1	2	2	5	6
Clarence Moore	18	2-4	0-2	2-6	8	0	1	0	2	6
Theodis Tarver	12	3-4	0-0	0-1	6	0	0	1	1	6
B.J. Elder	3	0-2	0-1	0-0	0	1	1	0	0	0
TOTALS	200	27-63	6-18	12-22	47	10	9	5	22	72
Percentages		42.9	33.3	54.5						

Coach: Paul Hewitt

NEVADA	MIN	FG	3FG	FT	REB	A	ST	BL	PF	TP
Kirk Snyder	34	6-20	1-6	8-8	5	3	1	0	2	21
Todd Okeson	34	5-19	2-10	1-1	10	0	1	0	4	13
Garry Hill-Thomas	36	3-10	0-0	3-4	6	1	0	0	2	9
Kevinn Pinkney	32	4-5	0-0	0-2	8	0	2	1	5	8
Nick Fazekas	23	1-6	1-3	3-4	5	0	0	0	3	6
Jermaine Washington	9	2-4	0-0	0-0	2	1	0	0	3	4
Sean Paul	22	0-3	0-0	3-5	6	0	0	2	2	3
Marcelus Kemp	10	1-2	1-1	0-0	0	0	0	0	1	3
TOTALS	200	22-69	5-20	18-24	42	5	4	3	22	67
Percentages		31.9	25.0	75.0						

Coach: Trent Johnson

Officials: Ed Corbett, Ed Hightower, Tor O'Neill **Technicals:** Nevada (Hill-Thomas) **Attendance:** 30,801

84-80 — 37 1H 38 / 47 2H 42 — SWEET 16

SAINT JOSEPH'S	MIN	FG	3FG	FT	REB	A	ST	BL	PF	TP
Jameer Nelson	40	9-23	1-5	5-8	3	7	3	0	4	24
Delonte West	40	8-15	2-5	6-6	4	3	1	0	2	24
Pat Carroll	34	6-8	5-7	0-0	8	2	1	2	3	17
Tyrone Barley	34	4-6	4-6	1-2	1	0	2	0	2	13
Dwayne Jones	27	1-3	0-0	2-5	7	1	1	1	4	4
Chet Stachitas	8	1-3	0-1	0-0	1	0	0	0	1	2
John Bryant	16	0-0	0-0	0-2	0	2	0	1	4	0
Dave Mallon	1	0-0	0-0	0-0	0	0	0	0	1	0
TOTALS	200	29-58	12-24	14-23	24	15	8	4	21	84
Percentages		50.0	50.0	60.9						

Coach: Phil Martelli

WAKE FOREST	MIN	FG	3FG	FT	REB	A	ST	BL	PF	TP
Justin Gray	38	9-18	4-8	1-2	0	1	1	-	4	23
Eric Williams	28	7-8	0-0	5-6	4	0	0	-	2	19
Chris Paul	33	2-6	1-2	7-8	0	8	3	-	4	12
Jamaal Levy	31	4-10	1-2	3-4	6	2	1	-	4	12
Taron Downey	25	3-5	2-4	0-0	4	3	1	-	1	8
Trent Strickland	23	1-2	0-0	0-1	6	1	0	-	3	2
Kyle Visser	11	1-2	0-0	0-0	3	0	0	-	2	2
Vytas Danelius	10	0-0	0-0	2-4	2	0	0	-	2	2
Todd Hendley	1	0-0	0-0	0-0	0	0	0	-	0	0
TOTALS	200	27-51	8-16	18-25	25	15	6	-	22	80
Percentages		52.9	50.0	72.0						

Coach: Skip Prosser

Officials: Curtis Shaw, Steve Welmer, Tim Higgins **Technicals:** None **Attendance:** 19,557

63-51 — 26 1H 28 / 37 2H 23 — SWEET 16

OKLAHOMA STATE	MIN	FG	3FG	FT	REB	A	ST	BL	PF	TP
Tony Allen	35	8-14	1-1	6-6	7	2	2	3	3	23
Joey Graham	35	4-9	0-1	1-2	6	1	1	0	3	9
Janavor Weatherspoon	22	2-3	0-0	4-4	3	0	0	0	1	8
John Lucas III	35	2-7	1-3	2-2	2	6	1	0	0	7
Ivan McFarlin	27	3-5	0-0	0-0	5	2	0	1	4	6
Daniel Bobik	21	2-3	2-2	0-0	1	2	1	0	4	6
Jason Miller	11	0-0	0-0	2-2	2	0	0	0	0	2
Stephen Graham	7	1-2	0-0	0-0	0	0	0	0	0	2
Terrence Crawford	7	0-2	0-1	0-0	1	0	1	1	1	0
TOTALS	200	22-45	4-8	15-16	27	13	6	5	16	63
Percentages		48.9	50.0	93.8						

Coach: Eddie Sutton

PITTSBURGH	MIN	FG	3FG	FT	REB	A	ST	BL	PF	TP
Carl Krauser	38	6-17	0-6	3-6	6	3	0	0	2	15
Jaron Brown	25	4-7	1-3	2-2	0	0	2	0	4	11
Chevon Troutman	32	4-8	0-2	0-0	8	0	2	0	3	8
Chris Taft	31	4-9	0-0	0-0	4	3	0	0	2	8
Julius Page	38	2-11	1-2	0-0	1	0	0	1	3	5
Mark McCarroll	16	1-4	1-3	1-2	5	1	0	0	1	4
Yuri Demetris	14	0-0	0-0	0-0	4	1	1	0	1	0
Antonio Graves	4	0-1	0-1	0-0	0	0	0	0	2	0
Toree Morris	2	0-1	0-0	0-0	1	0	0	0	0	0
TOTALS	200	21-58	3-17	6-10	29	8	5	1	18	51
Percentages		36.2	17.6	60.0						

Coach: Jamie Dixon

Officials: Gerald Boudreaux, Rick Hartzell, J.D. Collins **Technicals:** None **Attendance:** 19,557

72-62 — 31 1H 30 / 41 2H 32 — SWEET 16

DUKE	MIN	FG	3FG	FT	REB	A	ST	BL	PF	TP
Luol Deng	33	6-11	2-4	4-4	6	4	2	0	4	18
J.J. Redick	37	7-13	3-8	0-1	1	2	1	0	1	17
Shelden Williams	35	7-9	0-0	0-0	4	2	1	3	2	14
Daniel Ewing	37	5-11	1-4	0-1	2	2	2	0	2	11
Shavlik Randolph	12	3-5	0-0	1-3	3	1	1	2	4	7
Chris Duhon	36	0-1	0-1	4-4	10	8	1	0	0	4
Sean Dockery	9	0-1	0-1	1-2	2	0	2	0	1	1
Nick Horvath	1	0-0	0-0	0-0	0	0	0	0	0	0
TOTALS	200	28-51	6-18	10-15	28	19	10	5	14	72
Percentages		54.9	33.3	66.7						

Coach: Mike Krzyzewski

ILLINOIS	MIN	FG	3FG	FT	REB	A	ST	BL	PF	TP
Roger Powell	37	7-13	0-0	1-4	8	1	0	0	1	15
James Augustine	22	5-8	0-0	5-6	8	2	2	1	4	15
Dee Brown	39	6-10	2-4	0-1	3	2	1	0	0	14
Luther Head	40	4-11	1-4	0-0	8	3	0	0	1	9
Deron Williams	31	3-13	1-5	0-0	4	6	1	0	4	7
Nick Smith	9	1-5	0-0	0-0	1	1	0	0	0	2
Jack Ingram	12	0-2	0-0	0-0	0	1	1	1	4	0
Rich McBride	10	0-2	0-0	0-0	1	1	0	0	1	0
TOTALS	200	26-64	4-13	6-11	33	17	5	2	15	62
Percentages		40.6	30.8	54.5						

Coach: Bruce Weber

Officials: Dave Libbey, John Cahill, Mark Whitehead **Technicals:** None **Attendance:** 24,533

79-71 — 44 1H 41 / 35 2H 30 — SWEET 16

XAVIER	MIN	FG	3FG	FT	REB	A	ST	BL	PF	TP
Romain Sato	40	5-13	3-9	14-17	3	0	2	0	3	27
Lionel Chalmers	40	4-15	2-8	4-5	7	6	0	0	2	14
Dedrick Finn	29	3-7	2-5	3-4	3	1	3	0	1	11
Justin Doellman	22	4-9	1-3	1-1	6	1	0	2	4	10
Anthony Myles	29	4-10	0-0	1-5	7	1	0	0	3	9
Justin Cage	20	2-2	0-0	1-1	3	1	0	0	5	5
Keith Jackson	3	1-1	0-0	0-0	0	1	0	0	0	2
Brandon Cole	17	0-1	0-0	1-2	5	2	1	1	2	1
TOTALS	200	23-58	8-25	25-35	34	13	6	3	20	79
Percentages		39.7	32.0	71.4						

Coach: Thad Matta

TEXAS	MIN	FG	3FG	FT	REB	A	ST	BL	PF	TP
Brandon Mouton	30	9-15	2-4	1-3	7	1	0	1	5	21
Brian Boddicker	22	4-7	3-5	0-0	1	1	0	0	2	11
P.J. Tucker	31	4-10	0-0	2-2	10	1	0	0	4	10
Royal Ivey	37	2-6	0-1	5-6	4	6	0	0	2	9
Brad Buckman	16	3-6	0-0	1-2	1	0	0	4	1	7
Kenton Paulino	17	1-3	1-3	3-4	1	2	0	0	4	6
Sydmill Harris	13	2-3	1-2	0-0	0	0	0	0	2	5
Jason Klotz	20	1-10	0-0	0-0	8	0	0	1	2	2
Edgar Moreno	9	0-0	0-0	0-0	0	1	0	0	1	0
Kenny Taylor	3	0-1	0-1	0-0	0	0	1	0	0	0
James Thomas	2	0-1	0-0	0-0	0	0	0	0	2	0
TOTALS	200	26-62	7-16	12-17	32	12	1	6	25	71
Percentages		41.9	43.8	70.6						

Coach: Rick Barnes

Officials: Gary Maxwell, Karl Hess, Ted Valentine **Technicals:** Texas (bench) **Attendance:** 24,533

80-71

38	1H	36
42	2H	35

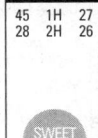

SWEET 16

ALABAMA	MIN	FG	3FG	FT	REB	A	ST	BL	PF	TP
Earnest Shelton	35	5-11	4-8	8-8	2	2	5	0	2	22
Chuck Davis	38	8-12	0-0	3-4	4	3	0	2	2	19
Kennedy Winston	37	6-12	3-7	4-5	3	5	3	0	1	19
Antoine Pettway	36	4-9	2-5	0-0	0	3	1	2	3	10
Emmett Thomas	16	2-6	0-2	2-2	2	0	0	0	0	6
Evan Brock	17	1-2	0-0	0-2	5	2	0	0	3	2
Jermareo Davidson	17	0-0	0-0	2-2	2	0	1	2	3	2
Demetrius Smith	4	0-0	0-0	0-0	0	1	1	0	3	0
TOTALS	200	26-52	9-22	19-23	18	16	11	6	17	80
Percentages		52.2	45.0	81.0						

Coach: Mark Gottfried

SYRACUSE	MIN	FG	3FG	FT	REB	A	ST	BL	PF	TP
Gerry McNamara	38	6-15	4-9	8-9	2	2	0	0	2	24
Hakim Warrick	40	8-15	0-0	5-7	8	1	1	0	3	21
Louie McCroskey	22	4-9	1-4	1-1	3	2	2	0	4	10
Josh Pace	38	3-7	0-0	0-3	4	7	2	1	3	6
Jeremy McNeil	27	2-3	0-0	0-0	5	0	0	3	3	4
Demetris Nichols	15	1-2	0-1	0-0	3	0	0	0	4	2
Terrence Roberts	13	1-1	0-0	0-0	2	0	0	0	1	2
Craig Forth	7	1-3	0-0	0-0	4	0	0	0	0	2
TOTALS	200	26-55	5-14	14-20	31	12	5	4	20	71
Percentages		47.3	35.7	70.0						

Coach: Jim Boeheim

Officials: Larry Rose, Jamie Luckie, Steven Skiles **Technicals:** Alabama (coach Gottfried) **Attendance:** 17,684

73-53

45	1H	27
28	2H	26

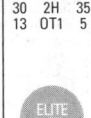

SWEET 16

CONNECTICUT	MIN	FG	3FG	FT	REB	A	ST	BL	PF	TP
Ben Gordon	39	7-16	3-9	3-3	9	5	0	0	1	20
Rashad Anderson	34	5-11	3-8	2-2	6	3	1	1	0	15
Taliek Brown	36	4-7	0-0	4-4	5	5	1	0	0	12
Emeka Okafor	32	4-7	0-0	4-6	11	0	2	0	3	12
Josh Boone	28	4-6	0-0	0-0	4	0	2	1	2	8
Charlie Villanueva	11	2-3	0-0	0-0	2	0	0	0	2	4
Hilton Armstorng	13	1-1	0-0	0-0	3	1	0	2	1	2
Denham Brown	7	0-0	0-0	0-0	1	0	0	0	1	0
TOTALS	200	27-51	6-17	13-15	41	14	6	4	10	73
Percentages		52.9	35.3	86.7						

Coach: Jim Calhoun

VANDERBILT	MIN	FG	3FG	FT	REB	A	ST	BL	PF	TP
Mario Moore	33	4-9	2-4	2-2	1	1	4	-	1	12
Corey Smith	29	4-9	3-6	1-2	0	0	1	-	1	12
Matt Freije	33	3-18	0-6	2-4	4	1	0	-	1	8
Dawid Przybyszewski	24	3-7	2-4	0-0	3	1	0	-	1	8
Adam Payton	12	2-2	0-0	0-0	1	1	0	-	1	4
Scott Hundley	14	1-1	1-1	0-0	1	2	1	-	0	3
Russell Lakey	25	1-5	0-2	0-0	1	1	2	-	3	2
Julian Terrell	19	1-2	0-0	0-0	6	4	0	-	4	2
Jason Holwerda	5	1-1	0-0	0-0	0	0	0	-	1	2
Ted Skuchas	4	0-2	0-0	0-0	0	0	0	-	1	0
Dan Cage	2	0-1	0-1	0-0	0	0	0	-	0	0
TOTALS	200	20-57	8-24	5-8	17	11	8	-	14	53
Percentages		35.1	33.3	62.5						

Coach: Kevin Stallings

Officials: Mike Sanzere, Reggie Cofer, Ted Hillary **Technicals:** None **Attendance:** 17,684

79-71

36	1H	31
30	2H	35
13	OT1	5

ELITE 8

GEORGIA TECH	MIN	FG	3FG	FT	REB	A	ST	BL	PF	TP
Jarrett Jack	38	8-12	0-2	13-14	9	6	4	1	2	29
Luke Schenscher	39	5-5	0-0	5-6	4	0	1	1	2	15
Clarence Moore	29	5-11	1-5	3-5	6	1	5	0	1	14
Isma'il Muhammad	31	2-6	0-0	4-7	9	2	1	0	3	8
Will Bynum	20	3-7	2-3	0-0	2	1	0	0	1	8
Anthony McHenry	18	2-5	0-1	0-0	4	1	2	1	4	4
Marvin Lewis	32	0-6	0-4	1-2	2	2	0	0	4	1
B.J. Elder	12	0-2	0-1	0-0	1	1	0	0	0	0
Theodis Tarver	6	0-2	0-0	0-0	2	0	0	0	0	0
TOTALS	225	25-56	3-16	26-34	39	14	13	3	17	79
Percentages		44.6	18.8	76.5						

Coach: Paul Hewitt

KANSAS	MIN	FG	3FG	FT	REB	A	ST	BL	PF	TP
J.R. Giddens	36	6-13	3-10	0-0	4	0	2	0	3	15
Keith Langford	34	4-11	0-2	7-9	3	2	4	1	5	15
Aaron Miles	43	4-11	1-3	2-2	3	8	2	0	3	11
Wayne Simien	43	4-14	0-0	3-4	11	2	0	0	3	11
Michael Lee	19	4-6	2-3	1-2	5	2	0	0	5	11
Jeff Graves	27	2-5	0-0	0-2	7	0	0	1	2	4
David Padgett	14	2-4	0-0	0-0	3	1	0	1	3	4
Christian Moody	5	0-0	0-0	0-0	0	0	0	0	1	0
Jeff Hawkins	2	0-0	0-0	0-0	0	0	0	0	0	0
Jeremy Case	1	0-1	0-1	0-0	0	0	0	0	1	0
Bryant Nash	1	0-0	0-0	0-0	0	0	0	0	0	0
TOTALS	225	26-65	6-19	13-19	36	15	8	3	26	71
Percentages		40.0	31.6	68.4						

Coach: Bill Self

Officials: Donnee Gray, James Burr, Tom Lopes **Technicals:** None **Attendance:** 30,648

64-62

27	1H	33
37	2H	29

ELITE 8

OKLAHOMA STATE	MIN	FG	3FG	FT	REB	A	ST	BL	PF	TP
John Lucas III	38	7-20	3-12	2-2	3	4	0	0	1	19
Joey Graham	28	7-8	0-1	3-6	11	1	0	0	4	17
Tony Allen	40	6-11	0-2	0-0	6	5	2	3	3	12
Ivan McFarlin	35	3-7	0-0	3-3	12	0	0	2	4	9
Janavor Weatherspoon	19	1-3	0-0	2-2	4	2	0	0	0	4
Daniel Bobik	23	1-2	1-2	0-2	1	1	0	0	3	3
Terrence Crawford	13	0-1	0-0	0-0	3	0	0	1	1	0
Jason Miller	3	0-0	0-0	0-0	1	0	0	0	0	0
Stephen Graham	1	0-1	0-0	0-0	0	0	0	0	0	0
TOTALS	200	25-53	4-17	10-15	41	13	2	6	16	64
Percentages		47.2	23.5	66.7						

Coach: Eddie Sutton

SAINT JOSEPH'S	MIN	FG	3FG	FT	REB	A	ST	BL	PF	TP
Delonte West	39	7-15	2-6	4-4	1	4	2	1	0	20
Jameer Nelson	40	6-18	3-6	2-2	8	8	4	0	2	17
Pat Carroll	30	3-11	3-11	0-0	3	0	1	0	1	9
Dwayne Jones	31	2-3	0-0	2-4	2	0	1	2	3	6
John Bryant	21	2-3	0-0	0-0	3	0	0	0	3	4
Tyrone Barley	25	1-4	0-2	1-2	3	3	0	0	2	3
Chet Stachitas	14	1-3	0-1	1-1	2	0	0	0	3	3
TOTALS	200	22-57	8-26	10-13	22	15	8	3	14	62
Percentages		38.6	30.8	76.9						

Coach: Phil Martelli

Officials: Bob Staffen, Dick Cartmell, Verne Harris **Technicals:** None **Attendance:** 19,779

66-63

28	1H	30
38	2H	33

ELITE 8

DUKE	MIN	FG	3FG	FT	REB	A	ST	BL	PF	TP
Luol Deng	30	7-13	2-4	3-5	7	3	1	0	4	19
J.J. Redick	38	4-14	3-9	2-2	7	1	2	0	4	13
Daniel Ewing	33	4-11	3-6	2-2	3	3	2	0	3	13
Shelden Williams	30	3-5	0-0	6-7	13	0	0	5	4	12
Chris Duhon	40	2-8	0-1	2-2	5	5	1	1	0	6
Shavlik Randolph	15	1-2	0-0	1-2	3	0	0	1	5	3
Sean Dockery	10	0-1	0-0	0-0	1	1	0	0	2	0
Nick Horvath	4	0-0	0-0	0-0	0	2	0	0	1	0
TOTALS	200	21-54	8-20	16-20	39	15	6	7	23	66
Percentages		38.9	40.0	80.0						

Coach: Mike Krzyzewski

XAVIER	MIN	FG	3FG	FT	REB	A	ST	BL	PF	TP
Lionel Chalmers	40	6-16	1-5	4-4	3	1	0	0	4	17
Anthony Myles	23	7-11	0-0	2-4	10	1	0	0	5	16
Romain Sato	40	2-10	0-3	6-9	11	4	1	0	4	10
Dedrick Finn	32	2-8	1-4	2-2	1	2	3	0	2	7
Justin Doellman	28	2-9	1-3	0-0	1	0	1	0	1	5
Justin Cage	26	2-4	0-0	1-2	5	0	0	0	2	5
Brandon Cole	11	1-5	0-0	1-2	2	0	0	0	3	3
TOTALS	200	22-63	3-15	16-23	33	8	5	0	21	63
Percentages		34.9	20.0	69.6						

Coach: Thad Matta

Officials: Michael Kitts, Olandis Poole, Pat Driscoll **Technicals:** None **Attendance:** 24,711

87-71

53	1H	29
34	2H	42

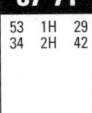

ELITE 8

CONNECTICUT	MIN	FG	3FG	FT	REB	A	ST	BL	PF	TP
Ben Gordon	39	11-19	4-7	10-11	2	2	2	0	2	36
Rashad Anderson	37	9-20	6-9	4-4	7	2	0	0	1	28
Charlie Villanueva	24	4-6	0-1	0-0	8	0	0	2	4	8
Josh Boone	24	2-4	0-0	2-9	5	0	0	0	3	6
Taliek Brown	39	1-3	0-0	1-2	4	10	1	0	2	3
Emeka Okafor	19	1-5	0-0	0-1	9	2	0	5	2	2
Hilton Armstorng	8	1-2	0-0	0-0	2	1	0	0	1	2
Denham Brown	8	0-1	0-0	2-2	1	0	0	0	2	2
Shamon Tooles	2	0-0	0-0	0-0	0	0	0	0	1	0
TOTALS	200	29-60	10-17	19-29	38	17	3	7	18	87
Percentages		48.3	58.8	65.5						

Coach: Jim Calhoun

ALABAMA	MIN	FG	3FG	FT	REB	A	ST	BL	PF	TP
Chuck Davis	40	8-14	0-0	8-9	9	2	0	1	2	24
Kennedy Winston	36	8-17	1-3	4-5	4	4	0	1	4	21
Emmett Thomas	19	4-7	3-5	0-0	3	0	0	0	4	11
Earnest Shelton	34	3-11	2-8	2-2	4	3	0	1	4	10
Evan Brock	14	1-5	0-0	0-0	4	0	2	0	1	2
Jermareo Davidson	13	1-3	0-0	0-0	2	0	0	2	4	2
Antoine Pettway	37	0-2	0-2	1-2	5	4	0	0	3	1
Demetrius Smith	7	0-1	0-1	0-0	0	1	0	0	1	0
TOTALS	200	25-60	6-19	15-18	31	14	2	5	23	71
Percentages		41.7	31.6	83.3						

Coach: Mark Gottfried

Officials: David Hall, Mike Wood, Randy McCall **Technicals:** None **Attendance:** 17,889

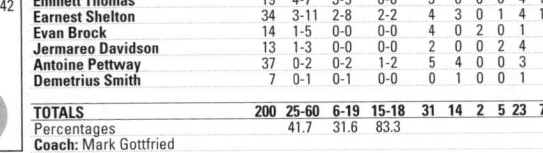

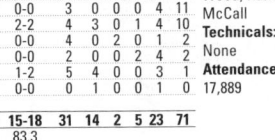

67-65 (FINAL 4)

	1H	2H
Georgia Tech	37	30
Oklahoma State	30	35

GEORGIA TECH	MIN	FG	3FG	FT	REB	A	ST	BL	PF	TP
Luke Schenscher	33	9-13	0-0	1-3	12	1	0	1	2	19
Marvin Lewis	28	5-9	5-9	0-0	2	3	0	0	4	15
Will Bynum	22	3-6	1-2	4-5	0	1	0	1	2	11
Jarrett Jack	36	2-6	1-2	5-6	3	5	0	0	2	10
Anthony McHenry	25	3-5	0-1	0-0	7	4	3	1	3	6
Isma'il Muhammad	15	1-3	0-0	2-2	1	1	3	0	1	4
B.J. Elder	19	1-4	0-3	0-0	2	1	1	0	2	2
Clarence Moore	15	0-1	0-0	0-0	0	0	0	0	3	0
Theodis Tarver	7	0-2	0-0	0-0	2	0	0	1	0	0
TOTALS	**200**	**24-49**	**7-17**	**12-16**	**29**	**16**	**7**	**4**	**19**	**67**
Percentages		49.0	41.2	75.0						

Coach: Paul Hewitt

OKLAHOMA STATE	MIN	FG	3FG	FT	REB	A	ST	BL	PF	TP
Joey Graham	37	6-12	0-1	5-7	10	1	0	-	1	17
Ivan McFarlin	34	6-11	0-0	4-7	8	1	0	-	4	16
Tony Allen	26	3-5	1-1	6-6	4	4	1	-	4	13
John Lucas III	39	4-14	2-8	1-2	1	2	0	-	1	11
Daniel Bobik	39	1-5	1-5	1-2	5	2	1	-	1	4
Janavor Weatherspoon	11	1-1	0-0	0-0	0	0	0	-	0	2
Stephen Graham	6	1-1	0-0	0-0	1	0	0	-	0	2
Terrence Crawford	7	0-1	0-0	0-0	0	0	1	-	3	0
Jason Miller	1	0-0	0-0	0-1	1	0	0	-	1	0
TOTALS	**200**	**22-50**	**4-15**	**17-25**	**30**	**10**	**3**	**-**	**15**	**65**
Percentages		44.0	26.7	68.0						

Coach: Eddie Sutton

Officials: Donnee Gr. James Burr Higgins
Technicals: None
Attendance: 44,417

79-78 (FINAL 4)

	1H	2H
Connecticut	34	45
Duke	41	37

CONNECTICUT	MIN	FG	3FG	FT	REB	A	ST	BL	PF	TP
Ben Gordon	38	5-12	1-3	7-8	3	2	2	0	4	18
Emeka Okafor	22	7-9	0-0	4-7	7	1	0	2	3	18
Rashad Anderson	30	3-5	3-5	5-5	3	1	2	0	4	14
Josh Boone	35	3-6	0-0	3-5	14	1	0	1	2	9
Denham Brown	16	3-4	1-1	1-2	1	0	0	0	1	8
Charlie Villanueva	14	3-8	1-2	1-2	6	0	0	2	1	8
Taliek Brown	35	2-8	0-0	0-0	3	3	1	0	3	4
Hilton Armstorng	9	0-0	0-0	0-1	5	1	0	1	2	0
Shamon Tooles	1	0-0	0-0	0-2	1	0	0	0	0	0
TOTALS	**200**	**26-52**	**6-11**	**21-32**	**43**	**9**	**5**	**6**	**20**	**79**
Percentages		50.0	54.5	65.6						

Coach: Jim Calhoun

DUKE	MIN	FG	3FG	FT	REB	A	ST	BL	PF	TP
Luol Deng	39	7-15	1-4	1-3	12	2	1	0	1	16
Chris Duhon	40	5-13	1-6	4-6	3	6	0	0	3	15
J.J. Redick	38	4-12	3-9	4-4	4	1	1	0	1	15
Shavlik Randolph	14	6-6	0-0	1-3	6	0	0	1	5	13
Daniel Ewing	27	4-12	1-2	2-3	1	1	2	0	3	11
Shelden Williams	19	1-9	0-0	2-4	6	0	0	2	5	4
Sean Dockery	15	1-3	0-1	0-0	2	1	4	0	1	2
Nick Horvath	8	1-1	0-0	0-0	2	0	0	0	5	2
TOTALS	**200**	**29-71**	**6-22**	**14-23**	**36**	**11**	**8**	**3**	**24**	**78**
Percentages		40.8	27.3	60.9						

Coach: Mike Krzyzewski

Officials: Dav Hall, Olandis Poole, Ted Hillary
Technicals: None
Attendance: 44,417

82-73 (NCAA FINAL 2004)

	1H	2H
Connecticut	41	41
Georgia Tech	26	47

CONNECTICUT	MIN	FG	3FG	FT	REB	A	ST	BL	PF	TP
Emeka Okafor	38	10-17	0-0	4-8	15	1	1	2	3	24
Ben Gordon	30	5-17	3-8	8-9	2	2	2	0	4	21
Rashad Anderson	31	5-10	2-7	6-8	6	1	2	0	1	18
Taliek Brown	37	2-6	0-0	5-8	6	4	0	0	3	9
Josh Boone	29	4-6	0-0	1-4	6	1	0	0	2	9
Hilton Armstorng	7	0-1	0-0	1-2	6	0	0	0	1	1
Denham Brown	19	0-4	0-2	0-0	6	0	0	0	3	0
Charlie Villanueva	7	0-0	0-0	0-0	1	1	0	0	1	0
Shamon Tooles	2	0-0	0-0	0-0	0	0	0	0	0	0
TOTALS	**200**	**26-61**	**5-17**	**25-39**	**48**	**10**	**5**	**2**	**18**	**82**
Percentages		42.6	29.4	64.1						

Coach: Jim Calhoun

GEORGIA TECH	MIN	FG	3FG	FT	REB	A	ST	BL	PF	TP
Will Bynum	23	6-11	3-6	2-6	2	5	1	0	4	17
B.J. Elder	28	4-15	3-8	3-4	4	0	0	0	4	14
Isma'il Muhammad	16	5-12	0-0	0-0	5	0	2	0	3	10
Luke Schenscher	28	4-7	0-0	1-2	11	0	0	0	2	9
Jarrett Jack	26	1-8	0-1	5-6	4	3	4	0	3	7
Clarence Moore	24	3-5	0-1	1-3	10	0	0	0	2	7
Marvin Lewis	23	3-9	0-5	0-0	1	1	1	0	3	6
Anthony McHenry	20	1-3	1-1	0-0	4	0	0	1	4	3
Theodis Tarver	11	0-1	0-0	0-0	2	0	2	0	1	0
Robert Brooks	1	0-0	0-0	0-0	0	0	0	0	0	0
TOTALS	**200**	**27-71**	**7-22**	**12-21**	**43**	**9**	**10**	**1**	**26**	**73**
Percentages		38.0	31.8	57.1						

Coach: Paul Hewitt

Officials: Dick Cartmell, Randy McCall, Verne Harris
Technicals: None
Attendance: 44,468

National Invitation Tournament (NIT)

Opening Round: Rhode Island d. Boston U. 80-52, West Virginia d. Kent State 65-54, Boise State d. UNLV 84-69, Wisconsin-Milwaukee d. Rice 91-53, George Mason d. Tennessee 58-55, Austin Peay d. Belmont 65-59, Nebraska d. Creighton 71-70, Niagara d. Troy 87-83

First Round: Villanova d. Drexel 85-70, Virginia d. George Washington 79-66, Rutgers d. Temple 76-71, West Virginia d. Rhode Island 79-72, Boise State d. Wisconsin-Milwaukee 73-70, Marquette d. Toledo 87-72, Florida State d. Wichita State 91-84 (2OT), Iowa State d. Georgia 82-74, Notre Dame d. Purdue 71-59, Saint Louis d. Iowa 70-69, Oregon d. Colorado 77-72 (OT), George Mason d. Austin Peay 66-60, Nebraska d. Niagara 78-70, Hawaii d. Utah State 85-74, Oklahoma d. LSU 70-61, Michigan d. Missouri 65-64

Second Round: Villanova d. Virginia 73-63, Rutgers d. West Virginia 67-64, Marquette d. Boise State 66-53, Iowa State d. Florida State 62-59, Notre Dame d. Saint Louis 77-66, Oregon d. George Mason 68-54, Hawaii d. Nebraska 84-83, Michigan d. Oklahoma 63-52

Third Round: Rutgers d. Villanova 72-60, Iowa State d. Marquette 77-69, Oregon d. Notre Dame 65-61, Michigan d. Hawaii 88-73

Semifinals: Rutgers d. Iowa State 84-81 (OT), Michigan d. Oregon 78-53

Championship: Michigan d. Rutgers 62-55

MVP: Daniel Horton, Michigan

2004-05: Roy's Joy

In 15 years as coach at Kansas, Roy Williams reached four Final Fours without winning a title. His first North Carolina team was bounced in the second round in 2004. This time the Tar Heels (33–4)—led by future NBA first-rounders Sean May, Raymond Felton, Rashad McCants and Marvin Williams—won it all by beating Illinois in the Final, 75-70. During the regular season, the Illini (37-2) held the nation's No. 1 ranking for 15 straight weeks. They beat Arizona, 90-89, in the Elite Eight after coming back from 15 down and forcing overtime.

Three of the four regional finals went to overtime. Louisville and Michigan State returned to the Final Four for the first time since 1986 and 2001, respectively.

Player of the Year honors went to Utah's Andrew Bogut, a seven-foot center from Australia, who became the first pick of the NBA draft (Milwaukee Bucks).

Major Conference Standings

AMERICA EAST	Conference W	L	Pct	Overall W	L	Pct
Vermont⊕	16	2	.889	25	7	.781
Northeastern□	15	3	.833	21	10	.677
Boston U.□	14	4	.778	20	9	.690
Albany (NY)	9	9	.500	13	15	.464
Maine	8	10	.444	14	15	.483
Binghamton	8	10	.444	12	17	.414
Stony Brook	6	12	.333	12	17	.414
UMBC	5	13	.278	11	18	.379
New Hampshire	5	13	.278	9	19	.321
Hartford	4	14	.222	8	20	.286

Tournament: **Vermont d. Northeastern 80-57**
Tournament MVP: **Taylor Coppenrath**, Vermont

ACC	Conference W	L	Pct	Overall W	L	Pct
North Carolina○	14	2	.875	33	4	.892
Wake Forest○	13	3	.813	27	6	.818
Duke⊕	11	5	.688	27	6	.818
Georgia Tech○	8	8	.500	20	12	.625
Virginia Tech□	8	8	.500	16	14	.533
NC State○	7	9	.438	21	14	.600
Maryland□	7	9	.438	19	13	.594
Miami (FL)□	7	9	.438	16	13	.552
Clemson□	5	11	.313	16	16	.500
Virginia	4	12	.250	14	15	.483
Florida State	4	12	.250	12	19	.387

Tournament: **Duke d. Georgia Tech 69-64**
Tournament MVP: **J.J. Redick**, Duke

ATLANTIC SUN	Conference W	L	Pct	Overall W	L	Pct
Gardner-Webb	13	7	.650	18	12	.600
Central Florida⊕	13	7	.650	24	9	.727
Belmont	12	8	.600	14	16	.467
Lipscomb	11	9	.550	16	12	.571
Mercer	11	9	.550	16	12	.571
Jacksonville	11	9	.550	16	13	.552
Georgia State	11	9	.550	14	15	.483
Troy	10	10	.500	12	18	.400
Florida Atlantic	10	10	.500	10	17	.370
Stetson	8	12	.400	10	17	.370
Campbell	0	20	.000	2	25	.074

Tournament: **Central Florida d. Gardner-Webb 63-54**
Tournament MVP: **Gary Johnson**, Central Florida

ATLANTIC 10	Conference W	L	Pct	Overall W	L	Pct
East Division						
Saint Joseph's□	14	2	.875	24	12	.667
Temple□	11	5	.688	16	14	.533
Massachusetts	9	7	.563	16	12	.571
Fordham	8	8	.500	13	16	.448
Rhode Island	4	12	.250	6	22	.214
St. Bonaventure	1	15	.063	2	26	.071
West Division						
George Washington⊕	11	5	.688	22	8	.733
Dayton	10	6	.625	18	11	.621
Xavier	10	6	.625	17	12	.586
Richmond	8	8	.500	14	15	.483
La Salle	5	11	.313	10	19	.345
Duquesne	5	11	.313	8	22	.267

Tournament: **George Washington d. Saint Joseph's 76-67**
Tournament MOP: **Pat Carroll**, Saint Joseph's

BIG EAST	Conference W	L	Pct	Overall W	L	Pct
Boston College○	13	3	.813	25	5	.833
Connecticut○	13	3	.813	23	8	.742
Syracuse⊕	11	5	.688	27	7	.794
Villanova○	11	5	.688	24	8	.750
Pittsburgh○	10	6	.625	20	9	.690
Notre Dame□	9	7	.563	17	12	.586
West Virginia○	8	8	.500	24	11	.686
Georgetown□	8	8	.500	19	13	.594
Providence	4	12	.250	14	17	.452
Seton Hall	4	12	.250	12	16	.429
St. John's	3	13	.188	9	18	.333
Rutgers	2	14	.125	10	19	.345

Tournament: **Syracuse d. West Virginia 68-59**
Tournament MVP: **Hakim Warrick**, Syracuse

BIG SKY	Conference W	L	Pct	Overall W	L	Pct
Portland State	11	3	.786	19	9	.679
Montana⊕	9	5	.643	18	13	.581
Montana State	9	5	.643	14	14	.500
Sacramento State	8	6	.571	12	16	.429
Weber State	7	7	.500	14	16	.467
Eastern Washington	5	9	.357	8	20	.286
Northern Arizona	4	10	.286	11	17	.393
Idaho State	3	11	.214	9	18	.333

Tournament: **Montana d. Weber State 63-61**
Tournament MVP: **Kamarr Davis**, Montana

BIG SOUTH	Conference W	L	Pct	Overall W	L	Pct
Winthrop⊕	15	1	.938	27	6	.818
Liberty	11	5	.688	13	15	.464
UNC Asheville	8	8	.500	11	17	.393
Birmingham Southern	7	9	.438	16	14	.533
Radford	7	9	.438	12	16	.429
Charleston Southern	7	9	.438	13	17	.433
High Point	7	9	.438	13	18	.419
Coastal Carolina	7	9	.438	10	19	.345
VMI	3	13	.188	9	18	.333

Tournament: **Winthrop d. Charleston Southern 68-46**
Tournament MVP: **Torrell Martin**, Winthrop

BIG TEN	Conference W	L	Pct	Overall W	L	Pct
Illinois⊕	15	1	.938	37	2	.949
Michigan State○	13	3	.813	26	7	.788
Wisconsin○	11	5	.688	25	9	.735
Minnesota○	10	6	.625	21	11	.656
Indiana□	10	6	.625	15	14	.517
Ohio State	8	8	.500	20	12	.625
Iowa○	7	9	.438	21	12	.636
Northwestern	6	10	.375	15	16	.484
Michigan	4	12	.250	13	18	.419
Purdue	3	13	.188	7	21	.250
Penn State	1	15	.063	7	23	.233

Tournament: **Illinois d. Wisconsin 54-43**
Tournament MOP: **James Augustine**, Illinois

BIG 12	Conference W	L	Pct	Overall W	L	Pct
Oklahoma○	12	4	.750	25	8	.758
Kansas○	12	4	.750	23	7	.767
Oklahoma State⊕	11	5	.688	26	7	.788
Texas Tech○	10	6	.625	22	11	.667
Texas○	9	7	.563	20	11	.645
Iowa State○	9	7	.563	19	12	.613
Texas A&M□	8	8	.500	21	10	.677
Nebraska	7	9	.438	14	14	.500
Missouri□	7	9	.438	16	17	.485
Kansas State	6	10	.375	17	12	.586
Colorado	4	12	.250	14	16	.467
Baylor	1	15	.063	9	19	.321

Tournament: **Oklahoma State d. Texas Tech 72-68**
Tournament MOP: **Joey Graham**, Oklahoma State

BIG WEST	Conference W	L	Pct	Overall W	L	Pct
Pacific○	18	0	1.000	27	4	.871
Utah State⊕	13	5	.722	24	8	.750
Cal State Fullerton□	12	6	.667	21	11	.656
Cal State Northridge	12	6	.667	18	13	.581
UC Irvine	8	10	.444	16	13	.552
UC Santa Barbara	7	11	.389	11	18	.379
Long Beach State	7	11	.389	10	20	.333
Idaho	6	12	.333	8	22	.267
UC Riverside	4	14	.222	9	19	.321
Cal Poly	3	15	.167	5	22	.185

Tournament: **Utah State d. Pacific 65-52**
Tournament MVP: **Jaycee Carroll**, Utah State

COLONIAL ATHLETIC	Conference W	L	Pct	Overall W	L	Pct
Old Dominion⊕	15	3	.833	28	6	.824
UNC Wilmington	13	5	.722	19	10	.655
VCU□	13	5	.722	19	13	.594
Hofstra□	12	6	.667	21	9	.700
Drexel□	12	6	.667	17	12	.586
George Mason	10	8	.556	16	13	.552
Delaware	7	11	.389	11	20	.355
William and Mary	3	15	.167	8	21	.276
James Madison	3	15	.167	6	22	.214
Towson	2	16	.111	5	24	.172

Tournament: **Old Dominion d. VCU 73-66 OT**
Tournament MVP: **Alex Loughton**, Old Dominion

C-USA	Conference W	L	Pct	Overall W	L	Pct
Louisville⊕	14	2	.875	33	5	.868
Cincinnati○	12	4	.750	25	8	.758
Charlotte○	12	4	.750	21	8	.724
UAB○	10	6	.625	22	11	.667
DePaul□	10	6	.625	20	11	.645
Memphis□	9	7	.563	22	16	.579
Houston□	9	7	.563	18	14	.563
TCU□	8	8	.500	21	14	.600
Marquette□	7	9	.438	19	12	.613
Saint Louis	6	10	.375	9	21	.300
South Florida	5	11	.313	14	16	.467
Tulane	4	12	.250	10	18	.357
East Carolina	4	12	.250	9	19	.321
Southern Miss	2	14	.125	11	17	.393

Tournament: **Louisville d. Memphis 75-74**
Tournament MVP: **Taquan Dean**, Louisville

HORIZON	Conference W	L	Pct	Overall W	L	Pct
Wisc.-Milwaukee⊕	14	2	.875	26	6	.813
Wisconsin-Green Bay	10	6	.625	17	11	.607
Detroit	9	7	.563	14	16	.467
Illinois-Chicago	8	8	.500	15	14	.517
Wright State	8	8	.500	15	15	.500
Loyola-Chicago	8	8	.500	13	17	.433
Butler	7	9	.438	13	15	.464
Cleveland State	6	10	.375	9	17	.346
Youngstown State	2	14	.125	5	23	.179

Tournament: **Wisconsin-Milwaukee d. Detroit 59-58**
Tournament MVP: **Joah Tucker**, Wisconsin-Milwaukee

IVY	Conference W	L	Pct	Overall W	L	Pct
Penn⊕	13	1	.929	20	9	.690
Cornell	8	6	.571	13	14	.481
Harvard	7	7	.500	12	15	.444
Yale	7	7	.500	11	16	.407
Dartmouth	7	7	.500	10	17	.370
Princeton	6	8	.429	15	13	.536
Brown	5	9	.357	12	16	.429
Columbia	3	11	.214	12	15	.444

Conference Standings Continue →

ANNUAL REVIEW

⊕ Automatic NCAA Tournament bid ○ At-large NCAA Tournament bid □ NIT appearance ⊗ Team record doesn't reflect games forfeited or vacated. For adjusted record, see p. 521.

MAAC

	Conference W	L	Pct	Overall W	L	Pct
Niagara ⊕	13	5	.722	20	10	.667
Rider	13	5	.722	19	11	.633
Fairfield	11	7	.611	15	15	.500
Saint Peter's	10	8	.556	15	13	.536
Manhattan	9	9	.500	15	14	.517
Iona	9	9	.500	15	16	.484
Marist	8	10	.444	11	17	.393
Canisius	8	10	.444	11	18	.379
Loyola (MD)	5	13	.278	6	22	.214
Siena	4	14	.222	6	24	.200

Tournament: **Niagara d. Rider 81-59**
Tournament MVP: **Juan Mendez**, Niagara

MID-AMERICAN

	Conference W	L	Pct	Overall W	L	Pct
East Division						
Miami (OH) □	12	6	.667	19	11	.633
Buffalo □	11	7	.611	23	10	.697
Ohio ⊕	11	7	.611	21	11	.656
Akron	11	7	.611	19	10	.655
Kent State State □	11	7	.611	20	13	.606
Marshall	3	15	.167	6	22	.214
West Division						
Toledo	11	7	.611	16	13	.552
Western Michigan □	11	7	.611	20	13	.606
Bowling Green	10	8	.556	18	11	.621
Ball State	10	8	.556	15	13	.536
Northern Illinois	7	11	.389	11	17	.393
Eastern Michigan	5	13	.278	12	18	.400
Central Michigan	4	14	.222	10	18	.357

Tournament: **Ohio d. Buffalo 80-79 OT**
Tournament MVP: **Leon Williams**, Ohio

MID-CONTINENT

	Conference W	L	Pct	Overall W	L	Pct
Oral Roberts □	13	3	.813	25	8	.758
UMKC	12	4	.750	16	12	.571
Valparaiso	10	6	.625	15	16	.484
IUPUI	9	7	.563	16	13	.552
Oakland ⊕	7	9	.438	13	19	.406
Western Illinois	7	9	.438	11	17	.393
Chicago State	7	9	.438	9	19	.321
Southern Utah	6	10	.375	13	15	.464
Centenary	1	15	.063	3	24	.111

Tournament: **Oakland d. Oral Roberts 61-60**
Tournament MVP: **Rawle Marshall**, Oakland

MEAC

	Conference W	L	Pct	Overall W	L	Pct
Delaware State ⊕	14	4	.778	19	14	.576
Hampton	13	5	.722	17	13	.567
Coppin State	13	5	.722	14	15	.483
South Carolina State	11	7	.611	19	12	.613
Norfolk State	11	7	.611	13	14	.481
Morgan State	10	7	.588	14	16	.467
Florida A&M	9	8	.529	14	15	.483
Bethune-Cookman	8	9	.471	13	17	.433
NC A&T	5	13	.278	6	24	.200
Howard	2	16	.111	5	23	.179
UMES	1	17	.056	2	26	.071

Tournament: **Delaware State d. Hampton 55-53**
Tournament MOP: **Jahsha Bluntt**, Delaware State

MISSOURI VALLEY

	Conference W	L	Pct	Overall W	L	Pct
Southern Illinois ○	15	3	.833	27	8	.771
Wichita State □	12	6	.667	22	10	.688
Creighton ⊕	11	7	.611	23	11	.676
Northern Iowa ○	11	7	.611	21	11	.656
Missouri State □	10	8	.556	19	13	.594
Illinois State	8	10	.444	17	13	.567
Drake	7	11	.389	13	16	.448
Bradley	6	12	.333	13	15	.464
Evansville	5	13	.278	11	17	.393
Indiana State	5	13	.278	11	20	.355

Tournament: **Creighton d. Missouri State 75-57**
Tournament MOP: **Johnny Mathies**, Creighton

MOUNTAIN WEST

	Conference W	L	Pct	Overall W	L	Pct
Utah ○	13	1	.929	29	6	.829
New Mexico ⊕	10	4	.714	26	7	.788
Air Force	9	5	.643	18	12	.600
UNLV □	7	7	.500	17	14	.548
Wyoming	7	7	.500	15	13	.536
San Diego State	4	10	.286	11	18	.379
Colorado State	3	11	.214	11	17	.393
BYU	3	11	.214	9	21	.300

Tournament: **New Mexico d. Utah 60-56**
Tournament MVP: **Danny Granger**, New Mexico

NORTHEAST

	Conference W	L	Pct	Overall W	L	Pct
Monmouth	14	4	.778	16	13	.552
Fairleigh Dickinson ⊕	13	5	.722	20	13	.606
Robert Morris	11	7	.611	14	15	.483
Saint Francis (PA)	10	8	.556	15	13	.536
Long Island	10	8	.556	14	15	.483
Wagner	10	8	.556	13	17	.433
St. Francis (NY)	9	9	.500	13	15	.464
Central Conn. State	8	10	.444	12	16	.429
Quinnipiac	6	12	.333	10	17	.370
Mount St. Mary's	5	13	.278	7	20	.259
Sacred Heart	3	15	.167	4	23	.148

Tournament: **Fairleigh Dickinson d. Wagner 58-52**
Tournament MVP: **Tamien Trent**, Fairleigh Dickinson

OHIO VALLEY

	Conference W	L	Pct	Overall W	L	Pct
Tennessee Tech	12	4	.750	18	11	.621
Eastern Kentucky ⊕	11	5	.688	22	9	.710
Murray State	11	5	.688	17	11	.607
Samford	10	6	.625	15	13	.536
SE Missouri State	9	7	.563	15	14	.517
Tennessee State	9	7	.563	14	17	.452
Austin Peay	9	7	.563	13	19	.406
Eastern Illinois	7	9	.438	12	16	.429
Morehead State	5	11	.313	11	16	.407
Tennessee-Martin	3	13	.188	6	21	.222
Jacksonville State	2	14	.125	7	22	.241

Tournament: **Eastern Kentucky d. Austin Peay 52-46**
Tournament MVP: **Michael Haney**, Eastern Kentucky

PAC-10

	Conference W	L	Pct	Overall W	L	Pct
Arizona ○	15	3	.833	30	7	.811
Washington ⊕	14	4	.778	29	6	.829
UCLA ○	11	7	.611	18	11	.621
Stanford ○	11	7	.611	18	13	.581
Oregon State □	8	10	.444	17	15	.531
Arizona State □	7	11	.389	18	14	.563
Washington State	7	11	.389	12	16	.429
Oregon	6	12	.333	14	13	.519
California	6	12	.333	13	16	.448
Southern California	5	13	.278	12	17	.414

Tournament: **Washington d. Arizona 81-72**
Tournament MOP: **Salim Stoudamire**, Arizona

PATRIOT LEAGUE

	Conference W	L	Pct	Overall W	L	Pct
Holy Cross □	13	1	.929	25	7	.781
Bucknell ⊕ ⊗	10	4	.714	23	10	.697
American ⊗	8	6	.571	16	12	.571
Lehigh ⊗	7	7	.500	14	15	.483
Colgate ⊗	7	7	.500	12	16	.429
Lafayette ⊗	5	9	.357	9	19	.321
Navy ⊗	5	9	.357	9	19	.321
Army ⊗	1	13	.071	3	24	.111

Tournament: **Bucknell d. Holy Cross 61-57**
Tournament MVP: **Charles Lee**, Bucknell

SEC

	Conference W	L	Pct	Overall W	L	Pct
Eastern						
Kentucky ○	14	2	.875	28	6	.824
Florida ⊕	12	4	.750	24	8	.750
Vanderbilt □	8	8	.500	20	14	.588
South Carolina □	7	9	.438	20	13	.606
Tennessee	6	10	.375	14	17	.452
Georgia	2	14	.125	8	20	.286
Western						
Alabama ○	12	4	.750	24	8	.750
LSU ○	12	4	.750	20	10	.667
Mississippi State ○	9	7	.563	23	11	.676
Arkansas	6	10	.375	18	12	.600
Auburn	4	12	.250	14	17	.452
Mississippi	4	12	.250	14	17	.452

Tournament: **Florida d. Kentucky 70-53**
Tournament MVP: **Matt Walsh**, Florida

SOUTHERN

	Conference W	L	Pct	Overall W	L	Pct
North						
Chattanooga ⊕	10	6	.625	20	11	.645
Appalachian State	9	7	.563	18	12	.600
UNC Greensboro	9	7	.563	18	12	.600
Elon	5	11	.313	8	23	.258
East Tennessee State	4	12	.250	10	19	.345
Western Carolina	3	13	.188	8	22	.267
South						
Davidson □	16	0	1.000	23	9	.719
Charleston	10	6	.625	18	10	.643
Georgia Southern	10	6	.625	18	13	.581
Furman	9	7	.563	16	13	.552
Wofford	7	9	.438	14	14	.500
The Citadel	4	12	.250	12	16	.429

Tournament: **Chattanooga d. UNC Greensboro 66-62**
Tournament MOP: **Mindaugas Katelynas**, Chattanooga

SOUTHLAND

	Conference W	L	Pct	Overall W	L	Pct
Northwestern St. (LA)	13	3	.813	21	12	.636
Southeastern La. ⊕	13	3	.813	24	9	.727
Sam Houston State	11	5	.688	18	12	.600
UTSA	10	6	.625	15	13	.536
Lamar	9	7	.563	18	11	.621
Texas State	8	8	.500	14	14	.500
McNeese State	8	8	.500	13	15	.464
Texas-Arlington	7	9	.438	13	15	.464
Stephen F. Austin	6	10	.375	12	15	.444
UL-Monroe	2	14	.125	8	19	.296
Nicholls State	1	15	.063	6	21	.222

Tournament: **Southeastern La. d. Northwestern State (LA) 49-42**
Tournament MVP: **Ricky Woods**, Southeastern La.

SWAC

	Conference W	L	Pct	Overall W	L	Pct
Alabama A&M ⊕	12	6	.667	18	14	.563
Grambling	11	7	.611	14	12	.538
Alabama State	11	7	.611	15	15	.500
Miss. Valley State	11	7	.611	13	15	.464
Southern U.	10	8	.556	14	15	.483
Jackson State ⊗	10	8	.556	15	17	.469
Texas Southern ⊗	8	9	.471	11	15	.423
Alcorn State	6	12	.333	7	22	.241
Arkansas-Pine Bluff ⊗	5	13	.278	7	21	.250
Prairie View A&M ⊗	5	14	.278	5	23	.179

Tournament: **Alabama A&M d. Alabama State 72-53**
Tournament MVP: **Obie Trotter**, Alabama A&M

SUN BELT

	Conference W	L	Pct	Overall W	L	Pct
East Division						
Arkansas-Little Rock	10	4	.714	18	10	.643
Western Kentucky □	9	5	.643	22	9	.710
Middle Tenn. State	7	7	.500	19	12	.613
Arkansas State	7	7	.500	16	13	.552
Florida Int'l ⊗	4	10	.286	13	17	.433
West Division						
Denver □	12	3	.800	20	11	.645
UL-Lafayette ⊕ ⊗	11	4	.733	20	11	.645
New Orleans	7	8	.467	13	17	.433
North Texas	6	9	.400	14	14	.500
South Alabama	6	9	.400	10	18	.357
New Mexico State	1	14	.067	6	24	.200

Tournament: **UL-Lafayette d. Denver 88-69**
Tournament MOP: **Tiras Wade**, UL-Lafayette

WEST COAST

	Conference W	L	Pct	Overall W	L	Pct
Gonzaga ⊕	12	2	.857	26	5	.839
Saint Mary's (CA) ○	11	3	.786	25	9	.735
Santa Clara	7	7	.500	15	16	.484
Pepperdine	6	8	.429	17	14	.548
San Diego	7	7	.500	16	13	.552
San Francisco □	6	8	.429	17	14	.548
Portland	4	10	.286	15	15	.500
Loyola Marymount	3	11	.214	11	17	.393

Tournament: **Gonzaga d. Saint Mary's (CA) 80-67**
Tournament MVP: **Adam Morrison**, Gonzaga

WAC

	Conference W	L	Pct	Overall W	L	Pct
Nevada ○	16	2	.889	25	7	.781
UTEP ⊕	14	4	.778	27	8	.771
Rice □	12	6	.667	19	12	.613
Fresno State	9	9	.500	16	14	.533
SMU	9	9	.500	14	14	.500
Louisiana Tech	9	9	.500	14	15	.483
Hawaii	7	11	.389	16	13	.552
Boise State	6	12	.333	16	18	.471
Tulsa	5	13	.278	9	20	.310
San Jose State	3	15	.167	6	23	.207

Tournament: **UTEP d. Boise State 91-78**
Tournament MVP: **Filiberto Rivera**, UTEP

INDEPENDENTS

	Overall W	L	Pct
Corpus Christi	20	8	.714
Texas-Pan American	12	16	.429
IPFW	7	22	.241
Savannah State	0	28	.000

ALL OTHERS

(Reclassifying & provisional teams that are not eligible for the NCAA tournament)

	Overall W	L	Pct
Utah Valley State	16	12	.571
UC Davis	11	17	.393
Northern Colorado	8	21	.276
Longwood	1	30	.032

INDIVIDUAL LEADERS—SEASON

SCORING	CL	POS	G	FG	3FG	FT	PTS	PPG
1 **Keydren Clark**, Saint Peter's	JR	G	28	230	109	152	721	**25.8**
2 **Taylor Coppenrath**, Vermont	SR	F	31	271	9	226	777	**25.1**
3 **Juan Mendez**, Niagara	SR	F	30	221	39	224	705	**23.5**
4 **Rob Monroe**, Quinnipiac	SR	G	26	173	72	171	589	**22.7**
5 **Bo McCalebb**, New Orleans	SO	G	30	261	25	132	679	**22.6**
6 **Ike Diogu**, Arizona State	JR	F	32	229	18	248	724	**22.6**
7 **Tim Smith**, East Tennessee State	JR	G	29	245	59	96	645	**22.2**
8 **Jose Juan Barea**, Northeastern	JR	G	30	233	68	131	665	**22.2**
9 **J.J. Redick**, Duke	JR	G	33	202	121	196	721	**21.8**
10 **Ryan Gomes**, Providence	SR	F	31	247	52	124	670	**21.6**

FIELD GOAL PCT	CL	POS	G	FG	FGA	PCT
1 **Bruce Brown**, Hampton	JR	C	30	178	269	**66.2**
2 **Nate Harris**, Utah State	JR	F	32	172	264	**65.2**
3 **Eric Williams**, Wake Forest	JR	C	33	201	319	**63.0**
4 **Chad McKnight**, Morehead State	SR	F	27	155	246	**63.0**
5 **Aaron Andrews**, Morgan State	SR	C	28	140	224	**62.5**

MINIMUM: 5 MADE PER GAME

THREE-POINT FG PER GAME	CL	POS	G	3FG	3PG
1 **Brendan Plavich**, Charlotte	SR	G	29	114	**3.9**
2 **Keydren Clark**, Saint Peter's	JR	G	28	109	**3.9**
3 **Pat Carroll**, Saint Joseph's	SR	G	35	135	**3.9**
4 **T.J. Sorrentine**, Vermont	SR	G	31	116	**3.7**
5 **J.J. Redick**, Duke	JR	G	33	121	**3.7**

THREE-POINT FG PCT	CL	POS	G	3FG	3FGA	PCT
1 **Salim Stoudamire**, Arizona	SR	G	36	120	238	**50.4**
2 **Will Whittington**, Marist	SO	G	28	97	197	**49.2**
3 **Dennis Trammell**, Ball State	SR	G	23	59	122	**48.4**
4 **Chris Lofton**, Tennessee	FR	G	31	93	200	**46.5**
5 **Drake Diener**, DePaul	SR	G	31	85	184	**46.2**

MINIMUM: 2.5 MADE PER GAME

FREE THROW PCT	CL	POS	G	FT	FTA	PCT
1 **Blake Ahearn**, Missouri State	SO	G	32	90	95	**94.7**
2 **J.J. Redick**, Duke	JR	G	33	196	209	**93.8**
3 **Vince Greene**, Illinois State	SR	G	30	81	88	**92.0**
4 **Salim Stoudamire**, Arizona	SR	G	36	122	134	**91.0**
5 **Jamaal Hilliard**, Lafayette	SO	G	28	91	100	**91.0**

MINIMUM: 2.5 MADE PER GAME

ASSISTS PER GAME	CL	POS	G	AST	APG
1 **Damitrius Coleman**, Mercer	JR	G	28	224	**8.0**
Will Funn, Portland State	SR	G	28	224	**8.0**
3 **Marcus Williams**, Connecticut	SO	G	31	243	**7.8**
4 **Walker Russell Jr.**, Jacksonville State	JR	G	29	211	**7.3**
5 **Jose Juan Barea**, Northeastern	JR	G	30	218	**7.3**
6 **Aaron Miles**, Kansas	SR	G	30	216	**7.2**
7 **Filiberto Rivera**, UTEP	SR	G	32	229	**7.2**
8 **Javier Mendiburu**, Wisconsin-Green Bay	SR	G	26	184	**7.1**
9 **Garrett Farha**, Saint Francis (PA)	JR	G	28	194	**6.9**
10 **Raymond Felton**, North Carolina	JR	G	36	249	**6.9**

REBOUNDS PER GAME	CL	POS	G	REB	RPG
1 **Paul Millsap**, Louisiana Tech	SO	F	29	360	**12.4**
2 **Andrew Bogut**, Utah	SO	F/C	35	427	**12.2**
3 **Lance Allred**, Weber State	SR	C	29	348	**12.0**
4 **Michael Harris**, Rice	SR	F	31	363	**11.7**
5 **Dwayne Jones**, Saint Joseph's	JR	C	36	418	**11.6**
6 **Shelden Williams**, Duke	JR	F	33	369	**11.2**
7 **Wayne Simien**, Kansas	SR	F	26	287	**11.0**
8 **Lawrence Roberts**, Mississippi State	SR	F	32	351	**11.0**
9 **Sean May**, North Carolina	JR	C	37	397	**10.7**
10 **Juan Mendez**, Niagara	SR	F	30	319	**10.6**

BLOCKED SHOTS PER GAME	CL	POS	G	BLK	BPG
1 **Deng Gai**, Fairfield	SR	F	30	165	**5.5**
2 **Shawn James**, Northeastern	FR	F	25	136	**5.4**
3 **Shelden Williams**, Duke	JR	F	33	122	**3.7**
4 **Kyle Hines**, UNC Greensboro	FR	F	30	106	**3.5**
5 **Dwayne Jones**, Saint Joseph's	JR	C	36	109	**3.0**

STEALS PER GAME	CL	POS	G	STL	SPG
1 **Obie Trotter**, Alabama A&M	JR	G	32	125	**3.9**
2 **Chakowby Hicks**, Norfolk State	SR	G	27	91	**3.4**
3 **Keydren Clark**, Saint Peter's	JR	G	28	93	**3.3**
4 **Hosea Butler**, Mississippi Valley State	SR	G	28	91	**3.3**
5 **Eddie Basden**, Charlotte	SR	G/F	29	93	**3.2**

INDIVIDUAL LEADERS—GAME

POINTS	CL	POS	OPP	DATE	PTS
1 **Joe Knight**, Lehigh	JR	G	Colgate	M4	**45**
2 **Elton Nesbitt**, Georgia Southern	JR	G	Chattanooga	J17	**43**
Keydren Clark, Saint Peter's	JR	G	Charleston	D30	**43**
4 **Jose Juan Barea**, Northeastern	JR	G	Stony Brook	M5	**41**
Jay Straight, Wyoming	SR	G	Colorado State	F26	**41**
Rob Monroe, Quinnipiac	SR	G	Longwood	J2	**41**

THREE-POINT FG MADE	CL	POS	OPP	DATE	3FG
1 **Elton Nesbitt**, Georgia Southern	JR	G	Chattanooga	J17	**11**
2 **Joe Knight**, Lehigh	JR	G	Colgate	M4	**10**
Elton Nesbitt, Georgia Southern	JR	G	The Citadel	F14	**10**
4 **Mario Moore**, Vanderbilt	JR	G	Wichita State	M21	**9**
Salim Stoudamire, Arizona	SR	G	Oregon State	F20	**9**
Sean Morris, Colorado State	FR	G	UNLV	J22	**9**
Ed McCants, Wisconsin-Milwaukee	SR	G	Detroit	J3	**9**
Levi Rost, Western Michigan	SR	F	Buffalo	D4	**9**

ASSISTS	CL	POS	OPP	DATE	AST
1 **Filiberto Rivera**, UTEP	SR	G	Louisiana Tech	F25	**18**
Ronald Steele, Alabama	FR	G	East Tennesee State	D1	**18**
3 **Jonathan Bluitt**, Oral Roberts	JR	G	Oakland	J20	**16**
4 **Rodney Billups**, Denver	SR	G	UL-Lafayette	F5	**15**
5 **Will Conroy**, Washington	SR	G	California	M3	**14**
Jeremy Long, Lamar	JR	G	Texas State	F19	**14**
Jose Juan Barea, Northeastern	JR	G	Hartford	F9	**14**
Acie Law IV, Texas A&M	SO	G	Missouri	F5	**14**
Johnny Miller, IUPUI	SR	G	Southern Utah	F5	**14**
Gary Ervin, Mississippi State	SO	G	Florida A&M	D20	**14**
Louis Ford, Howard	JR	G	UMES	D6	**14**
Jared Jordan, Marist	SO	G	Saint Peter's	D6	**14**
Javier Mendiburu, Wisc.-Green Bay	SR	G	Weber State	D4	**14**
Jeff Gardner, Idaho State	SR	G	Montana Tech	D1	**14**
Bucky McMillan, Birmingham-So.	SO	G	Tenn. Wesleyan	N27	**14**
Rob Monroe, Quinnipiac	SR	G	Longwood	N27	**14**
Marvin Lea, Pepperdine	SO	G	Siena	N18	**14**

REBOUNDS	CL	POS	OPP	DATE	REB
1 **Paul Millsap**, Louisiana Tech	SO	F	Boise State	F27	**25**
2 **Sean May**, North Carolina	JR	C	Duke	M6	**24**
Michael Harris, Rice	SR	F	Hawaii	F27	**24**
Aaron Johnson, Penn State	JR	F	Western Carolina	N15	**24**
5 **Dreike Bouldin**, Fresno State	SR	F	Louisiana Tech	J8	**23**
6 **Dillion Sneed**, East Tennesee State	JR	F	Georgia Southern	F26	**22**
Glen McGowan, Pepperdine	SR	F	Colorado State	J3	**22**
Louis Amundson, UNLV	JR	F	Auburn	D12	**22**

BLOCKED SHOTS	CL	POS	OPP	DATE	BLK
1 **Deng Gai**, Fairfield	SR	F	Siena	J22	**13**
Anthony King, Miami	SO	C	Florida Atlantic	N29	**13**
3 **Shawn James**, Northeastern	FR	F	Albany (NY)	F27	**11**
Mustafa Al-Sayyad, Fresno State	SR	C	Buffalo	F19	**11**
Shawn James, Northeastern	FR	F	Iona	D30	**11**

STEALS	CL	POS	OPP	DATE	STL
1 **Doron Perkins**, Santa Clara	SR	G	San Diego	F24	**10**
Louis Ford, Howard	JR	G	UMES	D6	**10**
3 **Obie Trotter**, Alabama A&M	JR	G	Jackson State	M5	**9**
Bryan Hopkins, SMU	JR	G	San Jose State	F10	**9**
Mardy Collins, Temple	JR	G	South Carolina	N27	**9**

TEAM LEADERS—SEASON

WIN-LOSS PCT	W	L	PCT
1 **Illinois**	37	2	.949
2 **North Carolina**	33	4	.892
3 **Pacific**	27	4	.871
4 **Louisville**	33	5	.868
5 **Gonzaga**	26	5	.839

SCORING OFFENSE	G	W-L	PTS	PPG
1 **North Carolina**	37	33-4	3,257	**88.0**
2 **Washington**	35	29-6	3,026	**86.5**
3 **Wake Forest**	33	27-6	2,801	**84.9**
4 **Niagara**	30	20-10	2,537	**84.6**
5 **Maryland**	32	19-13	2,620	**81.9**

SCORING MARGIN	G	W-L	PPG	OPP PPG	MAR
1 **North Carolina**	37	33-4	88.0	70.3	**17.8**
2 **Louisville**	38	33-5	80.7	64.1	**16.6**
3 **Illinois**	39	37-2	77.0	61.1	**15.9**
4 **Utah State**	32	24-8	72.3	57.8	**14.6**
5 **Oklahoma State**	33	26-7	78.3	65.2	**13.1**

FIELD GOAL PCT	G	W-L	FG	FGA	PCT
1 **Utah State**	32	24-8	851	1,621	**52.5**
2 **Utah**	35	29-6	837	1,628	**51.4**
3 **Samford**	28	15-13	616	1,224	**50.3**
4 **Gonzaga**	31	26-5	856	1,702	**50.3**
5 **North Carolina**	37	33-4	1,128	2,260	**49.9**

THREE-POINT FG PER GAME	G	W-L	3FG	3PG
1 **Troy**	30	12-18	338	**11.3**
2 **Belmont**	30	14-16	292	**9.7**
3 **Louisville**	38	33-5	361	**9.5**
4 **Vanderbilt**	34	20-14	322	**9.5**
5 **Furman**	29	16-13	267	**9.2**

FREE THROW PCT	G	W-L	FT	FTA	PCT
1 **UTEP**	35	27-8	606	765	**79.2**
2 **Oklahoma State**	33	26-7	521	668	**78.0**
3 **Michigan State**	33	26-7	543	699	**77.7**
4 **Arizona**	37	30-7	541	697	**77.6**
5 **Monmouth**	29	16-13	420	545	**77.1**

ASSISTS PER GAME	G	W-L	AST	APG
1 **North Carolina**	37	33-4	706	**19.1**
2 **Washington**	35	29-6	660	**18.9**
3 **Illinois**	39	37-2	727	**18.6**
4 **Corpus Christi**	28	20-8	514	**18.4**
5 **Sam Houston State**	30	18-12	535	**17.8**

REBOUND MARGIN	G	W-L	RPG	OPP RPG	MAR
1 **Connecticut**	31	23-8	45.5	34.3	**11.3**
2 **Chattanooga**	31	20-11	41.4	30.6	**10.8**
3 **Utah**	35	29-6	34.1	23.6	**10.5**
4 **Pittsburgh**	29	20-9	38.0	29.5	**8.6**
5 **Mississippi State**	34	23-11	40.9	32.4	**8.5**

Scoring Defense

	G	W-L	OPP PTS	OPP PPG
1 Air Force	30	18-12	1,629	**54.3**
2 Princeton	28	15-13	1,521	**54.3**
3 Boston U.	29	20-9	1,616	**55.7**
4 Southeastern La.	33	24-9	1,842	**55.8**
5 Holy Cross	32	25-7	1,817	**56.8**

Field Goal Pct Defense

	G	W-L	OPP FG	OPP FGA	OPP PCT
1 Boston U.	29	20-9	588	1,584	**37.1**
2 Cincinnati	33	25-8	749	2,008	**37.3**
3 Connecticut	31	23-8	761	2,011	**37.8**
4 Memphis	38	22-16	827	2,155	**38.4**
5 Kansas	30	23-7	663	1,712	**38.7**

Blocked Shots Per Game

	G	W-L	BLK	BPG
1 Connecticut	31	23-8	275	**8.9**
2 Cincinnati	33	25-8	225	**6.8**
3 Duke	33	27-6	220	**6.7**
4 Northeastern	31	21-10	202	**6.5**
5 Fairfield	30	15-15	192	**6.4**

Steals Per Game

	G	W-L	STL	SPG
1 UAB	33	22-11	382	**11.6**
2 Cal State Northridge	31	18-13	340	**11.0**
3 Alabama A&M	32	18-14	338	**10.6**
4 Houston	32	18-14	331	**10.3**
5 Troy	30	12-18	309	**10.3**

TEAM LEADERS—GAME

Points

	OPP	DATE	SCORE
1 Furman	Virginia Intermont	D29	126-33
2 Texas Tech	UNC Asheville	N19	119-55
3 Florida International	Arkansas-Little Rock	J30	118-114
High Point	Southeastern Florida	N20	118-66
5 Wisconsin-Milwaukee	Prairie View A&M	N20	117-55

Field Goal Pct

	OPPt	DATE	FG	FGA	PCT
1 Utah	Air Force	J24	24	30	**80.0**
2 Utah State	UC Davis	N27	28	36	**77.8**
3 Tex.-Arlington	Texas-Tyler	D22	34	47	**72.3**
4 Utah State	UC Santa Barbara	F5	32	45	**71.1**
5 Northern Arizona	Willamette	D11	33	47	**70.2**

Three-point FG Made

	OPP	DATE	3FG
1 Troy	Mercer	J31	**22**
Georgia Southern	Chattanooga	J17	**22**
3 Furman	Virginia Intermont	D29	**21**
4 Creighton	Chattanooga	F19	**20**
New Mexico	Santa Clara	N13	**20**

CONSENSUS ALL-AMERICAS

First Team

PLAYER	CL	POS	HT	SCHOOL	RPG	PPG
Andrew Bogut	SO	F/C	7-0	Utah	12.2	20.4
Dee Brown	JR	G	6-0	Illinois	2.7	13.3
Chris Paul	SO	G	6-0	Wake Forest	4.5	15.3
J.J. Redick	JR	G	6-4	Duke	3.3	21.8
Wayne Simien	SR	F	6-9	Kansas	11.0	20.3
Hakim Warrick	SR	F	6-9	Syracuse	8.6	21.4

Second Team

PLAYER	CL	POS	HT	SCHOOL	RPG	PPG
Ike Diogu	JR	F	6-8	Arizona State	9.8	22.6
Luther Head	SR	G	6-3	Illinois	4.0	15.9
Sean May	JR	C	6-9	North Carolina	10.7	17.5
Salim Stoudamire	SR	G	6-1	Arizona	2.3	18.4
Deron Williams	JR	G	6-3	Illinois	3.6	12.5

Selectors: AP, NABC, Sporting News, USBWA

AWARD WINNERS

Player of the Year

PLAYER	CL	POS	HT	SCHOOL	AWARD(S)
Andrew Bogut	SO	F/C	7-0	Utah	Naismith, AP, USBWA, Wooden, NABC
J.J. Redick	JR	G	6-4	Duke	Rupp, Sullivan†
Nate Robinson	JR	G	5-9	Washington	Frances Pomeroy Naismith*

* For the most outstanding senior player who is 6 feet or under

† Top amateur athlete in U.S.

Defensive Player of the Year

PLAYER	CL	POS	HT	SCHOOL
Shelden Williams	JR	F	6-9	Duke

Coach of the Year

COACH	SCHOOL	REC	AWARD
Bruce Weber	Illinois	37-2	Naismith, AP, USBWA, NABC, Sporting News, CBS/Chevrolet

Bob Gibbons' Top High School Senior Recruits

PLAYER	POS	HT	HIGH SCHOOL	A-A TEAMS	COLLEGE	CAREER NOTES
1 **Tyler Hansbrough**	PF	6-9	Poplar Bluff (MO) HS	McD, MJ, P	North Carolina	National POY, '08; 3-time, first-team All-America; No. 13 pick, '09 NBA draft (Pacers)
2 **Monta Ellis**	G	6-3	Lanier HS, Jackson, MS	McD, MJ, P, USA	None	Drafted straight out of HS; 2nd-round pick, '05 NBA draft (Warriors); 232 NBA games, 16.0 ppg, 4.3 rpg. 3.7 apg
3 **Martell Webster**	G/F	6-7	Seattle (WA) Preparatory School	McD, MJ, P	None	Drafted straight out of HS; No. 6 pick, '05 NBA draft (Blazers); 10.7 ppg in '07-08; injured '08-09
4 **Josh McRoberts**	PF	6-10	Carmel (IN) HS	McD, P, USA	Duke	ACC All-Defensive team, '07; 2nd-round pick,'07 NBA draft (Blazers); 2.4 ppg (Pacers '09)
5 **Gerald Green**	F	6-8	Gulf Shores Academy, Houston	McD	None	Drafted straight out of HS; No. 18 pick, '05 NBA draft (Celtics); NBA Slam Dunk champ, '07; 7.5 ppg (4 seasons)
6 **Louis Williams**	G	6-1	South Gwinnett HS, Snellville, GA	McD, MJ, P, USA	None	Drafted straight out of HS; 2nd-round pick, '05 NBA draft (Sixers); 11.5 ppg in '08; 12.8 ppg in '09
7 **Julian Wright**	P/F	6-8	Homewood-Flossmoor (IL) HS	McD, MJ, P	Kansas	All-Big 12 first-team, '06-07; No. 13 pick, '07 NBA draft (Hornets); 4.4 ppg in '09
8 **Richard Hendrix**	C	6-9	Athens (AL) HS	McD, MJ, P	Alabama	At Bama ('06-08), 14.0 ppg, 8.9 rpg, 2nd-round pick, '08 NBA draft (Warriors)
9 **C.J. Miles**	G	6-6	Skyline HS, Dallas	McD, MJ, P	None	Drafted straight out of HS; 2nd-round pick, '05 NBA draft (Jazz); avg. 9.1 ppg in '09
10 **Amir Johnson**	PF	6-9	Westchester HS, Los Angeles	McD, P	None	Drafted straight out of HS; 2nd-round pick, '05 NBA draft (Pistons); 3.7 ppg (4 seasons)
11 **Wilson Chandler**	PF	6-8	Benton Harbor (MI) HS	P	DePaul	14.6 ppg (2 seasons); No. 23 pick, '07 NBA draft (Knicks);14.4 ppg, 5.4 rpg in '09
12 **Brandon Costner**	PF	6-8	Seton Hall Prep, West Orange, NJ	McD, P	NC State	Led Wolfpack in ppg as Fr. (16.8), Jr. (13.3)
13 **Brandon Rush**	F	6-7	Mt. Zion Christian Academy, Durham, NC		Kansas	Led KU in scoring, 2 seasons; No. 13 pick, '08 NBA draft (Blazers); 8.1 ppg for Indiana ('09)
14 **Andrew Bynum**	C	7-0	St. Joseph HS, Metuchen, NJ	McD, MJ, P	None	Drafted straight out of HS; youngest player drafted by NBA; No. 10 pick, '05 NBA draft (Lakers); 8.8 ppg (4 seasons)
15 **Jamont Gordon**	G/F	6-4	Oak Hill Academy, Mouth of Wilson, VA	P	Mississippi State	First-team All-SEC ('08); 15.7 ppg, 6.8 rpg, 4.9 apg in 3 seasons; plays in Italy
16 **Jon Brockman**	PF	6-7	Snohomish (WA) HS	McD, MJ, P	Washington	At UW: 1,805 points,1,283 rebounds; 2nd-round pick, '09 NBA draft (Blazers)
17 **Tasmin Mitchell**	PF	6-7	Denham Springs (LA) HS	McD, P	LSU	First-team All-SEC as redshirt Jr. for LSU (16.3 ppg)
18 **Eric Devendorf**	G	6-4	Oak Hill Academy, Mouth of Wilson, VA	McD, P	Syracuse	14.8 ppg, 4.1 apg as Soph.; tore ACL in Dec '07; returned to score 15.7 ppg as Jr.
19 **Lewis Clinch**	G	6-3	Crisp County HS, Cordele, GA	MJ, P	Georgia Tech	Averaged 11.3 ppg in 4 seasons at GT, including 15.5 ppg as Sr.
20 **Korvotney Barber**	PF	6-7	Manchester (GA) HS	McD, P	Auburn	11.3 ppg, 6.6 rpg as Soph.; 12.8 ppg, 9.6 rpg as Sr.; second-team All-SEC

Other Standouts

PLAYER	POS	HT	HIGH SCHOOL	A-A TEAMS	COLLEGE	CAREER NOTES
22 **Mario Chalmers**	PG	6-2	Bartlett HS, Anchorage, AK	McD, P	Kansas	Clutch 3-pointer led Kansas to NCAA title in '08; 2nd-round pick '08 NBA draft (Wolves); 10.0 ppg for Miami Heat in '09
23 **Marcus Williams**	F	6-7	Roosevelt HS, Seattle		Arizona	Top UA scorer (16.6 ppg) as Soph.; 2nd-round pick, '07 NBA draft (Spurs); 6.1 ppg

Abbreviations: McD=McDonald's; MJ=Jordan Brand; P=Parade; USA=USA Today

Poll Progression

Preseason Poll

AP	ESPN/USA	SCHOOL
1	1	Kansas
2	2	Wake Forest
3	4	Georgia Tech
4	3	North Carolina
5	5	Illinois
6	6	Syracuse
7	8	Oklahoma State
8	7	Connecticut
9	9	Kentucky
10	11	Arizona
11	12	Duke
12	14	Mississippi State
13	10	Michigan State
14	13	Louisville
15	16	Maryland
16	15	Texas
17	17	Pittsburgh
18	18	Alabama
19	19	NC State
20	21	Notre Dame
21	20	Wisconsin
22	24	Washington
23	22	Florida
24	23	Memphis
25	—	Gonzaga
—	25	Stanford

Week of Nov 16

AP	SCHOOL	AP↓↑
1	Kansas (0-0)	
2	Wake Forest (0-0)	
3	Georgia Tech (0-0)	
4	North Carolina (0-0)	
5	Syracuse (2-0)	↑1
6	Illinois (0-0)	↓1
7	Oklahoma State (0-0)	
8	Connecticut (0-0)	
9	Kentucky (0-0)	
10	Arizona (0-0)	
11	Duke (0-0)	
12	Mississippi State (2-0)	
13	Michigan State (0-0)	
14	Louisville (0-0)	
15	Maryland (0-0)	
16	Texas (0-0)	
17	Pittsburgh (0-0)	
18	Alabama (0-0)	
19	NC State (0-0)	
20	Notre Dame (0-0)	
21	Wisconsin (0-0)	
22	Washington (0-0)	
23	Florida (0-0)	
24	Memphis (2-0)	
25	Gonzaga (0-0)	

Week of Nov 23

AP	ESPN/USA	SCHOOL	AP↓↑
1	1	Wake Forest (2-0)	↑1
2	2	Kansas (1-0)	↓1
3	3	Georgia Tech (1-0)	
4	5	Syracuse (4-0)	↑1
5	4	Illinois (2-0)	↑1
6	7	Oklahoma State (1-0)	↑1
7	6	Connecticut (1-0)	↑1
8	8	Kentucky (1-0)	↑1
9	10	Duke (1-0)	↑2
10	9	Michigan State (1-0)	↑3
11	12	North Carolina (0-1)	↓7
12	11	Louisville (1-0)	↑2
13	14	Maryland (1-0)	↑2
14	20	Mississippi State (4-1)	↓2
15	13	Texas (1-0)	↑1
16	15	Pittsburgh (1-0)	↑1
17	16	NC State (3-0)	↑2
18	17	Arizona (2-1)	↓8
19	19	Alabama (2-0)	↓1
20	17	Wisconsin (1-0)	↑1
21	21	Notre Dame (1-0)	↓1
22	23	Washington (1-0)	
23	22	Florida (1-0)	
24	25	Gonzaga (2-0)	↑1
25	24	Memphis (3-1)	↓1

Week of Nov 30

AP	ESPN/USA	SCHOOL	AP↓↑
1	1	Wake Forest (5-0)	
2	2	Kansas (2-0)	
3	5	Syracuse (5-0)	↑1
4	4	Georgia Tech (3-0)	↓1
5	3	Illinois (4-0)	
6	7	Oklahoma State (3-0)	
7	6	Connecticut (1-0)	
8	8	Kentucky (3-0)	
9	11	North Carolina (4-1)	↑2
10	10	Duke (3-0)	↓1
11	9	Michigan State (3-0)	↓1
12	12	Maryland (3-0)	↑1
13	14	Pittsburgh (3-0)	↑3
14	16	Washington (4-0)	↑8
15	21	Mississippi State (5-1)	↓1
16	13	NC State (4-0)	↑1
17	17	Louisville (3-1)	↓5
18	15	Texas (3-1)	↓3
19	18	Florida (3-0)	↑4
20	19	Notre Dame (3-0)	↑1
21	20	Arizona (3-2)	↓3
22	22	Alabama (4-1)	↓3
23	—	Iowa (3-1)	⤴
24	25	Virginia (4-0)	⤴
25	23	Wisconsin (2-1)	⤴
—	24	Cincinnati (3-0)	

Week of Dec 7

AP	ESPN/USA	SCHOOL	AP↓↑
1	1	Illinois (6-0)	⤴
2	2	Kansas (4-0)	⤴
3	3	Georgia Tech (5-0)	⤴
4	4	Syracuse (7-0)	⤴
5	5	Oklahoma State (5-0)	⤴
6	7	Wake Forest (6-1)	⤴
7	6	Connecticut (3-0)	⤴
8	8	North Carolina (6-1)	⤴
9	9	Duke (5-0)	⤴
10	11	Kentucky (4-1)	⤴
11	12	Pittsburgh (5-0)	⤴
12	10	NC State (6-0)	⤴
13	14	Louisville (4-1)	⤴
14	13	Texas (5-1)	⤴
15	15	Arizona (5-2)	⤴
16	21	Washington (5-1)	⤴
17	24	Iowa (6-1)	⤴
18	18	Alabama (6-1)	⤴
19	19	Virginia (6-0)	↑5
20	16	Michigan State (4-2)	⤴
21	25	George Washington (5-1)	⤴
22	23	Mississippi State (6-2)	⤴
23	17	Maryland (4-2)	⤴
24	22	Wisconsin (4-1)	↑1
25	—	Gonzaga (5-1)	⤴
—	20	Cincinnati (4-0)	

Week of Dec 14

AP	ESPN/USA	SCHOOL	AP↓↑
1	1	Illinois (9-0)	
2	2	Kansas (6-0)	
3	3	Georgia Tech (6-0)	
4	4	Oklahoma State (7-0)	↑1
5	6	North Carolina (7-1)	↑3
6	5	Wake Forest (6-1)	
7	7	Duke (6-0)	↑2
8	8	Syracuse (8-1)	↓4
9	11	Kentucky (6-1)	↑1
10	10	Pittsburgh (7-0)	↑1
11	13	Connecticut (4-1)	↓4
12	9	NC State (7-0)	
13	14	Louisville (5-1)	
14	12	Texas (6-1)	
15	16	Arizona (6-2)	
16	21	Iowa (8-1)	↑1
17	15	Alabama (6-1)	↑1
18	20	Washington (7-1)	↓2
19	22	George Washington (6-1)	↑2
20	24	Mississippi State (7-2)	↑2
21	18	Michigan State (5-2)	↓1
22	—	Gonzaga (7-1)	↑3
23	19	Maryland (5-2)	
24	23	Virginia (7-1)	↓5
25	17	Cincinnati (6-0)	⤴
—	25	Marquette (9-0)	

Week of Dec 21

AP	ESPN/USA	SCHOOL	AP↓↑
1	1	Illinois (10-0)	
2	2	Kansas (7-0)	
3	3	Oklahoma State (8-0)	↑1
4	5	North Carolina (8-1)	↑1
5	4	Wake Forest (9-1)	↑1
6	6	Duke (8-0)	↑1
7	8	Syracuse (9-1)	↑1
8	10	Kentucky (7-1)	↑1
9	9	Georgia Tech (7-1)	↓6
10	7	Pittsburgh (8-0)	
11	11	Connecticut (5-1)	
12	17	Washington (8-1)	↑6
13	23	Gonzaga (8-1)	↑9
14	15	Arizona (7-2)	↑1
15	12	Texas (7-2)	↓1
16	13	NC State (8-1)	↓4
17	19	Iowa (9-1)	↓1
18	18	Louisville (6-2)	↓5
19	14	Alabama (9-1)	↓2
20	22	George Washington (7-1)	↓1
21	24	Mississippi State (9-2)	↓1
22	16	Cincinnati (7-0)	↑3
23	20	Michigan State (6-2)	↓2
24	21	Maryland (6-2)	↓1
25	25	Virginia (7-1)	↓1

Week of Dec 28

AP	ESPN/USA	SCHOOL	AP↓↑
1	1	Illinois (11-0)	
2	2	Kansas (8-0)	
3	3	Oklahoma State (9-0)	
4	5	North Carolina (9-1)	
5	4	Wake Forest (10-1)	
6	6	Duke (8-0)	
7	8	Syracuse (11-1)	
8	10	Kentucky (8-1)	
9	9	Georgia Tech (8-1)	
10	7	Pittsburgh (9-0)	
11	11	Connecticut (6-1)	
12	21	Gonzaga (9-1)	↑1
13	16	Washington (10-1)	↓1
14	14	Arizona (8-2)	
15	12	Texas (8-2)	
16	18	Iowa (10-1)	↑1
17	15	NC State (9-1)	↓1
18	13	Alabama (10-1)	↑1
19	19	Louisville (8-2)	↓1
20	22	George Washington (8-1)	
21	24	Mississippi State (11-2)	
22	17	Cincinnati (9-0)	
23	20	Michigan State (7-2)	
24	23	Maryland (7-2)	
25	25	Virginia (8-1)	

Week of Jan 4

AP	ESPN/USA	SCHOOL	AP↓↑
1	1	Illinois (14-0)	
2	2	Kansas (9-0)	
3	4	North Carolina (12-1)	↑1
4	3	Wake Forest (12-1)	↑1
5	5	Duke (9-0)	↑1
6	7	Syracuse (13-1)	↑1
7	6	Oklahoma State (9-1)	↓4
8	8	Kentucky (9-1)	
9	10	Georgia Tech (9-2)	
10	9	Connecticut (8-1)	↑1
11	17	Gonzaga (10-2)	↑1
12	14	Washington (12-1)	↑1
13	13	Arizona (11-2)	↑1
14	15	Iowa (12-1)	↑2
15	11	Texas (10-2)	
16	12	Pittsburgh (10-1)	↓6
17	16	Louisville (11-2)	↑2
18	22	Mississippi State (12-2)	↑3
19	18	Alabama (11-2)	↓1
20	19	Michigan State (8-2)	↑3
21	23	West Virginia (10-0)	⤴
22	21	Maryland (8-2)	↑2
23	20	Cincinnati (11-1)	↓1
24	25	George Washington (8-2)	↓4
25	—	Boston College (11-0)	⤴
—	24	NC State (10-3)	⤵

Week of Jan 11

AP	ESPN/USA	SCHOOL	AP↓↑
1	1	Illinois (16-0)	
2	2	Kansas (11-0)	
3	4	North Carolina (13-1)	
4	3	Wake Forest (13-1)	
5	5	Duke (11-0)	
6	6	Oklahoma State (11-1)	↑1
7	7	Syracuse (15-1)	↓1
8	8	Georgia Tech (11-2)	↑1
9	10	Kentucky (10-2)	↓1
10	9	Texas (12-2)	↑5
11	15	Mississippi State (14-2)	↑7
12	11	Connecticut (9-2)	↓2
13	17	Boston College (13-0)	↑12
14	14	Washington (13-2)	↓2
15	12	Michigan State (10-2)	↑5
16	20	Gonzaga (11-3)	↓5
17	16	Arizona (12-3)	↓4
18	13	Cincinnati (13-1)	↑5
19	19	Louisville (12-3)	↓2
20	18	Pittsburgh (11-2)	↓4
21	22	George Washington (10-2)	↑3
22	—	Marquette (13-1)	⤴
23	21	Alabama (12-3)	↓4
24	23	Iowa (12-3)	↓10
25	25	Oklahoma (11-2)	⤴
—	24	West Virginia (11-1)	⤵

Week of Jan 18

AP	ESPN/USA	SCHOOL	AP↓↑
1	1	Illinois (18-0)	
2	2	Kansas (13-0)	
3	3	Wake Forest (15-1) (A)	↑1
4	4	Duke (13-0)	↑1
5	5	Oklahoma State (13-1)	↑1
6	6	North Carolina (14-2)	↓3
7	7	Syracuse (17-1)	
8	8	Kentucky (12-2)	↑1
9	9	Boston College (14-0)	↑4
10	10	Washington (15-2)	↑4
11	20	Gonzaga (13-3)	↑5
12	15	Georgia Tech (11-4)	↓4
13	12	Arizona (14-3)	↑4
14	14	Louisville (14-3)	↑5
15	11	Texas (13-3)	↓5
16	13	Connecticut (10-3)	↓4
17	19	Mississippi State (15-3)	↓6
18	21	Oklahoma (13-2)	↑7
19	16	Michigan State (10-3)	↓4
20	18	Cincinnati (14-2)	↓2
21	17	Pittsburgh (12-2)	↓1
22	22	Alabama (13-3)	↑1
23	24	Iowa (13-3)	↑1
24	23	Wisconsin (12-3)	⤴
25	25	Marquette (14-2)	↓3

Week of Jan 25

AP	ESPN/USA	SCHOOL	AP↓↑
1	1	Illinois (19-0)	
2	2	Duke (16-0)	↑2
3	3	North Carolina (16-2)	↑3
4	4	Syracuse (19-1)	↑3
5	5	Wake Forest (16-2)	↓2
6	7	Kansas (14-1) (B)	↓4
7	6	Kentucky (14-2)	↑1
8	8	Boston College (16-0)	↑1
9	9	Oklahoma State (14-2)	↓4
10	10	Washington (16-2)	
11	11	Arizona (16-3)	↑2
12	12	Louisville (18-3)	↑2
13	15	Oklahoma (15-2)	↑5
14	17	Alabama (15-3)	↑8
15	13	Michigan State (12-3)	↑4
16	13	Texas (14-4)	↓1
17	23	Gonzaga (14-4)	↓6
18	19	Wisconsin (13-3)	↑6
19	16	Connecticut (11-4)	↓3
20	18	Pittsburgh (13-3)	↑1
21	20	Cincinnati (15-3)	↓1
22	21	Georgia Tech (11-5)	↓10
23	24	Iowa (14-4)	
24	22	Mississippi State (16-4)	↓7
25	25	Utah (16-3)	⤴

Poll Progression Continues →

Week of Feb 1

AP	ESPN/USA	School	AP ↓↑
1	1	**Illinois** (21-0)	
2	2	**North Carolina** (17-2)	↑1
3	3	**Kansas** (16-1)	↑3
4	6	**Duke** (16-1)	↓2
5	5	**Boston College** (18-0)	↑3
6	4	**Kentucky** (16-2)	↑1
7	7	**Wake Forest** (17-3)	↓2
8	8	**Syracuse** (20-2)	↓4
9	9	**Louisville** (18-3)	↑3
10	11	**Oklahoma State** (15-3)	↓1
11	14	**Alabama** (17-3)	↑3
12	10	**Michigan State** (14-3)	↑3
13	12	**Washington** (17-3)	↓3
14	13	**Arizona** (17-4)	↓3
15	16	**Oklahoma** (16-3)	↓2
16	15	**Pittsburgh** (14-3)	↑4
17	21	**Gonzaga** (15-4)	
18	17	**Cincinnati** (17-3)	↑3
19	19	**Wisconsin** (14-4)	↓1
20	18	**Texas** (15-5)	↓4
21	22	**Utah** (17-3)	↑4
22	24	**Maryland** (13-5)	⤴
23	20	**Connecticut** (12-5)	↓4
24	25	**Villanova** (12-4)	⤴
25	23	**Georgia Tech** (12-6)	↓3

Week of Feb 8

AP	ESPN/USA	School	AP ↓↑
1	1	**Illinois** (23-0)	
2	2	**North Carolina** (19-2)	
3	3	**Kansas** (18-1)	
4	4	**Boston College** (20-0)	↑1
5	5	**Kentucky** (17-2)	↑1
6	6	**Wake Forest** (19-3)	↑1
7	8	**Duke** (17-2)	↓3
8	7	**Syracuse** (21-2) Ⓒ	
9	9	**Louisville** (20-3)	
10	10	**Oklahoma State** (17-3)	
11	11	**Washington** (19-3)	↑2
12	13	**Arizona** (19-4)	↑2
13	12	**Michigan State** (15-4)	↓1
14	17	**Gonzaga** (17-4)	↑3
15	15	**Utah** (19-3)	↑6
16	18	**Oklahoma** (17-4)	↓1
17	19	**Alabama** (17-4)	↓6
18	15	**Pittsburgh** (15-4)	↓2
19	14	**Connecticut** (14-5)	↑4
20	21	**Wisconsin** (15-5)	↓1
21	20	**Cincinnati** (17-5)	↓3
22	25	**Villanova** (13-5)	↑2
23	22	**Texas** (15-6)	↓3
24	24	**Pacific** (18-2)	⤴
25	23	**Texas Tech** (14-5)	⤴

Week of Feb 15

AP	ESPN/USA	School	AP ↓↑
1	1	**Illinois** (25-0)	
2	2	**Kansas** (20-1)	↑1
3	3	**Kentucky** (19-2)	↑2
4	4	**North Carolina** (20-3)	↓2
5	5	**Wake Forest** (21-3)	↑1
6	6	**Boston College** (20-1)	↓2
7	8	**Duke** (18-3)	
8	7	**Oklahoma State** (19-3)	↑2
9	9	**Syracuse** (22-3)	↓1
10	11	**Arizona** (21-4)	↑2
11	10	**Michigan State** (17-4)	↑2
12	12	**Louisville** (21-4)	↓3
13	16	**Gonzaga** (19-4)	↑1
14	13	**Utah** (21-3)	↑1
15	13	**Washington** (20-4)	↓4
16	17	**Alabama** (19-4)	↑1
17	15	**Pittsburgh** (17-4)	↑1
18	18	**Connecticut** (15-6)	↑1
19	19	**Pacific** (20-2)	↑5
20	20	**Wisconsin** (16-6)	
21	22	**Oklahoma** (17-6)	↓5
22	—	**Maryland** (15-7)	⤴
23	23	**Charlotte** (17-4)	⤴
24	21	**Cincinnati** (18-6)	↓3
25	—	**Villanova** (14-6)	↓3
—	24	**Florida** (15-6)	
—	25	**Texas Tech** (15-6)	↱

Week of Feb 22

AP	ESPN/USA	School	AP ↓↑
1	1	**Illinois** (27-0)	
2	2	**North Carolina** (22-3)	
3	3	**Boston College** (22-1)	
4	4	**Oklahoma State** (20-3)	
5	5	**Kentucky** (20-3)	
6	6	**Wake Forest** (22-4)	
7	10	**Duke** (19-4)	
8	7	**Kansas** (20-3)	
9	8	**Arizona** (23-4)	
10	9	**Michigan State** (19-4)	
11	11	**Louisville** (23-4)	
12	16	**Gonzaga** (21-4)	
13	12	**Utah** (23-3)	
14	13	**Washington** (21-4)	
15	15	**Syracuse** (22-5)	
16	14	**Alabama** (21-4)	
17	19	**Connecticut** (17-6)	↑
18	17	**Pittsburgh** (18-5)	↓
19	18	**Pacific** (22-2)	
20	20	**Wisconsin** (17-6)	
21	21	**Charlotte** (19-4)	↑
22	23	**Oklahoma** (19-6)	↓
23	24	**Villanova** (17-6)	↑
24	22	**Cincinnati** (20-6)	
25	—	**Nevada** (20-5)	⤴
—	25	**Texas Tech** (16-7)	

Week of Mar 1

AP	ESPN/USA	School	AP ↓↑
1	1	**Illinois** (28-0)	
2	2	**North Carolina** (24-3)	
3	3	**Kentucky** (22-3)	↑2
4	4	**Wake Forest** (24-4)	↑2
5	5	**Boston College** (23-2)	↓2
6	6	**Duke** (21-4)	↑1
7	7	**Kansas** (21-4)	↑1
8	8	**Oklahoma State** (20-5)	↓4
9	9	**Louisville** (24-4)	↑2
10	10	**Washington** (23-4)	↑4
11	11	**Arizona** (24-5)	↓2
12	13	**Gonzaga** (22-4)	
13	13	**Syracuse** (24-5)	↑2
14	12	**Michigan State** (20-5)	↓4
15	16	**Connecticut** (19-6)	↑2
16	15	**Utah** (24-4)	↓3
17	17	**Pacific** (23-2)	↑2
18	18	**Charlotte** (21-4)	↑3
19	22	**Villanova** (19-6)	↑4
20	20	**Oklahoma** (21-6)	↑2
21	19	**Alabama** (21-6)	↓5
22	21	**Cincinnati** (22-6)	↑2
23	23	**Wisconsin** (18-7)	↓3
24	24	**Pittsburgh** (18-7)	↓6
25	—	**Nevada** (22-5)	
—	25	**Southern Illinois** (24-6)	

Week of Mar 8

AP	ESPN/USA	School	AP ↓↑
1	1	**Illinois** (29-1) Ⓓ	
2	2	**North Carolina** (26-3)	
3	3	**Wake Forest** (26-4) Ⓔ	↑1
4	4	**Kentucky** (23-4)	↓1
5	5	**Duke** (22-5)	↑1
6	6	**Louisville** (26-4)	↑3
7	7	**Boston College** (24-3)	↓2
8	8	**Arizona** (25-5)	↑3
9	9	**Kansas** (22-5)	↓2
10	11	**Oklahoma State** (21-6)	↓2
11	12	**Gonzaga** (24-4)	↑1
12	14	**Connecticut** (21-6)	↑3
13	10	**Michigan State** (22-5)	↑1
14	13	**Washington** (24-5)	↓4
15	15	**Utah** (25-4)	↑1
16	18	**Syracuse** (24-6)	↓3
17	17	**Oklahoma** (23-6)	↑3
18	16	**Pacific** (25-2)	↓1
19	21	**Villanova** (21-6)	
20	19	**Alabama** (23-6)	↑1
21	20	**Cincinnati** (24-6)	↑1
22	23	**Pittsburgh** (20-7)	↑2
23	22	**Wisconsin** (20-7)	
24	—	**Nevada** (24-5)	↑1
25	24	**Charlotte** (21-6)	↓7
—	25	**Florida** (20-7)	

Week of Mar 15

AP	ESPN/USA	School	AP ↓↑
1	1	**Illinois** (32-1)	
2	3	**North Carolina** (27-4)	
3	2	**Duke** (25-5)	↑2
4	4	**Louisville** (29-4)	↑2
5	6	**Wake Forest** (26-5)	↓2
6	8	**Oklahoma State** (24-6)	↑4
7	5	**Kentucky** (25-5)	↓3
8	7	**Washington** (27-5)	↑6
9	9	**Arizona** (27-6)	↓1
10	11	**Gonzaga** (25-4)	↑1
11	13	**Syracuse** (27-6)	↑5
12	10	**Kansas** (23-6)	↓3
13	14	**Connecticut** (22-7)	↓1
14	12	**Boston College** (24-4)	↓7
15	15	**Michigan State** (26-6)	↓2
16	18	**Florida** (23-7)	⤴
17	16	**Oklahoma** (24-7)	
18	17	**Utah** (27-5)	↓3
19	22	**Villanova** (22-7)	
20	19	**Wisconsin** (22-8)	↑3
21	21	**Alabama** (24-7)	↓1
22	20	**Pacific** (26-3)	↓4
23	23	**Cincinnati** (24-7)	↓2
24	24	**Texas Tech** (20-10)	⤴
25	25	**Georgia Tech** (19-11)	⤴

Final Poll (Post-Tournament

ESPN/USA	School
1	**North Carolina** (33-4)
2	**Illinois** (37-2)
3	**Louisville** (33-5)
4	**Michigan State** (26-7)
5	**Kentucky** (28-6)
6	**Arizona** (30-7)
7	**Duke** (27-6)
8	**Oklahoma State** (26-7)
9	**Washington** (29-6)
10	**Wisconsin** (25-9)
11	**Wake Forest** (27-6)
12	**West Virginia** (24-11)
13	**Villanova** (24-8)
14	**Utah** (29-6)
15	**Kansas** (23-7)
16	**Texas Tech** (22-11)
17	**Connecticut** (23-8)
18	**Gonzaga** (26-5)
19	**Boston College** (25-5)
20	**Oklahoma** (25-8)
21	**Syracuse** (27-7)
22	**NC State** (21-14)
23	**Wisc.-Milwaukee** (26-6)
24	**Florida** (24-8)
25	**Cincinnati** (25-8)

Ⓐ Wake Forest sets an NCAA record by making 50 consecutive free throws over two games, against UNC and Florida State. When Taron Downey steps to the line for the Demon Deacons' 19th attempt against FSU with the game tied at 76 and :04 left, he misses and so does Wake Forest, losing the game in OT, 91-83.

Ⓑ Fans on Philadelphia's Main Line fight through a snowstorm to watch Villanova demolish Kansas, 83-62—easily the biggest Wildcats upset in a decade.

Ⓒ A crowd of 33,199—an NCAA record for an on-campus game—fills the Carrier Dome on Feb. 5 and watches as Syracuse takes down Notre Dame, 60-57. A year later, on March 5, 2006, 33,633 will cram into the same venue for star guard Gerry McNamara's final home game, which the Orangemen lose to Villanova, 92-82.

Ⓓ Ohio State hands Illinois its first loss, 65-64. It's the second time in two seasons that a team coached by Thad Matta has upset a No. 1. In 2003-04, Matta's Xavier squad knocked off top-ranked Saint Joseph's.

Ⓔ During a March 6 two-point victory over NC State in which Wake Forest's Chris Paul hits the game-winner at the buzzer, Paul punches Julius Hodge in the groin. Despite replays showing otherwise, Paul insists, "I don't believe I popped [Hodge] ... it was just the heat of the game." Wake Forest suspends Paul for the first round of the ACC tournament, which—talk about karma—Wake loses to NC State, 81-65.

Pre-Tournament Ratings Percentage Index (RPI)

Rank	School	W-L	Sched. Strg.	SS Rank	RPI
1	**Kansas**	23-6	.6577	1	.6693
2	**Illinois**	32-1	.5690	43	.6672
3	**Washington**	26-5	.5944	15	.6579
4	**Duke**	25-5	.6113	5	.6576
5	**Oklahoma State**	23-6	.6318	2	.6574
6	**North Carolina**	27-4	.5814	26	.6535
7	**Wake Forest**	26-5	.5937	17	.6534
8	**Arizona**	27-6	.5883	21	.6387
9	**Boston College**	24-4	.5740	35	.6375
10	**Gonzaga**	25-4	.5640	50	.6370
11	**Kentucky**	25-5	.5748	33	.6365
12	**Louisville**	27-4	.5654	48	.6273
13	**Connecticut**	22-7	.6118	4	.6264
14	**Wisconsin**	22-8	.6028	9	.6260
15	**Villanova**	22-7	.6046	7	.6251
16	**Oklahoma**	24-7	.5786	30	.6209
17	**Southern Illinois**	25-7	.5586	60	.6205
18	**Alabama**	23-7	.5828	24	.6204
19	**Florida**	23-7	.5892	19	.6191
20	**Syracuse**	27-6	.5556	66	.6173
21	**Michigan State**	22-6	.5491	75	.6100
22	**Pacific**	26-3	.5143	126	.6053
23	**Utah**	25-5	.5256	108	.6042
24	**Cincinnati**	24-7	.5668	46	.6034
25	**LSU**	20-9	.5816	25	.6015
26	**Vermont**	24-6	.5247	111	.6011
27	**Georgia Tech**	19-11	.5988	11	.5917
28	**Texas Tech**	20-10	.5795	28	.5913
29	**Mississippi State**	22-10	.5590	58	.5871
30	**Saint Mary's**	23-8	.5304	96	.5862
31	**Charlotte**	21-7	.5219	115	.5861
32	**Nevada**	23-6	.5265	104	.5851
33	**UTEP**	25-7	.5213	116	.5849
34	**West Virginia**	21-10	.5561	63	.5847
35	**Old Dominion**	27-5	.4808	193	.5812
36	**Pittsburgh**	20-8	.5526	69	.5807
37	**Northern Iowa**	20-10	.5548	67	.5804
38	**UCLA**	18-10	.5710	37	.5803
39	**Stanford**	18-12	.5791	29	.5802
40	**Miami (OH)**	18-10	.5474	79	.5797
41	**Minnesota**	21-10	.5618	52	.5783
42	**Texas**	19-10	.5613	54	.5779
43	**Iowa**	21-11	.5615	53	.5775
44	**Creighton**	23-10	.5477	78	.5758
45	**Wichita State**	20-9	.5368	93	.5757
46	**Buffalo**	22-9	.5222	114	.5736
47	**UL-Lafayette**	19-10	.5269	102	.5711
48	**Ohio**	21-10	.5211	117	.5693
49	**UAB**	21-10	.5344	94	.5692
50	**Utah State**	24-7	.4935	167	.5667

Source: Collegiate Basketball News

2005 NCAA Tournament

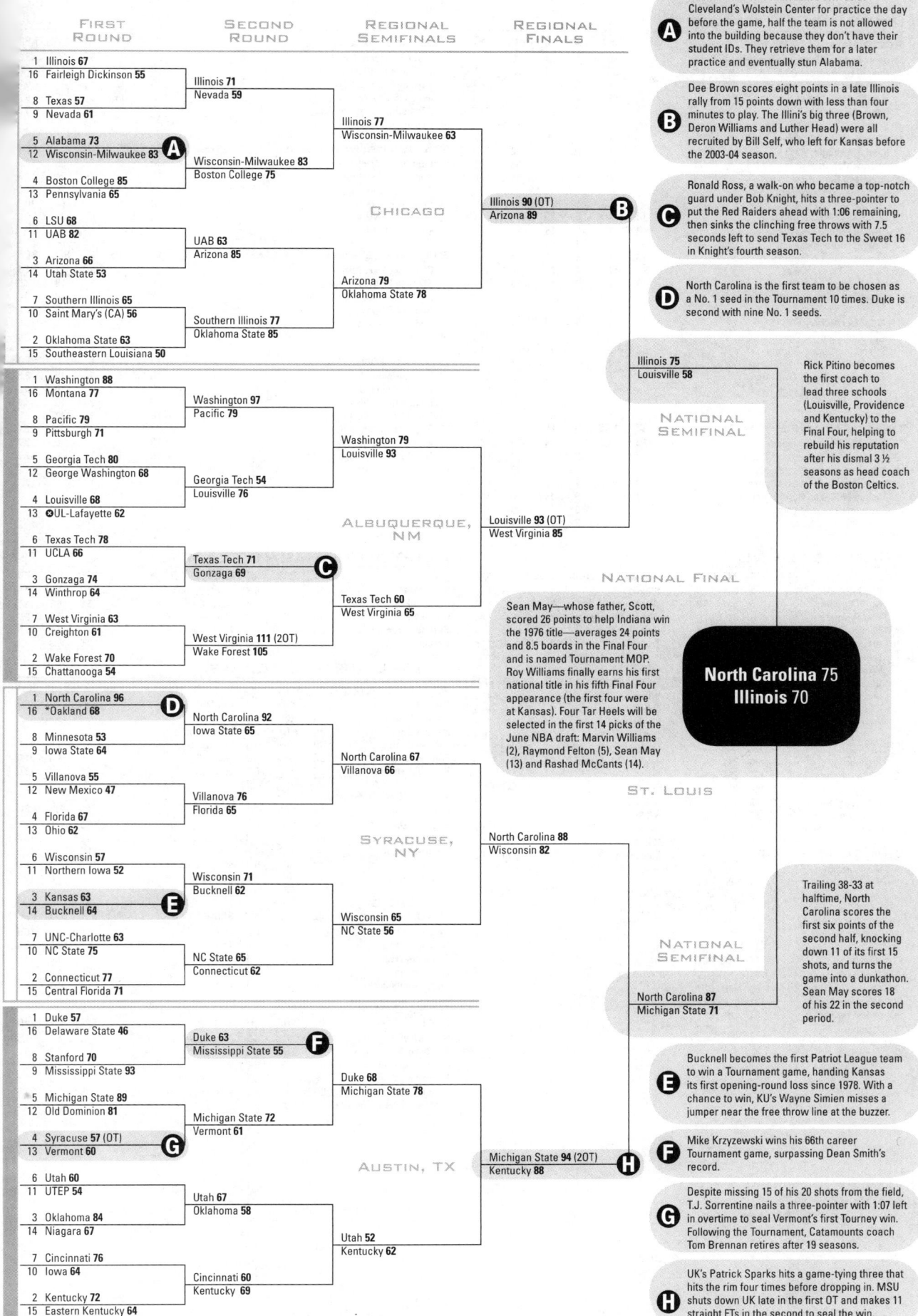

Chicago

First Round

1 Illinois **67**
16 Fairleigh Dickinson **55**

8 Texas **57**
9 Nevada **61**

5 Alabama **73**
12 Wisconsin-Milwaukee **83** (A)

4 Boston College **85**
13 Pennsylvania **65**

6 LSU **68**
11 UAB **82**

3 Arizona **66**
14 Utah State **53**

7 Southern Illinois **65**
10 Saint Mary's (CA) **56**

2 Oklahoma State **63**
15 Southeastern Louisiana **50**

Second Round

Illinois **71**
Nevada **59**

Wisconsin-Milwaukee **83**
Boston College **75**

UAB **63**
Arizona **85**

Southern Illinois **77**
Oklahoma State **85**

Regional Semifinals

Illinois **77**
Wisconsin-Milwaukee **63**

Arizona **79**
Oklahoma State **78**

Regional Finals

Illinois **90** (OT) (B)
Arizona **89**

Albuquerque, NM

First Round

1 Washington **88**
16 Montana **77**

8 Pacific **79**
9 Pittsburgh **71**

5 Georgia Tech **80**
12 George Washington **68**

4 Louisville **68**
13 ⊗UL-Lafayette **62**

6 Texas Tech **78**
11 UCLA **66**

3 Gonzaga **74**
14 Winthrop **64**

7 West Virginia **63**
10 Creighton **61**

2 Wake Forest **70**
15 Chattanooga **54**

Second Round

Washington **97**
Pacific **79**

Georgia Tech **54**
Louisville **76**

Texas Tech **71** (C)
Gonzaga **69**

West Virginia **111** (2OT)
Wake Forest **105**

Regional Semifinals

Washington **79**
Louisville **93**

Texas Tech **60**
West Virginia **65**

Regional Finals

Louisville **93** (OT)
West Virginia **85**

Syracuse, NY

First Round

1 North Carolina **96** (D)
16 *Oakland **68**

8 Minnesota **53**
9 Iowa State **64**

5 Villanova **55**
12 New Mexico **47**

4 Florida **67**
13 Ohio **62**

6 Wisconsin **57**
11 Northern Iowa **52**

3 Kansas **63** (E)
14 Bucknell **64**

7 UNC-Charlotte **63**
10 NC State **75**

2 Connecticut **77**
15 Central Florida **71**

Second Round

North Carolina **92**
Iowa State **65**

Villanova **76**
Florida **65**

Wisconsin **71**
Bucknell **62**

NC State **65**
Connecticut **62**

Regional Semifinals

North Carolina **67**
Villanova **66**

Wisconsin **65**
NC State **56**

Regional Finals

North Carolina **88**
Wisconsin **82**

Austin, TX

First Round

1 Duke **57**
16 Delaware State **46**

8 Stanford **70**
9 Mississippi State **93**

5 Michigan State **89**
12 Old Dominion **81**

4 Syracuse **57** (OT) (G)
13 Vermont **60**

6 Utah **60**
11 UTEP **54**

3 Oklahoma **84**
14 Niagara **67**

7 Cincinnati **76**
10 Iowa **64**

2 Kentucky **72**
15 Eastern Kentucky **64**

Second Round

Duke **63** (F)
Mississippi State **55**

Michigan State **72**
Vermont **61**

Utah **67**
Oklahoma **58**

Cincinnati **60**
Kentucky **69**

Regional Semifinals

Duke **68**
Michigan State **78**

Utah **52**
Kentucky **62**

Regional Finals

Michigan State **94** (2OT) (H)
Kentucky **88**

St. Louis

National Semifinal

Illinois **75**
Louisville **58**

Rick Pitino becomes the first coach to lead three schools (Louisville, Providence and Kentucky) to the Final Four, helping to rebuild his reputation after his dismal 3 ½ seasons as head coach of the Boston Celtics.

National Semifinal

North Carolina **87**
Michigan State **71**

Trailing 38-33 at halftime, North Carolina scores the first six points of the second half, knocking down 11 of its first 15 shots, and turns the game into a dunkathon. Sean May scores 18 of his 22 in the second period.

National Final

North Carolina 75
Illinois 70

Sean May—whose father, Scott, scored 26 points to help Indiana win the 1976 title—averages 24 points and 8.5 boards in the Final Four and is named Tournament MOP. Roy Williams finally earns his first national title in his fifth Final Four appearance (the first four were at Kansas). Four Tar Heels will be selected in the first 14 picks of the June NBA draft: Marvin Williams (2), Raymond Felton (5), Sean May (13) and Rashad McCants (14).

A When Wisconsin-Milwaukee arrives at Cleveland's Wolstein Center for practice the day before the game, half the team is not allowed into the building because they don't have their student IDs. They retrieve them for a later practice and eventually stun Alabama.

B Dee Brown scores eight points in a late Illinois rally from 15 points down with less than four minutes to play. The Illini's big three (Brown, Deron Williams and Luther Head) were all recruited by Bill Self, who left for Kansas before the 2003-04 season.

C Ronald Ross, a walk-on who became a top-notch guard under Bob Knight, hits a three-pointer to put the Red Raiders ahead with 1:06 remaining, then sinks the clinching free throws with 7.5 seconds left to send Texas Tech to the Sweet 16 in Knight's fourth season.

D North Carolina is the first team to be chosen as a No. 1 seed in the Tournament 10 times. Duke is second with nine No. 1 seeds.

E Bucknell becomes the first Patriot League team to win a Tournament game, handing Kansas its first opening-round loss since 1978. With a chance to win, KU's Wayne Simien misses a jumper near the free throw line at the buzzer.

F Mike Krzyzewski wins his 66th career Tournament game, surpassing Dean Smith's record.

G Despite missing 15 of his 20 shots from the field, T.J. Sorrentine nails a three-pointer with 1:07 left in overtime to seal Vermont's first Tourney win. Following the Tournament, Catamounts coach Tom Brennan retires after 19 seasons.

H UK's Patrick Sparks hits a game-tying three that hits the rim four times before dropping in. MSU shuts down UK late in the first OT and makes 11 straight FTs in the second to seal the win.

***Opening round:** Oakland d. Alabama A&M 79-69 ⊗ Team participation later vacated

TOURNAMENT LEADERS

INDIVIDUAL LEADERS

SCORING	CL	POS	G	PTS	PPG
1 **Joah Tucker**, Wisconsin-Milwaukee	SO	F	3	76	25.3
2 **Ronald Ross**, Texas Tech	SR	G	3	68	22.7
3 **Sean May**, North Carolina	JR	C	6	134	22.3
4 **Ivan McFarlin**, Oklahoma State	SR	F	3	64	21.3
5 **Randy Foye**, Villanova	JR	G	3	60	20.0
6 **Salim Stoudamire**, Arizona	SR	G	4	73	18.3
7 **Maurice Ager**, Michigan State	JR	G	5	91	18.2
8 **Kevin Pittsnogle**, West Virginia	JR	F/C	4	72	18.0
Andrew Bogut, Utah	SO	F/C	3	54	18.0
10 **Francisco Garcia**, Louisville	JR	F	5	88	17.6

MINIMUM: 3 GAMES

FIELD GOAL PCT	CL	POS	G	FG	FGA	PCT
1 **Devonne Giles**, Texas Tech	SR	F	3	16	21	76.2
2 **Ivan McFarlin**, Oklahoma State	SR	F	3	24	35	68.6
3 **Sean May**, North Carolina	JR	C	6	52	78	66.7
4 **Channing Frye**, Arizona	SR	C	4	26	40	65.0
5 **Brandon Roy**, Washington	JR	G	3	19	30	63.3

MINIMUM: 15 MADE AND 3 GAMES

FREE THROW PCT	CL	POS	G	FT	FTA	PCT
1 **Alan Anderson**, Michigan State	SR	G	5	21	22	95.5
2 **Salim Stoudamire**, Arizona	SR	G	4	16	17	94.1
Ivan McFarlin, Oklahoma State	SR	F	3	16	17	94.1
4 **Andrew Brackman**, NC State	FR	C	3	15	16	93.8
5 **Francisco Garcia**, Louisville	JR	F	5	21	23	91.3

MINIMUM: 15 MADE

THREE-POINT FG PCT	CL	POS	G	3FG	3FGA	PCT
1 **JamesOn Curry**, Oklahoma State	FR	G	3	8	12	66.7
2 **Joah Tucker**, Wisconsin-Milwaukee	SO	F	3	6	10	60.0
3 **Clayton Hanson**, Wisconsin	SR	G	4	11	19	57.9
4 **Kevin Pittsnogle**, West Virginia	JR	F/C	4	13	23	56.5
5 **Rashad McCants**, North Carolina	JR	F	6	15	30	50.0
Shannon Brown, Michigan State	SO	G	5	10	20	50.0
Engin Atsur, NC State	SO	G	3	7	14	50.0

MINIMUM: 6 MADE AND 3 GAMES

ASSISTS PER GAME	CL	POS	G	AST	APG
1 **Deron Williams**, Illinois	JR	G	6	50	8.3
2 **Will Conroy**, Washington	SR	G	3	21	7.0
3 **Raymond Felton**, North Carolina	JR	G	6	41	6.8
4 **Julius Hodge**, NC State	SR	G/F	3	20	6.7
5 **J.D. Collins**, West Virginia	JR	G	4	21	5.3

MINIMUM: 3 GAMES

REBOUNDS PER GAME	CL	POS	G	REB	RPG
1 **Paul Davis**, Michigan State	JR	C	5	58	11.6
2 **Andrew Bogut**, Utah	SO	F/C	3	34	11.3
Shelden Williams, Duke	JR	F	3	34	11.3
4 **Sean May**, North Carolina	JR	C	6	64	10.7
5 **Channing Frye**, Arizona	SR	C	4	39	9.8

MINIMUM: 3 GAMES

BLOCKED SHOTS PER GAME	CL	POS	G	BLK	BPG
1 **Channing Frye**, Arizona	SR	C	4	17	4.3
2 **Shelden Williams**, Duke	JR	F	3	9	3.0
3 **Francisco Garcia**, Louisville	JR	F	5	10	2.0
Andrew Bogut, Utah	SO	F/C	3	6	2.0
Andrew Brackman, NC State	FR	C	3	6	2.0

MINIMUM: 3 GAMES

STEALS PER GAME	CL	POS	G	STL	SPG
1 **Ilian Evtimov**, NC State	JR	F	3	10	3.3
Daniel Ewing, Duke	SR	G	3	10	3.3
Ronald Ross, Texas Tech	SR	G	3	10	3.3
4 **Rajon Rondo**, Kentucky	FR	G	4	12	3.0
5 **Engin Atsur**, NC State	SO	G	3	8	2.7
Kyle Lowry, Villanova	FR	G	3	8	2.7
Ivan McFarlin, Oklahoma State	SR	F	3	8	2.7

MINIMUM: 3 GAMES

TEAM LEADERS

SCORING	G	PTS	PPG
1 **Washington**	3	264	88.0
2 **North Carolina**	6	505	84.2
3 **West Virginia**	4	324	81.0
4 **Michigan State**	5	404	80.8
5 **Arizona**	4	319	79.8
6 **Louisville**	5	387	77.4
7 **Wisc.-Milwaukee**	3	229	76.3
8 **Oklahoma State**	3	226	75.3
9 **Illinois**	6	447	74.5
10 **Kentucky**	4	291	72.8

MINIMUM: 3 GAMES

FG PCT	G	FG	FGA	PCT
1 **Arizona**	4	116	214	54.2
2 **North Carolina**	6	184	358	51.4
3 **Kentucky**	4	106	208	51.0
4 **West Virginia**	4	109	214	50.9
5 **Texas Tech**	3	85	167	50.9

MINIMUM: 3 GAMES

3-PT FG PCT	G	3FG	3FGA	PCT
1 **Oklahoma State**	3	20	42	47.6
2 **West Virginia**	4	42	90	46.7
3 **Wisconsin**	4	33	77	42.9
4 **North Carolina**	6	48	115	41.7
5 **Wisc.-Milwaukee**	3	30	74	40.5

MINIMUM: 3 GAMES

FT PCT	G	FT	FTA	PCT
1 **NC State**	3	43	52	82.7
2 **Oklahoma State**	3	62	75	82.7
3 **Michigan State**	5	101	129	78.3
4 **West Virginia**	4	64	84	76.2
5 **Arizona**	4	60	79	75.9

MINIMUM: 3 GAMES

AST/TO RATIO	G	AST	TO	RAT
1 **Illinois**	6	114	61	1.87
2 **Washington**	3	51	32	1.59
3 **Wisc.-Milwaukee**	3	49	34	1.44
4 **North Carolina**	6	107	75	1.43
5 **Texas Tech**	3	49	36	1.36

MINIMUM: 3 GAMES

REBOUNDS	G	REB	RPG
1 **Villanova**	3	124	41.3
2 **North Carolina**	6	243	40.5
3 **Michigan State**	5	189	37.8
4 **Duke**	3	108	36.0
5 **Louisville**	5	173	34.6

MINIMUM: 3 GAMES

BLOCKS	G	BLK	BPG
1 **Arizona**	4	26	6.5
2 **NC State**	3	17	5.7
3 **Duke**	3	14	4.7
4 **Villanova**	3	13	4.3
5 **Louisville**	5	21	4.2

MINIMUM: 3 GAMES

STEALS	G	STL	SPG
1 **NC State**	3	34	11.3
2 **Villanova**	3	28	9.3
3 **Michigan State**	5	42	8.4
4 **Texas Tech**	3	25	8.3
5 **Oklahoma State**	3	24	8.0

MINIMUM: 3 GAMES

ALL-TOURNAMENT TEAM

PLAYER	CL	POS	HT	SCHOOL	RPG	APG	PPG
Sean May*	JR	C	6-9	North Carolina	10.7	1.8	22.3
Raymond Felton	JR	G	6-1	North Carolina	5.8	6.8	13.7
Luther Head	SR	G	6-3	Illinois	3.3	4.0	16.7
Rashad McCants	JR	F	6-4	North Carolina	3.2	2.7	17.0
Deron Williams	JR	G	6-3	Illinois	3.5	8.3	14.7

ALL-REGIONAL TEAMS

ALBUQUERQUE, NM

PLAYER	CL	POS	HT	SCHOOL	RPG	APG	PPG
Larry O'Bannon*	SR	G/F	6-4	Louisville	5.0	3.3	17.8
Patrick Beilein	JR	G	6-4	West Virginia	1.5	2.0	7.8
Taquan Dean	JR	G	6-3	Louisville	6.0	1.8	17.0
Francisco Garcia	JR	F	6-7	Louisville	2.5	4.3	21.0
Kevin Pittsnogle	JR	F/C	6-11	West Virginia	5.5	1.3	18.0

AUSTIN, TX

PLAYER	CL	POS	HT	SCHOOL	RPG	APG	PPG
Shannon Brown*	SO	G	6-3	Michigan State	3.3	0.8	13.5
Maurice Ager	JR	G	6-4	Michigan State	5.0	0.5	16.8
Andrew Bogut	SO	F/C	7-0	Utah	11.3	2.7	18.0
Paul Davis	JR	C	6-11	Michigan State	10.8	1.0	15.0
Chuck Hayes	SR	F	6-6	Kentucky	6.5	2.8	13.5

CHICAGO

PLAYER	CL	POS	HT	SCHOOL	RPG	APG	PPG
Deron Williams*	SR	G	6-3	Illinois	3.0	8.5	16.5
Hassan Adams	JR	F	6-4	Arizona	8.3	2.5	16.5
Channing Frye	SR	C	6-11	Arizona	9.8	2.0	15.5
Luther Head	SR	G	6-3	Illinois	2.3	4.0	14.8
Salim Stoudamire	SR	G	6-1	Arizona	2.8	4.3	18.3

SYRACUSE, NY

PLAYER	CL	POS	HT	SCHOOL	RPG	APG	PPG
Sean May*	JR	C	6-9	North Carolina	11.8	1.5	21.5
Randy Foye	JR	G	6-4	Villanova	5.3	2.3	20.0
Clayton Hanson	SR	G	6-5	Wisconsin	2.0	1.3	8.8
Rashad McCants	JR	F	6-4	North Carolina	2.8	2.8	17.8
Alando Tucker	SO	F	6-6	Wisconsin	3.8	2.0	17.5

* MOST OUTSTANDING PLAYER

2005 NCAA TOURNAMENT BOX SCORES

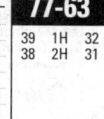

ILLINOIS	MIN	FG	3FG	FT	REB	A	ST	BL	PF	TP
Dee Brown	38	7-12	5-8	2-2	2	2	2	1	1	21
Deron Williams	37	8-12	2-5	3-4	3	8	1	0	4	21
Roger Powell	35	5-11	0-1	2-2	9	1	1	0	2	12
Luther Head	33	5-15	2-5	0-1	1	6	2	0	4	12
James Augustine	38	3-3	0-0	5-6	0	0	0	1	2	11
Rich McBride	8	0-1	0-1	0-0	0	0	0	0	2	0
Jack Ingram	5	0-2	0-0	0-0	2	0	1	0	4	0
Warren Carter	4	0-1	0-0	0-0	1	2	0	0	0	0
Nick Smith	2	0-0	0-0	0-0	0	1	0	0	1	0
TOTALS	**200**	**28-57**	**9-20**	**12-15**	**18**	**20**	**7**	**2**	**20**	**77**
Percentages		49.1	45.0	80.0						

Coach: Bruce Weber

77-63

39	1H	32
38	2H	31

SWEET 16

WISCONSIN-MILWAUKEE	MIN	FG	3FG	FT	REB	A	ST	BL	PF	TP
Joah Tucker	36	12-18	2-3	6-8	3	1	1	0	3	32
Ed McCants	32	4-17	4-14	1-2	4	3	2	0	1	13
Boo Davis	22	3-9	1-5	2-2	5	0	0	2	2	9
Jason McCoy	12	1-3	0-1	1-2	2	2	0	0	0	3
Chris Hill	36	0-3	0-3	2-3	4	4	0	0	3	2
Adrian Tigert	33	1-6	0-3	0-0	7	2	1	1	1	2
James Wright	25	1-1	0-0	0-1	5	0	0	0	1	2
Mark Pancratz	4	0-0	0-0	0-0	3	0	0	0	1	0
TOTALS	**200**	**22-57**	**7-29**	**12-18**	**33**	**12**	**4**	**3**	**12**	**63**
Percentages		38.6	24.1	66.7						

Coach: Bruce Pearl

Officials: Pat Driscoll, Tim Clougherty, Tom Lopes
Technicals: None
Attendance: 16,957

ARIZONA	MIN	FG	3FG	FT	REB	A	ST	BL	PF	TP
Hassan Adams	35	8-12	3-4	0-0	10	1	0	2	1	19
Salim Stoudamire	28	7-11	4-7	1-2	2	7	2	0	2	19
Channing Frye	40	7-12	0-1	1-2	10	4	0	3	3	15
Ivan Radenovic	28	5-5	0-0	3-5	3	1	1	0	4	13
Chris Rodgers	25	2-4	0-2	1-2	0	2	0	0	1	5
Mustafa Shakur	27	0-1	0-0	4-6	1	1	0	0	2	4
Jawann McClellan	13	2-2	0-0	0-0	3	0	0	0	2	4
Kirk Walters	4	0-0	0-0	0-0	1	1	0	0	2	0
TOTALS	**200**	**31-47**	**7-14**	**10-17**	**30**	**17**	**3**	**5**	**17**	**79**
Percentages		66.0	50.0	58.8						

Coach: Lute Olson

79-78

41	1H	38
38	2H	40

SWEET 16

OKLAHOMA STATE	MIN	FG	3FG	FT	REB	A	ST	BL	PF	TP
Joey Graham	35	9-19	3-5	5-6	8	1	0	0	2	26
Ivan McFarlin	31	6-12	0-0	3-3	5	4	4	0	2	15
John Lucas III	37	5-15	2-7	1-1	2	3	1	0	3	13
JamesOn Curry	35	4-9	3-6	0-0	2	7	2	0	2	11
Daniel Bobik	37	3-7	2-5	0-0	1	0	0	0	3	8
Stephen Graham	11	2-3	0-0	1-1	0	2	2	0	2	5
Terrence Crawford	14	0-1	0-0	0-2	0	0	1	0	3	0
TOTALS	**200**	**29-66**	**10-23**	**10-13**	**18**	**17**	**10**	**0**	**17**	**78**
Percentages		43.9	43.5	76.9						

Coach: Eddie Sutton

Officials: Duke Edsall, Jim Haney, Ted Valentine
Technicals: None
Attendance: 16,957

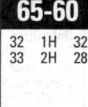

LOUISVILLE	MIN	FG	3FG	FT	REB	A	ST	BL	PF	TP
Francisco Garcia	38	8-16	5-8	2-2	2	3	1	3	1	23
Taquan Dean	34	5-10	5-10	4-6	9	2	3	0	2	19
Larry O'Bannon	37	6-11	0-4	6-9	6	4	2	0	3	18
Juan Palacios	33	6-11	1-4	1-1	4	0	0	0	4	14
Ellis Myles	28	2-4	0-0	4-6	13	6	1	1	4	8
Otis George	17	3-3	0-0	0-1	5	1	0	0	2	6
Perrin Johnson	2	1-1	0-0	1-1	0	0	0	0	1	3
Brandon Jenkins	9	0-0	0-0	2-2	0	1	1	0	1	2
Brad Gianiny	1	0-0	0-0	0-0	0	0	0	0	0	0
Lorrenzo Wade	1	0-0	0-0	0-0	0	0	0	0	0	0
TOTALS	**200**	**31-56**	**11-26**	**20-28**	**39**	**17**	**8**	**4**	**18**	**93**
Percentages		55.4	42.3	71.4						

Coach: Rick Pitino

93-79

47	1H	35
46	2H	44

SWEET 16

WASHINGTON	MIN	FG	3FG	FT	REB	A	ST	BL	PF	TP
Jamaal Williams	24	8-16	0-0	2-4	6	1	1	0	3	18
Brandon Roy	23	7-12	0-1	1-2	5	2	0	0	4	15
Will Conroy	35	4-7	3-6	3-4	1	8	2	0	4	14
Tre Simmons	19	3-6	2-4	2-2	1	0	1	0	4	10
Bobby Jones	29	2-6	1-2	3-7	9	1	0	0	5	8
Nate Robinson	26	1-7	0-5	6-9	3	3	2	0	4	8
Hakeem Rollins	13	2-3	0-0	0-0	1	0	0	0	0	4
Mike Jensen	16	1-6	0-4	0-0	0	0	0	0	1	2
Joel Smith	15	0-4	0-3	0-0	3	0	3	0	0	0
TOTALS	**200**	**28-67**	**6-25**	**17-28**	**29**	**15**	**9**	**0**	**25**	**79**
Percentages		41.8	24.0	60.7						

Coach: Lorenzo Romar

Officials: Frank Scagliotta, Karl Hess, Larry Rose
Technicals: None
Attendance: 15,792

WEST VIRGINIA	MIN	FG	3FG	FT	REB	A	ST	BL	PF	TP
Kevin Pittsnogle	23	7-13	2-3	6-8	8	0	0	1	2	22
Mike Gansey	27	4-7	3-4	0-2	4	2	1	0	0	11
Patrick Beilein	23	4-7	2-5	0-0	2	4	2	0	0	10
Tyrone Sally	33	3-9	1-3	1-1	3	3	0	1	3	8
D'or Fischer	17	2-3	0-0	1-2	5	1	0	0	2	5
J.D. Collins	29	1-2	1-2	0-0	3	3	1	0	4	3
Johannes Herber	29	1-7	0-4	0-0	2	1	1	0	2	2
Darris Nichols	12	1-1	0-0	0-0	0	0	0	0	2	2
Frank Young	7	1-2	0-1	0-0	2	0	0	0	0	2
TOTALS	**200**	**24-51**	**9-22**	**8-13**	**29**	**14**	**5**	**2**	**15**	**65**
Percentages		47.1	40.9	61.5						

Coach: John Beilein

65-60

32	1H	32
33	2H	28

SWEET 16

TEXAS TECH	MIN	FG	3FG	FT	REB	A	ST	BL	PF	TP
Ronald Ross	40	8-22	0-3	0-0	4	0	4	0	1	16
Devonne Giles	19	6-7	0-0	0-1	5	0	0	0	5	12
Darryl Dora	40	3-8	0-1	5-7	9	3	0	0	4	11
Curtis Marshall	21	3-5	1-1	3-3	2	1	2	0	1	10
Jarrius Jackson	40	3-11	0-3	3-3	5	0	3	0	1	9
Martin Zeno	31	1-3	0-0	0-2	3	4	1	0	2	2
LucQuente White	9	0-0	0-0	0-0	2	2	1	1	1	0
TOTALS	**200**	**24-56**	**1-8**	**11-16**	**30**	**10**	**11**	**1**	**15**	**60**
Percentages		42.9	12.5	68.8						

Coach: Bob Knight

Officials: John Clougherty, Mark Reischling, Tom Wood
Technicals: None
Attendance: 15,792

NORTH CAROLINA	MIN	FG	3FG	FT	REB	A	ST	BL	PF	TP
Rashad McCants	33	3-9	2-5	9-10	3	1	0	0	3	17
Marvin Williams	24	4-9	2-3	6-6	5	0	1	0	3	16
Sean May	28	6-9	0-0	2-3	10	1	1	0	4	14
Raymond Felton	34	4-12	3-7	0-2	11	5	0	0	5	11
Melvin Scott	15	1-1	1-1	2-2	2	2	0	0	4	5
Jackie Manuel	30	1-4	0-1	0-0	3	0	0	2	3	2
Jawad Williams	23	1-4	0-2	0-0	2	1	0	0	0	2
David Noel	13	0-0	0-0	0-1	2	1	1	1	1	0
TOTALS	**200**	**20-48**	**8-19**	**19-24**	**38**	**11**	**3**	**3**	**23**	**67**
Percentages		41.7	42.1	79.2						

Coach: Roy Williams

67-66

29	1H	33
38	2H	33

SWEET 16

VILLANOVA	MIN	FG	3FG	FT	REB	A	ST	BL	PF	TP
Randy Foye	36	9-21	5-12	5-7	3	2	2	0	5	28
Kyle Lowry	29	7-10	1-2	3-5	7	3	2	1	2	18
Allan Ray	34	2-14	1-10	2-2	3	1	0	0	2	7
Mike Nardi	32	2-8	1-4	1-2	1	1	0	0	5	6
Will Sheridan	36	2-3	0-0	0-0	5	0	0	2	3	4
Jason Fraser	26	1-4	0-0	1-3	6	0	1	2	3	3
Marcus Austin	7	0-1	0-0	0-0	4	0	0	0	1	0
TOTALS	**200**	**23-61**	**8-28**	**12-19**	**29**	**7**	**5**	**5**	**21**	**66**
Percentages		37.7	28.6	63.2						

Coach: Jay Wright

Officials: David Hall, Gerry Pollard, Tom O'Neill
Technicals: None
Attendance: 30,916

WISCONSIN	MIN	FG	3FG	FT	REB	A	ST	BL	PF	TP
Alando Tucker	39	9-17	0-2	4-6	1	1	1	0	1	22
Michael Wilkinson	31	5-8	0-0	7-8	5	1	0	0	3	17
Zach Morley	35	3-5	0-0	4-5	8	2	1	0	3	10
Sharif Chambliss	30	2-4	2-4	1-2	7	1	0	0	0	7
Clayton Hanson	32	2-5	2-4	0-0	3	2	0	0	1	6
Andreas Helmigk	5	0-1	0-0	2-2	1	0	0	0	1	2
Kammron Taylor	11	0-2	0-0	1-2	3	0	0	0	0	1
Ray Nixon	8	0-0	0-0	0-0	0	0	0	0	2	0
Jason Chappell	6	0-0	0-0	0-0	1	0	0	0	1	0
Brian Butch	3	0-0	0-0	0-0	0	0	0	0	2	0
TOTALS	**200**	**21-42**	**4-10**	**19-25**	**29**	**7**	**2**	**0**	**14**	**65**
Percentages		50.0	40.0	76.0						

Coach: Bo Ryan

65-56

21	1H	30
44	2H	26

SWEET 16

NC STATE	MIN	FG	3FG	FT	REB	A	ST	BL	PF	TP
Engin Atsur	40	6-12	4-8	0-0	0	3	4	0	4	16
Julius Hodge	36	4-16	0-2	6-8	5	5	2	0	3	14
Cameron Bennerman	31	4-6	2-3	0-1	3	1	0	0	3	10
Ilian Evtimov	38	2-10	2-7	2-2	4	3	3	0	4	8
Jordan Collins	19	1-1	1-1	0-0	2	0	0	1	2	3
Cedric Simmons	9	1-1	0-0	1-2	1	0	0	3	1	3
Gavin Grant	11	1-3	0-1	0-0	0	0	1	0	3	2
Andrew Brackman	14	0-1	0-0	0-0	2	0	0	1	5	0
Tony Bethel	2	0-0	0-0	0-0	0	0	0	0	0	0
TOTALS	**200**	**19-50**	**9-22**	**9-13**	**17**	**12**	**10**	**5**	**25**	**56**
Percentages		38.0	40.9	69.2						

Coach: Herb Sendek

Officials: Ed Corbett, Joe Lindsay, Verne Harris
Technicals: None
Attendance: 30,713

78-68

32	1H	32
46	2H	36

SWEET 16

MICHIGAN STATE	MIN	FG	3FG	FT	REB	A	ST	BL	PF	TP
Paul Davis	33	6-14	0-0	8-10	12	2	0	0	3	20
Alan Anderson	32	6-11	3-4	2-2	8	2	5	0	4	17
Maurice Ager	28	6-13	0-3	2-3	6	0	1	0	3	14
Shannon Brown	26	3-9	1-2	4-4	2	1	2	0	0	11
Kelvin Torbert	18	3-4	1-2	0-0	4	0	0	0	5	7
Drew Neitzel	21	2-5	0-0	1-2	0	3	0	0	2	5
Chris Hill	18	0-6	0-3	2-2	0	3	2	0	2	2
Matt Trannon	11	1-2	0-0	0-0	3	0	2	0	2	2
Tim Bograkos	9	0-0	0-0	0-0	0	1	1	0	0	0
Anthony Hamo	1	0-0	0-0	0-0	0	0	0	0	0	0
Andy Harvey	1	0-0	0-0	0-0	0	0	0	0	0	0
Drew Naymick	1	0-1	0-0	0-0	1	0	0	0	1	0
Delco Rowley	1	0-0	0-0	0-0	1	0	0	0	0	0
TOTALS	**200**	**27-65**	**5-14**	**19-23**	**37**	**12**	**13**	**0**	**22**	**78**
Percentages		41.5	35.7	82.6						

Coach: Tom Izzo

DUKE	MIN	FG	3FG	FT	REB	A	ST	BL	PF	TP
Shelden Williams	32	5-10	0-0	9-10	8	1	3	2	5	19
Daniel Ewing	38	7-16	2-7	2-4	5	2	5	0	3	18
J.J. Redick	39	4-14	3-9	2-2	3	2	0	0	0	13
DeMarcus Nelson	18	3-4	0-1	2-4	3	0	0	0	2	8
Lee Melchionni	22	2-5	1-4	2-2	5	1	0	0	2	7
Sean Dockery	26	1-2	1-2	0-0	1	1	1	0	3	3
Shavlik Randolph	18	0-0	0-0	0-2	2	0	1	0	3	0
Reggie Love	6	0-0	0-0	0-0	4	1	1	0	4	0
David McClure	1	0-0	0-0	0-0	0	0	0	0	0	0
TOTALS	**200**	**22-51**	**7-23**	**17-24**	**31**	**8**	**11**	**2**	**22**	**68**
Percentages		43.1	30.4	70.8						

Coach: Mike Krzyzewski

Officials: D Libbey, Mic Kitts, Reggi Greenwoo
Technicals: None
Attendance: 16,239

62-52

29	1H	24
33	2H	28

SWEET 16

KENTUCKY	MIN	FG	3FG	FT	REB	A	ST	BL	PF	TP
Chuck Hayes	24	5-6	0-0	2-5	4	2	3	0	2	12
Rajon Rondo	27	4-5	0-1	2-6	2	2	2	0	1	10
Kelenna Azubuike	25	2-5	0-2	5-6	2	1	0	0	2	9
Joe Crawford	11	3-4	1-2	0-0	3	0	0	0	1	7
Ramel Bradley	14	3-4	0-1	0-0	1	2	0	0	2	6
Ravi Moss	14	2-2	2-2	0-0	3	1	0	0	3	6
Lukasz Obrzut	20	2-3	0-0	0-0	5	0	0	0	4	4
Patrick Sparks	24	1-5	1-4	0-0	0	1	1	0	3	3
Bobby Perry	14	1-1	0-0	1-2	2	1	0	0	1	3
Randolph Morris	5	1-1	0-0	0-0	0	0	0	0	4	2
Shagari Alleyne	15	0-1	0-0	0-0	2	0	0	2	1	0
Jeff Carrier	5	0-1	0-1	0-0	1	0	0	0	0	0
Sheray Thomas	2	0-1	0-0	0-0	0	0	0	0	1	0
TOTALS	**200**	**24-39**	**4-13**	**10-19**	**25**	**10**	**6**	**2**	**25**	**62**
Percentages		61.5	30.8	52.6						

Coach: Tubby Smith

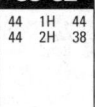

UTAH	MIN	FG	3FG	FT	REB	A	ST	BL	PF	TP
Andrew Bogut	40	8-19	0-1	4-11	12	0	1	0	3	20
Chris Jackson	39	2-6	1-4	5-6	1	2	0	0	5	10
Bryant Markson	37	3-7	1-2	2-4	1	2	0	0	3	9
Justin Hawkins	30	1-4	0-0	2-4	6	3	1	0	4	4
Tim Drisdom	27	1-1	1-1	0-0	2	2	2	0	3	3
Richard Chaney	17	1-2	0-0	1-2	2	0	1	0	2	3
Jonas Langvad	9	1-1	1-1	0-1	1	0	0	0	0	3
Jermaine Calvin	1	0-1	0-1	0-0	0	1	0	0	0	0
TOTALS	**200**	**17-41**	**4-10**	**14-28**	**25**	**10**	**5**	**-**	**20**	**52**
Percentages		41.5	40.0	50.0						

Coach: Ray Giacoletti

Officials: Cur Shaw, Reggie Cofer, Steve Welmer
Technicals: Utah (Bogut), Kentucky (Bradley)
Attendance: 16,239

90-89

38	1H	36
42	2H	44
10	OT1	9

ELITE 8

ILLINOIS	MIN	FG	3FG	FT	REB	A	ST	BL	PF	TP
Deron Williams	44	8-15	5-9	1-2	3	10	1	0	3	22
Luther Head	39	7-18	5-12	1-2	3	2	4	1	0	20
Roger Powell	30	6-11	1-3	3-3	5	0	0	1	4	16
Dee Brown	42	6-14	3-8	0-0	5	7	3	0	2	15
Jack Ingram	28	3-8	1-1	1-2	3	1	2	0	3	8
James Augustine	31	1-3	0-0	2-4	6	1	2	0	5	4
Rich McBride	8	1-2	1-2	0-0	1	0	0	0	1	3
Warren Carter	3	0-0	0-0	2-2	2	0	0	0	0	2
TOTALS	**225**	**32-71**	**16-35**	**10-15**	**28**	**21**	**12**	**2**	**18**	**90**
Percentages		45.1	45.7	66.7						

Coach: Bruce Weber

ARIZONA	MIN	FG	3FG	FT	REB	A	ST	BL	PF	TP
Channing Frye	44	11-14	1-1	1-2	12	1	0	6	1	24
Hassan Adams	37	9-13	1-3	2-3	8	5	1	0	3	21
Ivan Radenovic	29	4-6	1-1	4-4	5	2	4	1	2	13
Mustafa Shakur	37	4-6	2-3	2-2	2	4	2	0	1	12
Jawann McClellan	24	2-7	1-2	5-6	4	1	1	1	1	10
Salim Stoudamire	39	2-13	1-7	4-4	5	7	2	0	1	9
Chris Rodgers	14	0-2	0-1	0-0	0	1	1	0	1	0
Kirk Walters	1	0-0	0-0	0-0	0	0	0	0	0	0
TOTALS	**225**	**32-61**	**7-18**	**18-21**	**36**	**21**	**11**	**8**	**10**	**89**
Percentages		52.5	38.9	85.7						

Coach: Lute Olson

Officials: Doug Shows, Randy McCall, Bob Donato
Technicals: None
Attendance: 16,957

93-85

27	1H	40
50	2H	37
16	OT1	8

ELITE 8

LOUISVILLE	MIN	FG	3FG	FT	REB	A	ST	BL	PF	TP
Larry O'Bannon	39	6-10	2-5	10-11	3	4	0	1	1	24
Taquan Dean	39	8-20	7-17	0-0	6	2	0	0	2	23
Juan Palacios	35	6-8	1-2	0-4	6	1	3	0	2	13
Francisco Garcia	31	5-6	1-2	2-2	4	8	0	1	5	13
Ellis Myles	30	3-6	0-1	3-8	7	1	2	2	3	9
Otis George	24	4-4	0-0	0-0	1	0	0	0	4	8
Lorrenzo Wade	2	0-0	0-0	2-2	1	0	0	0	0	2
Brandon Jenkins	24	0-4	0-1	1-2	2	3	3	0	1	1
Brad Gianiny	1	0-0	0-0	0-0	1	0	0	0	0	0
TOTALS	**225**	**32-58**	**11-28**	**18-29**	**31**	**19**	**8**	**4**	**18**	**93**
Percentages		55.2	39.3	62.1						

Coach: Rick Pitino

WEST VIRGINIA	MIN	FG	3FG	FT	REB	A	ST	BL	PF	TP
Kevin Pittsnogle	34	9-15	6-9	1-2	5	1	0	0	2	25
Patrick Beilein	27	4-7	3-6	2-2	1	3	0	0	4	13
Mike Gansey	40	3-6	2-4	3-4	1	3	2	1	2	11
J.D. Collins	37	2-5	2-2	5-6	1	5	2	0	1	11
Johannes Herber	32	3-7	3-4	2-2	2	5	0	0	4	11
Tyrone Sally	27	2-3	0-0	0-1	3	1	1	0	5	4
D'or Fischer	11	1-1	0-0	2-2	4	2	0	1	0	4
Darris Nichols	9	1-1	1-1	0-0	0	2	0	0	1	3
Frank Young	8	1-2	1-1	0-0	0	1	0	0	0	3
TOTALS	**225**	**26-47**	**18-27**	**15-19**	**17**	**23**	**5**	**2**	**19**	**85**
Percentages		55.3	66.7	78.9						

Coach: John Beilein

Officials: Ed Hightower, J.D. Collins, Tim Higgins
Technicals: None
Attendance: 15,896

88-82

44	1H	44
44	2H	38

ELITE 8

NORTH CAROLINA	MIN	FG	3FG	FT	REB	A	ST	BL	PF	TP
Sean May	34	13-19	0-0	3-4	12	2	0	2	2	29
Rashad McCants	31	8-17	3-6	2-4	4	4	0	1	2	21
Raymond Felton	33	5-11	1-5	6-6	5	7	0	1	2	17
Jawad Williams	21	3-6	0-3	0-0	2	1	0	1	0	6
Marvin Williams	21	1-6	0-1	4-4	3	1	2	0	2	6
Jackie Manuel	27	2-2	0-0	0-0	2	1	3	0	3	4
Melvin Scott	15	1-1	1-1	0-0	0	1	0	0	1	3
David Noel	16	1-2	0-0	0-0	3	1	0	0	3	2
Quentin Thomas	2	0-0	0-0	0-0	0	1	0	0	0	0
TOTALS	**200**	**34-64**	**5-16**	**15-18**	**31**	**19**	**5**	**5**	**15**	**88**
Percentages		53.1	31.2	83.3						

Coach: Roy Williams

WISCONSIN	MIN	FG	3FG	FT	REB	A	ST	BL	PF	TP
Alando Tucker	33	9-17	0-4	7-9	2	2	1	0	4	25
Kammron Taylor	28	6-12	2-3	4-4	3	1	0	0	2	18
Clayton Hanson	32	5-8	5-8	0-0	2	1	1	0	0	15
Michael Wilkinson	39	5-11	1-2	0-0	7	5	2	0	4	11
Sharif Chambliss	26	3-7	3-6	0-0	3	4	0	0	2	9
Ray Nixon	6	1-2	0-0	0-0	1	0	0	0	2	2
Greg Stiemsma	3	1-1	0-0	0-0	0	0	0	0	0	2
Zach Morley	20	0-1	0-0	0-0	3	3	1	0	3	0
Michael Flowers	5	0-1	0-1	0-0	2	0	0	0	0	0
Brian Butch	4	0-0	0-0	0-0	1	0	0	0	0	0
Andreas Helmigk	4	0-1	0-0	0-0	1	1	0	0	0	0
TOTALS	**200**	**30-61**	**11-24**	**11-13**	**25**	**17**	**5**	**0**	**17**	**82**
Percentages		49.2	45.8	84.6						

Coach: Bo Ryan

Officials: Bruce Hicks, Dick Cartmell, John Cahill
Technicals: None
Attendance: 30,132

94-88

33	1H	37
42	2H	38
6	OT1	6
13	OT2	7

ELITE 8

MICHIGAN STATE	MIN	FG	3FG	FT	REB	A	ST	BL	PF	TP
Shannon Brown	36	8-10	5-6	3-4	4	1	0	0	3	24
Maurice Ager	39	6-13	2-4	7-8	8	1	1	1	1	21
Paul Davis	41	6-13	0-0	3-5	11	0	0	0	3	15
Alan Anderson	38	3-7	1-1	6-6	9	1	0	0	2	13
Chris Hill	27	3-7	1-4	0-0	1	4	2	0	4	7
Kelvin Torbert	25	1-8	0-3	5-6	2	3	1	1	2	7
Matt Trannon	17	2-2	0-0	0-1	1	1	2	1	3	4
Drew Neitzel	14	1-4	1-1	0-0	0	3	0	0	2	3
Tim Bograkos	6	0-0	0-0	0-0	0	0	0	0	0	0
Drew Naymick	4	0-0	0-0	0-0	1	1	0	0	0	0
Anthony Hamo	1	0-0	0-0	0-0	0	0	0	0	0	0
Andy Harvey	1	0-0	0-0	0-0	0	0	0	0	0	0
Delco Rowley	1	0-0	0-0	0-0	0	0	0	0	0	0
TOTALS	**250**	**30-64**	**10-19**	**24-30**	**37**	**15**	**6**	**3**	**20**	**94**
Percentages		46.9	52.6	80.0						

Coach: Tom Izzo

KENTUCKY	MIN	FG	3FG	FT	REB	A	ST	BL	PF	TP
Randolph Morris	35	6-12	0-0	8-10	3	0	0	2	3	20
Chuck Hayes	35	8-11	0-0	0-0	5	3	1	0	4	16
Patrick Sparks	30	5-12	5-9	0-1	3	1	1	0	2	15
Kelenna Azubuike	35	2-6	2-3	3-4	4	3	0	0	5	9
Rajon Rondo	27	3-8	0-0	1-3	5	3	3	0	3	7
Ravi Moss	21	2-4	2-3	0-0	6	0	1	0	3	6
Ramel Bradley	18	1-5	0-2	4-4	3	3	0	0	2	6
Joe Crawford	17	2-8	0-2	1-1	4	0	1	0	1	5
Sheray Thomas	8	2-2	0-0	0-0	1	1	0	0	1	4
Bobby Perry	17	0-1	0-0	0-0	2	0	0	1	1	0
Lukasz Obrzut	4	0-0	0-0	0-0	0	0	0	0	0	0
Shagari Alleyne	1	0-0	0-0	0-0	0	0	0	0	0	0
Preston LeMaster	1	0-0	0-0	0-0	0	0	0	0	0	0
Brandon Stockton	1	0-0	0-0	0-0	0	0	0	0	0	0
TOTALS	**250**	**31-69**	**9-19**	**17-23**	**36**	**14**	**7**	**3**	**25**	**88**
Percentages		44.9	47.4	73.9						

Coach: Tubby Smith

Officials: James Burr, Mark Whitehead, John Higgins
Technicals: None
Attendance: 16,239

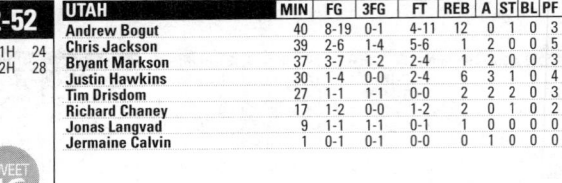

FINAL 4 — 72-57

	1H	2H
Illinois	31	41
Louisville	28	29

ILLINOIS	MIN	FG	3FG	FT	REB	A	ST	BL	PF	TP
Luther Head	37	6-13	6-11	2-2	6	5	2	0	1	20
Roger Powell	22	9-13	2-3	0-0	5	2	1	0	2	20
Jack Ingram	21	4-6	1-1	0-0	5	1	0	0	3	9
Dee Brown	36	3-10	2-9	0-0	3	4	1	0	2	8
James Augustine	31	1-3	0-0	4-6	11	0	0	0	1	6
Deron Williams	38	2-7	1-5	0-0	5	9	0	0	2	5
Nick Smith	6	2-3	0-0	0-0	0	0	0	0	1	4
Rich McBride	8	0-1	0-1	0-0	1	0	0	0	0	0
Warren Carter	1	0-0	0-0	0-0	0	0	0	0	0	0
TOTALS	**200**	**27-56**	**12-30**	**6-8**	**36**	**21**	**4**	**0**	**12**	**72**
Percentages		48.2	40.0	75.0						

Coach: Bruce Weber

LOUISVILLE	MIN	FG	3FG	FT	REB	A	ST	BL	PF	TP
Ellis Myles	37	8-12	0-0	1-1	7	2	2	3	3	17
Taquan Dean	36	4-15	2-9	2-2	1	1	1	0	3	12
Larry O'Bannon	31	4-10	2-5	2-2	4	4	0	0	1	12
Brandon Jenkins	19	2-3	2-2	2-2	2	0	1	0	1	8
Francisco Garcia	32	2-10	0-4	0-0	1	2	1	1	2	4
Otis George	22	1-4	0-0	2-5	6	0	0	0	2	4
Juan Palacios	21	0-0	0-0	0-0	4	1	0	0	1	0
Lorrenzo Wade	2	0-0	0-0	0-0	0	0	0	0	0	0
TOTALS	**200**	**21-54**	**6-20**	**9-12**	**25**	**10**	**5**	**4**	**13**	**57**
Percentages		38.9	30.0	75.0						

Coach: Rick Pitino

Officials: Doug Shows, Ed Hightower, James Burr
Technicals: None
Attendance: 47,754

FINAL 4 — 87-71

	1H	2H
North Carolina	33	54
Michigan State	38	33

NORTH CAROLINA	MIN	FG	3FG	FT	REB	A	ST	BL	PF	TP
Sean May	31	9-18	0-0	4-6	7	3	1	1	2	22
Jawad Williams	23	9-13	2-5	0-0	8	0	0	1	1	20
Rashad McCants	28	7-11	2-3	1-2	6	4	1	1	1	17
Raymond Felton	35	6-12	2-6	2-2	8	7	1	0	2	16
David Noel	21	2-5	0-1	0-3	4	2	1	2	2	4
Melvin Scott	16	0-2	0-2	4-4	2	0	0	0	1	4
Marvin Williams	23	1-6	0-1	0-0	8	1	0	1	3	2
Reyshawn Terry	3	1-2	0-1	0-0	0	0	0	0	0	2
Jackie Manuel	11	0-1	0-0	0-0	3	0	1	0	5	0
Quentin Thomas	5	0-0	0-0	0-0	1	1	0	0	0	0
Charlie Everett	1	0-0	0-0	0-0	0	0	0	0	0	0
Jesse Holley	1	0-1	0-1	0-0	1	0	0	0	0	0
CJ Hooker	1	0-0	0-0	0-0	0	0	0	0	0	0
Wes Miller	1	0-0	0-0	0-0	0	0	0	0	0	0
TOTALS	**200**	**35-71**	**6-20**	**11-17**	**48**	**18**	**5**	**6**	**17**	**87**
Percentages		49.3	30.0	64.7						

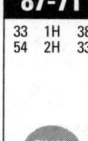

Coach: Roy Williams

MICHIGAN STATE	MIN	FG	3FG	FT	REB	A	ST	BL	PF	TP
Maurice Ager	28	6-18	2-6	10-10	3	1	0	1	1	24
Shannon Brown	29	6-14	3-6	0-0	1	1	1	0	2	15
Paul Davis	33	6-16	0-1	2-4	15	1	3	1	3	14
Kelvin Torbert	26	4-11	1-4	0-0	5	6	2	1	1	9
Matt Trannon	15	1-1	0-0	2-2	3	0	1	1	3	4
Chris Hill	18	1-6	1-5	0-0	1	2	2	0	2	3
Drew Neitzel	15	1-3	0-1	0-1	3	3	0	0	2	2
Alan Anderson	20	0-4	0-0	0-0	4	0	1	0	3	0
Drew Naymick	7	0-1	0-0	0-0	4	1	0	0	1	0
Tim Bograkos	6	0-0	0-0	0-1	1	0	0	0	1	0
Anthony Hamo	1	0-0	0-0	0-0	1	0	0	0	0	0
Andy Harvey	1	0-0	0-0	0-0	0	0	0	0	0	0
Delco Rowley	1	0-0	0-0	0-0	0	0	0	0	0	0
TOTALS	**200**	**25-74**	**7-23**	**14-18**	**41**	**15**	**10**	**4**	**19**	**71**
Percentages		33.8	30.4	77.8						

Coach: Tom Izzo

Officials: Randy McCall, Reggie Greenwood, Bob Donato
Technicals: None
Attendance: 47,754

NCAA FINAL 2005 — 75-70

	1H	2H
North Carolina	40	35
Illinois	27	43

NORTH CAROLINA	MIN	FG	3FG	FT	REB	A	ST	BL	PF	TP
Sean May	34	10-11	0-0	6-8	10	2	0	1	1	26
Raymond Felton	35	4-9	4-5	5-6	3	7	2	0	4	17
Rashad McCants	31	6-15	2-5	0-0	2	1	1	0	0	14
Jawad Williams	22	3-6	3-4	0-0	5	0	1	1	1	9
Marvin Williams	24	4-8	0-1	0-1	5	0	0	0	2	8
David Noel	20	0-0	0-0	1-2	3	0	0	0	0	1
Jackie Manuel	18	0-1	0-0	0-2	3	2	0	0	4	0
Melvin Scott	13	0-2	0-1	0-0	2	0	0	0	0	0
Reyshawn Terry	2	0-0	0-0	0-0	0	0	0	0	0	0
Quentin Thomas	1	0-0	0-0	0-0	1	0	0	0	1	0
TOTALS	**200**	**27-52**	**9-16**	**12-19**	**34**	**12**	**4**	**2**	**13**	**75**
Percentages		51.9	56.2	63.2						

Coach: Roy Williams

ILLINOIS	MIN	FG	3FG	FT	REB	A	ST	BL	PF	TP
Luther Head	37	8-21	5-16	0-0	5	3	2	1	1	21
Deron Williams	40	7-16	3-10	0-2	4	7	1	0	4	17
Dee Brown	38	4-10	2-8	2-2	4	7	3	0	1	12
Jack Ingram	30	4-9	1-3	2-2	7	0	0	0	4	11
Roger Powell	38	4-10	1-2	0-0	14	1	1	0	2	9
James Augustine	9	0-3	0-0	0-0	2	0	0	0	5	0
Warren Carter	5	0-1	0-1	0-0	1	0	1	0	1	0
Rich McBride	2	0-0	0-0	0-0	0	0	0	0	0	0
Nick Smith	1	0-0	0-0	0-0	0	0	0	0	0	0
TOTALS	**200**	**27-70**	**12-40**	**4-6**	**37**	**18**	**8**	**1**	**18**	**70**
Percentages		38.6	30.0	66.7						

Coach: Bruce Weber

Officials: Ed Corbett, John Cahill, Verne Harris
Technicals: None
Attendance: 47,262

National Invitation Tournament (NIT)

Opening Round: Missouri State d. Rice 105-82, Davidson d. VCU 77-62, Cal State Fullerton d. Oregon State 85-83 (OT), San Francisco d. Denver 69-67, Western Kentucky d. Kent State 88-80 (OT), Wichita State d. Houston 85-69, Buffalo d. Drexel 81-76 (OT), Saint Joseph's d. Hofstra 53-44

First Round: Western Michigan d. Marquette 54-40, TCU d. Miami (OH) 60-58, Maryland d. Oral Roberts 85-72, Davidson d. Missouri State 82-71, Cal State Fullerton d. San Francisco 85-69, Georgetown d. Boston U. 64-34, UNLV d. Arizona State 89-78, South Carolina d. Miami 69-67, Memphis d. Northeastern 90-65, Virginia Tech d. Temple 60-50, Vanderbilt d. Indiana 67-60, Wichita State d. Western Kentucky 84-81, Saint Joseph's d. Buffalo 55-50, Holy Cross d. Notre Dame 78-73, Texas A&M d. Clemson 82-74, DePaul d. Missouri 75-70

Second Round: TCU d. Western Michigan 75-76 (OT), Maryland d. Davidson 78-63, Georgetown d. Cal State Fullerton 74-57, South Carolina d. UNLV 77-66, Memphis d. Virginia Tech 83-62, Vanderbilt d. Wichita State 65-63, Saint Joseph's d. Holy Cross 68-60, Texas A&M d. DePaul 75-72

Third Round: Maryland d. TCU 85-73, South Carolina d. Georgetown 69-66, Memphis d. Vanderbilt 81-68, Saint Joseph's d. Texas A&M 58-51

Semifinals: South Carolina d. Maryland 75-67, Saint Joseph's d. Memphis 70-58

Championship: South Carolina d. Saint Joseph's 60-57

MVP: Carlos Powell, South Carolina

2005-06: Gator Raid I

Florida won the championship, but No. 11-seed George Mason (27–8) won many fans' hearts with its miraculous march to the Final Four, taking out No. 6-seed Michigan State, No. 3-seed North Carolina and No. 7-seed Wichita State before stunning No. 1-seed Connecticut, 86-84 in OT. GMU finally lost to No. 3-seed Florida, 73-58, in the first Final Four that did not include a single No. 1 seed since the field was expanded to 64 teams in 1985. Billy Donovan coached the Gators (33–6) to their first national title with a 73-57 win over UCLA. Tournament MOP Joakim Noah led the way for the Gators, who won their six games by an average margin of 16 points.

The Co-Players of the Year were Gonzaga's Adam Morrison and Duke's J.J. Redick, who became the ACC's all-time leading scorer while setting a national record for most three-pointers made (457) and an ACC mark for most consecutive free throws made (54).

Major Conference Standings

America East

	Conference			Overall		
	W	L	PCT	W	L	PCT
Albany (NY)⊕	13	3	.813	21	11	.656
Binghamton	12	4	.750	16	13	.552
Hartford	9	7	.563	13	15	.464
Boston U.	9	7	.563	12	16	.429
New Hampshire	8	8	.500	12	17	.414
Vermont	7	9	.438	13	17	.433
Maine	7	9	.438	12	16	.429
UMBC	5	11	.313	10	19	.345
Stony Brook	2	14	.125	4	24	.143

Tournament: **Albany (NY) d. Vermont 80-67**
Tournament MVP: **Jamar Wilson**, Albany (NY)

ACC

	Conference			Overall		
	W	L	PCT	W	L	PCT
Duke⊕	14	2	.875	32	4	.889
North Carolina○	12	4	.750	23	8	.742
Boston College○	11	5	.688	28	8	.778
NC State○	10	6	.625	22	10	.688
Florida State□	9	7	.563	20	10	.667
Maryland□	8	8	.500	19	13	.594
Clemson□	7	9	.438	19	13	.594
Miami (FL)□	7	9	.438	18	16	.529
Virginia□	7	9	.438	15	15	.500
Virginia Tech	4	12	.250	14	16	.467
Georgia Tech	4	12	.250	11	17	.393
Wake Forest□	3	13	.188	17	17	.500

Tournament: **Duke d. Boston College 78-76**
Tournament MVP: **J.J. Redick**, Duke

Atlantic Sun

	Conference			Overall		
	W	L	PCT	W	L	PCT
Lipscomb□	15	5	.750	21	11	.656
Belmont⊕	15	5	.750	20	11	.645
Gardner-Webb	14	6	.700	17	12	.586
Florida Atlantic	14	6	.700	15	13	.536
East Tenn State	12	8	.600	15	13	.536
Stetson	11	9	.550	14	18	.438
Kennesaw State	10	10	.500	12	17	.414
Campbell	9	11	.450	10	18	.357
Mercer	7	13	.350	9	19	.321
North Florida	3	17	.150	6	22	.214
Jacksonville	1	19	.050	1	26	.037

Tournament: **Belmont d. Lipscomb 74-69 OT**
Tournament MVP: **Justin Hare**, Belmont

Atlantic 10

	Conference			Overall		
	W	L	PCT	W	L	PCT
George Washington○	16	0	1.000	27	3	.900
Charlotte□	11	5	.688	19	13	.594
La Salle	10	6	.625	18	10	.643
Saint Louis	10	6	.625	16	13	.552
Saint Joseph's□	9	7	.563	19	14	.576
Fordham	9	7	.563	16	16	.500
Xavier⊕	8	8	.500	21	11	.656
Temple□	8	8	.500	17	15	.531
Rhode Island	8	8	.500	14	14	.500
Massachusetts	8	8	.500	13	15	.464
Dayton	6	10	.375	14	17	.452
Richmond	6	10	.375	13	17	.433
St. Bonaventure	2	14	.125	8	19	.296
Duquesne	1	15	.063	3	24	.111

Tournament: **Xavier d. Saint Joseph's 62-61**
Tournament MOP: **Justin Cage**, Xavier

Big East

	Conference			Overall		
	W	L	PCT	W	L	PCT
Connecticut○	14	2	.875	30	4	.882
Villanova○	14	2	.875	28	5	.848
West Virginia○	11	5	.688	22	11	.667
Pittsburgh○	10	6	.625	25	8	.758
Georgetown○	10	6	.625	23	10	.697
Marquette○	10	6	.625	20	11	.645
Seton Hall○	9	7	.563	18	12	.600
Cincinnati□	8	8	.500	21	13	.618
Syracuse⊕	7	9	.438	23	12	.657
Rutgers□	7	9	.438	19	14	.576
Louisville□	6	10	.375	21	13	.618
Notre Dame□	6	10	.375	16	14	.533
DePaul	5	11	.313	12	15	.444
Providence	5	11	.313	12	15	.444
St. John's	5	11	.313	12	15	.444
South Florida	1	15	.063	7	22	.241

Tournament: **Syracuse d. Pittsburgh 65-61**
Tournament MVP: **Gerry McNamara**, Syracuse

Big Sky

	Conference			Overall		
	W	L	PCT	W	L	PCT
Northern Arizona□	12	2	.857	21	11	.656
Montana⊕	10	4	.714	24	7	.774
Eastern Washington	9	5	.643	15	15	.500
Montana State	7	7	.500	15	15	.500
Sacramento State	5	9	.357	15	15	.500
Portland State	5	9	.357	12	16	.429
Idaho State	4	10	.286	13	14	.481
Weber State	4	10	.286	10	17	.370

Tournament: **Montana d. Northern Arizona 73-60**
Tournament MVP: **Virgil Matthews**, Montana

Big South

	Conference			Overall		
	W	L	PCT	W	L	PCT
Winthrop⊕	13	3	.813	23	8	.742
Birmingham-Southern	12	4	.750	19	9	.679
Coastal Carolina	12	4	.750	20	10	.667
Radford	9	7	.563	16	13	.552
High Point	8	8	.500	16	13	.552
Charleston Southern	7	9	.438	13	16	.448
UNC Asheville	6	10	.375	9	19	.321
Liberty	3	13	.188	7	23	.233
VMI	2	14	.125	7	20	.259

Tournament: **Winthrop d. Coastal Carolina 51-50**
Tournament MVP: **Torrell Martin**, Winthrop

Big Ten

	Conference			Overall		
	W	L	PCT	W	L	PCT
Ohio State○	12	4	.750	26	6	.813
Illinois○	11	5	.688	26	7	.788
Iowa⊕	11	5	.688	25	9	.735
Indiana○	9	7	.563	19	12	.613
Wisconsin○	9	7	.563	19	12	.613
Michigan□	8	8	.500	22	11	.667
Michigan State○	8	8	.500	22	12	.647
Penn State□	6	10	.375	15	15	.500
Northwestern	6	10	.375	14	15	.483
Minnesota□	5	11	.313	16	15	.516
Purdue	3	13	.188	9	19	.321

Tournament: **Iowa d. Ohio State 67-60**
Tournament MOP: **Jeff Horner**, Iowa

Big 12

	Conference			Overall		
	W	L	PCT	W	L	PCT
Texas○	13	3	.813	30	7	.811
Kansas⊕	13	3	.813	25	8	.758
Oklahoma○	11	5	.688	20	9	.690
Texas A&M○	10	6	.625	22	9	.710
Colorado□	9	7	.563	20	10	.667
Nebraska□	7	9	.438	19	14	.576
Kansas State	6	10	.375	15	13	.536
Iowa State	6	10	.375	16	14	.533
Oklahoma State□	6	10	.375	17	16	.515
Texas Tech	6	10	.375	15	17	.469
Missouri	5	11	.313	12	16	.429
Baylor	4	12	.250	4	13	.235

Tournament: **Kansas d. Texas 80-68**
Tournament MOP: **Mario Chalmers**, Kansas

Big West

	Conference			Overall		
	W	L	PCT	W	L	PCT
Pacific⊕	12	2	.857	24	8	.750
UC Irvine	10	4	.714	16	13	.552
Long Beach State✪	9	5	.643	18	12	.600
Cal Poly	7	7	.500	10	19	.345
UC Santa Barbara	6	8	.429	15	14	.517
Cal State Fullerton	5	9	.357	16	13	.552
Cal State Northridge	4	10	.286	11	17	.393
UC Riverside	3	11	.214	5	23	.179

Tournament: **Pacific d. Long Beach State 78-70**
Tournament MVP: **Johnny Gray**, Pacific

Colonial Athletic

	Conference			Overall		
	W	L	PCT	W	L	PCT
George Mason○	15	3	.833	27	8	.771
UNC Wilmington⊕	15	3	.833	25	8	.758
Hofstra□	14	4	.778	26	7	.788
Old Dominion□	13	5	.722	24	10	.706
Northeastern	12	6	.667	19	11	.633
VCU	11	7	.611	19	10	.655
Drexel	8	10	.444	15	16	.484
Towson	8	10	.444	12	16	.429
Delaware	4	14	.222	9	21	.300
William and Mary	3	15	.167	8	20	.286
Georgia State	3	15	.167	7	22	.241
James Madison	2	16	.111	5	23	.179

Tournament: **UNC Wilmington d. Hofstra 78-67**
Tournament MVP: **T.J. Carter**, UNC Wilmington

C-USA

	Conference			Overall		
	W	L	PCT	W	L	PCT
Memphis⊕	13	1	.929	33	4	.892
UAB○	12	2	.857	24	7	.774
UTEP□	11	3	.786	21	10	.677
Houston□	9	5	.643	21	10	.677
Central Florida	7	7	.500	14	15	.483
Rice	6	8	.429	12	16	.429
Tulane	6	8	.429	12	17	.414
Tulsa	6	8	.429	11	17	.393
Marshall	5	9	.357	12	16	.429
SMU	4	10	.286	13	16	.448
Southern Miss	3	11	.214	10	21	.323
East Carolina	2	12	.143	8	20	.286

Tournament: **Memphis d. UAB 57-46**
Tournament MVP: **Shawne Williams**, Memphis

Horizon

	Conference			Overall		
	W	L	PCT	W	L	PCT
Wisc.-Milwaukee⊕	12	4	.750	22	9	.710
Butler□	11	5	.688	20	13	.606
Loyola-Chicago	8	8	.500	19	11	.633
Illinois-Chicago	8	8	.500	16	15	.516
Detroit	8	8	.500	16	16	.500
Wisc.-Green Bay	8	8	.500	15	16	.484
Wright State	8	8	.500	13	15	.464
Cleveland State	5	11	.313	10	18	.357
Youngstown State	4	12	.250	7	21	.250

Tournament: **Wisc.-Milwaukee d. Butler 87-71**
Tournament MVP: **Adrian Tigert**, Wisc.-Milwaukee

⊕ Automatic NCAA Tournament bid ○ At-large NCAA Tournament bid □ NIT appearance ✪ Team record doesn't reflect games forfeited or vacated. For adjusted record, see p. 521.

IVY

	Conference			Overall		
	W	L	PCT	W	L	PCT
Penn⊕	12	2	.857	20	9	.690
Princeton	10	4	.714	12	15	.444
Cornell	8	6	.571	13	15	.464
Yale	7	7	.500	15	14	.517
Brown	6	8	.429	10	17	.370
Harvard	5	9	.357	13	14	.481
Columbia	4	10	.286	11	16	.407
Dartmouth	4	10	.286	6	21	.222

MAAC

	Conference			Overall		
	W	L	PCT	W	L	PCT
Manhattan□	14	4	.778	20	11	.645
Iona⊕	13	5	.722	23	8	.742
Marist	12	6	.667	19	10	.655
Siena	10	8	.556	15	13	.536
Saint Peter's	9	9	.500	17	15	.531
Loyola (MD)	8	10	.444	15	13	.536
Niagara	7	11	.389	11	18	.379
Fairfield	7	11	.389	9	19	.321
Canisius	6	12	.333	9	20	.310
Rider	4	14	.222	8	20	.286

Tournament: **Iona d. Saint Peter's 80-61**
Tournament MVP: **Steve Burtt Jr.**, Iona

MID-AMERICAN

	Conference			Overall		
	W	L	PCT	W	L	PCT
East Division						
Kent State⊕	15	3	.833	25	9	.735
Akron□	14	4	.778	23	10	.697
Miami (OH)□	14	4	.778	18	11	.621
Ohio	10	8	.556	19	11	.633
Buffalo	8	10	.444	19	13	.594
Bowling Green	5	13	.278	9	21	.300
West Division						
Northern Illinois	12	6	.667	17	11	.607
Toledo	10	8	.556	20	11	.645
Western Michigan	10	8	.556	14	17	.452
Ball State	6	12	.333	10	18	.357
Eastern Michigan	3	15	.167	7	21	.250
Central Michigan	1	17	.056	4	24	.143

Tournament: **Kent State d. Toledo 71-66**
Tournament MVP: **Kevin Warzynski**, Kent State

MID-CONTINENT

	Conference			Overall		
	W	L	PCT	W	L	PCT
IUPUI	13	3	.813	19	10	.655
Oral Roberts⊕	13	3	.813	21	12	.636
UMKC	11	5	.688	14	14	.500
Valparaiso	8	8	.500	17	12	.586
Chicago State	8	8	.500	11	19	.367
Southern Utah	8	8	.500	10	20	.333
Oakland	6	10	.375	11	18	.379
Western Illinois	3	13	.188	7	21	.250
Centenary	2	14	.125	4	23	.148

Tournament: **Oral Roberts d. Chicago State 85-72**
Tournament MVP: **Ken Tutt**, Oral Roberts

MEAC

	Conference			Overall		
	W	L	PCT	W	L	PCT
Delaware State□	16	2	.889	21	14	.600
Coppin State	12	6	.667	12	18	.400
Bethune-Cookman	11	7	.611	15	15	.500
South Carolina State	11	7	.611	14	16	.467
Hampton⊕	10	8	.556	16	16	.500
Florida A&M	10	8	.556	14	17	.452
Norfolk State	10	8	.556	13	18	.419
NC A&T	6	12	.333	6	23	.207
Howard	5	13	.278	7	22	.241
UMES	4	14	.222	7	22	.241
Morgan State	4	14	.222	4	26	.133

Tournament: **Hampton d. Delaware State 60-56**
Tournament MOP: **Rashad West**, Hampton

MISSOURI VALLEY

	Conference			Overall		
	W	L	PCT	W	L	PCT
Wichita State○	14	4	.778	26	9	.743
Missouri State□	12	6	.667	22	9	.710
Southern Illinois⊕	12	6	.667	22	11	.667
Creighton	12	6	.667	20	10	.667
Northern Iowa○	11	7	.611	23	10	.697
Bradley○	11	7	.611	22	11	.667
Drake	5	13	.278	12	19	.387
Evansville	5	13	.278	10	19	.345
Indiana State	4	14	.222	13	16	.448
Illinois State	4	14	.222	9	19	.321

Tournament: **Southern Illinois d. Bradley 59-46**
Tournament MOP: **Randal Falker**, Southern Illinois

MOUNTAIN WEST

	Conference			Overall		
	W	L	PCT	W	L	PCT
San Diego State⊕	13	3	.813	24	9	.727
Air Force○	12	4	.750	24	7	.774
BYU□	12	4	.750	20	9	.690
UNLV	10	6	.625	17	13	.567
New Mexico	8	8	.500	17	13	.567
Utah	6	10	.375	14	15	.483
Wyoming	5	11	.313	14	18	.438
Colorado State	4	12	.250	16	15	.516
TCU	2	14	.125	6	25	.194

Tournament: **San Diego State d. Wyoming 69-64**
Tournament MVP: **Marcus Slaughter**, San Diego State

NORTHEAST

	Conference			Overall		
	W	L	PCT	W	L	PCT
Fairleigh Dickinson□	14	4	.778	20	12	.625
Central Conn. State	13	5	.722	18	11	.621
Monmouth⊕	12	6	.667	19	15	.559
Mount St. Mary's	11	7	.611	13	17	.433
Robert Morris	10	8	.556	15	14	.517
Long Island	9	9	.500	12	16	.429
Sacred Heart	8	10	.444	11	17	.393
Quinnipiac	7	11	.389	12	16	.429
St. Francis (NY)	7	11	.389	10	17	.370
Wagner	6	12	.333	13	14	.481
Saint Francis (PA)	2	16	.111	4	24	.143

Tournament: **Monmouth d. Fairleigh Dickinson 49-48**
Tournament MVP: **Marques Alston**, Monmouth

OHIO VALLEY

	Conference			Overall		
	W	L	PCT	W	L	PCT
Murray State⊕	17	3	.850	24	7	.774
Samford	14	6	.700	20	11	.645
Tennessee Tech	13	7	.650	19	12	.613
Jacksonville State	12	8	.600	16	13	.552
Austin Peay	11	9	.550	17	14	.548
Eastern Kentucky	11	9	.550	14	16	.467
Tennessee State	11	9	.550	13	15	.464
Tennessee-Martin	9	11	.450	13	15	.464
Eastern Illinois	5	15	.250	6	21	.222
SE Missouri State	4	16	.200	7	20	.259
Morehead State	3	17	.150	4	23	.148

Tournament: **Murray State d. Samford 74-57**
Tournament MVP: **Pearson Griffith**, Murray State

PAC-10

	Conference			Overall		
	W	L	PCT	W	L	PCT
UCLA⊕	14	4	.778	32	7	.821
Washington○	13	5	.722	26	7	.788
California○	12	6	.667	20	11	.645
Arizona○	11	7	.611	20	13	.606
Stanford□	11	7	.611	16	14	.533
Southern California	8	10	.444	17	13	.567
Oregon	7	11	.389	15	18	.455
Oregon State	5	13	.278	13	18	.419
Arizona State	5	13	.278	11	17	.393
Washington State	4	14	.222	11	17	.393

Tournament: **UCLA d. California 71-52**
Tournament MVP: **Leon Powe**, California

PATRIOT LEAGUE

	Conference			Overall		
	W	L	PCT	W	L	PCT
Bucknell⊕	14	0	1.000	27	5	.844
Holy Cross	11	3	.786	20	12	.625
Lehigh	11	3	.786	19	12	.613
American	7	7	.500	12	17	.414
Lafayette	5	9	.357	11	17	.393
Colgate	4	10	.286	10	19	.345
Navy	3	11	.214	10	18	.357
Army	1	13	.071	5	22	.185

Tournament: **Bucknell d. Holy Cross 74-59**
Tournament MVP: **Charles Lee**, Bucknell

SEC

	Conference			Overall		
	W	L	PCT	W	L	PCT
Eastern						
Tennessee○	12	4	.750	22	8	.733
Florida⊕	10	6	.625	33	6	.846
Kentucky○	9	7	.563	22	13	.629
Vanderbilt□	7	9	.438	17	13	.567
South Carolina□	6	10	.375	23	15	.605
Georgia	5	11	.313	15	15	.500
Western						
LSU○	14	2	.875	27	9	.750
Arkansas○	10	6	.625	22	10	.688
Alabama○	10	6	.625	18	13	.581
Mississippi State	5	11	.313	15	15	.500
Mississippi	4	12	.250	14	16	.467
Auburn	4	12	.250	12	16	.429

Tournament: **Florida d. South Carolina 49-47**
Tournament MVP: **Taurean Green**, Florida

SOUTHERN

	Conference			Overall		
	W	L	PCT	W	L	PCT
North						
Elon	10	4	.714	15	14	.517
Chattanooga	8	6	.571	19	13	.594
Western Carolina	7	7	.500	13	17	.433
Appalachian State	6	8	.429	14	16	.467
UNC Greensboro	4	10	.286	12	19	.387
South						
Georgia Southern□	11	4	.733	20	10	.667
Davidson⊕	10	5	.667	20	11	.645
Charleston	9	6	.600	17	11	.607
Furman	8	7	.533	15	13	.536
Wofford	6	9	.400	11	18	.379
The Citadel	1	14	.067	10	21	.323

Tournament: **Davidson d. Chattanooga 80-59**
Tournament MOP: **Brendan Winters**, Davidson

SOUTHLAND

	Conference			Overall		
	W	L	PCT	W	L	PCT
Northwestern St. (LA)⊕	15	1	.938	26	8	.765
Sam Houston State	11	5	.688	22	9	.710
Southeastern Louisiana	10	6	.625	16	12	.571
Stephen F. Austin	9	7	.563	17	12	.586
Lamar	9	7	.563	17	14	.548
McNeese State	9	7	.563	14	14	.500
Texas-Arlington	7	9	.438	14	16	.467
UTSA	6	10	.375	11	17	.393
UL-Monroe	6	10	.375	10	18	.357
Nicholls State	5	11	.313	9	18	.333
Texas State	1	15	.063	3	24	.111

Tournament: **Northwestern St. (LA) d. Sam Houston State 95-87**
Tournament MVP: **Cilfton Lee**, Northwestern St. (LA)

SWAC

	Conference			Overall		
	W	L	PCT	W	L	PCT
Southern U.⊕	15	3	.833	19	13	.594
Grambling	11	7	.611	14	13	.519
Alabama A&M	11	7	.611	13	13	.500
Jackson State	10	8	.556	15	17	.469
Alabama State	10	8	.556	12	18	.400
Miss. Valley State	9	9	.500	9	19	.321
Arkansas-Pine Bluff	8	10	.444	13	16	.448
Alcorn State	8	10	.444	8	20	.286
Texas Southern	6	12	.333	8	22	.267
Prairie View A&M	2	16	.111	5	24	.172

Tournament: **Southern U. d. Arkansas-Pine Bluff 57-44**
Tournament MVP: **Peter Cipriano**, Southern U.

SUN BELT

	Conference			Overall		
	W	L	PCT	W	L	PCT
East Division						
Western Kentucky□	12	2	.857	23	8	.742
Middle Tenn State	8	6	.571	16	12	.571
Arkansas State	7	7	.500	12	18	.400
Arkansas-Little Rock	5	9	.357	14	15	.483
Florida International⊗	4	10	.286	8	20	.286
West Division						
South Alabama⊕	12	3	.800	24	7	.774
Denver	7	8	.467	16	15	.516
UL-Lafayette	7	8	.467	13	16	.448
North Texas	6	9	.400	14	14	.500
Troy	6	9	.400	14	15	.483
New Orleans	6	9	.400	10	19	.345

Tournament: **South Alabama d. Western Kentucky 95-70**
Tournament MOP: **Chey Christie**, South Alabama

WEST COAST

	Conference			Overall		
	W	L	PCT	W	L	PCT
Gonzaga⊕	14	0	1.000	29	4	.879
Saint Mary's (CA)	8	6	.571	17	12	.586
Loyola Marymount	8	6	.571	12	18	.400
San Francisco	7	7	.500	11	17	.393
San Diego	6	8	.429	18	12	.600
Santa Clara	5	9	.357	13	16	.448
Portland	5	9	.357	11	18	.379
Pepperdine	3	11	.214	7	20	.259

Tournament: **Gonzaga d. Loyola Marymount 68-67**
Tournament MVP: **Adam Morrison**, Gonzaga

WAC

	Conference			Overall		
	W	L	PCT	W	L	PCT
Nevada⊕	13	3	.813	27	6	.818
Utah State○	11	5	.688	23	9	.719
Louisiana Tech□	11	5	.688	20	13	.606
Hawaii	10	6	.625	17	11	.607
New Mexico State	10	6	.625	16	14	.533
Fresno State	8	8	.500	15	13	.536
Boise State	6	10	.375	14	15	.483
San Jose State	2	14	.125	6	25	.194
Idaho	1	15	.063	4	25	.138

Tournament: **Nevada d. Utah State 70-63**
Tournament MVP: **Nick Fazekas**, Nevada

INDEPENDENTS

	Overall		
	W	L	PCT
Corpus Christi	20	8	.714
IPFW	10	18	.357
Texas-Pan American	6	24	.200
Savannah State	2	28	.067

ALL OTHERS

(Reclassifying and provisional teams that are not eligible for the NCAA Tournament.)

	Overall		
	W	L	PCT
North Dakota State	16	12	.571
Utah Valley State	16	13	.552
Kennesaw State	12	17	.414
Longwood	10	20	.333
South Dakota State	9	20	.310
NJIT	8	19	.296
UC Davis	8	20	.286
North Florida	6	22	.214
Northern Colorado	5	24	.172

INDIVIDUAL LEADERS—SEASON

SCORING	CL	POS	G	FG	3FG	FT	PTS	PPG
1 **Adam Morrison**, Gonzaga	JR	F	33	306	74	240	926	**28.1**
2 **J.J. Redick**, Duke	SR	G	36	302	139	221	964	**26.8**
3 **Keydren Clark**, Saint Peter's	SR	G	32	273	105	189	840	**26.3**
4 **Andre Collins**, Loyola (MD)	SR	G	28	256	118	101	731	**26.1**
5 **Brion Rush**, Grambling	SR	G	21	189	54	109	541	**25.8**
6 **Quincy Douby**, Rutgers	JR	G	33	287	116	149	839	**25.4**
7 **Steve Burtt Jr.**, Iona	SR	G	31	258	96	168	780	**25.2**
8 **Rodney Stuckey**, Eastern Washington	FR	G	30	250	55	171	726	**24.2**
9 **Alan Daniels**, Lamar	SR	F	31	250	75	155	730	**23.5**
10 **Trey Johnson**, Jackson State	JR	G	32	255	67	174	751	**23.5**

FIELD GOAL PCT	CL	POS	G	FG	FGA	PCT
1 **Randall Hanke**, Providence	SO	C	27	149	220	**67.7**
2 **Cedric Smith**, Corpus Christi	JR	F	27	139	210	**66.2**
3 **Joakim Noah**, Florida	SO	F/C	39	202	322	**62.7**
4 **James Augustine**, Illinois	SR	F	33	174	279	**62.4**
5 **Michael Harrison**, Colorado State	JR	F	31	160	257	**62.3**

MINIMUM: 5 MADE PER GAME

THREE-PT FG PER GAME	CL	POS	G	3FG	3PG
1 **Andre Collins**, Loyola (MD)	SR	G	28	118	**4.2**
2 **Jack Leasure**, Coastal Carolina	SO	G	30	125	**4.2**
3 **Steve Novak**, Marquette	SR	F	31	121	**3.9**
4 **J. Robert Merritt**, Samford	SR	F	31	120	**3.9**
5 **J.J. Redick**, Duke	SR	G	36	139	**3.9**

THREE-PT FG PCT	CL	POS	G	3FG	3FGA	PCT
1 **Stephen Sir**, Northern Arizona	JR	G	32	93	190	**48.9**
2 **Josh Alexander**, Stephen F. Austin	FR	G	29	73	153	**47.7**
3 **J. Robert Merritt**, Samford	SR	F	31	120	252	**47.6**
4 **Ross Schraeder**, UC Irvine	SR	G	29	74	156	**47.4**
5 **Chris Hernandez**, Stanford	SR	G	30	75	159	**47.2**

MINIMUM: 2.5 MADE PER GAME

FREE THROW PCT	CL	POS	G	FT	FTA	PCT
1 **Blake Ahearn**, Missouri State	JR	G	31	117	125	**93.6**
2 **Jermaine Anderson**, New Hampshire	JR	G	26	68	74	**91.9**
3 **Shawan Robinson**, Clemson	SR	G	32	84	92	**91.3**
4 **Derek Raivio**, Gonzaga	JR	G	31	83	91	**91.2**
5 **Adam Vogelsberg**, Middle Tennessee State	JR	G	28	108	119	**90.8**

MINIMUM: 2.5 MADE PER GAME

ASSISTS PER GAME	CL	POS	G	AST	APG
1 **Jared Jordan**, Marist	JR	G	29	247	**8.5**
2 **Jose Juan Barea**, Northeastern	SR	G	29	244	**8.4**
3 **Terrell Everett**, Oklahoma	SR	G	29	199	**6.9**
4 **Walker Russell**, Jacksonville State	SR	G	29	197	**6.8**
5 **Kenny Grant**, Davidson	SR	G	31	208	**6.7**
6 **Bobby Dixon**, Troy	SR	G	29	192	**6.6**
7 **Aaron Fitzgerald**, UC Irvine	SR	G	29	190	**6.6**
8 **Chris Quinn**, Notre Dame	SR	G	29	187	**6.4**
9 **Carldell Johnson**, UAB	SR	G	31	194	**6.3**
10 **Will Blalock**, Iowa State	JR	G	30	184	**6.1**

REBOUNDS PER GAME	CL	POS	G	REB	RPG
1 **Paul Millsap**, Louisiana Tech	JR	F	33	438	**13.3**
2 **Kenny Adeleke**, Hartford	SR	F	28	366	**13.1**
3 **Rashad Jones-Jennings**, Arkansas-Little Rock	JR	F	29	329	**11.3**
4 **Curtis Withers**, Charlotte	SR	F	32	362	**11.3**
5 **Ivan Almonte**, Florida International	SR	F	25	281	**11.2**
6 **Marcus Slaughter**, San Diego State	JR	F	30	329	**11.0**
Justin Williams, Wyoming	SR	C	30	329	**11.0**
8 **Yemi Nicholson**, Denver	SR	C	31	339	**10.9**
9 **Harding Nana**, Delaware	SR	F	30	326	**10.9**
10 **Ricky Woods**, Southeastern Louisiana	SR	F	28	304	**10.9**

BLOCKED SHOTS PER GAME	CL	POS	G	BLK	BPG
1 **Shawn James**, Northeastern	SO	F	30	196	**6.5**
2 **Justin Williams**, Wyoming	SR	C	30	163	**5.4**
3 **Stephane Lasme**, Massachusetts	JR	F	28	108	**3.9**
4 **Shelden Williams**, Duke	SR	F	36	137	**3.8**
5 **Slim Millien**, Idaho State	SR	F	27	93	**3.4**

STEALS PER GAME	CL	POS	G	STL	SPG
1 **Tim Smith**, East Tennessee State	SR	G	28	95	**3.4**
2 **Oliver Lafayette**, Houston	JR	G	31	105	**3.4**
3 **Obie Trotter**, Alabama A&M	SR	G	26	87	**3.3**
4 **Ibrahim Jaaber**, Penn	JR	G	29	96	**3.3**
5 **Kevin Hamilton**, Holy Cross	SR	G	31	102	**3.3**

INDIVIDUAL LEADERS—GAME

POINTS	CL	POS	OPP	DATE	PTS
1 **Brion Rush**, Grambling	SR	G	Southern U.	F4	**53**
2 **Rodney Stuckey**, Eastern Washington	FR	G	Northern Arizona	J5	**45**
3 **Adam Morrison**, Gonzaga	JR	F	Loyola Marymount	F18	**44**
4 **Keydren Clark**, Saint Peter's	SR	G	Canisius	F24	**43**
Adam Morrison, Gonzaga	JR	F	Washington	D4	**43**
Adam Morrison, Gonzaga	JR	F	Michigan State	N22	**43**

THREE-PT FG MADE	CL	POS	OPP	DATE	3FG
1 **Josh Goodwin**, Belmont	JR	G	East Tennessee State	D1	**11**
2 **Chris Riouse**, Oral Roberts	SR	G	Oakland	F9	**10**
Jaycee Carroll, Utah State	SO	G	New Mexico State	F2	**10**
4 **Keydren Clark**, Saint Peter's	SR	G	Canisius	F24	**9**
Kyle Anslinger, Evansville	JR	G	Drake	F11	**9**
Chris Lofton, Tennessee	SO	G	Georgia	F11	**9**
Quincy Douby, Rutgers	JR	G	Syracuse	F1	**9**
Daniel Gibson, Texas	SO	G	Baylor	J21	**9**
Andre Collins, Loyola (MD)	SR	G	Marist	J8	**9**
Greg Sprink, Navy	SO	G	Brown	D22	**9**
Jack Leasure, Coastal Carolina	SO	G	Chowan	D19	**9**
Kevin Oleksiak, UNC Greensboro	SO	G	Greensboro	D16	**9**
J.J. Redick, Duke	SR	G	Texas	D10	**9**
Sean Morris, Colorado State	SO	G	Colorado	N21	**9**
Calvin Wooten, Oakland	JR	G	Albany (NY)	N9	**9**

ASSISTS	CL	POS	OPP	DATE	AST
1 **Bobby Dixon**, Troy	SR	G	Western Kentucky	J19	**16**
Jared Jordan, Marist	JR	G	Rider	J15	**16**
3 **Jejuan Plair**, Sam Houston State	JR	G	Stephen F. Austin	M4	**15**
Terrell Everett, Oklahoma	SR	G	Baylor	F11	**15**
Jared Jordan, Marist	JR	G	Iona	F5	**15**
Greg Paulus, Duke	FR	G	Valparaiso	D18	**15**
Dontell Jefferson, Arkansas	SR	G	Portland State	N18	**15**

REBOUNDS	CL	POS	OPP	DATE	REB
1 **Rashad Jones-Jennings**, Ark.-L.R.	JR	F	Arkansas-Pine Bluff	D13	**30**
2 **Paul Millsap**, Louisiana Tech	JR	F	San Jose State	F15	**28**
3 **Paul Millsap**, Louisiana Tech	JR	F	Hawaii	M4	**23**
Greg Brunner, Iowa	SR	F	Minnesota	J18	**23**
5 **Brad Nuckles**, East Tenn. State	SR	F	Campbell	J7	**22**
Jermaine Griffin, Texas-Arlington	SO	F	Tex. Permian Basin	D1	**22**

BLOCKED SHOTS	CL	POS	OPP	DATE	BLK
1 **Justin Williams**, Wyoming	SR	C	Utah	M10	**12**
2 **Justin Williams**, Wyoming	SR	C	BYU	F18	**11**
Shawn James, Northeastern	SO	F	James Madison	F15	**11**
Michael Southall, UL-Lafayette	SR	C	North Texas	J5	**11**
5 **Shawn James**, Northeastern	SO	F	Delaware	F23	**10**
Shawn James, Northeastern	SO	F	VCU	F4	**10**
Shawn James, Northeastern	SO	F	Hofstra	J21	**10**
Shelden Williams, Duke	SR	F	Maryland	J11	**10**
Eric Hicks, Cincinnati	SR	F	Marquette	J7	**10**
Steven Hill, Arkansas	SO	C	Texas State	D6	**10**
Shawn James, Northeastern	SO	F	Cal State Northridge	N25	**10**

STEALS	CL	POS	OPP	DATE	STL
1 **Carldell Johnson**, UAB	SR	G	South Carolina State	N27	**12**
2 **Ricky Woods**, Southeastern La.	SR	F	Lamar	M3	**10**
Obie Trotter, Alabama A&M	SR	G	Jarvis Christian	N26	**10**
Ricky Soliver, Iona	SR	G	Portland State	N25	**10**
5 **Al Stewart**, Drake	JR	G	Illinois State	F14	**9**
Tony Skinn, George Mason	SR	G	Northeastern	J19	**9**

TEAM LEADERS—SEASON

WIN-LOSS PCT	W	L	PCT
1 **George Washington**	27	3	.900
2 **Memphis**	33	4	.892
3 **Duke**	32	4	.889
4 **Connecticut**	30	4	.882
5 **Gonzaga**	29	4	.879

SCORING OFFENSE	G	W-L	PTS	PPG
1 **Long Beach State**	30	18-12	2,498	**83.3**
2 **Campbell**	28	10-18	2,319	**82.8**
3 **Corpus Christi**	28	20-8	2,307	**82.4**
4 **Washington**	33	26-7	2,706	**82.0**
5 **Connecticut**	34	30-4	2,781	**81.8**

SCORING MARGIN	G	W-L	PPG	OPP PPG	MAR
1 **Corpus Christi**	28	20-8	82.4	67.4	**15.0**
2 **Texas**	37	30-7	75.2	60.3	**14.9**
3 **Florida**	39	33-6	78.3	63.5	**14.8**
4 **Connecticut**	34	30-4	81.8	67.1	**14.7**
5 **Memphis**	37	33-4	80.0	65.5	**14.5**

FIELD GOAL PCT	G	W-L	FG	FGA	PCT
1 **Corpus Christi**	28	20-8	837	1,671	**50.1**
2 **Florida**	39	33-6	1,061	2,120	**50.0**
3 **Utah State**	32	23-9	853	1,714	**49.8**
4 **Belmont**	31	20-11	897	1,819	**49.3**
5 **Montana**	31	24-7	876	1,781	**49.2**

THREE-PT FG PER GAME	G	W-L	3FG	3PG
1 **Troy**	29	14-15	344	**11.9**
2 **West Virginia**	33	22-11	337	**10.2**
3 **Campbell**	28	10-18	276	**9.9**
4 **Samford**	31	20-11	298	**9.6**
5 **Notre Dame**	30	16-14	288	**9.6**

ASSISTS PER GAME	G	W-L	AST	APG
1 **Corpus Christi**	28	20-8	550	**19.6**
2 **Sam Houston State**	31	22-9	574	**18.5**
3 **Davidson**	31	20-11	567	**18.3**
4 **Montana**	31	24-7	565	**18.2**
5 **Kansas**	33	25-8	589	**17.8**

Rebound Margin

	G	W-L	RPG	OPP RPG	MAR
1 **Texas**	37	30-7	40.5	29.9	**10.6**
2 **Connecticut**	34	30-4	43.8	34.3	**9.5**
3 **Charleston**	28	17-11	41.9	32.8	**9.0**
4 **Oklahoma**	29	20-9	36.6	27.7	**8.9**
5 **North Carolina**	31	23-8	39.9	31.8	**8.1**

Scoring Defense

	G	W-L	OPP PTS	OPP PPG
1 **Air Force**	31	24-7	1,695	**54.7**
2 **Princeton**	27	12-15	1,500	**55.6**
3 **Bucknell**	32	27-5	1,785	**55.8**
4 **Southern Illinois**	33	22-11	1,864	**56.5**
5 **Delaware State**	35	21-14	2,011	**57.5**

Field Goal Pct Defense

	G	W-L	OPP FG	OPP FGA	OPP PCT
1 **Kansas**	33	25-8	702	1,896	**37.0**
2 **Memphis**	37	33-4	795	2,094	**38.0**
3 **Iowa**	34	25-9	732	1,924	**38.0**
4 **Connecticut**	34	30-4	842	2,200	**38.3**
5 **Texas**	37	30-7	805	2,097	**38.4**

Blocked Shots Per Game

	G	W-L	BLK	BPG
1 **Connecticut**	34	30-4	298	**8.8**
2 **Northeastern**	30	19-11	240	**8.0**
3 **Massachusetts**	28	13-15	202	**7.2**
4 **Wyoming**	32	14-18	221	**6.9**
5 **Idaho State**	27	13-14	179	**6.6**

Steals Per Game

	G	W-L	STL	SPG
1 **Houston**	31	21-10	385	**12.4**
2 **Clemson**	32	19-13	352	**11.0**
3 **UAB**	31	24-7	337	**10.9**
4 **East Tennessee State**	28	15-13	288	**10.3**
5 **Tennessee**	30	22-8	301	**10.0**

TEAM LEADERS—GAME

Points

	OPP	DATE	SCORE
1 **Houston**	Florida Tech	N22	131-62
2 **Connecticut**	Morehead State	D23	129-61
3 **The Citadel**	Atlanta Christian	D5	126-61
The Citadel	Florida Christian	N28	126-43
5 **Sam Houston State**	Paul Quinn	J4	124-70

Field Goal Pct

	OPP	DATE	FGM	FGA	PCT
1. **Florida Atlantic**	Kennesaw State	F18	32	46	**69.6**
2. **SMU**	Savannah State	D19	34	49	**69.4**
3. **Oral Roberts**	IUPUI	J14	29	42	**69.0**
4. **Air Force**	Utah	J19	26	38	**68.4**
5. **NC State**	Appalachian State	D10	31	46	**67.4**

Three-Pt FG Made

	OPP	DATE	3FG
1 **Utah State**	New Mexico State	F2	**20**
West Virginia	Marquette	J14	**20**
3 **Akron**	Denison	D7	**19**
Houston	Florida Tech	N22	**19**
5 **Butler**	Detroit	F25	**18**
Oral Roberts	Oakland	F9	**18**
Wofford	Virginia-Wise	D3	**18**

CONSENSUS ALL-AMERICAS

FIRST TEAM

PLAYER	CL	POS	HT	SCHOOL	RPG	PPG
Randy Foye	SR	G	6-4	Villanova	5.8	20.5
Adam Morrison	JR	F	6-8	Gonzaga	5.5	28.1
J.J. Redick	SR	G	6-4	Duke	2.0	26.8
Brandon Roy	SR	G	6-6	Washington	5.6	20.2
Shelden Williams	SR	F	6-9	Duke	10.7	18.8

SECOND TEAM

PLAYER	CL	POS	HT	SCHOOL	RPG	PPG
Dee Brown	SR	G	6-0	Illinois	3.1	14.2
Rodney Carney	SR	F	6-7	Memphis	4.3	17.2
Rudy Gay	SO	F	6-9	Connecticut	6.4	15.2
Tyler Hansbrough	FR	F	6-9	North Carolina	7.8	18.9
Leon Powe	SO	F	6-8	California	10.1	20.5
Allan Ray	SR	G	6-2	Villanova	3.6	18.5
P.J. Tucker	JR	F	6-5	Texas	9.3	16.3

SELECTORS: AP, NABC, SPORTING NEWS, USBWA

AWARD WINNERS

PLAYER OF THE YEAR

PLAYER	CL	POS	HT	AWARDS
Dee Brown	SR	G	6-0	Naismith, Frances Pomeroy Naismith*
J.J. Redick	SR	G	6-4	AP, USBWA, Wooden (shared), NABC (shared), Rupp, Sullivan‡
Adam Morrison	JR	F	6-8	Wooden (shared), NABC (shared)

* FOR THE MOST OUTSTANDING SENIOR PLAYER WHO IS 6 FEET OR UNDER
‡ TOP AMATEUR ATHLETE IN U.S.

DEFENSIVE PLAYER OF THE YEAR

PLAYER	CL	POS	HT	SCHOOL
Shelden Williams	SR	F	6-9	Duke

COACH OF THE YEAR

COACH	SCHOOL	REC	AWARDS
Jay Wright	Villanova	28-5	Naismith, NABC, CBS/Chevrolet
Roy Williams	North Carolina	23-8	AP, USBWA
Bruce Pearl	Tennessee	22-8	Sporting News

Bob Gibbons' Top High School Senior Recruits

PLAYER	POS	HT	HIGH SCHOOL	A-A TEAMS	COLLEGE	CAREER NOTES
1 **Greg Oden**	C	7-0	Lawrence North HS, Indianapolis	McD, MJ, P, USA	Ohio State	First-team All-America; No. 1 overall pick, '07 NBA draft (Blazers); 61 NBA games, 8.9 ppg
2 **Kevin Durant**	F	6-9	Montrose Christian School, Rockville, MD	McD, MJ, P, USA	Texas	College POY '07; No. 2 pick, '07 NBA draft (Sonics); NBA ROY '08; 25.3 ppg, '09
3 **Spencer Hawes**	C	7-0	Seattle (WA) Prepatory School	McD, MJ, P, USA	Washington	Pac-10 All-Freshman team; No. 10 pick, '07 NBA draft (Kings); 11.4 ppg, '09
4 **Brandan Wright**	PF	6-9	Brentwood (NC) Academy	McD, MJ, P	North Carolina	ACC ROY '07; No. 8 pick, '07 NBA draft (Bobcats); 77 NBA games, 6.2 ppg (2 seasons)
5 **Wayne Ellington**	G	6-4	The Episcopal Academy, Merion Station, PA	McD, MJ, P	North Carolina	3rd in scoring (15.8 ppg); NCAA title, '09; No. 28 pick, '09 NBA draft (Wolves)
6 **Chase Budinger**	F	6-8	La Costa Canyon HS, Carlsbad, CA	McD, P	Arizona	17.0 ppg, 5.8 rpg (3 seasons); 2nd-round pick, '09 NBA draft (Pistons)
7 **Mike Conley Jr.**	PG	6-1	Lawrence North HS, Indianapolis	McD, P	Ohio State	All-Big Ten '07, No. 4 pick, '07 NBA draft (Grizzlies); 10.9 ppg, 4.3 apg in '08-'09
8 **Thaddeus Young**	F	6-8	Mitchell HS, Memphis, TN	McD, MJ, P	Georgia Tech	ACC All-Rookie team honorable mention; No. 12 pick, '07 draft (76ers); 11.8 ppg (2 seasons)
9 **Ty Lawson**	PG	6-0	Oak Hill Academy, Mouth of Wilson, VA	McD, MJ, P, USA	North Carolina	'09 ACC POY, consensus All-America ('09); No. 18 pick, '09 NBA draft (Wolves)
10 **Daequan Cook**	G	6-5	Dunbar HS, Dayton, OH	McD, P	Ohio State	No. 21 pick '07 NBA draft (76ers); '09 NBA All-Star 3-point shootout winner
11 **Darrell Arthur**	PF	6-9	South Oak Cliff HS, Dallas	McD, P	Kansas	1 season at KU ('07); No. 27 pick '08 NBA draft (Hornets); 5.6 ppg for Grizzlies, '09
12 **Javaris Crittenton**	G	6-5	Southwest Atlanta Christian Academy	McD, P	Georgia Tech	ACC All-Rookie team, '07; No. 19 pick, '07 NBA draft (Lakers); 113 NBA games, 5.3 ppg
13 **Gerald Henderson**	G	6-5	The Episcopal Academy, Merion, PA	McD, P	Duke	12.7 ppg, 4.7 rpg as sophomore; 16.5 ppg, 4.9 rpg and All-ACC team as junior; No. 12 pick (Bobcats), '09 NBA draft
14 **Sherron Collins**	PG	5-11	Crane Tech Prep HS, Chicago	McD, MJ, P	Kansas	Big 12 All-Rookie team '07; All-Big 12, 3rd-team All-America in '09
15 **Derrick Caracter**	F/C	6-9	Notre Dame Prep, Fitchburg, MA		Louisville/UTEP	8.2 ppg in 53 games (2 seasons) for Louisville; transferred to UTEP
16 **Damion James**	PF	6-8	Nacogdoches (TX) HS	P	Texas	:ed team in rebounding (9.2 rpg), 2nd in scoring (15.4 ppg) as a Jr.
17 **Brook Lopez**	PF	7-0	San Joaquin Memorial HS, Fresno, CA	McD, P	Stanford	Pac-10 All-Freshman team; No.10 pick, '08 NBA draft (Nets); '09 NBA All-Rookie team
18 **Scottie Reynolds**	G	6-1	Herndon (VA) HS	McD, P	Villanova	'07 Big East ROY; 3 seasons,15.3 ppg, 3.5 apg
19 **DaJuan Summers**	P/F	6-8	McDonough School, Owings Mills, MD	MJ	Georgetown	11.1 ppg, 5.4 rpg as Soph.; 13.6 ppg as Jr.; 2nd-round pick, '09 NBA draft (Pistons)
20 **Jon Scheyer**	G	6-6	Glenbrook North HS, Northbrook, IL	McD, MJ, P	Duke	'07 ACC All-Rookie team (12.2 ppg); 14.9 ppg as junior; '09 ACC tourney MVP
21 **Duke Crews**	PF	6-7	Bethel HS, Hampton, VA	MJ, P	Tennessee	'07 SEC All-Freshman team with 8.4 ppg; 7.4 ppg as a Soph.; now at Bowie St.
22 **Stanley Robinson**	P/F	6-9	Huffman HS, Birmingham, AL	P	Connecticut	5.1 ppg as Fr.; 10.4 ppg, 6.5 rpg as soph.; 8.9 ppg, 5.9 rpg as Jr.
23 **Earl Clark**	F	6-9	Rahway (NJ) HS	McD, P	Louisville	3 seasons at Louisville, 10.6 ppg, 7.0 rpg; No. 14 pick, '09 NBA draft (Suns)
24 **Vernon Macklin**	PF	6-9	Hargrave Military Academy, Catham, VA	McD, MJ, P	Georgetown	3.2 ppg, 1.8 rpg in 65 games for Hoyas; transferred to Florida
25 **Obi Muonelo**	G/F	6-5	Santa Fe HS, Edmond, OK	MJ	Oklahoma State	10.1 ppg in 17 games as Fr.; 9.8 ppg as Soph.; 12.7 ppg, 7.2 rpg as Jr.

Other Standouts

PLAYER	POS	HT	HIGH SCHOOL	A-A TEAMS	COLLEGE	CAREER NOTES
82 **Patrick Beverly**	G	6-2	Marshall HS., Chicago		Arkansas	SEC FOY; 12.1 ppg, 6.6 rpg as Soph.; academically ineligible in '09
144 **Ryan Anderson**	PF	6-9	Oak Ridge HS, El Dorado Hills, CA		California	All-Pac-10 as Soph., '07; No. 21 pick, '08 NBA draft (Nets); 7.4 ppg for Nets, '09

Abbreviations: McD=McDonald's; MJ=Jordan Brand; P=Parade; USA=USA Today

Poll Progression

Preseason Poll

AP	ESPN/USA	School
1	1	**Duke**
2	3	**Texas**
3	2	**Connecticut**
4	5	**Michigan State**
5	4	**Villanova**
6	6	**Oklahoma**
7	8	**Louisville**
8	7	**Gonzaga**
9	10	**Kentucky**
10	9	**Arizona**
11	11	**Boston College**
12	12	**Memphis**
13	13	**Stanford**
14	15	**West Virginia**
15	14	**Alabama**
16	16	**Syracuse**
17	17	**Illinois**
18	18	**Wake Forest**
18	18	**UCLA**
20	20	**Iowa**
21	24	**George Washington**
22	25	**Nevada**
23	22	**Indiana**
24	21	**Maryland**
25	23	**Iowa State**

Week of Nov 15 (A)

AP	School	AP↓↑
1	**Duke** (0-0)	
2	**Texas** (0-0)	
3	**Connecticut** (0-0)	
4	**Michigan State** (0-0)	
5	**Villanova** (0-0)	
6	**Oklahoma** (0-0)	
7	**Louisville** (0-0)	
8	**Kentucky** (1-0)	↑1
9	**Gonzaga** (0-0)	↓1
10	**Arizona** (0-0)	
11	**Boston College** (0-0)	
12	**Memphis** (0-0)	
13	**Stanford** (0-0)	
14	**West Virginia** (2-0)	
15	**Alabama** (0-0)	
16	**Syracuse** (2-0)	
17	**Illinois** (0-0)	
18	**UCLA** (0-0)	
19	**Wake Forest** (2-0)	↓1
20	**Iowa** (0-0)	
21	**George Washington** (0-0)	
22	**Nevada** (0-0)	
23	**Indiana** (0-0)	
24	**Maryland** (0-0)	
25	**Iowa State** (0-0)	

Week of Nov 22

AP	ESPN/USA	School	AP↓↑
1	1	**Duke** (3-0)	
2	2	**Texas** (2-0)	
3	3	**Connecticut** (1-0)	
4	4	**Villanova** (1-0)	↑1
5	5	**Oklahoma** (1-0)	↑1
6	6	**Louisville** (1-0)	↑1
7	7	**Kentucky** (2-0)	↑1
8	9	**Gonzaga** (1-0)	↑1
9	8	**Arizona** (0-0)	↑1
10	10	**Boston College** (2-0)	↑1
11	11	**Memphis** (2-0)	↑1
12	12	**Michigan State** (0-1)	↓8
13	13	**West Virginia** (2-0)	↑1
14	15	**Florida** (4-0)	⤴
15	14	**Illinois** (2-0)	↑2
16	16	**UCLA** (3-0)	↑2
17	19	**Syracuse** (3-1)	↓1
18	17	**Iowa** (2-0)	↑2
19	18	**Alabama** (2-1)	↓4
20	21	**Indiana** (1-0)	↑3
21	22	**George Washington** (0-0)	
22	—	**Nevada** (1-0)	
23	20	**Maryland** (1-0)	↑1
24	24	**Wake Forest** (3-1)	↓5
25	—	**Washington** (4-0)	⤴
—	23	**Iowa State** (1-0)	⤵
—	25	**Stanford** (0-1)	⤵

Week of Nov 29

AP	ESPN/USA	School	AP↓↑
1	1	**Duke** (5-0)	
2	2	**Texas** (5-0)	
3	3	**Connecticut** (4-0)	
4	4	**Villanova** (2-0)	
5	5	**Oklahoma** (3-0)	
6	7	**Gonzaga** (3-1)	
7	6	**Louisville** (1-0)	
8	8	**Boston College** (5-0)	
9	9	**Memphis** (3-1)	[illegible]
10	10	**Kentucky** (4-1)	[illegible]
11	11	**Florida** (5-0)	[illegible]
12	12	**Illinois** (5-0)	[illegible]
13	14	**Michigan State** (3-2)	↓[illegible]
14	15	**Iowa** (4-1)	↑[illegible]
15	13	**Arizona** (2-2)	↓[illegible]
16	17	**UCLA** (4-1)	
17	16	**Indiana** (3-0)	↑[illegible]
18	19	**Washington** (6-0)	↑[illegible]
19	22	**George Washington** (2-0)	↑2
20	—	**Nevada** (3-0)	↑2
21	18	**Alabama** (2-1)	↓2
22	23	**Wake Forest** (5-1)	↑2
23	20	**Maryland** (4-1)	
24	21	**NC State** (5-0)	⤴
25	25	**LSU** (3-0)	⤴
—	24	**Syracuse** (4-2)	⤵

Week of Dec 6

AP	ESPN/USA	School	AP↓↑
1	1	**Duke** (7-0)	
2	2	**Texas** (7-0)	
3	3	**Connecticut** (6-0)	
4	4	**Villanova** (4-0)	
5	5	**Louisville** (3-0)	↑2
6	6	**Boston College** (6-0)	↑2
7	7	**Memphis** (6-1)	↑2
8	9	**Oklahoma** (4-1)	↓3
9	11	**Gonzaga** (4-2)	↓3
10	8	**Florida** (7-0)	↑1
11	10	**Illinois** (7-0)	↑1
12	13	**Iowa** (7-1)	↑2
13	12	**Washington** (7-0)	↑5
14	14	**Michigan State** (5-2)	↓1
15	15	**Kentucky** (5-2)	↓5
16	18	**UCLA** (6-1)	
17	22	**Nevada** (5-0)	↑3
18	16	**Indiana** (4-1)	↓1
19	20	**George Washington** (4-0)	
20	21	**Wake Forest** (7-1)	↑2
21	17	**Maryland** (5-1)	↑2
22	19	**Alabama** (4-1)	↓1
23	24	**North Carolina** (4-1)	⤴
24	25	**Arizona** (2-3)	↓9
25	23	**NC State** (5-1)	↓1

Week of Dec 13

AP	ESPN/USA	School	AP↓↑
1	1	**Duke** (9-0)	
2	2	**Connecticut** (7-0)	↑1
3	3	**Villanova** (6-0)	↑1
4	4	**Louisville** (5-0)	↑1
5	5	**Memphis** (7-1)	↑2
6	7	**Texas** (8-1)	↓4
7	6	**Florida** (9-0)	↑3
8	9	**Oklahoma** (5-1)	
9	8	**Illinois** (10-0)	↑2
10	11	**Gonzaga** (6-2)	↓1
11	10	**Washington** (8-0)	↑2
12	12	**Michigan State** (7-2)	↑2
13	13	**Boston College** (6-2)	↓7
14	14	**UCLA** (7-1)	↑2
15	15	**George Washington** (7-0)	↑4
16	16	**Wake Forest** (7-1)	↑4
17	17	**Maryland** (7-2)	↑4
18	18	**Indiana** (5-2)	
19	20	**North Carolina** (5-1)	↑4
20	21	**Nevada** (6-1)	↓3
21	19	**NC State** (6-1)	↑4
22	23	**Iowa** (7-3)	↓10
23	22	**Kentucky** (6-3)	↓8
24	—	**Arizona** (4-3)	
25	—	**Houston** (4-1)	⤴
—	24	**Wisconsin** (8-1)	
—	25	**Ohio State** (5-0)	

Week of Dec 20

AP	ESPN/USA	School	AP↓↑
1	1	**Duke** (10-0)	
2	2	**Connecticut** (8-0)	
3	3	**Villanova** (7-0)	
4	4	**Memphis** (8-1)	↑1
5	5	**Florida** (10-0)	↑2
6	6	**Illinois** (11-0)	↑3
7	8	**Oklahoma** (6-1)	↑1
8	9	**Gonzaga** (7-2)	↑2
9	7	**Washington** (9-0)	↑2
10	11	**Michigan State** (9-2)	↑2
11	10	**Louisville** (6-1)	↓7
12	12	**UCLA** (8-1)	↑2
13	13	**George Washington** (8-0)	↑2
14	14	**Boston College** (7-2)	↓1
15	15	**Texas** (8-2)	↓9
16	16	**Maryland** (7-2)	↑1
17	19	**North Carolina** (6-1)	↑2
18	17	**Indiana** (5-2)	
19	20	**Kentucky** (7-3)	↑4
20	21	**Nevada** (7-1)	
21	18	**NC State** (8-1)	
22	24	**Wake Forest** (8-2)	↓6
23	—	**Tennessee** (6-0)	⤴
24	22	**Ohio State** (7-0)	⤴
25	—	**Iowa** (8-3)	↓3
—	23	**Wisconsin** (9-1)	
—	25	**Pittsburgh** (8-0)	

Week of Dec 27

AP	ESPN/USA	School	AP↓↑
1	1	**Duke** (11-0)	
2	2	**Connecticut** (9-0)	
3	3	**Villanova** (8-0)	
4	4	**Memphis** (9-1)	
5	5	**Florida** (11-0) (B)	
6	6	**Illinois** (12-0)	
7	7	**Washington** (10-0)	↑2
8	8	**Gonzaga** (9-2)	
9	9	**Michigan State** (10-2)	↑1
10	10	**Louisville** (9-1)	↑1
11	11	**UCLA** (10-1)	↑1
12	12	**George Washington** (8-0)	↑1
13	13	**Boston College** (8-2)	↑1
14	15	**Oklahoma** (6-2)	↓7
15	16	**Texas** (9-2)	
16	14	**Maryland** (8-2)	
17	17	**Indiana** (7-2)	↑1
18	19	**Kentucky** (8-3)	↑1
19	18	**NC State** (9-1)	↑2
20	21	**Nevada** (8-1)	
21	20	**Ohio State** (8-0)	↑3
22	24	**Wake Forest** (9-2)	
23	25	**North Carolina** (6-2)	↓6
24	22	**Wisconsin** (9-1)	⤴
25	—	**West Virginia** (7-3)	⤴
—	23	**Pittsburgh** (9-0)	

Week of Jan 3

AP	ESPN/USA	School	AP↓↑
1	1	**Duke** (12-0)	
2	2	**Connecticut** (11-0)	
3	3	**Villanova** (9-0)	
4	4	**Memphis** (11-1)	
5	5	**Florida** (12-0)	
6	6	**Illinois** (14-0)	
7	7	**Michigan State** (12-2)	↑2
8	9	**Gonzaga** (10-3)	
9	8	**Louisville** (11-1)	↑1
10	10	**Washington** (11-1)	↓3
11	11	**Boston College** (10-2)	↑2
12	14	**Oklahoma** (8-2)	↑2
13	12	**NC State** (11-1)	↑6
14	12	**Maryland** (10-2)	↑2
15	16	**Texas** (10-2)	
16	15	**Indiana** (8-2)	↑1
17	17	**UCLA** (11-2)	↓6
18	18	**Ohio State** (10-0)	↑3
19	21	**Kentucky** (9-3)	↓1
20	19	**George Washington** (8-1)	↓8
21	23	**Arizona** (9-3)	⤴
22	20	**Pittsburgh** (11-0)	⤴
23	22	**Wake Forest** (10-2)	↓1
24	—	**West Virginia** (8-3)	↑1
25	25	**North Carolina** (7-2)	↓2
—	24	**Wisconsin** (10-2)	⤵

Week of Jan 10

AP	ESPN/USA	School	AP↓↑
1	1	**Duke** (14-0)	
2	2	**Florida** (14-0)	↑3
3	3	**Villanova** (10-1)	
4	4	**Connecticut** (12-1) (C)	↓2
5	5	**Memphis** (13-2)	↓1
6	7	**Gonzaga** (11-3)	↑2
7	6	**Illinois** (15-1)	↓1
8	9	**Texas** (12-2)	↑7
9	8	**Indiana** (10-2)	↑7
10	10	**Louisville** (12-2)	↓1
11	12	**UCLA** (13-2)	↑6
12	11	**Pittsburgh** (12-0)	↑10
13	13	**Washington** (12-2)	↓3
14	15	**Michigan State** (12-4)	↓7
15	14	**Boston College** (11-3)	↓4
16	23	**West Virginia** (10-3)	↑8
17	19	**George Washington** (10-1)	↑3
18	16	**NC State** (12-2)	↓5
19	16	**Ohio State** (11-1)	↓1
20	20	**North Carolina** (9-2)	↑5
21	17	**Wisconsin** (12-2)	⤴
22	22	**Oklahoma** (9-3)	↓10
23	21	**Maryland** (11-3)	↓9
24	25	**Arizona** (10-4)	↓3
25	—	**Cincinnati** (13-2)	⤴
—	24	**Syracuse** (13-2)	

Week of Jan 17

AP	ESPN/USA	School	AP↓↑
1	1	**Duke** (16-0)	
2	2	**Florida** (16-0)	
3	3	**Connecticut** (14-1)	↑1
4	4	**Memphis** (15-2)	↑1
5	6	**Texas** (14-2)	↑3
6	8	**Gonzaga** (13-3)	
7	5	**Illinois** (16-1)	
8	7	**Villanova** (11-2)	↓5
9	9	**Pittsburgh** (14-0)	↑3
10	10	**Washington** (14-2)	↑3
11	12	**Michigan State** (14-4)	↑3
12	17	**West Virginia** (12-3)	↑4
13	11	**Indiana** (10-3)	↓4
14	14	**NC State** (14-2)	↑4
15	13	**Wisconsin** (14-2)	↑6
16	18	**George Washington** (12-1)	↑1
17	15	**Louisville** (13-3)	⤴
18	16	**UCLA** (14-3)	↓7
19	19	**Ohio State** (12-2)	
20	20	**Syracuse** (15-2)	⤴
21	21	**Boston College** (12-4)	↓6
22	22	**Maryland** (12-4)	↑1
23	25	**Iowa** (13-4)	⤴
24	23	**North Carolina** (10-3)	↓4
25	24	**Oklahoma** (10-4)	↓3

Week of Jan 24

AP	ESPN/USA	School	AP↓↑
1	1	**Connecticut** (16-1)	↑2
2	2	**Duke** (17-1) (D)	↓1
3	3	**Memphis** (17-2)	↑1
4	5	**Texas** (16-2)	↑1
5	4	**Florida** (17-1)	↓3
6	6	**Villanova** (13-2)	↑2
7	7	**Gonzaga** (15-3)	↓1
8	7	**Illinois** (17-2)	↓1
9	13	**West Virginia** (14-3)	↑3
10	9	**Washington** (16-2)	
11	12	**Michigan State** (15-4)	
12	10	**Pittsburgh** (15-1)	↓3
13	11	**Indiana** (12-3)	
14	15	**George Washington** (14-1)	↑2
15	14	**NC State** (15-3)	↓1
16	16	**Ohio State** (14-2)	↑3
17	17	**UCLA** (15-4)	↑1
18	19	**Maryland** (13-4)	↑4
19	20	**Tennessee** (12-3)	⤴
20	18	**Boston College** (14-4)	↑1
21	—	**Georgetown** (12-4) (D)	⤴
22	23	**Louisville** (13-5)	⤴
23	21	**Wisconsin** (14-4)	↓8
24	22	**Oklahoma** (11-4)	↑1
25	24	**Syracuse** (15-4)	↓5
—	25	**North Carolina** (11-4)	⤵

Week of Jan 31

AP	ESPN/USA	SCHOOL	AP↓↑
	1	**Connecticut** (18-1)	
	2	**Duke** (19-1)	
	3	**Memphis** (19-2)	
	4	**Villanova** (15-2)	↑2
	5	**Gonzaga** (17-3)	↑2
	6	**Illinois** (19-2)	↑2
	8	**Texas** (17-3)	↓3
	7	**Florida** (18-2)	↓3
	9	**Pittsburgh** (17-1)	↑3
	10	**George Washington** (16-1)	↑4
	11	**West Virginia** (15-4)	↓2
	12	**Michigan State** (16-5)	↓1
	16	**Tennessee** (14-3)	↑6
	13	**UCLA** (17-4)	↑3
	14	**Boston College** (16-4)	↑5
	15	**Washington** (16-4)	↓6
	22	**Georgetown** (14-4)	↑4
	17	**NC State** (16-4)	↓3
	18	**Oklahoma** (13-4)	↑5
	19	**Ohio State** (14-3)	↓4
	20	**Michigan** (15-3)	⤴
22	21	**Indiana** (12-5)	↓9
23	—	**Iowa** (16-5)	⤴
24	—	**LSU** (14-5)	⤴
25	24	**Northern Iowa** (19-3)	⤴
—	23	**Maryland** (14-5)	⤵
—	25	**Colorado** (15-3)	

Week of Feb 7

AP	ESPN/USA	SCHOOL	AP↓↑
1	1	**Connecticut** (20-1)	
2	2	**Duke** (21-1)	
3	3	**Memphis** (21-2)	
4	4	**Villanova** (17-2)	
5	5	**Gonzaga** (18-3)	
6	7	**Texas** (19-3)	↑1
7	6	**Florida** (20-2)	↑1
8	8	**George Washington** (18-1)	↑2
9	10	**West Virginia** (17-4)	↑2
10	9	**Illinois** (20-3)	↓4
11	14	**Tennessee** (16-3)	↑2
12	11	**Michigan State** (17-5)	
13	12	**UCLA** (19-4)	↑1
14	13	**Pittsburgh** (17-3)	↓5
15	16	**Georgetown** (16-4)	↑2
16	15	**NC State** (18-4)	↑2
17	18	**Boston College** (17-5)	↓2
18	19	**Iowa** (18-5)	↑5
19	17	**Ohio State** (16-3)	↑1
20	20	**Oklahoma** (14-5)	↓1
21	23	**Washington** (16-5)	↓5
22	22	**Michigan** (16-4)	↓1
23	24	**North Carolina** (14-5)	⤴
24	21	**Indiana** (13-6)	↓2
25	—	**Northern Iowa** (20-4)	
—	25	**Colorado** (15-4)	

Week of Feb 14

AP	ESPN/USA	SCHOOL	AP↓↑
1	1	**Connecticut** (22-1)	
2	2	**Duke** (23-1) Ⓔ	
3	3	**Memphis** (22-2)	
4	4	**Villanova** (19-2)	
5	5	**Gonzaga** (20-3)	
6	6	**Texas** (21-3)	
7	8	**George Washington** (20-1)	↑1
8	10	**Tennessee** (18-3)	↑3
9	9	**Pittsburgh** (19-3)	↑5
10	7	**Florida** (21-3) Ⓕ	↓3
11	11	**West Virginia** (18-5)	↓2
12	12	**Ohio State** (18-3)	↑7
13	15	**Boston College** (19-5)	↑4
14	13	**Illinois** (20-4)	↓4
15	14	**UCLA** (20-5)	↓2
16	16	**Michigan State** (18-6)	↓4
17	17	**Georgetown** (17-5)	↓2
18	20	**Iowa** (19-6)	
19	19	**Oklahoma** (16-5)	↑1
20	21	**Washington** (18-5)	↑1
21	18	**NC State** (19-5)	↓5
22	22	**Kansas** (17-6)	⤴
23	23	**North Carolina** (15-6)	
24	24	**Bucknell** (20-3)	⤴
25	25	**LSU** (16-7)	⤴

Week of Feb 21

AP	ESPN/USA	SCHOOL	AP↓↑
1	1	**Duke** (25-1)	↑1
2	2	**Villanova** (21-2)	↑2
3	4	**Connecticut** (23-2)	↓2
4	3	**Memphis** (24-2)	↓1
5	5	**Gonzaga** (22-3)	
6	6	**George Washington** (22-1)	↑1
7	7	**Texas** (22-4)	↓1
8	8	**Illinois** (22-4)	↑6
9	10	**Pittsburgh** (20-4)	
10	11	**Tennessee** (19-4)	↓2
11	13	**Boston College** (21-5)	↑2
12	9	**Florida** (22-4)	↓2
13	12	**Ohio State** (19-4)	↓1
14	15	**West Virginia** (18-7)	↓3
15	14	**NC State** (21-5)	↑6
16	18	**Kansas** (19-6)	↑6
17	19	**Washington** (20-5)	↑3
18	16	**Michigan State** (19-7)	↓2
19	17	**UCLA** (20-6)	↓4
20	22	**Iowa** (20-7)	↓2
21	21	**North Carolina** (17-6)	↑2
22	20	**Oklahoma** (17-6)	↓3
23	23	**Georgetown** (17-7)	↓6
24	24	**LSU** (18-7)	↑1
25	—	**Northern Iowa** (22-6)	⤴
25	—	**Nevada** (20-5)	⤴
—	25	**George Mason** (21-5)	

Week of Feb 28

AP	ESPN/USA	SCHOOL	AP↓↑
1	1	**Duke** (27-1)	
2	2	**Connecticut** (25-2)	↑1
3	3	**Memphis** (26-2)	↑1
4	4	**Villanova** (22-3)	↓2
5	5	**Gonzaga** (24-3)	
6	7	**Texas** (24-4)	↑1
7	6	**George Washington** (24-1)	↓1
8	9	**Pittsburgh** (21-4)	↑1
9	8	**Ohio State** (21-4)	↑4
10	10	**Illinois** (23-5)	↓2
11	11	**Tennessee** (20-5)	↓1
12	12	**Boston College** (22-6)	↓1
13	15	**North Carolina** (19-6)	↑8
14	16	**Washington** (22-5)	↑3
15	13	**UCLA** (22-6)	↑4
16	18	**West Virginia** (19-8)	↓2
17	14	**Florida** (22-6)	↓5
18	22	**Kansas** (20-7)	↓2
19	17	**Oklahoma** (19-6)	↑3
20	20	**Georgetown** (19-7)	↑3
21	21	**LSU** (20-7)	↑3
22	19	**NC State** (21-7)	↓7
23	24	**Iowa** (20-8)	↓3
24	—	**Nevada** (22-5)	↑1
25	23	**Michigan State** (19-9)	↓7
—	25	**Wisconsin** (19-8)	

Week of Mar 7

AP	ESPN/USA	SCHOOL	AP↓↑
1	1	**Connecticut** (27-2)	↑1
2	2	**Villanova** (24-3)	↑2
3	3	**Duke** (27-3)	↓2
4	4	**Gonzaga** (26-3)	↑1
5	5	**Memphis** (27-3)	↓2
6	6	**George Washington** (26-1)	↑1
7	7	**Ohio State** (23-4)	↑2
8	8	**Texas** (25-5)	↓2
9	9	**Illinois** (25-5)	↑1
10	10	**North Carolina** (21-6)	↑3
11	11	**Boston College** (24-6)	↑1
12	13	**Washington** (24-5)	↑2
13	12	**UCLA** (24-6)	↑2
14	15	**Tennessee** (21-6)	↓3
15	16	**Pittsburgh** (21-6)	↓7
16	14	**Florida** (24-6) Ⓖ	↑1
17	17	**LSU** (22-7)	↑4
17	18	**Kansas** (22-7)	↑1
19	21	**West Virginia** (20-9)	↓3
20	20	**Iowa** (22-8)	↑3
21	24	**Nevada** (24-5)	↑3
22	19	**Oklahoma** (20-7)	↓3
23	23	**Georgetown** (19-8)	↓3
24	25	**UAB** (22-5)	⤴
25	22	**NC State** (21-8)	↓3

Week of Mar 14

AP	ESPN/USA	SCHOOL	AP↓↑
1	1	**Duke** (30-3)	↑2
2	2	**Connecticut** (27-3)	↓1
3	4	**Villanova** (25-4)	↓1
4	3	**Memphis** (30-3)	↑1
5	5	**Gonzaga** (27-3)	↓1
6	6	**Ohio State** (25-5)	↑1
7	7	**Boston College** (26-7)	↑4
7	8	**UCLA** (27-6)	↑6
9	9	**Texas** (27-6)	↓1
10	12	**North Carolina** (22-7)	
11	10	**Florida** (27-6)	↑5
12	13	**Kansas** (25-7)	↑5
13	14	**Illinois** (25-6)	↓4
14	11	**George Washington** (26-2)	↓8
15	15	**Iowa** (25-8)	↑5
16	16	**Pittsburgh** (24-7)	↓1
17	17	**Washington** (24-6)	↓5
18	19	**Tennessee** (21-7)	↓4
19	18	**LSU** (23-8)	↓2
20	21	**Nevada** (27-5)	↑1
21	22	**Syracuse** (23-11)	⤴
22	23	**West Virginia** (20-10)	↓3
23	24	**Georgetown** (21-9)	
24	20	**Oklahoma** (20-8)	↓2
25	25	**UAB** (24-6)	↓1

FINAL POLL (Post-Tournament)

ESPN/USA	SCHOOL
1	**Florida** (33-6)
2	**UCLA** (32-7)
3	**LSU** (27-9)
4	**Connecticut** (30-4)
5	**Villanova** (28-5)
6	**Memphis** (33-4)
7	**Duke** (32-4)
8	**George Mason** (27-8)
9	**Texas** (30-7)
10	**Gonzaga** (29-4)
11	**Boston College** (28-8)
12	**Washington** (26-7)
13	**Ohio State** (26-6)
14	**North Carolina** (23-8)
15	**West Virginia** (22-11)
16	**Georgetown** (23-10)
17	**Illinois** (26-7)
18	**Pittsburgh** (25-8)
19	**George Washington** (27-3)
20	**Tennessee** (22-8)
21	**Wichita State** (26-9)
22	**Kansas** (25-8)
23	**Iowa** (25-9)
24	**Bradley** (22-11)
25	**Bucknell** (27-5)

Ⓐ Columbia defeats New Hampshire, 64-61, on Nov. 18 as Lions guard K.J. Matsui becomes the first Japanese-born player to compete in Division I basketball. The Tokyo native goes 0-for-5 from the floor in 18 minutes of action.

Ⓑ In a Dec. 18 victory over Jacksonville, Florida's Corey Brewer gets 15 points, 10 rebounds and 13 assists—the first triple-double in Gator history.

Ⓒ In his first Big East game, Marquette's Steve Novak scores 41 points and grabs 16 boards in a stunning upset of Connecticut. It's the most points any player has scored in his Big East debut.

Ⓓ After eight straight losses to top-ranked teams dating back to 1985, Georgetown upends Duke, 87-84, on Jan. 21.

Ⓔ Duke's J.J. Redick knocks down four three-pointers in a win over Wake Forest, giving him 416 for his career—an NCAA record. He will end up with 457 treys.

Ⓕ South Carolina fans rush the floor after a 71-67 upset of Florida. The SEC fines South Carolina $5,000 and promises a $25,000 fine for any repeat, citing the rule that fans must be denied "access to the competition area."

Ⓖ Florida ruins Kentucky's Senior Day, drilling the Wildcats, 79-64, on March 5. It's the second victory in what will turn out to be an 11-game winning streak that carries the Gators to their first NCAA title.

Pre-Tournament Ratings Percentage Index (RPI)

RANK	SCHOOL	W-L	Sched. Strg.	SS Rank	RPI
1	**Duke**	29-3	.6288	2	.6809
2	**Villanova**	25-4	.6201	6	.6667
3	**Memphis**	30-3	.5889	26	.6511
4	**Connecticut**	27-3	.5649	50	.6509
5	**Ohio State**	25-4	.5802	31	.6459
6	**Tennessee**	21-7	.6276	3	.6341
7	**Texas**	27-5	.5684	46	.6338
8	**Gonzaga**	27-3	.5261	105	.6254
9	**UCLA**	27-6	.5875	27	.6253
10	**Iowa**	24-8	.5788	33	.6245
11	**Pittsburgh**	24-7	.5735	40	.6233
12	**North Carolina**	22-7	.6090	10	.6229
13	**LSU**	22-8	.6019	13	.6222
14	**Illinois**	25-6	.5569	60	.6205
15	**Oklahoma**	20-8	.5921	24	.6127
16	**Florida**	26-6	.5452	76	.6113
17	**Syracuse**	23-11	.6345	1	.6107
18	**Michigan State**	21-11	.6126	9	.6094
19	**Nevada**	26-5	.5267	103	.6063
20	**Missouri State**	20-8	.5770	35	.6030
21	**Boston College**	25-6	.5383	99	.6025
22	**Arizona**	19-12	.6204	5	.6018
23	**Wisconsin**	19-11	.6131	8	.6007
24	**Northern Iowa**	21-9	.5785	34	.5989
25	**Kansas**	23-7	.5537	64	.5986
26	**George Mason**	23-7	.5430	80	.5985
27	**UNC Wilmington**	25-7	.5269	102	.5982
28	**Wichita State**	23-8	.5607	54	.5982
29	**Southern Illinois**	22-9	.5585	68	.5980
30	**Hofstra**	24-6	.5148	133	.5971
31	**Marquette**	19-10	.5928	23	.5965
32	**UAB**	23-6	.5181	123	.5944
33	**Indiana**	18-11	.5958	19	.5939
34	**Bradley**	20-10	.5659	47	.5934
35	**West Virginia**	19-10	.5871	28	.5923
36	**Washington**	24-6	.5286	98	.5922
37	**George Washington**	26-2	.4599	243	.5919
38	**Georgetown**	21-9	.5441	77	.5919
39	**Creighton**	19-9	.5618	53	.5906
40	**Cincinnati**	18-12	.6179	7	.5896
41	**Kentucky**	21-12	.5949	20	.5892
42	**Bucknell**	25-4	.4812	192	.5865
43	**Saint Joseph's**	18-13	.6011	14	.5865
44	**Texas A&M**	21-8	.5535	65	.5858
45	**Arkansas**	22-9	.5395	86	.5830
46	**Michigan**	18-10	.5697	45	.5817
47	**Utah State**	22-8	.5296	97	.5813
48	**Maryland**	18-12	.6084	11	.5806
49	**Kent State**	24-8	.5299	96	.5805
50	**NC State**	21-9	.5518	68	.5796

Source: NCAA.

ANNUAL REVIEW

2006 NCAA Tournament

First Round	Second Round	Regional Semifinals	Regional Finals

Atlanta

First Round
1 Duke **70**
16 Southern **54**

8 George Washington **88** (OT)
9 UNC Wilmington **85**

5 Syracuse **58** (A)
12 Texas A&M **66**

4 LSU **80** (B)
13 Iona **64**

6 West Virginia **64**
11 Southern Illinois **46**

3 Iowa **63** (C)
14 Northwestern State **64**

7 California **52**
10 NC State **58**

2 Texas **60**
15 Pennsylvania **52**

Second Round
Duke **74**
George Washington **61**

Texas A&M **57**
LSU **58**

West Virginia **67**
Northwestern State **54**

NC State **54**
Texas **75**

Regional Semifinals
Duke **54**
LSU **62**

West Virginia **71**
Texas **74**

Regional Final
LSU **70** (OT)
Texas **60**

Oakland

First Round
1 Memphis **94**
16 Oral Roberts **78**

8 Arkansas **55**
9 Bucknell **59**

5 Pittsburgh **79**
12 Kent State **64**

4 Kansas **73**
13 Bradley **77**

6 Indiana **87**
11 San Diego State **83**

3 Gonzaga **79**
14 Xavier **75**

7 Marquette **85**
10 Alabama **90**

2 UCLA **78**
15 Belmont **44**

Second Round
Memphis **72**
Bucknell **56**

Pittsburgh **66** (D)
Bradley **72**

Indiana **80** (E)
Gonzaga **90**

Alabama **59**
UCLA **62**

Regional Semifinals
Memphis **80**
Bradley **64**

Gonzaga **71**
UCLA **73**

Regional Final
Memphis **45** (F)
UCLA **50**

Washington, DC

First Round
1 Connecticut **72**
16 Albany (NY) **59**

8 Kentucky **69**
9 UAB **64**

5 Washington **75**
12 Utah State **61**

4 Illinois **78**
13 Air Force **69**

6 Michigan State **65**
11 George Mason **75**

3 North Carolina **69**
14 Murray State **65**

7 Wichita State **86**
10 Seton Hall **66**

2 Tennessee **63**
15 Winthrop **61**

Second Round
Connecticut **87** (G)
Kentucky **83**

Washington **67**
Illinois **64**

George Mason **65**
North Carolina **60**

Wichita State **80**
Tennessee **73**

Regional Semifinals
Connecticut **98** (OT)
Washington **92**

George Mason **63**
Wichita State **55**

Regional Final
Connecticut **84** (OT) (H)
George Mason **86**

Minneapolis

First Round
1 Villanova **58**
16 *Monmouth **45**

8 Arizona **94**
9 Wisconsin **75**

5 Nevada **79**
12 Montana **87**

4 Boston College **88** (OT)
13 Pacific **76**

6 Oklahoma **74**
11 Wisconsin-Milwaukee **82**

3 Florida **76**
14 South Alabama **50**

7 Georgetown **54**
10 Northern Iowa **49**

2 Ohio State **70**
15 Davidson **62**

Second Round
Villanova **82**
Arizona **78**

Montana **56**
Boston College **69**

Wisconsin-Milwaukee **60**
Florida **82**

Georgetown **70**
Ohio State **52**

Regional Semifinals
Villanova **60** (OT)
Boston College **59**

Florida **57**
Georgetown **53**

Regional Final
Villanova **62**
Florida **75**

National Semifinal

LSU **45**
UCLA **59**

LSU's 45 points is its lowest Tournament output ever, and second-lowest in a Final Four game since the NCAA adopted the shot clock in 1986. Wisconsin holds the shot-clock era record low of 41, thanks to Michigan State's defense in the 2000 Final Four.

National Final

Florida 73
UCLA 57

The Gators literally slam UCLA, with seven of their last eight baskets being dunks. Tourney MOP Joakim Noah dominates with 16 points, 9 rebounds and a title-game record 6 blocks. Rick Pitino, who coached Billy Donovan at Providence and hired him as an assistant at Kentucky, watches from the stands wearing an orange Florida tie.

Indianapolis

National Semifinal

George Mason **58**
Florida **73**

For just the second time, no No. 1 seed reaches the Final Four. The last time all four fell short of the national semis was 1980. In this game, the Patriots' bombers go cold while the Gators shoot better from beyond the three-point arc (12 for 25, or 48%) than they do inside it (39%).

A The Orangemen earned an unexpected Tournament berth when Gerry McNamara carried them to the Big East Tournament title a week earlier. The ride ends abruptly when Texas A&M's Acie Law IV scores a dozen of his 23 points in the final 2:25.

B Iona's Steve Burtt Jr. gets 23 points to become the second-leading scorer in Gaels history, with 2,034 points. His father, Steve Burtt Sr., is No. 1 with 2,534. They become the NCAA's leading father-son career scoring leaders.

C In Northwestern State's second Tournament appearance in five years, the Demons fight back from a 17-point second-half deficit and Jermaine Wallace hits a fadeaway three-pointer with :01 left for the win.

D In Bradley's first Tournament in 10 years, Patrick O'Bryant gets 28 points and seven rebounds. With the win, the Braves advance to their first round of 16 in 51 years.

E The Hoosiers hold the Zags' Adam Morrison to 14 points, but five other Bulldogs score in double figures. It is Indiana's last game under embattled coach Mike Davis, who had announced his resignation earlier in the season.

F UCLA wins the lowest-scoring regional final of the shot-clock era. The Bruins tie North Carolina for the most Final Four appearances (16), although their 1980 appearance was vacated.

G This is the first meeting between the Huskies and Wildcats in 208 years of combined basketball history. In June, UConn will become the first team to have five players selected in the two-round NBA draft.

H After dropping traditional powers Michigan State and North Carolina (and upstart Wichita State), George Mason rallies from a nine-point deficit to become the first double-digit seed to crack the Final Four since LSU in 1986.

***Opening round:** Monmouth d. Hampton 71-49 ⊘Team participation later vacated

Tournament Leaders

Individual Leaders

Scoring	CL	POS	G	PTS	PPG
1 **Adam Morrison**, Gonzaga	JR	F	3	73	24.3
2 **Randy Foye**, Villanova	SR	G	4	95	23.8
3 **Brandon Roy**, Washington	SR	G	3	69	23.0
4 **Shelden Williams**, Duke	SR	F	3	69	23.0
5 **Craig Smith**, Boston College	SR	F	3	61	20.3
6 **Marcus Williams**, Connecticut	JR	G	4	80	20.0
7 **J.J. Redick**, Duke	SR	G	3	60	20.0
8 **Glen Davis**, LSU	SO	F	5	97	19.4
9 **Jared Dudley**, Boston College	JR	F	3	57	19.0
10 **Marcellus Sommerville**, Bradley	SR	F	3	57	19.0

Minimum: 3 games

Field Goal Pct	CL	POS	G	FG	FGA	PCT
1 **Ryan Hollins**, UCLA	SR	C	6	23	32	71.9
2 **Tyrus Thomas**, LSU	FR	F	5	21	31	67.7
3 **Folarin Campbell**, George Mason	SO	G/F	5	25	40	62.5
Roy Hibbert, Georgetown	SO	C	3	20	32	62.5
5 **Al Horford**, Florida	SO	F/C	6	29	51	56.9

Minimum: 15 made and 3 games

Free Throw Pct	CL	POS	G	FT	FTA	PCT
1 **Marcus Williams**, Connecticut	JR	G	4	22	23	95.7
2 **Marcellus Sommerville**, Bradley	SR	F	3	18	20	90.0
3 **Taurean Green**, Florida	SO	G	6	26	29	89.7
4 **Randy Foye**, Villanova	SR	G	4	24	28	85.7
Folarin Campbell, George Mason	SO	G/F	5	18	21	85.7
Ronald Steele, Alabama	SO	G	2	18	21	85.7

Minimum: 15 made

Three-Point FG Pct	CL	POS	G	3FG	3FGA	PCT
1 **Marcus Williams**, Connecticut	JR	G	4	10	18	55.6
2 **Corey Brewer**, Florida	SO	G/F	6	13	25	52.0
3 **Folarin Campbell**, George Mason	SO	G/F	5	9	18	50.0
Antonio Anderson, Memphis	FR	G	4	7	14	50.0
Ashanti Cook, Georgetown	SR	G	3	6	12	50.0

Minimum: 6 made and 3 games

Assists Per Game	CL	POS	G	AST	APG
1 **Marcus Williams**, Connecticut	JR	G	4	35	8.8
2 **Greg Paulus**, Duke	FR	G	3	18	6.0
3 **Louis Hinnant**, Boston College	SR	G	3	16	5.3
4 **Daniel Ruffin**, Bradley	SO	G	3	15	5.0
5 **J.D. Collins**, West Virginia	SR	G	3	13	4.3
Jeff Green, Georgetown	SO	F	3	13	4.3
Craig Smith, Boston College	SR	F	3	13	4.3

Minimum: 3 games

Rebounds Per Game	CL	POS	G	REB	RPG
1 **Shelden Williams**, Duke	SR	F	3	45	15.0
2 **Craig Smith**, Boston College	SR	F	3	43	14.3
3 **P.J. Tucker**, Texas	JR	G/F	4	50	12.5
4 **Patrick O'Bryant**, Bradley	SO	C	3	31	10.3
LaMarcus Aldridge, Texas	SO	F/C	4	41	10.3

Minimum: 3 games

Blocked Shots Per Game	CL	POS	G	BLK	BPG
1 **Shelden Williams**, Duke	SR	F	3	15	5.0
2 **Joakim Noah**, Florida	SO	F/C	6	29	4.8
3 **Tyrus Thomas**, LSU	FR	F	5	17	3.4
4 **Sean Williams**, Boston College	SO	C	3	9	3.0
5 **Roy Hibbert**, Georgetown	SO	C	3	7	2.3
Josh McRoberts, Duke	FR	F	3	7	2.3

Minimum: 3 games

Steals Per Game	CL	POS	G	STL	SPG
1 **Jamaal Williams**, Washington	SR	F	3	11	3.7
2 **Randy Foye**, Villanova	SR	G	4	11	2.8
3 **J.D. Collins**, West Virginia	SR	G	3	7	2.3
Greg Paulus, Duke	FR	G	3	7	2.3
5 **Kyle Lowry**, Villanova	SO	G	4	9	2.3
Darius Washington, Memphis	SO	G	4	9	2.3

Minimum: 3 games

Team Leaders

Scoring	G	PTS	PPG
1 **Connecticut**	4	341	85.3
2 **Gonzaga**	3	240	80.0
3 **Washington**	3	234	78.0
4 **Wichita State**	3	221	73.7
5 **Memphis**	4	291	72.8
6 **Florida**	6	436	72.7
7 **Boston College**	3	216	72.0
8 **Bradley**	3	213	71.0
9 **George Mason**	5	347	69.4
10 **West Virginia**	3	202	67.3

Minimum: 3 games

FG Pct	G	FG	FGA	PCT
1 **Connecticut**	4	116	225	51.6
2 **Memphis**	4	108	223	48.4
3 **Gonzaga**	3	78	162	48.1
4 **George Mason**	5	125	267	46.8
5 **Boston College**	3	79	169	46.7

Minimum: 3 games

3-Pt FG Pct	G	3FG	3FGA	PCT
1 **Bradley**	3	18	43	41.9
2 **Connecticut**	4	29	70	41.4
3 **George Mason**	5	28	73	38.4
4 **West Virginia**	3	33	87	37.9
5 **Florida**	6	45	119	37.8

Minimum: 3 games

FT Pct	G	FT	FTA	PCT
1 **Florida**	6	93	116	80.2
2 **Villanova**	4	72	90	80.0
3 **Gonzaga**	3	73	94	77.7
4 **Texas**	4	59	76	77.6
5 **Duke**	3	56	73	76.7

Minimum: 3 games

Ast/TO Ratio	G	AST	TO	RAT
1 **Georgetown**	3	48	29	1.66
2 **Boston College**	3	56	37	1.51
3 **West Virginia**	3	45	33	1.36
4 **Florida**	6	88	70	1.26
5 **Texas**	4	57	46	1.24

Minimum: 3 games

Rebounds	G	REB	RPG
1 **Texas**	4	170	42.5
2 **Florida**	6	242	40.3
3 **Duke**	3	118	39.3
4 **LSU**	5	194	38.8
5 **Wichita State**	3	113	37.7
Boston College	3	113	37.7

Minimum: 3 games

Blocks	G	BLK	BPG
1 **LSU**	5	40	8.0
2 **Duke**	3	23	7.7
3 **Florida**	6	44	7.3
4 **Boston College**	3	17	5.7
5 **Connecticut**	4	18	4.5

Minimum: 3 games

Steals	G	STL	SPG
1 **Washington**	3	35	11.7
2 **Memphis**	4	38	9.5
3 **Villanova**	4	36	9.0
4 **West Virginia**	3	24	8.0
5 **Duke**	3	22	7.3

Minimum: 3 games

All-Tournament Team

PLAYER	CL	POS	HT	SCHOOL	RPG	APG	PPG
Joakim Noah*	SO	F/C	6-11	Florida	9.5	3.2	16.2
Corey Brewer	SO	G/F	6-9	Florida	4.8	2.3	13.8
Jordan Farmar	SO	G	6-2	UCLA	1.8	4.0	12.5
Taurean Green	SO	G	6-0	Florida	3.0	3.8	10.5
Lee Humphrey	JR	G	6-2	Florida	2.0	1.5	12.8

All-Regional Teams

Atlanta

PLAYER	CL	POS	HT	SCHOOL	RPG	APG	PPG
Tyrus Thomas*	FR	F	6-9	LSU	9.3	1.0	11.5
LaMarcus Aldridge	SO	F/C	6-11	Texas	10.3	1.0	14.8
Glen Davis	SO	F	6-9	LSU	8.8	1.0	20.8
P.J. Tucker	JR	G/F	6-5	Texas	12.5	3.8	14.8
Shelden Williams	SR	F	6-9	Duke	15.0	0.3	23.0

Minneapolis

PLAYER	CL	POS	HT	SCHOOL	RPG	APG	PPG
Joakim Noah*	SO	F/C	6-11	Florida	10.0	3.5	17.3
Randy Foye	SR	G	6-4	Villanova	7.3	2.0	23.8
Taurean Green	SO	G	6-0	Florida	2.8	3.8	11.5
Al Horford	SO	F/C	6-10	Florida	10.0	2.0	12.8
Craig Smith	SR	F	6-7	Boston College	14.3	4.3	20.3

Oakland

PLAYER	CL	POS	HT	SCHOOL	RPG	APG	PPG
Ryan Hollins*	SR	C	7-0	UCLA	6.3	0.3	12.0
Arron Afflalo	SO	G	6-5	UCLA	3.5	0.5	12.5
Jordan Farmar	SO	G	6-2	UCLA	1.3	4.3	11.3
Adam Morrison	JR	F	6-8	Gonzaga	5.3	2.0	24.3
Darius Washington	SO	G	6-2	Memphis	2.5	1.8	13.3

Washington, DC

PLAYER	CL	POS	HT	SCHOOL	RPG	APG	PPG
Lamar Butler*	SR	G	6-2	George Mason	3.3	1.3	16.0
Folarin Campbell	SO	G/F	6-4	George Mason	5.0	3.3	16.8
Rudy Gay	SO	F	6-9	Connecticut	4.3	1.3	14.8
Jamaal Williams	SR	F	6-6	Washington	5.3	0.7	17.3
Marcus Williams	JR	G	6-3	Connecticut	3.5	8.8	20.0

* Most outstanding player

2006 NCAA TOURNAMENT BOX SCORES

LSU 62-54 Duke (Sweet 16)

31	1H	27
31	2H	27

LSU	MIN	FG	3FG	FT	REB	A	ST	BL	PF	TP
Darrel Mitchell	38	6-16	1-2	1-2	6	5	2	0	1	14
Glen Davis	27	3-12	0-0	8-13	5	0	0	0	4	14
Tasmin Mitchell	40	5-10	0-2	0-0	10	3	1	1	1	10
Darnell Lazare	18	5-8	0-0	0-0	3	2	1	0	1	10
Tyrus Thomas	25	3-5	0-0	3-6	13	1	1	5	4	9
Garrett Temple	40	1-6	1-3	0-0	2	3	2	1	3	3
Magnum Rolle	10	1-4	0-0	0-2	3	0	0	2	2	2
Ben Voogd	2	0-0	0-0	0-0	0	0	0	0	0	0
TOTALS	200	24-61	2-7	12-23	42	14	7	9	16	62
Percentages		39.3	28.6	52.2						

Coach: John Brady

DUKE	MIN	FG	3FG	FT	REB	A	ST	BL	PF	TP
Shelden Williams	39	8-18	0-1	7-8	13	0	0	4	4	23
J.J. Redick	39	3-18	3-9	2-2	2	1	3	0	0	11
Josh McRoberts	35	4-10	0-2	1-2	10	2	1	1	5	9
Greg Paulus	36	2-8	1-5	2-2	1	4	2	0	5	7
DeMarcus Nelson	16	1-5	1-4	1-2	5	2	0	0	0	4
Sean Dockery	26	0-4	0-4	0-0	4	2	3	0	3	0
Lee Melchionni	9	0-2	0-1	0-0	3	1	0	0	1	0
Eric Boateng	0	0-0	0-0	0-0	0	0	0	0	0	0
Jamal Boykin	0	0-0	0-0	0-0	0	0	0	0	0	0
Martynas Pocius	0	0-0	0-0	0-0	0	0	0	0	0	0
TOTALS	200	18-65	5-26	13-16	38	12	9	5	18	54
Percentages		27.7	19.2	81.2						

Coach: Mike Krzyzewski

Officials: J Burr, David Bruce Hick **Technicals:** None **Attendance:** 27,633

Texas 74-71 West Virginia (Sweet 16)

39	1H	27
35	2H	44

TEXAS	MIN	FG	3FG	FT	REB	A	ST	BL	PF	TP
LaMarcus Aldridge	37	11-15	0-0	4-8	13	2	0	0	2	26
P.J. Tucker	36	5-9	0-0	5-6	14	4	0	0	3	15
A.J. Abrams	29	3-10	1-5	2-2	0	7	2	0	3	9
Mike Williams	20	4-4	0-0	1-2	7	0	1	1	1	9
Kenton Paulino	30	3-9	2-7	0-0	1	1	0	0	0	8
Brad Buckman	17	1-3	0-1	2-2	4	1	2	0	0	4
Daniel Gibson	30	1-8	1-6	0-0	4	4	3	0	3	3
J.D. Lewis	1	0-0	0-0	0-0	0	0	0	0	0	0
TOTALS	200	28-58	4-19	14-20	43	19	8	1	12	74
Percentages		48.3	21.1	70.0						

Coach: Rick Barnes

WEST VIRGINIA	MIN	FG	3FG	FT	REB	A	ST	BL	PF	TP
Kevin Pittsnogle	36	7-15	5-9	0-0	3	0	1	0	3	19
Mike Gansey	29	6-12	3-7	3-3	5	1	0	0	0	18
Patrick Beilein	26	5-7	4-6	0-0	0	4	0	1	5	14
Johannes Herber	35	4-12	2-5	3-4	4	4	0	0	2	13
J.D. Collins	30	2-5	0-2	0-0	2	6	2	0	1	4
Frank Young	28	1-4	1-4	0-1	1	1	0	0	1	3
Darris Nichols	10	0-0	0-0	0-0	0	3	0	0	2	0
Rob Summers	4	0-0	0-0	0-0	0	0	0	0	0	0
Alex Ruoff	2	0-0	0-0	0-0	0	0	0	0	0	0
TOTALS	200	25-55	15-33	6-8	15	19	3	1	14	71
Percentages		45.5	45.5	75.0						

Coach: John Beilein

Officials: Ran McCall, Mike Sanzere, Gary Maxwell **Technicals:** None **Attendance:** 27,633

Memphis 80-64 Bradley (Sweet 16)

35	1H	30
45	2H	34

MEMPHIS	MIN	FG	3FG	FT	REB	A	ST	BL	PF	TP
Rodney Carney	35	7-12	2-5	7-8	4	1	3	0	2	23
Darius Washington	28	8-14	1-3	1-2	3	1	1	0	1	18
Shawne Williams	32	4-8	1-2	3-4	8	0	1	4	3	12
Antonio Anderson	28	3-6	2-4	0-0	5	1	1	1	2	8
Joey Dorsey	30	3-9	0-0	0-2	11	3	2	0	3	6
Chris Douglas-Roberts	12	2-3	0-0	0-0	1	0	0	0	0	4
Andre Allen	16	1-2	0-0	1-2	3	5	2	0	3	3
Kareem Cooper	8	1-2	0-1	0-0	2	0	0	0	1	2
Robert Dozier	6	1-2	0-0	0-0	0	0	0	1	3	2
Clyde Wade	1	1-1	0-0	0-0	1	0	0	0	0	2
Lamont Long	1	0-0	0-0	0-0	0	0	0	1	0	0
Chance McGrady	1	0-0	0-0	0-0	0	0	0	0	0	0
Jared Sandridge	1	0-1	0-0	0-0	0	0	0	0	0	0
Waki Williams	1	0-0	0-0	0-0	0	0	0	0	0	0
TOTALS	200	31-60	6-15	12-18	38	11	10	7	18	80
Percentages		51.7	40.0	66.7						

Coach: John Calipari

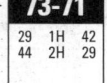

BRADLEY	MIN	FG	3FG	FT	REB	A	ST	BL	PF	TP
Marcellus Sommerville	28	4-13	1-4	9-10	8	0	1	1	4	18
Lawrence Wright	28	5-13	0-1	4-4	6	0	0	0	2	14
Tony Bennett	25	4-13	1-2	0-0	0	0	1	0	5	9
Patrick O'Bryant	33	3-7	0-0	2-5	14	0	0	1	2	8
Daniel Ruffin	30	2-5	1-2	2-4	1	4	1	0	3	7
Will Franklin	25	2-6	2-5	0-0	2	2	0	0	1	6
JJ Tauai	20	0-0	0-0	2-4	1	0	0	0	0	2
Zach Andrews	6	0-1	0-0	0-0	1	0	0	0	1	0
Jeremy Crouch	2	0-1	0-1	0-0	0	0	0	0	0	0
Danny Adams	1	0-0	0-0	0-0	0	0	0	0	0	0
Ray Brown	1	0-1	0-1	0-0	0	0	0	0	0	0
Brandyn Heemskerk	1	0-0	0-0	0-0	0	0	0	0	0	0
TOTALS	200	20-60	5-16	19-27	33	6	3	2	18	64
Percentages		33.3	31.2	70.4						

Coach: Jim Les

Officials: Bryan Kersey, Karl Hess, Ted Valentine **Technicals:** None **Attendance:** 19,596

UCLA 73-71 Gonzaga (Sweet 16)

29	1H	42
44	2H	29

UCLA	MIN	FG	3FG	FT	REB	A	ST	BL	PF	TP
Jordan Farmar	33	5-13	3-9	2-2	0	6	2	0	3	15
Arron Afflalo	28	5-13	2-6	3-6	2	1	0	0	4	15
Luc Richard Mbah a Moute	32	5-10	0-0	4-7	10	1	1	0	4	14
Ryan Hollins	30	3-5	0-0	6-6	8	0	0	1	3	12
Darren Collison	20	2-6	0-1	1-3	2	0	0	0	1	5
Cedric Bozeman	31	1-5	0-2	2-2	6	4	1	1	3	4
Lorenzo Mata-Real	10	0-0	0-0	3-4	1	0	0	1	2	3
Michael Roll	8	1-4	1-3	0-0	0	0	0	0	1	3
Alfred Aboya	8	1-1	0-0	0-0	1	0	0	1	1	2
TOTALS	200	23-57	6-21	21-30	30	12	4	4	22	73
Percentages		40.4	28.6	70.0						

Coach: Ben Howland

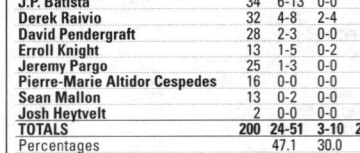

GONZAGA	MIN	FG	3FG	FT	REB	A	ST	BL	PF	TP
Adam Morrison	37	10-17	1-4	3-4	5	1	0	0	2	24
J.P. Batista	34	6-13	0-0	6-7	9	1	0	1	2	18
Derek Raivio	32	4-8	2-4	2-2	3	6	2	0	3	12
David Pendergraft	28	2-3	0-0	3-5	5	3	1	1	1	7
Erroll Knight	13	1-5	0-2	5-6	3	1	0	0	5	7
Jeremy Pargo	25	1-3	0-0	1-2	3	2	0	0	1	3
Pierre-Marie Altidor Cespedes	16	0-0	0-0	0-0	3	0	0	0	2	0
Sean Mallon	13	0-2	0-0	0-0	3	0	0	1	3	0
Josh Heytvelt	2	0-0	0-0	0-0	0	0	0	1	3	0
TOTALS	200	24-51	3-10	20-26	34	14	3	4	22	71
Percentages		47.1	30.0	76.9						

Coach: Mark Few

Officials: Curtis Shaw, Pat Driscoll, Gerry Pollard **Technicals:** None **Attendance:** 19,596

Connecticut 98-92 Washington (Sweet 16)

40	1H	45
42	2H	37
16	OT1	10

CONNECTICUT	MIN	FG	3FG	FT	REB	A	ST	BL	PF	TP
Marcus Williams	36	6-13	3-5	11-11	4	8	1	0	4	26
Rashad Anderson	31	6-12	5-10	2-2	2	1	1	0	2	19
Josh Boone	41	3-4	0-0	7-13	11	0	1	2	3	13
Hilton Armstorng	38	4-4	0-0	5-9	9	0	1	2	2	13
Rudy Gay	32	4-10	0-1	4-5	3	0	1	1	3	12
Denham Brown	21	4-6	2-3	2-2	2	2	0	0	4	12
Craig Austrie	15	0-2	0-0	2-3	5	4	2	0	1	2
Ed Nelson	6	0-0	0-0	1-2	1	0	0	0	1	1
Jeff Adrien	5	0-0	0-0	0-0	0	0	0	0	0	0
Rob Garrison	0	0-0	0-0	0-0	0	0	0	0	0	0
Marcus Johnson	0	0-0	0-0	0-0	0	0	0	0	0	0
TOTALS	225	27-51	10-19	34-47	37	15	7	5	20	98
Percentages		52.9	52.6	72.3						

Coach: Jim Calhoun

WASHINGTON	MIN	FG	3FG	FT	REB	A	ST	BL	PF	TP
Jamaal Williams	29	12-22	1-1	2-2	7	1	4	2	4	27
Brandon Roy	36	7-18	1-2	5-7	4	3	3	0	5	20
Jon Brockman	26	4-6	0-0	3-4	4	0	2	0	4	11
Ryan Appleby	20	3-6	2-4	2-2	2	0	2	0	0	10
Bobby Jones	32	4-8	1-3	0-0	5	1	2	1	5	9
Justin Dentmon	34	2-9	0-3	4-5	4	3	2	0	5	8
Joel Smith	18	1-4	0-1	2-3	3	0	0	0	5	4
Mike Jensen	28	1-6	1-5	0-0	5	1	4	0	5	3
Brandon Burmeister	2	0-1	0-1	0-0	0	0	0	0	0	0
Artem Wallace	0	0-0	0-0	0-0	0	0	0	0	0	0
TOTALS	225	34-80	6-20	18-23	34	9	19	3	33	92
Percentages		42.5	30.0	78.3						

Coach: Lorenzo Romar

Officials: John Higgins, Steven Skiles, Patrick Adams **Technicals:** Washington (Roy), Connecticut (Gay, bench) **Attendance:** 19,638

George Mason 63-55 Wichita State (Sweet 16)

35	1H	19
28	2H	36

GEORGE MASON	MIN	FG	3FG	FT	REB	A	ST	BL	PF	TP
Folarin Campbell	33	5-9	3-6	3-4	4	3	0	1	4	16
Lamar Butler	32	4-6	2-4	4-6	5	1	0	0	0	14
Tony Skinn	31	4-9	2-4	4-5	2	4	2	0	2	14
Will Thomas	34	4-12	0-0	2-4	10	1	0	0	3	10
Jai Lewis	27	2-6	0-1	0-2	2	1	1	2	5	4
Jordan Carter	9	1-1	1-1	0-0	2	1	1	0	1	3
Gabe Norwood	21	0-0	0-0	2-2	2	0	1	2	0	2
Sammy Hernandez	12	0-0	0-0	0-0	2	1	0	0	0	0
Chris Fleming	1	0-1	0-0	0-0	1	0	0	0	1	0
TOTALS	200	20-44	8-16	15-23	30	12	5	5	16	63
Percentages		45.5	50.0	65.2						

Coach: Jim Larranaga

WICHITA STATE	MIN	FG	3FG	FT	REB	A	ST	BL	PF	TP
Paul Miller	31	7-12	0-0	2-3	9	0	0	1	3	16
KaRon Bradley	26	5-14	1-6	2-2	5	2	2	0	1	13
Kyle Wilson	26	5-11	2-6	0-0	7	1	0	0	3	12
Ryan Martin	21	0-2	0-0	5-8	6	0	0	0	0	5
P.J. Couisnard	38	2-13	0-4	0-0	6	1	2	0	4	4
Sean Ogirri	35	1-8	0-5	2-2	6	3	0	0	4	4
Matt Braeuer	17	0-4	0-3	1-2	1	1	0	0	5	1
Wendell Preadom	4	0-0	0-0	0-0	0	0	0	0	1	0
Nick Rogers	2	0-0	0-0	0-0	0	0	0	0	0	0
TOTALS	200	20-64	3-24	12-17	40	8	4	1	21	55
Percentages		31.2	12.5	70.6						

Coach: Mark Turgeon

Officials: Bob Donato, John Hughes, Raymond Perone **Technicals:** None **Attendance:** 19,638

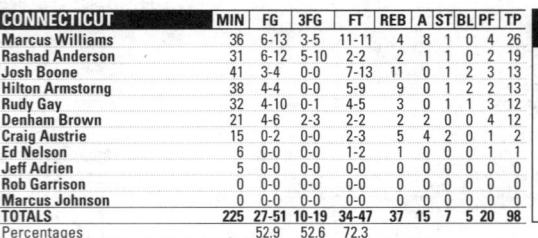

VILLANOVA	MIN	FG	3FG	FT	REB	A	ST	BL	PF	TP
Randy Foye	45	10-25	2-8	7-8	6	3	2	0	2	29
Allan Ray	37	3-15	2-9	1-2	3	0	0	0	2	9
Kyle Lowry	29	3-8	0-2	1-3	3	3	5	0	3	7
Will Sheridan	36	2-5	0-0	2-2	7	0	0	0	3	6
Dante Cunningham	36	1-1	0-0	2-3	8	3	4	1	3	4
Shane Clark	14	1-2	0-0	1-2	1	0	0	0	2	3
Jason Fraser	16	1-1	0-0	0-0	2	0	0	1	4	2
Mike Nardi	11	0-3	0-0	0-0	0	0	0	0	2	0
Chris Charles	1	0-0	0-0	0-0	0	0	0	0	0	0
TOTALS	225	21-60	4-19	14-20	30	9	11	2	21	60
Percentages		35.0	21.1	70.0						

Coach: Jay Wright

60-59

24	1H	28
27	2H	23
9	OT1	8

SWEET 16

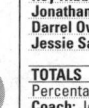

BOSTON COLLEGE	MIN	FG	3FG	FT	REB	A	ST	BL	PF	TP
Craig Smith	45	6-11	0-0	2-6	14	7	2	2	4	14
Jared Dudley	40	6-11	2-3	0-1	3	2	0	0	3	14
Sean Marshall	40	5-10	2-6	0-0	3	3	0	1	4	12
Sean Williams	24	2-2	0-0	3-6	7	0	1	3	3	7
Louis Hinnant	43	2-9	1-6	0-0	2	4	1	0	3	5
Tyrese Rice	11	0-3	0-3	3-4	0	2	1	0	0	3
John Oates	12	1-2	0-1	0-0	4	0	0	0	3	2
Akida McLain	9	1-1	0-0	0-0	1	0	0	0	1	2
Marquez Haynes	1	0-0	0-0	0-0	0	0	0	0	0	0
TOTALS	225	23-49	5-19	8-17	34	18	5	6	21	59
Percentages		46.9	26.3	47.1						

Coach: Al Skinner

Officials: Verne Harris, J.D. Collins, Hal Lusk
Technicals: None
Attendance: 22,293

FLORIDA	MIN	FG	3FG	FT	REB	A	ST	BL	PF	TP
Joakim Noah	35	6-13	0-0	3-4	10	0	0	5	3	15
Taurean Green	37	3-9	3-7	4-4	3	2	0	0	2	13
Al Horford	28	4-8	0-0	4-6	6	0	1	2	3	12
Corey Brewer	34	3-6	0-1	3-3	2	4	1	1	2	9
Lee Humphrey	34	2-7	2-5	0-0	4	1	0	0	0	6
Chris Richard	14	1-1	0-0	0-0	0	0	0	0	2	2
Walter Hodge	12	0-1	0-0	0-0	1	0	2	0	1	0
Adrian Moss	6	0-0	0-0	0-0	1	0	0	0	1	0
TOTALS	200	19-45	5-13	14-17	27	7	4	8	14	57
Percentages		42.2	38.5	82.4						

Coach: Billy Donovan

57-53

28	1H	30
29	2H	23

SWEET 16

GEORGETOWN	MIN	FG	3FG	FT	REB	A	ST	BL	PF	TP
Jeff Green	32	5-10	1-1	4-5	6	4	2	0	3	15
Ashanti Cook	35	4-8	2-5	2-2	0	3	2	0	2	12
Brandon Bowman	33	5-15	0-4	0-1	7	1	0	1	3	10
Roy Hibbert	28	5-9	0-0	0-0	7	0	0	3	4	10
Jonathan Wallace	31	1-5	1-4	0-0	4	2	2	0	1	3
Darrel Owens	25	1-6	1-6	0-0	2	4	2	0	2	3
Jessie Sapp	16	0-1	0-1	0-0	5	1	0	0	1	0
TOTALS	200	21-54	5-21	6-8	31	15	8	4	16	53
Percentages		38.9	23.8	75.0						

Coach: John Thompson III

Officials: Dave Libbey, Joe Lindsay, Tom O'Neill
Technicals: Florida (Noah)
Attendance: 22,293

LSU	MIN	FG	3FG	FT	REB	A	ST	BL	PF	TP
Glen Davis	39	11-19	1-2	3-5	9	2	1	1	1	26
Tyrus Thomas	39	10-14	0-0	1-3	13	1	1	3	2	21
Darrel Mitchell	45	2-10	1-6	6-6	4	5	3	1	1	11
Tasmin Mitchell	30	2-8	1-4	1-2	5	6	1	0	4	6
Garrett Temple	44	2-9	0-6	0-0	2	2	1	2	2	4
Magnum Rolle	7	1-2	0-0	0-0	0	1	0	0	1	2
Darnell Lazare	14	0-3	0-0	0-0	2	0	1	0	1	0
Ben Voogd	7	0-1	0-0	0-0	1	1	0	0	1	0
TOTALS	225	28-66	3-18	11-16	36	18	8	7	13	70
Percentages		42.4	16.7	68.8						

Coach: John Brady

70-60

26	1H	26
26	2H	26
18	OT1	8

ELITE 8

TEXAS	MIN	FG	3FG	FT	REB	A	ST	BL	PF	TP
Daniel Gibson	42	5-12	4-8	1-2	3	1	1	0	3	15
Brad Buckman	39	3-9	3-8	4-4	14	0	3	2	4	13
P.J. Tucker	44	4-11	1-2	1-3	13	6	1	0	1	10
Kenton Paulino	29	4-14	0-5	2-2	3	4	0	0	2	10
A.J. Abrams	19	2-7	2-6	0-0	1	1	0	0	0	6
LaMarcus Aldridge	44	2-14	0-0	0-0	10	2	2	5	3	4
Mike Williams	8	1-2	0-0	0-0	1	0	0	0	3	2
TOTALS	225	21-69	10-29	8-11	45	14	7	7	16	60
Percentages		30.4	34.5	72.7						

Coach: Rick Barnes

Officials: Dick Cartmell, Terry Wymer, John Cahill
Technicals: None
Attendance: 27,130

UCLA	MIN	FG	3FG	FT	REB	A	ST	BL	PF	TP
Arron Afflalo	35	2-9	2-4	9-10	3	0	0	0	1	15
Ryan Hollins	31	6-7	0-0	2-11	9	0	1	1	4	14
Jordan Farmar	36	1-9	0-2	2-4	3	3	1	0	0	4
Darren Collison	19	1-2	0-0	2-3	3	1	1	0	1	4
Alfred Aboya	13	2-2	0-0	0-2	2	0	0	0	0	4
Lorenzo Mata-Real	9	2-3	0-0	0-1	6	0	0	1	1	4
Cedric Bozeman	25	0-3	0-1	3-4	3	0	0	0	3	3
Luc Richard Mbah a Moute	27	0-4	0-0	2-4	7	1	1	0	3	2
Michael Roll	5	0-1	0-1	0-0	0	1	0	0	1	0
TOTALS	200	14-40	2-8	20-39	36	6	4	2	14	50
Percentages		35.0	25.0	51.3						

Coach: Ben Howland

50-45

28	1H	21
22	2H	24

ELITE 8

MEMPHIS	MIN	FG	3FG	FT	REB	A	ST	BL	PF	TP
Darius Washington	32	4-10	0-2	5-6	4	0	4	0	2	13
Shawne Williams	31	2-9	1-5	3-6	8	1	2	0	4	8
Chris Douglas-Roberts	14	3-5	0-0	0-0	6	0	1	0	1	6
Robert Dozier	11	3-4	0-0	0-0	8	0	0	0	4	6
Rodney Carney	26	2-12	1-5	0-0	2	0	1	0	4	5
Antonio Anderson	34	1-5	0-3	0-0	2	3	0	0	2	2
Joey Dorsey	21	1-3	0-0	0-0	6	0	0	2	5	2
Kareem Cooper	11	1-3	0-0	0-0	1	0	0	0	3	2
Andre Allen	14	0-3	0-2	1-3	0	1	0	0	3	1
Waki Williams	6	0-0	0-0	0-0	2	0	0	0	1	0
TOTALS	200	17-54	2-17	9-15	39	5	8	2	29	45
Percentages		31.5	11.8	60.0						

Coach: John Calipari

Officials: Tim Higgins, Tom Lopes, Reggie Greenwood
Technicals: None
Attendance: 19,689

GEORGE MASON	MIN	FG	3FG	FT	REB	A	ST	BL	PF	TP
Jai Lewis	41	6-12	0-0	8-14	7	3	0	0	2	20
Will Thomas	44	8-12	0-0	3-4	12	2	1	1	4	19
Lamar Butler	35	6-11	4-6	3-3	4	2	2	0	4	19
Folarin Campbell	41	5-10	2-5	3-3	2	3	1	1	2	15
Tony Skinn	39	4-11	2-5	0-1	5	2	2	0	4	10
Sammy Hernandez	5	1-2	1-2	0-0	2	0	0	0	0	3
Gabe Norwood	19	0-2	0-0	0-0	3	1	0	0	1	0
Jordan Carter	1	0-0	0-0	0-0	0	0	0	0	0	0
Chris Fleming	0	0-0	0-0	0-0	0	0	0	0	0	0
TOTALS	225	30-60	9-18	17-25	35	13	6	2	17	86
Percentages		50.0	50.0	68.0						

Coach: Jim Larranaga

86-84

34	1H	43
40	2H	31
12	OT1	10

ELITE 8

CONNECTICUT	MIN	FG	3FG	FT	REB	A	ST	BL	PF	TP
Rudy Gay	42	8-16	2-4	2-2	6	2	2	1	4	20
Jeff Adrien	25	7-8	0-0	3-4	7	0	0	1	3	17
Marcus Williams	41	5-12	2-5	1-1	3	11	1	0	2	13
Denham Brown	24	3-8	1-5	4-4	5	1	1	0	0	11
Hilton Armstorng	37	3-8	0-0	2-3	5	0	1	4	4	8
Josh Boone	20	2-4	0-0	2-4	4	0	0	1	3	6
Rashad Anderson	17	2-8	2-8	0-0	0	1	0	0	3	6
Ed Nelson	8	1-2	0-0	1-1	0	0	1	0	1	3
Craig Austrie	11	0-0	0-0	0-0	1	0	0	0	0	0
TOTALS	225	31-66	7-22	15-19	31	15	6	7	20	84
Percentages		47.0	31.8	78.9						

Coach: Jim Calhoun

Officials: Scott Thornley, Tony Greene, Zelton Steed
Technicals: None
Attendance: 19,718

FLORIDA	MIN	FG	3FG	FT	REB	A	ST	BL	PF	TP
Joakim Noah	36	4-8	0-0	13-15	15	1	1	5	1	21
Taurean Green	37	3-9	1-4	12-13	2	4	1	0	3	19
Al Horford	33	6-12	0-0	0-0	15	1	0	2	2	12
Corey Brewer	17	4-7	1-2	2-3	3	2	0	0	5	11
Lee Humphrey	38	3-12	2-9	0-0	2	4	0	0	2	8
David Huertas	14	1-2	0-1	0-0	3	1	0	0	3	2
Chris Richard	11	1-2	0-0	0-0	4	1	0	1	2	2
Walter Hodge	12	0-2	0-1	0-0	3	0	0	0	4	0
Adrian Moss	2	0-0	0-0	0-0	2	0	0	0	0	0
TOTALS	200	22-54	4-17	27-31	49	14	2	8	22	75
Percentages		40.7	23.5	87.1						

Coach: Billy Donovan

75-62

35	1H	30
40	2H	32

ELITE 8

VILLANOVA	MIN	FG	3FG	FT	REB	A	ST	BL	PF	TP
Randy Foye	37	7-18	2-8	9-10	8	0	2	0	5	25
Allan Ray	27	5-19	1-7	0-0	2	1	0	0	4	11
Jason Fraser	22	1-4	0-0	7-7	7	1	0	4	0	9
Mike Nardi	35	2-11	1-7	3-4	4	4	1	0	3	8
Kyle Lowry	29	1-9	0-0	1-1	4	2	2	1	5	3
Dante Cunningham	10	1-2	0-0	0-1	1	0	1	0	2	2
Shane Clark	6	1-2	0-0	0-0	4	0	0	0	1	2
Will Sheridan	30	0-6	0-0	1-2	5	0	0	1	4	1
Dwayne Anderson	1	0-2	0-1	1-2	1	0	0	0	0	1
Bilal Benn	1	0-0	0-0	0-0	0	0	0	0	0	0
Chris Charles	1	0-0	0-0	0-0	0	0	0	0	0	0
Baker Dunleavy	1	0-0	0-0	0-0	0	0	0	0	0	0
TOTALS	200	18-73	4-23	22-27	36	8	6	6	24	62
Percentages		24.7	17.4	81.5						

Coach: Jay Wright

Officials: Ed Hightower, Ed Corbett, Tom Eades
Technicals: Villanova (Ray)
Attendance: 21,613

59-45

39	1H	24
20	2H	21

FINAL 4

UCLA	MIN	FG	3FG	FT	REB	A	ST	BL	PF	TP
Luc Richard Mbah a Moute	30	5-9	0-1	7-8	9	1	2	0	5	17
Jordan Farmar	28	4-9	3-6	1-2	4	3	1	0	2	12
Arron Afflalo	25	3-11	1-5	2-2	6	1	0	0	2	9
Darren Collison	21	3-6	0-1	0-0	4	2	1	0	1	6
Ryan Hollins	17	2-2	0-0	2-2	3	1	0	1	4	6
Cedric Bozeman	25	2-6	0-1	0-0	5	1	2	0	3	4
Michael Roll	15	1-4	1-4	0-0	0	0	1	0	2	3
Lorenzo Mata-Real	17	1-2	0-0	0-3	8	1	2	2	1	2
Alfred Aboya	12	0-1	0-0	0-0	0	0	1	2	1	0
Janou Rubin	5	0-1	0-0	0-0	0	0	0	0	3	0
Michael Fey	2	0-0	0-0	0-0	0	0	0	0	0	0
Ryan Wright	2	0-0	0-0	0-0	0	0	0	0	0	0
DeAndre Robinson	1	0-0	0-0	0-0	0	0	0	0	0	0
TOTALS	**200**	**21-51**	**5-18**	**12-17**	**39**	**10**	**10**	**5**	**24**	**59**
Percentages		41.2	27.8	70.6						
Coach: Ben Howland										

LSU	MIN	FG	3FG	FT	REB	A	ST	BL	PF	TP
Glen Davis	31	5-17	0-0	4-10	7	0	3	0	5	14
Tasmin Mitchell	35	5-12	0-0	2-4	6	1	2	2	2	12
Darrel Mitchell	36	3-9	0-3	2-3	1	1	1	0	2	8
Tyrus Thomas	17	2-4	0-0	1-1	6	1	1	3	4	5
Magnum Rolle	14	1-1	0-0	0-2	8	0	0	1	1	2
Ben Voogd	11	0-1	0-1	2-2	0	0	1	0	1	2
Garrett Temple	38	0-5	0-2	1-2	1	1	1	0	3	1
Darnell Lazare	18	0-1	0-0	1-4	3	0	0	1	0	1
TOTALS	**200**	**16-50**	**0-6**	**13-28**	**32**	**4**	**9**	**7**	**18**	**45**
Percentages		32.0	0.0	46.4						
Coach: John Brady										

Officials: Karl Hess, Corbett, Ed Hightower
Technicals: None
Attendance: 43,822

73-58

31	1H	26
42	2H	32

FINAL 4

FLORIDA	MIN	FG	3FG	FT	REB	A	ST	BL	PF	TP
Corey Brewer	34	6-11	3-6	4-5	6	1	1	0	1	19
Lee Humphrey	34	6-12	6-12	1-3	3	0	1	0	2	19
Taurean Green	36	3-9	3-6	6-6	3	0	2	0	1	15
Joakim Noah	26	5-11	0-1	2-2	8	2	1	4	3	12
Al Horford	29	2-7	0-0	2-3	13	4	0	0	3	6
Chris Richard	24	1-1	0-0	0-0	3	1	0	0	1	2
Walter Hodge	10	0-1	0-0	0-0	0	0	0	0	1	0
David Huertas	4	0-0	0-0	0-0	0	0	0	0	0	0
Adrian Moss	3	0-1	0-0	0-0	0	0	0	0	0	0
TOTALS	**200**	**23-53**	**12-25**	**15-19**	**36**	**8**	**5**	**4**	**12**	**73**
Percentages		43.4	48.0	78.9						
Coach: Billy Donovan										

GEORGE MASON	MIN	FG	3FG	FT	REB	A	ST	BL	PF	TP
Jai Lewis	37	5-13	0-1	3-3	11	1	2	0	4	13
Tony Skinn	29	5-12	1-4	2-3	3	1	1	0	3	13
Will Thomas	34	4-12	0-0	2-5	3	0	3	1	2	10
Folarin Campbell	25	3-5	1-2	3-3	1	0	0	0	4	10
Lamar Butler	36	4-7	0-2	0-0	4	1	0	1	1	8
Gabe Norwood	25	1-4	0-2	0-0	1	3	2	0	0	2
Sammy Hernandez	4	1-3	0-0	0-0	2	0	0	0	1	2
Jordan Carter	7	0-0	0-0	0-0	0	0	0	0	0	0
Tim Burns	1	0-0	0-0	0-0	0	0	0	0	0	0
Chris Fleming	1	0-0	0-0	0-0	0	0	0	0	0	0
Milo Konate	1	0-0	0-0	0-0	0	0	0	0	0	0
TOTALS	**200**	**23-56**	**2-11**	**10-14**	**25**	**6**	**8**	**2**	**15**	**58**
Percentages		41.1	18.2	71.4						
Coach: Jim Larranaga										

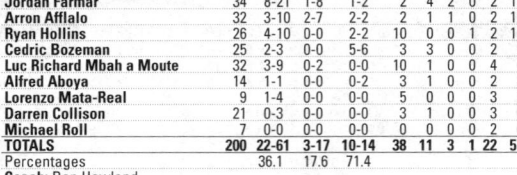

Officials: Dick Cartmell, Ted Valentine, Cur Shaw
Technicals: Florida (Green
Attendance: 43,822

73-57

36	1H	25
37	2H	32

NCAA FINAL 2006

FLORIDA	MIN	FG	3FG	FT	REB	A	ST	BL	PF	TP
Joakim Noah	33	7-9	0-0	2-2	9	3	1	6	2	16
Lee Humphrey	36	4-8	4-8	3-3	1	2	0	0	1	15
Al Horford	24	5-8	0-0	4-5	7	3	0	2	2	14
Corey Brewer	37	4-12	2-3	1-3	7	4	3	1	3	11
Adrian Moss	10	3-6	0-0	3-4	6	0	0	0	0	9
Chris Richard	12	2-3	0-0	2-2	0	0	0	1	3	6
Taurean Green	36	1-9	0-7	0-1	4	8	1	0	1	2
Walter Hodge	12	0-3	0-1	0-0	1	1	2	0	1	0
TOTALS	**200**	**26-58**	**6-19**	**15-20**	**35**	**21**	**7**	**10**	**13**	**73**
Percentages		44.8	31.6	75.0						
Coach: Billy Donovan										

UCLA	MIN	FG	3FG	FT	REB	A	ST	BL	PF	TP
Jordan Farmar	34	8-21	1-8	1-2	2	4	2	0	2	18
Arron Afflalo	32	3-10	2-7	2-2	2	1	1	0	2	10
Ryan Hollins	26	4-10	0-0	2-2	10	0	0	1	2	10
Cedric Bozeman	25	2-3	0-0	5-6	3	3	0	0	2	9
Luc Richard Mbah a Moute	32	3-9	0-2	0-0	10	1	0	0	4	6
Alfred Aboya	14	1-1	0-0	0-2	3	1	0	0	2	2
Lorenzo Mata-Real	9	1-4	0-0	0-0	5	0	0	0	3	2
Darren Collison	21	0-3	0-0	0-0	3	1	0	0	3	0
Michael Roll	7	0-0	0-0	0-0	0	0	0	0	2	0
TOTALS	**200**	**22-61**	**3-17**	**10-14**	**38**	**11**	**3**	**1**	**22**	**57**
Percentages		36.1	17.6	71.4						
Coach: Ben Howland										

Officials: James Burr, John Cahill, Tony Greene
Technicals: None
Attendance: 43,168

National Invitation Tournament (NIT)

Opening Round: Manhattan d. Fairleigh Dickinson 80-77, Rutgers d. Penn State 76-71, UTEP d. Lipscomb 85-66, Akron d. Temple 80-73 (OT), Delaware State d. Northern Arizona 58-53, Stanford d. Virginia 65-49, Charlotte d. Georgia Southern 77-61, Butler d. Miami (OH) 54-52
First Round: Manhattan d. Maryland 87-84, Old Dominion d. Colorado 79-61, Saint Joseph's d. Rutgers 71-62, Hofstra d. Nebraska 73-62, Michigan d. UTEP 82-67, Notre Dame d. Vanderbilt 79-69, Creighton d. Akron 71-60, Miami (FL) d. Oklahoma State 62-59, Louisville d. Delaware State 71-54, Clemson d. Louisiana Tech 69-53, Missouri State d. Stanford 76-67, Houston d. BYU 77-67, Cincinnati d. Charlotte 86-80, Minnesota d. Wake Forest 73-58, Florida State d. Butler 67-63, South Carolina d. Western Kentucky 74-55
Second Round: Old Dominion d. Manhattan 70-66, Hofstra d. Saint Joseph's 77-75 (OT), Michigan d. Notre Dame 87-84 (2OT), Miami (FL) d. Creighton 53-52, Louisville d. Clemson 74-68, Missouri State d. Houston 60-59, Cincinnati d. Minnesota 76-62, South Carolina d. Florida State 69-68 (OT)
Quarterfinals: Old Dominion d. Hofstra 61-51, Michigan d. Miami (FL) 71-65, Louisville d. Missouri State 74-56, South Carolina d. Cincinnati 65-62
Semifinals: Michigan d. Old Dominion 66-43, South Carolina d. Louisville 78-63
Championship: South Carolina d. Michigan 76-64
MVP: Renaldo Balkman, South Carolina

2006-07: Gator Raid II

Florida became just the seventh team to win back-to-back national championships and the first since Duke in 1991 and '92. Billy Donovan joined Kentucky legend Adolph Rupp as the only coaches in SEC history to win multiple national titles. Alone among all the repeat champs, Florida (35–5) started the same five players in both title games—2007 NBA first-rounders Al Horford (No. 3, Atlanta Hawks), Corey Brewer (No. 7, Minnesota Timberwolves) and Joakim Noah (No. 9, Chicago Bulls), along with Taurean Green and Lee Humphrey. The quintet accounted for 69 of Florida's points in the 84-75 Final win over Ohio State.

The season's most-talked-about players, freshmen Greg Oden of OSU and Kevin Durant of Texas—the national POY after averaging a double-double (25.8 ppg, 11.1 rpg)—ended up going 1-2 in the NBA draft, Oden to the Portland Trail Blazers and Durant to the Seattle SuperSonics. On New Year's Day, Texas Tech coach Bob Knight achieved his 880th career victory, passing North Carolina's Dean Smith for first place on the all-time wins list.

Major Conference Standings

America East

	Conference			Overall		
	W	L	Pct	W	L	Pct
Vermont□	15	1	.938	25	8	.758
Albany (NY)⊕	13	3	.813	23	10	.697
Boston U.	8	8	.500	12	18	.400
Maine	7	9	.438	12	18	.400
UMBC	7	9	.438	12	19	.387
Binghamton	6	10	.375	13	16	.448
Hartford	6	10	.375	13	18	.419
New Hampshire	6	10	.375	10	20	.333
Stony Brook	4	12	.250	9	20	.310

Tournament: **Albany (NY) d. Vermont 60-59**
Tournament MOP: **Jamar Wilson**, Albany (NY)

ACC

	Conference			Overall		
	W	L	Pct	W	L	Pct
North Carolina⊕	11	5	.688	31	7	.816
Virginia○	11	5	.688	21	11	.656
Maryland○	10	6	.625	25	9	.735
Virginia Tech○	10	6	.625	22	12	.647
Boston College○	10	6	.625	21	12	.636
Georgia Tech○	8	8	.500	20	12	.625
Duke○	8	8	.500	22	11	.667
Clemson□	7	9	.438	25	11	.694
Florida State□	7	9	.438	22	13	.629
NC State□	5	11	.313	20	16	.556
Wake Forest	5	11	.313	15	16	.484
Miami (FL)	4	12	.250	12	20	.375

Tournament: **North Carolina d. NC State 89-80**
Tournament MVP: **Brandan Wright**, North Carolina

Atlantic Sun

	Conference			Overall		
	W	L	Pct	W	L	Pct
East Tenn State□	16	2	.889	24	10	.706
Belmont⊕	14	4	.778	23	10	.697
Lipscomb	11	7	.611	18	13	.581
Jacksonville	11	7	.611	15	14	.517
Kennesaw State	9	9	.500	14	18	.438
Mercer	8	10	.444	13	17	.433
Campbell	7	11	.389	14	17	.452
Gardner-Webb	7	11	.389	9	21	.300
Stetson	6	12	.333	11	20	.355
North Florida	1	17	.056	3	26	.103

Tournament: **Belmont d. East Tennessee St. 94-67**
Tournament MVP: **Justin Hare**, Belmont

Atlantic 10

	Conference			Overall		
	W	L	Pct	W	L	Pct
Massachusetts□	13	3	.813	24	9	.727
Xavier○	13	3	.813	25	9	.735
George Washington⊕	11	5	.688	23	9	.719
Fordham	10	6	.625	18	12	.600
Rhode Island	10	6	.625	19	14	.576
Saint Joseph's	9	7	.563	18	14	.563
Dayton	8	8	.500	19	12	.613
Saint Louis	8	8	.500	20	13	.606
Charlotte	7	9	.438	14	16	.467
Temple	6	10	.375	12	18	.400
Duquesne	6	10	.375	10	19	.345
Richmond	4	12	.250	8	22	.267
St. Bonaventure	4	12	.250	7	22	.241
La Salle	3	13	.188	10	20	.333

Tournament: **George Washington d. Rhode Island 78-69**
Tournament MOP: **Maureece Rice**, George Washington

Big East

	Conference			Overall		
	W	L	Pct	W	L	Pct
Georgetown⊕	13	3	.813	30	7	.811
Pittsburgh○	12	4	.750	29	8	.784
Louisville○	12	4	.750	24	10	.706
Notre Dame○	11	5	.688	24	8	.750
Marquette○	10	6	.625	24	10	.706
Syracuse□	10	6	.625	24	11	.686
West Virginia□	9	7	.563	27	9	.750
Villanova○	9	7	.563	22	11	.667
DePaul□	9	7	.563	20	14	.588
Providence□	8	8	.500	18	13	.581
St. John's	7	9	.438	16	15	.516
Connecticut	6	10	.375	17	14	.548
Seton Hall	4	12	.250	13	16	.448
South Florida	3	13	.188	12	18	.400
Rutgers	3	13	.188	10	19	.345
Cincinnati	2	14	.125	11	19	.367

Tournament: **Georgetown d. Pittsburgh 65-42**
Tournament MVP: **Jeff Green**, Georgetown

Big Sky

	Conference			Overall		
	W	L	Pct	W	L	Pct
Weber State⊕	11	5	.688	20	12	.625
Northern Arizona	11	5	.688	18	12	.600
Montana	10	6	.625	17	15	.531
Portland State	9	7	.563	19	13	.594
Eastern Washington	8	8	.500	15	14	.517
Idaho State	8	8	.500	13	17	.433
Montana State	8	8	.500	11	19	.367
Sacramento State	5	11	.313	10	19	.345
Northern Colorado	2	14	.125	4	24	.143

Tournament: **Weber State d. Northern Arizona 88-80**
Tournament MVP: **David Patten**, Weber State

Big South

	Conference			Overall		
	W	L	Pct	W	L	Pct
Winthrop⊕	14	0	1.000	29	5	.853
High Point	11	3	.786	22	10	.688
Liberty	8	6	.571	14	17	.452
Coastal Carolina	7	7	.500	15	15	.500
UNC Asheville	6	8	.429	12	19	.387
VMI	5	9	.357	14	19	.424
Radford	3	11	.214	8	22	.267
Charleston Southern	2	12	.143	8	22	.267

Tournament: **Winthrop d. VMI 84-81**
Tournament MVP: **Craig Bradshaw**, Winthrop

Big Ten

	Conference			Overall		
	W	L	Pct	W	L	Pct
Ohio State⊕	15	1	.938	35	4	.897
Wisconsin○	13	3	.813	30	6	.833
Indiana○	10	6	.625	21	11	.656
Illinois○	9	7	.563	23	12	.657
Purdue○	9	7	.563	22	12	.647
Iowa	9	7	.563	17	14	.548
Michigan State○	8	8	.500	23	12	.657
Michigan□	8	8	.500	22	13	.629
Minnesota	3	13	.188	9	22	.290
Northwestern	2	14	.125	13	18	.419
Penn State	2	14	.125	11	19	.367

Tournament: **Ohio State d. Wisconsin 66-49**
Tournament MVP: **Greg Oden**, Ohio State

Big 12

	Conference			Overall		
	W	L	Pct	W	L	Pct
Kansas⊕	14	2	.875	33	5	.868
Texas A&M○	13	3	.813	27	7	.794
Texas○	12	4	.750	25	10	.714
Kansas State□	10	6	.625	23	12	.657
Texas Tech○	9	7	.563	21	13	.618
Missouri	7	9	.438	18	12	.600
Oklahoma State□	6	10	.375	22	13	.629
Nebraska	6	10	.375	17	14	.548
Oklahoma	6	10	.375	16	15	.516
Iowa State	6	10	.375	15	16	.484
Baylor	4	12	.250	15	16	.484
Colorado	3	13	.188	7	20	.259

Tournament: **Kansas d. Texas 88-84 (OT)**
Tournament MOP: **Kevin Durant**, Texas

Big West

	Conference			Overall		
	W	L	Pct	W	L	Pct
Long Beach State⊕	12	2	.857	24	8	.750
Cal State Fullerton	9	5	.643	20	10	.667
Cal Poly	9	5	.643	19	11	.633
UC Santa Barbara	9	5	.643	18	11	.621
UC Irvine	6	8	.429	15	18	.455
Cal State Northridge	5	9	.357	14	17	.452
Pacific	5	9	.357	12	19	.387
UC Riverside	1	13	.071	7	24	.226

Tournament: **Long Beach State d. Cal Poly 94-83**
Tournament MVP: **Aaron Nixon**, Long Beach State

Colonial Athletic

	Conference			Overall		
	W	L	Pct	W	L	Pct
VCU⊕	16	2	.889	28	7	.800
Old Dominion○	15	3	.833	24	9	.727
Hofstra□	14	4	.778	22	10	.688
Drexel□	13	5	.722	23	9	.719
George Mason	9	9	.500	18	15	.545
Northeastern	9	9	.500	13	19	.406
William and Mary	8	10	.444	15	15	.500
Towson	8	10	.444	15	17	.469
Georgia State	5	13	.278	11	20	.355
UNC Wilmington	4	14	.222	7	22	.241
James Madison	4	14	.222	7	23	.233
Delaware	3	15	.167	5	26	.161

Tournament: **VCU d. George Mason 65-59**
Tournament MOP: **Eric Maynor**, VCU

C-USA

	Conference			Overall		
	W	L	Pct	W	L	Pct
Memphis⊕	16	0	1.000	33	4	.892
Central Florida	11	5	.688	22	9	.710
Houston	10	6	.625	18	15	.545
Southern Miss	9	7	.563	20	11	.645
Tulsa	9	7	.563	20	11	.645
Tulane	9	7	.563	17	13	.567
Rice	8	8	.500	16	16	.500
UAB	7	9	.438	15	16	.484
Marshall	7	9	.438	13	19	.406
UTEP	6	10	.375	14	17	.452
SMU	3	13	.188	14	17	.452
East Carolina	1	15	.063	6	24	.200

Tournament: **Memphis d. Houston 71-59**
Tournament MVP: **Chris Douglas-Roberts**, Memphis

Horizon

	Conference			Overall		
	W	L	Pct	W	L	Pct
Wright State⊕	13	3	.813	23	10	.697
Butler○	13	3	.813	29	7	.806
Loyola-Chicago	10	6	.625	21	11	.656
Wisconsin-Green Bay	7	9	.438	18	15	.545
Youngstown State	7	9	.438	14	17	.452
Illinois-Chicago	7	9	.438	14	18	.438
Detroit	6	10	.375	11	19	.367
Wisconsin-Milwaukee	6	10	.375	9	22	.290
Cleveland State	3	13	.188	10	21	.323

Tournament: **Wright State d. Butler 60-55**
Tournament MVP: **DaShaun Wood**, Wright State

Conference Standings Continue →

⊕ Automatic NCAA Tournament bid ○ At-large NCAA Tournament bid □ NIT appearance ✪ Team record doesn't reflect games forfeited or vacated. For adjusted record, see p. 521.

IVY

	Conference			Overall		
	W	L	Pct	W	L	Pct
Penn⊕	13	1	.929	22	9	.710
Yale	10	4	.714	14	13	.519
Cornell	9	5	.643	16	12	.571
Columbia	7	7	.500	16	12	.571
Brown	6	8	.429	11	18	.379
Harvard	5	9	.357	12	16	.429
Dartmouth	4	10	.286	9	18	.333
Princeton	2	12	.143	11	17	.393

MAAC

	Conference			Overall		
	W	L	Pct	W	L	Pct
Marist□	14	4	.778	25	9	.735
Niagara⊕	13	5	.722	23	12	.657
Siena	12	6	.667	20	12	.625
Loyola (MD)	12	6	.667	18	13	.581
Manhattan	10	8	.556	13	17	.433
Fairfield	10	8	.556	13	19	.406
Rider	9	9	.500	16	15	.516
Canisius	6	12	.333	12	19	.387
Saint Peter's	3	15	.167	5	25	.167
Iona	1	17	.056	2	28	.067

Tournament: **Niagara d. Siena 83-79**
Tournament MVP: **Tyrone Lewis**, Niagara

MID-AMERICAN

	Conference			Overall		
	W	L	Pct	W	L	Pct
East Division						
Akron	13	3	.813	26	7	.788
Kent State	12	4	.750	21	11	.656
Miami (OH)⊕	10	6	.625	18	15	.545
Ohio	9	7	.563	19	13	.594
Buffalo	4	12	.250	12	19	.387
Bowling Green	3	13	.188	13	18	.419
West Division						
Toledo□	14	2	.875	19	13	.594
Western Michigan	9	7	.563	16	16	.500
Central Michigan	7	9	.438	13	18	.419
Eastern Michigan	6	10	.375	13	19	.406
Ball State	5	11	.313	9	22	.290
Northern Illinois	4	12	.250	7	23	.233

Tournament: **Miami (OH) d. Akron 53-52**
Tournament MVP: **Tim Pollitz**, Miami (OH)

MID-CONTINENT

	Conference			Overall		
	W	L	Pct	W	L	Pct
Oral Roberts⊕	12	2	.857	23	11	.676
Oakland	10	4	.714	19	14	.576
Valparaiso	9	5	.643	16	15	.516
IUPUI	7	7	.500	15	15	.500
Southern Utah	6	8	.429	16	14	.533
UMKC	6	8	.429	12	20	.375
Centenary	3	11	.214	10	21	.323
Western Illinois	3	11	.214	7	23	.233

Tournament: **Oral Roberts d. Oakland 71-67**
Tournament MVP: **Caleb Green**, Oral Roberts

MEAC

	Conference			Overall		
	W	L	Pct	W	L	Pct
Delaware State□	16	2	.889	21	13	.618
Florida A&M⊕	12	6	.667	21	14	.600
Hampton	10	8	.556	15	16	.484
NC A&T	10	8	.556	15	17	.469
SC State	10	8	.556	13	17	.433
Morgan State	10	8	.556	13	18	.419
Norfolk State	10	8	.556	11	19	.367
Coppin State	9	9	.500	12	20	.375
Bethune-Cookman	6	12	.333	9	21	.300
Howard	5	13	.278	9	22	.290
UMES	1	17	.056	4	27	.129

Tournament: **Florida A&M d. Delaware State 58-56**
Tournament MOP: **Brian Greene**, Florida A&M

MISSOURI VALLEY

	Conference			Overall		
	W	L	Pct	W	L	Pct
Southern Illinois○	15	3	.833	29	7	.806
Creighton⊕	13	5	.722	22	11	.667
Missouri State□	12	6	.667	22	11	.667
Bradley□	10	8	.556	22	13	.629
Northern Iowa	9	9	.500	18	13	.581
Wichita State	8	10	.444	17	14	.548
Drake	6	12	.333	17	15	.531
Illinois State	6	12	.333	15	16	.484
Evansville	6	12	.333	14	17	.452
Indiana State	5	13	.278	13	18	.419

Tournament: **Creighton d. Southern Illinois 67-61**
Tournament MVP: **Nate Funk**, Creighton

MOUNTAIN WEST

	Conference			Overall		
	W	L	Pct	W	L	Pct
BYU○	13	3	.813	25	9	.735
UNLV⊕	12	4	.750	30	7	.811
Air Force□	10	6	.625	26	9	.743
San Diego State□	10	6	.625	22	11	.667
Wyoming	7	9	.438	17	15	.531
Colorado State	6	10	.375	17	13	.567
Utah	6	10	.375	11	19	.367
New Mexico	4	12	.250	15	17	.469
TCU	4	12	.250	13	17	.433

Tournament: **UNLV d. BYU 78-70**
Tournament MVP: **Kevin Kruger, UNLV**

NORTHEAST

	Conference			Overall		
	W	L	Pct	W	L	Pct
Central Conn. State⊕	16	2	.889	22	12	.647
Sacred Heart	12	6	.667	18	14	.563
Quinnipiac	11	7	.611	14	15	.483
Robert Morris	9	9	.500	17	11	.607
Fairleigh Dickinson	9	9	.500	14	16	.467
Mount St. Mary's	9	9	.500	11	20	.355
Wagner	8	10	.444	11	19	.367
Monmouth	7	11	.389	12	18	.400
St. Francis (NY)	7	11	.389	9	22	.290
Long Island	6	12	.333	10	19	.345
Saint Francis (PA)	5	13	.278	8	21	.276

Tournament: **Central Conn. St. d. Sacred Heart 74-70**
Tournament MVP: **Javier Mojica**, Central Conn. St.

OHIO VALLEY

	Conference			Overall		
	W	L	Pct	W	L	Pct
Austin Peay□	16	4	.800	21	12	.636
Eastern Kentucky⊕	13	7	.650	21	12	.636
Tennessee Tech	13	7	.650	19	13	.594
Murray State	13	7	.650	16	14	.533
Samford	12	8	.600	16	16	.500
SE Missouri State	9	11	.450	11	20	.355
Morehead State	8	12	.400	12	18	.400
Tennessee State	8	12	.400	12	20	.375
Jacksonville State	7	13	.350	9	21	.300
Eastern Illinois	6	14	.300	10	20	.333
Tennessee-Martin	5	15	.250	8	23	.258

Tournament: **Eastern Kentucky d. Austin Peay 63-62**
Tournament MVP: **Mike Rose**, Eastern Kentucky

PAC-10

	Conference			Overall		
	W	L	Pct	W	L	Pct
UCLA○	15	3	.833	30	6	.833
Washington State○	13	5	.722	26	8	.765
Oregon⊕	11	7	.611	29	8	.784
Southern California○	11	7	.611	25	12	.676
Arizona○	11	7	.611	20	11	.645
Stanford○	10	8	.556	18	13	.581
Washington	8	10	.444	19	13	.594
California	6	12	.333	16	17	.485
Oregon State	3	15	.167	11	21	.344
Arizona State	2	16	.111	8	22	.267

Tournament: **Oregon d. Southern California 81-57**
Tournament MVP: **Tajuan Porter**, Oregon

PATRIOT LEAGUE

	Conference			Overall		
	W	L	Pct	W	L	Pct
Holy Cross⊕	13	1	.929	25	9	.735
Bucknell	13	1	.929	22	9	.710
American	7	7	.500	16	14	.533
Lehigh	7	7	.500	12	19	.387
Colgate	5	9	.357	10	19	.345
Army	4	10	.286	15	16	.484
Navy	4	10	.286	14	16	.467
Lafayette	3	11	.214	9	21	.300

Tournament: **Holy Cross d. Bucknell 74-66**
Tournament MOP: **Keith Simmons**, Holy Cross

SEC

	Conference			Overall		
	W	L	Pct	W	L	Pct
Eastern						
Florida⊕	13	3	.813	35	5	.875
Tennessee○	10	6	.625	24	11	.686
Vanderbilt○	10	6	.625	22	12	.647
Kentucky○	9	7	.563	22	12	.647
Georgia□	8	8	.500	19	14	.576
South Carolina	4	12	.250	14	16	.467
Western						
Mississippi State□	8	8	.500	21	14	.600
Mississippi□	8	8	.500	21	13	.618
Alabama□	7	9	.438	20	12	.625
Arkansas○	7	9	.438	21	14	.600
Auburn	7	9	.438	17	15	.531
LSU	5	11	.313	17	15	.531

Tournament: **Florida d. Arkansas 77-56**
Tournament MVP: **Al Horford**, Florida

SOUTHERN

	Conference			Overall		
	W	L	Pct	W	L	Pct
North						
Appalachian State□	15	3	.833	25	8	.758
UNC Greensboro	12	6	.667	16	14	.533
Western Carolina	7	11	.389	11	20	.355
Chattanooga	6	12	.333	15	18	.455
Elon	5	13	.278	7	23	.233
South						
Davidson⊕	17	1	.944	29	5	.853
Charleston	13	5	.722	22	11	.667
Furman	8	10	.444	15	16	.484
Georgia Southern	7	11	.389	15	16	.484
Wofford	5	13	.278	10	20	.333
The Citadel	4	14	.222	7	23	.233

Tournament: **Davidson d. Charleston 72-65**
Tournament MVP: **Stephen Curry**, Davidson

SOUTHLAND

	Conference			Overall		
	W	L	Pct	W	L	Pct
East						
Northwestern St. (LA)	10	6	.625	17	15	.531
McNeese State	9	7	.563	15	17	.469
Southeastern Louisiana	8	8	.500	16	14	.533
Lamar	8	8	.500	15	17	.469
Nicholls State	7	9	.438	8	22	.267
Central Arkansas	4	12	.250	10	20	.333
West						
Corpus Christi⊕	14	2	.875	26	7	.788
Sam Houston State	13	3	.813	21	10	.677
Stephen F. Austin	8	8	.500	15	14	.517
Texas-Arlington	8	8	.500	13	17	.433
Texas State	4	12	.250	9	20	.310
UTSA	3	13	.188	7	22	.241

Tournament: **Corpus Christi d. Northwestern St. (LA) 81-78**
Tournament MVP: **Chris Daniels**, Corpus Christi

SWAC

	Conference			Overall		
	W	L	Pct	W	L	Pct
Miss. Valley State□	13	5	.722	18	16	.529
Jackson State⊕	12	6	.667	21	14	.600
Grambling	10	8	.556	12	14	.462
Alcorn State	10	8	.556	11	19	.367
Texas Southern	9	9	.500	14	17	.452
Arkansas-Pine Bluff	9	9	.500	12	19	.387
Southern U.	9	9	.500	10	21	.323
Alabama State	8	10	.444	10	20	.333
Prairie View A&M	6	12	.333	8	22	.267
Alabama A&M	4	14	.222	10	20	.333

Tournament: **Jackson State d. Miss. Valley State 81-71**
Tournament MOP: **Trey Johnson**, Jackson State

SUN BELT

	Conference			Overall		
	W	L	Pct	W	L	Pct
Eastern Division						
South Alabama□	13	5	.722	20	12	.625
Western Kentucky	12	6	.667	22	11	.667
Florida Atlantic	10	8	.556	16	15	.516
Middle Tenn. State	8	10	.444	15	17	.469
Troy	8	10	.444	13	17	.433
Florida International	7	11	.389	12	17	.414
Western Division						
Arkansas State	11	7	.611	18	15	.545
UL-Monroe	11	7	.611	18	14	.563
North Texas⊕	10	8	.556	23	11	.676
New Orleans	9	9	.500	14	17	.452
Arkansas-Little Rock	8	10	.444	13	17	.433
UL-Lafayette	7	11	.389	9	21	.300
Denver	3	15	.167	4	25	.138

Tournament: **North Texas d. Arkansas State 83-75**
Tournament MOP: **Calvin Watson**, North Texas

WEST COAST

	Conference			Overall		
	W	L	Pct	W	L	Pct
Gonzaga⊕	11	3	.786	23	11	.676
Santa Clara	10	4	.714	21	10	.677
Saint Mary's (CA)	8	6	.571	17	15	.531
San Francisco	8	6	.571	13	18	.419
San Diego	6	8	.429	18	14	.563
Loyola Marymount	5	9	.357	13	18	.419
Portland	4	10	.286	9	23	.281
Pepperdine	4	10	.286	8	23	.258

Tournament: **Gonzaga d. Santa Clara 77-68**
Tournament MVP: **Derek Raivio**, Gonzaga

WAC

	Conference			Overall		
	W	L	Pct	W	L	Pct
Nevada○	14	2	.875	29	5	.853
New Mexico State⊕	11	5	.688	25	9	.735
Fresno State□	10	6	.625	22	10	.688
Utah State□	9	7	.563	23	12	.657
Hawaii	8	8	.500	18	13	.581
Boise State	8	8	.500	17	14	.548
Louisiana Tech	7	9	.438	10	20	.333
San Jose State	4	12	.250	5	25	.167
Idaho	1	15	.063	4	27	.129

Tournament: **New Mexico State d. Utah State 72-70**
Tournament MVP: **Justin Hawkins**, New Mexico State

INDEPENDENTS

	Overall		
	W	L	Pct
Texas-Pan American	14	15	.483
IPFW	12	17	.414
Savannah State	12	18	.400
Chicago State	9	20	.310

ALL OTHERS

(Reclassifying and provisional teams not eligible for the NCAA Tournament.)

	Overall		
	W	L	Pct
Utah Valley State	22	7	.759
North Dakota State	20	8	.714
Cal St. Bakersfield	15	14	.517
Kennesaw State	13	18	.419
Central Arkansas	10	20	.333
Longwood	9	22	.290
South Dakota State	6	24	.200
UC Davis	5	23	.179
NJIT	5	24	.172
Winston-Salem	5	24	.172
Northern Colorado	4	24	.143
North Florida	3	26	.103

INDIVIDUAL LEADERS—SEASON

SCORING	CL	POS	G	FG	3FG	FT	PTS	PPG
1 **Reggie Williams**, VMI	JR	F	33	338	76	176	928	**28.1**
2 **Trey Johnson**, Jackson State	SR	G	35	311	79	246	947	**27.1**
3 **Morris Almond**, Rice	SR	G	32	263	77	241	844	**26.4**
4 **Kevin Durant**, Texas	FR	F	35	306	82	209	903	**25.8**
5 **Gary Neal**, Towson	SR	G	32	267	93	183	810	**25.3**
6 **Bo McCalebb**, New Orleans	JR	G	31	287	26	176	776	**25.0**
7 **Rodney Stuckey**, Eastern Washington	SO	G	29	227	43	215	712	**24.6**
8 **Gerald Brown**, Loyola (MD)	JR	G	29	205	58	175	643	**22.2**
9 **Stephen Curry**, Davidson	FR	G	34	242	122	124	730	**21.5**
10 **Jaycee Carroll**, Utah State	JR	G	35	256	83	151	746	**21.3**

FIELD GOAL PCT	CL	POS	G	FG	FGA	PCT
1 **Mike Freeman**, Hampton	FR	F	30	162	239	**67.8**
2 **Roy Hibbert**, Georgetown	JR	C	37	186	277	**67.1**
3 **Florentino Valencia**, Toledo	SR	F	32	164	246	**66.7**
4 **Vladimir Kuljanin**, UNC Wilmington	JR	C	29	165	249	**66.3**
5 **Calvin Brown**, Norfolk State	SR	C	30	152	233	**65.2**

MINIMUM: 5 MADE PER GAME

THREE-PT FG PER GAME	CL	POS	G	3FG	3PG
1 **Stephen Sir**, Northern Arizona	SR	G	30	124	**4.1**
2 **Will Whittington**, Marist	SR	G	34	137	**4.0**
3 **Steven Rush**, NC A&T	JR	G	30	115	**3.8**
4 **Tristan Blackwood**, Central Connecticut St.	JR	G	34	122	**3.6**
Stephen Curry, Davidson	FR	G	34	122	**3.6**

THREE-PT FG PCT	CL	POS	G	3FG	3FGA	PCT
1 **Josh Carter**, Texas A&M	SO	G	34	86	172	**50.0**
Jeremy Crouch, Bradley	JR	G	27	83	166	**50.0**
3 **Stephen Sir**, Northern Arizona	SR	G	30	124	253	**49.0**
4 **Jimmy Baron**, Rhode Island	SO	G	32	97	203	**47.8**
5 **Josh Washington**, Corpus Christi	SR	G	32	90	189	**47.6**

MINIMUM: 2.5 MADE PER GAME

FREE THROW PCT	CL	POS	G	FT	FTA	PCT
1 **Derek Raivio**, Gonzaga	SR	G	34	148	154	**96.1**
2 **A.J. Graves**, Butler	JR	G	35	145	153	**94.8**
3 **Blake Ahearn**, Missouri State	SR	G	33	111	120	**92.5**
4 **Tristan Blackwood**, Central Connecticut St.	JR	G	34	97	105	**92.4**
5 **David Kool**, Western Michigan	FR	G	29	99	108	**91.7**

MINIMUM: 2.5 MADE PER GAME

ASSISTS PER GAME	CL	POS	G	AST	APG
1 **Jared Jordan**, Marist	SR	G	33	286	**8.7**
2 **Jason Richards**, Davidson	JR	G	34	249	**7.3**
3 **Mustafa Shakur**, Arizona	SR	G	31	215	**6.9**
4 **D.J. Augustin**, Texas	FR	G	35	233	**6.7**
5 **Eric Maynor**, VCU	SO	G	35	224	**6.4**
6 **Keenan Jones**, Northwestern State (LA)	SR	G	32	200	**6.3**
7 **Mike Conley Jr.**, Ohio State	FR	G	39	238	**6.1**
8 **Dwayne Foreman**, Ga. Southern	JR	G	29	176	**6.1**
9 **Josh Wilson**, Northern Arizona	SO	G	30	181	**6.0**
10 **Ishmael Smith**, Wake Forest	FR	G	31	186	**6.0**

REBOUNDS PER GAME	CL	POS	G	REB	RPG
1 **Rashad Jones-Jennings**, Arkansas-Little Rock	SR	F	30	392	**13.1**
2 **Chris Holm**, Vermont	SR	C	33	401	**12.2**
3 **Kentrell Gransberry**, South Florida	JR	C	23	263	**11.4**
4 **Kevin Durant**, Texas	FR	F	35	390	**11.1**
5 **Nick Fazekas**, Nevada	SR	F	32	354	**11.1**
6 **Obie Nwadike**, Central Conn. State	SR	F	31	331	**10.7**
7 **Ryvon Covile**, Detroit	SR	C	30	317	**10.6**
8 **Glen Davis**, LSU	JR	F	29	303	**10.4**
9 **Jason Smith**, Colorado State	JR	F	30	304	**10.1**
10 **Jason Thompson**, Rider	JR	F	31	312	**10.1**

BLOCKED SHOTS PER GAME	CL	POS	G	BLK	BPG
1 **Mickell Gladness**, Alabama A&M	JR	F/C	30	188	**6.3**
2 **Stephane Lasme**, Massachusetts	SR	F	33	168	**5.1**
3 **Hasheem Thabeet**, Connecticut	FR	C	31	118	**3.8**
4 **McHugh Mattis**, South Florida	SR	G	30	109	**3.6**
5 **Dominic McGuire**, Fresno State	JR	G	32	114	**3.6**

STEALS PER GAME	CL	POS	G	STL	SPG
1 **Travis Holmes**, VMI	SO	F	33	111	**3.4**
2 **Paul Gause**, Seton Hall	SO	G	29	90	**3.1**
3 **Ledell Eackles**, Campbell	SR	G	31	94	**3.0**
4 **Ibrahim Jaaber**, Penn	SR	G	31	90	**2.9**
5 **Chavis Holmes**, VMI	SO	G	32	90	**2.8**

INDIVIDUAL LEADERS—GAME

POINTS	CL	POS	OPP	DATE	PTS
1 **Trey Johnson**, Jackson State	SR	G	UTEP	D22	**49**
2 **Bobby Brown**, Cal St. Fullerton	SR	G	Bethune-Cookman	D16	**47**
3 **Al Thornton**, Florida State	SR	G	Miami (FL)	M3	**45**
Reggie Williams, VMI	JR	F	Virginia Intermont	N15	**45**
5 **Jaycee Carroll**, Utah State	JR	G	New Mexico State	F5	**44**
Morris Almond, Rice	SR	G	Vanderbilt	J2	**44**

THREE-PT FG MADE	CL	POS	OPP	DATE	3FG
1 **Michael Jenkins**, Winthrop	JR	G	North Greenville	N10	**12**
2 **Eric Moore**, Buffalo	SO	G	Bowling Green	J7	**11**
Bobby Brown, Cal St. Fullerton	SR	G	Bethune-Cookman	D16	**11**
4 **Tristan Blackwood**, Central Conn. St.	JR	G	Robert Morris	F22	**10**
Andy Wicke, Belmont	SO	G	Gardner-Webb	J20	**10**
Nathan Cranford, Appalachian State	SR	G	Chattanooga	J6	**10**
Leslie Robinson, Florida A&M	JR	G	Albany State (GA)	D9	**10**
Tajuan Porter, Oregon	FR	G	Portland State	N12	**10**
Daryl Cohen, Southeastern La.	SR	G	McNeese State	F1	**10**

ASSISTS	CL	POS	OPP	DATE	AST
1 **Jason Richards**, Davidson	JR	G	Mount St. Mary (NY)	D15	**19**
2 **Ryan Evanochko**, Wisc.-Green Bay	SR	G	Chicago State	D12	**16**
Jason Richards, Davidson	JR	G	Colby	N21	**16**
4 **Ishmael Smith**, Wake Forest	FR	G	Georgia Tech	M8	**15**
Jared Jordan, Marist	SR	G	Siena	F24	**15**
Darren Collison, UCLA	SO	G	Arizona	F17	**15**
Acie Law IV, Texas A&M	SR	G	Texas	F5	**15**
Eric Maynor, VCU	SO	G	Georgia State	F3	**15**
Charles Richardson Jr., Nebraska	SR	G	Rutgers	D2	**15**
Keenan Jones, Northwestern St.(LA)	SR	G	Utah State	N10	**15**

REBOUNDS	CL	POS	OPP	DATE	REB
1 **Arizona Reid**, High Point	JR	F	VMI	F24	**25**
2 **Kentrell Gransberry**, South Florida	JR	C	DePaul	M3	**23**
Kevin Durant, Texas	FR	F	Texas Tech	J31	**23**
4 **Jason Smith**, Colorado State	JR	F	Wyoming	F24	**22**
Josh Heytvelt, Gonzaga	SO	F	Pepperdine	F3	**22**
Moses Sonko, Coastal Carolina	SR	G	VMI	F3	**22**
Calvin Henry, Mercer	SO	F	VMI	D9	**22**
Paul Butorac, Eastern Washington	SR	F	Lewis-Clark State	N18	**22**

BLOCKED SHOTS	CL	POS	OPP	DATE	BLK
1 **Mickell Gladness**, Alabama A&M	JR	F/C	Texas Southern	F24	**16**
2 **Joel Anthony**, UNLV	SR	C	TCU	F7	**13**
Sean Williams, Boston College	JR	F	Duquesne	D28	**13**
4 **Brook Lopez**, Stanford	FR	F	Southern California	J25	**12**
Sean Williams, Boston College	JR	F	Providence	N22	**12**

STEALS	CL	POS	OPP	DATE	STL
1 **Travis Holmes**, VMI	SO	F	Bridgewater (VA)	J18	**11**
2 **Ledell Eackles**, Campbell	SR	G	UNC Pembroke	N11	**10**
3 **D.J. Thompson**, Appalachian State	SR	G	UNC Greensboro	F22	**9**
Kevin Bell, Fresno State	JR	G	Hawaii	F1	**9**
Chavis Holmes, VMI	SO	G	Bridgewater (VA)	J18	**9**
Damian Martin, Loyola Marymount	JR	G	Boise State	D19	**9**
Darren Collison, UCLA	SO	G	Long Beach State	N28	**9**

TEAM LEADERS—SEASON

WIN-LOSS PCT	W	L	PCT
1 **Ohio State**	35	4	**.897**
2 **Memphis**	33	4	**.892**
3 **Florida**	35	5	**.875**
4 **Kansas**	33	5	**.868**
5 **UCLA**	30	6	**.833**

SCORING OFFENSE	G	W-L	PTS	PPG
1 **VMI**	33	14-19	3,331	**100.9**
2 **North Carolina**	38	31-7	3,258	**85.7**
3 **Eastern Washington**	29	15-14	2,443	**84.2**
4 **Northern Arizona**	30	18-12	2,490	**83.0**
5 **Cal State Fullerton**	30	20-10	2,462	**82.1**

SCORING MARGIN	G	W-L	PPG	OPP PPG	MAR
1 **Florida**	40	35-5	79.8	62.6	**17.2**
2 **North Carolina**	38	31-7	85.7	68.6	**17.1**
3 **Kansas**	38	33-5	78.4	61.7	**16.7**
4 **Texas A&M**	34	27-7	75.6	59.4	**16.1**
5 **Memphis**	37	33-4	78.9	63.1	**15.8**

FIELD GOAL PCT	G	W-L	FG	FGA	PCT
1 **Florida**	40	35-5	1,125	2,138	**52.6**
2 **Corpus Christi**	33	26-7	912	1,747	**52.2**
3 **Georgetown**	37	30-7	923	1,826	**50.5**
4 **North Carolina**	38	31-7	1,187	2,379	**49.9**
5 **Texas A&M**	34	27-7	908	1,823	**49.8**

THREE-PT FG PER GAME	G	W-L	3FG	3PG
1 **VMI**	33	14-19	442	**13.4**
2 **West Virginia**	36	27-9	371	**10.3**
3 **Houston**	33	18-15	330	**10.0**
4 **Bradley**	35	22-13	349	**10.0**
5 **Wofford**	30	10-20	297	**9.9**

ASSISTS PER GAME	G	W-L	AST	APG
1 **VMI**	33	14-19	681	**20.6**
2 **Sam Houston State**	31	21-10	596	**19.2**
3 **North Carolina**	38	31-7	696	**18.3**
4 **Northern Arizona**	30	18-12	544	**18.1**
5 **Corpus Christi**	33	26-7	595	**18.0**

REBOUND MARGIN	G	W-L	RPG	OPP RPG	MAR
1 **Vermont**	33	25-8	40.7	31.1	**9.6**
2 **Washington**	32	19-13	38.3	29.3	**9.0**
3 **North Carolina**	38	31-7	40.8	32.3	**8.5**
Florida	40	35-5	37.6	29.1	**8.5**
5 **Massachusetts**	33	24-9	40.4	32.8	**7.7**

SCORING DEFENSE	G	W-L	OPP PTS	OPP PPG
1 **Princeton**	28	11-17	1,493	**53.3**
2 **Air Force**	35	26-9	1,960	**56.0**
3 **Southern Illinois**	36	29-7	2,023	**56.2**
4 **Illinois**	35	23-12	1,997	**57.1**
5 **Butler**	36	29-7	2,056	**57.1**

FIELD GOAL PCT DEFENSE	G	W-L	OPP FG	OPP FGA	OPP PCT
1 Connecticut	31	17-14	677	1,824	**37.1**
2 Texas A&M	34	27-7	672	1,793	**37.5**
3 Syracuse	35	24-11	834	2,223	**37.5**
4 Kansas	38	33-5	804	2,136	**37.6**
5 Georgetown	37	30-7	742	1,935	**38.3**

BLOCKED SHOTS PER GAME	G	W-L	BLK	BPG
1 Connecticut	31	17-14	264	**8.5**
2 Alabama A&M	30	10-20	236	**7.9**
3 Massachusetts	33	24-9	246	**7.5**
4 Syracuse	35	24-11	250	**7.1**
5 Maryland	34	25-9	233	**6.9**

STEALS PER GAME	G	W-L	STL	SPG
1 VMI	33	14-19	490	**14.8**
2 Sacramento State	29	10-19	320	**11.0**
3 Seton Hall	29	13-16	299	**10.3**
4 Northwestern State (LA)	32	17-15	326	**10.2**
5 Missouri	30	18-12	302	**10.1**

TEAM LEADERS—GAME

POINTS	OPP	DATE	SCORE
1 Cal State Northridge	Redlands	N15	**159-97**
2 VMI	Virginia Intermont	N15	**156-95**
3 VMI	Southern Virginia	N20	**144-127**
4 VMI	Lees-McRae	D6	**135-75**
5 Oklahoma State	Southwestern Okla.	J2	**129-77**
Penn State	VMI	D30	**129-111**

FIELD GOAL PCT	OPPt	DATE	FG	FGA	PCT
1 Ohio	Bellarmine	D9	32	44	**72.7**
2 Long Island	Old Westbury	N25	42	58	**72.4**
3 Richmond	Longwood	N20	28	39	**71.8**
4 Rice	Paul Quinn	N11	43	60	**71.7**
5 Cal State Northridge	Redlands	N15	62	87	**71.3**

THREE-PT FG MADE	OPP	DATE	3FG
1 VMI	Lees-McRae	D6	**22**
2 VMI	Charleston So.	J13	**21**
VMI	Va. Intermont	N15	**21**
Pepperdine	Nicholls State	N14	**21**
Nicholls State	Corpus Christi	F8	**21**

CONSENSUS ALL-AMERICAS

FIRST TEAM

PLAYER	CL	POS	HT	SCHOOL	RPG	PPG
Arron Afflalo	JR	G	6-5	UCLA	2.8	16.9
Kevin Durant	FR	F	6-9	Texas	11.1	25.8
Tyler Hansbrough	SO	F	6-9	North Carolina	7.9	18.4
Acie Law IV	SR	G	6-3	Texas A&M	3.3	18.1
Alando Tucker	SR	F	6-6	Wisconsin	5.4	19.9

SECOND TEAM

PLAYER	CL	POS	HT	SCHOOL	RPG	PPG
Jared Dudley	SR	F	6-7	Boston College	8.3	19.0
Nick Fazekas	SR	F	6-11	Nevada	11.1	20.4
Chris Lofton	JR	G	6-2	Tennessee	3.1	20.8
Joakim Noah	JR	F/C	6-11	Florida	8.4	12.0
Greg Oden	FR	C	7-0	Ohio State	9.6	15.7

SELECTORS: AP, NABC, SPORTING NEWS, USBWA

AWARD WINNERS

PLAYER OF THE YEAR

PLAYER	CL	POS	HT	SCHOOL	AWARDS
Kevin Durant	FR	F	6-9	Texas	Naismith, AP, USBWA, Wooden, NABC, Rupp
Tré Kelly	SR	G	6-0	South Carolina	Frances Pomeroy Naismith*

* FOR THE MOST OUTSTANDING SENIOR PLAYER WHO IS 6 FEET OR UNDER.

DEFENSIVE PLAYER OF THE YEAR

PLAYER	CL	POS	HT	SCHOOL
Greg Oden	FR	C	7-0	Ohio State

COACH OF THE YEAR

COACH	SCHOOL	REC	AWARDS
Tony Bennett	Washington State	26-8	Naismith, AP, USBWA, Sporting News, CBS/Chevrolet
Todd Lickliter	Butler	29-7	NABC

ESPNU CLASS OF 2007

RATING/PLAYER	POS	HT	HIGH SCHOOL	A-A TEAMS	COLLEGE	CAREER NOTES
99 Kevin Love	C	6-9	Lake Oswego (OR) HS	McD, P, USA	UCLA	First-team All-America; No. 5 pick, '08 NBA draft (Wolves); 11.1 ppg, 9.1 rpg
98 Eric Gordon	SG	6-5	North Central HS, Indianapolis	McD, MJ, P, USA	Indiana	First-team All-America; No. 7 pick, '08 NBA draft (Clippers); 16.1 ppg in '08-09
98 O.J. Mayo	SG	6-4	Huntington (WV) HS	McD, MJ, P, USA	USC	First-team All-Pac-10; No. 3 pick, '08 NBA draft (Wolves); 18.5 ppg in '08-09
98 Kyle Singler	SF	6-8	Camden (NJ) Catholic HS	McD, MJ, P, USA	Duke	ACC Rookie of the Year, '08; averaged 16.5 ppg for Duke as sophomore
98 Derrick Rose	PG	6-3	Simeon Career Academy HS, Chicago	McD, MJ, P, USA	Memphis	Memphis' No. 2 scorer in '07-08; No. 1 overall pick, '08 NBA draft (Bulls); NBA ROY, '09
98 Nolan Smith	SG	6-4	Oak Hill Academy, Mouth of Wilson, VA	McD, P, USA	Duke	Played in all 34 games, averaging 5.9 ppg; averaged 8.5 ppg as sophomore
98 Austin Freeman	SG	6-3	DeMatha Catholic HS Hyattsville, MD	McD, MJ, P, USA	Georgetown	All-Big East rookie selection; 9.1 ppg as freshman; 11.5 ppg as sophomore
98 Michael Beasley	PF	6-9	Notre Dame Prep, Fitchburg, MA	McD, USA	Kansas State	No. 2 pick, '08 NBA draft (Heat); first-team All-America, '08; 13.9 ppg in '08-09
97 Patrick Patterson	PF	6-8	Huntington (WV) HS	McD, MJ, P, USA	Kentucky	SEC co-Freshman of the Year; first-team All-SEC as sophomore; 17.9 ppg, 9.3 rpg
97 Nick Calathes	SG	6-5	Lake Howell HS, Winter Park, FL	McD, MJ, P, USA	Florida	SEC co-Freshman of the Year; led UF in scoring (17.2 ppg) as sophomore; 2nd-round pick, '09 NBA draft (Wolves)
97 Corey Fisher	PG	6-1	St. Patrick HS, Elizabeth, NJ	MJ, P, USA	Villanova	9.1 ppg, 2.7 apg as freshman; Big East Sixth Man of the Year as sophomore (10.8 ppg)
97 Kosta Koufos	C	7-1	Glen Oak HS, Canton, OH	McD, MJ, P, USA	Ohio State	Averaged 14.4 ppg, 6.5 rpg for OSU; No. 23 pick, '08 NBA draft (Jazz); 4.7 ppg (48 NBA games)
97 Cole Aldrich	C	6-10	Jefferson HS Bloomington, MN	McD, P	Kansas	Played in all 40 games of championship season; Big 12 Defensive Player of Year as sophomore
97 J.J. Hickson	C	6-8	Wheeler HS, Marietta, GA	McD, P	NC State	ACC All-Freshman team; No. 19 pick, '08 NBA draft (Cavs); 4.0 ppg in '08-09
97 Corey Stokes	SG	6-6	St. Benedict's Prep, Newark, NJ	McD, P	Villanova	Played in all 'Nova games his first 2 seasons; 6.4 ppg as freshman, 9.3 as sophomore
97 Taylor King	SF	6-7	Mater Dei HS Santa Ana, CA	McD, P	Duke/Villanova	Played in 34 games for Duke; 5.5 ppg; transferred to 'Nova
97 Donté Greene	PF	6-8	Towson (MD) Catholic HS	McD, MJ, P, USA	Syracuse	All-Big East 2nd team; No. 28 pick, '08 NBA draft (Grizzlies); 55 games for Kings
97 Blake Griffin	PF	6-9	Oklahoma Christian School, Edmond, OK	McD, MJ, P	Oklahoma	Consensus National Player of Year as sophomore; No. 1 pick, '09 NBA draft (Clippers)
97 Jai Lucas	PG	5-10	Bellaire (TX) HS	McD, MJ, P	Florida/Texas	Played in 36 games for UF; 8.5 ppg, 1.7 rpg; transferred to Texas, '09
97 E'Twaun Moore	PG	6-3	East Chicago (IN) Central HS	P	Purdue	2-time 2nd team All-Big Ten; 12.9 ppg as freshman; led team as sophomore (13.8 ppg)
97 James Harden	SG	6-5	Artesia HS, Lakewood, CA	McD, P	Arizona State	First-team All-Pac-10; Consensus first-team All-America (20.1 ppg as sophomore); No. 3 pick, '09 NBA draft (Thunder)
97 Gani Lawal	PF	6-8	Montgomery County HS, Mount Sterling, KY	McD, P	Georgia Tech	Led GT with 32 blocks as freshman; 15.1 ppg, 9.5 rpg as sophomore
97 Jonny Flynn	PG	6-0	Niagara Falls (NY) HS	McD, P	Syracuse	Big East co-Rookie of the Year; led SU with 17.4 ppg, 254 assists as sophomore; No. 6 pick, '09 NBA draft (Wolves)
97 James Anderson	SF	6-5	Junction City (AR) HS	McD, P	Oklahoma State	2nd team All Big 12; led OSU with 18.2 ppg as sophomore
97 DeAndre Jordan	C	7-0	Houston (TX) Christian HS	P	Texas A&M	2nd-round pick, '08 NBA draft (Clippers); 4.3 ppg in 53 NBA games

Abbreviations: McD=McDonald's; MJ=Jordan Brand; P=Parade; USA=USA Today

Poll Progression

Preseason Poll

AP	ESPN/USA	School
1	1	Florida
2	2	North Carolina
3	3	Kansas
4	5	Pittsburgh
5	7	LSU
6	5	UCLA
7	4	Ohio State
8	8	Georgetown
9	9	Wisconsin
10	10	Arizona
11	12	Alabama
12	11	Duke
13	13	Texas A&M
14	14	Memphis
15	15	Boston College
16	17	Marquette
17	16	Washington
18	18	Connecticut
19	23	Creighton
20	20	Syracuse
21	19	Texas
22	22	Kentucky
23	21	Georgia Tech
24	25	Nevada
25	24	Tennessee

Week of Nov 14

AP	ESPN/USA	School	AP↓↑
1	1	Florida (1-0)	
2	2	North Carolina (0-0)	
3	3	Kansas (1-0)	
4	5	Pittsburgh (1-0)	
5	4	Ohio State (3-0)	↑2
6	6	UCLA (0-0)	
7	7	LSU (0-0)	↓2
8	8	Georgetown (1-0)	
9	9	Wisconsin (1-0)	
10	11	Alabama (1-0)	↑1
11	10	Duke (1-0)	↑1
12	12	Texas A&M (1-0)	↑1
13	13	Memphis (0-0)	↑1
14	14	Boston College (1-0)	↑1
15	16	Arizona (0-1)	↓5
16	17	Marquette (1-0)	
17	15	Washington (1-0)	
18	20	Syracuse (3-0)	↑2
19	18	Texas (2-0)	↑2
20	25	Creighton (0-0)	↓1
21	19	Connecticut (1-0)	↓3
22	22	Kentucky (0-0)	
23	21	Georgia Tech (1-0)	
24	23	Nevada (1-0)	
25	24	Tennessee (1-0)	

Week of Nov 21

AP	ESPN/USA	School	AP↓↑
1	1	Florida (4-0)	
2	2	North Carolina (3-0)	
3	4	Pittsburgh (5-0)	↑1
4	3	Ohio State (4-0)	↑1
5	5	UCLA (1-0)	↑1
6	6	LSU (2-0)	↑1
7	7	Wisconsin (3-0)	↑2
8	9	Alabama (3-0)	↑2
9	8	Duke (3-0)	↑2
10	12	Kansas (2-1)	↓7
11	10	Texas A&M (4-0)	↑1
12	11	Memphis (1-0)	↑1
13	17	Marquette (4-0)	↑3
14	16	Georgetown (2-1)	↓6
15	15	Arizona (2-1)	
16	13	Washington (4-0)	↑1
17	14	Syracuse (4-0)	↑1
18	18	Connecticut (4-0)	↑3
19	19	Georgia Tech (3-0)	↑4
20	22	Kentucky (2-0)	↑2
21	20	Nevada (3-0)	↑3
22	21	Tennessee (4-0)	↑3
23	—	Boston College (1-1)	↓9
24	—	Wichita State (3-0)	⤴
25	24	Maryland (5-0)	⤴
—	23	Gonzaga (4-0)	
—	25	Texas (3-1)	⤵

Week of Nov 28

AP	ESPN/USA	School	AP↓↑
1	2	UCLA (4-0)	↑4
2	3	Pittsburgh (6-0)	↑1
3	1	Ohio State (6-0)	↑1
4	4	Florida (6-1)	↓3
5	5	Kansas (5-1)	↑5
6	7	Alabama (5-0)	↑2
7	6	North Carolina (4-1)	↓5
8	9	Marquette (6-0)	↑5
9	8	Texas A&M (5-0)	↑2
10	12	LSU (2-1)	↓4
11	10	Duke (5-1)	↓2
12	13	Wisconsin (5-1)	↓5
13	11	Washington (5-0)	↑3
14	17	Memphis (3-1)	↓2
15	14	Syracuse (6-0)	↑2
16	16	Arizona (3-1)	↓1
17	22	Wichita State (4-0)	↑7
18	23	Georgetown (3-1)	↓4
19	18	Butler (7-0)	⤴
20	15	Connecticut (5-0)	↓2
21	24	Georgia Tech (5-1)	↓2
22	21	Gonzaga (6-1)	⤴
23	19	Maryland (7-0)	↑2
24	20	Nevada (5-0)	↓3
25	—	Virginia (4-0)	⤴
—	25	Texas (4-1)	

Week of Dec 5

AP	ESPN/USA	School	AP↓↑
1	1	UCLA (6-0)	
2	2	Pittsburgh (8-0)	
3	3	North Carolina (6-1)	↑4
4	5	Alabama (7-0)	↑2
5	4	Ohio State (7-1) (A)	↓2
6	6	Texas A&M (7-0)	↑3
7	9	Duke (7-1)	↑4
8	7	Florida (7-2)	↓4
9	11	LSU (4-1)	↑1
10	16	Wichita State (6-0)	↑7
11	12	Wisconsin (7-1)	↑1
12	13	Kansas (6-2)	↓7
13	8	Washington (6-0)	
14	15	Arizona (5-1)	↑2
15	14	Butler (9-0)	↑4
16	17	Memphis (5-1)	↓2
17	20	Marquette (8-1)	↓9
18	18	Gonzaga (8-1)	↑4
19	10	Connecticut (7-0)	↑1
20	19	Nevada (7-0)	↑4
21	21	Syracuse (7-1)	↓6
22	24	Oklahoma State (9-0)	⤴
23	22	Maryland (8-1)	
24	—	Xavier (6-1)	⤴
25	—	Georgia Tech (6-2)	↓4
—	23	Air Force (8-1)	
—	25	Michigan State (7-2)	

Week of Dec 12

AP	ESPN/USA	School	AP↓↑
1	1	UCLA (8-0)	
2	2	Pittsburgh (10-0)	
3	3	North Carolina (7-1)	
4	4	Ohio State (8-1)	↑1
5	5	Florida (8-2)	↑3
6	6	Duke (9-1)	↑1
7	7	Wisconsin (9-1)	↑4
8	10	Wichita State (7-0)	↑2
9	9	Alabama (8-1)	↓5
10	11	Arizona (7-1)	↑4
11	12	Kansas (8-2)	↑1
12	15	LSU (5-2)	↓3
13	13	Texas A&M (7-2)	↓7
14	8	Connecticut (8-0)	↑5
15	17	Oklahoma State (11-0)	↑7
16	16	Gonzaga (9-2)	↑2
17	14	Washington (7-1)	↓4
18	18	Butler (10-1)	↓3
19	19	Memphis (7-2)	↓3
20	22	Marquette (9-2)	↓3
21	—	Notre Dame (7-1)	⤴
22	24	Oregon (7-0)	⤴
23	—	Syracuse (8-2)	↓2
24	20	Air Force (10-1)	⤴
25	21	Nevada (7-1)	↓5
—	23	Michigan State (9-2)	
—	25	Clemson (10-0)	

Week of Dec 19

AP	ESPN/USA	School	AP↓↑
1	1	UCLA (9-0)	
2	2	North Carolina (8-1)	↑1
3	3	Ohio State (9-1)	↑1
4	5	Wisconsin (11-1)	↑3
5	4	Florida (9-2)	
6	6	Duke (9-1)	
7	7	Pittsburgh (10-1)	↓5
8	8	Wichita State (8-0)	
9	9	Arizona (8-1)	↑1
10	10	Alabama (9-1)	↓1
11	12	Kansas (8-2)	
12	15	LSU (6-2)	
13	13	Texas A&M (9-2)	
14	11	Connecticut (9-0)	
15	14	Oklahoma State (11-0)	
16	16	Butler (11-1)	↑2
17	17	Washington (8-1)	
18	18	Memphis (8-2)	↑1
19	21	Marquette (10-2)	↑1
20	—	Notre Dame (8-1)	↑1
21	23	Oregon (10-0)	↑1
22	24	Gonzaga (9-3)	↓6
23	—	Syracuse (9-2)	
24	19	Air Force (11-1)	
25	20	Nevada (9-1)	
—	22	Clemson (10-0)	
—	25	Michigan State (10-2)	

Week of Dec 26

AP	ESPN/USA	School	AP↓↑
1	1	UCLA (11-0)	
2	2	North Carolina (10-1)	
3	3	Florida (11-2)	↑2
4	4	Wisconsin (12-1)	
5	5	Duke (11-1)	↑1
6	6	Ohio State (10-2)	↓3
7	7	Arizona (9-1)	↑2
8	8	Alabama (11-1)	↑2
9	10	Kansas (10-2)	↑2
10	11	Pittsburgh (11-2)	↓3
11	12	Texas A&M (10-2)	↑2
12	9	Connecticut (10-0)	↑2
13	14	Oklahoma State (12-1)	↑2
14	13	Washington (10-1)	↑3
15	15	Butler (12-1)	↑1
16	16	Wichita State (9-2)	↓8
17	19	LSU (7-3)	↓5
18	22	Marquette (12-2)	↑1
19	24	Notre Dame (10-1)	↑1
20	20	Oregon (11-0)	↑1
21	—	Tennessee (10-2)	⤴
22	23	Memphis (9-3)	↓4
23	17	Air Force (11-1)	↑1
24	18	Nevada (10-1)	↑1
25	21	Clemson (12-0)	⤴
—	25	Michigan State (12-2)	

Week of Jan 2 (B)

AP	ESPN/USA	School	AP↓↑
1	1	UCLA (13-0)	
2	2	North Carolina (12-1)	
3	3	Florida (12-2)	
4	4	Wisconsin (14-1)	
5	5	Duke (12-1)	
6	6	Ohio State (11-2)	
7	7	Arizona (11-1)	
8	8	Alabama (12-1)	
9	9	Kansas (12-2)	
10	10	Pittsburgh (12-2)	
11	11	Texas A&M (11-2)	
12	12	Oklahoma State (13-1)	↑1
13	13	Butler (13-1)	↑2
14	19	LSU (10-3)	↑3
15	21	Marquette (13-2)	↑3
16	17	Oregon (13-0)	↑4
17	22	Notre Dame (12-1)	↑2
18	14	Connecticut (11-1)	↓6
19	25	Tennessee (12-2)	↑2
20	16	Air Force (13-1)	↑3
21	15	Nevada (12-1)	↑3
22	23	Memphis (10-3)	
23	18	Clemson (14-0)	↑2
24	20	Washington (10-3)	↓10
25	—	West Virginia (11-1)	⤴
—	24	Michigan State (13-2)	

Week of Jan 9

AP	ESPN/USA	School	AP↓↑
1	1	North Carolina (14-1)	↑1
2	2	Florida (14-2)	↑1
3	4	Wisconsin (15-1)	↑1
4	3	UCLA (14-1)	↓3
5	5	Ohio State (13-2)	↑1
6	6	Kansas (13-2)	↑3
7	7	Pittsburgh (14-2)	↑3
8	9	Texas A&M (13-2)	↑3
9	10	Oklahoma State (15-1) (C)	↑3
10	8	Arizona (12-2)	↓3
11	11	Duke (13-2)	↓6
12	12	Butler (14-1)	↑1
13	18	LSU (11-3)	↑1
14	13	Alabama (13-2)	↓6
15	17	Oregon (14-1)	↑1
16	20	Tennessee (13-2)	↑3
17	14	Clemson (16-0)	↑6
18	15	Air Force (15-1)	↑2
19	15	Nevada (13-1)	↑2
20	19	Memphis (11-3)	↑2
21	21	West Virginia (13-1)	↑4
22	—	Notre Dame (13-2)	↓5
23	23	Washington State (14-2)	⤴
24	22	Connecticut (12-2)	↓6
25	—	Texas (11-3)	⤴
—	24	Washington (11-4)	⤵
—	25	Maryland (14-2)	

Week of Jan 16

AP	ESPN/USA	School	AP↓↑
1	1	Florida (16-2)	↑1
2	3	Wisconsin (17-1)	↑1
3	2	UCLA (15-1)	↑1
4	4	North Carolina (15-2)	↓3
5	5	Kansas (15-2)	↑1
6	6	Pittsburgh (16-2)	↑1
7	7	Ohio State (14-3)	↓2
8	8	Texas A&M (15-2)	
9	10	Oregon (16-1)	↑6
10	9	Alabama (14-2)	↑4
11	12	Arizona (13-3)	↓1
12	14	Oklahoma State (15-2)	↓3
13	11	Air Force (17-1)	↑5
14	17	Duke (14-3)	↓3
15	13	Nevada (16-1)	↑4
16	19	LSU (12-4)	↓3
17	18	Memphis (13-3)	↑3
18	15	Butler (15-2)	↓6
19	16	Clemson (17-1)	↓2
20	20	Notre Dame (15-2)	↑2
21	23	Texas (13-3)	↑4
22	24	Tennessee (13-4)	↓6
23	25	Virginia Tech (13-4)	⤴
24	—	Marquette (15-4)	⤴
25	—	Kentucky (14-3)	⤴
—	21	Washington State (15-3) (D)	⤵
—	22	Maryland (15-3)	

Week of Jan 23

AP	ESPN/USA	School	AP↓↑
1	1	Florida (17-2)	
2	3	Wisconsin (19-1)	
3	2	UCLA (17-1)	
4	4	North Carolina (17-2)	
5	5	Ohio State (16-3)	↑2
6	6	Texas A&M (16-2)	↑2
7	7	Oregon (18-1)	↑2
8	8	Kansas (16-3)	↓3
9	9	Pittsburgh (17-3)	↓3
10	10	Duke (16-3)	↑4
11	14	Memphis (15-3)	↑6
12	12	Alabama (15-3)	↓2
13	16	Oklahoma State (16-3)	↓1
14	11	Butler (17-2)	↑4
15	20	Marquette (17-4)	↑9
16	13	Air Force (18-2)	↓3
17	19	Arizona (13-5)	↓6
18	15	Nevada (17-2)	↓3
19	17	Clemson (18-2)	
20	18	Washington State (16-3)	⤴
21	22	LSU (13-5)	↓5
22	21	Notre Dame (16-3)	↓2
23	24	Indiana (14-4)	⤴
24	23	Virginia Tech (14-5)	↓1
25	—	USC (15-5)	⤴
—	25	Kentucky (15-4)	⤵

Poll Progression Continues →

ANNUAL REVIEW

Week of Jan 30

AP	ESPN/USA	School	AP↓↑
1	1	**Florida** (19-2)	
2	2	**Wisconsin** (21-1)	
3	3	**North Carolina** (19-2)	↑1
4	4	**Ohio State** (18-3)	↑1
5	5	**UCLA** (18-2)	↓2
6	6	**Kansas** (18-3)	↑2
7	7	**Pittsburgh** (19-3)	↑2
8	10	**Duke** (18-3)	↑2
9	9	**Oregon** (19-2)	↓2
10	8	**Texas A&M** (17-3)	↓4
11	12	**Memphis** (17-3)	
12	14	**Oklahoma State** (18-3)	↑1
13	11	**Butler** (19-2)	↑1
14	15	**Marquette** (19-4)	↑1
15	13	**Nevada** (19-2)	↑3
16	18	**Virginia Tech** (16-5)	↑8
17	16	**Air Force** (19-3)	↓1
18	17	**Washington State** (17-4)	↑2
19	20	**Alabama** (15-5)	↓7
20	22	**Arizona** (14-6)	↓3
21	19	**Notre Dame** (17-4)	↑1
22	23	**Texas** (15-5)	⤴
23	—	**Stanford** (14-5)	⤴
24	—	**Vanderbilt** (15-6)	⤴
25	21	**Clemson** (18-4)	↓6
—	24	**Kentucky** (16-5)	
—	25	**Indiana** (15-5)	⌐
—	25	**UNLV** (18-4)	

Week of Feb 6

AP	ESPN/USA	School	AP↓↑
1	1	**Florida** (21-2)	
2	2	**UCLA** (20-2)	↑3
3	3	**Ohio State** (20-3)	↑1
4	4	**Wisconsin** (22-2)	↓2
5	5	**North Carolina** (20-3)	↓2
6	7	**Texas A&M** (19-3)	↑4
7	6	**Pittsburgh** (20-3)	
8	10	**Memphis** (19-3)	↑3
9	8	**Kansas** (19-4)	↓3
10	9	**Butler** (22-2)	↑3
11	12	**Marquette** (20-4)	↑3
12	11	**Nevada** (21-2)	↑3
13	15	**Oregon** (19-4)	↓4
14	14	**Washington State** (19-4)	↑4
15	13	**Air Force** (20-3)	↑2
16	16	**Duke** (18-5)	↓8
17	17	**Oklahoma State** (18-4)	↓5
18	19	**Alabama** (17-5)	↑1
19	21	**USC** (18-6)	⤴
20	18	**Kentucky** (17-5)	⤴
21	20	**Southern Illinois** (19-5)	⤴
22	23	**Georgetown** (16-5)	⤴
23	—	**Vanderbilt** (16-7)	↑1
24	—	**Arizona** (15-7)	↓4
25	—	**Stanford** (15-6)	↓2
—	21	**Notre Dame** (18-5)	⌐
—	24	**Indiana** (16-6)	
—	25	**Texas** (16-6)	⌐

Week of Feb 13

AP	ESPN/USA	School	AP↓↑
1	1	**Florida** (23-2) (E)	
2	2	**Ohio State** (22-3)	↑1
3	3	**Wisconsin** (24-2)	↑1
4	4	**North Carolina** (22-3)	↑1
5	7	**UCLA** (21-3)	↓3
6	6	**Texas A&M** (21-3)	
7	5	**Pittsburgh** (22-3)	
8	9	**Memphis** (21-3)	
9	8	**Kansas** (21-4)	
10	11	**Washington State** (21-4)	↑4
11	10	**Nevada** (22-2)	↑1
12	13	**Marquette** (21-5)	↓1
13	12	**Butler** (23-3)	↓3
14	16	**Georgetown** (18-5)	↑8
15	17	**Oregon** (20-5)	↓2
16	15	**Southern Illinois** (21-5)	↑5
17	14	**Air Force** (21-4)	↓2
18	20	**Oklahoma State** (19-5)	↓1
19	24	**Arizona** (17-7)	↑5
20	18	**Kentucky** (18-6) (E)	
21	21	**Boston College** (18-6)	⤴
22	23	**USC** (18-7)	↓3
23	22	**West Virginia** (19-5)	⤴
24	19	**Indiana** (17-6)	⤴
25	—	**Alabama** (18-6)	↓7
—	25	**Virginia Tech** (17-7)	

Week of Feb 20

AP	ESPN/USA	School	AP↓↑
1	2	**Wisconsin** (26-2) (F)	
2	1	**Ohio State** (24-3) (F)	
3	3	**Florida** (24-3) (F)	
4	4	**UCLA** (23-3)	
5	5	**North Carolina** (23-4)	
6	6	**Kansas** (23-4)	
7	7	**Memphis** (23-3)	
8	9	**Texas A&M** (22-4)	
9	11	**Washington State** (22-4)	
10	8	**Pittsburgh** (23-4)	
11	10	**Nevada** (24-2)	
12	12	**Georgetown** (20-5)	
13	14	**Southern Illinois** (23-5)	
14	13	**Air Force** (23-4)	
15	15	**Butler** (24-4)	
16	16	**Marquette** (21-7)	↓
17	21	**Vanderbilt** (18-8)	
18	17	**Duke** (20-7)	
19	20	**Texas** (19-7)	
20	—	**Louisville** (19-8)	
21	22	**BYU** (20-6)	
22	18	**West Virginia** (20-6)	↑1
23	24	**Oregon** (20-7)	↓8
24	19	**Virginia** (18-7)	⤴
25	25	**Alabama** (19-7)	
—	23	**Notre Dame** (20-6)	

Week of Feb 27

AP	ESPN/USA	School	AP↓↑
1	1	**Ohio State** (26-3)	↑1
2	2	**UCLA** (25-3)	↑2
3	3	**Kansas** (25-4)	↑3
4	5	**Wisconsin** (26-4)	↓3
5	4	**Florida** (25-4)	↓2
6	7	**Memphis** (25-3)	↑1
7	6	**Texas A&M** (24-4)	↑1
8	8	**North Carolina** (24-5)	↓3
9	10	**Georgetown** (22-5)	↑3
10	9	**Nevada** (26-2)	↑1
11	11	**Southern Illinois** (25-5)	↑2
12	12	**Pittsburgh** (24-5)	↓2
13	13	**Washington State** (23-5)	↓4
14	14	**Duke** (22-7)	↑4
15	15	**Texas** (21-7)	↑4
16	19	**Louisville** (21-8)	↑4
17	18	**Oregon** (22-7)	↑6
18	16	**Butler** (26-5)	↓3
19	23	**Vanderbilt** (19-9)	↓2
20	21	**Marquette** (22-8)	↓4
21	21	**Virginia Tech** (20-8)	⤴
22	17	**Notre Dame** (22-6)	⤴
23	24	**USC** (21-8)	⤴
24	—	**Maryland** (22-7)	⤴
25	20	**Air Force** (23-6)	↓11
—	25	**Virginia** (19-8)	⌐

Week of Mar 6

AP	ESPN/USA	School	AP↓↑
1	1	**Ohio State** (27-3)	
2	2	**Kansas** (27-4)	↑1
3	4	**Wisconsin** (27-4)	↑1
4	3	**UCLA** (26-4)	↓2
5	5	**Memphis** (27-3)	↑1
6	6	**Florida** (26-5)	↓1
7	7	**Texas A&M** (25-5)	
8	8	**North Carolina** (25-6)	
9	9	**Georgetown** (23-6)	
10	10	**Nevada** (27-3)	
11	12	**Washington State** (24-6)	↑2
12	15	**Louisville** (22-8)	↑4
13	11	**Pittsburgh** (25-6)	↓1
14	13	**Southern Illinois** (27-6)	↓3
15	14	**Texas** (22-8)	
16	18	**Oregon** (23-7)	↑1
17	20	**Maryland** (24-7)	↑7
18	19	**Marquette** (23-8)	↑2
19	17	**Butler** (27-5)	↓1
20	16	**Notre Dame** (23-6)	↑2
21	21	**Duke** (22-9)	↓7
22	—	**Tennessee** (22-9)	⤴
23	23	**BYU** (23-7)	⤴
24	22	**Winthrop** (28-4)	⤴
25	25	**UNLV** (25-6)	⤴
—	24	**Virginia** (20-9)	

Week of Mar 13

AP	ESPN/USA	School	AP↓↑
1	1	**Ohio State** (30-3)	⤴
2	2	**Kansas** (30-4)	
3	3	**Florida** (29-5)	↑3
4	4	**North Carolina** (28-6)	↑4
5	5	**Memphis** (30-3)	
6	7	**Wisconsin** (29-5)	↓3
7	6	**UCLA** (26-5)	↓3
8	8	**Georgetown** (26-6)	↑1
9	9	**Texas A&M** (25-6)	↓2
10	12	**Oregon** (26-7)	↑6
11	11	**Texas** (24-9)	↑4
12	10	**Pittsburgh** (27-7)	↑1
13	13	**Washington State** (25-7)	↓2
14	15	**Southern Illinois** (27-6)	
15	13	**Nevada** (28-4)	↓5
16	16	**Louisville** (23-9)	↓4
17	17	**Notre Dame** (24-7)	↑3
18	22	**Maryland** (24-8)	↓1
19	18	**UNLV** (28-6)	↑6
20	20	**Marquette** (24-9)	↓2
21	19	**Butler** (27-6)	↓2
22	21	**Winthrop** (28-4)	↑2
23	25	**USC** (23-11)	⤴
24	23	**BYU** (25-8)	↓1
25	—	**Tennessee** (22-10)	↓3
—	24	**Creighton** (22-10)	

Final Poll (Post-Tournament

ESPN/USA	School
1	**Florida** (35-5)
2	**Ohio State** (35-4)
3	**UCLA** (30-6)
4	**Georgetown** (30-7)
5	**North Carolina** (31-7)
5	**Kansas** (33-5)
7	**Memphis** (33-4)
8	**Oregon** (29-8)
9	**Texas A&M** (27-7)
10	**Pittsburgh** (29-8)
11	**Southern Illinois** (29-7)
11	**Wisconsin** (30-6)
13	**Butler** (29-7)
14	**UNLV** (30-7)
15	**USC** (25-12)
16	**Texas** (25-10)
17	**Washington State** (26-8)
18	**Tennessee** (24-11)
19	**Vanderbilt** (22-12)
20	**Louisville** (24-10)
21	**Nevada** (29-5)
22	**Winthrop** (29-5)
23	**Maryland** (25-9)
24	**Virginia** (21-11)
25	**Virginia Tech** (22-12)

(A) Slow to recover from wrist surgery, Ohio State's 7-foot freshman, Greg Oden, finally makes his college debut on Dec. 2 against Valparaiso, registering a double-double (14 points, 10 rebounds) in a 78-58 Buckeyes victory.

(B) Texas Tech defeats New Mexico, 70-68, on Jan.1. For coach Bob Knight, it's career victory No. 880, passing North Carolina's Dean Smith as the winningest men's coach in Division I history.

(C) Oklahoma State, which led the nation in scoring defense seven times under legendary coach Henry Iba, whips Division II Southwestern Oklahoma State, 129-77—a school record for points scored in a game.

(D) In a 71-68 overtime loss at Stanford on Jan. 13, junior Kyle Weaver gets the first triple-double in Washington State history (14 points, 13 rebounds, 10 assists).

(E) Kentucky gives the defending national champs a scare on Feb. 10, but loses to Florida, 64-61, when Ramel Bradley—who hit two three-pointers in the final :20 to cut a nine-point Florida lead to three—misses a trey at the horn.

(F) A Florida loss to Vanderbilt allows two Big Ten teams to take over the top two spots in the polls—which differ on who is No. 1. Ohio State will settle the issue (but not by much) on Feb. 25 with a 49-48 win over Wisconsin in Columbus.

Pre-Tournament Ratings Percentage Index (RPI)

Rank	School	W-L	Sched. Strg.	SS Rank	RPI
1	**Ohio State**	30-3	.6010	15	.6720
2	**North Carolina**	28-6	.6250	6	.6610
3	**UCLA**	25-5	.6151	8	.6579
4	**Wisconsin**	29-5	.5844	25	.6466
5	**Pittsburgh**	27-7	.6277	4	.6464
6	**Florida**	29-5	.5736	43	.6433
7	**Southern Illinois**	26-6	.5784	34	.6400
8	**Memphis**	30-3	.5520	70	.6379
9	**Georgetown**	26-6	.5958	17	.6368
10	**UNLV**	27-6	.5812	29	.6349
11	**Kansas**	30-4	.5601	59	.6334
12	**Tennessee**	22-10	.6257	5	.6272
13	**Kentucky**	21-11	.6491	1	.6263
14	**Arizona**	20-10	.6487	2	.6241
15	**Duke**	22-10	.6388	3	.6182
16	**Maryland**	24-8	.6040	11	.6167
17	**Texas A&M**	25-6	.5636	54	.6156
18	**BYU**	24-8	.5647	52	.6146
19	**Villanova**	21-10	.6206	7	.6138
20	**Creighton**	22-10	.5937	19	.6121
21	**Oregon**	26-7	.5511	71	.6112
22	**Marquette**	23-9	.6006	16	.6054
23	**Nevada**	27-4	.5079	134	.6036
24	**Michigan State**	22-11	.6087	9	.6034
25	**Washington State**	25-7	.5282	107	.6031
26	**Texas**	24-9	.5648	51	.6018
27	**Butler**	25-6	.5301	101	.5966
28	**Indiana**	20-10	.5599	60	.5954
29	**Illinois**	23-11	.5896	23	.5948
30	**Air Force**	22-8	.5495	75	.5945
31	**Notre Dame**	24-7	.5185	114	.5943
32	**Boston College**	20-11	.6027	13	.5941
33	**Xavier**	24-8	.5466	84	.5940
34	**Virginia Tech**	20-11	.5898	22	.5936
35	**Arkansas**	21-13	.6058	10	.5907
36	**Missouri State**	21-10	.5763	39	.5897
37	**Louisville**	22-9	.5758	41	.5890
38	**Bradley**	20-12	.5929	21	.5884
39	**Drexel**	22-8	.5369	96	.5883
40	**Old Dominion**	24-8	.5477	80	.5822
41	**Florida State**	20-12	.5934	20	.5867
42	**Purdue**	21-11	.5726	46	.5857
43	**Utah State**	22-11	.5565	64	.5845
44	**VCU**	27-6	.5108	129	.5844
45	**Clemson**	21-10	.5630	55	.5833
46	**Vanderbilt**	19-11	.5874	24	.5827
47	**USC**	23-11	.5759	40	.5824
48	**Davidson**	27-4	.4704	215	.5821
49	**Alabama**	20-11	.5729	45	.5820
50	**Syracuse**	22-10	.5720	47	.5809

Source: NCAA

ANNUAL REVIEW

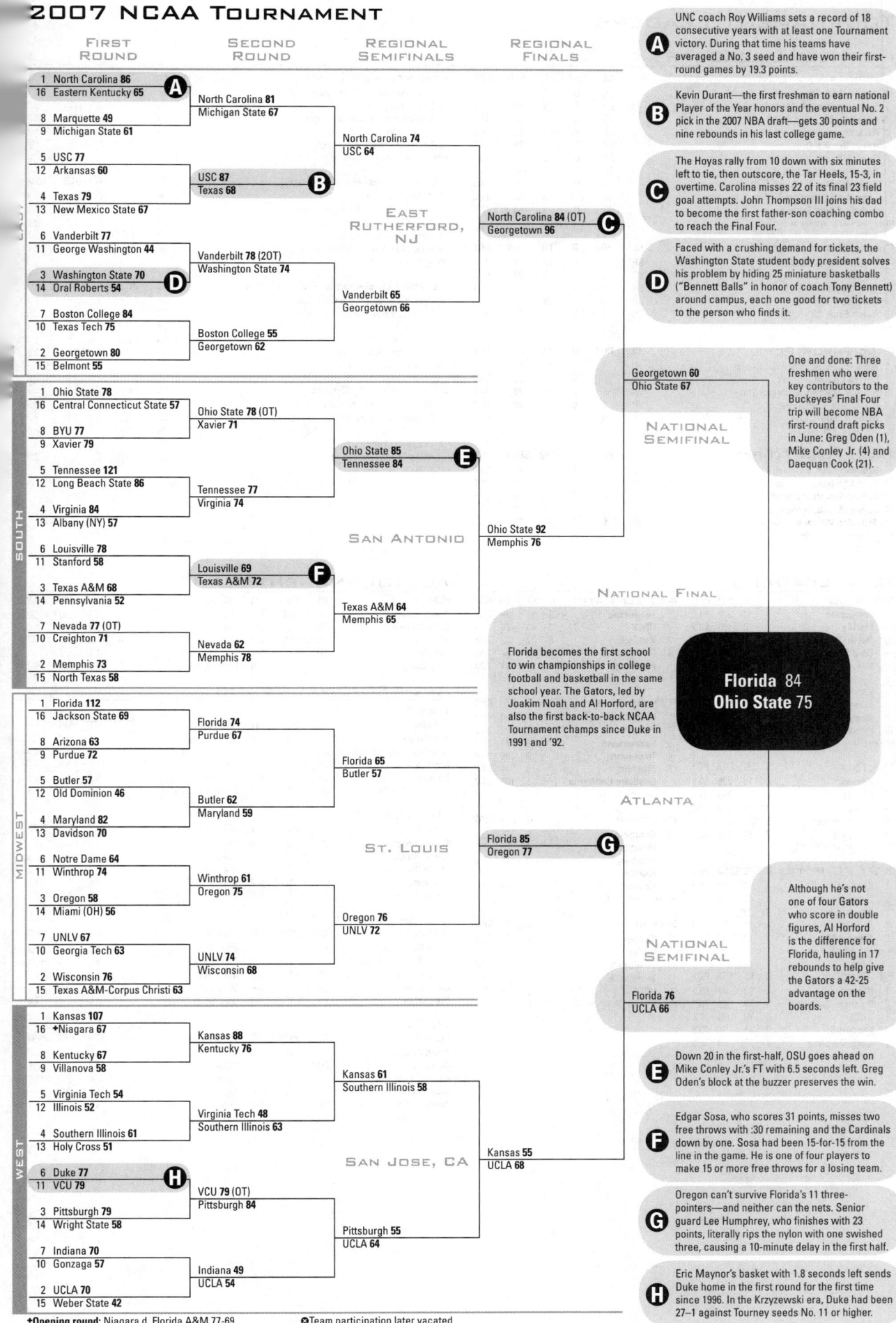

2007 NCAA Tournament

East (East Rutherford, NJ)

First Round
- 1 North Carolina **86**, 16 Eastern Kentucky **65** (A)
- 8 Marquette **49**, 9 Michigan State **61**
- 5 USC **77**, 12 Arkansas **60**
- 4 Texas **79**, 13 New Mexico State **67**
- 6 Vanderbilt **77**, 11 George Washington **44**
- 3 Washington State **70**, 14 Oral Roberts **54** (D)
- 7 Boston College **84**, 10 Texas Tech **75**
- 2 Georgetown **80**, 15 Belmont **55**

Second Round
- North Carolina **81**, Michigan State **67**
- USC **87**, Texas **68** (B)
- Vanderbilt **78** (2OT), Washington State **74**
- Boston College **55**, Georgetown **62**

Regional Semifinals
- North Carolina **74**, USC **64**
- Vanderbilt **65**, Georgetown **66**

Regional Finals
- North Carolina **84** (OT), Georgetown **96** (C)

South (San Antonio)

First Round
- 1 Ohio State **78**, 16 Central Connecticut State **57**
- 8 BYU **77**, 9 Xavier **79**
- 5 Tennessee **121**, 12 Long Beach State **86**
- 4 Virginia **84**, 13 Albany (NY) **57**
- 6 Louisville **78**, 11 Stanford **58**
- 3 Texas A&M **68**, 14 Pennsylvania **52**
- 7 Nevada **77** (OT), 10 Creighton **71**
- 2 Memphis **73**, 15 North Texas **58**

Second Round
- Ohio State **78** (OT), Xavier **71**
- Tennessee **77**, Virginia **74**
- Louisville **69**, Texas A&M **72** (F)
- Nevada **62**, Memphis **78**

Regional Semifinals
- Ohio State **85**, Tennessee **84** (E)
- Texas A&M **64**, Memphis **65**

Regional Finals
- Ohio State **92**, Memphis **76**

Midwest (St. Louis)

First Round
- 1 Florida **112**, 16 Jackson State **69**
- 8 Arizona **63**, 9 Purdue **72**
- 5 Butler **57**, 12 Old Dominion **46**
- 4 Maryland **82**, 13 Davidson **70**
- 6 Notre Dame **64**, 11 Winthrop **74**
- 3 Oregon **58**, 14 Miami (OH) **56**
- 7 UNLV **67**, 10 Georgia Tech **63**
- 2 Wisconsin **76**, 15 Texas A&M-Corpus Christi **63**

Second Round
- Florida **74**, Purdue **67**
- Butler **62**, Maryland **59**
- Winthrop **61**, Oregon **75**
- UNLV **74**, Wisconsin **68**

Regional Semifinals
- Florida **65**, Butler **57**
- Oregon **76**, UNLV **72**

Regional Finals
- Florida **85**, Oregon **77** (G)

West (San Jose, CA)

First Round
- 1 Kansas **107**, 16 +Niagara **67**
- 8 Kentucky **67**, 9 Villanova **58**
- 5 Virginia Tech **54**, 12 Illinois **52**
- 4 Southern Illinois **61**, 13 Holy Cross **51**
- 6 Duke **77**, 11 VCU **79** (H)
- 3 Pittsburgh **79**, 14 Wright State **58**
- 7 Indiana **70**, 10 Gonzaga **57**
- 2 UCLA **70**, 15 Weber State **42**

Second Round
- Kansas **88**, Kentucky **76**
- Virginia Tech **48**, Southern Illinois **63**
- VCU **79** (OT), Pittsburgh **84**
- Indiana **49**, UCLA **54**

Regional Semifinals
- Kansas **61**, Southern Illinois **58**
- Pittsburgh **55**, UCLA **64**

Regional Finals
- Kansas **55**, UCLA **68**

National Semifinal (Atlanta)
- Georgetown **60**, Ohio State **67**
- Florida **76**, UCLA **66**

National Final (Atlanta)

Florida 84
Ohio State 75

Florida becomes the first school to win championships in college football and basketball in the same school year. The Gators, led by Joakim Noah and Al Horford, are also the first back-to-back NCAA Tournament champs since Duke in 1991 and '92.

One and done: Three freshmen who were key contributors to the Buckeyes' Final Four trip will become NBA first-round draft picks in June: Greg Oden (1), Mike Conley Jr. (4) and Daequan Cook (21).

Although he's not one of four Gators who score in double figures, Al Horford is the difference for Florida, hauling in 17 rebounds to help give the Gators a 42-25 advantage on the boards.

+Opening round: Niagara d. Florida A&M 77-69

⊗Team participation later vacated

A UNC coach Roy Williams sets a record of 18 consecutive years with at least one Tournament victory. During that time his teams have averaged a No. 3 seed and have won their first-round games by 19.3 points.

B Kevin Durant—the first freshman to earn national Player of the Year honors and the eventual No. 2 pick in the 2007 NBA draft—gets 30 points and nine rebounds in his last college game.

C The Hoyas rally from 10 down with six minutes left to tie, then outscore, the Tar Heels, 15-3, in overtime. Carolina misses 22 of its final 23 field goal attempts. John Thompson III joins his dad to become the first father-son coaching combo to reach the Final Four.

D Faced with a crushing demand for tickets, the Washington State student body president solves his problem by hiding 25 miniature basketballs ("Bennett Balls" in honor of coach Tony Bennett) around campus, each one good for two tickets to the person who finds it.

E Down 20 in the first-half, OSU goes ahead on Mike Conley Jr.'s FT with 6.5 seconds left. Greg Oden's block at the buzzer preserves the win.

F Edgar Sosa, who scores 31 points, misses two free throws with :30 remaining and the Cardinals down by one. Sosa had been 15-for-15 from the line in the game. He is one of four players to make 15 or more free throws for a losing team.

G Oregon can't survive Florida's 11 three-pointers—and neither can the nets. Senior guard Lee Humphrey, who finishes with 23 points, literally rips the nylon with one swished three, causing a 10-minute delay in the first half.

H Eric Maynor's basket with 1.8 seconds left sends Duke home in the first round for the first time since 1996. In the Krzyzewski era, Duke had been 27–1 against Tourney seeds No. 11 or higher.

Tournament Leaders

INDIVIDUAL LEADERS

Scoring	CL	POS	G	PTS	PPG
1 Chris Lofton, Tennessee	JR	G	3	69	23.0
2 Tyler Hansbrough, North Carolina	SO	F	4	85	21.3
3 Acie Law IV, Texas A&M	SR	G	3	59	19.7
4 Nick Young, Southern California	JR	F	3	57	19.0
5 Aaron Brooks, Oregon	SR	G	4	75	18.8
6 Derrick Byars, Vanderbilt	SR	G	3	56	18.7
7 Ron Lewis, Ohio State	SR	G	6	108	18.0
Arron Afflalo, UCLA	JR	G	5	90	18.0
Shan Foster, Vanderbilt	JR	G/F	3	54	18.0
JaJuan Smith, Tennessee	JR	G	3	54	18.0

Minimum: 3 games

Field Goal Pct	CL	POS	G	FG	FGA	PCT
1 Chris Richard, Florida	SR	C	6	22	26	84.6
2 Brandon Rush, Kansas	SO	G	4	23	37	62.2
3 Greg Oden, Ohio State	FR	C	6	36	58	62.1
4 Al Horford, Florida	JR	F/C	6	26	43	60.5
5 Aaron Gray, Pittsburgh	SR	C	3	15	25	60.0

Minimum: 15 made and 3 games

Free Throw Pct	CL	POS	G	FT	FTA	PCT
1 Nick Young, Southern California	JR	F	3	15	15	100.0
2 Darren Collison, UCLA	SO	G	5	20	21	95.2
3 Raymar Morgan, Michigan State	FR	F	2	16	17	94.1
4 Ron Lewis, Ohio State	SR	G	6	28	30	93.3
5 Arron Afflalo, UCLA	JR	G	5	24	26	92.3

Minimum: 15 Made

Three-Point FG Pct	CL	POS	G	3FG	3FGA	PCT
1 Brandon Rush, Kansas	SO	G	4	9	11	81.8
2 Ryan Childress, Tennessee	SO	F	3	6	8	75.0
3 Ronald Ramon, Pittsburgh	JR	G	3	10	16	62.5
4 JaJuan Smith, Tennessee	JR	G	3	11	18	61.1
5 Jonathan Wallace, Georgetown	JR	G	5	14	25	56.0

Minimum: 6 made and 3 games

Assists Per Game	CL	POS	G	AST	APG
1 Dane Bradshaw, Tennessee	SR	F	3	20	6.7
2 Kevin Kruger, UNLV	SR	G	3	19	6.3
Gabe Pruitt, Southern California	JR	G	3	19	6.3
4 Ty Lawson, North Carolina	FR	G	4	25	6.3
5 Levance Fields, Pittsburgh	SO	G	3	17	5.7

Minimum: 3 games

Rebounds Per Game	CL	POS	G	REB	RPG
1 Al Horford, Florida	JR	F/C	6	68	11.3
2 Taj Gibson, Southern California	JR	F	3	34	11.3
3 Roy Hibbert, Georgetown	JR	C	5	52	10.4
4 Joakim Noah, Florida	JR	F/C	6	58	9.7
5 Randal Falker, Southern Illinois	JR	F	3	29	9.7

Minimum: 3 games

Blocked Shots Per Game	CL	POS	G	BLK	BPG
1 Taj Gibson, Southern California	JR	F	3	8	2.7
2 Robert Dozier, Memphis	SO	F	4	10	2.5
3 Roy Hibbert, Georgetown	JR	C	5	12	2.4
4 Aaron Gray, Pittsburgh	SR	C	3	7	2.3
5 Greg Oden, Ohio State	FR	C	6	13	2.2

Minimum: 3 games

Steals Per Game	CL	POS	G	STL	SPG
1 Mario Chalmers, Kansas	SO	G	4	14	3.5
2 Russell Robinson, Kansas	JR	G	4	13	3.3
3 Gabe Pruitt, Southern California	JR	G	3	9	3.0
4 Brandon Crone, Butler	SR	F	3	7	2.3
Mike Green, Butler	JR	G	3	7	2.3

Minimum: 3 games

TEAM LEADERS

Scoring	G	PTS	PPG
1 Tennessee	3	282	94.0
2 Florida	6	496	82.7
3 North Carolina	4	325	81.3
4 Ohio State	6	475	79.2
5 Kansas	4	311	77.8
6 Southern California	3	228	76.0
7 Vanderbilt	3	220	73.3
8 Memphis	4	292	73.0
9 Georgetown	5	364	72.8
10 Pittsburgh	3	218	72.7

Minimum: 3 games

FG Pct	G	FG	FGA	PCT
1 Kansas	4	118	225	52.4
2 Florida	6	154	295	52.2
3 Tennessee	3	95	189	50.3
4 Georgetown	5	139	278	50.0
5 Pittsburgh	3	81	167	48.5

Minimum: 3 games

3-Pt FG Pct	G	3FG	3FGA	PCT
1 Kansas	4	28	52	53.8
2 Tennessee	3	41	84	48.8
3 Pittsburgh	3	23	49	46.9
4 Oregon	4	37	84	44.0
5 Texas A&M	3	13	31	41.9

Minimum: 3 games

FT Pct	G	FT	FTA	PCT
1 Oregon	4	57	67	85.1
2 Southern California	3	57	72	79.2
3 UCLA	5	70	90	77.8
4 Vanderbilt	3	41	54	75.9
5 North Carolina	4	72	96	75.0

Minimum: 3 games

Ast/TO Ratio	G	AST	TO	RAT
1 Tennessee	3	51	28	1.82
2 UNLV	3	40	25	1.60
3 Vanderbilt	3	52	33	1.58
4 Georgetown	5	86	57	1.51
5 Pittsburgh	3	54	41	1.32

Minimum: 3 games

Rebounds	G	REB	RPG
1 North Carolina	4	160	40.0
2 Florida	6	229	38.2
3 Georgetown	5	177	35.4
4 Tennessee	3	105	35.0
5 Pittsburgh	3	104	34.7
Southern California	3	104	34.7

Minimum: 3 games

Blocks	G	BLK	BPG
1 Georgetown	5	28	5.6
2 Memphis	4	22	5.5
3 Pittsburgh	3	15	5.0
4 Florida	6	30	5.0
5 Kansas	4	19	4.8

Minimum: 3 games

Steals	G	STL	SPG
1 Kansas	4	47	11.8
2 Butler	3	23	7.7
3 Vanderbilt	3	23	7.7
4 Tennessee	3	22	7.3
5 UCLA	5	34	6.8

Minimum: 3 games

ALL-TOURNAMENT TEAM

PLAYER	CL	POS	HT	SCHOOL	RPG	APG	PPG
Corey Brewer*	JR	G/F	6-9	Florida	5.5	2.2	15.8
Mike Conley Jr.	FR	G	6-1	Ohio State	5.0	4.8	16.0
Al Horford	JR	F/C	6-10	Florida	11.3	2.2	13.5
Lee Humphrey	SR	G	6-2	Florida	1.2	0.7	12.5
Greg Oden	FR	C	7-0	Ohio State	9.2	0.5	16.2

ALL-REGIONAL TEAMS

EAST

PLAYER	CL	POS	HT	SCHOOL	RPG	APG	PPG
Jeff Green*	JR	F	6-9	Georgetown	7.0	2.0	15.8
Tyler Hansbrough	SO	F	6-9	North Carolina	8.5	1.8	21.3
Roy Hibbert	JR	C	7-2	Georgetown	11.5	2.3	13.0
DaJuan Summers	FR	F	6-8	Georgetown	5.3	1.5	11.5
Brandan Wright	FR	F	6-9	North Carolina	7.0	0.8	12.8

MIDWEST

PLAYER	CL	POS	HT	SCHOOL	RPG	APG	PPG
Taurean Green*	JR	G	6-0	Florida	2.5	4.5	14.5
Aaron Brooks	SR	G	6-0	Oregon	1.8	3.5	18.8
Malik Hairston	JR	G	6-6	Oregon	6.3	1.0	12.3
Lee Humphrey	SR	G	6-2	Florida	1.0	0.8	11.8
Tajuan Porter	FR	G	5-6	Oregon	3.3	1.3	16.3

SOUTH

PLAYER	CL	POS	HT	SCHOOL	RPG	APG	PPG
Mike Conley Jr.*	FR	G	6-1	Ohio State	5.5	4.3	15.3
Chris Douglas-Roberts	SO	G	6-7	Memphis	4.0	1.3	15.3
Jeremy Hunt	SR	G	6-5	Memphis	3.5	0.8	17.5
Ron Lewis	SR	G	6-4	Ohio State	5.0	0.8	21.8
Greg Oden	FR	C	7-0	Ohio State	8.5	0.5	14.8

WEST

PLAYER	CL	POS	HT	SCHOOL	RPG	APG	PPG
Arron Afflalo*	JR	G	6-5	UCLA	5.5	2.5	18.3
Darren Collison	SO	G	6-1	UCLA	2.3	3.8	13.8
Russell Robinson	JR	G	6-1	Kansas	2.0	3.8	11.3
Brandon Rush	SO	G	6-6	Kansas	4.3	3.3	14.5
Jamaal Tatum	SR	G	6-2	Southern Illinois	3.0	2.3	16.7

* Most outstanding player

2007 NCAA TOURNAMENT BOX SCORES

74-64

33	1H	42
41	2H	22

SWEET 16

NORTH CAROLINA	MIN	FG	3FG	FT	REB	A	ST	BL	PF	TP
Brandan Wright	35	9-15	0-0	3-4	9	1	0	1	0	21
Wayne Ellington	28	6-16	0-2	0-0	4	0	1	0	1	12
Marcus Ginyard	26	3-9	0-1	4-5	9	0	0	0	2	10
Reyshawn Terry	5	4-6	1-2	0-1	0	1	0	0	0	9
Danny Green	18	3-7	0-2	2-2	8	4	1	1	2	8
Tyler Hansbrough	29	1-6	0-0	3-4	4	0	0	0	3	5
Ty Lawson	32	2-10	0-3	0-1	7	4	3	1	2	4
Wes Miller	9	1-4	1-4	0-0	1	0	0	0	1	3
Deon Thompson	9	1-4	0-0	0-0	2	0	0	1	2	2
Bobby Frasor	5	0-0	0-0	0-0	1	0	1	0	1	0
Quentin Thomas	3	0-0	0-0	0-0	0	1	0	0	0	0
Alex Stepheson	1	0-0	0-0	0-0	0	0	0	0	0	0
TOTALS	**200**	**30-77**	**2-14**	**12-17**	**45**	**11**	**6**	**4**	**14**	**74**
Percentages		39.0	14.3	70.6						

Coach: Roy Williams

USC	MIN	FG	3FG	FT	REB	A	ST	BL	PF	TP
Taj Gibson	34	7-12	0-0	2-3	12	0	0	4	5	16
Lodrick Stewart	36	6-15	3-7	0-0	4	2	0	1	1	15
Nick Young	36	6-13	1-5	2-2	7	0	0	0	4	15
Gabe Pruitt	38	5-15	1-6	2-2	4	7	5	1	3	13
Daniel Hackett	29	2-4	0-0	1-2	1	3	0	0	1	5
Keith Wilkinson	14	0-0	0-0	0-0	1	0	0	1	2	0
Dwight Lewis	10	0-2	0-0	0-0	1	1	0	0	1	0
RouSean Cromwell	2	0-0	0-0	0-0	1	0	0	0	2	0
Abdoulaye N'Diaye	1	0-0	0-0	0-0	0	0	0	0	0	0
TOTALS	**200**	**26-61**	**5-18**	**7-9**	**31**	**13**	**5**	**7**	**19**	**64**
Percentages		42.6	27.8	77.8						

Coach: Tim Floyd

Officials: Mike Sanzere, Mike Roberts, Tom Lopes
Technicals: None
Attendance: 19,557

66-65

24	1H	32
42	2H	33

SWEET 16

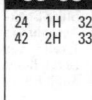

GEORGETOWN	MIN	FG	3FG	FT	REB	A	ST	BL	PF	TP
Jeff Green	40	7-11	0-2	1-1	4	3	1	0	3	15
DaJuan Summers	34	5-13	3-4	2-4	7	3	0	2	1	15
Roy Hibbert	27	5-7	0-0	2-4	10	0	1	0	5	12
Jonathan Wallace	33	3-8	2-5	0-0	3	4	0	0	1	8
Patrick Ewing Jr	17	2-5	1-1	2-2	3	1	0	0	3	7
Jessie Sapp	33	2-10	1-5	1-3	5	3	1	1	3	6
Tyler Crawford	8	1-2	1-2	0-0	2	0	0	0	2	3
Jeremiah Rivers	8	0-0	0-0	0-0	1	0	0	0	0	0
TOTALS	**200**	**25-56**	**8-19**	**8-14**	**35**	**14**	**3**	**3**	**18**	**66**
Percentages		44.6	42.1	57.1						

Coach: John Thompson III

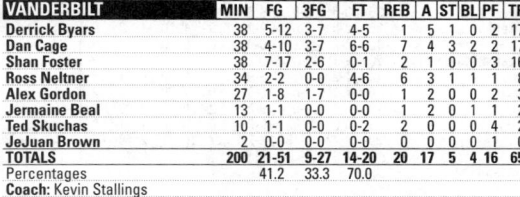

VANDERBILT	MIN	FG	3FG	FT	REB	A	ST	BL	PF	TP
Derrick Byars	38	5-12	3-7	4-5	1	5	1	0	2	17
Dan Cage	38	4-10	3-7	6-6	7	4	3	2	2	17
Shan Foster	38	7-17	2-6	0-1	2	1	0	0	3	16
Ross Neltner	34	2-2	0-0	4-6	6	3	1	1	1	8
Alex Gordon	27	1-8	1-7	0-0	1	2	0	0	2	3
Jermaine Beal	13	1-1	0-0	0-0	1	2	0	1	1	2
Ted Skuchas	10	1-1	0-0	0-2	2	0	0	0	4	2
JeJuan Brown	2	0-0	0-0	0-0	0	0	0	0	1	0
TOTALS	**200**	**21-51**	**9-27**	**14-20**	**20**	**17**	**5**	**4**	**16**	**65**
Percentages		41.2	33.3	70.0						

Coach: Kevin Stallings

Officials: Verne Harris, Dick Cartmell, Randy Mccall
Technicals: None
Attendance: 19,557

85-84

32	1H	49
53	2H	35

SWEET 16

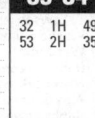

OHIO STATE	MIN	FG	3FG	FT	REB	A	ST	BL	PF	TP
Ron Lewis	36	9-17	3-9	4-4	5	1	0	0	1	25
Mike Conley Jr.	34	4-10	0-0	9-14	7	6	2	0	3	17
Ivan Harris	18	4-4	3-3	0-0	3	1	0	0	3	11
Greg Oden	18	2-2	0-0	5-6	3	0	1	4	4	9
David Lighty	20	2-3	1-2	2-5	2	1	0	0	1	7
Matt Terwilliger	14	1-3	0-1	3-4	3	0	0	0	0	5
Othello Hunter	16	2-2	0-0	0-2	5	1	0	1	4	4
Daequan Cook	8	2-4	0-1	0-0	0	1	0	0	0	4
Jamar Butler	36	1-6	1-6	0-0	2	2	0	0	1	3
TOTALS	**200**	**27-51**	**8-22**	**23-35**	**30**	**13**	**3**	**5**	**17**	**85**
Percentages		52.9	36.4	65.7						

Coach: Thad Matta

TENNESSEE	MIN	FG	3FG	FT	REB	A	ST	BL	PF	TP
Chris Lofton	33	9-18	6-13	0-0	5	1	0	0	1	24
Ramar Smith	33	6-10	0-0	3-7	3	4	1	0	3	15
JaJuan Smith	28	5-10	4-5	0-0	8	1	1	0	4	14
Ryan Childress	17	4-5	4-5	0-0	3	0	0	0	3	12
Wayne Chism	19	2-7	0-4	2-4	1	1	1	0	4	6
Dane Bradshaw	26	1-4	1-3	2-2	2	4	0	1	3	5
Duke Crews	17	2-5	0-0	1-4	3	0	0	0	3	5
Josh Tabb	18	1-3	1-1	0-0	6	2	1	0	2	3
Jordan Howell	9	0-0	0-0	0-0	2	1	0	0	1	0
TOTALS	**200**	**30-62**	**16-31**	**8-17**	**33**	**14**	**4**	**1**	**24**	**84**
Percentages		48.4	51.6	47.1						

Coach: Bruce Pearl

Officials: David Libbey, Jamie Luckie, Pat Driscoll
Technicals: None
Attendance: 26,776

65-64

37	1H	42
28	2H	22

SWEET 16

MEMPHIS	MIN	FG	3FG	FT	REB	A	ST	BL	PF	TP
Jeremy Hunt	26	6-12	3-7	4-5	4	2	1	1	0	19
Chris Douglas-Roberts	37	5-8	0-2	5-7	4	1	0	0	0	15
Joey Dorsey	28	4-6	0-0	0-0	4	0	1	1	5	8
Willie Kemp	14	3-5	1-2	0-0	0	1	0	0	2	7
Antonio Anderson	29	1-6	0-2	3-6	4	3	0	1	1	5
Andre Allen	24	1-5	0-2	2-3	4	1	0	0	1	4
Robert Dozier	21	2-6	0-1	0-0	5	0	0	2	3	4
Doneal Mack	6	1-2	1-1	0-0	0	0	0	0	0	3
Kareem Cooper	13	0-1	0-0	0-0	2	0	0	1	3	0
Pierre Niles	2	0-3	0-0	0-0	0	0	0	0	0	0
TOTALS	**200**	**23-54**	**5-17**	**14-21**	**27**	**8**	**2**	**6**	**15**	**65**
Percentages		42.6	29.4	66.7						

Coach: John Calipari

TEXAS A&M	MIN	FG	3FG	FT	REB	A	ST	BL	PF	TP
Antanas Kavaliauskas	32	7-13	0-0	3-3	8	2	0	0	2	17
Joseph Jones	29	7-11	0-1	0-1	5	1	1	0	3	14
Acie Law	37	6-17	1-3	0-0	5	1	0	0	2	13
Donald Sloan	21	2-6	0-1	1-2	2	1	0	0	2	5
Josh Carter	32	1-4	1-3	1-2	6	1	1	0	4	4
Dominique Kirk	28	2-4	0-1	0-2	2	7	1	0	3	4
Logan Lee	2	1-1	1-1	0-0	0	0	0	0	0	3
Marlon Pompey	10	1-2	0-0	0-0	1	0	1	0	3	2
Bryan Davis	7	1-1	0-0	0-0	1	1	0	0	1	2
Josh Johnston	2	0-0	0-0	0-0	0	0	0	0	0	0
TOTALS	**200**	**28-59**	**3-10**	**5-10**	**30**	**14**	**4**	**0**	**20**	**64**
Percentages		47.5	30.0	50.0						

Coach: Billy Gillispie

Officials: John Hughes, Karl Hess, Joe Lindsay
Technicals: None
Attendance: 26,060

65-57

35	1H	29
30	2H	28

SWEET 16

FLORIDA	MIN	FG	3FG	FT	REB	A	ST	BL	PF	TP
Taurean Green	38	5-8	5-8	2-3	1	1	0	0	2	17
Al Horford	34	4-5	0-0	8-10	7	2	0	4	2	16
Joakim Noah	32	2-4	0-0	9-11	9	2	0	1	1	13
Corey Brewer	36	3-10	1-6	4-4	5	2	1	0	3	11
Lee Humphrey	32	2-5	2-5	0-0	0	0	0	0	4	6
Chris Richard	12	1-2	0-0	0-0	2	1	0	1	2	2
Walter Hodge	14	0-0	0-0	0-0	0	1	0	0	2	0
Dan Werner	2	0-0	0-0	0-0	1	0	0	0	0	0
TOTALS	**200**	**17-34**	**8-19**	**23-28**	**25**	**9**	**1**	**6**	**16**	**65**
Percentages		50.0	42.1	82.1						

Coach: Billy Donovan

BUTLER	MIN	FG	3FG	FT	REB	A	ST	BL	PF	TP
Pete Campbell	19	5-9	4-6	0-0	1	0	0	0	3	14
Mike Green	26	4-12	0-3	4-6	6	3	3	0	4	12
A.J. Graves	38	4-13	1-6	2-3	3	2	1	0	2	11
Brandon Crone	28	4-9	2-3	0-0	4	1	2	0	5	10
Drew Streicher	28	1-2	0-1	4-4	3	0	0	0	3	6
Julian Betko	25	1-3	0-0	0-0	0	1	0	0	5	2
Brian Ligon	21	1-2	0-0	0-0	2	0	0	0	3	2
Marcus Nellems	12	0-0	0-0	0-0	1	1	1	0	0	0
Willie Veasley	3	0-0	0-0	0-0	1	0	0	0	0	0
TOTALS	**200**	**20-50**	**7-19**	**10-13**	**21**	**8**	**7**	**0**	**25**	**57**
Percentages		40.0	36.8	76.9						

Coach: Todd Lickliter

Officials: John Cahill, Mike Littlewood, J.D. Collins
Technicals: None
Attendance: 26,214

76-72

37	1H	33
39	2H	39

SWEET 16

OREGON	MIN	FG	3FG	FT	REB	A	ST	BL	PF	TP
Tajuan Porter	38	9-17	8-12	7-9	3	1	0	0	3	33
Malik Hairston	35	4-8	2-3	4-4	11	1	0	2	2	14
Maarty Leunen	34	4-8	3-5	0-2	10	1	0	0	4	11
Aaron Brooks	37	2-8	0-2	4-4	1	5	3	0	4	8
Bryce Taylor	25	2-4	0-1	2-3	0	2	0	1	4	6
Joevan Catron	24	2-2	0-0	0-0	7	1	1	0	2	4
Adam Zahn	4	0-1	0-0	0-0	2	0	0	0	0	0
Chamberlain Oguchi	2	0-0	0-0	0-0	1	0	0	0	1	0
Ray Schafer	1	0-0	0-0	0-0	0	0	0	0	0	0
TOTALS	**200**	**23-48**	**13-23**	**17-22**	**35**	**11**	**4**	**3**	**20**	**76**
Percentages		47.9	56.5	77.3						

Coach: Ernie Kent

UNLV	MIN	FG	3FG	FT	REB	A	ST	BL	PF	TP
Kevin Kruger	34	5-16	2-11	3-3	4	4	1	0	4	15
Michael Umeh	30	6-11	3-8	0-0	4	4	0	0	1	15
Joe Darger	14	5-6	3-4	0-0	2	0	0	0	1	13
Wendell White	24	4-11	0-0	1-1	4	1	0	0	3	9
Joel Anthony	20	4-5	0-0	0-1	5	1	2	1	4	8
Wink Adams	31	2-11	1-6	1-1	8	3	2	0	3	6
Gaston Essengue	17	2-6	0-0	1-3	4	0	1	2	1	5
Curtis Terry	13	0-7	0-4	1-2	1	0	2	0	0	1
Corey Bailey	6	0-1	0-0	0-1	2	0	0	0	0	0
Marcus Lawrence	6	0-0	0-0	0-0	1	0	0	0	0	0
Matt Shaw	3	0-0	0-0	0-0	0	0	0	0	2	0
Rene Rougeau	2	0-0	0-0	0-0	0	0	0	0	2	0
TOTALS	**200**	**28-74**	**9-33**	**7-12**	**35**	**13**	**8**	**3**	**21**	**72**
Percentages		37.8	27.3	58.3						

Coach: Lon Kruger

Officials: Reggie Greenwood, David Hall, Ed Corbett
Technicals: None
Attendance: 26,307

61-58 (Sweet 16)

	1H	2H
Kansas	27	34
Southern Illinois	24	34

KANSAS	MIN	FG	3FG	FT	REB	A	ST	BL	PF	TP
Brandon Rush	30	6-6	0-0	0-1	5	5	0	1	3	12
Russell Robinson	32	4-10	1-4	0-0	2	3	3	0	2	9
Mario Chalmers	27	2-6	0-1	5-8	0	3	1	0	3	9
Darrell Arthur	19	4-5	0-0	1-1	2	2	0	0	4	9
Darnell Jackson	21	3-3	0-0	2-2	5	0	1	0	1	8
Julian Wright	28	3-7	0-0	1-4	4	1	2	0	2	7
Rodrick Stewart	9	1-1	0-0	1-2	0	0	0	0	0	3
Sherron Collins	23	1-3	0-1	0-1	3	1	2	0	0	2
Sasha Kaun	11	1-1	0-0	0-0	1	1	0	0	1	2
TOTALS	**200**	**25-42**	**1-6**	**10-19**	**22**	**16**	**9**	**1**	**16**	**61**
Percentages		59.5	16.7	52.6						

Coach: Bill Self

SOUTHERN ILLINOIS	MIN	FG	3FG	FT	REB	A	ST	BL	PF	TP
Jamaal Tatum	36	7-19	1-8	4-4	3	1	2	0	2	19
Tony Young	32	5-16	4-11	0-0	2	0	2	1	4	14
Randal Falker	28	4-8	0-0	3-6	9	2	0	1	4	11
Matt Shaw	36	3-7	1-5	2-3	6	3	0	0	2	9
Tony Boyle	16	1-3	0-0	1-1	3	0	0	0	3	3
Tyrone Green	14	1-1	0-0	0-0	3	0	0	0	2	2
Bryan Mullins	31	0-3	0-1	0-0	1	2	2	0	4	0
Wesley Clemmons	7	0-0	0-0	0-0	1	1	0	0	0	0
TOTALS	**200**	**21-57**	**6-25**	**10-14**	**28**	**9**	**6**	**2**	**21**	**58**
Percentages		36.8	24.0	71.4						

Coach: Chris Lowery

Officials: R[illegible] Perone, Do[illegible] Shows, Ton[illegible] Greene
Technicals: None
Attendance: 18,102

64-55 (Sweet 16)

	1H	2H
UCLA	32	32
Pittsburgh	26	29

UCLA	MIN	FG	3FG	FT	REB	A	ST	BL	PF	TP
Arron Afflalo	37	3-11	1-5	10-10	7	2	0	0	2	17
Josh Shipp	33	4-10	3-6	5-6	5	2	1	0	2	16
Darren Collison	36	3-5	0-0	6-6	2	4	0	0	2	12
Lorenzo Mata-Real	26	3-6	0-0	2-2	9	1	0	1	3	8
Michael Roll	10	2-2	1-1	0-0	0	0	0	0	0	5
Luc Richard Mbah a Moute	20	1-1	0-0	0-2	2	0	0	0	3	2
James Keefe	10	1-2	0-1	0-0	0	0	0	0	1	2
Russell Westbrook	6	1-1	0-0	0-0	0	1	0	0	1	2
Alfred Aboya	19	0-4	0-0	0-0	2	0	0	0	3	0
Ryan Wright	3	0-0	0-0	0-0	0	0	0	1	1	0
TOTALS	**200**	**18-42**	**5-13**	**23-26**	**27**	**10**	**1**	**2**	**18**	**64**
Percentages		42.9	38.5	88.5						

Coach: Ben Howland

PITTSBURGH	MIN	FG	3FG	FT	REB	A	ST	BL	PF	TP
Ronald Ramon	26	4-8	4-7	0-0	0	1	1	0	3	12
Levance Fields	30	4-8	3-5	0-0	3	4	0	0	4	11
Aaron Gray	32	5-11	0-0	0-0	6	1	0	2	4	10
Sam Young	22	3-10	0-1	3-5	3	0	1	0	2	9
Mike Cook	29	3-9	0-1	1-2	4	2	1	0	2	7
Antonio Graves	29	1-3	0-0	3-5	2	1	2	0	3	5
Tyrell Biggs	5	0-1	0-0	1-2	0	1	0	0	1	1
Levon Kendall	22	0-4	0-1	0-0	5	3	0	0	2	0
Keith Benjamin	5	0-1	0-1	0-0	1	0	0	0	2	0
TOTALS	**200**	**20-55**	**7-16**	**8-14**	**24**	**13**	**5**	**2**	**23**	**55**
Percentages		36.4	43.8	57.1						

Coach: Jamie Dixon

Officials: Sco[illegible] Thornley, Tom[illegible] Eades, Larry Rose
Technicals: None
Attendance: 18,049

96-84 (Elite 8)

	1H	2H	OT1
Georgetown	44	37	15
North Carolina	50	31	3

GEORGETOWN	MIN	FG	3FG	FT	REB	A	ST	BL	PF	TP
Jeff Green	42	10-17	1-1	1-3	9	3	2	1	1	22
DaJuan Summers	35	7-10	2-3	4-4	6	0	1	2	1	20
Jonathan Wallace	38	7-11	3-4	2-2	3	7	0	0	1	19
Jessie Sapp	36	5-9	2-4	3-5	4	8	0	0	3	15
Roy Hibbert	31	6-10	0-0	1-1	11	4	1	6	4	13
Patrick Ewing Jr	17	2-5	0-2	0-0	2	2	0	1	4	4
Vernon Macklin	9	1-3	0-0	0-1	1	0	0	0	3	2
Jeremiah Rivers	17	0-1	0-0	1-2	1	2	0	1	1	1
TOTALS	**225**	**38-66**	**8-14**	**12-18**	**37**	**26**	**4**	**11**	**18**	**96**
Percentages		57.6	57.1	66.7						

Coach: John Thompson III

NORTH CAROLINA	MIN	FG	3FG	FT	REB	A	ST	BL	PF	TP
Tyler Hansbrough	32	6-15	0-0	14-16	11	3	0	0	4	26
Brandan Wright	26	4-8	0-0	6-6	6	0	0	1	4	14
Deon Thompson	21	6-7	0-0	2-2	6	0	1	2	1	14
Reyshawn Terry	29	4-13	2-5	0-0	6	0	1	0	2	10
Ty Lawson	40	2-9	1-4	0-0	0	6	1	0	3	5
Wayne Ellington	24	2-11	1-6	0-0	2	0	0	0	2	5
Wes Miller	14	1-1	1-1	0-0	0	1	0	0	0	3
Danny Green	9	0-6	0-4	3-4	1	0	2	1	2	3
Marcus Ginyard	18	0-0	0-0	2-2	3	2	0	0	0	2
Alex Stepheson	8	0-1	0-0	2-4	6	0	0	0	1	2
Bobby Frasor	2	0-0	0-0	0-0	0	1	0	0	0	0
Quentin Thomas	2	0-0	0-0	0-0	0	2	0	0	0	0
TOTALS	**225**	**25-71**	**5-20**	**29-34**	**41**	**15**	**5**	**4**	**19**	**84**
Percentages		35.2	25.0	85.3						

Coach: Roy Williams

Officials: Mike Scyphers, Curtis Shaw, John Higgins
Technicals: None
Attendance: 19,557

92-76 (Elite 8)

	1H	2H
Ohio State	41	51
Memphis	38	38

OHIO STATE	MIN	FG	3FG	FT	REB	A	ST	BL	PF	TP
Ron Lewis	37	5-12	2-6	10-10	6	0	2	0	1	22
Mike Conley Jr.	40	5-11	0-2	9-10	4	2	2	0	3	19
Greg Oden	24	7-8	0-0	3-6	9	0	0	1	4	17
Jamar Butler	39	2-6	2-6	6-6	3	4	1	0	2	12
Daequan Cook	16	2-4	1-3	4-4	3	0	2	0	0	9
David Lighty	19	2-4	0-0	3-5	6	3	1	0	3	7
Othello Hunter	11	2-3	0-0	0-0	2	0	0	1	2	4
Matt Terwilliger	4	1-1	0-0	0-0	0	0	0	0	0	2
Ivan Harris	10	0-2	0-0	0-0	0	0	0	0	0	0
TOTALS	**200**	**26-51**	**5-17**	**35-41**	**33**	**9**	**8**	**2**	**15**	**92**
Percentages		51.0	29.4	85.4						

Coach: Thad Matta

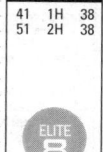

MEMPHIS	MIN	FG	3FG	FT	REB	A	ST	BL	PF	TP
Jeremy Hunt	35	6-16	5-11	9-10	4	0	1	0	4	26
Chris Douglas-Roberts	24	6-10	0-1	2-4	4	1	1	2	5	14
Willie Kemp	22	4-10	4-5	0-0	1	1	0	0	0	12
Antonio Anderson	29	5-14	0-4	0-0	3	4	1	0	4	10
Robert Dozier	33	3-8	0-0	3-4	11	2	1	1	3	9
Doneal Mack	17	1-2	1-1	0-0	0	0	0	0	2	3
Kareem Cooper	7	1-2	0-0	0-0	3	0	1	0	2	2
Joey Dorsey	19	0-0	0-0	0-2	3	0	0	0	4	0
Andre Allen	14	0-3	0-0	0-0	3	2	0	0	5	0
TOTALS	**200**	**26-65**	**10-22**	**14-20**	**32**	**10**	**5**	**3**	**29**	**76**
Percentages		40.0	45.5	70.0						

Coach: John Calipari

Officials: Tim Higgins, Donnee Gray, Mike Kitts
Technicals: None
Attendance: 26,260

85-77 (Elite 8)

	1H	2H
Florida	40	45
Oregon	38	39

FLORIDA	MIN	FG	3FG	FT	REB	A	ST	BL	PF	TP
Lee Humphrey	38	8-15	7-13	0-0	0	0	1	0	0	23
Taurean Green	38	5-12	4-8	7-10	2	3	0	0	1	21
Corey Brewer	34	3-7	0-3	8-12	5	3	2	2	3	14
Joakim Noah	30	4-9	0-0	6-7	14	1	2	1	2	14
Al Horford	30	1-3	0-0	4-8	7	2	0	2	3	6
Walter Hodge	4	1-1	0-0	2-4	0	0	0	0	0	4
Chris Richard	22	1-1	0-0	1-2	6	1	0	0	3	3
Dan Werner	4	0-0	0-0	0-0	1	0	0	0	2	0
TOTALS	**200**	**23-48**	**11-24**	**28-43**	**35**	**10**	**5**	**5**	**14**	**85**
Percentages		47.9	45.8	65.1						

Coach: Billy Donovan

OREGON	MIN	FG	3FG	FT	REB	A	ST	BL	PF	TP
Aaron Brooks	34	11-19	3-6	2-2	2	4	1	0	4	27
Malik Hairston	35	7-13	0-1	4-4	5	1	2	0	5	18
Tajuan Porter	37	2-12	2-10	4-4	1	4	1	0	3	10
Maarty Leunen	29	2-4	1-1	4-4	4	1	2	2	5	9
Bryce Taylor	39	3-6	1-2	0-0	8	2	1	0	3	7
Chamberlain Oguchi	6	1-3	1-2	0-0	0	0	0	0	1	3
Ray Schafer	5	1-1	0-0	0-0	0	0	0	0	0	2
Adam Zahn	5	0-0	0-0	1-2	1	0	0	0	4	1
Joevan Catron	10	0-0	0-0	0-0	0	1	1	0	5	0
TOTALS	**200**	**27-58**	**8-22**	**15-16**	**21**	**13**	**8**	**2**	**30**	**77**
Percentages		46.6	36.4	93.8						

Coach: Ernie Kent

Officials: Tom O'Neill, Mike Stuart, Terry Wymer
Technicals: None
Attendance: 25,947

68-55 (Elite 8)

	1H	2H
UCLA	35	33
Kansas	31	24

UCLA	MIN	FG	3FG	FT	REB	A	ST	BL	PF	TP
Arron Afflalo	36	10-15	3-7	1-2	4	3	0	0	1	24
Darren Collison	36	4-8	2-3	4-4	1	1	5	0	3	14
Josh Shipp	35	2-7	2-4	3-4	6	5	4	2	1	9
Luc Richard Mbah a Moute	35	3-8	0-2	2-2	6	2	4	1	1	8
Alfred Aboya	25	1-2	0-0	2-2	6	0	1	0	4	4
Russell Westbrook	5	2-2	0-0	0-0	1	1	1	0	0	4
Michael Roll	9	1-1	1-1	0-2	1	0	0	0	0	3
Lorenzo Mata-Real	18	1-2	0-0	0-2	3	0	0	0	4	2
James Keefe	1	0-0	0-0	0-0	0	0	0	0	0	0
TOTALS	**200**	**24-45**	**8-17**	**12-18**	**28**	**12**	**15**	**3**	**14**	**68**
Percentages		53.3	47.1	66.7						

Coach: Ben Howland

KANSAS	MIN	FG	3FG	FT	REB	A	ST	BL	PF	TP
Brandon Rush	36	7-16	2-3	2-2	5	1	0	2	3	18
Russell Robinson	32	4-8	2-2	1-2	2	1	5	1	4	11
Julian Wright	29	4-7	0-0	0-2	5	4	4	0	2	8
Darnell Jackson	14	3-3	0-0	2-5	4	0	2	0	1	8
Darrell Arthur	24	2-6	0-0	0-0	4	0	0	2	3	4
Sasha Kaun	13	2-4	0-0	0-0	1	2	0	1	1	4
Mario Chalmers	33	1-8	0-2	0-0	3	7	6	0	2	2
Sherron Collins	15	0-4	0-1	0-0	1	2	0	0	3	0
Rodrick Stewart	4	0-0	0-0	0-0	0	0	0	0	0	0
TOTALS	**200**	**23-56**	**4-8**	**5-11**	**25**	**17**	**17**	**6**	**19**	**55**
Percentages		41.1	50.0	45.5						

Coach: Bill Self

Officials: Mark Whitehead, Paul Janssen, Ted Valentine
Technicals: None
Attendance: 18,102

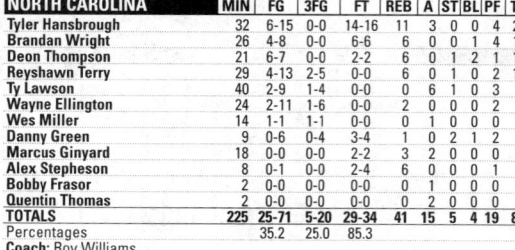

67-60

	1H	2H
Ohio State	27	40
Georgetown	23	37

OHIO STATE	MIN	FG	3FG	FT	REB	A	ST	BL	PF	TP
Mike Conley Jr.	39	7-12	1-3	0-0	5	6	0	0	1	15
Greg Oden	20	6-11	0-0	1-4	9	0	1	1	4	13
Jamar Butler	34	4-9	2-6	0-0	0	4	0	0	1	10
Ron Lewis	34	1-8	0-3	7-8	5	2	3	0	0	9
Ivan Harris	15	3-7	1-1	2-4	7	1	1	0	0	9
David Lighty	25	2-3	0-0	1-1	3	0	2	0	2	5
Othello Hunter	16	1-2	0-0	0-0	4	0	0	1	1	2
Matt Terwilliger	10	1-1	0-0	0-0	3	0	1	1	1	2
Daequan Cook	7	0-4	0-1	2-2	0	0	0	0	0	2
TOTALS	**200**	**25-57**	**4-14**	**13-19**	**36**	**13**	**8**	**3**	**10**	**67**
Percentages		43.9	28.6	68.4						

Coach: Thad Matta

GEORGETOWN	MIN	FG	3FG	FT	REB	A	ST	BL	PF	TP
Jonathan Wallace	37	7-12	5-9	0-0	1	1	1	0	1	19
Roy Hibbert	24	9-13	0-0	1-4	6	1	0	1	4	19
Jessie Sapp	30	4-9	2-7	0-0	2	4	1	0	2	10
Jeff Green	40	4-5	0-0	1-2	12	3	0	0	4	9
DaJuan Summers	30	1-10	0-4	1-2	3	3	1	1	0	3
Patrick Ewing Jr	17	0-2	0-1	0-0	2	3	0	0	3	0
Jeremiah Rivers	13	0-0	0-0	0-0	1	2	0	1	1	0
Vernon Macklin	6	0-0	0-0	0-0	2	0	0	0	0	0
Tyler Crawford	3	0-0	0-0	0-0	0	0	0	0	0	0
TOTALS	**200**	**25-51**	**7-21**	**3-8**	**29**	**17**	**3**	**3**	**15**	**60**
Percentages		49.0	33.3	37.5						

Coach: John Thompson III

Officials: Dick Cartmell, Ted Valentine, Mike Kitts
Technicals: None
Attendance: 53,510

76-66

	1H	2H
Florida	29	47
UCLA	23	43

FLORIDA	MIN	FG	3FG	FT	REB	A	ST	BL	PF	TP
Corey Brewer	32	5-7	4-5	5-6	2	1	0	2	3	19
Chris Richard	21	7-7	0-0	2-2	4	0	1	0	2	16
Lee Humphrey	39	5-9	4-8	0-1	2	0	0	0	1	14
Taurean Green	33	2-9	1-7	5-6	4	3	0	0	2	10
Al Horford	27	2-3	0-0	5-9	17	3	0	0	4	9
Joakim Noah	33	3-7	0-0	2-7	11	2	1	4	2	8
Walter Hodge	13	0-2	0-1	0-0	2	1	0	0	3	0
Dan Werner	2	0-1	0-1	0-0	0	0	0	0	0	0
TOTALS	**200**	**24-45**	**9-22**	**19-31**	**42**	**10**	**2**	**6**	**17**	**76**
Percentages		53.3	40.9	61.3						

Coach: Billy Donovan

UCLA	MIN	FG	3FG	FT	REB	A	ST	BL	PF	TP
Josh Shipp	34	7-14	0-4	4-4	4	5	4	0	2	18
Arron Afflalo	22	5-14	3-9	4-4	3	0	0	0	5	17
Darren Collison	36	3-14	1-6	2-2	0	5	0	0	1	9
Lorenzo Mata-Real	22	3-6	0-0	0-0	2	0	0	0	5	6
Alfred Aboya	26	2-4	0-0	1-2	3	0	2	0	4	5
Luc Richard Mbah a Moute	17	2-4	0-0	0-0	5	1	0	0	5	4
Michael Roll	19	1-5	1-4	0-0	1	1	0	0	0	3
James Keefe	15	1-1	0-0	0-1	6	0	0	0	3	2
Russell Westbrook	8	1-2	0-0	0-0	0	0	0	0	1	2
Ryan Wright	1	0-0	0-0	0-0	1	0	0	0	0	0
TOTALS	**200**	**25-64**	**5-23**	**11-13**	**25**	**12**	**6**	**0**	**26**	**66**
Percentages		39.1	21.7	84.6						

Coach: Ben Howland

Officials: Verne Harris, Curtis Shaw, Tom O'Neil
Technicals: None
Attendance: 53,510

84-75

	1H	2H
Florida	40	44
Ohio State	29	46

FLORIDA	MIN	FG	3FG	FT	REB	A	ST	BL	PF	TP
Al Horford	34	6-15	0-0	6-8	12	3	0	2	3	18
Taurean Green	38	4-6	3-3	5-5	3	6	0	0	0	16
Lee Humphrey	34	5-8	4-7	0-0	1	1	0	0	1	14
Corey Brewer	36	4-12	3-8	2-2	8	1	3	1	2	13
Joakim Noah	21	1-3	0-0	6-6	3	0	1	0	4	8
Chris Richard	20	3-5	0-0	2-3	8	0	0	0	5	8
Walter Hodge	11	2-2	0-0	1-1	1	0	1	0	1	5
Marreese Speights	6	1-2	0-0	0-0	2	0	0	0	3	2
TOTALS	**200**	**26-53**	**10-18**	**22-25**	**38**	**11**	**5**	**3**	**19**	**84**
Percentages		49.1	55.6	88.0						

Coach: Billy Donovan

OHIO STATE	MIN	FG	3FG	FT	REB	A	ST	BL	PF	TP
Greg Oden	38	10-15	0-0	5-8	12	1	1	4	4	25
Mike Conley Jr.	34	7-13	1-3	5-6	3	6	4	0	3	20
Ron Lewis	34	6-13	0-4	0-1	3	0	1	0	3	12
Ivan Harris	26	2-8	2-8	1-2	5	0	1	0	2	7
David Lighty	13	2-3	0-1	0-0	0	1	1	0	1	4
Jamar Butler	36	1-7	1-6	0-0	2	1	2	0	3	3
Daequan Cook	9	1-2	0-1	0-0	0	1	1	0	1	2
Matt Terwilliger	5	1-1	0-0	0-0	0	0	0	0	1	2
Othello Hunter	5	0-2	0-0	0-0	2	0	0	0	2	0
TOTALS	**200**	**30-64**	**4-23**	**11-17**	**27**	**10**	**11**	**4**	**20**	**75**
Percentages		46.9	17.4	64.7						

Coach: Thad Matta

Officials: Karl Hess, Tony Greene, Edward Corbett
Technicals: None
Attendance: 51,458

National Invitation Tournament (NIT)

First Round: Florida State d. Toledo 77-61, Michigan d. Utah State 68-58, Mississippi State d. Miss. Valley St. 82-63, Bradley d. Providence 90-78 (OT), NC State d. Drexel 63-56, Massachusetts d. Alabama 89-87 (OT), Marist d. Oklahoma State 67-64, West Virginia d. Delaware State 74-50, Georgia d. Fresno State 88-78, Kansas State d. Vermont 59-57, DePaul d. Hofstra 83-71, Air Force d. Austin Peay 75-51, Clemson d. East Tenn. St. 64-57, Syracuse d. South Alabama 79-73, Mississippi d. Appalachian State 73-59, San Diego St. d. Missouri State 74-70
Second Round: Florida State d. Michigan 87-66, Mississippi State d. Bradley 101-72, West Virginia d. Massachusetts 90-77, NC State d. Marist 69-62, Air Force d. Georgia 83-52, DePaul d. Kansas State 70-65, Clemson d. Mississippi 89-68, Syracuse d. San Diego St. 80-64
Quarterfinals: Mississippi State d. Florida State 86-71, West Virginia d. NC State 71-66, Clemson d. Syracuse 74-70, Air Force d. DePaul 52-51
Semifinals: West Virginia d. Mississippi State 63-62, Clemson d. Air Force 68-67
Championship: West Virginia d. Clemson 78-73
MVP: Frank Young, West Virginia

2007-08: JAYHAWKS' TREY

Memphis, 38–1 (its only loss to Tennessee in February), was leading Kansas (37-3) by nine with 2:12 left in the NCAA Final. But the Jayhawks came back—with Tourney MOP Mario Chalmers' three-pointer forcing overtime—then prevailed, 75-68. KU was now a three-time national champ and Memphis 0-for-3 in Final Fours. It was the first time since seeding began in 1979 that all four No. 1s—UNC and UCLA were the others—reached the Final Four. Memphis guard Derrick Rose was the first pick in the NBA draft (Chicago). The second pick (Miami) was another freshman, Kansas State's Michael Beasley, who averaged a double-double—26.2 ppg and 12.4 rpg. North Carolina junior Tyler Hansbrough, who averaged 22.6 ppg and 10.2 rpg, was the unanimous player of the year. On Feb. 4, Bob Knight abruptly resigned as coach at Texas Tech, leaving the team in the care of his son, Pat—and leaving the game as the winningest coach of all time (902).

MAJOR CONFERENCE STANDINGS

AMERICA EAST

	Conference			Overall		
	W	L	PCT	W	L	PCT
UMBC⊛	13	3	.813	24	9	.727
Hartford	10	6	.625	18	16	.529
Albany (NY)	10	6	.625	15	15	.500
Vermont	9	7	.563	16	15	.516
Binghamton	9	7	.563	14	16	.467
Boston U.	9	7	.563	14	17	.452
New Hampshire	6	10	.375	9	20	.310
Maine	3	13	.188	7	23	.233
Stony Brook	3	13	.188	7	23	.233

Tournament: **UMBC d. Hartford 82-65**
Tournament MOP: **Jay Greene**, UMBC

ACC

	Conference			Overall		
	W	L	PCT	W	L	PCT
North Carolina⊛	14	2	.875	36	3	.923
Duke○	13	3	.813	28	6	.824
Clemson○	10	6	.625	24	10	.706
Virginia Tech□	9	7	.563	21	14	.600
Miami (FL)○	8	8	.500	23	11	.676
Maryland□	8	8	.500	19	15	.559
Wake Forest	7	9	.438	17	13	.567
Florida State□	7	9	.438	19	15	.559
Georgia Tech	7	9	.438	15	17	.469
Virginia	5	11	.313	17	16	.515
NC State	4	12	.250	15	16	.484
Boston College	4	12	.250	14	17	.452

Tournament: **North Carolina d. Clemson 86-81**
Tournament MVP: **Tyler Hansbrough**, North Carolina

ATLANTIC SUN

	Conference			Overall		
	W	L	PCT	W	L	PCT
Belmont⊛	14	2	.875	25	9	.735
Jacksonville	12	4	.750	18	13	.581
East Tenn. State	11	5	.688	19	13	.594
Stetson	11	5	.688	16	16	.500
Gardner-Webb	9	7	.563	16	16	.500
Lipscomb	9	7	.563	15	16	.484
Kennesaw State	7	9	.438	10	20	.333
Mercer	6	10	.375	11	19	.367
Florida Gulf Coast	6	10	.375	10	21	.323
Campbell	5	11	.313	10	20	.333
SC Upstate	5	11	.313	7	23	.233
North Florida	1	15	.063	3	26	.103

Tournament: **Belmont d. Jacksonville 79-61**
Tournament MVP: **Shane Dansby**, Belmont

ATLANTIC 10

	Conference			Overall		
	W	L	PCT	W	L	PCT
Xavier○	14	2	.875	30	7	.811
Temple⊛	11	5	.688	21	13	.618
Massachusetts□	10	6	.625	25	11	.694
Saint Joseph's○	9	7	.563	21	13	.618
Charlotte□	9	7	.563	20	14	.588
Richmond	9	7	.563	16	15	.516
Dayton□	8	8	.500	23	11	.676
La Salle	8	8	.500	15	17	.469
Rhode Island□	7	9	.438	21	12	.636
Duquesne	7	9	.438	17	13	.567
Saint Louis	7	9	.438	16	15	.516
Fordham	6	10	.375	12	17	.414
George Washington	5	11	.313	9	17	.346
St. Bonaventure	2	14	.125	8	22	.267

Tournament: **Temple d. Saint Joseph's 69-64**
Tournament MOP: **Dionte Christmas**, Temple

BIG EAST

	Conference			Overall		
	W	L	PCT	W	L	PCT
Georgetown○	15	3	.833	28	6	.824
Notre Dame○	14	4	.778	25	8	.758
Louisville ○	14	4	.778	27	9	.750
Connecticut○	13	5	.722	24	9	.727
Marquette○	11	7	.611	25	10	.714
West Virginia○	11	7	.611	26	11	.703
Pittsburgh⊛	10	8	.556	27	10	.730
Villanova○	9	9	.500	22	13	.629
Syracuse□	9	9	.500	21	14	.600
Cincinnati	8	10	.444	13	19	.406
Seton Hall	7	11	.389	17	15	.531
Providence	6	12	.333	15	16	.484
DePaul	6	12	.333	11	19	.367
St. John's	5	13	.278	11	19	.367
South Florida	3	15	.167	12	19	.387
Rutgers	3	15	.167	11	20	.355

Tournament: **Pittsburgh d. Georgetown 74-65**
Tournament MVP: **Sam Young**, Pittsburgh

BIG SKY

	Conference			Overall		
	W	L	PCT	W	L	PCT
Portland State⊛	14	2	.875	23	10	.697
Northern Arizona	11	5	.688	21	11	.656
Weber State	10	6	.625	16	14	.533
Montana	8	8	.500	14	16	.467
Idaho State	8	8	.500	12	19	.387
Montana State	7	9	.438	15	15	.500
Northern Colorado	6	10	.375	13	16	.448
Eastern Washington	6	10	.375	11	19	.367
Sacramento State	2	14	.125	4	24	.143

Tournament: **Portland State d. Northern Arizona 67-51**
Tournament MVP: **Deonte Huff**, Portland State

BIG SOUTH

	Conference			Overall		
	W	L	PCT	W	L	PCT
UNC Asheville□	10	4	.714	23	10	.697
Winthrop⊛	10	4	.714	22	12	.647
High Point	8	6	.571	17	14	.548
Liberty	7	7	.500	16	16	.500
VMI	6	8	.429	14	15	.483
Coastal Carolina	6	8	.429	13	15	.464
Radford	5	9	.357	10	20	.333
Charleston Southern	4	10	.286	10	20	.333

Tournament: **Winthrop d. UNC Asheville 66-48**
Tournament MVP: **Michael Jenkins**, Winthrop

BIG TEN

	Conference			Overall		
	W	L	PCT	W	L	PCT
Wisconsin⊛	16	2	.889	31	5	.861
Purdue○	15	3	.833	25	9	.735
Indiana○	14	4	.778	25	8	.758
Michigan State○	12	6	.667	27	9	.750
Ohio State□	10	8	.556	24	13	.649
Minnesota□	8	10	.444	20	14	.588
Penn State	7	11	.389	15	16	.484
Iowa	6	12	.333	13	19	.406
Illinois	5	13	.278	16	19	.457
Michigan	5	13	.278	10	22	.313
Northwestern	1	17	.056	8	22	.267

Tournament: **Wisconsin d. Illinois 61-48**
Tournament MOP: **Marcus Landry**, Wisconsin

BIG 12

	Conference			Overall		
	W	L	PCT	W	L	PCT
Texas○	13	3	.813	31	7	.816
Kansas⊛	13	3	.813	37	3	.925
Kansas State○	10	6	.625	21	12	.636
Oklahoma○	9	7	.563	23	12	.657
Baylor○	9	7	.563	21	11	.656
Texas A&M○	8	8	.500	25	11	.694
Nebraska□	7	9	.438	20	13	.606
Texas Tech	7	9	.438	16	15	.516
Oklahoma State□	7	9	.438	17	16	.515
Missouri	6	10	.375	16	16	.500
Iowa State	4	12	.250	14	18	.438
Colorado	3	13	.188	12	20	.375

Tournament: **Kansas d. Texas 84-74**
Tournament MOP: **Brandon Rush**, Kansas

BIG WEST

	Conference			Overall		
	W	L	PCT	W	L	PCT
UC Santa Barbara□	12	4	.750	23	9	.719
Cal State Fullerton⊛	12	4	.750	24	9	.727
Cal State Northridge	12	4	.750	20	10	.667
Pacific	11	5	.688	21	10	.677
UC Irvine	9	7	.563	18	16	.529
Cal Poly	7	9	.438	12	18	.400
UC Riverside	4	12	.250	9	21	.300
Long Beach State	3	13	.188	6	25	.194
UC Davis	2	14	.125	9	22	.290

Tournament: **Cal State Fullerton d. UC Irvine 81-66**
Tournament MVP: **Josh Akognon**, Cal State Fullerton

COLONIAL ATHLETIC

	Conference			Overall		
	W	L	PCT	W	L	PCT
VCU□	15	3	.833	24	8	.750
George Mason⊛	12	6	.667	23	11	.676
UNC Wilmington	12	6	.667	20	13	.606
Old Dominion	11	7	.611	18	16	.529
William and Mary	10	8	.556	17	16	.515
Delaware	9	9	.500	14	17	.452
Northeastern	9	9	.500	14	17	.452
Hofstra	8	10	.444	12	18	.400
Towson	7	11	.389	13	18	.419
James Madison	5	13	.278	13	17	.433
Drexel	5	13	.278	12	20	.375
Georgia State	5	13	.278	9	21	.300

Tournament: **George Mason d. William and Mary 68-59**
Tournament MOP: **Folarin Campbell**, George Mason

C-USA

	Conference			Overall		
	W	L	PCT	W	L	PCT
Memphis⊛	16	0	1.000	38	2	.950
UAB□	12	4	.750	23	11	.676
Houston	11	5	.688	24	10	.706
Southern Miss	9	7	.563	19	14	.576
Central Florida	9	7	.563	16	15	.516
Tulsa	8	8	.500	25	14	.641
UTEP	8	8	.500	19	14	.576
Marshall	8	8	.500	16	14	.533
Tulane	6	10	.375	17	15	.531
East Carolina	5	11	.313	11	19	.367
SMU	4	12	.250	10	20	.333
Rice	0	16	.000	3	27	.100

Tournament: **Memphis d. Tulsa 77-51**
Tournament MVP: **Antonio Anderson**, Memphis

HORIZON

	Conference			Overall		
	W	L	PCT	W	L	PCT
Butler⊛	16	2	.889	30	4	.882
Wright State	12	6	.667	21	10	.677
Cleveland State□	12	6	.667	21	13	.618
Valparaiso	9	9	.500	22	14	.611
Ill.-Chicago	9	9	.500	18	15	.545
Wisc.-Green Bay	9	9	.500	15	15	.500
Wisc.-Milwaukee	9	9	.500	14	16	.467
Loyola-Chicago	6	12	.333	12	19	.387
Youngstown State	5	13	.278	9	21	.300
Detroit	3	15	.167	7	23	.233

Tournament: **Butler d. Cleveland State 70-55**
Tournament MVP: **Mike Green**, Butler

IVY

	Conference			Overall		
	W	L	PCT	W	L	PCT
Cornell⊛	14	0	1.000	22	6	.786
Brown⊗	11	3	.786	19	10	.655
Penn	8	6	.571	13	18	.419
Columbia	7	7	.500	14	15	.483
Yale	7	7	.500	13	15	.464
Dartmouth	3	11	.214	10	18	.357
Harvard	3	11	.214	8	22	.267
Princeton	3	11	.214	6	23	.207

⊛ Automatic NCAA Tournament bid ○ At-large NCAA Tournament bid □ NIT appearance ⊗ Team record doesn't reflect games forfeited or vacated. For adjusted record, see p. 521.

MAAC

	Conference			Overall		
	W	L	PCT	W	L	PCT
Siena⊕	13	5	.722	23	11	.676
Rider	13	5	.722	23	11	.676
Niagara	12	6	.667	19	10	.655
Loyola (MD)	12	6	.667	19	14	.576
Fairfield	11	7	.611	14	16	.467
Marist	11	7	.611	18	14	.563
Iona	8	10	.444	12	20	.375
Manhattan	5	13	.278	12	19	.387
Saint Peter's	3	15	.167	6	24	.200
Canisius	2	16	.111	6	25	.194

Tournament: **Siena d. Rider 74-53**
Tournament MVP: **Kenny Hasbrouck**, Siena

MID-AMERICAN

	Conference			Overall		
	W	L	PCT	W	L	PCT
East						
Kent State⊕	13	3	.813	28	7	.800
Akron□	11	5	.688	24	11	.686
Ohio	9	7	.563	20	13	.606
Miami (OH)	9	7	.563	17	16	.515
Bowling Green	7	9	.438	13	17	.433
Buffalo	3	13	.188	10	20	.333
East						
Western Michigan	12	4	.750	20	12	.625
Central Michigan	8	8	.500	14	17	.452
Eastern Michigan	8	8	.500	14	17	.452
Toledo	7	8	.467	11	19	.367
Ball State	5	11	.313	6	24	.200
Northern Illinois	3	12	.200	6	22	.214

Tournament: **Kent State d. Akron 74-55**
Tournament MVP: **Haminn Quaintance**, Kent State

MEAC

	Conference			Overall		
	W	L	PCT	W	L	PCT
Morgan State□	14	2	.875	22	11	.667
Hampton	11	5	.688	18	12	.600
Norfolk State	11	5	.688	16	15	.516
Delaware State	10	6	.625	14	16	.467
NC A&T	9	7	.563	15	16	.484
Florida A&M	9	7	.563	15	17	.469
Coppin State⊕	7	9	.438	16	21	.432
South Carolina State	7	9	.438	13	20	.394
Bethune-Cookman	5	11	.313	11	21	.344
Howard	3	13	.188	6	26	.188
UMES	2	14	.125	4	28	.125

Tournament: **Coppin State d. Morgan State 62-60**
Tournament MOP: **Tywain McKee**, Coppin State

MISSOURI VALLEY

	Conference			Overall		
	W	L	PCT	W	L	PCT
Drake⊕	15	3	.833	28	5	.848
Illinois State□	13	5	.722	25	10	.714
Southern Illinois□	11	7	.611	18	15	.545
Creighton□	10	8	.556	22	11	.667
Northern Iowa	9	9	.500	18	14	.563
Bradley	9	9	.500	21	17	.553
Missouri State	8	10	.444	17	16	.515
Indiana State	8	10	.444	15	16	.484
Wichita State	4	14	.222	11	20	.355
Evansville	3	15	.167	9	21	.300

Tournament: **Drake d. Illinois State 79-49**
Tournament MVP: **Adam Emmenecker**, Drake

MOUNTAIN WEST

	Conference			Overall		
	W	L	PCT	W	L	PCT
BYU○	14	2	.875	27	8	.771
UNLV⊕	12	4	.750	27	8	.771
New Mexico□	11	5	.688	24	9	.727
San Diego State□	9	7	.563	20	13	.606
Air Force	8	8	.500	16	14	.533
Utah	7	9	.438	18	15	.545
TCU	6	10	.375	14	16	.467
Wyoming	5	11	.313	12	18	.400
Colorado State	0	16	.000	7	25	.219

Tournament: **UNLV d. BYU 76-61**
Tournament MVP: **Wink Adams**, UNLV

NORTHEAST

	Conference			Overall		
	W	L	PCT	W	L	PCT
Robert Morris□	16	2	.889	26	8	.765
Wagner	15	3	.833	23	8	.742
Sacred Heart	13	5	.722	18	14	.563
Mount St. Mary's⊕	11	7	.611	19	15	.559
Quinnipiac	11	7	.611	15	15	.500
Central Conn. State	10	8	.556	14	16	.467
Long Island	7	11	.389	15	15	.500
Fairleigh Dickinson	4	14	.222	8	20	.286
St. Francis (NY)	4	14	.222	7	22	.241
Monmouth	4	14	.222	7	24	.226
Saint Francis (PA)	4	14	.222	6	23	.207

Tournament: **Mount St. Mary's d. Sacred Heart 68-55**
Tournament MVP: **Jean Cajou**, Mount St. Mary's

OHIO VALLEY

	Conference			Overall		
	W	L	PCT	W	L	PCT
Austin Peay⊕	16	4	.800	24	11	.686
Murray State	13	7	.650	18	13	.581
Morehead State	12	8	.600	15	15	.500
Tennessee-Martin	11	9	.550	17	16	.515
Tennessee State	10	10	.500	15	17	.469
Eastern Kentucky	10	10	.500	14	16	.467
Samford	10	10	.500	14	16	.467
Tennessee Tech	10	10	.500	13	19	.406
Southeast Mo. State	7	13	.350	12	19	.387
Eastern Illinois	6	14	.300	7	22	.241
Jacksonville State	5	15	.250	7	22	.241

Tournament: **Austin Peay d. Tennessee State 82-64**
Tournament MVP: **Todd Babington**, Austin Peay

PAC-10

	Conference			Overall		
	W	L	PCT	W	L	PCT
UCLA⊕	16	2	.889	35	4	.897
Stanford○	13	5	.722	28	8	.778
Washington State○	11	7	.611	26	9	.743
Southern California○	11	7	.611	21	12	.636
Arizona State□	9	9	.500	21	13	.618
Oregon○	9	9	.500	18	14	.563
Arizona○	9	9	.500	19	15	.559
Washington	7	11	.389	16	17	.485
California□	6	12	.333	17	16	.515
Oregon State	0	18	.000	6	25	.194

Tournament: **UCLA d. Stanford 67-64**
Tournament MVP: **Darren Collison**, UCLA

PATRIOT

	Conference			Overall		
	W	L	PCT	W	L	PCT
American⊕	10	4	.714	21	12	.636
Navy	9	5	.643	16	14	.533
Colgate	7	7	.500	18	14	.563
Lehigh	7	7	.500	14	15	.483
Lafayette	6	8	.429	15	15	.500
Army	6	8	.429	14	16	.467
Bucknell	6	8	.429	12	19	.387
Holy Cross	5	9	.357	15	14	.517

Tournament: **American d. Colgate 52-46**
Tournament MOP: **Garrison Carr**, American

SEC

	Conference			Overall		
	W	L	PCT	W	L	PCT
Eastern						
Tennessee○	14	2	.875	31	5	.861
Kentucky○	12	4	.750	18	13	.581
Vanderbilt○	10	6	.625	26	8	.765
Florida□	8	8	.500	24	12	.667
South Carolina	5	11	.313	14	18	.438
Georgia⊕	4	12	.250	17	17	.500
Western						
Mississippi State○	12	4	.750	23	11	.676
Arkansas○	9	7	.563	23	12	.657
Mississippi□	7	9	.438	24	11	.686
LSU	6	10	.375	13	18	.419
Alabama	5	11	.313	17	16	.515
Auburn	4	12	.250	14	16	.467

Tournament: **Georgia d. Arkansas 66-57**
Tournament MVP: **Sundiata Gaines**, Georgia

SOUTHERN

	Conference			Overall		
	W	L	PCT	W	L	PCT
North						
Appalachian State	13	7	.650	18	13	.581
Chattanooga	13	7	.650	18	13	.581
UNC Greensboro	12	8	.600	19	12	.613
Elon	9	11	.450	14	19	.424
Western Carolina	6	14	.300	10	21	.323
South						
Davidson⊕	20	0	1.000	29	7	.806
Georgia Southern	13	7	.650	20	12	.625
Charleston	9	11	.450	16	17	.485
Wofford	8	12	.400	16	16	.500
Furman	6	14	.300	7	23	.233
The Citadel	1	19	.050	6	24	.200

Tournament: **Davidson d. Elon 65-49**
Tournament MVP: **Stephen Curry**, Davidson

SOUTHLAND

	Conference			Overall		
	W	L	PCT	W	L	PCT
East						
Lamar	13	3	.813	19	11	.633
Southeastern La.	9	7	.563	17	13	.567
Northwestern St. (LA)	9	7	.563	15	18	.455
McNeese State	7	9	.438	13	16	.448
Nicholls State	5	11	.313	10	21	.323
Central Arkansas	4	12	.250	14	16	.467
West						
Stephen F. Austin□	13	3	.813	26	6	.813
Sam Houston St.	10	6	.625	23	8	.742
Texas-Arlington⊕	7	9	.438	21	12	.636
UTSA	7	9	.438	13	17	.433
Texas State	6	10	.375	13	16	.448
Corpus Christi	6	10	.375	9	20	.310

Tournament: **Tex.-Arlington d. Northwestern St. (LA) 82-79**
Tournament MVP: **Anthony Vereen**, Texas-Arlington

SWAC

	Conference			Overall		
	W	L	PCT	W	L	PCT
Alabama State□	15	3	.833	20	11	.645
Miss. Valley State⊕	12	6	.667	17	16	.515
Alabama A&M	11	7	.611	14	15	.483
Jackson State	10	8	.556	14	20	.412
Southern U.	9	9	.500	11	19	.367
Arkansas-Pine Bluff	8	10	.444	13	18	.419
Grambling	7	11	.389	7	19	.269
Prairie View A&M	6	12	.333	8	22	.267
Alcorn State	6	12	.333	7	24	.226
Texas Southern	6	12	.333	7	25	.219

Tournament: **Miss. Valley State d. Jackson State 59-58**
Tournament MOP: **Carl Lucas**, Miss.Valley State

SUMMIT

	Conference			Overall		
	W	L	PCT	W	L	PCT
Oral Roberts⊕	16	2	.889	24	9	.727
IUPUI	15	3	.833	26	7	.788
Oakland	11	7	.611	17	14	.548
North Dakota State	10	8	.556	16	13	.552
IPFW	9	9	.500	13	18	.419
Southern Utah	9	9	.500	11	19	.367
Western Illinois	7	11	.389	12	18	.400
UMKC	6	12	.333	11	21	.344
Centenary	4	14	.222	10	21	.323
South Dakota State	3	15	.167	8	21	.276

Tournament: **Oral Roberts d. IUPUI 71-64**
Tournament MVP: **Moses Ehambe**, Oral Roberts

SUN BELT

	Conference			Overall		
	W	L	PCT	W	L	PCT
Eastern Division						
Western Kentucky⊕	16	2	.889	29	7	.806
South Alabama○	16	2	.889	26	7	.788
Middle Tenn. State	11	7	.611	17	15	.531
Florida Atlantic	8	10	.444	15	18	.455
Florida International	6	12	.333	9	20	.310
Troy	4	14	.222	12	19	.387
Western Division						
Arkansas-Little Rock	11	7	.611	20	11	.645
UL-Lafayette	11	7	.611	15	15	.500
North Texas	10	8	.556	20	11	.645
New Orleans	8	10	.444	19	13	.594
Denver	7	11	.389	11	19	.367
Arkansas State	5	13	.278	10	20	.333
UL-Monroe	4	14	.222	10	21	.323

Tournament: **Western Kentucky d. Middle Tenn. St. 67-57**
Tournament MOP: **Jeremy Evans**, Western Kentucky

WEST COAST

	Conference			Overall		
	W	L	PCT	W	L	PCT
Gonzaga○	13	1	.929	25	8	.758
Saint Mary's (CA)○	12	2	.857	25	7	.781
San Diego⊕	11	3	.786	22	14	.611
Santa Clara	6	8	.429	15	16	.484
San Francisco	5	9	.357	10	21	.323
Pepperdine	4	10	.286	11	21	.344
Portland	3	11	.214	9	22	.290
Loyola Marymount	2	12	.143	5	26	.161

Tournament: **San Diego d. Gonzaga 69-62**
Tournament MVP: **Brandon Johnson**, San Diego

WAC

	Conference			Overall		
	W	L	PCT	W	L	PCT
Utah State□	12	4	.750	24	11	.686
Boise State⊕	12	4	.750	25	9	.735
Nevada	12	4	.750	21	12	.636
New Mexico State	12	4	.750	21	14	.600
Hawaii	7	9	.438	11	19	.367
Fresno State	5	11	.313	13	19	.406
Idaho	5	11	.313	8	21	.276
San Jose State	4	12	.250	13	19	.406
Louisiana Tech	3	13	.188	6	24	.200

Tournament: **Boise State d. New Mexico St. 107-102 (3OT)**
Tournament MVP: **Reggie Larry**, Boise State

INDEPENDENTS

	Overall		
	W	L	PCT
Texas-Pan American	18	13	.581
Savannah State	13	18	.419
Chicago State	11	17	.393
Longwood	9	22	.290

ALL OTHERS

(Reclassifying and provisional teams not eligible for the NCAA Tournament.)

	Overall		
	W	L	PCT
North Dakota State	16	13	.552
Utah Valley State	15	14	.517
Central Arkansas	14	16	.467
Winston-Salem	12	18	.400
Kennesaw State	10	20	.333
Fla. Gulf Coast	10	21	.323
Cal State Bakersfield	8	21	.276
South Dakota State	8	21	.276
SC Upstate	7	23	.233
Presbyterian	5	25	.167
North Florida	3	26	.103
NC Central	4	26	.133
NJIT	0	29	.000

INDIVIDUAL LEADERS—SEASON

Scoring	CL	POS	G	FG	3FG	FT	PTS	PPG
1 **Reggie Williams**, VMI	SR	F	25	269	43	114	695	**27.8**
2 **Charron Fisher**, Niagara	SR	F	29	256	69	219	800	**27.6**
3 **Michael Beasley**, Kansas State	FR	F	33	307	36	216	866	**26.2**
4 **Stephen Curry**, Davidson	SO	G	36	317	162	135	931	**25.9**
5 **Lester Hudson**, Tenn.-Martin	JR	G	33	291	124	141	847	**25.7**
6 **Arizona Reid**, High Point	SR	F	31	304	34	100	742	**23.9**
7 **Stefon Jackson**, UTEP	JR	G	33	261	35	221	778	**23.6**
8 **Robert McKiver**, Houston	SR	G	34	233	145	190	801	**23.6**
9 **Bo McCalebb**, New Orleans	SR	G	32	261	47	173	742	**23.2**
10 **David Holston**, Chicago State	JR	G	28	202	130	112	646	**23.1**

Field Goal Pct	CL	POS	G	FG	FGA	PCT
1 **Kenny George**, UNC Asheville	JR	C	28	151	217	**69.6**
2 **Vladimir Kuljanin**, UNC Wilmington	SR	C	33	188	282	**66.7**
3 **Matt Nelson**, Boise State	SR	F	33	202	312	**64.7**
4 **Ahmad Nivins**, Saint Joseph's	JR	F	33	165	255	**64.7**
5 **Will Thomas**, George Mason	SR	F	34	208	324	**64.2**

Minimum: 5 made per game

Three-Pt FG Per Game	CL	POS	G	3FG	3PG
1 **David Holston**, Chicago State	JR	G	28	130	**4.6**
2 **Stephen Curry**, Davidson	SO	G	36	162	**4.5**
3 **Robert Vaden**, UAB	JR	G	33	142	**4.3**
4 **Robert McKiver**, Houston	SR	G	34	145	**4.3**
5 **Garrison Carr**, American	JR	G	33	135	**4.1**

Three-Pt FG Pct	CL	POS	G	3FG	3FGA	PCT
1 **Jaycee Carroll**, Utah State	SR	G	35	114	229	**49.8**
2 **Chad Toppert**, New Mexico	JR	G	33	85	177	**48.0**
3 **Shawn Huff**, Valparaiso	SR	G	36	91	190	**47.9**
4 **Darnell Harris**, La Salle	SR	G	32	123	257	**47.9**
5 **Henry Salter**, TCU	JR	G	24	62	130	**47.7**

Minimum: 2.5 made per game

Free Throw Pct	CL	POS	G	FT	FTA	PCT
1 **Tyler Relph**, St. Bonaventure	SR	G	29	75	80	**93.8**
2 **Jaycee Carroll**, Utah State	SR	G	35	137	149	**91.9**
3 **Jack McClinton**, Miami (FL)	JR	G	32	114	124	**91.9**
4 **Justin Hare**, Belmont	SR	G	33	112	122	**91.8**
5 **Julio Anthony**, Eastern Illinois	SR	G	27	75	82	**91.5**

Minimum: 2.5 made per game

Assists Per Game	CL	POS	G	AST	APG
1 **Jason Richards**, Davidson	SR	G	36	293	**8.1**
2 **TeeJay Bannister**, Liberty	SR	G	31	224	**7.2**
Paul Stoll, Texas-Pan American	SR	G	31	224	**7.2**
4 **Jay Greene**, UMBC	JR	G	33	236	**7.2**
5 **Mike Jefferson**, High Point	SR	G	31	216	**7.0**
6 **Nikola Stojakovic**, Morehead State	SR	G	30	204	**6.8**
7 **Greivis Vasquez**, Maryland	SO	G	34	231	**6.8**
8 **Adam Emmenecker**, Drake	SR	G	33	213	**6.5**
9 **Kris Clark**, Utah State	SR	G	35	224	**6.4**
10 **Tony Lee**, Robert Morris	SR	G	34	217	**6.4**

Rebounds Per Game	CL	POS	G	REB	RPG
1 **Michael Beasley**, Kansas State	FR	F	33	408	**12.4**
2 **Jason Thompson**, Rider	SR	F	34	412	**12.1**
3 **Jon Brockman**, Washington	JR	F	32	370	**11.6**
4 **Durell Vinson**, Wagner	SR	F	31	358	**11.5**
5 **Marqus Blakely**, Vermont	SO	F	29	320	**11.0**
6 **Arizona Reid**, High Point	SR	F	31	342	**11.0**
7 **Boubacar Coly**, Morgan State	SR	F	33	361	**10.9**
8 **Ryan Bright**, Sam Houston State	SR	F	31	337	**10.9**
9 **Kentrell Gransberry**, South Florida	SR	C	30	325	**10.8**
10 **Thomas Sanders**, Gardner-Webb	SR	F	32	346	**10.8**

Blocked Shots Per Game	CL	POS	G	BLK	BPG
1 **Jarvis Varnado**, Mississippi State	SO	F	34	157	**4.6**
2 **Mickell Gladness**, Alabama A&M	SR	F/C	29	131	**4.5**
3 **Hasheem Thabeet**, Connecticut	SO	C	33	147	**4.5**
4 **Kleon Penn**, McNeese State	JR	C	29	117	**4.0**
5 **Shawn James**, Duquesne	JR	F	28	111	**4.0**

Steals Per Game	CL	POS	G	STL	SPG
1 **Devin Gibson**, UTSA	FR	G	28	93	**3.3**
2 **Devan Downey**, South Carolina	SO	G	32	103	**3.2**
3 **Chris Gaynor**, Winthrop	SR	G	34	97	**2.9**
4 **Lester Hudson**, Tenn.-Martin	JR	G	33	94	**2.8**
5 **Tony Lee**, Robert Morris	SR	G	34	95	**2.8**

INDIVIDUAL LEADERS—GAME

Points	CL	POS	OPP	DATE	PTS
1 **Robert McKiver**, Houston	SR	G	Southern Miss	F27	**52**
2 **Tyrese Rice**, Boston College	JR	G	North Carolina	M1	**46**
3 **Charron Fisher**, Niagara	SR	F	Loyola (MD)	F10	**45**
4 **Michael Beasley**, Kansas State	FR	F	Baylor	F23	**44**
Justin Jonas, Troy	SR	F	Paul Quinn	N14	**44**

Three-Pt FG Made	CL	POS	OPP	DATE	3FG
1 **Gary Patterson**, IUPUI	JR	G	Southern Utah	J31	**11**
2 **Justin Jonas**, Troy	SR	F	South Alabama	F10	**10**
Andre Smith, George Mason	JR	G	James Madison	J19	**10**
Samuel Haanpää, Valparaiso	SO	G	Chicago State	D15	**10**
Steven Rush, NC A&T	SR	G	DePaul	N24	**10**

Assists	CL	POS	OPP	DATE	AST
1 **Brandon Brooks**, Alabama State	JR	G	Jackson State	M8	**20**
2 **Mitch Johnson**, Stanford	JR	G	Marquette	M22	**16**
3 **Greivis Vasquez**, Maryland	SO	G	NC State	F9	**15**
TeeJay Bannister, Liberty	SR	G	Coastal Carolina	J21	**15**
Mike Jefferson, High Point	SR	G	Anderson	D14	**15**

Rebounds	CL	POS	OPP	DATE	REB
1 **Jason Thompson**, Rider	SR	F	Siena	F10	**24**
Michael Beasley, Kansas State	FR	F	Sacramento State	N9	**24**
3 **J.J. Hickson**, NC State	FR	F	Clemson	F16	**23**
Richard Hendrix, Alabama	JR	F	Troy	N9	**23**
5 6 players tied at 22					

Blocked Shots	CL	POS	OPP	DATE	BLK
1 **Shawn James**, Duquesne	JR	F	Oakland	N20	**12**
2 **Tyrelle Blair**, Boston College	SR	C	Maryland	D9	**11**
3 **Shawn James**, Duquesne	JR	F	Saint Joseph's	F6	**10**
Jarvis Varnado, Mississippi State	SO	F	Kentucky	J15	**10**
Jarvis Varnado, Mississippi State	SO	F	Georgia	J12	**10**
Hasheem Thabeet, Connecticut	SO	C	Notre Dame	J5	**10**
Jarvis Varnado, Mississippi State	SO	F	Miami (FL)	D13	**10**
Kenny George, UNC Asheville	JR	C	Campbell	N17	**10**
Kenny George, UNC Asheville	JR	C	Lees-McRae	N11	**10**
Mickell Gladness, Alabama A&M	SR	F/C	Oakwood	N10	**10**

Steals	CL	POS	OPP	DATE	STL
1 **Lester Hudson**, Tenn.-Martin	JR	G	Central Baptist	N13	**10**
2 **Jerome Dyson**, Connecticut	SO	G	St. John's	J8	**9**
3 **Chris Gaynor**, Winthrop	SR	G	VMI	F20	**8**
Ryan Bright, Sam Houston State	SR	F	McNeese State	J17	**8**
Marcus Hall, Colorado	SR	G	Tulsa	J7	**8**
Russell Robinson, Kansas	SR	G	Yale	D29	**8**
Paul Gause, Seton Hall	JR	G	James Madison	D22	**8**
Travis Holmes, VMI	JR	F	William and Mary	D20	**8**
Trae Clark, Cal Poly	JR	G	Menlo	D2	**8**
DeWayne Reed, Auburn	SO	G	George Washington	D2	**8**
Paul Gause, Seton Hall	JR	G	Monmouth	N11	**8**

TEAM LEADERS—SEASON

Win-Loss Pct	W	L	PCT
1 **Memphis**	38	2	**95.0**
2 **Kansas**	37	3	**92.5**
3 **North Carolina**	36	3	**92.3**
4 **UCLA**	35	4	**89.7**
5 **Butler**	30	4	**88.2**

Scoring Offense	G	W-L	PTS	PPG
1 **VMI**	29	14-15	2,649	**91.3**
2 **North Carolina**	39	36-3	3,454	**88.6**
3 **Texas State**	29	13-16	2,423	**83.6**
4 **Duke**	34	28-6	2,830	**83.2**
5 **Duquesne**	30	17-13	2,470	**82.3**

Scoring Margin	G	W-L	PPG	OPP PPG	MAR
1 **Kansas**	40	37-3	80.5	61.5	**19.0**
2 **Memphis**	40	38-2	79.9	61.9	**18.0**
3 **North Carolina**	39	36-3	88.6	72.5	**16.1**
4 **Davidson**	36	29-7	77.9	63.2	**14.7**
5 **UCLA**	39	35-4	73.5	59.0	**14.5**

Field Goal Pct	G	W-L	FG	FGA	PCT
1 **Utah State**	35	24-11	923	1,797	**51.4**
2 **Kansas**	40	37-3	1,176	2,314	**50.8**
3 **Boise State**	34	25-9	994	1,956	**50.8**
4 **IUPUI**	33	26-7	883	1,754	**50.3**
5 **Pacific**	31	21-10	772	1,569	**49.2**

Three-Pt FG Per Game	G	W-L	3FG	3PG
1 **VMI**	29	14-15	336	**11.6**
2 **Houston**	34	24-10	375	**11.0**
3 **Troy**	31	12-19	335	**10.8**
4 **Belmont**	34	25-9	357	**10.5**
5 **Lafayette**	30	15-15	299	**10.0**

Assists Per Game	G	W-L	AST	APG
1 **Notre Dame**	33	25-8	608	**18.4**
2 **Sam Houston State**	31	23-8	564	**18.2**
3 **Duquesne**	30	17-13	542	**18.1**
4 **Kansas**	40	37-3	721	**18.0**
5 **VMI**	29	14-15	518	**17.9**

Rebound Margin	G	W-L	RPG	OPP RPG	MAR
1 **North Carolina**	39	36-3	43.5	32.5	**11.0**
2 **New Mexico State**	35	21-14	41.7	32.8	**8.9**
3 **Kansas State**	33	21-12	41.3	32.9	**8.4**
4 **UCLA**	39	35-4	36.7	28.5	**8.2**
5 **Kansas**	40	37-3	38.7	30.8	**7.9**

Scoring Defense

	G	W-L	OPP PTS	OPP PPG
1 Wisconsin	36	31-5	1,958	**54.4**
2 Stephen F. Austin	32	26-6	1,805	**56.4**
3 Washington State	35	26-9	1,975	**56.4**
4 Air Force	30	16-14	1,715	**57.2**
5 Iowa	32	13-19	1,857	**58.0**

Field Goal Pct Defense

	G	W-L	OPP FG	OPP FGA	OPP PCT
1 Georgetown	34	28-6	669	1,827	**36.6**
2 Mississippi State	34	23-11	790	2,137	**37.0**
3 Kansas	40	37-3	853	2,249	**37.9**
4 VCU	32	24-8	647	1,698	**38.1**
5 Wisconsin	36	31-5	719	1,879	**38.3**

Blocked Shots Per Game

	G	W-L	BLK	BPG
1 Connecticut	33	24-9	285	**8.6**
2 Mississippi State	34	23-11	267	**7.9**
3 Massachusetts	36	25-11	264	**7.3**
Duquesne	30	17-13	220	**7.3**
5 Maryland	34	19-15	224	**6.6**

Steals Per Game

	G	W-L	STL	SPG
1 VMI	29	14-15	369	**12.7**
2 Robert Morris	34	26-8	337	**9.9**
3 Pepperdine	32	11-21	316	**9.9**
4 Clemson	34	24-10	334	**9.8**
5 Austin Peay	35	24-11	335	**9.6**

TEAM LEADERS—GAME

Points

	OPP	DATE	SCORE
1 VMI	Columbia Union	N28	**156-91**
2 VMI	W. Virginia Wesleyan	N14	**135-81**
3 Troy	Paul Quinn	N14	**133-131**
4 The Citadel	Daniel Webster	N9	**131-79**
5 Duquesne	Howard	N9	**129-59**

Field Goal Pct

	OPP	DATE	FG	FGA	PCT
1 Syracuse	East Tennessee St.	D15	47	62	**75.8**
2 Radford	Emory and Henry	J7	49	65	**75.4**
3 Arizona State	Saint Francis (PA)	D29	31	43	**72.1**
4 Santa Clara	Sacramento State	N25	28	39	**71.8**
5 Ohio State	Presbyterian College	D15	35	49	**71.4**

3-Pt FG Made

	OPP	DATE	3FG
1 Louisville	Hartford	N17	**22**
2 The Citadel	Daniel Webster	N9	**21**
3 Florida State	Maine	D8	**20**
VMI	Columbia Union	N28	**20**
5 VMI	Radford	F5	**19**
IUPUI	Southern Utah	J31	**19**
Jacksonville State	Tenn. Temple	N12	**19**
Davidson	Emory	N9	**19**

CONSENSUS ALL-AMERICAS

FIRST TEAM

PLAYER	CL	POS	HT	SCHOOL	RPG	PPG
D.J. Augustin	SO	G	6-0	Texas	2.9	19.2
Michael Beasley	FR	F	6-10	Kansas State	12.4	26.2
Chris Douglas-Roberts	JR	G	6-7	Memphis	4.1	18.1
Tyler Hansbrough	JR	F	6-9	North Carolina	10.2	22.6
Kevin Love	FR	C	6-10	UCLA	10.6	17.5

SECOND TEAM

PLAYER	CL	POS	HT	SCHOOL	RPG	PPG
Stephen Curry	SO	G	6-3	Davidson	4.6	25.9
Shan Foster	SR	G/F	6-6	Vanderbilt	4.9	20.3
Luke Harangody	SO	F	6-8	Notre Dame	10.6	20.4
Roy Hibbert	SR	C	7-2	Georgetown	6.4	13.4
Chris Lofton	SR	G	6-2	Tennessee	3.2	15.6
D.J. White	SR	F/C	6-9	Indiana	10.3	17.4

Selectors: AP, NABC, Sporting News, USBWA

AWARD WINNERS

PLAYER OF THE YEAR

PLAYER	CL	POS	HT	SCHOOL	AWARDS
Tyler Hansbrough	JR	F	6-9	North Carolina	Naismith, AP, USBWA, Wooden, NABC, Rupp
Mike Green	SR	G	6-0	Butler	Frances Pomeroy Naismith*

*For the most outstanding senior player who is 6 feet or under

DEFENSIVE PLAYER OF THE YEAR

PLAYER	CL	POS	HT	SCHOOL
Hasheem Thabeet	SO	C	7-3	Connecticut

COACH OF THE YEAR

COACH	SCHOOL	REC	AWARDS
Keno Davis	Drake	28-5	AP, USBWA, Sporting News, CBS/Chevrolet
John Calipari	Memphis	38-2	Naismith
Bob McKillop	Davidson	29-7	NABC

ESPNU Class of 2008

RATING/PLAYER	POS	HT	HIGH SCHOOL	A-A TEAMS	COLLEGE	CAREER NOTES
99 Brandon Jennings	PG	6-2	Oak Hill Academy, Mouth of Wilson, VA	McD, MJ, P, USA	None	Naismith and Parade POY, '08; one pro season in Italy, No. 10 pick, '09 NBA draft (Bucks)
98 Samardo Samuels	C	6-8	St. Benedict's Prep, Newark, NJ	McD, MJ, P, USA	Louisville	USA Today National High School POY, '08; 11.8 ppg as freshman starter at Louisville
98 Tyreke Evans	SG	6-5	American Christian School, Aston, PA	McD, MJ, P, USA	Memphis	17.1 ppg in 1 season at Memphis; No. 4 pick, '09 NBA draft (Kings)
98 Jrue Holiday	SG	6-3	Campbell Hall, North Hollywood, CA	McD, MJ, P, USA	UCLA	8.5 ppg, 3.8 apg, 3.7 rpg as freshman; No. 17 pick, '09 NBA draft (76ers)
98 B.J. Mullens	C	7-0	Canal Winchester (OH) HS	McD, MJ, P, USA	Ohio State	8.8 ppg and 64% FG Pct as OSU freshman; No. 24 pick, '09 NBA draft (Mavericks)
96 JaMychal Green	PF	6-8	St. Jude HS, Montgomery, AL	McD, MJ, P	Alabama	Alabama Mr. Basketball, '08; 10.3 ppg, 7.6 rpg as freshman starter at Alabama
96 Tyler Zeller	PF	6-11	Washington (IN) HS	McD, P, USA	North Carolina	Indiana Mr. Basketball, '08; played 15 games for '09 NCAA champs before wrist injury
96 DeMar DeRozan	SF	6-6	Compton (CA) HS	McD, MJ, P, USA	USC	13.9 ppg, 5.7 rpg as freshman; No. 9 pick, '09 NBA draft (Raptors)
96 Scotty Hopson	SF	6-5	University Heights Academy, Hopkinsville, KY	McD, MJ, P, USA	Tennessee	AP Kentucky Boys POY, '08; at Tennessee, 9.2 ppg as freshman starter
96 Willie Warren	SG	6-4	North Crowley HS, Fort Worth, TX	McD, MJ, P, USA	Oklahoma	Texas Gatorade POY '08; at Oklahoma, No. 2 in scoring (14.6 ppg), 67 3-pointers
96 Ed Davis	PF	6-8	Benedictine HS Richmond, VA	McD, MJ, P	North Carolina	Virginia Mr. Basketball, '08; 2nd in rebounding (6.6 rpg) for '09 NCAA champs
96 William Buford	SG	6-5	Libbey HS, Toledo, OH	McD, MJ, P	Ohio State	Ohio Mr. Basketball, '08; at OSU, No. 2 in scoring (11.3 ppg) as freshman
96 Luke Babbitt	PF	6-7	Galena HS, Reno, NV	McD, P	Nevada	2-time Nevada Gatorade POY; led Nevada in scoring (16.9), rebounding (7.4) as freshman
96 Kemba Walker	PG	6-1	Rice HS, New York	McD, MJ, P	Connecticut	MVP of FIBA Americas tourney, '08; at UConn, 8.9 ppg, 2nd in assists (104) as freshman
96 Delvon Roe	PF	6-8	St. Edward HS, Lakewood, OH	MJ	Michigan State	Played 1 game as HS senior due to injury; started 31 games as freshman at MSU
96 Mike Rosario	SG	6-3	St. Anthony HS Jersey City, NJ	McD, P, USA	Rutgers	1st McDonald's All-America in Rutgers history; led Rutgers with 15.2 ppg as freshman
96 Al-Farouq Aminu	SF	6-9	Norcross (GA) HS	McD, MJ, P, USA	Wake Forest	Georgia Mr. Basketball, '08; 10 double-doubles as freshman at Wake; 12.9 ppg, 8.2 rpg
96 Elliot Williams	SG	6-4	St. George Independent School, Memphis, TN	McD, P	Duke/Memphis	Division II-A Tennessee Mr. Basketball, '08; 4.2 ppg, 2.3 rpg as freshman;
96 Sylven Landesberg	SF	6-6	Holy Cross HS Flushing, NY	McD, P	Virginia	All-time leading scorer at Holy Cross; led UVA with 16.6 ppg as freshman
96 Greg Monroe	PF	6-10	Helen Cox HS, Harvey, LA	McD, MJ, P, USA	Georgetown	Morgan Wooten Award winner, '08; at Georgetown, 12.7 ppg, 6.5 rpg as freshman
96 Howard Thompkins	PF	6-9	Wesleyan School, Norcross, GA/ Oak Hill Academy, Mouth of Wilson, VA	P	Georgia	Led Oak Hill Academy with 15.8 ppg as a Jr.; 12.6 ppg as freshman at UGA Transferred to Memphis
96 Michael Dunigan	C	6-10	Farragut Academy, Chicago	McD, MJ, P, USA	Oregon	In only 19.9 mpg, finished third in scoring (8.4) and second in rebounding (4.6) for Oregon
96 Emmanuel Negedu	PF	6-7	Brewster Academy, Wolfeboro, NH		Tennessee	Gatorade POY in New Hampshire; played in 33 games as freshman at Tennessee
96 Drew Gordon	PF	6-9	Archbishop Mitty HS, San Jose, CA	MJ	UCLA	Played in only 11 games as HS senior because of an ankle injury; at UCLA, 3.6 ppg as freshman
96 Chris Singleton	PF	6-8	Dunwoody HS, Atlanta		Florida State	Averaged 21.0 ppg and 13.0 rpg as HS senior; 8.1 ppg as freshman starter at FSU

Abbreviations: McD=McDonald's; MJ=Jordan Brand; P=Parade; USA=USA Today

Poll Progression

Preseason Poll

AP	ESPN/USA	SCHOOL
1	1	**North Carolina**
2	2	**UCLA**
3	3	**Memphis**
4	4	**Kansas**
5	5	**Georgetown**
6	6	**Louisville**
7	7	**Tennessee**
8	8	**Michigan State**
9	9	**Indiana**
10	10	**Washington State**
11	12	**Marquette**
12	13	**Oregon**
13	11	**Duke**
14	14	**Gonzaga**
15	16	**Texas**
16	14	**Texas A&M**
17	17	**Arizona**
18	18	**USC**
19	19	**Arkansas**
20	22	**Kentucky**
21	24	**NC State**
22	20	**Pittsburgh**
23	21	**Stanford**
24	23	**Southern Illinois**
25	—	**Kansas State**
—	25	**Villanova**

Week of Nov 12

AP	ESPN/USA	SCHOOL	AP ↓↑
1	1	**North Carolina** (0-0)	
2	2	**UCLA** (1-0)	
3	3	**Memphis** (2-0)	
4	4	**Kansas** (2-0)	
5	5	**Georgetown** (1-0)	
6	6	**Louisville** (0-0)	
7	7	**Tennessee** (1-0)	
8	8	**Indiana** (0-0)	↑1
9	9	**Washington State** (1-0)	↑1
10	11	**Marquette** (1-0)	↑1
11	13	**Oregon** (2-0)	↑1
12	12	**Michigan State** (0-0)	↓4
13	10	**Duke** (1-0)	
14	14	**Gonzaga** (1-0)	
15	15	**Texas A&M** (1-0)	↑1
16	16	**Texas** (0-0)	↓1
17	17	**Arizona** (0-0)	
18	18	**Arkansas** (1-0)	↑1
19	19	**Pittsburgh** (3-0)	↑3
20	20	**Stanford** (3-0)	↑3
21	22	**NC State** (0-0)	
22	24	**Kansas State** (2-0)	↑3
23	21	**Southern Illinois** (0-0)	↑1
24	23	**Villanova** (1-0)	⤴
25	—	**Butler** (1-0)	⤴
—	25	**Syracuse** (0-0)	

Week of Nov 19

AP	ESPN/USA	SCHOOL	AP ↓↑
1	1	**North Carolina** (2-0)	
2	2	**UCLA** (3-0)	
3	3	**Memphis** (4-0)	
4	4	**Kansas** (3-0)	
5	5	**Georgetown** (2-0)	
6	6	**Louisville** (2-0)	
7	7	**Tennessee** (3-0)	
8	8	**Indiana** (2-0)	
9	9	**Washington State** (3-0)	
10	11	**Michigan State** (2-0)	↑2
11	13	**Marquette** (2-0)	↓1
12	11	**Oregon** (4-0)	↓1
13	10	**Duke** (2-0)	
14	14	**Gonzaga** (3-0)	
15	16	**Texas** (3-0)	↑1
16	15	**Texas A&M** (4-0)	↓1
17	17	**Pittsburgh** (4-0)	↑2
18	20	**Kansas State** (3-0)	↑4
19	18	**Southern Illinois** (1-0)	↑4
20	19	**Villanova** (2-0)	↑4
21	21	**Syracuse** (3-0)	⤴
22	23	**Butler** (3-0)	↑3
23	—	**Virginia** (3-0)	⤴
24	22	**Clemson** (3-0)	⤴
25	24	**Florida** (4-0)	⤴
—	25	**Davidson** (1-1)	

Week of Nov 26

AP	ESPN/USA	SCHOOL	AP ↓↑
1	2	**North Carolina** (5-0)	
2	1	**UCLA** (6-0)	
3	3	**Memphis** (5-0)	
4	4	**Kansas** (5-0)	
5	5	**Georgetown** (3-0)	
6	6	**Washington State** (6-0)	↑[illegible]
7	7	**Duke** (6-0)	↑[illegible]
8	8	**Texas** (5-0)	↑[illegible]
9	9	**Texas A&M** (6-0)	↑[illegible]
10	13	**Michigan State** (4-1)	
11	12	**Tennessee** (5-1)	↓[illegible]
12	10	**Louisville** (4-1)	↓[illegible]
13	14	**Marquette** (4-1)	↓2
14	11	**Pittsburgh** (5-0)	↑3
15	15	**Indiana** (4-1)	↓7
16	16	**Butler** (6-0)	↑6
17	17	**Oregon** (5-1)	↓5
18	18	**Clemson** (5-0)	↑6
19	19	**Gonzaga** (5-1)	↓5
20	20	**Wisconsin** (5-0)	⤴
21	23	**BYU** (5-1)	⤴
22	24	**USC** (5-1)	⤴
23	25	**Xavier** (4-1)	⤴
24	—	**NC State** (4-1)	⤴
25	—	**Kansas State** (5-1)	↓7
—	21	**Villanova** (4-1)	⤵
—	22	**Southern Illinois** (3-1)	⤵

Week of Dec 3

AP	ESPN/USA	SCHOOL	AP ↓↑
1	1	**North Carolina** (7-0)	
2	2	**Memphis** (6-0)	↑1
3	3	**Kansas** (7-0)	↑1
4	5	**Texas** (7-0)	↑4
5	4	**Georgetown** (5-0)	
6	7	**Duke** (8-0)	↑1
7	8	**UCLA** (7-1)	↓5
8	6	**Washington State** (7-0)	↓2
9	10	**Michigan State** (6-1)	↑1
10	12	**Tennessee** (7-1)	↑1
11	15	**Marquette** (5-1)	↑2
12	9	**Pittsburgh** (7-0)	↑2
13	13	**Butler** (7-0)	↑3
14	11	**Louisville** (5-1)	↓2
15	15	**Indiana** (6-1)	
16	14	**Texas A&M** (7-1)	↓7
17	19	**Gonzaga** (7-1)	↑2
18	17	**Clemson** (7-0)	
19	18	**Oregon** (6-1)	↓2
20	22	**BYU** (6-1)	↑1
21	20	**Xavier** (6-1)	↑2
22	24	**Arizona** (5-2)	⤴
23	25	**Vanderbilt** (7-0)	⤴
24	—	**USC** (6-2)	↓2
25	21	**Villanova** (5-1)	⤴
—	23	**Wisconsin** (5-1)	⤵

Week of Dec 10

AP	ESPN/USA	SCHOOL	AP ↓↑
1	1	**North Carolina** (8-0)	
2	2	**Memphis** (7-0)	
3	3	**Kansas** (9-0)	
4	5	**Texas** (9-0)	
5	4	**Georgetown** (7-0)	
6	7	**Duke** (9-0)	
7	6	**Washington State** (9-0)	↑1
8	8	**UCLA** (8-1)	↓1
9	10	**Michigan State** (8-1)	
10	13	**Marquette** (6-1)	↑1
11	9	**Pittsburgh** (9-0)	↑1
12	11	**Tennessee** (8-1)	↓2
13	14	**Indiana** (8-1)	↑2
14	12	**Texas A&M** (8-1)	↑2
15	15	**Clemson** (8-0)	↑3
16	16	**Oregon** (7-1)	↑3
17	17	**Xavier** (7-1)	↑4
18	19	**Butler** (8-1)	↓5
19	23	**Gonzaga** (8-2)	↓2
20	21	**Vanderbilt** (9-0)	↑3
21	22	**Arizona** (6-2)	↑1
22	20	**Louisville** (5-2)	↓8
23	18	**Villanova** (7-1)	↑2
24	24	**Saint Mary's (CA)** (7-0)	⤴
25	25	**BYU** (7-2)	↓5

Week of Dec 17

AP	ESPN/USA	SCHOOL	AP ↓↑
1	1	**North Carolina** (9-0)	
2	2	**Memphis** (8-0)	
3	3	**Kansas** (10-0)	
4	5	**Texas** (10-0)	
5	4	**Georgetown** (8-0)	
6	7	**Duke** (9-0)	
7	6	**Washington State** (9-0)	
8	8	**UCLA** (9-1)	
9	10	**Michigan State** (9-1)	
10	13	**Marquette** (7-1)	
11	9	**Pittsburgh** (10-0)	
12	12	**Tennessee** (9-1)	
13	14	**Indiana** (9-1)	
14	11	**Texas A&M** (9-1)	
15	15	**Clemson** (8-0)	
16	18	**Butler** (9-1)	↑2
17	17	**Vanderbilt** (10-0)	↑3
18	20	**Gonzaga** (8-2)	↑1
19	19	**Arizona** (7-2)	↑2
20	16	**Villanova** (8-1)	↑3
21	23	**BYU** (9-2)	↑4
22	22	**Miami (FL)** (9-0)	⤴
23	21	**Oregon** (8-2)	↓7
24	—	**West Virginia** (8-1)	⤴
25	—	**USC** (6-3)	⤴
—	24	**Xavier** (8-2)	⤵
—	25	**Stanford** (8-1)	

Week of Dec 24

AP	ESPN/USA	SCHOOL	AP ↓↑
1	1	**North Carolina** (11-0)	
2	2	**Memphis** (10-0)	
3	3	**Kansas** (12-0)	
4	4	**Washington State** (11-0)	↑3
5	5	**UCLA** (11-1)	↑3
6	6	**Pittsburgh** (11-0)	↑5
7	7	**Michigan State** (11-1)	↑2
8	8	**Georgetown** (8-1)	↓3
9	9	**Texas** (11-1)	↓5
10	10	**Duke** (10-0)	↓4
11	12	**Tennessee** (11-1)	↑1
12	13	**Marquette** (9-1)	↓2
13	14	**Indiana** (10-1)	
14	11	**Texas A&M** (11-1)	
15	15	**Vanderbilt** (11-0)	↑2
16	17	**Butler** (11-1)	
17	18	**Arizona** (9-2)	↑2
18	16	**Villanova** (9-1)	↑2
19	19	**Miami (FL)** (12-0)	↑3
20	21	**BYU** (10-2)	↑1
21	20	**Clemson** (10-1)	↓6
22	24	**Mississippi** (11-0)	⤴
23	23	**West Virginia** (10-1)	↑1
24	—	**USC** (8-3)	↑1
25	25	**Rhode Island** (11-1)	⤴
—	22	**Stanford** (11-1)	

Week of Dec 31

AP	ESPN/USA	SCHOOL	AP ↓↑
1	1	**North Carolina** (13-0)	
2	2	**Memphis** (11-0)	
3	3	**Kansas** (13-0)	
4	4	**Washington State** (12-0)	
5	5	**UCLA** (12-1)	
6	6	**Michigan State** (12-1)	↑1
7	7	**Georgetown** (9-1)	↑1
8	9	**Tennessee** (12-1)	↑3
9	8	**Duke** (10-1)	↑1
10	11	**Marquette** (10-1)	↑2
11	12	**Indiana** (11-1)	↑2
12	10	**Texas A&M** (12-1)	↑2
13	13	**Pittsburgh** (11-1)	↓7
14	14	**Texas** (11-2)	↓5
15	15	**Vanderbilt** (12-0)	
16	17	**Butler** (12-1)	
17	16	**Villanova** (10-1)	↑1
18	18	**Mississippi** (12-0)	↑4
19	19	**Clemson** (11-1)	↑2
20	23	**Dayton** (11-1)	⤴
21	21	**Arizona** (9-3)	↓4
22	—	**USC** (9-3)	↑2
23	22	**Rhode Island** (13-1)	↑2
24	20	**Stanford** (11-1)	⤴
25	24	**Wisconsin** (10-2)	⤴
—	24	**Saint Mary's (CA)** (12-1)	

Week of Jan 7 (A)

AP	ESPN/USA	SCHOOL	AP ↓↑
1	1	**North Carolina** (15-0)	
2	2	**Memphis** (13-0)	
3	3	**Kansas** (14-0)	
4	4	**Washington State** (13-0)	
5	5	**UCLA** (14-1)	
6	6	**Michigan State** (13-1)	
7	8	**Georgetown** (11-1)	
8	9	**Tennessee** (12-1)	
9	7	**Duke** (11-1)	
10	11	**Indiana** (12-1)	↑1
11	10	**Texas A&M** (14-1)	↑1
12	13	**Texas** (13-2)	↑2
13	12	**Vanderbilt** (15-0)	↑2
14	14	**Butler** (13-1)	↑2
15	16	**Marquette** (11-2)	↓5
16	15	**Mississippi** (13-0)	↑2
17	22	**Dayton** (12-1)	↑3
18	19	**Clemson** (12-2)	↑1
19	17	**Villanova** (11-2)	↓2
20	18	**Pittsburgh** (12-2)	↓7
21	21	**Wisconsin** (12-2)	↑4
22	20	**Rhode Island** (14-1)	↑1
23	23	**Stanford** (12-2)	↑1
24	25	**Xavier** (12-3)	⤴
25	—	**Miami (FL)** (13-1)	⤴
—	24	**Arizona** (10-4)	⤵

Week of Jan 14

AP	ESPN/USA	SCHOOL	AP ↓↑
1	1	**North Carolina** (17-0)	
2	2	**Memphis** (15-0)	
3	3	**Kansas** (16-0)	
4	4	**UCLA** (16-1)	↑1
5	6	**Georgetown** (13-1)	↑2
6	7	**Tennessee** (14-1)	↑2
7	5	**Duke** (13-1)	↑2
8	8	**Washington State** (14-1)	↓4
9	10	**Indiana** (14-1)	↑1
10	9	**Texas A&M** (15-1)	↑1
11	11	**Michigan State** (14-2)	↓5
12	12	**Butler** (16-1)	↑2
13	13	**Marquette** (13-2)	↑2
14	18	**Dayton** (14-1)	↑3
15	16	**Pittsburgh** (14-2)	↑5
16	14	**Vanderbilt** (16-1)	↓3
17	17	**Wisconsin** (13-2)	↑4
18	15	**Mississippi** (14-1)	↓2
19	19	**Texas** (13-3)	↓7
20	20	**Xavier** (14-3)	↑4
21	24	**Miami (FL)** (14-1)	↑4
22	25	**Arizona State** (13-2)	⤴
23	21	**Rhode Island** (15-2)	↓1
24	23	**Clemson** (13-3)	↓6
25	21	**Villanova** (11-3)	↓6

Week of Jan 21

AP	ESPN/USA	SCHOOL	AP ↓↑
1	1	**Memphis** (17-0)	↑1
2	2	**Kansas** (18-0)	↑1
3	5	**Tennessee** (16-1)	↑3
4	3	**Duke** (15-1)	↑3
5	4	**North Carolina** (18-1)	↓4
6	6	**Washington State** (16-1)	↑2
7	8	**Indiana** (16-1)	↑2
8	7	**UCLA** (16-2)	↓4
9	9	**Georgetown** (14-2)	↓4
10	10	**Michigan State** (16-2)	↑1
11	11	**Wisconsin** (15-2)	↑6
12	12	**Texas** (14-3)	↑7
13	17	**Pittsburgh** (15-3)	↑2
14	13	**Vanderbilt** (17-2)	↑2
15	14	**Butler** (17-2)	↓3
16	19	**Dayton** (14-2)	↓2
17	15	**Mississippi** (15-2)	↑1
18	16	**Texas A&M** (15-3)	↓8
19	18	**Villanova** (13-3)	↑7
20	21	**Stanford** (15-3)	⤴
21	20	**Marquette** (13-4)	↓8
22	23	**Drake** (16-1)	⤴
23	22	**Xavier** (15-4)	↓3
24	—	**Arizona State** (14-3)	↓2
25	—	**Baylor** (15-2)	⤴
—	24	**Saint Mary's (CA)** (15-2)	
—	25	**Clemson** (14-4)	⤵

[We]ek of Jan 28

AP	ESPN/USA	SCHOOL	AP ↓↑
	1	**Memphis** (19-0)	
	2	**Kansas** (20-0)	
	3	**Duke** (17-1)	↑1
	4	**North Carolina** (19-1)	↑1
	5	**UCLA** (18-2)	↑3
	6	**Georgetown** (16-2)	↑3
	8	**Tennessee** (17-2)	↓4
	7	**Michigan State** (18-2)	↑2
	9	**Washington State** (17-2)	↓3
	10	**Texas** (16-3)	↑2
	11	**Indiana** (17-2)	↓4
[illegible]	12	**Butler** (19-2)	↑3
[illegible]	13	**Wisconsin** (16-3)	↓2
[illegible]	14	**Stanford** (16-3)	↑6
[illegible]	15	**Xavier** (17-4)	↑8
16	17	**Drake** (18-1)	↑6
17	16	**Marquette** (14-4)	↑4
18	21	**Pittsburgh** (16-4)	↓5
19	18	**Vanderbilt** (17-3)	↓5
20	19	**Florida** (18-3)	⤴
21	20	**Saint Mary's (CA)** (17-2)	⤴
22	24	**Kansas State** (14-4)	⤴
23	23	**Texas A&M** (16-4)	↓5
24	22	**Mississippi** (15-3)	↓7
25	—	**Baylor** (16-3)	
—	25	**Mississippi State** (14-5)	

Week of Feb 4

AP	ESPN/USA	SCHOOL	AP ↓↑
1	1	**Memphis** (21-0)	
2	2	**Duke** (19-1)	↑1
3	3	**North Carolina** (21-1)	↑1
4	5	**Kansas** (21-1)	↓2
5	4	**UCLA** (20-2)	
6	6	**Georgetown** (18-2)	
7	7	**Tennessee** (19-2)	
8	8	**Wisconsin** (18-3)	↑5
9	9	**Stanford** (18-3)	↑5
10	11	**Butler** (19-2)	↑2
11	10	**Michigan State** (19-3)	↓3
12	12	**Texas** (17-4)	↓2
13	14	**Xavier** (18-4)	↑2
14	13	**Indiana** (18-3)	↓3
15	15	**Drake** (20-1)	↑1
16	16	**Marquette** (16-4)	↑1
17	17	**Washington State** (17-4)	↓8
18	18	**Texas A&M** (18-4)	↑5
19	19	**Connecticut** (16-5)	⤴
20	24	**Kansas State** (15-5)	↑2
21	25	**Pittsburgh** (17-5)	↓3
22	21	**Notre Dame** (16-4)	⤴
23	20	**Vanderbilt** (18-4)	↓4
24	—	**Purdue** (17-5)	⤴
25	23	**Saint Mary's (CA.)** (18-3)	↓4
—	22	**Florida** (18-4)	⤵

Week of Feb 11 Ⓑ

AP	ESPN/USA	SCHOOL	AP ↓↑
1	1	**Memphis** (23-0)	
2	2	**Duke** (21-1)	
3	3	**Kansas** (23-1)	↑1
4	4	**Tennessee** (21-2)	↑3
5	5	**North Carolina** (22-2)	↓2
6	6	**UCLA** (21-3)	↓1
7	7	**Stanford** (20-3)	↑2
8	8	**Georgetown** (19-3)	↓2
9	10	**Butler** (21-2)	↑1
10	9	**Michigan State** (20-3)	↑1
11	11	**Texas** (19-4)	↑1
12	13	**Xavier** (20-4)	↑1
13	12	**Indiana** (20-3)	↑1
14	15	**Drake** (22-1)	↑1
15	14	**Wisconsin** (19-4)	↓7
16	16	**Texas A&M** (20-4)	↑2
17	17	**Connecticut** (18-5)	↑2
18	22	**Kansas State** (17-5)	↑2
19	23	**Purdue** (19-5)	↑5
20	18	**Notre Dame** (18-4)	↑2
21	20	**Washington State** (18-5)	↓4
22	24	**Pittsburgh** (18-5)	↓1
23	—	**Louisville** (18-6)	⤴
24	19	**Vanderbilt** (20-4)	↓1
25	21	**Saint Mary's (CA)** (20-3)	
—	25	**Marquette** (16-6)	⤵

Week of Feb 18

AP	ESPN/USA	SCHOOL	AP ↓↑
1	1	**Memphis** (25-0)	
2	2	**Tennessee** (23-2)	↑2
3	3	**North Carolina** (24-2) Ⓒ	↑2
4	5	**Kansas** (24-2)	↓1
5	4	**Duke** (22-2)	↓3
6	6	**UCLA** (22-3)	
7	7	**Texas** (21-4)	↑4
8	8	**Butler** (24-2)	↑1
9	9	**Stanford** (21-4)	↓2
10	12	**Xavier** (21-4)	↑2
11	10	**Wisconsin** (21-4)	↑4
12	11	**Georgetown** (20-4)	↓4
13	13	**Connecticut** (20-5)	↑4
14	15	**Purdue** (21-5)	↑5
15	14	**Indiana** (21-4)	↓2
16	18	**Drake** (23-2)	↓2
17	19	**Washington State** (20-5)	↑4
18	23	**Louisville** (20-6)	↑5
19	17	**Michigan State** (20-5)	↓9
20	16	**Vanderbilt** (22-4)	↑4
21	21	**Notre Dame** (19-5)	↓1
22	22	**Texas A&M** (20-5)	↓6
23	20	**Saint Mary's (CA)** (22-3)	↑2
24	25	**Kansas State** (18-6)	↓6
25	24	**Marquette** (18-6)	⤴

Week of Feb 25

AP	ESPN/USA	SCHOOL	AP ↓↑
1	1	**Tennessee** (25-2) Ⓓ	↑1
2	3	**Memphis** (26-1) Ⓓ	↓1
3	2	**North Carolina** (26-2)	
4	4	**UCLA** (24-3)	↑2
5	5	**Texas** (23-4)	↑2
6	7	**Kansas** (24-3)	↓2
7	6	**Duke** (23-3)	↓2
8	8	**Stanford** (22-4)	↑1
9	11	**Xavier** (24-4)	↑1
10	9	**Wisconsin** (23-4)	↑1
11	10	**Georgetown** (22-4)	↑1
12	12	**Indiana** (23-4)	↑3
13	18	**Louisville** (22-6)	↑5
14	13	**Butler** (25-3)	↓6
15	16	**Connecticut** (21-6)	↓2
16	19	**Purdue** (21-6)	↓2
17	17	**Notre Dame** (21-5)	↑4
18	14	**Vanderbilt** (23-4)	↑2
19	15	**Michigan State** (22-5)	
20	20	**Drake** (24-3)	↓4
21	21	**Marquette** (20-6)	↑4
22	22	**Washington State** (21-6)	↓5
23	24	**Kent State** (23-5)	⤴
24	—	**Gonzaga** (21-6)	⤴
25	23	**Saint Mary's (CA)** (23-4)	↓2
—	25	**BYU** (21-6)	

Week of Mar 3

AP	ESPN/USA	SCHOOL	AP ↓↑
1	1	**North Carolina** (27-2)	↑2
2	3	**Memphis** (28-1)	
3	2	**UCLA** (26-3)	↑1
4	4	**Tennessee** (26-3)	↓3
5	6	**Kansas** (26-3) Ⓔ	↑1
6	5	**Duke** (25-3)	↑1
7	7	**Stanford** (24-4)	↑1
8	11	**Xavier** (25-4)	↑1
9	9	**Texas** (24-5)	↓4
10	8	**Wisconsin** (24-4)	
11	10	**Georgetown** (24-4)	
12	13	**Louisville** (24-6)	⤴
13	14	**Connecticut** (23-6)	↑2
14	12	**Butler** (27-3)	
15	15	**Purdue** (23-6)	↑1
16	16	**Vanderbilt** (24-5)	↑2
17	18	**Michigan State** (23-6)	↑2
18	17	**Indiana** (24-5)	↓6
19	19	**Notre Dame** (22-6)	↓2
20	21	**Drake** (25-4)	
21	20	**Marquette** (21-7)	
22	23	**Gonzaga** (23-6)	↑2
23	22	**Washington State** (22-7)	↓1
24	—	**Clemson** (21-7)	⤴
25	—	**Davidson** (23-6)	⤴
—	24	**BYU** (23-6)	
—	25	**Mississippi State** (23-8)	

Week of Mar 10

AP	ESPN/USA	SCHOOL	AP ↓↑
1	1	**North Carolina** (29-2)	
2	3	**Memphis** (30-1)	
3	2	**UCLA** (28-3)	
4	4	**Tennessee** (28-3)	
5	5	**Kansas** (28-3)	
6	8	**Texas** (26-5)	↑3
7	7	**Duke** (26-4)	↓1
8	6	**Wisconsin** (26-4)	↑2
9	9	**Georgetown** (25-4)	↑2
10	12	**Xavier** (26-5)	↓2
11	11	**Stanford** (24-6)	↓4
12	10	**Butler** (28-3)	↑2
13	13	**Louisville** (24-7)	⤴
14	14	**Notre Dame** (24-6)	↑5
15	15	**Connecticut** (24-7)	↓2
16	18	**Drake** (28-4)	↑4
17	16	**Purdue** (24-7)	↓2
18	17	**Vanderbilt** (25-6)	↓2
19	19	**Michigan State** (24-7)	↓2
20	22	**Gonzaga** (25-6) Ⓕ	↑2
21	21	**Washington State** (23-7)	↑2
22	20	**Indiana** (25-6)	↓4
23	25	**Davidson** (25-6)	↑2
24	23	**BYU** (25-6)	⤴
25	24	**Marquette** (22-8)	↓4

Week of Mar 17

AP	ESPN/USA	SCHOOL	AP ↓↑
1	1	**North Carolina** (32-2)	
2	3	**Memphis** (33-1)	
3	2	**UCLA** (31-3)	
4	4	**Kansas** (31-3)	↑1
5	6	**Tennessee** (29-4)	↓1
6	5	**Wisconsin** (29-4)	↑2
7	7	**Texas** (28-6)	↓1
8	8	**Georgetown** (27-5)	↑1
9	9	**Duke** (27-5)	↓2
10	11	**Stanford** (26-7)	↑1
11	10	**Butler** (29-3)	↑1
12	12	**Xavier** (27-6)	↓2
13	13	**Louisville** (24-8)	
14	14	**Drake** (28-4)	↑2
15	15	**Notre Dame** (24-7)	↓1
16	17	**Connecticut** (24-8)	↓1
17	19	**Pittsburgh** (26-9)	⤴
18	20	**Michigan State** (25-8)	↑1
19	16	**Vanderbilt** (26-7)	↓1
20	18	**Purdue** (24-8)	↓3
21	21	**Washington State** (24-8)	
22	22	**Clemson** (24-9)	⤴
23	23	**Davidson** (26-6)	
24	—	**Gonzaga** (25-7)	↓4
25	24	**Marquette** (24-9)	
—	24	**Indiana** (25-7)	⤵

Final Poll (Post-Tournament)

ESPN/USA	SCHOOL
1	**Kansas** (35-3)
2	**Memphis** (37-1)
3	**North Carolina** (36-2)
4	**UCLA** (35-3)
5	**Texas** (31-7)
6	**Louisville** (27-9)
7	**Tennessee** (31-5)
8	**Xavier** (30-7)
9	**Davidson** (29-7)
10	**Wisconsin** (31-5)
11	**Stanford** (28-8)
12	**Georgetown** (28-6)
13	**Michigan State** (27-9)
14	**Butler** (30-4)
15	**Washington State** (26-9)
16	**Duke** (28-6)
17	**West Virginia** (26-11)
18	**Pittsburgh** (27-10)
19	**Notre Dame** (25-8)
20	**Purdue** (25-9)
21	**Marquette** (25-10)
22	**Western Kentucky** (29-7)
23	**Drake** (28-5)
24	**Villanova** (22-13)
25	**Vanderbilt** (26-8)

Ⓐ Kansas State pounds Savannah State, 85-25, on Jan. 7 in Manhattan. In the second half, K-State holds Savannah to one field goal in 23 attempts—an NCAA record for futility in a half—and a total of four points, the lowest for a half since the advent of the shot clock in 1986.

Ⓑ On Feb. 4, just two days after picking up career victory No. 902—the most in D1 history—with a 67-60 win over Oklahoma State, Texas Tech's Bob Knight abruptly announces that he is retiring. He is succeeded by his son, Pat.

Ⓒ On Feb. 10, Clemson sets an NCAA record for futility on the road against a single opponent when North Carolina defeats the Tigers, 103-93, in double overtime. It's Clemson's 53rd consecutive loss in Chapel Hill, surpassing Brown's 52 straight losses at Princeton (1929-2002).

Ⓓ In the first battle between top-ranked teams from Tennessee, coach Bruce Pearl's Volunteers beat Memphis, 66-62. Although the game is sloppy, it's the most-watched regular-season game in ESPN history (until it is surpassed by North Carolina's 76-68 win over Duke on March 8).

Ⓔ Kansas gets its most lopsided victory ever over a Big 12 opponent, ripping Pat Knight's Texas Tech, 109-51. (It's also the biggest margin of defeat in Tech history.) The Jayhawks go 20–0 in Allen Fieldhouse, the 14th time they've gone unbeaten at home since the arena opened in 1955.

Ⓕ Gonzaga fails to get a three-pointer in its 69-62 loss to San Diego in the WCC tournament final, ending its NCAA-record streak of 491 consecutive games with at least one trey.

Pre-Tournament Ratings Percentage Index (RPI)

RANK	SCHOOL	W-L	Sched. Strg.	SS Rank	RPI
1	**Tennessee**	28-4	.6325	1	.6765
2	**North Carolina**	31-2	.6130	3	.6722
3	**Memphis**	33-1	.5853	21	.6644
4	**UCLA**	30-3	.5849	22	.6535
5	**Texas**	27-5	.6052	5	.6523
6	**Duke**	27-5	.5979	8	.6481
7	**Kansas**	29-3	.5504	65	.6457
8	**Georgetown**	27-5	.5702	42	.6424
9	**Xavier**	27-6	.5845	24	.6345
10	**Drake**	26-4	.5485	70	.6283
11	**Wisconsin**	28-4	.5517	64	.6276
12	**Vanderbilt**	26-7	.5704	40	.6247
13	**Louisville**	24-8	.6032	7	.6224
14	**Stanford**	26-7	.5544	61	.6174
15	**Pittsburgh**	25-9	.5809	25	.6160
16	**Michigan State**	25-8	.5706	38	.6153
17	**Butler**	29-3	.5011	155	.6120
18	**Connecticut**	24-8	.5775	31	.6107
19	**Clemson**	23-8	.5690	45	.6097
20	**Marquette**	23-9	.5872	17	.6056
21	**Kent State**	28-6	.5231	108	.6050
22	**Indiana**	25-7	.5562	58	.6032
23	**Washington State**	24-8	.5709	37	.6021
24	**UNLV**	25-7	.5605	55	.6020
25	**BYU**	27-7	.5333	97	.6018
26	**Arkansas**	22-10	.5847	23	.6005
27	**Notre Dame**	24-7	.5343	94	.5986
28	**Oklahoma**	22-11	.5928	12	.5956
29	**USC**	21-11	.5934	11	[illegible]
30	**West Virginia**	23-10	.5665	49	[illegible]
31	**Gonzaga**	25-7	.5323	100	[illegible]
32	**Dayton**	21-10	.5808	26	[illegible]
33	**Illinois State**	23-9	.5485	71	[illegible]
34	**Miami**	21-10	.5703	41	[illegible]
35	**Davidson**	25-6	.5174	119	[illegible]
36	**St. Mary's (CA)**	24-6	.5068	148	[illegible]
37	**Arizona**	18-14	.6235	2	[illegible]
38	**South Alabama**	24-6	.5153	120	[illegible]
39	**Mississippi State**	22-10	.5562	59	[illegible]
40	**Western Kentucky**	25-6	.5078	143	[illegible]

Source: NC

Tournament Leaders

Individual Leaders

Scoring

	CL	POS	G	PTS	PPG
1 **Stephen Curry**, Davidson	SO	G	4	128	32.0
2 **Tyrone Brazelton**, Western Kentucky	SR	G	3	79	26.3
3 **Chris Douglas-Roberts**, Memphis	JR	G	6	140	23.3
4 **Derrick Rose**, Memphis	FR	G	6	125	20.8
5 **Courtney Lee**, Western Kentucky	SR	G	3	62	20.7
6 **A.J. Abrams**, Texas	JR	G	4	81	20.3
7 **Tyler Hansbrough**, North Carolina	JR	F	5	101	20.2
8 **Brook Lopez**, Stanford	SO	F	3	60	20.0
9 **Kevin Love**, UCLA	FR	C	5	99	19.8
10 **Scottie Reynolds**, Villanova	SO	G	3	57	19.0

Minimum: 3 games

Field Goal Pct

	CL	POS	G	FG	FGA	PCT
1 **Derrick Brown**, Xavier	SO	F	4	20	27	74.1
2 **Aron Baynes**, Washington State	JR	C	3	17	24	70.8
3 **Deon Thompson**, North Carolina	SO	F	5	24	34	70.6
4 **Goran Suton**, Michigan State	JR	F	3	21	30	70.0
5 **Sasha Kaun**, Kansas	SR	C	6	16	24	66.7

Minimum: 15 made and 3 games

Free Throw Pct

	CL	POS	G	FT	FTA	PCT
1 **Kenny Hasbrouck**, Siena	JR	G	2	16	16	100.0
2 **Jack McClinton**, Miami (FL)	JR	G	2	15	15	100.0
3 **Brook Lopez**, Stanford	SO	F	3	18	19	94.7
4 **Jon Scheyer**, Duke	SO	G	2	15	16	93.8
5 **Ty Lawson**, North Carolina	SO	G	5	21	23	91.3

Minimum: 15 made

Three-Point FG Pct

	CL	POS	G	3FG	3FGA	PCT
1 **Kenny Brown**, Stanford	JR	G	3	7	9	77.8
2 **Darren Collison**, UCLA	JR	G	5	10	16	62.5
Scottie Reynolds, Villanova	SO	G	3	10	16	62.5
4 **Tyrone Brazelton**, Western Kentucky	SR	G	3	14	26	53.8
Willie Kemp, Memphis	SO	G	6	7	13	53.8

Minimum: 6 made and 3 games

Assists Per Game

	CL	POS	G	AST	APG
1 **Mitch Johnson**, Stanford	JR	G	3	29	9.7
2 **Jason Richards**, Davidson	SR	G	4	36	9.0
3 **D.J. Augustin**, Texas	SO	G	4	26	6.5
4 **Taylor Rochestie**, Washington State	JR	G	3	19	6.3
5 **Derrick Rose**, Memphis	FR	G	6	36	6.0
Drew Lavender, Xavier	SR	G	4	24	6.0

Minimum: 3 games

Rebounds Per Game

	CL	POS	G	REB	RPG
1 **Kevin Love**, UCLA	FR	C	5	53	10.6
2 **Luc Richard Mbah a Moute**, UCLA	JR	F	4	41	10.3
3 **Joe Alexander**, West Virginia	JR	F	3	29	9.7
4 **Tyler Hansbrough**, North Carolina	JR	F	5	47	9.4
5 **Joey Dorsey**, Memphis	SR	F	6	54	9.0
Aron Baynes, Washington State	JR	C	3	27	9.0
Goran Suton, Michigan State	JR	F	3	27	9.0

Minimum: 3 games

Blocked Shots Per Game

	CL	POS	G	BLK	BPG
1 **Kevin Love**, UCLA	FR	C	5	20	4.0
2 **Connor Atchley**, Texas	JR	F	4	11	2.8
3 **Jeremy Evans**, Western Kentucky	SO	F	3	8	2.7
Robin Lopez, Stanford	SO	C	3	8	2.7
5 **Joey Dorsey**, Memphis	SR	F	6	14	2.3

Minimum: 3 games

Steals Per Game

	CL	POS	G	STL	SPG
1 **Stephen Curry**, Davidson	SO	G	4	13	3.3
2 **Mario Chalmers**, Kansas	JR	G	6	17	2.8
3 **Courtney Lee**, Western Kentucky	SR	G	3	8	2.7
4 **Andre McGee**, Louisville	JR	G	4	10	2.5
5 **Dwayne Anderson**, Villanova	JR	G	3	7	2.3
Tyrone Brazelton, Western Kentucky	SR	G	3	7	2.3

Minimum: 3 games

Team Leaders

Scoring

	G	PTS	PPG
1 **North Carolina**	5	438	87.6
2 **Western Kentucky**	3	251	83.7
3 **Memphis**	6	487	81.2
4 **Louisville**	4	309	77.3
5 **Kansas**	6	450	75.0
6 **Texas**	4	298	74.5
7 **West Virginia**	3	223	74.3
8 **Stanford**	3	221	73.7
9 **Xavier**	4	294	73.5
10 **Villanova**	3	216	72.0

Minimum: 3 games

FG Pct

	G	FG	FGA	PCT
1 **Louisville**	4	116	211	55.0
2 **Kansas**	6	172	327	52.6
3 **North Carolina**	5	167	319	52.3
4 **Michigan State**	3	80	165	48.5
5 **Memphis**	6	165	354	46.6

Minimum: 3 games

3-Pt FG Pct

	G	3FG	3FGA	PCT
1 **Stanford**	3	21	49	42.9
2 **Western Kentucky**	3	29	68	42.6
3 **Louisville**	4	31	74	41.9
4 **Texas**	4	39	98	39.8
5 **West Virginia**	3	16	41	39.0

Minimum: 3 games

FT Pct

	G	FT	FTA	PCT
1 **Michigan State**	3	36	44	81.8
2 **North Carolina**	5	76	97	78.3
3 **West Virginia**	3	45	58	77.6
4 **Villanova**	3	54	71	76.1
5 **UCLA**	5	65	88	73.9

Minimum: 3 games

Ast/TO Ratio

	G	AST	TO	RAT
1 **Davidson**	4	63	32	1.97
2 **Memphis**	6	92	54	1.70
3 **Texas**	4	63	38	1.66
4 **Washington State**	3	43	26	1.65
5 **Stanford**	3	56	37	1.51

Minimum: 3 games

Rebounds

	G	REB	RPG
1 **UCLA**	5	195	39.0
2 **Stanford**	3	115	38.3
3 **Texas**	4	147	36.8
4 **North Carolina**	5	181	36.2
5 **Memphis**	6	214	35.7

Minimum: 3 games

Blocks

	G	BLK	BPG
1 **UCLA**	5	42	8.4
2 **Memphis**	6	37	6.2
3 **Texas**	4	22	5.5
4 **Louisville**	4	21	5.3
5 **Stanford**	3	15	5.0

Minimum: 3 games

Steals

	G	STL	SPG
1 **Western Kentucky**	3	29	9.7
2 **Tennessee**	3	28	9.3
3 **Kansas**	6	51	8.5
4 **Villanova**	3	24	8.0
5 **Davidson**	4	31	7.8

Minimum: 3 games

All-Tournament Team

PLAYER	CL	POS	HT	SCHOOL	RPG	APG	PPG
Mario Chalmers*	JR	G	6-1	Kansas	3.2	3.0	14.8
Darrell Arthur	SO	F	6-9	Kansas	6.5	1.0	11.0
Chris Douglas-Roberts	JR	G	6-7	Memphis	4.2	2.3	23.3
Derrick Rose	FR	G	6-3	Memphis	6.5	6.0	20.8
Brandon Rush	JR	G	6-6	Kansas	6.0	2.0	15.8

All-Regional Teams

East

PLAYER	CL	POS	HT	SCHOOL	RPG	APG	PPG
Tyler Hansbrough*	JR	F	6-9	North Carolina	9.5	1.3	21.0
Earl Clark	SO	G/F	6-8	Louisville	8.3	1.0	14.5
Wayne Ellington	SO	G	6-4	North Carolina	5.5	1.0	15.5
Ty Lawson	SO	G	5-11	North Carolina	3.0	5.0	15.8
Jerry Smith	SO	G	6-1	Louisville	2.3	1.5	13.5

Midwest

PLAYER	CL	POS	HT	SCHOOL	RPG	APG	PPG
Stephen Curry*	SO	G	6-3	Davidson	3.3	3.5	32.0
Mario Chalmers	JR	G	6-1	Kansas	3.0	3.0	15.0
Sasha Kaun	SR	C	6-11	Kansas	5.5	0.0	7.3
Jason Richards	SR	G	6-2	Davidson	2.0	9.0	13.3
Brandon Rush	JR	G	6-6	Kansas	5.8	2.0	14.5

South

PLAYER	CL	POS	HT	SCHOOL	RPG	APG	PPG
Derrick Rose*	FR	G	6-3	Memphis	6.0	6.0	20.5
D.J. Augustin	SO	G	6-0	Texas	3.3	6.5	14.3
Joey Dorsey	SR	F	6-9	Memphis	9.3	0.5	8.3
Chris Douglas-Roberts	JR	G	6-7	Memphis	5.0	3.3	22.5
Brook Lopez	SO	F	7-0	Stanford	5.3	1.3	20.0

West

PLAYER	CL	POS	HT	SCHOOL	RPG	APG	PPG
Kevin Love*	FR	C	6-10	UCLA	11.0	2.5	21.8
Tyrone Brazelton	SR	G	6-0	Western Kentucky	3.7	5.0	26.3
Darren Collison	JR	G	6-1	UCLA	1.8	2.5	12.3
Josh Duncan	SR	F	6-9	Xavier	5.3	0.8	18.3
Russell Westbrook	SO	G	6-3	UCLA	5.5	4.5	11.3

* Most outstanding player

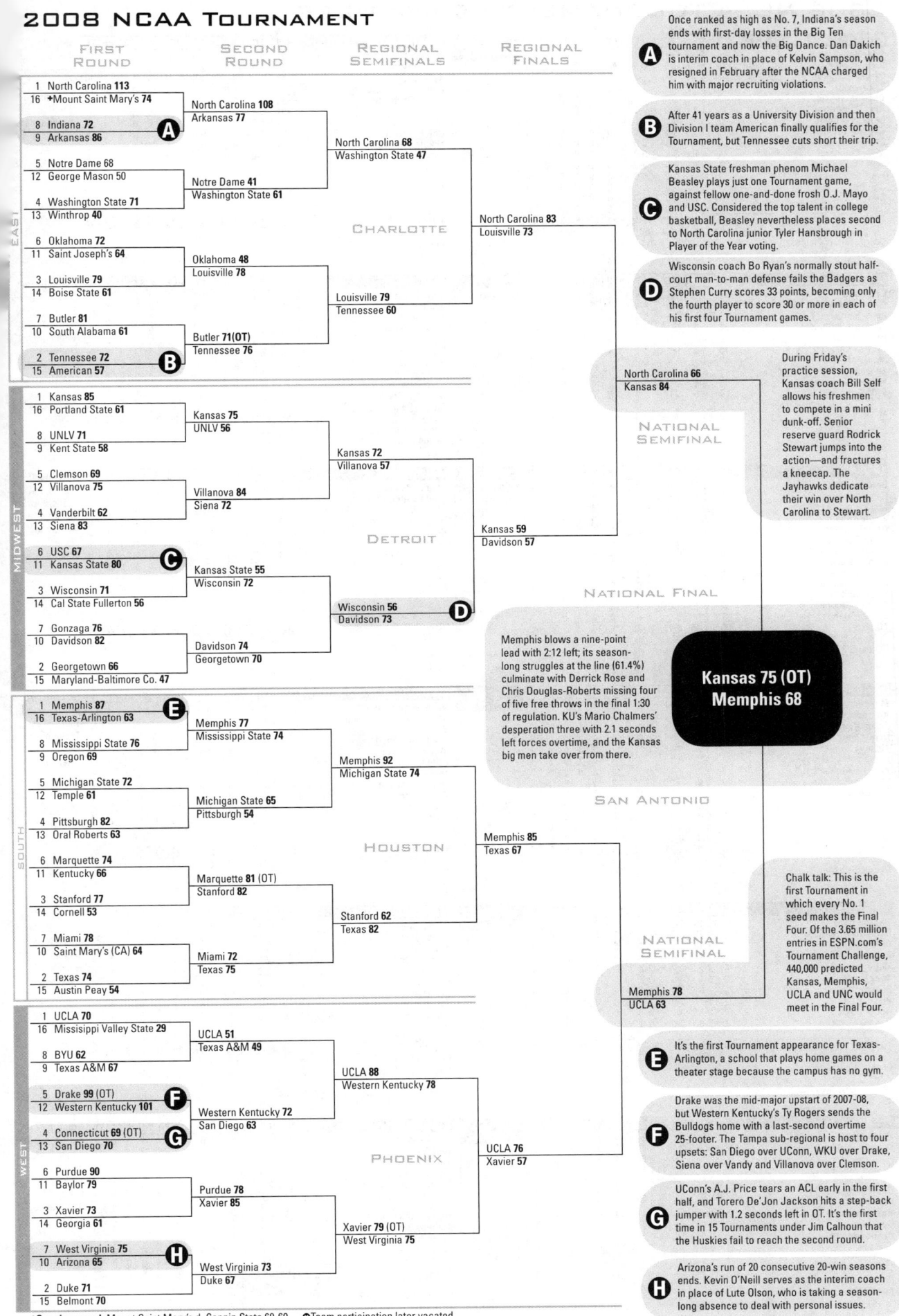

2008 NCAA Tournament

East — Charlotte

First Round
- 1 North Carolina **113** — 16 +Mount Saint Mary's 74
- 8 Indiana 72 — 9 Arkansas **86** (A)
- 5 Notre Dame 68 — 12 George Mason 50
- 4 Washington State **71** — 13 Winthrop **40**
- 6 Oklahoma **72** — 11 Saint Joseph's **64**
- 3 Louisville **79** — 14 Boise State **61**
- 7 Butler **81** — 10 South Alabama **61**
- 2 Tennessee **72** — 15 American **57** (B)

Second Round
- North Carolina **108** — Arkansas **77**
- Notre Dame **41** — Washington State **61**
- Oklahoma **48** — Louisville **78**
- Butler **71(OT)** — Tennessee **76**

Regional Semifinals
- North Carolina **68** — Washington State **47**
- Louisville **79** — Tennessee **60**

Regional Finals
- North Carolina **83** — Louisville **73**

Midwest — Detroit

First Round
- 1 Kansas **85** — 16 Portland State **61**
- 8 UNLV **71** — 9 Kent State **58**
- 5 Clemson **69** — 12 Villanova **75**
- 4 Vanderbilt **62** — 13 Siena **83**
- 6 USC **67** — 11 Kansas State **80** (C)
- 3 Wisconsin **71** — 14 Cal State Fullerton **56**
- 7 Gonzaga **76** — 10 Davidson **82**
- 2 Georgetown **66** — 15 Maryland-Baltimore Co. **47**

Second Round
- Kansas **75** — UNLV **56**
- Villanova **84** — Siena **72**
- Kansas State **55** — Wisconsin **72**
- Davidson **74** — Georgetown **70**

Regional Semifinals
- Kansas **72** — Villanova **57**
- Wisconsin **56** — Davidson **73** (D)

Regional Finals
- Kansas **59** — Davidson **57**

South — Houston

First Round
- 1 Memphis **87** — 16 Texas-Arlington **63** (E)
- 8 Mississippi State **76** — 9 Oregon **69**
- 5 Michigan State **72** — 12 Temple **61**
- 4 Pittsburgh **82** — 13 Oral Roberts **63**
- 6 Marquette **74** — 11 Kentucky **66**
- 3 Stanford **77** — 14 Cornell **53**
- 7 Miami **78** — 10 Saint Mary's (CA) **64**
- 2 Texas **74** — 15 Austin Peay **54**

Second Round
- Memphis **77** — Mississippi State **74**
- Michigan State **65** — Pittsburgh **54**
- Marquette **81** (OT) — Stanford **82**
- Miami **72** — Texas **75**

Regional Semifinals
- Memphis **92** — Michigan State **74**
- Stanford **62** — Texas **82**

Regional Finals
- Memphis **85** — Texas **67**

West — Phoenix

First Round
- 1 UCLA **70** — 16 Mississippi Valley State **29**
- 8 BYU **62** — 9 Texas A&M **67**
- 5 Drake **99** (OT) — 12 Western Kentucky **101** (F)
- 4 Connecticut **69** (OT) — 13 San Diego **70** (G)
- 6 Purdue **90** — 11 Baylor **79**
- 3 Xavier **73** — 14 Georgia **61**
- 7 West Virginia **75** — 10 Arizona **65** (H)
- 2 Duke **71** — 15 Belmont **70**

Second Round
- UCLA **51** — Texas A&M **49**
- Western Kentucky **72** — San Diego **63**
- Purdue **78** — Xavier **85**
- West Virginia **73** — Duke **67**

Regional Semifinals
- UCLA **88** — Western Kentucky **78**
- Xavier **79** (OT) — West Virginia **75**

Regional Finals
- UCLA **76** — Xavier **57**

San Antonio

National Semifinal
- North Carolina **66** — Kansas **84**

During Friday's practice session, Kansas coach Bill Self allows his freshmen to compete in a mini dunk-off. Senior reserve guard Rodrick Stewart jumps into the action—and fractures a kneecap. The Jayhawks dedicate their win over North Carolina to Stewart.

National Final

Kansas 75 (OT)
Memphis 68

Memphis blows a nine-point lead with 2:12 left; its season-long struggles at the line (61.4%) culminate with Derrick Rose and Chris Douglas-Roberts missing four of five free throws in the final 1:30 of regulation. KU's Mario Chalmers' desperation three with 2.1 seconds left forces overtime, and the Kansas big men take over from there.

National Semifinal
- Memphis **78** — UCLA **63**

Chalk talk: This is the first Tournament in which every No. 1 seed makes the Final Four. Of the 3.65 million entries in ESPN.com's Tournament Challenge, 440,000 predicted Kansas, Memphis, UCLA and UNC would meet in the Final Four.

+Opening round: Mount Saint Mary's d. Coppin State 69-60 ✪Team participation later vacated

---

A Once ranked as high as No. 7, Indiana's season ends with first-day losses in the Big Ten tournament and now the Big Dance. Dan Dakich is interim coach in place of Kelvin Sampson, who resigned in February after the NCAA charged him with major recruiting violations.

B After 41 years as a University Division and then Division I team American finally qualifies for the Tournament, but Tennessee cuts short their trip.

C Kansas State freshman phenom Michael Beasley plays just one Tournament game, against fellow one-and-done frosh O.J. Mayo and USC. Considered the top talent in college basketball, Beasley nevertheless places second to North Carolina junior Tyler Hansbrough in Player of the Year voting.

D Wisconsin coach Bo Ryan's normally stout half-court man-to-man defense fails the Badgers as Stephen Curry scores 33 points, becoming only the fourth player to score 30 or more in each of his first four Tournament games.

E It's the first Tournament appearance for Texas-Arlington, a school that plays home games on a theater stage because the campus has no gym.

F Drake was the mid-major upstart of 2007-08, but Western Kentucky's Ty Rogers sends the Bulldogs home with a last-second overtime 25-footer. The Tampa sub-regional is host to four upsets: San Diego over UConn, WKU over Drake, Siena over Vandy and Villanova over Clemson.

G UConn's A.J. Price tears an ACL early in the first half, and Torero De'Jon Jackson hits a step-back jumper with 1.2 seconds left in OT. It's the first time in 15 Tournaments under Jim Calhoun that the Huskies fail to reach the second round.

H Arizona's run of 20 consecutive 20-win seasons ends. Kevin O'Neill serves as the interim coach in place of Lute Olson, who is taking a season-long absence to deal with personal issues.

2008 NCAA TOURNAMENT BOX SCORES

North Carolina 68, Washington State 47 (Sweet 16)

NORTH CAROLINA	MIN	FG	3FG	FT	REB	A	ST	BL	PF	TP
Tyler Hansbrough	36	6-15	0-1	6-10	9	1	1	1	3	18
Danny Green	23	6-10	3-5	0-0	5	1	3	1	1	15
Wayne Ellington	31	4-13	1-4	4-4	8	0	1	0	3	13
Ty Lawson	26	5-11	1-3	1-2	5	0	0	0	1	12
Deon Thompson	19	3-5	0-0	0-0	8	1	0	0	4	6
Alex Stepheson	18	1-1	0-0	2-3	5	0	0	3	1	4
Marcus Ginyard	27	0-1	0-0	0-0	2	4	0	0	2	0
Quentin Thomas	13	0-1	0-1	0-0	0	4	0	0	1	0
Marc Campbell	1	0-1	0-1	0-0	0	0	0	0	0	0
Mike Copeland	1	0-0	0-0	0-0	0	0	0	0	0	0
Will Graves	1	0-0	0-0	0-0	0	0	0	0	0	0
Patrick Moody	1	0-0	0-0	0-0	0	0	0	0	0	0
J.B. Tanner	1	0-0	0-0	0-0	0	0	0	0	0	0
Surry Wood	1	0-0	0-0	0-0	0	0	0	0	0	0
Jack Wooten	1	0-0	0-0	0-0	0	0	0	0	0	0
TOTALS	**200**	**25-58**	**5-15**	**13-19**	**42**	**11**	**5**	**5**	**16**	**68**
Percentages		43.1	33.3	68.4						

Coach: Roy Williams

68-47

	1H	
35	1H	21
33	2H	26

SWEET 16

WASHINGTON STATE	MIN	FG	3FG	FT	REB	A	ST	BL	PF	TP
Derrick Low	37	6-16	2-9	0-0	0	1	0	0	2	14
Aron Baynes	27	6-8	0-0	2-4	8	0	2	0	5	14
Kyle Weaver	37	3-13	0-3	4-8	7	5	1	3	2	10
Daven Harmeling	12	0-2	0-2	3-3	3	0	0	0	0	3
Taylor Rochestie	38	1-8	0-1	0-0	1	2	2	0	2	2
Robbie Cowgill	31	1-7	0-0	0-0	8	0	1	0	5	2
Chris Henry	1	1-2	0-0	0-0	0	0	0	0	0	2
Caleb Forrest	12	0-1	0-1	0-0	0	0	0	2	1	0
Nikola Koprivica	4	0-0	0-0	0-0	1	1	0	0	1	0
Jeremy Cross	1	0-0	0-0	0-0	0	0	0	0	0	0
TOTALS	**200**	**18-57**	**2-16**	**9-15**	**28**	**9**	**6**	**5**	**18**	**47**
Percentages		31.6	12.5	60.0						

Coach: Tony Bennett

Officials: Jo[illegible] Hughes, Ray Perone, Tim Higgins **Technicals:** None **Attendance:** 19,092

Louisville 79, Tennessee 60 (Sweet 16)

LOUISVILLE	MIN	FG	3FG	FT	REB	A	ST	BL	PF	TP
Earl Clark	28	7-10	0-1	3-4	12	2	2	4	2	17
Andre McGee	32	4-10	1-5	4-4	3	3	1	0	2	13
Jerry Smith	24	3-6	2-3	5-6	4	0	1	1	3	13
Terrence Williams	38	4-7	0-1	4-7	8	3	1	2	0	12
David Padgett	25	4-5	0-0	2-4	8	3	0	0	4	10
Derrick Caracter	15	3-6	0-0	3-3	5	0	0	0	1	9
Juan Palacios	13	1-1	1-1	0-0	2	1	0	0	1	3
Edgar Sosa	7	0-1	0-0	2-2	0	0	1	0	5	2
Preston Knowles	16	0-4	0-3	0-0	0	2	0	0	4	0
Will Scott	2	0-0	0-0	0-0	0	0	0	0	1	0
TOTALS	**200**	**26-50**	**4-14**	**23-30**	**42**	**14**	**6**	**7**	**23**	**79**
Percentages		52.0	28.6	76.7						

Coach: Rick Pitino

79-60

37	1H	30
42	2H	30

SWEET 16

TENNESSEE	MIN	FG	3FG	FT	REB	A	ST	BL	PF	TP
Chris Lofton	34	3-15	2-11	7-7	3	2	2	0	1	15
JaJuan Smith	28	5-11	2-5	0-0	6	2	4	0	5	12
Tyler Smith	27	3-9	0-1	5-8	4	1	1	0	4	11
Wayne Chism	24	3-4	1-1	2-2	4	0	0	1	4	9
Ramar Smith	28	2-9	0-0	2-7	0	3	2	0	4	6
Duke Crews	16	2-4	0-0	1-1	1	2	0	0	3	5
J.P. Prince	27	1-3	0-1	0-0	1	2	2	0	4	2
Brian Williams	7	0-0	0-0	0-0	2	0	0	0	0	0
Josh Tabb	4	0-0	0-0	0-0	1	0	0	0	0	0
Ryan Childress	3	0-1	0-1	0-0	0	0	0	0	1	0
Steven Pearl	2	0-0	0-0	0-0	2	0	0	0	0	0
TOTALS	**200**	**19-56**	**5-20**	**17-25**	**24**	**12**	**11**	**1**	**26**	**60**
Percentages		33.9	25.0	68.0						

Coach: Bruce Pearl

Officials: Dick Cartmell, Gerry Pollard, Verne Harris **Technicals:** None **Attendance:** 19,092

Kansas 72, Villanova 57 (Sweet 16)

KANSAS	MIN	FG	3FG	FT	REB	A	ST	BL	PF	TP
Brandon Rush	28	6-12	2-6	2-2	4	1	1	1	3	16
Russell Robinson	33	4-7	3-5	4-4	3	5	1	0	2	15
Mario Chalmers	28	3-7	2-5	6-6	3	4	3	0	4	14
Sasha Kaun	29	3-4	0-0	3-5	7	0	0	3	1	9
Darrell Arthur	24	3-4	0-0	1-2	3	0	0	1	3	7
Darnell Jackson	24	2-5	0-0	0-0	6	1	1	0	1	4
Sherron Collins	20	2-5	0-2	0-1	2	4	2	0	3	4
Jeremy Case	8	1-1	1-1	0-0	1	0	0	0	1	3
Cole Aldrich	2	0-0	0-0	0-0	1	1	0	0	0	0
Matt Kleinmann	1	0-0	0-0	0-0	0	0	0	0	0	0
Tyrel Reed	1	0-0	0-0	0-0	0	0	0	0	0	0
Rodrick Stewart	1	0-0	0-0	0-0	0	0	0	0	0	0
Conner Teahan	1	0-0	0-0	0-0	0	0	0	0	0	0
TOTALS	**200**	**24-45**	**8-19**	**16-20**	**30**	**16**	**8**	**5**	**18**	**72**
Percentages		53.3	42.1	80.0						

Coach: Bill Self

72-57

41	1H	22
31	2H	35

SWEET 16

VILLANOVA	MIN	FG	3FG	FT	REB	A	ST	BL	PF	TP
Scottie Reynolds	37	4-13	2-4	1-1	2	0	2	0	2	11
Dante Cunningham	35	3-8	0-0	4-6	7	0	1	0	3	10
Shane Clark	25	5-10	0-1	0-0	7	0	0	0	2	10
Dwayne Anderson	30	4-9	0-3	0-1	3	0	4	2	3	8
Corey Stokes	22	2-5	1-4	1-2	0	0	0	0	1	6
Corey Fisher	19	2-8	0-4	2-2	0	4	1	0	3	6
Reggie Redding	18	1-2	0-1	2-4	3	1	2	0	0	4
Antonio Pena	12	0-4	0-0	2-2	2	0	0	0	3	2
Jason Colenda	1	0-0	0-0	0-0	0	0	0	0	0	0
Frank Tchuisi	1	0-0	0-0	0-0	0	0	0	0	0	0
TOTALS	**200**	**21-59**	**3-17**	**12-18**	**24**	**5**	**10**	**2**	**17**	**57**
Percentages		35.6	17.6	66.7						

Coach: Jay Wright

Officials: Doug Shows, Pat Evans, Ted Valentine **Technicals:** None **Attendance:** 57,028

Davidson 73, Wisconsin 56 (Sweet 16)

DAVIDSON	MIN	FG	3FG	FT	REB	A	ST	BL	PF	TP
Stephen Curry	37	11-22	6-11	5-5	3	4	4	0	4	33
Andrew Lovedale	23	5-5	0-0	2-3	4	0	0	0	3	12
Jason Richards	39	4-13	3-8	0-0	3	13	1	0	2	11
Bryant Barr	10	2-5	2-3	0-0	2	0	0	0	1	6
Thomas Sander	25	2-2	0-0	0-1	2	0	0	0	3	4
Max Paulhus Gosselin	24	1-3	0-1	2-2	6	1	2	0	3	4
William Archambault	7	1-2	1-1	0-1	0	0	0	0	0	3
Stephen Rossiter	20	0-0	0-0	0-0	2	0	1	0	2	0
Boris Meno	11	0-1	0-0	0-0	3	0	1	0	1	0
Can Civi	1	0-0	0-0	0-0	0	0	0	0	0	0
Brendan McKillop	1	0-0	0-0	0-0	0	0	0	0	0	0
Dan Nelms	1	0-0	0-0	0-0	0	0	0	0	0	0
Mike Schmitt	1	0-0	0-0	0-0	0	0	0	0	0	0
TOTALS	**200**	**26-53**	**12-24**	**9-12**	**25**	**18**	**9**	**0**	**19**	**73**
Percentages		49.1	50.0	75.0						

Coach: Bob McKillop

73-56

36	1H	36
37	2H	20

SWEET 16

WISCONSIN	MIN	FG	3FG	FT	REB	A	ST	BL	PF	TP
Michael Flowers	40	4-14	3-9	1-1	6	2	1	0	2	12
Jason Bohannon	34	3-8	2-4	3-4	2	3	1	1	2	11
Brian Butch	29	4-9	2-6	1-4	2	1	0	0	1	11
Joe Krabbenhoft	35	4-5	1-1	1-2	3	2	0	0	2	10
Marcus Landry	31	1-4	0-1	5-6	6	1	0	0	3	7
Greg Stiemsma	16	1-3	0-0	3-4	5	0	0	2	3	5
Trevon Hughes	11	0-3	0-2	0-0	2	0	0	0	0	0
Tanner Bronson	1	0-0	0-0	0-0	0	0	0	0	0	0
Tim Jarmusz	1	0-0	0-0	0-0	0	0	0	0	0	0
Jon Leuer	1	0-0	0-0	0-0	0	0	0	0	0	0
Keaton Nankivil	1	0-0	0-0	0-0	0	0	0	0	0	0
TOTALS	**200**	**17-46**	**8-23**	**14-21**	**26**	**9**	**2**	**3**	**13**	**56**
Percentages		37.0	34.8	66.7						

Coach: Bo Ryan

Officials: David Hall, Paul Faia, Tom Eades **Technicals:** None **Attendance:** 57,028

Memphis 92, Michigan State 74 (Sweet 16)

MEMPHIS	MIN	FG	3FG	FT	REB	A	ST	BL	PF	TP
Derrick Rose	26	10-16	1-3	6-7	4	5	0	0	1	27
Chris Douglas-Roberts	31	7-12	0-2	11-12	5	2	2	1	2	25
Antonio Anderson	37	3-10	1-4	3-3	5	4	2	1	2	10
Robert Dozier	21	3-7	0-0	3-6	10	0	0	2	4	9
Willie Kemp	16	2-2	2-2	2-2	0	1	0	0	0	8
Joey Dorsey	29	3-4	0-0	0-2	4	1	3	2	2	6
Shawn Taggart	22	2-6	0-1	1-2	4	0	1	1	3	5
Pierre Niles	2	1-1	0-0	0-0	0	0	0	0	0	2
Andre Allen	14	0-1	0-1	0-1	0	0	1	0	2	0
Doneal Mack	2	0-0	0-0	0-0	0	0	0	0	0	0
TOTALS	**200**	**31-59**	**4-13**	**26-35**	**32**	**13**	**9**	**7**	**16**	**92**
Percentages		52.5	30.8	74.3						

Coach: John Calipari

92-74

50	1H	20
42	2H	54

SWEET 16

MICHIGAN STATE	MIN	FG	3FG	FT	REB	A	ST	BL	PF	TP
Goran Suton	29	11-14	1-1	0-0	9	0	0	1	3	23
Chris Allen	22	8-15	2-8	2-3	4	0	0	0	5	20
Kalin Lucas	23	3-7	0-1	5-6	1	4	1	0	5	11
Raymar Morgan	31	2-6	0-0	3-6	7	2	1	1	3	7
Drew Neitzel	29	2-8	2-7	0-0	1	7	0	0	3	6
Drew Naymick	23	2-5	0-1	0-0	1	1	0	1	1	4
Durrell Summers	14	1-3	0-0	1-2	0	1	0	0	1	3
Travis Walton	20	0-1	0-0	0-0	0	3	0	0	4	0
Idong Ibok	6	0-0	0-0	0-0	2	0	0	0	3	0
Isaiah Dahlman	2	0-0	0-0	0-0	0	0	0	0	0	0
Marquise Gray	1	0-0	0-0	0-0	0	0	0	0	0	0
TOTALS	**200**	**29-59**	**5-18**	**11-17**	**25**	**18**	**2**	**3**	**28**	**74**
Percentages		49.2	27.8	64.7						

Coach: Tom Izzo

Officials: Bert Smith, Karl Hess, Tom O'Neill **Technicals:** None **Attendance:** 32,931

Texas 82, Stanford 62 (Sweet 16)

TEXAS	MIN	FG	3FG	FT	REB	A	ST	BL	PF	TP
D.J. Augustin	37	10-18	2-4	1-2	5	7	2	0	0	23
Damion James	27	6-13	1-4	5-7	4	1	2	0	3	18
A.J. Abrams	36	5-14	2-8	0-0	4	1	1	0	1	12
Connor Atchley	28	4-5	1-2	1-1	4	1	0	2	3	10
Justin Mason	36	2-8	1-4	2-3	8	6	1	1	3	7
Dexter Pittman	10	2-4	0-0	0-2	6	0	0	2	1	4
Clint Chapman	7	2-2	0-0	0-0	2	0	1	0	0	4
Harrison Smith	1	1-1	0-0	1-1	0	0	0	0	0	3
Gary Johnson	10	0-0	0-0	1-2	2	0	0	0	2	1
Alexis Wangmene	6	0-0	0-0	0-0	1	0	0	0	1	0
J.D. Lewis	1	0-0	0-0	0-0	1	0	0	0	0	0
Ian Mooney	1	0-0	0-0	0-0	0	0	0	0	0	0
TOTALS	**200**	**32-65**	**7-22**	**11-18**	**37**	**16**	**7**	**5**	**14**	**82**
Percentages		49.2	31.8	61.1						

Coach: Rick Barnes

82-62

43	1H	34
39	2H	28

SWEET 16

STANFORD	MIN	FG	3FG	FT	REB	A	ST	BL	PF	TP
Brook Lopez	33	10-22	0-0	6-6	10	0	1	2	0	26
Landry Fields	14	3-6	2-4	3-4	2	0	0	1	1	11
Mitch Johnson	38	2-10	2-7	0-2	5	8	1	0	1	6
Robin Lopez	21	3-9	0-0	0-0	5	0	1	0	4	6
Lawrence Hill	15	2-5	1-2	0-0	1	0	0	1	2	5
Taj Finger	22	1-2	0-0	2-2	7	0	1	0	1	4
Kenny Brown	9	1-1	1-1	0-0	0	2	0	0	2	3
Fred Washington	22	0-2	0-0	1-4	7	1	0	0	2	1
Anthony Goods	22	0-7	0-3	0-0	2	1	1	0	0	0
Peter Prowitt	2	0-1	0-0	0-0	1	0	0	0	1	0
Josh Owens	1	0-0	0-0	0-0	0	0	0	0	0	0
Drew Shiller	1	0-0	0-0	0-0	0	1	0	0	0	0
TOTALS	**200**	**22-65**	**6-17**	**12-18**	**40**	**13**	**5**	**4**	**14**	**62**
Percentages		33.8	35.3	66.7						

Coach: Trent Johnson

Officials: J.D. Collins, John Cahill, Leslie Jones **Technicals:** None **Attendance:** 32,931

88-78 (Sweet 16)

	1H	2H
UCLA	41	47
Western Kentucky	20	58

UCLA	MIN	FG	3FG	FT	REB	A	ST	BL	PF	TP
Kevin Love	38	10-14	0-2	9-12	14	4	0	4	2	29
James Keefe	26	7-9	0-0	4-5	12	2	0	4	3	18
Josh Shipp	33	5-9	2-3	2-4	3	1	0	0	4	14
Russell Westbrook	32	3-15	1-2	7-8	11	5	1	0	4	14
Luc Richard Mbah a Moute	36	2-4	0-0	3-4	7	4	1	0	1	7
Darren Collison	28	1-6	1-2	1-2	2	1	3	0	5	4
Alfred Aboya	5	1-1	0-0	0-0	0	0	1	0	3	2
Lorenzo Mata-Real	2	0-0	0-0	0-0	0	0	0	0	0	0
TOTALS	**200**	**29-58**	**4-9**	**26-35**	**49**	**17**	**6**	**8**	**22**	**88**
Percentages		50.0	44.4	74.3						

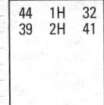

Coach: Ben Howland

WESTERN KENTUCKY	MIN	FG	3FG	FT	REB	A	ST	BL	PF	TP
Tyrone Brazelton	34	10-21	6-10	5-7	3	5	2	0	4	31
Courtney Lee	37	7-29	2-8	2-3	8	1	4	3	2	18
Boris Siakam	28	1-4	0-0	5-6	7	0	1	0	5	7
A.J. Slaughter	18	1-4	1-3	4-6	1	3	2	0	1	7
Ty Rogers	28	2-6	0-2	1-1	3	1	1	0	4	5
Jeremy Evans	17	2-3	0-0	0-1	6	1	0	1	4	4
D.J. Magley	15	1-2	0-0	0-0	3	0	1	0	2	2
Orlando Mendez-Valdez	14	0-1	0-1	2-2	2	1	0	0	2	2
Desire Gabou	1	1-1	0-0	0-0	0	0	0	0	0	2
Steffphon Pettigrew	5	0-1	0-0	0-0	0	0	0	0	0	0
B.J. Frazier	1	0-0	0-0	0-0	0	0	0	0	0	0
Adam Howard	1	0-0	0-0	0-0	0	0	0	0	0	0
Matt Maresca	1	0-0	0-0	0-0	0	0	0	0	0	0
TOTALS	**200**	**25-72**	**9-24**	**19-26**	**33**	**12**	**11**	**4**	**24**	**78**
Percentages		34.7	37.5	73.1						

Coach: Darrin Horn

Officials: Curtis Shaw, J.B. Caldwell, Zelton Steed
Technicals: None
Attendance: 18,103

79-75 (Sweet 16)

	1H	2H	OT1
Xavier	32	32	15
West Virginia	25	39	11

XAVIER	MIN	FG	3FG	FT	REB	A	ST	BL	PF	TP
Josh Duncan	31	7-15	3-4	9-10	5	1	0	1	4	26
C.J. Anderson	34	6-12	0-0	0-2	10	0	1	1	5	12
Drew Lavender	38	3-11	3-6	0-0	3	7	1	0	0	9
Derrick Brown	30	3-4	1-2	2-4	3	2	0	1	5	9
Stanley Burrell	35	3-7	1-2	1-2	5	5	0	0	4	8
B.J. Raymond	18	3-5	2-4	0-2	2	0	0	1	1	8
Jason Love	21	2-4	0-0	0-1	10	0	0	1	4	4
Dante' Jackson	18	1-1	1-1	0-0	1	1	1	0	2	3
TOTALS	**225**	**28-59**	**11-19**	**12-21**	**39**	**16**	**3**	**5**	**25**	**79**
Percentages		47.5	57.9	57.1						

Coach: Sean Miller

WEST VIRGINIA	MIN	FG	3FG	FT	REB	A	ST	BL	PF	TP
Joe Alexander	31	8-18	0-1	2-4	10	3	0	1	5	18
Da'Sean Butler	36	7-15	1-4	1-1	7	1	2	0	4	16
Alex Ruoff	38	6-11	0-2	2-3	5	1	1	0	2	14
Joe Mazzulla	31	2-7	0-1	6-9	5	5	0	0	1	10
Wellington Smith	29	3-8	0-0	2-4	3	1	1	5	5	8
Darris Nichols	41	1-6	0-3	4-4	4	4	1	0	4	6
Jamie Smalligan	9	1-1	0-0	0-0	1	0	0	0	0	2
Cam Thoroughman	4	0-0	0-0	1-2	0	0	0	0	0	1
Ted Talkington	6	0-0	0-0	0-0	0	0	0	0	0	0
TOTALS	**225**	**28-66**	**1-11**	**18-27**	**34**	**16**	**5**	**6**	**21**	**75**
Percentages		42.4	9.1	66.7						

Coach: Bob Huggins

Officials: Kelly Self, Mark Whitehead, Rick Hartzell
Technicals: None
Attendance: 18,103

83-73 (Elite 8)

	1H	2H
North Carolina	44	39
Louisville	32	41

NORTH CAROLINA	MIN	FG	3FG	FT	REB	A	ST	BL	PF	TP
Tyler Hansbrough	38	12-17	0-0	4-5	13	1	2	0	3	28
Wayne Ellington	36	5-14	1-4	2-2	5	0	1	0	1	13
Ty Lawson	31	2-5	1-3	6-6	2	9	1	0	0	11
Danny Green	23	2-6	1-4	6-6	2	1	2	0	4	11
Deon Thompson	18	5-9	0-0	0-0	2	1	1	0	4	10
Marcus Ginyard	35	3-5	0-0	0-2	7	2	2	0	3	6
Alex Stepheson	9	2-2	0-0	0-0	0	0	0	0	1	4
Quentin Thomas	10	0-0	0-0	0-0	0	2	0	0	1	0
TOTALS	**200**	**31-58**	**3-11**	**18-21**	**31**	**16**	**9**	**0**	**17**	**83**
Percentages		53.4	27.3	85.7						

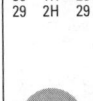

Coach: Roy Williams

LOUISVILLE	MIN	FG	3FG	FT	REB	A	ST	BL	PF	TP
Jerry Smith	32	7-12	3-7	0-1	1	1	1	0	2	17
Terrence Williams	35	6-12	1-3	1-1	4	3	1	1	3	14
Earl Clark	29	5-7	0-0	2-4	9	1	0	1	1	12
Edgar Sosa	15	5-7	1-3	1-1	0	2	0	0	5	12
David Padgett	34	1-5	0-0	4-4	8	6	2	2	3	6
Preston Knowles	13	3-4	0-1	0-1	0	0	0	1	2	6
Andre McGee	25	1-3	1-3	1-2	1	1	3	0	1	4
Derrick Caracter	5	1-3	0-0	0-2	3	0	0	0	2	2
Juan Palacios	11	0-2	0-2	0-0	0	1	0	0	0	0
Terrance Farley	1	0-0	0-0	0-0	0	0	0	0	0	0
TOTALS	**200**	**29-55**	**6-19**	**9-16**	**26**	**15**	**7**	**5**	**19**	**73**
Percentages		52.7	31.6	56.2						

Coach: Rick Pitino

Officials: Ed Corbett, Scott Thornley, Terry Wymer
Technicals: None
Attendance: 19,092

59-57 (Elite 8)

	1H	2H
Kansas	30	29
Davidson	28	29

KANSAS	MIN	FG	3FG	FT	REB	A	ST	BL	PF	TP
Mario Chalmers	33	5-10	3-4	0-0	3	2	2	1	2	13
Sasha Kaun	20	6-6	0-0	1-3	6	0	0	1	3	13
Brandon Rush	36	4-14	1-5	3-3	7	2	0	1	2	12
Darnell Jackson	23	4-6	0-0	1-4	7	3	1	1	1	9
Darrell Arthur	31	3-5	0-0	1-2	5	1	1	1	3	7
Sherron Collins	28	1-8	1-3	2-2	3	3	0	0	2	5
Russell Robinson	22	0-3	0-2	0-0	1	1	1	0	2	0
Cole Aldrich	5	0-0	0-0	0-0	1	0	0	0	1	0
Jeremy Case	2	0-0	0-0	0-0	0	0	0	0	0	0
TOTALS	**200**	**23-52**	**5-14**	**8-14**	**33**	**12**	**5**	**5**	**16**	**59**
Percentages		44.2	35.7	57.1						

Coach: Bill Self

DAVIDSON	MIN	FG	3FG	FT	REB	A	ST	BL	PF	TP
Stephen Curry	40	9-25	4-16	3-3	4	3	1	0	1	25
Bryant Barr	14	4-6	3-4	0-0	1	0	0	0	1	11
Thomas Sander	26	3-6	1-1	1-4	4	2	1	0	2	8
Jason Richards	34	3-9	0-4	1-2	1	9	2	0	1	7
Andrew Lovedale	32	3-8	0-0	0-1	5	1	1	2	5	6
Max Paulhus Gosselin	24	0-1	0-1	0-0	5	2	2	0	2	0
Boris Meno	12	0-0	0-0	0-0	1	0	0	0	1	0
Stephen Rossiter	11	0-0	0-0	0-2	3	0	0	0	2	0
William Archambault	7	0-2	0-1	0-0	0	0	0	0	0	0
TOTALS	**200**	**22-57**	**8-27**	**5-12**	**24**	**17**	**7**	**2**	**15**	**57**
Percentages		38.6	29.6	41.7						

Coach: Bob McKillop

Officials: Doug Sirmons, Randy Mccall, Tony Greene
Technicals: None
Attendance: 57,563

85-67 (Elite 8)

	1H	2H
Memphis	39	46
Texas	28	39

MEMPHIS	MIN	FG	3FG	FT	REB	A	ST	BL	PF	TP
Chris Douglas-Roberts	34	5-12	1-3	14-17	3	3	1	1	0	25
Derrick Rose	34	7-10	0-1	7-8	6	9	1	1	3	21
Shawn Taggart	18	5-7	0-0	2-2	3	0	0	1	1	12
Joey Dorsey	36	5-7	0-0	1-1	12	0	1	1	0	11
Antonio Anderson	38	3-5	2-3	1-2	2	4	1	0	1	9
Andre Allen	12	0-1	0-0	3-4	1	2	0	0	0	3
Robert Dozier	18	1-6	0-0	0-0	7	0	0	1	5	2
Willie Kemp	7	0-2	0-2	2-2	0	0	0	0	1	2
Doneal Mack	2	0-2	0-2	0-0	0	0	0	0	1	0
Pierre Niles	1	0-0	0-0	0-0	0	0	0	0	1	0
TOTALS	**200**	**26-52**	**3-11**	**30-36**	**34**	**18**	**4**	**5**	**13**	**85**
Percentages		50.0	27.3	83.3						

Coach: John Calipari

TEXAS	MIN	FG	3FG	FT	REB	A	ST	BL	PF	TP
A.J. Abrams	38	6-16	5-10	0-0	5	3	2	0	4	17
D.J. Augustin	39	4-18	2-6	6-6	2	3	1	0	3	16
Damion James	24	4-12	0-5	0-0	5	3	0	0	5	8
Gary Johnson	16	3-4	0-0	2-2	1	0	0	0	2	8
Justin Mason	35	3-8	1-2	0-0	7	3	1	0	5	7
Connor Atchley	23	2-8	1-5	0-0	6	1	1	3	4	5
Dexter Pittman	15	2-2	0-0	0-1	4	0	0	0	0	4
J.D. Lewis	3	1-1	0-0	0-0	0	0	0	0	0	2
Clint Chapman	3	0-0	0-0	0-0	0	0	0	1	0	0
Alexis Wangmene	3	0-0	0-0	0-0	1	0	0	0	0	0
Ian Mooney	1	0-0	0-0	0-0	0	0	0	0	2	0
TOTALS	**200**	**25-69**	**9-28**	**8-9**	**31**	**13**	**5**	**4**	**25**	**67**
Percentages		36.2	32.1	88.9						

Coach: Rick Barnes

Officials: Bob Donato, Mike Kitts, Pat Driscoll
Technicals: None
Attendance: 32,798

76-57 (Elite 8)

	1H	2H
UCLA	33	43
Xavier	24	33

UCLA	MIN	FG	3FG	FT	REB	A	ST	BL	PF	TP
Darren Collison	37	7-12	3-3	2-2	2	5	0	0	1	19
Kevin Love	33	7-11	2-4	3-4	10	4	0	2	3	19
Russell Westbrook	36	7-11	1-3	2-3	3	3	3	0	3	17
Luc Richard Mbah a Moute	35	5-9	0-0	3-6	13	3	3	1	3	13
Josh Shipp	35	1-7	0-4	3-3	2	1	0	2	3	5
Chace Stanback	1	1-1	1-1	0-0	0	0	0	0	0	3
James Keefe	13	0-0	0-0	0-0	1	0	0	0	2	0
Lorenzo Mata-Real	6	0-1	0-0	0-0	1	0	0	1	2	0
Alfred Aboya	2	0-0	0-0	0-0	1	1	0	0	2	0
Mustafa Abdul-Hamid	1	0-0	0-0	0-0	0	0	0	0	0	0
Nikola Dragovic	1	0-0	0-0	0-0	1	0	0	0	0	0
TOTALS	**200**	**28-52**	**7-15**	**13-18**	**34**	**17**	**6**	**6**	**19**	**76**
Percentages		53.8	46.7	72.2						

Coach: Ben Howland

XAVIER	MIN	FG	3FG	FT	REB	A	ST	BL	PF	TP
Derrick Brown	30	6-8	0-1	1-3	6	2	1	1	1	13
Josh Duncan	28	4-11	1-6	2-3	3	1	1	0	3	11
C.J. Anderson	27	4-10	0-0	2-2	2	0	1	0	1	10
Stanley Burrell	34	2-6	1-2	3-4	4	3	0	0	1	8
Drew Lavender	31	2-9	1-3	0-0	6	6	1	0	4	5
Jason Love	18	1-4	0-0	3-4	2	0	1	0	2	5
B.J. Raymond	20	1-4	1-3	0-0	3	0	1	0	1	3
Dante' Jackson	10	1-5	0-3	0-0	0	0	0	0	2	2
Charles Bronson	1	0-0	0-0	0-0	0	0	0	0	0	0
Adrion Graves	1	0-1	0-1	0-0	0	0	0	0	0	0
TOTALS	**200**	**21-58**	**4-19**	**11-16**	**26**	**12**	**6**	**1**	**15**	**57**
Percentages		36.2	21.1	68.8						

Coach: Sean Miller

Officials: Ed Hightower, Gary Maxwell, Jamie Luckie
Technicals: None
Attendance: 18,103

84-66

44	1H	27
40	2H	39

FINAL 4

KANSAS	MIN	FG	3FG	FT	REB	A	ST	BL	PF	TP
Brandon Rush	32	11-17	2-7	1-2	7	2	0	1	2	25
Darnell Jackson	17	5-6	0-0	2-2	4	2	2	0	3	12
Mario Chalmers	31	5-10	1-3	0-2	4	3	3	0	3	11
Sherron Collins	29	4-9	1-1	2-2	4	4	1	0	4	11
Cole Aldrich	16	2-4	0-0	4-4	7	0	1	4	1	8
Russell Robinson	30	2-5	1-4	2-2	4	4	3	0	2	7
Darrell Arthur	32	3-9	0-0	0-0	9	2	0	4	2	6
Sasha Kaun	9	2-4	0-0	0-0	0	0	0	0	3	4
Jeremy Case	1	0-0	0-0	0-0	0	0	0	0	1	0
Matt Kleinmann	1	0-0	0-0	0-0	0	0	0	0	0	0
Tyrel Reed	1	0-0	0-0	0-0	0	0	0	0	0	0
Conner Teahan	1	0-0	0-0	0-0	0	0	0	0	0	0
TOTALS	**200**	**34-64**	**5-15**	**11-14**	**39**	**17**	**10**	**9**	**21**	**84**
Percentages		53.1	33.3	78.6						

Coach: Bill Self

NORTH CAROLINA	MIN	FG	3FG	FT	REB	A	ST	BL	PF	TP
Wayne Ellington	33	8-21	1-9	1-1	6	0	3	1	3	18
Tyler Hansbrough	36	6-13	0-1	5-6	9	1	2	0	3	17
Danny Green	20	6-13	3-9	0-0	5	0	1	1	3	15
Ty Lawson	28	2-8	1-2	4-4	3	2	0	0	1	9
Deon Thompson	25	2-4	0-0	3-4	4	0	0	0	2	7
Marcus Ginyard	32	0-3	0-2	0-0	3	2	0	0	1	0
Quentin Thomas	13	0-2	0-0	0-0	1	2	1	0	1	0
Alex Stepheson	6	0-1	0-0	0-0	0	0	0	1	0	0
Will Graves	2	0-2	0-1	0-0	1	0	0	0	0	0
Marc Campbell	1	0-0	0-0	0-0	0	0	0	0	0	0
Mike Copeland	1	0-0	0-0	0-0	0	0	0	0	0	0
J.B. Tanner	1	0-0	0-0	0-0	0	0	0	0	0	0
Surry Wood	1	0-0	0-0	0-0	0	0	0	0	0	0
Jack Wooten	1	0-0	0-0	0-0	0	0	0	0	0	0
TOTALS	**200**	**24-67**	**5-24**	**13-15**	**32**	**7**	**7**	**3**	**14**	**66**
Percentages		35.8	20.8	86.7						

Coach: Roy Williams

Officials: T
Eades, Tony
Greene, Ve
Harris
Technicals:
None
Attendance:
43,718

78-63

38	1H	35
40	2H	28

FINAL 4

MEMPHIS	MIN	FG	3FG	FT	REB	A	ST	BL	PF	TP
Chris Douglas-Roberts	35	9-17	1-3	9-11	4	0	2	1	2	28
Derrick Rose	37	7-16	0-0	11-12	9	4	1	0	4	25
Antonio Anderson	38	5-11	2-5	0-0	3	3	0	0	0	12
Shawn Taggart	22	3-7	1-2	0-0	7	1	0	0	3	7
Robert Dozier	30	3-7	0-0	0-0	3	0	3	3	2	6
Joey Dorsey	27	0-3	0-0	0-0	15	2	1	2	3	0
Doneal Mack	6	0-2	0-1	0-0	1	0	0	0	0	0
Willie Kemp	4	0-1	0-1	0-0	0	0	0	0	0	0
Pierre Niles	1	0-0	0-0	0-0	0	0	0	0	0	0
TOTALS	**200**	**27-64**	**4-12**	**20-23**	**42**	**10**	**7**	**6**	**14**	**78**
Percentages		42.2	33.3	87.0						

Coach: John Calipari

UCLA	MIN	FG	3FG	FT	REB	A	ST	BL	PF	TP
Russell Westbrook	36	10-19	2-3	0-0	3	2	2	0	4	22
Kevin Love	36	4-11	0-2	4-4	9	1	2	3	1	12
Luc Richard Mbah a Moute	34	5-13	0-0	2-2	13	0	0	1	0	12
Josh Shipp	37	3-9	2-6	1-3	2	0	0	0	3	9
James Keefe	11	0-1	0-1	4-4	2	0	0	0	1	4
Darren Collison	33	1-9	0-1	0-0	4	4	2	0	5	2
Alfred Aboya	6	1-2	0-0	0-0	0	1	0	0	1	2
Lorenzo Mata-Real	7	0-0	0-0	0-0	2	0	0	0	2	0
TOTALS	**200**	**24-64**	**4-13**	**11-13**	**35**	**8**	**6**	**4**	**17**	**63**
Percentages		37.5	30.8	84.6						

Coach: Ben Howland

Officials: Curt
Shaw, J.D.
Collins, Karl
Hess
Technicals:
None
Attendance:
43,718

75-68

33	1H	28
30	2H	35
12	OT1	5

NCAA FINAL 2008

KANSAS	MIN	FG	3FG	FT	REB	A	ST	BL	PF	TP
Darrell Arthur	35	9-13	0-0	2-2	10	1	1	0	3	20
Mario Chalmers	40	5-13	2-6	6-6	3	3	4	0	3	18
Brandon Rush	42	5-9	0-2	2-3	6	2	1	1	3	12
Sherron Collins	34	4-10	1-4	2-2	4	6	3	0	3	11
Darnell Jackson	29	3-4	0-0	2-2	8	1	1	0	1	8
Sasha Kaun	21	2-5	0-0	0-0	2	0	0	0	2	4
Russell Robinson	20	1-1	0-0	0-0	4	1	1	0	3	2
Cole Aldrich	4	0-0	0-0	0-0	0	0	0	0	0	0
TOTALS	**225**	**29-55**	**3-12**	**14-15**	**37**	**14**	**11**	**1**	**18**	**75**
Percentages		52.7	25.0	93.3						

Coach: Bill Self

MEMPHIS	MIN	FG	3FG	FT	REB	A	ST	BL	PF	TP
Chris Douglas-Roberts	42	7-16	2-5	6-9	1	1	1	0	4	22
Derrick Rose	45	7-17	1-6	3-4	6	8	2	0	1	18
Robert Dozier	39	4-11	1-2	2-3	10	3	1	1	2	11
Antonio Anderson	42	3-9	2-7	1-3	5	1	4	0	3	9
Joey Dorsey	26	3-3	0-0	0-0	2	1	1	2	5	6
Shawn Taggart	24	1-5	0-1	0-0	3	0	1	0	2	2
Willie Kemp	4	0-0	0-0	0-0	0	0	1	0	0	0
Doneal Mack	2	0-1	0-1	0-0	0	0	0	0	0	0
Pierre Niles	1	0-0	0-0	0-0	0	0	0	0	0	0
TOTALS	**225**	**25-62**	**6-22**	**12-19**	**27**	**14**	**11**	**3**	**17**	**68**
Percentages		40.3	27.3	63.2						

Coach: John Calipari

Officials: Ed
Corbett, Ed
Hightower, John
Cahill
Technicals:
None
Attendance:
43,257

National Invitation Tournament (NIT)

First Round: Massachusetts d. Stephen F. Austin 80-60, Ohio State d. UNC Asheville 84-66, Syracuse d. Robert Morris 87-81, Akron d. Florida State 65-60 (OT), Southern Illinois d. Oklahoma State 69-53, Maryland d. Minnesota 68-58, Creighton d. Rhode Island 74-73, Arizona State d. Alabama State 64-53, Dayton d. Cleveland State 66-57, Virginia Tech d. Morgan State 94-62, UAB d. VCU 80-77, Mississippi d. UC Santa Barbara 83-68, Nebraska d. Charlotte 67-48, Florida d. San Diego St. 73-49, Illinois State d. Utah State 61-57, California d. New Mexico 68-66

Second Round: Syracuse d. Maryland 88-72, Arizona State d. Southern Illinois 65-51, Florida d. Creighton 82-54, Massachusetts d. Akron 68-63, Ohio State d. California 73-56, Dayton d. Illinois State 55-48, Virginia Tech d. UAB 75-49, Mississippi d. Nebraska 85-75

Quarterfinals Massachusetts d. Syracuse 81-77, Florida d. Arizona State 70-57, Mississippi d. Virginia Tech 81-72, Ohio State d. Dayton 74-63

Semifinals: Massachusetts d. Florida 78-66, Ohio State d. Mississippi 81-69

Championship: Ohio State d. Massachusetts 92-85

MVP: Kosta Koufos, Ohio State

2008-09: Carolina Finer

In one 11-week stretch of the season, the No. 1 ranking changed eight times—thrice among ACC foes North Carolina, Duke and Wake Forest. The Big East put three No. 1 seeds in the Tournament, but Carolina blitzed the field, taking all six of its games by double digits, including a 72-60 win over Oklahoma and national POY Blake Griffin. The Final was an 89-72 thrashing of Michigan State—in what was practically a home game for MSU at Detroit's Ford Field. The new all-time ACC scoring leader Tyler Hansbrough (18 points), Tourney MOP Wayne Ellington (19) and Ty Lawson (21) brought coach Roy Williams his second championship in five years.

Major Conference Standings

AMERICA EAST	Conference			Overall		
	W	L	Pct	W	L	Pct
Vermont	13	3	.813	24	9	.727
Binghamton⊛	13	3	.813	23	9	.719
Boston U.	11	5	.688	17	13	.567
Stony Brook	8	8	.500	16	14	.533
New Hampshire	8	8	.500	14	16	.467
UMBC	7	9	.438	15	17	.469
Albany (NY)	6	10	.375	15	16	.484
Maine	4	12	.250	9	21	.300
Hartford	2	14	.125	7	26	.212

Tournament: **Binghamton d. UMBC 61-51**
Tournament MOP: **D.J. Rivera**, Binghamton

ACC	Conference			Overall		
	W	L	Pct	W	L	Pct
North Carolina○	13	3	.813	34	4	.895
Duke⊛	11	5	.688	30	7	.811
Wake Forest○	11	5	.688	24	7	.774
Florida State○	10	6	.625	25	10	.714
Clemson○	9	7	.563	23	9	.719
Boston College○	9	7	.563	22	12	.647
Maryland○	7	9	.438	21	14	.600
Miami (FL)□	7	9	.438	19	13	.594
Virginia Tech□	7	9	.438	19	15	.559
NC State	6	10	.375	16	14	.533
Virginia	4	12	.250	10	18	.357
Georgia Tech	2	14	.125	12	19	.387

Tournament: **Duke d. Florida State 79-69**
Tournament MVP: **Jon Scheyer**, Duke

ATLANTIC SUN	Conference			Overall		
	W	L	Pct	W	L	Pct
Jacksonville□	15	5	.750	18	14	.563
East Tenn. State⊛	14	6	.700	23	11	.676
Belmont	14	6	.700	20	13	.613
Lipscomb	12	8	.600	17	14	.548
Mercer	11	9	.550	17	15	.531
Campbell	11	9	.550	14	16	.467
Stetson	9	11	.450	13	17	.434
SC Upstate	8	12	.400	9	21	.300
Florida Gulf Coast	7	13	.350	11	20	.355
North Florida	6	14	.300	8	22	.267
Kennesaw State	3	17	.150	7	22	.241

Tournament: **East Tenn. State d. Jacksonville 85-68**
Tournament MVP: **Kevin Tiggs**, East Tenn. St.

ATLANTIC 10	Conference			Overall		
	W	L	Pct	W	L	Pct
Xavier○	12	4	.750	27	8	.771
Dayton○	11	5	.688	27	8	.771
Rhode Island	11	5	.688	23	11	.676
Temple⊛	11	5	.688	22	12	.647
Duquesne□	9	7	.563	21	13	.618
La Salle	9	7	.563	18	13	.581
Richmond	9	7	.563	20	16	.556
Saint Joseph's	9	7	.563	17	15	.531
Saint Louis	8	8	.500	18	14	.563
Massachusetts	7	9	.438	12	18	.400
St. Bonaventure	6	10	.375	15	15	.500
Charlotte	5	11	.313	11	20	.355
George Washington	4	12	.250	10	18	.357
Fordham	1	15	.063	3	25	.107

Tournament: **Temple d. Duquesne 69-64**
Tournament MOP: **Dionte Christmas**, Temple

BIG EAST	Conference			Overall		
	W	L	Pct	W	L	Pct
Louisville⊛	16	2	.889	31	6	.838
Connecticut○	15	3	.883	31	5	.861
Pittsburgh○	15	3	.883	31	5	.861
Villanova○	13	5	.722	30	8	.789
Marquette○	12	6	.667	25	10	.714
Syracuse○	11	7	.611	28	10	.737
West Virginia○	10	8	.556	23	12	.657
Providence□	10	8	.556	19	14	.576
Notre Dame□	8	10	.444	21	15	.583
Cincinnati	8	10	.444	18	14	.563
Seton Hall	7	11	.389	17	15	.531
Georgetown□	7	11	.389	16	15	.516
St. John's	6	12	.333	16	18	.471
South Florida	4	14	.222	9	22	.290
Rutgers	2	16	.111	11	21	.344
DePaul	0	18	.000	9	24	.273

Tournament: **Louisville d. Syracuse 76-66**
Tournament MVP: **Jonny Flynn**, Syracuse

BIG SKY	Conference			Overall		
	W	L	Pct	W	L	Pct
Weber State□	15	1	.938	21	10	.677
Portland State⊛	11	5	.688	23	10	.697
Montana	11	5	.688	17	12	.586
Idaho State	9	7	.563	13	19	.406
Northern Colorado	8	8	.500	14	18	.438
Montana State	6	10	.375	14	17	.452
Eastern Washington	6	10	.375	12	18	.400
Northern Arizona	5	11	.313	8	19	.296
Sacramento State	1	15	.063	2	27	.069

Tournament: **Portland State d. Montana State 79-77**
Tournament MVP: **Jeremiah Dominguez**, Portland State

BIG SOUTH	Conference			Overall		
	W	L	Pct	W	L	Pct
Radford⊛	15	3	.833	21	12	.636
VMI	13	5	.722	24	8	.750
Liberty	12	6	.667	23	12	.657
UNC Asheville	10	8	.556	15	16	.484
Gardner-Webb	9	9	.500	13	17	.433
Winthrop	9	9	.500	11	19	.367
Coastal Carolina	5	13	.278	11	20	.355
Charleston Southern	4	14	.222	9	20	.310
High Point	4	14	.222	9	21	.300

Tournament: **Radford d. VMI 108-94**
Tournament MVP: **Artsiom Parakhouski**, Radford

BIG TEN	Conference			Overall		
	W	L	Pct	W	L	Pct
Michigan State○	15	3	.833	31	7	.816
Purdue⊛	11	7	.611	27	10	.730
Illinois○	11	7	.611	24	10	.706
Penn State□	10	8	.556	27	11	.711
Ohio State○	10	8	.556	22	11	.667
Wisconsin○	10	8	.556	20	13	.606
Minnesota○	9	9	.500	22	11	.667
Michigan○	9	9	.500	21	14	.600
Northwestern□	8	10	.444	17	14	.548
Iowa	5	13	.278	15	17	.469
Indiana	1	17	.056	6	25	.194

Tournament: **Purdue d. Ohio State 65-61**
Tournament MOP: **Robbie Hummel**, Purdue

BIG 12	Conference			Overall		
	W	L	Pct	W	L	Pct
Kansas○	14	2	.875	27	8	.771
Oklahoma○	13	3	.813	30	6	.833
Missouri⊛	12	4	.750	31	7	.816
Texas A&M○	9	7	.563	24	10	.704
Oklahoma State○	9	7	.563	23	12	.657
Texas○	9	7	.563	23	12	.657
Kansas State□	9	7	.563	22	12	.647
Nebraska□	8	8	.500	18	13	.581
Baylor□	5	11	.313	24	15	.615
Iowa State	4	12	.250	15	17	.469
Texas Tech	3	13	.188	14	19	.424
Colorado	1	15	.063	9	22	.290

Tournament: **Missouri d. Baylor 73-60**
Tournament MOP: **DeMarre Carroll**, Missouri

BIG WEST	Conference			Overall		
	W	L	Pct	W	L	Pct
Cal State Northridge⊛	11	5	.688	17	14	.548
Pacific	10	6	.625	21	13	.636
Long Beach State	10	6	.625	15	15	.500
UC Riverside	8	8	.500	17	13	.567
UC Santa Barbara	8	8	.500	16	15	.516
UC Irvine	8	8	.500	12	19	.387
Cal State Fullerton	7	9	.438	15	17	.469
UC Davis	7	9	.438	13	19	.406
Cal Poly	3	13	.188	7	21	.250

Tournament: **Cal State Northridge d. Pacific 71-66 (OT)**
Tournament MVP: **Rodrigue Mels**, Cal State Northridge

COLONIAL ATHLETIC	Conference			Overall		
	W	L	Pct	W	L	Pct
VCU⊛	14	4	.778	24	10	.706
George Mason□	13	5	.722	22	11	.667
Old Dominion	12	6	.667	25	10	.714
Northeastern	12	6	.667	19	13	.594
Hofstra	11	7	.611	21	11	.656
Drexel	10	8	.556	15	14	.517
James Madison	9	9	.500	21	15	.583
Georgia State	8	10	.444	12	20	.375
Delaware	6	12	.333	13	19	.406
Towson	5	13	.278	12	22	.353
William and Mary	5	13	.278	10	20	.333
UNC Wilmington	3	15	.167	7	25	.219

Tournament: **VCU d. George Mason 71-50**
Tournament MOP: **Eric Maynor**, VCU

C-USA	Conference			Overall		
	W	L	Pct	W	L	Pct
Memphis⊛	16	0	1.000	33	4	.892
Tulsa□	12	4	.750	25	11	.694
UAB□	11	5	.688	22	12	.647
Houston	10	6	.625	21	12	.636
UTEP	10	6	.625	23	14	.622
Central Florida	7	9	.438	17	14	.548
Marshall	7	9	.438	15	17	.469
Tulane	7	9	.438	14	17	.452
East Carolina	5	11	.313	13	17	.433
Southern Miss	4	12	.250	15	17	.469
Rice	4	12	.250	10	22	.313
SMU	3	13	.188	9	21	.300

Tournament: **Memphis d. Tulsa 64-39**
Tournament MVP: **Tyreke Evans**, Memphis

HORIZON	Conference			Overall		
	W	L	Pct	W	L	Pct
Butler○	15	3	.833	26	6	.813
Wisconsin-Green Bay	13	5	.722	22	11	.667
Cleveland State⊛	12	6	.667	26	11	.703
Wright State	12	6	.667	20	13	.606
Wisconsin-Milwaukee	11	7	.611	17	14	.548
Illinois-Chicago	7	11	.389	16	15	.516
Youngstown State	7	11	.389	11	19	.367
Loyola-Chicago	6	12	.333	14	18	.438
Valparaiso	5	13	.278	9	22	.290
Detroit	2	16	.111	7	23	.233

Tournament: **Cleveland State d. Butler 57-54**
Tournament MVP: **Cedric Jackson**, Cleveland State

IVY	Conference			Overall		
	W	L	Pct	W	L	Pct
Cornell⊛	11	3	.786	21	10	.677
Princeton	8	6	.571	13	14	.481
Yale	8	6	.571	13	15	.464
Columbia	7	7	.500	12	16	.429
Dartmouth	7	7	.500	9	19	.321
Harvard	6	8	.429	14	14	.500
Penn	6	8	.429	10	18	.357
Brown	3	11	.214	9	19	.321

Conference Standings Continue →

ANNUAL REVIEW

⊛ Automatic NCAA Tournament bid ○ At-large NCAA Tournament bid □ NIT appearance ⊗ Team record doesn't reflect games forfeited or vacated. For adjusted record, see p. 521.

MAAC

	Conference			Overall		
	W	L	Pct	W	L	Pct
Siena⊕	16	2	.889	27	8	.771
Niagara□	14	4	.778	26	9	.743
Rider	12	6	.667	19	13	.594
Manhattan	9	9	.500	16	14	.533
Fairfield	9	9	.500	17	15	.531
Saint Peter's	8	10	.444	11	19	.367
Iona	7	11	.389	12	19	.387
Loyola (MD)	7	11	.389	12	20	.375
Canisius	4	14	.222	11	20	.355
Marist	4	14	.222	10	23	.303

Tournament: **Siena d. Niagara 77-70**
Tournament MVP: **Kenny Hasbrouck**, Siena

MID-AMERICAN

	Conference			Overall		
	W	L	Pct	W	L	Pct
East Division						
Buffalo	11	5	.688	21	12	.636
Bowling Green□	11	5	.688	19	14	.576
Akron⊕	10	6	.625	23	13	.657
Miami (OH)	10	6	.625	17	13	.567
Kent State	10	6	.625	19	15	.559
Ohio	7	9	.438	15	17	.469
West Division						
Ball State	7	9	.438	14	17	.452
Central Michigan	7	9	.438	12	19	.387
Western Michigan	7	9	.438	10	21	.323
Eastern Michigan	6	10	.375	8	24	.250
Northern Illinois	5	11	.313	10	20	.333
Toledo	5	11	.313	7	25	.219

Tournament: **Akron d. Buffalo 65-53**
Tournament MVP: **Nate Linhart**, Akron

MEAC

	Conference			Overall		
	W	L	Pct	W	L	Pct
Morgan State⊕	13	3	.813	23	12	.657
South Carolina State	10	6	.625	17	14	.548
Bethune-Cookman	9	7	.563	17	16	.515
NC A&T	9	7	.563	16	16	.500
Norfolk State	9	7	.563	13	18	.419
Coppin State	9	7	.563	13	19	.406
Hampton	8	8	.500	16	16	.500
Florida A&M	6	10	.375	10	21	.323
Howard	6	10	.375	8	23	.258
Delaware State	6	10	.375	8	24	.250
UMES	3	13	.188	7	23	.233

Tournament: **Morgan State d. Norfolk State 83-69**
Tournament MOP: **Reggie Holmes**, Morgan State

MISSOURI VALLEY

	Conference			Overall		
	W	L	Pct	W	L	Pct
Creighton□	14	4	.778	27	8	.771
Northern Iowa⊕	14	4	.778	23	11	.714
Illinois State□	11	7	.611	24	10	.706
Bradley	10	8	.556	21	15	.583
Evansville	8	10	.444	17	14	.548
Wichita State	8	10	.444	17	17	.500
Southern Illinois	8	10	.444	13	18	.419
Drake	7	11	.389	17	16	.484
Indiana State	7	11	.389	11	21	.344
Missouri State	3	15	.167	11	20	.355

Tournament: **Northern Iowa d. Illinois State 60-57 (OT)**
Tournament MVP: **Osiris Eldridge**, Illinois State

MOUNTAIN WEST

	Conference			Overall		
	W	L	Pct	W	L	Pct
BYU○	12	4	.750	25	8	.758
Utah⊕	12	4	.750	24	10	.706
New Mexico□	12	4	.750	22	12	.647
San Diego State□	11	5	.688	26	10	.722
UNLV□	9	7	.563	21	11	.656
Wyoming	7	9	.438	19	14	.576
TCU	5	11	.313	14	17	.452
Colorado State	4	12	.250	9	22	.290
Air Force	0	16	.000	10	21	.323

Tournament: **Utah d. San Diego State 52-50**
Tournament MVP: **Luke Nevill**, Utah

NORTHEAST

	Conference			Overall		
	W	L	Pct	W	L	Pct
Robert Morris⊕	15	3	.833	24	11	.686
Mount St. Mary's	12	6	.667	19	14	.576
Sacred Heart	12	6	.667	17	14	.548
Long Island	12	6	.667	16	14	.533
Quinnipiac	10	8	.556	15	16	.484
Wagner	8	10	.444	16	14	.533
Central Conn. State	8	10	.444	13	17	.433
St. Francis (NY)	7	11	.389	10	20	.333
Monmouth	6	12	.333	8	23	.258
Fairleigh Dickinson	6	12	.333	7	23	.233
Saint Francis (PA)	3	15	.167	6	23	.207

Tournament: **Robert Morris d. Mount St. Mary's 48-46**
Tournament MVP: **Jeremy Chappell**, Robert Morris

OHIO VALLEY

	Conference			Overall		
	W	L	Pct	W	L	Pct
Tennessee-Martin□	14	4	.778	22	10	.689
Murray State	13	5	.722	19	12	.613
Austin Peay	13	5	.722	19	14	.576
Morehead State⊕	12	6	.667	20	16	.555
Eastern Kentucky	10	8	.556	18	13	.581
Tennessee State	9	9	.500	12	18	.400
Eastern Illinois	8	10	.444	12	18	.400
Tennessee Tech	6	12	.333	12	18	.400
Jacksonville State	5	13	.278	11	17	.393
Southeast Mo. State	0	18	.000	3	27	.100

Tournament: **Morehead State d. Austin Peay 67-65 (2OT)**
Tournament MVP: **Kenneth Faried**, Morehead State

PAC-10

	Conference			Overall		
	W	L	Pct	W	L	Pct
Washington○	14	4	.778	26	9	.743
UCLA○	13	5	.722	26	9	.743
Arizona State○	11	7	.611	25	10	.714
California○	11	7	.611	22	11	.667
Southern California⊕	9	9	.500	22	13	.629
Arizona○	9	9	.500	21	14	.600
Washington State□	8	10	.444	17	16	.515
Oregon State	7	11	.389	18	18	.500
Stanford	6	12	.333	20	14	.588
Oregon	2	16	.111	8	23	.258

Tournament: **Southern California d. Arizona State 66-63**
Tournament MOP: **DeMar DeRozan**, Southern California

PATRIOT

	Conference			Overall		
	W	L	Pct	W	L	Pct
American⊕	13	1	.929	24	8	.750
Holy Cross	11	3	.786	18	14	.563
Navy	8	6	.571	19	11	.633
Army	6	8	.429	11	19	.367
Lehigh	5	9	.357	15	14	.517
Colgate	5	9	.357	10	20	.333
Lafayette	4	10	.286	8	22	.267
Bucknell	4	10	.286	7	23	.233

Tournament: **American d. Holy Cross 73-57**
Tournament MOP: **Garrison Carr**, American

SEC

	Conference			Overall		
	W	L	Pct	W	L	Pct
East Division						
South Carolina□	10	6	.625	21	10	.677
Tennessee○	10	6	.625	21	13	.618
Florida□	9	7	.563	25	11	.694
Vanderbilt	8	8	.500	19	12	.613
Kentucky□	8	8	.500	22	14	.611
Georgia	3	13	.188	12	20	.375
West Division						
LSU○	13	3	.813	27	8	.771
Auburn□	10	6	.625	24	12	.667
Mississippi State⊕	9	7	.563	23	13	.639
Alabama	7	9	.438	18	14	.563
Mississippi	7	9	.438	16	15	.516
Arkansas	2	14	.125	14	16	.467

Tournament: **Mississippi State d. Tennessee 64-61**
Tournament MVP: **Jarvis Varnado**, Mississippi

SOUTHERN

	Conference			Overall		
	W	L	Pct	W	L	Pct
North Division						
Western Carolina	11	9	.550	16	15	.516
Chattanooga⊕	11	9	.550	18	17	.514
Samford	9	11	.450	16	16	.500
Appalachian State	9	11	.450	13	18	.419
Elon	7	13	.350	11	20	.355
UNC Greensboro	4	16	.200	5	25	.167
West Division						
Davidson□	18	2	.900	27	8	.806
Charleston	15	5	.750	27	9	.750
The Citadel	15	5	.750	20	13	.606
Wofford	12	8	.600	16	14	.533
Georgia Southern	5	15	.250	8	22	.267
Furman	4	16	.200	6	24	.200

Tournament: **Chattanooga d. Charleston 80-69**
Tournament MOP: **Stephen McDowell**, Chattanooga

SOUTHLAND

	Conference			Overall		
	W	L	Pct	W	L	Pct
East Division						
Stephen F. Austin⊕	13	3	.813	24	8	.750
Nicholls State	12	4	.750	20	11	.645
Southeastern La.	7	9	.438	13	17	.433
McNeese State	5	11	.313	11	18	.379
Northwestern St. (LA)	3	13	.188	11	20	.355
Central Arkansas	3	13	.188	10	19	.345
West Division						
Sam Houston State	12	4	.750	18	12	.600
Corpus Christi	11	5	.688	18	15	.545
Texas-Arlington	9	7	.563	16	14	.533
UTSA	8	8	.500	19	13	.594
Texas State	7	9	.438	14	16	.467
Lamar	6	10	.375	15	15	.500

Tournament: **Stephen F. Austin d. UTSA 68-57**
Tournament MVP: **Matt Kingsley**, Stephen F. Austin

SWAC

	Conference			Overall		
	W	L	Pct	W	L	Pct
Alabama State⊕	16	2	.889	22	10	.688
Jackson State	15	3	.833	18	15	.545
Prairie View A&M	12	6	.667	17	16	.515
Arkansas-Pine Bluff	11	7	.611	13	18	.419
Southern U.	8	10	.444	8	23	.258
Miss. Valley State	7	11	.389	7	25	.219
Texas Southern	7	11	.389	7	25	.219
Alabama A&M	6	12	.333	8	19	.296
Grambling	4	14	.222	6	23	.207
Alcorn State	4	14	.222	6	25	.194

Tournament: **Alabama State d. Jackson State 65-58**
Tournament MOP: **Andrew Hayles**, Alabama State

SUMMIT

	Conference			Overall		
	W	L	Pct	W	L	Pct
North Dakota State⊕	16	2	.889	26	7	.788
Oral Roberts	14	4	.778	16	15	.516
Oakland	13	5	.722	23	13	.639
IUPUI	9	9	.500	16	14	.533
IPFW	8	10	.444	13	17	.433
Southern Utah	8	10	.444	11	20	.355
South Dakota State	7	11	.389	13	20	.394
Western Illinois	6	12	.333	9	20	.310
Centenary	6	12	.333	8	23	.258
UMKC	3	15	.167	7	24	.226

Tournament: **North Dakota St. d. Oakland 66-64**
Tournament MVP: **Ben Woodside**, North Dakota St.

SUN BELT

	Conference			Overall		
	W	L	Pct	W	L	Pct
Eastern Division						
Western Kentucky⊕	15	3	.833	25	9	.735
Troy	14	4	.778	19	13	.594
South Alabama	10	8	.556	20	13	.606
Middle Tenn. State	10	8	.556	18	14	.563
Florida International	7	11	.389	13	20	.394
Florida Atlantic	2	16	.111	6	26	.188
Western Division						
Arkansas-Little Rock	15	3	.833	23	8	.742
North Texas	11	7	.611	20	12	.625
Denver	9	9	.500	15	16	.484
UL-Lafayette	7	11	.389	10	20	.333
New Orleans	6	12	.333	11	19	.367
UL-Monroe	6	12	.333	10	20	.333
Arkansas State	5	13	.278	13	17	.433

Tournament: **Western Kentucky d. South Alabama 64-56**
Tournament MOP: **A.J. Slaughter**, Western Kentucky

WEST COAST

	Conference			Overall		
	W	L	Pct	W	L	Pct
Gonzaga⊕	14	0	1.000	28	6	.824
Saint Mary's (CA)□	10	4	.714	28	7	.800
Portland	9	5	.643	19	13	.594
Santa Clara	7	7	.500	16	17	.485
San Diego	6	8	.429	16	16	.500
Pepperdine	5	9	.357	9	23	.281
San Francisco	3	11	.214	11	19	.367
Loyola Marymount	2	12	.143	3	28	.097

Tournament: **Gonzaga d. Saint Mary's (CA)** 83-58
Tournament MVP: **Micah Downs**, Gonzaga

WAC

	Conference			Overall		
	W	L	Pct	W	L	Pct
Utah State⊕	14	2	.875	30	5	.857
Nevada	11	5	.688	21	13	.618
Boise State	9	7	.563	19	13	.594
New Mexico State	9	7	.563	17	15	.531
Idaho	9	7	.563	17	16	.515
Louisiana Tech	6	10	.375	15	18	.455
San Jose State	6	10	.375	13	17	.433
Hawaii	5	11	.313	13	17	.433
Fresno State	3	13	.188	13	21	.382

Tournament: **Utah State d. Nevada 72-62**
Tournament MVP: **Gary Wilkinson**, Utah State

INDEPENDENTS

	Overall		
	W	L	Pct
Chicago State	19	13	.594
Longwood	17	14	.548
Savannah State	15	14	.517
Texas-Pan American	10	17	.370
Cal State Bakersfield	8	21	.276

ALL OTHERS

(Reclassifying and provisional teams not eligible for the NCAA Tournament)

	Overall		
	W	L	Pct
Seattle	21	8	.724
South Dakota	20	9	.690
Utah Valley	17	11	.607
North Dakota	16	12	.571
Presbyterian	12	17	.414
Central Arkansas	10	19	.345
SIU Edwardsville	10	20	.333
Bryant	8	21	.276
Winston-Salem	8	22	.267
Houston Baptist	5	25	.167
NC Central	4	27	.129
NJIT	1	30	.032

INDIVIDUAL LEADERS—SEASON

SCORING	CL	POS	G	FG	3FG	FT	PTS	PPG
1 **Stephen Curry**, Davidson	JR	G	34	312	130	220	974	**28.6**
2 **Lester Hudson**, Tenn.-Martin	SR	G	32	313	106	148	880	**27.5**
3 **Jermaine Taylor**, Central Florida	SR	G	31	291	92	138	812	**26.2**
4 **David Holston**, Chicago State	SR	G	32	269	147	145	830	**25.9**
5 **Stefon Jackson**, UTEP	SR	G	37	282	32	312	908	**24.5**
6 **Josh Akognon**, Cal State Fullerton	SR	G	32	248	136	132	764	**23.9**
7 **Jodie Meeks**, Kentucky	JR	G	36	263	117	211	854	**23.7**
8 **Luke Harangody**, Notre Dame	JR	F	34	300	14	178	792	**23.3**
9 **Ben Woodside**, North Dakota State	SR	G	33	234	67	231	766	**23.2**
10 **Jeremy Hazell**, Seton Hall	SO	G	32	235	105	151	726	**22.7**
Blake Griffin, Oklahoma	SO	F	35	300	3	191	794	**22.7**

FIELD GOAL PCT	CL	POS	G	FG	FGA	PCT
1 **Jeff Pendergraph**, Arizona State	SR	F	35	198	300	**66.0**
2 **Blake Griffin**, Oklahoma	SO	F	35	300	459	**65.4**
3 **Joey Henley**, Sacred Heart	SR	F	31	196	313	**62.6**
4 **Keith Benson**, Oakland	SO	C	36	191	307	**62.2**
5 **Ahmad Nivins**, Saint Joseph's	SR	F	32	205	335	**61.2**

MINIMUM: 5 MADE PER GAME

THREE-PT FG PER GAME	CL	POS	G	3FG	3PG
1 **David Holston**, Chicago State	SR	G	32	147	**4.6**
2 **Josh Akognon**, Cal State Fullerton	SR	G	32	136	**4.3**
3 **Erik Kangas**, Oakland	SR	G	35	135	**3.9**
Stephen McDowell, Chattanooga	SR	G	35	135	**3.9**
5 **Stephen Curry**, Davidson	JR	G	34	130	**3.8**

THREE-PT FG PCT	CL	POS	G	3FG	3FGA	PCT
1 **Mike Rose**, Eastern Kentucky	SR	G	31	99	206	**48.1**
2 **Booker Woodfox**, Creighton	SR	G	34	91	191	**47.6**
3 **Jared Stohl**, Portland	SO	G	32	89	195	**45.6**
4 **Ryan Tillema**, Wisconsin-Green Bay	SR	G	26	74	163	**45.4**
5 **Jimmy Baron**, Rhode Island	SR	G	34	118	260	**45.4**

MINIMUM: 2.5 MADE PER GAME

FREE THROW PCT	CL	POS	G	FT	FTA	PCT
1 **Brett Harvey**, Loyola (MD)	JR	G	32	142	156	**91.0**
2 **Josh White**, North Texas	SO	G	32	96	106	**90.6**
3 **Jodie Meeks**, Kentucky	JR	G	36	211	234	**90.2**
4 **Darren Collison**, UCLA	SR	G	35	113	126	**89.7**
5 **Alan Voskuil**, Texas Tech	SR	G	33	86	96	**89.6**

MINIMUM: 2.5 MADE PER GAME

ASSISTS PER GAME	CL	POS	G	AST	APG
1 **Johnathon Jones**, Oakland	JR	G	36	290	**8.1**
2 **Brock Young**, East Carolina	SO	G	30	227	**7.6**
3 **Levance Fields**, Pittsburgh	SR	G	36	270	**7.5**
4 **DiJuan Harris**, Charlotte	JR	G	31	223	**7.2**
5 **Ashton Mitchell**, Sam Houston State	JR	G	30	205	**6.8**
6 **Jonny Flynn**, Syracuse	SO	G	38	254	**6.7**
7 **Brandon Brooks**, Alabama State	SR	G	32	212	**6.6**
8 **Ty Lawson**, North Carolina	JR	G	35	230	**6.6**
9 **Chris Lowe**, Massachusetts	SR	G	30	193	**6.4**
10 **John Roberson**, Texas Tech	SO	G	33	212	**6.4**

REBOUNDS PER GAME	CL	POS	G	REB	RPG
1 **Blake Griffin**, Oklahoma	SO	F	35	504	**14.4**
2 **John Bryant**, Santa Clara	SR	C	33	467	**14.2**
3 **Kenneth Faried**, Morehead State	SO	C	36	468	**13.0**
4 **DeJuan Blair**, Pittsburgh	SO	F	35	432	**12.3**
5 **Ahmad Nivins**, Saint Joseph's	SR	F	32	378	**11.8**
6 **Luke Harangody**, Notre Dame	JR	F	34	401	**11.8**
7 **Jon Brockman**, Washington	SR	F	34	391	**11.5**
8 **Joseph Harris**, Coastal Carolina	SR	F	31	352	**11.4**
9 **Artsiom Parakhouski**, Radford	JR	C	33	369	**11.2**
10 **Cole Aldrich**, Kansas	SO	C	35	387	**11.1**

BLOCKED SHOTS PER GAME	CL	POS	G	BLK	BPG
1 **Jarvis Varnado**, Mississippi State	JR	F	36	170	**4.7**
2 **Hasheem Thabeet**, Connecticut	JR	C	36	152	**4.2**
3 **Tony Gaffney**, Massachusetts	SR	F	30	115	**3.8**
4 **Kleon Penn**, McNeese State	SR	C	29	102	**3.5**
5 **Taj Gibson**, Southern California	JR	F	35	100	**2.9**

STEALS PER GAME	CL	POS	G	STL	SPG
1 **Chavis Holmes**, VMI	SR	G	31	105	**3.4**
2 **Travis Holmes**, VMI	SR	F	27	87	**3.2**
3 **Devin Gibson**, UTSA	SO	G	27	82	**3.0**
4 **David Holston**, Chicago State	SR	G	32	97	**3.0**
5 **Cedric Jackson**, Cleveland State	SR	G	37	112	**3.0**

INDIVIDUAL LEADERS—GAME

POINTS	CL	POS	OPP	DATE	PTS
1 **Ben Woodside**, North Dakota State	SR	G	Stephen F. Austin	D12	**60**
2 **Jodie Meeks**, Kentucky	JR	G	Tennessee	J13	**54**
3 **Aaron Jackson**, Duquesne	SR	G	Virginia Tech	F18	**46**
Jodie Meeks, Kentucky	JR	G	Appalachian State	D20	**46**
5 **Jermaine Taylor**, Central Florida	SR	G	Rice	F25	**45**
Jodie Meeks, Kentucky	JR	G	Arkansas	F14	**45**

THREE-PT FG MADE	CL	POS	OPP	DATE	3FG
1 **Joey Mundweiler**, Wagner	SR	G	Monmouth	F28	**11**
2 **Roburt Sallie**, Memphis	SO	G	Cal St. Northridge	M19	**10**
Courtney Pigram, East Tenn. St.	SR	G	Mercer	F28	**10**
Jodie Meeks, Kentucky	JR	G	Tennessee	J13	**10**
Kyle McAlarney, Notre Dame	SR	G	North Carolina	N26	**10**

ASSISTS	CL	POS	OPP	DATE	AST
1 **Michael Vogler**, Troy	JR	G	Northwestern State (LA)	N29	**17**
2 **Levance Fields**, Pittsburgh	SR	G	DePaul	F7	**16**
3 **Johnathon Jones**, Oakland	JR	G	IUPUI	F21	**15**
DiJuan Harris, Charlotte	JR	G	George Washington	F14	**15**
Johnathon Jones, Oakland	JR	G	IPFW	F14	**15**
Chad Tomko, UNC Wilmington	SO	G	Towson	J24	**15**
Ashton Mitchell, Sam Houston St.	JR	G	Wright State	N29	**15**

REBOUNDS	CL	POS	OPP	DATE	REB
1 **John Bryant**, Santa Clara	SR	C	San Diego	M7	**27**
2 **Chris Gadley**, Canisius	JR	C	Maine	D30	**25**
3 **Kenneth Faried**, Morehead State	SO	C	Florida A&M	N23	**24**
4 **DeJuan Blair**, Pittsburgh	SO	F	Connecticut	F16	**23**
Blake Griffin, Oklahoma	SO	F	Texas Tech	F14	**23**

BLOCKED SHOTS	CL	POS	OPP	DATE	BLK
1 **C. Kickingstallionsims**, Alabama State	SR	C	Ark.-Pine Bluff	F7	**11**
2 **Cole Aldrich**, Kansas	SO	C	Dayton	M22	**10**
Hasheem Thabeet, Connecticut	JR	C	Providence	J31	**10**
4 **Leon Spencer**, Drexel	JR	F	Loyola (MD)	F21	**9**
Hasheem Thabeet, Connecticut	JR	C	Seton Hall	F14	**9**
Jay Brown, Lamar	SR	F	A&M-Corpus Christi	J21	**9**
Calvin Henry, Mercer	SR	F	Fla. Gulf Coast	J16	**9**
Andrew Nicholson, St. Bonaventure	FR	F	Bucknell	D30	**9**
Alvin Mofunanya, Fairleigh Dickinson	JR	F	Saint Peter's	D23	**9**
Tony Gaffney, Massachusetts	SR	F	Boston College	D6	**9**
Jarvis Varnado, Mississippi State	JR	F	UL-Monroe	N17	**9**
Colton Iverson, Minnesota	FR	C	Bowling Green	N15	**9**

STEALS	CL	POS	OPP	DATE	STL
1 **Stephen Curry**, Davidson	JR	G	Guilford	N14	**9**
2 **Ty Lawson**, North Carolina	JR	G	Michigan State	A6	**8**
Keith Gabriel, VMI	FR	G	High Point	J24	**8**
Aaron Linn, Gardner-Webb	SR	G	Coastal Carolina	J17	**8**
Lester Hudson, Tenn.-Martin	SR	G	Tennessee State	J10	**8**
Dominique Sutton, Kansas State	SO	F	Idaho State	J3	**8**
Chris Singletary, Kent State	JR	G	UNC Greensboro	D18	**8**
Kevin Thomas, Murray State	SR	G	Missouri	D13	**8**
Chavis Holmes, VMI	SR	G	Maryland Bible	N18	**8**
Lester Hudson, Tenn.-Martin	SR	G	Maryville (MO)	N14	**8**
Max Paulhus Gosselin, Davidson	SR	G	Guilford	N14	**8**
Chad Tomko, UNC Wilmington	SO	G	Appalachian State	N14	**8**

TEAM LEADERS—SEASON

WIN-LOSS PCT	W	L	PCT
1 **North Carolina**	34	4	**89.5**
2 **Memphis**	33	4	**89.2**
3 **Pittsburgh**	31	5	**86.1**
Connecticut	31	5	**86.1**
5 **Utah State**	30	5	**85.7**

SCORING OFFENSE	G	W-L	PTS	PPG
1 **VMI**	32	24-8	3,002	**93.8**
2 **North Carolina**	38	34-4	3,413	**89.8**
3 **Chicago State**	32	19-13	2,693	**84.2**
4 **Texas State**	30	14-16	2,445	**81.5**
5 **Missouri**	38	31-7	3,096	**81.5**

SCORING MARGIN	G	W-L	PPG	OPP PPG	MAR
1 **North Carolina**	38	34-4	89.8	72.0	**17.8**
2 **Memphis**	37	33-4	75.1	58.8	**16.3**
3 **Gonzaga**	34	28-6	78.9	63.0	**15.9**
4 **Connecticut**	36	31-5	78.3	64.3	**14.1**
5 **Missouri**	38	31-7	81.5	67.7	**13.8**

FIELD GOAL PCT	G	W-L	FG	FGA	PCT
1 **Utah State**	35	30-5	899	1813	**49.6**
2 **Oklahoma**	36	30-6	982	1997	**49.2**
3 **UCLA**	35	26-9	967	1973	**49.0**
4 **Wake Forest**	31	24-7	906	1849	**49.0**
5 **Gonzaga**	34	28-6	967	1982	**48.8**

THREE-PT FG PER GAME	G	W-L	3FG	3PG
1 **VMI**	32	24-8	438	**13.7**
2 **Eastern Kentucky**	31	18-13	320	**10.3**
3 **Belmont**	33	20-13	336	**10.2**
4 **Portland State**	33	23-10	317	**9.6**
5 **Oklahoma State**	35	23-12	327	**9.3**

ASSISTS PER GAME	G	W-L	AST	APG
1 **Missouri**	38	31-7	699	**18.4**
2 **Sam Houston St.**	30	18-12	546	**18.2**
3 **VMI**	32	24-8	581	**18.2**
4 **Syracuse**	38	28-10	687	**18.1**
5 **North Carolina**	38	34-4	685	**18.0**

Rebound Margin	G	W-L	RPG	OPP RPG	MAR
1 Michigan State	38	31-7	39.0	29.7	**9.3**
Pittsburgh	36	31-5	39.8	30.5	**9.3**
3 Connecticut	36	31-5	43.3	34.4	**8.9**
4 Albany (NY)	31	15-16	38.9	30.2	**8.7**
5 Xavier	35	27-8	39.4	31.1	**8.3**

Scoring Defense	G	W-L	OPP PTS	OPP PPG
1 Washington State	33	17-16	1,829	**55.4**
2 Stephen F. Austin	32	24-8	1,795	**56.1**
3 Illinois	34	24-10	1,944	**57.2**
4 Princeton	27	13-14	1,545	**57.2**
5 Wright State	33	20-13	1,897	**57.5**

Field Goal Pct Defense	G	W-L	OPP FG	OPP FGA	OPP PCT
1 Memphis	37	33-4	755	2,033	**37.1**
2 Stephen F. Austin	32	24-8	615	1,634	**37.6**
3 Connecticut	36	31-5	888	2,353	**37.7**
4 Gonzaga	34	28-6	748	1,981	**37.8**
5 Kansas	35	27-8	773	2,019	**38.3**

Blocked Shots Per Game	G	W-L	BLK	BPG
1 Connecticut	36	31-5	280	**7.8**
2 Mississippi State	36	23-13	271	**7.5**
3 Kentucky	36	22-14	238	**6.6**
4 Minnesota	33	22-11	201	**6.1**
5 LSU	35	27-8	212	**6.1**

Steals Per Game	G	W-L	STL	SPG
1 VMI	32	24-8	453	**14.2**
2 Missouri	38	31-7	388	**10.2**
3 Chicago State	32	19-13	321	**10.0**
4 Longwood	31	17-14	310	**10.0**
5 Niagara	35	26-9	346	**9.9**

TEAM LEADERS—GAME

Points	OPP	DATE	SCORE
1 Texas Tech	East Central	N20	167-115
2 UTSA	East Central	N22	136-68
3 VMI	Stevenson	N20	133-72
4 North Dakota State	Mayville State	N18	128-64
5 Syracuse	Connecticut	M12	127-117

Field Goal Pct	OPP	DATE	FG	FGA	PCT
1 Navy	UTSA	D2	25	35	**71.4**
2 Northern Iowa	Missouri State	J10	31	44	**70.5**
3 Arizona	Stanford	M7	35	50	**70.0**
Green Bay	North Dakota	D20	35	50	**70.0**
5 Georgetown	Savannah State	D8	37	53	**69.8**

Three-Pt FG Made	OPP	DATE	3FG
1 VMI	Southern Virginia	J29	**24**
2 VMI	Coastal Carolina	F14	**19**
Notre Dame	South Dakota	D2	**19**
VMI	Campbell	N24	**19**
VMI	Stevenson	N20	**19**

CONSENSUS ALL-AMERICAS

FIRST TEAM

PLAYER	CL	POS	HT	SCHOOL	RPG	PPG
DeJuan Blair	SO	F	6-7	Pittsburgh	12.3	15.7
Stephen Curry	JR	G	6-3	Davidson	4.4	28.6
Blake Griffin	SO	F	6-10	Oklahoma	14.4	22.7
Tyler Hansbrough	SR	F	6-9	North Carolina	8.1	20.7
James Harden	SO	G	6-5	Arizona State	5.6	20.1

SECOND TEAM

PLAYER	CL	POS	HT	SCHOOL	RPG	PPG
Sherron Collins	JR	G	5-11	Kansas	2.9	18.9
Luke Harangody	JR	F	6-8	Notre Dame	11.8	23.3
Ty Lawson	JR	G	5-11	North Carolina	3.0	16.6
Jodie Meeks	JR	G	6-4	Kentucky	3.4	23.7
Jeff Teague	SO	G	6-2	Wake Forest	3.3	18.8
Hasheem Thabeet	JR	C	7-3	Connecticut	10.8	13.6

Selectors: AP, NABC, Sporting News, USBWA

AWARD WINNERS

PLAYER OF THE YEAR

PLAYER	SCHOOL	CL	POS	HT	AWARD(S)
Blake Griffin	Oklahoma	SO	F	6-10	Wooden, Naismith, AP, USBWA, NABC, CBS/Chevrolet, Rupp
Darren Collison	UCLA	SR	G	6-0	Frances Pomeroy Naismith*

*For the most outstanding senior player who is 6 feet or under.

COACH OF THE YEAR

COACH	SCHOOL	REC	AWARDS
Bill Self	Kansas	27-8	AP, USBWA, CBS/Chevrolet, Sporting News
Jamie Dixon	Pittsburgh	31-5	Naismith
Mike Anderson	Missouri	31-7	NABC (shared)
John Calipari	Memphis	33-4	NABC (shared)

ESPNU Class of 2009

RATING/PLAYER	POS	HT	HIGH SCHOOL	A-A TEAMS	COLLEGE	CAREER NOTES
98 Avery Bradley	SG	6-3	Findlay College Prep, Las Vegas	McD, MJ, P, USA	Texas	Led No. 1 Findlay to unbeaten season (33-0); avg. 18.8 pts on 54% shooting
98 Derrick Favors	PF	6-9	South Atlanta HS, Atlanta	McD, MJ, P, USA	Georgia Tech	USA Today National High School POY, '09; Parade Player of the Year, '09
98 Xavier Henry	SG	6-6	Putnam City HS, Oklahoma City, OK	McD, MJ, P, USA	Kansas	Okla. Gatorade POY, '09; avg. 26.8 ppg; both parents played at Kansas
98 DeMarcus Cousins	C	6-9	LeFlore HS, Mobile, AL	McD, MJ, P, USA	Kentucky	Avg. 26.0 and 12.0, '09; followed John Calipari from Memphis to Kentucky
98 John Wall	PG	6-3	Word of God Academy, Raleigh, NC	MJ, USA	Kentucky	Averaged 22.1 ppg, 5.5 apg, 5.2 rpg, 2.0 spg
98 John Henson	PF	6-10	Sickles HS, Tampa, FL	McD, MJ, P, USA	North Carolina	Family left Texas for Fla. in '08; averaged 17.6 ppg, 12.2 rpg, '09
98 Renardo Sidney	PF	6-9	Fairfax HS, Los Angeles	McD, MJ, P, USA	Mississippi State	Native of Jackson, Miss.; 3-time all-state; averaged 24.8 ppg, '09
98 Jordan Hamilton	SF	6-7	Dominguez HS, Compton, CA	MJ	Texas	Did not play in '09 due to California transfer rules
98 Kenny Boynton Jr.	SG	6-3	American Heritage School, Plantation, FL	McD, MJ, P, USA	Florida	No. 3 all-time scorer in Florida; shot 58%, averaged 31.0 ppg, '09
98 Mason Plumlee	C	6-11	Christ School, Arden, NC	McD, MJ, P	Duke	Older brother is PF at Duke; 3 straight NCISSA titles at Christ School
97 Keith Gallon	C	6-9	Oak Hill Academy, Mouth of Wilson, VA	McD, MJ, P, USA	Oklahoma	Virginia Gatorade POY, '09; averaged 16.2 ppg and 10.3 rpg, '09
97 Lance Stephenson	SG	6-5	Lincoln HS, Brooklyn, NY	McD, P, USA	Cincinnati	All-time leading scorer in N.Y. (2,946 points); won 4 straight city titles
97 Daniel Orton	C	6-10	Bishop McGuiness HS, Oklahoma City, OK	MJ, USA	Kentucky	Missed all but 3 games as HS senior because of knee surgery
97 Abdul Gaddy	PG	6-3	Bellarmine Prep, Tacoma, WA	McD, MJ, P	Washington	Washington Gatorade POY, '08 as HS junior
97 Wallace Judge	PF	6-8	Arlington Country Day, Jacksonville, FL	McD, MJ, P	Kansas State	Won back-to-back Class 2A state championships at Arlington Country Day
97 Dante Taylor	PF	6-9	National Christian Academy, Ft. Washington, MD	McD, P	Pittsburgh	1st McDonald's All-America since 1987 for Pitt; 24.0 ppg, 10.0 rpg
97 Ryan Kelly	PF	6-10	Ravenscroft School, Raleigh, NC	McD, MJ, P; USA	Duke	25.3 ppg, 10.2 rpg, '09; 4th generation college player in his family
97 Mouphtaou Yarou	PF	6-9	Montrose Christian School, Rockville, MD	MJ, P, USA	Villanova	Native of Benin, Africa; averaged 19.6 points, 11.2 rebounds, '09
96 Dominic Cheek	SG	6-6	St. Anthony HS, Jersey City, NJ	McD, MJ, P	Villanova	Averaged 14.2 ppg, 9.0 rpg, 4.0 apg for legendary coach Bob Hurley
96 Alex Oriakhi	C	6-8	The Tilton School, Tilton, NH	McD, MJ, P	Connecticut	New Hampshire Gatorade POY, '09; led Tilton to National Prep Championship
96 John Jenkins	SG	6-4	Station Camp HS, Gallatin, TN	P	Vanderbilt	Led country in scoring as HS senior (42.8 ppg); Tennessee Gatorade POY, '09
96 Michael Snaer	SG	6-5	Rancho Verde HS, Moreno Valley, CA	McD	Florida State	Averaged 28.1 ppg, 10.8 rpg, 5.2 apg as HS senior; California Gatorade POY, '09
96 Maalik Wayns	PG	6-0	Roman Catholic HS, Philadelphia	McD, P	Villanova	Pennsylvania Gatorade POY, '09; averaged 28.1 ppg, 10.8 rpg, 5.2 apg, '09
96 Tommy Mason-Griffin	PG	5-10	Madison HS, Houston	McD, MJ	Oklahoma	Texas Gatorade POY, '09; averaged 22.8 ppg, shot 45.5% from 3pt
96 Peyton Siva	PG	5-11	Franklin HS, Seattle	McD, P, USA	Louisville	Washington Gatorade POY, '09; Led Franklin to 3A title (19.4 ppg), '09

Abbreviations: McD=McDonald's; MJ=Jordan Brand; P=Parade; USA=USA Today

POLL PROGRESSION

PRESEASON POLL

AP	ESPN/USA	SCHOOL
1	1	**North Carolina**
2	2	**Connecticut**
3	3	**Louisville**
4	4	**UCLA**
5	6	**Pittsburgh**
6	7	**Michigan State**
7	8	**Texas**
8	5	**Duke**
9	9	**Notre Dame**
10	11	**Gonzaga**
11	10	**Purdue**
12	14	**Oklahoma**
13	12	**Memphis**
14	13	**Tennessee**
15	15	**Arizona State**
16	17	**Marquette**
17	16	**Miami (FL)**
18	21	**USC**
19	19	**Florida**
20	20	**Davidson**
21	24	**Wake Forest**
22	18	**Georgetown**
23	25	**Villanova**
24	23	**Kansas**
25	21	**Wisconsin**

WEEK OF NOV 17

AP	ESPN/USA	SCHOOL	AP↓↑
1	1	**North Carolina** (1-0)	
2	2	**Connecticut** (1-0)	
3	3	**Louisville** (0-0)	
4	4	**UCLA** (2-0)	
5	7	**Michigan State** (1-0)	↑1
6	6	**Pittsburgh** (1-0)	↓1
7	8	**Texas** (1-0)	
8	9	**Notre Dame** (1-0)	↑1
9	11	**Gonzaga** (1-0)	↑1
10	5	**Duke** (3-0)	↓2
11	10	**Purdue** (1-0)	
12	14	**Oklahoma** (1-0)	
13	12	**Memphis** (1-0)	
14	13	**Tennessee** (1-0)	
15	15	**Arizona State** (1-0)	
16	17	**Marquette** (1-0)	
17	16	**Miami (FL)** (1-0)	
18	19	**Florida** (2-0)	↑1
19	20	**USC** (1-0)	↓1
20	25	**Wake Forest** (1-0)	↑1
21	21	**Davidson** (1-0)	↓1
22	18	**Georgetown** (0-0)	
23	23	**Villanova** (1-0)	
24	24	**Kansas** (1-0)	
25	22	**Wisconsin** (1-0)	

WEEK OF NOV 24

AP	ESPN/USA	SCHOOL	AP↓↑
1	1	**North Carolina** (3-0)	
2	2	**Connecticut** (4-0)	
3	3	**Louisville** (2-0)	
4	4	**Pittsburgh** (4-0)	↑2
5	6	**Michigan State** (2-0)	
6	7	**Texas** (2-0)	↑1
7	5	**Duke** (6-0)	↑3
8	8	**Notre Dame** (2-0)	
9	10	**Gonzaga** (2-0)	
10	9	**Purdue** (4-0)	↑1
11	13	**Oklahoma** (4-0)	↑1
12	12	**Tennessee** (3-0)	↑2
13	11	**UCLA** (3-1)	↓9
14	14	**Arizona State** (3-0)	↑1
15	15	**Marquette** (3-0)	↑1
16	20	**Xavier** (5-0)	⅃
17	18	**Florida** (3-0)	↑1
18	17	**Memphis** (4-1)	↓5
19	24	**Wake Forest** (2-0)	↑1
20	22	**Villanova** (3-0)	↑3
21	16	**Georgetown** (2-0)	↑1
22	21	**Miami (FL)** (2-1)	↓5
23	23	**Kansas** (2-0)	↑2
24	25	**Davidson** (3-1)	↓3
25	19	**Wisconsin** (4-0)	

WEEK OF DEC 1

AP	ESPN/USA	SCHOOL	AP↓↑
1	1	**North Carolina** (7-0)	
2	2	**Connecticut** (6-0) Ⓐ	
3	3	**Pittsburgh** (7-0)	↑1
4	4	**Duke** (7-0)	↑3
5	5	**Gonzaga** (5-0)	↑4
6	6	**Oklahoma** (6-0)	↑5
7	7	**Notre Dame** (5-1)	↑1
8	8	**Texas** (5-1)	↓2
9	10	**Purdue** (5-1)	↑1
10	13	**Tennessee** (5-1) Ⓑ	↑2
11	11	**Louisville** (2-1)	↓8
12	9	**UCLA** (4-1)	↑1
13	12	**Michigan State** (4-1)	↓8
14	14	**Xavier** (6-0)	↑2
15	17	**Wake Forest** (6-0)	↑4
16	20	**Syracuse** (6-0)	⅃
17	16	**Villanova** (6-0)	↑3
18	15	**Memphis** (4-1)	
19	19	**Arizona State** (5-1)	↓5
20	18	**Georgetown** (4-1)	↑1
21	22	**Miami (FL)** (4-1)	↑1
22	24	**Davidson** (5-1)	↑2
23	21	**Florida** (5-1)	↓6
24	—	**Baylor** (6-1)	⅃
25	—	**Marquette** (5-1)	↓10
—	22	**Wisconsin** (5-1)	Γ
—	25	**Kansas** (4-1)	Γ

WEEK OF DEC 8

AP	ESPN/USA	SCHOOL	AP↓↑
1	1	**North Carolina** (8-0)	
2	2	**Connecticut** (8-0)	
3	3	**Pittsburgh** (9-0)	
4	4	**Gonzaga** (6-0)	↑1
5	5	**Oklahoma** (8-0)	↑1
6	6	**Texas** (6-1)	↑2
7	7	**Duke** (8-1)	↓3
8	8	**Tennessee** (6-1)	↑2
9	10	**Louisville** (4-1)	↑2
10	9	**Xavier** (7-0)	↑4
11	11	**Wake Forest** (8-0)	↑4
12	13	**Notre Dame** (6-2)	↓5
13	16	**Syracuse** (8-0)	↑3
14	17	**Purdue** (6-2)	↓5
15	12	**Villanova** (8-0)	↑2
16	14	**UCLA** (5-2)	↓4
17	15	**Memphis** (5-1)	↑1
18	20	**Michigan State** (5-2) Ⓒ	↓5
19	19	**Georgetown** (5-1)	↑1
20	18	**Arizona State** (7-1)	↓1
21	21	**Ohio State** (5-0)	⅃
22	—	**Baylor** (7-1)	↑2
23	22	**Davidson** (6-1)	↓1
24	24	**Marquette** (7-1)	↑1
25	23	**Kansas** (7-1)	⅃
—	25	**Miami (FL)** (5-2)	Γ

WEEK OF DEC 15

AP	ESPN/USA	SCHOOL	AP↓↑
1	1	**North Carolina** (9-0)	
2	2	**Connecticut** (8-0)	
3	3	**Pittsburgh** (10-0)	
4	4	**Oklahoma** (10-0)	↑1
5	5	**Texas** (8-1)	↑1
6	6	**Duke** (8-1)	↑1
7	7	**Xavier** (9-0)	↑3
8	7	**Gonzaga** (7-1)	↓4
9	9	**Louisville** (6-1)	
10	10	**Wake Forest** (9-0)	↑1
11	11	**Syracuse** (9-0)	↑2
12	14	**Notre Dame** (7-2)	
13	18	**Purdue** (8-2)	↑1
14	12	**UCLA** (6-2)	↑2
15	13	**Georgetown** (7-1)	↑4
16	19	**Tennessee** (6-2)	↓8
17	16	**Ohio State** (6-0)	↑4
18	15	**Villanova** (10-1)	↓3
19	22	**Michigan State** (6-2)	↓1
20	17	**Arizona State** (8-1)	
21	24	**Baylor** (8-1)	↑1
22	20	**Davidson** (8-1)	↑1
23	21	**Memphis** (5-2)	↓6
24	23	**Marquette** (8-1)	
25	25	**Clemson** (10-0)	⅃

WEEK OF DEC 22

AP	ESPN/USA	SCHOOL	AP↓↑
1	1	**North Carolina** (11-0)	
2	2	**Connecticut** (10-0)	
3	3	**Pittsburgh** (12-0)	
4	4	**Oklahoma** (11-0)	
5	5	**Duke** (10-1)	↑1
6	6	**Wake Forest** (10-0)	↑4
7	7	**Gonzaga** (8-2)	↑1
8	11	**Notre Dame** (8-2)	↑4
9	8	**Texas** (9-2)	↓4
10	15	**Purdue** (9-2)	↑3
11	18	**Michigan State** (8-2)	↑8
12	9	**Georgetown** (8-1)	↑3
13	10	**UCLA** (8-2)	↑1
14	12	**Xavier** (9-1)	↓7
15	13	**Ohio State** (8-0)	↑2
16	21	**Tennessee** (8-2)	
17	14	**Syracuse** (11-1)	↓6
18	16	**Villanova** (10-1)	
19	19	**Louisville** (7-2)	↓10
20	17	**Arizona State** (9-1)	
21	22	**Baylor** (9-1)	
22	20	**Clemson** (12-0)	↑3
23	23	**Minnesota** (10-0)	⅃
24	—	**Michigan** (8-2)	⅃
25	—	**Missouri** (9-1)	⅃
—	24	**Memphis** (6-3)	Γ
—	25	**Marquette** (9-2)	Γ

WEEK OF DEC 29

AP	ESPN/USA	SCHOOL	AP↓↑
1	1	**North Carolina** (12-0)	
2	2	**Connecticut** (11-0)	
3	3	**Pittsburgh** (12-0)	
4	4	**Oklahoma** (12-0)	
5	5	**Duke** (10-1)	
6	6	**Wake Forest** (11-0)	
7	10	**Notre Dame** (9-2)	↑1
8	7	**Texas** (10-2)	↑1
9	11	**Purdue** (11-2)	↑1
10	15	**Michigan State** (9-2)	↑1
11	8	**Georgetown** (9-1)	↑1
12	9	**UCLA** (10-2)	↑1
13	12	**Syracuse** (12-1)	↑4
14	18	**Tennessee** (8-2)	↑2
15	13	**Villanova** (11-1)	↑3
16	17	**Gonzaga** (8-3)	↓9
17	14	**Arizona State** (10-1)	↑3
18	18	**Louisville** (8-2)	↑1
19	20	**Baylor** (10-1)	↑2
20	16	**Clemson** (12-0)	↑2
21	21	**Minnesota** (12-0)	↑2
22	22	**Xavier** (9-2)	↓8
23	24	**Michigan** (9-2)	↑1
24	23	**Ohio State** (9-1)	↓9
25	—	**Butler** (10-1)	⅃
—	25	**Marquette** (11-2)	

WEEK OF JAN 5

AP	ESPN/USA	SCHOOL	AP↓↑
1	1	**Pittsburgh** (14-0) Ⓓ	↑2
2	2	**Duke** (12-1)	↑3
3	3	**North Carolina** (13-1)	↓2
4	4	**Wake Forest** (13-0)	↑2
5	5	**Connecticut** (12-1)	↓3
6	6	**Oklahoma** (13-1)	↓2
7	7	**Texas** (11-2)	↑1
8	12	**Michigan State** (11-2)	↑2
9	10	**Georgetown** (10-2)	↑2
10	7	**UCLA** (12-2)	↑2
11	9	**Syracuse** (14-1)	↑2
12	11	**Clemson** (14-0)	↑8
13	13	**Notre Dame** (10-3)	↓6
14	14	**Purdue** (11-3)	↓5
15	25	**Tennessee** (9-3)	↓1
16	18	**Xavier** (11-2)	↑6
17	24	**Boston College** (13-2)	⅃
18	15	**Marquette** (13-2)	⅃
19	17	**Villanova** (12-2)	↓3
20	16	**Arizona State** (12-2)	↓3
21	20	**Butler** (12-1)	↑4
22	19	**Minnesota** (13-1)	↓1
23	21	**Louisville** (9-3)	↓5
23	23	**Baylor** (12-2)	↓4
25	22	**West Virginia** (11-2)	⅃

WEEK OF JAN 12

AP	ESPN/USA	SCHOOL	AP↓↑
1	1	**Pittsburgh** (15-0)	
2	3	**Wake Forest** (14-0)	↑2
3	2	**Duke** (14-1)	↓1
4	4	**Connecticut** (14-1)	↑1
5	6	**North Carolina** (14-2)	↓2
6	5	**Oklahoma** (15-1)	
7	10	**Michigan State** (13-2)	↑1
8	8	**Syracuse** (16-1)	↑3
9	7	**UCLA** (13-2)	↑1
10	9	**Clemson** (16-0)	↑2
11	11	**Texas** (12-3)	↓4
12	13	**Notre Dame** (12-3)	↑1
13	12	**Georgetown** (11-3)	↓4
14	14	**Marquette** (15-2)	↑4
15	16	**Xavier** (13-2)	↑1
16	15	**Arizona State** (14-2)	↑4
17	18	**Butler** (14-1)	↑4
18	17	**Minnesota** (15-1)	↑4
19	19	**Purdue** (12-4)	↓5
20	20	**Louisville** (11-3)	↑3
21	21	**Baylor** (13-2)	↑2
22	23	**California** (15-2)	⅃
23	22	**Villanova** (13-3)	↓5
24	—	**Tennessee** (10-4)	↓9
25	24	**Michigan** (13-3)	⅃
—	25	**Saint Mary's (CA)** (15-1)	

WEEK OF JAN 19

AP	ESPN/USA	SCHOOL	AP↓↑
1	1	**Wake Forest** (16-0) Ⓔ	↑1
2	2	**Duke** (16-1)	↑1
3	3	**Connecticut** (16-1)	↑1
4	4	**Pittsburgh** (16-1)	↓3
5	6	**North Carolina** (16-2)	
6	5	**Oklahoma** (17-1)	
7	7	**Michigan State** (15-2)	
8	8	**Syracuse** (17-2)	
9	12	**Louisville** (13-3)	↑11
10	9	**Clemson** (16-1)	
11	10	**Marquette** (16-2)	↑3
12	14	**Georgetown** (12-4)	↑1
13	11	**UCLA** (14-3)	↓4
14	15	**Texas** (13-4)	↓3
15	13	**Xavier** (15-2)	
16	17	**Butler** (16-1)	↑1
17	16	**Arizona State** (15-3)	↓1
18	18	**Purdue** (14-4)	↑1
19	19	**Notre Dame** (12-5)	↓7
20	21	**Villanova** (14-3)	↑3
21	20	**Minnesota** (16-2)	↓3
22	24	**Memphis** (14-3)	⅃
23	—	**Gonzaga** (12-4)	⅃
24	—	**Florida** (16-2)	⅃
25	24	**Illinois** (15-3)	⅃
—	22	**Saint Mary's (CA)** (17-1)	
—	23	**Baylor** (14-3)	Γ

WEEK OF JAN 26

AP	ESPN/USA	SCHOOL	AP↓↑
1	1	**Duke** (18-1)	↑1
2	2	**Connecticut** (18-1)	↑1
3	3	**Pittsburgh** (18-1)	↑1
4	5	**Oklahoma** (19-1)	↑2
5	6	**North Carolina** (17-2)	
6	4	**Wake Forest** (16-1)	↓5
7	7	**Louisville** (15-3)	↑2
8	8	**Marquette** (17-2)	↑3
9	9	**Michigan State** (16-3)	↓2
10	10	**Xavier** (17-2)	↑5
11	12	**Texas** (14-4)	↑3
12	11	**Clemson** (17-2)	↓2
13	13	**Butler** (18-1)	↑3
14	14	**Arizona State** (16-3)	↑3
15	15	**Syracuse** (17-4)	↓7
16	17	**Purdue** (15-4)	↑2
17	16	**UCLA** (15-4)	↓4
18	19	**Memphis** (16-3)	↑4
19	20	**Illinois** (17-3)	↑6
20	25	**Gonzaga** (14-4)	↑3
21	21	**Villanova** (15-4)	↓1
22	18	**Saint Mary's (CA)** (18-1)	⅃
23	—	**Washington** (15-4)	⅃
24	—	**Kentucky** (16-4)	⅃
25	23	**Georgetown** (12-6)	↓13
—	22	**Notre Dame** (12-6)	Γ
—	24	**Minnesota** (17-3)	Γ

Poll Progression Continues →

Week of Feb 2

AP	ESPN/USA	School	AP ↓↑
1	1	**Connecticut** (20-1)	↑1
2	2	**Oklahoma** (21-1)	↑2
3	4	**North Carolina** (19-2)	↑2
4	3	**Duke** (19-2)	↓3
5	7	**Louisville** (17-3)	↑2
6	5	**Pittsburgh** (19-2)	↓3
7	6	**Wake Forest** (17-2)	↓1
8	8	**Marquette** (19-2)	
9	9	**Xavier** (19-2)	↑1
10	10	**Clemson** (18-2)	↑2
11	11	**Butler** (19-1)	↑2
12	13	**Purdue** (17-4)	↑4
13	14	**Michigan State** (17-4)	↓4
14	15	**Memphis** (18-3)	↑4
15	12	**UCLA** (17-4)	↑2
16	17	**Texas** (15-5)	↓5
17	16	**Villanova** (17-4)	↑4
18	18	**Gonzaga** (16-4)	↑2
19	19	**Minnesota** (18-3)	⤴
20	20	**Syracuse** (17-5)	↓5
21	24	**Kansas** (17-4)	⤴
22	25	**Washington** (16-5)	↑1
23	21	**Illinois** (18-4)	↓4
24	23	**Arizona State** (16-5)	↓10
25	22	**Utah State** (21-1)	⤴

Week of Feb 9

AP	ESPN/USA	School	AP ↓↑
1	1	**Connecticut** (22-1)	
2	2	**Oklahoma** (23-1)	
3	3	**North Carolina** (21-2)	
4	4	**Pittsburgh** (21-2)	↑2
5	7	**Louisville** (18-4)	
6	5	**Duke** (20-3)	↓2
7	8	**Wake Forest** (18-3)	
8	10	**Memphis** (20-3)	↑6
9	9	**Michigan State** (19-4)	↑4
10	12	**Marquette** (20-3)	↓2
11	6	**UCLA** (19-4)	↑4
12	11	**Clemson** (19-3)	↓2
13	13	**Villanova** (19-4)	↑4
14	14	**Xavier** (20-3)	↓5
15	15	**Butler** (21-2)	↓4
16	16	**Kansas** (19-4)	↑5
17	19	**Missouri** (20-4)	⤴
18	18	**Arizona State** (18-5)	↑6
19	21	**Gonzaga** (17-5)	↓1
20	23	**Purdue** (17-6)	↓8
21	17	**Utah State** (23-1)	↑4
22	20	**Illinois** (19-5)	↑1
23	22	**Syracuse** (18-6)	↓3
24	—	**Ohio State** (17-5)	⤴
25	25	**Florida State** (18-5)	⤴
—	24	**Washington** (17-6)	⤵

Week of Feb 16

AP	ESPN/USA	School	AP ↓↑
1	1	**Connecticut** (24-1)	
2	2	**Oklahoma** (25-1)	
3	3	**North Carolina** (23-2)	
4	4	**Pittsburgh** (23-2)	
5	6	**Memphis** (22-3)	↑3
6	5	**Michigan State** (20-4)	↑3
7	7	**Louisville** (19-5)	↓2
8	8	**Wake Forest** (19-4)	↓1
9	9	**Duke** (20-5)	↓3
10	11	**Marquette** (21-4)	
11	10	**Missouri** (22-4)	↑6
12	14	**Villanova** (20-5)	↑1
13	13	**Clemson** (20-4)	↓1
14	11	**Arizona State** (20-5)	↑4
15	18	**Kansas** (20-5)	↑1
16	17	**Xavier** (21-4)	↓2
17	20	**Gonzaga** (19-5)	↑2
18	16	**Illinois** (21-5)	↑4
19	21	**Purdue** (19-6)	↑1
20	15	**UCLA** (19-6)	↓9
21	22	**Butler** (22-3)	↓6
22	19	**Washington** (19-6)	⤴
23	24	**LSU** (21-4)	Ⓕ ⤴
24	25	**Syracuse** (19-7)	↓1
25	—	**Dayton** (23-3)	⤴
—	23	**Utah State** (24-2)	⤵

Week of Feb 23

AP	ESPN/USA	School	AP ↓↑
1	1	**Pittsburgh** (25-2)	Ⓖ
2	2	**Connecticut** (25-2)	Ⓖ
3	3	**Oklahoma** (25-2)	
4	5	**North Carolina** (24-3)	
5	4	**Memphis** (24-3)	
6	6	**Louisville** (21-5)	Ⓖ
7	7	**Duke** (22-5)	
8	10	**Marquette** (23-4)	Ⓖ
9	9	**Michigan State** (21-5)	
10	12	**Villanova** (22-5)	Ⓖ
11	8	**Missouri** (23-4)	
12	13	**Clemson** (22-4)	[illegible]
13	14	**Wake Forest** (20-5)	[illegible]
14	11	**Arizona State** (21-5)	
15	15	**Kansas** (22-5)	
16	16	**Purdue** (21-6)	↑
17	17	**Gonzaga** (21-5)	
18	18	**LSU** (23-4)	↑[illegible]
19	22	**Xavier** (22-5)	↓[illegible]
20	20	**Illinois** (22-6)	↓[illegible]
21	21	**Washington** (20-7)	↑1
22	19	**UCLA** (20-7)	↓2
23	25	**Florida State** (21-6)	⤴
24	23	**Butler** (23-4)	↓3
25	24	**Texas** (18-8)	⤴

Week of Mar 2

AP	ESPN/USA	School	AP ↓↑
1	1	**Connecticut** (27-2)	↑1
2	2	**North Carolina** (25-3)	↑2
3	4	**Pittsburgh** (26-3)	↓2
4	5	**Oklahoma** (26-3)	↓1
5	3	**Memphis** (26-3)	
6	6	**Louisville** (23-5)	
7	7	**Duke** (24-5)	
8	8	**Michigan State** (23-5)	↑1
9	9	**Kansas** (24-5)	Ⓗ ↑6
10	10	**Wake Forest** (22-5)	↑3
11	16	**Villanova** (23-6)	↓1
12	11	**LSU** (25-4)	↑6
13	15	**Marquette** (23-6)	↓5
14	14	**Gonzaga** (23-5)	↑3
15	12	**Missouri** (24-5)	↓4
16	13	**Washington** (22-7)	↑5
17	18	**Xavier** (23-5)	↑2
18	19	**Clemson** (22-6)	↓6
19	20	**Purdue** (22-7)	↓3
20	17	**UCLA** (22-7)	↑2
21	21	**Arizona State** (21-7)	↓7
22	22	**Butler** (25-4)	↑2
23	23	**Illinois** (23-7)	↓3
24	24	**Florida State** (22-7)	↓1
25	25	**Syracuse** (21-8)	⤴

Week of Mar 9

AP	ESPN/USA	School	AP ↓↑
1	5	**Louisville** (25-5)	Ⓘ ↑5
2	1	**North Carolina** (27-3)	
3	3	**Memphis** (28-3)	↑2
4	2	**Pittsburgh** (28-3)	↓1
5	4	**Connecticut** (27-3)	Ⓘ ↓4
6	8	**Duke** (25-6)	↑1
7	7	**Oklahoma** (27-4)	↓3
8	6	**Michigan State** (25-5)	
9	15	**Missouri** (25-6)	↑6
10	12	**Gonzaga** (25-5)	↑4
11	13	**Villanova** (25-6)	
12	9	**Wake Forest** (24-5)	↓2
13	20	**Syracuse** (23-8)	↑12
14	11	**Kansas** (25-6)	↓5
15	10	**Washington** (24-7)	↑1
16	22	**Florida State** (23-8)	↑8
17	24	**Purdue** (22-9)	↑2
18	14	**UCLA** (24-7)	↑2
19	23	**Arizona State** (22-8)	↑2
20	19	**Xavier** (24-6)	↓3
21	16	**LSU** (25-6)	↓9
22	17	**Butler** (26-4)	
23	21	**Marquette** (23-8)	↓10
24	18	**Clemson** (23-7)	↓6
25	—	**Utah** (21-9)	⤴
—	25	**Illinois** (23-8)	⤵

Week of Mar 16

AP	ESPN/USA	School	AP ↓↑
1	1	**Louisville** (28-5)	
2	3	**North Carolina** (28-4)	
3	2	**Memphis** (31-3)	
4	4	**Pittsburgh** (28-4)	
5	6	**Connecticut** (27-4)	
6	5	**Duke** (28-6)	
7	8	**Oklahoma** (27-5)	
8	7	**Michigan State** (26-6)	
9	9	**Missouri** (28-6)	
10	10	**Gonzaga** (26-5)	
11	12	**Villanova** (26-7)	
12	11	**Wake Forest** (24-6)	
13	15	**Syracuse** (26-9)	
14	13	**Kansas** (25-7)	
15	14	**Washington** (25-8)	
16	16	**Florida State** (25-9)	
17	18	**Purdue** (25-9)	
18	17	**UCLA** (25-8)	
19	19	**Arizona State** (24-9)	
20	22	**Xavier** (25-7)	
21	20	**LSU** (26-7)	
22	23	**Butler** (26-5)	
23	24	**Marquette** (24-9)	
24	21	**Clemson** (23-8)	
25	—	**Utah** (24-9)	
—	25	**Utah State** (30-4)	

Final Poll (Post-Tournament)

ESPN/USA	School
1	**North Carolina** (32-4)
2	**Michigan State** (30-6)
3	**Connecticut** (31-4)
4	**Villanova** (30-7)
5	**Louisville** (31-6)
6	**Pittsburgh** (31-5)
7	**Oklahoma** (30-6)
8	**Missouri** (31-7)
9	**Memphis** (33-4)
10	**Kansas** (27-8)
11	**Duke** (30-7)
12	**Syracuse** (28-10)
13	**Gonzaga** (28-6)
14	**Purdue** (27-10)
15	**Xavier** (27-8)
16	**Washington** (26-9)
17	**LSU** (27-8)
18	**UCLA** (26-9)
19	**Arizona State** (25-10)
20	**Wake Forest** (24-7)
21	**Marquette** (25-10)
22	**Florida State** (25-10)
23	**Texas** (23-12)
24	**Arizona** (21-14)
25	**Butler** (26-6)

Ⓐ Connecticut is tops among eight Big East teams in the Top 25. The conference will have at least four teams in every poll during the season.

Ⓑ Tennessee begins a two-week run in the Top 10. The Vols are the only SEC team to crack the Top 10 all season.

Ⓒ On Dec. 3, Michigan State loses, 98-63, to North Carolina and over the next two weeks drops to No. 19, the lowest the Spartans will be ranked all season. MSU will lose again to UNC in the national championship game.

Ⓓ After improving to 14–0, Pitt supplants North Carolina, which loses, 92-89, at Wake Forest, to assume the No. 1 spot for first time in the history of the program.

Ⓔ Wake Forest gets to 16–0 with wins against North Carolina, Boston College and Clemson, and replaces Pitt at No. 1. Over a four-week period between Jan. 12 and Feb. 2, there is a different No. 1 each week.

Ⓕ Between Tennessee's drop-out the week of Jan. 19 and LSU's arrival the week of Feb. 16, the SEC has zero representatives in the Top 25 for the first time since March 7, 1989.

Ⓖ The Big East is the first conference ever to have five of its members in the Top 10.

Ⓗ The defending national champion Jayhawks make their first appearance of the season in the Top 10 after beating Missouri, 90-65.

Ⓘ Louisville reaches the No. 1 spot for the first time in the program's history after winning at West Virginia, 62-59. UConn drops out of the top spot after a 70-60 loss at Pittsburgh.

Pre-Tournament Ratings Percentage Index (RPI)

Rank	School	W-L	Sched. Strg.	SS Rank	RPI
1	**Duke**	28-6	.6322	3	.6677
2	**Pittsburgh**	27-4	.6110	8	.6670
3	**North Carolina**	27-4	.5870	27	.6531
4	**Louisville**	28-5	.6027	15	.6463
5	**Oklahoma**	27-5	.5919	25	.6459
6	**Michigan State**	26-6	.6137	6	.6449
7	**Memphis**	31-3	.5704	39	.6440
8	**Connecticut**	27-4	.5832	31	.6433
9	**Utah**	24-8	.6009	17	.6320
10	**Missouri**	27-6	.5709	38	.6310
11	**Kansas**	25-7	.5936	22	.6296
12	**Syracuse**	25-9	.6125	7	.6253
13	**Villanova**	26-7	.5836	30	.6244
14	**Washington**	24-8	.6023	16	.6213
15	**Florida State**	25-9	.5962	19	.6201
16	**Wake Forest**	24-6	.5520	69	.6184
17	**Xavier**	25-7	.5688	41	.6174
18	**Siena**	26-7	.5615	55	.6122
19	**Oklahoma State**	22-11	.6228	4	.6110
20	**Purdue**	25-9	.5869	28	.6109
21	**West Virginia**	23-11	.6039	14	.6106
22	**Illinois**	24-9	.5880	26	.6101
23	**Utah State**	29-4	.5126	133	.6090
24	**Butler**	25-5	.5412	85	.6084
25	**Tennessee**	21-12	.6368	2	.6082
26	**Gonzaga**	25-5	.5359	93	.6041
27	**Dayton**	26-7	.5393	88	.6037
28	**Clemson**	23-8	.5676	47	.6026
29	**BYU**	24-7	.5549	62	.6028
30	**Temple**	22-11	.5798	34	.6010
31	**Arizona State**	24-9	.5700	40	.6005
32	**Ohio State**	22-10	.5868	29	.6002
33	**UCLA**	25-8	.5502	72	.5991
34	**San Diego State**	21-9	.5803	33	.5975
35	**Marquette**	24-9	.5635	52	.5974
36	**Texas A&M**	22-9	.5638	51	.5927
37	**LSU**	26-7	.5420	84	.5922
38	**USC**	21-12	.5979	18	.5908
39	**California**	22-10	.5684	43	.5904
40	**Creighton**	26-7	.5262	111	.5900
41	**Texas**	22-11	.5685	42	.5899
42	**Minnesota**	21-10	.5731	37	.5883
43	**Western Kentucky**	23-8	.5230	117	.5860
44	**Michigan**	19-13	.6055	11	.5850
45	**Wisconsin**	18-12	.5947	21	.5840
46	**UAB**	22-11	.5515	71	.5812
47	**Illinois State**	24-9	.5319	101	.5804
48	**Saint Mary's (CA)**	24-6	.5001	158	.5799
49	**Niagara**	26-8	.5047	149	.5790
50	**VCU**	24-9	.5296	105	.5784

Source: NCAA

2009 NCAA Tournament

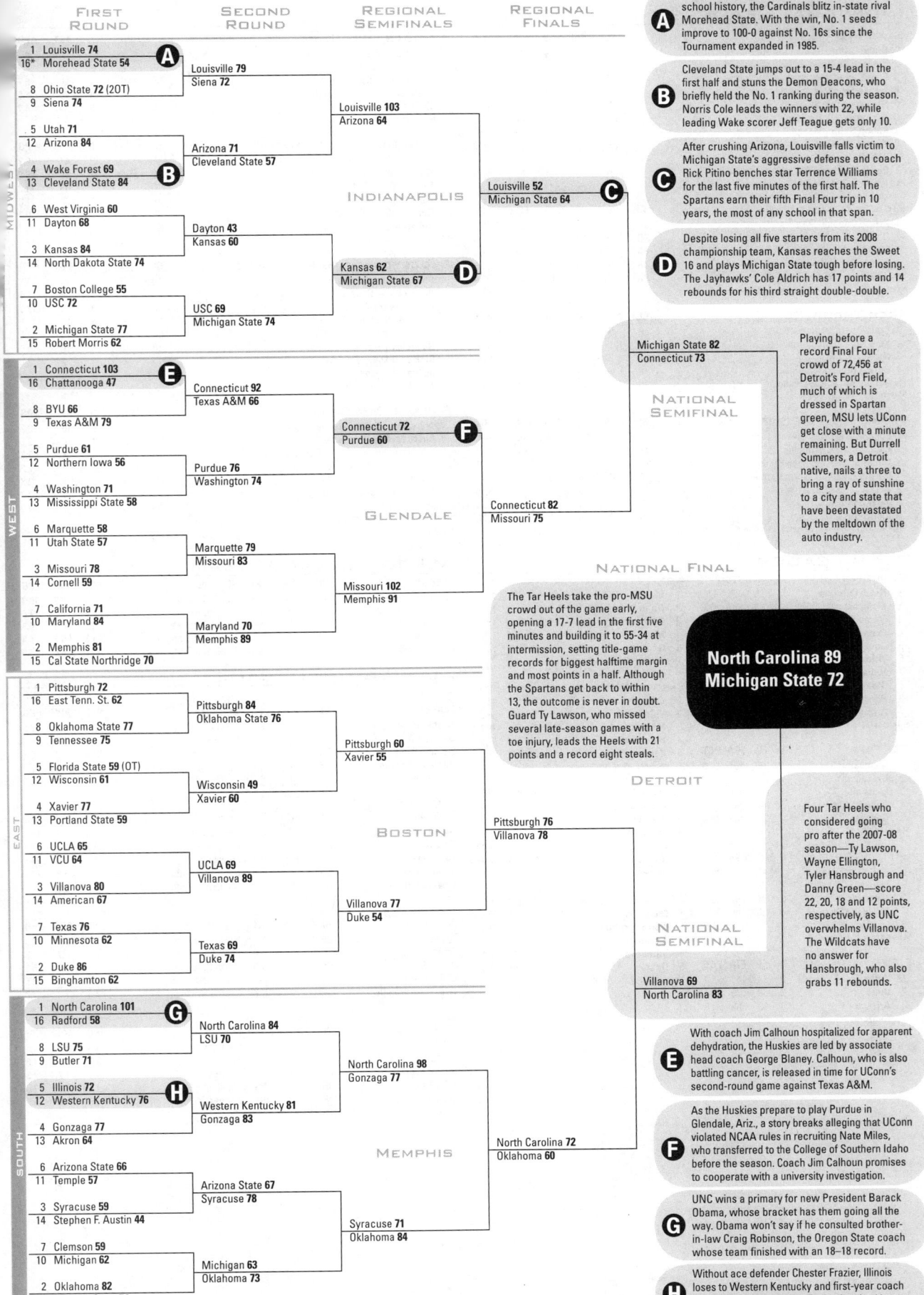

Midwest — Indianapolis

First Round
- 1 Louisville **74**, 16* Morehead State **54** (A)
- 8 Ohio State **72** (2OT), 9 Siena **74**
- 5 Utah **71**, 12 Arizona **84**
- 4 Wake Forest **69**, 13 Cleveland State **84** (B)
- 6 West Virginia **60**, 11 Dayton **68**
- 3 Kansas **84**, 14 North Dakota State **74**
- 7 Boston College **55**, 10 USC **72**
- 2 Michigan State **77**, 15 Robert Morris **62**

Second Round
- Louisville **79**, Siena **72**
- Arizona **71**, Cleveland State **57**
- Dayton **43**, Kansas **60**
- USC **69**, Michigan State **74**

Regional Semifinals
- Louisville **103**, Arizona **64**
- Kansas **62**, Michigan State **67** (D)

Regional Finals
- Louisville **52**, Michigan State **64** (C)

West — Glendale

First Round
- 1 Connecticut **103**, 16 Chattanooga **47** (E)
- 8 BYU **66**, 9 Texas A&M **79**
- 5 Purdue **61**, 12 Northern Iowa **56**
- 4 Washington **71**, 13 Mississippi State **58**
- 6 Marquette **58**, 11 Utah State **57**
- 3 Missouri **78**, 14 Cornell **59**
- 7 California **71**, 10 Maryland **84**
- 2 Memphis **81**, 15 Cal State Northridge **70**

Second Round
- Connecticut **92**, Texas A&M **66**
- Purdue **76**, Washington **74**
- Marquette **79**, Missouri **83**
- Maryland **70**, Memphis **89**

Regional Semifinals
- Connecticut **72**, Purdue **60** (F)
- Missouri **102**, Memphis **91**

Regional Finals
- Connecticut **82**, Missouri **75**

East — Boston

First Round
- 1 Pittsburgh **72**, 16 East Tenn. St. **62**
- 8 Oklahoma State **77**, 9 Tennessee **75**
- 5 Florida State **59** (OT), 12 Wisconsin **61**
- 4 Xavier **77**, 13 Portland State **59**
- 6 UCLA **65**, 11 VCU **64**
- 3 Villanova **80**, 14 American **67**
- 7 Texas **76**, 10 Minnesota **62**
- 2 Duke **86**, 15 Binghamton **62**

Second Round
- Pittsburgh **84**, Oklahoma State **76**
- Wisconsin **49**, Xavier **60**
- UCLA **69**, Villanova **89**
- Texas **69**, Duke **74**

Regional Semifinals
- Pittsburgh **60**, Xavier **55**
- Villanova **77**, Duke **54**

Regional Finals
- Pittsburgh **76**, Villanova **78**

South — Memphis

First Round
- 1 North Carolina **101**, 16 Radford **58** (G)
- 8 LSU **75**, 9 Butler **71**
- 5 Illinois **72**, 12 Western Kentucky **76** (H)
- 4 Gonzaga **77**, 13 Akron **64**
- 6 Arizona State **66**, 11 Temple **57**
- 3 Syracuse **59**, 14 Stephen F. Austin **44**
- 7 Clemson **59**, 10 Michigan **62**
- 2 Oklahoma **82**, 15 Morgan State **54**

Second Round
- North Carolina **84**, LSU **70**
- Western Kentucky **81**, Gonzaga **83**
- Arizona State **67**, Syracuse **78**
- Michigan **63**, Oklahoma **73**

Regional Semifinals
- North Carolina **98**, Gonzaga **77**
- Syracuse **71**, Oklahoma **84**

Regional Finals
- North Carolina **72**, Oklahoma **60**

National Semifinal — Detroit

- Michigan State **82**, Connecticut **73**

Playing before a record Final Four crowd of 72,456 at Detroit's Ford Field, much of which is dressed in Spartan green, MSU lets UConn get close with a minute remaining. But Durrell Summers, a Detroit native, nails a three to bring a ray of sunshine to a city and state that have been devastated by the meltdown of the auto industry.

- Villanova **69**, North Carolina **83**

Four Tar Heels who considered going pro after the 2007-08 season—Ty Lawson, Wayne Ellington, Tyler Hansbrough and Danny Green—score 22, 20, 18 and 12 points, respectively, as UNC overwhelms Villanova. The Wildcats have no answer for Hansbrough, who also grabs 11 rebounds.

National Final

North Carolina 89
Michigan State 72

The Tar Heels take the pro-MSU crowd out of the game early, opening a 17-7 lead in the first five minutes and building it to 55-34 at intermission, setting title-game records for biggest halftime margin and most points in a half. Although the Spartans get back to within 13, the outcome is never in doubt. Guard Ty Lawson, who missed several late-season games with a toe injury, leads the Heels with 21 points and a record eight steals.

A As the No. 1 overall seed for the first time in school history, the Cardinals blitz in-state rival Morehead State. With the win, No. 1 seeds improve to 100-0 against No. 16s since the Tournament expanded in 1985.

B Cleveland State jumps out to a 15-4 lead in the first half and stuns the Demon Deacons, who briefly held the No. 1 ranking during the season. Norris Cole leads the winners with 22, while leading Wake scorer Jeff Teague gets only 10.

C After crushing Arizona, Louisville falls victim to Michigan State's aggressive defense and coach Rick Pitino benches star Terrence Williams for the last five minutes of the first half. The Spartans earn their fifth Final Four trip in 10 years, the most of any school in that span.

D Despite losing all five starters from its 2008 championship team, Kansas reaches the Sweet 16 and plays Michigan State tough before losing. The Jayhawks' Cole Aldrich has 17 points and 14 rebounds for his third straight double-double.

E With coach Jim Calhoun hospitalized for apparent dehydration, the Huskies are led by associate head coach George Blaney. Calhoun, who is also battling cancer, is released in time for UConn's second-round game against Texas A&M.

F As the Huskies prepare to play Purdue in Glendale, Ariz., a story breaks alleging that UConn violated NCAA rules in recruiting Nate Miles, who transferred to the College of Southern Idaho before the season. Coach Jim Calhoun promises to cooperate with a university investigation.

G UNC wins a primary for new President Barack Obama, whose bracket has them going all the way. Obama won't say if he consulted brother-in-law Craig Robinson, the Oregon State coach whose team finished with an 18–18 record.

H Without ace defender Chester Frazier, Illinois loses to Western Kentucky and first-year coach Ken McDonald. WKU has Danced under 11 different coaches—the most in NCAA history.

*Opening round: Morehead State d. Alabama State 58-43

⊗Team participation later vacated

ANNUAL REVIEW

Tournament Leaders

Individual Leaders

Scoring

		CL	POS	G	PTS	PPG
1	**Blake Griffin**, Oklahoma	SO	F	4	114	28.5
2	**Sherron Collins**, Kansas	JR	G	3	77	25.7
3	**Sam Young**, Pittsburgh	SR	F	4	93	23.3
4	**Tyreke Evans**, Memphis	FR	G	3	67	22.3
5	**Nic Wise**, Arizona	JR	G	3	64	21.3
6	**Ty Lawson**, North Carolina	JR	G	5	104	20.8
7	**Robert Sallie**, Memphis	JR	G	3	60	20.0
8	**Wayne Ellington**, North Carolina	JR	G	6	115	19.2
9	**A.J. Price**, Connecticut	SR	G	5	95	19.0
	Chase Budinger, Arizona	JR	F	3	57	19.0

Minimum: 3 games

Field Goal Pct

		CL	POS	G	FG	FGA	PCT
1	**Arinze Onuaku**, Syracuse	JR	F	3	15	19	79.0
2	**Blake Griffin**, Oklahoma	SO	F	4	46	59	78.0
3	**Draymond Green**, Michigan State	FR	F	6	19	28	67.9
	Robert Sallie, Memphis	JR	G	3	19	28	67.9
5	**Jeremy Pargo**, Gonzaga	SR	G	3	17	26	65.4

Minimum: 15 made and 3 games

Free Throw Pct

		CL	POS	G	FT	FTA	PCT
1	**Craig Austrie**, Connecticut	SR	G	5	16	16	100.0
2	**Sam Young**, Pittsburgh	SR	F	4	15	16	93.8
3	**Nic Wise**, Arizona	JR	G	3	21	23	91.3
4	**Gerald Henderson**, Duke	JR	G	3	21	24	87.5
5	**Scottie Reynolds**, Villanova	JR	G	5	18	21	85.7

Minimum: 15 made

Three-Point FG Pct

		CL	POS	G	3FG	3FGA	PCT
1	**Edgar Sosa**, Louisville	JR	G	4	7	10	70.0
2	**Robert Sallie**, Memphis	JR	G	3	16	24	66.7
3	**Goran Suton**, Michigan State	SR	C	6	8	15	53.3
4	**Wayne Ellington**, North Carolina	JR	G	6	17	32	53.1
5	**Ty Lawson**, North Carolina	JR	G	5	9	18	50.0
	Jerry Smith, Louisville	JR	G	4	7	14	50.0
	Kim English, Missouri	FR	G	4	6	12	50.0

Minimum: 6 made and 3 games

Assists Per Game

		CL	POS	G	AST	APG
1	**Antonio Anderson**, Memphis	SR	G	3	25	8.3
2	**Ty Lawson**, North Carolina	JR	G	5	34	6.8
3	**Jonny Flynn**, Syracuse	SO	G	3	20	6.7
4	**Levance Fields**, Pittsburgh	SR	G	4	26	6.5
5	**Kalin Lucas**, Michigan State	SO	G	6	34	5.7

Minimum: 3 games

Rebounds Per Game

		CL	POS	G	REB	RPG
1	**Cole Aldrich**, Kansas	SO	C	3	47	15.7
2	**Blake Griffin**, Oklahoma	SO	F	4	60	15.0
3	**DeJuan Blair**, Pittsburgh	SO	F	4	55	13.8
4	**Jordan Hill**, Arizona	JR	F	3	33	11.0
5	**Goran Suton**, Michigan State	SR	F	6	64	10.7
	Robert Dozier, Memphis	SR	F	3	32	10.7

Minimum: 3 games

Blocked Shots Per Game

		CL	POS	G	BLK	BPG
1	**Cole Aldrich**, Kansas	SO	C	3	16	5.3
2	**Austin Daye**, Gonzaga	SO	F	3	8	2.7
	Kenny Frease, Xavier	FR	C	3	8	2.7
4	**Samardo Samuels**, Louisville	FR	F	4	10	2.5
5	**Reggie Redding**, Villanova	JR	G	5	10	2.0
	Hasheem Thabeet, Connecticut	JR	C	5	10	2.0
	Rick Jackson, Syracuse	SO	F	3	6	2.0
	JaJuan Johnson, Purdue	SO	F	3	6	2.0

Minimum: 3 games

Steals Per Game

		CL	POS	G	STL	SPG
1	**Ty Lawson**, North Carolina	JR	G	5	16	3.2
2	**Andre McGee**, Louisville	SR	G	4	10	2.5
3	**Tyler Hansbrough**, North Carolina	SR	F	6	14	2.3
	Tyreke Evans, Memphis	FR	G	3	7	2.3
	Kyle Fogg, Arizona	FR	G	3	7	2.3
	Dantea' Jackson, Xavier	SO	G	3	7	2.3
	Jon Scheyer, Duke	JR	G	3	7	2.3

Minimum: 3 games

Team Leaders

Scoring

		G	PTS	PPG
1	**North Carolina**	6	527	87.8
2	**Memphis**	3	261	87.0
3	**Missouri**	4	338	84.5
4	**Connecticut**	5	422	84.4
5	**Gonzaga**	3	237	79.0
6	**Villanova**	5	393	78.6
7	**Louisville**	4	308	77.0
8	**Oklahoma**	4	299	74.8
9	**Pittsburgh**	4	292	73.0
	Arizona	3	219	73.0

Minimum: 3 games

FG Pct

		G	FG	FGA	PCT
1	**Memphis**	3	95	181	52.5
2	**Oklahoma**	4	110	212	51.9
3	**Louisville**	4	117	228	51.3
4	**Connecticut**	5	147	296	49.7
5	**Gonzaga**	3	80	162	49.4

Minimum: 3 games

3-Pt FG Pct

		G	3FG	3FGA	PCT
1	**North Carolina**	6	43	94	45.7
2	**Louisville**	4	39	89	43.8
3	**Memphis**	3	24	62	38.7
4	**Michigan State**	6	36	99	36.4
5	**Gonzaga**	3	21	59	35.6

Minimum: 3 games

FT Pct

		G	FT	FTA	PCT
1	**Villanova**	5	98	118	83.0
2	**Duke**	3	59	76	77.6
3	**Arizona**	3	53	69	76.8
4	**Gonzaga**	3	56	73	76.7
5	**Michigan State**	6	100	131	76.3

Minimum: 3 games

Ast/TO Ratio

		G	AST	TO	RAT
1	**Missouri**	4	71	29	2.45
2	**North Carolina**	6	95	62	1.53
3	**Connecticut**	5	90	64	1.41
4	**Memphis**	3	56	40	1.40
5	**Gonzaga**	3	43	31	1.39

Minimum: 3 games

Rebounds

		G	REB	RPG
1	**Connecticut**	5	221	44.2
2	**Villanova**	5	196	39.2
3	**North Carolina**	6	232	38.7
4	**Pittsburgh**	4	150	37.5
5	**Kansas**	3	111	37.0

Minimum: 3 games

Blocks

		G	BLK	BPG
1	**Connecticut**	5	32	6.4
2	**Kansas**	3	18	6.0
3	**Louisville**	4	19	4.8
4	**Gonzaga**	3	14	4.7
	Xavier	3	14	4.7

Minimum: 3 games

Steals

		G	STL	SPG
1	**Memphis**	3	28	9.3
2	**North Carolina**	6	54	9.0
3	**Arizona**	3	26	8.7
4	**Villanova**	5	37	7.4
5	**Duke**	3	22	7.3

Minimum: 3 games

All-Tournament Team

PLAYER	CL	POS	HT	SCHOOL	RPG	APG	PPG
Wayne Ellington*	JR	G	6-4	North Carolina	5.7	2.7	19.2
Tyler Hansbrough	SR	F	6-9	North Carolina	7.8	1.3	17.5
Ty Lawson	JR	G	5-11	North Carolina	4.2	6.8	20.8
Kalin Lucas	SO	G	6-0	Michigan State	1.3	5.7	14.3
Goran Suton	SR	C	6-10	Michigan State	10.7	1.8	13.0

All-Regional Teams

East

PLAYER	CL	POS	HT	SCHOOL	RPG	APG	PPG
Scottie Reynolds*	JR	G	6-2	Villanova	2.0	1.3	12.5
Dwayne Anderson	SR	G/F	6-6	Villanova	8.0	1.5	15.0
DeJuan Blair	SO	F	6-7	Pittsburgh	13.8	1.8	16.8
Dante Cunningham	SR	F	6-8	Villanova	8.3	1.5	17.8
Sam Young	SR	F	6-6	Pittsburgh	7.8	0.8	23.3

Midwest

PLAYER	CL	POS	HT	SCHOOL	RPG	APG	PPG
Goran Suton*	SR	C	6-10	Michigan State	11.5	2.3	14.3
Cole Aldrich	SO	C	6-11	Kansas	15.7	1.7	17.7
Earl Clark	JR	G/F	6-9	Louisville	7.8	3.3	15.5
Kalin Lucas	SO	G	6-0	Michigan State	1.5	5.5	12.8
Travis Walton	SR	G	6-2	Michigan State	2.0	2.5	7.0

South

PLAYER	CL	POS	HT	SCHOOL	RPG	APG	PPG
Ty Lawson*	JR	G	5-11	North Carolina	3.3	6.7	20.3
Jonny Flynn	SO	G	6-0	Syracuse	2.3	6.7	16.3
Danny Green	SR	F/G	6-6	North Carolina	5.5	2.8	13.5
Blake Griffin	SO	F	6-10	Oklahoma	15.0	2.3	28.5
Tyler Hansbrough	SR	F	6-9	North Carolina	7.3	1.3	17.3

West

PLAYER	CL	POS	HT	SCHOOL	RPG	APG	PPG
A.J. Price*	SR	G	6-2	Connecticut	4.5	5.3	20.0
DeMarre Carroll	SR	F	6-8	Missouri	6.3	3.5	14.3
Tyreke Evans	FR	G	6-6	Memphis	4.0	4.7	22.3
J.T. Tiller	JR	G	6-3	Missouri	4.5	4.3	13.0
Kemba Walker	FR	G	6-1	Connecticut	3.3	4.8	11.5

* Most outstanding player

2009 NCAA TOURNAMENT BOX SCORES

103-64

Louisville	Half	Arizona
49	1H	28
54	2H	36

SWEET 16

LOUISVILLE	MIN	FG	3FG	FT	REB	A	ST	BL	PF	TP
Earl Clark	31	7-12	2-3	3-3	9	2	0	0	3	19
Jerry Smith	18	6-10	4-8	0-0	1	2	1	0	1	16
Terrence Williams	33	5-12	4-7	0-0	7	6	2	0	2	14
Samardo Samuels	26	4-5	0-0	6-6	5	2	1	2	2	14
Edgar Sosa	21	5-6	2-3	1-1	2	6	1	0	2	13
Terrence Jennings	10	3-3	0-0	1-2	5	0	2	1	0	7
Jared Swopshire	5	2-2	0-0	2-2	1	1	0	0	1	6
Andre McGee	19	1-3	1-3	0-0	1	3	2	0	2	3
Reginald Delk	9	1-3	1-2	0-0	1	1	0	0	1	3
Preston Knowles	13	1-4	0-1	0-0	0	2	0	0	1	2
Will Scott	9	1-4	0-2	0-0	0	3	1	0	0	2
George Goode	4	1-1	0-0	0-0	1	0	0	0	0	2
Kyle Kuric	2	1-1	0-0	0-0	0	1	0	0	0	2
TOTALS	**200**	**38-66**	**14-29**	**13-14**	**33**	**29**	**10**	**3**	**15**	**103**
Percentages		57.6	48.3	92.9						

Coach: Rick Pitino

ARIZONA	MIN	FG	3FG	FT	REB	A	ST	BL	PF	TP
Chase Budinger	36	9-15	2-6	2-3	2	3	0	1	1	22
Nic Wise	36	4-14	2-8	4-6	5	4	1	0	2	14
Jordan Hill	32	6-18	0-0	2-2	11	2	1	0	3	14
Kyle Fogg	29	1-4	1-2	0-0	2	2	0	0	1	3
Zane Johnson	18	1-4	1-4	0-0	1	1	1	0	1	3
David Bagga	1	1-1	1-1	0-0	0	0	1	0	0	3
Jamelle Horne	28	1-5	0-2	0-0	5	2	0	0	3	2
Fendi Onobun	9	1-1	0-0	0-0	2	0	0	0	2	2
Brendon Lavender	5	0-1	0-1	1-2	0	1	0	0	0	1
Alex Jacobson	4	0-0	0-0	0-0	0	0	0	0	0	0
D.J. Shumpert	2	0-0	0-0	0-0	0	0	1	0	0	0
TOTALS	**200**	**24-63**	**7-24**	**9-13**	**28**	**15**	**5**	**1**	**13**	**64**
Percentages		38.1	29.2	69.2						

Coach: Russ Pennell

Officials: Doug Shows, Steve Skiles, Steve Olson
Technicals: None
Attendance: 33,780

67-62

Michigan State	Half	Kansas
29	1H	36
38	2H	26

SWEET 16

MICHIGAN STATE	MIN	FG	3FG	FT	REB	A	ST	BL	PF	TP
Goran Suton	33	8-16	1-3	3-3	9	0	5	1	3	20
Kalin Lucas	35	5-15	1-4	7-7	2	7	4	0	0	18
Durrell Summers	26	3-4	2-3	1-2	5	0	1	0	3	9
Draymond Green	21	3-6	0-0	1-1	1	0	2	0	1	7
Chris Allen	20	2-7	1-4	2-2	3	3	0	0	1	7
Raymar Morgan	13	1-6	0-1	2-2	1	0	0	0	2	4
Travis Walton	29	1-5	0-0	0-0	5	5	1	0	3	2
Delvon Roe	10	0-0	0-0	0-0	1	2	0	0	0	0
Idong Ibok	7	0-0	0-0	0-0	0	0	0	1	2	0
Korie Lucious	4	0-0	0-0	0-0	0	0	0	0	1	0
Marquise Gray	2	0-0	0-0	0-0	0	0	0	0	0	0
TOTALS	**200**	**23-59**	**5-15**	**16-17**	**27**	**17**	**13**	**2**	**16**	**67**
Percentages		39.0	33.3	94.1						

Coach: Tom Izzo

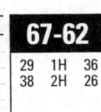

KANSAS	MIN	FG	3FG	FT	REB	A	ST	BL	PF	TP
Sherron Collins	38	9-13	2-5	0-1	2	3	0	0	2	20
Cole Aldrich	34	6-13	0-0	5-6	14	4	2	4	1	17
Tyshawn Taylor	28	2-4	0-1	4-4	1	2	1	0	3	8
Brady Morningstar	34	3-8	0-2	0-0	3	2	2	0	0	6
Marcus Morris	14	1-4	0-0	2-2	2	0	1	0	3	4
Tyrel Reed	21	1-2	1-2	0-0	1	0	0	0	5	3
Markieff Morris	24	1-7	0-2	0-0	7	0	0	0	1	2
Mario Little	7	1-2	0-0	0-0	1	0	1	0	2	2
TOTALS	**200**	**24-53**	**3-12**	**11-13**	**31**	**11**	**7**	**4**	**17**	**62**
Percentages		45.3	25.0	84.6						

Coach: Bill Self

Officials: Jamie Luckie, Doug Sirmons, Michael Stephens
Technicals: None
Attendance: 33,780

72-60

Connecticut	Half	Purdue
30	1H	25
42	2H	35

SWEET 16

CONNECTICUT	MIN	FG	3FG	FT	REB	A	ST	BL	PF	TP
Craig Austrie	32	4-6	3-3	6-6	2	4	1	0	2	17
Hasheem Thabeet	36	6-7	0-0	3-6	15	0	1	4	1	15
A.J. Price	34	5-15	0-3	5-9	4	7	2	0	2	15
Stanley Robinson	37	5-9	0-0	0-1	11	2	0	0	0	10
Jeff Adrien	28	3-13	0-0	2-4	6	2	0	1	2	8
Kemba Walker	19	1-3	0-0	3-4	3	4	2	0	2	5
Gavin Edwards	9	1-1	0-0	0-0	1	0	0	0	3	2
Donnell Beverly	2	0-1	0-1	0-0	0	0	0	0	0	0
Scottie Haralson	2	0-1	0-1	0-0	0	0	0	0	0	0
Jim Veronick	1	0-0	0-0	0-0	0	0	0	1	0	0
TOTALS	**200**	**25-56**	**3-8**	**19-30**	**42**	**19**	**6**	**6**	**12**	**72**
Percentages		44.6	37.5	63.3						

Coach: Jim Calhoun

PURDUE	MIN	FG	3FG	FT	REB	A	ST	BL	PF	TP
Robbie Hummel	35	7-17	3-10	0-0	5	1	3	0	5	17
JaJuan Johnson	29	5-12	0-0	3-4	7	3	1	1	4	13
Lewis Jackson	25	3-5	0-0	2-4	5	2	0	0	4	8
E'Twaun Moore	32	3-10	1-4	0-0	3	0	0	1	2	7
Chris Kramer	27	2-4	0-1	1-3	1	3	2	0	4	5
Keaton Grant	22	1-8	1-4	0-0	4	1	0	0	5	3
Bobby Riddell	1	1-1	1-1	0-0	0	0	0	0	0	3
Nemanja Calasan	14	1-5	0-2	0-0	4	1	0	0	1	2
Marcus Green	13	1-4	0-1	0-0	2	1	1	0	1	2
Chris Reid	1	0-0	0-0	0-0	0	0	0	0	0	0
Ryne Smith	1	0-0	0-0	0-0	0	0	0	0	0	0
TOTALS	**200**	**24-66**	**6-23**	**6-11**	**31**	**12**	**7**	**2**	**26**	**60**
Percentages		36.4	26.1	54.5						

Coach: Matt Painter

Officials: Ed Corbett, Timothy Kitts, Michael Reed
Technicals: None
Attendance: 20,101

102-91

Missouri	Half	Memphis
49	1H	36
53	2H	55

SWEET 16

MISSOURI	MIN	FG	3FG	FT	REB	A	ST	BL	PF	TP
J.T. Tiller	35	10-16	1-2	2-4	4	3	3	0	2	23
DeMarre Carroll	29	6-11	0-1	5-8	6	6	2	1	4	17
Leo Lyons	29	2-9	0-0	11-18	12	2	0	2	5	15
Zaire Taylor	22	5-7	0-1	4-5	4	1	2	0	2	14
Matt Lawrence	27	4-7	3-6	2-4	3	1	1	0	1	13
Justin Safford	13	3-3	1-1	0-0	0	0	0	0	1	7
Kim English	12	0-3	0-2	6-6	1	2	0	0	1	6
Marcus Denmon	11	2-3	1-2	0-0	1	0	0	0	1	5
Laurence Bowers	6	1-1	0-0	0-0	0	1	0	0	3	2
Miguel Paul	13	0-2	0-1	0-0	1	1	1	0	1	0
Keith Ramsey	3	0-0	0-0	0-0	0	0	0	0	3	0
TOTALS	**200**	**33-62**	**6-16**	**30-45**	**32**	**17**	**9**	**3**	**24**	**102**
Percentages		53.2	37.5	66.7						

Coach: Mike Anderson

MEMPHIS	MIN	FG	3FG	FT	REB	A	ST	BL	PF	TP
Tyreke Evans	39	12-25	0-3	9-9	5	4	2	0	1	33
Robert Dozier	36	8-11	0-0	3-6	16	2	2	1	4	19
Antonio Anderson	38	8-13	0-1	2-7	5	5	0	1	5	18
Roburt Sallie	28	3-5	3-5	3-4	0	3	3	2	5	12
Shawn Taggart	32	4-8	0-1	1-2	8	0	1	1	5	9
Doneal Mack	18	0-7	0-5	0-4	3	2	0	1	1	0
Wesley Witherspoon	6	0-0	0-0	0-0	1	0	0	0	4	0
Willie Kemp	3	0-0	0-0	0-0	0	0	0	0	0	0
TOTALS	**200**	**35-69**	**3-15**	**18-32**	**38**	**16**	**8**	**6**	**25**	**91**
Percentages		50.7	20.0	56.2						

Coach: John Calipari

Officials: Kelly Self, Ted Valentine, Brian O'Connell
Technicals: Memphis (team)
Attendance: 20,101

60-55

Pittsburgh	Half	Xavier
29	1H	37
31	2H	18

SWEET 16

PITTSBURGH	MIN	FG	3FG	FT	REB	A	ST	BL	PF	TP
Sam Young	40	7-16	1-2	4-4	3	1	1	0	1	19
Levance Fields	33	5-11	2-5	2-5	2	6	2	0	2	14
DeJuan Blair	35	5-16	0-0	0-1	17	1	3	2	3	10
Gilbert Brown	23	2-5	1-2	2-2	6	1	0	0	3	7
Brad Wanamaker	20	1-5	0-1	4-7	4	0	1	0	0	6
Jermaine Dixon	27	2-9	0-3	0-0	3	0	1	1	1	4
Tyrell Biggs	11	0-0	0-0	0-0	3	0	1	0	2	0
Ashton Gibbs	8	0-3	0-2	0-0	0	0	0	0	0	0
Gary McGhee	3	0-0	0-0	0-0	0	0	0	0	1	0
TOTALS	**200**	**22-65**	**4-15**	**12-19**	**38**	**9**	**9**	**3**	**13**	**60**
Percentages		33.8	26.7	63.2						

Coach: Jamie Dixon

XAVIER	MIN	FG	3FG	FT	REB	A	ST	BL	PF	TP
B.J. Raymond	36	6-19	1-8	2-2	3	0	0	0	3	15
Derrick Brown	32	6-15	2-6	0-0	9	2	2	2	2	14
Dante' Jackson	29	4-7	1-3	0-0	3	0	2	0	5	9
C.J. Anderson	27	2-9	0-0	2-2	8	3	0	0	2	6
Kenny Frease	17	1-3	0-0	2-2	2	1	0	5	1	4
Brad Redford	9	1-4	1-4	0-0	0	0	0	0	1	3
Jamel McLean	15	1-4	0-0	0-0	5	0	0	0	0	2
Jason Love	19	0-0	0-0	1-2	6	1	0	0	2	1
Terrell Holloway	16	0-3	0-2	1-2	2	2	0	0	1	1
TOTALS	**200**	**21-64**	**5-23**	**8-10**	**38**	**9**	**4**	**7**	**17**	**55**
Percentages		32.8	21.7	80.0						

Coach: Sean Miller

Officials: Bob Donato, Rick Hartzell, Joe Lindsay
Technicals: None
Attendance: 18,831

77-54

Villanova	Half	Duke
26	1H	23
51	2H	31

SWEET 16

VILLANOVA	MIN	FG	3FG	FT	REB	A	ST	BL	PF	TP
Scottie Reynolds	32	5-15	2-6	4-4	3	1	2	1	2	16
Dante Cunningham	33	5-13	0-0	4-6	11	0	1	1	4	14
Reggie Redding	32	4-7	1-2	2-2	9	4	1	2	3	11
Dwayne Anderson	26	4-8	0-2	0-0	7	2	0	0	4	8
Shane Clark	22	3-5	0-1	1-1	5	1	0	0	5	7
Corey Stokes	21	2-7	1-4	2-2	4	1	0	1	3	7
Corey Fisher	24	1-6	0-3	4-6	3	0	1	0	2	6
Antonio Pena	8	1-1	0-0	2-2	3	0	0	0	0	4
Frank Tchuisi	1	2-2	0-0	0-0	1	0	0	0	0	4
Jason Colenda	1	0-0	0-0	0-0	0	0	0	0	0	0
TOTALS	**200**	**27-64**	**4-18**	**19-23**	**46**	**9**	**5**	**5**	**23**	**77**
Percentages		42.2	22.2	82.6						

Coach: Jay Wright

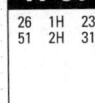

DUKE	MIN	FG	3FG	FT	REB	A	ST	BL	PF	TP
Kyle Singler	36	5-13	1-6	4-7	6	1	2	0	3	15
Jon Scheyer	36	3-18	2-10	5-7	2	2	3	0	0	13
Gerald Henderson	28	1-14	1-5	4-4	9	1	0	1	4	7
Elliot Williams	23	1-3	0-1	3-3	1	1	1	0	2	5
Nolan Smith	16	2-6	0-3	0-0	2	1	1	0	4	4
Brian Zoubek	14	2-2	0-0	0-0	2	0	0	1	2	4
Lance Thomas	21	1-2	0-0	1-3	5	0	0	0	4	3
Greg Paulus	10	1-2	1-2	0-0	0	1	0	0	4	3
David McClure	14	0-0	0-0	0-0	5	0	1	0	1	0
Olek Czyz	1	0-0	0-0	0-0	0	0	0	0	0	0
Martynas Pocius	1	0-0	0-0	0-0	0	0	0	0	0	0
TOTALS	**200**	**16-60**	**5-27**	**17-24**	**32**	**7**	**8**	**2**	**24**	**54**
Percentages		26.7	18.5	70.8						

Coach: Mike Krzyzewski

Officials: Mike Stuart, Karl Hess, J.D. Collins
Technicals: None
Attendance: 18,831

98-77 (1H: 53–42; 2H: 45–35) — SWEET 16

NORTH CAROLINA	MIN	FG	3FG	FT	REB	A	ST	BL	PF	TP
Tyler Hansbrough	34	8-10	0-0	8-9	10	0	2	0	2	24
Wayne Ellington	30	7-13	2-6	3-4	7	4	0	0	2	19
Ty Lawson	27	7-9	3-4	2-3	4	9	1	0	3	19
Danny Green	28	5-11	3-6	0-0	3	7	4	2	4	13
Bobby Frasor	20	2-2	2-2	0-0	3	1	0	1	1	6
Ed Davis	20	2-6	0-0	1-4	5	1	1	1	0	5
Deon Thompson	18	2-8	0-0	1-4	3	0	0	0	2	5
Tyler Zeller	5	2-4	0-0	0-0	2	0	0	0	0	4
Larry Drew II	8	1-2	1-1	0-3	0	0	0	0	1	3
Justin Watts	3	0-0	0-0	0-0	1	0	0	0	0	0
Mike Copeland	2	0-2	0-0	0-0	2	0	0	0	1	0
J.B. Tanner	2	0-1	0-0	0-0	0	1	0	0	1	0
Jack Wooten	2	0-0	0-0	0-0	0	0	0	0	0	0
Marc Campbell	1	0-0	0-0	0-0	0	0	0	0	0	0
TOTALS	200	36-68	11-19	15-27	40	23	8	4	17	98
Percentages		52.9	57.9	55.6						

Coach: Roy Williams

GONZAGA	MIN	FG	3FG	FT	REB	A	ST	BL	PF	TP
Jeremy Pargo	29	6-10	1-3	3-4	3	2	1	0	4	16
Josh Heytvelt	29	5-9	0-1	4-8	0	0	0	0	4	14
Micah Downs	28	5-7	2-4	0-0	4	2	3	1	3	12
Austin Daye	32	3-8	2-3	2-2	11	2	0	4	4	10
Matt Bouldin	30	3-10	0-5	1-1	4	0	1	0	1	7
Steven Gray	26	3-9	1-5	0-0	1	3	1	0	0	7
Ira Brown	4	1-1	1-1	4-4	3	0	0	0	0	7
Demetri Goodson	19	1-3	0-0	1-2	2	1	0	0	3	3
Andrew Sorenson	2	0-1	0-1	1-2	0	0	0	0	0	1
Will Foster	1	0-0	0-0	0-0	0	0	0	0	0	0
TOTALS	200	27-58	7-23	16-23	28	10	6	5	19	77
Percentages		46.6	30.4	69.6						

Coach: Mark Few

Officials: M Whitehead, Scott Thorn John Higgin **Technicals:** None **Attendance:** 17,103

84-71 (1H: 39–26; 2H: 45–45) — SWEET 16

OKLAHOMA	MIN	FG	3FG	FT	REB	A	ST	BL	PF	TP
Blake Griffin	33	12-15	0-0	6-10	14	3	1	0	2	30
Tony Crocker	37	9-17	6-11	4-6	3	2	3	1	0	28
Austin Johnson	38	4-8	1-2	0-0	5	6	3	1	3	9
Taylor Griffin	37	4-8	0-0	1-2	5	3	3	0	3	9
Willie Warren	36	2-7	2-5	0-0	4	5	1	0	1	6
Cade Davis	7	1-3	0-2	0-0	0	0	0	0	2	2
Orlando Allen	5	0-0	0-0	0-0	2	0	0	1	1	0
Juan Pattillo	2	0-0	0-0	0-0	1	0	0	0	0	0
Ryan Wright	2	0-0	0-0	0-0	0	0	0	0	2	0
T.J. Franklin	1	0-0	0-0	0-0	0	0	0	0	0	0
Beau Gerber	1	0-0	0-0	0-0	1	0	0	0	0	0
Ray Willis	1	0-1	0-1	0-0	0	0	0	0	0	0
TOTALS	200	32-59	9-21	11-18	35	19	11	3	14	84
Percentages		54.2	42.9	61.1						

Coach: Jeff Capel III

SYRACUSE	MIN	FG	3FG	FT	REB	A	ST	BL	PF	TP
Jonny Flynn	39	9-16	1-4	3-3	2	6	0	0	1	22
Andy Rautins	28	4-12	3-10	1-1	2	2	3	0	1	12
Eric Devendorf	35	3-12	2-7	0-0	2	2	4	0	2	8
Rick Jackson	31	4-5	0-0	0-2	3	0	2	1	1	8
Arinze Onuaku	24	3-4	0-0	1-2	6	0	0	1	2	7
Paul Harris	24	1-5	0-1	4-4	6	1	0	0	0	6
Kris Joseph	8	2-3	1-1	1-1	1	0	1	0	1	6
Justin Thomas	1	1-3	0-1	0-1	1	0	0	0	0	2
Kristof Ongenaet	7	0-0	0-0	0-0	2	1	0	0	2	0
Jake Presutti	1	0-0	0-0	0-0	0	0	0	0	0	0
Brandon Reese	1	0-0	0-0	0-0	1	1	0	0	0	0
Sean Williams	1	0-0	0-0	0-0	0	0	0	0	0	0
TOTALS	200	27-60	7-24	10-14	26	13	10	2	10	71
Percentages		45.0	29.2	71.4						

Coach: Jim Boeheim

Officials: Dick Cartmell, Paul Janssen, Gary Maxwell **Technicals:** None **Attendance:** 17,103

64-52 (1H: 30–27; 2H: 34–25) — ELITE 8

MICHIGAN STATE	MIN	FG	3FG	FT	REB	A	ST	BL	PF	TP
Goran Suton	32	7-15	3-5	2-4	10	4	1	1	2	19
Durrell Summers	25	4-6	2-3	2-2	3	1	0	0	1	12
Kalin Lucas	30	3-7	2-4	2-3	3	5	1	0	2	10
Travis Walton	30	3-8	0-0	2-2	2	2	2	0	3	8
Draymond Green	24	3-6	0-0	0-0	10	3	2	0	3	6
Korie Lucious	5	1-1	1-1	0-0	0	0	1	0	0	3
Chris Allen	18	1-5	0-2	0-0	4	3	0	0	2	2
Delvon Roe	14	1-1	0-0	0-0	0	1	0	0	2	2
Marquise Gray	7	1-1	0-0	0-0	1	0	0	0	3	2
Raymar Morgan	10	0-2	0-1	0-0	2	0	0	0	4	0
Jon Crandell	1	0-0	0-0	0-0	0	0	0	0	0	0
Isaiah Dahlman	1	0-0	0-0	0-0	0	0	0	0	0	0
Tom Herzog	1	0-0	0-0	0-0	0	0	0	0	0	0
Idong Ibok	1	0-0	0-0	0-0	0	0	0	0	0	0
Austin Thornton	1	0-0	0-0	0-0	0	0	0	0	0	0
TOTALS	200	24-52	8-16	8-11	35	19	7	1	22	64
Percentages		46.2	50.0	72.7						

Coach: Tom Izzo

LOUISVILLE	MIN	FG	3FG	FT	REB	A	ST	BL	PF	TP
Earl Clark	40	8-17	2-5	1-4	5	2	0	1	3	19
Preston Knowles	24	4-7	2-3	1-2	2	2	2	0	1	11
Jerry Smith	16	3-5	1-2	1-2	1	0	1	0	4	8
Terrence Williams	35	1-7	0-3	3-4	6	4	0	1	0	5
Edgar Sosa	16	1-1	1-1	2-2	1	2	0	0	2	5
Terrence Jennings	18	1-2	0-0	2-4	2	0	2	0	0	4
Andre McGee	24	0-1	0-1	0-0	2	1	2	0	1	0
Samardo Samuels	22	0-6	0-0	0-0	7	0	0	2	3	0
Reginald Delk	4	0-1	0-1	0-0	0	1	0	1	1	0
Jared Swopshire	1	0-0	0-0	0-0	1	0	0	0	0	0
TOTALS	200	18-47	6-16	10-18	27	12	7	5	15	52
Percentages		38.3	37.5	55.6						

Coach: Rick Pitino

Officials: David Hall, Curtis Shaw, Tony Greene **Technicals:** None **Attendance:** 36,084

82-75 (1H: 44–38; 2H: 38–37) — ELITE 8

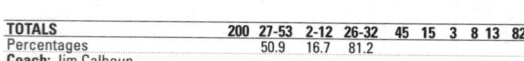

CONNECTICUT	MIN	FG	3FG	FT	REB	A	ST	BL	PF	TP
Kemba Walker	25	7-9	0-1	9-10	5	5	0	0	1	23
A.J. Price	34	6-17	1-6	5-7	3	3	0	0	1	18
Stanley Robinson	34	4-7	0-1	5-6	6	0	0	4	2	13
Jeff Adrien	39	5-8	0-0	2-2	10	4	2	3	2	12
Craig Austrie	27	1-4	1-4	4-4	1	1	1	0	2	7
Hasheem Thabeet	26	2-4	0-0	1-3	13	2	0	0	3	5
Gavin Edwards	13	1-3	0-0	0-0	7	0	0	1	1	2
Donnell Beverly	2	1-1	0-0	0-0	0	0	0	0	1	2
TOTALS	200	27-53	2-12	26-32	45	15	3	8	13	82
Percentages		50.9	16.7	81.2						

Coach: Jim Calhoun

MISSOURI	MIN	FG	3FG	FT	REB	A	ST	BL	PF	TP
Matt Lawrence	27	5-12	3-7	0-0	3	2	1	0	1	13
Leo Lyons	25	5-11	0-1	3-4	2	4	2	0	4	13
DeMarre Carroll	24	6-14	0-3	0-0	4	0	0	0	4	12
Justin Safford	15	4-8	1-2	0-1	3	0	0	0	1	9
Zaire Taylor	36	3-13	1-4	1-2	2	4	2	0	2	8
J.T. Tiller	26	3-4	0-0	2-4	5	5	2	0	5	8
Keith Ramsey	17	4-5	0-0	0-1	3	3	2	1	3	8
Marcus Denmon	14	1-3	0-1	0-0	2	2	0	0	2	2
Miguel Paul	5	1-2	0-0	0-0	0	1	0	0	0	2
Kim English	8	0-4	0-0	0-0	2	0	0	0	1	0
Laurence Bowers	2	0-0	0-0	0-0	0	0	1	0	0	0
Michael Anderson Jr.	1	0-0	0-0	0-0	0	0	0	0	1	0
TOTALS	200	32-76	5-18	6-12	26	21	10	1	24	75
Percentages		42.1	27.8	50.0						

Coach: Mike Anderson

Officials: John Cahill, Mike Littlewood, Les Jones **Technicals:** None **Attendance:** 18,886

78-76 (1H: 32–34; 2H: 46–42) — ELITE 8

VILLANOVA	MIN	FG	3FG	FT	REB	A	ST	BL	PF	TP
Dwayne Anderson	28	5-10	2-6	5-5	6	0	4	0	3	17
Scottie Reynolds	33	4-11	0-3	7-7	2	1	0	0	3	15
Dante Cunningham	30	6-11	0-0	2-2	5	2	0	1	4	14
Shane Clark	26	4-7	3-4	0-0	4	0	0	0	4	11
Corey Fisher	18	1-7	0-3	7-7	4	2	0	0	3	9
Corey Stokes	23	3-4	1-2	0-0	2	0	0	1	1	7
Reggie Redding	36	2-6	0-2	1-2	6	4	2	3	4	5
Antonio Pena	6	0-0	0-0	0-0	0	0	0	0	2	0
TOTALS	200	25-56	6-20	22-23	29	9	6	5	24	78
Percentages		44.6	30.0	95.7						

Coach: Jay Wright

PITTSBURGH	MIN	FG	3FG	FT	REB	A	ST	BL	PF	TP
Sam Young	38	10-17	3-7	5-5	7	0	0	1	1	28
DeJuan Blair	34	9-9	0-0	2-6	10	2	2	0	3	20
Levance Fields	37	2-8	2-5	4-4	3	6	0	0	2	10
Gilbert Brown	21	2-4	0-0	4-6	2	2	0	1	1	8
Brad Wanamaker	29	1-3	0-1	3-4	1	2	2	0	5	5
Jermaine Dixon	20	1-6	0-2	3-4	1	2	1	0	3	5
Tyrell Biggs	15	0-2	0-0	0-0	2	0	0	1	2	0
Ashton Gibbs	6	0-3	0-3	0-0	1	0	1	0	1	0
TOTALS	200	25-52	5-18	21-29	27	14	4	3	18	76
Percentages		48.1	27.8	72.4						

Coach: Jamie Dixon

Officials: Tom O'Neill, Pat Driscoll, Randy Mccall **Technicals:** None **Attendance:** 18,871

72-60 (1H: 32–23; 2H: 40–37) — ELITE 8

NORTH CAROLINA	MIN	FG	3FG	FT	REB	A	ST	BL	PF	TP
Ty Lawson	36	6-13	2-4	5-6	5	5	3	1	2	19
Danny Green	32	6-9	2-4	4-4	3	1	1	1	2	18
Deon Thompson	26	5-9	0-0	0-0	1	2	1	0	3	10
Wayne Ellington	34	3-9	1-5	2-2	3	1	0	0	0	9
Tyler Hansbrough	26	2-4	0-0	4-4	6	3	2	0	2	8
Ed Davis	16	2-4	0-0	0-0	3	0	2	0	4	4
Tyler Zeller	6	1-1	0-0	0-2	2	1	0	0	0	2
Larry Drew II	2	1-2	0-1	0-0	1	0	0	0	0	2
Bobby Frasor	13	0-0	0-0	0-0	3	0	0	0	4	0
Justin Watts	4	0-0	0-0	0-0	0	0	0	0	0	0
Marc Campbell	2	0-0	0-0	0-0	0	0	0	0	0	0
Mike Copeland	1	0-0	0-0	0-0	0	0	0	0	0	0
Patrick Moody	1	0-0	0-0	0-0	0	0	0	0	0	0
J.B. Tanner	1	0-0	0-0	0-0	0	0	0	0	0	0
TOTALS	200	26-51	5-14	15-16	27	13	9	2	19	72
Percentages		51.0	35.7	93.8						

Coach: Roy Williams

OKLAHOMA	MIN	FG	3FG	FT	REB	A	ST	BL	PF	TP
Blake Griffin	38	9-12	0-0	5-8	16	1	0	0	4	23
Willie Warren	36	6-16	2-9	4-4	1	3	1	0	1	18
Juan Pattillo	24	4-5	0-0	1-4	6	0	1	0	1	9
Taylor Griffin	37	2-6	0-1	0-0	2	0	0	0	5	4
Tony Crocker	25	2-8	0-5	0-0	1	1	3	0	3	4
Austin Johnson	29	1-5	0-2	0-0	1	3	1	0	4	2
Omar Leary	5	0-1	0-1	0-0	0	1	0	0	1	0
Cade Davis	4	0-1	0-1	0-0	0	0	0	0	0	0
Orlando Allen	2	0-0	0-0	0-0	0	0	0	0	0	0
TOTALS	200	24-54	2-19	10-16	27	9	6	0	20	60
Percentages		44.4	10.5	62.5						

Coach: Jeff Capel III

Officials: Verne Harris, John Hughes, Tom Eades **Technicals:** None **Attendance:** 17,025

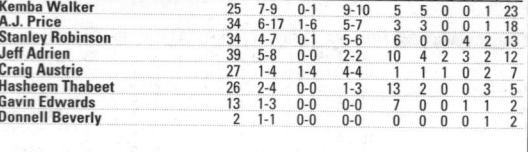

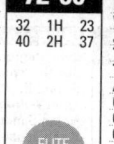

MICHIGAN STATE	MIN	FG	3FG	FT	REB	A	ST	BL	PF	TP
Kalin Lucas	33	7-15	3-6	4-6	2	5	0	0	1	21
Raymar Morgan	30	7-13	0-0	4-6	9	1	5	0	3	18
Korie Lucious	9	3-8	2-5	3-3	0	0	0	0	0	11
Durrell Summers	23	4-9	1-5	1-1	6	1	1	0	2	10
Draymond Green	12	3-4	0-0	2-4	2	1	1	0	5	8
Goran Suton	28	2-5	0-1	0-0	7	2	2	1	4	4
Delvon Roe	21	2-4	0-0	0-0	8	0	0	2	2	4
Travis Walton	23	1-6	0-0	0-0	0	8	2	0	3	2
Chris Allen	9	1-6	0-2	0-0	2	0	0	0	1	2
Marquise Gray	6	1-2	0-0	0-0	2	0	0	0	1	2
Idong Ibok	6	0-0	0-0	0-0	2	0	0	0	3	0
TOTALS	**200**	**31-72**	**6-19**	**14-20**	**40**	**18**	**11**	**3**	**25**	**82**
Percentages		43.1	31.6	70.0						

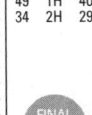

Coach: Tom Izzo

82-73

38	1H	36
44	2H	37

FINAL 4

CONNECTICUT	MIN	FG	3FG	FT	REB	A	ST	BL	PF	TP
Hasheem Thabeet	36	6-13	0-0	5-7	6	1	1	2	3	17
A.J. Price	32	5-20	1-3	4-4	6	1	2	0	3	15
Stanley Robinson	31	5-6	1-1	4-4	13	0	0	2	3	15
Jeff Adrien	32	5-10	0-0	3-7	7	1	0	2	2	13
Craig Austrie	37	2-4	0-2	2-2	3	2	0	0	2	6
Kemba Walker	20	1-5	0-0	3-9	2	2	1	0	4	5
Gavin Edwards	10	1-1	0-0	0-0	4	1	1	1	1	2
Donnell Beverly	2	0-0	0-0	0-0	0	0	0	0	0	0
TOTALS	**200**	**25-59**	**2-6**	**21-33**	**41**	**8**	**5**	**7**	**18**	**73**
Percentages		42.4	33.3	63.6						

Coach: Jim Calhoun

Officials: John Cahill, Mike Stuart, Les Jones
Technicals: None
Attendance: 72,456

NORTH CAROLINA	MIN	FG	3FG	FT	REB	A	ST	BL	PF	TP
Ty Lawson	34	5-11	2-4	10-17	7	8	2	0	3	22
Wayne Ellington	35	7-14	5-7	1-2	9	4	0	0	0	20
Tyler Hansbrough	33	5-13	0-1	8-12	11	1	4	0	4	18
Danny Green	27	4-11	4-10	0-0	3	1	0	3	4	12
Deon Thompson	20	2-6	0-0	2-3	4	0	0	2	4	6
Ed Davis	22	2-5	0-0	1-3	5	0	0	1	2	5
Bobby Frasor	19	0-1	0-0	0-0	7	1	0	0	2	0
Larry Drew II	7	0-0	0-0	0-0	0	1	0	0	0	0
Tyler Zeller	3	0-1	0-0	0-0	0	0	0	0	1	0
TOTALS	**200**	**25-62**	**11-22**	**22-37**	**46**	**16**	**6**	**6**	**20**	**83**
Percentages		40.3	50.0	59.5						

Coach: Roy Williams

83-69

49	1H	40
34	2H	29

FINAL 4

VILLANOVA	MIN	FG	3FG	FT	REB	A	ST	BL	PF	TP
Scottie Reynolds	34	6-18	3-11	2-3	4	5	1	0	3	17
Reggie Redding	29	5-9	2-3	3-3	4	0	0	1	3	15
Corey Fisher	25	5-19	0-4	3-6	7	2	0	0	2	13
Dante Cunningham	35	5-13	0-0	2-2	12	1	1	0	5	12
Dwayne Anderson	31	2-12	0-6	2-2	11	0	3	0	5	6
Shane Clark	18	3-4	0-0	0-0	6	0	1	1	4	6
Corey Stokes	20	0-3	0-3	0-0	3	0	1	0	2	0
Antonio Pena	8	0-1	0-0	0-0	3	0	0	1	2	0
TOTALS	**200**	**26-79**	**5-27**	**12-16**	**50**	**8**	**7**	**3**	**26**	**69**
Percentages		32.9	18.5	75.0						

Coach: Jay Wright

Officials: Scott Thornley, Karl Hess, Pat Driscoll
Technicals: None
Attendance: 72,456

NORTH CAROLINA	MIN	FG	3FG	FT	REB	A	ST	BL	PF	TP
Ty Lawson	37	3-10	0-3	15-18	4	6	8	0	0	21
Wayne Ellington	35	7-12	3-3	2-2	4	0	0	0	2	19
Tyler Hansbrough	34	6-14	0-2	6-10	7	2	0	0	3	18
Ed Davis	14	5-7	0-0	1-4	8	0	0	0	4	11
Deon Thompson	23	3-8	0-0	3-4	3	0	0	0	4	9
Danny Green	24	2-4	2-3	0-0	3	4	1	0	5	6
Bobby Frasor	23	1-2	0-1	0-0	1	1	0	0	3	2
Justin Watts	1	1-2	0-0	0-0	1	0	0	0	0	2
Tyler Zeller	1	0-0	0-0	1-2	1	0	0	0	1	1
Larry Drew II	4	0-1	0-0	0-0	0	0	0	0	0	0
Marc Campbell	1	0-1	0-0	0-0	1	0	0	0	0	0
Mike Copeland	1	0-0	0-0	0-0	0	0	0	0	0	0
Patrick Moody	1	0-0	0-0	0-0	0	0	0	0	0	0
J.B. Tanner	1	0-0	0-0	0-0	0	0	0	0	0	0
TOTALS	**200**	**28-61**	**5-12**	**28-40**	**33**	**13**	**9**	**0**	**22**	**89**
Percentages		45.9	41.7	70.0						

Coach: Roy Williams

89-72

55	1H	34
34	2H	38

NCAA FINAL 2009

MICHIGAN STATE	MIN	FG	3FG	FT	REB	A	ST	BL	PF	TP
Goran Suton	31	7-10	3-4	0-0	11	0	0	2	3	17
Kalin Lucas	35	4-12	0-1	6-8	0	7	0	0	2	14
Durrell Summers	21	4-10	2-6	3-4	5	2	0	1	1	13
Draymond Green	12	2-2	0-0	3-5	7	0	1	0	3	7
Korie Lucious	14	2-5	2-5	0-0	0	0	0	0	3	6
Raymar Morgan	19	1-2	0-0	2-2	1	0	0	0	5	4
Chris Allen	17	0-8	0-7	3-5	1	1	0	0	2	3
Travis Walton	24	0-2	0-0	2-2	1	3	0	0	3	2
Delvon Roe	17	1-1	0-0	0-1	8	0	0	1	3	2
Austin Thornton	3	0-1	0-0	2-2	3	0	0	0	1	2
Isaiah Dahlman	1	1-1	0-0	0-0	1	0	0	0	0	2
Marquise Gray	3	0-1	0-0	0-0	1	0	0	0	2	0
Jon Crandell	1	0-0	0-0	0-0	0	0	0	0	0	0
Tom Herzog	1	0-0	0-0	0-0	0	0	0	1	0	0
Idong Ibok	1	0-0	0-0	0-0	1	0	0	0	0	0
TOTALS	**200**	**22-55**	**7-23**	**21-29**	**40**	**13**	**1**	**5**	**28**	**72**
Percentages		40.0	30.4	72.4						

Coach: Tom Izzo

Officials: Tom O'Neill, Curtis Shaw, Tony Greene
Technicals: None
Attendance: 72,922

National Invitation Tournament (NIT)

First Round: San Diego St. d. Weber State 65-49, Kansas State d. Illinois State 83-79 (OT), Davidson d. South Carolina 70-63, Saint Mary's (CA) d. Washington State 68-57, Auburn d. Tennessee-Martin 87-82, Tulsa d. Northwestern 68-59, Baylor d. Georgetown 74-72, Virginia Tech d. Duquesne 116-108 (2OT), Creighton d. Bowling Green 73-71, Kentucky d. UNLV 70-60, New Mexico d. Nebraska 83-71, Notre Dame d. UAB 70-64, Florida d. Jacksonville 84-62, Miami d. Providence 78-66, Rhode Island d. Niagara 68-62, Penn State d. George Mason 77-73 (OT)

Second Round: San Diego St. d. Kansas State 70-52, Saint Mary's (CA) d. Davidson 80-68, Auburn d. Tulsa 74-55, Baylor d. Virginia Tech 84-66, Kentucky d. Creighton 65-63, Notre Dame d. New Mexico 70-68, Florida d. Miami 74-60, Penn State d. Rhode Island 83-72

Quarterfinals: San Diego St. d. Saint Mary's (CA) 70-66, Baylor d. Auburn 74-72, Notre Dame d. Kentucky 77-67, Penn State d. Florida 71-62

Semifinals: Baylor d. San Diego State 76-62, Penn State d. Notre Dame 67-59

Finals: Penn State d. Baylor 69-63

MVP: Jamelle Cornley, Penn State

RANKINGS AND RECORDS

The Ratings Are In

How the Polo Grounds and MIT prepared a lifelong sports fan for the task of determining the all-time king of college basketball

BY JEFF SAGARIN

Wondering how it is that we determined Kentucky is the greatest college basketball program of all time? It all goes back to the Polo Grounds.

In the spring of 1957, my dad took me to my first baseball game, between the Dodgers and the Giants, at the venerable (and long-since torn down) stadium in upper Manhattan. I was 8 at the time, and that 1957 season was the first one I truly followed day to day, reading box scores and rooting for the Dodgers. By the fall of 1958, I was thoroughly mesmerized by sports—baseball, football, basketball, hockey, boxing, Olympic track and field, tennis, golf. I also loved doing arithmetic, in particular figuring out batting averages.

So it was only natural that I started entering a weekly college football contest published in the New York *Daily News*. Not only did you have to pick the winners of 15 college games, you also had to predict the score of each game in the event a tiebreaker was needed. That started me thinking about the whole idea of how to determine which team was better than the other.

Now, I had just turned 10, so my method wasn't exactly rigorous. I simply would get the weekly *New York Times* summary of all the teams, grouped by conference, with their win-loss-tie and points for–points against records listed. And I figured that if a team was 4–0 with an average winning margin of 20 points per game, it was a "sure thing" to defeat a team that was 2–2 with an average margin of zero per game. Unfortunately, such a simple method of picking outcomes never won me the $500 weekly first prize! I was simply mystified that so many shocking—to me—upsets occurred. Of course, what was actually going on was that the 4–0 team might have played a bunch of patsies, all at home, while the 2–2 team might have played four tough opponents, with three of those games on the road.

The week-by-week experience of entering that contest over the next four years primed the thought process that resulted in my rating system for sports teams. When I took my love of math and sports to MIT, I eventually came to realize that the key elements of rating a team were *who, what, where* and, to some extent, *when. Who* did they play? *What* was the result in terms of score, win, loss or tie? *Where* was the game played, home or away? You can also factor in the *when* by giving extra weight to postseason events like bowls, tournaments and playoff games.

And so in the fall of 1971, at age 23, I started fooling around with my first real mathematical system to rate NFL teams. In retrospect, my methodology wasn't that advanced; I could actually do it with paper and pencil once I calculated a detailed "adjustment chart." The idea for the adjustment chart was kind of simple, and yet it worked quite well: Give each team a reasonable initial rating based on human opinion, and then, beginning in the first week of the season, determine the predicted outcome for each game. Then factor in the results to adjust each team's rating. And of course, I took into account the location of the game in making the prediction. So, for example, if the Raiders at home had been expected to beat the Chargers by seven points and won by only three, the Raiders' rating would decline somewhat and the Chargers' would rise.

In the spring of 1972 I wrote to more than 100 newspapers, hoping that someone would want to publish my ratings. I got one response. William Wallace, a reporter for *The New York Times,* called to interview me about my system. His story appeared in *Pro Quarterback* magazine and I was hired to be the weekly prognosticator for a publication called *Insiders Pro Football Newsletter,* published by *Pro Football Weekly*. By then, an old MIT friend had showed me how a computer language called FORTRAN could do all the work of my chart-paper-pencil formula. FORTRAN wasn't exactly the height of sophistication—all the data and programming was on IBM punch cards.

Over the years, I've made many improvements to my formula, and my current program is probably about 30 times longer in code than the original. As I mastered my pro football formula, I added ratings systems for NBA teams in the fall of 1972, college football in 1973 and college basketball in 1974. My systems are now so complex that I couldn't possibly do the calculations with paper and pencil anymore. But the underpinnings are still the same—*who, what, where* and sometimes *when.*

That brings me to April 2007, when the editors of the *ESPN College Basketball Encyclopedia* asked me if I could generate all-time ESPN/Sagarin ratings for all of the Division I basketball programs active through the 2008-09 season. I pointed out the difficulty of gathering all the scores from all the teams, some going back 100 years. No such collection existed and there was no central source for reliable information. It turned out that there were many contradictory results in the schools' media guides from old seasons. For instance, both Arkansas and Texas Tech claimed they won their matchup on Feb. 6, 1968, by a score of 61-56. But the NCAA lists Texas Tech's record for that year as 9–15 instead of the 10–14 that the school lists in its season records. Thus, we concluded that the Razorbacks must have actually won that game. Credit for reconciling these differences goes to ESPN's Doug Kern and the rest of the Stats & Information Group, which persevered against all obstacles and did a phenomenal job compiling a master database of scores.

In compiling the database and weeding out as many errors as possible, we made a number of remarkable discoveries. None was more meaningful to me than the case of Sal Sclafani. In the summer of 1958, a year after my first trip to the Polo Grounds, I learned to hit a curveball thanks to Sclafani, who ran the outdoor activities at my elementary school. One of the stories Sal told us was that he had played basketball for Rhode Island in the NIT when some guy hit a 60-foot shot at the end of a game. None of us had any idea what he was talking about or any way to check his story—no ESPN, no Internet and certainly no time to scour libraries for old newspaper clippings. While working on this project, I discovered that, yes indeed, Sal Sclafani played at Rhode Island and was on the 1946 team that lost the NIT championship game to Kentucky, 46-45. And yes, in that tournament Rhode Island beat Bowling Green, 82-79, in overtime after Ernie Calverly indeed hit a 62-foot shot to tie it at the end of regulation (okay, so Sal was off by two feet).

As you scour our all-time ratings, and the just-for-kicks custom ratings that follow (best programs by decade, best teams never to win a national championship, worst champions of all time), I'm sure a flood of memories will come back to you, as well. That's perhaps the best thing about what I do: For all the math that goes into my ratings, it's really about making history come alive.

My systems are now so complex that I couldn't possibly do the calculations with paper and pencil anymore. But the underpinnings are still the same—who, what, where and sometimes when.

THE ESPN/SAGARIN ALL-TIME RANKINGS

We know what you're thinking: How in the world did UCLA not come out on top? Well, as dominant as the Bruins were under John Wooden, they didn't even rank as a top-40 program in the 1940s. Meanwhile, Kentucky hasn't finished lower than 10th in any decade. We're guessing you're nearly as shocked by Northwestern's No. 77 ranking—pretty remarkable for a team that's never made the NCAA Tournament. But with eight Big Ten programs in the Top 20, the Wildcats have faced some of college basketball's toughest conference slates for more than seven decades. Just goes to show how much strength of schedule matters. **About the Rankings:** Only active Division I programs are listed in the all-time ranking. CHESS (named for the system of rating chess players) considers only a school's wins and losses. PREDICTOR considers only its scoring margin. RATING is a combination of the two. YRS indicates the number of seasons in which the program qualified for ranking, beginning in 1937-38 (the maximum number is 72). Schools that played fewer than five games against other qualified schools during a season did not qualify for that season, nor did schools that did not field teams or were on NCAA probation. A small penalty was assessed to a team's rating for every season in which it failed to qualify.

		RATING	CHESS	PREDICTOR	YRS
1	Kentucky	**89.81**	89.56	89.65	71
2	UCLA	**87.57**	87.45	87.36	72
3	Kansas	**87.27**	86.85	87.18	72
4	North Carolina	**87.19**	87.33	86.70	72
5	Indiana	**87.17**	87.02	86.93	72
6	Illinois	**86.79**	86.36	86.75	72
7	Duke	**86.65**	86.49	86.43	72
8	Purdue	**85.09**	84.87	84.70	72
9	Ohio State	**84.85**	85.04	84.16	72
10	Iowa	**84.60**	84.47	84.24	72
11	Louisville	**84.11**	83.87	83.82	71
12	Notre Dame	**84.04**	83.78	83.78	72
13	Michigan	**83.90**	83.79	83.42	72
14	Minnesota	**83.46**	83.42	82.89	72
15	Michigan State	**83.43**	83.11	83.18	71
16	St. John's	**83.22**	83.36	82.59	72
17	Cincinnati	**83.09**	82.58	83.12	72
18	Oklahoma State	**83.04**	82.46	83.01	72
19	Utah	**82.59**	82.32	82.32	72
20	Oklahoma	**82.57**	82.20	82.36	72
21	Villanova	**82.55**	82.50	82.01	72
22	NC State	**82.53**	82.44	82.08	72
23	Syracuse	**82.28**	81.92	82.07	71
24	Marquette	**82.23**	81.67	82.22	72
25	Southern California	**82.22**	81.49	82.44	72
26	DePaul	**82.11**	81.79	81.84	72
27	Kansas State	**81.86**	81.40	81.72	72
28	Wisconsin	**81.56**	81.34	81.18	72
29	Missouri	**81.53**	81.18	81.23	72
30	Stanford	**81.33**	80.90	81.29	70
31	Temple	**81.32**	81.08	80.96	72
32	Arkansas	**81.27**	80.90	81.09	72
33	Tennessee	**81.19**	80.94	80.86	71
34	California	**81.16**	80.65	81.24	72
35	Washington	**80.89**	80.65	80.59	71
36	West Virginia	**80.83**	80.67	80.40	72
37	Wake Forest	**80.81**	80.73	80.22	71
38	Maryland	**80.65**	80.44	80.18	72
39	Bradley	**80.59**	80.45	80.23	70
40	Oregon State	**80.52**	80.24	80.27	71
41	Brigham Young	**80.51**	79.91	80.45	72
42	Georgetown	**80.44**	79.97	80.35	70
43	Alabama	**80.20**	80.34	79.42	71
44	Western Kentucky	**80.03**	79.86	79.63	72
45	Alabama-Birmingham	**79.88**	79.66	79.81	32
46	Vanderbilt	**79.69**	79.48	79.23	72
47	Texas	**79.49**	79.24	79.09	72
48	Dayton	**79.47**	79.41	78.97	70
49	Arizona	**79.40**	78.65	79.50	71
50	Oregon	**79.32**	79.05	79.07	71
51	Colorado	**79.23**	79.02	78.84	70
52	Iowa State	**79.16**	78.83	78.85	72
53	Saint Louis	**79.11**	78.80	78.76	71
54	Connecticut	**79.11**	78.55	79.03	72
55	Houston	**78.87**	78.57	78.59	64
56	Saint Joseph's	**78.78**	78.80	78.20	72
57	Nebraska	**78.76**	78.67	78.16	72
58	UNLV	**78.74**	78.99	76.96	50
59	Xavier	**78.68**	78.08	78.66	70
60	Pittsburgh	**78.60**	78.30	78.26	72
61	Memphis	**78.38**	78.29	77.77	70
62	Louisiana State	**78.31**	78.23	77.75	72
63	Wyoming	**78.26**	77.68	78.24	71
64	Florida	**78.26**	77.86	78.02	71
65	Georgia Tech	**78.21**	77.86	77.83	72
66	Tulsa	**78.18**	77.96	77.71	72
67	Duquesne	**78.06**	77.84	77.71	69
68	Virginia	**78.04**	77.67	77.72	72
69	Miami (OH)	**77.82**	77.53	77.42	72
70	Washington State	**77.82**	77.53	77.52	71
71	La Salle	**77.80**	77.43	77.48	72
72	Utah State	**77.79**	77.45	77.48	71
73	Boston College	**77.64**	77.50	77.17	65
74	Florida State	**77.63**	77.39	77.26	62
75	San Francisco	**77.63**	77.53	77.20	67
76	Seton Hall	**77.61**	77.51	77.15	69
77	Northwestern	**77.60**	77.10	77.41	72
78	Providence	**77.54**	77.15	77.28	71
79	Santa Clara	**77.43**	77.06	77.22	70
80	Auburn	**77.36**	77.23	76.74	71
81	Wichita State	**77.31**	76.78	77.14	71
82	Penn State	**77.25**	76.78	77.10	72
83	Toledo	**77.16**	76.92	76.74	72
84	Southern Illinois	**77.15**	76.78	76.87	72
85	Princeton	**77.05**	76.52	76.90	72
86	Creighton	**76.87**	76.69	76.47	70
87	Pennsylvania	**76.79**	76.66	76.31	72
88	Ohio University	**76.59**	76.47	76.05	72
89	Texas Tech	**76.56**	75.94	76.35	72
90	Mississippi State	**76.43**	76.41	75.78	71
91	South Carolina	**76.36**	76.32	75.80	72
92	Southern Methodist	**76.29**	75.98	75.94	72
93	Bowling Green	**76.16**	75.59	75.94	72
94	Arizona State	**76.04**	75.23	76.05	71
95	Loyola-Chicago	**76.03**	75.68	75.68	72
96	St. Bonaventure	**75.99**	75.78	75.58	70
97	George Washington	**75.92**	75.58	75.59	70
98	Butler	**75.84**	75.76	75.27	71
99	Murray State	**75.81**	75.51	75.45	72
100	Holy Cross	**75.69**	75.56	75.16	70
101	Georgia	**75.68**	75.40	75.21	72
102	Colorado State	**75.65**	74.79	75.71	71
103	Clemson	**75.61**	75.13	75.37	72
104	Drake	**75.54**	75.17	75.21	72
105	Virginia Tech	**75.51**	74.95	75.37	72
106	Evansville	**75.36**	74.98	75.09	72
107	Detroit	**75.34**	74.83	75.13	72
108	Marshall	**75.29**	74.91	74.98	72

		RATING	CHESS	PREDICTOR	YRS
109	UTEP	**75.13**	74.55	75.00	71
110	New Mexico	**75.09**	74.63	74.80	72
111	Texas A&M	**74.98**	74.84	74.36	72
112	Missouri State	**74.64**	73.67	74.88	70
113	Illinois State	**74.60**	74.31	74.19	72
114	Rhode Island	**74.51**	73.87	74.50	72
115	Mississippi	**74.38**	74.18	73.85	71
116	Weber State	**74.26**	74.25	72.72	58
117	Baylor	**74.23**	73.92	73.79	72
118	Oral Roberts	**74.22**	73.64	74.33	40
119	New Mexico State	**74.17**	73.86	73.74	70
120	Western Michigan	**74.16**	73.87	73.71	72
121	New Orleans	**74.16**	74.17	73.75	40
122	Niagara	**74.06**	73.60	73.84	70
123	Tulane	**74.02**	73.97	73.36	68
124	Pepperdine	**73.99**	73.38	73.73	69
125	Indiana State	**73.98**	73.33	73.92	72
126	Fresno State	**73.86**	73.16	74.04	71
127	Gonzaga	**73.70**	73.25	73.45	71
128	South Florida	**73.70**	73.31	73.71	38
129	Rice	**73.56**	73.25	73.14	72
130	South Alabama	**73.54**	73.30	73.32	42
131	Manhattan	**73.53**	72.93	73.41	70
132	Miami (FL)	**73.52**	73.56	72.69	54
133	Fordham	**73.45**	73.00	73.17	71
134	Wisconsin-Green Bay	**73.39**	73.37	73.03	40
135	Texas Christian	**73.36**	72.83	73.13	72
136	Eastern Kentucky	**73.11**	72.84	72.66	71
137	Tennessee State	**73.11**	71.28	77.37	63
138	Pacific	**73.05**	72.02	73.85	72
139	Saint Mary's (CA)	**72.93**	72.13	73.45	72
140	San Diego State	**72.72**	71.77	72.79	72
141	Kent State	**72.64**	72.06	72.42	71
142	UC Santa Barbara	**72.62**	71.91	72.53	70
143	San Jose State	**72.62**	71.78	73.00	72
144	Akron	**72.62**	71.67	72.86	72
145	Canisius	**72.45**	71.94	72.21	72
146	Navy	**72.45**	71.77	72.37	72
147	Idaho	**72.44**	72.22	71.94	71
148	Ball State	**72.44**	72.03	72.06	71
149	Rutgers	**72.35**	71.67	72.27	71
150	Hawaii	**72.29**	72.11	71.74	66
151	Montana	**72.21**	71.69	71.97	71
152	Charlotte	**72.09**	71.65	71.23	49
153	Louisiana-Lafayette	**72.00**	71.54	71.66	69
154	Loyola Marymount	**71.98**	71.76	71.50	69
155	Southern Miss	**71.92**	71.59	71.46	66
156	Long Beach State	**71.77**	71.29	71.43	60
157	Massachusetts	**71.60**	71.14	71.30	70
158	Richmond	**71.43**	71.35	70.75	72
159	Morehead State	**71.43**	71.07	71.01	72
160	Old Dominion	**71.42**	69.75	71.57	61
161	Boise State	**71.14**	70.68	70.84	49
162	Louisiana Tech	**71.13**	70.40	70.87	70
163	Denver	**70.98**	70.45	70.51	63
164	Iona	**70.93**	70.27	70.81	65
165	Air Force	**70.83**	69.96	71.14	53
166	Nevada	**70.83**	70.57	70.33	70
167	VCU	**70.75**	69.47	70.50	57
168	Lamar	**70.74**	69.88	70.86	59
169	Montana State	**70.63**	70.25	70.28	71
170	Wright State	**70.55**	70.64	69.85	39
171	Northern Illinois	**70.49**	70.04	70.17	72
172	Valparaiso	**70.46**	69.95	70.16	72
173	East Tennessee State	**70.35**	69.85	70.14	65
174	Davidson	**70.35**	69.71	70.13	72
175	Long Island	**70.32**	69.75	70.24	66
176	UC Irvine	**70.19**	70.07	69.79	44
177	Saint Peter's	**70.18**	69.61	69.99	69
178	Portland	**70.17**	70.11	69.55	67
179	Cornell	**70.13**	69.67	69.83	72
180	North Texas	**70.05**	69.61	69.72	71
181	Idaho State	**69.98**	69.37	69.71	72
182	Tennessee Tech	**69.90**	69.88	69.04	72
183	Central Michigan	**69.89**	69.53	69.46	72
184	Hofstra	**69.89**	69.26	69.82	70
185	Yale	**69.74**	69.06	69.61	72
186	SE Missouri State	**69.59**	69.23	69.16	70
187	Saint Francis (PA)	**69.55**	69.36	68.98	69
188	McNeese State	**69.54**	68.94	69.48	59
189	Eastern Illinois	**69.54**	68.89	69.41	72
190	William and Mary	**69.47**	68.87	69.23	72
191	Portland State	**69.33**	69.42	68.42	45
192	Columbia	**69.32**	68.80	69.08	72
193	Jacksonville	**69.18**	68.65	68.89	57
194	Cal State Fullerton	**69.14**	68.95	67.60	51
195	Northern Iowa	**69.11**	68.82	68.57	70
196	Arkansas State	**68.93**	68.63	68.23	70
197	San Diego	**68.93**	68.66	68.48	54
198	Army	**68.82**	68.50	68.37	72
199	Fairfield	**68.77**	68.09	68.70	61
200	Lafayette	**68.74**	68.02	68.67	72
201	Texas-San Antonio	**68.73**	68.59	68.51	28
202	Stephen F. Austin	**68.72**	68.02	68.59	70
203	Siena	**68.67**	67.85	68.63	69
204	Alcorn State	**68.61**	67.50	70.64	44
205	Jackson State	**68.59**	68.56	68.44	46
206	Centenary	**68.59**	68.33	67.99	69
207	Texas Southern	**68.57**	66.95	70.26	52
208	Eastern Washington	**68.51**	68.59	67.69	67
209	Wisconsin-Milwaukee	**68.47**	68.83	67.31	67
210	Western Illinois	**68.45**	68.05	68.07	72
211	American	**68.45**	67.26	68.71	72
212	Austin Peay	**68.43**	68.25	67.69	70
213	Alabama State	**68.43**	67.31	70.11	53
214	Gardner-Webb	**68.37**	68.48	67.68	29
215	Middle Tennessee St.	**68.36**	68.33	67.46	69
216	Texas State	**68.35**	67.66	68.21	71
217	Dartmouth	**68.28**	67.96	67.79	72
218	NC Wilmington	**68.28**	67.70	68.18	49
219	Norfolk State	**68.27**	67.77	68.18	44
220	Boston University	**68.21**	67.43	68.09	71
221	James Madison	**68.11**	67.83	67.40	43
222	Youngstown State	**67.91**	66.99	67.95	69
223	Furman	**67.84**	67.60	67.25	70
224	Northwestern State	**67.79**	66.98	67.56	70
225	East Carolina	**67.75**	66.39	68.01	67
226	South Dakota State	**67.57**	66.66	67.32	56
227	Eastern Michigan	**67.54**	67.08	67.06	72
228	Monmouth	**67.46**	66.70	67.53	57
229	Georgia Southern	**67.44**	66.88	67.09	68
230	Central Florida	**67.35**	67.23	67.00	39
231	North Carolina A&T	**67.27**	66.52	67.63	57
232	Bucknell	**67.25**	66.46	67.12	72
233	Illinois-Chicago	**67.23**	67.08	66.04	57
234	Missouri-Kansas City	**67.05**	66.74	66.75	36
235	Colgate	**67.04**	66.27	66.94	72
236	Harvard	**67.01**	66.40	66.79	72
237	Rider	**67.01**	66.38	66.78	72
238	Texas-Pan American	**66.95**	66.03	67.16	56
239	Sam Houston State	**66.92**	66.34	66.61	70
240	Southern University	**66.81**	65.81	67.71	58
241	St. Francis (NY)	**66.60**	66.06	66.28	72
242	Fairleigh Dickinson	**66.58**	65.65	66.53	59
243	Mount St. Mary's	**66.55**	65.63	66.52	71
244	Chattanooga	**66.50**	66.47	65.35	70

		RATING	CHESS	PREDICTOR	YRS
245	Cal Poly	**66.47**	65.68	66.22	63
246	Brown	**66.42**	66.14	65.88	72
247	Grambling	**66.42**	65.60	67.94	49
248	Cal State Northridge	**66.41**	65.83	66.17	50
249	Alabama A&M	**66.38**	65.33	67.83	27
250	Northern Arizona	**66.36**	65.84	65.98	71
251	Stetson	**66.29**	65.60	66.13	68
252	George Mason	**66.28**	66.30	64.84	42
253	South Carolina State	**66.19**	65.79	66.44	49
254	Northeastern	**66.17**	65.81	65.35	72
255	Drexel	**66.12**	65.64	65.52	69
256	Radford	**65.99**	66.27	65.33	34
257	Louisiana-Monroe	**65.99**	66.77	64.83	10
258	Ark.-Little Rock	**65.98**	65.19	65.27	52
259	Mississippi Valley St.	**65.89**	65.14	66.24	39
260	Florida A&M	**65.87**	64.96	66.41	50
261	Winthrop	**65.87**	66.15	65.02	31
262	Appalachian State	**65.76**	65.19	65.52	71
263	Buffalo	**65.72**	65.00	65.50	65
264	Robert Morris	**65.66**	65.41	65.48	33
265	Cleveland State	**65.39**	65.11	64.14	71
266	North Dakota State	**65.27**	64.26	65.04	55
267	Loyola (MD)	**65.11**	64.11	65.11	72
268	Delaware	**65.08**	64.57	64.32	72
269	Texas-Arlington	**65.06**	64.47	64.96	50
270	High Point	**65.04**	64.25	64.79	62
271	Southern Utah	**64.98**	64.91	63.09	47
272	Oakland (MI)	**64.91**	63.77	65.02	37
273	Texas A&M-C.C.	**64.83**	63.29	65.11	32
274	Northern Colorado	**64.69**	63.70	63.94	57
275	Vermont	**64.66**	64.55	63.86	70
276	SE Louisiana	**64.61**	64.18	64.13	65
277	Fla. International	**64.51**	64.84	63.59	28
278	IUPUI	**64.47**	62.96	64.23	27
279	Western Carolina	**64.41**	63.31	64.25	69
280	Hampton	**64.30**	62.42	64.90	52
281	Sacred Heart	**64.26**	62.89	64.67	35
282	Wagner	**64.24**	63.28	64.19	68
283	Mercer	**64.21**	64.15	63.31	69
284	Elon	**64.18**	63.45	63.72	60
285	Chicago State	**64.16**	63.79	62.86	58
286	Maine	**64.14**	63.94	63.13	72
287	UNC Asheville	**64.03**	64.13	63.12	45

		RATING	CHESS	PREDICTOR	YRS
288	Samford	**63.84**	63.86	62.76	68
289	Tennessee-Martin	**63.75**	63.26	63.42	52
290	Prairie View A&M	**63.74**	63.40	63.92	50
291	Campbell	**63.68**	63.00	63.44	56
292	Nicholls State	**63.64**	63.45	63.06	51
293	The Citadel	**63.43**	63.25	62.54	72
294	Coastal Carolina	**63.39**	63.22	62.77	35
295	Jacksonville State	**63.35**	63.40	62.06	62
296	Troy	**63.34**	63.75	61.79	59
297	VMI	**63.16**	62.90	62.41	72
298	Central Conn. State	**63.13**	61.48	63.61	65
299	Savannah State	**63.05**	61.91	63.84	36
300	Longwood	**63.04**	62.49	62.43	18
301	Md. Eastern Shore	**63.01**	62.61	62.50	61
302	Coppin State	**62.86**	62.80	61.69	45
303	UC Riverside	**62.71**	62.66	61.46	44
304	Liberty	**62.67**	62.60	61.80	35
305	Arkansas-Pine Bluff	**62.60**	62.01	62.76	45
306	Bethune-Cookman	**62.57**	61.13	64.60	49
307	Belmont	**62.51**	62.27	61.36	49
308	Marist	**62.16**	60.99	62.31	47
309	Charleston Southern	**62.16**	62.24	61.32	43
310	Sacramento State	**62.13**	61.49	61.77	61
311	Florida Atlantic	**62.10**	61.91	61.78	18
312	Lehigh	**62.01**	61.03	61.88	72
313	Lipscomb	**61.79**	61.42	60.45	61
314	Towson State	**61.73**	60.89	61.35	51
315	Delaware State	**61.62**	60.53	61.40	57
316	Albany	**61.60**	59.34	61.76	53
317	Howard	**61.55**	60.12	61.70	57
318	Quinnipiac	**61.47**	59.21	61.89	46
319	UNC Greensboro	**61.43**	62.05	59.74	38
320	Morgan State	**61.43**	60.47	61.30	57
321	UC Davis	**61.01**	60.40	60.37	55
322	Hartford	**60.93**	59.71	61.06	52
323	Wofford	**60.56**	60.26	59.63	65
324	IPFW	**60.34**	59.53	58.98	23
325	New Hampshire	**59.82**	59.33	59.09	71
326	Georgia State	**59.14**	58.71	57.67	54
327	Md.-Baltimore County	**59.14**	59.49	57.95	29
328	Stony Brook	**58.66**	56.38	59.63	37
329	College of Charleston	**58.51**	58.53	55.81	70
330	Binghamton	**54.98**	52.74	54.37	46

THE TOP 40 PROGRAMS OF EACH DECADE

THE 1940s (1937-38 THROUGH '48-49)

		RATING	CHESS	POINTS
1	Oklahoma State	**91.59**	91.80	91.11
2	Kentucky	**91.53**	90.82	92.32
3	Illinois	**91.43**	91.15	91.50
4	Notre Dame	**90.84**	91.11	90.42
5	Indiana	**89.27**	89.36	88.98
6	DePaul	**89.02**	88.94	88.74
7	Purdue	**88.57**	88.35	88.45
8	Ohio State	**88.24**	88.51	87.78
9	Long Island	**87.39**	87.63	87.07
10	Michigan	**87.27**	87.20	87.02
11	Holy Cross	**86.83**	86.73	86.67
12	NYU	**86.56**	86.32	86.54
13	Wisconsin	**86.56**	86.87	86.07
14	Minnesota	**86.51**	87.02	85.70
15	Southern California	**86.43**	85.51	87.17
16	Iowa	**86.43**	86.96	85.57
17	Western Kentucky	**86.10**	85.83	86.36
18	Utah	**86.02**	85.32	86.58
19	Duquesne	**85.97**	86.84	84.87
20	Hamline	**85.80**	85.36	85.90
21	St. John's	**85.50**	84.93	85.86
22	Arkansas	**85.48**	86.06	84.66
23	Northwestern	**85.19**	84.47	85.62
24	Colorado	**85.10**	84.15	85.94
25	Kansas	**85.09**	84.86	84.93
26	West Virginia	**84.86**	84.55	84.89
27	Loyola-Chicago	**84.81**	84.40	84.79
28	Wyoming	**84.50**	83.90	84.80
29	California	**84.26**	83.27	84.88
30	Oklahoma	**84.10**	83.52	84.33
31	Bowling Green	**84.10**	83.10	84.11
32	Oregon	**84.01**	83.54	84.39
33	Oregon State	**84.01**	83.94	83.83
34	Bradley	**83.75**	83.87	83.20
35	Dartmouth	**83.71**	83.67	83.38
36	Temple	**83.46**	83.28	83.20
37	Penn State	**83.43**	82.60	84.05
38	Washington State	**83.32**	83.87	82.57
39	Toledo	**83.27**	83.03	83.11
40	Stanford	**83.22**	82.54	83.80

THE 1950s

		RATING	CHESS	POINTS
1	Kentucky	**93.50**	92.99	94.20
2	Illinois	**90.44**	90.06	90.76
3	Kansas State	**90.25**	89.54	91.05
4	Kansas	**89.97**	89.78	90.00
5	Indiana	**88.78**	89.00	88.37
6	UCLA	**88.40**	88.33	88.29
7	Dayton	**88.23**	88.22	88.28
8	Iowa	**87.37**	88.01	86.64
9	Louisville	**87.25**	87.17	87.20
10	Cincinnati	**86.59**	85.66	87.46
11	Minnesota	**86.44**	86.38	86.27
12	Oklahoma State	**86.36**	85.59	86.92
13	Duquesne	**86.33**	86.24	86.22
14	Saint Louis	**86.27**	86.05	86.21
15	La Salle	**86.24**	85.98	86.28
16	NC State	**86.20**	86.49	85.88
17	Notre Dame	**85.78**	85.75	85.55
18	California	**85.36**	85.08	85.36
19	Tennessee State	**85.30**	84.52	86.31
20	Bradley	**85.19**	84.98	85.14
21	Michigan State	**85.17**	84.91	85.19
22	San Francisco	**84.87**	85.29	84.62
23	Western Kentucky	**84.65**	84.42	84.65
24	Holy Cross	**84.24**	83.62	84.87
25	Ohio State	**84.09**	84.15	83.80
26	Washington	**84.08**	83.70	84.21
27	Southern California	**84.04**	83.93	83.93
28	Missouri	**83.54**	83.10	83.75
29	St. John's	**83.11**	83.41	82.68
30	Purdue	**83.08**	83.17	82.87
31	Duke	**83.07**	82.89	83.10
32	Brigham Young	**82.86**	82.21	83.35
33	Niagara	**82.63**	81.70	83.37
34	Xavier	**82.29**	81.86	82.54
35	Oklahoma City	**82.28**	81.97	82.39
36	Utah	**82.25**	81.68	82.62
37	DePaul	**82.19**	81.98	82.09
38	Colorado	**82.18**	82.58	81.61
39	Seattle	**81.83**	81.88	81.47
40	Fordham	**81.63**	81.16	81.90

THE 1960s

		RATING	CHESS	POINTS
1	UCLA	**94.32**	94.09	94.78
2	Cincinnati	**90.66**	90.63	90.68
3	Duke	**89.80**	89.62	89.71
4	Ohio State	**89.57**	90.09	88.83
5	Kentucky	**87.84**	87.24	88.26
6	North Carolina	**87.31**	87.43	87.02
7	Dayton	**87.00**	87.27	86.52
8	Bradley	**86.97**	87.11	86.61
9	Kansas	**86.75**	85.88	87.37
10	Villanova	**86.20**	85.84	86.29
11	Kansas State	**85.69**	85.11	86.06
12	Illinois	**85.50**	84.91	85.87
13	Wichita State	**85.49**	85.39	85.28
14	Louisville	**85.40**	85.01	85.57
15	Vanderbilt	**84.67**	85.23	83.94
16	Houston	**84.59**	84.32	84.60
17	St. John's	**84.41**	84.87	83.72
18	Saint Louis	**84.36**	83.76	84.66
19	Providence	**84.24**	85.77	82.94
20	Iowa	**84.17**	84.12	83.91
21	Southern California	**84.10**	83.18	84.91
22	Saint Joseph's	**84.03**	84.95	83.11
23	Utah	**83.98**	83.97	83.86
24	Loyola-Chicago	**83.91**	83.49	84.04
25	Princeton	**83.87**	83.55	83.95
26	Drake	**83.77**	83.73	83.57
27	Indiana	**83.76**	83.46	83.81
28	Purdue	**82.96**	82.74	82.88
29	Oregon State	**82.81**	82.82	82.54
30	Tennessee	**82.60**	81.60	83.54
31	Colorado	**82.49**	82.48	82.25
32	Wake Forest	**82.38**	82.26	82.15
33	West Virginia	**82.26**	82.84	81.44
34	Minnesota	**82.19**	82.53	81.59
35	Colorado State	**82.05**	81.28	82.69
36	St. Bonaventure	**81.99**	82.03	81.72
37	Michigan	**81.95**	81.84	81.75
38	Utah State	**81.85**	81.29	82.12
39	Auburn	**81.82**	81.90	81.43
40	Stanford	**81.81**	81.18	82.18

THE 1970s

		RATING	CHESS	POINTS
1	UCLA	**96.31**	96.79	96.15
2	North Carolina	**91.70**	90.93	92.42
3	Marquette	**90.49**	90.72	90.10
4	Kentucky	**89.80**	89.78	89.65
5	Indiana	**89.16**	89.03	89.61
6	NC State	**88.98**	88.84	89.48
7	Maryland	**87.38**	87.10	87.47
8	Notre Dame	**87.23**	86.50	87.81
9	Louisville	**86.84**	86.50	86.95
10	Purdue	**86.47**	85.81	86.85
11	Michigan	**86.41**	86.58	86.12
12	Southern California	**84.87**	84.92	84.63
13	South Carolina	**84.86**	84.48	85.08
14	Duke	**84.79**	83.96	85.37
15	Long Beach State	**84.78**	84.68	84.61
16	Tennessee	**84.68**	84.61	84.56
17	Minnesota	**84.30**	84.40	83.90
18	Alabama	**84.30**	84.88	83.44
19	Florida State	**84.23**	83.59	84.72
20	Pennsylvania	**84.07**	84.23	83.94
21	San Francisco	**83.94**	83.77	83.91
22	Houston	**83.74**	83.61	83.63
23	St. John's	**83.72**	83.65	83.59
24	Kansas State	**83.66**	83.65	83.47
25	Kansas	**83.47**	83.16	83.60
26	Syracuse	**83.40**	83.46	83.21
27	Washington	**83.34**	83.15	83.31
28	Cincinnati	**83.05**	82.41	83.50
29	Oregon State	**83.00**	82.63	83.33
30	Wake Forest	**82.91**	82.46	83.16
31	Providence	**82.85**	83.30	82.14
32	Michigan State	**82.77**	82.90	82.46
33	Virginia	**82.68**	82.32	82.73
34	Utah	**82.56**	82.84	81.99
35	Arizona State	**82.36**	81.84	82.67
36	Missouri	**82.32**	82.66	81.72
37	New Mexico	**82.13**	81.83	82.12
38	Oregon	**82.12**	81.94	82.03
39	Iowa	**82.11**	81.54	82.53
40	UNLV	**82.05**	82.50	81.43

THE 1980s

		RATING	CHESS	POINTS
1	North Carolina	**92.69**	92.82	92.59
2	Georgetown	**89.88**	90.32	89.58
3	Indiana	**89.66**	89.13	90.40
4	Illinois	**89.23**	88.25	90.48
5	Kentucky	**88.48**	88.46	88.22
6	Louisville	**88.22**	88.62	87.83
7	Syracuse	**88.11**	88.11	88.12
8	Iowa	**88.05**	87.05	89.10
9	Virginia	**88.05**	88.33	87.55
10	Purdue	**87.73**	87.72	87.62
11	Duke	**87.37**	87.56	87.19
12	Oklahoma	**87.07**	86.64	87.31
13	Michigan	**86.97**	86.28	87.44
14	Missouri	**86.68**	85.91	87.27
15	DePaul	**86.67**	86.93	86.27
16	NC State	**86.67**	86.59	86.54
17	UNLV	**86.50**	86.71	86.18
18	St. John's	**86.50**	87.53	85.50
19	Kansas	**85.70**	85.37	85.84
20	Alabama	**85.58**	85.45	85.49
21	Louisiana State	**85.58**	85.96	85.01
22	Ohio State	**85.18**	85.02	85.06
23	Villanova	**84.88**	85.80	84.04
24	Memphis	**84.66**	84.95	84.22
25	Oregon State	**84.63**	84.03	85.08
26	UCLA	**84.55**	83.76	85.14
27	Arkansas	**84.41**	83.94	84.71
28	Maryland	**83.97**	84.22	83.55
29	Georgia	**83.81**	82.98	84.43
30	Notre Dame	**83.72**	83.38	83.87
31	Kansas State	**83.57**	83.19	83.65
32	Tennessee	**83.56**	83.41	83.55
33	Clemson	**83.11**	82.43	83.61
34	Temple	**82.76**	82.96	82.40
35	Houston	**82.65**	82.42	82.82
36	Auburn	**82.43**	81.93	82.66
37	Pittsburgh	**82.37**	82.66	81.97
38	UTEP	**82.33**	82.27	82.20
39	Minnesota	**82.25**	81.80	82.42
40	Wake Forest	**82.20**	81.63	82.54

THE 1990s

		RATING	CHESS	POINTS
1	Kentucky	**93.16**	92.84	93.54
2	Duke	**93.02**	92.78	93.66
3	North Carolina	**92.51**	92.37	92.47
4	Kansas	**92.04**	91.22	92.86
5	Arizona	**90.61**	90.13	91.03
6	Connecticut	**89.61**	89.86	89.41
7	Indiana	**88.69**	88.09	89.24
8	Arkansas	**88.53**	88.89	88.34
9	Cincinnati	**87.68**	86.48	88.89
10	UCLA	**87.60**	88.82	86.71
11	Purdue	**86.80**	87.19	86.21
12	Michigan	**86.73**	87.21	86.25
13	Michigan State	**86.48**	86.62	86.28
14	Syracuse	**86.44**	86.88	85.98
15	Wake Forest	**86.20**	86.76	85.51
16	Oklahoma State	**85.83**	85.00	86.56
17	Maryland	**85.83**	85.52	85.93
18	Massachusetts	**85.62**	85.87	85.45
19	Temple	**85.30**	85.02	85.38
20	Georgetown	**85.27**	84.75	85.70
21	Minnesota	**85.24**	84.76	85.55
22	Iowa	**84.99**	84.28	85.75
23	Utah	**84.95**	85.30	84.65
24	Georgia Tech	**84.72**	85.43	83.95
25	Louisville	**84.65**	84.66	84.50
26	Oklahoma	**84.63**	83.85	85.32
27	Stanford	**84.60**	84.12	84.94
28	Virginia	**84.24**	84.67	83.71
29	Illinois	**84.18**	83.90	84.37
30	Missouri	**83.97**	84.57	83.45
31	Villanova	**83.65**	83.34	83.77
32	St. John's	**83.37**	83.11	83.53
33	Clemson	**83.25**	83.15	83.20
34	Georgia	**83.25**	82.24	84.31
35	Florida State	**83.21**	83.35	82.88
36	Alabama	**82.94**	83.05	82.69
37	Texas	**82.47**	82.04	82.67
38	Xavier	**82.44**	81.99	82.78
39	Providence	**82.27**	81.75	82.61
40	California	**82.25**	82.09	82.23

THE 2000s

		RATING	CHESS	POINTS
1	Duke	**92.63**	91.86	93.48
2	Kansas	**91.02**	90.41	91.69
3	North Carolina	**89.35**	89.07	89.55
4	Florida	**88.81**	88.06	89.63
5	Michigan State	**88.64**	88.57	88.65
6	Illinois	**88.33**	87.89	88.84
7	Arizona	**87.91**	87.55	88.24
8	Texas	**87.91**	87.83	87.98
9	Connecticut	**87.82**	87.83	87.78
10	Kentucky	**87.74**	87.54	87.74
11	Wisconsin	**87.25**	87.21	87.08
12	Oklahoma	**86.75**	86.81	86.73
13	Pittsburgh	**86.58**	86.98	86.05
14	Maryland	**86.48**	86.06	86.97
15	Memphis	**86.47**	86.44	86.49
16	Stanford	**86.27**	86.30	86.16
17	Gonzaga	**86.15**	86.21	86.08
18	Syracuse	**85.71**	86.52	85.01
19	Louisville	**85.71**	84.97	86.41
20	UCLA	**85.68**	86.05	85.20
21	Oklahoma State	**85.33**	85.04	85.47
22	Ohio State	**85.08**	85.71	84.41
23	Wake Forest	**84.91**	84.82	84.88
24	Xavier	**84.41**	84.07	84.57
25	Villanova	**84.35**	84.58	84.04
26	Tennessee	**84.33**	84.55	84.02
27	Cincinnati	**84.27**	83.37	85.12
28	Notre Dame	**84.24**	83.94	84.39
29	Georgetown	**84.24**	83.94	84.42
30	Mississippi State	**83.39**	83.03	83.67
31	Indiana	**83.37**	83.12	83.46
32	Marquette	**83.24**	83.35	83.01
33	Louisiana State	**82.85**	82.48	83.12
34	NC State	**82.76**	82.42	82.92
35	Boston College	**82.70**	83.23	82.03
36	Alabama	**82.65**	82.57	82.51
37	Missouri	**82.38**	82.17	82.41
38	Southern California	**82.15**	81.86	82.28
39	Butler	**82.07**	81.51	82.59
40	Purdue	**82.06**	81.46	82.51

The 10 Best Teams That Didn't Win The NCAA Tournament

Many UNLV fans still can't believe Larry Johnson & Co. lost in the 1991 NCAA Final Four. But, according to my ratings, those Runnin' Rebels rank as only the eighth-best team—relative to its competition—that failed to win its season's NCAA Tournament. No. 1? The 1944-45 DePaul Blue Demons. Ray Meyer's team split two games with that season's NCAA champ, Oklahoma A&M (today's Oklahoma State) and won the NIT, earning a 103.88 season rating. (The Cowboys finished just a tick behind at 103.73.) In fact, DePaul's rating is the third-highest of all time, behind two John Wooden title teams: the 1967-68 (104.86) and 1971-72 Bruins (105.23).

	YEAR	TEAM	RECORD	SEASON RANK	RATING	NOTES
1	**1944-45**	**DePaul**	21-3	1	**103.88**	Led by George Mikan, won NIT; did not participate in NCAA.
2	**1943-44**	**Army**	15-0	1	**103.57**	Military rules prevented Cadets from playing in NCAA Tournament.
3	**1998-99**	**Duke**	37-2	1	**101.82**	Outscored opponents 91.8-67.2; lost to UConn by three in NCAA Final.
4	**1956-57**	**Kansas**	24-3	1	**100.67**	Wilt & Co. lost to North Carolina in three OTs in title game.
5	**1953-54**	**Kentucky**	25-0	1	**100.60**	Declined NCAA bid after starters were declared ineligible for NCAA.
6	**1960-61**	**Ohio State**	27-1	1	**100.53**	Jerry Lucas scored 27 in OT Final loss to Cincinnati.
7	**1974-75**	**Indiana**	31-1	1	**98.98**	One and only loss came to Kentucky in Mideast Regional final, 92-90.
8	**1990-91**	**UNLV**	34-1	1	**98.94**	Tark's high-scoring crew won first four Tourney games by 17.8 per.
9	**1942-43**	**Illinois**	17-1	1	**98.69**	Declined NCAA bid because AD didn't want to pull players from classes.
10	**1997-98**	**Duke**	32-4	1	**97.76**	Won 12 ACC games by double digits but lost in Elite Eight to Kentucky.

The 10 Worst Teams That Won The NCAA Tournament

Here's what is perhaps most amazing about that 1984-85 Villanova team that won the NCAA title: Even after taking into account its six Tournament wins, by my ratings the Wildcats still trailed Georgetown (the team they beat for the title) and six other teams at the end of the season.

	YEAR	TEAM	RECORD	SEASON RANK	RATING	NOTES
1	**1984-85**	**Villanova**	25-10	7	**89.95**	Lowest seed (No. 8) to win it all.
2	**1982-83**	**NC State**	26-10	7	**90.05**	Dropped six of eight in one early-season stretch.
3	**1987-88**	**Kansas**	27-11	10	**90.31**	Lost five games by double digits.
4	**1940-41**	**Wisconsin**	20-3	5	**91.16**	Blown out by Minnesota, 44-27, in Big Ten opener, then didn't lose again.
5	**1946-47**	**Holy Cross**	27-3	5	**92.00**	Started 4-3; first two losses were by a combined 26 points.
6	**1979-80**	**Louisville**	33-3	1	**92.25**	Almost lost in first *and* second rounds of Tournament.
7	**1953-54**	**La Salle**	26-4	9	**92.34**	Part of worst Final Four ever in terms of team winning percentage.
8	**1976-77**	**Marquette**	25-7	4	**92.46**	First team to win NCAA title with seven or more losses.
9	**2002-03**	**Syracuse**	30-5	5	**92.53**	Carmelo Anthony's bunch lost to 12–16 Rutgers in January.
10	**1941-42**	**Stanford**	28-4	3	**92.82**	Rating suffers because of 43-39 loss to an outfit called Athens Club.

ALL CONTENTS COPYRIGHT © 2009 JEFF SAGARIN

ALL-TIME NCAA DIVISION I RECORDS

SINGLE-GAME RECORDS

INDIVIDUAL

POINTS (By D1 players against D1 opponents)	OPP	DATE	PTS
1 **Kevin Bradshaw**, U.S. International	Loyola Marymount	1/5/1991	72
2 **Pete Maravich**, LSU	Alabama	2/7/1970	69
3 **Calvin Murphy**, Niagara	Syracuse	12/7/1968	68
4 **Jay Handlan**, Washington and Lee	Furman	2/17/1951	66
Pete Maravich, LSU	Tulane	2/10/1969	66
Anthony Roberts, Oral Roberts	NC A&T	2/19/1977	66
7 **Anthony Roberts**, Oral Roberts	Oregon	3/9/1977	65
Scott Haffner, Evansville	Dayton	2/18/1989	65
9 **Pete Maravich**, LSU	Kentucky	2/21/1970	64
10 **Johnny Neumann**, Mississippi	LSU	1/30/1971	63
Hersey Hawkins, Bradley	Detroit	2/22/1988	63

POINTS (Any division, any opponent)	DIV	OPP	DATE	PTS
1 **Clarence "Bevo" Francis**, Rio Grande	II	Hillsdale	2/2/1954	113
2 **Frank Selvy**, Furman	I	Newberry	2/13/1954	100
3 **Paul Arizin**, Villanova	I	Philadelphia NAMC	2/12/1949	85
4 **Clarence "Bevo" Francis**, Rio Grande	II	Alliance	1954	84
5 **Clarence "Bevo" Francis**, Rio Grande	II	Bluffton	1954	82

THREE-POINT FG MADE	OPP	DATE	3FG
1 **Keith Veney**, Marshall	Morehead State	12/14/1996	15
2 **Dave Jamerson**, Ohio	Charleston (WV)	12/21/1989	14
Askia Jones, Kansas State	Fresno State	3/24/1994	14
Ronald Blackshear, Marshall	Akron	3/1/2002	14
5 8 players tied at 12			

ASSISTS	OPP	DATE	AST
1 **Tony Fairley**, Charleston Southern	Armstrong Atlantic	2/19/1987	22
Avery Johnson, Southern U.	Texas Southern	1/25/1988	22
Sherman Douglas, Syracuse	Providence	1/28/1989	22
4 **Mark Wade**, UNLV	Navy	12/29/1989	21
Kelvin Scarborough, New Mexico	Hawaii	2/13/1987	21
Anthony Manuel, Bradley	UC Irvine	12/19/1987	21
Avery Johnson, Southern U.	Alabama State	1/16/1988	21

REBOUNDS	OPP	DATE	REB
1 **Bill Chambers**, William and Mary	Virginia	2/14/1953	51
2 **Charlie Slack**, Marshall	Morris Harvey	1/12/1954	43
3 **Tom Heinsohn**, Holy Cross	Boston College	3/1/1955	42
4 **Art Quimby**, Connecticut	Boston U.	1/11/1955	40
John Tresvant, Seattle	Montana	2/8/1963	40

REBOUNDS (Since 1972-73)	OPP	DATE	REB
1 **Larry Abney**, Fresno State	SMU	2/17/2000	35
2 **David Vaughn**, Oral Roberts	Brandeis	1/8/1973	34
3 **Rudy Macklin**, LSU	Tulane	11/26/1976	32
Jervaughn Scales, Southern U.	Grambling	2/7/1994	32
5 **Jim Bradley**, Northern Illinois	Milwaukee	2/19/1973	31
Calvin Natt, UL-Monroe	Georgia Southern	12/29/1976	31

BLOCKED SHOTS	OPP	DATE	BLK
1 **Mickell Gladness**, Alabama A&M	Texas Southern	2/24/2007	16
2 **David Robinson**, Navy	UNC Wilmington	1/4/1986	14
Shawn Bradley, BYU	Eastern Kentucky	12/7/1990	14
Roy Rogers, Alabama	Georgia	2/10/1996	14
Loren Woods, Arizona	Oregon	2/3/2000	14

STEALS	OPP	DATE	STL
1 **Mookie Blaylock**, Oklahoma	Centenary	12/12/1987	13
Mookie Blaylock, Oklahoma	Loyola Marymount	12/17/1988	13
3 **Kenny Robertson**, Cleveland State	Wagner	12/3/1988	12
Terry Evans, Oklahoma	Florida A&M	2/20/1999	12
Richard Duncan, Middle Tennessee State	Eastern Kentucky	1/27/1993	12
Greedy Daniels, TCU	Arkansas-Pine Bluff	12/30/2000	12
Jehiel Lewis, Navy	Bucknell	1/12/2002	12
Carldwell Johnson, UAB	South Carolina State	11/27/2005	12

TEAM

POINTS	OPP	DATE	SCORE
1 **Loyola Marymount**	U.S. International	1/5/1991	186-140
2 **Loyola Marymount**	U.S. International	1/31/1989	181-150
3 **Long Island**	Medgar Evers	11/26/1997	179-62
4 **Oklahoma**	U.S. International	11/29/1989	173-101
5 **Oklahoma**	Loyola Marymount	12/15/1990	172-112

FIELD GOAL PCT	OPP	DATE	FG	FGA	PCT
1 **Maryland**	South Carolina	1/9/1971	15	18	83.3
2 **New Mexico**	Oregon State	11/30/1985	35	43	81.4
3 **Fresno State**	Portland State	12/3/1977	34	42	81.0
Saint Peter's	Utica	12/4/1984	34	42	81.0
5 **Fordham**	Fairfield	2/27/1984	33	41	80.5

THREE-POINT FG MADE	OPP	DATE	3FG
1 **Troy**	George Mason	12/10/1994	28
2 **Troy**	Oakwood	11/24/2003	26
3 **Cincinnati**	Oakland	12/5/1998	24
VMI	Southern Virginia	1/29/2009	24
5 4 teams tied at 23			

SEASON RECORDS

INDIVIDUAL

SCORING	SEASON	G	FG	3FG	FT	PTS
1 **Pete Maravich**, LSU	1969-70	31	522	-	337	1,381
2 **Elvin Hayes**, Houston	1967-68	33	519	-	176	1,214
3 **Frank Selvy**, Furman	1953-54	29	427	-	355	1,209
4 **Pete Maravich**, LSU	1968-69	26	433	-	282	1,148
5 **Pete Maravich**, LSU	1967-68	26	432	-	274	1,138
6 **Bo Kimble**, Loyola Marymount	1989-90	32	404	92	231	1,131
7 **Hersey Hawkins**, Bradley	1987-88	31	377	87	284	1,125
8 **Austin Carr**, Notre Dame	1969-70	29	444	-	218	1,106
9 **Austin Carr**, Notre Dame	1970-71	29	430	-	241	1,101
10 **Otis Birdsong**, Houston	1976-77	36	452	-	186	1,090

POINTS PER GAME	SEASON	G	FG	3FG	FT	PTS	PPG
1 **Pete Maravich**, LSU	1969-70	31	522	-	337	1,381	44.5
2 **Pete Maravich**, LSU	1968-69	26	433	-	282	1,148	44.2
3 **Pete Maravich**, LSU	1967-68	26	432	-	274	1,138	43.8
4 **Frank Selvy**, Furman	1953-54	29	427	-	355	1,209	41.7
5 **Johnny Neumann**, Mississippi	1970-71	23	366	-	191	923	40.1
6 **Freeman Williams**, Portland State	1976-77	26	417	-	176	1,010	38.8
7 **Billy McGill**, Utah	1961-62	26	394	-	221	1,009	38.8
8 **Calvin Murphy**, Niagara	1967-68	24	337	-	242	916	38.2
9 **Austin Carr**, Notre Dame	1969-70	29	444	-	218	1,106	38.1
10 **Austin Carr**, Notre Dame	1970-71	29	430	-	241	1,101	38.0

FIELD GOAL PCT	SEASON	G	FG	FGA	PCT
1 **Steve Johnson**, Oregon State	1980-81	28	235	315	74.6
2 **Dwayne Davis**, Florida	1988-89	33	179	248	72.2
3 **Keith Walker**, Utica	1984-85	27	154	216	71.3
4 **Steve Johnson**, Oregon State	1979-80	30	211	297	71.0
5 **Adam Mark**, Belmont	2001-02	26	150	212	70.8

THREE-POINT FG PER GAME	SEASON	G	3FG	3PG
1 **Darrin Fitzgerald**, Butler	1986-87	28	158	5.6
2 **Terrence Woods**, Florida A&M	2002-03	28	139	5.0
3 **Demon Brown**, Charlotte	2002-03	29	137	4.7
4 **Timothy Pollard**, Mississippi Valley State	1987-88	28	132	4.7
5 **Chris Brown**, UC Irvine	1993-94	26	122	4.7

THREE-POINT FG PCT	SEASON	G	3FG	3FGA	PCT
1 **Glenn Tropf**, Holy Cross	1987-88	29	52	82	63.4
2 **Sean Wightman**, Western Michigan	1991-92	30	48	76	63.2
3 **Keith Jennings**, East Tennessee State	1990-91	33	84	142	59.2
4 **Dave Calloway**, Monmouth	1988-89	28	48	82	58.5
5 **Steve Kerr**, Arizona	1987-88	38	114	199	57.3

FREE THROW PCT	SEASON	G	FT	FTA	PCT
1 **Blake Ahearn**, Missouri State	2003-04	33	117	120	97.5
2 **Derek Raivio**, Gonzaga	2006-07	34	148	154	96.1
3 **Craig Collins**, Penn State	1984-85	27	94	98	95.9
4 **J.J. Redick**, Duke	2003-04	37	143	150	95.3
5 **Steve Drabyn**, Belmont	2002-03	29	78	82	95.1

ASSISTS PER GAME	SEASON	G	AST	APG
1 **Avery Johnson**, Southern U.	1987-88	30	399	13.3
2 **Anthony Manuel**, Bradley	1987-88	31	373	12.0
3 **Avery Johnson**, Southern U.	1986-87	31	333	10.7
4 **Mark Wade**, UNLV	1986-87	38	406	10.7
5 **Nelson Haggerty**, Baylor	1994-95	28	284	10.1

REBOUNDS PER GAME	SEASON	G	REB	RPG
1 **Charlie Slack**, Marshall	1954-55	21	538	25.6
2 **Leroy Wright**, Pacific	1958-59	26	652	25.1
3 **Art Quimby**, Connecticut	1954-55	25	611	24.4
4 **Charlie Slack**, Marshall	1955-56	22	520	23.6
5 **Ed Conlin**, Fordham	1952-53	26	612	23.5

REBOUNDS PER GAME (Since 1972-73)	SEASON	G	REB	RPG
1 **Kermit Washington**, American	1972-73	25	511	20.4
2 **Marvin Barnes**, Providence	1972-73	30	571	19.0
3 **Marvin Barnes**, Providence	1973-74	32	597	18.7
4 **Pete Padgett**, Nevada	1972-73	26	462	17.8
5 **Jim Bradley**, Northern Illinois	1972-73	24	426	17.8

BLOCKED SHOTS PER GAME	SEASON	G	BLK	BPG
1 **Shawn James**, Northeastern	2005-06	30	196	6.5
2 **Adonal Foyle**, Colgate	1996-97	28	180	6.4
3 **Keith Closs**, Central Connecticut State	1995-96	28	178	6.4
4 **Mickell Gladness**, Alabama A&M	2006-07	30	188	6.3
5 **David Robinson**, Navy	1985-86	35	207	5.9

STEALS PER GAME	SEASON	G	STL	SPG
1 **Desmond Cambridge**, Alabama A&M	2001-02	29	160	5.5
2 **Darron Brittman**, Chicago State	1985-86	28	139	5.0
3 **Aldwin Ware**, Florida A&M	1987-88	29	142	4.9
4 **John Linehan**, Providence	2001-02	31	139	4.5
5 **Ronn McMahon**, Eastern Washington	1989-90	29	130	4.5

EAM

IN-LOSS PCT	SEASON	W	L	PCT
North Carolina	1956-57	32	0	1.000
Indiana	1975-76	32	0	1.000
UCLA	1963-64	30	0	1.000
UCLA	1966-67	30	0	1.000
UCLA	1971-72	30	0	1.000
UCLA	1972-73	30	0	1.000
San Francisco	1955-56	29	0	1.000
NC State	1972-73	27	0	1.000
Kentucky	1953-54	25	0	1.000
Long Island	1938-39	24	0	1.000
Seton Hall	1939-40	19	0	1.000
Army	1943-44	15	0	1.000

SCORING OFFENSE	SEASON	G	PTS	PPG
1 Loyola Marymount	1989-90	32	3,918	122.4
2 Loyola Marymount	1988-89	31	3,486	112.5
3 UNLV	1975-76	31	3,426	110.5
4 Loyola Marymount	1987-88	32	3,528	110.3
5 UNLV	1976-77	32	3,426	107.1

SCORING MARGIN	SEASON	PPG	OPP PPG	MAR
1 UCLA	1971-72	94.6	64.3	30.3
2 NC State	1947-48	75.3	47.2	28.1
3 Kentucky	1953-54	87.5	60.3	27.2
4 Kentucky	1951-52	82.3	55.4	26.9
5 UNLV	1990-91	97.7	71.0	26.7

FIELD GOAL PCT	SEASON	FG	FGA	PCT
1 Missouri	1979-80	936	1,635	57.2
2 Michigan	1988-89	1,325	2,341	56.6
3 Oregon State	1980-81	862	1,528	56.4
4 UC Irvine	1981-82	920	1,639	56.1
5 Michigan State	1985-86	1,043	1,860	56.1

THREE-POINT FG PER GAME	SEASON	G	3FG	3PG
1 VMI	2008-09	32	438	13.7
2 VMI	2006-07	33	442	13.4
3 Troy	2005-06	29	344	11.9
4 Troy	2003-04	31	364	11.7
5 VMI	2007-08	29	336	11.6

FREE THROW PCT	SEASON	FT	FTA	PCT
1 Harvard	1983-84	535	651	82.2
2 BYU	1988-89	527	647	81.5
3 Harvard	1984-85	450	555	81.1
4 Ohio State	1969-70	452	559	80.9
5 Siena	1997-98	574	715	80.3

ASSISTS PER GAME	SEASON	G	AST	APG
1 UNLV	1990-91	35	863	24.7
2 Loyola Marymount	1989-90	32	762	23.8
3 North Carolina	1985-86	34	800	23.5
4 UNLV	1989-90	40	926	23.2
5 SMU	1986-87	29	655	22.6

REBOUND MARGIN (Since 1972-73)	SEASON	RPG	OPP RPG	MAR
1 Manhattan	1972-73	56.5	38.0	18.5
2 American	1972-73	56.7	40.3	16.4
3 Alcorn State	1977-78	52.3	36.0	16.3
4 Oral Roberts	1972-73	65.9	50.3	15.6
5 Alcorn State	1979-80	49.2	33.8	15.4
Michigan State	2000-01	42.5	27.1	15.4

SCORING DEFENSE	SEASON	G	OPP PTS	OPP PPG
1 Oklahoma State	1947-48	31	1,006	32.5
2 Oklahoma State	1948-49	28	985	35.2
3 Oklahoma State	1949-50	27	1,059	39.2
4 Alabama	1947-48	27	1,070	39.6
5 Creighton	1947-48	23	925	40.2

FG PCT DEFENSE (Since 1977-78)	SEASON	OPP FG	OPP FGA	PCT
1 Stanford	1999-2000	667	1,893	35.2
2 Marquette	1993-94	750	2,097	35.8
3 Marquette	1996-97	628	1,735	36.2
4 Temple	1999-2000	633	1,747	36.2
5 Wake Forest	1996-97	667	1,832	36.4

BLOCKED SHOTS PER GAME	SEASON	G	BLK	BPG
1 Georgetown	1988-89	34	309	9.1
2 Connecticut	2004-05	31	275	8.9
3 Connecticut	2005-06	34	298	8.8
4 Connecticut	2007-08	33	285	8.6
5 Connecticut	2006-07	31	264	8.5

STEALS PER GAME	SEASON	G	STL	SPG
1 Long Island	1997-98	32	478	14.9
2 VMI	2006-07	33	490	14.9
3 UTSA	1990-91	29	430	14.8
4 Cleveland State	1986-87	33	473	14.3
5 VMI	2008-09	32	453	14.2

CAREER RECORDS

INDIVIDUAL

SCORING	SEASONS	G	FG	3FG	FT	PTS
1 **Pete Maravich**, LSU	1967-1970	83	1,387	-	893	3,667
2 **Freeman Williams**, Portland State	1974-1978	106	1,369	-	511	3,249
3 **Lionel Simmons**, La Salle	1986-1990	131	1,244	56	673	3,217
4 **Alphonso Ford**, Mississippi Valley State	1989-1993	109	1,121	333	590	3,165
5 **Harry Kelly**, Texas Southern	1979-1983	110	1,234	-	598	3,066
6 **Keydren Clark**, Saint Peter's	2002-2006	118	967	435	689	3,058
7 **Hersey Hawkins**, Bradley	1984-1988	125	1,100	118	690	3,008
8 **Oscar Robertson**, Cincinnati	1957-1960	88	1,052	-	869	2,973
9 **Danny Manning**, Kansas	1984-1988	147	1,216	10	509	2,951
10 **Alfredrick Hughes**, Loyola-Chicago	1981-1985	120	1,226	-	462	2,914

POINTS PER GAME	SEASONS	G	FG	3FG	FT	PTS	PPG
1 **Pete Maravich**, LSU	1967-70	83	1,387	-	893	3,667	44.2
2 **Austin Carr**, Notre Dame	1968-71	74	1,017	-	526	2,560	34.6
3 **Oscar Robertson**, Cincinnati	1957-60	88	1,052	-	869	2,973	33.8
4 **Calvin Murphy**, Niagara	1967-70	77	947	-	654	2,548	33.1
5 **Dwight Lamar**, UL-Lafayette	1971-73	57	768	-	326	1,862	32.7
6 **Frank Selvy**, Furman	1951-54	78	922	-	694	2,538	32.5
7 **Rick Mount**, Purdue	1967-70	72	910	-	503	2,323	32.3
8 **Darrell Floyd**, Furman	1953-56	71	868	-	545	2,281	32.1
9 **Nick Werkman**, Seton Hall	1961-64	71	812	-	649	2,273	32.0
10 **Willie Humes**, Idaho State	1969-71	48	565	-	380	1,510	31.5

MINIMUM: 1,400 POINTS

FIELD GOAL PCT	SEASONS	G	FG	FGA	PCT
1 **Steve Johnson**, Oregon State	1976-81	116	828	1,222	67.8
2 **Michael Bradley**, Kentucky, Villanova	1997-99, 2000-01	100	441	651	67.7
3 **Murray Brown**, Florida State	1976-80	106	566	847	66.8
4 **Lee Campbell**, Middle Tenn. St., Missouri St.	1986-88, '89-90	88	411	618	66.5
5 **Warren Kidd**, Middle Tennessee St.	1990-93	83	496	747	66.4

MINIMUM: 400 MADE AND 4 PER GAME

THREE-POINT FG PER GAME	SEASONS	G	3FG	3PG
1 **Timothy Pollard**, Mississippi Valley State	1987-89	56	256	4.57
2 **Sydney Grider**, UL-Lafayette	1988-90	58	253	4.36
3 **Stephen Curry**, Davidson	2006-09	104	414	3.98
4 **Brian Merriweather**, Texas-Pan American	1998-2001	84	332	3.95
5 **Josh Heard**, Tennessee Tech	1998-2000	55	210	3.82

THREE-POINT FG PCT	SEASONS	G	3FG	3FGA	PCT
1 **Tony Bennett**, Wisconsin-Green Bay	1988-92	118	290	584	49.7
2 **Stephen Sir**, San Diego St., Northern Arizona	2002-04, '04-07	111	323	689	46.9
3 **David Olson**, Eastern Illinois	1988-92	111	262	562	46.6
4 **Jaycee Carroll**, Utah State	2004-08	134	369	793	46.5
5 **Ross Land**, Northern Arizona	1996-2000	117	308	664	46.4

MINIMUM: 200 MADE AND 2 PER GAME

FREE THROWS MADE	SEASONS	G	FT	FTA	PCT
1 **Tyler Hansbrough**, North Carolina	2005-09	142	982	1,241	79.1
2 **Dickie Hemric**, Wake Forest	1951-55	104	905	1,359	66.6
3 **Pete Maravich**, LSU	1967-70	83	893	1,152	77.5
4 **Oscar Robertson**, Cincinnati	1957-60	88	869	1,114	78.0
5 **Caleb Green**, Oral Roberts	2003-07	128	852	1,134	75.1

FREE THROW PCT	SEASONS	G	FT	FTA	PCT
1 **Blake Ahearn**, Missouri State	2003-07	129	435	460	94.6
2 **Derek Raivio**, Gonzaga	2003-07	127	343	370	92.7
3 **Gary Buchanan**, Villanova	1999-2003	122	324	355	91.3
4 **J.J. Redick**, Duke	2002-06	139	662	726	91.2
5 **Greg Starrick**, Kentucky, Southern Illinois	1968-69, '70-72	72	341	375	90.9

MINIMUM: 300 MADE AND 2.5 PER GAME

ASSISTS PER GAME	SEASONS	G	AST	APG
1 **Avery Johnson**, Southern U.	1986-88	61	732	12.0
2 **Sam Crawford**, New Mexico State	1991-93	67	592	8.8
3 **Mark Wade**, Oklahoma, UNLV	1983-84, '85-87	79	693	8.8
4 **Chris Corchiani**, NC State	1987-91	124	1,038	8.4
5 **Taurence Chisholm**, Delaware	1984-88	110	877	8.0

MINIMUM: 550 ASSISTS

REBOUNDS PER GAME	SEASONS	G	REB	RPG
1 **Artis Gilmore**, Jacksonville	1969-71	54	1,224	22.7
2 **Charlie Slack**, Marshall	1952-56	88	1,916	21.8
3 **Paul Silas**, Creighton	1961-64	81	1,751	21.6
4 **Leroy Wright**, Pacific	1957-60	67	1,442	21.5
5 **Art Quimby**, Connecticut	1951-55	80	1,716	21.5

MINIMUM: 800 REBOUNDS

REBOUNDS PER GAME (Since 1972-73)	SEASONS	G	REB	RPG
1 **Glenn Mosley**, Seton Hall	1973-77	83	1,263	15.2
2 **Bill Campion**, Manhattan	1972-75	74	1,070	14.6
3 **Pete Padgett**, Nevada	1972-76	104	1,464	14.1
4 **Bob Warner**, Maine	1972-76	96	1,304	13.6
5 **Shaquille O'Neal**, LSU	1989-92	90	1,217	13.5

Blocked Shots Per Game

		SEASONS	G	BLK	BPG
1	**Keith Closs**, Central Connecticut State	1994-96	54	317	5.9
2	**Adonal Foyle**, Colgate	1994-97	87	492	5.7
3	**David Robinson**, Navy	1985-87	67	351	5.2
4	**Mickell Gladness**, Alabama A&M	2005-08	85	396	4.7
5	**Wojciech Mydra**, UL-Monroe	1998-2002	115	535	4.7

Minimum: 225 blocked shots

Steals Per Game

		SEASONS	G	STL	SPG
1	**Desmond Cambridge**, Alabama A&M	1999-2002	84	330	3.9
2	**Mookie Blaylock**, Oklahoma	1987-89	74	281	3.8
3	**Ronn McMahon**, Eastern Washington	1988-90	64	225	3.5
4	**Eric Murdock**, Providence	1987-91	117	376	3.2
5	**Van Usher**, Tennessee Tech	1989-92	85	270	3.2

Minimum: 225 steals

COACHING RECORDS

Most Victories

		YEARS	WINS
1	**Bob Knight**, Army 1965-71, Indiana 1971-2000, Texas Tech '01-08	42	902
2	**Dean Smith**, North Carolina 1961-97	36	879
3	**Adolph Rupp**, Kentucky 1930-52, '53-72	41	876
4	➡**Mike Krzyzewski**, Army 1975-80, Duke 1980-2009	34	833
5	**Jim Phelan**, Mount St. Mary's 1954-2003	49	830†
6	➡**Jim Calhoun**, Northeastern 1972-86, Connecticut 1986-2009	37	805†
7	**Eddie Sutton**, Creighton 1969-74, Arkansas '74-85, Kentucky '85-89, Oklahoma St. 1990-2006, San Francisco '07-08	37	804†
8	➡**Jim Boeheim**, Syracuse 1976-2009	33	799
9	**Lefty Driesell**, Davidson 1960-69, Maryland '69-86, James Madison '88-97, Georgia State 1997-2003	41	786
10	**Lute Olson**, Long Beach St. 1973-74, Iowa '74-83, Arizona 1983-2007	34	780†
11	**Lou Henson**, Hardin-Simmons 1962-66; New Mexico St. '66-75, 1997-2005; Illinois '75-96	41	779†
12	**Hank Iba**, NW Missouri St. 1929-33, Colorado '33-34, Oklahoma St. '34-70	41	764
13	**E.A. Diddle**, Western Kentucky, 1922-64	42	759
14	**Phog Allen**, Baker 1905-08; Kansas '07-09, '19-56; Haskell '08-09; Central Missouri '12-19	50	746
15	**John Chaney**, Cheyney 1972-82, Temple 1982-2006	34	741

Minimum: 10 Division I seasons as head coach

†Totals adjusted for forfeited and vacated games; see p. 521.

Highest Percentage

		YEARS	W	L	PCT
1	**Clair Bee**, Rider 1928-31, Long Island 1931-43, '45-51	21	412	88	.824
2	**Adolph Rupp**, Kentucky 1930-52, '53-72	41	876	190	.822
3	➡**Roy Williams**, Kansas 1988-2003, North Carolina '03-09	21	594	138	.811
4	**John Wooden**, Indiana St. 1946-48, UCLA '48-75	29	664	162	.804
5	➡**Mark Few**, Gonzaga 1999-2009	10	264	66	.800

Minimum: 10 seasons as head coach in Division I

Most Games

		NO.
1	**Jim Phelan**, Mount St. Mary's 1954-2003	1,354
2	**Bob Knight**, Army 1965-71, Indiana 1971-2000, Texas Tech '01-08	1,273
3	**Lou Henson**, Hardin-Simmons 1962-66; New Mexico St. '66-75, 1997-2005; Illinois '75-96	1,191
4	**Lefty Driesell**, Davidson 1960-69, Maryland '69-86, James Madison '88-97, Georgia State 1997-2003	1,180
5	➡**Jim Calhoun**, Northeastern 1972-86, Connecticut 1986-2009	1,147

Most Seasons

		NO.
1	**Phog Allen**, Baker 1905-08; Kansas '07-09, '19-56; Haskell '08-09; Cent. Missouri '12-19	50
2	**Jim Phelan**, Mount St. Mary's 1954-2003	49
3	**Frank Hill**, Seton Hall 1911-18, '19-30, Rutgers '16-43	46
4	**E.A. Diddle**, Western Kentucky, 1922-64	42
	Bob Knight, Army 1965-71, Indiana 1971-2000, Texas Tech '01-08	42
	Ray Meyer, DePaul 1942-84	42

Most Seasons at One School

		NO.
1	**Jim Phelan**, Mount St. Mary's 1954-2003	49
2	**E.A. Diddle**, Western Kentucky, 1922-64	42
	Ray Meyer, DePaul 1942-84	42
4	**Tony Hinkle**, Butler 1926-42, '45-70	41
	Adolph Rupp, Kentucky 1930-52, '53-72	41

Most Consecutive 20-Win Seasons

		NO.
1	**Dean Smith**, North Carolina 1970-97	27
2	**Lute Olson**, Arizona 1987-2007	20
3	➡**Tubby Smith**, Tulsa 1993-95, Georgia '95-97, Kentucky 1997-2007, Minnesota '07-09	16
4	➡**Jim Boeheim**, Syracuse 1982-96	14
	➡**Roy Williams**, Kansas 1989-2003	14

Most 30-Win Seasons

		NO.
1	➡**Mike Krzyzewski**, Army 1975-80, Duke 1980-2009	10
2	➡**Roy Williams**, Kansas 1988-2003, North Carolina '03-09	9
3	➡**Jim Calhoun**, Northeastern 1972-86, Connecticut 1986-2009	7
4	➡**John Calipari**, Massachusetts 1987-96, Memphis 1999-2009	6
5	➡**Rick Pitino**, Boston U. 1977-83, Providence '84-87, Kentucky '89-97, Louisville 2001-09	5

➡ Active through 2008-09

All-Time NCAA D1 Tournament Records

SINGLE-GAME RECORDS

INDIVIDUAL

Points

		OPP	ROUND & DATE	PTS
1	**Austin Carr**, Notre Dame	Ohio	First, 3/7/1970	61
2	**Bill Bradley**, Princeton	Wichita State	National Third Place, 3/20/1965	58
3	**Oscar Robertson**, Cincinnati	Arkansas	Regional Third Place, 3/15/1958	56
4	**Austin Carr**, Notre Dame	Kentucky	Regional Semifinals, 3/12/1970	52
	Austin Carr, Notre Dame	TCU	First, 3/13/1971	52
6	**David Robinson**, Navy	Michigan	First, 3/12/1987	50
7	**Elvin Hayes**, Houston	Loyola-Chicago	First, 3/9/1968	49
8	**Hal Lear**, Temple	SMU	National Third Place, 3/23/1956	48
9	**Austin Carr**, Notre Dame	Houston	Regional Third Place, 3/15/1971	47
10	**Dave Corzine**, DePaul	Louisville	Regional Semifinals, 3/17/1978 (2OT)	46

Three-Pt FG Made

		OPP	ROUND & DATE	3FG
1	**Jeff Fryer**, Loyola Marymount	Michigan	Second, 3/18/1990	11
2	**Freddie Banks**, UNLV	Indiana	National Semifinals, 3/28/1987	10
	Roburt Sallie, Memphis	CS Northridge	First, 3/19/2009	10
4	**Garde Thompson**, Michigan	Navy	First, 3/12/1987	9
	Johnny Miller, Temple	Cincinnati	First, 3/16/1995	9
	Johnny Hemsley, Miami (FL)	Lafayette	First 3/12/1999	9
	Ricky Paulding, Missouri	Marquette	Second, 3/22/2003 (OT)	9
	Gerry McNamara, Syracuse	BYU	First, 3/18/2004	9

Assists

		OPP	ROUND & DATE	AST
1	**Mark Wade**, UNLV	Indiana	National Semifinals, 3/28/1987	18
2	**Sam Crawford**, New Mex. St.	Nebraska	First, 3/19/1993	16
3	**Earl Watson**, UCLA	Maryland	Second, 3/18/2000	16
4	**Kenny Patterson**, DePaul	Syracuse	First, 3/15/1985	15
	Keith Smart, Indiana	Auburn	Second, 3/14/1987	15
	Pepe Sanchez, Temple	Lafayette	First, 3/17/2000	15

Rebounds

		OPP	ROUND & DATE	REB
1	**Fred Cohen**, Temple	Connecticut	Regional Semifinals, 3/16/1956	34
2	**Nate Thurmond**, Bowling Green	Miss. State	Regional Third Place, 3/16/1963	31
3	**Jerry Lucas**, Ohio State	Kentucky	Regional Finals, 3/18/1961	30
4	**Toby Kimball**, Connecticut	Saint Joseph's	First, 3/8/1965	29
5	**Elvin Hayes**, Houston	Pacific	Regional Third Place, 3/12/1966	28

Rebounds (Since 1972-73)

		OPP	ROUND & DATE	REB
1	**Phil Hubbard**, Michigan	Detroit	Regional Semifinals, 3/17/1977	26
2	**Tom Burleson**, NC State	Providence	Regional Semifinals, 3/14/1974	24
3	**Kent Benson**, Indiana	Kentucky	Regional Semifinals, 3/22/1975	23
4	**Larry Kenon**, Memphis	Providence	National Semifinals, 3/26/1973	22
	Hakeem Olajuwon, Houston	Louisville	National Semifinals, 4/2/1983	22
	Tim Duncan, Wake Forest	Oklahoma St.	Regional Semifinals, 3/24/1995	22
	Tim Duncan, Wake Forest	St. Mary's (CA)	First, 3/14/1997	22
	Luke Harangody, Notre Dame	Washington St.	Second, 3/22/2008	22

Blocked Shots

		OPP	ROUND & DATE	BLK
1	**Shaquille O'Neal**, LSU	BYU	First, 3/19/1992	11
2	**Shawn Bradley**, BYU	Virginia	First, 3/14/1991	10
	Cole Aldrich, Kansas	Dayton	Second, 3/22/2009	10
4	**David Robinson**, Navy	Cleveland State	Regional Semifinals, 3/21/1986	9
	D'or Fisher, Northwestern St.	Winthrop	Opening, 3/13/2001	9

Steals

		OPP	ROUND & DATE	STL
1	**Darrell Hawkins**, Arkansas	Holy Cross	First, 3/18/1993	8
	Grant Hill, Duke	California	Second, 3/20/1993	8
	Duane Clemens, Ball State	UCLA	First, 3/16/2000	8
	Ty Lawson, North Carolina	Michigan State	Final, 4/6/2009	8
5	13 players tied with 7			

TEAM

Points

		ROUND & DATE	SCORE
1	**Loyola Marymount**	Second, 3/18/1990	149-115
2	**UNLV**	Regional Finals, 3/25/1990	131-101
3	**Saint Joseph's**	National Third Place, 3/25/1961 (4OT)	127-120
4	**Oklahoma**	Second, 3/18/1989	124-81
5	**North Carolina**	Second, 3/19/1988	123-97

Field Goal Pct

		ROUND & DATE	FG	FGA	PCT
1	**Oklahoma State**	Second, 3/22/1992	28	35	80.0
2	**North Carolina**	Second, 3/19/1988	49	62	79.0
3	**Villanova**	National Final, 4/1/1985	22	28	78.6
4	**Northeastern**	First, 3/16/1984	33	44	75.0
5	**Georgetown**	Regional Finals, 3/20/1982	29	39	74.4

Three-Pt FG Made

		ROUND & DATE	3FG
1	**Loyola Marymount**	Second, 3/18/1990	21
2	**Duke**	First, 3/15/2001	18
	West Virginia	Regional Finals, 3/26/2005 (OT)	18
4	**Loyola Marymount**	Regional Finals, 3/25/1990	17
5	Six tied with 16		

SINGLE-TOURNAMENT RECORDS

THREE-GAME MINIMUM FOR ALL AVERAGES AND PERCENTAGES

INDIVIDUAL

POINTS PER GAME	YEAR	G	PTS	PPG
1 **Austin Carr**, Notre Dame	1970	3	158	52.7
2 **Austin Carr**, Notre Dame	1971	3	125	41.7
3 **Jerry Chambers**, Utah	1966	4	143	35.8
Bo Kimble, Loyola Marymount	1990	4	143	35.8
5 **Bill Bradley**, Princeton	1965	5	177	35.4
6 **Clyde Lovellette**, Kansas	1952	4	141	35.3
7 **Gail Goodrich**, UCLA	1965	4	140	35.0
Jerry West, West Virginia	1960	3	105	35.0
9 **Bob Houbregs**, Washington	1953	4	139	34.8
10 **Elvin Hayes**, Houston	1968	5	167	33.4

FIELD GOAL PCT	YEAR	G	FG	FGA	PCT
1 **Arinze Onuaku**, Syracuse	2009	3	15	19	78.9
2 **Christian Laettner**, Duke	1989	5	26	33	78.8
3 **Heyward Dotson**, Columbia	1968	3	22	28	78.6
4 **Winston Bennett**, Kentucky	1988	3	18	23	78.3
5 **Kevin Gamble**, Iowa	1987	4	32	41	78.0

MINIMUM: 5 MADE PER GAME

THREE-POINT FG MADE	YEAR	G	3FG
1 **Glen Rice**, Michigan	1989	6	27
2 **Freddie Banks**, UNLV	1987	5	26
3 **Dennis Scott**, Georgia Tech	1990	5	24
4 **Jeff Fryer**, Loyola Marymount	1990	4	23
Jason Williams, Duke	2001	6	23
Luther Head, Illinois	2005	6	23
Lee Humphrey, Florida	2007	6	23

THREE-POINT FG PCT	YEAR	G	3FG	3FGA	PCT
1 **Ranzino Smith**, North Carolina	1987	4	6	6	100.0
2 **Mike Chappell**, Duke	1998	4	6	7	85.7
3 **Brandon Rush**, Kansas	2007	4	9	11	81.8
4 **John Crotty**, Virginia	1989	4	8	10	80.0
5 **Corey Williams**, Oklahoma State	1992	3	7	9	77.8

MIN. 1.5 3FG MADE PER GAME BEFORE 2001, 2.0 3FG MADE AFTER

FREE THROW PCT	YEAR	G	FT	FTA	PCT
1 **Arthur Lee**, Stanford	1998	5	35	35	100.0
2 **Richard Morgan**, Virginia	1989	4	23	23	100.0
3 **Keith Van Horn**, Utah	1997	4	21	21	100.0
4 **Shammond Williams**, North Carolina	1998	5	20	20	100.0
5 **Lynn Greer**, Temple	2001	4	33	34	97.1

MINIMUM: 20 MADE

ASSISTS PER GAME	YEAR	G	AST	APG
1 **Mark Wade**, UNLV	1987	5	61	12.2
2 **Earl Watson**, UCLA	2000	3	33	11.0
3 **Mark Wade**, UNLV	1986	3	32	10.7
4 **Jason Kidd**, California	1993	3	31	10.3
5 **T.J. Ford**, Texas	2003	5	51	10.2
6 **John Crotty**, Virginia	1989	4	39	9.8
7 **Drew Barry**, Georgia Tech	1996	3	29	9.7
Reggie Geary, Arizona	1996	3	29	9.7
Mitch Johnson, Stanford	2008	3	29	9.7
10 **Rumeal Robinson**, Michigan	1989	6	56	9.3
Steve Bucknall, North Carolina	1989	3	28	9.3
Sam Crawford, New Mexico State	1992	3	28	9.3

REBOUNDS PER GAME	YEAR	G	REB	RPG
1 **Nate Thurmond**, Bowling Green	1963	3	70	23.3
2 **Howard Jolliff**, Ohio	1960	3	65	21.7
3 **Elvin Hayes**, Houston	1968	5	97	19.4
4 **Johnny Green**, Michigan State	1957	4	77	19.3
5 **Paul Silas**, Creighton	1964	3	57	19.0

REBOUNDS PER GAME (Since 1972-73)	YEAR	G	REB	RPG
1 **Marvin Barnes**, Providence	1974	3	51	17.0
2 **Mike Franklin**, Cincinnati	1975	3	49	16.3
3 **Tom Burleson**, NC State	1974	4	61	15.3
4 **Phil Hubbard**, Michigan	1977	3	45	15.0
Shelden Williams, Duke	2006	3	45	15.0
Blake Griffin, Oklahoma	2009	4	60	15.0

BLOCKED SHOTS PER GAME	YEAR	G	BLK	BPG
1 **David Robinson**, Navy	1986	4	23	5.8
2 **Tim Duncan**, Wake Forest	1995	3	16	5.3
Erick Dampier, Mississippi State	1995	3	16	5.3
Cole Aldrich, Kansas	2009	3	16	5.3
5 **Tim Perry**, Temple	1988	4	20	5.0
Shelden Williams, Duke	2006	3	15	5.0

STEALS PER GAME	YEAR	G	STL	SPG
1 **Ricky Grace**, Oklahoma	1987	3	14	4.7
2 **Mookie Blaylock**, Oklahoma	1988	6	23	3.8
3 **Edgar Padilla**, Massachusetts	1996	5	19	3.8
Mike Kelley, Wisconsin	2000	5	19	3.8
5 **Scott Burrell**, Connecticut	1991	3	11	3.7
Damian Owens, West Virginia	1998	3	11	3.7
Jason Hart, Syracuse	1998	3	11	3.7
Jamaal Williams, Washington	2006	3	11	3.7

TEAM

SCORING OFFENSE	YEAR	G	PTS	PPG
1 **Loyola Marymount**	1990	4	423	105.8
2 **Notre Dame**	1970	3	317	105.7
3 **UNLV**	1977	5	505	101.0
4 **UCLA**	1965	4	400	100.0
5 **UL-Lafayette**	1972	3	296	98.7

SCORING MARGIN	YEAR	G	MAR
1 **UCLA**	1967	4	23.8
2 **Loyola-Chicago**	1963	5	23.0
3 **Indiana**	1981	5	22.6
4 **Kentucky**	1996	6	21.5
5 **UCLA**	1968	4	21.3

FIELD GOAL PCT	YEAR	G	FG	FGA	PCT
1 **North Carolina**	1975	3	113	187	60.4
2 **Michigan**	1988	3	96	161	59.6
3 **Michigan State**	1978	3	92	156	59.0
4 **Alabama**	1987	3	99	169	58.6
5 **Wake Forest**	1993	3	85	146	58.2

THREE-POINT FG PCT	YEAR	G	FG	FGA	PCT
1 **Indiana**	1989	3	14	23	60.9
2 **St. John's**	1991	4	16	27	59.3
3 **Virginia**	1989	4	27	50	54.0
4 **Kansas**	2007	4	28	52	53.8
5 **Miami (OH)**	2000	3	23	43	53.5

MINIMUM: 12 MADE

FREE THROW PCT	YEAR	G	FT	FTA	PCT
1 **St. John's**	1969	3	47	54	87.0
2 **Utah**	1996	3	36	42	85.7
3 **Notre Dame**	1987	3	47	55	85.5
4 **Oklahoma State**	1958	3	69	81	85.2
5 **Oregon**	2007	4	57	67	85.1

ASSISTS	YEAR	G	AST
1 **Kentucky**	1996	6	143
2 **UNLV**	1990	6	140
3 **Oklahoma**	1988	6	136
4 **Michigan**	1989	6	125
5 **Louisville**	1986	6	120

REBOUNDS	YEAR	G	REB
1 **Houston**	1968	5	306
2 **Western Kentucky**	1971	5	289
3 **New Mexico State**	1970	5	268
4 **Connecticut**	2004	6	264
5 **UNLV**	1990	6	262

BLOCKED SHOTS	YEAR	G	BLK
1 **Kentucky**	1998	6	48
2 **Florida**	2006	6	44
3 **Arizona**	2001	6	42
UCLA	2008	5	42
5 **LSU**	2006	5	40

STEALS	YEAR	G	STL
1 **Oklahoma**	1988	6	72
2 **Kentucky**	1996	6	71
3 **Arkansas**	1995	6	65
4 **Kentucky**	1997	6	64
5 **Arkansas**	1990	5	57
Massachusetts	1996	5	57
Syracuse	2003	6	57

CAREER

TWO-YEAR MINIMUM FOR ALL AVERAGES AND PERCENTAGES

INDIVIDUAL

SCORING	YEARS	G	PTS
1 **Christian Laettner**, Duke	1989-92	23	407
2 **Elvin Hayes**, Houston	1966-68	13	358
3 **Danny Manning**, Kansas	1985-88	16	328
4 **Tyler Hansbrough**, North Carolina	2005-09	17	325
5 **Oscar Robertson**, Cincinnati	1958-60	10	324
6 **Glen Rice**, Michigan	1986-89	13	308
7 **Lew Alcindor**, UCLA	1967-69	12	304
8 **Bill Bradley**, Princeton	1963-65	9	303
Corliss Williamson, Arkansas	1993-95	15	303
10 **Juan Dixon**, Maryland	1999-2002	16	294

SCORING AVERAGE	YEARS	G	PTS	PPG
1 **Austin Carr**, Notre Dame	1969-71	7	289	41.3
2 **Bill Bradley**, Princeton	1963-65	9	303	33.7
3 **Oscar Robertson**, Cincinnati	1958-60	10	324	32.4
4 **Jerry West**, West Virginia	1958-60	9	275	30.6
5 **Bob Pettit**, LSU	1953, '54	6	183	30.5
6 **Dan Issel**, Kentucky	1968-70	6	176	29.3
Jim McDaniels, Western Kentucky	1970, '71	6	176	29.3
8 **Dwight Lamar**, UL-Lafayette	1972, '73	6	175	29.2
9 **Bo Kimble**, Loyola Marymount	1988-90	7	204	29.1
10 **David Robinson**, Navy	1985-87	7	200	28.6

MINIMUM: 6 GAMES

Field Goal Pct

	Years	G	FG	FGA	PCT
1 **Bill Walton**, UCLA	1972-74	12	109	159	68.6
2 **Stephen Thompson**, Syracuse	1987-90	15	78	114	68.4
3 **Brad Daugherty**, North Carolina	1983-86	12	70	103	68.0
4 **Andre Hutson**, Michigan State	1998-2001	19	86	132	65.2
5 **Hakeem Olajuwon**, Houston	1982-84	15	95	146	65.1

Minimum: 70 made

Three-Point FG Pct

	Years	G	3FG	3FGA	PCT
1 **William Scott**, Kansas State	1987, '88	5	26	40	65.0
2 **Sam Cassell**, Florida State	1992, '93	7	20	32	62.5
3 **Steve Alford**, Indiana	1984, '86-87	10	21	34	61.8
4 **Brian Boddicker**, Texas	2001-04	12	25	42	59.5
5 **Glen Rice**, Michigan	1986-89	13	35	62	56.5

Minimum: 20 made

Free Throw Pct

	Years	G	FT	FTA	PCT
1 **Keith Van Horn**, Utah	1995-97	8	42	43	97.7
2 **LaBradford Smith**, Louisville	1988-90	8	45	47	95.7
3 **Phil Ford**, North Carolina	1975-78	10	37	39	94.9
4 **Lawrence Moten**, Syracuse	1992, '94-95	7	33	35	94.3
5 **John McCarthy**, Notre Dame	1957, '58	6	46	49	93.9

Minimum: 30 made

Assists Per Game

	Years	G	AST	APG
1 **Mark Wade**, UNLV	1986, '87	8	93	11.6
2 **Sam Crawford**, New Mexico State	1992, '93	5	51	10.2
3 **T.J. Ford**, Texas	2002, '03	8	69	8.6
4 **Rumeal Robinson**, Michigan	1988-90	11	93	8.5
5 **Sherman Douglas**, Syracuse	1986-89	14	106	7.6

Minimum: 50 assists

Rebounds (Since 1973)

	Years	G	REB
1 **Nick Collison**, Kansas	2000-03	16	181
2 **Christian Laettner**, Duke	1989-92	23	169
3 **Tim Duncan**, Wake Forest	1994-97	11	165
4 **Derrick Coleman**, Syracuse	1987-90	14	155
5 **Hakeem Olajuwon**, Houston	1982-84	15	153

Rebounds Per Game

	Years	G	REB	RPG
1 **Johnny Green**, Michigan State	1957, '59	6	118	19.7
2 **Artis Gilmore**, Jacksonville	1970, '71	6	115	19.2
3 **Paul Silas**, Creighton	1962-64	6	111	18.5
4 **Len Chappell**, Wake Forest	1961, '62	8	137	17.1
5 **Elvin Hayes**, Houston	1966-68	13	222	17.1

Minimum: 6 games

Rebounds Per Game (Since 1973)

	Years	G	REB	RPG
1 **Tim Duncan**, Wake Forest	1994-97	11	165	15.0
2 **Marvin Barnes**, Providence	1972-74	7	99	14.1
3 **Bill Walton**, UCLA	1972-74	8	112	14.0
4 **Phil Hubbard**, Michigan	1976, '77	8	106	13.3
5 **David Robinson**, Navy	1985-87	7	86	12.3

Minimum: 85 rebounds

Blocked Shots Per Game

	Years	G	BLK	BPG
1 **Shaquille O'Neal**, LSU	1990-92	5	29	5.8
2 **David Robinson**, Navy	1986, '87	5	25	5.0
3 **Tim Duncan**, Wake Forest	1994-97	11	50	4.6
4 **Marcus Camby**, Massachusetts	1994-96	11	43	3.9
5 **Ken Johnson**, Ohio State	1999, 2000	7	27	3.9

Minimum: 25 blocked shots

Steals Per Game

	Years	G	STL	SPG
1 **Mookie Blaylock**, Oklahoma	1988, '89	9	32	3.6
2 **Ricky Grace**, Oklahoma	1987, '88	9	28	3.1
Pepe Sanchez, Temple	1997-2000	9	28	3.1
4 **Mario Chalmers**, Kansas	2005-08	11	34	3.1
5 **Scott Burrell**, Connecticut	1990-92	9	26	2.9

Minimum: 20 steals

TEAM

Appearances

	No.
1 **Kentucky**	49
2 **North Carolina**	41
UCLA	41
4 **Kansas**	38
5 **Indiana**	35
Louisville	35

Wins

	No.
1 **North Carolina**	102
2 **Kentucky**	98†
3 **UCLA**	94†
4 **Duke**	88
5 **Kansas**	84

†Vacated wins not included: Kentucky 2; UCLA 5

Winning Percentage

	Wins	Losses	PCT
1 **Duke**	88	30	.746
2 **UCLA**	94	34	.734†
3 **North Carolina**	102	39	.723
4 **Florida**	26	10	.722†
5 **Kansas**	84	37	.694

Minimum: 20 games

†Vacated games not included: UCLA 5-2; Florida 3-2

Consecutive Wins

	Seasons	No.
1 **UCLA**	1964-74	38
2 **Duke**	1991-93	13
3 **Cincinnati**	1960-63	12
Florida	2006-07	12
Kentucky	1945-52	12

COACHING RECORDS

Championships

	No.
1 **John Wooden**, UCLA	10
2 **Adolph Rupp**, Kentucky	4
3 **Bob Knight**, Indiana	3
➡ **Mike Krzyzewski**, Duke	3
5 Nine tied with 2	

Final Fours

	No.
1 **John Wooden**, UCLA	12
2 **Dean Smith**, North Carolina	11
3 ➡ **Mike Krzyzewski**, Duke	10
4 **Denny Crum**, Louisville	6
Adolph Rupp, Kentucky	6
➡ **Roy Williams**, Kansas, North Carolina	6

Appearances

	No.
1 **Bob Knight**, Indiana, Texas Tech	28
2 **Lute Olson**, Iowa, Arizona	27†
Dean Smith, North Carolina	27
4 ➡ **Jim Boeheim**, Syracuse	26
5 **Eddie Sutton**, Creighton, Arkansas, Kentucky, Oklahoma State	25†
➡ **Mike Krzyzewski**, Duke	25

†Vacated appearances not included; see p. 521.

Wins

	No.
1 ➡ **Mike Krzyzewski**, Duke	71
2 **Dean Smith**, North Carolina	65
3 ➡ **Roy Williams**, Kansas, North Carolina	55
4 **John Wooden**, UCLA	47
5 **Lute Olson**, Iowa, Arizona	46†

†Vacated wins not included; see p. 521.

➡ Active through 2008-09

Miscellaneous NCAA Tournament Records

Note: Seeding began in 1979

Consecutive Appearances

SCHOOL	NO.	YEARS
North Carolina	27	1975-2001
Arizona	25	1985-2009
Kansas	20	1990-2009
Indiana	18	1986-2003
Kentucky	17	1992-2008

Most No. 1 Seedings

SCHOOL	NO.
North Carolina	13
Duke	10
Kentucky	9
Kansas	8
Connecticut	5
Arizona	5
Georgetown	5
Oklahoma	5

Champions by Conference (Since 1979)

CONFERENCE	NO.
ACC	9
Big Ten	5
Big East	5
SEC	5
Pac-10	2
Others	5

Champions by Seed

SEED	TITLES	LAST
1	17	2009 UNC
2	6	2004 Connecticut
3	4	2006 Florida
6	2	1988 Kansas
4	1	1997 Arizona
8	1	1985 Villanova

Lowest-Seeded Champions (Since 1979)

YEAR	SCHOOL	SEED
1985	Villanova	8
1988	Kansas	6
1983	NC State	6
1997	Arizona	4
1981	Indiana	3
1989	Michigan	3
2003	Syracuse	3
2006	Florida	3

Consecutive Final Fours

SCHOOL	NO.	SPAN
UCLA	10	1967-76
Duke	5	1988-92
Cincinnati	5	1959-63

Defending Champion in Final Four (Since 1979)

YEAR	SCHOOL	RESULT
2007	Florida	Won championship
2001	Michigan State	Lost in national semifinals
1997	Kentucky	Lost in Final
1995	Arkansas	Lost in Final
1992	Duke	Won championship
1991	UNLV	Lost in national semifinals
1985	Georgetown	Lost in Final

Lowest Seeds to Reach Final Four (Since 1979)

YEAR	SCHOOL	SEED	RESULT
2006	George Mason	11	Lost in national semifinals
1986	LSU	11	Lost in national semifinals
1979	Penn	9	Lost in national semifinals
2000	North Carolina	8	Lost in national semifinals
2000	Wisconsin	8	Lost in national semifinals
1985	Villanova	8	Won championship
1980	UCLA	8	Lost in Final
1984	Virginia	7	Lost in national semifinals

No. 1 vs. No. 16 Games Decided by Five Points or Fewer (Since 1985)

YEAR	SCORE
1996	Purdue 73, Western Carolina 71
1990	Michigan State 75, Murray State 71 (OT)
1989	Oklahoma 72, East Tennessee St. 71
1989	Georgetown 50, Princeton 49
1985	Michigan 59, Fairleigh Dickinson 55

Wins Against Higher Seeds

SCHOOL	NO.
Villanova	15
UCLA	11
Temple	9
Boston College	9
Kansas	9
LSU	9

Multiple Teams from One Conference in Final Four (Since 1985)

YEAR	CONFERENCE	SCHOOLS (NCAA champs in bold)
1985	Big East	Georgetown, St. John's, **Villanova**
1987	Big East	Providence, Syracuse
1988	Big Eight	**Kansas**, Oklahoma
1989	Big Ten	Illinois, **Michigan**
1990	ACC	Duke, Georgia Tech
1991	ACC	**Duke**, North Carolina
1992	Big Ten	Indiana, Michigan
1994	SEC	**Arkansas**, Florida
1996	SEC	**Kentucky**, Mississippi State
1999	Big Ten	Michigan State, Ohio State
2000	Big Ten	**Michigan State**, Wisconsin
2001	ACC	**Duke**, Maryland
2002	Big 12	Kansas, Oklahoma
2003	Big 12	Kansas, Texas
2004	ACC	Duke, Georgia Tech
2005	Big Ten	Illinois, Michigan State
2006	SEC	**Florida**, LSU
2009	Big East	Connecticut, Villanova

Consecutive Years Without a First-Round Win, by Conference

CONFERENCE	YEARS	SPAN
Northeast	27	1982-2009
Southland	20	1986-2005
Ohio Valley	20	1990-2009
SWAC	16	1994-2009
Big South	14	1991-2006
Big Sky	14	1980-94

Most Wins Without a Championship

SCHOOL	WINS
Illinois	38
Oklahoma	35
Texas	33
Memphis	32
Purdue	31
Temple	31
Notre Dame	30
Kansas State	28
Wake Forest	27
Iowa	27
St. John's	27

Most Wins Without Reaching Final Four

SCHOOL	WINS
Boston College	22
Missouri	21
Alabama	20
Xavier	17
Gonzaga	14
Arizona State	13
Tennessee	13
Auburn	12
Tulsa	12
BYU	11

Most Appearances Without Reaching Final Four

SCHOOL	NO.
BYU	24
Missouri	22
Xavier	20
Alabama	19
Boston College	18
Utah State	18
Miami (OH)	17
Creighton	16

Deep Runs by Double-Digit Seeds (Since 1985)

SEED	SWEET 16	ELITE 8	FINAL FOUR
10	18	7	0
11	11	4	2
12	17	1	0
13	4	0	0
14	2	0	0

Double-Digit Seeds in Sweet 16 (Since 1985)

YEAR	SCHOOLS (Seed)
2009	Arizona (12)
2008	Western Kentucky (12), Villanova (12), Davidson (10)
2007	None
2006	Bradley (13), George Mason (11)
2005	Wisconsin-Milwaukee (12), NC State (10)
2004	Nevada (10)
2003	Butler (12), Auburn (10)
2002	Missouri (12), Southern Illinois (11), Kent State (10)
2001	Gonzaga (12), Temple (11), Georgetown (10)
2000	Gonzaga (10), Seton Hall (10)
1999	Oklahoma (13), Southwest Missouri St. (12), Gonzaga (10), Miami of Ohio (10), Purdue (10)
1998	Valparaiso (13), Washington (11), West Virginia (10)
1997	Chattanooga (14), Texas (10), Providence (10)
1996	Arkansas (12)
1995	None
1994	Tulsa (12), Maryland (10)
1993	George Washington (12)
1992	New Mexico State (12)
1991	Eastern Michigan (12), Connecticut (11), Temple (10)
1990	Ball State (12), Loyola Marymount (11), Texas (10)
1989	Minnesota (11)
1988	Richmond (13), Rhode Island (11)
1987	Wyoming (12), LSU (10)
1986	Cleveland State (14), DePaul (12), LSU (11)
1985	Kentucky (12), Boston College (11), Auburn (11)

Mid-Major Teams with At-Large Bids to Reach Sweet 16 (Since 1985)

YEAR	SCHOOLS (CONF.)	SEED	SWEET 16 RESULT
2007	Butler (Horizon)	5	Lost by 8
2007	Southern Illinois (MVC)	4	Lost by 3
2006	Bradley (MVC)	13	Lost by 16
2006	George Mason (CAA)	11	Won by 8
2006	Wichita State (MVC)	7	Lost by 8
2003	Butler (Horizon)	12	Lost by 11
2002	Southern Illinois (MVC)	11	Lost by 12
1999	Southwest Missouri St. (MVC)	12	Lost by 17
1999	Miami of Ohio (MAC)	10	Lost by 15
1995	Tulsa (MVC)	6	Lost by 25
1994	Tulsa (MVC)	12	Lost by 19
1990	Xavier (MCC)	6	Lost by 13
1986	Cleveland State (Mid-Con)	14	Lost by 1

Most One-Point Wins

SCHOOL	NO.
Duke	6
UCLA	5
Indiana	5
Notre Dame	5
North Carolina	5
Ohio State	5
Kansas	4
Saint Joseph's	4

Most One-Point Losses

TEAM	NO.
Kansas	6
Louisville	5
Duke	4
Kentucky	4

First-Round Records of Low Seeds (Since 1985)

SEED NO. (vs. opp. seed)	W	L	PCT
16 (vs. 1)	0	100	.000
15 (vs. 2)	4	96	.040
14 (vs. 3)	15	85	.150
13 (vs. 4)	21	79	.210
12 (vs. 5)	32	68	.320

Coaches Taking Four Different Schools to the Tournament

COACH	SCHOOLS
John Beilein	Canisius, Richmond, West Virginia, Michigan
Lefty Driesell	Davidson, Maryland, James Madison, Georgia State
Lon Kruger	Kansas State, Florida, Illinois, UNLV
Jim Harrick	Pepperdine, UCLA, Rhode Island, Georgia
Rick Pitino	Boston University, Providence, Kentucky, Louisville
Tubby Smith	Tulsa, Georgia, Kentucky, Minnesota
Eddie Sutton	Creighton, Arkansas, Kentucky, Oklahoma State

ACKNOWLEDGMENTS

The effort to put this book together—and to create the first comprehensive database of college basketball statistics—began in the winter of 2006-07, at about the time that Greg Oden and Ohio State were taking over the top spot in the AP poll. (Temporarily, as the Florida Gators ensured.) Indeed, the whole process has been a little like preparing for and playing through a college basketball season: years of careful planning, one talented and committed person after another entering the fray, everyone stepping up with a bright idea or a heroic effort to help ensure a W. As the clock ticked down, the days grew longer and the tempers grew shorter, but there was a constant pride in the frenzy. Madness? You could call it that. Except that ours began immediately after the 2009 NCAA version ended with North Carolina's victory in the Tournament Final over Michigan State on April 6.

ESPN The Magazine founding editor **John Papanek** was the head coach of the operation, orchestrating the different arms of ESPN to produce a multiplatform database that could be drawn on for the *Encyclopedia*, by TV producers and by ESPN.com. He also convinced Bill Bradley, Kareem Abdul-Jabbar and the other Springfield-worthy essayists to contribute. *ESPN The Magazine* senior editor **Scott Burton** was the sharpshooting guard, roping in dozens of writers to contribute hundreds of team profiles and national season wrap-ups. ESPN Books senior editor **Bill Vourvoulias** played the point, coordinating the editors, the research staff and the folks at Scribe Inc., who helped set up the database and provided the editorial production for the *Encyclopedia*.

The big men in the blocks were the leaders of the *ESPN The Magazine*'s research department, **Craig Winston** and **Roger Jackson.** To gather, organize and verify the tens of thousands of data nuggets in this book, they and the rest of the research staff spent endless days combing through media guides and news reports, talking with sports information directors and checking thousands of proofs. Much of the research was entirely original; and thanks to these efforts, the NCAA has altered portions of its own record books. Our roster of researchers for the *Encyclopedia* was as strong as it was deep: **Amanda Angel, Sanford Appell, Sean Bartlett, Tim Bella, Tom Biersdorfer, Sara Brady, Dale Brauner, Gerry Brown, Kevin Collier, LaRue Cook, Tommy Craggs, Mike Dempsey, Matt Giles, Ian Gordon, Eric Hinton, Mike Hume, Chris Khorey, Adesina Koiki, John Mastroberardino, Gueorgui Milkov, Doug Mittler, Lou Monaco, Mike Morrison, Barry Petchesky, Greg Segal, Jim Weber, Bill Weisbrod** and **Jared Zwerling.** They relied on the knowledge and experience of experts such as **Gary Johnson** at the NCAA, Kentucky basketball historian **Jon Scott** and researchers **Pat Premo** and **Phil Porretta.** The list of miscellaneous NCAA Tournament records on page 1,207 is the brainchild and product of the legwork of ESPN's **Chris Fallica.**

Essential to the enterprise were **Doug Kern, Ben Lerner** and the entire ESPN Stats & Information Group in Bristol, Conn., including **Eric Bolin, Hank Gargiulo** and **Mike Landrigan.** Together, they logged the result of every game in major college basketball history from 1937-38 to 2008-09, so that **Jeff Sagarin** could develop the ESPN/Sagarin rankings. Helping beyond the call of duty with the planning stages of the book and database were ESPN's **Jim Barger, Rob Gallace, Mike McManus, Noel Nash, Jim Noel, Bob Ryan** and **Chris Terry.**

At Scribe, many thanks to **David Rech** and **Andy Brown. Brandon Smith** and **Stephen Maris** were tireless in their struggles with, respectively, the layouts and the database. And, as with many of ESPN Books' titles, the *Encyclopedia* has benefited from the close attention and sharp minds at Random House—**Mark Maguire, Paul Taunton** and **Mark Tavani.**

The principal page designer was **Gabriel Ruegg**, who patiently manipulated columns of text and numbers in tiny type and managed to make it not just comprehensible, but also pleasing to the eye. A deep debt of gratitude is owed to veteran ESPN designer **Henry Lee,** who again proved he is a genius of the hardback, if not the hardwood, with a clear, crisp cover that belies the adage about judging a book.

Former ESPN Books editor-in-chief **Chris Raymond** was instrumental in getting the *Encyclopedia* off the ground. The current chief, **Steve Wulf,** stepped in and provided a level head and keen judgment. ESPN Publishing is profoundly grateful to **John Skipper, John Walsh, Gary Hoenig** and **Keith Clinkscales** for their unwavering enthusiasm for the project; to **Sandy DeShong** for a thousand different essential acts of support; to **Glen Waggoner,** who never tired of reading yet another team profile; to **John Glenn,** who provided technical know-how and a sense of cool to dozens of apparently insurmountable problems; and to *ESPN The Magazine* editor-in-chief **Gary Belsky,** for allowing the *Encyclopedia* to soak up much of the magazine staff's time. Providing key editorial assists spot-checking, spot-writing and spot-anything-they-were-asked were **David Duberstein, Kathleen Fieffe, Jonathan Katz, Mickey Steiner, Craig Thompson** and **Bo Wulf.** Every word of the *Encyclopedia* was copyedited by the marvelous **Beth Adelman**—a fact as stunning in its way as "Pistol" Pete Maravich's 44.2 career NCAA scoring average.

Our Reference Shelf

The research staff wishes to thank some of the sports information directors, librarians and archivists who assisted in compiling or verifying information for the encyclopedia, and to recognize the previously published works that have documented the history of the NCAA Tournament and college basketball.

AP Poll Archive (www.appollarchive.com) Keith Meador

Association for Professional Basketball Research (www.apbr.org)

Berkeley (Calif.) Public Library

BigBlueHistory.net Jon Scott

The Classic: The History of the NCAA Basketball Championship by Ken Rappoport

Drexel University sports information Mike Tuberosa

Encyclopedia of College Basketball by Mike Douchant

The Encyclopedia of the NCAA Basketball Tournament by Jim Savage

International Association of Approved Basketball Officials Tom Lopes

Ivy League media relations department Wesley Harris

Joyce Sports Research Collection at Notre Dame George Rugg

LA84 Foundation Sports Library

La Salle University archives Brother Joseph L. Grabenstein

Marquette University sports information Scott Kuykendall

NAIA media relations Chad Waller

The National Invitation Tournament by Ray Floriani

The NCAA Men's Basketball and Final Four Record Books researched and compiled by Gary Johnson

New Mexico State University Library

Oklahoma City University archives Christina Wolf

Oklahoma State sports information Mike Noteware

Ronald Basketball Encyclopedia by Bill Mokray

Saint Joseph's University sports information Marie Wozniak

Spartanburg (S.C.) Public Library

University of Kansas sports information Chris Theisen

University of Utah archives

Villanova University Library

CONTRIBUTORS

Kareem Abdul-Jabbar ("One Sport, Two Games," page 12) is considered by many to be the greatest basketball player of all time. The 7′2″ Hall-of-Fame center was twice national Player of the Year (when he was known as Lew Alcindor) and led UCLA to three straight NCAA championships and a phenomenal 88–2 three-year record. He went on to be a six-time NBA Most Valuable Player and a 19-time All-Star, and set league career records in nine categories. His NBA total of 38,387 points may never be surpassed. But as Abdul-Jabbar himself says, "I can do more than shoot a ball through a hoop." A lifelong passion for history inspired him to write six best-selling books on various historical subjects. His knowledge and love of jazz resulted in *On the Shoulders of Giants: My Journey Through the Harlem Renaissance*, not only as a hardcover and audio book, but also as an upcoming documentary film featuring Samuel L. Jackson, Quincy Jones and Maya Angelou. Abdul-Jabbar, who serves as a Los Angeles Lakers assistant coach, maintains the Kareem Abdul-Jabbar Foundation; its mission is to promote and support literacy and sports programs as a way to improve the lives of disadvantaged youth and communities around the globe.

Eric Adelson ("The Women's Game," page 40) wrote for *ESPN The Magazine* for 10 years, since its inception in 1998, covering seven women's basketball NCAA Final Fours, beginning in 2000. He has degrees from Harvard and Columbia and is the author of *The Sure Thing: The Making and Unmaking of Golf Phenom Michelle Wie*, which was published in 2009 by ESPN Books. He lives with his family in Orlando, Fla.

Morty Ain (team profiles) is a contributing writer for *ESPN The Magazine*. A screenwriter and comedian, he is a graduate of Brandeis, which is absent from these pages but ranks as the 489th best party school according to *Playboy*.

William Bendetson (team profiles) covers the New England Patriots for cbssports.com. He previously wrote for ESPN.com and contributed to *ESPN The Magazine*. A 2008 graduate of Tufts, he is currently writing a book about the New York Giants.

Bill Bradley (Introduction, page xiii) was a three-time All-America at Princeton (1962-65), a Rhodes Scholar, an Olympic gold medalist and a member of the two-time NBA champion New York Knicks. In 1983 he was inducted into the Naismith Hall of Fame. From 1979 to '97, Bradley served three terms as a U.S. senator, representing New Jersey. In 2000, he was a candidate for the Democratic nomination for president of the United States. He has also been an essayist for CBS News and has been a visiting professor at Stanford, Notre Dame and the University of Maryland. He is currently a managing director of Allen & Company, LLC, in New York City. He has written seven books on American politics, culture and economics, including his latest, *The New American Story*. Currently, Senator Bradley hosts *American Voices*, a weekly show on Sirius XM Satellite Radio that highlights the remarkable accomplishments of Americans both famous and unknown.

Dale Brauner (team profiles) is a freelance writer whose work has appeared in *ESPN The Magazine*, ESPN.com, *DanceView* and *USA Today*.

Jordan Brenner (team profiles) is an associate editor at *ESPN The Magazine* and ESPN Insider. He has covered college basketball for five years at the magazine. He is a graduate of Tufts and of Columbia University's Graduate School of Journalism.

Jason Catania (team profiles) is a contributing research editor at *ESPN The Magazine*. A graduate of NYU, he lives in Rockville Centre, Long Island.

LaRue Cook (research) began his journalism career by covering prep and Division II sports for the *News Sentinel* in Knoxville, Tenn., where he sat in a half-empty Thompson-Boling Arena watching bad basketball. Luckily, his junior year of college coincided with the arrival of Bruce Pearl.

Charles Curtis (team profiles) is a contributing researcher and freelance writer for *ESPN The Magazine*. A graduate of Haverford, he lives in New York City with his wife.

t Forde ("The Sweetest 16," page 28) has been a senior :iter at ESPN.com since 2004. Before that, he worked for ' years at the Louisville *Courier-Journal*, after graduating om the University of Missouri. In 2008 he co-wrote a book rith Rick Pitino, *Rebound Rules: The Art of Success 2.0*. He as covered every Final Four since 1990 and makes his home n the college basketball mecca of Louisville.

Cal Fussman ("They Were There," page 44) is a writer-at-large for *Esquire* and a contributor to *ESPN The Magazine*. He is the as-told-to author of *The New York Times* best-selling autobiography of Larry King, *My Remarkable Journey*. He also wrote *After Jackie*, a look at the African-American players who followed Jackie Robinson into Major League Baseball, published by ESPN Books in 2007. He lives in Los Angeles.

Matt Giles (research) is a lifelong fan of St. John's basketball and still believes Erick Barkley was fouled by Scoonie Penn in the Red Storm's 1999 Elite Eight appearance. He attended Saint Joseph's in Philadelphia and spent four years chanting "The Hawk Will Never Die." He was an original member of Delonte West's Wild Wild West fan club.

Ian Gordon (team profiles) is a former contributing editor to *ESPN The Magazine*, where he covered college basketball. A graduate of the University of North Carolina, he currently lives in the San Francisco Bay Area.

John Gustafson (team profiles) is a freelancer and a former staff writer for *ESPN The Magazine*.

Travis Haney (team profiles) is a college sports reporter for *The Post and Courier* in Charleston, S.C. A graduate of the University of Tennessee, Haney has won a variety of awards for his writing and had his work featured in *The Best American Sports Writing* series.

Darryl Howerton (team profiles) is a freelance writer living in Fresno, Calif. He has written for dozens of magazines, among them *Sport* in the 1990s and *Hoop* in the 2000s.

Donald Hunt ("Shadow Play," page 20) is a staff sportswriter for *The Philadelphia Tribune*.

Gary K. Johnson (NCAA historian) lettered in baseball at the University of Arizona and went on to work in the SID offices at Arizona and Northwestern. Since 1984, Gary has been the NCAA's basketball historian in charge of statistics, records and the RPI. He and his wife, Annie, have three grown children: Cory, Amanda and Tyler. He's been involved with the Kansas Special Olympics for 10 years, has coached 30 seasons of youth baseball, takes part in mentoring and reading programs, volunteers with his church high school youth group and builds homes with Habitat for Humanity. He lives in Greenwood, Ind.

Jason Jordan (team profiles) writes for ESPNRISE.com, *Dime Magazine* and *ESPN The Magazine*.

Doug Kern (ESPN Stats & Information Group associate) joined ESPN in 2006 after several years in the information technology field. Originally from Manassas, Va., he started his stats career as a high school stringer for *The Washington Post*. He's a 1996 graduate of Virginia Tech, where he was involved in coverage and statistics for all sports for the athletics communications department.

Paul Kix (team profiles) is a contributing writer for *ESPN The Magazine* and a senior editor at *Boston* magazine. His work has also appeared in *Men's Journal*, *Salon* and *The Chicago Tribune*.

John Mastroberardino (research) has nearly 30 years of experience as a sportswriter, reporter and operations director at SportsTicker, the now-defunct sports wire service. The long days and nights in SportsTicker's newsroom included coverage of the epic 19-inning Mets-Braves battle on July 4, 1985, Great Alaska Shootouts and Maui Invitationals.

Doug Mittler (team profiles) is a freelance writer whose work has appeared in *ESPN The Magazine*, ESPN.com, *The Baltimore Sun* and *The Providence Journal*.

Mike Ogle (team profiles) is a freelance writer whose work has appeared regularly in *The New York Times, ESPN The Magazine*, ESPN.com, SI.com and *Sports Illustrated*. A graduate of the University of North Carolina, he lives in New York City with his wife.

William F. Reed ("The Teachers," page 2; poll progression and Tournament bracket notes), commonly known as Billy in his native Kentucky, began covering college basketball in 1962. A 1966 graduate of Transylvania University, he is a former senior writer for *Sports Illustrated*, a former sports editor of the Louisville *Courier-Journal* and a member of the U.S. Basketball Writers Association Hall of Fame. He has covered 21 Final Fours, and considers Bill Walton the best college player he's seen and "Pistol" Pete Maravich the most entertaining. *The Final Four,* a book he wrote, edited and compiled with photographer Rich Clarkson, was presented in 1988 to all guests at the NCAA's Golden Salute to the Final Four, a celebration of the 50th anniversary of the Tournament.

John Roach (team profiles) is a Philadelphia-area freelance writer whose work has appeared in *ESPN The Magazine*, *The Philadelphia Inquirer*, ESPN.com and several national and regional media outlets.

Steve Rushin ("The Bracket Racket," page 24) is the author of the forthcoming novel *The Pint Man*, and two non-fiction books, *Road Swing: One Fan's Journey Into the Soul of America's Sports* and *The Caddie Was a Reindeer and Other Tales of Extreme Recreation*. While on staff at *Sports Illustrated*, he was voted National Sportswriter of the Year by his peers. He is a graduate of Marquette, which awarded him an honorary doctor of letters for "his unique gift of documenting the human condition through his writing." His website is www.steverushin.com.

Jeff Sagarin ("The Ratings Are In," page 1,194) has been rating sports teams in public print since September 1972. Born in New York City in 1948 and raised in New Rochelle, N.Y., he earned an S.B. in mathematics from MIT and an MBA in quantitative business analysis from the Indiana University School of Business. He'd like to remember his mom, Sherry, for always making sure he did his homewo[rk] and his dad, Fred, for passing on his love of sports. Witho[ut] them, there wouldn't be any Jeff Sagarin Ratings today.

Jim Savage (database provider) has been a passionat[e] observer of the college hoops scene for decades. He i[s] the author of the seminal work on March Madness, *The Encyclopedia of the NCAA Basketball Tournament,* and other books, including *The Force*, a biography of David Robinson. He is also a devotee of rock 'n' roll and the American musical theater.

David Scott ("In the Beginning," page 526; team profiles) is the site editor for CoachCal.com and has been covering college basketball for nearly 20 years. A graduate of the University of Massachusetts, his first book, *Bounce Back: Overcoming Setbacks to Succeed in Business and in Life*, written with Kentucky coach John Calipari, was released in September 2009.

Anthony Tao (team profiles) is a freelance writer, travel enthusiast and ultimate Frisbee player living in Beijing, China. His work has appeared in *ESPN The Magazine*, *Sports Illustrated* and *Pharmaceutical Executive*.

Jim Weber (team profiles) is a freelance writer and researcher living in New York City. His work has appeared in *ESPN The Magazine*, *Sports Illustrated Kids* and *The Detroit Free Press*.

Gene Wojciechowski ("Too Many Fouls," page 34) is the senior national columnist for ESPN.com and a senior writer for *ESPN The Magazine*. He has played pick-up games with and against Michael Jordan (and lost both times). He has played at Allen Fieldhouse. And he considers the 1992 East Regional final between Duke and Kentucky to be the greatest college game ever played.

Michael Woods (team profiles) is a boxing writer and editor of thesweetscience.com. Woods worked at *Newsday* from 1999 to 2003, and has written for *GQ*, *ESPN The Magazine*, ESPN.com and *The Huffington Post*.

ABOUT THE EDITORS

nn Papanek is the founding editor-in-chief of *ESPN The agazine* and former editor-in-chief of ESPN.com. He was so a longtime basketball writer for *Sports Illustrated* before ecoming its managing editor.

cott Burton is a senior editor at *ESPN The Magazine* nd is the former managing editor of *Dick Vitale's College Basketball Yearbook.*

Bill Vourvoulias is a senior editor at ESPN Books. Along with Michael MacCambridge, he edited the *ESPN Big Ten Football Encyclopedia* and the *ESPN Southeastern Conference Football Encyclopedia.*

Craig Winston is the director of research for ESPN Publishing. He has been an editor at *Newsday*, *The National Sports Daily* and *The Hartford Courant.* He supervised research for the *ESPN College Football Encyclopedia.*

Roger Jackson is the deputy research chief at *ESPN The Magazine.* He covered college basketball for *Sports Illustrated* for many years.